THE ENCYCLOPEDIA OF FANTASTIC FILM

Other Film Titles from Applause

Absolute Power: The Screenplay by William Goldman

Acting in Film by Michael Caine

The Adventures of Baron Munchausen by Terry Gilliam and Charles McKeown

The Battle of Brazil by Jack Matthews

The Big Picture by William Goldman

Bob Hope: The Road Well Travelled by Laurence J. Quirk

The Cinematic Century by Harry Haun

Fear and Loathing in Las Vegas: The Screenplay by Terry Gilliam & Tony Grisoni

A Fish Called Wanda by John Cleese

The Fisher King by Richard LaGravenese

The Ghost and the Darkness by William Goldman

The Graham Greene Film Reader

Jacob's Ladder: The Book of the Film by Bruce Joel Rubin

James Stewart: Behind the Scenes of a Wonderful Life by Laurence J. Quirk

JFK: The Book of the Film by Oliver Stone and Zachary Sklar

The Life and Death of Peter Sellers by Roger Lewis

Lolita: The Book of the Film by Stephen Schiff

Losing the Light: Terry Gilliam and the Munchausen Saga by Andrew Yule

John Willis' Screen World: The Definitive Film Annual

Terminator 2: The Book of the Film by James Cameron and William Wisher

William Goldman Four Screenplays

William Goldman Five Screenplays

THE ENCYCLOPEDIA OF FANTASTIC FILM

Ali Baba to Zombies

R. G. Young

 **APPLAUSE**
NEW YORK • LONDON

An Applause Original

THE ENCYCLOPEDIA OF FANTASTIC FILM

By R.G. Young

Copyright © 2000 Applause Books

ISBN 1-55783-269-2 (trade paperback)

Photo Research and assistance
by John Cocchi

Library of Congress Cataloging-In-Publication Data

Library of Congress Card Number: 99-068372

British Library Catalogue in Publication Data
A catalogue record for this book is available from the British Library

APPLAUSE BOOKS

1841 Broadway
New York, NY 10023
Phone (212) 765-7880
Fax: (212) 765-7875

Combined Book Services Ltd.
Units I/K, Paddock Wood Distribution Centre
Paddock Wood, Tonbridge Kent TN 12 6UU
Phone (44) 01892 837171
Fax: (44) 01892 837272

10   9   8   7   6   5   4   3   2   1

Contents

The Phantom of the Opera: LON CHANEY

Aaron's Magic Village

1997, (USA), color, 80 mins.
VOICE: Tommy Michaels
From a story by Isaac Bashevis Singer
Standard animated musical-fantasy: Orphan saves European hamlet from evil sorcerer

Abbott and Costello Go to Mars

1953, (USA), Univ, b&w, 76 mins.
W: Bud Abbott (*Lester*), Lou Costello (*Orville*), Martha Hyer (*Janie*), Robert Paige (*Dr. Wilson*), Mari Blanchard (*Queen Allura*), Horace McMahon (*Mugsy*), Jean Willes (*The Captain*), Jack Kruschen (*Harry*), Joe Kirk (*Dr. Orvilla*), Ruth Hampton, Anita Ekberg, James Flavin, Jeanne Thompson, Jackie Loughery, Valerie Jackson, Judy Hatula, Renate Huy, Elea Edsman, Jeri Miller
P: Howard Christie **D:** Charles Lamont **SCR:** John Grant & D.D. Beauchamp **STORY:** Howard Christie & D.D. Beauchamp **PHOTOG:** Clifford Stine **SPCL-FX:** David Horsley & Charlie Baker **MUSIC:** Joseph Gershenson
edited-down (10-min.) version known as **Rocket and Roll**
Juvenile SF-comedy: Two bunglers launched into space

Abbott and Costello in Rocket and Roll

see **Abbott and Costello Go to Mars**

Abbott and Costello Meet Boris Karloff

see **Abbott and Costello Meet the Killer**

Abbott and Costello Meet Captain Kidd

1952, (USA), WB, color, 70 mins.
W: Bud Abbott, Lou Costello, Charles Laughton (*Capt. Kidd*), Hillary Brooke (*Capt. Bonney*), Bill Shirley (*Bruce*), Leif Erickson (*Capt. Morgan*), Fran Warren (*Jane*)
P: Alex Gottlieb **D:** Charles Lamont **SCR:** Howard Dimsdale & John Grant **PHOTOG:** Stanley Cortez **MUSIC:** Raoul Kraushaar
Routine adventure-comedy: Two servants acquire treasure map

Abbott and Costello Meet Dr. Jekyll and Mr. Hyde

1953, (USA), Univ, b&w, 82 mins.
W: Bud Abbott (*Slim*), Lou Costello (*Tubby*), Boris Karloff (*Dr. Jekyll*), Craig Stevens (*Bruce Adams*), Helen Westcott (*Vicky Edwards*), John Dierkes (*Batley*), Reginald Denny (*The Inspector*), Ed Parker (*doubling for Karloff as Mr. Hyde*)
P: Howard Christie **D:** Charles Lamont **SCR:** Leo Loeb & John Grant, from a story by Sidney Fields & Grant Garrett **PHOTOG:** George Robinson **SPCL-FX:** David Horsley **MUSIC:** Joseph Gershenson
Juvenile comedy-thriller: Cops befriend doctor's ward

Abbott and Costello Meet Doctor Jekyll and Mr. Hyde: BORIS KARLOFF

Abbott and Costello Meet Frankenstein

1948, (USA), Univ, b&w, 82 mins.
W: Bud Abbott (*Chick Young*), Lou Costello (*Wilbur*), Bela Lugosi ("*Dr. Lahos*"/*Count Dracula*), Lon Chaney Jr. (*Lawrence Talbot/The Wolfman*), Lenore Aubert (*Dr. Sandra Mornay*), Jane Randolph (*Joan Raymond*), Glenn Strange (*The Frankenstein Monster*), Charles Bradstreet (*Prof. Stevens*), Frank Ferguson (*McDougal*)
P: Robert Arthur **D:** Charles T. Barton **SCR:** Robert Lees, Frederic Rinaldo & John Grant **PHOTOG:** Charles Van Enger **SPCL-FX:** David S. Horsley & Jerome Ash **MUSIC:** Frank Skinner
orig. to be titled **The Brain of Frankenstein**

GB retitle, **Abbott and Costello Meet the Ghosts**
"...a surprisingly bright spoof, but a sad end to the once great monster tradition"—William K. Everson, *The Bad Guys*
"To Universal's credit, they staged the horror sequences with all the care of old. The visuals were extremely handsome...some vampiric bat-into-human transformations being as good as anything Universal's horror, special effects technicians had done in their heyday"—William K. Everson, *Classics of the Horror Film*
Entertaining horror-comedy: Vampire and lady scientist seek to revive immortal monster

Abbott and Costello Meet the Ghosts

see **Abbott and Costello Meet Frankenstein**

Abbott and Costello Meet the Invisible Man

1951, (USA), Univ, b&w, 82 mins.
W: Bud Abbott (*Bud Alexander*), Lou Costello (*Lou Francis*), Nancy Guild (*Helen Gray*), Arthur Franz (*Tommy Nelson*), Adele Jergens (*Boots Marsden*), William Frawley (*Det. Roberts*), Sam Balter (*The Radio Announcer*), Sheldon Leonard (*Morgan*), Gavin Muir (*Dr. Philip Gray*), John Day (*Rocky Hanlon*)
P: Howard Christie **D:** Charles Lamont **SCR:** Robert Lees, et al. **PHOTOG:** George Robinson **SPCL-FX:** David Horsley **MUSIC:** Joseph Gershenson
Standard comedy-fantasy: Fledgling detectives involved with persecuted boxer

Abbott and Costello Meet the Killer

1949, (USA), Univ, b&w, 94 mins.
W: Bud Abbott, Lou Costello, Boris Karloff, Lenore Aubert, Gar Moore, Victoria Horne, Alan Mowbray, Nicholas Joy, Roland Winters, James Flavin, Donna Martell
P: Robert Arthur **D:** Charles T. Barton **SCR:** John Grant, Hugh Wedlock Jr. & Howard Snyder **PHOTOG:** Charles Van Enger **SPCL-FX:** David Horsley **MUSIC:** Milton Schwarzwald
GB retitle, **Abbott and Costello Meet Boris Karloff**
Standard comedy-thriller: House detective and bumbling bellboy encounter murder at posh resort

Abbott and Costello Meet the Mummy

1955, (USA), Univ, b&w, 79 mins.
W: Bud Abbott (*Pete Patterson*), Lou Costello (*Freddie Franklin*), Marie Windsor (*Mme. Rontru*), Michael Ansara (*Charlie*), Richard Deacon (*Semu*), Eddie Parker (*Klaris, the Mummy*), Dan Seymour (*Josef*), Richard Karlan (*Hetsut*), George Khoury (*Habid*), Kurt Katch (*Dr. Zoomer*), Mel Welles (*Iben*), Peggy King (in a cameo role, singing *You Came a Long Way from St. Louis*), The Mazzone-Abbott Dancers
P: Howard Christie **D:** Charles Lamont **SCR:** John Grant **STORY:** Leo Loeb **PHOTOG:** George Robinson **SPCL PHOTOG:** Clifford Stine **MUSIC:** Joseph Gershenson
Standard comedy-thriller: Two soldiers-of-fortune menaced by fanatical cult

Abby

1974, (USA), Mid-America/AIP, color, 91 mins.
W: William Marshall (*Garnet Williams*), Carol Speed (*Abby*), Terry Carter (*Emmett*), Austin Stoker (*Cass*), Juanita Moore (*Momma*), Charles Kissinger (*Dr. Hennings*), Elliott Moffitt (*Russell*), Nathan Cook (*Tafa*), Nancy Lee Owen (*Mrs. Wiggins*), Bob Holt (*The Voice of the Demon*)
D: William Girdler **SCR:** G. Cornell Layne **STORY:** William Girdler & G. Cornell Layne **PHOTOG:** William Asman
Standard **Exorcist** *imitation: Girl possessed by African devil*

Abduction

1975, (USA), color, 100 mins.
W: Judith-Marie Bergman, David Pendleton, Gregory Rozakis, Leif Erickson, Dorothy Malone, Lawrence Tierney
D: Joseph Zito, from Harrison James' novel *Abductors*
Minor thriller: Tycoon's daughter kidnapped

The Abductors

1957, (USA), Regal/20th-Fox, b&w, 80 mins.
W: Victor McLaglen, George Macready, Fay Spain, Gavin Muir
D: Andrew V. McLaglen **PHOTOG:** Joseph La Shelle
Minor fact-based melodrama: Plot to steal Lincoln's remains

Abdullah's Harem

1956, (USA), 20th-Fox, color, 88 mins.
W: Gregory Ratoff, Kay Kendall, Sydney Chaplin
Standard romance-satire, (broad spoof of Egypt's King Farouk): Potentate falls for model
A.k.a. **Abdullah the Great**

Abide with Me

1916, (GB), Grenville-Taylor/Kin-Ex, b&w, 4,200 ft. (1280.2m)
W: Austin Camp (*Ralph Stoneham*), George Foley (*Father Eustace*), Vera Cornish (*Amy*), Jack Berry (*Hubert Stoneham*), N. Watts-Phillips (*Denham Thorpe*), Mme. d'Esterre (*Miss Stoneham*)
D: Tom Watts **STORY:** H. Grenville-Taylor
Standard crime-thriller: Rich man kills brother, dares monk to reveal his confession

Abismos de Pasion

see **Cumbres Borrascosas**

The Abominable Dr. Hichcock

see **Raptus**

The Abominable Dr. Phibes
1971, (GB), AIP, color, 93 mins.
W: Vincent Price *(Dr. Anton Phibes)*, Joseph Cotten *(Dr. Vesalius)*, Terry-Thomas *(Dr. Longstreet)*, Virginia North *(Vulnavia)*, Peter Jeffrey *(Insp. Trout)*, Hugh Griffith *(The Rabbi)*, John Cater *(Waverley)*, Derek Godfrey *(Crow)*, Norman Jones *(Schenley)*, Susan Travers *(Nurse Allan)*, Aubrey Woods *(Goldsmith)*, Alex Scott *(Dr. Hargreaves)*, Edward Burnham *(Dr. Dunwoody)*, Peter Gilmore *(Dr. Kitaj)*, Maurice Kaufmann *(Dr. Whitcombe)*, Barbara Keogh *(Mrs. Frawley)*, Sean Bury *(Lem)*, Walter Horsborough *(Ross)*, David Hutcheson *(Dr. Hedgepath)*, Alister Williamson *(A Policeman)*, Thomas Heathcote *(A Policeman)*, Caroline Munro *(Victoria Phibes)*, Charles Farrell, James Grout, John Laurie, Alan Zipson, Dallas Adams
P: Louis M. Heyward & Ron Dunas D: Robert Fuest SCR: James Whiton & William Goldstein PHOTOG: Norman Warwick SPCL-FX: George Blackwell MUSIC: Basil Kirchin & Jack Nathan
"Dr. Phibes is just what a horror movie should be, outrageously hammy and frightfully funny"—Kathleen Carroll, New York Daily News
"one of the most luscious horror stories you will ever see"—Judith Crist
Stylish horror-comedy (billed as Vincent Price's 100th film): Madman enacts bizarre vengeance. cf. **Dr. Phibes Rises Again**

The Abominable Snowman of the Himalayas
1957, (GB), Exclusive/20th-Fox, b&w, 85 mins.
W: Peter Cushing *(Dr. John Rollason)*, Forrest Tucker *(Tom Friend)*, Maureen Connell *(Helen Rollason)*, Richard Wattis *(Peter Fox)*, Arnold Marle *(The Lhama)*, Robert Brown, Wolfe Morris, Michael Brill, Anthony Chinn
D: Val Guest SCR: Nigel Kneale (from his play *The Creature*)
PHOTOG: Arthur Grant MUSIC: Humphrey Searle MUSIC DIR: John Hollingsworth
Superior SF-thriller: Scientific expedition thwarted by non-humans

The Abomination
1988, (USA), color, 100 mins.
W: Van Connery, Victoria Chaney, Gaye Bottoms, Suzy Meyer, Jude Johnson, Blue Thompson, Scott Davis
D: Max Raven
Standard horror-fantasy: Boy possessed by 5,000-year-old creature

About Two Persons Who Stole the Moon
see **O Dwoch Takich Co Ukradli Ksiezyc**

Above Suspicion
1943, (USA), MGM, b&w, 91 mins.
W: Fred MacMurray *(Richard Myles)*, Joan Crawford *(Frances Myles)*, Conrad Veidt *(Hassert Seidel)*, Basil Rathbone *(Sig von Aschenhausen)*, Reginald Owen *(Dr. Mespelbrunn)*, Richard Ainley *(Peter Galt)*, Peter Lawford *(The Student)*, Ann Shoemaker *(Aunt Ellen)*, Sara Haden *(Aunt Hattie)*, Felix Bressart *(Mr. A. Werner)*, Lotte Palfi *(Ottillie)*, Bruce Lester *(Thornley)*, Johanna Hofer *(Frau Kleist)*, Cecil Cunningham *(The Countess)*, Alex Papana *(The Man in Paris)*, Rex Williams *(The Gestapo Leader)*, William Yetter *(Hauptman)*, Steven Geray *(Anton)*, William "Wee Willie" Davis *(Hans)*, Lisa Golm *(Frau Schultz)*, Ludwig Stossel *(Herr Schultz)*, Henry Glynn *(The Chauffer)*, Eily Malyon *(The Manageress)*, Frank Lackteen *(The Arab Vendor)*, Marcelle Corday *(The Maid)*, Egon Brecher *(The Gestapo Official)*, Steven Muller *(The German Boy)*, Sven-Hugo Borg *(The German Guard)*, Arthur Shields, Nicholas Vehr, Ferdinand Schumann-Heink, Peter Seal, Otto Reichow, Edit Angold
P: Victor Saville D: Richard Thorpe SCR: Keith Winter, Melville Baker & Patricia Coleman, from Helen MacInnes' novel
PHOTOG: Robert Planck SPCL-FX: Warren Newcombe MUSIC: Bronislau Kaper
Standard melodrama: Newlyweds pressed into espionage

Abrakadabra
1957, (Yugo), color
D: Dusan Vukotic
Animated fantasy: Magic amazes

Abraxas, Guardian of the Universe
1991, (Can), HBO-TV, color, 90 mins.
W: Jesse Ventura, Marjorie Bransfield, Sven Ole-Thorsen, James Belushi
Made-for-Cable, minor SF-thriller: Galactic policeman opposes turncoat

The Absent-Minded Professor
1907, (GB), Clarendon/Gaumont, b&w, 550 ft. (167.6m)
D: Percy Stow STORY: Langford Reed
Standard comedy-fantasy short: Math master has weird dream

The Absent-Minded Professor
1961, (USA), Walt Disney/Buena Vista, b&w, 97 mins.
W: Fred MacMurray *(Prof. Ned Brainard)*, Nancy Olson *(Betsy Carlisle)*, Keenan Wynn *(Alonzo Hawk)*, Elliott Reid *(Prof. Shelby Ashton)*, Tommy Kirk *("Biff" Hawk)*, Ed Wynn *(A.J. Allen)*, Leon Ames *(Pres. Rufus Daggett)*, Edward Andrews, Belle Montrose, Wally Brown, Forrest Lewis, Alan Carney, Jack Mullaney, David Lewis, Gage Clarke
D: Robert Stevenson SCR: Bill Walsh, from a story by Samuel W. Taylor
PHOTOG: Edward Colman MUSIC: George Bruns
Amusing comedy-fantasy: Teacher discovers anti-gravity substance. cf. **Son of Flubber**

Absolution
1981, (GB), Bulldog/Enterprise, color, 95 mins.
W: Richard Burton *(Father Goddard)*, Dominic Guard *(Benjie Stanfield)*, Dai Bradley *(Arthur Dyson)*, Bill Connolly *(Blakey)*, Andrew Keir *(The Headmaster)*, Willoughby Gray *(Brig Walsh)*, Hilda Fenemore *(Mrs. Hoskins)*, Robert Addie *(Cawley)*, Sharon Duce *(Louella)*, James Ottaway *(Father Matthews)*, Hilary Mason *(Mrs. Froggatt)*, Trevor Martin *(Gladstone)*, Preston Lockwood *(Father Hibbert)*, Robin Soans *(Father Henryson)*, Jon Plowman *(Father Piers)*, Brook Williams *(Father Clarence)*, Kevin Hart *(Petersen)*, Brian Glover *(A Constable)*, Dan Meaden *(A Constable)*
D: Anthony Page SCR: Anthony Shaffer PHOTOG: John Coquillon MUSIC: Billy Connolly
Minor thriller (filmed in 1978): Priest involved in murder, A.k.a. **Murder by Confession**

An Absorbing Tale
1909, (GB), Urban Trading Co., b&w, 300 ft. (91.4m)
D: Walter R. Booth
Standard comedy-fantasy: Man absorbed in book, is eventually blown up

The Abyss
1989, (USA), Gale Anne Hurd/20th-Fox, color, 136 mins.
W: Ed Harris *(Bud Brigman)*, Mary Elizabeth Mastrantonio *(Lindsey)*, Michael Biehn *(Lt. Coffey)*, Todd Graff *(Alan "Hippy" Carnes)*, Leo Burmester, John Bedford Lloyd, Kimberly Scott, J.C. Quinn
WRIT & D: James Cameron PHOTOG: Mikael Salomon MUSIC: Alan Silvestri
Superior SF-thriller: Alien life-form found in sea depths

Les Abysses (The Depths)
1963, (Fr), Kanawha, b&w, 96 mins.
W: Francine Berge, Colette Berge, Paul Bonifas, Pascale de Boysson
D: Nico Papatakis SCR: Jean Vauthier
Gripping thriller: Two demented maids commit atrocities

Act Of Aggression: CATHERINE DENEUVE AND JEAN-LOUIS TRINTIGNANT

Abysses of Passion
see **Cumbres Borrascosas**

Accidental Death
1963, (GB), Merton Park/Anglo-Amalgamated, b&w, 57 mins.
W: John Carson *(Paul Lanson)*, Jacqueline Ellis *(Henriette)*, Derrick Sherwin *(Alan)*, Richard Vernon *(Johnnie Paxton)*, Jean Lodge *(Brenda)*, Jacqueline Lacey *(Milly)*, Gerald Case *(The Inspector)*
D: Geoffrey Nethercott SCR: Arthur la Bern, from an Edgar Wallace story
Standard thriller: Man seeks revenge for wartime treachery

An Accident Victim Revives
1896, (GB), R.W. Paul, b&w
Standard short fantasy

The Accident
1962, (Fr), b&w, 91 mins.
W: George Riviere *(The Husband)*, Magali Noel *(The Wife)*, Danik Patisson *(The New Assistant)*
D: Edmond T. Greville PHOTOG: Jean Badal
Minor thriller: Philandering teacher plots wife's murder

Accidental Death
1963, (GB), Merton Park/Anglo-Amalgamated, b&w, 57 mins.
W: John Carson *(Paul Lanson)*, Jacqueline Ellis *(Henriette)*, Derrick Sherwin *(Alan)*, Richard Vernon *(Johnnie Paxton)*, Jean Lodge *(Brenda)*, Jacqueline Lacey *(Milly)*, Gerald Case *(The Inspector)*
P: Jack Greenwood D: Geoffrey Nethercott SCR: Arthur la Bern, from Edgar Wallace's novel *Judgement*

Accomplice
1946, (USA), PRC, b&w, 68 mins.
<u>W</u>: Richard Arlen, Veda Ann Borg, Tom Dugan, Francis Ford
<u>D</u>: Walter Colmes
Standard melodrama: Detective hoodwinked in bank-heist plot

Account Rendered
1957, (GB), Major/RFD, b&w, 61 mins.
<u>W</u>: Griffith Jones (*Robert Ainsworth*), Ursula Howells (*Lucille Ainsworth*), Honor Blackman (*Sarah Hayward*), Robert Raikes (*Sgt. Berry*), Ewen Solon (*Insp. Marshall*), John Van Eyssen (*Clive Franklin*), Philip Gilbert (*John Langford*), Carl Bernard (*Gilbert Morgan*)
<u>P</u>: John Temple-Smith & Francis Edge   <u>D</u>: Peter Graham Scott   <u>SCR</u>: Barbara S. Harper, from a novel by Pamela Barrington
Minor crime-thriller: Man accused of killing faithless wife

Accumulator 1
1994, (Czech), color, 102 mins.
<u>W</u>: Petr Forman, Edita Brychta, Zdenek Sverak
<u>D</u>: Jan Sverak
Unusual SF-romance-comedy: Allegory about complacency and the vampiric effects of TV

The Accursed
1958, (GB), Fantur/AA, b&w, 78 mins.
<u>W</u>: Donald Wolfit, Robert Bray, Jane Griffiths, Anton Diffring, Carl Jaffe, Karel Stepanek, Oscar Quitak, Frederick Schiller, Christopher Lee, Rupert Davies, John Van Eyssen, Colin Croft
<u>D, STORY & SCR</u>: Michael McCarthy   <u>MUSIC</u>: Jackie Brown   <u>SOLO PIANIST</u>: Dennis Wilson
Standard thriller: Mystery unfolds at reunion

The Accused
1948, (USA), Para, b&w, 101 mins.
<u>W</u>: Loretta Young (*Dr. Wilma Tuttle*), Robert Cummings (*Warren Ford*), Wendell Corey (*Lt. Ted Dorgan*), Sam Jaffe (*Dr.Romley*), Douglas Dick (*Bill Perry*), Sara Allgood (*Mrs. Conner*), Mickey Knox, Francis Pierlot, Carole Mathews
<u>P</u>: Hal Wallis   <u>D</u>: William Dieterle   <u>SCR</u>: Ketti Frings, from a novel by June Truesdell
<u>PHOTOG</u>: Milton Krasner   <u>MUSIC</u>: Victor Young
A.k.a. Strange Deception
Standard melodrama: Attractive teacher kills amorous student, tries to conceal crime

Accused of Murder
1956, (USA), Rep, color, 74 mins.
<u>W</u>: David Brian, Vera Ralston, Sidney Blackmer, Virginia Grey
<u>D</u>: Joseph Kane
Standard melodrama: Singer involved in underworld killing

The Acquittal
1923, (USA), Univ, b&w, 1988m (6,522.3 ft.)
<u>D</u>: Clarence Brown   <u>STORY</u>: Jules Furthman
Standard melodrama

Across the Atlantic
see The Secret of the Air

Across The Bridge
1957, (GB), IPF/RFD, b&w, 103 mins.
<u>W</u>: Rod Steiger (*Carl Schaffer*), David Knight (*Johnny*), Noel Willman (*The Police Chief*), Marla Landi (*Mary*), Bernard Lee (*Insp. Hadden*), Eric Pohlmann (*The Sgt.*), IngeborgWells (*Mrs. Scarff*), Alan Gifford (*Cooper*), Faith Brook (*Kay*), Bill Nagy (*Paul Scarff*), Marianne Deeming (*Anne*)
<u>P</u>: John Stafford   <u>D</u>: Ken Annakin   <u>SCR</u>: Guy Elmes & Denis Freeman, from a novel by Graham Greene
Standard crime-thriller: Fugitive financier poses as man he killed

Acting on Impulse
1993, (USA), Made for Cable, color, 93 mins.
<u>W</u>: Linda Fiorentino, C. Thomas Howell, Nancy Allen, Judith Hoag, Paul Bartel, Isaac Hayes, MaryWoronov, Patrick Bauchau, Dick Sargent, Miles O'Keefe, Cassandra Peterson, Peter Lupus, Don Most, Adam Ant
<u>D</u>: Sam Irvin
Standard thriller: Killer stalks movie "scream queen"

Action Stations
see Hi-Jack

Act of Aggression (L'Agression)
1975, (Fr-It), Gaumont-Int'l/Joseph Green, color
<u>W</u>: Jean-Louis Trintignant, Catherine Deneuve (*Sara*), Philippe Brigaud (*Escudero*), Claude Brasseur (*Andre*), Michelle Grellier
Minor thriller: Man pursues thugs who murdered family

An Act of Murder
1948, (USA), Univ, b&w, 91 mins.
<u>W</u>: Fredric March, Edmond O'Brien, Geraldine Brooks, Clarence Muse, Florence Eldridge
<u>D</u>: Michael Gordon   <u>SCR</u>: Michael Blankfort & Ernest Thoren, from Ernst Lothar's novel *The Mills of God*   <u>PHOTOG</u>: Hal Mohr   <u>MUSIC</u>:

Amfitheatrof
A.k.a. Live Today for Tomorrow
Superior melodrama: Judge tried for mercy killing of wife

Act of Murder
1964, (GB), Merton Park/Anglo-Amalgamated, b&w, 62 mins.
<u>W</u>: John Carson (*Tim Ford*), Anthony Bate (*Ralph Longman*), Justine Lord (*Anne Longman*), Duncan Lewis (*Will Peterson*), Richard Burrell (*John Quick*), Dandy Nichols (*Maud Peterson*), Sheena Marshe (*Pauline*), Norman Scace (*Watson*)
<u>P</u>: Jack Greenwood   <u>D</u>: Alan Bridges   <u>STORY</u>: Lewis Davidson
Standard thriller: Actor uses crook's plot to steal antiques, lure ex-mistress from her husband

Adam and Eve
1956, (Mex), color, 76 mins.
<u>W</u>: Carlos Baena (*Adam*), Christine Martel (*Eve*)
<u>D</u>: Albert Gout   <u>PHOTOG</u>: Alex Phillips
Standard fantasy: Loose adaptation of Genesis love story

Adam's Rib
1923, (USA), Famous Players-Lasky, b&w, 9,528 ft. (2904m)
<u>W</u>: Milton Sills, Pauline Garon, Wallace Reid, Elliott Dexter, Anna Q. Nilsson, Theodore Kosloff
<u>P & D</u>: Cecil B. DeMille
Standard fantasy-adventure: Problems of prehistoric man

The Addams Family
1991, (USA), Scott Rudin/Para, color, 102 mins.
<u>W</u>: Anjelica Huston (*Morticia Addams*), Raul Julia (*Gomez Addams*), Christopher Lloyd (*Uncle Fester*), Christina Ricci (*Wednesday Addams*), Jimmy Workman (*Pugsley Addams*), Judith Malina (*Granny*), Carel Struycken (*Lurch*), Dan Hedaya (*Alford*), Dana Ivey (*Margaret*), Paul Benedict (*Judge Womack*), Christopher Hart (*Thing*), Elizabeth Wilson, John Franklin
<u>D</u>: Barry Sonnenfeld   <u>SCR</u>: Caroline Thompson & Larry Wilson, from characters created by Charles Addams   <u>PHOTOG</u>: Owen Roizman   <u>MUSIC</u>: Marc Shaiman
Superior comedy-fantasy: Bizarre clan finds long-lost uncle

The Addams Family: ANJELICA HUSTON AND RAUL JULIA

Addams Family Reunion
1998, (USA), WB, color
<u>W</u>: Daryl Hannah
from characters created by Charles Addams
Made-for-Cable, standard comedy-fantasy

Addams Family Values
1993, (USA), Para, color, 94 mins.
<u>W</u>: Anjelica Huston (*Morticia Addams*), Raul Julia (*Gomez Addams*), Christina Ricci (*Wednesday Addams*), Christopher Lloyd (*Uncle Fester*), Carol Kane (*Grandmama*), Jimmy Workman (*Pugsley Addams*), Joan Cusack (*Debbie*), Carel Struycken (*Lurch*), Kaitlin & Kristen Hooper (*Pubert Addams*), David Krumholtz, Christopher Hart, Dana Ivey, Peter MacNicol, Christine Baranski, Mercedes McNab, Sam McMurray, Harriet Sansom Harris, Julie Halston, Barry Sonnenfeld, John Franklin, Nathan Lane, Charles Busch, Laura Esterman, Maureen Sue Levin, Darlene Levin, Carol Hankins, Vickilyn Reynolds, Steven M. Martin, Edye Byrde, Douglas Brian Martin, Cynthia Ryan Holihan, Lois deBanzie, David Hyde Pierce, Rick Scarry, Adreana Weiner, Peter Graves, Francis Coady, Monet Mazur, Zack Phifer, Ian Abercrombie, Tony Shalhoub, Chris Ellis, Camille Saviola, Jeffrey Van Hoose, Matthew Beebe, Micah Winkelspecht, Kristy Shirvani, Jamie Gordon, Micah Hata, Jason Fife, Karl David-Djerf, Haley Peel
<u>P & SCR</u>: Paul Rudnick   <u>D</u>: Barry Sonnenfeld, from characters created by Charles Addams   <u>PHOTOG</u>: Donald Peterman   <u>VS-FX SPRVSR</u>: Alan Munro   <u>MUSIC</u>: Marc Shaiman
Standard comedy-fantasy: Demonic nanny upsets weird family

The Addiction
1995, (USA), b&w, 85 mins.
<u>W</u>: Lili Taylor, Annabella Sciorra, Christopher Walken, Edie Falco, Paul

Calderone, Fredro Star, Kathryn Erbe, Michael Imperioli
D: Abel Ferrera   **SCR:** Nicholas St. John   **MUSIC:** Joe Delia
Standard horror-fantasy: New York grad student becomes vampiress

The Adding Machine
1968, (GB), Regional/Univ, color, 99 mins.
W: Milo O'Shea (*Zero*), Phyllis Diller (*Mrs. Zero*), Phil Brown (*Don*), Billie
    Whitelaw (*Daisy*), Sydney Chaplin (*Lt. Charles*), Julian Glover (*Shrdlu*),
    Libby Morris (*Ethel*), Raymond Huntley (*Smithers*), Hugh McDermott
    (*Harry*), Paddie O'Neil (*Mabel*), Carol Cleveland (*Judy*), Bruce Boa (*The
    Detective*), John Brandon (*The 1st Cell Jailer*), Hal Galili (*The 2nd Cell Jailer*),
    Tony Caunter (*The 3rd Cell Jailer*), Kenny Damon (*Joe*), Bill Hutchinson
    (*Judy's Lover*), C. Denier Warren (*The Jury Foreman*), Bill Nagy (*The Lawyer*),
    Tommy Duggan (*The Judge*), Nicholas Stuart (*The District Attorney*), George
    Margo (*The Gateman*), Lola Lloyd (*The Coffee Girl*), Janet Brown (*The Fat &
    Thin Woman*), John Cook (*The Husband*), Cal McCord (*The Tenant*), John
    Bloomfield, Helena Stevens, Alan Surtees, Mike Reed, Christine Pryor,
    Shirley Conklin, Anthony Harwood, Gordon Sterne, Mike Reed
D & SCR: Jerome Epstein from Elmer Rice's 1923 play   **PHOTOG:** Walter
    Lassally   **MUSIC:** Mike Leander & Lambert Williamson
Unusual thriller: Neurotic bookkeeper commits murder

Address Unknown
1944, (USA), Col, b&w, 72 mins.
W: Paul Lukas, Carl Esmond, Mady Christians
P & D: William Cameron Menzies   **PHOTOG:** Rudolph Mate
Superior thriller: Businessman in Germany embraces Nazi cause

Adrenalin
1996, (USA), Dimension, color, 80 mins.
W: Christopher Lambert, Natasha Henstridge, Norbert Weisser (*Cuzco*), Elizabeth
    Barondes (*Wocek*)
A.k.a. Adrenalin: Fear the Rush
Made-for-Video, standard SF-thriller: Infectious lab subject escapes

The Adulteress
see Yoru No Tsuzumi

The Advanced Guard
1998, (USA), SCI-TV, Made-for-Cable, color
W: Isabella Hofmann (*Harper*), Michael Weatherly (*Kevin*), James Avery (*Fred*)
Standard SF-thriller: Space aliens abduct four people for mind-control tests

The Advantages of Hypnotism
1911, (GB), Cricks & Martin, b&w, 445 ft. (135.6m)
D: A.E. Coleby
Minor comedy-fantasy short: Spurned suitor mesmerizes girl's father

Adventure at the Center of the Earth
1965, (Mex), color
Minor SF-fantasy: Standard terrors at Earth's core

Adventure Island
1947, (USA), Para, color, 66 mins.
W: Rory Calhoun, Rhonda Fleming, John Abbott, Paul Kelly, Alan Napier
P: William Fine & William Thomas   **D:** Peter Stewart, based on Robert Louis
    Stevenson's novel *Ebb Tide* (remake of 1937 film)   **PHOTOG:** Jack
    Greenhalgh   **MUSIC:** Darrell Calker
Minor adventure-thriller: Shipwrecked sailors on isle ruled by madman

The Adventure of Nemo
see Captain Nemo and the Underwater City

The Adventure of Lyle Swann
see Timerider

Adventurer of Tortuga
1964, (It), color
W: Guy Madison, Nadia Gray
Standard melodrama: Pirate aids lady

Adventures in Dinosaur City
1992, (USA), color, 94 mins.
W: Omri Katz, Tiffanie Poston Pete Koch, Tony Doyle, Mimi Maynard, Sharon
    Hoffman, Megan Hughes, Steven Anderson
D: Brett Thompson   **SCR:** Willie Baronet & Lisa Morton   **PHOTOG:** Rick
    Fichter   **MUSIC:** Fredric Teetsel
Standard juvenile fantasy: Dinosaur war traps three children

The Adventures of a Football
1914, (GB), Urban Trading Co., b&w, 250 ft (76.2m)
D: Stuart Kinder
Standard comedy-fantasy: Crowd chases football that runs up tree

The Adventures of Baron Munchausen (1943)
see Die Avonturen de Baron Munchhausen

The Adventures of Baron Munchausen
1989, (GB), Col, color, 126 mins.
W: John Neville (*Baron Munchausen*), Eric Idle (*Desmond/Berthold*), Sarah Polley
    (*Sally Salt*), Oliver Reed (*Vulcan*), Uma Thurman (*Venus/Rose*), Charles
    McKeown (*Rupert/Adolphus*), Winston Dennis (*Bill/Albrecht*), Jack Purvis
    (*Jeremy/Gustavus*), Valentina Cortese (*Queen Ariadne/Violet*), Jonathan Pryce
    (*Horatio Jackson*), Bill Paterson (*Henry Salt*), Sting (*The Heroic Officer*), Alison
    Steadman (*Daisy*), "Ray D. Tutto" [Robin Williams] (*King of the Moon*)
D: Terry Gilliam   **SCR:** Charles McKeown & Terry Gilliam   **PHOTOG:**
    Giuseppe Rotunno   **SPCL-FX:** Richard Conway   **MUSIC:** Michael Kamen
    DESIGN: Dante Ferretti
Lavish fantasy-adventure: Life and times of notorious liar

The Adventures of Big and Little Willie
1915, (GB), Haselden Mario-Toons, b&w, 355 ft. (108.2m)
STORY: W.K. Haselden
Standard fantasy: Marionettes' exploits

The Adventures of Buckaroo Banzai
1984, (USA), Sherwood/20th-Fox, color, 102 mins.
W: Peter Weller (*Buckaroo Banzai*), Ellen Barkin (*Penny Priddy*), John Lithgow
    (*Dr. Emilio Lizardo*), Jeff Goldblum (*New Jersey*), Christopher Lloyd (*John
    Bigboote*), Lewis Smith (*Perfect Tommy*), Rosalind Cash, Robert Ito, Pepe
    Serna, Ronald Lacey, Matt Clark, Clancy Brown, William Traylor, Read
    Morgan, Dan Hedaya
D: W.D. Richter   **SCR:** Earl Mac Rauch   **PHOTOG:** Fred J. Koenekamp
    MUSIC: Michael Boddicker
Uneven SF-satire: Hero-scientist uncovers invasion of invisible aliens

Adventures of Captain Fabian
1951, (USA), Rep, b&w, 100 mins.
W: Errol Flynn, Micheline Presle, Vincent Price, Victor Francen, Agnes
    Moorehead, Howard Vernon, Reggie Nalder
P & D: William Marshall   **SCR:** Errol Flynn
Standard adventure-thriller: Sea captain in New Orleans rescues vengeful Creole servant girl

The Adventures of Captain Marvel
1966, (USA), Rep, b&w, 100 mins.
W: Tom Tyler (*Capt. Marvel*), Frank Coghlan Jr. (*Billy Batson*)
D: William Witney & John English   **SCR:** Ronald Davidson, Norman S. Hall,
    Arch B. Heath, Joseph Poland & Sol Shor
A.k.a. The Return of Captain Marvel
*Classic SF-fantasy (feature culled from 1941 serial): Superhero opposes villain who seeks
    magical lenses*

The Adventures of Captain Zoom in Outer Space
1995, (USA), Tony Dow, color
W: Daniel Riordan, Ron Perlman, Liz Vassey, Duane Davis, Gregory Smith
D: Max Tash   **PHOTOG:** Jan Kiessler   **MUSIC:** Shirley Walker
Standard juvenile SF-adventure: Tempermental TV hero transported to far planet

Adventures of Casanova
1948, (USA), Eagle Lion, b&w, 83 mins.
W: Arturo de Cordova, Lucille Bremer, Turhan Bey, John Sutton
D: Roberto Gavaldon
Standard adventure-romance

The Adventures of Dick Turpin—A Deadly Foe, A Pack of Hounds, and some Merry Monks
1912, (GB), B&C/MP, b&w, 1,198 ft. (365.1m)
W: Percy Moran (*Dick Turpin*), Harry Missouri (*Peters*)
D: Charles Raymond   **STORY:** Harold Brett
Standard adventure-thriller: Highwayman poses as monk

The Adventures of Dick Turpin—The Gunpowder Plot
1912, (GB), B&C/MP, b&w, 1,133 ft. (345.3m)
W: Percy Moran (*Dick Turpin*), Douglas Payne (*George II*), George Foley (*Sir Robert
    Walpole*), Jack Houghton (*Sir Hugh Melville*), W. Gladstone Haley, Olympia
    Sumner, Harold Brett, Herbert Trumper
D: Charles Raymond   **STORY:** Harold Brett
Standard adventure-thriller: Highwayman saves king from assassination

The Adventures of Dick Turpin—The King of Highwaymen
1912, (GB), B&C/MP, b&w, 1,132 ft. (345m)
W: Percy Moran (*Dick Turpin*), Frank Pollard (*Tom King*), Bert Murray (*Blueskin*),
    Madge Thorpe (*Moonlight Nell*), Raymond Cox (*O'Phelyn*), Ernest A.
    Trimingham (*Beetles*), Harry Missouri (*Peters*), Herbert Trumper (*Ridgeway*),
    Harold Houghton (*Hitchen*)
D: Charles Raymond   **STORY:** Harold Brett
Standard adventure-thriller: Countryman steals cow, turns highwayman

The Adventures of Dick Turpin—200 Guineas Reward, Dead or Alive
1912, (GB), B&C/MP, b&w, 1,147 ft. (349.6m)
W: Percy Moran (*Dick Turpin*), Harry Paulo (*Constable Puffin*), Tom Shelford (*Sir
    Mortimer Biggott*), Mabel Clarke (*Lady Dennis*), Dorothy Foster (*Lady Dennis'
    Daughter*), Frank Pollard (*Tom King*), Bert Murray (*Blueskin*), Raymond Cox
    (*O'Phelyn*), Ernest A. Trimingham (*Beetles*), Harry Missouri (*Peters*)
D: Charles Raymond   **STORY:** Harold Brett
Standard adventure-thriller: Highwayman eludes justice

The Adventures of Don Juan
1949, (USA), WB, color, 110 mins.
<u>W</u>: Errol Flynn (*Don Juan*), Viveca Lindfors (*Queen Margaret*), Romney Brent (*Phillip*), Robert Douglas (*Duke de Lorca*), Alan Hale, Jerry Austin, Robert Warwick, Douglas Kennedy, Raymond Burr, Una O'Connor, Aubrey Mather
<u>P</u>: Jerry Wald   <u>D</u>: Vincent Sherman   <u>SCR</u>: George Oppenheimer & Harry Kurnitz   <u>PHOTOG</u>: Elwood Bredell   <u>MUSIC</u>: Max Steiner
*GB retitle, **The New Adventures of Don Juan***
Standard adventure-thriller: Rogue seeks beauty's love

The Adventures of Don Quixote
see Les Aventures de Don Quichotte

The Adventures of Galgameth
1996, (USA), Walt Disney, color, 100 mins.
<u>W</u>: Devin Oatway, Stephen Macht, Johna Stewart, Time Winters, Tom Dugan, Ken Thorley, Richard Horvitz, Brendan O'Brien, Lou Wagner
<u>D</u>: Sean McNamara   <u>STORY</u>: Simon Sheen   <u>PHOTOG</u>: Christian Sebaldt   <u>MUSIC</u>: Richard Marvin
Juvenile action-fantasy: Prince teams with magical creature, opposes usurper

The Adventures of Hajji Baba
1954, (USA), 20th-Fox, color, 94 mins.
<u>W</u>: John Derek (*Hajji Baba*), Elaine Stewart (*Fawzia*), Thomas Gomez (*Osman Aga*), Amanda Blake (*Banah*), Donald Randolph (*The Caliph*), Paul Picerni (*Nur-El-Din*), Rosemarie Bowe (*Ayesha*), Melinda Markey (*Touareg*), Peter Mamakos (*The Executioner*), Kurt Katch (*Caoush*), Robert Bice (*Musa*), Carl Milletaire (*The Captain*), Robert Bice (*Musa*), Leo Mostovoy, Joann Arnold, Veronika Pataky, Linda Danson, Laurette Luez, Eugenia Paul, Barbara James
<u>P</u>: Walter Wanger   <u>D</u>: Don Weis   <u>SCR</u>: Richard Collins, based on James Morier's novel *The Adventures of Hajji Baba of Ispahan*   <u>PHOTOG</u>: Harold Lipstein   <u>MUSIC</u>: Dimitri Tiomkin
Standard adventure-fantasy: Daring barber rescues Caliph's daughter

The Adventures of Hal 5
1958, (GB), Bushey, b&w, 59 mins.
<u>W</u>: Peter Godsell (*Charles*), William Russell (*The Vicar*), John Glyn-Jones (*Mr. Goorlie*), Janina Faye (*Moira*), David Morrell (*Dicey*), John Charlesworth (*Ralph*), Edwin Richfield (*Cooper*)
<u>P</u>: Gilbert Church   <u>D & SCR</u>: Don Sharp, from Henry Donald's novel *Hal 5 and the Haywards*
Minor fantasy: Endearing auto has mind of it's own

The Adventures of Hercules
1985, (USA-It), Cannon, color, 88 mins.
<u>W</u>: Lou Ferrigno (*Hercules*), Milly Carlucci (*Urania*), William Berger (*King Minos*), Sonia Viviani (*Glaucia*), Carlotta Green (*Athena*), Claudio Cassinelli (*Zeus*), Nando Poggi (*Poseidon*), Maria Rosario Omaggio (*Hera*), Venantino Venantini (*The High Priest*), Laura Lenzi (*Flora*), Margi Newton (*Aphrodite*), Raf Baldassarre (*Atreus*), Cindy Leadbetter (*Ilia*), Serena Grandi (*Euryale*), Eva Robbins (*Dedalos*), Sandra Venturini (*Teti*), Andrea Nicole (*The 1st Amazon*), Alessandra Canale (*Deianira*), Pamela Prati (*Aracne*), Cristina Basili (*The Little People*)
<u>WRIT & D</u>: Lewis Coates   <u>PHOTOG</u>: Alberto Spagnoli   <u>SPCL-FX</u>: Giovanni Corridori   <u>MUSIC</u>: Pino Donaggio
*A.k.a. **Hercules II***
Minor myth-fantasy: Demigod quells Olympian rebellion

The Adventures of Ichabod and Mr. Toad
1949, (USA), Walt Disney, color, 68 mins.
<u>VOICES</u>: Bing Crosby, Basil Rathbone, Eric Blore, Claude Allister, Pat O'Malley, John Ployardt, Colin Campbell
<u>D</u>: Jack Kinney, Clyde Geronimi & James Algar   <u>MUSIC DIR</u>: Oliver Wallace
2-part animated feature: Washington Irving's "The Legend of Sleepy Hollow" & Kenneth Grahame's "Willows"

Adventures of Kitty O'Day
1945, (USA), Mono, b&w, 62 mins.
<u>W</u>: Jean Parker, Peter Cookson
*Standard thriller. cf. **Detective Kitty O'Day***

The Adventures of Lieutenant Darning, RN, in a South American Port
1911, (GB), B&C/Cosmo, b&w, 760 ft. (231.6m)
<u>W</u>: Clifford Marle (*Lt. Daring*), Dorothy Foster (*The Girl*), Fred Paul (*The Villain*)
<u>D</u>: Dave Aylott   <u>STORY</u>: Harold Brett
Standard crime-thriller: Lieutenant rescues kidnapped girl, escapes torture

The Adventures of Mandrin
1960, (It), color
<u>W</u>: Raf Vallone, Silvana Pampanini
*A.k.a. **Captain Adventure***
Standard action-adventure: Champion leads revolt against oppressive Spanish dukedom

The Adventures of Mowgli
1996, (USA), color, 90 mins.
<u>W</u>: Charlton Heston, Sam Elliott, Dana Delany, Ian Corlett
from stories by Rudyard Kipling
Made-for-Video, standard adventure-thriller: Jungle boy vs. sinister tiger

The Adventures of Nick Carter
1972, (USA), Univ/ABC-TV, color, 73 mins.
<u>W</u>: Robert Conrad (*Nick Carter*), Shelley Winters, Broderick Crawford, Dean Stockwell, Pat O'Brien, Neville Brand, Pernell Roberts, Sean Garrison, Brooke Bundy, Laraine Stephens, Jaye P. Morgan, Joseph P. Marcos, Ned Glass, Paul Mantee, Arlene Martell, Leon Lontoc, Larry Watson, William Benedict, Sorrell Booke
<u>D</u>: Paul Krasny   <u>TELEPLAY</u>: Ken Bettus, from characters created by John R. Coryell
TVM, minor thriller: Sleuth seeks playboy's missing wife

The Adventures of PC Sharpe
1911, (GB), Cricks & Martin, b&w, 830 ft. (253m)
<u>D</u>: A.E. Coleby
Standard crime-thriller: Disguised policeman trails girl counterfeiter

The Adventures of PC Sharpe—The Stolen Child
1911, (GB), Cricks & Martin, b&w, 930 ft. (283.5m)
<u>D</u>: A.E. Coleby
Standard crime-thriller: Constable trails crooked governess

The Adventures of Pinocchio
1978, (USA), G.G. Communications, color
<u>D</u>: Jesse Vogel   <u>SCR</u>: Albert D'Angelo, from a story by Carlo Collodi   <u>PHOTOG</u>: Ralph Cenci   <u>MUSIC</u>: Victor Thomas
Standard fantasy: Marionette roams free

The Adventures of Pinocchio
1996, (USA), Savoy/New Line, color, 90 mins.
<u>W</u>: Martin Landau (*Gepetto*), Jonathan Taylor Thomas (*Pinocchio*),Rob Schneider (*Volpe*), Udo Keir (*Lorenzini*), David Doyle (*Voice of Pepe the Cricket*), Bebe Neuwirth (*Felinet*), Genevieve Bujold (*Leona*), Corey Carrier (*Lampwick*)
<u>D</u>: Steve Barron   <u>SCR</u>: Sherry Mills, Steve Barron, Tom Benedek & Barry Berman, from Carlo Collodi's 1883 classic *Pinocchio*   <u>PHOTOG</u>: Juan Ruiz-Anchia   <u>MUSIC</u>: Rachel Portman
Standard juvenile fantasy (with dark overtones): Woodcarver creates living marionette

The Adventures of Robin Hood
1938, (USA), WB, color, 102 mins.
<u>W</u>: Errol Flynn (*Robin Hood*), Olivia de Havilland (*Maid Marian*), Basil Rathbone (*Sir Guy of Gisbourne*), Claude Rains (*Prince John*), Eugene Pallette (*Friar Tuck*), Alan Hale (*Little John*), Melville Cooper (*The High Sheriff of Nottingham*), Herbert Mundin (*Much, the Miller's Son*), Una O'Connor (*Bess*), Montagu Love (*The Bishop of Black Canon*), Robert Warwick (*Sir Geoffrey*), Ian Hunter (*King Richard*), Howard Hill (*The Captain of Archers*), Patric Knowles (*Will Scarlett*), Harry Cording (*Dicken Malbott*), Robert Noble (*Sir Ralfe*), Kenneth Hunter (*Sir Mortimer*), Ivan F. Simpson (*The Proprietor of Kent Road Tavern*), Leonard Willey (*Sir Essex*), Lester Mathews (*Sir Ivor*), Colin Kenny (*Sir Baldwin*), Charles McNaughton (*Crippen*), Lionel Belmore (*Humility Prin, the Tavern Keeper*), Janet Shaw (*Humility's Daughter*), Austin Fairman (*Sir Nigel*), Crauford Kent (*Sir Norbert*), Hal Brazeale (*The High Sheriff's Squire*), Marten Lamont (*Sir Guy's Squire*), Joe North (*The Friar*), Leonard Mudie (*The Town Crier*), Herbert Evans (*The Senechal*), Thomas R. Mills (*The Priest*), George Bunny (*The Butcher*), Dave Thursby (*The Archer*), Jack Richardson (*The Serf*), Claude Wisberg (*The Blacksmith*), Bob St. Angelo (*Pierre de Caan*), Lowden Adams (*The Old Crusader*), Holmes Herbert (*The Referee*), Reginald Sheffield (*The Herald*), D'Arcy Corrigan (*The Villager*), Val Stanton, Ernie Stanton, Olaf Hytten, Peter Hobbes, Alec Hartford, Edward Dew, Sidney Baron, John Sutton, Paul Power, Ivor Henderson, Jack Deery, Denis d'Auburn, Cyril Thornton, Gerald Rogers, Charles Irwin, Connie Leon, Phyllis Coghlan, Frank Hagney, James Baker
<u>P</u>: Hal Wallis   <u>D</u>: Michael Curtiz   <u>SCR</u>: Norman Reilly Raine & Seton I. Miller   <u>PHOTOG</u>: Sol Polito & Tony Gaudio   <u>OSCAR-WINNING MUSIC SCORE</u>: Erich Wolfgang Korngold
Classic adventure: Forest outlaw battles oppression

The Adventures of Robinson Crusoe (1902)
see Les Aventures de Robinson Crusoe

The Adventures of Robinson Crusoe
1952, (Mex), Tepeyac/UA, color, 85 mins.
<u>W</u>: Dan O'Herlihy (*Robinson Crusoe*), James Fernandez (*Friday*), Felipe De Alba (*Capt. Oberzo*), Chel Lopez (*The Bos'n*), Jose Chavez, Emilio Garibay
<u>D</u>: Luis Bunuel   <u>ADAPT</u>: Phillip Roll & Luis Bunuel, from Daniel Defoe's novel   <u>PHOTOG</u>: Alex Phillips   <u>MUSIC</u>: Anthony Collins
Standard adventure-melodrama: Marooned man copes

The Adventures of Sherlock Holmes
1905, (USA), Vitagraph, b&w
<u>D</u>: J. Stewart Blackton, from Sir Arthur Conan Doyle's short stories
Standard thriller: Famed sleuth faces challenges

The Adventures of Sherlock Holmes
1939, (USA), 20th-Fox, b&w, 83 mins.
<u>W</u>: Basil Rathbone (*Sherlock Holmes*), Nigel Bruce (*Dr. John Watson*), George Zucco (*Prof. Moriarty*), Ida Lupino (*Ann*), Mary Forbes (*Mrs. Hudson*), Alan Marshal, Terry Kilburn, E.E. Clive, Henry Stephenson
<u>D</u>: Alfred Werker   <u>SCR</u>: Edwin Blum & William Drake, from Sir Arthur Conan Doyle's short stories   <u>PHOTOG</u>: Leon Shamroy   <u>MUSIC</u>: Cyril Mockridge

GB retitle, Sherlock Holmes
Modest mystery-thriller: Sleuth foils plot to steal England's Crown Jewels

The Adventures of Sherlock Holmes' Smarter Brother
1976, (USA), 20th-Fox, color
W: Gene Wilder, Madeline Kahn, Marty Feldman, Leo McKern, Douglas Wilmer, Thorley Walters, Dom DeLuise, Roy Kinnear
P: Richard A. Roth D & SCR: Gene Wilder
Modest comedy-thriller: Detective aids music-hall entertainer

The Adventures of the American Rabbit
1986, (USA), color, 85 mins.
VOICES: Bob Arbogast, Pat Freley
Standard animated fantasy: Mild-mannered bunny vs. evil forces

The Adventures of the Great Mouse Detective
see *The Great Mouse Detective*

Adventures of the Queen
1975, (USA), color
W: Robert Stack, Ralph Bellamy, David Hedison, Bradford Dillman, Russell Johnson, Sorrell Booke
P: Irwin Allen D: David Lowell Rich TELEPLAY: John Gay
TVM, standard thriller: Sabotage threatens luxury liner

The Adventures of Ulysses
1969, (It), Franco Rossi/CBS-TV, color
D: Mario Bava, et al., based on Homer's *Odyssey*
Standard myth-adventure, feature culled from 8-part Italian mini-series: Hero battles mortals and monsters

The Adventures of William Tell
1898, (Fr), Star, b&w, 20m (65.6 ft./1.1 mins.)
WRIT, P & D: Georges Melies
Action short: Tale of Swiss hero

Adventures of Willie Woodbine and Lightning Larry—A Joyride to the Cannibal Islands
1915, (GB), New Agency, b&w, 700 ft. (213.4m)
WRIT & D: Sidney Aldridge
Minor fantasy: Tramps use magic to visit cannibal isles

The Adventures of Young Robin Hood
1983, (GB), color
W: Peter Demin (*Robin Hood*), Amanda Jones (*Maid Marian*)
Minor action-adventure, feature culled from British teleseries "Unbroken Arrow:" Outlaw hero matches wits with King Richard's enemies

An Adventuress Outwitted
1912, (GB), Clarendon, b&w, 715 ft. (217.9m)
D: Wilfred Noy
Standard crime-thriller: Woman spy foiled by officer's young brother

The Adventurous Blonde
1937, (USA), First Nat'l, b&w, 61 mins.
W: Glenda Farrell (*Torchy Blane*), Barton MacLane (*Steve McBride*), Anne Nagel (*Grace Brown*), Tom Kennedy (*Gahagan*), George E. Stone (*Pete*), Natalie Moorehead (*Theresa Gray*), William Hopper (*Matt*), Anderson Lawlor (*Hugo Brand*), Charles Foy (*Dud*), Bobby Watson (*Mugsy*), Charles Wilson (*Mortimer Gray*), Virginia Brissac (*Mrs. Hammond*), Leland Hodgson (*Harvey Hammond*), Frank Shannon (*Capt. McTavish*), Raymond Hatton (*Maxie*), James Conlin (*Dr. Bolger*), Granville Owen (*Dr. Nolly*), Walter Young (*The Lawyer*), George Guhl (*The Desk Sergeant*), Al Herman (*Herman*)
D: Frank MacDonald SCR: Robertson White & David Diamond, from characters created by Frederick Nebel PHOTOG: Arthur Todd
A.k.a. Torchy Blane, the Adventurous Blonde
3rd "Torchy Blane" mystery-thriller: Girl reporter investigates puzzling murder

Adventurous Voyage of 'The Arctic'
1903, (GB), R.W. Paul, b&w, 600 ft. (182.9m)
W: Fred Farren (*Capt. Kettle*) D: Walter R. Booth
Standard fantasy short (in 12 scenes): Amazing discoveries at South Pole

Aelita
1924, (Russ), Mezhrabpom-Russ, b&w, 6,040 ft. (1841m),113 mins.
W: Igor Ilinsky, Yulia Solntseva, Nikolai Tseretelly, Valentina Kuinzhi, Yuri Zavadsky, V. Orlova, Nikolai Batalov, Konstantin Eggert
D: Jacob Protazanov SCR: Fyodor Otzep & Alexei Falko, from Alexei Tolstoy's novel PHOTOG: E. Schonemann & Yuri Zheliabuzhky
SF classic: Problems in robotic civilization on Mars

The Aerial Anarchists
1911, (GB), Kineto, partially tinted, 700 ft. (213.4m)
D: Walter R. Booth
Standard SF: Futuristic mayhem in skies. cf. Master of the World *and* The Airship Destroyer

The Aerial Submarine
1910, (GB), Kineto, b&w, 750 ft. (228.6m)
D: Walter R. Booth
reissued 1915
Standard adventure-fantasy: Flying pirates terrorize

Aerial Torpedo
see *The Airship Destroyer*

Aerial Warfare
see *The Airship Destroyer*

Aesop
see *Esop*

The Affair at No. 26
1915, (GB), British Oak, b&w, 1,070 ft. (326.1m)
D: Ernest G. Batley
Standard crime-thriller: Man kills wrong woman, frames his brother

An Affair of Honour
1904, (GB), Gaumont, b&w, 250 ft. (76.2m)
W: Percy Murray
D: Alf Collins SCR: Percival H.T. Sykes
Minor crime-thriller: 18th-century gambler kills daughter's suitor in duel

An Affair of State
1966, (W. Ger), color, 95 mins.
W: Curt Jurgens, Lilli Palmer
Minor spoof of "James Bond" genre: Spy shenanigans

Affairs of Messalina
1954, (It), Col, b&w, 106 mins.
W: Maria Felix, Georges Marchal
Standard melodrama: Wicked empress plots intrigue

Affair with a Stranger
1953, (USA), RKO, b&w, 87 mins.
W: Victor Mature, Jean Simmons
Standard romantic drama

Afraid of the Dark
1992, (GB), Fine Line Features, color, 92 mins.
W: James Fox (*Frank*), Fanny Ardant (*Miriam*), Paul McGann (*Tony Dalton*), Clare Holman (*Rose*), Robert Stephens (*Dan Burns*), Susan Woolridge (*Lucy Trent*), Ben Keyworth (*Lucas*), David Thewlis
D: Mark Peploe SCR: Mark Peploe & Frederick Seidel PHOTOG: Bruno de Keyzer MUSIC: Jason Osborn
Unusual thriller: Slasher menaces blind women

African Manhunt
1955, (USA), Rep, b&w, 65 mins.
W: Myron Healey, Karin Booth
Minor adventure-thriller

African Treasure
1952, (USA), Mono, b&w, 70 mins.
W: Johnny Sheffield, Laurette Luez, Leonard Mudie, Lyle Talbot, Lane Bradford, Arthur Space, Martin Garralaga, James Adamson, Robert Whitfield, Jack Williams, Woody Strode
WRIT & D: Ford Beebe, from characters created by Roy Rockwood
blurb: "Jungle drums echo the dangers of ruthless fortune seekers!"
Standard "Bomba, the Jungle Boy" adventure: Jungle riches lure unsavory types

Africa Screams
1949, (USA), Huntington Hartford/Nassour/UA, b&w, 80 mins.
W: Bud Abbott (*Buzz*), Lou Costello (*Stanley*), Hillary Brooke (*Diana*), Frank Buck, Clyde Beatty, Buddy Baer, Max Baer, Joe Besser, Shemp Howard, Burton Wenland
D: Charles T. Barton STORY & SCR: Earl Baldwin PHOTOG: Charles Van Enger SPCL-FX: Carl Lee MUSIC: Walter Schumann
Juvenile comedy-adventure: Safari seeks fortune in diamonds

After Dark
1932, (GB), Fox British, b&w, 45 mins.
W: Horace Hodges (*Thaddeus C. Brompton*), Grethe Hansen (*Alva Lea*), Hugh Williams (*Richard Morton*), George Barraud (*George Harvey*), Ian Fleming (*Henry Lea*), Henry Oscar (*Higgins*), Pollie Emery (*Mrs. Thirkettle*), Lucille Lisle (*Vivienne Roberts*)
D: Albert Parker SCR: John Barrow, from a play by J. Jefferson Farjeon
Standard comedy-thriller: Crooks seek stolen emeralds

After Dark, My Sweet
1990, (USA), color, 111 mins.
W: Jason Patric, Rachel Ward, Bruce Dern, George Dickerson, James Cotton, Rocky Giordani, Corey Carrier
D: James Foley SCR: Robert Redlin & James Foley STORY: Jim Thompson MUSIC: Maurice Jarre
Unusual thriller: Drifter involved in kidnapping

After Jenny Died
see **Revenge** *(1971, GB)*

Aftermath
1985, (USA), color, 96 mins.
W: Steve Barkett, Larry Latham, Lynne Margulies, Sid Haig, Forrest J. Ackerman
D: Ted V. Mikels
Minor SF-thriller: Astronauts return to Earth, find world ravaged by nuclear war

After Midnight
1989, (USA), Made-for-Video, color, 95 mins.
W: Jillian McWhirter (*Allison*), Pamela Segall (*Cheryl*), Ramy Zade, Nadine Van Der Velde, Marc McClure, Billy Ray Sharkey, Marg Helgenberger, Alan Rosenberg
D: Ken & Jim Wheat
Minor thriller: Ghost stories become reality for coeds

After Midnight with Boston Blackie
1943, (USA), Col, b&w, 64 mins.
W: Chester Morris (*Boston Blackie*), Ann Savage (*Betty Barnaby*), Richard Lane (*Insp. Farraday*), George E. Stone (*Runt*), George McKay (*Marty Beck*), Cy Kendall (*Joe Herschel*), Al Hill (*Sammy Walsh*), Walter Sande (*Det. Matthews*), Walter Baldwin (*Diamond Ed Barnaby*), Jan Buckingham (*Dixie Rose Blossom*), Don Barclay (*The Cigar Clerk*), Lloyd Corrigan (*Arthur Manleder*), Dick Elliott (*The Justice of the Peace*), John Harmon (*The Fence*)
D: Lew Landers   SCR: Howard J. Green & Aubrey Wisberg, from characters created by Jack Boyle   PHOTOG: L.W. O'Connell   MUSIC: Morris Stoloff
Minor thriller: Sleuth helps girl retrieve stolen jewels

After Pilkington
1988, (GB), BBC-TV, color, 100 mins.
W: Bob Peck, Miranda Richardson, Barry Foster
D: Christopher Morahan
TVM, standard thriller: Oxford professor searches for missing archeologist

Aftershock
1988, (USA), color, 90 mins.
W: Jay Roberts Jr., Elizabeth Kaitan, Chris Mitchum, John Saxon, Richard Lynch, Russ Tamblyn, Michael Berryman, Chris De Rose, Chuck Jeffreys
D: Frank Harris
Minor SF-thriller: Mysterious stranger and beautiful alien oppose evil government

After the Fall of New York
1985, (It-Fr), color, 95 mins.
W: Michael Sopkiw (*Parsifal*), Valentine Monnier (*Giaiada*), Anna Kanakis, Roman Geer, Edmund Purdom, George Eastman
D: Martin Dolman
Minor SF-adventure: Post-nuke mission to save humankind

After the Thin Man
1936, (USA), MGM, b&w, 110 mins.
W: William Powell (*Nick Charles*), Myrna Loy (*Nora Charles*), Elissa Landi (*Salma Landis*), Joseph Calleia (*Dancer*), James Stewart (*David Graham*), Jessie Ralph (*Aunt Katherine Forrest*), Alan Marshal (*Robert Landis*), Sam Levene (*Lt. Abrams*), Dorothy McNulty later Penny Singleton(*Polly Byrnes*), Dorothy Vaughan (*Charlotte*), Teddy Hart (*Floyd Casper*), Maude Turner Gordon (*Helen*), William Law (*Lum Kee*), William Burress (*Lucius*), Thomas Pogue (*William*), George Zucco (*Dr. Adolph Kammer*), Tom Ricketts (*The Butler*), Paul Fix (*Phil Byrnes*), Joe Caits (*Joe*), Joe Phillips (*Willie*), Edith Kingdon (*Hattie*), John T. Murray (*Jerry*), John Kelly (*Harold*), Zeffie Tilbury (*Aunt Lucy*), Alice H. Smith (*Emily*), Mary Gordon (*Rose*), George Taylor (*Eddie*), Harlan Briggs (*Burton Forrest*), Murray Alper (*The Kid*), Richard Loo (*The Headwaiter*), Vince Barnett (*The Wrestling Manager*), Harry Tyler (*Fingers*), Bobby Watson, Clarence Kolb, George Guhl, Guy Usher, Jack Norton, Dick Rush, Eric Wilton
D: W.S. Van Dyke   SCR: Frances Goodrich & Albert Hackett, from a novel by Dashiell Hammett   PHOTOG: Oliver T. Marsh   MUSIC: Herbert Stothart & Edward Ward
2nd "Nick & Nora Charles" mystery-thriller: Weapons manufacturer fears for his life, calls in urbane sleuth

Against All Odds
see **The Blood of Fu Manchu**

Agatha
1979, (GB), Sweetwall-Casablanca Filmworks/First Artists/WB, color, 98 mins.
W: Vanessa Redgrave (*Agatha Christie*), Dustin Hoffman (*Wally Stanton*), Timothy Dalton (*Archibald Christie*), Celia Gregory (*Nancy Neele*), Helen Morse (*Evelyn*), Paul Brooke (*John Foster*), Carolyn Pickles (*Charlotte Fisher*), Timothy West (*Ken Ward*), Tony Britton (*William Collins*), Alan Badel (*Lord Brackenbury*), Robert Longden (*Pettelson*), Donald Nithsdale (*Uncle Jones*), Yvonne Gilan (*Mrs. Braithwaite*), Sandra Voe (*The Therapist*), Barry Hart (*Supt. MacDonald*), David Hargreaves (*Sgt. Jarvis*), Tim Seely (*Capt. Rankin*), Jill Summers (*Nancy's Aunt*), Chris Fairbank (*Luland*), Liz Smith (*Flora*), Peter Arne (*The Hotel Manager*), D. Geoff Tomlinson (*The Hotel Receptionist*), John Joyce (*The Hotel Waiter*), Irene Sutcliffe (*The Dress Shop Manageress*), Ann Francis (*Jane*), John Ludlow, Ray Gatenby, Hope Johnstone, Hubert Rees, Tommy Hunter, Pamela Austin, Bert Ward, Harry Segal, Howard Blake, Jim Archer, Reginald Kilbey
P: Jarvis Astaire & Gavrik Losey   D: Michael Apted   SCR: Kathleen Tynan & Arthur Hopcraft   STORY: Kathleen Tynan   PHOTOG: Vittorio Storaro   MUSIC: Johnny Mandel   SONG: *Close Enough for Love* (lyric by Paul Williams, sung by Pattie Brooks)
Unusual thriller: Fictional reconstruction of Agatha Christie's actual 1926 disappearance

L'Age d'Or (The Golden Age)
1930, (Sp), b&w, 62 mins.
W: Max Ernst (*The Bandit Chief*), Marie Berthe Ernst, Lya Lys (*The Woman*), Gaston Modot (*The Man*), Pierre Prevert (*The Bandit*), Madame Noizet, Lionel Salem, Caridad de Laberdesque, Ibanez, Roland Penrose, Paul Eduard, Jacques Brunius, Jose Artigas
WRIT & D: Luis Bunuel   PHOTOG: Albert Duverger   MUSIC: Georges Van Parys
Bizarre classic: Fantasy meets eroticism

Agency
1981, (Can), color, 94 mins.
W: Robert Mitchum, Lee Majors, Valerie Perrine, Alexandra Stewart, Saul Rubinek, Anthony Parr
D: George Kaczender   MUSIC: Lewis Furey
A.k.a. **Mind Games**
Minor thriller: Sinister political group puts subliminal messages into commercials.

Agent 8 3/4
see **Hot Enough for June**

Agent for H.A.R.M.
1965, (USA), Univ, color, 84 mins.
W: Mark Richman, Wendell Corey, Barbara Bouchet, Carl Esmond Martin Kosleck, Wendell Quarry, Donna Michelle, Rafael Campos, Aliza Gur, Robert Christopher
P: Joseph F. Robertson   D: Gerd Oswald   SCR: Blair Robertson   PHOTOG: James Crabe   MUSIC: Gene Kauer
orig. to be titled **The H.A.R.M. Machine**
Minor SF-thriller: Foreign spies seek life-destroying organism from outer space

Agent of Doom
1959, (Fr), color
W: Annette Stroyberg [later Annette Vadim], Jean Servais, Pierre Brasseur, Michel le Royer
Routine spy-tale: Scientist recovers from accident, finds himself in house of strange happenings

Agent 383/Passport to Hell
1964, (It), color, 101 mins.
W: George Ardisson, Georges Riviere
Minor spy-thriller: Secret agent pursues "Black Scorpion"

Agent 255/Desperate Mission
1964, (Jap), color, 112 mins.
W: Jerry Cobb, Yoko Tani
Minor spy-thriller: American agent seeks nuclear physicist in Hong Kong

The Age of Gold
see **L'Age d'Or**

Agi Murad, Il Diavolo Blanco (Agi Murad, The White Devil)
1958, (It), WB, color, 98 mins.
W: Steve Reeves
D: Riccardo Freda   PHOTOG: Mario Bava, from Leo Tolstoy's novel
USA retitle (1961), **The White Warrior**
Standard action-adventure: Conflict on Russian steppes

A-Haunting We Will Go
1942, (USA), 20th-Fox, b&w, 68 mins.
W: Stan Laurel, Oliver Hardy, Dante the Magician, Sheila Ryan, Henry [Harry] Morgan, Willie Best, Ed Gargan, John Shelton, Elisha Cook Jr.
D: Alfred Werker   SCR: Lou Breslow   PHOTOG: Glen Macdonald
Standard comedy-thriller: Two innocents accompany coffin on train trip

L'Aigle a Deux Tetes (The Eagle Has Two Heads)
1947, (Fr), b&w, 93 mins.
W: Jean Marais, Edwige Feuillere
WRIT & D: Jean Cocteau   PHOTOG: Christian Matras   MUSIC: Georges Auric
Avant-garde classic: Artistic fantasies

Aimez-Vous Les Femmes? (Do You Like Women?)
1964, (It-Fr), Les Films Number One/Productions/Cinematografica Federiz S.p.A./ComacicoFrancoriz, b&w
W: Sophie Daumier, Guy Bedos, Edwige Feuillere, Gerard Sety, Gregoire Aslan, Guido Alberti, Maria Rosa Rodriguez, Gordon Felio, Graziella Granata, Leo Baron, Roger Blin, Marc Eyraud, Jacques Rispal, Georges Adet, Roger Trapp, Colette Castel, Philippe Castelli, Fernand Berset, Raoul Delfosse, Ernest Menzer, Willy Braque, Andre Katelbach
P: Pierre Kalfon   D: Jean Leon   SCR: Roman Polanski, from a story by George Bardawil (*Gallimard*)   ADAPT: Jean Leon   PHOTOG: Sacha Vierny   MUSIC: Ward Swingle
Odd "black comedy": Men's club promotes cannibalism

The Airman's Children
1915, (GB), Neptune/Browne, b&w, 1,400 ft. (426.7m)
<u>W:</u> Douglas Payne   <u>D:</u> Jack Denton
Standard crime-thriller: German pilot kidnaps detective's children

The Airship Destroyer
1909, (GB), Charles Urban, b&w, 685 ft. (208.8m)
<u>D:</u> Walter Booth, based on ideas of Rudyard Kipling, Jules Verne, & H.G. Wells
*A.k.a. **Aerial Warfare** and **Battle in the Clouds***
*Semi-adaptation of Jules Verne's novel **Master of the World**: Super-ship dominates skies*
*cf. **The Aerial Anarchists***

The Airship, or 100 Years Hence
1908, (USA), Vitaphone, b&w
<u>P & D:</u> J. Stuart Blackton
Standard SF short: Glimpse at 2008, when machines rule the skies

The Airtight Safe
1910, (GB), Cricks & Martin, b&w, 825 ft. (252.5m)
<u>D:</u> A.E. Coleby
Standard thriller: Old man sees young wife's lover hide in safe, locks him in

Akira
1989, (Jap), color
<u>VOICES:</u> Mitsuo Iwara, Nozomu Sasaki
Standard animated SF-fantasy: Youth discovers he has telepathic powers

Alabama's Ghost
1972, (USA), Bremson Int'l, color, 96 mins.
<u>W:</u> Christopher Brooks, E. Kerrigan Scott
<u>WRIT, P & D:</u> Fredric Hobbs
blurb: "A super hip horror movie"
Minor horror-fantasy: Vampire rock group on motorcycles

A la Conquete du Pole (At the Conquest of the Pole)
1912, (Fr), Star, b&w, 650m (2,112 ft./30.3 mins.)
<u>D:</u> Georges Melies
USA retitle, **Conquest of the Pole**
Fantasy short: Expedition reaches North Pole

Aladdin
1915, (GB), Piccadilly/Browne, b&w, 1,280 ft. (390.1m)
<u>W:</u> Fred Evans   <u>WRIT & D:</u> Fred & Joe Evans
Standard fantasy: Chinese boy's magic lamp helps him foil evil uncle, win princess

Aladdin: BUD SPENCER AND LUCA VENANTINI

Aladdin
1987, (It), <u>Media</u> color, 100 mins.
<u>W:</u> Bud Spencer, Luca Venantini, Janet Agren, Julian Voloshin, Umberto Raho
<u>D:</u> Bruno Corbucci
*A.k.a. **Superfantagenio***
Minor fantasy: Modern youth meets genie

Aladdin
1992, (USA), Walt Disney, color, 90 mins.
<u>VOICES:</u> Scott Weinger (*Aladdin*), Robin Williams (*Genie*), Linda Larkin
(*Princess Jasmine*), Gilbert Gottfried (*Iago*), Jonathan Freeman, Frank Welker,
Brad Kane
<u>D:</u> J h M k   & R n Cl m   <u>SCR:</u> R n Clements John Musker Ted Elliot
& Terry Rossio
Well-made animated fantasy: Street urchin aided by genie

Aladdin and His Lamp
1952, (USA), Mono, color, 67 mins.
<u>W:</u> John Sands, Patricia Medina, Richard Erdman, Noreen Nash
Standard fantasy: Youth loves princess, genie assists

Aladdin and His Magic Lamp
1967, (Russ), color
Animated feature, standard fantasy: Lad meets genie

Aladdin and His Wonderful Lamp
1917, (USA), Fox, b&w
<u>W:</u> Buddy Messinger, Virginia Corbin, Gertrude Messinger, Violet Radcliffe
Standard fantasy: Genie helps youth realize dreams

Aladdin and His Wonderful Lamp
1899, (GB), G.A.S. Films, b&w, 75 ft. (22.9m)
<u>D:</u> George Albert Smith
Standard fantasy short: Genie enriches youth

Aladdin and the King of Thieves
1996, (USA-Jap), Walt Disney, Made-for-Video, color, 78 mins.
<u>VOICES:</u> Scott Weinger (*Aladdin*), Robin Williams (*Genie*), Linda Larkin
(*Jasmine*), Gilbert Gottfried (*Iago*), Val Bettin, Jim Cummings, Jerry
Orbach, John Rhys-Davies, Frank Welker, Jeff Bennett, Corey Burton, Jess
Harnell, Clyde Kusatsu, Rob Paulsen, C.C.H. Pounder
<u>D:</u> Kazuo Teroda   <u>SCR:</u> Mark McCorkle & Robert Schooley   <u>MUSIC:</u> Mark
Watters & Carl Johnson   <u>SONGS:</u> Party in Agraba, Out of Thin Air, Welcome
to the Forty Thieves, Are You In or Out & Father and Son
*Standard animated fantasy: Youth enters lair of Forty Thieves, seeks long-lost father. **cf.**
Aladdin (1992) and **The Return of Jaffar***

Aladdin in Pearlies
1912, (GB), British Anglo-American/Gerrard, b&w, 795 ft. (242.3m)
<u>W:</u> Fred Rains   <u>D:</u> Fred Rains
Minor fantasy: Magic lamp summons Mephistopheles

Aladdin: or, A Lad Out
1914, (GB), Hepworth, b&w, 925 ft. (281.9m)
<u>W:</u> Tom Powers (*The Lad*), Alma Taylor (*The Girl*)
<u>D:</u> Hay Plumb   <u>STORY:</u> Tom Powers
Minor fantasy: Art student dreams uncle's present is magic lamp

Aladdin's Lantern
1938, (USA), Hal Roach, MGM, b&w, 1 reel
<u>D:</u> Gordon Douglas
Fantasy short: Youth pursues love, riches (Hal Roach)

Alakazam the Great
1961, (Jap), AIP, color, 84 mins.
<u>VOICES:</u> Jonathan Winters, Frankie Avalon, Dodie Stevens, Arnold Stang,
Sterling Holloway
<u>SCR:</u> Lou Rusoff, Osamu Tezuka & Lee Kresel   <u>PHOTOG:</u> Komei Ishikawa &
Kenji Sugiyama   <u>MUSIC:</u> Al Simms
Animated feature, standard fantasy: Arrogant royal monkey misuses magic powers

The Alchemist
1985, (USA), Lawrence Applebaum/Empire, color, 84 mins.
<u>W:</u> Robert Ginty, Lucinda Dooline, John Sanderford, Viola Kate Stimpson
(*Esther*), Robert Glaudini (*Delgatto*), Billy Scudder, Tony Abatemarco
<u>D:</u> James Amante   <u>SCR:</u> Alan J. Adler   <u>PHOTOG:</u> Andrew W. Friend   <u>SPCL-</u>
<u>FX:</u> Doug White   <u>MUSIC:</u> Richard H. Band
Minor horror-fantasy, filmed in 1981: Demons plague immortal

The Alchemist's Hallucination
*see **L'Hallucination de l'Alchemiste***

Alcofrisbas, the Master Magician
*see **L'Enchanteur Alcofrisbas***

Alfred Packer: The Musical
1993, (USA), color
<u>W:</u> Trey Parker   <u>WRIT, D, & MUSIC:</u> Trey Parker
Unusual musical-satire: Fact-based saga of cannibalism in 1870s Colorado Rockies

Alfred Hitchcock Presents
1985, (USA), NBC-TV, color, 95 mins.
<u>W:</u> Ned Beatty, John Huston, Steven Bauer, Bianca Rose, Tippi Hedren, Annette
O'Toole, Kim Novak, Bruce Davison, Melanie Griffith, Helena Kallianiotes,
Lyman Ward, Walter Klenhard, Gail Youngs, Billy Mumy, Owen Bush, Lee
Ving, John Shearin, Tony Frank, Arthur Taxier, Richard Lineback, Jack
Thibeau, Gene Ross, Jerry Curtin, Cynthia Hartley, Danny De La Paz,
Jonathan Goldsmith, Mark L. Taylor, Kale Browne, Linda Hoy, David Held,
Gregory Levinson, Douglas Emerson, Gail Barle, Christina Lange, Gigi
Vorgan, Ross Elliott, Nancy Burnett
remakes of episodes from TV's "Alfred Hitchcock Presents" (1955-1962) and
"Alfred Hitchcock Hour" (1962-1965), with orig. intros color-enhanced by
            (1) I   S   ll   il   <u>D & TELEPLAY:</u> Joel Oliansky
from Henry Slesar's teleplay; <u>PHOTOG:</u> Mario DiLeo; <u>MUSIC:</u> John Goux

(2) *Man from the South*—**D & TELEPLAY:** Steve DeJarnatt; based on William Fay's teleplay; from a story by Roald Dahl; **PHOTOG:** Mario DiLeo; **MUSIC:** Basil Poledouris (3) *Bang! You're Dead*—**D:** Randa Haines; **TELEPLAY:** Harold Swanton & Christopher Crowe; from a story by Margery Vosper; **PHOTOG:** Mario DiLeo; **MUSIC:** Craig Safan. (4) *An Unlocked Window*—**D & TELEPLAY:** Fred Walton; based on a teleplay by James Bridges; from a story by Ethel Lina White; **PHOTOG:** Mario DiLeo; **MUSIC:** Craig Safan

TVM, 4 terror tales: (1) Traveling salesman mistaken for murderer, (2) Codger proposes bizarre wager, (3) Child obtains gun, & (4) Nurse stalked by mad strangler

Alf's Button
1920, (GB), Hepworth, b&w, 7,050 ft. (2148.8m)
W: Leslie Henson *(Alf Higgins)*, Alma Taylor *(Liz)*, Gerald Ames *(Lt. Denis Allen)*, James Carew *(Eustace the Genie)*, Eileen Dennes *(Lady Isobel Fitzpeter)*, John McAndrews *(Bill Grant)*, Gwynne Herbert *(Lady Fitzpeter)*, Jean Cadell *(The Vicar's Wife)*
D: Cecil M. Hepworth   **SCR:** Blanche McIntosh, from a play by W.A. Darlington
reissued 1921
Standard comedy-fantasy: Soldier's tunic button made from Aladdin's lamp, grants wishes

Alf's Button
1930, (GB), Gaumont, b&w & color, 96 mins.
W: Tubby Edlin *(Alf Higgins)*, Alf Goddard *(Bill Grant)*, Nora Swinburne *(Lady Isobel Fitzpeter)*, Polly Ward *(Liz)*, Gypsy Rhouma *(Lucy)*, Humberstone Wright *(Eustace)*, Annie Esmond *(Mrs. Gaskins)*, Peter Haddon *(Lt. Allen)*, Spencer Trevor *(Lord Dunwater)*, Cyril McLaglen *(The Sgt.Major)*, Bruce Winston *(Mustapha)*, The Gotham Quartette
D: W.P. Kellino   **SCR:** L'Estrange Fawcett, from a play by W.A. Darlington
Standard comedy-fantasy: Soldier discovers button made from Aladdin's lamp

Alf's Button Afloat
1938, (GB), Gainsborough/GFD, b&w, 89 mins.
W: Bud Flanagan *(Alf Higgins)*, Chesney Allen *(Ches)*, Jimmy Nervo *(Cecil)*, Teddy Knox *(Teddy)*, Charlie Naughton *(Charlie)*, Jimmy Gold *(Jimmy)*, Alastair Sim *(Eustace)*, Wally Patch *(Sgt. Hawkins)*, Peter Gawthorne *(Capt. Driscol)*, Agnes Lauchlan *(Lady Driscol)*, Glennis Lorrimer *(Frankie Driscol)*, James Carney *(Lt. John Hardy)*, Wilson Coleman *(The Doctor)*, J.H. Roberts *(Aladdin)*, Bruce Winston *(Mustapha)*, Richard Cooper *(Lord Wimbledon)*
D: Marcel Varnel   **SCR:** Marriott Edgar, Val Guest & Ralph Smart, from W.A. Darlington's play *Alf's Button*
Standard comedy-fantasy: Marine's button made from Aladdin's lamp. Reissued 1943

Alf's Button Afloat: GLENNIS LORRIMER

Alf's Carpet
1929, (GB), BIP/Wardour, b&w, 65 mins.
W: Pat *(Bill)*, Patachon *(Alf)*, Janice Adair *(Joan)*, Gerald Rawlinson *(Jimmy Donaldson)*, Gladys Hamer *(Lizzie Fletcher)*, Philip Hewland *(The Djinn)*, Edward O'Neill *(Father)*, Frank Perfitt *(The Caliph)*
D: W.P. Kellino   **SCR:** Val Valentine, Arthur Leclerq & Blanche Metcalfe, from a novel by W.A. Darlington
Standard comedy-fantasy: Busmen find magic carpet

Algol
1920, (Ger), b&w
D: Hans Werkmeister
Early SF classic: Lure of outer space

Alias Boston Blackie
1942, (USA), Col, b&w, 67 mins.
W: Chester Morris *(Boston Blackie)*, Adele Mara *(Eve Sanders)*, Richard Lane *(Insp. Farraday)*, George E. Stone *(Runt)*, Lloyd Corrigan *(Arthur Manleder)*, Walter Sande *(Det. Matthews)*, Ben Taggart *(The Warden)*, Larry Parks *(Joe Trilby)*, George McKay *(Roggi)*, Cy Kendall *(Jumbo Madigan)*, Paul Fix *(Steve Caveroni)*, Lloyd Bridges *(The Bus Driver)*, Ernie Adams *(The Doorman)*, Bud Geary *(The Cop)*, Edmund Cobb *(The Police Sgt.)*, Sidney Miller *(The Bellhop)*, Duke York *(Johnson)*
D: Lew Landers   **SCR:** Paul Yawitz, from characters created by Jack Boyle   **PHOTOG:** Philip Tanura
Minor mystery-thriller: Sleuth framed for prison escape

Alias Bulldog Drummond
see Bulldog Jack

Alias John Preston
1955, (GB), Danziger/British Lion, b&w, 71 mins.
W: Betta St. John *(Sally Sandford)*, Alexander Knox *(Dr. Walton)*, Christopher Lee *(John Preston)*, Sandra Dorne *(Maria)*, Patrick Holt *(The Stranger)*, Betty Ann Davies *(Mrs. Sandford)*, John Longden *(Mr. Sandford)*, Bill Fraser *(Joe Newton)*, John Stuart *(Dr. Underwood)*
P: Edward J. & Harry Lee Danziger   **D:** David MacDonald   **STORY:** Paul Tabori   **PHOTOG:** Jack Cox
Standard thriller: Psychiatrist finds schizophrenic's dream of murder was true

Alias Nick Beal
1949, (USA), Para, b&w, 93 mins.
W: Ray Milland, Audrey Totter, Thomas Mitchell, Fred Clark, George Macready, Darryl Hickman, King Donovan
D: John Farrow   **SCR:** Jonathan Latimer   **STORY:** Mindret Lord   **PHOTOG:** Lionel Lindon   **MUSIC:** Franz Waxman
A.k.a. The Contact Man
Unusual fantasy-thriller: Satanic gentleman retrieves woman of the streets, uses her in scheme to corrupt honest politician

Alias Sherlock Holmes
see The Return of the World's Greatest Detective

Alias the Doctor
1932, (USA), First Nat'l, b&w, 69 mins.
W: Richard Barthelmess, Boris Karloff, Norman Foster
D: Michael Curtiz
Minor thriller: Mysterious killer strikes

Alias the Lone Wolf
1927, (USA), Col, b&w, 7 reels
W: Bert Lytell *(Michael Lanyard)*, Lois Wilson *(Eve de Montalais)*, William V. Mong *(Whitaker Monk)*, Ned Sparks *(Phinuit)*, Paulette Duval *(Liane De Lorme)*, James Mason *(Popinot)*, Ann Brody *(Fifi)*, Alphonse Ethier *(Insp. Crane)*
D: Edward H. Griffith   **SCR:** Dorothy Howell & Edward H. Griffith, from a novel by Joseph Louis Vance   **PHOTOG:** J.O. Taylor
Standard thriller: Rogue encounters jewel smugglers

Ali-Baba
see Ali-Baba et Les Quarante Voleurs

Ali Baba and the Forty Thieves
1943, (USA), Univ, color, 87 mins.
W: Jon Hall, Maria Montez, Frank Puglia, Andy Devine, Turhan Bey, Yvette Dugay, Scotty Beckett, Kurt Katch, Ramsay Ames
D: Arthur Lubin   **SCR:** Edmund L. Hartmann   **PHOTOG:** George Robinson   **MUSIC:** Edward Ward
Major adventure-romance: Conflict in "Arabian Nights" kingdom. cf. The Sword of Ali Baba

Ali Baba and the Forty Thieves (1954)
see Ali-Baba et Les Quarante Voleurs

Ali Baba and the 400 Thieves
see Ali Baba et Les 400 Voleurs

Ali Baba and the Sacred Crown
1960, (It), color
W: Rod Flash *(Ilush)*, Bella Cortez
Minor adventure-thriller: Desert hero battles sinister youth and his henchmen

Ali Baba and the Seven Saracens
1963, (It), color
W: Dan Harrison, Bella Cortez, Gordon Mitchell
Minor "Arabian Nights" adventure: Hero opposes tyrant

Ali Baba et Les 400 Voleurs (Ali Baba and the 400 Thieves)
1901, (Fr), Pathe, b&w, 164 ft. (50m)

WRIT & D: Ferdinand Zecca
Standard fantasy-adventure: Turmoil in Oriental kingdom

Ali-Baba et Les Quarante Voleurs (Ali Baba and the Forty Thieves)
1954, (Fr), color, 90 mins.
W: Fernandel, Samia Gamel
D: Jacques Becker   **MUSIC:** Paul Misraki
A.k.a. Ali-Baba
Uneven "Arabian Nights" farce: Bumbler finds treasure

Ali Baba Goes to Town
1937, (USA), 20th-Fox, b&w, 81 mins.
W: Eddie Cantor, Tony Martin, June Lang, Roland Young, Gypsy Rose Lee, John
   Carradine, Lee J. Cobb
D: David Butler   **SCR:** Harry Tugend & Jack Yelten   **PHOTOG:** Ernest Palmer
Standard comedy-fantasy: Youth meets genie

Alibi
1931, (GB), Twickenham/W&F, b&w, 75 mins.
W: Austin Trevor (*Hercule Poirot*), Franklin Dyall (*Sir Roger Ackroyd*), Elizabeth
   Allan (*Ursula Browne*), J.H. Roberts (*Dr. Sheppard*), John Deverell (*Lord
   Halliford*), Mercia Swinburne (*Caryll Sheppard*), Ronald Ward (*Ralph
   Ackroyd*), Mary Jerrold (*Mrs. Ackroyd*), Harvey Braban (*Insp. Davis*)
D: Leslie Hiscott   **SCR:** H. Fowler Mear, from a play by Michael Morton &
   Agatha Christie
Standard mystery-thriller: Detective exposes faked suicide

Alibi
1942, (GB), Corona/Rep, b&w, 82 mins.
W: Margaret Lockwood (*Helene Ardouin*), Hugh Sinclair (*Insp. Calas*), James
   Mason (*Andre Laurent*), Raymond Lovell (*Prof. Winkler*), Enid Stamp-Taylor
   (*Dany*), Hartley Power (*Gordon*), Jane Carr (*Delia*), Rodney Ackland (*Kretz*),
   Edana Romney (*The Ass't*), Elizabeth Welch (*The Singer*), Olga Lindo (*Mme.
   Laureau*), Muriel George (*Mme. Bertonnet*), George Merritt (*Bourdille*), Derek
   Bloomfield
D: Brian Desmond Hurst   **SCR:** Lesley Storm, Jacques Companeez, Justine &
   Carter, from a novel by Marcel Archard   **PHOTOG:** Otto Heller   **MUSIC:**
   Jack Beaver
Reissued 1945
Standard thriller: Inspector and night-club hostess trap murderous mind-reader

Alice
1988, (Czech), First Run Features, color, 84 mins.
W: Kristyna Kohoutova (*Alice*)
WRIT, D & EDITED: Jan Svankmajer, from characters created by Lewis Carroll
Avant-garde fantasy combining live action & animation: Girl enters nightmarish world

Alice In Wonderland: GARY COOPER

Alice in Wonderland
1903, (GB), Hepworth, b&w, 800 ft. (243.8m)
W: May Clark (*Alice*), Cecil Hepworth (*The Frog*), Mrs. Hepworth (*The White
   Rabbit/The Queen*), Norman Whitten (*The Fish/The Mad Hatter*), Stanley
   Faithfull (*A Card*), Geoffrey Faithfull (*A Card*)
D: Cecil Hepworth & Percy Stow   **SCR:** Cecil Hepworth, from Lewis Carroll's
   novel
Standard fantasy short (in 16 scenes): Girl follows rabbit down hole, has strange adventures

Alice in Wonderland
1920, (USA), b&w
W: Mabel Taliaferro (*Alice*)
from Lewis Carroll's stories
Standard fantasy: Girl's surreal adventures

Alice in Wonderland
1933, (USA), Para, b&w, 90 mins.
W: Charlotte Henry (*Alice*), W.C. Fields (*Humpty Dumpty*), Gary Cooper (*The
   White Knight*), Alison Skipworth (*The Duchess*), Edna May Oliver (*The Red
   Queen*), Cary Grant (*The Mock Turtle*), Leon Errol (*The Uncle*), Jack Oakie
   (*Tweedledum*), Ned Sparks (*The Caterpillar*), Charles Ruggles (*The March
   Hare*), Edward Everett Horton (*The Mad Hatter*), May Robson (*The Queen of
   Hearts*), Louise Fazenda (*The White Queen*), Ethel Griffies, Richard Arlen,
   Roscoe Ates, William Austin, Polly Moran, Ford Sterling
P: Louis D. Lighton   **D:** Norman Z. McLeod   **SCR:** Joseph L. Mankiewicz &
   William Cameron Menzies, from Lewis Carroll's classic   **PHOTOG:** Henry
   Sharp & Bert Glennon   **MUSIC:** Dimitri Tiomkin
Stilted rendering of famed fantasy: Girl falls down rabbit hole, meets grotesques

Alice in Wonderland
1950, (GB), Bunin, b&w, 83 mins.
W: Carole Marsh (*Alice*), Felix Aylmer, Pamela Brown, The Bunin Puppets
D: Dallas Bowers, from Lewis Carroll's story
Animated puppets enhance classic fantasy: Girl has adventures in dream-world

Alice in Wonderland
1951, (USA), Walt Disney/RKO, color, 75 mins.
VOICES: Verna Felton, Kathryn Beaumont, Ed Wynn (*The Mad Hatter*), Jerry
   Colonna (*The March Hare*), Richard Haydn (*The Caterpillar*), Sterling
   Holloway (*The Cheshire Cat*), Bill Thompson, James MacDonald, Heather
   Angel, Queenie Leonard, Pat O'Malley, Larry Grey, Doris Lloyd, Dink Trout
D: Clyde Geronimi, Hamilton Luske & Wilfred Jackson   **SCR:** Milt Banta, Joe
   Grant, Del Connell, William Cottrell, Tom Oreb, Bill Peet, Ted Sears, John
   Walbridge, Winston Hibler, Joe Rinaldi, Dick Kelsey & Erdman Penner
   MUSIC SCORE: Oliver Wallace   **SONGS:** *I'm Late* & *The Unbirthday Song*
Classic animated fantasy: Girl pursues rabbit, has adventures

Alice in Wonderland
1985, (USA), Irwin Allen/Col-TV, color, Part I, 93 mins.; Part II, 90 mins.
W: Natalie Gregory (*Alice*), Sheila Allen (*The Mother*), Sharee Gregory (*The Sister*),
   Red Buttons (*The White Rabbit*), Sherman Hemsley (*The Mouse*), Donald
   O'Connor (*The Lory Bird*), Charles Dougherty (*The Duck*), Scott Baio (*Pat the
   Pig*), Martha Raye (*The Duchess*), Shelley Winters (*The Dodo Bird*), Billy
   Braver (*The Eaglet*), Ernie Orsatti (*Bill the Lizard*), Sammy Davis Jr. (*The
   Caterpillar/"Father William"*), Scotch Byerley (*The Fish Footman*), Robert
   Axelrod (*The Frog Footman*), Imogene Coca (*The Cook*), Telly Savalas (*The
   Cheshire Cat*), Anthony Newley (*The Mad Hatter*), Roddy McDowall (*The
   March Hare*), Arte Johnson (*The Dormouse*), Michael Chieffo (*The Two of
   Spades*), Jeffrey Winner (*The Five of Spades*), John Walter Davis (*The Seven of
   Spades*), Jayne Meadows (*The Queen of Hearts*), Robert Morley (*The King of
   Hearts*), James Joseph Galante (*The Knave of Hearts*), Selma Archerd (*The
   Queen of Diamonds*), George Savalas (*The Courtier*), Sid Caesar (*The Gryphon*),
   Candace Savalas (*The Lady in Waiting*), Ringo Starr (*The Mock Turtle*), Troy
   Jordan (*The Black Cat*), Tom McLoughlin (*The Jabberwocky*), Steve Lawrence
   (*Tweedledum*), Eydie Gorme (*Tweedledee*), Louis Nye (*The Carpenter*), Karl
   Malden (*The Walrus*), Ann Jillian (*The Red Queen*), Carol Channing (*The
   White Queen*), Lloyd Bridges (*The White Knight*), Harvey Korman (*The White
   King*), Jonathan Winters (*Humpty Dumpty*), Donna Mills (*The Rose*), Ernest
   Borgnine (*The Lion*), Sally Struthers (*The Tiger Lily*), Beau Bridges (*The
   Unicorn*), Jack Warden (*The Gentleman in the Paper
   Suit*), Patrick Duffy (*The Goat*), George Gobel (*The Gnat*), Pat Morita (*The
   Horse*), Merv Griffin (*The Conductor*), John Stamos (*The Messenger*), Don
   Matheson, Kristi Lynes, Desiree Szabo, Barbie Alison, Janie Walton, Dee
   Brantlinger
D: Harry Harris   **TELEPLAY:** Paul Zindel, from Lewis Carroll's classic   **PHO-
   TOG:** Fred J. Koenekamp   **SPCL-FX:** John Dykstra   **MUSIC SCORE:**
   Morton Stevens   **LYRICS:** Steve Allen
2-part TVM, modest fantasy: Little girl's bizarre adventures in dream-world

Alice in Wonderland
1999, (USA), Hallmark/NBC-TV, color, approx. 133 mins.
W: Tina Majorino (*Alice*), Miranda Richardson (*The Queen of Hearts*), Martin Short
   (*The Mad Hatter*), Adrian Gettley (*The March Hare*), Ben Kingsley (*Maj
   Caterpillar*), Whoopi Goldberg (*The Cheshire Cat*), Christopher Lloyd (*The
   White Knight*), Gene Wilder (*The Mock Turtle*), Peter Ustinov (*The Walrus*),
   Pete Postlethwaite (*The Carpenter*), George Wendt (*Tweedledee*), Robbie
   Coltrane (*Tweedledum*), Ken Dodd, Liz Smith, Elizabeth Spriggs
D: Nick Willing   **TELEPLAY:** Peter Barnes, from stories by Lewis Carroll

PHOTOG: Giles Nuttgens **VS-FX SPRVSR:** David Booth **MUSIC:** Richard Hartley
TVM, well-made fantasy: Girl visits bizarre world

Alice's Adventures in Wonderland
1910, (USA), Edison, b&w
D: Edwin S. Porter, from Lewis Carroll's story

Alice's Adventures in Wonderland
1972, (GB), American Nat'l, color, 101 mins.
W: Fiona Fullerton (*Alice*), Michael Crawford (*The White Rabbit*), Flora Robson (*The Queen of Hearts*), Ralph Richardson (*The Caterpillar*), Peter Sellers (*The March Hare*), Dudley Moore (*The Dormouse*), Michael Jayston (*Dodgson*), Robert Helpmann (*The Mad Hatter*), Dennis Price (*The King of Hearts*), Spike Milligan (*The Gryphon*), Rodney Bewes (*The Knave of Hearts*), Michael Hordern (*The Mock Turtle*), Peter Bull (*The Duchess*), Hywel Bennett (*Duckworth*), Davy Kaye (*The Mouse*), Ray Brooks (*The Five of Spades*), Julian Chagrin (*Bill*), Freddie Earle (*The Guinea Pig*), Roy Kinnear (*The Chesire Cat*), Patsy Rowlands (*The Cook*), Dennis Waterman (*The Two of Spades*), Frank Cox (*Tweedledee*), Freddie Cox (*Tweedledum*)
P: Derek Horne **D & ADAPT:** William Sterling, based on Lewis Carroll's classic stories **PHOTOG:** Geoffrey Unsworth **MUSIC:** John Barry **LYRICS:** Don Black
Musical fantasy: Girl visits bizarre world

Alice, Sweet Alice
1977, Made in America, AA, color, 108 mins.
W: Paula Sheppard (*Alice*), Brooke Shields (*Karen*), Jane Lowry (*Aunt Annie*), Linda Miller (*Catherine*), Mildred Clinton (*Mrs. Tredoni*), Alphonso DeNoble (*Alphonso*), Niles McMaster (*Dom Spages*), Randolph Willrich (*Father Tom*), Michael Hardstark (*The Detective*), Gary Allen (*The Uncle*), Tom Signorelli (*Brenner*), Louisa Horton (*The Psychiatrist*), Antonino Rocca (*The Funeral Attendant*), Lillian Roth (*The Pathologist*)
D: Alfred Sole **SCR:** Rosemary Ritvo & Alfred Sole **PHOTOG:** John Friberg **MUSIC:** Stephen Lawrence
A.k.a. Communion, distrib. (1981) as Holy Terror
Minor thriller: Girl brutally slain on day of first communion

Alice Through the Looking Glass
1988, (USA), color, 75 mins.
based on Lewis Carroll's writings
Standard animated fantasy: Girl has amazing adventures

Alien
1979, (USA), Brandywine-Ronald Shusett Prod./20th-Fox, color, 124 mins.
W: Sigourney Weaver (*Ripley*), Tom Skerritt (*Dallas*), Ian Holm (*Ash*), Veronica Cartwright (*Lambert*), Harry Dean Stanton (*Brett*), John Hurt (*Kane*), Yaphet Kotto (*Parker*), Helen Horton (*Voice of "Mother"*)
P: Gordon Carrol & David Giler **D:** Ridley Scott **SCR:** Dan O'Bannon, Walter Hill & David Giler **STORY:** Dan O'Bannon & Ronald Shusett **PHOTOG:** Derek Vanlint **MUSIC:** Jerry Goldsmith
Superior SF-horror, blends elements from films of yore (e.g., It!—The Terror from Beyond Space, The Thing from Another World, Terrore Nello Spazio, Queen of Blood, Silent Running, Night of the Blood-Beast, et al): Horrific life-form stalks crew of space freighter

Alien Abduction: Intrimate Secrets
see Forbidden Zone: Alien Abduction

Alienator
1989, (USA), Amazing Movies, color, 92 mins.
W: Teagan Clive, Jan-Michael Vincent, John Phillip Law, Robert Clarke, Ross Hagen, Dyana Ortelli, Jesse Dabson, Dawn Wildsmith, P.J. Soles, Richard Wiley, Fox Harris, Leo V. Gordon, Robert Quarry, Hoke Howell
D: Fred Olen Ray **SCR:** Paul Garson **PHOTOG:** Gary Graver **MUSIC:** Chuck Cirino
Minor SF-adventure: Female android assigned to terminate killer

Alien Avengers
1996, (USA), SHO-TV, color, 90 mins.
W: George Wendt, Shanna Reed, Christopher Brown (*Joseph*), Anastasia Sakelaris (*Daphne*)
Made-for-Cable, standard SF-comedy: Space aliens vacation in Los Angeles

Alien Avengers II
1997, (USA), color
W: George Wendt, Julie Brown
Minor SF-comedy

Alien Cargo
1999, (USA), UPN-TV, color, 95 mins.
W: Jason London, Missy Crider, Simon Westaway, Alan Dale, Elizabeth Alexander, Warwick Young
D: Mark Haber **TELEPLAY:** Carla Jean Wagner **PHOTOG:** John Stokes **MUSIC:** Patrick O'Hearn
TVM, standard SF-thriller: Insanity virus infects spaceship crew

Alien Contamination
1981, (It), Cannon, color
W: Ian McCulloch, Louise Monroe, Martin Mase, Siegfried Rauch, Lisa Hahn, Carl Major, Carl Money
D: Lewis Coates **SCR:** Lewis Coates & Eric Tomek **PHOTOG:** Joseph Pinori **SPCL-FX:** John Corridori **MUSIC:** Goblin
A.k.a. Alien...On Earth! and Contamination
Minor SF-horror with elements of Alien and It Conquered the World: Monstrous Martian eggs threaten Earth

Alien Dead
see It Fell from the Sky

The Alien Factor
see Nightbeast

Aliens From Another Planet
1966, (USA), color, 100 mins.
W: James Darren, Robert Colbert
TVM, standard SF-thriller (culled from teleseries "Time Tunnel"): Scientists vs. space-alien saboteur

Alien from LA
1988, (USA), color, 87 mins.
W: Thom Matthews, William R. Moses, Don Michael Paul, Richard Haines, Linda Kerridge, Janie du Plessis, Simon Poland
D: Albert Pyun **SCR:** Albert Pyun, Debra Ricci & Regina Davis **PHOTOG:** Tom Fraser
Minor SF-thriller

Alien Nation: JAMES CAAN AND MANDY PATIAKIN

Alien High
1987, (Can), Jack Bravman/Gold Gems, color, 87 mins.
W: Roy Thinnes (*Principal Borden*), Skip Lackey (*Frankie Lawrence*), Lee Tergesen (*Crash Hopkins*), David Kener (*Calvin Howell*), Miranda de Pencier (*Julie Freeman*), Bill Curry (*Dr. Gunbow*), Robert Dubac (*The French Teacher*), Brian Rabey (*Mr. Frommer*), Steve Dunnington (*The Coach*), Alecia Munn (*Miss Knight*), Nathalie Gauthier (*Lauren*), Frank Potvin (*Steve*), Robert Mercier (*Mark*), Keith Connor (*Roy*), Leslie Sellers (*Rosalie*), Sophie Lanza (*Ginette*), Merrily Gauthier, Alexandre Aumont, Sylvie Hachey, Manon Turbide, Lee Dempsey, Francoise Robertson, Jason Robert, Diane Ager, Greg Calpakis, Patrick Kerton, Gordon Speirs, Belle Richardson, Patricia Rodriguez, Mitchell Krystantos, Richard Fucco, Paul Leblanc, George Thomas, Stephanie Levesque, Marie-Claude Beauvais, Victoria Barkoff, Al Cruise, Nancy Bravman, Zarya Rubin, Talya Rubin, Virginia Ferguson, Sarah Hayward, Beverly Lowe, Robert Bruni, Alexandra Innes, Andrea Sadle, Michael Whitehead
D: Eugenie Joseph **PHOTOG:** Christian Racine **SPCL-FX:** Arnold Gargiulo **MUSIC:** Diane Bulgarelli **SONG:** Mind Benders
A.k.a. Mind Benders
Standard SF-comedy: Evil space aliens turn hyperactive students into zombies

Alien Intruder
1993, (USA), color, 90 mins.
W: Billy Dee Williams
Standard SF-thriller: Interplanetary convicts fall under spell of computer-spawned temptress

Alien Massacre
see Gallery of Horror

Alien Nation
1988, (USA), 20th-Fox, color, 89 mins.
W: James Caan (*Matthew Sykes*), Mandy Patinkin (*Sam Francisco*), Terence Stamp

(*William Harcourt*), Kevyn Major Howard (*Kipling*), Leslie Bevis (*Cassandra*), Peter Jason (*Fedorchuk*), George Jenesky (*Quint*), Jeff Kober, Roger Aaron Brown, Tony Simotes, Michael David Simms, Ed Krieger, Tony Perez, Brian Thompson, Frank McCarthy, Keone Young, Don Hood, Earl Boen, William E. Dearth, Robert Starr, Bobby Sargent, Bebe Drake-Massey, Edgar Small, Thomas Wagner, Abraham Alvarez, Diana James, Jessica James, Frank Collison, Tom DeFranco, Angela O'Neill, Tom Morga, Seth Marten, Kendall Conrad, Brian Lando, Reggie Parton, Tom Finnegan, Doug MacHugh, Lawrence Kopp, Alec Gillis, Shuko Akune, Stephanie Shroyer, Frank Wagner, Clarence Landry, Van Ling, Mark Murphey, Kirsten Graham, George Robotham, Douglas Cameron, Debra Seitz, James De Closs
D: Graham Baker **SCR:** Rockne S. O'Bannon **PHOTOG:** Adam Greenberg **MUSIC:** Curt Sobel
orig. to be titled **Outer Heat**
Unusual SF-thriller: Earth cop teamed with extraterrestrial

Alien Nation: Body and Soul
1996, (USA), Fox-TV, color, 95 mins.
W: Gary Graham (*Sikes*), Eric Pierpoint (*Sam Francisco*), Michele Scarabelli, Terri Treas, Lauren Woodland, Sean Six, Ron Fassler, Jeff Marcus, Jenny Gago, Leon Russom, Pamela Gordon, Danielle Warren, Kristin Davis, Aimee Warren
D: Kenneth Johnson **PHOTOG:** Shelley Johnson **SPCL-FX:** Dream Quest
TVM, standard SF-thriller: Space aliens breed with humans

Alien Nation: Dark Horizon
1994, (USA), Fox-TV, color, 90 mins.
W: Gary Graham, Eric Pierpoint, Scott Patterson, Michelle Scarabelli, Terri Treas, Lee Bryant, Sean Six, Lauren Woodland, Ron Fassier, Jeff Marcus
D: Kenneth Johnson **TELEPLAY:** Diane Frolov & Andrew Schneider **MUSIC:** David Kurtz
TVM, standard SF-thriller: Virus attacks immigrants from space

Alien Nation: Millennium
1996, (USA), Fox-TV, color, 95 mins.
W: Hary Graham (*Sikes*), Eric Pierpoint (*Sam Francisco*), Kerrie Keane (*Jennifer*), Herta Ware (*Alana*), Steven Flynn (*Calaban*), Susan Diol (*Marina del Rey*), Brian Markinson (*Jason Webster*), Michele Scarabelli, Terri Treas, Lauren Woodland, Sean Six, Jeff Marcus, Jason Behr, Ron Fassler, Jenny Gago, Ellis Williams, David Faustino
D & TELEPLAY: Kenneth Johnson **PHOTOG:** Shelley Johnson **MUSIC:** David Kurtz
TVM, standard SF-thriller: Cult leader lures space-alien settlers on Earth

Alien Nation: The Enemy Within
1996, (USA), Fox-TV, color, 95 mins.
W: Gary Graham (*Sikes*), Eric Pierpoint (*Sam Francisco*), Joe Lando, Kerrie Keane, Terri Treas, Michele Scarabelli, Tiny Ron, Sean Six, Jeff Marcus, Ron Fassler, Lauren Woodland, Dana Anderson, Bridgitta Dau
D: Kenneth Johnson **TELEPLAY:** Diane Frolov & Andrew Schneider **PHOTOG:** Ron Garcia **MUSIC:** Steve Dorff
TVM standard SF-thriller: Outcast space aliens breed monsters

Alien Nation: The Udara legacy
1996, (USA), Fox-TV, color, 95 mins.
TVM, standard SF-thriller

Alien...On Earth!
see Alien Contamination

The Alien Oro
1973, (Can), color
W: Keir Dullea
TVM, reedited from teleseries "Starlost": Adventures of Earth's last survivor, c. 2790
cf. **The Beginning**

Alien Predators
1987, (USA-Sp), Edward & Helen Sarlui/Hal Roach, color, 92 mins.
W: Dennis Christopher (*Damon*), Martin Hewitt (*Michael*), Luis Prendes (*Dr. Tracer*), Lynn-Holly Johnson (*Samantha*), J.O. Bosso (*Capt. J.J. Wells*), Yousaf Bokhari (*Mr. Bodi*), Christina Augustin (*Baby Bodi*), Yolanda Palomo (*Mrs. Bodi*), Pablo Garcia, Christina San Juan, Carlos Ramirez
WRIT & D: Deran Sarafian **PHOTOG:** Tote Trenas **SPCL-FX:** John Balandin **MUSIC:** Chase/Rucker Prods.
Minor SF-horror: Strange plague descends on Earth

Alien Prey
see Prey

Alien Private Eye
1987, (USA), color, 90 mins.
W: Nikki Fastinetti **D:** Nik Rubenfeld
Minor SF-thriller: Alien cop hunts magic disk

Aliens
1986, (USA), Brandywine/20th-Fox, color, 137 mins.
W: Sigourney Weaver (*Ripley*), Michael Biehn (*Hicks*), Paul Reiser (*Burke*), Lance Henriksen (*Bishop*), Carrie Henn (*Newt*), Jenette Goldstein (*Vasquez*), Bill Paxton (*Hudson*), William Hope, Blain Fairman, Ricco Ross, Barbara Coles,

Al Matthews
D: James Cameron, from characters created by Dan O'Bannon & Ronald Shusett
PHOTOG: Adrian Biddle **SPCL-FX SPRVSR:** John Richardson
MUSIC: James Horner
Superior SF-horror, rousing sequel to **Alien***: Astronauts vs. carnivorous space monsters*

Alien 3
1992, (USA), Brandywine/20th-Fox, color.
W: Sigourney Weaver (*Ripley*), Charles S. Dutton (*Dillon*), Charles Dance (*Clemens*), Lance Henriksen (*Bishop*), Brian Glover (*The Warden*), Paul McGann, Ralph Brown, Danny Webb, Christopher John Fields, Carl Chase, Chris Fairbank
P: Gordon Carroll, David Giler & Walter Hill **D:** David Fincher **SCR:** David Giler, Walter Hill & Larry Ferguson **STORY:** Vincent Ward, based on characters created by Dan O'Bannon & Ronald Shusett **PHOTOG:** Alex Thomson **VS-FX:** Richard Edlund **SPCL-FX SPRVSR:** George Gibbs **MUSIC:** Elliot Goldenthal
Standard SF-horror: Female astronaut stranded on prison-world, menaced by monster

Alien 4
see Alien Resurrection

Alien Resurrection
1997, (USA), 20th-Fox, color, 109 mins.
W: Sigourney Weaver (*Ripley*), Winona Ryder (*Call*), Dominique Pinon (*Vriess*), Ron Perlman (*Johner*), Brad Dourif, Leland Orser
D: Jean-Pierre Jeunet **SCR:** Joss Whedon
orig. to be titled **Alien 4**
Exciting SF-horror: Woman astronaut cloned, does battle with monstrous archenemies

The Aliens are Coming
1980, (USA), QM-Woodruff/NBC-TV, color, 95 mins.
W: Tom Mason (*Scott Dryden*), Max Gail (*Russ Garner*), Caroline Mc-Williams (*Sue Garner*), Fawne Harriman (*Joyce Cummings*), Ron Masak (*Harve Nelson*), Matthew Laborteaux (*Timmy Garner*), Eric Braeden (*Nero*), Melinda Fee (*O'Brien*), John Milford (*Eldon Gates*), Tom Lowell, Gerald McRaney, Ed Harris, Laurie Beach, Hank Brandt, Laurence Haddon, Curtis Credel, John Gilgreen, Richard Lockmiller, Nancy Priddy, Lorna Thayer, Tom Pittman, Sean Griffin, Peter Schuck, Chris O'Brien, Dirk Olthof
D: Harvey Hart **TELEPLAY:** Robert W. Lenski **PHOTOG:** Jacques R. Marquette **MUSIC:** William Goldstein
TVM, standard SF: Alien energy beings possess human bodies

Aliens Attack Tokyo
see Uchujin Tokyo No Arawaru

Aliens From Spaceship Earth
1977, (USA), color, 107 mins.
W: Donovan, Lynda Day George **D:** Don Como
Minor speculation-docmantry: Do outerspace beings threaten Earth?

The Alien's Return
1980, (USA), Samuel Goldwyn, color, 89 mins.
W: Jan-Michael Vincent (*Wayne*), Cybill Shepherd (*Jennifer*), Martin Landau (*Niles Buchanan*), Raymond Burr (*Dr. Kramer*), Neville Brand (*Walt*), Brad Rearden (*Eddie*), Ernest Anderson (*Dr. Mortorff*), Vincent Schiavelli (*The Prospector*), Steven Hirsch (*Dr. Parkfield*), Darby Hinton (*Darren*), Susan Kiger (*Joyce*), Ken Minyard (*Federal Agent #1*), Roger Hampton (*Homer*), Hilary Labow (*Lee Ann*), Candy Castillo (*Federal Agent #2*), Dorothy Constantine (*The Motel Manager*), Michael R. Starita (*Grandfather*), Robert M. Magnus (*The Town Drunk*), Farah Bunch (*Young Jennifer*), Zachary Vincent (*Young Wayne*), Lynda Clark (*The Girl*), Buck Allen (*The Truck Driver*), Jacob Bresler (*The Cafe Patron*), Mike Tillman, Rock Walker, John Moio, Dee Cooper, Diane Carter, Pat Allphin, Mickey Epps, Robert Bradford, Diane de Moye, Gabrielle Bottcher, Neil Bottcher, James de Moye, Tom Franckhauser, Donna Gaffe, James Gaffe, Gary Goldberg, Ronald Kimmich, J.R. Green, Barbara Kimmich, Mary Ann Roedel, Edythe Magnus, John Roedel, Barbara Starita, Bill Womble
P & D: Greydon Clark **SCR:** Ken Wheat, Jim Wheat & Curtis Burch **PHOTOG:** Daniel Pearl **SPCL-FX:** Dana Rheaume **MUSIC:** Dan Wyman
Minor SF-thriller: Space beings mutilate cattle

Alien Seed
1989, (USA), color, 88 mins
W: Erik Estrada, Heidi Paine, Steven Blade **D:** Bob James
Minor SF-thriller: UFO specialist embroiled in government cover-up

Alien Space Avenger
1991, (USA), AIP, color, 88 mins.
W: Robert Prichard, Mike McClerie, Charity Staley, Angela Nicholas, Gina Mastrogiacomo, Kick Fairbanks Fogg, Marty Roberts, James Gillis
D: Richard W. Haine **SCR:** Richard W. Haines & Linwood Sawyer **MUSIC:** Richard Fiocca
A.k.a. **Space Avenger**
Minor SF-thriller: Space-alien convicts crashland in New York City

Alien Terminator
1995, (USA), New Horizons, color, 95 mins.
W: Maria Ford (*McKay*), Rodger Halston (*Dean Taylor*), Cassandra Leigh (*Rachel*)

Hutchinson), Kevin Alber, Emile Levisetti
D: Dave Payne
Minor SF-horror: Genetically-engineered mutant stalks scientists trapped five miles underground

Alien Warrior
1985, (Can), Ben Tavi-Hunt-Coe/Samuel Goldwyn, color, 87 mins.
W: Brett Clark, Pamela Saunders, Reggie DeMorton, Nelson D. Anderson, Norman Budd, Elodie McKee, Bill Woods Jr., Rameon Witt, Tony Williams
D: Edward Hunt   **SCR:** Edward Hunt, Rueben Gordon, Steven Schoenberg & Barry Pearson   **PHOTOG:** Richard Gale, Luis Santiago & Joe Pennella   **MUSIC:** Bax   **SONGS:** *Smooth & Cool, Flesh, Read to Break, Whatever's Fair and Usual, King of the Streets & Hold the Light*
Minor SF-adventure: Extraterrestrial fights Earth crime

The Alien Within
1991, (USA), color
W: Richard Harrison (*Max Adrian*), Gordon Mitchell (*Dan Thorn*), Jay Richardson (*Samanski*), Suzanne Ager (*Erin West*), Melissa Moore (*Monica Roarke*), Crystal Shaw (*The Sec'y*), Bobbie Bresee (*Lynn Roman*), Drew Godderis (*Ross Anderson*), John Terrence (*Brent Price*), Donna Shock (*Evelyn Avery*), Jerry Fox (*Harry Fox*), Pamela Gilbert (*Elaine Talbot*), Mark Anthony (*Mark Randall*), Leslie Eve (*Tracy*), Chris Kobin (*Will*), Sue Mashaw (*Betty*), Gary J. Levinson (*Dr. Leibowitz*), Michael S. Deak (*Symanski*), Roger McCoin (*Bordona*), Forrest J. Ackerman (*The Pool Man*), John Carradine (*Dr. Zeitman*)
PHOTOG: Scott Ressler & Frank Isaacs   **SPCL-FX:** Dan Bordona & Christopher Ray
Minor horror-thriller: Anti-aging drug creates monsters

Alien Women
1969, (GB), color, 86 mins.
W: James Robertson Justice, Charles Hawtrey, Robin Hawdon, Anna Gael, Brigitte Skay, Dawn Addams, Yutte Stensgaard, Valerie Leon, Wendy Lingham, Rita Webb, Caroline Hawkins
D: Michael Cort
Minor soft-core SF: Special agent investigates otherworld beauties

Alive by Night
see Evil Spawn

All-American Murder
1992, (USA), color, 95 mins.
W: Charlie Schlatter, Josie Bissett, Christopher Walken (*P.J.*), Joanna Cassidy, Richard Kind, Amy Davis, Woody Watson, J.C. Quinn
D: Anson Williams   **SCR:** Barry Sandler
Minor thriller: College student accused of killing coed

Allan Field's Warning
1913, (GB), Barker, b&w, 667 ft. (203.3m)
W: Fred Paul (*Allan Field*), Blanche Forsythe (*Mrs. Field*), Kenneth Barker (*Master Field*)
D: Bert Haldane   **STORY:** Rowland Talbot
Standard crime-thriller: Gambler dreams of criminal life

Allan Quatermain and the Lost City of Gold
1987, (USA), Cannon, color, 103 mins.
W: Richard Chamberlain (*Allan Quatermain*), Sharon Stone (*Jesse Huston*), James Earl Jones (*Umslopogaas*), Henry Silva (*Agon*), Robert Donner (*Swarma*), Robert Rabbett
D: Gary Nelson   **SCR:** Gene Quintano, from H. Rider Haggard's novel   **PHOTOG:** Alex Phillips   **MUSIC:** Michael Linn
Minor adventure: Great White Hunter seeks legendary treasure

All Clear: No Need to Take Cover
1917, (GB), Denvirose Films, b&w, 1,000 ft. (304.8m)
W: Jane Denison (*The Fairy*), Anne Bolt (*The Child*)
P & D: Jane Denison
Minor fantasy: Fairy shows marvels to child

All Hallowe'en
1953, (GB), Joan Maude-Michael Warre/ABFD, b&w, 34 mins.
W: Sally Gilmour (*Rowena*), Oleg Briansky (*Gervase*), Jane Baxter (*Lady Delville*), Diane Cilento (*Harriet*), Walter Hudd (*Mr. Wilberforce*), Clive Morton (*Sir Arthur*), Ferdy Mayne (*The Soldier*), Hattie Jacques (*Miss Quibble*)
D: Michael Gordon   **STORY:** Joan Maude & Michael Warre
Standard short fantasy: Lovers born 200 years apart united on Halloween

Alley of Nightmares
see She Freak

Alligator (1976)
see Eaten Alive! (1976)

Alligator
1981, (USA), Avco Embassy, color, 92 mins.
W: Sue Lyon, Robert Forster (*David Maison*), Perry Lang (*Kelly*), Dean Jagger (*Slade*), Jack Carter (*The Mayor*), Henry Silva (*Brock*), Bart Braverman (*The Reporter*), Pat Petersen, Sidney Lassick
D: Lewis Teague   **SCR:** John Sayles   **PHOTOG:** Joseph Mangine   **MUSIC:** Craig Hundley

Amusing SF-thriller: Giant reptile in sewer system

The Alligator People
1959, (USA), 20th-Fox, b&w, 74 mins.
W: Beverly Garland (*Jane*), Frieda Inescort (*Mrs. Hawthorne*), George Macready (*Sinclair*), Bruce Bennett (*Lorimer*), Richard Crane (*Paul*), Lon Chaney Jr., Douglas Kennedy, Ruby Goodwin, Lee Warren, Vince Townsend Jr., Boyd Stockman, John Merrick
P: Jack Leewood   **D:** Roy Del Ruth   **SCR:** Orville H. Hampton, from a story by Orville H. Hampton & Charles O'Neal   **PHOTOG:** Karl Struss   **SPCL-FX:** Fred Etcheverry   **MUSIC:** Irving Gertz
orig. co-billed with Return of the Fly
Standard SF-horror: Woman finds husband turned into scaly monstrosity, uncovers ghastly reptile-hormone experiments

Alligator II: The Mutation
1991, (USA), Group 1, color, 92 mins.
W: Joseph Bologna, Dee Wallace Stone, Richard Lynch, Woody Brown, Holly Gagnier, Bill Dailey, Brock Peters, Steve Railsback, Julian Reyes
D: Jon Hess   **SCR:** Curt Allen   **PHOTOG:** Joseph Mangine   **MUSIC:** Jack Tillar
Standard horror-satire

Allison's Birthday
1979, (USA), color, 99 mins.
W: Joanne Samuel, Lou Brown, Bunny Brooke
D: Ian Coughlan
Minor fantasy-thriller: Teen girl finds family harbors Satan worshipper

All of Me
1984, (USA), Kings Road/Univ, color, 91 mins.
W: Steve Martin (*Roger Cobb*), Lily Tomlin (*Edwina Cutwater*), Victoria Tennant (*Terry Hoskins*), Richard Libertini (*Prahka Lasa*), Jason Bernard, Madolyn Smith, Dana Elcar, Selma Diamond, Eric Christmas, Neva Patterson, Michael Ensign
D: Carl Reiner   **SCR:** Phil Alden Robinson   **ADAPT:** Henry Olek, from Ed Davis' novel *Me Two*   **PHOTOG:** Richard H. Kline   **MUSIC:** Patrick Williams
Unusual comedy-fantasy: Dying woman's soul transferred to man's body

All That Jazz
1979, (USA), 20th-Fox/Col, color, 123 mins.
W: Roy Scheider (*Joe Gideon*), Ann Reinking (*Kate Jagger*), Ben Vereen (*O'Connor*

All Of Me: Steve Martin and Lily Tomlin

Flood), Jessica Lange (*Angelique*), Leland Palmer (*Audrey Paris*), Cliff Gorman (*Davis Newman*), Michael Tolan (*Dr. Ballinger*), John Lithgow (*Lucas Sargeant*), Erzebet Foldi (*Michelle*), Keith Gordon (*Young Joe*), Deborah Geffner (*Victoria*), Max Wright (*Joshua Penn*), William Le Massena (*Jonesy Hecht*), Chris Chase (*Leslie Perry*), Anthony Holland (*Paul Dann*), Kathryn Doby (*Kathryn*), David Margulies (*Larry Goldie*), Robert Hitt (*Ted Christopher*), Sue Paul (*Stacy*), Ben Masters (*Dr. Garry*), Frankie Man (*The Comic*), Sloane Shelton (*Mother*), Alan Heim (*Eddie*), Sandahl Bergman
P: Robert Alan Aurthur   **D:** Bob Fosse   **SCR:** Robert Alan Aurthur & Bob Fosse   **PHOTOG:** Giuseppe Rotunno   **MUSIC SPRVSR & CONDUCTOR:** Ralph Burns   **FANTASY DESIGNER:** Tony Walton
Lavish psychodrama: Choreographer flirts with Death

All That Money Can Buy
1941, (USA), RKO, b&w, 112 mins.
W: Edward Arnold (*Daniel Webster*), Walter Huston (*Satan*), Simone Simon (*Belle*), James Craig (*Jabez Stone*), Anne Shirley (*Mary Stone*), Jane Darwell (*Ma Stone*), Gene Lockhart (*Squire Slossum*), John Qualen (*Miser Stevens*), H.B. Warner (*Justice Hawthorne*), Frank Conlan, George Cleveland, Lindy Wade, Jeff Corey
P & D: William Dieterle   **SCR:** Stephen Vincent Benet & Dan Totheroh, from Stephen Vincent Benet's *The Devil and Daniel Webster*   **PHOTOG:** Joseph August   **SPCL-FX:** Vernon L. Walker   **MUSIC:** Bernard Herrmann
*A.k.a. **The Devil and Daniel Webster**, **Daniel and the Devil** and **Here is a Man***
Classic fantasy: New England farmer sells soul to Satan, soon regrets transaction

Allures
1966, (USA), Belson, color, 8 mins.
Fantasy short: "A trip into the interstices of the internal cosmos"

Almost Dead
1994, (USA), color, 92 mins.
W: Shannen Doherty, Costas Mandylor, John Diehl, William R. Moses
D: Ruben Preuss
Standard thriller: Woman psychiatrist haunted

Aloma of the South Seas
1926, (USA), Famous Players-Lasky/Para, b&w, 2094m (6,870.1 ft.)
W: Warner Baxter, William Powell
P & D: Maurice Tourneur
Standard adventure-thriller

Aloma of the South Seas
1941, (USA), para, color, 77 mins.
W: Dorothy Lamour, Jon Hall, Lynne Overman, Philip Reed, Katherine DeMille
D: Alfred Santell   PHOTOG: Karl Struss
Standard adventure-thriller: Island girl faces volcanic cataclysm

Alone in London
1915, (GB), Turner Films/Ideal, b&w, 4,525 ft. (1379.2m)
W: Florence Turner (*Nan Meadows*), Henry Edwards (*John Biddlecombe*), Edward Lingard (*Redcliffe*), Amy Lorraine (*Mrs. Burnaby*), James Lindsay (*Chick*)
D: Larry Trimble, from a play by Robert Buchanan & Harriet Jay
Standard crime-thriller: Crook tries to make thief of boss' son, ties flower girl to lock gates of canal

Alone in the Dark
1982, (USA), Robert Shaye/New Line Cinema, color, 92 mins.
W: Jack Palance (*Frank Hawkes*), Donald Pleasence (*Dr. Leo Bain*), Martin Landau (*Byron "Preacher" Sutcliff*), Dwight Schultz (*Dr. Dan Potter*), Erland Van Lidth ("*Fatty*"), Deborah Hedwall
WRIT & D: Jack Sholder   PHOTOG: Joseph Mangine   MUSIC: Renato Serio
Minor thriller: Four psychopaths flee asylum

The Alphabet Murders
1965, (GB), MGM, b&w, 90 mins.
W: Tony Randall (*Hercule Poirot*), Anita Ekberg (*Amanda Beatrice Cross*), Robert Morley (*Capt. Hastings*), Maurice Denham (*Insp. Japp*), Duncan Doncaster*), James Villiers (*Franklin*), Clive Morton ("*X*"), Margaret Rutherford (*in cameo role as "Miss Jane Marple"*), Sheila Allen (*Lady Diane*), Julian Glover (*Don Fortune*), Grazina Frame (*Betty Barnard*), Richard Wattis (*Wolf*), Cyril Luckham (*Sir Carmichael Clarke*), Austin Trevor (*Justin*)
D: Frank Tashlin   SCR: David Pursall & Jack Seddon, based on Agatha Christie's novel *The A.B.C. Murders*   PHOTOG: Desmond Dickinson   MUSIC: Ron Goodwin
A.k.a. **Amanda**
Minor mystery-comedy: Belgian sleuth solves murders tied to alphabet

The Alpha Incident
1977, (USA), Wisconsin Film Group, color, 85 mins.
W: Ralph Meeker (*Charlie*), Stafford Morgan (*Dr. Sorensen*), John Goff (*Jack Tiller*), Carol Irene Newell (*Jenny*), Buck Flower (*Hank*), Paul Bentzen (*Dr. Farrell*), John Alderman (*Dr. Rogers*), Ray Szmanda (*The Official*), Sir Lawrence Ripp (*The Guard*), Harry Youstos (*Alvin*)
D: Bill Rebane   MUSIC: Richard A. Girvin
Minor SF-thriller: Gov't tries to contain extraterrestrial virus

Alphaville, Une Etrange Aventure de Lemmy Caution (Alphaville, A Strange Adventure of Lemmy Caution)
1965, (Fr), Chaumiane/Pathe-Contemp, b&w, 100 mins.
W: Eddie Constantine (*Lemmy Caution*), Anna Karina (*Natacha von Braun*), Howard Vernon (*Prof. Leonard Nosferatu, a.k.a. Prof. von Braun*), Akim Tamiroff (*Henry Dickson*), Laszlo Szabo (*The Chief Engineer*), Michel Delahaye (*Prof. von Braun's Ass't*), Jean-Andre Fieschi (*Prof. Heckell*), Jean-Louis Comolli (*Prof. Jeckell*)
P: Andre Michelin   WRIT & D: Jean-Luc Godard   PHOTOG: Raoul Coutard   MUSIC: Paul Misraki
orig. to be titled **Tarzan vs IBM**
Adult SF-fantasy: Super-macho hero pits forces against Alpha 60, an all-powerful computer

Alraune
1928, (Ger), Ufa, b&w, 10,978 ft. (3346m)
W: Brigitte Helm, Paul Wegener, Ivan Petrovich
WRIT & D: Henrik Galeen, from a novel by H.H. Ewers   PHOTOG: Franz Planer   DESIGN: Walter Reimann
USA retitle, **Unholy Love***, A.k.a.* **Daughter of Destiny** *and* **Mandragore**
Classic fantasy: Artificial impregnation produces beautiful, soulless creature

Alraune
1952, (GB W. Ger), b&w, 90 mins.
W: Brigitte Helm, Harry Meyer, Denise Vernac, Harry Helm, Julia Koschka
D: Richard Oswald   PHOTOG: Gunther Krampf   MUSIC: Bronislau Kaper, from a novel by H.H. Ewers
Sound remake of fantasy classic: Scientist creates woman

Alraune
1952, (W. Ger), DCA, color

W: Erich von Stroheim, Hildegarde Neff, Karl Boehm
D: Arthur Maria Robenalt   SCR: Fritz Rotter, from a novel by H.H. Ewers
USA retitle, **Unnatural**
Updated version of classic fantasy: Scientist creates soulless beauty

Altar Chains
1916, (GB), London/Jury, b&w, 4,600 ft. (1402.1m)
W: Dawson Millward (*Capt. Kerr*), Heather Thatcher (*Alice Vaughan*), Philip Hewland (*Harry Avery*), Edward O'Neill (*Philip Anson*), Minna Grey (*Mrs. Anson*), Hubert Willis (*Charles Vaughan*), Fred Volpe (*Harky*), Donald Calthrop
D & STORY: Bannister Merwin
Standard crime-thriller: Captain with month to live forces usurer to join him in drinking poison

The Altar Stairs
1922, (USA), Univ, b&w, 5 reels (4,641 ft./1414.6m)
W: Frank Mayo (*Rod McLean*), Louise Lorraine (*Joie Malet*), Lawrence Hughes (*Tony Heritage*), J.J. Lanoe (*Capt. Jean Malet*), Harry De Vere (*Blundell*), Hugh Thompson (*John Strickland*), Boris Karloff (*Hugo*), Dagmar Godowsky (*Parete*), Nick De Ruiz (*Tulli*)
D: Lambert Hillyer   SCR: George Hively, Doris Schroeder & George Randolph Chester, from G.B. Lancaster's 1908 story   PHOTOG: Dwight Warren
Standard melodrama: Unrest on South Seas isle

Altered States
1980, (USA), WB, color, 101 mins.
W: William Hurt (*Eddie Jessup*), Blair Brown (*Emily Jessup*), Bob Balaban (*Arthur*), Charles Haid (*Mason*), Thaao Penghlis (*Eccheverria*), Miguel Godreau (*The Primal Man*), Dori Brenner (*Sylvia*), Peter Brandon (*Hobart*), Charles White Eagle (*The Brujo*), Drew Barrymore (*Margaret Jessup*), Megan Jeffers (*Grace Jessup*), Jack Murdock (*Hector Ortego*), Frank McCarthy (*Obispo*), Deborah Baltzell (*The Schizophrenic Patient*), Evan Richards (*Young Rosenberg*), John Walter Davis (*The Medical Technician*), Hap Lawrence (*The Endocrinology Fellow*), Cynthia Burr (*Parrish's Girl*) Susan Bredhoff (*Eccheverria's Girl*), George Gaynes (*Dr. Wissenschaft*), John Larroquette (*The X-Ray Technician*), Ora Rubinstein, Paul Larson, Eric Forst, Adriana Shaw, Martin Fiscoe, Olivia Michelle, M. James Arnett
P: Howard Gottfried   D: Ken Russell   SCR: "Sidney Aaron" (Paddy Chayefsky), from Paddy Chayefsky's novel   PHOTOG: Jordan Cronenweth   SPCL VS-FX: Bran Ferren   MUSIC: John Corigliano
"A powerful, terrifying, suspenseful, mind-blowing movie that gives the audience a jolt of electricity they won't soon forget. The result will fry your hair"—Rex Reed, New York Daily News
"The screen explodes in fantastic, artful montages. The special effects are spectacular. This is Russell's best movie. At least once he will scare you right out of your socks"—Stewart Klein, WNEW-TV
"This one has everything: sex, violence, comedy, thrills, tenderness. Laugh with it, scream at it, think about it. You may leave the theatre in an altered state"—Richard Corliss, Time
"The climax of the film...and the film's effects...is simply amazing, it's totally absorbing. The most dramatic and novel film to play Boston in ages. An extraordinary picture"—Bruce McCabe, Boston Globe
"The film lays siege to the senses with a powerful arsenal of images. It will make your capillaries restrict and your pulse thump"—Alan Berger, Boston Herald American
Classic SF-thriller: Scientist regresses self

Always

Always: RICHARD DREYFUSS AND HOLLY HUNTER

1989, (USA), Univ, color, 123 mins.
W: Richard Dreyfuss (*Pete Sandich*), Holly Hunter (*Dorinda Durston*), Brad Johnson (*Ted Baker*), John Goodman (*Al Yackey*), Audrey Hepburn (*Hap*), Keith David (*Powerhouse*), Ed Van Nuys (*Nails*), Roberts Blossom (*Dave*), Marg Helgenberger (*Rachel*), Dale Dye (*The Fire Boss*), Brian Haley (*Alex*), James Lashly (*Charlie*), Michael Steve Jones (*Grey*), Kim Robillard (*The Air Traffic Controller*), Jim Sparkman (*The Dispatcher*), Doug McGrath (*The Bus Driver*), Shereil L. Bowens, Acencion Fuentes, Todd Jacobson, DeMarious T. Morganfield, Joseph McCrossin, Mike O'Neal, Larry Landless, Steve Shatynski, James Pruitt, J.D. Souther, David Jackson, David Kitay, Gene Strimling, Roy Harrison, Ted Grossman, Gerry Rothschild, Loren Smothers, Taleena Ottwell
D: Steven Spielberg SCR: Jerry Belson & Diane Thomas, from a screenplay by Dalton Trumbo PHOTOG: Mikael Salomon VS-FX SPRVSR: Bruce Nicholson MUSIC: John Williams
Sentimental fantasy (remake of 'A Guy Named Joe'): Flier's ghost benefits living

Amador
1965, (Sp-Fr), Jet Films/Champs-Elysees Prods., color
W: Maurice Ronet (*Amador*), Amparo Soler Leal (*Laura*), Maria Asquerino (*Ana*), Yelena Samarina (*Julia*), Maria Luisa Ponte (*Aunt Aurora*), Medeleine Dehecq (*The Chambermaid*), Jose Maria Prada (*Jesus*), Elsa Zabala (*Ketty*), Robert Llamas (*Sergid*), Maria Paz Ballesteros (*Pilar*), Coral Pellicer, Chiro Bermejo
D: Francisco Regueiro SCR: Francisco Regueiro, Angelion Fons & Jacques Lagneau, from an adaptation by Francisco Regueiro & Manuel Lopez Yubero, based on a subject by Francisco Regueiro PHOTOG: Francisco Sempere MUSIC: Daniel White
Standard fantasy: Love meets philosophy

Amanda
see *The Alphabet Murders*

Amanda and the Alien
1995, (USA), Century Group/SHO-TV, color, 94 mins.
W: Nicole Eggert (*Amanda*), Stacy Keach (*Mallory*), Michael Dorn (*Vint*), John Diehl, David Millbern, Alex Meneses, Michael C. Bendetti
WRIT & D: Jon Kroll PHOTOG: Gary Tieche, from a story by Robert Silverberg
Made-for-Cable, standard SF-thriller: California girl befriends cannibalistic space-alien

L'Amante del Vampiri (Love of the Vampires)
1961, (It), Lopert/UA, b&w
W: Walter Brandi, Helene Remy, Maria Luisa Rolando, John Turner, Tina Gloriani, Isarco Ravaioli
P: Bruno Bolognesi D: Renato Polselli SCR: Renato Polselli, Giuseppe Pellegrini & Ernesto Gastaldi MUSIC: Aldo Piga
USA retitle, **The Vampire and the Ballerina**
orig. to be titled **The Dancer and the Vampire** or **The Vampire's Lover**
Standard horror-thriller: Dancers visit castle, master vampire preys

Amante d'Oltretomba (Lovers Beyond the Grave)
1965, (It), color
W: Barbara Steele, Raf Vallone, Paul Miller
D: Mario Caiano
GB retitle, **The Faceless Monster**, USA retitle, **Nightmare Castle**, A.k.a. **Night of the Doomed**
Minor horror-thriller: Eerie tale of ghosts that return for vengeance

Amarcord (I Remember)
1973, (It-Fr), New World, color, 127 mins.
W: Magali Noel (*Gradisca*), Bruno Zanin (*Titta*), Pupella Maggio (*Titta's Mother*), Armando Brancia (*Titta's Father*), Nando Orfei (*Pataca*), Luigi Rossi (*The Lawyer*), Ciccio Ingrassia (*Uncle Teo*), Gennaro Ombra (*Bisein*), Josiane Tanzilli (*Volpina*), Dina Adorni (*The Math Teacher*), Antonietta Beluzzi (*The Tobacconist*), Gianfilippo Carcano (*Don Baravelli*), Ferruccio Brembilla (*The Fascist Leader*), Antonino Faa'DiBruno, Ferdinando Villella, Aristide Caporale, Domenico Pertica, Mauro Misul, Bruno Lenzi, Antonino Spaccatini, Stefano Proietti, Marcello DiFalco, Bruno Scagnetti
D: Federico Fellini SCR: Federico Fellini & Tonino Guerra PHOTOG: Giuseppe Rotunno MUSIC: Nino Rota
Oscar-winner (Best Foreign Film): Humorous, surrealistic remembrances of Italian life during rule of Mussolini

The Amazing Captain Nemo
1978, (USA), WB, color, 95 mins.
W: Jose Ferrer (*Capt. Nemo*), Burgess Meredith (*Prof. Cunningham*), Tom Hallick (*Cmdr. Tom Franklin*), Lynda Day George (*Kate*), Burr DeBenning (*Lt. Jim Porter*), Warren Stevens (*Miller*), Mel Ferrer (*Dr. Cook*), Horst Buchholz (*The King of Atlantis*), Yale Summers, Richard Angarola, Med Flory, Anthony Geary, Peter Jason
D: Alex March PHOTOG: L.B. Abbott MUSIC: Richard LaSalle STORY: Robert Bloch
A.k.a **The Return of Captain Nemo**
TVM, juvenile SF-adventure: Legendary sea captain revived from suspended animation, opposes 20th-century villain

The Amazing Colossal Man
1957, (USA), Malibu/AIP, b&w, 81 mins.

W: Glenn Langan (*Col. Glenn Manning*), William Hudson (*Dr. Paul Lindstrom*), Cathy Downs (*Carol Forrest*), Russ Bender (*Richard Kingman*), James Seay (*Col. Hallock*), Larry Thor (*Dr. Eric Coulter*), Lyn Osborn (*Sgt. Taylor*), Diana Darrin (*The Typist*), William Hughes (*The Control Officer*), Hank Patterson (*Henry*), Scott Peters (*Sgt. Lee Carter*), Myron Cook (*Capt. Thomas*), Jack Kosslyn, Jean Moorhead, June Jocelyn, Harry Raybould, Jimmy Cross, Frank Jenks, Stanley Lachman, Judd Holdren, Ed Cobb, Michael Harris, Bill Cassady, Dick Nelson, Keith Heatherington, Paul Hahn
P, D & SPCL-FX: Bert I. Gordon SCR: Mark Hanna & Bert I. Gordon PHOTOG: Joseph Biroc MUSIC: Albert Glasser
orig. co-billed with Cat Girl
Minor SF classic: Plutonium-bomb blast turns man into giant. cf. War of the Colossal Beast

The Amazing Dr. G
see *Two Mafia Guys vs. Goldginger*

The Amazing Dr. Jekyll
1976, (USA), Webster, color
W: Harry Reems, Bobby Astyr, C.J. Laing, Susan Sparkle, Sue Rowan, Zebedy Colt, Terri Hall
D: Tim McCoy, inspired by Robert Louis Stevenson's *The Strange Case of Dr. Jekyll and Mr. Hyde*
Low-budget X-rated sex-farce

The Amazing Mr. Blunden
1972, (GB), Hemdale/Hemisphere, color, 99 mins.
W: Laurence Naismith (*Mr. Blunden*), Lynne Frederick (*Lucy Allen*), Garry Miller (*James Allen*), Rosalyn Landor (*Sarah*), Marc Granger (*George*), Diana Dors (*Mrs. Wickens*), Madeleine Smith (*Bella*), James Villiers (*Uncle Bertie*), David Lodge (*Wickens*), Dorothy Alison (*Mrs. Allen*), Stuart Lock (*Tom*), Deddie Davis (*Meakin*)
WRIT & D: Lionel Jeffries, based on Antonio Barker's story *The Ghosts* PHOTOG: Gerry Fisher MUSIC: Elmer Bernstein
Juvenile fantasy: Children time-travel to aid ghosts

The Amazing Mr. X
1948, (USA), Eagle Lion, b&w, 78 mins.
W: Cathy O'Donnell, Turhan Bey, Lynn Bari, Richard Carlson, Donald Curtis, Virginia Gregg
P: Ben Stoloff D: Bernard Vorhaus SCR: Muriel Roy Boulton & Ian Hunter ORIG. STORY: Crane Wilbur
A.k.a. **The Spiritualist**
Minor melodrama: Fake medium takes advantage of widow

The Amazing Partnership
1921, (GB), Stoll, b&w, 5,153 ft. (1570.6m)
W: Milton Rosmer (*Pryde*), Gladys Mason (*Grace Burton*), Arthur Walcott (*Julius Hatten*), Temple Bell (*Stella*), Teddy Arundell (*Baron Feldemay*), Robert Vallis (*Feldemay's Confederate*), Harry J. Worth (*Jean Marchand*), Charles Barnett (*M. Dupay*)
D: George Ridgwell SCR: Charles Barnett, from a novel by E. Phillips Oppenheim
Standard crime-triler: Reporter and girl detective recover stolen jewels hidden in Chinese idol

The Amazing Spider-Man
see *Spider-Man*

Amazing Stories
1985, (USA), Univ, color, 110 mins.
W: Kevin Costner, Casey Siemaszko, Tom Harrison, Christopher Lloyd, Bronson Pinchot, Scott Coffey, Jeffrey Jay Cohen, Mary Stuart Masterson
D: Steven Spielberg, William Dear & Robert Zemeckis
Standard fantasy trilogy (culled from teleseries): (1) Doomed cartoonist saved by imagination, (2) Rednecks mistake actor for living mummy, & (3) Teacher terrorizes pupils

Amazing Stories II
1987, (USA), Univ, color, 70 mins.
W: Danny DeVito, Rhea Perlman, John Lithgow, Roberts Blossom, Lukas Haas
Standard fantasy tales (culled from teleseries)

The Amazing Transparent Man
1960, (USA), AIP, b&w, 59 mins.
W: Marguerite Chapman, Douglas Kennedy, James Griffith, Ivan Triesault, Read Morgan, Norman Smith, Cormel Daniel, Jonathan Ledford, Edward Erwin, Patrick Cranshaw
P: Lester D. Guthrie D: Edgar G. Ulmer SCR: Jack Lewis
Minor SF: Scientist tries to create invisible army

The Amazing World of Psychic Phenomena
1977, (USA), color
W: Raymond Burr (*host*)
Standard speculation-docu: Supernatural events around the world

The Amazon Queen
see *La Regina delle Amazzoni*

Amazon Quest
1949, (USA), Agay/Film Classics, b&w, 75 mins.
W: Tom Neal, Carole Matthews, Carol Donne, Don Zelaya, Ralph Graves, Joseph

Crehan, Jack George, Joe Granby, Edward Clark, Julian Rivero, Lester Sharpe, Z. Yaconelli
D: S.K. Seeley **SCR:** Al Martin **ORIG. STORY:** Irwin Gielgud **PHOTOG:** Guy Rowe **MUSIC DIR:** Alexander Laszlo
Minor adventure-thriller: Perilous trek through Brazilian jungle

Amazons
1984, (USA), Circle/ABC-TV, color, 90 mins.
W: Madeline Stowe (*Sharon*), Jennifer Warren (*Diane*), Stella Stevens (*Kathryn*), Jack Scalia (*Tony Monaco*), Tamara Dobson (*Rosalund*), Peter Scolari (*Jerry Menzies*), Nicholas Pryor (*Dr. Thompson*), Leslie Bevis (*Vivian Todd*), Jordan Charney (*Stowe*), Greg Monaghan (*James*), Stephen Shellen (*Kevin*), Hansford Rowe (*Gov. Price*), Suzanne Kent (*Nurse Franklin*), Jessie Lawrence Ferguson (*Baker*), Robert Harrison (*Roger*), Paul Cross (*Martin*), Morgan Lofting (*Marge Webster*), Carl LaRocco (*Rossi*), Wesley Thompson (*The Attendant*), Paula Russell (*The Woman Newscaster*), John Walsh (*The Reporter*), Edward Beimfohr (*The Anchorman*), Nick DeMauro (*The Victim*), Donald Craig (*The Moderator*), Ron Prince (*The Desk Sgt.*), Fred Dennis (*The Mailman*), Heather Hepler (*Tracy*), Crystal DeWoody (*Amy*), Misty Hall (*Deidre*), Jessica Weisman (*Christine*), Amy Benesh (*Kelly*), Danielle Michonne (*Marsha*)
D: Paul Michael Glaser **TELEPLAY:** David Solomon, from a story by David Solomon & Guerdon Trueblood **PHOTOG:** Dean Cundey **SPCL-FX:** Steve Gauch & Ray Beetz **MUSIC:** Basil Poledouris
TVM, standard thriller: Females plot world domination

Amazons
1986, (USA-Mex), New Horizons/Aries/Concorde, color, 76 mins.
W: Windsor Taylor Randolph (*Dyala*), Willie Nelson, Penelope Reed, Joseph Whipp, Danitza Kingsley, Wolfram Hoechst, Jacques Arndt, Frank Cocza, Charles Finch, Santiago Mallo, Annie Larronde, Mary Fournery, Armand Capo, Noelle Balfour, Esther Velazquez, Fabiana Smith, Marc Woinsky, Lena Marie Johansson, Linda Guzman, Albert Marty, William Reta
D: Alex Sessa **SCR:** Charles Saunders **PHOTOG:** Leonard Solis **SPCL-FX:** Willy Smith **MUSIC:** Oscar Camp
Minor adventure-fantasy: Warrior women oppose machinations of evil wizard

The Amazons' March and Evolutions
1902, (GB), G.A.S. Films/WTC, b&w, 75 ft. (22.9m)
D: G.A. Smith
A.k.a. ***The March of the Amazons***
Standard comedy short: Dance scene from pantomime "Robinson Crusoe"

Amazons of Rome
see ***La Regina delle Amazzoni***

Amazon Women on the Moon
1987, (USA), Univ, color, 85 mins.
W: Lou Jacobi, Steve Forrest, Rosanna Arquette, Sybil Danning, Michelle Pfeiffer, Griffin Dunne, B.B. King, Forrest J. Ackerman, Joe Pantoliano, Joey Travolta, Rip Taylor, Angel Tompkins, Steve Allen, Steven Guttenberg, David Alan Grier, Mary Reid, Henny Youngman, Russ Meyer, Charlie Callas, Jackie Vernon, Paul Bartel, Slappy White, Carrie Fisher, Ralph Bellamy, Henry Silva, Robert Colbert, Monique Gabrielle, Arsenio Hall, Kelly Preston, Howard Hesseman, Ed Begley Jr.
P: Robert K. Weiss **D:** Joe Dante, Carl Gottlieb, Peter Horton, John Landis & Robert K. Weiss **SCR:** Michael Barrie & Jim Mulholland
Standard comedy-fantasy: Satire on "B" flicks of 1950's

The Ambulance
1990, (USA), Epic Prods., color, 95 mins.
W: Eric Roberts, James Earl Jones, Megan Gallagher, Janine Turner, Richard Bright, Eric Braeden, Red Buttons, Nichlas Chinlund, Laurene Landon, Jill Gatsby, Jim Dixon, Stan Lee
D & SCR: Larry Cohen **PHOTOG:** Jacques Haitkin **MUSIC:** Jay Chattaway
Standard thriller: Cartoonist seeks woman who mysteriously vanished from ambulance

The Ambushers
1967, (USA), Meadway/Col, color, 102 mins.
W: Dean Martin (*Matt Helm*), Senta Berger, Janice Rule, James Gregory, Beverly Adams, Albert Salmi, Kurt Kasznar, Roy Jenson, David Mauro, Edit Angold
P: Irving Allen **D:** Henry Levin **SCR:** Herbert Baker, from a novel by Donald Hamilton **PHOTOG:** Burnett Guffey & Edward Colman **SPCL-FX:** Danny Lee **MUSIC:** Hugo Montenegro
Standard spy-comedy: Super-agent trails power-mad espionage chief. cf. ***Murderers' Row,*** ***The Silencers*** *(1966) and* ***The Wrecking Crew***

Ambush In Leopard Street
1962, (GB), Bill & Michael Luckwell/Col, b&w, 60 mins.
W: James Kenney (*Johnny*), Michael Brennan (*Harry*), Bruce Seton (*Nimmo*), Norman Rodney (*Kegs*), Jean Harvey (*Jean*), Pauline Delany (*Cath*), Marie Conmee (*Myra*)
P: Bill Luckwell & Jock MacGregor **D:** J. Henry Piperno **SCR:** Bernard Spicer & Ahmed Faroughy **STORY:** Bernard Spicer
Standard crime-thriller: Retired crook plans to ambush diamond consignment

An American Christmas Carol
1979, (USA), Primetime/ABC-TV, color, 95 mins.
W: Henry Winkler (*Benedict Slade*), Chris Wiggins (*Brewster*), Susan Hogan

(*Helen*), Gerard Parkes (*Jessup*), Linda Goranson (*Mrs. Thatcher*), Kenneth Pogue (*Jack Latham*), Dorian Harewood, R.H. Thomson, Arlene Duncan, David Wayne, Tammy Bourne, Chris Crabb, James B. Douglas, Cec Linder, Derrick Jones, Michael Wincott, Sylvia Llewellyn, Sammy Snyders, Frank Gibbs, Marie Pirie, Justine Till, William Ballantyne
D: Eric Till **TELEPLAY:** Jerome Coopersmith, inspired by Charles Dickens' *A Christmas Carol* **PHOTOG:** Richard Ciupka **MUSIC:** Hagood Hardy
TVM, minor fantasy: Spirits reform skinflint in "Americanized" version of durable classic

American Cyborg: Steel Warrior
1994, (USA), Global Pictures, color, 94 mins.
W: Joe Lara (*Austin*), Nicole Hansen (*Mary*), John Ryan, Yoseph Shiloa, Andrea Litt, Kevin Patterson, Eric Storch
D: Boaz Davidson **STORY:** Boaz Davidson & Christopher Pearce **PHOTOG:** Avi Karpick **MUSIC:** Blake Leyh **SCR:** Bill Crounse
Minor SF-thriller: Killer cyborg hunts last fertile woman on Earth

American Gothic
1988, (GB), Manor Ground/Vidmark, color, 90 mins.
W: Rod Steiger (*Pa*), Yvonne DeCarlo (*Ma*), Fiona Hutchison (*Lynn*), Michael J. Pollard (*Woody*), Sarah Torgov (*Cynthia*), Mark Lindsay Chapman (*Rob*), Terry Kelly (*The Psychiatrist*), Mark Ericksen (*Jeff*), Caroline Barclay (*Terri*), Janet Wright (*Fanny*), Stephen Shellen (*Paul*), William Hootkins (*Teddy*)
D: John Hough **SCR:** Burt Wetanson & Michael Vines **PHOTOG:** Harvey Harrison **MUSIC:** Alan Parker
Standard thriller: Vacationers meet murderous family

The American Heiress
1917, (GB), Hepworth/Harma, b&w, 2,800 ft. (853.4m)
W: Alma Taylor (*Bessie*), Violet Hopson (*Cynthia Hunks*), Stewart Rome (*Parker*), Lionelle Howard (*Bob Summers*), John MacAndrews (*Viper Smith*), Johnny Butt (*Sir John Higgins*)
D: Cecil M. Hepworth **STORY:** Blanche McIntosh
Standard crime-thriller: Maid poses as heiress, is abducted by thieves

An American Tale
1986, (USA), Univ, color, 80 mins.
VOICES: Cathianne Blore, Dom DeLuise, John Finnegan, Amy Green, Phillip Glasser, Madeline Kahn, Will Ryan, Pat Musick, Christopher Plummer, Nehemiah Persoff
D: Don Bluth **SCR:** Judy Freudberg & Tony Geiss **PHOTOG:** David R. Ankey, Joe Juiliano, Karl Bredendieck, Rocky Solotoff, Ralph Migliori, Stan Miller & Marilyn, O'Connor **MUSIC:** James Horner **SONG:** *Somewhere Out There*
Entertaining animated fantasy: Immigrant mouse searches for family

An American Tale: Fievel Goes West
1991, (USA), Univ, color, 74 mins.
VOICES: Phillip Glasser, James Stewart, Erica Yohn, Cathy Cavadini, Nehemiah Persoff, Dom DeLuise, Amy Irving, John Cleese, Jon Lovitz
D: Phil Nibbelink & Simon Wells
Standard animated fantasy: Further adventures of immigrant mouse

An American Werewolf in London
1981, (GB), Lycanthrope Films Ltd./Polygram/Univ, color, 98 mins.
W: David Naughton (*David Kessler*), Jenny Agutter (*Alex*), Griffin Dunne (*Jack Goodman*), John Woodvine (*Dr. Hirsch*), Brian Glover (*A Chess Player*), David Schofield (*The Dart Player*), Lila Kaye (*The Barmaid*), Paul Kember (*Sgt. McManus*), Don McKillop (*Insp. Villiers*), Frank Oz (*Collins*), Paula Jacobs (*Mrs. Kessler*), Anne-Marie Davies (*Nurse Gallagher*), Mark Fisher (*Max*), Gordon Sterne (*Mr. Kessler*), Michele Brisigotti (*Rachel*), Rik Mayall (*A Chess Player*), Paddy Ryan (*The Werewolf*), Colin Fernandes (*Benjamin*), Nina Carter (*Naughty Nina*), Geoffrey Burridge (*Harry Berman*), Brenda Cavendish (*Judith Browns*), Christopher Scoular (*Sean*), Sydney Bromley (*Alf*), Frank Siguineau, Rufus Deakin, Michael Carter, Will Leighton, Elizabeth Bradley, Lesley Ward, George Hilsdon, Gerry Lewis, Dennis Fraser, Claudine Bowyer, Joe Belcher, Sean Baker, Johanna Crayden, Albert Moses, Mary Tempest, Cynthia Powell
P: George Folsey Jr. **WRIT & D:** John Landis **PHOTOG:** Robert Paynter **SPCL MAKEUP FX:** Rick Baker **MUSIC:** Elmer Bernstein
Well-made horror-comedy: Yank student, bitten on moors by local lycanthrope, has astounding adventures

An American Werewolf in Paris
1997, (USA), Disney, color, 99 mins.
W: Julie Delpy, Tom Everett Scott, Pierre Cosso, Julie Bowen, Phil Buckman, Vince Vieluf
D: Anthony Waller **MUSIC:** Wilbert Hirsch
Unusual horror-fantasy: Student proves lycanthropic after meeting with French werewolves

Americathon
1979, (USA), UA, color
W: John Ritter, Harvey Korman, Fred Willard, Elvis Costello, Chief Dan George
P: Joe Roth **D:** Neil Israel **SCR:** Michael Mislove & Monica Johnson
Standard SF-comedy: 1998 telethon to save USA

America 3000
1986, (USA), Cannon, color, 94 mins.
W: Chuck Wagner, Laurene Landon, Camilla Sparv (*Rhea*), Steve Malovic

D & SCR: David Engelbach
Minor SF-thriller: Post-nuke rebel opposes female dictator

The Amityvillie Curse
1990, (Can), color, 91 mins.
W: Kim Coates, Dawna Wightman, Helen Hughes, Jan Rubes, David Stein, Anthony Dean Rubes, Cassandra Gava
D: Tom Berry, from Hans Holzer's book, *The Amityville Horror*
A.k.a. **Maniac Mansion** *and* **Replica of a Crime**
Made-for-Video, standard horror-fantasy: House has life of its own

The Amityville Horror
1979, (USA), Professional/AIP, color, 117 mins.
W: James Brolin (*George Lutz*), Margot Kidder (*Kathleen Lutz*), Rod Steiger (*Father Delaney*), Murray Hamilton (*Father Ryan*), John Larch (*Father Nuncio*), Natasha Ryan (*Amy*), Michael Sacks (*Jeff*), K.C. Martel (*Greg*), Helen Shaver (*Carolyn*), Val Avery (*Sgt. Gion-friddo*), Irene Dailey (*Aunt Helena*), Elsa Raven (*Mrs. Townsend*), Amy Wright (*Jackie*), Marc Vahanian (*Jimmy*), Ellen Saland (*The Bride*), Eddie Barth (*Agucci*)
P: Ronald Saland & Elliot Geisinger **D:** Stuart Rosenberg **SCR:** Sandor Stern, based on book by Jay Anson **PHOTOG:** Fred J. Koenekamp **MUSIC:** Lalo Schifrin
Entertaining but loose cinemadaptation of creepy best-seller: Spooks bother family in notorious house

Amityville: Dollhouse
1997, (USA), Gramercy, color
Made-for-Video, minor horror-fantasy

Amityville II: The Possession
1982, (USA), Dino De Laurentiis/Orion, color, 110 mins.
W: James Olson (*Father Frank Adamski*), Burt Young (*Montelli*), Rutanya Alda (*Dolores Montelli*), Jack Magner (*Sonny Montelli*), Diane Franklin (*Patricia Montelli*), Andrew Prine, Moses Gunn, Ted Ross
P: Ira N. Smith & Steven R. Greenwald **D:** Damiano Damiani **SCR:** Tommy Lee Wallace, based on Hans Holzer's novel *Murder in Amityville* **PHOTOG:** Franco DiGiacomo **SPCL-FX SPRVSR:** Glen Robinson **MUSIC:** Lalo Schifrin
Standard horror-thriller: Spooks, demonic possession, and incest plague unsuspecting family

Amityville 3-D
1983, (USA), Dino De Laurentiis/Orion, 3D, color, 92 mins.
W: Tony Roberts (*John Baxter*), Tess Harper (*Nancy Baxter*), John Beal (*Harold Caswell*), Robert Joy (*Elliot West*), Candy Clark (*Melanie*), Meg Ryan, Leora Dana (*Emma*), John Harkins (*Clifford*), Lori Loughlin (*Susan*), Meg Ryan (*Lisa*), Neill Barry (*Jeff*), Rikke Borge (*Elliot's Ass't*), Pete Kowanko (*Roger*), Carlos Romano (*David*), Josephina Echanove (*Dolores*), Jorge Zepeda (*The Van Driver*), Raquel Pankowsky (*The Sensory Woman*), Paco Pharres (*The Maintenance Man*)
D: Richard Fleischer **SCR:** William Wales **PHOTOG:** Fred Schuler **SPCL-FX SPRVSR:** Jeff Jarvis **MUSIC:** Howard Blake
Minor horror-thriller: Writer purchases maligned mansion

Amityville: The Evil Escapes
1989, (USA), NBC-TV, color, 95 mins.
W: Patty Duke (*Nancy Evans*), Jane Wyatt (*Alice Leacock*), Fredric Lehne (*Father Kibbler*), Brandy Gold (*Jessica Evans*), Norman Lloyd (*Father Manfred*), Geri Betzler (*Amanda Evans*), Aaron Eisenberg (*Brian Evans*)
TVM, standard fantasy-thriller: Satanic forces travel across country

Amityville 1992: It's About Time
1992, (USA), TV Movie, color, 95 mins.
W: Stephen Macht, Shawn Weatherly, Megan Ward, Damon Martin, Nita Talbot, Dick Miller
D: Tony Randel
TVM, standard fantasy-thriller: Antique clock from haunted estate engenders new horror

Amityville: The New Generation
1993, (USA), color, 92 mins.
W: Ross Partridge, Julia Nickson-Soul, David Naughton, Richard Roundtree, Terry O'Quinn
D: John Murlowski **SCR:** Christopher DeFaria & Antonio Toro
Standard horror-fantasy: Evil mirror influences photographer and his roommates

Amok (1976)
see **Eaten Alive!** *(1976)*

Amok (1977)
see **Schizo** *(1977)*

Among the Living
1941, (USA), Para, b&w, 68 mins.
W: Albert Dekker, Susan Hayward, Harry Carey, Frances Farmer, Gordon Jones, Jean Phillips, Maude Eburne
P: Sol C. Siegel **D:** Stuart Heisler **SCR:** Lester Cole & Garrett Fort **PHOTOG:** Theodor Sparkuhl
Modest melodrama: Madman terrorizes small community

El Amor Brujo (Love, the Magician)
1972, (Sp), Espana, color, 101 mins.
W: Antonio Gades (*Antonio*), La Polaca (*Candela*), Morucha (*Lucia*), Rafael de Cordova (*Diego*)
P & D: Rovira-Beleta, based on a musical by Don Manuel de Falla
Unusual fantasy: Mystery bedevils lovers

El Amor Brujo (Love, the Magician)
1986, (Sp), Orion, color, 100 mins.
W: Antonio Gades (*Carmelo*), Cristina Hoyos (*Candela*), Laura del Sol (*Lucia*), Juan Antonio Jimenez (*Jose*), Emma Penella (*Aunt Rosario*), La Polaca (*Pastora*), Gomez de Jerez (*El Lobo*), Enrique Ortega (*Jose's Father*), Giovana (*Rocio*), Candy Roman (*Chulo*), Diego Pantoja (*Candela's Father*)
D: Carlos Saura **SCR:** Carlos Saura & Antonio Gades, based on a musical by Don Manuel de Falla **PHOTOG:** Teo Escamilla **MUSIC:** Manuel de Falla
Unusual musical-fantasy: Ghost lover fascinates beauty

Gli Amori di Ercole (The Loves of Hercules)
1960, (It-Fr), Walter Manley Enterprises, color, 98 mins.
W: Mickey Hargitay (*Hercules*), Jayne Mansfield, Massimo Serato, Rossella Como, Tina Gloriani, Giulio Donnini, Andrea Aureli, Arturo Bragaglia, Andrea Scotti, Moira Orfei, Rene Dary, Olga Solbelli, Sandrine, Antonio Gradoli, Cesare Fantoni, Giovanna Galletti, Barbara Florian, Gianni Loti
D: Carlo Ludovico Bragaglia **SCR:** Alessandro Continenza & Luciano Doria **STORY:** Alberto Manca **PHOTOG:** Enzo Serafin **SPCL-FX:** Augusto Vivani & Nino Battistelli **MUSIC:** Carlo Innocenzi
USA retitle, **Hercules vs. the Hydra**
Standard myth-adventure: Legendary hero tempted by fair sex as he seeks to avenge wife's death

Un Amour de Poche (A Pocket Love)
1957, (Fr), Madeleine, b&w, 85 mins.
W: Jean Marais, Genevieve Page, Agnes Laurent, Regine Lovi, Amedee
P: Gilbert Goldschmidt **D:** Pierre Kast, based on Waldemar Kaempffert's *The Diminishing Draft* **PHOTOG:** Ghislain Clouquet
USA retitle, **Girl in His Pocket**
Standard comedy-fantasy: Professor uses secret shrinking formula as solution to his romantic problems

Anaconda: ERIC STOLTZ

The Amphibian Man
1964, (Russ), NTA, color, 96 mins.
W: William Koren, Anastasia Virten, K. Korieniev, M. Virzinskaya
D: Gennadi Kazansky & Vladimir Chebotaryov **SCR:** Alexander Xenofontov, Alexei Kapler & Akiba Golburt
Fr retitle, **Tarzan des Mers (Tarzan of the Seas)**
Standard SF-thriller: Scientist studies mutant son

Am Rande der Welt (At the Edge of the World)
1927, (Ger), Ufa, b&w
W: Max Schreck, Brigitte Helm
D: Karl Grune
Unusual melodrama: Star-crossed lovers find mystery

Amsterdam Affair
1968, (GB), Trio-Group W/London Independent Producers, color, 91 mins.
W: Wolfgang Kieling (*Insp. Van Der Valk*), William Marlowe (*Martin Ray*), Catherine Von Schell (*Sophie Ray*), Pamela Ann Davey (*Elsa de Charmoy*), Josef Dubin-Behrman (*Eric de Charmoy*), Will Van Hensbergen (*The Magistrate*), Guido de Moor (*Piet Ulbricht*)
P: William Gell & Howard Barnes   **D:** Gerry O'Hara   **SCR:** Edmund Ward, from Nicholas Freeling's novel *Amsterdam*
Standard crime-thriller: Novelist accused of killing mistress

The Amsterdam Kill
1977, (Hong Kong), Golden Harvest/Col, color, 132 mins.
W: Robert Mitchum (*Quinlan*), Bradford Dillman (*Odums*), Keye Luke (*Chung Wei*), Richard Egan (*Ridgeway*), Leslie Nielsen (*Knight*), George Cheung (*Jimmy Wong*), Chan Sing (*The Assassin*)
D: Robert Clouse   **SCR:** Robert Clouse & Gregory Teifer   **STORY:** Gregory Teifer   **PHOTOG:** Alan Hume   **MUSIC:** Hal Schaefer
Minor thriller: Drug dealer seeks retirement

Amuck
1978, (It), Group 1 Films, color, 98 mins.
W: Farley Granger, Barbara Bouchet
P & D: Jurgen Goslar
*A.k.a. **Maniac Mansion***
Minor eroto-thriller: Man kidnaps women, forces them to perform sex acts

Anaconda
1997, (USA), Col, color, 90 mins.
W: Jennifer Lopez (*Terri Flores*), Ice Cube (*Danny Rich*), Jon Voight (*Paul Sarone*), Eric Stoltz (*Steven Cale*), Jonathan Hyde (*Warren Westridge*), Owen Wilson (*Gary Dixon*), Kari Wuhrer (*Denise Kalberg*), Vincent Castellanos (*Mateo*), Danny Trejo
D: Luis Llosa   **SCR:** Hans Bauer, Jim Cash & Jack Epps Jr.   **PHOTOG:** Bill Butler   **MUSIC:** Randy Edelman   **SPCL-FX:** John Nelson   **SONGS:** *Foe Life* & *Tipsy Dazy*
Standard thriller: Giant snake menaces documentary filmmakers in Amazon

An American does London in 10 Minutes
1908, (GB), Walter Tyler, b&w, 580 ft. (179.3m)

And Now The Screaming Starts: STEPHANIE BEACHAM

Standard fantasy: Speeded-up tour of London sights

Anastasia
1997, (USA), 20th-Fox, color
VOICES: Meg Ryan (*Anastasia*), Christopher Lloyd (*Rasputin*), John Cusack (*Dimitri*), Angela Lansbury (*Marie*)
D: Don Bluth & Gary Goldman
Animated adventure-fantasy: Princess flees revolution

The Anatomist
1961, (GB), b&w, 73 mins.
W: Alastair Sim, George Cole, Margaret Gordon
D: Leonard William

Minor melodrama: Scottish doctor procures corpses for medical experiments

Anatomy of a Psycho
1961, (USA), Unitel of California, b&w
W: Ronnie Burns, Judy Howard, Darrell Howe, Pamela Lincoln, Russ Bender, Don Devlin, Robert W. Stabler, Pat McMahon
P & D: Brooke L. Peters   **SCR:** Jane Mann & Larry Lee
Standard thriller: Convict's brother seeks revenge

Anatomy of Terror
1973, (USA-GB), ABC-TV, color, 74 mins.
W: Paul Burke, Polly Bergen, William Job, Roger Hume
TVM, minor thriller: Brainwashed man reveals sinister secret

An Andalousian Dog
see Un Chien Andalou

Der Andere (The Other)
1913, (Ger), b&w
W: Albert Bassermann
D: Max Mack, based on Paul Lindau's stage play
*Unusual psychodrama: After falling from horse, Berlin lawyer experiences split-personality
cf. **Dr. Hallers***

And Comes the Dawn. . . But Colored Red
see Web of the Spider

—And Now the Screaming Starts!
1973, (GB), Amicus/Harbor/CRC/Fox-Rank, color, 87 mins.
W: Peter Cushing (*Dr. Pope*), Herbert Lom (*Henry Fengriffen*), Patrick Magee (*Dr. Whittle*), Stephanie Beacham (*Catherine Fengriffen*), Ian Ogilvy (*Charles Fengriffen*), Gillian Lind (*Aunt Edith*), Guy Rolfe (*Maitland*), Rosalie Crutchley (*Mrs. Luke*), Geoffrey Whitehead (*Woodsman Silas*), Sally Harrison (*Sarah*), Janet Key (*Bridget*), Lloyd Lamble (*Sir John Westcliffe*), Norman Mitchell (*The Constable*), Kay Adrian, John Sharp, David Barclay, Blake Butler, Frank Forsyth, Daniel Jones, Vic Chapman, Beth Owen, Hilary Martin, Elsa Smith, Sylvester Morand, Toni Sinclair, John Stamp, Larry Taylor, Drew Wood, Rocky Taylor, Gloria Walker
P: Max J. Rosenberg & Milton Subotsky   **D:** Roy Ward Baker   **SCR:** Roger Marshall, based on David Case' novel *Fengriffen*   **PHOTOG:** Denys Coop   **MUSIC:** Douglas Gamley
Static horror-thriller: Ghost rapes new bride

Androcles and the Lion
1952, (USA), RKO, b&w, 98 mins.
W: Alan Young (*Androcles*), Jean Simmons (*Lavinia*), Victor Mature (*The Captain*), Robert Newton (*Ferrovius*), Gene Lockhart (*The Menagerie Keeper*), Maurice Evans (*Caesar*), Elsa Lanchester (*Megaera*), John Hoyt (*Cato*), Alan Mowbray (*The Editor*), Reginald Gardiner (*Lentulus*), Noel Willman (*Spintho*), Jim Backus (*The Centurian*), Lowell Gilmore (*Metellus*)
P: Gabriel Pascal   **D:** Chester Erskine   **SCR:** Noel Langley & Chester Erskine, from George Bernard Shaw's play   **PHOTOG:** Harry Stradling   **MUSIC:** Frederick Hollander
Modest satire: Lion befriends slave

Android
1984, (USA), Rupert Harvey-Barry Opper/SHO, color, 80 mins.
W: Klaus Kinski (*Dr. Daniel*), Don Opper (*Max 404*), Brie Howard (*Maggie*), Norbert Weisser (*Keller*), Crofton Hardester (*Mendes*), Kendra Kirchner (*Cassandra*), Gary Corarito, Mary Ann Fisher, Darrell Larson, Ian Scheibel, Wayne Springfield, Julia Gibson, Randy Connor, Roger Kelton, Rachel Talalay, Johanne Todd
D: Aaron Lipstadt   **SCR:** James Reigle & Don Opper   **PHOTOG:** Tim Suhrstedt   **SPCL-FX:** New World Effects   **MUSIC:** Don Preston
Modest SF-satire: Cyborg faces obsolescence

The Android Affair
1995, (USA), USA-TV, color, 95 mins.
W: Harley Jane Kozak, Griffin Dunne, Ossie Davis, Saul Rubinek, Peter Outerbridge, Natalie Radford
D & TELEPLAY: Richard Kletter   **PHOTOG:** Bernard Salzman   **MUSIC:** Simon Boswell
TVM, minor SF-thriller: Woman physician falls in love with android

The Andromeda Nebula
1968, (Russ), color
from Ivan Efremov's novel
Minor SF-adventure: Saga of space exploration

The Andromeda Strain
1971, (USA), Univ, color, 137 mins.
W: Arthur Hill (*Dr. Jeremy Stone*), James Olson (*Dr. Mark Hall*), David Wayne (*Dr. Charles Dutton*), Kate Reid (*Dr. Ruth Leavitt*), George Mitchell (*Jackson*), Mark Jenkins (*Shawn*), Paula Kelly (*Dr. Karen Anson*), Kermit Murdock (*Dr. Robertson*), Richard O'Brien (*Grimes*), Ramon Bieri (*Maj. Manchek*), Eric Christmas (*The Sen. from Vermont*), Peter Hobbs (*Gen. Sparks*), Joe Dirreda, Ken Swofford, Carl Reindel, Frances Reid, Richard Bull, John Carter
P & D: Robert Wise   **SCR:** Nelson Gidding, from Michael Crichton's novel
   PHOTOG: Richard H. Kline   **MUSIC:** Gil Melle & Boris Leven

"...trim, fast, suspenseful, just plain superb thriller, completely absorbing in its technology. It's perhaps the most thoroughly satisfying cinematic adaptation of a bestseller since Rosemary's Baby—Mark Stevens, Cinefantastique
Lavish production values, good performances in gripping SF-thriller: Satellite brings deadly alien virus to Earth

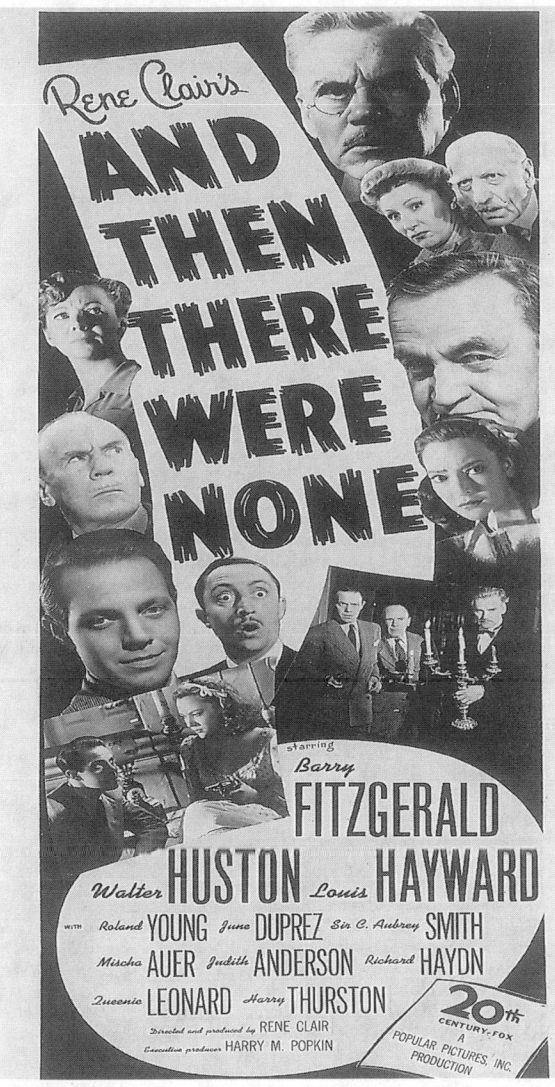

And Soon the Darkness
1970, (GB), Assoc. British/Anglo-EMI/Levitt-Pickman, color, 99 mins.
<u>W:</u> Pamela Franklin (*Jane*), Michele Dotrice (*Cathy*), Sandor Eles (*Paul*), John Nettleton (*The Gendarme*), Hana-Maria Pravda (*Mme. Lassal*), Clare Kelly (*The Schoolmistress*), Claude Bertrand (*Lassal*), John Franklyn (*The Old Man*), Jean Carmet (*Renier*)
<u>D:</u> Robert Fuest <u>STORY & SCR:</u> Brian Clemens & Terry Nation <u>MUSIC:</u> Laurie Johnson
Minor thriller: Nurse on holiday slain by sex maniac

And Suddenly It's Murder
1964, (It), Royal, b&w, 90 mins.
<u>W:</u> Alberto Sordi, Dorian Gray
Minor comedy-thriller

And Then He Woke Up
1915, (GB), I.B. Davidson-St. George/Browne, b&w, 1,025 ft. (312.4m)
<u>D:</u> A.E. Coleby
Standard comedy-fantasy: Man rejected by army dreams his bed transports him to France

And Then There Were None
1945, (USA), Popular/20th-Fox, b&w, 97 mins.
<u>W:</u> Walter Huston (*Dr. Armstrong*), Louis Hayward (*Philip Lombard*), Roland Young (*Blore*), June Duprez (*Vera Claythorne*), Richard Haydn (*Rogers*), Barry Fitzgerald (*Judge Quincannon*), Mischa Auer (*Prince Nikki Starloff*), Queenie Leonard (*Mrs. Rogers*), Judith Anderson (*Emily Brent*), C. Aubrey Smith (*Gen. Mandrake*), Harry Thurston
<u>P & D:</u> Rene Clair <u>SCR:</u> Dudley Nichols, from Agatha Christie's novel <u>PHOTOG:</u> Lucien Andriot <u>MUSIC:</u> Charles Previn
A.k.a. Ten Little Niggers, cf. Ten Little Indians (1965, 1974, & 1989).
Classic thriller: Members of stranded group systematically murdered by unknown assassin

And the Wall came Tumbling Down
1985, (GB), color
<u>W:</u> Barbi Benton, Gareth Hunt, Brian Deacon
Standard thriller: Demolition crew unearths 300-year-old remains of satanic cult

And to Die of Pleasure
see Et Mourir de Plaisir

And Women Shall Weep
1960, (GB), Ethiro/RFD, b&w, 65 mins.
<u>W:</u> Ruth Dunning (*Mrs. Lumsden*), Max Butterfield (*Terry Lumsden*), Gillian Vaughan (*Brenda Wilkes*), Richard O'Sullivan (*Godfrey Lumsden*), Claire Gordon (*Sadie MacDougall*), David Gregory (*Desmond Peel*), David Rose (*Woody Forrest*), Leon Garcia (*Ossie Green*)
<u>P:</u> Norman Williams <u>D:</u> John Lemont <u>STORY:</u> John Lemont & Leigh Vance
Standard crime-thriller: Widow saves teen son from life of crime

And You Thought Your Parents Were Weird
1991, (USA), Trimark, color, 92 mins.
<u>W:</u> Marcia Strassman (*Sarah Carson*), Joshua Miller (*Josh Carson*), Edan Gross (*Max Carson*), John Quade (*Walter Kotzwinkle*), Sam Behrens (*Steve Franklin*), Alan Thicke (*The Voice of Matthew Carson*), Susan Gibney (*Alice Woods*), Gustav Vintas, Eric Walker, Richard Libertini (*Voice*)
<u>MUSIC:</u> Randy Miller <u>WRIT & D:</u> Tony Cookson <u>PHOTOG:</u> Paul Elliott
Minor SF-fantasy: Father's soul inhabits robot

L'Ange de Noel (The Christmas Angel)
1905, (Fr), Star, b&w, 158m (518.4 ft./8.8 mins.)
<u>W:</u> Rachel Gillet, Georges Melies
<u>D:</u> Georges Melies
A.k.a. The Beggar Maiden
Standard fantasy (in 7 scenes): Supernatural being brightens holiday

Angel, Angel, Down We Go
1969, (USA), AIP, color
<u>W:</u> Jennifer Jones, Jordan Christopher, Roddy McDowall, Lou Rawls, Holly Near
<u>P:</u> Jerome F. Katzman <u>D & SCR:</u> Robert Thom <u>SONGS:</u> Mother Lover & Hey, Hey, and a Hi Ho
A.k.a. Cult of the Damned
Minor melodrama: Musicians corrupt family.

Angel Dust
1996, (Jap), Northern Arts Entertainment, color, 116 mins.
<u>W:</u> Kaho Minami (*Setsuko Suma*), Takeshi Wakamatsu (*Rei Aku*), Etshushi Toyokawa (*Tomoo*)
<u>D:</u> Sogo Ishii <u>SCR:</u> Yorozu Ikute & Sogo Ishii <u>PHOTOG:</u> Norimichi Kasamatsu <u>MUSIC:</u> Hiroyuki Nagashima
Unusual thriller: Serial killer targets young women on Tokyo commuter line

El Angel Exterminador (The Exterminating Angel)
1962, (Mex), Altura, b&w, 95 mins.
<u>W:</u> Silvia Pinal, Enrique Rambal, Jose Baviera, Jacqueline Andre, Luis Beristein, Augusto Benedico, Claudio Brook, Antonio Bravo, Cesar Del Campo
<u>D:</u> Luis Bunuel <u>SCR:</u> Luis Bunuel & Luis Alcoriza, from a play by Jose Bergamin <u>MUSIC:</u> Alessandro Scarlatti & Pietro Domenico <u>D & SCR:</u> Luis Bunuel <u>STORY:</u> Luis Bunuel & Luis Alcoriza <u>PHOTOG:</u> Gabriel Figueroa
distrib. in USA in 1967
Standard melodrama: Somber allegory of life and death

Angel Face
1952, (USA), RKO, b&w, 90 mins.
<u>W:</u> Jean Simmons, Robert Mitchum, Herbert Marshall, Barbara O'Neil, Mona Freeman, Leon Ames
<u>D:</u> Otto Preminger <u>SCR:</u> Frank S. Nugent <u>PHOTOG:</u> Harry Stradling (Sr.) <u>MUSIC:</u> Dimitri Tiomkin
Unusual thriller: Psychotic girl menaces stepmother

An Angel for Satan
see Un Angelo per Satan

Angel Heart
1987, (USA), Winkast-Union/Carolco, color, 112 mins.
<u>W:</u> Mickey Rourke (*Harry Angel*), Robert De Niro (*Louis Cyphre*), Lisa Bonet (*Epiphany Proudfoot*), Charlotte Rampling (*Margaret Krusemark*), Stocker Fontelieu (*Ethan Krusemark*), Dann Florek (*Winesap*), Brownie McGhee (*Toots Sweet*), Michael Higgins (*Dr. Fowler*), Elizabeth Whitcraft (*Connie*), Elliott Keener (*Sterne*), Charles Gordone (*Spider Simpson*), Kathleen Wilhoite (*The Nurse*), George Buck (*Izzy*), Judith Drake (*Izzy's Wife*), Peggy Severe (*Mammy Carter*), Gerald L. Orange (*Pastor John*), Pruitt Taylor Vince (*Deimos*), David Petitjean, Rick Washburn, Oakley Dalton, Neil Newlon, Yvonne Bywaters, Loys T. Bergeron, Joshua Frank, Karmen Harris, Nicole Burdette, Kendall Lupe, Jarrett Narcisse, Percy Martin, Viola Dunbar, Murray Bandel, Webster Whinery, Ernest Watson, Rickie Monte, Felix Mauras, Jeff Ward, Perry Nichols, Roy Thomas, Joy Hooper, Shirley Walker, Franklyn Scott, Andy Duppin, Bufort McClerkins, Sugar Blue, Joel Adam, Pinetop Perkins, W. Alonzo Stewart, Deacon John Moore, Darrel Beasley, Richard Payne, Lillian Boutte, Stephen Beasley, Louis Freddie Kohlman, Jerome Reddick, Stephen Kenyatta Simon, Oscar Best, Curtis

Pierre, Kufaru Aaron Mouton, Rosclyn Lionheart, Marilyn Banks, Lula Elzy, Francesca J. Ridge, Hope Clarke, Noel Jones, Sarita Allen, Valerie Jackson, Greer Goff, Arlena Rolant, Karen Davis, Shirleta Jones, Mark Taylor
D & SCR: Alan Parker, from William Hjortsberg's novel *Fallen Angel* **PHOTOG:** Michael Seresin **SPCL-FX SPRVSR:** J.C. Brotherhood **MUSIC:** Trevor Jones
Unusual thriller: 1950's gumshoe faces murder and voodoo

An Angelic Servant
1908, (Fr), Star, b&w, 147.2m (483 ft./8.2 mins.)
D: Georges Melies
Standard fantasy

The Angel Levine
1970, (USA), UA, color, 105 mins.
W: Zero Mostel (*Morris Mishkin*), Harry Belafonte (*Alexander Levine*), Ida Kaminska (*Fanny Mishkin*), Milo O'Shea (*Dr. Arnold Berg*), Eli Wallach (*The Store Clerk*), Anne Jackson (*The Lady in the Store*), Gloria Foster (*Sally*), Barbara Ann Teer (*The Welfare Lady*)
D: Janos Kadar **SCR:** Bill Gunn & Ronald Ribman, adapted from an allegorical story by Bernard Malamud **PHOTOG:** Richard Kratina **MUSIC:** Zdenek Liska
Uneven blend of philosophy & whimsy: Elderly Jewish tailor aided by black angel

The Angel of Christmas
see *L'Ange de Noel*

The Angel of the Ward
1915, (GB), Barker/Gerrard, b&w, 3,000 ft. (914.4m)
W: Evelyn Cecil (*Barbara*), Arthur Chisholm (*Gentleman Jack*), Herbert Trumper (*Philip*)
D: Tom Watts **SCR:** Langford Reed, from a novel by Murray Herbert
Standard crime-thriller: Surgeon's son tries to kill amnesiac heir

Angel on Earth
see *Angel on Wheels*

Angel on My Shoulder
1946, (USA), UA, b&w, 101 mins.
W: Paul Muni, Claude Rains, Anne Baxter, George Cleveland, Hardie Albright, Erskine Sanford, Onslow Stevens, James Flavin, Marion Martin
D: Archie Mayo **SCR:** Roland Kibbee & Harry Segall **PHOTOG:** James Van Trees **SPCL-FX:** Harry Redmond Jr. **MUSIC:** Dimitri Tiomkin
Classic fantasy: Deceased gangster makes deal with Satan, returns to Earth as respected judge

Angel on My Shoulder
1980, (USA), Beowulf/ABC-TV, color, 96 mins.
W: Peter Strauss (*Eddie Kagel*), Richard Kiley (*Satan*), Janis Paige (*Dolly Blaine*), Barbara Hershey (*Julie*), Seymour Cassel (*Smiley Mitchell*), Frank Campanella (*Giannelli*), Anne Seymour (*Mrs. Martin*), Scott Colomby (*Tony*), Terry Alexander (*Luke*), Peter MacLean (*Gregg Harlowe*), Charles Cooper (*Matt*), Billy Jacoby (*Joe Navotny*), Janis Hansen (*Cissy*), Murray Matheson (*The Stranger*)
D: John Berry **SCR:** George Kirgo **PHOTOG:** Gayne Rescher **SPCL-FX:** Knott Ltd. **MUSIC:** Artie Butler
TVM, inept remake of 1946 classic: Gangster makes deal with Devil

Angel on Wheels
1961, (Fr), color
W: Romy Schneider, Jean-Paul Belmondo, Henri Vidal
A.k.a. Angel on Earth
Minor fantasy: Heavenly envoy prevents race-car driver's death

Un Angelo per Satan (An Angel for Satan)
1966, (It), b&w
W: Barbara Steele
Minor horror-fantasy: Woman possessed by strange power

An Angel Passed Over Brooklyn
see *The Man Who Wagged His Tail*

Angels
1991, (GB), color
W: Tom Bell (*Michael*)
TVM, standard fantasy: Heavenly spirits guide souls to afterlife

Angels and Pirates
see *Angels in the Outfield* (1951)

Angels From Hell
1968, (USA), AIP, color, 86 mins.
W; Ted Markland, Arlene Martel, Stephen Oliver, Paul Bertoya, Tom Stern, James Murphy, Jack Starrett, Pepper Martin, Luana Talltree
D: Bruce Kessler
Standard thriller: Violent bikers roam

Angels in the Outfield
1951, (USA), UA, b&w, 102 mins.
W: Paul Douglas, Janet Leigh, Lewis Stone, Bruce Bennett, Keenan Wynn, Spring

Byington, Donna Corcoran
P & D: Clarence Brown **SCR:** Dorothy Kingsley & George Wells **PHOTOG:** Paul C. Vogel **MUSIC:** Amfitheatrof
GB retitle, Angels and Pirates
Modest fantasy: Baseball team becomes involved with orphan who sees angels

Angels in the Outfield
1994, (USA), Walt Disney, color,105 mins.
W: Danny Glover, Tony Danza, Christopher Lloyd, Taylor Negron
D: William Dear **SCR:** Holly Goldberg Sloan
Standard comedy-fantasy about baseball

Angels of Darkness
1957, (It), Excelsior, b&w, 84 mins.
W: Anthony Quinn, Linda Darnell, Valentina Cortese, Lea Padovani
D: Giuseppe Amato
Standard melodrama

Angel Street
see *Gaslight* (1940)

Angels' Wild Women
1972, (USA), Independent Int'l, color, 85 mins.
W: Ross Hagen, Kent Taylor, Regina Carrol, Vicki Volante, Preston Pierce, Jill Woelfel, William Bonner, Maggie Bemby
P & D: Al Adamson **SCR:** D. Dixon Jr.
Standard thriller: Four female bikers visit "free love colony," meet devil worshippers

The Angel Who Pawned Her Harp
1954, (GB), Assoc. Artists/Dominant, b&w, 76 mins.
W: Diane Cilento (*The Angel*), Felix Aylmer (*Joshua Webman*), Jerry Desmonde (*Parker*), Joe Linnane (*Ned Sullivan*), Robert Eddison (*The Voice*), Sheila Sweet (*Jenny Lane*), Alfie Bass (*Lennox*), Philip Guard (*Len Burrows*), Genitha Halsey (*Mrs. Burrows*), Edward Evans (*Sgt. Lane*), Elaine Wodson (*Mrs. Lane*), Thomas Gallagher (*Boyd*), Phyllis Morris (*Mrs. Trap*), David Kossoff (*Schwartz*), Raymond Rollett, June Ellis, Herbert C. Walton, Freddie Watts, Cyril Smith, Jean Aubrey, Thomas Moore, Maurice Kaufmann
D: Alan Bromly **SCR:** Sidney Cole & Charles Terrot, from Charles Terrot's novel **PHOTOG:** Arthur Grant **MUSIC:** Antony Hopkins
Whimsical fantasy: Beautiful angel visits Earth to do good deeds

An' Good in the Worst of Us
1911, (GB), Hepworth, b&w, 550 ft. (167.6m)
D: Bert Haldane
Standard crime-thriller: Ex-convict battles thieves, daughter fetches police

The Angry Red Planet
1959, (USA), Sino/AIP, color, 94 mins.
W: Gerald Mohr (*O'Banion*), Nora (*Naura*) Hayden (*Iris*), Les Tremayne (*Gettell*), Jack Kruschen (*Jacobs*), Edward Innes, Paul Mahn, J. Edward McKinley, Gordon Barnes, Tom Daly, Jack Haddock, Don Lamond, Brandy Bryan, Fred Ross, Arline Hunter, David DeHaven
P: Sid Pink & Norman Maurer **D:** Ib Melchior **SCR:** Sid Pink & Ib Melchior **STORY:** Sid Pink **PHOTOG:** Stanley Cortez **SPCL-FX:** Mel Sternlight, Art Wasson & Herman Townsley **MUSIC:** Paul Dunlap
Standard SF-adventure: First spaceship to Mars beset by horrors

Anguish
1988, (Sp), Ramaco Anstalt/Spectrafilm, color, 89 mins.
W: Zelda Rubinstein (*Mother*), Michael Lerner (*John*), Talia Paul (*Patty*), Angel Jove (*The Killer*), Clara Pastor (*Linda*), Isabel Garcia Lorca (*Caroline*), Edward Ledden, Gustavo Gili, Nat Baker, Antonio Regueiro, Joaquin Ribas, Patricia Manget, Janet Porter, Merche Gascon, Antonella Murgia, Michael Heat, Josephine Borchaca, Georgie Pinkley, Francesc Rabella, Diane Pinkley, Benito Pocino, Victor Guillen, Evelyn Rosenka, John Garcia, Michael Chandler, Vicente Gil, Pedro Vidal, Alberto Merelles, Robert Long, Miguel Montfort, Jordi Estivill, Joy Blackburn, Javier Moya, Kit Kincannon, Tatiana Thauven, Rose Sherpac, Jasmine Parker, Marc Maloney, Javier Duran, Randall Stewart, Eva Heald, Marc Aliba, Emi Matias, May Vives, Elisa Crehuet, Mingo Rafols, Maribel Martinez, Frank Craven, Mario Fernandez, Gustavo Guarino, Anita Shemanski, Craig Hill, John Shelly, Ricardo Azulay, Joe Wolberg, Steven Brown, Fabia Matas, Mark Parker, Philip Rodgers, Joan Lloveras, Ignacio Garcia, Jorge Ferrer, John Heald, Tito Alvarez, Elvira Salles
WRIT & D: Bigas Luna **SCR DIALOG:** Michael Berlin **PHOTOG:** J.M. Civit **MUSIC:** J.M. Pagan
Modest horror-satire: Audience watches "splatter" film, killer stalks theater

Animal Farm
1954, (GB), Louis de Rochemont/DCA, color, 75 mins.
VOICES: Maurice Denham
D: John Halas & Joy Batchelor **SCR:** Lothar Wolff, Borden Mace, Philip Stapp, John Halas & Joy Batchelor, from George Orwell's novel **PHOTOG:** S.G. Griffiths, J. Gurr, W. Taylor & R. Turk **MUSIC:** Matyas Sieber
Animated feature: World paralleled to farm in satiric view of communism

The Animal World
1956, (USA), Windsor/WB, color, 82 mins.
NARRATORS: Theodor Von Eltz & John Storm

WRIT, P, & D: Irwin Allen **PHOTOG**: Harold Wellman **SPCL-FX**: Willis O'Brien, Ray Harryhausen & Arthur S. Rhoades **MUSIC**: Paul Sawtell

blurb: "Two Billion Years in the Making!"

Modest overview of Evolution: Stop-motion dinosaurs provide main interest in poorly-constructed "nature" film

Animated Clown Portrait
1898, (GB), G.A.S. Films, b&w, 75 ft. (22.9m)
D: George Albert Smith
Minor fantasy short: Picture of clown comes to life

The Animated Costumes
see Les Costumes Animes

Animated Cotton
1909, (GB), Urban, b&w, 340 ft. (103.6m)
D: Walter R. Booth
reissued 1913
Minor fantasy short: Stocking darns itself

Animated Matches
1908, (GB), Alpha Trading Co./Williamson, b&w, 250 ft. (76.2m)
WRIT & D: Arthur Cooper
Minor fantasy short: Matches come to life, perform tricks

Animated Toys
1912, (GB), Urban Trading Co., b&w, 365 ft. (111.3m)
D: Walter R. Booth
reissued 1915
Standard fantasy: Squares and circles dissolve into wooden toys

Annabel Lee
1921, (USA), Joan Film Sales, b&w, 5 reels (4,800 ft./1463m)
W: Jack O'Brien (*David Martin*), Lorraine Harding (*Annabel Lee*), Florida Kingsley (*Mother Martin*), Louis Stearns (*Col. Lee*), Ben Grauer (*David Martin, as a Child*), Arline Blackburn (*Annabel Lee, as a Child*), Ernest Hilliard (*David Grainger*)
D: William J. Scully **SCR**: Arthur Brilliant, inspired by Edgar Allan Poe's poem
Romantic melodrama: Fisherman seeks sunken treasure, returns to true love

Anna Boleyn (Anne Boleyn)
1920, (Ger), Ufa, b&w, 100 mins.
W: Emil Jannings, Henny Porten **D**: Ernst Lubitsch **PHOTOG**: Theodor Sparkuhl
USA retitle, *Deception*
Sumptuous historical melodrama: Queen faces executioner's axe

Anna the Adventuress
1920, (GB), Hepworth/National, b&w, 6,280 ft. (1914.1m)
W: Alma Taylor (*Anna/Annabel Pelissier*), James Carew (*Montagu Hill*), Gerald Ames (*Nigel Ennison*), Gwynne Herbert (*Aunt*), Christine Rayner (*Mrs. Ellicote*), Ronald Colman (*Brendan*), Jean Cadell (*Mrs. White*), James Annand (*Sir John Ferringhall*)
D: Cecil M. Hepworth **SCR**: Blanche McIntosh, from a novel by E. Phillips Oppenheim
Standard crime-thriller: Parisian dancer poses as twin, plots crooked husband's murder

L'Année Derniere a Marienbad (Last Year at Marienbad)
1961, (Fr), Astor, b&w, 94 mins.
W: Delphine Seyrig (*The Woman*), Sacha Pitoeff (*The "Husband"*), Giorgio Albertazzi (*The Stranger*), Francoise Bertin, Luce Garcia-Ville, Helena Kornel, Jean Lanier, Karin Toeche-Mittler, Pierre Barbaud, Wilhelm von Deek, Gerard Lorin, Davide Montemuri, Gilles Queant, Gabriel Werner
D: Alain Resnais **SCR**: Alain Resnais & Alain Robbe-Grillet **PHOTOG**: Sacha Vierny **MUSIC**: Francis Seyrig
Allegorical psychodrama: Three people meet at lonely spa

Anne of the Indies
1951, (USA), 20th-Fox, color, 81 mins.
W: Jean Peters, Louis Jourdan, Herbert Marshall, Debra Paget, Thomas Gomez, James Robertson Justice
D: Jacques Tourneur **MUSIC**: Franz Waxman
Standard adventure-thriller: Lady pirate has agenda

The Annihilator
1986, (USA), NBC-TV, color, 96 mins.
W: Mark Lindsay Chapman (*Robert Armor*), Catherine Mary Stewart (*Angela*), Susan Blakely (*Layla*), Lisa Blount (*Cindy*), Nicole Eggert (*Elyse*), Earl Boen (*Sid*), Geoffrey Lewis (*Prof. Alan Jeffries*), Paul Brinegar (*Pops*), Brion James, Channing Chase, Barry Pearl, Barbara Townsend, Christopher Johnston, Richard Partlow, Glen Vernon, Biff Yeager, Toni Attell, Greg Collins, James Parkes, Rodger LaRue, Stanley Bennett Clay, Jerry Boyd, Lola Fisher, Robert Beaulieu, Al Pugliese, Martin Clark, John Durbin, Donald Hayes, Helen Anderson, William B. Jackson, Gary Burden
D: Michael Chapman **TELEPLAY**: Roderick Taylor & Bruce A. Taylor **PHOTOG**: Paul Goldsmith **MUSIC**: Sylvester LeVay
TVM, standard SF-thriller: Humans replaced by murderous robot lookalikes

The Anniversary
1968, (GB), Hammer-7Arts/20th-Fox, color, 95 mins.
W: Bette Davis (*Mrs. Taggart*), Jack Hedley (*Terry Taggart*), Christian Roberts (*Tom Taggart*), Timothy Bateson (*Mr. Bird*), Sheila Hancock (*Karen Taggart*), James Cossins (*Henry Taggart*), Elaine Taylor (*Shirley Blair*), Arnold Diamond (*The Headwaiter*), Albert Shepherd, Ralph Watson, Sally-Jane Spencer
D: Roy Ward Baker **SCR**: Jimmy Sangster, from Bill MacIlwraith's play **PHOTOG**: Harry Waxman **MUSIC**: Philip Martell
Gritty psychodrama: "Monster" mother dominates sons' lives

Another Man's Poison
1952, (GB), Eros/UA, b&w, 89 mins.
W: Bette Davis (*Jane Frobisher*), Gary Merrill (*George Bates*), Emlyn Williams (*Dr. Henderson*), Anthony Steel (*Larry Stevens*), Barbara Murray (*Chris Dale*), Reginald Beckwith (*Mr. Bigley*), Edna Morris (*Mrs. Bunting*)
P: Daniel Angel & Douglas Fairbanks Jr. **D**: Irving Rapper **SCR**: Val Guest, from Leslie Sands' play *Deadlock*
Standard thriller: Woman novelist plots to kill bankrobber husband

Another Thin Man
1939, (USA), MGM, b&w, 105 mins.
W: William Powell (*Nick Charles*), Myrna Loy (*Nora Charles*), C. Aubrey Smith (*Col. Burr MacFay*), Otto Kruger (*Van Slack*), Nat Pendleton (*Lt. John Guild*), Virginia Grey (*Lois MacFay*), Tom Neal (*Freddie Coleman*), Muriel Hutchison (*Smitty*), Ruth Hussey (*Dorothy Waters*), Sheldon Leonard (*Sam Church*), Harry Bellaver (*Creeps Binder*), Phyllis Gordon (*Mrs. Bellam*), Don Costello (*Diamond Back Vogel*), Patric Knowles (*Dudley Horn*), Abner Biberman (*Dum-Dum*), Marjorie Main (*Mrs. Dolley*), Frank Sully (*Pete*), Martin Garralaga (*Pedro*), Nell Craig (*The Maid*), Alex D'Arcy (*The South American*), Horace McMahon (*MacFay's Chauffeur*), William Anthony Poulsen (*Nicky*), Milton Kibbee (*Les*), Thomas Jackson (*The Detective*), Edward Gargan (*Quinn*), Bert Roach (*Cookie*), Shemp Howard (*Wacky*), Nellie V. Nichols (*Mrs. Wacky*), Claire Rochelle (*The Telephone Operator*), Joe Devlin (*Barney*), Milton Parsons (*The Medical Examiner*), Dick Elliott (*The Investigator*), Nestor Paiva (*The Proprietor*), Roy Barcroft, Joseph Dowling, Marty Fain, Doodles Weaver, Gladden James, Edwin Parker, Murray Alper, Lee Bowman
D: W.S. Van Dyke **SCR**: Frances Goodrich & Albert Hackett, from a novel by Dashiell Hammett **PHOTOG**: Oliver T. Marsh & William Daniels **MUSIC**: Edward Ward
Third "Nick & Nora Charles" mystery-thriller: Sleuthing couple meets man with prophetic dreams of death

Another Thin Man
VIRGINIA GREY, PATRIC KNOWLES, WILLIAM POWELL, MYRNA LOY, TOM NEAL

Ansiktet (The Face)
1958, (Swed), Svensk Filmindustri/Janus, b&w, 101 mins.
W: Max von Sydow (*Volger*), Bibi Andersson (*Sara*), Ingrid Thulin (*Manda*), Sif Ruud, Gunnar Bjornstrand, Bengt Ekerot, Lars Ekborg, Naima Wifstrand, Birgitta Pettersson, Erland Josephson, Gertrud Fridh, Toivo Pawlo, Ulla Sjoblom, Ake Fridell, Oscar Ljung, Axel Duberg, Sif Ruud (*Sofia*), Gunnar Bjornstrand (*Vergerus*), Bengt Ekerot (*Spegel*), Lars Ekborg (*Simson*), Naima Wifstrand (*Grandmother*), Birgitta Pettersson (*Sanna*), Erland Josephson (*Egerman*), Gertrud Fridh (*Ottilia*), Toivo Pawlo (*Starbeck*), Ulla Sjoblom (*Henrietta*), Ake Fridell (*Tubal*), Oscar Ljung (*Antonsson*), Axel Duberg (*Rustan*)
P: Carl-Henry Cagarp **WRIT & D**: Ingmar Bergman **PHOTOG**: Gunnar Fischer
*Moody fantasy: Magic troupe detained at home of rich merchant. A.k.a.***The Magician**

The Answer
1916, (GB), Broadwest-Black Cat/Browne, b&w, 4,604 ft. (1403.3m)
W: Muriel Martin-Harvey (*The Lonely Woman*), George Foley (*Justin Siddeley*),

Dora Barton (*The Lost Magdalene*), George Bellamy (*The Clerk*), J.R. Tozer, Gregory Scott, Arthur M. Cullin
<u>D</u>: Walter West   <u>SCR</u>: Dane Stanton, from Newman Flower's novel *Is God Dead?*
Standard fantasy-melodrama: Spirit shows bankrupt three tales of faith overcoming distress

Anthropophagus
see **The Grim Reaper**

Anticristo (Antichrist)
1974, (It), Avco Embassy, color, 96 mins.
<u>W</u>: Carla Gravina (*Ippolita*), Mel Ferrer (*Massimo*), Arthur Kennedy (*The Bishop*), Alida Valli (*Irene*), Anita Strinberg (*Gretel*), George Coulouris (*Father Mittner*), Mario Scaccia (*The Faith Healer*), Umberto Orsini (*The Psychiatrist*)
<u>P</u>: Edmondo Amati   <u>D</u>: Alberto DeMartino   <u>SCR</u>: Alberto DeMartino, Vincenzo Mannino & Gianfranco Clerici   <u>MUSIC</u>: Ennio Morricone   <u>PHOTOG</u>: Aristide Massaccesi
USA retitle, **The Tempter**
Standard horror-fantasy (minor **Exorcist** *imitation): Crippled girl possessed by witch ancestor.*

Antigone
1961, (Greece), b&w, 86 mins.
<u>D</u>: George Tzavellas, from Sophocles' play
Standard melodrama: Girl defies law, gives brother proper burial

Antinea, L'Amante della Citta Sepolta (Antinea, Lover of the Buried City)
1960, (It-Fr), CCM-Fides/Embassy, color, 100 mins.
<u>W</u>: Haya Harareet (*Antinea*), Jean-Louis Trintignant, George Riviere, Rad Fulton
<u>EXEC-P</u>: Nat Wachsberger   <u>D</u>: Edgar G. Ulmer & Giuseppi Masini   <u>SCR</u>: Edgar G. Ulmer, from a novel by Pierre Benoit   <u>MUSIC SCORE</u>: Carlo Rustichelli
USA retitle, **Journey Beneath the Desert**, *A.k.a.* **Atlantis** *and* **The Lost Kingdom**
Unusual adventure-fantasy: Lost, subterranean civilization threatened by A-bomb testing
cf. **Die Herrin von Atlantis**

The Antique Brooch
1914, (GB), Edison, b&w, 2,060 ft. (627.9m)
<u>W</u>: Marc McDermott (*Jack Morley*), Miriam Nesbitt (*Veronica*), Kathleen Russell (*Lady Stanley*)
<u>D</u>: Charles J. Brabin   <u>STORY</u>: Bannister Merwin
Standard crime-thriller: Lord's disowned nephew takes blame when cousin steals brooch

Ants
see **It Happened at Lake Wood Manor**

Antz
1998, (USA), DreamWorks, color
<u>VOICES</u>: Woody Allen, Sharon Stone, Gene Hackman, Sylvester Stallone, Jennifer Lopez, Anne Bancroft, Danny Glover, Jane Curtin, Christopher Walken
Amusing animated fantasy: Adventures of non-conformist bug

The Anxious Years
see **Dark Journey**

Apartment on the Thirteenth Floor
1974, (Sp), Atlas Int'l, color
<u>W</u>: Vincent Parra, Emma Cohen   <u>P</u>: Joe Truchado   <u>D</u>: Eloy De La Iglesia
Minor horror-thriller: Slaughterhouse employee goes mad, enacts gory murders

Apartment Zero
1989, (GB), color, 125 mins.
<u>W</u>: Colin Firth, Hart Bochner, Dora Bryan, Liz Smith, Fabrizio Bentivoglio, James Telfer, Juan Vitali, Mirella D'Angelo
<u>D</u>: Martin Donovan   <u>SCR</u>: Martin Donovan & David Koepp
Bizarre thriller: Mysterious roommate generates tension

The Ape
1940, (USA), Mono, b&w, 63 mins.
<u>W</u>: Boris Karloff (*Dr. Bernard Adrian*), Maris Wrixon (*Frances*), Gene O'Donnell, Dorothy Vaughan, Gertrude W. Hoffman, Selmer Jackson, Henry Hall
<u>D</u>: William Nigh   <u>SCR</u>: Kurt Siodmak & Richard Carroll, remake of *House of Mystery*, (1939)   <u>ADAPT</u>: Kurt Siodmak, suggested by Adam Hull Shirk's play   <u>PHOTOG</u>: Harry Neumann   <u>MUSIC DIR</u>: Edward Kay
Minor thriller: Doctor seeks polio cure, murders while disguised as gorilla (Not recommended by Dr. Salk)

A*P*E
1976, (USA), Worldwide/Jack H. Harris, 3D, color, 87 mins.
<u>W</u>: Rod Arrants, Joanna DeVarona (later Joanna Kerns), Alex Nicol
<u>D</u>: Paul Leder   <u>SCR</u>: Paul Leder & Reuben Leder   <u>MUSIC</u>: Bruce MacRae
blurb: "Ten Tons of Animal Fury Leaps from the Screen"
Minor **King Kong** *imitation: Giant gorilla strikes*

The Ape Creature
1968, (W. Ger), Rialto/Independent-Int'l, color, 90 mins.
<u>W</u>: Horst Tappert, Uschi Glas, Uwe Friedrichsen, Hubert von Meyerinck, Herbert Fux, Inge Langen, Albert Lieven, Beate Hasenau, Ilse Page, Hilde Sessak, Ralf Schermuly, Maria Litto, Claus Holm, Ingrit Back, Franz Otto Kruger,

Calna Cayetano, Eric Vaessen
<u>D</u>: Alfred Vohrer   <u>SCR</u>: Freddy Greger   <u>MUSIC</u>: Peter Thomas
Minor, confused thriller: Gorilla prowls London waterfront

The Ape Man
1943, (USA), Banner/Favorite/Monogram, b&w, 64 mins.
<u>W</u>: Bela Lugosi (*James Brewster*), Louise Currie (*Billie Mason*), Wallace Ford (*Jeff Carter*), Henry Hall (*Dr. George Randall*), Minerva Urecal (*Agatha Brewster*), Emil Van Horn (*The Ape*), J. Farrell MacDonald (*The Captain*), Wheeler Oakman, Jack Mulhall, Ralph Littlefield
<u>P</u>: Sam Katzman & Jack Dietz   <u>D</u>: William Beaudine   <u>SCR</u>: Barney Sarecky   <u>ORIG. STORY</u>: Karl Brown   <u>PHOTOG</u>: Mack Stengler   <u>MUSIC</u>: Edward Kay
GB retitle, **Lock Your Doors**
Minor horror-thriller: Scientist seeks human spinal fluid to counteract ape-like condition
cf. **Return of the Ape Man** *and* **Lock Up Your Daughters**

Ape Man of the Jungle
1962, (It), b&w
Minor thriller: Bizarre creature lurks in jungle lair

The Ape Woman
see **La Donna Scimmia**

An Ape's Devotion
1913, (GB), Clarendon, b&w, 870 ft. (265.2m)
<u>D</u>: Wilfred Noy
Standard thriller: Spaniard wounds pet ape he mistakes for camper

A.P.E.X.
1994, (USA), Made-for-Video, color, 103 mins.
<u>W</u>: Richard Keats, Mitchell Cox, Lisa Ann Russell, Marcus Aurelius, David Jean Thomas, Adam Lawson, Anna B. Choi, Kristin Norton, Mitchell Cox
<u>D</u>: Phillip J. Roth   <u>SCR</u>: Phillip J. Roth & Ronald Schmidt   <u>MUSIC</u>: Jim Goodwin
Standard SF-thriller: Scientist's time experiments change present, create world where robot armies hunt humans

The Apocalypse
1997, (USA), color
<u>W</u>: Sandra Bernhard, Cameron Dye, Matt McCoy, Laura San Giacomo
Unusual SF-thriller: Salvage spaceship finds abandoned freighter headed for Earth with super-bomb

Apollo 13
1995, (USA), Imagine/Univ, color, 109 mins.
<u>W</u>: Tom Hanks (*Jim Lovell*), Kevin Bacon (*Jack Swigert*), Bill Paxton (*Fred Haise*), Gary Sinise (*Ken Mattingly*), Ed Harris (*Gene Kranz*), Kathleen Quinlan (*Marilyn Lovell*), Tracy Reiner (*Mary Haise*), Miko Hughes, Mary Kate Schellhardt, Jean Speegle Howard, Max Elliott Slade, Roger Corman
<u>P</u>: Brian Grazer   <u>D</u>: Ron Howard   <u>SCR</u>: William Broyles Jr. & Al Reinert, from the book *Lost Moon* by Jim Lovell, Jeffrey Kluger   <u>PHOTOG</u>: Dean Cundey   <u>SPCL VIS-FX</u>: Digital Domain   <u>MUSIC</u>: James Horner
Exciting, fact-based thriller: Saga of doomed space mission

Apology for Murder
1945, (USA), PRC, b&w, 67 mins.
<u>W</u>: Hugh Beaumont, Ann Savage
Standard melodrama

The Apparition
see **Le Revenant**

The Apparition: or, Mr.Jones' Comical Experience with a Ghost
see **Le Revenant**

Apparitions Fantomatiques
see **Le Roi des Mediums**

Les Apparitions Fugitives (The Fugitive Apparitions)
1904, (Fr), Star, b&w, 33m (108.3 ft./1.8 mins.)
<u>D</u>: Georges Melies
Standard fantasy

The Apple of Discord
1907, (GB), Urban, b&w, 240 ft. (73.2m)
<u>D</u>: Walter R. Booth
Minor fantasy short: Wizard shows love scene acted within apple slice

Appointment for a Killing
1993, (USA), ACI, color, 93 mins.
<u>W</u>: Markie Post, Corbin Bernsen, Kelsey Grammer, Don Swayze, Jeanne Cooper, Laurie O'Brien, Suzanne Barnes, Danielle von Zerneck, Matthew Best, John Putch, Melissa Pace, Janet Graham, Geoff Hansen, Anna Maria Sistare, Harry Murphy, Marjorie Hilton, Jack North, Sharon Clark, Thom Dillon, Steven W. Anderson, Brad Steinke, Michele Wilson, Donre' Sampson
<u>D</u>: William A. Graham   <u>TELEPLAY</u>: Karen Clark, from Susan Crain Bakos' book *Appointment Murder*   <u>PHOTOG</u>: Denis Lewiston   <u>MUSIC</u>: Chris Boardman
TVM, standard fact-based crime-thriller: Woman helps Feds nail murdering husband

Appointment in Honduras
1953, (USA), RKO, color, 75 mins.
W: Glenn Ford, Ann Sheridan, Zachary Scott, Jack Elam, Ric Roman, Rodolpho Acosta, Rico Alaniz
D: Jacques Tourneur   PHOTOG: Joseph Biroc
Standard melodrama

Appointment with a Killer
1975, (GB), TV Movie, color
W: Joanna Pettet (*Jody*), Tony Anholt (*Johnny*), Freddie Jones (*Tully*), Norman Rodway (*Ingram*), Brian Blessed (*Briggs*)
TVM, minor mystery: Old murder case resurfaces

Appointment with a Shadow
1958, (USA), Univ, b&w, 73 mins.
W: George Nader, Joanna Moore, Brian Keith, Virginia Field, Frank DeKova
D: Richard Carlson
Standard melodrama: Reporter beats booze, scoops big story

Appointment with Danger
1951, (USA), Para, b&w, 89 mins.
W: Alan Ladd, Phyllis Calvert, Jan Sterling, Paul Stewart, Jack Webb, Henry (Harry) Morgan, Stacy Harris
Standard thriller: Post-office investigator foils robbery

Appointment with Murder
1948, (USA), Film Classics, b&w, 67 mins.
W: John Calvert (*Mike Waring*), Catherine Craig (*Lorraine*), Jack Reitzen (*Norton*), Lyle Talbot (*Fred Muller*), Robert Conte (*Count Dalo*), Peter Brocco (*Donatti*), Ben Welden (*Minecci*), Carlos Schipa (*Farella*), Ann Demitri (*The Italian Woman*), Pat Lane (*The Customs Officer*), Eric Wilson (*The Butler*), Carole Donne (*Miss Connors*), Robert Nadell, Michael Mark, Jack Chefe, Gene Garrick, Frank Richards, Jay Griffith, Carl Sklover
P & D: Jack Bernhard   SCR: Joel Malone & Harold Swanton, from characters created by Michael Arlen   PHOTOG: Walter Strange   MUSIC: Karl Hajos
Standard "Falcon" mystery-thriller: Determined agent tracks stolen paintings

Apprentice to Murder
1988, (USA), Hot Int'l A.S./New World, color, 94 mins.
W: Donald Sutherland (*John Reese*), Chad Lowe (*Billy*), Mia Sara (*Alice*), Knut Husebo (*Lars Hoeglin*)
D: R.L. Thomas   SCR: Allan Scott & Wesley Moore   PHOTOG: Kelvin Pike   MUSIC: Charles Gross
Unusual fact-based thriller: Satanic forces surround faith healer

April Fool's Day
1986, (USA), Hometown/Para, color, 91 mins.
W: Jay Baker (*Harvey*), Deborah Foreman (*Muffy*), Ken Olandt (*Rob*), Deborah Goodrich (*Vikki*), Griffin O'Neal (*Skip*), Amy Steel, Clayton Rohner, Leah King Pinsent, Pat Barlow, Lloyd Berry, Thomas F. Wilson, Tom Heaton
D: Fred Walton   SCR: Danilo Bach   PHOTOG: Charles Minsky   MUSIC: Charles Bernstein   SONG: *Too Bad You're Crazy*
Minor thriller: College students have murder-filled vacation

The Aquarians
1970, (USA), Ivan Tors/Univ, color, 96 mins.
W: Ricardo Montalban, Jose Ferrer, Leslie Nielsen, Kate Woodville
D: Don McDougall   SCR: Leslie Stevens & Winston Miller   MUSIC: Lalo Schifrin
TVM, routine SF-adventure: Scientists face underwater perils

The Aqua Sex
see *Mermaids of Tiburon*

Arabella
1925, (Ger), Ufa, b&w
D: Karl Grune
Unusual melodrama: Life seen through eyes of a horse

Arabian Adventure
1979, (GB), EMI/WB/AFD, color, 98 mins.
W: Christopher Lee (*Alquazar*), Peter Cushing (*Wazir Al Wuzara*), Oliver Tobias (*Prince Hasan*), Emma Samms (*Princess Zuleira*), Mickey Rooney (*DeadalShur*), Capucine (*Vahishta*), Puneet Sira (*Majeed*), Milo O'Shea (*Khasim*), John Wyman (*Bah lour*), Shane Rimmer (*Abu*), John Ratzenberger (*Achmed*), Hal Galili (*Asaf*), Elizabeth Welch (*The Beggarwoman*), Athar Malik (*Mahmoud*), Jacob Witkin (*Omar, the Goldsmith*), Suzanne Danielle (*The Eastern Dancer*), Milton Reid (*The Genie*)
P: John Dark   D: Kevin Connor   SCR: Brian Hayles   PHOTOG: Alan Hume   MUSIC: Ken Thorne
Juvenile fantasy: Prince meets genie

Arabian Nights
1942, (USA), Univ, color, 86 mins.
W: Jon Hall (*Caliph Haroun*), Maria Montez (*Sheherazade*), Sabu (*Ali*), Turhan Bey (*The Captain*), Leif Erickson (*Kamal*), Shemp Howard (*Sinbad*), Richard Lane (*The Corporal*), Billy Gilbert (*Ahmed*), Thomas Gomez (*Hakim*), William "Wee Willie" Davis, Edgar Barrier, John Qualen, Robert Greig, Jeni LeGon, Emory Parnell
P: Walter Wanger   D: John Rawlins   STORY & SCR: Michael Hogan   PHOTOG: Milton Krasner   MUSIC: Frank Skinner
Colorful fantasy-adventure: Beautiful dancing girl causes division between two royal brothers

Arabian Nights
1974, (It-Fr), UA, color, 128 mins. (orig. 155 mins.)
W: Ninetto Davoli, Franco Merli, Ines Pellegrini, Luigina Rocchi, Francesco Paola Governale, Zeudi Biasolo, Abadit Ghidel, Elisabetta Vito Genovesi, Salvatore Verdetti, Christian Allgny, Luigi Antonio Gurra, Tessa Bouche, Margarethe Clementi, Franco Citti
D & SCR: Pier Paolo Pasolini   PHOTOG: Giuseppe Ruzzolini   MUSIC: Ennio Morricone
Standard adventure-fantasy

The Arab's Curse
1915, (GB), Planet/YCC, b&w, 399 ft. (121.6m)
D: A. Kiralfy
Standard comedy-fantasy: Mishaps pursue man who insulted Arab

Arachnophobia
1990, (USA), Amblin/Hollywood/Buena Vista, color, 103 mins.
W: Jeff Daniels (*Ross Jennings*), Harley Jane Kozak (*Molly Jennings*), John Goodman (*Delbert McClintock*), Julian Sands (*Dr. James Atherton*), Stuart Pankin (*Sheriff Parsons*), Brian McNamara (*Chris Collins*), Mark L. Taylor (*Jerry Manley*), Mary Carver (*Margaret Hollins*), Henry Jones (*Dr. Sam Metcalf*), Peter Jason (*Henry Beechwood*), James Handy (*Milton Briggs*), Roy Brocksmith (*Irv Kendall*), Kathy Kinney (*Blaire Kendall*), Garette Patrick Ratliff, Jane Marla Robbins, Marlene Katz, Theo Schwartz, Cori Wellins, Chance Boyer, Brandy, Frances Bay, Lois de Banzie, Warren Rice, Robert Frank Telfer, Michael Steve Jones, Fiona Walsh, Terese Del Piero, Nathaniel Spitzley, Jay Scorpio, Robert "Bobby Z" Zajonc, Mai-Lis Kunholm
D: Frank Marshall   SCR: Don Jakoby & Wesley Strick   STORY: Don Jakoby & Al Williams   PHOTOG: Michael Salomon   MUSIC: Trevor Jones   SONGS: *Goin' Ahead & Don't Bug Me*
Superior comedy-thriller: Dangerous spiders terrorize town

The Arc
1919, (Ger), b&w, 85 mins.
D: Richard Oswald
Standard SF-fantasy: End of world allegory

Arcade
1993, (USA), Para, color, 85 mins.
W: Megan Ward, Peter Billingsley, John de Lancie, Sharon Farrell, Seth Green, Humberto Ortiz, Jonathan Fuller, Norbert Weisser
D: Albert Pyun   SCR: David S. Goyer   MUSIC: Alan Howarth
Minor SF-thriller: Woman links teen disappearances to virtual reality game

The Archer
see *Fugitive from the Empire*

Are You Lonesome Tonight?
1992, (USA), color, 95 mins.
W: Jane Seymour, Parker Stevenson, Beth Broderick, Robert Pine, Joel Brooks
D: E.W. Swackhamer   TELEPLAY: Wesley Moore   PHOTOG: Billy Dickson   MUSIC: J. Peter Robinson
TVM, standard thriller: Socialite's husband involved with phone-sex operator

La Ardilla Roja (The Red Squirrel)
1993, (Sp), color, 104 mins.
W: Nancho Novo, Emma Suarez, Maria Barranco, Carmelo Gomez, Karra Elejalde, Cristina Marcos
D & SCR: Julio Medem
Unusual romance-mystery: Washed-up rock singer convinces amnesiac girl that she is his lover

The Arena
1973, (USA), New World, color
W: Pam Grier, Margaret Markov   P: Mark Damon   D: Steve Carver
SCR: Joyce & John Corrington
blurb: "See wild women fight to the death!"
Minor thriller (filmed in Italy): Female slaves forced into gladiatorial battle

Arena
1989, (USA), color, 97 mins.
W: Paul Satterfield, Claudia Christian, Steve Wong
Minor SF-adventure: Gladiatorial games 2000 years in future

Are You Dying Young Man?
1970, (GB), Tigon-Leander/Cannon, color, 87 mins.
W: Flora Robson (*Joyce*), Beryl Reid (*Ellie*), Tessa Wyatt (*The Nurse*), John Hamill (*Alan*), T.P. McKenna (*Det. Paddick*), John Kelland (*Sgt. Young*), Dafydd Havard (*Stephen*), Roberta Tovey (*The Paper Girl*), David Dodimead (*Dr. Spencer*), Reg Lever (*The Young Joyce*), Gail Lidstone (*Young Ellie*), Merlin Ward (*Young Stephen*), Christopher Chittell (*Baker*), Anabel Littledale (*Gloria*), Anthony Heaton (*Anderson*), Peter Craze (*Roy*), Howard Rawlinson (*The Young Soldier*), Robert Wilde
P: Graham Morris   D & SC: James Kelly   PHOTOG: Harry Waxman & Desmond Dickinson   MUSIC: Tony Macaulay
*USA retitle: **The Beast in the Cellar**, USA TV-retitle: **The Cellar***
Performances by veteran actresses enliven standard thriller: Old maids keep brother prisoner

Are You in the House Alone?

1978, (USA), Stonehenge/Charles Fries, color, 94 mins.
<u>W</u>: Kathleen Beller *(Gail)*, Scott Colomby *(Steve)*, Dennis Quaid *(Phil)*, Blythe Danner, Tony Bill, Robin Mattson, Tricia O'Neil, Alan Fudge, Ellen Travolta, Lois Areno, Randy Stumpf, Michael Bond, Magda Harout, Sandra Sharp, Ted Gehring, Sandra Giles, Richard Molinaro, Jayne Lyn Martin, David Leon, Art Kimbro
<u>D</u>: Walter Grauman   <u>TELEPLAY</u>: Judith Parker, from Richard Peck's novel-Edgar Mystery Award Winner   <u>PHOTOG</u>: Jack Swain   <u>MUSIC</u>: Charles Bernstein
TVM, standard thriller: Sex-psycho stalks student

The Argonauts
see Giants of Thessaly

The Argyle Secrets
1948, (USA), Film Classics, b&w, 63 mins.
<u>W</u>: William Gargan, Marjorie Lord
Standard thriller

The Aristocats
1970, (USA), Walt Disney, color, 79 mins.
<u>VOICES</u>: Eva Gabor, Hermione Baddeley, Scatman Crothers, RoddyMaude-Roxby, Phil Harris, Sterling Holloway, Bill Thompson, Carol Shelley, Pat Buttram, Nancy Kulp, Paul Winchell
<u>D</u>: Wolfgang Reitherman   <u>MUSIC</u>: George Bruns
Standard animated fantasy: Butler tries to bilk cats in 1910 Paris

Arizona Ripper
see Bridge Across Time

Ark of the Sun God
1982, (It), color, 95 mins.
<u>W</u>: David Warbeck, John Steiner, Susie Sudlow, Alan Collins, Riccardo Palacio
<u>D</u>: Antonio Margheriti
Minor adventure-thriller (Raiders of the Lost Ark imitation): Ancient relic sought in Sahara

Armageddon
1998, (USA), Touchstone, color, 144 mins.
<u>W</u>: Bruce Willis, Ben Affleck, Steve Buscemi, Liv Tyler, Will Patton, Billy Bob Thornton, Peter Stormare, Keith David, Michael Clarke Duncan
<u>D</u>: Michael Bay   <u>SCR</u>: Jonathan Hensleigh & J.J. Abrams   <u>ADAPT</u>: Tony Gilroy & Shane Salerno   <u>PHOTOG</u>: John Schwartzman   <u>MUSIC</u>: Trevor Rabin
<u>SONGS</u>: *I Don't Want to Miss a Thing* (performed by Aerosmith)
Lavish apocalyptic science-fiction: Meteor threatens Earth

The Armchair Detective
1952, (GB), Meridian/Apex, b&w, 60 mins.
<u>W</u>: Ernest Dudley *(himself)*, Hartley Power *(Nicco)*, SallyNewton *(Penny)*, Derek Elphinstone *(Insp. Carter)*, Iris Russell *(Jane)*, David Oxley *(Terry)*, Lionel Grose *(The Sgt.)*
<u>D</u>: Brendan J. Stafford   <u>SCR</u>: Ernest Dudley & Derek Elphinstone, from a radio-series by Ernest Dudley
Standard crime-thriller: Radio detective proves nightclub singer did not slay employer

L'Armoire des Freres Davenport (The Cabinet of the Davenport Brothers)
1902, (Fr), Star, b&w, 65m (213.3 ft./3.6 mins.)
<u>W</u>: Georges Melies   <u>D</u>: Georges Melies
A.k.a. The Cabinet Trick of the Davenport Brothers and The Mysterious Cabinet
Standard fantasy: Stage magicians perform.

Armored Car Robbery
1950, (USA), RKO, b&w, 68 mins.
<u>W</u>: Charles McGraw *(Lead)*, Adele Jergens, Steve Brodie, Douglas Fowley, Don McGuire, Gene Evans
Standard melodrama

Arms of the Avenger
1963, (It), color
<u>W</u>: John Barrymore Jr., Scilla Gabel, Ross Stuart
A.k.a. Weapons for Vengeance
Minor action-adventure: Leonardo da Vinci's former apprentice uses master's weapons to help cause of Italian noblemen.

Army of Darkness
1993, (USA), Renaissance/Univ, color, 80 mins.
<u>W</u>: Bruce Campbell, Marcus Gilbert, Ian Abercrombie, Richard Grove, Michael Earl Reid, Timothy Patrick Quill, Bridget Fonda, Ivan Raimi, Patricia Tallman,Theodore Raimi, Brad Bradbury, Embeth Davidtz
<u>D</u>: Sam Raimi   <u>SCR</u>: Sam & Ivan Raimi   <u>PHOTOG</u>: Bill Pope   <u>MUSIC</u>: Joseph LoDuca
orig. to be titled Evil Dead III
Bizarre fantasy-satire: Modern man transported to magic-haunted Middle Ages

Arnold
1973, (USA), Bing Crosby Prods./CRC, color, 94 mins.
<u>W</u>: Stella Stevens *(Karen)*, Roddy McDowall *(Robert)*, Farley Granger *(Evan Lyons)*, Elsa Lanchester *(Hester)*, Shani Wallis *(Jocelyn)*, Bernard Fox *(Constable*

Hooks), Victor Buono *(The Minister)*, John McGiver *(The Governor)*, Patric Knowles *(Douglas Whitehead)*, Jamie Farr *(Dybbi)*, Norman Stuart *(Arnold)*, Ben Wright *(Jonesy)*, Wanda Bailey *(Flo)*, Steven Marlo *(A Dart Player)*, Leslie Thompson *(A Dart Player)*
<u>P</u>: Andrew J. Fenady   <u>D</u>: Georg Fenady   <u>SCR</u>: Jameson Brewer & John Fenton Murray   <u>PHOTOG</u>: William Jurgensen   <u>MUSIC</u>: George Duning
Minor comedy-thriller: Death complicates honeymoon

The Arnelo Affair
1947, (USA), MGM, b&w, 86 mins.
<u>W</u>: John Hodiak, George Murphy, Frances Gifford, Eve Arden, Dean Stockwell
<u>WRIT & D</u>: Arch Oboler
Minor thriller: Attorney's bored wife drawn to charismatic murderer

The Arrival: RON SILVER AND CHARLIE SHEEN

Around the World in 80 Days
1956, (USA), UA, color, 178 mins.
<u>W</u>: David Niven *(Phileas Fogg)*, Cantinflas *(Passepartout)*, Shirley MacLaine *(Aouda)*, Robert Newton *(Mr. Fix)*, Charles Boyer, John Carradine, Martine Carol, Charles Coburn, Ronald Colman, Sir John Gielgud, Noel Coward, Fernandel, Melville Cooper, Trevor Howard, Marlene Dietrich, Peter Lorre, Buster Keaton, Joe E. Brown, Gilbert Roland, Cesar Romero, John Mills, Jose Greco, Victor McLaglen, George Raft, Frank Sinatra, Ava Gardner, Basil Sydney, Finlay Currie, Harcourt Williams, Tim McCoy, Edmund Lowe, Luis Dominguin, Reginald Denny, Jack Oakie, Andy Devine, A.E. Matthews, Mike Mazurki, Beatrice Lillie, Robert Morley, Alan Mowbray, Glynis Johns, Evelyn Keyes, Red Skelton, Ronald Squire
<u>P</u>: Mike Todd   <u>D</u>: Michael Anderson   <u>SCR</u>: S.J. Perelman, James Poe & John Farrow, from Jules Verne's novel   <u>PHOTOG</u>: Lionel Lindon   <u>MUSIC</u>: Victor Young
Lavish adventure-spectacle: English gentleman attempts to circle Earth in record time

Around the World Under the Sea
1966, (USA), Ivan Tors/MGM, color, 117 mins.
<u>W</u>: Lloyd Bridges *(Dr. Doug Standish)*, Brian Kelly *(Dr. Craig Mosby)*, Shirley Eaton *(Dr. Maggie Hanford)*, Gary Merrill *(Dr. August Boren)*, David McCallum *(Dr. Phil Volker)*, Keenan Wynn *(Hank Stahl)*, Marshall Thompson *(Dr. Orn Hillyard)*, Ron Hayes *(Brinkman)*, George Shibata *(Prof. Hamuru)*, Frank Logan, Jack Ewalt, Joey Carter, Don Wells, George DeVries, Celeste Yarnall, Paul Gray, Donald Linton, Tony Gulliver
<u>P & D</u>: Andrew Marton   <u>SCR</u>: Arthur Weiss & Art Arthur   <u>PHOTOG</u>: Clifford Poland & Lamar Boren   <u>SPCL-FX</u>: Project Unlimited, Inc.   <u>MUSIC</u>: Harry Sukman
Standard SF-adventure: Submarine plants devices for control of sub-oceanic volcanic activity

The Arousers
see Sweet Kill

The Arp Statue
1971, (GB), b&w, 70 mins.
<u>W</u>: Mel Lamb, Francois Hugo, Monique Hugo, James L. Fox
<u>D</u>: Alan Sekers
Bizarre melodrama: Model has arm eaten by lion

Arrest Bulldog Drummond
1939, (USA), Para, b&w, 60 mins.
<u>W</u>: John Howard *(Hugh "Bulldog" Drummond)*, H.B. Warner *(Col. Neilson)*, Heather Angel *(Phyllis Clavering)*, Reginald Denny *(Algy Longworth)*, E.E. Clive *(Tenny)*, Jean Fenwick *(Lady Beryl Ledyard)*, Zeffie Tilbury *(Aunt Meg)*, George Zucco *(Rolf Alferson)*, Leonard Mudie *(Robin Gannett)*, Neil Fitzgerald *(Sir Malcolm McLeonard)*, Evan Thomas *(Smith)*, George Regas *(Soongh)*, Clyde Cook *(Constable Sacker)*, David Clyde *(Constable McThane)*, Claud Allister *(Sir Basil Leghorne)*, Ferdinand Munier *(Old Maj. Trumleigh)*, John Sutton *(Insp. Tredennis)*, Forrester Harvey *(Constable Severn)*, John Rogers *(Cabbie)*, Frank Baker *(The Cop)*, John Davidson *(Gunda), Dill)*, Bevan *(The Aquarium Guard)*, Harold Garrison *(The Pickaninny)*, Jimmie

Aubrey *(The Steward)*, Ruth Rogers *(The Maid)*, Eugene Jackson *(The Page Boy)*, Gerald Rogers *(The Desk Sgt.)*, Sam Savitsky, Hercules Mendes, Kathryn Bates, Nell Craig, Grace Hayle, Olaf Hytten, Steve Clemento, Frank Lackteen, Joyce Mathews, Dolores Casey, Sheila D'Arcy
D: James Hogan **SCR:** Stuart Palmer, from Sapper's novel *The Final Count* **PHOTOG:** Ted Tetzlaff
Standard mystery-thriller: Sleuth accused of stealing valuable ray machine, pursues real culprit

Arrival
1990, (USA), color, 107 mins.
W: John Saxon, Joseph Culp, Robert Sampson, David Schmoeller, Michael J. Pollard, Stuart Gordon
D & SCR: David Schmoeller **MUSIC:** Richard Band
Minor horror-fantasy: Alien parasite turns old man into vampiric young stud

The Arrival
1996, (USA), Steelwork Films-Thomas G. Smith/Orion, color, 109 mins.
W: Charlie Sheen *(Zane)*, Lindsay Crouse *(Iliana Green)*, Ron Silver *(Phil Gordion)*, Teri Polo, Richard Schiff, Leon Rippy, Alan Coates, Tony T. Johnson, Shane, Phyllis Applegate, Buddy Joe Hooker, Angel De La Pena, Catalina Botello, Georg Lillitsch, Maria Luisa Coronel, Ellen Bradley, Jose Garcia, Javier Morga, Luisa Huertas, Jorge Zepeda, Monica Dionne, Dave Galasso
WRIT & D: David Twohy **PHOTOG:** Hiro Narita **MUSIC:** Arthur Kempel
Standard SF-thriller: Radio astronomer detects space-alien transmission, uncovers deadly intrigue

Arsene Lupin
1916, (GB), London/Jury, b&w, 6,400 ft. (1950.7m)
W: Gerald Ames *(Arsene Lupin)*, Manora Thew *(Savia)*, Kenelm Foss *(Insp. Guerchard)*, Douglas Munro *(Gournay-Martin)*, Margala Rubia, Philip Hewland
D: George L. Tucker **SCR:** Kenelm Foss, from a play by Maurice le Blanc & Francois de Crosset
Standard crime-thriller: Paris inspector tries to catch gentleman thief

Arsen Lupin Contre Arsene Lupin (Arsene Lupin vs. Arsene Lupin)
1962, (Fr), b&w, 110 mins.
W: Jean-Claude Brialy **D:** Edouard Molinaro
Standard melodrama

Arsenic and Old Lace
1944, (USA), WB, b&w, 118 mins.
W: Cary Grant *(Mortimer Brewster)*, Priscilla Lane *(Elaine Harper)*, Josephine Hull *(Abby Brewster)*, Peter Lorre *(Dr. Einstein)*, Jean Adair *(Martha Brewster)*, Raymond Massey *(Jonathan Brewster)*, Jack Carson *(O'Hara)*, James Gleason *(Lt. Rooney)*, John Alexander *("Teddy Roosevelt" Brewster)*, Edward Everett Horton *(Mr. Witherspoon)*, Grant Mitchell *(Rev. Harper)*, Edward McNamara *(Brophy)*, John Ridgely *(Saunders)*, Garry Owen *(The Taxi Driver)*, Vaughan Glaser *(Judge Cullman)*, Chester Clute *(Dr. Gilchrist)*, Charles Lane *(The Reporter)*, Edward McWade *(Gibbs)*
D: Frank Capra **SCR:** Julius J. Epstein & Philip G. Epstein, from Joseph Kesselring's play **PHOTOG:** Sol Polito **SPCL-FX:** Byron Haskin & Robert Burks **MUSIC:** Max Steiner
Classic murder-comedy: Two sweet old ladies put lonely "gentleman callers" out of their misery

Arson for Hire
1959, (USA), AA, b&w, 67 mins.
W: Steve Brodie, Lyn Thomas
Minor melodrama

The Arsonists
see Les Incendiaires

Arthur the King
1985, (GB), Martin Poll-Comworld/CBS-TV, color, 140 mins.
W: Malcolm McDowell *(Arthur)*, Candice Bergen *(Morgan Le Fay)*, Dyan Cannon *(Katherine)*, Edward Woodward *(Merlin)*, Liam Neeson *(Prince Grak)*, Lucy Gutteridge *(Niniane)*, Ann Thornton *(Lady Ragnell)*, Rosalyn Landor *(Guinevere)*, Rupert Everett *(Lancelot)*, Joseph Blatchley *(Mordred)*, Denis Lill *(King Pellinore)*, Terry Torday *(The Enchanted Queen)*, Patrick Ryecart *(Gawain)*, Philip Sayer *(Agravain)*, Michael Gough *(The Archbishop)*, John Quarmby *(Sir Kai)*, Milance Avramovic *(Gorgo)*, Mary Stavin, Pat Starr, Alison Worth, Carole Ashby, Peter Blythe, Marie Elise, Maryam d'Abo, Tina Robinson, Pia Constance-Churcher, Linda Fontana, Cia Ford, Christine Hunt, Miro Pfeiffer, Vlado Spindler, Mise Martinovic, Tom Vukusic
D: Clive Donner **TELEPLAY:** J. David Wyles **PHOTOG:** Denis Lewiston **MUSIC:** Charles Gross
Video retitle: *(94 mins.)*, **Merlin and the Sword**
TVM, elaborate adventure-fantasy: King Arthur's sorceress half-sister plots his downfall

Artistic Creation
1901, (GB), R.W. Paul, b&w, 85 ft. (25.9m)
D: Walter R. Booth
Minor fantasy short: Pierrot draws lady in sections, and parts come alive

The Artist's Dream
see La Reve d'Artiste

Artists in the Circus Tent/Perplexed
1968, (W. Ger), color, 103 mins.

WRIT, P & D: Alexander Kluge
Avant-garde psychodrama: Bemused girl inherits circus when her father, an owner/performer, falls to his death

Aschenputtel (Cinderella)
1922, (Ger), b&w, 358 ft. (109m)
D: Lotte Reiniger
Standard fantasy: Fairy godmother aids oppressed girl - animated

Ashes
1930, (GB), Gainsborough/Ideal, b&w, 23 mins.
W: Ernset Thesiger *(The Announcer)*, Babs Valerie *(A Girl)*, Elsa Lanchester *(A Girl)*, Herbert Mundin *(A Cricketeeer)*, M.D. Lyon *(A Cricketeer)*
D: Frank Birch **SCR:** Angus Macphail **STORY:** M.D. Lyon & Claude Soman
Standard comedy-fantasy short: Cricket match starts in 1940, ends in 2000

The Ashes of Revenge
1915, (GB), London/Jury, b&w, 3,600 ft. (1097.3m)
W: Edna Flugrath *(Bess)*, Philip Hewland *(Hugh Graydon)*, Gwynne Herbert *(Lady Graydon)*
D: Harold Shaw **SCR:** Bannister Merwin, from a novel by R.C. Carton
Standard melodrama: Widowed lady rejects businessman, so he buys gypsy girl and contrives to have her marry the lady's son

Ashik Kereb
1988, (Russ), color, 75 mins.
W: Yiur Mgoyan, Veronkia Metonidze, Levan Natroshvili, Sofiko Chiaureli
D: Dodo Abashidze & Sergei Paradjanov **SCR:** Giya Badridze, from a story by Mikhail Lermontov **MUSIC:** Djavashir Kuliev
Unusual adventure-fantasy: Poor minstrel seeks love of merchant's daughter, travels to obtain wealth

As in Days of Yore
1917, (GB), Gaiety, b&w, 2,000 ft. (609.6m)
W: Bob Reed *(The Caveman)*
D: Maurice Sandground
Standard satire: Problems of Stone Age man

The Asphyx
1972, (GB), Glendale-Titan/Scotia-Barber/Paragon, color, 99 mins.
W: Robert Stephens *(Sir Hugo)*, Robert Powell *(Giles)*, Jane Lapotaire *(Christina)*, Alex Scott *(The President)*, Ralph Arliss *(Clive)*, Fiona Walker *(Anna)*, Terry Scully *(The Pauper)*, John Lawrence *(Mason)*, Tony Caunter *(The Warden)*, David Grey *(The Vicar)*, Paul Bacon *(The First Member)*
D: Peter Newbrook **SCR:** Brian Comfort **PHOTOG:** Freddie Young **SPCL-FX:** Ted Samuels **MUSIC:** Bill McGuffie
reissued *(1974, 87 mins.)* as **The Horror of Death**, video-cassette retitle:**Spirit of the Dead**
Unusual horror-thriller: Victorian scientists trap elusive "spirit of death"

The Assassin (1952)
see Venetian Bird

The Assassin (1961)
see L'Assassino

The Assassin (1992)
see Point of No Return

Assassin
1973, (GB), Pemini Org./Col-WB, color, 83 mins.
W: Ian Hendry *(The Assassin)*, Edward Judd *(The Control)*, Frank Windsor *(John Stacey)*, Ray Brooks *(Edward Craig)*, John Hart Dyke *(Janik)*, Verna Harvey *(The Girl)*, Frank Duncan *(Luke)*, Mike Pratt *(Matthew)*, Paul Whitsun-Jones *(A Drunk)*, Mike Shannon *(A Drunk)*, Molly Weir *(A Drunk)*, Andrew Lodge *(The Man)*, Peter Hawkins *(The Official)*
P: Peter Crane & Michael Sloan **D:** Peter Crane **STORY:** Michael Sloan **PHOTOG:** Brian Johnson **MUSIC:** Zack Laurence
Standard thriller: M15 discover suspect innocent after hiring assassin to kill him

Assassin
1986, (USA), Sankan/CBS-TV, color, 95 mins.
W: Robert Conrad *(Henry Stanton)*, Robert Young *(Robert Golem)*, Karen Austin *(Mary)*, Robert Webber *(Calvin Lantz)*, Jonathan Banks *(Dickman)*, Jessica Nelson *(Ann Walsh)*, Len Birman *(Sen. Corbin)*, Ben Frank *(Franklin)*, Nick Angotti *(Kreiger)*, Nancy Lenehan *(Grace Decker)*, Allan Graff *(Wheeler)*, Robert F. Hoy *(Becker)*, Grace Simmons *(The Secretary)*, Scott Lincoln *(Todd)*,Richard Newton *(Oliver)*, John H. Evans *(Slocum)*, Mark Lindsay *(The Hotel Clerk)*, Patrick Gorman *(Agent One)*, Chuck Courtney *(The Corridor Agent)*, Leonard A. Mazzola *(Marcus Baines)*, Jamie Stern *(The Teenager)*
WRIT & D: Sandor Stern **PHOTOG:** Chuck Arnold **MUSIC:** Anthony Guefen
*TVM, standard SF-thriller (**Terminator** imitation): Former secret agent stalks murderous runaway robot*

Assassin For Hire
1951, (GB), Merton Park/Anglo-Amalgamated, b&w, 67 mins.
W: Sydney Tafler *(Antonio Riccardi)*, Ronald Howard *(Insp.Carson)*, John Hewer *(Giuseppi Riccardi)*, Kathryn Blake *(Maria Riccardi)*, Gerald Case *(Sgt. Stott)*, Ian Wallace *(Charlie)*, Martin Benson *(Catesby)*, Ewen Solon *(Fred)*

P: Julian Wintle   **D:** Michael McCarthy   **SCR:** Rex Rienits, from his teleplay
Standard crime-thriller: Inspector tricks professional killer

The Assasin Has Fear Of The Night
see L'Assassin a Peur de la Nuit

Assassination
1967, (It), color
W: Henry Silva, Fred Beir
Minor melodrama: CIA agent faces spy intrigue in Germany

The Assassination Bureau
1969, (GB), Michael Relph-Basil Dearden/Para, color, 110 mins.
W: Oliver Reed (*Ivan*), Diana Rigg (*Sonya*), Telly Savalas (*Lord Bostwick*), Kenneth Griffith (*Popescu*), Curt Jurgens (*Gen. Von Pinck*), Clive Revill (*Cesare*), Philippe Noiret (*Lucoville*), Beryl Reid (*Mme. Otero*), Annabella Incontrera (*Eleanora*), Warren Mitchell (*Herr Weiss*), Vernon Dobtcheff (*Muntzov*), Jess Conrad (*Angelo*), George Coulouris (*The Peasant*), Ralph Michael (*The Editor*), Olaf Pooley (*The Cashier*), Katherine Kath (*Mme. Lucoville*), William Kendall (*The Client*), Eugene Deckers (*The Clerk*)
WRIT, P & DESIGN: Michael Relph   **P:** Michael Relph   **D:** Basil Dearden, from an idea found in *The Assassination Bureau, Ltd.* by Jack London & Robert Fish   **PHOTOG:** Geoffrey Unsworth   **MUSIC:** Ron Grainer   **SONG:** *Life is a Precious Thing*
Modest comedy-thriller: Daring young woman investigates secret organization

The Assassination of the Duc de Guise
1908, (Fr), Films D'Art, b&w
Minor thriller: Nobleman meets foul play

The Assassination of the King and Queen of Servia
1903, (GB), Harrison, b&w, 110 ft. (33.5m)
D: Dicky Winslow
Standard historical melodrama (in 3 scenes): Attack on palace; murders; throwing out the bodies

L'Assassino (The Assassin)
1961, (It), b&w, 105 mins.
W: Marcello Mastroianni, Micheline Presle
D: Elio Petri   **SCR:** Elio Petri, Ruy Guerra & Pasquale Festa Campanile   **PHOTOG:** Carlo Di Palma   **MUSIC:** Piero Piccioni
Minor melodrama: Paid killer faces entanglements

Assault
see In the Devil's Garden

Assault on Dome 4
1997, (USA), SCI-TV, color, 95 mins.
W: Bruce Campbell, Joseph Culp, Brion James, Raymond Baker, Jocelyn Seagrave
TVM, standard SF-thriller: Interglactic criminal holds planet hostage

As Seen Through a Telescope
1900, (GB), G.A.S. Films, b&w, 75 ft. (22.9m)
D: George Albert Smith
Minor "gimmick" short: Man uses telescope to spy on girl tying shoelace

Assigned to Danger
1948, (USA), Eagle Lion, b&w, 66 mins.
W: Gene Raymond, Noreen Nash
D: Oscar "Budd" Boetticher Jr.   **PHOTOG:** L. William O'Connell
Standard melodrama

Assignment: Istanbul
see The Castle of Fu Manchu

Assignment K
1967, (GB), Mazurka/Col, color, 97 mins.
W: Stephen Boyd (*Philip Scott*), Camilla Sparv (*Toni Peters*), Leo McKern (*Smith*), Robert Hoffmann (*Paul Spiegler*), Michael Redgrave (*Harris*), Jan Werich (*Dr. Spiegler*), Jeremy Kemp (*Hall*), Jane Merrow (*Martine*), Vivi Bach (*Erika Herschel*), David Healy (*David*), Geoffrey Bayldon (*Boffin*), Carl Mohner (*The Inspector*), Werner Peters (*Kramer*), Friedrich von Ledebur (*The Proprietor*), Ursula Howells (*Estelle*)
D: Val Guest   **SCR:** Val Guest, William Strutton & Maurice Foster, from Hartley Howard's novel *Department K*   **PHOTOG:** Ken Hodges   **MUSIC:** Basil Kirchin
Minor thriller: Spy seeks microfilm holding names of enemy agents

Assignment—Outer Space
1960, (It), Titanus/Ultra, color, 73 mins.
W: Archie Savage, Gaby Farinon, Rik Van Nutter, Alain Dijon, Dave Montresor
D: Antonio Margheriti   **SCR:** Vasily Petrov   **SPCL-FX:** Caesar Peace
A.k.a. Space Men, distrib in USA (1962) by AIP
Minor SF-adventure: Wayward spaceship threatens Earth

Assignment—Paris
1952, (USA), Col, b&w, 85 mins.
W: Dana Andrews, Marta Toren, George Sanders
D: Robert Parrish   **MUSIC:** George Duning
Standard thriller

Assignment Redhead
1956, (GB), Butcher's Films, b&w, 79 mins.
W: Richard Denning (*Keen*), Carole Matthews (*Hedy*), Ronald Adam (*Scammel*), Danny Green (*Yottie*), Elwyn Brook-Jones (*Mitchell*), Brian Worth (*Ridgway*), Jan Holden (*Sally*), Hugh Moxey (*Sgt. Coutts*)
P: W.G. Chalmers   **D & SCR:** Maclean Rogers   **STORY:** Lindsay Hardy
Standard crime-thriller: Gang seeks millions counterfeited by Nazis

Assignment to Kill
1967, (USA), WB-7Arts, color, 99 mins.
W: Patrick O'Neal (*Richard Cutting*), Joan Hackett (*Dominique*), Eric Portman (*The Notary*), Sir John Gielgud (*Valayan*), Oscar Homolka (*The Inspector*), Herbert Lom (*Matt Wilson*), Peter Van Eyck (*Walter Green*), Leon Greene (*The Big Man*), Kent Smith (*Eversley*), Philip Ober (*Bohlen*), Fifi D'Orsay (*Mrs. Hennie*), Eve Soreny (*The Landlady*)
D & SCR: Sheldon Reynolds   **PHOTOG:** Harold Lipstein   **MUSIC:** William Lava
Minor thriller: Gumshoe checks corporate fraud in Switzerland

The Assistant
1969, (GB), Armada/British Lion, color, 37 mins.
W: Richard Poore (*Jimmy*), Susan Drury (*The Model*), Tessa Roberts, Tom Georgeson
P: D & STORY: John Dooley   **SCR:** John Pitt
Standard short fantasy: Photographer's assistant dreams of loving model

Asterix in Britain
1986, (Fr), Palace, color, 89 mins.
VOICES: Jack Beaber, Bill Kearns, Graham Bushnell, Herbert Baskind, Jimmy Shuman, Ed Marcus, Sean O'Neil, Gordon Heath
D: Pino Van Lamsweerde   **SCR:** Pierre Tchernia, from cartoon strip by Rene Goscinny & Alberto Uderzo   **PHOTOG:** Philippe Laine   **MUSIC:** Vladimir Cosma
Standard animated adventure: Celts and Gauls vs. Romans

Asteroid
1997, (USA), Davis Entertainment/NBC-TV, color, approx. 190 mins.
w: Michael Biehn (*Jack Wallach*), Annabella Sciorra (*Dr. Lily McKee*), Denis Arndt (*The President*), Zachary B. Charles (*Elliot McKee*), Don Franklin, Carlos Gomez, Michael Weatherly, Jensen Daggett, Anne-Marie Johnson, John Lindsey, Frank McRae, Gerry Becker, Anthony Zerbe (*Dr. Charles Napier*), David Underwood, Brian Alan Hill, Gregory Wheeler, Christopher Murphy, Stephanie Marie, Jon Cedar, Eileen Witt, John Scott Clough, Michael Flynn, Laurence Curry, Dane Witherspoon, Norm Silver, Kathryn Christopher, Sarah Levy Arbess, Leslie Wing, Peter Ware, Jim Dirker, Rich Beall
D: Bradford May   **TELEPLAY:** Robbyn Burger & Scott Sturgeon   **PHOTOG:** Tom Del Ruth & David Hennings   **MUSIC:** Shirley Walker
2-part TVM, standard SF-thriller: Collision with asteroid threatens Earth

Asthore
1917, (GB), Clarendon/Ideal, b&w, 4,745 ft. (1446.3m)
W: Hayford Hobbs (*Lord Frederick Armitage*), Violet Marriott (*Elsa*)
D: Wilfred Noy   **STORY:** Kenelm Foss
Standard crime-thriller: Lady promises to wed man if he disfigures her ex-fiance

The Astounding Giant Woman
see Attack of the 50-Foot Woman (1958)

The Astounding She-Monster
1957, (USA), Hollywood-Int'l/AIP, b&w
W: Robert Clarke, Marilyn Harvey, Kenne Duncan, Jeanne Tatum, Ewing Brown, Shirley Kilpatrick (*The She-Monster*)
P & D: Ronnie Ashcroft   **STORY & SCR:** Frank Hall   **PHOTOG:** William C. Thompson   **MUSIC:** Guenther Kauer
*GB retitle, **Mysterious Invader**, orig. co-billed with **The Viking Women and the Sea Serpent***
*Minor SF-thriller: Glowing space-woman from Antares terrorizes kidnappers and their hostages. cf. **Monstroid***

The Astral Factor
1978, (USA), Cougar, color, 91 mins.
W: Frank Stell (*Rodger*), Robert Foxworth (*Berret*), Percy Rodriguez (*The Police Captain*), Mark Slade (*Holt*), Elke Sommer (*Chris*), Stefanie Powers (*Candy*), Leslie Parrish, (*Colleen*), Sue Lyon (*Darlene*), Marianna Hill (*Bambi*)
D: John Floria   **SCR:** Arthur Pierce & Earle Lyon   **MUSIC:** Bill Marx
Minor SF-thriller

Astrologie
1952, (Fr), color, 22 mins.
D: Jean Gremillon
*A.k.a. **Miroir de la Vie (Mirror of Life)***
Fantasy short: Stars predict

Astromati (Astromuts)
1963, (Yugo), color
D: Dusan Vukotic
Animated SF-fantasy: Satire of space exploration

Astromuts
see Astromati

The Astronaut
1971, (USA), Univ, color, 74 mins.
<u>W</u>: Monte Markham *(The Impersonator),* Susan Clark *(Gail),* Jackie Cooper *(Kurt Anderson),* Robert Lansing *(John Phillips),* Walter Brooke, Richard Anderson, John Lupton, James Sikking, Loretta Leversee, Paul Kent
<u>D</u>: Robert Michael Lewis   <u>TELEPLAY</u>: Gerald di Pego, Charles R. Kuenstle, Robert S. Biheller, Harve Bennet
TVM, standard SF-thriller: U.S. gov't hires man to impersonate dead astronaut

The Astronomer's Dream: or, The Man in the Moon
see L'Homme dans la Lune

Astro Zombies
1968, (USA), Ram Ltd./Geneni, color
<u>W</u>: Wendell Corey, John Carradine, Tura Satana, Tom Pace, Rafael Campos, Joan Patrick, Joseph Hoover, Wally Moon, Vincent Barbi, Victor Izay
<u>P & D</u>:Ted V. Mikels   <u>SCR</u>: Ted V. Mikels & Wayne Rogers   <u>PHOTOG</u>: Robert Maxwell   <u>MUSIC</u>: Nico Karaski
A.k.a. Space Vampires
Minor SF-horror: Alien defectives steal human organs

Asylum
1972, (GB), Amicus/Harbor/CRC, color, 88 mins.
<u>W</u>: Peter Cushing *(Smith),* Richard Todd *(Walter),* Barbara Parkins *(Bonnie),* Britt Ekland *(Lucy),* Megs Jenkins *(Miss Higgins),* Charlotte Rampling *(Barbara),* Herbert Lom *(Byron),* Barry Morse *(Bruno),* Patrick Magee *(Dr. Rutherford),* Geoffrey Bayldon *(Max),* Sylvia Syms *(Ruth),* Robert Powell *(Dr. Martin),* James Villiers *(George),* Ann Firbank *(Anna),* John Franklyn-Robbins *(Stebbins),* Tony Wall, Dan Jones, Sylvia Marriott, Frank Forsyth
<u>P</u>: Max J. Rosenberg & Milton Subotsky   <u>D</u>: Roy Ward Baker   <u>SCR</u>: Robert Bloch—from his stories   <u>PHOTOG</u>: Denys Coop   <u>MUSIC</u>: Douglas Gamley
A.k.a. House of Crazies
blurb: "You have nothing to lose but your mind"
4 tales of madness & terror: *Frozen Fear, The Weird Tailor, Lucy Comes to Stay & Mannikins of Horror*
Above-average anthology thriller: New madhouse doctor must identify insane predecessor

Asylum
1996, (USA), color, 90 mins.
<u>W</u>: Robert Patrick, Sarah Douglas, Henry Gibson
Standard thriller: Detective hunts psychiatrist's killer

Asylum Erotica
see Slaughter Hotel (1972)

Asylum for a Spy
1967, (USA), Univ, color, 74 mins.
<u>W</u>: Robert Stack, Felicia Farr, George Macready, Martin Milner
<u>D</u>: Stuart Rosenberg   <u>TELEPLAY</u>: Robert L. Joseph
TVM, talky thriller; orig. 2-parts on TV's "Chrysler Theatre": Spy has brain picked by counterspy

Asylum of Satan
1972, (USA), Studio One, color, 87 mins.
<u>W</u>: Carla Borelli, Nick Jolly, Sherry Steiner, Charles Kissinger
<u>P</u>: J. Patrick Kelly III   <u>D & SCR.</u>: William Girdler
Minor horror-thriller: Satanist runs hospital

Atlas In The Land Of Cyclops: GORDON MITCHELL AS ATLAS

Asylum of the Insane
see The Flesh and Blood Show

As You Desire Me
1932, (USA), MGM, b&w, 71 mins.
<u>W</u>: Greta Garbo, Melvyn Douglas, Erich von Stroheim, Owen Moore, Hedda Hopper, Rafaela Ottiano, William Ricciardi, Albert Conti, Warburton Gamble, Roland Varno
<u>D</u>: George Fitzmaurice   <u>ADAPT & DIALOG</u>: Gene Markey, from Luigi Pirandello's stage play   <u>PHOTOG</u>: William Daniels
Static melodrama: Man's wife, believed killed in World War I, is discovered alive but amnesiac

El Ataque de los Muertos sin Ojos (Attack of the Blind Dead)
1973, (Sp), color
<u>W</u>: Tony Kendall   <u>D</u>: Armando De Ossorio
USA retitle, **Return of the Blind Dead**
Standard horror-fantasy (1st sequel to **Tombs of the Blind Dead***): Eyeless ghouls menace unwary. cf.* **Horror of the Zombies**

El Ataud del Vampiro (The Vampire's Coffin)
1958, (Mex), Abel Salazar-Cinematografica ABSA/Azteca/AIP, b&w, 86 mins.
<u>W</u>: Abel Salazar *(Dr. Henry Heatherford),* German Robles *(Count Lavud),* Ariadne Welter *(Martha),* Guillermo Oras, Yeire Beirute, Alicia Montoya, Carlos Ancira
<u>P</u>: Abel Salazar   <u>D</u>: Fernando Mendez   <u>SCR</u>: Ramon Obon, from an idea by Raul Centeno   <u>PHOTOG</u>: Kurt Dayton & Rosalio Solano   <u>MUSIC</u>: Gustavo C. Carrion
Minor horror-thriller (sequel to **El Vampiro***): Vengeful vampire pursues doctor's fiancee*

L'Atlantide (Atlantis)
1920, (Fr), Thalman, b&w
<u>W</u>: Stacia Napierkowska, Jean Angelo, Georges Melchior
<u>D & SCR</u>: Jacques Feyder, from a novel by Pierre Benoit   <u>PHOTOG</u>: Victor Morin & Georges Specht
Moody fantasy: Ageless girl rules lost kingdom

L'Atlantide (1932)
see Die Herrin von Atlantis

L'Atlantide (1960)
see Antinea, l'Amante della Citta Sepolta

Atlantis
1913, (Ger), b&w
<u>D & SCR</u>: August Blom, from the play by Gerhardt Hauptman

Atlantis (1932)
see Die Herrin von Atlantis

Atlantis
1948, (USA), Nebenzal/UA, b&w, 75 mins.
<u>W</u>: Maria Montez, Dennis O'Keefe, Jean-Pierre Aumont, Henry Daniell, Allan Nixon, Henry Daniell, Morris Carnovsky
<u>D</u>: Gregg R. Tallas, Arthur Ripley (uncredited), Douglas Sirk (uncredited) & John Brahm (uncredited)   <u>SCR</u>: Roland Leigh & Robert Lay   <u>PHOTOG</u>: Karl Struss
Standard fantasy-thriller: Two Frenchmen find lost civilization. A.k.a. **Siren of Atlantis**

Atlantis (1960)
see Antinea, l'Amante della Citta Sepolta

The Atlantis Interceptors
see Raiders of Atlantis

Atlantis, the Lost Continent
1961, (USA), Galaxy/MGM, color, 91 mins.
<u>W</u>: Anthony Hall *(Demetrius),* Joyce Taylor *(Princess Antillea),* John Dall *(Zaran),* Frank de Kova *(The Astrologer),* Edgar Stehli *(The King),* Edward C. Platt *(Azore),* Jay Novello, Buck Maffei, Wolfe Barzell, Berry Kroeger
<u>P & D</u>: George Pal   <u>SCR</u>: Daniel Mainwaring, based on a celebrated play by Sir Gerald Hargreaves   <u>PHOTOG</u>: Harold Wellman   <u>SPCL-FX</u>: A. Arnold Gillespie, Gene Warren, Wah Chang & Tim Barr, with stock-footage from **Quo Vadis?***(1951)
Entertaining SF-fantasy: Young Greek braves terrors of deep to return shipwrecked Atlantean princess to her homeland

Atlas
1961, (USA), Filmgroup/AA/Realart, b&w, 79 mins.
<u>W</u>: Michael Forest *(Atlas),* Frank Wolff, Barboura Morris, Jean Moore, Walter Maslow, William Jolley, Christos Exarchos, Kent Whitley, Andreas Filippidis, Robert Hudson, Miranda Kounelaki, James Carleton, Theodore Dimitriou, Charles Stirling, Sascha Dario
<u>P & D</u>: Roger Corman   <u>SCR</u>: Charles Griffith   <u>PHOTOG</u>: Basil Maros   <u>MUSIC</u>: Ronald Stein
"Sword & Sandal" semi-satire: Muscleman vs. tyrant. Filmed in Greece

Atlas Against the Cyclops
see Atlas in the Land of Cyclops

Atlas Against the Czar
1964, (It), color
<u>W</u>: Kirk Morris, Gloria Milland
Minor myth-adventure: Muscleman opposes Tartar hordes

Atlas in the Land of Cyclops
1961, (It), Medallion, color
<u>W</u>: Gordon Mitchell, Chelo Alonso
A.k.a. **Atlas Against the Cyclops**
Minor "Sword & Sandal" fantasy: Hero battles mythical monsters

A Toi de Faire, Migonne (You Do It, Cutie)
1963, (Fr), Films Borderie, b&w, 93 mins.
<u>W</u>: Eddie Constantine *(Lemmy Caution)*, Christiane Minazzoli, Elga Andersen, Henri Cogan, Gaia Germani, Philippe Lemaire, Noel Roquevert
<u>D</u>: Bernard Borderie <u>SCR</u>: Bernard Borderie & Marc-Gilbert Sauvajon, from Peter Cheyney's novel *Your Deal, My Lovely*
USA TV-retitle, **Your Turn, Darling**
7th "Lemmy Caution" action-thriller: Secret agent seeks killer of female spy

Atoll K
1950, (It-Fr), Fortezza Film-Films Sirius/Exploitation Prods., b&w, 93 mins.
<u>W</u>: Stan Laurel, Oliver Hardy, Suzy Delair, M. Dalmatoff, Max Elloy, A. Rimoldi
<u>D</u>: Leo Joannon <u>SCR</u>: John Klorer, F. Kohner, R. Wheeler & P. Tellini, from an idea by Leo Joannon <u>DIALOG</u>:, John Klorer, Monty Collins & I. Kloucowsky <u>GAGS</u>: Monty Collins <u>PHOTOG</u>: Armand Thirard <u>MUSIC</u>: Paul Misraki
USA retitle, **Robinson Crusoeland** *recut & reissued as* **Utopia**, *GB retitle,* **Escapade**
Screen 'swan song' for Laurel & Hardy, standard adventure-comedy: Two bumblers find uncharted isle, form new gov't

Atom Age Vampire
1960, (It-Fr), Lion's Films/Topaz, b&w, 87 mins.
<u>W</u>: Alberto Lupo, Susanne Loret, Franca Parisi, Sergio Fantoni, Andrea Scotti, Roberto Bertea, Rina Franchetti, Ivo Garrani
<u>P</u>: Mario Bava <u>D</u>: Anton Giulio Majano <u>SCR</u>: Piero Monviso, Gino deSantis, Alberto Bevilacqua, Anton Giulio Majano & John Hart <u>PHOTOG</u>: Aldo Giordano <u>SPCL-FX</u>: Ugo Amadoro <u>MUSIC</u>: Armando Trovajoli
GB retitle, **Seddok, Son of Satan**
Unusual horror-thriller: Scientist turns self into monster while repairing dancer's scarred face

Atomic Agent
1959, (Fr), color
<u>W</u>: Martine Carol, Felix Marten, Dany Saval
Minor thriller: Parisian model suspected of being spy

The Atomic Brain
see Monstrosity

The Atomic Cafe
1982, (USA), Libra/Archives Project, b&w, 89 mins.
<u>P & D</u>: Kevin Rafferty, Jayne Loader & Pierce Rafferty
Celebrated docu: Bizarre views on nuclear threat (edited from 1950s U.S. Gov't films)

The Atomic City
1952, (USA), Para, b&w, 85 mins.
<u>W</u>: Gene Barry *(Dr. Frank Addison)*, Lee Aaker *(Tommy Addison)*, Lydia Clarke *(Martha Addison)*, Bert Freed *(Jablons)*, Michael Moore *(Russ Farley)*, Milburn Stone *(Insp. Mann)*, Nancy Gates *(Ellen Haskell)*, Bonny Kay Eddy

Attack Of The Crab Monsters: RICHARD GARLAND, RUSSELL JOHNSON, PAMELA DUNCAN

(Peggy Marston), Norman Budd *(Driscoll)*, Houseley Stevenson Jr. *(Gregory)*, Leonard Strong, Frank Cady, Anthony Warde, John Damler, George M. Lynn, Jerry Hausner, Olan Soule

Attack of the 50-Foot Woman: ALLISON HAYES AND ROY GORDON

<u>P</u>: Joseph Sistrom <u>D</u>: Jerry Hopper <u>SCR</u>: Sydney Boehm <u>PHOTOG</u>: Charles B. Lang <u>SPCL-FX</u>: Gordon Jennings <u>MUSIC</u>: Leith Stevens
Superior SF-melodrama: H-bomb spies kidnap physicist's son

Atomic Dog
1997, (USA), USA-TV, color, 95 mins.
<u>W</u>: Daniel Hugh-Kelly, Isabella Hofmann, Cindy Pickett, Katie Stuart, Micah Gardener
<u>D</u>: Brian Trenchard-Smith <u>TELEPLAY</u>: Miguel Tejada-Flores <u>PHOTOG</u>: David Lewis <u>MUSIC</u>: Peter Bernstein
TVM, standard thriller: Mutant pooch menaces family

The Atomic Kid
1954, (USA), Rep, b&w, 86 mins.
<u>W</u>: Mickey Rooney *(Blix Waterberry)*, Elaine Davis *(Audrey Nelson)*, Robert Strauss *(Stan Cooper)*, Hal March *(Ray)*, Bill Goodwin *(Dr. Rodell)*, Whit Bissell *(Dr. Edgar Pangborn)*, Joey Forman *(The M.P. in the Hospital)*, Peter Leeds *(Bill)*, Fay Roope *(Gen. Lawler)*, Stanley Adams *(Wildcat Hooper)*, Robert Emmett Keane *(Mr. Reynolds)*
<u>D</u>: Leslie H. Martinson <u>SCR</u>: Benedict Freedman & John Fenton Murray, from a story by Blake Edwards <u>MUSIC</u>: Van Alexander
Juvenile SF-comedy: Uranium prospectors imperiled by A-bomb testing

The Atomic Man
see Timeslip

The Atomic Monster
see Man-Made Monster

Atomic Rulers of the World
1964, (Jap), color
<u>W</u>: Ken Utsui, Minoru Takada, Junko Ikeuchi
<u>P</u>: Mitsugi Okura <u>D</u>: Teruo Ishii, Akira Mitsuwa & Koreyoshi Akasaka <u>SCR</u>: Ichiro Miyagawa
Juvenile SF-fantasy: Orphaned children assist sleuth in foiling A-bomb smugglers

The Atomic Submarine
1959, (USA), Gorham/AA, b&w, 73 mins.
<u>W</u>: Arthur Franz, Brett Halsey, Dick Foran, Tom Conway, Paul Dubov, Bob Steele, Joi Lansing, Jack Mulhall, Victor Varconi, Sid Melton, Selmer Jackson, Jean Moorhead, Richard Tyler, Ken Becker
<u>P</u>: Alex Gordon <u>D</u>: Spencer G. Bennet <u>SCR</u>: Orville H. Hampton
Modest SF-thriller: Atom sub destroys unearthly invader beneath polar ice cap

Atom Man vs. Superman
1950, (USA), Columbia, b&w, 15 chaps. (130 mins.)
<u>W</u>: Kirk Alyn, Lyle Talbot, Noel Neill <u>D</u>: Spencer G. Bennet

Atonement of Gosta Berling
see **The Story of Gosta Berling**

Ator, the Blademaster
1984, (USA-It), color, 90 mins.
W: Miles O'Keeffe (*Ator*)
Minor "Sword & Sorcery" adventure: Hero battles evil forces. A.k.a. **Blademaster**

Ator: The Fighting Eagle
1983, (USA-It), Helen Sarlui, color, 88 mins.
W: Miles O'Keeffe (*Ator*), Sabrina Siani (*Roon*), Ritza Brown (*Sunya*), Edmund Purdom (*Griba*), Laura Gemser (*Indun*), Dakkar (*High Priest of the Spider*), Chandra Vazzoler (*The Woman in the Tavern*), Nat Williams, Olivia Goods, Jean Lopez
WRIT & D: David Hills   PHOTOG: Frederick Slonisco   MUSIC: Carlo Maria Cordio
Minor "Sword & Sorcery" adventure: Barbarian hero hunts for bride abducted by Spider Kingdom

Atragon
1964, (Jap), Toho/AIP, color, 96 mins.
W: Tadao Takashima, Yu Fujiki, Yoko Fujiyama, Hiroshi Koizumi, Jun Tazaki, Kenji Sawara, Ken Uehara
D: Inoshiro Honda   SCR: Shinichi Sekizawa   SPCL-FX: Eiji Tsuburaya
   MUSIC: Akira Ifukube
Juvenile SF-fantasy: Burrowing super-ship disturbs denizens of submerged continent

At Sword's Point
1951, (USA), RKO Radio, color, 81 mins.
W: Cornel Wilde, Maureen O'Hara, Dan O'Herlihy, Robert Douglas, Alan Hale Jr., Gladys Cooper, Blanche Yurka, Nancy Gates
D: Lewis Allen   SCR: Walter Ferris & Joseph Hoffman   PHOTOG: Ray Rennahan   MUSIC: Roy Webb
GB retitle, **Sons of the Musketeers**
Standard action-adventure: Queen rescued by sons of the Three Musketeers

The Attached Balloon
see **Privarzaniat Balon**

Attack of the Blind Dead
see **El Ataque de los Muertos sin Ojos**

Attack of the Blood-Leeches
see **Attack of the Giant Leeches**

Attack of the Crab Monsters
1957, (USA), AA, b&w, 64 mins.
W: Richard Garland, Pamela Duncan, Russell Johnson, Leslie Bradley, Mel Welles, Ed Nelson, Tony Miller, Richard Cutting, Beech Dickerson
P & D: Roger Corman   SCR: Charles B. Griffith   PHOTOG: Floyd Crosby
   MUSIC: Ronald Stein
orig. co-billed with **Not of this Earth** *(1957)*
Modest SF-thriller: Giant mutated crabs terrorize island

Attack of the 50-Foot Woman
1958, (USA), AA, b&w, 72 mins.
W: Allison Hayes (*Nancy Archer*), John Hudson (*Harry Archer*), Yvette Vickers (*Honey Parker*), Roy Gordon (*Dr. Cushing*), Ken Terrell (*Jessup Stout*), George Douglas (*Sheriff Dubbitt*), Eilene Stevens (*The Nurse*), Frank Chase (*Charlie*), Mike Ross (*Tony*), Otto Waldis (*Dr. Von Loeb*), Dale Tate
P: Bernard Woolner   D: Nathan Hertz   SCR: Mark Hanna   PHOTOG: Jacques R. Marquette   MUSIC: Ronald Stein
pre-release title, **The Astounding Giant Woman**
blurb: "See a female colossus...her mountainous torso, skyscraper limbs, giant desires!"
Minor SF-thriller: Space alien causes woman to become giant

Attack of the 50-Foot Woman
1993, (USA), WB/HBO-TV, color, 95 mins.
W: Daryl Hannah (*Nancy Archer*), Daniel Baldwin (*Harry Archer*), William Windom (*Hamilton Cobb*), Paul Benedict, Frances Fisher, Cristi Conaway, Lewis Arquette, Xander Berkeley, Hamilton Camp, Richard Edson, Victoria Haas, O'Neal Compton
MUSIC: Nicholas Pike   D: Christopher Guest   TELEPLAY: Joseph Dougherty
VS-FX SPRVSR: Gene Warren Jr.   SONGS: Stand Tall, Too Many Nights & Down in Louisiana.
TVM, remake of camp SF-melodrama: Beauty becomes giantess after close encounter with alien spaceship

Attack of the Giant Leeches
1959, (USA), Balboa/AIP, b&w, 62 mins.
W: Ken Clark (*Steve*), Jan Shepard (*Nan*), Yvette Vickers (*Liz*), Michael Emmet (*Cal*), Gene Roth (*The Sheriff*), Tyler McVey (*Doc*), Bruno Ve Sota (*Dave Walker*), George Cisar, Dan White
P: Gene Corman   D: Bernard L. Kowalski   SCR: Leo Gordon
orig. to be titled **Attack of the Blood-Leeches**, *orig. co-billed with* **A Bucket of Blood** *(1959), GB retitle,* **Demons of the Swamp**
Minor SF-horror: Rocket-launching radiation mutates swamp leeches

Attack of the Jungle Women
1959, (USA), Barjul Int'l, color, 72 mins.

W: William Phillips
Minor adventure-thriller

Attack of the Killer Bees
see **The Savage Bees**

Attack of the Killer Tomatoes
1978, (USA), Four Square, color, 87 mins.
W: David Miller (*Mason Dixon*), George Wilson (*Jim Richardson*), Sharon Taylor (*Lois Fairchild*), Eric Christmas (*Sen. Polk*), "Rock" Peace (*Lt. Wilbur Finletter*), Al Sklar (*Ted Swann*), Don Birch (*The Old Man*), Ernie Meyers (*The President*), Paul Oya (*Dr. Nokitofa*), Ron Shapiro (*The Newspaper Editor*), Rebecca Birch (*The Old Woman*), Jerry Anderson (*Maj. Mills*), John Qualls (*The Captain*), Tom Coleman (*The Singing Soldier*), Art Koustik (*The FIA Director*), Jack Nolen (*Sen. McKinley*), Gary Smith (*Sam Smith*), Alan Scharf (*Roberts*), Doug Vernon (*The Scientist*), Byron Teegarden (*Dr. Morrison*), Cindy Charles (*The Housewife*), Joe Price (*Detective #1*), Gordon Ross (*Detective #2*), D. Wayne Cyphert (*The Husband*), Efemia Dillon (*The Wife*), Nigel Barber (*The Guard at the Gate*), John De Bello (*The Janitor*), Paul Abbot (*A Sergeant*), Wayne Wynne (*Mr. Mikkelson*), Chad Demmon (*Bobby Drake*), Ellen Drexler (*The President's Sec'y*), Burt Miller (*The Admiral*), David Hall (*Bruce*), Richard Curtis (*General #1*), Hal Chidnoff (*General #2*), Benita Barton (*Gretta Attenbaum*), Steve Cates (*Greg Colburn*), Linda Hannibal (*The Receptionist*), Brian Cantwell (*Superman*), Richard Buresh (*The Hotel Clerk*), James De Bello (*The Deaf/Blind Cop*), Dan Walsh (*Billy*), Hutch the Dog (*Spot the Dog*), Greg Berger (*A Sergeant*), Riba Nolan (*The Lady in the Supermarket*), C.J. "Clark" Dillon (*The Man in the Library*), Mike Niederman (*The Soldier at the Phone*), Jim Hess (*The TV Reporter*), D.J. Sullivan (*Mrs.*

Attack of the 50-Foot Woman (1993): DARYL HANNAH

Williams), Jack Riley, Robert Matzenauer, Dean Grell, Von Schauer
D: John De Bello   SCR: Costa Dillon, John De Bello & Steve Peace   PHOTOG: John K. Culley   SPCL-FX: Greg Auer   MUSIC SCORE: Paul Sundfor & Gordon Goodwin   SONGS: Puberty Love, Tomato Stomp & The Mindmaker Song
Classic SF-satire: Monstrous "love apples" terrorize. cf. **Return of the Killer Tomatoes**

Attack of the Mayan Mummy
1963, (Mex), b&w, 77 mins.
W: Nina Knight, Richard Webb, John Burton
Minor horror-thriller: Moldy Mexican mummy makes mucho misery

Attack of the Monsters
1968, (Jap), Daiei/AIP, color, 72 mins.
W: Nobuhiro Kajima (*Akio*), Miyuki Akiyama (*Tomoko*), Christopher Murphy (*Tom*)
D: Noriaki Yuasa   SCR: Fumi Takahashi   PHOTOG: Akira Kitazaki   MUSIC: Shunsuke Kikuchi
Juvenile SF-fantasy: Two boys have space adventure

Attack of the Monsters (1969)
see **Gammera vs. Guiron**

29

Attack of the Mushroom People
see Matango

Attack of the Phantoms
see Kiss Meets the Phantom of the Park

Attack of the Puppet People
1958, (USA), AIP, b&w, 79 mins.
W: John Agar (*Bob*), June Kenney (*Sally*), John Hoyt, Michael Mark, Jack Kosslyn, Laurie Mitchell, June Jocelyn, Marlene Willis, Susan Gordon, Scott Peters, Ken Miller, Hal Bogart, Jean Moorhead, Hank Patterson, Bill Giorgio, Troy Patterson, George Diestel, Jaime Forster, Mark Lowell
P, D & STORY: Bert I. Gordon   SCR: George Worthington Yates   PHOTOG: Ernest Laszlo   MUSIC: Albert Glasser   SONGS: I'm Your Living Doll
orig. co-billed with War of the Colossal Beast
Modest SF-thriller: Doll-maker shrinks humans with ray

Attack of the Robots
see Cartes sur Table

Attack of the 60 Foot Centerfold
1995, (USA), New Horizons, color, 85 mins.
W: J.J. North, Ted Monte, Raelyn Saalman (*Inga*), Tammy Park (*Betty*), Tom Abell, Michelle Bauer, George Stover, Nikki Fritz, Ross Hagen, Jay Richardson, Russ Tamblyn, Tommy Kirk, Stanley Livingston, John LaZar
P & D: Fred Olen Ray   SCR: Steve Armogida   PHOTOG: Gary Graver   MUSIC: Jeffrey Walton
Standard SF-spoof: Beauty-enhancement formula turns woman into giant

Attack of the Swamp Creature
1975, (USA), color, 96 mins.
W: Frank Crowell, David Robertson
D: Arnold Stevens
Minor SF-horror: Mad scientist transforms self into monster

The Attack on the Agent
1906, (GB), b&w, 540 ft. (165m)
W: Jennie Green (*The Wife*)
D: Tom Green
Standard crime-thriller (in 8 scenes): Irish moonlighters tie eviction agent to railroad tracks

Attempted Murder in a Railway Train
1904, (GB), Clarendon/Gaumont, b&w, 225 ft. (68.6m)
D: Percy Stow
Standard crime-thriller (in 7 scenes): Criminal cardsharp captured

Attempt to Kill
1961, (GB), Merton Park/Anglo-Amalgamated, b&w, 57 mins.
W: Derek Farr (*Insp. Minter*), Tony Wright (*Gerry Hamilton*), Richard Pearson (*Frank Weyman*), Freda Jackson (*Mrs. Weyman*), Patricia Mort (*Elisabeth Gray*), J.G. Devlin (*Elliott*), Clifford Earl (*Sgt. Bennett*), Denis Holmes (*Fraser*), Allan Jeayes

At The Earth's Core: CAROLINE MUNRO

P: Jack Greenwood   D: Royston Morley   SCR: Richard Harris, from Edgar Wallace's novel *The Lone House Mystery*
Standard thriller: Confidence tricksters scheme to kill business man

At the Conquest of the Pole
see A la Conquete du Pole

At the Earth's Core
1976, (GB), Max J. Rosenberg-Milton Subotsky/Amicus/AIP, color, 89 mins.
W: Doug McClure (*David Innes*), Peter Cushing (*Dr. Abner Perry*), Caroline Munro (*Dia*), Cy Grant (*Ra*), Godfrey James (*Ghak*), Sean Lynch (*Hooja*), Michael Crane (*Jubal*), Bobby Parr (*The Chief*), Keith Barron (*Dowsett*), Helen Gill (*Maisie*), Anthony Verner (*Gadsby*), Andree Cromarty (*The Slave*), Robert Gillespie (*The Photographer*)
P: John Dark   D: Kevin Connor   SCR: Milton Subotsky, from Edgar Rice Burroughs' novel   PHOTOG: Alan Hume   SPCL-FX SPRVSR: Ian Wingrove   MUSIC: Mike Vickers
Juvenile SF-adventure: Professor and star pupil discover savage world at center of Earth

At the Edge of the World
see Am Rande der Welt

At the Eleventh Hour
1912, (GB), Hepworth, b&w, 975 ft. (297.2m)
W: Gladys Sylvani (*Gladys Henderson*), Alec Worcester (*Reggie Wells*)
D: Warwick Buckland
Standard thriller: Girl saves lover from murder charge

At the Foot of the Scaffold
1913, (GB), Hepworth, b&w, 1,925 ft. (586.7m)
W: Alec Worcester (*John West*), Chrissie White (*Emily West*), Harry Royston (*The Convict*), Harry Gilbey (*The Banker*), Ruby Belasco (*The Banker's Wife*)
D: Warwick Buckland
Standard crime-thriller: Escaped convict's dying confession clears clerk convicted of stabbing banker

At the Hour of Three
1912, (GB), Clarendon, b&w, 875 ft. (241.3m)
W: Dorothy Bellew (*The Girl*)
D: Wilfred Noy
Standard crime-thriller: Debtor accused of shooting father

At the Mercy of the Tide
1910, (GB), Cricks & Martin, b&w, 555 ft. (169.2m)
D: Dave Aylott
Standard adventure-thriller: Girl rescues sweetheart trapped in sea

At the Midnight Hour
1995, (GB), color
W: Patsy Kensit, Simon MacCorkindale
Standard thriller: Nanny finds mystery when hired by famous scientist

At the Prompting of the Devil
see His Evil Genius

At the Stroke of Nine
1957, (GB), Tower/Grand Nat'l, b&w, 72 mins.
W: Patricia Dainton (*Sally Bryant*), Stephen Murray (*Stephen Garrett*), Patrick Barr (*Frank*), Dermot Walsh (*MacDonnell*), Clifford Evans (*Insp. Hudgell*), Leonard White (*Thompson*), Reg Green (*Toby*), Frank Atkinson
P & SCR: Harry Booth & Micheal Deeley   D: Lance Comfort   STORY: Tony O'Grady
Minor thriller: Girl reporter kidnapped by madman

At the Villa Rose
1920, (GB), Stoll, b&w, 7,038 ft. (2145.2m)
W: Manora Thew (*Celia Harland*), Langhorne Burton (*Harry Weathermill*), Teddy Arundell (*Insp. Hanaud*), Norman Page (*Julius Ricardo*), Joan Beverley (*Adele Rossignol*), Kate Gurney (*Helene*), Eva Westlake (*Mme. Dauvray*), J.L. Boston (*Besnard*), Armand Lenders (*Perichet*)
D: Maurice Elvey   SCR: Sinclair Hill, from a novel by A.E.W. Mason
Standard crime-thriller: Jewel thieves kidnap fraudulent medium, frame her for strangling widow

At the Villa Rose
1939, (GB), ABPC, b&w, 74 mins.
W: Keneth Kent (*Insp. Hanaud*), Judy Kelly (*Celia Harland*), Peter Murray-Hill (*Harry Wethermill*), Walter Rilla (*Ricardo*), Clifford Evans (*Tace*), Antoinette Cellier (*Adele Rossignol*), Ronald Adam (*Besnard*), Martita Hunt (*Helen Vaquier*), Ruth Maitland
D: Walter Summers   SCR: Doreen Montgomery, from a novel by A.E.W. Mason
USA retitle, House of Mystery
Standard thriller: Gem thieves frame fake medium

The Attic
1980, (USA), Forum-Attic Assocs./Samuel Goldwyn, color, 93 mins.
W: Carrie Snodgress (*Louise Elmore*), Ray Milland (*Wendell Elmore*), Michael Rhodes (*The Sailor*), Ruth Cox (*Emily Perkins*), Rosemary Murphy (*Mrs. Perkins*), Frances Bay (*The Librarian*), Fern Barry (*Mrs. Mooney*), Marjorie Eaton (*Mrs. Fowler*), Angel (*Dickie*), Dick Welsbacher (*The Missing Persons Agent*), Joyce Cavarozzi (*The Secretary*), Phil Speary (*The Travel Agent*), Ron Luce (*Young Robert*), Patrick Brennan (*David Perkins*), Mark Andrews (*Marty*), Terry Troutt (*Donald*), Zale Kessler (*The Mailman*), Mason Armin James (*The Gorilla*)
D: George Edwards   SCR: Tony Crechales & George Edwards   PHOTOG: Gary Graver   MUSIC: Hod David Schudson   SONGS: Who Cares, Come Love Me Again & The Ticket
Standard thriller: Spinster obsessed by memory of vanished fiance

L'Auberge Ensorcelee (The Bewitched Inn)
1897, (Fr), Star, b&w, 40m (131.2 ft./2.2 mins.)
<u>D</u>: Georges Melies
Standard fantasy: Fatigued traveler finds his clothes have life of their own

L'Auberge Rouge (The Red Inn)
1951, (Fr), Arthur Davis Release, b&w, 100 mins.
<u>W</u>: Fernandel (*The Monk*), Francoise Rosay (*Marie*), Lud Germain (*The Novice*), Julien Carette (*Martin*), Andre Cheff (*The Dandy*), Marie Claire Olivia (*Mathilde*), A. Vialla (*Fetiche*), N. Germon (*The Englishman*), D. D'Yd (*The Marchioness*), G. Aslan (*The Lady Passenger*), Caussimon (*The Gentleman Passenger*)
<u>D</u>: Claude Autant-Lara   <u>SCR</u>: Jean Aurenche & Pierre Bost   <u>STORY</u>: Jean Aurenche
Grotesque comedy-thriller: Monk finds travelers who stop at inn are being robbed and murdered

Au Coeur de la Vie (In the Midst of Life)
1962, (Fr), Franco-London-Sinfonia-Films du Centaure, b&w, 94 mins.
<u>W</u>: Edwin Moatti, Francois Frankiel, Stephane Fey, Frederique Ruchaud, Eric Frankiel, Roger Jacquet, Anne Cornaly
<u>WRIT & D</u>: Robert Enrico, trilogy of Ambrose Bierce short stories about the American Civil War: ***Chickamauga, The Mocking Bird,*** & the Oscar-winning La Riviere du Hibou (Owl River)—based on Bierce's ***An Occurrence at Owl Creek Bridge***   <u>PHOTOG</u>: Jean Boffety   <u>MUSIC</u>: Henri Lance

Audrey Rose
1977, (USA), UA, color, 113 mins.
<u>W</u>: Marsha Mason (*Janice Templeton*), Anthony Hopkins (*Elliot Hoover*), John Beck (*Bill Templeton*), Robert Walden (*Brice Mack*), Susan Swift (*Ivy Templeton*), Norman Lloyd (*Dr. Lipscomb*), John Hillerman (*Scott Velie*), Philip Sterling (*Judge Langley*), Mary Jackson, Richard Lawson
<u>P</u>: Joe Wizan & Frank De Felitta   <u>D</u>: Robert Wise   <u>SCR</u>: Frank De Felitta, from his novel   <u>PHOTOG</u>: Charles H. Maguire   <u>MUSIC</u>: Michael Small
Static fantasy-thriller: Young girl is reincarnated

Die Augen der Mumie Ma (The Eyes of the Mummy)
1918, (Ger), Ufa, b&w, 55 mins.
<u>W</u>: Apolinia Chalupetz [Pola Negri], Emil Jannings, Harry Liedtke
<u>D</u>: Ernst Lubitsch   <u>PHOTOG</u>: Theodor Sparkuhl
Moody melodrama: Murder amid archeological treasures

Auntie Lee's Meat Pies
1992, (USA), color, 100 mins.
<u>W</u>: Karen Black, Noriyuki "Pat" Morita, Pat Paulsen, Huntz Hall, Michael Berryman, David Parry, Stephen Quadros
<u>D</u>: Joseph F. Robertson
Minor horror-satire: Nieces lure men, provide aunt with secret ingredient for popular pies

Aurora Encounter
1986, (USA), New World, color
<u>W</u>: Jack Elam, Peter Brown, Carol Bagdasarian, Dottie West
<u>D</u>: Jim McCullough Sr.
Minor SF-adventure: Astronauts meet aliens

Automan
1983, (USA), color, 89 mins.
<u>W</u>: Desi Arnaz Jr.
Minor SF-thriller: Police computer expert and crime-fighting creation break up int'l kidnapping ring

Los Automatas de la Muerte (The Death Robots)
1961, (Mex), Commonwealth United-TV, b&w
<u>W</u>: Wolf Rubinskis, Julio Aleman, Armando Silvestre
<u>P</u>: Luis Garcia de Leon   <u>D</u>: Federico Curiel   <u>SCR</u>: Alfredo Ruanova
*USA retitle, **Neutron vs. the Death Robots***
Minor SF-thriller: Superhero battles human robots and a monstrous blood-consuming brain

Automatic
1994, (USA), HBO-TV, color, 90 mins.
<u>W</u>: Olivier Gruner, Daphne Ashbrook
Made-for-Cable, standard SF-thriller: Home-security android develops own personality

The Automatic Motorist
1911, (GB), Kineto, b&w, 610 ft. (185.9m)
<u>D</u>: Walter R. Booth
Standard fantasy short: Robot chaeffeur drives honeymooners to Saturn and under the sea

Autopsia de un Fantasma (Autopsy of a Ghost)
1967, (Mex), Peclicalas Nacionales, color
<u>W</u>: John Carradine, Basil Rathbone, Cameron Mitchell
<u>P & D</u>: Ismael Rodriguez
Minor horror-fantasy: Satan meets mad scientist and lovelorn ghost

Autopsy
1978, (It-Sp), Pisces Partners/Leonardo Pescarolo/Joseph Brenner, color, 89 mins.
<u>W</u>: Mimsy Farmer, Barry Primus, Ray Lovelock, Angela Goodwin
<u>P</u>: Leonardo Pescarola   <u>D</u>: Armando Crispino   <u>PHOTOG</u>: Carlo Carlini   <u>MUSIC</u>: Ennio Morricone
Minor thriller: Brutal murders terrify

Autopsy of a Ghost
see ***Autopsia de un Fantasma***

Avalanche
1978, (USA), New World, color, 91 mins.
<u>W</u>: Rock Hudson (*David Shelby*), Mia Farrow (*Caroline Brace*), Robert Forster (*Nick Throne*), Jeanette Nolan (*Florence Shelby*), Anthony Carbone (*Leo the Coach*),Rick Moses (*Bruce Scott*), Steve Franken (*Henry McDade*), Barry Primus (*Mark Elliott*), Cathey Paine (*Tina Elliott*), Jerry Douglas (*Phil Prentiss*), Peggy Browne (*AnnetteRivers*), Pat Egan (*Cathy Jordan*), Joby Baker (*The TV Director*), X Brands (*Marty Brenner*), Cindy Luedke (*Susan Maxwell*),

Autopsy: MIMSY FARMER

John Cathey (*Ed the Pilot*), Angelo Lamonea (*Bruce's Coach*), Buzz Bundy, Bill Catching, Fred Hice, Dottie Catching, Sandy Gimpel, Leslie Hoffman, Keith Lane Jensen, Dennis Madalone, Cindy Perpiche, Jeremy Summers, Sandy Robertson, Chuck Tamburro, Allen Wyatt Jr.
P: Roger Corman **D:** Corey Allen **SCR:** Claude Pola & Corey Allen **STORY:** Frances Doel **PHOTOG:** Pierre-William Glenn **MUSIC:** William Kraft
blurb: "6 million tons of icy terror"
Standard "disaster" thriller: Jet crash causes avalanche that imperils resort

Avalanche: ROCK HUDSON

Avalanche Express
1979, (GB-Ire-Bavaria), Lorimar/20th-Fox, color, 88 mins.
W: Robert Shaw (*Gen. Malenkov*), Lee Marvin (*Col. HarryWargrave*), Linda Evans (*Elsa Lang*), Maximilian Schell (*Nikolai Bunin*), Mike Connors (*Haller*), Horst Buchholz (*Scholten*), Joe Namath (*Leroy*), David Hess (*Geiger*), Arthur Brauss (*Neckermann*), Kristine Nel (*Helga Mann*), Sylva Langova (*Olga*), Gunter Meissner (*Muehler*), Cyril Shaps (*Sedov*), Claudio Cassinelli (*Molinari*), Vladek Sheybal (*Zarubin*)
P & D: Mark Robson **SCR:** Abraham Polonsky, from a novel by Colin Forbes **PHOTOG:** Jack Cardiff **MUSIC:** Allyn Ferguson
Standard thriller: U.S. agent helps Soviet defector

The Avaricious Monk
1912, (GB), Hepworth, b&w, 750 ft. (228.6m)
D: Warwick Buckland
Standard adventure-thriller: King pardons Robin Hood

The Avenger (1960)
see Der Raecher

The Avenger (1961)
see La Leggendi di Enea

The Avengers
1998, (USA-GB), WB, color, 88 mins.
W: Ralph Fiennes (*John Steed*), Uma Thurman (*Emma Peel*), Sean Connery (*Sir August De Wynter*), Fiona Shaw, Jim Broadbent, Eddie Izzard, Eileen Atkins, John Wood
D: Jeremiah Chechik
Energetic thriller (inspired by 1960's BBC teleseries): Suave British agent and beautiful assistant fight madman out to control world weather

Avengers of the Reef
1971, (Austral), color
W: Tim Elliot, Noel Ferrier, Biu Rarawa
Standard thriller: Killer pursues scientist and his son

The Avenging Conscience
1914, (USA), Mutual, b&w, 6 reels/92 mins.
W: Henry B. Walthall, Dorothy Gish, Mae Marsh, Donald Crisp, Blanche Sweet, Spottiswoode Aitken, George Siegmann, Ralph Lewis
D & ADAPT: D.W. Griffith, from Edgar Allan Poe trilogy: *The Tell-Tale Heart, The Pit and the Pendulum,& Annabel Lee* **PHOTOG:** G.W. "Billy" Bitzer
A.k.a. **Thou Shalt Not Kill**
Standard trilogy of terror tales

The Avenging Hand (1915)
see The Wraith of the Tomb

The Avenging Hand
1943, (USA), b&w, 56 mins.
W: Noah Beery Jr., Kathleen Kelly, Louis Borell, Reginald Long, James Harcourt,

Charles Oliver
D: Victor Hanbury
Minor thriller: Thieves seek stolen loot

Les Aventures de Don Quichotte (The Adventures of Don Quixote)
1908, (Fr), Star, b&w, 109m (357.6 ft./6 mins.)
D: Georges Melies
A.k.a. **Incident from Don Quixote**
Standard fantasy: Spanish knight has bizarre dream

Les Aventures de Robinson Crusoe (The Adventures of Robinson Crusoe)
1902, (Fr), Star, b&w, 280m (910 ft./15.4 mins.)
W: Georges Melies **D:** Georges Melies, from Daniel Defoe's novel Robinson Crusoe
Standard adventure (in 25 scenes): Man shipwrecked. A.k.a. **Robinson Crusoe**

Les Aventures du Baron de Munchausen
see Les Hallucinations du Baron de Munchausen

Les Aventures Extraordinaires de Jules Verne (The Extraordinary Adventures of Jules Verne)
1952, (Fr), b&w, 31 mins.
D: Jean Aurel
Short adventure-fantasy: Pastiche of fabulous events

L'Aveu (The Confession)
1970, (It-Fr), Para, color, 160 mins.
W: Yves Montand (*Gerard*), Simone Signoret (*Lise*), Gabriele Ferzetti (*Kohoutek*), Michel Vitold (*Smola*), Jean Bouise (*Boss*), Laszlo Szabo
D: Costa-Gavras **SCR:** Jorge Semprun **PHOTOG:** Raoul Coutard, from a story by Lise & Arthur London
Standard melodrama: Couple enmired by communism

Die Avonturen von Baron Munchausen (The Adventures of Baron Munchausen)
1943, (Ger), Ufa, color
W: Hans Albers, Ilse Werner, Brigitte Horney **D:** Josef Von Baky
Standard adventure-fantasy: Life of eccentric nobleman

The Awakening
1980, (USA), Robert Solo/Orion/WB, color, 100 mins.
W: Charlton Heston (*Matthew Corbeck*), Susannah York (*Jane*), Stephanie Zimbalist (*Margaret/Kara*), Jill Townsend (*Anne*), Patrick Drury (*Paul Whittier*), Bruce Myers (*Dr. Khalid*), Ian McDiarmid (*Dr. Richter*), Nadim Sawalha (*Dr. El Sadek*), Ahmed Osman (*Yussef*), Michael Mellinger (*Hamid*), Leonard Maguire (*John Matthews*), Ishia Bennison (*The Nurse*), Miriam Margolyes (*Dr. Kadira*), Madhau Sharma, Michael Halphie, Roger Kemp, Chris Fairbank
D: Mike Newell **SCR:** Allan Scott, Chris Bryant & Clive Exton, from Bram Stoker's novel *The Jewel of Seven Stars* **PHOTOG:** Jack Cardiff **MUSIC:** Claude Bolling **MUSIC CONDUCTED BY:** Marcus Dods
Japanese retitle:*Pyramid*
Well-made horror-fantasy: Archeologist disturbs tomb of ancient Egyptian witch
cf. **Blood from the Mummy's Tomb**

The Awakening Hour
1957, (GB), Falcon/Anglo-Amalgamated, b&w, 21 mins.
W: Donovan Winter (*The Man*)
WRIT, P & D: Donovan Winter
Standard short crime-thriller: Burglars shoot policeman

The Awakening of Candra
1983, (USA), CBS-TV, color, 96 mins.
W: Blanche Baker (*Candra*), Cliff De Young (*Brown*), Paul Regina (*Julio*), Richard Jaeckel, Jeffrey Tambor
D: Paul Wendkos **TELEPLAY:** Tom Lazarus **PHOTOG:** Richard C. Glouner
TVM, minor thriller (filmed in 1981): Widowed newlywed has eerie nightmares

The Awakening of Chrysis
1899, (Fr), Pathe, b&w
Standard fantasy

Awake to Danger
1995, (USA), color, 95 mins.
W: Tori Spelling, Reed Diamond
TVM, standard thriller: Amnesiac woman tries to recall identity of mother's killer

The Awful Dr. Orlof
1961, (Sp-Fr), Sigma III, b&w, 95 mins.
W: Howard Vernon, Conrado San Martin, Perla Cristal, Diana Lorys
P: Serge Newman **D & SCR:** Jesus Franco
Minor horror-thriller: Tale of wicked scientist

The Ayah's Revenge
1908, (GB), Williamson, b&w, 660 ft. (201.2m)
W: Florence Williamson **D:** James Williamson
Standard thriller: Discharged Hindu nurse steals officer's children

The Aztec Mummy
see La Momia

Babar: the Movie
1989, (Can-Fr), color, 76 mins.
VOICES: Gordon Pinsent, Elizabeth Hanna, Marsha Moreau, Lisa Yamanaka, Gavin Magrath, Sarah Polley, Chris Wiggins
D: Alan Bunce **SCR:** Alan Bunce & John deKlein, from stories by Jean and Laurent de Brunhoff
Standard animated fantasy: Adventures of young elephant king

Babe
1995, (USA), Univ, color, 91 mins.
W: James Cromwell (*Farmer Hoggett*), Magda Szubanski (*Esme*)
VOICES: Christine Cavanaugh (*Babe*), Danny Mann (*Ferdinand*), Miriam Margolyes (*Fly*), Hugo Weaving (*Rex*)
D: Chris Noonan **SCR:** Chris Noonan & George Miller, from Dick King-Smith's book *Sheep-Pig* **PHOTOG:** Andrew Lesnie **MUSIC:** Nigel Westlake
Celebrated fantasy: Precocious pig learns to herd sheep

Babe: Pig in the City
1998, (USA), Univ, color
W: James Cromwell, Mickey Rooney, Magda Szubanski
VOICE: Steven Wright **D:** George Miller **SCR:** George Miller, Judy Morris & Mark Lamprell, from characters created by Dick King-Smith **PHOTOG:** Andrew Lesnie **MUSIC:** Nigel Westlake
Standard fantasy: Pig has urban adventures

Babes in Bagdad
1952, (USA-Sp), UA, color, 72 mins.
W: Paulette Goddard, John Boles, Carmen Sevilla, Gypsy Rose Lee, Raphael Duran, Jose Calvo, Richard Ney, Sebastian Cabot, Thomas Gallagher, Macdonald Parke, Hugh Dempster, Natalie Benesh, Peter Bathurst, Christopher Lee
D: Edgar G. Ulmer & Jeronimo Mihura **SCR:** Felix Feist & Joe Anson
French retitle: Les Mille et Une Filles de Bagdad' (The Thousand and One Girls of Bagdad)
Standard adventure-fantasy: Parody of "Arabian Nights" tales

The Babes in the Wood
1905, (GB), Hepworth, b&w, 700 ft. (213.4m)
D: Lewin Fitzhamon
Standard fantasy short: Wicked uncle hires robbers to kill orphan heirs

Babes in Toyland
1934, (USA), Federal Films/Hal Roach/MGM, b&w, 77 mins.
W: Stan Laurel (*Stannio Dum*), Oliver Hardy (*Ollie Dee*), Henry Kleinbach (later Brandon) (*Silas Barnaby*), Charlotte Henry (*Little Bo-Peep*), Johnny Downs (*Tom-Tom*), Marie Wilson, Florence Roberts, Felix Knight, Virginia Karns
D: Gus Mines & Charles Rogers **SCR:** Nick Grinde & Frank Butler from the operetta by Victor Herbert & Glenn McDonough **PHOTOG:** Art Lloyd & Francis Corby
TV retitle March of the Wooden Soldiers
*A.k.a. **Laurel and Hardy in Toyland** and **Wooden Soldiers, Revenge is Sweet***
Standard comedy-fantasy: Nitwits save town from villain

Babes in Toyland
1961, (USA), Walt Disney/Buena Vista, color, 105 mins.
W: Ray Bolger (*Mr. Barnaby*), Annette Funicello (*Mary Contrary*), Tommy Sands (*Tom Piper*), Ed Wynn (*The Toymaker*), Ann Jillian (*Bo Peep*), Tommy Kirk (*Grumio*), Henry Calvin (*Gonzorgo*), Gene Sheldon (*Roderigo*), Kevin Corcoran (*Little Boy Blue*), Brian Corcoran (*Wee Willie Winkie*), Mary McCarty (*Mother Goose*)
D: Jack Donohue **SCR:** Joe Rinaldi, Lowell S. Hawley & Ward Kimball, from the operetta by Victor Herbert & Glenn McDonough **PHOTOG:** Edward Colman **MUSIC:** George Bruns **SONGS:** *Castle in Spain, Toyland, Floretta, I Can't Do the Sum, Just a Whisper Away, March of the Toys, Go to Sleep, The Workshop Song, Slowly He Sank into the Sea, & The Forest of No Return*
Juvenile fantasy: Ruthless miser pursues girl

Babes in Toyland
1986, (USA-W. Ger), NBC-TV, color, 143 mins.
W: Drew Barrymore, Richard Mulligan, Eileen Brennan, Keanu Reeves, Pat Morita, Jill Schoelen, Googy Gress, Shari Weiser, Walter Buschoff, Rolf Knie, Gaston Haeni, Pipo Sosman, Chad Carlson, Jean Moake, Bill Marcus
P: Tony Ford & Neil T. Maffeo **D:** Clive Donner **TELEPLAY:** Paul Zindel, from the popular stage production **PHOTOG:** Arthur Ibbetson **SPCL-FX SPRVSR:** Willi Neuner **MUSIC:** Victor Herbert **LYRICS & BOOK:** Glenn McDonough **MUSIC & LYRICS:** Leslie Bricusse **MUSIC SPRVSD & CONDUCT:** Ian Fraser
TVM, standard fantasy: Girl visits enchanted kingdom

Babes in Toyland
1997, (USA-GB-Thai-Nat'list China), MGM, color
VOICES: James Belushi, Lacey Chabert, Bronson Pinchot, Ike Eisenmann, Christopher Plummer, Charles Nelson Reilly, Joseph Ashton, Raphael Sbarge, Mitch Carter
TELEPLAY: John Loy, from the operetta by Victor Herbert & Glen MacDonough **MUSIC SCORE:** Mark Watters
Standard animated fantasy: Toyland menaced

The Baby
1981, (USA), Scotia-Int'l, color, 80 mins.
W: Ruth Roman, Anjanette Comer, Marianna Hill, Tod Andrews, Suzanne Zenor, Michael Pataki, Erin O'Reilly, Joseph Bernard, Dan Mallon, Beatrice Manley Blau, Virginia Vincent, David Manzy (*Baby*)
D: Ted Post **SCR:** Abe Polsky **PHOTOG:** Michael Margulies **MUSIC:** Gerald Fried
Minor melodrama: Social worker takes excessive interest in retarded adult

The Baby and the Bomb
1911, (GB), Hepworth, b&w, 525 ft. (160m)
D: Bert Haldane
Standard crime-thriller: Baby removes bomb, saves procession

Baby Blood
see The Evil Within

The Baby Doll Murders
1992, (USA), color, 90 mins.
W: Jeff Kober, John Saxon, Melanie Smith, Bobby DiCicco, Tom Hodges
D & SCR: Paul Leder
Minor thriller: Los Angeles cops track serial killer

Baby: Secret of the Lost Legend
1985, (USA), Touchstone/Buena Vista, color, 91 mins.
W: William Katt (*George*), Sean Young (*Susan*), Patrick McGoohan, Julian Fellowes, Edward Hardwicke, Kyalo Mativo, Hugh Quarshie, Olu Jacobs, Julian Curry, Eddie Tagoe, Alexis Meless, Susie Nottingham, Jeannot Banny, Stephane Krora, Anthony Sarfoh, Roger Carlton, Therese Taba
D: B.W.L. Norton **SCR:** Clifford Green & Eileen Green **PHOTOG:** John Alcott **MUSIC:** Jerry Goldsmith
Modest adventure-fantasy: Paleontologists vie for possession of infant brontosaurus

Babylon 5: A Call to Arms
1999, (USA), TNT-TV, color, 95 mins.
W: Bruce Boxleitner, Jerry Doyle, Jeff Conaway, Tony Todd, Peter Woodward, Tracy Scoggins, Tony Maggio, Endre Hules, Michael Harris, Wayne Alexander, Scott MacDonald, Carlos Bernard, Tim O'Hare
D: Mike Vejar **TELEPLAY:** J. Michael Straczynski **PHOTOG:** Frederick V. Murphy II **MUSIC:** Evan H, Chen
TVM, standard SF-thriller: Surprise attack threatens Earth

Babylon 5: In the Beginning
1998, (USA), TNT-TV, color, 95 mins.
W: Bruce Boxleitner (*Sheridan*), Theodore Bikel (*Lenonn*), Reiner Schone (*Dukhat*),Michael O'Hare, Tamlyn Tomita, Jerry Doyle, Mira Furlan, Blaire Baron, John Fleck, Paul Hampton, Peter Jurasik, Andreas Katsulas, Johnny Sekka, Patricia Tallman
D: Richard Compton **TELEPLAY:** J. Michael Straczynski **PHOTOG:** Billy Dickson **MUSIC:** Christopher Franke
TVM (edited teleseries pilot), standard SF-adventure: 23rd-century space station hosts interplanetary summit. "Prequel" to teleseries recounts creation of space station

The Babysitter
1980, (USA), Moonlight Prods./Filmways/ABC-TV, color, 96 mins.
W: Stephanie Zimbalist (*Joanna*), Patty Duke Astin (*Liz*), Quinn Cummings (*Tara*), William Shatner (*Jeff*), Richard Ty Haller (*The Minister*), John Houseman (*Doc*), Frank Birney (*Farragut*), David Wallace (*Scotty*), Hildy Brooks (*Barbara*), Kenneth Tigar, Virginia Kiser
P: David Garcia **D:** Peter Medak **SCR:** Jennifer Miller **PHOTOG:** Rexford Metz
Modest thriller: Live-in housekeeper disrupts family

The Babysitter
1995, (USA), Spelling Films Int'l, color, 90 mins.
W: Alicia Silverstone, J.T. Walsh (*Harry*), Lee Garlington (*Dolly*), Nicky Katt (*Mark*), Jeremy London (*Jack*), Lois Chiles, Tuesday Knight, Ryan Slater, George Segal, Eric Menyuk, Jane Alden
PHOTOG: Rick Bota **MUSIC:** Loek Dikker **WRIT & D:** Guy Ferland, from a short story by Robert Coover
Standard thriller: Seductive teen inspires obsession

The Babysitter Murders
see Halloween

The Bacchantes
1961, (It), Medallion, color, 100 mins.
W: Taina Elg, Pierre Brice, Akim Tamiroff, Alessandra Panaro, Alberto Lupo from Euripedes' play
Minor myth-adventure: Greek god returns to Thebes

Backfire!
1962, (GB), Merton Park/Anglo-Amalgamated, b&w, 59 mins.
W: Alfred Burke (*Mitchell Logan*), Zena Marshall (*Pauline Logan*), Oliver Johnston (*Bernard Curzon*), Suzanne Neve (*Shirley Curzon*), Noel Trevarthen (*Jack Bryce*), Derek Francis (*Arthur Tilsley*), John Cazabon (*Willy Kyser*), Madeleine Christie (*Hannah Chenko*)
P: Jack Greenwood **D:** Paul Almond **SCR:** Robert Stewart, from an Edgar Wallace novel
Standard crime-thriller: Insurance investigator saves girl from arsonist

Back from the Dead
1957, (USA), Regal-Emirau/20th-Fox, b&w, 79 mins.
<u>W</u>: Peggie Castle, Arthur Franz, Marsha Hunt, Marianne Stewart, Don Haggerty, Otto Reichow, Ned Glass, Evelyn Scott, Jeanne Bates, Helen Wallace, Jeane Wood, James Bell, Joan Bradshaw, Frances Turner
<u>D</u>: Charles Marquis Warren   <u>SCR</u>: Catherine Turney, from her novel *The Other One*
<u>PHOTOG</u>: Ernest Haller   <u>SPCL-FX</u>: Jack Rabin & Louis DeWitt   <u>MUSIC</u>: Raoul Kraushaar
Standard fantasy-thriller: Soul of man's satanist first wife takes possession of second wife's body

The Bacchantes: PIERRE BRICE AND TAINA ELG

Background to Danger
1943, (USA), WB, b&w, 80 mins.
<u>W</u>: George Raft, Brenda Marshall, Sydney Greenstreet, Peter Lorre, Osa Massen, Turhan Bey, Kurt Katch, Willard Robertson
<u>P</u>: Jerry Wald   <u>D</u>: Raoul Walsh   <u>PHOTOG</u>: Tony Gaudio   <u>MUSIC</u>: Frederick Hollander   <u>SCR</u>: W.R. Burnett, from Eric Ambler's novel *Uncommon Danger*
Standard "Cloak & Dagger" thriller: American agent has forged documents that might sway Turkey from Nazi cause

Backlash: Oblivion 2
1996, (USA), color, 82 mins.
<u>W</u>: Andrew Divoff, Musetta Vander, Meg Foster, Isaac Hayes, Julie Newmar, Carel Struycken, George Takei, James F. Skaggs, Irwin Keyes, Maxwell Caulfield
<u>D</u>: Sam Irvin   <u>SCR</u>: Peter David   <u>MUSIC</u>: Pino Donaggio
Made-for-Video, minor SF-western: Marshal faces whip-wielding villainess

Back of Beyond
1995, (Austral), color, 85 mins.
<u>W</u>: Paul Mercurio
Minor thriller

Back to the Future
1985, (USA), AmblinUniv, color, 116 mins.
<u>W</u>: Michael J. Fox (*Marty McFly*), Christopher Lloyd (*Dr. Emmett*), Lea Thompson (*Lorraine*), Thomas F. Wilson (*Biff Tannen*), Marc Mc-Clure, Crispin Glover, Claudia Wells, Jeff O'Haco, Elsa Raven, Will Hare, Billy Zane, Wende Jo Sperber, George DiCenzo, Lisa Freeman, Ivy Bethune, Read Morgan, Gary Riley
<u>D</u>: Robert Zemeckis   <u>SCR</u>: Robert Zemeckis & Bob Gale   <u>PHOTOG</u>: Dean Cundey   <u>MUSIC</u>: Alan Silvestri   <u>SONGS</u>: *The Power of Love* (sung by Huey Lewis and the News), *Heaven is One Step Away*, *Back in Time* & *Time Bomb Town*
Elaborate SF-comedy: Scientist's time machine transports youth to 1955

Back to the Future, Part II
1989, (USA), Univ, color, 105 mins.
<u>W</u>: Michael J. Fox (*Marty McFly*), Christopher Lloyd (*Dr. Emmett*), Lea Thompson (*Lorraine*), Thomas F. Wilson (*Biff Tannen*), Harry Waters Jr. (*Marvin Berry*), Charles Fleischer (*Terry*), Joe Flaherty, James Tolkan, Casey Siemaszko, Billy Zane, Crispin Glover, Jeffrey Weissman, J.J. Cohen, Darlene Vogel, Jason Scott Lee, Ricky Dean Logan, James Ishida, Charles Fleischer, Wesley Mann
<u>D</u>: Robert Zemeckis   <u>SCR</u>: Bob Gale   <u>PHOTOG</u>: Dean Cundey   <u>MUSIC</u>: Alan Silvestri
Entertaining SF-comedy: Youth must mend time warp

Back to the Future, Part III
1990, (USA), Amblin/Univ, color, 119 mins.
<u>W</u>: Michael J. Fox (*Marty McFly*), Christopher Lloyd (*Dr. Emmett*), Mary Steenburgen, Thomas F. Wilson, Lea Thompson, Elizabeth Shue, Matt Clark, Richard Dysart, Harry Carey Jr., Dub Taylor
<u>D</u>: Robert Zemeckis   <u>SCR</u>: Bob Gale   <u>STORY</u>: Robert Zemeckis & Bob Gale   MUSIC: Alan Silvestri   SONG: Doubleback (performed by ZZ Top)
Well-made SF-comedy: Time-traveling youth visits Old West

Back to the Planet of the Apes
1974, (USA), 20th-Fox, color
<u>W</u>: Roddy McDowall (*Galen*), Ron Harper (*Alan*), James Naughton (*Ted*)
based on characters created by Pierre Boulle
TVM, feature culled from teleseries: Time-warped astronauts face simian-controlled future
cf. Farewell to the Planet of the Apes, Forgotten City of the Planet of the Apes, Treachery and Greed on the Planet of the Apes, and Life, Liberty and Pursuit on the Planet of the Apes

Backwoods
1987, (USA), color, 90 mins.
<u>W</u>: Jack O'Hara, Dick Kreusser, Brad Armacot
<u>D</u>: Dea Crow
Minor thriller: Mountain man menaces two campers

Backwoods Massacre
see Midnight (1980)

Bad Blonde
see The Flanagan Boy

Bad Channels
1992, (USA), color, 88 mins.
<u>W</u>: Paul Hipp Martha Quinn, Aaron Lustig, Ian Patrick William Thomerson, Charles Spradling
<u>D</u>: Ted Nicolaou   <u>SCR</u>: Jackson Barr
Standard SF-thriller: Space alien poses as disc jockey, seeks human female specimens

Bad Dreams
1988, (USA), No Frills/20th-Fox, color, 84 mins.
<u>W</u>: Jennifer Rubin (*Cynthia*), Bruce Abbott (*Dr. Alex Karmen*), Richard Lynch (*Harris*), Dean Cameron (*Ralph*), Harris Yulin (*Dr. Berrisford*), Susan Barnes (*Connie*), Damita Jo Freeman (*Gilda*), E.G. Daily (*Lana*), Louis Giambalvo (*Ed*), Susan Ruttan (*Miriam*), John Scott Clough, Sy Richardson, Ben Kronen, Missy Francis, Kristina Loggia
<u>D & SCR</u>: Andrew Fleming   <u>STORY</u>: Andrew Fleming, Michael Dick, P.J. Pettiette & Yuri Zeltser   <u>PHOTOG</u>: Alexander Gruszynski   <u>MUSIC</u>: Jay Ferguson
Standard horror-thriller: Evil guru haunts sole survivor of cult massacre

The Bad Flower
1961, (S. Korea), color
Oriental remake of Horror of Dracula

Bad Girls From Mars
1990, (USA), color, 86 mins.
<u>W</u>: Edy Williams, Brinke Stevens, Jay Richardson, Oliver Darrow
<u>D</u>: Fred Olen Ray   <u>SCR</u>: Sherman Scott & Mark Thomas McGee
Minor sleaze-satire: Murders plague filming of SF movie

Back To The Future II: MICHAEL J. FOX AND CHRISTOPHER LLOYD

The Bad Lord Byron
1948, (GB), Triton/Rank, b&w, 85 mins.
<u>W</u>: Dennis Price (*Lord Byron/The Judge*), Mai Zetterling (*Teresa Guiccioli*), Joan Greenwood (*Lady Caroline Lamb*), Sonia Holm (*Anna Milbanke*), Linden Travers (*Augusta Leigh*), Denis O'Dea (*The Prosecution*), Raymond Lovell (*John Hobhouse*), Leslie Dwyer (*Fletcher*), Irene Browne (*Lady Melbourne*), Ernest Thesiger (*Count Guiccioli*), Leo Texera (*Pietro Gamba*), Robert Harris (*Dallas*), Cyril Chamberlain (*The Defense*), Henry Oscar (*Count Gamba*), Nora Swinburne (*Lady Jersey*), Wilfrid Hyde-White (*Mr. Hopton*), Barry Jones (*Col. Stanhope*), Ronald Adam (*The Judge*), Archie Duncan (*John Murray*), Liam Gaffney (*Tom Moore*), Betty Lynne (*Signora Segati*), John Salew (*Samuel Rogers*), Audrey Mallalieu (*The Member*), Zena Marshall (*The Italian*), Henry

Mollison (*The Prince*)
P: Aubrey Baring & Sydney Box   **D:** David MacDonald   **SCR:** Terence Young, Anthony Thorne, Peter Quennell, Laurence Kitchin & Paul Holt   **PHOTOG:** Stephen Dade   **MUSIC:** Cedric Thorpe Davie
Classy film-bio: As he lies dying in Greece, people from Lord Byron's naughty past return in a vision

Bad Moon
1996, (USA), WB, color
W: Michael Pare, Mariel Hemingway, Mason Gamble, Primo
D: Eric Red   **MUSIC:** Daniel Licht
blurb: "Half man. Half wolf. Total Terror"
Standard horror-fantasy: Man becomes werewolf

Bad Moon: MARIEL HEMINGWAY AND MICHAEL PARE

The Bad One
see *Sorority Girl* (1957)

Bad Ronald
1974, (USA), Lorimar/ABC-TV, color, 74 mins.
W: Scott Jacoby (*Ronald Wilby*), Kim Hunter (*Mrs. Wilby*), Linda Watkins (*Mrs. Schumacher*), Dabney Coleman (*Mr. Wood*), Pippa Scott (*Mrs. Wood*), John Fiedler (*Mr. Roscoe*), Cindy Eilbacher (*Althea Wood*), Cindy Fisher (*Babs Wood*), Lisa Eilbacher (*Ellen Wood*), Ted Eccles (*Duane Matthews*), Lesley Woods (*Aunt Margaret*), Aneta Corsaut (*Mrs. Matthews*), Roger Aaron Brown (*Sgt. Carter*), Angela Hoffman (*Carol Matthews*), Karen Purcil (*Wanda*), Shelley Spurlock (*Laurie Matthews*), John Larch
D: Buzz Kulik   **TELEPLAY:** Andrew Peter Marin, from a novel by John Holbrook Vance   **PHOTOG:** Charles F. Wheeler   **MUSIC:** Fred Karlin
TVM, modest thriller: Boy accidentally kills girl, goes into hiding in secret room

The Bad Seed
1956, (USA), WB, b&w, 129 mins.
W: Nancy Kelly (*Christine*), Patty McCormack (*Rhoda*), Eileen Heckart (*Mrs. Daigle*), Henry Jones (*LeRoy*), Paul Fix (*Bravo*), William Hopper (*Kenneth*), Evelyn Varden (*Monica*), Jesse White (*Emory*), Gage Clarke (*Tasker*), Joan Croydon (*Miss Fern*), Frank Cady (*Mr. Daigle*)
P & D: Mervyn LeRoy   **SCR:** John Lee Mahin, from the stage play by Maxwell Anderson & the novel by William March   **PHOTOG:** Hal Rosson   **MUSIC:** Alex North
Classic melodrama: Woman fears daughter has inherited criminal traits

The Bad Seed
1985, (USA), Hajeno-WB/ABC-TV, color, 100 mins.
W: Blair Brown (*Christine Penmark*), Lynn Redgrave (*Monica*), David Carradine (*LeRoy*), David Ogden Stiers (*Emory Breedlove*), Carrie Wells (*Rachel Penmark*), Richard Kiley (*Richard Bravo*), Anne Haney (*Miss Fern*), Carol Locatell (*Rita Daigler*), Weldon Bleiler, Chad Allen, Christa Denton, Eve Smith, Sarah Fairfax, Katharine Tobin
P & TELEPLAY: George Eckstein, from Maxwell Anderson's play & the novel by William March   **D:** Paul Wendkos   **PHOTOG:** Ted Voigtlander   **MUSIC:** Paul Chihara
TVM, tepid remake of classic thriller: Woman finds daughter is juvenile murderess

Bad Sister
1948, (GB), Univ, b&w, 90 mins.
W: Margaret Lockwood, Ian Hunter
Standard melodrama

Bad Taste
1988, (New Zealand), color, 90 mins.
D: Peter Jackson
W: Peter Jackson, Pete O'Herne, Mike Minett, Terry Potter, Craig Smith, Doug Wren, Dean Lawrie
Standard SF-satire: Space-alien zombies terrorize

Baffled!
1972, (GB), Arena/ITC/ABC-TV, color, 90 mins.
W: Leonard Nimoy (*Tom Kovack*), Susan Hampshire (*Michele Brent*), Vera Miles

(Andrea Glenn), Jewel Blanch (*Jennifer Glenn*), Ray Brooks (*George Tracewell*), Rachel Roberts (*Mrs. Farraday*), Al Mancini (*The Interviewer*), Valerie Taylor (*Louise Sandford*), Angharad Rees (*Peggy Tracewell*), Christopher Benjamin (*Verelli*), Mike Murray (*Parrish/Sandford*), Ewan Roberts (*Hopkins*), Milton Johns (*Dr. Reed*), John Rae (*The Stage Doorman*), Patsy Smart (*The Cleaner*), Shane Rimmer (*The Announcer*), Dan Meaden (*The Policeman*)
P & D: Philip Leacock   **TELEPLAY:** Theodore Apstein   **PHOTOG:** Ken Hodges   **MUSIC:** Richard Hill
TVM, standard thriller: Race-car driver has visions of people in trouble

Bagdad
1949, (USA), Univ, color, 82 mins.
W: Maureen O'Hara, Vincent Price, Paul Christian, John Sutton, Jeff Corey, Otto Waldis, Frank Puglia, Fritz Leiber
P: Robert Arthur   **D:** Charles Lamont   **SCR:** Robert Hardy Andrews   **PHOTOG:** Russell Metty
Standard action-adventure: Girl vows to avenge father's death

A Bag of Monkey Nuts
1911, (GB), Cricks & Martin, b&w, 405 ft. (123.4m)
D: A.E. Coleby
USA retitle: *The Mad Monkey*
Standard comedy-fantasy: Eating peanuts causes workman to act like monkey

Bait
1954, (USA), Col, b&w, 79 mins.
W: Hugo Haas, Cleo Moore, John Agar, Bruno Ve Sota, Sir Cedric Hardwicke (*The Devil*)
P & D: Hugo Haas   **SCR:** Samuel W. Taylor & Hugo Haas
Standard melodrama: Old prospector instigates deadly love triangle

Balaoo
1913, (Fr), b&w
D: Victorin Jasset, from Gaston Leroux's play
PHOTOG: Lucien Andriot
Standard thriller, cf. **The Wizard**

The Balcony
1963, (USA), Walter Reade/Sterling/Allen Hodgdon/City Film/Continental, b&w, 86 mins.
W: Shelley Winters, Peter Falk, Lee Grant, Ruby Dee (*The Thief*), Kent Smith (*The General*), Peter Brocco (*The Judge*), Jeff Corey, Leonard Nimoy, Arnette Jens, Joyce Jameson
P: Joseph Strick & Ben Maddow   **D:** Joseph Strick   **PHOTOG:** George Folsey   **SCR:** Ben Maddow, from Jean Genet's play   **MUSIC:** Igor Stravinsky
Adult psychodrama: Brothel is house of illusions

Le Bal des Vampires
see **The Fearless Vampire Killers** or **Pardon Me, But Your Teeth Are in My Neck**

The Balcony: KENT SMITH AND ARNETTE JENS

The Ballet Master's Dream
see *Le Reve du Maitre de Ballet*

Bambi
1942, (USA), Walt Disney/RKO, color, 72 mins.

VOICES: Bobby Stewart (*Bambi*), Peter Behn (*Thumper*), Cammie King (*Faline*), Paula Winslowe (*Bambi's Mother*), Stan Alexander (*Flower*)
D: David Hand   **SCR:** Larry Morey   **STORY:** Felix Salten   **MUSIC:** Frank Churchill & Edward Plumb
Classic animated fantasy: Young deer learns about life

The Bamboo Saucer
1968, (USA), Harris Associates/NTA World Entertainment Corp., color, 103 mins.
W: Dan Duryea (*Hank*), Lois Nettleton, John Ericson Nan Leslie, Bob Hastings
D: Frank Telford
A.k.a. **Collision Course, Operation Bluebook**
Cold-War thriller: Soviets and Americans wrestle over downed "flying saucer" in Red China

The Banana Monster
see **Schlock**

Banana Peel
1965, (Fr), Pathe-Cont'l, b&w, 97 mins.
W: Jean-Paul Belmondo (*Michel*), Jeanne Moreau (*Cathy*), Gert Frobe (*Lachard*), Claude Brasseur (*Charlie*), Jean-Pierre Marielle (*Reynaldo*), Alain Cuny (*Bontemps*)
D: Marcel Ophuls   **SCR:** Marcel Ophuls & Claude Sautet   **PHOTOG:** Jean Rabier
Standard comedy-thriller: Rogues swindle millionaire

The Bandit of Sherwood Forest
1946, (USA), Col, b&w, 87 mins.
W: Cornel Wilde, Anita Louise, Jill Esmond, Henry Daniell, John Abbott, Edgar Buchanan, Russell Hicks, George Macready, Miles Mander, Eva Moore, Ray Teal, Lloyd Corrigan
P: Leonard S. Picker & Clifford Sanforth   **D:** George Sherman   **SCR:** Wilfrid H. Pettit & Melvin Levy, from Paul Castleton's novel *Son of Robin Hood*   **PHOTOG:** Tony Gaudio, George B. Meehan, & William Snyder   **MUSIC:** M.W. Stoloff
Standard action-adventure: Robin Hood's son aids Queen

The Bandit's Daughter
1912, (GB), Cricks & Martin, b&w, 975 ft. (297m)
W: Una Tristram (*The Daughter*)
D: Edwin J. Collins
Standard adventure-thriller: Bandit's daughter brings troops to rescue captive lieutenant

The Bandits of Corsica
1953, (USA), UA, b&w, 82 mins.
W: Raymond Burr (*Jonatto*), Richard Greene (*Mario, Carlos, & Lucien*), Paula Raymond (*Christina*), Dona Drake (*Zelda*), Lee Van Cleef (*Nerva*), Raymond Greenleaf (*Paoli*), Frank Puglia (*Riggio*), Peter Mamakos (*Diegas*), Peter Brocco (*Angelo*), Paul Cavanagh (*Dianza*), George Lewis (*Arturo*), Nestor Paiva (*Lorenzo*), Clayton Moore, Virginia Brissac, Michael Ansara, Francis J. McDonald, William Forrest, John Pickard
D: Ray Nazzaro   **SCR:** Richard Schayer   **STORY:** Frank Burt, inspired by Alexander Dumas' novel *The Corsican Brothers*   **MUSIC:** Irving Gertz
Standard action-adventure: Siamese twins join forces, oppose tyranny

The Bang-Bang Kid
1967, (It), West Side Int'l/Group W, color, 69 mins.
W: Guy Madison, Tom Bosley, Sandra Milo, Riccardo Garrone, Joe Cafarell
D: Stanley Prager   **ORIG. STORY & SCR:** Howard Berk   **PHOTOG:** Anthony Macasoli   **MUSIC:** Nico Fidenco
Minor western-SF-comedy: Gunslinging robot aids town

Bang, Bang, You're Dead
see **Our Man in Marrakesh**

Bang!, You're Dead
1954, (GB), Wellington/British Lion, b&w, 88 mins.
W: Jack Warner (*Percy Bonsell*), Derek Farr (*Supt. Grey*), Veronica Hurst (*Hilda*), Michael Medwin (*Bob Carter*), Gordon Harker (*Mr. Hare*), Anthony Richmond (*Cliff Bonsell*), Sean Barrett (*Willy Moxted*), John Warwick (*Sgt. Gurney*), Beatrice Varley (*Mrs. Moxted*), Philip Saville (*Ben Jones*), Toke Townley (*Jimmy Knuckle*), Edmund Hockridge
P & D: Lance Comfort   **SCR:** Guy Elmes & Ernest Bornemann   **STORY:** Guy Elmes
A.k.a. **Game of Danger**
Standard crime-thriller: Boy accidentally shoots man

The Bank Breaker
see **Kaleidoscope**

The Banker
1989, (USA), color, 95 mins.
W: Robert Forster (*Sgt. Jefferson*), Duncan Regehr (*Spalding*)
Minor thriller: Financier suspected of ritual killings

The Bank Raiders
1958, (GB), Film Workshop/RFD, b&w, 60 mins.
W: Peter Reynolds (*Terry*), Sandra Dorne (*Della*), Sydney Tafler (*Shelton*), Lloyd Lamble (*Insp. Mason*), Arthur Mullard (*Linders*), Rose Hill (*Mrs. Marling*)
P: Geoffrey Goodhart   **D:** Maxwell Munden   **STORY:** Brandon Fleming
Standard crime-thriller: Petty crook joins gang of bank robbers, becomes involved in kidnapping

Baraka X-77
1966, (Fr), color
W: Gerard Barray, Sylva Koscina, Jose Suarez, Yvette Lebon, Agnes Spaak
Minor spy-thriller: Secret agents vs. diabolical doctors

Baran
see **Varan the Unbelievable**

Barbados Quest
1955, (GB), Cipa/RKO, b&w, 70 mins.
W: Tom Conway (*Tom "Duke" Martin*), Delphi Lawrence (*Jean Larsen*), Brian Worth (*Geoffrey Blake*), Michael Balfour (*Barney*), Campbell Cotts (*Coburn*), John Horsley (*Insp. Taylor*), Ronan O'Casey (*Stefan Gordoni*), Launce Maraschal (*Everleigh*), Colin Tapley (*Lord Valcrist*)
P: Robert Baker & Monty Berman   **D:** Bernard Knowles   **STORY:** Kenneth R. Hayles
USA retitle, **Murder on Approval**
Standard crime-thriller: Private detective exposes forgery of rare stamp

Barbarella
1968, (It-Fr), Dino De Laurentiis-Cinematografica S.p.A.-Marianne Prods./Para, color, 98 mins.
W: Jane Fonda (*Barbarella*), John Phillip Law (*Pygar, the Blind Angel*), Ugo Tognazzi (*Markan, the Catch-Man*), Milo O'Shea (*Duran Duran*), Marcel Marceau (*Prof. Ping*), Anita Pallenberg (*The Black Queen*), David Hemmings (*Dildano*), Veronique Vendell, Claude Dauphin
P: Dino De Laurentiis   **D:** Roger Vadim   **SCR:** Terry Southern, Roger Vadim, Brian Degas, Clement Wood, Jean-Claude Forest, Tudor Gates & Vittorio Bonicelli, based on book by Jean-Claude Forest   **PHOTOG:** Claude Renoir   **MUSIC & LYRICS:** Bob Crewe & Charles, performed by Bob Crewe Generation Orchestra   **SONGS:** *An Angel is Love, Black Queen's Beads*, et al.
"...defending his $3 million film from censors, Vadim said that there is no reference whatsoever in the picture to moral concepts as we know them. 'It would be difficult for any censor to discover objectionable scenes in futuristic fiction...totally unrelated to the present day'...Vadim states, 'I make sensuous pictures, but I don't make dirty pictures.'"—Philip B. Moshcovitz, "Future Fantasy Films," *Castle of Frankenstein*, Vol. IV, No. 1 (Spring, 1969), p. 6
Erotic SF-fantasy: Spacewoman seeks missing inventor of devastating "positronic ray"

Barbarella: JOHN PHILLIP LAW AND JANE FONDA

The Barbarian
see **El Barbaro**

El Barbaro (The Barbarian)
1984, (Sp), color, 88 mins.
W: Andrea Occhipinti, Maria Scola, Violeta Cela, Sabrina Sellers
Minor "Sword & Sorcery": Hero rescues world from sorcerer's evil power

Barbarian Queen
1985, (USA), color, 71 mins.
W: Lana Clarkson, Frank Zagarino, Katt Shea Ruben, Susana Traverso, Dawn Dunlap
D: Hector Olivera

Minor "Sword & Sorcery"

Barbarian Queen II (The Empress Strikes Back)
1991, (USA), color, 87 mins.
<u>W</u>: Lana Clarkson, Greg Wrangler, Rebecca Wood, Elizabeth Jaegen, Roger Cundy
<u>D</u>: Joe Finley
Minor "Sword & Sorcery"

The Barbarians
see Revak, Lo Schiavo di Cartagine

The Barbaric Beast of Boggy Creek, Part II
see Boggy Creek II—The Legend Continues

Barbe-Bleue (Bluebeard)
1901, (Fr), Star, b&w, 210m (689 ft./11.6 mins.)
<u>W</u>: Bluette Bernon, Jehanne d'Alcy
<u>D</u>: Georges Melies
Standard thriller: Murderer preys

Barbed Wire Dolls
1975, (W. Ger), Burbank Int'l, color
<u>W</u>: Lina Romay <u>P</u>: E.C. Dietrich <u>D</u>: Jesus Franco
A.k.a. Caged Women
Standard thriller: Bondage, beatings, rape, humiliation, and sadism in a women's prison

Barb Wire
1996, (USA), Propaganda-Dark Horse/Polygram/Gramercy, color, 98 mins.
<u>W</u>: Pamela Anderson Lee, Temuera Morrison, Victoria Rowell, Jack Noseworthy, Xander Berkeley, Steve Railsback, Udo Keir, Clint Howard, Tony Bill
<u>D</u>: David Hogan <u>SCR</u>: Chuck Pfarrer & Ilene Chaiken <u>STORY</u>: Ilene Chaiken <u>PHOTOG</u>: Rick Bota <u>MUSIC</u>: Michel Colombier <u>MUSIC SPRVSR</u>: Barklie K. Griggs
Standard action-SF: Buxom mercenary caught in future US civil war

The Barefoot Boy
1938, (USA), Mono, b&w
<u>W</u>: Jackie Moran, Marcia Mae Jones
Juvenile comedy-thriller: Racketeers in "haunted house"

The Barefoot Executive
1971, (USA), Walt Disney/Buena Vista, color, 96 mins.
<u>W</u>: Kurt Russell *(Steven Post)*, Wally Cox *(Mertons)*, Joe Flynn *(Francis X. Wilbanks)*, Harry Morgan *(E.J. Crampton)*, Heather North *(Jennifer Scott)*, Alan Hewitt *(Farnsworth)*, John Ritter *(Roger)*, Hayden Rorke *(Clifford)*, Raffles *(Raffles)*, George N. Neise *(A Network Executive)*, Jack Bender *(Tom)*, Ed Reimers *(The Announcer)*, Tom Anfinsen *(Dr. Schmidt)*, Morgan Farley *(The Advertising Executive)*, J.B. Douglas *(A Network Executive)*, Fabian Dean *(The Jackhammer Man)*, Jack Smith *(Clatworthy)*, Iris Adrian *(The Woman Shopper)*, Eve Brent *(Mrs. Crampton)*, Sandra Gould *(Mrs. Wilbanks)*, James Flavin *(Father O'Leary)*, Anthony Teague *(The TV Salesman)*, Bill Daily *(The Navigator)*, Edward Faulkner *(The Reporter)*, Dave Willock *(The Doorman)*, Robert Shayne, Glen Dixon, Ed Prentiss, Tris Coffin, Pete Renoudet, Judson Pratt, Vince Howard, Hal Baylor, Raffles
<u>D</u>: Robert Butler <u>SCR</u>: Joseph L. McEveety <u>PHOTOG</u>: Charles F. Wheeler <u>MUSIC</u>: Robert F. Brunner
Standard comedy-fantasy: Chimpanzee predicts hit TV programs

The Bargain
1921, (GB), Hepworth, b&w, 5,800 ft. (1767.8m)
<u>W</u>: Henry Edwards *(Dennis Trevor)*, Chrissie White *(Mary)*, Rex McDougall *(Dick Wentworth)*, Henry Vibart *(Grosvenor Wentworth)*, Mary Dibley *(Bella Wentworth)*, James Annand *(Tamplin)*, John McAndrews *(Murphy)*, John East *(Longhurst)*
<u>D & SCR</u>: Henry Edwards, from a play by Henry Edwards & Edward Irwin
Standard crime-thriller: Rescued man impersonates convicted heir

Bariera (Barrier)
1966, (Pol), b&w, 83 mins.
<u>W</u>: Jan Nowicki, Joanna Szczerbic, Tadeusz Lomnicki, Ryszard Pietruski, Malgorzata Lorentowicz, Maria Malicka
<u>WRIT & D</u>: Jerzy Skolimowski <u>PHOTOG</u>: Jan Laskowski <u>MUSIC</u>: Krzysztof Komeda
Allegorical fantasy

Barney's Great Adventure
1998, (USA), Lyrick/Polygram, color, 87 mins.
<u>W</u>: George Hearn, Shirley Douglas, Trevor Morgan, Diana Rice
<u>D</u>: Steve Gomer <u>SCR</u>: Stephen White <u>STORY</u>: Stephen White, Sheryl Leach & Dennis DeShazer <u>PHOTOG</u>: Sandi Sissel
Standard juvenile fantasy: Dinosaur befriends children

Barn of the Naked Dead
1976, (USA), Twin World, color, 86 mins.
<u>W</u>: Andrew Prine, Manuella Theiss, Sherri Alberoni, Gyl Roland, Al Cormier, Jennifer Ashley
<u>P & SCR</u>: Gerald Cormier <u>D</u>: Alan Rudolf
A.k.a. Terror Circus and Nightmare Circus
Minor "splatter" satire: Bad doings in countryside

Barnum
see Freaks

Baron Blood
see Gli Orrori del Castello di Noremberga

Le Baron de Crac
see Baron Prasil

El Baron del Terror (The Baron of Terror)
1961, (Mex), Azteca/AIP-TV, b&w, 76 mins.
<u>W</u>: Abel Salazar, Ariadne Welter, David Silvia, German Robles, Louis Aragon, Mauricio Garces, Ofelia Guilmain, Rene Cardona, Ruben Rojo, Rosa Maria Gallardo
<u>P</u>: Abel Salazar <u>D</u>: Chano Urueta <u>SCR</u>: Adolpho Portillo & Frederick Curiel <u>MUSIC</u>: Gustavo Cesar Carrion
USA retitle, The Brainiac
Minor horror-thriller: Evil nobleman reborn, seeks revenge.

Le Baron Fantome (The Phantom Baron)
1943, (Fr), b&w, 100 mins.
<u>WRIT & D</u>: Serge de Poligny <u>DIALOG</u>: Jean Cocteau
Moody fantasy: Wanderings of mysterious nobleman, with the voice of Jean Cocteau

Baron Gregor
see The Black Room

Baron Munchausen
see Les Hallucinations du Baron de Munchausen

The Baron of Arizona
1950, (USA), Lippert, b&w, 93 mins.
<u>W</u>: Vincent Price, Ellen Drew, Reed Hadley, Vladimir Sokoloff, Beulah Bondi, Robert Barrat, Robin Short, Barbara Woodell, Tina Rome, Margia Dean, Edward Keane, Tristram Coffin, Gene Roth, Karen Kester, Joseph Green, Fred Kohler Jr., Zachary Yaconelli, Angelo Rossitto, I. Stanford Jolley, Terry Frost, Adolfo Ornelas, Wheaton Chambers, Stephen Harrison, Robert O'Neil
<u>WRIT & D</u>:Samuel Fuller <u>PHOTOG</u>: James Wong Howe <u>SPCL-FX</u>: Ray Mercer <u>MUSIC</u>: Paul Dunlap
Superior historical melodrama (one of Vincent Price's best roles): Avaricious scoundrel forges Spanish land grant

The Baron of Terror
see El Baron del Terror

Baron Prasil
1961, (Czech), color, 80 mins.
<u>W</u>: Milos Kopecky, Jana Brajchova, Rudolf Jelinek, Karel Effa, Karel Hogel, Jan Werich, Nadezda Blazickova, Bohus Zahorsky, Rudolf Hrusinsky, Eduard Kohout
<u>D & SCR</u>: Karel Zeman, from Gottfried Burger's novel and illustrations by Gustave Doré <u>PHOTOG</u>: Jiri Tarantik <u>MUSIC</u>: Zdenek Liska <u>CHOREOGRAPHY</u>: Jiri Nemecek
French retitle, Le Baron de Crac, USA retitle, The Fabulous Baron Munchausen
Standard adventure-fantasy: Astronaut meets legendary noble man on surface of moon

The Barony
see The Ultimate Warrior

Barracuda
1976, (USA), Manfred Menz/Rep, color, 93 mins.
<u>W</u>: Wayne David Crawford, Jason Evers, William Kerwin, Bert Freed, Roberta Leighton, Cliff Emmich, Matt King, Robert G. Noe, Harry Kerwin, Rick Rhodes, Ray Michel, Denise Taylor, William Roundebush, Leigh Walsh, David Kenier, Jerry Rhodes, Burt Richards, Dick Sterling, Bob Hiers, Scott Wohrman, Bob J. Shields, Elizabeth Michel, Julian Byrd, Jill Shakoor, Kim Nichols, Bobbie-Ellyne Kosstrin, Scott Avery, Ruth Miller, Willis Knickerbocker, Daniel L. Fitzgerald, Frank Logan, Ed Lupinski
<u>WRIT & P</u>: Wayne Crawford <u>D</u>: Harry Kerwin <u>PHOTOG</u>: H. Edmund Gibson <u>MUSIC</u>: Klaus Schulze
A.k.a. The Lucifer Project
Minor SF-thriller: Biologist uncovers plot to control populace by chemicals

Barrier
see Bariera

Bar Sinister
see It's a Dog's Life

The Barton Mystery
1920, (GB), Stoll, b&w, 6,158 ft. (1877m)
<u>W</u>: Lyn Harding *(Beverley)*, Hilda Bayley *(Ethel Standish)*, Maud Cressall *(Mrs. Barton)*, Vernon Jones *(Phyllis Grey)*, Edward O'Neill *(Richard Standish)*, Arthur Pusey *(Harry Maitland)*, Ernest A. Cox *(Sir Everard Marshall)*, Austen Camp *(Gerald Barton)*, Eva Westlake *(Lady Marshall)*
<u>D</u>: Harry Roberts <u>SCR</u>: R. Byron-Webber, from a play by Walter Hackett
Standard mystery: Fake medium involved in murder

The Barton Mystery

1932, (GB), B&D/Para British, b&w, 77 mins.
W: Ursula Jeans (*Ethel Standish*), Lyn Harding (*Beverley*), Ion Swinley (*Richard Standish*), Ellis Jeffreys (*Lady Marshall*), Wendy Barrie (*Phyllis Grey*), Joyce Bland (*Helen Barton*), Tom Helmore (*Harry Maitland*), O.B. Clarence (*Sir Everard Marshall*), Franklyn Bellamy (*Gerald Barton*), Wilfred Noy (*Griffiths*)
D: Henry Edwards, from a play by Walter Hackett
Standard thriller: Fake medium exposes crime

The Basilisk

1914, (GB), Hepworth, b&w, 2,500 ft. (762m)
W: Tom Powers (*Eric Larne*), Alma Taylor (*Freda Hampton*), William Felton (*Basil Reska*), Chrissie White, Cyril Morton
WRIT & D: Cecil M. Hepworth
Standard thriller: Hypnotist weaves evil spell

Basket Case

1983, (USA), Rugged Films, color, 89 mins.
W: Kevin van Hentenryk, Terri Susan Smith, Beverly Bonner, Robert Vogel, Joe Clarke, Bill Freeman, Lloyd Pace, Richard Pierce, Ruth Neuman
WRIT & D: Frank Henenlotter **PHOTOG:** Bruce Torbet **MUSIC:** Gus Russo
blurb: "The tenant in room 7 is very small, very twisted and very mad"
Standard horror-satire: Weirdo conceals mutant

Basket Case 2

1990, (USA), Shapiro Glickenhaus/IGE, color, 91 mins.
W: Kevin van Hentenryk (*Duane*), Annie Ross (*Granny Ruth*), Kathryn Meisle (*Marcie Elliott*), Jason Evers, Ted Sorel, Heather Rattray
WRIT & D: Frank Henenlotter **PHOTOG:** Robert M. Baldwin **MUSIC:** Joe Renzetti
Standard horror-satire: Youth harbors mutant twin

Basket Case 3: The Progeny

1992, (USA), Shapiro Glickenhaus, color, 90 mins.
W: Kevin van Hentenryk, Annie Ross, Gil Roper, Tina Louise Hilbert, Dan Biggers, Jim O'Doherty
Standard horror-satire: Genetic mutant plagues cops who kidnapped his offspring

The Bat: AGNES MOOREHEAD

The Bat

1926, (USA), UA, b&w, 9 reels (8,219 ft./2505.2m)
W: Andre de Beranger (*Gideon Bell*), Charles W. Herzinger (*The Man in the Blue Mask*), Emily Fitzroy (*Miss Cornelia Van Gorder*), Louise Fazenda (*Lizzie Allen*), Robert McKim (*Dr. Wells*), Lee Shumway (*The Unknown*), Arthur Houseman (*Richard Fleming*), Eddie Gribbon (*Det. Anderson*), K. Sojin

(*Billy*), Tullio Carminatti (*Moletti*), Jewel Carmen (*Miss Dale Ogden*), Jack Pickford (*Brooks Bailey*)
D: Roland West **SCR:** Julien Josephson, from stage play by Mary Roberts Rinehart & Avery Hopwood, based on Miss Rinehart's novel *The Circular Staircase* **PHOTOG:** Arthur Edeson
Classic mystery-comedy: Killer prowls mansion

The Bat

1959, (USA), Liberty/AA, b&w, 78 mins.
W: Vincent Price, Agnes Moorehead, Lenita Lane, John Sutton, Elaine Edwards, Gavin Gordon, John Bryant, Darla Hood, Mike Steele, Harvey Stephens, Riza Royce, Robert B. Williams
P: C.J. Tevlin **D & SCR:** Crane Wilbur, from the play by Mary Roberts Rinehart & Avery Hopwood, based on Miss Rinehart's novel *The Circular Staircase, filmed under that name by Selig in 1915* **PHOTOG:** Joseph Biroc **MUSIC:** Louis Forbes
French retitle, **Le Masque (The Mask)**
blurb: "Make a double date! People in pairs don't mind the scares!"
Standard mystery-thriller: Maniacal killer prowls mansion being rented by spinster mystery writer

Le Bataillon Elastique (The Elastic Battalion)

1902, (Fr), Star, b&w, 20m (65.6 ft./1.1 mins.)
D: Georges Melies
Standard fantasy

Bates Motel

1987, (USA), Univ/NBC-TV, color, 96 mins.
W: Bud Cort (*Alex West*), Lori Petty (*Willie*), Jason Bateman (*Tony*), Moses Gunn (*Henry*), Gregg Henry (*Tom*), Kerrie Keane (*Barbara Peters*), Khrystyne Haje (*Sam*), Robert Picardo (*Dr. Goodman*), Lee DeBroux (*The Sheriff*), Kurt Paul (*Norman Bates*), Marla Frumkin (*Dr. Phillip*), Kelly Ames (*Beth*), Timothy Fall (*Terry Miller*), Rick Lieberman (*The Architect*), Peter Dobson (*Billy Parks*), Paula Irvine (*Rebecca*), Scott St. James (*The Radio Reporter*), Carmen Filpi (*Buddy*), David Wakefield (*The Macho Chicken*), Greg Finley (*The Attorney*), Nat Bernstein (*The Salesman*), Buck Flower (*The Vagrant*), Andy Albin (*Mr. Yokey*), Gary Ballard (*The Pastor*), Dolores Albin (*Mrs. Fisher*), Peter A. Stelzer (*The Bank Customer*), Hardy Rawls (*Charlie Waters*), George J. Woods (*The Minister*), Jack Ross Obney (*The Workman*), John Kenton Shull (*The Gas Station Attendant*), George Skinta (*The Theater Marquee Man*), Robert Axelrod (*The Sheepskin Salesman*), Pedro Gonzales-Gonzales (*The Mexican Gardener*), Chad Jonas (*The Promnighter*)
D & TELEPLAY: Richard Rothstein, suggested by Robert Bloch's novel *Psycho* **PHOTOG:** Bill Butler **MUSIC:** J. Peter Robinson
TVM-pilot, standard thriller: Former mental patient inherits infamous murder scene

Batman

1966, (USA), Greenway/20th-Fox, color, 105 mins.
W: Adam West (*Bruce Wayne/Batman*), Burt Ward (*Robin, the Boy Wonder*), Lee Meriwether (*The Catwoman*), Cesar Romero (*The Joker*), Burgess Meredith (*The Penguin*), Frank Gorshin (*The Riddler*), Alan Napier (*Alfred*), Neil Hamilton (*Commissioner Gordon*), Stafford Repp (*Chief O'Hara*), Madge Blake (*Aunt Harriet*), Reginald Denny, Ivan Triesault
P: William Dozier **D:** Leslie H. Martinson **SCR:** Lorenzo Semple Jr., from characters created by Bob Kane **PHOTOG:** Howard Schwartz **MUSIC:** Nelson Riddle
Feature-film extension of "camp" teleseries: Superhero faces combined forces of arch-enemies

Batman

1989, (USA), WB, color, 124 mins.
W: Michael Keaton (*Bruce Wayne/Batman*), Jack Nicholson (*Jack Napier/The Joker*), Kim Basinger (*Vicki Vale*), Robert Wuhl (*Alexander Knox*), Pat Hingle (*Commissioner Gordon*), Michael Gough (*Alfred*), Billy Dee Williams (*Harvey Dent*), Jerry Hall (*Alicia*), Jack Palance (*Gus Grissom*), Tracey Walter (*Bob the Goon*), Lee Wallace, William Hootkins, Richard Strange, Carl Chase, George Lane Cooper, Terrence Plummer, Vincent Wong, Philip Tan, John Sterland, Edwin Craig, Joel Cutrara, John Dair, Christopher Fairbank, George Roth, Kate Harper, Leon Herbert, Bruce McGuire, Richard Durden, Jit Hollerbach, Del Baker, Lachelle Carl, Jazzer Jeyes, Wayne Michaels, Steve Plytas, Valentino Musetti, Rocky Taylor, Keith Edwards, Jon Soresi, Anthony Wellington, Amir Korangy, Charles Roskilly, Hugo F. Blick, Philip O'Brien, Michael Balfour, Liza Ross, Garrick Hagon, Adrian Meyers, David Baxt, Sharon Holm, Sam Douglas, Clyde Gatell, Elliott Stein, Dennis Lill, Paul Birchard, Paul Michael
D: Tim Burton **SCR:** Sam Hamm & Warren Skaaren **STORY:** Sam Hamm, from characters created by Bob Kane **PHOTOG:** Roger Pratt **SPCL VS-FX:** Derek Meddings **MUSIC:** Danny Elfman
Lavish adventure-thriller: Caped Crusader fights crime

Batman and Mr. Freeze: Subzero

1998, (USA), WB, color, 70 mins.
VOICES: Marilu Henner, Kevin Conroy
Standard animated adventure-fantasy: Caped Crusader vs. frosty madman

Batman and Robin

1997, (USA), WB, color
W: George Clooney (*Bruce Wayne/Batman*), Chris O'Donnell (*Robin*), Alicia Silverstone (*Batgirl*), Arnold Schwarzenegger (*Mr. Freeze*), Uma Thurman (*Poison Ivy*), Michael Gough (*Alfred*), Pat Hingle (*Commissioner Gordon*), Vivica A. Fox, Eric Lloyd, Elle Macpherson

D: Joel Schumacher **SCR:** Akiva Goldsman, from characters created by Bob Kane **PHOTOG:** Stephen Goldblatt **VS-FX:** John Dykstra **MUSIC:** Elliot Goldenthal
Lavish adventure-thriller

Batman Forever
1995, (USA), WB, color, 121 mins.
W: Val Kilmer (*Bruce Wayne/Batman*), Tommy Lee Jones (*Two Face*), Nicole Kidman (*Dr. Chase Meridian*), Jim Carrey (*The Riddler*), Drew Barrymore (*Sugar*), Debi Mazar (*Spice*), Chris O'Donnell (*Robin, the Boy Wonder*), Michael Gough (*Alfred*), Pat Hingle (*Commissioner Gordon*), Elizabeth Sanders (*Gossip Gertie*), Joe Grifasi, Rene Auberjonois, Philip Moon, Jessica Tuck, Ed Begley Jr.
D: Joel Schumacher **SCR:** Lee Batchler, Janet Scott Melniker, & Akiva Goldsman, from characters created by Bob Kane **PHOTOG:** Stephen Goldblatt **VS-FX SPRVSR:** John Dykstra **MUSIC:** Elliot Goldenthal
"A THRILL-PACKED JOY RIDE! There's no fun machine this summer that packs more surprises. Jim Carrey's Riddler is comic combustion that sets the film ablaze. Val Kilmer is utterly disarming and deftly understated. Uproarious"—Peter Travers, Rolling Stone
Rousing adventure-thriller

Batman: Mask of the Phantasm
1993, (USA), WB, color, 76 mins.
VOICES: Kevin Conroy (*Batman*), Dana Delany (*Andrea Beaumont*), Mark Hamill (*The Joker*), Hart Bochner, Stacy Keach Jr., Efrem Zimbalist Jr., Abe Vigoda, Dick Miller, John P. Ryan
D: Eric Radomski & Bruce W. Timm **SCR:** Michael Reeves, Alan Burnett, Paul Dini & Martin Pako, from characters created by Bob Kane **MUSIC:** Shirley Walker
Standard animated thriller

Batman Returns
1992, (USA), WB, color, 125 mins.
W: Michael Keaton (*Bruce Wayne/Batman*), Michelle Pfeiffer (*The Catwoman/Selina Kyle*), Danny DeVito (*The Penguin/Oscar Cobblepot*), Christopher Walken (*Max Shreck*), Michael Gough (*Alfred*), Pat Hingle (*Commissioner Gordon*), Michael Murphy (*Mayor of Gotham City*), Vincent Schiavelli (*The Organ Grinder*), Cristi Conaway (*The Ice Princess*), Jan Hooks (*Jen*), Andrew Bryniarski (*Chip Shreck*), Steve Witting (*Josh*), Paul Reubens (aka PeeWee Herman) (*The Penguin's Father*), Diane Salinger (*The Penguin's Mother*), Marlon Wayans
D: Tim Burton **SCR:** Daniel Waters **STORY:** Daniel Waters & Sam Hamm, from characters created by Bob Kane **PHOTOG:** Stefan Czapsky **MUSIC:** Danny Elfman
*Lavish adventure-thriller: Dark Knight fights for Justice. Orig. to be titled **Batman II***

Batman Dracula
1964, (USA), b&w, 16mm silent, 120 mins.
D: Andy Warhol
Experimental horror-fantasy: Hero opposes villains

Batman Fights Dracula
1967, (Phil), color
Minor horror-thriller

Batman II
see ***Batman Returns***

Batmen of Africa
1966, (USA), Rep, b&w, 100 mins.
W: Clyde Beatty, Elaine Shepard, Manuel King
P: Barney Sarecky **D:** B. Reeves Eason & Joseph Kane **SCR:** John Rathmell, Barney Sarecky & Ted Parsons
*A.k.a. **Batmen of Africa** and **King of the Jungleland***
*Minor adventure-thriller (feature version of 15-chapter 1936 serial **Darkest Africa**): Animal trainer finds hidden city, rescues boy's sister*

The Bat People
1974, (USA), AIP, color, 95 mins.
W: Stewart Moss (*Dr. John Beck*), Marianne McAndrew (*Cathy*), Michael Pataki (*The Sergeant*), Paul Carr (*Dr. Kipling*), Pat Delany (*Ms. Jax*), Arthur Space (*The Tramp*), George Paulsin (*The Youth in the Car*), Robert Berk (*The Motel Owner*), Bonnie Van Dyke (*The Girl in the Car*), Jeni Kulik, Laurie Brooks Jefferson
D: Jerry Jameson **SCR:** Lou Shaw **PHOTOG:** Matthew Leonetti **MUSIC:** Artie Kane
*orig. to be titled **It Lives by Night***
Unusual horror-thriller: Bat bites convert humans to Legions of Undead

La Battaglia di Maratona (The Battle of Marathon)
1959, (It), color, 92 mins.
W: Steve Reeves **P:** Bruno Vailati **D:** Bruno Vailati, Jacques Tourneur, & Mario Bava **SCR:** Ennio De Concini, Augusto Frassinetti, & Bruno Vailati
PHOTOG: Mario Bava **MUSIC:** Roberto Nicolosi
*USA retitle, **The Giant of Marathon***
Standard "Sword & Sandal" epic: Greeks repel invaders

The Batallion Shot
1912, (GB), B&C/MP, b&w, 890 ft. (271.3m)
W: James Russell (*Cpl. Farrell*), Dorothy Foster (*Daisy Williams*), Edward Durrant (*Sgt. Delaney*), Fred Rains, Alfred Wood, Harold Brett
D: H.O. Martinek **STORY:** Harold Brett
Standard crime-thriller: Mad sergeant abducts girl

*Batteries Not Included
1987, (USA), Steven Spielberg/Amblin/Univ, color, 105 mins.
W: Hume Cronyn (*Frank Riley*), Jessica Tandy (*Faye Riley*), Frank McRae (*Harry*), Elizabeth Pena (*Marisa*), Michael Carmine (*Carlos*), Dennis Boutsikaris (*Mason*), Tom Aldredge (*Sid*), Jane Hoffman (*Muriel*), John DiSanti (*Gus*), Michael Greene (*Lacey*), John Pankow (*Kovacs*), MacIntyre Dixon (*DeWitt*), Jose Santana, Doris Belack, Wendy Schaal, Alice Beardsley
D: Matthew Robbins **SCR:** Brad Bird, Matthew Robbins, Brent Maddock, & S.S. Wilson **STORY:** Mick Garris **PHOTOG:** John McPherson **VS-FX:** Industrial Light & Magic **MUSIC:** James Horner
Sentimental SF-fantasy: Tiny flying robots help tenants fight developers

Battle Beneath the Earth
1967, (GB), Reynolds-Vetter/MGM, color, 92 mins.
W: Kerwin Mathews (*Cdr. Jonathan Shaw*), Viviane Ventura (*Tila Yung*), Robert Ayres (*Adm. Hillebrand*), Martin Benson (*Gen. Chan Lu*), Peter Arne (*Arnold Kramer*), Edward Bishop (*Lt.-Cdr. Vance Cassidy*), Al Mulock (*Sgt. Marvin Mulberry*), Earl Cameron (*Sgt. Seth Hawkins*), Peter Elliott (*Kengh Lee*), Peter Brandon (*Maj. Frank Cannon*), Bill Nagy (*Col. Talbot Wilson*), Sarah Brackett (*Meg Webson*), Carl Jaffe (*Dr. Galissi*), Bessie Love (*The Matron*), David Spenser, Bee Duffell
P: Charles Reynolds **D:** Montgomery Tully **ORIG. STORY & SCR:** L.Z. Hargreaves **PHOTOG:** Kenneth Talbot **SPCL-FX:** Tom Howard **MUSIC:** Ken Jones
Juvenile SF-adventure: Enemy Orientals burrow under USA

Battle Beyond the Stars (1968)
see ***The Green Slime***

Battle Beyond the Stars
1980, (USA), New World, color, 104 mins.
W: Richard Thomas (*Shad*), Robert Vaughn (*Gelt*), George Peppard (*Cowboy*), John Saxon (*Sador*), Darlanne Fluegel (*Nanelia*), Sybil Danning (*St. Exmin*), Sam Jaffe, Morgan Woodward, Jeff Corey, Marta Kristen, Sam Jaffe (*Dr. Hephaestus*), Jeff Corey (*Zed*), Morgan Woodward (*Cayman*), Steve Davis (*Quopeg*), Earl Boen, John McGowans, Larry Meyers, Laura Cody, Lynne Carlin, Julia Duffy, Eric Morris, Doug Carleson, Ron Ross, Terrence McNally, Don Thompson, Daniel Carlin, Ansley Carlin, Whitney Rydbeck, Dallas Clarke, Dan Vincent, Ron Henschel, Rick Davidson, Brian Coventry, Kerry Frank
D: Jimmy T. Murakami **SCR:** John Sayles **STORY:** John Sayles & Ann Dyer **PHOTOG:** Daniel Lacambre **MUSIC:** James Horner
Standard SF-satire: Space tyrant threatens Earth

Battle Beyond the Sun
see ***The Heavens Call***

Battle for the Planet of the Apes
1973, (USA), Arthur P. Jacobs/20th-Fox, color, 86 mins.
W: Roddy McDowall (*Caesar*), Claude Akins (*Aldo*), Natalie Trundy (*Lisa*), Lew Ayres (*Mandemus*), Severn Darden (*Kolp*), Noah Keen (*The Teacher*), Austin Stoker (*McDonald*), Paul Williams (*Virgil*), France Nuyen (*Alma*), John Huston ("*The Lawgiver*"), Pat Cardi (*The Young Chimp*), Richard Eastham (*The Mutant Captain*), Paul Stevens (*Mendez*), Heather Lowe (*The Doctor*), Cal Wilson (*The Soldier*), Bobby Porter (*Cornelius*), Michael Stearns (*Jake*), Andy Knight (*The Mutant on the Motorcycle*), John Landis (*Jake's Friend*)
D: J. Lee Thompson **SCR:** John William Corrington & Joyce Hooper Corrington **STORY:** Paul Dehn, based on characters created by Pierre Boulle **PHOTOG:** Richard H. Kline **MUSIC:** Leonard Rosenman
5th & last installment in popular "Apes" series, standard SF adventure: Intelligent simians of far future battle human mutants

Battle in Outer Space
1960, (Jap), Toho/Col, color, 93 mins.
W: Ryo Ikebe, Koreya Senda, Kyoko Anzai, Kisaya Ito, Yoshio Tsuchiya, Fuyuki Murakami, Minoru Takada, Kozo Nomura
P: Tomoyuki Tanaka **D:** Inoshiro Honda **SCR:** Shinichi Sekizawa, based on a story by Jotaro Okami **PHOTOG:** Hajime Koizumi **SPCL-FX:** Eiji Tsuburaya **MUSIC:** Akira Ifukube
Standard SF-fantasy: Earth wars with space aliens

Battle in the Clouds
see ***The Airship Destroyer***

The Battle of Marathon
see ***La Battaglia di Maratona***

Battle of the Amazons
1973, (It-Sp), AIP, color, 92 mins.
W: Lincoln Tate (*Zeno*), Lucretia Love (*Eraglia*), Mirta Miller (*Melanippe*), Robert Vidmark (*Ilio*), Solvy Stubing (*Sinade*), Paola Tedesco (*Valeria*), Benito

Stefanelli (*Erno*), Giancarlo Bastianoni (*Filodos*), Genia Woods (*Antiope*), Luigi Ciavarro (*Turone*), Pilar Clement (*Elperia*), Sonia Ciuffi (*Fara*), Marco Stefanelli (*Medio*), Riccardo Pizzuti (*Medonte*), Franco Ukmar (*Artemio*)
D: Al Bradley **SCR:** Mario Amendola, Bruno Corbucci, & Fernando Izcaino Casas **PHOTOG:** Fausto Rossi **MUSIC:** Franco Micalizzi
Standard "Sword & Sandal" adventure: Greek tribes war at dawn of history

Battle of the Astros
see Monster Zero

Battle of the Worlds
see Il Planeta degli Uomini Spenti

The Battles of Chief Pontiac
1952, (USA), Realart, b&w, 72 mins.
W: Lex Barker, Helen Westcott, Lon Chaney Jr.
Minor adventure-thriller-western

Battlestar Galactica
1979, (USA), Glen Larson/Univ, color, 125 mins.
W: Richard Hatch (*Capt. Apollo*), Dirk Benedict (*Lt. Starbuck*), Lorne Greene (*Cdr. Adams*), Maren Jensen (*Athena*), Ray Milland (*Uri*), Lew Ayres (*Adar*), Jane Seymour (*Serina*), John Colicos (*Count Baltar*), Wilfrid Hyde-White (*Anton*), Tony Swartz (*Lt. Jolly*), Terry Carter (*Col. Tighe*), John Fink (*Dr. Paye*), Herb Jefferson Jr. (*Lt. Boomer*), Laurette Spang (*Cassiopea*), Noah Hathaway (*Boxey*), Ed Begley Jr. (*Ensign Greenbean*), Norman Stuart (*The Statesman*), Rick Springfield (*Lt. Zac*), David Greenan (*The Bridge Officer*), Randi Oakes (*The Young Woman*), Sarah Rush (*The Woman on Duty*), David Matthau (*The Operative*), Chip Johnson, Paul Coufos, Geoffrey Binney, Bruce Wright
P: John Dykstra & Leslie Stevens **D:** Richard A. Colla **SCR:** Glen A. Larson **PHOTOG:** Ben Colman **MUSIC:** Stu Phillips
A.k.a. **Mission Galactica: The Cyclon Attack**
Theatrical pilot-feature for teleseries, standard SF-adventure: Alien humans seek new world

The Bat Whispers: CHESTER MORRIS AND UNA MERKEL

Battletruck
see Warlords of the 21st Century

The Bat Whispers
1930, (USA), UA, b&w, 70 mins. (10 reels/7,991 ft./2435.7m)
W: Chester Morris (*Det. Anderson/The Bat*), Una Merkel (*Dale Van Gorder*), Maude Eburne (*Lizzie Allen*), Chance Ward (*The Police Lt.*), Hugh Huntley (*Richard Fleming*), Ben Bard (*The Unknown*), Gustav von Seyffertitz (*Dr. Venrees*), Richard Tucker (*Mr. Bell*), Grayce Hampton (*Cornelia Van Gorder*), William Bakewell (*Brook*), Spencer Charters (*The Caretaker*), Wilson Benge (*The Butler*), DeWitt Jennings (*The Police Capt.*), Sidney D'Albrook (*The Police Sgt.*), S.E. Jennings (*The Man in the Black Mask*), Charles Dow Clark (*Det. Jones*)
D & SCR: Roland West, based on stage play *The Bat* by Mary Roberts Rinehart & Avery Hopwood, from Miss Rinehart's novel *The Circular Staircase* **PHOTOG:** Ray June & Robert Planck
First talking version of Rinehart's classic thriller: Insane murderer strikes

Bat Woman
1967, (Mex), color
W: Maura Monti
Minor thriller: Enigmatic female involved in high crimes

Bay Coven
1987, (USA), Guber-Peters/Phoenix/NBC-TV, color, 95 mins.
W: Pamela Sue Martin (*Linda*), Tim Matheson (*Jerry*), Barbara Billingsley (*Beatrice*), James Sikking (*Nicholas Kline*), Inga Swenson (*Matty Kline*), Susan

Ruttan (*Debbi McGwin*), John Dee (*Old Man Kline*), Woody Harrelson (*Slater*), Jeff Conaway (*Josh McGwin*), Paul Horruzey (*Edward*), Susan Jay (*Sarah*), Patrick Brymer (*The Store Clerk*), Nigel Bennett (*Mr. Bob Holden #1*), Michael Caruana (*The Priest*), Cree Summer Francks (*The Jazz Singer*), David Harvey (*Tom Holden*), Marsha Moreau (*Rachel*), Eric Murphy (*Barret*), Neil Vipond (*Mr. Wesley*)
D: Carl Schenkel **TELEPLAY:** R. Timothy Kring **PHOTOG:** Jack Steyn **SPCL-FX:** Frank C. Carrere **MUSIC:** Shuki Levy
A.k.a. **Strangers in Town**
TVM, standard thriller: Yuppie couple finds satanism on small New England isle

Bay of Blood
see Twitch of the Death Nerve

Beach Babes from Beyond
1993, (USA), color, 78 mins.
W: Joe Estevez
D: Ellen Cabot
Minor SF-comedy: Three intergalactic beauties visit California coast

Beach Girls and the Monster
1965, (USA), American Academy Productions/U.S. Films, color & b&w, 70 mins.
W: Jon Hall, Sue Casey, Walker Edmiston, Elaine Dupont, Read Morgan, Arnold Lessing, Gloria Neil, Clyde Adler, Dale Davis
D: Jon Hall **SCR:** Joan Gardner **MUSIC:** Frank Sinatra Jr.
orig. to be titled **The Invisible Monster** *or* **Dr. Doom**
TV retitles, **The Surf Terror** *and* **Monster from the Surf**
Minor horror-fantasy: Beach bunnies menaced by mutant

Beanstalk
1994, (USA), color, 80 mins.
W: J.D. Daniels, Margot Kidder, Richard Moll, Patrick Renna, Amy Stock-Poynton, Richard Paul, David Naughton, Stuart Pankin, Cathy McAuley
D & SCR: Michael Paul Davis **MUSIC:** Kevin Bassinson
Standard fantasy: Rustic meets giant

The Bear
see L'Ours

Bear Island
1980, (USA-GB-Can), Selkirk Films/Taff International, color, 118 mins.
W: Donald Sutherland (*Frank Lansing*), Christopher Lee (*Prof. Lechinski*), Lloyd Bridges (*Smithy*), Richard Widmark (*Prof. Otto Gervan*), Vanessa Redgrave (*Hedi Lindquist*), Barbara Parkins (*Judith Roben*),Christopher Lee, Lloyd Bridges, Richard Widmark, Vanessa Redgrave, Barbara Parkins, Lawrence Dane (*Paul Hartman*), Patricia Collins (*Inge Von Zipper*), Michael Reynolds (*Hexter*), Nicholas Cortland (*Jungbeck*), Candace O'Connor (*The Ass't*), Michael Collins (*The Captain*), Hagen Beggs, August Schellenberg, Joseph Golland, Bruce Greenwood, Terry Kelly, Terry Waterhouse
P: Peter Snell **D:** Don Sharp **SCR:** Don Sharp, David Butler & Murray Smith from Alistair MacLean's novel **PHOTOG:** Alan Hume **MUSIC:** Robert Farnon
Minor thriller: Intrigue at remote U.N. outpost on frozen North Sea

The Beast (1933)
see King Kong (1933)

The Beast (1970)
see Equinox

The Beast
1974, (Fr), Argos, color, 102 mins.
W: Sirpa Lane, Lisabeth Hummel, Elisabeth Kahson, Marcel Dalio, Pierre Benedetti
P: Anatole Dauman **D & SCR:** Walerian Borowczyk
Unusual erotic fantasy (orig. intended as a segment for Contes Immoraux): Reworking of "Beauty & the Beast" legend

The Beast
1996, (USA), NBC-TV, color
W: William Petersen (*Whip Dalton*), Karen Sillas (*Katherine Marcus*), Larry Drake (*Lucas Coven*), Charles Martin Smith (*Schuyler Graves*), Ronald Guttman (*Herbert Talley*), Missy Crider, Sterling Macer Jr., Denis Arndt, Murray Bartlett, Laura Vazquez
D: Jeff Bleckner **TELEPLAY:** J.B. White, from Peter Benchley's novel **PHOTOG:** Geoff Burton **VS-FX:** Gene Warren Jr. **MUSIC:** Don Davis
2-part TVM, unusual thriller: Enormous squid plagues seaside community

Beast from Blood Island
see Bloodlust!

Beast from Haunted Cave
1959, (USA), Marathon/AA Filmgroup, b&w, 70 mins.
W: Michael Forrest (*Gil Jackson*), Sheila Carol (*Gypsy*), Frank Wolff (*Alex*), Wally Campo, Richard Sinatra, Linne Ahlstrand, Christopher Robinson, Kay Jennings
P: Gene Corman **D:** Monte Hellman **ORIG. STORY & SCR:** Charles B. Griffith **PHOTOG:** Andrew Costikyan **MUSIC:** Alexander Laszlo
blurb: "See screaming young girls sucked into a labyrinth of horror by a blood starved ghoul from hell!"
Minor horror-thriller: Ancient monster stalks gangsters. Orig. co-billed with **The Wasp Woman**

The Beast from Space
see 20 Million Miles to Earth

The Beast from 20,000 Fathoms
1953, (USA), WB, b&w, 80 mins.
W: Paul Christian (*Tom Nesbitt*), Paula Raymond (*Lee Hunter*), Cecil Kellaway (*Prof. Thurgood Elson*), Kenneth Tobey (*Col. Evans*), Jack Pennick (*Jacob*), Donald Woods (*Capt. Jackson*), King Donovan (*Dr. Ingersoll*), Steve Brodie (*Sgt. Loomis*), Lee Van Cleef (*Cpl. Stone*), Ray Hyke (*Sgt. Willistead*), Michael Fox (*The Doctor*), Ross Elliott (*George Ritchie*), Mary Hill (*Nesbitt's Sec'y*), Alvin Greenman (*The 1st Radar Man*), Frank Ferguson (*Dr. Morton*), James Best
P: Jack Dietz   **CO-P:** Bernard W. Burton & Hal Chester   **D:** Eugene Lourie
SCR: Lou Morheim & Fred Friedberger, suggested by Ray Bradbury's short story *The Foghorn*   **PHOTOG:** Jack Russell   **SPCL-FX:** Willis Cook   **TECH-FX:** Ray Harryhausen **MUSIC:** David Buttolph
French retitle, **The Monster from the Past,** *German retitle,* **Panic in New York**
blurb: "The King of Prehistoric Sea-Giants raging up from ages past to tear a city apart!"
Classic SF-thriller: Prehistoric monster, carrying ancient disease, rampages through New York City

The Beast in the Cellar
see Are You Dying Young Man?

The Beastmaster
1982, (USA), Leisure Investment/MGM/UA, color, 119 mins.
W: Marc Singer (*Dar*), Tanya Roberts (*Kiri*), Rip Torn (*Maax*), Josh Milrad (*Tal*), John Amos (*Seth*), Rod Loomis
P: Paul Pepperman & Sylvio Tabet   **D:** Don Coscarelli   **SCR:** Don Coscarelli & Paul Pepperman   **PHOTOG:** John Alcott   **MUSIC:** Lee Holdridge
'Conan'-type adventure-fantasy: Muscular youth communicates with animals, opposes evil high priest

Beastmaster 2: Through the Portal of Time
1991, (USA), Films 21, color, 110 mins.
W: Marc Singer (*Dar*), Wings Hauser (*Arklon*), Kari Wuhrer (*Jackie*), Sarah Douglas (*Lyranna*), James Avery, Arthur Malet, Jim Eagle, Robert Fieldsteel, Robert Z'Dar, Michael Berryman, Larry Dobkin, Vic Trevino
P & D: Sylvio Tabet, from characters created by Don Coscarelli & Paul Pepperman   **PHOTOG:** Ronn Schmidt   **VS-FX SPRVSR:** Frank H. Isaacs   **MUSIC:** Robert Folk   **SONGS:** (by Bill Wray) *I Will Be Your Hero, Keep On Rockin'* & *Hollywood Girls*
Standard SF-adventure: Primitive brothers time-travel to modern Los Angeles

Beastmaster III: The Eye of Braxus
1996, (USA), Univ/MCA, color, 92 mins.
W: Marc Singer (*Dar*), Tony Todd, Keith Coulouris, Sandra Hess, Casper Van Dien, David Warner (*Lord Agon*), Patrick Kilpatrick, Lesley-Anne Down
D: Gabrielle Beaumont   **SCR:** David Wise, from characters created by Don Coscarelli & Paul Pepperman   **PHOTOG:** Barbara Claman   **MUSIC:** Jan Hammer
Made-for-Video, standard "Sword & Sorcery"

The Beast Must Die
1974, (GB), Amicus/CRC, color, 93 mins.
W: Calvin Lockhart (*Tom Newcliffe*), Marlene Clark (*Caroline Newcliffe*), Peter Cushing (*Dr. Christopher Lundgren*), Anton Diffring (*Pavel*), Charles Gray (*Arthur Bennington*), Andrew Lodge (*The Pilot*), Michael Gambon (*Jan Jarmakowski*), Ciaran Madden (*Divina Gilmore*), Tom Chadbon (*Paul Foote*), Sam Mansaray (*The Butler*), Eric Carte, Carol Bohun
P: Max J. Rosenberg & Milton Subotsky   **D:** Paul Annett   **SCR:** Michael Winner, from James Blish's short story *There Shall Be No Darkness*   **PHOTOG:** Jack Hildyard   **MUSIC:** Douglas Gamley
Standard horror-thriller: Millionaire hunter unmasks werewolf among house guests. Video title, **Black Werewolf**

Beast of Babylon Against the Son of Hercules
1964, (It-Fr), Embassy, color, 98 mins
W: Gordon Scott, Moira Orfei, Michael Lane, Genevieve Grad, Piero Lulli
A.k.a. **The Hero of Babylon** *(L'Eroe di Babilonia)*
Standard "Sword & Sandal" adventure: Evil ruler sacrifices maidens

Beast of Blood
1970, (Phil), Sceptre/Marvin/Hemisphere, color, 90 mins.
W: John Ashley (*Bill*), Eddie Garcia (*Dr. Lorca*), Celeste Yarnall (*Myra*), Alfonso Carvajal (*Ramu*), Lisa Belmonte (*Laida*), Bruno Punzalan (*Razak*), Angel Buenaventura, Beverly Miller, Johnny Long
P, D, & SCR: Eddie Romero, Beverly Miller   **PHOTOG:** Justo Paulino   **MUSIC:** Tito Arevaloa   **STORY:** Beverly Miller
A.k.a. **Blood Devils, Horrors of Blood Island, Beast of the Dead** *and* **Return to the Horrors of Blood Island**
Minor horror-thriller: Gruesome experiments cause disaster

The Beast of Hollow Mountain
1956, (USA), Nassour/UA, color, 79 mins.
W: Guy Madison (*Jim*), Patricia Medina (*Sarila*), Carlos Rivas, Eduardo Noriega, Mario Navarro, Julio Villarreai, Jose Chavez, Manuel Arvide, Margarita Luna, Roberto Contreras, Lobo Negro, Jorge Trevino, Armando Gutierrez, Pascual Garcia Pena, Lupe Carriles

Beast Of Babylon Against The Son Of Hercules: GORDON SCOTT

P: William Nassour & Edward Nassour   **D:** Edward Nassour & Ismael Rodriguez   **SCR:** Robert Hill,,based on an idea conceived by Willis O'Brien   **PHOTOG:** Jorge Stahl Jr.   **SPCL-FX:** Jack Rabin & Louis DeWitt
German retitle, **The Haunted Monte Bravo**
Standard SF-adventure: Prehistoric monster terrorizes village

The Beast of Morocco
see The Hand of Night

Beast of Paradise Isle
see Port Sinister

Beast of the Dead
see Beast of Blood

Beast of the Yellow Night
1970, (Phil), New World, color, 87 mins.
W: John Ashley (*Joseph Langdon*), Mary Wilcox, Eddie Garcia, Vic Diaz, Ken Metcalfe
WRIT, P, & D: Eddie Romero
Minor horror-thriller: Man enters satanic pact

Beasts
see The Twilight People

The Beast of Yucca Flats
1961, (USA), Cardoza/Crown Int'l, b&w, 53 mins.
W: Larry Aten, Tor Johnson, Barbara Francis, Douglas Meller, Conrad Brooks, Tony Cardoza
D & SCR: Coleman Francis
Minor horror-thriller: Mutant haunts desert

Beasts of Marseilles
see Seven Thunders

The Beast That Killed Women
1965, (USA), Mahon, color, 60 mins.
P, D, & SCR: Barry Mahon
A.k.a. **Beast That Molested Women** *and* **Beast That Ruined Women**
Minor "splatter" thriller: Misogynist gorilla slays female nudists

Beast That Molested Women
see The Beast That Killed Women

Beast That Ruined Women
see The Beast That Killed Women

The Beast with a Million Eyes
1955, (USA), San Mateo/American Releasing Corp., b&w, 71 mins.
W: Paul Birch, Lorna Thayer, Dona Cole, Richard Sargent, Chester Conklin, Leonard Tarver
P: Roger Corman   **D:** David Kramarsky   **SCR:** Tom Filer   **PHOTOG:** Everett Baker
blurb: "Screaming Terror!"
Minor but engrossing SF-thriller: Space-alien controls minds

The Beast with Five Fingers

1946, (USA), WB, b&w, 88 mins.
W: Robert Alda, Peter Lorre, Andrea King, J. Carrol Naish, Victor Francen, Charles Dingle, Barbara Brown, David Hoffman, John Alvin, Patricia White [later Patricia Barry], Pedro de Cordoba, Ray Walker, Belle Mitchell, William Edmunds
P: William Jacobs   D: Robert Florey   SCR: Curt Siodmak, from W.F. Harvey's novel   PHOTOG: Wesley Anderson   MUSIC: Max Steiner
Gripping horror-fantasy: Madness and terror when it seems a murdered pianist is gaining fiendish revenge. cf. **The Hand** *(1981)*

The Beast Within

1982, (USA), Harvey Bernhard-Gabriel Katzka/MGM-UA, color, 96 mins.
W: Ronny Cox (*Eli*), Bibi Besch (*Caroline*), Don Gordon (*Curwin*), Paul Clemens, R.G. Armstrong, Kitty Moffat, L.Q. Jones, Logan Ramsey
D: Philippe Mora   SCR: Tom Holland, from Edward Levy's novel   PHOTOG: Jack L. Richards   MUSIC: Les Baxter
Standard horror-fantasy: Youth begins to mutate

Beat the Devil

1953, (USA), Santana-Romulus/UA b&w, 100 mins.
W: Humphrey Bogart (*Billy Dannreuther*), Gina Lollobrigida (*Maria Dannreuther*), Robert Morley (*Petersen*), Jennifer Jones (*Gwendolen Chelm*), Peter Lorre (*O'Hara*), Edward Underdown (*Harry Chelm*), Bernard Lee (*The C.I.D. Inspector*), Marco Tulli (*Ravello*), Ivor Barnard (*Maj. Ross*), Alex Pochet (*The Hotel Manager*), Marrio Perroni (*The Purser*), Aldo Silvani (*Charles*), Manuel Serano, Giulio Donnini, Saro Urzi, Juan De Landa, Mimo Poli
P & D: John Huston   SCR: John Huston & Truman Capote, from James Halvick's novel   PHOTOG: Oswald Morris & Freddie Francis   MUSIC: Franco Mannino
Intellectual satire-thriller: Crooks and fortune-hunters seek uranium

La Beauté du Diable (Beauty of the Devil)

1950, (It-Fr), UA, b&w, 96 mins.
W: Gerard Philipe, Martine Carol, Michel Simon, Gaston Modot, Raymond Cordy, Paolo Stoppa, Nicole Besnard, Simone Valere, Carlo Ninchi
D: Rene Clair   PHOTOG: Michel Kelber
A.k.a. **Beauty and the Devil**
Unusual fantasy-romance: Disillusioned composer finds solace in dream worlds spanning time and space.

Beauties of the Night

see **La Beauté du Diable**

Beautiful Jim

1914, (GB), B&C/Renters, b&w, 3,253 ft. (991.5m)
W: Elizabeth Risdon (*Nancy Earle*), Fred Groves (*Lt. Jim Beresford*), Bootles Winter (*Capt. Owen*), M. Gray Murray (*Col. Earle*), A.V. Bramble (*Lt. Tommy Earle*)
D: Maurice Elvey   SCR: Eliot Stannard, from a novel by John Strange Winter.
USA retitle, **The Price of Justice**
Standard crime-thriller: Colonel's son kills sister's fiancee

Beautiful Stranger

1954, (GB), Marksman/British Lion, b&w, 89 mins.
W: Ginger Rogers (*Johnny Victor*), Herbert Lom (*Emil Landosh*), Stanley Baker (*Louis Galt*), Jacques Bergerac (*Pierre Clement*), Margaret Rawlings (*Marie Galt*), Eddie Byrne (*Luigi*), Coral Browne (*Helen*), Lisa Gastoni (*Yvette*), Lily Kann (*Nicole*), Ferdy Mayne (*The Police Chief*), Keith Pyott (*Georges*)
P: Maxwell Setton & John R. Sloan   D: David Miller   SCR: Robert Westerby & Carl Nystrom   STORY: David Miller & Rip Van Ronkel
USA retitle, **Twist of Fate**
Standard crime-thriller: Counterfeiter kills mistress' lover, frames artist

Beauty and the Beast

1905, (GB), Clarendon/Gaumont, b&w, 665 ft. (202.7m)
D: Percy Stow
Standard fantasy (in 15 scenes): Beast reverts to prince after kiss from merchant's daughter

Beauty and the Beast (1946)

see **La Belle et la Bete**

Beauty and the Beast

1962, (USA), Harvard/UA, color
W: Joyce Taylor, Mark Damon, Michael Pate, Eduard Franz, Tom Cound, Merry Anders, Dayton Lummis, Charles Wagenheim, Walter Burke, Herman Rudin
P: Robert E. Kent   D: Edward L. Cahn   SCR: George Bruce & Orville H. Hampton, as suggested by the ancient legend
Standard fantasy: Prince plagued by lycanthropy

Beauty and the Beast

1985, (Czech), color
W: Zdena Studenkova, Vaclav Voska, Vlastimil Harapes
WRIT & D: Juraj Herz
Standard fantasy: Girl meets monstrous suitor

Beauty and the Beast

1991, (USA), Walt Disney/Buena Vista, color, 84 mins.
VOICES: Paige O'Hara, Robby Benson, Angela Lansbury, David Ogden Stiers, Richard White, Jerry Orbach, Jesse Corti, Rex Everhart, Bradley Michael Pierce, Jo Anne Worley, Kimmy Robertson
D: Gary Trousdale & Kirk Wise   SONGS: *Be Our Guest*
Superior animated fantasy: Inepndent girl imprisoned by cursed nobleman

Beauty and the Beast: The Enchanted Christmas

1997, (USA), Walt Disney, color
VOICES: Tim Curry, Bernadette Peters, Robby Benson, Paige O'Hara, Paul Reubens, Angela Lansbury
D: Andy Knight   SCR: Flip Kobler   MUSIC: Rachel Portman
Made-for-Video, standard juvenile musical-fantasy: Evil pipe organ threatens lovers

Beauty and the Brain

see **Sex Kittens Go to College**

Beauty and the Robot

see **Sex Kittens Go to College**

Beauty of the Devil

see **La Beauté du Diable**

Beauty's Revenge

1995, (USA), color
W: Tracey Gold, Courtney Thorne-Smith, Kyle Secor

Because of Cats

1974, (GB), color, 90 mins.
W: Bryan Marshall, Alexandra Stewart, Alex Van Rooyen, Sylvia Kristel, Sebastian Graham Jones
D: Fons Rademakers
Minor thriller: Police inspector uncovers evil cult

The Becket Affair

1966, (It), color
W: Lang Jeffries, Ivan Desny
Minor action-thriller: Secret agent spies in Paris

Beckwith's Gun

1910, (GB), Barker, b&w, 788 ft. (240m)
Standard crime-thriller: Gamekeeper shoots squire with rival's gun

Bedazzled

1967, (GB), 20th-Fox, color, 103 mins.
W: Peter Cook (*George Spiggott*), Dudley Moore (*Stanley Moone*), Eleanor Bron (*Margaret Spencer*), Raquel Welch (*Lilian Lust*), Michael Bates (*Insp. Clarke*), Bernard Spear (*Irving Moses*), Parnell McGarry (*Gluttony*), Howard Goorney (*Sloth*), Daniele Noel (*Avarice*), Alba (*Vanity*), Barry Humphries (*Envy*), Robert Russell (*Anger*), Michael Trubshawe (*Lord Dowdy*), Robin Hawdon
P & D: Stanley Donen   SCR: Peter Cook, based on an idea by Peter Cook & Dudley Moore   PHOTOG: Austin Dempster   MUSIC: Dudley Moore
SONG: *Love Me*
Amusing mod-version of "Faust" legend: Short-order cook sells soul to Satan, lives several amazing incarnations

Bedelia

1946, (GB), John Corfield/Eagle Lion, b&w, 90 mins.
W: Margaret Lockwood (*Bedelia Carrington*), Ian Hunter (*Charles Carrington*), Barry K. Barnes (*Ben Chaney*), Anne Crawford (*Ellen Walker*), Jill Esmond (*Nurse Harris*), Barbara Blair (*Sylvia Johnstone*), Ellen Pollock (*The Housekeeper*), Louise Hampton (*Hannah*), Julien Mitchell (*Dr. McAbee*), Kynaston Reeves (*Mr. Bennett*), Beatrice Varley (*Mary*), Olga Lindo (*Mrs. Bennett*), John Salew (*Alec Johnstone*)
P: Isadore Goldsmith   D: Lance Comfort   SCR: Vera Caspary, Herbert Victor, Moie Charles, Roy Ridley, & Isadore Goldsmith, from Vera Caspary's novel-   PHOTOG: Frederick A. Young
Standard thriller: Female "Bluebeard" lures men. reissued 1948

The Bedford Incident

1965, (USA-GB), James B. Harris-Richard Widmark/Col, b&w, 102 mins.
W: Richard Widmark (*Capt. Eric Finland*), Sidney Poitier (*Ben Munceford*), James MacArthur (*Ensign Ralston*), Martin Balsam (*Lt.-Cdr. Chester Potter*), Wally Cox (*Sonar Man*), Phil Brown (*CMM McKinley*), Eric Portman (*Cdr. Wolfgang Schrepke*), Gary Cockrell (*Lt. Bascombe*), Michael Kane (*Cdr. Allison*), Brian Davies (*Lt. Beckman*), Paul Carson, Glen Beck, Bill Edwards, Colin Maitland, Paul Tamarin, Clint Maitland (*Seaman Jones*), Warren Stanhope (*Pharmacist Mate Strauss*), Donald Sutherland (*Pharmacist Mate Nerney*), Edward Bishop (*Lt. Burger*)
D: James B. Harris   SCR: James Poe, from Mark Rascovich's novel   PHOTOG: Gilbert Taylor   MUSIC: Gerard Schurmann
Tense thriller: Soviet sub invades Greenland's territorial waters, World War III threatened

Bedknobs and Broomsticks

1971, (USA), Walt Disney/Buena Vista, color, 117 mins.
W: Angela Lansbury (*Eglantine Price*), David Tomlinson (*Emelius Browne*), Roddy McDowall (*Mr. Jelk*), Sam Jaffe (*The Bookman*), John Ericson (*Col. Heller*),

Bruce Forsyth (*Swinburne*), Cindy O'Callaghan (*Carrie*), Reginald Owen (*Gen. Teagler*), Roy Smart (*Paul*), Tessie O'Shea (*Mrs. Hobday*), Arthur E. Gould-Porter (*Capt. Greer*), Ben Wrigley (*The Street Sweeper*), John Orchard (*The Vendor*), Ian Weighall (*Charlie*), Rick Traeger (*A German Sergeant*), Manfred Lating (*A German Sergeant*), Robert Holt (*The Voice of the Codfish*), Lennie Weinrib (*The Voice of the Secretary Bird & Lion*)
P: Bill Walsh   **D:** Robert Stevenson   **SCR:** Bill Walsh & Don DaGradi, from a novel by Mary Norton   **PHOTOG:** Frank Phillips   **SPCL-FX:** Eustace Lycett, Alan Maley, & Danny Lee   **MUSIC & LYRICS:** Richard M. Sherman & Robert B. Sherman
Unusual fantasy: Novice witch repels Nazi invasion of Britain

Bedlam
1946, (USA), RKO, b&w, 79 mins.
W: Boris Karloff, Anna Lee (*Nell Bowen*), Jason Robards Sr. (*Todd*), Billy House (*Lord Mortimer*), Ian Wolfe (*Long*), Richard Fraser (*Hannay*), Glenn Vernon (*The Gilded Boy*), Robert Clarke (*Dan*), Ellen Corby (*Betty*), Skelton Knaggs, Elizabeth Russell, Joan Newton, Leyland Hodgson
P: Val Lewton   **D:** Mark Robson   **SCR:** Carlos Keith (Val Lewton)   **PHOTOG:** Nicholas Musuraca   **MUSIC:** Roy Webb
Outstanding melodrama: Young woman unjustly imprisoned in England's notorious 18th-century insane asylum

The Bed-Sitting Room
1969, (GB), Oscar Lewenstein/UA/Lopert, color, 91 mins.
W: Rita Tushingham (*Penelope*), Ralph Richardson (*Lord Fortnum*), Dandy Nichols (*Ethyl*), Spike Milligan (*Mate*), Mona Washbourne (*Mother*), Michael Hordern (*Bules*), Peter Cook (*The Inspector*), Dudley Moore (*The Sergeant*), Roy Kinnear (*Plastic Mac Man*), Richard Warwick (*Allan*), Arthur Lowe (*Father*), Ronald Fraser (*The Field Marshall Sgt.*), Frank Thornton (*The BBC Man*), Ron Moody (*The Dwarf*), Gordon Rollings (*The Patient*), Henry Woolf (*The Electricity Man*), Marty Feldman (*The National Health Service*), Jimmy Edwards (*Nigel*), Harry Secombe (*The Shelter Man*)
D: Richard Lester   **SCR:** John Antrobus & Charles Wood, from a play by Spike Milligan & John Antrobus   **PHOTOG:** David Watkin   **MUSIC:** Ken Thorne
Surreal SF-satire: Atom war mutates survivors

Bedtime for Bonzo
1951, (USA), Univ, b&w, 83 mins.
W: Ronald Reagan, Diana Lynn, Walter Slezak, Lucille Barkley, Jesse White, Herbert Heyes, Brad Johnson, Bill Mauch, Herburt Vigran
P: Michel Kraike   **D:** Frederick de Cordova   **SCR:** Val Burton & Lou Breslow   **PHOTOG:** Carl Guthrie   **MUSIC:** Frank Skinner
Standard comedy: Professor adopts chimpanzee, tries to disprove theories of inherited criminal tendencies. cf. Bonzo Goes to College

Beelzebub's Daughters
see Les Filles du Diable

The Bees
1978, (USA-Mex), New World/CBS-TV, color, 86 mins.
W: John Saxon (*John*), Angel Tompkins (*Sandra*), Claudio Brook (*Dr. Miller*), John Carradine (*Dr. Hummel*), Julio Cesar (*Julio*), Alicia Encinas (*Alicia*), Armand Martin (*Arthur*), Jose Chavez Trowe (*The Father*), George Bellanger (*Undersecretary Brennan*), Deloy White (*Winkler*), Roger Cudney (*Blankeley*), Julia Yallop (*The Model*), Chad Hastings (*Gray*), Elizabeth Wallace (*The Sec'y*), Gray Johnson, Al Jones, Whitey Hughes, Alfred Melhem, David Silverkleit, Don Maxwell, Brian Hanna, Eddie Alexander, Bill Bordy, Walter Hanna
WRIT: P & D: Alfredo Zacharias   **PHOTOG:** Leon Sanchez   **MUSIC:** Richard Gillis
TVM, minor SF-thriller: Vicious insects threaten world

The Beetle
1919, (GB), Barker/Urban, b&w, 5,600 ft. (1706.9m)
W: Maudie Dunham (*Dora Greyling*), Hebden Foster (*Paul Lessingham*), Fred Morgan (*Neces*), Nancy Benyon (*Marjorie Linden*), Frank Reade (*Sidney Atherton*), Rolf Leslie (*Holt*), Leal Douglas (*The High Priestess*)
P: Jack W. Smith   **D:** Alexander Butler   **SCR:** Helen Blizzard from a novel by Richard Marsh
Standard horror-thriller: Soul of Egyptian priestess inhabits monstrous insect

Beetlejuice
W: Alec Baldwin, Geena Davis, Michael Keaton, Catherine O'Hara, Gleen Shadix   **SCR:** Michael McDowell & Warren Skaaren   **DIR:** Tim Burton   **PHOTOG:** Thomas Ackerman   **MUSIC:** Danny Elfman   **VS-FX SPRVSR:** Alan Munro McDowell & Larry Wilson
Elaborate and outrageous comedy-fantasy: "Bio-exorcist" aids recently-deceased couple

Before Dawn
1933, (USA), RKO, b&w, 60 mins.
W: Stuart Erwin, Dorothy Wilson, Warner Oland, Jane Darwell, Dudley Digges
D: Irving Pichel
Standard thriller: Mad scientist involved in murder

Before I Die
see The Sorcerers

Before I Hang
1940, (USA), Col, b&w, 71 mins.
W: Boris Karloff, Evelyn Keyes, Bruce Bennett, Edward Van Sloan, Pedro de Cordoba, Don Beddoe, Wright Kramer, Kenneth MacDonald, Robert Fiske, Frank Richards, Bertram Marbrugh, Ben Taggart
D: Nick Grinde   **SCR:** Robert D. Andrews   **PHOTOG:** Benjamin Kline
Unusual horror-thriller, vintage Karloff: Negative results when doctor injects himself with murderer's blood

Before I Wake
1955, (GB), Gibraltar/Grand Nat'l, b&w, 78 mins.
W: Mona Freeman (*April Haddon*), Jean Kent (*Florence Haddon*), Maxwell Reed (*Dr. Simon Elder*), Frederick Leister (*Dr. Elder*), Hugh Miller (*Driscoll*), Gretchen Franklin (*Elsie*), Alexander Gauge (*The Sergeant*), Josephine Middleton (*Mrs. Harrison*), Frank Forsyth, Stanley van Beers, Frank Atkinson, Philip Ray, Robert Sansom, Phyllis Cornell
P: Steven Pallos & Charles A. Leeds   **D:** Albert S. Rogell   **SCR:** Robert Westerby   from a novel by Hal Debrett   **MUSIC:** Leonard Salzedo
USA retitle, Shadow of Fear, United Artists
Standard thriller: Nurse kills husband, tries to kill stepdaughter

The Beggar Girl's Wedding
1915, (GB), British Empire, b&w, 4,500 ft. (1371.6m)
W: Henry Lonsdale (*Gilbert Lindsay*), Ethel Bracewell (*Bessie Webster*), Lauderdale Maitland (*Jack Cunningham*), Cecil du Gue (*Dr. Millbank*), Nina Lynn (*Maud Villiers*), Wilfred Payne (*Norman Marsh*), J.C. MacMillian (*Joe Webster*), George Mitchell (*Robert Grimshaw*), Bernice Walters (*Tina*), Harry Hartley (*Dodger*), Fred Ingram (*Dicky Storm*)
D: Leedham Bantock, from a play by Walter Melville
Standard crime-thriller: Wastrel heir forced to wed thief's daughter, is put in mad doctor's asylum by cousin

The Beggar Maiden
see L'Ange de Noel

The Beggar's Dream
see Le Reve du Pauvre

The Beginning
1973, (Can) TV Movie, color
W: Keir Dullea
TVM, reedited from teleseries "Starlost": Earth's last survivor, circa A.D. 2790. cf. The Alien Oro

The Beginning of the End
1957, (USA), AB-PT/Rep, b&w, 74 mins.
W: Peter Graves, Peggie Castle, Morris Ankrum, Than Wyenn, Richard Benedict, Thomas B. Henry, James Seay, Don C. Harvey, Paul Grant, John Close, Larry J. Blake, Pierre Watkin, Frank Chase, Steve Warren, Frank Connor, Don Eitner, Frank Wilcox, Eilene Janssen, Alan Reynolds, Alan Wells, Patricia Dean, Hylton Socher, Douglas Evans, Richard Emory, Hank Patterson, Rayford Barnes
P, D & SPCL-FX: Bert I. Gordon   **SCR:** Fred Friedberger & Lester Gorn   **PHOTOG:** Jack Marta   **MUSIC:** Albert Glasser   **SONG:** *Natural, Natural Baby*
blurb: "The screen's first full-length science-fiction thriller with real live creatures!"
Minor SF-thriller: Giant locusts invade Chicago

The Beginning or the End?
1947, (USA), MGM, b&w, 112 mins.
W: Brian Donlevy (*Maj.-Gen. Leslie R. Groves*), Hume Cronyn (*Dr. J. Robert Oppenheimer*), Tom Drake (*Matt Cochran*), John Litel (*K.T. Keller*), Beverly Tyler (*Anne Cochran*), Robert Walker Sr. (*Col. Jeff Nixon*), Audrey Totter (*Jean O'Leary*), Joseph Calleia (*Dr. Enrico Fermi*), Hurd Hatfield (*Dr. John Wyatt*), Godfrey Tearle (*Pres. Franklin D. Roosevelt*), Victor Francen (*Dr. Marre*), Richard Haydn (*Dr. Chisholm*), Jonathan Hale (*Dr. Vannevar Bush*), Henry O'Neill (*Gen. Thomas F. Farrell*), Warner Anderson (*Capt. William S. Parsons, USN*), Art Baker (*Pres. Harry S. Truman*), Barry Nelson (*Col. Paul Tibbets Jr.*), Ludwig Stossel (*Dr. Albert Einstein*), John Hamilton (*Dr. Harold C. Urey*), Frank Ferguson (*Dr. James B. Conant*), John Gallaudet (*Dr. Leo Szilard*), Tom Stevenson (*Dr. E.P. Wigner*), Edward Earle (*Charles G. Ross*), Nella Walker (*Grace Tully*), Jim Davis (*The Pilot at Tinian*), Moroni Olsen (*Dr. Arthur H. Compton*), Norman Lloyd (*Dr. Troyanski*), Charles Trowbridge (*Walter S. Carpenter Jr.*), Frank Wilcox (*Dr. W.H. Zinn*), Henry Hall (*Gen. Brehan Somervell*), Paul Harvey (*Lt.-Gen. W.D. Styer*), Larry Johns (*The Quaker Scientist*), Robert Emmett Keane (*Dr. Rand*), James Bush (*Dr. Ernest O. Lawrence*), Trevor Bardette (*The Clinic Doctor*), William Wright (*Col. John Lansdale*), Damian O'Flynn (*C.D. Howe*)
P: Samuel Marx   **D:** Norman Taurog   **SCR:** Frank Wead, from a story by Robert Considine   **PHOTOG:** Ray June   **SPCL-FX:** Warren Newcombe, A. Arnold Gillespie, & Donald Jahraus   **MUSIC:** Daniele Amfitheatrof
Semi-SF documentary (loaded with incorrect science): Account of first A-bomb

The Beguiled
1971, (USA), Malpaso/Univ, color, 105 mins.
W: Clint Eastwood (*John McBurney*), Geraldine Page (*Martha Farnsworth*), Jo Ann Harris (*Carol*), Elizabeth Hartman (*Edwina*), Darleen Carr (*Doris*), Mae Mercer (*Hallie*), Pattye Mattick (*Jamie*), Pamelyn Ferdin (*Amy*), Melody Thomas (*Abigail*), Peggy Drier (*Lizzie*)

P & D: Donald Siegel   **SCR:** John B. Sherry & Grimes Grice, from Thomas Cullinan's novel   **PHOTOG:** Bruce Surtees   **MUSIC:** Lalo Schifrin
"The most terrifying film since Rosemary birthed her baby"—Jan Cocks, Time
"A must for sadists and woman-haters"—Judith Crist
Gothic tale of jealousy, lust, and revenge set in Civil War South: Union soldier disrupts Confederate girl's school

Behemoth, the Sea Monster
1959, (GB), Eros/AA, b&w, 79 mins.
W: Gene Evans (*Steve Karnes*), Andre Morell (*Prof. James Bickford*), Leigh Madison (*Jeanie Trevethan*), John Turner (*Ian Duncan*), Jack MacGowran (*Dr. Sampson*), Maurice Kaufmann (*The Officer*), Henry Vidon (*Tom MacDougal*), Leonard Sachs (*The Scientist*), Neal Arden (*The Announcer*), Patrick Jordan, Robert Gallico
P: David Diamond   **D & SCR:** Eugene Lourie, from a story by Robert Abel & Allen Adler   **PHOTOG:** Ken Hodges   **SPCL-FX:** designed & engineered by Jack Rabin, Irving Block, & Louis DeWitt   **SPCL-FX SPRVSR:** Willis O'Brien
*Standard SF-thriller: Prehistoric horror terrorizes British Isles. USA retitle, **The Giant Behemoth***

Behind City Lights
1945, (USA), Rep, b&w, 68 mins.
W: Lynne Roberts, William Terry
Minor melodrama

Behind Convent Walls
1977, (It), color, 95 mins.
W: Loredana Martinez, Marina Pierro, Gabriella Giacobe, Ligia Branice
D: Walerian Borowczyk
Minor eroto-melodrama: Passion in nunnery

Behind Locked Doors
1948, (USA), Arc/Eagle Lion, b&w, 62 mins.
W: Richard Carlson (*Ross Stewart*), Tor Johnson (*"Champ"*), Tom Browne Henry (*Dr. Porter*), Lucille Bremer (*Kathy Lawrence*), Douglas Fowley, Ralf Harolde, Herbert Heyes, Gwen Donovan, Kathleen Freeman
D: Oscar "Budd" Boetticher Jr.   **SCR:** Malvin Wald & Eugene Ling   **STORY:** Malvin Wald   **PHOTOG:** Huy Roe   **PHOTO-FX:** George J. Teague
*A.k.a. **Human Gorilla***
Minor thriller: Detective trapped in madhouse

Behind That Curtain
1929, (USA), Fox, b&w, 72 mins. (10 reels/8,320 ft.)
W: Warner Baxter (*John Beetham*), Lois Moran (*Eve Mannering*), Gilbert Emery (*Sir Frederick Bruce*), Claude King (*Sir George Mannering*), Philip Strange (*Eric Durand*), Boris Karloff (*The Soudanese Servant*), Jamiel Hassan (*Habib Hanna*), John Rogers (*Alf Pornick*), Peter Gawthorne (*The Scotland Yard Inspector*), Montague Shaw (*Hilary Galt*), Frank Finch-Smiles (*The Clerk*), Mercedes De Velasco (*Nunah*), E.L. Park (*Charlie Chan*)
D: Irving Cummings   **SCR:** Sonya Levien & Clarke Silvernail, from Earl Derr Biggers' novel, remake of **Charlie Chan's Chance**   **PHOTOG:** Conrad Wells, Dave Ragin, & Vincent Farrar
Standard "Charlie Chan" mystery-thriller: Nobleman hires sleuth to check on prospective son-in-law's past.

Behind the Curtain
1915, (GB), Hepworth/Renters, b&w, 2,750 ft. (838.2m)
W: Stewart Rome (*Sir Geoffrey Atherton*), Chrissie White, Henry Vibart, Lionelle Howard, Violet Hopson
D: Frank Wilson   **STORY:** Kate Murray
*A.k.a. **The Curtain's Secret***
Standard thriller: Cousin tries to kill heir

Behind the Curtain
1924, (USA), Univ, b&w, 5 reels (4,875 ft./1485.9m)
W: Lucille Ricksen (*Sylvia Bailey*), Johnny Harron (*Hugh Belmont*), Winifred Bryson (*Laura Bailey*), Charles Clary (*George Belmont*), Eric Mayne (*Prof. Gregorius*), George Cooper (*"Slug" Gorman*), Clarence Geldert (*The D.A.*), Pat Harmon (*"Spike"*)
D: Chester M. Franklin   **SCR:** Emil Forest & Harvey Gates   **STORY:** William J. Flynn   **PHOTOG:** Jackson Rose
Standard thriller: Fake spiritualist exposed as assassin

Behind the Door
*see **The Man with Nine Lives***

Behind the Doors of Horror
*see **The Strange Door***

Behind the Headlines
1956, (GB), Kenilworth/RFD, b&w, 67 mins.
W: Paul Carpenter (*Paul Banner*), Hazel Court (*Maxine*), Adrienne Corri (*Pam Barnes*), Alfie Bass (*Sammy*), Ewen Solon (*Supt. Faro*), Harry Fowler (*Alfie*), Trevor Reid (*Mr. Bunting*), Olive Gregg (*Mrs. Bunting*)
P: Guido Coen   **D:** Charles Saunders   **SCR:** Allan Mackinnon, from a novel by Robert Chapman
Standard crime thriller: Reporter probes murder of blackmailer

Behind the Mask
1932, (USA), Col, b&w
W: Boris Karloff, Constance Cummings, Jack Holt, Edward Van Sloan, Claude King, Joseph Crehan
D: John Francis Dillon   **SCR:** Jo Swerling & Dorothy Howell
Standard thriller: Killer strikes

Behind the Mask
1946, (USA), Mono, b&w, 67 mins.
W: Kane Richmond, Barbara Reed, George Chandler, Dorothy Kent, Robert Shayne, June Clyde
D: Phil Karlson
Minor thriller: Lamont Cranston, the sleuthing "Shadow", accused of blackmailer's murder

Behind the Mask of Zorro
1962, (It-Sp), color
W: Tony Russel, Maria Jose Alfonso, Robert Paoletti, Mirella Maravidi, Jesus Puente, Jose Rubio, Angela Rho, Rosita Yarza, Augustin Gonzales, Felix Sancho Gracia, Aldo Cecconi, Jose Maria Seoane
D: Ricardo Blasco   **SCR:** Mario Amendola, Lucas Gallardo & Daniel Ribera
Minor action-adventure: Masked rider foils tyrant

Behind the Scenes
1913, (GB), Clarendon, b&w, 2,390 ft. (728.5m)
W: Dorothy Bellew (*Flo*)
D: Wilfred Noy   **STORY:** Marchioness of Townshend
Standard crime-thriller: Cowboy actor mistakenly uses real bullets, kills faithless actress

Behind the Wall
*see **The Cold Room***

The Being
1983, (USA), Bill Osco/Jackie Kong, color, 81 mins.
W: Martin Landau (*Garson Jones*), Ruth Buzzi (*Virginia Lane*), Jose Ferrer (*Mayor Gordon Lane*), Dorothy Malone (*Marge Smith*), Rexx Coltrane (Bill Osco) (*Lutz*), Marianne Gordon (*Laurie*), Murray Langston (*Arn*), Kinky Friedman (*Willis*), Johnny Dark (*John*), Ellen Blake (*Jenny*), Kent Perkins (*Officer Dudley*), Roxanne Cybelle Osco (*Suzie*), Johny Commander (*Mortimer Lutz*), Eric Helland (*Doper #1*), Bill Rawlinson (*Doper #2*), Jerry Maren (*The Monster*), Richard Marcus (*Joe the Lab Ass't*), Nancy Osco (*The Woman Motorist*), Jay Sherlock, James Simmerman, John Elliott, Brian Swain, Tracy Barry, Patrick Cunningham, Jefferson Jewell, Mary Hold, Cory Germann, Roger Smith, Brad Ginther, Roland Onffrey, Larry Babcock, Chief Sherwin, Dave Clark
WRIT & D: Jackie Kong   **PHOTOG:** Robert Ebinger & Hanania Baer   **MUSIC:** Don Preston
*A.k.a. **Easter Sunday***
Minor SF-horror: Nuclear-pollution monster prowls Idaho town

Being Human
1994, (USA), Enigma/WB, color
W: Robin Williams, John Turturro, Anna Galiena (*Beatrice*). Vincent D'Onofrio, Hector Elizondo, Lindsay Crouse, Lorraine Bracco, Jonathan Hyde, William H. Macy
WRIT & D: Bill Forsyth   **PHOTOG:** Michael Coulter   **MUSIC:** Michael Gibbs
Standard fantasy: Gentle "Everyman" meanders through history

Bela Lugosi Meets a Brooklyn Gorilla
*see **The Boys from Brooklyn***

The Believers
1987, (USA), Orion, color, 112 mins.
W: Martin Sheen, Helen Shaver, Robert Loggia, Richard Masur, Elizabeth Wilson, Lee Richardson, Harris Yulin, Jimmy Smits, Harley Cross, Carla Pinza, Raul Davila, Malik Bowens
D: John Schlesinger   **SCR:** Mark Frost   **PHOTOG:** Robby Muller   **MUSIC:** J. Peter Robinson
Modest thriller: Widower fears magic of Santeria

Belinda's Dream
1913, (GB), H&W Films/Prieur, b&w, 400 ft. (121.9m)
D: Stuart Kinder
Minor comedy-fantasy short: Maid dreams of changing places with mistress

Bella Donna
1923, (USA), Famous Players-Lasky/Para, b&w, 8 reels (7,895 ft./2406.4m)
W: Pola Negri (*Bella Donna*), Conway Tearle (*Mahmoud Baroudi*), Conrad Nagel (*Nigel Armine*), Claude King (*Dr. Meyer Isaacson*), Adolphe Menjou (*Mr. Chepstow*), Lois Wilson (*Patricia*), Macey Harlam (*Ibrahim*), Robert Schable (*Dr. Hartley*)
D: George Fitzmaurice   **SCR:** Ouida Bergere   **STORY:** Robert Smythe Hichens   **PHOTOG:** Arthur C. Miller
Standard melodrama: Adventuress involved in Egyptian intrigue

Bella Donna
1934, (GB), Twickenham/Gaumont, b&w
W: Conrad Veidt (*Mahmoud Baroudi*), Mary Ellis (*Mona Chepstow*), Cedric Hardwicke (*Dr. Isaacson*), John Stuart (*Nigel Armine*), Jeanne Stuart (*Lady*

Harwick), Michael Shepley (*Dr. Hartley*), Rodney Millington (*Ibrahim*), Eve (*The Dancer*)
<u>D</u>: Robert Milton   <u>SCR</u>: H. Fowler Mear, from a play by James B. Fagan, based on a novel by Robert Hichens
Standard thriller (Conrad Veidt's English-language film debut): Woman plots husband's murder

Bell, Book and Candle
1958, (USA), Phoenix/Col, color, 103 mins.
<u>W</u>: Kim Novak (*Gillian Holroyd*), James Stewart (*Shepherd Henderson*), Ernie Kovacs (*Sidney Redlitch*), Jack Lemmon (*Nicky Holroyd*), Elsa Lanchester (*Queenie*), Hermione Gingold (*Mrs. De Pass*), Janice Rule (*Merle Kittridge*), Philippe Clay (*The French Singer*), Howard McNear (*Andy White*), Bek Nelson (*The Sec'y*), Wolfe Barzell (*The Proprietor*), Joe Barry (*The Exterminator*), Gail Bonney (*Merle's Maid*), Monty Ash (*The Herb Store Owner*), The Brothers Candoli (*The Musicians*)
<u>P</u>: Julian Blaustein   <u>D</u>: Richard Quine   <u>SCR</u>: Daniel Taradash, from John Van Druten's stage play   <u>PHOTOG</u>: James Wong Howe   <u>MUSIC</u>: George Duning
*German retitle, **My Bride is Supernatural**, Italian retitle, **A Witch in Paradise***
Superior comedy-fantasy: Beautiful witch entrances neighbor

Belle de Jour
1967, (Fr), Hakim/AA, color, 100 mins.
<u>W</u>: Catherine Deneuve (*Severine Serizy*), Genevieve Page (*Mme. Anais*), Jean Sorel (*Pierre Serizy*), Michel Piccoli (*Henri Husson*), Pierre Clementi (*Marcel*), Macha Meril (*Renee*), Francisco Rabal (*Hyppolite*)
<u>D</u>: Luis Bunuel, from Joseph Kessel's story   <u>PHOTOG</u>: Sacha Vierny
Classic blend of fantasy, reality, surrealism, & erotica: Beauty feels compelled to work in brothel. reissued 1995

La Belle et la Bete (Beauty and the Beast)
1946, (Fr), Andre Paulve/Lopert, b&w, 89 mins.
<u>W</u>: Jean Marais (*The Beast*), Josette Day (*Belle*), Marcel Andre, Mila Parely, Michel Auclair, Christian Marquand, Nane Germo, Marcel Andre (*The Merchant*), Mila Parely (*Adelaide*), Nane Germon (*Felicie*), Michel Auclair (*Ludovic*)
<u>D & SCR</u>: Jean Cocteau, from Mme. LePrince de Beaumont's classic fairy tale
<u>PHOTOG</u>: Henri Alekan   <u>MUSIC</u>: Georges Auric
"...free from whimsy and sugar; whose plot evinced the dark power of the best fantasy and whose visual production in scene after scene brought forth the sense of wonder—pure magic unfolding before your eyes"—Baird Searles, "Films," The Magazine of Fantasy and Science Fiction, Vol. 49, No. 2 (August, 1975), p. 107
Fantasy classic: To redeem father's life, maiden must live with grotesque

A Bell from Hell
1974, (Sp), Avco-Embassy TV, color, 93 mins.
<u>W</u>: Renaud Verley (*Juan*), Viveca Lindfors (*Aunt Marta*), Alfredo Mayo (*Don Pedro*), Maribel Martin, Nuria Gimeno, Christine Betzner
<u>P & D</u>: Claudio Guerin Hill   <u>SCR</u>: Santiago Moncada
Modest horror-thriller with dark humor: Vengeful youth, out of asylum, plays murderous practical jokes

La Belle Et La Bete: JOSETTE DAY AND JEAN MARAIS

The Bells
1923, (GB), B&C/Walturdaw, b&w, 2,100 ft. (640.1m)
<u>W</u>: Russell Thorndike (*Matthias*), Arthur Walcott (*The Hypnotist*), Daisy Agnew (*The Farmer's Wife*)
<u>D</u>: Edwin Greenwood   <u>SCR</u>: Eliot Stannard, from Leopold Lewis' play
Standard thriller (episode from "Gems of Literature" series): Mesmerist weaves web of intrigue

The Bells
1926, (USA), Chadwick, b&w, 7 reels (6,300 ft./1920.2m)
<u>W</u>: Lionel Barrymore (*Mathias*), Eddie Phillips (*Christian*), Lola Todd (*Annette*), Gustav von Seyffertitz (*Frantz*), Fred Warren (*Kowelski*), Boris Karloff (*The Mesmerist*), Otto Lederer, Lorimer Johnston
<u>D & SCR</u>: James Young, from Erckmann-Chatrian's stage play   <u>PHOTOG</u>: L. William O'Connell
Modest thriller: Innkeeper murders rich traveler

The Bells
1931, (GB), British Sound Film/Producers Distrib. Corp., b&w, 75 mins.
<u>W</u>: Donald Calthrop (*Mathias*), Jane Welsh (*Annette*), Edward Sinclair (*Sgt. Christian Nash*), O.B. Clarence (*The Watchman*), Wilfred Shine (*The Philosopher*), Ralph Truman (*The Blacksmith*)
<u>D</u>: Oscar M. Werndorff & Harcourt Templeman   <u>SCR</u>: C.H. Dand, from a play by Erckmann & Chatrian
Standard thriller: Burgomeister kills Jew, is tormented by conscience

The Bells
1983, (Can), color
<u>W</u>: Richard Chamberlain, John Houseman
Minor thriller: Killer transmits death by telephone

Beloved
1998, (USA), Touchstone, color, 175 mins.
<u>W</u>: Oprah Winfrey (*Sethe*), Danny Glover (*Paul D*), Thandie, Newton (*Beloved*), Kimberly Elise (*Denver*), Beah Richards (*Baby Suggs*), Lisa Gay Hamilton (*Young Sethe*)
<u>D</u>: Jonathan Demme   <u>SCR</u>: Richard LaGravenese, Adam Brooks & Akosua Busia, from Toni Morrison's novel
Unusual fantasy-thriller: Former slave haunted by her daughter's ghost

Below the Deadline
1946, (USA), Mono, b&w, 65 mins.
<u>W</u>: Warren Douglas, Ramsay Ames
Minor melodrama

Be My Valentine Or Else
see Hospital Massacre

Ben
1972, (USA), Bing Crosby Prods./CRC, color, 95 mins.
<u>W</u>: Joseph Campanella (*Cliff Kirtland*), Rosemary Murphy (*Beth Garrison*), Lee Harcourt Montgomery (*Danny Garrison*), Arthur O'Connell (*Billy Hatfield*), Meredith Baxter (*Eve Garrison*), Kaz Garas (*Joe Greer*), Kenneth Tobey (*The Engineer*), Richard Van Fleet (*Reade*), James Luisi (*Ed*), Lee Paul (*Carey*), Norman Alden (*The Policeman*), Arlen Stuart (*Mrs. Gray*), Scott Garrett (*Henry Gray*), Richard Drasin (*George*)
<u>P</u>: Mort Briskin   <u>D</u>: Phil Karlson   <u>SCR</u>: Gilbert A. Ralston, from characters created by Stephen Gilbert   <u>PHOTOG</u>: Russell Metty   <u>MUSIC</u>: Walter Scharf   <u>SONGS</u>: *Ben's Song* & *Start the Day*, title sung by Michael Jackson
"Superior follow-up to 'Willard.' Imaginative and enormously effective"—Donald J. Mayerson, Cue
*Unusual thriller: Ailing boy befriends rats. Sequel to **Willard***

Beneath the Mask
1915, (GB), Barker/Award, b&w, 2,246 ft. (684.6m)
<u>D</u>: Bert Haldane   <u>STORY</u>: Rowland Talbot
Standard crime-thriller: Chemist regains sight in time to see assistant poisoning his drink

Beneath the Planet of the Apes
1970, (USA), Arthur P. Jacobs/20th-Fox, color, 108 mins.
<u>W</u>: James Franciscus (*Brent*), Kim Hunter (*Zira*), Maurice Evans (*Dr. Zaius*), Linda Harrison (*Nova*), Charlton Heston (*Taylor*), Paul Richards (*Mendez*), James Gregory (*Ursus*), Victor Buono (*The Fat Man*), Thomas Gomez (*The Minister*), Don Pedro Colley (*The Negro*), Natalie Trundy (*Albina*), David Watson (*Cornelius*), Tod Andrews (*Skipper*), Gregory Sierra (*Verger*), Eldon Burke (*The Gorilla Sgt.*), Lou Wagner (*Lucius*), Jeff Corey (*Caspay*)
<u>D</u>: Ted Post   <u>SCR</u>: Paul Dehn   <u>STORY</u>: Paul Dehn & Mort Abrahams, from characters created by Pierre Boulle   <u>PHOTOG</u>: Milton Krasner
*Standard SF-adventure (1st sequel to **Planet of the Apes**): Astronaut breaks space-time barrier, searches for missing comrades.   cf. **Escape from the Planet of the Apes***

Beneath the 12 Mile Reef
1953, (USA), 20th-Fox, color, 102 mins.
<u>W</u>: Robert Wagner, Terry Moore, Gilbert Roland, Peter Graves, J. Carrol Naish, Richard Boone
<u>D</u>: Robert D. Webb   <u>MUSIC</u>: Bernard Herrmann
Standard adventure-thriller: Conflict among Florida sponge fishermen

The Beneficiary
1996, (USA), color
W: Ron Silver *(Guy)*, Stacy Haiduk *(Lena)*, Suzy Amis *(Connie)*, Linden Ashby *(Jimmy)*, Steven Ford *(Bill)*
Standard thriller: Woman plots against philandering husband

Benefit of the Doubt
1993, (USA-Ger), color, 91 mins.
W: Donald Sutherland, Amy Irving, Rider Strong, Christopher McDonald, Graham Greene, Theodore Bikel
D: Jonathan Heap
Contrived thriller: Paroled wife-murderer returns to family

The Benson Murder Case
1930, (USA), Para, b&w, 65 mins.
W: William Powell *(Philo Vance)*, Natalie Moorhead *(Fanny Del Roy)*, Eugene Pallette *(Sgt. Ernest Heath)*, Paul Lukas *(Adolph Mohler)*, William (Stage) Boyd• *(Harry Gray)*, E.H. Calvert *(D.A. John F.X. Markham)*, May Beatty *(Paula Benning)*, Otto Yamaoka *(Sam)*, Mischa Auer *(Albert)*, Charles McMurphy *(Burke)*, Richard Tucker *(Anthony Benson)*, Dick Rush *(Welch)*, Perry Ivins *(The Dealer)*
D: Frank Tuttle **SCR:** Bartlett Cormack, from S.S. Van Dine's novel
PHOTOG: A.J. Stout
Superior "Philo Vance" mystery-thriller: Suave sleuth seeks murderer at posh hunting lodge
cf. **El Cuerpo del Lito** • not the William Boyd who was Hopalong Cassidy

Berenice
1954, (Fr), b&w, 15 mins.
W: Eric Rohmer
WRIT, D, & EDITED: Eric Rohmer, from Edgar Allan Poe's short story **PHOTOG:** Jacques Rivette
16mm horror short: Eerie tale of grave robbing

Berkeley Square
1933, (USA), Fox, b&w, 87 mins.
W: Leslie Howard, Heather Angel, Beryl Mercer, Irene Browne, Valerie Taylor, Colin Keith-Johnston, Alan Mowbray
D: Frank Lloyd **SCR:** Sonya Levien, from John L. Balderston's stage play **PHOTOG:** Ernest Palmer **MUSIC:** Louis de Francesco & William Carling
Modest fantasy-romance: London house transports man to 18th century. cf. 'The House in the Square'

Berlin Appointment for the Spy
see **Berlino Appuntamento per le Spie**

The Berlin Conspiracy
1991, (USA), color, 83 mins.
W: Marc Singer, Mary Crosby, Stephen Davies, Richard Leparmentier, Terence Henry
D: Terence H. Winkless
Minor thriller: Saboteurs steal killer bacteria

Berlin Express
1948, (USA), RKO, b&w, 87 mins.
W: Merle Oberon, Robert Ryan, Paul Lukas, Charles Korvin, Otto Waldis, Robert Coote
D: Jacques Tourneur **SCR:** Harold Medford **PHOTOG:** Lucien Ballard **MUSIC:** Frederick Hollander
Modest spy-thriller: Allied agents counter Nazi fanatics

Berlino Appuntamento per le Spie (Berlin Appointment for the Spy)
1965, (It), AIP, color, 105 mins.
W: Brett Halsey *(Morris)*, Pier Angeli *(Paula)*, Dana Andrews
D: Vittorio Sala
USA retitle, **Spy in Your Eye**
Minor thriller: US and Soviet agents pursue secret formula

The Bermuda Depths
1978, (USA), Arthur Rankin Jr.-Jules Bass, ABC-TV, color, 88 mins.
W: Leigh McCloskey *(Magnus)*, Connie Selleca *(Jennie)*, Carl Weathers *(Eric)*, Burl Ives *(Dr. Paulis)*, Julie Woodson, Ruth Attaway, Elise Frick, Nicholas Ingham, Kevin Petty, Jonathan Ingham, Nicole Marsh, John Instone, George Richards, Patricia Rego, Doris Riley, Tracy Anne Sadler
D: Tom Kotani **SCR:** William Overgard **STORY:** Arthur Rankin Jr. **PHOTOG:** Jeri Sopanen **MUSIC:** Maury Laws
A.k.a. **It Came Up from the Bermuda Depths**
Minor adventure-fantasy: Marine biologists pursue mysterious sea creature, made for TV Movie

Bermuda Mystery
1944, (USA), 20th-Fox, b&w, 65 mins.
W: Preston Foster, Ann Rutherford
Standard melodrama

The Bermuda Triangle
1978, (USA), Sunn Classic, color
W: Brad Crandall, Donald Albee, Lin Berlitz, Larry Bisman, Howard W. Bishop Jr., Jim Bohan, R.J. Bohner, Vince Davis, David C. Ellzey, Steve Farrell,

Bobbie Faye Ferguson, Ed Fry, Tony Frank, John William Galt, Anne Galvan, Michael Glanfield, Albert Hall, Brian Herskowitz, Robert Hibbard, Leland Holmes, Joe Houde, Charles E. Houston, Tom Matts, Ron Jackson, Harlan Jordan, Warren Kemmerling, Warren A. Munson III, Tommy Kendrick, Joel P. Kenney, James Logan, Fritz Leiber, Bob Magruder, Hedley Mattingly, John Pochna, Harriet Medin, Paul Menzel, Richard M. Mills, Thalmus Rasulala, Glenn Morshower, Arthur Roberts, Roxie Roker, Clement St. George, Kimo Schulze, Oliver Seale, Jeremiah Todd, Vickery Turner, Michael Vam Dalsem, Jim Wiggins, Warren Vanders, Don Wiseman
D: Richard Friedenberg **SCR:** Stephen Lord **PHOTOG:** Henning Schellerup **MUSIC:** John Cameron
Minor speculation-documentary

Bermuda Triangle
1996, (USA), ABC-TV, color, 95 mins.
W: Sam Behrens *(John)*, Susanna Thompson *(Grace)*, Lisa Jakub *(Annie)*, David Gallagher *(Sam)*, Michael Reilly Burke *(Michael)*, Jerry Hardin *(Slick)*, Naomi Watts *(Amanda)*
TVM, standard SF-thriller: Shipwrecked family trapped in "27th dimension"

Bernard and the Genie
1991, (GB), Made for TV Movie., color, 70 mins.
W: Alan Cumming, Lenny Henry *(The Genie)*, Rowan Atkinson *(Pinkworth)*
D: Paul Welland
TVM, standard comedy-fantasy: Genie helps victimized art broker plot revenge

Bernardo's Confession
1914, (GB), Planet Films/Hibbert, b&w, 1,000 ft. (304.8m)
W: Bransby Williams *(Count Bernardo)*, Sidney Kearns
D: Charles Vernon, from a sketch by Bransby Williams
Standard crime-thriller: Italian count, framed for anarchy, kills wife and her lover

Berserk
1968, (GB), Herman Cohen/Col, color, 96 mins.
W: Joan Crawford *(Monica Rivers)*, Ty Hardin *(Frank Hawkins)*, Michael Gough *(Dorando)*, Judy Geeson *(Angela Rivers)*, Diana Dors *(Matilda)*, Geoffrey Keen *(Commissioner Dalby)*, Robert Hardy *(Det.-Supt. Brooks)*, Sydney Tafler *(Harrison Liston)*, George Claydon *(Bruno)*, Philip Madoc *(Lazlo)*, Peter Burton *(Gustavo)*, Ambrosine Phillpotts *(Miss Burrows)*, Golda Casimir *(The Bearded Lady)*, Ted Lune *(The Skeleton Man)*, Byron Pringle *(Sgt. Bradford)*, Milton Reid *(The Strong Man)*, Thomas Cimarro *(Gaspar)*, Marianne Stone *(Wanda)*, Howard Goorney *(Emil)*, Miki Iveria *(The Gypsy Fortune-Teller)*, Reginald Marsh *(Sgt. Hutchins)*, The Billy Smart Circus
P: Herman Cohen **D:** Jim O'Connolly **ORIG. STORY & SCR:** Aben Kandel & Herman Cohen **PHOTOG:** Desmond Dickinson **MUSIC:** John Scott
orig. to be titled **Circus of Blood**
Standard thriller: Woman's circus plagued by grisly "accidents"

Beware The Blob !: CAROL LYNLEY AND JACK HARRIS

Bertie's Book of Magic
1912, (GB), Hepworth, b&w, 325 ft. (99.1m)
D: Frank Wilson
Standard comedy-fantasy: Boarder turns landlady into black cat

The Beryl Coronet
1912, (GB-Fr), Franco-British Film Co.-Eclair/Fenning, b&w, 2,300 ft. (701m)
W: Georges Treville *(Sherlock Holmes)*, Mr. Moyse *(Dr. John Watson)*
D: Georges Treville, from a story by Sir Arthur Conan Doyle
Standard thriller

Berseker

1987, (USA), color, 85 mins.
W: Joseph Alan Johnson, Valerie Sheldon, Greg Dawson
D: Jef Richard
Minor thriller: Psycho attacks camping college students

The Beryl Coronet

1921, (GB), Stoll, b&w, 2,340 ft. (713.2m)
W: Eille Norwood (*Sherlock Holmes*), Hubert Willis (*Dr. John Watson*), Henry Vibart (*Alexander Holder*), Molly Adair (*Mary*), Lawrence Anderson (*Arthur*), Jack Selfridge (*Sir George Burnwell*), Mme. d'Esterre (*Mrs. Hudson*)
D: Maurice Elvey **SCR:** Charles Barnett, from the writings of Sir Arthur Conan Doyle
Standard crime-thriller (episode in "Adventures of Sherlock Holmes" series)

The Bespoke Overcoat

1955, (GB), Remus/IFD, b&w, 37 mins.
W: Alfie Bass (*Fender*), David Kossoff (*Morry*), Alan Tilvern (*Ranting*), Alfie Dean (*The Gravedigger*)
P & D: Jack Clayton **SCR:** Wolf Mankowitz, from Nikolai Gogol's short story *The Cloak*
Reissued 1965
Standard short fantasy: Old Jew dies from cold, returns for promised overcoat. cf. Shinel and The Overcoat.

The Best Man Wins

1934, (USA), Col, b&w
W: Bela Lugosi, Jack Holt, Edmund Lowe
D: Erle C. Kenton **SCR:** Ethel Hill & Bruce Manning
Standard thriller: Fisherman unmasked as gem smuggler

The Best of Sex and Violence

1981, (USA), Wizard, color
W: John Carradine (*narrator*), David Carradine, Keith Carradine
P: Charles Band **D:** Ken Dixon
Standard cinema docu: Clips from 40 trailers of 1970s films (e.g., Tourist Trap, Terminal Island, et al)

Be Sure Your Sins

1915, (GB), Hepworth/KTC, b&w, 2,900 ft. (886.5m)
W: Alma Taylor (*Maggie White*), Stewart Rome (*Dr. Wynne*), Tom Powers (*Leo Garth*), Eric Desmond (*Reggie Wynne*), Violet Hopson (*Mrs. Wynne*), Ruby Belasco (*Mrs. White*)
D: Cecil M. Hepworth **STORY:** Blanche McIntosh
A.k.a. The Canker of Jealousy
Standard crime-thriller: Doctor strangles wife's lover

Betrayal

1974, (USA), CBS-TV, color, 74 mins.
W: Amanda Blake, Tisha Sterling, Sam Groom, Lucille Benson, Dick Haymes, Edward Marshall
D: Gordon Hessler **TELEPLAY:** James Miller **MUSIC:** Ernest Gold
A.k.a. The Companion
TVM, Minor thriller: Widow errs in hiring young companion

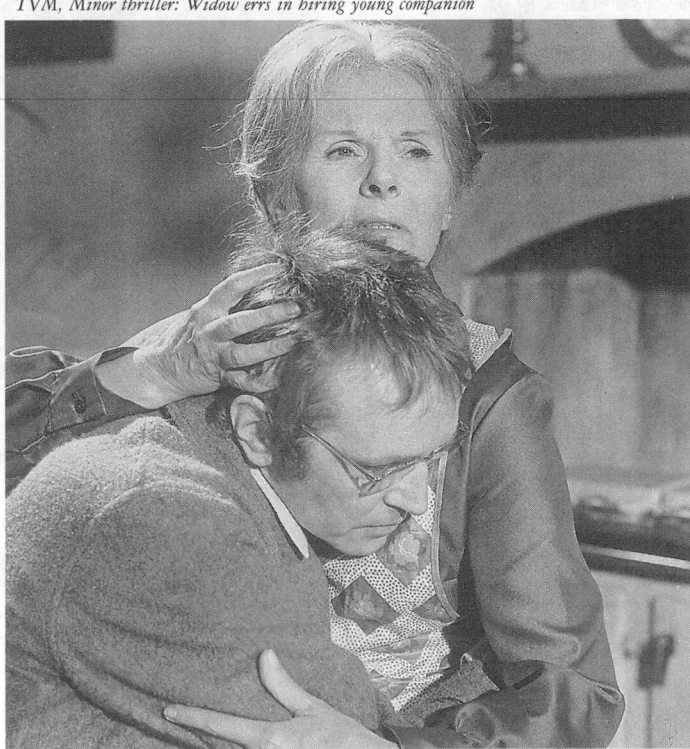

Beware My Brethren: TONY BECKLEY AND ANN TODD

Betrayal from the East

1944, (USA), b&w, 82 mins.
W: Lee Tracy, Nancy Kelly, Richard Loo, Abner Biberman, Regis Toomey, Philip Ahn, Addison Richards, Victor Sen Young, Drew Pearson
D: William Berke
Standard wartime-propaganda thriller: Carnival barker saves Panama Canal from Japanese war machine

Betrayal of the Dove

1993, (USA), color, 93 mins.
W: Helen Slater
Minor thriller: Divorcee convinced someone is trying to kill her

The Betrayal

1958, (GB), Danziger/UA, b&w, 82 mins.
W: Philip Friend (*Michael McCall*), Diana Decker (*Janet Hillyer*), Philip Saville (*Bartel*), Peter Bathurst (*Insp. Baring*), Peter Burton (*Tony Adams*), Ballard Berkeley (*Lawson*), Harold Lang (*Clay*)
P: Edward J. & Harry Lee Danziger **D:** Ernest Morris **STORY:** Brian Clemens & Eldon Howard
Standard crime-thriller: Model helps blind pilot locate traitor

Betrayed Women

1955, (USA), AA, b&w, 70 mins.
W: Carole Matthews, Tom Drake, Beverly Michaels, Peggy Knudsen, Sara Haden
D: Edward L. Cahn
Minor melodrama

Beware Spooks !: JOE E. BROWN AND MARY CARLISDLE

Between Midnight and Dawn

1950, (USA), Col, b&w, 89 mins.
W: Edmond O'Brien, Gale Storm, Mark Stevens, Donald Buka, Gale Robbins, Anthony Ross, Roland Winters, Grazia Narciso, Tito Vuolo, Madge Blake, Lora Lee Michel, Jack Del Rio, Tony Barr, Philip Van Zandt, Cliff Bailey, Peter Mamakos, Frances Morris, Wheaton Chambers, Earl Breitbard
D: Gordon M. Douglas **SCR:** Eugene Ling **STORY:** Gerald Drayson Adams & Leo Katcher
Routine melodrama: Cop pursues escaped gangster

Between Two Worlds

1944, (USA), WB, b&w, 112 mins.
W: John Garfield, Eleanor Parker, Lester Matthews, John Emery, Faye Emerson, Edmund Gwenn, Sydney Greenstreet, Sara Allgood, Paul Henreid, George Coulouris, Dennis King, George Tobias, Isobel Elsom
D: Edward A. Blatt **SCR:** Daniel Fuchs, from Sutton Vane's play *Outward Bound*
PHOTOG: Carl Guthrie **MUSIC:** Erich Wolfgang Korngold
Moody fantasy: Remake of 1930 film. Phantom ship sails to Eternity with cargo of deceased souls

Between Worlds

see Der Mude Tod

Beverly Hills Bodysnatchers

1989, (USA), Hess-Kallberg Assocs./McGuffin Prods./Shapiro Glickenhaus Entertainment, color, 85 mins.
W: Vic Tayback (*Lou*), Frank Gorshin (*The Doctor*), Seth Jaffe (*Don Carlo*), Rodney Eastman (*Freddie*), Warren Selko (*Vincent*), Brooke Bundy (*Mrs. Darren*), Keone Young (*Don Ho*), Art Metrano (*Vito*), Steven Field (*Nunz*), Christian Hoff (*Stu*), Allison Barron (*Julie*), Linda Carol (*Heather*), Milt Tarver (*Det. Rice*), Judy Jernudd (*The Reporter*), Jodi Peterson (*The Golf Brat*), Charles C. Stevenson Jr. (*The Priest*), Alan Berger (*Robber #1*), James Fredericks (*Robber #2*), Ted Davis (*The Male Nurse*), Tom Bate (*The Plugger*), Harold Shapiro (*Mr. Smithers*), Terrence Tierney (*Goon*), Mitchell French (*The Security*

Guard), Virginia Gilbert (*The French Maid*), Barry Zetlin (*The Assassin*), Paul Verdugo (*The Limo Driver*), Jim Noble (*The Heavy Metal Rocker*), Penny Hamilton (*The Society Dame*), Vincent Van Lenhoff (*Mr. Stiff*), Mac F. Williams (*The Motorcycle Cop*), Manuel Portela (*The Man with the Teddy Bear*), Leslie Hess, John T. Hess, Tim Toomay, Rob Brooks, P.K. Simonds Jr., Jon Mostow
<u>D</u>: Jon Mostow   <u>SCR</u>: P.K. Simonds Jr.   <u>STORY</u>: Jon Mostow & P.K. Simonds Jr.   <u>PHOTOG</u>: Zoran Hochstatter   <u>MUSIC</u>: Arthur Barrow   <u>SONG</u>: *Let's Take a Drive to Beverly Hills, This Is the Beat, Surfomatic 2000, Kinda Insane, All Noshed Out, The Don is Alive!, Hearse Burnin' Rubber, & Hey, There's a Bikini in My Casket*
Minor horror-comedy: Greedy mortician and mad scientist revive wealthy dead

Beverly Hills Vamp
1989, (USA), color, 90 mins.
<u>W</u>: Eddie Deezen (*Kyle*), Britt Ekland, Debra Lamb
<u>D</u>: Fred Olen Ray
Standard horror-comedy: Vampiresses prey on film makers

Beware, My Brethren
1972, (GB), World Arts media/Miracle/Cinerama, color, 87 mins.
<u>W</u>: Patrick Magee, Ann Todd, Tony Beckley
<u>P & D</u>: Robert Hartford-Davis   <u>SCR</u>: Brian Comfort
Standard fantasy-thriller: Murderous youth tries to contact dead mother aka **The Fiend**

Beware, My Lovely
1952, (USA), RKO, b&w, 77 mins.
<u>W</u>: Ida Lupino (*Mrs. Gordon*), Robert Ryan (*Howard*), Barbara Whiting (*Ruth Williams*), Taylor Holmes (*Mr. Armstrong*), O.Z. Whitehead (*Mr. Franks*), James Willmas (*Mr. Steven*), Dee Pollock (*The Grocery Boy*)
<u>P</u>: Collier Young   <u>D</u>: Harry Horner   <u>SCR</u>: Mel Dinelli, from his radio-play *The Man*   <u>PHOTOG</u>: George E. Diskant   <u>MUSIC</u>: Leith Stevens
Tense thriller: Widow hires mentally-disturbed handyman

Beware, Spooks!
1939, (USA), Col, b&w, 68 mins
<u>W</u>: Joe E. Brown, Mary Carlisle, Don Beddoe, Clarence Kolb, Marc Lawrence
<u>D</u>: Edward Sedgwick
Minor comedy-thriller: "Ghosts" cause consternation

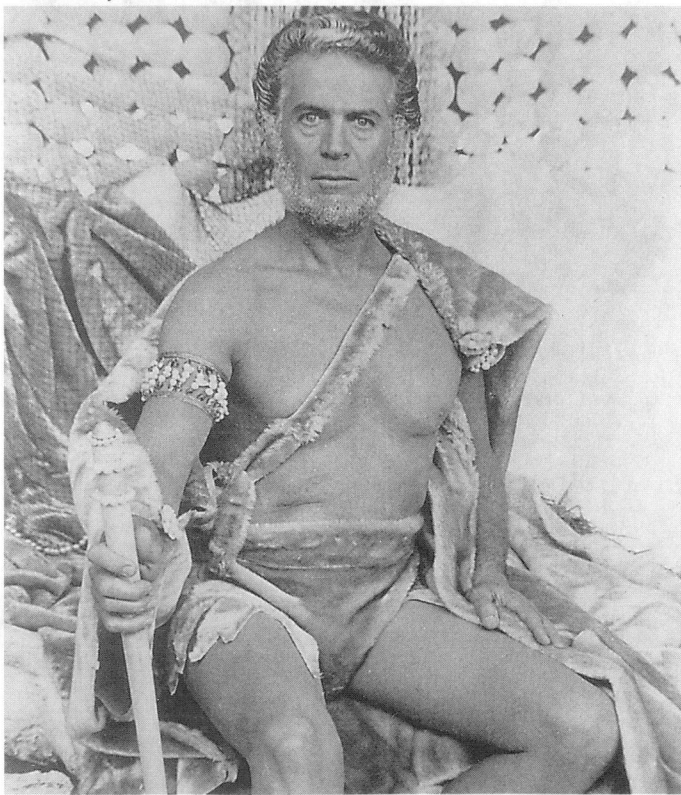
Beyond Atlantis: GEORGE NADER

Beware The Blob !
1971, (USA), Jack H. Harris, color, 88 mins.
<u>W</u>: Robert Walker Jr., Gwynne Gilford, Godfrey Cambridge, Carol Lynley, Richard Stahl, Richard Webb, Larry Hagman, Del Close, Burgess Meredith, Shelley Berman, Fred Smoot, Marlene Clark, Rockne Tarkington
<u>P</u>: Anthony Harris   <u>D</u>: Larry Hagman   <u>SCR</u>: Jack Woods & Anthony Harris, from a story by Richard Clair   <u>PHOTOG</u>: Al Hamm   <u>MUSIC</u>: Mort Garson   <u>SONG</u>: *Captain Coke*
GB retitle and US release, Son of Blob
Minor SF-satire: Gelatinous horror returns to menace cf. **The Blob** (1958)

The Bewildering Cabinet
1907, (Fr), Star, b&w, 114m (374 ft./6.3 mins.)
<u>D</u>: Georges Melies
Standard fantasy

Bewildering Transformations
1912, (GB), Urban, b&w, 335 ft. (102.1m)
<u>WRIT & D</u>: F. Perry Smith
Minor fantasy short: Lizard melts into boot; midget boxers melt into grapes

Bewitched
1945, (USA), MGM, b&w, 65 mins.
<u>W</u>: Phyllis Thaxter, Edmund Gwenn, Addison Richards, Kathleen Lockhart
<u>WRIT & D</u>: Arch Oboler, from his radio-play *Alter Ego*   <u>PHOTOG</u>: Charles Salerno Jr.
Minor thriller: Psychiatrist uses hypnosis on woman with split-personality

Bewitched
1985, (GB), BBC-TV, color, 60 mins.
<u>W</u>: Eileen Atkins, Alfred Lynch
<u>D</u>: Edmund Oboler
TVM, standard thriller: Dead woman suspected of plaguing elderly couple

The Bewitched Boxing Gloves
1910, (GB), Kineto, b&w, 567 ft. (172.8m)
<u>D</u>: Walter R. Booth
reissued 1913
Minor fantasy short: Man dons magic boxing gloves, smashes motor-cars

The Bewitched Dungeon
see **La Tour Maudite**

The Bewitched Inn
see **L'Auberge Ensorcelee**

The Bewitched Manor House
1909, (Fr), b&w
Minor fantasy: Supernatural events

Bewitched Matches
1913, (Fr), b&w
Minor fantasy: Matches refuse to be extinguished

Bewitched Place
see **Zvenigora**

The Bewitched Traveller
see **The Jonah Man** *or,* **The Traveller Bewitched**

The Bewitched Trunk
see **Le Coffre Enchante**

Beyond a Reasonable Doubt
1956, (USA), RKO, b&w, 80 mins.
<u>W</u>: Dana Andrews (*Tom Garrett*), Joan Fontaine (*Susan Spencer*), Shepperd Strudwick (*Wilson*), Arthur Franz (*Hale*), Sidney Blackmer (*Austin Spencer*), Edward Binns (*Lt. Kennedy*), Robin Raymond (*Terry*), Philip Bourneuf (*Thompson*), Barbara Nichols (*Sally*), William Leicester (William Lester) (*Charlie Miller*), Carleton Young (*Kirk*), Dan Seymour (*Greco*), Rusty Lane (*Judge*), Joyce Taylor (*Joan*), Trudy Wroe (*The Hat Check Girl*), Joe Kirk (*The Clerk*), Charles Evans (*The Governor*), Wendell Niles (*The Announcer*)
<u>D</u>: Fritz Lang   <u>SCR</u>: Douglas Morrow   <u>PHOTOG</u>: William Snyder   <u>MUSIC</u>: Herschel Burke Gilbert
Minor thriller: Man becomes guinea pig to prove fallibilty of circumstantial evidence

Beyond and Back
1978, (USA), Sunn Classics, color, 93 mins.
<u>W</u>: Brad Crandall (*The Narrator*), Vern Adix (*Plato*), Shelley Osterloh (*Louisa May Alcott*), Beverly Rowland (*Mrs. Houdini*), Linda Bishop, Janet Bylund, Richard Cannaday, Ian Flynn, Maxilyn Capell, Bill Carroll, David Chandler, Jan Noyes, Hyde Clayton, Elaine Daniels, Lori Davis, Stewart Falconer, James Fleming, Margaret Gibson, Carol Hertford, John F. Hart, Mary Ethel Gregory, Rick Jury, Donna K.W. Johnson, Myron Peter Griffen, Bruce Hertford, Alan Nash, Norman Keefer, Thomas Kelley, Diana Kozlowski, Anthony Mannino, Charon Levitan, Marie Lillo, Anna Louise, Tony Romano, Barta Lee Heiner, Robert Macri, James Montgomery, Jean Stringam Oswald, Lucia Pappas, Kate Petley, H.E.D. Redford, Walt Price, Steve Riley, Bruce Robinson, Larry Roupe, Joe Robinson, Oscar Rowland, Stanley Russon, M. Scott Wilkinson, Michael Ruud, Malinda St. James, Craig Shipler, Craig Stephenson, Jim Strong
<u>D</u>: James L. Conway   <u>SCR</u>: Stephen Lord, from a book by Ralph Wilkerson   <u>PHOTOG</u>: Henning Schellerup   <u>MUSIC</u>: Bob Summers
Minor speculation-docu: Life-after-death experiences

Beyond Atlantis
1973, (Phil), Dimension, color, 90 mins.
<u>W</u>: Patrick Wayne (*Vic Mathias*), John Ashley (*Logan*), Lenore Stevens (*Kathy Vernon*), Leigh Christian (*Syrene*), Sid Haig (*East Eddie*), George Nader

(*Nereus*), Vic Diaz (*Manuel*), Kim Ramos, Eddie Garcia, Ken Warren, Andy Centenera, Gil Arceo, Angelo Ventura
<u>D</u>: Eddie Romero <u>SCR</u>: Charles Johnson <u>STORY</u>: Stephanie Rothman <u>PHOTOG</u>: Justo Paulino & Michael J. Dugan
A.k.a. ***Sea Creatures*** and ***Sea People***
Minor action-thriller: Fortune hunters find lost continent

Beyond Belief
1976, (USA), color
Standard speculation-docu: Paranormal probed

Beyond Darkness
1992, (USA) color, 111 mins.
<u>W</u>: Gene Le Brock, David Brandon, Barbara Bingham, Michael Stephenson, Stephen Brown
<u>D</u>: Clyde Anderson
Minor horror-fantasy: Dead witches seek revenge

Beyond Dream's Door
1988, (USA), color, 86 mins.
<u>W</u>: Nick Baldasare, Rick Kesler, Susan Pinsky, Norm Singer
<u>D</u>: Jay Woelfel
Minor horror-fantasy: Collegian's nightmares become reality

Beyond Evil
1983, (USA), Milano/IFI/Scope III, color, 93 mins.
<u>W</u>: John Saxon (*Larry Andrews*), Lynda Day George (*Barbara Andrews*), Michael Dante (*Del*), David Opatoshu (*Dr. Solomon*), Mario Milano (*Dr. Frank Albanos*), Janice Lynde (*Alma*), Anne Marisse (*Leia Solomon*), Zitto Kazann (*Esteban*), Allan Caillou (*The Inspector*), Beverly Dixon (*The Nurse*), Jennifer Italiano (*Jennifer*), Edward An-sara, Peggy Stewart, Chuck Hicks, Mickey Carouso, Lisa Antille, Richard Herkert, Verkina Flower, Kiku Hamaoa, Kuinise Leiataua, Anne Gaybis, Anna Marlow, Johnny Mendez, Lisona Leiataua
<u>D</u>: Herb Freed <u>SCR</u>: Paul Rose & Herb Freed <u>PHOTOG</u>: Ken Plotin <u>SPCL-FX</u>: Joe Quinlivan <u>MUSIC</u>: Pino Donaggio
Minor fantasy-thriller: Spirit of 19th-century sorceress torments modern couple

Beyond the Bermuda Triangle
1975, (USA), Playboy/NBC-TV, color, 74 mins.
<u>W</u>: Fred MacMurray (*Harry*), Sam Groom (*Jed*), Donna Mills, Dan White, Suzanne Reed, Dana Plato, Woody Woodbury, Ric O'Feldman, John DiSanti
<u>P</u>: Ron Roth <u>D</u>: William A. Graham <u>SCR</u>: Charles A. McDaniel
TVM, minor adventure-thriller: "Satan's Triangle" explored

Beyond the Blue Horizon
1942, (USA), Para, color, 76 mins.
<u>W</u>: Dorothy Lamour, Richard Denning, Patricia Morison, Walter Abel, Jack Haley, Helen Gilbert, Elizabeth Patterson
<u>D</u>: Alfred Santell <u>SCR</u>: Frank Butler <u>PHOTOG</u>: William C. Mellor <u>MUSIC</u>: Victor Young
Standard adventure-romance: Jungle girl leads scoffers to island paradise

Beyond the Door
1975, (USA-It), Edward L. Montoro/Film Ventures, color, 92 mins.
<u>W</u>: Juliet Mills (*Jessica*), Richard Johnson (*Dimitri*), David Conlin Jr., Elizabeth Turner, Barbara Fiorini, Gabriele Lavia
<u>D</u>: Oliver Hellman <u>SONG</u>: *Bargain with the Devil*
Minor horror-thriller: Unsuspecting housewife carries demonic child

Beyond the Door III
1990, (USA), color, 94 mins.
<u>W</u>: Mary Kohnert, Sarah Conway Ciminera, William Geiger, Renee Rancourt, Alex Vitale, Victoria Zinny, Savina Gersak, Bo Svenson
<u>D</u>: Jeff Kwitny
Minor horror-thriller: Exchange students find demonic terror in Serbia

Beyond the Fog
see ***Tower of Evil***

Beyond the Gate
see ***Human Experiments***

Beyond the Living
1978, (USA), Independent-Int'l, color, 85 mins.
<u>W</u>: Jill Jacobson (*Sherry*), Geoffrey Land (*Dr. Peter Desmond*), Marilyn Joi, Mary Kay Pass, Prentiss Moulden, Erwin Fuller, Bill Roy, J.C. Wells, Clayton Foster
<u>P</u>: Mark Sherwood <u>D</u>: Al Adamson <u>SCR</u>: Michael Bockman & Greg Tittinger <u>PHOTOG</u>: Roger Michaels
A.k.a. ***Nurse Sherri***
Minor horror-thriller: Nurse possessed by dead man's evil spirit

Beyond the Living Dead
see ***La Orgia de los Muertos***

Beyond the Moon
1954, (USA), Reed, b&w
<u>W</u>: Richard Crane (*Rocky Jones*), Sally Mansfield

---

reedited from 1950s teleseries ***Rocky Jones, Space Ranger***
Minor space-opera: Hero battles off-Earth injustice

Beyond Obsession
1994, (USA), Lifetime, color, 95 mins.
<u>W</u>: Victoria Principal, Emily Warfield (*Traci*), Henry Thomas (*John*), Donnelly Rhodes, Joe Regalbuto, Garry Chalk, Vince Metcalfe
<u>D</u>: David Greene, from a book by Richard Hammer <u>PHOTOG</u>: Richard Leiterman <u>MUSIC</u>: Peter Manning Robinson
TVM, standard fact-based thriller: Woman pianist persuades boyfriend to kill her mother

Beyond the Poseidon Adventure
1979, (USA), WB, color, 122 mins.
<u>W</u>: Michael Caine (*Capt. Mike Turner*), Sally Field (*Celeste Whitman*), Telly Savalas (*Dr. Stefan Svevo*), Peter Boyle (*Frank Mazzetti*), Jack Warden (*Harold Meredith*), Karl Malden (*Wilbur*), Shirley Knight (*Hannah Meredith*), Angela Cartwright (*Theresa Mazzetti*), Veronica Hamel (*Suzanne*), Slim Pickens (*Hopkins*), Shirley Jones (*Gina Rowe*), Mark Harmon (*Larry Simpson*), Patrick Culliton (*Doyle*), Paul Picerni (*Kurt*), Dean Ferrandini (*Castorp*), Paul Stader, George Wilbur, Rick Wilson, Peter Stader, Tony Epper, Ayn Cavellini, Hubie Kerns Jr., Gary Taraman, Fred Shaw, Sheree Kerns, Peter Peterson, Janet Brady, Justin DeRosa, Bob Bralver, Joe Cirillo, Marneen Fields, Jimmy Stader, Henry Wills, Kay Kimler, Vince Deadrick, Pamela Estrom, Fred Zendar
<u>D</u>: Irwin Allen <u>SCR</u>: Nelson Gidding, from characters created by Paul Gallico <u>PHOTOG</u>: Joseph Biroc <u>SPCL FX</u>: Howard Jensen <u>MUSIC</u>: Jerry Fielding
Sequel to ***The Poseidon Adventure***, *minor thriller: Criminals and adventurers seek fortune on overturned ship*

Beyond Sanity
1997, (USA), Salt City, color
<u>D</u>: Kevin J. Lindenmuth
Minor horror anthology

Beyond the Stars
1989, (USA), color, 94 mins
<u>W</u>: Martin Sheen, Christian Slater, Olivia d'Abo, F. Murray Abraham, Robert Foxworth, Sharon Stone
<u>D</u>: David Saperstein
Standard SF-thriller: Astronaut conceals moon-mission secret

Beyond the Time Barrier
1959, (USA), AIP, b&w, 75 mins.
<u>W</u>: Robert Clarke, Darlene Tompkins, Vladimir Sokoloff, Don Flourney, Arianne Arden, Stephen Bekassy, Read Morgan, Tom Ravick, John Van Dreelen, Ken Knox
<u>P</u>: Robert Clarke <u>D</u>: Edgar G. Ulmer <u>STORY & SCR</u>: Arthur C. Pierce
Standard SF-adventure (incorporating footage from ***Journey to the Lost City***)*: Jet pilot breaks time barrier, finds grim world of future*

Beyond the Universe
1981, (USA), Sandler Institutional Films, color
<u>W</u>: David Ladd, Jacqueline Ray, Christopher Cary, Stephanie Faulkner, John Dewey-Carter, Frank A. Miller, C.M. Gampel, Hamilton Mitchell, Michael Twain, Peter Jason, Clare Peck, Deborah Greene, Mary Ellen O'Neill, Larry Curran, Agi Terree, Henry Darrow
<u>D & MUSIC</u>: Robert Emenegger <u>SCR</u>: Allan Sandler, Robert Emenegger, Steven Posner, & Seth Marshall <u>ORIG & CONCEPT</u>: Robert Emenegger & Allan Sandler <u>PHOTOG</u>: Jose Luis Mignone
Standard SF-adventure: Scientist seeks contact with advanced aliens

Beyond the Veil
see ***The Secret Kingdom***

Beyond This Place
1959, (GB), Georgefield/Renown/AA, b&w, 88 mins.
<u>W</u>: Van Johnson (*Paul Mathry*), Vera Miles (*Lena Anderson*), Emlyn Williams (*Enoch Oswald*), Bernard Lee (*Patrick Mathry*), Jean Kent (*Louise Burt*), Leo McKern (*McEvoy*), Ralph Truman (*Sir Matthew Sprott*), Rosalie Crutchley (*Ella Mathry*), Vincent Winter (*Paul as a Child*), Moultrie Kelsall (*Insp. Dale*), Geoffrey Keen (*The Governor*), Jameson Clark (*Swann*), Joyce Heron (*Lady Catherine Sprott*), Henry Oscar (*Sharpe*)
<u>P</u>: Maxwell Setton & John R. Sloan <u>D</u>: Jack Cardiff <u>SCR</u>: Kenneth Taylor. from A.J. Cronin's novel <u>PHOTOG</u>: Wilkie Cooper <u>MUSIC</u>: Douglas Gamley
USA retitle, ***Web of Evidence***
Standard thriller: Man seeks truth about father's death

Beyond Tomorrow
1940, (USA), RKO, b&w, 84 mins.
<u>W</u>: Harry Carey (*Melton*), C. Aubrey Smith (*Chadwick*), Charles Winninger (*O'Brien*), Jean Parker (*Jean*), Richard Carlson (*James*), Maria Ouspenskaya (*Tanya*), Alex Melesh (*Josef*), Rod La Rocque (*Hubert*), Robert Homans, J. Anthony Hughes, William Bakewell, Virginia McMullen, James Bush
<u>D</u>: A. Edward Sutherland <u>SCR</u>: Adele Comandini <u>ORIG. STORY</u>: Mildred Cram & Adele Comandini <u>PHOTOG</u>: Lester White <u>SPCL-FX</u>: Ned Mann & Jack Cosgrove <u>MUSIC</u>: Frank Tours <u>SONG</u>: *It's Raining Dreams*
Minor sentimental fantasy: Ghosts of three old men aid young couple

Bill And Ted's Excellent Adventure: ALEX WINTER AND KEANU REEVES

Bezludna Planeta (Inhabited Planet)
1962, (Pol), Film Polski, b&w
D: Krzysztof Debowski   **SCR:** Stanislaw Lem   **PHOTOG:** Jan Tkaczyk
    MUSIC: Krzysztof Penderecki
Minor SF-fantasy

The Bible
1966, (USA-It), 20th-Fox, color, 175 mins.
W: George C. Scott (*Abram/Abraham*), Ava Gardner (*Sarai/Sarah*), Michael Parks
    (*Adam*), Ulla Bergryd (*Eve*), John Huston (*Noah/The Voice of God*), Stephen
    Boyd (*Nimrod*), Gabriele Ferzetti (*Lot*), Eleonora Rossi-Drago (*Lot's Wife*),
    Peter O'Toole (*The Three Angels*), Richard Harris (*Cain*), Franco Nero (*Abel*),
    Zoe Sallis (*Hagar the Egyptian*), Roger Beaumont, Pupella Maggio, Adriana
    Ambesi
P: Dino De Laurentiis   **D:** John Huston   **SCR:** Christopher Frye   **PHOTOG:**
    Giuseppe Rotunno   **SPCL-FX:** Linwood Dunn   **MUSIC:** Toshiro
    Mayuzumi
"When De Laurentiis first embarked on his epic, he envisioned a ten-hour film,
    costing $25 million and depicting nearly all the still waters and flaming
    furnaces, from Creation to Gethsemane. When he actually started shooting
    the picture in Rome last May [1964], he had boiled it down to a mere
    three-hour, $15 million Technicolor frieze of episodes from Genesis 1-
    22..."—"Show Business," Time, LXXXV (Jan. 15, 1965), p. 70
"...a respectful and unexciting $18,000,000 star-studded adaptation of the first 22
    chapters of Genesis"—Judith Crist, TV Guide
*Lavish biblical romance: Events from Creation to the fulfillment of Abraham (film omits
    Abraham & Sarah's sojourn in Egypt)*

Beyond the Living
W: Richard Travis, Anne Gillis
D: William C. Thomas
A.k.a. **Hands of Death, Hospital of Terror, Killer's Curse, Nurse Sherri, Terror
    Hospital, Big Town After Dark, Underworld After Dark**
Minor melodrama: Journalists probe crime ring

Beyond the Rising Moon
see **Star Quest** *(1989)*

A Bid for Fortune
1911, (GB), Hepworth, b&w, 900 ft. (274.3m)
D: Bert Haldane
Standard crime-thriller: Usurper poses as heir to fortune

A Bid for Fortune
1917, (GB), Unity-Super, b&w, 4,000 ft. (1219.2m)
W: A. Harding Steerman (*Dr. Nikola*), Violet Graham (*Phyllis Wetherall*), Sydney
    Vautier (*Dick Hattaras*)
D & SCR: Sidney Morgan, from a novel by Guy Boothby
Standard crime-thriller: Occult scientist tries to steal Chinese artifact

Big
1988, (USA), 20th-Fox, color, 104 mins.
W: Tom Hanks (*Josh Baskin*), Elizabeth Perkins (*Susan*), Robert Loggia
    (*MacMillan*), John Heard (*Paul*), Jared Rushton (*Billy*), David Moscow
    (*Young Josh*), Jon Lovitz (*Scotty Brennen*), Josh Clark (*Mr. Baskin*), Mercedes
    Ruehl (*Mrs. Baskin*), Kimberlee M. Davis (*Cynthia Benson*), Oliver Block
    (*Freddie Benson*), Allan Wasserman (*The Gym Teacher*)
D: Penny Marshall   **SCR:** Gary Ross & Anne Spielberg   **PHOTOG:** Barry
    Sonnenfeld   **MUSIC:** Howard Shore
Superior comedy-fantasy: Wish turns 13-year-old into adult

Big & Hairy
1998, (USA), color, 95 mins.
W: Robert Burke, Trevor Jones, Richard Thomas (*Victor*), Donnelly Rhodes (*Bumstock*)
Made-for-Cable, minor comedy-fantasy: Boy recruits sasquatch for high-school basketball team

Big, Big and Highest
see **Wielka, Wielka I Najwieksza**

The Big Chance
1957, (GB), Major/RFD, b&w, 61 mins.
W: Adrienne Corri (*Diana*), William Russell (*Bill*), Ian Colin (*Adam*), Penelope
    Bartley (*Betty*), John Rae (*Jarvis*), Ferdy Mayne (*Alpherghis*), Douglas Ives
    (*Stan Willett*), Robert Raglan (*The Inspector*)
P: John Temple-Smith & Francis Edge   **D & SCR:** Peter Graham Scott, from a
    novel by Pamela Barrington
Standard crime-thriller: Clerk robs travel agency, flees to Panama

The Big Clock
1948, (USA), Para, b&w, 95 mins.
W: Ray Milland (*George Stroud*), Charles Laughton (*Earl Janoth*), Maureen
    O'Sullivan (*Georgette Stroud*), Rita Johnson (*Pauline York*), George Macready
    (*Steve Hagen*), Elsa Lanchester (*Louise Patterson*), Harold Vermilyea (*Don
    Klausmeyer*), Dan Tobin (*Roy Cordette*), Hen-ry (Harry) Morgan (*Bill
    Womack*), Elaine Riley (*Lily Gold*), Richard Webb (*Nat Sperling*), Luis Van
    Rooten (*Edwin Orlin*), Frank Orth (*Burt*), Bobby Watson (*Morton Spaulding*),
    Margaret Field (Later Maggie Mahoney) (*The 2nd Sec'y*), Philip Van Zandt
    (*Sidney Kislav*), Henri Letondal (*The Antique Dealer*), Douglas Spencer (*Bert
    Finch*), B.G. Norman (*George Jr.*), Joey Ray (*Joe Talbot*), James Burke
    (*O'Brien*), Frances Morris (*Grace Adams*), Lucille Barkley (*The Hatcheck Girl*),
    Harry Rosenthal (*Charlie*), Erno Verebes (*The Waiter*), Lloyd Corrigan, Noel
    Neill
P: Richard Maibaum   **D:** John Farrow   **SCR:** Jonathan Latimer, from Kenneth
    Fearing's novel   **PHOTOG:** John F. Seitz   **SPCL-FX:** Gordon Jennings
    MUSIC: Victor Young
*Classic film-puzzle, complicated thriller: Magnate kills his mistress, inadvertently impli-
    cates innocent employee. cf.* **No Way Out**

The Big Cube
1969, (USA-Mex), WB, color
W: Lana Turner, Richard Egan, Karin Mossberg, George Chakiris, Regina Thorne,
    Dan O'Herlihy

P: Lindsley Parsons **D:** Tito Davison **SCR:** William Douglas Lansford
Minor thriller: Retired actress lands in asylum after stepdaughter spikes her sedatives with LSD

Big Duel in the North
see Ebirah, Horror of the Deep

Big Foot
1972, (USA), Ellman Enterprises, color
W: Chris Mitchum, John Carradine, Joi Lansing, Lindsay Crosby, Ken Maynard, John Mitchum, Doodles Weaver, Haji
P: Anthony Cardoza **D:** Robert F. Slatzer **SCR:** James Gordon White & Robert F. Slatzer
Minor horror-thriller: Missing link seeks human women for breeding purposes

Bigfoot: The Unforgettable Encounter
1994, (USA), color, 89 mins.
W: Zachary Ty Brown, Matt McCoy, Barbara Willis Sweete, Clint Howard, Rance Howard, David Rasche
D & SCR: Corey Michael Eubanks **MUSIC:** Shimon Arama
Standard SF-thriller: Boy meets sasquatch

The Big Frame
see The Lost Hours

The Big Funk
see Tender Dracula

The Big Game
1972, (USA), Atlantic Film & Comet Film, color
W: Stephen Boyd, Ray Milland, France Nuyen, Cameron Mitchell, Brendon Boone, John Stacy, John Van Dreelen, Ian Yule, George Wang, Michael Kirner, Bill Brewer
P: Stanley Norman **D:** Robert Day, from Ralph Anders' novel *The Two Sides* **PHOTOG:** Mario Fioretti **SONG:** *Tomorrow is Another Land*
Minor thriller: Spies seek thought-control device

Biggles: Adventures in Time
1986, (GB), Compact Yellowbill, color, 90 mins.
W: Neil Dickson, Alex Hyde-White, Fiona Hutchison, Peter Cushing
D: John Hough **SCR:** John Groves & Kent Walwin, from characters created by Capt. W.E. Johns **PHOTOG:** Ernest Vincze **MUSIC:** Stanislas
Minor adventure-fantasy: Man time-travels to World War I

Big Ben's Dream of Greatness
1912, (GB), Britannia Films/Pathe, b&w, 660 ft. (201.2m)
D: A.E. Coleby
Standard fantasy: Man dreams he is Caesar, awakens with power to change objects

The Big Heart
see Miracle on 34th Street (1947)

Big Meat Eater
1985, (USA), color, 81 mins.
W: George Dawson, Big Miller, Andrew Gillies
D: Chris Windsor
Standard musical gore-comedy: Space aliens use butcher's radioactive discards for ship fuel

The Big Sleep
1946, (USA), WB, b&w, 114 mins.
W: Humphrey Bogart, Lauren Bacall, John Ridgely, Martha Vickers, Elisha Cook Jr., Dorothy Malone, Peggy Knudsen, Charles Waldron, Regis Toomey, Bob Steele, Charles D. Brown
P & D: Howard Hawks **SCR:** William Faulkner, Leigh Brackett & Jules Furthman, from Raymond Chandler's novel **PHOTOG:** Sidney Hickox **MUSIC:** Max Steiner
Classic thriller: Wealthy invalid hires gumshoe to help with wayward daughter, plot thickens

The Big Sleep
1978, (GB), Winkast/ITC, color, 99 mins.
W: Robert Mitchum (*Philip Marlowe*), Sarah Miles (*Charlotte Regan*), Richard Boone (*Lash Canino*), Candy Clark (*Camilla Sternwood*), Joan Collins (*Agnes Lozelle*), Edward Fox (*Joe Brody*), John Mills (*Insp. Jim Carson*), James Stewart (*Gen. Guy Sternwood*), Oliver Reed (*Eddie Mars*), Richard Todd (*Cdr. Barker*), Harry Andrews (*Vincent Norris*), Colin Blakely (*Harry Jones*), Diana Quick (*Mona Mars*), James Donald (*Insp. Gregory*), John Justin (*Arthur Geiger*), Simon Turner (*Karl Lundgren*), Martin Potter (*Owen Taylor*), David Saville (*Rusty Regan*), Dudley Sutton (*Lanny*), David Jackson (*Rusty Willis*), Norman Lumsden (*Lord Smethurst*), Don Henderson (*Lou*), Joe Ritchie (*The Taxi Driver*), Nik Forster (*The Croupier*), Patrick Durkin (*Reg*), Derek Deadman (*The Man in the Bookstore*)
D & SCR: Michael Winner, from Raymond Chandler's novel **PHOTOG:** Robert Paynter **MUSIC:** Jerry Fielding
Minor remake of classic thriller: Detective investigates blackmailer's murder

The Big Switch
1968, (GB), Pete Walker/Miracle, color, 81 mins.
W: Sebastian Breaks (*John Carter*), Virginia Wetherell (*Karen*), Erika Raffael (*Samantha*), Jack Allen (Hornsby Smith), Roy Stone (*Al*), Derek Aylward (*Carl Mendez*), Douglas Blackwell (*Bruno*), Julie Shaw (*Cathy*), Jane Howard

(*Jane*), Tracey Yorke (*A Stripper*), Lena Ellis (*A Stripper*), Brian Weske (*Mike*)
WRIT, P & D: Pete Walker
Standard crime-thriller: Plot to kill playboy, replace him with gangster. A.k.a. Strip Poker

Big Town After Dark
1947, (USA), Para, b&w, 69 mins.
W: Philip Reed, Hillary Brooke
Minor melodrama

Big Trouble in Little China
1986, (USA), Taft-Barish-Monash/20th-Fox, color, 98 mins.
W: Kurt Russell (*Jack Burton*), Kim Cattrall (*Gracie Law*), Dennis Dun (*Wang Chi*), James Hong (*Lo Pan*), Suzie Pai (*Miao Yin*), Al Leong (*Wing Kong*), Victor Wong, Kate Burton, Jeff Imada, Donald Li
D & MUS: John Carpenter **SCR:** Gary Goldman & David Weinstein **ADAPT:** W.D. Richter **PHOTOG:** Dean Cundey **VS-FX:** Richard Edlund
Standard fantasy-adventure: Truck driver opposes ancient Chinese magician

The Big World of Little Children
see Wielka, Wielka I Najwieksza

Bikini Genie
see Wildest Dreams

Bill and Coo
1948, (USA), Rep, color, 61 mins.
D: Dean Riesner
Ken Murray's Oscar-winner: Two lovebirds threatened by crow

Bill & Ted's Bogus Journey
1991, (USA), Orion, color, 98 mins.
W: Keanu Reeves (*Ted*), Alex Winter (*Bill*), William Sadler (*Death*), George Carlin (*Rufus*), Joss Ackland (*De Nomolos*), Hal Landon Jr. (*Capt. Logan*), Pam Grier (*Mrs. Wardroe*), Dennis C. Ott, Amy Stock-Poynton, Annette Acuy, Sarah Trigger, Chelcie Ross, Roy Brocksmith, Taj Mahal, William Shatner
D: Peter Hewitt **SCR:** Ed Solomon & Chris Matheson **PHOTOG:** Oliver Wood **MUSIC:** David Newman
Standard comedy-fantasy: Teens time-travel, meet Grim Reaper

Bill & Ted's Excellent Adventure
1989, (USA), Interscope/Nelson/Orion, color, 90 mins.
W: Keanu Reeves (*Ted Logan*), Alex Winter (*Bill S. Preston*), George Carlin (*Rufus*), Dan Shor, Tony Steedman
D: Stephen Herek **SCR:** Chris Matheson & Ed Solomon **PHOTOG:** Timothy Suhrstedt **MUSIC:** David Newman **SONGS:** *I Can't Break Away*
Standard comedy-fantasy: Teens time-travel, meet great figures of history

Billiards Mad
1912, (GB), Hepworth, b&w, 400 ft. (121.9m)
D: Frank Wilson
Minor comedy-fantasy short: Man dreams of playing billiards in unlikely places

Billion Dollar Brain
1967, (GB), Jivara-Lowndes/UA, color, 111 mins.
W: Michael Caine (*Harry Palmer*), Karl Malden (*Leo Newbigen*), Ed Begley (*Gen. Midwinter*), Oscar Homolka (*Col. Stok*), Milo Sperber (*Basil*), Guy Doleman (*Col. Ross*), Francoise Dorleac (*Anya*), Vladek Sheybal (*Dr. Eiwort*), Donald Sutherland (*The Scientist*), Mark Elwes (*Birkinshaw*), Susan George (*The Girl*), Janos Kurutz, Paul Tamarin, Alexei Jawdokimov, Gregg Palmer, Iza Teller, Stanley Caine, John Herrington, Fred Griffiths, Hans De Vries, John Brandon, Tony Harwood, George Roubicek, Peter Forest, Michael Stayner, Alex Marchevsky, James Woolf, Brandon Brady, Reed de Rouen, Miki Iveria, Jill Mai Meredith, Mark Moss, Dolly Brennan, Frederick Schrecker, Bill Mitchell, Steve Emerson, Max Kirby
P: Albert Saltzman **D:** Ken Russell **SCR:** John McGrath, from Len Deighton's novel **PHOTOG:** Billy Williams **MUSIC:** Richard Rodney Bennett
Modest spy-thriller: Secret agent finds intrigue in Finland

Billion Dollar Threat
1979, (USA), ABC-TV, color
W: Dale Robinette (*Robert Sands*), Patrick Macnee (*Horatio Black*), Beth Specht (*Holly*), Keenan Wynn (*Ely*), Ronnie Carol (*Marcia*), Ralph Bellamy (*Miles Larson*), Stephen Keep (*Darling*), Karen Specht (*Ivy*), Robert Tessier (*Benjamin*), William Bryant (*Harry*)
TVM, minor SF-thriller: Agent probes Utah UFO sightings

Billy the Kid vs. Dracula
1966, (USA), Circle/Embassy, color, 72 mins.
W: Chuck Courtney (*Billy the Kid*), John Carradine (*Dracula*), Melinda Plowman (*Betty Bentley*), Virginia Christine, Marjorie Bennett, Bing Russell, George Cisar, Charlita, William Forrest, Olive Carey, Harry Carey Jr., Hannie Landman, Lennie Geer, Roy Barcroft, Jack Williams, Walter Janovitz, Richard Reeves, William Challee, Max Kleven
P: Carroll Case **D:** William Beaudine **SCR:** Karl Hittleman **PHOTOG:** Lothrop Worth **MUSIC:** Raoul Kraushaar
Minor horror-thriller: Reforming gunslinger discovers girlfriend's uncle is vampire

Bio-Dome

1996, (USA), Weasel/3 Arts/MGM, color, 94 mins.
W: Henry Gibson, Kevin West, Denise Dowse, Pauly Shore, Stephen Baldwin, William Atherton, Joey Adams, Kylie Minogue, Teresa Hill, Dara Tomanovich, Patricia Hearst
D: Jason Bloom   **SCR:** Kip Koenig & Scott Marcano   **STORY:** Adam Leff, Mitchell Peck & Jason Blumenthal   **PHOTOG:** Phedon Papamichael
MUSIC: Andrew Gross
blurb: "The fate of our planet is in their hands"
Standard SF-comedy: Nerds cause havoc in biosphere lab

Bio-Force I

1995, (USA), color, 100 mins.
W: Ted Prior, Denise Crosby, Leo Rossi, Powers Boothe, Wilford Brimley
D & CO-SCR: David A. Prior
*video retitle, **Mutant Species***
Standard SF-horror: Biological weapon contaminates soldiers

Biohazard

1984, (USA), 21st Century, color, 84 mins.
W: Aldo Ray, Angelique Pettyjohn, Bill Faire, Loren Crabtree, Richard Hench, Carol Borland
D: Fred Olen Ray
Minor SF-horror: Parallel universe found, monster released

Biohazard: The Alien Force

1995, (USA), color, 88 mins.
W: Steve Zurk, Chris Mitchum, Susan Fronsoe, Tom Ferguson, Patrick Moran, John Maynard
D: Steve Latshaw
Minor SF-horror: Reptilian mutant hunted

Bionic Ever After ?

1994, (USA), color, 95 mins.
W: Lee Majors, Lindsay Wagner
TVM, minor SF-thriller: Spies and terrorists disrupt marriage of bionic man and woman

The Bionic Woman

1975, (USA), color, 96 mins.
W: Lindsay Wagner, Lee Majors, Richard Anderson, Alan Oppenheimer
D: Richard Moder
TVM (teleseries pilot), standard SF-adventure: Injured tennis pro gets rebuilt body

The Birds

1963, (USA), Univ, color, 120 mins.
W: Rod Taylor *(Mitch Brenner)*, Tippi Hedren *(Melanie Daniels)*, Jessica Tandy *(Lydia Brenner)*, Suzanne Pleshette *(Annie Hayworth)*, Veronica Cartwright *(Cathy Brenner)*, Ethel Griffies *(Mrs. Bundy)*, Ruth McDevitt *(Mrs. MacGruder)*, Charles McGraw *(Sebastian Sholes)*, Joe Mantell, Elizabeth Wilson, Doreen Lang, Karl Swenson, John McGovern, Malcolm Atterbury, Lonny Chapman, Doodles Weaver, Richard Deacon
P & D: Alfred Hitchcock   **SCR:** Evan Hunter. loosely based on Daphne du Maurier's short story   **PHOTOG:** Robert Burks   **SPCL-FX:** Lawrence Hampton   **SOUND CONSULTANT:** Bernard Herrmann
"Hitchcock at the height of his artistic powers"—Andrew Sarris, Sight and Sound
"Enough to make you kick the next pigeon you come across"—Judith Crist
Impressive SF-thriller: Birds of world attack mankind

The Birds II: Land's End

1994, (USA), SHO-TV, color, 83 mins.
W: Brad Johnson, Chelsea Field, Tippi Hedren
Made-for-Cable, standard thriller: Feathered fiends mount new attack on humans

Birds Do It

1966, (USA), Col, color, 88 mins.
W: Soupy Sales *(Melvyn Byrd)*, Tab Hunter *(Porter)*, Arthur O'Connell *(Prof. Wald)*, Edward Andrews, Beverly Adams, Doris Dowling, Louis Quinn
P: Stanley Colbert   **D:** Andrew Marton   **SCR:** Archie Kogen & Art Arthur   **STORY:** Leonard Kaufman   **PHOTOG:** Howard Winner   **MUSIC:** Samuel Matlovsky
Juvenile fantasy: Young man acquires ability to fly

Birds of Prey

1930, (GB), ATP/Radio, b&w, 98 mins.
W: Robert Loraine *(Carter)*, Warwick Ward *(Laverick)*, C. Aubrey Smith *(Arthur Hilton)*, Frank Lawton *(Jimmy Hilton)*, Dorothy Boyd *(Mollie)*, Ellis Jeffrys *(Mrs. Green)*, Nigel Bruce *(The Manager)*, Jack Hawkins *(Alfred)*, David Hawthorne, Tom Reynolds
P &D: Basil Dean   **SCR:** A.A. Milne & Basil Dean, from A.A. Milne's play *The Fourth Wall*
*USA retitle, **The Perfect Alibi***
Standard thriller: Young couple solves murder in country house

The Bird with the Crystal Plumage

see L'Uccello delle Piume di Cristallo

Birgitt Haas Must be Killed

1983, (Fr), color, 105 mins.
W: Philippe Noiret, Jean Rochefort, Elisabeth Kreuzer

D: Laurent Heynemann
Standard thriller: German female terrorist marked for death

The Birthday Present

1957, (GB), Whittingham/British Lion, b&w, 100 mins.
W: Tony Britton *(Simon Scott)*, Sylvia Syms *(Jean Scott)*, Jack Watling *(Bill Thompson)*, Geoffrey Keen *(Col. Wilson)*, Walter Fitzgerald *(Sir John Dell)*, Howard Marion Crawford *(George Bates)*, David Hutcheson *(Traveller)*, John Welsh *(The Customs Officer)*, Thorley Walters *(Bunch)*, Richard Leech *(Hawkins)*, Ian Bannen *(The Ass't)*, Ralph Michael *(Crowther)*
P: George Pitcher & Jack Whittingham   **D:** Pat Jackson   **STORY:** Jack Whittingham
Standard crime-thriller: Toy salesman smuggles watches

The Birth of the Robot

1936, (GB), Shell-Mex, color, 6 mins.
D: Len Lye   **MUSIC:** Holst
Fantasy short: Automaton amazes

The Bishop Murder Case

1930, (USA), MGM, b&w, 91 mins.
W: Basil Rathbone *(Philo Vance)*, Leila Hyams *(Belle Dillard)*, Roland Young *(Arneson)*, George Marion *(Adolph Drukker)*, Alec B. Francis *(Prof. Bertrand Dillard)*, Bodil Rosing *(Grete Menzel)*, Zelda Sears *(Miss Drukker)*, Carroll Nye *(John E. Sprigg)*, Charles Quartermaine *(John Pardee)*, James Donlan *(Sgt. Ernest Heath)*, Sidney Bracy *(Pyne)*, Clarence Geldert *(D.A. John F.X. Markham)*, Delmer Daves *(Raymond Sperling)*, Nellie Bly Baker *(Beddle)*
D: Nick Grinde & David Burton   **SCR:** Lenore J. Coffee, from characters created by S.S. Van Dine   **PHOTOG:** Roy Overbaugh
Standard "Philo Vance" mystery-thriller: Suave sleuth seeks assassin known as "The Bishop"

The Bishop's Silence

1914, (GB), Regent/MP, b&w, 3,000 ft. (914.4m)
W: Arthur Finn *(Bishop Lawrence)*, Rowland Moore, Gordon Begg, Cissie Elen
P: Charles Weston & Arthur Finn   **D:** Charles Finn
Standard crime-thriller: Bishop dies after confessing he framed actor for murder of seduced girl's father

The Bishop's Wife

1947, (USA), RKO, b&w, 108 mins.
W: Cary Grant *(Dudley)*, Loretta Young *(Julia Brougham)*, David Niven *(Bishop Henry Brougham)*, Monty Woolley *(Prof. Wutheridge)*, Elsa Lanchester *(Matilda)*, Gladys Cooper *(Mrs. Hamilton)*, James Gleason *(Sylvester)*, Sara Haden, Regis Toomey, Tito Vuolo, Karolyn Grimes, Isabel Jewell, Erville Alderson, Teddy Infuhr, Almira Sessions
P: Samuel Goldwyn   **D:** Henry Koster   **SCR:** Robert E. Sherwood & Leonardo Bercovici, from Robert Nathan's novel   **PHOTOG:** Gregg Toland   **SPCL-FX:** John P. Fulton   **MUSIC:** Hugo Friedhofer   **MUSIC DIR:** Emil Newman
*Modest fantasy: Angel aids cleric and his wife. cf. **The Preacher's Wife***

Bits of Life

1921, (USA), First Nat'l, b&w, 6 reels (6,339 ft./1932m)
W: Lon Chaney Sr. *(Chin Gow)*, Rockliffe Fellowes *(Tom Levitt)*, Wesley Barry *(Tom Levitt, a Boy)*, Noah Beery *(The Hindoo)*, Anna May Wong *(Chin Gow's Wife)*, John Bowers *(The Dentist's Patient)*, Teddy Sampson, Dorothy Mackaill, Tammany Young, Edythe Chapman, Frederick Burton, Scott Welsh, James Bradbury Jr., Harriet Hammond, James Neill
D: Marshall A. Neilan   **SCR:** Lucita Squier   **PHOTOG:** David Kesson
Standard anthology of 4 melodramas (Chaney episode concerns Chinaman who plots murder of wife and unwanted daughter)

Bittersweet

see The Shock (1923)

B.J. Lang Presents

1971, (USA), CoBurt Prods./Maron, color, 85 mins.
W: Mickey Rooney, Keenan Wynn, Luana Anders   **D & SCR:** Yabo Yablonsky, from a story by John Durin
Minor thriller: Insane ex-movie director acts out fantasies, terrorizes girl

The Black Abbot

1934, (GB), Real Art/Radio, b&w, 56 mins.
W: John Stuart *(Frank Brooks)*, Judy Kelly *(Sylvia Hillcrist)*, Richard Cooper *(Lord Jerry Pilkdown)*, Drusilla Wills *(Mary Hillcrist)*, Ben Welden *(Charlie Marsh)*, Edgar Norfolk *(Brian Heslewood)*, Farren Soutar *(John Hillcrist)*, Cyril Smith *(Alf Higgins)*, John Turnbull *(Insp. Lockwood)*
D: George A. Cooper   **SCR:** H. Fowler Mear, from Philip Godfrey's novel *The Grange Mystery*
Standard thriller: Crooks hold rich man for ransom

The Black Abbot

1961, (W. Ger), CCC, b&w, 95 mins
W: Joachim Fuchsberger, Dieter Borsche, Gritt Bottcher
translated Der Schwarze Abbot
Standard thriller: Mysterious killer strikes

Black and White

1913, (GB), H&W Films, b&w, 350 ft. (106.7m)

D: Stuart Kinder
Minor fantasy short: Boy's magic powder turns black objects white

Black Angel
1946, (USA), Univ, b&w, 80 mins.
W: Dan Duryea, June Vincent, Wallace Ford, Broderick Crawford, Peter Lorre, Constance Dowling, Hobart Cavanaugh, John Banner, Ben Bard, Freddie Steele
P: Tom McKnight & Roy William Neill   D: Roy William Neill   SCR: Roy Chanslor, from Cornell Woolrich's novel   PHOTOG: Paul Ivano   MUSIC: Frank Skinner
Intense mystery: Blacked-out alcoholic accused of murder

Black Angel
1980, (GB), Painted Lady/Fox, color, 25 mins.
W: Tony Vogel (*Sir Maddox*), James Gibb (*Anselm*), Patricia Christian (*The Maiden*), John Young (*The Old Man*)
P: Roger Christian & Leslie Dilley   WRIT & D: Roger Christian   PHOTOG: Roger Pratt   MUSIC: Trevor Jones
Standard short fantasy: Knight fights to free magic maiden from phantom's thrall

Black Art
see *Magie Diabolique*

Blackbeard's Ghost
1967, (USA), Walt Disney/Buena Vista, color, 107 mins.
W: Peter Ustinov, Dean Jones, Suzanne Pleshette, Richard Deacon, Elsa Lanchester
D: Robert Stevenson   SCR: Bill Walsh & Don DaGradi   PHOTOG: Edward Colman   MUSIC: Robert F. Brunner
Ponderous comedy-fantasy: Pirate returns as ghost, aids old ladies running hotel

Blackbeard the Pirate
1952, (USA), RKO, color, 99 mins.
W: Robert Newton (*Blackbeard*), Linda Darnell (*Edwina*), Keith Andes (*Maynard*), William Bendix (*Worley*), Torin Thatcher (*Sir Henry Morgan*), Richard Egan (*Briggs*), Irene Ryan (*Alvina*), Alan Mowbray (*Noll*), Skelton Knaggs (*Gilly*), Anthony Caruso (*Pierre La Garde*), Dick Wessel (*Dutchman*), Jack Lambert (*Tom Whetstone*), Noel Drayton (*Jeremy*), Pat Flaherty (*Job Maggot*)
D: Raoul Walsh   SCR: Alan LeMay   PHOTOG: William E. Snyder   MUSIC: Victor Young
Modest adventure-thriller: Wicked buccaneer keeps girl captive

The Black Belly of the Tarantula
1972, (It), MGM, color, 88 mins.
W: Giancarlo Giannini (*The Inspector*), Stefania Sandrelli (*Anna*), Claudine Auger (*Laura*), Barbara Bouchet (*Maria Zani*), Rossella Falk (*The Woman with the Mole*), Silvano Tranquilli (*Paolo*), Annabella Incontrera (*Mirta*), Barbara Bach (*Jenny*), Ezio Marano (*The Masseur*), Giancarlo Prete (*Mario*), Anna Saia (*Amica*), Eugene Walter (*The Waiter*), Nino Vingelli (*The Commisario*), Daniele Dublino (*The Entymologist*), Carla Mancini (*The Beauty Parlor Client*), Fulvio Mingozzi (*The Director of the Clinic*), Giuseppe Fortis (*The Psychiatrist*), Guerrino Crivello (*The Informer*), Giorgio Dolfin (*The Policeman*)
P: Marcello Danon   D: Paolo Cavara   SCR: Lucile Laks   STORY: Marcello Danon   PHOTOG: Marcello Gatti   MUSIC: Ennio Morricone
Standard thriller: Mysterious murders baffle

The Black Bird
1926, (USA), MGM, b&w, 7 reels (6,688 ft./2038.5m)
W: Lon Chaney Sr. (*The Black Bird/The Bishop of Limehouse*), Renee Adoree (*Fifi*), Owen Moore (*West End Bertie*), Doris Lloyd (*Polly*), Andy MacLennan (*Ghost*), William Weston (*Red*), Eric Mayne (*A Sightseer*), Sidney Bracy (*Bertie's #1 Man*), Ernie S. Adams (*Bertie's #2 Man*), Lionel Belmore, Billy Mack, Peggy Best
D & STORY: Tod Browning   ADAPT: Waldemar Young   PHOTOG: Percy Hilburn
Standard melodrama: Limehouse gangsters vie for girl's affections

The Black Bird
1975, (USA), Col, color, 98 mins.
W: George Segal (*Sam Spade Jr.*), Stephane Audran (*Anna Kemidon*), Lionel Stander (*Andrew Jackson Immelman*), Lee Patrick (*Effie Cook*), Elisha Cook Jr. (*Wilmer Cook*), Felix Silla (*Litvak*), Signe Hasso (*Dr. Crippen*), John Abbott (*Du Quai*), Connie Kreski (*The Girl*), Ken Swafford (*Brad McGregor*), Richard B. Small (*Prizer*), Howard Jeffrey (*Kerkorian*), Titus Napoleon, Harry Kenoi
D: David Giler   SCR: David Giler, Don Mankiewicz & George Cotler, inspired by Dashiell Hammett's novel *The Maltese Falcon*   PHOTOG: Philip Lathrop   MUSIC: Jerry Fielding
Minor mystery-comedy: Dangerous hunt for fabulous statue

The Black Book
1949, (USA), Eagle Lion, b&w, 91 mins.
W: Robert Cummings, Arlene Dahl, Richard Basehart, Norman Lloyd, Beulah Bondi, Arnold Moss, Richard Hart
D: Anthony Mann   SCR: Philip Yordan & Aeneas Mackenzie   PHOTOG: John Alton   MUSIC: Sol Kaplan
GB and US retitle, **Reign of Terror**
Modest mystery-adventure: Intrigue surrounds cryptic volume during dark days of French Revolution

The Black Buccaneer
see *Rage of the Buccaneers*

Black Butterflies
1953, (Mex), b&w
Minor melodrama

The Black Camel
1931, (USA), Fox, b&w, 71 mins.
W: Victor Varconi, Warner Oland (*Charlie Chan*), Sally Eilers (*Julie O'Neil*), Bela Lugosi (*Tarnevero*), Dorothy Revier (*Shela Fane*), Robert Young (*Jimmy Bradshaw*), C. Henry Gordon (*Van Horn*), Marjorie White (*Rita Ballou*), Richard Tucker (*Wilkie Ballou*), William Post Jr. (*Alan Jaynes*), J.M. Kerrigan (*Thomas MacMaster*), Mary Gordon (*Mrs. MacMaster*), Violet Dunn (*Anna*), Dwight Frye (*Jessop*), Murray Kinnell (*Smith*), Otto Yamaoka (*Kashimo*), Rita Roselle (*Luana*), Robert Homans (*The Chief of Police*), Louise Mackintosh (*The Housekeeper*)
D: Hamilton MacFadden   SCR: Hugh Strange, Barry Connors, & Philip Klein, from characters created by Earl Derr Biggers   PHOTOG: Dan Clark
Standard "Charlie Chan" mystery: Swami helps Oriental detective solve puzzling case

Black Carrion
1985, (GB), Hammer/Fox MysteryTheatre, Made for TV, color, 69 mins.
W: Season Hubley (*Cora*), Leigh Lawson (*Paul*)
TVM, minor thriller: Investigation into odd disappearance of 1960s rock group

The Black Castle
1952, (USA), Univ, b&w, 81 mins.
W: Boris Karloff (*Dr. Meissen*), Richard Greene (*Beckett*), Paula (Rita) Corday (*Elga*), Stephen McNally (*Von Bruno*), Michael Pate (*Herr von Melcher*), John Hoyt (*Herr Stieken*), Lon Chaney Jr. (*Gargon*), Henry Corden (*Fender*), Tudor Owen (*Romley*), Otto Waldis (*Krantz*), Nancy Valentine
P: William Alland   D: Nathan Juran   SCR: Jerry Sackheim   PHOTOG: Irving Glassberg   MUSIC: Joseph Gershenson
French retitle, **The Mystery of the Black Castle**
Modest thriller: Evil excesses in Black Forest castle of mad count

The Black Cat
1934, (USA), Univ, b&w, 66 mins.
W: Boris Karloff (*Hjalmar Poelzig*), Bela Lugosi (*Dr. Vitus Verdegast*), David Manners (*Peter Alison*), Jacqueline Wells [later Julie Bishop], Lucille Lund, Egon Brecher, Anna Duncan, Albert Conti, Andre Cheron, Henry Armetta, Alphonse Martell, Harry Cording, Tony Marlow, George Davis, Paul Weige, John Carradine (aka Peter Richmond)
P: E.M. Asher   D: Edgar G. Ulmer   SCR: Peter Ruric, inspired by Edgar Allan Poe's short story   PHOTOG: John Mescall   MUSIC: Heinz Roemheld
reissed (1947) as **The Vanishing Body**
GB retitle, **The House of Doom**
"...the story...is a sadistically 'sick' and complicated one. Karloff—who marries both Lugosi's wife and his daughter (consecutively, not concurrently)— winds up as Bela's son-in law. Thus, Bela's ultimate revenge (skinning Karloff alive on an embalming rack, prior to blowing him up) is not only medically drastic, but paternally tactless, to say the least"—William K. Everson, Classics of the Horror Film
Classic thriller: Revenge and satanism in eastern Europe

The Black Cat
1941, (USA), Univ, b&w, 70 mins.
W: Basil Rathbone, Broderick Crawford, Hugh Herbert, Anne Gwynne, Bela Lugosi, Gale Sondergaard, Cecilia Loftus, John Eldredge, Claire Dodd, Gladys Cooper, Alan Ladd
ASSOC-P: Burt Kelly   D: Albert S. Rogell   SCR: Robert Lees, Frederic Rinaldo, Robert Neville & Eric Taylor   PHOTOG: Stanley Cortez   SPCL-FX: John P. Fulton
Minor comedy-thriller: Rich cat-fancier stirs conflict with her last will and testament

The Black Cat
1965, (USA), Falcon-Int'l, b&w
W: Robert Frost, Robyn Bider, Sadie French
P: Patrick Simms   D & SCR: Harold Hoffman, loosely based on Edgar Allan Poe's short story
Minor fantasy-thriller: Ghostly feline avenges itself on sadistic master

The Black Cat
1980, (It), Selenia/World Northal, color, 90 mins.
W: Patrick Magee (*Miles*), Mimsy Farmer (*Jill*), David Warbeck (*Insp. Gorley*), Al Cliver, Dagmar Lassander, Daniela Dorio, Bruno Corazzari, Geoffrey Copleston
D: Lucio Fulci   SCR: Biaggio Proietti & Lucio Fulci   STORY: Biaggio Proietti, inspired by Edgar Allan Poe's short story   PHOTOG: Sergio Salvati   SPCL-FX: Paolo Ricci   MUSIC: Pino Donaggio   MUSIC DIR: Natale Massara
blurb:"When you hear this cat breathing down your neck start praying...before you finish your Amen...you're dead!"
Minor horror-thriller: Parapsychologist tries to contact Dead; demonic pet spreads terror

The Black Cat
1990, (USA), color, 119 mins.

W: Caroline Munro, Brett Halsey
D & SCR: Luigi Cozzi
Minor horror-fantasy: Vengeful witch stalks film crew

The Black Cauldron
1985, (USA), Walt Disney, color, 80 mins.
VOICES: Grant Bardsley, Susan Sheridan, Freddie Jones, John Byner, John Hurt
D: Ted Berman & Richard Rich
Standard animated fantasy

Black Christmas
see Silent Night, Evil Night

The Black Circle Gang
1916, (GB), British Oak/New Agency, b&w, 1,090 ft. (332.2m)
D: Ernest G. Batley
Standard crime-thriller: Detective thwarts Chinaman's plans to rob solicitor

Black Cloak
see Dark Intruder

The Black Cobra
1961, (W. Ger), b&w
W: Adrian Hoven, Ann Smyrner
Minor thriller: Detective tracks mysterious killer

The Black Cross Gang
1914, (GB), B&C/DFSA, b&w, 1,828 ft. (557.2m)
W: Lillian Wiggins (*The Gypsy*), Fred Morgan (*Dr. Kish*)
WRIT & D: James Youngdeer
Standard crime-thriller: Gang kidnaps doctor for safe's combination; gypsy girl saves him

The Black Crown
see La Corona Negra

Black Day Blue Night
1995, (USA), color, 100 mins.
W: Gil Bellows, Michelle Forbes
Made-for-Video, standard thriller: Two women join forces with sinister stranger

The Black Devil (1905)
see Le Diable Noir

The Black Devil
1963, (It), Embassy, color
W: Gerard Landry, Milly Vitale
Minor adventure-thriller: Italian "Zorro" fights evil

Black Devil Doll From Hell
1984, (USA), color, 70 mins.
W: Shirley Jones, Rickey Roach
D: Chester Turner
Minor fantasy-thriller (shot-on-video): Voodoo doll kills owners

Black Devils of Kali
1955, (It), Cosmopolitan/Rep, b&w, 72 mins.
W: Lex Barker, Paul Muller, Jane Maxwell, Luigi Tosi, Jack Rex, Pamela Palma
D: Ralph Murphy **SCR:** Ralph Murphy & Jean Paul Callegari, from a novel by Emilio Salgari **MUSIC:** Georges Tzipine & Giovanni Fusco
A.k.a. Mystery of the Black Jungle
Minor adventure-thriller: Sacrifices to bloodthirsty goddess

The Black Doll
1938, (USA), Univ, b&w
W: Nan Grey (*Marion*), Edgar Kennedy (*Renick*), Donald Woods (*Nick*), William Lundigan (*Rex*)
Clever "Crime Club" thriller: Murders center on child's doll

Black Dragons
1942, (USA), Banner/Mono, b&w, 61 mins.
W: Bela Lugosi (*Cologne*), Joan Barclay (*Alice*), Clayton Moore (*Dick Martin*), George Pembroke, Robert Frazer, Max Hoffman Jr., Edward Piel Sr., Robert Fiske, Kenneth Harlan, Irving Mitchell, Frank Melton, Joseph Eggenton, I. Stanford Jolley
P: Sam Katzman & Jack Dietz **D:** William Nigh **SCR:** Harvey M. Gates
Minor horror-thriller: Plastic surgeon disguises Japanese infiltrators

Black Eliminator
see Death Dimension

Blackenstein
1973, (USA), Exclusive Int'l, color, 89 mins.
W: John Hart, Ivory Stone, Andrea King, Liz Renay, Roosevelt Jackson, James Cougar, Cardella Di Milo, Joe De Sue, Andy C., Nick Bolin
A.k.a. Black Frankenstein
Minor "blaxploitation" horror-thriller: Ghetto surgeon performs transplants

Black Flowers for the Bride
see Something for Everyone

Black Frankenstein
see Blackenstein

Black Friday
1940, (USA), Univ, b&w, 70 mins.
W: Boris Karloff, Bela Lugosi, Anne Nagel (*Sunny*), Anne Gwynne (*Jean*), Stanley Ridges (*Kingsley*), Edmund MacDonald (*Miller*), Virginia Brissac (*Margaret*), Jack Mulhall, Manly P. Hall, Joe King, Paul Fix, Murray Alper
D: Arthur Lubin **SCR:** Curt Siodmak & Eric Taylor **PHOTOG:** Elwood Bredell
French retitle, Friday the 13th
Unusual thriller: Doctor puts portion of criminal brain into body of injured college professor

The Black Glove
1954, (UK), Lippert/Hammer/Exclusive, b&w, 84 mins.
W: Alex Nicol, Eleanor Summerfield
Standard melodrama, UK title, Face the Music

The Black Harvest of Countess Dracula
1972, (It), color
Minor horror-thriller: Vampiress spreads woe

The Black Hole
1979, (USA), Walt Disney/Buena Vista, color, 97 mins.
W: Maximilian Schell (*Dr. Hans Reinhardt*), Joseph Bottoms (*Lt. Charles Pizer*), Robert Forster (*Capt. Dan Holland*), Anthony Perkins (*Alex Durant*), Yvette Mimieux (*Kate McCrae*), Ernest Borgnine (*Harry Booth*), Tommy McLoughlin (*Capt. S.T.A.R.*)
P: Ron Miller **D:** Gary Nelson **SCR:** Jeb Rosebrook & Gerry Day. from a story by Jeb Rosebrook, Richard Landau, & Bob Barbash **PHOTOG:** Frank Phillips **MUSIC:** John Barry
Expensive ($20 million) but juvenile SF-fantasy: Nemo-type causes distress on distant space station. Originally to be titled Space Probe

Blackie's Redemption
1919, (USA), Metro, b&w, 5 reels

The Black Room: BORIS KARLOFF AND CATHERINE DeMILLE

W: Bert Lytell (*Boston Blackie*), Alice Lake (*Mary Dawson*), Henry Kolker (*Fred the Count*), Bernard Durning (*Sober Dent*), Jack Duffy (*The Dove*), William Musgrave (*Little Squirrel*), Gertrude Short (*Baby Doll*), Don Daily (*Chief of Detectives*), Wilton Taylor (*Det. Mack*), Joseph Kilgour (*The Warden*), Ah Toy (*The Chinese Waiter*)
D: John Ince **SCR:** Ferris Fox, from a story by Jack Boyle
A.k.a. Boston Blackie's Mary
Standard mystery-thriller: Rogue framed for theft

The Black Imp
see *Le Diable Noir*

The Black Knight
1954, (GB), Warwick/Col, color, 85 mins.
<u>W</u>: Alan Ladd (*John*), Patricia Medina (*Linet*), Andre Morell (*Sir Ontzlake*), Harry Andrews (*Earl of Yeonil*), Ronald Adam (*The Abbot*), Peter Cushing (*Sir Palamides*), Anthony Bushell (*King Arthur*), Laurence Naismith (*The Major Domo*), Patrick Troughton (*King Mark*), Basil Appleby (*Sir Hal*), Jean Lodge (*Queen Guinevere*), John Laurie (*James*), David Paltenghi (*The High Priest*), Elton Hayes (*The Troubadour*), Pauline Jameson (*Lady Yeonil*), Bill Brandon (*Bernard*), Olwen Brookes (*Lady Ontzlake*), Thomas Moore (*The Apprentice*), John Kelly (*The Woodchopper*)
<u>P</u>: Irving Allen, Albert Broccoli, & Phil C. Samuel <u>D</u>: Tay Garnett <u>SCR</u>: Alec Coppel, Dennis O'Keefe, & Bryan Forbes <u>STORY</u>: Alec Coppel <u>PHOTOG</u>: John Wilcox <u>MUSIC</u>: John Addison
reissued 1961
Standard action-adventure: Sword-maker poses as knight, unmasks traitors

Black Limelight
1938, (GB), ABPC/Film Alliance, b&w, 70 mins.
<u>W</u>: Raymond Massey (*Peter Charrington*), Walter Hudd (*Lawrence Crawford*), Joan Marion (*Mary Charrington*), Henry Oscar (*Insp. Tanner*), Coral Browne (*Lily James*), Diana Beaumont (*Gwen*), Elliot Mason (*Jemima*), Dan Tobin (*The Reporter*), Leslie Bradley (*The Detective*), Renee Asherson
<u>D</u>: Paul Stein <u>SCR</u>: Dudley Leslie & Walter Summers, from a play by Gordon Sherry, *reissued 1942*
Standard thriller: Convicted man's wife hunts insane killer

Black Magic (1898)
see *Le Magicien*

Black Magic
1944, (USA), Mono, b&w, 67 mins.
<u>W</u>: Sidney Toler (*Charlie Chan*), Mantan Moreland (*Birmingham Brown*), Joseph Crehan (*Matthews*), Jacqueline de Wit (*Justine Bonner*), Ralph Peters (*Rafferty*), Richard Gordon (*Bonner*), Helen Beverly (*Norma Duncan*), Frank Jacquet (*Paul Hamlin*), Charles Jordan (*Tom Starkey*), Claudia Dell (*Vera Starkey*), Geraldine Wall (*Harriett Green*), Edward Earle (*Dawson*), Harry Depp (*Charles Edwards*)
<u>D</u>: Phil Rosen <u>SCR</u>: George Callahan, from characters created by Earl Derr Biggers <u>PHOTOG</u>: Arthur Martinelli <u>MUSIC</u>: Alexander Laszlo
reissued as Meeting at Midnight
Minor "Charlie Chan" mystery: Oriental sleuth encounters murder and spiritualism

Black Magic
1949, (USA), Edward Small/UA, b&w, 104 mins.
<u>W</u>: Orson Welles (*Cagliostro*), Nancy Guild, Raymond Burr, Akim Tamiroff, Valentina Cortese, Frank Latimore, Silvana Mangano, Margot Grahame, Charles Goldner, Stephen Bekassy
<u>P & D</u>: Gregory Ratoff, Uncredited Director was Orson Welles <u>SCR</u>: Charles Bennett, from Alexandre Dumas' novel *Memoires d'un Medecin (Memoirs of a Doctor)* <u>PHOTOG</u>: Ubaldo Arata & Anchise Brizzi- Filmed in Italy <u>MUSIC</u>: Paul Sawtell
Unusual costume-thriller: Infamous hypnotist tries to supplant Marie Antoinette with innocent girl who is her double

Black Magic
1992, (USA), Made-for-Cable, color, 94 mins.
<u>W</u>: Rachel Ward, Judge Reinhold, Brion James, Anthony LaPaglia
<u>D & TELEPLAY</u>: Daniel Taplitz
Minor thriller: Man suspects lover dabbles in witchcraft

Black Magic II
see *Revenge of the Zombies (1981)*

Black Magic Mansion
1991, (GB), color, 88 mins.
<u>W</u>: Frank Finlay
Minor horror-fantasy: Evil forces unleashed when thugs invade aging magician's eerie estate

Black Magic Woman
1991, (USA), color, 91 mins.
<u>W</u>: Appolonia Kotero (*Cassandra*), Mark Hamill (*Brad*), Amanda Wyss (*Diane*), Gwen Willson, Marilyn Pitzer, Stella Pacific, Phyllis Flax, Elizabeth Robinson, Jaqueline Coon, Abidah Viera, Larry Hankin, Thomas Meurer, F. Cameron MacRae, Bonnie Ebsen, Michael Halpin, Kyle Fredericks, Alan Toy, John Warner Williams, Victor Rivers, Carmen More, John C. Slade, Ray Quiroga, John Reno, Marina Ferrier
<u>D</u>: Deryn Warren <u>SCR</u>: Gerry Daly <u>MUSIC</u>: Randy Miller <u>SONGS</u>: "Listening for Your Love" & "Vintage Love"
Minor horror-fantasy: Innocent bedeviled by evil beauty

Blackmail
1912, (GB), Cricks & Martin, b&w, 1,070 ft. (326.1m)
<u>D</u>: Edwin J. Collins
Standard crime-thriller: Knight saves daughter from clutches of blackmailers

Blackmail
1929, (GB), BIP/Wardour, b&w, 96 mins.
<u>W</u>: Anny Ondra (*Alice White*), John Longden (*Frank Webber*), Sara Allgood (*Mrs. White*), Donald Calthrop (*Tracy*), Cyril Ritchard (*The Artist*), Charles Paton (*Mr. White*), Phyllis Monkman (*The Gossip*), Harvey Braban (*The Inspector*), Johnny Butt (*The Sgt.*), Hannah Jones (*The Landlady*), Percy Parsons (*The Crook*), John Stuart
<u>D</u>: Alfred Hitchcock <u>SCR</u>: Charles Bennett, Benn W. Levy, Garnett Weston, & Alfred Hitchcock, from Charles Bennett's play <u>PHOTOG</u>: Jack Cox <u>MUSIC</u>: Campbell & Connelly
First British "talkie," standard thriller: Detective's fiancee blackmailed

Blackmail
1947, (USA), Rep, b&w, 87 mins.
<u>W</u>: William Marshall, Adele Mara
Standard thriller

Blackmailed
1951, (GB), HH Films/GFD, b&w, 85 mins.
<u>W</u>: Mai Zetterling (*Carol Edwards*), Dirk Bogarde (*Stephen Mundy*), Fay Compton (*Mrs. Christopher*), Robert Flemyng (*Dr. Giles Freeman*), Michael Gough (*Maurice Edwards*), Joan Rice (*Alma*), James Robertson Justice (*Mr. Sine*), Wilfrid Hyde-White (*Lord Dearsley*), Harold Huth (*Hugh Saintsbury*), Bruce Seton (*Supt. Crowe*), Cyril Chamberlain (*The PC*)
<u>P</u>: Harold Huth <u>D</u>: Marc Allegret <u>SCR</u>: Hugh Mills & Roger Vadim, from Elizabeth Myers' novel *Mrs. Christopher*
Standard thriller: Victims of dead blackmailer conspire to conceal crime

The Blackmailer
1907, (GB), Sheffield Photo Co., b&w, 585 ft. (178.3m)
<u>D</u>: Frank Mottershaw
Standard crime-thriller: Detective nabs blackmailer

The Blackmailers
1915, (GB), I.B. Davidson-St. George/LIFT, b&w, 3,000 ft. (914.4m)
<u>W</u>: Arthur Rooke (*John Drew*), Joan Legge (*Pickles*)
<u>D</u>: A.E. Coleby
Standard crime-thriller: Detective escapes pitfalls

Black Market Babies
1945, (USA), Mono, b&w, 71 mins.
<u>W</u>: Ralph Morgan, Jayne Hazard
Minor melodrama

Black Midnight
1949, (USA), Mono, b&w, 68 mins.
<u>W</u>: Roddy McDowall, Damian O'Flynn
<u>D</u>: Oscar "Budd" Boetticher Jr.
Standard melodrama

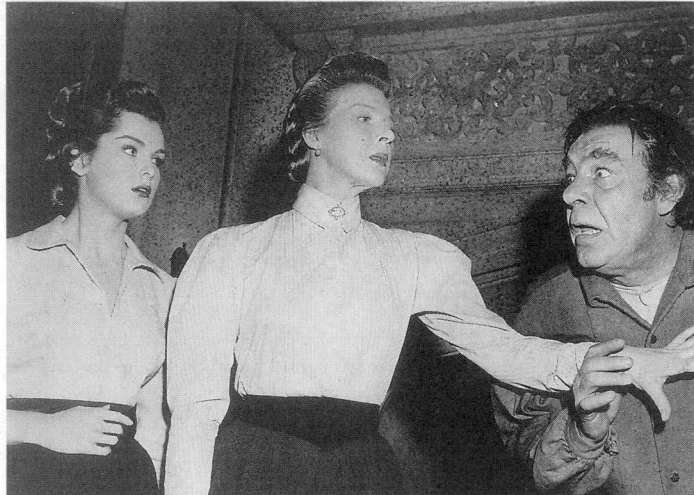

The Black Sleep: PATRICIA BLAKE, PHYLLIS STANLEY AND LON CHANEY JR.

Black Moon
1934, (USA), Col, b&w
<u>W</u>: Fay Wray
Standard melodrama

Black Moon
1975, (Fr-W. Ger), 20th Century-Fox, color, 92 mins.
<u>W</u>: Cathryn Harrison, Therese Giehse, Alexandra Stewart, Joe Dallesandro
<u>D</u>: Louis Malle <u>SCR</u>: Louis Malle, Ghislain Uhry & Joyce Bunuel <u>PHOTOG</u>: Sven Nykvist
Unusual SF-fantasy: Girl flees civil war between men and women

B

Black Narcissus
1947, (GB), Archers/Rank/Walter Reade/IP/U-1, color, 100 mins.
<u>W</u>: Deborah Kerr (*Sister Clodagh*), David Farrar (*Mr. Dean*), Sabu (*Dulip Rai*), Flora Robson (*Sister Philippa*), Kathleen Byron (*Sister Ruth*), Esmond Knight (*The General*), Jenny Laird (*Sister Honey*), Jean Simmons (*Kanchi*), Judith Furse (*Sister Briony*), May Hallatt (*Angu Ayah*), Nancy Roberts (*Mother Dorothea*), Shaun Noble (*Con*)
<u>WRIT, P, & D</u>: Michael Powell & Emeric Pressburger, from Rumer Godden's novel <u>PHOTOG</u>: Jack Cardiff <u>MUSIC</u>: Brian Easdale
Off-beat melodrama: Anglican nuns fall under disquieting spell of Mother India

The Black Night
1916, (GB), Broadwest, b&w, 4,124 ft. (1257m)
<u>W</u>: Gregory Scott (*Lord Dupois*), J.R. Tozer (*Lord Somerdans*)
<u>D & SCR</u>: Harold Weston, from a novel by Andrew Soutar
Standard crime-thriller: Lord assumes identity of dead jewel thief, tries to steal wife's letters back from blackmailer

Black Noon
1971, (USA), Col/Screen Gems, Made for TV, color, 73 mins.
<u>W</u>: Roy Thinnes (*Rev. Jonathan Keyes*), Lyn Loring (*Lorna Keyes*), Ray Milland (*Caleb Hobbes*), Yvette Mimieux (*Deliverance*), Henry Silva (*Moon*), Gloria Grahame (*Bethia*), Hank Worden, William Bryant, Joshua Bryant
<u>D</u>: Bernard L. Kowalski
TVM, standard horror-fantasy: Witchcraft proves rife in small town of Old West

Black Orchid
1953, (GB), Kenilworth/GFD, b&w, 60 mins.
<u>W</u>: Ronald Howard (*Dr. John Winnington*), Olga Edwards (*Christine Shaw*), John Bentley (*Eric Blair*), Mary Laura Wood (*Sophie Winnington*), Patrick Barr (*Vincent Humphries*), Sheila Burrell (*Annette Durrant*), Russell Napier (*Insp. Markham*), Mary Jones (*Mrs. Humphries*)
<u>P</u>: Robert Baker & Monty Berman <u>D</u>: Charles Saunders <u>STORY</u>: John Temple-Smith & Francis Edge
Standard thriller: Doctor accused of poisoning wife

Black Orchids
1916, (USA), Bluebird, b&w, 5 reels
<u>W</u>: Cleo Madison, Wedgewood Nowell, Howard Crampton, Francis McDonald
<u>WRIT & D</u>: Rex Ingram <u>PHOTOG</u>: Duke Hayward
*Standard melodrama. GB retitle, **The Fatal Orchids***

Black Orpheus
1958, (Fr-Brz), Lopert, color, 105 mins.
<u>W</u>: Breno Mello (*Orpheus*), Marpessa Dawn (*Eurydice*), Lourdes de Oliveira, Lea Garcia, Maria Alica
<u>P</u>: Sacha Gordini <u>D</u>: Marcel Camus <u>PHOTOG</u>: Jean Bourgoin <u>THEME</u>: *A Day in the Life of a Fool*
Celebrated fantasy-melodrama: Confusion of Carnival frames re-telling of Orpheus & Eurydice legend

Blackout (1955)
*see **Murder by Proxy***

Blackout
1978, (Fr-Can), New World, color, 89 mins.
<u>W</u>: Robert Carradine (*Christie*), Jim Mitchum (*Dan*), Ray Milland (*Mr. Stafford*), Jean-Pierre Aumont (*Henry Lee*), June Allyson (*Mrs. Grant*), Belinda Montgomery (*Annie*)
<u>P</u>: Nicole Boisuert & Eddy Matalon <u>D</u>: Eddy Matalon <u>SCR</u>: John Saxton <u>PHOTOG</u>: J.J. Tarbes <u>MUSIC</u>: Didier Vasseur
Minor thriller: Violence during New York's 1977 blackout

Blackout
1988, (USA), color, 91 mins.
<u>W</u>: Carol Lynley, Gail O'Grady, Michael Keys Hall, Joanna Miles, Joseph Gian
<u>D</u>: Doug Adams
Standard thriller: Childhood memories haunt woman fighting for life

Blackout
1995, (USA), color, 100 mins.
<u>W</u>: Brian Bosworth, Brad Dourif (*Payne*), Claire Yarlett (*Jenny*)
Standard thriller: Amnesiac banker suspected of killing wife

Black Panther of Ratana
1962, (W. Ger), color, 65 mins.
<u>W</u>: Brad Harris, Marianne Cook, Heinz Drache
Minor thriller: Secret agent follows trail of stolen ruby

The Black Parachute
1944, (USA), Col, b&w
<u>W</u>: John Carradine
Standard World War II propaganda

The Black Pearl
1928, (USA), Famous Authors/Trem Carr/Rayart, b&w, 6 reels (5,134 ft./1564.8m)
<u>W</u>: Lila Lee (*Eugenie Bromley*), Ray Hallor (*Robert Lathrop*), Carlton Stockdale

(*Ethelbert/Bertram Chisolm*), Howard Lorenz (*Dr. Drake*), Adele Watson (*Sarah Runyan*), Thomas Curran (*Silas Lathrop*), Sybil Grove (*Miss Sheen*), Baldy Belmont (*Wiggenbottom*), Lew Short (*Eugene Bromley*), Art Rowlands (*Claude Lathrop*)
<u>D</u>: Scott Pembroke <u>SCR</u>: Arthur Hoerl <u>PHOTOG</u>: Hap Depew
Standard thriller: Gem stolen from brow of Hindu idol brings evil to all possessors

The Black Pirate
1926, (USA), UA, color, 9 reels (8,488 ft./2587.1m)
<u>W</u>: Douglas Fairbanks Sr. (*The Black Pirate/Michel*), Billie Dove (*The Princess*), Donald Crisp (*McTavish*), Anders Randolf (*The Pirate Leader*), Tempe Pigott (*The Duenna*), Sam De Grasse (*The Lt.*), Charles Stevens (*The Powder Man*), Charles Belcher (*The Chief Passenger*), Fred Becker, John Wallace, E.J. Ratcliffe
<u>D</u>: Albert Parker <u>STORY</u>: "Elton Thomas" (Douglas Fairbanks Sr.) <u>ADAPT</u>: Jack Cunningham <u>PHOTOG</u>: Henry Sharp
Standard action-thriller: Rogue buccaneer has adventures

The Black Pirates
1954, (USA), Lippert, color, 74 mins.
<u>W</u>: Anthony Dexter, Lon Chaney, Jr. Martha Roth, Robert Clarke
<u>D</u>: Allen H. Miner
Standard adventure-thriller

The Black Pit of Dr. M
*see **Misterios del Ultratumba***

Black Rainbow
1989, (GB), color, 103 mins.
<u>W</u>: Rosanna Arquette, Jason Robards Jr., Tom Hulce, Mark Joy, Ron Rosenthal, John Bennes, Linda Pierce
<u>WRIT & D</u>: Mike Hodges
Standard thriller: Medium "witnesses" murder before it happens

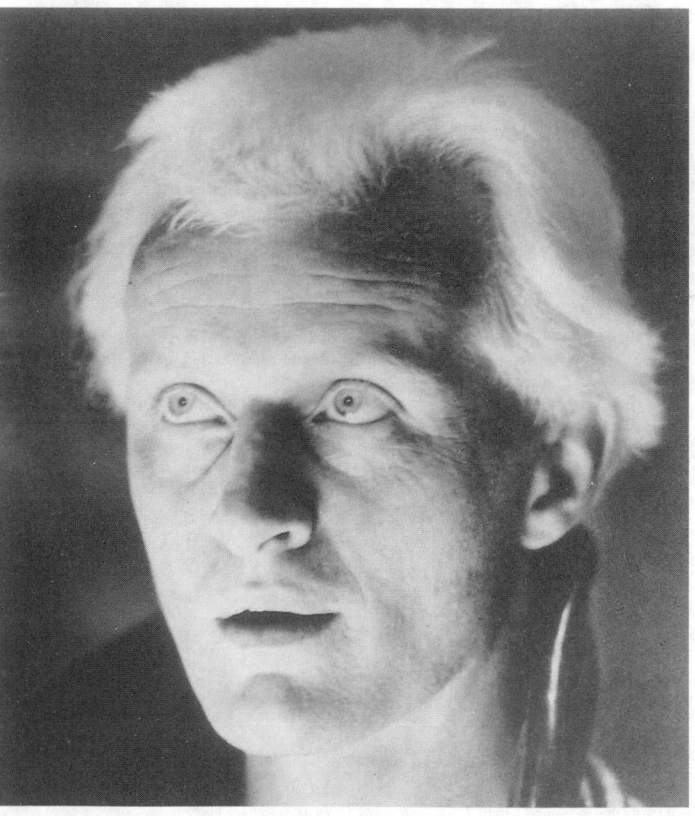

Blade Runner: RUTGER HAUER

The Black Raven
1943, (USA), PRC, b&w, 65 mins
<u>W</u>: George Zucco, Wanda McKay, Charles Middleton, Noel Madison, Glenn Strange, Robert Livingston (aka Randall)Byron Foulger, I. Stanford Jolley
<u>D</u>: Sam Newfield <u>SCR</u>: Fred Myton
Minor thriller: Stranded travelers murdered

The Black Rider
1954, (GB), Butcher/NTA, b&w, 66 mins.
<u>W</u>: Jimmy Hanley (*Jerry Marsh*), Rona Anderson (*Mary*), Leslie Dwyer (*Robert*), Lionel Jeffries (*Brennan*), Beatrice Varley (*Mrs. Marsh*), Michael Golden (*Rakov*), Valerie Hanson (*Karen*), Vincent Ball (*Ted Lintott*), Edwin Richfield (*Geoff Morgan*), Kenneth Connor (*George Amble*)
<u>WRIT & P</u>: A.R. Rawlinson <u>D</u>: Wolf Rilla
Minor comedy-thriller: Atom-saboteurs frightened by "ghost"

The Black Room
1935, (USA), Col, b&w, 70 mins.
W: Boris Karloff (*Anton & Gregor*), Katherine DeMille (*Mashka*), Marian Marsh (*Thea*), Robert Allen, John Buckler, Torben Meyer, Frederick Vogeding, Thurston Hall, Edward Van Sloan, Herbert Evans, Egon Brecher, Colin Tapley, Lois Lindsey, John Bleifer, Henry Kolker
D: Roy William Neill   **SCR:** Henry Meyers & Arthur Strawn   **STORY:** Arthur Strawn   **PHOTOG:** Al Siegler
*French retitle, **Baron Gregor***
Superior thriller: Nobleman murders twin, impersonates him.

The Black Rose
1950, (GB), 20th-Fox, color, 121 mins.
W: Tyrone Power (*Walter of Gurnie*), Orson Welles (*Bayan*), Jack Hawkins (*Tristram*), Cecile Aubry (*Miriam*), Laurence Harvey (*Edmond*), Finlay Currie (*Alfgar*), Herbert Lom (*Anemus*), Henry Oscar (*Friar Roger Bacon*), Michael Rennie (*King Edward*), Mary Clare (*Countess of Lessford*), Alfonso Bedoya (*Lu Chung*), James Robertson Justice (*Simeon Beautrie*), Bobby Blake (*Mahmoud*), Gibb McLaughlin (*Wilderkin*), Valery Inkijinoff (*The Minister*)
P: Louis D. Lighton   **D:** Henry Hathaway   **SCR:** Talbot Jennings, from Thomas B. Costain's novel   **PHOTOG:** Jack Cardiff   **MUSIC:** Richard Addinsell
reissued 1954 (30 mins. cut)
Opulent action-thriller: Saxon leader flees England, has many adventures in Orient

Black Roses
1989, (USA), Rayvan/Shapiro Glickenhaus, Made for cable, color, 90 mins.
W: John Martin, Ken Swofford, Julie Adams, Carla Ferrigno, Frank Dietz, David Crichton, E.K. Miller, Karen Planden, Pat Strelioff, Jesse D'Angelo, Robin Stapler, Anthony Bua, Sal Viviano, Carmine Appice
D: John Fasano   **TELEPLAY:** Cindy Sorrell   **PHOTOG:** Paul Mitchnick   **MUSIC:** Elliot Solomon
Made-for-Cable, minor fantasy-thriller: Ghoulish rock group mesmerizes

Black Sabbath
*see **I Tre Volti Della Paura***

The Black Scorpion
1957, (USA), WB, b&w, 88 mins.
W: Richard Denning (*Hank Scott*), Mara Corday (*Teresa Alvarez*), Carlos Rivas (*Arturo Ramos*), Mario Navarro, Arturo Martinez, Carlos Muzquiz, Pascual Garcia Pena, Fanny Schiller, Pedro Galvan   **P:** Frank Melford & Jack Dietz   **D:** Edward Ludwig   **SCR:** David Duncan & Robert Blees, from a story by Paul Yawitz   **PHOTOG:** Lionel Lindon   **SPCL-FX:** Willis O'Brien   **MUSIC:** Paul Sawtell
*Standard SF-thriller (with footage from unfinished 'Gwangi'): Giant scorpions emerge from fissures during volcanic upheaval in Mexico. cf. **Gwangi, Mighty Joe Young** and **The Valley of Gwangi***

Black Scorpion
1995, (USA), Roger Corman, Made-for-Cable, color
W: Joan Severance, Garrett Morris, Casey Siemaszko, Rick Rossovich
D: Jonathan Winfrey
Standard SF-fantasy: Woman cop becomes superhero

The Black Shield of Falworth
1954, (USA), Univ, color, 99 mins.
W: Tony Curtis (*Myles Falworth*), Janet Leigh (*Lady Anne*), David Farrar (*Earl of Alban*), Barbara Rush (*Meg Falworth*), Herbert Marshall (*Earl of Mackworth*), Dan O'Herlihy (*Prince Hal*), Ian Keith (*King Henry IV*), Torin Thatcher (*Sir James*), Rhys Williams (*Diccon Bow-man*), Patrick O'Neal (*Walter Blunt*), Craig Hill (*Francis Gascoyne*)
P: Robert Arthur   **D:** Rudolph Maté   **SCR:** Oscar Brodney, from Howard Pyle's novel *Men of Iron*   **PHOTOG:** Irving Glassberg   **MUSIC:** Joseph Gershenson
Standard action-thriller. Noble youth assailed by enemies

The Black Skull
*see **La Calavera Negra***

The Black Sleep
1956, (USA), Bel-Air/UA, b&w, 81 mins.
W: Basil Rathbone, Herbert Rudley, Patricia Blake, Lon Chaney Jr., Akim Tamiroff, Tor Johnson, Phyllis Stanley, Bela Lugosi, George Sawaya, Claire Carleton, Sally Yarnell, Clive Morgan, Peter Gordon, Louanna Gardner
P: Howard W. Koch   **D:** Reginald LeBorg   **SCR:** John C. Higgins   **PHOTOG:** Gordon Avil   **MUSIC:** Les Baxter
*German retitle, **The Horror Chamber of Dr. Thosti***
*reissued (1963) as **Dr. Cadman's Secret***
Standard horror-thriller: Fanatical doctor creates monsters

The Black Spider
1920, (GB), B&C/Butcher, b&w, 5,800 ft. (1767.8m)
W: Lydia Kyasht (*Angela Carfour*), Bertram Burleigh (*Archie Lowndes*), Sam Livesey (*Reginald Conway*), Ronald Colman (*Vicomte de Beauvais*), Hayden Coffin (*Lord Carfour*), Adeline Hayden Coffin (*Lady Carfour*), Mary Clare (*Coralie Mount*), Dorothy Cecil (*Marjorie West*)
P: Edward Godal   **D & SCR:** William J. Humphrey, from a novel by Carlton Dawe
Standard crime-thriller: Girl poses as masked thief

The Black Spot
1914, (GB), London, b&w, 2,417 ft. (736.7m)
W: Jane Gail (*Olga Scerloff*), Arthur Holmes-Gore (*Duke Paul*), Charles Rock (*Prof. Scerloff*), Gerald Ames (*Serge Malkow*)
D: George Loane Tucker   **SCR:** Bannister Merwin, from a story by John Alwin
Standard crime-thriller: Duke dons disguises to save Russian professor's daughter from assassination

Black Sunday (1960)
*see **La Maschera del Demonio***

Black Sunday
1977, (USA), Para, color, 143 mins.
W: Robert Shaw (*Maj. David Kabakov*), Marthe Keller (*Dahlia Iyad*), Bruce Dern (*Michael Lander*), Fritz Weaver (*FBI Agent Corley*), Steven Keats (*Robert Moshevsky*), Walter Gotell (*Col. Riyadh*), Michael V. Gazzo (*Muzi*), Walter Brooke (*Fowler*), Than Wyenn, William Daniels, Bekim Fehmiu, Victor Campos, Frank Logan
P: Robert Evans   **D:** John Frankenheimer, from Thomas Harris' novel   **PHOTOG:** John A. Alonzo   **MUSIC:** John Williams
Standard thriller: Terrorists plot presidential assassination

The Black Swan
1942, (USA), 20th-Fox, color, 85 mins.
W: Tyrone Power, Maureen O'Hara, Laird Cregar, Anthony Quinn, Thomas Mitchell, George Sanders, John Carradine, George Zucco, Frederick Worlock, Edward Ashley
D: Henry King   **SCR:** Ben Hecht & Seton I. Miller, from a novel by Rafael Sabatini   **PHOTOG:** Leon Shamroy   **MUSIC:** Alfred Newman
Standard action-adventure: Pirate's tumultuous life

Black 13
1953, (GB), Archway/Vandyke/20th-Fox, b&w, 77 mins.
W: Peter Reynolds (*Stephen Barclay*), Rona Anderson (*Claire Barclay*), Patrick Barr (*Robert*), Lana Morris (*Marion*), Genine Graham (*Stella*), Michael Balfour (*Joe*), Viola Lyel (*Mrs. Barclay*), John Forrest (*Wally*), Martin Walker (*Prof. Barclay*), John LeMesurier (*The Inspector*)
P: Roger Proudlock   **D & SCR:** Ken Hughes, from a story by Pietro Germi
Standard thriller: Sister of neurotic girl-killer loves detective on case

Black Torment
1964, (GB), Compton/Col, color, 85 mins.
W: Heather Sears (*Lady Elizabeth Fordyke*), John Turner (*Sir Richard Fordyke*), Ann Lynn (*Diane*), Norman Bird (*Harris*), Peter Arne (*Seymour*), Raymond Huntley (*Col. Wentworth*), Joseph Tomelty (*Sir Giles Fordyke*), Patrick Troughton (*The Ostler*), Francis De Wolff (*Black John*)
P: Tony Tenser & Michael Klinger, & Robert Hartford-Davis   **D:** Robert Hartford-Davis   **STORY:** Donald Ford & Derek Ford
Eerie thriller: Plot to drive nobleman insane

The Black Triangles
1916, (GB), Clarendon, b&w, 695 ft. (211.8m)
D: Percy Stow
Standard thriller: Bachelor joins secret society, falls in love

The Black Tulip
1921, (GB), Granger-Binger, b&w, 5,269 ft. (1606m)
W: Zoe Palmer (*Rosa*), Gerald McCarthy (*Cornelius van Baerle*), Frank Dane (*Prince William*), Harry Walter (*Isaac Boxtel*), Dio Huysmans (*John de Witt*), Edward Verkade (*Cornelius de Witt*), Coen Hissink (*Gryphus*)
D: Frankland A. Richardson   **SCR:** Marjorie Bowen, from Alexander Dumas' novel
Standard adventure: Royalist jails ruler's son to obtain secret of black tulips

The Black Tulip
1937, (GB), Fox British, b&w, 57 mins.
W: Patrick Waddington (*Cornelius*), Ann Soreen (*Rosa*), Wilson Coleman (*Cornelius de Witte*), Jay Laurier (*Gryphus*), Campbell Gullan (*Boxtel*), Bernard Lee (*William of Orange*), Florence Hunt (*Julia Boxtel*), Ronald Shiner (*Hendrik*), Aubrey Mallalieu (*Col. Marnix*)
D: Alex Bryce, from Alexander Dumas' novel
Standard adventure: Merchant frames cultivator to get secret of black tulips

The Black Tulip (1963)
*see **La Tulipe Noire***

Black Voodoo
*see **Voodoo Woman***

Black Waters
1929, (GB), British & Dominions/Sono Art World Wide, b&w, 79 mins.
W: James Kirkwood (*Tiger Larabee/Kelly*), Mary Brian (*Eunice*), John Loder (*Charles*), Hallam Cooley (*Elmer*), Lloyd Hamilton (*Temple*), Frank Reicher (*Randall*), Robert Ames (*Darcy*), Ben Hendricks (*Olaf*), Noble Johnson (*Jeelo*)
D: Marshall Neilan, based on John Willard's play *Fog*
Standard thriller (made in USA): Mad captain poses as cleric, commits murder on fog-bound ship

Blackwater Trail
1995, (USA), color, 100 mins.
W: Judd Nelson, Dee Smart
Made-for-Video, minor thriller: Writer pursues serial killer

Black Werewolf
see The Beast Must Die

Black Widow
1951, (GB), Hammer/Exclusive, b&w, 62 mins.
W: Christine Norden (*Christine Sherwin*), Robert Ayres (*Mark Sherwin*), Anthony
   Forwood (*Paul*), Jennifer Jayne (*Sheila Kemp*), John Longden (*Kemp*), John
   Harvey (*Dr. Wallace*)
P: Anthony Hinds   D: Vernon Sewell   SCR: Allan Mackinnon, from Lester
   Powell's radio-serial *Return Darkness*
Standard crime-thriller: Amnesiac finds wife and her lover plot his murder

Black Widow
1954, (USA), 20th-Fox, color, 95 mins.
W: Ginger Rogers (*Lottie*), Van Heflin (*Peter*), George Raft (*Det. Bruce*), Gene
   Tierney (*Iris*), Peggy Ann Garner (*Nancy Ordway*), Reginald Gardiner
   (*Brian*), Skip Homeier (*John*), Virginia Leith (*Claire Amberly*), Otto Kruger
   (*Ling*), Hilda Simms (*Anne*), Cathleen Nesbitt (*Lucia*), Harry Carter (*Welch*),
   Geraldine Wall (*Miss Mills*), Richard Cutting (*Sgt. Owens*), Mabel Albertson
   (*Sylvia*), Aaron Spelling (*Mr. Oliver*), Wilson Wood (*The Costume Designer*),
   Tony De Mario (*The Bartender*), Virginia Maples (*The Model*), Frances Driver
   (*The Maid*), James F. Stone (*The Stage Doorman*), Michael Vallon (*The Coal
   Dealer*),
WRIT, P & D: Nunnally Johnson, from Patrick Quentin's novel *Fatal Woman*
   PHOTOG: Charles G. Clarke   MUSIC: Leigh Harline
Dynamic cast in transparent murder mystery: Innocent New York socialite accused of murder

Black Widow
1987, (USA), 20th-Fox, color, 100 mins.
W: Debra Winger (*Alex Barnes*), Theresa Russell (*Catherine*), Sami Frey (*Paul
   Nuytten*), Nicol Williamson (*Macauley*), Diane Ladd (*Rita*), Dennis Hopper
   (*Ben Dumers*), James Hong (*Det. Shin*), Terry O'Quinn (*Alex's Boss*)
D: Bob Rafelson   SCR: Ronald Bass   PHOTOG: Conrad L. Hall   MUSIC:
   Michael Small
Standard thriller: Homicidal beauty marries, murders

The Black Windmill
1974, (GB), Univ, color, 106 mins.
W: Michael Caine (*Maj. John Tarrant*), Janet Suzman (*Alex Tarrant*), Donald
   Pleasence (*Cedric Harper*), Delphine Seyrig (*Ceil Burrows*), Clive Revill (*Alf
   Chesterman*), John Vernon (*McKee*), Joseph O'Conor (*Sir Edward Julyan*),
   Joss Ackland (*Chief Supt. Wray*), Edward Hardwicke (*Mike McCarthy*), Mark
   Praid (*James Stroud*), David Daker (*The Thickset M.I. 5 Man*), Denis Quilley
   (*Bateson*), Paul Moss (*David Tarrant*), George Cooper (*Pincus*), Derek
   Newark (*The Monitoring Policeman*), John Rhys-Davies (*The Special
   Policeman*), Brenda Cowling (*The Pleasant Sec'y*), Nancy Gabrielle (*The
   Manageress*), Preston Lockwood (*Ilkeston*), Derek Lord (*Sollars*), Murray
   Brown (*The Doctor*), Frank Henson (*The S.P. Driver*), Hilary Sesta (*Ilkeston's
   Sec'y*), Michael Segal (*The Postman*), Catherine Schell (*Lady Julyan*), Maureen
   Pryor (*Jane Harper*), Paul Humpoletz (*Tomkins*), Hermione Baddeley (*Hetty*),
   Patrick Barr (*Gen. St. John*), Russell Napier (*Adm. Ballentyne*), John Harvey
   (*Heppenstal*), Anthony Verner (*Magnus*), Joyce Carey (*The Secretary*), Robert
   Dorning (*The Jeweller*), Jon Croft (*The Officer*), Mollie Urquhart (*Margaret*),
   Jacques Ciron (*The Prison Official*), Christopher Hawkings (*The Auctioneer*),
   Billy Milton (*The Pianist*), Golda Casimir (*The Barmaid*), Peter Halliday
   (*The Customs Official*), Del Baker (*The M.I. 5 Driver*), Jessie Robins (*The Fat
   Lady*), Yves Afonso (*Jacques*), Roger Lumont (*The Prison Guard*), Jean
   Michaud (*The Doctor*), Michel Norman (*The Paddy Wagon Driver*), Jean-
   Pierre Allais (*The Passenger in the Truck*), Roland Neunreuther (*The Motorcycle
   Cop*), Mme. Vagenende (*The Hurdy Gurdy Woman*)
D: Don Siegel   SCR: Leigh Vance, from Clive Egleton's novel *Seven Days to a
   Killing*   PHOTOG: Ousama Rawi   MUSIC: Roy Budd
Unusual thriller: Spy's son is abducted

Black Zoo
1963, (USA), AA, color
W: Michael Gough, Jeanne Cooper, Elisha Cook Jr., Rod Lauren, Jerome Cowan,
   Virginia Grey, Oren Curtis, Mariana Hill, Eric Stone, Edward C. Platt,
   Warene Ott, Eilene Janssen, Claudia Brack, Susan Slavin, Jerry Douglas,
   Dani Lynn, Byron Morrow, Douglas Henderson, Daniel Kurlick, Michael St.
   Angel (*Steve Flagg*)
P: Herman Cohen   D: Robert Gordon   SCR: Herman Cohen   PHOTOG: Floyd
   Crosby   MUSIC: Paul Dunlap
Minor thriller: Zookeeper has animals commit murder

Blacula
1972, (USA), AIP, color, 93 mins.
W: William Marshall (*Blacula*), Denise Nicholas (*Michelle*), Vonetta McGee
   (*Tina*), Thalmus Rasulala (*Gordon*), Emily Yancy (*Nancy*), Charles Macaulay
   (*Count Dracula*), Ted Harris (*Bobby*), Logan Field (*Barnes*), Rick Metzler
   (*Billy*), Lance Taylor Sr. (*Swenson*), Ji-Tu Cumbuka (*Skillet*), Ketty Lester
   (*Juanita*), Eric Brotherson (*The Real Estate Agent*), Elisha Cook Jr. (*Sam*)
P: Joseph T. Naar   D: William Crain   SCR: Joan Torres & Raymond Koenig

PHOTOG: John Stevens   MUSIC: Gene Page   LYRICS: Wally Holmes
SONG: Main Chance
Unusual "blaxploitation" horror-satire: African prince made Undead. cf. Scream,
Blacula, Scream

Blade
1973, (USA), Joseph Green, color
W: John Marley, William Prince, Keene Curtis, Marshall Efron
P: George Mansse   D: Ernest Pintoff   SCR: Ernest Pintoff & Jeff Lieberman
blurb: "A psycho-karate killer brutalizes his victims and your emotions!"
Minor thriller: New York detective stalks psycho-killer

Blade
1998, (USA), New Line, color, 118 mins.
W: Wesley Snipes, Traci Lords, Tim Guinee, Stephen Dorff, Kris Kristofferson,
   N'Bushe Wright
D: Stephen Norrington
Standard action-horror: Vampiric crimefighter

Blade af Satans Bog (Pages from Satan's Book)
1919, (Den), Nordisk Films Kompagni, b&w, 9,902 ft. (3018m)
W: Helge Nissen, Halvard Hoff, Erling Hansson, Jacob Texeire, Elith Pio, Karina
   Bell, Tenna Kraft, Clara Pontoppidan, Ebon Strandin
D: Carl Dreyer   SCR: Edgar Hoyer, from Marie Corelli's novel   PHOTOG:
   George Schneevoight
Classic silent fantasy: Exploration of witchcraft & satanism

A Blade in the Dark
1983, (It), color, 96 mins.
W: Anny Papa, Andrea Occhipinti
D: Lamberto Bava
A.k.a. **La Casa Con La Scala Nel Buiom** *(House of the Dark Stairway)*
Minor thriller: Composer haunted by strange visions.

Blademaster
see Ator: The Blademaster

Blade of the Ripper
1984, (Fr), color, 90 mins.
W: George Hilton, Edwige Fenech
Standard thriller: Razor-wielding madman menaces jet-set beauties

Blade Runner
1982, (USA), Ladd Co./WB, color, 118 mins.
W: Harrison Ford (*Rick Deckard*), Rutger Hauer (*Roy*), Sean Young (*Rachel*), Daryl
   Hannah (*Pris*), Edward James Olmos (*Gaff*), William Sanderson (*Sebastian*),
   Joanna Cassidy (*Zhora*), Brion James (*Leon*), M. Emmet Walsh (*Bryant*), Joe
   Turkel (*Tyrell*), James Hong (*Chew*), Morgan Paull (*Holden*), Kevin
   Thompson (*Bear*)
D: Ridley Scott   SCR: Hampton Fancher & David Peoples, from Philip K. Dick's
   novel *Do Androids Dream of Electric Sheep?*   PHOTOG: Jordan Cronenweth
   MUSIC: Vangelis
Outstanding SF-thriller: 21st-century detective hunts for runaway androids

Blades
1989, (USA), color, 100 mins.
W: Robert North, Jeremy Whelan, Victoria Scott, Jon McBride
Minor horror-spoof: Runaway lawnmower terrorizes

Bladestorm
1986, (USA), color, 87 mins.
Minor fantasy-adventure

Blake of Scotland Yard
1937, (USA), Bon Ami/Sam Katzman/Victory, b&w, 70 mins.
W: Ralph Byrd, Joan Barclay, Bob Terry, Herbert Rawlinson, Lloyd Hughes
D: Robert F. Hill
Minor action-thriller, feature-version of serial: Crime fighter seeks stolen death ray

Blake the Lawbreaker
1928, (GB), British Filmcraft/Para, b&w, 1,888 ft. (575.5m)
W: Langhorne Burton (*Sexton Blake*), Mickey Brantford (*Tinker*), Fred Raynham,
   Thelma Murray, Leslie Perrins, Philip Desborough
D: George A. Cooper
Standard "Sexton Blake" mystery: Detective confronts judicial dilemma

The Blancheville Monster
see Horror

Blankman
1994, (USA), color, 96 mins
W: Damon Wayans, David Alan Grier, Jason Alexander, Sol Polito
D: Mike Binder   SCR: Damon Wayans & J.P. Lawton
Standard comedy-adventure: Inner-city superhero

Blastfighter
1984, (It), color, 93 mins.
W: Michael Sopkiw, Valerie Blake, George Eastman
D: Lamberto Bava
Standard SF-adventure: Cop seeks revenge

Blast-Off!
see *Those Fantastic Flying Fools*

Das Blaue Licht (The Blue Light)
1931, (Ger), Sokal, b&w, 86 mins.
W: Leni Riefenstahl, Mathias Weimann, Beni Fuhrer, Max Holzboer
P: Leni Riefenstahl, Bela Balazs & Hans Schneeberger D: Leni Riefenstahl, from an old legend of the Italian Dolomites PHOTOG: Hans Schneeberger
Fantasy classic: Strange lights in Dolomite Mountains lure young people

Bleak House
1920, (GB), Ideal, b&w, 6,400 ft. (1950.7m)
W: Constance Collier (*Lady Dedlock*), Berta Gellardi (*Esther Summerson*), E. Vivian Reynolds (*Tulkinghorne*), Clifford Heatherley (*Bucket*), Norman Page (*Guppy*), Ion Swinley (*Capt. Hawdon*), Anthony St. John (*Jo*), Helen Haye (*Miss Barbay*), A. Harding Steerman (*Sir Leicester Dedlock*), Teddy Arundell (*George*), Beatrix Templeton (*Rachel*)
D: Maurice Elvey SCR: William J. Elliott, from Charles Dickens' novel
Standard crime-thriller: Noblewoman is suspect in murder of blackmailing lawyer. cf. Jo the Crossing Sweeper

Blind Alley
1939, (USA), Col, b&w, 61 mins.
W: Chester Morris, Ralph Bellamy, Ann Dvorak, Rose Stradner, Melville Cooper, Marc Lawrence, Joan Perry
D: Charles Vidor SCR: Philip MacDonald, Albert Blankfort, & Michael Duffy from a play by James Warwick PHOTOG: Lucien Ballard MUSIC: Morris Stoloff
Unusual thriller: Psychiatrist probes killer's mind. Remake of The Dark Past (1948)

A Blind Bargain
1922, (USA), Goldwyn, b&w, 5 reels (4,473 ft./1363.4m)
W: Lon Chaney Sr. (*Dr. Arthur Lamb/The Hunchback*), Raymond McKee (*Robert Sandell*), Virginia True Boardman (*Mrs. Sandell*), Jacqueline Logan (*Angela Marshall*), Fontaine La Rue (*Mrs. Lamb*), Aggie Herring (*Bessie*), Virginia Madison (*Angela's Mother*)
D: Wallace Worsley SCR: J.G. Hawks, from Barry Pain's *The Octave of Claudius* PHOTOG: Norbert Brodine
Standard SF-horror: Scientist attempts to create ape men

Blind Corner
1963, (GB), Blakeley's Films/Mancunian, b&w, 80 mins.
W: William Sylvester (*Paul Gregory*), Barbara Shelley (*Anne Gregory*), Elizabeth Shepherd (*Joan Marshall*), Alexander Davion (*Rickie Seldon*), Ronnie Carroll (*Ronnie*), Barry Aldis (*Compere*), Mark Eden (*Mike Williams*), Edward Evans (*The Chauffeur*), Frank Forsyth (*The Policeman*)
P: Tom Blakeley D: Lance Comfort SCR: James Kelly & Peter Miller STORY: Vivian Kemble
Standard crime-thriller: Woman urges artist lover to kill her blind husband

Blind Date
1959, (GB), Independent Artists/RFD, b&w, 95 mins.
W: Hardy Kruger (*Jan Van Rooyen*), Robert Flemyng (*Sir Brian Lewis*), Micheline Presle (*Jacqueline Cousteau*), Stanley Baker (*Insp. Morgan*), Gordon Jackson (*The Sgt.*), George Roubicek (*The Constable*), John Van Eyssen (*Westover*), Jack MacGowran (*The Postman*)
P: David Deutsch D: Joseph Losey SCR: Ben Barzman & Millard Lampell, from a novel by Leigh Howard PHOTOG: Christopher Challis
A.k.a. *Chance Meeting*
Standard crime-thriller: Diplomat's wife frames artist for murder

Blind Date
1984, (GB-Greece), Omega, color, 100 mins.
W: Joseph Bottoms (*Jonathon Ratcliff*), Kirstie Alley (*Claire Simpson*), James Daughton (*Dave*), Lana Clarkson (*Rachel*), Keir Dullea (*Dr. Steiger*), Michael Howe, Gerald Kelly, Kathy Hill, Jerry Sundquist, Marina Sirtis, Noelle Simpson, Jan Geneen, Antigone Amanitis, Ankie Grelson, Louis Sheldon, Chris Paps, Charles Nicklin, Danos Lygizos, Spyros Papafrantzis, Agatha Visviki, V. Kloufetos, Brian Walker, Mirella Vardi, Beatrice Vetterly, Carol Shideler, Christy Keenan, Valeria Golino, Ali Spanoghe, Maria Marinelli, Yvette Jarvis, Laura Rozos, Alice Amoruzo, Godfrey Holdsworth, Karen Lee, E. Spanos, A. Uslar, David Platt, Andrew Johnson, V. Papadopoulou, K. Bourlessi, E. Kouerini, M. Roberts, R. Cunniffe, S. Papageorgiou, D. Ballos
P & D: Nico Mastorakis SCR: Nico Mastorakis & Fred C. Perry STORY: Nico Mastorakis PHOTOG: Andrew Bellis MUSIC: Stanley Myers ORIG SONGS: John Kongos
Minor thriller: Computer wizardry helps blind man stalk mad killer

The Blind Dead
see *Tombs of the Blind Dead*

Blind Fate
1914, (GB), Hepworth, b&w, 2,000 ft. (609.6m)
W: Alma Taylor (*Molly*), Alec Worcester, Jamie Darling
D: Cecil M. Hepworth STORY: Blanche McIntosh
Standard crime-thriller: Blind girl exposes father's killer

Blind Fear
1989, (Can), color, 95 mins.

W: Shelley Hack, Jack Langedijk (*Bo*), Kim Coates (*Ed*), Heidi von Palleske (*Marla*)
Standard thriller: Sightless telephone operator terrorized at Maine lodge

Blindfold
1965, (USA), Univ, color, 102 mins.
W: Rock Hudson, Claudia Cardinale, Guy Stockwell, Jack Warden, Brad Dexter, Anne Seymour
D: Philip Dunne PHOTOG: Joe MacDonald MUSIC: Lalo Schifrin
Modest thriller (Philip Dunne's final directorial effort): Unexpected complications in international plot

The Blind Heroine
1912, (GB), Hepworth, b&w, 475 ft. (144.8m)
D: Bert Haldane
Standard crime-thriller: Blind orphan detects burglars, calls police

Blind Man's Bluff
1936, (GB), Fox British, b&w, 72 mins.
W: Basil Sydney (*Dr. Peter Fairfax*), Enid Stamp-Taylor (*Sylvia Fairfax*), Barbara Greene (*Vicki Sheridan*), Warburton Gamble (*Tracy*), James Mason (*Stephen Neville*), Iris Ashley (*Claire*), Ian Colin (*Philip Stanhope*), Wilson Coleman (*Dr. Franz Morgenhardt*)
D: Albert Parker SCR: Cecil Maiden, from the play *Smoked Glasses* by William Foster & B. Scott Elder
Standard thriller: Blind scientist cured by secret ray

Blind Man's Bluff
1952, (GB), Present Day/Apex, b&w, 67 mins.
W: Zena Marshall (*Christine Stevens*), Sydney Tafler (*Rikki Martin*), Anthony Pendrell (*Roger Morley*), Russell Napier (*Stevens*), Norman Shelley (*Insp. Morley*), Anthony Doonan (*Charley*), John LeMesurier (*Lefty Jones*), Barbara Shaw (*Clare Raven*)
D: Charles Saunders STORY: John Gilling
Standard crime-thriller: Inspector's novelist son breaks up boarding-house crime ring

Blind Man's Bluff (1968)
see *Cauldron of Blood*

Blind Spot
1932, (GB), WB-First Nat'l, b&w, 75 mins.
W: Percy Marmont (*Holland Janney*), Muriel Angelus (*Marilyn Janney*), Warwick Ward (*Hugh Conway*), Laura Cowie (*Anna Wiltone*), Ivor Barnard (*Mull*), George Merritt (*Insp. Cadbury*), Mary Jerrold (*Mrs. Herriott*)
P: Irving Asher D: John Daumery STORY: Roland Pertwee & John Hastings Turner
Standard crime-thriller: Gentleman thief's amnesiac daughter weds policeman

Blind Spot
1947, (USA), Col, b&w, 73 mins.
W: Chester Morris, Constance Dowling
Standard melodrama

Blind Spot
1958, (GB), Butcher's Films, b&w, 71 mins.
W: Robert Mackenzie (*Dan Adams*), Delphi Lawrence (*Yvonne*), Gordon Jackson (*Chalky*), Anne Sharp (*June*), Ernest Clark (*Fielding*), John LeMesurier (*Brent*), George Pastell (*Schreider*), Ronan O'Casey (*Rushford*), Andrew Faulds (*The Inspector*), John Crawford (*Dr. Kirkland*), Michael Caine (*Johnny Brent*)
P: Monty Berman D: Peter Maxwell SCR: Kenneth R. Hayles STORY: Robert Baker & John Gilling
Standard crime-thriller: Army officer tails gem smugglers

Blind Terror
1971, (GB), Filmways/Col, color, 89 mins.
W: Mia Farrow (*Sarah*), Brian Rawlinson (*Barker*), Norman Eshley (*Steve Reding*), Robin Bailey (*George Rexton*), Paul Nicholas (*Jacko*), Dorothy Alison (*Betty Rexton*), Diane Grayson (*Sandy Rexton*), Chris-topher Matthews (*Frost*), Michael Elphick (*Gypsy Tom*), Barrie Houghton (*Gypsy Jack*), Donald Bissett (*The Doctor*), Lila Kaye (*The Gypsy Mother*), Max Faulkner, Scott Fredericks, Reg Harding
P: Martin Ransohoff & Leslie Linder D: Richard Fleischer SCR: Brian Clemens PHOTOG: Gerry Fisher MUSIC: Elmer Bernstein
USA retitle, *See No Evil*
Standard melodrama: Murderous drifter menaces blind girl

Blind Vision
1990, (USA), color, 92 mins.
W: Lenny Von Dohlen, Deborah Shelton
Standard thriller: Psychotic mail clerk kills neighbor's lovers

Blink
1994, (USA), New Line, color, 106 mins
W: Madeleine Stowe (*Emma Brady*), Aidan Quinn (*Det. John Hollstrom*), James Remar (*Thomas Ridgely*), Laurie Metcalf (*Candice*), Bruce A. Young (*Lt. Mitchell*), Peter Friedman (*Dr. Ryon Pierce*), Matt Roth (*Crowe*), Paul Dillon (*Neal Booker*), Michael P. Byrne (*Barry*), Anthony Cannata (*Ned*), Greg Noonan (*Frank*), Heather Schwartz (*Young Emma*), Sean C. Cleland (*Sean*), Marilyn Dodds Frank (*Emma's Mother*), Michael Stuart Kirkpatrick (*Michael*), Craig Winston Damon (*Winston*), David Callahan (*David*), Jackie

Moran (*Jackie*), Mary Ann Thebus (*Mrs. Davison*), Joy E. Gregory (*Valerie Wheaton*), Lucy Childs (*Margaret Tattersall*), Blake Whealy (*Mark Tattersall*), Tim Monsion (*Mr. Tattersall*), Shirley Spiegler Jacobs (*The Grandmother*), Debra Dusay (*The Female Detective*), Don Forston (*The Priest*), Mario Tanzi (*Cuchetto*), Lia D. Mortensen (*The Reporter*), Sam Sanders (*Bobby*), Kate Buddeke (*Mrs. Whitney*), Adele Robbins (*The Davison Doctor*), Rick Lefevour (*The Driver*), Darryl Rocky Davis (*Forensics*), Dallas J. Crawford (*The Kid*), Lucina Paquet (*Mrs. Goldman*), Mark Nagel (*The Parking Guard*), Les Podewell (*The Old Man*), Glendon Gabbard (*Mr. Goldman*), Gene Janson (*Mr. Getz*), Renee Lockett-Lawson (*The Admitting Nurse*), Mary Seidel (*The Records Nurse*), Dr. Donna Alexander (*The Animal Veterinarian*), Valerie Spencer (*A Children's Nurse*), Kathryn Miller (*A Children's Nurse*), Jackie Samuel (*The Woman Conductor*), Kevin B. Swerdlow (*The Receiving Cop*), Ted Gilbert (*Ted*), Kevin Matthews (*The Man on the Train*), Joe McConnell (*A Basketball Announcer*), Bob Lanier (*A Basketball Announcer*), Ray Clay (*A Basketball Announcer*), Chantal Wentworth (*The Backup Singer*)
D: Michael Apted   **SCR:** Dana Stevens   **PHOTOG:** Dante Spinotti   **MUSIC:** Brad Fiedel   **SONGS:** *Insulated Man, When Fortune Turns Her Wheel, The Boys and the Babies, Love Won't Be, & Jerusalem Ridge*
Engrossing thriller: Blind woman regains sight, is stalked by killer

Blink of an Eye
1992, (USA), color, 90 mins.
W: Michael Pare
Minor SF-thriller: Terrorists seek plutonium, face agent trained as psychic warrior

Blithe Spirit
1945, (GB), Cineguild/Two Cities/GFD/UA, color, 96 mins.
W: Rex Harrison (*Charles Condomine*), Constance Cummings (*Ruth Condomine*), Kay Hammond (*Elvira Condomine*), Margaret Rutherford (*Mme. Arcati*), Hugh Wakefield (*George Bradman*), Joyce Carey (*Violet Bradman*), Jacqueline Clark (*Edith*)
P: Noel Coward   **D:** David Lean   **SCR:** David Lean, Anthony Havelock-Allan, & Ronald Neame, from Noel Coward's play   **PHOTOG:** Ronald Neame   **MUSIC:** Richard Addinsell
Classic comedy-fantasy: Man's second marriage upset by return of first wife's ghost

The Blob
1958, (USA), Tonylyn/Para, color, 85 mins.
W: Steve McQueen, Aneta Corseaut, Steven Chase, Olin Howlin, Earl Rowe, John Benson, George Karis, Elbert Smith, Robert Fields, Lee Payton, James Bonnet, Anthony Franke, Tom Ogden, Hugh Graham, Audrey Metcalf, Vince Barbi, George Gerbereck, Jasper Deeter, Ralph Roseman, Elinor Hammer, Josh Randolph, David Metcalf, Keith Almoney, Pamela Curran, Julie Cousins, Charlie Overdorff, Eugene Sabel, Molly Anne Bourne, Diane Tabban
P: Jack H. Harris   **D:** Irvin Yeaworth Jr.   **SCR:** Kate Phillips & Ted Simonson   **PHOTOG:** Thomas Spaulding   **MUSIC:** Ralph Carmichael
French retile, **Terreur sans Nom (Terror without Name)**, *German retile,* **The Nameless Terror**, *reissued 1964*
Classic SF-horror: Alien life-form devours humans, filemd in Valley Forge, Pa. cf. **Beware! The Blob**

The Blob
1988, (USA), Andre Blay-Elliott Kastner/Tri-Star, color, 93 mins.
W: Kevin Dillon (*Brian Flagg*), Shawnee Smith (*Meg Penny*), Donovan Leitch (*Paul Taylor*), Jeffrey DeMunn (*Sheriff Herb Geller*), Ricky Paull Goldin (*Scott Jeskey*), Candy Clark (*Fran Hewitt*), Del Close (*Rev. Meeker*), Joe Seneca (*Dr. Meddows*), Paul McCrane, Art La Fleur, Beau Billingslea, Billy Beck, Michael Kenworthy
D: Chuck Russell   **SCR:** Chuck Russell & Frank Darabont   **PHOTOG:** Mark Irwin   **MUSIC:** Michael Hoenig
Excellent remake of 1958 SF-horror cult classic: Amorphous monstrosity terrorizes small town

Blonde Bait
1956, (USA/GB), Screen Guild/Hammer/Exclusive/AFD, b&w, 71 mins.
W: Beverly Michaels, Richard Travis, Jim Davis, Joan Rice, Paul Cavanagh
UK Title: **Women Without Men**
Minor melodrama

Blonde Blackmailer
1958, (USA), AA, b&w, 58 mins.
W: Richard Arlen, Susan Shaw
Minor thriller. See **Stolen Time**

Blonde Cobra
1963, (USA), Bob Fleishner, color, 25 mins.
W: Jack Smith
EDITED: Ken Jacobs
Underground film, not in general release: Man entranced by child's doll

Blonde for a Day
1946, (USA), PRC, b&w, 68 mins.
W: Hugh Beaumont (*Michael Shayne*), Kathryn Adams (*Phyllis Hamilton*), Cy Kendall, Marjorie Hoshelle, Paul Bryar, Frank Ferguson, Richard Fraser, Mauritz Hugo, Charles Wilson, Sonia Sorel, Claire Rochelle
D: Sam Newfield   **SCR:** Fred Myton, from characters created by Brett Halliday   **PHOTOG:** Jack Greenhalgh   **MUSIC:** Leo Erdody
Standard "Michael Shayne" detective-thriller: Sleuth pursues murderous racketeers

Blonde Heaven
1995, (USA), color, 80 mins.
W: Julie Strain, Michelle Bauer, Joe Estevez
Minor fantasy-thriller: Young woman gets job at Hollywood escort service staffed by supernatural predators

Blondes at Work
1938, (USA), WB, b&w, 63 mins.
W: Glenda Farrell (*Torchy Blane*), Barton MacLane (*Steve McBride*), Tom Kennedy (*Gahagan*), Donald Briggs (*Maitland Greer*), Rosella Towne (*Louisa Revelle*), John Ridgely Betty Compson (*Blanche Revelle*), Thomas E. Jackson (*Parker*), Frank Shannon (*Capt. McTavish*), Jean Benedict (*The Sales Girl*), Carole Landis (*Carol*), Theodore von Eltz (*The D.A.*), Suzanne Kaaren (*Olive*), Charles Richman (*Judge Wilson*), George Guhl (*The Desk Sergeant*), Robert Middlemas (*Boylan*), Kenneth Harlan (*Marvin Spencer*), Joe Cunningham (*Maxie*), Milton Owen (*The Fashion Director*), Ralph Sanford (*Healy*)
D: Frank McDonald   **SCR:** Albert De Mond, from characters created by Frederick Nebel   **PHOTOG:** Warren Lynch
4th "Torchy Blane" mystery-thriller: Girl reporter nabs criminal

Blonde Savage
1947, (USA), Eagle Lion, b&w, 62 mins.
W: Leif Erickson, Gale Sherwood, Veda Ann Borg, Douglass Dumbrille, Frank Jenks, Matt Willis, Ernest Whitman
D: Steve Sekely
Minor action-thriller: Two pilots bring jungle princess to USA

Blonde Sinner
see **Yield to the Night**

Blond Gorilla
see **White Pongo**

Blood!
1974, (USA), Bryanston, color
P: Walter Kent   **D & SCR:** Andy Milligan
Minor horror-fantasy: Wolfman's son weds Dracula's daughter

Blood and Black Lace
see **Sei Donne per l'Assassino**

Blood and Concrete
1990, (USA), color, 99 mins.
W: Billy Zane (*Joey Turks*), Jennifer Beals (*Mona*), Darren McGavin (*Hank Dick*), James Le Gros (*Lance*), Nicholas Worth, William Bastiani, Harry Shearer
D & SCR: Jeffrey Reiner
Standard satire-thriller: Small-time criminal involved with addictive aphrodisiac drug

Blood & Donuts
1996, (Can), color, 90 mins.
W: Gordon Currie, Justin Louis
Standard horror-fantasy: Reawakened vampire haunts all-night donut shop

Blood and Lace
1971, (USA), Contemporary Filmakers-Carlin C./AIP, color, 87 mins.
W: Gloria Grahame (*Mrs. Deere*), Melody Patterson (*Ellie*), Len Lesser (*Tom*), Milton Selzer (*Mullins*), Vic Tayback (*Calvin*), Terri Messina (*Bunch*), Ronald Taft (*Walter*), Peter Armstrong (*Ernest*), Dennis Christopher (*Pete*), Maggie Corey (*Jennifer*), Mary Strawberry (*The Nurse*), Louise Sherrill (*Edna*)
P: Ed Carlin & Gil Lasky   **D:** Philip Gilbert   **SCR:** Gil Lasky   **PHOTOG:** Paul Hipp   **MUSIC:** John Rons
Minor thriller: Murder and mayhem at sinister orphanage

Blood and Roses
see **Et Mourir de Plaisir**

Blood Bath
1966, (USA), AIP, b&w, 69 mins.
W: William Campbell, Linda Saunders, Marissa Mathes, Sandra Knight, Jonathan Haze, Sid Haig
P: Jack Hill   **WRIT & D:** Jack Hill & Stephanie Rothman
TV retitle, **Track of the Vampire**
Minor horror-thriller (with footage from 'Portrait in Terror'): Tale of vampiric artist

Blood Bath
1975, (USA), Trans Orient, color
W: Harve Presnell, Jack Somack, Curt Dawson, Doris Roberts, Jerry Lacy, Stefan Schnabel, Norman Bush, Lee Moore, Richard Niles, P.J. Soles, Tom Tammi, Sharon Shayne
WRIT & D: Joel M. Reed   **MUSIC:** Michael Sahl
Amateurish anthology-thriller

Blood Bath at the House of Death
1982, (GB), Wildwood, color, 92 mins.
W: Vincent Price (*The Sinister Man*), Pamela Stephenson (*Barbara Coyle*), Kenny Everett (*Lucas Mandeville*), Gareth Hunt (*Elliot Broome*), Don Warrington (*Stephen Wilson*), John Fortune (*John Harrison*), Sheila Steafel (*Sheila Finch*), John Stephen Hill (*Henry Noland*), Cleo Rocos (*Deborah Rudling*), Graham

Stark (*The Blind Man*), Pat Ashton (*The Barmaid*), David Lodge (*Insp. Goule*), Davilia David (*Sheila's Mother*), Debbie Linden (*The Attractive Girl*), Tim Barrett (*A Doctor*), Oscar Quitak (*A Doctor*), Ellis Dale (*The Patient*), Anna Dawson (*The Nurse*), Barry Cryer (*The Police Inspector*), Gordon Rollings (*The Man at the Bar*), Jack Le White (*The Old Man*), Ray Cameron (*The Policeman*), Sandy Donaldson (*The Dog*)
P & D: Ray Cameron SCR: Ray Cameron & Barry Cryer PHOTOG: Brian West & Dusty Miller MUSIC: Mike Moran & Mark London
Minor horror-spoof: Parapsychologists probe murder mansion

Blood Beach
1980, (USA), Sir Run Run Shaw & Sidney Beckerman/Jerry Gross, color, 88 mins.
W: David Huffman (*Harry*), Mariana Hill (*Catherine*), John Saxon (*Pearson*), Burt Young (*Royko*), Stefan Gierasch (*Dimitrios*), Otis Young (*Piantadosi*), Darrell Fetty (*Hoagy*), Lynne Marta (*Jo*), Eleanor Zee (*Mrs. Selden*), Lena Pousette (*Marie*), Mickey Fox (*Moose*), Pamela McMyler (*Mrs. Hench*), Harriet Medin (*Ruth*), Laura Burkett, Marleta Giles, Charles Rowe Rook, Julie Dolan, Jacqueline Randall, John Joseph Thomas, Christopher Franklin, Sandra Friebel, Bobby Bass, Read Morgan, Robert Newirth, Mary Jo Catlett, James Ogg, Judy Walker, Norton Buffalo, Yancy E. Burns III, Michael Lewis, Laurin Rinder
P: Steven Nalevansky D & SCR: Jeffrey Bloom STORY: Jeffrey Bloom & Steven Nalevansky PHOTOG: Steve Poster MUSIC: Gil Melle
Minor horror-thriller: Mutant terror resides beneath beach

Blood Beast from Hell
see The Deathshead Vampire

Blood Beast from Outer Space
see Night Caller from Outer Space

The Blood Beast Terror
see The Deathshead Vampire

Blood Brides
see Brides of Blood

Blood Ceremony
see Ceremonia Sangrienta

Blood Couple
see Ganja and Hess

The Blood Creature
see Terror is a Man

Blood Cult
1985, (USA), color, 92 mins.
W: Chuck Ellis, Julie Andelman, Jim Vance, Joe Hardt
D: Christopher Lewis
Made-for-Video, minor thriller: Murder-mutilations on a midwestern campus. cf Revenge (1986)

The Blood Cult of Shangri-La
see The Thirsty Dead

Blood Hunt
see The Thirsty Dead

Blood Demon
see Die Schlangengrube und das Pendel

Blood Diner
1987, (USA), PMS Filmworks/Lightning, color, 88 mins.
W: Rick Burks (*Michael Tutman*), Carl Crew (*George Tutman*), Roger Dauer (*Mark Shepard*), LaNetta La France (*Sheba Jackson*), Lisa Guggenheim (*Connie Stanton*), Max Morris (*Chief Miller*), Roxanne Cybelle (*Little Michael*), Sir Rodenheaver (*Little George*), Dino Lee (*King of White Trash*), The Luv Johnsons (*The White Trash Review*), Drew Godderis (*Anwar*), Alan Corona (*Paul Stanton*), Bob Loya (*Stan Saidin*), Tanya Papanicolas (*Sheetar & Bitsy*), Deseree Rose (*Mrs. Stanton*), Laurie Guzda (*Joanne*), Karen Hazelwood (*Babs*), Cynthia Baker (*Cindy*), Effie Bilbrey (*Peggy*), Michael Barton (*Vitamin*), John Randall (*Buzz*), Jane Cantillion (*Mrs. Namtut*), John Barton Shields (*Jimmy Hitler*), Alisa Alvarez, Bonnie Bradigan, Cynthia Cantrell, Cathy Cooper, Deanne McCain, Eva Swidereka, Carol Katz, Joe Barton, Barbara Babbins, Bob Avacado, Aron Illa, Sean Holton, L'Ronald Smith, Gary Scherzer, David Dressel, Anthony McFarland, Nichol Paris, Mark Smith, Eric Williams, Samuel Cambell, Sabrina Brooks, Art Weeks, Brick Schmidt, Erick Amidor, Parnell Davison, Aric Levit, Harold Hager, Steve Donemeyer, Dennis Logan, Reynaldo Anaya, Eric Snyder, Michael Lucie, Les Robin, Michael Boshears, Tony Smith, Jared Chandler, Brad Biggart, Teresa Stone, Debra Wolf, Jeff Poduvski, Jeff Harris, Terry Thompson, Simon Alexander, Ted Guggenheim, Jerry Mascot, Mang Doung, Sydney Kato, Maritza Morales, Steve Jenson, Joanne Taylor, Herman Senac, Don Barris, Peter Honig, Beautiful Bobby, Rhett Bartlett, William Kempton, Tony Defillipis, Patrick Kelly Mack, Sonya Baez, Candye Kane
D: Jackie Kong SCR: Michael Sonye PHOTOG: Jurg Walther SPCL-FX: Bruce Zahlava MUSIC: Don Preston SONGS: *Stud Party, Everybody Get Some, Shake It Out, Ay Si Si, Lost Incas, Love Will Make Your Mind Go Wild, Let Me Give You Money, Baby Let's Make Love, Crazy Over You, Heaven in*

Paradise, '59 Volvo, & Putting the Night on Hold
Minor horror-satire: Nerds revive pagan goddess

Blood Doctor
see Mad Doctor of Blood Island

The Blood Drinkers
1966, (Phil), Hemisphere, color, 86 mins.
W: Amalia Fuentes, Eddie Fernandez, Eva Montes, Renato Robles, Celia Rodriguez, Mary Walter, Ronald Remy, Fred Param, Paquito Salcedo, Felisa Salcedo, Andres Benitez, Eddie Arce, Conchita Cruz, Vicky Velasquez, Jess Roma, Cesar Aguilar, Ric Paulino, Frank Saavedra, Evelyn Shreve, Tiva Lava, Renato Murado Jr., Rudy Bugarin, Ricardo Rivera, Ernesto David, Luis Benedicto, Felix Dionisio, Mona del Cielo, Eriberto Amazan Jr., Frankie Lastimoso, Jess Buenaflor, Philip Antivo
D: Gerardo de Leon SCR: Cesar Amigo STORY: Rico Bello Omagap PHOTOG: Felipe J. Sacdalan SPCL-FX: Hilario Brothers MUSIC: Tito Arevalo
Minor horror-thriller: Master vampire seeks girl's life. USA TV-retitle, Vampire People

Bloodeaters
1980, (USA), Parker Nat'l, color, 84 mins.
W: John Amplas (*Phillips*), Charles Austin (*Cole*), Beverly Shapiro (*Polly*), Dennis Helfend (*The Hermit*), Paul Haskin (*Briggs*)
P, D, & SCR: Chuck McCann PHOTOG: David Sperling MUSIC: Ted Shapiro
A.k.a. Forest of Fear
Minor horror-thriller: Drug dealers become cannibal-zombies

Blood Evil
see Demons of the Mind

Blood Feast
1963, (USA), Boxoffice Spectaculars, color, 70 mins.
W: Thomas Wood, Connie Mason, Mal Arnold, Lyn Bolton, Scott H. Hall, Ashlyn Martin P: David F. Friedman D & PHOTOG: Herschell G. Lewis SCR: A. Louis Downe
Legendary schlock-exploitation epic: Demented fiend performs grisly ritual murders

Blood Fiend
see Theatre of Death

Blood Frenzy
1987, (USA), color, 90 mins.
W: John Montero, Lisa Loring, Hank Garrett, Wendy MacDonald
D: Hal Freeman
Made-for-Video, minor thriller: Psychologist's patients take trip to desert; things get nasty

Blood from the Mummy's Tomb
1971, (GB), Hammer/AIP, color, 94 mins.
W: Andrew Keir (*Prof. Julian Fuchs*), Valerie Leon (*Margaret/Queen Tera*), James Villiers (*Corbeck*), Hugh Burden (*Dandridge*), George Coulouris (*Berigan*), Mark Edwards (*Tod Browning*), Joan Young (*Mrs. Caporal*), Rosalie Crutchley (*Helen Dickerson*), James Cossins (*A Nurse*), David Jackson (*A Nurse*), Tamara Ustinov (*Veronica*), Jonathan Burne (*The Man*), Penelope Holt (*A Nurse*), Madina Luis (*The Priest*), Aubrey Morris (*Dr. Putnam*)
P: Howard Brandy D: Seth Holt SCR: Christopher Wicking, from Bram Stoker's novel *The Jewel of Seven Stars* PHOTOG: Arthur Grant MUSIC: Tristam Cary
Modest horror-fantasy: Archeologist opens tomb of ancient Egyptian witch, grief follows cf. The Awakening

Blood Harvest
1973, (USA), color, 90 mins.
W: Tiny Tim
Minor thriller: Murders mar girl's homecoming

Blood Hook
1987, (USA), color, 85 mins.
W: Mark Jacobs, Lisa Todd, Patrick Danz
D: James Mallon
Minor horror-thriller: Insane fisherman turns tournament into bloodbath

Bloodhounds
1996, (USA), Made for Cable, color
W: Christine Hamos, Corbin Bernsen
Made-for-Cable, standard thriller: Woman detective teams with author to capture murderer

Blood Island
see The Shuttered Room

Blood is My Heritage
see Blood of Dracula

Bloodknot
1995, (USA), Showtime/Para, Made for Cable, color, 98 mins.
W: Patrick Dempsey, Kate Vernon, Margot Kidder, Craig Sheffer
D: Jorge Montesi SCR: Randy Kornfield PHOTOG: Philip Linzey MUSIC: Ian Thomas
Standard thriller

Blood Lake

1987, (USA), color, 90 mins
Minor thriller: Psycho stalks teens

Blood Legacy

see Legacy of Blood

The Bloodless Vampire

1965, (USA), Journey, b&w
<u>W:</u> Charles Macaulay, Helen Thompson
<u>D:</u> Michael du Pont
Minor horror-thriller

Blood Link

1983, (It), color, 98 mins
<u>W:</u> Geraldine Fitzgerald, Sarah Langenfeld, Michael Moriarty, Penelope Milford
(*Julie*), Cameron Mitchell (*Waldo*)
<u>D:</u> Alberto DeMartino
Minor horror-thriller: Doctor tormented by visions of murder connected to twin brother

Blood Simple: JOHN GETZ

Bloodlust!

1961, (USA), Cinegraf/Crown-Int'l, b&w, 68 mins.
<u>W:</u> Wilton Graff, Robert Reed, June Kenny, Lilyan Chauvin, Gene Persson,
Walter Brooke
<u>WRIT, P, & D:</u> Ralph Brooke, inspired by Richard Connell's novella *The Most Dangerous Game*
TV retitle, Beast from Blood Island
Minor thriller: Bearded weirdo on drugs stalks unfortunates

Bloodlust: Subspecies III

1993, (USA), color, 83 mins.
<u>W:</u> Anders Hove
Minor horror-thriller: Woman battles sadistic vampire to save sister's soul

Blood Mania

1971, (USA), Jude/Crown-Int'l, color, 88 mins.
<u>W:</u> Paul Carpenter (*Cooper*), Vicki Peters (*Gail*), Maria de Aragon (*Victoria*),
Reagan Wilson, Eric Allison, Alex Rocco, Arell Blanton, Leslie Simms, Reid
"Chip" Smith
<u>D:</u> Robert O'Neil   <u>SCR:</u> Toby Sacher & Tony Crechales
Minor thriller: Plotless mix of seduction, blackmail, & murder

Blood Money

1921, (GB), Granger-Binger, b&w, 4,722 ft. (1439.3m)
<u>W:</u> Adelqui Migliar (*Le Grand*), Dorothy Fane (*Felice Deschanel*), Frank Dane
(*Sarne*), Arthur Cullin (*Matthew Harper*), Colette Brettel (*Marguerite Deschanel*), Harry Ham (*Insp. Bell*), Fred Goodwins (*Bruce Harper*)
<u>D:</u> Fred Goodwins, from a novel by Cecil Bullivant
Standard crime-thriller: Gambler kidnaps mistress' husband

Blood Moon

see La Noche de Walpurgis

Bloodmoon

1990, (Austral), color, 104 mins.
<u>W:</u> Leon Lissek, Christine Amor, Ian Patrick Williams, Anya Molina, Helen
Thomson, Hazel Howson, Craig Cronin
<u>D:</u> Alec Mills   <u>SCR:</u> Richard Brennan   <u>MUSIC:</u> Brian May
Minor thriller: Mad killer slays randy students

Blood of a Poet

see Le Sang d'un Poete

Blood of Dracula

1957, (USA), Carmel/AIP, b&w, 69 mins.
<u>W:</u> Sandra Harrison (*Nancy Perkins*), Gail Ganley (*Myra*), Louise Lewis (*Miss
Branding*), Jerry Blaine (*Tab*), Heather Ames (*Nola*), Craig Duncan (*Glenn*),
Thomas B. Henry (*Mr. Perkins*), Mary Adams, Don Devlin, Paul Maxwell, Richard Devon, Barbara Wilson, Michael Hall,
Jeanne Dean, Carlyle Mitchell, Voltaire Perkins
<u>P:</u> Herman Cohen   <u>D:</u> Herbert L. Strock   <u>STORY & SCR:</u> Ralph Thornton
<u>PHOTOG:</u> Monroe Askins   <u>MUSIC:</u> Paul Dunlap
British retitle, Blood is My Heritage, Canadian retitle, Blood of the Demon
orig. co-billed with I Was a Teenage Frankenstein
blurb: "In her eyes—desire! In her veins—the blood of a monster!"
Minor but effective horror-thriller: Chemistry teacher turns troubled teen into vampiress

Blood of Dracula's Castle

1969, (USA), Paragon-Int'l/Crown-Int'l, color, 81 mins.
<u>W:</u> John Carradine (*George*), Paula Raymond (*Countess Townsend*), Alex D'Arcy
(*Count Townsend/Dracula*), Gene O'Shane (*Glen Cannon*), Barbara Bishop
(*Liz*), Robert Dix (*Johnny*), Vicki Volante (*Ann*), Ray Young (*Mango*), John
Cardos, Ken Osborne
<u>P:</u> Al Adamson & Rex Carlton   <u>D:</u> Al Adamson   <u>SCR:</u> Rex Carlton   <u>PHOTOG:</u>
Leslie Kovacs   <u>SONG:</u> *The Next Train Out*
orig. to be titled Feast of Blood, TV retitle, Dracula's Castle
Minor horror-thriller: Couple inherits desert estate, find it occupied by vampires

Blood of Frankenstein

see Dracula vs. Frankenstein

The Blood of Fu Manchu

1968, (GB-Sp), Hammer/Anglo-Amalgamated, color, 91 mins.
<u>W:</u> Christopher Lee (*Dr. Fu Manchu*), Gotz George (*Carl Janson*), Tsai Chin (*Lin
Tang*), Richard Greene (*Nayland Smith*), Howard Marion-Crawford (*Dr.
Petrie*), Maria Rohm (*Ursula*), Richard Palacios (*Sancho Lopez*), Shirley Eaton
(*Black Widow*), Frances Kahn (*Carmen*), Loni von Friedl (*Celeste*), Isaura de
Olivera (*Yuma*)
<u>P:</u> Harry Alan Towers   <u>D:</u> Jesus Franco   <u>SCR:</u> Peter Welbeck [Harry Alan
Towers], from characters created by Sax Rohmer   <u>PHOTOG:</u> Manuel
Merino   <u>MUSIC:</u> Daniel White
A.k.a. Against All Odds and Kiss and Kill
Standard thriller: Oriental villain poisons heads of state

Blood of Ghastly Horror

1971, (USA), Hemisphere, color, 87 mins.
<u>W:</u> John Carradine (*Dr. Vannard*), Kent Taylor, Regina Carrol, Tommy Kirk, Roy
Morton, Tacey Robbins, Richard Smedley, John Armond, Arne Warda, Kirk
Duncan, Tanya Maree, Barney Gelfan, Lyle Felice, Joey Benson, John
Talbert, K.K. Riddle
<u>P & D:</u> Al Adamson   <u>SCR:</u> Dick Poston & Chris Martino   <u>STORY:</u> Al Adamson
& Samuel M. Sherman   <u>PHOTOG:</u> Vilmos Zsigmond & Louis Horvath
<u>ORIG. MUSIC:</u> Jimmy Roosa & Don McGinnis
*orig. released (1965) as Psycho-A-Go-Go!, reissued (1969, with added scenes) as
Fiend with the Electronic Brain, A.k.a. Blood of Ghastly Terror, Man
with the Synthetic Brain, The Fiend with the Atomic Brain, and The
Love Maniac*
Minor horror-thriller: Doctor creates monstrosities

Blood of Ghastly Terror

see Blood of Ghastly Horror

The Blood of Heroes

1990, (USA), New Line, color, 90 mins.
<u>W:</u> Rutger Hauer (*Sallow*), Joan Chen (*Kidda*), Anna Katarina (*Big Cimber*),
Vincent D'Onofrio (*Young Gar*), Gandhi MacIntyre (*Gand-hai*), Delroy
Lindo (*Mbulu*), Justin Monjo (*Doy Boy*)
<u>WRIT & D:</u> David Peoples   <u>PHOTOG:</u> David Eggby   <u>MUSIC:</u> Todd
Boekelheide
Standard SF-thriller: Post-nuke warriors clash. Australian retitle, Salute of the Juggers

Blood of Jesus

1941, (USA), b&w, 60 mins.
<u>W:</u> Spencer Williams Jr., Kathryn Craviness
<u>D & SCR:</u> Spencer Williams Jr.
Minor religious fantasy: Man accidentally shoots wife

Blood of Nostradamus

1960, (Mex), b&w
<u>W:</u> German Robles, Domingo Soler, Julio Aleman, Aurora Alvarado
*Minor horror-fantasy, feature comprised of 3 episodes (The Apparition in the Convent,
The Black Bird & The Last Victim) from 1959 serial. Vampire rises from
grave, carries out vendetta against police inspector. cf. Nostradamus y el
Destructor de Monstruos, Nostradamus y el Genio de la Tinieblas and La
maldicion de Nostradamus*

Blood of the Demon

see Blood of Dracula

Blood of the Devil Man
see House of the Black Death

Blood of the Undead
see Schizo (1977)

Blood of the Vampire
1958, (GB), Eros/Univ, color, 87 mins.
<u>W:</u> Donald Wolfit (*Dr. Callistratus*), Vincent Ball (*Dr. John Pierre*), Barbara Shelley (*Madeleine*), Victor Maddern (*Carl*), William Devlin (*Kurt Urach*), Andrew Faulds (*Wetzler*), John LeMesurier (*The Chief Justice*), George Murcell (*The Guard*), Bryan Coleman (*Herr Auron*), Bernard Bresslaw (*The Sneakthief*), Colin Tapley (*The Judge*), Cameron Hall, John Stuart, Henry Vidon
<u>P:</u> Robert S. Baker & Monty Berman   <u>D:</u> Henry Cass   <u>STORY & SCR:</u> Jimmy Sangster   <u>PHOTOG:</u> Monty Berman   <u>MUSIC:</u> Stanley Black
*German retitle, **The Demon with Bloody Hands***
Well-made thriller: Fiend runs prison for criminally insane, experiments on inmates to find cure for his blood malady

Blood on His Lips
see The Hideous Sun Demon

Blood on His Sword
1961, (Fr), color
<u>W:</u> Jean Marais, Rosanna Schiaffino
Minor action-thriller: King's daughter accused of witchcraft

The Blood on Satan's Claw
1970, (GB), Tigon/Cannon, color, 93 mins.
<u>W:</u> Patrick Wymark (*The Judge*), Linda Hayden (*Angel*), Barry Andrews (*Ralph*), Avice Landon (*Isobel*), Anthony Ainley (*Rev. Fallowfield*), Tamara Ustinov (*Rosalind*), Michele Dotrice (*Margaret*), Wendy Padbury (*Cathy*), James Hayter (*Middleton*), Charlotte Mitchell (*Ellen*), Simon Williams (*Peter*), Howard Goorncy (*The Doctor*), Robin Davies (*Mark*), Milton Reid
<u>D:</u> Piers Haggard   <u>SCR:</u> Robert Wynne-Simmons & Piers Haggard   <u>PHOTOG:</u> Dick Bush   <u>MUSIC:</u> Marc Wilkinson
*A.k.a. **Satan's Skin***
Modest horror-fantasy: Demon summoned forth

Blood Orgy
see The Gore-Gore Girls

Blood Orgy of the She-Devils
1972, (USA), Geneni, color, 74 mins.
<u>W:</u> Lila Zaborin, Tom Pace
<u>P, D, & SCR:</u> Ted V. Mikels
Minor horror-fantasy: Witch queen appropriates deserted castle

Blood Pen
1975, (USA), Ursus/Classic, color, 85 mins.
<u>W:</u> Marc Lawrence (*Zambrini*), Toni Lawrence (*Lynn Webster*), Jesse Vint (*The Sheriff*), Katharine Ross (*Miss Macy*), Iris Korn (*Annette*), Walter Barnes (*The Doctor*), William Michael (*The Deputy*), Erik Holland (*Hoagy*), Jim Antonio (*The Man from the Hospital*), Bone Adams (*The Truck Farmer*), Don Skylar (*The Oil Worker*), Larry Hussmann (*The Gas Attendant*), Paul Hickey
<u>P &D:</u> Marc Lawrence   <u>SCR:</u> F.A. Foss   <u>PHOTOG:</u> Glenn R. Roland Jr.   <u>SPCL-FX:</u> Bruce Adams   <u>MUSIC:</u> Charles Bernstein
*A.k.a. **Pigs** and **Daddy's Deadly Darling***
Minor thriller: Murderous pig-farmer befriends psychotic girl

Blood Rage
1987, (USA), color, 87 mins.
<u>W:</u> Louise Lasser, Mike Soper
<u>D:</u> John Grissmer   <u>SCR:</u> Richard Einhorn
*A.k.a. **Nightmare at Shadow Woods***
Minor thriller: Maniac twin goes on killing spree.

Blood Relatives
1977, (Can-Fr), Filmcorp/SNC, color, 94 mins.
<u>W:</u> Donald Sutherland (*Carella*), Aude Landry (*Patricia*), Lisa Langlois (*Muriel*), Laurent Malet (*Andrew*), Micheline Lanctot (*Mrs. Carella*), Stephane Audran (*Mother*), Donald Pleasence (*Doniac*), David Hemmings (*Armstrong*)
<u>D:</u> Claude Chabrol   <u>SCR:</u> Claude Chabrol & R. Sydney, from a novel by Ed McBain   <u>PHOTOG:</u> Jean Rabier   <u>MUSIC:</u> Paul Jensen
Standard thriller: Detective probes young girl's murder. USA release, 1981

Blood Relations
1988, (Can), color, 90 mins.
<u>W:</u> Jan Rubes, Lydie Dernier (*Marie*), Kevin Hicks (*Thomas*), Lynne Adams (*Sharon*)
Minor horror-thriller: Surgeon seeks body for dead wife's brain

The Blood Rose
1969, (Fr), Transatlantic/AA, color
<u>W:</u> Philippe Lemaire (*Frederic*), Annie Duperey (*Anne*), Howard Vernon (*Prof. Rohmer*), Elisabeth Tessier (*Barbara*)
<u>P:</u> Edgar Oppenheimer   <u>D:</u> Claude Mulot   <u>SCR:</u> Edgar Oppenheimer, Claude Mulot, & Jean Carriaga   <u>PHOTOG:</u> Roger Fellous   <u>MUSIC:</u> J.P. Dorsay
Standard eroto-horror: Doctor kills to restore woman's face

Blood Run
1995, (USA), color
<u>W:</u> Anna Thomson, David Bradley, Steven H. Gagnon, Ashley Laurence
Standard melodrama: Police detective attracted to murder suspect

Blood Salvage
1990, (USA), color, 98 mins.
<u>W:</u> Danny Nelson, Lori Birdsong, John Saxon, Ray Walston, Evander Holyfield
<u>D:</u> Tucker Johnston
Minor horror-thriller: Man runs body-parts junkyard

Blood Screams
1988, (USA), color, 75 mins.
<u>W:</u> Ran Sands, James Garnett
Minor horror-fantasy: Spooks in Mexican town

The Blood Seekers
see Dracula vs. Frankenstein

Bloodshed
1983, (USA), Gravity Films, color, 88 mins
<u>W:</u> Laslo Papas, Beverly Ross
<u>D:</u> Richard Cassidy
Minor horror-thriller: Psycho conceals dead girl's body

Blood Simple
1983, (USA), River Road, Circle Releasing, color, 96 mins.
<u>W:</u> John Getz (*Ray*), Frances McDormand (*Abby*), M. Emmet Walsh (*The Private Detective*), Dan Hedaya (*Julian Marty*), Samm-Art Williams (*Meurice*), Deborah Neumann (*Debra*), Van Brooks (*The Man from Lubbock*), Raquel Gavia (*The Landlady*), Senor Marco (*Mr. Garcia*), William Creamer (*The Old Cracker*), Loren Bivens (*The Strip Bar Exhorter*), Bob McAdams (*The Strip Bar Senator*), Shannon Sedwick (*The Stripper*), Nancy Finger (*The Girl on Overlook*), Rev. William Preston Robertson (*The Radio Evangelist*)
<u>D:</u> Joel Coen   <u>SCR:</u> Joel Coen & Ethan Coen   <u>PHOTOG:</u> Barry Sonnenfeld   <u>SPCL-FX:</u> Loren Bivens   <u>MUSIC:</u> Carter Burwell
Acclaimed low-budget thriller: Man conspires against wife and her lover

Blood Sisters
1986, (USA), color, 85 mins.
<u>W:</u> Amy Brentano, Marla MacHart, Brigete Cossu, Randy Mooers
<u>D:</u> Roberta Findlay
Minor thriller: Sorority babes in haunted house

Blood Song
1982, (USA), Allstate, color, 82 mins.
<u>W:</u> Frankie Avalon (*Paul*), Antoinette Bower (*Bea*), Dane Clark (*Sheriff Gibbons*), Richard Jaeckel (*Frank*), Jennifer Enskat (*Judith*), William Kirby Cullen (*Joey*), Victor Izay (*The Doctor*), Lenny Montana Jr. (*Skipper*), Noelle North (*Cathy*), Christopher Scarano (*Deputy Wilkins*), Donna Wilkes (*Marion*), David Arnot (*The First Boy*), Norman Brecke (*Norm*), Candace Dickey (*Betty*), Roydon Clark (*The Watchman*), Carla McKizzick (*The Desk Nurse*), Joseph Stanfill (*The 2nd Boy*), Robert Diedrich, Erick Fischer, Jeffery Isham, Dennis P. Karroll, Jim Kimball, Kit Lewis, Don Perry, Beverly Saukko, Elliott Silverstein
<u>D:</u> Alan J. Levi   <u>SCR:</u> James Fargo, Frank Avianca & Lenny Montana, from orig. short story by Joseph M. Shink & George Hart   <u>PHOTOG:</u> Steve Posey   <u>SPCL-FX:</u> Rick Hatcher   <u>MUSIC:</u> Rob Walsh   <u>SONGS:</u> All in Your Mind (sung by Lainie Kazan)
*A.k.a. **Dream Slayer***
Minor thriller: Girl has psychic link with axe-murderer

The Blood Spattered Bride
1972, (Sp), Morgana/Europix, color, 77 mins.
<u>W:</u> Simon Andreu (*He*), Maribel Martin (*Susan*), Dean Selmier (*The Doctor*), Alexandra Bastedo (*Carmilla*), Montserrat Julio (*The Maid*), Rosa M. Rodriguez (*Carol*), Angel Lombarte (*The Servant*)
<u>P:</u> Antonio Perez Olea   <u>WRIT & D:</u> Vicente Aranda, from Sheridan LeFanu's novel *Carmilla* (remake)   <u>PHOTOG:</u> Fernando Arribas   <u>SPCL-FX:</u> Antonio Molina   <u>MUSIC:</u> Antonio Perez Olea
*USA TV retitle, **Till Death Do Us Part***
Modest tale of lesbian-vampirism: Newlyweds encounter mystery woman

Bloodspell
1988, (USA), Feifer-Miller/Vista Street, color, 87 mins.
<u>W:</u> Anthony Jenkins (*Daniel*), Aarin Teich (*Charlie*), Alexandra Kennedy (*Debbie*), Theodora Louise (*Jenny*), John Reno (*Luther*), Edward Dloughy (*Tony*), Jacque J. Coon (*Delores*), Heather Green (*Peggy*), Kimble Jemison (*Georgie*), Christopher G. Venuti (*Joe*), Susan Bu-chanan (*Mrs. Redding*), Douglas Vale (*Dr. Nelson*), Geri Elkus (*Dr. Scott*), Arthur Alexander (*Dr. Moyers*), James English (*The Fire Chief*), Jam (*The Police Chief*), Rick "The Cheese" Jacobson (*Logger #1*), Todd "Shred" Szabo (*Logger #2*), Chris Munson (*Paramedic #1*), Tia Lachelle (*Claudia*), Jock Peterson (*Paramedic #2*)
<u>D:</u> Deryn Warren   <u>SCR:</u> Gerry Daly   <u>PHOTOG:</u> Ron Schmidt   <u>MUSIC:</u> Randy Miller
Made-for-Video, minor horror-thriller: Telekinetic teen bedevils students

The Bloodstained Shoe
1914, (GB), Urban Trading Co., b&w, 2,200 ft. (670.6m)
W: Henri Houry *(Barnet-Parker)*
Standard crime-thriller: French detective, blamed for killing blackmailer, poses as woman to find missing witness

The Bloodstained Witch
see La Sanglante Sorciere

Bloodstalkers
1976, (USA), color, 91 mins.
W: Kenny Miller, Celea Ann Cole, Jerry Albert
D: Robert W. Morgan
Minor thriller: Two vacationers meet swamp lunatics

Bloodstone
1988, (USA), color, 90 mins.
W: Charlie Brill, Christopher Neame, Jack Kehler, Brett Stimely
D: Dwight Little   SCR: Nico Mastorakis & Curt Allen
Standard comedy-thriller: Honeymooners involved with jewel thieves

Bloodstone: Subspecies II
1993, (USA), color, 90 mins.
W: Anders Hove, Kevin Blair, Denice Duff, Melanie Shatner
Standard horror-fantasy: Two sisters pursued by vampire

Bloodsucker
see Doctors Wear Scarlet

The Blood Suckers
see Gallery of Horror

Bloodsuckers from Outer Space
1983, (USA), color, 80 mins.
W: Thom Meyer, Laura Ellis, Billie Keller, Kim Braden
D: Glenn Coburn
Minor SF-horror: Space aliens cause Texas farmers to become bloodsucking zombies

Blood Sucking Freaks
see The Incredible Torture Show

Bloodsucking Pharaohs in Pittsburgh
see Picking Up the Pieces

Bloodthirsty Butchers
1970, (USA), Mishkin/Constitution, color, 80 mins.
W: John Miranda, Annabella Wood, Berwick Kaler
P: William Mishkin   D, SCR, & PHOTOG: Andy Milligan
*orig. co-billed with **Torture Dungeon***
*Minor thriller (remake of **The Demon Barber of Fleet Street**): Psychos commit atrocities*

Bloodthirsty Eyes
see Lake of Dracula

Blood Tide
1982, (USA), color, 82 mins.
W: James Earl Jones, Jose Ferrer, Lila Kedrova, Mary Louise, Weller, Martin Kove, Deborah Shelton
D: Richard Jeffries   SCR: Nico Mastorakis
*A.k.a. **The Red Tide**.*
Minor horror-thriller: Aquatic monster unleashed in Greek isles

Blood Tracks
1986, (USA), color, 82 mins.
W: Jeff Harding, Michael Fitzpatrick, Naomi Kaneda
D: Mike Jackson
Minor thriller: Cannibal family lurks in mountains, menaces members of music-video shoot

Blood Virgin
see Symptoms

Blood Waters of Dr. Z
1975, (USA), Capital, color
W: Marshall Grauer, Nancy Lien, Paul Galloway, Gerald Cruse, Sanna Ringhaver, Wade Popwell
P & D: Don Barton   SCR: Lee O. Larew & Ron Kivett   PHOTOG: Jack McGowan   MUSIC: Jami De Frates & Barry Hodgin
*released (by Horizon Films) in limited areas as **Zaat**, orig. filmed in 1972*
Minor horror-thriller: Experiments have monstrous results

Bloody Birthday
1986, (USA), color, 85 mins.
W: Susan Strasberg, Jose Ferrer, Lori Lethin, Joe Penny, Melinda Cordell, Julie Brown, Billy Jacoby, Michael Dudikoff
D: Ed Hunt
Minor horror-thriller (filmed in 1980): Born during lunar eclipse, three 10-year-old kids go on murder spree

Bloody Birthday
1980, (USA), color, 92 mins.
W: Susan Strasberg, Jose Ferrer, Lori Lethin, Joe Penny, Melinda Cordell, Ellen Geer, Julie Brown, Billy Jacoby, Michael Dudikoff
D: Edward Hunt
*Minor thriller: Three hellions commit murder. A.k.a. **Creeps***

Bloody Judge
see Night of the Blood Monster

Bloody Moon
1983, (Sp), color, 84 mins.
W: Olivia Pascal, Christopher Brugger
D: Jesus Franco
Minor horror-thriller: Tourists murdered in Spanish village

Bloody New Year
1987, (GB), color, 90 mins.
W: Suzy Aitchison, Colin Heywood
D: Norman J. Warren
Minor horror-fantasy: Spirits trap guests at year-end party

The Bloody Pit of Horror
see Il Boia Scarlatto

The Bloody Vampire
see El Vampiro Sangriento

Bloody Wednesday
1987, (USA), color, 89 mins.
W: Raymond Elmendorf, Pamela Baker, Navarre Perry
D: Mark Gilhuis   SCR: Philip Yordan   MUSIC: Al Sendry
Standard thriller: Hotel caretaker goes mad

Blow Out
1981, (USA), George Litto/Filmways, color, 107 mins.
W: John Travolta *(Jack Terri)*, Nancy Allen *(Sally)*, Dennis Franz *(Manny Karp)*, John Lithgow *(Burke)*, Peter Boyden *(Sam)*, Curt May *(Frank Donohue)*, John Aquino *(The Detective)*, Dave Roberts *(Anchorman #1)*, Ernest McClure *(Jim)*, Claire Carter *(Joan, the Anchorwoman)*, Maurice Copeland *(Jack Manners)*, John Hoffmeister *(McRyan)*, Patrick McNamara *(Officer Nelson)*, Tom McCarthy *(The Policeman)*, Terrence Currier *(Lawrence Henry)*, Dean Bennett *(The Campus Guard)*
WRIT & D: Brian De Palma   PHOTOG: Vilmos Zsigmond   MUSIC: Pino Donaggio
Modest thriller, imitation of Hitchcock: Sound mixer witnesses murder

Blow-Up
1966, (GB), Carlo Ponti/Bridge/MGM, color, 111 mins.
W: David Hemmings *(Thomas)*, Vanessa Redgrave *(Jane)*, Sarah Miles *(Patricia)*, Peter Bowles *(Ron)*, John Castle *(The Painter)*, Gillian Hills *(A Girl)*, Harry Hutchinson *(The Dealer)*, Verushka *(The Model)*, Julian Chagrin *(The Mime)*, Jill Kennington, Rosaleen Murray, Ann Norman, Melanie Hampshire
D: Michelangelo Antonioni   STORY: Julio Cortazar   SCR: Michelangelo Antonioni, Tonino Guerra & Edward Bond   PHOTOG: Carlo Di Palma
Celebrated thriller: Photographer suspects murder

Bluebeard (1901)
see Barbe-Bleue

Bluebeard
1944, (USA), PRC, b&w, 73 mins.
W: John Carradine *(Gaston)*, Jean Parker *(Lucille)*, Nils Asther *(Insp. Lefevre)*, George Pembroke, Ludwig Stossel, Sonia Sorel, Teala Loring, Henry Kolker, Iris Adrian
D: Edgar G. Ulmer   SCR: Pierre Gendron   PHOTOG: Jockey A. Feindel   MUSIC COMPOSED AND CONDUCT.: Erdody
blurb: "To love him meant death!"
Standard thriller, classic Carradine performance: Psychotic puppeteer kills women

Bluebeard (1962)
see Landru

Bluebeard
1972, (It), CRC, color, 125 mins.
W: Richard Burton *(Baron von Sepper/"Bluebeard")*, Raquel Welch *(Magdalena)*, Joey Heatherton *(Anne)*, Virna Lisi *(Elga)*, Karin Schubert *(Greta)*, Nathalie Delon *(Brigitte)*, Agostina Belli *(Caroline)*, Edward Meeks *(Sergio)*, Sybil Danning *(The Prostitute)*, Jean Lefebvre *(Greta's Father)*, Mathieu Carriere *(The Violinist)*
P: Alexander Salkind   D: Edward Dmytryk   STORY & SCR:, Ennio De Concini, Edward Dmytryk, & Maria Pia Fusco   PHOTOG: Gabor Pogany   MUSIC: Ennio Morricone
"For Burton there have been assembled eight very beautiful actresses, each and every one of them endowed far beyond the ordinary... (They are) spectacular"—Archer Winsten, New York Post

Bluebeard's Ten Honeymoons
1960, (GB), Anglo-Allied/WPD, b&w, 92 mins.
<u>W</u>: George Sanders (*Henri Landru*), Corinne Calvet (*Odette*), Jean Kent (*Julienne Guillin*), Patricia Roc (*Vivienne Dureaux*), Greta Gynt (*Jeannette Tissot*), Maxine Audley (*Cynthia Phillips*), Ingrid Hafner (*Giselle*), Selma Vas Diaz (*Mme. Boyer*), Peter Illing (*Lefevre*), George Coulouris (*Lacoste*), Sheldon Lawrence (*Pepi*), Jack Melford (*The Concierge*), Harold Berens (*The Jeweller*)
<u>P</u>: Roy Parkinson   <u>D</u>: W. Lee Wilder   <u>STORY</u>: Myles Wilder
Standard thriller: Antique dealer murders his wealthy wives

The Blue Bird
1910, (GB), Gaumont, b&w, 1,380 ft. (420.6m)
<u>W</u>: Pauline Gilmer (*Mytyl*), OLive Walter (*Tyltyl*), Margaret Murray (*Mummy Tyl*), E.A. Warburton (*Daddy Tyl*), Norma Page (*Tylette*), Ernest Hendrie (*Tylo*), Carlotta Addison (*The Fairy*), Edward Rigby (*Bread*), H.R. Hignett (*Sugar*), C.V. France (*Time*), Doris Lytton (*Milk*), Saba Raleigh (*Night*), Roy Travers (*The Cow*)
from Maurice Maeterlinck's 1908 fairy play
Standard fantasy: Fairy helps selfish children find bird of happiness

The Blue Bird
1918, (USA), Famous Players-Lasky, b&w
<u>W</u>: Robin MacDougall, Gertrude McCoy, Tula Belle
<u>D</u>: Maurice Tourneur, from Maurice Maeterlinck's 1908 fairy play
Standard fantasy: Girl seeks true meaning of happiness

The Blue Bird
1940, (USA), Darryl F. Zanuck/20th-Fox, color, 98 mins.
<u>W</u>: Shirley Temple, Spring Byington, Gale Sondergaard, Nigel Bruce, Laura Hope Crews, Eddie Collins, Al Shean, Cecilia Loftus, Johnny Russell, Russell Hicks, Sterling Holloway, Scotty Beckett, Helen Ericson (*Light*), Sybil Jason, Jessie Ralph
<u>D</u>: Walter Lang   <u>SCR</u>: Ernest Pascal, from Maurice Maeterlinck's 1908 fairy play   <u>PHOTOG</u>: Arthur C. Miller   <u>SPCL-FX</u>: Fred Sersen   <u>MUSIC</u>: Alfred Newman
Lavish but ponderous fantasy (20th-Fox's answer to MGM's 1939 'Wizard of Oz'): Self-centered girl reformed by magic adventure

The Blue Bird
1976, (USA-Russ), Edward Lewis-Lenfilm/20th-Fox, color, 100 mins.
<u>W</u>: Elizabeth Taylor (*Mother/Maternal Love/Light/Witch*), Todd Lookinland (*Tyltyl*), Patsy Kensit (*Mytyl*), Jane Fonda (*Night*), Cicely Tyson (*The Cat*), Ava Gardner (*Luxury*), Harry Andrews (*The Oak King*), Robert Morley (*Father Time*), Nadezda Pavlova (*The Blue Bird*), George Cole (*The Dog*), Will Geer (*Grandfather*), Mona Washbourne (*Grandmother*), Maya Plisetskaya (*Water*), Oleg Popov (*The Clown*), Richard Pearson (*Bread*), Margarate Terechova (*Milk*), George Vitzin (*Sugar*), Leonid Nevedomsky (*Father*), Yevgeny Scherbakov (*Fire*), Leningrad Kirov Ballet
<u>P</u>: Paul Maslansky   <u>D</u>: George Cukor   <u>SCR</u>: Hugh Whitemore, from Maurice Maeterlinck's 1908 fairy play   <u>PHOTOG</u>: Freddie Young & Ionas Gritzus   <u>MUSIC</u>: Irwin Kostal
Unforgivable editing (ballet sequences butchered) makes first US-Soviet co-production a sorry hodgepodge: Two small children seek elusive embodiment of joy

Blue Blood
1974, (GB), Mallard/Impact Quadrant/Nationwide, color, 86 mins.
<u>W</u>: Oliver Reed (*Tom*), Fiona Lewis (*Lily*), Derek Jacobi (*Gregory*), Anna Gael (*Carlotta*), John Rainer (*Clurman*), Meg Wynn Owen (*Beate Krug*), Richard Davies (*Jones*), Tim Wylton (*Morrell*), Gwyneth Owen (*Agnes*), Patrick Carter (*Cocky*), Elaine Ives-Cameron (*Serena*), Hubert Rees (*Dr. Barrett*), Dilys Price (*Mrs. Barrett*), Sally Anne Newton (*Susannah*)
<u>P</u>: Kent Walwin & John Trent   <u>D & SCR</u>: Andrew Sinclair, from Alexander Thynne's novel *The Carry Cot*   <u>PHOTOG</u>: Harry Waxman   <u>MUSIC</u>: Brian Gascoigne
Standard horror-thriller: Evil butler and German governess employ black magic to usurp aristocrat's estate

The Blue Dahlia
1946, (USA), Para, b&w, 98 mins.
<u>W</u>: Alan Ladd, Veronica Lake, William Bendix, Howard Da Silva, Hugh Beaumont, Doris Dowling, Tom Powers, Howard Freeman, Don Costello
<u>D</u>: George Marshall   <u>SCR</u>: Raymond Chandler   <u>PHOTOG</u>: Lionel Lindon   <u>MUSIC</u>: Victor Young
Modest thriller: War veteran seeks wife's killer

The Blue Demon
1966, (Mex), b&w
Minor SF-fantasy: Monstrous creature wreaks havoc

Blue Desert
1991, (USA), color
<u>W</u>: Courtney Cox, D.B. Sweeney (*Smith*)
Made-for-Video, standard thriller: New York rape victim finds peril in desert town

Blue Flame
1993, (USA), color, 88 mins.
<u>W</u>: Brian Wimmer, Ian Buchanan, Kerri Green, Cecilia Peck, Jad Mager
<u>D & SCR</u>: Cassian Elwes
Standard SF-thriller: Vigilante cop tracks humanoid aliens

The Blue Gardenia
1953, (USA), WB, b&w, 90 mins.
<u>W</u>: Anne Baxter, Richard Conte, Ann Sothern, Raymond Burr, Jeff Donnell, Richard Erdman, Nat King Cole
<u>D</u>: Fritz Lang   <u>STORY</u>: Vera Caspary   <u>PHOTOG</u>: Nicholas Musuraca
Modest thriller : Woman fears she has murdered

Blue Ice
1992, (USA), HBO-TV, color, 96 mins.
<u>W</u>: Michael Caine (*Harry Anders*), Sean Young (*Stacy Mansdorf*), Ian Holm (*Sir Hector*), Bobby Short (*Buddy*), Alun Armstrong (*Osgood*), Sam Kelly (*George*), Jack Shepherd (*Stevens*), Phillip Davis (*Westy*), Patricia Hayes (*The Old Woman*), Bob Hoskins (*Garcia*), Alan MacNaughton (*Lewis Mansdorf*), Mac Andrews (*The Cab Driver*), Todd Boyce (*Kyle*), Peter Forbes (*The Medic*), Peter Gordon (*The Mortuary Attendant*), Oliver Haden (*Stacy's Driver*), Nigel Harrison (*Fleming*), Philip Whitchurch (*Blackner*)
<u>D</u>: Russell Mulcahy   <u>SCR</u>: Ron Hutchinson   <u>MUSIC</u>: Michael Kamen
Made-for-Cable, standard thriller: Ex-spy probes friends' death

The Blue Light
see Das Blaue Licht

The Blue Lightning
1986, (Australian), The 7 Network/Roadshow/CBS-TV, color, 95 minutes
<u>W</u>: Sam Elliott
TV Movie; Standard melodrama: Detective trails international jewelry criminal from San Francisco to Australia

Blue Monkey
1987, (Can), Sandy Howard/Spectrafilm, color, 98 mins.
<u>W</u>: Steve Railsback (*Det. Jim Bishop*), Gwynyth Walsh (*Dr. Rachel Carson*), Susan Anspach (*Dr. Judith Glass*), John Vernon (*Roger Levering*), Joe Flaherty (*George Baker*), Ivan E. Roth (*The Creature*), Robin Duke (*Sandra Baker*)
<u>D</u>: William Fruet   <u>SCR</u>: George Goldsmith   <u>PHOTOG</u>: Brenton Spencer   <u>MUSIC</u>: Patrick Coleman & Paul Novotny
Modest SF-horror: Ghastly larvae rampage. Laser-disc retitle, **Insect**

Blue Movie Blackmail
1973, (GB-It), Monymusk/Clodio/Italian Int'l/Hemdale, color,, 97 mins.
<u>W</u>: Ivan Rassimov (*Insp. Cliff*), Stephanie Beacham (*Joanne*), Patricia Hayes (*Momma the Turk*), Red Carter (*Morrel*), Cec Linder (*The Ambassador*), Verna Harvey, Luciano Catenacci, Giacomo Rossi-Stuart, Leon Vitali
<u>P</u>: Ross MacKenzie & Leonardo Pescarolo   <u>D</u>: Massimo Dellamano   <u>STORY</u>: Massimo Dellamano & Sandy MacRae   <u>PHOTOG</u>: Jack Hildyard   <u>MUSIC</u>: Riz Ortolani
Standard crime-thriller: Inspector loves girl involved with drug ring, reissue retitle, **Superbitch**

The Blue Panther
1965, (Fr), color
<u>W</u>: Akim Tamiroff, Marie Laforet, Roger Hanin
<u>D</u>: Claude Chabrol
Fast-moving thriller: International jewel thieves operate in Switzerland

The Blue Parrot
1953, (GB), ACT Films/Monarch, b&w, 69 mins.
<u>W</u>: Dermot Walsh (*Bob Herrick*), Jacqueline Hill (*Maureen*), Ballard Berkeley (*Supt. Chester*), Ferdy Mayne (*Stevens*), Valerie White (*Eva West*), Richard Pearson (*Quincey*), John LeMesurier (*Carson*), June Ashley (*Gloria*), Diane Watts (*Carena*), Edwin Richfield (*Taps Campbell*), Arthur Rigby (*Charlie*)
<u>P</u>: Stanley Haynes   <u>D</u>: John Harlow   <u>SCR</u>: Allan Mackinnon, from Percy Hoskins' story "Gunman"
Standard crime-thriller: American detective and woman cop solve nightclub killing

Blue Lightning: SAM ELLIOT AND REBECCA GILLING

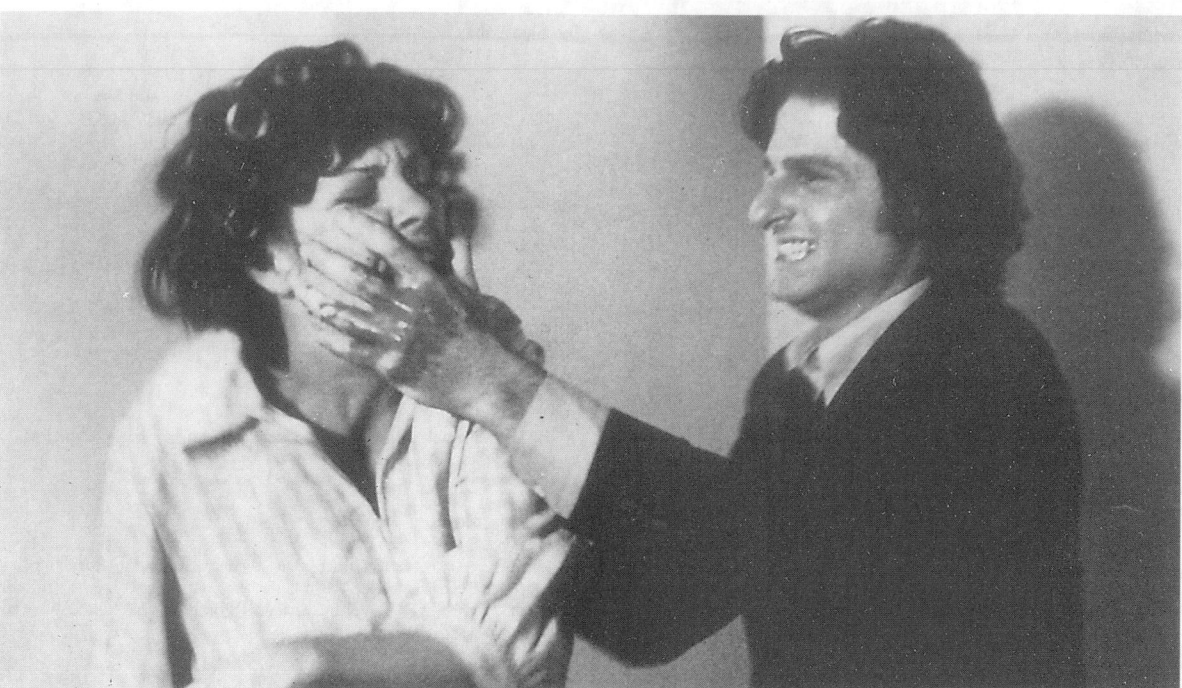

Blue Sunshine: BARBARA QUINN AND ZALMAN KING

A Blueprint for Murder
1953, (USA), 20th-Fox, b&w, 77 mins.
W: Joseph Cotten, Jean Peters, Catherine McLeod, Gary Merrill, Jack Kruschen, Walter Sande
WRIT & D: Andrew L. Stone   **PHOTOG:** Leo Tover   **MUSIC:** Lionel Newman
Standard "perfect crime" thriller: Man proves sister-in-law is murderess

Blue Sunshine
1978, (USA), Cinema Shares, color, 95 mins.
W: Zalman King (*Zipkin*), Robert Walden, Alice Ghostley, Mark Goddard, Deborah Winters, Charles Siebert, Ann Cooper, Ray Young, Stefan Gierasch, Bill Cameron, Richard Crystal
P: George Manasse   **D & SCR:** Jeff Lieberman   **MUSIC:** Charles Gross
Standard thriller: Bad LSD causes outbreak of psychosis

Blue Velvet
1986, (USA), DEG, color, 120 mins.
W: Kyle MacLachlan, Isabella Rossellini, Dennis Hopper, Dean Stockwell, Laura Dern, Hope Lange, George Dickerson, Frances Bay, Priscilla Pointer, Brad Dourif, Jack Harvey, Ken Stovitz
WRIT & D: David Lynch   **PHOTOG:** Frederick Elmes   **MUSIC:** Angelo Badalamenti
Erotic thriller: Youth fascinated by psycho-killer

Blue, White and Perfect
1941, (USA), 20th-Fox, b&w, 75 mins.
W: Lloyd Nolan (*Michael Shayne*), Mary Beth Hughes (*Merle Garland*), Helene Reynolds (*Helen Shaw*), George Reeves (*Juan Arturo O'Hara*), Steven Geray (*Vanderhoffen*), Henry Victor (*Hagerman*), Curt Bois (*Nappy*), Marie Blake (*Ethel*), Emmett Vogan (*Charlie*), Mae Marsh (*Mrs. Toby*), Frank Orth (*Mr. Toby*), Ivan Lebedeff (*Alexis Fournier*), Wade Boteler (*The Judge*), Charles Trowbridge (*The Captain*), Edward Earle (*Richards*), Cliff Clark (*The Inspector*), Arthur Loft (*Capt. McCordy*), Ann Doran (*Miss Hoffman*), Charles Williams (*The Printer*)
D: Herbert I. Leeds   **SCR:** Samuel G. Engel, from orig. story by Borden Chase and characters created by Brett Halliday   **PHOTOG:** Glen MacWilliams   **MUSIC:** Emil Newman
Standard "Michael Shayne" thriller: Gumshoe foils Axis agents

The Blue Yonder
see **Time Flyer**

Bluff
1921, (GB), Hardy/Gaul, b&w, 6,240 ft. (1902m)
W: Lewis Willoughby (*Courtenay Boscawen*), Marjorie Hume (*Dorothy Channing*), Lawrence Anderson (*James Legge*), Guy Graham (*Lord Landassyl*), Sydney Paxton (*Everard Wade*), A. Harding Steerman (*Geoffrey Channing*), Mme. d'Esterre (*Mrs. Channing*)
P: Sam Hardy   **D:** Geoffrey H. Malins   **SCR:** Rafael Sabatini—from his novel
Standard crime-thriller: Ex-embezzler foils blackmailer. Reissued 1930

Boadicea
1926, (GB), British Instructional/New Era, b&w, 7,915 ft. (2412.5m)
W: Phyllis Neilson-Terry (*Boadicea*), Clifford McLaglen (*Marcus*), Lilian Hall Davis (*Emmelyn*), Sybil Rhoda (*Blondicca*), Clifford Heatherley (*Catus Decianus*), Fred Raynham (*Badwallon*), Edward O'Neill (*Caradoc*), Humberston Wright (*Prasutagas*), Roy Raymond (*Burrus*), Cyril McLaglen (*Madoc*)
D: Sinclair Hill   **STORY:** Sinclair Hill & Anthony Asquith
Standard adventure: Celtic queen opposes Roman invaders

Boarding House
1982, (USA), Comet/Blustarr/Paragon Video, color, 99 mins.
W: Hawk Adley (*Jim Royce/The Gardener*), Kalassu Kay (*Victoria*), Alexandra Day (*Debbie Hoffman*), Joel McGinnis Riordan (*Joel Weintraub*), Brian Bruderlin (*Richard*), Belma Kora (*Sandy*), Tom Mones (*The Agent*), Tracy O'Brian (*Suzie*), Rosane Woods (*Gloria*), Mary McKinley (*Cindy*), Cindy Williamson (*Pam*), Elizabeth Hall (*Terri*), Christopher Conlan (*Christopher*), Elliot Van Koghbe (*Officer Weston*), Dean Disico (*Harris*), A'Ryen Winter (*Nurse Sherry*), John Chase (*The Orderly*), Victoria Herron (*Su Ling*), Michael Burke (*The Lawyer*), Jim Vincioni (*Officer Paul*), Carla Nansel (*The Girl in the Car*), Allen R. Warren (*The Uncle*), Tim Campbell (*The Bass Player*), Michele Krieger (*The Photographer*), Jon Buxer (*The Keyboard Player*), Chris Cristin (*The Guitar Player*), Mark Prines (*The Magician*)
D: Johnn Wintergate   **SCR:** Jonema   **PHOTOG:** Jan Lucas & Obee Ray   **MUSIC:** Teeth   **SONGS:** by 33 1/3
Made-for-Video, minor horror-fantasy: Beauties butchered by mysterious assassin

Bobbikins
1959, (GB), 20th-Fox, b&w, 90 mins.
W: Shirley Jones (*Betty Barnaby*), Max Bygraves (*Benjamin Barnaby*), Billie Whitelaw (*Lydia Simmons*), Barbara Shelley (*Valerie*), Colin Gordon (*Dr. Phillips*), Charles Tingwell (*Luke Packer*), Lionel Jeffries (*Gregory Mason*), Rupert Davies (*Jock Fleming*), Charles Carson (*Sir Jason Crandall*), Steven Stocker (*Bobbikins Barnaby*), Charles Lloyd-Pack (*Stebbins*)
WRIT & P: Oscar Brodney   **D:** Robert Day   **PHOTOG:** Geoffrey Hawkes   **MUSIC:** Philip Green
Amusing comedy-fantasy: Entertainer finds infant son can converse like adult

The Bobby's Nightmare
1905, (GB), Gaumont, b&w, 200 ft. (60.9m)
D: Alf Collins
Standard comedy-fantasy: Policeman has bad dream

Bobby's Dream of Battle
1907, (GB), Warwick Trading Co., b&w, 385 ft. (117.3m)
Standard comedy-fantasy: Boy dreams he is sentry shooting bypassers

Bobby Wideawake
1909, (GB), Urban Trading Co., b&w, 500 ft. (152.4m)
D: Walter R. Booth
Standard fantasy: Boy dreams motorized bed travels under sea to Arctic

Bodily Harm
1995, (USA), Rysher Entertainment, color, 95 mins.
W: Linda Fiorentino, Daniel Baldwin, Gregg Henry (*J.D.*), Bill Smitrovich (*Lt. Stewart*), Troy Evans (*Oscar*), Joe Regalbuto (*Stan*), Millie Perkins, Todd Susman, Shannon Kenny, Ken Lerner, William Utay, Casey Biggs, Mark Morrow
D: James Lemmo   **SCR:** James Lemmo, Joseph Whaley & Rhoda Barehase

PHOTOG: Doyle Smith   MUSIC: Robert Sprayberry
Minor thriller: Woman homicide detective probes stripper's murder, finds ex-lover is suspect

Body Armor
1997, (USA), color, 100 mins.
W: Matt McColm, Ron Perlman (*Dr. Krago*), Annabel Schofield (*Marisa*), Morgan
   Brittany (*Sloane*), Clint Howard (*Hutch*), John Rhys-Davies (*Rashee*)
Made-for-Video, minor SF-thriller: Special agent injected with deadly virus

Body Bags
1993, (USA), Made for Cable, color, 95 mins.
W: Alex Datcher, Stacy Keach, Mark Hamill, Robert Carradine, David Warner,
   David Naughton, Twiggy, Sheena Easton, Tobe Hooper, John Agar, Deborah
   Harry, Roger Corman, Sam Raimi, Wes Craven, Tom Arnold, John
   Carpenter
D: John Carpenter & Tobe Hooper   SCR: Billy Brown & Dan Angel   MUSIC:
   John Carpenter
Standard trio of terror tales: Unleaded, Hair, & Baseball Man

The Body Beneath
1971, (USA), Nova Int'l, color
W: Gavin Reed, Jackie Skarvellis
P, D, SCR, & PHOTOG: Andy Milligan
Minor horror-fantasy: Reverend heads family of 19th-century vampires

Body Count
1987, (USA), color, 90 mins.
W: Marilyn Hassett, Dick Sargent, Steven Ford, Thomas Ryan, Greg Mullavey,
   Bernie White
D: Paul Leder
A.k.a. The 11th Commandment
Minor thriller: Murder and cannibalism as weird family seeks to enhance fortune.

The Body Disappears
1941, (USA), WB, b&w, 72 mins.
W: Edward Everett Horton, Jane Wyman, Jeffrey Lynn, Marguerite Chapman,
   Willie Best
D: Ross Lederman
Minor SF-comedy: Corpse injected with "invisibility formula"

Body Double
1984, (USA), Col, color, 115 mins.
W: Craig Wasson (*Jake Scully*), Gregg Henry (*Sam*), Melanie Griffith (*Holly*),
   Deborah Shelton (*Gloria*), David Haskell, Guy Boyd, Dennis Franz, Al
   Israel
P & D: Brian De Palma   SCR: Robert J. Avrech & Brian De Palma   STORY:
   Brian De Palma   PHOTOG: Stephen H. Burum   MUSIC: Pino Donaggio
SONGS: *Relax*
De Palma's modest homage to Hitchcock's Dial M for Murder, Rear Window and
   Vertigo: House-sitting actor spies on mysterious beauty, becomes involved in murder

Body Heat
1981, (USA), Ladd Co./WB, color, 113 mins.
W: William Hurt (*Ned Racine*), Kathleen Turner (*Matty Walker*), Richard Crenna
   (*Edmund Walker*), Mickey Rourke (*Teddy Lewis*), J.A. Preston (*Oscar Grace*),
   Ted Danson (*Peter Lowenstein*), Kim Zimmer (*Mary Ann*), Jane Hallaren
   (*Stella*), Lanna Saunders (*Roz Kraft*), Michael Ryan (*Miles Hardin*), Carola
   McGuinness (*Heather Kraft*), Larry Marko (*Judge Costanza*), Deborah
   Lucchessi (*Beverly*), Lynn Hallowell (*Angela*), Thom J. Sharp (*Michael
   Glenn*), Ruth Thom (*Mrs. Singer*), Diane Lewis IRobert Traynor (*The Prison
   Trustee*), Meg Kasdan (*The Nurse*), Ruth P. Strahan (*Betty the Housekeeper*),
   Bruce A. Lee (*The Man on the Beach*), Filomena Triscari (*The Hostess at
   Tulios*), Tomas Choy, Ramiro Velasco, Servio T. Moreno
D & SCR: Lawrence Kasdan   PHOTOG: Richard H. Kline   MUSIC: John Barry
Erotic (with echoes of Double Jeapordy): Beauty draws lawyer into murder plot

Body Melt
1993, (USA), color, 82 mins.
W: Gerard Kennedy, Andrew Daddo, Ian Smith, Vincent Gil, Regina Gaigalas
D & MUSIC: Philip Brophy   SCR: Philip Brophy & Rod Bishop
Standard SF-thriller: Crazed doctor eliminates small-town residents

Body Parts
1990, (USA), color, 96 mins.
W: Teri Lee, Dick Monda, Johnny Mandel
Minor thriller: Psycho dismembers strippers

Body Parts
1991, (USA), Frank Mancuso Jr./Para, color, 89 mins.
W: Jeff Fahey (*Chrushank*), Lindsay Duncan (*Dr. Agatha Webb*), Brad Dourif (*Remo
   Lacey*), Kim Delaney (*Karen Chrushank*), Zakes Mokae (*Det. Sawchuk*), Paul
   Benvictor (*Ray Kolberg*), Lindsay Merrithew (*Roger*), Nathaniel Moreau (*Bill
   Jr.*), Sarah Campbell (*Samantha*), Arlene Duncan (*Nurse #1*), Allan Price (*TV
   Reporter #1*), Hal Eisen (*TV Reporter #2*), Taia Red (*The Female Reporter*),
   James Kidnie (*Det. Jackson*), Peter Murnik (*Mark Draper*), Andy Humphrey
   (*Ricky*), Gene Dinovi (*The Bartender*), Lynn Remus (*Nurse #2*), Peter
   MacNeill (*The Drunk*), Larry McLean, John Stoneham Sr., Gene Mack, John
   Walsh
D: Eric Red   SCR: Eric Red & Norman Snider   SCREEN STORY: Patricia

Herskovic, from Pierre Boileau & Thomas Narcejac's novel *Choice Cuts*
PHOTOG: Theo Van de Sande   MUSIC: Loek Dikker
Standard horror-fantasy: Man bedeviled by arm transplant

The Body Shop
1972, (USA), color, 91 mins.
W: Pat Patterson, Jenny Driggers, Ron Mehaffey, Candy Furr, Linda Faile
D: Pat Patterson
Minor horror-thriller: Man pieces together dismembered wife. A.k.a. Doctor Gore

The Body Snatcher
1945, (USA), RKO, b&w, 77 mins.
W: Boris Karloff, Henry Daniell, Edith Atwater (*Meg*), Rita Corday (*Mrs. Marsh*),
   Bela Lugosi (*Joseph*), Russell Wade (*Fettes*), Sharyn Moffett, Donna Lee,
   Robert Clarke, Bill Williams
P: Val Lewton   D: Robert Wise   SCR: Philip MacDonald & Carlos Keith, from
   Robert Louis Stevenson's short story   PHOTOG: Robert De Grasse
MUSIC: Roy Webb
"...one of the most literate of horror films"—William K. Everson, The Bad Guys
Classic melodrama: Scottish doctor involved with sinister grave-robber. cf. The Doctor and
   the Devils and The Flesh and the Fiends

The Body Snatcher (1956)
see El Ladron de Cadaveres

Body Snatcher from Hell
1969, (Jap), Pacemaker, color, 84 mins
W: Hideo Ko, Teruo Yoshida, Tomomi Sato, Eizo Kitamura, Masay Takahashi,
   Cathy Horlan, Kazuo Kato, Yuko Kusonoki
D: Hajime Sato   SCR: Susumu Tataku & K. Kobayashi
A.k.a. Goke, the Body Snatcher from Hell
Standard SF-horror: Plane-crash survivors slain by space vampire

The Body Snatchers
1993, (USA), WB, color, 87 mins.
W: Terry Kinney (*Steve Malone*), Meg Tilly (*Carol Malone*), Gabrielle Anwar (*Marti
   Malone*), Billy Wirth (*Tim Young*), Reilly Murphy (*Andy Malone*), Christine
   Elise (*Jenn Platt*), R. Lee Ermey (*Gen. Platt*), Kathleen Doyle (*Mrs. Platt*),
   Forest Whitaker (*Dr. Collins*), G. Elvis Phillips (*Pete*), Stanley Small (*Platt's
   Aide*), Tonea Stewart (*The Teacher*), Keith Smith, Winston E. Grant, Phil
   Neilson, Sylvia Small, Timothy P. Brown, Thurman L. Combs, Adrian
   Unveragh, Allen Perada, Johnny L. Smith, Candy Orsini, Marty Lyons,
   Darien Taylor, Rick Kangrga, Michael Cohen, James P. Monoghan,
   Kimberly L. Cole, Craig Lockhart
P: Robert H. Solo   D: Abel Ferrara   SCR: Stuart Gordon, Dennis Paoli &
   Nicholas St. John   SCR STORY: Raymond Cistheri & Larry Cohen, based
   on Jack Finney's novel   PHOTOG: Bojan Bazelli   MUSIC: Joe Delia
Standard SF-horror: Angst on army base as pod people supplant humans

The Body Stealers
1969, (GB), Tigon-Sagittarius/AA, color, 91 mins.
W: George Sanders (*Gen. Armstrong*), Maurice Evans (*Dr. Matthews*), Patrick Allen
   (*Bob Megan*), Neil Connery (*Jim Radford*), Hilary Dwyer (*Julie Slade*), Robert
   Flemyng (*Baldwin*), Lorna Wilde (*Lorna*), Allan Cuthbertson (*Hindsmith*),
   Sally Faulkner (*Joanna*), Michael Culver (*Lt. Bailes*), Shelagh Fraser (*Mrs.
   Thatcher*), Carl Rigg (*Briggs*), Jan Miller (*Sally*), Carol-Anne Hawkins
   (*Paula*)
P: Tony Tenser   D: Gerry Levy   STORY: Michael St. Clair & Peter Marcus
   PHOTOG: Peter Henry
A.k.a. Invasion of the Body Stealers and Thin Air
Standard SF-thriller: Space-alien abductions of parachutists

The Body Vanishes
1939, (GB), Venture/New Realm, b&w, 45 mins.
W: Anthony Hulme (*Rodney Paine*), Ernest Sefton (*Sgt. Hopkins*), C. Denier
   Warren (*Pip Piper*), Eve Foster (*Miss Casson*), Frank Atkinson (*Hobbleberry*),
   Wilfred Noy (*Snelling*)
D: Walter Tennyson   STORY: Ian Walker
Minor thriller: Art thief fakes own death to escape partner's vengeance

Bog
1983, (USA), Bog-Nelsen Communications/Marshall, color, 87 mins.
W: Gloria De Haven (*Ginny Glenn/Arianna*), Aldo Ray (*Sheriff Neal Rydholm*),
   Marshall Thompson (*Dr. Brad Wednesday*), Leo Gordon (*Dr. John Warren*),
   Glen Voros (*Alan Tanner*), Lou Hunt (*Kim Pierce*), Rojay North (*Chuck
   Pierce*), Carol Terry (*May Tanner*), Ed Clark (*Deputy Jensen*), Robert Fry
   (*Wallace Fry*), Leroy Winbush (*Terry Taylor*), Dan Killian (*Bill Beckley*), Don
   Daniels (*Hotchkiss*), Charles Pitt (*Deputy Corbett*), Richard Nygaard (*The
   Townsman*), Chris Harris (*Deputy Siegel*), Glen Hopkins (*Deputy Macweeny*),
   Pat Hop-kins (*1st Girl on Bike*), Dino Stroppa (*Potter the Poacher*), Jeff
   Schwaab (*The Bug Monster*)
D: Don Keeslar   ORIG. SCR: Carl N. Kitt   PHOTOG: Wings   SPCL-FX,
   MUSIC DIR: Richard Albain & Gerald Winchell Bill Walker   SONGS:
   Walk with Me (sung by Pat Hopkins)

The Bogey Man
1980, (Ind), color, 90 mins.
W: Ramunni, Master Ashokan, Vilasini
D: G. Aravindan
Standard mix of fantasy & folklore: Pied piper visits small village

Boggy Creek II—The Legend Continues
1985, (USA), color
<u>W</u>: Charles B. Pierce, Cindy Butler (*Leslie Ann*), Serene Hedin (*Tanya*)
<u>WRIT & D</u>: Charles B. Pierce
*Minor horror-thriller: Professor pursues bizarre creature. cf. **The Legend of Boggy Creek***

Bogus
1996, (USA), Regency Enterprises/WB, color, 112 mins.
<u>W</u>: Whoopi Goldberg (*Harriet Franklin*), Gerard Depardieu (*Bogus*), Haley Joel Osment (*Albert*), Nancy Travis, Denis Mercier
<u>D</u>: Norman Jewison <u>SCR</u>: Alvin Sargent <u>STORY</u>: Jeff Rothberg & Francis X. McCarthy <u>PHOTOG</u>: David Watkin <u>MUSIC</u>: Marc Shaiman
Standard romance-fantasy: Imaginary playmate becomes real

Bogus: GÉRARD DEPARDIEU AND WHOOPI GOLDBERG

Il Boia Scarlatto (The Crimson Executioner)
1965, (It), Pacemaker, color, 74 mins.
<u>W</u>: Mickey Hargitay
<u>P</u>: Francesco Merli <u>D</u>: Massimo Pupillo <u>SCR</u>: Roberto Natale & Romano Migliorini
*A.k.a. **The Bloody Pit of Horror** and **The Red Hangman***
Minor horror-thriller: Laughable torture scenes when demented body-builder comes to believe he is reincarnation of infamous medieval inquisitor

A Bold Adventuress
1915, (GB), Broadwest/Award, b&w, 3,446 ft. (1056.4m)
<u>W</u>: Nell Emerald (*Clara Blythe*), Walter West (*James Ridgeway*)
<u>D & STORY</u>: Walter West
Standard crime-thriller: Earl's fiancee hires burglar to steal letters from blackmailer

The Bold Caballero
1936, (USA), Rep, color, 69 mins.
<u>W</u>: Robert Livingston, Heather Angel, Sig Rumann, Robert Warwick
<u>D</u>: Wells Root
Minor thriller: Masked hero fights corrupt California governor (Zorro)

A Bold Venture
1912, (GB), Hepworth, b&w, 1,050 ft. (320m)
<u>D</u>: Warwick Buckland
<u>STORY</u>: Muriel Alleyne
Standard crime-thriller: Bank robbers pose as rag pickers, frame clerk for theft

Bombshell
1997, (USA), SCI-TV, color
<u>W</u>: Henry Thomas, Madchen Amick
TVM, standard SF-thriller: Research scientist's experiments with microscopic robots go awry

Bomba and the Elephant Stampede
1951, (USA), Mono, b&w, 71 mins.
<u>W</u>: Johnny Sheffield, Donna Martell, Myron Healey, John Kellogg
from characters created by Roy Rockwood.
*TV retitle, **Elephant Stampede***
Minor adventure-thriller: Jungle boy opposes villains

Bomba and the Hidden City
1950, (USA), Mono, b&w, 71 mins.
<u>W</u>: Johnny Sheffield, Sue England, Paul Guilfoyle, Charles La Torre, Damian O'Flynn, Leon Belasco, Smoki Whitfield
<u>D</u>: Ford Beebe <u>SCR</u>: Carroll Young, from characters created by Roy Rockwood
  <u>PHOTOG</u>: William Sickner <u>MUSIC</u>: Ozzie Caswell
blurb: "Ruthless killers stalk human prey in Africa's citadel of mystery!"
Standard adventure-thriller: Jungle boy helps girl flee concealed African city

Bomba and the Jungle Girl
*see **The Jungle Girl***

Bomba and the Lion Hunters
*see **The Lion Hunters***

Bomba on Panther Island
*see **Panther Island***

Bomba, the Jungle Boy
1949, (USA), Mono, b&w, 71 mins.
<u>W</u>: Johnny Sheffield, Peggy Ann Garner, Onslow Stevens, Smoki Whitfield, Charles Irwin, Martin Wilkins
<u>D</u>: Ford Beebe <u>SCR</u>: Jack de Witt, from the popular comic strip by Roy Rockwood <u>PHOTOG</u>: William Sickner <u>MUSIC DIR.</u>: Edward Kay
Standard adventure-thriller: White boy raised in Africa

Bomb in High Street
1961, (GB), Foxwarren-Elthea/RFD, b&w, 60 mins.
<u>W</u>: Ronald Howard (*Capt. Manning*), Suzanne Leigh (*Jackie*), Terry Palmer (*Mike*), Jack Allen (*Supt. Haley*), Peter Gilmore (*Shorty*), Russell Waters (*Trent*), Jack Lambert (*The Sgt.*), Maurice Good (*Feeney*), Geoffrey Bayldon (*Clay*), Humphrey Lestocq (*The Reporter*)
<u>P</u>: Ethel Linder Reiner, T.B.R. Zichy & Henry Passmore <u>D</u>: Terence Bishop & Peter Bozencenet <u>STORY</u>: Benjamin Simcoe
Standard crime-thriller: Eloping teenagers foil bank-robbing gang

Bon Baisers de Hong Kong (From Hong Kong with Love)
1975, (Fr), Films Christian Fechner-Renn Prods., color, 97 mins.
<u>W</u>: Les Charlots, Mickey Rooney, Huguette Funfrok, David Tomlinson, Clifton James, Jean Manson
<u>D</u>: Yvan Chiffre <u>SCR</u>: Christian Fechner & Yvan Chiffre
Standard spy-spoof: Mad millionaire kidnaps queen of Great Britain

Bond of Fear
1956, (GB), Mid-Century/Eros, b&w, 66 mins.
<u>W</u>: Dermot Walsh (*John Sewell*), Jane Barrett (*Mary Sewell*), John Colicos (*Dewar*), Jameson Clark (*Scotty*), Anthony Pavey (*Michael Sewell*), John Horsley (*The Constable*), Marulyn Baker (*Ann Sewell*), Avril Angers (*The Hiker*)
<u>P</u>: Robert Baker & Monty Berman <u>D</u>: Henry Cass <u>SCR</u>: John Gilling & Norman Hudis <u>STORY</u>: Digby Wolfe
Standard crime-thriller: Escaped killer takes family hostage

The Bone Yard
1990, (USA), color, 98 mins.
<u>W</u>: Ed Nelson, Deborah Rose, Norman Fell, Jim Eustermann, Denise Young, Willie Stratford Jr., Phyllis Diller
<u>D & SCR</u>: James Cummins
Minor thriller: Mortuary murder

The Bonnie Parker Story
1958, (USA), AIP, b&w, 79 mins.
<u>W</u>: Dorothy Provine, Jack Hogan, Richard Bakalyan, Douglas Kennedy, Joseph Turkel, Stanley Livingston
<u>WRIT & P.</u>: Stanley Shpetner <u>D</u>: William Witney
Standard melodrama: Highly-fictionalized bio of notorious 1930's criminal

Bonzo Goes to College
1952, (USA), Univ, b&w, 80 mins.
<u>W</u>: Maureen O'Sullivan (*Marion Drew*), Charles Drake (*Malcolm Drew*), Edmund Gwenn (*Pop Drew*), Gene Lockhart (*Clarence B. Gateson*), Gigi Perreau (*Betsy Drew*), Irene Ryan (*Nancy*), Guy Williams (*Ronald Calkins*), John Miljan (*Wilbur Crane*), Jerry Paris (*Lefty Edwards*), David Janssen (*Jack*), Frank Nelson (*Dick*), Paul Birch, Kathleen Freeman, Bonzo
<u>P</u>: Ted Richmond <u>D</u>: Frederick de Cordova <u>SCR</u>: Leo Lieberman & Jack Henley <u>PHOTOG</u>: Carl Guthrie <u>MUSIC</u>: Frank Skinner
*Minor comedy-fantasy: Chimp gets educated. cf. **Bedtime for Bonzo***

Booby Trap
1957, (GB), Jaywell/Eros, b&w, 71 mins.
<u>W</u>: Sydney Tafler (*Hunter*), Patti Morgan (*Jackie*), Harry Fowler (*Sammy*), Tony Quinn (*Prof. Hasdane*), Jacques Cey (*Bentley*), Richard Shaw (*Richards*), John Watson (*Maj.Cunliffe*), Michael Moore (*The Curate*)
<u>P</u>: Bill Luckwell & Derek Winn <u>D</u>: Henry Cass <u>SCR</u>: Peter Bryan & Bill Luckwell <u>STORY</u>: Peter Bryan
Standard crime-thriller: Drug peddler unknowingly takes explosive pen

The Boogens
1981, (USA), Jensen Farley Pictures/Taft-Int'l, color, 95 mins.
<u>W</u>: Rebecca Balding (*Trish*), Fred McCarren (*Kinner*), Jeff Harlan (*Roger*), Anne-Marie Martin (*Jessica*), Peg Stewart, Med Flory, John Crawford
<u>D</u>: James L. Conway <u>SCR</u>: David O'Malley & Bob Hunt <u>STORY</u>: Tom Chapman & David O'Malley <u>PHOTOG</u>: Paul Hipp <u>MUSIC</u>: Bob Summers
Standard horror-thriller: Subterranean creatures strike

The Boogeyman
1980, (USA), Ulli Lommel/Interbest/Jerry Gross, color, 81 mins.
<u>W</u>: Suuzanna Love (*Lacey*), Ron James (*Jake*), John Carradine (*Dr. Warren*), Nicholas Love (*Willy*), Raymond Boyden (*Kevin*), Felicite Morgan (*Helen*), Jay Wright (*Young Willy*), Bill Rayburn (*Uncle Ernest*), Llewelyn Thomas (*Father Reilly*), Natasha Schiano (*Young Lacey*), Gillian Gordon (*Mother*), Howard Grant (*The Lover*), Jane Pratt (*Jane*), Lucinda Ziesing (*Susan*), David Swim, Katie Casey, Ernest Meier, Stony Richards, Claudia Porcelli

Catherine Tambini
WRIT, P, & D: Ulli Lommel   **SCR:** Ulli Lommel, Suzanna Love & David Herschel   **PHOTOG:** David Sperling & Jochen Breitenstein   **MUSIC:** Tim Krog
Minor horror-fantasy: Murderous spirit escapes mirror

Boogeyman II
1981, (USA), Ulli Lommel/Interbest/Jerry Gross, color
W: Ulli Lommel, Suzanna Love, Shannah Hall
WRIT, P & D: Ulli Lommel
Minor horror-fantasy: Little girl haunted by mirror

The Boogie Man Will Get You
1942, (USA), Col, b&w, 66 mins.
W: Boris Karloff, Jeff Donnell, Peter Lorre, Maxie Rosenbloom, Larry Parks, Maude Eburne, Don Beddoe
P: Colbert Clark   **D:** Lew Landers   **SCR:** Edwin Blum   **PHOTOG:** Henry Freulich
Modest comedy-fantasy: Mad doctor drugs traveling salesmen, hustles them into "superman" machine

The Book
1913, (GB), Hepworth, b&w, 1,200 ft. (365.8m)
W: Alec Worcester (*Jack Arkwright*), Maria de Solla (*Mrs. Arkwright*)
D: Warwick Buckland
Standard crime-thriller: Cashier gambles, robs bank

Boots from Bootle
1916, (GB), Martin/DFSA, b&w, 718 ft. (218.8m)
D: Edwin J. Collins
Minor fantasy short: Sailor's boots kick people and make them vanish

Boris and Natasha: The Movie
1988, (USA), color, 92 mins.
W: Dave Thomas (*Boris*), Sally Kellerman (*Natasha*), Christopher Neame (*Fearless Leader*), Andrea Martin (*Toots*), Alex Rocco (*Kaufman*), Paxton Whitehead (*Anton/Kregor*) Larry Cedar, Arye Gross, Anthony Newley, John Candy, John Travolta, Charles Martin Smith
D: Charles Martin Smith
*Standard comedy-satire (characters from **Rocky & Bullwinkle** cartoon teleseries): Inept spies vs. mad scientist, debuted on cable in 1992*

Born to Kill
1947, (USA), RKO, b&w, 92 mins.
W: Lawrence Tierney, Claire Trevor, Walter Slezak, Audrey Long, Phillip Terry, Elisha Cook Jr., Tommy Noonan, Isabel Jewell, Esther Howard, Grandon Rhodes
D: Robert Wise
*A.k.a. **Lady of Deceit***
Standard thriller: Society woman involved with professional killer.

The Borrower
1989, (USA), Cannon, color, 97 mins.
W: Rae Dawn Chong (*Diana Pierce*), Don Gordon (*Charles Krieger*), Tom Towles (*Bob Laney*), Pam Gordon (*Connie*), Antonio Fargas (*Julius Caesar Roosevelt*), Neil Giuntoli, Larry Pennell, Tony Amendola, Madchen Amick, Stuart Cornfeld
D: John McNaughton   **SCR:** Mason Nage & Richard Fire, from a story by Mason Nage
PHOTOG: Julio Macat & Robert New   **MUSIC:** Robert McNaughton & Steven A. Jones   **SONGS:** *Blood Money, Chain Me Down & Fatal Strike*
Modest SF-satire: Space alien seeks human heads

The Borrowers
1973, (USA), NBC-TV/Charles M. Schulz/Walt DeFaria/20th Fox, color
W: Eddie Albert, Tammy Grimes, Dame Judith Anderson (*Aunt Sophy*), Beatrice Straight (*Mrs. Crampfurl*), Karen Pearson (*Arrietta*), Dennis Larson
D: Walter C. Miller, from Mary Norton's children's book
TVM, standard fantasy: Little people live under floorboards of Victorian mansion

The Borrowers
1993, (GB), color, 199 mins.
W: Ian Holm, Penelope Wilton, Rebecca Callard
D: John Henderson   **TELEPLAY:** Richard Carpenter
TVM, standard fantasy

The Borrowers
1998, (USA), Working Title/Polygram, color, 83 mins.
W: John Goodman (*Ocious P. Potter*), Jim Broadbent (*Pod Clock*), Celia Imrie (*Homily Clock*), Flora Newbigin (*Arrietty Clock*), Tom Felton (*Peagreen Clock*), Mark Williams (*Exterminator Jeff*), Hugh Laurie (*Officer Steady*), Bradley Pierce (*Pete Lender*)
D: Peter Hewitt   **SCR:** Gavin Scott & John Kamps, from novels by Mary Norton
PHOTOG: John Fenner & Trevor Brooker   **VS-FX SPRVSR:** Peter Chiang
MUSIC: Harry Gregson-Williams   **SCORE:** Hans Zimmer
Standard juvenile fantasy: Diminuitive people infest house

Boston Blackie
1923, (USA), Fox, b&w, 5 reels
W: William Russell (*Boston Blackie*), Eva Novak (*Mary Carter*), Frank Brownlee (*Warden Benton*), Otto Matieson (*Danny Carter*), Spike Robinson (*Shorty*

McNutt), Frederick Esmelton (*John Gilmore*)
D: Scott Dunlap   **SCR:** Paul Schofield, from Jack Boyle's novel   **PHOTOG:** George Schneiderman
Minor thriller: Rogue opposes brutal prison warden

Boston Blackie Booked on Suspicion
1945, (USA), Col, b&w, 70 mins.
W: Chester Morris, Lloyd Corrigan, George E. Stone, Richard Lane
Standard thriller: Man fleeced in rare-book deal

Boston Blackie Goes Hollywood
1942, (USA), Col, b&w, 68 mins.
W: Chester Morris (*Boston Blackie*), Constance Worth (*Gloria Lane*), George E. Stone (*Runt*), Richard Lane (*Insp. Farraday*), Forrest Tucker (*Whipper*), William Wright (*Slick Barton*), John Tyrrell (*Steve*), Lloyd Corrigan (*Arthur Manleder*), Ralph Dunn (*The Sergeant*), Walter Sande (*Det. Matthews*), Shirley Patterson (*The Stewardess*), Al Herman, Charles Sullivan, Cy Ring, Jessie Arnold
D: Michael Gordon   **SCR:** Paul Yawitz, from characters created by Jack Boyle
PHOTOG: Henry Freulich   **MUSIC:** Morris Stoloff
Standard mystery-thriller: Rogue hunts stolen diamonds

Boston Blackie's Appointment with Death
*see **One Mysterious Night***

Boston Blackie's Chinese Venture
1949, (USA), Col, b&w, 59 mins.
W: Chester Morris (*Boston Blackie*), Maylia (*Mei Ling*), Joan Woodbury (*Red*), Richard Lane (*Insp. Farraday*), Don McGuire (*The Bus Guide*), Frank Sully (*Sgt. Matthews*), Luis Van Rooten (*Bill Craddock*), Sid Tomack (*Runt*), Charles Arnt (*Pop Gerard*), Benson Fong (*Ah Hing*), Philip Ahn (*Wong*), Peter Brocco (*Rolfe*), Edgar Dearing
P: Rudolph C. Flothar   **SCR:** Maurice Tombragel   **PHOTOG:** Vincent Farrar
MUSIC: Mischa Bakaleinikoff
Standard mystery-thriller: Rogue seeks Chinatown murderer

Boston Blackie's Little Pal
1918, (USA), Metro, b&w, 5 reels
W: Bert Lytell (*Boston Blackie*), Rhea Mitchell (*Mary*), Frank Whitson (*Martin Wilmerding*), Rosemary Theby (*Mrs. Wilmerding*), Joey Jacobs (*Martin Wilmerding Jr.*), John Burton (*Jackson*), Howard Davies (*Donald Lavelle*)
D: E. Mason Hopper   **SCR:** Albert Shelby Le Vino, from a story by Jack Boyle
First "Boston Blackie" mystery-thriller: Suave thief covets jewels

Boston Blackie's Rendezvous
1945, (USA), Col, b&w, 64 mins.
W: Chester Morris (*Boston Blackie*), Nina Foch (*Sally Brown*), Steve Cochran (*James Cook*), Richard Lane (*Insp. Farraday*), George E. Stone (*Runt*), Frank Sully (*Sgt. Matthews*), Adelle Roberts (*Patricia Powers*), Iris Adrian (*Martha*), Harry Hayden (*Arthur Manleder*), Joe Devlin (*Steve Caveroni*), Dan Stowell (*The Hotel Clerk*), Philip Van Zandt (*Dr. Fagle*), Marilyn Johnson (*The Chambermaid*), Robert Williams, Joseph Palma, John Tyrrell, Richard Alexander
D: Arthur Dreifuss   **SCR:** Edward Dein & Fred Schiller, from characters created by Jack Boyle   **PHOTOG:** George B. Meehan Jr.   **MUSIC:** Mischa Bakaleinikoff
Best of "Boston Blackie" mystery-thrillers: Maniac flees prison, searches for mythical girl

The Boston Strangler
1968, (USA), 20th-Fox, color, 114 mins.
W: Tony Curtis, Henry Fonda, Hurd Hatfield, George Kennedy, Jeff Corey, Mike Kellin, George Voskovec, Sally Kellerman, Almira Sessions, William Marshall, William Hickey, James Brolin
P: Robert Fryer   **D:** Richard Fleischer   **SCR:** Edward Anhalt, based on Gerold Frank's book   **PHOTOG:** Richard Kline   **MUSIC:** Lionel Newman
Unusual docu-thriller: Search for infamous slayer

The Bottle Imp
1917, (USA), Para-Artcraft, b&w, 5 reels
W: James Neill, Sessue Hayakawa
D: Marshall A. Neilan, from Robert Louis Stevenson's classic short story
Modest fantasy-thriller: Magical artifact brings grief

Le Boucher (The Butcher)
1969, (It-Fr), CRC, color, 93 mins.
W: Stephane Audran (*Helene*), Antonio Passalia (*Angelo*), Jean Yanne (*Popaul the Butcher*), Mario Beccaria (*Leon Hamel*), Pasquale Ferone (*Pere Cahrpy*), Roger Rudel (*The Police Inspector*), William Gerrault (*Charles*)
WRIT & D: Claude Chabrol   **PHOTOG:** Jean Rabier   **MUSIC:** Pierre Jansen
"*Alfred Hitchcock, move over...Claude Chabrol has not only earned the title of 'master of suspense-thriller' but also has added a new dimension to that genre!*"—Robert Lauder, America
Gripping thriller: Woman suspects lover is murderer

Boundary House
1918, (GB), Hepworth/Moss, b&w, 5,250 ft. (1600.2m)
W: Alma Taylor (*Jenny Gay*), Gerald Ames (*Cherry Ricardo*), William Felton (*Old Fob*), Victor Prout (*Henry Gay*), John MacAndrews (*Ricardo*), Gwynne Herbert (*Miss Gay*)

69

D: Cecil M. Hepworth, from a novel by Peggy Webling
Standard melodrama: Miser forces girl to marry him and pose as dead wife who was her double

Bounty Hunter 2002
see Rape of Eden

Bourbon St. Shadows
see The Invisible Avenger

Bowery at Midnight
1942, (USA), Astor/Banner/Mono, b&w
W: Bela Lugosi, Wanda McKay *(Judy)*, Tom Neal *(Frankie)*, John Archer *(Dennison)*, Vince Barnett, Lucille Vance, Lew Kelly, Anna Hope, Wheeler Oakman, Ray Miller
P: Sam Katzman & Jack Dietz   **D:** Wallace Fox   **SCR:** Gerald Schnitzer   **PHOTOG:** Mack Stengler
Standard horror-crime thriller: Madman revives dead, scheming professor uses Bowery mission as front

The Bowery Boys Meet the Monsters
1954, (USA), AA, b&w, 66 mins.
W: Leo Gorcey *(Slip)*, Huntz Hall *(Sach)*, Bernard Gorcey *(Louie)*, John Dehner *(Derek)*, Lloyd Corrigan *(Anton)*, Ellen Corby *(Amelia)*, Paul Wexler
D: Edward Bernds   **SCR:** Elwood Ullman & Edward Bernds
Minor comedy-thriller: Dead End Kids meet mad scientist

Bowery to Bagdad
1954, (USA), AA, b&w, 64 mins.
W: Leo Gorcey *(Slip)*, Huntz Hall *(Sach)*, Joan Shawlee *(Velma)*, Eric Blore *(The Genie)*, Bernard Gorcey, Jean Willes, Richard Wessel, Rick Vallin, Robert Bice, Rayford Barnes, David Condon, Michael Ross, Paul Marion, Bennie Bartlett
D: Edward Bernds   **SCR:** Edward Bernds & Elwood Ullman   **PHOTOG:** Harry Neumann
Standard comedy-fantasy: Bowery Boys obtain Aladdin's lamp

A Boy and His Dog
1975, (USA), LQ/Jaf, color, 89 mins.
W: Don Johnson *(Vic)*, Susanne Benton *(Quilla June)*, Jason Robards Jr. *(Lew)*, Ron Feinberg *(Fellini)*, Tim McIntire *(The Voice of Blood)*, Alvy Moore, Helene Winston, Charles McGraw, Hal Baylor
P: Alvy Moore   **D & SCR:** L.Q. Jones, from Harlan Ellison's novella
PHOTOG: John Arthur Morrill   **SPCL-FX:** Frank Rowe   **MUSIC:** Tim McIntire & Jaime Mendoza-Nava
shown at 42nd St. theater (NYC) as *Psycho Boy and His Killer Dog*
R-rated (cult favorite) SF tale of survival in A.D. 2024: Post-nuke youth and telepathic canine have serio-comic adventures

The Boy and the Convict
1909, (GB), Williamson, b&w, 750 ft. (228.6m)
D: Dave Aylott
Standard crime-thriller: Blacksmith's boy frees convict

The Boy and the Pirates
1960, (USA), UA, color, 90 mins.
W: Charles Herbert, Susan Gordon, Murvyn Vye, Paul Guilfoyle, Than Wyenn, Joseph Turkel, Mickey Finn, Archie Duncan, Morgan Jones, Al Cavens, Timothy Carey
P & D: Bert I. Gordon   **SCR:** Lillie Hayward & Jerry Sackheim, from a story by Bert I. Gordon   **PHOTOG:** Ernest Haller   **MUSIC:** Albert Glasser
*orig. to be titled **The Boy in the Bottle***
Juvenile adventure-fantasy: Boy opens bottle found on beach, is transported several centuries into past

The Boy Cried Murder
1965, (USA), Univ, color, 86 mins.
W: Fraser MacIntosh, Phil Brown, Veronica Hurst, Tim Barrett, Beba Loncar
D: George Breakston
*Standard melodrama: Small boy witnesses crime, no one will believe him remake of **The Window**, (1949); remake of **Cloak and Dagger** (1989)*

The Boy from Andromeda
1990, (USA), color, 93 mins.
W: Katrina Hobbs, Jane Cresswell
Standard SF-adventure: Earth teens involved in intergalactic wars

The Boy in the Bottle
see The Boy and the Pirates

The Boy Scout Detective
1914, (GB), Conqueror Films, b&w, 714 ft. (217.6m)
Standard crime-thriller: Girl's boy-scout brother tracks counterfeiters

A Boy Scout's Dream: Or, How Billie Captured The Kaiser
1917, (GB), Brum Films, b&w, 2,000 ft. (6096m)
D: Bert Haldane
Standard comedy-fantasy: Scout dreams he nabs German leader

The Boys
1962, (GB), Galaworldfilm-Atlas/Gala, b&w, 123 mins.
W: Richard Todd *(Victor Webster)*, Robert Morley *(Montgomery)*, Felix Aylmer *(The Judge)*, Dudley Sutton *(Stan Coulter)*, Jess Conrad *(Barney Lee)*, Ronald Lacey *(Billy Herne)*, Tony Garnett *(Ginger Thompson)*, Wilfred Brambell *(Robert Brewer)*, Allan Cuthbertson *(Randolph St. John)*, Wensley Pithey *(Mr. Coulter)*, Colin Gordon *(Gordon Lonsdale)*, Kenneth J. Warren *(George Tanner)*, Betty Marsden *(Mrs. Herne)*, Patrick Magee *(Mr. Lee)*, Roy Kinnear *(Charles Salmon)*
P: Kenneth Rive & Sidney J. Furie   **D:** Sidney J. Furie   **STORY:** Stuart Douglass
   MUSIC: The Shadows
Standard crime-thriller: Four teens tried for garage-man's murder

The Boys from Brazil
1978, (USA), 20th-Fox, color, 124 mins.
W: Gregory Peck *(Dr. Josef Mengele)*, Sir Laurence Olivier *(Ezra Lieberman)*, James Mason *(Eduard Seibert)*, Lilli Palmer *(Esther Lieberman)*, Uta Hagen *(Frieda Maloney)*, Steven Guttenberg *(Barry Kohler)*, Denholm Elliott *(Sidney Beynon)*, John Dehner *(Henry Wheelock)*, Rosemary Harris *(Mrs. Doring)*, Anne Meara *(Mrs. Curry)*, John Rubinstein *(David Bennett)*, Jeremy Black *(Jack Curry/Simon Harrington/Erich Doring/Bobby Wheelock)*, David Hurst *(Strasser)*, Bruno Ganz *(Prof. Bruckner)*, Wolfgang Preiss *(Lofquist)*, Walter Gotell *(Mundt)*, Michael Gough *(Harrington)*, Joachim Hansen *(Fassler)*, Guy Dumont *(Hessen)*, Carl Duering *(Trausteiner)*, Richard Marner *(Doring)*, Linda Hayden *(Nancy)*, Georg Marischka *(Gunther)*, Gunter Meisner *(Farnbach)*, Prunella Scales *(Mrs. Harrington)*, Jurgen Anderson *(Kleist)*, Raul Faustino Saldanha *(Ismael)*, David Brandon *(Schmidt)*, Wolf Kahler *(Schwimmer)*, Monica Gearson *(Gertrud)*, Mervyn Nelson *(Stroop)*, Gerti Gordon *(Berthe)*
D: Franklin J. Schaffner   **SCR:** Heywood Gould, from Ira Levin's novel   **PHOTOG:** Henri Decae   **MUSIC:** Jerry Goldsmith
Superior thriller: Nazi-hunter seeks Adolph Hitler clones

The Boys from Brooklyn
1952, (USA), Jack Broder/Realart, b&w, 65 mins.
W: Bela Lugosi, Duke Mitchell, Sammy Petrillo, Muriel Landers, Charlita, Mickey Simpson
P: Maurice Duke   **D:** William Beaudine   **SCR:** Tim Ryan   **PHOTOG:** Charles Van Enger
*A.k.a. **Bela Lugosi Meets a Brooklyn Gorilla***
Cornball comedy-fantasy: Mad scientist turns humans into apes

The Boys from Syracuse
1940, (USA), Univ, b&w, 74 mins.
W: Martha Raye, Allan Jones, Rosemary Lane, Joe Penner, Irene Hervey, Charles Butterworth, Alan Mowbray
D: A. Edward Sutherland   **SCR:** Leonard Spigelgass, Charles Grayson & Paul Gerard Smith, from George Abbott's play   **PHOTOG:** Joseph Valentine   **MUSIC:** Charles Previn   **SONGS:** Rodgers & Hart
Historical farce: Burlesque of Shakespeare's The Comedy of Errors

Boys of the City
see The Ghost Creeps

The Boy Who Could Fly
1986, (USA), Lorimar/20th-Fox, color, 114 mins.
W: Lucy Deakins *(Milly)*, Jay Underwood *(Eric)*, Colleen Dewhurst *(Mrs. Sherman)*, Bonnie Bedelia *(Charlene)*, Fred Savage *(Louis)*, Fred Gwynne *(Uncle Hugo)*, Louise Fletcher *(The Psychiatrist)*, Mindy Cohn, Janet MacLachlan, Jennifer Michas, Aura Pithart
WRIT & D: Nick Castle   **PHOTOG:** Steven Poster & Adam Holender   **VS-FX SPRVSR:**. Richard Edlund   **MUSIC:** Bruce Broughton
Sentimental fantasy: Girl befriends autistic youth

The Boy Who Cried Werewolf
1973, (USA), RKF/Univ, color, 93 mins.
W: Kerwin Mathews *(Robert)*, Elaine Devry *(Sandy)*, Scott Sealey *(Richie)*, Robert J. Wilke *(The Sheriff)*, Geoge Gaynes *(Dr. Marderosian)*, Bob Homel *(Brother Christopher)*, Susan Foster *(Jenny)*, Jack Lucas *(Harry)*, Dave Cass *(The Deputy)*, Loretta Temple *(Monica)*, Harold Goodwin *(Duncan)*, Tim Haldeman *(The 1st Guard)*, John Logan *(The 2nd Guard)*, Eric Gordon *(The Hippy Jesus Freak)*, Paul Baxley *(The First Werewolf)*
P: Aaron Rosenberg   **D:** Nathan Juran   **SCR:** Bob Homel   **PHOTOG:** Michael P. Joyce   **MUSIC:** Ted Stovall
Standard horror-thriller: Young boy finds estranged father is lycanthrope

The Boy Who Never Was
1980, (GB), Monument/CFF, color, 58 mins.
W: Gordon Hagan *(Salu/Ubu)*, Paul Atlantis *(Charlie)*, Melissa Wilkes *(Audrey)*, Christian Bulloch *(Nobby)*, Eddie Tagoe *(Ngalo)*, Robert La Bassiere *(Awudu)*, Jules Walter *(Okara)*, Terence Alexander *(The Major)*, Derek Benfield *(The Inspector)*, Harcourt Curacao *(The President)*, Beryl Cooke *(The Lady)*, Cinnamon *(The Nurse)*
P & MUSIC: Harry Robinson   **D:** Frank Godwin   **STORY:** H. McLeod Robertson   **PHOTOG:** Ray Orton
Standard juvenile thriller: Boys thwart assassination plot

The Boy Who Turned Yellow

1972, (GB), Cherrill/CFF, color, 55 mins.
<u>W</u>: Mark Dignam (*John*), Robert Eddison (*Nick*), Helen Weir (*Mrs. Saunders*), Brian Worth (*Mr. Saunders*), Esmond Knight (*The Doctor*), Laurence Carter (*The Teacher*), Patrick McAlinney (*The Beefeater*), Lem Kitaj (*Munro*)
<u>P</u>: Roger Cherrill <u>D</u>: Michael Powell <u>STORY</u>: Emeric Pressburger <u>PHOTOG</u>: Christopher Challis <u>MUSIC</u>: Patrick Gowers
Standard juvenile fantasy: Boy loses pet mouse, is turned yellow by extraterrestrial

Boy With A Flute

1964, (GB), Grand Nat'l, b&w, 30 mins.
<u>W</u>: Freda Jackson (*Anne Winters*), Ursula Jeans (*Dorothy Winters*), Andree Melly (*Caroline Naser*), Richard Bidlake (*Charles*), Bill Nagy (*Conrad Barstow*), Ernest Clark (*Sir George Noble*), Guy Doleman (*Supt. Fitch*), Gerard Heinz (*Duclos*)
<u>WRIT, P & D</u>: Montgomery Tully
Standard short crime-thriller: Collector plots art theft

Brain Dead

1990, (USA), Concorde, color, 85 mins
<u>W</u>: Bill Pullman, Bill Paxton, Bud Cort, Patricia Charbonneau, Nicholas Pryor, George Kennedy
<u>D</u>: Adam Simon <u>SCR</u>: Charles Beaumont & Adam Simon <u>STORY</u>: Charles Beaumont
Standard thriller: Doctor performs brain surgery on psychotic

The Brain Eaters

1958, (USA), AIP, b&w, 60 mins.
<u>W</u>: Edwin Nelson (*Dr. Kettering*), Alan Frost, Jody Fair, Jack Hill (aka Cornelius Keefe), Joanna Lee, Leonard Nimoy, Orville Sherman, Doug Banks, David Hughes, Greigh Phillips, Henry Randolph
<u>P</u>: Edwin Nelson <u>D</u>: Bruno Ve Sota <u>SCR</u>: Gordon Urquhart, loosely based on Robert A. Heinlein's novel *The Puppet Masters* <u>MUSIC</u>: Tom Jonson
orig. co-billed with **The Spider** *(1958), reissued 1961*
Unusual SF-horror: Slimy parasites from Earth's depths control human hosts. cf. **The Puppet Masters**

The Brain From Planet Arous: JOYCE MEADOWS AND JOHN AGAR

The Boy with Green Hair

1948, (USA), RKO, color, 82 mins.
<u>W</u>: Pat O'Brien (*Gramp*), Robert Ryan (*Dr. Evans*), Barbara Hale (*Miss Brand*), Dean Stockwell (*Peter*), Samuel S. Hinds (*Dr. Knudson*), Richard Lyon (*Michael*), Walter Catlett ("*The King*"), Regis Toomey (*Mr. Davis*), Charles Meredith (*Mr. Piper*), David Clarke (*The Barber*), Billy Sheffield (*Red*), John Calkins (*Danny*), Teddy Infuhr (*Timmy*), Dwayne Hickman (*Joey*), Eilene Jannsen (*Peggy*), Curtis Jackson (*The Classmate*)
<u>P</u>: Stephen Ames <u>D</u>: Joseph Losey <u>SCR</u>: Alfred Lewis Levitt & Ben Barzman, from a story by Betsy Beaton <u>PHOTOG</u>: George Barnes <u>MUSIC</u>: Leigh Harline <u>SONG</u>: *Nature Boy* by Eden Ahbez
Classic anti-war allegory: Orphaned boy finds society regards him differently when his hair turns green

The Brahmin and the Butterfly

1901, (Fr), Star, b&w, 40m (131.2 ft./2.2 mins.)
<u>W</u>: Georges Melies
<u>D</u>: Georges Melies
Standard fantasy: Caterpillar becomes princess

The Brain (1962)

see Vengeance

The Brain

1988, (USA), color
<u>W</u>: David Gale
<u>D</u>: Ed Hunt
Minor SF-horror: Alien creature tries to control Earthlings via hit TV show

Brain Damage

1987, (USA), Brain Damage Co./Palisades Entertainment, color, 89 mins.
<u>W</u>: Rick Herbst (*Brian*), Gordon Macdonald (*Mike*), Jennifer Lowry (*Barbara*), Theo Barnes. Lucille Saint-Peter (*Martha*)
<u>WRIT & D</u>: Frank Henenlotter <u>PHOTOG</u>: Bruce Torbert <u>MUSIC</u>: Gus Russo & Clutch Reiser
Minor horror-thriller: Cerebrum-sucking parasites

The Brain from Planet Arous

1958, (USA), Marquette/Howco-Int'l, b&w, 71 mins.
<u>W</u>: John Agar, Joyce Meadows, Robert Fuller, Thomas B. Henry, Kenneth Terrell, Dale Tate, E. Leslie Thomas, Henry Traver, Tim Graham
<u>P & PHOTOG</u>: Jacques Marquette <u>D</u>: Nathan Hertz <u>SCR</u>: Ray Buffum <u>STORY</u>: Jacques Marquette <u>MUSIC</u>: Walter Greene
blurb: "Science-fiction's most astounding story!"
Standard SF-horror: Alien entity controls man's body

The Brainiac (1936)

see The Man Who Changed His Mind

The Brainiac (1961)

see El Baron del Terror

The Brain Machine

1955, (GB), Merton Park/Anglo-Amalgamated, b&w, 83 mins.
<u>W</u>: Patrick Barr (*Dr. Geoffrey Allen*), Elizabeth Allan (*Dr. Philippa Roberts*), Maxwell Reed (*Frank Smith*), Russell Napier (*Insp. Dur-ham*), Gibb McLaughlin (*Spencer Simon*), Neil Hallett (*Sgt. John Harris*), Edwin Richfield (*Ryan*), Bill Nagy (*Charlie*), Vanda Godsell (*Mae*)
<u>P</u>: Alec Snowden <u>D & SCR</u>: Ken Hughes
Minor thriller: Psychopath kidnaps woman psychiatrist

The Brain Machine (1972)

see Mind Warp *(1972)*

Brain of Blood

1971, (USA), Hemisphere, color, 85 mins.
<u>W</u>: Grant Williams (*Bob*), Kent Taylor (*Dr. Trenton*), Regina Carrol (*Tracy*), Reed Hadley (*Amir*), John Bloom (*Gor*), Vicki Volante (*Katherine*), Angelo Rossitto (*Derro*), Zandor Vorkov (*Mohammed*), Gus Peters (*Charlie*), Margo Hope (*The Pale Girl*), Richard Smedley (*Angel*), Bruce Kimball (*Jim*), Ervin Saunders (*The Victim*)
<u>D</u>: Al Adamson <u>SCR</u>: Joe Van Rodgers & Kane W. Lynn <u>STORY</u>: Samuel M. Sherman <u>PHOTOG</u>: Louis Horvath

TV retitle, **The Creature's Revenge**
blurb: "A Blood-dripping Brain Transplant turns a Maniac into a Monster"
Minor horror-thriller: Potentate's brain is transplanted

The Brain of Frankenstein
see *Abbott and Costello Meet Frankenstein*

Brainscan
1994, (USA), Triumph/Col, color, 96 mins.
W: Edward Furlong (*Michael*), Frank Langella (*Det. Hayden*), Amy Hargreaves (*Kimberly*), T. Ryder Smith (*The Trickster*), Jamie Marsh (*Kyle*), Victor Ertmanis (*Martin*), David Hemblen (*Dr. Fromberg*), Vlasta Vrana (*Frank*), Dom Fiore (*Ken*), Tod Fennel (*Young Michael*), Claire Riley (*The News Anchor*), Don Jordan (*Cop #1*), Michele-Barbara Pelletier (*Stacie*), Dean Hagopian (*Mr. Keller*), Donna Bacalla (*Mrs. Keller*), Jerome Thiberghian (*Mr. Tebb*), Pete White (*The Dog Owner*), Peter Colvey (*John*), Paul Stewart (*Bob*), Richard Zeman (*The Police Officer*), Zak (*The Dog*)
P: Michel Roy   D: John Flynn   SCR: Andrew Kevin Walker   STORY: Brian Owens   PHOTOG: Francois Protat   MUSIC: George S. Clinton
Standard SF-fantasy: Interactive video game encourages acts of murder

Brain Smasher...A Love Story
1993, (USA), color, 88 mins.
W: Andrew Dice Clay, Teri Hatcher
D: Albert Pyun
Minor SF-fantasy-satire: Model and bouncer vs. evil Chinese monks who possess mystical lotus

The Brainsnatcher
see *The Man Who Changed His Mind*

The Brain Snatchers
see *Monstrosity*

Brainstorm
1965, (USA), WB, b&w, 105 mins.
W: Jeffrey Hunter (*Jim Grayam*), Anne Francis (*Lorrie Benson*), Dana Andrews (*Cort Benson*), Kathie Brown (*Angie DeWitt*), Viveca Lindfors (*Dr. E. Larstadt*), Michael Pate (*Dr. Mills*), Stacy Harris (*Josh Reynolds*), Phillip Pine (*Dr. Ames*), Pat Cardi (*Bobby*), Strother Martin (*Mr. Clyde*), Robert McQueeney (*Sgt. Dawes*), Stephen Roberts (*The Judge*), Joan Swift (*Clara*), George Pelling (*The Butler*), Victoria Meyerink (*Julie*), James Lydon
P & D: William Conrad   SCR: Mann Rubin   STORY: Larry Marcus   PHOTOG: Sam Leavitt   MUSIC: George Duning
"A sub-B potboiler for those who find comic books too intellectual"—Judith Crist
Minor melodrama: Computer programmer kills lover's husband, fakes insanity

Brainstorm
1983, (USA), J F Prods.-Douglas Trumbull/MGM-UA, color, 105 mins.
W: Christopher Walken (*Michael Brace*), Natalie Wood (*Karen Brace*), Louise Fletcher (*Lillian Reynolds*), Cliff Robertson (*Alex Terson*), Jordan Christopher (*Gordy Forbes*), Joe Dorsey (*Hal Abramson*), Donald Hotton (*Landon Marks*), Georgianne Walken (*Wendy Abramson*), Alan Fudge, Jason Lively, Darrell Larson, Bill Morey, Lou Walker (*Chef*), Stacey Kuhne-Adams (*Andrea*), John Hugh (*The Animal Lab Technician*), David Wood (*Barry*), Keith Colbert (*Dr. Ted Harris*), Jerry Bennett (*Dr. Janet Bock*), Mary-Fran Lyman (*The Realtor*), Jim Boyd (*Col. Howe*), Charlie Briggs (*Col. Easterbrook*), Jack Harmon, Kelly W. Brown, Nina Axelrod, Desiree Ayres, Debbie Porter, Allen G. Butler, Robert Bloodworth, Ann Lincoln, Robert Terry Young, Bill Willens, Jim Burk, Jimmy Casino, John Galdstein, Robert Hippard, Herbert Hirschman, Glen Lee, John Vidor, Bill Couch, Robert Gooden, Wallace Merck, Ernie Robinson, Roger Black, Tommy Huff, Peter Harrell, May Raymond Boss, Clay Boss, Susan Kampe
P & D: Douglas Trumbull   SCR: Robert Stitzel & Philip Frank Messina, from a story by Bruce Joel Rubin   PHOTOG: Richard Yuricich   MUSIC: James Horner
Unusual SF-thriller (Natalie Wood's last film): Electronic device transfers sensory perceptions from one individual to another

The Brain That Wouldn't Die
1962, (USA), Rex Carlton-Mort Landsberg/AIP, b&w, 81 mins.
W: Jason Evers, Virginia Leith, Adele Lamont, Bruce Brighton, Lola Mason, Doris Brent, Paula Maurice, Bruce Kerr, Les lie Daniel, Bonnie Shari, Audrey Devereau, Eddie Carmel
P: Rex Carlton   D & SCR: Joseph Green, from orig. story by Rex Carlton & Joseph Green   PHOTOG: Stephen Hajnal   SPCL-FX: Byron Baer
blurb: "Alive...without a body... Fed by an unspeakable horror from hell!"
Minor SF-thriller: Scientist keeps alive fiancee's severed head

Brainwashed
1960, (W. Ger), Luggi Waldleitner-Roxy/AA, b&w, 102 mins.
W: Curt Jurgens, Claire Bloom, Jorg Felmy
P: Luggi Waldleitner   D: Gerd Oswald   SCR: Harold Medford & Gerd Oswald, from Stefan Zweig's novel *The Royal Game*   PHOTOG: Gunther Senftleben   MUSIC: Hans-Martin Majewski
Odd melodrama: Imprisoned man becomes chess master

Brainwaves
1983, (USA), MGM, color, 81 mins.
W: Keir Dullea (*Julian Bedford*), Suzanna Love (*Kaylie*), Vera Miles (*Marian*),

---

Percy Rodrigues (*Dr. Tobinson*), Tony Curtis (*Dr. Clavius*), Paul Wilson (*Dr. Schroder*), Ryan Seitz (*Danny*), Nicholas Love (*Willy*), Corinne Alphen (*Lelia*), Eve Brent Ashe (*Miss Simpson*)
WRIT, P & D: Ulli Lommel   PHOTOG: Jon Kranhouse   MUSIC: Robert O. Ragland
Minor thriller

Bram Stoker's 'Dracula'
1992, (USA), Col, color, 130 mins.
W: Gary Oldman (*Dracula*), Anthony Hopkins (*Prof. Van Helsing*), Winona Ryder (*Mina Murray/Elisabeta*), Keanu Reeves (*Jonathan Harker*), Cary Elwes (*Lord Arthur Holmwood*), Bill Campbell (*Quincey P. Morris*), Richard E. Grant (*Dr. Jack Seward*), Tom Waits (*R.M. Renfield*), Sadie Foster (*Lucy Westenra*), Jay Robinson (*Mr. Hawkins*), I.M. Hobson (*Hobbs*), Laurie Franks (*Lucy's Maid*), Monica Bellucci, Robert Getz, Michaela Bercu, Florina Kendrick, Maud Winchester, Dagmar Stanec, Octavian Cadia, Eniko Oss, Nancy Linehan Charles, Tatiana von Furstenberg, Jules Sylvester, Daniel Newman, Hubert Wells, Honey Lauren, Judi Diamond, Robert Buckingham, Cully Fredricksen
D: Francis Ford Coppola   SCR: James V. Hart, from Bram Stoker's novel *Dracula: A Tale*   PHOTOG: Michael Ballhaus   MUSIC: Wojciech Kilar   DESIGN: Thomas Sanders
Superior horror-fantasy: Vampire seeks reborn love. Orig. to be titled **Dracula: The Untold Story**

Bram Stoker's 'The Mummy'
1998, (USA), A-Pix, color, 100 mins.
W: Lou Gossett Jr., Amy Locane
from Bram Stoker's novel
Minor horror-fantasy. cf. **The Awakening** *and* **Blood From the Mummy's Tomb**

Bram Stoker's 'ShadowBuilder'
1998, (USA), color
W: Michael Rooker, Tony Todd
From a story by Bram Stoker
Made-for-Cable, standard horror-fantasy

The Branded Soul
see *The Iron Stair*

The Brasher Doubloon
1947, (USA), 20th-Fox, b&w, 72 mins.
W: George Montgomery (*Philip Marlowe*), Nancy Guild, Conrad Janis, Florence Bates, Roy Roberts, Fritz Kortner, Reed Hadley
P: Robert Bassler   D: John Brahm   SCR: Dorothy Bennett, from Raymond Chandler's novel *The High Window*   PHOTOG: Lloyd Aherne   MUSIC: David Buttolph
Classic mystery: Rare coin inspires murder. Remake of **Time to Kill** *(1942)*

The Brass Bottle
1914, (GB), Theatre & General, b&w, 3,600 ft. (1097.3m)
W: Holman Clark (*Fakrash-al-Amash*), Alfred Bishop (*Prof. Futvoye*), Doris Lytton (*Sylvia Futvoye*), Lawrence Grossmith (*Horace Ventmire*), Tom Mowbray (*Samuel Wackerbath*), J.R. Tozer (*King Solomon*), Mary Brough (*Mrs. Futvoye*), Vane Featherstone, Rudge Harding, Molly Farrell
P: Nicholson Ormsby-Scott   D & SCR: Sidney Morgan, from a play by F. Anstey
Standard fantasy: Genie aids poor architect

The Brass Bottle
1923, (USA), First Nat'l, b&w, 6 reels (5,290 ft./1612.4m)
W: Harry Myers (*Horace Ventimore*), Tully Marshall (*Prof. Hamilton*), Ernest Torrence (*Fakresh-el-Aamash*), Clarissa Selwyn (*Mrs. Hamilton*), Ford Sterling (*Rapkin*), Charlotte Merriam (*Sylvia Hamilton*), Aggie Herring (*Mrs. Rapkin*), Edward Jobson (*Samuel Wackerbath*), Barbara La Marr (*The Queen*), Otis Harlan (*The Captain of the Guard*), Julanne Johnston, Hazel Keener
D: Maurice Tourneur   SCR: Fred Kennedy Myton, from a play by F. Anstey   PHOTOG: Arthur Todd
Standard fantasy: Architect acquires genie

The Brass Bottle
1964, (USA), Scarus/Univ, color, 89 mins.
W: Tony Randall, Barbara Eden, Burl Ives (*The Genie*), Edward Andrews, Ann Doran, Kamala Devi, Parley Baer, Philip Ober, LuLu Porter, Jan Arvan
D: Harry Keller   SCR: Oscar Brodney, from a play by F. Anstey   PHOTOG: Clifford Stine   SPCL-FX: Roswell Hoffman   MUSIC: Bernard Green
Standard comedy-fantasy: Genie complicates architect's life

Brave Children: or, The Little Thief Catchers
1908, (GB), Cricks & Martin, b&w, 420 ft. (128m)
D: A.E. Coleby
Standard crime-thriller: Child holds burglar at bay, brother fetches police

The Brave Little Toaster
1987, (USA), Disney, color, 80 mins.
VOICES: Deanna Oliver (*Toaster*), Jon Lovitz (*Radio*), Timothy E. Day (*Blanky*), Tim Stack (*Lamp*), Thurl Ravenscroft (*Vacuum*), Phil Hartman, Joe Ranft, Judy Toll, Colette Savage, Wayne Kaatz, Randy Bennett, Louis Conti
D: Jerry Rees   SCR: Jerry Rees & Joe Ranft, from a story by Thomas M. Disch   MUSIC: David Newman   SONGS: *City of Lights, Cutting Edge, It's a B-*

Movie & Worthless
Standard animated fantasy: Household appliances seek young owner of abandoned summer cabin

Brave Little Toaster Goes to Mars
1998, (USA), Hyperion/Walt Disney, color
<u>VOICES:</u> Deanna Oliver (*Toaster*), Thurl Ravencroft (*Vacuum*), Fyvush Finkel (*Hearing Aid*), Alan King (*Supreme Commander*), Farrah Fawcett (*Faucet*), Wayne Knight (*Microwave*), DeForest Kelley (*Viking 1*)
<u>SONGS:</u> *Home Again, A New You, Floating & Humans*
Made-for-Video, standard animated fantasy: Toaster meets mechanical expatriates on red planet

Brave New World
1980, (USA), NBC-TV, color
<u>W:</u> Dick Anthony Williams (*Helmholtz Watson*), Marcia Strassman (*Lenina Disney*), Kristoffer Tabori (*John Savage*), Bud Cort (*Bernard Marx*), Keir Dullea (*Thomas Grahmbell*), Ron O'Neal (*Mustapha Mond*), Valerie Curtin (*Stalina Shell*), Julie Cobb (*Linda Lysenko*), Trish O'Neil (*Maoina Krupps*), Patrick Cronin (*The Gamma Male*), Beatrice Colen (*The Gamma Female*)
<u>D:</u> Burt Brinckerhoff <u>TELEPLAY:</u> Robert E. Thompson, from Aldous Huxley's classic novel
TVM, ambitious SF-melodrama: Conformity and discontent in sterile, totalitarian world of future

Brave New World
1998, (USA), NBC-TV, color
<u>W:</u> Peter Gallagher, Miguel Ferrer, Leonard Nimoy, Sally Kirkland, Tim Guinee, Rya Kihlstedt, Jacob Chase, Aron Eisenberg
from Aldous Huxley's novel
TVM, modest SF-thriller: Life in totalitarian future

Bravestarr—The Movie
1988, (USA),Filmatron/Taurus Entertainment, color, 91 mins.
<u>P:</u> Lou Scheimer <u>D:</u> Tom Tataranowicz <u>SCR:</u> Bob Forward & Steve Hayes
Unusual animated SF-adventure: Hero awakes from cybernetic sleep, opposes evil forces

Brazil
1984, (GB), Arnon Milchan/Univ, color, 131 mins.
<u>W:</u> Jonathan Pryce (*Sam Lowry*), Robert De Niro (*Harry Tuttle*), Katherine Helmond (*Mrs. Ida Lowry*), Michael Palin (*Jack Lint*), Ian Holm (*Mr. Kurtzmann*), Bob Hoskins (*Spoor*), Peter Vaughan (*Mr. Helpmann*), Ian Richardson (*Mr. Warren*), Kim Greist (*Jill Layton*), Barbara Hicks (*Mrs. Terrain*), Charles McKeown (*Lime*), Bryan Pringle (*Spiro*), Sheila Reid (*Mrs. Buttle*), Brian Miller (*Buttle*), Derrick O'Connor (*Dowser*), Kathryn Pogson (*Shirley*), John Flanagan (*The Interviewer*), Terence Bayler (*The Presenter*), Bill Wallis (*The Lurker*), Winston Dennis (*The Warrior*), Oscar Quitak (*The Official*), Elizabeth Spender (*Alison Lint*), Ray Cooper, Prudence Oliver, Simon Nash, Derek Deadman, Gorden Kaye, Simon Jones, Nigel Planer, Tony Portacio, Diana Martin, Jack Purvis, Antony Brown, Ann Way, Myrtle Devenish, Howard Lew Lewis, Holly Gilliam, John Pierce Jones, Don Henderson, Terry Forrestal, Roger Ashton-Griffiths, Patrick Connor
<u>P:</u> Arnon Milchan & Patrick Cassavetti <u>D:</u> Terry Gilliam <u>SCR:</u> Terry Gilliam, Tom Stoppard, & Charles McKeown <u>PHOTOG:</u> Roger Pratt <u>SPCL-FX:</u> George Gibbs <u>ORIG. MUSIC:</u> Michael Kamen
Superior SF-satire: Two people trapped in totalitarian world

Brazil
ROBERT DeNiro

The Break
1962, (GB), Blakeley's Films/Planet, b&w, 76 mins.
<u>W:</u> Tony Britton (*Greg Parker*), William Lucas (*Jacko Thomas*), Eddie Byrne (*Judd Tredegar*), Robert Urquhart (*Pearson*), Sonia Dresdel (*Sarah*), Edwin Richfield

(*Moses*), Gene Anderson (*Jean Tredegar*), Christina Gregg (*Sue Thomas*)
<u>P:</u> Tom Blakeley <u>D:</u> Lance Comfort <u>STORY:</u> Pip & Jane Baker
Standard crime-thriller: Mixed guests at smuggler's farm

Breakaway
1956, (GB), Cipa/RKO, b&w, 72 mins.
<u>W:</u> Tom Conway (*Tom "Duke" Martin*), Honor Blackman (*Paula Grant*), Michael Balfour (*Barney*), Bruce Seton (*Webb*), Brian Worth (*Johnny Matlock*), Freddie Mills (*Pat*), Alexander Gauge (*McAllister*), John Horsley (*Michael Matlock*)
<u>P:</u> Robert Baker & Moty Berman <u>D:</u> Henry Cass <u>SCR:</u> Norman Hudis <u>STORY:</u> Manning O'Brine
Standard crime-thriller: Gang kidnaps girl, seeks formula for elimination of mental fatigue

The Breaking Point
1914, (GB), Hepworth, b&w, 1,275 ft. (388.6m)
<u>W:</u> Stewart Rome (*Howard Esmond*), Chrissie White (*Clarice Armitage*), Lionelle Howard (*Croyle*)
<u>D:</u> Frank Wilson
Standard crime-thriller: Framed man's fiancee gains confession by filming reconstruction of murder

Breakout
1959, (GB), Independent Artists/Anglo-Amalgamated, b&w, 62 mins.
<u>W:</u> Lee Patterson (*George Munro*), Hazel Court (*Rita Arkwright*), Terence Alexander (*Farrow*), Dermot Kelly (*O'Quinn*), John Paul (*Arkwright*), Billie Whitelaw (*Rose Munro*), William Lucas (*Chandler*), Estelle Brody (*Maureen O'Quinn*)
<u>P:</u> Julian Wintle & Leslie Parkyn <u>D:</u> Peter Graham Scott <u>SCR:</u> Peter Barnes, from a book by Frederick Oughton
Standard crime-thriller: Architect helps embezzler break jail

Breeders
1985, (USA), Empire, color
<u>W:</u> Lance Lewman (*Det. Dale Andriotti*), Teresa Farley (*Gamble Pace*), Ed French, Frances Raines, Lee Anne Baker, Adriane Lee, Amy Bren-tano
<u>D:</u> Tim Kincaid
Minor SF-horror: Insectoid aliens mate with Earth virgins

Brenda Starr
1976, (USA), David Wolper/ABC-TV, color, 74 mins.
<u>W:</u> Jill St. John (*Brenda Starr*), Jed Allan (*Roger Randall*), Victor Buono (*Lance O'Toole*), Barbara Luna (*Luisa Santamaria*), Sorrell Booke (*A.J. Livwright*), Joel Fabiani (*Carlos Varga*), Torin Thatcher (*Willis Lassiter*), Judith Wright (*Susan Lynn*), Art Roberts (*Dax*), Marcia Strassman (*Kentucky Smith*), Harold Oblong (*The Photographer*)
<u>D:</u> Mel Stuart <u>SCR:</u> George Kirgo, from Dale Messick's comic strip
TVM, minor adventure: Girl faces foreign intrigue and voodoo

Brenda Starr
1992, (USA), Triumph, color, 96 mins.
<u>W:</u> Brooke Shields (*Brenda Starr*), Timothy Dalton (*Basil St. John*), Tony Peck (*Mike Randall*), Diana Scarwid (*Libby "Lips" Lipscomb*), Nestor Serrano (*Jose*), Jeffrey Tambor (*Vladimir*), June Gable (*Luba*), Charles Durning (*Francis I. Livright*), Ed Nelson (*Pres. Harry S. Truman*), Eddie Albert (*Police Chief Maloney*), Henry Gibson (*Prof. Gerhardt Von Kreutzer*), Kathleen Wilhoite, Mary Lou Rosato, Pola Miller, Ramon Saldana, Erik Cord
<u>D:</u> Robert Ellis Miller <u>SCR:</u> Jenny Wolkind, Noreen Stone & James David Buchanan, from Dale Messick's comic strip <u>PHOTOG:</u> Freddie Francis <u>MUSIC:</u> Johnny Mandel
Standard adventure-romance (filmed in 1986): Courageous girl finds intrigue

Brenn, Hexe, Brenn
see Mark of the Devil (1972)

The Bribe
1949, (USA), MGM, b&w, 98 mins.
<u>W:</u> Robert Taylor, Ava Gardner, Charles Laughton, Vincent Price, John Hodiak, John Hoyt
<u>P:</u> Pandro S. Berman <u>D:</u> Robert Z. Leonard <u>SCR:</u> Marguerite Roberts
Standard thriller: Federal agent vs. post-war weapons ring

The Bride
1973, (Can), Unisphere, color, 85 mins.
<u>W:</u> Robin Strasser (*Barbara*), Arthur Roberts (*David*), John Beal (*Father*), Ivan Jean Saraceni (*Ellen*)
<u>P:</u> John Grissmer <u>D:</u> Jean-Marie Pelissie <u>SCR:</u> John Grissmer & Jean-Marie Pelissie <u>PHOTOG:</u> Geoffrey Stephenson <u>MUSIC:</u> Peter Bernstein
A.k.a. The House That Cried Murder
Standard melodrama: Woman torments faithless husband

The Bride
1985, (GB), Col, color, 119 mins.
<u>W:</u> Sting (*Baron Charles Frankenstein*), Jennifer Beals (*Eva*), Anthony Higgins (*Clerval*), Clancy Brown (*Viktor*), Geraldine Page (*Mrs. Baumann*), David Rappaport (*Rinaldo*), Phil Daniels (*Bela*), Alexei Sayle (*Magar*), Verushka (*The Countess*), Tony Haygarth (*The Tavern Keeper*), Quentin Crisp (*Dr. Zahlus*), John Sharp (*The Bailiff*), Andrew De La Tour (*The Priest*), Matthew Guinness (*The Patron*), Jack Birkett (*The Blind Man*), Harold Coyne (*The Butler*), Andy Barratt (*The Ringmaster*), Stromboli (*A Performer*), Miss Irta (*A*

Performer), Tim Spall
P: Victor Drai & Chris Kenny   **D:** Franc Roddam   **SCR:** Lloyd Fonvielle, from Mary W. Shelley's novel *Frankenstein*   **PHOTOG:** Stephen H. Burum   **MUSIC:** Maurice Jarre
Standard horror-thriller: Scientist creates liberated woman

The Bride and the Beast
1958, (USA), AA, b&w, 78 mins.
W: Charlotte Austin, Lance Fuller, Gil Frye, William Justine, Slick Slavin, Johnny Roth, Shogwan Singh, Steve Calvert, Jean Ann Lewis, Jeanne Gerson
P & D: Adrian Weiss   **SCR:** Edward D. Wood Jr., from a story by Adrian Weiss   **PHOTOG:** Roland Price   **MUSIC:** Les Baxter
*Belgian retitle, **The Fiancee of the Jungle**, A.k.a. **Queen of the Gorillas***
Minor fantasy-thriller: Hunter's bemused wife finds she is reincarnated gorilla

The Bride in Black
1990, (USA), New World/Lifetime, color, 95 mins.
W: Susan Lucci, David Soul, Reginald Veljohnson, Robert Gunton, Tom Signorelli, Melissa Leo, Irma St. Paule, Stephen Liska, Finola Hughes, Cecil Goffmann, Robert Katims, Tony Todd
D: James Goldstone   **TELEPLAY:** Claire Labine   **STORY:** Claire Labine & Jack Laird   **PHOTOG:** Ron Garcia   **MUSIC:** Joe Conlan
TVM, standard thriller: Woman's artist-bridegroom slain on wedding day, art-forgery plot unravels

Bride of Boogedy
1987, (USA), Walt Disney, color, 100 mins.
W: Richard Masur, Mimi Kennedy, Tammy Lauren, David Faustino, Howard Witt, Eugene Levy
D: Oz Scott
Standard juvenile fantasy: 300-year-old ghost seeks wife

Bride of Chucky
1998, (USA), color
W: Jennifer Tilly
D: Ronny Yu
Standard fantasy-thriller: Demonic doll selects mate

Bride of Frankenstein
1935, (USA), Univ, b&w, 80 mins.
W: Colin Clive (*Baron Henry Frankenstein*), Boris Karloff (*The Monster*), Valerie Hobson (*Elizabeth*), Ernest Thesiger (*Dr. Praetorious*), Elsa Lanchester ("*The Bride*"/*Mary W. Shelley*), Douglas Walton (*Percy Bysshe Shelley*), Gavin Gordon (*Lord Byron*), O.P. Heggie (*The Blind Hermit*), Dwight Frye (*Fritz*), Reginald Barlow (*Hans*), Una O'Connor (*Minnie*), Mary Gordon (*Hans' Wife*), Ann Darling (*The Shepherdess*), E.E. Clive, Rollo Lloyd, Neil Fitzgerald, Lucien Prival, Ted Billings, John Carradine, Tempe Piggott, Grace Cunard
P: Carl Laemmle Jr.   **D:** James Whale   **SCR:** William Hurlbut & John L. Balderston, from characters created by Mary W. Shelley   **PHOTOG:** John D. Mescall   **MUSIC:** Franz Waxman
"...a lavish and enjoyable fairy tale, which has genuine pathos to offer along with all its thrills. Karloff's performance remains one of his best, although not surprisingly, Ernest Thesiger steals the whole show with a marvelously written and played performance as the mad Dr. Praetorious"—William K. Everson, Classics of the Horror Film
"Tilted cameras suspensefully involve the viewer in the reality of creating the bride"—Roy Huss, Focus on the Horror Film
Engrossing fantasy-thriller, generally considered 'The Great American Horror Film': Scientist persuaded to create mate for his famous monster

Bride of Re-Animator
1991, (USA), Troma, color, 95 mins.
W: Jeffrey Combs (*Herbert West*), Bruce Abbott (*Dr. Dan Cain*), David Gale (*Dr. Carl Hill*), Kathleen Kinmont (*Gloria*), Claude Earl Jones (*Lt. Chapman*), Fabiana Udenio (*Francesca*), Irene Forrest, Mel Stewart, Michael Strasser
P & D: Brian Yuzna   **SCR:** Woody Keith & Ricky Fry, based on H.P. Lovecraft's short story "Herbert West-The Reanimator"   **PHOTOG:** Rick Fichter   **MUSIC:** Richard Band
*Standard horror-fantasy: Scientist creates female monstrosity. cf. **Re-Animator***

Bride of the Atom
*see **Bride of the Monster***

Bride of the Gorilla
1951, (USA), Realart, b&w, 70 mins.
W: Barbara Payton (*Dina*), Tom Conway (*Dr. Viet*), Raymond Burr (*Barney Chavez*), Lon Chaney Jr. (*Taro*), Paul Cavanagh (*Van Gelder*), Woody Strode, Carol Varga, Paul Maxey
P: Jack Broder   **WRIT & D:** Curt Siodmak   **PHOTOG:** Charles Van Enger   **SPCL-FX:** Lee Zavitz
Minor but effective were-gorilla thriller: Man believes he is turning into jungle beast because of voodoo curse

Bride of the Monster
1955, (USA), Rolling M/Banner, b&w, 69 mins.
W: Bela Lugosi (*Dr. Stroesser*), Loretta King (*Janet Lawton*), Tor Johnson (*Lobo*), Tony McCoy (*Lt. Dick Craig*), Don Nagel (*Martin*), Harvey B. Dunn (*Capt. Robbins*), George Becwar (*Prof. Strowski*), Paul Marco (*Kelton*), Ann Wilner (*Tillie*), Dolores Fuller (*Margie*), Bud Osborne (*Mac*), John Warren (*Jake*),

Ben Frommer (*The Drunk*), William Benedict (*The Newsboy*)
P & D: Edward D. Wood Jr.   **ORIG. STORY & SCR:** Edward D. Wood Jr. & Alex Gordon   **PHOTOG:** William C. Thompson & Ted Allan   **SPCL-FX:** Pat Dinga   **MUSIC:** Frank Worth
*orig. to be titled **Bride of the Atom**, orig. co-billed with **Macumba***
Notorious low-budget horror-thriller: Cardboard sets and an ailing Lugosi as mad doctor tries to create supermen

Bride of Vengeance
1949, (USA), Para, b&w, 91 mins.
W: Paulette Goddard (*Lucretia Borgia*), John Lund (*Alfonso*), Macdonald Carey (*Cesare Borgia*), Albert Dekker (*Vanetti*), John Sutton, Ray-mond Burr, Billy Gilbert, Charles Dayton, Fritz Leiber, Rose Hobart, Nicholas Joy, Anthony Caruso
P: Richard Maibaum   **D:** Mitchell Leisen   **SCR:** Cyril Hume & Michael Hogan   **PHOTOG:** Daniel Fapp   **SPCL-FX:** Gordon Jennings   **MUSIC:** Hugo Friedhofer
Costume thriller: Life and times of infamous Lucretia Borgia

Brides of Blood
1968, (Phil), Hemisphere, color, 85 mins.
W: John Ashley (*Jim Farrell*), Beverly Hills, Kent Taylor, Eva Darren, Mario Montenegro
D: Eddie Romero & Gerardo de Leon
*A.k.a. **Blood Brides, Brides of Blood Island, Brides of Death, The Cursed Brides, The Island of Living Horror, Orgy of Blood,** and **Terror on Blood Island**. Reissued as **Grave Desires***
Minor SF-horror: Atom tests mutate island's flora and fauna

Brides of Blood Island
*see **Brides of Blood***

Brides of Death
*see **Brides of Blood***

Brides of Dracula
1960, (GB), Hammer/Univ, color, 85 mins.
W: Peter Cushing (*Dr. Van Helsing*), Freda Jackson (*Greta*), Martita Hunt (*Baroness Meinster*), Yvonne Monlaur (*Marianne Danielle*), Andree Melly (*Gina*), Miles Malleson (*Dr. Tobler*), Henry Oscar (*Lang*), Mona Washbourne (*Mrs. Lang*), David Peel (*Baron Meinster*), Victor Brooks (*Hans*), Michael Mulcaster (*Latour*), Marie Devereaux, Fred Johnson, Vera Cook, Harold Scott, Michael Ripper, Henry Scott
P: Michael Carreras   **D:** Terence Fisher   **SCR:** Jimmy Sangster, Peter Bryan & Edward Percy   **PHOTOG:** Jack Asher   **MUSIC:** John Hollingsworth
*Elaborate semi-sequel to **Horror of Dracula**: Vampirologist aids girl stalked by Undead baron*

The Brides of Fu Manchu
1966, (GB), 7Arts-Hallam/AA, color, 94 mins.
W: Christopher Lee (*Dr. Fu Manchu*), Douglas Wilmer (*Nayland Smith*), Howard Marion-Crawford (*Dr. Petrie*), Marie Versini (*Marie Lentz*), Heinz Drache (*Franz Baumer*), Rupert Davies (*Jules Merlin*), Roger Hanin (*Pierre*), Tsai Chin (*Lin Tang*), Kenneth Fortescue (*Sgt. Spicer*), Joseph Furst (*Otto Lentz*), Carole Gray (*Michele Merlin*), Harald Leipnitz (*Nikki Sheldon*), Denis Holmes, Tommy Yapp
P: Harry Alan Towers   **D:** Don Sharp   **SCR:** Peter Welbeck, from Sax Rohmer's *Fu Manchu* novels
Standard thriller: Oriental villain kidnaps daughters of world leaders

The Brides Wore Black
1984, (USA), color, 86 mins.
Minor horror-fantasy: Dead bride revived, becomes vampire's mate

The Bride Wore Black
*see **La Mariee etait en Noir***

Bridge Across Time
1985, (USA), Fries Ent./NBC-TV, color, 96 mins.
W: David Hasselhoff (*Don Gregory*), Stepfanie Kramer (*Angie*), Randolph Mantooth (*Joe*), Adrienne Barbeau (*Lynn*), Lane Smith (*Anson Whitfield*), Lindsay Bloom (*Elaine Gardner*), Clu Gulager (*Chief Pete Dawson*), Paul Rossilli (*The Ripper*), David Fox-Brenton (*Mr. Latting*), Rose Marie, Barbara Bingham, Jim Hodge, Michael Boyle, Cameron Milzer, Charles Benton, Nancy Skillen, Ray Ravero, Peter Vernon, Mike Wilkins, Stephanie Ann Stone, Steve Archer
D: E.W. Swackhamer   **TELEPLAY:** William F. Nolan   **SPCL-FX:** John C. Hartigan   **MUSIC:** Lalo Schifrin
*retitle (1986), **Arizona Ripper**, A.k.a. **Terror at London Bridge***
TVM, minor fantasy-thriller: Jack the Ripper menaces Arizona home of London Bridge

The Bridge Destroyer
1914, (GB), Hepworth, b&w, 1,075 ft. (327.7m)
W: Violet Hopson (*The Girl*), Lionelle Howard (*The Spy*), Eric Desmond (*The Scout*), William Felton (*The Vicar*), Johnny Butt
D: Frank Wilson
Standard thriller: Scout and vicar's daughter stop spy from blowing up bridge

The Bridge of San Luis Rey
1929, (USA), MGM, b&w, 10 reels (7,890 ft./2404.9m/88 mins.)
W: Lili Damita (*Camila*), Ernest Torrence (*Uncle Pio*), Don Alvarado (*Manuel*), Raquel Torres (*Pepita*), Duncan Renaldo (*Esteban*), Henry B. Walthall (*Father Juniper*), Michael Vavitch (*The Viceroy*), Emily Fitzroy (*The Marquesa*), Gordon Thorpe (*Jaime*), Jane Winton (*Dona Clara*), Mitchell Lewis (*Capt. Alvarado*), Paul Ellis (*Don Vicente*), Tully Marshall (*The Townsman*), Eugenic Besscrcr (*The Nun*)
D: Charles Brabin **ADAPT:** Alice D.G. Miller, from Thornton Wilder's novel **PHOTOG:** Merritt B. Gerstad
Standard melodrama: Old bridge collapses, lives of victims examined

The Bridge of San Luis Rey
1944, (USA), Bogeans/UA, b&w, 85 mins.
W: Lynn Bari (*Michaela*), Akim Tamiroff (*Pio*), Louis Calhern (*The Viceroy*), Francis Lederer, Nazimova, Donald Woods, Joan Lorring, Barton Hepburn, Blanche Yurka, Abner Biberman, Emma Dunn, Minerva Urecal
P: Benedict Bogeaus **D:** Rowland V. Lee **SCR:** Howard Estabrook, from Thornton Wilder's novel **PHOTOG:** John W. Boyle **MUSIC:** Dmitri Tiomkin
Unusual melodrama: Flashbacks on lives of people involved in Peruvian bridge collapse

Bridge of Time
1997, (USA), RHI/ABC-TV, color, 95 mins.
W: Susan Dey, Cicely Tyson, Nigel Havers, Josette Simon, Robert Whitehead, Cotter Smith
D: Jorge Montesi **TELEPLAY:** Drew Hunter & Christopher Canaan **PHOTOG:** David Geddes **MUSIC:** Irwin Fisch
*TVM, standard fantasy-thriller (blatant plagiarsm of **Lost Horizon**):Mixed group shanghaied to African paradise*

The Bridge to Nowhere
1986, (New Zeal), color, 82 mins.
W: Bruno Lawrence, Alison Routledge, Margaret Umbers, Philip Gordon
D: Ian Mune
Standard thriller: Mad backwoodsman stalks campers

Brigadier Gerard
1915, (GB), Barker/Walturdaw, b&w, 5,260 ft. (1603.5m)
W: Lewis Waller (*Brigadier Gerard*), A.E. George (*Napoleon*), Madge Titheradge (*Countess de Rochequelaune*), Blanche Forsythe (*Agnes*), Austin Leigh (*Gen. Coulaincourt*), Frank Cochrane (*Pierre*), Fernand Mailly (*Talleyrand*), R.F. Symons (*Maj. Olivier*), Philip Renouf (*Jacques*)
D: Bert Haldane **SCR:** Rowland Talbot, based on Sir Arthur Conan Doyle's novel
Standard adventure-thriller: French captain and countess save emperor's secret papers

Brigadoon
1954, (USA), MGM, color, 108 mins.
W: Gene Kelly, Van Johnson, Cyd Charisse, Elaine Stewart, Barry Jones, Hugh Laing
D: Vicente Minnelli **PHOTOG:** Joseph Ruttenberg **MUSIC:** Alan Jay Lerner & Frederick Lowe **SONGS:** Almost Like Being in Love & Heather on the Hill
Classic musical-fantasy: Vacationers find enchanted Scottish village

The Brigand of Kandahar
1965, (GB), Hammer/Col color, 81 mins.
W: Oliver Reed (*Eli Khan*), Ronald Lewis (*Lt. Case*), Duncan Lamont (*Col. Drewe*), Yvonne Romain (*Ratina*), Walter Brown (*Hitala*), Catherine Woodville (*Elsa Connolly*), Glyn Houston (*Marriott*), Sean Lynch (*Rattu*), Inigo Jackson (*Capt. Boyd*), Jeremy Burnham (*Capt. Connolly*)
P: Anthony Nelson Keys **D & SCR:** John Gilling **PHOTOG:** Reg Wyer **MUSIC:** Don Banks
Standard thriller, action-adventure in 19th-century India: British officer seeks to clear name, joins warring tribe

The Brigand's Daughter
1907, (GB), Williamson, b&w, 806 ft. (245.7m)
W: Winnie Barton (*The Girl*)
D: James Williamson
Standard thriller: Girl helps artist escape from bandits; they are chased onto bridge which is struck by lightning

The Brigand's Daughter
1911, (GB), Cricks & Martin, b&w, 725 ft. (221m)
D: A.E. Coleby
Standard crime-thriller: Soldier saves girl from Italian brigands

The Brighton Strangler
1945, (USA), RKO, b&w, 67 mins
W: John Loder, June Duprez (*April*), Michael St. Angel (aka Steve Flagg) (*Bob*), Miles Mander (*Allison*), Rose Hobart (*Dorothy*), Gilbert Emery (*Manby*), Olaf Hytten, Ian Wolfe, Rex Evans
P: Herman Schlom **D:** Max Nosseck **ORIG STORY & SCR:** Arnold Phillips & Max Nosseck
Standard thriller: Actor begins to live stage role of murderer

Das Brillanten Schiff
*see **Die Spinnen***

Brimstone & Treacle
1982, (GB), Namara/Salke/Solow/Pennies from Heaven/Brent Walker, color, 87 mins.
W: Sting (*Martin Taylor*), Denholm Elliott (*Thomas Bates*), Joan Plowright (*Norma Bates*), Suzanna Hamilton (*Patricia Bates*), Benjamin Whitrow (*The Businessman*), Tim Preece (*The Cleric*), Dudley Sutton (*The Stroller*), Elizabeth Bradley (*The Passerby*), Mary MacLeod (*Miss Holdsworth*), Hugh Walters (*The Man*), Christopher Fairbanks (*The Drunk*)
P: Kenith Trodd **D:** Richard Loncraine **SCR:** Dennis Potter, from his teleplay **PHOTOG:** Peter Hannan **MUSIC:** Sting
Unusual thriller: Wastrel rapes poet's crippled daughter

Bring Me the Vampire
1965, (Mex), b&w, 100 mins
W: Carlos Riquelme, Mary Eugenia St. Martin, Hector Godoy, Joaquin Vargas
D: Carlos Riquelme
Minor comedy-thriller: Heirs must spend time in eerie castle

Britain's Naval Secret
1915, (GB), Lieut. Moran Films/DFSA, b&w, 1,197 ft. (364.8m)
W: Percy Moran (*Lt. Jack Moran*), Noel Grahame
D: Percy Moran
Standard adventure-thriller: Naval lieutenant saves secret plans from spies

Britain's Secret Treaty
1914, (GB), I.B. Davidson/KTC, b&w, 3,000 ft. (916.9m)
W: Philip Kay (*Sexton Blake*), Lewis Carlton (*Tinker*), Thomas Canning (*The Count*)
D & SCR: Charles Raymond, from a story by Andrew Murray
Minor crime-thriller: Count nabs detective posing as foreign war minister

British Agent
1934, (USA), First Nat'l/WB, b&w, 81 mins.
W: Leslie Howard, Kay Francis, J. Carrol Naish, Cesar Romero, William Gargan, Irving Pichel, Philip Reed, Halliwell Hobbes, Walter Byron
D: Michael Curtiz **SCR:** Laird Doyle, from a novel by H. Bruce Lockhart **PHOTOG:** Ernest Haller
Modest melodrama: Britisher falls for lady spy

British Intelligence
1940, (USA), WB, b&w, 62 mins
W: Boris Karloff, Margaret Lindsay, Holmes Herbert, Maris Wrixon, Leonard Mudie, Bruce lester
D: Terry Morse **SCR:** Lee Katz
*Standard melodrama. Remake: **Three Faces East**, (1930)*

Brock's Last Case
1973, (USA), Univ/CBS-TV, color, 98 mins.
W: Richard Widmark, Beth Brickell, Will Geer, John Anderson, Henry Darrow, Michael Burns
D: David Lowell Rich **TELEPLAY:** Martin Donaldson & Alex Gordon **MUSIC:** Charles Gross
TVM, talky melodrama: Retired detective aids Indian foreman facing murder rap

Broken Barrier
1917, (GB), Zeitlin & Dewhurst, b&w, 5,612 ft. (1710.5m)
W: George Dewhurst (*Dick Ransom*), Vera Cornish (*Mary Barton*), George Bellamy (*Sir Gilbert Foster*), Minna Grey (*Mrs. Dowling*), Mercy Hatton (*Flossie*), Douglas Munro (*George Parsons*), J. Hastings Batson (*Rev. Barton*), Hayford Hobbs, Wyndham Guise, Nelson Ramsey, Mrs. Sterling McKinlay
D: George Bellamy **SCR:** George Dewhurst, from Ben Landeck's play *Guilty Mother*. A.k.a. **Quicksands**
Standard crime-thriller: Forger blackmails wife who married elderly knight

The Broken Chisel
1913, (GB), B&C/DFSA, b&w, 2,986 ft. (910.1m)
W: Ernest G. Batley (*Jack Hinton*), Marie Pickering (*May Caversham*), Dorothy Batley (*Eva Barker*)
D: Charles Weston **STORY:** Ernest G. Batley
*USA retiTle, **Escape from Broadmoor***
Standard crime-thriller: Man flees jail by balloon

Broken Goddess
1973, (USA), Immortal Films, b&w, 24 mins.
W: Holly Woodlawn
D: Peter Dallas
Bizarre opus, underground film not in general release: Transvestite romp in manner of silent screen

Broken Threads
1917, (GB), Hepworth/Butcher, b&w
W: Henry Edwards (*Jack Desmond*), Chrissie White (*Helen Desmond*), A.V. Bramble (*Pierre*), Harry Gilbey (*Murray*), Gwynne Herbert (*The Housekeeper*), Fred Johnson (*The Stepfather*), W.G. Saunders (*Boniface*), John MacAndrews (*The Confederate*)
D: Henry Edwards **STORY:** Harold Bartholomew
Standard melodrama: Girl presumed drowned flees lighthouse keeper, finds husband insane

The Bronze Idol
1914, (GB), Hepworth, b&w, 1,300 ft. (396.2m)
W: Stewart Rome *(The Secretary)*, Harry Royston *(The Burglar)*
D: Frank Wilson
Standard crime-thriller: Rich man's secretary catches burglar who exposes him as ex-convict

The Brood
1979, (Can), Mutual-Elgin/New World, color, 91 mins.
W: Oliver Reed *(Dr. Hal Raglan)*, Art Hindle *(Frank Carveth)*, Samantha Eggar *(Nola Carveth)*, Nuala Fitzgerald *(Julianna Kelly)*, Henry Beckman *(Barton Kelly)*, Susan Hogan *(Ruth Mayer)*, Cindy Hinds *(Candice Carveth)*, Gary McKeehan *(Mike)*, Michael McGhee *(The Inspector)*, Bob Silverman *(Jan)*, Joseph Shaw *(Dr. Desborough)*, Felix Silla *(The Child)*, Larry Solway *(Resnikoff)*, Rainer Schwartz *(Birkin)*, Nicholas Campbell *(Chris)*
WRIT & D: David Cronenberg   PHOTOG: Mark Irwin   MUSIC: Howard Shore
Standard SF-fantasy: Unethical "psycho-plasmic" experiments turn unbalanced woman into mother of horrors

The Brother from Another Planet
1984, (USA), A-Train/Cinecom Int'l, color, 109 mins.
W: Joe Morton *(The Brother)*, Rosanna Carter *(The West Indian Woman)*, Ray Ramirez *(The Hispanic Man)*, Yves Rene *(The Haitian Man)*, Peter Richardson *(The Islamic Man)*, Darryl Edwards *(Fly)*, Ginny Yang *(The Korean Shopkeeper)*, Steve James *(Odell)*, Bill Cobbs *(Walter)*, Leonard Jackson *(Smokey)*, Tom Wright *(Sam)*, Maggie Renzi *(Noreen)*, Olga Merediz *(Noreen's Client)*, Minnie Gentry *(Mrs. Brown)*, Ren Woods *(Bernice)*, Reggie Rock Bythewood *(Rickey)*, Alvin Alexis *(Willis)*, Caroline Aaron *(Randy Sue)*, John Sayles *(A Man in Black)*, David Strathairn *(A Man in Black)*, Herbert Newsome *(Little Earl)*, Rosetta Le Noire *(Mama)*, Michael Albert Mantel *(Mr. Lowe)*, Dee Dee Bridgewater *(Malverne)*, Jaime Tirelli *(Hector)*, Liane Curtis *(Ace)*, Fisher Stevens *(The Card Trickster)*, Chip Mitchell *(Ed)*, David Babcock *(Phil)*, Sidney Sheriff Jr. *(Virgil)*, Randy Frazier *(The Bouncer)*, Marisa Smith *(The White Hooker)*, Copper Cunningham *(The Black Hooker)*, Kim Staunton *(The Teacher)*, Ishmael Houston-Jones *(The Dancer)*, Leon W. Grant *(A Basketball Player)*, Carl Gordon *(Mr. Price)*, Dwania Kyles *(The Waitress)*, Anthony Thomas *(A Basketball Player)*, Andre Robinson Jr. *(The Pusher)*, John Griesemer *(The White Cop)*, Ellis Williams *(The Watcher)*, Edward Baran *(Mr. Vance)*, Deborah Taylor *(Vance's Receptionist)*, Josh Mostel *(The Casio Vendor)*, Herb Downer *(The Floor Buffer)*
WRIT, D, & EDIT: John Sayles   PHOTOG: Ernest R. Dickerson   ORIG SCORE: Mason Darling   SONGS: *Homeboy Dinero, You Can't Get to Heaven from Here, Burning My Heart Out, Boss of the Block, Two People in the World, Getaway, & Promised Land*
Celebrated SF-fantasy: Black extraterrestrial meets Harlem

Brother Future
1991, (USA), Made for TV, color, 110 mins
W: Phill Lewis, Carl Lumbly, Frank Converse, Vonetta McGee
TVM, standard fantasy: Modern black teen transported to 1822, where he's enslaved

The Brotherhood of Satan
1970, (USA), LQ-Jaf/Four Star Excelsior/Col, color, 93 mins.
W: Strother Martin *(Doc)*, L.Q. Jones *(The Sheriff)*, Charles Bateman *(Ben)*, Ahna Capri *(Nicky)*, Alvy Moore *(Tobey)*, Geri Reischl *(Kiti)*, Charles Robinson *(The Priest)*, Helene Winston *(Dame Alice)*, Joyce Easton *(Mildred)*, Debi Storm *(Billy Jo)*, Jeff Williams *(Stuart)*, Robert Ward *(Mike)*, Judy McConnell *(Phyllis)*, John Barclay, Patrick Sullivan Burke, Elsie Moore, Ysabel MacCloskey, Cicely Walper, Phillis Coughlan, Margaret Wheeler, Anthony Jochim, Donald Journeaux, Lenore Shaenwise, Kevin McEveety, Alyson Moore, Sheila McEveety, Brian McEveety, Grant McGregor, Jonathan Eisley, Cindy Holden, Debbie Judith, Scott Aguilar, Robyn Grei, Linda Riffany
D: Bernard McEveety   SCR: William Welch   PHOTOG: John Arthur Morrill   MUSIC: Jaime Mendoza-Nava
Minor horror-thriller: Village isolated by diabolism

The Brotherhood of the Bell
1970, (USA), Cinema Center 100, Made for TV, color, 100 mins.
W: Glenn Ford, Dean Jagger, Rosemary Forsyth, Maurice Evans, Will Geer, William Conrad, Bill Smithers, Logan Field, Scott Graham, Eduard Franz, Robert Pine
WRIT & P: David Karp   D: Paul Wendkos   PHOTOG: Robert B. Hauser   MUSIC: Jerry Goldsmith
TVM, standard thriller: Insidious fraternity spreads terror and ruin

A Brother's Atonement
1914, (GB), Barker/Walturdaw, b&w, 2,000 ft. (609.6m)
W: Roy Travers *(George Harding)*
D: Bert Haldane   STORY: Rowland Talbot
Standard crime-thriller: Framed gamekeeper flees jail, gets revenge

Brown Bewitched
1911, (GB), Cricks & Martin, b&w, 440 ft. (134.1m)
D: A.E. Coleby
Minor fantasy short: Man buys eggs, oranges, cheese, rabbit, and sausages that come to life

Una Bruja sin Escoba
see A Witch without a Broom

La Brulure de Mille Soleils (The Burn of a Thousand Suns)
1965, (Fr), Argos, color, 25 mins.
WRIT, P, & D: Pierre Kast   PHOTOG: Jacques Maillet   MUSIC & SOUND FX: Bernard Parmeggiani
Animated short, arty SF-fantasy: Extraterrestrial race faces problems

The Brutal Burglar
1900, (GB), R.W. Paul, b&w
Standard crime-thriller

The Brute Man
1946, (USA), Univ/PRC, b&w, 58 mins.
W: Rondo Hatton, Tom Neal, Jane Adams, Peter Whitney, Donald MacBride, Jan Wiley
P: Ben Pivar   D: Jean Yarbrough   SCR: George Bricker & M. Coates Webster   PHOTOG: Maury Gertsman
blurb: "His brain cried Kill! Kill! Kill!"
Minor thriller: Blind pianist's love redeems disfigured madman

The Bubble
1966, (USA), Monarch/Midwestern Magic-Vuers/Oboler, 3D, color, 112 mins.
W: Michael Cole, Deborah Walley, Johnny Desmond, Chester Jones, Virginia Gregg
WRIT, P, & D: Arch Oboler
reissued (1976) as **Fantastic Invasion of Planet Earth**
Minor SF-thriller: Space aliens trap small community under force field in Space-Vision

Buccaneer's Girl
1950, (USA), Univ, color, 77 mins.
W: Yvonne DeCarlo, Philip Friend, Robert Douglas, Jay C. Flippen, Elsa Lanchester, Andrea King, Henry Daniell, Douglass Dumbrille
D: Frederick de Cordova   SPCL-FX: David S. Horsley   MUSIC: Walter Scharf
Standard adventure-thriller: Pirate rescues maiden from merchant ship, she returns favor

Die Buchse Der Pandora (Pandora's Box)
1928, (Ger), Nero, b&w, 3254m (10,675.1 ft.)
W: Louise Brooks, Fritz Kortner, Franz Lederer, Carl Goetz, Krafft Raschig, Alice Roberts, Gustav Diessl
D: G.W. Pabst   PHOTOG: Gunther Krampf
Classic melodrama: Girl has many lovers, meets Jack the Ripper

Buckaroo Banzai
see **The Adventures of Buckaroo Banzai**

A Bucket of Blood (1934)
see **The Tell-Tale Heart (1934)**

A Bucket of Blood
1959, (USA), AIP, b&w, 65 mins.
W: Dick Miller, Barboura Morris, Antony Carbone, Julian Burton, Ed Nelson, John Brinkley, Myrtle Domerel, John Shaner, Bruno Ve Sota, Judy Bamber, Burt Convy, Jean Burton
P & D: Roger Corman   SCR: Charles B. Griffith   PHOTOG: Jack Marquette   MUSIC: Fred Katz
orig. co-billed with **Attack of the Giant Leeches**
Minor horror-melodrama: Beatnik artist commits murder

A Bucket of Blood
1995, (USA), color
W: Anthony Michael Hall, Justine Bateman
Made-for-Cable, standard thriller (remake of 1950s cult film)

Buck Rogers
see **Destination Saturn**

Buck Rogers in the 25th Century
1979, (USA), Glen A. Larson/Univ, color, 89 mins.
W: Gil Gerard *(Buck Rogers)*, Erin Gray *(Wilma Deering)*, Tim O'Connor *(Dr. Huer)*, Pamela Hensley *(Princess Ardala)*, Duke Butler *(Tigerman)*, Henry Silva *(Kane)*, Joseph Wiseman *(Draco)*, Felix Silla *(Twiki)*, Mel Blanc *(The Voice of Twiki)*, Caroline Smith *(The Young Woman)*, Kevin Coates *(The Pilot)*, Gil Serna *(The Technician)*, John Dewey-Carter *(The Supervisor)*, David Cadiente *(The Comtel Officer)*, Colleen Kelly *(Wrather)*, H.B. Haggerty, Larry Duran, Kenny Endoso, Steve Jones, Eric Lawrence, David Buchanan, Burt Marshall
P: Richard Caffey & Leslie Stevens   D: Daniel Haller   SCR: Glen A. Larson & Leslie Stevens   PHOTOG: Frank Beascoechea   MUSIC: Stu Phillips   SONGS: *Suspension* (sung by Kipp Hamilton)
Standard SF-adventure, spawned teleseries: Astronaut-type in suspended animation, awakens in warring future

Buddha
1963, (Jap), Daiei/UA, color
W: Kojiro Hongo, Charito Solis, Fujiko Yamamoto, Shintaro Katsu, Ma-chiko Kyo, Raizo Ichikawa, Keizo Kawasaki, Hiroshi Kawaguchi
P: Masaichi Nagata   D: Kenji Misumi   SCR: Fuji Yahiro   PHOTOG: Hiroshi Imai   COLOR CONSULTANT: Yoshiaki Kiara
Lavish adventure-fantasy: Sinful pre-Buddhist paganism

Buddha's Lock

1987, (Hong Kong-Red China), color, 96 mins.
W: John X. Heart, Zhang Lutong, Yan Bide, Sun Feihu, Wei Zongwan, Steve Horowitz
D: Yim Ho
Standard melodrama: Crashed American pilot enslaved by backward Chinese tribe during World War II

Bud the C.H.U.D. II

1989, (USA), Lightning/Vestron, color, 84 mins
W: Brian Robbins *(Steve)*, Bill Calvert *(Kevin)*, Tricia Leigh Fisher *(Katie)*, Gerrit Graham *(Bud the Chud)*, Larry Cedar, Bianca Jagger, Larry Linville, Judd Omen, Norman Fell, Jack Riley, Sandra Kerns, June Lockhart, Robert Vaughn, Rich Hall, Robert Symonds, Priscilla Pointer, Jo Ann Dearing, Jami Lynn Grenham, Frank Birney, Mr. Marvin J. McIntyre, Clive Revill, Ritch Shydner, James F. Dean, Gregory Phelan, Peter Beckman, Tony Edwards, Zachariah Sage Kerns, Winifred Freedman, Barah Berry, Mark S. Lane, Jonathan Farwell, Mary Margaret Patts, Andy Pelish
D: David Irving **SCR:** M. Kane Jeeves **PHOTOG:** Arnie Sirlin **MUSIC:** Nicholas Pike **SONGS:** *Bud the Chud, Guys Like Girls, For Love, Brave New Dance, Nearer to Morning, Man Talk, & I'm a Hungry Man*
Made-for-Video, minor horror-satire: Army of zombies attacks

Buffalo Bill on the Brain

1911, (GB), Kineto, b&w, 445 ft. (135.6m)
D: Theo Bouwmeester
Standard comedy-fantasy: Old man reads cowboy story, dreams of fighting Indians

Buffet Froid (Cold Buffet)

1979, (Fr), color, 95 mins.
W: Gerard Depardieu, Bernard Blier, Jean Carmet, Genevieve Page, Denise Gence, Carole Bouquet, Michel Serrault, Jean Benguigui
D & SCR: Bertrand Blier
Surreal thriller: Innocent suspected of murder

Buffy, the Vampire Slayer

1992, (USA), 20th Fox, color, 98 mins.
W: Kristy Swanson *(Buffy)*, Donald Sutherland *(Merrick)*, Luke Perry *(Pike)*, Rutger Hauer *(Lothos)*, Paul Reubens (Paul Reubens) *(Amilyn)*, Michelle Abrams *(Jennifer)*, Hilary Swank *(Kimberly)*, Paris Vaughan *(Nicole)*, Candy Clark *(Buffy's Mom)*, Mark DeCarlo *(The Coach)*
D: Fran Rubel Kuzui **SCR:** Joss Whedon **PHOTOG:** James Hayman **MUSIC:** Carter Burwell **SONGS:** *In the Wind, Man Smart, Woman Smarter, We Close Our Eyes, Silent City & Inner Mind*
Standard horror-satire: Valley Girl enlisted to stalk Undead (Later a TV series)

Buffy The Vampire Slayer: LUKE PERRY AND KRISTY SWANSON

Bug

1975, (USA), Para, color, 101 mins.
W: Bradford Dillman *(James Parmiter)*, Joanna Miles *(Carrie Parmiter)*, Richard Gilliland *(Gerald Metbaum)*, Jamie Smith Jackson *(Norma Tacker)*, Alan Fudge *(Mark Ross)*, Jesse Vint *(Tom Tacker)*, Patty McCormack *(Sylvia Ross)*, Sam Jarvis *(The Taxi Driver)*, Jim Poyner *(Kenny Tacker)*, Fred Downs *(Henry Tacker)*, Brendan Dillon *(Charlie)*, James Greene *(Rev. Kern)*, Bard Stevens *(The Security Guard)*, Georgiana Castle
P: William Castle **D:** Jeannot Szwarc **SCR:** Thomas Page & William Castle from Thomas Page's novel *The Hephaestus Plague* (film orig. to be titled same)
PHOTOG: Michel Hugo **SPCL-FX:** Phil Cory **ELECTRONIC MUSIC:** Charles Fox
Effective SF-horror: Teacher breeds vicious super-roaches

Bug Goes to Town

see Hoppity Goes to Town

A Bug's Life

1998, (USA), Walt Disney, color, 94 mins.
VOICES: Kevin Spacey, Dave Foley, Julia Louis-Dreyfus, John Ratzenberger, Dennis Leary, Jonathan Harris, David Hyde Pierce, Madeline Kahn, Phyllis Diller, Richard Kind, Roddy McDowall *(Mr. Soil)*,
SONGS: Randy Newman
Amusing animated fantasy (Roddy McDowall's last film): Ants vs. grasshoppers

Bulldog Drummond

1922, (GB), Astra-Nat'l/Hodkinson, b&w, 6,000 ft. (1828.8m)
W: Carlyle Blackwell *(Hugh "Bulldog" Drummond)*, Dorothy Fane *(Irma Peterson)*, Evelyn Greely *(Phyllis Benton)*, Warwick Ward *(Dr. Lakington)*, Horace de Vere *(Carl Peterson)*, Gerald Dean *(Algy Longworth)*, Harry Bogarth *(Sparring Partner)*, William Browning *(James Handley)*
D: Oscar Apfel **SCR:** C.B. Doxat-Pratt, from Sapper's novel
Standard thriller: Sleuth seeks kidnapped millionaire. Filmed in Holland

Bulldog Drummond

1929, (USA), Samuel Goldwyn/UA, b&w, 90 mins.
W: Ronald Colman *(Hugh "Bulldog" Drummond)*, Lilyan Tashman *(Irma Peterson)*, Joan Bennett *(Phyllis Benton)*, Montagu Love *(Carl Peterson)*, Lawrence Grant *(Dr. Lakington)*, Wilson Benge *(Danny)*, Claud Allister *(Algy Longworth)*, Tetsu Komai *(Chong)*, Adolph Milar *(Marcovitch)*, Charles Sellon *(John Travers)*, Donald Novis *(Singer)*, Tom Ricketts *(The Colonel)*, Gertrude Short *(The Barmaid)*
P & D: F. Richard Jones **SCR:** Wallace Smith & Sidney Howard, from Sapper's novel & the play by Gerald du Maurier **PHOTOG:** George Barnes & Gregg Toland
"Great melodrama, intelligently produced with a great performance by Ronald Colman"—Photoplay
Superior thriller: Sleuth rescues girl's uncle from asylum

Bulldog Drummond Again

see Bulldog Drummond Escapes

Bulldog Drummond at Bay

1937, (GB), Wardour/Rep, b&w, 78 mins.
W: John Lodge *(Hugh "Bulldog" Drummond)*, Dorothy Mackaill *(Doris)*, Victor Jory *(Gregory)*, Leslie Perrins *(Grayson)*, Claud Allister *(Algy Longworth)*, Brian Buchel *(Meredith)*, Hugh Miller *(Ivan Kalinsky)*, Marie O'Neill *(Norah)*, Richard Bird *(Caldwell)*, Jim Gerald *(Veight)*, Frank Cochrane *(Dr. Belfus)*, Annie Esmond *(Mrs. Caldwell)*, Wilfrid Hyde-White *(Conrad)*, William Dewhurst *(Reginald Portside)*
P: Walter C. Mycroft **D:** Norman Lee **SCR:** Patrick Kirwan & James Parrish, from Sapper's novel **PHOTOG:** Walter Harvey
Standard thriller: Sleuth prevents theft of robot plane

Bulldog Drummond At Bay: RON RANDELL, TERRY KILBURN AND PAT O'MOORE

Bulldog Drummond at Bay

1947, (USA), Col, b&w, 70 mins.
W: Ron Randell (*Bulldog Drummond*), Anita Louise (*Doris*), Pat O'Moore (*Algy Longworth*), Terence Kilburn (*Seymour*), Holmes Herbert (*Insp. Melvar*), Lester Matthews (*Shannon*), Leonard Mudie (*Meredith*), Dave Thursby (*Tommy*), Oliver Thorndike (*Richard Hamilton*), Aminta Dyne (*Mrs. Eskdale*)
D: Sidney Salkow   **SCR:** Frank Gruber, from Sapper's novel   **PHOTOG:** Philip Tannura   **MUSIC:** Mischa Bakaleinikoff
Standard thriller: Sleuth trails diamond thief

Bulldog Drummond Comes Back

1937, (USA), Para, b&w, 64 mins.
W: John Barrymore (*Col. Nielson*), John Howard (*Hugh "Bulldog" Drummond*), Louise Campbell (*Phyllis Clavering*), Reginald Denny (*Algy Longworth*), E.E. Clive (*Tenny*), J. Carrol Naish (*Mikhail Valdin*), Helen Freeman (*Irena Soldanis*), John Rogers (*Blanton*), Ivor Henderson (*Morris*)
P: Stuart Walker   **D:** Louis King   **SCR:** Edward T. Lowe, from Sapper's novel *The Female of the Species*   **PHOTOG:** William C. Mellor   **MUSIC:** Boris Morros
Standard thriller: Sleuth pursues kidnappers

Bulldog Drummond Escapes

1937, (USA), Para, b&w, 65 mins.
W: Ray Milland (*Hugh "Bulldog" Drummond*), Sir Guy Standing (*Insp. Nielson*), Heather Angel (*Phyllis Clavering*), Porter Hall (*Norman Merridew*), Reginald Denny (*Algy Longworth*), E.E. Clive (*Tenny*), Fay Holden (*Natalie Selden*), Clyde Cook (*Alf, the Constable*), Walter Kingsford (*Prof. Stanton*), David Clyde (*Gower*), Patrick Kelly (*Stiles, the Butler*), Frank Elliott (*Bailey*), Charles McNaughton (*Constable Higgins*), Doris Lloyd (*The Nurse*), Colin Tapley (*Dixon*), Zeffie Tilbury (*The Drunken Woman*), John Power (*The Customs Officer*), Barry Macollum (*Blodgson*), Robert Adair (*Woolsey*), Pat Sommerset, Bobbie Hale, Ernie Stanton, Gunnis Davis
D: James Hogan   **SCR:** Edward T. Lowe, from Sapper's novel *Bulldog Drummond Again*   **PHOTOG:** Victor Milner
Standard thriller: Rogue sleuth encounters mystery. Working title, **Bulldog Drummond Again**

Bulldog Drummond in Africa

1938, (USA), Para, b&w, 60 mins.
W: John Howard (*Hugh "Bulldog" Drummond*), H.B. Warner (*Col. Nielson*), Heather Angel (*Phyllis Clavering*), J. Carrol Naish (*Richard Lane*), Reginald Denny (*Algy Longworth*), E.E. Clive (*Tenny*), Anthony Quinn (*Deane Fordine*), Rollo Lloyd (*Acris*), Matthew Boulton (*Maj. Grey*), Michael Brooks (*Baron Newsky*), William von Bricken (*Dr. Stern*), Forrester Harvey (*Constable Jenkins*)
D: Louis King   **SCR:** Garnett Weston, from Sapper's novel *The Challenge*
Standard thriller: Sleuth pursues spies seeking radio-wave disintegrator

Bulldog Drummond's Bride

1939, (USA), Para, b&w, 55 mins.
W: John Howard (*Hugh "Bulldog" Drummond*), H.B. Warner (*Col. Neilson*), Heather Angel (*Phyllis Clavering*), Reginald Denny (*Algy Longworth*), Elizabeth Patterson (*Aunt Blanche*), E.E. Clive (*Tenny*), Eduardo Ciannelli (*Henry Armides*), John Sutton (*Prof. Tredennis*), Gerald Hamer (*Garvey*), Jacques Lory (*The Clerk*), Adrienne d'Ambricourt (*Therese*), Adia Kuznetzoff (*Gaston*), Louis Mercier (*Dupree*), George Davis (*The Turnkey*)
P: Stuart Walker   **D:** James Hogan   **SCR:** Stuart Palmer & Garnett Weston, from Sapper's novel *Bulldog Drummond and the Oriental Mind*
Standard thriller: Sleuth pursues bank robber. Working title, **Mr. and Mrs. Bulldog Drummond**

Bulldog Drummond's Peril

1938, (USA), Para, b&w, 66 mins.
W: John Barrymore (*Col. Nielson*), John Howard (*Hugh "Bulldog" Drummond*), Louise Campbell (*Phyllis Clavering*), E.E. Clive (*Tenny*), Reginald Denny (*Algy Longworth*), Porter Hall (*Dr. Botulian*), Elizabeth Patterson (*Aunt Blanche*), Nydia Westman (*Gwen Longworth*), Michael Brooks (*Anthony Greer*), Halliwell Hobbes (*Prof. Bernard Goodman*), Matthew Boulton (*Sir Raymond Blantrye*), Zeffie Tilbury (*Mrs. Weavens*)
D: James Hogan   **SCR:** Stuart Palmer, from Sapper's novel *The Third Round*
Standard thriller: Sleuth battles gangsters for synthetic diamond formula

Bulldog Drummond's Revenge

1937, (USA), Para, b&w, 60 mins.
W: John Barrymore (*Col. Nielson*), John Howard (*Hugh "Bulldog" Drummond*), Louise Campbell (*Phyllis Clavering*), E.E. Clive (*Tenny*), Reginald Denny (*Algy Longworth*), Nydia Westman (*Gwen Longworth*), Frank Puglia (*Draven Negais*), Lucien Littlefield (*Smith*), John Sutton (*Nielson's Sec'y*), Miki Morita (*Sumio Kanda*), Robert Gleckler (*Hardcastle*), Ronnie Bartlett (*The Cabin Boy*)
D: Louis King   **SCR:** Edward T. Lowe, from Sapper's novel *The Return of Bulldog Drummond*   **PHOTOG:** Harry Fischbeck
Standard thriller: Sleuth opposes transvestite thief of formula for new explosive

Bulldog Drummond's Secret Police

1939, (USA), Para, b&w, 56 mins.
W: John Howard (*Hugh "Bulldog" Drummond*), H.B. Warner (*Col. Nielson*), Heather Angel (*Phyllis Clavering*), Reginald Denny (*Algy Longworth*), Elizabeth Patterson (*Aunt Blanche*), Leo G. Carroll (*Borjei Islanyani*), E.E. Clive (*Tenny*), David Clyde (*Constable Jenkins*), Forrester Harvey (*Prof.*

Downie), Gerald Rogers (*Sgt. Peters*), Clyde Cook (*Constable Hawkins*), Elspeth Dudgeon (*The Housekeeper*), Neil Fitzgerald (*The Station Master*), Wyndham Standing (*Master of Ceremonies*), Dutch Hendrian, Dick Rush
D: James Hogan   **SCR:** Garnett Weston, from Sapper's novel *Temple Tower*   **PHOTOG:** Merritt Gerstad
Standard thriller: Sleuth seeks professor's killer

Bulldog Drummond's Third Round

1925, (GB), Astra-Nat'l, b&w, 7,300 ft. (2225m)
W: Jack Buchanan (*Hugh "Bulldog" Drummond*), Betty Faire (*Phyllis*), Juliette Compton (*Irma Peterson*), Allan Jeayes (*Carl Peterson*), Austin Leigh (*Prof. Goodman*), Phil Scott (*Sparring Partner*), Frank Goldsmith (*Sir Raymond Blayntree*), Edward Sorley (*Julius Freyder*)
D & SCR: Sidney Morgan, from Sapper's novel *The Third Round*
Minor thriller: Sleuth seeks formula for synthetic diamonds

Bulldog Drummond Strikes Back

1934, (USA), 20th Century Pictures/UA, b&w, 84 mins.
W: Ronald Colman (*Hugh "Bulldog" Drummond*), Loretta Young (*Lola Field*), Warner Oland (*Prince Achmed*), C. Aubrey Smith (*Insp. Nielsen*), Mischa Auer (*Hassan*), Charles Butterworth (*Algy Longworth*), Una Merkel (*Gwen*), Kathleen Burke (*Jane Sothern*), George Regas (*Singh*), Arthur Hohl (*Dr. Sothern*), Ethel Griffies (*Mrs. Field*), Douglas Gerrard (*Parker*), H.N. Clugston (*Mr. Field*), Charles Irwin (*The Drunk*), Gunnis Davis (*The Man with the Harsh Voice*), William O'Brien (*The Servant at the Banquet*), Wilson Benge (*Nielsen's Valet*), Lucille Ball (*The Girl*), Robert Kortman (*The Henchman*), Doreen Monroe (*The Woman in the Hotel Room*), Vernon Steele, Creighton Hale, Pat Somerset, E.E. Clive, Halliwell Hobbes, Yorke Sherwood
P: Darryl F. Zanuck   **D:** Roy Del Ruth   **SCR:** Nunnally Johnson, from characters created by Sapper   **PHOTOG:** J. Peverell Marley   **MUSIC:** Alfred Newman
Superior thriller: Sleuth craves excitement

Bulldog Drummond Strikes Back

1947, (USA), Col, b&w, 65 mins.
W: Ron Randell (*Hugh "Bulldog" Drummond*), Pat O'Moore (*Algy Longworth*), Gloria Henry (*Phyllis*), Terence Kilburn (*Seymour*), Anabel Shaw (*Ellen Curtiss*), Holmes Herbert (*Insp. Melvar*), Wilton Graff (*Cedric Mason*), Barry Bernard (*Vincent Cummings*), Matthew Boulton (*William Cosgrove*), Elspeth Dudgeon (*Nanny*), Carl Harbord (*Insp. Sanderson*), Leslie Denison (*Sgt. Schubeck*)
D: Frank McDonald   **SCR:** Edna Anhalt, Edward Anhalt & L.E. Taylor, from Sapper's novel   **PHOTOG:** Henry Freulich   **MUSIC:** Mischa Bakaleinikoff
Standard thriller: Sleuth seeks heiress' impersonator

Bulldog Jack

1935, (GB), Gaumont, b&w, 72 mins.
W: Jack Hulbert (*Jack Pennington*), Fay Wray (*Ann Manders*), Athole Fleming (*Hugh "Bulldog" Drummond*), Ralph Richardson (*Morelle*), Claude Hulbert (*Algy Longworth*), Gibb McLaughlin (*Denny*), Paul Graetz (*Salvini*), Harvey Braban (*Sgt. Robinson*), Cyril Smith (*The Duke*)
D: Walter Forde   **SCR:** H.C. McNeile ("Sapper"), Gerard Fairlie, J.O.C. Orton, & Sidney Gilliat, from characters created by Sapper
USA retitle, **Alias Bulldog Drummond**
Standard thriller: Jewel heist is foiled

Bulldog Sees It Through

1940, (GB), ABPC, b&w, 77 mins.
W: Jack Buchanan (*Bill Watson*), Greta Gynt (*Jane Sinclair*), Sebastian Shaw (*Derek Sinclair*), David Hutcheson (*Freddie Caryll*), Googie Withers (*Toots*), Robert Newton (*Watkins*), Arthur Hambling (*Insp. Horn*), Polly Ward (*Miss Fortescue*), Wylie Watson (*The Dancing Professor*), Nadine March (*Gladys*), Ronald Shiner (*Pug*), Aubrey Mallalieu (*The Magistrate*)
D: Harold Huth   **SCR:** Doreen Montgomery, from Gerard Fairlie's novel *Scissors Cut Paper*
Standard thriller: Test pilot and secret-agent butler unmask armaments saboteur

Bullet from the Past

1957, (GB), Merton Park/Anglo-Amalgamated, b&w, 33 mins.
W: Ballard Berkeley, Robert Sansom, Philippa Hiatt
P: Alec Snowden   **D:** Kenneth Hume   **STORY:** Donovan Winter, from a novel by Edgar Lustgarten
Standard short crime-thriller: 27-year-old murder surfaces when insurance agent is shot

Bullet to Beijing

1995, (GB), color
W: Michael Caine (*Harry Palmer*), Jason Connery
from characters created by Len Deighton
Stanadrd thriller: British spy chases deadly virus on train
cf. **Billion Dollar Brain, Funeral in Berlin** & **The Ipcress File**

The Bullet Train

1975, (Jap), color, 89 mins. (orig. 155 mins.)
W: Ken Takakura, Shinichi Chiba, Akira Oda, Kei Yamamoto, Fumio Watanabe
D: Junya Sato
Standard thriller: Bomb planted on high-speed train

Bumbles' Diminisher

1913, (GB), EcKo, b&w, 500 ft. (152.4m)
W: Phillipi (*Bumbles*)

D: W.P. Kellino
Minor comedy-fantasy short: Magic powder shrinks beer, fat circus child

Bump in the Night
see *The Final Terror*

Bunny Lake is Missing
1965, (USA-GB), Col, b&w, 107 mins.
W: Laurence Olivier (*Supt. Newhouse*), Carol Lynley (*Ann Lake*), Keir Dullea (*Steven Lake*), Noel Coward (*Horatio Wilson*), Anna Massey (*Elvira Smollett*), Martita Hunt (*Ada Ford*), Adrienne Corri (*Dorothy*), Clive Revill (*Sgt. Andrews*), Finlay Currie (*The Dollmaker*), Lucie Mannheim (*The Cook*), Delphi Lawrence (*Mother*), Megs Jenkins (*Sister*), Jill Melford (*The Teacher*), Richard Wattis (*The Clerk*), Victor Maddern (*The Taxi Driver*), Fred Emney (*The Man*), Damarys Hayman (*Daphne*), Suky Appleby (*Bunny Lake*), Percy Herbert, Suzanne Neve, Patrick Jordan, David Oxley, The Zombies (*singing group*)
P & D: Otto Preminger   **SCR:** John & Penelope Mortimer, from Evelyn Piper's novel   **PHOTOG:** Denys Coop   **MUSIC:** Paul Glass   **DESIGN:** Don Ashton
Standard melodrama: Woman fails to prove existence of kidnapped daughter

The 'Burbs
1989, (USA), Imagine/Univ, color, 101 mins.
W: Tom Hanks (*Ray Peterson*), Bruce Dern (*Mark Rumsfield*), Carrie Fisher (*Carol Peterson*), Corey Feldman (*Ricky Butler*), Rick Ducommun (*Art Weingartner*), Henry Gibson (*Dr. Werner Klopek*), Brother Theodore (*Uncle Reuben Klopek*), Courtney Gains (*Hans Klopek*), Wendy Schaal, Gale Gordon, Robert Picardo, Franklyn Ajaye, Bill Stevenson, Heather Haase, Kevin Gage, Brenda Benner, Patrika Darbo, Dick Miller, Nick Katt, Rance Howard, Gary Hays, Dana Olsen, Cory Danziger
D: Joe Dante   **SCR:** Dana Olsen   **PHOTOG:** Robert Stevens   **SPCL-FX SPRVSR:** Ken Pepiot   **MUSIC:** Jerry Goldsmith   **SONGS:** *Machine, Bloodstone, Questa O Quella, Locked in a Cage,* & *Make Some Noise*
Standard comedy-thriller: Surburbanites leery of weird neighbors

The Burglar
1957, (USA), Col, b&w, 90 mins.
W: Jayne Mansfield, Dan Duryea, Stewart Bradley, Martha Vickers, Mickey Shaughnessy, Peter Capell, Phoebe Mackay
P: Louis W. Kellman   **D:** Paul Wendkos   **SCR:** David Goodis
Standard film noir: Woman and half-brother steal diamond necklace from spiritualist. cf. **The Burglars**

The Burglar and the Child
1909, (GB), Hepworth, b&w, 450 ft. (137.2m)
D: Theo Bouwmeester
Standard crime-thriller: Burglar kidnaps girl, frames father

The Burglar and the Clock
1908, (GB), Hepworth, b&w, 550 ft. (167.6m)
W: Thurston Harris (*The Burglar*)
D: Lewin Fitzhamon
Standard fantasy-thriller: Burglar steals wristwatch which turns into pocket watch and then into alarm clock, etc.

A Burglar for a Night
1911, (GB), Hepworth, b&w, 775 ft. (236.2m)
W: Flora Morris (*Mary*), John McAndrews (*The Man*)
D: Bert Haldane
Standard crime-thriller: Unemployed man robs house

The Burglars
1972, (Fr), color
W: Jean-Paul Belmondo, Omar Shariff, Dyan Cannon, Robert Hossein
D: Henri Verneuil
Standard film noir (remake of **The Burglar***): Thieves steal necklace*

The Burglar's Daughter
1912, (GB), Hepworth, b&w, 475 ft. (144.8m)
D: Lewin Fitzhamon
Standard crime-thriller: Policeman helps maid nab her burglar father

The Burglar's Misfortune
1910, (GB), Acme Films/C&M, b&w, 525 ft. (160m)
W: Fred Rains (*The Burglar*)
D: Fred Rains
Standard thriller: Burglar mistaken for escaped lunatic

Burial Ground
1980, (It), Esteban Cinematografica/FCG, color, 84 mins.
W: Karen Well, Peter Bark
D: Andrea Bianchi   **SCR:** Piero Regnoli   **PHOTOG:** Gianfranco Maioletti   **SPCL-FX:** Gino de Rossi
Minor horror-fantasy: Etruscan corpses revive, USA release, 1985

Burial of the Rats
1995, (USA), color, 85 mins.

W: Adrienne Barbeau, Maria Ford, Kevin Alber
Made-for-Cable, minor thriller: Cult kidnaps man. From a story by Bram Stoker

Buried Alive
1940, (USA), Producers Pictures Corp., b&w, 69 mins.
W: Beverly Roberts (*Joan Wright*), Paul McVey (*Jim Henderson*), Robert Wilcox (*Johnny Martin*), Ted Osborn (*Ira Hanes*), George Pembroke (*Ernie Matthews*), Alden Chase (*Dr. Robert Lee*), Ben Alexander (*Riley*), Peter Lynn (*Gus Barth*), Bob McKenzie (*Al Garrity*), Wheeler Oakman (*Manning*), Norman Budd (*The Kid*), Don Rowan (*Big Billy*), Boyd Irwin (*Rutledge*), Edward Earle (*Charlie Blake*), Dave O'Brien (*Carson*)
D: Victor Halperin   **SCR:** George Bricker   **ORIG. STORY:** William A. Ullman Jr.   **PHOTOG:** Jack Greenhalgh   **MUSIC DIR.:** David Chudnow
Minor melodrama: Convict finds love, faces execution

Buried Alive (1951)
see *The Strange Door*

Buried Alive
1981, (It), color, 90 mins.
W: Kieran Canter, Cinzia Monreale, Franca Stoppi
D: Joe D'Amato
Standard thriller: Taxidermist goes mad

Buried Alive
1990, (USA), Made-for-Cable, color, 97 mins.
W: Robert Vaughn, Donald Pleasence, Karen Witter, Hoyt Axton, John Carradine, Ginger Lynn Allen
D: Frank Darabont, Gerard Kikione   **WRIT:** Mark Patrick Carducci & Jake Clesi   **MUSIC:** Michel Colombier
Minor thriller: Students disappear at school for delinquent girls

Buried Alive II
1997, (USA), USA-TV, color, 95 mins.
W: Ally Sheedy (*Laura*), Stephen Caffrey (*Randy*), Tracey Needham (*Roxanne*), Tim Matheson (*Clint*), Brian Libby, J.C. Quinn, Tommy Hinkley, Keith Flippen
D: Tim Matheson   **TELEPLAY:** Walter Klenhard   **PHOTOG:** Jacques Haitkin   **MUSIC:** Michel Colombier
TVM, standard thriller: Heiress marked for death by cheating husband

Buried Secrets
1996, (USA), NBC-TV, color, 95 mins.
W: Tiffani-Amber Thiessen, Tim Matheson (*Clay*), Erika Flores (*Mary*), Melinda Culea (*Laura*), Kelly Rutherford, Channon Roe
D: Michael Toshiyuko Uno   **TELEPLAY:** John Leekley   **PHOTOG:** Richard Quinlan   **MUSIC:** J. Peter Robinson
TVM, minor fantasy-thriller: Ghost seeks vengeance, possesses young woman's body

Buried Treasure
1921, (USA), Famous Players-Lasky/Para, b&w, 6,964 ft. (2122.6m)
W: Marion Davies (*Pauline Vandermueller*), Norman Kerry (*Dr. John Grant*), Anders Randolf (*William Vandermueller*), Edith Shayne (*Mrs. Vandermueller*), John Charles (*Duc de Chavannes*), Thomas Findlay (*The Capt.*)
WRIT & D: George D. Baker   **PHOTOG:** Hal Rosson
Standard fantasy-melodrama: Reincarnated girl finds fabulous Caribbean treasure

Burke and Hare
1972, (GB), Shipman/Armitage/UA, color, 91 mins.
W: Derren Nesbitt (*Burke*), Glyn Edwards (*Hare*), Harry Andrews (*Dr. Knox*), Dee Shenderey (*Mrs. Burke*), Yootha Joyce (*Mrs. Hare*), Francoise Pascal (*Marie*), Alan Tucker (*Arbuthnot*), Paul Greaves (*Ferguson*), Joan Carol (*Mme. Thompson*), Thomas Heathcote (*Paterson*), David Pugh (*Jamie*), Robin Hawdon (*Angus*), Yutte Stensgaard (*Janet*)
P: Guido Coen   **D:** Vernon Sewell   **STORY:** Ernie Bradford   **PHOTOG:** Desmond Dickinson   **MUSIC:** Roger Webb
USA retitle, **The Horrors of Burke and Hare**
Standard thriller: Irishmen commit murders, supply surgeon with corpses

Burned at the Stake
see *The Coming*

The Burning
1982, (USA), Miramax/Filmways/Orion, color, 88 mins.
W: Brian Matthews (*Todd*), Leah Ayres (*Michelle*), Brian Backer (*Alfred*), Larry Joshua (*Glazer*), Carrick Glenn (*Sally*), Ned Eisenberg (*Eddie*), Carolyn Houlihan (*Karen*), Lou David (*Cropsy*), Holly Hunter
D: Tony Maylam   **SCR:** Peter Lawrence & Bob Weinstein   **PHOTOG:** Harvey Harrison   **MUSIC:** Rick Wakeman   **MAKEUP:** Tom Savini
Minor thriller: Human monster stalks young campers

The Burning Court
1961, (It-Fr-W. Ger), Int'l Prods./Ufa-Comacico/Trans-Lux, b&w, 110 mins.
W: Nadja Tiller, Jean-Claude Brialy, Perrette Pradier, Claude Rich, Antoine Balpetre, Rene Genin, Edith Scob, Walter Giller, Duvalles, Helena Manson, Dany Jacquet
P: Yvon Guezel   **D:** Julien Duvivier   **SCR:** Charles Spaak & Julien Duvivier, from John Dickson Carr's novel   **MUSIC:** Georges Auric

GB retitle, *The Curse and the Coffin*
Engrossing fantasy-thriller: Witch returns from death, gains revenge

Burnin' Love
see *Love at Stake*

The Burn of a Thousand Suns
see *La Brulure de Mille Soleils*

Burn Out
see *Journey into Fear (1975)*

Burnt Evidence
1954, (GB), ACT Films/Monarch, b&w, 61 mins.
W: Jane Hylton (*Diana Taylor*), Duncan Lamont (*Jack Taylor*), Donald Gray (*Jimmy Thompson*), Meredith Edwards (*Bob Edwards*), Cyril Smith (*Alf Quinney*), Irene Handl (*Mrs. Raymond*), Hugo Shuster (*Hartl*), Kynaston Reeves (*The Pathologist*)
P: Ronald Kinnoch   **D:** Dan Birt   **SCR:** Ted Willis, from Percy Haskins' story "Burn the Evidence"
Standard crime-thriller: Husband accidentally shoots wife's lover

Burnt Offerings
1976, (USA), P.E.A./UA, color, 116 mins.
W: Karen Black (*Marian Rolfe*), Oliver Reed (*Ben Rolfe*), Bette Davis (*Aunt Elizabeth*), Burgess Meredith (*Arnold Allardyce*), Eileen Heckart (*Roz Allardyce*), Lee Harcourt Montgomery (*David Rolfe*), Dub Taylor (*Walker*), Anthony James (*The Chauffeur*), Orin Cannon (*The Minister*), James T. Myers (*Dr. Ross*), Todd Turquand (*The Young Ben*), Joseph Riley (*Ben's Father*)
P & D: Dan Curtis   **SCR:** William F. Nolan & Dan Curtis, from a novel by Robert Marasco   **PHOTOG:** Jacques Marquette   **SPCL-FX:** Cliff Wenger   **MUSIC:** Robert Cobert
Modest horror-thriller: Vampiric house destroys vacationing family

Burn, Witch, Burn (1962)
see *Night of the Eagle*

Burn, Witch, Burn (1972)
see *Mark of the Devil (1972)*

Bury Me an Angel
1972, (USA), New World, color, 86 mins
W: Dixie Peabody, Terry Mace, Clyde Ventura, Joanne Jordan, Dan Haggerty, Beech Dickerson, Stephen Whittaker, Gary Littlejohn
P: Paul Norbert   **WRIT & D:** Barbara Peeters
blurb: "A howling hellcat humping a hot steel hog on a roaring rampage of revenge"
Standard thriller (1st "biker" film directed by a woman): Six-foot blonde hunts brother's killer

Bury Me Dead
1947, (USA), Eagle Lion, b&w, 71 mins.
W: Mark Daniels, June Lockhart
Minor thriller

Busman's Honeymoon
1940, (GB), MGM, b&w, 99 mins.
W: Robert Montgomery (*Lord Peter Wimsey*), Constance Cummings (*Harriet Vane*), Leslie Banks (*Insp. Kirk*), Robert Newton (*Frank Crutchley*), Seymour Hicks (*Bunter*), Googie Withers (*Polly*), Frank Pettingell (*Puffett*), Joan Kemp-Welch (*Aggie Twitterton*), Aubrey Mallalieu (*Rev. Simon Goodacre*), Roy Emerton (*Noakes*), James Carney (*PC Sellon*), Louise Hampton (*Mrs. Ruddle*), Eliot Makeham (*Simpson*), Reginald Purdell (*McBride*), Gordon McLeod (*The Coroner*)
D: Arthur Woods   **SCR:** Monckton Hoffe, Angus Macphail, & Harold Goldman, from a play by Dorothy L. Sayers & Muriel St. Clare Byrne
USA retitle, *Haunted Honeymoon*
Standard thriller: Sleuthing newlyweds uncover murder

Busman's Honeymoon: ROBERT MONTGOMERY AND ROBERT NEWTON

The Busy Body
1966, (USA), Para, color, 102 mins.
W: Sid Caesar, Robert Ryan, Anne Baxter, Kay Medford, Godfrey Cambridge, Arlene Golonka, Richard Pryor, Charles McGraw, Jan Murray, Ben Blue, George Jessel, Dom DeLuise, Marty Ingels, Bill Dana
P & D: William Castle   **SCR:** Ben Starr, from a novel by Donald Westlake.   **PHOTOG:** Harold Stine   **MUSIC:** Vic Mizzy
Minor comedy-thriller: Problems keeping track of corpse

The Busy Man
1907, (GB), Hepworth, b&w, 525 ft. (160m)
D: Lewin Fitzhamon
Standard fantasy: Speeded-up scenes of businessman's day

The Butcher (1983)
see *Psycho from Texas*

The Butcher (1969)
see *Le Boucher*

Butcher, Baker (Nightmare Maker)
1982, (USA), Int'l Film Marketing, color
W: Jimmy McNichol, Susan Tyrrell, Bo Svenson
P: Stephen Breimer & Eugene Mazzola   **D:** William Asher   **SCR:** Stephen Breimer, Alan Jay Glueckman & Boon Collins
A.k.a. *Night Warning* & *Nightmare Maker*
Standard thriller: Boy's aunt becomes psycho-killer.

The Butcher's Wife
1991, (USA), Para, color, 104 mins.
W: Demi Moore (*Marina*), Jeff Daniels (*Alex*), George Dzundza (*Leo*), Mary Steenburgen (*Stella*), Frances McDormand (*Grace*), Christopher Durang (*Mr. Liddle*), Margaret Colin, Max Perlich, Miriam Margolyes, Diane Salinger
D: Terry Hughes   **SCR:** Ezra Litwak & Marjorie Schwartz   **PHOTOG:** Frank Tidy   **MUSIC:** Michael Gore
Minor fantasy: Beautiful clairvoyant changes lives

The Butterfly Revolution
see *Summer Camp Nightmare*

Buttons
1915, (GB), G.B. Samuelson/Moss, b&w, 2,000 ft. (609.6m)
W: Gerald Royston (*Crummings*), Fred Paul (*Mr. Alendale*)
D: George Pearson   **SCR:** Harry Engholm   **STORY:** G.B. Samuelson
Standard crime-thriller: Page trails burglars, is saved by dog

Bwana Devil
1952, (USA), Oboler/UA, 3D, color, 79 mins.
W: Robert Stack, Barbara Britton, Nigel Bruce, Paul McVey, Pat Aherne
WRIT: P & D: Arch Oboler   **PHOTOG:** Joseph F. Biroc   **MUSIC:** Gordon Jenkins
Standard adventure-thriller (first feature film in 3D): Railroad workers plagued by lions.
      Remake : *The Ghost and the Darkness*

By a Brother's Hand
see *By the Hand of a Brother*

By Candlelight
1933, (USA), Univ, b&w, 70 mins.
W: Paul Lukas, Elissa Landi, Nils Asther, Dorothy Revier, Lawrence Grant, Esther Ralston
D: James Whale
Standard comedy-thriller: Butler impersonates master

By Dawn's Early Light
1990, (USA), color, 100 mins.
W: Powers Boothe, Rebecca DeMornay, James Earl Jones, Rip Torn, Martin Landau, Darren McGavin, Peter MacNichol
D: Jack Sholder   **TELEPLAY:** Bruce Gilbert, from William Prochnau's novel *Trinity's*
Made-for-Cable, above-average thriller: USA and USSR on brink of nuclear war

By His Father's Orders
1914, (GB), Barker, b&w, 1,455 ft. (443.5m)
D: Bert Haldane   **STORY:** Rowland Talbot
Standard crime-thriller: Man shot robbing father's office

By Rocket to the Moon
see *Cat-Women of the Moon*

By the Hand of a Brother
1915, (GB), Broadwest/Gerrard, b&w, 2,000 ft. (609.6m)
W: Jack Jarman (*The Man*), Pauline Peters (*The Girl*)
P & D: Walter West
A.k.a. *By a Brother's Hand*
Standard crime-thriller: Ruined man shoots burglar, finds he is brother who has secretly helped him.

By Whose Hand?
see *The Mystery of Mr. Marks*

The Cabby's Dream
1906, (GB), Warwick Trading Co., b&w, 320 ft. (97.5m)
D: Charles Raymond
Minor fantasy short (in 7 scenes): Cabman dreams of bizarre ride with magician

La Cabeza Viviente (The Living Head)
1959, (Mex), Azteca/K. Gordon Murray, b&w, 75 mins.
W: German Robles, Abel Salazar, Ana Luisa Peluffo, Rosita Arenas, Mauricio Garces
P: Abel Salazar   **D:** Chano Urueta   **SCR:** Frederick Curiel & A. Lopez Portillo
Minor horror-fantasy: Aztec head comes to life, puts woman under spell

Le Cabinet de Mephistopheles (The Cabinet of Mephistopheles)
1897, (Fr), Star, b&w, 60m (196.9 ft./3.3 mins)
D: Georges Melies
Minor fantasy short: Conjurer produces marvels

The Cabinet of Caligari
1962, (USA), Lippert/20th-Fox, b&w, 105 mins.
W: Glynis Johns, Dan O'Herlihy, Dick Davalos, Constance Ford, Estelle Winwood, J. Pat O'Malley, Lawrence Dobkin, Phyllis Teagardin, Doreen Lang, Vicki Trickett, Charles Fredericks
P & D: Roger Kay   **SCR:** Robert Bloch   **PHOTOG:** John Russell   **MUSIC:** Gerald Fried
Not a remake of 1919's Das Kabinett des Dr. Caligari; engrossing, well-acted thriller: Woman stranded in house of eerie happenings

The Cabinet of Dr. Caligari
see Das Kabinett des Dr. Caligari

The Cabinet of Mephistopheles
see Le Cabinet de Mephistopheles

The Cabinet of the Davenport Brothers
see L'Armoire des Freres Davenport

The Cabinet of Wax Figures
see Das Wachsfigurenkabinett

The Cabinet Trick of the Davenport Brothers
see L'Armoire des Freres Davenport

Cabin in the Sky
1943, (USA), MGM, b&w, 99 mins.
W: Lena Horne, Ethel Waters (*Petunia*), Rex Ingram (*Lucifer Jr.*), Eddie "Rochester" Anderson (*Joe*), Butterfly McQueen, Cab Calloway, Clinton Rosemond, Louis Armstrong, Ella Fitzgerald, Duke Ellington, John W. Sublett ('Bubbles')
D: Vincente Minelli   **SCR:** Joseph Schrank, from Lynn Root's musical play
   PHOTOG: Sidney Wagner   **MUSIC:** George Stoll   **LYRICS & MUSIC:** E.Y. Harburg & Harold Arlen
Classic Negro fantasy: Satan duels with heaven

The Cable Guy: JIM CARREY

The Cable Car Murders
see Crosscurrent

The Cable Guy
1996, (USA), Col, color, 91 mins.
W: Jim Carrey (*Cable Guy*), Matthew Broderick (*Steven Kovacs*), Leslie Mann (*Robin*), Ben Stiller (*Sam Sweet*), Diane Baker (*Mrs. Kovacs*), Janeane Garofalo (*The Waitress*), Eric Roberts (*himself*), George Segal
P: Andrew Licht, Jeffrey A. Mueller & Judd Apatow   **D:** Ben Stiller   **SCR:** Lou Holtz Jr.   **PHOTOG:** Robert Brinkmann   **MUSIC:** John Ottman
Bizarre comedy-thriller: Man menaced by obsessed Cable TV installer

La Caduta di Troia (The Fall of Troy)
1910, (It), b&w, 1,969 ft. (600m)
D: Giovanni Pastrone
Standard adventure-thriller: Ancient metropolis beseiged by Achean warriors

The Cage
1914, (GB), London, b&w, 2,010 ft. (612.6m)
W: Lillian Logan (*Adrienne*), Gerald Ames (*Comte de Lavalle*), Charles Rock (*Baron de Tartas*), George Bellamy (*The Monk*)
D: George Loane Tucker   **SCR:** Bannister Merwin   **STORY:** Hesketh Pearson
Standard adventure: Knight foils wicked baron, wins lady

Caged Heat!
1974, (USA), New World, color, 84 mins
W: Juanita Brown, Roberta Collins, Erica Gavin, Rainbeaux Smith, Bar-bara Steele, Ella Reid, Desiree Cousteau
P: Evelyn Purcell   **WRIT & D:** Jonathan Demme   **MUSIC:** John Cale
A.k.a. **Renegade Girls**
Unusual thriller (Jonathan Demme's first film): Female convicts flee abuse and "corrective physical therapy"

Caged Heat II: Stripped of Freedom
1994, (USA), color, 85 mins.
W: Jewel Shepard
Minor thriller: CIA agent infiltrates hellish women's prison

Caged Virgins
see Vierges et Vampires

Caged Women
see Barbed Wire Dolls

Cage of Evil
1960, (USA), UA, b&w, 70 mins.
W: Ronald Foster, Pat Blair
Standard thriller

Cage of Gold
1950, (GB), Ealing, b&w, 83 mins.
W: Jean Simmons (*Judith*), David Farrar (*Bill Brennan*), James Donald (*Dr. Alan Kearn*), Madeleine Lebeau (*Madeleine*), Maria Mauban (*Antoinette*), Herbert Lom (*Rahman*), Bernard Lee (*Insp. Gray*), Gladys Henson (*Nanny*), Harcourt Williams (*Dr. Kearn Sr.*), Gregoire Aslan (*Duport*), Martin Boddey (*Adams*), Arthur Howard (*The Registry Office Bridegroom*), Campbell Singer (*The Constable*), Michael Balfour (*The GI*), George Benson (*The Clerk*)
P: Michael Balcon   **D:** Basil Dearden   **SCR:** Jack Whittingham   **PHOTOG:** Douglas Slocombe   **MUSIC:** Georges Auric
Intense thriller: Remarried girl blackmailed by first spouse. Working title, **Sacrifice**

The Cage of Stone
1968, (Fr), color
Fantasy short

Cagliostro
1928, (Ger), b&w
D: Richard Oswald
Standard thriller: Evil hypnotist spreads ruin

Cagliostro's Mirror
see Le Miroir de Cagliostro

The Cakes of Khandipore
1915, (GB), Martin/DFSA, b&w, 500 ft. (152.4m)
D: Dave Aylott
Standard comedy-fantasy: Boy gives away Indian cakes that cause eaters' mouths to stick

La Calavera Negra (The Black Skull)
1960, (Mex), b&w
Standard horror-thriller

The Callbox Mystery
1932, (GB), Samuelson/UA, b&w, 73 mins.
W: Warwick Ward (*Leo Mount*), Harold French (*Insp. Layton*), Wendy Barrie (*Iris Banner*), Gerald Rawlinson (*David Radnor*), Harvey Braban (*Insp. Brown*), Daphne Mowbray (*Rose*)
D: G.B. Samuelson, from a story by Joan Wentworth Wood (*Morgan*)
Standard thriller: Inspector proves suicides are murders

Called Back
1914, (GB), London/Fenning, b&w, 3,536 ft. (1077.8m)
W: Henry Ainley *(Gilbert Vaughan)*, Charles Rock *(Macari)*, Jane Gail *(Pauline March)*, George Bellamy *(Dr. Manuel Ceneri)*, Vincent Clive *(Anthony March)*, Ackerman May *(Petroff)*, Judd Green *(The Drunk)*
D: George L. Tucker, from a play by Comyns Carr, based on a novel by Hugh Conway,
Standard crime-thriller: Blind husband of Italian doctor's mad ward "sees" her brother murdered during a trance. Reissued 1918

Call Him Mr. Shatter
1974, (GB-Hong Kong), Hammer/Avco Embassy, color, 90 mins
W: Stuart Whitman, Anton Diffring, Peter Cushing
P: Michael Carreras & Vee King Shaw   **D:** Michael Carreras   **SCR:** Don Houghton
A.k.a. **Shatter**
Minor spy-kung fu thriller

Calling Bulldog Drummond
1951, (GB), MGM, b&w, 80 mins.
W: Walter Pidgeon *(Hugh "Bulldog" Drummond)*, Margaret Leighton *(Sgt. Helen Smith)*, Peggy Evans *(Molly)*, David Tomlinson *(Algy Longworth)*, Robert Beatty *(Guns)*, Bernard Lee *(Col. Webson)*, Charles Victor *(Insp. McIver)*, Patric Doonan *(Alic)*, Harold Lang *(Stan)*, James Hayter *(Bill)*
P: Hayes Goetz   **D:** Victor Saville   **SCR:** Howard Emmett Rogers, Gerard Fairlie & Arthur Wimperis, from Gerard Fairlie's novel, based on characters created by Sapper   **PHOTOG:** Graham Kelly
Standard thriller: Sleuth comes out of retirement

Calling Dr. Death
1943, (USA), Univ, b&w, 63 mins.
W: Lon Chaney Jr. *(Dr. Steel)*, Ramsay Ames *(Maria Steel)*, J. Carrol Naish *(Insp. Gregg)*, David Bruce *(Robert Duval)*, Fay Helm *(Mrs. Duval)*, Patricia Morison *(Stella)*, Fred Gierman *(Father)*, Lisa Golm *(Mother)*, Mary Hale *(Marion)*, Alec Craig *(The Watchman)*, Holmes Herbert *(The Butler)*, Charles Wagenheim *(The Coroner)*, John Elliott *(The Priest)*, George Eldredge *(The D.A.)*
D: Reginald LeBorg   **SCR:** Edward Dein   **PHOTOG:** Virgil Miller
Well-made "Inner Sanctum" mystery: Neurologist fears he may be murderer

Calling Homicide
1956, (USA), AA, b&w, 61 mins.
W: Bill Elliott, Kathleen Case
Standard melodrama

Calling Philo Vance
1940, (USA), WB, b&w, 62 mins.
W: James Stephenson *(Philo Vance)*, Margot Stevenson *(Hilda Lake)*, Henry O'Neill *(D.A. John F.X. Markham)*, Edward Brophy *(Ryan)*, Ralph Forbes *(Tom MacDonald)*, Donald Douglas *(Philip Wrede)*, Martin Kosleck *(Gamble)*, James Conlin *(Dr. Doremus)*, Edward Raquello *(Grassi)*, George Irving *(Avery)*, Wedgewood Nowell *(Brisbane Coe)*, Creighton Hale *(Hennessey)*, Richard Kipling *(Archer Coe)*, Bo Ling *(Ling Toy)*, DeWolf (William) Hopper *(The Hotel Clerk)*, George Reeves *(The Steamship Clerk)*
D: William Clemens   **SCR:** Tom Reed, from characters created by S.S. Van Dine   **PHOTOG:** L.W. O'Connell
Minor "Philo Vance" mystery-thriller: Remake of **The Kennel Murder Case**

Call Me Bwana
1963, (GB), Rank/Eon/UA, color, 103 mins.
W: Bob Hope *(Matt Merryweather)*, Anita Ekberg *(Luba)*, Edie Adams *(Frederica Larsen)*, Lionel Jeffries *(Dr. Ezra Mungo)*, Percy Herbert *(A Henchman)*, Paul Carpenter *(Col. Spencer)*, Orlando Martins *(The Chief)*, Al Mulock *(A Henchman)*, Peter Dyneley *(Williams)*, Arnold Palmer [cameo role]
D: Gordon M. Douglas   **SCR:** Johanna Harwood & Nate Monaster   **PHOTOG:** Ted Moore   **MUSIC:** Monty Norman
Humor & marginal SF: Confused search for space capsule

Call of the Flesh
see **The Old Dark House** *(1932)*

Call of the Jungle
1944, (USA), Mono, b&w, 60 mins.
W: Ann Corio, James Bush
Minor adventure-thriller

Caltiki, Il Mostro Immortale (Caltiki, the Immortal Monster)
1959, (It), Galatea/Bruno Vailati/AA, b&w, 75 mins.
W: John Merivale, Didi Perego [Didi Sullivan in USA release], Daniela Rocca, Gerald Haerter, Daniele Vargas, Victor Andree, Arturo Dominici, Giacomo Rossi-Stuart
P: Samuel Schneider   **D:** Robert Hampton [Riccardo Freda]   **SCR:** Philip Just [Filippo Sanjust], from a Mexican legend   **PHOTOG:** John Foam [Mario Bava]
German retitle, **The Mysterious Horror**
Standard SF-horror: **Blob***-type terror revives*

Calypso
see **Manfish**

Camelot
1967, (USA), WB, color, 179 mins.
W: Richard Harris *(King Arthur)*, Vanessa Redgrave *(Guinevere)*, Franco Nero *(Lancelot)*, David Hemmings *(Mordred)*, Gary Marshal *(Sir Lionel)*, Lionel Jeffries *(King Pellinore)*, Laurence Naismith *(Merlyn)*, Estelle Winwood *(Lady Clarinda)*, Pierre Olaf *(Dap)*, Peter Bromilow *(Sir Sagramore)*, Anthony Rogers
P: Jack Warner   **D:** Joshua Logan   **SCR & LYRICS:** Alan Jay Lerner, from the stage play by Alan Jay Lerner & Frederick Loewe, based on T.H. White's novel *The Once and Future King*   **PHOTOG:** Richard Kline   **SONGS:** *Camelot, I Wonder What the King is Doing Tonight, Follow Me, If Ever I Would Leave You, How to Handle a Woman, What Do the Simple Folks Do?, C'est Moi, The Simple Joys of Maidenhood, I Loved You Once in Silence, The Lusty Month of May, Guenevere, Take Me to the Fair*
Lavish musical: Forbidden love of Lancelot and Guinevere precipitates destruction of King Arthur's Round Table

Cameron's Closet
1989, (USA), SVS, color, 87 mins.
W: Cotter Smith *(Sam Talliaferro)*, Mel Harris *(Nora Haley)*, Scott Curtis *(Cameron)*, Chuck McCann *(Ben Majors)*, Leigh McCloskey *(Pete Groom)*, Kim Lankford *(Dory Lansing)*, Gary Hudson *(Bob Froelich)*, Tab Hunter *(Owen Lansing)*, David Estruado *(Capt. Navarro)*, Dort Donald Clark *(Alan Wilson)*, Wilson Smith *(Joe Crespy)*, Kerry Nakagawa *(The Policeman)*, Raymond Patterson *(The Physician)*, Skip E. Lowe *(The Newscaster)*, Frank Pesce *(Ed Wallace)*, Paul W. Zecevic *(The Reporter)*, Doc D. Charbonneau *(The Little Demon)*
P: Luigi Cingolani   **D:** Armand Mastroianni   **SCR:** Gary Brandner, from his novel   **PHOTOG:** Russell Carpenter   **VS-FX SPRVSR:** Ermanno Biamonte   **MUSIC:** Harry Manfredini
Standard horror-thriller: Closet materializes boy's worst fears

The Camp on Blood Island
1958, (GB), Hammer/Col, b&w, 81 mins.
W: Andre Morell *(Col. Lambert)*, Carl Mohner *(Piet van Elst)*, Edward Underdown *(Maj. Dawes)*, Barbara Shelley *(Kate Keiller)*, Walter Fitzgerald *(Cyril Beattie)*, Phil Brown *(Lt. Bellamy)*, Michael Goodliffe *(Father Anjou)*, Mary Merrall *(Mrs. Beattie)*, Richard Wordsworth *(Dr. Keiller)*, Wolfe Morris, Ronald Radd, Michael Gwynn, Marne Maitland, Michael Ripper, Lee Montague, Edwin Richfield, Barry Lowe, Max Butterfield, Michael Brill, Liliane Scottane, Peter Wayn, Jack McNaughton, Betty Cooper, Jan Holden, Anne Ridler, Barbara Lee, Grace Denbeigh-Russell, Jacqueline Curtiss
P: Anthony Hinds   **D:** Val Guest   **SCR:** Jon Manchip White & Val Guest   **PHOTOG:** Jack Asher   **MUSIC:** Gerard Schurmann
Standard action-melodrama: Brutal doings in Japanese prison camp
cf. **The Secret of Blood Island.** *Reissued 1961*

The Canary Murder Case
1929, (USA), Para, b&w, 82 mins.
W: William Powell *(Philo Vance)*, James Hall *(Jimmie Spotswoode)*, Louise Brooks *(Margaret O'Dell)*, Eugene Pallette *(Sgt. Ernest Heath)*, Jean Arthur *(Alice LaFosse)*, Gustav von Seyffertitz *(Dr. Ambrose Linquist)*, Charles Lane *(Charles Spotswoode)*, Ned Sparks *(Tony Skeel)*, Lawrence Grant *(John Cleaver)*, Louis John Bartels *(Louis Mannix)*, E.H. Calvert *(D.A. John F.X. Markham)*, Oscar Smith *(The Stuttering Hallboy)*, Tim Adair *(George Y. Harvey)*
D: Malcolm St. Clair   **SCR:** Florence Ryerson & Albert S. Le Vino, from S.S. Van Dine's *Philo Vance* novel   **PHOTOG:** Harry Fischbeck
Well-made thriller: Broadway singer murdered, suave sleuth investigates

Candidate for Murder
1962, (GB), Merton Park/Anglo-Amalgamated, b&w, 60 mins.
W: Michael Gough *(Donald Edwards)*, Erika Remberg *(Helena Edwards)*, Hans Borsody *(Kersten)*, John Justin *(Robert Vaughan)*, Paul Whitsun-Jones *(Phillips)*, Vanda Godsell *(Betty Conlon)*, Jerold Wells *(The Inspector)*, Annika Wills *(Jacqueline)*
P: Jack Greenwood   **D:** David Villiers   **SCR:** Lukas Heller, from Edgar Wallace's story "The Best Laid Plans of a Man in Love"
Compact thriller: Professional assassin hired to kill man's wife

The Candlelight Murder
1953, (GB), Merton Park/Anglo-Amalgamated, b&w, 32 mins.
W: Jack Lambert *(Supt. Rawson)*, Gerald Case *(Supt. Carron)*, Robert Cawdron *(The Sgt.)*, Clifford Buckton *(Parrish)*, Denis Shaw *(Joe Hawkins)*
P: Alec C. Snowden   **WRIT & D:** Ken Hughes, from a novel by Edgar Lustgarten
Standard short thriller: Inspector unmasks blacksmith as killer of old hermit

Candles at Nine
1944, (GB), British Nat'l, b&w, 86 mins.
W: Jessie Matthews *(Dorothea Capper)*, John Stuart *(William Gordon)*, Beatrix Lehmann *(Miss Carberry)*, Winifred Shotter *(Brenda Tem-pest)*, Reginald Purdell *(Charles Lacey)*, Joss Ambler *(Garth Hope)*, Hugh Dempster *(Hugh Lacey)*, Eliot Makeham *(Everard Hope)*, Vera Boggetti *(Lucille Hope)*, Ernest Butcher *(The Gardener)*, Guy Fielding, Gerry Wilmot
D: John Harlow   **SCR:** John Harlow & Basil Mason, from Anthony Gilbert's novel *The Mouse Who Wouldn't Play Ball*
Standard thriller: Heiress menaced in old mansion

Candyman
1992, (USA), Polygram/Tri-Star, color, 101 mins.
<u>W</u>: Virginia Madsen *(Helen Lyle)*, Tony Todd *(Candyman)*, Xander Berkeley *(Trevor Lyle)*, Kasi Lemmons *(Bernadette Walsh)*, Vanessa Williams *(Anne-Marie McCoy)*, Bernard Rose *(Archie Walsh)*
<u>WRIT & D</u>: Bernard Rose, from Clive Barker's novel *The Forbidden*   <u>PHOTOG</u>: Anthony B. Richmond   <u>MUSIC</u>: Philip Glass
Unusual horror-fantasy: Spectral killer pursues woman

Candyman: Farewell to the Flesh
1995, (USA), Propaganda/Polygram/Gramercy, color, 99 mins.
<u>W</u>: Tony Todd *(Candyman)*, Kelly Rowan *(Annie)*, Timothy Carhart *(Paul McKeever)*, Veronica Cartwright *(Octavia)*, Bill Nunn *(Rev. Ellis)*, Caroline Barclay, Michael Bergeron, Nate Bynum, Brianna Blanchard, Clotiel Bordellier, Sandy Byrd, Russell Buchanan, Eric Cadora, Carl N. Ciafalio, Michael Culkin, Matt Clark, Stephen Dunn, Daniel Dupont, Margaret Howell, David Gianopoulos, Glen Gomez, Steven Hartman, Fay Hauser, Ralph Joseph, Erin LaBranche, Carl LeBlanc, George Lemore, Maria Mason, Joshua Gibran Mayweather, Monica I. Monica, Brian Joseph Moore, William O'Leary, Randy Oglesby, Steve Picerni, Eric Pierson, Terrence Rosemore, Carol Sutton, Amy Ryder, Patricia Sansone, Hunt Scarritt
<u>D</u>: Bill Condon   <u>SCR</u>: Rand Ravich & Mark Kruger   <u>STORY</u>: Clive Barker   <u>PHOTOG</u>: Tobias A. Schliessler   <u>MUSIC</u>: Philip Glass
Standard horror-fantasy: Spirit of murdered slave seeks vengeance

The Candy Web
see 13 Frightened Girls

Cannibal
1976, (It), color
<u>W</u>: Mei Mei Lay
<u>D</u>: Ruggero Deodato
Minor thriller

Cannibal Attack
1954, (USA), Col, b&w, 69 mins.
<u>W</u>: Johnny Weissmuller *(Himself)*, David Bruce *(Arnold)*, Judy Walsh *(Luora)*, Bruce Cowling *(Rovak)*, Charles Evans, Joseph A. Allen Jr., Steve Darrell
<u>D</u>: Lee Sholem   <u>SCR</u>: Carroll Young
Standard adventure-thriller: Cobalt thefts investigated. Continuation of 'Jungle Jim' series.

Cannibal Campout
1988, (USA), color
Minor horror-thriller: Campers terrorized

Cannibal Girls
1972, (Can), Scary Pictures/AIP, color, 84 mins.
<u>W</u>: Eugene Levy *(Cliff)*, Andrea Martin *(Gloria)*, Ronald Ulrich *(The Reverend)*, Randall Carpenter *(Anthea)*, Bob McHeady *(The Sheriff)*, Bonnie Neilson *(Clarissa)*, Mira Pawluk *(Leona)*, May Jarvis *(Mrs. Wainwright)*, Alan Gordon *(The 1st Victim)*, Allan Price *(The 2nd Victim)*, Earl Pomerantz *(The 3rd Victim)*
<u>P</u>: Daniel Goldberg   <u>D</u>: Ivan Reitman   <u>SCR</u>: Robert Sandler   <u>PHOTOG</u>: Robert Saad   <u>SPCL FX</u>: Richard Whyte & Michael Lotosky   <u>MUSIC</u>: Doug Riley
Minor horror-satire: Moderns fall prey to ugly appetites

Cannibal Holocaust
see Queen of the Cannibals

Cannibal in the Streets
1982, (It), Almi Cinema 5, color
<u>W</u>: John Saxon
<u>P</u>: Maurizio Amati & Sandro Amati   <u>D & SCR</u>: Antonio Margheriti
*A.k.a. **Invasion of the Flesh Hunters***
Standard horror-thriller: Virus turns ex-Green Beret into cannibal

Cannibal Orgy, or The Maddest Story Ever Told
see Spider Baby

The Canterville Ghost
1944, (USA), MGM, b&w, 96 mins.
<u>W</u>: Robert Young, Margaret O'Brien, Charles Laughton, Peter Lawford, Rags Ragland, William Gargan, Reginald Owen, Mike Mazurki, Una O'Connor
<u>D</u>: Jules Dassin, from a story by Oscar Wilde   <u>PHOTOG</u>: Robert Planck   <u>MUSIC</u>: George Bassman
Classic comedy-fantasy: Cowardly ghost cursed to haunt castle

The Canterville Ghost
1986, (USA, GB), ABC-TV/Col, color, 96 mins.
<u>W</u>: Sir John Gielgud *(Sir Simon de Canterville)*, Ted Wass *(Harry Canterville)*, Alyssa Milano *(Jennifer)*, Andrea Marcovicci *(Lucy)*, Harold Innocent *(Umney)*, Lila Kaye *(Mrs. Umney)*, Bill Wallis
<u>D</u>: Paul Bogart, from a story by Oscar Wilde
TVM, standard fantasy: Cursed ghost haunts castle. Also made for TV in 1996

The Cape Canaveral Monsters
1960, (USA), CCM, b&w, 69 mins
<u>W</u>: Scott Peters, Katherine Victor, Linda Connell, Jason Johnson, Frank Smith
<u>P</u>: Richard Greer   <u>D & SCR</u>: Phil Tucker
Minor SF-thriller: Energy beings possess human bodies

Cape Fear
1961, (USA), Univ, b&w, 103 mins.
<u>W</u>: Gregory Peck *(Sam Bowden)*, Robert Mitchum *(Max Cady)*, Polly Bergen *(Peggy Bowden)*, Martin Balsam *(Mark Dutton)*, Lori Martin *(Nancy Bowden)*, Barrie Chase *(Diane Taylor)*, Edward C. Platt *(The Judge)*, Jack Kruschen *(Dave Grafton)*, Paul Comi *(Garner)*, Telly Savalas *(Charles Sievers)*, Ward Ramsey *(Officer Brown)*, Joan Staley *(The Waitress)*, John McKee *(Marconi)*, Will Wright *(Dr. Pearsall)*, Page Slattery *(Deputy Kersek)*, Mack Williams *(Dr. Lowney)*, Thomas Newman *(Lt. Gervasi)*, Carol Sydes *(Betty)*, Bunny Rhea *(The Pianist)*, Norma Yost, Alan Reynolds, Alan Wells, Paul Levitt, Herb Armstrong
<u>D</u>: J. Lee Thompson   <u>SCR</u>: James R. Webb, from John D. MacDonald's novel *The Executioners*   <u>PHOTOG</u>: Sam Leavitt   <u>MUSIC</u>: Bernard Herrmann
Tense melodrama: Ex-convict terrorizes lawyer's family

Cape Fear
1992, (USA), Amblin-Cappa Films-Tribeca Prods./Univ, color, 123 mins.
<u>W</u>: Robert De Niro *(Max Cady)*, Nick Nolte *(Sam Bowden)*, Jessica Lange *(Leigh Bowden)*, Juliette Lewis *(Danielle Bowden)*, Robert Mitchum *(Lt. Elgart)*, Joe Don Baker *(Claude Kersek)*, Gregory Peck *(Lee Heller)*, Martin Balsam *(The Judge)*
<u>D</u>: Martin Scorsese   <u>SCR</u>: Wesley Strick, from a screenplay by James R. Webb based on John D. MacDonald's novel *The Executioners*   <u>PHOTOG</u>: Freddie Francis   <u>MUSIC</u>: Bernard Herrmann (adapted by Elmer Bernstein)
Excellent remake of taut thriller: Vicious ex-con on path of vengeance

The Cap of Invisibility
1911, (GB), Natural Colour Kinematograph Co., color, 325 ft. (99.1m)
<u>D</u>: Walter R. Booth & Theo Bouwmeester
Minor fantasy short: Boy dreams conjurer gives him cap that makes objects disappear

Capricorn One
1978, (USA), Lazarus-Hyams/Assoc. General/Sir Lew Grade/WB, color, 127 mins.
<u>W</u>: Elliott Gould, James Brolin *(Charles Brubaker)*, Hal Holbrook *(Dr. Kelloway)*, Brenda Vaccaro *(Kay Brubaker)*, Sam Waterston *(Peter Willis)*, O.J. Simpson *(John Walker)*, Karen Black *(Judy Drinkwater)*, Telly Savalas *(Albain)*, David Huddleston *(Hollis Peaker)*, David Doyle *(Walter Loughlin)*, Alan Fudge *(The Capsule Communicator)*, Denise Nicholas, Robert Walden *(Elliot Whittier)*, Lee Bryant *(Sharon Willis)*, Norman Bartold, Paul Picerni, Milton Selzer, Lou Frizzell
<u>P</u>: Paul N. Lazarus III   <u>WRIT & D</u>: Peter Hyams   <u>PHOTOG</u>: Bill Butler   <u>MUSIC</u>: Jerry Goldsmith
Modest SF-intrigue: Bizarre coverup in U.S. space program

Captain Adventure
see The Adventures of Mandrin

Captain America
1978, (USA), Univ/CBS-TV, color, 98 mins.
<u>W</u>: Reb Brown *(Steve Rogers/Capt. America)*, Heather Menzies *(Dr. Wendy Day)*, Len Birman *(Dr. Simon Mills)*, Steve Forrest *(Brackett)*, Lance LeGault *(Harley)*, Joseph Ruskin *(Sandrini)*, Robin Mattson *(Tina)*, Frank Marth *(Barber)*, Chip Johnson
<u>P</u>: Martin Goldstein   <u>D</u>: Rod Holcomb   <u>TELEPLAY</u>: Don Ingalls, from characters created by Joe Simon & Jack Kirby   <u>PHOTOG</u>: Ronald W. Browne
*TVM, standard SF-adventure: Super-hero saves Phoenix from neutron bomb cf. **Captain America II***

Captain America
1992, (USA), 21st Century, color, 95 mins.
<u>W</u>: Matt Salinger *(Steve Rogers/Captain America)*, Ned Beatty *(Sam)*, Scott Paulin *("Red Skull")*, Ronny Cox *(Pres. Tom Kimball)*, Darren McGavin *(Gen. Fleming)*, Michael Nouri, Wayde Preston, Melinda Dillon, Francesca Neri, Kim Gillingham, Bill Mumy, Massimilio Massimi, Norbert Weisser, Bernarda Oman, Garette Ratliff, Robert Egon
<u>P</u>: Menahem Golan   <u>D</u>: Albert Pyun   <u>SCR</u>: Stephen Tolkin   <u>STORY</u>: Stephen Tolkin & Lawrence J. Block, from characters created by Joe Simon & Jack Kirby   <u>PHOTOG</u>: Philip Alan Waters   <u>SPCL VS-FX</u>: Fantasy II Film Effects   <u>MUSIC</u>: Barry Goldberg
Standard SF-adventure: Superhero comes out of suspended animation, battles archvillain

Captain America II
1979, (USA), Univ/CBS-TV, color, 96 mins.
<u>W</u>: Reb Brown *(Steve Rogers/Capt. America)*, Connie Selleca *(Dr. Wendy Day)*, Len Birman *(Dr. Simon Mills)*, Christopher Lee *(Miguel)*, Katherine Justice *(Helen)*, Christopher Cary *(Prof. Ilson)*, Stanley Kamel *(Kramer)*, John Waldron *(Peter)*, Arthur Rosenberg, Bill Mims, Alex Hyde-White, Lachelle Chamberlain, Susan French, Peter Moore, Ken Swofford, Bill Lucking, Lana Wood
<u>P</u>: Allan Balter   <u>D</u>: Ivan Nagy   <u>TELEPLAY</u>: Wilton Schiller & Patricia Payne, from Marvel Comics character created by Joe Simon & Jack Kirby   <u>PHOTOG</u>: Vincent A. Martinelli   <u>MUSIC SCORE</u>: Mike Post & Pete Carpenter
TVM, standard SF-adventure: Mastermind terrorizes with aging formula

Captain Clegg

1962, (GB), Hammer-Major/Univ, color, 82 mins.
<u>W:</u> Peter Cushing (*Dr. Blyss*), Oliver Reed (*Harry Crabtree*), Yvonne Romain (*Imogene*), Patrick Allen (*Capt. Collier*), Michael Ripper (*Mipps*), Martin Benson (*Rash*), David Lodge (*The Bosun*), Daphne Anderson (*Mrs. Rash*), Derek Francis (*The Squire*), Milton Reid (*The Mulatto*), Jack MacGowran (*The Man*), Sydney Bromley (*Tom Ketch*), Bob Head, Peter Halliday, Terry Scully, Rupert Osborn, Gordon Rollings, Colin Douglas
<u>P:</u> John Temple-Smith <u>D:</u> Peter Graham Scott <u>SCR:</u> John Elder [Anthony Hinds] & Barbara S. Harper, based on Russell Thorndyke's 1915 novel *Dr. Syn* <u>PHOTOG:</u> Arthur Grant <u>MUSIC:</u> Don Banks
*USA retitle, **Night Creatures** French retitle, **Le Fascinant Capitaine Clegg (The Fascinating Captain Clegg)***
*Standard action-thriller: Vicar unmasked as "dead" pirate. cf. **Dr. Syn***

Capt. John Smith and Pocahontas

1953, (USA), UA, color, 75 mins.
<u>W:</u> Anthony Dexter, Jody Lawrance
Standard adventure-thriller: Indian princess saves European's life

Captain Kidd

1945, (USA), UA, b&w, 90 mins.
<u>W:</u> Charles Laughton (*Capt. Kidd*), Randolph Scott, Barbara Britton, John Carradine, Reginald Owen, Ray Teal, Gilbert Roland, John Qualen, Sheldon Leonard, Henry Daniell, Abner Biberman, Norman Reilly Raine
<u>P:</u> Benedict Bogeaus <u>D:</u> Rowland V. Lee <u>SCR:</u> Norman Reilly Raine from a story by Robert H. Lee <u>PHOTOG:</u> Archie Stout <u>SPCL-FX:</u> Lee Zavitz <u>MUSIC SCORE:</u> Werner Janssen <u>MUSIC DIR:</u> David Chudnow
Melodramatic semi-bio: Old pirate tries to acquire "class"

Captain Kidd and the Slave Girl

1954, (USA), Reliance/UA, color, 83 mins.
<u>W:</u> Anthony Dexter, Eva Gabor, Alan Hale Jr., Richard Karlan, James Seay, Noel Cravat, Lyle Talbot, Jack Reitzen, Robert Long, Sonia Sorel, Mike Ross, Bill Cottrell, John Crawford, Bill Tannen
<u>WRIT & P:</u> Aubrey Wisberg & Jack Pollexfen <u>D:</u> Lew Landers
Standard adventure-thriller: Pirate finds love

Captain Kronos: Vampire Hunter

1974, (GB), Hammer/Para, color, 91 mins.
<u>W:</u> Horst Janson (*Capt. Kronos*), Caroline Munro (*Carla*), John Carson (*Dr. Marcus*), Shane Briant (*Paul Durward*), John Cater (*Prof. Hier-onymous Grost*), Lois Daine (*Sara Durward*), Wanda Ventham (*Lady Durward*), Ian Hendry (*Kerro*), Paul Greenwood (*Giles*), William Hobbs (*Hagen*), Brian Tully (*George Sorell*), Robert James (*Pointer*), Perry Soblosky (*Barlow*), Lisa Collings (*Vanda Sorell*), John Hollis (*The Barman*), Susanna East (*Isabella Sorell*),Elizabeth Dear (*Ann Sorell*), Joanna Ross (*Myra*), Stafford Gordon (*Barton Sorell*), Neil Seiler (*The Priest*), Olga Anthony (*Lilian*), Terence Sewards (*Tom*), Gigi Gurpinar (*The Blind Girl*), Jacqui Cook (*The Barmaid*), Peter Davidson (*The Big Man*), Trevor Lawrence (*Deke*), Penny Price (*The Whore*), Caroline Villiers (*Petra*)
<u>P:</u> Brian Clemens & Albert Fennell <u>WRIT & D:</u> Brian Clemens <u>PHOTOG:</u> Ian Wilson <u>MUSIC:</u> Laurie Johnson <u>MUSIC SPRVSR:</u> Philip Martell
*orig. to be titled **Kronos***
Modest horror-thriller: Dashing destroyer of Undead unmasks vampiric nobles

Captain Mephisto and the Transformation Machine

1966, (USA), Rep, b&w, 100 mins.
<u>W:</u> Richard Bailey, Linda Stirling, Roy Barcroft
<u>D:</u> Spencer G. Bennet, Wallace Grissell, & Yakima Canutt <u>SCR:</u> Albert DeMond, Basil Dickey, Jesse Duffy, Alan James, Grant Nel-son, & Joseph Poland
Standard adventure-thriller (feature culled from 1945 serial 'Manhunt on Mystery Island'): Villain seeks control of radioatomic power transmitter

Captain Nemo and the Floating City

*see **Captain Nemo and the Underwater City***

Captain Nemo and the Underwater City

1969, (GB), Omnia/MGM, color, 106 mins.
<u>W:</u> Robert Ryan (*Capt. Nemo*), Chuck Connors (*Robert Fraser*), Luciana Paluzzi (*Mala*), John Turner (*Joab*), Nanette Newman (*Helena*), Kenneth Connor (*Swallow*), Allan Cuthbertson (*Lomax*), Vincent Harding (*The Mate/Navigator*), Bill Fraser (*Barnaby*), Christopher Hartstone (*Philip*), Ralph Nosseck (*The Engineer*), Margot Ley, Ann Patrice, Michael McGovern, Alan Barry, Anthony Bailey, Patsy Snell
<u>P:</u> Bertram Ostrer <u>D:</u> James Hill <u>SCR:</u> Pip Baker, Jane Baker & R. Wright Campbell, inspired by the works of Jules Verne <u>PHOTOG:</u> Alan Hume <u>UNDERWATER PHOTOG:</u> Egil Woxholt <u>MUSIC:</u> Walter Stott
*orig. to be titled **The Adventure of Nemo, or Captain Nemo and the Floating City***
Juvenile SF-adventure: Shipwreck survivors visit underwater empire

Captain Pirate

1952, (USA), Col, color, 85 mins.
<u>W:</u> Louis Hayward, Patricia Medina
Standard adventure-thriller

Captain Scarlet vs. the Mysterons

1982, (GB), color, 90 mins.
*GB title: **Captain Blood, Fugitive***
<u>SPCL-FX:</u> Derek Meddings & Brian Johnson
Juvenile fantasy; animated puppets: Earth heroes battle Martians

Captain Scarlett

1953, (USA), UA, color, 75 mins.
<u>W:</u> Richard Greene, Leonora Amar, Isobel Del Puerto, Nedrick Young, Manolo Fabregas
<u>D:</u> Thomas Carr
Standard adventure-thriller

Captain Sinbad

1963, (W. Ger), King Bros./MGM, color, 88 mins.
<u>W:</u> Guy Williams (*Sinbad*), Heidi Bruehl, Pedro Armendariz, Guy Doleman, Abraham Sofaer, James Dobson, Walter Barnes, Margaret Jahnen, Bernie Hamilton, Helmut Schneider, Lawrence Montaigne, Rolf Wanka, Maurice Marsac, Charles Fawcett, Geoffrey Toone, Henry Brandon, John Crawford, Anna Luisa Schubert (*The Spider Dancer*)
<u>P:</u> Frank & Herman King <u>D:</u> Byron Haskin <u>STORY & SCR:</u> Samuel B. West & Harry King <u>PHOTOG:</u> Gunther Senftleben & Eugen Shuftan <u>MUSIC:</u> Michel Michelet
Lavish action-fantasy: Hero battles to save princess from clutches of evil magician

La Captive du Desert (Captive of the Desert)

1990, (Fr), color, 101 mins.
<u>W:</u> Sandrine Bonnaire, Dobi Kor, Fadi Taha, Dobi Wachink, Badel Barka
<u>D & PHOTOG:</u> Raymond Depardon
Unusual fact-based melodrama: Woman lives in captivity with desert tribe

Captive

1991, (USA), color, 95 mins.
<u>W:</u> Barry Bostwick, Joanna Kerns
TVM, standard thriller: Crazed men abduct couple and infant

Captive Girl

1950, (USA), Col, b&w, 73 mins.
<u>W:</u> Johnny Weissmuller (*Jungle Jim*), Buster Crabbe (*Barton*), Anita Lhoest, Rick Vallin, John Dehner, Nelson Leigh, Rusty Wescoatt
<u>P:</u> Sam Katzman <u>D:</u> William Berke <u>SCR:</u> Carroll Young
Standard action-adventure: Search for underwater treasure

Captive of the Desert

*see **La Captive du Desert***

Captive Planet

1978, (USA), color, 95 mins.
<u>W:</u> Sharon Baker, Chris Auram, Anthony Newcastle
<u>D:</u> Al Bradley
Minor SF-thriller: Earth threatened with obliteration

Captive Wild Woman

1943, (USA), Univ, b&w, 61 mins.
<u>W:</u> John Carradine (*Dr. Sigmund Walters*), Evelyn Ankers, Milburn Stone, Acquanetta, Fay Helm, Lloyd Corrigan, Paul Fix, Vince Barnett, Martha MacVicar [later Martha Vickers]
<u>D:</u> Edward Dmytryk <u>SCR:</u> Griffin Jay & Henry Sucher <u>PHOTOG:</u> George Robinson
*Standard horror-thriller, first installment in Universal's **Ape Woman** series: Scientist transforms female ape into beautiful woman cf **Jungle Captive** and **The Jungle Woman***

Captive Women

1952, (USA), American/RKO, b&w, 65 mins.
<u>W:</u> Robert Clarke, Margaret Field (later Maggie Mahoney), Gloria Saunders, Ron Randell, Eric Colmar, Stuart Randall, Robert Bice, Chili Williams, Paula Dorety, William Schallert
<u>WRIT & P:</u> Aubrey Wisberg & Jack Pollexfen <u>D:</u> Stuart Gilmore <u>PHOTOG:</u> Paul Ivano <u>MUSIC:</u> Charles Koff
*A.k.a. **1,000 Years from Now** working title, **3000 A.D.***
Minor SF-thriller: Post-nuke tribes war for supremacy

The Capture of Bigfoot

1979, (USA), Studio Film, color, 93 mins.
<u>W:</u> Stafford Morgan (*Dave Garrett*), Katherine Hopkins (*Karen*), Richard Kennedy (*Harvey Olsen*), Otis Young (*Jason*), George Buck Flower (*Jake*), John Goff (*Burt*), John Eimerman (*Jimmy*), Randolph Scott (*Randy*), Durwood McDonald (*John*), Greg Gault (*Kevin*), Wally Flaherty (*Sheriff Cooper*), Nelson C. Sheppo (*Daniels*), William Dexter (*Hank*), Harry Youstos (*Harry*), Doug Ibold (*Trapper*), Verkina Flower (*Linda*), Mitzi Kress (*Elsie*), Woody Jarvis (*Woody*), Bill Cannon (*Carlsen*), Patty Holzmann (*A Singer*), Mitch Irish (*A Singer*), Jeana Tomasino (*A Dancer*), Janus Raudkivi (*The Legendary Creature of Arak*), Randolph Rebane (*Little Bigfoot*)
<u>P & D:</u> Bill Rebane <u>ORIG. SCR:</u> Ingrid Neumeyer & Bill Rebane <u>SONGS:</u> *My Spirit Runs Free* & *Sensuous Tiger*

Capture That Capsule!
1961, (USA), Riviera/AIP, b&w, 70 mins.
W: Richard Miller *(Novak)*, Dick O'Neil *(Al)*, Richard Jordahl, Pat Bradley, Carl Rogers, Ed Siani, Doug Hughes, Ron Wright, Wylie Carter, Ed Gangel, Michael David, Web Smith, Dorothy Schiller, John Treacy, Dick Twohy
P & D: Will Zens   **SCR:** Jan Elbein & Will Zens   **PHOTOG:** Vilis Lapenieks Jr.   **MUSIC:** Art Hopkins
orig. co-billed with **The Pit and the Pendulum** *(1961)   TV retitle,* **Spy Squad**
Minor SF-melodrama: Spies seek space capsule

Captured by Boy Scouts
1909, (GB), London Cinematograph Co., b&w, 440 ft. (134.1m)
Standard crime-thriller: Boy scouts track thieving tramp

The Car
1977, (USA), Univ, color, 95 mins
W: James Brolin *(Wade Parent)*, Kathleen Lloyd *(Lauren)*, John Marley *(Everett Peck)*, Ronny Cox *(Luke Johnson)*, John Rubenstein *(John Morris)*, R.G. Armstrong *(Amos Clements)*, Elizabeth Thompson
P: Marvin Birdt & Elliot Silverstein   **D:** Elliot Silverstein   **SCR:** Dennis Shryack & Michael Butler   **MUSIC:** Leonard Rosenman
Modest fantasy-thriller: Demonic auto terrorizes Southwest community

La Cara del Terror (The Face of Terror)
1962, (Sp), Documento/Futuramic/Cinema-Video, b&w, 81 mins
W: Lisa Gaye, Fernando Rey, Virgilio Teixeira, Gerard Tichy, Conchita Cuetos, Carlos Casaravilla
D: Isidoro Martinez Ferry   **SCR:** Monroe Maning   **PHOTOG:** Jose F. Aguayo
SONG: My Lonely Life
Minor thriller: Doctor repairs psychotic girl's scarred face

Caravan to Vaccares
1974, (GB-Fr), Crowndale/Reeve/Societe Nouvelle/Fox/Rank, color, 98 mins.
W: Charlotte Rampling *(Lila)*, David Birney *(Neil Bowman)*, Michel Lonsdale *(Duc de Croytor)*, Marcel Bozzuffi *(Henri Czerda)*, Serge Marquand *(Ferenc)*, Michael Bryant *(Stefan Zuger)*, Francoise Brion *(Stella)*, Manitas de Plata *(Ricardo)*, Graham Hill *(The Pilot)*, Marianne Eggericks *(Cecile)*, Vania Vilers *(The Guardian)*, Jean-Pierre Castaldi *(Pierre)*, Gordon Tanner *(The American)*, Jean-Pierre Cargol
P: Geoffrey Reeve & Richard Morris-Adams   **D:** Geoffrey Reeve   **SCR:** Paul Wheeler, from a novel by Alistair MacLean   **PHOTOG:** Frederic Tammes   **MUSIC:** Stanley Myers
Standard action-melodrama: Scientist abducted

Card Manipulations
1912, (GB), Natural Colour Kinematograph Co., color, 500 ft. (152.4m)
D: Walter R. Booth
reissued 1916
Standard fantasy short: Playing card characters come to life

The Care Bears Movie
1985, (USA), color, 76 mins.
VOICES: Mickey Rooney, Georgia Engel, Harry Dean Stanton, Jackie Burroughs, Sunny Besen Thrasher
D: Arna Selznick
Standard animated fantasy

Care Bears Movie II: A New Generation
1986, (Can), color, 77 mins.
VOICES: Maxine Miller, Pam Hyatt, Hadley Kay   **D:** Dale Schott
Standard animated fantasy: Bruins help girl at summer camp

Careful
1993, (Can), color, 100 mins.
D: Guy Maddin
Bizarre surrealistic classic: Inhabitants of avalanche-prone Alpine village must maintain silence

The Caretakers
1963, (USA), UA, b&w, 97 mins.
W: Polly Bergen, Robert Stack, Joan Crawford, Janis Paige, Susan Oliver, Robert Vaughn, Van Williams, Barbara Barrie, Herbert Marshall, Ellen Corby, Jerry Paris
P & D: Hall Bartlett   **SCR:** Henry F. Greenberg
Unusual psychodrama: Woman becomes demented, is institutionalized

Carlota
1959, (Sp), Bosco-Ana Mariscal, b&w
W: Ana Mariscal, Jorge Rigaud, Juan Jose Menendez
D: Enrique Cahen Salaverri   **SCR:** Miguel Mihura   **PHOTOG:** Valentin Javier
Standard melodrama

Carmen
1918, (Ger), Ufa, First National b&w, 5,413 ft. (1650m)
W: Pola Negri, Emil Jannings, Harry Liedtke
D: Ernst Lubitsch   **SCR:** Hans Kraly   **PHOTOG:** Theodor Sparkuhl
USA retitle, **Gypsy Blood** *,1921*
Romantic melodrama: Gypsy beauty causes grief

Carmen (1931)
see **Gipsy Blood**

Carmen
1942, (Fr), Superfilm, b&w, 107 mins.
W: Viviane Romance, Jean Marais
D: Christian-Jaque   **SCR:** Henri Jeanson
Romantic melodrama: Gypsy beauty foments disaster

Carnage
1984, (USA), color, 91 mins.
W: Lesie Den Dooven, Michael Chiodo, Deeann Veeder
D: Andy Milligan
Minor fantasy-thriller: House eats inhabitants

The Carnation Killer
1973, (GB),Made for TV, color
W: Katharine Schofield, Norman Eshley, Garrick Hagon, Derek Smith
TVM, standard thriller: Lawyer's assistant mistakes murderer for client

Carnival of Blood
1970, (USA), Kirt Films Int'l, color, 89 mins.
W: Earle Edgerton *(Tom)*, Judith Resnick *(Laura)*, Kaly Mills *(The Fortuneteller)*, Martin Barolsky *(Dan)*, Glen Kimberley *(The Sailor)*, Linda Kurtz, "John Harris" [Burt Young], Eve Packer, William Grinell, Gloria Spivak
WRIT, P, & D: Leonard Kirtman   **PHOTOG:** David Howe   **MUSIC:** The Brooks Group   **SONGS:** (written & sung by Patrice Barnett), *Don't Ever Go Away* & *Carousel World*
Minor thriller: Murders on boardwalk

Carnival of Sinners
see **La Main du Diable**

Carnival of Souls
1962, (USA), Harcourt/Herts-Lion, b&w, 80 mins.
W: Candace Hilligoss *(Mary Henry)*, Sidney Berger *(John)*, Herk Harvey *(The Ghoul)*, Frances Feist, Stanley Leavitt, Forbes Caldwell, Art Ellison, Tom McGinnis
P & D: Herk Harvey   **SCR:** John Clifford   **PHOTOG:** Maurice Prather   **MUSIC:** Gene Moore
Semi-classic fantasy-thriller: Girl escapes car crash, is haunted by phantom figure

Carnival Of Souls: CANDACE HILLIGOSS

Carnivore
see **The Final Terror**

Carnosaur
1993, (USA), Caravan, color, 85 mins.
W: Diane Ladd, Raphael Sbarge, Jennifer Runyon *(Thrush)*
D: Adam Simon
Standard SF-thriller: Woman scientist creates killer dinosaur

Carnosaur 2
1995, (USA), Caravan, color, 90 mins.
W: John Savage, Cliff DeYoung, Don Stroud, Rick Dean, Ryan Thomas Johnson, Arabella Holzbog, Miguel A. Nunez Jr.
D: Louis Morneau
Standard SF-thriller: Dinosaurs found in mining tunnels

Carnosaur 3: Primal Species
1996, (USA), color, 85 mins.
<u>W:</u> Scott Valentine (*Rance*), Janet Gunn (*Dr. Hodges*), Rick Dean (*Polchek*), Justina Vail (*Proudfoot*), Morgan Englund (*Rossi*)
Made-for-Video, standard SF-thriller: Police and dinosaurs trapped in warehous

Caroline at Midnight
1993, (USA), color, 89 mins.
<u>W:</u> Tim Daly, Mia Sara
Minor mystery-thriller: "Dead" woman phones

Carousel
1956, (USA), 20th-Fox, color, 128 mins.
<u>W:</u> Gordon MacRae (*Billy Bigelow*), Shirley Jones (*Julie*), Gene Lockhart (*The Starkeeper*), Cameron Mitchell (*Jigger*), Audrey Christie (*Mrs. Mullin*), Barbara Ruick (*Carrie*), Susan Luckey (*Louise*), Claramae Turner (*Cousin Nettie*), Robert Rounseville (*Mr. Snow*), William Le Massena (*The Heavenly Friend*), Jacques D'Amboise (*Louise's Dancing Partner*), John Dehner (*Mr. Bascombe*), Frank Tweddell (*Capt. Watson*), Richard Deacon (*The Policeman*), Dee Pollock (*Enoch Snow Jr.*), Sylvia Stanton, Tor Johnson, Mary Orozco, Marion Dempsey, Harry "Duke" Johnson, Ed Mundy, Angelo Rossitto
<u>P:</u> Henry Ephron <u>D:</u> Henry King <u>SCR:</u> Phoebe & Henry Ephron, adapted from the musical play by Rodgers & Hammerstein, based on Ferenc Molnar's fantasy stage play *Liliom*, <u>PHOTOG:</u> Charles G. Clarke <u>MUSIC:</u> Alfred Newman <u>SONGS:</u> *If I Loved You, You'll Never Walk Alone, June is Bustin' Out All Over, My Boy, Bill,* et al.
Lavish fantasy: Departed spirit allowed to visit Earth. Filmed in Maine

The Carpet of Horror
1962, (W. Ger, It.-Sp.), b&w, 92 mins
<u>W:</u> Joachim Fuchsberger, Eleonora Rossi-Drago, Karin Dor
<u>D:</u> Dr. Harald Reinl   from an Edgar Wallace thriller
Minor mystery: Special agent murdered while investigating international crime syndicate

Carrie
1976, (USA), UA, color, 97 mins.
<u>W:</u> Sissy Spacek (*Carrie White*), Piper Laurie (*Margaret White*), John Travolta (*Billy Nolan*), William Katt (*Tommy Ross*), Nancy Allen (*Chris Hargenson*), Amy Irving (*Sue Snell*), P.J. Soles (*Norman*), Sydney Lassick (*Mr. Fromm*), Priscilla Pointer (*Mrs. Snell*), Betty Buckley (*Miss Collins*), Doug Cox (*The Beak*), Stefan Gierasch (*Mr. Morton*), Michael Talbot (*Freddy*), Harry Gold (*George*), Noelle North (*Frieda*), Cindy Daly (*Cora*), Rory Stevens (*Kenny*), Dierdre Berthron (*Thonda*), Cameron De Palma (*The Boy on the Bicycle*), Anson Downes (*Ernest*), Edie McClurg (*Helen*)
<u>P:</u> Paul Monash <u>D:</u> Brian De Palma <u>SCR:</u> Lawrence D. Cohen, from Stephen King's novel <u>PHOTOG:</u> Mario Tosi <u>MUSIC:</u> Pino Donaggio <u>SONG:</u> *Born to Have It All* (sung by Katie Irving)
Superior horror-fantasy: Girl uses telekinetic powers for ghastly revenge

Carry On Screaming
1966, (GB), Anglo-Amalgamated/Warner-Pathe, color, 93 mins.
<u>W:</u> Harry Corbett (*Det. Sgt. Bung*), Jim Dale (*Albert Potter*), Kenneth Williams (*Dr. Orlando Watt*), Fenella Fielding (*Valeria*), Joan Sims (*Emily*), Charles Hawtrey (*Dan Dann*), Peter Butterworth (*Slobo-tham*), Angela Douglas (*Doris Mann*), Bernard Bresslaw (*Sockett*), Jon Pertwee (*Fettle*), Tom Clegg (*Odbodd*), Billy Cornelius (*Odbodd Jr.*), Denis Blake (*Rubbatiti*), Frank Thornton, Michael Ward, Norman Mitchell, Frank Forsyth, Sally Douglas, Anthony Sagar, Marianne Stone
<u>D:</u> Gerald Thomas <u>SCR:</u> Talbot Rothwell <u>PHOTOG:</u> Alan Hume <u>MUSIC:</u> Eric Rogers
Standard horror-comedy: Victorian detectives seek missing girls

Carry On Spying
1964, (GB), Adder/AA, b&w, 88 mins.
<u>W:</u> Kenneth Williams (*Desmond Simkins*), Barbara Windsor (*Daphne Honeybutt*), Bernard Cribbins (*Harold Crump*), Charles Hawtrey (*Charlie Bind*), Eric Barker (*The Chief*), Jim Dale (*Carstairs*), Dilys Laye (*Lila*), Richard Wattis (*Cobley*), Eric Pohlmann (*Emil Fauzak*), Victor Maddern (*Milchmann*), Judith Furse (*Dr. Crow*), John Bluthal (*The Headwaiter*), Renee Houston (*Madame*), Frank Forsythe, Gertan Klauber, Jill Mai Meredith, Nora Gordon, Angela Ellison, Norman Mitchell, Hugh Futcher, Tom Clegg, Derek Sydney, Jack Taylor, Bill Cummings, Anthony Baird, Patrick Durkin
<u>P:</u> Peter Rogers <u>D:</u> Gerald Thomas <u>STORY:</u> Sid Colin & Talbot Rothwell <u>SCR:</u> Donald & Derek Ford <u>PHOTOG:</u> Alan Hume <u>MUSIC:</u> Eric Rogers
Standard mystery-comedy: Spoof of "James Bond" genre

The Cars That Ate Paris
1976, (Austral), Australian Film Co./Royce Smeal/New Line, color, 90 mins.
<u>W:</u> John Meillon (*The Mayor*), Kevin Miles (*The Doctor*), Terry Camilleri (*Arthur*), Rick Scully (*George*), Danny Adcock (*The Policeman*), Max Gillies (*Metcalf*), Bruce Spence (*Charlie*), Joe Burrow (*Ganger*), Kevin Golsby (*The Insurance Man*), Max Phipps (*Rev. Mulray*), Chris Haywood (*Darryl*), Peter Armstrong (*Gorman*), Deryck Barnes (*Smedley*), Edward Howell (*Tringham*), Herbie Nelson, Melissa Jaffers, Tim Robertson
<u>D & SCR:</u> Peter Weir, from a story by Peter Weir, Keith Gow, & Piers Davies <u>MUSIC:</u> Bruce Smeaton
A.k.a. (USA) The Cars That Eat People
Innovative fantasy-satire: Drifter finds town dominated by automobiles

The Cars That Eat People
see The Cars That Ate Paris

Cartes sur Table (Cards on the Table)
1962, (Sp-Fr), AIP, b&w, 93 mins.
<u>W:</u> Eddie Constantine (*Lemmy Caution*), Sophie Hardy, Fernando Rey, Francoise Brion
<u>D:</u> Jesus Franco
USA retitle, Attack of the Robots
Standard SF-thriller: Interpol agent probes organization controlling people with O-type blood.

Les Cartes Vivantes (The Living Playing Cards)
1905, (Fr), Star, b&w, 48m (157.5 ft./2.7 mins.)
<u>D:</u> Georges Melies
Standard fantasy

Carthage in Flames
1959, (It), Col, color, 115 mins.
<u>W:</u> Anne Heywood, Pierre Brasseur, Jose Suarez, Daniel Gelin
<u>P & D:</u> Carmine Gallone <u>SCR:</u> Duccio Tessari, Carmine Gallone & Ennio De Concini, from Emilio Salgari's novel <u>PHOTOG:</u> Piero Portalupi <u>MUSIC:</u> Mario Nascimbene
Lavish "Sword & Sandal" melodrama: Slave girl avenges death of Carthaginian rescuer

Le Carton Fantastique (The Fantastic Sketch)
1907, (Fr), Star, b&w, 74m (242.8 ft./4.1 mins.)
<u>D:</u> Georges Melies
A.k.a. A Mischievous Sketch
Standard fantasy: Drawing assumes life of its own.

Cartouche
1957, (GB), RKO, b&w, 73 mins.
<u>W:</u> Richard Basehart, Patricia Roc
Minor melodrama

Cartouche
1962, (Fr), color, 106 mins.
<u>W:</u> Jean-Paul Belmondo, Claudia Cardinale, Odile Versois, Marcel Dalio Philippe Lemaire
<u>D:</u> Philippe De Broca <u>SCR:</u> Philippe De Broca & Charles Spaak <u>PHOTOG:</u> Christian Matras <u>MUSIC:</u> Georges Delerue
A.k.a. Swords of Blood
Fast-paced swashbuckler spoof: Nobleman's son must clear himself of crime

La Casa Con La Scala Nel Buio (House Of The Dark Stairway)
1983, (It), color, 99 mins.
<u>W:</u> Andrea Occhipinti, Anny Papa
<u>D:</u> Lamberto Bava
Standard thriller: mysterious murder inspires composer. USA retitle, A Blade in the Dark

La Casa del Terror (The House of Terror)
1959, (Mex), DesFuentes/ADP, b&w
<u>W:</u> Lon Chaney Jr., Donald Barron, Yolanda Varela, Steve Conte, Ray-mond Gaylord, Tin Tan
<u>D:</u> Gilberto Martinez Solares <u>SCR:</u> Alfred Salimar & Gilberto Martinez Solares
USA retitle (1964; d, Jerry Warren), Face of the Screaming Werewolf
Minor horror-potboiler with added USA-made scenes: Mad doctor, monstrous happenings

Casanova's Big Night
1954, (USA), Para, color, 86 mins.
W: Bob Hope, Joan Fontaine, Vincent Price, Hugh Marlowe, Lon Chaney Jr., Audrey Dalton, Basil Rathbone, Raymond Burr, John Carradine, Primo Carnera, Hope Emerson, John Hoyt, Frieda Inescort, Frank Puglia, Robert Hutton, Henry Brandon
<u>D:</u> Norman Z. McLeod <u>SCR:</u> Hal Kanter <u>PHOTOG:</u> Lionel Lindon <u>SPCL-FX:</u> John P. Fulton <u>MUSIC:</u> Lyn Murray
Standard costume comedy: Tailor impersonates great lover

A Case for PC-49
1951, (GB), Hammer/Exclusive, b&w, 80 mins.
<u>W:</u> Brian Reece (*Archibald Berkeley-Willoughby*), Christine Norden (*Della Dainton*), Gordon McLeod (*Insp. Wilson*), Leslie Bradley (*Victor Palantine*), Campbell Singer (*Sgt. Wright*), Jack Stewart (*Cutler*), Michael Balfour (*Chubby Price*), Michael Ripper (*George Steele*)
<u>P:</u> Anthony Hinds <u>D:</u> Francis Searle <u>SCR:</u> Alan Stranks & Vernon Harris (from a radio-series)
Standard crime-thriller: Constable proves artist's model killed millionaire

A Case for Sherlock Holmes
1911, (GB), Cricks & Martin, b&w, 410 ft. (125m)
<u>D:</u> A.E. Coleby
from characters created by Sir Arthur Conan Doyle
Standard adventure short: Bagsnatcher dons disguises to elude pursuers. Reissued 1915

The Case of a Doped Actress
1919, (GB), Life Dramas/National, b&w, 2,000 ft. (609.6m)
<u>W:</u> Clare Barrington (*Dobbie Barton*), Walter Drake (*Dr. Edwards*), F.E. Harrison

(Hubert Van Dorl), Ella Dore (Mrs. Van Dorl)
D: Wilfred Carlton
Standard thriller: Agent causes actress' death by inducing her to take opium

A Case of Identity
1921, (GB), Stoll, b&w, 2,610 ft. (795.5m)
W: Eille Norwood (*Sherlock Holmes*), Hubert Willis (*Dr. John Watson*), Edna
   Flugrath (*Mary Sutherland*), Nelson Ramsey (*Hosmer Angel*)
D: Maurice Elvey   **SCR:** William J. Elliott, from the writings of Sir Arthur Conan Doyle
Standard crime-thriller (episode in "Adventures of Sherlock Holmes" series)

The Case of Jonathan Drew
see The Lodger (1926)

The Case of Lady Camber
1920, (GB), Broadwest/Walturdaw, b&w, 6,000 ft. (1828.8m)
W: Violet Hopson (*Esther Yorke*), Stewart Rome (*Dr. Harley Napier*), Gregory Scott
   (*Lord Camber*), Mercy Hatton (*Lady Camber*), C.M. Hallard (*Sir Bedford
   Slufter*), Pollie Emery (*Peach*)
D: Walter West   **SCR:** Benedict James, from a play by H.A. Vachell
*Standard crime-thriller: Doctor proves nurse did not give strychnine to invalid wife of phi-
   landering nobleman*

The Case Of The Frightened Lady: PATRICK BARR

The Case of the Curious Bride
1935, (USA), First Nat'l/WB, b&w, 80 mins.
W: Warren William, Errol Flynn
D: Michael Curtiz, from Erle Stanley Gardner's novel
Standard melodrama

The Case of the Frightened Lady
1940, (GB), Pennant/British Lion/Associated Artists, b&w, 81 mins.
W: Marius Goring (*Lord Lebanon*), Penelope Dudley Ward (*Isla Crane*), Helen
   Haye (*Lady Lebanon*), Patrick Barr (*Dick Ferraby*), Felix Aylmer (*Dr.
   Amersham*), John Warwick (*Studd*), Roy Emerton (*Gilder*), George Merritt
   (*Insp. Tanner*), Ronald Shiner (*Sgt. Totty*)
P & D: George King   **SCR:** Edward Dryhurst, from a novel by Edgar Wallace
USA retitle, *The Frightened Lady* , 1941.
reissued 1944 & 1946
*Standard thriller: Lady's mad son tries to strangle cousin. Remake :***The Indian Scarf**

Case of the Full Moon Murders
1971, (USA), Newport, color
W: Harry Reems
P & D: Sean Cunningham   **SCR:** Bud Talbot & Jerry Hayling
A.k.a. Sex on the Groove Tube &Case of the Smiling Stiffs
Minor eroto-horror: Vampiress' adventures

The Case of the Howling Dog
1934, (USA), WB, b&w, 75 mins.
W: Mary Astor, Warren William (*Perry Mason*)
D: Alan Crosland, from Erle Stanley Gardner's novel
Standard mystery-thriller

The Case of the Missing Blonde
see Lady in the Morgue

The Case of the Missing Brides
see The Corpse Vanishes

The Case of the Old Rope Man
1952, (GB), G.B. Instructional/GFD, b&w, 18 mins.
W: James Carney (*Ken Casey*), Howell Davies (*Jack Spice*), David Tearle (*Kroller*),
   Phillip Lennard (*Snaith*), Brian Campbell (*Insp. Dunwoodie*)
P: Frank Wells   **D:** Darrell Catling   **STORY:** Alastair Scobie
Standard short crime-thriller: Reporter solves murder of dockside nightwatchman

The Case of the Red Monkey
see Little Red Monkey

The Case of the River Morgue
1956, (GB), Merton Park/Anglo-Amalgamated, b&w, 34 mins.
W: Hugh Moxey (*The Inspector*), Gordon Needham (*Hiller*), Jane Welsh (*Mrs.
   Hiller*)
P: Alec Snowden   **D & SCR:** Montgomery Tully, from a novel by Edgar
   Lustgarten
Standard short crime-thriller: Diabetic steals corpse, "drowns" it to get insurance money

Case of the Smiling Stiffs
see Case of the Full Moon Murders

The Case of the Smiling Widow
1957, (GB), Merton Park/Anglo-Amalgamated, b&w, 31 mins.
W: Russell Napier (*Insp. Duggan*), Carl Jaffe (*Christopher Nicholls*), Sylvia Marriott
   (*Mrs. Nicholls*)
P: Alec Snowden   **D:** Montgomery Tully   **STORY:** Gil Saunders, from a novel
   by Edgar Lustgarten
Standard short crime-thriller: Collector's wife gasses blackmailing artist

Cash on Demand
1961, (GB), Hammer-Woodpecker/Col, b&w, 84 mins.
W: Peter Cushing (*Fordyce*), Andre Morell (*Hepburn*), Richard Vernon (*Pearson*),
   Barry Lowe (*Harvill*), Norman Bird (*Sanderson*), Edith Sharpe (*Miss Pringle*),
   Charles Morgan (*Collins*), Kevin Stoncy (*Insp. Mason*)
P: Michael Carreras   **D:** Quentin Lawrence   **SCR:** David T. Chantler & Lewis
   Greifer, from Jacques Gillies' TV-play *The Gold Inside*
Modest melodrama: Strict bank manager forced to commit robbery

The Casino Murder Case
1935, (USA), MGM, b&w, 85 mins.
W: Paul Lukas (*Philo Vance*), Rosalind Russell (*Doris*), Ted Healy (*Sgt. Heath*),
   Alison Skipworth (*Mrs. Llewellyn*), Eric Blore (*Currie*), Donald Cook (*Lynn*),
   Arthur Byron (*Kincaid*), Isabel Jewell (*Amelia*), Louise Fazenda (*Becky*),
   Louise Henry (*Virginia*), Leslie Fenton (*Dr. Kane*), Leo G. Carroll (*Smith*),
   Purnell Pratt (*Insp. Markham*), Keye Luke (*Taki*), Grace Hayle (*The Fat
   Lady*), Charles Sellon (*Dr. Doremus*), Edna Bennett (*The Nurse*), William
   Demarest (*The Auctioneer*), Ernie Adams (*The Husband of the Fat Lady*),
   Milton Kibbee, Tom Herbert
P: Lucien Hubbard   **D:** Edwin L. Marin   **SCR:** Florence Ryerson & Edgar Allan
   Woolf, from S.S. Van Dine's novel   **PHOTOG:** Charles Clarke   **MUSIC:**
   Dimitri Tiomkin
Modest "Philo Vance" mystery-thriller: Gambler receives death threat, suave sleuth investigates

The Casino Murder Case: PAUL LUKAS, TED HEALY AND ROSALIND RUSSELL

Casino Royale
1967, (GB), Famous Artists/Col, color, 131 mins.
W: Peter Sellers (*Evelyn Tremble*), Ursula Andress (*Vesper Lynd*), David Niven (*Sir
   James Bond*), Orson Welles (*Le Chiffre*), Joanna Pettet (*Mata Bond*), Dahlia

Lavi (*The Detainer*), Woody Allen (*Jimmy Bond*), Deborah Kerr (*Mimi*), John Huston ("*M*"), William Holden (*Ransome*), Charles Boyer (*Le Grand*), Jean-Paul Belmondo (*The Legionnaire*), Kurt Kasznar (*Smernov*), Terence Cooper (*Cooper*), Barbara Bouchet (*Miss Moneypenny*), Angela Scoular (*Buttercup*), Tracey Crisp (*Heather*), Gabriel la Licudi (*Eliza*), Elaine Taylor (*Peg*), Anna Quayle (*Frau Hoffner*), Derek Nimmo (*Hadley*), Peter O'Toole (*The Piper*), Stirling Moss (*The Driver*), Colin Gordon (*The Director*), Bernard Cribbins (*The Taxi Driver*), Duncan Macrae (*Insp. Mathis*), Richard Wattis (*The Officer*), Valentine Dyall (*The Voice of Dr. Noah*), Jacqueline Bisset (*Miss Goodthighs*), Tracy Reed, Vladek Sheybal, Geoffrey Bayldon, Dave Prowse, John LeMesurier, David McCallum, Ronnie Corbett
P: Charles K. Feldman & Jerry Bresler **D:** Ken Hughes, Val Guest, John Huston, Robert Parrish, Joseph McGrath & Richard Talmadge **SCR:** Wolf Mankowitz, John Law & Michael Sayers, suggested by Ian Fleming's "James Bond" novels **PHOTOG:** Jack Hildyard **MUSIC:** Burt Bacharach **SONG:** *The Look of Love* (Burt Bacharach, Hal David)
Amusing spy-spoof: Secret agent comes out of retirement to match wits with megalomaniac

Casper
1995, (USA), Amblin/Univ., color, 96 mins.
W: Christina Ricci (*Kat*), Bill Pullman (*Dr. Harvey*), Cathy Moriarty (*Carrigan*), Eric Idle (*Dibs*), Malachi Pearson (*The Voice of Casper*), Amy Brenneman (*Amelia Harvey*), Brad Garrett (*The Voice of Fatso*), Dan Aykroyd, Devon Sawa, Don Novello, Chauncey Leopardi, Spencer Vrooman, Rodney Dangerfield, Terry Murphy, Ernestine Mercer, Joe Alaskey, John Kassir, Jessica Wesson, Micah Winkelspecht, Michael McCarty, Wesley Thompson, Michael Dubrow, J.J. Anderson, Jess Harnell
D: Brad Silberling **SCR:** Sherri Stoner & Deanna Oliver **PHOTOG:** Dean Cundey **MUSIC:** James Horner **SONG:** *Remember Me This Way*
Standard comedy-fantasy: Adventures of friendly ghost

Casper: A Spirited Beginning
1998, (USA), Saban/Fox-TV, color, 95 mins.
W: Brendon Ryan Barrett, Steve Guttenberg, Lori Loughlin, Rodney Dangerfield, Michael McKean, Shannon Chandler, Logan Robbins, Richard Moll, Edie McClurg, Bill Farmer, Jeremy Foley, Pauly Shore (*voice*), James Earl Jones (*voice*)
D: Sean McNamara **PHOTOG:** Christian Sebaldt **MUSIC:** Udi Harpaz
TVM, standard juvenile fantasy: Ghost's adventures

Casper the Friendly Ghost: A Spirited Beginning
1997, (USA), 20th-Fox, color
Made-for-Video, standard fantasy

Cassandra
1987, (GB), color, 94 mins.
W: Tessa Humphries, Shane Briant, Brionny Behets, Kit Taylor, Lee James
D: Colin Eggleston
Minor thriller: Psychic girl taps killer's mind

Cast a Dark Shadow
1955, (GB), Frobisher/Eros, b&w, 82 mins.
W: Dirk Bogarde (*Edward Bare*), Margaret Lockwood (*Freda Jeffries*), Kay Walsh (*Charlotte Young*), Robert Flemyng (*Peter Mortimer*), Kathleen Harrison (*Emmie*), Walter Hudd (*The Coroner*), Mona Washbourne (*Monica Bare*), Philip Stainton (*Charlie Mann*) Lita Roza (*The Singer*)
P: Daniel Angel **D:** Lewis Gilbert **SCR:** John Cresswell, from Janet Green's play *Murder Mansion*
Standard crime-thriller: Clerk kills rich wife

Cast a Deadly Spell
1991, (USA), HBO, color, 96 mins.
W: Fred Ward (*H. Phillip Lovecraft*), Julianne Moore (*Connie Stone*), David Warner (*Amos Hackshaw*), Clancy Brown (*Harry Bordon*), Al-exandra Powers (*Olivia Hackshaw*), Arnetia Walker (*Hypolite Kropotkin*), Peter Allas (*Det. Grimaldi*), Charles Hallahan (*Bradbury*), Raymond O'Connor (*Tugwell*)
D: Martin Campbell **TELEPLAY:** Joseph Dougherty & Dave Edison **PHOTOG:** Alexander Gruszyski **MUSIC:** Curt Sobel
Made-for-Cable, standard fantasy-thriller: 1948 gumshoe encounters supernatural

The Castaways
see *In Search of the Castaways*

El Castello dell'Orrore (The Castle of Horror)
1973, (It), Classic-Int'l/Boxoffice-Int'l, color, 86 mins.
W: Rossano Brazzi (*Count Frankenstein*), Edmund Purdom (*The Prefect*), Michael Dunn (*Genz*), Gordon Mitchell (*Igor*), Alan Collins (*Hans*), Boris Lugosi (*Ook*), Simone Blondell (*Maria*), Xiro Papas (*Kreegin*), Eric Mann (*Eric*), Christiane Royce (*Krista*), Robert Marx (*Koerner*), Perrella Alessandro (*The Doctor*), Loren Ewing (*Goliath*), Laura De Benedittis (*Valda*), Tornello Annamaria (*The Raped Girl*), Aristide Caporale (*The Grave-Digger*), Palumbo Nicola (*The Agent*), Ozzic Raghct (*Almut*), Walter Saxer (*Warner*), Margaret Oliver, Mike Monty, Bob Fiz, Rossella Ferrero
P & D: Robert H. Oliver **SCR:** Mark Smith, William Rose & Roberto Spano **PHOTOG:** Mario Mancini **MUSIC:** Marcello Gigante
A.k.a. Frankenstein's Castle of Freaks, House of Freaks & Monsters of Dr. Frankenstein

El Castillo de las Bofetadas (The Castle of Slaps)
1945, (Sp), b&w
W: Dolores Paris, Elena de Castilla, Domingo Bronchalo, Jose Zaro, Antonio Martinez, Miguel Alonso
WRIT & P: Juan Arajol **D:** J. de Orazal **MUSIC:** Juan Hernandez
Standard melodrama

El Castillo de los Monstruos (The Castle of Monsters)
1962, (Mex), Producciones Sotomayor-S.A., b&w
W: Evangelina Elizondo, Clavillazo
Standard horror-thriller

The Castle
see *Das Schloss*

Castle Freak
1995, (USA), color, 95 mins.
W: Jeffrey Combs, Barbara Crampton, Jonathan Fuller (*Giorgio*), Jessica Dollarhide (*Rebecca*), Massimo Sarchielli (*Giannetti*)
D: Stuart Gordon **SCR:** Dennis Paoli **PHOTOG:** Mario Vulpiani **MUSIC:** Richard Band
*Standard horror-fantasy (reminiscent of **The Maze**): American family inherits Italian castle inhabited by grotesque creature*

Castle in the Desert
1942, (USA), 20th-Fox, b&w, 62 mins.
W: Sidney Toler (*Charlie Chan*), Richard Derr (*Carl Detheridge*), Arleen Whalen (*Brenda Hartford*), Henry Daniell (*Watson King*), Douglass Dumbrille (*Manderley*), Ethel Griffies (*Mme. Saturnie*), Edmund MacDonald (*Walter Hartford*), Milton Parsons (*Fletcher*), Victor Sen Yung (*Jimmy Chan*), Lenita Lane (*Lucretia Manderley*), Steven Geray (*Dr. Retling*), Lucien Littlefield (*Prof. Gleason*), Paul Kruger (*The Bodyguard*), George Chandler (*The Bus Driver*), Oliver Prickett (*Blake Wigley*)
D: Harry Lachman **SCR:** John Larkin, from characters created by Earl Derr Biggers **PHOTOG:** Virgil Miller
Minor "Charlie Chan" mystery: Oriental sleuth finds murder plot in Mojave Desert

Castle Keep
1969, (USA), Martin Ransohoff/Col, color, 107 mins.
W: Burt Lancaster (*Maj. Abraham Falconer*), Peter Falk (*Sgt. Orlando Rossi*), Jean-Pierre Aumont (*Henri Tixier, Comte de Maldorais*), Patrick O'Neal (*Capt. Lionel Beckman*), Tony Bill (*Lt. Adam Amberjack*), Michael Conrad (*Sgt. DeVaca*)Al Freeman Jr. (*Pfc. Alistair Benjamin*), Astrid Heeren (*Ther-ese, Comtesse de Maldorais*), Scott Wilson (*Cpl. Ralph Clearboy*), Caterina Boratto (*The Red Queen*), Bruce Dern (*Lt. Billy Buron Bix*), James Patterson (*Pvt. Henry Three Ears of an Elk*), Ernest Clark (*British Colonel*), Harry Baird (*The Dancing Soldier*), Dave Jones (*The One-Eared Soldier*), Jean Gimello (*The First Puerto Rican*), Jancika Kovac (*David*), Bisera Vukotic, Karen Blanguernon, Maria Danube, Elizabeth Darius, Marja Allanen, Anne Marie Moskovenko, Elizabeth Teissier, Eya Calley
P: Martin Ransohoff & John Calley **D:** Sydney Pollack **SCR:** David Taradash & David Rayfiel, from William Eastlake's novel **PHOTOG:** Henri Decae **MUSIC:** Michel Legrand
Unusual melodrama: World War II soldiers come under strange spell of ancient French castle. Filmed in Yugoslavia

Castle of Blood
see *La Danza Macabra*

The Castle of Cagliostro
1980, (Jap), color, 100 mins.
Standard animated fantasy: Hero-thief rescues princess

Castle of Crimes
see *The House of the Arrow* (1940)

Castle of Doom
see *Vampyr*

Castle of Evil
1966, (USA), United Pictures, color, 81 mins.
W: Scott Brady, Virginia Mayo, David Brian, Hugh Marlowe, Lisa Gaye
D: Francis D. Lyon
Minor SF-horror: Group summoned for reading of will

The Castle of Fu Manchu
1970, (GB-W. Ger), Terra Filmkunst-Balcazar-Towers of London/MGM-EMI, color, 92 mins.
W: Christopher Lee (*Dr. Fu Manchu*), Richard Greene (*Nayland Smith*), Howard Marion-Crawford (*Dr. Petrie*), Tsai Chin (*Lin Tang*), Gunther Stoll (*Dr. Curt Kessler*), Jose Manuel Martin (*Omar Pasha*), Rosalba Neri (*Lisa*), Werner Aprelat (*Melnik*), Maria Perschy (*Marie*)
P: Harry Alan Towers **D:** Jess Franco **SCR:** Peter Welbeck (Harry Alan Towers), from characters created by Sax Rohmer **PHOTOG:** Manuel Merino **MUSIC:** Charles Camilleri
A.k.a. Assignment: Istanbul
Minor thriller: Oriental villain seeks invention that turns water into ice

The Castle of Horror
see *El Castello delle'Orrore*

The Castle of Monsters
see *El Castillo de los Monstruos*

The Castle of Slaps
see *El Castillo de las Bofetadas*

The Castle of Terror (1951)
see *The Strange Door*

Castle of Terror (1964)
see *La Danza Macabra*

Castle of Terrors
1964, (GB), color
W: Aub Marks
Standard horror-thriller: Grotesque prowls. Amateur film, not in general release

Castle of the Living Dead
1963, (Fr), Dandi/AIP, b&w, 90 mins.
W: Christopher Lee, Gaia Germani, Philippe Leroy, Mirko Valentin, Donald Sutherland
P: Paul Maslansky   D: Warren Keifer
Standard horror-thriller: Troupe of performers involved with mad nobleman

The Castle of the Spider's Web
see *Throne of Blood*

Castle of the Walking Dead
see *Die Schlangengrube und das Pendel*

Castle Rock
1981, (Can), color
W: Cindy Girling, James C. Burge, Margaret Phillips
D: John Desmond   SCR: Mel Brez & Ethel Brez
Minor thriller: Girl encounters mystery

Castle Sinister
1932, (GB), Delta/Filmophone, b&w, 50 mins.
W: Haddon Mason (*Ronald Kemp*), Eric Adeney (*Prof. Bandov*), Wally Patch (*Jorkins*), Ilsa Kilpatrick (*Jean*), Edmund Kennedy (*The Father*)
D: Widgey R. Newman
Standard horror-thriller: Mad doctor tries to place girl's brain into apeman's head

Castle Sinister
1948, (GB), Unicorn/Equity British Film Prods., b&w, 49 mins.
W: Mara Russell-Tavernan (*Lady Glennye*), Robert Essex (*Nigel Craven*), Karl Mier (*Maj. Selwyn*), Alastair Hunter (*McTavish*), John Gauntley (*Michael*), James Liggatt (*Neale*), Maureen O'Moor (*Maggie*)
P: W. Howard Borer   D: Oscar Burn
Standard thriller: Marchioness' stepson unmasks Nazi spy

Castle Vogelod
see *Schloss Vogelod*

Cataclysm
1981, (USA), color, 94 mins.
W: Cameron Mitchell, Marc Lawrence, Faith Clift, Charles Moll
D: Tom McGowan, Greg Tallas & Philip Marshak
Standard fantasy-thriller: Sadistic demon terrorizes. Video title, Satan's Supper

Catacombs
1964, (GB), Parroch-McCallum/WB, b&w, 84 mins.
W: Gary Merrill (*Raymond Garth*), Jane Merrow (*Alice Taylor*), Neil McCallum (*Dick Corbett*), Georgina Cookson (*Ellen Garth*), Rachel Thomas (*Christine*), Jack Train (*The Solicitor*), Frederick Piper (*The Inspector*)
P: Jack Parsons & Neil McCallum   D: Gordon Hessler   SCR: Daniel Mainwaring, from Jay Bennett's novel   PHOTOG: Arthur Lavis   MUSIC: Carlo Martelli
USA retitle, The Woman Who Wouldn't Die
Standard thriller: Man murders wife, corpse vanishes

Catacombs
1989, (USA), color, 112 mins.
W: Timothy Van Patten, Laura Schaefer, Ian Abercrombie, Jeremy West
D: David Schmoeller   SCR: C. Courtey Joyner   MUSIC: Pino Donaggio
Minor fantasy-thriller: Centuries-old evil power uncovered

Cat and Mouse
1958, (GB), Anvil/Eros, b&w, 79 mins.
W: Lee Patterson (*Rod Fenner*), Ann Sears (*Ann Coltby*), Victor Maddern (*Supt. Harding*), Hilton Edwards (*Mr. Scruby*), Roddy McMillan (*Mr. Pomeroy*), George Rose (*The Dealer*)
D & SCR: Paul Rotha, from a novel by Michael Halliday
A.k.a. The Desperate Men
Standard crime-thriller: G.I. deserter seeks gems, frames girl for killing blackmailer

Cat and Mouse
1974, (GB), Associated London/EMI, color, 89 mins.
W: Kirk Douglas (*George Anderson*), Jean Seberg (*Laura Anderson*), John Vernon (*David Richardson*), Sam Wanamaker (*The Inspector*), James Bardford (*The Detective*), Bessie Love (*Mrs. Richardson*), Beth Porter (*Sandra*), Suzanne Lloyd (*Nancy*), Mavis Villiers (*Martha*), Elliott Sullivan (*Harry*), James Berwick (*The Headmaster*), Valerie Colgan (*Miss Wainwright*), Margo Alexis (*Miss Carter*), Stewart Chandler (*Simon Anderson*)
P: Aida Young   D: Daniel Petrie   STORY: John Peacock   PHOTOG: Jack Hildyard   MUSIC: Ron Grainer
Standard crime-thriller: Mad biology teacher tries to kill ex-wife

Cat and Mouse
1978, (Fr), color, 107 mins.
W: Michele Morgan, Serge Reggiani, Jean-Pierre Aumont
D: Claude Lelouch
Well-made mystery: Inspector probes millionaire's death

The Cat and the Canary
1927, (USA), Univ, b&w, 70 mins. (7,717 ft./2352m)
W: Creighton Hale (*Paul Jones*), Laura La Plante (*Annabelle West*), Tully Marshall (*Lawyer Crosby*), Flora Finch (*Susan*), Forrest Stanley (*Charles Wilder*), Gertrude Astor (*Cecily*), Lucien Littlefield (*The Doctor*), Arthur Edmund Carewe (*Harry*), Martha Mattox (*Mammy Pleasant*), George Siegmann (*Hendricks*), Billie Engel (*The Taxi Driver*), Joe Murphy (*The Milkman*)
P: Carl Laemmle   D: Paul Leni   SCR: Robert F. Hill & Alfred A. Cohn, from John Willard's stage play   PHOTOG: Gilbert Warrenton
"...a blueprint of its own species. The format has now been repeated so many times since, the sliding panels and clutching hands degenerating through the years into such casual cliches that the original just doesn't have the same punch it had in 1927. The cards have rather been stacked against this one, but nevertheless it's still a striking and fascinating mystery thriller"—Joe Franklin, Classics of the Silent Screen (William K. Everson)
Classic silent thriller: Heirs summoned to mansion of dying man learn murderous maniac has escaped from nearby asylum

The Cat and the Canary
1939, (USA), Para, b&w, 72 mins.
W: Bob Hope, Paulette Goddard, Gale Sondergaard, John Beal, George Zucco, Douglass Dumbrille, Elizabeth Patterson, John Wray, Nydia Westman, George Regas
D: Elliott Nugent   SCR: Walter DeLeon & Lynn Starling, from John Willard's stage play   PHOTOG: Charles Lang   MUSIC: Dr. Ernst Toch
French retitle, Le Mystere de la Maison Norman (The Mystery of Norman House)
Chills & laughs in remake of silent classic: Heirs plagued by mad assassin

The Cat and the Canary
1978, (GB), Richard Gordon/Grenadier/Audubon?Cinema Shares, color, 90 mins.
W: Honor Blackman (*Susan*), Michael Callan (*Paul*), Edward Fox (*Dr. Hendrix*), Carol Lynley (*Annabelle*), Wendy Hiller (*Crosby*), Olivia Hussey (*Cecily*), Daniel Massey (*Harry*), Peter McEnery (Charlie), Wilfrid Hyde-White (*Cyrus West*), Beatrix Lehmann (*Mrs. Pleasant*)
P: Richard Gordon   WRIT & D: Radley Metzger, from John Willard's stage play   PHOTOG: Alex Thomson   MUSIC: Steve Cagan
Standard remake of silent classic: Heirs summoned for will reading, maniacal killer stalks

The Cat And The Canary: DANIEL MUSSEY, MICHAEL CALLAN, PETER MCENERY, OLIVIA HUSSEY, WENDY HILLER, CAROL LYNLEY, BEATRIX LEFMANN, HONOR BLACKMAN

The Cat and the Chestnuts
1913, (GB), Hepworth, b&w, 800 ft. (243.8m)
W: Flora Moris (*The Girl*), Cyril Morton (*Gerald*)
D: Warwick Buckland
Standard crime-thriller: Girl thief foils debtor who stole uncle's necklace

Catastrophe 1999: The Prophecies of Nostradamus
1974, (Jap), Toho, color
W: Kenji Kobayashi, Hiroshi Fujioka
D: Shiro Moritani **SCR:** Shinobu Hashimoto
A.k.a. **Last Days of Planet Earth**
Standard SF-thriller: End of world ensues

Catch Me a Spy
1971, (GB-Fr), Ludgate/Capitole/Films de la Pleiade/Bryna/Rank, color, 94 mins.
W: Kirk Douglas (*Andrej*), Marlene Jobert (*Fabienne*), Trevor Howard (*Sir Trevor Dawson*), Tom Courtenay (*Baxter Clarke*), Patrick Mower (*John Fenton*), Bernardette Lafont (*Simone*), Sacha Pitoeff (*Stefan*), Bernard Blier (*Webb*), Robert Raglan (*The Ambassador*), Richard Pearson (*Haldane*), Angharad Rees (*Victoria*), Garfield Morgan (*The Husband*), Isabel Dean (*Celia*), Jonathan Cecil (*The Attache*), Trevor Peacock (*The Passenger*), Sheila Steafel (*The Woman*)
P: Steven Pallos & Pierre Braunberger **D:** Dick Clement **SCR:** Dick Clement & Ian La Frenais, from a novel by George Marton & Tibor Meray **PHOTOG:** Christopher Challis **MUSIC:** Claude Bolling
Standard thriller: Romanian spy smuggles Russian documents

The Cat Creature
1973, (USA), Col/ABC-TV, color, 74 mins.
W: David Hedison (*Roger Edmunds*), Meredith Baxter (*Rena*), Gale Sondergaard (*Hester Black*), Stuart Whitman (*Lt. Marco*), Renne Jarrett (*Sherry Hastings*), Keye Luke (*The Thief*), Kent Smith (*Frank Lucas*), John Abbott (*Dr. Reinhart*), Milton Parsons (*The Deputy Coroner*), John Carradine (*The Hotel Clerk*), Peter Lorre Jr., Virgil Frye
P: Douglas S. Cramer **D:** Curtis Harrington **TELEPLAY:** Robert Bloch **STORY:** Douglas S. Cramer, Wilford Lloyd Baums & Robert Bloch **PHOTOG:** Charles Rosher **MUSIC:** Leonard Rosenman
TVM, unusual horror-fantasy: Deaths linked to cult of ancient cat-goddess

The Cat Creeps
1930, (USA), Univ, b&w, 72 mins.
W: Helen Twelvetrees, Raymond Hackett, Jean Hersholt, Montagu Love, Lilyan Tashman, Theodore von Eltz, Elizabeth Patterson, Lawrence Grant, Blanche Frederici, Neil Hamilton
D: Rupert Julian **SCR:** Gladys Lehman & William Hurlbut, adapted from John Willard's stage play *The Cat and the Canary* **PHOTOG:** Jerry Ash & Hal Mohr
Spanish-speaking version (starring Antonio Moreno) was also leased for release in Spanish-speaking countries
Standard thriller: Mysterious killer stalks heirs

The Cat Creeps
1946, (USA), Univ, b&w, 58 mins.
W: Fred Brady, Lois Collier, Iris Clive, Douglass Dumbrille, Noah Beery Jr., Paul Kelly, Rose Hobart, Jonathan Hale, Vera Lewis
D: Erle C. Kenton **SCR:** Edward Dein & Jerry Warner **PHOTOG:** George Robinson
Minor thriller: Murder-plagued hunt for stolen loot

The Cat from Outer Space
1978, (USA), Walt Disney/Buena Vista, color, 103 mins.
W: Ken Berry (*Dr. Frank Wilson*), Sandy Duncan (*Dr. Elizabeth Bartlett*), Harry Morgan (*Gen. Stilton*), McLean Stevenson (*Dr. Carl Link*), Roddy McDowall (*Stallwood*), Jesse White (*Earnest Ernie*), Hans Conried (*Dr. Heffel*), Alan Young (*Dr. Wenger*), Ronnie Schell (*Sgt. Duffy*), James Hampton (*Capt. Anderson*), Howard T. Platt (*Col. Woodruff*), William Prince (*Mr. Olympus*), Ralph Manza (*Weasel*), Tom Pedi (*Honest Harry*), Hank Jones (*The Officer*), Rick Hurst (*The Dydee Guard*), John Alderson (*Mr. Smith*), Tiger Joe Marsh (*Omar*), Arnold Soboloff (*The NASA Executive*), Mel Carter, Dallas McKennon, Alice Backes, Richard Warlock, Henry Slate, Roger Pancake, Roger Price, Jim Begg, Jerry Fujikawa, Pete Renaday, Rick Sorensen, Fred L. Whalen, Tom Jackman, Joe Medalis, Jana Milo, Gil Stratton
P: Ron Miller **D:** Norman Tokar **SCR:** Ted Key **PHOTOG:** Charles F. Wheeler **MUSIC:** Lalo Schifrin
Juvenile SF-comedy: Alien feline causes complications

Cat Girl
1957, (GB), Insignia/Nat Cohen-Stuart Levy/AIP, b&w, 75 mins.
W: Barbara Shelley (*Leonora*), Robert Ayres (*Dr. Marlowe*), Kay Callard (*Dorothy Marlowe*), Paddy Webster (*Cathy*), Lily Kann (*Anna*), Ernest Milton (*Edmund Brandt*), Jack May (*Richard*), Edward Harvey, John Lee, Selma Vaz Dias, John Watson, Frank Atkinson, John Baker, Geoffrey Tyrrell
P: Herbert Smith & Peter Rogers **D:** Alfred Shaughnessy **SCR:** Lou Rusoff **PHOTOG:** Peter Hennessy
orig. co-billed with *The Amazing Colossal Man*, reissued 1963
Standard but unusual horror-fantasy: Young woman ("To caress me is to tempt death") inherits weird leopard family curse

Catharsis
see Katharsis

Cathy's Curse
see Cauchemares

The Catman of Paris
1946, (USA), Rep, b&w, 65 mins.
W: Carl Esmond, Lenore Aubert, Douglass Dumbrille, Robert Wilke, Adele Mara, George Renavent, Gerald Mohr
D: Lesley Selander **PHOTOG:** Reggie Lanning **SPCL-FX:** Howard & Theodore Lydecker **MUSIC:** Dale Butts
Minor thriller: Killings blamed on "cat-monster"

The Cat O' Nine Tails
1971, (USA-It), Nat'l General, color, 112 mins.
W: Karl Malden (*Franco Arno*), Catherine Spaak (*Anna Terzi*), James Franciscus (*Carlo Giordani*), Cinzia De Carolis (*Lori*), Carlo Alighiero (*Dr. Calabresi*), Pier Paolo Capponi (*The Police Supt.*), Vittorio Congia (*The Cameraman*), Corrado Olmi (*Morsella*), Tino Carraro (*Terzi*), Horst Frank (*Dr. Braun*), Aldo Reggiani (*Dr. Casoni*), Emilio Marchesini (*Dr. Mombelli*), Tom Felleghy (*Dr. Esson*), Werner Pochat (*Manuel*), Rada Rassimov (*Bianca Merusi*)
D & SCR: Dario Argento **STORY:** Dario Argento, Luigi Collo & Dardano Sacchetti **PHOTOG:** Enrico Menczer **MUSIC:** Ennio Morricone
Standard thriller: Journalists pursue psychotic killer who has chromosome imbalance

Cat People
1942, (USA), RKO, b&w, 73 mins.
W: Simone Simon (*Irena*), Kent Smith (*Oliver*), Jane Randolph (*Alice*), Tom Conway (*Dr. Judd*), Alan Napier (*The Commodore*), Jack Holt (*Doc*), Elizabeth Russell, Jeni LeGon, Elizabeth Dunne, Mary Jane Halsey
P: Val Lewton **D:** Jacques Tourneur **SCR:** DeWitt Bodeen **PHOTOG:** Nicholas Musuraca **MUSIC:** Roy Webb **DESIGN:** A.S. D'Agostino & Walter E. Keller
Classic horror-fantasy: Beautiful bride rejects love, fears were-panther curse
cf. **Curse of the Cat People**. French retitle, **La Feline**

Cat People
1982, (USA), Univ, color, 118 mins.
W: Nastassia Kinski (*Irena Gallier*), Malcolm McDowell (*Paul Gallier*), John Heard (*Oliver Yates*), Annette O'Toole (*Alice Perrin*), Ruby Dee (*Female*), Ed Begley Jr. (*Joe Creigh*), Ron Diamond (*Det. Ron Diamond*), Frankie Faison (*Det. Brandt*), Scott Paulin (*Bill Searle*), John Larroquette (*Bronte Judson*), Lynn Lowry (*Ruthie*), Tessa Richarde (*Billie*), Patricia Perkins (*The Taxi Driver*), Berry Berenson, Fausto Barajas, John H. Fields, Emery Hollier, Stephen Marshal, Julie Denney, Robert Pavlovitch, Arione de Winter, David Showacre, Francine Segal, Don Hood, Neva Gage, Danelle Hand, Marisa Folse, Roger Reid, John C. Isbell, Marco St. John, Charles Joseph Konya Jr., Ray Wise, Brett Alexander, Gregory Gatto, Terc Martinez, Harold D. Hauss, David Ross McCarty, James Deeth, Jo Ann Dearing
D: Paul Schrader **SCR:** Alan Ormsby, from a story by DeWitt Bodeen **PHOTOG:** John Bailey **SPCL-FX:** Tom Del Genio, Pat Domenico & Karl Miller **MUSIC:** Giorgio Moroder, **THEME:** David Bowie
Erotic semi-remake of classic horror-fantasy: Young woman learns terrible secret of her lineage

The Cats
see Les Felins

The Cat's Cup Final
1912, (GB), Empire Films/MP, b&w, 360 ft. (109.7m)
WRIT & D: Arthur Cooper
Standard fantasy short: Toy cats play football match

Cat's Eye
1985, (USA), Dino De Laurentiis/MGM, color, 92 mins.
W: Drew Barrymore, James Woods, Alan King, Kenneth McMillan, Robert Hays, Candy Clark, James Naughton, Jesse Doran, Court Miller
D: Lewis Teague **SCR:** Stephen King—from his stories **PHOTOG:** Jack Cardiff **MUSIC:** Alan Silvestri
Modest trilogy of comedy-fantasy tales

Cat-Women of the Moon
1954, (USA), Savino/Astor, 3D, b&w, 64 mins.
W: Marie Windsor (*Helen*), Sonny Tufts (*Grainger*), Victor Jory (*Kip*), Bill Phipps, Susan Morrow, Carol Brewster
P: Al Zimbalist **D:** Arthur Hilton **SCR:** Roy Hamilton **STORY & SPCL-FX:** Jack Rabin & Al Zimbalist **MUSIC:** Elmer Bernstein
A.k.a. **By Rocket to the Moon**
Amusing SF-thriller: Disappearing-reappearing feline dames found on dark side of moon cf. **Missile to the Moon**.

Le Cauchemar (The Nightmare)
1897, (Fr), Star, b&w, 20m (65.6 ft./1.1 mins.)
D: Georges Melies
Fantasy short

Le Cauchemar de Dracula
see Horror of Dracula

Cauchemares (Nightmares)
1977, (Can), 21st Century, color
W: Randi Allen, Alan Scarfe, Beverly Murray
D: Eddy Matalon **SCR:** Myra Clement, Eddy Matalon, & A. Sens-Cazenave
USA retitle, Cathy's Curse
Minor fantasy: Girl owns possessed rag doll

Caught
1949, (USA), Enterprise/MGM, b&w, 88 mins.
<u>W</u>: James Mason, Barbara Bel Geddes, Robert Ryan, Curt Bois, Natalie Schafer, Frank Ferguson, Ruth Brady, Art Smith
<u>P</u>: Wolfgang Reinhardt <u>D</u>: Max Ophuls <u>SCR</u>: Arthur Laurents, based on Libbie Block's novel *Wild Calendar* <u>PHOTOG</u>: Lee Garmes <u>MUSIC</u>: Frederick Hollander
Tense melodrama: Girl realizes she has wed sadist

Caught
1996, (USA), color, 110 mins.
<u>W</u>: Edward James Olmos, Maria Conchita Alonso, Arie Verveen, Steven Schub (*Danny*), Bitty Schram (*Amy*)
Standard thriller: Couple befriends mysterious drifter

Caught by a Child
1910, (GB), Walturdaw, b&w, 350 ft. (106.7m)
Standard crime-thriller: Child traps tramp in cellar

Caught in his Own Net
1912, (GB), Cricks & Martin, b&w, 990 ft. (301.8m)
<u>W</u>: Charles Vane (*The Squire*)
<u>D</u>: Edwin J. Collins
Standard crime-thriller: Detective poses as tramp, catches crook

Cauldron of Blood
1971, (USA-Sp), Cannon, color, 101 mins.
<u>W</u>: Boris Karloff (*Badulescu*), Jean-Pierre Aumont (*Marchand*), Viveca Lindfors (*Tania*), Rosenda Monteros (*Valerie*), Dianik Zurakowska (*Elga*), Milo Quesada (*Shanghai*), Ruben Rojo (*Pablo*), Mercedes Rojo, Jacqui Speed
<u>P</u>: Robert D. Weinbach <u>D</u>: Edward Mann [S. Alcocer] <u>SCR</u>: John Melson & Edward Mann <u>PHOTOG</u>: Francisco Sempere <u>MUSIC</u>: Ray Ellis
Sp title, El Colleccionista de Cadaveres (The Collector of Cadavers)
A.k.a. Blind Man's Bluff
Minor thriller (filmed in 1967): Grim tale of blind sculptor and his sadistic wife

The Cauldron of Death
1979, (It), Edward L. Montoro/Film Ventures, color
<u>W</u>: Chris Mitchum, Arthur Kennedy, Barbara Bouchet, Melisa Longo, Edward Fajardo, Angel Alvarez
<u>D</u>: Tulio Demicheli <u>SCR</u>: Joe Maesso
Minor thriller: Mafia intrigue

Il Cavaliere di Ferro
see Il Conte Ugolino

The Cavaliers of the Demon
see The Hell-Fire Club

The Cave Dwellers
see One Million B.C.

The Cave Girl
1921, (USA), First Nat'l, b&w, 5 reels (4,405 ft./1342.6m)
<u>W</u>: Teddie Gerard (*Margot*), Charles Meredith (*Divvy Bates*), Wilton Taylor (*J.T. Bates*), Eleanor Hancock (*Mrs. Georgia Case*), Lillian Tucker (*Elsie Case*), Frank Coleman (*Rufus Patterson*), Boris Karloff (*Baptiste*), Jake Abrahams (*Prof. Orlando Sperry*), John Beck (*Rogers*)
<u>D</u>: Joseph J. Franz <u>SCR</u>: William Parker, from a play by Guy Bolton & George Middleton <u>PHOTOG</u>: Victor Milner
Standard melodrama: Professor studies primitive modes of living

Cavegirl
1985, (USA), Crown-Int'l, color, 85 mins.
<u>W</u>: Daniel Roebuck (*Rex*), Cindy Ann Thompson (*Eba*), Saba Moor (*Saba*), Darren Young (*Dar*), Jeff Chayette (*Argh*), Bill Adams (*Bill*), Charles Mitchell (*Char*), Cynthia Rullo (*Aka*), Chris Noble (*Hank*), Tom Hamil (*Casey*), Bill Sehres (*Ralph*), Sydni King (*Karen*), Stacey Swain (*Brenda*), A.A. Cavallaro (*Rex's Father*), Maggie Ostroff (*Rex's Mother*), Larry Gabriel (*The Professor*), Valerie Greybe, David Castro, Bob Verne, Robert Nathan Field, Kent Jorgensen, Jerry Day, Craig S. Leary, Ken Willingham, Shane Kelly, Jennifer Keel, Tim Berry, Nathaniel Bratton, Debbie Wright, Olivia De Anda, Paul Enns, Michelle Bauer, Kathy Mehling, Bonita Samek, David Alvedrez, Susanne Mierisch, Barry Hibbard, Jasae, Pamela Powers, Susie Lynch
<u>WRIT, P, D, & PHOTOG</u>: David Oliver, adapted from Phil Groves' screenplay *Primal Urge* <u>SPCL-FX</u>: Gregory C. Landerer <u>MUSIC</u>: Jon St. James
Minor comedy-fantasy: Nerd time-warped to Stone Age

Cave Girl Island
1995, (USA), color, 80 mins.
<u>W</u>: Sara Bellomo, Tina Hollimon, Rodrigo Botero, Stephanie Hudson
Standard SF-fantasy: Space-traveling women land on isle populated by cavemen and dinosaurs

Cave Man (1940)
see One Million B.C.

Caveman
1981, (USA), Turman-Foster Co./UA, color, 94 mins.
<u>W</u>: Ringo Starr (*Atouk*), Barbara Bach (*Lana*), Shelley Long (*Tala*), Jack Gilford (*Og*), Dennis Quaid (*Lar*), John Matuszak (*Tonda*), Avery Schreiber (*Ock*), Richard Moll (*The Abominable Snowman*), Cork Hubbert (*Ta*), Mark King (*Ruck*), Paco Morayta (*Flok*), Evan Kim (*Nook*), Ed Greenberg (*Kalta*), Carl Lumbly (*Bork*), Jack Scalici (*Folg*), Erica Carlson (*Folg's Mate*), Gigi Vorgan (*Folg's Daughter*), Sara Lopez Sierra (*Folg's Youngest Daughter*), Esteban Valdez (*Folg's Son*), Juan Ancona Figueroa (*Folg's Younger Son*), Juan Omar Ortiz (*Folg's Youngest Son*), Anais de Melo (*Meeka*), Miguel Angel Fuentes (*Grot*), Gerardo Zepeda (*Boola*), Tere Alvarez (*Ock's Mate*), Ana de Sade (*Grot's Mate*), Hector Moreno (*Noota*), Pamela Gual (*Noota's Mate*)
<u>P</u>: Lawrence Turman & David Foster <u>D</u>: Carl Gottlieb <u>SCR</u>: Rudy De Luca & Carl Gottlieb <u>PHOTOG</u>: Alan Hume <u>MUSIC</u>: Lalo Schifrin
Modest comedy: Tale of prehistoric humans

The Cave of the Demons
see La Caverne Maudite

Cave of the Living Dead
1964, (W. Ger), Schneider/Objective/Film Development/Trans Lux, b&w, 86 mins.
<u>W</u>: Adrian Hoven, Carl Mohner, Erika Remberg, Wolfgang Preiss, Karin Field, John Kitzmiller, Tito Strozzi, Emmerich Schrenk, Danilo Turk, Vida Juvan, Laci Cigoj, Stane Sever
<u>D</u>: Akos V. Rathony <u>SCR</u>: C.V. Rock <u>PHOTOG</u>: H. Saric <u>MUSIC</u>: Herbert Jarczyk
Minor horror-thriller: Detective looks into baffling murders

The Cavern
see Sette Contro la Morte

La Caverne Maudite (The Cursed Cave)
1898, (Fr), Star, b&w, 20m (65.6 ft./1.1 mins.)
<u>D</u>: Georges Melies
USA retitle, The Cave of the Demons
Standard fantasy: Spirits infest cavern

Celia
1949, (GB), Exclusive, b&w, 67 mins.
<u>W</u>: Hy Hazell (*Celia*), Bruce Lister (*Larry Peters*), John Bailey (*Lester Martin*), James Raglan (*Insp. Parker*), Elsie Wagstaffe (*Aunt Nora*), Lockwood West (*Dr. Cresswell*)
<u>P</u>: Anthony Hinds <u>D</u>: Francis Searle <u>SCR</u>: Francis Searle, Edward J. Mason & A.R. Rawlinson, from a radio-serial by Edward J. Mason
Standard thriller: Actress poses as aunt to prove her step-uncle is murderer

The Cellar (1970)
see Are You Dying Young Man?

The Cellar
1989, (USA), color, 90 mins.
<u>W</u>: Chris Miller, Patrick Kilpatrick, Suzanne Savoy, Ford Rainey
<u>D</u>: Kevin S. Tenney
Standard fantasy: Indian spirit haunts boy

Cellar Dweller
1988, (USA-It), Dove/Empire, color, 78 mins.
<u>W</u>: Debrah Mullowney, Brian Robbins, Vince Edwards, Cheryl Ann Wilson, Jeffrey Combs, Yvonne DeCarlo, Pamela Bellwood, Floyd Levine, Michael S. Deak
<u>D</u>: John Carl Buechler <u>SCR</u>: Kit DuBois <u>PHOTOG</u>: Sergio Salvati <u>MUSIC</u>: Carl Dante <u>SONGS</u>: *Nothing Changes, Master Dancer, Mystery Baby, & Death Knell*
Standard horror-fantasy: Cartoonist's monster comes to life

The Cellar of Death
1916, (GB), Cricks/Apex, b&w, 2,500 ft. (762m)
<u>D</u>: Charles Calvert
Standard crime-thriller

Cellblock Sisters: Banished Behind Bars
1995, (USA), color, 95 mins.
<u>W</u>: Gail Harris, Annie Wood, Jenna Bodnar
Minor melodrama: Innocent imprisoned for murder committed by sister

Cell 2455, Death Row
1955, (USA), Col, b&w, 77 mins.
<u>W</u>: William Campbell, Kathryn Grant, Vince Edwards, Robert Campbell
<u>P & D</u>: Fred F. Sears <u>SCR</u>: Jack DeWitt
Standard fact-based thriller: Exploits of sex-killer Caryl Chessman

Cemetery Girls
see Gran Amore del Conde Dracula

Cemetery Man
1996, (It-Fr), October Films, color, 100 mins.
<u>W</u>: Rupert Everett (*Francesco Dellamorte*), Francos Hadji-Lazaro (*Gnaghi*), Anna Falchi ("*She*")
<u>D</u>: Michele Soavi <u>SCR</u>: Gianini Romoli <u>PHOTOG</u>: Mauro Marchetti

MUSIC: Manuel De Sica
Gothic black comedy: Cemetery keeper contends with living dead

Cendrillon (Cinderella)
1899, (Fr), Star/Pathe, b&w & color (hand-tinted), 295m (967 ft.)
D: Georges Melies, from Charles Perrault's classic fairytale
Standard fantasy: Drudge becomes princess

Central Park Driver
see Graveyard Shift (1987)

C'era Una Volta (Once Upon a Time)
1967, (It-Fr), Les Films Concordia-C.C. Champion/MGM, color, 103 mins.
W: Sophia Loren, Omar Sharif, Dolores Del Rio, George Wilson, Leslie French, Marina Malfatti
P: Carlo Ponti   **D:** Francesco Rosi   **SCR:** Francesco Rosi, Tonino Guerra, Raffaele La Capria & Peppino Pa-troni Griffi, based on a story by Tonino Guerra   **PHOTOG:** Piero Poletto   **MUSIC:** Piero Piccioni
*USA retitle, **More Than a Miracle**. A.k.a. **Cinderella, Italian Style***
Modest fantasy: Witch helps peasant girl snare prince

C'Era Una Volta: SOPHIA LOREN

Ceremonia Sangrienta (Blood Ceremony)
1972, (It-Sp), Film Ventures, color
W: Lucia Bose, Ewa Aulin
P: Jose Maria Gonzalez Sinde   **D:** Jorge Grau   **SCR:** Juan Tebar & Sando Continenza
*USA retitle, **The Female Butcher**. A.k.a. **Legend of Blood Castle***
blurb: "She butchered 610 nubile virgins!"
*Standard horror-thriller: To keep her youth, Countess Elizabeth Bathory bathes in blood of virgins. cf. **Countess Dracula***

Cesare Borgia
1923, (Ger), b&w, 83 mins.
W: Conrad Veidt
D: Richard Oswald
Standard melodrama: Dastardly deeds of Pope Alexander VI's son

Cesta Do Praveku (Journey into Primeval Times)
1954, (Czech), color, 92 mins.
WRIT & D: Karel Zeman
released in USA (1966) as ***Journey to the Beginning of Time***
Modest fantasy-adventure: Time-travel to prehistoric world

Cet Homme est Dangereux (This Man is Dangerous)
1953, (Fr), Lutetia/Edic/Sonofilms, b&w, 84 mins.
W: Eddie Constantine (*Lemmy Caution*), Colette Dercal, Claude Borelli, Guy Decomble, Gregoire Aslan, Jacqueline Pierreux
D: Jean Sacha   **SCR:** Andre Duhamel & Jacques Berland, from Peter Cheyney's novel
released in USA in 1956, USA TV-retitle, ***Dangerous Agent***
2nd "Lemmy Caution" action-thriller: Underworld hero rounds up crime gangs

Chained for Life
1950, (USA), Classic Films, b&w, 81 mins.
W: Violet Hilton, Daisy Hilton, Allen Jenkins
P: George Moscov   **D:** Harry L. Fraser   **SCR:** Nat Tanchuck
Minor exploitation melodrama: One of Siamese twins is accused of murder

Chained Heat
1983, (USA), Jensen Farley, color, 93 mins.
W: Linda Blair (*Carol*), John Vernon (*Warden Backman*), Sybil Danning (*Ericka*), Tamara Dobson (*Dutchess*), Stella Stevens (*Capt. Taylor*), Sharon Hughes (*Val*), Henry Silva (*Lester*), Edy Williams, Nita Talbot, Michael Callan, Louisa Moritz

D: Paul Nico:las   **SCR:** Vincent Mongol & Paul Nicolas   **PHOTOG:** Mac Ahlberg
Exciting action: Girls in prison

Chain of Circumstance
1951, (USA), Col, b&w, 68 mins.
W: Richard Grayson, Margaret Field (Maggie Mahoney)
Minor melodrama

Chain of Events
1958, (GB), Beaconsfield/British Lion, b&w, 62 mins.
W: Dermot Walsh (*Quinn*), Susan Shaw (*Jill*), Lisa Gastoni (*Simone*), Jack Watling (*Freddie*), Alan Gifford (*Lord Fenchurch*), Harold Lang (*Jimmy Boy*), Kenneth Griffith (*Clarke*), Ballard Berkeley (*Stockman*), Freddie Mills (*Tiny*), John Stuart (*The Manager*)
P: Peter Rogers   **D:** Gerald Thomas   **SCR:** Patrick Brawn, from Leo McKern's radio-play *London*
Standard crime-thriller: Bank clerk involved in blackmail and death

Chain of Evidence
1957, (USA), AA, b&w, 64 mins.
W: Bill Elliott, James Lydon
Minor thriller

The Chain Reaction
1980, (Austral), color, 92 mins.
W: Steve Bisley, Anna-Maria Winchester, Ross Thompson, Ralph Cotterill, Hugh Keays-Byrne
D: Ian Barry
*A.k.a. **Nuclear Run***
Standard thriller: Corporate coverup of nuclear contamination

Chain Reaction
1996, (USA), Zanuck-Chicago Pacific/20th-Fox, color, 106 mins.
W: Keanu Reeves (*Eddie Kasalivich*), Morgan Freeman (*Paul Shan non*), Fred Ward (*FBI Agent Ford*), Rachel Weisz (*Lily Sinclair*),Kevin Dunn (*FBI Agent Doyle*), Brian Cox (*Lyman Earl Collier*), Joanna Cassidy (*Maggie McDermott*), Chelcie Ross (*Ed Rafferty*), Nicholas Rudall (*Dr. Alistair Barkley*), Tzi Ma (*Lu Chen*), Daniel H. Friedman, Julie R. Pearl, Krzysztof Pieczynski, Gene Barge, Nathan Davis, Aaron Williams, Johnny Lee Davenport, James Sie, Juan Ramirez, Joan Kohn
D: Andrew Davis   **SCR:** J.F. Lawton & Michael Bortman   **STORY:** Arne L. Schmidt, Rick Seaman & Josh Friedman   **PHOTOG:** Frank Tidy   **MUSIC:** Jerry Goldsmith
*A.k.a. **Dead Drop***
Unusual SF-thriller: dangerous intrigue when young scientist deveops cold fusion

Chainsaw Hookers
*see **Hollywood Chainsaw Hookers***

La Chaise a Porteurs Enchantee (The Enchanted Sedan Chair)
1905, (Fr), Star, b&w, 56m (183.7 ft./3.1 mins)
D: Georges Melies
Standard fantasy

Chain Reaction: KEANU REEVES

The Challenge

1948, (USA), Reliance/20th-Fox, b&w, 64 mins.
W: Tom Conway (*Hugh "Bulldog" Drummond*), June Vincent (*Vivian Bailey*), Richard Stapley (*Cliff Sonnenberg*), John Newland (*Algy Longworth*), Eily Malyon (*Kitty*), Terence Kilburn (*Seymour*), Stanley Logan (*Insp. Melvar*), Leland Hodgson (*Sgt. Schubeck*), James Fairfax (*Blinky Henderson*), Oliver Blake (*Arno*), Houseley Stevenson (*Capt. Sonnenberg*), Pat Aherne (*Jerome Roberts*)
D: Jean Yarbrough   **SCR:** Frank Gruber & Irving Elman, from Sapper's novel-
   PHOTOG: George Robinson   **MUSIC:** Milton Rosen
Standard mystery-thriller: Famed sleuth becomes embroiled in murderous search for casket of gold

A Challenge for Robin Hood

1967, (GB), Hammer-7Arts/20th-Fox, color, 96 mins.
W: Barrie Ingham (*Robin Hood*), James Hayter (*Friar Tuck*), Leon Greene (*Little John*), Gay Hamilton (*Lady Marian Fitzwarren*), Peter Blythe (*Roger de Courtenay*), Jenny Till (*Lady Marian*), John Arnatt (*The Sheriff of Nottingham*), Reg Lye (*Much*), Eric Flynn (*Alan-a-Dale*), Alfie Bass (*The Merchant*), William Squire (*Sir John de Courtenay*), Douglas Mitchell (*Will Scarlett*)
D: C. Pennington-Richards   **SCR:** Peter Bryan   **PHOTOG:** Arthur Grant
   MUSIC: Gary Hughes
Minor romance-adventure: Retelling of Robin Hood legend

Challenge of the Gladiators

1964, (It), color
W: Rock Stevens, Gloria Milland, Massimo Serato
Minor "Sword & Sandal" adventure: Spartacus revolts against Nero's corrupt reign

Chamber of Fear

*see **The Fear Chamber***

Chamber of Horrors

1929, (GB), British Instructional/PDC, b&w, 5,014 ft. (1528.3m)
W: Frank Stanmore (*James Budgeforth*), Elizabeth Hempel (*Ninette*), Joan Maude (*The Reporter*), Leslie Holland (*The Deaf Mute*), Fanny Wright (*The Lecturer*)
D & SCR: Walter Summers
Standard horror-thriller: Man dreams he murders mistress

Chamber of Horrors (1940)

*see **The Door with Seven Locks** (1940)*

Chamber of Horrors

1966, (USA), WB, color, 99 mins.
W: Cesare Danova (*Anthony Draco*), Laura Devon (*Marie Champlain*), Wilfrid Hyde-White (*Harold Blount*), Patrick O'Neal (*Cravette/Jason Carroll*), Tun Tun (*Pepe de Reyes*), Jeanette Nolan, Marie Windsor, Suzy Parker, Patrice Wymore, Philip Bourneuf, Tony Curtis
P & D: Hy Averback   **SCR:** Stephen Kandel   **STORY:** Ray Russell & Stephen Kandel   **PHOTOG:** Richard Kline   **MUSIC:** William Lava
Standard thriller, orig. pilot-film for unsold teleseries: Detective tracks fiendish murderer

Chameleon

1998, (USA), UPN-TV, color, 95 mins.
W: Bobbie Phillips (*Kam*), Eric Lloyd (*Ghen*), Nicholas Bell, John Adam, Jerome Ehlers, Philip Casnoff
D: Stuart Cooper   **TELEPLAY:** Bennett Cohen   **PHOTOG:** John Stokes
   MUSIC: Wendy Blackstone
TVM, standard SF-thriller: Genetically-altered woman turns on her creators

The Chameleon Man

*see **The Lightning Change Artist***

Champagne

1928, (GB), BIP/Wardour, b&w, 8,038 ft. (2450m)
W: Betty Balfour (*Betty*), Jean Bradin (*Jean*), Gordon Harker (*The Father*), Theodore von Alten (*The Baron*), Jack Trevor (*The Officer*), Clifford Heatherley (*The Manager*), Claude Hulbert (*A Guest*), Sunday Wilshin (*A Girl*), Balliol & Merton (*The Dancers*), Alex D'Arcy
D: Alfred Hitchcock   **SCR:** Eliot Stannard & Alfred Hitchcock, from a story by Walter C. Mycroft
Standard comedy: Millionaire feigns bankruptcy

Champagne for Caesar

1950, (USA), Cardinal/UA, b&w, 99 mins.
W: Ronald Colman (*Beauregard Bottomley*), Barbara Britton (*Gwen Bottomley*), Vincent Price (*Burnbridge Waters*), Art Linkletter (*Happy Hogan*), Celeste Holm (*Flame O'Neil*), Gabriel Heater (*An Announcer*), George Fisher (*An Announcer*), Douglas Evans (*The Radio Announcer*), Byron Foulger (*Gerald*), Vici Raaf (*Waters' Sec'y*), Ellye Marshall (*Frosty*), John Eldredge (*Executive #1*), Lyle Talbot (*Executive #2*), George Leigh (*Executive #3*), John Hart (*Executive #4*), Mel Blanc (*Voice of Caesar*), Brian O'Hara (*Buck*), Peter Brocco (*The Fortune Teller*), Jack Daly (*Scratch*), Gordon Nelson (*The Lecturer*), Herbert Lytton (*Chuck Johnson*), George Meader (*Mr. Brown*)
D: Richard Whorf   **SCR:** Hans Jacoby & Fred Brady   **PHOTOG:** Paul Ivano
   MUSIC: Dimitri Tiomkin
Classic comedy: Genius decides to ruin obnoxious quiz show

The Champagne Murders

*see **Le Scandale***

Chance Meeting

*see **Blind Date** (1959)*

The Chance of a Lifetime

1943, (USA), Col, b&w, 56 mins.
W: Chester Morris (*Boston Blackie*), Erik Rolf (*Dooley Watson*), Jeanne Bates (*Mary Watson*), George E. Stone (*Runt*), Richard Lane (*Insp. Farraday*), Walter Sande (*Matthews*), Cy Kendall (*Jumbo Madigan*), Lloyd Corrigan (*Arthur Manleder*), Douglas Fowley (*Nails Banton*), Larry Joe Olson (*Johnny Watson*), Sally Cairns (*Richie Adair*), Arthur Hunnicutt (*Tex*), Harry Semels (*Egypt Hines*), Trevor Bardette (*Manny Vogel*), Eddie Bruce (*Sandy*), Heinie Conklin (*The Desk Sgt.*), Marie de Becker (*Miss Bailey*), Maude Eburne (*Miss Couniham*), Ray Teal, Frank O'Connor, Jack Carr, George Magrill, Pierre Watkin, Eddy Chandler, Jessie Arnold, Jack Alexander, Minta Durfee, John Harmon
D: William Castle   **SCR:** Paul Yawitz, from characters created by Jack Boyle
   PHOTOG: Ernie Miller   **MUSIC:** Morris W. Stoloff
Standard "Boston Blackie" mystery-thriller

Chances Are

1989, (USA), Lobell-Bergman/Tri-Star, color, 108 mins.
W: Cybill Shepherd (*Corinne Jeffries*), Robert Downey Jr. (*Alex Finch*), Ryan O'Neal (*Philip Train*), Mary Stuart Masterson (*Miranda*)
D: Emile Ardolino   **SCR:** Perry Howze & Randy Howze   **PHOTOG:** William A. Fraker   **MUSIC:** Maurice Jarre
Standard comedy-fantasy: Reincarnated reporter pursues his widow

Chances Are: ROBERT DOWNEY JR. AND CYBILL SHEPHERD

Chandu

1934, (USA), Principal, b&w, 67 mins.
W: Bela Lugosi, Maria Alba, Dean Benton, Bryant Washburn, Clara Kimball Young
*A.k.a. **Chandu on the Magic Isle***
*Standard fantasy-thriller (feature culled from 1934 serial **Return of Chandu**): Mystic fights crime*

Chandu on the Magic Isle

*see **Chandu***

Chandu the Magician

1932, (USA), Fox, b&w, 74 mins.
W: Edmund Lowe (*Chandu*), June Lang, Bela Lugosi, Irene Ware, Herbert Mundin, Henry B. Walthall
D: William Cameron Menzies & Marcel Varnel   **SCR:** Philip Klein & Barry Conners   **PHOTOG:** James Wong Howe
Minor thriller: Mystic vs. mad scientist with monstrous heat ray

The Changeling

1980, (Can), AFD, color, 104 mins.
W: George C. Scott (*John Russell*), Trish Van Devere (*Claire Norman*), Melvyn Douglas (*Sen. Carmichael*), John Colicos (*Capt. DeWitt*), Madeleine Thornton Sherwood (*Mrs. Norman*), Jean Marsh (*Joanna Russell*), Hagan Beggs (*The Coroner*), Bernard Behrens (*Robert Lingstrom*), Barry Morse (*Dr. Pemberton*), Helen Burns (*Leah Harmon*), Frances Hyland, Eric Christmas (*Eric Harmon*), Roberta Maxwell (*Eva Lingstrom*), Chris Gampel (*Tuttle*), James B. Douglas (*Eugene Carmichael*), Ruth Springford (*Minnie Huxley*)
P: Joel B. Michaels & Garth H. Drabinsky   **D:** Peter Medak   **SCR:** William Gray & Diana Maddox, based on a story by Russell Hunter   **PHOTOG:** John Coquillon   **MUSIC:** Rick Williams
Standard fantasy-thriller: Widowed composer rents old house possessed by restless haunt

Change of Mind
1969, (USA), Sagittarius/CRC, color, 103 mins.
W: Raymond St. Jacques (*David Rowe*), Susan Oliver (*Margaret Rowe*), Donnelly Rhodes (*Roger Morrow*), Leslie Nielsen (*Sheriff Webb*), Janet MacLachlan (*Elizabeth Dickson*), Clarisse Taylor (*Rose Landis*), Jack Creley (*Bill Chambers*), Larry Reynolds (*Judge Forrest*), David Bailey (*Tommy Benson*), Rudy Challenger (*Howard Culver*), Cosette Lee (*Angela Rowe*), Hope Clarke (*Nancy*), Andre Womble (*Scupper*), Tony Kamreither (*Dr. Bornear*), Henry Ramer (*Chief Enfield*), Ron Hartman (*Dr. Kelman*), Franz Russell (*Mayor Farrell*), Sean Sullivan (*Mr. Robinson*), Joseph Shaw (*Gov. LaTourette*), Sydney Brown (*Attorney Nash*), Charles Elder (*Mako*), Murray Westgate (*Judge Stanton*), Horace Bailey (*Moorland*), Don Crawford (*Callicot*), Buddy Ferens (*The Officer*), Vivian Reis (*Gloria*), Pat Collins (*Mrs. Robinson*), Joseph Wynn, Clarence Haynes, Guy Sanvido, Chuck Shamata, Dan MacDonald
WRIT & CO-P: Seeleg Lester & Dick Wesson D: Robert Stevens PHOTOG: Arthur Ornitz MUSIC: Duke Ellington
Modest "blaxploitation" thriller: White D.A.'s brain transplanted to body of dead black man

Change Partners
1965, (GB), Merton Park/Anglo-Amalgamated, b&w, 63 mins.
W: Zena Walker (*Anna Arkwright*), Kenneth Cope (*Joe Trent*), Basil Henson (*Ricky Gallen*), Jane Barrett (*Betty Gallen*), Anthony Dawson (*Ben Arkwright*), Pamela Ann Davey (*Jean*), Peter Bathurst (*McIvor*), Josephine Pritchard (*Sally Morrison*)
P: Jack Greenwood D: Robert Lynn STORY: Doanal Giltinian
Standard crime-thriller: Alcoholic's wife plots murder

The Channeler
1989, (USA), color, 90 mins.
W: Dan Haggerty, Richard Harrison, Jay Richardson, David Homb, Oliver Darrow, Robin Sims, Charles Solomon
D: Grant Austin Waldman
Minor horror-fantasy: Demons in Colorado mine

Le Chapeau á Surprises (The Hat of Surprises)
1901, (Fr), Star, b&w, 50m (164 ft./2.8 mins.)
D: Georges Melies
Standard fantasy. USA retitle, The Hat with Many Surprises

Chappaqua
1966, (USA), Regional/Univ, color & b&w, mixture of 35mm & 16mm film 82 mins.
W: Conrad Rooks (*Russell Harwick*), Jean-Louis Barrault (*Dr. Benoit*), William Burroughs (*Opium Jones*), Allen Ginsberg, Ornette Coleman, Ravi Shankar, The Fugs
WRIT, P & D, Conrad Rooks PHOTOG: Robert Frank
Unusual semi-documentary: Vivid depiction of drug addicts' hallucination-world

Charade
Univ, 113 mins.
W: Paul Bonifas, Ned Glass, Dominique Minot

Chariots of the Gods?
1969, (W. Ger), Sunn Classics, color, 98 mins.
P: Guentler Eulau D: Harald Reinl SCR: Wilhelm Pogersdorff, from Erich Von Daniken's book
A.k.a. Memories of the Future
Standard docu: Speculation on Earth's visitation by ancient astronauts

The Charlatan
1916, (GB), Famous Authors/Crown, b&w, 4,363 ft. (1329.8m)
W: Eille Norwood (*Dr. O'Kama*), Violet Graham (*Isobel Arlington*), Anna Mather (*Mme. Obnowsky*), Frederick de Lara (*The Earl of Wansborough*), Ernest A. Dagnall (*Col. Arlington*), R. Courtland (*Lord Dewsbury*)
D: Sidney Morgan SCR: Austin Fryers, from a play by Robert Buchanan
Standard thriller: Fake occultist, reformed by colonel's daughter, saves earl from his ex-partner

Charley and the Angel
1973, (USA), Walt Disney/Buena Vista, color, 93 mins.
W: Fred MacMurray (*Charley Appleby*), Cloris Leachman (*Nettie Appleby*), Harry Morgan (*The Angel*), Kurt Russell (*Ray Ferris*), Kathleen Cody (*Leonora Appleby*), Vincent Van Patten (*Willie Appleby*), Scott Kolden (*Rupert Appleby*), Kelly Thordsen (*The Policeman*), George Lindsey (*Pete*), Edward Andrews (*The Banker*), Richard Bakalyan (*Buggs*), Barbara Nichols (*Sadie*), Liam Dunn (*Dr. Sprague*), Larry D. Mann (*Felix*), George O'Hanlon (*The Police Chief*), Susan Tolsky (*Miss Partridge*), Ed Begley Jr. (*Derwood Moseby*), Mills Watson (*Frankie Zuto*), Roy Engel (*The Driver*), Christina Anderson (*Susie*), Pat Delany (*The Girl in Sadie's Palace*), Bob Hastings (*The News Reporter*), Jack Griffin (*Policeman #2*)
D: Vincent McEveety SCR: Roswell Rogers, from a story by Will Stanton PHOTOG: Charles F. Wheeler MUSIC: Buddy Baker
Juvenile fantasy: Heavenly visitor complicates family's life

Charlie Boy/The Thirteenth Reunion
1980, (GB), color, 120 mins.
W: Leigh Lawson (*Graham*), Marius Goring (*Heinz*)
TVM: standard thriller: Two episodes from British teleseries House of Horror

Charlie Chan and the Curse of the Dragon Queen
1981, (USA), American Cinema, color, 97 mins.
W: Peter Ustinov (*Charlie Chan*), Lee Grant (*Mrs. Lupowitz*), Angie Dickinson (*The Dragon Queen*), Brian Keith (*The Police Chief*), Richard Hatch (*Lee Chan Jr.*), Rachel Roberts (*Mrs. Dangers*), Roddy McDowall (*Gillespie*), Johnny Sekka (*Stefan*), Michelle Pfeiffer (*Cordelia Farrington III*), Bennett Ohta (*The Hawaiian Police Chief*), Paul Ryan (*Masten*), James Ray (*Haynes*), David Hirokane (*Lee Chan Sr.*), Momo Yashima (*Dr. Yu Sing*), Karlene Crockett (*Brenda Lupowitz*), Michael Fairman (*Bernard Lupowitz*), Alison Hong (*Maysie Ling*), Jerry Loo, Kael Blackwood, Laurence Cohen, Robin Hoff, Kathie Kei, John Hugh, James Bacon, Frank Michael, George Chiang, David Chow, Duane Tucker, Dewi Yee, Joe Bellan, Garrick Huey, Don Parker, Kai Wong, Kenneth Snell, Nicholas Gunn, Miya, Gerald Okamura, Vic Hunsberger, Lonny Carbajal, Peter Michas, Larry Duran, Trevor Hook, Kay Kimler, Jim Winburn, Pavla Ustinov, Molly Roden, Paul Sanderson
D: Clive Donner SCR: Stan Burns & David Axelrod STORY: Jerry Sherlock, from characters created by Earl Derr Biggers PHOTOG: Paul Lohmann MUSIC: Patrick Williams
Modest comedy-thriller: Oriental sleuth stalks crime czaress

Charlie Chan and the Red Dragon
see The Red Dragon (1945)

Charlie Chan at Monte Carlo
1937, (USA), 20th-Fox, b&w, 71 mins.
W: Warner Oland (*Charlie Chan*), Virginia Field (*Evelyn Gray*), Keye Luke (*Lee Chan*), Sidney Blackmer (*Karnoff*), Kay Linaker (*Joan Karnoff*), Harold Huber (*The Inspector*), Robert Kent (*Gordon Chase*), Edward Raquello (*Paul Savarin*), George Lynn (*Al Rogers*), Louis Mercier (*The Cab Driver*), John Bleifer (*Ludwig*), George Davis (*Pepito*), George Renavent (*Renault*), George Sorrel (*The Gendarme*)
D: Eugene Forde SCR: Charles S. Belden, Jerry Cady, Robert Ellis & Helen Logan, from characters created by Earl Derr Biggers PHOTOG: Dan Clark MUSIC: Samuel Kaylin
Minor thriller: Oriental sleuth suspected of murder when several people are killed at famed resort

Charlie Chan at the Circus
1936, (USA), 20th-Fox, b&w, 72 mins.
W: Warner Oland (*Charlie Chan*), George Brasno (*Tim*), Keye Luke (*Lee Chan*), Olive Brasno (*Tiny*), J. Carrol Naish (*Tom Holt*), Francis Ford (*Gaines*), Shirley Deane (*Louise Norman*), Maxine Reiner (*Marie Norman*), John McGuire (*Hal Blake*), Paul Stanton (*Joe Kinney*), Boothe Howard (*Dan Farrell*), Drue Leyton (*Nellie Farrell*), Franklyn Farnum (*Mike*), Wade Boteler (*Lt. Macy*), Shia Jung (*Su Toy*)
D: Harry Lachman SCR: Robert Ellis & Helen Logan, from characters created by Earl Derr Biggers PHOTOG: Dan Clark MUSIC: Samuel Kaylin
Standard mystery-thriller: Oriental sleuth visits Big Top, finds murder most foul

Charlie Chan at the Olympics
1937, (USA), 20th-Fox, b&w, 71 mins.
W: Warner Oland (*Charlie Chan*), Katherine DeMille (*Yvonne Roland*), Pauline Moore (*Betty Adams*), Allan Lane (*Richard Masters*), Keye Luke (*Lee Chan*), John Eldredge (*Cartwright*), C. Henry Gordon (*Arthur Hughes*), Morgan Wallace (*Zaraka*), Jonathan Hale (*Hopkins*), Layne Tom Jr. (*Charlie Chan Jr.*), Frederick Vogeding (*Insp. Strasser*), Andrew Tombes (*Chief Scott*), Howard Hickman (*Dr. Burton*), Edward Keane (*The Colonel*), Selmer Jackson (*The Navy Commander*), Don Brodie (*The Radio Announcer*), George Chandler (*The Ship's Radio Announcer*)
D: H. Bruce Humberstone SCR: Paul Burger, Robert Ellis & Helen Logan, from characters created by Earl Derr Biggers PHOTOG: Dan Clark MUSIC: Samuel Kaylin
Standard "Chan" mystery-thriller: Top-secret airplane device stolen, Oriental sleuth trails suspects to Olympic games

Charlie Chan at the Opera
1936, (USA), 20th-Fox, b&w, 66 mins.
W: Warner Oland (*Charlie Chan*), Boris Karloff (*Gravelle*), Keye Luke (*Lee Chan*), Charlotte Henry (*Kitty*), Thomas Beck (*Phil Childers*), Margaret Irving (*Lilli Rochelle*), Nedda Harrigan (*Anita Barelli*), Gregory Gay (*Enrico Barelli*), Frank Conroy (*Whitley*), Guy Usher (*Insp. Regan*), Harland Tucker (*The Private Detective*), William Demarest (*Sgt. Kelly*), Billy Wayne (*The Electrician*), Maurice Cass (*Arnold*), Tom McGuire (*Morris*), Dodo Newton (*The Bar Maid*), Gladden James (*The Secretary*), Eddie Tamblyn (*The Call Boy*), Anthony Hughes (*The Ambulance Doctor*), Fred Kelsey, Bud Geary, Lee Shumway, Stanley Blystone, Richard Powell, Larry Fisher, Ed Parker, Harry Strang, Hilda Vaughn, Jane Keckey, Tony Merlo, Myrtie Bonnilias, Marjorie May Timm, Milton Gowman, Herschel Graham, Leonard Mellon, Pat Cunning, Mary Louise Smith, Tony Roux
D: H. Bruce Humberstone SCR: Scott Darling & Charles S. Belden, from a story by Bess Meredyth, from characters created by Earl Derr Biggers PHOTOG: Lucien Andriot MUSIC: Oscar Levant, William Kernell & Samuel Kaylin
Modest mystery-thriller: Oriental sleuth seeks link between escaped mental patient and threatening notes being received by opera star

Charlie Chan at the Race Track
1936, (USA), 20th-Fox, b&w, 70 mins.
W: Warner Oland (*Charlie Chan*), Helen Wood (*Alice Fenton*), Keye Luke (*Lee*

Chan), Thomas Beck *(Bruce Rogers)*, Gloria Roy *(Catherine Chester)*, Alan Dinehart *(George Chester)*, George Irving *(Maj. Kent)*, Gavin Muir *(Bagley)*, Jonathan Hale *(Warren Fenton)*, G.P. Huntley Jr. *(Denny Barton)*, Frankie Darro *(Tip Collins)*, Junior Coghlan *(Eddie Brill)*, John Rogers *(Mooney)*, John H. Allen *(Streamline Jones)*, Harry Jans *(Al Meers)*, Jack Mulhall *(The 2nd Purser)*, Robert Warwick *(The Police Chief)*, Paul Fix *(The Gangster)*
D: H. Bruce Humberstone SCR: Robert Ellis, Helen Logan & Edward T. Lowe STORY: Lou Breslow & Saul Elkins, from characters created by Earl Derr Biggers PHOTOG: Harry Jackson MUSIC: Samuel Kaylin
Standard "Chan" mystery-thriller: Oriental sleuth arrives in Honolulu to meet racetrack owner, finds him dead

Charlie Chan at the Opera: WARNER OLAND, GREGORY GAY, THOMAS BECK, GUY USHER, FRANK CONROY

Charlie Chan at the Wax Museum
1940, (USA), 20th-Fox, b&w, 63 mins.
W: Sidney Toler *(Charlie Chan)*, Victor Sen Yung *(Jimmy Chan)*, C. Henry Gordon *(Dr. Cream)*, Marc Lawrence *(Steve McBirney)*, Joan Valerie *(Lily Latimer)*, Marguerite Chapman *(Mary Bolton)*, Ted Osborn *(Tom Agnew)*, Michael Visaroff *(Dr. Otto von Brom)*, Hilda Vaughn *(Mrs. Rocke)*, Charles Wagenheim *(Willie Fern)*, Archie Twitchell *(Carter Lane)*, Edward Marr *(Grenock)*, Harold Goodwin *(Edwards)*, Joe King *(Insp. Matthews)*
D: Lynn Shores SCR: John Larkin, from characters created by Earl Derr Biggers PHOTOG: Virgil Miller
Standard "Chan" mystery-thriller: Criminal escapes on way to prison, hides out in wax museum

Charlie Chan at Treasure Island
1939, (USA), 20th-Fox, b&w, 59 mins.
W: Sidney Toler *(Charlie Chan)*, Cesar Romero *(Fred Rhadini)*, Pauline Moore *(Eve Cairo)*, Victor Sen Yung *(Lee Chan)*, June Gale *(Myra Rhadini)*, Douglas Fowley *(Pete Lewis)*, Douglass Dumbrille *(Thomas Gregory/Stuart Salsbury)*, Charles Halton *(Redley)*, Billie Seward *(Bessie Sibley)*, Sally Blane *(Stella Essex)*, Wally Vernon *(Elmer Keiner)*, Donald MacBride *(Chief Kilvaine)*, Trevor Bardette *(Abdul)*, Louis Jean Heydt *(Paul Essex)*, Gerald Mohr *(Dr. Zodiac)*, John Elliott *(The Doctor)*
D: Norman Foster SCR: John Larkin, from characters created by Earl Derr Biggers PHOTOG: Virgil Miller
Standard "Chan" mystery-thriller: Famed Oriental sleuth meets blackmailing mystic at San Francisco Exposition

Charlie Chan Carries On
1931, (USA), Fox, b&w, 76 mins.
W: Warner Oland *(Charlie Chan)*, Marguerite Churchill *(Pamela Potter)*, John Garrick *(Mark Kenaway)*, Marjorie White *(Sadie)*, Warren Hymer *(Max Minchin)*, C. Henry Gordon *(John Ross)*, John T. Murray *(Dr. Lofton)*, George Brent *(Capt. Ronald Keane)*, Peter Gawthorne *(Insp. Duff)*, John Sworn *(Elmer Benbow)*, Jason Robards Sr. *(Walter Honeywood)*, Lumsden Hare *(Insp. Hanley)*, Zeffie Tilbury *(Mrs. Luce)*, Betty Francisco *(Sybil Conway)*, Harry Beresford *(Kent)*, John Rogers *(Martin)*, J.Gunnis Davis *(Eben)*
D: Hamilton MacFadden SCR: Philip Klein & Barry Conners, from Earl Derr Biggers' novel PHOTOG: George Schneiderman
*Early "Chan" mystery-thriller: Murder on around-world cruise. Spanish version **Eran Trece**. Remake of **Charlie Chan's Murder Cruise***

Charlie Chan: Happiness is a Warm Clue
1971, (USA), Univ, color, TV Movie, 96 mins.
W: Ross Martin *(Charlie Chan)*, Leslie Nielsen, Virginia Lee, Rocky Gunn, Louise Sorel, Kathleen Widdoes, Richard Haydn, Don Gordon, Joseph Hindy, Peter Donat, Pearl Hong, Soon-Taik Oh, Pat Gage, Ernest Harada, Adele Yoshioka
D: Daryl Dukes TELEPLAY: Gene Kearney STORY: Simon Last & Gene Kearney, from characters created by Earl Derr Biggers PHOTOG: Richard C. Glouner MUSIC: Robert Prince

A.k.a. **The Return of Charlie Chan**
TVM, standard mystery-thriller: Strange events aboard yacht

Charlie Chan in Castle in the Desert
see Castle in the Desert

Charlie Chan in City in Darkness
1939, (USA), 20th-Fox, b&w, 75 mins.
W: Sidney Toler *(Charlie Chan)*, Lynn Bari *(Marie Dubon)*, Richard Clarke *(Tony Madero)*, Harold Huber *(Marcel)*, Dorothy Tree *(Charlotte Rondell)*, Pedro de Cordoba *(Antoine)*, Leo G. Carroll *(Louis Sentinelli)*, C. Henry Gordon *(Romaine)*, Noel Madison *(Belescu)*, Douglass Dumbrille *(Petroff)*, Lon Chaney Jr. *(Pierre)*, Louis Mercier *(Max)*, Barbara Leonard *(Lola)*, George Davis *(Alex)*, Adrienne d'Ambricourt *(The Landlady)*, Frederick Vogeding *(The Captain)*, Paul Irving *(The Doctor)*, Tommy Seidel *(Phillip)*, George Sorrel *(The Plainclothesman)*, Anita Pike *(The Telegraph Operator)*, Albert Conti *(The Manager)*, Frank Puglia *(The Porter)*, Michael Mark *(The Mechanic)*, Gino Corrado *(The Wine Cellar Owner)*, Major Fred Farrell *(The Man)*, Harry Fleischmann *(Batiste)*, Veola Vonn *(The French Girl)*, Albert Pollett, Jean Del Val, Marek Windheim, Eugene Borden, Alphonse Martell
D: Herbert I. Leeds SCR: Robert Ellis, Helen Logan, Gina Kaus & Ladislas Fodor, from characters created by Earl Derr Biggers PHOTOG: Virgil Miller
Standard "Chan" mystery-thriller: Spies and con men utilize Paris blackouts

Charlie Chan in Egypt
1935, (USA), Fox, b&w, 72 mins.
W: Warner Oland *(Charlie Chan)*, Pat Paterson *(Carol Arnold)*, Thomas Beck *(Tom Evans)*, Rita Cansino (Hayworth) *(Nayda)*, Frank Conroy *(Prof. Thurston)*, Nigel de Brulier *(Edfu Ahmad)*, James Eagles *(Barry Arnold)*, Paul Porcasi *(Fouad Soueida)*, Stepin Fetchit *(Snowshoes)*, Arthur Stone *(Dragoman)*, Anita Brown *(Snowshoes' Girlfriend)*, George Irving *(Prof. Arnold)*, John Davidson *(The Chemist)*, Gloria Roy, Jameson Thomas
D: Louis King SCR: Robert Ellis & Helen Logan, from characters created by Earl Derr Biggers PHOTOG: Daniel B. Clark MUSIC: Samuel Kaylin
Above-average "Chan" mystery-thriller: Oriental sleuth finds trouble pyramiding along Nile when he investigates murder on archeological expedition

Charlie Chan in Honolulu
1938, (USA), 20th-Fox, b&w, 65 mins.
W: Sidney Toler *(Charlie Chan)*, Phyllis Brooks *(Judy Hayes)*, Victor Sen Yung *(Jimmy Chan)*, John King *(Randolph)*, Claire Dodd *(Carol Wayne)*, Eddie Collins *(Al Hogan)*, George Zucco *(Dr. Cardigan)*, Robert Barrat *(Capt. Johnson)*, Marc Lawrence *(Johnnie McCoy)*, Philip Ahn *(Wing Foo)*, Layne Tom Jr. *(Tommy Chan)*, Richard Lane *(Det. Arnold)*, Richard Alexander *(The Sailor)*, Paul Harvey *(The Detective)*
D: H. Bruce Humberstone SCR: Charles S. Belden, from characters created by Earl Derr Biggers PHOTOG: Charles Clarke MUSIC: Samuel Kaylin
Clever "Chan" mystery-thriller: Oriental sleuth stops departure of USA-bound tramp steamer after passenger is shot

Charlie Chan in London
1934, (USA), Fox, b&w, 80 mins.
W: Warner Oland *(Charlie Chan)*, Drue Leyton *(Pamela Gray)*, Douglas Walton *(Paul Gray)*, Mona Barrie *(Lady Mary Bristol)*, Alan Mowbray *(Geoffrey Richmond)*, Ray Milland *(Neil Howard)*, George Barraud *(Maj. Jardine)*, E.E. Clive *(Det. Sgt. Thacker)*, Paul Englund *(Bunny Fothergill)*, Madge Bellamy *(Becky Fothergill)*, Walter Johnson *(Jerry Garton)*, Elsa Buchanan *(Alice Perkins)*, Murray Kinnell *(Philips)*, John Rogers *(Lake)*, David Torrance *(Sir Lionel Bashford)*, Reginald Sheffield *(Flight Cmdr. King)*, Claude King *(The RAF Commandant)*, Montague Shaw *(The Doctor)*, Perry Ivins *(Kemp)*, Helena Grant *(Miss Johnson)*, Phyllis Coghlan *(The Nurse)*, Margaret Mann *(The Maid)*, Arthur Clayton *(The Warden)*, Ann Doran, Carli Taylor, Doris Stone
D: Eugene Forde SCR: Philip MacDonald, from characters created by Earl Derr Biggers PHOTOG: L.W. O'Connell MUSIC: Samuel Kaylin
Well-made "Chan" mystery-thriller: Oriental sleuth has three days to prevent execution of man he believes to be innocent

Charlie Chan in Panama
1940, (USA), 20th-Fox, b&w, 67 mins.
W: Sidney Toler *(Charlie Chan)*, Jean Rogers *(Kathi Lenesch)*, Lionel Atwill *(Cliveden Compton)*, Mary Nash *(Jennie Finch)*, Victor Sen Yung *(Jimmy Chan)*, Kane Richmond *(Richard Cabot)*, Chris-Pin Martin *(Lt. Montero)*, Jack LaRue *(Manolo)*, Edwin Stanley *(Gov. Webster)*, Don Douglas *(Capt. Lewis)*, Addison Richards *(Godley)*, Frank Puglia *(Achmed Halide)*, Eddie Acuff *(The Suspicious Sailor)*, Edward Keane *(Dr. Fredericks)*, Lane Chandler *(The Officer)*, Edward Gargan *(The Plant Worker)*, Jimmie Aubrey *(The Drunken Sailor)*, Wally Vernon *(The Man)*
D: Norman Foster SCR: John Larkin & Lester Ziffren, from characters created by Earl Derr Biggers PHOTOG: Virgil Miller
*Standard "Chan" mystery-thriller: Saboteurs plot to blow up Panama Canal. Remake of **Marie Galante** (1934)*

Charlie Chan in Paris
1935, (USA), Fox, b&w, 70 mins.
W: Warner Oland *(Charlie Chan)*, Mary Brian *(Yvette Lamartine)*, Erik Rhodes *(Max Corday)*, John Miljan *(Dufresne)*, Thomas Beck *(Victor)*, Ruth Peterson *(Renee)*, Minor Watson *(Renaud)*, Murray Kinnell *(Henri Latouche)*, Keye Luke *(Lee Chan)*, Henry Kolker *(Lamartine)*, Perry Ivins *(Bedell)*, John Qualen *(The Concierge)*, Dorothy Appleby *(Nardi)*, Harry Cording *(The Gendarme)*

D: Lewis Seiler   SCR: Philip MacDonald, Edward T. Lowe & Stuart Anthony, from characters created by Earl Derr Biggers   PHOTOG: Ernest Palmer   MUSIC: Samuel Kaylin
Minor "Chan" mystery-thriller: Oriental sleuth investigates bond forgeries

Charlie Chan in Reno
1939, (USA), 20th-Fox, b&w, 70 mins.
W: Sidney Toler (*Charlie Chan*), Ricardo Cortez (*Dr. Ainsley*), Phyllis Brooks (*Vivian Wells*), Victor Sen Yung (*Jimmy Chan*), Slim Summerville (*Sheriff Tombstone Fletcher*), Kane Richmond (*Curtis Whitman*), Pauline Moore (*Mary Whitman*), Eddie Collins (*The Cab Driver*), Kay Linaker (*Mrs. Russell*), Louise Henry (*Jeanne Bently*), Charles D. Brown (*The Police Chief*), Robert Lowery (*Wally Burke*), Iris Wong (*Choy Wong*), Morgan Conway (*George Bently*), Hamilton MacFadden (*The Night Clerk*)
D: Norman Foster   SCR: Philip Wylie, Frances Hyland, Albert Ray & Robert E. Kent, from characters created by Earl Derr Biggers   PHOTOG: Virgil Miller
Minor "Chan" mystery-thriller: Oriental sleuth searches for clues when divorcee is murdered

Charlie Chan in Rio
1941, (USA), 20th-Fox, b&w, 60 mins.
W: Sidney Toler (*Charlie Chan*), Cobina Wright Jr. (*Grace Ellis*), Mary Beth Hughes (*Joan Reynolds*), Ted (Michael) North (*Clark Denton*), Victor Jory (*Alfredo Marana*), Harold Huber (*Chief Souto*), Victor Sen Yung (*Jimmy Chan*), Jacqueline Dalya (*Lola Dean*), Richard Derr (*Ken Reynolds*), Kay Linaker (*Helen Ashby*), Truman Bradley (*Paul Wagner*), Hamilton MacFadden (*Bill Kellogg*), Leslie Denison (*Rice*), Iris Wong (*Lili*), Ann Codee (*Margo*), Eugene Borden (*Armando*)
D: Harry Lachman   SCR: Samuel G. Engel & Lester Ziffren, from characters created by Earl Derr Biggers   PHOTOG: Joseph P. MacDonald   MUSIC: Mack Gordon
Minor "Chan" mystery-thriller: Oriental sleuth finds accused murderess slain

Charlie Chan in Shanghai
1935, (USA), 20th-Fox, b&w, 70 mins.
W: Warner Oland (*Charlie Chan*), Irene Hervey (*Diana Woodland*), Charles Locher (Jon Hall) (*Philip Nash*), Keye Luke (*Lee Chan*), Halliwell Hobbes (*The Police Chief*), Russell Hicks (*James Andrews*), Neil Fitzgerald (*Dakin*), Frederick Vogeding (*Burke*), Harry Strang (*The Chauffeur*), Max Wagner (*The Taxi Driver*), Pat O'Malley (*Belden*)
D: James Tinling   SCR: Robert Ellis, Helen Logan & Joseph Hoffman, from characters created by Earl Derr Biggers   PHOTOG: Rudolph Maté
Standard "Chan" mystery-thriller: Oriental sleuth breaks up opium ring

Charlie Chan in the Chinese Cat
see The Chinese Cat

Charlie Chan in the Secret Service
1944, (USA), Mono, b&w, 63 mins.
W: Sidney Toler (*Charlie Chan*), Mantan Moreland (*Birmingham Brown*), Gwen Kenyon (*Inez*), Arthur Loft (*Jones*), Benson Fong (*Tommie Chan*), Marianne Quon (*Iris Chan*), Lelah Tyler (*Mrs. Winters*), Gene Stutenroth (*Luis Vega*), George Lewis, Barry Bernard, Eddy Chandler, George Lessey, Muni Seroff, Sarah Edwards, Gene Oliver, Dave Clark
D: Phil Rosen   SCR: George Callahan, from characters created by Earl Derr Biggers   PHOTOG: Ira Morgan   MUSIC: Karl Hajos
Standard "Chan" mystery-thriller: Oriental sleuth pursues thief of plans for new torpedo

Charlie Chan on Broadway
1937, (USA), 20th-Fox, b&w, 68 mins.
W: Warner Oland (*Charlie Chan*), Joan Marsh (*Joan Wendall*), Keye Luke (*Lee Chan*), J. Edward Bromberg (*Murdock*), Louise Henry (*Billie Bronson*), Joan Woodbury (*Marie Collins*), Marc Lawrence (*Thomas Mitchell*), Donald Woods (*Speed Patton*), Leon Ames (*Buzz Moran*), Douglas Fowley (*Johnny Burke*), Toshia Mori (*Ling Tse*), Harold Huber (*Insp. Nelson*), Creighton Hale (*The Reporter*), Lon Chaney Jr. (*The Desk Man*), Sidney Fields (*The Porter*), Eugene Borden (*Louis*), Charles Williams (*Meeker*), William Jeffrey (*The Coroner*), Norman Ainsley (*The Steward*), Philip Morris (*The Customs Officer*), George Regas (*The Hindu*), George Guhl (*Smitty*), Beulah Hutton (*The Telephone Operator*), Sam Ash (*The Waiter*), Harry Depp (*Snapper*), Sherry Hall, Don Brodie, Billy Wayne, Paddy O'Flynn, Franklin Parker, Charles Haefeli, Allen Fox, Lester Dorr, Robert Middlemass, Art Miles, Victor Adams
D: Eugene Forde   SCR: Art Arthur, Robert Ellis, Helen Logan, Charles S. Belden & Jerry Cady, from characters created by Earl Derr Biggers   PHOTOG: Harry Jackson
Standard "Chan" mystery-thriller: Smuggler involves Oriental sleuth

Charlie Chan's Chance
1932, (USA), Fox, b&w, 73 mins.
W: Warner Oland (*Charlie Chan*), Alexander Kirkland (*John Douglas*), Marian Nixon (*Shirley Marlowe*), H.B. Warner (*Insp. Fife*), Ralph Morgan (*Barry Kirk*), Linda Watkins (*Gloria Garland*), James Kirkwood (*Insp. Flannery*), James Todd (*Kenneth Dunwood*), Charles McNaughton (*Paradise*), Edward Piel Sr. (*Li Gung*), Herbert Bunston (*Garrick Enderly*), Jimmy Wang
D: John Blystone   SCR: Barry Connors & Philip Klein, from Earl Derr Biggers' novel *Behind That Curtain*
Standard "Chan" mystery-thriller: Oriental sleuth solves murder of Scotland Yard inspector. Remake of 1929 film

Charlie Chan's Courage
1934, (USA), Fox, b&w, 72mins.
W: Warner Oland (*Charlie Chan*), Drue Leyton (*Paula Graham*), Donald Woods (*Bob Crawford*), Murray Kinnell (*Martin Thorne*), Paul Harvey (*J.P. Madden/Jerry Delaney*), Harvey Clark (*Prof. Gamble*), Si Jenks (*Will Holley*), Jerry Jerome (*Maydorff*), Jack Carter (*Victor Jordan*), James Wang (*Wong*), DeWitt C. Jennings (*Constable Brackett*), Reginald Mason (*Mr. Crawford*), Virginia Hammond (*Mrs. Jordan*), Francis Ford (*Hewitt*)
D: George Hadden & Eugene Forde   SCR: Seton I. Miller, from Earl Derr Biggers' novel *The Chinese Parrot*   PHOTOG: Hal Mohr   MUSIC: Samuel Kaylin
Standard "Chan" mystery-thriller: Oriental sleuth finds precious necklace inspires murder cf. The Chinese Parrot

Charlie Chan's Greatest Case
1933, (USA), Fox, b&w, 71 mins.
W: Warner Oland (*Charlie Chan*), Heather Angel (*Carlotta Eagan*), Roger Imhoff (*The Beachcomber*), Walter Byron (*Harry Jennison*), John Warburton (*John Quincy Winterslip*), Virginia Cherrill (*Barbara Winterslip*), Ivan Simpson (*Brade*), Francis Ford (*Capt. Hallett*), Robert Warwick (*Dan Winterslip*), Clara Blandick (*Minerva Winter-slip*), William Stack (*James Eagan*), Claude King (*Capt. Arthur Cope*), Gloria Roy (*Arlene Compton*), Cornelius Keefe (*Steve Letherbee*)
D: Hamilton MacFadden   SCR: Lester Cole & Marion Orth, from Earl Derr Biggers' novel *The House Without a Key*   PHOTOG: Ernest Palmer   MUSIC: Samuel Kaylin
Standard "Chan" mystery-thriller: Oriental sleuth investigates theft of treasure chest. Remake of 1926 Pathe serial

Charlie Chan's Murder Cruise
1940, (USA), 20th-Fox, b&w, 75 mins.
W: Sidney Toler (*Charlie Chan*), Lionel Atwill (*Dr. Suderman*), Marjorie Weaver (*Paula Drake*), Victor Sen Yung (*Jimmy Chan*), Robert Lowery (*Dick Kenyon*), Don Beddoe (*James Ross*), Leo G. Carroll (*Prof. Gordon*), Kay Linaker (*Mrs. Pendleton*), Charles Middleton (*Mr. Walters*), Cora Witherspoon (*Susie Watson*), Harlan Briggs (*The Coroner*), Claire DuBrey (*Mrs. Walters*), Leonard Mudie (*Walter Pendleton*), James Burke (*Wilkie*), Layne Tom Jr. (*Willie Chan*), Richard Keene (*Buttons*), Cliff Clark (*The Policeman*), Montague Shaw (*Insp. Duff*), Walter Miller (*The Officer*), Harry Strang (*The Guard*)
D: Eugene Forde   SCR: Robertson White & Lester Ziffren, from characters created by Earl Derr Biggers   PHOTOG: Virgil Miller
Clever "Chan" mystery-thriller: Oriental sleuth pursues masked strangler on world cruise. Remake of Charlie Chan Carries On

Charlie Chan's Secret
1936, (USA), 20th-Fox, b&w, 71 mins.
W: Warner Oland (*Charlie Chan*), Rosina Lawrence (*Alice Lowell*), Charles Quigley (*Dick Williams*), Edward Trevor (*Fred Gaige*), Astrid Allwyn (*Janice Gaige*), Jerry Miley (*Allen Coleby*), Ivan "Dusty" Miller (*Morton*), Henrietta Crossman (*Henrietta Lowell*), Herbert Mundin (*Baxter*), Gloria Roy (*Carlotta*), Jonathan Hale (*Warren T. Phelps*), Arthur Edmund Carewe (*Prof. Bowan*), James T. Mack (*The Fingerprint Man*), Egon Brecher (*Ulrich*), William N. Bailey (*Harris*), Landers Stevens (*The Coroner*), Francis Ford (*The Boat Captain*)
D: Gordon Wiles   SCR: Robert Ellis, Helen Logan & Joseph Hoffman, from characters created by Earl Derr Biggers   PHOTOG: Rudolph Maté
Good "Chan" mystery-thriller: Heir to fortune disappears

Charlie's Ghost Story
1994, (USA), SHO-TV, color, 90 mins.
W: Cheech Marin, Anthony Edwards
Made-for-Cable, minor fantasy: Ghost helps boy deal with bully

Charlotte's Web
1973, (USA-Jap), Para, color, 94 mins.
VOICES: Debbie Reynolds (*Charlotte*), Henry Gibson (*Wilbur*), Paul Lynde (*Templeton*), Agnes Moorehead (*The Goose*), Rex Allen (*The Narrator*), Martha Scott (*Mrs. Arable*), Danny Bonaduce (*Avery*), Dave Madden (*The Old Sheep*), William B. White (*Henry Fussy*), Don Messick (*Geoffrey*), Robert Holt (*Homer Zuckerman*), Herb Vigran (*Lurvy*), Pam Ferdin (*Fern Arable*), Joan Gerber (*Mrs. Zuckerman/Mrs. Fussy*), John Stephenson (*Arable*)
D: Charles A. Nichols & Iwao Takamoto   SCR: Earl Hamner Jr., from a story by E.B. White   PHOTOG: Roy Wade, Dick Blundell, Ralph Migliori, Dennis Weaver & George Epperson   MUSIC & LYRICS: Richard M. & Robert B. Sherman
Well-made animated fantasy: Spider advises piglet

Charly
1968, (USA), Selmur Pictures-Robertson Assocs./CRC, color, 103 mins.
W: Cliff Robertson (*Charly*), Claire Bloom (*Alice*), Dick Van Patten (*Bert*), Leon Janney (*Dr. Nemur*), Ruth White (*The Landlady*), Lilia Skala (*Dr. Straus*), Ralph Nelson, Barney Martin
P & D: Ralph Nelson   SCR: Stirling Silliphant, from Daniel Keye's short story & Nebula Award-winning novel *Flowers for Algernon*, and TV play
PHOTOG: Arthur Ornitz   MUSIC: Ravi Shankar
SF classic with Oscar-winning performance by Cliff Robertson: Scientists advance retarded man to state of genius

The Charm That Charmed
1915, (GB), Martin/DFSA, b&w, 680 ft. (207.3m)

D: Dave Aylott
Minor fantasy: Man dreams he finds magic charm

The Chase
1946, (USA), Nero/UA, b&w, 84 mins.
W: Peter Lorre, Robert Cummings, Michele Morgan, Jack Holt, Steve Cochran, Lloyd Corrigan, Don Wilson
P: Seymour Nebenzal   **D:** Arthur Ripley   **SCR:** Philip Yordan, from Cornell Woolrich's novel *The Black Path of Fear*   **PHOTOG:** Franz Planer   **MUSIC:** Michel Michelet
Standard melodrama: Shell-shocked ex-serviceman foils criminal, falls for his wife

Chase a Crooked Shadow
1957, (GB), Douglas Fairbanks Jr.-Assoc. Dragon/WB, b&w, 87 mins.
W: Anne Baxter (*Kimberly*), Richard Todd (*Ward*), Herbert Lom (*Vargas*), Alexander Knox (*Chandler Bridson*), Faith Brook (*Mrs. Whitman*), Alan Tilvern (*Carlos*), Thelma d'Aguilar (*Maria*)
P: Douglas Fairbanks Jr. (also in epilogue)   **D:** Michael Anderson   **SCR:** David Osborn & Charles Sinclair   **PHOTOG:** Erwin Hillier   **MUSIC:** Matyas Sieber
Taut thriller: Man claims to be heiress' dead brother

Le Chateau Hante (The Haunted Castle)
1897, (Fr), Star, b&w, 20m (65.6 ft./1.1 mins.)
WRIT, P & D: Georges Melies
A.k.a. **Le Manoir Maudit (The Cursed Mansion)** *USA & GB retitle,* **The Devil's Castle**
Standard fantasy

Le Chaudron Infernal (The Infernal Cauldron)
1903, (Fr), Star, b&w, 36m (118.1 ft./2 mins.)
D: Georges Melies
A.k.a. **The Infernal Cauldron and the Phantasmal Vapours**
Standard fantasy

The Chauffeur's Dream
1908, (GB), Urban Trading Co., b&w, 420 ft. (128m)
D: W.R. Booth
Standard fantasy: Chauffeur dreams of driving under sea, down volcano, etc. reissued 1915

Cheaters at Play
1932, (USA), Fox, b&w, 7 reels
W: Thomas Meighan (*Michael Lanyard*), Charlotte Greenwood (*Mrs. Crozier*), William Bakewell (*Maurice Parry*), James Kirkwood (*Det. Crane*), Barbara Weeks (*Fenno Crozier*), William Pawley (*Wally*), Ralph Morgan (*Freddie Isquith*), Linda Watkins (*Tess Boyer*), Olin Howland (*The Secretary*), Andres Van Haden (*The Captain*), Dewey Robinson (*Strong Arm Algy*)
D: Hamilton MacFadden   **SCR:** Malcolm Stuart Boylan, from Joseph Louis Vance's novel *First Cabin*
Standard "Lone Wolf" melodrama: Detective and rogue investigate jewel theft at sea

The Checkered Flag
1963, (USA), Mercury, color, 110 mins.
W: Evelyn King, Joe Morrison, Charles G. Martin, Peggy Vendig
P: Herb Vendig   **D & SCR:** William Grefe
Minor melodrama: Lust and murder on hot-wheels circuit

Cheerleader Camp
1988, (USA), color, 89 mins.
W: Betsy Russell, leif Garrett, Lucinda Dickey, Rebecca Ferratti, Lorie Griffin, George Flower, Teri Weigel
D: John Quinn
A.k.a. **Bloody Pom Poms**
Minor thriller: Psycho stalks sumer-camp beauties.

Cheese Mites
1903, (GB), Urban Trading Co.-Micro Bioscope, b&w, 150 ft. (45.7m)
D: F. Martin Duncan
Standard comedy: Diner examines cheese through magnifying glass, sees mites magnified "30 diameters"

The Cheese Mites: or, Lilliputians in a London Restaurant
1901, (GB), R.W. Paul, b&w, 70 ft. (21.3m)
D: Walter R. Booth
Minor fantasy short: Six-inch high sailors dance upon diner's cheese

The Chef's Revenge
1907, (GB), R.W. Paul, b&w, 238 ft. (72.5m)
D: J.H. Martin
Minor fantasy short: Chef's love rival baked in oven, shrunk

Chelsea Bird
1971, (GB), Freeman/Saxon, color, 10 mins.
W: Fred Marshall (*The Man*), Leslie Miller (*The Girl*)
Standard short fantasy: Fashion model's make-believe world

Chemical Portraiture
1909, (GB), Urban Trading Co., b&w, 260 ft. (79.2m)
D: F. Percy Smith
Standard fantasy: Liquid screen changes Czar Nicholas' face into that of King Alfonso

Cherry 2000
1988, (USA), Orion, color, 100 mins.
W: Melanie Griffith (*E. Johnson*), David Andrews (*Sam Treadwell*), Pamela Gidley (*Cherry 2000*)
D: Steve DeJarnatt
Standard SF-adventure: Desert guide vs. futuristic villains

Le Chevalier Mystère (The Mysterious Knight)
1899, (Fr), Star, b&w, 40m (131.2 ft./2.2 mins.)
D: Georges Melies
Standard fantasy

Les Chevaliers du Demon
see **The Hell-Fire Club**

Chicago May, The Adventuress
1909, (GB), Anglo-American Films, b&w, 985 ft. (300.2m)
Standard crime-thriller (in 26 scenes): Girl leaves home, becomes criminal

Un Chien Andalou (An Andalousian Dog)
1928, (Fr), b&w, 24 mins.
W: Luis Bunuel, Salvadore Dali, Pierre Batcheff, Simone Marevil, Jaime Miravilles
WRIT, P & D: Luis Bunuel & Salvadore Dali
Classic short: Exploration of distortion as artistic technique

The Child
1977, (USA), Valiant Int'l, color, 95 mins.
W: Rosalie Cole, Laurel Barnett
P: Robert Dadashian   **D:** Robert Voskanian   **SCR:** Ralph Lucas   **MUSIC:** Michael Quatro
A.k.a. **Kill and Go Hide!**
Minor horror-fantasy: Little girl makes dead rise

A Child, A Wand And A Wish
1912, (GB), B&C/MP, b&w, 825 ft. (254m)
W: Helen Beresford (*Molly Grey*), Maudie Dagmar (*Babs*), Dick Tyrrell (*The Shopkeeper*)
D: H.O. Martinek
Standard melodrama: Sick widow's daughter steals pantomime magic wand, is helped by rich neighbors

The Child and the Fiddler
1910, (GB), Hepworth, b&w, 750 ft. (228.6m)
D: Theo Bouwmeester
Standard crime-thriller: Amnesiac girl kidnapped, forced to dance

The Child and the Killer
1959, (GB), Danziger/UA, b&w, 65 mins.
W: Patricia Driscoll (*Peggy Martin*), Robert Arden (*Capt. Joe Marsh*), Richard Williams (*Tommy Martin*), Gordon Sterne (*The Sgt.*), Ryck Rydon (*Mather*), Robert Raglan (*The Inspector*), John McLaren (*Maj. Finch*)
P: Edward J. & Harry Lee Danziger   **D:** Max Varnel   **STORY:** Brian Clemens & Eldon Howard
Standard crime-thriller: Army deserter forces widow's young son to aid him

The Child Detective
1912, (GB), Hepworth, b&w, 600 ft. (182.9m)
D: Bert Haldane
Standard crime-thriller: Blind man's daughter leads police to burglars

Child in the House
1956, (GB), Laureate/Eros, b&w, 88 mins.
W: Phyllis Calvert (*Evelyn Acheson*), Eric Portman (*Henry Acheson*), Stanley Baker (*Stephen Lorimer*), Mandy Miller (*Elizabeth Lorimer*), Dora Bryan (*Cassie*), Percy Herbert (*Sgt. Taylor*), Joan Benham (*Vera McNally*), Martin Miller (*Prof. Topolsky*), Victor Maddern (*Bert*), Joan Hickson, Alfie Bass
P: S. Benjamin Fisz   **D:** C. Raker Endfield & Charles de la Tour   **SCR:** C. Raker Endfield, from a novel by Janet McNeil
Standard crime-thriller: Rich woman tricks niece, gets her to reveal fugitive father

Child of Darkness, Child of Light
1991, (USA), Wilshire Court/USA-TV, color, 95 mins.
W: Anthony John Denison, Brad Davis, Sela Ward, Claudette Nevins, Viveca Lindfors, Paxton Whitehead, Kristin Dattilo, Sydney Penny, Alan Oppenheimer, Eric Christmas, John DeMita, Richard McKenzie, Joshua Lucas, Mark Tassoni, Peter Holden, Patrick Ryan, Vana O'Brien, Michelle Guthrie, Betty Moyer, Brendan Fraser, Joe Ivy, Barbara Irvin, Mary Marsh, Russ Fast, Lance Rosen, Hank Cartwright, Mark Allen, Richard Wiltshire, Karen Trumbo, Julie Emery, Al Strobel, Lindsey Smith-Sands, Steven Clark Pachosa
D: Marina Sargenti   **TELEPLAY:** Brian Taggart, from James Patterson's novel *Virgin*   **PHOTOG:** Tobias Schliessler   **SPCL-FX:** Roy Downey   **MUSIC:** Jay Gruska
TVM, minor fantasy-thriller: Priest investigates sinister virgin pregnancies

Child of Glass
Walt Disney, 93 mins.
W: Nina Foch, Olivia Barash
D: John Erman

97

Child of Glass
1978, (USA), Made for TV, color
W: Steve Shaw, Katy Kurtzman (*Blossom*), Anthony Zerbe (*Timmons*), Barbara Barrie (*Emily*), Biff McGuire (*Joe*)
TVM, standard fantasy: Girl's ghost haunts plantation

Child of Satan
see To the Devil a Daughter

The Children
1980, (USA), Albright Films/Red Northal, color, 89 mins.
W: Gil Rogers, Martin Shakar, Gale Garnett, Jessie Abrams, Joy Glaccum, Tracy Griswold, Michelle LeMothe, June Berry, Suzanne Barnes, Rita Montone, John Codiglia, Michael Carrier, Martin Brennan, Diane Deckard, David Platt, Arthur Chase, Edward Terry, J.D. Clarke, James Klawin, X. Ben Fakackt, Clara Evans, Ray Delmolino, Peter Maloney, Jeptha Evans, Julie Carrier, Shannon Bolin, Nathanael Albright, Sarah Albright
D: Max Kalmanowicz **SCR:** Carlton J. Albright & Edward Terry **PHOTOG:** Barry Abrams **MUSIC:** Harry Manfredini
Minor SF-horror: Pollution turns kids into zombies

Children of the Corn
1984, (USA), Gatlin/New World, color, 87 mins.
W: Peter Horton (*Burt*), Linda Hamilton (*Vicky*), R.G. Armstrong (*Diehl*), Courtney Gains, Robby Kiger, John Franklin, Jonas Marlowe, Annemarie McEvoy, Julie Maddalena, John Philbin
P: Donald P. Borchers & Terrence Kirby **D:** Fritz Kiersch **SCR:** George Goldsmith, from Stephen King's story **PHOTOG:** Raoul Lomas **SPCL-FX:** Max W. Anderson **MUSIC:** Jonathan Elias
Minor thriller: Cult of murderous youths menaces strangers

Children of the Corn II: The Final Sacrifice
1993, (USA), Dimension, color, 93 mins.
W: Terence Knox, Paul Scherrer, Ryan Bollman (*Micah*), Christie Clark (*Lacey*), Ned Romero, Rosalind Allen, Ted Travelstead
D: David Price **SCR:** Gilbert Adler & A.L. Katz, from Stephen King's short story "Children of the Corn" **PHOTOG:** Levie Isaacks
Standard thriller

Children of the Corn III: Urban Sacrifice
1995, (USA), Dimension, video, color, 103 mins.
W: Daniel Cerny, Ron Melendez, Mari Morrow, Duke Stroud, Jim Metzler, Nancy Lee Grahn
D: James D.R. Hickox **SCR:** Dode Levenson, from characters created by Stephen King **PHOTOG:** Gerry Lively **MUSIC:** Daniel Licht
Made-for-Video, standard thriller

Children of the Corn IV
1996, (USA), color, 85 mins.
W: Naomi Watts, Karen Black, Brent Jennings, William Windom, Jaime Renee Smith
from characters created by Stephen King
Made-for-Video, standard fantasy-thriller: Coed returns to home town, finds children controlled by mysterious youth

Children of the Damned
1963, (GB), Lawrence P. Bachmann/MGM, b&w, 90 mins.
W: Ian Hendry (*Dr. Tom Lewellin*), Alan Badel (*Dr. David Neville*), Barbara Ferris (*Susan Elliott*), Alfred Burke (*Colin Webster*), Sheila Allen (*Diana Looran*), Ralph Michael (*The Defense Minister*), Martin Miller (*Prof. Gruber*), Harold Goldblatt (*Harib*), Clive Powell (*Paul*), Lee Yoke-Moon (*Mi Ling*), Bessie Love, Patrick White, Andre Mikhelson, Gerald Delsol, Roberta Rex, Mahdu Mathen, Frank Summerscale
P: Ben Arbeid **D:** Anton M. Leader **SCR:** Jack Briley **PHOTOG:** David Boulton **MUSIC:** Ron Goodwin
*Modest SF-thriller, semi-sequel to **The Village of the Damned** (1960): Psychic children regarded as threat to national security*

Children of the Forest
1912, (GB), Fitz Films/Western Import, b&w, 425 ft. (129.5m)
W: Roy Royston (*The Boy*), Marie Royston (*The Girl*)
WRIT & D: Lewin Fitzhamon
Standard adventure-thriller: Boy and dog trail gypsy who kidnapped sister

Children of the Full Moon
1984, (GB), color, 60 mins.
W: Christopher Cazenove, Celia Gregory, Diana Dors, Robert Urquhart, Jacof Witken
D: Tom Clegg
Minor horror-fantasy: Couple meets werewolf family

Children of the Night (1970)
*see **Daughters of Darkness** (1970)*

Children of the Night
1992, (USA), Fangoria Films, color, 95 mins.
W: Karen Black, Ami Dolenz (*Lucy*), Maya McLaughlin (*Cindy*), David Sawyer (*Czakyr*), Peter DeLuise (*Mark Gardner*), Garrett Morris (*Matty*), Evan

MacKenzie (*Father Frank Aldin*)
D: Tony Randel **PHOTOG:** Richard Michalak
Minor horror-fantasy: Evil priest imprisons vampiric mother and daughter

Children Shouldn't Play with Dead Things
1972, (USA), Brandywine-Motionarts/Geneni, color, 70 mins.
W: Alan Ormsby (*Alan*), Anya Ormsby (*Anya*), Valerie Mamches (*Val*), Jeffrey Gillen (*Jeff*), Jane Daly, Paul Cronin, Seth Sklarey, Roy Engleman, Robert Philip, Bruce Solomon, Robert Sherman, Alecs Baird, Curtis Bryant, Gordon Gilbert, Peter Burke, Robert Smedley
D: Benjamin Clark **SCR:** Benjamin Clark & Alan Ormsby **PHOTOG:** Jack McGowan **MUSIC:** Carl Zittrer
Amateurish horror-thriller: Troupe of actors disturbs burial ground

A Child's Dream of Christmas
1912, (GB), GS Films/Hepworth, b&w, 750 ft. (228.6m)
D: Gilbert Southwell
Standard fantasy: Girl dreams of fairy-tale characters

Child's Play
1954, (GB), Group 3/British Lion, b&w, 68 mins.
W: Mona Washbourne (*Miss Goslett*), Peter Martyn (*PC Parker*), Dorothy Alison (*Margery Chappell*), Ingeborg Wells (*Lea Blotz*), Carl Jaffe (*Carl Blotz*), Ballard Berkeley (*Dr. Nightingale*), Joan Young (*Mrs. Chizzler*), Robert Raglan (*The Superintendent*), Christopher Beeny (*Horatio Flynn*), Wendy Westcott (*Mary Huxley*), Ian Smith (*Tom Chizzler*), Patrick Wells (*Hans Einstein Blotz*)
P: Herbert Mason **D:** Margaret Thomson **SCR:** Peter Blackmore **STORY:** Don Sharp
Standard SF-comedy: Research scientist's son invents atomic popcorn

Child's Play
1985, (GB), color, 90 mins.
W: Mary Crosby (*Ann*), Nicholas Clay (*Mike*), Debbie Chasen (*Sarah*), Joanna Joseph (*The Child*), Suzanne Church (*The Mother*)
Standard SF-thriller: Impenetrable wall traps family

Child's Play
1988, (USA), David Kirschner/MGM/UA, color, 88 mins.
W: Catherine Hicks (*Karen Barclay*), Chris Sarandon (*Mike Norris*), Alex Vincent (*Andy Barclay*), Brad Dourif (*Charles Lee Ray*), Dinah Manoff (*Maggie Peterson*), Jack Colvin (*Dr. Ardmore*), Tommy Swerdlow (*Jack Santos*), Neil Giunioli (*Eddie Capputo*), Juan Ramirez (*The Peddler*), Alan Wilder (*Mr. Criswell*), Richard Baird (*The News Reporter at the Toy Store*), Raymond Oliver (*Dr. Death*), Aaron Osborne (*The Orderly*), Tyler Hard (*Mona*), Ted Liss (*George*), Roslyn Alexander (*Lucy*), Robert Kane (*The Male Newscaster*), Leila Hee Olsen (*The Female Newscaster*)
D: Tom Holland **SCR:** Don Mancini, John Lafia & Tom Holland **PHOTOG:** Bill Butler **MUSIC:** Joe Renzetti
Modest horror-fantasy: Doll possessed by murderer's spirit

Child's Play 2
1990, (USA), Univ, color, 95 mins.
W: Alex Vincent (*Andy Barclay*), Christine Elise (*Kyle*), Brad Dourif (*Voice of*

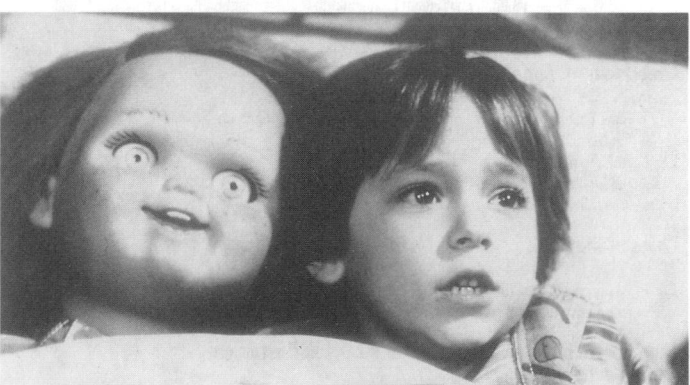

Child's Play: CHUCKY AND ALEX VINCENT

Chucky), Jenny Agutter (*Joanne Simpson*), Gerrit Graham (*Phil Simpson*), Beth Grant (*Miss Kettlewell*), Grace Zabriskie (*Grace Poole*), Peter Haskell, Bill Stevenson
D: John Lafia **SCR:** Don Mancini **PHOTOG:** Stefan Czapsky **MUSIC:** Graeme Ravell **SONG:** New China
Standard fantasy-thriller: Demonic doll returns for revenge

Child's Play 3
1991, (USA), Univ, color, 90 mins.
W: Justin Whalin (*Andy Barclay*), Perrey Reeves (*De Silva*), Jeremy Sylvers (*Tyler*), Travis Fine (*Shelton*), Brad Dourif (*Voice of Chucky*), Dean Jacobson (*Whitehurst*), Dakin Matthews, Peter Haskell, Andrew Robinson, Matthew Walker
D: Jack Bender **SCR:** Don Mancini **PHOTOG:** John R. Leonetti **MUSIC:**

Cory Lerios & John D'Andrea
Standard fantasy-thriller: Demonic doll commits more mayhem

A Child's Strategy
1912, (GB), HB Films/Cosmo, b&w, 635 ft. (193.6m)
<u>W:</u> Dorothy Batley (*The Girl*), Ernest G. Batley (*The Father*)
<u>D & STORY:</u> Ernest G. Batley
Standard crime-thriller: Girl trails robber

Chiller
1985, (USA), Polar/CBS-TV, color, 95 mins.
<u>W:</u> Michael Beck (*Miles Creighton*), Beatrice Straight (*Marion Creighton*), Laura Johnson (*Leigh Kenyon*), Paul Sorvino (*Rev. Penny*), Jill Schoelen (*Stacey*), Dick O'Neill (*Clarence Beeson*), Alan Fudge (*Dr. Stricklin*), Anne Seymour, Russ Marin, Kenneth White, Craig Richard Nelson, Jerry Lacy, Edward Blackoff, Ned Wertimer, Wendy Goldman, Joseph Whipp, Brian Libby, Melanie F. Williams, Karen Huie, Perla Walter, Starletta DuPois, Mimi Meyer-Craven, Bill Dearth, William Forward, Clare Nono, Roger Hampton
<u>WRIT & P:</u> J.D. Feigelson   <u>D:</u> Wes Craven   <u>PHOTOG:</u> Frank Thackery
   <u>SPCL-FX:</u> Ken Pepiot   <u>MUSIC:</u> Dana Kaproff
TVM, modest SF-horror: Woman's son returns from suspended animation, is evil incarnate

Chillers
1988, (USA), color, 90 mins.
<u>W:</u> Jesse Emery, Marjorie Fitzsimmons, Laurie Pennington, Jim Wolfe, David Wohl
<u>D & SCR:</u> Daniel Boyd
Minor horror-fantasy: Travellers attacked by vampires and zombies

The Chill Factor
see A Cold Night's Death

Chilling
1981, (Austral), Filmco Ltd., color, 91 mins.
<u>W:</u> Diana McLean, Jon Blake, Guy Doleman, Jan Kingsbury, Kit Taylor, David Franklin, Joanne Samuel, Danny Adcock, Daniel Cumerford, Raoul Teague, Aaron Nitties, John Higgins, Chris Bench, Stuart Fryd-man, Alan Baskin, Gerry Sont, Gabby Mason, Mardi Kennedy, Brita Kingsbury
<u>WRIT:</u> Terry O'Connor   <u>PHOTOG:</u> David Eggby   <u>MUSIC:</u> Mike Harvey
<u>SONGS:</u> *Can't We Start Over, Safe Beneath the Water, Cutting Loose, Danger Danger, The Key, Good Time Lady, Theme for Valerie, Turn Out the Light, & Always Let Him Know*
Standard thriller: Insurance investigator uncovers brutal murders

The Chilling
1989, (USA), color, 91 mins.
<u>W:</u> Linda Blair, Dan Haggerty, Troy Donahue, Jack A. De Rieux, Ron Vincent
<u>D:</u> Deland Nuse & Jack A. Sunseri
Minor horror-thriller: Carnivorous zombies attack Kansas City

The Chimes
1914, (GB), Hepworth/Renters, b&w, 2,500 ft. (762m)
<u>W:</u> Stewart Rome (*Richard*), Violet Hopson (*Meg Veck*), Warwick Buckland (*Trotty Veck*), Harry Gilbey (*Sir Richard Bowley*), Johnny Butt (*Alderman Cute*), Muriel Smith (*Lilian*), John Mc Andrews (*Will Fern*)
<u>D & SCR:</u> Thomas Bentley, from a story by Charles Dickens
Standard fantasy: Father Time reveals tragic future

The Chimney's Secret
1915, (USA), Univ, b&w, 1 reel
<u>W:</u> Lon Chaney Sr.
<u>WRIT & D:</u> Lon Chaney Sr.
Standard thriller: Murder uncovered

The Chimney Sweep
see Jack le Ramoneur

A Chinaman's First Day in London
1912, (GB), Gaumont, b&w, 320 ft. (97.5m)
Standard comedy-fantasy: Chinaman thwarts boys by electrifying pigtail

The China Syndrome
1979, (USA), Michael Douglas/IPC Films/Col, color, 122 mins.
<u>W:</u> Jack Lemmon (*Jack Godell*), Jane Fonda (*Kimberly Wells*), Michael Douglas (*Richard Adams*), Peter Donat (*Don Jacovich*), Scott Brady (*Herman DeYoung*), James Hampton (*Bill Gibson*), Wilford Brimley (*Ted Spindler*), Richard Herd (*Evan McCormack*), Daniel Valdez (*Hector Salas*), Stan Bohrman (*Pete Martin*), Tom Eure (*Tommy*), James Karen (*Mac Churchill*), Donald Hotton (*Dr. Lowell*), Michael Alaimo (*Greg Minor*), Khalilah Ali (*Marge*), Paul Larson (*D.B. Royce*), Ron Lombard (*Barney*), Daniel Lewk (*Donny*), Nick Pellegrino (*Borden*), Allan Chinn (*Holt*), Martin Fiscoe (*The Control Guard*), Alan Kaul (*The TV Director*), E. Hampton Beagle (*Mort*), Dennis McMullen (*Robertson*), James Hall (*Harmon*), David Pfeiffer (*David*), Lewis Arquette (*Hatcher*), Rita Taggart (*Rita Jacovich*), Michael Mann, David Eisenbise, Frank Cavestani, Reuben Collins, Carol Helvey, David Arnsen, Trudy Lane, Jack Smith Jr., Betty Harford, Diandra Morrell, Donald Bishop, Al Baietti, Darrell Larson, Roger Pancake, Joe Lowry, Dennis Barker, Harry M. Williams, Joseph Garcia, James Kline, Alan Beckwith, Clay Hodges, Val Clenard
<u>P:</u> Michael Douglas   <u>D:</u> James Bridges   <u>SCR:</u> Mike Gray, T.S. Cook & James Bridges   <u>PHOTOG:</u> James Crabe   <u>SONG:</u> (by Stephen Bishop), *Somewhere in Between*
Celebrated melodrama: Woman reporter investigates coverup of near-disaster at nuclear plant

Chinatown at Midnight
1950, (USA), Col, b&w, 67 mins.
<u>W:</u> Hurd Hatfield, Jean Willes
Standard thriller

Chinese Boxes
1985, (GB-W. Ger), Road Movies/Palace, color, 87 mins.
<u>W:</u> Will Patton (*Langdon Marsh*), Gottfried John (*Zwemmer*), Adelheid Arndt (*Sarah*), Robbie Coltrane (*Harwood*), Beate Jensen (*Donna*), Susanne Meierhofer (*Eva*), Martin Muller (*Frank Wolf*), Jonathan Kinsler (*Alan*), Chris Sievernich (*Snake*), L.M. Kit Carson (*Crewcut*), Christopher Petit (*The Gunman*), Jochen von Vietinghoff, Ben De Jong, Edgar Hinz, Michael Buttner, Michael Maichle
<u>P:</u> Chris Sievernich   <u>D:</u> Christopher Petit   <u>STORY:</u> Christopher Petit & Kit Carson   <u>PHOTOG:</u> Peter Harvey   MUSIC: Gunther Fischer, et al.
Standard thriller: Heroin smuggler involved in girl's murder

The Chinese Cat
1944, (USA), Mono, b&w, 65 mins.
<u>W:</u> Sidney Toler (*Charlie Chan*), Mantan Moreland (*Birmingham Brown*), Benson Fong (*Tommie Chan*), Weldon Heyburn (*Harvey Dennis*), Joan Woodbury (*Leah Manning*), Ian Keith (*Recknick*), Sam Flint (*Thomas Manning*), Anthony Warde (*Catlen*), Betty Blythe (*Mrs. Manning*), Cy Kendall (*Walter Deacon*), I. Stanford Jolley (*The Henchman*), Dewey Robinson (*Salos*), John Davidson (*Carl/Kurt*), Jack Norton (*The Hotel Clerk*), George Chandler (*The Doorman*), Luke Chan
<u>D:</u> Phil Rosen   <u>SCR:</u> George Callahan, from characters created by Earl Derr Biggers   <u>PHOTOG:</u> Ira Morgan
Minor "Chan" mystery-thriller: Asian figurine holds key to diamond smuggling and murder

The Chinese Cat: SIDNEY TOLER AND BENSON FONG

A Chinese Ghost Story
1987, (Hong Kong), color, 93 mins.
<u>W:</u> Leslie Cheung, Wong Tsu Hsien, Wu Ma
<u>D:</u> Ching Siu Tung
Standard fantasy: Spectre seduces scholar

A Chinese Ghost Story II
1990, (Hong Kong), color, 104 mins.
<u>W:</u> Leslie Cheung, Wong Tsu Hsien, Michelle Li, Wu Ma, Jacky Cheung
<u>D:</u> Ching Siu-Tung
Standard fantasy: Satanic forces attack

Chinese Magic
1900, (GB), R.W. Paul, b&w, 100 ft. (30.5m)
<u>D:</u> Walter Booth
A.k.a. Yellow Peril
Minor fantasy short: Chinese conjurer changes girl into butterfly, himself into giant bat

The Chinese Parrot

1927, (USA), Univ, b&w, 7 reels
W: Marian Nixon (*Sally Phillimore*), Florence Turner (*Mrs. Sally Phillimore*), Hobart Bosworth (*Philip Madden/Jerry Delaney*), Edmund Burns (*Robert Eden*), K. Sojin (*Charlie Chan*), Albert Conti (*Martin Thorne*), Fred Esmelton (*Alexander Eden*), Edgar Kennedy (*Maydorf*), George Kuwa (*Louie Wong*), Etta Lee (*The Gambler*), Jack Trent (*Jordan*), Slim Summerville, Anna May Wong, Dan Maxon
D: Paul Leni **SCR:** J. Grubb Alexander, from Earl Derr Biggers' novel **PHOTOG:** Ben Kline
Standard "Chan" mystery-thriller: Priceless necklace stolen. cf. **Charlie Chan's Courage**

The Chinese Puzzle

1919, (GB), Ideal, b&w, 5,000 ft. (1524m)
W: Leon M. Lion (*Marquis Li Chung*), Lilian Braithwaite (*Lady de la Haye*), Milton Rosmer (*Sir Roger de la Haye*), Charles Rock (*Sir Aylmer Brent*), Sybil Arundale (*Naomi Melsham*), Sam Livesey (*Paul Markatel*), Dora de Winton (*Mrs. Melsham*), Reginald Bach (*Henrik Stroom*), Alexander Sarner (*Raoul d'Armand*)
D & SCR: Fred Goodwins, from a play by Leon M. Lion & Marion Bower
Standard crime-thriller: Mandarin takes blame when wife of friend's son steals secret papers

The Chinese Ring

1947, (USA), Mono, b&w, 68 mins.
W: Roland Winters (*Charlie Chan*), Mantan Moreland (*Birmingham Brown*), Warren Douglas (*Sgt. Bill Davidson*), Victor Sen Yung (*Tommie Chan*), Louise Currie (*Peggy Cartwright*), Byron Foulger (*Armstrong*), Philip Ahn (*Capt. Kong*), Jean Wong (*Princess Mei Ling*), Thayer Roberts (*Capt. Kelso*), Chabing (*Lilly Mae Wong*), Paul Bryar (*The Sergeant*), Charmienne Harker (*The Stenographer*), George L. Spaulding (*Dr. Hickey*), Thornton Edwards (*The Hotel Clerk*), Lee Tung Foo, Richard Wang, Spencer Chan, Kenneth Chuck
D: William Beaudine **SCR:** Scott Darling, from characters created by Earl Derr Biggers **PHOTOG:** William A. Sickner **MUSIC:** Edward J. Kay
remake of **Mr. Wong in Chinatown**, *working title,* **The Red Hornet**
Minor "Chan" mystery-thriller: Chinese princess comes to USA to purchase airplanes, is found murdered in Oriental sleuth's den

A Chinese Vengeance

1914, (GB), Phoenix Film Agency, b&w, 3,000 ft. (914.4m)
Standard crime-thriller: Chinese priest kidnaps daughter of collector who bought stolen idol

The Chinese Web

1978, (USA), CBS-TV, color, 96 mins.
W: Nicholas Hammond, Robert F. Simon, Chip Fields, Rosalind Chao, Benson Fong, Ellen Bry, Ted Danson
D: Donald McDougall
TVM culled from "Amazing Spider-Man" teleseries: Superhero prevents World War III

Ching-Ching's Revenge

1910, (GB), Walturdaw, b&w, 665 ft. (202.7m)
Standard thriller: Discharged Chinese servant poisons employer's sugar and ties his daughter to mill wheel

The Chipmunk Adventure

1987, (USA), Orion, color, 76 mins.
D: Janice Karman **SCR:** Janice Karman & Ross Bagdasarian **MUSIC:** Randy Edelman
Standard animated fantasy: Furry trio involved with diamond smugglers

Chitty Chitty Bang Bang

1968, (GB), Warfield-D.F.I./UA, color, 145 mins.
W: Dick Van Dyke (*Caractacus Potts*), Sally Ann Howes (*Truly Scrumptious*), Lionel Jeffries (*Grandpa Potts*), Gert Frobe (*Baron Bomburst*), Anna Quayle (*Baroness Bomburst*), Robert Helpmann (*The Child Catcher*), Benny Hill (*The Toymaker*), Davy Kaye (*The Admiral*), James Robertson Justice (*Lord Scrumptious*), Heather Ripley (*Jemima Potts*), Adrian Hall (*Jeremy Potts*), Barbara Windsor (*The Blonde*), Stanley Unwin (*The Chancellor*), Peter Arne (*The Captain*), Victor Maddern (*The Junkman*), Max Bacon (*The Orchestra Leader*), Felix Felton (*The Minister*), Totti Truman Taylor (*The Duchess*), Richard Wattis (*The Secretary*), Max Wall (*The Inventor*), Alexander Dore
P: Albert Broccoli **D:** Ken Hughes **SCR:** Roald Dahl & Ken Hughes, from Ian Fleming's novel **PHOTOG:** Christopher Challis **SPCL-FX:** John Stears **MUSIC & LYRICS:** Robert B. Sherman & Richard M. Sherman **MUSIC SPRVSR & CONDUCT:** Irwin Kostal **SONGS:** Toots Sweets, The Old Bamboo, Hushabye Mountain, & Truly Scrumptious
Juvenile fantasy: Inventor and children transported to sinister country

A Choice of Weapons

1976, (GB), Combat/WB, color, 90 mins.
W: John Mills (*Bertie Cook*), Donald Pleasence (*Sir Giles Marley*), Barbara Hershey Marion Evans), David Birney (*Sir John Gifford*), Margaret Leighton (*Ma Gore*), Brian Glover (*Sidney Gore*), Peter Cushing (*Sir Edward Gifford*), John Savident (*Oliver Griggs*), John Hallam (*Sir Roger Monckton*), Keith Buckley The Herald), Neil McCarthy (*Ben Willoughby*), Thomas Heathcote (*The Tramp*), Bernard Hill (*Blind Freddie*), Diane Langton (*Ruby*), Kevin Lloyd (*Little Willie*), Una Brandon-Jones (*Martha Willoughby*), Max Faulkner (*Sir Harold Carslake*), Bill Weston (*Sir Anthony Beeson-White*), Mike Horsburgh (*Sir Thomas Hartwell*)

P & STORY: Fred Weintraub & Paul Heller **D:** Kevin Connor **SCR:** Julian Bond, Steven Rossen & Mitchell Smith **PHOTOG:** Alan Hume **MUSIC:** Frank Cordell
A.k.a. **Trail by Combat**
Modest crime-thriller: Secret society executes escaped felons.

C.h.o.m.p.s.

1979, (USA), AIP, color
W: Wesley Eure, Valerie Bertinelli, Jim Backus, Chuck McCann, Red Buttons, Regis Toomey
P: Joseph Barbera **D:** Don Chaffey **SCR:** Dick Robbins & Duane Poole
Standard SF-comedy: Electronics genius invents robot dog

Chopper Chicks in Zombietown

1991, (USA), Troma, color, 84 mins.
W: Jamie Rose (*Dede*), Catherine Carlen (*Rox*), Vicki Frederick (*Jewel*), Lycia Naff (*T.C.*), Kristina Loggia (*Jojo*), Don Calfa (*Ralph Willum*), Billy Bob Thornton, Martha Quinn
WRIT & D: Dan Hoskins **PHOTOG:** Tom Fraser **MUSIC:** Daniel Day
Minor SF-adventure: Future femmes battle monsters

Chopping Mall

1986, (USA), Concorde/Trinity, color, 77 mins.
W: Kelli Maroney, John Terlesky, Tony O'Dell, Russell Todd, Karrie Emerson, Barbara Crampton, Suzee Slater, Mary Woronov, Nick Segal, Paul Bartel, Dick Miller, Gerrit Graham, Angela Aames, Mel Welles, Paul Coufos, Arthur Roberts, Toni Naples, Morgan Douglas, Ace Mask, Will Gill Jr., Lawrence Guy, Lenny Juliano, Robert Greenberg, Maurie Gallagher
D: Jim Wynorski **SCR:** Jim Wynorski & Steve Mitchell **PHOTOG:** Tom Richmond **MUSIC:** Chuck Cirino
Modest SF-thriller: Malfunctioning security robots stalk youths. orig. to be titled **Killbots**

The Chosen

see **Holocaust 2000**

Chosen Survivors

1974, (USA), Metromedia/Col, color, 99 mins.
W: Alex Cord (*Steven Mayes*), Diana Muldaur (*Alana Fitzgerald*), Jackie Cooper (*Raymond Couzins*), Richard Jaeckel (*Gordon Ellis*), Bradford Dillman (*Peter Macomber*), Pedro Armendariz Jr. (*Luis Cabral*), Barbara Babcock (*Lenore Chrisman*), Gwen Mitchell (*Carrie Draper*), Lincoln Kilpatrick (*Woody Russo*), Christina Moreno (*Kristin Lerner*), Nancy Rodman (*Claire Farraday*), Kelly Lange (*Mary Louise Borden*)
D: Sutton Roley **SCR:** H.B. Cross & Joe Reb Moffly **PHOTOG:** Gabriel Torres **MUSIC:** Fred Karlin
Standard SF-melodrama: Occupants of underground bunker menaced by vampire bats

Christine

1983, (USA), Polar/Col, color, 107 mins.
W: Keith Gordon (*Arnie Cunningham*), John Stockwell (*Dennis Guilder*), Alexandra Paul (*Leigh Cabot*), Harry Dean Stanton (*Junkins*), Roberts Blossom (*George LeBay*), John Ostrander (*Buddy Repperton*), Robert Prosky (*Will Darnell*), Christine Belford (*Regina Cunningham*), David Spielberg (*Mr. Casey*), Malcolm Danare (*Moochie*), Steven Tash (*Rich*), Kelly Preston (*Roseanne*), Stuart Charno (*Vandenberg*), Marc Poppel (*Chuck*), Robert Barnell (*Michael Cunningham*)
D: John Carpenter **SCR:** Bill Phillips, from Stephen King's novel **PHOTOG:** Donald M. Morgan **SPCL-FX:** Roy Arbogast **MUSIC:** John Carpenter & Alan Howarth
Superior horror-fantasy: Demonic auto transforms life of awkward teen

The Christmas Angel

see **L'Ange de Noel**

A Christmas Card: or, A Story of Three Homes

1905, (GB), R.W. Paul, b&w, 215 ft. (65.5m)
D: J.H. Martin
Standard fantasy short: Fairy takes children to visit Santa, reissued 1906

A Christmas Carol

1914, (GB), London/Fenning, b&w, 1,340 ft. (408.4m)
W: Charles Rock (*Ebenezer Scrooge*), Edna Flugrath (*Belle*), George Bellamy (*Bob Cratchit*), Mary Brough (*Mrs. Cratchit*), Franklyn Bell-amy (*Fred*), Edward O'Neill (*Jacob Marley*), Arthur Cullin (*Christmas Past*), Wyndham Guise (*Christmas Present*), Assheton Tonge (*Christmas Future*)
D & SCR: Harold Shaw, from Charles Dickens' story
Standard fantasy: Spirits reform miser

A Christmas Carol

1938, (USA), MGM, b&w, 69 mins.
W: Reginald Owen (*Ebenezer Scrooge*), Terry Kilburn (*Tiny Tim*), Gene Lockhart (*Bob Cratchit*), Leo G. Carroll (*Marley's Ghost*), Barry Mackay (*Fred*), Kathleen Lockhart (*Mrs. Cratchit*), Lynne Carver (*Bess*), Ann Rutherford (*Ghost of Christmas Past*), Lionel Braham (*Ghost of Christmas Present*), Ronald Sinclair (*Young Scrooge*), D'Arcy Corrigan (*Ghost of Christmas Future*), June Lockhart, Ronald Squire
P: Joseph L. Mankiewicz **D:** Edwin L. Marin **SCR:** Hugo Butler, from Charles Dickens' classic **PHOTOG:** Sidney Wagner **MUSIC:** Franz Waxman
Modest version of yuletide fantasy: Spirits transform miser

A Christmas Carol (1951)
see Scrooge (1951)

A Chrsitmas Carol: TERRY KILBURN AND REGINALD OWEN

A Christmas Carol
1960, (GB), Alpha/Anglo-Amalgamated, b&w, 28 mins.
<u>W</u>: John Hayter, Stewart Brown, Gordon Mulholland
<u>P & D</u>: Robert Hartford-Davis, from Charles Dickens' story
Standard short fantasy: Ghosts reform miser

A Christmas Carol
1982, (Austral), color
Animated version of Dickens' classic

A Christmas Carol
1984, (USA-GB), Entertainment Partners/CBS-TV, color, 102 mins.
<u>W</u>: George C. Scott *(Ebenezer Scrooge)*, Roger Rees *(Fred Holywell)*, Frank Finlay *(Marley's Ghost)*, Angela Pleasence *(Ghost of Christmas Past)*, Edward Woodward *(Ghost of Christmas Present)*, David Warner *(Bob Cratchit)*, Anthony Walters *(Tiny Tim)*, Susannah York *(Mrs. Cratchit)*, Lucy Gutteridge *(Belle)*, Nigel Davenport *(Silas Scrooge)*, Mark Strickson *(Young Scrooge)*, Timothy Bateson *(Fezziwig)*, Peter Woodthorpe *(Old Joe)*, John Quarmby *(Mr. Hacking)*, Michael Carter *(Ghost of Christmas Yet to Come)*, Caroline Langrishe *(Janet Holywell)*, Michael Gough *(Mr. Poole)*, Liz Smith *(Mrs. Dilber)*, Joanne Whalley *(Fan)*, Brian Pettifer *(Ben)*, Spencer Banks *(Dick Wilkins)*, Danny Davies *(Forbush)*, Cathrine Hall *(Meg)*, John Sharp *(Tipton)*, Derck Francis *(Pemberton)*
<u>P</u>: William Storke & Alfred Kelman   <u>D</u>: Clive Donner   <u>TELEPLAY</u>: Roger O. Hirson, from Charles Dickens' classic   <u>PHOTOG</u>: Tony Imi   <u>SPCL-FX</u>: Martin Gutteridge   <u>MUSIC</u>: Nick Bicat   <u>SONG</u>: *God Bless Us Every One*
TVM, good rendering of yuletide favorite: Spirits help miser reform

A Christmas Carol
1997, (USA), color, 70 mins.
<u>VOICE</u>: Tim Curry
from Charles Dickens' classic
Standard animated musical-fantasy: Miser reforms

The Christmas Dream
see Le Reve de Noel

Christmas Every Day
1996, (USA), Goodman-Rosen/MTM/Fox-TV, color, 95 mins.
<u>W</u>: Erik von Detten, Robert Hays, Bess Armstrong, Yvonne Zima, Robert Curtis-Brown, Robin Riker, Julia Whelan, Kara Woods
<u>D</u>: Larry Peerce   <u>TELEPLAY</u>: Stephen Alix & nancey Silver   <u>STORY</u>: Stephen Alix   <u>PHOTOG</u>: Gideon Porath   <u>MUSIC</u>: Billy Goldenberg
TVM, standard comedy-fantasy: Boy finds he is constantly reliving Christmas Day

Christmas Evil
1983, (USA), Edward R. Pressman, color, 100 mins.
<u>W</u>: Brandon Maggart *(Harry)*, Dianne Hull *(Jackie)*, Scott McKay *(Fletcher)*, Joe Jamrog *(Frank)*, Peter Friedman *(Grosch)*, Ray Barry *(Gleason)*, Bobby Lesser *(Gottlieb)*, Sam Gray *(Grilla)*, Ellen McElduff *(Harry's Mother)*, Patty Richardson
<u>D & SCR</u>: Lewis Jackson   <u>PHOTOG</u>: Ricardo Aronovich
A.k.a. **You Better Watch Out**
Standard thriller: Terror haunts Yuletide

The Christmas That Almost Wasn't
1966, (USA-It), Childhood Productions, color, 89 mins.
<u>W</u>: Rossano Brazzi, Paul Tripp, Mischa Auer, Sonny Fox
<u>D</u>: Rossano Brazzi   <u>SCR</u>: Paul Tripp
Juvenile fantasy-adventure: Meanie buys North Pole, tries to evict Santa Claus

Chronicle of a Death Foretold
1987, (It Fr), color, 110 mins.
<u>W</u>: Rupert Everett, Ornella Muti, Gian Maria Volonte, Irene Papas, Lucia Bose, Alain Cuny
<u>D</u>: Francesco Rosi, from Garcia Marquez' novel
Unusual melodrama: South American villagers kill man who deflowered girl

Chronicle of the Gray House
see Chronik von Grieshuus

Chronik von Grieshuus (Chronicle of the Gray House)
1923, (Ger), Union-Ufa, b&w, 9,731 ft. (2966m)
<u>W</u>: Paul Hartmann, Lil Dagover, Gertrud Arnold, Rudolph Forster, Ar-thur Kraussneck, Gertrud Welcker
<u>D</u>: Arthur von Gerlach   <u>SCR</u>: Thea von Harbou, from a story by Theodor Storm   <u>PHOTOG</u>: Karl Drews, Fritz Arno Wagner & Erich Nietzchmann
Unusual melodrama: Mansion has unsavory past

Chronopolis
1982, (Fr), color, 70 mins.
<u>D</u>: Piotr Kamier
Standard SF-fantasy: Aliens manipulate time

Chu Chin Chow
1923, (GB-Ger), Graham-Wilcox, b&w, 12,250 ft. (3733.8m)
<u>W</u>: Betty Blythe *(Zahrat)*, Herbert Langley *(Abou Hassan)*, Eva Moore *(Alcolma)*, Randle Ayrton *(Kasim Baba)*, Jameson Thomas *(Omar)*, Judd Green *(Ali Baba)*, Olaf Hytten *(Mukbill)*, Jeff Barlow *(Mustafa)*, Dora Levis *(Mahbubah)*, Dacia *(The Dancer)*
<u>D & SCR</u>: Herbert Wilcox, from the play by Oscar Asche & Frederick Norton
Standard fantasy: Girl flees robber-sheikh

Chu Chin Chow
1934, (GB), Gainsborough/Gaumont, b&w, 102 mins.
<u>W</u>: George Robey *(Ali Baba)*, Fritz Kortner *(Abu Hassan)*, Anna May Wong *(Zahrat)*, John Garrick *(Nur-al-din)*, Pearl Argyle *(Marjanah)*, Malcolm MacEachern *(Abdullah)*, Lawrence Hanray *(Kasim Baba)*, Dennis Hoey *(Rakham)*, Francis L. Sullivan *(The Caliph)*, Sydney Fairbrother *(Mahbubah)*, Frank Cochrane *(Mustafa)*, Thelma Tuson *(Alcolom)*, Kyoshi Takase *(The Entertainer)*
<u>D</u>: Walter Forde   <u>SCR</u>: Edward Knoblock, L. DuGarde Peach & Sidney Gilliat, from the play by Oscar Asche & Frederick Norton
Standard musical-fantasy: Slave girl foils thief. US: 1934; reissue **Ali Baba Nights** *(Lippert, 1953)*

C.H.U.D.
1984, (USA), Bonime Assocs./New World, color, 85 mins.
<u>W</u>: John Heard, Daniel Stern, Christopher Curry, Kim Greist, Laure Mattos, Brenda Currin, Ivan Brogger
<u>D</u>: Douglas Cheek   <u>SCR</u>: Parnell Hall   <u>STORY</u>: Shepard Abbott   <u>PHOTOG</u>: Peter Stein   <u>MUSIC</u>: Cooper Hughes
Minor SF-thriller: Subterranean cannibals attack

A Chump at Oxford
1940, (USA), Hal Roach/UA, b&w, 63 mins.
<u>W</u>: Stan Laurel, Oliver Hardy, Forrester Harvey, Wilfred Lucas, James Finlayson, Peter Cushing
<u>D</u>: Alfred Goulding   <u>SCR</u>: Charles Rogers, Felix Adler & Harry Langdon   <u>PHO-TOG</u>: Art Lloyd
Good comedy, Laurel & Hardy's answer to Robert Taylor vehicle **A Yank at Oxford***: Nitwits upset order of distinguished school*

The Church
1990, (It), color, 110 mins.
<u>W</u>: Tomas Arana, Hugh Quarshie, Feodor Chaliapin Jr.
<u>D</u>: Michele (Michael), Soavi   <u>SCR</u>: Dario Argento   <u>MUSIC</u>: Keith Emerson
Unusual horror-fantasy: Demons plague cathedral renovation

Chusingura
1932, (Jap), b&w
<u>W</u>: Teinosuke Kinugasa
<u>WRIT & D</u>: Teinosuke Kinugasa
A.k.a. **The Loyal 47 Ronin** *and* **The Vengeance of the 47 Ronin**
Classic action-thriller: Crime and revenge in ancient Nippon

Chusingura
1963, (Jap), Toho, color, 204 mins.
<u>W</u>: Koshiro Matsumoto, Chusha Ichikawa, Yuzo Kayama, Toshiro Mi-fune, Yoko Tsukasa, Setsuko Hara, Tatsuya Mihashi, Akira Takarada
<u>D</u>: Hiroshi Inagaki   <u>SCR</u>: Toshio Yasumi, from old Samurai legends   <u>PHOTOG</u>: Kazuo Yamada   <u>MUSIC</u>: Akira Ifukube
Colorful remake of durable adventure: Nipponese warlords seek revenge

La Chute de la Maison Usher (The Fall of the House of Usher)
1927, (Fr), A.C.E., b&w, 45 mins.
<u>W</u>: Jean Dubencourt, Margaret Gance, Charles Lamay
<u>D</u>: Jean Epstein, from Edgar Allan Poe's short story   <u>PHOTOG</u>: Lucas
*Arty version of Poe classic: Man's sister entombed alive. cf. **House of Usher***

La Cigale et la Fourmi (The Grasshopper and the Ant)
1897, (Fr), Star, b&w, 20m (65.6 ft./1.1 mins.)
<u>D</u>: Georges Melies
Standard fantasy

Cinder-Elfred
1914, (GB), Hepworth, b&w, 950 ft. (289.6m)
<u>W</u>: Tom Powers *(Elfred)*
<u>D</u>: Hay Plumb   <u>STORY</u>: Percy Darmstatter
Standard comedy-fantasy: Poor artist dreams fairy gives him dress suit to wear to American girl's ball

Cinderella (1899)
*see **Cendrillon***

Cinderella
1907, (GB), Hepworth, b&w, 1,200 ft. (365.8m)
<u>W</u>: Frank Wilson *(Prince Charming)*, Dolly Lupone *(Cinderella)*, Gertie Potter *(The Fairy)*, Thurston Harris *(The Baron)*
<u>D</u>: Lewin Fitzhamon
Standard fantasy: Fairy godmother helps drudge attend royal ball

Cinderella
1911, (USA), Selig, b&w
<u>W</u>: Mabel Taliaferro *(Cinderella)*, Lillian Leighton, Thomas J. Carrigan, Olive Cox, Josephine Miller, Frank Weed
based on Charles Perrault's fairy-tale classic

Cinderella
1911, (USA), Thanhouser, b&w
based on Charles Perrault's fairy-tale classic

Cinderella
1912, (GB), Empire Films/MP, b&w, 997 ft. (303.9m)
<u>WRIT & D</u>: Arthur Cooper, from Charles Perrault's fairy-tale classic
Standard fantasy: Fairy story enacted by toys

Cinderella
1913, (GB), Hepworth, b&w, 8 ft. (2.4m)
<u>W</u>: Gertie Potter *(Cinderella)*
<u>D</u>: Harry Buss, from a sketch by Herbert C. Rideout
Standard fantasy short with sound: Fairy aids drudge

Cinderella (1922)
*see **Aschenputtel***

Cinderella (1923)
*see **Der Verlorene Schuh***

Cinderella
1950, (USA), Walt Disney, color, 74 mins.
<u>VOICES</u>: Ilene Woods *(Cinderella)*, William Phipps *(The Prince)*, Eleanor Audley *(The Stepmother)*, Rhoda Williams, Lucille Bliss, Verna Felton
<u>SONGS</u>: *A Dream Is a Wish Your Heart Makes & Bibbidi Bobbidi Boo*
Classic animated fantasy: Drudge becomes princess

Cinderella
1961, (Russ), Janus, color, 81 mins.
<u>W</u>: The Bolshoi Ballet, Gennady Ledyakh, Raisa Struchkova, Elena Vanke
<u>P & D</u>: Rostislav Zakharov & Alexander Row   <u>SCR</u>: Alexander Row, Alexander Ginzburg, & Rostislav Zakharov, from Charles Perrault's fairy-tale classic

Cinderella
1966, (Mex), Childhood, color
based on Charles Perrault's fairy-tale classic

Cinderella
1997, (USA), ABC-TV, color
<u>W</u>: Brandy *(Cinderella)*, Whitney Houston *(The Fairy Godmother)*, Bernadette Peters *(The Stepmother)*, Whoopi Goldberg *(The Queen)*, Victor Garber *(The King)*, Paolo Montalban *(The Prince)*, Jason Alexander *(The Valet)*, Veanne Cox, Natalie Desselle
<u>D</u>: Robert Iscove   <u>TELEPLAY</u>: Robert L. Freedman, from the Rodgers & Hammerstein musical   <u>PHOTOG</u>: Ralf Bode
TVM, lavish musical-fantasy

Cinderella and the Fairy Godmother
1898, (GB), b&w, 75 ft. (22.9m)
<u>W</u>: Laura Bayley *(Cinderella)*
<u>D</u>: George Albert Smith
from Charles Perrault's fairy-tale classic "Cinderella"

Cinderella: or, The Glass Slipper
1912, (Fr), Star/Pathe, b&w, 615m (2,017.7 ft./34.1 mins.)
<u>W</u>: Louise Lagrange *(Cinderella)*
<u>D</u>: Georges Melies
Standard fantasy: Drudge finds royal love

Cinderella, Italian Style
*see **C'era Una Volta***

Cinderella's Glass Slipper
*see **The Glass Slipper***

Cinderella 2000
1977, (USA), Independent Int'l, color, 95 mins (also 86 mins.)
<u>W</u>: Catharine Erhardt, Jay B. Larson, Vaughn Armstrong
<u>P & D</u>: Al Adamson   <u>SCR</u>: Bud Donnelly   <u>MUSIC</u>: Sparky Sugarman
Minor eroto-fantasy: Mistreated beauty meets bizarre creatures

Cinderella Up-to-Date
1909, (Fr), Star, b&w, 292m (958 ft./16.2 mins.)
<u>D</u>: Georges Melies
Standard fantasy: Modern drudge finds true love

Cinderfella
1960, (USA), Para, color, 91 mins.
<u>W</u>: Jerry Lewis *(Fella)*, Anna Maria Alberghetti *(Princess Charmaine)*, Judith Anderson *(The Stepmother)*, Ed Wynn *(The Fairy Godfather)*, Henry Silva, Robert Hutton, Count Basie, Joe Williams
<u>P</u>: Jerry Lewis   <u>WRIT & D</u>: Frank Tashlin   <u>PHOTOG</u>: Haskell Boggs   <u>SPCL-FX</u>: John P. Fulton   <u>MUSIC</u>: Walter Scharf   <u>SONGS</u>: *Let Me Be a People, Count Basie's Cute,* et al.
Entertaining spoof of Cinderella: Fairy godfather aids youth in pursuit of princess

Cinq Survivants
*see **Five***

Cinque Tombe per un Medium (Five Tombs for a Medium)
1965, (It), M.B.S. Cinematografica-Int'l Entertainment, b&w, 85 mins.
<u>W</u>: Barbara Steele *(Clio Hauff)*, Alfred Rice *(Dr. Nemek)*, Walter Brandi *(Albert Kovaks)*, Tilde Till *(Luise)*, Alan Collins *(Kurt)*, Marilyn Mitchell *(Corinna Hauff)*, Richard Garrett *(Riccardo Garrone)*, Ennio Balbo *(The Paralytic)*, Steve Robinson
<u>P & D</u>: Ralph Zucker   <u>SCR</u>: Roberto Natale & Romano Migliorini   <u>PHOTOG</u>: Charles Brown   <u>MUSIC</u>: Aldo Piga
*USA retitle (1974), **Terror-Creatures from the Grave**. A.k.a. **The Tombs of Horror**
Standard horror-thriller: Dead occultist gains revenge on his murderers*

The Circle
*see **The Vicious Circle** (1957)*

Circle of Danger
1951, (GB), Coronado/RKO, b&w, 86 mins.
<u>W</u>: Ray Milland *(Clay Douglas)*, Patricia Roc *(Elspeth Graham)*, Marius Goring *(Sholto Lewis)*, Hugh Sinclair *(Hamish McArran)*, Naunton Wayne *(Reggie Sinclair)*, Marjorie Fielding *(Mrs. McArran)*, Edward Rigby *(Idwal Llewellyn)*, Dora Bryan *(Bubbles)*, John Bailey *(Pape Llewellyn)*, Colin Gordon *(Col. Fairbairn)*, Michael Brennan *(Bert Oakshott)*, Reginald Beckwith *(Oliver)*, David Hutcheson *(Tony Wrexham)*
<u>P</u>: David E. Rose & Joan Harrison   <u>D</u>: Jacques Tourneur   <u>SCR</u>: Philip MacDonald, from his novel   <u>PHOTOG</u>: Oswald Morris   <u>MUSIC</u>: Robert Farnon
Standard mystery: American probes brother's death in England

Circle of Death
1960, (Mex), b&w
<u>W</u>: Sarita Montiel, Raul Ramirez
Minor thriller: Businessman tries murder to gain control of wife's fortune

Circle of Deceit
1998, (USA), ABC-TV, color, 95 mins.
<u>W</u>: Janine Turner, Esai Morales *(Jeff)*, Dean Wray *(Walker)*, Robert Wisden *(Coopersmith)*, Tracy Griffith *(Donna)*, Joanna Cassidy *(Elaine)*, Matthew Prior *(Jackson)*, Jerry Wasserman *(Leo Pappas)*, L. Harvey Gold, Marcy Goldberg, Norma Jean Wick, B.J. Harrison, Nadia Leigh
<u>D</u>: Alan Metzger   <u>TELEPLAY</u>: Karen Clark   <u>PHOTOG</u>: Ron Stannett   <u>MUSIC</u>: Brian Adler
TVM, standard thriller: Wife of abusive husband fakes her murder

Circle of Iron
1978, (GB), Avco Embassy, color, 102 mins.
<u>W</u>: David Carradine, Jeff Cooper, Christopher Lee, Eli Wallach, Roddy McDowall, Erica Creer
<u>P</u>: Paul Maslansky & Sandy Howard   <u>D</u>: Richard Howard   <u>SCR</u>: Stirling Silliphant & Stanley Mann
*Standard martial arts-fantasy: Naive pilgrim seeks "Book of Enlightenment." A.k.a. **The Silent Flute***

Circuitry Man

1990, (USA), IRS Media/Skourascolor, 93 mins.
<u>W</u>: Jim Metzler (*Danner*), Dana Wheeler-Nicholson (*Lori*), Dennis Christopher (*Leech*), Lu Leonard, Vernon Wells, Barbara Alyn Woods, Dennis Christopher
<u>D & SCR</u>: Steven Lovy   <u>MUSIC</u>: Deborah Holland
Standard SF-thriller: Diabolic crook pursues post-apocalypse bodyguard and her android companion. cf. **Plughead Rewired: Circuitry Man II**

Circumstances Unknown

1995, (USA), color, 91 mins.
<u>W</u>: Judd Nelson, Isabel Glasser, William R. Moses, Phillip MacKenzie, Rhys Huber, William B. Davis, Sheila Moore, Garry Chalk, Duncan Fraser
<u>D</u>: Robert Lewis   <u>SCR</u>: Thomas Hood & Emily Shoemaker, from a novel by Jonellen Heckler   <u>PHOTOG</u>: Bruce Worrall   <u>MUSIC</u>: Joseph Conlan
Minor thriller: Jealous killer targets unhappily-married friends

Circumstantial Evidence

1910, (GB), Hepworth, b&w, 600 ft. (182.9m)
<u>D</u>: Bert Haldane
Standard crime-thriller: Tramp sees girl steal traveler's bag

Circumstantial Evidence

1945, (USA), 20th-Fox, b&w, 67 mins.
<u>W</u>: Michael O'Shea, Lloyd Nolan
Standard thriller

Circumstantial Evidence

1952, (GB), ACT Films/Monarch, b&w, 61 mins.
<u>W</u>: Rona Anderson (*Linda Harrison*), Patrick Holt (*Michael Carteret*), John Arnatt (*Steve Harrison*), John Warwick (*Pete Hanken*), Frederick Leister (*Sir Edward Carteret*), Ronald Adam (*Sir William Harrison*), June Ashley (*Rita Hanken*), Peter Swanwick (*Charley Pott*), Ballard Berkeley (*Insp. Hall*), Lisa Lee Gladys Vavasour)
<u>P</u>: Phil Brandon   <u>D</u>: Dan Birt   <u>SCR</u>: Allan Mackinnon, from his story "The Judge Sees the Light"
Standard crime-thriller: Blackmailed doctor accused of killing fiancee's husband

Circus Angel

1965, (Fr), b&w, 80 mins.
<u>W</u>: Philippe Avron, Mirielle Negre
<u>D</u>: Albert Lamorisse
Unusual fantasy: Nightgown transforms burglar into angel

Circus of Blood

see *Berserk*

Circus of Fear

1965, (GB), Amalgamated/AIP, color, 83 mins.
<u>W</u>: Christopher Lee (*Gregor*), Leo Genn (*Insp. Elliott*), Eddi Arent (*Eddie*), Anthony Newlands (*Barberini*), Heinz Drache (*Carl*), Klaus Kinski (*Manfred*), Margaret Lee (*Gina*), Cecil Parker (*Sir John*), Suzy Kendall (*Natasha*), Maurice Kaufmann (*Mario*), Victor Maddern (*Mason*), Skip Martin (*Mr. Big*)
<u>P</u>: Harry Alan Towers   <u>D</u>: John Moxey   <u>SCR</u>: Peter Welbeck
USA retitle, **Psycho-Circus**, *released in USA in b&w*
Minor thriller: Brutal murders in circus milieu

Circus of Horrors

1960, (GB), Lynx/Independent Artists/Herman Cohen/AIP, color, 91 mins.
<u>W</u>: Anton Diffring (*Rossiter/Dr. Bernard Schuler*), Erika Remberg (*Elissa*), Donald Pleasence (*Vanet*), Yvonne Monlaur (*Nicole Vanet*), Jane Hylton (*Angela Webb*), Kenneth Griffith (*Martin Webb*), Conrad Phillips (*Insp. Arthur Ames*), Yvonne Romain (*Melina*), Jack Gwillim (*Supt. Andrews*), Vanda Hudson (*Magda von Meck*), Colette Wilde, John Merivale, Kenny Baker
<u>P</u>: Julian Wintle & Leslie Parkyn   <u>D</u>: Sidney Hayers   <u>SCR</u>: George Baxt   <u>PHOTOG</u>: Douglas Slocombe   <u>MUSIC</u>: Franz Reizenstein & Muir Mathieson   <u>SONG</u>: Look for a Star, reissued 1962
Entertaining thriller: Fugitive plastic surgeon turns disfigured criminals into circus of beauty

Cisaruv Pekar, Pekaruv Cisar (The Emperor's Baker, The Baker's Emperor)

1951, (Czech), State Film Studios, color, 125 mins.
<u>W</u>: Frantisek Cerny, Marie Vasova, Jan Werich, Natasa Gollova, Jiri Plachy, Zdenek Stepanek
<u>D</u>: Martin ("Mac") Fric   <u>SCR</u>: Jan Werich, Martin Fric & Jiri Brdecka   <u>PHOTOG</u>: Jan Stallich & Bohumil Haba
A.k.a. **The Emperor and the Golem** *and* **The Golem and the Emperor's Baker**
Standard fantasy-thriller: Automaton becomes royal servant. cf. **Der Golem** *and* **The Curse of the Golem**

Cisaruv Slavik (The Emperor's Nightingale)

1948, (Czech), color, 73 mins.
<u>W</u>: The Jiri Trnka Puppets
<u>D</u>: Jiri Trnka   <u>SCR</u>: Jiri Trnka & Jiri Brdecka, from the story by Hans Christian Andersen   <u>ANIMATION</u>: Bretislav Pojar
released in USA (1951, Rembrandt Films) with voice of Boris Karloff, released in France (1951), with voice of Jean Cocteau, under title **Le Rossignol de l'Empereur de Chine** *(The Chinese Emperor's Nightingale)*

Standard fantasy: Asian ruler fascinated by bird

La Citta delle Donne (City of Women)

1981, (It), Gaumont-Opera/New Yorker, color, 139 mins.
<u>W</u>: Marcello Mastroianni (*Snaporaz*), Ettore Manni (*Dr. Xavier Zuberkock*), Anne Prucnal (*Elena*), Bernice Stegers (*The Woman on the Train*), Jole Silvani (*The Old Woman on the Motorcycle*), Dominique Labourier (*The Feminist*), Mara Ciukleva (*Zuberkock's Elderly Maid*), Alessandra Panelli (*The Housewife in the Skit*), Gabriella Giorgelli (*The Fishwoman of San Leo*), Donatella Damiani (*The Feminist on Roller Skates*), Sara Tafuri (*The Other Dancing Girl*), Carla Terizzi (*Dr. Zuberkock's Conquest*), Katren Gabelein (*Enderbreith Small*), Tatiana Petronio, Brigitte Petronio, Armando Parracino, Umberto Zuanelli, Pietro Fumagalli
<u>D</u>: Federico Fellini   <u>SCR</u>: Federico Fellini, Bernardino Zapponi & Brunello Rondi   <u>PHOTOG</u>: Giuseppe Rotunno   <u>MUSIC</u>: Luis Bacalov

City After Midnight

1959, (USA), Monarch/British Lion/RKO, b&w, 84 mins.
<u>W</u>: Phyllis Kirk (*Eve Atwood*), Dan O'Herlihy (*Dermott Kincross*), Wilfrid Hyde-White (*Sir Maurice Lawes*), Jack Watling (*Toby*), Petula Clark (*Janice*), William Franklyn (*Ned*), Guido Lorraine (*Goron*), Margaret Withers (*Lady Lawes*), Balbina (*Prue*)
<u>P</u>: William Gell   <u>D & SCR</u>: Compton Bennett, from John Dickson Carr's novel *Emperor's Snuffbox*
UK Title: **That Woman Opposite**
Standard crime-thriller: Jewel thief's ex-wife accused of murder

City Beneath the Sea

1953, (USA), Univ, color, Made for TV, 87 mins.
<u>W</u>: Robert Ryan, Anthony Quinn (*Terry*), George Mathews (*Meade*), Suzan Ball, Hilo Hatti, Lalo Rios, Barbara Morrison, Karel Stepanek, Woody Strode, Bernie Gozier, Leon Lontoc, John Warburton
<u>D</u>: Oscar "Budd" Boetticher Jr.   <u>SCR</u>: Jack Harvey & Ramon Romero   <u>PHOTOG</u>: Charles P. Boyle
Minor melodrama: Search for sunken metropolis

City Beneath the Sea

1970, (USA), WB/Kent/Motion Pic-Int'l, color, 98 mins.
<u>W</u>: Stuart Whitman, Robert Colbert, Rosemary Forsyth, James Darren, Paul Stewart, Whit Bissell, Joseph Cotten, Richard Basehart, Robert Wagner, Tom Drake, Sugar Ray Robinson, Burr DeBenning, Susana Miranda, Larry Pennell
<u>P & D</u>: Irwin Allen   <u>SCR</u>: John Meredyth Lucas   <u>PHOTOG</u>: Kenneth Peach   <u>SPCL-FX</u>: L.B. Abbott & Art Cruickshank   <u>MUSIC</u>: Richard LaSalle
GB theatrical title, **One Hour to Doomsday**
TVM, standard adventure-thriller: Scheme to steal gold and nuclear supplies from submerged metropolis

City in Darkness

see *Charlie Chan in City in Darkness*

City in the Sea

see *The City Under the Sea*

City of Angels

1998, (USA), Taurus/Regency/WB, color, 114 mins.
<u>W</u>: Nicholas Cage (*Seth*), Meg Ryan (*Dr. Maggie Rice*), Dennis Franz (*Nathaniel Messenger*), Andre Braugher
<u>D</u>: Brad Silberling   <u>SCR</u>: Dana Stevens   <u>PHOTOG</u>: John Seale   <u>MUSIC</u>: Gabriel Yared
Modest fantasy-romance (Hollywood version of **Wings of Desire**): *Angel falls in love with woman doctor*

City of Fear

1965, (GB-W. Ger), Towers of London/Planet/AA, b&w, 75 mins.
<u>W</u>: Paul Maxwell (*Mike Foster*), Terry Moore (*Suzan*), Marisa Mell (*Ilona*), Albert Lieven (*Paul*), Pinkas Braun (*Ferenc*), Zsu Zsu Banki (*Magda*), Maria Takacs (*Marika*), Birgit Heiberg, Maria Rohm
<u>P</u>: Harry Alan Towers   <u>D</u>: Peter Bezencenet   <u>SCR</u>: Peter Welbeck & Max Bourne   <u>STORY</u>: Peter Welbeck
Standard crime-thriller: Scientist smuggled across border

The City of Lost Children

1995, (Fr/Span/Germ), Sony/Lumiere/Le Studio Canal/ France 3, color, 114 mins.
<u>W</u>: Ron Perlman (*One*), Judith Vittet (*Miette*), Joseph Lucien (*Denree*), Daniel Emilfork (*Krank*), Mireille Moss (*Miss Bismuth*), Dominique Pinon (*The Clones*), Genevieve Brunet & Odile Mallet (*The Octopus*), Jean-Louis Trintignant (*Voice of Irvin the Brain*), Jean-Claude Dreyfus
<u>D</u>: Marc Caro & Jean-Pierre Jeunet   <u>PHOTOG</u>: Darius Khondji   <u>MUSIC</u>: Angelo Badalamenti   <u>SCR</u>: Jean-Marie Jeunet, Marc Caro & Giles Adrien
Superior fantasy: Mad scientist kidnaps children

City of Shadows

1955, (USA), Rep, b&w, 78 mins.
<u>W</u>: Victor McLaglen, John Baer
Minor melodrama

City of Shadows

1986, (USA), color, 97 mins.
<u>W</u>: John P. Ryan, Paul Coufos, Tony Rosato

D: David Mitchell   **MUSIC:** tangerine Dream
Standard thriller:Evil mind unites separated twins

City of the Dead
1960, (GB), Vulcan/Trans Lux, b&w, 78 mins.
W: Christopher Lee (*Prof. Driscoll*), Dennis Lotis (*Richard Barlow*), Betta St. John (*Patricia Russell*), Venetia Stevenson (*Nan Barlow*), Valentine Dyall (*Jethrow Keane*), Norman Macowan (*Rev. Russell*), Patricia Jessel (*Elizabeth Selwyn*), Tom Naylor (*Bill Maitland*), Fred Johnson
P: Donald Taylor   **D:** John Moxey   **SCR:** George Baxt   **STORY:** Milton Subotsky   **PHOTOG:** Desmond Dickinson   **MUSIC:** Douglas Gamley & Ken Jones
USA retitle, **Horror Hotel** *(1962), reissued 1964*
Effective horror-thriller: College girl researches witchcraft, becomes human sacrifice

City of the Living Dead
see **The Gates of Hell**

City of the Walking Dead
1983, (It-Sp), Dialchi-Lotus/21st Century, color, 92 mins.

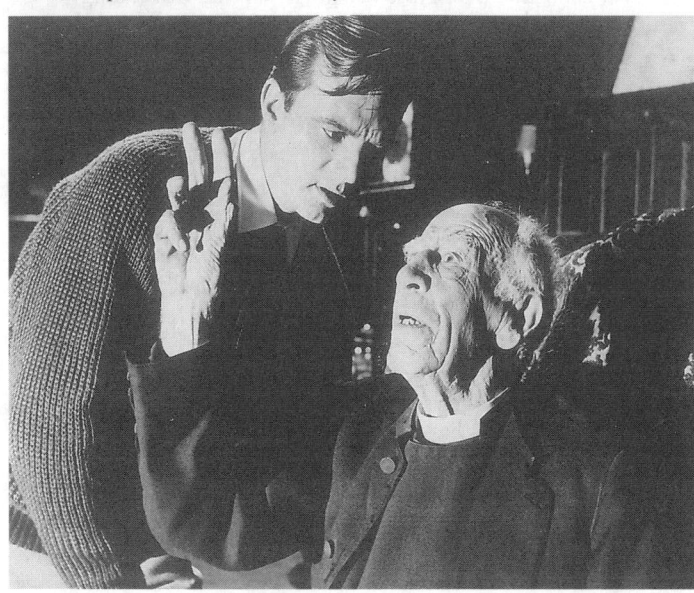

City of the Dead

W: Hugo Stiglitz, Laura Trotter, Francisco Rabal, Mel Ferrer (*Gen. Murchison*), Maria Rosario Omaggio, Sonia Viviani, Ugo Bologna, Tom Felleghy
D: Umberto Lenzi   **SCR:** Piero Regnoli, Tony Corti & Jose Luis Delgado   **PHOTOG:** Hans Burman   **MUSIC:** Stelvio Cipriani
A.k.a. **Nightmare** *and* **Nightmare City**
Minor horror-fantasy: Immortal zombies pillage

City of Women
see **La Citta delle Donne**

City on Fire
1979, (Can), Sandy Howard-Harold Greenberg/Avco Embassy, color, 105 mins.
W: Barry Newman (*Dr. Frank Whitman*), Susan Clark (*Diana*), Ava Gardner (*Maggie Grayson*), Shelley Winters (*Nurse Harper*), Cec Linder (*Paley*), James Franciscus (*Jimbo*), Henry Fonda (*Fire Chief Risley*), Leslie Nielsen (*Mayor Dudley*), Jonathan Welsh (*Herman*), Mavor Moore (*John*), Richard Donat (*The Captain*), Ken James (*Andrew*), Donald Pilon (*Fox*), Terry Haig (*Terry*), Hilary LeBow (*Mrs. Adams*), Jeff Mappin (*Beezer*), Sonny Forbes (*Tom*), Earl Pennington (*Clark*), Lee Murray (*Tony*), Janice Chaikelson (*Debbie*), Bronwen Mantel (*Sarah*), Steven Chaikelson (*Gerald*), Jerome Tiberghien (*The Fireman*)
D: Alvin Rakoff   **SCR:** Jack Hill, David P. Lewis, & Celine La Freniere   **PHOTOG:** Rene Verzier   **MUSIC:** William McCauley & Matthew McCauley
Standard melodrama: Holocaust threatens metropolis

The City Under the Sea
1965, (GB), Bruton/AA/AIP, color, 85 mins.
W: Vincent Price (*Sir Hugh Tregathion*), Tab Hunter (*Ben Harris*), David Tomlinson (*Harold Tufnell-Jones*), Susan Hart (*Jill Tregellis*), John LeMesurier (*Rev. Jonathan Ives*), Anthony Selby (*George*), Henry Oscar (*Mumford*), Derek Newark (*Dan*), Roy Patrick (*Simon*)
P: Daniel Haller   **D:** Jacques Tourneur   **SCR:** Charles Bennett & Louis M. Heyward, inspired by Edgar Allan Poe's poem *The City in the Sea*   **PHOTOG:** Stephen Dade   **SPCL-FX:** Frank George & Les Bowie   **MUSIC:** Stanley Black
USA retitle, **War-Gods of the Deep**
Standard SF-fantasy: Nemo-type rules aquatic humanoids

La Civilisation a Travers Les Ages (Civilization Through the Ages)

1908, (Fr), Star, b&w, 380m (1,246.7 ft.)
D: Georges Melies
Fanciful historical retrospective (in 11 parts)

Civilization Through the Ages
see **La Civilisation a Travers les Ages**

The Clairvoyant
1934, (GB), Gainsborough/Gaumont, b&w, 80 mins.
W: Claude Rains (*Maximus*), Fay Wray (*Rene*), Mary Clare (*Topsy*), Ben Field (*Simon*), Jane Baxter (*Christine*), Athole Stewart (*Lord Southwood*), C. Denier Warren (*James Bimiter*), Frank Cellier (*MacGregor*), Donald Calthrop (*The Derelict*), Jack Raine (*The Customs Officer*), Felix Aylmer (*The Counsel*), Graham Moffatt (*The Page*), George Merritt (*The Guard*), Eliot Makeham (*The Man*), Percy Parsons (*The Showman*)
D: Maurice Elvey   **SCR:** Charles Bennett, Bryan Edgar Wallace & Robert Edmunds, from Ernst Lothar's novel   **PHOTOG:** Gen. Mac Williams   **MUSIC:** Arthur Benjamin   **MUSIC DIR:** Louis Levy
A.k.a. **The Evil Mind**
Modest thriller: Fake medium develops true powers

The Clairvoyant
1985, (USA), Lansbury-Beruh/20th-Fox, color
W: Perry King, Elizabeth Kemp, Norman Parker, Barbara Quinn, Ken-neth McMillan, Jon Polito, Joe Morton, Antone Pagan
D: Armand Mastroianni   **SCR:** B. Jonathan Ringkamp   **STORY:** B. Jonathan Ringkamp & Armand Mastroianni   **PHOTOG:** Larry Pizer   **MUSIC:** Alexander Peskanov
Minor thriller: Artist sketches future murder victims

The Clan of the Cave Bear
1986, (USA), Jozak-Decade/WB, color, 98 mins.
W: Daryl Hannah (*Ayla*), Pamela Reed (*Iza*), James Remar (*Creb*), Thomas G. Waites (*Broud*), John Doolittle (*Brun*), Martin Doyle (*Grod*), Curtis Armstrong (*Goov*), Adel C. Hammond (*Vorn*), Tony Montanaro, Mike Muscat, John Wardlow, Keith Wardlow, Barbara Duncan, Karen Austin, Gloria Lee, Janne Mortil, Penny Smith, Lycia Naff, Linda Quibell, Bernadette Sabath, Joey Cramer, Amy Cyr, Rory L. Crowley, Nicole Eggert, Emma Floria, Mary Reid, Pierre Lamielle, Samantha Ostry, Shane Punt, Christiane Boyce, Catherine Flather, Guila Chiesa, Shauna Fanara, Alan Waltman, Colin Doyle, Natino Bellantino, Rick Valiquette, Paul Carafotes
D: Michael Chapman   **SCR:** John Sayles, from Jean M. Auel's novel   **MUSIC:** Alan Silvestri
Standard prehistory melodrama: Cro-Magnon beauty abides with Neanderthals

Clarence
1990, (Can-New Zeal), Atlantic-South Pacific/Northstar,Made For TV, color, 95 mins.
W: Robert Carradine (*Clarence*), Kate Trotter, Louis Del Grande, Richard Fitzpatrick, Barbara Hamilton, Jamie Rainey, Nicholas Van Burek, Jason McSkimming, Larry Aubrey, Rachel Blanchard, Chris Campbell, Claire Celluci, Conrad Coates, Alvin Crawford, Murray Cruchley, Kevin Frank, Marvin Karon, Shawn Lawrence, Deborah Kirshenbaum, Bruce McFee, Jeff McGibbon, B.J. McQueen, Jack Newman, James O'Regan, Paul Rainville, Julian Reed, Todd Schroeder, Julian Richings, Robbie Rox, Philip Williams, Harvey Sokoloff
D: Eric Till   **TELEPLAY:** Lorne Cameron & David Hoselton   **PHOTOG:** Glen MacPherson   **MUSIC DIR:** Louis Natale
TVM, minor fantasy: Angel aids mortals

Clash by Night
1963, (GB), Eternal/Grand Nat'l/AA, b&w, 75 mins.
W: Terence Longdon (*Martin Lord*), Jennifer Jayne (*Nita Lord*), Harry Fowler (*Doug Roberts*),Peter Sallis (*Victor Lush*), Arthur Lovegrove (*Ernie Peel*), Hilda Fenemore (*Mrs. Peel*), Alan Wheatley (*Ronald Grey-Simmons*), Vanda Godsell (*Mrs. Grey-Simmons*), Mark Dignam (*Sydney Selwyn*), John Arnatt (*Insp. Croft*)
P: Maurice J. Wilson   **D:** Montgomery Tully   **SCR:** Maurice J. Wilson & Montgomery Tully, from a novel by Rupert Croft-Cooke
USA retitle, **Escape by Night**
Standard crime-thriller: Crooks capture busload of prisoners in attempt to free convict

Clash of the Titans
1981, (GB), MGM-UA, color, 118 mins.
W: Harry Hamlin (*Perseus*), Sir Laurence Olivier (*Zeus*), Judy Bowker (*Andromeda*), Sian Phillips (*Cassiopeia*), Claire Bloom (*Hera*), Burgess Meredith (*Ammon*), Maggie Smith (*Thetis*), Neil McCarthy (*Calibos*), Ursula Andress (*Aphrodite*), Jack Gwillim (*Poseidon*), Susan Fleetwood (*Athena*), Pat Roach (*Hephaestus*), Donald Houston (*Acrisius*), Vida Taylor (*Danae*), Harry Jones (*The Huntsman*), Tim Pigott-Smith (*Thallo*), Flora Robson (*A Stygian Witch*), Freda Jackson (*A Stygian Witch*), Anna Manahan (*A Stygian Witch*)
P: Charles H. Schneer & Ray Harryhausen   **D:** Desmond Davis   **SCR:** Beverly Cross   **PHOTOG:** Ted Moore   **SPCL-FX:** Ray Harryhausen   **MUSIC:** Laurence Rosenthal
"...a lavish vehicle for the talents of Effects Wizard Ray Harryhausen"—Richard Corliss, Time
Well-made but overlong adventure-fantasy: Hero battles mythical foes to free princess from dreadful curse

Class of '01
1982, (Can), United Film Distribution, color, 98 mins.

W: Perry King, Roddy McDowall, Timothy Van Patten, Steven Arngrim, Merrie Lynn Ross, Michael J. Fox
P: Arthur Kent   D: Mark Lester   SCR: John Saxton & Tom Holland   MUSIC: Lalo Schifrin & Alice Cooper
*Intense thriller: Ultra-violence in high school. Sequel: **Class of 1999***

Class of 1999
1990, (USA), Lightning/Taurus, color, 98 mins.
W: Bradley Gregg (*Cody Culp*), Traci Lin (*Christie Langford*), Malcolm McDowell (*Dr. Miles Langford*), Stacy Keach (*Dr. Bob Forrest*), Patrick Kilpatrick (*Mr. Bryles*), John P. Ryan (*Mr. Hardin*), Pam Grier (*Ms. Connors*), Darren E. Burrows (*Sonny*)
P & D: Mark L. Lester   SCR: C. Courtney Joyner, from a story by Mark L. Lester   PHOTOG: Mark Irwin   MUSIC: Michael Hoenig
Standard SF-satire: Robot teachers brutally enforce school discipline

Class of 1999 II: The Substitute
1993, (USA), Lightning/Taurus, color, 91 mins.
W: Sasha Mitchell
Standard SF-thriller: Deadly android poses as substitute teacher

Class of Nuke 'Em High
1986, (USA), Lloyd Kaufman-Michael Herz/Troma, color, 84 mins.
W: Janelle Brady, Gilbert Brenton, Robert Prichard, James Nugent Vernon, R.L. Ryan, Brad Dunker, Gary Schneider, Theo Cohan, Gary Rosenblatt, Mary Taylor, Heather McMahan, Rick Howard, Chris McNamee, Anthony Ventola, Seth Oliver Hawkins, Arthur Lorenz, Donald O'Toole, Lerae Dean, Lauraine Austin, Reuben Guss, Diana DeVries, Dianna-Jean Flaherty, Lilly Hayes Kaufman, Sloane Herz, Don Costello
D: Richard W. Haines & Samuel Weil   SCR: Richard W. Haines, Mark Rudnitsky, Lloyd Kaufman, & Stuart Strutin, from an orig. story by Richard W. Haines   PHOTOG: Michael Mayers   SPCL-FX: Scott Coulter & Brian Quinn   MUSIC: Michael Lattanzi
Minor "Sci-Fi-Action-Terror-Comedy": Juvenile delinquency in radiation-plagued community

Class of Nuke 'Em High, Part 2: Subhumanoid Meltdown
1991, (USA), Troma, color, 99 mins.
W: Brick Bronsky (*Roger Smith*), Lisa Gaye (*Prof. Holt*), Leesa Rowland (*Victoria*), Michael Kurtz (*Yoke*), Scott Resnick (*Dean Okra*), Shelby Shepard (*Prof. Jones*)
D: Eric Louzil   SCR: Lloyd Kaufman, Eric Louzil, Carl Morano, Marcus Roling, Jeffrey W. Sass & Matt Unger   PHOTOG: Ron Chapman   MUSIC: Bob Mithoff
Minor SF-spoof: Genetically-engineered menials run amok

Class Reunion Massacre
*see **The Redeemer***

The Claw Monsters
1966, (USA), Rep, b&w, 100 mins.
W: Phyllis Coates, Myron Healey, Arthur Space, John Day, Mike Ragan
D: Franklin Adreon
*Standard adventure-thriller (feature culled from 12-chapter 1955 serial {Republic's next-to-last serial} **Panther Girl of the Congo**): Mad chemist guards diamond mine with giant crawfish*

The Clay Pigeon
1949, (USA), RKO, b&w, 63 mins.
W: Bill Williams, Barbara Hale, Richard Loo, Richard Quine, Frank Fenton, Martha Hyer
D: Richard Fleischer   SCR: Carl Foreman
Standard melodrama: Amnesiac ex-POW accused of treason

The Claydon Treasure Mystery
1938, (GB), Fox British, b&w, 63 mins.
W: John Stuart (*Peter Kerrigan*), Evelyn Ankers (*Rosemary Claydon*), Garry Marsh (*Sir George Ilford*), Campbell Gullan (*Tollemach*), Annie Esmond (*Lady Caroline*), Aubrey Mallalieu (*Lord Claydon*), Finlay Currie (*Rubin*), Joss Ambler (*Insp. Fleming*), Vernon Harris (*Rhodes*)
D: Manning Haynes   SCR: Edward Dryhurst, from Neil Gordon's novel *The Shakespeare Murders*
*Standard crime-thriller: Novelist solves murder, finds hidden treasure cf. **The Third Clue***

Clean Shaven
1993, (USA), color, 80 mins.
W: Robert Albert, Jennifer MacDonald, Peter Greene, Megan Owen, Molly Castelloe
D & SCR: Lodge Kerrigan   PHOTOG: Teodoro Maniaci   MUSIC: Hahn Rowe
Unusual thriller: Detective tracks schizophrenic

Cleaver and Haven
*see **Future Cop***

Clegg
1969, (GB), Sutton-Shinteff/Tigon, color, 87 mins.
W: Gilbert Wynne (*Harry Clegg*), Garry Hope (*Francis Wildman*), Gilly Grant (*Suzy the Slag*), Norman Claridge (*Lord Cruik Shank*), A.J. Brown (*Joseph Valentine*), Noel Davis (*The Manager*), Michael Nightingale (*Col. Sullivan*), Ronald Leigh-Hunt (*Insp. Kert*), Jenny Robbins (*Shirley*)

P: Herbert Alpert & Lewis Force   D: Lindsay Shonteff   STORY: Lewis J. Hagleton
Standard thriller: Man-hating whore commits murders

Cleopatra
*see **Cleopatre***

Cleopatre (Cleopatra)
1899, (Fr), Star, b&w, 40m (131.2 ft./2.2 mins.)
D: Georges Melies
*USA retitle, **Robbing Cleopatra's Tomb***
Standard thriller: Tomb-robbers get comeuppance

Clever Egg Conjuring
1912, (GB), Natural Colour Kinematograph Co., color
D: Walter R. Booth
Minor fantasy short: Conjurer does tricks with eggs

The Climax
1944, (USA), Univ, color, 86 mins.
W: Boris Karloff (*Dr. Hohner*), Susanna Foster (*Angela*), Gale Sonder-gaard (*Luise*), Turhan Bey (*Franz*), June Vincent (*Marcellina*), Jane Farrar (*Carmila Vadek*), Dorothy Lawrence (*Miss Metzger*), William Edmunds (*Leon*), George Dolenz (*Roselli*), Thomas Gomez (*Count Seebruck*), Ludwig Stossel (*Baumann*), Erno Verebes (*Brunn*), Scotty Beckett (*The King*), Lotte Stein (*Mama Hinzl*), Maxwell Hayes
D: George Waggner   SCR: Curt Siodmak & Lynn Starling, from a play by Edward Locke   PHOTOG: Hal Mohr   MUSIC: Edward Ward
*Belgian retitle, **The Passion of Dr. Hohner***
*Standard thriller (utilizing sets from 1943's **Phantom of the Opera**): Svengali-like impresario mesmerizes beautiful girl*

The Cloak
*see **Shinel** (1926 & 1965)*

Cloak and Dagger
1946, (USA), WB, b&w, 106 mins.
W: Gary Cooper, Lilli Palmer, Robert Alda, Vladimir Sokoloff, J. Ed-ward Bromberg, Ludwig Stossel, Marjorie Hoshelle, Marc Lawrence, Helene Thimig
P: Milton Sperling   D: Fritz Lang   SCR: Albert Maltz   PHOTOG: Sol Polito   MUSIC: Max Steiner
Standard thriller: Scientist spies on Nazis

Cloak and Dagger
1984, (USA), Allan Carr/Univ, color, 99 mins.
W: Henry Thomas (*David Osborne*), Dabney Coleman (*Jack Flak/Hal Osborne*), Michael Murphy (*Rice*), Jeanette Nolan (*Eunice MacCready*), Christina Nigra (*Kim Gardener*), John McIntire (*George MacCready*)
D: Richard Franklin   STORY & SCR: Tom Holland   PHOTOG: Victor J. Kemper   MUSIC: Brian May
*Standard melodrama (reminiscent of **The Window**): Boy involved with murderous spies. Remake of **The Boy Cried Murder** (1965)*

Cloak Without Dagger
1956, (GB), Balblair/Butcher, b&w, 69 mins.
W: Philip Friend (*Felix Gretton*), Mary Mackenzie (*Kyra Gabaine*), Leslie Dwyer (*Fred Borcombe*), Allan Cuthbertson (*Col. Packham*), John G. Heller (*Peppi Gilroudian*), Chin Yu (*Yan Chu*), Bill Nagy (*Mario Oromonda*), Patrick Jordan (*Capt. Wallis*)
WRIT & P: A.R. Rawlinson   D: Joseph Stirling
*USA retitle, **Operation Conspiracy** (Republic 1957)*
Standard thriller: Intelligence man and fashion reporter nab spies

The Clockmaker's Dream
*see **Le Reve de l'Horloger***

A Clockwork Orange
1971, (GB), Polaris/WB, color, 137 mins.
W: Malcolm McDowell (*Alex*), Patrick Magee (*Mr. Alexander*), Warren Clarke (*Dim*), John Clive (*The Stage Actor*), Adrienne Corri (*Mrs. Alexander*), Dave Prowse (*The Bodyguard*), Miriam Karlin (*The Cat Lady*), Michael Bates (*The Chief Guard*), Carl Duering (*Brodsky*), Aubrey Morris (*Deltold*), Godfrey Quigley (*The Chaplain*), James Marcus (*Georgie*), Michael Tarn (*Pete*), Sheila Raynor (*Mum*), Philip Stone (*Dad*), Clive Francis (*The Lodger*), Madge Ryan (*Dr. Branum*), Paul Farrell (*The Tramp*), Michael Glover (*The Prison Governor*), Pauline Taylor (*The Psychiatrist*), Anthony Sharpe (*The Minister*), John Savident (*A Conspirator*), Margaret Tyzack (*A Conspirator*), Lindsay Campbell (*The Inspector*), Carol Drinkwater (*Nurse Feeley*), Virginia Wetherell (*The Actress*), Katya Wyeth (*The Girl*), Gaye Brown, Peter Burton, John J. Carney, Vivienne Chandler, Neil Wilson, Richard Connaught, Prudence Drage, Lee Fox, Cheryl Grunwald, Gillian Hills, Craig Hunter, Barbara Scott, Shirley Jaffe, Barrie Cookson, Jan Adair, Steven Berkoff
WRIT, P, & D, Stanley Kubrick, from Anthony Burgess' novel   PHOTOG: John Alcott   MUSIC: Walter Carlos
"...one of the few perfect movies I have seen in my lifetime"—Rex Reed
Hard-hitting, mature SF-drama: Juvenile delinquency in the sordid world of future

The Cloister and the Woman
1913, (GB), Searchlight/MP, b&w, 1,995 ft. (608.1m)

W: Eva Stuart (*Adele*), Wallace Aldridge (*Andre*), Bernard Vaughan (*The Abbe*), George Ashley (*Michael*), Rosamund Tatton (*Rose*)
Standard melodrama: Jealous abbe imprisons monk

The Clone Master
1978, (USA), Mel Ferber-Para/NBC-TV, color, 95 mins.
W: Art Hindle (*Dr. Simon Shane*), Robyn Douglass (*Gussie*), John Van Dreelen (*Salt*), Ed Lauter (*Bender*), Ralph Bellamy (*Dr. Ezra Louthin*), Mario Roccuzzo, Phillip Pine, Betty Lou Robinson, Stacy Keach, Trent Dolan, Lew Brown, Ken Sansom, Bill Sorrells, Robert Karnes, Vernon Weddle, Steve Eastin, Kirk Duncan, Ian Sullivan, Bonwitt St. Claire, Richard Lapp, James O'Connell, Steve Ross, William Whitaker
WRIT & P: John D.F. Black   D: Don Medford   PHOTOG: Joseph Biroc
SPCL-FX: Joe Mercurio   MUSIC: Glenn Paxton
TVM, standard SF-thriller: Scientist's cloning experiments generate dangerous intrigue

The Clones
1973, (USA), Hunt-Card/Filmakers Int'l/CBS-TV, color, 94 mins.
W: Michael Greene (*Appleby*), Otis Young (*Sawyer*), Gregory Sierra (*Nemo*), Susan Hunt, Stanley Adams, Barbara Burgdorph, John Barrymore Jr., Bruce Bennett, Angelo Rossitto
P: Paul Hunt   D: Paul Hunt & Lamar Card   TELEPLAY: Steve Fisher   PHOTOG: Gary Graver   MUSIC: Allen D. Allen
TVM, minor SF-thriller: Government scientist investigates lab-grown human duplicates

The Clonus Horror
1979, (USA), Schreibman-Fiveson, color, 90 mins
W: Peter Graves (*Jeff Knight*), Rick DiAngelo (*Guide #1*), Gene Glazier (*Guide #2*), Keith Langsdale (*Guide #3*), Eileen Dietz (*Dana*), Paulette Breen (*Lena*), Timothy Donnelly (*Richard*), Frank Ashmore (*George*), Dick Sargent (*Dr. Jameson*), William Bufkin (*The Clone*), Zale Kessler (*Dr. Nelson*), Larry Manning (*Guide #4*), Tony Haig (*Jack*), Boyd Holister (*The Senator*), Eddy Carroll (*The Doctor*), John Donovan (*Guide #5*), Greg Brickman (*The Motorcycle Rider*), Keenan Wynn (*Jake Noble*), Lurene Tuttle (*Anna Noble*), James Mantell (*Ricky*), Joel Lawrence (*Guide #6*), David Hooks (*Richard Knight*), George Wilbur, Chuck Hayward, Amanda Davies, Frank Birney
A.k.a. **Parts**
Standard SF-thriller: Human clone flees sinister institute

A Close Call for Boston Blackie
1946, (USA), Col, b&w, 60 mins.
W: Chester Morris (*Boston Blackie*), Lynn Merrick (*Gerry Peyton*), Richard Lane (*Insp. Farraday*), George E. Stone (*Runt*), Frank Sully (*Sgt. Matthews*), Claire Carleton (*Mamie Kirwin*), Erik Rolf (*Smiley Slade*), Charles Lane (*Hack Hagen*), Russell Hicks (*Harcourt*), Robert Scott (*John Peyton*), Emmett Vogan (*The Coroner*), Doris Houck (*Josie*), Ruth Warren (*The Milk Woman*), Jack Gordon (*The Cab Driver*)
D: Lew Landers   SCR: Ben Markson & Paul Yawitz, from characters created by Jack Boyle   PHOTOG: Burnett Guffey   MUSIC: Mischa Bakaleinikoff
Standard mystery-thriller: Sleuth suspected of murder

Close Call for Ellery Queen
1942, (USA), Col, b&w, 65 mins.
W: William Gargan (*Ellery Queen*), Margaret Lindsay (*Nikki Porter*), Charley Grapewin (*Insp. Queen*), Ralph Morgan (*Alan Rogers*), Kay Linaker (*Margo Rogers*), Edward Norris (*Stewart Cole*), James Burke (*Sgt. Velie*), Addison Richards (*Lester Younger*), Charles Judels (*Corday*), Ben Welden (*The Fisherman*), Andrew Tombes (*Bates*), Claire DuBrey (*The Housekeeper*), Micheline Cheirel (*Marie Dubois*), Milton Parsons (*The Butler*)
D: James Hogan   SCR: Eric Taylor, loosely based on Ellery Queen's novel *The Dragon's Teeth: A Problem in Deduction*   PHOTOG: James S. Brown Jr.
Minor mystery-thriller: Two blackmailers murdered

Close Encounters of the Third Kind
1977, (USA), Col/EMI, Made for Cable, color, 135 mins. (TV: 143 mins.)
W: Richard Dreyfuss (*Roy Neary*), Teri Garr (*Ronnie Neary*), Francois Truffaut (*LaCombe*), Melinda Dillon (*Jillian Guiler*), Carl Guffey (*Barry Guiler*), Bob Balaban (*David*), J. Patrick McNamara (*The Project Leader*), Warren Kemmerling (*Wild Bill*), George DiCenzo (*Maj. Benchley*)
P: Julia Phillips & Michael Phillips   WRIT & D: Steven Spielberg   PHOTOG: Vilmos Zsigmond   VS-FX: Douglas Trumbull   MUSIC: John Williams
SF classic: Space aliens contact earthlings

Closer and Closer
1996, (USA), Lifetime, Made for Cable, color, 95 mins.
W: Kim Delaney, John J. York
Made-for-Cable, standard thriller: Copycat killer targets woman novelist

Cloudburst
1951, (GB), Exclusive/UA, b&w, 92 mins.
W: Robert Preston (*John Graham*), Elizabeth Sellars (*Carol Graham*), Colin Tapley (*Insp. Davis*), Sheila Burrell (*Lorna*), Harold Lang (*Mickie Fraser*), Mary Germaine (*Peggy*), George Woodbridge (*Sgt. Ritchie*), Lyn Evans (*Chuck Peters*), Daphne Anderson (*Kate*), Edward Lexy (*Cardew*), Thomas Heathcote, Edith Sharpe, James Mills, Noel Howlett, Gerald Case, Robert Brown, Charles Saynor, Fredric Steger, Stanley Baker, Martin Boddey
D: Francis Searle   SCR: Francis Searle & Leo Marks, from a play by Leo Marks
MUSIC: Frank Spencer
Modest melodrama: Man vows to avenge wife's murder

The Clouded Crystal
1948, (GB), Grossman-Cullimore-Arbeid/Butcher, b&w, 57 mins.
W: Patrick Waddington (*Jack*), Lind Joyce (*Cathy Butler*), Dorothy Bramhall (*Paula*), Frank Muir (*Frank Butler*), Dino Galvani (*Manzetti*), Ethel Coleridge (*Mme. Zamba*)
P: Ben Arbeid & A. Grossman   D: Alan Cullimore   STORY: Donald Ginsberg
Standard comedy: Fortune teller predicts girl's husband has month to live

Clown and His Dogs
see Clown et Ses Chiens

The Clown and His Donkey
1910, (GB), Armstrong/Urban, b&w, 265 ft. (81m)
D & STORY: Charles Armstrong
Minor fantasy: Animated paper silhouettes depict adventuresv of clown and donkey

The Clown and the Enchanted Candle
1900, (GB), Warwick Trading Co., b&w, 50 ft. (15.2m)
Minor fantasy short: Candle grows large and shrinks as clown reads book

Clown and the Policeman
1900, (GB), Hepworth, b&w, 100 ft. (30.5m)
W: Cecil Hepworth (*The Clown*)
D: Cecil Hepworth
Minor fantasy short: Clown blows cop to pieces, fits him together again

The Clown Barber
1898, (GB), Williamson, b&w, 70 ft. (21.3m)
D: James Williamson
Minor fantasy short: Clown barber beheads customer

La Clownesse Fantome (The Phantom Clown-Girl)
1902, (Fr), Star, b&w, 30m (98.4 ft./1.7 mins.)
D: Georges Melies
A.k.a. **The Shadow-Girl** *and* **Twentieth Century Conjuring**
Standard comedy-fantasy

Clown et Ses Chiens (Clown and His Dogs)
1892, (Fr), b&w
approx. 15 mins.
D: Emile Reynaud
Animated "praxinoscope" short, standard fantasy: Harlequin trains pets

Clownhouse
1989, (USA), color, 85 mins.
W: Nathan Forrest Winters (*Casey*), Brian McHugh (*Geoffrey*), Sam Rockwell, Viletta Skillman, Timothy Enos
D: Victor Salva
Standard thriller: Brothers terrorized by killer clowns

The Clown versus Satan
see Guguste et Belzebuth

The Club (1984)
see Invitation to Hell

The Club (1994)
1994, (USA), color, 94 mins.
W: Kim Coates, Joel Wyner, Andrea Roth, Rino Romano, Zack Ward, Kelli Taylor, Matthew Ferguson
D: Benton Spencer   SCR: Robert Cooper   MUSIC: Paul Zaza
Standard thriller: Student initiates classmates into society of evil

Club Extinction
see Dr. M

Clubhouse Detectives
1996, (USA), color, 85 mins.
W: Michael Ballam, Michael Galeota
Made-for-Video, standard adventure-thriller: Kids form detective agency, hunt suspected killer

The Club of Pharos
1915, (GB), Martin/DFSA, b&w, 565 ft. (172.2m)
D: Dave Aylott
Minor fantasy short: Burglar steals Egyptian club that makes objects disappear

The Clue of the Cigar Band
1915, (GB), Big Ben/Pathe, b&w, 3,453 ft. (1052.5m)
W: H.O. Martinek (*The Officer*), Ivy Montford (*The Girl*)
D: H.O. Martinek   STORY: L.C. MacBean
Standard crime-thriller: Customs officer poses as blind skipper, saves girl from cigar smugglers

Club Vampire
1999, (USA), Roger Corman, color
Minor horror-fantasy

The Clue of the New Pin
1929, (GB), British Lion/PDC, b&w, 7,292 ft. (2222.6m)

W: Benita Hume (*Ursula Ardfern*), Kim Peacock (*Tab Holland*), Donald Calthrop (*Yeh Ling*), John Gielgud (*Rex Trasmere*), H. Saxon-Snell (*Walters*), Johnny Butt (*Wellington Briggs*), Colin Kenney (*Insp. Carver*), The Hippodrome Chorus
D: Arthur Maude **SCR:** Kathleen Hayden, from a novel by Edgar Wallace
Standard thriller: Rich recluse killed by nephew

The Clue of the New Pin
1961, (GB), Merton Park/Anglo-Amalgamated, b&w, 58 mins.
W: Paul Daneman (*Rex Lander*), Bernard Archard (*Supt. Carver*), James Villiers (*Tab Holland*), Catherine Woodville (*Jane Ardfern*), Clive Morton (*Ramsey Brown*), Wolfe Morris (*Yeh Ling*), David Horne (*John Trasmere*), Leslie Sands (*Sgt. Harris*), Ruth Kettlewell (*Mrs. Rushby*)
P: Jack Greenwood **D:** Allan Davis **SCR:** Philip Mackie, from a novel by Edgar Wallace
Standard mystery-thriller: Sleuth investigates murder in locked room

The Clue of the Second Goblet
1928, (GB), British Filmcraft/Para, b&w, 2,246 ft. (684.6m)
W: Langhorne Burton (*Sexton Blake*), Fred Raynham (*George Marsden Plummer*), Mickey Brantford (*Tinker*), Gabrielle Morton (*Helen*), Leslie Perrins (*Fairbairn*)
D: George A. Cooper **STORY:** G.H. Teed
Standard "Sexton Blake" mystery: Detective probes murder

The Clue of the Silver Key
1961, (GB), Merton Park/Anglo-Amalgamated, b&w, 59 mins.
W: Bernard Lee (*Supt. Meredith*), Lyndon Brook (*Gerry Dornford*), Finlay Currie (*Harvey Lane*), Jennifer Daniel (*Mary Lane*), Patrick Cargill (*Binny*), Derrick Sherwin (*Quigley*), Anthony Sharp (*Mike Hennessey*), Stanley Morgan (*Sgt. Anson*), Sam Kydd (*Tickler*)
P: Jack Greenwood **D:** Gerard Glaister **SCR:** Philip Mackie, from a novel by Edgar Wallace
Minor mystery-thriller: Scotland Yard probes moneylender's murder

Clue of the Twisted Candle
1960, (GB), Merton Park/Anglo-Amalgamated, b&w, 61 mins.
W: Bernard Lee (*Supt. Meredith*), David Knight (*Lexman/Griswold*), Colette Wilde (*Grace*), Francis De Wolff (*Karadis*), Richard Caldicott (*Fisher*), Stanley Morgan (*Anson*), Richard Vernon (*Viney*), Gladys Henson (*The landlady*), Christine Shaw (*Belinda Holland*)
P: Jack Greenwood **D:** Allan Davis **SCR:** Philip Mackie, from a novel by Edgar Wallace
Minor mystery-thriller: Wealthy man implicated in murder

The Clutching Hand
1936, (USA), Weiss/Stage & Screen, b&w, 65 mins.
W: Jack Mulhall (*Craig Kennedy*), Marion Schilling, William Farnum, Ruth Mix, Yakima Canutt, Reed Howes, Rex Lease, Mae Busch, Bryant Washburn, Olin Francis, Robert Frazer, William Desmond, Gaston Glass, Robert Russell, Mahlon Hamilton, John Ince, Robert Walker, Joseph W. Girard, Artemus Nigolian, Art Howard, Frank Leigh, Ethel Grove, Charles Locher (later John Hall), Gordon S. Griffith, Franklyn Farnum, Roger Williams, Richard Alexander, Knute Erickson, Milburn Moranti, John Elliot, George Morrell, Vera Steadman, Snub Pollard, Henry Hall, Eugene Burr, Willard Kent, Bert Howard, Gil Patrick, Bull Montana, Slim Whittaker, Tom London, Art Felix, George Allen, Robert Kortman, Roy Cardona
D: Albert Herman **SCR:** Louis d'Usseau & Dallas Fitzgerald, from Arthur B. Reeves' novel
Minor thriller, feature culled from 15-chapter serial: Master criminal kidnaps scientist

The Cobra
1967, (It-Sp), AIP, color, 93 mins.
W: Dana Andrews, Anita Ekberg, Peter Martell, Elisa Montes
P: Fulvio Lucisano **D:** Mario Sequi
Minor thriller: Master criminal pursued

The Cobra Strikes
1948, (USA), Eagle Lion, b&w, 62 mins
W: Leslie Brooks, Sheila Ryan
Minor thriller

Cobra Woman
1944, (USA), Univ, color, 71 mins.
W: Maria Montez (*Tollea/Naja*), Jon Hall (*Ramu*), Sabu (*Kado*), Edgar Barrier (*Martok*), Mary Nash (*The Queen*), Lois Collier (*Veeda*), Samuel S. Hinds (*Father Paul*), Lon Chaney Jr. (*Hava*), Moroni Olsen (*MacDonald*)
P: George Waggner **D:** Robert Siodmak **SCR:** Richard Brooks & Gene Lewis, from a story by W. Scott Darling **PHOTOG:** George Robinson & Howard Greene **SPCL-FX:** John P. Fulton **MUSIC:** Edward Ward
Exciting South Seas adventure-fantasy: Twin sisters vie for control of island paradise

The Cobweb
1917, (GB), Hepworth/Harma, b&w, 5,700 ft. (1737.4m)
W: Henry Edwards (*Stephen Mallard*), Alma Taylor (*Irma Brian*), Stewart Rome (*Merton Forsdyke*), Margaret Blanche (*Miss Debb*), Violet Hopson (*Dolorosa*), Molly Hamley-Clifford (*Mrs. Brian*), John MacAndrews (*Insp. Beall*), Charles Vane (*Sir George Gillingham*), Lionelle Howard (*The Poacher*)
D: Cecil M. Hepworth **SCR:** Blanche McIntosh, from a play by Leon M. Lion &

Naunton Davies
Standard crime-thriller: Millionaire thinks he strangled his blackmailing Mexican wife

Cobweb Castle
see **Throne of Blood**

Cock-A-Doodle-Doo
1910, (GB), Clarendon, b&w, 540 ft. (164.6m)
D: Percy Stow
Standard comedy-fantasy: Couple eats noisy cockerel and start crowing

The Cockeyed Miracle
1946, (USA), MGM, b&w, 81 mins.
W: Frank Morgan, Audrey Totter, Keenan Wynn, Cecil Kellaway, Gladys Cooper, Marshall Thompson, Leon Ames, Morris Ankrum, Jane Green, Arthur Space
D: S. Sylvan Simon **PHOTOG:** Ray June
A.k.a. **Mr. Griggs Returns**
Sentimental fantasy: Ghosts look after family

Cocoon
1985, (USA), Zanuck-Brown/20th-Fox, color, 114 mins.
W: Don Ameche (*Art*), Wilford Brimley (*Ben*), Brian Dennehy (*Walter*), Hume Cronyn (*Joe*), Jack Gilford (*Bernie*), Maureen Stapleton (*Mary*), Steve Guttenberg (*Jack Bonner*), Jessica Tandy (*Alma*), Gwen Verdon (*Bess*), Tahnee Welch (*Kitty*), Herta Ware (*Rose*), Linda Harrison (*Susan*), Charles Lampkin (*Pops*), Barret Oliver (*David*), Tyrone Power Jr. (*Pillsbury*), Mike Nomad, Clint Howard
D: Ron Howard **SCR:** David Saperstein **PHOTOG:** Don Peterman **VS-FX, SPRVSR:** Mitch Suskin **MUSIC:** James Horner **SONG:** "Gravity"
Entertaining SF-fantasy: Benevolent alien beings rejuvenate old-timers

Cocoon: The Return
1988, (USA), Zanuck-Brown/20th-Fox, color, 116 mins.
W: Don Ameche (*Art Selwyn*), Wilford Brimley (*Ben Luckett*), Courtney Cox (*Sara*), Hume Cronyn (*Joe Finley*), Jack Gilford (*Bernie Lefkowitz*), Steve Guttenberg (*Jack Bonner*), Maureen Stapleton (*Mary Luckett*), Barret Oliver (*David*), Gwen Verdon (*Bess McCarthy*), Elaine Stritch (*Ruby*), Jessica Tandy (*Alma Finley*), Tahnee Welch (*Kitty*), Tyrone Power Jr. (*Pillsbury*), Linda Harrison (*Susan*), Brian Dennehy (*Walter*), Wendy Cooke (*Phil/Antareans*), Mike Nomad (*Doc*), Herta Ware (*Rose*), Brian C. Smith (*Dr. Baron*), Fred Buch (*Alma's Doctor*), Iris Acker (*Mrs. Cushman*), Harold Bergman (*Dr. Erwin*), Tom Kouchalakos (*Doug*), Glenn Scherer (*Bess' Doctor*), Alan R. Jordan (*The Orderly*), Fritz Dominique (*Orderly #2*), Will Marchetti (*Gen. Jefferds*), Shelley Spurlock (*Rebecca*), Ted Milford (*Kid #1*), Chris Fuxa (*Kid #2*), Bill Wohrman (*The Coach*), Jay Smith (*The Catcher*), Tony Vila Jr. (*The Umpire*), Brian J. Andrews (*The Visiting Catcher*), David Easton (*Player #1*), Matt Ford (*Player #2*), Jack McDermott (*The Spectator*), Darcy Shean (*The Woman in the Restaurant*), Barrie Mizurski (*The Waiter*), Madeline Lee (*The Impatient Woman*), Mal Jones (*The Man at the Kiosk*), Ryan Szurgot (*Little Boy #1*), Anthony Finazzo (*Little Boy #2*), Kelly Jasen (*Little Girl #1*), Stephanie Oldziej (*Little Girl #2*), Priscilla Ashley Behne (*Little Girl #3*), Patricia Rainier (*The Wife of the Man at the Kiosk*), Richard Jasen (*The Little Boy*), Patricia Winters (*The Lamaze Teacher*), Rachel Renick (*Janet*), Glenn L. Robbins (*Mr. Srydlo*), Bruce McLaughlin (*The Man on the Glass Bottom Boat*), Buddy Reynolds (*The Airforce Policeman*), Carlos Gonzalez (*The Janitor*), Kevin Corrigan (*The Security Guard*), Robert Gwaltney (*The Clerk*), Robert Short (*The Technician*)
D: Daniel Petrie **SCR:** Stephen McPherson **STORY:** Stephen McPherson & Elizabeth Bradley, from characters created by David Saperstein **PHOTOG:** Tak Fujimoto **VS-FX:** Industrial Light & Magic **MUSIC:** James Horner
Modest SF-fantasy: Benevolent aliens revisit Earth

Code Name: Dancer
1987, (USA), color, 93 mins.
W: Kate Capshaw, Jeroen Krabbe, Gregory Sierra, Cliff DeYoung
TVM, standard thriller: Woman spy quits retirement, finds Cuban intrigue

Code Name: Jaguar
1965, (Fr), color
W: Ray Danton, Pascale Petit (*Chaton*)
Minor thriller: CIA agent brainwashed by communists

Code Name: Minus One
1976, (USA), HarveBennett/Univ-TV, color, 98 mins.
W: Ben Murphy (*Sam Casey*), Katherine Crawford (*Abby*), Richard A. Dysart (*Leonard Driscoll*), Paul Shenar (*Charles Edward Royce*), Dana Elcar, Quinn Redeker, Gregory Walcott, Michael Lane, Len Wayland, Cheryl Miller, H.M. Wynant, Dave Shelley, Austin Stoker, Robert Forward, Jim Raymond
D: Alan J. Levi **TELEPLAY:** Leslie Stevens, based on a novel by H.G. Wells **PHOTOG:** Enzo A. Martinelli **MUSIC:** Billy Goldenberg
TVM, minor SF (feature-film pilot for short-lived TV series **Gemini Man**): *Daredevil made invisible by radiation. A.k.a.* **Gemini Man**

Code Name: Tiger
1964, (Fr), color
W: Roger Hanin, Daniela Bianchi
D: Claude Chabrol
Minor spy-thriller: Secret agent guards diplomat's family

Code Name Trixie
1973, (USA), Cambist, color, 103 mins.
__W:__ Lane Carroll (*Judy*), W.G. McMillan (*David*), Lloyd Hollar (*The Colonel*), Harold Wayne Jones (*Clank*), Richard Liberty (*Artie*), Lynn Lowry (*Kathie*), Richard France (*Dr. Watts*), Harry Spillman (*Maj. Rider*)
__D:__ George A. Romero   __SONG:__ *Heaven Help Us*
A.k.a. __The Crazies__
Minor SF-horror: Polluting biochemicals spread insanity.

The Code of Scotland Yard
see __The Shop at Sly Corner__

Code 7...Victim 5
see __Victim Five__

Codename: Icarus
1985, (GB), color, 106 mins.
__W:__ Barry Angel, Jack Galloway
__D:__ Marilyn Fox
TVM, standard thriller: Genius student uncovers evil gov't plot

The Codicil
1912, (GB), Hepworth, b&w, 1,050 ft. (320m)
__W:__ Harry Royston
__D:__ Warwick Buckland
Standard crime-thriller: Grandfather foils greedy couple, posts will before death

The Coed Murders
1980, (It), Primex Italiana/NMD, color, 96 mins.
__W:__ Giovanna Ralli, Claudio Cassinelli, Mario Adorf, Franco Fabrizi, Farley Granger
__D:__ Massimo Dallamano   __MUSIC:__ Stelvio Cipriani
Standard thriller

The Coffin of the Vampire
see __El Ataud del Vampiro__

Le Coffre Enchante (The Enchanted Trunk)
1904, (Fr), Star, b&w, 68m (223.1 ft./3.8 mins.)
__D:__ Georges Melies
A.k.a. __The Bewitched Trunk__
Standard fantasy.

The Coiners
1904, (GB), Sheffield Photo Co., b&w, 280 ft. (85.6m)
__D:__ Frank Mottershaw
Standard thriller: Police raid counterfeiters

The Coiner's Den
1912, (GB): Hepworth, b&w, 850 ft. (259.1m)
__W:__ Alec Worcester (*The Detective*), Gladys Sylvani (*The Girl*), Harry Royston (*The Cashier*)
__D:__ Frank Wilson
Standard crime-thriller: Detective poses as cabby, drives counterfeiters to police station

Cold Blood
see __The Ice House__

Cold Buffet
see __Buffet Froid__

The Cold Equations
1996, (USA), SCI-TV, color, 95 mins.
__W:__ Bill Campbell, Poppy Montgomery, Daniel Roebuck (*Mitch*)
Made-for-Cable, standard SF-thriller: Stowaway imperils space mission

The Cold Heart
see __Das Kalte Herz__

A Cold Night's Death
1973, (USA), Spelling-Goldberg/20th-Fox-TV, color, 73 mins.
__W:__ Robert Culp (*Robert Jones*), Eli Wallach (*Frank Enari*), Michael C. Gwynne (*Val Adams*)
__D:__ Jerrold Freedman   __WRIT:__ Christopher Knopf   __ELECTRONIC SCORE:__ Gil Melle
A.k.a. __The Chill Factor__
TVM, standard SF-melodrama: Mystery besets scientists at isolated simian research center

The Cold Room
1984, (GB), Jethro Film/Home Box Office, color, 95 mins.
__W:__ George Segal (*Hugh Martin*), Amanda Pays (*Carla Martin/Christa Bruckner*), Renee Soutendijk (*Lili*), Warren Clarke (*Bruckner*), An-thony Higgins (*Erich*), Clifford Rose (*Moltke*), Elizabeth Spriggs (*Frau Hoffman*), Ursula Howells (*The Headmistress*), Lucy Hornack (*Sophie*), Gertan Klauber (*The Older Nazi*), Tristram Wymark (*The Young Nazi*), Stuart Wolfe (*The Young Man*), Wolf Rudiger Reutermann (*The Customs Officer*), Judich Melische (*The Young Woman*)
__WRIT & D:__ James Dearden, from Jeffrey Caine's novel   __PHOTOG:__ Tony Pierce-

Roberts   __MUSIC:__ Michael Nyman
Cable-TVM, standard thriller: Girl relives drama of World War II lookalike

The Cold Sun
1954, (USA), Reed, b&w
__W:__ Richard Crane
Minor SF-adventure, feature culled 1950's teleseries __Rocky Jones, Space Ranger__

Cold Sweat
1993, (USA), color
__W:__ Shannon Tweed
Minor fantasy: Hit man haunted by victim's ghost

El Colleccionista de Cadaveres
see __Cauldron of Blood__

The Collector
1965, (USA-GB), Col, color, 119 mins.
__W:__ Terence Stamp (*Freddie Clegg*), Samantha Eggar (*Miranda Grey*), Mona Washbourne (*Aunt Annie*), Maurice Dallimore (*The Neighbor*)
__P:__ Jud Kinberg   __D:__ William Wyler   __SCR:__ Stanley Mann & John Kohn, from John Fowles' novel   __PHOTOG:__ Robert L. Surtees & Robert Krasker   __MUSIC:__ Maurice Jarre   __DESIGN:__ John Stoll
French retitle, __L'Obsede (The Obsessed)__
Superior, award-winning melodrama: Disturbed youth kidnaps woman, holds her prisoner

The Collector of Cadavers
see __Cauldron of Blood__

Collision Course (1968)
see __The Bamboo Saucer__

Collision Course
1990, (USA), color, 100 mins.
__W:__ Jay Leno, Pat Morita, Chris Sarandon (*Philip*), Ernie Hudson (*Shortcut*)
Standard thriller: Japanese investigator and Detroit cop team to find stolen turbocharger prototype

Colonel Bogey
1948, (GB), Production Facilities/GFD, b&w, 51 mins.
__W:__ Jack Train (*Voice of Uncle James*), Mary Jerrold (*Aunt Mabel*), Jane Barrett (*Alice Graham*), Ethel Coleridge (*Emily*), John Stone (*Wilfred Barriteau*), Hedli Anderson (*Millicent*)
__P:__ John Croydon   __D:__ Terence Fisher   __SCR:__ William Fairchild & John Baines   __STORY:__ William Fairchild
Standard fantasy: Uncle's ghost refuses to leave his home

Colonel March Investigates
1953, (GB), Criterion/Panda, b&w
__W:__ Boris Karloff, Joan Sims, Dana Wynter
__P:__ Donald Ginsberg   __SCR:__ Led Davis
Minor mystery-thriller (culled from episodes of British teleseries __Colonel March of Scotland Yard__*): One-eyed sleuth faces perplexing case*

Colonel March of Scotland Yard
1953, (GB), Criterion/Panda, b&w
__W:__ Boris Karloff
Minor mystery-thriller: British sleuth's powers of deduction are sorely tried

Colony
1997, (Switz), color
__D:__ Thomas Berna
A.k.a. __Colony Mutation__
Minor SF-horror

The Colony
1995, (USA), USA-TV, color, 93 mins.
__W:__ John Ritter, Hal Linden, Mary Page Keller, Frank Bonner, Marshall Teague, Michelle Scarabelli, June Lockhart, Todd Jeffries, Alexandra Picatto, Cody Dorkin
__D & TELEPLAY:__ Rob Hedden
TVM, standard thriller: Security-systems designer discovers totalitarian community

Colony Mutation
see __Colony (1997)__

Color Him Dead
1974, (GB), TV Movie, color
__W:__ Gayle Hunnicutt, Stephen Rea, Christopher Cazenove
TVM, minor thriller: Husband & wife detectives try to prevent millionaire's murder

Color Me Blood Red
1965, (USA), Boxoffice Spectaculars, color, 78 mins.
__W:__ Don Joseph, Sandi Conder
__D, SCR & PHOTOG,__ Herschell Gordon Lewis
A.k.a. __Model Massacre__
Minor thriller: Mad artist slays beauties, paints with blood

Color Me Dead
1969, (Austral), Commonwealth, color, 97 mins.

W: Tom Tryon (*Frank*), Carolyn Jones (*Paula*), Patricia Connolly (*Maria*), Rick Jason (*Bradley*), Tony Ward (*Halliday*), Michael Lawrence (*George*), Penny Sugg (*Miss Foster*), Margot Reid (*Mrs. Phillips*), Reg Gillam (*Eugene*), Peter Sumner (*Stanley*), Sandy Harbott (*Chester*)
D: Eddie Davis, based on a screenplay by Russell Rouse & Clarence Greene
    PHOTOG: Mick Borneman   **MUSIC:** Bob Young
A.k.a. D.O.A. II
Inferior remake of D.O.A. (1949): Poisoned man seeks killer

Color Me Perfect
1996, (USA), Lifetime, color, 95 mins.
W: Robin Thomas, Michele Lee (*Dina Blake*), Susan Blakely (*Linda*), Stan Cahill (*Andy*), Nathaniel Deveaux (*Elisha*)
D & CO-TELEPLAY: Michele Lee
Standard SF-melodrama (similar to Charly): DNA injections raise I.Q. of retarded woman

Color of Night
1994, (USA), Hollywood Pictures/Buena Vista, color, 123 mins.
W: Bruce Willis, Jane March, Ruben Blades, Lesley Ann Warren, Brad Dourif, Scott Bakula, Lance Henriksen, Kevin J. O'Connor, Jeff Corey Andrew Lowery, Eriq La Salle, Shirley Knight, Kathleen Wilhoite
D: Richard Rush   **SCR:** Matthew Chapman, Billy Ray & Richard Rush
    MUSIC: Dominic Frontiere
Bizarre eroto-thriller: Psychiatrist seeks friend's killer

Colossus and the Amazon Queen
see La Regina delle Amazzoni

Colossus and the Headhunters
1960, (It), IDS/Alta Vista, color
W: Kirk Morris, Laura Brown, Frank Leroy, Alfredo Zammi, Ines Holder
D: Guido Malatesta   **PHOTOG:** Dominico Scala
Minor "Sword & Sandal" adventure: Muscleman lends aid to deposed queen

Colossus and the Huns
1960, (It), color
W: Jerome Courtland, Lisa Gastoni
Minor adventure-thriller: Barbarian hordes threaten, hero aids king

The Colossus of New York
1958, (USA), Para, b&w, 70 mins.
W: Mala Powers, John Baragrey, Charles Herbert, Otto Kruger, Robert Hutton, Ross Martin, Ed Wolff (*The Colossus*)
P: William Alland   **D:** Eugene Lourie   **SCR:** Thelma Schnee, based on a story by Willis Goldbeck   **PHOTOG:** Jack Warren   **SPCL-FX:** John P. Fulton
Standard SF: Scientist's brain placed in android body

The Colossus of Rhodes
1961, (It-Fr), Cineproduzioni/Procusa/C.F.P.C./C.T.I./MGM, color, 129 mins.
W: Rory Calhoun (*Dario*), Lea Massari (*Diala*), Georges Marchal (*Peliocles*), Conrado San Martin (*Thar*), Roberto Camardiel, Angel Aranda, Mabel Karr, Mimmo Palmara, Carlo Tamberlani, Jorge Rigaud, Felix Fernandez, Alfio Caltaviano
P: Michael Scaglione   **D:** Sergio Leone   **SCR:** Ennio De Concini & Cesare Seccia
    PHOTOG: Antonio Ballesteros   **MUSIC:** Angelo Francisco Lavagnino
"Sword & Sandal" spectacular: Intrigue inside and outside mighty Wonder of the ancient world

Colossus of the Arena
1960, (It), color
W: Mark Forest, Scilla Gabel
Minor "Sword & Sandal": Gladiator rescues princess

Colossus: The Forbin Project
1970, (USA), Univ, color, 100 mins.
W: Eric Braeden (*Forbin*), Susan Clark (*Clea*), Gordon Pinsent (*The President*), William Schallert (*Grauber*), Leonid Rostoff (*First Chairman*), Willard Sage (*Blake*), Sid McCoy (*Secretary of Defense*), Georg Stanford Brown (*Fisher*), Dolph Sweet (*The Missile Commander*), Alex Rodine (*Kuprin*), Marion Ross (*Angela*), Martin Brooks (*Johnson*), Byron Morrow (*The Secretary of State*), Lew Brown (*Peterson*), Tom Basham (*Harrison*), Sergei Tschernisch (*The Translator*), James Hong, Robert Cornthwaite
P: Stanley Chase   **D:** Joseph Sargent   **SCR:** James Bridges, based on D.F. Jones' novel *Colossus*   **PHOTOG:** Gene Polito   **MUSIC:** Michel Columbier
orig. to be titled Mighty Colossus, televised as The Forbin Project
Superior SF-thriller: Sentient computer manipulates humans

Coma
1978, (USA), MGM-UA, color, 113 mins.
W: Genevieve Bujold (*Dr. Susan Wheeler*), Michael Douglas (*Dr. Mark Bellows*), Richard Widmark (*Dr. Harris*), Elizabeth Ashley (*Mrs. Emerson*), Rip Torn (*Dr. George*), Tom Selleck (*Murphy*), Lois Chiles (*Nancy Greenly*), Harry Rhodes (*Dr. Morelind*), Gary Barton (*The Computer Technician*), Lance LeGault (*Vince*), Alan Haufrect (*Dr. Marcus*), Frank Downing (*Kelly*), Richard Doyle (*Jim*), Michael MacRae (*The Chief Resident*), Charles Siebert (*Dr. Goodman*), Betty McGuire (*The Nurse*), William Wintersole (*The Lab Technician*), Harry Basch, Ernest Anderson, Joni Palmer, Maury Cooper, Joanna Keekis, Kay Cole

P: Max Ehrlichman   **D & SCR:** Michael Crichton, from Robin Cook's novel
    PHOTOG: Victor J. Kemper   **SPCL-FX:** Joe Day   **MUSIC:** Jerry Goldsmith
Standard thriller: Woman doctor uncovers gruesome traffic in body parts

The Comeback
see The Day the Screaming Stopped

Comedy Cartoons
1907, (GB), Urban, b&w, 200 ft. (60.1m)
D: Walter R. Booth
Minor fantasy short: Artist's hand draws cartoons that come to life

The Comedy of Terrors
1963, (USA), AIP, color, 88 mins.
W: Vincent Price, Peter Lorre, Basil Rathbone, Boris Karloff, Joyce Jameson, Beverly Hills, Joe E. Brown, Paul Barselow, Linda Rogers, Luree Nicholson, Buddy Mason, Rhubarb the Cat
P: Anthony Carras   **D:** Jacques Tourneur   **SCR:** Richard Matheson   **PHOTOG:** Floyd Crosby   **MUSIC:** Les Baxter
reissued (1965) as The Graveside Story
Standard horror-comedy: Undertakers revive failing business

Come in, Children
see The Brotherhood of Satan

Come Out, Come Out, Wherever You Are
1974, (GB), Made for TV, color
W: Lynda Day George, John Carson (*Arthur*), Peter Jeffrey (*Dexter*), Bernard Holley (*Paul*), Colette O'Neil (*Alice*)
TVM, minor thriller: Tourist's cousin disappears

The Comfort of Strangers
1990, (GB-It), color, 104 mins.
W: Christopher Walken, Rupert Everett, Natasha Richardson, Helen Mirren, Manfredi Aliquo
D: Paul Schrader   **SCR:** Harold Pinter, from Ian McEwan's novel   **PHOTOG:** Dante Spinotti
Unusual melodrama: Mysterious aristocrat lures couple on second honeymoon

Comical Conjuring
see Jack et Jim

The Coming
1980, (USA), Alan Landsburg Prods., color, 95 mins.
W: Susan Swift (*Loreen Graham/Ann Putnam*), Guy Stockwell (*Dr. Grossinger*), Tisha Sterling (*Karen Graham*), Lauren Downing (*Sarah Goode*), Albert Salmi (*The Captain*), Beverly Ross (*Merlina*), David Rounds (*William Goode*), John Peters (*Rev. Parris*), Jennine Babo (*Dorcas Goode*), Dana Hardwick (*Justice Hathorne*), Frank Dolan (*Kevin O'Neil*), Terese Giammarco (*Gwyneth*), Judy Dodd (*Nancy*), David Golia (*The Driver*), Nina Marten (*Rebecca Nurse*), Harold Jackson (*The Library Guard*), Richard Kneeland (*Giles Corey*), Janice Wayne (*Miss Williams*)
WRIT, P, & D: Bert I. Gordon   **PHOTOG:** Daniel Yarussi   **SPCL-FX,** Fred Yawnick   **MUSIC:** Arthur Kempel
A.k.a. Burned at the Stake
Minor fantasy-thriller: 1692 witchcraft mania has repercussions in modern Salem

The Coming of Santa Claus
1906, (GB), Walturdaw, b&w, 550 ft. (167.6m)
Standard fantasy short: Fairies help St. Nick deliver toys

Comment Qu'ella Est! (Women Are Like That!)
1960, (Fr), Films Borderie, b&w, 91 mins.
W: Eddie Constantine (*Lemmy Caution*), Andre Luget, Francoise Brion, Alfred Adam, Francoise Prevost, Renaud Mary
D: Bernard Borderie   **SCR:** Bernard Borderie & Marc-Gilbert Sauvajon, from Peter Cheyney's novel *I'll Say She Does*
5th "Lemmy Caution" adventure, standard thriller: Secret agent captures dangerous spy

Committed
1991, (USA), color, 90 mins.
W: Jennifer O'Neill, Robert Forster, Ron Palillo (*Ronnie*), William Windom, Sydney Lassick
D: William A. Levey
Minor thriller: Nurse held prisoner in psychiatric hospital

The Committee
1968, (GB), Craytic/Planet, b&w, 58 mins.
W: Paul Jones (*The Central Figure*), Pauline Munro (*The Girl*), Robert Lloyd (*The Director*), Tom Kempinski (*The Victim*), Jimmy Gardner (*The Boss*)
P & STORY: Max Steuer   **D:** Peter Sykes   **SCR:** Max Steuer & Peter Sykes
Standard fantasy: Strange convocation summons homicidal hitchhiker

The Commuter
1967, (GB), Norland/Contemporary, b&w, 16 mins.
WRIT, P & D: Tom Misha Norland
Standard short fantasy: Commuter's dress dummy turns illusions into reality

Communion

1989, (USA), Pheasantry-Allied Visions Ltd. Picture Property Co./New Line, color, 107 mins.
W: Christopher Walken *(Whitley Strieber)*, Lindsay Crouse *(Anne Strieber)*, Frances Sternhagen *(Dr. Janet Duffy)*, John Dennis Johnston *(The Fireman)*, Andreas Katsulas *(Alex)*, Basil Hoffman *(Dr. Friedman)*, Terri Hannauer *(Sarah)*, Joel Carlson *(Andrew Strieber)*, Dee Dee Rescher *(Mrs. Greenberg)*, Holly Fields *(The Praying Mantis Girl)*, Aileen Fitzpatrick *(Mother)*, R.J. Miller *(Father)*, Tifni Twitchell *(The Teacher)*, Paula Shaw *(The Woman from the Apt.)*, Juliet Sorcey *(The 2nd-Grade Girl)*, Joshua John Miller *(The Tall Boy)*, Diane Behrens *(The Nurse)*, Johnny Dark *(The Lab Technician)*, Kate Stern *(The Woman on the Bus)*, Jonathan Fromdahl *(Whitley, Age 5 yrs.)*, Andrew Margarian *(The Man in the Hallway)*, Madeleine Mora *(The Baby Girl)*, Maggie Egan *(Nancy)*, Paul Clemens *(Patrick)*, Irene Forrest *(Sally)*, Sally Kemp *(Laurie)*, Vince McKewin *(Bob)*
D: Philippe Mora   **SCR:** Whitley Strieber, from his book   **PHOTOG:** Louis Irving, **THEME:** Eric Clapton   **MUSIC:** Allan Zavod
Unusual SF-thriller: Space aliens visit author

The Companion (1974)
*see **Betrayal***

The Companion

1994, (USA), Univ, color, video, 94 mins.
W: Kathryn Harrold *(Gillian)*, Bruce Greenwood *(Geoffrey)*, Talia Balsam *(Charlene)*, Brion James *(Ron Cocheran)*, Joely Fisher *(Stacy)*, Bryan Cranston *(Alan)*, James Karen *(Peter Franklin)*, Brenda Leigh *(Ellen)*, Earl Boen *(Marty Bailin)*, Julian Brams *(The Technician)*, Courtney Taylor *(Shelley)*, Stacie Randall *(The Saleswoman)*, Tracey Walter *(Leo Mirita)*
P: Richard Brams   **D:** Gary Fleder   **WRIT:** Ian Seeberg   **PHOTOG:** Rick Bota   **MUSIC:** David Shire
Made-for-Video, unusual SF-thriller: Woman writer held captive by over-programmed android

Company of Fools

1966, (GB), Merton Park/Anglo-Amalgamated, color, 33 mins.
W: Barrie Ingham *(Maj. MacDonald)*, Jacqueline Jones *(Liz Jason)*, Maurice Kaufmann *(Kasabis)*, Garfield Morgan *(Jason)*, Barry Keegan *(Webb)*, Frank Williams *(Price)*
P: Jack Greenwood   **D:** Peter Duffell   **STORY:** James Eastwood, from a novel by Edgar Lustgarten
Standard short crime-thriller: Ex-major poses as sheik to ruin crooked financier

The Company of Wolves

1985, (GB), Palace/ITC/Cannon, color, 93 mins.
W: Angela Lansbury *(Granny)*, David Warner *(Father)*, Graham Crowden *(The Old Priest)*, Shane Johnstone *(The Amorous Boy)*, Brian Glover *(The Amorous Boy's Father)*, Susan Porrett *(The Amorous Boy's Mother)*, Kathryn Pogson *(The Young Bride)*, Stephen Rea *(The Young Groom)*, Tusse Silberg *(Mother)*, Micha Bergese *(The Huntsman)*, Sarah Patterson *(Rosaleen)*, Georgia Slowe *(Alice)*, Dawn Archibald *(The Witch Woman)*, Danielle Dax *(The Wolfgirl)*, Richard Morant *(The Wealthy Groom)*, Vincent McClaren *(The Devil Boy)*, Ruby Buchanan *(The Dowager)*, Jimmy Gardner *(The Ancient)*, Roy Evans *(Eyepatch)*, Terence Stamp *(The Prince of Darkness)*, Edward Marksen, Jimmy Brown
P: Chris Brown & Stephen Woolley   **D:** Neil Jordan   **SCR:** Angela Carter & Neil Jordan, from a story by Angela Carter   **PHOTOG:** Brian Loftus   **MUSIC:** George Fenton
*Adult, horrific reworking of **Little Red Riding Hood**: Girl dreams of werewolves*

Compelled

1960, (GB), Danziger/UA, b&w, 56 mins.
W: Ronald Howard *(Paul Adams)*, Beth Rogan *(Carol)*, Richard Shaw *(Jug)*, John Gabriel *(Fenton)*, Colin Tapley *(The Inspector)*, Jack Melford *(Grimes)*, Mark Singleton *(Derek)*
P: Brian Taylor   **D:** Ramsey Harrington   **STORY:** Mark Grantham
Standard crime-thriller: Ex-convict blackmailed into helping jewel thieves

Le Compositeur Toque (The Crazy Composer)

1905, (Fr), Star, b&w, 103m (337.9 ft./5.7 mins.)
D: Georges Melies
Standard comedy-fantasy: Pianist commits suicide

Computercide

1982, (USA), NBC-TV, color
W: Joseph Cortese *(Michael Stringer)*, Susan George *(Lisa Korter)*, Donald Pleasence *(Dettler)*, David Huddleston *(Sorenson)*
TVM (orig. produced in 1977), standard SF-thriller: World's last private eye finds puzzling case in year 1996

Computer Killers
*see **Horror Hospital***

The Computer Wore Tennis Shoes

1970, (USA), Walt Disney/Buena Vista, color, 91 mins
W: Kurt Russell *(Dexter Riley)*, Cesar Romero *(A.J. Arno)*, Joe Flynn *(Dean Higgins)*, William Schallert *(Prof. Quigley)*, Alan Hewitt *(Dean Collingsgood)*, Richard Bakalyan *(Chillie Walsh)*, Debbie Paine *(Annie)*, Frank Webb *(Pete)*, Frank Welker *(Henry)*, Michael McGreevey *(Schuyler)*, Fritz Feld *(Sigmund Van Dyke)*, Jon Provost *(Bradley)*, Alexander Clarke *(Myles)*, Bing Russell *(Angelo)*, Pat Harrington *(The Moderator)*, Fabian Dean *(Little Mac)*, Pete

Renoudet *(Lt. Hannah)*, Hillyard Anderson *(J. Reedy)*
D: Robert Butler   **SCR:** Joseph L. McEveety   **PHOTOG:** Frank Phillips   **MUSIC:** Robert F. Brunner
*Juvenile SF-comedy: Shock from computer turns failing student into superbrain. Sequel: **Now You See Him, Now You Don't**, remade for TV in 1995.*

The Computer Wore Tennis Shoes

1995, (USA), Walt Disney, color, 95 mins.
W: Kirk Cameron, Larry Miller, Jason Bernard, Jeff Maynard, Andrew Woodworth, Dean Jones
D: Peyton Reed   **SCR:** Joseph L. McEveety & Ryan Rowe   **PHOTOG:** Russ Alsobrook   **MUSIC:** Philip Giffin
Standard comedy-fantasy (remake)

Le Comte de Monte Cristo (The Count of Monte Cristo)

1960, (Fr), Vital-Modiano/WB, color, 130 mins.
W: Louis Jourdan *(Edmund Dantes)*, Yvonne Furneaux *(Mercedes)*, Pierre Mondy *(Caderousse)*, Franco Silva *(Mario)*, Jean-Claude Michel *(Fernand de Montcerf)*, Jean Martinelli *(Vidocq)*, Yves Renier *(Albert de Montcerf)*, Bernard Dheran *(Villefort)*, Henri Guisol *(Abbe Faria)*, Marie Mergey *(Mme. Caderousse)*, Claudine Coster *(Haydee)*, Alain Ferral *(Benedetto)*
D: Claude Autant-Lara   **SCR:** Jean Halain, from Alexander Dumas' novel   **MUSIC:** Rene Cloerec
*A.k.a. **The Story of the Count of Monte Cristo***
Lavish melodrama: Prison escapee gains revenge and riches

Conan: King of Thieves
*see **Conan the Destroyer***

Conan the Barbarian

1982, (USA), Dino De Laurentiis-Edward R. Pressman/Univ, color, 115 mins.
W: Arnold Schwarzenegger *(Conan)*, Sandahl Bergman *(Valeria)*, James Earl Jones *(Thulsa Doom)*, Ben Davidson *(Rexor)*, Max von Sydow *(King Osric)*, Mako *(Akiro)*, Cassandra Gaviola *(The Witch)*, Gerry Lopez, William Smith
P: Buzz Feitshans & Raffaela De Laurentiis   **D:** John Milius   **SCR:** John Milius & Oliver Stone, from characters created by Robert E. Howard   **PHOTOG:** Duke Callaghan   **MUSIC:** Basil Poledouris
Superior adventure-fantasy: Hero battles cultists at dawn of civilization

Conan the Destroyer

1984, (USA), Dino De Laurentiis-Edward R. Pressman/Univ, color, 100 mins.

Conan the Destroyer: ARNOLD SCHWARTZENEGGER

W: Arnold Schwarzenegger (*Conan*), Grace Jones (*Zula*), Olivia D'Abo (*Princess Jehnna*), Wilt Chamberlain (*Bombaata*), Tracey Walter (*Malak*), Mako (*Akiro*), Sarah Douglas (*Queen Taramis*), Ferdinand Mayne (*The Leader*), Pat Roach, Jeff Corey
D: Richard Fleischer **SCR:** Stanley Mann **STORY:** Roy Thomas & Gerry Conway, from characters created by Robert E. Howard **PHOTOG:** Jack Cardiff **MUSIC:** Basil Poledouris
orig. to be titled **Conan: King of Thieves**
Standard adventure-fantasy: Hero seeks fabled treasure and return of lost love

Con Caper/Curse of Rava
1978, (USA), CBS-TV, color
W: Nicholas Hammond
TVM, minor fantasy-thriller culled from teleseries **SpiderMan:** *Superhero vs. criminals and cultists*

The Concrete Jungle (1960)
see **The Criminal**

The Concrete Jungle
1982, (USA), Col, color, 106 mins.
W: Jill St. John, Nita Talbot, Tracy Bregman, Peter Brown, Barbara Luna
D: Tom De Simone **SCR:** Alan Adler
Standard exploitation thriller: Girl faces prison terrors

The Condemnation of Faust
see **Faust aux Enfers**

Condemned
1929, (USA), UA, b&w, 86 mins.
W: Ronald Colman (*Michel*), Ann Harding (*Mme. Vidal*), Louis Wol-heim (*Jacques*), Dudley Digges (*Vidal*), William Elmer (*Pierre*), Albert Kingsley (*Felix*), William Vaughn (*Vidal's Orderly*)
P: Samuel Goldwyn **D:** Wesley Ruggles **SCR:** Sidney Howard, from Blair Niles' novel *Condemned to Devil's Island* **PHOTOG:** George Barnes & Gregg Toland
Modest melodrama: Man tries to escape prison camp

Condemned to Death
1932, (GB), Twickenham/W&F, b&w, 75 mins.
W: Arthur Wontner (*Sir Charles Wallington*), Gordon Harker (*Sam Knudge*), Edmund Gwenn (*Banting*), Jane Welsh (*Sonia Wallington*), Cyril Raymond (*Jim Wrench*), Nora Howard (*Gwen Banting*), Bernard Brunel (*Tobias Lantern*), Griffith Humphreys (*Prof. Michaels*), H. St. Barbe West (*Sir Rudolph Cantler*)
D: Walter Forde **SCR:** Bernard Merivale, Brock Williams & H. Fowler Mear, from George Goodchild's play *Jack O'Lantern*
A.k.a. **Jack O'Lantern Murders**
Standard thriller: Condemned killer hypnotizes judge

Condemned to Live
1935, (USA), Chesterfield-Invincible, b&w, 68 mins.
W: Mischa Auer, Maxine Doyle, Ralph Morgan, Russell Gleason, Pedro de Cordoba
P: Maury M. Cohen **D:** Frank Strayer **SCR:** Karen de Wolfe **PHOTOG:** M.A. Anderson **MUSIC DIR:** Abe Meyer
Minor horror-fantasy: Woman bitten by vampire bat, conceives monstrous child

Condom of Terror
see **Kondom des Grauens**

Condor
1986, (USA), Orion TV/ABC-TV, color, 69 mins.
W: Ray Wise (*Christopher Proctor*), Wendy Kilbourne (*Lisa Hampton*), Craig Stevens (*Cyrus Hampton*), Carolyn Seymour (*Rachel Hawkins*), Vic Polizos (*Ward*), Cassandra Gava (*Sumiko*), James Avery (*Cass*), Shawn Michaels (*The Watch Commander*), Mario Roccuzzo (*Manny*), Catherine Battistone, Barbara Beckley, Wendell W. Wright, Diana Bellamy, Gene Bicknell, Myra Chason, Karen Montgomery, Tony Epper, Brad Fisher, Mike Freeman, Jay Scorpio, Phil Fondacaro
D: Virgil W. Vogel **TELEPLAY:** Len Janson & Chuck Menville **PHOTOG:** Thom Neuwirth **MUSIC:** Ken Heller
TVM (feature-film pilot for unsold teleseries), minor SF adventure: Anti-terrorist agent pursues prison escapee

Condorman
1981, (USA-GB), Walt Disney/Buena Vista, color, 90 mins.
W: Michael Crawford (*Woody*), Oliver Reed (*Krokov*), Barbara Carrera (*Natalia*), James Hampton (*Harry*), Dana Elcar (*Russ*), Jean-Pierre Kalfon (*Morovich*), Vernon Dobtcheff (*The Russian Agent*), Robert Arden (*The CIA Chief*)
D: Charles Jarrott **SCR:** Marc Stirdivant, based on Robert Sheckley's *The Game of X* **PHOTOG:** Charles F. Wheeler **SPCL-FX:** Colin Chilvers & Art Cruickshank **MUSIC:** Henry Mancini
Standard comedy-thriller: Complications arise when comic book author is mistaken for secret agent

Coneheads
1993, (USA), Paramount, color, 88 mins.
W: Dan Aykroyd, Jane Curtin, Jon Lovitz, Michelle Burke, Michael McKean,
Julia Sweeney, David Spade, Chris Farley, Phil Hartman, Michael Richards, Adam Sandler, Sinbad, Drew Carey, Kevin Nealon, Laraine Newman, Danielle Aykroyd, Jason Alexander, Jan Hooks, Dave Thomas, Garrett Morris, Chris Rock, Lisa Jane Persky
D: Steve Barron **SCR:** Tom Davis, Dan Aykroyd, Bonnie Turner & Terry Turner **PHOTOG:** Francis Kenny **ORIG. SCORE:** David Newman
Standard SF-comedy: Space aliens pose as suburbanites

Confess, Dr. Corda
1961, (W. Ger), CCC/President, b&w, 81 mins.
W: Hardy Kruger, Elisabeth Muller, Lucie Mannheim, Eva Pflug, Hans Nielsen, Fritz Tillman, Rudolf Fernau, Siegfried Lowitz, Albert Bessler, Emmy Burg, Lore Hartling, Ernst Sattler, Paul Edwin Roth, Jochen Blume, Alfred Balthoff, Roma Bahn, Werner Butler, Reinhard Kolldehoff, Georg Gutlich, Barbara Wieczik, Hans Binner, Siegrid Hackenberg, Maria Krasna
D: Joseph Von Baky **SCR:** R.A. Stemmle **MUSIC:** George Haentzchel
Standard thriller: Doctor has blackout, becomes suspect in girl's murder

Confession
1955, (GB), Anglo-Guild/Anglo-Amalgamated, b&w, 90 mins.
W: Sydney Chaplin (*Mike Nelson*), Peter Hammond (*Alan*), John Bentley (*Insp. Kessler*), Audrey Dalton (*Louise Nelson*), John Welsh (*Father Neil*), Jefferson Clifford (*Pop*), Pat McGrath (*Williams*), Robert Raglan (*Becklan*), Patrick Allen (*Corey*)
P: Alec Snowden **D & SCR:** Ken Hughes, from a play by Don Martin
USA retitle, **The Deadliest Sin**
Standard crime-thriller: Thief tries to kill priest who knows his secret

The Confession
1915, (GB), Hepworth, b&w, 1,000 ft. (304.8m)
W: Stewart Rome (*Edward Clavering*), Chrissie White (*Pauline Allington*), Lionelle Howard (*Rupert Hartley*), Harry Gilbey (*Mr. Allington*)
D: Frank Wilson
Standard crime-thriller: Girl extracts confession from gambler who framed her fiance for murder

The Confession
1920, (USA), b&w, 78 mins.
W: Henry B. Walthall, Francis McDonald, William H. Clifford, Margaret McWade, Margaret Landis
D: Bertram Bracken
Standard thriller: Priest knows killer's identity

The Confession (1970)
see **L'Aveu**

The Confessional
see **House of Mortal Sin**

Confessions of a Nazi Spy
1939, (USA), WB, b&w, 102 mins.
W: Edward G. Robinson, Francis Lederer, George Sanders, Paul Lukas, Lya Lys, Henry O'Neill, James Stephenson, Ward Bond
D: Anatole Litvak
Well-made thriller: Man duped into becoming spy

Confessions of an Opium Eater
1962, (USA), Photoplay/AA, b&w, 85 mins.
W: Vincent Price (*DeQuincey*), Linda Ho (*Ruby Low*), Richard Loo (*George Wah*), June Kim (*Lotus*), Caroline Kido (*Lo Tsen*), Philip Ahn (*Ching Foon*), Miel Saan (*Look Gow*), Yvonne Moray (*The Child*), Gerald Jann (*The Fat Chinese*), Terence de Marney (*The Scrawny Man*), Vivianne Manku (*The Catatonic Girl*), John Mamo (*The Auctioneer*), Victor Sen Yung (*Wing Young*), Arthur Wong (*Kwai Tong*), Ralph Ahn (*Wah Chan*), Alicia Li (*Ping Toy*), Charles Horvath
P & D: Albert Zugsmith **SCR:** Robert Hill, based on Thomas DeQuincey's novel *Confessions of an English Opium Eater* **PHOTOG:** Joseph Biroc **MUSIC:** Albert Glasser
GB retitle, **Evils of Chinatown,** *A.k.a.* **Souls for Sale**
Standard melodrama: Slave trade and vice among Chinese immigrants of 1800's

Confessions of a Serial Killer
1992, (USA), HBO-TV, color, 92 mins.
W: Robert A. Burns
Made-for-Cable, standard thriller: Fact-based story of murderer Henry Lee Lucas

Confessions of Boston Blackie
1941, (USA), Col, b&w, 65 mins.
W: Chester Morris (*Boston Blackie*), Richard Lane (*Insp. Farraday*), Harriet Hilliard (*Diane Parrish*), George E. Stone (*Runt*), Lloyd Corrigan (*Arthur Manleder*), Walter Sande (*Det. Matthews*), Joan Woodbury (*Mona*), Ralph Theodore (*Buchanan*), Kenneth MacDonald (*Caulder*), Walter Soderling (*Eric Allison*), Billy Benedict (*The Ice Cream Man*), Jack Clifford (*The Motor Cop*), Mike Pat Donovan (*The Policeman*), Eddie Laughton (*The Express Man*), Jack O'Malley (*The Taxi Driver*)
D: Edward Dmytryk **SCR:** Paul Yawitz & Jay Dratler, from characters created by Jack Boyle **PHOTOG:** Philip Tanura
Minor thriller: Man murdered at New York art auction

Confidence Girl
1952, (USA), UA, b&w, 81 mins.
W: Tom Conway, Hillary Brooke
P,D & SCR.: Andrew L. Stone
Standard melodrama

Confidential Agent
1945, (USA), WB, b&w, 118 mins.
W: Charles Boyer, Lauren Bacall, Peter Lorre, George Coulouris, George Zucco, Victor Francen, Wanda Hendrix
P & SCR: Robert Buckner **D:** Herman Schumlin, from Graham Greene's novel-
PHOTOG: James Wong Howe
Standard thriller: Spanish loyalist involved in intrigue

Confidential Report
see Mr. Arkadin

Confidentially Yours
1983, (Fr), Spectrafilms, b&w, 111 mins.
W: Fanny Ardant, Jean-Louis Trintignant, Philippe Laudenbach, Caroline Sihol, Philippe Morier-Genoud, Xavier Saint Macary
D: Francois Truffaut **SCR:** Francois Truffaut, Suzanne Schiffman & Jean Aurel from Charles Williams' novel *Saturday* **PHOTOG:** Nestor Almendros
MUSIC: Georges Delerue
Unusual whodunit (Truffaut's last film): Ex-secretary tries to clear boss of murder charge

Congo
1995, (USA), Para, color
W: Dylan Walsh (*Peter Eliot*), Laura Linney (*Karen Ross*), Ernie Hudson (*Monroe Kelly*), Joe Don Baker (*R.B. Travis*), Tim Curry (*Herkermer Homolka*), Grant Heslov (*Richard*), Bruce Campbell (*Charles Travis*), Lorene Noh & Misty Rosas (*Amy*), James Karen, Taylor Nichols, Adewale, Mary Ellen Trainor, Stuart Pankin, Jimmy Buffett, Carolyn Seymour, Romy Rosemont, Bill Pugin, Lawrence T. Wentz, Robert Almodovar, Joel Weiss, Kathleen Connors, John Hawkes, Thom Barry, Peter Jason, James R. Paradise, William John Murphy, M. Darnell Suttles, Ayo Adejugbe, Kevin Grevioux, Kahara Muhoro, Michael Chinyamurindi, Willie Amakye, Jay Speed Forney, Malang, Guy Toley, Shelton Mack, David Mungai, Sylvester Mwangi, E.J. Callahan, Nelson Shalita, Les Robinson, Jackson Gitonga, Fidel Bateke, Andrew Kamuyu
D: Frank Marshall **SCR:** John Patrick Shanley, from Michael Crichton's novel **PHOTOG:** Allen Daviau **SPCL-FX SPRVSR:** Scott Farrar **MUSIC:** Jerry Goldsmith
Unusual SF-thriller: Techno-intrigue and intelligent gorillas in Central Africa

Congo Crossing
1956, (USA), Univ, color, 83 mins.
W: George Nader, Virginia Mayo, Peter Lorre, Rex Ingram, Michael Pate, Robin Raymond, Carmen D'Antonio, Tudor Owen, George Ramsey
P: Howard Christie **D:** Joseph Pevney **SCR:** Richard Alan Simmons
Standard melodrama: Crooks and tsetse flies at African construction site

The Conjurer
1900, (GB), G.A.S. Films, b&w, 50 ft. (15.2m)
D: George Albert Smith
Minor fantasy short: Magician makes girl vanish, produces kittens from handkerchief

The Conjurer and the Boer
1900, (GB), Hepworth, b&w, 75 ft. (22.9m)
W: Cecil Hepworth
D: Cecil Hepworth
Minor fantasy short: Conjurer turns Boer soldier into Britannia

Conjurer Making Ten Hats in Sixty Seconds
see Dix Chapeaux en 60 Secondes

The Conjurer's Pupil
1906, (GB), Urban, b&w, 300 ft. (91.4m)
D: Walter R. Booth
Minor fantasy short: Conjurer's son's tricks go awry

The Conjurer with a Hundred Tricks
see L'Homme aux Cent Trucs

Conjuring
see Seance de Prestidigitation

The Conjuring Clown
see The Pierrot and the Devil's Dice

The Conjuring Tramps
1912, (GB), Cosmopolitan, b&w, 400 ft. (121.9m)
Minor comedy-fantasy short: Hobos steal conjurer's devices

The Conjuror as a Good Samaritan
1912, (GB), Natural Colour Kinematograph Co., color
D: Walter R. Booth
Minor fantasy: Magician hypnotizes bailiffs, saves widow's children

A Connecticut Yankee
1931, (USA), Fox, b&w, 96 mins.
W: Will Rogers, Maureen O'Sullivan, William Farnum, Frank Albertson, Myrna Loy
D: David Butler **SCR:** William Conselman, based on Mark Twain's novel *A Connecticut Yankee in King Arthur's Court* **PHOTOG:** Ernest Palmer
Standard adventure-fantasy: Rube visits Celtic Britain

A Connecticut Yankee in King Arthur's Court
1921, (USA), Fox, b&w, 8,291 ft. (2527m)
W: Harry C. Myers, Pauline Starke
D: Emmett J. Flynn, from Mark Twain's novel **PHOTOG:** Lucien Andriot
Standard adventure-fantasy: American transported to ancient Great Britain

A Connecticut Yankee in King Arthur's Court
1949, (USA), Para, color, 107 mins.
W: Bing Crosby, Sir Cedric Hardwicke (*King Arthur*), Murvyn Vye (*Merlin*), Rhonda Fleming, William Bendix, Richard Webb, Ann Carter, Virginia Field, Henry Wilcoxon, Joseph Vitale, Alan Napier, Julia Faye, Mary Field
P: Robert Fellows **D:** Tay Garnett **SCR:** Edmund Beloin,, musical based on Mark Twain's novel **PHOTOG:** Ray Rennahan **MUSIC:** Victor Young
GB retitle, A Yankee in King Arthur's Court
Tuneful but loose adaptation of Twain's classic: American mechanic visits Dark-Age Britain

A Connecticut Yankee in King Arthur's Court
1989, (USA), Consolidated/NBC-TV, color, 94 mins.
W: Keshia Knight Pulliam (*Karen*), Jean Marsh (*Morgana*), Rene Au-berjonois (*Merlin*), Michael Gross (*King Arthur*), Emma Samms (*Queen Guinevere*), Whip Hubley (*Sir Lancelot*), Hugo E. Blick (*Mordred*), Bryce Hamnet, Berlinda Tolbert, Marissa Lindsay, William Nunn, William Jongeneel, Cardew Robinson, Natasha Williams, Bernard McKenna, Camilla Dempster
D: Mel Damski **TELEPLAY:** Paul Zindel, from Mark Twain's novel **PHOTOG:** Harvey Harrison **SPCL-FX:** Gabor Budahazi **MUSIC:** William Goldstein **SONG:** (performed by Tracie Spencer), *Cross My Heart*
TVM, minor fantasy: Girl visits Arthurian times

The Conquering Power
1922, (USA), Metro-Goldwyn, b&w, 7 reels (6,348 ft./1935m)
W: Rudolph Valentino (*Charles Grandet*), Alice Terry (*Eugenie Grandet*), Eric Mayne (*Victor Grandet*), Ralph Lewis (*Pere Grandet*), Carrie Daumery (*Pere Grandet's Wife*), Ward King (*Adolph*), Edward Connelly (*Notary Cruchot*), George Atkinson (*Cruchot's Son*), Willard Lee Hall (*The Abbe*), Mark Fenton (*Msr. des Grassins*), Bridgetta Clark (*des Grassins' Wife*), Mary Hearn (*Nanon*), Eugene Pouyet (*Cornoiller*), Andree Tourneur (*Annette*)
D: Rex Ingram **SCR:** June Mathis, based on Honore de Balzac's novel *Eugenie Grandet* **PHOTOG:** John F. Seitz
Standard romance: Passion and torment in 19th-century France

Conqueror of Atlantis
1964, (It), color
W: Kirk Morris, Luciana Gilli
Minor "Sword & Sandal": Shadow People kidnap Bedouins

Conqueror Worm
see Witch-Finder General

Conquest
1984, (It), UFD, color, 92 mins.
W: George Rivero, Andrea Occhipinti, Violeta Cela, Sabrina Sellers, Jose Gras Palau, Maria Scola
D: Lucio Fulci **SCR:** Gino Capone, Jose de La Loma Sr. & Carlos Vasallo **STORY:** Giovanni Di Clemente **MUSIC:** Claudio Simonetti
Minor SF-sorcery: Witch controls planet's sun

The Conquest of Mycenae
1960, (It-Fr), Explorer-Comptoir/Embassy, color, 95 mins.
W: Gordon Scott (*Glaucus*), Alessandra Panaro (*Medea*), Arturo Dominici (*Pentheus*), Rosalba Neri (*Demetra*), Michel Lemoine, Jany Clair, Nerio Bernardi, Pietro Marascalchi, Giovanni Pazzafini, Gaetano Scala, Mario Lodolini
D: Giorgio Ferroni **STORY & SCR:** Arrigo Equini, Remigio Del Grosso, & Giorgio Ferroni **PHOTOG:** Augusto Tiezzi **MUSIC:** Carlo Rustichelli
A.k.a. Hercules Against Moloch
Standard "Sword & Sandal" adventure-thriller: King's son leads revolt against evil queen and pagan god

Conquest of Space
1955, (USA), Para, color, 80 mins.
W: Walter Brooke (*Sam*), Eric Fleming (*Barney*), Phil Foster (*Siegel*), William Hopper (*Fenton*), Mickey Shaughnessy (*Mahoney*), Ross Martin (*Fodor*), Benson Fong (*Imoto*), William Redfield (*Cooper*), Joan Shawlee (*Rosie*), Vito Scotti (*Sanella*), Michael Fox (*Elsbach*), Iphigenie Castiglioni (*Mrs. Fodor*), John Dennis (*Donkersgoed*)
P: George Pal **D:** Byron Haskin **SCR:** James O'Hanlon, from the book by Chesley Bonestell & Willy Ley **PHOTOG:** Lionel Lindon **SPCL-FX:** John P. Fulton, Irmin Roberts, Paul Lerpae, Ivyl Burks & Jan Domela **MUSIC:** Van Cleave

Vintage SF-adventure: Personality clashes on first spaceship to Mars

The Conquest of the Air
see **La Conquete de l'Air**

Conquest of the Planet of the Apes
1972, (USA), Arthur P. Jacobs/20th-Fox, color, 87 mins.
W: Roddy McDowall (*Caesar*), Don Murray (*Breck*), Hari Rhodes (*Mac-Donald*), Ricardo Montalban (*Armando*), John Randolph (*The Com-mission Chairman*), Natalie Trundy (*Lisa*), Severn Darden (*Kolp*), Lou Wagner (*The Busboy*), David Chow (*Aldo*), Asa Maynor (*Mrs. Riley*), H.M. Wynant (*Hoskyns*), Buck Kartalian (*Frank, the Gorilla*), John Dennis (*The Policeman*), Paul Comi (*The 2nd Policeman*), Joyce Haber (*Zelda*), Gordon Jump (*The Auctioneer*), Dick Spangler (*The Announcer*), Hector Soucy (*The Ape on a Chain*)
P: Arthur P. Jacobs   **D:** J. Lee Thompson   **SCR:** Paul Dehn, based on characters created by Pierre Boulle   **PHOTOG:** Bruce Surtees   **MUSIC:** Tom Scott
SF-thriller, 4th installment in popular "Apes" series: Child of intelligent apes leads revolt against human masters. cf. **Battle for the Planet of the Apes**

Conquest of the Pole
see **A la Conquete du Pole**

La Conquete de l'Air (The Conquest of the Air)
1901, (Fr), Pathe, b&w, 164 ft. (50m)
WRIT & D: Ferdinand Zecca
SF-fantasy short: Imaginative efforts to rule skies

The Conspiracy of Fear
1994, (USA), color
W: Leslie Hope, Andrew Lowery
Standard thriller: Tomboy and scientist's son flee assassins

The Conspiracy of Torture
1976, (It), Film Ena/Athena, color, 95 mins.
W: Thomas Milian, Adrienne LaRossa, George Wilson
D: Lucio Fulci
Minor thriller: Ghastly murders

The Conspirators
1944, (USA), WB, b&w, 101 mins.
W: Paul Henreid, Hedy Lamarr, Sydney Greenstreet, Peter Lorre, Victor Francen, Carol Thurston
P: Jack Chertok   **D:** Jean Negulesco   **SCR:** Vladimir Pozner & Leo Rosten
Standard thriller: Wartime intrigue in Lisbon

Constable Smith and the Magic Baton
1912, (GB), Cricks & Martin, b&w, 600 ft. (182.9m)
W: Kelly Storrie (*PC Smith*)
D: Edwin J. Collins
Minor fantasy: Fairy gives cop enchanted truncheon

Constable Smith in Trouble Again
1912, (GB), Cricks & Martin, b&w, 335 ft. (102.1m)
W: Kelly Storrie (*PC Smith*)
D: A.E. Coleby
Standard comedy-fantasy: Cop has trouble with disappearing burglar

Constable Smith on the Warpath
1912, (GB), Cricks & Martin, b&w, 560 ft. (170.7m)
W: Kelly Storrie (*PC Smith*)
D: Edwin J. Collins
Standard comedy-fantasy: Cop uses magic baton to track down lord's stolen watch

Contact
1997, (USA), South Side Amusement Co./WB, color, 150 mins.
W: Jodie Foster, Matthew McConaughey, James Woods, Tom Skerritt, John Hurt, Rob Lowe, Angela Bassett, David Morse
D: Robert Zemeckis   **SCR:** James V. Hart & Michael Goldenberg   **STORY:** Carl Sagan & Ann Druyan, from Carl Sagan's novel   **MUSIC:** Alan Silvestri
Superior SF-thriller: Humans find other intelligent life in universe

The Contact Man
see **Alias Nick Beal**

Contamination
see **Alien Contamination**

Il Conte Ugolino (Count Ugolino)
1949, (It), b&w, 90 mins.
D: Riccardo Freda
SCR: Riccardo Freda & Mario Bonicelli, based on *The Inferno* of Dante's *La Divina Comedia.*
A.k.a. **Il Cavaliere di Ferro** *(The Iron Knight)*
Standard thriller: Regal sins cry out for atonement

Contes Immoraux (Immoral Tales)
1974, (Fr), New Line, color, 103 mins.
W: Paloma Picasso
P: Anatole Dauman   **D & SCR:** Walerian Borowczyk

Standard adult anthology: Four erotic stories, including one about "vampiric" Countess Erzebet Bathory. cf. **The Beast** *(1974)*

Continent in Panic
see **The Deadly Mantis**

Contraband Spain
1955, (GB), Diadem/ABP, color, 82 mins.
W: Richard Greene (*Lee Scott*), Anouk Aimee (*Elena Vargas*), Michael Denison (*Ricky Melcalfe*), Jose Nieto (*Pierre*), John Warwick (*Bryan*), Philip Saville (*Martin Scott*), Alfonso Estella (*Marcos*), G.H. Mulcaster (*Col. Ingleby*), Robert Ayres (*The Official*)
P: Ernest Gartside   **D & STORY:** Lawrence Huntington
Standard crime-thriller: Spanish singer helps FBI agent collar forgers who killed his brother

Conundrum
1996, (USA), SHO-TV, color, 100 mins.
W: Marg Helgenberger, Michael Biehn, Harvey Chao, Von Flores, Karen Waddell
Made-for-Cable, standard thriller: Woman cop tries to crack Vietnamese syndicate, suspects partner is wife-killer

The Convent
1995, (GB-Port-Fr), color, 90 mins.
W: John Malkovich, Catherine Deneuve, Luis Miguel Cintra
D: Manoel de Oliveira
"an exceedingly odd morality play, a whimsical blend of theological chess and erotic cat-and-mouse"—Stephen Holden
Unusual thriller, metaphysical mystery: Satan sought in old Spanish convent

Convict 762
1998, (USA), SCI-TV, color
W: Shannon Sturges, Billy Drago
TVM, minor SF-thriller: Escaped convict menaces spaceship's all-female crew

The Convict and the Curate
1904, (GB), Clarendon/Gaumont, b&w, 250 ft. (76.2m)
D: Percy Stow
USA retitle, **The Convict's Escape**
Standard thriller (in 6 scenes): Escaped convict changes clothes with cleric

Convict 99
1909, (GB), Gaumont, b&w, 1,060 ft. (320.6m)
W: Frank Beresford (*Laurence Grey*)
D: Arthur Gilbert
Standard crime-thriller: Framed clerk cleared by dying confession

The Convict's Dream
1909, (GB), Cricks & Martin, b&w, 650 ft. (198.1m)
D: A.E. Coleby
Minor fantasy short: Convict dreams of life of luxury

The Convict's Escape
see **The Convict and the Curate**

The Convict's Sister
1911, (GB), Hepworth, b&w, 625 ft. (190.5m)
W: Flora Morris (*Mary Robbins*)
D: Bert Haldane
Standard crime-thriller: Policeman's wife shelters her brother, an escaped convict

Convicted
1932, (USA), b&w, 57 mins.
W: Aileen Pringle, Jameson Thomas, Harry Myers, Dorothy Christy, Richard Tucker
D: Christy Cabanne
Standard thriller: Woman involved in murder enigma

The Cook in Trouble
see **Sorcellerie Culinaire**

The Cook's Dream
1907, (GB), R.W. Paul, b&w, 320 ft. (97.5m)
D: J.H. Martin
Minor fantasy short: Cook dreams of exploding pie, etc.

Cool World
1992, (USA), Frank Mancuso Jr./Para, color, 95 mins.
W: Gabriel Byrne (*Jack Deebs*), Kim Basinger (*Holli Would*), Brad Pitt (*Det. Frank Harris*), Michele Abrams, Deirdre O'Connell, William Frankfather, Joey Camen, Carrie Hamilton, Frank Sinatra Jr.
D: Ralph Bakshi   **SCR:** Michael Grais & Mark Victor   **PHOTOG:** John A. Alonzo   **MUSIC:** Mark Isham   **SONG:** *Sex On Wheels*
Standard fantasy: Cartoonist enters animated dimension. Live action and animation

Coppelia: or, The Animated Doll
see **Coppelia ou la Poupee Animee**

Coppelia ou la Poupee Animee (Coppelia: or, The Animated Doll)
1900, (Fr), Star, b&w, 40m (131.2 ft./2.2 mins.)

D: Georges Melies
USA retitle, Coppelia, the Animated Doll
Standard fantasy: Female automaton bewitches

Coppelia, the Animated Doll
see Coppelia ou la Poupee Animee

The Copper Beeches
1912, (GB-Fr), Franco-British Film Co.-Eclair/Fenning, b&w, 1,700 ft. (518.2m)
W: Georges Treville (*Sherlock Holmes*), Mr. Moyse (*Dr. John Watson*)
D: Georges Treville, from a story by Sir Arthur Conan Doyle
Standard thriller

The Copper Beeches
1921, (GB), Stoll, b&w, 2,193 ft. (668.4m)
W: Eille Norwood (*Sherlock Holmes*), Hubert Willis (*Dr. John Watson*), Madge White (*Violet Hunter/Ada*), Lyell Johnson (*Jephro Rucastle*), Fred Raynham (*Toller*), Eve McCarthy (*Mrs. Toller*), William J. Elliott Jr. (*Japhat*), Lottie Blackford (*Mrs. Rucastle*), Bobbie Harwood (*Roger Wilson*)
D: Maurice Elvey **SCR:** William J. Elliott, from the writings of Sir Arthur Conan Doyle
Standard crime-thriller (episode in "Adventures of Sherlock Holmes" series)

Coppers and Cutups
1915, (GB), Martin/DFSA, b&w, 557 ft. (169.7m)
D: Dave Aylott
Standard comedy-fantasy: Strange fluid gives strength to rejected suitor

Copycat
1995, (USA), Regency/WB, color, 110 mins.
W: Sigourney Weaver (*Dr. Helen Hudson*), Holly Hunter (*Insp. Mary Jane Monahan*), Dermot Mulroney (*Robert Goetz*), Harry Connick Jr. (*Daryll Lee Cullum*), William McNamara, Will Patton, John Rothman, J.E. Freeman, Bob Greene, Tony Haney, Shannon O'Hurley, Dennis Richmond, Danny Kovacs, Tahmus Rounds, Diane Amos, Scott De Venney, David Michael Silverman, Richard Conti, Bert Kinyon, Rebecca Jane Klingler, Nick Scoggin, Kelly de Martino, Rob Nisson, Kenny K'Gong, Kathleen Stefano, Terry Brown, Corie Henninger, Bill Bonham, Chris Beale, Hansford Prince, Don West, Jay Jacobus, Ron Kaell, John Charles Morris, Keith Phillips, Johnetta Shearer, Damon Lawner, Lee Kopp, Kelvin Han Yee, Victor Talmadge, James Cunningham, Brian Russell, Russ Christoff, Jeni Chia, Stuart W. Yee, Doug Morrisson, Edith Bryson, William Oates, Floyd Gale Holland, Thomas J. Fieweger, Anthony Moore, S.J. Spinalli, Vincenetta Gunn, David Ferguson, Eleva Singleton, Gena Bingham
P: Arnon Milchan & Mark Tarlov **D:** Jon Amiel **SCR:** Ann Biderman & David Madsen **PHOTOG:** Laszlo Kovacs **MUSIC:** Christopher Young **SONG:** *Murder by Numbers* (sung by The Police)
Gripping thriller: Madman commits crimes based on serial killers of past

La Coquille et le Clergyman (The Seashell and the Clergyman)
1926, (Fr), b&w, 44 mins.
D: Germaine Dulac, based on a script by Antonin Artaud
Minor fantasy: Seashell reveals new vistas to cleric

Le Corbeau (The Crow)
1943, (Fr), b&w, 92 mins.
W: Pierre Fresnay, Ginette Leclerc, Pierre Larquey, Helena Manson, Micheline Francey
D: Henri-Georges Clouzot **SCR:** Louis Chavance **DIALOG:** Henri-Georges Clouzot & Louis Chavance **PHOTOG:** Nicholas Hayer **MUSIC:** Tony Aubin **DESIGN:** Andre Andrejew
distrib. in Nazi Germany as A Little Town in France
Unusual melodrama: Poison-pen letters spread fear and hatred in Gallic village. cf. The Thirteenth Letter

La Corbeille Enchantée (The Enchanted Basket)
1903, (Fr), Star, b&w, 25m (82 ft./1.4 mins.)
D: Georges Melies
Standard fantasy: Man battles demon

Cornered
1945, (USA), RKO, b&w, 102 mins.
W: Dick Powell, Micheline Cheirel, Luther Adler
D: Edward Dmytrik
Standard thriller

The Corner House Burglary
1914, (GB), Big Ben Films-Union/Pathe, b&w, 2,385 ft. (726.9m)
W: James Carew (*Henry Arnold*), Ivy Montford (*Dolores*), Mr. Jackson (*Fred Creston*), H. Maligny (*James Heron*), H. Nicholson (*Dr. Nash*)
D: H.O. Martinek **STORY:** L.C. MacBean
Standard crime-thriller: "Gang of the Pointing Finger" robs doctor by planting maid and using poison gas

A Cornish Romance
1912, (GB), B&C/MP, b&w, 1,000 ft. (302.3m)
W: Wallett Waller (*Sir Ralph Chetwynd*), Dorothy Foster (*Sybilla Chetwynd*), O'Neil Farrell (*Jules Marx*), Ruth Sampson (*Miss Baston*), Sidney Northcote (*Dark Davy*)

D: Sidney Northcote **STORY:** Harold Brett
Standard crime-thriller: Usurer's pawn kidnaps knight's sister

La Corona Negra (The Black Crown)
1950, (Sp), Suevia, b&w, 94 mins.
W: Rossano Brazzi, Maria Felix, Vittorio Gassman, Antonio Plana, Jose M. Lado, Julia C. Alba, Pieral
D: Luis Saslavsky **SCR:** Miguel Mihura, from an idea by Jean Cocteau **PHOTOG:** Antonio Ballesteros & Valentin Javier **MUSIC:** M. Quitero
Standard melodrama: Passion and crime breed tragedy

Corporate Ladder
1997, (USA), color, 115 mins.
W: Anthony Dennison
Made-for-Cable, standard thriller: Deranged assistant bedevils ad executive

The Corpse
1970, (GB), London Cannon-Abacus/Grand Nat'l, color, 91 mins.
W: Michael Gough (*Walter Eastwood*), Yvonne Mitchell (*Edith Eastwood*), Sharon Gurney (*Jane Eastwood*), Simon Gough (*Rupert Eastwood*), Olaf Pooley (*Reid*), David Butler (*Gregson*), Mary Hignett (*Mrs. Roberts*), Benjie (*Benjie*), Howard Goorney (*The Petrol Pump Attendant*), Sam ("*Sam*" the Dog)
P: Dennis Friedland, Christopher Dewey, & Gabrielle Beaumont **D:** Viktors Ritelis **SCR:** Olaf Pooley **PHOTOG:** John Mackey **MUSIC:** John Hotchkis
USA retitle, Crucible of Horror, A.k.a. Velvet House
Standard thriller: Woman and daughter poison tyrannical patriarch

The Corpse Grinders
1971, (USA), Geneni, color, 73 mins.
W: Sean Kenney (*Dr. Howard Glass*), J. Byron Foster (*Maltby*), Monika Kelly (*Angie*), Warren Ball (*Caleb*), Sanford Mitchell (*Landau*), Ann Noble (*Cleo*), Vince Barbi (*Monk*), Earl Burnam (*DeSisto*), Ray Dannis (*Babcock*), Harry Lovejoy (*The Neighbor*), Zenna Foster (*Mrs. Babcock*), Drucilla Hoy (*Tessie*), Don Ellis (*The Workman*), George Bowden (*David*), Charles Fox (*Willie*), Stephen Lester (*The Mortician*), Curt Mason (*Paul*), William Kirschner (*B.K.*), Mike Garrison (*DeSisto's Ass't*), Mary Ellen Burke (*Annie*), Andy Collings (*The Secretary*)
P & D: Ted V. Mikels **SCR:** Arch Hall & Joseph L. Cranston **PHOTOG:** Bill Anneman
Minor horror-thriller: Strange cat food turns household pets into man-eaters

A Corpse Hangs in the Web
see Horrors of Spider Island

The Corpse Makers
see Twice-Told Tales

The Corpse Thief
see El Ladron de Cadaveres

The Corpse Vanishes
1942, (USA), Banner/Mono, b&w, 64 mins.
W: Bela Lugosi (*Dr. Lorenz*), Luana Walters (*Patricia Hunter*), Tris Coffin (*Dr. Foster*), Minerva Urecal (*Fagah*), Elizabeth Russell (*Countess Lorenz*), Angelo Rossitto (*Toby*), Kenneth Harlan (*Keenan*), Joan Barclay (*Alice Wentworth*), Frank Moran (*Angel*), Gwen Kenyon (*Peggy*), Vince Barnett (*Sandy*), George Eldredge (*Mike*)
P: Sam Katzman & Jack Dietz **D:** Wallace Fox **SCR:** Harvey Gates **ORIG. STORY:** Sam Robins & Gerald Schnitzer **PHOTOG:** Art Reed
GB retitle, The Case of the Missing Brides
blurb: "Horror to make your hair stand on end!"
Standard horror-thriller: Mad scientist sends poisoned flowers to brides, steals bodies for weird experiments

The Corpus Delicti
see El Cuerpo del Lito

Corridor of Mirrors
1948, (GB), Apollo/Rank/GFD/U-I, b&w, 105 mins.
W: Eric Portman (*Paul Mangin*), Edana Romney (*Mifanwy Conway*), Barbara Mullen (*Veronica*), Hugh Sinclair (*Owen Rhys*), Bruce Bel-frage (*Sir David Conway*), Joan Maude (*Caroline Hart*), Alan Wheatley (*Edgar Orsen*), Leslie Weston (*Mortimer*), Lois Maxwell (*Imogen*), Christopher Lee (*Charles*), Valentine Dyall (*The Defense*), Noel Howlett
P: Rudolph Cartier **D:** Terence Young **SCR:** Rudolph Cartier & Edana Romney from a novel by Chris Massie **PHOTOG:** Andre Thomas **MUSIC:** Georges Auric
Standard thriller: Eccentric art collector thinks he and mistress are reincarnated lovers in 400-year-old painting. Christopher Leef debut

Corridors of Blood
see Doctor of Seven Dials

Corruption
1967, (GB), Titan/Col, color, 91 mins.
W: Peter Cushing (*Sir John Rowan*), Sue Lloyd (*Lynn Nolan*), David Lodge (*Groper*), Noel Trevarthen (*Steve Harris*), Kate O'Mara (*Val Nolan*), Anthony Booth (*Mike Orme*), Jan Waters (*The Girl in the Flat*), Wendy Varnals (*Terry*),

Valerie Van Ost (*The Girl on the Train*), Billy Murray (*Rik*), Vanessa Howard (*Kate*), Phillip Manikum (*George*), Victor Baring (*The Mortuary Attendant*), Diana Ashley (*Claire*), Alexandra Dane (*Sandy*), Shirley Stelfox (*The Girl at the Party*)
D: Robert Hartford-Davis **SCR:** Donald Ford & Derek Ford **PHOTOG:** Peter Newbrook **SPCL-FX:** Michael Albrechtsen **MUSIC:** Bill McGuffie
Minor thriller: Doctor kills to gain glands for disfigured fiancee

The Corsican Brothers
1897, (GB), b&w, 75 ft. (22.9m)
D: George Albert Smith, from Alexandre Dumas' novel
Standard melodrama: Siamese twins share intrigue

The Corsican Brothers
1902, (GB), Harrison, b&w, 300 ft. (91.4m)
W: A.W. Fitzgerald (*Fabian & Louis de Franchi*)
D & SCR: Dicky Winslow, from Alexandre Dumas' novel
Standard melodrama: Twin dies after brother perishes in duel

The Corsican Brothers
1941, (USA), Edward Small/UA, b&w, 112 mins.
W: Douglas Fairbanks Jr., Ruth Warrick, Akim Tamiroff, Henry Wil-coxon, H.B. Warner, J. Carrol Naish, John Emery, William Farnum, Gloria Holden, Veda Ann Borg, Walter Kingsford, Nana Bryant, Pedro de Cordoba
D: Gregory Ratoff **SCR:** George Bruce, from Alexandre Dumas' novel **PHOTOG:** Harry Stradling **MUSIC:** Dimitri Tiomkin
Definitive film-version of Dumas' romance: Twins share psychic link

The Corsican Brothers
1960, (Fr), b&w
W: Jean Servais, Geoffrey Horne
Inferior rendering of Dumas' classic: Siamese twins share mystic bond

The Corsican Brothers
1985, (GB), Rosemont, color, 100 mins.
W: Trevor Eve, Geraldine Chaplin, Olivia Hussey, Jean Marsh, Nicholas Clay, Benedict Taylor, Donald Pleasence, Simon Ward, James Hazeldine, Patsy Kensit, Mark Ryan, Margaret Tyzack, Kevork Malikyan, Jennie Linden, Daniel Auguste, Peter Howell, Anthony Pedley, Peter Cellier, Joe Maalouf, Toby Salaman, Raynald Bandry, Flora Alberti, Lise Roy, Mirelle Chaulet, Mark Brooks, David Brooks, Nancy Mooy, Bernard Fontaine, Francoise Trumpette, Liselote Palm, Marc Estrada De Tourmiel, Marina Bonin, Abbe Fantozzi, Anne Bruner, Louis LaLanne, Rosette Jaubert, Pietro Jianni, Mike Bainsborough
D: Ian Sharp **TELEPLAY:** Robin Miller, from Alexandre Dumas' novel **PHO-TOG:** Frank Watts **MUSIC:** Allyn Ferguson
TVM, standard adventure-thriller: Twins unite for justice

Cosh Boy
1953, (GB), Daniel Angel/Romulus/Lippert, b&w, 75 mins.
W: James Kenney (*Roy Walsh*), Joan Collins (*Rene Collins*), Hermione Baddeley (*Mrs. Collins*), Hermione Gingold (*Queenie*), Betty Ann Davies (*Elsie Walsh*), Nancy Roberts (*Gran Walsh*), Robert Ayres (*Bob Stevens*), Ian Whittaker (*Alfie Collins*), Stanley Escane (*Pete*), Sean Lynch (*Darkey*), Edward Evans (*Sgt. Woods*), Michael McKeag (*Brian*), Laurence Naismith (*Insp. Donaldson*), Frederick Piper (*Mr. Easter*), Walter Hudd (*The Magistrate*), Sidney James (*The Sgt.*)
D: Lewis Gilbert **SCR:** Lewis Gilbert & Vernon Harris, from Bruce Walker's play *Master Crook*
*USA retitle, **The Slasher***
Standard melodrama: Teen gang leader robs old woman

The Cosmic Eye
1971, (USA), color, 71 mins.
VOICES: Dizzy Gillespie, Maureen Stapleton, Benny Carter
D: Faith Hubley
Standard animated SF: Space-alien musicians bring peace message to Earth

Cosmic Killer
*see **Miami Golem***

The Cosmic Man
1959, (USA), AA, b&w, 72 mins.
W: John Carradine, Bruce Bennett, Angela Greene, Paul Langton, Lyn Osborn, Scotty Morrow, Walter Maslow, Herbert Lytton
P: Robert A. Terry **D:** Herbert Greene **SCR:** Arthur C. Pierce
Minor, low-budget SF-thriller: Invisible being from outer space spreads terror

The Cosmic Man Appears in Tokyo
*see **Uchujin Tokyo Ni Arawaru***

The Cosmic Monster
*see **The Strange World of Planet X***

Cosmos-War of the Planets
*see **War of the Planets***

Les Costumes Animes (The Animated Costumes)
1904, (Fr), Star, b&w, 50m (164 ft./2.8 mins.)

D: Georges Melies
Standard comedy-fantasy: Apparel has life of its own

The Cosmic Man

The Couch
1962, (USA), WB, b&w, 100 mins.
W: Grant Williams (*Charles Campbell*), Shirley Knight (*Terry Ames*), Onslow Stevens (*Dr. W.L. Janz*), William Leslie (*Dr. David Lindsey*), Anne Helm (*Jean*), Hope Summers (*Mrs. Quimby*), Simon Scott (*Lt. Kritzman*), Michael Bachus (*Sgt. Bonner*), John Alvin (*Sloan*), Tracy Olsen, Harry Holcombe, Sandra Harrison
P & D: Owen Crump **SCR:** Robert Bloch, based on a story by Blake Edwards & Owen Crump **PHOTOG:** Harold Stine **MUSIC:** Francis Perkins
Minor thriller: Psychotic killer terrorizes city

The Council of Three
1909, (GB), London Cinematograph Co., b&w
From a character created by Harry Blyth
Standard crime-thriller: Detective Sexton Blake poses as gang's messenger, saves kidnapped girl

Countdown
1968, (USA), WB, color, 101 mins.
W: James Caan, Joanna Moore (*Mickey*), Robert Duvall (*Chiz*), Barbara Baxley (*Jean*), Charles Aidman (*Gus*), Michael Murphy, Ted Knight, Steve Ihnat
P: William Conrad **D:** Robert Altman **SCR:** Loring Mandel, from Henry Searles' novel *The Pilgrim Project* **PHOTOG:** William M. Spencer **MUSIC:** Leonard Rosenman
Standard SF-adventure: Soviet & U.S. spaceships race for moon. Production title: **Moonshot**

Countdown to Danger
1967, (GB), Wallace/CFF, color, 63 mins.
W: David Macalister (*Mike*), Paul Martin (*Tony*), Angela Lee (*Sandie*), Peny Spencer (*Sue*), Richard Coleman (*Capt. Wright*), Lane Meddick (*Sgt. Thompson*), Frank Williams (*Harry*)
P: A. Frank Bundy **D & STORY:** Peter Seabourne
Standard juvenile thriller: Boy trapped in cache of German explosives

Count Dracula
1970, (GB-Sp.-Ital.-Germ.), Tigon/Commonwealth/Rep/Crystal, color, 94 mins.
W: Christopher Lee (*Dracula*), Herbert Lom (*Dr. Van Helsing*), Klaus Kinski (*Renfield*), Maria Rohm (*Mina*), Soledad Miranda (*Lucy*), Jack Taylor (*Quincey*), Frederick Williams, Paul Muller
P: Harry Alan Towers **D:** Jesus Franco **SCR:** Peter Welbeck, from Bram Stoker's novel *Dracula: A Tale* **PHOTOG:** Manuel Merino **MUSIC:** Bruno Nicolai
French retitle, **Les Nuits de Dracula (The Nights of Dracula)**
Modest horror-fantasy: Vampire count goes to England

Count Dracula and His Vampire Bride
*see **The Satanic Rites of Dracula***

Count Dracula's Great Love
*see **Gran Amore del Conde Dracula***

Counterblast
1948, (GB), British Nat'l/Pathe, b&w, 99 mins.
W: Robert Beatty (*Dr. Rankin*), Mervyn Johns (*Dr. Bruckner*), Nova Pilbeam (*Tracy Shaw*), Margaretta Scott (*Sister Johnson*), Sybilla Binder (*Martha*), Marie Lohr (*Mrs. Coles*), Alan Wheatley (*Kennedy*), Karel Stepanek (*Prof. Inman*), Antony Eustrel (*Dr. Forrester*), Gladys Henson (*Mrs. Plum*), Ronald Adam (*Col. Ingram*), John Salew (*The Padre*), Martin Miller (*The Seaman*), Karl Jaffe (*Heinz*), Peter Madden
P: Louis H. Jackson **D:** Paul Stein **SCR:** Jack Whittingham **STORY:** Guy Morgan
A.k.a. **The Devil's Plot**

Standard thriller: Nazis seek germ-warfare secrets

Counter-Espionage
1942, (USA), Col, b&w, 72 mins.
W: Warren William (*Michael Lanyard*), Hillary Brooke (*Pamela*), Eric Blore (*Jamison*), Thurston Hall (*Insp. Crane*), Forrest Tucker (*Anton Schugg*), Fred Kelsey (*Dickens*), Matthew Boulton (*Insp. Stephens*), Kurt Katch (*Gustave Sossel*), Morton Lowry (*Kent Wells*), Leslie Denison (*Harvey Leeds*), Clyde Cook (*The Huckster*), Billy Bevan (*George Barrow*), Stanley Logan (*Sir Stafford Hart*), Tom Stevenson (*Constable Hopkins*), William von Brincken (*Von Ruhoff*), Keith Hitchcock (*Williams*), Eddie Laughton (*The Orchestra Leader*), Wyndham Standing (*The Head Waiter*), William Yetter (*The Operator*), Eric Wilson (*Thomas*), Guy Kingsford (*Carter*), Robert Hale (*The News-boy*), Heather Wilde (*Gertie*), Frank Baker, Herbert Clifton
D: Edward Dmytryk   SCR: Aubrey Wisberg, from characters created by Joseph Louis Vance   PHOTOG: Philip Tanura   MUSIC: Morris Stoloff
Standard "Lone Wolf" melodrama: Gentleman rogue becomes spy for British intelligence

The Counterfeit Plan
1957, (GB), Merton Park/Anglo-Amalgamated, b&w, 87 mins.
W: Zachary Scott (*Max Brandt*), Peggie Castle (*Carol*), Lee Patterson (*Duke*), Mervyn Johns (*Louis*), Sydney Tafler (*Flint*), Chili Bouchier (*The Housekeeper*), John Welsh (*Insp. Grant*), Eric Pohlmann (*Wandermann*), David Lodge (*Watson*), Robert Arden (*Bob*), Alvar Lidell (*The Newsreader*)
P: Alec Snowden   D: Montgomery Tully   STORY: James Eastwood
Standard crime-thriller: Escaped murderer forces ex-forger to counterfeit money

The Counterfeiters
1915, (GB), I.B. Davidson-St. George/KTC, b&w, 2,600 ft. (792.5m)
W: Harry Lorraine (*Sexton Blake*), Bert Rex (*Tinker*), Jack Jarman, N. Watts-Phillips
D & SCR: Charles Raymond, from a story by John W. Bobin, based on characters created by Harry Blyth
Standard crime-thriller: Counterfeiters using old mill tie detective to waterwheel

The Counterfeiters of Paris
1962, (Fr), MGM, b&w, 90 mins.
W: Jean Gabin, Bernard Blier
Standard thriller

Counterplot
1959, (USA), UA, b&w, 76 mins.
D: Kurt Newman
W: Forrest Tucker, Allison Hayes
Standard thriller. Filmed in Puerto Rico

Counterspy
1953, (GB), Merton Park/Anglo-Amalgamated/Lippert, b&w, 88 mins.
W: Dermot Walsh (*Manning*), Hazel Court (*Clare Manning*), Hermione Baddeley (*Del Mar*), Alexander Gauge (*Smith*), Bill Travers (*Rex*), James Vivian (*Larry*), Archie Duncan (*Jim*), Frederick Schrecker (*Plattnauer*), Hugh Latimer (*Barlow*), Beryl Baxter (*The Girl*)
P: W.H. Williams   D: Vernon Sewell   SCR: Guy Elmes & Michael le Fevre, from Julian Symons' novel *Criss Cross Code*
USA retitle, **Undercover Agent**
Standard crime-thriller: Auditor becomes involved with spy ring running nursing home

Counterspy Meets Scotland Yard
1951, (USA), Col, b&w, 67 mins.
W: Howard St. John, Amanda Blake
Minor thriller

Countess Dracula
1970, (GB), Hammer/20th-Fox, color, 94 mins.
W: Ingrid Pitt (*Countess Elizabeth Nadasdy*), Nigel Green (*Capt. Dobi*), Sandor Eles (*Imre Toth*), Maurice Denham (*Master Fabio*), Patience Collier (*Julia*), Peter Jeffrey (*Capt. Balogh*), Lesley-Anne Down (*Ilona*), Leon Lissek (*Capt. Bailiff*), Jessie Evans (*Rosa*), Andrea Lawrence (*Zizi*), Nike Arrighi (*The Gypsy*), Hulya Babus (*The Belly Dancer*), Charles Farrell, Peter May
P: Alexander Paal   D: Peter Sasdy   SCR: Jeremy Paul, from a story by Alexander Paal & Peter Sasdy, based on an idea by Gabriel Ronay   PHOTOG: Ken Talbot   MUSIC: Harry Robinson
Standard horror-thriller: Sanguine noblewoman seeks immortality. cf. Ceremonia Sangrienta

The Count of Monte Cristo
1912, (USA), Famous Players, b&w, 90 mins.
W: James O'Neill
D: Edwin S. Porter, from Alexandre Dumas' novel
Standard melodrama: Wronged man seeks revenge and riches

The Count of Monte Cristo
1934, (USA), Edward Small/Reliance/UA, b&w, 115 mins.
W: Robert Donat (*Edmund Dantes*), Elissa Landi (*Mercedes*), Louis Calhern (*Villefort*), Sidney Blackmer, Raymond Walburn, O.P. Heggie, William Farnum
P: Philip Dunne   D: Rowland V. Lee   SCR: Philip Dunne, Dan Totheroh, & Rowland V. Lee, from Alexandre Dumas' novel   PHOTOG: J. Peverell Marley   MUSIC: Alfred Newman
Definitive film-version of Dumas' classic: Prisoner escapes confinement, seeks revenge and

fabled treasure

The Count of Monte Cristo
1955, (Fr), color, 97 mins.
W: Pierre-Richard Willm (*Edmund Dantes*), Michele Alfa
D: Robert Vernay, from Alexandre Dumas' novel
Inferior film-version of literary classic: Man flees prison, finds fabulous treasure

The Count of Monte Cristo (1960)
see Le Comte de Monte Cristo

The Count of Monte Cristo
1975, (GB), ITC/Rosemont/ABC-TV, color, 104 mins.
W: Richard Chamberlain (*Edmund Dantes*), Tony Curtis (*Mondego*), Louis Jourdan (*De Villefort*), Kate Nelligan (*Mercedes*), Taryn Power (*Valentine*), Trevor Howard (*Abbe Faria*), Donald Pleasence (*Danglars*), Dominic Guard (*Albert Mondego*), Angelo Infanti (*Jacopo*), Harold Bromley (*Morrell*), Alessio Orano (*Caderousse*), Carlo Puri (*Andrea Benedetto*), Isabelle de Valvert (*Haydee*), Ralph Michael (*Dantes*), George Willing (*Andre Morrell*), Anthony Dawson (*Noirtier De Villefort*), Eddy Fay (*Casimir*)
P: Norman Rosemont   D: David Greene   TELEPLAY: Sidney Carroll, from Alexandre Dumas' novel   PHOTOG: Aldo Tonti   MUSIC: Allyn Ferguson
TVM, standard adventure-thriller: Ex-prisoner gains revenge on enemies

Count Ugolino
see Il Conte Ugolino

Count Yorga, Vampire
1970, (USA), Erica/AIP, color, 92 mins.
W: Robert Quarry (*Yorga*), Michael Macready (*Michael*), Donna Anders (*Donna*), Roger Perry (*Hayes*), Julie Conners (*Cleo*), Michael Murphy (*Paul*), Paul Hansen (*Peter*), Sybil Scotford (*Judy*), Edward Walsh (*Brudah*), Judith Lang (*Erica*), Deborah Darnell (*The Vampiress*), Erica Macready (*The Nurse*), Marsha Jordan (*Mother*)
P: Michael Macready   WRIT & D: Bob Kelljan, narrated by George Macready   PHOTOG: Arch Archambault   MUSIC: William Marx
orig. to be titled Loves of Count Yorga
Standard horror-thriller (now considered minor classic): Undead nobleman prowls Los Angeles. cf. The Return of Count Yorga

The Courage of a Coward
1914, (GB),B&C/DFSA, b&w, 911 ft. (277.7m)
W: Elizabeth Risdon (*The Wife*), A.V. Bramble (*The Burglar*), Ernest Cox (*The Husband*), M. Gray Murray (*The Doctor*)
D & STORY: Eliot Stannard
Standard crime-thriller: Frightened woman stabs burglar

The Courtyard
1995, (USA), SHO-TV, color, 105 mins.
W: Andrew McCarthy, Madchen Amick, Richard "Cheech" Marin
Made-for-Cable, standard thriller: Architect investigates murders in upscale apartment complex

Les Cousines (The Cousins)
1971, (Fr), Cinemation, color
USA retitle, **From Ear to Ear**
Standard thriller: Bisexual female cousins torture girl

Covenant
1985, (USA), 20th-Fox/NBC-TV, color, 71 mins.
W: Jane Badler (*Dana Noble*), Charles Frank (*David Wyman*), Whitney Kershaw (*Angelica*), Barry Morse (*Zachariah*), Jose Ferrer (*Victor Noble*), Michelle Phillips (*Claire*), Bradford Dillman (*Eric*), Kevin Conroy, Judy Parfitt, Lenore Kasdorf, Laurence Guittard, John Van Dreelen, Jan Merlin, Will Gerard, Tia Carrere, Ji-Tu Cumbuka, Fred Lerner, Mike Runyard, Scott Utley, James Saito, Jon Sharp, Erica Todd, Charles Walker
D: Walter Grauman   TELEPLAY: J.D. Feigelson & Dan DiStefano   PHOTOG: James Crabe   MUSIC: Charles Bernstein
TVM, standard fantasy-thriller (feature-pilot for unsold teleseries): Ruthless banking family derives power from occult

Cover Girl Killer
1960, (GB), Butcher-Paroch/Eros, b&w, 61 mins.
W: Harry H. Corbett (*The Man*), Felicity Young (*June Rawson*), Spencer Teakle (*John Mason*), Victor Brooks (*Insp. Brunner*), Tony Doonan (*The Sgt.*), Bernardette Milne (*Gloria*), Christina Gregg (*Joy*), Charles Lloyd-Pack (*Capt. Adams*)
P: C. Jack Parsons   WRIT & D: Terry Bishop
Standard thriller: Pinup-magazine publisher and model help police trap maniac

The Cover Girl Murders
1993, (USA), color, 87 mins.
W: Lee Majors, Jennifer O'Neill, Beverly Johnson, Vanessa Angel, Adrian Paul
D: James A. Contner   TELEPLAY: Douglas Barr & Bernard Maybeck   MUSIC: Rick Marotta
TVM, standard thriller: Magazine photo shoot on remote island plagued by accidents

Cover Me
1995, (USA), color, 95 mins.
W: Courtney Taylor, Rick Rossovich

Made-for-Video, standard thriller: Woman cop poses as adult-magazine model, tries to nab killer

Cover Up
see **Frightmare** (1974)

The Cow on the Moon
see **Krava na Mjesecu**

Cracked Nuts
1931, (USA), RKO, b&w, 8 reels (75 mins.)
<u>W</u>: Edna May Oliver, Dorothy Lee, Bert Wheeler, Robert Woolsey, Boris Karloff, Stanley Fields, Leni Stengel, Ben Turpin
<u>D</u>: Edward Cline   <u>PHOTOG</u>: Nicholas Musuraca
Standard comedy: Zanies win mythical kingdom in crap game

Cracked Nuts
1941, (USA), Univ, b&w
<u>W</u>: Stu Erwin, Mischa Auer, Una Merkel, Hugh Herbert
Minor comedy: Robot inventor's misadventures

Crack in the World
1964, (GB), Philip Yordan/Security/Para, color, 96 mins.
<u>W</u>: Dana Andrews (*Dr. Stephen Sorensen*), Kieron Moore (*Ted Rampion*), Janette Scott (*Maggie Sorensen*), Alexander Knox (*Sir Charles Eggerston*), Jim Gillen (*Rand*), Peter Damon (*Masefield*), Gary Lasdun (*Markov*), Todd Martin (*Simpson*), Mike Steen (*Steele*)
<u>P</u>: Bernard Glasser & Lester A. Sansom   <u>D</u>: Andrew Marton   <u>SCR</u>: Jon Manchip White & Julian Halevy, based on a story by Jon Manchip White   <u>PHOTOG</u>: Manuel Berenguer   <u>SPCL-FX</u>: Alec Weldon & Eugene Lourie   <u>MUSIC</u>: John Douglas
French retitle, **Quand la Terre s'Entrouvrira (When the Earth is Opening)**
Standard SF-thriller: Underground nuclear blast threatens Earth's stability

Crackle of Death
1974, (USA), Francy Prods./Univ/ABC-TV, color
<u>W</u>: Darren McGavin, Phil Carey, Simon Oakland, Fred Beir, Tom Drake, William Smith, Elaine Giftos, David Doyle, Michael Strong, Robert Yuro, Joyce Jillson, Madlyn Rhue, Virginia Vincent, Jack Grinnage, Ruth McDevitt, John Alvin, Robert Cornthwaite, Michael Fox, Carol Ann Susi, Patricia Estrin, Carol Veazie, John Mitchum, Melissa Greene, Dianne Harper, Ella Edwards, Barbara Graham
<u>P</u>: Cy Chermak   <u>D</u>: Don Weis & Alex Grasshoff   <u>TELEPLAY</u>: Bill S. Ballinger, Arthur Rowe, & Rudolph Borchert   <u>STORY</u>: Bill S. Ballinger & Arthur Rowe, from characters created by Jeff Rice   <u>PHOTOG</u>: Ronald W. Browne   <u>MUSIC SCORE</u>: Jerry Fielding & Luchi De Jesus   <u>THEME</u>: Gil Melle
TVM, minor thriller culled from **Night Stalker** *teleseries: Reporter investigates bizarre murders in Chicago. cf.* **The Night Stalker** (1971) *and* **The Night Strangler**

Crack-Up
1936, (USA), 20th-Fox, b&w, 70 mins.
<u>W</u>: Peter Lorre, Brian Donlevy, Ralph Morgan, Helen Wood, J. Carrol Naish
<u>P</u>: Samuel G. Engels   <u>D</u>: Malcolm St. Clair   <u>SCR</u>: Charles Kenyon & Sam Mintz
Standard thriller: Pilot plans to steal design of new war plane

The Cradle will Fall
1983, (USA), Cates Films/CBS-TV, color, 100 mins.
<u>W</u>: Lauren Hutton, James Farentino, Ben Murphy (*Richard Carroll*), Charita Bauer (*Bert Bauer*), Joe Ponazecki (*Det. Larry Wyatt*), Carolyn Ann Clark (*Lesley Ann*), Jerry verDorn (*Ross Marler*), Elvera Roussel, Peter Simon, Doris Belack, Michael Higgins, Ralph Byers, Debra Mooney, W.H. Macy, Frieda Bauer, Cindy Cash, Audrey Jo Campbell, Robin Jo Coleman, Danielle DuClos, Dianne Dixon, Peggy Dobson, Ezra Eichelberger, Mary Timoney, Terri M. Gardner, Gerry House, Barbara B. Shepherd, Michael Torrey, Jackie Welch
<u>D</u>: John Llewellyn Moxey   <u>TELEPLAY</u>: Jerome Coopersmith, from Mary Higgins Clark's novel   <u>PHOTOG</u>: Steven Poster   <u>SPCL-FX</u>: J.B. Jones   <u>MUSIC</u>: Elliot Lawrence
TVM, standard thriller: Murderous gynecologist experiments on patients

The Craft
1996, (USA), Col, color, 101 mins.
<u>W</u>: Robin Tunney (*Sarah*), Fairuza Balk (*Nancy*), Neve Campbell (*Bonnie*), Rachel True (*Rochelle*), Skeet Ulrich (*Chris*), Assumpta Serna, Cliff DeYoung, Christine Taylor, Breckin Meyer, Nathaniel Marston, Helen Shaver, Jeanine Jackson, Mark Conlon, Elizabeth Guber, Rod Britt, Brenda Strong, Jennifer Greenhut, Arthur Senzy, Erin Tavin, Brogan Roche, Endre Hules, Christine Louise Berry, William Newman, Jason Filardi, Rebecca McLaughlin, Tony Genaro, Danielle Koenig, Janet Rotblatt, Karyn J. Dean, Janet Eilber, Esther Scott
<u>D</u>: Andrew Fleming   <u>SCR</u>: Andrew Fleming & Peter Filardi   <u>STORY</u>: Peter Filardi   <u>PHOTOG</u>: Alexander Gruszynski   <u>MUSIC</u>: Graeme Revell
<u>SONGS</u>: *Tomorrow Never Knows, How Soon is Now!, I Have the Touch, All This and Nothing, Under the Water, Sick Child, Witches Song, Jump into the Fire, Dangerous Type, Warning, Dark Secret, Scorn The Horror & Spastica*
Modest horror-fantasy: High-school girls dabble in witchcraft

Crash! (1977)
see **Death Ride**

Crash
1996, (Can), Fine Line Features, color, 98 mins.
<u>W</u>: James Spader (*James Ballard*), Holly Hunter (*Dr. Helen Remington*), Elias Koteas (*Vaughan*), Deborah Kara Unger (*Catherine Ballard*), Rosanna Arquette (*Gabrielle*)
<u>WRIT, P & D</u>: David Cronenberg, from J.G. Ballard's 1973 novel   <u>PHOTOG</u>: Peter Suschitzky   <u>MUSIC</u>: Howard Shore
USA release, 1997
Bizarre, controversial tale of "auto-eroticism" (winner of 6 Genies {Canadian "Oscars"} & "Golden Reel" for highest-grossing Canadian film of 1996): Car wrecks stimulate sexual appetites

Crash and Burn
1990, (USA), Full Moon/Para, color, 85 mins.
<u>W</u>: Paul Ganus (*Tyson Keen*), Megan Ward (*Arren*), Ralph Waite (*Lathan Hooks*), Bill Moseley (*Quinn*), Eva Larue (*Parice*), Jack McGee (*Winston Wickett*), Elizabeth MacLellan (*Sandra*), Katherine Armstrong (*Christie*), John Chandler (*Bud*), Kristopher Logan (*Scratch*)
<u>D</u>: Charles Band   <u>SCR</u>: J.S. Cardone   <u>PHOTOG</u>: Mac Ahlberg   <u>SPCL-FX</u>: Players Special Effects   <u>MUSIC</u>: Richard Band
Standard SF-thriller: Relentless android stalks remote TV station

Crashing Las Vegas
1956, (USA), AA, b&w, 62 mins.
<u>W</u>: Huntz Hall, Leo Gorcey, Don Haggerty, Mary Castle, David Condon, Mort Mills, Terry Frost, Jimmy Murphy, Doris Kemper, Jack Rice, Nicky Blair
<u>D</u>: Jean Yarbrough   <u>STORY & SCR</u>: Jack Townley   <u>MUSIC</u>: Marlin Skiles
Minor comedy: Bowery Boy finds he can predict future

Crash Landing
1958, (USA), Col, b&w, 77 mins
<u>W</u>: Gary Merrill, Nancy Davis, Roger Smith, Irene Hervey
<u>P</u>: Sam Katzman   <u>D</u>: Fred F. Sears   <u>SCR</u>: Fred Freiberger
Minor thriller: Plane threatens to crash in ocean

The Crash of Moons
1954, (USA), Reed, b&w
<u>W</u>: Richard Crane
Minor SF-adventure, feature culled from **Rocky Jones, Space Ranger** *teleseries*

The Crater Lake Monster
1977, (USA), Crown Int'l, color, 84 mins.
<u>W</u>: Richard Cardella (*Steve Hanson*), Glenn Roberts (*Arnie Chabot*), Mark Siegel (*Mitch Kowalski*), Bob Hyman (*Richard Calkins*), Richard Garrison (*Dan Turnor*), Kacey Cobb (*Susan Patterson*), Michael Hoover (*Ross Conway*), Marv Eliot (*Jack Fuller*), Suzanne Lewis (*Paula Conway*), Garry Johnston (*The Blackmailer*), Sonny Shepard (*The Robber*), John Crowder (*The Mechanic*), Susy Claycomb (*The Waitress*), Mike Simmons (*The Store Clerk*), Hal Scharn (*The Birdwatcher*), Jim Goeppinger (*The Villager*), Mary Winford (*The Lady Customer*), Joe Sasway (*Ferguson*)
<u>P & D</u>: William R. Stromberg   <u>ORIG. STORY & SCR</u>: William R. Stromberg & Richard Cardella   <u>PHOTOG</u>: Paul Gentry   <u>SPCL-FX</u>: Bikk Dickenson   <u>SONGS</u>: by James West
Minor SF-thriller: Pleisiosaur prowls, panics perplexed populace

The Craving
1980, (Sp), Dalmata Films/Film Concept Group, color, 91 mins.
<u>W</u>: Paul Naschy, Julie Saly
<u>D</u>: Jack Molina
Minor horror-fantasy: Werewolf and vampiress revived. USA release: 1986

The Crawlers
1993, (USA), color, 94 mins.
<u>W</u>: Jason Saucier, Mary Sellers
<u>D</u>: Martin Newlin   <u>SCR</u>: Dan Price & Martin Newlin
Standard SF-horror: Ravenous organisms seek human prey

The Crawling Eye
see **The Trollenberg Terror**

The Crawling Hand
1963, (USA), Hansen/AIP, b&w, 89 mins.
<u>W</u>: Peter Breck, Allison Hayes, Rod Lauren, Kent Taylor, Syd Saylor, Sirry Steffen, Alan Hale Jr., Richard Arlen, Arline Judge, Tristram Coffin, Ross Elliott, Jock Putnam, G. Stanley Jones, Andy Andrews
<u>D</u>: Herbert L. Strock   <u>SCR</u>: William Idelson & Herbert L. Strock   <u>STORY</u>: Joseph Cranston, Malcolm Young & William Idelson   <u>PHOTOG</u>: Willard Van Der Veer
orig. to be titled **Don't Cry Wolf, Tomorrow** *Minor horror-thriller: Astronaut's severed hand gains life of its own*

The Crawling Monster
see **The Creeping Terror**, A.k.a. **Demon Monster**

Crawlspace
1986, (USA-It), Altar/Empire, color, 80 mins.
<u>W</u>: Klaus Kinski, Talia Balsam, Barbara Whinnery, Carol Francis, Tane Sally Brown, Kenneth Robert Shippy

WRIT & D: David Schmoeller   **PHOTOG:** Sergio Salvati   **MUSIC:** Pino
 Donaggio
Minor thriller: Maniacal landlord stalks female tenants

Craze
1973, (GB), Harbour/EMI/WB, color, 96 mins.
W: Jack Palance *(Neal Mottram)*, Trevor Howard *(Supt. Bellamy)*, Suzy Kendall
 (Sally), Diana Dors *(Dolly Newman)*, Michael Jayston *(Det. Sgt. Wall)*, Julie
 Ege *(Helena)*, Edith Evans *(Aunt Louise)*, Martin Potter *(Ronnie)*, Hugh
 Griffith *(The Solicitor)*, Percy Herbert *(Det. Russet)*, Kathleen Byron *(Muriel
 Sharp)*, David Warbeck *(Det. Wilson)*, Venecia Day *(The Dancer)*, Anita Sharp
 Bolster *(Mary Lonsdale)*, Marianne Stone *(The Barmaid)*, Dean Harris
 (Ronnie's Friend)
P: Herman Cohen   **D:** Freddie Francis   **SCR:** Aben Kandel & Herman Cohen,
 from Henry Seymour's novel *Infernal Idol*   **PHOTOG:** John Wilcox
 MUSIC: John Scott
Minor horror-fantasy: African fetish inspires murder

Crazed
1982, (USA), color, 88 mins.
W: Laslo Papas, Belle Mitchell, Beverly Ross
D: Richard Cassidy
Minor thriller: Psycho secretes dead girl's body

Crazed Vampire
*see **Vierges et Vampires***

The Crazies
*see **Code Name Trixie***

The Crazy Composer
*see **Le Compositeur Toque***

The Crazy Family
1986, (Jap), color
W: Katsuya Kobayashi, Mitsuko Baisho, Yuki Kudo, Yoshiki Arizono, Hitoshi Ueki
D: Sogo Ishii   **SCR:** Sogo Ishii, Yoshinori Kobayashi & Fumio Kohnami
Bizarre satire: Family disintegrates after moving into new house

Crazy House
1943, (USA), Univ, b&w, 80 mins.
W: Chic Johnson, Ole Olsen, Cass Daley, Lon Chaney Jr., Hans Conried, Martha
 O'Driscoll, Marion Hutton, Patric Knowles, Percy Kilbride, Thomas
 Gomez, Edgar Kennedy, Robert Emmett Keane, Basil Rathbone, Nigel
 Bruce, Shemp Howard, Franklin Pangborn, Billy Gilbert, Fiorello La
 Guardia, Count Basie Band
D: Edward Cline   **SCR:** Robert Lees & Frederick I. Rinaldo   **PHOTOG:** Charles
 Van Enger   **MUSIC DIR:** George Hale
Standard comedy-fantasy: Outrageous burlesque routines

Crazy Fat Ethel II
1985, (USA), color, 90 mins.
W: Priscilla Alden, Michael Flood, Jane Lambert, Robert Copple
D: Nick Phillips
*Minor thriller (sequel to **Criminally Insane**): Female psycho released from prison,
 goes on cannibalistic rampage*

Crazy House (1973)
*see **The House in Nightmare Park***

Crazy Knights
*see **Ghost Crazy***

Crazy Music
*see **The 5000 Fingers of Dr. T***

Crazy Paradise
1965, (Den), Sherpix, color, 95 mins.
W: Dirch Passer, Hans Peterson, Ove Sprogoe, Ghita Norby, Paul Hagen, Bodil
 Steen, Karl Stegger, Lone Hertz, Kjeld Petersen, Gunnar Lemvigh, Arthur
 Jensen, Elsebeth Larsen
D & SCR: Gabriel Axel, from a novel by Ole Juul
Standard sex-fantasy: Exploration of Scandinavian libidos

The Crazy Ray
*see **Paris Qui Dort***

Creation
1931, (USA), RKO, b&w
*production abandoned after several months, but Willis O'Brien's miniatures inspired ma-
king of **King Kong** (1933): **Creation** would have illustrated evolution of life on Earth*

La Creation du Monde (The Creation of the World)
1962, (Fr), Jean Effel, color,
Animated feature

Creation of the Humanoids
1962, (USA), Genie/Emerson, color, 75 mins.
W: Don Megowan, Erika Elliot, Frances McCann, Don Doolittle, David Cross,
 George Milan
D: Wesley E. Barry   **SCR:** Jay Simms   **PHOTOG:** Hal Mohr
Standard but unusual SF-adventure (hailed by Andy Warhol, et al): Tale of future race of robots

The Creation of the World
*see **La Creation du Monde***

Creations Spontanées (Spontaneous Creations)
1898, (Fr), Star, b&w, 20m (65.6 ft./1.1 mins.)
D: Georges Melies
*Standard fantasy. A.k.a. **Illusions Fantastiques (Fantastic Illusions)***

Creator
1985, (USA), Kings Road/Univ, color, 108 mins.
W: Peter O'Toole *(Harry Wolper)*, Mariel Hemingway *(Meli)*, Vincent Spano
 (Boris), Virginia Madsen *(Barbara)*, Kenneth Tigar *(Pavlo)*, David Ogden
 Stiers *(Sid)*, John Dehner *(Paul)*, Karen Kopins *(Lucy)*, Elsa Raven *(Mrs.
 Mallory)*, Lee Kessler *(Mrs. Pruitt)*, Rance Howard *(Mr. Spencer)*, Ellen Geer
 (Mrs. Spencer), Ian Wolfe *(Prof. Bracer)*, Mike Jolly *(Boom-Boom)*, Burton
 Collins *(Lyman)*, Judith Hansen *(Karen)*, Byrne Piven *(Krauss)*, Doug Cox
 (Arthur), Anthony Peck *(Norman)*, Crawford Binion *(Fred)*, Vincent Cobb
 (Hamberg), Gary Bayer *(Bovi)*, Jordan Charney *(Dr. Whitaker)*, Sandy Ignon
 (Dr. Franklin), William H. Bassett *(Dr. Sutter)*, Jeff Corey *(Dean Harrington)*,
 Michael McGrady *(Larry)*, Eve McVeagh *(The Woman with the Monkey)*, Al
 Fann *(A Guard)*, Michael Green *(A Guard)*
D: Ivan Passer   **SCR:** Jeremy Leven—from his novel   **PHOTOG:** Robbie
 Greenberg   **MUSIC:** Sylvester LeVay
Modest comedy with SF overtones: Professor tries to clone dead wife

Creation of the Hunmanoids: DON MEGOWAN AND ERIKA ELLIOT

Creature
1984, (USA), Trans World Entertainment, color, 100 mins.
W: Klaus Kinski *(Hans Rudy Hofner)*, Stan Ivar *(Mike Davison)* Wendy Schaal
 (Beth Sladen), Lyman Ward *(David Perkins)*, Diane Salinger *(Melanie Bryce)*,
 Annette McCarthy *(Dr. Wendy H. Oliver)*, Robert Jaffe *(Jon Fennel)*, Marie
 Laurin *(Susan Delambre)*, John Stinson, Jim McKeny, Buckley Morris,
 Thomas C. James, Ray Bickel, Michael Griswold, David Moses, Earle
 Dugan, Randy Popplewell, Eileen Seeley, Michael Jones
D: William Malone   **SCR:** William Malone & Alan Reed   **PHOTOG:** Harry
 Mathias   **SPCL-FX:** The L.A. Effects Group, Inc.   **MUSIC:** Thomas Chase
 & Steve Rucker
*Award-winning SF-horror, impressive Alien imitation: Nasty boogen found on Saturn
 moon. Orig. to be titled **Titan Find***

Creature from Black Lake
1976, (USA), Jim McCullough/Howco-Int'l, color, 95 mins.
W: John David Carson, Jack Elam, Dennis Fimple, Dub Taylor, Bill Thurman
D: Joy Houck Jr.   **SCR:** Jim McCullough Jr.   **PHOTOG:** Dean Cundey
 MUSIC: Jaime Mendoza-Nava   **SONG:** *Exits and Truck Stops*
Minor horror-thriller: Nightmare hunt for swamp monster

The Creature from Galaxy 27
*see **Night of the Blood-Beast***

Creature from the Black Lagoon
1954, (USA), Univ, 3D, b&w, 79 mins.
W: Richard Carlson *(Dr. David Reed)*, Julia Adams *(Kay)*, Richard Denning *(Dr.
 Mark Williams)*, Antonio Moreno *(Dr. Carl Maia)*, Lucas), Whit Bissell *(Dr. Thompson)*, Henry Escalante *(Chico)*,
 Bernie Gozier *(Zee)*, Whit Bissell *(Dr. Thompson)*, Henry Escalante *(Chico)*,
 Rodd Redwing *(Louis)*, Julio Lopez *(Tomas)*, Sydney Mason *(Dr. Matos)*, Ben
 Chapman *(The Gill-Man)*, Ned Lefevre
P: William Alland   **D:** Jack Arnold   **SCR:** Harry Essex & Arthur Ross   **STORY:**

Maurice Zimm   **PHOTOG:** William E. Snyder & Charles S. Welbourne
MUSIC DIR: Joseph Gershenson
French retitle, The Strange Creature of the Black Lake
"...brilliant underwater photography and the miraculous mime of Ben Chapman
   as the Gill-Man convert the depths of the lagoon into a world of mystery as
   subtly beautiful as that Cocteau conceived for his fantastic creations"—John
   Baxter, Science Fiction in the Cinema
blurb: "Centuries of Passion Pent Up in His Savage Heart!"
*Classic SF-fantasy: Living fossil imperils paleontologists. cf. Revenge of the Creature
   and The Creature Walks Among Us*

Creature from the Haunted Sea
1961, (USA), Filmgroup/AA, b&w, 72 mins.
W: Antony Carbone, Betsy Jones-Moreland, Edward Wain (Robert Tome), Beech
   Dickerson, Robert Bean, Esther Sandoval, Edmundo Rivera Alvarez, Sonia
   Noemi Gonzalez, Blanquita Romero, Terry Nevin, Elisio Lopez, Tanner
   Hunt
P & D: Roger Corman   **SCR:** Charles B. Griffith   **PHOTOG:** Jack Marquette
MUSIC: Fred Katz
Minor classic, horror-melodrama satire: Motley seagoers meet marine menace

Creature of the Devil
see Dead Men Walk

Creature of the Walking Dead
1963, (Mex-USA), Jerry Warren/ADP, b&w, 70 mins.
W: Rock Madison, Ann Wells, George Todd, Bruno Ve Sota, Willard Gross, Lloyd
   Nelson, Katherine Victor
P: Alfred Ripstein   **D:** Frederic Corte [Fernando Cortes]   **SCR:** Alfredo Varela Jr.
   & Fernando Cortes (USA: Joseph Unsain)   **PHOTOG:** Richard Wallace
SPCL-FX: Nicolas Reye
*Minor horror-thriller (USA scenes added to 1960 film La Marca del Muerto' {The
   Mark of the Dead}): Scientist revives father's corpse*

Creatures
see From Beyond the Grave

The Creatures from Beyond the Grave
see From Beyond the Grave

Creatures of Clay
1914, (GB), Hepworth, b&w, 2,350 ft. (716.3m)
W: Alice de Winton (Vasca de Lisle), Stewart Rome (Stuart Finlay), Jack Raymond
   (Michael Trevis), Harry Gilbey (Mr. Trevis), Rachel de Solla (Mrs. Trevis),
   Henry Vibart (Hilary Sinclair)
D: Frank Wilson
Standard crime-thriller: Actress' ex-lover takes blame when she steals mother's gems

Creature From the Haunted Sea: BETSY JONES-MORELANDF AND ANTONY CARBONE

Creatures of Destruction
1968, (USA), Azalea/AIP, color, 80 mins
W: Les Tremayne, Pat Delany, Aron Kincaid, Neil Fletcher, Ann McAdams
P & D: Larry Buchanan   **SCR:** Enrique Touceda
*Minor horror-fantasy, remake of The She-Creature: Hypnotist calls forth prehistoric
   beast*

Creatures of the Prehistoric Planet
see Horror of the Blood Monsters

The Creature's Revenge
see Brain of Blood

Creatures the World Forgot
1970, (GB), Hammer/Col, color, 95 mins.
W: Julie Ege (The Girl), Marcia Fox (The Dumb Girl), Brian O'Shaughnessy (The
   Father), Rosalie Crutchley (The Old Crone), Robert John (The Dark Boy),
   Tony Bonner (The Fair Boy), Gerard Bonthuys (The Young Fair Boy), Sue
   Wilson (The Mother), Josje Kiesouw (The Young Dumb Girl), Hans Kiesouw
   (The Young Dark Boy), Don Leonard (The Old Leader), Rosita Moulan (The
   Dancer), Frank Hayden (The Murderer), Fred Swart (The Marauder Leader),
   Ken Hare (The Fair Tribe Leader), Beverly Blake, Doon Baide
P: Michael Carreras   **D:** Don Chaffey   **SCR:** Michael Carreras   **PHOTOG:**
   Vincent Cox   **MUSIC:** Mario Nascimbene
Standard SF-fantasy: Sibling rivalry in caveman clan

The Creature Walks Among Us
1956, (USA), Univ, b&w, 78 mins.
W: Jeff Morrow (Barton), Rex Reason (Morgan), Leigh Snowden, Gregg Palmer,
   Maurice Manson, James Rawley, Lillian Molieri, David McMahon, Paul
   Fierro, Larry Hudson, Frank Chase, Ricou Browning, Don Megowan
P: William Alland   **D:** John Sherwood   **SCR:** Arthur Ross   **PHOTOG:** Maury
   Gertsman   **MUSIC:** Joseph Gershenson
*Standard SF-horror, 3rd& last entry in "Creature" series: Scientists turn gill-man into air-
   breather. German retitle, The Horror is Among Us
cf. Creature from the Black Lagoon and Revenge of the Creature*

The Creature Wasn't Nice
1981, (USA), Mark Haggard/Creature Features, color, 88 mins.
W: Cindy Williams (McHugh), Bruce Kimmel (John), Patrick Macnee (Stark),
   Leslie Nielsen (Jameson), Ron Kurowski (The Creature), Gerrit Graham
   (Rodzinski)
WRIT & D: Bruce Kimmel   **PHOTOG:** Denny Lavil   **MUSIC:** David Spear
SONGS: I Want to Eat Your Face
Minor SF-spoof: Mission to locate interstellar life. TV retitle, Spaceship

Creature with the Atom Brain
1955, (USA), Clover/Col, b&w, 70 mins.
W: Richard Denning, Angela Stevens, Michael Granger, Tyler McVey, Gregory
   Gay, Charles Evans, Harry Lauter, Linda Bennett, Larry Blake, Tristram
   Coffin, Pierre Watkin, Nelson Leigh, Lane Chandler, Don C. Harvey, Paul
   Hoffman, Edward Coch, Karl Davis
D: Edward L. Cahn   **STORY & SCR:** Curt Siodmak   **PHOTOG:** Fred Jackman
Minor SF-horror: Corpses animated by remote control

Creature with the Blue Hand
1967, (W. Ger), New World, color, 74 mins (also 92 mins.)
W: Klaus Kinski, Diana Kerner, Harald Leipnitz
P: Horst Wendlandt   **D:** Alfred Vohrer   **SCR:** Alex Berg
Minor thriller: Which twin is diabolic killer?

The Creeper
1948, (USA), Edward Small/20th-Fox, b&w, 64 mins.
W: Onslow Stevens, Ralph Morgan, Eduardo Ciannelli, June Vincent, Philip Ahn
P: Bernard Small & Ben Pivar   **D:** Jean Yarbrough   **SCR:** Maurice Tombragel
Minor thriller: Scientist transformed into cat-like killer

The Creeper (1978)
see Rituals

The Creeper (1986)
see Dark Side of Midnight

The Creepers (1966)
see Island of Terror

The Creepers (1985)
see Phenomena

The Creeping Flesh
1973, (GB), World Film Services/Col, color, 91 mins.
W: Christopher Lee (James Hildern), Peter Cushing (Emmanuel Hildern), Lorna
   Heilbron (Penelope Hildern), George Benson (Waterlow), Kenneth J. Warren
   (Lenny), Duncan Lamont (The Inspector), Harry Locke (The Barman), Michael
   Ripper (Carter), Hedger Wallace (Dr. Perry), Catherine Finn (Emily),
   Marianne Stone (The Ass't), Robert Swann (The Aristocrat), Tony Wright
   (The Sailor), David Bailie (The Doctor), Maurice Bush (Karl), Alexandra
   Dane (The Whore)
P: Michael Redbourne   **D:** Freddie Francis   **SCR:** Peter Spenceley & Jonathan
   Rumbold   **PHOTOG:** Norman Warwick   **MUSIC:** Paul Ferris
Effective horror-fantasy: Rain restores life to evil, prehistoric skeleton. cf. D.N.A.

Creeping Shadows
1931, (GB), BIP/Wardour, b&w, 79 mins.
W: Franklin Dyall (Disher), Arthur Hardy (Sir Edwin Paget), Margot Grahame
   (Gloria Paget), Lester Matthews (Brian Nash), Jeanne Stuart (Olga Hoyt),
   Gerald Rawlinson (Paul Tegle), David Hawthorne (Peter Hoyt), Charles
   Farrell (Chicago Joe), Henrietta Watson (Lady Paget), Matthew Boulton (Insp.

Potter), Percy Parsons (*The Limping Man*)
D & SCR: John Orton, from Will Scott's play *The Limping Man*
Modest thriller: Three victims plot to kill retired informer

The Creeping Terror
1964, (USA), Metropolitan Int'l Crown International/Teledyn, b&w, 70 mins.
W: Vic Savage (*Martin*), Shannon O'Neil (*Brett*), William Thourlby (*Thorpe*) (*Dr. Bradford*), John Caresio, Norman Boone, Byrd Holland, Jack King, Pierre Kopp, Mark Field, Les La Marr, Ken Savage, Mary Price, Louise Lawson, Myra Lee, Al Lewis, Buddy Mize, Lewis Lawson, Robin James, Ray Wickman, Connie Valoie, Rita Tubin, Kelly Adams, Karl Goldenberg
P & D: A.J. Nelson **PHOTOG:** Irving Phillips **MUSIC:** Frederick Kopp
A.k.a. **The Crawling Monster** *and* **Dangerous Charter**
Amateurish SF-horror: Alien beast terrorizes small community. Filmed at Lake Tahoe, NV

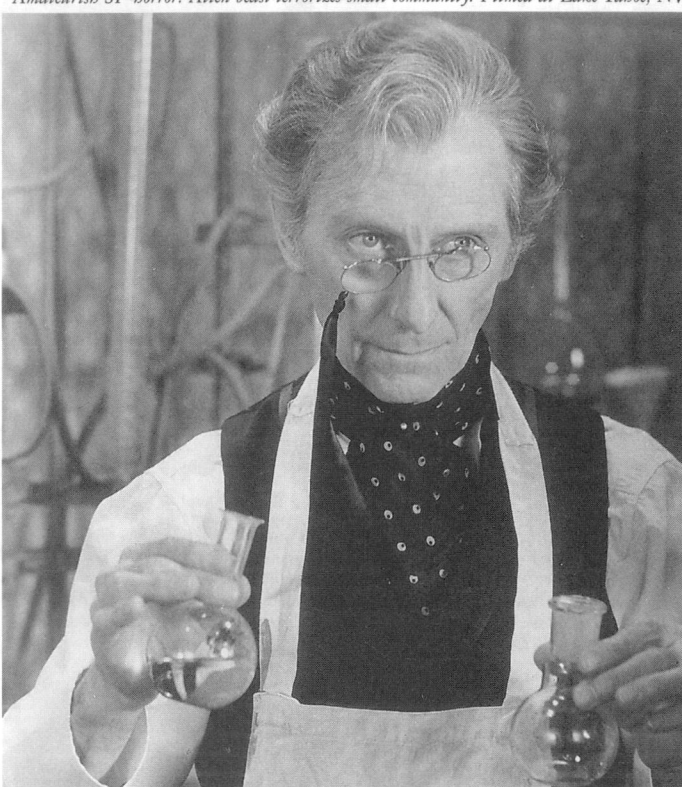

The Creeping Flesh: PETER CUSHING

The Creeping Unknown
see **The Quatermass Experiment**

Creepozoids
1987, (USA), Titan/Urban Classics, color, 72 mins.
W: Linnea Quigley, Ken Abraham, Michael Aranda, Joi Wilson, Richard Hawkins, Kim McKamy
D: David DeCoteau **SCR:** Burford Hauser & David DeCoteau **PHOTOG:** Thomas Callaway **MUSIC:** Guy Moon
orig. co-billed with **Slavegirls from Beyond Infinity**
Minor SF-horror: Botched experiment releases bloodthirsty mutants

Creepshow
1982, (USA), Laurel/WB, color, 118 mins.
W: Hal Holbrook (*Henry Northrup*), Adrienne Barbeau (*Wilma Northrup*), E.G. Marshall (*Upson Pratt*), Stephen King (*Jordy Verrill*), Leslie Nielsen (*Richard Vickers*), Viveca Lindfors (*Aunt Bedelia*), Ted Danson (*Harry Wentworth*), Fritz Weaver (*Prof. Dexter Stanley*), Carrie Nye (*Sylvia*), Ed Harris, Tom Savini, Gaylen Ross
D: George A. Romero **SCR:** Stephen King **PHOTOG:** Michael Gornick **MAKEUP:** Tom Savini
Standard anthology of terror tales

Creepshow 2
1987, (USA), Laurel/New World, color, 90 mins.
W: Lois Chiles, George Kennedy, Dorothy Lamour, Tom Savini (*The Creep*), Richard Parks, Philip Dore, Tom Wright, David Holbrook, Domenick John, Daniel Beer, Stephen King
P: David Ball **D:** Michael Gornick **SCR:** George A. Romero, from stories by Stephen King **MUSIC:** Les Reed & Rick Wakeman
Standard anthology of terror tales

La Cremation (The Cremation)
1899, (Fr), Star, b&w, 20m (65.6 ft./1.1 mins.)

D: Georges Melies
USA retitle, **The Spanish Inquisition**
Standard thriller: Heretic burned at stake

The Cremator
1968, (Czech), color, 90 mins.
W: Rudolph Hrusinsky, Vlasta Chramostova
D: Juraj Herz
Gripping thriller: Crematorium director becomes killer

The Cremators
1972, (USA), Arista/New World, color, 90 mins.
W: Maria Di Aragon, Marvin C. Howard, Eric Allison, Barney Bossick, Mason Caulfield, Cecil Redick, R.N. Bullard, Chuck Hillig, Tim Frawley, Jax Jason Carroll, Olga Kauffman, Jim Ragan, Al Ward
WRIT, P & D: Harry Essex **STORY:** Judy Ditky **PHOTOG:** Robert Caramico **SPCL-FX:** Doug Beswick **MUSIC:** Albert Glasser
Minor SF-thriller: Alien sphere absorbs humans

Crescendo
1969, (GB), Hammer/WB, color, 95 mins.
W: Stefanie Powers (*Susan Roberts*), James Olson (*Georges/Jacques*), Margaretta Scott (*Danielle Ryman*), Jane Lapotaire (*Lilliane*), Joss Ackland (*Carter*), Kirsten Betts (*Catherine*)
P: Michael Carreras **D:** Alan Gibson **SCR:** Jimmy Sangster & Alfred Shaughnessy **PHOTOG:** Paul Beeson **MUSIC:** Malcolm Williamson
not distrib. in USA until 1972
Standard thriller: Student researches dead composer, finds his son has mad twin

The Crew
1995, (USA), color, 100 mins.
W: Viggo Mortensen, Donal Logue, Pamela Gidley, Jeremy Sisto, Laura Del Sol, Grace Zabriskie, John Philbin
WRIT & D: Carl Colpaert
Standard psychodrama: Armed intruder holds pleasure cruisers hostage

Crime and Punishment
1935, (Fr), b&w, 110 mins.
W: Harry Baur, Pierre Blanchar, Madeleine Ozeray, Marcelle Geniat, Lucienne Lemarchand
D: Pierre Chenal **SCR:** Marcel Ayme, Pierre Chenal, Christian Stengel & Waldimir Strijewski, from Dostoevski's novel
Standard melodrama: Crime of murder plagues youth

Crime and Punishment
1935, (USA), Col, b&w, 89 mins.
W: Peter Lorre (*Raskolnikov*), Marian Marsh (*Sanya*), Edward Arnold (*Porfiri*), Tala Birell, Elisabeth Risdon, Douglass Dumbrille, Robert Allen, Sara Haden, Charles Waldron, Mrs. Patrick Campbell, Gene Lockhart, Thurston Hall
D: Josef von Sternberg **SCR:** S.K. Lauren & Joseph Anthony, from Dostoevski's novel **PHOTOG:** Lucien Ballard **MUSIC:** Arthur Honegger
Best film-version of classic novel: Murderer tormented by his conscience

Crime and Punishment
1958, (Fr), b&w
W: Jean Gabin, Robert Hossein
D: Georges Lampin, from Dostoevski's novel
Minor rendering of literary classic: Killer pursued by police and own conscience

Crime and Punishment
1970, (Russ), color, 220 mins.
W: Georgi Taratorkin (*Raskolnikov*), Innokenty Smoktonovsky, Victoria Fyodorova
D: Lev Julianov, from Dostoevski's novel
Faithful rendering of classic novel: Conscience bothers murderer

Crime and Punishment
1998, (USA), NBC-TV, color, 95 mins.
W: Patrick Dempsey (*Raskolnikov*), Julie Delpy, Ben Kingsley
D: Joseph sargent **TELEPLAY:** David Stevens, from Dostoevski's novel
TVM, standard melodrama: Impoverished student kills

Crime and Punishment, U.S.A.
1959, (USA), AA, b&w, 96 mins.
W: George Hamilton, Mary Murphy, Frank Silvera, John Harding, Marian Seldes
P & D: Terry & R. Denis Sanders **SCR:** Walter Newman, from Dostoevski's novel *Crime and Punishment* **PHOTOG:** Floyd Crosby **MUSIC:** Herschel Burke Gilbert
Minor thriller: Young man commits murder

Crime and the Penalty
1916, (GB), Martin/DFSA, b&w, 3,400 ft. (1036.3m)
W: Alesia Leon (*Mildred*), Jack Lovatt (*Jack*), Louis Nanten (*Jabez Burke*)
D: R. Harley West
Standard thriller: Crook hires scientist to kidnap cousin's wife with aid of chimpanzee that strangles when hypnotized

The Crime at Blossoms
1933, (GB), B&D/Para-British, b&w, 77 mins.
W: Hugh Wakefield (*Chris Merryman*), Joyce Bland (*Valerie Merryman*), Eileen

Munro (*Mrs. Woodman*), Ivor Barnard (*A Late Visitor*), Frederick Lloyd (*George Merryman*), Maud Gill (*Mrs. Merryman*), Iris Baker (*Lena Denny*), Wally Patch (*Palmer*), Arthur Stratton (*Mr. Woodman*), Barbara Gott (*The Fat Lady*), Moore Marriott (*The Driver*), George Ridgwell (*The Process Server*)
<u>D</u>: Maclean Rogers, from a play by Mordaunt Shairp
Standard thriller: Wife obsessed by country cottage's previous tenant

Crime at the Dark House
1940, (GB), Pennant/British Lion, b&w, 69 mins.
<u>W</u>: Tod Slaughter (*Sir Percival Glyde*), Sylvia Marriott (*Laura Fairlie*), Hilary Eaves (*Marian Fairlie*), Hay Petrie (*Dr. Fosco*), Geoffrey Wardwell (*Paul Hartwright*), Margaret Yarde (*Mrs. Bullen*), David Horne (*Mr. Fairlie*), Rita Grant (*Anne Catherick*)
<u>P & D</u>: George King   <u>SCR</u>: Edward Dryhurst, Frederick Hayward & H.F. Maltby, from Wilkie Collins' novel *The Woman in White*
reissued 1944 & 1947
Standard thriller: Inheritance scheme involves lookalikes

Crime at the Mill
1913, (GB), Dart Films/Anderson, b&w, 1,800 ft. (548.7m)
<u>D</u>: Stuart Kinder
Standard thriller: Wealthy miller abducts girl

Crime Beneath the Sea
see *Undersea Girl*

Crime by Night
1944, (USA), WB, b&w, 72 mins.
<u>W</u>: Jane Wyman, Jerome Cowan
Minor melodrama

Crime Casebook
see *The Hand of Fate*

Crime Doctor
1943, (USA), Col, b&w, 66 mins.
<u>W</u>: Warner Baxter (*Dr. Robert Ordway*), Margaret Lindsay (*Grace Fielding*), John Litel (*Three Fingers*), Don Costello (*Nick*), Ray Collins (*Dr. Carey*), Harold Huber (*Joe*), Constance Worth (*Betty*), Dorothy Tree (*Pearl*), Vi Athens (*Myrtle*), Leon Ames (*Capt. Wheeler*)
<u>D</u>: Michael Gordon   <u>SCR</u>: Graham Baker & Louis Lantz, from characters created by Max Marcin   <u>PHOTOG</u>: James S. Brown Jr.   <u>MUSIC</u>: Lee Zahler
Standard mystery-thriller: Amnesiac criminal becomes famous crime-fighter. Remake: The Man Who Lived Twice (1936), remade: The Man in The Dark (1953)

Crime Doctor's Courage
1945, (USA), Col, b&w, 70 mins.
<u>W</u>: Warner Baxter (*Dr. Robert Ordway*), Jerome Cowan (*Jeffers Jerome*), Hillary Brooke (*Kathleen Carson*), Robert Scott (*Rob Rencoret*), Lloyd Corrigan (*John Massey*), Charles Arnt (*The Butler*), Emory Parnell (*Capt. Birch*), Stephen Crane (*Gordon Carson*), Anthony Caruso (*Miguel Bragga*), Dennis Moore (*David Lee*), Lupita Tovar (*Dolores Bragga*), Jack Carrington (*Det. Fanning*), King Kong Kashay (*Luga*)
<u>D</u>: George Sherman   <u>SCR</u>: Eric Taylor, from characters created by Max Marcin   <u>PHOTOG</u>: L.W. O'Connell
Standard mystery-thriller: Crime-psychiatrist probes death of girl's spouse

Crime Doctor's Diary
1949, (USA), Col, b&w, 61 mins.
<u>W</u>: Warner Baxter (*Dr. Robert Ordway*), Stephen Dunne (*Steve Carter*), Lois Maxwell (*Jane Darrin*), Robert Armstrong (*Goldie Harrigan*), Adele Jergens (*Inez Grey*), George Meeker (*Anson*), Don Beddoe (*Philip Bellem*), Whit Bissell (*Pete Bellem*), Sid Tomack (*Blane*), Cliff Clark (*Insp. Manning*), Claire Carleton (*Louise*), Crane Whitley (*Mac*), Lois Fields (*Roma*), Selmer Jackson (*The Warden*), Robert Emmett Keane
<u>D</u>: Seymour Friedman   <u>SCR</u>: David Dressler & Edward Anhalt, from characters created by Max Marcin   <u>PHOTOG</u>: Vincent Farrar
Standard mystery-thriller: Crime-psychiatrist aids parolee framed for arson and murder

Crime Doctor's Gamble
1947, (USA), Col, b&w, 66 mins.
<u>W</u>: Warner Baxter (*Dr. Robert Ordway*), Steven Geray (*Jules Daudet*), Micheline Cheirel (*Mignon*), Roger Dann (*Henri Jardin*), Marcel Journet (*Jacques Morrell*), Eduardo Ciannelli (*Maurice Duval*), Maurice Marsac (*Anton Geroux*), Jean Del Val (*Theodore*), Henri Letondal (*Louis Chabonet*), Emory Parnell (*O'Reilly*), George Davis (*Paul Romaine*), Wheaton Chambers, Leon Lenoir
<u>D</u>: William Castle   <u>SCR</u>: Edward Boch & Raymond L. Schrock, from characters created by Max Marcin   <u>PHOTOG</u>: Philip Tannura   <u>MUSIC</u>: Mischa Bakaleinikoff
Standard mystery-thriller: Crime-psychiatrist hobnobs with European art collectors, encounters murder

Crime Doctor's Manhunt
1946, (USA), Col, b&w, 61 mins.
<u>W</u>: Warner Baxter (*Dr. Robert Ordway*), Ellen Drew (*Irene Cotter*), William Frawley (*Insp. Manning*), Claire Carleton (*Ruby Farrell*), Frank Sully (*Bigger*), Ivan Triesault (*Alfredi*), Bernard Nedell (*Waldo*), Jack Lee (*Sgt. Bradley*), Francis Pierlot (*Gerald Cotter*), Mary Newsom (*Martha*), Olin Howlin (*Marcus Leblanc*), Myron Healey (*Philip Armstrong*), Paul E. Burns (*Tom*), Leon Lenoir (*Herrera*)

<u>D</u>: William Castle   <u>SCR</u>: Eric Taylor & Leigh Bracketz, from characters created by Max Marcin   <u>PHOTOG</u>: Philip Tannura   <u>MUSIC</u>: Mischa Bakaleinikoff
Standard mystery-thriller: Crime-psychiatrist tackles murder and disappearance of "twin sister"

Crime Doctor's Strangest Case
1943, (USA), Col, b&w, 68 mins.
<u>W</u>: Warner Baxter (*Dr. Robert Ordway*), Lloyd Bridges (*Jimmy Trotter*), Lynn Merrick (*Mrs. Trotter*), Barton MacLane (*Rief*), Rose Hobart (*Mrs. Burns*), Reginald Denny (*Paul Ashley*), Sam Flint (*Addison Burns*), Virginia Brissac (*Patricia Cornwell*), Gloria Dickson (*Mrs. Keppler*), Constance Worth (*Betty Watson*), Jerome Cowan (*Malory*), George Lynn (*Walter Burns*), Thomas Jackson (*Yarnell*)
<u>D</u>: Eugene Forde   <u>SCR</u>: Eric Taylor, from characters created by Max Marcin   <u>PHOTOG</u>: James S. Brown Jr.
Standard mystery-thriller: Crime-psychiatrist aids man accused of killing former employers

Crime Doctor's Vacation
see *The Millerson Case*

Crime Doctor's Warning
1945, (USA), Col, b&w, 69 mins.
<u>W</u>: Warner Baxter (*Dr. Robert Ordway*), Dusty Anderson (*Connie Mace*), John Litel (*Insp. Dawes*), Coulter Irwin (*Frederick Malone*), Miles Mander (*Frederick Malone*), John Abbott (*Jimmy Gordon*), Alma Kruger (*Mrs. Wellington*), Franco Corsaro (*Joseph Duval*), Eduardo Ciannelli (*Nick Petroni*), J.M. Kerrigan (*Robert Mac Pherson*)
<u>D</u>: William Castle   <u>SCR</u>: Eric Taylor, from characters created by Max Marcin   <u>PHOTOG</u>: L.W. O'Connell   <u>MUSIC</u>: Paul Sawtell
Standard mystery-thriller: Crime-psychiatrist seeks killer of Parisian artist's model

The Crime of Dr. Crespi
1935, (USA), Rep, b&w
<u>W</u>: Erich von Stroheim, Harriet Russell, Edward Van Sloan, Dwight Frye
<u>P & D</u>: John Auer   <u>SCR</u>: Lewis Graham & Edwin Olmstead, based on Edgar Allan Poe's short story *The Premature Burial*
Standard thriller: Doctor has rival buried alive

The Crime of Monsieur Lange
1936, (Fr), b&w, 80 mins.
<u>W</u>: Rene Lefevre (*Monsieur Lange*), Florelle (*Valentine*), Henri Guisol (*Meinier*), Marcel Levesque (*Bessard*), Odette Talazac (*Mme. Besard*), Maurice Baquet (*Charles*), Nadia Sibirskaia (*Estelle*), Sylvia Battille (*Edith*), Jules Berry (*Batala*)
<u>D</u>: Jean Renoir   <u>SCR</u>: Jean Renoir & Jacques Prevert   <u>PHOTOG</u>: Jean Bachelet
Amusing comedy-thriller: Publisher vanishes

Crime on the Hill
1933, (GB), BIP/Wardour, b&w, 69 mins.
<u>W</u>: Sally Blane (*Sylvia Kennett*), Nigel Playfair (*Dr. Moody*), Lewis Casson (*Rev. Michael Gray*), Judy Kelly (*Alice Green*), Anthony Bushell (*Tony Fields*), Phyllis Dare (*Claire Winslow*), George Merritt (*Insp. Wolf*), Reginald Purdell (*The Reporter*), Gus McNaughton (*Collins*), Hal Gordon (*Sgt. Granger*), Kenneth Kove (*The Tourist*), Jimmy Godden (*The Landlord*), Hay Petrie (*Jevons*)
<u>D</u>: Bernard Vorhaus   <u>SCR</u>: Michael Hankinson, Vera Allinson, E.M. Delafield & Bernard Vorhaus, from a play by Jack De Leon & Jack Celestin
Standard crime-thriller: Vicar proves convicted man did not poison fiancee's rich uncle

Crime on the Riviera
see *Juggernaut*

Crime Over London
1936, (GB), Criterion/UA, b&w, 80 mins.
<u>W</u>: Margot Grahame (*Pearl Dupres*), Paul Cavanagh (*Insp. Gary*), Joseph Cawthorn (*Sherwood/Riley*), Basil Sydney (*Joker Finnegan*), Rene Ray (*Joan Vane*), Bruce Lister (*Ronald Martin*), David Burns (*Sniffy*), Edmon Ryan (*Spider*), John Darrow (*Jim*), Danny Green (*Klemm*), Googie Withers (*Miss Dupree*)
<u>P</u>: Marcel Hellman & Douglas Fairbanks Jr.   <u>D</u>: Alfred Zeisler   <u>SCR</u>: Norman Alexander & Harold French, from Louis de Wohl's novel *Thousand Windows*,
reissued 1944 & 1946 (cut)
Standard crime-thriller: Blackmailer turns to theft

Les Crimes au Musee des Horreurs
see *Horrors of the Black Museum*

Crimes in the Museum of Horrors
see *Horrors of the Black Museum*

Crimes in the Wax Museum
see *Nightmare in Wax*

The Crimes of Stephen Hawke
1936, (GB), George King/MGM, b&w, 69 mins.
<u>W</u>: Tod Slaughter (*Stephen Hawke*), Marjorie Taylor (*Julia Hawke*), Eric Portman (*Matthew Trimble*), Gerald Barry (*Miles Archer*), Ben Soutten (*Nathaniel*), D.J. Williams (*Joshua Trimble*), Charles Penrose (*Sir Franklyn*), Norman Pierce (*The Landlord*)
<u>D</u>: George King & Paul White   <u>SCR</u>: H.F. Maltby, from a story by Jack Celestin

USA retitle, **Strangler's Morgue** (Hoffberg, 1953)
Standard thriller: Usurer is notorious "Spinebreaker". reissued 1940

Crime Zone
1989, (USA), Concorde, color, 87 mins.
<u>W</u>: David Carradine (*Jason*), Peter Nelson (*Bone*), Sherilyn Fenn (*Helen*), Michael Shaner (*Creon*)
<u>P & D</u>: Luis Llosa   <u>SCR</u>: Daryl Haney   <u>PHOTOG</u>: Cusi Barrio
Minor SF-thriller: Brutal adventure in post-nuke world

The Criminal
1960, (GB), Merton Park/Anglo-Amalgamated, b&w, 97 mins.
<u>W</u>: Stanley Baker (*Johnny Bannion*), Margit Saad (*Suzanne*), Sam Wanamaker (*Mike Carter*), Gregoire Aslan (*Frank Saffron*), Jill Bennett (*Maggie*), Laurence Naismith (*Town*), Noel Willman (*The Governor*), Patrick Magee (*Barrows*), Derek Francis (*The Priest*), Rupert Davies (*Edwards*), Kenneth J. Warren (*Clobber*), Patrick Wymark (*Sol*), Edward Judd
<u>P</u>: Jack Greenwood   <u>D</u>: Joseph Losey   <u>SCR</u>: Alun Owen   <u>STORY</u>: Jimmy Sangster   <u>PHOTOG</u>: Robert Krasker
USA retitle, **The Concrete Jungle**
Standard crime-thriller: Gang helps jailed leader escape, seeks buried loot

Criminal at Large
see **The Frightened Lady** (1932)

I Criminali della Galassia (The Galaxy Criminals)
1965, (It), Ram/MGM, color, 93 mins.
<u>W</u>: Franco Nero (*Jake*), Massimo Serato (*Nurmi*), Carlo Giustini (*Ken*), Lisa Gastoni, Tony Russel
<u>P</u>: Joseph Fryd & Antonio Margheriti   <u>D</u>: Antonio Margheriti   <u>SCR</u>: Ivan Reiner & Renato Moretti   <u>PHOTOG</u>: Richard Pallton   <u>MUSIC</u>: Francisco Lavagnino
USA retitle, **Wild, Wild Planet**
Standard SF-adventure: Humans shrunk by female agents of alien mad scientist

Criminally Insane
1975, (USA), color, 61 mins.
<u>W</u>: Priscilla Alden, Michael Flood
<u>D</u>: Nick Phillips
Minor thriller: Madwoman craves blood. cf. **Crazy Fat Ethel II**

Criminals of the Galaxy
see **I Criminali della Galassia**

Criminals Within
1941, (USA), b&w, 67 mins.
<u>W</u>: Eric Linden, Ann Doran, Constance Worth, Donald Curtis, Weldon Heyburn, Ben Alexander
<u>D</u>: Joseph H. Lewis
Minor wartime thriller: Spies kill scientist working on top-secret formula

The Crimson Affair
see **Curse of the Crimson Altar**

The Crimson Altar
see **Curse of the Crimson Altar**

The Crimson Blade
see **The Scarlet Blade**

The Crimson Canary
1945, (USA), Univ, b&w, 64 mins.
<u>W</u>: Noah Beery Jr., Lois Collier
Standard thriller

The Crimson Candle
1934, (GB), Mainwaring/MGM, b&w, 48 mins.
<u>W</u>: Eve Gray (*Mavis*), Eliot Makeham (*The Doctor*), Kenneth Kove (*Hon. Horatius Chillingsbotham*), Eugene Leahy (*The Detective*), Audrey Cameron (*The Maid*), Kynaston Reeves, Derek Williams, Arthur Goullet
<u>P & D</u>: Bernard Mainwaring
Minor thriller: Doctor proves maid engineered "curse" murder

The Crimson Circle
1922, (GB), Kinema Club/Granger, b&w, 5,378 ft. (1639.2m)
<u>W</u>: Madge Stuart (*Thalia Drummond*), Fred Groves (*Insp. Parr*), Rex Davis (*Jack Beardmore*), Clifton Boyne (*Derrick Yale*), Eva Moore (*Aunt Prudence*), Robert English (*Felix Marl*), Lawford Davidson (*Raphael Willings*), Sydney Paxton (*Harvey Froyant*), Harry J. Worth, Bertram Burleigh, Mary Odette, Victor McLaglen, Joan Morgan, Henry Victor, Olaf Hytten, George Dewhurst, Jack Hobbs, Henry Vibart, Eille Norwood, Kathleen Vaughan, Flora le Breton, Malcolm Tod, Sir Simeon Stuart
<u>D</u>: George Ridgwell   <u>SCR</u>: Patrick L. Mannock, from a novel by Edgar Wallace
Standard thriller: Detective heads blackmail gang

The Crimson Circle
1936, (GB), Wainwright/Univ, b&w, 76 mins.
<u>W</u>: Hugh Wakefield (*Derrick Yale*), Alfred Drayton (*Insp. Parr*), Noah Beery (*Felix Marl*), June Duprez (*Sylvia Howard*), Renee Gadd (*Millie MacRoy*), Basil

Gill (*James Beardmore*), Niall MacGinnis (*Jack Beardmore*), Paul Blake (*Sgt. Webster*), Gordon McLeod (*Insp. Brabazon*), Ralph Truman (*Lawrence Fuller*)
<u>D</u>: Reginald Denham   <u>SCR</u>: Howard Irving Young, from a novel by Edgar Wallace
Standard thriller: Inspector unmasks mysterious criminal

The Crimson Cult
see **Curse of the Crimson Altar**

The Crimson Executioner
see **Il Boia Scarlatto**

The Crimson Key
1947, (USA), 20th-Fox, b&w, 76 mins.
<u>W</u>: Kent Taylor, Doris Dowling
Minor thriller

The Crimson Triangle
1915, (GB), Martin/Ogden, b&w, 4,000 ft. (1219.2m)
<u>W</u>: R. Harley West (*Marcus Plane*), Jack Jarman
<u>D</u>: Dave Aylott
Standard thriller: Embassy attache forced to join secret society

Cristobal's Gold
see **L'Or du Cristobal**

Critters
1986, (USA), SHO/Smart Egg/New Line, color, 85 mins.
<u>W</u>: Dee Wallace Stone (*Helen Brown*), Billy Green Bush (*Jay Brown*), Scott Grimes (*Brad Brown*), Nadine Van Der Velde (*April Brown*), M. Emmet Walsh, Don Opper, Terrence Mann, Lin Shaye, Ethan Phillips, Billy Zane, Jeremy Lawrence, Art Frankel, Douglas Koth
<u>D</u>: Stephen Herek   <u>SCR</u>: Domonic Muir & Stephen Herek   <u>PHOTOG</u>: Tim Suhrstedt   <u>MUSIC</u>: David Newman   <u>SONG</u>: Power of the Night
Modest SF-fantasy: Carnivorous aliens attack farm family

Critters 2: The Main Course
1988, (USA), SHO/New Line, color, 87 mins.
<u>W</u>: Scott Grimes (*Bradley Brown*), Terrence Mann (*Ug*), Don Opper (*Charlie*), Cynthia Garris, Al Stevenson, Tom Hodges, Douglas Rowe, Liane Curtis, Lindsay Parker, Sam Anderson, Herta Ware, Lin Shaye, Barry Corbin, Frank Birney, Gregory Patrick, David Ursin, Roxane Kernichan, Tom McLoughlin, J. Christopher Sullivan, Patrick Campbell, Candace Laughlin, Gary Cashdollar, Montrose Hagins
<u>D</u>: Mick Garris   <u>SCR</u>: D.T. Twohy & Mick Garris   <u>PHOTOG</u>: Russell Carpenter   <u>MUSIC</u>: Nicholas Pike
Modest SF-comedy: Flesh-eating space beasties return to plague small town

Critters 3
1992, (USA), color
<u>W</u>: Aimee Brooks
Standard SF-comedy: Los Angeles apartment-house tenants repel alien invasion

Critters 4
1992, (USA), color, 94 mins.
<u>W</u>: Don Opper, Paul Whitthorne, Angela Bassett
Minor SF-comedy: Space salvagers find alien eggs

Crocodile
1979, (Hong Kong), Cobra Media/Herman Cohen, color, 91 mins (also 95 mins.)
<u>W</u>: Tany Tim, Nat Puvanai
<u>P</u>: Dick Randall & Robert Chan   <u>D</u>: Sompote Sands
Minor SF-thriller: Monster reptile wreaks havoc

Cronos
1993, (Mex), color, 92 mins.
<u>W</u>: Ron Perlman, Federico Luppi, Claudio Brook
<u>WRIT & D</u>: Guillermo del Toro
Stylish, award-winning horror-fantasy: Antiques dealer finds device that imparts immortality, but turns users into vampires

Crooked Alley
1923, (USA), Univ, b&w, 5 reels
<u>W</u>: Thomas Carrigan (*Boston Blackie*), Laura La Plante (*Norine Tyrell/Olive Sloan*), Tom S. Guise (*Judge Milnar*), Owen Gorine (*Rudy Milnar*), Albert Hart (*Kaintuck*), Kate Lester, Lillian Worth, Sidney Bracy
<u>D</u>: Robert F. Hill   <u>SCR</u>: Adrian Johnson   <u>ADAPT</u>: Robert F. Hill, from a story by Jack Boyle   <u>PHOTOG</u>: Harry Fowler
working title, **The Daughter of Crooked Alley**
Standard thriller: Merciless judge targeted for revenge

The Crooked Road
1964, (GB), Argo-Triglav-Trident/Gala, b&w, 92 mins.
<u>W</u>: Robert Ryan (*Richard Ashley*), Stewart Granger (*The Duke of Organga*), Nadia Gray (*Cosima*), Catherine Woodville (*Elena*), Marius Goring (*Harlequin*), George Coulouris (*Carlos*), Robert Rietty (*The Police Chief*)
<u>P</u>: Jack O. Lamont & David Henley   <u>D</u>: Don Chaffey   <u>SCR</u>: Don Chaffey & J. Garrison, from Morris L. West's novel

Standard crime-thriller: Embezzling duke poisons reporter

The Crooked Sky
1957, (GB), Luckwin/RFD, b&w, 77 mins.
W: Wayne Morris (*Mike Conlin*), Karin Booth (*Sandra Hastings*), Anton
  Diffring (*Fraser*), Bruce Seton (*Mac*), Frank Hawkins (*Robson*),
  Sheldon Lawrence (*Bill*), Collette Barthrop (*Penny*), Murray Kash
  (*Lewis*), Wally Peterson (*Wilson*)
P: Bill Luckwell & Derek Winn **D:** Henry Cass **SCR:** Norman Hudis **STORY:**
  Lance Z. Hargreaves & Maclean Rogers
Standard crime-thriller: Detective unmasks gambler as head of counterfeiters

The Crooked Web
1955, (USA), Col, b&w, 77 mins.
W: Frank Lovejoy, Mari Blanchard
Standard melodrama

Cross Channel
1955, (GB), Republic Prods., b&w, 61 mins.
W: Wayne Morris (*Tex Parker*), Yvonne Furneaux (*Jacqueline Moreau*), Arnold
  Marle (*Papa Moreau*), Carl Jaffe (*Otto Dagoff*), Patrick Allen (*Hugo Platt*),
  Charles Lawrence (*Jean-Pierre*), Peter Sinclair (*Soapy*), Michael Golden
  (*Carrick*)
P: William N. Boyle **D:** R.G. Springsteen **STORY:** Rex Rienits
Standard crime-thriller: Jewel smugglers frame boat skipper for faked murder

Crosscurrent
1970, (USA), WB/CBS-TV, color, 96 mins.
W: Robert Hooks, Carol Lynley, Robert Wagner, Jeremy Slate, Jose Ferrer, Simon Oak

The Crow
(USA), Miramax, color, 102 mins.
W: Brandon Lee, Ernie Hudson, Michael Wincott, Graeme Revell, Sofia Shinas,
  Rochelle Davis
D: Alex Proyas, from James O'Barr's comic-book character
*Unusual fantasy-thriller (Brandon Lee's last film; he was killed on the set): Revived corpse
  becomes superhero*

The Crow: City of Angels
1996, (USA), Miramax/Dimension, color, 84 mins
W: Vincent Perez, Mia Kirshner, Richard Brooks, Iggy Pop, Ian Dury
P: Edward R. Pressman & Jeff Most **D:** Tim Pope **SCR:** David S. Goyer, from
  James O'Barr's comic-book character **PHOTOG:** Jean Yves Escoffier
  MUSIC: Graeme Revell
Standard action-fantasy

Crowhaven Farm
1970, (USA), Aaron Spelling/ABC-TV, color, 72 mins.
W: Hope Lange, Paul Burke, Lloyd Bochner, John Carradine, Cyril Delevanti,
  Virginia Gregg
D: Walter Grauman **TELEPLAY:** John McGreevey
TVM, standard horror-thriller: Young couple swept into nightmare world of witchcraft

Crow Hollow
1952, (GB), Merton Park-Bruton/Anglo-Amalgamated, b&w, 69 mins.
W: Donald Houston (*Robert*), Natasha Parry (*Ann*), Esma Cannon (*Judith*), Nora
  Nicholson (*Opal*), Susan Richmond (*Hester*), Pat (Patricia) Owens (*Willow*),
  Melissa Stribling (*Diana*)
P: William Williams **D:** Michael McCarthy **STORY:** Vivian Milroy
Standard thriller: Bride seeks would-be murderers

The Crucible (1957)
see *Les Sorcieres de Salem*

The Crucible
1996, (USA), 20th-Fox, color, 123 mins.
W: Daniel Day-Lewis, Winona Ryder, Emma Thompson, Joan Allen, Paul
  Scofield (*Rev. Danforth*), Bruce Davison, Jeffrey Jones, Rob Campbell
D: Nicholas Hytner **SCR:** Arthur Miller, from his play **PHOTOG:** Andrew
  Dunn **MUSIC:** George Fenton
Well-made melodrama: Repressed passions fuel Salem witch hunt

Crucible of Horror
see *The Corpse*

Crucible of Terror
1972, (GB), Glendale/Scotia-Barber, color, 91 mins.
W: Mike Raven (*Victor Clare*), Mary Maude (*Millie*), Ronald Lacey (*Michael Clare*),
  James Bolam (*John Davies*), Betty Alberge (*Dorothy Clare*), John Arnatt
  (*Bill*), Beth Morris (*Jane Clare*), Judy Matheson (*Marcia*), Melissa Stribling
  (*Joanna Brent*), Kenneth Keeling (*George Brent*), Mei Mei Lay (*Chi-San*)
P: Tom Parkinson **D:** Ted Hooker **STORY:** Ted Hooker & Tom Parkinson
  PHOTOG: Peter Newbrook **MUSIC:** Paris Rutherford
Minor horror-thriller: Sculptor makes statues of female corpses

The Crucifer of Blood
1991, (USA), TNT-TV, color, 105 mins.
W: Charlton Heston (<u>Sherlock Holmes</u>), Richard Johnson (<u>Dr. JohnWatson</u>),
  Susannah Harker, John Castle, Clive Wood, Simon Callow, Edward Fox

D: Fraser Heston, from Sir Arthur Conan Doyle's *The Sign of Four*
TVM, standard thriller: British soldiers share accursed secret

Cruel Swamp
see *Swamp Women*

Cruise into Terror
1978, (USA), Aaron Spelling/20th Fox/ABC TV, color, 95 mins.
W: Dirk Benedict (*Simon*), Frank Converse (*Matt Lazarus*), Hugh O'Brian (*Andy*),
  John Forsythe (*Rev. Charles Mather*), Christopher George (*Neal Barry*), Lynda
  Day George (*Sandra Barry*), Lee Meriwether (*Lil Mather*), Stella Stevens
  (*Marilyn Magneson*), Ray Milland (*Dr. Isaiah Bakkun*), Jo Ann Harris (*Judy
  Haines*), Marshall Thompson (*Bennett*), Ruben Moreno (*Emanuel*), Roger E.
  Mosley, Hilary Thompson
D: Bruce Kessler **TELEPLAY:** Michael Braverman **PHOTOG:** Arch Dalzell
  SPCL-FX: Dick Albain **MUSIC:** Gerald Fried
TVM, standard fantasy-thriller: Demonic sarcophagus disrupts ocean trip

Crusoe
1988, (USA), color, 94 mins.
W: Sandy Ward (*Bannerman*), Jerry Hardin (*Masen*), Aidan Quinn, Ade
  Sapara, Warren Clarke, Hepburn Graham, Shane Rimmer, Elvis Payne,
  Jimmy Nail, Tim Spall
D: Caleb Deschanel, from Daniel Defoe's novel "Robinson Crusoe"
Unusual melodrama: Slave-trader shipwrecked

The Cry Baby Killer
1958, (USA), AA, b&w, 62 mins.
W: Jack Nicholson, Harry Lauter, Leo Gordon, Brett Halsey, Carolyn Mitchell, Ed
  Nelson, Mitzi McCall, Roger Corman
P: Roger Corman **D:** Justus Addiss **SCR:** Leo Gordon **SONG:** (sung by Dick
  Kallman), *Cry Baby Cry*
Minor thriller (Jack Nicholson's first film): Sociopath takes hostages at drive-in theater

Cry Danger
1951, (USA), RKO, b&w, 79 mins.
W: Dick Powell, Rhonda Fleming
Standard thriller

The Cry for Justice
1919, (GB), Vanity/J&S, b&w, 5,000 ft. (1524m)
W: Amy Brandon Thomas (*Myra Stuart*), Norman Page (*Bruce Stuart*), Mary
  Glynne (*Jeannette*), Geoffrey Wilmer (*Beveridge*), Charles Childerstone (*Jim*),
  Victor Lusk (*Mr. Stuart*)
D: A.G. Frenguelli
*Standard crime-thriller: Inventor jailed when assistant fakes his own murder to steal plans
  and wife*

Cry for the Strangers
1982, (USA), David Gerber-MGM/CBS-TV, color, 86 mins.
W: Patrick Duffy (*Dr. Russell*), Cindy Pickett (*Elaine Russell*), Brian Keith (*Chief
  Whalen*), Lawrence Pressman (*Glen Palmer*), Shawn Carson (*Robby Palmer*),
  Claire Malis (*Rebecca Palmer*), Robin Ignico, Jeff Corey, Taylor Lacher, Parley
  Baer, Anita Dangler, Martin Kove, J.V. Bradley, Jerry-Mac Johnston, Josef
  James
D: Peter Medak **TELEPLAY:** J.D. Feigelson, from John Saul's novel **PHO-
  TOG:** Frank W. Stanley **SPCL-FX:** John Frazier **MUSIC:** John Cacavas
TVM, minor thriller: Outsiders killed in Northwest village

The Crying Child
1996, (USA), USA-TV, color, 95 mins.
W: Kin Shriner, Mariel Hemingway, George DelHoyo, Finola Hughes
TVM, standard thriller

Cry Danger
W: William Conrad, Richard Erdman
D: Robert Parrish **PHOTOG:** Joseph Biroc
Standard thriller: Falsely-imprisoned man seeks revenge

A Cry in the Night
1915, (GB), New Agency, b&w, 1,200 ft. (365.8m)
W: James Russell (*The Thing*)
D: Ernest G. Batley
Standard horror-thriller: Man killed by scientist's winged gorilla

A Cry in the Night
1956, (USA), WB, b&w, 75 mins.
W: Raymond Burr, Natalie Wood, Brian Donlevy, Richard Anderson, Edmond
  O'Brien
WRIT & P: David Dortort **D:** Frank Tuttle
blurb: "A frenzied search, a madman's whim, a girl's life in the balance!"
Standard but suspenseful thriller: Psychopath abducts policeman's daughter

Cry Murder
1950, (USA), Film Classics, b&w, 63 mins.
W: Carole Matthews, Jack Lord
Standard thriller

Cry of the Banshee
1970, (GB), MGM-EMI/AIP, color, 87 mins.
W: Vincent Price (*Lord Whitman*), Essy Persson (*Lady Patricia*), Hugh Griffith (*Mickey*), Elisabeth Bergner (*Oona*), Hilary Dwyer (*Maureen*), Sally Geeson (*Sarah*), Carl Rigg (*Harry*), Patrick Mower (*Roderick*), Pamela Farbrother (*Margaret*), Marshall Jones (*Father Tom*), Stephen Chase (*Sean*), Michael Elphick (*Burke*), Andrew McCulloch (*Bully Boy*), Gertan Klauber (*The Landlord*), Robert Hutton (*The Guest*), Godfrey James, Terry Martin, Quinn O'Hara, Richard Everett, Jan Rossini, Peter Forest, Joyce Mandre
P & D: Gordon Hessler   SCR: Tim Kelly & Christopher Wicking   PHOTOG: John Coquillon   MUSIC: Les Baxter
Standard horror-thriller: Witch avenges death of her children

Cry of the Bewitched
1956, (Mex), Yates/John Alexander Film Associates, color, 79 mins
W: Ninon Sevilla, Ramon Gay
A.k.a. *Young and Evil* (US title, 1962)
Standard fantasy-melodrama: Girl uses witchcraft to entice plantation owner

The Cry of the Captive
1914, (GB), Hepworth, b&w, 2,075 ft. (632.5m)
W: Stewart Rome (*Thornley Vibart*), Violet Hopson (*Zorah Vibart*), James Lindsay (*Charles Glenney*), Edward Lingard (*The Cardsharper*)
D: Frank Wilson   STORY: Percy Manton
Standard crime-thriller: Cardsharper uses man's cowardice to force sister to act as his decoy

Cry of the Werewolf
1944, (USA), Col, b&w, 65 mins.
W: Nina Foch, Stephen Crane (*Bob*), Osa Massen (*Elsa*), Barton MacLane, Blanche Yurka, Fritz Leiber, Milton Parsons, Ivan Triesault, John Abbott
P: Wallace MacDonald   D: Henry Levin   SCR: Griffin Jay & Charles O'Neal
French retitle, Cry of the Werewolf's Daughter
Standard horror-fantasy: Gypsy princess discovers mother was lycanthrope

Cry of the Werewolf's Daughter
see Cry of the Werewolf

Crypt of Dark Secrets
1976, (USA), color, 100 mins.
W: Maureen Chan, Ronald Tanet, Wayne Mack, Herbert G. Jahncke
D: Jack Weis
Minor fantasy-thriller: Indian spirit saves war vet from death

Crypt of Horror
see La maldicion de los Karnsteins

Crypt of the Living Dead
1972, (USA), Coast Industries/Atlas, color, 79 mins.
W: Andrew Prine (*Chris*), Mark Damon (*Peter*), Patty Sheppard (*Mary*), Teresa Gimpera (*Hannah*), Ihsan Genik (*The Wild Man*), Frank Brana (*The Blind Sailor*), Mariano Rey (*Prof. Bolton*), Jack La Rue Jr. (*Adnan*), Edward Walsh (*Adnan's Father*), Jem Osmanoglu (*The Little Boy*), Shera Osman (*The Little Girl*), John Alderman (*The First Fisherman*)
D: Ray Danton   SCR: Lou Shaw   STORY: Lois Gibson   PHOTOG: Juan Gelpi   SPCL-FX: A. Molina   MUSIC: Phillip Lambro
blurb: "She's 700 Years Old And Still Going Strong!"
Minor horror-thriller: Vampiress released from island tomb

The Crystal Casket
see Le Phenix ou le Coffret de Cristal

The Crystal Gazer
1912, (GB), Cosmopolitan, b&w, 640 ft. (195.1m)
Minor thriller: Adventures of female clairvoyant

Cry Terror!
1958, (USA), MGM, b&w, 96 mins.
W: James Mason (*Jim Molner*), Inger Stevens (*Joan Molner*), Rod Steiger (*Paul Hoplin*), Angie Dickinson (*Kelly*), Barney Phillips (*Pringle*), Neville Brand (*Steve*), Kenneth Tobey (*Frank Cole*), Jack Klugman (*Vince*), Jack Kruschen (*Charles Pope*), Carleton Young (*Robert Adams*), William Schallert (*Henderson*), Harlan Warde, Ed Hinton, Chet Huntley, Mae Marsh, Roy Neal, Portland Mason, Terry Ann Ross
P: Andrew & Virginia Stone   WRIT & D: Andrew Stone   PHOTOG: Walter Strenge   MUSIC: Howard Jackson
Taut thriller: Psychopath forces technician to build bombs for airplane sabotage

Cry Wolf
1947, (USA), WB, b&w, 83 mins.
W: Barbara Stanwyck (*Sandra Marshall*), Errol Flynn (*Mark Caldwell*), Richard Basehart (*James Demarest*), Jerome Cowan (*Sen. Caldwell*), Geraldine Brooks (*Julie Demarest*), Barry Bernard (*Roberts, the Groom*), John Ridgely (*Jackson Laidell*), Patricia Barry (*White*) (*Angela*), Rory Mallinson (*Becket*), Lisa Golm (*Mrs. Laidell*), Paul Stanton (*Davenport*), John Elliott (*The Clergyman*), Helene Thimig (*Marta*), Jack Mower (*Watkins*), Paul Panzer (*The Gatekeeper*), Creighton Hale (*Dr. Reynolds*)
P: Henry Blanke   D: Peter Godfrey   SCR: Catherine Turney, from Marjorie Carleton's novel   PHOTOG: Carl Guthrie   MUSIC: Franz Waxman

MUSIC DIR: Leo F. Forbstein
Standard thriller: Distraught woman suspects brother-in-law of skullduggery. Film debuts of Basehart and Brooks

Cry Wolf
1980, (GB), Picture Partnership/Para, color, 31 mins.
W: Paul Maxwell (*Dr. Jack Russell*), Rosalind Ayres (*Maria Moore*), Stephen Greif (*Prof. Ion Porphiriou*), James Bree (*The Inspector*), Chris Fairbank (*The Sgt.*), Gabrielle Day (*Mrs. Taylor*), Joseph Brady (*The Scotsman*)
P: Brian Eastman   D: Lezlek Burzynski   STORY: Stan Hey   PHOTOG: Robert Krasker   MUSIC: Leith Stevens
Standard short horror-thriller: Canine serum turns doctor into werewolf

Cthulhu Mansion
1991, (USA), color, 95 mins.
W: Frank Finlay, Marcia Layton, Brad Fisher, Luis Fernando Alves, Melanie Shatner, Kaethe Cherney, Paul Birchard, Francisco Brana
D & SCR: J. Piquer Simon
Minor horror-fantasy: Delinquents unleash evil spirits

Las Cuatro Noches de la Luna Llena (The Four Nights of the Full Moon)
1964, (Sp), Gustav Unger/Documento b&w
W: Gene Tierney, Analia Gade, Dan Dailey, Perla Cristal, Nini Montian, Jaime de Mora y Aragon [*Fabiolo*]
D: Sobey Martin   PHOTOG: Juan Marine
Standard melodrama: Woman's love precipitates tragedy

Cuentos de Hadas (Fairy Tale)
1951, (Sp), b&w
W: Conchita Montez, Manuel Gomez Burr, Nini Polan, Ismael Merlo, Julia Lajos, Mariana Larrabeiti
WRIT & D: Edgar Neville   PHOTOG: Enrique Guerner
Standard fantasy: Enchantment comes to life

El Cuerpo del Lito (The Corpus Delicti)
1930, (USA), Para, b&w
W: Ramon Pereda (*Philo Vance*), Maria Alba (*Fanny*), Antonio Moreno (*Mohler*), Barry Norton (*Sgt. Heath*), Carlos Villarias (*Markham*), Andres de Segurola, Maria Calvo, Vincente Padula
D: Cyril Gardner & A. Washington Pezet   SCR: W. Tuchinski & J. Carrara Rebalta, from S.S. Van Dine's novel *The Benson Murder Case*
Standard thriller, Spanish-speaking version of The Benson Murder Case*: Suave sleuth stalks killer at hunting lodge*

La Cuisine de l'Ogre (The Ogre's Cuisine)
1908, (Fr), Star, b&w, 107m (351 ft./5.9 mins.)
D: Georges Melies
A.k.a. *In the Bogie Man's Cave*
Standard fantasy: Ogre eats boy

Cujo
1983, (USA), Daniel H. Blatt-Robert Singer/Taft/WB, color, 96 mins.
W: Dee Wallace (*Donna Trenton*), Danny Pintauro (*Tad Trenton*), Daniel Hugh-Kelly (*Vic Trenton*), Christopher Stone (*Steve Kemp*), Ed Lauter (*Joe Camber*), Kauilani Lee (*Mrs. Camber*), Billy Jacoby (*Brett Camber*), Mills Watson (*Gary Pervier*), Sandy Ward
D: Lewis Teague   SCR: Don Carlos Dunaway & Lauren Currier, from Stephen King's novel   PHOTOG: Jan DeBont   MUSIC: Charles Bernstein
Tense thriller: Rabid dog terrorizes mother and child

Cul-de-Sac
1965, (GB), Compton/Tekli, b&w, 111 mins.
W: Donald Pleasence (*George*), Francoise Dorleac (*Teresa*), Lionel Stander (*Richard*), Jack MacGowran (*Albert*), Geoffrey Sumner (*Father*), Iain Quarrier (*Christopher*), Renee Houston (*Mother*), Robert Dorning (*Mr. Fairweather*), Marie Kean (*Marion Fairweather*), William Franklyn (*Cecil*), Jacqueline (Jackie) Bisset (*Jacqueline*)
D: Roman Polanski   SCR: Roman Polanski & Gerard Brach   PHOTOG: Gilbert Taylor   MUSIC: Krzysztof Komeda-Trczcinski
Eccentric "black comedy": Fugitive gangsters find uneasy refuge in old castle

Culinary Sorcery
see Sorcellerie Culinaire

Cult of the Cobra
1955, (USA), Univ, b&w, 80 mins.
W: Faith Domergue, Marshall Thompson, Jack Kelly, William Reynolds, Kathleen Hughes, Richard Long, David Janssen, James Dobson, Myrna Hansen, Leonard Strong, Walter Coy, Edward C. Platt [unbilled]
P: Howard Pine   D: Francis D. Lyon   SCR: Richard Collins, Jerry Davis, & Cecil Maiden   PHOTOG: Russell Metty   MUSIC: Joseph Gershenson
orig. co-billed with Revenge of the Creature
Modest horror-fantasy: Asian snake-worshippers avenge temple desecration

Cult of the Damned
see Angel, Angel, Down We Go

Cult of the Dead
see Isle of the Snake People

Cumbres Borrascosas (Hidden Mysteries)
1953, (Sp), b&w, 90 mins.
<u>W</u>: Jorge Mistral, Irasema Dilian, Lilia Prado
<u>WRIT & D</u>: Luis Bunuel, loosely based on Emily Bronte's novel *Wuthering Heights*
A.k.a. Abismos de Pasion (Abysses of Passion)
reissued (1984) by Plexus Films
Unusual film-version of Bronte classic: Passion and death separate lovers

Cupid and the Widow
1906, (GB), Hepworth, b&w, 150 ft. (45.7m)
<u>D</u>: Lewin Fitzhamon
Minor fantasy short: Cupid shows young widow how love outweighs gold

Curdled
1996, (USA), Band Apart-Tinderbox/Quentin Tarantino/Miramax, color, 94 mins.
<u>W</u>: William Baldwin *(Paul Guell)*, Angela Jones *(Gabriela)*, Bruce Ramsay
  (Eduardo), Mel Gorham *(Elena)*, Barry Corbin, Lois Chiles, Daisy Fuentes
<u>D</u>: Reb Braddock <u>SCR</u>: John Maass & Reb Braddock <u>PHOTOG</u>: Steven
  Bernstein <u>MUSIC</u>: Joseph Julian Gonzalez
blurb: "After the killer kills... Somebody has to clean up the mess"
Standard thriller: Woman works for post-forensic cleaning service, discovers killer's identity

Curfew
1988, (USA), color, 86 mins.
<u>W</u>: John Putch, Kyle Richards, William Wellman Jr., Bert Remsen
<u>D</u>: Gary Winick
Standard thriller: Young woman meets two killers

Curfew Must Not Ring Tonight
1912, (GB), Hepworth, b&w, 1,100 ft. (335.3m)
<u>W</u>: Alec Worcester *(Basil Underwood)*, Alma Taylor *(Bessie)*
<u>D</u>: Hay Plumb, from a poem by Rose Thorpe
Standard adventure-thriller: Girl prevents execution of cavalier

Curfew Shall Not Ring Tonight
1906, (GB), Gaumont, b&w, 730 ft. (222.5m)
<u>D</u>: Alf Collins, from Rose H. Thorpe's poem
Standard adventure-romance (in 8 scenes): Girl ties herself to bell clapper to stop lover's execution

The Curious Dr. Humpp
1970, (Argent), b&w, 87 mins.
<u>W</u>: Ricardo Bauleo, Aldo Barbero
<u>D</u>: Emilio Vieyra
Minor eroto-SF: Mad scientist seeks eternal youth, drains exotic dancers' libidos

The Curious Female
1969, (USA), Fanfare, color, 87 mins
<u>W</u>: Bunny Allister, David Westberg, Angelique Pettyjohn
<u>P & D</u>: Paul Rapp <u>SCR</u>: Winston R. Paul
Minor eroto-SF: Computer runs sexually liberated world of 2177

Curiousity Kills
1990, (USA), color, 86 mins.
<u>W</u>: Rae Dawn Chong, C. Thomas Howell, Courtenay Cox, Paul Guilfoyle, Jeff Fahey
<u>D</u>: Colin Bucksey <u>SCR</u>: Joe Batteer & John Rice
Made-for-Cable, standard thriller: Tenant's death probed

The Curse
1987, (USA), Ovidio G. Assonitis/Trans World, color, 92 mins.
<u>W</u>: Wil Wheaton *(Zachary Hayes)*, Claude Akins *(Nathan Crane)*, Malcolm Danare
  (Cyrus Crane), John Schneider *(Carl Willis)*, Amy Wheaton *(Alice Hayes)*,
  Cooper Huckabee *(Dr. Alan Forbes)*, Kathleen Jordon Gregory *(Frances)*,
  Steve Davis *(Mike)*, Hope North *(Esther)*, Steve Carlisle *(Davidson)*
<u>D</u>: David Keith <u>SCR</u>: David Chaskin, based on H.P. Lovecraft's short story *The
  Colour Out of Space* <u>PHOTOG</u>: Robert D. Forges <u>VS-FX</u>: Kevin Erham
  <u>MUSIC</u>: John Debney
Aka The Farm
*Modest SF-horror: Space object poisons water supply, mutates, and maddens rural family..
  cf. Monster of Terror*

Curse II: The Bite
1989, (USA), Trans World, color, 96 mins.
<u>W</u>: Jill Schoelen *(Lisa Snipes)*, J. Eddie Peck *(Clark Newman)*, Jamie Farr *(Harry
  Morton)*, Savina Gersak *(Iris)*, Marianne Muellerleile *(Big Flo)*, Al Fann *(The
  Gas Station Attendant)*, Sydney Lassick *(George)*, Terrence Evans *(Farmer
  Dave)*, Sandra Sexton, Bruce Marchiano, Shiri Appleby, Jose Garcia, Bo
  Svenson, Tiny Welles, Sommer Betsworth, Barbara Glover, Suzanne Celeste,
  David Ode, Ana Maria Auther, Deke Anderson, Shawn Tierney
<u>D</u>: Fred Goodwin <u>ORIG. SCR</u>: Susan Zelouf & Federico Prosperi, from a short
  story by H.P. Lovecraft <u>PHOTOG</u>: Roberto D'Ettore Piazzoli <u>SPCL-FX</u>:
  Screaming Mad George <u>MUSIC</u>: Carlo Maria Cordio
Minor SF-horror: Snake venom mutates youth

Curse III: Blood Sacrifice
1991, (USA), color, 90 mins.
<u>W</u>: Christopher Lee, Jenilee Harrison
Minor horror-thriller: Voodoo in 1950 East Africa

Curse IV: The Ultimate Sacrifice
1992, (USA), color
<u>W</u>: Timothy Van Patten, Laura Schaefer, Jeremy West, Ian Abercrombie
<u>D</u>: David Schmoeller
Minor horror-thriller: Teacher and priest unearth Beast of Apocalypse

The Curse and the Coffin
see The Burning Court

The Cursed Brides
see Brides of Blood

The Cursed Cave
see La Caverne Maudite

The Cursed Mansion
see Le Manoir Maudit

The Cursed Medallion
1975, (GB-It), Film Ventures, color
<u>W</u>: Nicole Elmi, Richard Johnson, Joanna Cassidy
<u>P</u>: William C. Reich <u>D</u>: Max Dallamano <u>SCR</u>: Massimo Dallamano & Franco
  Marrottax
A.k.a. Night Child
*Minor fantasy-thriller (inept Exorcist imitation): Little girl possessed by murderous spirit
  of evil child, ghastly events ensue*

The Cursed Mountain Mystery
1993, (USA), color, 87 mins.
<u>W</u>: Phillip Avalon, Tom Richards, Joe Bugner
<u>D</u>: Vince Martin <u>SCR</u>: Denis Whitburn
Minor fantasy-thriller: Petty thieves steal cursed jewel, immortal warrior pursues

The Cursed Tower
see La Tour Maudite

Curse of the Alpha Stone
1985, (USA), color, 90 mins.
Minor horror-thriller: Experiment creates murderous maniac

The Curse of Bigfoot
1975, (USA), Universal Entertainment, color
<u>W</u>: William Simonsen, Robert Clymire
<u>D</u>: Don Fields <u>SCR</u>: J.T. Fields
blurb: "The story of five students who will never be the same!"
Minor horror-thriller: Students on field trip meet monster

Curse of Dracula
see The Return of Dracula

The Curse of Frankenstein
1957, (GB), Clarion/Hammer/WB, color, 83 mins.
<u>W</u>: Peter Cushing *(Baron Victor Frankenstein)*, Robert Urquhart *(Paul Krempe)*,
  Hazel Court *(Elizabeth)*, Christopher Lee *(The Creature)*, Valerie Gaunt
  (Justine), Hugh Dempster *(The Burgomaster)*, Paul Hardtmuth *(Prof.
  Bernstein)*, Melvyn Hayes *(Young Victor)*, Noel Hood *(Aunt Sophia)*, Marjorie
  Hume *(Mother)*, Ann Blake, Michael Mulcaster, Fred Johnson, Middleton
  Woods, Claude Kingston, Alex Gallier, Sally Walsh, Ernest Jay, Raymond
  Ray, Andrew Leigh
<u>P</u>: Anthony Hinds <u>D</u>: Terence Fisher <u>SCR</u>: Jimmy Sangster, from characters
  created by Mary W. Shelley <u>PHOTOG</u>: Jack Asher <u>MUSIC</u>: James
  Bernard <u>DESIGN</u>: Ted Marshall
French retitle, Frankenstein s'est Echappe (Frankenstein is Escaping)
*reissued (by 7Arts) with Horror of Dracula in 1965 & 1968, orig. co-billed with
  X...The Unknown*
*Impressive horror-thriller, first installment in Hammer's Frankenstein series: Nobleman
  labors to revive dead tissue*

The Curse of King Tut's Tomb
1980, (USA), Col/NBC-TV, color, 98 mins.
<u>W</u>: Robin Ellis *(Howard Carter)*, Raymond Burr *(Sebastian)*, Eva Marie Saint
  (Sarah), Harry Andrews *(The Earl of Carnarvon)*, Faith Brook *(Lady Almina
  Carnarvon)*, Tom Baker *(Daoud)*, John Palmer *("Fish-bait")*, Angharad Rees
  (Lady Evelyn Carnarvon), Barbara Murray *(Giovanna)*, Wendy Hiller *(The
  Princess)*, Patricia Routledge
<u>D</u>: Philip Leacock <u>SCR</u>: Herb Meadow <u>PHOTOG</u>: Bob Edwards <u>MUSIC</u>:
  Gil Melle
TVM, modest docudrama: Sensational events surrounding opening of Tutankhamun's tomb

The Curse of Nostradamus
see La Maldicion de Nostradamus

Curse of Simba
1964, (GB), Galaworldfilm/AA, b&w, 77 mins.
<u>W</u>: Bryant Halliday *(Mike Stacey)*, Dennis Price *(Maj. Lomas)*, Lisa Daniely *(Janet
  Stacey)*, Mary Kerridge *(Mother)*, Ronald Leigh-Hunt *(The Doctor)*, Jean
  Lodge *(Mrs. Lomas)*, Andy Myers *(Tommy Stacey)*, Dennis Alaba Peters
  (Saidi), Tony Thawnton *(Radlett)*, Beryl Cunningham, The Bobby Breen

Quintet
P: Kenneth Rive **D:** Lindsay Shontoff **SCR:** Tony O'Grady **PHOTOG:** Gerald Gibbs
orig. to be titled **The Lion Man** *or* **Voodoo Blood Death**, *USA retitle,* **The Curse of the Voodoo**
Tense horror-thriller: Scoundrel pursued by African mysteries

The Curse of the Aztec Mummy
see **La Momia**

Curse of the Beast
see **La Maldicion de la Bestia**

Curse of the Black Widow
1977, (USA), ABC-TV, color, 97 mins.
W: Donna Mills *(Leigh Lockridge)*, Patty Duke Astin *(Laura Lockridge)*, Anthony Franciosa *(Higbie)*, June Allyson *(Olga)*, Vic Morrow *(Lt. Conti)*, Roz Kelly *(Flaps)*, Jeff Corey *(Aspa Soldano)*, Robert Burton *(Jeff Wallace)*, Max Gail *(Ragsdale)*, Sid Caesar *(Lazlo Cozart)*, June Lockhart *(Mrs. Lockridge)*, H.B. Haggerty *(Popeye)*, Rosanna Locke *(Jennifer)*, Michael DeLano, Bruce French
P: Steven North **D:** Dan Curtis **TELEPLAY:** Robert Blees & Earl Wallace **PHOTOG:** Paul Lohmann **SPCL-FX:** Ray Downey **MUSIC:** Robert Cobert
TVM, standard horror-fantasy: Woman infected by spiders undergoes monstrous transformations. retelevised (1979) as **Love Trap**

Curse of the Blood-Ghouls
see **La Strage dei Vampiri**

Curse of the Blue Lights
1988, (USA), color, 93 mins.
W: Brent Ritter
D: John H. Johnson
Minor horror-fantasy: Ghoul raises dead

Curse of the Cat People
1944, (USA), RKO, b&w, 70 mins.
W: Simone Simon *(Irena)*, Kent Smith *(Oliver)*, Jane Randolph *(Alice)*, Ann Carter *(Amy)*, Julia Dean, Eve March, Elizabeth Russell, Erford Gage, Juanita Alvarez, Sir Lancelot, Joel Davis
P: Val Lewton **D:** Robert Wise & Gunther V. Fritsch **SCR:** DeWitt Bodeen **PHOTOG:** Nicholas Musuraca **MUSIC:** Roy Webb
blurb: "A tender tale of terror!"
Unusual, psychological fantasy-thriller; critically-acclaimed sequel to **Cat People** *(1942): Solitary girl wishes for playmate, finds supernatural friend*

Curse of the Crimson Altar
1968, (GB), Tigon/AIP, color, 89 mins.
W: Boris Karloff *(Prof. Marsh)*, Christopher Lee *(J.D. Morley)*, Barbara Steele *(Lavinia)*, Virginia Wetherell *(Eve)*, Rupert Davies *(The Vicar)*, Michael Gough *(Elder)*, Rosemarie Reede *(Esther)*, Derek Tansley *(The Judge)*, Denys Peek *(Peter Manning)*, Mark Eden *(Robert Manning)*, Millicent Scott *(The Stripper)*, John Clifford
P: Tony Tenser & Louis M. Heyward **D:** Vernon Sewell **SCR:** Mervyn Haisman & Henry Lincoln, from a story by Jerry Sohl, suggested by H.P. Lovecraft's short story *The Dreams in the Witch-House* **PHOTOG:** John Coquillon **MUSIC:** Peter Knight
orig. to be titled **The Crimson Altar, Dreams in the Witch House, Reincarnation** *or* **Witch House**
USA retitle, **The Crimson Cult,** *A.k.a.* **The Crimson Affair**
Frustratingly confusing (many script changes during filming) horror-fantasy: Beautiful but ineffably evil witch is reincarnated

The Curse of the Crying Woman
see **La Maldicion de la Llorona**

Curse of the Crystal Eye
1993, (USA), color, 90 mins.
W: Jameson Parker, Cynthia Rhodes, Mike Lane, David Sherwood, Andre Jacobs
D: Joe Tornatore
Minor adventure-thriller: Gunrunner seeks Ali Baba's treasure

Curse of the Dead
see **Operazione Paura**

Curse of the Demon
see **Night of the Demon** *(1957)*

Curse of the Devil
see **El Retorno de la Walpurgis**

The Curse of the Doll People
1961, (Mex), Azteca, b&w, 83 mins.
W: Elvira Quintana, Ramon Gay, Roberto G. Rivera
Minor horror-fantasy: Four men encounter witchcraft and zombies while investigating voodoo curse

Curse of the Faceless Man
1958, (USA), Vogue/UA, b&w, 66 mins.

W: Richard Anderson *(Dr. Paul Mallon)*, Elaine Edwards *(Tina)*, Adele Mara *(Maria)*, Luis Van Rooten *(Insp. Fiorillo)*, Felix Locher *(Dr. Emanuel)*, Bob Bryant *(The "Faceless Man")*, Gar Moore, Jan Arvan
P: Robert Kent **D:** Edward L. Cahn **SCR:** Jerome Bixby **PHOTOG:** Kenneth Peach **SPCL-FX:** Ira Anderson **MUSIC:** Gerald Fried
Minor fantasy-thriller: Ossified Pompeiian priest revives

Curse of the Fly
1964, (GB), Lippert/20th-Fox, b&w, 86 mins.
W: Brian Donlevy *(Henri Delambre)*, George Baker *(Martin Delambre)*, Carole Gray *(Patricia Stanley)*, Yvette Rees *(Wan)*, Mary Manson *(Judith Delambre)*, Michael Graham *(Albert Delambre)*, Rachel Kempson *(Mme. Fournier)*, Jeremy Wilkin *(Insp. Ranet)*, Burt Kwouk *(Tai)*, Charles Carson *(Insp. Charas)*, Stan Simmons *(The Creature)*, Arnold Bell, Warren Stanhope
P: Robert L. Lippert & Jack Parsons **D:** Don Sharp **SCR:** Harry Spalding **PHOTOG:** Basil Emmett **MUSIC:** Bert Shefter
Minor SF-thriller (last entry in **Fly** *series): Woman flees mental hospital, meets unsavory scientists*

The Curse of the Golem
1967, (GB), Gold Star/WB-7Arts, color, 96 mins.
W: Roddy McDowall *(Pimm)*, Jill Haworth *(Ellen)*, Paul Maxwell *(Perkins)*, Aubrey Richards *(Weal)*, Noel Trevarthen *(Insp. White)*, Ernest Clark *(Grove)*, Oliver Johnston *(Trimmingham)*, Ian McCulloch *(Wayne)*, Richard Goolden *(The Old Man)*, Steve Kirby *(Ellis)*, Tom Chatto *(The Captain)*, Dorothy Frere *(Miss Swanson)*, Russell Napier *(The Boss)*, Brian Haines *(Joe Hill)*, Frank Sieman *(The Workman)*, Mark Burns *(The 1st Officer)*, Ray Adamson *(The 2nd Officer)*, John Baker *(The Guard)*, Alan Sellers *(The Golem)*, Lindsay Campbell *(The Policeman)*
WRIT, P & D: Herbert J. Leder **PHOTOG:** David Boulton **MUSIC:** Carlo Martell **MUSIC DIR:** Philip Martell
USA retitle, **It!**
Modest horror-fantasy: Museum curator reanimates legendary automaton. cf. **Der Golem.**

Curse of the Headless Horseman
1972, (USA), color, 80 mins.
W: Don Carrara, Claudia Dean, B.G. Fisher, Margo Dean, Lee Byers, Joe Cody
D: John Kirkland
Standard fantasy: Spectre rides again

The Curse of the Hidden Vault
1964, (W. Ger), b&w
W: Judith Dornys, Harald Lieb
based on an Edgar Wallace story
Minor thriller: Gangsters seek dead gambler's treasure

The Curse of the Karnsteins
see **La Maldicion de los Karnsteins**

The Curse of the Living Corpse
1964, (USA), Iselin-Tenney/20th-Fox, b&w, 83 mins.
W: Helen Waren *(Abigail)*, Roy R. Scheider, Margot Hartman, Robert Milli, Hugh Franklin, Jane Bruce, Candace Hilligoss, Dino Narizzano, Linda Donovon, J. Frank Lucas, Paul Haney, William Blood, George Cotton
WRIT, P & D: Del Tenney **PHOTOG:** Richard L. Hilliard **MUSIC:** Bill Holmes
orig. co-billed with **The Horror of Party Beach**
Minor horror-thriller (Roy Scheider's film debut): Heirs find bloody legacy

Curse of the Living Dead (1966)
see **Operazione Paura**

Curse of the Living Dead
1989, (USA), color, 90 mins.
D: Lawrence Foldes
Minor horror-thriller: Siblings cursed with cannibalism

The Curse of the Mummy's Tomb
1964, (GB), Hammer-Swallow/Col, color, 80 mins.
W: Terence Morgan *(Adam Beauchamp)*, Ronald Howard *(John Bray)*, Jeanne Roland *(Annette Dubois)*, Dickie Owen *(The Mummy)*, Fred Clark *(Alexander King)*, George Pastell *(Hashmi Bey)*, Jack Gwillim *(Sir Giles Dalrymple)*, John Paul *(Insp. Mackenzie)*, Jill Mai Meredith *(Jenny)*, Marianne Stone *(The Landlady)*, Michael McStay *(Ra-Antef)*, Harold Goodwin *(Fred)*, Vernon Smythe *(Jessop)*, Michael Ripper *(Achmed)*, Bernard Rebel *(Prof. Dubois)*
P & D: Michael Carreras **SCR:** Henry Younger **PHOTOG:** Otto Heller **MUSIC:** Carlo Martelli
French retitle, **Les Malefices de la Momie** *(Evils of the Mummy)*
Standard horror-fantasy: Victorian cad seeks immortality

Curse of the Mushroom People
see **Matango**

Curse of the Pharaohs
see **The Mummy** *(1959)*

Curse of the Puppet Master
1998, (USA), color, 79 mins.
W: George Peck, Emily Harrison

Minor fantasy-thriller

Curse of the Queerwolf
1987, (USA), color, 90 mins.
<u>W</u>: Michael Palazzolo, Kent Butler, Taylor Whitney
<u>D</u>: Mark Pirro
Stadard horror-comedy: Man becomes gay lycanthrope

Curse of the Screaming Dead
1984, (USA), color, 90 mins.
Minor horror-thriller: Zombies prowl

Curse of the Stone Hand
1959, (Mex), Azteca/ADP, b&w, 72 mins
<u>W</u>: John Carradine, Sheila Bon, Ernst Walch, Charles Cores, Katherine Victor, Lloyd Nelson
<u>D</u>: Hugo Christensen   <u>SCR</u>: F. Amos Powell & Marie Laurent
released in USA (1965) with added direction by Jerry Warren
Minor thriller: Evil spell spans generations

Curse of the Swamp Creature
1966, (USA), Azalea/AIP-TV, color, 69 mins.
<u>W</u>: John Agar, Francine York, Jeff Alexander, Shirley McLine, Cal Duggan, Charles McLine, Bill McGee, Ted Mitchell, Gayle Johnson, Rodger Ready, Bill Thurman, Tony Houston, Annabelle Weenick, Michael Tolden, Pat Cranshaw, Naomi Bruton, J.V. Lee
<u>P & D</u>: Larry Buchanan   <u>SCR</u>: Tony Houston   <u>PHOTOG</u>: Ralph K. Johnson
Minor SF-horror: Doctor seeks to create fish-men

The Curse of the Undead
1959, (USA), Univ, b&w, 79 mins.
<u>W</u>: Eric Fleming, Kathleen Crowley, Michael Pate, John Hoyt, Bruce Gordon, Edward Binns, Jimmy Murphy, Helen Kleeb, John Truax, Jay Adler, Edwin Parker, Frankie Van, Rush Williams
<u>P</u>: Joseph Gershenson   <u>D</u>: Edward Dein   <u>SCR</u>: Edward & Mildred Dein   <u>PHO-TOG</u>: Ellis W. Carter   <u>MUSIC</u>: Irving Gertz
orig. co-billed with The Mummy (1959)
Modest horror-fantasy: Vampiric cowboy stalks lady rancher

Curse of the Vampire (1960)
see L'Ultima Preda del Vampiro

Curse of the Vampires
1970, (Phil), Marvin, color, 90 mins.
<u>W</u>: Amalia Fuentes (*Leonora*), Romeo Vasquez, Eddie Garcia, Johnny Monteiro, Rosario Del Pilar, Mary Walter, Paquito Salcedo, Francisco Cruz, Quiel Mendoza, Andres Benitez, Luz Angeles, Tessie Hernandez, Linda Rivers
<u>D</u>: Gerardo de Leon   <u>SCR</u>: Ben Feleo & Pierre L. Salas   <u>STORY</u>: Ben Feleo   <u>PHOTOG</u>: Mike Accion   <u>MUSIC</u>: Tito Arevalo
Minor horror-fantasy: Family skeletons exhumed, old bloodlust revived

The Curse of the Voodoo
see Curse of Simba

The Curse of the Werewolf
1961, (GB), Hammer/Univ, color, 92 mins.
<u>W</u>: Oliver Reed (*Leon*), Clifford Evans (*Don Alfredo Carido*), Yvonne Romain (*The Jailer's Daughter*), Catherine Feller (*Christina Fernando*), Anthony Dawson (*Marques Siniestro*), Ann Blake (*Rosa Valiente*), Warren Mitchell (*Pepe Valiente*), Michael Ripper (*The Drunk*), Ewen Solon (*Don Fernando*), Hira Talfrey (*Teresa*), Justin Walters (*Leon, as a Child*), Richard Wordsworth (*The Beggar*), Sheila Brennan, Josephine Llewellyn, Charles Lamb, Desmond Llewelyn, John Gabriel, George Woodbridge, Joy Webster, Renny Lester, Denis Shaw
<u>P</u>: Anthony Hinds   <u>D</u>: Terence Fisher   <u>SCR</u>: John Elder [Anthony Hinds]
based on Guy Endore's novel *The Werewolf of Paris*
<u>PHOTOG</u>: Arthur Grant   <u>SPCL-FX</u>: Les Bowie   <u>MUSIC</u>: Benjamin Frankel
French retitle, **La Nuit du Loup-Garou** *(Night of the Werewolf)*
"...came closer to the mark than both of Universal's (earlier) forays into the same theme, giving back to the lycanthrope many suggestive traits"—Carlos Clarens, An Illustrated History of the Horror Film
Superior horror-fantasy (banned in Spain until 1976): Doctor raises lycanthropic orphan

The Curse of the Wraydons
1946, (GB), Bushey/Ambassador, b&w, 94 mins.
<u>W</u>: Tod Slaughter (*Phillip Wraydon*), Bruce Seton (*Capt. Jack Clayton*), Gabriel Toyne (*Lt. Payne*), Lorraine Clewes (*Helen Sedgefield*), Andrew Laurence (*George Heeningham*), Pearl Cameron (*RoseWraydon*), Ben Williams (*John Rickers*), Barry O'Neill (*George Wraydon*)
<u>D</u>: Victor M. Gover   <u>SCR</u>: Michael Barringer, from the play *Springheeled*

Curse of the Yellow Snake
1963, (W. Ger), RB, b&w, 99 mins.
<u>W</u>: Joachim Fuchsberger, Brigette Grothum, Werner Peters, Pinkas Braun
<u>D</u>: Frank Gottlieb. from an Edgar Wallace story
Minor thriller: Boy uncovers ring of fanatics

The Curtain
1914, (GB), Hepworth, b&w, 1,150 ft. (350.5m)

<u>W</u>: Chrissie White (*Mary*), Cyril Morton (*Philip*), Harry Royston (*Nils Fillsen*)
<u>D</u>: Warwick Buckland
Standard crime-thriller: Amnesiac robs fiancee's house, saves her from attack

Curtain Call
1998, (USA), color, 94 mins.
<u>W</u>: James Spader, Maggie Smith, Michael Caine
Standard comedy-fantasy: Actors haunt publisher's new home

Curtains
1983, (Can), Simcom/Jensen Farley Pictures, color, 88 mins.
<u>W</u>: John Vernon (*Jonathan Stryker*), Linda Thorson (*Brooke*), Anne Ditchburn (*Laurian*), Lynne Griffin (*Patti O'Connor*), SandraWarren (*Tara*), Lesleh Donaldson (*Christie*), Joann McIntyre (*The Sec'y*), Deborah Burgess (*Amanda*), Michael Wincott (*Matthew*), Maury Chaykin (*Monty*), Calvin Butler (*Dr. Pendleton*), Kate Lynch (*The Receptionist*), William Marshall, Booth Savage, James Kidnie, Jeremy Jenson, Donald Adams, Diane Godwin, Janelle Hutchison, Virginia Laight, Kay Griffin, Bunty Webb, Daisy White, Suzanne Russell, Vivian Reis, Sheila Currie, Frances Gunn, Jenna Louise, Anna Migliarese, Elaine Crosley, Alison Lawrence, Janie Nicholson, Mary Darkin, Angela Carrol, Teresa Tova, Julie Massie, Pat Carroll Brown, Jo-Anne Hannah Samantha Eggar (*Samantha*), Anne Ditchburn, Deborah Burgess, Lynne Griffin, Sandra Warren, Lesleh Donaldson, Kate Lynch, Michael Wincott, Booth Savage, Calvin Butler
<u>D</u>: Jonathan Stryker   <u>SCR</u>: Robert Guza Jr.   <u>PHOTOG</u>: Robert Paynter   <u>ADDITIONAL PHOTOG</u>: Fred Guthe   <u>MUSIC</u>: Paul Zaza
Minor thriller: Masked murderer stalks actress

The Curtain's Secret
see Behind the Curtain

Curucu, Beast of the Amazon
1956, (USA), Univ, color, 76 mins.
<u>W</u>: John Bromfield, Beverly Garland, Tom Payne, Harvey Chalk, Larri Thomas, Sergio De Oliveira, Wilson Vianna
<u>P</u>: Richard Kay & Harry Rybnick   <u>WRIT & D</u>: Curt Siodmak
orig. co-billed with The Mole People
Minor adventure-thriller: Search for legendary river monster

Cutthroat Island
1995, (USA), Carolco/MGM, color, 118 mins.
<u>W</u>: Geena Davis (*Morgan Adams*), Matthew Modine (*William Shaw*), Frank Langella (*Dawg Brown*), Harris Yulin (*Black Harry*), Rex Linn, Stan Shaw, Maury Chaykin, Patrick Malahide
<u>P & D</u>: Renny Harlin   <u>SCR</u>: Robert King & Marc Norman   <u>STORY</u>: Michael Frost Beckner, James Gorman, Bruce A. Evans & Raynold Gideon   <u>MUSIC</u>: John Debney   <u>PHOTOG</u>: Peter Levy

Lavish but financially disastrous adventure-thriller (cost, $92 million; gross, $11 million): Lady pirate seeks treasure

Cutting Class
1989, (USA), Republic, color, 90 mins.
<u>W</u>: Donovan Leitch (*Brian*), Jill Schoelen (*Paula*), Brad Pitt (*Dwight*)
Minor thriller: Murderer terrorizes high-school students

Cyber Bandits
1995, (USA), color, 86 mins.
<u>W</u>: Alexandra Paul, Martin Kemp, Robert Hays, Adam Ant, Grace Jones
<u>D</u>: Erik Fleming   <u>SCR</u>: James Robinson & Winston Beard
Minor SF-thriller: Plans for deadly virtual-reality weapon stolen

Cyber Chic
1989, (USA), color, 90 mins
<u>W</u>: Kathy Shower, Jack Carter, Burt Ward, Lyle Waggoner
<u>D</u>: Ed Hansen & Jeffrey Mandel
A.k.a. Robo-Chic
Minor SF-thriller: Curvaceous android foils madman's reign of terror

Cyberella: Forbidden Passion
1996, (USA), color
<u>W</u>: Debra Beatty
Minor eroto-SF

Cyber Jack
see Virtual Assassin

Cyber Ninja
1994, (Jap), color, 80 mins.
<u>W</u>: Hanbel Kawai, Hiroki Ida
Standard action-SF: Warrior princess captured by Dark Overlord

Cybernetic Grandma
see Kyberneticka Babicka

The Cyber Stalking
1999, (Can-Luxem), Alliance Atlantis, color
<u>W</u>: Jean Louisa Kelly (*Holly*), Noah Huntley, Beatie Edney, Claudine Wilde, Daniel Caltagirone, Martin East, Indra Ove, Jason Hildebrandt, Marcus Testory, Robert Crippen, Jerrol Leitterboom, Luce Botte
<u>D</u>: Brian Grant   <u>TELEPLAY</u>: Joe Gannon, from Pat Cadigan's short story *Pretty Boy Crossover*   <u>PHOTOG</u>: Richard Wincenty   <u>VS-FX SPRVSR</u>: Tom Turnbull   <u>MUSIC</u>: Donald Quan
TVM, standard SF-thriller: Computer program taps into nightmares

Cyber-Tracker
1994, (USA), color, 91 mins.
<u>W</u>: Don "The Dragon" Wilson, Richard Norton, Stacie Foster, Steve Burton, Abby Dalton, Jim Maniaci, Joseph Ruskin, John Aprea
<u>D</u>: Richard Pepin
Minor SF-thriller: Secret agent pursued by android executioners

Cybertracker 2
1995, (USA), color, 100 mins.
<u>W</u>: Don "The Dragon" Wilson, Stacie Foster, Tony Burton, Stephen Rowe, Jim Maniaci, John Kassar
Minor SF-thriller: Secret agent battles arms dealer bent on creating cyborg army

Cyberzone
1995, (USA), color, 90 mins.
<u>W</u>: Marc Singer, Matthias Hues, Rochelle Swanson (*Beth*), Robin Clarke (*Humberstone*), Kin Shriner (*Walsh*)
Standard SF-adventure: 21st-century bounty hunter seeks four stolen androids

Cyborg (1973)
see The Six Million Dollar Man

Cyborg
1989, (USA), Golan-Globus/Cannon, video, color, 87 mins.
<u>W</u>: Jean-Claude Van Damme (*Rickenbacker*), Deborah Richter (*Nady Simmons*), Vincent Klyn (*Fender Tremolo*), Alex Daniels (*Marshall Strat*), Dayle Haddon (*Pearl Prophet*), Haley Peterson (*Haley*), Rolf Muller, Jackson "Rock" Pinckney, Blaise Loong (*Furman Vox*), Terrie Batson (*Mary*), Janice Grase (*Vorg*), Robert Pentz, Sharon K. Tew, Chuck Allen, Stefanos Miltsakakis, Kristina Sebastian, Thomas Barley, Dale Frye, Jophery Brown, Jim Creech, Matt McColm, KarenSpell, James G. Irwin, Johnny Grady Jr., Bill Morrison, Michael Craig Halford, O.D. Wilson, Bruce Frye, Tommy Evans, Tim Gilbert
<u>D</u>: Albert Pyun   <u>SCR</u>: Kitty Chalmers   <u>PHOTOG</u>: Philip Waters   <u>MUSIC</u>: Kevin Bassinson
Minor SF-adventure: Power struggle in 21st century

Cyborg 2: Glass Shadow
1993, (USA), Anglo-American/Vidmark, color, 99 mins.
<u>W</u>: Elias Koteas, Angelina Jolie, Jack Palance, Jim Youngs, Billy Drago, Karen Sheperd, Allen Garfield, Ric Young, Sven Thorsen, Renee Griffin, Tracey Walter, Robert Dryer, Sheryl Mary Lewis, John Durbin, Patrick O'Connell,

Lori Michelle, Elizabeth Sung, Matthew DeMeritt, Alain Joel Silver, Galen Yuen, William Colon, Irving Bonios, David Schroeder, Linus Huffman, Rick Hill
<u>D</u>: Michael Schroeder   <u>SCR</u>: Ron Yanover, Mark Geldman & Michael Schroeder   <u>STORY</u>: Ron Yanover & Mark Geldman   <u>PHOTOG</u>: Jamie Thompson   <u>VS-FX SPRVSR</u>: Dan Schmit   <u>MUSIC</u>: Peter Allen   <u>SONGS</u>:, *Nothing That is Possible* & *Crystal Hearts*
Made-for-Video, minor SF-thriller: Evil corporation employs dangerous cyborg

Cyborg 3
1995, (USA), color, 90 mins.
<u>W</u>: Richard Lynch, Khrystyne Haje (*Cash*), Zack Galligan (*Evans*), Andre Bryniarski (*Jocko*), Malcolm McDowell
<u>D</u>: Michael Schroeder   <u>SCR</u>: Barry Victor & Troy Bolotnick
A.k.a. Cyborg III, the Recycler
Minor SF-thriller: Future bounty hunters track cyborgs

Cyborg 3: The Recycler
see Cyborg 3

Cyborg Cop
1993, (USA), Nu Image, color, 93 mins.
<u>W</u>: David Bradley, John Rhys-Davies, Todd Jenson, Alona Shaw, Rufus Swart
<u>P</u>: Danny Lerner   <u>D</u>: Sam Firstenberg   <u>SCR</u>: Greg Latter   <u>PHOTOG</u>: Joseph Wein   <u>MUSIC</u>: Paul Fishman
Minor SF-thriller: Druglord turns DEA agent's brother into robot

Cyborg Cop II
1994, (USA), color, 97 mins.
<u>W</u>: David Bradley, Morgan Hunter, Jill Pierce, Victor Mellaney, Doug-las Bristow
<u>D</u>: Sam Firstenberg   <u>SCR</u>: Jon Stevens
A.k.a. Cyborg II- the Soldier
Minor SF-thriller: Cyborg plots extermination of human race

Cyborg Cop III
1995, (USA), color, 100 mins.
<u>W</u>: Frank Zagarino, Bryan Genesse
Minor SF-thriller

Cyborg Soldier
see Cyborg Cop II

Cyborg 2087
1966, (USA), United Pictures, color, 87 mins.
<u>W</u>: Michael Rennie (*Garth*), Karen Steele (*Dr. Sharon Mason*), Warren Stevens (*Dr. Carl Zellar*), Harry Carey Jr. (*Jay C.*), Wendell Corey (*The Sheriff*), John Beck (*Skinny*), Adam Roarke (*Deputy Dan*), Eduard Franz (*Prof. Marx*), Richard Travis (*The General*), James Kline, Troy Melton, Jo Ann Pflug
<u>D</u>: Franklin Adreon   <u>SCR</u>: Arthur C. Pierce   <u>PHOTOG</u>: Alan Stensvold   <u>SPCL-FX</u>: Roger George   <u>MUSIC</u>: Paul Dunlap
Standard SF-thriller: Cyborg arrives from future

Cycle Psycho
1972, (USA), color, 80 mins.
<u>W</u>: Joe Turkel, Tom Drake, Stephen Oliver
<u>D & SCR</u>: John Lawrence
A.k.a. Numbered Days and Savage Abduction
Minor thriller: Serial killer blackmails businessman

Cyclone
1987, (USA), color
<u>W</u>: Jeffrey Combs, Heather Thomas, Ashley Ferrare (*Carla*)
Minor thriller: Inventor killed, girlfiend protects invention from spies

Cyclone Cavalier
1925, (USA), b&w, 58 mins.
<u>W</u>: Reed Howes
<u>D</u>: Albert Rogell
Standard adventure-thriller: Hero travels through Central America

The Cyclops
1957, (USA), AA, b&w, 72 mins.
<u>W</u>: Gloria Talbott (*Susan Winters*), James Craig (*Russ*), Lon Chaney Jr. (*Marty*), Duncan Parkin (*The Cyclops*), Tom Drake (*Lee*), Vincent Padula, Marlene Kloss, Manuel Lopez
<u>WRIT, P, D & TECH-FX</u>: Bert I. Gordon   <u>PHOTOG</u>: Ira Morgan   <u>MUSIC</u>: Albert Glasser
orig. co-billed with Daughter of Dr. Jekyll
Standard SF-thriller: Adventurers find mutant horrors

Cyclotrode X
1966, (USA), Rep, b&w, 100 mins.
<u>W</u>: Charles Quigley, Linda Stirling, Clayton Moore, Forrest Taylor, I. Stanford Jolley, Kenne Duncan, Emmett Vogan, Sam Flint, Joe Forte, Stanley Price, Wheaton Chambers, Dale Van Sickel, Tom Steele, Rex Lease, Fred Graham, Bud Wolfe
<u>D</u>: William Witney & Fred C. Brannon   <u>ORIG. SCR</u>: Albert DeMond, Basil Dickey, Jesse Duffy & Sol Shor   <u>PHOTOG</u>: Bud Thackery   <u>SPCL-FX</u>: Howard & Theodore Lydecker   <u>MUSIC DIR</u>: Mort Glickman
Minor thriller culled from 1946 serial The Crimson Ghost: Masked villain covets atomic device

D. Devant, Conjurer
1897, (Fr), Star, b&w, 20m (65.6 ft./1.1 mins.)
W: David Devant
D: Georges Melies
Standard fantasy: English illusionist performs. cf. David Devant, Conjurer

Daddy's Deadly Darling
see Blood Pen

Daddy's Girl
1996, (USA), color, 95 mins.
W: William Katt, Michelle Greene
Standard thriller: Adopted daughter suspected of malevolence

Daddy's Gone A-Hunting
1969, (USA), Red Lion/Nat'l General, color, 100 mins.
W: Carol White (*Cathy*), Paul Burke (*Jack*), Scott Hylands (*Kenneth*), Andrea King (*Brenda*), Mala Powers (*Meg*), Barry Cahill (*An FBI Agent*), Rachel Ames (*The Nurse*), Gene Lyons (*The Doctor*), Matilda Calnan (*Ilsa*), James Sikking (*An FBI Agent*), Ron Masak (*Paul*), Dennis Patrick (*Dr. Parkington*)
P & D: Mark Robson   SCR: Larry Cohen & Lorenzo Semple Jr.   PHOTOG: Ernest Laszlo   MUSIC: John Williams
"The best Hitchcock-type suspense thrill in years!"—Joyce Haber
Lively thriller: Mother and child threatened by deranged ex-husband

Dad, the Angel & Me
1995, (USA),Fox-TV color, 96 mins.
W: Judge Reinhold, Stephi Lineburg, Carol Kane (*Gloria*), Shirley Knight, Eve Gordon, Betsy Brantley, Jane Carr, Caroline Aaron
D: Rick Wallace   TELEPLAY: Josh Goldstein   PHOTOG: Sandi Sissel
Standard fantasy: Unconventional guardian angel helps girl adjust to life without mother

Daffy Duck's Quackbusters
1988, (USA), WB, color, 80 mins.
Standard animated comedy-fantasy: Compilation of cartoon horror-spoofs, including The Night of the Living Duck

Dagora, the Space Monster
see Dogora, the Space Monster

The Dain Curse
1978, (USA), color, 138 mins.
W: James Coburn, Jason Miller, Jean Simmons, Nancy Addison, Beatrice Straight, Hector Elizondo
D: E.W. Swackhamer, from Dashiell Hammett's novel
Standard thriller, edited-down TV miniseries (orig. 312 mins.): Private eye searches for stolen diamonds

Daisy's Adventures in the Land of Chrysanthemums
1904, (GB), Mutoscope & Biograph/Gaumont, b&w, 265 ft. (80.8m)
Standard fantasy short: Fairy takes girl to land of flowers and distortion

Daleks Invasion Earth 2150 A.D.
1966,(GB), AARU/Walter Reade-Sterling/Amicus/Continental, color, 84 mins.
W: Peter Cushing (*Dr. Who*), Bernard Cribbins (*Tom Campbell*), Ray Brooks (*David*), Jill Curzon (*Louise*), Andrew Keir (*Wyler*), Roberta Tovey (*Susan*), Roger Avon (*Wells*), Geoffrey Chesire (*Roboman*), Godfrey Quigley (*Dortmun*), Keith Marsh (*Conway*), Steve Peters (*Leader Roboman*), Robert Jewell (*Leader Dalek*), Philip Madoc, Peter Reynolds
P: Milton Subotsky & Max J. Rosenberg   D: Gordon Flemyng   SCR: Milton Subotsky, from an orig. BBC-TV serial by Terry Nation   PHOTOG: John Wilcox   SPCL-FX: Ted Samuels   MUSIC: Barry Gray
Standard SF-fantasy: Alien brains in robot bodies try to enslave Earth of future. cf. Dr. Who and the Daleks

La Dame Dans L'auto avec des Luneties et un Fusil (The Lady in the Car with Glasses and a Gun)
1969, (Fr), Col, color, 105 mins.
W: Samantha Eggar, Oliver Reed, John McEnery, Billie Dixon, Stephane Audran, Bernard Fresson, Jacques Fabbri
D: Anatole Litvak   PHOTOG: Claude Renoir   MUSIC: Michel Legrand
Unusual thriller: Secretary encounters nightmarish events on the Riviera

La Dame Fantome (The Phantom Lady)
1904, (Fr), Star, b&w, 53m (173.9 ft./2.9 mins.)
D: Georges Melies
A.k.a. The Shadow Lady
Standard fantasy

Damien—Omen II
1978, (USA), Harvey Bernhard-Mace Neufeld/20th-Fox, color, 107 mins.
W: William Holden (*Richard Thorn*), Lee Grant (*Ann Thorn*), Jonathan Scott-Taylor (*Damien Thorn*), Leo McKern (*Bugenhagen*), Robert Foxworth (*Paul Buher*), Lew Ayres (*Bill Atherton*), Lucas Donat (*Mark Thorn*), Sylvia Sidney (*Aunt Marion*), Nicholas Pryor (*Charles Warren*), Elizabeth Shepherd (*Joan Hart*),Lance Henriksen (*Sgt. Neff*), Alan Arbus (*Pasarian*), Fritz Ford (*Murray*), Meshach Taylor (*Dr. Kane*), John J. Necombe (*Teddy*), John Charles Burns (*The Butler*), Paul Cook (*The Colonel*), Diane Daniels (*Jane*),

Robert E. Ingham (*The Teacher*), William B. Fosser (*The Minister*), Russel P. Delia (*The Truck Driver*), Corney Morgan (*The Greenhouse Technician*), Judith Dowd (*The Maid*), Thomas O. Erhart Jr (*The Sgt.*), Anthony Hawkins (*Pasarian's Ass't*), Robert J. Jones Jr. (*The Guide*), Rusdi Lane (*Jim*), Charles Mountain (*The Priest*), Cornelia Sanders (*The Girl*), Felix Shuman (*Dr. Fiedler*), James Spinks (*The Technician*), Owen Sullivan (*Byron*), William J. Whelehan (*The Guard*)
P: Harvey Bernhard   D: Don Taylor   SCR: Stanley Mann & Michael Hodges   STORY: Harvey Bernhard, from characters created by David Seltzer   PHOTOG: Bill Butler   MUSIC: Jerry Goldsmith
Modest horror-fantasy: Anti-Christ moves into puberty cf. The Omen and The Final Conflict

Damnation Alley
1977, (USA), Landers-Roberts-Zeitman/20th-Fox, color, 95 mins.
W: George Peppard (*Denton*), Jan-Michael Vincent (*Tanner*), Dominique Sanda (*Janice*), Paul Winfield (*Keegan*), Jackie Earle Haley (*Billy*), Kip Niven (*Perry*), Robert Donner, Murray Hamilton [unbilled]
D: Jack Smight   SCR: Alan Sharp based on Roger Zelazny's novel   PHOTOG: Harry Stradling Jr.   SPCL-FX: Linwood Dunn, Milt Rice & Don Weed   MUSIC: Jerry Goldsmith
film includes stock-footage from Operation Crossbow
Standard SF-adventure: Humans and mutant animals vie for survival after World War III

Damnation of Doctor Faust
1904, (Fr), Star, b&w, 261m (856.3 ft./14.5 mins.)
D: Georges Melies
A.k.a. Faust and Faust and Marguerite
Standard fantasy

The Damnation of Faust
1898, (Fr), Star, b&w, 20m (65.6 ft./1.1 mins.)
P & D: Georges Melies
Short fantasy: Alchemist sells soul to Satan

The Damnation of Faust (1903)
see Faust aux Enfers

The Damned
1961, (GB), Hammer-Swallow/Col, b&w, 87 mins.
W: Macdonald Carey (*Simon Wells*), Shirley Anne Field (*Joan*), Viveca Lindfors (*Freya Nielsen*), Alexander Knox (*Prof. Bernard*), Oliver Reed (*King*), Brian Oulton (*Mr. Dingle*), James Villiers (*Capt. Gregory*), Walter Gotell (*Maj. Holland*), Kenneth Cope (*Sid*), Barbara Everest (*Miss Lamont*), Christopher Witry, Thomas Kempinski, David Palmer, Caroline Sheldon, Kit Williams, Rebecca Dignam, Siobhan Taylor, James Maxwell
P: Anthony Hinds   D: Joseph Losey   SCR: Evan Jones based on H.L. Lawrence's novel *The Children of Light*   PHOTOG: Arthur Grant   MUSIC: James Bernard   DESIGN: Don Mingaye
USA retitle, These Are the Damned
Outstanding SF-thriller: Children raised under radioactive conditions

Damn Yankees
1958, (USA), WB, color, 109 mins.
W: Tab Hunter (*Joe Hardy*), Gwen Verdon (*Lola*), Ray Walston (*Applegate*), Russ Brown (*Van Buren*), Nathaniel Frey (*Smokey*), Jean Stapleton (*Sister*), Shannon Bolin (*Meg*), Jimmie Komack (*Rocky*), Rae Allen (*Gloria*), Robert Shafer (*Joe Boyd*), Albert Linville (*Vernon*), Nesdon Booth
P & D: George Abbott & Stanley Donen   SCR: George Abbott, based on the play from Douglass Wallop's novel *The Year the Yankees Lost the Pennant*   PHOTOG: Harold Lipstein   MUSIC: Richard Adler & Jerry Ross   SONGS: Heart, Whatever Lola Wants, We've Got Each Other, & Those Were the Good Old Days
GB retitle, What Lola Wants
Entertaining musical-fantasy: Aged baseball fan sells soul to Devil

Dance Macabre
see La Danza Macabra

The Dance of Death
1938, (GB), Glenrose/Fidelity, b&w, 64 mins.
W: Vesta Victoria (*Lady Lander*), Julie Suedo (*Mara Gessner*), Stewart Rome (*Armand Chabrier*), Elizabeth Kent, Jimmy Godden, Betty Norton, Billy Merrin and his Commanders
D: Gerald Blake   STORY: Ralph Dawson
Standard thriller: Ex-convict steals Lord's cursed jewel

Dance of Death (1971)
see House of Evil

Dance of the Damned
1988, (USA), color, 83 mins.
W: Starr Andreef, Cyril O'Reilly Deborah Ann Nassar, Maria Ford, Athena Worthy, Tom Ruben
D: Katt Shea Ruben   SCR: Katt Shea Ruben & Andy Ruben
Standard horror-fantasy: Mystery man seeks to turn stripper into vampire

Dance of the Dwarfs
1983, (USA), Dove, color, 89 mins.
W: Deborah Raffin (*Dr. Evelyn Howard*), Peter Fonda (*Harry Bediker*), John Amos (*Esteban*), Carlos Palomino, Jun Turko, Arthur "Turko" Cervantes, Ike Arpuco, Angel Buenaventura, Sammy Brilliante, Ed-ward Martinez, Racquel Vera, Gil Arceo, Mario Teodoro, Venchito Galvez, Iliany Vitales, Telly Babasa, Theresa Reyes, Cherron Hoye, Chiquita the Wonder Chicken
D: Gus Trikonis **SCR:** Gregory Weston King, Larry Johnson & Michael Viner, from Geoffrey Household's novel **PHOTOG:** Michael Butler **MUSIC:** Perry Botkin **SONG:** Defiance
A.k.a. **Jungle Heat**
Minor SF-thriller: Helicopter pilot and lady anthropologist discover weird creatures

The Dancer and the Vampire
see **L'Amante del Vampiri**

The Dancer of the Nile
1923, (USA), Film Booking Offices of America, b&w, 6 reels (5,787 ft./1763.9m)
W: Carmel Myers (*Arvia*), Malcolm McGregor (*Karmet*), Sam De Grasse (*Pasheri*), Bertram Grassby (*Prince Tut*), June Eldridge (*The Princess*), Iris Ashton (*Mimitta*)
D & ADAPT: William P.S. Earle **STORY:** Blanche Taylor Earle **PHOTOG:** Jules Cronjager
Standard melodrama: Love triangle in ancient Egypt

The Dancer's Dream
1905, (GB), Bakros International, R.W. Paul, b&w, 180 ft. (54.9m)
D: J.H. Martin
Minor fantasy short: Ballerina dreams of dancing under sea

The Dancing Heart
1958, (W. Ger), color, 91 mins.
W: Gertrud Kueckelmann, Herta Staal
D: Wolfgang Liebeneiner
Standard musical-fantasy: Puppet-maker creates replica of daughter

The Dancing Midget
see **La Danseuse Microscopique**

Dandy Dick of Bishopsgate
1911, (GB), Natural Colour Kinematograph Co., color, 645 ft. (196.6m)
D: Theo Bouwmeester
Standard melodrama: 18th-century madman locks dead fiancee's room for 40 years, dies after seeing vision of her

A Dandy in Aspic
1967, (GB), Col, color, 107 mins.
W: Laurence Harvey (*Alexander Eberlin*), Mia Farrow (*Caroline*), Tom Courtenay (*Gatiss*), Lionel Stander (*Sobakevich*), Harry Andrews (*Fraser*), Peter Cook (*Prentiss*), Per Oscarsson (*Pavel*), Barbara Murray (*Heather Vogler*), Norman Bird (*Copperfield*), John Bird (*Henderson*), Michael Trubshawe (*Flowers*), Richard O'Sullivan (*Nevil*), Michael Pratt (*Greff*)
P & D: Anthony Mann (due to Mann's death, direction completed by Laurence Harvey) **STORY & SCR:** Derek Marlowe **PHOTOG:** Christopher Challis **MUSIC:** Quincy Jones
Standard spy-thriller: Double agent hired to kill himself

The Danger
see **Niebezpieczenstwo**

Danger by My Side
1962, (GB), Butcher's Films, b&w, 63 mins.
W: Anthony Oliver (*Willoughby*), Maureen Connell (*Lynne Marsdon*), Alan Tilvern (*Nicky Venning*), Tom Naylor (*Sgt. Roberts*), Bill Nagy (*Sam Warren*), Sonya Cordeau (*Francine Dumont*), Brandon Brady (*Bernie Hewson*), Wally Patch (*The Timekeeper*), John Stuart (*The Governor*), Kim Darvos (*The Singer*)
P: John I. Phillips **D:** Charles Saunders **STORY:** Ronald C. Liles & Aubrey Cash
Minor thriller: Detective killed, sister seeks murderer

Danger: Diabolik
see **Diabolik**

Danger Island
see **Mr. Moto in Danger Island**

A Dangerous Affair
1995, (USA), color, 95 mins.
W: Connie Selleca, Gregory Harrison, Christopher Meloni (*Tommy Moretti*), Robin Bartlett (*Martha*), Rosalind Cash (*Dr. Robertson*), John Marshall Jones (*Det. Webber*), Ryan Todd (*Eric*), Eileen Seeley, Jo de Winter, Gerald Berns, Brian Evers, Frank Novak
D: Alan Metzger **TELEPLAY:** Alan Rosen Photog: Zoltan David **MUSIC:** David Mansfield
TVM, standard thriller: Disturbed man stalks woman executive

Dangerous Afternoon
1961, (GB), Theatrecraft/Bry, b&w, 62 mins.
W: Ruth Dunning (*Miss Frost*), Nora Nicholson (*Mrs. Sprule*), Joanna Dunham (*Freda*), Howard Pays (*Jack Loring*), May Hallatt (*Miss Burge*), Gwenda Wilson (*Miss Berry*), Ian Colin (*Rev. Everard Porson*), Barbara Everst (*Mrs. Jackson*), Gladys Henson (*Miss Cassell*)
P: Guido Coen **D:** Charles Saunders **SCR:** Brandon Fleming, from a play by Gerald Anstruther
Standard crime-thriller: Escaped convict poisons blackmailer

Dangerous Agent
see **Cet Homme est Dangereux**

Dangerous Business
1946, (USA), Col, b&w, 59 mins.
W: Forrest Tucker, Lynn Merrick
Minor melodrama

Dangerous Charter
see **The Creeping Terror**

Dangerous Female
see **The Maltese Falcon** (1931)

Dangerous Fingers
1937, (GB), Rialto/Pathe, b&w, 79 mins.
W: James Stephenson (*Fingers*), Betty Lynne (*Doris*), D.A. Clarke-Smith (*Insp. Williams*), Leslie Perrins (*Standish*), Nadine March (*Mabel*), Sally Stewart (*Molly*), George Merritt (*Charlie*), Phil Ray (*Ben*)
D: Norman Lee **SCR:** Vernon Clancey, from his novel *Man Hunt*
USA retitle, **Wanted by Scotland Yard**
Standard thriller: Man framed for murder

A Dangerous Friend
see **The Todd Killings**

Dangerous Intruder
1945, (USA), PRC, b&w, 65 mins.
W: Charles Arnt, Veda Ann Borg
Standard thriller

Dangerous Ground
1934, (GB), B&D/Para British, b&w, 68 mins.
W: Malcolm Keen (*Mark Lyndon*), Jack Raine (*Philip Tarry*), Joyce Kennedy (*Claire Breedon*), Martin Lewis (*John Breedon*), Kathleen Kelly (*Joan Breedon*), Gordon Begg (*Holford*), Henry Longhurst (*Insp. Hurley*)
D: Norman Walker **SCR:** Dion Titheradge & Dorothy Rowan **STORY:** Dion Titheradge
Standard thriller: Dead detective's fiancee unmasks killer

The Dangerous Lunatic
see **Le Fou Assassin**

Dangerous Millions
1946, (USA), 20th-Fox, b&w, 69 mins.
W: Kent Taylor, Dona Drake
Minor melodrama

Dangerous Mission
1954, (USA), RKO, 3D, color, 75 mins.
W: Victor Mature, Piper Laurie, Vincent Price, William Bendix, Betta St. John
P: Irwin Allen **D:** Louis King **SCR:** Horace McCoy, W.R. Burnett & Charles Bennett
Standard thriller: Woman witnesses gangland murder, flees to Glacier National Park

Dangerous Money
1946, (USA), Mono, b&w, 66 mins.
W: Sidney Toler (*Charlie Chan*), Victor Sen Yung (*Tommie Chan*), Willie Best (*Chattanooga Brown*), Dick Elliott (*P.T. Burke*), Joseph Crehan (*Capt. Black*), Elaine Lange (*Cynthia Martin*), Amira Moustafa (*Laura Erickson*), Joe Allen Jr. (*George Brace*), Gloria Warren (*Rona Simmonds*), Rick Vallin (*Tao Erickson*), Bruce Edwards (*Harold Mayfair*), John Harmon (*Freddie Kirk*), Emmett Vogan (*Prof. Martin*), Tristram Coffin (*Scott Pearson*), Leslie Denison (*Rev. Whipple*), Rito Punay (*Pete*), Dudley Dickerson (*Big Ben*), Selmer Jackson (*The Ship's Doctor*)
D: Terry Morse **SCR:** Miriam Kissinger, from characters created by Earl Derr Biggers **PHOTOG:** William A. Sickner **MUSIC:** Edward J. Kay
Modest thriller: Oriental sleuth confronts art thieves and counterfeiters

Dangerous Prey
1995, (USA), color, 90 mins.
W: Shannon Whirry, Ciara Hunter
Made-for-Video, minor thriller: Stuntwoman imprisoned in training camp for assassins

A Dangerous Summer
1981, (Austral), color, 100 mins.
W: Tom Skerritt, Ian Gilmour, Wendy Hughes, Ray Barrett, James Mason, Guy Doleman
D: Quentin Masters
Minor thriller: Sabotage at resort project

Dangerous Touch
1993, (USA), Cinetel-Facet/Trimark, color, 92 mins.
W: Lou Diamond Phillips (*Mick Burroughs*), Kate Vernon (*Amanda Grace*), Max Gail (*Jasper Stone*), Berlinda Tolbert (*Sasha Taylor*), Mitch Pileggi (*Vince*), Robert Prentiss (*Charlie*), Adam Roarke (*Robert Turner*), Grey Stone (*Graham*), William Lawrence Allen (*Slim*), Stacie Bourgeois (*Sharon*), Andrew Divoff (*Johnnie*), Karla Montana (*Maria*), Shanti Kahn (*The Female Fan*), Efran Figueroa (*The Home Owner*), Ira Heiden (*Benny*), Richard D'Alessandro (*Dino*), Michael Welden (*The Male Fan*), Monique Parent (*Nicole*), Jeff Nokes (*Wade*), Irene Forrest (*The Maid*), Tom Dugan (*Freddie*), Dale Duck (*The Waiter*), Janet Zappata (*herself*)
D: Lou Diamond Phillips   SCR: Kurt Voss & Lou Diamond Phillips   PHOTOG: James Lemmo   SPCL-FX: Bruno Stempel & David Domeyer   MUSIC: Terry Plumeri   SONGS: *When You Want Me* (sung by Roberta Flack)
Standard eroto-thriller: Ex-con menaces woman sex therapist

Dangerous Voyage
see *Terror Ship*

Danger Route
1967, (GB), Amicus/UA, color, 92 mins.
W: Richard Johnson (*Jonas Wilde*), Carol Lynley (*Jocelyn*), Barbara Bouchet (*Mari*), Sylvia Syms (*Barbara Canning*), Diana Dors (*Rhoda Gooderich*), Gordon Jackson (*Stern*), David Bauer (*Bennett*), Maurice Denham (*Peter Ravenspur*), Robin Bailey (*Parsons*), Sam Wanamaker (*Lucinda*), Leslie Sands (*The Man*), Harry Andrews (*Chief Canning*)
P: Max Rosenberg & Milton Subotsky   D: Seth Holt   SCR: Meade Roberts & Robert Stewart, from Andrew York's novel *The Eliminator*
Standard thriller: Secret agent ordered to kill defected Czech scientist

Danger Signal
1945, (USA), WB, b&w, 80 mins.
W: Zachary Scott, Faye Emerson
D: Robert Florey
Standard thriller

Danger Street
1947, (USA), Para, b&w, 66 mins.
W: Jane Withers, Robert Lowery
Standard thriller

Danger Tomorrow
1960, (GB), Parroch/AA, b&w, 61 mins.
W: Zena Walker (*Ginny Murray*), Robert Urquhart (*Bob Murray*), Rupert Davies (*Dr. Robert Campbell*), Annabel Maule (*Helen*), Russell Waters (*Steve*), Lisa Daniely (*Marie*)
P: C. Jack Parsons   D: Terry Bishop   SCR: Guy Deghy   STORY: Frank Charles
Standard fantasy: Doctor's wife has ESP, envisions murder in attic

Danger Woman
1946, (USA), Univ, b&w, 60 mins.
W: Brenda Joyce, Don Porter, Patricia Morison
Minor thriller: Female sleuth encounters intrigue

Danger Zone
1951, (USA), Lippert, b&w, 56 mins.
W: Richard Travis, Hugh Beaumont, Virginia Dale, Tom Neal
Minor melodrama: Auctioned saxophone contains stolen jewels

Daniel and the Devil
see *All That Money Can Buy*

La Danse de Feu (The Fire Dance)
1899, (Fr), Star, b&w, 20m (65.6 ft./1.1 mins.)
D: Georges Melies, from H. Rider Haggard's novel *She*
USA retitle, *Haggard's "She"—The Pillar of Fire*
Standard fantasy: Immortal beauty bathes in magic flame

La Danseuse Microscopique (The Microscopic Dancer)
1902, (Fr), Star, b&w, 60m (196.9 ft./3.3 mins.)
D: Georges Melies
GB retitle, *Marvellous Egg Producing with Surprise Developments* USA retitle, *The Dancing Midget*
Standard fantasy

Danse Vampiresque
1912, (Den), b&w
Fantasy short

Dante's Inferno
1912, (It), b&w
based on Dante's *La Divina Comedia*
Standard fantasy: Graphic depiction of Hell's torments

Dante's Inferno
1924, (USA), Fox, b&w, 6 reels (5,484 ft./1671.5m)
W: Pauline Starke (*Marjorie Vernon*), Ralph Lewis (*Mortimer Judd*), Lawson Butt

(*Dante*), Gloria Grey (*Mildred Craig*), Winifred Landis (*Mrs. Judd*), Josef Swickard (*Eugene Craig*), Howard Gaye (*Virgil*), Bud Jamison (*The Butler*), Robert Klein (*The Fiend*), William Scott (*Ernest Judd*), Lon Poff (*The Secretary*), Lorimer Johnston (*The Doctor*), Diana Miller
D: Henry Otto   SCR: Edmund Goulding & Cyrus Wood   inspired by Dante's *La Divina Comedia*   PHOTOG: Joseph August
Allegorical melodrama: Miserly tenement owner dreams of Hades

Dante's Inferno
1935, (USA), Fox, b&w, 89 mins.
W: Spencer Tracy, Claire Trevor, Henry B. Walthall, Robert Gleckler, Alan Dinehart, Scotty Beckett, Morgan Wallace, Ray Corrigan, Rita Cansino (Hayworth), Willard Robertson, Gary Leon
D: Henry Lachman   SCR: Philip Klein & Robert M. Yost   PHOTOG: Rudolph Maté, film contains stock-footage from 1924 *Dante's Inferno*
Superior melodrama: Amusement-park operator runs extremely dangerous ride

Dante's Peak
1997, (USA), Pacific Western/Univ, color, 112 mins.
W: Pierce Brosnan, Linda Hamilton, Charles Hallahan, Elizabeth Hoffman, Hansford Rowe, Grant Heslov, Jeffrey L. Ward, Peter Jason, Lee Garlington, Bill Bolender, Justin Williams, Kirk Trutner, Ed Stone, Heather Stephens, Susie Spear, Tammy L. Smith, Jamie Renee Smith, Brian Reddy, Christopher Murray, Tom Magnuson, Tzi Ma, Marilyn Leubner, Tim Holdeman, Jeremy Foley, R.J. Burns, Arabella Field, Donna Deshon, Carol Androsky, Walker Brandt
P: Gale Anne Hurd & Joseph Singer   D: Roger Donaldson   SCR: Leslie Bohem   MUSIC: John Frizzell   THEME: James Newton Howard
Exciting, big-budget ($100 million) thriller: Volcanic eruption threatens small town

La Danza Macabra (Dance Macabre)
1964, (GB-It), Woolner Bros., b&w, 77 mins.
W: Barbara Steele, George Riviere, Margrete Robsahm, Henry Kruger, Montgomery Gleen, Sylvia Sorent
P: Frank Belty & Walter Sarch
D: Anthony Dawson [Antonio Margheriti]   SCR: Jean Grimaud & Gordon Wilson Jr.   suggested by a short story by Edgar Allan Poe
USA retitle, *Castle of Blood*, A.k.a. *Castle of Terror*
Modest eroto-horror: Writer spends night in haunted house, meets two venal lady ghosts. cf. **Web of the Spider**

La Danza Macabra (Dance Macabre): BARBRA STEELE, MARGRETE ROBSAHM

Daphne and the Pirate
1916, (USA), Triangle, b&w, 5 reels
W: Lillian Gish
reissued 1924
Standard melodrama

Darby O'Gill and the Little People
1959, (USA), Walt Disney/Buena Vista, color, 93 mins.
W: Albert Sharpe (*Darby O'Gill*), Janet Munro, Sean Connery, Estelle Winwood, Kieron Moore, Walter Fitzgerald, Farrell Pelly, Jimmy O'Dea, Denis O'Dea, Jack MacGowran, J.G. Devlin, Nora O'Mahony
D: Robert Stevenson   SCR: Lawrence Edward Watkin, suggested by H.T. Kavanagh's *Darby O'Gill* stories   PHOTOG: Winton C. Hoch   MUSIC: Oliver Wallace
Well-made fantasy: Old Irishman meets Leprechaun king

The Daredevil
1972, (USA), George Montgomery/Trans-International/Visualscope/Gold Key, color, 70 mins
W: George Montgomery, Terry Moore
D: Robert W. Stringer
blurb: "I'm waiting for you to die! Die!"
Minor thriller: Voodoo plagues stock-car driver

The Dark (1968)
see *The Haunted House of Horror*

The Dark
1979, (USA), Film Ventures, color, 92 mins.
W: William Devane (*Roy*), Cathy Lee Crosby (*Zoe*), Keenan Wynn (*Moss*), Richard Jaeckel (*Mooney*), Warren Kemmerling (*Capt. Speer*), Biff Elliot (*Bresler*), Jacquelyn Hyde (*DeRenzey*), Casey Kasem (*The Pathologist*), John Bloom (*The Killer*), Jay Lawrence (*Jim*), Vivian Blaine (*Courtney*), William Derringer (*Herman*), Russ Marin (*Dr. Baranowski*), Roberto Contreras (*The Bartender*), Vernon Washington (*Henry*), Erik Howell (*Antwine*), Ron Iglesias (*Rudy*), William Lampley (*The Young Man*), Sandra Walker McCulley (*The Carhop*), Ken Menyard (*The Sportscaster*), Valla Rae McDade (*Camille*), Monica Peterson (*Mrs. Lydell*), Penny Ann Phillips (*Zelza*), Jeffrey Reese (*Randy*), Kathie Richards (*Shelly*), Mel Anderson, John Dresden, Morton Willis, Paula Crist, Joann Kirk
D: John Cardos   SCR: Stanford Whitmore   PHOTOG: John Morrill   MUSIC: Roger Kellaway
video title, The Mutilator
Minor SF-horror: Alien creature commits fiendish murders

The Dark
1994, (USA), color, 90 mins.
W: Brion James, Cynthia Belliveau, Jaimz Woolvett, Stephen McHattie
D: Craig Pryce
Minor horror-fantasy: Graveyard creature holds power to heal or destroy

Dark Age
1988, (Austral), color, 90 mins.
W: John Jarratt, Nikki Coghill, Gulpilil
D: Arch Nicholson
Standard thriller: Giant crocodile prowls

Dark Alibi
1946, (USA), Mono, b&w, 61 mins.
W: Sidney Toler (*Charlie Chan*), Mantan Moreland (*Birmingham Brown*), Ben Carter (*Ben Brown*), Teala Loring (*June Harley*), Benson Fong (*Tommie Chan*), George Holmes (*Hugh Kenzie*), Ray Walker (*Danvers*), Edward Earle (*Thomas Harley*), Joyce Compton (*Emily Evans*), Janet Shaw (*Miss Petrie*), Edna Holland (*Mrs. Foss*), John Eldredge (*Morgan*), William Ruhl (*Thompson*), Tim Ryan (*Foggy*), Milton Parsons (*Johnson*), Russell Hicks (*Warden Cameron*), Anthony Warde (*Jimmy Slade*), Frank Marlowe (*Barker*), George Eldredge (*Brand*), Meyer Grace
D: Phil Karlson   SCR: George Callahan, from characters created by Earl Derr Biggers   PHOTOG: William A. Sickner   MUSIC: Edward J. Kay
Modest mystery-thriller: Oriental sleuth tries to save man from electric chair

The Dark Alibi: SIDNEY TOLER, EDNA HOLLAND, JOYCE COMPTON

Dark Angel (1990)
see *I Come in Peace*

The Dark Angel
1991, (GB), color, 150 mins.
W: Peter O'Toole, Beatie Edney, Jane Lapotaire, Barbara Shelley, Tim Woodward, Alan MacNaughton, Guy Rolfe
D: Peter Hammond, from Sheridan LeFanu's novel
TVM, well-made thriller: Young heiress menaced by uncle

Dark Angel
1996, (USA), Fox-TV, color, 95 mins.
W: Eric Roberts, Ashley Crow, Linden Ashby, Gina Torres, Nicholas Pryor, Paul Calderon, V.P. Oliver, Wayne Pere, Joel Polis, Margo Moorer, Ray Baker
P & D: Robert Iscove   TELEPLAY: John Romano   PHOTOG: Francis Kenny

MUSIC: Michael Wolff
TVM, standard thriller: Serial killer targets unfaithful wives

Dark Angel: The Ascent
1994, (USA), color, 84 mins.
W: Angela Featherstone, Daniel Markel, Charlotte Stewart, Michael Genovese Michael C. Mahon, Nicholas Worth, Milton James
D: Linda Hassani   SCR: Matthew Bright   MUSIC: Fuzzbee Morse
Minor fantasy-thriller: Bored female demon rises from hell, torments wicked

Dark August
1976, (USA), color, 87 mins.
W: J.J. Barry, Carole Shelyne, Kim Hunter, William Robertson
D: Martin Goldman
Standard thriller: Urbanite accidentally kills Vermont girl, is cursed by her grandfather

The Dark Backward
1991, (USA), Greycat Films, color, 101 mins.
W: Judd Nelson, Bill Paxton, Wayne Newton, Lara Flynn Boyle, James Caan, King Moody, Rob Lowe, Claudia Christian, Adam Rifkin
D & SCR: Adam Rifkin
Standard horror-satire: Stand-up comic grows third arm

Dark Breed
1996, (USA), Color, 105 mins.
W: Jack Scalia (*Nick*), Lance LeGault (*Cutter*)
Standard action-SF-horror: Astronauts become hosts to alien parasites

Dark City
1998, (USA), Mystery Clock/New Line, color, 103 mins.
W: Rufus Sewell, Kiefer Sutherland, Jennifer Connelly, Ian Richardson, Richard O'Brien, William Hurt
WRIT & D: Alex Proyas
Bizarre, innovative fantasy: Man finds himself in surreal urban setting, breaks out to Eden

The Dark Crystal
1982, (GB), Lord Grade/ITC/Univ, color, 93 mins.
VOICES: Stephen Garlick, Lisa Maxwell, Billie Whitelaw, Percy Edwards, Barry Dennen, Brian Muehl, Jerry Nelson, Michael Kilgarriff, Steve Whitmire, Thick Wilson, David Buck, John Baddeley, Sean Barrett
P: Jim Henson & Gary Kurtz   D: Jim Henson & Frank Oz   SCR: David Odell   STORY: Jim Henson   PHOTOG: Oswald Morris   MUSIC: Trevor Jones   NARRATOR: Joseph O'Conor
Unusual fantasy-adventure enacted by puppets: Good vs. evil in mythical world

The Dark Dancer
1995, (USA), color, 98 mins.
W: Shannon Tweed, Jason Carter, Lisa Pescia, Andrew Prine, Francesco Quinn
Standard thriller: Woman psychologist moonlights as stripper, is linked to murders

The Dark Dealer
1995, (USA), color, 85 mins.
W: Mark Fickert, Richard Hull, Vincet Gaskins, Gordon Fox, Rocky Patterson
D: Tom Alexander
Standard horror anthology: Trio in limbo dealt three unsettling fates

Dark Delusion
1947, (USA), MGM, b&w, 90 mins.
W: James Craig, Lucille Bremer, Lionel Barrymore
Minor thriller. Last of Dr. Gillespie-Kildare series.

Darkened Rooms
1929, (USA), Para, b&w, 7 reels (6,066 ft./1848.9m)
W: Neil Hamilton (*Emory Jago*), Evelyn Brent (*Ellen*), Doris Hill (*Joyce Clayton*), David Newell (*Billy*), Blanche Craig (*Mrs. Fogarty*), Gale Henry (*Mme. Silvera*), Wallace MacDonald (*Bert Nelson*), E.H. Calvert (*Mr. Clayton*), Sammy Bricker (*The Sailor*)
D: Louis Gasnier   ADAPT: Patrick Kearney & Melville Baker, from a story by Philip Hamilton Gibbs   PHOTOG: Archie J. Stout
Standard melodrama: Fake spiritualists prey on chorus girl

The Darker Side of Terror
1979, (USA), Shaner-Ramrus/Bob Banner/CBS-TV, color, 94 mins.
W: Robert Forster (*Paul Corwin/The Clone*), Adrienne Barbeau (*Margaret Corwin*), Ray Milland (*Prof. Meredith*), John Lehne (*Lt. Merholz*), David Sheiner (*Prof. Hillstrom*), John Shaner, Denise DuBarry, Thomas Bellin, Heather Hobbs, Eddie Quillan, Raye Sheffield, Russell Shannon, Jim Nolan, Madeleine Shaner, Johnny Hock, Tom Elliott
WRIT & P: John Herman Shaner & Al Ramrus   D: Gus Trikonis   PHOTOG: Donald M. Morgan   MUSIC: Paul Chihara
TVM, standard SF-thriller: Cloning produces scientist's duplicate

Darkest London: or, The Dancer's Romance
1915, (GB), Barker/Renters, b&w, 4,000 ft. (1219.2m)
W: Ivy Close (*Mabel Carstairs*)
D: Bert Haldane
Standard crime-thriller: Abducted heiress leaves crooked husband, becomes dancer, loves blackmailed earl

Dark Eyes
see *Satan's Mistress*

Dark Eyes of London
1939, (GB), Argyle/British Pathe, b&w, 75 mins.
W: Bela Lugosi (*Dr. Orloff*), Greta Gynt (*Diana Stewart*), Hugh Williams (*Insp. Holt*), Wilfrid Walter (*Jake*), Edmon Ryan (*Lt. O'Reilly*), Julie Suedo (*The Sec'y*), Alexander Field (*Grogan*), Arthur E. Owen (*Dumb Lew*), Gerald Pring (*Henry Stuart*), Charles Penrose (*The Drunk*), May Hallatt, B. Herbert
D: Walter Summers   SCR: Patrick Kirwin, Walter Summers & J.F. Argyle, from Edgar Wallace's novel   PHOTOG: Bryan Langly
USA retitle, **The Human Monster** *(Monogram, 1940), reissued 1945 & 1950*
Grim chiller: Fiend murders blind to collect insurance. cf. Die Toten Augen von London

The Dark Half
1992, (USA), Orion, color, 122 mins.
W: Timothy Hutton (*Thad Beaumont/George Stark*), Amy Madigan (*Liz Beaumont*), Julie Harris (*Reggie Delesseps*), Robert Joy (*Fred Clawson*), Chelsea Field (*Annie Pangborn*), Royal Dano (*Digger Holt*), Rutanya Alda (*Miriam Cowley*), Beth Grant (*Shayla Beaumont*), Kent Broadhurst (*Mike Donaldson*), Tom Mardirosian (*Rick Cowley*), Glenn Colerider (*Homer Gamache*), Michael Rooker (*Alan Pangborn*), Patrick Brannan (*Young Thad Beaumont*), Larry John Meyers (*Doc Pritchard*), Christina Romero (*The Little Girl*), Rohn Thomas (*Dr. Albertson*), Molly Renfroe (*Hilary*), Judy Grafe (*The Head Nurse*), Erik Jensen (*The Male Student*), John Machione (*The Male Nurse*), Nardi Novak (*Pangborn's Receptionist*), Christine Forrest (*Trudy Wiggins*), Zachary Bill Mott (*Norris Ridgewick*), William Cameron (*Officer Hamilton*), David Butler (*Trooper #1*), Curt De Bor (*Trooper #2*), Drinda LaLumia (*Dodie*), Lamont Arnold (*NYC Cop #1*), Lee Hayes (*NYC Cop #2*), John Ponzio (*Todd Pangborn*), Jack Skelly (*The Man in the Hallway*), Marc Field (*Donaldson Cop #1*), Rik Billock (*Donaldson Cop #2*), Bruce Kirkpatrick (*Officer #1*), David Early (*Officer #2*), Melissa Papp (*Rosalie*), Jeff Monahan (*Wes*), Jeffery Howell (*Dave*), J. Michael Hunter (*Garrison*), Therese Courtney (*The Receptionist*), Marty Roppelt (*The Young Officer*), Sarah & Elizabeth Parker (*Wendy & William Beaumont*)
P: Declan Baldwin   WRIT & D: George A. Romero, from Stephen King's novel   PHOTOG: Tony Pierce-Roberts   MUSIC: Christopher Young
Standard horror-fantasy: Writer's murderous creation given form

The Dark Hour
1936, (USA), Chesterfield, b&w 72 mins.
W: Ray Walker, Irene Ware, Berton Churchill, Hedda Hopper, Hobart Bosworth, E.E. Clive
D: Charles Lamont, from a story by Sinclair Gluck
Minor thriller: Murder involves multiple suspects

Dark Interval
1950, (GB), Present Day/Apex, b&w, 60 mins.
W: Zena Marshall (*Sonia Jordan*), Andrew Osborn (*Walter Jordan*), John Barry (*Trevor*), John LeMesurier, Mona Washbourne, Wallas Eaton, Charmian Innes
P: Charles Reynolds   D: Charles Saunders   STORY: John Gilling
Standard thriller: Bride learns husband is jealous madman

Dark Intruder
1965, (USA), Univ, b&w, 59 mins.
W: Leslie Nielsen, Mark Richman, Judi Meredith, Bill Quinn, Peter Brocco, Gilbert Green, Charles Bolender, Ken Hooker, Vaughn Taylor, Werner Klemperer
P: Jack Laird   D: Harvey Hart   SCR: Barre Lyndon   PHOTOG: John F. Warren   MUSIC: Stanley Wilson
orig. co-billed with I Saw What You Did (1965)
Standard fantasy-thriller, orig. intended as feature-pilot for unsold teleseries **Black Cloak**: *Sumerian magic spreads terror in turn-of-century San Francisco*

Dark Journey
1937, (GB), London-Victor Saville/UA, b&w, 77 mins.
W: Conrad Veidt (*Baron Karl von Marwitz*), Vivien Leigh (*Madeleine Goddard*), Anthony Bushell (*Bob Carter*), Ursula Jeans (*Gertrude*), Margery Pickard (*Colette*), Eliot Makeham (*Anatole*), Austin Trevor (*Dr. Muller*), Sam Livesey (*Maj. Schaffer*), Edmund Willard (*German Intelligence*), Cecil Parker (*The Captain*), Charles Carson (*The Fifth Bureau*), Reginald Tate (*The Mate*), Henry Oscar (*The Magistrate*), Robert Newton (*The Officer*), William Dewhurst (*The Killer*), Cyril Smith (*The Valet*)
D: Victor Saville   SCR: Arthur Wimperis, from a story by Lajos Biro   PHOTOG: Georges Perinal & Harry Stradling
reissued (1953) as **The Anxious Years**
Standard thriller: Beautiful French spy vs. suave German spy during World War I

The Dark Light
1951, (GB), Hammer/Exclusive, b&w, 66 mins.
W: Albert Lieven (*Mark*), David Greene (*Johnny*), Norman MacOwan (*Rigby*), Martin Benson (*Luigi*), Catherine Blake (*Linda*), Jack Stewart (*Matt*), John Longden (*Stephen*), John Harvey (*Roger*)
P: Michael Carreras   D & SCR: Vernon Sewell
Standard crime-thriller: Lighthouse keeper aids bank robbers

The Dark Man
1951, (GB), Independent Artists/GFD, b&w, 91 mins.
W: Edward Underdown (*Insp. Jack Viner*), Natasha Parry (*Molly Lester*), Maxwell Reed (*The Dark Man*), William Hartnell (*The Supt.*), Barbara Murray (*Carol Burns*), Cyril Smith (*Samuel Denny*), Leonard White (*Det. Evans*), John Singer (*The Adjutant*), Geoffrey Sumner (*The Major*)
P: Julian Wintle   WRIT & D: Jeffrey Dell
Standard thriller: Woman witnesses murder, killer pursues

Darkman
1990, (USA), Renaissance/Univ, color, 106 mins.
W: Liam Neeson (*Dr. Peyton Westlake/Darkman*), Colin Friels (*Louis Strack Jr.*), Frances McDormand (*Julie Hastings*), Larry Drake (*Robert G. Durant*), Nelson Mashita (*Yakitito*), Jessie Lawrence Ferguson (*Eddie Black*), Danny Hicks (*Skip*), Rafael H. Robledo (*Rudy Guzman*), Theodore Raimi (*Rick*), Aaron Lustig (*Martin Katz*), Dan Bell (*Smiley*), Nicholas Worth (*Pauly*), Arsenio "Sonny" Trinidad (*Hung Fat*), Said Faraj (*The Convenience Store Clerk*), Nathan Jung (*The Chinese Warrior*), Prof. Toru Tanaka (*Chinese Warrior #2*), John Lisbon Wood (*The Carnival Booth Attendant*), Frank Noon (*The Side Show Barker*), William Dear (*The Limo Driver*), Julius Harris (*The Gravedigger*), Carl Bresk (*Policeman #1*), Sean Daniel (*Policeman #2*), Bridget Hoffman (*The Computer Voice*), Philip A. Gillis (*The Priest*), John Cameron (*The Bartender*), Maggie Moore (*The Nurse*), John Landis (*The Physician*), Craig Hosking (*The Helicopter Pilot*), Carrie Hall (*The Screaming Woman*), Karl Wickman, Cliff Fleming, Andy Bale, Neal McDonough, Stuart Cornfeld, William Lustig, Charles W. Young, Scott Spiegel, Cary Tyler, Bruce Campbell
D: Sam Raimi   SCR: Chuck Pfarrer, Sam Raimi, Ivan Raimi, Daniel Goldin, & Joshua Goldin   STORY: Sam Raimi   PHOTOG: Bill Pope   MUSIC: Danny Elfman
Superior satire-thriller: Disfigured scientist eliminates criminals

Darkman II: The Return of Durant
1995, (USA), Renaissance/MCA/Univ, video, color, 93 mins.
W: Arnold Vosloo (*Darkman/Peyton Westlake*), Larry Drake (*Durant*), Renee O'Connor (*Laurie Brinkman*), Kim Delaney (*Jill Randall*), Lawrence Dane (*Dr. Alfred Hathaway*), Rod Wilson (*Druganov*), Jesse Collins (*Dr. David Brinkman*), David Ferry (*Eddie*), Jack Langedijk (*Rollo Latham*), James Millington (*Mr. Perkins*), Steve Mousseau (*Roy*), Sten Eirik (*Whitey*), Phillip Jarrett (*Dan*), Kevin Rushton, Graham Rowatt, Chris Gillett, David Clement, Catherine Swing, Anne Marie Loder, Adam Bramble, Harry Spiegel, Candice Beaulieu, Donna Mullin
D & PHOTOG: Bradford May   SCR: Steven McKay   STORY: Robert Eisele & Lawrence Hertzog, from characters created by Sam Raimi   MUSIC: Randy Miller   THEMES: Danny Elfman
Made-for-Video, standard SF-thriller: Disfigured scientist vs. archenemy's super-weapon

Darkman III: Die Darkman Die
1995, (USA), Univ, color, video, 90 mins.
W: Arnold Vosloo (*Darkman/Peyton Westlake*), Jeff Fahey, Darlanne Fluegel, Nigel Bennett, Roxann Biggs-Dawson
D: Bradford May   SCR: Mike Werb   MUSIC: Randy Miller
Made-for-Video, minor SF-thriller: Superhero imperiled by evil businessman

Dark Mansions
1986, (USA), Aaron Spelling/ABC-TV, color, 95 mins.
W: Joan Fontaine (*Margaret Drake*), Michael York (*Jason Drake*), Paul Shenar (*Phillip Drake*), Lois Chiles (*Jessica Drake*), Dan O'Herlihy (*Alexander Drake*), Linda Purl (*Shellane Victor*), Melissa Sue Anderson (*Noelle Drake*), Steve Inwood (*Jerry Mills*), Nicollette Sheridan (*Banda Drake*), Byron Morrow (*David Forbes*), Lee Corrigan (*Capt. Hemmings*), Raymond St. Jacques, Yves Andre Martin, Vincent Pandoliano, Grant Aleksander
P & D: Jerry London   TELEPLAY: Robert L. McCullough   STORY: Anthony Lawrence, Nancy Lawrence, & Robert L. McCullough   PHOTOG: Paul Lohmann   SPCL-FX: John Gray   MUSIC: Ken Harrison
TVM, aimless melodrama (feature-pilot for unsold teleseries): Rich family conceals secrets

The Dark Mirror
1946, (USA), Univ, b&w, 85 mins.
W: Olivia de Havilland (*Terry Collins/Ruth Collins*), Lew Ayres (*Dr. Scott Elliott*), Thomas Mitchell (*Lt. of Detectives Stevenson*), Richard Long (*Rusty*), Lela Bliss (*Mrs. Didriksen*), Charles Evans (*D.A. Girard*), Garry Owen (*Franklin*), Ida Moore (*Mrs. O'Brien, the Cleaning Lady*), Marta Mitrovich (*Miss Beade*), Lester Allen (*George Benson*), William Halligan (*Sgt. Temple*), Jack Cheatham (*The Policeman*), Amelita Ward (*The Photo-Double*), Charles McAvoy (*Janitor O'Brien*), Lane Chandler (*The Intern*), Jack Gargan (*The Waiter*), Lane Watson (*Mike, the Ass't*), Ralph Peters (*The Dumb Cop*)
WRIT & P: Nunnally Johnson, from a story by Vladimir Pozner   D: Robert Siodmak   PHOTOG: Milton Krasner   SPCL-FX: J. Devereaux Jennings & Paul Lerpae   MUSIC: Dmitri Tiomkin
Classic mystery-thriller: Twin sisters implicated in murder

Dark Mirror
1984, (USA), Aaron Spelling/ABC-TV, color, 94 mins.
W: Jane Seymour (*Lee Cullen/Tracey Cullen*), Stephen Collins (*Dr. James Eiseley*), Vincent Gardenia (*Al Church*), Robert DoQui (*Higgens*), Hank Brandt (*Girard*), Ty Henderson (*Wittman*), Jack Kruschen (*Smithson*), Reid Cruickshanks (*Avery*), Bill Quinn (*Mr. Bennett*), Cathleen Cordell (*Mrs.*

Bennett), Sandy Freeman (*Dorothy Francis*), Tim Haldeman (*The Policeman*), Patti Been (*The Policewoman*), Cis Rundle (*The Receptionist*), Alma Beltran (*A Woman*)
D: Richard Lang **TELEPLAY**: Corey Blechman based on the screenplay by Nunnally Johnson **PHOTOG**: Frank Stanley **SPCL-FX**: Dutch Van Der Byl **MUSIC**: Dominic Frontiere **SONGS**: *Touch Me One More Time*
TVM, standard thriller: Which twin sister is mad murderess?

The Dark Mirror (1946): OLIVIA DE HAVILLAND IN BOTH ROLES

Dark Night of the Scarecrow
1981, (USA), Wizan/CBS-TV, color, 100 mins.
W: Charles Durning (*Otis*), Tonya Crowe (*Marylee*), Robert F. Lyons (*Skeeter*), Lane Smith (*Harless*), Jocelyn Brando (*Mrs. Ritter*), Claude Earl Jones (*Philby*), Larry Drake (*Bubba*), Tom Taylor, Ivy Jones, Richard McKenzie, Jim Tartan, David Adams, Ed Call, Alice Nunn, John Steadman, Dennis Robertson, Jetta Scelza, Ivy Bethune, Modi Frank
D: Frank DeFelitta **TELEPLAY**: J.D. Feigelson **PHOTOG**: Vincent Martinelli **SPCL-FX**: Cliff Wenger
TVM, modest thriller: Vigilantes face eerie retribution for slaying of retarded man

Dark of the Night
1985, (New Zeal), Preston-Laing/Quartet, color, 87 mins.
W: Heather Bolton (*Meg*), David Letch (*The Man*), Suzanne Lee (*Val*), Perry Piercy (*Mary Carmichael*), Danny Mulheron (*Wayne*), Margaret Umbers (*Samantha*), Gary Stalker (*Bruce*), Jan Fisher (*Edith*), Michael Haugh (*Mr. Whitehorn*), Kate Harcourt (*Meg's Mother*), Phillip Gordon (*Clive*), Meriol Buchanan (*The Woman with the Dog*), Ross Jolly (*The Neighbor*), Don Linke (*Martin*), John Bullock (*Meg's Father*), Rebecca Gibney (*Clive's Sec'y*), Jonathan Crayford (*The Petrol Pump Attendant*), Lew Martin, Les Stone, Frank Slobbe, Ken Saville, Phillip Mills, Matty
D: Gaylene Preston **SCR**: Gaylene Preston, Geoff Murphy, & Graeme Tetley, from Elizabeth Jane Howard's story **PHOTOG**: Thom Burstyn **MUSIC**: Jonathan Crayford
A.k.a. Mr. Wrong
Standard fantasy-thriller: Woman buys haunted auto

Dark Passage
1947, (USA), WB, b&w, 106 mins.
W: Humphrey Bogart, Lauren Bacall, Agnes Moorehead, Bruce Bennett, Tom D'Andrea, Clifton Young, Douglas Kennedy
D & SCR: Delmer Daves, from David Goodis' novel **PHOTOG**: Sidney Hickox **MUSIC**: Franz Waxman
Standard thriller: Innocent man flees murder rap, has plastic surgery

The Dark Past
1949, (USA), Col, b&w, 75 mins.
W: William Holden, Lee J. Cobb
D: Rudolph Mate **PHOTOG**: Joseph Walker **MUSIC**: George Duning
*Standard thriller (remake of **Blind Alley**): Psychiatrist foils criminal*

Dark Places
1973, (GB), James Hannah Jr./CRC, color, 91 mins.
W: Robert Hardy (*Edward/Andrew*), Joan Collins (*Sarah*), Roy Evans (*Baxter*), Christopher Lee (*Dr. Mandeville*), Herbert Lom (*Prescott*), Jane Birkin (*Alta*), Martin Boddey (*The Police Sgt.*), Jean Marsh (*Victoria*), Carleton Hobbs (*Old Marr*), John Glyn-Jones (*The Bank Manager*), Jennifer Thanisch (*Jessica*), Barry Linehan (*The Gatekeeper*), John Levene (*The Doctor*), Linda Gray (*The Woman on the Hill*), Lysandre de-la Haye, Earl Rhodes
P: James Hannah Jr. **D**: Don Sharp **SCR**: Ed Brennan & Joseph Van Winkle **PHOTOG**: Ernest Steward **MUSIC**: Wilfred Josephs
Standard thriller: Ghosts, madness, and a hidden fortune

Dark Purpose
see L'Intrigo

Dark Reflection
1994, (USA), Fox-TV, color
W: C. Thomas Howell
TVM, standard thriller: Man stalked by murderous double

The Dark Ride
1984, (USA), color, 83 mins.
W: James Luisi, Susan Sullivan, Martin Speer
D: Jeremy Hoenack
Sordid thriller (based on career of serial killer Ted Bundy): Lunatic rapes and kills women

Dark Secret
1949, (GB), Nettlefold/Butcher, b&w, 85 mins.
W: Dinah Sheridan (*Valerie Merryman*), Emrys Jones (*Chris Merryman*), Irene Handl ("*Woody*" *Woodman*), Hugh Pryse (*A Very Late Visitor*), Barbara Couper (*Mrs. Barrington*), Percy Marmont (*The Vicar*), Geoffrey Sumner (*Jack Farrell*), Mackenzie Ward (*The Artist*), Charles Hawtrey (*Arthur Figson*), John Salew (*Mr. Barrington*), George Merritt (*Mr. Lumley*), Stanley Vilven (*Mr. Woodman*)
P: Ernest G. Roy **D**: Maclean Rogers **SCR**: A.R. Rawlinson & Moie Charles, from Mordaunt Shairp's play *Crime at Blossoms*
reissued 1952 (10 mins. cut)
Standard thriller: Ex-pilot's wife obsessed by murder of their cottage's previous tenant

The Dark Secret of Black Bayou
see Mistress of Paradise

The Dark Secret of Harvest Home
1978, (USA), NBC-TV, color, 118 mins.
W: Bette Davis (*Widow Fortune*), David Ackroyd (*Nick Constantine*), Rosanna Arquette (*Kate Constantine*), Michael O'Keefe (*Worthy Pettinger*), John Calvin (*Justin Hooke*), Joanna Miles (*Beth Constantine*), Laurie Prange (*Sophie Hooke*), Lina Raymond (*Tamar Penrose*), Norman Lloyd (*Amys Penrose*), Rene Auberjonois (*Jack Stump*), Linda Marsh, Richard Venture
P: Jack Laird **D**: Leo Penn, from Thomas Tryon's novel *Harvest Home*
TVM (orig. in 2 parts), unusual thriller: Urban family finds terrifying mysteries in small New England town

Dark Side of Midnight
1986, (USA), color, 108 mins.
W: James Moore, Wes Olsen, Sandy Schemmel, Dave Bowling
A.k.a. The Creeper
Minor thriller: Detective trails psycho-killer

The Dark Side of the Moon
1990, (USA), color, 95 mins.
W: William Bledsoe, Alan Blumenfeld, John Diehl, Robert Sampson, Wendy MacDonald, Camilla More, Joe Turkel
D: D.J. Webster
Minor SF-thriller: Demonic spirit possesses spaceship crew

The Dark Stairway
1938, (GB), WB, b&w, 72 mins.
W: Hugh Williams (*Dr. Thurlow*), Chili Bouchier (*Betty Trimmer*), Garry Marsh (*Dr. Mortimer*), Reginald Purdell (*Askew*), James Stephenson (*Insp. Clarke*), Glen Alyn (*Isabel Simmonds*), John Carol (*Merridew*), Lesley Brook (*Mary Cresswell*), Robert Rendel (*Dr. Fletcher*)
D: Arthur Woods **SCR**: Brock Williams & Basil Dillon, from Mignon G. Eberhart's novel *From What Dark Stairway*
Standard thriller: Doctor murdered for new anesthetic

Dark Star
1975, (USA), Jack H. Harris/Bryanston, color, 91 mins.
W: Dan O'Bannon (*Pinback*), Brian Narelle (*Doolittle*), Dre Pahich (*Talby*), Cal Kuniholm (*Boiler*), Joe Saunders
P & D: John Carpenter
SCR: John Carpenter & Dan O'Bannon **PHOTOG**: Douglas Knapp **SPCL-FX**: John Walsh, Bob Greenberg, Greg Jein, Harry Walton & Ron Cobb **VS-FX CONSULTANT & OP-FX**: Bill Taylor **MUSIC**: John Carpenter **SONG**: *Benson Arizona* (lyrics, Bill Taylor)
"It would be hard to imagine a sharper, funnier, scarier picture of the direction our technology could take us" —Margaret Ronan, Scholastic Magazine
Unusual SF-fantasy: Astronauts eliminate "unstable" planets

Dark Streets of Cairo
1940, (USA), Univ, b&w
W: George Zucco, Katherine DeMille, Sigrid Gurie, Eddie Quillan, Ralph Byrd
Minor thriller: Intrigue in Egypt

The Dark Tower
1943, (GB), WB, b&w, 93 mins.
W: Ben Lyon (*Phil Danton*), Anne Crawford (*Mary*), Herbert Lom (*Torg*), David Farrar (*Tom Danton*), Billy Hartnell (*Towers*), Frederick Burtwell (*Willie*), Josephine Wilson (*Mme. Shogun*), Elsie Wagstaff (*Eve*), J.H. Roberts (*Dr. Wilson*)
D: John Harlow **SCR**: Brock Williams & Reginald Purdell, from a play by Alexander Woolcott & George S. Kaufman
reissued 1949
*Standard thriller: Hypnotist controls circus girl. Remake: **Man With Two Faces***

Dark Tower
1987, (USA), color, 91 mins.
W: Michael Moriarty, Jenny Agutter, Carol Lynley, Theodore Bikel, Anne Lockhart, Kevin McCarthy, Patch Mackenzie
D: Ken Barnett (Freddie Francis) **SCR:** Robert J. Avrech & Kenneth G. Blackwell
Standard thriller

Darkened Rooms: EVELYN BRENT AND NEIL HAMILTON

Dark Universe
1993, (USA), Sharan/American Independent, color, 83 mins.
W: Blake Pickett Cherie Scott, Bently Tittle, John Maynard, Paul Austin Sanders, Pat Moran, Tom Ferguson, Steve Barkett, Joe Estevez
D: Steve Latshaw **SCR:** Pat Moran **PHOTOG:** Maxwell J. Beck **MUSIC:** Jeffrey Walton
Minor SF-horror: Space aliens try to harvest humans for food

Dark Venture
1956, (USA), First Nat'l Film Distributors, color, 81 mins.
W: John Trevlac [John Calvert], Ann Cornell, John Carradine
D & SCR: John Calvert
Minor thriller: Adventurer in Africa meets deranged white mystic

Dark Water
1980, (GB), Dragonfly/ITC, color, 28 mins.
W: Gwyneth Strong (*Jo*), Philip Davis (*Eddie*), David Beames (*The Killer*), Bruce White (*Bob*), Tony Caunter (*The Manager*), Jane Freeman (*The Wife*), Derek Martin (*The Guard*), Gillian Martell (*The Cashier*)
P: Tony Grisoni **D:** Andrew Bogle **STORY:** Andrew Bogle & Tony Grisoni **PHOTOG:** Gale Tattersall **MUSIC:** Rory Forsyth
Standard short thriller: Escaped murderer kills swimmers at baths

Dark Waters
1944, (USA), UA, b&w, 90 mins.
W: Merle Oberon, Franchot Tone, Elisha Cook Jr., Thomas Mitchell, Fay Bainter, John Qualen, Rex Ingram, Odette Myrtil
P: Benedict Bogeaus **D:** Andre de Toth **SCR:** Joan Harrison & Marian Cockrell, from the novel by Frank & Marian Cockrell **PHOTOG:** John Mescall **MUSIC:** Miklos Rozsa
Standard melodrama: Fortune thieves target heiress

Dark World
1935, (GB), Fox British, b&w, 73 mins.
W: Tamara Desni (*Brigitta*), Leon Quartermaine (*Stephen*), Hugh Brooke (*Philip*), Olga Lindo (*Eleanor*), Morton Selten (*The Colonel*), Fred Duprez (*Schwartz*), Viola Compton (*Auntie*), Googie Withers (*Annie*), Kynaston Reeves (*John*)
D: Bernard Vorhaus **SCR:** Hugh Brooke, from a story by Leslie Landau & Selwyn Jepson
Standard thriller: Jealous brother plots sibling's electrocution, kills wrong man

D'artagnan
see The Three Musketeers (1916)

D.A.R.Y.L.
1985, (USA), John Heyman-Burtt Harris/Para, color, 98 mins.
W: Mary Beth Hurt (*Joyce Richardson*), Michael McKean (*Andy Richardson*), Barret Oliver (*Daryl*), Danny Corkill (*Turtle*), Kathryn Walker (*Dr. Ellen Lamb*), Josef Sommer (*Dr. Jeffrey Stuart*), Colleen Camp, David Wohl, Steve Ryan, Ron Frazier, Amy Linker, Ed L. Grady, Tucker McGuire, Dalton Poole, Kevin O'Neill
D: Simon Wincer **SCR:** David Ambrose, Allan Scott, & Jeffrey Ellis **PHOTOG:** Frank Watts **VS-FX:** Michael Fink **MUSIC:** Marvin Hamlisch **SONG:** Somewhere I Belong
Modest SF: Small boy revealed to be robot

A Dash for Help
1909, (GB), Williamson, b&w, 515 ft. (157m)
D & STORY: Dave Aylott
Standard thriller: Messenger penetrates Hindu native lines, Highlanders rescue fort

Date at Midnight
1960, (GB), Danziger/Para, b&w, 57 mins.
W: Paul Carpenter (*Bob Dillon*), Jean Aubrey (*Paula Burroughs*), Harriette Johns (*Lady Leyton*), Ralph Michael (*Sir Edward Leyton*), John Charlesworth (*Tommy*), Robert Ayres (*Gordon Baines*), Philip Ray (*Jenkins*), Howard Lang (*The Inspector*)
P: Edward J. & Harry Lee Danziger **D:** Godfrey Grayson **STORY:** Mark Grantham
Standard thriller: American reporter proves lawyer's nephew did not kill girl

Date with an Angel
1987, (USA), DEG, color, 105 mins.
W: Michael E. Knight (*Jim Sanders*), Phoebe Cates (*Patty Winston*), Emmanuelle Beart (*Angel*), Phil Brock (*George*), David Dukes (*Ed Winston*), Albert Macklin (*Don*), Pete Kowanko (*Rex*), Vinny Argiro (*Ben Sanders*)
WRIT & D: Tom McLoughlin **PHOTOG:** Alex Thomson **VS-FX:** Richard Edlund **MUSIC:** Randy Kerber
Minor fantasy: Heavenly envoy causes confusion

A Date with Death
1959, (USA), Pacific Int'l, color, 81 mins
W: Gerald Mohr, Liz Renay, Harry Lauter, Robert Clarke, Stephanie Farnay
P: William S. Edwards **D:** Harold Daniels
Minor thriller: Vagrant borrows identity of murdered police agent. In psychorama, filmed in Arizona

A Date with Destiny
see The Mad Doctor

Date with Disaster
1957, (GB), Fortress/Eros, b&w, 61 mins.
W: Tom Drake (*Miles*), William Hartnell (*Tracy*), Shirley Eaton (*Sue*), Maurice Kaufmann (*Don*), Michael Golden (*Insp. Matthews*), Richard Shaw (*Ken*)
P: Guido Coen **D:** Charles Saunders **STORY:** Brock Williams
Standard crime-thriller: Car salesman suspected of being safecracker

A Date with the Falcon
1941, (USA), RKO, b&w, 63 mins.
W: George Sanders (*Gay Lawrence*), Wendy Barrie (*Helen Reed*), James Gleason (*Mike O'Hara*), Mona Maris (*Rita Mara*), Allen Jenkins (*Jonathan G. "Goldy" Locke*), Victor Kilian (*Max*), Frank Moran (*Dutch*), Russ Clark (*Needles*), Alec Craig (*Waldo Sampson/H. Sampson*), Edward Gargan (*Bates*), Frank Martinelli (*Louie*), Hans Conreid (*The Hotel Clerk*), Elizabeth Russell (*The Girl on the Airplane*)
D: Irving Reis **SCR:** Lynn Root & Frank Fenton, from characters created by Michael Arlen **PHOTOG:** Robert De Grasse
Standard mystery-thriller, 2nd entry in Falcon *series: Inventor of synthetic diamond is murdered*

The Daughter of Crooked Alley
see Crooked Alley

Daughter of Darkness
1948, (GB), Kenilworth/Alliance/Para, b&w, 91 mins.
W: Anne Crawford (*Bess Stanforth*), Siobhan McKenna (*Emily Beaudine*), Maxwell Reed (*Dan*), George Thorpe (*Mr. Tallent*), Barry Morse (*Robert Stanforth*), Liam Redmond (*Father Corcoran*), Honor Blackman (*Julie Tallent*), Grant Tyler (*Larry Tallent*), David Greene (*David Price*), Denis Gordon (*Saul Trevethick*), Arthur Hambling (*Jacob*)
P: Victor Hanbury **D:** Lance Comfort **SCR:** Max Catto, from his play *They Walk Alone*
Standard thriller: Irish peasant murders her lovers. reissued 1955

Daughter of Darkness
1990, (GB-Hung), Accent-King Phoenix/CBS-TV, color, 95 mins.
W: Mia Sara (*Catherine*), Anthony Perkins (*Anton Crainic*), Jack Coleman (*Jack Devlin*), Dezso Garas (*Max*), Robert Reynolds (*Grigore*), Erika Bodnar (*Nicole*), Kati Rak, Attila Lute, Istvan Hunyadkurty
D: Stuart Gordon **TELEPLAY:** Andrew Laskos **PHOTOG:** Ivan Mark **SPCL-FX:** Peter Szilayyi **MUSIC:** Colin Towns
TVM, standard horror-thriller: Girl finds father is Undead

Daughter of Death
see Julie Darling

Daughter of Destiny
see Alraune (1928)

Daughter of Dr. Jekyll
1957, (USA), Film Ventures/AA, b&w, 69 mins.
W: Gloria Talbott (*Janet Smith*), John Agar (*George Hastings*), Arthur Shields (*Dr. Lomas*), John Dierkes (*Jacob*), Mollie McCard (*Maggie*), Martha Wentworth (*Mrs. Merchant*), Marel Page, Marjorie Stapp, Rita Greene

WRIT & P: Jack Pollexfen   **D:** Edgar G. Ulmer   **PHOTOG:** John F. Warren   **SPCL-FX:** Jack Rabin & Louis DeWitt   **MUSIC SPRVSR:** Melvyn Lenard
orig. co-billed with **The Cyclops**
Standard horror-fantasy (interesting as an Edgar G. Ulmer effort): Girl finds she was sired by fiend

Daughter of the Mind: DON MURPHY, RAY MILLARD

Daughter of Frankenstein
see **La Figlia di Frankenstein**

Daughter of Horror
see **Dementia**

The Daughter of Mata Hari
see **Mata Hari's Daughter**

The Daughter of Romany
1913, (GB), Edison, b&w, 1,000 ft. (304.8m)
W: Marc McDermott (*Capt. Courtney*), Miriam Nesbitt (*Mona*), Winifred Albion (*The Daughter*)
D: Charles Brabin   **STORY:** Anne Merwin & Bannister Merwin
Standard melodrama: Nobleman deserts secret gypsy wife, later their child weds gypsy

A Daughter of Satan
1913, (USA), Cricks & Martin, b&w
W: Fred Dunning
Minor melodrama: Temptress lures innocent

A Daughter of Satan
1914, (GB), Cricks/Ruffells, b&w, 2,895 ft. (882.4m)
W: Jack Leigh (*Jack Fortescue*), Una Tristram (*Alicia Fortescue*), Lionel d'Aragon (*Ralph Merivale*)
D: Edwin J. Collins
Standard thriller: Divers fight beneath sea for stolen plans

Daughter of Shanghai
1937, (USA), Para, b&w
W: Anna May Wong, Anthony Quinn, Philip Ahn
Standard melodrama

Daughter of the Dragon
1931, (USA), Para, b&w 70 mins.
W: Anna May Wong, Warner Oland, Sessue Hayakawa Bramwell Fletcher, Frances Dade, Holmes Herbert
D: Lloyd Corrigan, from characters created by Sax Rohmer
Standard thriller: Fu Manchu's daughter hatches plot

Daughter of the Gods
1916, (USA), Univ, b&w, 10 reels
W: Annette Kellermann, Stuart Holmes
WRIT & D: Herbert Brenon
Standard fantasy-adventure: Sea siren has problems

Daughter of the Jungle
1949, (USA), Rep, b&w, 69 mins.
W: Lois Hall, James Cardwell, Sheldon Leonard, Jim Nolan, William Wright, Frank Lackteen, Jim Bannon, George Piltz, George Carleton, Francis McDonald, Al Kikume, Alex Montoya, Charles Soldani, Leo C. Richmond
D: George Blair   **SCR:** William Lively   **ORIG. STORY:** Sol Shor   **PHOTOG:** John MacBurnie   **SPCL-FX:** Howard & Theodore Lydecker   **MUSIC:** Stanley Wilson
Minor action-thriller: Pilot meets female "Tarzan"

Daughter of the Mind
1969, (USA), 20th-Fox, color, 92 mins.
W: Don Murray (*Dr. Alexander Lauder*), Ray Milland (*Prof. Samuel Hale Constable*), Gene Tierney (*Lenore Constable*), Barbara Dana (*Tina Cryder*), Edward Asner (*Saul Wiener*), Pamelyn Ferdin (*Mary Constable*), William Beckley (*Arnold Bessmer*), George Macready (*Dr. Frank Ferguson*), Virginia Christine (*Helga*), John Carradine (*Mr. Bosch*), Ivor Barry (*Dr. Paul Cryder*), Cecile Ozorio (*Devi Bessmer*), Frank Maxwell (*Gen. Augstadt*), Bill Hickman (*The Enemy Agent*), Hal Frederick (*The C.I.C. Technician*)
P & D: Walter Grauman   **TELEPLAY:** Luther Davis, from Paul Gallico's novel *The Hand of Mary Constable*   **PHOTOG:** Jack Woolf   **OPTICAL SPCL-FX:** L.B. Abbott & Art Cruickshank   **MUSIC:** Robert Drasnin   **MUSIC SPRVSR:** Lionel Newman
TVM, standard thriller: Scientist claims contact with dead

Daughter of the Tong
1939, (USA), b&w, 56 mins.
W: Evelyn Brent, Grant Withers, Dorothy Short, Dave O'Brien
D: Raymond K. Johnson
Minor melodrama: Woman runs smuggling ring

Daughters of Darkness
1970, (Belg-Fr-W. Ger-It), Gemini/Maron, color, 87 mins.
W: Delphine Seyrig (*Elisabeth*), Daniele Ouimet (*Valerie*), John Karlen (*Stefan*), Andrea Rau (*Ilona*), Fons Rademakers, Georges Jamin, Paul Esser, Joris Collet
P: Alain Guilleaume & Paul Collet   **D:** Harry Kumel   **SCR:** Pierre Drouot & Harry Kumel   **PHOTOG:** Edward van Der Enden   **MUSIC:** Francois De Roubiax
A.k.a. **Children of the Night**
Minor horror-thriller: Evil countess resurrected as blooddrinking succubus

Daughters of Satan
1972, (USA), UA, color, 90 mins.
W: Tom Selleck (*James Robertson*), Barra Grant (*Chris Robertson*), Tani Phelps Guthrie (*Kitty Duarte*), Vic Salayan (*Dr. Dangal*), Paraluman (*Juana Rios*), Gina Laforteza (*Andrea*), Vic Diaz (*Carlos Ching*), Ben Rubio (*Tommy Tantuico*), Chito Reyes (*The Guerilla*), Paquito Salcedo (*The Mortician*), Bobby Greenwood (*Mrs. Postelwaite*)
P: Aubrey Schenck   **D:** Hollingsworth Morse   **SCR:** John C. Higgins   **STORY:** John Bushelman   **PHOTOG:** Nonong Rasca   **MUSIC:** Richard LaSalle
Minor fantasy-thriller: Couple tormented by witch coven

David and Goliath
1959, (It), Ansa/Beaver-Champion/Embassy, color, 95 mins.
W: Orson Welles (*King Saul*), Ivo Payer (*David*), Eleonora Rossi-Drago (*Merab*), Edward Hilton (*The Prophet Samuel*), Massimo Serato (*Abner*), Giulia Rubini (*Michael*), Umberto Fiz (*Lazar*), Pierre Cressoy (*Jonathan*), Furio Meniconi (*Asrod, King of Philistines*), Kronos (*Goliath*), Dante Maggio (*Cret*), Luigi Tosi (*Benjamin*), Ugo Sasso (*Huro*)
D: Richard Pottier & Ferdinando Baldi   **SCR:** Umberto Scarpelli, Gino Mangini, Ambrogio Molteni, & Emimmo Salvi   **PHOTOG:** Carlo Fiore & Cristiano Civirani   **ORIG. MUSIC:** Carlo Innocenzi   **MUSIC CONDUCT:** Giuseppe Savagnone
USA release, 1961
Modest "Sword & Sandal" rendering of biblical tale: Shepherd boy vs. enemy giant

Dave Craggs, Detective
1910, (GB), Hepworth, b&w, 850 ft. (259m)
D: Lewin Fitzhamon
Standard crime-thriller: Detective chases jewel thieves

David Devant, Conjuror
1903, (GB), Mutoscope & Biograph, b&w
W: David Devant
Minor fantasy short: Conjuror performs The Incubated Head & The Fairy Dancer.
cf. **D.Devant, Conjuror**

David Harding, Counterspy
1950, (USA), Col, b&w, 71 mins.
W: Willard Parker, Audrey Long, Howard St. John (*David Harding*)
Standard thriller

Dawn of the Dead
1979, (USA), Herbert R. Steinmann & Billy Baxter/Laurel, color, 126 mins.
W: David Emge (*Stephen*), Ken Foree (*Peter*), Scott H. Reiniger (*Roger*), Gaylen Ross (*Francine*)
D & SCR: George A. Romero   **PHOTOG:** Michael Gornick   **MUSIC:** Goblin
Euro-retitle, **Zombi**
Modest sequel to orig. **Night of the Living Dead**: *Zombie bites spread plague of Undead*
cf. **Day of the Dead**

Dawn of the Mummy
1981, (It-Egypt), Frank Agrama/Harmony Gold, color, 92 mins.
W: Brenda King, Barry Sattels, George Peck, Ibrahim Khan, John Salvo, Joan Levy, Ellene F aison, Diane Beatty, Ali Gohar, Ahmed Ratib, Baher Saied, Ali Azab, Ahmed Laban, Laila Nasr
D: Frank Agrama   **SCR:** Daria Price, Ronald Dobrin, & Frank Agrama   based on

a story by Ronald Dobrin, & Daria Price **PHOTOG:** Sergio Rubini & Massoud Issa **SPCL-FX:** Luigi Batistelli, Farid Abdoul Hai & Tony DiDio Jr. **MUSIC:** Shuki Y. Levy **MUSIC ORCHESTRATION:** Steve Rucker
Minor horror-thriller: Treasure-hunters and fashion models disturb mean-tempered mummy

The Day After
1983, (USA), ABC-TV, color, 126 mins.
W: Jason Robards Jr. (*Dr. Russell Oakes*), JoBeth Williams (*Nancy Bauer*), John Cullum (*Jim Dahlberg*), William Allen Young (*Airman McCoy*), John Lithgow (*Joe Huxley*), Bibi Besch (*Eve Dahlberg*), Georgann Johnson (*Helen Oakes*), Lori Lethin (*Denise Dahlberg*), Steve Guttenberg (*Stephen Klein*), Calvin Jung (*Dr. Sam Hachiya*), Kyle Aletter (*Marilyn Oakes*), Lin McCarthy (*Dr. Austin*), Doug Scott, Jeff East, Clayton Day, Dennis Lipscomb, Ellen Anthony
D: Nicholas Meyer **TELEPLAY:** Edward Hume **PHOTOG:** Gayne Rescher **ORIG. SCORE:** David Raksin
TVM, unusual SF-thriller: Aftermath of nuclear war

Dawn of the Dead: GAYLEN ROSS

The Day After Halloween
1980, (Austral), Australian Int'l, color, 92 mins.
W: Chantal Contouri, Robert Bruning, Sigrid Thornton, Hugh Keays-Byrne, Denise Drysdale, Vincent Gil, Jon Sidney, Peter Stratford, Jacqui Gordon, Julia Blake, Christine Amord,
D: Simon Wincer **SCR:** Chris & Everett DeRoche **PHOTOG:** Vincent Monton **MUSIC:** Brian May **SONG:** *Angela*
A.k.a. Snapshot
Minor melodrama: Model hounded by old boyfriend.

Daybreak
1993, (USA), Made for Cable color, 88 mins.
W: Cuba Gooding Jr., Moira Kelly, Omar Epps, Martha Plimpton
Made-for-Cable, minor SF-thriller: Young lovers oppose future quarantine

Daydreams
1913, (GB), Cricks & Martin, b&w, 425 ft. (129.5m)
D: Edwin J. Collins
Minor fantasy: Tramp dreams he owns magic cane

The Day It Came to Earth
1977, (USA), Rainbow/Atlas, color, 88 mins.
W: Wink Roberts, Roger Manning, Bob Ginnaven, George Gobel (*Prof. Bartholomew*), DeLight DeBruine, Rita Wilson, Ed Love
D: Harry Thomason **SCR:** Paul J. Fiske **PHOTOG:** Mike Varner **MUSIC:** Joe Southerland
orig. **The Creature from North of Midnight**
Amateurish SF-horror: Meteorite animates corpses. Rita Wilson's debut

Daylight
1996, (USA), Univ, color, 109 mins.
W: Sylvester Stallone (*Kit Latura*), Amy Brenneman (*Madelyne Thompson*), Viggo Mortensen (*Roy Nord*), Jay O. Sanders (*Steven Crighton*), Karen Young (*Sarah Crighton*), Danielle Harris (*Ashley Crighton*), Claire Bloom (*Eleanor Trilling*), Colin Fox (*Roger Trilling*), Vanessa Bell Calloway (*Grace*), Stan Shaw (*George Tyrell*), Sage Stallone (*Vincent*), Dan Hedaya, Barry Newman, Jo Anderson, Renoly Santiago, Trina McGee-Davis, Marcello Thedford, Mark Rolston, Rosemary Forsyth, Luoyong Wang, Lee Oakes, Marc Chadwick, Candace Miller, Sakina Jaffrey, Albert Macklin, Tony Munafo, John Lees, Joseph Ragno, Nestor Serrano, Harold Bradley, Robert Sommer, Stephen Nalewicki, Lenore Lohman, Mark DeAlessandro, Madison, Lisa McCullough, Penny Crone, Ed Wheeler, Dan Daily, Stephen James, Isis Mussenden
D: Rob Cohen **SCR:** Leslie Bohem **PHOTOG:** David Eggby **MUSIC:** Randy Edelman **SONG:** *Whenever There is Love* (sung by Donna Summer & Bruce Roberts)
Standard disaster-thriller: Mixed group trapped in Holland Tunnel

The Day Mars Invaded Earth
1963, (USA), Assoc. Prods./20th-Fox, b&w, 70 mins.
W: Kent Taylor (*Dr. David Fielding*), Marie Windsor (*Claire Fielding*), William Mims (*Webb*), Betty Beall (*Judi Fielding*), Lowell Brown, Gregg Shank, Henrietta Moore, George Riley, Troy Melton
P & D: Maury Dexter **SCR:** Harry Spalding **PHOTOG:** John Nickolaus Jr. **MUSIC:** Richard LaSalle
Minor but effective SF-chiller: Alien beings try to supplant Earth family

Day of the Animals: MICHAEL ANSARA

Day of the Animals
1977, (USA), Edward L. Montoro/Film Ventures, color, 97 mins.
W: Christopher George (*Steve Buckner*), Lynda Day George (*Terry Marsh*), Leslie Nielsen (*Jensen*), Richard Jaeckel (*MacGregor*), Michael Ansara (*Santee*), Ruth Roman (*Shirley Goodwin*), Paul Mantee (*Roy Moore*), Jon Cedar (*Frank Young*), Walter Barnes, Andrew Stevens, Bobby Porter, Garrison True, Michelle Stacy, Gil Lamb, Michael Andreas, Gertrude Lee, Jan Andrew Scott
D: William Girdler **SCR:** William Norton & Eleanor Norton **PHOTOG:** Robert Sorrentino **MUSIC:** Lalo Schifrin
Gripping SF-thriller: Earth's ozonosphere damaged, cosmic rays drive animals mad

Day of the Dead
1985, (USA), Laurel/UFD, color, 102 mins.
W: Lori Cardille (*Sarah*), Terry Alexander, Richard Liberty, Joe Pilato, Howard Sherman, Jarlath Conroy, G. Howard Klar, Antone DiLeo, Don Brockett, William Cameron
D & SCR: George A. Romero **PHOTOG:** Michael Gornick **MUSIC:** John Harrison
Standard horror-thriller, conclusion of Romero's **Living Dead** *trilogy: Scientists bottle cannibalistic corpses. cf.* **Night of the Living Dead** *(1968) and* **Dawn of the Dead**

The Day of the Dolphin
1974, (USA), Joseph E. Levine/Avco Embassy, color, 104 mins.
W: George C. Scott (*Dr. Jake Terrell*), Trish Van Devere (*Maggie Terrell*), Paul Sorvino (*Mahoney*), Edward Herrmann (*Mike*), Fritz Weaver (*Harold DeMilo*), William Roerick (*Dunhill*), Jon Korkes (*David*), Leslie Charleson (*Maryanne*), John Dehner (*Wallingford*), Victoria Racimo (*Lana*), Phyllis Davis (*The Sec'y*), John David Carson (*Larry*), Elizabeth Wilson (*Mrs. Rome*), Severn Darden (*Schwinn*), Julie Follansbee (*The 1st Woman at Club*), Florence Stanley (*The 2nd Woman at Club*), Brooke Hayward (*The 3rd Woman at Club*), Willie Meyers
P: Robert E. Relyea **D:** Mike Nichols **SCR:** Buck Henry, from Robert Merle's novel **PHOTOG:** William A. Fraker **SPCL-FX:** Jim White **MUSIC:** Georges Delerue
Superior SF-thriller: Political intrigue clouds dolphin experiments

Day of the Nightmare
1965, (USA), Herts-Lion, b&w
W: John Ireland, Elena Verdugo, John Hart, Liz Renay
P: Leon Bleiberg **D:** John Bushelman **SCR:** Leonard Goldstein **PHOTOG:** Ted V. Mikels
Minor thriller: Artist plots murders

The Day of the Triffids
1963, (GB), Security/AA, color, 95 mins.
W: Howard Keel (*Bill Mason*), Nicole Maurey (*Christine Durrant*), Janette Scott (*Karen Goodwin*), Kieron Moore (*Tom Goodwin*), Mervyn Johns (*Mr. Coker*), Alison Leggatt (*Mrs. Coker*), Ewan Roberts (*Dr. Soames*), Janina Faye (*Susan*), Geoffrey Matthews (*Luis de la Vega*), Gilgi Hauser (*Teresa de la Vega*), Carole Ann Ford, Colette Wilde, Victor Brooks, Ian Wilson
P: George Pitcher **D:** Steve Sekely **SCR:** Philip Yordan, from John Wyndham's novel **PHOTOG:** Ted Moore **SPCL-FX:** Wally Veevers **MUSIC:** Ron Goodwin
Standard thriller: Meteor shower mutates plants

Day of the Woman
see *I Spit on Your Grave*

Day of Wrath
see *Vredens Dag*

The Day the Earth Caught Fire
1961, (GB), Val Guest/British Lion-Pax/Univ, b&w, 99 mins.
W: Edward Judd (*Peter Stenning*), Janet Munro (*Jeannie*), Leo McKern (*Bill Maguire*), Michael Goodliffe (*The Night Editor*), Reginald Beckwith (*Harry*), Renee Asherson (*Angela*), Bernard Braden (*The News Editor*), Austin Trevor (*Sir John Kelly*), Gene Anderson (*May*), Arthur Christiansen (*The Editor*), Edward Underdown
P & D: Val Guest   SCR: Wolf Mankowitz & Val Guest   PHOTOG: Harry Waxman   SPCL-FX: Les Bowie   MUSIC: Stanley Black
Modest SF-thriller: Atom tests disrupt Earth's orbit

The Day the Earth Froze
see *Sampa*

The Day the Earth Stood Still
1951, (USA), 20th-Fox, b&w, 92 mins.
W: Michael Rennie (*Klaatu*), Patricia Neal (*Helen Benson*), Hugh Marlowe (*Tom Stevens*), Billy Gray (*Bobby Benson*), Sam Jaffe (*Prof. Jacob Bernhardt*), Lock Martin (*Gort the Robot*), Frances Bavier, James Seay, Frank Conroy, Carleton Young, Robert Osterloh, Edith Evanson, Fay Roope, Tyler McVey, Dorothy Neumann
P: Julian Blaustein   D: Robert Wise   SCR: Edmund H. North   based on Harry Bates' short story *Farewell to the Master*   PHOTOG: Leo Tover   SPCL-FX: Fred Sersen   MUSIC: Bernard Herrmann
Spanish retitle, *Ultimatum to Earth*
"...a beautiful movie. The simple-yet-effective special effects have a dignified, restrained quality about them, and (the) musical score captures the precise mood of awe and mystery inherent in the visuals"—Gary Gerani, "The Space Monster Book—Chapter Two: The Universe Next Door," Monster Fantasy, Vol. 1, No. 4 (August, 1975), p. 26
"...one of the very best SF films"—Jim Harmon, "The Coming of the Robots," Fantastic Monsters of the Films, Vol. 1, No. 5 (1963), p. 56
Major SF classic: Earthlings amazed by alien spaceman and his robot companion

The Day the Fish Came Out
1967, (GB-Greece), Int'l Classics/20th-Fox, color, 109 mins.
W: Tom Courtenay (*The Navigator*), Colin Blakely (*The Pilot*), Sam Wanamaker (*Elias*), Candice Bergen (*Electra*), Ian Ogilvy (*Peter*), Patricia Burke (*Mrs. Mavroyannis*), Dimitris Nicolaides (*The Dentist*), Tom Klunis (*Mr. French*), Nicos Alexiou (*The Goatherd*), Costas Papaconstantinou (*Manolias*)
WRIT, P & D: Michael Cacoyannis   PHOTOG: Walter Lassally   MUSIC: Mikis Theodorakis
Standard SF-comedy: A-bombs lost over Aegean Sea

The Day the Screaming Stopped
1978, (GB), Bedford, colorWalker/Heritage/Enterprise/Bedford, 100 mins.
W: Jack Jones (*Nick Cooper*), David Doyle (*Webster Jones*), Richard Johnson (*Dr. Macauley*), Sheila Keith (*Mrs. B*), Pamela Stephenson (*Linda Everett*), Bill Owen (*Mr. B*), Holly Palance (*Gail Cooper*), Peter Turner (*Harry*), Patrick Brock (*Dr. Paulsen*), June Chadwick (*The Nurse*), Penny Irving (*The Singer*)
P & D: Pete Walker   SCR: Murray Smith   PHOTOG: Peter Jessop   MUSIC: Stanley Myers
USA retitle, *The Comeback*
Unusual thriller: Singer goes insane

The Day the Sky Exploded
see *Death Comes from Space*

Day the World Ended
1955, (USA), Golden State/AIP, b&w, 81 mins.
W: Richard Denning, Lori Nelson, Paul Birch, Adele Jergens, "Touch" [Michael] Connors, Paul Dubov, Raymond Hatton, Paul Blaisdell (*The Mutant*), Jonathan Haze
P & D: Roger Corman   SCR: Lou Rusoff   PHOTOG: Jock Feindel
blurb: "A new high in naked shrieking terror!"
*Standard SF-thriller: Atom-war strands mixed group in remote canyon. cf. **In the Year 2889***

Day the World Ended (1980)
see *When Time Ran Out*

The Day Time Ended
1978, (Sp), Compass Int'l, color 79 mins.
W: Jim Davis (*Grant*), Chris Mitchum (*Richard*), Dorothy Malone (*Ana*), Marcy Lafferty (*Beth*), Natasha Ryan (*Jenny*), Scott Kolden (*Steve*)
D: John "Bud" Cardos   SCR: Wayne Schmidt, J. Larry Carroll & David Schmoeller   STORY: Steve Neill   PHOTOG: John Murill   MUSIC: Richard Band
A.k.a. *Vortex*
Standard SF-thriller: Family enters time warp

Dead Again
1991, (USA), Mirage/Para, color, 108 mins.
W: Kenneth Branagh (*Roman Strauss/Mike Church*), Andy Garcia (*Gray Baker*), Emma Thompson (*Margaret Strauss/Grace*), Derek Jacobi (*Franklyn Madison*), Robin Williams (*Dr. Cozy Carlisle*), Hanna Schygulla (*Inga*), Campbell Scott (*Doug*), Christine Ebersole (*Lydia Larson*), Lois Hall (*Sister Constance*), Richard Easton (*Father Timothy*), Jo Anderson (*Sister Madeleine*), Erik Kilpatrick, Raymond Cruz, Patrick Montes, Wayne Knight, Obba Babatunde, Patrick Doyle, Gordon Rashovich, Vasek C. Simek, Gregor Hesse, John Gould Rubin, Steven Culp, Yvette Freeman
D: Kenneth Branagh   SCR: Scott Frank   PHOTOG: Matthew F. Leonetti   MUSIC: Patrick Doyle
Offbeat psychodrama: Old murder clouds reincarnation

Dead Air
1994, (USA), color, 91 mins.
W: Gregory Hines, Debrah Farentino, Gloria Reuben, Michael Harris, Beau Starr, Laura Harrington, W. Earl Brown, Veronica Cartwright
D: Fred Walton   SCR: David Amann   MUSIC: Dana Kaproff
Standard thriller: Mystery woman menaces deejay

Dead Alive
1992, (New Zealand), Trimark, color, 97 mins.
W: Timothy Balme, Diana Penalver, Elizabeth Moody, Ian Watkin, Jed Brophy, Brenda Kendall, Jamie Selkirk, Jim Booth, Stuart Devenie, Nick Ward, James Grant, Michelle Turner
D: Peter Jackson   SCR: Peter Jackson, Frances Walsh & Stephen Sinclair   Photog: Murray Milne   MUSIC: Peter Dasent   SONGS *The Moon and Stars & 29 Steps*
Standard horror-thriller: Animal bite transforms mother into ravenous zombie

Dead and Buried
1981, (USA), Ronald Shusett/Richard R. St. Johns/Avco Embassy, color, 95 mins.
W: James Farentino (*Dan*), Melody Anderson (*Janet*), Jack Albertson (*Dobbs*), Dennis Redfield (*Ron*), Nancy Locke Hauser (*Linda*), Lisa Blount (*The Girl on the Beach*), Barry Corbin (*Phil*), Bill Quinn (*Ernie*), Robert Englund (*Harry*), Michael Currie (*Herman*), Lisa Marie (*The Hitchhiker*), Estelle Omens (*Betty*), Christopher Allport (*George Le Moyne/"Freddie"*), Ed Bakey (*The Fisherman*), Joe Medalis (*The Doctor*), Jill Fosse (*The Nurse*), Macon McCalman (*Ben*), Linda Turley (*The Waitress*), Glenn Morshower (*Jimmy*), Robert Boler (*Mr. Haskell*), Mark & Michael Courtney (*Jamie*), Renee McDonnell (*Girl #1*), Dottie Catching (*The Lady Car Passenger*), Colby Smith (*The Female Stranger*), Judy Ashton (*Joyce*), Michael Pataki (*Sam*), Charles Couch, Bill Couch, Bill Couch Jr., Tony Cecere, Angelo DeMeo
D: Gary A. Sherman   SCR: Ronald Shusett & Dan O'Bannon, from a story by Jeff Millar & Alex Stern   PHOTOG: Steve Poster   SPCL-FX: Knott Limited   MUSIC: Joe Renzetti
Modest horror-thriller: Strange murders and corpse disappearances in small New England town

The Dead and the Deadly
1982, (Hong Kong), color, 90 mins.
W: Samo Hung, Yuen Biao
D: Wu Ma
Standard action-fantasy: Youth dabbles in sorcery

The Dead Are Alive
1972, (It), Nat'l General, color, 98 mins.
W: Alex Cord (*Jason*), Samantha Eggar (*Myra*), Nadja Tiller (*Leni*), John Marley (*Nikos*), Horst Frank (*Stephan*), Carlo de Mejo (*Igor*), Enzo Tarascio (*Giuranna*), Enzo Cerusico (*Alberto*), Vladan Milasinovic (*Otello*), Christiane Von Blank (*Velia*), Daniela Surina (*Irene*), Mario Maranzana (*Vitanza*), Pier Luigi D'Orazio (*Minelli*), Wendy D'Olive (*Giselle*), Ivan Pavicevac (*The Policeman*)
D: Armando Crispino   SCR: Lucio Battistrada & Armando Crispino   PHOTOG: Enrico Menczer   MUSIC: Riz Ortolani
Modest horror-fantasy: Predations of Etruscan demon-god

Dead as a Doorman
1985, (USA), color, 83 mins.
W: Bradley Whitford, Sharon Schlarth, Bruce Taylor
D: Gary Youngman
Minor thriller: Murderous psycho targets doorman

Dead Bang
1989, (USA), color, 102 mins.
W: Don Johnson, Penelope Ann Miller, William Forsythe, Bob Balaban, Frank Military, Tate Donovan
D: John Frankenheimer
Routine thriller: Homicide cop meets neo-Nazis

Deadbolt
1992, (USA), Pierre David/Allegro-Image, color, 95 mins.
W: Justine Bateman (*Marty*), Adam Baldwin (*Alex*), Michele Scarabelli (*Theresa*), Chris Mulkey (*Jordan*), Amy Fulco (*Michelle*), Cyndi Pass (*Diana*), Ellen Cohen (*Lani*), Colin Fox (*Prof. Rhodes*), Anthony Sherwood, Griffith Brewer, Mark Camacho, Isabelle Truchon, Gordon Masten, Shirley Merovitz, Don Jordan, Bernadette Li, Philip Spensley, Dominique Perreault, Nancy Boulanger, Bree Asher, Paul Valade

D: Douglas Jackson **SCR:** Mara Trafficante & Frank Rehwaldt **PHOTOG:** Rodney Gibbons **SPCL-FX SPRVSR:** Ryal Cosgrove **MUSIC:** Milan Kymlicki **SONGS:** *Better Get Ready & Got Me a True Love*
Standard thriller: Female medical student gets male psychopath for roommate

Dead Calm
1989, (Austral), Kennedy Miller/WB, color, 96 mins.
W: Sam Neill, Nicole Kidman, Billy Zane
D: Phillip Noyce **SCR:** Terry Hayes, from Charles Williams novel **PHOTOG:** Dean Semler **ORIG. MUSIC:** Graeme Revell
Unusual thriller: Psychotic imperils yachting couple

The Dead Can't Lie
see **Gotham**

Dead Certain
1992, (USA), color, 93 mins.
W: Brad Dourif, Francesco Quinn, Karen Russell, Joel Kaiser
D & SCR: Anders Palm
*Minor thriller (**Silence of the Lambs** imitation): Serial killer aids police*

Dead Cold
1995, (USA), Image, color, 90 mins.
W: Lysette Anthony, Chris Mulkey, Peter Dobson, Michael Champion, Alina Thompson, Anneliza Scott, Apache Moon
SPCL-FX: Kevin McCarthy
Made-for-Video, standard thriller: Mysterious stranger disturbs writer and his wife

The Dead Don't Die
1975, (USA), NBC-TV, color, 75 mins.
W: George Hamilton (*Don Drake*), Ray Milland (*Jim Moss*), Linda Cristal (*Vera La Valle*), Joan Blondell (*Levenia*), James McEachin (*Frankie Specht*), Ralph Meeker (*Lt. Reardon*), Reggie Nalder (*Perdido*), Jerry Douglas (*Ralph Drake*), Milton Parsons (*The Undertaker*), William O'Connell (*The Priest*), Yvette Vickers
P: Henry Colman **D:** Curtis Harrington **TELEPLAY:** Robert Bloch **PHOTOG:** James Crabe
TVM, unusual horror-thriller: Sailor confronts zombies

The Dead Do Not Forgive
see **Los Muertos No Perdonan**

Dead Drop
see **Chain Reaction** *(1996)*

Dead Dudes in the House
1991, (USA), color, 95 mins.
W: Mark Zobian, Victor Verhaeghe, Doug Gibson
Minor thriller: Killer granny slays occupants of rundown house

Dead End Drive-In
1986, (Austral), Apringvale-New South Wales Film Corp./New World, color, 92 mins.
W: Ned Manning, Natalie McCurry (*Carmen*), Wilbur Wilde (*Hazza*), Peter Whitford

Deadlier than The Male: NIGEL GREEN

Dead Connection
1993, (USA), Propaganda/Polygram, color, 93 mins.
W: Michael Madsen, Lisa Bonet, Gary Stretch, Damian Chapa, Tim Russ, Carmen Argenziano, Clarence Landry, Nicholas Kenny, Lisa Sinclair, Simon Kenny, Andrew Shaw, Parker Posey, Connie Blankenship, John Clayton Schafer, Jimmy Ortega, Paul Leslie Disley, Eric DaRe, Brenda Swanson, Julio Oscar Mechoso, Alan Toy, Shawne Rowe, Ava Dupree, Curt Smith, Dr. John Ciambotti, Ernesto Hernandez, Rick Marotta, Thunderwolf, Alex Desia, Ben Bray, Sonny Mascar, Ernie Lee Banks, Susan Byun, John Robert Clark, Shawn Huff, Carl Mueller
D: Nigel Dick **SCR:** Larry Golin **STORY:** Jonathan Tydor Photog: David Bridges **SPCL-FX SPRVSR:** Mike Schorr **MUSIC:** Rolfe Kent **SONGS:** *You Got What It Takes, Man to Man,"No Two Bit Judge & Now Is the Time*
Standard thriller

D: Brian Trenchard-Smith **SCR:** Peter Smalley **PHOTOG:** Paul Murphy **ORIG. MUSIC:** Frank Strangio
Minor thriller: Teens trapped in satanic outdoor theater

Dead Eyes of London
see **Die Toten Augen von London**

Deadfall
1967, (GB), Salamanda/20th-Fox, color, 120 mins.
W: Michael Caine (*Henry Clarke*), Giovanna Ralli (*Fe Moreau*), Eric Portman (*Richard Moreau*), Nanette Newman (*The Girl*), David Buck (*Salinas*), Carlos Pierre (*Antonio*), Vladek Sheybal (*Dr. Delgado*), Leonard Rossiter (*Fillmore*), John Barry (*The Conductor*), Carmen Dene (*The Masseuse*), Emilio Rodriguez (*Insp. Ballasteros*)
WRIT & D: Bryan Forbes, from a novel by Desmond Cory **MUSIC:** John Barry, **TITLE:** Shirley Bassey
Minor thriller: Jewel thief involved with unsavory types

Dead Fire
1998, (USA), SCI-TV, color, 95 mins.
W: Matt Frewer, Colin Cunningham, C. Thomas Howell
Made-for-Cable, standard SF-thriller: Space station orbits fatally-polluted Earth

The Dead Heart
1914, (GB), Hepworth/Walturdaw, b&w, 3,225 ft. (983m)
W: Alice de Winton (*Catherine*), Lionelle Howard (*St. Valery*), Harry Gilbey (*Robert Landy*), William Felton (*Abbe Latour*), Edward Lingard (*Count St. Valery*), Claire Pridelle (*Cerisette*), John McAndrews (*Jocrisse*), James Lindsay
D: Hay Plumb **SCR:** Muriel Alleyne & Reginald Hargreaves, from a play by Watts Phillips
Standard adventure: 18th-century Frenchman avenges himself on count's son

Dead Heat
1988, (USA), Helpern-Meltzer/New World, color, 87 mins.
W: Treat Williams (*Roger Mortis*), Joe Piscopo (*Doug Bigelow*), Lindsay Frost (*Randi James*), Darren McGavin (*Dr. Ernest McNab*), Vincent Price (*Arthur P. Loudermilk*), Clare Kirkconnell (*Rebecca Smythers*), Keye Luke, Robert Picardo, Mel Stewart
D: Mark Goldblatt **SCR:** Terry Black **PHOTOG:** Robert D. Yeoman **MUSIC:** Ernest Troost
Minor SF-comedy: Slain cops revived

Dead Image
see *Dead Ringer*

Dead Kids
see *Strange Behavior* (1981)

Deadlier Than the Male
1967, (GB), Rank/Univ, color, 98 mins.
W: Richard Johnson (*Hugh "Bulldog" Drummond*), Elke Sommer (*Irma Eckman*), Sylva Koscina (*Penelope*), Nigel Green (*Carl Peterson/Weston*), Suzanna Leigh (*Grace*), Laurence Naismith (*Sir John Bledlow*), Virginia North (*Brenda*), Steve Carlson (*Robert Drummond*), Justine Lord (*Miss Asheden*), Lee Montague (*Boxer*), Zia Moyheddin (*King Fedra*), George Pastell (*Carloggio*), Yasuko Nagazumi (*Mitsouko*), Leonard Rossiter (*Bridgenworth*), Milton Reid (*Chang*)
P: Betty E. Box **D:** Ralph Thomas **SCR:** Jimmy Sangster, David Osborn, & Liz Charles-Williams, from characters created by Sapper **PHOTOG:** Ernest Steward **MUSIC:** Malcolm Lockyer
Modest thriller: Master criminal uses female assassins

The Deadliest Sin
1955, (GB), AA, b&w, 75 mins.
W: Sydney Chaplin, Audrey Dalton
Standard melodrama. UK title: Confession

The Deadliest Sin
see *Confession* (1955)

Deadline
1982, (USA), color, 85 mins.
W: Stephen Young, Sharon Masters, Phillip Leonard, Cindy Hinds
D: Mario Azzopardi
Stadard fantasy-thriller: Horror writer's life begins to reflect his latest story

Deadline at Dawn
1946, (USA), RKO, b&w, 83 mins.
W: Susan Hayward, Bill Williams, Osa Massen, Lola Lane, Paul Lukas, Joseph Calleia, Jerome Cowan, Marvin Miller, Roman Bohnen, Steven Geray
D: Harold Clurman **SCR:** Clifford Odets Photog: Nicholas Musuraca **MUSIC:** Hanns Eisler
Standard thriller: Dance-hall girl involved with sailor accused of murder

Deadline for Murder
1946, (USA), 20th-Fox, b&w, 65 mins.
W: Paul Kelly, Kent Taylor
Standard thriller

Deadlock
1991, (USA), color, 103 mins.
W: Rutger Hauer, Mimi Rogers, Joan Chen, Stephen Tobolowsky, James Remar, Basil Wallace
D: Lewis Teague
Made-for-Cable, standard SF: convicts of future pursued

Deadlock 2
1994, (USA), color, 120 mins.
W: Esai Morales, Nia Peeples, Stephen McHattie, Jon Cuthbert
D: Graeme Campbell
Made-for-Cable, standard SF: Inmates in prison of future

Deadlock: A Passion for Murder
1996, (USA), color, 85 mins.
W: Doug Jeffrey, Shauna O'Brien
Made-for-Video, standard thriller: Detective hired to protect pornography magnate

Dead Lucky
1960, (GB), ACT Films/British Lion, b&w, 64 mins.
W: Vincent Ball (*Mike Billings*), Betty McDowall (*Jenny Drew*), John LeMesurier (*Insp. Corcoran*), Alfred Burke (*Knocker Parsons*), Michael Ripper (*Percy Simpson*), Sam Kydd (*Harry Winston*), Brian Worth (*Lucky Lewis*), John Charlesworth (*Hon. Stanley Dewsbury*), Joan Heal (*The Barmaid*), Frederick Piper (*Harvey Walters*), Chili Bouchier (*Mrs. Winston*)
P: Ralph Bond & Robert Dunbar **D:** Montgomery Tully **STORY:** Sidney Nelson & Maurice Harrison
Standard crime-thriller: Reporter's girlfriend accused of killing gambler

Deadly
1991, (Austral), color, 101 mins.
W: Jerome Ehlers, Frank Gallagher, John Moore
D: Esben Storm
Standard thriller: Cop probes Aborigine's "suicide"

Deadly Advice
1993, (GB), color, 91 mins.
W: Jane Horrocks, Brenda Fricker, Imelda Staunton, Jonathan Pryce, Edward Woodward, Ian Abbey, John Mills, Billie Whitelaw, Hywel Bennett, Eleanor Bron
D: Mandie Fletcher **SCR:** Glenn Chandler
Unusual fantasy-satire: Woman contemplates mother's murder, is given advice by literary characters

The Deadly Affair
1967, (GB), Col, color, 107 mins.
W: James Mason (*Charles Dobbs*), Simone Signoret (*Elsa Fennan*), Maximilian Schell (*Dieter Frey*), Harriet Anderson (*Anna Dobbs*), Harry Andrews (*Insp. Mendel*), Kenneth Haigh (*Bill Appleby*), Roy Kinnear (*Adam Scarr*), Max Adrian (*The Adviser*), Lynn Redgrave (*Miss Bumpus*), Robert Flemyng (*Samuel Fennan*), Leslie Sands (*The Inspector*), Corin Redgrave (*David*), Les White (*Harek*), June Murphy (*Witch*), Sheraton Blount (*Eunice Scarr*), David Warner (*Edward II*), Michael Bryant (*Gaveston*), Stanley Lebor (*Lancaster*), Paul Hardwick (*Mortimar*)
P & D: Sidney Lumet **SCR:** Paul Dehn based on John Le Carre's novel *Call for the Dead* **PHOTOG:** Frederick A. Young **MUSIC:** Quincy Jones
Standard thriller: Civil servant trails murderer

The Deadly Bees
1966, (GB), Amicus/Para, color, 84 mins.
W: Guy Doleman (*Ralph Hargrove*), Suzanna Leigh (*Vicky Robbins*), Frank Finlay (*Manfred*), Catherine Finn (*Mary Hargrove*), John Harvey (*Thompson*), Michael Ripper (*Dave Hawkins*), Katy Wild (*Doris*), Tim Barrett (*Harcourt*), Michael Gwynn (*Dr. Lang*), James Cossins, Anthony Bailey
P: Milton Subotsky & Max J. Rosenberg **SCR:** Robert Bloch & Anthony Marriott, based on H.F. Heard's novel *A Taste for Honey* **PHOTOG:** John Wilcox **MUSIC:** Wilfred Josephs
Modest thriller: Bee-keeper trains his charges to kill

Deadly Blessing
1981, (USA), Inter Planetary/Polygram/UA, color, 102 mins.
W: Maren Jensen (*Martha*), Ernest Borgnine (*Isaiah*), Sharon Stone (*Lana*), Lois Nettleton (*Louisa*), Jeff East (*Schmidt*), Susan Buckner (*Vicky*), Doug Barr (*Jim*), Michael Berryman (*Gluntz*), Lisa Hartman (*Faith*), Kevin Cooney (*The Sheriff*), Coleen Riley (*Melissa*), Bobby Dark (*The Theatre Manager*), Kevin Farr (*The Fat Boy*), Neil Fletcher (*The Gravedigger*), Jonathan Gulla (*Tom*), Chester Kulas Jr. (*Leopold*), Lawrence Montaigne (*Matthew*), Lucky Mosley (*Sammy*), Dan Shackelford (*The Medic*), Annabelle Weenick (*Ruth*), Jenna Worthen (*Mrs. Gluntz*), Percy Rodrigues (*The Narrator*)
D: Wes Craven **SCR:** Glenn M. Benest, Matthew Barr, & Wes Craven **STORY:** Glenn M. Benest & Matthew Barr **PHOTOG:** Robert Jessup **MUSIC:** James Horner
Minor thriller: Madness and murder in Amish countryside

The Deadly Circle
see *Honeymoon of Horror*

Deadly Daphne's Revenge
1993, (USA), Troma, color, 98 mins.
Minor thriller: Rapist pursued by victims

The Deadly Diaphanoids
1966, (It), color
W: Tony Russel, Lisa Gastoni
D: Anthony Dawson [Antonio Margheriti]
Minor SF-thriller: Terror from outer space

The Deadly Dream
1971, (USA), Univ/CBS-TV, color, 73 mins.
W: Lloyd Bridges, Janet Leigh, Richard Jaeckel, Carl Betz, Leif Erick-son, Don Stroud
D: Alf Kjellin **TELEPLAY:** Barry Oringer
TVM, minor thriller with echoes of Kafka: Scientist is persecuted for unexplained crime

Deadly Dreams

1988, (USA), color 79 mins.
<u>W</u>: Mitchell Anderson, Xander Berkeley, Thom Babbes, Juliette Cummins
<u>D</u>: Kristine Peterson   <u>SCR</u>: Thom Babbes
Standard thriller: Maniac slays boy's parents

Deadly Dust

1978, (USA), CBS TV, color, 93 mins.
<u>W</u>: Nicholas Hammond, Robert Alda, JoAnna Cameron, Michael Pataki, Randy Powell
<u>D</u>: Ron Satlof
TVM, minor SF-fantasy culled from Amazing Spider-Man teleseries: Superhero tries to retrieve A-bomb

Deadly Eyes

1983, (Can), Filmtrust/Golden Harvest/WB, color, 85 mins.
<u>W</u>: Sam Groom, *(Paul)*, Sara Botsford, *(Kelly)*, Scatman Crothers, *(George)*, Cec Linder, *(Dr. Spenser)*, Lisa Langlois, *(Trudy)*, Lesleh Donaldson, *(Martha)* James B. Douglas, *(Mel)*, David Cardoza
<u>D</u>: Robert Clouse   <u>SCR</u>: Charles Eglee, based on James Herbert's novel *The Rats*
   <u>PHOTOG</u>: Rene Verzier   <u>SPCL-FX</u>: Malivoire Prods. & Allan Apone
   <u>MUSIC</u>: Anthony Guefen
Modest SF-thriller: Steroid mishap creates super-rodents

The Deadly Females

1976, (GB), Donwin/Monarch, color, 105 mins.
<u>W</u>: Tracy Reed *(Joan)*, Bernard Holley *(Roger)*, Scott Fredericks *(Mark)*, Heather Chasen *(Frances)*, Roy Purcell *(Sir Charles)*, Brian Jackson *(Tony)*, Jean Harrington *(Mary Adams)*, Olivia Munday *(Diana)*, Jean Rimmer *(Elizabeth)*, Raymond Young *(Michael)*, Lana Travers *(Josie)*, Angela Jay *(Samantha)*, Gennie Nevison *(Vickie)*, Rula Lenska *(Luisa)*
<u>WRIT, P, & D</u>: Donovan Winter   <u>PHOTOG</u>: Austin Parker
Standard thriller: Woman antiquarian runs assassination bureau

Deadly Friend

1986, (USA), Pan Arts-Layton/WB, color, 92 mins.
<u>W</u>: Matthew Laborteaux *(Paul)*, Kristy Swanson *(Samantha)*, Michael Sharrett *(Tom)*, Anne Twomey *(Jeanne Conway)*, Lee Paul *(Police Sgt. Volcheck)*, Richard Marcus *(Harry)*, Anne Ramsey *(Elvira Williams)*, Andrew Roperto *(Carl Denton)*, Russ Marin *(Dr. Johanson)*
<u>D</u>: Wes Craven   <u>SCR</u>: Bruce Joel Rubin, based on Diana Henstell's novel *Friend*
   <u>PHOTOG</u>: Philip Lathrop   <u>MUSIC</u>: Charles Bernstein
Standard SF-horror: Robotics whiz animates dead girlfriend

Deadly Game

1991, (USA), Wilshire Court/USA-TV, color, 95 mins.
<u>W</u>: Michael Beck, Jenny Seagrove, Roddy McDowall, Marc Singer, Mitchell Ryan, Abdul Salaam El Razzac, Fredric Lehne, Joseph Arias, Steven Leigh, Soon-Teck Oh, John Pleshette, Brittany Almond, Jerry Basham, Larry Boothby, Richard Duran, Russ Fast, Tom Enyart, Sombra Forrest, Rick Jones, Lisa Sigel, T. Julian Wright, Jacqui Sutton, Prof. Toru Tanaka
<u>D</u>: Thomas J. Wright   <u>TELEPLAY</u>: Wes Claridge   <u>PHOTOG</u>: Frank Beascoeche   <u>SPCL-FX</u>: Rick Josephsen   <u>MUSIC</u>: Tim Truman
TVM, standard thriller: Madman hunts humans

Deadly Harvest

1976, (Can), color, 86 mins.
<u>W</u>: Clint Walker, Nehemiah Persoff, Kim Cattrall
Minor SF-thriller: Revenge sought in famine-plagued future

Deadly Intent

1988, (USA), color 83 mins.
<u>W</u>: Steve Railsback, Maud Adams, Fred Williamson, Persis Khambatta, Lance Henriksen Lisa Eilbacher
<u>D</u>: Nigel Dick
Minor thriller: Greedy group seeks priceless gem

Deadly Intruder

1984, (USA), color, 86 mins.
<u>W</u>: Chris Holder, Molly Creek
Minor thriller: Escaped maniac disrupts vacation

Deadly Invasion: The Killer Bee Nightmare

1995, (USA), Fox-TV, color, 95 mins.
<u>W</u>: Robert Hays *(Chad Ingram)*, Nancy Stafford *(Karen Ingram)*, Dennis Christopher *(Beauchamp)*, Ryan Phillippe *(Tom Redman)*, Gina Philips *(Tracy Ingram)*
TVM, standard thriller: Africanized honeybees attack an agrarian California community

Deadly Lessons

1983, (USA), ABC-TV, color, 95 mins.
<u>W</u>: Donna Reed *(Miss Wade)*, David Ackroyd *(Ferrar)*, Larry Wilcox *(Det. Kemper)*, Diane Franklin *(Stefanie)*, Donald Hotton *(Hardigan)*, Ally Sheedy *(Marita)*
<u>D</u>: William Wiard   <u>TELEPLAY</u>: Jennifer Miller
TVM, standard thriller: Murders at girl's boarding school

Deadly Love

1995, (USA), Lifetime, color, 95 mins.
<u>W</u>: Susan Dey, Stephen McHattie
Minor horror-fantasy: Vampiric woman photographer loves cop

The Deadly Mantis

1957, (USA), Univ, b&w, 78 mins.
<u>W</u>: Craig Stevens *(Col. Parkman)*, William Hopper *(Dr. Ned Jackson)*, Alix Talton *(Marjorie Blaine)*, Donald Randolph, Florenz Ames, Pat Conway, Floyd Simmons, Phil Harvey, Paul Smith, Helen Jay, Paul Campbell
<u>P</u>: William Alland   <u>D</u>: Nathan Juran   <u>SCR</u>: Martin Berkeley, from writings by William Alland   <u>PHOTOG</u>: Ellis W. Carter   <u>MUSIC</u>: Joseph Gershenson
French retitle, The Thing That Leapt from Nowhere, Swedish retitle, Continent in Panic, A.k.a. The Incredible Praying Mantis
Standard SF-thriller: Giant insect emerges from polar ice

Deadly Messages

1985, (USA), Col/ABC-TV, color, 96 mins.
<u>W</u>: Kathleen Beller *(Laura Daniels)*, Michael Brandon *(Michael Krasnick)*, Dennis Franz *(Dr. Lucas)*, Scott Paulin *(Dr. Roger Kelton)*, Elizabeth Huddle *(Nurse Crenshaw)*, Michael Cassidy *(Mark Banning)*, Charles Tyner *(George Clark)*, Patricia Gaul *(Madge)*, Michael Miller *(The Pawn Broker)*, Wally Dalton *(Fire Chief Jack Branch)*, Rion Hunter *(Lester)*, Troy Evans *(Jessup)*, Terry Wills *(Hal)*, Rod Gist *(Sgt. Murray)*, Doris Singleton *(Marge)*, Erwin Fuller *(Harry)*, Janet Raney *(The Woman on the Escalator)*, Henry G. Sanders *(The Gym Attendant)*, Edgy Lee *(The Nurse)*, George Wyner, Raye Birk, Sherri Stoner, Kurtwood Smith, Kit McDonough, Joseph G. Medalis, Barbara Collentine, Marc Silver, Dennis Redfield, Pattie Pierce, Bill DeLand, Ted Haler, Teresa Ligier, Tim Wade, Cynthia-Gail Wilson, J. Stephen Burton
<u>D</u>: Jack Bender   <u>TELEPLAY</u>: Bill Bleich   <u>PHOTOG</u>: Rexford Metz   <u>SPCL-FX</u>: Eddie Surkin   <u>MUSIC</u>: Brad Fiedel
TVM, modest thriller: Ouija board warns girl of murder

The Deadly Model

1915, (GB), Big Ben-Union/Pathe, b&w, 2,575 ft. (784.9m)
<u>W</u>: H.O. Martinek, Ivy Montford
<u>D</u>: H.O. Martinek   <u>STORY</u>: L.C. MacBean
Standard thriller: German spies covet inventor's model gun

Deadly Nightshade

1953, (GB), Kenilworth/GFD, b&w, 61 mins.
<u>W</u>: Emrys Jones *(Matthews/Barlow)*, John Horsley *(Insp. Clements)*, Zena Marshall *(Ann Farrington)*, Joan Hickson *(Mrs. Fenton)*, Hector Ross *(Canning)*, Victor Platt *(The Sgt.)*, Roger Maxwell *(Col. Smythe)*, Lesley Deane *(Mrs. Smythe)*
<u>P</u>: Robert Baker & Monty Berman   <u>D</u>: John Gilling   <u>STORY</u>: Lawrence Huntington
Standard crime-thriller: Escaped convict poses as dead double

Deadly Obsession

1988, (USA), color
Minor horror-thriller: Sadist tortures coed

Deadly Reactor

1989, (USA), color, 88 mins.
<u>W</u>: David Heavener, Stuart Whitman, Darwyn Swalve, Allyson Davis
<u>D</u>: David Heavener
Standard SF-adventure: Post-nuke preacher turns vigilante

The Deadly Ray from Mars

1965, (USA), Univ, b&w
<u>W</u>: Larry "Buster" Crabbe *(Flash Gordon)*, Carol Hughes *(Dale Arden)*, Frank Shannon *(Dr. Zarkoff)*, Anne Gwynne *(Sonja)*, Charles Middleton *(Ming the Merciless)*, John Hamilton, Lee Powell, Shirley Deane, Edgar Edwards, Don Rowan
<u>D</u>: Ford Beebe & Ray Taylor   <u>SCR</u>: George H. Plympton, Basil Dickey & Barry Shipman
Standard SF-adventure, feature culled from 1940 serial Flash Gordon Conquers the Universe: Earth hero opposes murderous alien dictator

Deadly Record

1959, (GB), Independent Artists/Anglo-Amalgamated, b&w, 58 mins.
<u>W</u>: Lee Patterson *(Trevor Hamilton)*, Barbara Shelley *(Susan Webb)*, Jane Hylton *(Ann Garfield)*, Peter Dyneley *(Dr. Morrow)*, Geoffrey Keen *(Supt. Ambrose)*, John Paul *(Phil Gamage)*, Everley Gregg *(Mrs. Mac)*, Edward Cast *(PC Ryder)*, George Pastell *(Angelo)*, Ferdy Mayne *(Ramon Casadas)*, April Olrich *(Carmela)*
<u>P</u>: Vivian A. Cox   <u>D</u>: Lawrence Huntington   <u>SCR</u>: Vivian A. Cox & Lawrence Huntington, from a novel by Nina Warner Hooke
Standard thriller: Accused pilot proves jealous receptionist killed wife

Deadly Sins

1995, (USA), Barbour-Langley Prods./Libra, color, 95 mins.
W: Alyssa Milano, David Keith, Terry David Mulligan, Corrie Clark, Heidi Lenhart, Pamela Perry, Ann Warn-Pegg, Peter Hanlon, Jo Bates, Joely Collins, Robert Jones, Mary McDonald
<u>D</u>: Michael Robison   <u>SCR</u>: John Langley & Malcolm Barbour   <u>PHOTOG</u>: Barry Gravelle   <u>MUSIC</u>: Barron Abramovitch
Made-for-Video, standard thriller: Female detective poses as student, probes murders at convent school

The Deadly Spawn

1983, (USA), 21st Century, color, 78 mins.
W: Charles George Hildebrandt (*Charles*), Tom DeFranco (*Tom*), Richard Lee Porter (*Frankie*), Jean Tafler (*Ellen*), Karen Tighe (*Kathy*), Elissa Neil (*Barbara*), James Brewster (*Sam*), John Schmerling (*Uncle Herb*), Ethel Michelson (*Aunt Millie*)
D & SCR: Douglas McKeown STORY: Douglas McKeown, Ted Bohus & John Dods PHOTOG: Harvey Birnbaum MUSIC: Michael Perilstein, Ken Walker & Paul Cornell
Minor SF-thriller

Deadly Strangers

1974, (GB), Silhouette/Rank, color, 93 mins.
W: Hayley Mills (*Belle Adams*), Simon Ward (*Stephen Slade*), Sterling Hayden (*Malcolm Robarts*), Peter Jeffrey (*Uncle*), Ken Hutchison (*Jim Nichols*), Hubert Tucker (*The Owner*), Nina Francis (*The Attendant*), George Collis (*The Motorcyclist*), Juliet Ackroyd (*The Girlfriend*)
P: Peter Miller D: Sidney Hayers SCR: Philip Levene PHOTOG: Graham Edgar MUSIC: Ron Goodwin
Minor melodrama: Hitchhiking girl meets mad strangler

Deadly Sting

see Evil Spawn

The Deadly Trap

1971, (Fr-Ital), Nat'l General, color, 93 mins.
W: Faye Dunaway, Frank Langella, Barbara Parkins, Maurice Ronet, Michele Lourie, Patrick Vincent, Karen Blanguernon, Raymond Gerome
D: Gene Clement
Orognial title: The House Under the Trees. Fr retitle, La Maison Sous les Arbes (The House Under the Trees) Aka Death Scram
Standard thriller: Sinister organization hounds couple.

Deadly Treasure of the Piranha

see Killer Fish

A Deadly Vision

1997, (USA), ABC-TV, color, 95 mins.
W: Kristin Davis, Matthew Settle, Peter Boyle (*Det. Salvatore DaVinci*), Ellen Burstyn (*Yvette Watson*), James McDaniel (*Dr. Tony Natale*), Matthew Ross (*The Killer*), Deirdre O'Connell (*Marilyn Middleton*),Tari Signor (*Linda Lowry*), Jennie Nauman (*Beverly Rachlin*)
D: Bill L. Norton TELEPLAY: Dan Greenburg—from his novel *Love Kills*
PHOTOG: Alan Caso MUSIC: Chris Walden
TVM, standard thriller: Psychic waitress helps cop find serial killer

Deadly Weapon

1988, (USA), color, 89 mins.
W: Rodney Eastman, Gary Frank, Michael Horse, Kim Walker, Ed Nelson
D & SCR: Michael Miner
Minor SF-adventure: Teen finds gov't anti-matter weapon

Deadly Web

1996, (USA), NBC-TV, color, 95 mins.
W: Gigi Rice, Ed Marinaro, Andrew Lawrence (*Spence Lawrence*), John Wesley Shipp (*Dr. Stanton*), Ted McGinley (*Peter Lawrence*), Raphael Sbarge (*Barry*), Robin Quivers (*Lee Aaron*)
TVM, standard thriller: Single mother targeted by cyber-stalker

Dead Man's Chest

1965, (GB), Merton Park/Anglo-Amalgamated, b&w, 59 mins.
W: John Thaw (*David Jones*), Ann Firbank (*Mildred Jones*), John Meillon (*Johnnie Gordon*), Peter Bowles (*Arthur*), John Collin (*Insp. Briggs*), John Abineri (*Arthur*), Arthur Brough (*Groves*), Graham Crowden (*Murchie*), Michael Robbins (*Sgt. Harris*), Geoffrey Bayldon (*Laine*)
P: Jack Greenwood D: Patrick Dromgoole STORY: Donal Giltinian
Standard thriller: Reporter fakes colleague's murder to expose weakness of circumstantial evidence

Dead Man's Evidence

1962, (GB), Bayford-RCH/British Lion, b&w, 67 mins.
W: Conrad Phillips (*David Baxter*), Jane Griffiths (*Linda Howard*), Veronica Hurst (*Gay Clifford*), Alex Mackintosh (*Paul Kay*), Ryck Rydon (*Fallon*), Godfrey Quigley (*Insp. O'Brian*), Bruce Seton (*Col. Somerset*)
P: Francis Searle & Ryck Rydon D: Francis Searle SCR: Arthur la Bern & Gordon Wellesley STORY: Arthur la Bern
Standard crime-thriller: Secret agent probes frogman's death

Dead Man's Eyes

1944, (USA), Univ, b&w, 64 mins.
W: Lon Chaney Jr., Jean Parker, Acquanetta, Thomas Gomez, Paul Kelly, Jonathan Hale, George Meeker, Pierre Watkin, Eddie Dunn, Edward Fielding
D: Reginald LeBorg SCR: Dwight V. Babcock PHOTOG: Paul Ivano
Standard "Inner Sanctum" thriller: Eye-transplant operation clouded by murder

Dead Man's Folly

1986, (USA-GB), CBS-TV, color, 95 mins.
W: Peter Ustinov (*Hercule Poirot*), Jean Stapleton (*Ariadne Oliver*), Susan Wooldridge (*Miss Brewis*), Constance Cummings (*Mrs. Folliot*), Timothy Pigott-Smith (*Sir George Stubbs*), Nicollette Sheridan (*Lady Hattie Stubbs*), Kenneth Cranham (*Insp. Bland*), Jonathan Cecil (*Hastings*), Christopher Guard (*Alec Legge*), Ralph Arliss (*Michael Weyman*), Jimmy Gardner (*Merdell*), Caroline Langrishe (*Sally Legge*)
D: Clive Donner, from a story by Agatha Christie
TVM, minor thriller: Sleuth finds murder at English manor

Dead Man's Island

1996, (USA), CBS-TV, color, 95 mins.
W: Barbara Eden (*Henrietta O. Collins*), William Shatner (*Chase Prescott*), Morgan Fairchild (*Valerie St. Vincent*), Roddy McDowall (*Trevor Dunnaway*), Jameson Parker (*Lyle Stedman*), Christopher Atkins (*Roger Prescott*), Traci Lords (*Miranda*), David Faustino (*Haskell*), Olivia Hussey (*Rosie*), Christopher Cazenove (*Milo*), Don Most (*Burton Andrews*)
D: Peter Hunt TELEPLAY: Peter S. Fischer, from Carolyn G. Hart's novel
PHOTOG: Robert D. Hayes MUSIC: Arthur Rubenstein
TVM, standard thriller: Woman investigative journalist aids former lover who fears for his life

Dead Man Walking

1988, (USA), Rep, video, color
W: Wings Hauser, Jeffrey Combs, Brion James,Pamela Ludwig, Sy Richardson, Leland Crooke
D: Gregory Brown SCR: R.J. Marx
Standard SF-adventure: Post-nuke mercenary attempts to rescue woman from plague zone

Dead Men are Dangerous

1939, (GB), Welwyn/Pathe, b&w, 69 mins.
W: Robert Newton (*Aylmer Franklyn*), Betty Lynne (*Nina*), John Warwick (*Goddard*), Peter Gawthorne (*Conroy*), Merle Tottenham (*Gladys*), John Turnbull (*Insp. Roberts*), John Salew (*The Tramp*), Aubrey Mallalieu (*The Coroner*), Cyril Chamberlain (*George Franklin*), Kynaston Reeves (*James Franklin*), Anita Sharp Bolster (*The Woman*)
D: Harold French SCR: Victor Kendall, Harry Hughes & Vernon Clancey, from H.C.Armstrong's novel *Hidden*
Standard thriller: Author changes clothes with tramp, is accused of murder. reissued 1942

Dead Men Don't Die

1991, (USA), color, 94 mins.
W: Elliott Gould, Melissa Anderson, Mark Moses, Mabel King, Philip Bruns, Jack Betts
D & SCR: Malcolm Marmorstein
Minor horror-comedy: Anchorman revived as zombie

Dead Men Tell

1941, (USA), 20th-Fox, b&w, 60 mins.
W: Sidney Toler (*Charlie Chan*), Sheila Ryan (*Kate Ransome*), Robert Weldon (*Steve Daniels*), Victor Sen Yung (*Jimmy Chan*), Don Douglas (*Jed Thomason*), Paul McGrath (*Charles Thursday*), Katharine (Kay) Aldridge (*Laura Thursday*), Truman Bradley (*Capt. Kane*), George Reeves (*Bill Lydig*), Ethel Griffies (*Patience Nodbury*), Lenita Lane (*Dr. Anne Bonney*), Stanley Andrews (*The Inspector*), Milton Parsons (*Gene La Farge*)
D: Harry Lachman SCR: John Larkin, from characters created by Earl Derr Biggers PHOTOG: Charles Clarke
Standard thriller: Killer sought on treasure hunt

Dead of Night: JEAN HACKETT

Dead Men Tell No Tales

1971, (USA), 20th-Fox/CBS-TV, color, 74 mins.
W: Christopher George, Judy Carne, Richard Anderson, Patricia Barry, Larry D. Mann (*Sam Mirakian*), Kevin Hagen (*Karl*), Joan Shawlee (*Polly Grant*), Fred Sadoff (*Sgt. Corso*), Ella Edwards (*Mrs. Carter*), Mike Lookinland (*Bud Riley*), Scott Ellsworth (*The Director*), Judith DeHart (*Mrs. Riley*), Bill

Quinn (*The Bartender*), Lincoln Kilpatrick Jr. (*Mike Carter*), Len Weyland (*Darrow*), John Dennis (*Mack*), Thom Carney (*Fatso*), David Frank (*The Escort*), Lorna Thayer (*The Suntan Lady*), Richard O'Brien (*Mr. Riley*), Tom Hernandez (*The Spanish Bartender*)
<u>D</u>: Walter Grauman **TELEPLAY**: Robert Dozier, from a novel by Kelly Ross **PHOTOG**: Jack Woolf **MUSIC**: David Grusin **MUSIC DIR**: Lionel Newman
TVM, standard thriller: Killers pursue wrong man

Dead Men Walk
1943, (USA), PRC, b&w, 63 mins.
<u>W</u>: George Zucco (*Elwyn Clayton/Dr. Lloyd Clayton*), Dwight Frye (*Zolarr*), Mary Carlisle (*Gail*), Nedrick Young
<u>D</u>: Sam Newfield **SCR**: Frank Myton **PHOTOG**: Jack Greenhalgh **MUSIC**: Erdody
*French retitle, **Creature of the Devil**, A.k.a. **The Vampire***
Minor horror-thriller: Doctor has vampiric twin brother

The Dead Next Door
1989, (USA), color, 84 mins.
<u>W</u>: Scott Spiegel, Peter Terry
SCR: J.R. Bookwalter
Minor SF-horror: Virus reanimates corpses

Dead of Night
1945, (GB), Ealing/Univ, b&w, 104 mins.
<u>W</u>: Mervyn Johns (*Walter Craig*), Roland Culver (*Eliot Foley*), Mary Merrall (*Mrs. Foley*), Frederick Valk (*Dr. Van Straaten*), Renee Gadd (*Mrs. Craig*), Antony Baird (*Hugh Grainger*), Judy Kelly (*Joyce Grainger*), Sally Ann Howes (*Sally O'Hara*), Miles Malleson (*The Hearse Driver*), Michael Allen (*Jimmy Watson*), Robert Wyndham (*Dr. Albury*), Googie Withers (*Joan Courtland*), Ralph Michael (*Peter Courtland*), Esme Percy (*The Dealer*), Michael Redgrave (*Maxwell Frere*), Elizabeth Welch (*Beulah*), Hartley Power (*Sylvester Kee*), Magda Kun (*Mitzi*), Garry Marsh (*Harry Parker*), Basil Radford (*George Parratt*), Naunton Wayne (*Larry Potter*), Peggy Bryan (*Mary Lee*), Allan Jeayes, Barbara Leakey
<u>D</u>: Michael Balcon **DIRS**: Cavalcanti ("*Christmas Party*" & "*Ventriloquist*" sequences), Charles Crichton ("*Golfing*" sequence), Basil Dearden ("*Hearse*" sequence), & Robert Hamer ("*Mirror*" sequence) **SCR**: John Baines, Angus Macphail & T.E.B. Clarke, from stories by John Baines, Angus Macphail, E.F. Benson & H.G. Wells **PHOTOG**: Jack Parker & Douglas Slocombe **MUSIC**: Georges Auric
*German retitle, **Dream Without End**, reissued 1949 (with 10 mins. cut)*
Classic fantasy-thriller: Visitors in English countryside relate strange and prophetic happenings

Dead of Night (1972)
see Deathdream

Dead of Night
1977, (USA), NBC-TV, color, 95 mins.
<u>W</u>: Ed Begley Jr. (*Frank*), Christina Hart (*Helen*), Anjanette Comer (*Alexis*), E.J. Andre (*McCauley*), Patrick Macnee (*Dr. Gheria*), Lee H. Montgomery (*Bobby*), Horst Buchholz (*Michael*), Elisha Cook Jr. (*Karel*), Joan Hackett
*TVM, standard trilogy of terror tales adapted by Richard Matheson: **Second Chance**, **No Such Thing as a Vampire**, & **Bobby***

Dead of Night
1987, (USA), Feifer-Miller/Vista Street, color, 84 mins.
<u>W</u>: Julie Merrill (*Sura/Sara*), Kuri Browne (*April*), John Reno (*Bobby*), J.K. Dumont (*Richard*), Isaac Allan (*David*), Aarin Teich (*Charles*), Bob Kip (*John Smith*), Jack Castro (*Napoleon*), Jordan Brown (*Mensa*), Stanla Shirley (*The Bag Lady*), Abigail Lenz (*The Actress*), Micheal McGuire (*The Actor*), Thom Spadero (*A Policeman*), Bobby Bird (*A Policeman*)
<u>D</u>: Deryn Warren **SCR**: Gerry Daly **PHOTOG**: Ronn Schmidt **MUSIC**: David Frank
*A.k.a. **Mirror of Death***
Minor fantasy-thriller: Girl possessed by murderous spirit

Dead of Night
1998, (USA), color, 110 mins.
<u>W</u>: John Enos, Kathleen Kinmont
Standard horror-fantasy: Vampire seeks long-dead wife

Dead of Winter
1987, (USA), MGM, color, 100 mins.
<u>W</u>: Mary Steenburgen (*Katie*), Roddy McDowall (*Mr. Murray*), Jan Rubes (*Dr. Lewis*), William Russ (*Rob Sweeney*), Mark Malone (*Ro-land*), Ken Pogue (*Officer Mullavy*), Sam Malkin, Wayne Robson, Michael Copeman
<u>D</u>: Arthur Penn **SCR**: Marc Shmuger & Mark Malone **PHOTOG**: Jan Weincke **MUSIC**: Richard Einhorn
Modest thriller: Actress terrorized at secluded estate

Dead On
1993, (USA), color
<u>W</u>: Matt McCoy
Minor thriller: Illicit lovers plot murders of respective spouses

The Dead One
1962, (USA), Mardi Gras, color, 71 mins
<u>W</u>: Linda Ormond, John MacKay, Clyde Kelly, Monica Davis
blurb: "See the voodoo princess call on the dead ones to Kill! Kill! Kill!"
Minor fantasy-thriller: Woman seeks inheritance, utilizes zombie

The Dead One: LINDA ORMOND

Dead on Sight
1994, (USA), color, 96 mins.
<u>W</u>: Jennifer Beals, Daniel Baldwin, Kurtwood Smith, William H. Macy
<u>D</u>: Ruben Preuss **SCR**: Lewis Green **MUSIC**: Harry Manfredini
Standard thriller: Coed's nightmares come true

Dead on Time
1955, (GB), Vandyke/Archway, b&w, 27 mins.
<u>W</u>: Patrick Allen, Greta Gynt, John Loder
<u>P</u>: Roger Proudlock <u>D</u>: Don Chaffey
Standard short crime-thriller: Secret agent tracks atomic spies

Dead People
1974, (USA), Bedford, color
<u>W</u>: Marianna Hill, Joy Bang, Royal Dano, Elisha Cook Jr., Michael Greer
P D, & SCR: Gloria Katz & Willard Huyck
*A.k.a. **Messiah of Evil, Return of the Living Dead, The Second Coming** and **Revenge of the Screaming Dead***
Minor horror-thriller: Zombies in California coastal town

Dead Pigeon on Beethoven Street
1972, (W. Ger), color, 103 mins.
<u>W</u>: Glenn Corbett, Christa Lang, Anton Diffring, Alex D'Arcy Eric P. Caspar, Sieghart Rupp, Anthony Chin
<u>D</u>: Samuel Fuller
TVM, bizarre crime-thriller: American agent in Germany seeks partner's killer

Dead Pit
1989, (USA), color, 90 mins.
<u>W</u>: Jeremy Slate, Steffen Gregory Foster
<u>D</u>: Brett Leonard
Minor horror-thriller: Mad scientist brought back from death

Dead Reckoning
1947, (USA), Col, b&w, 100 mins.
<u>W</u>: Humphrey Bogart, Lizabeth Scott, Morris Carnovsky, Charles Cane, William Prince, Marvin Miller, Wallace Ford
<u>D</u>: John Cromwell
Standard thriller: Ex-paratrooper probes friend's vanishing

Dead Ringer
1964, (USA), WB, b&w, 115 mins.
<u>W</u>: Bette Davis (*Margaret de Lorca/Edith Philips*), Peter Lawford (*Tony Collins*), Karl Malden (*Sgt. Jim Hobbson*), Jean Hagen (*Dede Marshall*), Philip Carey (*Sgt. Hoag*), Ken Lynch (*Capt. Johnson*), George Macready (*Paul Harrison*), Estelle Winwood (*The Matriarch*), Charles Watts (*The Apt. Manager*), Mario Alcalde (*Garcia*), George Chandler (*George*), Bert Remsen (*Dan*), Monika Henreid (*Janet*), Cyril Delevanti (*Henry*)
<u>P</u>: William H. Wright <u>D</u>: Paul Henreid **SCR**: Albert Beich & Oscar Millard, from Rian James' novel **PHOTOG**: Ernest Haller **MUSIC**: Andre Previn
*remake of **La Otra**, GB retitle, **Dead Image***
blurb: "Double Davis Means Double Dynamite!"
Modest thriller: Woman murders twin, impersonates her

Dead Ringers
1988, (Can), 20th-Fox, color, 115 mins.
W: Jeremy Irons (*Beverly Mantle/Elliot Mantle*), Genevieve Bujold (*Claire Niveau*), Heidi von Palleske (*Cary*), Barbara Gordon (*Danuta*), Shirley Douglas (*Laura*), Nick Nichols (*Leo*), Stephen Lack (*Anders Wolleck*), Lynn Cormack (*Arlene*)
D: David Cronenberg   **SCR:** David Cronenberg & Norman Snider, from the book *Twins* by Bari Wood & Jack Geasland   **PHOTOG:** Peter Suschitzky
MUSIC: Howard Shore
Unusual thriller: Twin gynecologists descend into madness

Dead Sleep
1991, (Austral), color, 95 mins.
W: Linda Blair, Tony Bonner
D: Alec Mills
Standard thriller: Patients used as guinea pigs

Dead Space
1991, (USA), Concorde, color, 78 mins.
W: Bryan Cranston, Judith Chapman Marc Singer, Laura Tate
D: Fred Gallo
Minor SF-horror: Vaccine mutates into monster

Deadtime Stories
1987, (USA), Bill Paul/Cinema Group, color, 83 mins.
W: Scott Valentine (*Peter*), Michael Mesmer (*Uncle Mike*), Brian De-Persia (*Little Brian*), Phyllis Craig (*Hanagobl*), Anne Redfern (*Florinda*), Nicole Picard (*Rachel*), Melissa Leo (*Judith "Mama" Baer*), Kathy Fleig (*Miranda*), Casper Roos (*The Vicar*), Matt Mitler (*Willie*), Barbara Seldon (*A Seductress*), Leigh Kilton (*A Seductress*), Lesley Sank (*The Reviving Magoga*), Lisa Cain (*The Living Magoga*), Michael Berlinger (*Greg*), Jeff Delman (*The Strangling Man*), Fran Lopate (*Grandma*), John Bachelder (*The Drugstore Clerk*), Caroline Carrigan (*The Nurse*), Heather L. Baley (*The Girl in the Store*), Oded Carmi (*The Groundskeeper/The Postman*), Cathryn DePrume (*Goldi Lox*), Kevin Hannon (*Beresford "Papa" Baer*), Timothy Rule (*Wilmont "Baby" Baer*), Robert Trimboli (*Lt. Jack B. Nimble*), Harvey Pierce (*Capt. Jack B. Quick*), Rondell Sheridan (*The Looney Bin Guard*), Michele Mars (*The Waitress*), Beth Felty (*The Reporter*), Pat McCord (*The Anchorman*), Ron Bush (*The Bank Guard*), Bryant Tausek, Jim Nocell, Suzanna Vaucher, Leif Wennerstrom
D: Jeffrey Delman   **SCR:** Jeffrey Delman, Charles F. Shelton, & J. Edward Kiernan   **STORY:** Jeffrey Delman   **PHOTOG:** Daniel B. Canton
MUSIC: Taj
Minor horror-satire: Uncle tells trio of terror tales

Dead Weekend
1995, (USA), color, 84 mins.
W: Stephen Baldwin David Rasche, Damian Jones
D: Amos Poe   **TELEPLAY:** Joel Rose
Made-for-Cable, standard SF: Female space alien assumes different guises

Dead Women in Lingerie
1990, (USA), color, 87 mins.
W: June Lockhart, Lyle Waggoner, John Romo, Jerry Orbach, Maura Tierney
D: Enka Fox
Minor thriller: Models turn up dead

The Dead Zone
1983, (Can), Dino De Laurentiis/Para, color, 104 mins.
W: Christopher Walken (*John Smith*), Tom Skerritt (*Sheriff Bannerman*), Brooke Adams (*Sarah*), Martin Sheen (*Greg Stillson*), Herbert Lom (*Dr. Sam Weizak*), Colleen Dewhurst (*Mrs. Dodd*), Nicholas Campbell (*Frank Dodd*), Anthony Zerbe (*Roger*), Sean Sullivan (*Herb*), Roberta Weiss (*Alma*), Jackie Burroughs (*Vera*), Simon Craig (*Chris*), Geza Kovacs (*Elliman*), JulieAnn Heathwood (*Amy*), Peter Dvorsky (*Dardis*), Les Carlson
D: David Cronenberg   **SCR:** Jeff Boam, from Stephen King's novel   **PHOTOG:** Mark Irwin   **MUSIC:** Michael Kamen
Modest SF-thriller: Head injury enables man to see future

Deafula
1975, (USA), Diversity/Signscope, b&w
P: Gary Holstrom
D & SCR: Peter Wechsberg
Standard horror-fantasy (first feature film in sign language): Vampire's adventures

A Deal with the Devil
1916, (GB), Hepworth, b&w, 1,025 ft. (312.4m)
D: Frank Wilson
Standard fantasy: Old chemist makes satanic pact to regain youth

Dean Koontz' 'Mr. Murder'
1999, (USA), ABC-TV, color, 95 mins.
W: Stephen Baldwin, Julie Warner, Thomas Haden Church, James Coburn, Bill Smitrovich, Don McManus, Dan Lauria, Kaley Cuoco, Don Hood, K Callan, Dean Norris, Brandon Smith
D: Dick Lowry   **TELEPLAY:** Stephen Tolkin, from Dean Koontz' novel
PHOTOG: Greg Gardiner
2-part TVM, standard thriller: Dangerous clone besets author and his family

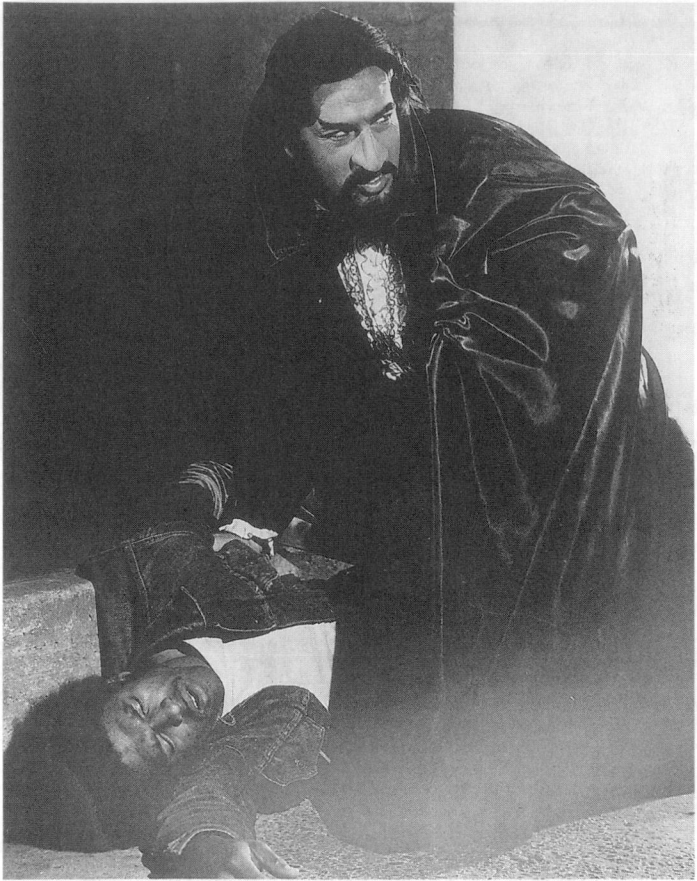

Deafula: WILLIAM GLENN AND PETER WEX

Dean R. Koontz' 'Whispers'
1990, (USA), color, 90 mins.
W: Victoria Tennant, Chris Sarandon, Jean Leclerc, Peter MacNeill, Linda Sorenson, Eric Christmas
D: Douglas Jackson   **SCR:** Anita Doohan & Don Carmody, from Dean R. Koontz' novel *Whispers*
Standard thriller: Maniac stalks woman

Dear, Dead Delilah
1972, (USA), Southern Star/Avco Embassy, color, 95 mins.
W: Agnes Moorehead (*Delilah*), Patricia Carmichael (*Luddy*), Will Geer (*Ray Jurroe*), Michael Ansara (*Morgan*), Anne Gibbs (*Young Luddy*), Dennis Patrick (*Alonzo*), Anne Meacham (*Grace*), Robert Gentry (*Richard*), Elizabeth Eis (*Ellen*), John Marriott (*Marshall*), Ruth Baker (*Buffy*)
WRIT & D: John Farris   **PHOTOG:** William R. Johnson   **MUSIC:** Bill Justis
*Crude, low-budget rehash of **Hush...Hush, Sweet Charlotte** and **Strait-Jacket**: Woman matricide released from prison, encounters greed and axe-murders*

Dear Detective
1978, (Fr), Cinema 5, color, 105 mins.
W: Annie Girardot, Philippe Noiret
D: Philippe De Broca
*Standard comedy-thriller: Beautiful police inspector tracks dangerous killer. A.k.a. **Dear Inspector***

Dear Murderer
1947, (GB), Gainsborough/GFD/U-I, b&w, 94 mins.
W: Eric Portman (*Lee Warren*), Greta Gynt (*Vivien Warren*), Dennis Price (*Richard Fenton*), Jack Warner (*Insp. Pembury*), Maxwell Reed (*Jimmy Martin*), Hazel Court (*Avis Fenton*), Andrew Crawford (*Sgt. Fox*), Jane Hylton (*Rita*), John Blythe (*Ernie*), Ernest Butcher, Charles Rolfe, Howard Douglas, Helene Burls, Judith Carol, Valerie Ward
D: Arthur Crabtree   **SCR:** Muriel Box, Sydney Box, & Peter Rogers, from St. John L. Clowes' play   **PHOTOG:** Stephen Dade
Grim melodrama: Businessman suspects wife of infidelity, plots her lover's demise

Death at Broadcasting House
1934, (GB), Phoenix/ABFD, b&w, 71 mins.
W: Ian Hunter (*Insp. Gregory*), Austin Trevor (*Leopold Dryden*), Mary Newland (*Joan Dryden*), Henry Kendall (*Rodney Fleming*), Val Gielgud (*Julian Caird*), Peter Haddon (*Guy Bannister*), Betty Ann Davies (*Poppy Levine*), Jack Hawkins (*Herbert Evans*), Donald Wolfit (*Sydney Parsons*), Robert Rendel (*Sir Herbert Farquharson*), Gordon McLeod (*The Superintendent*), Bruce Lister (*Peter Ridgwell*), Arthur Hambling (*The Receptionist*), Ivor Barnard (*Higgins*), Hannen Swaffer, Vernon Bartlett, Eric Dunstan, Gillie Potter, Eve Becke, Elizabeth Welch, The Gershom Parkington Quintet, Percival Mackey & His

Band, Ord Hamilton
D: Reginald Denham   **SCR:** Basil Mason, from a novel by Val Gielgud & Holt Marvel
Standard thriller: Radio actor strangled

Death at Love House
1976, (USA), ABC-TV, color, 75 mins.
W: Robert Wagner *(Joel Gregory)*, Kate Jackson *(Donna Gregory)*, Sylvia Sidney *(Mrs. Josephs)*, Joan Blondell *(Marcella Gefenhardt)*, John Carradine *(Conan Carroll)*, Dorothy Lamour *(Denise Christian)*, Bill Macy *(Oscar Payne)*, Joe Bernard *(The Bus Driver)*, Mariana Hill *(Lorna Love)*, Robert Gibbons *(Eric Herrmann)*, Crofton Hardester, Al Hansen
P: Hal Sitowitz   **D:** E.W. Swackhammer   **TELEPLAY:** Jim Barnett   **PHOTOG:** Dennis Dalzell   **MUSIC:** Laurence Rosenthal
TVM, standard thriller: Writer obsessed by legend of 1930s actress. Made on Harold Lloyd's estate as **The Shrine of Lorna Love**

Death Becomes Her
1992, (USA), Univ, color, 105 mins.
W: Meryl Streep *(Madeline Ashton)*, Bruce Willis *(Dr. Ernest Menville)*, Goldie Hawn *(Helen Sharp)*, Isabella Rossellini *(Lisle)*, Ian Ogilvy (Chagall) ,Adam Storke *(Dakota)*, Nancy Fish *(Rose)*, Sydney Pollack *(The Doctor)* Alaina Reed Hall, Michelle Johnson, Mimi Kennedy, Fabio, Jonathan Silverman
D: Robert Zemeckis   **SCR:** Martin Donovan & David Koepp   **PHOTOG:** Dean Cundey   **SPCL VS-FX:** Industrial Light & Magic   **MUSIC:** Alan Silvestri
Bizarre comedy-fantasy: Elixir of Youth causes conflict

Death Benefit
1996, (USA),Made for Cable, color
W: Peter Horton, Carrie Snodgress Wendy Makkena *(Wynn)*
TVM, standard thriller: Murder case involves corporate attorney with psychopathic man

Death Bite
see Spasms

Death by Invitation
1971, (USA), Paragon, color
D & SCR: Ken Friedman
Minor horror-fantasy: Witch decapitates killers' descendants

Death Collector
1989, (USA), color, 90 mins.
W: Daniel Chapman, Ruth Collins
D: Tom Gniazdowski
Minor SF-thriller: Future insurance companies inflict death when premiums not forthcoming

Death Comes from Space
1958, (W. Ger-It-Fr.), Excelsior, b&w, 80 mins.
W: Paul Hubschmid, Giacomo Rossi-Stuart, Madeleine Fischer, Ivo Garrani, Fiorella Mari, Dario Michaelis, Annie Berval, Sam Galter, Jean Jacques Delbo, Peter Meersman
D: Paolo Heusch
USA retitle, **The Day the Sky Exploded** *(Excelsior, 1961), Orig. Ital. title:* **La Morte Viene Dallo Spazio**
Minor SF-thriller: Meteors bombard Earth

Death Corps
see Shock Waves

Death Cruise
1974, (USA), Spelling-Goldberg,, Made fir TV, color, 74 mins.
W: Edward Albert, Kate Jackson, Richard Long, Tom Bosley, Polly Bergen, Celeste Holm, Michael Constantine, Cesare Danova
D: Ralph Senensky   **TELEPLAY:** Jack Sowards
TVM, standard thriller: Luxury cruise members murdered

Death Curse of Tartu
1966, (USA), Falcon/Thunderbird-Int'l, color, 88 mins.
W: Fred Pinero *(Ed)*, Babbette Sherrill *(Julie)*, Frank Weed *(Sam)*, Sherman Hayes *(Johnny)*, Mayra Gomez, Maurice Stewart, Doug Hobart, Bill Marcus, Gary Holtz
WRIT & D: William Grefe   **PHOTOG:** Julio C. Chavez   **SONGS:** Al Greene & Al Jacobs
Minor horror-thriller: Indian apparition strikes

Death Dive
see Fer-de-Lance

Death Dorm
see Pranks

Deathdream
1972, (Can), Europix, color, 98 mins.
W: John Marley, Lynn Carlin, Richard Backus
P & D: Bob Clark   **SCR:** Alan Ormsby
A.k.a. **Dead of Night, Night Walk** *and* The Veteran
Unusual fantasy-thriller (reworking of W.W. Jacobs' short story "The Monkey's Paw"): Vietnam-veteran son returns from death

Death Dreams
1991, (USA), Lifetime, Made for TV, color, 95 mins.
W: Christopher Reeve, Marg Helgenberger, Fionnula Flanagan, George Dickerson *(Dr. Drake)*, Conor O'Farrell *(Bennett Massell)*, Cec Verrell *(Denise Massell)*, Jim Jarrett *(Fromme)*, Jan Devereaux *(Mimi)*, Pat Atkins *(Mrs. Parker)*, Kevin Page *(Dr. Holvag)*, Robert Ward *(Dr. Green)*, Harry Johnson *(Judge Wiley)*, Richard Morrison *(The Jury Foreman)*, Wendell Grayson *(The Bailiff)*, Jack Angeles *(The Priest)*, John Rubinow *(The Ambulance Ass't)*, Tom Mustin *(The Guard)*, Taylor Fry *(Jennie)*
D: Martin Donovan   **TELEPLAY:** Robert Glass, from William Katz' novel   **PHOTOG:** James Chressanthis   **MUSIC:** Gerald Gouriet
TVM, standard thriller: Woman communicates with murdered daughter

Death Drums Along the River
1963, (GB), Big Ben-Hallam/Planet, color, 83 mins.
W: Richard Todd *(Insp. Harry Sanders)*, Marianne Koch *(Dr. Inge Jung)*, Albert Lieven *(Dr. Weiss)*, Walter Rilla *(Dr. Schneider)*, Vivi Bach *(Marlene)*, Jeremy Lloyd *(Hamilton)*, Robert Arden *(Hunter)*, Bill Brewer *(Pearson)*
P: Harry Alan Towers   **D:** Lawrence Huntington   **SCR:** Harry Alan Towers, Nicolas Roeg, Kevin Kavanagh & Lawrence Huntington, from Edgar Wallace's novel *Sanders*
Standard crime-thriller: Inspector probes murder in African hospital, finds hidden diamond mine

Death from a Distance
1935, (USA), Invincible, b&w, 73 mins.
W: Creighton Hale, Lola Lane, Russell Hopton, John St. Polis, Lee Kohlmar, Lew Kelly, Wheeler Oakman, Robert Frazer, Cornelius Keefe
Minor thriller: Murder at astronomical observatory

Death Game
1996, (USA), SHO-TV, color, 90 mins.
W: Timothy Bottoms
Made-for-Cable, standard SF-thriller: Future detective aids street kids forced to battle cyborgs

Death Goes to School
1953, (GB), Independent Artists/Eros, b&w, 65 mins.
W: Barbara Murray *(Miss Shepherd)*, Gordon Jackson *(Insp. Campbell)*, Pamela Allan *(Helen Cooper)*, Jane Aird *(Miss Halstead)*, Beatrice Varley *(Miss Hopkinson)*, Stanley Rose *(Insp. Burgess)*, Robert Long *(Mr. Lawley)*, Sam Kydd *(Sgt. Harvey)*
P: Victor Hanbury   **D:** Stephen Clarkson   **SCR:** Maisie Sharman & Stephen Clarkson, from a novel by Maisie Sharman
Standard thriller: Girls' school music teacher proves colleague is strangler

Deathhead Virgin
1974, (USA), color, 94 mins.
W: Jock Gaynor, Larry Ward, Diane McBain, Vic Diaz
Minor fantasy-thriller: Evil spirit harasses treasure seekers

Death House
see Silent Night, Bloody Night

Death in Small Doses
1957, (USA), AA, b&w, 79 mins.
W: Peter Graves, Mala Powers
Standard thriller

Death in Small Doses
1973, (GB), Made for TV, color
W: Michael Jayston, Barry Nelson, Nyree Dawn Porter
TVM, minor thriller: Butler manipulates rich widow's life

Death in the Hand
1948, (GB), Four Star/GFD, b&w, 43 mins.
W: Esme Percy *(Cosmo Vaughan)*, Ernest Jay *(MacRae)*, Cecile Chevreau *(Sylvia Mottram)*, Carleton Hobbs *(The Chairman)*, John LeMesurier *(Jack Mottram)*, Shelagh Fraser *(Penelope MacRae)*, Norman Shelley *(The Businessman)*, Wilfred Caithness *(Rowlandson)*
P: A. Barr-Smith & Roger Proudlock   **D:** A. Barr-Smith   **SCR:** Douglas Cleverdon, from a story by Max Beerbohm
Standard thriller: Neurotic reads passengers' palms, predicts train crash

Death is a Number
1951, (GB), Delman/Adelphi, b&w, 50 mins.
W: Terence Alexander *(Alan Robert)*, Lesley Osmond *(Joan Robert)*, Denis Webb *(John Bridgnorth)*, Ingeborg Wells *(The Gipsy)*, Peter Gawthorne *(James Gregson)*, Isabel George *(The Nurse)*
P: Phyllis Shepherd   **D:** Horace Shepherd   **STORY:** Charles K. Shaw
Standard fantasy: Racing driver's death in car crash fulfills 300-year-old curse

Death is a Woman
1966, (GB), AB-Pathe/WPD, color, 81 mins.
W: Patsy Ann Noble *(Francesca)*, Mark Burns *(Dennis)*, Shaun Curry *(Joe)*, Wanda Ventham *(Priscilla)*, Terence de Marney *(Jacomini)*, Caron Gardner *(Mary)*, William Dexter *(Malo)*, Anita Harris
P: Harry Field   **D:** Frederic Goode   **STORY:** Wally Bosco
Standard thriller: Agent proves girl killed nightclub partners to obtain heroin

The Death Kiss

1932, (USA), Tiffany/World Wide, b&w & color tinted, 72 mins.
W: David Manners (*Franklyn Drew*), Adrienne Ames (*Marcia Lane*), Bela Lugosi (*Joseph Steiner*), John Wray (*Det. Lt. Sheehan*), Edward Van Sloan (*Tom Avery*), Barbara Bedford (*The Script Girl*), Vince Barnett (*Officer Gulliver*), Wade Boteler (*Sgt. Hilliker*), Harold Minjir (*Howell*), Alexander Carr (*Leon A. Grossmith*), Harold Waldridge (*Charlie*), Al Hill (*The Ass't Director*), Lee Moran (*Todd*), Mona Maris, Edmund Burns, Alan Roscoe, Jimmy Donlan
D: Edwin L. Marin   **SCR:** Gordon Kahn & Barry Barringer, from a book by Madelon St. Denis   **PHOTOG:** Norbert Brodine
Minor mystery-thriller: Actor murdered on movie set

Deathline

1972, (GB), K.L. Prods./AIP, color, 88 mins.
W: Donald Pleasence (*Insp. Colquhoun*), Christopher Lee (*Stratton-Villers*), David Ladd (*Alex Campbell*), Sharon Gurney (*Patricia Wilson*), Norman Rossington (*Det. Rogers*), June Turner ("*The Woman*"), Hugh Armstrong ("*The Man*"), James Cossins (*James Manfred*), Hugh Dickson (*Dr. Bacon*), Clive Swift (*Insp. Richardson*), Jack Woolgar (*The Inspector*), Heather Stoney (*Alice Marshall*), Ron Pember (*The Collector*), Suzanne Winkler (*The Prostitute*), Colin McCormack, Gary Winkler, James Culliford, Gerry Crampton, Terry Plummer, Gordon Petrie
D: Gary Sherman   **SCR:** Ceri Jones   **STORY:** Gary Sherman   **PHOTOG:** Alex Thomson   **MUSIC:** Jeremy Rose & Wil Mallone
USA retitle, **Raw Meat**
Grisly horror-thriller: Cannibalism in London subway

Death Machine

1995, (USA), color, 100 mins.
W: Brad Dourif, Ely Pouget, William Hootkins, John Sharian
WRIT & D: Stephen Norrington
Standard SF-thriller: Psychotic weapons designer unleashes fearsome android

Death Magic

1992, (USA), color, 93 mins.
W: Ane Coffrey, Keith DeGreen, Jack Dunlap, Danielle Frons, Norman Stone
D & SCR: Paul E. Clinco
Standard fantasy-thriller: Magicians revive American Civil War soldier; murders ensue

The Deathmaster

1972, (USA), AIP, color, 88 mins.
W: Robert Quarry (*Khorda*), Brenda Dickson (*Rona*), Betty Ann Rees (*Esslin*), Bill Ewing (*Pico*), John Fiedler (*Pop*), John Lasell (*The Detective*), William Jordan (*Monk*), LaSesne Hilton (*Barbado*), Freda T. Vanterpool (*The Dancer*), Tari Tabakin (*Mavis*)
P: Fred Sadoff   **D:** Ray Danton   **SCR:** R.L. Grove   **PHOTOG:** Wilmer C. Butler   **MUSIC:** Bill Marx
orig. to be titled **Khorda**
Standard horror-thriller: Vampire poses as guru, enslaves hippies

Death May Be Your Santa Claus

1969, (GB), Space-Soul-Creative Enterprises/Amanda, color, 50 mins.
W: Ken Gajadhar (*Raymond*), Donnah Dolce (*The White Girl*), Merdel Jordine (*Georgina*)
WRIT, P & D: Frankie Dymon Jr.
Standard fantasy: Hallucinations of Negro who loves both black and white girls

Deathmoon

1978, (USA), Roger Gimbel-EMI/CBS-TV, color, 93 mins.
W: Robert Foxworth (*Jason Palmer*), Barbara Trentham (*Diane May*), Joe Penny (*Rick Bladen*), Dolph Sweet (*Lt. Russ Cort*), France Nuyen (*Tapulua*), Debralee Scott (*Sherry Weston*), Don Pomes (*Dr. Eckworth*), Mitch Mitchell (*Jennings*), Carole Kai (*Tami Wimea*), Charles Haid (*Earl Wheelie*), Carol Avery (*Kay*), Branscombe Richmond (*Vince Tatupu*), Lydia Lei Kayahara (*Julie Chin*), Joan Freeman (*Mrs. Jennings*), Terry Takada (*Judy*), Albert Harris (*Dr. Restin*), Robert Witthans (*Harry Phillips*), Donna White (*Dora*)
P: Jay Benson   **D:** Bruce Kessler   **TELEPLAY:** George Schenck   **STORY:** George Schenck & Jay Benson   **PHOTOG:** Jack Whitman   **MUSIC:** Paul Chihara
TVM, standard horror-fantasy: Werewolfry on tourist isle

Death Nurse

1987, (USA), color, 80 mins.
W: Priscilla Alden, Michael Flood
D: Nick Phillips
Standard thriller: Evil nurse extorts money from patients

Death Occurred Last Night

see **La Mort Risale a Ieri Sera**

Death of an Angel

1952, (GB), Hammer-Lesser, b&w, 64 mins.
W: Jane Baxter (*Mary Welling*), Patrick Barr (*Robert Welling*), Julie Somers (*Judy Welling*), Jean Lodge (*Ann Marlow*), Katie Johnson (*Sarah Oddy*), Raymond Young (*Chris Boswell*), Russell Waters (*Walter Grannage*), Russell Napier (*Supt. Walshaw*)
P: Anthony Hinds & Julian Lesser   **D:** Charles Saunders   **SCR:** Reginald Long from Frank King's play *This Is Mary's Chair*
Standard thriller: Village doctor's wife is poisoned

The Death of Mario Ricci

1983, (Switz-Fr-W. Ger), color, 101 mins.
W: Gian Maria Volonte, Magali Noel, Heinz Bennent, Michel Robin, Mimsy Farmer, Jean-Michel Dupuis
D: Claude Goretta
Unusual thriller: TV journalist uncovers intrigue

Death of Siegfried

see **Die Nibelungen**

The Death of the Incredible Hulk

1990, (USA), Bixby-Brandon/New World TV, color, 95 mins.
W: Bill Bixby (*Dr. David Banner*), Lou Ferrigno (*The Hulk*), Elizabeth Gracen, Philip Sterling, Barbara Tarbuck, Carla Ferrigno, Andreas Katsulas, Anna Katerina, Chilton Crane, John Novak, Duncan Fraser, Dwight McFee, Mina E. Mina, Garwin Sanford, Lindsay Bourne, Marlane O'Brien, Justin di Pego, Fred Henderson, Judith Maxie, French Tickner
D: Bill Bixby   **TELEPLAY:** Gerald di Pego   **PHOTOG:** Chuck Colwell   **MUSIC:** Lance Rubin   **SONGS:** *And Something Ends*
TVM, standard SF-fantasy: Scientist tries to eradicate his violent alter ego

The Death of the Sun

see **Le Mort du Soleil**

Death on the Nile

1978, (GB), Mersham/EMI/Para, color, 140 mins.
W: Peter Ustinov (*Hercule Poirot*), Bette Davis (*Mrs. Van Schuyler*), Jane Birkin (*Louise Bourget*), Lois Chiles (*Linnet Ridgeway*), Mia Farrow (*Jacqueline de Bellefort*), Angela Lansbury (*Mrs. Salome Otterbourne*), Jon Finch (*Mr. Ferguson*), Olivia Hussey (*Rosalie Otterbourne*), George Kennedy (*Andrew Pennington*), I.S. Johar (*The Manager of the Karnak*), Maggie Smith (*Miss Bowers*), Jack Warden (*Dr. Ludwig Bessner*), David Niven (*Col. Rice*), Simon MacCorkindale (*Simon Doyle*), Sam Wanamaker (*Rockford*), Harry Andrews (*Barnstaple*)
P: John Brabourne & Richard Goodwin   **D:** John Guillermin   **SCR:** Anthony Shaffer, from Agatha Christie's novel   **PHOTOG:** Jack Cardiff   **MUSIC:** Nino Rota
Superior mystery-thriller: Belgian sleuth seeks ruthless killer plaguing Egyptian tour

Death Over my Shoulder

1958, (GB), Vicar/Orb, b&w, 89 mins.
W: Keefe Brasselle (*Jack Regan*), Bonar Colleano (*Joe Longo*), Jill Adams (*Evelyn Connors*), Arlene de Marco (*Julie*), Charles Farrell (*Shiv Maitland*), Sonia Dresdel (*Miss Upton*), Al Mulock (*Brainy Peterson*)
P: Frank Beis   **D:** Arthur Crabtree   **SCR:** Norman Hudis   **STORY:** Alyce Canfield
Standard crime-thriller: Detective hires thug to kill him so his insurance will pay for sick son's cure

Death Promise

1978, (USA), color, 90 mins.
W: Charles Bonet
Minor horror-thriller: Murderous landlord seeks to evict tenants

Death Race 2000

1975, (USA), New World, color, 79 mins.
W: David Carradine ("*Frankenstein*"), Mary Woronov (*Calamity Jane*), Sylvester Stallone (*Machine Gun Joe Viterbo*), Simone Griffeth (*Annie*), Louisa Moritz (*Myra*), Sandy McCallum (*Mr. President*), Martin Kove (*Nero the Hero*), Don Steele (*Junior Bruce*), Joyce Jameson (*Grace Pander*), Carle Bensen (*Harold*), Roberta Collins (*Matilda the Hun*), Paul Laurence (*The Special Agent*), Harriet Medin (*Thomasina Paine*), Vince Trankina (*Lt. Fury*), Bill Morey (*Deacon*), Fred Grandy (*Herman the German*), William Shephard (*Pete*), Leslie McRay (*Cleopatra*), Wendy Bartel (*Laurie*), Jack Favorite (*Henry*), Roger Rook (*The Radio Operator*), Sandy Ignon (*The FBI Agent*), John Landis (*The Mechanic*), Darla McDonell (*Rhonda Bainbridge*)
D: Paul Bartel   **SCR:** Robert Thom & Charles Griffith   **STORY:** Ib Melchior   **PHOTOG:** Tak Fujimoto   **OPTICAL SPCL-FX:** Jack Rabin   **MUSIC:** Paul Chihara
Modest SF-satire: Future race-car driving becomes blood sport

Death Rage

1977, (It), S.J. Int'l, color, 98 mins
W: Yul Brynner, Massimo Ranieri, Barbara Bouchet, Giancarlo Sbragia, Martin Balsam
D: Anthony Dawson [Antonio Margheriti]
Minor thriller: Mafia hitman seeks vengeance

The Death Ray

see **Luch Smerti**

Death Ride

1977, (USA), Band Ltd., color, 85 mins
W: Jose Ferrer, Sue Lyon, John Carradine, John Ericson, Leslie Parrish
P: Brandon Chase   **D:** Charles Band   **SCR:** Marc Marais
A.k.a. **Crash!**
Minor Fantasy-thriller: Woman uses idol to cause car wrecks

Death Ring
1992, (USA), Trans Atlantic/New Line, color, 95 mins.
<u>W:</u> Mike Norris, Billy Drago, Chad McQueen, Isabel Glasser, Don Swayze, Elizabeth Fong Sung, Branscombe Richmond, Kelly Bennett
<u>D:</u> R.J. Kizer <u>SCR:</u> George T. LeBrun <u>PHOTOG:</u> Glenn Kershaw <u>MUSIC:</u> John Massari
Made-for-Video, minor thriller: Athlete hunted by millionaire

The Death Robots
see Los Automatas de la Muerte

Death Row Diner
1988, (USA), color 90 mins.
<u>W:</u> Michelle Bauer, Jay Richardson, John Content, Dennis Mooney, Tom Schell, Frank Sarcinello Sr., Dana Mason
Minor horror-thriller: Film producer returns from grave

Deathrow Gameshow
1987, (USA), Pirromount/Crown Int'l, color, 90 mins.
<u>W:</u> John McCafferty (*Chuck Teodan*), Robin Blythe (*Gloria Stern-virgin*), Darwyn Carson (*Trudy*), Beano (*Luigi Pappalardo*) Mark Lasky
<u>WRIT & D:</u> Mark Pirro <u>PHOTOG:</u> Craig Bassuk <u>MUSIC:</u> Greg Gross
Minor SF-satire: TV show gives criminals one more chance

Death Screams
1983, (USA), color, 88 mins.
<u>W:</u> Susan Kiger, Jennifer Chase, Jody Kay, William T. Hicks, Martin Tucker
Minor horror-thriller: Coeds meet machete-wielding maniac

The Deathshead Vampire
1968, (GB), Tigon, color, 88 mins.
<u>W:</u> Peter Cushing (*Insp. Quennell*), Robert Flemyng (*Prof. Mallinger*), Wanda Ventham (*Clare Mallinger*), David Griffin (*William*), Vanessa Howard (*Meg Quennell*), Russell Napier (*The Landlord*), Roy Hudd (*The Morgue Attendant*), John Paul (*Warrander*), Kevin Stoney (*Grainger*), Glynn Edwards (*Sgt. Allan*), Malcolm Rogers, Joan Ingram
<u>P:</u> Tony Tenser & Arnold Miller <u>D:</u> Vernon Sewell <u>STORY:</u> Peter Bryan
USA retitle (1974), **The Vampire-Beast Craves Blood.** A.k.a. **Blood Beast from Hell** and **The Blood Beast Terror**
Modest horror-fantasy: Scientist's "daughter" undergoes nocturnal changes, becomes blood-thirsty moth

Death Ship
1980, (GB-Can), Sandy Howard-Harold Greenberg/Astral Bellevue Pathe/Bloodstar/Lamitas/Avco Embassy, color, 91 mins.
<u>W:</u> Richard Crenna (*Trevor Marshall*), George Kennedy (*Capt. Ashland*), Sally Ann Howes (*Margaret Marshall*), Nick Mancuso (*Nick*), Kate Reid (*Mrs. Morgan*), Jennifer McKinney (*Robin Marshall*), Danny Higham (*Ben Marshall*), Victoria Burgoyne (*Lori*), Saul Rubineck (*Jackie*), Lee Murray (*Parsons*), Doug Smith (*The Seaman*)
<u>P:</u> Derek Gibson & Harold Greenberg <u>D:</u> Alvin Rakoff <u>SCR:</u> John Robins <u>STORY:</u> Jack Hill & David P. Lewis <u>PHOTOG:</u> Rene Verzier <u>MUSIC:</u> Ivor Slaney
Standard horror-thriller: Weird events on Nazi "death ship"

Deaths in Tokimeki
1984, (Jap), color, 105 mins.
<u>W:</u> Kenji Sawada, Kanaka Higuchi, Naoki Sugiura
<u>D:</u> Yoshimitsu Morita
Standard thriller: Hit man targets cult leader

Death Smiles on a Murderer
1973, (W. Ger-It), Avco Embassy TV, color
<u>W:</u> Ewa Aulin (*Charlotte*), Klaus Kinski (*Walter*), Angela Bo, Giacomo Rossi-Stuart
<u>D:</u> Aristide Massaccesi
Minor horror-thriller: Dead return to life

Death Spa
1987, (USA), color, 87 mins.
<u>W:</u> William Bumiller, Brenda Bakke, Merritt Butrick
<u>D:</u> Michael Fischa
Minor horror-thriller: Health club possessed by woman's vengeful spirit

Deathsport
1978, (USA), New World, color, 82 mins
<u>W:</u> David Carradine, Claudia Jennings, Richard Lynch, Will Walker, William Smithers, David McLean, Jesse Vint, Peter Hooper, H.B. Haggerty, John Himes, Jim Galante, Brenda Venus
<u>D:</u> Henry Suso & Alan Arkush <u>SCR:</u> Henry Suso & Donald Stewart <u>STORY:</u> Frances Doel <u>PHOTOG:</u> Gary Graver <u>MUSIC:</u> Andrew Stein
Standard SF-adventure: Future nomad leader vs. evil cyclists

Deathstalker
1983, (USA-Mex), Palo Alto/New World, color, 80 mins.
<u>W:</u> Richard Hill, Barbi Benton, Richard Brooker, Lillian Ker, Lana Clarkson
<u>D:</u> John Watson <u>SCR:</u> Howard Cohen
Minor fantasy-adventure: Muscleman ousts tyrant magician

Deathstalker II: Duel of the Titans
1987, (USA), New Horizons, color, 96 mins.
<u>W:</u> John Terlesky, Monique Gabrielle, John LaZar, Douglas Mortimer, Carina Davi, Toni Naples, Maria Socas, William Feldman, Marcos Wolinsky, Jake Arnt, Queen Kong, Arch Stanton, Leo Nichols, Maria Luisa Carnivani, Frank Sisty, Red Sands, Dan Savio, Nick Sardansky
<u>D & STORY:</u> Jim Wynorski <u>SCR:</u> Neil Ruttenberg <u>PHOTOG:</u> Leonard Solis <u>SPCL-FX:</u> Nicky Morgan <u>MUSIC:</u> Chuck Cirino
Made-for-Video, minor adventure-fantasy: Hero aids deposed princess

Deathstalker III: Warriors from Hell
1988, (USA), New Horizons, video, color, 85 mins.
<u>W:</u> John Allen Nelson, Carla Herb, Thom Christopher, Terri Treas
<u>D:</u> Alfonso Corona <u>SCR:</u> Howard R. Cohen
Made-for-Video, minor adventure-fantasy: Hero faces despot's demonic minions

Deathstalker 4: Match of the Titans
1992, (USA), color, 85 mins.
<u>W:</u> Richard Hill, Maria Ford, Michelle Moffett, Brent Baxter Clark
<u>D:</u> Howard R. Cohen

Death Takes a Holiday
1934, (USA), Para, b&w, 78 mins.
<u>W:</u> Fredric March (*Count Sirki/"Death"*), Katharine Alexander, Sir Guy Standing, Evelyn Venable, Edward Van Sloan, Kathleen Howard, Gail Patrick, Kent Taylor, Helen Westley, Henry Travers, Otto Hoffman, Anna Delinsky, G.P. Huntley Jr., Frank Yaconelli
<u>D:</u> Mitchell Leisen <u>SCR:</u> Maxwell Anderson, Gladys Lehman & Walter Ferris, from Alberto Casella's stage play <u>PHOTOG:</u> Charles Lang
*Classic fantasy: Death takes human form, pursues love. Remake: **Meet Joe Black** (1998)*

Death Takes a Holiday
1971, (USA), Univ, Made for TV, color, 73 mins.
<u>W:</u> Monte Markham, Yvette Mimieux, Myrna Loy, Burt Convy, Melvyn Douglas, Kerwin Mathews, Austin Willis, Priscilla Pointer, Colby Chester, Maureen Reagan
<u>P:</u> George Eckstein <u>D:</u> Robert Butler <u>TELEPLAY:</u> Rita Lakin, from Alberto Casella's stage play
TVM, standard fantasy: Death in human form pursues maiden

Death Trap
1962, (GB), Merton Park/Anglo-Amalgamated, b&w, 56 mins.
<u>W:</u> Albert Lieven (*Paul Heindrick*), Barbara Shelley (*Jean Anscombe*), John Meillon (*Ross Williams*), Mercy Haystead (*Carol Halston*), Kenneth Cope (*Derek Maitland*), Gladys Henson (*The Housekeeper*), Leslie Sands (*Insp. Simons*), Richard Bird (*Ted Cupps*), Barbara Windsor (*Babs Newton*)
<u>P:</u> Jack Greenwood <u>D:</u> John Moxey <u>SCR:</u> John Roddick, from a novel by Edgar Wallace
Modest mystery: Girl seeks deceased sister's vanished money

Death Trap (1976)
see Eaten Alive! (1976)

Death Valley
1982, (USA), Univ, color, 90 mins.
<u>W:</u> Paul LeMat, Catherine Hicks, Stephen McHattie, A. Wilford Brimley, Peter Billingsley, Edward Herrmann, Jack O'Leary, Mary Steelsmith, Gina Christian, Kirk I. Kiskella, Frank J. Cimorelli, Arnold C. Waterman, Fred W.S. Newton, J.P.S. Brown, Roy S. Gunsburg, Merritt Holloway
<u>D:</u> Dick Richards <u>SCR:</u> Richard Rothstein <u>PHOTOG:</u> Stephen H. Burum <u>MUSIC:</u> Dana Kaproff
Minor thriller: Murderer stalks desert

Deathwatch: LEONARD NIMOY

Death Warmed Over
*see **Death Warmed Up***

Death Warmed Up
1984, (New Zeal), Skouras, color 83 mins.
W: Gary Day (*Archer Howell*), Michael Hurst, Bruno Lawrence, Margaret Umbers, David Letch
D: David Blyth   **SCR:** David Blyth & Michael Heath   **PHOTOG:** James Bartle
   ELECTRONIC MUSIC SCORE: Mark Nicholas
A.k.a. Death Warmed Over
Award-winning SF-horror (Golden Unicorn, Paris Horror Festival): Scientist turns
   humans into killing machines

Deathwatch
1966, (USA), Beverly/Altura, b&w, 88 mins
W: Leonard Nimoy, Michael Forrest, Paul Mazursky
D: Vic Morrow
Minor melodrama: War-time atrocity breeds murder

Deathwatch
1980, (Fr-W. Ger), Selta Films-Little Bear, color, 128 mins.
W: Romy Schneider, Harvey Keitel, Harry Dean Stanton, Max von Sydow, Therese Liotard, Bernhard Wicki
D: Bertrand Tavernier **-SCR:** Bertrand Tavernier & David Rayfiel, from David Compton's novel Continuous Katherine Mortenhoe   **PHOTOG:** Pierre-William Glenn
Unusual SF-drama: Dying authoress secretly filmed

Death Weekend
see The House by the Lake

The Death Wheelers
see Psychomania (1972)

Deborah
1974, (It), Paola/Lorimar, color, 101 mins.
W: Bradford Dillman (*Michael*), Marina Malfatti (*Deborah*), Gig Young (*Herman*), Delia Boccardo, Michela Esdra, Mario Garibba, Lucretia Love, Adriano Amidei Migliano, Vittorio Mangano, Gigi Casellato, Luigi Atonio Guerra, Raffaele Di Mario, Matilde Dell'Acqua, Rita Lo Verde, Giuseppe Castelli
D: Marcello Andrei   **SCR:** Piero Regnoli, Marcello Andrei, Alvaro Fabrizio, & Giuseppe Pulieri   **PHOTOG:** Claudio Racca   **MUSIC:** Albert Verrecchia
Standard thriller: Psychic woman has hallucinations

The Debt of Gambling
1913, (GB), Barker, b&w, 780 ft. (237.7m)
W: Thomas H. MacDonald (*Jack Argyll*), Doreen O'Connor (*Bertha Argyll*), Tom Coventry (*Mrs. Marks*), Rachel de Solla (*Mrs. Marks*), May Morton (*The French Maid*)
D: Bert Haldan   **STORY:** Rowland Talbot
Standard crime-thriller: Gambling wife steals bracelet, kills herself

Le Decapité Vivant
see The Thing That Couldn't Die

Deceived
1991, (USA), color, 108 mins.
W: Goldie Hawn, John Heard, Robin Bartlett, Ashley Peldon, Tom Irwin, Beatrice Straight, Kate Reid, Maia Filar, Jan Rubes, Amy Wright
D: Damian Harris   **PHOTOG:** Jack Green
Standard thriller: Woman fears husband is killer

The Deceivers
1988, (GB-Ind), color, 103 mins.
W: Pierce Brosnan, Saeed Jaffrey, Shashi Kapoor, Helena Mitchell, Keith Michell, David Robb, Tariq Yunus
D: Nicholas Meyer, from a novel by John Masters
Standard adventure-thriller: British spy disguised as Hindu

Deceit (1976)
see Family Plot

Deceit
1993, (USA), color, 92 mins.
W: Scott Paulin, Norbert Weisser, Samantha Phillips
D: Albert Pyun   **SCR:** Kitty Chalmers
Standard SF-comedy: Libidinous space aliens assigned to vaporize Earth

The Deception
1912, (GB), Hepworth, b&w, 975 ft. (297.2m)
W: Gladys Sylvani (*Esme*), Alec Worcester (*Hugh Mortimer*), Chrissie White (*Fay*)
D: Bert Haldane
Standard melodrama: Girl takes place of sister who deserted blind scientist

Deception (1920)
see Anna Boleyn

La Decima Vittima (The Tenth Victim)
1965, (It-Fr), C.C. Champion-Les Filmes Concordia/Carlo Ponti/Embassy, color, 92 mins.
W: Marcello Mastroianni, Ursula Andress, Elsa Martinelli, Salvo Randone, Evi Rigano, Massimo Serato, Milo Quesada, Luce Bonifassy, Mickey Knox,

---

Richard Armstrong, Anita Sanders, Walter Williams, George Wang
P: Carlo Ponti   **D:** Elio Petri   **SCR:** Elio Petri, Ennio Flaiano, Tonina Guerra & Giorgio Salvioni, based on Robert Sheckley's novel *The Seventh Victim*
   PHOTOG: Gianni Di Venenzo   **MUSIC:** Piero Piccioni
Wry SF-comedy: Murder legalized in overpopulated future

The Decision of Christopher Blake
1948, (USA), WB, b&w, 75 mins.
W: Ted Donaldson, Alexis Smith, John Hoyt, Cecil Kellaway, Art Baker, Mary Wickes, Robert Douglas, Lois Maxwell, Harry Davenport, Bert Hanlon, Douglas Kennedy
WRIT & P: Ranald MacDougall   **D:** Peter Godfrey, from a play by Moss Hart
   PHOTOG: Karl Freund   **MUSIC:** Max Steiner
Confused melodrama: Divorce trial affects young boy

Decoy
1946, (USA), Mono, b&w, 76 mins.
W: Jean Gillie, Edward Norris
Minor melodrama

Decoy: JEAN GILLIE

Decoy for Terror
1970, (Can), color 85 mins.
W: William Kerwin, Jean Christopher, Neil Sedaka, Andree Champagne, Mary Lou Collier
D: Erick Santamaria
A.k.a. Playgirl Killer
Minor thriller: Demented artist kills female models

The Deep
1977, (USA), Casablanca-Filmworks/Col/EMI, color, 124 mins.
W: Robert Shaw (*Romer Treece*), Jacqueline Bisset (*Gail Berke*), Nick Nolte (*David Sanders*), Lou Gossett (*Henri Cloche*), Dick Anthony Williams (*Slake*), Robert Tessier (*Kevin*), Earl Maynard (*Ronald*), Eli Wallach (*Adam Coffin*), Teddy Tucker (*The Harbor Master*), Bob Minor (*Wiley*), Lee McClain (*Johnson*)
P: Peter Guber   **D:** Peter Yates   **SCR:** Peter Benchley & Tracy Keenan Wynn, from Peter Benchley's novel   **PHOTOG:** Christopher Challis   **MUSIC:** John Barry, title sung by Donna Summer   **SPCL-FX:** Ira Anderson
Major adventure-thriller: Intrigue surrounds sunken ship with cargo of morphine

Deep Freeze
1958, (USA), AA, b&w
W: Gerald Mohr, Allison Hayes, Charles Bronson, John Shepodd
Minor but engrossing SF-thriller: Beautiful but deadly space alien tries to appropriate Antarctica

Deep Impact
1998, (USA), Amblin/Dreamworks/Para, color
W: Vanessa Redgrave, Robert Duvall, Morgan Freeman, Tea Leoni, Maximilian Schell, Elijah Wood, Jon Favreau
D: Mimi Leder   **SCR:** Michael Tolkin & Bruce Joel Rubin
Impressive SF-thriller (remake of When Worlds Collide): Rogue comet on collision course with Earth

Deep Red (1976)
see Profundo Rosso

Deep Red
1994, (USA), Univ, video color, 85 mins.
W: Michael Biehn (*Joe Keyes*), Joanna Pacula (*Monica Qwik*), Lisa Collins (*Mrs. Rickman*), John de Lancie (*Thomas Newmeyer*), Tobin Bell (*Warren Rickman*), John Kapelos (*Mack Waters*), Steven Williams (*Eldon James*), Michael Des

D

Barres (*Lew Ramirez*), Lindsey Haun (*Gracie Rickman*), Daniel Barringer (*Milkman #1*), John Alden (*Milkman #2*), Kevin Page (*The Patrolman*), Chayse Dacoda (*Lydia*), Hank Cheyne (*Bradley Parker*), Jesse Vint (*Det. Rhodes*), Jack Andreozzi (*The Janitor*), Eric Fleeks, Jose Rey
<u>SPCL-FX SPRVSR</u>: B. Russell Hessey
Made-for-Video, standard SF-thriller: Villains seek bio-engineered immortality factor

Deep Rising
1998, (USA), Hollywood, color
<u>W</u>: Treat Williams, Famke Janssen, Clifton Powell, Wes Studi, Anthony Heald, Kevin J. O'Connor, Derrick O'Connor, Jason Flemyng
<u>WRIT & D</u>: Stephen Sommers <u>PHOTOG</u>: Howard Atherton <u>MUSIC</u>: Jerry Goldsmith
Exciting SF-thriller: Band of thieves meets sea monster

Deep Space
1988, (USA), Trans World, color, 90 mins.
<u>W</u>: Charles Napier, Ann Turkel, Ron Glass, James Booth, Bo Svenson, Norman Burton, Julie Newmar, Anthony Eisley, Peter Palmer
<u>D</u>: Fred Olen Ray <u>SCR</u>: Fred Olen Ray & T.L. Lankford
Minor SF-thriller: Alien life found on moon

Deepstar Six
1989, (USA), Carolco/Tri-Star, color, 100 mins.
<u>W</u>: Taurean Blacque (*Laidlaw*), Nancy Everhard (*Joyce Collins*), Greg Evigan (*McBride*), Miguel Ferrer (*Snyder*), Cindy Pickett (*Diane Norris*), Nia Peeples (*Scarpelli*), Matt McCoy (*Richardson*), Marius Meyers, Elya Baskin, Thom Bray, Ronn Carroll
<u>D</u>: Sean S. Cunningham <u>SCR</u>: Lewis Abernathy & Geof Miller <u>STORY</u>: Lewis Abernathy <u>PHOTOG</u>: Mac Ahlberg <u>VS-FX SPRVSR</u>: James Isaac <u>MUSIC</u>: Harry Manfredini
Standard SF-horror: Sea monster threatens underwater base

Deep Star Six: Greg Evigan and Nancy Everhard

Def by Temptation
1990, (USA), Bonded Filmworks/Orpheus/Troma, color, 95 mins.
<u>W</u>: James Bond III (*Joel*), Kadeem Hardison ("K"), Samuel L. Jackson (*Minister Garth*), Bill Nunn (*Dougy*), Minnie Gentry (*Grandma*), Rony Clanton (*The Married Man*), Stephen Van Cleef (*Jonathan*), John Canada Terrell (*Bartender #1*), Guy Davis (*Bartender #2*), Cynthia Bond (*The Temptress*), Melba Moore (*Madame Sonya*), Freddie Jackson, Najee, Z Wright, Starlina Young, Michael Rivera, Sundra Jean Williams, Angela Stokes, Beth Latty, Lahaina Kameha, Ellis Williams, Michael Michelle, Robin Harmon
<u>WRIT, P, & D</u>: James Bond III <u>PHOTOG</u>: Ernest Dickerson <u>MUSIC</u>: Paul Laurence <u>SONGS</u>: *All Over You, Hungry for Me Again, Face to Face, In a Sexy Mood, What Makes You Feel That Way About Me, In and Out, On a Mission, & Sex and the Single Man*
Standard horror-fantasy: Demoness lures men

Def Con 4
1985, (USA), Salter Street Films/New World, color, 86 mins.
<u>W</u>: Lenore Zann, Maury Chaykin, Kate Lynch, Kevin King, Tim Choate, John Walsch, Jeff Pustil, Donna King, Karen Kenedy, Al Foster, Ken Ryan, Peter Falconer
<u>D & SCR</u>: Paul Donovan <u>MUSIC</u>: Chris Young
Minor SF-thriller: Astronauts face post-nuke barbarism

The Defilers
1965, (USA), Boxoffice Spectaculars/Sonney Amusement Enterprises, color
<u>W</u>: Mae Johnson
<u>P</u>: David F. Friedman <u>D</u>: R.L. Frost
Minor shocker: Punks on violent rampage

A Degree of Murder
1967, (W. Ger), Univ, color
<u>W</u>: Anita Pallenberg
<u>P</u>: Rob Houwer <u>D & SCR</u>: Volker Schlondorff <u>MUSIC</u>: Brian Jones
Standard thriller: Waitress accidentally kills ex-lover

Deja Vu
1985, (GB), Golan-Globus/Cannon, color, 95 mins.
<u>W</u>: Jaclyn Smith (*Brooke/Maggie*), Nigel Terry (*Michael/Greg*), Shelley Winters (*Olga*), Claire Bloom (*Eleanor*), Richard Kay (*William Tanner, 1935*), Frank Gatliff (*William Tanner, 1984*), Michael Ladkin (*Willmer*), David Lewin (*The Reporter*), David Adams (*The Chauffeur*), Marianne Stone (*Mabel*), Virginia Guy (*The Lead Dancer*), Josephine Buchan (*The Research Ass't*), Richard Graydon (*Capt. Wilson*), Claire Bayliss
<u>D</u>: Anthony Richmond <u>SCR</u>: Ezra Rappaport, Anthony Richmond & Arnold Schmidt <u>ADAPT</u>: Joane A. Gil, from Trevor Meldal-Johnson's novel *Always* <u>PHOTOG</u>: David Holmes <u>MUSIC</u>: Pino Donaggio
Standard thriller: Playwright encounters reincarnation

Delerium
1977, (USA), color, 94 mins.
<u>W</u>: Turk Cekovsky, Debi Shanley, Terry Ten Broeck
<u>D</u>: Peter Maris
A.k.a. **Psycho Puppet**
Minor thriller: Homicidal maniac goes on killing spree.

Delerium in a Studio
1907, (Fr), Star, b&w, 93m (305.1 ft./5.2 mins.)
<u>D</u>: Georges Melies
Standard fantasy

The Delphic Oracle
see L'Oracle de Delphes

Deluge
1933, (USA), RKO, b&w, 70 mins
<u>W</u>: Peggy Shannon, Lois Wilson, Sidney Blackmer, Samuel S. Hinds, Ralfe Harolde, Matt Moore, Fred Kohler, Edward Van Sloan
<u>D</u>: Felix Feist Jr. <u>SCR</u>: John Goodrich & Warren B. Duff, based on a story by S. Fowler Wright <u>PHOTOG</u>: Norbert Brodine & William B. Williams
Classic SF-thriller: Vision of apocalypse

Delusion
1978, (USA), New Line, color, 83 mins.
<u>W</u>: Patricia Pearcy, David Hayward, John Dukakis, Joseph Cotten
<u>D</u>: Alan Beattie <u>SCR</u>: Jack Viertel
Minor thriller: Nurse falls under spell of strange teenager

Dementia
1955, (USA), Van Wolf-API, b&w, 60 mins.
<u>W</u>: Adrienne Barrett, Bruno Ve Sota
<u>P D, & SCR</u>: John Parker <u>NARRATOR</u>: Ed McMahon
A.k.a. **Daughter of Horror**
"...inhuman, indecent, and the quintessence of gruesomeness"—NY State Board of Censors
Unusual expressionistic horror-fantasy: Distraught girl commits atrocities

Dementia 13
1963, (USA-Irish), Filmgroup/AIP, b&w, 81 mins.
<u>W</u>: William Campbell (*Richard Haloran*), Luana Anders (*Louise Haloran*), Bart Patton (*Billy Haloran*), Mary Mitchel (*Kane*), Patrick Magee (*Justin Caleb*), Eithne Dunn (*Lady Haloran*), Peter Read (*John Haloran*), Karl Schanzer (*Simon*), Barbara Dowling (*Kathleen*), Ron Perry (*Arthur*), Derry O'Donavan (*Lillian*)
<u>P</u>: Roger Corman <u>WRIT & D</u>: Francis Coppola <u>PHOTOG</u>: Charles Hanawalt <u>MUSIC</u>: Ronald Stein <u>DESIGN</u>: Albert Locatelli
A.k.a. **The Haunted and the Hunted**
Minor but impressive thriller: Murders on Irish estate

Demented
1980, (USA), color, 92 mins.
<u>W</u>: Sallee Elyse, Bruce Gilchrist
Minor thriller: Gang-raped woman gets revenge

The Demolitionist
1995, (USA), color, 95 mins.
<u>W</u>: Nicole Eggert, Richard Grieco, Bruce Abbott, Susan Tyrrell
Standard SF-thriller: Bio-engineering resurrects woman cop

Demolition Man
1993, (USA), Silver Pictures/WB, color, 114 mins.
<u>W</u>: Sylvester Stallone (*John Spartan*), Wesley Snipes (*Simon Phoenix*), Sandra Bullock (*Lenina Huxley*), Nigel Hawthorne (*Dr. Raymond Cocteau*), Denis Leary (*Edgar Friendly*), Benjamin Bratt, Bob Gunton, Glenn Shadix, Bill Cobbs, Troy Evans, Andre Gregory, Jesse Ventura, Grand L. Bush, Pat Skipper, Steve Kaman, John Enos, Dan Cortese
<u>D</u>: Marco Brambilla <u>SCR</u>: Daniel Waters, Robert Reneau & Peter M. Lenkov <u>STORY</u>: Peter M. Lenkov & Robert Reneau <u>PHOTOG</u>: Alex Thomson <u>MUSIC</u>: Elliot Goldenthal
Standard SF-thriller: 20th-century cop pursues villain in pacified 21st century

The Demon (1963)
see Il Demonio

Demon
1976, (USA), Georgia/New World, color, 89 mins.
W: Tony Lo Bianco, Sandy Dennis, Sylvia Sidney, Sam Levene, Robert Drivas, Mike Kellin, Richard Lynch, Deborah Raffin, Harry Bellaver, James Dixon, Andy Kaufman, Sammy Williams, Jo Flores Chase, Sherry Steiner, Adrian James
WRIT, P & D: Larry Cohen   MUSIC: Frank Cordell
A.k.a. **God Told Me To**
Modest SF-thriller: Detective stalks instigator of senseless killings

The Demon
1981, (GB), Hollard, color, 94 mins.
W: Jennifer Holmes, Cameron Mitchell, Zoli Markey, Peter J. Elliott, Craig Gardner, Moira Winslow, Mark Tanous, Diane Burmeister, George Korelin, Vera Blacker, Ashleigh Sendin, John Parsonson, Graham Kennard, April Galetti, Jannie Wienand, Amanda Wildman
WRIT, P, & D: Percival Rubens   PHOTOG: Vincent Cox   MUSIC: Nick Labuschagne
Minor horror-thriller: Fiendish killer prowls

Demon and the Mummy
1975, (USA), Francy/Univ/ABC-TV, color, 93 mins.
W: Darren McGavin (*Kolchak*), Simon Oakland (*Vincenzo*), Erik Estrada (*Pepe Torres*), Carolyn Jones (*The Registrar*), Andrew Prine (*Dr. C. Evans Speight*), Keenan Wynn (*Capt. Joe Siska*), Jackie Vernon (*Coach Toomey*), Ruth McDevitt (*Emily Cowles*), Sorrell Booke (*The Taxidermist*), Ramon Bieri, Jack Grinnage, Kristina Holland, Pippa Scott, Victor Campos, Carlos Romero, Ben Masters, John Elerick, Udana Power, Sondra Currie, Davis Roberts, Donald Mantooth, Robert Casper
D: Don Weis & Don McDougall   TELEPLAY: Stephen Lord, Michael Kozoll, Arthur Rowe & David Chase   STORY: Arthur Rowe & Stephen Lord, from characters created by Jeff Rice   PHOTOG: Ronald W. Browne   MUSIC: Jerry Fielding & Gil Melle
TVM, minor horror-fantasy culled from 2 episodes of **Night Stalker** *teleseries: Rogue reporter probes occult murders*

The Demon Barber of Fleet Street
1936, (GB), George King/MGM, b&w, 68 mins.
W: Tod Slaughter (*Sweeney Todd*), Stella Rho (*Mrs. Lovatt*), Johnny Singer (*Tobias*), Eve Lister (*Johanna*), Bruce Seton (*Mark*), D.J. Williams (*Stephen Oakley*), Davina Graig (*Nan*), Jerry Verno (*Pearley*), Ben Soutten (*Beadle*), Billy Holland (*Mr. Parsons*), Norman Pierce (*Mr. Findlay*), Ben Williams (*Capt. Stevenson*), Aubrey Mallalieu (*Trader Patterson*)
D: George King   SCR: Frederick Hayward & H.F. Maltby, from a play by George Dibdin-Pitt. Basis for Musical *Sweeney Todd*   PHOTOG: Jack Parker
U.S. Release:1939
Aka **Sweeney Todd, the Demon Barber of Fleet Street.**
Standard thriller: Murderous barber preys on unwary. cf. **Bloodthirsty Butchers**

Demon Cavaliers
see **The Hell-Fire Club**

Demon City Shinjuku
1993, (Jap), color 82 mins.
Standard animated SF-fantasy: Evil forces beset Nipponese city

The Demon Doctor (1936)
see **Juggernaut**

The Demon Doctor (1964)
see **El Secreto del Dr. Orlof**

The Demon Dog
1911, (GB), Hepworth, b&w, 400 ft. (121.9m)
W: Hay Plumb (*The Father*)
D: Lewin Fitzhamon
Minor fantasy short: Father dreams toy bulldog grows bigger

The Demon from Devil's Lake
1964, (USA), Phillips-Marker, b&w
W: Dave Heath
P D & SCR: Russ Marker
Minor SF-horror: "Noah's Ark" spaceship crashes, animal inhabitants transmute into one monstrous beast

Demon Hunter
1988, (USA), color, 90 mins.
W: George Ellis, Erin Fleming, Marrianne Gordon
D: Massey Cramer
Minor thriller: Deranged killer stalks

Demoniac
1957, (Fr), UMPO, b&w, 97 mins.
W: Jeanne Moreau, Micheline Presle, Francois Perier
D: Luis Saslavsky
Standard melodrama: Mistaken identities in World War II

Demonic Toys
1992, (USA), Para, video, color, 86 mins
W: Tracy Scoggins, Bentley Mitchum, Michael Russo, Pete Schrum, Jeff Weston, Daniel Cerny, Ellen Dunning, Barry Lynch
D: Peter Manoogian
Made-for-Video, standard fantasy-thriller: Evil dolls kill. sequel: **Dollman vs. Demonic Toys**

Il Demonio (The Demon)
1963, (It), Vox Films-Titanus, b&w, 100 mins.
W: Daliah Lavi, Frank Woolf
D: Brunello Rondi   MUSIC: Piero Piccioni
Minor horror-thriller: Terrors of possession

Demon Island
1982, (GB-Greece), video, color
W: James Earl Jones, Jose Ferrer
Minor horror-thriller: Monster terrorizes Greek isle

Demon Keeper
1994, (USA), New Horizons, color, 90 mins.
W: Dirk Benedict, Edward Albert
Made-for-Video, standard horror-fantasy: Swindler meets satanic fiend

Demon Knight
1995, (USA), Univ, color, 92 mins.
W: William Sadler, Billy Zane, Jada Pinkett, CCH Pounder, Dick Miller, Brenda Bakke, Charles Fleischer, Thomas Haden Church, Dale Swann, John Schuck, Gary Farmer, Tim de Zarn, Sherrie Rose, Tony Salome, Ryan Sean O'Donohue, Ken Baldwin, Mark D. Kennerly, John Kassir (*Voice of the Crypt Keeper*), John Larroquette, Tiffany Anne, Traci Bingham, Reda Beebe, Fonti Butler, Veronica Culver, Tina Hollimon, Elaine Marks, Mim Parker
D: Ernest Dickerson   SCR: Ethan Reiff, Cyrus Voris & Mark Bishop   PHOTOG: Rick Bota   MUSIC: Ed Shearmur
Standard horror-fantasy: Soul "collector" pursues man

The Demon Lover
1976, (USA), 21st-Century/Wolf Lore, color 87 mins.
W: Gunnar Hansen, Val Mayerick, Christmas Robbins, Tom Hutton, David Howard
P D & SCR: Donald Jackson & Jerry Younkins
A.k.a. **Devil Master** *and* **Master of Evil**
Minor horror-fantasy

Demon Monster
see **Craze**

The Demon Murder Case
1983, (USA), Dick Clark Cinema Prod./NBC-TV, color, 95 mins.
W: Kevin Bacon (*Kenny*), Andy Griffith (*Harris*), Eddie Albert (*Fr. Dietrich*), Liane Langland (*Nancy*), Cloris Leachman (*Joan*), Joyce Van Patten (*Connie*), Ken Kercheval (*Richard*), Frank Hamilton (*Fr. Eagon*), Beverlee McKinsey (*Charlotte*), Richard Masur (*Mariono*), Charlie Fields (*Brian*), Harvey Fierstein (*Voice of Demon*)
D: Billy Hale   TELEPLAY: William Kelley   PHOTOG: John Lindley   MUSIC: George Aliceson Tipton
TVM, standard thriller: Fact-based tale of demonic possession

Demon of Paradise
1987, (USA), color, 84 mins.
W: Kathryn Witt, William Steis, Leslie Huntly, Laura Banks
D: Cirio H. Santiago
Minor SF-horror: Dynamite fishing rouses aquatic monster

Demonoid
1981, (USA), American Panorama, color, 85 mins.
W: Stuart Whitman (*Father Cunningham*), Samantha Eggar (*Jennifer Baines*), Roy Cameron Jenson (*Mark Baines*), Ted White (*Frankie*), Narciso Busquets (*Dr. Julian Rivkin*), Haji Catton (*Angela*), Erika Carlsson (*Nurse Morgan*), Lew Saunders (*Sgt. Leo Matson*), Jose Chavez Trowe (*Pepe*), Whitey Hughes (*The Gambler*), George Soviak (*Sgt. Needham*), Al Jones (*Patrolman Yates*)
P & D: Alfred Zacharias   SCR: David Lee Fein, Alfred Zacharias, & F. Amos Powell, from an orig. story by Alfred Zacharias   PHOTOG: Alex Phillips Jr.   MUSIC: Richard Gillis
A.k.a. **Demonoid: Messenger of Death** *and* **Macabra**
Minor horror-fantasy: Ancient severed hand exerts evil influence

Demonoid: Messenger of Death
see **Demonoid**

The Demon Planet
see **Terrore Nello Spazio**

Demon Rage
see **Satan's Mistress**

The Demons
1974, (USA), color, 90 mins.
W: Anne Libert, Britt Nichols, Doris Thomas
Minor horror-thriller: Dying woman curses torturers

Demons
1985, (It), Dacfilm/Ascot, color, 85 mins.
W: Natasha Hovey (*Sharel*), Paola Cozzo (*Kathy*), Fabiola Toledo, Urbano Barberini, Karl Zinny, Fiore Argento
D: Lamberto Bava **SCR:** Dardano Sacchetti **PHOTOG:** Gianlorenzo Battaglia **MUSIC:** Claudio Simonetti **ADDITIONAL MUSIC:** Billy Idol, Motley Crue, Pretty Maids, Rick Springfield, Go West, The Adventures, Accept, and Saxon
Standard horror-fantasy: Fiends trap theater patrons

Demons 2
1988, (It), Dario Argento/Dacfilm, color, 88 mins.
W: David Knight, Nancy Brilli, Coralina Cataldi Tassoni, Asia Argento, Bobby Rhodes, Virginia Bryant, Marco Vivio, Anita Bartolucci, Antonio Cantafora, Luisa Passega, Lina Salemme, Davide Marotta, Michele Mirabella, Lorenzo Gioielli, Luca De Nardo, Maria Chara Sasso, Dario Casalini, Andrea Garinei, Angela Frondaroli, Caroline Christina Lund, Karen Gennaro, Marina Loi, Silvia Rosa, Lorenzo Flaherty, Monica Umena, Andrea Spera, Fabio Poggiali, Eliana Hoppe, Pascal Persiano, Robert Chilcott, Yvonne Fraschetti, Bruno Bilotta, Giovanna Pini, Furio Bilotta, Kim Rhone, Stefano Molinari, Pasquale Valente, Annalie Harrison
D: Lamberto Bava **SCR:** Dario Argento, Lamberto Bava, Franco Perrini & Dardano Sacchetti **PHOTOG:** Gianlorenzo Battaglia **MUSIC:** Simon Boswell, The Smiths, The Cult, Art of Noise, Peter Murphy & Dead Can Dance
Standard horror-fantasy: Ghouls rampage in high-rise

Demon Seed
1977, (USA), Herb Jaffe/MGM, color, 94 mins.
W: Julie Christie (*Susan Harris*), Fritz Weaver (*Alex Harris*), Gerrit Graham (*Walter Gabler*), Lisa Lu (*Soon Yen*), Larry J. Blake (*Came-ron*), John O'Leary (*Royce*), Berry Kroeger (*Petrosian*), Davis Roberts, Alfred Dennis, Patricia Wilson, Monica MacLean, E. Hampton Beagle, Michael Glass, Barbara O. Jones, Dana Laurita, Harold Oblong, Georgie Paul, Michelle Stacy, Tiffany Potter, Felix Silla, Robert Vaughn (*Voice of "Proteus IV"*)
D: Donald Cammell, from Dean R. Koontz' novel **PHOTOG:** Bill Butler **SPCL-FX:** Tom Fisher **MUSIC:** Jerry Fielding
Superior SF-thriller: Computer terrorizes scientist's wife

Demons of the Dead
1977, (It), Lea Film-Rational Cinematografica/Independent Int'l, color, 82 mins.
W: George Hilton, Edwige Fenech, Ivan Rassimov, Dominique Bochero, Julian Ugarte, George Rigaud, Susan Scott, Maria Cumari Quasimodo, Marina Malfatti, Renato Chiantoni, Alan Collins, Lisa Leonardi, Tom Felleghy, Gianni Pulone, Carla Mancini, Vera Drudi
D: Sergio Martino
Minor thriller: Disturbed woman joins satanic cult

Demons of Ludlow
1975, (USA), color, 83 mins.
W: Paul von Hauser, Stephanie Cushna, James Robinson, Carol Perry
D: Steven Kuether
Minor horror-fantasy: Demons attend small town's bicentennial celebration

Demons of the Mind
1972, (GB), Hammer/Int'l Co-Prods., color, 89 mins.
W: Paul Jones (*Carl*), Gillian Hills (*Elizabeth*), Kenneth J. Warren (*Klaus*), Patrick Magee (*Falkenberg*), Michael Hordern (*The Priest*), Yvonne Mitchell (*Hilda*), Shane Briant (*Emil*), Robert Hardy (*Friedrich*), Virginia Wetherell (*Inge*), Robert Brown (*Fischinger*), Deirdre Costello (*Magda*), Barry Stanton (*Ernst*), Sidonie Bond (*The Baroness*), Thomas Heathcote (*The Coachman*), Sheila Raynor (*The Crone*)
P: Frank Godwin **D:** Peter Sykes **SCR:** Christopher Wicking **STORY:** Frank Godwin & Christopher Wicking **PHOTOG:** Arthur Grant **MUSIC:** Harry Robinson
A.k.a. **Blood Evil**
Standard melodrama: Hereditary insanity in Viennese family

Demons of the Swamp
see **Attack of the Giant Leeches**

Demonstone
1989, (USA), color, 90 mins.
W: R. Lee Ermey, Jan-Michael Vincent, Nancy Everhard
D: Andrew Prowse
A.k.a. **Heartstone**
Minor fantasy-thriller: Filipino demon possesses TV reporter

Demonwarp
1988, (USA), Vidmark, color, 91 mins.
W: George Kennedy (*Crafton*), David Michael O'Neill, Pamela Gilbert, Billy

Jacoby, Hank Stratton, Emmett Alston
D: Emmett Alston, from a story by John Buechler **PHOTOG:** R. Michael Stringer
Minor SF-fantasy: Vacationers meet yeti, zombies

Demon Wind
1990, (USA), color, 100 mins.
W: Eric Larson, Francine Lapensee, Rufus Norris
D: Charles Philip Moore
Minor fantasy-thriller: Mayhem at haunted house

Demon Witch Child
1974, (Sp), Coliseum, color
D: Armando De Ossorio
Minor horror-fantsy (Exorcist imitation): Satanic child becomes old witch

The Demon with Bloody Hands
see **Blood of the Vampire**

Den of Doom
see **The Glass Cage**

The Dentist
1996, (USA), color, 90 mins.
W: Corbin Bernsen (*Dr. Feinman*), Linda Hoffman (*Brooke*), Ken Foree (*Harry Gibbs*)
Standard horror-thriller: Mad dentist discovers wife's infidelity, tirns office into torture chamber

The Dentist II
1998, (USA), color, 100 mins.
W: Corbin Bernsen, Jillian McWhirter, Linda Hoffman, Wendy Robie, Jim Antonio
Made-for-Video, standard thriller: Mad dentist flees asylum

Deported
1950, (USA), Univ, b&w, 87 mins.
W: Jeff Chandler, Marta Toren, Claude Dauphin, Carlo Rizzo
D: Robert Siodmak **PHOTOG:** William H. Daniels
Standard melodrama

The Depraved
1957, (GB), Danziger/UA, b&w, 70 mins.
W: Anne Heywood (*Laura Wilton*), Robert Arden (*Dave Dillon*), Carroll Levis (*Maj. Kellaway*), Basil Dignam (*Tom Wilton*), Denis Shaw (*Insp. Flynn*), Robert Ayres (*The Colonel*), Gary Thorne (*Kaufmann*)
P: Edward J. & Harry Lee Danziger **D:** Paul Dickson **SCR:** Brian Clemens **STORY:** Edith Dell
Standard crime-thriller: Army officer helps his lover kill her alcoholic husband

The Depths
see **Les Abysses**

Depths of the Unknown
see **The Time Travelers (1964)**

Deranged
1974, (Can), Karr Int'l/AIP, color, 83 mins.
W: Roberts Blossom (*Ezra*), Cosette Lee (*Ma*), Robert Warner (*Harlan*), Marcia Diamond (*Jenny*), Jack Mather (*The Drunk*), Brian Sneagle (*Brad*), Arlene Gillen (*Miss Johnson*), Robert McHeady (*The Sheriff*), Marian Waldman (*Maureen*), Pat Orr (*Sally*), Micki Moore (*Mary*), Leslie Carlson (*The Narrator*)
P: Tom Karr [Bob Clark] **D:** Bob Clark, Jeff Gillen & Alan Ormsby **SCR:** Alan Ormsby **PHOTOG:** Jack McGowan **MUSIC:** Carl Zittrer
Minor thriller: Madman kills and stuffs people

Deranged
1987, (USA), Platinum Pictures, color, 85 mins.
W: Jane Hamilton (*Joyce*), Paul Siederman (*Frank*), Jennifer Delora (*Maryann*), Jill Cumer (*Sheila*), John Brett (*Darren*), Loretta Palma (*Margaret*)
P & D: Chuck Vincent **SCR:** Craig Horrall **PHOTOG:** Larry Revene **MUSIC:** Bill Heller
Minor thriller: Woman descends into madness

Le Dernier Combat (The Last Battle)
1983, (Fr), b&w 90 mins.
W: Pierre Jolivet, Fritz Wepper, Jean Reno, Jean Bouise, Christiane Kruger
D: Luc Besson
Unusual SF-thriller: War among post-nukers

Les Derniers Jours de Pompeii (The Last Days of Pompeii)
1948, (Fr), b&w, 110 mins.
W: Micheline Presle
D & DIALOG: Marcel L'Herbier, from Bulwer-Lytton's classic novel
Standard melodrama: Intrigue and romance in Antiquity's doomed city

Le Dernier Voyage de Gulliver (The Last Voyage of Gulliver)
1960, (Fr), color
WRIT & D: Walerian Borowcyzk, based on Jonathan Swift's satire *Gulliver's Travels*
Unfinished animated feature, standard adventure-fantasy: Man visits bizarre societies

De Sade
1969, (USA-W. Ger), CCC-Trans Cont'l/AIP, color, 113 mins.
W: Keir Dullea *(Marquis de Sade)*, John Huston *(The Abbe)*, Senta Berger *(Anne de Montreuil)*, Uta Levka *(Rose Keller)*, Lilli Palmer *(Mme. de Montreuil)*, Anna Massey *(Renee de Montreuil)*, Sonja Ziemann *(La Beauvoisin)*, Max Kiebach *(The Young de Sade)*, Herbert Weissbach *(M. de Montreuil)*, Christiane Kruger *(The Marquis' Mistress)*, Barboura Morris
P: James H. Nicholson & Samuel Z. Arkoff **D:** Cy Endfield **SCR:** Richard Matheson **PHOTOG:** Heinz Pehlke **MUSIC:** Billy Strange
Ambitious but static melodrama: Kaleidoscopic biography of infamous degenerate

The Desert Island
1914, (GB), Captain Kettle/A&C, b&w, 1,340 ft. (408.4m)
STORY: C.J. Cutcliffe-Hyne
Standard adventure-fantasy: Child dreams of being shipwrecked, fighting pirates

Desert Legion
1953, (USA), Univ, color, 87 mins.
W: Alan Ladd *(Paul Lartal)*, Arlene Dahl *(Morjana)*, Richard Conte *(Crito)*, Anthony Caruso *(Lt. Messaoud)*, Oscar Beregi *(Si Khalil)*, Akim Tamiroff *(Pvt. Plevko)*, Leon Askin *(Maj. Vasil)*, Ivan Triesault *(Cpl. Schmidt)*, Ted Hecht *(Tabban)*, Don Blackman *(Kumbaba)*, Dave Sharpe *(Alyoun)*, Henri Letondal *(The General)*, George J. Lewis *(Lt. Lopez)*, Peter Coe *(Lt. Doudelet)*, Sujata & Asoka *(The Dancers)*
P: Ted Richmond **D:** Joseph Pevney **SCR:** Irving Wallace & Lewis Meltzer based on George Surdez' novel *Demon Caravan* **PHOTOG:** John Seitz **MUSIC:** Frank Skinner
Standard adventure-romance: Beautiful ruler of hidden city rescues only survivor of Foreign Legion patrol

Desert Raiders
*see **Hercules of the Desert***

Desert Warrior
1988, (USA), color, 89 mins.
W: Lou Ferrigno, Shari Shattuck, Kenneth Peer, Anthony East
D: Jim Goldman **SCR:** Frederick Bailey
Minor action-SF: Post-nuke hero roams devastated Earth

Des Filles pour un Vampire
*see **L'Ultima Preda del Vampiro***

Le Deshabillage Impossible (Impossible Undressing)
1900, (Fr), Star, b&w, 40m (131.2 ft./2.2 mins.)
D: Georges Melies
*GB retitle, **An Increasing Wardrobe**, USA retitle, **Going to Bed Under Difficulties***
Standard comedy-fantasy

Design for Murder
*see **Trunk Crime***

Desire
1920, (GB), B&C/Butcher, b&w, 4,460 ft. (1359.4m)
W: Dennis Neilson-Terry *(Raphael Valentin)*, Yvonne Arnaud *(Pauline)*, Christine Maitland *(Fedora)*, G.W. Anson *(Duval)*, Chris Walker *(Jonathon)*, Pardoe Woodman *(Emile)*, Austin Leigh *(Andre Valentin)*, Saba Raleigh *(Mother)*
P: Edward Godal **D & SCR:** George Edwards Hall, from a story by Honore de Balzac
*USA retitle, **The Magic Skin***
Standard fantasy: Author dreams asst's skin grants wishes

Desire and Hell at Sunset Motel
1992, (USA), SHO-TV, color, 90 mins.
W: Sherrilyn Fenn Whip Hubley, David Hewlett, David Johansen, Paul Bartel
D & SCR: Allen Castle
Made-for-Cable, standard thriller: Paranoid salesman and seductive wife encounter lust, betrayal, and murder at seedy California motel

Desire: The Vampire
*see **I, Desire***

Desk Set
1957, (USA), 20th-Fox, color, 103 mins.
W: Spencer Tracy *(Richard Sumner)*, Katharine Hepburn *(Bunny Watson)*, Joan Blondell *(Peg Costello)*, Gig Young *(Mike Cutler)*, Dina Merrill *(Sylvia)*, Sue Randall *(Ruthie)*, Nicholas Joy *(Azae)*, Diane Jergens *(Alice)*, Harry Ellerbe *(Smithers)*, Rachel Stevens *(The Receptionist)*, Merry Anders *(Cathy)*, Ida Moore *(The Old Lady)*, Neva Patterson *(Miss Warringer)*, Dick Gardner *(Fred)*, Sammy Ogg *(Kenny)*, Jesslyn Fax *(Mrs. Hewitt)*, Shirley Mitchell *(Myra Smithers)*, Hal Taggart, Renny McEvoy, King Mojave, Charles Heard, Harry Evans, Jack M. Lee, Bill Duray
P: Henry Ephron **D:** Walter Lang **SCR:** Phoebe & Henry Ephron, from

William Marchant's play **PHOTOG:** Leon Shamroy **SPCL-FX:** Ray Kellogg **MUSIC:** Lionel Newman
*GB retitle, **His Other Woman***
Amusing comedy: Computerization causes pandemonium in research department

Desperate
1947, (USA), RKO, b&w, 73 mins.
W: Steve Brodie, Audrey Long, Raymond Burr, Douglas Fowley, William Challee, Jason Robards Sr.
D: Anthony Mann
Minor melodrama Racketeers victimize truck driver

A Desperate Chance for Ellery Queen
1942, (USA), Col, b&w, 70 mins.
W: William Gargan *(Ellery Queen)*, Margaret Lindsay *(Nikki Porter)*, Charley Grapewin *(Insp. Queen)*, James Burke *(Sgt. Velie)*, John Litel *(Norman Hadley)*, Lillian Bond *(Adele Belden)*, Jack LaRue *(Tommy Gould)*, Morgan Conway *(Ray Stafford)*, Noel Madison *(George Belden)*, Charlotte Wynters *(Mrs. Norman Hadley)*, Frank Thomas *(Capt. Daley)*
D: James Hogan **SCR:** Eric Taylor, from characters created by Ellery Queen **PHOTOG:** James S. Brown Jr.
Minor mystery-thriller: Detective seeks missing man, finds several homicides

A Desperate Crime
*see **Les Incendiaires***

The Desperate Man
1959, (GB), Merton Park/Anglo-Amalgamated, b&w, 57 mins.
W: Jill Ireland *(Carol Bourne)*, Conrad Phillips *(Curtis)*, William Hartnell *(Smith)*, Charles Gray *(Lawson)*, John Warwick *(Insp. Cobley)*, Peter Swanwick *(Hoad)*, Arthur Gomez *(The Landlord)*, Patricia Burke *(Miss Prew)*, Ernest Butcher *(The Grocer)*
P: Jack Greenwood **D:** Peter Maxwell **SCR:** James Eastwood, from Paul Somers' novel
Beginner's Modest crime-thriller: Gem thief holds girl hostage in old castle

The Desperate Men
*see **Cat and Mouse** (1958)*

Desperate Mission
*see **Agent 255/Desperate Mission***

Desperate Motive
1992, (USA), color, 95 mins.
W: David Keith, William Katt, Mel Harris
Standard thriller: Psychopath insinuates himself into home of relative

A Desperate Stratagem
1914, (GB), Big Ben-Union/Pathe, b&w, 1,125 ft. (342.9m)
W: H.O. Martinek, Ivy Montford
D: H.O. Martinek **STORY:** L.C. MacBean
Standard crime-thriller: Engineer unmasks counterfeiters, aids oppressed girl

Destination Death
1956, (GB), Merton Park/Anglo-Amalgamated, b&w, 31 mins.
W: Russell Napier *(Insp. Duggan)*, Paula Byrne *(Mrs. Carden)*, Melissa Stribling

Destination Innerspace

(Helen Challoner), Arthur Gomez *(Supt. Mason)*, Raymond Young *(Mr. Carden)*
P: Alec Snowden **D:** Montgomery Tully **SCR:** James Eastwood **STORY:** Colin S. Reid, from a novel by Edgar Lustgarten
Standard crime thriller: Scotland Yard tracks currency smugglers

Destination Fury
1961, (Fr), b&w, 85 mins.
W: Eddie Constantine, Renato Rascel, Dorian Gray, Pierre Grasset
D: Giorgio Bianchi
Inane spy spoof: Double agent involved with Interpol

Destination Inner Space
1966, (USA), United Pictures, color, 82 mins.
W: Scott Brady, Sheree North, Gary Merrill, Wende Wagner, Mike Road, John Howard, Richard Niles, Biff Elliot, James Hong, Glen Sipes, Roy Barcroft, Ed Charles Sweeny, Ken Delo, Ron Burke
D: Francis D. Lyon   SCR: Arthur C. Pierce   PHOTOG: Brick Marquard
SPCL-FX: Roger George   MUSIC: Paul Dunlap
Minor SF-thriller: Underwater-lab scientists find UFO and aquatic space monstrosity

Destination Moon
1950, (USA), Eagle Lion/UA, color, 91 mins.
W: John Archer (*Barnes*), Warner Anderson (*Cargraves*), Dick Wesson (*Sweeney*), Tom Powers (*Gen. Thayer*), Erin O'BrienMoore (*Mrs. Cargraves*)
P: George Pal   D: Irving Pichel   SCR: Robert A. Heinlein, Rip Van Ronkel, & James O'Hanlon inspired by Robert A. Heinlein's novel *Rocketship Galileo*
PHOTOG: Lionel Lindon   SPCL-FX: Lee Zavitz   MUSIC: Leith Stevens
Modest SF classic: First manned expedition to moon

Destination Moonbase Alpha
1975, (USA), color, 93 mins.
W: Martin Landau, Barbara Bain, Barry Morse
TVM, standard SF-adventure (pilot for teleseries "Space 1999"): Moon-based scientists search for life in space

Destination Murder
1950, (USA), RKO, b&w, 70 mins.
W: Joyce MacKenzie, Stanley Clements
D: Edward L. Cahn
Standard thriller

Destination Saturn
1965, (USA), Univ, b&w, 70 mins.
W: Buster Crabbe (*Buck Rogers*), C. Montague Shaw (*Dr. Huer*), Constance Moore (*Wilma Deering*), Anthony Warde (*Killer Kane*), Jackie Moran (*Buddy Wade*), Philip Ahn (*Prince Tallen*), Jack Mulhall (*Capt. Rankin*), Carleton Young (*Scott*), Henry Brandon (*Capt. Lasca*), Kenne Duncan (*Lt. Lacy*), Guy Usher (*Aldar*), William Gould (*Marshall Kragg*), Wheeler Oakman (*Patten*), Reed Howes (*Roberts*)
D: Ford Beebe & Saul Goodkind   STORY & SCR: Norman S. Hall & Ray Trampe   PHOTOG: Jerry Ash
reissued (1979) as Buck Rogers, *A.k.a.* Planet Outlaws
Minor SF-adventure, feature culled from 1939 serial 'Buck Rogers': Man awakens from suspended animation, finds dangerous 25th century

Destiny (1921)
see Der Mude Tod

Destiny (1941)
see The Wolf Man (1941)

Destiny
1944, (USA), Univ, b&w, 65 mins.
W: Alan Curtis, Gloria Jean, Grace McDonald, Frank Craven
D: Reginald LeBorg   SCR: Roy Chanslor   PHOTOG: George Robinson
Sentimental melodrama, deleted portion of Flesh and Fantasy: *Escaped convict finds refuge with blind girl*

Destroy All Monsters
1968, (Jap), Toho/AIP, color, 87 mins.
W: Akiro Kubo (*Yamabe*), Kyoko Ai (*The Queen*), Jun Tazaki, Yokiko Kobayashi, Notari Sojak, Yoshio Tsuchiya, Andrew Hughs, Kenji Sahara
P: Tomoyuki Tanaka   D: Ishiro (Inoshiro) Honda   SCR: Kaoru Mabuchi & Inoshiro Honda   PHOTOG: Taiichi Kankura   SPCL-FX: Eiji Tsuburaya
MUSIC: Akira Ifukube
Modest SF-fantasy: Aliens cause monsters to invade Tokyo

Destroy All Planets
see Gammera vs. Viras

Destroyer
1988, (USA), Back East Money-Wind River/TMS, color, 90 mins.
W: Lyle Alzado (*Ivan Moser*), Clayton Rohner, Deborah Foreman, Anthony Perkins
D: Robert Kirk   SCR: Rex Hauck & Peter Garrity   PHOTOG: Chuy Elizondo
MUSIC: Patrick O'Hearn   SONG: *Kiss My Stinky White Ass*
Standard horror-fantasy: Filmmakers in former prison are haunted by dead inmate

The Destructors
1968, (USA), United Pictures, color, 93 mins.

W: Richard Egan (*Dan Street*), Patricia Owens (*Charlie*), John Ericson (*Dutch Holland*), Michael Ansara (*Count Mario Romano*), Joan Blackman (*Stassa*), David Brian (*Hogan*), Jim Adams (*Agent Wayne*), Johnny Seven (*Spaniard*), Olan Soule (*Mace*), Khigh Dhiegh (*King Chou Lai*), Gregory Morton (*Dr. Frazer*), John Howard (*Ernest Bushnell*), Eddie Firestone (*Dr. Barnes*), Michael Dugan (*Parkhouse*), King Moody (*Patch*), Linda Kirk (*Prissy*), Rick Traeger (*Hans Gertmann*), Tommy McDonald (*Agent Dewey*), Cal Currens, Jayne Massey, Lennie Geer, Karen Norris, Mary Lou Cook, Adele Claire, Jim Kline, Dodie Warren, Virginia Wood, Capt. Horace Brown, James Seay, Tex Armstrong, John Lawrence, Douglas Kennedy, Walter Reed, Robert Riordan, Richard Norris
P: Earle Lyon   D: Francis D. Lyon   SCR: Arthur C. Pierce & Larry E. Jackson
PHOTOG: Alan Stensvold   SPCL-FX: Roger George   MUSIC: Paul Dunlap
Minor SF-thriller: Spies seek laser rubies

Desvio al Parasio (Shortcut to Paradise)
1994, (Sp), color, 97 mins.
W: Charles Dance, Assumpta Serna, Morgan Weisser, Katrina Gibson
D: Gerardo Herrero
Schlocky psycho-thriller: Janitor commits murder

The Detective and the Jewel Trick
1911, (GB), Hepworth, b&w, 850 ft. (259m)
D: Lewin Fitzhamon
Standard crime-thriller: Crook poses as noblewoman, steals gems

Detective Daring and the Thames Coiners
1914, (GB), Daring Films/Cosmo, b&w, 2,450 ft. (746.8m)
W: Harry Lorraine (*Det. Daring*), Arthur Mavity (*Barney*), Bert Berry (*Spider*), Claude Winn (*Flash Harry*), Eileen Daybell (*Eileen*), Will Discombe (*Grandfather*)
P: Harry Lorraine   D: Sidney Northcote   STORY: B. Harold Brett
Standard crime-thriller: Detective nabs counterfeiters, proves girl's grandfather innocent

Detective Ferris
1912, (GB), GS Films/Hepworth, b&w, 925 ft. (281.9m)
D: Gilbert Southwell
Standard thriller: Detective poses as crone, saves prince from anarchists

Detective Finn and the Foreign Spies
1914, (GB), Regent/MP, b&w, 3,000 ft. (914.4m)
W: Arthur Finn (*Det. Finn*), Alice Inward
P: Charles Weston & Arthur Finn   D: Arthur Finn
USA retitle, The Foreign Spies *(Paul H. Cromelin, 1914)*
Standard crime-thriller: Detective poses as crook, catches butler who stole inventor's gun plans

Detective Finn: or, In the Heart of London
1914, (GB), Regent Films/Gaumont, b&w, 2,800 ft. (853.4m)
W: Arthur Finn (*Det. Finn*), Alice Inward (*Slippery Kate*), Charles Weston (*Silk Hat Harry*)
P: Charles Weston & Arthur Finn   WRIT & D: Charles Weston
USA retitle, The Society Detective *(A.B. Carnick, 1914)*
Standard crime-thriller: Detective chases crooks who stole lord's di-amond

Detective Geronimo
see The Mad Bomber

The Detective in Peril
1910, (GB), Hepworth, b&w, 750 ft. (228.6m)
W: Lewin Fitzhamon (*The Detective*)
D & STORY: Lewin Fitzhamon
Standard thriller: Dog saves detective captured by crooks

Detective Kitty O'Day
1944, (USA), Mono, b&w, 65 mins.
W: Jean Parker, Tim Ryan, Peter Cookson, Veda Ann Borg
Standard thriller

Detour
1945, (USA), PRC, b&w, 69 mins.
W: Tom Neal, Ann Savage
D: Edgar G. Ulmer
Minor but classic film noir: Drifter swept into vortex of crime

A Deuce of a Girl
1916, (GB), Martin/DFSA, b&w, 760 ft. (231.6m)
D: Edwin J. Collins
Standard comedy-fantasy: Employer dreams that girl typist changes into devil

Os Deuses e os Mortos (The Gods and the Dead)
1970, (Yugo-W. Ger-It), Daga Films/New Yorker, color, 129 mins.
W: Othon Bastos (*The Man*), Norma Bengell (*Soledad*), Itala Nandi (*Ereno*), Ruy

Potanah (*Urbano*), Nelson Xavier (*Valu*), Fredi Kleeman (*The Man in White*), Jorge Chaia (*Santana*)
P: Freddy Rozemberg D: Ruy Guerra SCR: Ruy Guerra, Flavio Imperio & Paulo Jose PHOTOG: Dib Lutfi MUSIC: Milton Nascimento
Minor fantasy-thriller: Mysteries of death and rebirth

Deux Cent Mille Lieues sous les Mers (20,000 Leagues under the Sea)
1907, (Fr), Star, b&w, 286m (938.3 ft./15.9 mins.)
D: Georges Melies, from Jules Verne's novel
A.k.a. **Under the Seas** *(Melies 1907)*
Standard adventure-fantasy: Mad submarine captain terrorizes sea lanes

Le Deuxième Souffle (Second Breath)
1965, (Fr), b&w, 150 mins.
W: Lino Ventura, Paul Meurisse, Raymond Pellegrin, Christina Fabrega, Pierre Zimmer, Michel Constantin, Denis Manuel
D & SCR: Jean-Pierre Melville , from a novel by Jose Giovanni
Unusual melodrama: Aging gangster escapes jail

Devi (The Goddess)
1962, (India), Harrison, b&w, 94 mins.
W: Sharmila Tagore (*Doyamoyee*), Chhabi Biswas (*Kalikinkar*), Soumitra Chatterjee (*Umaprasad*), Arpen Choudhury (*Khoka*), Purnendu Mukherjee (*Taraorasad*), Karuna Bannerjee (*Harasundari*), Anil Chatterjee (*Bhudev*), Kali Sarkar (*Prof. Jarkar*), Mohamed Ibn Israel (*The Sick Boy's Father*), Nagendra Nath (*The Priest*), Khagesh Chakravarty (*The Doctor*)
P D & ADAPT, Satyajit Ray, based on a story by Prabhat Kumer Mukherjee, from a theme suggested by Rabindranath Tagore, PHOTOG: Subrata Mitra MUSIC: Alik Akbar Khan
Classic semi-fantasy: Girl's belief in her divinity leads to tragedy

The Devil
1909, (USA), Biograph, b&w

The Devil
1909, (USA), Edison, b&w

The Devil
1921, (USA), Pathe, b&w, 6 reels (5,682 ft./1731.9m)
W: George Arliss (*Dr. Muller*), Sylvia Breamer (*Mimi*), Edmund Lowe (*Paul de Veaux*), Lucy Cotton (*Marie Matin*), Roland Bottomley (*Georges Roben*), Mrs. George Arliss (*Marie's Aunt*)
D: James Young STORY & SCR: Edmund Goulding, from Ferenc Molnar's play PHOTOG: Harry A. Fischbeck
Satirical melodrama: Society cad enjoys corrupting virtuous

The Devil
1984, (USA), color, 90 mins.
Minor horror-thriller: Last surviving humans fight demonic lifeforms

The Devil and Max Devlin
1981, (USA), Walt Disney/Buena Vista, color, 96 mins.
W: Elliott Gould (*Max Devlin*), Bill Cosby (*Barney Satin*), Susan Ans-pach (*Penny Hart*), Adam Rich (*Toby Hart*), Julie Budd (*Stella Sum-mers*), Ted Zeigler (*Billings*), David Knell (*Nerve Nordlinger*), Sonny Shroyer (*Big Billy Hunniker*), Charles Shamata (*Jerry*), Deborah Baltzell (*Heidi*), Ronnie Schell (*Greg*), Jeannie Wilson (*Laverne*), Stanley Brock (*The Counterman*), Vic Dunlop (*Brian*), Stu Gilliam (*The Orderly*), Reggie Nalder (*The Chairman*), Julie Parrish (*Sheila*), Denise DuBarry (*The Sec'y*), Lillian Muller (*Veronica*), Sally K. Marr (*Mrs. Gormley*), Madelyn Cates (*Mrs. Trent*), Ruth Manning (*Mrs. Davis*)
D: Steven Hilliard Stern SCR: Mary Rodgers STORY: Mary Rodgers & Jimmy Sangster PHOTOG: Howard Schwartz MUSIC: Buddy Baker LYRICS: Marvin Hamlisch & Carole Bayer Sager
Minor juvenile fantasy: Modern Faust bargains with Satan

The Devil and Miss Sarah
1971, (USA), Universal/ABC-TV, color, 90 mins
W: Gene Barry, Janice Rule, James Drury, Slim Pickens
P: Stan Shpetner D: Michael Caffey TELEPLAY: Calvin Clements
TVM, minor occult-western: Outlaw uses hypnotism to possess woman's soul

The Devil and the Cornet
1908, (GB), Hepworth, b&w, 250 ft. (76.2m)
D: Lewin Fitzhamon
Minor fantasy short: Man's magic cornet forces girl's father to dance until he agrees to her marriage

The Devil and the Nun
see **Matka Joanna Od Aniolow**

The Devil and the Statue
see **Le Diable Geant ou le Miracle de la Madonne"**

The Devil and the Ten Commandments
see **Le Diable et les Dix Commandements**

The Devil Bat
1940, (USA), PRC, b&w, 70 mins.

W: Bela Lugosi (*Dr. Paul Carruthers*), Dave O'Brien (*Johnny Layton*), Suzanne Kaaren (*Mary*), Guy Usher (*Henry Morton*), Edmund Mortimer (*Martin Heath*), Yolande Mallott (*Donlan*) (*Maxine*), Donald Kerr ("*One-Shot*" *McGuire*), John Ellis (*Ray Heath*), Alan Baldwin (*Tommy Heath*), Gene O'Donnell (*Dan Morton*), Hal Price (*Chief Wilkins*), Arthur Q. Bryan (*Joe McGinty*), John Davidson (*Prof. Raines*), Billy Griffith (*The Coroner*), Wally Rairdon (*Walter King*)
D: Jean Yarbrough SCR: George Bricker PHOTOG: Arthur Martinelli MUSIC DIR: David Chudnow
TV retitle, **Killer Bats**
Standard thriller: Scientist creates monstrous bat, gains revenge on former employers

Devil Bat's Daughter
1946, (USA), PRC, b&w, 66 mins.
W: Rosemary LaPlanche, Edward Cassidy, John James, Michael Hale
P & D: Franck Wisbar SCR: Griffin Jay, from an idea by Leo T. McCarthy, Franck Wisbar & Ernst Jaeger
Minor thriller: Murdering physician throws blame for crimes onto daughter of infamous Devil Bat doctor

The Devil Bear
1929, (Can), Thunder Bay, b&w
D: Louis Chaudet
Standard melodrama: Curious happenings perplex comedy-fantasy: Boy meets Satan

The Devil Commands
1941, (USA), Col, b&w, 65 mins.
W: Boris Karloff (*Dr. Julian Blair*), Richard Fiske (*Richard Sayles*), Amanda Duff (*Anne Blair*), Anne Revere (*Mrs. Walters*), Dorothy Adams, Shirley Warde, Walter Baldwin, Ralph Penney, Kenneth MacDonald
D: Edward Dmytryk SCR: Robert D. Andrews & Milton Gunzburg, based on William Sloane's novel *The Edge of Running Water* PHOTOG: Allen G. Siegler
orig. to be titled **The Devil Said No**
Classic SF-fantasy: Scientist tries to contact dead

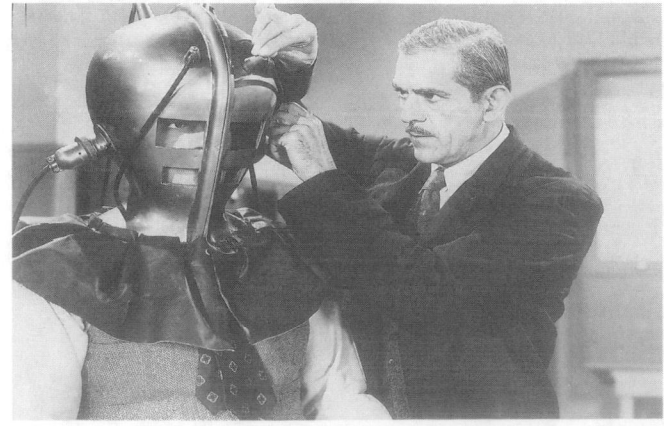

The Devil Commands: RICHARD FISKE, BORIS KARLOFF

Devil Diamond
1937, (USA), b&w
W: Kane Richmond, Frankie Darro
Minor thriller: Amateur detectives track jewel thieves

The Devil's Daughter: JOSEPH COTTEN AND BELINDA MONTGOMERY

Devil Dog: The Hound of Hell
1978, (USA), CBS-TV, color, 95 mins.
W: Richard Crenna (*Mike Barry*), Kim Richards (*Bonnie Barry*), Yvette Mimieux (*Betty Barry*), Victor Jory (*The Shaman*), Ike Eisenmann (*Charlie Barry*), Ken Kercheval (*Miles Amory*), Lou Frizzell (*George Baskins*), R.G. Armstrong (*Dunworth*), Tina Menard (*Maria*), Martine Beswick (*The Red-Haired Lady*), Bill Zuckert, Gertrude Flynn, Jack Carol
D: Curtis Harrington
TVM, minor fantasy-thriller: Pooch does Satan's bidding

Devil Doll
1936, (USA), MGM, b&w, 79 mins.
W: Lionel Barrymore (*Paul Lavond*), Maureen O'Sullivan (*Lorraine*), Henry B. Walthall (*Marcel*), Rafaela Ottiano (*Malita*), Frank Lawton (*Toto*), Grace Ford (*Lachna*), Pedro de Cordoba (*Matin*), Lucy Beaumont (*Mme. Lavond*), Rollo Lloyd (*The Detective*), Juanita Quigley (*Marguerita*), Arthur Hohl (*Radin*), Robert Greig (*Coulvet*), Claire DuBrey (*Mme. Coulvet*), E. Alyn Warren
D: Tod Browning **SCR:** Tod Browning, Garrett Fort, Erich von Stroheim, & Guy Endore, based on A. Merritt's novel *Burn, Witch, Burn* **PHOTOG:** Leonard Smith **MUSIC:** Franz Waxman
French retitle, **Les Poupees du Diable (The Dolls of the Devil)**
Classic fantasy-thriller: Devil's Island escapee shrinks humans, gains revenge

Devil Doll
1963, (GB), Galaworldfilm-Gordon/Associated Film Dist., b&w, 80 mins.
W: William Sylvester (*Mark English*), Bryant Halliday (*The Great Vorelli*), Yvonne Romain (*Marian*), Karel Stepanek (*Dr. Heller*), Nora Nicholson (*Aunt Eva*), Francis De Wolff (*Dr. Keisling*), Philip Ray (*Uncle Walter*), Heidi Erich (*Grace*), Alan Gifford (*Bob Garrett*), Sandra Dorne
P: Kenneth Rive, Richard Gordon & Lindsay Shonteff **D:** Lindsay Shonteff **SCR:** George Barclay & Lance Z. Hargreaves **STORY:** Frederick E. Smith
Standard fantasy-thriller, similar to **The Great Gabbo**: *Ventriloquist's dummy gains diabolical life*

Devilfish
1984, (It), color, 92 mins.
D: Lamberto Bava
Minor thriller: Seaside community attacked by manta rays

Devil Girl from Mars
1954, (GB), Gigi/British Lion/Spartan, b&w, 78 mins.
W: Hugh McDermott (*Michael Carter*), Hazel Court (*Eileen Prestwick*), Patricia Laffan (*Nyah*), Adrienne Corri (*Doris*), Peter Reynolds (*Albert*), Joseph Tomelty (*Prof. Hennessey*), Sophie Stewart (*Mrs. Jamieson*), John Laurie (*Mr. Jamieson*), Anthony Richmond (*Tommy*), James Edmond
P: Edgar J. & Harry Lee Danziger **D:** David MacDonald **SCR:** James Eastwood **STORY:** John C. Maher **PHOTOG:** Jack Cox
Modest SF-thriller: Uncompromising space-woman traps Brits behind force field

Devil Goddess
1955, (USA), Col, b&w, 76 mins.
W: Johnny Weissmuller, Angela Stevens, William Tannen, Ed Hinton, Selmer Jackson, William Griffith, Frank Lackteen, Abel Fernandez, Vera Francis, George Berkely
P: Sam Katzman **D:** Spencer G. Bennet **SCR:** George H. Plympton **STORY:**

Dwight V. Babcock
Minor adventure-thriller (last of 16 "Jungle Jim"/Weissmuller films): Jungle hero leads explorer to land of volcano worshippers

The Devil in a Convent
see **Le Diable au Couvent**

Devil in the Flesh
1997, (USA), color, 95 mins.
W: Rose McGowan, Phil Morris, Robert Silver
Made-for-Video, standard thriller: Teen girl slays love rivals

The Devil in Love
see **Il Diavolo Innamorato**

The Devil in the Studio
1901, (GB), R.W. Paul, b&w, 100 ft. (30.5m)
D: W.R. Booth
Standard fantasy short: Mephistopheles causes artist's model to disappear

Devil Kiss
1977, (USA), color, 93 mins.
W: Oliver Mathews, Evelyn Scott
Minor horror-fantasy: Living dead prey

Devilish Magic
see **Magie Diabolique**

Devil Master
see **The Demon Lover**

The Devil May Well Laugh
1960, (Switz), b&w
Minor thriller: Fiendish killer hunted

Devil Men from Space
see **Planet on the Prowl**

Devil Monster
1946, (USA), Weiss, b&w 65 mins.
W: Barry Norton, Blanche Mehaffey
D: S. Edwin Graham
UK : **The Sea Fiend** *original release as* **The Great Manta** *(1935)*
Minor thriller: South seas adventure,

A Devil of a Honeymoon
1915, (GB), Cherry Kearton, b&w, 550 ft. (167.6m)
D: Walter R. Booth
Standard fantasy short: Satan drives honeymooners' car via volcano to North Pole

Devil of the Desert Against the Son of Hercules
1964, (It), Avco Embassy, color, 93 mins
W: Kirk Morris, Michele Girardon, Mario Felicianni
Minor "Sword & Sandal" adventure: Muscleman saves princess from assassins

Devil Pirates
see **The Devil-Ship Pirates**

The Devil Rides Out
1968, (GB), Hammer-7Arts/20th-Fox, color, 95 mins.
W: Christopher Lee (*Duc de Richleau*), Nike Arrighi (*Tanith*), Charles Gray (*Mocata*), Leon Greene (*Rex Van Ryn*), Patrick Mower (*Simon Aron*), Sarah Lawson (*Marie Eaton*), Rosalyn Landor (*Peggy Eaton*), Gwen Ffrangcon-Davies (*Countess D'Urfe*), Paul Eddington (*Richard Eaton*), Russell Waters (*Malin*)
P: Anthony Nelson Keys **D:** Terence Fisher **SCR:** Richard Matheson, from Dennis Wheatley's novel **PHOTOG:** Arthur Grant **SPCL-FX:** Michael Stainer-Hutchins **MUSIC:** James Bernard **MUSIC SPRVSR:** Philip Martell
USA retitle, **The Devil's Bride**
Standard fantasy: Scientists marshall evil forces

Devil Rider
1991, (USA), color, 90 mins.
Minor horror-fantasy: Monster from hell seeks victims at western ranch

Devil Woman
1976, (Phil), Hallmark, color
P: Jimmy Pasqual
D: Albert Yu & Felix Vila
Minor horror-fantasy: Gorgon slays villagers

The Devils
1971, (GB), Russo/WB, color, 111 mins.
W: Vanessa Redgrave (*Sister Jeanne*), Oliver Reed (*Father Grandier*), Dudley Sutton (*Baron de Laubardemont*), Murray Melvin (*Philippe*), Max Adrian (*Ibert*), Gemma Jones (*Madeleine*), Michael Gothard (*Father Barre*), Christopher Logue (*Richelieu*), Georgina Hale (*Mignon*), John Woodvine (*Trincant*), Brian Murphy (*Adam*), Graham Armitage (*Louis XIII*), Andrew Faulds (*Rangier*),

Kenneth Colley (*Legrand*), Judith Paris (*Sister Judith*), Iza Teller (*Sister Iza*), Catherine Willmer (*Sister Catherine*)
WRIT & D: Ken Russell, from the play by John Whiting & the book by Aldous Huxley, *The Devils of Loudun* **PHOTOG:** David Watkin **MUSIC:** Peter Maxwell Davies
Historical melodrama: Satanic possession in French convent

The Devil's Agent
1962, (GB-W. Ger), Emmet Dalton/British Lion, b&w, 77 mins.
W: Peter Van Eyck (*George Droste*), Marianne Koch (*Nora Gulden*), Macdonald Carey (*Mr. Smith*), Christopher Lee (*Baron von Staub*), Billie Whitelaw (*Piroska*), David Knight (*Father Zombary*), Marius Goring (*Gen. Greenhahn*), Peter Vaughan (*The Police Chief*), Helen Cherry (*Countess Cosimano*), Colin Gordon (*Count Dezsepalvy*), Niall MacGinnis (*Paul Vass*), Michael Brennan (*Horvat*), Eric Pohlmann (*Bloch*), Albert Lieven, Peter Cushing
P: Victor Lyndon **D:** John Paddy Carstairs **SCR:** Robert Westerby, from a novel by Hans Habe
Modest thriller: Wine salesman pressed into espionage

The Devil Doll: LIONEL BARRYMORE

The Devil Said No
see The Devil Commands

Devil's Advocate
1997, (USA), WB, color, 144 mins.
W: Al Pacino (*John Milton*), Keanu Reeves (*Kevin Lomax*), Charlize Theron, Jeffrey Jones, Craig T. Nelson, Judith Ivey, Don King, Ruben Santiago-Hudson
D: Taylor Hackford **SCR:** Jonathan Lemkin & Tony Gilroy **MUSIC:** James Newton Howard

Devil's Angel
1922, (USA), Clark-Cornelius Corp., b&w, 5 reels
W: Helen Gardner (*Cymba Roget*), Templar Saxe (*The Hindoo Hypnotist*), Peggy O'Neil (*The Artist's Model*), C.D. Williams, Lejarena Hiller, Marc Connelly
D: Lejaren a'Hiller
Standard melodrama: Model escapes hypnotist's influence

The Devil's Assistant
1916, (USA), Mutual, b&w
W: Margarita Fischer, Jack Mower
D & SCR:, Harry Pollard, from a story by F. Edward Hungerford
Minor melodrama: Underworld intrigue

The Devil's Bargain
1908, (GB), Cricks & Martin, b&w, 530 ft. (161.5m)
D: A.E. Coleby
Standard fantasy short: Artist sells soul to Satan for month's wages, girl in painting comes to rescue him

The Devil's Beauty
see La Beaute du Diable

The Devil's Bedroom
1964, (USA), Manson, color, 78 mins
W: Valerie Allen, Dick Jones, Alvy Moore, John Lipton (star), Morgan Woodward
P: George Gunter & L.Q. Jones **D:** L.Q. Jones **SCR:** Claude Hall & Morgan Woodward
Minor thriller: Couple seeks brother's Western property, attempts to drive him insane. released in b&w but shot in color

The Devil's Bondman
1915, (GB), Transatlantic, b&w, 3,892 ft. (1186.3m)
W: George Bellamy (*Morton Masters*), Gregory Scott (*Gerald Carstairs*), Fay Temple (*Peggy Lofting*), J. Hastings Batson (*The Bishop of Lowden*), Douglas Payne (*Satan*), Daisy Cordell (*Myra*), Arthur M. Cullin (*Rev. Hughes*)
D: Percy Nash **STORY:** Rowland Talbot
USA retitle, The Scorpion's Sting
Standard fantasy: Ex-convict sells soul to Satan

The Devil's Bride
see The Devil Rides Out

The Devil's Cargo
1948, (USA), Film Classics, b&w, 61 mins.
W: John Calvert (*Mike Waring*), Rochelle Hudson (*Margo*), Lyle Talbot (*Morello*), Roscoe Karns (*Lt. Hardy*), Theodore von Eltz (*Tom Mallon*), Tom Kennedy (*Naga*), Paul Marion (*Ramon Delgado*), Paul Regan (*Bernie*)
D: John F. Link **SCR:** Don Martin, Robert Tallman & Jason James, from characters created by Michael Arlen **PHOTOG:** Walter Strange **MUSIC:** Karl Hajos
Minor "Falcon" thriller: Sleuth helps man accused of killing racetrack operator

The Devil's Castle (1897, Fr)
see Le Chateau Hante

The Devil's Castle
1963, (Turk), b&w
W: Ahmet Mekin, Nilufer Avdan, Mahir Ozerdem
Minor horror-thriller: Vampire stalks

The Devil's Commandment
see I Vampiri

The Devil's Crypt
see The Devil's Wedding Night

The Devil's Daffodil
1962, (GB), Omnia-Rialto/Britannia, b&w, 86 mins.
W: Christopher Lee (*Ling Chu*), Marius Goring (*Oliver Milburgh*), Albert Lieven (*Raymond Lyne*), Penelope Horner (*Anne Rider*), Ingrid Van Bergen (*Gloria*), William Lucas (*Jack Tarling*), Jan Hendricks (*Charles*), Colin Jeavons (*Peter Keene*), Peter Illing (*Jan Putek*), Walter Gotell (*Supt. Whiteside*), Lance Percival (*The Gendarme*), Irene Prador (*Maisie*)
P: Steven Pallos & Donald Taylor **D:** Akos Rathony **SCR:** Donald Taylor & Basil Dawson, from Edgar Wallace's novel *The Daffodil Mystery*
Standard thriller: Airline investigator and Chinese detective track down maniacal heroin smuggler

Devil's Daughter (1939)
see Pocomania

The Devil's Daughter
1973, (USA), Miller-Milkis/Para/ABC-TV, Made for TV, color, 74 mins.
W: Shelley Winters, Belinda J. Montgomery, Martha Scott (*Mrs. Stone*), Robert Foxworth (*Steve*), Jonathan Frid (*Howard*), Joseph Cotten (*Judge*), Ian Wolfe, Barbara Sammeth, Diane Ladd, Robert Cornthwaite, Lucille Benson, Thelma Carpenter
P: Thomas L. Miller & Edwin K. Milkis **D:** Jeannot Szwarc **TELEPLAY:** Colin Higgins
TVM, standard fantasy-thriller: Evil forces surround girl

The Devil's Daughter
1995, (USA), video, color 112 mins.
W: Kelly Curtis, Herbert Lom, Maria Agela Giordano, Michel Hans Adatte, Carla Cassola, Agelika Maria Boeck, Tomas Arana
D: Michele Soavi **SCR:** Dario Argento **MUSIC:** Pino Donaggio
Made-for-Video, standard horror-fantasy

The Devil's Daughters
see Les Filles du Diable

Devil's Envoys
see Les Visiteurs du Soir

Devil's Express
1975, (USA), Mahler Films, color
W: Warhawk Tanzania, Sam DeFazio
P: Nick Patton & Steve Madoff **D:** Barry Rosen
A.k.a. Gang Wars
Minor action-horror: Kung fu student unleashes demon

The Devil's Eye
1960, (Swed), Svensk Filmindustri/Janus, b&w, 90 mins.
W: Jari Kulle (*Don Juan*), Bibi Andersson (*Britt-Marie*), Axel Duberg (*Britt-Marie's Fiance*), Stig Jarrell (*Satan*), Nils Poppe (*The Pastor*), Sture Lagerwell (*Pablo*), Gertrud Fridh (*The Pastor's Wife*), Georg Funkquist, Allan Edwall, Kristina Adolphson, Gunnar Bjornstrand, Gunnar Sjoberg
WRIT, P & D: Ingmar Bergman **PHOTOG:** Gunnar Fischer
Classic fantasy: Satan tempts engaged girl

Devil's Food
1996, (USA), SHO-TV, color, 95 mins.
W: Suzanne Somers, Dabney Coleman
Made-for-Cable, standard fantasy: Overweight woman sells soul to Satan

The Devil's Foot
1921, (GB), Stoll, b&w, 2,514 ft. (715.5m)
W: Eille Norwood (*Sherlock Holmes*), Hubert Willis (*Dr. John Watson*), Harvey Braban (*Mortimer Tregennis*), Hugh Buckler (*Dr. Sterndale*)
D: Maurice Elvey   SCR: William J. Elliott, from the writings of Sir Arthur Conan Doyle
Standard crime-thriller (episode in "Adventures of Sherlock Holmes" series)

The Devil's 400 Farces
see Les 400 Farces du Diable

Devils from Space
see I Diavoli della Spazio

The Devil's Gift
1984, (USA), Windridge/Zenith Int'l/Cinema Shares, color, 91 mins.
W: Bob Mendlesohn (*David*), Vicki Saputo (*Susan*), Struan Robertson (*Michael*), Bruce Parry (*Pete*), Madelon Phillips (*Adrianne*), J. Renee Gilbert (*Gramma*), Stuart White (*The Manager*), Marlene Ryan (*Marge*), Barry Chandler (*The Guy in the Car*), Caris Palm (*The Girl in the Store*), Olwen Morgan (*Elmira Johnson*), Angeles Olazabal (*The Girl on the Bike*)
D: Kenneth J. Berton   SCR: Hayden O'Hara, Jose Vergelin, & Kenneth J. Berton   STORY: Kenneth J. Berton & Jose Vergelin   PHOTOG: Karil Daniels & Caris Palm   MUSIC: Todd Hayen   SONGS: Fire Doesn't Burn & Only Roses for You
Minor horror-thriller: Demonic toy monkey causes death

The Devil's Hand: LINDA CHRISTIAN AND ROBERT ALDA

The Devil's Hand (1941)
see La main du Diable

The Devil's Hand
1961, (USA), Bubis-Katz/Rex Carlton/Crown-Int'l, b&w, 71 mins.
W: Linda Christian (*Bianca Milan*), Robert Alda (*Rick Turner*), Neil Hamilton (*Francis Lamont*), Ariadna Welter (*Donna Trent*), Gere Craft, Jeannie Carmen, Diana Spears, Julie Scott, Bruno Ve Sota, Gertrude Astor, Coleen Vico, Dick Lee, Jim Knight, Roy Wright, Romona Ravez, Tony Rock
D: William Hole Jr.   SCR: Jo Heims   PHOTOG: Meredith Nicholson   MUSIC DIR: Manuel Francisco
A.k.a. The Naked Goddess, Live to Love, & Devil's Doll
Minor thriller: Satanic sect snares skeptic

The Devil's Henchmen
1949, (USA), Col, b&w, 69 mins.
W: Warner Baxter, Mary Beth Hughes
Minor melodrama

Devil's Island
62 mins.
W: Adia Kuznetzoff, Will Stanton, Edward Keane

The Devil-Ship Pirates
1963, (GB), Hammer/Col, color, 86 mins.
W: Christopher Lee (*Capt. Robles*), John Cairney (*Harry*), Ernest Clark (*Sir Basil Smeeton*), Barry Warren (*Manuel*), Natasha Pyne (*Jane*), Andrew Keir (*Tom*), Duncan Lamont (*The Bosun*), Suzan Farmer (*Angela*), Charles Houston (*Antonio*), Michael Ripper (*Pepe*), Harry Locke (*Bragg*), Peter Howell (*The First Mate*), Michael Newport (*Smiler*), Barry Linehan (*Gustavo*), Jack Rodney (*Mandrake*), Johnny Briggs (*Pablo*), Bruce Beeby (*Pedro*), Michael Peake (*Grande*), Philip Latham (*Miller*), Leonard Fenton (*Quintana*), Annette Whiteley (*Meg*), Joseph O'Conor (*Don Jose*), June Ellis (*Mrs. Blake*)
P: Anthony Nelson Keys   D: Don Sharp   SCR: Jimmy Sangster   PHOTOG: Michael Reed   SPCL-FX: Les Bowie   MUSIC: Gary Robinson & Don Mingaye
French retitle, Les Pirates du Diable (Pirates of the Devil)
Standard action-thriller: Spanish captain captures girl, forces Cornish villagers to repair crippled ship

The Devil's House
see The Haunting

Devil's Island
1940, (USA), WB, b&w, 65 mins
W: Boris Karloff, James Stephenson, Nedda Harrigan, Will Stanton, Stuart Holmes
D: William Clemens   SCR: Kenneth Gamet & Don Ryan   PHOTOG: George Barnes
Good Karloff performance in stilted melodrama: Brutality and terror at infamous prison camp

The Devil's Jest
1954, (GB), Terra Nova/Equity British, b&w, 60 mins.
W: Mara Russell-Tavernan (*Lady Irma Enderby*), Ivan Craig (*Maj. Seton*), Derek Aylwood (*Victor*), Valentine Dyall (*The Intelligence Director*), Julian Sherrier (*Tony*), Lee Fox (*Maj. Malcolm*), Hamilton Keene (*Col. Lorimer*), Edward Leslie (*Capt. Blynne*)
P: Paul King   D: Alfred Goulding   STORY: Vance Uhden
Standard crime-thriller: Noblewoman's ex-lover is Nazi spy

The Devil's Laboratory of Dr. Rambow
see Frankenstein—1970

The Devil's Locksmith
1919, (Austria), b&w
Minor thriller

The Devil's Mansion
see Le Manoir du Diable

The Devil's Mask
1946, (USA), Col, b&w, 66 mins.
W: Jim Bannon, Barton Yarborough, Anita Louise, Michael Duane, Mona Barrie
P: Wallace MacDonald   D: Henry Levin   SCR: Charles O'Neal & Dwight V. Babcock
Minor mystery-thriller: Sleuth team probes murder. ('I Love a Mystery' Series)

The Devil's Men
1976, (GB-USA), Poseidon/Getty Pictures, color, 94 mins.
W: Donald Pleasence (*Father Roche*), Luan Peters (*Laurie Gordon*), Niklos Verlakis (*Ian*), Costas Skouras (*Miko Kay*), Peter Cushing (*Baron Corofax*), Vanna Revilli (*Beth*), Bob Behling (*Tom Gifford*), Fernando Bislani (*Sgt. Vendris*), Anna Mentgosrani (*The Widow*)
P: Frixos Constantine   D: Costas Carayiannis   STORY: Arthur Rowe   PHOTOG: Aris Stavrou   MUSIC: Brian Eno
A.k.a. Land of the Minotau & Minotaur
Minor horror-thriller: Archeologist uncovers cult

The Devil's Messenger
1959, (Swed), Herts-Lion, b&w, 72 mins.
W: Lon Chaney Jr., Karen Kadler, John Crawford, Michael Hinn, Ralph Brown, Bert Johnson, Chalmers Goodlin, Jan Blomberg, Gunnel Brostrom, Tammy Newmara, Ingrid Bedoya, Eve Hossner
D: Curt Siodmak & (uncredited) Herbert L. Strock   SCR: Leo Guild   PHOTOG: William Troiano   MUSIC: Alfred Gwynn
distrib. in USA in 1962
Standard thriller anthology, 3-part film culled from Curt Siodmak's unsold teleseries "#13 Demon Street:" Supernatural events astound

The Devil's Money Bags
see Les Tresors de Satan

The Devil's Nightmare
1971, (Belg-It), Hemisphere, color, 87 mins.
W: Erika Blanc (*Hilse*), Daniel Emilfork (*Alban*), Jean Servais, Ivana Novak, Lucien Raimbourg, Jacques Monseau, Colette Emmanuelle, Shirley Corrigan, Frederique Hender
P: Charles Lecocq   D: Jean Brismee   SCR: Patrice Rhomm, Charles Lecocq & Andre Hunebelle   SPCL-FX: Paul Defru   MUSIC: Alessandro Alessandrini
A.k.a. Vampire Playgirls
USA release, 1974
Standard horror-thriller: Tourists stranded at castle, succubus preys

Devils of Darkness

1964, (GB), Planet/20th-Fox, color, 86 mins.

<u>W:</u> William Sylvester (*Paul Baxter*), Hubert Noel (*Count Sinistre*), Tracy Reed (*Karen*), Carole Gray (*Tania*), Rona Anderson (*Anne Forrest*), Diana Decker (*Madeleine Braun*), Peter Illing (*Insp. Malin*), Gerard Heinz (*Bouvier*), Avril Angers (*Midge*), Victor Brooks (*Insp. Hardwicke*), Julie Mendes (*The Dancer*), Eddie Byrne, Brian Oulton

<u>P:</u> Tom Blakely   <u>D:</u> Lance Comfort   <u>SCR:</u> Lyn Fairhurst   <u>PHOTOG:</u> Reg Wyer

Devil's Partner

<u>MUSIC:</u> Bernie Fenlon
Standard horror-thriller: Man runs afoul of vampire cult

The Devil's Own

see The Witches (1966)

The Devil's Partner

1961, (USA), Huron/Filmgroup/AIP, b&w, 75 mins (also 61 mins)

<u>W:</u> Ed Nelson, Edgar Buchanan, Richard Crane, Jean Allison, Spencer Carlisle, Byron Foulger

<u>P:</u> Hugh M. Hooker   <u>D:</u> Charles R. Rondeau   <u>SCR:</u> Stanley Clements, Laura J. Mathews, Dorrell McGowan

Standard horror-fantasy: Warlock reborn

The Devil's Plot

see Counterblast

The Devil's Possesed

1974, (Argent-Sp), color, 90 mins.

<u>W:</u> Paul Naschy
<u>D:</u> Leon Klimovsky
Minor thriller: Middle-Ages despot tortures peasants

The Devil's Profession

1915, (GB), Arrow/YCC, b&w, 3,300 ft. (1005.8m)

<u>W:</u> Rohan Clensy (*Dr. Felix Emerson*), Alesia Leon (*Lionne*), Sidney Strong (*Clifford*

Carton*), May Lynn, Nancy Roberts

<u>D</u> & <u>SCR:</u> F.C.S. Tudor, from Gertie de S. Wentworth James' novel
Standard thriller: Doctor paid to inject rich people with madness simulant

Devil's Son-In-Law

1977, (USA), color, 95 mins.

<u>W:</u> Rudy Ray Moore
<u>D:</u> Cliff Roguemore
Minor fantasy-satire: Black stand-up comic makes satanic pact

The Devil's Rain

1975, (USA), Sandy Howard/Bryanston, color, 86 mins.

<u>W:</u> Ernest Borgnine (*Corbis*), Eddie Albert (*Dr. Samuel Richards*), William Shatner (*Mark Preston/Martin Fyffe*), Keenan Wynn (*Sheriff Owens*), Lisa Todd (*Lilith*), Joan Prather (*Julie Preston*), Tom Skerritt (*Dr. Tom Preston*), Ida Lupino (*Mrs. Preston*), Woodrow Chambliss (*Tom*), John Travolta (*Danny*), George Sawaya

<u>D:</u> Robert Fuest   <u>SCR:</u> Gabe Essoe, James Ashton, & Gerald Hopman   <u>PHOTOG:</u> Alex Phillips Jr.   <u>MUSIC:</u> Al de Lory

"...one of those satanic-cult hackeries that is badly written, badly directed and badly produced but boasts some gee-whiz special effects"—Judith Crist, TV Guide

"A satanic thriller with ingenious special effects" —Motion Picture Digest
Standard horror-fantasy: Satanic cult in Western ghost town

Devil Times Five

see The Horrible House on the Hill

The Devil's Trap

1964, (Czech), Salisbury, b&w, 85 mins.

<u>W:</u> Vitezlan Vejrazka, Vit Olmer
Minor thriller: Dark motives inspire murder

Devil's Triangle

1976, (USA), UFO Distribution, color, 55 mins.

<u>W:</u> Vincent Price (*narrator*)
<u>WRIT, P & D:</u> Richard Winer   <u>MUSIC:</u> King Crimson
Minor speculation-docu: Investigation of Bermuda Triangle

The Devil Strikes at Night

1957, (W. Ger), b&w, 104 mins.

<u>W:</u> Mario Adorf, Claus Holm
<u>P & D:</u> Robert Siodmak
Standard thriller based on Bruno Luedke case: Serial killer terrorizes

The Devil's Undead

see Nothing But the Night

The Devil's Wanton

1948, (Swed), Joseph E. Levine/Embassy, b&w, 80 mins.

<u>W:</u> Doris Svedlund (*Birgitta Karolina*), Eva Henning (*Sefi*), Birger Malmsten (*Thomas*), Anders Henriksson (*Paul*), Hasse Ekman (*Martin*), Stig Olin (*Peter*), Marianne Lofgren (*Mrs. Bolin*), Irma Christenson (*Linnea*), Curt Masreliez (*Alf*), Carl-Henrik Fant (*Arne*)

<u>WRIT & D:</u> Ingmar Bergman   <u>PHOTOG:</u> Goran Strindberg   <u>MUSIC:</u> Erland Von Koch

A.k.a. Prison
Unusual allegorical thriller: Young woman seeks happiness with man who killed his former wife's lover

The Devil's Rain: WILLIAM SHATNER

Devil's Web
1975, (GB), Made for TV , color, 73 mins.
W: Diana Dors, Andrea Marcovicci, Michael Culver, Linda Liles
TVM, standard thriller: Nurse heals with occult powers

The Devil's Wedding Night
1972, (Sp), Virginia/Dimension, color, 79 mins.
W: Mark Damon (*Franz Schiller/Karl Schiller*), Sara Bay (*The Countess Dracula*), Esmeralda Barras (*The Zombie*), Alexander Getty (*The Mysterious Man*), Ciro Papas (*The Vampire Monster*), Francesca Romana (*The Innkeeper's Daughter*), Mort Baxter (*The Innkeeper*), George Dolfin (*The 1st Villager*), Stephen

Devils of Darkness

Hopper (*The 2nd Villager*)
D: Paul Solvay **SCR:** Alan M. Harris & Ralph Zucker, based on orig. story *The Brides of Countess Dracula* by Ralph Zucker & Ian Danby **PHOTOG:** Michael Holloway **MUSIC:** Vasil Kojucharov
A.k.a. **The Devil's Crypt**
Standard horror-thriller: Twin brothers seek legendary ring, meet sinister noblewoman

The Devil's Widow
see **Tam Lin**

The Devil's Women
1972, (Mex), color
Minor thriller

The Devil Thumbs a Ride
1947, (USA), RKO, b&w, 65 mins.
W: Lawrence Tierney, Nan Leslie
Minor melodrama

The Devil to Pay
1915, (GB), Martin/DFSA, b&w, 585 ft. (178.3m)
W: Jack Jarman (*The Man*)
D: Edwin J. Collins
Standard fantasy short: Mephistopheles grants youth to old alchemist

The Devil Within Her
see **I Don't Want to be Born**

Devil Woman
1976, (Phil), color, 79 mins.
W: Rosemarie Gil
D: Albert Yu & Felix Vilars
Minor horror-fantasy: Gorgon-woman seeks reptilian revenge

Devjani
1939, (India), b&w
Unusual fantasy: War between gods and demons

The Devonsville Terror
1983, (USA), Atlantic/MPM, color, 82 mins.
W: Suzanna Love (*Jenny*), Robert Walker Jr. (*Matthew*), Donald Pleasence (*Dr. Warley*), Paul Willson (*Walter*)
D & PHOTOG: Ulli Lommel **SCR:** Ulli Lommel, George T. Lindsey & Suzanna Love **MUSIC:** Ray Colcord & Ed Hill
Minor horror-fantasy: Supernatural events in small town

The Devoted Ape
1910, (GB), Cricks & Martin, b&w, 560 ft. (170.7m)
W: Jack Miller (*The Miner*), Johnny Butt (*The Ape*)
D: Dave Aylott
Standard thriller: Pet ape saves kidnapped girl

Devotion
1946, (USA), WB, b&w, 107 mins.
W: Olivia de Havilland (*Charlotte Brontë*), Ida Lupino (*Emily Brontë*), Nancy Coleman (*Anne Brontë*), Arthur Kennedy (*Branwell Brontë*), Odette Myrtil (*Mme. Heger*), Sydney Greenstreet (*Thackeray*), Paul Henreid (*Nichols*), Dame May Whitty (*Lady Thornton*), Montagu Love (*Rev. Brontë*), Victor Francen (*Msr. Heger*), Ethel Griffies (*Aunt Branwell*), Reginald Sheffield (*Dickens*), Edmund Breon (*Sir John Thornton*), Maric dc Becker (*Tabby*), Forrester Harvey (*Hoggs*), Donald Stuart (*Butcher*), Billy Bevan (*The Draper*), John Meredith (*The Draper's Ass't*), David Thursby (*The Farmer*), P.J. Kelly (*The Shepherd*), David Clyde (*The Land Agent*), Doris Lloyd (*Mrs. Ingham*), Brandon Hurst (*The Duke of Wellington*), Howard Davies (*The Englishman*), Violet Seton (*Mrs. Crump*), Yorke Sherwood, Anne Goldthwaite, Sylvia Opert, Elyane Lima, Irina Semochenko, Hartney Arthur, Elspeth Dudgeon
D: Curtis Bernhardt **SCR:** Keith Winter, from a story by Theodore Reeves **PHOTOG:** Ernest Haller **SPCL-FX:** Jack Holden, Jack Okey & Rex Wimpy **MUSIC:** Erich Wolfgang Korngold
Fictionalized film-bio melodrama: Turbulent lives of tormented Brontës

Devyat'dney Odnogo Goda (Nine Days in One Year)
1961, (Russ), color, 110 mins.
W: Alexei Batalov (*Dimitri*), Innokenty Smoktonovsky (*Ilya*), Tamara Lavrova (*Lelya*), Nikolai Polotnikov (*Prof. Sintsov*)
P & D: Mikhail Romm **SCR:** Mikhail Romm & Danily Khrabovitsky
PHOTOG: German Lavrov
Unusual SF: Vision of future

Le Diable au Couvent (The Devil in a Convent)
1899, (Fr), Star, b&w, 60m (196.9 ft./3.3 mins.)
W: Georges Melies
WRIT & D: Georges Melies
USA retitle, **The Sign of the Cross**
Standard fantasy: Hellish events inspire laughs

Le Diable et les Dix Commandements (The Devil and the Ten Commandments)
1962, (It-Fr), color, 120 mins.
W: Michel Simon, Francoise Arnoul, Micheline Presle, Alain Delon, Charles Aznavour, Fernandel, Gaston Modot, Louis de Funes, Jean-Claude Brialy, Danielle Darrieux, Lino Ventura, Germaine Kerjean, Claude Dauphin, Mel Ferrer
D: Julien Duvivier
Standard comedy-fantasy: Love and sin, parable-style

Le Diable Geant ou le Miracle de la Madonne (The Gigantic Devil: or, The Miracle of the Madonna)
1902, (Fr), Star, b&w, 40m (131.2 ft./2.2 mins.)
W: Georges Melies
D: Georges Melies
GB retitle, **The Gigantic Devil***, USA retitle,* **The Devil and the Statue**
Standard fantasy

Le Diable Noir (The Black Devil)
1905, (Fr), Star, b&w, 68m (223.1 ft./3.8 mins.)
D: Georges Melies
A.k.a. **The Black Imp**
Standard fantasy

Diablo Nightmare
1907, (GB), Urban, b&w, 385 ft. (117.3m)
D: Walter R. Booth
Minor fantasy short in 22 scenes: Clerk, addicted to game of Diablo, dreams of playing under sea

Diabolic Magic
see **Magie Diabolique**

The Diabolical Dr. Mabuse
see **Die Tausend Augen des Dr. Mabuse**

The Diabolical Dr. Z
1965, (Fr-Sp-W. Ger), U.S. Films, b&w, 86 mins.
W: Howard Vernon, Estella Blain, Mabel Karr, Fernando Montes
D: Jesus Franco **SCR:** Jesus Franco & Jean-Claude Carriere
A.k.a. **Miss Muerte (Miss Death)**
Minor thriller: Good Doctor's daughter mesmerizes female dancer, uses her to avenge slain father

The Diabolical Invention
1957, (Czech), Joseph E. Levine/Embassy/WB, b&w, 83 mins.
W: Louis Tock (*Simon*), Ernest Navara, Francis Sherr, Jane Zalata, Milo Holl, Van Kissling
D: Karel Zeman **SCR:** Karel Zeman & Francis Gross, from Jules Verne's writings
PHOTOG: George Taran **MUSIC:** Sydney Fox
USA retitle (1961) as **The Fabulous World of Jules Verne.** *A.k.a.* **An Invention for Destruction** *and* **The Wonderful Invention**
Arty SF-fantasy: Mastermind's super-cannon rules sea lanes

159

Diabolically Yours
1967, (Fr), color, 94 mins.
W: Alain Delon, Senta Berger
D: Julien Duvivier
French title: Diaboliquement Votre
Minor mystery: Amnesiac tries to unravel his past

The Diabolical Place
see Le Locataire Diabolique

The Diabolic Axe
1964, (Mex), color
W: Santo
Minor adventure-fantasy: Muscleman vs. evildoers

Diabolik
1967, (It-Fr), Para, color, 105 mins.
W: John Phillip Law, Marisa Mell, Michel Piccoli, Adolfo Celi, Terry-Thomas
P: Dino De Laurentiis   D: Mario Bava   SCR: Dino Maiuri, Brian Degas, Tudor Gates & Mario Bava, from the European comic strip   PHOTOG: Antonio Rinaldi   MUSIC: Ennio Morricone
A.k.a. Danger: Diabolik
Standard spy-fantasy: Adventures of superhero

Diabolique
1955, (Fr), UMPO, b&w, 115 mins.
W: Simone Signoret (*Nicole Horner*), Vera Clouzot (*Christina Delasalle*), Charles Vanel (*Insp. Fichet*), Paul Meurisse (*Michel Delasalle*), Noel Roquevert (*Msr. Herboux*), Pierre Larquey (*Msr. Drain*), Therese Dorny (*Mme. Herboux*), Michel Serrault (*Msr. Raymond*), Jean Brochard (*Plantiveau*), Jean Pierre Bonnefous (*De Gascuel*), Jacques Varennes (*Prof. Bridoux*), Georges Chamarat (*Dr. Loisy*), Roberto Rodrigo (*Jose*), Michel Dumur (*Ritberger*), Henri Humbert (*Patard*), Georges Poujouly
P & D: Henri-Georges Clouzot   SCR & DIALOG,:Henri-Georges Clouzot, from a novel by Pierre Boileau & Thomas Narcejac   PHOTOG: Armand Thirard   MUSIC: Georges Van Parys
winner of French Motion Picture Critics' Award
Classic thriller: Wife and mistress plot man's murder. cf. Reflections of Murder

Diabolique
1996, (USA), Morgan Creek/WB, color, 107 mins.
W: Sharon Stone (*Nicole*), Isabelle Adjani (*Mia*), Chazz Palminteri(*Guy*), Kathy Baker (*Shirley*), Spalding Gray, Allen Garfield, Adam Hahn-Byrd, Shirley Knight, Clea Lewis, Donal Logue, Jeffrey Abrams, Diana Bellamy
D: Jeremiah Chechik   SCR: Don Roos, from a novel by Pierre Boileau & Thomas Narcejac   PHOTOG: Peter James   MUSIC: Randy Edelman
blurb: "Two Perfect Women. One Perfect Crime. The Perfect Thriller"
"A rare intelligent remake. Sharon Stone is sensational"—Gene Siskel
Unusual thriller: Two women plot murder

El Dia de la Bestia (The Day of the Beast)
1995, (Sp), color
W: Santiago Segura, Alex Angulo, Terele Pavez, Armando de Razza, Maria Grazia Cucinotta, Juan Inciarte, Saturnino Garcia
D: Alex de la Iglesia   PHOTOG: Flavio Martinez
Minor horror-thriller

Diagnosis: Murder
1975, (GB), Silhouette/CIC, color, 90 mins.
W: Jon Finch (*Insp. Lomax*), Judy Geeson (*Helen*), Christopher Lee (*Dr. Stephen Hayward*), Tony Beckley (*Sgt. Green*), Dilys Hamlett (*Julia Hayward*), Jane Merrow (*Mary Dawson*), Adrian Cairns (*Morgan*), Colin Jeavons (*Bob Dawson*), David Trevina (*Johnson*), Hugh Smith-Marriott (*Dr. Chapman*), Daphne Neville (*Nurse Fisher*)
P: Peter Miller   D: Sidney Hayers   STORY: Philip Levene   PHOTOG: Bob Edwards   MUSIC: Laurie Johnson
Standard thriller: Psychiatrist plots wife's murder

Dial 1119
1950, (USA), b&w, 75 mins.
W: Marshall Thompson, Virginia Field, Andrea King, Keefe Brasselle, Sam Levene
D: Gerald Mayer
Modest thriller: Killer holds bar patrons hostage

Dial a Deadly Number
1975, (GB), Made for TV, color
W: Gary Collins, Gemma Jones
TVM, standard thriller: Actor impersonates psychiatrist

Dial 999
1955, (GB), Merton Park/Anglo-Amalgamated, b&w, 86 mins.
W: Gene Nelson (*Greg Carradine*), Mona Freeman (*Terry Carradine*), John Bentley (*Sgt. Seagrave*), Sydney Tafler (*Cressett*), Michael Goodliffe (*John Moffatt*), Charles Victor (*Tom Smithers*), Paula Byrne (*Vera Bellamy*), Michael Golden (*Insp. Keyes*), Arthur Lovegrove (*George*), Charles Mortimer (*Harding*)
P: Alec Snowden   D & SCR: Montgomery Tully, from Bruce Graeme's novel
USA retitle, The Way Out

Standard crime-thriller: Bookie's killer tries to flee England

Dial Help
1988, (It), color, 94 mins.
W: Charlotte Lewis, Marcello Modugno, Mattia Sbragia, Victor Cavallo
D: Ruggero Deodato
Minor thriller: Ghostly phone calls plague model

Dial M for Murder
1954, (USA), WB, 3D, color, 105 mins.
W: Ray Milland (*Tony Wendice*), Grace Kelly (*Margot Wendice*), Robert Cummings (*Mark*), John Williams (*Chief Insp. Hubbard*), Anthony Dawson (*Swan*), Leo Britt (*The Storyteller*), Patrick Allen (*Pearson*), Robin Hughes, George Leigh, George Alderson
P & D: Alfred Hitchcock   SCR: Frederick Knott, from his stage play   PHOTOG: Robert Burks   MUSIC: Dimitri Tiomkin
"Mr. Hitchcock has presented this mental material on the screen with remarkable visual definition of developing intrigue and mood. He needed good actors and he got them!" —New York Times
Cerebral thriller: Man plots death of faithless wife. cf. Body Double. Remake: A Perfet Murder

Dial M for Murder
1981, (USA), NBC-TV, color, 95 mins.
W: Christopher Plummer (*Tony Wendice*), Angie Dickinson (*Margot Wendice*), Michael Parks (*Max Halliday*), Anthony Quayle, Ron Moody
D: Boris Sagal   TELEPLAY: John Gay, from Frederick Knott's play
TVM, minor remake of classic thriller: Man plots wife's death

The Diamond
1954, (GB), Gibraltar/UA, b&w, 83 mins.
W: Dennis O'Keefe (*Joe Dennison*), Margaret Sheridan (*Marlene Miller*), Philip Friend (*Insp. McLaren*), Francis De Wolff (*Yeo*), Alan Wheatley (*Thompson Blake*), Ann Gudrun (*Sgt. Smith*), Eric Berry (*Hunzinger*), Paul Hardtmuth (*Dr. Eric Miller*), Colin Tapley (*Sir Stafford Beach*), Donald Gray (*Cdr. Gillies*), Cyril Chamberlain (*Castle*), Michael Balfour, Seymour Green
P: Steven Pallos   D: Montgomery Tully   SCR: John C. Higgins, from Maurice Procter's novel *Rich is the Treasure*
USA retitle, The Diamond Wizard
Standard thriller: Intrigue surrounds scientist's diamond-making process

Diamond Cut Diamond
1914, (GB), Hepworth, b&w, 1,075 ft. (327.7m)
W: Claire Pridelle (*Grace Lewin*)
D: Warwick Buckland
Standard crime-thriller: Inventor kidnaps daughter of capitalist who stole his plans

Diamond Hunters
see La Mort en Ce Jardin

The Diamond Mercenaries
1975, (Switz), color, 101 mins.
W: Telly Savalas, Peter Fonda, O.J. Simpson, Maude Adams, Hugh O'Brian, Christopher Lee
D: Val Guest
Minor thriller: Crooks plan desert heist

The Diamond Queen
1953, (USA), WB, color, 80 mins.
W: Fernando Lamas, Arlene Dahl, Gilbert Roland, Michael Ansara, Jay Novello, Sheldon Leonard, Paul Guilfoyle, Richard Hale, Sujata & Asoka
D: John Brahm   PHOTOG: Stanley Cortez
Modest adventure-thriller: Fictionalized account of Hope Diamond's discovery

Diamonds Are Forever
1971, (GB), Eon/UA, color, 119 mins.
W: Sean Connery (*James Bond*), Jill St. John (*Tiffany Case*), Charles Gray (*Ernst Stavros Blofeld*), Jimmy Dean (*Willard Whyte*), Lana Wood (*Plenty O'Toole*), Bruce Cabot (*Albert R. Saxby*), Bruce Glover (*Wint*), Putter Smith (*Kydd*), Bernard Lee ("M"), Lois Maxwell (*Miss Moneypenny*), Norman Burton (*Felix Leiter*), Desmond Llewelyn ("Q"), Joe Robinson (*Peter Franks*), Leonard Barr (*Shady Tree*), Donna Garratt (*Bambi*), Trina Parks (*Thumper*), Margaret Lacey (*Mrs. Whistler*), Edward Bishop (*Klaus Hergersheimer*), Nicky Blair (*The Doorman*), Henry Rowland (*The Dentist*), Marc Lawrence (*The Crook*), Joseph Furst (*Dr. Metz*), Laurence Naismith (*Sir Donald Munger*), David De Keyser (*The Doctor*), David Bauer (*Slumber*), Larry Blake, Constantin De Goguel
P: Harry Saltzman & Albert R. Broccoli   D: Guy Hamilton   SCR: Richard Maibaum & Tom Mankiewicz, from Ian Fleming's novel   PHOTOG: Ted Moore   MUSIC: John Barry, title sung by Shirley Bassey
Lavish adventure-thriller: Stolen diamonds fuel super-laser that could enslave world. Cabot's last film

The Diamond Ship
see Die Spinnen

The Diamond Star
1913, (GB), Cricks & Martin, b&w, 1,280 ft. (390.1m)
D: Edwin J. Collins
Standard crime-thriller: Gypsy poacher joins criminal gang

The Diamond Thieves
1908, (GB), Warwick Trading Co., b&w, 660 ft. (201.2m)
D: Charles Raymond
Standard crime-thriller: Thieves rob jeweler

Diamond's Edge
see Just Ask for Diamond

Diamonds on Wheels
1973, (GB), Walt Disney, color, 85 mins.
W: Patrick Allen (*Insp. Cook*), George Sewell (*Henry Stewart*), Derek Newark
(*Mercer*), Dudley Sutton (*Finch*), Christopher Malcolm (*Jock*), Barry Jackson
(*Wheeler*), Richard Wattis (*Sir Hilary Stanton*), Allan Cuthbertson (*Ashley*),
Peter Firth (*Robin Stewart*), Cynthia Lund (*Susan Stewart*), Spencer Banks
(*Charlie Todd*), George Woodbridge, Edwin Richfield, Ambrosine Philpotts,
Tom Bowman, Patrick Holt, Joe Robinson, Douglas Robinson, Royston
Tickner
D: Jerome Courtland **SCR:** William R. Yates, from Pierre Castex' novel
Nightmare **PHOTOG:** Michael Reed **MUSIC:** Ron Goodwin
Standard juvenile thriller: Stolen diamonds hidden in racing car

The Diamond Wizard
see The Diamond

Diane the Zebra Woman
1963, (USA), Sheldon Rochlin-Diane Cramer, color
Fanciful "underground" yarn: Capricious girl is actually zebra in human form

Diario Secreto da un Carcere Femminile (Secret Diary of an Imprisioned Girl)
1972, (It), color, 100 mins.
W: Annita Strindberg, Eva Czemerys, Jenny Tamburi, Paolo Senatore, Olga Bisera
D: Rino Di Silvestro
A.k.a. Love in a Women's Prisio
Minor melodrama: Gang violence in women's lockup

Diary of a High School Bride
1959, (USA), AIP, b&w, 80 mins.
W: Anita Sands, Ron Foster, Chris Robinson
WRIT, P & D: Burt Topper **TITLE:** Tony Casanova
orig. co-billed with The Ghost of Dragstrip Hollow
Standard melodrama: Unbalanced youth tries to sabotage former girlfriend's marriage

Diary of an Imprisoned Girl
see Diario Segreto da un Carcere Femminile

Diary of a Madman
1962, (USA), Admiral/UA, color, 96 mins.
W: Vincent Price, Nancy Kovack, Chris Warfield, Stephen Roberts, Elaine Devry,
Lewis Martin, Edward Colmans, Ian Wolfe, Harvey Stephens, Mary Adams,
Dick Wilson, Gloria Clark, Nelson Olmsted, Joseph Ruskin (*The Voice of the
"Horla"*)
WRIT & P: Robert E. Kent **D:** Reginald LeBorg, based on Guy de
Maupassant's short story *The Horla* (orig. to be titled same) **PHOTOG:**
Ellis W. Carter **MUSIC:** Richard LaSalle
*French retitle, L'Etrange Histoire du Juge Cordier (The Strange Story of Judge
Cordier)*
Standard fantasy-thriller: Evil force possesses respectable judge, compels him to kill

Diary of a Serial Killer
1998, (USA), SHO-TV, color, 95 mins.
W: Gary Busey, Arnold Vosloo
Made-for-Video, minor thriller: Writer involved with killer

Diary of a Space Virgin
see The Sexplorer

I Diavoli della Spazio (Devils from Space)
1965, (It), Mercury Int'l/Southern Cross/MGM, color, 92 mins
W: Giacomo Rossi-Stuart, Ombretta Colli, Wilbert Bradley
P: Joseph Fryd & Antonio Margheriti **D:** Antonio Margheriti from a story by
Aubrey Wisberg
USA retitle, Snow Devils, A.k.a. Snow Demons'
Standard SF-thriller

Il Diavolo Innamorato (The Devil in Love)
1966, (It), Fair, color, 97 mins.
W: Vittorio Gassman, Mickey Rooney, Claudine Auger, Gabriele Ferzetti, Ettore
Manni, Liana Orfei, Giorgia Moll, Annabella Incontrera
D: Ettore Scola **SCR:** Ettore Scola & Ruggero Maccari
USA release, 1968, Warner Brothers-7 Arts
Standard comedy-fantasy: Satan's emissary stirs discord between Medicis and Papal State.
Original Italian title: L'Arcidiavolo

Dick Barton at Bay
1950, (GB), Marylebone-Hammer/Exclusive, b&w, 68 mins.
W: Don Stannard (*Dick Barton*), Tamara Desni (*Anna*), Percy Walsh (*Prof.
Mitchell*), George Ford (*Snowey White*), Joyce Linden (*Mary Mitchell*),
Meinhart Maur (*Serg Volkoff*), John Arnatt (*Jackson*), Campbell Singer (*Insp.*

Cavendish), Richard George (*Insp. Slade*), Sebastian Cabot. Patrick Macnee
P: Henry Halstead **D:** Godfrey Grayson **SCR:** Ambrose Grayson, from a radio
serial by Edward J. Mason
Standard thriller: Anarchist kidnaps inventer, installs death ray

Dick Barton, Special Agent
1948, (GB), Marylebone/Exclusive, b&w, 70 mins.
W: Don Stannard (*Dick Barton*), George Ford (*Snowey White*), Jack Shaw (*Jock*),
Gillian Maude (*Jean Hunter*), Geoffrey Wincott (*Dr. Caspar*), Beatrice Kane
(*Miss Horrock*), Ivor Danvers (*Snub*)
P: Henry Halstead **D:** Alfred Goulding **SCR:** Alan Stranks & Alfred Goulding,
from a radio serial by Edward J. Mason
Standard thriller: British detective foils foreign agents bearing germ bombs

Dick Barton Strikes Back
1949, (GB), Exclusive, b&w, 71 mins.
W: Don Stannard (*Dick Barton*), Jean Lodge (*Tina*), Sebastian Cabot (*Fouracada*),
James Raglan (*Lord Armadale*), Humphrey Kent (*Col. Gardner*), Bruce
Walker (*Snowey White*), John Harvey (*Maj. Henderson*)
P: Anthony Hinds & Mae Murray **D:** Godfrey Grayson **SCR:** Ambrose
Grayson, from a radio serial by Edward J. Mason
Standard thriller: Foreign agents beam atomic rays

Dick Carson Wins Through
see The Failure

A Dickensian Fantasy
1933, (GB), Gee Films, b&w, 10 mins.
W: Lawrence Hanray
D: Aveling Ginever, based on Charles Dickens' *A Christmas Carol*
Standard fantasy short: Man dreams book characters come to life

Dick Tracy
1937, (USA), Rep, b&w, serial
W: Ralph Byrd (*Dick Tracy*), Kay Hughes (*Gwen*), Carleton Young (*Gordon Tracy,
after*), Lee Van Atta (*Junior*), John Piccori (*Moloch*), Smiley Burnette (*Mike
McGurk*), Francis X. Bushman (*Chief Anderson*), Fred Hamilton (*Steve*), John
Dilson (*Brewster*), Richard Beach (*Gordon Tracy, before*), Theodore Lorch
(*Paterno*), Wedgewood Nowell (*Clayton*), Edwin Stanley (*Odette*), Herbert
Weber (*Martino*), Harrison Greene (*Cloggerstein*), Buddy Roosevelt (*Burke*),
George DeNormand (*Flynn*), Byron Foulger (*Korvitch*)
D: Ray Taylor & Alan James **SCR:** Barry Shipman, Winston Miller, Morgan
Cox, & George Morgan, from characters created by Chester Gould
PHOTOG: William Nobles & Edgar Lyons **MUSIC:** Harry Grey
15-chapter serial: Crimefighter vs. terrorist gang

Dick Tracy
1945, (USA), RKO, b&w, 62 mins.
W: Morgan Conway (*Dick Tracy*), Mike Mazurki (*Splitface*), Anne Jeffreys (*Tess
Trueheart*), Jane Greer (*Judith Owens*), Joseph Crehan (*Chief Brandon*), Lyle
Latell (*Pat Patton*), Mickey Kuhn (*Junior*), Trevor Bardette (*Prof. Lynwood P.
Starling*), Morgan Wallace (*Steven Owens*), Milton Parsons (*Deathridge*),
William Halligan (*The Mayor*), Mary Currier (*Dorothy Stafford*), Edythe
Elliott (*Mrs. Caraway*), Edmund Glover (*The Radio Announcer*), Ralph Dunn
(*Det. Manning*), Bruce Edwards (*The Sgt.*), Tanis Chandler (*Miss Stanley*),
Jimmy Jordan, Carl Hanson, Franklyn Farnum, Carl Faulkner, Jack Gargan,
Sam Ash, Harry Strang, Frank Meredith, George Magrill, Bob Reeves, Tom
Noonan, Alphonse Martell, Robert Douglass, Gertrude Astor, Jack Chefe,
Wilbur Mack, Florence Pepper
D: William Berke **SCR:** Eric Taylor, from characters created by Chester Gould
PHOTOG: Frank Redman **MUSIC:** C. Bakaleinikoff & Roy Webb
*First **Dick Tracy** feature film: Crimefighter stalks brutal killer. A.k.a. **Dick Tracy,
Detective***

Dick Tracy
1990, (USA), Touchstone/Buena Vista, color, 106 mins, also 110 mins
W: Warren Beatty (*Dick Tracy*), Madonna (*Breathless Mahoney*), Al Pacino (*Big Boy
Caprice*), Glenne Headly (*Tess Trueheart*), Charlie Korsmo (*The Kid*), Mandy
Patinkin (*88 Keys*), Charles Durning (*Chief Brandon*), Dick Van Dyke (*D.A.
Fletcher*), Paul Sorvino (*Lips Manlis*), Estelle Parsons (*Mrs. Trueheart*), Ed
O'Ross (*Itchy*), Dustin Hoffman (*Mumbles*), William Forsythe (*Flattop*), R.G.
Armstrong (*Pruneface*) Michael J. Pollard (*Bug Bailey*), Henry Silva
(*Influence*), James Caan (*Spaldoni*), Seymour Cassel (*Sam Catchem*), James
Keane (*Pat Patton*), Tom Signorelli (*Mike*), Allen Garfield (*The Reporter*),
James Tol kan (*Numbers*), Michael Donovan O'Donnell, Jim Wilkey, Stig
Eldred, Neil Summers, Chuck Hicks, Lawrence Steven Meyers, Marvelee
Cariaga, Michael Gallup, John Schuck, Jack Kehoe, Charles Fleischer,
Robert Costanzo, Marshall Bell, Michael G. Hagerty, Lew Horn, Arthur
Malet, Tony Epper, Kathy Bates, Jack Goode Jr., Ray Stoddard, Hamilton
Camp, Robert Beecher, Ed McCready, Colm Meaney, Catherine O'Hara,
Bing Russell, Bert Remsen, Frank Campanella, Sharmagne Leland-St. John,
Tom Finnegan, Billy Clevenger, Ned Claflin, Mary Woronov, John
Moschitta Jr., Neil Ross, Walker Edmiston, Ian Wolfe, Henry Jones, Mike
Mazurki, Rita Bland, Lada Boder, Karyne Ortega, Dee Hengstler, Liz
Imperio, Karen Russell, Michelle Johnston
P & D: Warren Beatty **SCR:** Jim Cash & Jack Epps Jr., from Chester Gould's
comic-strip character **PHOTOG:** Vittorio Storaro **SPCL-FX:** Casey
Cavanaugh, Dave Kelsey, Joe Montenegro, John Stirber, Ron MacInnes & Ed
Felix **MUSIC:** Danny Elfman **SONGS:** (by Stephen Sondheim), *Sooner or*

Later (I Always Get My Man)-Oscar winner, Move, What Can You Lose, Live Alone and Like It, & Back in Business
Standard adventure: Cop vs. crime syndicate

Dick Tracy Meets Gruesome
1947, (USA), RKO, b&w, 64 mins.
<u>W:</u> Ralph Byrd (*Dick Tracy*), Anne Gwynne (*Tess Trueheart*), Boris Karloff (*Gruesome*), Joseph Crehan (*Chief Brandon*), Edward Ashley (*L.E. Thal*), Lyle Latell (*Pat Patton*), Jim Nolan (*Dan Sterne*), June Clayworth (*Dr. I.M. Learned*), Tony Barrett (*Melody*), Skelton Knaggs (*X-Ray*), Milton Parsons (*Dr. A. Tomic*), Robert Clarke, Lex Barker, Sean McClory
<u>D:</u> John Rawlins <u>SCR:</u> Robertson White, Eric Taylor, William H. Graffis & Robert E. Kent, from characters created by Chester Gould <u>PHOTOG:</u> Frank Redman <u>SPCL-FX:</u> Russell A. Cully <u>MUSIC:</u> Paul Sawtell & C. Bakaleinikoff
*French retitle, **Dick Tracy vs. the Gang**, GB retitle, **Dick Tracy's Amazing Adventure***
Standard thriller: Crimefighter pursues escaped criminal

Dick Tracy Returns
1938, (USA), Rep, b&w, serial
<u>W:</u> Ralph Byrd (*Dick Tracy*), Lynne Roberts (*Gwen*), Charles Middleton (*Pa Stark*), Jerry Tucker (*Junior*), David Sharpe (*Ron Merton*), Lee Ford (*Mike McGurk*), Ned Glass (*The Kid*), Michael Kent (*Steve*), John Merton (*Champ*), Raphael (Ray) Bennett (*Trigger*), Jack Roberts (*Dude*), Edward Foster (*Joe Hanner*), Alan Gregg (*Snub*), Reed Howes (*Rance*), Tom Seidel (*Hunt*), Robert Terry (*Reynolds*), Jack Ingram (*Slasher*)
<u>D:</u> William Witney & John English <u>SCR:</u> Barry Shipman, Franklin Adreon, Ronald Davidson, Rex Taylor & Sol Shor, from characters created by Chester Gould <u>PHOTOG:</u> William Nobles <u>MUSIC:</u> Alberto Columbo
15-chapter serial, standard thriller: Crimefighter trails murderous family

Dick Tracy vs. The Spider
1937, (USA), b&w
<u>W:</u> Ralph Byrd, Kay Hughes
Minor thriller

Dick Tracy's Amazing Adventure
*see **Dick Tracy Meets Gruesome***

Dick Tracy's Dilemma
1947, (USA), RKO, b&w, 60 mins.

Dick Tracy's Dilemma: JACK LAMBERT

<u>W:</u> Ralph Byrd (*Dick Tracy*), Kay Christopher (*Tess Trueheart*), Lyle Latell (*Pat Patton*), Jack Lambert (*The Claw*), Ian Keith (*Vitamin Flintheart*), Bernadene Hayes (*Longshot Lillie*), Jimmy Conlin (*Sightless*), William B. Davidson (*Peter Premium*), Tony Barrett (*Jam*), Richard Powers (*Tom Keene*) (*Fred*)
<u>D:</u> John Rawlins <u>SCR:</u> Robert Stephen Brodie, from characters created by Chester Gould <u>PHOTOG:</u> Frank Redman <u>MUSIC:</u> Paul Sawtell
*A.k.a. **Mark of the Claw***
Standard thriller: Crimefighter stalks fur thief

Dick Tracy's G-Men
1939, (USA), Rep, b&w, serial
<u>W:</u> Ralph Byrd (*Dick Tracy*), Irving Pichel (*Zarnoff*), Ted Pearson (*Steve*), Walter Miller (*Robal*), Kenneth Harlan (*Anderson*), Phylis Isley (*Jennifer Jones*) (*Gwen*), George Douglas (*Sandoval*), Joe McGuinn (*Tommy*), Robert Carson (*Scott*), Julian Madison (*Foster*), Kenneth Terrell (*Ed*), Harrison Greene (*Baron*), Harry Humphrey (*Warden Stover*), William Stahl, Robert Wayne, Ted Mapes
<u>D:</u> William Witney & John English <u>SCR:</u> Barry Shipman, Franklin Adreon, Ronald Davidson, Rex Taylor, & Sol Shor, from characters created by Chester Gould <u>PHOTOG:</u> William Nobles <u>MUSIC:</u> William Lava

15-chapter serial, standard thriller: Crimefighter pursues head of int'l spy ring

Dick Tracy vs. Crime, Inc.
1941, (USA), Rep, b&w, serial
<u>W:</u> Ralph Byrd (*Dick Tracy*), Jan Wiley (*June Chandler*), Ralph Morgan (*Morton/Metzicoff*), Michael Owen (*Bill Carr*), Kenneth Harlan (*Lt. Cosgrove*), Jack Mulhall (*Wilson*), Anthony Warde (*Corey*), John Dilson (*Weldon*), Robert Frazer (*Brewster*), Robert Fiske (*Cabot*), John Davidson (*Lucifer*), Frank Alten (*Drage*), Chuck Morrison (*Trask*), Hooper Atchley (*Trent*), C. Montague Shaw (*Dr. Jonathan Martin*), Marjorie Kane (*The Cigarette Girl*), Max Waizman (*The Telegrapher*), Edmund Cobb (*Kelly*), Selmer Jackson (*The Marine Officer*), Griff Barnett (*The Watchman*), Nora Lane (*Ella Gilbert*), Stanley Price (*Jackson*), Howard Hickman (*Stephen Chandler*), Walter McGrail (*The Marine Captain*)
<u>D:</u> William Witney & John English <u>SCR:</u> Ronald Davidson, Norman S. Hall, Joseph O'Donnell, William Lively, & Joseph Poland, from characters created by Chester Gould <u>PHOTOG:</u> Reggie Lanning <u>SPCL-FX:</u> Howard Lydecker <u>MUSIC:</u> Cy Feuer
*reissued (1952) as **Dick Tracy vs. the Phantom Empire***
15-chapter serial, standard thriller: Crimefighter battles master criminal armed with invisibility secret

Dick Tracy vs. Cueball
1946, (USA), RKO, b&w, 62 mins.
<u>W:</u> Morgan Conway (*Dick Tracy*), Anne Jeffreys (*Tess Trueheart*), Lyle Latell (*Pat Patton*), Dick Wessel (*Cueball*), Rita Corday (*Mona Clyde*), Ian Keith (*Vitamin Flintheart*), Esther Howard (*Flora*), Douglas Walton (*Priceless*), Joseph Crehan (*Chief Brandon*), Byron Foulger (*Little*), Skelton Knaggs (*Rudolph*), Jimmy Crane (*Junior*), Milton Parsons (*Higby*)
<u>D:</u> Gordon Douglas <u>SCR:</u> Dane Lussier & Robert E. Kent, from characters created by Chester Gould <u>PHOTOG:</u> George E. Diskant <u>MUSIC:</u> Phil Ohman
Minor thriller: Crimefighter pursues murderous gem thief

Dick Tracy vs. the Gang
*see **Dick Tracy Meets Gruesome***

Dick Tracy vs. the Phantom Empire
*see **Dick Tracy vs. Crime, Inc.***

Dick Turpin
1925, (USA), Fox, b&w, 7 reels (73 mins.)
<u>W:</u> Tom Mix, Kathleen Myers, Philo McCullough, Alan Hale, Bull Montana
<u>D:</u> John G. Blystone
Entertaining adventure-thriller: Highwayman's exploits

Dick Turpin--Highwayman
1956, (GB), Hammer, color, 25 mins.
<u>W:</u> Philip Friend (*Dick Turpin*), Diane Hart (*Liz*), Raymond Rollett (*Hawkins*), Hal Osmond (*Mac*), Allan Cuthbertson (*Jonathan Redgrove*), Norman Mitchell (*Rooks*), Gabrielle May (*Genevieve*)
<u>P:</u> Michael Carreras <u>D:</u> David Paltenghi <u>STORY:</u> Joel Murcott
Standard short adventure-thriller: Highwayman steals girl's dowry

Dick Turpin's Last Ride to York
1906, (GB), Warwick Trading Co., b&w, 500 ft. (152.4m)
<u>W:</u> Fred Ginnett (*Dick Turpin*), Mrs. Ginnett (*Susan Truelove*)
<u>D:</u> Charles Raymond <u>SCR:</u> fred Ginnett
Standard adventure-thriller (in 10 scenes): 18th-century highwayman pursued

Dick Turpin's Ride to York
1906, (GB), Hepworth, b&w, 1,000 ft. (304.8m)
<u>W:</u> Lewin Fitzhamon (*Dick Turpin*), Dorothy Lupone (*The Innkeeper's Daughter*), Louis Stanislaus (*Maj. Mowbray*), Cliff Bing (*Mr. Tyrconnell*), Claude Whitten (*Sir Luke Rookwood*), Tom Mowbray (*The Innkeeper*), Willie Hartill (*Mr. Coates*), Emily Cistance (*The Maid*), Elco Mearson (*Mr. Patterson*), Frank Cousins (*The Postilllion*), Nathaniel Menzies (*The Ostler*), George Curtiss (*The Horse Boy*)
<u>D:</u> S. Lewin Fitzhamon
Standard adventure-thriller (Britain's first "one-reel" feature): Highwayman pursued as he carries message to knight

Dick Turpin's Ride to York
1913, (GB), Walturdaw/B&C, b&w, 1,737 ft. (529.4m)
<u>W:</u> Percy Moran (*Dick Turpin*)
<u>D:</u> Charles Raymond
Standard adventure-thriller: Highwayman betrayed by jealous wife

Dick Turpin's Ride to Yorke
1913, (GB), Foly Films/Phoenix, b&w, 695 ft. (211.8m)
<u>W:</u> Fred Evans (*Dicke Turpin*)
<u>WRIT & D:</u> Fred Evans & Joe Evans
*Standard adventure-comedy: Burlesque of **Dick Turpin's Ride to York** (1913, Walturdaw/B&C/Univ)*

Dick Whittington
1899, (GB), G.A.S. Films, b&w, 75 ft. (22.9m)
<u>D:</u> George Albert Smith
Standard fantasy short: Fairy shows sleeping youth three visions of future

Die! Die! My Darling!
see **Fanatic** *(1965)*

Die, Monster, Die!
see **Monster of Terror**

Die Screaming, Marianne
1970, (GB), Pete Walker/London Screen, color, 104 mins.
W: Susan George (*Marianne*), Christopher Sandford (*Sebastian Smith*), Leo Genn (*The Judge*), Barry Evans (*Eli Frome*), Judy Huxtable (*Hildegarde*), Kenneth Hendel (*Rodriguez*), Anthony Sharp (*The Registrar*), Martin Wyldeck (*The Policeman*)
P & D: Pete Walker   **STORY:** Murray Smith
Minor thriller: Nightclub dancer pursued by killers

Die Sister, Die!
1978, (USA), Cinema Shares Int'l, color
W: Jack Ging, Edith Atwater, Antoinette Bower, Kent Smith, Robert Emhardt, Burt Santos
P & D: Randall Hood   **SCR:** Tony Sawyer   **PHOTOG:** Michael Lonzo   **MUSIC:** Hugo Friedhofer
Minor thriller

Die Watching
1993, (USA), color, 88 mins.
W: Christopher Atkins, Tim Thomerson
Minor thriller: Psychotic director kills aspiring actresses

Digby—The Biggest Dog in the World
1973, (GB), Walter Shenson/Fox-Rank/CRC, color, 88 mins.
W: Jim Dale (*Jeff*), Angela Douglas (*Janine*), John Bluthal (*Jerry*), Spike Milligan (*Harz*), Norman Rossington (*Tom*), Milo O'Shea (*Jameson*), Richard Beaumont (*Billy*), Dinsdale Landon (*Masters*), Garfield Morgan (*Rogerson*), Harry Towb (*The Ringmaster*), Victor Spinetti (*Ribart*), Sandra Caron (*The General's Aide*), Kenneth J. Warren (*The General*), Bob Todd (*Manzini*), Margaret Stuart (*The Ass't*), Ben Aris (*The Captain*), Molly Urquhart (*Aunt Ina*), Victor Maddern (*The Dog Home Manager*), Frank Thornton (*The Estate Agent*), Rob Stewart (*The Train Driver*), Edward Underdown (*Grandfather*), Sheila Steafel (*The Control Operator*), Clovissa Newcombe (*Bunny*), Henry McGee (*The Announcer*)
P: Walter Shenson   **D:** Joseph McGrath   **SCR:** Michael Pertwee   **STORY:** Charles Isaacs, from a book by Ted Key   **PHOTOG:** Harry Waxman   **MUSIC:** Edwin T. Astley
Standard juvenile fantasy: Scientist turns dog into giant

Digital Man
1995, (USA), color, 95 mins.
W: Ken Olandt Adam Baldwin, Ed Lauter, Matthias Hues, Kristen Dalton, Paul Gleason
D: Phillip J. Roth   **SCR:** Phillip J. Roth & Ronald Schmidt
Minor SF-thriller: Super-soldier prototype has programming sabotaged

Dig That Uranium!
1955, (USA), AA, b&w, 61 mins.
W: Leo Gorcey, Huntz Hall, Bernard Gorcey, David Condon (*Gorcey*), Raymond Hatton, Mary Beth Hughes, Harry Lauter, Richard Powers (*Tom Keene*), Myron Healey, Bennie Bartlett, Paul Fierro, Carl Switzer
P: Ben Schwalb   **D:** Edward Bernds   **SCR:** Elwood Ullman & Bert Lawrence
Standard comedy with SF elements: Bowery Boys buy fake uranium mine

Dilemma
1962, (GB), ACT Films/Bry, b&w, 70 mins.
W: Peter Halliday (*Harry Barnes*), Ingrid Haffner (*Jean Barnes*), Patricia Burke (*Edna Jones*), Jean Heath (*Mrs. Barnes*), Patrick Jordan (*Insp. Murray*), Alan Rolfe (*Arthur Jones*), Robert Dean (*The Doctor*)
P: Edward Lloyd   **D & SCR:** Peter Maxwell   **STORY:** Pip & Jane Baker
USA retitle, **The Man With Two Faces**
Stadard crime-thriller (shown on TV only): Teacher suspects missing wife killed bather

Dimension 5
1966, (USA), United Pictures, color, 91 mins.
W: Jeffrey Hunter, France Nuyen, Donald Woods, Linda Ho, Harold Sakata, Robert Ito, David Chow, Jon Lormer, Bill Walker, Virginia Lee, Tad Horino, Lee Kolima, Kam Tong, Gerald Jann, Carol Byron, Maggie Thrett, Marianna Case, Kay Michaels, Ken Spalding, Deanna Lund, Robert Phillips, Allen Jung, John McKee, Ruth Foster, Tex Armstrong, Tita Marsell, Ed Parker
P: Earle Lyon   **D:** Franklin Adreon   **SCR:** Arthur C. Pierce   **PHOTOG:** Alan Stensvold   **SPCL-FX:** Roger George   **MUSIC:** Paul Dunlap
Minor SF-thriller: Secret agent uses time-altering device

Le Diner Impossible (The Impossible Dinner)
1904, (Fr), Star, b&w, 41m (134.5 ft./2.3 mins.)
D: Georges Melies
Standard fantasy

The Dinosaur and the Missing Link
1917, (USA), Edison, b&w, 5 mins.
Stop-motion short conceived & executed by Willis O'Brien: Life in prehistory

Dinosaur Island
1966, (Mex), color
Minor SF-adventure (with stock footage from 'One Million B.C.'): Humans vs. prehistoric beasts

Dinosaur Island
1994, (USA), color, 85 mins.
W: Ross Hagen, Richard Gabai
Standard SF-thriller: Five downed pilots face prehistoric beasts, lusty cavewomen

Dinosaurus!
1960, (USA), Fairview/Univ, color, 85 mins.
W: Ward Ramsey (*Bart Thompson*), Kristina Hanson (*Betty*), Paul Lukather (*Hacker*), Gregg Martell (*The Cro-Magnon Man*), Fred Engleberg, Alan Roberts, Jack Younger, Luci Blain
P: Jack H. Harris   **CO-P & D:** Irvin S. Yeaworth Jr.   **SCR:** Jean Yeaworth & Dan E. Weisburd   **PHOTOG:** Stanley Cortez   **SPCL-FX:** Tim Barr, Wah Chang & Gene Warren   **MUSIC:** Ronald Stein
reissued 1965
Juvenile SF: Excavation revives prehistoric beasts

Dinosaur Valley Girls
1995, (USA), color, 95 mins.
W: Jeff Rector
Minor SF-adventure: Movie star transported to primeval world

The Diplomatic Corpse
1958, (GB), ACT Films/RFD, b&w, 65 mins.
W: Robin Bailey (*Mike Billings*), Susan Shaw (*Jenny Drew*), Liam Redmond (*Insp. Corcoran*), Harry Fowler (*Knocker Parsons*), Maya Koumani (*Marian Weaver*), Andre Mikhelson (*Hamid*), Bill Shine (*Hum-phrey Garrad*), Charles Farrell (*Percy Simpson*)
P: Francis Searle   **D:** Montgomery Tully   **STORY:** Sidney Nelson & Maurice

Dirigible: JACK HOLT AND RALPH GRAVES

Harrison
Standard thriller: Reporter solves diplomat's murder, rescues fiancee from foreign embassy

Le Dirigeable Fantastique ou le Cauchemar d'un Inventeur (The Fantastic Dirigible: or, An Inventor's Nightmare)
1906, (Fr), Star, b&w, 60m (196.9 ft./3.3 mins.)
D: Georges Melies
A.k.a. **The Inventor Crazybrains and His Wonderful Airship**
Minor SF-fantasy: Aerial escapades

Dirigible
1931, (USA), Col, b&w, 102 mins.
W: Jack Holt, Fay Wray, Ralph Graves, Hobart Bosworth, Richard Loo, Roscoe Karns
D: Frank Capra   **SCR:** Jo Swerling & Dorothy Howell, from a story by "Spig" Wead   **PHOTOG:** Joe Wilbur & Elmer Dyer
Modest SF-adventure: Perilous Antarctic exploration

The Disappearance
1977, (GB-Can), Trofar/Tiberius/Cinegate, color, 102 mins.
W: Donald Sutherland (*Jay Mallory*), Francine Racette (*Celandine*), David Hemmings (*Edward*), John Hurt (*Atkinson*), David Warner (*Burbank*), Peter Bowles (*Jeffries*), Michele Magny (*Melanie*), Virginia McKenna (*Catherine Deverell*), Christopher Plummer (*Deverell*), Duane Howard (*James*), Robert Korne (*Dominic*), Michael Kramer (*Peter*), Danny Galivan (*The Commentator*), Patricia Hodge (*The Wife*)
D: Stuart Cooper   **P:** David Hemmings & Gerry Arbeid   **SCR:** Paul Mayersberg from a novel by Derek Marlowe *Echoes of Celandine*
Glossy thriller: Hired killer's wife vanishes

The Disappearance of Flight 412
1974, (USA), NBC-TV, color, 74 mins.
W: Glenn Ford, Bradford Dillman, Guy Stockwell, David Soul, Stanley Clay,

The Disappearance: FRANCINE RACETTE

Robert F. Lyons, Kent Smith, Greg Mullavey
D: Jud Taylor   **SCR:** George Simpson & Neal Burger
orig. to be titled **Something in the Air**
TVM, minor thriller: Air Force jets vanish chasing UFO

The Disappearance of Nora
1993, (USA), Made for TV, color, 96 mins.
W: Veronica Hamel, Dennis Farina (*Denton*), Stephen Collins (*Fremont*), Stan Ivar (*Sinclair*), David Sheen (*Ernie*)
TVM, standard thriller: Nightmares of murder plague amnesiac

The Disappearance of the Judge
1919, (GB), Barker/Globe, b&w, 5,000 ft. (1524m)
W: James Lindsay (*Judge Moultrie/Augustus*), Florence Nelson (*Mme. Julia*), Mark Melford (*Capt. Hayter*), Joan Lockton (*Miss Moultrie*), Wilfred Benson, Daisy Cordell
P: Jack W. Smith   **D:** Alexander Butler, from a novel by Guy Thorne
Standard crime-thriller: German gang kidnaps judge to obtain aero-engine plans

Disaster, Launching of HMS Albion
1898, (GB), Robert William Paul, b&w, 40 ft. (12.2m)
Standard historical recreation: Abortive ship launching

Disaster in Time
Wild Street/Channel Comunications
W: Nicholas Guest, Robert Colbert, Marily Lightstone, Time Winters, Thomas Kent, Anna Neill, Mimi Craven, Lori Lively
D & SCR: David N. Twohy, from the novella *Vintage Season* by Lawrence O'Donnell & C.L. Moore   **PHOTOG:** Harry Mathias   **MUSIC:** Gerald Gouriet
A.k.a. **The Grand Tour**

Disaster in Time
1992, (USA), Made for Cable, color, 98 mins.
W: Jeff Daniels, Ariana Richards (*Hilary*), Emilia Crow (*Reeve*), Jim Haynie (*Oscar*), George Murdock (*The Judge*), David Wells (*Quish*)
Made-for-Cable, standard SF-thriller: Time travelers visit small Ohio town

Disciple of Death
1972, (GB), Chromage/Target Int'l/Allan King Assocs., color, 84 mins.
W: Mike Raven (*The Stranger*), Marguerite Hardiman (*Julia*), Ronald Lacey (*The Parson*), Stephen Bradley (*Ralph*), George Belbin (*The Squire*), Virginia Wetherell (*Ruth*), Nick Amer (*The Cabalist*), Betty Alberge (*Dorothy*), Rusty Goffe (*The Dwarf*), Louise Jameson (*Betty*), Daisika (*The Gypsy*), Joe Dunlop (*Mathew*)
WRIT & P: Tom Parkinson & Churton Fairman   **D:** Tom Parkinson   **PHOTOG:** William Brayne
Minor horror-thriller: Demonic cultist invokes evil

Disciple of Dracula
see **Dracula, Prince of Darkness**

Discipline
1935, (GB), Monarch/Zenifilms, b&w, 18 mins.
W: Charles Mortimer (*The Businessman*), A.B. Imeson (*The Watchman*), April Vivian, Eric Dance, Mary Mackintosh, Clifford Cobbe, Natalie Nova
D: James Riddell, A.B. Imeson, John Gladstone, & Lawrence Barrett   **SCR:** James Riddell, from a story by Lesley Storm
Standard short thriller: Psychic warns businessman of train crash

Il Disco Volante (The Flying Saucer)
1961, (It), Dino De Laurentiis/Embassy, color, 93 mins.
W: Alberto Sordi, Monica Vitti, Silvana Mangano, Eleonora Rossi-Drago
P: Dino De Laurentiis   **D:** Tinto Brass   **SCR:** Rudolpho Sonego   **MUSIC:** Piero Piccioni
Sordi plays 4 roles in minor SF-comedy: Earthlings abducted by Martians

The Discreet Charm of the Bourgeoisie
1972, (Fr), 20th-Fox, color, 100 mins.
W: Fernando Rey (*The Ambassador*), Delphine Seyrig (*Mrs. Thevenot*), Stephane Audran (*Mrs. Senechal*), Bulle Ogier (*Florence*), Paul Frankeur (*Mr. Thevenot*), Julien Bertheau (*The Bishop*), Jean-Pierre Cassel (*Mr. Senechal*), Michel Piccoli (*The Home Sec'y*), Claude Pieplu (*The Colonel*), Muni (*The Peasant Girl*)
P: Serge Silberman   **D:** Luis Bunuel   **STORY & SCR:** Luis Bunuel & Jean-Claude Carriere   **PHOTOG:** Pierre Lary
Classic satire: Civilization's corruptions exposed

The Disembodied
1957, (USA), AA, b&w, 65 mins.
W: Paul Burke (*Tom Maxwell*), Allison Hayes (*Tonda/Metz*), John Wengraf (*Dr. Karl Metz*), Joel Marston (*Norman*), Eugenia Paul (*Lara*), Robert Christopher (*Joe*), Paul Thompson (*Gogi*), Norman Frederic (*Suba*), A.E. Okunu (*The Voodoo Drum Leader*), Otis Greene
P: Ben Schwalb   **D:** Walter Grauman   **SCR:** Jack Townley   **PHOTOG:** Harry Neumann   **MUSIC:** Marlin Skiles
orig. co-billed with **From Hell It Came**
Minor thriller with "'50's eroticism": Jungle doctor's wife practices voodoo

The Disinherited Nephew
1912, (GB), Barker, b&w, 1,010 ft. (307.9m)
D: Bert Haldane
Standard crime-thriller: Child kidnapped by disowned cousin

Dislocation Extraordinary
see **Dislocation Mysterieuse**

Dislocation Mysterieuse (Mysterious Dislocation)
1901, (Fr), Star, b&w, 40m (131.2 ft./2.2 mins.)
W: Andre Deed
D: Georges Melies
A.k.a. **Dislocation Extraordinary**
Standard fantasy: Clown disassemble

A Distant Scream
1985, (GB), Hammer/Fox Mystery Theatre, Made for TV, color, 69 mins.
W: David Carradine (*Michael/Harris*), Stephanie Beacham (*Rosemary Richardson*), Stephen Greif (*Clifford*), Fanny Carby (*Mrs. Kimble*), Stephen Chase (*Gary*), Bernard Horsfall (*The Doctor*), Lesley Dunlop (*Sarah*), Edward Peel (*The Prison Officer*), Ewan Stuart (*Robin*)
D: John Hough   **TELEPLAY:** Martin Worth   **PHOTOG:** Brian West   **MUSIC:** Paul Patterson   **MUSIC SPRVSR:** Philip Martell
TVM, minor thriller: Aged ghost haunts

Distortions
1987, (USA), Jackelyn Giroux, color, 98 mins.
W: Olivia Hussey (*Amy Marks*), Steve Railsback (*Scott Marshall*), Piper Laurie (*Margot Caldwell*), Rita Gam (*Mildred Tyson*), June Chadwick (*Kelly Powell*), Edward Albert (*Jason Marks*), Terence Knox (*Paul Elliott*), Tom Castronova (*Harry Cory*), Leon Smith (*Dan Jackson*), Don Clark (*Gary Walker*), John Goff (*Coroner Tomplins*), Christopher Hayes (*Ralph*), Cathleen Chin (*Receptionist Tie Lyn*), Moya Goodwin (*Amy's Mother*), Joseph Colgan (*Amy's Father*), Cary Scott (*The Male Hustler*), Nina M. Aguirre (*Little Amy*), Rafael Narbaez (*The Chauffeur*), Anne Pouliot (*Janice*), Rocky Slaymaker, Warren Reingold, Randy Earl, Herb Reingold, Melanie Reingold, Ashley Hester, Randy Braverman, Caren Avedon, Claude Roberts, Hilary Jacobs, Gene Leoni, Susan Fischer, Richard Bennett Warsk, Richard Rush, Jackie Giroux
D: Armand Mastroianni   **SCR:** John Goff   **PHOTOG:** John Dirlam   **MUSIC DIR:** Brian Leahy   **MUSIC COMPOSER:** David Morgan
Standard mystery-thriller: Young widow has eerie visions

Disturbance
1989, (USA), color, 81 mins.
W: Timothy Greeson, Lisa Goffreion
D: Cliff Guest
Minor thriller: Schizophrenic youth involved in murders

Disturbed
1990, (USA), Live Entertainment/Odyssey Distributors, color, 96 mins.
W: Malcolm McDowell, Geoffrey Lewis, Pamela Gidley, Irwin Keyes Peter Murnik Priscilla Pointer, Deep Roy, Clint Howard, Kim McGuire
D: Charles Winkler   **SCR:** Emerson Bixby & Charles Winkler
Standard black comedy: Perverted psychiatrist's sins come back to haunt him

Disturbing Behavior
1998, (USA), MGM, color, 82 mins.
W: James Marsden (*Steve Clark*), Katie Holmes, Nick Stahl, Bruce Greenwood
D: David Nutter   **SCR:** Scott Rosenberg   **MUSIC:** Mark Snow

Standard SF-thriller: New boy in town finds teens strangely docile

Diving For Treasure
1900, (GB), R.W. Paul, b&w, 45 ft. (13.7m)
<u>D</u>: Walter Booth
Standard thriller: Divers find sunken riches

Dix Chapeaux en 60 Secondes (Ten Hats in Sixty Seconds)
1896, (Fr), Star, b&w, 20m (65.6 ft./1.1 mins.)
<u>WRIT, P, & D</u>: Georges Melies
*USA retitle, **Conjurer Making Ten Hats in Sixty Seconds***
Fantasy short: Examples of prestidigitation

D.N.A.
1996, (USA), color, 95 mins.
<u>W</u>: Jurgen Prochnow (*Dr. Wessinger*), Mark Dacascos
*Standard SF-horror: Evil scientist revives monstrous jungle beast. cf. **The Creeping Flesh***

D.O.A.
1949, (USA), Cardinal/UA, b&w, 83 mins.
<u>W</u>: Edmond O'Brien (*Frank Bigelow*), Pamela Britton (*Paula*), Luther Adler (*Majak*), William Ching (*Halliday*), Henry Hart (*Stanley Philips*), Beverly (Campbell) Garland (*Miss Foster*), Neville Brand (*Chester*), Lynn Baggett (*Mrs. Philips*), Laurette Luez (*Marla Rakubian*), Jess Kirkpatrick (*Sam*), Cay Forrester (*Sue*), Virginia (*Lindley*) Lee (*Jeanie*), Michael Ross (*Dave*), Larry Dobkin
<u>D</u>: Rudolph Maté <u>SCR</u>: Russell Rouse & Clarence Greene <u>PHOTOG</u>: Ernest Laszlo <u>MUSIC</u>: Dimitri Tiomkin
*Semi-classic "film noir": Dying man seeks his murderer. cf. **Color Me Dead***

D.O.A.
1988, (USA), Ziskin-Sander/Silver ScreenPartners II/Touchstone, color, 98 mins.
<u>W</u>: Dennis Quaid (*Dexter Cornell*), Meg Ryan (*Sydney Fuller*), Charlotte Rampling (*Mrs. Fitzwaring*), Rob Knepper (*Nicholas Lang*), Daniel Stern (*Hal Petersham*), Jane Kaczmarek (*Gail Cornell*), Christopher Neame (*Bernard*), Jay Patterson (*Graham Carey*), Robin Johnson (*Cookie Fitzwaring*), Brion James (*Det. Ulmer*), Jack Kehoe (*Det. Brockton*), Karen Radcliffe (*Jane Carey*), Elizabeth Arlen (*Elaine Wells*), Bill Bolender (*Nicholas Lang Sr.*), William Forward (*The Chief President*), Lee Gideon (*Mr. Fitzwaring*), Hillary Hoffman, John Hawkes, Marco Perella, Michael Costello, William Johnson, Joye Swan, Brent Anderson, Wendye Clarendon, Charles Beecham, Gabriel Folse, Matt Thompson
<u>D</u>: Rocky Morton & Annabel Jankel <u>SCR</u>: Charles Edward Pogue <u>STORY</u>: Charles Edward Pogue, Russell Rouse, & Clarence Greene <u>PHOTOG</u>: Yuri Nevman <u>ORIG. SCORE</u>: Chaz Jankel
Modest thriller remake: College prof hunts his assassin

D.O.A. II
see Color Me Dead

The Docks of New Orleans
1948, (USA), Mono, b&w, 64 mins.
<u>W</u>: Roland Winters (*Charlie Chan*), Virginia Dale (*Rene La Fontaine*), Mantan Moreland (*Birmingham Brown*), Victor Sen Yung (*Tommie Chan*), John Gallaudet (*Capt. McNally*), Carol Forman (*Nita Aguirre*), Douglas Fowley (*Grock*), Boyd Irwin (*La Fontaine*), Harry Hayden (*Swendstrom*), Stanley Andrews (*Theodore Von Scherbe*), Howard Negley (*Pereaux*), George J. Lewis (*Dansiger*), Emmett Vogan (*Henri Castanaro*), Rory Mallinson (*Simon Thompson*), Diane Fauntele, Forrest Matthews, Ferris Taylor, Wally Walker, Eric Wilson, Frank Stephens, Haywood Jones, Larry Steers, Paul Conrad, Fred Miller
<u>D</u>: Derwin Abrahams <u>SCR</u>: Scott Darling, from characters created by Earl Derr

Doctor Butcher

Biggers <u>PHOTOG</u>: William A. Sickner
*Minor mystery-thriller, remake of **Mr. Wong, Detective**: Oriental sleuth probes deaths of three men who shared secret formula*

Doc Savage, the Man of Bronze
1975, (USA), WB, color, 100 mins.
<u>W</u>: Ron Ely (*Doc Savage*), Pamela Hensley (*Maria*), Paul Gleason (*Long Tom*), Bill Lucking (*Renny*), Mike Miller, Darrell Zwerling, Robert Tessier, Michael Berryman, Eldon Quick
<u>P</u>: George Pal <u>D</u>: Michael Anderson <u>SCR</u>: George Pal & Joe Morhaim, based on the *Doc Savage* novels by "Kenneth Robeson" (Lester Dent) <u>PHOTOG</u>: Fred Koenekamp <u>MUSIC</u>: John Phillip Sousa
Minor SF-fantasy, George Pal's last production: Superhero seeks missing father

Docteur Petiot
1990, (Fr), b&w & color, 102 mins.
<u>W</u>: Michel Serrault, Pierre Romans, Zbigniew Horoks, Berangere Bonvoisin, Aurore Prieto, Andre Chaumeau, Axel Bogousslavski
<u>D</u>: Christian de Chalonge
Unusual fact-based thriller: Homicidal physician in WW II occupied France

The Doctor and the Devils
1985, (GB), color, 93 mins.
<u>W</u>: Timothy Dalton (*Dr. Rock*), Jonathan Pryce (*Fallon*), Stephen Rea (*Broom*), Twiggy, Sian Phillips, Beryl Reid
<u>D</u>: Freddie Francis, from a story by Dylan Thomas <u>ADAPT</u>: Ronald Harwood
*Standard thriller: Saga of graverobbers based on case of Burke & Hare. cf. **The Body Snatcher** (1945) and **The Flesh and the Fiends***

Dr. Alien
1988, (USA), color, 87 mins.
<u>W</u>: Judy Landers, Billy Jacoby, Olivia Barash, Raymond O'Connor, Stuart Fratkin, Arlene Golonka, Edy Williams, Linnea Quigley, Troy Donahue, Ginger Lynn Allen
<u>D</u>: David DeCoteau
Standard SF-comedy: Space-alien female disguised as college professor

Dr. Black Mr. Hyde
1976, (USA), Walker-Bernhard/Dimension, color, 87 mins.
<u>W</u>: Bernie Casey (*Dr. Henry Pride/Hyde*), Rosalind Cash (*Dr. Billie Worth*), Marie O'Henry (*Linda*), Milt Kogan (*Lt. O'Connors*), Ji-Tu Cumbuka (*Lt. Jackson*), Cora Lee Day (*The Old Woman*), Stu Gilliam (*Silky*), Marc Alaimo (*Preston*), Sam Laws (*The Bartender*), Gwyn Karon (*Gwyn*), Elizabeth Robinson (*Cissy*), Pamela Serpe (*Mary Beth*), Virginia Lynne (*Brenda*), Della Thomas (*Bernice*), Judith Angeline (*A Nurse*), Janet Dey (*A Nurse*), Kejo Thomas (*Cathy*), Nancy Middleton (*Betty*), LaVerne Jackson (*A Student*), Wilson Bryant III (*Jimmy*), Sam Nudell (*The Doctor*), Angel Colbert (*A Student*), Rai Tasco (*The Indian Doctor*), Manfred Bernhard (*The German Doctor*), Gregory Awosika (*The African Doctor*), Daniel Spelling (*An Orderly*), Erik Washington (*An Orderly*), Roma Alvarez (*The Cleaning Lady*), Phillip Roye, Gene Massey, Joy Lee, Val Loring, Shirley Harding, Joseph M. Reynolds, Bobby Angelle, Adrian Ricard, Bob Minor, Buff Brady
<u>D</u>: William Crain <u>SCR</u>: Larry LeBron <u>PHOTOG</u>: Tak Fujimoto <u>SPCL-FX</u>: Harry Woolman <u>MUSIC;</u>Johnny Pate
*A.k.a. **The Watts Monster***
Standard horror-fantasy: Black physician frees alter ego

Dr. Blood's Coffin
1961, (GB), Caralan/UA, color, 92 mins.
<u>W</u>: Kieron Moore (*Dr. Peter Blood*), Hazel Court (*Linda Parker*), Ian Hunter (*Dr. Blood*), Fred Johnson (*Tregaye*), Gerald C. Lawson (*Morton*), Paul Hardtmuth (*The Professor*), Paul Stockman (*Steve Parker*), Andy Alston (*Beale*), Kenneth J. Warren
<u>P</u>: George Fowler <u>D</u>: Sidney J. Furie <u>SCR</u>: Jerry Juran <u>PHOTOG</u>: Stephen Dade <u>MUSIC</u> Buxton Orr
*orig. co-billed with **The Snake Woman***
Standard horror-thriller: Doctor raises dead, terrorizes beautiful widow

Dr. Breedlove: or, How I Learned to Stop Worrying and Love
see Kiss Me Quick

Dr. Brian Pellie and the Bank Robbery
1911, (GB), Clarendon, b&w, 785 ft. (239.3m)
<u>D</u>: Wilfred Noy
Standard thriller: Crook captures bank manager, poses as him and robs safe

Dr. Brian Pellie and the Baronet's Bride
1911, (GB), Clarendon, b&w, 680 ft. (207.3m)
<u>D</u>: Wilfred Noy
Standard thriller: Crook kidnaps millionaire's bride

Dr. Brian Pellie and the Secret Despatch
1912, (GB), Clarendon, b&w, 745 ft. (227.1m)
<u>D</u>: Wilfred Noy
Standard thriller: Crook chased by tram

Dr. Brian Pellie and the Spanish Grandees
1912, (GB), Clarendon, b&w, 870 ft. (265.2m)

D: Wilfred Noy
Standard thriller: Gang captures duchess

Dr. Brian Pellie and the Wedding Gifts
1913, (GB), Clarendon, b&w, 935 ft. (285m)
D: Wilfred Noy
Standard thriller: Crook poses as policeman, robs sugar king

Dr. Brian Pellie Escapes from Prison
1912, (GB), Clarendon, b&w, 575 ft. (175.3m)

TVM, standard thriller: Small-town G.P. eliminates patients

Doctor? Coppelius!!
1966, (Sp), Childhood, color, 96 mins.
W: Walter Slezak, Claudia Corday, Carmen Rojas
WRIT & D: Ted Kneeland   **PHOTOG:** Cecillo Paniagua   **MUSIC:** Leo Delibes
Minor fantasy: Artisan creates living doll

Dr. Crippen
1962, (GB), Torchlight/WPD/WB, b&w, 98 mins.

Doctor Dolittle: REX HARRISON

D: Wilfred Noy
Standard thriller: Crook flees justice disguised as chaplain

Dr. Brian Pellie, Thief and Coiner
1910, (GB), Clarendon, b&w, 710 ft. (216.4m)
D: Wilfred Noy
Standard thriller: Crook hypnotizes heiress on train, waif fetches fiance and police

Dr. Butcher, M.D. (Medical Deviate)
see Queen of the Cannibals

Dr. Cadman's Secret
see The Black Sleep

Dr. Caligari
1989, (USA), Joseph F. Robertson/Steiner Films, color, 80 mins.
W: Madeleine Reynal (*Dr. Caligari*), Fox Harris (*Dr. Avol*), Laura Albert (*Mrs. Van Houten*), Barry Phillips (*Cesare*), Jennifer Balgobin (*Ramona Lodger*), Jennifer Miro (*Miss Koonce*), John Durbin (*Gus Pratt*), Gene Zerna (*Les Van Houten*), David Parry (*Dr. Lodger*), Magie Song (*The Patient in the Strait-Jacket*), Stephen Quadros (*The Scarecrow*), Carol Albright (*The Screaming Patient*), Lori Chacko (*A Patient in Bed*), Marjean Holden (*A Patient in Bed*), Catherine Case (*The Patient with Extra Hormones*), Debra Deliso (*Grace Butter*), Salvador R. Espinoza (*The Spanish Patient/Baby Man*), Vera Butler (*The Human Lamp*), Joseph Baratelli (*The Shoe Salesman on Video*), Anthony Robertson (*The Patient in the Doorway*), April Hartz (*The Shoe Customer on Video*), Tequila Mockingbird (*The Door Tongue*), Brad Durham, Cathy Durham, Tommy Wright, Martin Corbin, Ray Mullins, Annette Karcher, Megan Berglevist, Ky Moffet, Tracey Mirmer, Kim Kruger, Anastasia Steiner, Charles Prior, Honey Davis, Randy Cook, Brian Balrice, Lisa La Mel, Jodie Davis, Carol Ercolono, Texacala Jones, Renee Le
D: Stephen Sayadian   **SCR:** Jerry Stahl & Stephen Sayadian   **PHOTOG:** Ladi von Jansky   **MUSIC:** Mitchell Froom
Surreal horror-satire: Woman scientist experiments on asylum patients

Dr. Cook's Garden
1971, (USA), Para-TV, color, 74 mins.
W: Bing Crosby (*Dr. Cook*), Blythe Danner, Frank Converse, Abby Lewis, Fred Burrell, Barney Hughes, Bethel Leslie, Carol Morley, Staats Cotsworth, Thomas Barbour, Jordan Reed, Helen Stenborg
P: Bob Markell   **D:** Ted Post   **TELEPLAY:** Art Wallace, based on Ira Levin's stage play   **PHOTOG:** Urs Furrer   **MUSIC:** Robert Drasnin

W: Donald Pleasence (*Dr. Crippen*), Coral Browne (*Belle Crippen*), Samantha Eggar (*Ethel le Neve*), Donald Wolfit (*R.D. Muir*), James Robertson Justice (*Capt. Kendall*), Geoffrey Toone (*Mr. Tobin*), Oliver Johnston (*The Lord Chief Justice*), Elspeth March (*Mrs. Jackson*), Edward Underdown (*The Governor*), Olga Lindo (*Clara Arditti*), Paul Carpenter (*Bruce Martin*), John Arnatt (*Insp. Dew*), Basil Henson (*Paul Arditti*)
P: John Clein   **D:** Robert Lynn   **STORY:** Leigh Vanc
Standard thriller: Exploits of murderous physician, USA release, 1964

Dr. Cut'emup
1904, (GB), Gaumont, b&w, 190 ft. (57.9m)
D: Alf Collins
Minor fantasy short: Tramp sells "dead" friend to doctor

Dr. Cyclops
1940, (USA), Para, color, 76 mins.
W: Albert Dekker (*Dr. Alex Thorkel*), Janice Logan (*Mary Phillips*), Charles Halton (*Dr. Rupert Bullfinch*), Tom Coley (*Bill Stockton*), Bill Wilkerson, Paul Fix, Victor Kilian, Frank Yaconelli, Allen Fox, Frank Reicher
P: Dale van Every   **D:** Ernest B. Schoedsack   **SCR:** Tom Kilpatrick, from Charles Strong's novel   **PHOTOG:** Ellsworth Hoagland   **SPCL-FX:** Farciot Edouart & Wallace Kelley   **MUSIC:** Ernst Toch, Gerard Carbonera & Albert Hay Malotte
"...the film has good moments, such as the efforts of the (little people) to train a rifle on the sleeping Cyclops"—Ivan Butler, The Horror Film
"...a fascinating film"—Francois Truffaut, Cahiers du Cinema
Classic SF-fantasy. Scientist uses ray to shrink humans

Dr. Death
see Madhouse

Doctor Death: Seeker of Souls
1973, (USA), Freedom Arts/CRC, color, 93 mins.
W: John Considine (*Dr. Death*), Barry Coe (*Fred*), Stewart Moss (*Greg*), Cheryl Miller (*Sandy*), Leon Askin (*Thor*), Jo Morrow (*Laura*), Athena Lorde (*The Spiritualist*), Florence Marly (*Tana*), Sivi Aberg (*Venus*), Jim Boles (*Franz*), Moe Howard (*The Volunteer*), Robert F. Ball (*The Old Wizard*), Lin Henson (*The TV Watcher*), Barbara Boles (*Alice*), Anna Bernard (*The Girl in the Phonebooth*), Eric Boles (*The Man at the Seance*), Patrick Dennis-Leigh (*The Old Man*), Larry Rogers (*The Young Man in the Park*), Jeffrey Herman (*The Man Wanting a New Body*), Denise Denise (*The Girl with the Flat Tire*), Leon Williams (*The Man to Arrange the Seance*), Larry "Seymour" Vincent (*The

Strangler)
P & D: Eddie Saeta   SCR: Sal Ponti   PHOTOG: Kent Wakeford & Emil Oster
MUSIC: Richard LaSalle
Minor horror-fantasy: Man claims power to raise dead

Dr. Dolittle
1967, (USA), 20th-Fox, color, 152 mins.
W: Rex Harrison (*Dr. Dolittle*), Richard Attenborough (*Mr. Blossom*), Samantha
   Eggar (*Emma*), Anthony Newley (*Matthew*), Norma Varden, Peter Bull,
   William Dix, Geoffrey Holder, Portia Nelson, Muriel Landers
D: Richard Fleischer, from stories by Hugh Lofting   PHOTOG: Robert L. Surtees
   SPCL-FX: L.B. Abbott   SONGS: *Talk to the Animals, When I Look in Your
   Eyes & My Friend the Doctor*
Juvenile musical fantasy: Eccentric probes languages of animals. Remade in 1998 with Eddie Murphy

Dr. Dolittle
1998, (USA), 20th-Fox, color, 85 mins.
W: Eddie Murphy, Ossie Davis, Oliver Platt, Raven-Symone, Jeffrey Tambor,
   Kristin Wilson, Richard Schiff, Peter Boyle
VOICES: Albert Brooks, Chris Rock, Ellen DeGeneres, Julie Kavner, Garry
   Shandling, Norm MacDonald, Reni Santoni, John Leguizamo, Jenna Elfman
D: Betty Thomas   SCR: Nat Mauldin & Larry Levin, from Hugh Lofting's stories

Dr. Mabuse: GERTRUDE WELCKER, RUDOLF KLIEN-ROGGE, ALFRED ABEL

PHOTOG: Russell Boyd   MUSIC: Richard Gibbs   MUSIC SPRVSR:
Pilar McCurry
Standard comedy-fantasy: Doctor distressed by telepathic communication with animals

Dr. Doom
see *Beach Girls and the Monster*

Dr. Dracula
1977, (USA), Rafael Film Assocs./Independent-Int'l, color, 86 mins.
W: John Carradine, Donald Barry, Jane Brunel-Cohen, Larry Hankin, Geoffrey
   Land, Regina Carrol, Norman Pierce, Noel Welch, Vic Kirk, Susan McIver,
   Tweed Morris, Emily Smith, Michael Renner, Robert Carr, Susan Catherine
D: Al Adamson & Paul Aratow   PHOTOG: Gary Graver & Robbie Greenberg
   SPCL-FX: Doug Jones & Larry Todd
Minor horror-fantasy: Evil spirit takes possession of author, vampire prowls

Dr. Faustus
1968, (GB), Oxford Univ.-Nassau-Venfilms/Col, color, 93 mins.
W: Richard Burton (*Dr. Faustus*), Elizabeth Taylor (*Helen of Troy/ "Woman"*),
   Andreas Teuber (*Mephistopheles*), David McIntosh (*Lucifer*), Ian Marter (*The
   Emperor*), Ram Chopra (*Valdes*), Elizabeth Donovan (*The Empress*), Jeremy
   Eccles (*Beelzebub*), Richard Carwardine (*Cornelius*), Nevill Coghill (*The
   Professor*), Hugh Williams (*The Scholar*), Bridget Coghill (*Gluttony*),
   Ambrose Coghill (*Avarice*)
P: Richard Burton & Richard McWhorter   D: Richard Burton & Nevill Coghill
   SCR: Nevill Coghill, from Christopher Marlowe's play *The Tragical History
   of Doctor Faustus*   PHOTOG: Gabor Pogany   MUSIC: Mario Nascimbene
"Richard Burton's performance burns with a demonic fire and soars with the
   magic of his voice!"—Arthur Knight, Saturday Review
"Richard Burton has stamped Faustus with a swirl of color, mood and intensity!"
   —William Wolf, Cue
Lavish fantasy: Aged doctor sells soul for wine, women and special effects

Dr. Fenton's Ordeal
1914, (GB), Hepworth, b&w, 2,100 ft. (640.1m)
W: Tom Powers (*Rupert Harding*), Stewart Rome (*Guy Fenton*), Chrissie White
   (*Sybil Harding*), Henry Vibart (*Mr. Harding*)
D: Frank Wilson
Standard thriller: Thief becomes oculist, cures blind girl witness

Doctor Franken
1980, (USA), Herbert Brodkin/Titus-Janus/NBC-TV, color, 92 mins.
W: Robert Vaughn (*Dr. Arno Franken*), Teri Garr (*Kelli Fisher*), Robert Perault

(*John Doe in Rm. #841*), David Selby (*Dr. Mike Foster*), Cynthia Harris
(*Anita Franken*), Josef Sommer (*Mr. Parker*), Addison Powell, Stranja Lowe,
Randolph Willrich, Sam Schacht, Theodore Sorel, Nicolas Surovy, Claiborne
Cary, Tokayo Doran, Roger Hill, Debra Mooney, Alan Cabal
D: Marvin J. Chomsky   TELEPLAY: Lee Thomas   STORY: Jeff Lieberman &
   Lee Thomas   suggested by Mary W. Shelley's novel *Frankenstein*
   PHOTOG: Alan Metzger   MUSIC: John Morris
orig. to be titled The Franken Project
TVM, minor SF-thriller: Modern scientist creates human

Dr. Frankenstein on Campus
1970, (Can), Medford, color, 81 mins
W: Robin Ward
P: Bill Marshall   D: Gil Taylor   SCR: David Cobb, Bill Marshall & Gil Taylor
A.k.a. **Flick**
Minor SF-horror: Student turns classmates into zombies

Dr. Giggles
1992, (USA), Dark Horse Prods./Largo-JVC/Univ, color, 93 mins.
W: Larry Drake (*Dr. Evan Rendell*), Holly Marie Combs (*Jennifer Campbell*), Cliff
   De Young (*Tom Campbell*), Michelle Johnson (*Tamara*), Glenn Quinn (*Max
   Anderson*), Nancy Fish (*Elaine Henderson*), Keith Diamond (*Officer Joe Reitz*),
   Richard Bradford (*Officer Hank Magruder*), John Vickery (*Dr. Chamberlain*),
   Sara Melson (*Coreen*)
D: Manny Coto   SCR: Manny Coto & Graeme Whifler   PHOTOG: Robert
   Draper   MUSIC: Brian May
Standard horror-satire: Mad physician takes revenge on small town

Dr. Goldfoot and the Bikini Machine
1965, (USA), AIP, color, 90 mins.
W: Vincent Price (*Dr. Goldfoot*), Frankie Avalon, Dwayne Hickman, Susan Hart,
   Fred Clark, Jack Mullaney, William Baskin, Patti Chandler, Salli Sachse,
   Aron Kincaid, Sue Hamilton, Troy Milton, Annette Funicello, Harvey
   Lembeck, Deborah Walley, Alberta Nelson, Milton Frome, Hal Riddle, Kay
   Elhardt, William Baskin, Vincent L. Barnett, Joe Ploski, Sally Frei,
   Marianne Gaba, Issa Arnal, Pam Rodgers, Leslie Summers, Jan Watson,
   Mary Hughes, Luree Holmes, China Lee, Laura Nicholson, Deanna Lund,
   Arlene Charles, Kay Michaels
P: James H. Nicholson & Samuel Z. Arkoff   D: Norman Taurog   SCR: Elwood
   Ullman & Robert Kaufman   STORY: James Hartford   PHOTOG: Sam
   Leavitt   MUSIC: Les Baxter
orig. to be titled Dr. Goldfoot and the Sex Machine. *GB retitle,* Professor G. and
   the Bikini Machine
Standard SF-comedy: Mad scientist creates female robots

Dr. Goldfoot and the Girl Bombs
1966, (USA-It), AIP, color, 85 mins.
W: Vincent Price (*Dr. Goldfoot*), Fabian, Franco Franchi, Ciccio Ingrassia, Laura
   Antonelli, Francesco Mule
D: Mario Bava   SCR: Louis M. Heyward & Robert Kaufman   STORY: James
   Hartford
sequel to both Dr. Goldfoot and the Bikini Machine *and* Two Mafia Guys vs.
   Goldginger
orig. to be titled Dr. Goldfoot and the Sex Bomb *or* Dr. Goldfoot and the "S" Bomb
Ital title, Two Mafia Guys from the FBI
Minor SF-comedy: Bumblers meet criminal genius

Dr. Goldfoot and the "S" Bomb
see *Dr. Goldfoot and the Girl Bombs*

Dr. Goldfoot and the Sex Bomb
see *Dr. Goldfoot and the Girl Bombs*

Dr. Goldfoot and the Sex Machine
see *Dr. Goldfoot and the Bikini Machine*

Doctor Gore
see *The Body Shop*

Dr. Hackenstein
1988, (USA), color
W: Phyllis Diller, Anne Ramsey
Standard horror-spoof

Dr. Hallers
1930, (Ger), b&w
W: Fritz Kortner
D: Robert Wiene
Standard thriller, remake of Der Andere: *Man develops split personality*

Dr. Heckyl & Mr. Hype
1980, (USA), Golan-Globus/Cannon, color, 100 mins.
W: Oliver Reed (*Dr. Heckyl/Mr. Hype*), Sunny Johnson (*Coral*), Maia Danziger
   (*Miss Finegum*), Virgil Frye (*Il Topo*), Mel Welles (*Dr. Hunkle*), Sharon
   Compton (*Mrs. Quivel*), Kedric Wolfe (*Dr. Hoo*), Jackie Coogan (*Sgt.
   Fleacollar*), Corinne Calvet (*Pizelle*), Denise Hayes (*Liza*), Dick Miller, Jack
   Warford, Charles Howerton, Lucretia Love, Ben Frommer, Mickey Fox,
   Catalaine Knell, Jacque Lynn Colton, Duane Thomas, Lisa Zebro, Stan Ross,
   Joe Anthony Cox, Michael Ciccone, Steve Ciccone, Candi Brough, Randi

Brough, Dan Sturkie, Yehuda Efroni, Herta Ware, Samuel Livneh, Dana Feller, Katherine Kirkpatrick, Carin Berger, Merle Ann Taylor, Ed Randolph, Cindy Riegel
D & SCR: Charles B. Griffith, "with apologies to Robert Louis Stevenson"
PHOTOG: Robert Garras **MUSIC:** Richard Band
Minor comedy-thriller: Ugly podiatrist becomes playboy

Dr. Jekyll and Mr. Hyde (1920): JOHN BARRYMORE, BRANDON HURST

The Doctor in the Nude
see Traitement de Choc

Doctor Jekyll (1951)
see IL DOTTOR JEKYLL

Doctor Jekyll
1964, (It), color
W: Franco Andrei
based on Robert Louis Stevenson's novel Dr. Jekyll and Mr. Hyde
Minor thriller: Scientist releases his evil alter ego

Dr. Jekyll and Mr. Hyde
1908, (USA), Selig, b&w
from Robert Louis Stevenson's novel

Dr. Jekyll and Mr. Hyde
1910, (Den), Nordisk, b&w
W: Alwin Neuss
from Robert Louis Stevenson's novel

Dr. Jekyll and Mr. Hyde
1912, (USA), Thanhouser, b&w
W: Harry Benham, Marguerite Snow, James Cruze
D: Lucius Henderson
from Robert Louis Stevenson's novel

Dr. Jekyll and Mr. Hyde
1913, (GB), Kineto-Kinemacolor, b&w
from Robert Louis Stevenson's novel

Doomsday Gun: FRANK LANGELLA

Dr. Jekyll and Mr. Hyde
1913, (USA), IMP, b&w
W: King Baggot, Jane Gail
from Robert Louis Stevenson's novel

Dr. Jekyll and Mr. Hyde
1920, (USA), Pioneer/Pathe, b&w
W: Sheldon Lewis, Gladys Field
P: Louis B. Mayer
1st full-length cinemadaptation of Robert Louis Stevenson's classic novel

Dr. Jekyll and Mr. Hyde
1920, (USA), Famous Players/Para, b&w, 63 mins.
W: John Barrymore (*Dr. Henry Jekyll/Mr. Hyde*), Nita Naldi (*Miss Gina*), Martha Mansfield (*Millicent Carewe*), Brandon Hurst (*Sir George Carewe*), Louis Wolheim (*The Music Hall Proprietor*), Charles Lane (*Dr. Lanyon*)
D: John S. Robertson **SCR:** Clara S. Beranger **Photog:** Roy Overbough
2nd major film-version of Robert Louis Stevenson's classic novel

Dr. Jekyll and Mr. Hyde
1920, (USA), Arrow, b&w
W: Hank Mann
Minor spoof of Robert Louis Stevenson's novel

Dr. Jekyll and Mr. Hyde
1925, (USA), Standard Cinema, b&w
Take-off on Robert Louis Stevenson's novel

Dr. Jekyll and Mr. Hyde
1931, (USA), Para/MGM, b&w, 81 mins.
W: Fredric March, Miriam Hopkins, Holmes Herbert, Arnold Lucy, Rose Hobart, Halliwell Hobbes, Tempe Piggott, Edgar Norton
D: Rouben Mamoulian **SCR:** Samuel Hoffenstein & Percy Heath, from Robert Louis Stevenson's novel **PHOTOG:** Karl Struss **DESIGN:** Hans Dreier
Major horror-fantasy, definitive film-version of literary classic (Best Actor Oscar to Fredric March): Doctor chemically alters his personality

Dr. Jekyll and Mr. Hyde
1939, (USA), Pixilated Pic, b&w
from Robert Louis Stevenson's novel

Dr. Jekyll and Mr. Hyde
1941, (USA), MGM, b&w, 122 mins.
W: Spencer Tracy (*Dr. Henry Jekyll/Mr. Hyde*), Lana Turner (*Beatrice*), Ingrid Bergman (*Ivy*), Ian Hunter (*Dr. John Lanyon*), Donald Crisp (*Sir Charles Emery*), Frederic Worlock (*Dr. Heath*), Peter Godfrey (*Poole*), Barton MacLane, Sara Allgood, C. Aubrey Smith, Billy Bevan, Frances Robinson, Lumsden Hare
P & D: Victor Fleming **SCR:** John Lee Mahin, from Robert Louis Stevenson's novel **PHOTOG:** Joseph Ruttenberg **SPCL-FX:** Warren Newcombe **MUSIC:** Franz Waxman **DESIGN:** Cedric Gibbons & Daniel Cathcart
Excellent horror-fantasy-psychodrama: Doctor releases alter ego

Dr. Jekyll and Ms. Hyde
1995, (USA-Can), Savoy, color, 90 mins.
W: Sean Young (*Helen Hyde*), Tim Daly (*Richard Jacks*), Lysette Anthony (*Sarah Carver*), Stephen Tobolowsky (*Oliver Mintz*), Harvey Fierstein (*Yves Dubois*), Jeremy Piven (*Pete*), Polly Bergen (*Mrs.Unterveldt*), Thea Vidale (*Valerie*), Aron Tager (*The Lawyer*), John Franklyn-Robbins (*Prof. Manning*), Stephen Shellen (*Larry*), Sheena Larkin (*Mrs. Mintz*), Julie Cobb (*Dubois' Psychiatrist*), Jane Connell(*Aunt Agatha*), Kim Morgan Greene (*Paparazzi Lady/Party Lady*),Robert Wuhl (*The Man with the Lighter*), Victor Knight (*Bill*), Mark Camacho (*The Waiter*), Susan Trustman (*The Cocktail Party Woman*),Manon Deschenes (*The Gorgeous Female Model*), Donna Barnes (*TheYoung Woman*), Jean-Claude Page (*The Gorgeous Male Model*), MariaStanton (*Dress Admirer 1 & 2*), Rachel Bertrand (*The PneumaticYoung Woman*), Marie-Helene Pierre (*The Helen Body Double*), Herb Goldstein (*Nose #1*), Michael Rudder (*Nose #2*), Susan Glover (*Nose#3*), Kate Asner (*The Female Admirer*), Liz Larson (*Carson*), DonnaS arrasin (*Mintz' Sec'y*), Mike Hodge (*Eagleton*), Stephane Lefebvre (*The Bus Boy*), Don Jordan (*The Driver*)
P: Robert Shapiro & Jerry Leider **D & STORY**, David Price **SCR:** Tim John, Oliver Butcher, William Davies & William Osborne inspired by Robert Louis Stevenson's *Jekyll and Hyde* **PHOTOG:** Tom Priestley **VS-FX:** Dream Quest Images **VS-FX SPRVSR:** Tim Landry **MUSIC:** Mark McKenzie **SONGS:** Brand New Me, Chemistry, Girl U Want, If I Could Fool My Heart, The Habaneros, It Might Get Hot Tonight & We're in a Partyin' Mood
Standard comedy-fantasy: Experiments of infamous doctor's great-grandson induce sex change

Dr. Jekyll and Sister Hyde
1971, (GB), Hammer/AIP, color, 97 mins.
W: Ralph Bates (*Dr. Jekyll*), Martine Beswick (*Sister Hyde*), Lewis Fi-ander (*Howard*), Gerald Sim (*Prof. Robertson*), Ivor Dean (*Burke*), Tony Calvin (*Hare*), Susan Brodrick (*Susan*), Dorothy Alison (*Mrs. Spencer*), Virginia Wetherell (*Betsy*), Philip Madoc (*Byker*), Julia Wright (*The Street Singer*), Dan Meaden (*The Town Crier*), Paul Whitsun-Jones (*Sgt. Danvers*), Irene Bradshaw (*A Street Walker*), Neil Wilson (*The Policeman*), Anna Brett (*Julie*), Jackie Poole (*Margie*), Rosemary Lord (*Marie*), Petula Portell (*Petra*), Will

Stampe (*The Host*), Jeannette Wilde (*Jill*), Roy Evans (*The Knife Grinder*)
P: Albert Fennell & Brian Clemens **D:** Roy Ward Baker **SCR:** Brian Clemens inspired by Robert Louis Stevenson's novel *Dr. Jekyll and Mr. Hyde*
PHOTOG: Norman Warwick **MUSIC:** David Whitaker **SONG:** *He'll Be There*
Modest horror-fantasy: Young doctor's elixir of life causes sex change

Dr. Jekyll and Mr. Hyde (1931): FREDIC MARCH

Dr. Jekyll and the Wolfman
see Dr. Jekyll y el Hombre Lobo

Dr. Jekyll's Dungeon of Darkness
see Dr. Jekyll's Dugeon of Death

Dr. Jekyll's Dungeon of Death
1982, (USA), Rochelle, color 90 mins.
W: James Mathers, Daw Carver Kelly, John Kearney, Jake Pearson
P & D: James Wood **SCR:** James Mathers
video title, **Dr. Jekyll's Dungeon of Darkness**
Minor horror-thriller: Mad doctor injects captives with aggression serum

Dr. Jekyll's Hide
1932, (USA), Univ, b&w, 1 reel
Minor spoof of Robert Louis Stevenson's novel Dr. Jekyll and Mr. Hyde

Dr. Jekyll y el Hombre Lobo (Dr. Jekyll and the Wolfman)
1971, (Sp), Int'l Cinema Films, color 85 mins.
W: Paul Naschy, Jack Taylor Shirley Corrigan
P: Jose Frade **D:** Leon Kaminsky **SCR:** Jacinto Molina
Standard horror-fantasy: Lycanthrope seeks cure

Dr. Jerry et Mr. Love
see The Nutty Professor (1963)

Dr. M
1989, (Ger-Fr), color, 105 mins.
W: Alan Bates, Jennifer Beals, Andrew McCarthy
D: Claude Chabrol
A.k.a. **Club Extinction**
Standard thriller, reworking of Fritz Lang's "Dr. Mabuse" scripts

Doctor Mabuse
1922, (Ger), Ullstein-UCO Films/Ufa, b&w; Part 1 = 8596 ft. (2620m), Part 2 = 9032 ft. (2753m)
W: Rudolf Klein-Rogge (*Dr. Mabuse*), Aud Egede Nissen (*Cara Carozza*), Gertrud Welcker (*Countess Told*), Alfred Abel (*Count Told*), Bernhard Goetzke (*Von Wenck*), Julius Falkenstein (*Karsten*), Forster Larinaga (*Spoerri*), Paul Richter

(*Edgar Hull*), Georg John (*Pesch*), Greta Berger (*Fine*), Karl Huszar (*Hawasch*), Hans Adalbert von Schlettow (*Georg, the Chauffeur*), Anita Berber (*The Dancer*), Max Adalbert, Lydia Potechina, Adele Sandrock, Karl Platen, Auguste Prasch-Grevenberg, Paul Biensfeldt, Hans J. Junkermann
P: Erich Pommer **D:** Fritz Lang **SCR:** Fritz Lang & Thea von Harbou, from Norbert Jacques' novel **PHOTOG:** Carl Hoffmann **SETS,** Otto Hunte & Stahl-Urach
in 2 parts: [1] *Der Spieler (The Gambler)*, USA retitle **The Great Gambler** and [2] *Menschen der Zeit (Men of Time)*, USA retitles—**Inferno** and **Dr. Mabuse, King of Crime**
"...bizarre but rather rambling affair, held together primarily by the spellbinding personality of Rudolph Klein Rogge, Lang's favorite villain, and a sort of German forerunner of Karloff and Chaney"—William K. Everson, The Bad Guys
Classic thriller: Criminal genius baffles authorities

Dr. Mabuse, King of Crime
see Doctor Mabuse

Dr. Mabuse vs. Scotland Yard
1964, (W. Ger), CCC/Omnia, b&w, 90 mins
W: Peter Van Eyck, Walter Rilla, Dieter Borsche
Standard thriller: Criminal genius seeks world domination, mesmerizes mental specialist

Dr. Maniac
see The Man Who Changed His Mind

Doctor Mordrid
1992, (USA), color, 75 mins.
W: Jeffrey Combs, Yvette Nipar, Brian Thompson, Jay Acovone, Keith Coulouris, Murray Rubin, Ritch Brinkley, Pearl Shear, Jeff Austin, John Apicella
D: Albert & Charles Band **MUSIC:** Richard Band
Minor fantasy: Sorcerers battle over fate of Earth

Dr. No
1962, (GB), Eon/UA, color, 105 mins.
W: Sean Connery (*James Bond*), Ursula Andress (*Honey Ryder*), Joseph Wiseman (*Dr. No*), Jack Lord (*Felix Leiter*), Anthony Dawson (*Prof. Dent*), Bernard Lee ("*M*"), Lois Maxwell (*Miss Moneypenny*), Zena Marshall (*Miss Taro*), Peter Burton (*Maj. Boothroyd*), Eunice Gayson (*Sylvia*), Margaret LeWars (*The Photographer*), John Kitzmiller (*Quarrel*), Reginald Carter (*Jones*), Dolores Keator (*Mary*), Michel Mok (*Sister Rose*), Yvonne Shima (*Sister Lily*), William Foster-Davis (*The Superintendent*), Louis Blaazer (*Playdell-Smith*), Colonel Burton (*Gen. Potter*)
P: Harry Saltzman & Albert R. Broccoli **D:** Terence Young **SCR:** Richard Maibaum, Johanna Harwood, & Berkeley Mather, from Ian Fleming's novel **PHOTOG:** Ted Moore **SPCL-FX:** Frank George **MUSIC:** Monty Norman **SONGS:** *Underneath the Mango Tree*
reissued (1965) with **From Russia with Love**
1st "James Bond" film, modest thriller: Master criminal aborts US missile launchings

Doctor of Doom
1960, (Mex), Azteca/Young America, b&w, 77 mins.
W: Lorena Velazquez, Armando Silvestre, Chucho Salinas, Elizabeth Campbell, Robert Canedo, Sonia Infante, Martha "Guera" Solis, Chabela Romero, Magdalena Caballero, Irma Rodriguez
D: Rene Cardona **STORY & SCR,** Alfred Salazar **PHOTOG:** Henry Wallace **MUSIC:** Antonio Diaz Conde
French retitle, Sex Monsters
Minor horror-thriller: Obsessed surgeon seeks human females for brain transplants

Doctor of Seven Dials
1962, (GB), Amalgamated/Altura Films International MGM, b&w, 86 mins.
W: Boris Karloff (*Dr. Thomas Bolton*), Christopher Lee (*Ressurection Joe*), Betta St. John (*Susan*), Finlay Currie (*Dr. Matheson*), Francis Matthews (*Dr. Jonathan Bolton*), Francis De Wolff (*Black Ben*), Adrienne Corri (*Rachel*), Basil Dignam (*The Chairman*), Frank Pettingell (*Dr. Blount*), Nigel Green (*Insp. Donovan*), Marian Spencer (*Mrs. Matheson*), Carl Bernard (*Ned the Crow*)
P: John Croydon **D:** Robert Day **SCR:** Jean Scott Rogers **PHOTOG:** Geoffrey Faithfull **MUSIC:** Buxton Orr
released in USA (1963) as **Corridors of Blood**. *Made in 1958, UK release 1962*
Modest thriller: Victorian surgeon seeks anesthesia, mixes with sordid types

Dr. Orloff's Invisible Horror
1972, (Sp), color
W: Howard Vernon
Minor horror-thriller: Scientist creates invisible ape-monster

Dr. Orlof's Monster
see El Secreto del Dr. Orlof

Dr. Paxton's Last Crime
1914, (GB), P&M Films, b&w, 2,170 ft. (661.4m)
P: John M. Payne **WRIT & D,** Sidney Morgan
Standard thriller

Dr. Phibes Rises Again
1972, (GB), AIP, color, 89 mins.
W: Vincent Price (*Dr. Anton Phibes*), Robert Quarry (*Darius Biederbeck*), Valli

Kemp (*Vulnavia*), Gerald Sim (*Hackett*), Terry Thomas (*Lombardo*), Fiona Lewis (*Diana*), Beryl Reid (*Mrs. Ambrose*), Peter Cushing (*The Captain*), Hugh Griffith (*Harry Ambrose*), John Cater (*Waverly*), Peter Jeffrey (*Insp. Trout*), Lewis Fiander (*Baker*), Keith Buckley (*Stewart*), John Shaw (*Shavers*), Milton Reid (*The Man-servant*)
P: Louis M. Heyward **D:** Robert Fuest **SCR:** Robert Fuest & Robert Blees, from characters created by James Whiton & William Goldstein
PHOTOG: Alex Thomson **MUSIC:** John Gale
"...the wittiest, most stylish horror film ever made"—Baird Searles, "Films," *Magazine of Fantasy and Science Fiction*, Vol. 50, No. 5 (May, 1976), p. 96
Unusual horror-satire, sequel to 'The Abominable Dr. Phibes': Vengeful fiend causes biblical"plagues" to descend upon enemies

Dr. Renault's Secret
1942, (USA), 20th-Fox, b&w
W: George Zucco (*Dr. Renault*), Lynne Roberts, J. Carrol Naish, John Shepperd (*Shepperd Strudwide*), Mike Mazurki, Arthur Shields, Jack Norton, Eugene Borden
D: Harry Lachman **SCR:** William Bruckner & Robert F. Metzler **PHOTOG:** Virgil Miller
*Standard horror-thriller: Scientist turns ape into "human." cf. **Terror is a Man***

Dr. Satan
1966, (Mex), color
Minor SF-thriller: Evil genius plots

Dr. Satan and Black Magic
1967, (Mex), color
Minor SF-thriller: Evil genius enlists unholy forces

Dr. Satan's Robot
1966, (USA), Rep, b&w, 100 mins.
W: Eduardo Ciannelli, Robert Wilcox, Ella Neal, C. Montague, Shaw William Newell
D: William Witney & John English **SCR:** Franklin Adreon, Ronald Davidson, Norman S. Hall, Sol Shor & Joseph Poland
Standard thriller (feature version of 1940 serial 'Mysterious Dr. Satan'): Master criminal seeks power

Dr. Scorpion
1978, (USA), Stephen J. Cannell/Univ/ABC-TV, color, 94 mins.
W: Nick Mancuso (*Jonathan Shackelford*), Christine Lahti (*Tania*), Sandra Kerns (*Sharon Shackelford*), Denny Miller (*The Dane*), Richard T. Herd (*Worthington*), Granville Van Dusen (*Batlinger*), Roscoe Lee Browne (Dr. Cresus), James Murtaugh (*Dave Steel*), Michael Cavanaugh (*Whitey*), Zitto Kazann (*Arubella*), James Hong (*Ho Chin*), Bob Minor (*Jean Claud Ammatt*), Eric Server (*Agent Shelby*), Harvey Fisher (*Tony*), Richmond Hoxie (*Morrison*), Philip Sterling, Bill Lucking, Joseph Ruskin, Lincoln Kilpatrick
D: Richard Lang **TELEPLAY:** Stephen J. Cannell **PHOTOG:** Charles Correll
MUSIC: Mike Post & Pete Carpenter
TVM, standard SF-fantasy: Evil genius plots to dominate world, former secret agent opposes him

The Doctor's Crime
1914, (GB), Regent/MP, b&w, 3,000 ft. (914.4m)
W: Charles Weston
P: Charles Weston & Arthur Finn
Standard thriller

Dr. Sin Fang
1937, (GB), Victory/MGM, b&w, 60 mins.
W: H. Agar Lyons (*Dr. Sin Fang*), Anne Grey (*Sonia Graham*), Robert Hobbs (*John Byrne*), George Mozart (*Bill*), Arty Ash (*Prof. Graham*), Nell Emerald (*Mrs. Higgins*), Louis Darnley, Ernest Sefton
D: Tony Frenguelli **SCR:** Nigel Byass & Frederick Reynolds **STORY:** Kaye Mason
Standard crime-thriller: Chinese crook seeks formula for cancer cure

The Doctor's Secret
see Le Secret du Medecin

Dr. Strange
1978, (USA), Univ/ABC-TV, color, 94 mins.
W: Peter Hooten (*Dr. Stephen Strange*), John Mills (*Linmer*), Jessica Walter (*Morgan le Fay*), Clyde Kusatsu (*Wong*), David Hooks ("*The Nameless One*"), Eddie Benton (*Clea Lake*), Diana Webster (*The Head Nurse*), Bob Delegall (*The Intern*), Philip Sterling (*Dr. Frank Taylor*), Larry Anderson (*The Magician*), Blake Marion (*The Deputy Chief*), Lady Rowlands (*Mrs. Sullivan*), Inez Pedroza (*The Announcer*), Michael Clark (*The Taxi Driver*), Frank Catalano (*The Orderly*), June Barrett, Sarah Rush
D & TELEPLAY: Philip DeGuere, from the Marvel comic book **PHOTOG:** Enzo A. Martinelli **MUSIC:** Paul Chihara
TVM, modest fantasy-thriller: Modern wizard battles ancient sorceress

Dr. Strangelove: or, How I Learned to Stop Worrying and Love the Bomb
1963, (GB), Hawk/Col, b&w, 94 mins.
W: Peter Sellers (*Dr. Strangelove/Mandrake/Pres. Muffley*), George C. Scott (*Gen. "Buck" Turgidson*), Sterling Hayden (*Gen. Jack D. Ripper*), Tracy Reed (*Miss Scott*), Keenan Wynn (*Col. "Bat" Guano*), Slim Pickens (*Maj. T.J. "King" Kong*), Peter Bull (*Amb. de Sadesky*), James Earl Jones (*Lt. Lothar Zogg*), Jack Creley (*Mr. Staines*), Shane Rimmer (*Capt. G.A. "Ace" Owens*), Frank Berry

(*Lt. H.R. Dietrich*), Glenn Beck (*Lt. W.D. Kivel*), Paul Tamarin (*Lt. B. Goldberg*), Gordon Tanner (*Gen. Faceman*), Robert O'Neil (*Adm. Randolph*), Roy Stephens (*Frank*), John McCarthy
P & D: Stanley Kubrick **SCR:** Stanley Kubrick, Terry Southern, & Peter George based on a book by Peter Bryant (published in GB as *Two Hours to Doom* and in USA as *Red Alert*) **PHOTOG:** Gilbert Taylor **MUSIC:** Laurie Johnson
Classic satire-thriller: World totters on brink of nuclear destruction. James Earl Jones' film debut

Doctors Wear Scarlet
1970, (GB),Lucinda-Titan Int'l/Grand Nat'l/Cevron-Paragon, color, 87 mins.
W: Patrick Macnee (*Maj. Derek Longbow*), Peter Cushing (*Dr. Goodrich*), Alex Davion (*Tony Seymour*), Johnny Sekka (*Bob Kirby*), Madeleine Hinde (*Penelope*), Patrick Mower (*Richard Fountain*), Imogen Hassall (*Chriseis Constandinidi*), David Lodge (*The Colonel*), Edward Woodward (*Holmstrom*), William Mervyn (*Honeydew*)
P: Peter Newbrook **D:** Robert Hartford-Davies **SCR:** Julian More, from a novel by Simon Raven
*USA retitle, **Bloodsucker** A.k.a. **Incense for the Damned***
Standard horror-thriller: Foreign Secretary's son becomes a vampire

Dr. Syn
1937, (GB), Gaumont/GFD, b&w, 80 mins.
W: George Arliss (*Dr. Syn*), Margaret Lockwood (*Imogene*), John Loder (*Denis Cobtree*), Graham Moffatt (*Jerry Jerk*), Roy Emerton (*Capt. Howard Collyer*), Frederick Burtwell (*Rash*), George Merritt (*Mipps*), Wally Patch (*The Bosun*), Athole Stewart (*Sir Anthony Cobtree*), Meinhart Maur (*The Mulatto*), Muriel George (*Mrs. Waggetts*), Wilson Coleman (*Dr. Pepper*), Robert Newton
D: Roy William Neill **SCR:** Michael Hogan & Roger Burford, from a novel by Russell Thorndyke
*A.k.a. **Dr. Syn, the Pirate***
*Vintage melodrama: Revenue agent unmasks "dead" buccaneer. Arliss' last film. cf. **Captain Clegg***

Dr. Syn—Alias the Scarecrow
1963, (GB), Walt Disney, color, 98 mins.
W: Patrick McGoohan (*Dr. Syn*), George Cole (*Sexton Mipps*), Tony Britton (*Simon Bates*), Michael Hordern (*Sir Thomas Banks*), Geoffrey Keen (*Gen. Pugh*), Kay Walsh (*Mrs. Waggett*), Eric Pohlmann (*George III*), Patrick Wymark (*Joe Ransley*), Alan Dobie (*Fragg*), Sean Scully (*John Banks*), Eric Flynn (*Phillip Brackenbury*), Richard O'Sullivan (*George Ransley*), David Buck (*Harry Banks*)
P: William Anderson **D:** James Neilson **SCR:** Robert Westerby, from novel *Christopher Syn* by Russell Thorndike & William Buchanan,
reissued 1976 (23 mins. cut)
Standard adventure-thriller: 18th-century vicar secretly leads smugglers, foils traitor

Dr. Syn, the Pirate
see Dr. Syn

Dr. Tarr's Torture Dungeon
1975, (Mex), Catalina, color, 88 mins.
W: Claudio Brook, Arthur Hansel, Ellen Sherman, Martin LaSalle, David Silva, Monica Serna, Max Kerlow, Susana Kamini, Francisco Cordoba, Henry West, Roberto Dumont, Rene Alis, Jorge Bektis, Mario Castillon Bracho, Oscar Saro, Abraham Stabans, Diane Shay, Paloma Zozaya, Jose Antonio Alcaraz, Julia Marichal, Nadine Markova, Peter Jones, Iya Engel, Virgilio Leos, Sofia Solorio, Javier Batiz-Macaria, Victorio Blanco, Ramon Barragan, Miguel Santamaria, Kevin McCormick, Guillermo Maldonado, Juan Garza, Emanuele Olea, Antonio Zubiaga, Joan Mary, Tita Arroyo, Fernando Rosales, Gerardo Zepeda, Leon Singer, Alexis Arroyo, Rene Barrera, Beatriz Belo, Simon Alkon, German Castro, Roberto Hernandez
D: Juan Lopez Moctezuma **SCR:** Charles Illescas inspired by Edgar Allan Poe's short story "The System of Dr. Tarr and Professor Fether" **PHOTOG:** Rafael Corkidi **MUSIC:** Racho Mendez
Minor thriller: Socialite encounters bizarre mental asylum

Dr. Terror's Gallery of Horror
see Gallery of Horror

Dr. Terror's House of Horrors
1943, (USA), Nat'l Road Show, b&w
blurb: "Now together for the first time on any screen! Zombies, vampires, ghouls, werewolves, voodoo rites, weird creatures, and the living dead!"
*Standard anthology: Film clips from **Le Golem** (1936), **Vampyr, Living Dead** (1932), **White Zombie and The Return of Chandu***

Dr. Terror's House of Horrors
1964, (GB), Amicus/Para, color, 98 mins.
W: Peter Cushing (*Dr. Sandor Schreck*), Roy Castle (*Biff Bailey*), Christopher Lee (*Franklyn Marsh*), Michael Gough (*Eric Landor*), Max Adrian (*Dr. Blake*), Neil McCallum (*Jim Dawson*), Ann Bell (*Ann Rogers*), Jennifer Jayne (*Nicolle*), Bernard Lee (*Hopkins*), Alan Freeman (*Bill Rogers*), Peter Madden (*Caleb*), Kenny Lynch (*Sammy Coin*), Ursula Howells (*Deirdre Biddulph*), Jeremy Kemp (*Drake*), Donald Sutherland (*Bob Carroll*), Edward Underdown (*Tod*), Harold Lang (*Shine*), Katy Wild (*Valda*), Isla Blair, Irene Richmond, Thomas Baptiste, Frank Forsyth, Christopher Carlos, Sarah Nicholls, Walter Sparrow

P: Max J. Rosenberg & Milton Subotsky **D:** Freddie Francis **SCR:** Milton Subotsky **PHOTOG:** Alan Hume **MUSIC:** Elizabeth Lutyens **SONG:** *Give Me Love* **DESIGN,** Bill Constable
Modest anthology of terror tales: (1) Architect meets werewolf, (2) Intelligent plants menace family, (3) Musician encounters voodoo, (4) Art critic tormented by severed hand, & (5) Bride proves vampiric

Dr. Trimball's Verdict
1913, (GB), Hepworth, b&w, 1,100 ft. (335.3m)
W: Alec Worcester (*Dr. Trimball*), Chrissie White (*Alice*)
D: Frank Wilson
Standard thriller: Doctor kills rival

Doctor Who
1996, (USA), Univ/Fox-TV, color, 96 mins.
W: Paul McGann (*Dr. Who*), Daphne Ashbrook (*Grace Holloway*), Eric Roberts (*The Master*), John Novak, Yee Jee Tso, Sylvester McCoy
D: Geoffrey Sax **TELEPLAY:** Matthew Jacobs, from an orig. BBC-TV serial by Terry Nation **PHOTOG:** Glen MacPherson **VS-FX,** Tony Dow **MUSIC:** John Debney
TVM, standard SF-fantasy

Dr. Who and the Daleks
1965, (GB), Regal Films/AARU/Lion-Int'l/Continental/Walter Reade-Sterling, color, 85 mins.
W: Peter Cushing (*Dr. Who*), Roy Castle (*Ian*), Jennie Linden (*Barbara*), Roberta Tovey (*Susan*), Barrie Ingham (*Alydon*), Michael Coles (*Ganatus*), Geoffrey Toone (*Temmosus*), Mark Peterson (*Elydon*), John Bown (*Antodus*), Yvonne Antrobus (*Dyoni*), Ken Garady, Michael Lennox
P: Max J. Rosenberg & Milton Subotsky **D:** Gordon Flemyng **SCR:** Milton

Doctor Who and The Daleks: JENNIE LINDEN

Subotsky, from an orig. BBC-TV serial by Terry Nation **PHOTOG:** John Wilcox **SPCL-FX:** Ted Samuels **MUSIC:** Malcolm Lockyer
Standard SF-fantasy: Earth invaded by robotic aliens. cf. **Daleks' Invasion Earth 2150 A.D.**

Doctor X
1932, (USA), WB, color, 80 mins.
W: Lionel Atwill (*Dr. Xavier*), Fay Wray (*Joan Xavier*), Lee Tracy (*Lee Taylor*), Preston Foster (*Dr. Wells*), Robert Warwick (*Police Commissioner Stevens*), Arthur Edmund Carewe (*Dr. Rowitz*), Willard Robertson (*Insp. Halloran*), George Rosener (*Otto*), Harry Beresford, Mae Busch, John Wray, Tom Dugan, Leila Bennett, Harry Holman
D: Michael Curtiz **SCR:** Earl Baldwin & Robert Tasker, from the story by Howard W. Comstock & Allen C. Miller **PHOTOG:** Richard Tower & Ray Rennahan
Classic mystery-thriller: Police hunt monstrous murderer

The Dodgers Dodged
1907, (GB), Sheffield Photo Co., b&w, 276 ft. (84.1m)
D: Frank Mottershaw
Standard comedy-fantasy short: Cops chase vanishing robbers. reissued 1911

Does Dracula Really...?
see **Guess What Happened to Count Dracula**

Does Dracula Suck?
see **Guess What Happened to Count Dracula**

A Dog, a Mouse and a Sputnik
1961, (Fr), Films Around the World, b&w, 85 mins.(also 92 mins)
W: Denis Gray, Mischa Auer, Noel Noel, Darry Cowl, Noel Roquevert
D: Jean Dreville
Standard sci-fi comedy. Russian and Frenchman in orbit. A.k.a. **Sputnik**

Dog Eat Dog
1963, (USA-W. Ger-It), Ajay, b&w, 84 mins.
W: Cameron Mitchell, Jayne Mansfield
P: Carl Szokol **D:** Ray Nazarro & Albert Zugsmith, Gustav Gavrin **SCR:** Robert Hill & Michael Elkins
Minor thriller: Embezzler and moll flee to Adriatic island

Dog Eat Dog
1976, (USA), color, 90 mins.
W: Dody Heath, Ivor Salter, Isa Miranda, Werner Peters, Pinkas Braun, David McCallum, George Wyner, Eric Server, Sandra McCabe, Sterling Swanson, Linda Gray
D: Burt Brinckerhof (some sources list Gustav Gavrin as director)
A.k.a. **Slaughter**
Minor thriller: Canines stalk collegians

The Dogfighters
1996, (USA), Hess Kallberg/Live, color
W: Robert Davi (*Rowdy Wells*), Ben Gazzara, Alexander Godunov, Lara Harris, David Gautreaux, Patricia Rive
D: Barry Zetlin **SCR:** Anthony Stark & Sean Smith **STORY:** Barry Zetlin & Richard Boehm **PHOTOG:** Levie Isaacks **MUSIC:** Jimmie Haskell
Made-for-Video, standard thriller: Ex-Air Force pilot vs. mad scientist

Dogora, the Space Monster
1963, (Jap), Toho/AIP, color, 80 mins
W: Yoko Fujiyama, Yosuke Natsuki, Akiko Wakabayashi, Hiroshi Koizumi
D: Inoshiro Honda **SCR:** Inoshiro Honda **PHOTOG:** Hajime Koizumi **SPCL-FX:** Eiji Tsuburaya
distrib. in USA (1965) as **Dogora, the Space Monster**
Standard SF-fantasy: Space creatures seek diamonds

Dogs
1976, (USA), La Quinta Prods/Mar Vista., color, 85 mins.
W: David McCallum, George Wyner, Eric Server, Linda Gray, Holly Harris, Barry Greenberg, Dean Santoro, Cathy Austin, Sterling Swanson
D: Burt Brinckerhoff **SCR:** O'Brien Tomalin **PHOTOG:** Bob Steadman **MUSIC:** Alan Oldfield
Minor thriller: Domestic dogs become vicious. Video title: **Slaughter**

Dog's Best Friend
1997, (USA), Regent/FAM-TV, color, 95 mins.
W: Adam Zolotin (*Wiley*), Shirley Jones (*Ethel*), Richard Mulligan (*Fred*), Bobcat Goldthwait, Adrienne Carter
VOICES: Edward Asner, Meredith Baxter, James Belushi, John Ratzenberger, Roger Clinton, Valerie Harper, Markie Post
D: Allen A. Goldstein **TELEPLAY:** Nancey Silvers **PHOTOG:** Rod Parkhurst

Dr. X: FAY WRAY LEE TRACY

MUSIC: David Lawrence
TVM, minor comedy-fantasy: Boy communes with animals

Dogs of Hell
1983, (USA), color, 90 mins.
W: Earl Owensby, Bill Gribble, Jerry Rushing
D: Worth Keeter
Minor thriller: Killer canines upset resort community

Dog Star Man
1962-64, (USA), Stan Brakhage, color; in 4 parts: I (1962), 30 mins.; II (1963), 7

mins.; III (1964), 11 mins.; & IV (1964), 5 mins.
Silent, "underground" 16mm film not in general release: Dissertation on mysteries of Creation

Doings in Dolly Land
1905, (GB), Urban, b&w, 375 ft. (114.3m)
Minor fantasy short: Adventures of animated dolls

Doin' Time on Planet Earth
1988, (USA), Cannon, color, 85 mins.
W: Nicholas Strouse, Hugh Gillin (*Richmond*), Hugh O'Brian (*Camalier*), Kellie Martin, Andrea Thompson, Adam West, Candice Azzara, Matt Adler, Timothy Patrick Murphy, Roddy McDowall, Maureen Stapleton
D: Charlie Matthau
Minor SF: Teen meets extraterrestrial

The Doll (1919)
see Die Puppe

The Doll (1962)
see La Poupee

Dollars for Sale
1955, (GB), Ascot House/Adelphi, b&w, 35 mins.
W: Robert Ayres (*Ray Blanchard*), Earl Cameron (*Earl Rutters*), John Slater (*Loudmouth Willetts*), Victor Platt (*Insp. Mann*), Magda Miller (*The Girl*), Robert Hartford-Davis (*The Cop*), Larry Cross (*Mike Stevens*), Bernie Winters (*The Suspect*)
P & STORY: Robert Hartford-Davis   **D & SCR:** Denis Kavanagh
Standard short crime-thriller: FBI agent tracks counterfeiter

The Doll
1963, (Swed), Kanawha, b&w, 94 mins.
W: Per Oscarsson, Gio Petre, Ric Axberg
D: Arne Mattsson
Standard psychodrama: Tale of displaced personality

Dollman
1991, (USA), Full Moon, color, 86 mins.
W: Tim Thomerson, Kamela Lopez, Jackie Earle Haley, Humberto Ortiz, Nicholas Guest, Michael Halsey, Eugene Glazer, Judd Omen, Frank Collison, Vincent Klyn
D: Albert Pyun
Minor fantasy-thriller: 13-inch-tall alien cop in South Bronx gang war

Dollman vs. Demonic Toys
1993, (USA), Full Moon, color, 65 mins.
W: Tim Thomerson, Tracy Scoggins, Melissa Behr, Phil Brock Phil Fondacaro
D: Charles Band   **SCR:** Craig Hamann   **MUSIC:** Richard Band
Standard SF-fantasy: Miniature alien cop battles lethal playthings

Dolls
1986, (USA-It), Charles Band/Empire, color, 77 mins.
W: Ian Patrick Williams (*David Bower*), Carrie Lorraine (*Judy Bower*), Carolyn Purdy-Gordon (*Rosemary Bower*), Guy Rolfe (*Gabriel Hartwicke*), Bunty Bailey (*Isabel*), Hilary Mason (*Hilary Hartwicke*), Cassie Stewart (*Enid*), Stephen Lee (*Ralph Morris*)
D: Stuart Gordon   **SCR:** Ed Naha   **PHOTOG:** Mac Ahlberg   **MUSIC:** Fuzzbee Morse, additional music, Victor Spiegel   **MUSIC SPRVSR,** Richard Band
Minor horror-fantasy: Stranded travelers in sinister home of elderly dollmakers

The Dolls of the Devil
see Devil Doll (1936)

The Doll Squad
1973, (USA), Geneni, color, 101 mins
W: Anthony Eisley, Tura Satana, Michael Ansara, Francine York, Herb Robbins, John Carter, Rafael Campos, Lisa Todd
P & D: Ted V. Mikels
A.k.a. Hustler Squad
Minor adventure-satire: CIA hires female assassins to stop foreign rocket saboteurs

The Doll's Revenge
1907, (GB), Hepworth, b&w, 225 ft. (68.6m)
W: Gertie Potter (*The Girl*), Bertie Potter (*The Brother*)
D: Lewin Fitzhamon
Minor fantasy short: Doll broken by boy regenerates, eats youth

The Doll's Secret
1910, (GB), Walturdaw, b&w, 615 ft. (187.5m)
Standard crime-thriller: Workman's child finds stolen necklace hidden in doll

Dolly Dearest
1991, (USA), Trimark, color 94 mins.
W: Denise Crosby, Sam Bottoms, Rip Torn
D & SCR, Maria Lease   **STORY,** Maria Lease, Rod Nave & Peter Sutcliffe   **VS-FX SPRVSR,** Alan G. Markowitz   **MUSIC:** Mark Snow
Standard horror-fantasy: Demonic puppet kills

Dolly's Toys
1901, (GB), R.W. Paul, b&w, 80 ft. (24.4m)
D: Arthur Cooper
Minor fantasy short: Child dreams toys come to life

Dolores Claiborne
1995, (USA), Castle Rock/Col, color, 131 mins.
W: Kathy Bates, Jennifer Jason Leigh, Christopher Plummer, David Strathairn, John C. Reilly, Eric Bogosian, Judy Parfitt, Ellen Muth, Bob Gunton
P: Taylor Hackford & Charles Mulvehill   **D:** Taylor Hackford   **SCR:** Tony Gilroy, from Stephen King's novel   **PHOTOG:** Gabriel Beristain   **MUSIC:** Danny Elfman
blurb: "Sometimes an accident can be an unhappy woman's best friend"
"The Best Psychological Thriller Of The Year!...A Must See!"—Jim Ferguson, The Preview Channel
Standard thriller: Woman reveals old murder

The Dolphin
1987, (Brz), color, 95 mins.
W: Cassia Kiss Carlos Alberto Riccelli, Ney Latorraca
D & SCR: Walter Lima Jr.   **PHOTOG:** Pedro Farkas
Standard eroto-fantasy: Dolphin-man excites passions

The Domino Killings
see The Domino Principle

The Domino Principle
1977, (USA), color, 100 mins.
W: Gene Hackman, Candice Bergen, Richard Widmark, Eli Wallach, Mickey Rooney, Edward Albert Jr.
D: Stanley Kramer
A.k.a. The Domino Killings
Minor conspiracy thriller: Gov't springs Viet vet from prison to undertake sniping mission

Dominion
1995, (USA), color, 95 mins.
W: Brad Johnson, Brion James, Tim Thomerson, Woody Brown, Glen Morshower, Richard Riehle, Geoffrey Blake
D: Mickey Kehoe   **SCR:** Woody Brown & Michael Kehoe
Standard thriller: Psycho stalks six vacationers

Dominique
1979, (GB), Sword & Sorcery/Grand Prize/Barber Dann, color, 100 mins.
W: Cliff Robertson (*David Ballard*), Jean Simmons (*Dominique Ballard*), Jenny Agutter (*Ann Ballard*), Simon Ward (*Tony Calvert*), Ron Moody (*Dr. Rogers*), Michael Jayston (*Arnold Craven*), Judy Geeson (*Marjorie Craven*), Leslie Dwyer (*The Man*), Flora Robson (*Mrs. Davis*), Jack Warner (*George*), David Tomlinson (*The Solicitor*)
P: Milton Subotsky & Andrew Donally   **D:** Michael Anderson   **SCR:** Edward Abraham & Valerie Abraham, from Harold Lawlor's story "What Beckoning Ghost"   **PHOTOG:** Ted Moore   **MUSIC:** David Whitaker
A.k.a. Dominique is Dead
Minor thriller: Girl impersonates suicide's ghost

Dominique is Dead
see Dominique

Don Juan
1926, (USA), WB, b&w, 10 reels (10,018 ft./3053.5m)
W: John Barrymore (*Don Juan/Don Jose*), Mary Astor (*Adriana Della Varnese*), Willard Louis (*Pedrillo*), Estelle Taylor (*Lucretia Borgia*), Helene Costello (*Rena, Adriana's Maid*), Myrna Loy (*Maia, Lucretia's Maid*), Jane Winton (*Beatrice*), John Roche (*Leandro*), June Marlowe (*Trusia*), Yvonne Day (*Don Juan, 5 yrs. old*), Philippe de Lacey (*Don Juan, 10 yrs. old*), John George (*The Hunchback*), Helena D'Algy (*The Murderess of Jose*), Warner Oland (*Caesar Borgia*), Montagu Love (*Donati*), Josef Swickard (*Duke Della Varnese*), Lionel Brahm (*Duke Margoni*), Phyllis Haver (*Imperia*), Nigel de Brulier (*Marquis Rinaldo*), Hedda Hopper (*Marquise Rinaldo*), Helen Lee Worthing (*Eleanora*), Emily Fitzroy (*The Dowager*), Gustav von Seyffertitz (*The Alchemist*), Sheldon Lewis (*A Gentleman of Rome*), Gibson Gowland (*A Gentleman of Rome*), Dick Sutherland (*A Gentleman of Rome*)
D: Alan Crosland   **SCR:** Bess Meredyth   **PHOTOG:** Byron Haskins
Standard melodrama: Notorious lover surrounded by intrigue

Don Juan
1956, (W. Ger), Times, color, 85 mins.
W: Cesare Danova, Josef Neinrad, John Berry
Standard adventure-thriller: Exploits of infamous lover

Don Juan et Faust
1922, (Fr), b&w
D: Marcel L'Herbier
Minor fantasy-thriller: Satanic pact is regretted

Don Juan's End
see La Fin de Don Juan

Don Juan's Night of Love
1955, (It), Rep, b&w, 71 mins.

172

W: Raf Vallone, Silvana Pampanini
Standard adventure-romance

Donkey Skin
see *Peau d'Ane*

La Donna Scimmia (The Ape Woman)
1964, (It/Fr), Champion/Embassy, b&w
W: Ugo Tognazzi, Ermelinda De Felice, Annie Girardot, Antonio Cianci
P: Carlo Ponti **D:** Mario Ferreri
A.k.a. A Most Unusual Woman
Philosophical melodrama: Promoter finds extremely hirsute girl, exploits her in side show, but comes to love her

Donor
1990, (USA), CBS-TV, color, 95 mins.
W: Melissa Gilbert-Brinkman, Jack Scalia, Pernell Roberts, Wendy Hughes, Gregory Sierra, Gale Mayron, Marc Lawrence, Wendy Cooke, Michael Boatman, Hari Rhodes, Carol Ann Susi, Virginia Capers, Larry Cedar, Don Alan Croll, Robert Kim, David Crowley, Ruth Ekholm, Gregory Daven, Toni Lawrence, Gail Fisher, Pedro Gonzalez-Gonzalez, Emily Kuroda, Liana Odalys, Michael Matthews, Dorothy Neumann, Jeff Olan, Sunni Walton, Al Scheckwitz
D: Larry Shaw **TELEPLAY:** Michael Braverman **PHOTOG:** Neil Roach
SPCL-FX: Art Brewer **MUSIC:** Gary Chang
TVM, standard thriller: Woman intern uncovers dangerous hospital intrigue

Do Not Fold, Spindle or Mutilate
1971, (USA), Aaron Spelling/CBS-TV, color, 73 mins.
W: Helen Hayes, Sylvia Sidney, Myrna Loy, Mildred Natwick, Vince Edwards, John Beradino, Larry D. Mann, Diane Shalet
D: Ted Post **SCR:** John D.F. Black, from a novel by Doris Miles Disney
TVM, standard thriller: Old ladies meet psychopath

Donovan's Brain
1953, (USA), Dowling/UA, b&w, 83 mins.
W: Lew Ayres, Nancy Davis, Gene Evans, Steve Brodie, Tom Powers, Lisa Howard, Michael Colgan, Kyle James (*James Anderson*), William Cottrell, Stapleton Kent, Peter Adams, Victor Sutherland, John Hamilton, Paul Hoffman, Harlan Warde, Faith Langley, Tony Merrill, Mark Lowell, Shimen Ruskin
P: Tom Gries **D:** Felix Feist Jr. adapted by Hugh Brooke from Curt Siodmak's novel **PHOTOG:** Joseph Biroc **MUSIC:** Eddie Dunstedter
blurb: "A dead man's brain told him to kill kill kill kill kill..."
*Modest SF classic: Doctor keeps human brain alive. Remake: **Lady and the Monster***

Don Q and the Artist
1912, (GB), B&C/MP, b&w, 1,170 ft. (356.6m)
W: Charles Raymond (*Don Q*)
D: H.O. Martinek **SCR:** Harold Brett **STORY:** Hesketh Pearson
Standard adventure-thriller

Don Q--How He Outwitted Don Luis
1912, (GB), B&C/MP, b&w, 1,113 ft. (339.3m)
W: Charles Raymond (*Don Q*), Ivy Martinek (*Isabelilla*), Percy Moran (*Don Luis*), W. Gladstone Haley (*Felipe*)
D: H.O. Martinek **SCR:** Harold Brett **STORY:** Hesketh Pearson
Standard adventure-thriller: Hired assassins thwarted

Don Q--How He Treated the Parole of Gevil Hay
1912, (GB), B&C/MP, b&w, 958 ft. (292m)
W: Charles Raymond (*Don Q*), H.O. Martinek (*Gevil Hay*)
D: H.O. Martinek **SCR:** Harold Brett **STORY:** Hesketh Pearson
Standard adventure-thriller: Bandit chief ensnares British agent

Don Q, Son of Zorro
1925, (USA), Elton Corp./UA, b&w, 11 reels (10,266 ft./3129m)
W: Douglas Fairbanks Sr. (*Don Cesar de Vega/Zorro*), Mary Astor (*Dolores de Muro*), Jean Hersholt (*Don Fabrique*), Jack McDonald (*Gen. de Muro*), Donald Crisp (*Don Sebastian*), Stella De Lanti (*The Queen*), Warner Oland (*The Archduke*), Albert MacQuarrie (*Col. Matsado*), Juliette Belanger (*The Dancer*), Lottie Pickford Forrest (*Lola*), Charles Stevens (*Robledo*), Tote Du Crow (*Bernardo*), Roy Coulson (*The Dancer's Admirer*), Martha Franklin (*The Duenna*), Enrique Acosta (*Ramon*)
D: Donald Crisp **SCR:** Jack Cunningham, from a story by Hesketh Prichard & Kate Prichard **PHOTOG:** Henry Sharp
Standard adventure-thriller: Nobleman accused of assassination

Don Quixote's Dream
1908, (GB), Hepworth, b&w, 250 ft. (76.2m)
D: Lewin Fitzhamon
Minor comedy-fantasy short: Don dreams of kidnapped girl

Don't Answer the Phone!
1980, (USA), Scorpion/Crown-Int'l, color, 93 mins.
W: James Westmoreland (*Chris*), Flo Gerrish (*Dr. Gale*), Ben Frank (*Hatcher*), Nicholas Worth (*Kirk*), Stan Haze (*Adkins*), Gary Allen (*Feldon*), Pamela Bryant (*Sue*), Ted Chapman (*The Bald Man*), Denise Galick (*Lisa*), Dale Kalberg, Deborah Leah Land, Tom Lasswell, Ellen Karston, Mike Levine, Chuck Mitchell, Victor Mohica, Susanna Severeid, Paula Warner, Chris

Wallace
WRIT, P & D, Robert Hammer **PHOTOG:** James Carter **MUSIC:** Byron Allred *Minor thriller: Hunt for slob-murderer of young women*

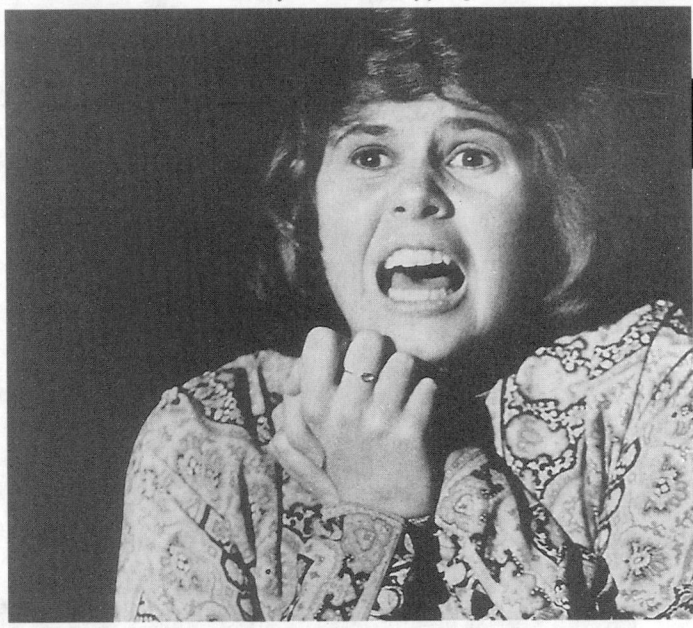

Don't be Afraid of the Dark: KIM DARBY

Don't Bother to Knock
1952, (USA), 20th-Fox, b&w, 76 mins.
W: Richard Widmark, Marilyn Monroe, Anne Bancroft, Jeanne Cagney, Donna Corcoran, Lurene Tuttle, Gloria Blondell
Standard thriller: Demented babysitter imperils child. cf. 'The Sitter'

Don't Be Afraid of the Dark
1973, (USA), Lorimar/ABC-TV, color, 74 mins.
W: Kim Darby, Jim Hutton, Pedro Armendariz Jr., William Demarest (*Harris*), Barbara Anderson (*Joan*), William Sylvester, Lesley Woods, Robert Cleaves, Sterling Swanson
P: Allen S. Epstein **D:** John Newland **TELEPLAY:** Nigel McKeand
TVM, standard fantasy-thriller: Bride finds gremlins in woodwork

Don't Cry Wolf
see *The Crawling Hand*

Don't Get Me Started
1994, (GB-Ger), British Film Institute, color, 76 mins.
W: Trevor Eve, Steve Waddington, Marion Bailey, Ralph Brown
D: Arthur Ellis
A.k.a. Psycotherapy
Minor comedy-thriller: Insurance salesman gives up smoking, takes up murder

Don't Go in the House
1979, (USA), Turbine/Film Ventures, color, 80 mins.
W: Dan Grimaldi (*Donny*), Ruth Dardick (*Mrs. Kohler*), Robert Osth (*Bobby*), Charlie Bonet (*Ben*), Bill Ricci (*Vito*), Dennis M. Hunter, John Hedberg, Johanna Brushay, Mary AnnChin, Darcy Shean, Jim Donnegan, Claudia Folts, Denise Woods, Pat Williams, Colin McInness, Ralph D. Bowman, Joey Peschl, Connie Oaks, David McComb, Jean Manning, Louis Grimaldi, Ken Kelsch, Tom Brumberger, Nikki Kollins, Kim Roberts, Gloria Szymkovicz, David Brody, O'Mara Leary, Gail Turner, Eileen Dunn, Christian Isodore
D: Joseph Ellison **SCR:** Joseph Ellison, Ellen Hammill & Joseph R. Masefield **STORY:** Joseph R. Masefield **PHOTOG:** Oliver Wood **MUSIC:** Richard Einhorn
Minor thriller: Psycho manacles and incinerates beauties

Don't Go in the Woods
1981, (USA), color, 88 mins.
Minor thriller: Crazed axe-murderer stalks young campers

Don't Go to Sleep
1982, (USA), ABC-TV, color, 95 mins.
W: Valerie Harper (*Flora*), Dennis Weaver (*Philip*), Ruth Gordon (*Grandma*), Robin Ignico (*Mary*), Kristin Cumming (*Jennifer*), Robert Webber (*Dr. Cole*), Claudette Nevins (*The Psychiatrist*), Oliver Robins (*Kevin*)
P & D: Richard Lang **TELEPLAY:** Ned Wynn **PHOTOG:** Chuck Arnold
TVM, standard thriller: Dead girl's spirit wracks family

Don't Joke with Martians
see *Please, Don't Joke with Martians*

Don't Look Down
1998, (USA), ABC-TV, color, 95 mins.
W: Megan Ward, Billy Burke (*Mark*), Angela Moore (*Jocelyn*), Terry Kinney (*Dr. Sadowski*), Kate Robbins, Adam Smolinski
D: Larry Shaw   TELEPLAY: Gregory Goodell   PHOTOG: David Geddes
MUSIC: J. Peter Robinson
TVM, standard thriller: Woman traumatized by sister's fatal fall

Don't Look in the Basement
1973, (USA), Camera 2-Century Studios/Hallmark, color, 89 mins.
W: Rosie Holotik (*Charlotte*), Ann McAdams (*Dr. Masters*), William "Bill" McGhee (*Sam*)
P & D: S.F. Brownrigg   ORIG. SCR: Tim Pope   PHOTOG: Robert Alcott

THE MAKERS OF LAST HOUSE ON THE LEFT
WARN YOU AGAIN TO KEEP REPEATING...
TO AVOID FAINTING KEEP REPEATING, IT'S ONLY A MOVIE ...ONLY A MOVIE ...ONLY A MOVIE ...ONLY A MOVIE ...ONLY A MOVIE ...ONLY A MOVIE
HALLMARK RELEASING CORP. presents
"DON'T LOOK IN THE BASEMENT"
...THE DAY THE INSANE TOOK OVER THE ASYLUM!
WARNING NOT RECOMMENDED FOR PERSON OVER 30!
· THEATRE IMPRINT ·
R RESTRICTED Under 17 requires accompanying Parent or Adult Guardian

SPCL-FX: Jack Bennett   MUSIC: Robert Farrar
Minor thriller: Inmates run mental asylum

Don't Look Now
1973, (GB-It), Casey/Eldorado/British Lion/Para, color, 110 mins.
W: Julie Christie (*Laura Baxter*), Donald Sutherland (*John Baxter*), Hilary Mason (*Heather*), Renato Scarpa (*The Inspector*), Clelia Matania (*Wendy*), Giorgio Trestini (*The Workman*), Massimo Serato (*The Bishop*), Leopoldo Trieste (*The Hotel Manager*), David Tree (*Anthony Babbage*), Bruno Cattaneo (*Det. Sabbione*), Ann Rye (*Mandy Babbage*), Adelina Poerio (*The Dwarf*), Sharon Williams (*Christine Baxter*), Nicholas Salter (*Johnny Baxter*), Bourvil
P: Peter Katz   D: Nicolas Roeg   SCR: Allan Scott & Chris Bryant   based on Daphne du Maurier's novella   PHOTOG: Anthony Richmond   MUSIC: Pino Donaggio
"The fanciest, most carefully assembled enigma yet seen on the screen"—New Yorker
Unusual thriller: Visions of dead child haunt couple

Don't Open the Window
see The Living Dead at Manchester Morgue

Don't Open Till Christmas
1984, (GB), color, 86 mins.
W: Edmund Purdom, Caroline Munro, Alan Lake, Belinda Mayne, Mark Jones, Gerry Sundquist
D: Edmund Purdom
Minor thriller: Killer stalks Santa Clauses

Don't Play with Fire
1980, (Hong Kong), color, 95 mins.
W: Lo Lieh, Lin Chen-Chi, Albert Au, Paul Che
D: Tsui Hark
Bizarre thriller: Violent tale of arms-dealing Vietnam vets, Triad gangsters & urban terrorists

Don't Talk to Strange Men
1962, (GB), Derick Williams/Bry, b&w, 65 mins.
W: Christina Gregg (*Jean Painter*), Conrad Phillips (*Ron*), Cyril Raymond (*Mr. Painter*), Gillian Lind (*Mrs. Painter*), Janina Faye (*Ann Painter*), Dandy Nicholls (*Molly*), Gwen Nelson (*Mrs. Mason*)

P: Derick Williams   D: Pat Jackson   STORY: Gwen Cherrill
Standard crime-thriller: Country girl has blind date with sex maniac

Don't Tempt the Devil
1964, (Fr), UMPO, b&w, 106 mins.
W: Marina Vlady, Bourvil
Standard thriller

Don't Touch My Sister
see The Glass Cage

Doom Asylum
1987, (USA), color, 77 mins.
W: Patty Mullen, Ruth Collins, Kristen Davis, William Hay, Kenny L. Price, Dawn Alvan, Harrison White, Michael Rogan
D: Richard S. Friedman
Minor horror-comedy: Madhouse frights

Doomed to Die
1940, (USA), Mono, b&w, 63 mins.
W: Boris Karloff (*James Lee Wong*), Grant Withers (*Capt. Sam Street*), Marjorie Reynolds (*Bobby Logan*), Guy Usher (*Fleming*), Melvin Lang (*Cyrus Wentworth*), Kenneth Harlan (*Ludlow*), Catherine Craig (*Cynthia Wentworth*), William Sterling (*Dick Fleming*), Wilbur Mack (*Matthews*), Henry Brandon (*Martin*), Gibson Gowland (*Doctor*)
P: Paul Malvern   D: William Nigh   SCR: Michel Jacoby & Ralph Gilbert Bettinson, from characters created by Hugh Wiley   PHOTOG: Harry Neumann
GB retitle, The Mystery of Wentworth Castle
Minor thriller: Chinese sleuth hunts shipowner's killer ('Mr. Wong' series)

Doom Runners
1997, (USA), Millennium/Showtime/Nickelodeon, color, 95 mins.
W: Lea Moreno, Tim Curry, Dean O'Gorman, Bradley Pierce, Nathan Jones, Rebecca Smart
D: Brendan Maher   PHOTOG: Steve Arnold   MUSIC: Braedy Neal
Made-for-Cable, standard SF-thriller: Teen girl opposes evil dictator

Doomsday Gun
1994, (USA), HBO-TV, color, 106 mins.
W: Frank Langella (*Gerald Bull*), Alan Arkin (*Yossi*) Kevin Spacey, Tony Goldwyn, James Fox, Michael Kitchen, Francesca Annis, Marianne Denicourt
D: Robert Young   WRIT: Lionel Chetwynd & Walter Bernstein
Made-for-Cable, standard docu-drama thriller: Inventor works on super-cannon to aid warring Arabs

Doomsday Machine
1972, (USA), Harry Hope, color, 83 mins.
W: Bobby Van, Ruta Lee, Mala Powers, James Craig, Grant Williams, Henry Wilcoxon, Essie Lin Chia, Mike Farrell, Denny Miller, Casey Kasem, Lorri Scott, Raymond Mayo, Anthony Loder, Scott Miller, Mark Bailey, Winston DeLugo, Leo Ramirez, Mary Meade French, Michael Christian, John Cestare, Ted Markland, Gabor Curtiz, Frank Gambina, Josh Peine, Karl Bruck, Steven Roberts, Robert Swan, Skip Battyn
P: Harvey Rope   D: Lee Sholem & Harry Hope   ORIG. STORY & SCR: Stuart James Byrne   PHOTOG: Stanley Cortez   SPCL-FX: David L. Hewitt & William C. Davies
video title, Escape from Planet Earth
Minor SF-melodrama: Survivors of Earth's nuclear destruction head for Venus

Doomsday Rock
1997, (USA), Regent/FAM-TV, color, 95 mins.
W: William Devane, Connie Sellaca, Ed Marinaro, Jessica Walter, Marsha Warfield, Kent McCord, Andrew Airlie, Howard Dell, Roger R. Cross, Dale Wilson
D: Brian Trenchard-Smith   PHOTOG: Rod Parkhurst   MUSIC: Sam Winans
TVM, standard SF-thriller: Asteroid threatens Earth

Doomsday Voyage
1972, (GB), Futuramic-Int'l, color, 88 mins.
W: Joseph Cotten (*Jason*), Ann Randall (*Katherine*), John Gabriel (*Wilson*)
P: Al Adamson   WRIT & D: John Vidette
Minor melodrama: Political assassin stows away on ship

Doomwatch
1972, (GB), Tigon/Embassy, color, 92 mins.
W: Ian Bannen (*Dr. Del Shaw*), John Paul (*Dr. Quist*), Judy Geeson (*Victoria Brown*), Simon Oates (*Dr. Ridge*), George Sanders (*The Admiral*), Percy Herbert (*Hartwell*), Geoffrey Keen (*Sir Henry Layton*), Joseph O'Conor (*The Vicar*), Jean Trend (*Dr. Fay Chantry*), Shelagh Fraser (*Mrs. Straker*), Joby Blanshard (*Bradley*), George Woodbridge (*The Skipper*), Brian Anthony (*Brian Murray*), Rita Davies (*Mrs. Murray*), James Cosmo (*Bob Gillette*), Michael Brennan (*Tom Straker*), Norman Bird (*Brewer*), Constance Chapman (*Miss Johnson*), Cyril Cross
P: Tony Tenser   D: Peter Sasdy   SCR: Clive Exton   STORY Dr. Kit Pedler & Gerry Davis, from teleseries   PHOTOG: Kenneth Talbot   MUSIC: John Scott
Minor ecological-thriller: Pollution disfigures inhabitants of Cornish village

D

The Door in the Wall
1956, (GB), BFI/ABP, color, 29 mins.

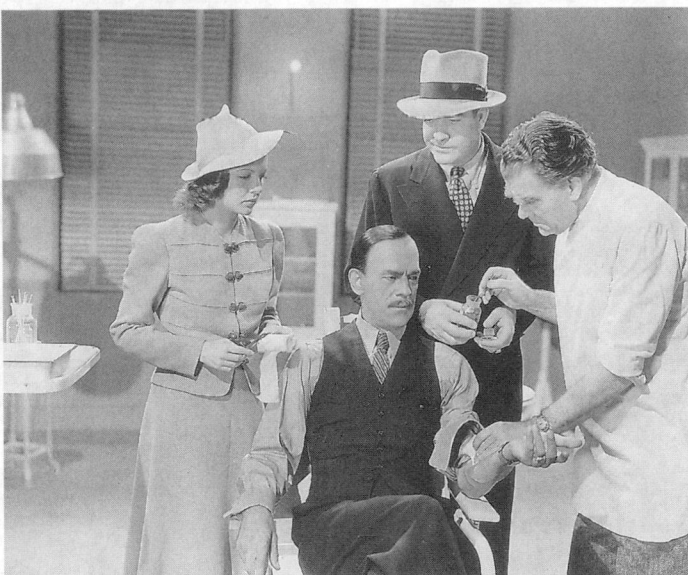

Doomed to Die: MARJORIE REYNOLDS, BORIS KARLOFF, GRANT WITHERS, GIBSON GOWLAND

<u>W:</u> Stephen Murray (*Sir Frank Wallace*), Ian Hunter (*Henry Redmond*), Leonard Sachs (*Father*), Anne Blake (*Aunt*), Kit Terrington (*Frank as a Child*), Brian Leslie (*Henry as a Child*)
<u>P:</u> Howard Thomas <u>D & SCR,</u> Glenn H. Alvey Jr., from a story by H.G. Wells
Standard short fantasy: Minister's childhood memory of enchanted garden causes his death

The Door with Seven Locks
1940, (GB), Rialto/Pathe/Mono, b&w, 89 mins.
<u>W:</u> Leslie Banks (*Dr. Manetta*), Lilli Palmer (*June Landsdowne*), Romilly Lunge (*Dick Martin*), David Horne (*Edward Havelock*), Gina Malo (*Glenda Blake*), Richard Bird (*Insp. Sneed*), Cathleen Nesbitt ^, J.H. Roberts (*Luis Silva*), Aubrey Mallalieu (*Lord Selford*), Harry Hutchinson (*Bevan Cody*), Ross Landon (*John Selford*)
<u>P:</u> John Argyle <u>D:</u> Norman Lee <u>SCR:</u> Norman Lee, John Argyle & Gilbert Gunn, from a novel by Edgar Wallace
USA retitle, **Chamber of Horrors**
Standard thriller: Inspector unmasks villainous mad doctor

The Door with Seven Locks (1962)
see Die Tur mit den Sieben Schlossern

Doppelganger
1969, (GB), Century 21/Univ, color, 101 mins.
<u>W:</u> Roy Thinnes (*Col. Glen Ross*), Patrick Wymark (*Jason*), Lyn Loring (*Sharon Ross*), Herbert Lom (*Dr. Hasler*), Ian Hendry (*Dr. John Kane*), Loni von Friedl (*Lise*), Franco Derosa (*Paulo*), George Sewell (*Mark Neuman*), Edward Bishop (*David Poulson*)
<u>P:</u> Gerry & Sylvia Anderson <u>D:</u> Robert Parrish <u>SCR:</u> Gerry Anderson, Sylvia Anderson & Donald James, from a story by Gerry & Sylvia Anderson
<u>PHOTOG:</u> John Read <u>SPCL-FX:</u> Derek Meddings & Harry Oakes
<u>MUSIC:</u> Barry Gray
USA retitle, 'Journey to the Far Side of the Sun'
Standard SF-adventure: Astronaut discovers "mirror" Earth

Doppelganger: The Evil Within
1993, (USA), color, 104 mins.
<u>W:</u> Drew Barrymore, George Newbern, Dennis Christopher, Leslie Hope, Sally Kellerman, George Maharis, Luana Anders, Jaid Barrymore
<u>D & SCR:</u> Avi Nesher
Standard fantasy-thriller: Ghostly double haunts woman

Dorian Gray
1970, (It-Lichtenstein-W. Ger), Towers of London/Commonwealth/AIP, color, 93 mins.
<u>W:</u> Helmut Berger (*Dorian Gray*), Richard Todd (*Basil*), Margaret Lee (*Gwendolyn*), Herbert Lom (*Henry*), Renato Romano (*Alan*), Maria Rohm (*Alice*), Isa Miranda (*Mrs. Ruxton*), Marie Liljedahl (*Sybil*), Beryl Cunningham (*Adrienne*), Eleonora Rossi-Drago (*Esther*), Stewart Black (*James*)
<u>D:</u> Massimo Dallamano <u>SCR:</u> Marcello Coscia & Massimo Dallamano based on Oscar Wilde's novel The Picture of Dorian Gray <u>PHOTOG:</u> Otello Spila
<u>MUSIC:</u> Peppino DeLuca & Carlo Pes
USA retitle, **The Secret of Dorian Gray**
Modest fantasy-thriller: Playboy gains eternal youth

The Dorm that Dripped Blood
see Pranks

Dorothy's Dream
1903, (GB), G.A.S. Films/Urban, b&w, 600 ft. (182.9m)
<u>D:</u> George Albert Smith
Standard fantasy short (in 8 scenes): Girl dreams of Dick Whittington, Robinson Crusoe, Forty Thieves, Aladdin, Cinderella, Bluebeard and Red Riding Hood

Dot and Keeto
1985, (Austral), color, 75 mins.
Animated fantasy: Girl shrinks to insect size

Dot and Santa Claus
1981, (Austral), color, 73 mins.
Minor juvenile fantasy, blend of live-action & animation: Santa aids small girl in search for baby kangaroo

Dot and the Kangaroo
1972, (Austral), Satori, color, 75 mins.
<u>VOICES:</u> Spike Milligan, Nola Brooks <u>SCR:</u> John Palmer & Yoram Gross, from a novel by Ethel Pedley
Minor juvenile fantasy, blend of live-action & animation: Forest animals aid lost girl

Dot and the Whale
1986, (Austral), color, 75 mins.
Minor juvenile fantasy, blend of live-action & animation: Girl befriends leviathan

Il Dottor Jekyll (Doctor Jekyll)
1951, (It), Sono, b&w
<u>W:</u> Mario Scoffi, Anna Maria Campoy
<u>D:</u> Mario Scoffi, from Robert Louis Stevenson's novella

The Double
1963, (GB), Merton Park/Anglo-Amalgamated, b&w, 56 mins.
<u>W:</u> Jeanette Sterke (*Mary Winston*), Alan MacNaughton (*John Cleeve*), Robert Brown (*Richard Harrison*), Jane Griffiths (*Jane Winton*), Basil Henson (*Derreck Alwyn*), Diane Clare (*Selena Osmond*), Anne Lawson (*Sally Carter*), Llewellyn Rees (*Bradshaw*), Hamilton Dyce (*Insp. Ames*)
<u>P:</u> Jack Greenwood <u>D:</u> Lionel Harris <u>SCR:</u> Lindsay Galloway & John Roddick, from a novel by Edgar Wallace
Minor thriller: Cad steals business partner's identity

The Double Agents
1962, (Fr), b&w
<u>W:</u> Robert Hossein, Marina Vlady
Minor melodrama: Young man and woman suspect each other of being enemy spies

Double Alibi
1937, (GB), Fox British, b&w, 40 mins.
<u>W:</u> Ernest Sefton (*Crayshaw*), John Warwick (*Charlie*), Paul Neville (*Dawkin*), Linden Travers (*Rita*), Mavis Villiers (*Miss Grant*), Margaret Scudamore (*Mrs. Havilland*), Eric Hales (*The Chauffeur*), Charles Eaton (*Davidson*)
<u>D:</u> David MacDonald <u>SCR:</u> Edward Dryhurst & Laurie Webb, from a story by Harold Weston
reissued 1941
Minor crime-thriller: Factory robber's alibi ruined by rival's girlfriend

Double Confession
1950, (GB), Reynolds/ABP, b&w, 86 mins.
<u>W:</u> Derek Farr (*Jim Medway*), Joan Hopkins (*Ann Corday*), Peter Lorre (*Paynter*), William Hartnell (*Charlie Durham*), Kathleen Harrison (*Kate*), Naunton Wayne (*Insp. Tenby*), Ronald Howard (*Hilary Boscombe*), Leslie Dwyer (*Leonard*), Edward Rigby (*Church*), George Woodbridge (*Sgt. Sawnton*), Henry Edwards (*The Man in the Shelter*), Vida Hope (*Mme. Zilia*), Esma Cannon (*Mme. Cleo*), Roy Plomley (*The Collector*)
<u>P:</u> Harry Reynolds <u>D:</u> Ken Annakin <u>SCR:</u> William Templeton & Ralph Keene, from John Garden's novel All on a Summer's Day
Minor thriller: Murder and blackmail at seaside resort

Double Crossbones
1951, (USA), Univ, color, 75 mins.
<u>W:</u> Donald O'Connor, Helena Carter
Standard pirate spoof

The Double Door
1934, (USA), Para, b&w, 70 mins.
<u>W:</u> Evelyn Venable, Sir Guy Standing, Mary Morris
<u>D:</u> Charles Vidor
Standard thriller: Murderer sought

Double Dragon
1994, (USA), color
<u>W:</u> Mark Dacascos, Robert Patrick
Standard SF-fantasy (inspired by video game): Megalomaniac covets ancient Chinese medallion

Double, Double, Toil and Trouble
1993, (USA), Walt Disney, color, 93 mins.
<u>W:</u> Ashley Olsen, Mary-Kate Olsen, Cloris Leachman, Meshach Taylor
<u>D & TELEPLAY:</u> Jeff Franklin

TVM, standard juvenile fantasy: Twins break witch's spell

Double Exposure
1944, (USA), b&w, 63 mins.
W: Chester Morris, Nancy Kelly, Jane Farrar, Richard Gaines
D: William Berke
Modest thriller: Girl unwittingly photographs murder

Double Exposure
1954, (GB), Kenilworth/GFD, b&w, 63 mins.
W: John Bentley (*Pete Fleming*), Rona Anderson (*Barbara Leyland*), Garry Marsh (*Daniel Beaumont*), Alexander Gauge (*Denis Clayton*), Ingeborg Wells (*Maxine Goldner*), John Horsley (*Lamport*), Ryck Ridon (*Trixon*), Frank Forsyth (*Insp. Grayle*)
P: Robert Baker & Monty Berman   D & SCR: John Gilling   STORY: John Roddick
Modest crime-thriller: Bookmaker fakes suicide of executive's wife

Double Exposure
1977, (GB), Westwind/Col-WB, color, 81 mins.
W: Anouska Hempel (*Simone*), David Baron (*James Compton*), Alan Brown (*Howard Townsend*), Julia Vidler (*Rhoda*), Dean Harris (*O'Hara*), Robert Russell (*The Kidnapper*), Deacon Mulholland (*Joe*), Alan Hay (*Ian Paterson*), Hugh Martin (*Ed*), Graham Mallard (*David Green*), Mary Maude (*Nicki*), Trevor Ainsley (*The Butler*), Ali Baba (*The Arab*), Hazel O'Connor (*Shirley*)
WRIT, P & D: William Webb   PHOTOG: Alan Pudney
Standard crime-thriller: Photographer hunts arms magnate's kidnapped mistress

Double Exposure
1982, (USA), color, 95 mins.
W: Michael Callan, James Stacy, Joanna Pettet, Cleavon Little, Pamela Hensley, Seymour Cassel
D: William B. Hillman
Minor thriller: Photographer's nightmares become real

Double Indemnity
1944, (USA), Para, b&w, 107 mins.
W: Barbara Stanwyck (Phyllis Dietrichson), Fred MacMurray (Walter Neff), Edward G. Robinson (Barton Keyes), Jean Heather (Lola Dietrichson), Porter Hall (Mr. Jackson), Tom Powers (Mr. Dietrichson), Fortunio Bonanova (Sam Gorlopis), Richard Gaines (Mr. Norton), Byron Barr (Nino Zachette)
D: Billy Wilder   SCR: Billy Wilder & Raymond Chandler, from James N. Cain's novel   MUSIC: Miklos Rozsa
Classic thriller: Scheming wife involves insurance agent in murder plot

Double Indemnity
1973, (USA), color, 73 mins.
W: Richard Crenna, Lee J. Cobb, Samantha Eggar, Kathleen Cody, Arch Johnson, John Fiedler, Robert Webber
D: Jack Smight, from James N. Cain's novel
TVM, standard thriller: Woman plans husband's murder

The Double Illusionist and the Living Head
see L'Illusioniste Double et la Tete Vivante

Double Jeopardy
1955, (USA), Rep, b&w, 70 mins.
W: Rod Cameron, Gale Robbins
Standard melodrama

A Double Life
1912, (GB), Hepworth, b&w, 800 ft. (243.8m)
W: Flora Morris (*Nellie Gray*), Harry Royston (*Insp. Gray*)
D: Warwick Buckland
Standard crime-thriller: Constable unmasks thieving inspector, his fiancee's father

A Double Life
1913, (GB), Barker, b&w, 880 ft. (268.2m)
W: Fred Paul (*Walter Clare*), Blanche Forsythe (*Madge Clare*), Thomas H. MacDonald (*Frank Norman*), Rachel de Solla (*Mrs. Norman*), Roy Travers (*Logan*)
D: Bert Haldane   STORY: Rowland Talbot
Standard crime-thriller: Husband jailed for theft

A Double Life
1947, (USA), Kanin/Univ, b&w, 101 mins.
W: Ronald Colman, Shelley Winters, Edmond O'Brien, Ray Collins, Sig-ne Hasso, Millard Mitchell, Joe Sawyer, Fay Kanin, Charles La Torre, Whit Bissell, Peter Thompson, Philip Loeb, Claire Carleton, Elizabeth Dunne
P: Michael Kanin   D: George Cukor   SCR: Garson Kanin & Ruth Gordon   PHOTOG: Milton Krasner   MUSIC: Miklos Rozsa
Classic psychodrama: Actor lives stage role of murderer. cf. The Brighton Strangler

The Double Man
1967, (GB), Albion/WB, color, 105 mins.
W: Yul Brynner (*Dan Slater/Kalmar*), Britt Ekland (*Gina*), Clive Revill (*Frank Wheatley*), Anton Diffring (*Berthold*), Moira Lister (*Mrs. Carrington*), Lloyd Nolan (*Edwards*), George Mikell (*Max Gruner*), Julia Arnall (*Anna*),

Brandon Brady (*Gregori*), Franklin J. Schaffner (*The Man*), Kenneth J. Warren (*The Police Chief*), Ulla Jacobsson, Carl Jaffe
P: Hal E. Chester   D: Franklin J. Schaffner   SCR: Frank Tarloff & Alfred Hayes based on Henry S. Maxfield's novel *Legacy for a Spy*   PHOTOG: Denys Coop   MUSIC: Ernie Freeman
Standard thriller: CIA agent investigates son's death

Double Negative
1986, (Can), color, 96 mins.
W: Michael Sarrazin, Susan Clark, Anthony Perkins, Howard Duff, Kate Reid, Al Waxman, Elizabeth Shepherd
D: George Bloomfield, based on Ross MacDonald's novel
video title, **Deadly Companion**
Minor thriller: Photojournalist hunts wife's killer

Double Possession
see Ganja and Hess

A Double Tour
see Leda

Dougal and the Blue Cat
1970, (Fr), color, 82 mins.
VOICES: Eric Thompson, Fenella Fielding
D: Serge Danot
Bizarre animated fantasy: Mysterious cat communes with disembodied voice

Douglas Fairbanks in Robin Hood
see Robin Hood (1922)

Doulos--The Finger Man
1962, (It-Fr), Pathe, b&w, 108 mins.
W: Jean-Paul Belmondo, Michel Piccoli, Serge Reggiani, Jean Desailly, Rene Lafevre, Fabienne Dali, Marcel Cuvelier, Monique Hennessy, Daniel Crohen
WRIT, P & D: Jean-Pierre Melville   PHOTOG: Nicholas Hayer   MUSIC: Paul Misraki
Standard melodrama: Informer juggles friendship

Downfall
1964, (GB), Merton Park/Anglo-Amalgamated, b&w, 59 mins.
W: Maurice Denham (*Sir Harold Crossley*), Nadja Regin (*Suzanne Crossley*), T.P. McKenna (*Martin Somers*), Iris Russell (*Mrs. Webster*), Peter Barkworth (*Tom Cotterell*), G.H. Mulcaster (*The Elderly Man*), Ellen McIntosh (*Jane Meldrum*), Victor Brooks (*Insp. Royd*)
P: Jack Greenwood   D: John Moxey   SCR: Robert Stewart, from a story by Edgar Wallace
Standard thriller: Lawyer acquits murderer, hires him to kill faithless wife

The Dover Road Mystery
1960, (GB), Merton Park/Anglo-Amalgamated, b&w, 30 mins.
W: Geoffrey Keen (*Supt. Graham*), Leonard Sachs (Herbert Roberts), Cyril Chamberlain (*Jack Chambers*)
P: Jack Greenwood   D: Gerard Bryant   STORY: James Eastwood, from a novel by Edgar Lustgarten
Minor short crime-thriller: Police unmask thieving motoris

Downhill
1927, (GB), Gainsborough, b&w, 7,600 ft. (2316.5m)
W: Ivor Novello (*Roddy Berwick*), Isabel Jeans (*Julia*), Ian Hunter (*Archie*), Ben Webster (*Dr. Dawson*), Norman McKinnel (*Sir Thomas Berwick*), Lilian Braithwaite (*Lady Berwick*), Robin Irvine (*Tim Walkeley*), Sybil Rhoda (*Sybil Walkeley*), Annette Benson (*Mabel*), Alf Goddard (*The Swede*), Jerrold Robertshaw (*Rev. Henry Walkeley*), Violet Fairbrother (*The Poetess*), Barbara Gott (*Mme. Michet*)
P: Michael Balcon   D: Alfred Hitchcock   SCR: Eliot Stannard, from a play by Ivor Novello & Constance Collier
USA retitle, **When Boys Leave Home** *(World Wide, 1928)*
Standard melodrama: Disowned youth becomes gigolo

Down Three Dark Streets
1954, (USA), UA, b&w, 84 mins.
W: Broderick Crawford, Ruth Roman, Martha Hyer, Marisa Pavan, Casey Adams, Kenneth Tobey, Gene Reynolds, Claude Akins
D: Arnold Laven
Standard thriller

Down to Earth
1947, (USA), Col, color, 101 mins.
W: Rita Hayworth (*Terpsichore*), Larry Parks, Marc Platt, James Gleason, Edward Everett Horton, George Macready, Roland Culver, Adele Jergens, William Frawley, James Burke, Fred F. Sears, Lynn Merrick, Myron Healey
D: Alexander Hall   SCR: Edwin Blum & Don Hartman   PHOTOG: Rudolph Maté   MUSIC: Heinz Roemheld   LYRICS: Allan Roberts & Doris Fisher   SONGS: People Have More Fun Than Anyone & Let's Stay Young Forever
Superior musical fantasy: Terpsichore, Goddess of Dance, gets job in chorus line of Broadway show. cf. Xanadu

Do You Keep a Lion at Home?
1964, (Czech), Ceskoslovensky Film-Export/Brandon, color, 81 mins.

W: Josef Filip, Ladislav Ocenasek, Jan Brychta
D: Pavel Hobl **SCR:** Sheila Ochova, Bohumil Sobotka, Pavel Hobl, from a story by Sheila Ochova **PHOTOG:** Jiri Vojta **MUSIC:** Wiliam Bukovy **ANIMATION:** Vojta, Trmal, Novak & Vinklarek
Standard fantasy-satire

Do You Like Women?
see Aimez-Vous Les Femmes?

Do You Know This Voice?
1964, (GB), Parroch-McCallum-Lippert/British Lion, b&w, 75 mins.
W: Dan Duryea (*Joe Hopta*), Isa Miranda (*Rosa Marotta*), Gwen Watford (*Jackie Hopta*), Peter Madden (*Supt. Hume*), Barry Warren (*Sgt. Bob Connor*), Jean Aubrey (*Judy*), Shirley Cameron (*Mrs. Wilson*), Alan Edwards (*Colin Wilson*)
P: C. Jack Parsons **D:** Frank Nesbitt **SCR:** Neil McCallum, from a novel by Evelyn Berckman
Standard crime-thriller (shown only on TV): Italian widow nabs kidnapper

Dracos
1956, (Greece), b&w, 110 mins.
D: Nikos Koundouros
A.k.a. The Ogre of Athens
Standard melodrama

Dracula (1921)
see Drakula

Dracula
1931, (USA, English-speaking version), Univ, b&w, 84 mins.
W: Bela Lugosi (*Count Dracula*), Helen Chandler (*Mina Seward*), Edward Van Sloan (*Dr. Abraham Van Helsing*), David Manners (*Jonathan Harker*), Dwight Frye (*Renfield*), Frances Dade (*Lucy Weston*), Herbert Bunston (*Dr. Seward*), Charles Gerrard (*Martin*), Joan Standing (*Briggs*), Moon Carroll (*The Maid*), Donald Murphy, Carla Laemmle (*Coach Passenger*), Ted Browning (*Harbormaster*), Josephine Velez (*Grace-nurse*), Geraldine Dvorak, Dorothy Tree, Cornelia Thaw (*Dracula's Brides*)
D: Tod Browning **SCR:** Garrett Fort, from the play by Hamilton Deane & John L. Balderston based on Bram Stoker's novel *Dracula: A Tale* **PHOTOG:** Karl Freund **MUSIC:** Tchaikovsky **DESIGN:** Charles D. Hall
"Brooding, slow, relying heavily on atmosphere and set design, 'Dracula' is nevertheless a true horror classic and a breakthrough for the genre, although its cinematic worth is at best uncertain. Most film critics will admit, however, that the opening scenes in Dracula's cobweb-filled castle are among the most frightening sequences ever put on film"—Gary Gerani, "The Vampire Book—Chapter Three: Lugosi the Great," Monster Fantasy, Vol. I, No. 1 (April, 1975), p. 25
"...Dracula...launched the full vogue of horror films. What made Dracula a turning-point was that it did not attempt to explain away its tale of vampirism and supernatural horrors. Something in the air of the early Thirties made audiences believe and enjoy believing what they would have scoffed at ten years earlier"—Richard Griffith & Arthur Mayer, The Movies
"If Dracula, the film, has retained any power to impress after 35 years of repeated showings, it is due in the main to Lugosi himself. It is useless to debate whether he was a good actor or not; Lugosi was Dracula: the actor's identification is complete...he left an indelible mark on the role and consequently, on the horror film as well"—Carlos Clarens, An Illustrated History of the Horror Film
Classic horror-fantasy: Vampire leaves Transylvania, comes to hunt England's fog-shrouded streets

Dracula
1931, (USA, Spanish-speaking version), Univ, b&w, 102 mins
W: Carlos Villarias, Carmen Guerrero, Lupita Tovar, Barry Norton, Pablo Alvarez Rubio, Eduardo Arozamena, Manuel Arbo
D: George Melford, from Bram Stoker's novel *Dracula: A Tale*

Dracula (1958)
see Horror of Dracula

Dracula (1931): FRANCES DADE AND BELA LUGOSI

Dracula

1973, (USA-Can), Latglen/Curtis/Universal-TV/CBS-TV, color, 105 mins.

<u>W</u>: Jack Palance (*Count Dracula*), Nigel Davenport (*Dr. Abraham Van Helsing*), Simon Ward (*Arthur Holmwood*), Penelope Horner (*Mina Seward*), Fiona Lewis (*Lucy Westenra*), Pamela Brown (*Mrs. Westenra*), Murray Brown (*Jonathan Harker*), Virginia Wetherell (*A Vampire*), Gita Denise (*Mme. Kristoff*), Reg Lye (*The Zoo Keeper*), Barbara Lindley (*A Vampire*), Sarah Douglas (*A Vampire*), George Pravda (*The Innkeeper*), Fred Stone (*The Priest*), Sandra Caron (*The Maid*)

<u>P & D</u>:Dan Curtis   <u>SCR</u>: Richard Matheson, from Bram Stoker's novel *Dracula: A Tale*   <u>PHOTOG</u>: Oswald Morris   <u>MUSIC</u>: Robert Cobert   <u>DESIGN</u>, Trevor Williams

TVM, standard horror-fantasy: Vampire's reign of terror

Dracula

1974, (USA-It-W. Ger), Carlo Ponti-Braunsberg-Rassam/Bryanston/Paul Morrissey/Andy Warhol, color, 93 mins.

<u>W</u>: Joe Dallesandro (*Mario, the Field Man*), Udo Keir (*Count Dracula*), Vittorio De Sica (*Lord Difiore*), Gil Cagne (*The Townsman*), Dominique Darrell (*Rubinia*), Arno Juerging (*The Count's Ass't*), Maxime McKendry (*Lady Difiore*), Stefania Cassini (*Safiria*), Roman Polanski (*The Man at the Inn*), Milena Ukovich (*Esmeralda*)

<u>WRIT & D</u>, Paul Morrissey, from Bram Stoker's novel *Dracula: A Tale*   <u>PHOTOG</u>: Luigi Kuveiller

A.k.a. **Blood for Dracula** *and* **Young Dracula**

Standard sex-farce horror-fantasy: Vampire king requires blood of virgins

Dracula

1979, (USA), Mirisch/Univ, color, 115 mins.

<u>W</u>: Frank Langella (*Count Dracula*), Kate Nelligan (*Lucy*), Laurence Olivier (*Dr. Abraham Van Helsing*), Jan Francis (*Mina Van Helsing*), Donald Pleasence (*Dr. Seward*), Trevor Eve (*Jonathan Harker*), Tony Haygarth (*Renfield*), Janine Duvitski (*Annie*), Teddy Turner (*Swales*), Sylveste McCoy (*Walter*), Kristine Howarth (*Mrs. Galloway*), Joe Belcher (*Tom Hindley*), Gabor Vernon (*The Captain*), Peter Wallis (*The Priest*)

<u>P</u>: Walter Mirisch   <u>D</u>: John Badham   <u>SCR</u>: W.D. Richter   based on the stage play by Hamilton Deane & John L. Balderston, from Bram Stoker's novel *Dracula: A Tale*   <u>PHOTOG</u>: Gilbert Taylor   <u>SPCL-FX SPRVSR</u>, Albert Whitlock   <u>MUSIC</u>: John Williams

Lavish horror-fantasy: Vampire becomes enamored of mortal woman

Dracula (1992)

see **Bram Stoker's 'Dracula'**

Dracula A.D. 1972

1972, (GB), Hammer/WB/Col, color, 95 mins.

<u>W</u>: Christopher Lee (*Count Dracula*), Peter Cushing (*Prof. Van Helsing*), Stephanie Beacham (*Jessica Van Helsing*), Christopher Neame (*Johnny Alucard*), Michael Coles (*Insp. Murray*), William Ellis (*Joe Mitchum*), Philip Miller (*Bob*), Marsha Hunte (*Gaynor*), Caroline Munro (*Laura*), Lally Bowers (*The Matron*), Janet Key (*Anna*), Michael Kitchen (*Greg*), David Andrews (*Sgt. Pearson*), Stoneground (*The Rock Group*)

<u>P</u>: Josephine Douglas   <u>D</u>: Alan Gibson   <u>SCR</u>: Don Houghton   <u>PHOTOG</u>: Dick Bush   <u>MUSIC</u>: Michael Vickers   <u>DESIGN</u>, Don Mingaye

orig. to be titled **Dracula Today**

Standard horror-fantasy: Mod teens dabble in black magic, conjure up blood-lusting fiend

Dracula and Son

see **Dracula, Pere et Fils**

Dracula and the Seven Golden Vampires

see **Legend of the Seven Golden Vampires**

Dracula Blows His Cool

1983, (W. Ger), Martin Films, color, 90 mins.

<u>W</u>: Gianni Garko (*Stan/Count Stanislaus*), Betty Verges (*Countess Olivia*), Giacomo Rizzo (*Mario*), Linda Grondier (*Linda*), Bea Fiedler, Ralf Wolter, Alexander Grill, Herta Worell, Tobias Meister, Ellen Umlauf, Laurence Kaesermann, Herbert Stiny

<u>D</u>: Carlo Ombra   <u>SCR</u>: Grunbach & Rosenthal   <u>PHOTOG</u>: Heinz Holscher   <u>MUSIC</u>: Gerhard Heinz

Minor horror-comedy

Dracula: Dead and Loving It

1995, (USA), Brooksfilms/Castle Rock/Col, color, 90 mins

<u>W</u>: Leslie Nielsen (*Count Dracula*), Peter MacNicol (*Renfield*), Harvey Korman (*Dr. Seward*), Mel Brooks (*Dr. Van Helsing*), Steven Weber, Amy Yasbeck, Lysette Anthony, Anne Bancroft (*Mme. Ouspenskaya*) Mark Blankfield, Clive Revill, Chuck McCann

<u>D</u>: Mel Brooks   <u>SCR</u>: Mel Brooks, Rudy DeLuca & Steve Haberman   <u>STORY</u>: Rudy DeLuca & Steve Haberman   <u>PHOTOG</u>: Michael D. O'Shea   <u>MUSIC</u>: Hummie Mann

Standard horror-spoof

Dracula Has Risen from the Grave

1968, (GB), Hammer/WB-7Arts, color, 92 mins.

<u>W</u>: Christopher Lee (*Count Dracula*), Rupert Davies (*Msgr. Ernst Muller*), Veronica Carlson (*Maria*), Barry Andrews (*Paul*), Barbara Ewing (*Zena*), Michael

Ripper (*Max*), Ewan Hooper (*The Priest*), Marion Mathie (*Anna Muller*), Norman Bacon (*The Boy*), John D. Collins (*The Student*), George A. Cooper (*The Landlord*), Chris Cunningham

<u>P</u>: Aida Young   <u>D</u>: Freddie Francis   <u>SCR</u>: John Elder [Anthony Hinds]   <u>PHOTOG</u>: Arthur Grant   <u>SPCL-FX</u>: Frank George   <u>MUSIC</u>: James Bernard   <u>DESIGN</u>, Bernard Robinson

orig. to be titled **Dracula's Revenge**

Standard horror-fantasy, sequel to **Dracula, Prince of Darkness***: Vampire puts young priest under evil spell*

Dracula in Istanbul

see **Drakula Istanbulda**

Dracula in the Castle of Blood

see **Web of the Spider**

Dracula: CARLOS VILLARIAS, PABLO ALVAREZ RUBIO

Dracula is Dead and Well and Living in London

see **The Satanic Rites of Dracula**

Dracula Meets the Outer Space Chicks

1968, (USA), Independent, color

Minor sex-horror farce: Bimbos encounter bloodsucker

Dracula, Pere et Fils (Dracula, Father and Son)

1979, (Fr), Production 2000/Gaumont/Quartet Films, color, 96 mins.

<u>W</u>: Christopher Lee (*Dracula*), Bernard Menez (*Dracula's Son*), Marie-Helene Breillat (*Nicole*), Catherine Breillat (*The Wife*), Anna Gael (*The Woman*), Jean-Claude Dauphin (*The Young Man*)

<u>P</u>: Alain Poire   <u>D</u>: Edouard Molinaro   <u>SCR</u>: Edouard Molinaro, Jean-Marie Poire & Alain Godard, from a book by Claude Klotz   <u>PHOTOG</u>: Alan Levent   <u>MUSIC</u>: Vladimir Cosma

USA retitle, **Dracula and Son**

Standard horror-spoof: Vampire wants son to continue family tradition

Dracula, Prince of Darkness

1966, (GB), Hammer-7Arts/20th-Fox, color, 90 mins.

<u>W</u>: Christopher Lee (*Count Dracula*), Andrew Keir (*Father Shandor*), Barbara Shelley (*Helen*), Suzan Farmer (*Diana*), Francis Matthews (*Charles*), Philip Latham (*Klove*), Thorley Walters (*Ludwig*), Charles Tingwell (*Alan*), Walter Brown (*Brother Mark*), George Woodbridge (*The Landlord*), Joyce Hemson (*Girl*), Peter Cushing (*Van Helsing*, clip from **Horror of Dracula**)

<u>P</u>: Anthony Nelson Keys   <u>D</u>: Terence Fisher   <u>SCR</u>: John Sansom [Jimmy Sangster]—from his property titled *Disciple of Dracula*   <u>PHOTOG</u>: Michael Reed   <u>SPCL-FX</u>: Bowie Films Ltd.   <u>MUSIC</u>: James Bernard   <u>DESIGN</u>: Don Mingaye

*Modest horror-fantasy, first direct sequel to '***Horror of Dracula***': Servant revives vampiric master*

Dracula Rising

1993, (USA), color, 85 mins.

<u>W</u>: Christopher Atkins

<u>D</u>: Fred Gallo

Minor horror-fantasy: Art historian finds new employer is vampiric

Dracula Saga
see The Saga of the Draculas

Dracula's Castle
see Blood of Dracula's Castle

Dracula's Daughter
1936, (USA), Univ, b&w, 70 mins.
<u>W</u>: Gloria Holden, Marguerite Chapman, Edward Van Sloan, Otto Kruger, Irving Pichel, Halliwell Hobbes, Nan Grey, Edgar Norton, Gilbert Emery, Hedda Hopper, Billy Bevan, E.E. Clive, Claud Allister, Douglas Wood, Eily Malyon, Christian Rub
<u>D</u>: Lambert Hillyer   <u>SCR</u>: Garrett Fort   suggested by Oliver Jeffries   based on Bram Stoker's short story "Dracula's Guest" (a deleted chapter from ***Dracula: A Tale***)   <u>PHOTOG</u>: George Robinson
"...a thoughtful, well constructed film...a follow up that one can both enjoy and respect"—William K. Everson, Classics of the Horror Film
*Modest horror-fantasy, only direct sequel to **Dracula** (1931): Female offspring of legendary fiend tries to escape vampiric heritage*

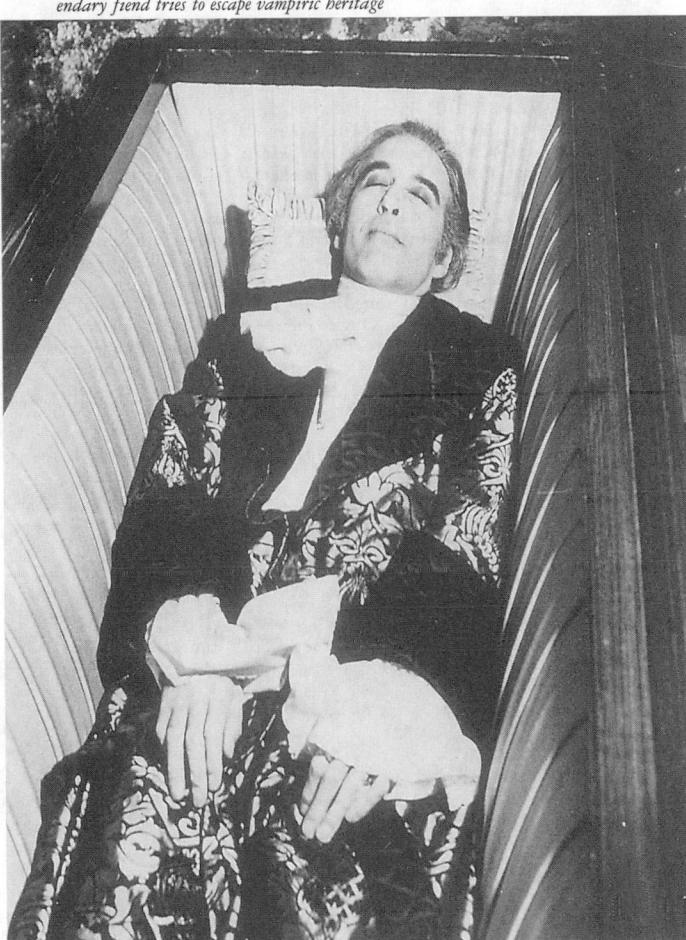

Dracula, Pere et Fils: CHRISTOPHER LEE

Dracula's Dog
1978, (USA), Crown Int'l, color, 90 mins.
<u>W</u>: Michael Pataki (*Drake/Dracula*), Jose Ferrer (*Insp. Branco*), Reggie Nalder (*Veidt-Smith*), Jan Shutan (*Marla*), Libbie Chase (*Linda*), John Levin (*Steve*), Cleo Harrington (*Mrs. Parks*), Simmy Bow, JoJo D'Amore, Tom Gerrard, Roger Pancake, Gordon McGill, Bob Miller, Al Ferrara, Katherine Fitzpatrick, Sally Marr, Merryl Jay, Jackie Drake, Dwight Krizman, John Kirby, Darlene Craviotta, Chris George, Lou Schumacher, Carl Morrison, Dimitri Logothetis, Joan Leone, Roger Schumacher, Dominic Ferlan, Arlene Martell
<u>D</u>: Albert Band   <u>SCR</u>: Frank Ray Perilli   <u>PHOTOG</u>: Bruce Logan   <u>MUSIC</u>: Andrew Belling
*A.k.a. **Zoltan: Hound of Dracula***
Minor horror-fantasy: Soviet soldiers disturb tomb, unleash terror

Dracula's Great Love
see Gran Amore del Conde Dracula

Dracula's Last Rites
see Last Rites

Dracula's Lust for Blood
see Lake of Dracula

Dracula's Nightmare
see Horror of Dracula

Dracula's Revenge
see Dracula Has Risen from the Grave

Dracula Sucks
1980, (USA), Kodiak Films, Color, 91 mins.
<u>W</u>: Jamie Gillis (*Dracula*), Serena (*Lucy*), Annette Haven (*Mina*), John Leslie (*Seward*), Richard Bulik (*Renfield*), John Holmes (*Stoker*), Paul Thomas (*Harker*), Kay Parker (*Sybil*), Bill Margold (*Henry*), Detlef Van Berg (*Helsing*), Pat Manning (*Irene*), Mike Ranger (*Bradley*), Seka (*Lawson*), David Lee Bynum (*Jarvis*), Irene Best (*The Maid*), George Lee (*The Cowboy*), Kurt Sjoberg (*Hitler*), Renee Andre (*A Handmaiden*), Slavica (*A Handmaiden*), Martin L. Dorf (*Martin*), Nancy Hoffman (*Baby Jane*), Ken Michaels (*A Patient*), Mitch Morrill (*A Patient*)
<u>D</u>: Philip Marshak   <u>SCR</u>: Darryl A. Marshak & David J. Kern   <u>PHOTOG</u>: Hanania Baer   <u>MUSIC</u>: Lionel Thomas
Standard eroto-horror-satire

Dracula's Vampire Lust
1970, (Switz), color
Minor sex-horror farce

Dracula's Widow
1988, (USA), color 85 mins
<u>W</u>: Sylvia Kristel, Josf Sommer (*Lannon*), Lenny Von Dohlen (*Everett*), Marc Coppola (*Brad*)
<u>D</u>: Christopher Coppola
Minor horror-fantasy: Vampiress prowls L.A. night life

Dracula: Up in Harlem
1983, (USA), color, 90 mins.
Minor horror-satire: Vampire visits NYC, disturbs Pentagon

Dracula: The Bloodline Continues...
see The Saga of the Draculas

Dracula (The Dirty Old Man)
1969, (USA), Whit Boyd/Art Films, color
<u>W</u>: Vince Kelly
<u>P,D & SCR</u>: Williams Edwards
Minor eroto-horror-comedy: Vampire kidnaps naked virgins

Dracula: The Untold Story
see Bram Stoker's 'Dracula'

Dracula Today
see Dracula A.D. 1972

Dracula vs. Frankenstein
1971, (USA), Independent-Int'l, color, 90 mins.
<u>W</u>: Lon Chaney Jr., Regina Carrol, Russ Tamblyn, Zandor Voikov, J. Carrol Naish, Anthony Eisley, John Bloom, Jim Davis, Angelo Rossitto, Forrest J. Ackerman
<u>P & D</u>: Al Adamson   <u>STORY & SCR</u>: William Pugsley & Samuel M. Sherman
*A.k.a. **The Blood Seekers, Blood of Frankenstein, Frankenstein's Bloody Horror, Frankenstein's Bloody Terror, They're Coming to Get You, Satan's Blood Freaks, The Revenge of Dracula***
*video title, **The Revenge of Dracula***
Minor horror-fantasy: Vampire forces doctor to revive manmade monster

Dragonheart
1996, (USA), Rafaella DeLaurentiis/Univ, 103 mins, color
<u>W</u>: Dennis Quaid (*Bowen*), Julie Christie, David Thewlis, Dina Meyer, Pete Postlethwaite, Sean Connery (*Voice of Draco the Dragon*), Jason Isaacs, Brian Thompson, Wolf Christian, Terry O'Neill, Sir John Gielgud (*voice*)
<u>D</u>: Rob Cohen   <u>SCR</u>: Charles Edward Pogue   <u>STORY</u>: Patrick Read Johnson & Charles Edward Pogue   <u>PHOTOG</u>: David Eggby   <u>SPCL VS-FX</u>: Industrial Light & Magic   <u>VS-FX SPRVSR</u>: Scott Squires   <u>MUSIC</u>: Randy Edelman
Lavish adventure-fantasy ($58 million budget): Hero travels with talking dragon

The Dragon Murder Case
1934, (USA), WB, b&w, 68 mins.
<u>W</u>: Warren William (*Philo Vance*), Margaret Lindsay (*Bernice*), Lyle Talbot (*Leland*), Helen Lowell (*Mrs. Stamm*), Eugene Pallette (*Sgt. Ernest Heath*), Etienne Girardot (*Doremus*), Dorothy Tree (*Ruby*), Robert McWade (*D.A. John F.X. Markham*), Robert Barrat (*Stamm*), Robert Warwick (*Dr. Holliday*), William B. Davidson (*Greeff*), George E. Stone (*Tatum*), George Meeker (*Montague*), Charles Wilson (*Hennessey/Snitkin*)
<u>D</u>: H. Bruce Humberstone   <u>SCR</u>: F. Hugh Herbert & Robert N. Lee, from characters created by S.S. Van Dine   <u>PHOTOG</u>: Tony Gaudio
Engrossing mystery-thriller: Legendary monster blamed for grisly murder, suave sleuth investigates

The Dragon of Pendragon Castle

1950, (GB), Elstree Independent/GFD, b&w, 52 mins.
W: Robin Netscher (*Peter Fielding*), Hilary Rennie (*Judy Fielding*), Jane Welsh (*Mrs. Fielding*), J. Hubert Leslie (*Sir William Magnus*), Graham Moffatt (*Paddy*), C. Denier Warren (*Mr. Morgan*), Lily Lapidus (*Mrs. Morgan*), Leslie Bradley (*Mr. Ferber*), David Hannaford (*Bobby*)
P & D: John Baxter SCR: Mary Cathcart Borer STORY, Janet M. Smith
reissued 1972 (17 mins. cut)
Standard juvenile fantasy: Impoverished knight's children find sea dragon

The Dragon's Blood

1963, (It), Ferrigno, color
W: Rolf Tasna, Katharina Mayberg
Minor adventure-fantasy: Legend of Siegfried

Dragon's Gold

1953, (USA), UA, b&w, 70 mins.
W: John Archer, Hillary Brooke
Standard thriller: Treasure hunt in Chinatown

Dragonslayer

1981, (GB), Walt Disney-Para, color, 111 mins.
W: Ralph Richardson (*Ulrich*), Peter MacNicol (*Galen Bradwardyn*), Caitlin Clarke (*Valerian*), Albert Salmi (*Greil*), Peter Eyre (*King Cas-iodorus*), John Hallam (*Tyrian*), Chloe Salaman (*Princess Elspeth*), Roger Kemp (*Horsrik*), Sydney Bromley (*Hodge*), Ian McDiarmid (*Brother Jacopus*), Emrys James (*Simon*), Jason White, Ken Shorter, Yolanda Palfrey, Douglas Cooper, Alf Mangon, David Mount, James Payne, Chris Twinn
P: Hal Barwood D: Matthew Robbins SCR: Hal Barwood & Matthew Robbins
PHOTOG: Derek Vanlint SPCL-FX: Brian Johnson & Dennis Muren
MUSIC: Alex North
Standard adventure-fantasy: Sorcerer helps boy free village from pillaging monster

The Dragon that Wasn't...or Was He

1983, (Holl), color, 81 mins.
Minor animated fantasy: Bear adopts dragon

Dragonworld

1994, (GB), color, 86 mins.
W: Sam Mackenzie, Brittney Powell, Courtland Mead, John Calvin, Lila Kaye, John Woodvine
D: Ted Nicolaou SCR: Ted Nicolaou & Suzanne Glazener Naha MUSIC: Richard Band
Standard fantasy: Youth saves fire-breathing friend from unscrupulous amusement park owner

Dragonworld: The Legend Continues

1996, (USA), color, 85 mins.
W: Drake Bell (*Johnny*), Andrew Keir (*Angus*)
Made-for-Video, standard fantasy: Fairies entrust boy with baby dragon

Dragonwyck

1946, (USA), 20th-Fox, b&w, 103 mins.
W: Gene Tierney, Vincent Price, Walter Huston, Spring Byington, Anne Revere, Glenn Langan, Jessica Tandy (*Peggy*), Henry (Harry) Morgan (*Bleecker*), Connie Marshall (*Katrine*), Vivienne Osborne
P: Darryl F. Zanuck D: Joseph L. Mankiewicz, from a novel by Anya Seton
PHOTOG: Arthur Miller SPCL-FX: Fred Sersen MUSIC: Alfred Newman
Superior melodrama: Amish girl finds mystery and sadness with haughty lord of large estate

Drakula (Dracula)

1921, (Hung), b&w
based on Bram Stoker's novel *Dracula: A Tale*

Drakula Istanbulda (Dracula in Istanbul)

1953, (Turk), Demirag, b&w
W: Atif Kaptan
P: Turgut Demirag D: Mehmet Muhtar SCR: Umit Deniz
based on Riza Seyfi's novel *The Impaling Voivode*
Standard horror-fantasy: Vampire prowls Asia Minor

The Drawing Lesson: or, The Living Statue

see *La Statue Animee*

A Dream

see *His Prehistoric Past*

Dream a Little Dream

1989, (USA), Lightning, color, 100 mins.
W: Jason Robards Jr. (*Coleman Ettinger*), Corey Feldman (*Bobby Keller*), Piper Laurie (*Gene Ettinger*), Meredith Salenger (*Lainie Diamond*), Corey Haim (*Dinger*), Harry Dean Stanton (*Ike Baker*), William McNamara (*Joel*), Susan Blakely (*Cherry Diamond*), Matt Adler (*Dumas*), Alex Rocco (*Gus Keller*), Victoria Jackson (*Kit Keller*), Ria Pavia (*Maureen*), Lala (*Shelley*), Mickey Thomas (*Mr. Pattison*), Laura Lee Norton (*Marge*), Russell Livingstone (*The Neighbor Next Door*), John Ward (*Derek*), Fran Taylor (*Sheila Baker*), John

Grissom (*The P.E. Coach*), John Ford Coley (*Ron*), Josh Evans (*Low Life #1*), Jody Smith (*Low Life #2*), Kent Faulcon (*Low Life #3*)
D: Marc Rocco SCR: D.F. Eisenberg & Marc Rocco ORIG. STORY: Daniel Jay Franklin PHOTOG: King Baggott ORIG. SCORE, John William Dexter SONGS: *The Future's So Bright, I Gotta Wear Shades, Time Runs Wild, Into the Mystic, Where Is She?, Dress to Kill, It's the End of the World as We Know It (And I Feel Fine), You'd Better Wait, Dreams to Remember, Whenever There's a Night, & Never Turn Away*
Minor fantasy: Teen's body occupied by mystic's mind

Dream a Little Dream 2

1994, (USA), color, 90 mins.
W: Corey Feldman, Corey Haim
Minor fantasy: Two guys seek magic sunglasses

Dream a Little Evil

1991, (USA), color
W: Lyle Waggoner, Tom Alexander, Stacie Randall, Michael Nicolosi, James Lemmo
SCR: David Weissman & Susan Forman
Minor SF-thriller: Inventor creates sinister "dreamgirl"

DreamChild

1985, (GB), PFH/Thorn-EMI/Univ, color, 90 mins.
W: Coral Browne (*Mrs. Hargreaves*), Ian Holm (*Rev. Charles Dodgson*), Peter Gallagher (*Jack Dolan*), Jane Asher (*Mrs. Liddell*), Caris Corfman (*Sally Mackeson*), Nicola Cowper (*Lucy*), Amelia Shankley (*Little Alice*), Rupert Wainwright (*Hargreaves*), Imogen Boorman (*Lorina*), Peter Whitman (*The Radio Producer*), Roger Ashton-Griffiths (*Rev. Duckworth*), James Wilby (*Baker*), Shane Rimmer (*Mr. Marl*), Ken Campbell (*The Radio Sound Effects Man*), William Hootkins (*The 1st Radio Actor*), Jeffrey Chiswick (*The 2nd Radio Actor*), Pat Starr (*The Radio Actress*), Alan Sherman (*The 1st Reporter*), Johnny M (*The 1st Crooner*), Danny Brainin (*The 3rd Reporter/Photographer*), Sam Douglas (*The 4th Reporter*), Olivier Pierre (*The Pres. of the University*), Peter Banks (*The 1st Editor*), Derek Hoxby (*The 2nd Editor*), Ron Berglas (*The 3rd Editor*), Ron Travis (*The 4th Editor*), Thomasine Heiner (*The Announcer/Chairman*), Tony Mansell (*The Waldorf Astoria Crooner*)
D: Gavin Millar SCR: Dennis Potter PHOTOG: Billy Williams MUSIC: Stanley Myers
Unusual fantasy-melodrama: Inspiration for Alice in Wonderland relives her past

Dream Circus

1939, (GB), b&w
D: Lotte Reiniger MUSIC: Igor Stravinsky
Unfinished animated fantasy

Dream Demon

1988, (GB), color, 89 mins.
W: Jemma Redgrave, Kathleen Wilhoite, Timothy Spall, Jimmy Nail, Mark Greenstreet
D: Harley Cokliss
Minor thriller: American visits spooky British manor

The Dream Doctor

1936, (GB), Bernard Smith-Widgey Newman/MGM, b&w, 41 mins.
W: Sydney Monckton (*The Doctor*), Julie Suedo (*The Gipsy*), Yvonne Murray (*The Patient*), Leo Genn (*The Husband*)
D: R.W. Lotinga
Minor fantasy: Psychic gypsy interprets dreams

Dream Girl

1948, (USA), Para, b&w, 86 mins.
W: Betty Hutton, Macdonald Carey, Patric Knowles, Lowell Gilmore, Virginia Field, Walter Abel, Peggy Wood
D: Mitchell Leisen SCR: Arthur Sheekman, from Elmer Rice's play (later produced on stage as musical *Skyscraper*) PHOTOG: Daniel Fapp MUSIC: Victor Young
Amusing comedy with fantasy sequences: Daydreams of wistful young woman

Dreamhouse

1981, (GB), Salon Films/Alpha, color, 36 mins.
W: Robert Dorning, Lally Bowers, Ian Saynor, Yvonne Nicholson
D: Al Beresford
Standard short crime-thriller: Couple's new house was scene of violent murder

Dream House

1998, (USA), UPN-TV, color, 95 mins.
W: Timothy Busfield, Jennifer Dale (*Laura*), Brennan Elliot (*Ray*), Daniel Petronijevic (*Michael*), Lisa Jakub (*Jenny*)
TVM, standard SF-thriller

The Dreaming

1989, (Austral), color, 87 mins.
Minor fantasy-thriller: Young doctor enters weird dimension

The Dream Killer

see *The Night Walker*

Dreamland Adventures
1907, (GB), Urban, b&w, 540 ft. (164.6m)
<u>D</u>: Walter R. Booth
Standard fantasy short: Doll and gollywog take children to Arctic

A Dreamland Frolic
1919, (GB), Globe, b&w, 2,000 ft. (609.6m)
<u>W</u>: Lupino Lane (*Nipper*)
Standard comedy-fantasy: Schoolboy dreams he dons father's clothes, has night out on town

Dream Lover
1986, (USA), MGM-UA, color, 104 mins.
<u>W</u>: Kristy McNichol, Paul Shenar, Justin Deas, Ben Masters
<u>D</u>: Alan J. Pakula   <u>SCR</u>: Jon Boorstin   <u>PHOTOG</u>: Sven Nykvist
Modest thriller: Nightmares plague young woman

Dream Man
1995, (USA), Cinemax, Made for TV, color, 94 mins.
<u>W</u>: Patsy Kensit, Bruce Greenwood, Andrew McCarthy
TVM, standard thriller: Clairvoyant policewoman drawn to murder suspect

Dream Master: The Erotic Invador
1998, (USA), color, 90 mins.
<u>W</u>: Patrick Ahern, Cassandra Leigh
Minor eroto-SF: Research scientist helps coeds overcome erotic dreams

Dream No Evil
1975, (USA), color, 93 mins.
<u>W</u>: Edmond O'Brien, Brooke Mills, Marc Lawrence, Arthur Franz
<u>D</u>: John Hughes
Minor thriller: Disturbed woman commits bizarre murders

The Dream of a Hindu Beggar
see Le Reve du Pariah

The Dream of an Opium Fiend
see Le Reve d'un Fumeur d'Opium

The Dream of an Opium Smoker
see Le Reve d'un Fumeur d'Opium

The Dream of a Rarebit Fiend
1906, (USA), Edison, b&w
<u>W</u>: John P. Brown
<u>D</u> & <u>PHOTOG</u>: Edwin S. Porter, from a story by Winsor McCay
Modest adventure fantasy: Overeater's nightmare

Dream of Olwen
see While I Live

The Dream of Shakespeare
see Le Reve de Shakespeare

Dream Paintings
1912, (GB), Ivy Close Films/Butcher, b&w, 1,000 ft. (304.8m)
<u>W</u>: Ivy Close (*The Model*), Austin Melford (*The Artist*)
<u>WRIT & D</u>: Elwin Neame
Standard fantasy: Artist dreams model poses as famous paintings

Dreamscape
1984, (USA), Zupnik-Curtis/20th-Fox, color, 106 mins.
<u>W</u>: Dennis Quaid (*Alex Gardner*), Max von Sydow (*Dr. Paul Novotny*), Christopher Plummer (*Bob Blair*), Eddie Albert (*The President*), Kate Capshaw (*Jane DeVries*), David Patrick Kelly (*Tommy Ray Glatman*), George Wendt (*Charlie Prince*), Larry Gelman (*Mr. Webber*), Cory "Bumpers" Yothers (*Buddy*), Larry Cedar (*The Snakeman*), Jana Taylor, Redmond Gleeson, Peter Jason, Chris Mulkey
<u>D</u>: Joseph Ruben   <u>SCR</u>: David Loughery, Chuck Russell & Joseph Ruben   <u>STORY</u>: David Loughery   <u>PHOTOG</u>: Brian Tufano   <u>VS-FX</u>, Peter Kuran   <u>MUSIC</u>: Maurice Jarre
Modest SF-fantasy: Secret experiments enable telepath to enter dreams of others

Dreams Come True
1984, (USA), color, 95 mins.
<u>W</u>: Michael Sanville, Stephanie Shuford
<u>D</u>: Max Kalmanowicz
Minor comedy-romance: Young lovers master out-of-body travel

Dreams in the Witch House
see Curse of the Crimson Altar

Dream Slayer
see Blood Song

Dreams of Toyland
1908, (GB), Alpha Trading Co./Walturdaw, b&w, 350 ft. (106.7m)
<u>WRIT & D</u>: Arthur Cooper
Minor fantasy short: Boy dreams toys come to life

Dreams That Money Can Buy
1944-46, (USA), Hans Richter Prods., b&w, 84 mins.
<u>W</u>: Julien Levy, Max Ernst, Darius Milhaud
<u>D & SCR</u>: Hans Richter, Fernand Leger, Max Ernst, Man Ray, et al.   <u>MUSIC</u>: John Cage
Anthology of short subjects celebrating surrealism: **Desire, The Girl with the Prefabricated Heart, Ballet and Circus, Narcissus,** *3 others*

Dream Without End
see Dead of Night (1945)

Die Dreizehn Koffer des Herrn O.F. (The Thirteen Trunks of Mr. O.F.)
1931, (Ger), Tobis, b&w
<u>W</u>: Peter Lorre, Hedy Kiesler (*Lamarr*)
<u>D</u>: Alexis Granowski
Standard thriller: Mystery man suspected of murder

Dressed to Kill
1941, (USA), 20th-Fox, b&w, 72 mins.
<u>W</u>: Lloyd Nolan (*Michael Shayne*), William Demarest (*Insp. Pierson*), Mary Beth Hughes (*Joanne La Marr*), Sheila Ryan (*Connie Earle*), Ben Carter (*Rusty*), Milton Parsons (*Max Allaron*), Virginia Brissac (*Emily*), Henry Daniell (*Julian Davis*), Erwin Kalser (*Otto Kuhn*), Charles Arnt (*Hal Brennon*), Charles Trowbridge (*David Earle*), Dick Rich (*Al*), Charles Wilson, Hamilton MacFadden, Mantan Moreland, May Beatty
<u>D</u>: Eugene Forde   <u>SCR</u>: Stanley Rauh & Manning O'Connor   based on Richard Burke's novel *The Dead Take No Bows* and characters created by Brett Halliday   <u>PHOTOG</u>: Glen MacWilliams
Standard thriller: Detective probes theatrical producer's murder ('Michael Shayne' series)

Dressed to Kill
1946, (USA), Univ, b&w, 72 mins.
<u>W</u>: Basil Rathbone (*Sherlock Holmes*), Nigel Bruce (*Dr. John Watson*), Patricia Morison (*Hilda Courtney*), Carl Harbord, Edmund Breon, Harry Cording, Holmes Herbert, Frederic Worlock, Ian Wolfe, Patricia Cameron
<u>P & D</u>:Roy William Neill   <u>SCR</u>: Leonard Lee, from characters created by Sir Arthur Conan Doyle   <u>PHOTOG</u>: Maury Gertsman   <u>MUSIC</u>: Milton Rosen
A.k.a. Sherlock Holmes and the Secret Code
Minor thriller, Universal's final "Sherlock Holmes" film: Music box holds clue to mystery

Dressed to Kill
1980, (USA), Samuel Z. Arkoff-Geo. Litto/Filmways, color, 102 mins.
<u>W</u>: Michael Caine (*Dr. Robert Elliott*), Angie Dickinson (*Kate Miller*), Nancy Allen (*Liz*), Keith Gordon (*Peter*), Susanna Clemm (*Bobbi*), Dennis Franz (*Det. Marino*), Ken Baker (*Warren Lockman*), Brandon Maggart (*Cleveland Sam*), David Margulies (*Dr. Levy*), Anthony Boyd Scriven, Mary Davenport (*The Woman in the Coffee Shop*), Robert Lee Rush (*Hood #1*), Fred Weber (*Mike Miller*), Sean O'Rinn (*The Museum Cabbie*), Bill Randolph (*The Chase Cabbie*)
<u>P</u>: George Litto   <u>WRIT & D</u>: Brian De Palma   <u>PHOTOG</u>: Ralf Bode   <u>MUSIC</u>: Pino Donaggio
Major thriller: Assassin stalks women

The Drifter
1988, (USA), Pacific Trust/Concorde, color, 90 mins
<u>W</u>: Kim Delaney, Timothy Bottoms, Al Shannon, Miles O'Keeffe, Larry Brand (*Detective*) Loren Haines, Thomas Wagner
<u>WRIT & D</u>: Larry Brand   <u>MUSIC</u>: Rick Conrad
Minor thriller: Murderous wanderer menaces girl

Driller Killer
1979, (USA), Rochelle, color, 90 mins.
<u>W</u>: Carolyn Marz, Jimmy Laine, Baybi Day, Peter Yellen, Bob DeFrank, Harry Schultz, Tony Coca Cola & The Roosters
<u>P</u>: Rochelle Weisberg   <u>D</u>: Abel Ferrera   <u>SCR</u>: Nicholas St. John   <u>PHOTOG</u>: Ken Kelsch   <u>MUSIC</u>: Joseph Delia
blurb: "Several pints of blood will spill when teenage girls confront his drill!"
Standard gore-fest: Psycho stalks beauties

Drink
1907, (GB), Hepworth, b&w, 200 ft. (60.1m)78 mins.
<u>D</u>: Lewin Fitzhamon
Minor comedy-fantasy short: Drunkard dreams motorist in fur coat is bear

Drive-In Massacre
1976, (USA), New American, color
<u>W</u>: Adam Lawrence
<u>P & D</u>: Stuart Segall, Jake Barnes   <u>SCR</u>: John Goff & Buck Flower
Minor horror-thriller: Madman kills drive-in theater patrons

Drop Dead Fred
1991, (USA), Polygram/Working Title/New Line, color, 99 mins.
<u>W</u>: Phoebe Cates, Rik Mayall, Marsha Mason, Tim Matheson, Carrie Fisher, Keith Charles, Ron Eldard, Ashley Peldon, Daniel Gerroll
<u>D</u>: Ate De Jong   <u>SCR</u>: Carlos Davis & Anthony Fingleton, from a story by Elizabeth Livingston   <u>PHOTOG</u>: Peter Deming   <u>MUSIC</u>: Randy Edelman
Standard comedy-fantasy: Fantasy playmate returns to plague grown woman

Drowsy Dick's Dream
1909, (GB), B&C/Cosmo, b&w, 510 ft. (155.4m)
<u>W:</u> Nelson Keys (*Drowsy Dick*), Ivy Martinek (*The Queen*)
<u>D:</u> H.O. Martinek
Minor fantasy short: Tramp dreams he rescues queen, is crowned king

The Drum
1938, (GB), London-Denham/UA, color, 104 mins.
<u>W:</u> Sabu (*Prince Azim*), Raymond Massey (*Prince Ghul*), Valerie Hobson (*Marjorie Brook*), Roger Livesey (*Tony Carruthers*), David Tree (*Lt. Escott*), Desmond Tester (*Bill Holder*), Archibald Batty (*Maj. Bond*), Francis L. Sullivan (*The Governor*), Amid Taftazani (*Mohammed Khan*), Frederick Culley (*Dr. Murphy*), Martin Walker (*Herrick*), Edward Lexy (*Sgt.-Maj. Kernel*), Roy Emerton (*Wafadar*), Charles Oliver (*Rejab*), Julien Mitchell (*The Sgt.*), Alf Goddard (*Pte. Kelly*), Gerald Campion (*The Boy*), Leo Genn
<u>P:</u> Alexander Korda <u>D:</u> Zoltan Korda <u>STORY:</u> Lajos Biro, Arthur Wimperis, Patrick Kirwin & Hugh Gray, from a novel by A.E.W. Mason
*USA retitle, **Drums**, reissued 1944*
Standard adventure-thriller: Boy prince thwarts usurping uncle

Drums of Africa
1963, (USA), MGM, color, 92 mins.
<u>W:</u> Frankie Avalon, Mariette Hartley
*Standard adventure-thriller. Remake: **King Solomon's Mines***

Drums of Fu Manchu
1940, (USA), b&w, 150 mins.
<u>W:</u> Henry Brandon, Robert Kellard, George Cleveland, Gloria Franklin, Dwight Frye, Tom Chatterton
<u>D:</u> William Witney & John English, from characters created by Sax Rohmer
Standard thriller (culled from 15-chapter serial): Oriental mastermind seeks Genghis Khan's sceptre

The Drums of Jeopardy
1923, (USA), Hoffman Prods./Truart, b&w, 7 reels (6,529 ft./1990m)
<u>W:</u> Elaine Hammerstein (*Dorothy Burrows*), Jack Mulhall (*Jerome Hawksley*), Wallace Beery (*Gregor Karlov*), David Torrence (*Cutty*), Maude George (*Olga Andrevich*), Forrest Seabury (*Stefani*), Eric Mayne (*Banker Burrows*)
<u>D:</u> Edward Dillon <u>ADAPT:</u> Arthur Hoerl, from a 1920 story by Harold MacGrath <u>PHOTOG:</u> James Diamond
Standard thriller: Emeralds, inserted in drums, exert sinister power

Drums of Jeopardy
1931, (USA), Tiffany, b&w, 75 mins.
<u>W:</u> Warner Oland (*Gregor Karlov*), June Collyer, Lloyd Hughes, Ann Brody, George Fawcett, Ernest Hilliard, Florence Lake, Wallace MacDonald, Hale Hamilton, Mischa Auer, Clara Blandick
<u>D:</u> George B. Seitz <u>SCR:</u> Florence Ryerson, from Harold MacGrath's novel <u>PHOTOG:</u> Arthur Reed
Standard melodrama: Lust for revenge drives doctor mad

Drums of Tahiti
1954, (USA), Col, color, 73 mins.
<u>W:</u> Dennis O'Keefe, Patricia Medina, Francis L. Sullivan, George Keymas, Sylvia Lewis
<u>P:</u> Sam Katzman <u>D:</u> William Castle <u>SCR:</u> Robert E. Kent & Douglas Heyes <u>PHOTOG:</u> Lester H. White <u>MUSIC DIR:</u> Mischa Bakaleinikoff
Standard adventure-thriller: Romance and gun-running, hurricane and volcanic eruption in South Seas paradise

Drums of the Congo
1942, (USA), Univ, b&w, 59 mins
<u>W:</u> Stu Erwin, Ona Munson, Don Terry, Peggy Moran, Dorothy Davidridge
Standard adventure-thriller: Explorers vs. green hell

Drums O'Voodoo
1934, (USA), b&w, 70 mins.
<u>W:</u> Laura Bowman, J. Augustus Smith, Edna Barr
<u>D:</u> Arthur Hoerl
*A.k.a. **She Devil***
Minor thriller (all-Black feature): Voodoo princess fights town villain

The Drunkard's Conversion
1901, (GB), R.W. Paul, b&w, 80 ft. (24.4m)
<u>D:</u> Walter R. Booth
*A.k.a. **The Horrors of Drink***
Minor fantasy short: Drunk sees gnome, snake and Spirit of Temperance

The Drunkard's Dream
1908, (GB), Gaumont, b&w, 312 ft. (95.1m)
<u>D:</u> Alf Collins
Standard melodrama: Sot reforms after dreaming of killing wife and her lover

Dual Alibi
1947, (GB), British Nat'l/Pathe, b&w, 81 mins.
<u>W:</u> Herbert Lom (*Jules/Georges de Lisle*), Phyllis Dixey (*Penny*), Terence de Marney (*Mike Bergen*), Ben Williams (*Charlie*), Ronald Frankau (*Vincent Barney*), Abraham Sofaer (*The Judge*), Eugene Deckers (*The Ringmaster*), Beryl Measor

(*Gwen*), Clarence Wright (*Mangin*), Harold Berens (*Ali*), Sebastian Cabot (*The Official*), Cromwell Brothers Trapeze Act
<u>P:</u> Louis H. Jackson <u>D:</u> Alfred Travers <u>SCR:</u> Alfred Travers, Stephen Clarkson, & Vivienne Ades <u>STORY:</u> Renault Capes
Standard thriller: Trapeze star poses as twin to recoup stolen lottery ticket

The Duality of Man
1910, (GB), Wrench Films, b&w, 580 ft. (176.8m)
based on Robert Louis Stevenson's *Dr. Jekyll and Mr. Hyde*
Standard horror-thriller: Doctor's potion makes him steal bank notes and kill fiancee's father

Dublin Nightmare
1958, (GB), Pennington-Eady/RFD, b&w, 64 mins.
<u>W:</u> William Sylvester (*John Kevin*), Marla Landi (*Anna*), Richard Leech (*Steven Lawlor*), William Sherwood (*Edward Dillon*), Harry Hutchinson (*The Vulture*), Pat O'Sullivan (*O'Callaghan*), Jack Cunningham (*Insp. O'Connor*)
<u>P:</u> Jon Pennington & David Eady <u>D:</u> John Pomeroy <u>STORY:</u> John Tully
Standard thriller: Photographer finds "murdered" friend is IRA leader

Duel
1972, (USA), Univ, color, 90 mins.
<u>W:</u> Dennis Weaver (*David Mann*), Eddie Firestone (*The Cafe Owner*), Gene Dynarski (*The Man in the Cafe*), Tim Herbert (*The Gas Station Attendant*), Charles Seel (*The Old Man*), Alexander Lockwood (*The Old Man in the Car*), Amy Douglas (*The Old Woman in the Car*), Shirley O'Hara (*The Waitress*), Lucille Benson (*The Lady at Snakerama*), Cary Loftin (*The Truck Driver*), Dale Van Sickle (*The Car Driver*), Lou Frizzell
<u>D:</u> Steven Spielberg <u>SCR:</u> Richard Matheson <u>PHOTOG:</u> Jack A. Marta <u>MUSIC:</u> Billy Goldenberg
TVM (but also shown theatrically), classic thriller: Mysterious truck murderously pursues motorist

Duel at the Rio Grande
1962, (It), Teleworld/Astral-TV, color, Dyaliscope, 93 mins
<u>W:</u> Sean Flynn, Gaby Andre, Armando Calvo, Folco Lulli, Danielle De Metz
<u>D:</u> Mario Caiano
*Standard adventure-thriller, remake of **The Mark of Zorro**: Debonair swordsman opposes tyrannical governor*

Le Duel d'Hamlet (Hamlet's Duel)
1900, (Fr), b&w
<u>W:</u> Sarah Bernhardt
<u>D:</u> Clement Maurice, from Shakespeare's play *Hamlet*
Classic short: Prince routs kingdom's evil influences

Duel in Space
1954, (USA), Reed, b&w, 78 mins
<u>W:</u> Richard Crane
*A.k.a. **Silver Needle in the Sky***
Standard space-opera, feature culled from 1950's teleseries "Rocky Jones, Space Ranger:" Ambassadors escorted to space conference

Duel in the Jungle
1954, (GB), WB, color, 102 mins.
<u>W:</u> Dana Andrews, Jeanne Crain, David Farrar
<u>D:</u> George Marshall
Standard adventure-thriller

Duel of the Space Monsters
*see **Frankenstein Meets the Space Monster***

Duel of the Titans
*see **Romolo e Remo***

Due to an Act of God
1983, (W. Ger), color, 106 mins.
<u>W:</u> Renate Schroeter, Wigand Witting, Johanna Rudolph, Antje Hagen, Mathias Nitschke
<u>D:</u> Rainer Boldt
Gripping thriller: German village imperiled when carriers of liquid nitrogen and radioactive waste collide

The Duke's Gold
*see **L'Or du Duc***

The Dumb Girl of Portici
1916, (USA), Univ, b&w, 10 reels
<u>W:</u> Anna Pavlova [Pavlova's only film], Rupert Julian, Lois Wilson, Boris Karloff (debut)
<u>D:</u> Lois Weber
Standard melodrama

The Dumb Man of Manchester
1908, (GB), Haggar & Sons, b&w
<u>W:</u> Will Haggar Jr., Jenny Linden, Will Desmond
<u>D:</u> William Haggar, from a play by Barnabus Rayner
Standard ??? thriller: ??? locates locket and witness to save mute from murder charge

Dumbo
1941, (USA), Walt Disney, color, 64 mins.
VOICES: Edward Brophy, Herman Bing, Sterling Holloway, Cliff Edwards, Verna Felton
D: Ben Sharpsteen   SCR: Joe Grant & Dick Huemer

Dummy of Death
see Hipnosis

The Dummy Talks
1943, (GB), British Nat'l, b&w, 85 mins.
W: Jack Warner (*Jack*), Claude Hulbert (*Victor Harbord*), Beryl Orde (*Beryl*), Derna Hazel (*Maya*), Manning Whiley (*Russell Warren*), Ivy Benson (*Ivy*), Charles Carson (*Marvello*), G.H. Mulcaster (*Piers Har-riman*), John Carol (*Jimmy Royce*)
D: Oswald Mitchell   SCR: Michael Barringer, from a story by Con West & Jack Clifford
Standard crime-thriller: Midget poses as dummy, unmasks killer

Dunderklumpen
1974, (Swed), color
W: Beppe Wolgers
Minor musical fantasy, blend of live action & animation: Fairytale characters have adventure

Dune
1984, (USA), Dino De Laurentiis/Univ, color, 136 mins.(also 190 mins)
W: Max von Sydow (*Dr. Kynes*), Kyle MacLachlan (*Paul Atreides*), Silvana Mangano (*Rev. Mother Ramallo*), Sean Young (*Chani Kynes*), Jose Ferrer (*The Emperor*), Francesca Annis (*Lady Jessica*), Kenneth McMillan (*Baron Harkonnen*), Linda Hunt (*The Shadout Mapes*), Everett McGill (*Stilgar*), Jack Nance (*Nefud*), Patrick Stewart (*Gurney Halleck*), Richard Jordan (*Duncan*), Sian Phillips (*Rev. Mother Heuen Mohian*), Sting (*Feyd*), Jurgen Prochnow (*Duke Atreides*), Judd Omen (*Jamis*), Dean Stockwell (*Dr. Yueh*), Paul Smith (*"Beast" Rabban*), Freddie Jones (*Thufir Hawat*), Virginia Madsen, Brad Dourif, Alicia Roanne Witt
D & SCR, David Lynch, from Frank Herbert's classic SF novel   PHOTOG: Freddie Francis   SPCL-FX: Barry Nolan & Albert J. Whitlock   MUSIC: Toto
Lavish but confused, overly-ambitious SF-adventure: Futuristic messiah leads planetary revolt

Dune Warriors
1992, (USA), color, 80 mins.
W: David Carradine, Rick Hill, Luke Askew, Blake Boyd(*William*), Jillian McWhirter (*Val*)
D: Cirio H. Santiago
Minor SF-thriller: Wandering mercenary helps futuristic village battle warlord

The Dungeon
1922, (USA), Micheaux Film Corp., b&w, 7 reels (6,300 ft./1920.2m)
W: William E. Fountaine, Shingzie Howard, J. Kenneth Goodman, W.B.F. Crowell, Earle Browne Cook, Blanche Thompson
Standard thriller: Villainous "Bluebeard" hypnotizes woman. (All-black cast)

The Dungeonmaster
1985, (USA), Empire, color, 85 mins.
W: Jeffrey Byron (*Paul Bradford*), Richard Moll (*Mestema*), Leslie Wing (*Gwen*), Gina Calabrese, Daniel Dion, Barbara Mueller, Ed Dorini, Bill Bestolarides, P.J. Miller, Nina Baker, Scott Campbell, Don Moss, Alanna Roth, Jack Reed, Kim Connell, Janet Welsh, Carol Solomon, Cleve Hall, Ken Hall, Jackie Gross, Guy Simmons, Jeff Rayburn, James Di Mino, Lonnie Hashimoto, E. Lee Nation, David Karp, James Chestnut, Curtis Lee Garrick, Beverly Miko, Randy Piper, Peter Kent, Blackie Lawless, Chris Holmes, Eddie Zammit, Tony Richards, Sal Fondacaro, Phil Fondacaro, Anthony T. Genova III, Mack Ademia, Danny Dick, Kurt Braun, Suzanne Lelong, Marika Zoll, Brian R. Carson, Diane Carter, Jerri Plinthus, Michael Jones, Randy Popplewell, Felix Cilla, De Ette Adams
D: Rosemarie Turko, John Buechler, Charles Band, David Allen, Steve Ford, Peter Manoogian & Ted Nicolaou   SCR: Rosemarie Turko, John Buechler, Charles Band, David Allen, Jeffrey Byron, Peter Manoogian & Ted Nicolaou   ORIG. STORY: Allen Actor   PHOTOG: Mac Ahlberg   VS-FX: David Allen   MUSIC: Richard Band & Shirley Walker
Minor episodic SF-fantasy: Computer whiz challenged by alien villain

The Dungeon of Death
1915, (GB), Weston Feature Film/Gaumont, b&w, 3,100 ft. (944.9m)
W: George Keen, Alice Inward, Lily Saxby, James Lindsay, Gordon Begg
D: Charles Weston
Standard thriller: Mad actor captures blackmailing producer

Dungeons of Harrow
see Dungeons of Horror

Dungeons of Horror
1962, (USA), Herts-Lion, color, 74 mins.
W: Russ Harvey, Helen Hogan, Eunice Grey, Don Russell, Bill McNulty, Maurice Harris, Lee Morgan, Pat Boyette
D: Pat Boyette   SCR: Henry Garcia
A.k.a. Dungeons of Harrow
Minor thriller: Castaways trapped by evil count

Dungeons of Terror
see Vierges et Vampires

The Dunwich Horror
1970, (USA), AIP, color, 90 mins.
W: Sandra Dee (*Nancy*), Dean Stockwell (*Wilbur*), Sam Jaffe (*Shateley*), Lloyd Bochner (*Dr. Cary*), Joanne Moore Jordan (*Lavinia*), Ed Begley (*Dr. Armitage*), Jason Wingreen (*The Police Chief*), Donna Baccala (*Elizabeth*), Barboura Morris (*Mrs. Cole*), Michael Fox (*Dr. Raskin*), Michael Haynes (*The Guard*), Talia Coppola (Shire) (*Cora*), Beech Dickerson
P: James H. Nicholson & Samuel Z. Arkoff   D: Daniel Haller   SCR: Curtis Lee Hanson, Henry Rosenbaum & Ronald Silkosky, from H.P. Lovecraft's short story, 1933   PHOTOG: Richard C. Glouner   MUSIC: Les Baxter
Modest horror-fantasy, most effective of Lovecraft cinemadaptations: College student summons demon gods

The Dusseldorf Vampire
see Le Vampire de Dusseldorf

Dust Devil
1993, (USA-GB) color, 108 mins.
W: Robert Burke, Chelsea Field, Zakes Mokae, Rufus Swart, John Matskikiza, William Hootkins, Marianne Sagebrecht
D & SCR: Richard Stanley   MUSIC: Simon Boswell
Standard fantasy-thriller: Three travelers meet demon in Namibia's desert

Dusting Cliff Seven
1996, (USA), color, 90 mins.
W: Nancy Allen, Lance Henriksen

The Dustman's Nightmare
1915, (GB), EcKo/YCC, b&w, 541 ft. (164.9m)
W: Albert Egbert (*Bill*), Seth Egbert (*Walter*)
D: W.P. Kellino   STORY, Albert & Seth Egbert
Minor comedy-fantasy short: Dustman buys rubber face, dreams about it

The Dust of Egypt
1915, (USA), Vitagraph, b&w
W: Antonio Moreno, Edith Storey
Standard melodrama

The Dwarf and the Giant
1902, (Fr), Star, b&w, 20m (65.6 ft./1.1 mins.)
D: Georges Melies
A.k.a. 'The Long and Short of It
Standard fantasy

The Dybbuk
1938, (Pol), b&w, 123 mins.
W: Leon Liebgold, Lili Liliana, Max Bozyk, Dina Halpern, Abraham Morevsky, Isaac Samberg, Moshe Lipman
D: Michael Waszynsky, from a story by Sholom Anski
Classic fantasy: Evil spirit released

The Dying Detective
1921, (GB), Stoll, b&w, 2,273 ft. (692.8m)
W: Eille Norwood (Sherlock Holmes), Hubert Willis (Dr. John Watson), Cecil Humphreys (Culverton Smith), Mme. d'Esterre (Mrs. Hudson)
D: Maurice Elvey   SCR: William J. Elliott, from the writings of Sir Arthur Conan Doyle
Standard crime-thriller (episode in "Adventures of Sherlock Holmes" series)

Dying Game
1994, (USA), color, 85 mins.
W: Michael Hughes, Mathea Webb, D.J. Boozer
D: Kris Hughes
Standard thriller: Stalker slays sorority girls

Dying Room Only
1973, (USA), Lorimar/ABC-TV, color, 73 mins.
W: Cloris Leachman, Ross Martin, Louise Latham, Dabney Coleman, Ned Beatty, Ron Feinberg
D: Philip Leacock   STORY & TELEPLAY, Richard Matheson
TVM, standard thriller: Woman seeks vanished husband

Dying to Remember
1993, (USA), UPN-TV, color, 87 mins.
W: Melissa Gilbert, Ted Shackelford, Scott Plank, Christopher Stone, Jay Robinson, Kat Green, Wade Anderson, Sandra Nelson
D: Arthur Allan Seidelman   TELEPLAY: George Schenck, Frank Cardea & Brian L. Ross   PHOTOG: Glen MacPherson   MUSIC: Jay Gruska
TVM, standard thriller: Hypnotherapy regresses woman to past life

The Dying Truth
1991, (USA), color, 80 mins.
W: David Carradine, Stephanie Beacham, Stephen Greif, Larr Carby, Stephan Chase, Lesley Dunlop
D: John Hough
Standard thriller: Dying prisoner seeks crime's solution

The Eagle Has Two Heads
see *L'Aigle a Deux Tetes*

The Eagle's Nest
see *Rescued From an Eagle's Nest*

Earth Angel
1991, (USA), ABC-TV, color
W: Cathy Podewell, Cindy Williams (*Judith*), Mark Hamill (*Wayne*), Erik Estrada (*Duke*), Rainbow Harvest (*Cindy*), Roddy McDowall (*Tatum*), Brian Krause (*Mike*), Alan Young, Dustin Nguyen
D: Joe Napolitano **TELEPLAY:** Nina Shengold **PHOTOG:** Stan Taylor **MUSIC:** Kevin Klingler
TVM, minor fantasy: Heavenly envoy causes distress

Earthbound
1940, (USA), 20th-Fox, b&w, 67 mins.
W: Warner Baxter, Andrea Leeds
D: Irving Pichel **MUSIC:** Alfred Newman
Standard melodrama, dead man returns. Remake of 1920 film

Earthbound
1981, (USA), Taft Int'l, color, 94 mins.
W: Burl Ives (*Ned*), Christopher Connelly (*Zef*), Meredith MacRae (*Lara*), Joseph Campanella (*Conrad*), Elissa Leeds (*Teva*), Marc Gilpin (*Dalem*), Todd Porter (*Tommy*), Stuart Pankin (*The Deputy*), John Schuck (*The Sheriff*), Doodles Weaver (*Sterling*), Joey Forman (*Madden*), Peter Isacksen (*Willy*), John Hansen (*The 1st Rider*), Mindy Dow (*Rosie*), Tiger Thompson (*Butch*), Daryl Bingham (*Pudge*), Michael Witt (*Snodgrass*), April Gilpin (*Bridgette*), Michael Ruud (*The Coach*), H.E.D. Redford (*The General*), Jesse Bennett, H.M. Wynant, David Chambers, Craig Clyde, Melvin Hampton, Bill Couch, Travis DeCastro, Tim Eisenhart, Cindy Epple, William Bruce Estey, Jerry Fleck, Richard Hoag, Craig R. Larsen, Gregg R. Larsen, Rick Jury, Zane Parker, Marcia Reider, Kevin Parr, Marc Raymond, Max Robinson, William Howell, Beverly Rowland, Oscar Rowland, Steven Sherman, Dennis Saylor
WRIT & P: Michael Fisher **D:** James Conway **PHOTOG:** Paul Hipp **SPCL-FX:** Harry Woolman **MUSIC:** Bob Summers
Whimsical SF-fantasy: Extraterrestrial family stranded in small-town America

The Earth Dies Screaming
1964, (GB), Lippert/20th-Fox, b&w, 62 mins.
W: Willard Parker (*Jeff Nolan*), Virginia Field (*Peggy Taggett*), Dennis Price (*Quinn Taggett*), Thorley Walters (*Edgar Otis*), Vanda Godsell (*Violet Courtland*), David Spenser (*Mel*), Anna Palk (*Lorna*)
P: Robert L. Lippert & Jack Parsons **D:** Terence Fisher **SCR:** Henry Cass **PHOTOG:** Arthur Lavis **MUSIC:** Elisabeth Lutyens **DESIGN:** George Provis
Standard SF-thriller: Robots from space kill humans, revive corpses as mindless slaves

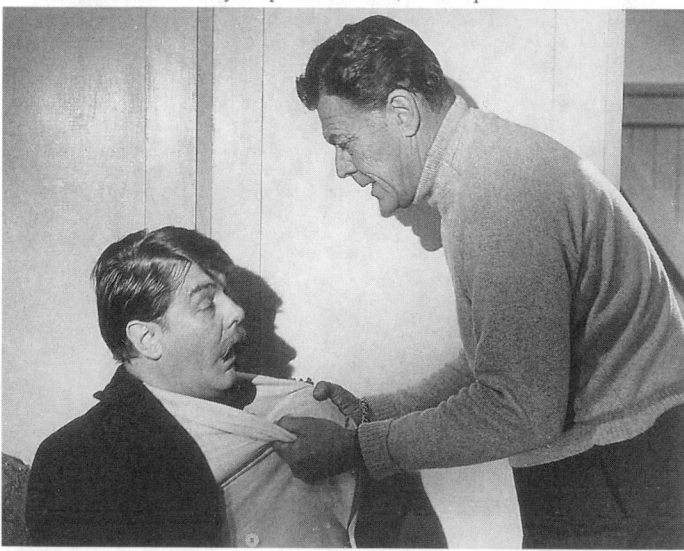

The Earth Dies Screaming: THORLEY WALTERS AND WILLARD PARKER

Earth Girls Are Easy
1989, (USA), Kestrel/Vestron, color, 100 mins.
W: Geena Davis (*Valerie*), Jeff Goldblum (*Mac*), Jim Carrey (*Wiploc*), Damon Wayans (*Zeebo*), Julie Brown (*Candy*), Rick Overton (*Dr. Rick*), Michael McKean (*Woody*), Felix Montano (*Ramon*), Charles Rocket (*Ted*), Larry Linville (*Dr. Bob*), Diane Stilwell (*Robin*), June C. Ellis (*Mrs. Merkin*), Tita Omeze (*Tanya*), Richard Hurst (*Joe the Cop*), Leslie Morris (*Mike the Cop*), Lisa Fuller (*Kikki*), Stacey Travis (*Tammy*), Nicole Kramer (*Missy*), Wayne "Crescendo" Ward (*Demone*), T.C. Diamond, Victor Garron, Steve Lundquist, Jory Husain, Angelyne, Jake Jundeff, Susan Krebs, Lucy Lee Flippin, Rob Large, Gail Neely, Terrence E. McNally, Nedra Volz, April Giuffria, Cristy

Dawson, Carol Infield Sender, Helen Infield Siff, Yetta, Crystal Lujan, Ismael Araujo Jr.
D: Julien Temple **SCR:** Julie Brown, Charlie Coffey, & Terrence E. McNally **PHOTOG:** Oliver Stapleton **MUSIC:** Nile Rodgers **MUSIC-SPRVSR:** Peter Afterman **SONGS:** *Cause I'm a Blond, Summer of Love, I Like 'em Big and Stupid, Brand New Girl, The Ground You Walk On, Throb, Animal Attraction, Hit Me & Body to Body*
Modest SF-comedy-musical: Valley Girl meets space aliens

Earthquake
1974, (USA), Mark Robson-Filmakers/Univ, color, 129 mins.
W: Charlton Heston (*Stuart Graff*), Genevieve Bujold (*Denise Marshall*), Ava Gardner (*Remy Graff*), George Kennedy (*Lew Slade*), Lorne Greene (*Sam Royce*), Richard Roundtree (*Miles Quade*), Barry Sullivan (*Dr. Stockle*), Lloyd Nolan (*Dr. Vance*), Victoria Principal (*Rosa*), Kip Niven (*Walter Russel*), John Randolph (*The Mayor*), Marjoe Gortner (*Jody*), Walter Matthau (*The Drunk*), Gabriel Dell (*Sal*), Monica Lewis (*Barbara*), Pedro Armendariz Jr. (*Chavez*), John S. Ragin (*The Chief Inspector*), Lloyd Gough (*Cameron*), Alan Vint (*Ralph*), Jesse Vint (*Buck*), Scott Hylands (*The Ass't Caretaker*), Tiger Williams (*Corry*), Donald Moffat (*Dr. Harvey Johnson*), Lionel Johnston (*Hank*), George Murdock (*The Colonel*), John Elerick (*Carl Leeds*), Alex A. Brown (*A Pool Player*), Donald Mantooth (*Sid*), Bob Cunningham (*Dr. Frank Ames*), Michael Richardson (*Sandy*), John Dennis (*The Brawny Foreman*), Gene Dynarski (*The Dam Caretaker*), Bob Gravage (*Farmer Mr. Griggs*), Dave Morick (*The Technician*), H.B. Haggerty (*A Pool Player*), Inez Pedroza (*Laura*)
P & D: Mark Robson **SCR:** George Fox & Mario Puzo **PHOTOG:** Philip Lathrop **SPCL-FX:** Albert Whitlock **MUSIC:** John Williams
Standard thriller: Mother Nature levels Los Angeles

Earthquake in New York
1998, (USA), Fox-TV, color, 95 mins.
W: Greg Evigan, Cynthia Gibb, Michael Sarrazin, Gotz Otto, Michael Moriarty, Dylan Provencher, Bryn McAuley, Page Fletcher, Vanessa Evigan, Dan Warry-Smith, Catherine Disher, Eugene A. Clark, Robert Nicholson, Melissa Anderson
D: Terry Ingram **TELEPLAY:** Michael Sloan & D. Brent Mote **PHOTOG:** Barry Bergthorsen **MUSIC:** Christophe Beck
TVM, standard thriller: Nature's upheaval disrupts cop's family

Earth's Final Fury
see *When Time Ran Out*

Earth II
1971, (USA), Wabe/MGM, Made for TV, color, 97 mins.
W: Gary Lockwood (*David*), Anthony Franciosa (*Frank*), Mariette Hartley (*Lisa*), Gary Merrill (*Dietrich*), Inga Swenson (*Ilyana*), Scott Hylands, Hari Rhodes, Lew Ayres
D: Tom Gries **TELEPLAY:** William Read Woodfield & Allan Balter **PHOTOG:** Michel Hugo **MUSIC:** Lalo Schifrin
TVM, standard SF: American space station menaced by Red Chinese

Earth vs. the Flying Saucers
1956, (USA), Col, b&w, 83 mins.
W: Hugh Marlowe, Joan Taylor, Donald Curtis, Morris Ankrum, John Zaremba, Grandon Rhodes, Tom Browne Henry [Thomas B. Henry], Larry Blake, Harry Lauter, Charles Evans, Clark Howat, Frank Wilcox, Alan Reynolds
P: Charles H. Schneer **D:** Fred F. Sears **SCR:** George Worthington Yates, Raymond T. Marcus, & Curt Siodmak, suggested by Maj. Donald Keyhoe's book *Flying Saucers from Outer Space* **PHOTOG:** Fred Jackman **SPCL-FX:** Ray Harryhausen
*orig. co-billed with **The Werewolf** (1956)*
Engrossing SF-thriller (some of Harryhausen's best b&w special effects): Space aliens attack world, scientists race to perfect defense

Earth vs. the Spider
see *The Spider (1958)*

East of Borneo
1931, (USA), b&w, 76 mins.
W: Charles Bickford, Rose Hobart, George Renavent
D: George Melford
Minor melodrama: Wife hunts physician-husband "lost" in jungle

East of Piccadilly
1941, (GB), ABPC/Pathe, b&w, 79 mins.
W: Judy Campbell (*Penny Sutton*), Sebastian Shaw (*Tamsie Green*), Henry Edwards (*The Inspector*), Niall MacGinnis (*Joe*), George Pughe (*Oscar Juloff*), Martita Hunt (*Ma*), George Hayes (*Mark Struberg*), Edana Romney (*Sadie Jones*), Cameron Hall (*George*), Charles Victor (*The Editor*), Bunty Payne (*Tania*)
D: Harold Huth **SCR:** Lesley Storm & J. Lee Thompson, from a novel by Gordon Beckles
*USA retitle, **The Strangler** (PRC, 1941), reissued 1945*
Standard thriller: Novelist and girl reporter unmask silk-stocking strangler

East of Shanghai
see *Rich and Strange*

Earthbound: WARNER BAXTER

The East Side Kids Meet Bela Lugosi
see Ghosts on the Loose

Easy Prey
1986, (USA), color
W: Gerald McRaney
Standard thriller: Teen held captive by psychotic serial killer

Eat and Run
1986, (USA), New World, color, 85 mins.
W: Ron Silver (*Mickey McSorely*), Sharon Schlarth (*Judge Cheryl Cohen*), R.L. Ryan (*Murray Creature*), Robert Silver (*The Pusher*), John J. Fleming (*The Police Captain*), Derek Murcott (*Sorely Mc Sorely*), Tony Moundroukas (*The Zepoli Kid*), Mimi Cecchini (*Grandmother*), Peter Waldren (*Dinkleman*), Frank Nastasi (*The Pick-Up Driver*), George Peter Ryan (*The Narcotics Cop*), Lou Criscuolo (*The Italian Ices Vendor*), Gabriel Barre (*The Mime*), Ruth Jaroslow (*The Crossing Guard*), Tom Mardirosian (*Scarpetti*), Louis Turenne (*Dr. Gretel*), Matt Fischel (*The District Att'y*), Joe Barrett (*The Bartender*), Brian Evers (*The Man on the Phone*), Malachi Throne (*The Opera Announcer*), Anthony Bishop (*The Old Man*)
D: Christopher Hart   **SCR:** Stan Hart & Christopher Hart   **PHOTOG:** Dyanna Taylor   **MUSIC:** Scott Harper
Minor SF-satire: Space alien hungers for Manhattanites

Eaten Alive!
1976, (USA), Virgo-Int'l/New World, color, 96 mins
W: Neville Brand, Stuart Whitman, Carolyn Jones, William Finley, Mel Ferrer, Marilyn Burns, Robert Englund
D: Tobe Hooper   **SCR:** Alvin Fast & Mardi Rustam   **MUSIC:** Wayn Bell
A.k.a. Amok, Death Trap, Horror Hotel Massacre, Legend of the Bayou, Murder on the Bayou, Slaughter Hotel and Starlight Slaughter, orig. to be titled Alligator
Minor thriller: Innkeeper feeds guests to pet crocodiles

Eaten Alive
1980, (It), color, 96 mins
W: Janet Agren, Ivan Rassimov, Mei Mei Lay
D: Umberto Lenzi
Standard horror-thriller

Eaters of the Dead
1998, (USA), color
W: Antonio Banderas, Omar Sharif, Diane Venora
D: John McTiernan, from Michael Crichton's novella
Unusual adventure-melodrama: Arab courtier joins Viking band, circa 900 A.D.

Eaters of the Dead
1999, (USA), Touchstone, color

W: Antonio Banderas
D: John McTiernan   **SCR:** William Wisher & Warren Lewis, from Michael Crichton's 1976 novella
Unusual melodrama: Wanderer joins Viking band

Eating Raoul
1983, (USA), 20th-Fox, color, 87 mins.
W: Paul Bartel, Mary Woronov, Robert Beltran, Richard Paul, Buck Henry, Susan saiger, Ed Begley Jr., Dan Barrows
D: Paul Bartel   **SCR:** Paul Bartel & Richard Blackburn   **PHOTOG:** Gary Thieltges
Minor classic, amusing black comedy: Couple entertains, kills unwary

Ebbie
1995, (USA), Lifetime, Made for TV, color, 95 mins.
W: Susan Lucci, Taran Noah Smith
loosely based on Charles Dickens' A Christmas Carol
TVM, standard fantasy: Businesswoman confronts her past, present and future

Ebenezer
1998, (USA), Nomadic/TNT-TV, color, 95 mins.
W: Jack Palance, Rick Schroder, Amy Locane, Richard Comar, Darcy Dunlop, Susan Coyne, Daryl Shuttleworth, Albert Schultz, Aaron Pearl
D: ken Jubenvill   **TELEPLAY:** Donald Martin, based on Charles Dickens' Christmas Carol   **PHOTOG:** Henry Lebo   **MUSIC:** Bruce Leitl
TVM, standard fantasy: Spirits reform Old West miser

Ebirah, Horror of the Deep
1966, (Jap), Toho/AIP, color, 86 mins.
W: Akira Takarada, Hideo Sunazuka, Toru Watanabe
A.k.a. Godzilla vs. the Sea Monster
Minor SF-thriller: Islanders plagued by prehistoric beasts

An Eccentric Burglary
1905, (GB), Sheffield Photo Co., b&w, 400 ft. (121.9m)
D: Frank Mottershaw
Minor action short: Cops chase vanishing acrobatic thieves

The Eccentric Dancer
1900, (GB), Hepworth, b&w, 50 ft. (15.2m)
D: Cecil M. Hepworth
Standard fantasy: Clown's impossible dance

An Eccentric Sportsman
1912, (GB), Urban Trading Co., b&w, 415 ft. (126.5m)
WRIT & D,: Walter R. Booth
Standard comedy-fantasy: Magical sportsman's troubles with artist, fish, and dog

The Eccentric Thief
1906, (GB), Sheffield Photo Co., b&w, 340 ft. (103.6m)
D: Frank Mottershaw
Standard fantasy short: Fat cop pursues thin thief who vanishes at will

The Eccentric Uncle's Will
1912, (GB), Barker, b&w, 980 ft. (298.7m)
D: Bert Haldane   **STORY:** Rowland Talbot
Standard crime-thriller: Heiress finds codicil, cousin tries to steal it

Ecco
see World by Night No. 2

Echoes
1983, (USA), Herberval/Barry E. Rosenthal, color, 90 mins.
W: Richard Alfieri (*Michael Durant/Alberto Serrano*), Ruth Roman (*Michael's Mother*), Nathalie Nell (*Christine*), Mercedes McCambridge (*Lillian Gerber*), Gale Sondergaard (*Mrs. Edmunds*), Mike Kellin (*Sid Berman*), Barbara Monte-Britton (*The Woman in the Dreams*), John Spencer (*Stephen*), Duncan Quinn (*The Man in the Dreams*), Paul Joynt (*Ed*), Leonard Crofoot (*Danny*), Julie Burger (*Susan*), David M. Brezniak (*The Art Student*), Sheila Coonan (*Rose*), James Dunne (*The Dancer Backstage*), Robin Karfo (*Sheila*), Ron Asher (*1st Stage Manager*), Barry Eric (*2nd Stage Manager*), Leib Lensky (*The Backstage Doorman*), Raaf Baldwin (*The Theatre Doorman*), Damien Akhan (*Damien*), Dennis Wayne (*Christine's Dance Partner*), John Teitsort (*Ropert*), Jan Winarsky (*The Girl in the Red Dress*), Joe Zaloom (*The Truck Driver*), Mike Brown, Ricky Paul, Suzanne McBride, Dickson Lane
D: Arthur Allan Seidelman   **SCR:** Richard J. Anthony   **PHOTOG:** Hanania Baer   **SPCL-FX:** Peter Kunz   **ORIG. MUSIC:** Stephen Schwartz   **SONGS:** *Time Out of Mind, Tailspin, & A Night on the Town*
Minor psychodrama: Visions of past haunt artist

The Echo Murders
1945, (GB), British Nat'l-Strand, b&w, 75 mins.
W: David Farrar (*Sexton Blake*), Pamela Stirling (*Stella Duncan*), Dennis Price (*Dick Warren*), Ferdi Mayne (*Dacier*), Julien Mitchell (*James Duncan*), Patric Curwen (*Dr. Grey*), Dennis Arundell (*Rainsford*), Cyril Smith (*PC Morgan*), Kynaston Reeves (*Beales*)
P: Louis H. Jackson   **D & SCR,** John Harlow, from John Sylvester's novel *Terror of Tregarwyth*

Standard thriller: Detective trails Nazis. 'Sexton Blake' series

Echo of Barbara
1961, (GB), Independent Artists/RFD, b&w, 58 mins.
<u>W:</u> Mervyn Johns (*Sam Roscoe*), Maureen Connell (*Paul Brown*), Paul Stassino (*Caledonia*), Ronald Hines (*Mike Roscoe*), Tom Bell (*Ben*), Brian Peck (*Ted*), Beatrice Varley (*Mrs. Roscoe*), Eddie Leslie (*The Aide*)
<u>P:</u> Arthur Alcott <u>D:</u> Sidney Hayers <u>SCR:</u> John Kruse, from a novel by Jonathan Burke
Standard crime-thriller: Wastrel and stripper seek hidden loot

Echo of Diana
1963, (GB), Butcher's Films, b&w, 61 mins.
<u>W:</u> Vincent Ball (*Bill Vernon*), Betty McDowall (*Joan Scott*), Geoffrey Toone (*Col. Justin*), Clare Owen (*Pam Jennings*), Peter Illing (*Kovali*), Marianne Stone (*Miss Green*), Raymond Adamson (*George*)
<u>P:</u> John I. Phillips <u>D:</u> Ernest Morris STORY: Reginald Hearne
Standard crime-thriller: Reporters expose spy ring

The Eclipse
1907, (Fr), Star, b&w, 172m (564.3 ft./9.5 mins.)
<u>D:</u> Georges Melies
Standard fantasy: Sun and moon have romantic tryst

Eclipse
1977, (GB), Celandine/Gala, color, 85 mins.
<u>W:</u> Tom Conti (*Tom/Geoffrey*), Gay Hamilton (*Cleo*), Gavin Wallace (*Giles*), Paul Cormack (*The Procurator*), David Steuart (*The Sheriff*), Jennie Paul (*The Lady*), Patrick Cadell (*The Lighthouse Keeper*)
<u>P:</u> David Munro <u>D & SCR:</u> Simon Perry, from a novel by Nicholas Wollaston <u>PHOTOG:</u> Mike Berwick <u>MUSIC:</u> Adrian Wagner
Standard thriller: Man kills his twin, makes love to widow

An Eclipse of the Moon
1905, (GB), Williamson/Urban, b&w, 170 ft. (51.8m)
<u>D:</u> James Williamson
USA retitle, **Moonbeams**
Standard comedy short: Page peeps through end of telescope, fools astrologer

Ed and His Dead Mother
1993, (USA), ITC/IRS, color and b&w, 89 mins.
<u>W:</u> Steve Buscemi, Ned Beatty, Miriam Margolyes
<u>D:</u> Jonathan Wacks
A.k.a. **Bon Appetit Mama**
Standard horror-comedy: Cryogenics salesman revives youth's deceased mother.

Edgar Allan Poe
1909, (USA), American Mutoscope & Biograph, b&w, 1 reel
<u>W:</u> Herbert Yost, Linda Arvidson [Mrs. D.W. Griffith]
<u>D:</u> D.W. Griffith
Fictionalized bio of literary genius

Edgar Allan Poe's Tales of Terror
see **Tales of Terror**

The Edge
1997, (USA), color, 118 mins.
<u>W:</u> Anthony Hopkins (Charles Morris), Alec Baldwin (Bob Green), Elle MacPherson, Harold Perrineau

Earthquake: GEORGE KENNEDY

<u>D:</u> Lee Tamahori STORY: David Mamet
Unusual thriller: Love rivals meet vicious bear

Edge of Fear
see **Ella y el Miedo**

Edge of Fury
1958, (USA), UA, b&w, 77 mins.
<u>W:</u> Michael Higgins, Jean Allison, Lois Holmes, Malcolm Lee Beggs, Doris Fesette
P & SCR: Robert Gurney Jr. <u>D:</u> Irving Lerner & Robert Gurney Jr.
Minor thriller: Beachcomber slaughters family

The Edge of Hell
1987, (Can), Thunder/Shapiro, color, 77 mins.
<u>W:</u> Jon-Miki Thor (*John Triton*), Jillian Peri (*Lou Anne*), Frank Dietz (*Roger Eburt*), Dave Lane (*Max*), Clara Pater (*The Mother*), Teresa Simpson (*Randy*), Rusty Hamilton (*The Seductress*), Denise DiCandia (*Dee Dee*), Chris Finkel (*The Father*), Jesse D'Angelo (*The Little Boy*), Carrie Schiffler (*Cindy Connelly*), Liane Abel (*Mary Eburt*), Jim Cirile (*Stig*), Gene Kroth (*Karl*), Tralle O'Farrell, Layra Deans, Nancy Bush, Adam Fried
WRIT & P: Jon-Miki Thor <u>D:</u> John Fasano PHOTOG: Mark MacKay <u>MUSIC:</u> The Tritonz <u>SONGS:</u>, *We Live to Rock, Energy, Danger, Live It Up, Steal Your Thunder, The Challenge, Heads Will Turn & Maybe It's Love*
A.k.a. **Rock 'N' Roll Nightmare**
Minor fantasy-thriller: Gremlins eliminate heavy-metal musicians

Edge of Sanity
1989, (GB-Hung), Allied Vision, color, 86 mins.
<u>W:</u> Anthony Perkins (*Dr. Henry Jekyll/Jack Hyde*), Glynis Barber (*Elizabeth Jekyll*), Sarah Maur-Thorp (*Susannah*), David Lodge (*Underwood*), Ben Cole (*Johnny*), Ray Jewers (*Newcomen*), Jill Melford (*Flora*), Briony McRoberts (*Ann Underwood*), Lisa Davis (*Maria*), Mark Elliot (*Lamont*), Noel Coleman (*Egglestone*), Harry Landis (*The Coroner*), Jill Pearson (*Mrs. Egglestone*), Ruth Burnett (*Margot*), Basil Hoskins (*Mr. Bollingham*), Cathy Murphy (*The Cockney Prostitute*), Carolyn Cortez (*Maggie*), Claudia Udy (*Liza*)
<u>P:</u> Edward Simons & Harry Alan Towers <u>D:</u> Gerard Kikoine <u>SCR:</u> J.P. Felix & Ron Raley, from Robert Louis Stevenson's *The Strange Case of Dr. Jekyll and Mr. Hyde* <u>PHOTOG:</u> Tony Spratling SPCL-FX SPRVSR: Ian Wingrove <u>MUSIC:</u> Frederic Talgorn
Standard eroto-horror: Drug turns Victorian doctor into lecherous monster

Edge of the Axe
1989, (USA), color, 91 mins.
<u>W:</u> Barton Faulks, Christina Marie Lane, Page Moseley, Fred Hollyday
<u>D:</u> Joseph Braunstein
Minor thriller: Mad slasher terrorizes small town

Edipo Re (Oedipus Rex)
1967, (It), color, 110 mins.
<u>W:</u> Silvana Mangano, Alida Valli, Pier Paolo Pasolini
WRIT & D: Pier Paolo Pasolini, based on Sophocles' plays *Oedipus Rex and Oedipus at Colonus*
Classic tragedy: Patricide unknowingly commits incest

Edward Scissorhands
1990, (USA), 20th-Fox, color, 100 mins.
<u>W:</u> Johnny Depp (*Edward Scissorhands*), Winona Ryder (*Kim*), Dianne Wiest (*Peg*), Anthony Michael Hall (*Jim*), Conchata Ferrell (*Helen*), Kathy Baker (*Joyce*), Vincent Price (*The Inventor*), Robert Oliveri (*Kevin*), Dick Anthony Williams (*Officer Allen*), Caroline Aaron (*Marge*), Marti Greenberg (*Suzanne*), O-Lan Jones (*Esmeralda*), Linda Perry (*Cissy*), Alan Arkin (*Bill*), John Davidson (*The TV Host*), Vic-toria Price (*The TV Newswoman*), Biff Yeager (*George*), Susan J. Blommaert (*Tinka*), Bryan Larkin (*Max*), Stuart Lancaster (*The Retired Man*), John McMahon (*Denny*), Gina Gallagher (*The Granddaughter*), Alan Fudge (*The Loan Officer*), Peter Palmer (*The Editor*), Aaron Lustig (*The Psychologist*), Steven Brill (*The Dishwasher Man*), Marc Macaulay, Carmen J. Alexander, Brett Rice, Andrew Clark, Linda Jean Hess, Kelli Crofton, Rosalyn Thomson, Lee Ralls, Kathy Dombo, Eileen Meurer, Bea Albano, Donna Pieroni, Tricia Lloyd, Ken DeVaul, Michael Gaughan, Rex Fox, Sherry Ferguson, Tabetha Thomas
<u>D:</u> Tim Burton <u>SCR:</u> Caroline Thompson STORY: Tim Burton & Caroline Thompson PHOTOG: Stefan Czapsky SPCL-FX: Michael Arbogast, James Reedy, Gary Schaedler, David Wood, & Brian Wood SPCL-FX SPRVSR: Michael Wood <u>MUSIC:</u> Danny Elfman
Superior fantasy-satire: Android seeks human acceptance

Ed Wood
1994, (USA), Touchstone/Buena Vista, b&w, 127 mins.
<u>W:</u> Johnny Depp (*Edward D. Wood Jr.*), Martin Landau (*Bela Lugosi*), Sarah Jessica Harper (*Dolores Fuller*), Bill Murray (*Bunny Breckinridge*), George "The Animal" Steele (*Tor Johnson*), Jeffrey Jones (*Criswell*), Lisa Marie (*Vampira*), Patricia Arquette (*Kathy O'Hara*), G.D. Spradlin (*Reverend Lemon*), Vincent D'Onofrio (*Orson Welles*), Mike Starr (*Georgie Weiss*), Max Casella (*Paul Marco*), Brent Hinkley (*Conrad Brooks*), Juliet Landau (*Loretta King*), Clive Rosengren (*Ed Reynolds*), Norman Alden (*Cameraman Bill*), Leonard Termo (*Make-up Man Harry*), Ned Bellamy (*Dr. Tom Mason*), John Ross (*The Camera Ass't*), Danny Dayton (*The Soundman*), Bill Cusack (*Tony McCoy*), Aaron Nelms (*The Teenage Kid*), Joseph R. Gannascoli (*The Security Guard*),

Biff Yeager (*The Rude Boss*), Carmen Filpi (*The Old Crusty Man*), Lisa Malkiewicz (*Sec'y #1*), Melora Walters (*Sec'y #2*), Conrad Brooks (*The Bartender*), Don Amendolia (*The Salesman*), Tommy Bertelsen (*The Tough Boy*), Reid Cruickshanks (*The Stage Guard*), Gene LeBell (*The Ring Announcer*), Stanley DeSantis (*Mr. Feldman*), Lionel Decker (*Executive #1*), Edmund L. Shaff (*Executive #2*), Jesse Hernandez (*The Wrestling Opponent*), John Rice (*The Conservative Man*), Catherine Butterfield (*The Conservative Wife*), Bobby Slayton (*The TV Show Host*), Gretchen Becker (*The TV Host's Ass't*), King Cotton (*The Hick Backer*), Mary Portzer (*The Backer's Wife*), Don Hood (*The Southern Backer*), Frank Echols (*The Doorman*), Matthew Barry (*The Valet*), Ralph Monaco (*The Waiter*), Anthony Russell (*The Busboy*), Tommy Bush (*The Stage Manager*), Gregory Walcott (*The Potential Backer*), Charles C. Stevenson Jr. (*Another Backer*), Rance Howard (*Old Man McCoy*), Vasek C. Simek (*Prof. Strowski*), Alan Martin (*Vampira's Ass't*), Salwa Ali (*Vampira's Girlfriend*), Rodney Kizziah (*Vampira's Friend*), Korla Pandit (*The Indian Musician*), Hannah Eckstein (*Greta Johnson*), Luc De Schepper (*Karl Johnson*), Vinny Argiro (*The TV Horror Show Director*), Patti Tippo (*The Nurse*), Louis Lombardi (*The Rental House Manager*), Ray Baker (*The Doctor*), James Reid Boyce (*The Theatre Manager*), Ben Ryan Ganger (*The Angry Kid*), Ryan Holihan (*The Frantic Usher*), Charlie Holliday (*The Tourist*), Marc Revivo (*The High School Punk*), Adam Drescher (*Photographer #1*), Ric Mancini (*Photographer #2*), Daniel Riordan (*The Pilot/Strapping Young Man*), Mickey Cottrell (*The Hammy Alien*), Christopher George Simpson (*The Organist*), Robert Binford, Herbert Boche, Linda Rae Brienza, Sylvia Coussa, Joseph Golightly, Marlene Cook, Carrie Starner Hummel, Audrey Cuyler, Ramona Kemp-Blair, Carolyn Kessinger, Matthew Nelson, Nancy Longyear, William Michael Short, Robert Nuffer, George F. Sterne, Cheri A. Williams, Susan Eileen Simpson, Charles Alan Stephenson, Cynthia Ann Wilson **D:** Tim Burton **SCR:** Scott Alexander & Larry Karaszewski **PHOTOG:** Stefan

Edward Scissorhands: JOHNNY DEPP

Czapsky **MUSIC:** Howard Shore
Superior film-bio: Bizarre life of transvestite "B-movie" director

Eegah!
1962, (USA), Fairway-Int'l, color, 93 mins.
W: Arch Hall Jr., Marilyn Manning, Richard Kiel (*Eegah*), William Watters
WRIT & D: Nicholas Merriweather
Minor SF-adventure: Teenaged cave man found in desert

Eerie Midnight Horror Show
see The Tormented (1977)

Effects
1980, (USA), Image Works/International Harmony, color, 87 mins
W: Tom Savini, John Harrison
P: John Harrison & Pasquale Buba   **D & SCR:** Dusty Nelson   **SPCL-FX:** Tom Savini

---

A.k.a. The Manipulator
Standard thriller: Mad film director plots mayhem

The Effects of Too Much Scotch
1903, (GB), Gaumont, b&w, 160 ft. (48.8m)
D: Alf Collins
Minor fantasy short: Scot undresses, clothes come to life

Egghead's Robot
1970, (GB), Interfilm/CFF, color, 56 mins.
W: Keith Chegwin (*Egghead Wentworth*), Jeffrey Chegwin (*Eric*), Kathryn Dawe (*Elspeth*), Roy Kinnear (*The Park Keeper*), Richard Wattis (*Paul Wentworth*), Patricia Routledge (*Mrs. Wentworth*)
D: Milo Lewis   **STORY:** Leif Saxon
Juvenile SF-fantasy: Inventor's son uses father's robot as double

The Egg in Black Art
see L'Oeuf du Sorcier

The Egg-Laying Man
1896, (GB), R.W. Paul, b&w, 50 ft. (15.2m)
W: David Devant
Minor fantasy short: Conjurer produces eggs from head and arms

The Eiger Sanction
1975, (USA), Zanuck-Brown/Malpaso/Univ, color, 125 mins.
W: Clint Eastwood (*Hemlock*), George Kennedy (*Ben Bowman*), Vonetta McGee (*Jemima Brown*), Thayer David (*Dragon*), Heidi Bruehl (*Anna Montaigne*), Jack Cassidy (*Miles Mellough*), Gregory Walcott, Dan Howard, Reiner Schoene, Brenda Venus
D: Clint Eastwood   **SCR:** Warren B. Murphy, Hal Dresner, & Rod Whitaker, from Trevanian's novel   **PHOTOG:** Frank Stanley, John Cleare, Peter Pilafian, Jeff Schoolfield, & Pete White   **MUSIC:** John Williams
Standard action-thriller: Former hit man lured out of retirement, forced to take deadly assignment

8-Man After
1993, (Jap), color
Standard animated SF-thriller: Cyborg detective combats crime

8 1/2
1963, (It), Joseph E. Levine/Embassy, b&w, 135 mins.
W: Marcello Mastroianni, Claudia Cardinale, Anouk Aimee, Sandra Milo, Rossella Falk, Barbara Steele, Mario Pisu, Guido Alberti, Madeleine Lebeau, Jean Rougeul
P: Angelo Rizzoli   **D:** Federico Fellini   **SCR:** Federico Fellini, Tullio Pinelli, Brunello Rondi & Ennio Flaiano   **PHOTOG:** Gianni Di Venanzo   **MUSIC:** Nino Rota
Celebrated psychodrama: Strange fantasies of world-weary movie-maker

18 Again!
1988, (USA), Walter Coblenz/New World, color, 99 mins.
W: George Burns (*Jack Watson*), Charlie Schlatter (*David Watson*), Tony Roberts (*Arnold*), Anita Morris (*Madelyn*), Miriam Flynn (*Betty*), Jennifer Runyon (*Robin*), Red Buttons (*Charlie*), George DiCenzo, Bernard Fox, Kenneth Tigar, Pauly Shore, Anthony Starke
D: Paul Flaherty   **SCR:** Josh Goldstein & Jonathan Prince   **PHOTOG:** Stephen M. Katz   **MUSIC:** Billy Goldenberg
Modest comedy-fantasy: Teen and grandfather switch bodies

The Eighth Wonder
see King Kong (1933)

The Elastic Battalion
see Le Bataillon Elastique

Electra
1961, (Greece), Finos Films/Lopert, b&w, 113 mins.
W: Irene Papas (*Electra*), Aleka Catseli (*Clytemnestra*), Yannis Fertis (*Orestes*), Theano Ioannidou (*The Chorus Leader*), Notis Peryalis (*Electra's Husband*), Takis Emmanouil (*Pylades*), Phoebus Rhazis (*Aegisthus*), Theodore Demetriou (*Agamemnon*), Manos Katrakis (*The Tutor*), Elsie Pitta
WRIT, P & D: Michael Cacoyannis, from Sophocles' play   **PHOTOG:** Walter Lassally   **MUSIC:** Mikis Theodorakis
Brilliant cinemadaptation of timeless classic: Forced to marry beneath her station, princess awaits her brother's vengeful return

Electra
1995, (USA), color, 90 mins.
W: Joe Tab, Shannon Tweed (*Lorna*), Sten Eirik (*Roach*), Katie Griffin (*Mary*)
D: Julian Grant
Standard SF-thriller: Evil scientist pursues teen whose blood contains regenerative properties

Electrical House-Building
1912, (GB), Clarendon, b&w, 495 ft. (150.9m)
D: Percy Stow
Standard fantasy: House built by electrical invention

The Electric Belt

1912, (GB), Cosmopolitan, b&w, 650 ft. (198.1m)
Standard comedy-fantasy: Lazy maid's soldier-suitor becomes electrified, shocks people with sword

The Electric Doll

1914, (GB), Cricks/DFSA, b&w, 485 ft. (147.8m)
<u>D</u>: Edwin J. Collins
Minor comedy-fantasy short: Automaton causes trouble

Electric Dreams

1984, (GB), Virgin/MGM, color, 98 mins.
<u>W</u>: Lenny Von Dohlen (*Miles Harding*), Virginia Madsen (*Madeline*), Maxwell
  Caulfield (*Bill*), Bud Cort (*The Voice of "Edgar"*), Don Fellows (*Ryley*), Alan
  Polonsky (*Frank*), Wendy Miller (*The Clerk*), Harry Rabinowitz (*The
  Conductor*), Miriam Margolyes (*The Ticket Girl*), Holly De Jong (*The
  Receptionist*), Stella Maris (*The Woman*), Mary Doran (*Millie*), Diana Choy
  (*The Checkout Girl*), Koo Stark (*The Actress*), Giorgio Moroder (*The Producer*),
  Dr. Ruth Westheimer (*The Host*), Frazer Smith (*The Discjockey*), Howland
  Chamberlin, Jim Steck, Gary Pettinger, Patsy Smart, Bob Coffey, Mac
  McDonald, Regina Walden
<u>P</u>: Rusty Lemorande & Larry De Way <u>D</u>: Steve Barron <u>SCR</u>: Rusty
  Lemorande <u>PHOTOG</u>: Alex Thomson <u>ORIG. SCORE</u>, Giorgio
  Moroder <u>MUSIC</u>: Culture Club, Heaven 17, Philip Oakey, Jeff Lynne,
  Giorgio Moroder <u>SONGS</u>: *Love is Love & Together in Electric Dreams*
Standard SF-comedy: Home computer controls owner's life

Electric Eskimo

1979, (GB), Monument/CFF, color, 57 mins.
<u>W</u>: Derek Francis (*Kroll*), Diana King (*Aunt Agatha*), Tom Chadbon (*Jenks*),
  David Rowlands (*Prof. Pringle*), Charles Pemberton (*The Constable*), Roger
  Avon (*The Commissioner*), Victor Brooks (*The Sgt.*), Norman Mitchell (*The
  Workman*), Kris Emmerson (*Poochook*), Ian Sears (*Peter*), Debbie Padbury
  (*Kate*), Ivor Danvers (*Dr. Fielding*), Richard Wren (*Newson*), Kenneth
  Kendall (*The Newsreader*)
<u>P & D</u>: Frank Godwin <u>STORY</u>: Frank Godwin & H. MacLeod
  Robertson <u>PHOTOG</u>: Ray Orton <u>MUSIC</u>: Harry Robinson
Standard juvenile thriller: Crooks capture Eskimo boy charged with electrical powers

The Electric Goose

1905, (GB), Gaumont, b&w, 300 ft. (91.4m)
<u>D</u>: Alf Collins
Minor comedy-fantasy short: Boy revives roast goose with father's shock machine

The Electric Leg

1912, (GB), Clarendon, b&w, 500 ft. (152.4m)
<u>D</u>: Percy Stow
Minor comedy-fantasy short: Professor's electrified leg carries one-legged man into girl's dormitory

The Electric Man

see Man-Made Monster

The Electric Servant

1909, (GB), Urban, b&w, 440 ft. (134.1m)
<u>D</u>: Walter R. Booth
Minor SF-fantasy short: Prof. Puddenhead's robot wreaks havoc

Electric Transformation

1909, (GB), Clarendon, b&w, 425 ft. (129.5m)
<u>D</u>: Percy Stow
Minor fantasy short: Professor's invention melts metal and people's faces

The Electric Vitalizer

1910, (GB), Kineto, b&w
<u>D</u>: Walter R. Booth
Minor fantasy short: Man's invention revives waxworks

The Electronic Monster

see Zex

Elektra

see Electra (1961)

The Element of Crime

1984, (Den), Per Holst Filmproduktion/Danish Film Inst./ Palace, color, 104 mins.
<u>W</u>: Michael Elphick, Esmond Knight, Jerold Wells, Me Me Lai, Astrid Henning-
  Jensen, Preben Leerdorff-Rye, Ahmed El Shenawi, Gotha Andersen, Janos
  Hersko, Lars von Trier, Stig Larsson, Harry Harper, Roman Moszkowicz,
  Frederik Casby, Duke Addabayo, Jon Bang Carlsen, Leif Magnusson,
  Camilla Overbye
<u>D</u>: Lars von Trier <u>SCR</u>: Lars von Trier & Niels Vorsel <u>PHOTOG</u>: Tom Elling
  <u>MUSIC</u>: Bo Holton
Bizarre psychodrama: Sex crime detected

Elephant Boy

1937, (GB), London/UA, b&w, 80 mins.
<u>W</u>: Sabu (*Toomai*), Walter Hudd (*Petersen*), Allan Jeayes (*Machua Appa*), Bruce
  Gordon (*Ram Lal*), W.E. Holloway (*Father*), Wilfrid Hyde-White (*The
  Commissioner*), D.J. Williams (*The Hunter*)
<u>P</u>: Alexander Korda <u>D</u>: Robert Flaherty & Zoltan Korda <u>SCR</u>: John Collier

Akos Tolnay & Marcia de Sylva, from Rudyard Kipling's story "Toomai of
the Elephants" <u>MUSIC</u>: John Greenwood
*Standard adventure: Boy leads gov't agents to dancing ground of migrating pachyderms.
Film debut of Sabu. reissued 1943 & 1946*

8¹/₂: MARCELLO MASTROIANNI

Elephant Stampede

see Bomba and the Elephant Stampede

Elevator to the Gallows

see Frantic

The 11th Commandment

see Body Count

The Eleventh Hour

1916, (GB), British Oak/New Agency, b&w, 1,195 ft. (364.2m)
<u>W</u>: James Russell
<u>D</u>: Ernest G. Batley
*Standard crime-thriller: Cinematographer proves gambler framed cousin for murdering their
  stepfather*

The Eleventh Hour

1923, (USA), Fox, b&w, 7 reels (6,820 ft./2078.7m)
<u>W</u>: Shirley Mason (*Barbara Hackett*), Charles (Buck) Jones (*Brick McDonald*),
  Richard Tucker (*Herbert Glenville*), Alan Hale (*Prince Stefan de Bernie*), Walter
  McGrail (*Dick Manley*), June Elvidge (*Estelle Hackett*), Fred Kelsey (*The
  Submarine Cmdr.*), Nigel De Brulier (*Mordecai Newman*), Fred Kohler
  (*Barbara's Uncle*)
<u>D</u>: Bernard J. Durning <u>SCR</u>: Louis Sherwin, from a play by Lincoln J. Carter
  <u>PHOTOG</u>: Don Short
Standard thriller: Mad prince seeks new explosive, intends to conquer world

The Eliminator

1980, (USA), Great Plains Entertainment/Samuel Goldwyn, color, 93 mins.
<u>W</u>: Sam Groom (*Roger*), Jo Ann Harris (*Keegan*), Alexandra Morgan (*Linda*), Steve
  Railsback (*Billy*), Saul Sindell (*Tom*), Dick Butkus (*Joe*), June Lockhart
  (*Marge Lawrence*), Denise Galik (*Mary*), Christine Tudor (*Chris*), Robin Hoff
  (*Carol*), Jere Lea Rae (*Sooty*), Colleen Camp (*Randy*), Bill Johnson (*Bob*)
<u>WRIT & D</u>: Scott Mansfield <u>PHOTOG</u>: Michael Stringer <u>MUSIC</u>:
  Hod David Schudson & Richard S. Thompson <u>SONGS</u>: *Lost in Love Again,
  Back Home, You're the Best that I Remember, Gamblin', Lover's Language, Yesterday
  and You, Long Summer, The Stranger & Orion*
Standard thriller: Killer panics town

The Eliminators
1986, (USA-Sp), Charles Band/Empire, color, 96 mins.
W: Andrew Prine (*Harry Fontana*), Denise Crosby (*Nora Hunter*), Pa-trick
    Reynolds (*John Mandroid*), Conan Lee (*Kuji*), Roy Dotrice (*Abbott Reeves*)
D: Peter Manoogian   SCR: Paul DeMeo & Danny Bilson   PHOTOG: Mac
    Ahlberg
Standard SF-thriller: Android, mercenary, scientist and Ninja team up to fight evil

The Elixir of Life
1901, (GB), Williamson, b&w, 90 ft. (27.4m)
W: Sam Dalton
D: James Williamson
Minor fantasy short: Old man drinks elixir, becomes young

Ella y el Miedo (She and the Fear)
1963, (Sp), C.I.T.A., b&w
W: Virgilio Teixeira, May Heatherly, Georges Rigaud, Luis Marin, Jesus Puente,
    Mario Vico
D: Leon Klimovsky   SCR: Antonio F. Fos   PHOTOG: Manuel Hernandez
    MUSIC: Jose Pagan
USA retitle, Edge of Fear
Standard thriller: Killer stalks

Ellery Queen
1975, (USA), Univ/NBC-TV, color, 100 mins.
W: Jim Hutton (*Ellery Queen*), David Wayne (*Insp. Richard Queen*), Ray Milland
    (*Carson McKell*), Kim Hunter (*Marion McKell*), Monte Markham (*Tom*

Ellery Queen: DAVID WAYNE AND JIM HUTTON

McKell), John Hillerman (*Simon Bremmer*), Gail Strickland (*Gail Stevens*),
    Tom Reese (*Sgt. Velie*), Tim O'Connor (*Ben Waterson*), Franny Michel
    (*Penny*), Vic Mohica (*Ramon*), Nancy (Kovack) Mehta (*Monica Gray*), John
    Larch, Warren Berlinger, Dawn Smith, James Lydon
D: David Greene   TELEPLAY: Richard Levinson & William Link, from charac-
    ters created by Ellery Queen   PHOTOG: Harold Schwartz   MUSIC:
    Elmer Bernstein
TVM, feature pilot for short-lived teleseries: Detective trails killer of famous fashion designer

Ellery Queen and the Murder Ring
1941, (USA), Col, b&w, 70 mins.
W: Ralph Bellamy (*Ellery Queen*), Margaret Lindsay (*Nikki Porter*), Charley
    Grapewin (*Insp. Queen*), George Zucco (*Dr. Janney*), Mona Barrie (*Miss
    Tracy*), James Burke (*Sgt. Velie*), Paul Hurst (*Page*), Blanche Yurka (*Mrs.
    Stack*), Tom Dugan (*Thomas*), Leon Ames (*John Stack*), Jean Fenwick (*Alice
    Stack*), Olin Howland (*Dr. Williams*), Dennis Moore (*Dr. Dunn*), Charlotte
    Wynters (*Miss Fox*)
D: James Hogan   SCR: Eric Taylor & Gertrude Purcell, loosely based on Ellery
    Queen's novel *The Dutch Shoe Mystery*   PHOTOG: James S. Brown Jr.
    MUSIC: Lee Zahler

Routine thriller: Strange events at private hospital

Ellery Queen and the Perfect Crime
1941, (USA), b&w, 68 mins.
W: Ralph Bellamy (*Ellery Queen*), Margaret Lindsay (*Nikki Porter*), Charley
    Grapewin (*Insp. Queen*), Spring Byington (*Carlotta Emerson*), H.B. Warner
    (*Ray Jardin*), James Burke (*Sgt. Velie*), Douglass Dumbrille (*John Mathews*),
    Charles Lane (*Dr. Prouty*), John Beal (*Walter Mathews*), Honorable Wu (*Lee*),
    Sidney Blackmer (*Anthony Rhodes*), Walter Kingsford (*Henry*)
D: James Hogan   SCR: Eric Taylor, from characters created by Ellery Queen
    PHOTOG: James S. Brown Jr.   MUSIC: Lee Zahler
Standard thriller: Detective seeks man's missing son

Ellery Queen: Don't Look Behind You
1971, (USA), Univ/NBC-TV, color, 100 mins.
W: Peter Lawford (*Ellery Queen*), Harry Morgan (*Insp. Richard Queen*), E.G.
    Marshall (*Dr. Cazalis*), Stefanie Powers (*Celeste*), Skye Aubrey (*Christy*),
    Coleen Gray (*Mrs. Cazalis*), Morgan Sterne (*The Police Commissioner*), Bill
    Zuckert (*Sgt. Velie*), Bob Hastings (*Hunter*), Than Wyenn, Tim Herbert,
    Robin Raymond, Buddy Lester, Sid Melton, William Lucking, Pat Delany
D: Barry Shear   TELEPLAY: Ted Leighton from Ellery Queen's novel *Cat of
    Many Tails*
TVM, minor thriller: Crazed strangler terrorizes NYC

Ellery Queen, Master Detective
1940, (USA), Col, b&w, 69 mins.
W: Ralph Bellamy (*Ellery Queen*), Margaret Lindsay (*Nikki Porter*), Charley
    Grapewin (*Insp. Queen*), Michael Whalen (*Dr. James Rogers*), James Burke
    (*Sgt. Velie*), Fred Niblo (*John Braun*), Marsha Hunt (*Barbara Braun*),
    Katherine DeMille (*Valerie Norris*), Charles Lane (*Dr. Prouty*), Byron Foulger
    (*Amos*), Ann Shoemaker (*Lydia Braun*), Lee Phelps (*Flynn*), Marion Martin
    (*Cornelia*), Douglas Fowley (*Rocky Taylor*), Morgan Wallace (*Zachary*)
D: Kurt Neumann   SCR: Eric Taylor, loosely based on Ellery Queen's novel *The
    Door Between*   PHOTOG: James S. Brown
Standard thriller: Detective probes murder of physical culturist

Ellery Queen's Penthouse Mystery
1941, (USA), Col, b&w, 69 mins.
W: Ralph Bellamy (*Ellery Queen*), Margaret Lindsay (*Nikki Porter*), Charley
    Grapewin (*Insp. Queen*), Anna May Wong (*Lois Ling*), James Burke (*Sgt.
    Velie*), Eduardo Ciannelli (*Count Brett*), Frank Albertson (*Sanders*), Russell
    Hicks (*Walsh*), Ann Doran (*Sheila Cobb*), Theodore von Eltz (*Jim Ritter*),
    Noel Madison (*Gordon Cobb*), Charles Lane (*Dr. Prouty*), Tom Dugan
    (*McGrath*), Mantan Moreland (*Roy*)
D: James Hogan   SCR: Eric Taylor, from characters created by Ellery Queen
    PHOTOG: James S. Brown
Complicated thriller: Jewel smuggler murdered in penthouse suite

The Elm-Chanted Forest
1986, (USA), color, 82 mins.
Standard animated fantasy: Animals oppose evil king

Elstree Calling
1930, (GB), BIP/Wardour, b&w, 86 mins.
W: Will Fyffe, Lily Morris, Tommy Handley, Teddy Brown, Anna May Wong,
    Gordon Harker, Bobbie Comber, Ivor McLaren, Hannah Jones, Cicely
    Courtneidge, Jack Hulbert, Helen Burnell, Donald Calthrop, Ted Ray, John
    Stuart, Jameson Thomas, John Longden, The Three Eddies, The Adelphi
    Girls, The Kasbek Singers, The Charlot Girls, The Berkoff Dancers
D: Adrian Brunel, Alfred Hitchcock, Andre Charlot, Jack Hulbert, & Paul
    Murray   SCR: Adrian Brunel, Val Valentine & Walter C. Mycroft
Standard revue: Film studio makes TV broadcast

The Elusive Pimpernel
1919, (GB), Stoll, b&w, 5,143 ft. (1567.6m)
W: Cecil Humphreys (*Sir Percy Blakeney*), Marie Blanche (*Lady Mar-guerite*),
    Norman Page (*Chauvelin*), Fotheringham Lysons (*Robespierre*), Teddy
    Arundell (*Colet d'Herbois*), Madge Stuart (*Juliette Marny*), A. Harding
    Steerman (*Abbe Jouquet*), Dorothy Hanson (*Mlle. Cardeille*)
D: Maurice Elvey   SCR: Frederick Blatchford, from Baroness Orczy's novel *The
    Scarlet Pimpernel*
Standard adventure: To save wife from guillotine, fop confesses to spying

The Elusive Pimpernel
1950, (GB), Carroll/London-Archers/British Lion, color, 109 mins.
W: David Niven (*Sir Percy Blakeney*), Margaret Leighton (*Marguerite Blakeney*),
    Jack Hawkins (*Prince of Wales*), Cyril Cusack (*Chauvelin*), Arlette Marchal
    (*Comtesse de Tournai*), Robert Coote (*Sir Andrew Ffoulkes*), Danielle Godet
    (*Suzanne de Tournai*), Arthur Wontner (*Lord Grenville*), David Hutcheson
    (*Lord Anthony Dewhurst*), John Longden (*The Abbot*), Eugene Deckers (*Capt.
    Merieres*), Charles Victor (*Col. Winterbotham*), Robert Griffiths (*Trubshawe*),
    Edmond Audran (*Armand St. Juste*), Gerard Nery (*Philippe de Tournai*),
    Patrick Macnee (*Bristow*), Philip Stainton (*Jellyband*)
P: Samuel Goldwyn & Alexander Korda   D & SCR: Michael Powell &
    Emeric Pressburger, from Baroness Orczy's novel *The Scarlet Pimpernel*
    PHOTOG: Christopher Challis   MUSIC: Brian Easdale
A.k.a. The Fighting Pimpernel and The Scarlet Pimpernel
*Colorful adventure-thriller: English fop dons disguises to save French aristocrats
    from the guillotine*

Elvira, Mistress of the Dark

1988, (USA), Queen "B"/NBC Prods./New World, color, 96 mins.

W: Cassandra Peterson (*Elvira*), Susan Kellermann (*Patty*), W. Morgan Sheppard (*Vince Talbot*), Jeff Conaway (*Travis*), Daniel Greene (*Bob Redding*), Edie McClurg (*Chastity Pariah*), Kurt Fuller (*Mr. Glotter*), Frank Collison (*Billy*), William Duell (*Mr. Meeker*), Mario Celario (*Rudy*), Robert Benedetti (*Calvin Cobb*), Lee McLaughlin (*Earl Hooter*), Jack Fletcher (*Mr. Bigelow*), Hugh Gillin (*The Sheriff*), Bill Morey (*Mr. Rivers*), William Cort (*The Lawyer/Game Show Host*), Ellen Dunning (*Robin Meeker*), Scott Morris (*Sean*), Ira Heiden (*Bo*), Kris Kamm (*Randy*), Lynn Stewart (*The Bartender*), Charles Woolf (*Manny*), Phil Rubenstein (*The Director*), Edwina Moore (*The Hairdresser*), Damita Jo Freeman (*The Assoc. Producer*), Bill Swearingen (*The Cameraman*), Larry Flash Jenkins (*The Technical Advisor*), Tress MacNeille (*The Anchorwoman*), Sharon Hays (*The Game Show Girl*), William Dance (*The

Elvira, Mistress of the Dark: CASSANDRA PETERSON

Messenger*), John Paragon (*The Gas Station Attendant*), Bill Cable (*The Cop*), Kate Brown (*Anita*), Joseph Arias (*The Hitchhiker*), Eve Smith (*The Little Old Lady*), Deryl Carroll (*Charlie*), Raleigh Bond (*The Minister*), Marie Sullivan (*Mrs. Morissey*)

D: James Signorelli **SCR:** Sam Egan, John Paragon, & Cassandra Peterson **PHOTOG:** Hanania Baer **MUSIC:** James Campbell

Standard horror-spoof: Noncomformist beauty seeks inheritance

Emanuelle E Glii Ultimi Canabali (Emanuelle and the Last Cannibals)

1977, (It), color, 87 mins.

W: Laura Gemser, Gabriele Tinti, Susan Scott, Donald O'Brien

D: Aristide Massaccesi

Minor thriller: Woman journalist meets savage tribe

The Embalmer

see *Il Mostro di Venezia*

Embassy

1972, (GB), Mel Ferrer/Hemdale, color, 90 mins.

W: Max von Sydow (*Gorenko*), Richard Roundtree (*Shannon*), Chuck Connors (*Kesten*), Broderick Crawford (*Dunninger*), Ray Milland (*The Ambassador*), Larry Cross (*Gamble*), David Bauer (*Kadish*), Marie-Jose Nat (*Laure*), Edmund Bannonio (*The Man in Black*), David Healy (*Phelan*), Sara Marshall (*Miss Harding*), Karl Held (*Rylands*), Dee Pollock (*Stacy*), Afif Boulos (*The

Foreign Minister*), Leila Buheiry (*Leila*), Gail Clymer (*The Switchboard Operator*), Mounir Maassri (*Michel*), Saladin Nader (*Roge*), David Parker (*Tula*), Dean Turner (*Clem*), Peter Smith (*The Clerk*)

P: Mel Ferrer **D:** Gordon Hessler **SCR:** William Fairchild, from Stephen Coulter's novel **PHOTOG:** Raoul Coutard **MUSIC:** Jonathan Hodge **SONGS:**, *Somebody Stop This Madness*

video title, *Target: Embassy*

Minor, confused melodrama: Soviet official seeks political asylum in Beirut

Embezzled Heaven

1959, (Austria), Rhombus-Ufa/Louis de Rochemont, color, 91 mins.

W: Annie Rosar, Hans Holt, Kurt Meisel

WRIT & D: Ernest Marischka, from Franz Werfel's novel

PHOTOG: Bruno Mondi **MUSIC:** Anton Profes

Maudlin semi-fantasy: Cook tries to buy "seat in heaven" by helping nephew become priest

Embrace of the Vampire

see *The Nosferatu Diaries: Embrace of the Vampire*

Embroidery Extraordinary

1910, (GB), Hepworth, b&w, 225 ft. (68.6m)

D: Cecil Hepworth

Standard fantasy: Designs embroider themselves and end with "goodbye"

Embryo

1976, (USA), Sandy Howard Prods./Cine Artists, color, 106 mins.

W: Rock Hudson (*Dr. Paul Holliston*), Barbara Carrera (*Victoria*), Diane Ladd (*Martha*), Roddy McDowall (*Riley*), Ann Schedeen (*Helen*), John Elerick (*Gordon*), Jack Colvin (*Dr. Wiston*), Vincent Bagetta (*Collier*), Dick Winslowe (*Forbes*), Lina Raymond (*Janet Novak*), Joyce Spitz, Dr. Joyce Brothers

P: Arnold H. Orgolini & Anita Doohan **D:** Ralph Nelson **SCR:** Anita Doohan & Jack W. Thomas, from a story by Jack W. Thomas **PHOTOG:** Fred Koenekamp **MUSIC:** Gil Melle

A.k.a. ***Created to Kill***

Modest SF-thriller: Doctor clones woman, tragedy ensues. cf. **Alraune**

The Emerald of Artatama

1967, (Sp-W. Ger), Sid Pink/Westside Int., color, 84 mins.

W: Rory Calhoun, James Philbrook, Nuria Torrey, Charles Fawcett, Brigitte Saint John, Pilar Arenas

D: Joe Lacy **ORIG. SCR:** M. Martin & Joe Lacy **PHOTOG:** Alfonso Nieva **MUSIC:** Fernando Garcia Morcillo

Minor adventure-thriller: Quest for Egyptian treasure

Emma's Wish

1998, (USA), CBS-TV, color, 95 mins.

W: Joanna Kerns, Harley Jane Kozak, Della Reese (*Mona*), William Moses (*Bryan*), Seymour Cassel (*Harry Bridges*), Courtland Mead (*Danny Bookman*), Jeanne Allen (*Iris Bookman*)

TVM, minor fantasy

The Emperor and the Golem

see *Cisaruv Pekar, Pekaruv Cisar*

The Emperor of China's Nightingale

see *Cisaruv Slavik*

The Emperor's Baker, The Baker's Emperor

see *Cisaruv Pekar, Pekaruv Cisar*

The Emperor's Candlesticks

see *Die Leuchter des Kaisers*

The Emperor's New Clothes

1989, (USA), Cannon, color, 85 mins.

W: Sid Caesar

D: David Irving

Standard fantasy: Monarch deceived by phony weavers

The Emperor's Nightingale

see *Cisaruv Slavik*

Empire of Ash III

1989, (Can), North American, color, 89 mins.

W: William Smith (*Lucas*), Melanie Kilgour (*Danielle*), Ken Farmer (*Chuck*), Scott Andersen (*Harris*), Michael Metcalfe (*Ozzie*), Nancy Pataki (*Baalca*), Tanya Orton (*Claudia*), Joe Maffei (*Iodine*), Nick Amoroso (*Dax*), Andrew MacGregor (*Zak*), Dave Gregg (*Rocket Man*), Judy Reynolds (*June*), Darline DeVink (*April*), Paul Hogan (*Jack*), Curt Bonn (*Arco*), Richard Hendery (*The 1st Shepherd*), Serge Houde (*The 2nd Shepherd*), Andy Graffitti (*The Grand Shepherd*), Gordon Cook, Tom Felcan, Paul Dignard, John Haines, Lee Hatch, Bruce Huggett, Bruce Hystad, Jeff Hystad, Adam Longworth, Ken Ralph, David Napio, Helmut Peters, Gary Renfree, Ken Lester, Gary Taylor, Willis Taylor, Carmen Vacchiann, Merlin Bowe, Rick Worthington, Bob Lessard, Urbain Chartier, John Bussani, Rob Berridge, Tim Chapman, Alex Pankiw, Scott McDonald, Pat McDonald, Pat McGarrigle, Charlie Drummond-May, Don Ferrier, Wayne Coffey, Adam Jones Palmer, John Diablo, Jim Dyck, Steve Gumbert, Patrick Robinson, Cecil Drummond

Hay, Del Lambert, Ross Feltron, Taylor Prince, Dan Robinson, Dave Stubbs, Micki Sacchari, Don Wilson, Dave Wetson, John Woodcock, Art Yates, Ken Kryeger, Brian Phillips, Brett Jones, Fred Reber, Harold Wyerch, Steve Franklin, William Kelley, Bill Murray, Nestor Garandza, Andra Brown, Christine Peters, Leslie Gmur, Lisa Larson, Marny McKewan, Lisa Clarke, Minna Setala, Laurie Martin, John Cowin, Dale Loewen, Susan Arnold, Debra King, Robin Rasberry, Don Demille, Patricia Maywood, Larissa Mai, Lesley Wiebe, Carson Ferguson, John Isaac, Robert McNarland, Gerald Dyck, Robby Berner, Derek Renfrey, Laura McNarland, Andrew Long, Lauretta MacCarron, Debra Renfrey, Brad Stewart, Gwyneth Williams, Phaeder Williams, August Buquet, Ed Buquet, Rick Thompson, Camillia Mahal, Art Watkins
D & STORY: Louis A. Simandl   SCR: Chris Maruna, developed by John Eyres
   PHOTOG: Danny Nowak   SPCL-FX COORD, Al Benjamin
   MUSIC: John Serenda & The Gore Avenue Sound Project
Minor SF-thriller: Warring post-plague tribes

The Empire of Dracula
1967, (Mex), color
Standard horror-fantasy

Empire of the Ants
1977, (USA), AIP, color, 87 mins.
W: Joan Collins, Robert Lansing, John David Carson, Albert Salmi, Robert Pine, Jacqueline Scott, Pamela Shoop, Irene Tedrow, Edward Power, Brooke Palance, Harry Holcombe
P, D, SCR & SPCL-FX: Bert I. Gordon   STORY, Jack Turley, based on a portion of H.G. Wells' novel The Food of the Gods
Modest SF-fantasy: Giant, intelligent ants enslave humans. cf. Village of the Giants and The Food of the Gods

The Empire Strikes Back
1980, (USA), 20th-Fox, color, 123 mins. (Special Edition {1997}: 124 mins.)
W: Mark Hamill (Luke Skywalker), Carrie Fisher (Princess Leia Organa), Harrison Ford (Han Solo), Anthony Daniels (C3PO), Kenny Baker (R2D2), Billy Dee Williams (Lando Calrissian), Peter Mayhew (Chewbacca), Frank Oz (Yoda), Alec Guinness (Obi Wan "Ben" Kenobi), Dave Prowse (Darth Vader), James Earl Jones (The Voice of Darth Vader), Jeremy Bulloch (Boba Fett), John Hollis (Lando's Aide), Jack Purvis (Chief Ugnaught), Kathryn Mullen (Performing Ass't for Yoda), Des Webb (The Snow Creature), Kenneth Colley (Adm. Piett), Julian Glover (Gen. Veers), Clive Revill (The Voice of the Emperor), Michael Sheard (Adm. Ozzel), Michael Culver (Capt. Needa), Bruce Boa (Gen. Rieekan), Christopher Malcolm (Zev), Richard Oldfield (Hobbie), Dennis Lawson (Wedge), John Morton (Dak), Ian Liston (Janson), John Ratzenberger (Maj. Derlin), Jerry Harte (The Head Controller), Jack McKenzie (The Deck Lt.), John Dicks, Milton Johns, Mark Jones, Robin Scoby, Oliver Maguire, Norman Chancer, Norwich Duff, Brigitte Kahn, Ray Hassett, Burnell Tucker
P: Gary Kurtz   D: Irvin Kershner   SCR: Leigh Brackett & Lawrence Kasdan   STORY: George Lucas   MUSIC: John Williams
Classic SF-fantasy, sequel to Star Wars:. Youth masters psychic powers, confronts galactic villain

L'Empreinte du Loup-Garou
see The Werewolf (1956)

The Empty House
1921, (GB), Stoll, b&w, 1,800 ft. (548.6m)
W: Eille Norwood (Sherlock Holmes), Hubert Willis (Dr. John Watson), Austin Fairman (Ronald Adair), Cecil Kerr (Sir Charles Ridge), Arthur Bell (Insp. Lestrade), Mme. d'Esterre (Mrs. Hudson)
D: Maurice Elvey   SCR: William J. Elliott from the writings of Sir Arthur Conan Doyle
Standard crime-thriller (episode in "Adventures of Sherlock Holmes" series)

The Enchanted Basket
see La Corbeille Enchantee

The Enchanted Cottage
1924, (USA), Inspiration/First Nat'l, b&w, 7 reels (7,120 ft./2170.2m)
W: Richard Barthelmess (Oliver Bashforth), May McAvoy (Laura Pennington), Ida Waterman (Mrs. Smallwood), Alfred Hickman (Rupert Smallwood), Florence Short (Ethel Bashforth), Marion Coakley (Beatrice Vaughn), Ethel Wright (Mrs. Minnett), Holmes E. Herbert (Maj. Hillgrove), Harry Allen
D: John S. Robertson   ADAPT & SCR: Josephine Lovett, from a play by Arthur Wing Pinero   PHOTOG: George Folsey
Standard romance-fantasy: Cottage seems to transform young lovers

The Enchanted Cottage
1945, (USA), RKO, b&w, 92 mins.
W: Robert Young, Dorothy McGuire, Herbert Marshall, Mildred Natwick, Spring Byington
D: John Cromwell   SCR: Herman Mankiewicz & DeWitt Bodeen, from the play by Sir Arthur Wing Pinero   PHOTOG: Ted Tetzlaff   MUSIC: Roy Webb
Modest romance-fantasy: Bungalow's strange aura transforms homely bride and war-scarred veteran

The Enchanted Cup
1902, (GB), R.W. Paul, b&w, 300 ft. (91.4m)
D: Walter R. Booth
Standard fantasy short in 7 scenes: Peasant rescues sweetheart from dwarfs

The Enchanted Forest
1945, (USA), PRC, color, 78 mins.
W: Edmund Lowe, Harry Davenport, Brenda Joyce, Billy Severn
D: Lew Landers   SCR: Robert Lee Johnson, John Le Bar & Lou Brock
   PHOTOG: Marcel LePicard   MUSIC: Alfred Hay Malotte
Standard semi-fantasy: Lost boy raised by forest hermit

Enchanted Island
1958, (USA), Benedict Bogeaus/RKO/WB, color, 94 mins.
W: Dana Andrews, Jane Powell, Don Dubbins, Arthur Shields, Ted de Corsia, Friedrich Ledebur
D: Allan Dwan   SCR: James Leicester & Harold Jacob Smith, from Herman Melville's novel Typee   PHOTOG: George Stahl   MUSIC: Raul Lavista
Minor adventure-thriller: Ship deserters on cannibal isle

The Enchanted Sedan Chair
see La Chaise a Poteurs Enchantee

The Enchanted Sword
1960, (Sp), 20th-Fox, color
Animated fantasy

The Enchanted Toymaker
1904, (GB), Alpha Trading Co., b&w, 190 ft. (57.9m)
D: Arthur Cooper
A.k.a. The Old Toymaker's Dream
Minor fantasy short: Old man dreams fairy enlarges his Noah's Ark, animals enter it

The Enchanted Trunk
see Le Coffre Enchante

The Enchanted Well
1903, (Fr), Star, b&w, 50m (164 ft./2.8 mins.)
P & D: Georges Melies
Standard fantasy short: Witch curses peasant's well

The Enchanter
see L'Enchanteur Alcofrisbas

The Enchanter Alcofrisbas
see L'Enchanteur Alcofrisbas

L'Enchanteur Alcofrisbas (The Enchanter Alcofrisbas)
1903, (Fr), Star, b&w, 70m (229.7 ft./3.9 mins.)
D: Georges Melies
A.k.a. The Enchanter and Alcofrisbas, the Master Magician
Standard fantasy

Enchantment
1916, (USA), Mutual, b&w
W: Alfred Vosburgh, Vivian Rich
Minor melodrama

The Enchantress
1984, (Greece), color, 93 mins.
W: Alkis Kourkoulos, Sofia Aliberti, Lily Kokodi, Antigone Amanitou, Vicky Koulianou, Nicols Papaconstantinou, Stratos Pachis
D: Manoussos Manoussakis
Standard fantasy: Youth traverses supernatural worlds in pursuit of mythica beauty

Encino Man
1992, (USA), Hollywood Pictures, color, 89 mins.
W: Sean Astin (Dave Morgan), Brendan Fraser (Link), Pauly Shore (Stoney Brown), Megan Ward (Robyn Sweeney), Richard Masur, Mariette Hartley, Robin Tunney, Rick Ducommun, Michael DeLuise
P: George Zaloom   D: Les Mayfield   SCR: Shawn Schepps   STORY: George Zaloom & Shawn Schepps   PHOTOG: Robert Brinkmann   ORIG. SCORE: J. Peter Robinson
Standard SF-comedy: Teens revive frozen caveman

Encino Woman
1996, (USA), ABC-TV, color, 95 mins.
W: Katherine Kousi, Corey Parker, Jay Thomas (Marvin), Ric Overton (Raji), John Kassir (Jean Michel), Joel Murray (Mr. Jones), Annabelle Gurwitch (Chris)
TVM, standard SF-comedy: Earthquake frees frozen cave woman

Encounter at Raven's Gate
1990, (Austral), John Daly-Derek Gibson/Hemdale, color, 89 mins.
W: Steven Vidler (Eddie), Celine Griffin (Rachel), Ritchie Singer (Richard), Max Cullen (Taylor), Terry Camilleri (Hemmings), Vince Gil, Saturday Rosenberg, Eddie Cleary
D: Rolf de Heer   SCR: Rolf de Heer & Marc Rosenberg, from an orig. scr by James Michael Vernon   PHOTOG: Richard Michalak
Modest SF-thriller: Space aliens visit Aussie Outback

Encounter with the Unknown
1973, (USA), Centronics Int'l, color, 90 mins.

<u>W</u>: Rosie Holotik, Gene Ross
<u>P</u>: Joe Glass <u>D</u>: Harry Thomason **NARRATOR**, Rod Serling
Minor horror anthology: (1) Trio of cursed teenagers, (2) Mysterious hole in Earth, & (3) Ghost on bridge

Endangered Species
1982, (USA), MGM-UA, color, 94 mins.
<u>W</u>: Robert Urich (*Ruben Castle*), JoBeth Williams (*Harriet Purdue*), Paul Dooley (*Joe Hiatt*), Peter Coyote (*Steele*), Hoyt Axton (*Ben Morgan*), Gailard Sartain (*The Mayor*), Dan Hedaya (*Peck*), Marin Kanter (*Mackenzie Castle*), Michelle Davison (*Mrs. Haskins*), Harry Carey Jr. (*Dr. Emmer*), Ned Dowd (*Dep. Bobby*), John Considine (*Burnside*), Joseph G. Medalis (*The Lawyer*), Margery Bond (*Judy Hiatt*), Patrick Houser (*Chester*), Alvin Crow (*Dep. Wayne*), Vernon Weddle (*Varney*), Kent Rizley (*Dep. Ray*), Henry G. Sanders (*Dr. Ross*), Heather Menzies (*Susan*), John Perry Barlow, Steve Tannen, Mark Carlton, Darrell Fetty, Fred Lerner, Billie Kirkland, Bruce Paul Barbour, Greg Elam, Dave Cass, John Binder, Steve Bassett, George Fisher, Zalman King, Joyce Rudolph, Tracy Smith, Ellen Flitner, Bill Moseley, Olive Joyce Lee, Richard Jury, Raymond Dixion, Kerrie Cullen, Gail Glover, Pat Mahoney, Connie Camino, Robyn Lundin, Bernie Welch, Bob Sargent, Rock Walker, Rick Seaman, Roger Creed
<u>D</u>: Alan Rudolph <u>SCR</u>: Alan Rudolph & John Binder <u>STORY</u>: Judson Klinger & Richard Woods <u>PHOTOG</u>: Paul Lohmann <u>SPCL-FX</u>: Jonnie Burke & Steve Galich <u>MUSIC</u>: Gary Wright <u>SONGS</u>: *Boozers are Losers*
Standard SF-melodrama: Lady sheriff and New York cop investigate baffling cattle mutilations

Endgame
1984, (USA-It), Filmirage/Cinema 80/American Nat'l, color, 96 mins.
<u>W</u>: Al Cliver (*Shannon*), Moira Chen (*Lilith*), Jack Davis (*Prof. Levin*), George Eastman (*Karnak*), Gus Stone (*Bull*), Al Yamanouchi (*Ninja*), Mario Pedone (*Kovack*), Frank Ukmar (*Stark*), Gordon Mitchell (*Col. Morgan*), Nat Williams (*Kijawa*), Christopher Walsh (*Tommy*), Richard Novak (*The TV Technician*), Bobby Rhodes (*Woody Smith*), Al Waterman (*Kid Hitchkoc*), David Brown (*The Speaker*), Peter Brighton (*The Blue Mutant*), Carlos Valles (*The Committee Member*)
<u>D</u>: Steven Benson <u>SCR</u>: Alex Carver <u>ORIG. SCR</u>: Steven Benson & Alex Carver <u>PHOTOG</u>: Federico Slonisco <u>SPCL-FX</u>: James Davies, Robert Gold, & Peter Gray <u>MUSIC</u>: Carlo Maria Cordio
Minor SF-adventure: Post-nuke gladiators

Endless Descent
1989, (USA-Sp), Dister, color, 79 mins.
<u>W</u>: Jack Scalia (*Wick Hayes*), R. Lee Ermey (*Capt. Phillips*), Ray Wise (*Robbins*), Deborah Adair (*Nina*), Ely Pouget (*Ana Rivera*), John Toles Bey (*Skeets*), Emilio Linder (*Phillippe*), Tony Isbert (*Fleming*), Alvaro Labra (*Carlo*), Luis Lorenzo (*Francisco*), Frank Brana (*Muller*), Edmund Purdom (*Steensland*), J. Martinez Bordiu (*Sven*), Garick Hagon (*Barton*), James Aubrey (*Contek 1*), Derrick Vopelka (*Contek 2*), Jed Downey (*Man on Tapes*)
<u>D</u>: J.P. Simon <u>SCR</u>: David Coleman <u>STORY</u>: J.P. Simon & Mark Klein <u>PHOTOG</u>: Juan Marine <u>SPCL-FX</u>: Basilio Cortijo <u>MUSIC</u>: Joel Goldsmith
Minor SF-thriller: Submarine crew finds mutant horrors

Endless Night
1972, (GB), British Lion/EMI, color, 99 mins.
<u>W</u>: Hayley Mills (*Ellie*), Hywel Bennett (*Michael*), Britt Ekland (*Greta*), George Sanders (*Lippincott*), Per Oscarsson (*Santonix*), Peter Bowles (*Reuben*), Aubrey Richards (*Dr. Philpott*), Ann Way (*Mrs. Philpott*), Lois Maxwell (*Cora*), Patience Collier (*Miss Townsend*), Robert Keegan (*The Innkeeper*), Madge Ryan (*Mother*), Helen Horton (*Aunt Beth*), Walter Gotell (*Constantine*), Mischa de la Motte (*Maynard*), David Bauer (*Uncle Frank*), Leo Genn (*The Psychiatrist*), Geoffrey Chater (*The Coroner*), David Healey (*Jason*)
<u>P</u>: Leslie Gilliat <u>D & SCR</u>: Sidney Gilliat, from a novel by Agatha Christie <u>PHOTOG</u>: Harry Waxman <u>MUSIC</u>: Bernard Herrmann
Standard thriller: Scheming chauffeur weds millionairess

The End of All Things
see Making Sausages

End of August at the Hotel Ozone
1967, (Czech), color
Standard SF-melodrama

The End of Don Juan
see La Fin de Don Juan

The End of the Line
1957, (GB), Fortress/Eros, b&w, 64 mins.
<u>W</u>: Barbara Shelley (*Lilliane Crawford*), Alan Baxter (*Mike Selby*), Ferdy Mayne (*Edwards*), Jennifer Jayne (*Ann Bruce*), Arthur Gomez (*John Crawford*), Geoffrey Hibbert (*Max Perrin*), Jack Meltord (*Insp. Gates*), Marianne Braun (*The Desk Clerk*)
<u>P</u>: Guido Coen <u>D</u>: Charles Saunders <u>STORY</u>: Paul Erickson
Standard thriller: Evil dame lures man into murder plot

The End of the World (1930)
see La Fin du Monde

The End of the World (1962)
see Panic in Year Zero

End of World
1977, (USA), Charles Band/Irwin Yablans, color, 88 mins.
<u>W</u>: Christopher Lee (*Father Pergado/Zindar*), Dean Jagger (*Collins*), Sue Lyon (*Sylvia Boran*), Kirk Scott (*Andrew Boran*), Lew Ayres (*Beckerman*), Macdonald Carey (*John Davis*), Liz Ross, Jon Van Ness, Kathy Cunha, Jane Wilbur, Mary Daugherty, Evelyn Lipton, Pat Wylie, George Soviak, Roscoe Born, John Dennis, Simmy Bow, Ron Carter, Michael Frank Leo, Gene Walker, David Gold, Bennah Burton, Frank Pendergast, John Hayes, Jeff Burtt, Lynn Robertson, Meda Band, Jackie Band, Frank Ray Perilli, Bertha Band, Laura Robertson, Gordon McGill, Dick Stenta, Dick Shore, Maria Wedin, Deborah Higgins, Marc Perilli

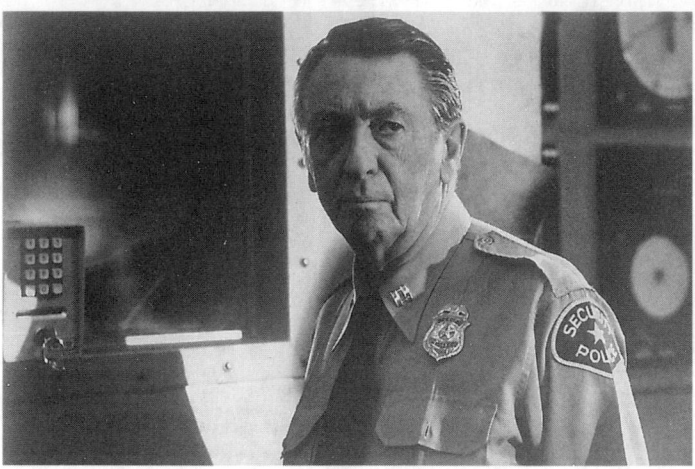

End of the World: MACDONALD CAREY

<u>D</u>: John Hayes <u>SCR</u>: Frank Ray Perilli <u>PHOTOG</u>: John Huneck <u>SPCL-FX</u>: Harry Woolman <u>MUSIC</u>: Andrew Belling
Minor SF-thriller: Space aliens plan Earth's destruction

Endplay
1975, (Austral), color, 110 mins.
<u>W</u>: George Mallaby, John Waters, Ken Goodiet, Delvene Delaney Charles Tingwell, Robert Hewett, Kevin Miles
<u>D</u>: Tim Burstall, from a novel by Russell Braddon
Standard thriller: Two brothers involved in murders

Endstation 13 Sahara
see Station Six—Sahara

Enemy Agents Meet Ellery Queen
1942, (USA), Col, b&w, 64 mins.
<u>W</u>: William Gargan (*Ellery Queen*), Margaret Lindsay (*Nikki Porter*), Charley Grapewin (*Insp. Queen*), Gale Sondergaard (*Mrs. Von Dorn*), Gilbert Roland (*Paul Gillette*), Sig Rumann (*Heinrich*), James Burke (*Sgt. Velie*), John Hamilton (*Commissioner Bracken*), Ernst Dorian (*Morse*), Felix Basch (*Helm*), Minor Watson (*Commodore Bang*), James Seay (*Sgt. Stevens*), Louis (*Ludwig*) Donath (*Reece*), Dick Wessel (*The Sailor*)
<u>D</u>: James Hogan <u>SCR</u>: Eric Taylor, from characters created by Ellery Queen <u>PHOTOG</u>: James S. Brown Jr.
Standard thriller: Detective vs. diamond-smuggling Nazis

The Enemy Amongst Us
1916, (GB), British Oak/NA, b&w, 1,120 ft. (341.4m)
<u>D</u>: Ernest G. Batley
Standard thriller: Detectives unmask spies

Enemy from Space
see Quatermass II

The Enemy in our Midst
1914, (GB), Clarendon/Argus. b&w, 2,360 ft. (719.3m)
<u>D</u>: Wilfred Noy
Standard crime-thriller: "Dr. Brian Pellie" bombs bullion cars, is betrayed to Navy

An Enemy in the Camp
1908, (GB), Hepworth, b&w, 175 ft. (53.3m)
<u>D</u>: Lewin Fitzhamon
Standard thriller: Child telephones soldiers, thwarts dispatch-stealing spy

Enemy Mine
1985, (USA-W. Ger), Kings Road/20th-Fox, color, 106 mins.
<u>W</u>: Dennis Quaid (*Davidge*), Louis Gossett Jr. (*The Drac*), Brion James (*Stubbs*), Richard Marcus (*Arnold*), Carolyn McCormick (*Morse*), Bumper Robinson (*Zammis*), Lance Kerwin (*Wooster*), Jim Mapp (*The Old Drac*), Lou Michaels (*Bates*), Scott Kraft (*Jonathan*), Andy Geer (*Wilson*), Colin Gilder (*Cohen*),

Henry Stolow (*Cates*), Herb Andress (*Hopper*), Doug Robinson (*Walker*), Danmar (*Wise Guy*), Mandy Hausenberger (*The Medic*), Emily Woods (*Simpson*), Barry Stokes (*Huck*), Charly Huber (*Kranzer*), Ulrich Gunther (*Daggett*), Jazzer Jeyes (*Scarbreath*), Frank Henson (*Lump*), Balog Menyert (*Mills*), Mark McBride (*Hensler*), Tony Moore, Kevin Taylor
D: Wolfgang Petersen **SCR:** Edward Khmara, from a story by Barry Longyear
PHOTOG: Tony Imi **MUSIC:** Maurice Jarre
Standard SF-thriller: Earthman and alien stranded on desolate planetoid

The Enemy Within
1994, (USA), HBO-TV, color, 86 mins.
W: Forest Whitaker, Sam Waterston, Josef Sommer, George Dzundza, Jason Robards Jr., Dana Delany
D: Jonathan Darby **WRIT:** Daryl Ponicsan & Ronald Bass
Made-for-Cable, stadard thriller

L'Enfant Sauvage (The Wild Child)
1970, (Fr), UA, color, 85 mins.
W: Francois Truffaut (*Jean Itard*), Jean Dante (*Prof. Pinel*), Jean-Pierre Cargol (*Victor, the child*), Francoise Seigner (*Mme. Guerin*), Paul Ville (*Remy*), Claude Miler (*Msr. Lemeri*), Annie Miler (*Mme. Lemeri*)
D: Francois Truffaut **SCR:** Francois Truffaut & Jean Gruault, from a novel by Jean Itard **PHOTOG:** Nestor Almendros **MUSIC:** Antonio Vivaldi
Superior semi-docu: Domestication of famous "wolf-child"

Les Enfants Terribles (The Terrible Children)
1950, (Fr), Mayer-Kingsley, b&w, 107 mins.
W: Nicole Stephane (*Elizabeth*), Edouard Dermithe (*Paul*), Renee Cosima (*Agatha*), Jacques Bernard (*Gerard*), Melvyn Martin (*Michael*), Roger Gaillard (*The Uncle*), Jean-Marie Revel (*The Maid*), Marie Cyliakus (*Mother*)
P & D: Jean-Pierre Melville **WRIT, ADAPT & NARRATED:** Jean Cocteau **PHOTOG:** Henri Decae **MUSIC:** J.S. Bach & A Vivaldi
*GB retitle, **The Strange Ones***
Classic melodrama: Children create somber fantasy world

England's Future Safeguard
1916, (GB), British Oak/New Agency, b&w, 1,080 ft. (329.2m)
D: Ethyle Batley
Standard thriller: Bus driver and conductress save anti-zeppelin gun from spies

The English Rose
1920, (GB), British Standard/Whincup, b&w, 4,890 ft. (1490.5m)
W: Fred Paul (*Father Michael*), Humbertson Wright (*Capt. MacDonnell*), Sydney Folker (*Harry O'Malley*), Mary Morton, Jack Raymond, Amy Brandon Thomas, George Turner, Clifford Desborough
P: John Robyns **D:** Fred Paul **SCR:** Paul Rooff, from a play by George R. Sims & Robert Buchanan
Standard crime-thriller: Irish priest learns truth of murder, but is unable to save framed man

Enigma
1982, (GB-Fr), Embassy, color, 101 mins.
W: Martin Sheen (*Alex Holbeck*), Sam Neill (*Dimitri Vasilkov*), Brigitte Fossey (*Karen*), Derek Jacobi (*Kurt Limmer*), Michel Lonsdale (*Bodley*), Frank Finlay (*Canarsky*), David Baxt (*Melton*), Kevin McNally (*Bruno*), Michael Williams (*Hirsch*), Warren Clarke (*Konstantin*)
D: Jeannot Szwarc **SCR:** John Briley, from a novel by Michael Barak **PHOTOG:** Jean-Louis Picavet
Minor thriller: KGB plans murders of Soviet dissidents

L'Enigmatique M. Moto
see ***Think Fast, Mr. Moto***

Enough Rope
1966, (Fr), Artixo, b&w, 104 mins.
W: Gert Frobe, Marina Vlady
Standard thriller

The Ensorcelled Prince
see ***El Principe Encadenado***

Enter Arsene Lupin
1944, (USA), Univ, b&w, 72 mins.
W: Charles Korvin, Ella Raines, J. Carrol Naish, George Dolenz, Gale Sondergaard
D: Ford Beebe
Standard thriller

Enter Inspector Duvall
1961, (GB), Bill & Michael Luckwell/Col, b&w, 64 mins.
W: Anton Diffring (*Insp. Duvall*), Diane Hart (*Jackie*), Mark Singleton (*Insp. Wilson*), Charles Mitchell (*Brossier*), Aiden Grennell (*Mark Sinclair*), Susan Hallinan (*Doreen*), Charles Roberts (*Charley*)
P: Bill Luckwell & Jock MacGregor **D:** Max Varnel **SCR:** J. Henry Piperno **STORY:** Jacques Monteux
Standard crime-thriller: Jewel thief kills socialite

The Entity
1983, (USA), Pelleport Investors/American Cinema/20th-Fox, color, 113 mins.
W: Barbara Hershey (*Carla Moran*), Ron Silver (*Phil Sneiderman*), David Labiosa

(*Billy*), George Coe (*Dr. Weber*), Jacqueline Brookes (*Dr. Cooley*), Michael Alldredge (*George Nash*), Margaret Blye (*Cindy Nash*), Richard Brestoff (*Gene Kraft*), Raymond Singer (*Joe Mehan*), Natasha Ryan (*Julie*), Melanie Gaffin (*Kim*), Allan Rich (*Dr. Walcott*), Alex Rocco (*Jerry Anderson*), Sully Boyar (*Mr. Reisz*), Paula Victor (*Dr. Chevalier*), Curt Lowens (*Dr. Wilkes*), Lee Wilkof (*Dr. L. Hase*), Tom Stern (*Woody Browne*), Lisa Gurley (*The Receptionist*), Chris Howell (*The Guard*), Deborah Stevenson (*An Intern*), Mark Weiner (*An Intern*), John Branagan (*A Student*), Amy Kirkpatrick (*A Student*), Todd Kutches (*A Student*), Pauline Lomas (*A Student*), Renee Neimark (*A Student*), Donna Garrett, John Ashby, Ron Burke, Bill Burton, Kenny Endoso, Thomas Huff, Eddy Donno, Janet Gibbs, Buddy Joe Hooker, Gary McLarty, Shawn Howell, Linda Jacobs, Ernie Orsatti, Harry Wowchuck
P: Harold Schneider **D:** Sidney Furie **SCR:** Frank De Felitta—from his novel **PHOTOG:** Stephen H. Burum **SPCL-FX:** Joe Lombardi **MUSIC:** Charles Bernstein
Modest horror-thriller "based on a true story:" Invisible being molests woman

An Episode of the Derby
1906, (GB), Hepworth, b&w, 300 ft. (91.4m)
D: Lewin Fitzhamon
Standard crime-thriller: Girl threatened with kidnapping

Epitaph
1987, (USA), color, 90 mins.
D: Joseph Merhi
Minor thriller: Axe-murdering mother disrupts family

Equalizer 2000
1987, (USA-Phil), Premiere (video), color, 85 mins.
W: Richard Norton, Corinne Wahl, William Steis, Frederick Bailey, Robert Patrick, Rex Cutter, Warren McLean, Peter Shilton, Don Gordon, Ramon D'Salva, Vic Diaz, Steve Cook, Bobbie Greenwood, Henry Strzalskowski, Schorber Sagarbarria, Daniel De Long
D: Cirio H. Santiago **SCR:** Frederick Bailey **STORY:** Frederick Bailey & Joe Mari Avellana **PHOTOG:** Johnny Araojo **MUSIC DIR:** Edward Achacoso
Made-for-Video, minor SF-adventure: Warring factions in post-nuke Alaska

L'Equilibre Impossible (The Impossible Balancing Feat)
1902, (Fr), Star, b&w, 25m (98.4 ft./1.7 mins.)
D: Georges Melies
Standard fantasy

Equinox
1970, (USA), Tonylyn/Jack H. Harris, color, 82 mins.
W: Edward Connell (*Dave*), Barbara Hewitt (*Susan*), Robin Christopher (*Vicki*), Jack Woods (*Asmodeus*), Frank Boers Jr. (*Jim*), Fritz Leiber Jr., Jim Phillips, Jim Duran, Patrick Burke
WRIT & D: Jack Woods, from a story by Mark Thomas McGee **PHOTOG:** Mike Hoover **SPCL-FX:** Dennis Muren, David Allen & Jim Danforth **MUSIC:** John Caper
*A.k.a. **The Beast***
Minor horror-fantasy: Monsters, supernatural hokum and devil worship

Eraser
1996, (USA), WB, color, 115 mins.
W: Arnold Schwarzenegger (*John Kruger*), Vanessa Williams (*Lee Cullen*), James Caan (*Robert Deguern*), James Coburn (*Beller*), Andy Romano (*Harper*), Robert Pastorelli (*Johnny C.*), James Cromwell (*Donahue*), Danny Nucci (*Monroe*), Nick Chinlund (*Calderon*), Joe Viterelli (*Tony*), Michael Papajohn (*Schiff*), Mark Rolston (*J. Scar*), Tony Longo (*Little Mike*), Roma Maffia (*Claire*), John Slattery (*Corvan*), Gerry Becker (*Morehart*), Robert Miranda (*Frediano*), Rocco Sisto (*Pauley*), John Snyder (*Sal*), Melora Walters (*Darleen*), Olek Krupa (*Sergei*), K. Todd Freeman (*Dutton*), Cylk Cozart (*Darryl*), Gerald Berns (*The Young Agent*), Rick Batalla (*The Bartender*), Ismael "East" carlo (*The Priest*), Steve Ford (*Knoland*), James Short (*The Crane Sniper*), Thomas J. Huff (*Soves*), Michael Gregory (*Leivan*), A.J. Nay (*Sniper #2*), Patrick Kilpatrick (*Haggerty*), Camryn Manheim (*The Nurse*), Skipp Sudduth (*The Watchcommander*), Anthony Fusco, Gregory McKinney, Craig Barnett, Brian Libby, Dan Wynands, Corey Joshua Taylor, Rick Marzan, Sonny H. King, David Wolos-Fonteno, Edward Rote, Michael Cameron, Tim Colceri, Dieter R. Trippel, Matthew Mahaney, Michael Stone, Denis Forest, Richie Varga, Christopher Mankiewicz, Kevin Fry, Sam Scarber, Clayton Landey, Diana Morgan, Ben Shenkman, Dorin Seymour, Dominic Marcus, Pat Collins, Vic Polizos, Terry Beeman, Camille Winbush, Michael Gregory Gong, James Clark, Sebastian LaCause, Frank Minitello, Charles Chiquete, Al Cerullo, Glenndon Chatman, David Bilson, Rick Shuster
P: Arnold & Anne Kopelson **D:** Charles Russell **SCR:** Tony Puryear & Walon Green **STORY:** Tony Puryear, Walon Green & Michael S. Chernuchin **PHOTOG:** Adam Greenberg **VS-FX SPRVSR:** John E. Sullivan **MUSIC:** Alan Silvestri **SONGS:** Where Do We Go from Here, & Caught a Train
blurb: "He will erase your past to protect your future"
"The best action movie of the summer by far. Schwarzenegger proves he is the biggest, baddest and best action hero alive. Vanessa Williams is a revelation"—John Corcoran, KCAL-TV
Exciting action-thriller: Specialist erases identities of people in Witness Protection Program

Eraserhead
1977, (USA), Libra/Col/AFI, b&w, 90 mins.
W: Jack Nance (*Henry Spencer*), Charlotte Stewart (*Mary X*), Allen Joseph (*Mr. X*), Jeanne Bates (*Mrs. X*), Judith Anna Roberts (*The Beautiful Girl Across the Hall*), Laurel Near (*The Lady in the Radiator*), V. Phipps-Wilson (*The Landlady*), Jack Fisk (*The Man in the Planet*), Jean Lange (*The Grandmother*), Thomas Coulson (*The Boy*), Neil Moran (*The Boss*), John Monez (*The Bum*), Darwin Jostin (*Paul*), Brad Keeler (*The Little Boy*), Hal Landon Jr. (*The Pencil Machine Operator*), Jennifer Lynch (*The Little Girl*), Gill Dennis, Peggy Lynch, Doddie Keeler, Toby Keeler, Raymond Walsh
WRIT, P & D: David Lynch
Bizarre fantasy, cult classic: Nerd sires monstrosity

Ercole al Centro della Terra (Hercules at the Center of the Earth)
1961, (It), Omnia/Woolner Bros., color, 83 mins.
W: Reg Park (*Hercules*), Eleonora Ruffo, Christopher Lee, Giorgio Ardisson, Ely Draco

Ercolee La Regina Di Lidia: SYLVIA KOSCINA

P: Achille Piazzi   D: Mario Bava   SCR: Alessandro Continenza, Mario Bava, Duccio Tessari & Franco Prosperi
US title: **Hercules in the Haunted World**
Modest "Sword & Sandal" with horror themes: Muscleman meets vampire

Ercole alla Conquista della Atlantide (Hercules at the Conquest of Atlatis)
1961, (It-Fr), Woolner Bros., color, 87 mins.
W: Reg Park (*Hercules*), Fay Spain, Ettore Manni, Luciano Marin, Laura Altan, Mario Petri, Maria Salerno
P: Achille Piazzi   D: Vittorio Cottafavi   SCR: Alessandro Continenza, Vittorio Cottafavi & Duccio Tessari
USA retitle, **Hercules and the Captive Women** *A.k.a.* **Hercules and the Conquest of Atlantis** *and* **Hercules and the Haunted Women**
Standard "Sword & Sandal": Hero vs. evil Atlantean queen

Ercole Contro i Figli del Sole (Hercules Against the Sons of the Sun)
1963, (It-Sp), Wonder, color, 91 mins.
W: Mark Forest, Anna Maria Pace, Andrea Scotti, Angela Rho
P, D, & SCR: Oswaldo Civirani
Standard "Sword & Sandal": Muscleman vs. King of Incas

Ercole Contro i Tiranni di Babilonia (Hercules Against the Tyrants of Babylon)
1964, (It), AIP-TV, color
W: Rock Stevens (*Hercules*), Helga Line, Mario Petri
D: Domenico Paolella   SCR: L. Martino & Domenico Paolella
USA retitle, **Hercules and the Tyrants of Babylon**
Standard "Sword & Sandal": King of Assyria learns that Babylonian despots have enslaved Queen of Helledes

Ercole Contro Roma (Hercules Against Rome)
1964, (It-Fr), AIP-TV, color
W: Alan Steel [Sergio Ciani], Wandisa Guida, Daniele Vargas
D: Piero Pierotti   SCR: Arpad De Riso & Nino Scolaro
Minor "Sword & Sandal": Strongman opposes tyranny

Ercole e la Regina di Lidia (Hercules and the Queen of Lydia)
1959, (It-Fr), Lux-Galatea/Embassy/WB, color, 105 mins.
W: Steve Reeves (*Hercules*), Sylva Koscina (*Iole*), Sylvia Lopez (*Omphale*), Primo Carnera (*Antaeus*), Gabriele Antonioni (*Ulysses*), Carlo D'Angelo (*Creon*), Patrizia Della Rovere (*Penelope*), Mimmo Palmara, Sergio Fantoni, Andrea Fantasia, Cesare Fantoni
P: Bruno Vailati   D: Pietro Francisci   SCR: Ennio De Concini & Pietro Francisci, from a story by Pietro Francisci, based on the legends of Hercules and Omphale
USA retitle, **Hercules Unchained**
Standard "Sword & Sandal", sequel to **Hercules**: *Muscleman lured by slimy queen*

Erik the Conqueror
see **Gli Invasori**

Erik the Viking
1989, (GB), Prominent Features/Orion, color, 104 mins.
W: Tim Robbins (*Erik*), Mickey Rooney (*Erik's Grandfather*), Eartha Kitt (*Freya*), Terry Jones (*King Arnulf*), Tim McInnerny (*Sven the Berserk*), John Cleese (*Halfdan the Black*), Imogen Stubbs (*Princess Aud*), Tsutomu Sekine, Anthony Sher, Anthony Sher (*Loki*), Gary Cody (*Keitel Blacksmith*), Charles McKeown (*Sven's Dad*), John Gordon Sinclair (*Ivar the Boneless*), Richard Ridings (*Thorfinn Skullsplitter*), Freddie Jones (*Harald the Missionary*), Samantha Bond (*Helga*), Danny Schiller (*Snorri the Miserable*), Jim Broadbent, Jim Carter, Jay Simpson, Matyelox Gibbs, Tilly Vosburgh, John Scott Martin, Sian Thomas, Sarah Crowden, Bernard Padden, Bernard Latham, Julia McCarthy, Allan Surtees, Sandra Voe, Sally Jones, Angela Connolly, Andrew Maclachlan, Tim Killick, Cyril Shaps, Graham McTavish, Peter Geeves, Paddy Joyce, Neil Innes, Colin Harper, Harry Jones, Barry McCarthy, Simon Evans, Matthew Baker, Dave Duffy, Frank Bednash
WRIT & D: Terry Jones   PHOTOG: Ian Wilson
Standard comedy-fantasy: Norse warrior seeks gods' aid

Ernest Scared Stupid
1991, (USA), Touchstone, color, 92 mins.
W: Jim Varney (*Ernest*), Eartha Kitt, Austin Nagler, Jonas Moscartolo, Shay Astar
D & SCR: John R. Cherry III   MUSIC: Bruce Arntson
Standard juvenile comedy: Moron meets monsters

Ernest Saves Christmas
1988, (USA), Touchstone/Buena Vista, color, 89 mins.
W: Jim Varney (*Ernest P. Worrell*), Douglas Seale (*Santa*), Oliver Clark (*Joe Carruthers*), Noelle Parker (*Harmony*), Gailard Sartain (*Chuck*), Billie Bird (*Mary Morrissey*), Bill Byrge (*Bobby*), Robert Lesser (*Marty*), Key Howard, Jack Swanson, Patty Maloney, Bill Cordell, Jesse Stone, Bob Barnes
D: John Cherry   SCR: B. Kline & Ed Turner   PHOTOG: Peter Stein
   MUSIC: Mark Snow   SPCL-FX SPRVSR: Tim McHugh
Juvenile comedy-fantasy: Nerdish yahoo aids tired Santa

The Erotic Adventures of Snow White
see **Grimm's Fairy Tales for Adults**

The Erotic Adventures of the Three Musketeers
1971, (W. Ger), color, 80 mins.
W: Achim Hammer, Peter Graf, Ingrid Steeger, Jurg Coray
A.k.a. **The Three Musketeers and Their Sexual Adventures** *and* **Sex Adventures of the Three Musketeers**
Minor soft-porn thriller: Swordsmen dally

The Erotic Experiences of Frankenstein
see **Les Experiences Erotiques de Frankenstein**

Erotic House of Wax
1998, (USA), color, 75 mins.
Mior eroto-horror

Erratic Power
1910, (GB), Cricks & Martin, b&w, 405 ft. (123.4m)
D: Dave Aylott
Minor fantasy short: Prof's magic wand reverses things and people

The Eruption of Mont-Pele
1902, (Fr), Star, b&w, 30m (98.4 ft./1.7 mins.)
D: Georges Melies
Standard docu-thriller: Volcano devastates

Escapade
see **Atoll K**

Escape
1971, (USA), ABC-TV/Paramount TV, color, 90 mins

Escape From L.A.: HARRY DEAN STANTON, ADRIENNE BARBEU, KURT RUSSELL AND DONALD PLEASENCE

W: Christopher George, Avery Schreiber, Gloria Grahame, Huntz Hall, William Schallert, William Windom
P: Bruce Lansbury   **D:** John Llewellyn Moxey   **TELEPLAY:** Paul Playdon
TVM, standard thriller: Magician-escape artist stops egomaniac from conquering world

Escape by Night
see Clash by Night

Escape by Night
1954, (GB), Tempean/Eros, b&w, 79 mins.
W: Bonar Colleano (*Tom Buchan*), Andrew Ray (*Joey Weston*), Sidney James (*Gino Rossi*), Ted Ray (*Mr. Weston*), Peter Sinclai (*MacNaughton*), Patrick Barr (*Insp. Frampton*), Simone Silva (*Rosetta Mantania*), Avice Landone (*Mrs. Weston*), Ronald Adam (*Tallboy*)
P: Robert Baker & Monty Berman   **D & SCR:** John Gilling
Standard crime-thriller: Reporter nabs fugitive vice king

Escape Clause
1996, (USA), color, 100 mins.
W: Andrew McCarthy, Paul Sorvino
Made-for-Video, standard thriller: Executive suspected of killing wife

Escape from Atlantis
1997, (USA), color, 95 mins.
W: Jeff Speakman, Mercedes McNab (*Claudia*)
Standard adventure-thriller: Father and three teens find uncharted land

Escape from Broadmoor (1913)
see The Broken Chisel

Escape from Broadmoor
1948, (GB), Int'l Motion Pictures/Grand Nat'l, b&w, 37 mins.
W: John Stuart (*Insp. Thornton*), Victoria Hopper (*Susan*), John Le-Mesurier (*Pendicot*), Frank Hawkins (*Roger Trent*), Anthony Doonan (*Jenkins*), T. Gilly Fenwick (*Sandy*)
P: Harry Reynolds   **WRIT & D:** John Gilling
Standard fantasy: Murdered girl's ghost seeks vengeance on madman

Escape from Hell
1964, (USA), Crown Int'l, b&w, 80 mins.
W: Mark Stevens
Minor melodrama

Escape from L.A.
1996, (USA), Para, color, 101 mins
W: Kurt Russell, Cliff Robertson, Pam Grier, Steve Buscemi, George Corraface, A.J. Langer, Peter Fonda, Leland Orser
D: John Carpenter   **SCR:** John Carpenter, Kurt Russell & Debra Hill
Standard SF-thriller: Theocracy vs. anarchy in Los Angeles of 2013

Escape from New York
1981, (USA), Debra Hill/Int'l Film Investors/Avco Embassy, color, 96 mins.
W: Kurt Russell (*S.D. "Snake" Plissken*), Lee Van Cleef (*Bob Hauk*), Isaac Hayes (*"The Duke"*), Donald Pleasence (*The President*), Ernest Borgnine (*Cabbie*),

Adrienne Barbeau (*Maggie*), Harry Dean Stanton (*"Brain"*), Tom Atkins (*Rehme*), Charles Cyphers (*The Sec'y of State*), Season Hubley (*The Girl in Chock Full O' Nuts*), John Strobel
P: Larry Franco & Debra Hill   **D:** John Carpenter   **SCR:** John Carpenter & Nick Castle   **PHOTOG:** Dean Cundey   **MUSIC:** John Carpenter & Alan Howarth
Standard SF-thriller: Criminal must rescue U.S. president from prison island of Manhattan

Escape from Planet Earth
see Doomsday Machine

Escape from Terror
1960, (USA), Coogan-Rogers, color, 70 mins.
W: Jackie Coogan, Mona Knox
Standard thriller

Escape from the Bronx
1985, (It), New Line Cinema, color, 80 mins.
W: Mark Gregory (*Trash*), Henry Silva (*Wangler*), Valeria D'Obici (*Moon*), Timothy Brent, Paolo Malco, Moana Pozzi, Thomas Moore, Antonio Sabato, Alessandro Prete, Massimo Vanni, Andrea Coppola, Eva Czemerys, Salvatore Furnari, Romano Puppo, Carla Brait, Thomas Felleghy, Maurizio Fardo
D: Enzo G. Castellari   **SCR:** Tito Carpi & Enzo G. Castellari, from a story by Tito Carpi   **PHOTOG:** Blasco Giurato   **SPCL-FX:** Corridori   **MUSIC:** Francesco De Masi
TV retitle, Escape 2000
Minor SF-thriller: Exterminator ousts tenants

Escape from the Planet of the Apes
1971, (USA), Arthur P. Jacobs/20th-Fox, color, 98 mins.
W: Roddy McDowall (*Cornelius*), Kim Hunter (*Zira*), Eric Braeden (*Dr. Otto Hasslein*), Bradford Dillman (*Dr. Louis Dixon*), Ricardo Montalban (*Armando*), Natalie Trundy (*Dr. Stephanie Branton*), Sal Mineo (*Dr. Milo*), William Windom (*The President*), Jason Evers (*E-2*), John Randolph (*The Chairman*), Albert Salmi (*E-1*), Harry Lauter (*Gen. Winthrop*), Tom Lowell (*The Orderly*), Roy E. Glenn Sr. (*The Lawyer*), James Bacon (*Gen. Faulkner*), Peter Forster (*The Cardinal*), M. Emmet Walsh (*The Aide*), Norman Burton (*The Army Officer*), William Woodson (*The Naval Officer*), Gene Whittington (*The Marine Captain*), Army Archerd (*The Referee*), Donald Elson (*The Curator*), Bill Bonds (*The TV Newscaster*), Karl Bruck
D: Don Taylor   **SCR:** Paul Dehn, from characters created by Pierre Boulle   **PHOTOG:** Joseph Biroc   **SPCL-FX:** Howard A. Anderson Co.   **MUSIC:** Jerry Goldsmith
Standard SF-adventure, 3rd installment in popular Apes series: Intelligent simians from future arrive in 20th century. cf. **Conquest of the Planet of the Apes**

Escape in the Fog
1945, (USA), Col, b&w, 63 mins.
W: Otto Kruger, Nina Foch, William Wright, Konstantin Shayne
D: Oscar "Budd" Boetticher Jr.
Standard melodrama: Girl dreams of murder, meets victim in real life

The Escape of Mechagodzilla

see Terror of Mechagodzilla

Escape Route
1953, (GB), Banner/Eros/Lippert, b&w, 79 mins.
<u>W:</u> George Raft (*Steve Rossi*), Sally Gray (*Joan Miller*), Clifford Evans (*Michael Grand*), Reginald Tate (*Col. Wilkes*), Patricia Laffan (*Miss Brooks*), Frederick Piper (*Insp. Reed*), Roddy Hughes, June Ashley, John Warwick
<u>D:</u> Seymour Friedman & Peter Graham Scott   <u>SCR:</u> John Baines & Nicholas Phipps   <u>STORY:</u> John Baines

Escape From The Planet of the Apes: KIM HUNTER AND CHIMP

USA retitle, **I'll Get You**
Standard crime-thriller: FBI agent poses as fugitive, saves kidnapped scientists

Escapes
1986, (USA), color, 72 mins.
<u>W:</u> Vincent Price, Jerry Grisham, Lee Canfield, Gil Reade, John Mitchum
<u>D:</u> David Steensland
Standard anthology of 5 short thrillers: Aliens, time travel, telepathy etc.

Escape to Danger
1943, (GB), RKO, b&w, 92 mins.
<u>W:</u> Eric Portman (*Arthur Lawrence*), Ann Dvorak (*Joan Grahame*), Karel Stepanek (*Franz von Brinkman*), Ronald Ward (*Rupert Chessman*), Ronald Adam (*George Merrick*), Charles Victor (*PO Flanagan*), Lily Kann (*Karin Moeller*), David Peel (*Lt. Peter Leighton*), Felix Aylmer (*Sir Alfred Horton*), Brefni O'Rorke (*The Security Officer*), Marjorie Rhodes (*Mrs. Pickles*), A.E. Matthews (*Sir Thomas Leighton*), Frederick Cooper (*Goesta*), Ivor Barnard (*Henry Waud*)
<u>P:</u> William Sistrom   <u>D:</u> Lance Comfort & Mutz Greenbaum   <u>SCR:</u> Wolfgang Wilhelm & Jack Whittingham   <u>STORY:</u> Patrick Kirwin
Standard thriller: English schoolmistress poses as Danish quisling, helps catch German agent

Escape to Nowhere
1974, (Fr), Peppercorn-Wormser, color, 118 mins.
<u>W:</u> Lino Ventura, Lea Massari
Standard melodrama

Escape to Witch Mountain
1975, (USA), Walt Disney/Buena Vista, color, 97 mins.
<u>W:</u> Eddie Albert (*Jason O'Day*), Ray Milland (*Aristotle Bolt*), Donald Pleasence (*Lucas Deranian*), Kim Richards (*Tia*), Ike Eisenmann (*Tony*), Denver Pyle (*Uncle Bene*), Walter Barnes (*Sheriff Purdy*), Reta Shaw (*Mrs. Grindley*), Paul Sorensen (*Sgt. Foss*), Dan Seymour, Lawrence Montaigne, Alfred Ryder, Harry Holcombe
<u>P:</u> Jerome Courtland   <u>D:</u> John Hough   <u>SCR:</u> Robert Malcolm Young, from a book by Alexander Key   <u>PHOTOG:</u> Frank Phillips   <u>SPCL-FX:</u> Art Cruickshank & Danny Lee   <u>MUSIC:</u> Johnny Mandel
Standard SF-fantasy: Extraterrestrial children flee from authorities and villains. cf. Return from Witch Mountain

Escape to Witch Mountain
1995, (USA), Walt Disney, color, 95 mins.

<u>W:</u> Erik von Detten, Elisabeth Moss, Robert Vaughn, Vincent Schiavelli, Lynne Moody, Perrey Reeves, Henry Gibson, Kevin Tighe, Brad Dourif
<u>D & TELEPLAY:</u> Peter Rader   <u>PHOTOG:</u> Russ Alsobrook   <u>MUSIC:</u> Richard Marvin
TVM, standard SF-fantasy remake

Escape 2000
1983, (Austral), Filmco/New World, color, 80 mins.
<u>W:</u> Steve Railsback (*Paul*), Olivia Hussey (*Chris*), Michael Craig (*Thatcher*), Noel Ferrier (*Mallory*), Carmen Duncan (*Jennifer*), Lynda Stoner (*Rita*), Roger Ward (*Ritter*), Michael Petrovich (*Tito*), Gus Mercurio (*Red*), John Ley (*Dodge*), Steve Rackmann (*Alph*), Marina Finaly (*Melinda*), John Godden (*Andy*), Bill Young (*Griff*)
<u>D:</u> Brian Trenchard-Smith   <u>SCR:</u> Jon George & Neill Hicks, from a story by George Schenck, Robert Williams & David Lawrence   <u>PHOTOG:</u> John McClean   <u>MUSIC:</u> Brian May
A.k.a. Turkey Shoot
Standard SF-thriller: Future "social deviants" hunted by behavior-modification agents

Escape 2000 (1985)
see Escape from the Bronx

Les Escargots (The Snails)
1965, (Fr), color
Animated feature, runner-up for Best Documentary in SF Field at Trieste's 4th International Science-Fiction Festival

Esclave des Amazones
see Love Slaves of the Amazons

The Escort
1997, (USA), color, 95 mins.
<u>W:</u> Shauna O'Brien, Landon Hall, Scott Coppola
Made-for-Video, standard thriller: Past haunts proprietor of escort service

Escort for Hire
1960, (GB), danziger/MGM, color, 66 mins.
<u>W:</u> June Thorburn (*Terry Kennedy*), Noel Trevarthen (*Steve Walker*), Peter Murray (*Buzz Jenkins*), Guy Middleton (*Arthur Vickers*), Jan Holden (*Elizabeth Quinn*), Peter Butterworth (*Insp. Bruce*), Mar Laura Wood (*Barbara*), Derek Blomfield (*Jack*), Jill Melford (*Nadia*), Patricia Plunkett (*Eldon Baker*), C. Denier Warren (*Porter*)
<u>P:</u> Brian Taylor   <u>D:</u> Godfrey Grayson   <u>STORY:</u> Mark Grantham
Standard crime-thriller: Unemployed actor becomes escort, is framed for rich client's death

Esmeralda
1922, (GB), Master Films/BEF, b&w, 1,100 ft. (335.3m)
<u>W:</u> Sybil Thorndike (*Esmeralda*), Booth Conway (*Quasimodo*), Arthur Kingsley (*Phoebus*), Annesley Hely (*The Priest*)
<u>D:</u> Edwin J. Collins   <u>SCR:</u> Frank Miller, from Victor Hugo's novel *Notre Dame de Paris*
A.k.a. The Hunchback of Notre Dame
Standard melodrama: Hunchback loves gypsy girl

Esop (Aesop)
1968, (Bulgar-Czech), color
<u>D:</u> Rangel Vulchanov
Minor fantasy: Fables enacted

El Espejo de la Bruja (The Witch's Mirror)
1961, (Mex), b&w, 75 mins.
<u>W:</u> Rosita Arenas, Armando Calvo, Isabella Corona, Dino de Marco
<u>D:</u> Chano Urueto
Standard horror-fantasy: Skilled witch, mad surgeon, grisly murder, and a mirror possessing unearthly powers

Espionage
1937, (USA), MGM, b&w, 67 mins.
<u>W:</u> Edmund Lowe, Madge Evans, Paul Lukas, Skeets Gallagher, Ketti Gallion, Leonid Kinskey, Billy Gilbert
<u>D:</u> Kurt Neumann
Modest thriller: Rival reporters trail arms tycoon on Orient Express

Espy
1975, (Jap), Toho, color
Standard SF-thriller

Eternal Evil
1987, (USA-Can), color, 85 mins.
<u>W:</u> Winston Rekert, Karen Black (*Janus*), John Novak (*Kaufman*), Andrew Bednarski (*Matthew*), Lois Maxwell
<u>D:</u> George Mihalka
Minor thriller: Beautiful occultist snares innocent

Eternal Love
see L'Eternel Retour

The Eternal Return
see L'Eternel Retour

L'Eternel Retour (The Eternal Return)
1942, (Fr), Andre Paulve/Discina, b&w, 111 mins.
W: Jean Marais, Madeleine Sologne, Alexandre Rignault
D: Jean Delannoy   SCR: Jean Cocteau   MUSIC: Georges Auric
A.k.a. Eternal Love
Classic fantasy-melodrama: Mystery surrounds lovers

Et Mourir de Plaisir (And to Die of Pleasure)
1960, (It-Fr), E.G.E./Documento/Para, color, 90 mins. (edited, 84 mins.)
W: Mel Ferrer (*Leopoldo von Karnstein*), Elsa Martinelli (*Georgia Monteverdi*),
   Annette Vadim (*Carmilla von Karnstein*), Serge Marquand (*Giuseppe*),
   Jacques-Rene Chauffard (*Dr. Valeri*), Marc Allegret (*Signor Monteverdi*),
   Camilla Stroyberg (*Marthe*), Gabriella Farinon (*Lisa*), Alberto Bonucci
   (*Carlo Ruggieri*)
P: Raymond Eger   D: Roger Vadim   SCR: Roger Vadim & Roger Vailland
   ADAPT: Claude Brule & Claude Martin, from Sheridan LeFanu's novel
   Carmilla   PHOTOG: Claude Renoir   MUSIC: Jean Prodromides
USA retitle, Blood and Roses
Adult horror-fantasy (USA release deleted scenes of vampire-lesbian eroticism):
   Spirit of dead vampiress takes possession of modern girl's body

L'Etrange Histoire du Juge Cordier
see Diary of A Madman

E.T.—The Extra-Terrestrial
1982, (USA), Univ, color, 112 mins.
W: Henry Thomas (*Elliott*), Dee Wallace, Drew Barrymore, Peter Coyote (*"Keys"*),
   Robert Macnaughton
P: Steven Spielberg & Kathleen Kennedy   D: Steven Spielberg   SCR:
   Melissa Mathison   PHOTOG: Allen Daviau   MUSIC: John Williams
SF-fantasy classic: Earth boy befriends space alien

Ethel's Danger
1912, (GB), Barker, b&w, 760 ft. (231.6m)
D: Bert Haldane
Standard crime-thriller: Girl saved from Soho kidnapper

Eugene Aram
1914, (GB), Cricks, b&w, 4,300 ft. (1310.6m)
W: Jack Leigh (*Eugene Aram*), Mary Manners (*Madeleine Lester*), John Sargent
   (*Richard Houseman*), Stewart Patterson (*Walter Lester*), Wingold Lawrence
   (*Geoffrey Lester*), Antonia Reith (*Elinor Lester*), Frank Melrose (*Rowland
   Lester*), Lionel d'Aragon (*The Judge*), Fred Southern (*Peter Dealtry*), Henry
   Foster (*Cpl. Bunting*), Harold Snell (*Mr. Courtland*)
D & SCR, Edwin J. Collins, from a novel by Edward Bulwer-Lytton
Standard thriller (75 scenes): Respected 18th-century scholar blackmailed by ex-partner in
   robbery, is executed for crime he did not commit

Eugenie...The Story of Her Journey into Perversion
1969, (GB-Sp-W. Ger), Distinction Films, color. 91 mins
W: Christopher Lee, Maria Rohm, Marie Liljedahl, Jack Taylor
WRIT & P: Harry Alan Towers   D: Jesus Franco
A.k.a. Philosophy in the Boudoir
Standard eroto-thriller: Jaded female De Sade fan seduces virgin

Eve
see The Face of Eve

The Evening Visitors
see Les Visiteurs du Soir

Eve of Destruction
1991, (USA), Interscope/Nelson/New Line, color, 101 mins.
W: Gregory Hines (*Jim McQuade*), Renee Soutendijk (*Eve Simmons/ Eve VIII*),
   Michael Greene (*Gen. Curtis*), Kurt Fuller (*Schneider*), John M. Jackson (*Peter
   Arnold*), David Hayward (*Cal*), Dakin Matthews (*Singleton*), Richard
   Cummings Jr. (*Lt. Frankel*), Christopher Kriesa (*Korman*), Larry Anderson
   (*The BMW Businessman*), Maryedith Burrell (*Dawn Perlin*), Ross Malinger
   (*Timmy Arnold*), Nelson Mashita (*The Scientist/Waiter*), Loren Haynes (*Steve,
   the Robot*), Alan Haufrect (*Dr. Heller*), Norman Merrill Jr. (*The 1st Scientist*),
   Craig Oldfather (*The Young Man on the Train*), Greg Collins (*Skaaren*), Tim
   Russ (*Carter*), Ed Matthews (*Bank Robber #1*), Tom Morga (*Bank Robber #2*),
   Mike Jolly (*Stevenson*), Marga Chavez (*Elvira*), Sharon Sebastian (*The News
   Anchor*), Coleen Maloney (*The Bartender*), Daryk Christian (*Lt. Griffin*),
   Daniel O'Haco (*Buddy #1*), Eugene Robert Glazer (*Buddy #2*), Carl Ciarfalio
   (*The Trooper Sgt.*), Thomas Lupo, Jeff McCarthy, George P. Wilbur, Bill
   Gratton, Thomas Knickerbocker, Nancy Locke, Bethany Richards, Jay
   Pickett, Joe Kane, Jim Antonio, Paul Tuerpe, Ronald William Lawrence,
   Dan Barringer, Randy Hall, Derek Barton, John Moio, Richard Collier, Sue
   Burke
D: Duncan Gibbins   SCR: Duncan Gibbins & Yale Udoff   PHOTOG:
   Alan Hume   SPCL-FX: Jeff Frink & Steve Riley   MUSIC:
   Philippe Sarde   SONGS: Acapulco, Got to Have It, Second Wind, &
   Round and Round
Standard SF-thriller: Female android runs amok

Event Horizon
1997, (USA), Para, color

W: Laurence Fishburne, Kathleen Quinlan, Sam Neill, Joely Richardson
D: Paul Anderson   SCR: Philip Eisner   MUSIC: Michael Kamen
Unusual SF-horror: Ancient spaceship harbors terror

Ever After: A Cinderella Story
1998, (USA), 20th-Fox, color
W: Drew Barrymore, Anjelica Huston, Dougray Scott, Jeanne Moreau
D: Andy Tennant
Unusual fantasy: Drudge meets prince

Every Man His Own Cigar Lighter
see Un Pea de Feu, S.V.P.

Everything's Ducky
1961, (USA), Barbroo/Col, b&w, 81 mins.
W: Mickey Rooney, Buddy Hackett, Joanie Sommers, Jackie Cooper, Gene
   Blakely, Roland Winters, Richard Deacon, Elizabeth MacRae, James
   Milhollin, Gordon Jones, Walker Edmiston (*The Voice of "Scuttlebut"*)
P: Red Doff   D: Don Taylor   SCR: John Fenton Murray & Benedict
   Freedman   PHOTOG: Carl Guthrie   MUSIC: Harold Spina
   SONG: Moonlight Music
Juvenile comedy-fantasy: Sailors find talking duck

Eve the Wild Woman
see Kong Island

The Evictors
1979, (USA), AIP, color, 92 mins.
W: Vic Morrow, Michael Parks, Jessica Harper, Sue Ane Langdon,
   Dennis Fimple
P & D: Charles B. Pierce   SCR: Charles B. Pierce & Gary Rusoff
Minor thriller: Real estate agent is killer

Evidence in Concrete
1960, (GB), Merton Park/Anglo-Amalgamated, b&w, 30 mins.
W: Russell Napier (*Supt. Duggan*), Howard Pays (*Sgt. Adams*), Jill
   Hyem (*Sandra*), Derek Sydney (*Jellineck*), Frederick Piper (*Ellis*),
   Kenneth Kendall (*The Announcer*)
P: Jack Greenwood   D: Gordon Hales   STORY: James Eastwood, from a novel
   by Edgar Lustgarten
Standard short crime-thriller: Whiskey hijackers connected with girl's death

The Evil
1978, (USA), Rangoon/New World, color, 90 mins.
W: Richard Crenna (*C.J.*), Joanna Pettet (*Caroline*), Andrew Prine (*Raymond*),
   Cassie Yates (*Mary*), Gorge O'Hanlon Jr. (*Pete*), Lynne Moody (*Felecia*),
   George Viharo (*Dwight*), Ed Bakey (*Sam*), Mary Louise Weller (*Laurie*),
   Victor Buono (*The Devil*), Milton Selzer (*The Realtor*), Galen Thompson
   (*Vargas*), Emory Souza (*The Demon*)
D: Gus Trikonis   SCR: Donald G. Thompson   PHOTOG: Mario DiLeo
   MUSIC: Johnny Harris
laser-disc title, House of Evil
Standard horror-fantasy: House harbors satanic force

Evil Altar
1989, (USA), color, 90 mins.
W: William Smith, Robert Z'Dar, Pepper Martin, Ryan Rao, Theresa
   Cooney
D: James R. Winburn
Minor fantasy-thriller: Satan worshipper controls small town

Evil Below
1989, (USA), Raedon Entertainment, color, 90 mins.
W: Wayne Crawford, June Chadwick
D: Jean-Claude Dubois
Minor adventure-thriller: Hunt for legendary shipwreck

Evil Brain from Outer Space
1964, (Jap), Shintoho/Manly TV, color
W: Junko Ikeuchi, Ken Utsui
P: Mitsugi Okora   D: Teruo Ishii, Akira Mitsuwa & Koreyoshi Akasaka
   SCR: Ichiro Miyagawa
Minor SF-fantasy: Superhero vs. deformed space men

Evil Clutch
1989, (It), color, 88 mins.
W: Coralina Cataldi Tassoni, Diego Riba, Elena Cantarone, Luciano Crovato,
   Stafano Molinari
D & SCR: Andreas Marfori
Minor horror-thriller: Young people finds terror in haunted Alpine forest

The Evil Dead
1983, (USA), Renaissance/New Line, color, 80 mins.
W: Bruce Campbell, Ellen Sandweiss
WRIT & D: Sam Raimi   MUSIC: Joe Lo Duca
Horror-fantasy, minor classic: Students ressurect Sumerian demon

Evil Dead 2: Dead by Dawn
1987, (USA), Renaissance/Rosebud, color, 85 mins.

W: Bruce Campbell (*Ash*), Sarah Berry (*Annie*), Theodore Raimi (*Henrietta*), Dan Hicks, Kassie Wesley, Denise Bixler
D: Sam Raimi **SCR:** Sam Raimi & Scott Spiegel **MUSIC:** Joseph Lo Duca
Lively horror-satire: Ancient tome generates modern mayhem. cf. Army of Darkness

Evil Dead III
see Army of Darkness

An Evil-Doer's Sad End
1903, (GB), Williamson, b&w, 125 ft. (38.1m)
D: James Williamson
Minor fantasy short: Cop tears tramp to pieces

Evil Eden
see La Mort en Ce Jardin

The Evil Force
see 4D Man

Evil in the Deep
1977, (USA), Selected, color, 96 mins
W: Stephen Boyd, Rosey Grier, Cheryl Stoppelmoor [Cheryl Ladd]
P: Virginia Stone & J.A.S. McCombie **D:** Virginia Stone
blurb: "Rips your nerves to shreds!"
A.k.a. The Treasure of Jamaica Reef
Minor thriller (Jaws imitation): Scuba divers face terror

Evil Laugh
1986, (USA), color, 90 mins.
W: Tony Griffin, Kim McKamy, Jody Gibson, Dominick Brascia
D: Dominick Brascia
Minor thriller: Medical students meet serial killer

The Evil Mind
see The Clairvoyant (1934)

Evil Obsession
1996, (USA), color
W: Kimberly Stevens
Minor horror-fantasy

Evil of Dracula
1978, (Jap), color
Minor horror-fantasy: Vampire count's sinister deeds

Evil of Frankenstein
1964, (GB), Hammer/Univ, color, 86 mins.
W: Peter Cushing (*Baron Victor Frankenstein*), Sandor Eles (*Hans*), Peter Woodthorpe (*Zoltan*), Katy Wild (*The Beggar Girl*), Duncan Lamont (*The Police Chief*), Kiwi Kingston (*The Monster*), David Hutcheson, Caron Gardner, Tony Arpino, Kenneth Cove, James Maxwell, Frank Forsyth, Alister Williamson, Michele Scott, David Conville, Howard Goorney, Anthony Blackshaw, Timothy Bateson
P: Anthony Hinds **D:** Freddie Francis **SCR:** John Elder [Anthony Hinds]
PHOTOG: John Wilcox **SPCL-FX:** Les Bowie **MUSIC:** Don Banks
Standard horror-thriller: Fugitive scientist revives his monstrous creation

Evil's Commandment
1956, (It), b&w
W: Gianna Maria Canale
D: Riccardo Freda
Standard horror-fantasy (started the classic Italian horror cycle): Countess requires blood to maintain youth

Evils of Chinatown
see Confessions of an Opium Eater

Evils of the Mummy
see The Curse of the Mummy's Tomb

Evils of the Night
1984, (USA), Aquarius, color, 85 mins.
W: John Carradine, Neville Brand, Julie Newmar, Aldo Ray, Tina Lou-ise, Karrie Emerson, Bridget Hollman
P & D: Mardi Rustam **SCR:** Philip Dennis Connors & Mardi Rustam
Minor SF-horror: Cannibalistic space aliens trap campers

Evilspeak
1982, (USA), Leisure Investment Co.-Coronet Film/New World, color, 90 mins.
W: Clint Howard (*Stanley Coopersmith*), R.G. Armstrong, Don Stark, Joseph Cortese, Claude Earl Jones, Haywood Nelson, Charles Tyner, Hamilton Camp, Louie Gravance, Sue Casey, Jim Greenleaf, Lynn Hancock, Loren Lester, Kathy McCullen, Lenny Montana, Leonard O'John, Bennett Liss, Richard Moll, Katherine Kelly Lang, Robert Ta-fur, Kristine Alskog, Jane Bartelme, Thomas Hilliard, Nadine Reimers, Deborah Dawes, DeForest Covan, Alan Harris, Kenny Ferrugiaro, Sam Baldoni, Dick Drake, Victor Hunsberger Jr.
D: Eric Weston **SCR:** Joseph Garofalo & Eric Weston **STORY:** Joseph

Garofalo **PHOTOG:** Irv Goodnoff **MUSIC:** Roger Kellaway
Standard horror-fantasy: Satanism at military academy

Evil Spirits
1990, (USA), color, 95 mins.
W: Karen Black, Arte Johnson, Virginia Mayo, Michael Berryman, Martine Beswick, Bert Remsen, Yvette Vickers, Robert Quarry, Debra Lamb, Mikel Angel
D: Gary Graver **SCR:** Mikel Angel
Minor satire-thriller: Deranged landlady kills boarders

Evil Stalks This House
1981, (Can), Gaylord/Jack Barry-Dan Enright/Global, color
W: Jack Palance, Helen Hughes, Frances Hyland (*Maggie*), Michael Starr (*Tom*), Reginald Love (*Adams*)
D: Gordon Hessler **TELEPLAY:** Louis M. Heyward
TVM, minor thriller: Interloper terrorizes elderly women

Evil Toons
1991, (USA), color, 86 mins.
W: Suzanne Ager, David Carradine, Dick Miller, Monique Gabrielle, Michelle Bauer, Stacy Nix, Madison Stone, Don Dowe, Arte Johnson
D: Fred Olen Ray
Minor fantasy-satire: Sorority girls agree to renovate a "haunted" mansion

Evil Town
1987, (USA), color, 88 mins.
W: Dean Jagger, James Keach, Robert Walker Jr., Doria Cook, Michele Marsh
D: Edward Collins
Minor horror-thriller: Mad doctor creates zombies

The Evil Trap
1975, (It-Fr), color, 95 mins.
W: Marlene Jobert, Tomas Milian, Victor Lanoux, Jean Bouix, Michel Lonsdale
D: Yves Boisset, from a novel by Jean-Patrick Manchette
Modest thriller: Governess caught in kidnap and murder plot

Evil Under the Sun
1982, (GB), Mersham/Titan/WB, color, 117 mins.
W: Peter Ustinov (*Hercule Poirot*), Colin Blakely (*Sir Horace Blatt*), Jane Birkin (*Christine Redfern*), Maggie Smith (*Daphne Castle*), Nicholas Clay (*Patrick Redfern*), Roddy McDowall (*Rex Brewster*), Sylvia Miles (*Myra Gardner*), James Mason (*Odell Gardner*), Dennis Quilley (*Kenneth Marshall*), Diana Rigg (*Arlena Marshall*), Barbara Hicks (*The Sec'y*), Emily Hone (*Linda Marshall*), Cyril Conway (*The Surgeon*), John Alderson (*The Sgt.*), Paul Antrim (*The Inspector*), Richard Vernon (*Flewitt*), Dimitri Andreas (*Gino*), Robert Dorning (*The Concierge*)
P: John Brabourne & Richard Goodwin **D:** Guy Hamilton **SCR:** Anthony Shaffer, from a novel by Agatha Christie **PHOTOG:** Christopher Challis **MUSIC:** Cole Porter
Modest thriller: Belgian sleuth solves Yorkshire strangling

The Evil Within
1994, (Fr), color, 88 mins.
W: Emmanuelle Escourrou, Jean-Francois Guillotte
D: Alain Robak **SCR:** Alain Robak & Serge Cukier
A.k.a. Baby Blood
Minor horror-fantasy

Evocation Spirite (Spirit Summoning)
1899, (Fr), Star, b&w, 20m (65.6 ft./1.1 mins.)
D: Georges Melies
A.k.a. 'Summoning the Spirits'
Standard fantasy

Evolution
1923, (USA), Red Seal, b&w, 6 reels
Standard science docu: Development of life on Earth and man's attempts to control environment

Evolution
1931, (USA), Ideal, b&w, short

Evolver
1994, (USA), color, video, 95 mins.
W: Ethan Randall, Cassidy Rae, Eugene Williams, John de Lancie, Cindy Pickett, Paul Dooley, William H. Macy (*Voice*)
D: Mark Rosman
Mde-for-Video, standard SF-thriller: Aggressive robot terrorizes computer whiz

The Ewok Adventure
1984, (USA), Lucasfilm/ABC-TV, color, 97 mins.
W: Eric Walker (*Mace*), Aubree Miller (*Cindel*), Warwick Davis (*Wicket*), Dan Frishman (*Deej*), Fionnula Flanagan (*Catarine Towani*), Guy Boyd (*Jeremitt Towani*), Tony Cox (*Widdle*), Debbie Carrington (*Weechee*), Kevin Thompson (*Chukha-Trok*), Margarita Fernandez (*Kaink*), Pam Grizz (*Shodu*), Bobby Bell (*Logray*)
D & PHOTOG: John Korty **TELEPLAY:** Bob Carrau **STORY:** George Lucas **MUSIC:** Peter Bernstein **NARRATION:** Burl Ives
TVM, SF adventure: Crash-landed on alien moon, two children seek missing parents

Ewoks: The Battle for Endor

1985, (USA), Lucasfilm/ABC-TV, color, 97 mins.
W: Wilford Brimley *(Noa)*, Warwick Davis *(Wicket)*, Aubree Miller *(Cindel)*, Niki Botholo *(Teek)*, Sian Phillips *(Charal)*, Carel Struycken *(Terak)*, Daniel Frishman *(Deej)*, Pam Grizz *(Shodu)*, Tony Cox *(Willy)*, Paul Gleason *(Jeremitt)*, Eric Walker *(Mace)*, Roger Johnson *(The Lieutenant)*, Marianne Horine, Michael Pritchard, Johnny Weissmuller Jr.
D & TELEPLAY: Ken Wheat & Jim Wheat   STORY: George Lucas
PHOTOG: Isidore Mankofsky   SPCL-FX: Industrial Light & Magic   MUSIC: Peter Bernstein   SONG: *My Star*
TVM, modest SF-fantasy: Innocents face lizardlike fiends on moon of alien world

The Ex

1996, (USA), color, 90 mins.
W: Nick Mancuso *(David Kenyon)*, Suzy Amis *(Molly)*, Yancy Butler *(Diedre)*
Standard thriller: Architect plagued by psychotic first wife

Excalibur

1981, (GB), Orion/WB, color, 140 mins.
W: Nicol Williamson *(Merlin)*, Nigel Terry *(Arthur)*, Helen Mirren *(Morgana)*, Cherie Lunghi *(Guenevere)*, Nicholas Clay *(Lancelot)*, Paul Geoffrey *(Perceval)*, Gabriel Byrne *(Uther Pendragon)*, Keith Buckley *(Uryens)*, Liam Neeson *(Gawain)*, Clive Swift *(Ector)*, Corin Redgrave *(Cornwall)*, Katrine Boorman *(Igrayne)*, Robert Addie *(Mordred as a Young Man)*, Charley Boorman *(Mordred as a Boy)*, Niall O'Brien *(Kay)*, Patrick Stewart *(Leondegrance)*, Ciarin Hinds *(Lot)*, Liam O'Callaghan, Michael Muldoon, Mannix Flynn, Emmet Bergin, Garrett Keogh, Barbara Byrne, Kay McLaren, Eamonn Kelly, Brid Brennan
P & D:John Boorman   SCR: Rospo Pallenberg & John Boorman
ADAPT: Rospo Pallenberg, from Sir Thomas Malory's *Le Mort D'Arthur*
PHOTOG: Alex Thomson   SPCL-FX: Peter Hutchinson & Alan Whibley   MUSIC: Trevor Jones
orig. to be titled **Merlin and the Knights of King Arthur**
blurb: "Forged by a god. Foretold by a wizard. Found by a king"
Classic fantasy, elegant retelling of Arthurian legend: Celtic king unites ancient Britain

Excelsior!

1901, (Fr), Star, b&w, 40m (131.2 ft./2.2 mins.)
D: Georges Melies
GB retitle, **The Prince of Magicians**
Standard fantasy

Excursion in the Cosmos

see **Wycieczka w Kosmos**

L'Execution d'un Espion (The Execution of a Spy)

1897, (Fr), Star, b&w, 20m (65.6 ft./1.1 mins.)
D: Georges Melies
Standard melodrama

The Executioner

see **Not on Your Life!**

The Executioner

1970, (GB), Ameran/Col, color, 111 mins.
W: George Peppard *(John Shay)*, Joan Collins *(Sarah Booth)*, Judy Geeson *(Polly Bendel)*, Oscar Homolka *(Racovsky)*, Charles Gray *(Vaughan Jones)*, Alexander Scourby *(Prof. Parker)*, Nigel Patrick *(Col. Scott)*, Keith Michell *(Adam Booth)*, George Baker *(Philip Crawford)*, Peter Bull *(Butterfield)*, Peter Dyneley *(Balkov)*
P: Charles H. Schneer   D: Sam Wanamaker   SCR: Jack Pulman
STORY: Gordon McDonell
Standard thriller: British spy probes counter-espionage

The Execution of a Spy

see **L'Execution d'un Espion**

The Execution of Mary, Queen of Scots

1895, (USA), Edison, b&w, running time: Under 1 min.
Short melodrama, first known film with "special effects" (beheading): Scottish queen goes to Tower of London

Exile Express

1939, (USA), Grand Nat'l, b&w, 70 mins
W: Anna Sten, Alan Marshal, Ed Brophy, Jerome Cowan
Minor melodrama: Intrigue on train

Exit to Eden

1994, (USA), Savoy, color, 113 mins.
W: Dana Delany, Paul Mercurio, Rosie O'Donnell, Dan Aykroyd, Hector Elizondo, Iman, Stuart Wilson, Sandi Korn
D: Garry Marshall   SCR: Deborah Amelon & Bob Brunner, from Anne Rice's novel
MUSIC: Patrick Doyle
Standard eroto-comedy: Exclusive island resort caters to bizarre sexual tastes

Exo-Man

1977, (USA), Univ/NBC-TV, color, 95 mins.
W: David Ackroyd *(Nick Conrad)*, Ann Schedeen *(Emily Frost)*, A Martinez *(Raphael)*, Jose Ferrer *(Kermit Haas)*, Jonathan Segal *(Eddie Rubenstein)*, Kevin McCarthy *(Kamenski)*, Harry Morgan *(Travis)*, Jack Colvin *(Martin)*, John Moio *(Leandro)*, Richard Narita *(Jim Yamaguchi)*, George Sperdakos *(Dr. Garrick)*, Martin Speer *(Ted Kamenski)*, Randy Faustino *(Larry)*, Nick David *(Jack)*, Wina Sturgeon *(The TV Newswoman)*, Donald Moffat
D: Richard Irving   TELEPLAY: Henri Simoun & Lionel E. Siegel
STORY: Martin Caidin & Henri Simoun   PHOTOG: Enzo A. Martinelli   MUSIC: Dana Kaproff
TVM, standard SF-thriller: Electronic suit turns crippled physics professor into superhero

Exorcism at Midnight

see **Naked Evil**

Exorcism's Daughter

1974, (Sp), Howard Mahler/Nat'l Forum Corp., color, 93 mins.
W: Analia Gade, Francisco Rabal, Espartaco Santoni
WRIT & D: Rafael Morena Alba
A.k.a. **House of Insane Women**
Minor horror-fantasy: Girl driven mad by mother's death during attempted exorcism

The Exorcist

1973, (USA), Hoya/WB, color, 122 mins.
W: Ellen Burstyn *(Chris MacNeil)*, Linda Blair *(Regan MacNeil)*, Jason Miller *(Father Karras)*, Max von Sydow *(Father Merrin)*, Lee J. Cobb *(Lt. Kinderman)*, Kitty Winn *(Sharon)*, Jack MacGowran *(Burke Dennings)*, Titos Vandis *(Karras' Uncle)*, Rev. William O'Malley *(Father Dyer)*, Vasiliki Maliaros *(Karras' Mother)*, Wallace Rooney *(The Bishop)*, Rev. T. Bermingham *(The Pres. of the University)*, Ron Faber *(The Ass't Director)*, Barton Heyman, Peter Masterson, William Peter Blatty, Rudolf Schundler, Robert Gerringer, Mercedes McCambridge *(The Voice of the Demon)*
WRIT & P: William Peter Blatty, from his novel   D: William Friedkin   PHOTOG: Owen Roizman   SPCL-FX: Marcel Vercoutere   MUSIC: Krzysztof Penderecki
"...a serious attempt at a contemporary handling of a classic supernatual/horror theme"—Baird Searles, "Films," Magazine of Fantasy and Science Fiction, Vol. 49, No. 6 (Dec., 1975), p. 61
Classic horror-fantasy: Demon possesses young girl

Exorcist II: The Heretic

1977, (USA), WB, color, 117 mins.
W: Linda Blair *(Regan MacNeil)*, Richard Burton *(Father Lamond)*, Louise Fletcher *(Jean)*, Max von Sydow *(Father Merrin)*, James Earl Jones *(The Older Kokumo)*, Paul Henreid *(The Cardinal)*, Ned Beatty *(Edwards)*, Kitty Winn *(Sharon)*, George Skaff, Rose Portillo, Joey Green
P: John Boorman & Richard Lederer   D: John Boorman   SCR: William Goodhart, from characters created by William Peter Blatty   PHOTOG: William A. Fraker   MUSIC: Ennio Morricone
Standard thriller: Experiments in psychic research lead to revival of demonic forces

The Exorcist III

1990, (USA), Morgan Creek/20th-Fox, color, 105 mins.
W: George C. Scott *(Police Lt. Kinderman)*, Ed Flanders *(Father Dyer)*, Jason Miller *(Father Damien Karras)*, Nicol Williamson *(Father Morning)*, Scott Wilson *(Dr. Temple)*, Brad Dourif, Barbara Baxley, Viveca Lindfors, Don Gordon, Nancy Fish, George DiCenzo, Lee Richardson, Mary Jackson, Grand L. Bush, Ken Lerner, Tracy Thorne, Harry Carey Jr., Zohra Lampert, Sherrie Wills, Edward Lynch, Tyra Ferrell, Clifford David, Alexander Zuckerman, Lois Foraker, Father John Durkin, James Burgess, Kevin Corrigan, Peggy Alston, Bobby Deren, Jan Neuberger, Alexis Chieffet, David Dwyer, Debra Port, Walt MacPherson, Daniel Epper, Patrick Ewing, William Preston, Chuck Kinlaw, Demetrios Pappageorge, Jan Smook, Nina Hansen, Shane Wexel, John A. Coe, Ryan Paul Amick, Jodi Long, Kathy Gerber, Samuel L. Jackson, Amelia Campbell, Cherie Baron, Larry King, C. Everett Koop
WRIT & D: William Peter Blatty—from his novel *Legion*   PHOTOG: Gerry Fisher   MUSIC: Barry DeVorzon
orig. to be titled **The Exorcist 1990**
Standard horror-fantasy: Demonic spirit returns to wreak havoc

The Exotic Ones

1968, (USA), Ormond, b&w, 60 mins
W: Ron Ormond, June Ormond
P D & SCR: Ron Ormond
Minor horror-thriller: Marijuana monster terrorizes New Orleans' strippers

Expedition Moon

see **Rocketship X-M**

Les Experiences Erotiques de Frankenstein (The Erotic Experiences of Frankenstein)

1975, (Fr), color
W: Fernando Bilbao
Soft-porn horror-fantasy

Experiment in Evil

see **Le Testament du Dr. Cordelier**

Experiment in Terror

1962, (USA), Col, b&w, 122 mins.
W: Glenn Ford *(John Ripley)*, Lee Remick *(Kelly Sherwood)*, Stefanie Powers *(Toby)*,

Anita Soong (*Lisa*), Ross Martin (*Red Lynch*), Roy Poole (*Brad*), Ned Glass (*Popcorn*), Dick Crockett (*The FBI Agent*), Patricia Huston (*Nancy*), James Lanphier (*The Landlord*), Clifton James (*Capt. Moreno*), Gilbert Green (*The Special Agent*), William Bryant (*Chuck*), Sidney Miller (*The Drunk*), Sherry O'Neil (*Edna*), William Sharon (*Raymond Burkgardt*), Harvey Evans (*Dave*), Mari Lynn (*Penny*)
P & D: Blake Edwards **SCR:** The Gordons, from their novel *Operation Terror* **PHOTOG:** Philip H. Lathrop **MUSIC:** Henry Mancini
GB retitle, **Grip of Fear**
Tense thriller: Psychotic blackmails bank teller

Explorers
1985, (USA), Edward S. Feldman/Para, color, 110 mins.
W: Ethan Hawke (*Ben Crandall*), River Phoenix (*Wolfgang Muller*), Jason Presson (*Darren Woods*), Amanda Peterson (*Lori Swenson*), Dick Miller (*Charlie Drake*), Dana Ivey (*Mrs. Muller*), Robert Picardo (*Wak/Starkiller*), Leslie Rickert (*Neek*), James Cromwell (*Mr. Muller*), Bobby Fite (*Steve Jackson*), Meshach Taylor (*Gordon Miller*), Frank Welker (*An Alien Voice*), Fred Newman (*An Alien Voice*), Joanie Gerber (*An Alien Voice*), Belinda Balaski (*An Alien Voice*), Roger Behr (*An Alien Voice*), Neil Ross (*An Alien Voice*), Roger Peltz (*An Alien Voice*), Jay Stewart (*An Alien Voice*), Marilyn Schreffler (*An Alien Voice*), Bill Ratner (An *Alien Voice*), Robert Holt (*An Alien Voice*), Jane Kean (*An Alien Voice*), Tricia Bartholme, Bradley Gregg, George Olden, Chance Schwass, Eric Luke, Brooke Bundy, Taliesin Jaffe, Robert F. Boyle, Deborah A. Paddock, Karen Mayo-Chandler, Mary Hillstead, John P. Navin Jr., Simone Blue, Christa Denton, Angela Lee, Elaine Pagnozzi
D: Joe Dante **SCR:** Eric Luke **PHOTOG:** John Hora **VS-FX:** Industrial Light & Magic **SPCL MAKEUP FX:** Rob Bottin **MUSIC:** Jerry Goldsmith
Modest SF-fantasy: Teens meet friendly space creatures

Explosion
1970, (USA), AIP, color, 96 mins.
W: Don Stroud, Gordon Thomson
Minor melodrama

The Explosion of a Motor Car
1900, (GB), Hepworth, b&w, 100 ft. (30.5m)
W: Cecil Hepworth (*The Driver*), Henry Lawley (*The Passenger*)
D: Cecil M. Hepworth
USA retitle, **The Delights of Automobiling**
Standard fantasy: Car explosion blows passengers into pieces

Exposed
1947, (USA), Rep, b&w, 59 mins.
W: Adele Mara, Robert Scott
Minor melodrama

Exquisite Tenderness
see **The Surgeon**

The Exterminating Angel
see **El Angel Exterminador**

The Exterminator
1980, (USA), Avco Embassy, color, 101 mins.
W: Christopher George (*Det. Dalton*), Samantha Eggar (*Dr. Stewart*), Robert Ginty (*John Eastland*), Steve James (*Michael*), Tony Di Benedetto (*The Chicken Pimp*), Dick Boccelli (*Gino*), Patrick Farrelly (*The CIA Agent*), Michele Harrell (*Maria*), David Lipman (*The State Senator*), Cindy Wilks (*Candy*), Dennis Boutsikaris (*Frankie*)
D & SCR: James Glickenhaus **PHOTOG:** Robert M. Baldwin **MUSIC:** Joe Renzetti
Standard thriller: Vigilante hunted

Exterminator II
1984, (USA), color, 88 mins.
W: Robert Ginty, Mario Van Peebles, Deborah Geffner, Scott Randolph, Frankie Faison, Arye Gross, John Turturro
D: Mark Buntzman
Minor thriller: Blowtorch wielder pursues crime gang

Exterminators of the Year 3000
1984, (It-Sp), 2T-Globe/Samuel Goldwyn, color, 101 mins.

The Extraordinary Seaman: FAYE DUNAWAY

W: Robert Jannucci, Alicia Moro, Alan Collins, Eduardo Fajardo, Fred Harris, Beryl Cunningham, Riccardo Mioni, Luca Ventantini, Anna Orso, Ventantino Venantini, Roman Ariz Navarreta, Sergio Mioni, Jose Chinchilla, Garcia Monserrat, Franco Salamon
D: Jules Harrison ORIG. STORY & SCR: Elisa Briganti, Dardano Sacchetti, & Jose Truchado Reyes PHOTOG: Alejandro Ulloa SPCL-FX: Gino de Rossi & Edmondo Natali MUSIC: Detto Mariano
Minor SF-adventure: Post-nuke barbarians war over water supplies

El Extrano Case del Dr. Fausto (The Strange Case of Dr. Faustus)
1969, (Sp), color
D: Gonzalo Suarez
Minor horror-thriller

Extranos Caminos (Strange Roads)
1992, (Mex), color
W: Julian Pastor, Pedro Armendariz Jr., Claudia Fernandez, Wolf Rubinskis
Minor thriller

The Extraordinary Adventures of Jules Verne
see *Les Aventures Extraordinaires de Jules Verne*

An Extraordinary Cab Accident
1903, (GB), R.W. Paul, b&w, 50 ft. (15.2m)
D: Walter R. Booth
Standard fantasy short: Horsedrawn four-wheeler runs over man, who then revives

Extraordinary Illusions
1903, (Fr), Star, b&w, 41m (134.5 ft./2.3 mins.)
W: Georges Melies
D: Georges Melies
A.k.a. The 20th Century Illustrationist
Standard fantasy

The Extraordinary Seaman
1968, (USA), MGM, color, 98 mins.
W: David Niven (*Finchhaven*), Faye Dunaway (*Jennifer*), Alan Alda (*Krim*), Mickey Rooney (*Oglethorpe*), Jack Carter (*Toole*), Juano Hernandez (*Ali Shar*), Manu Tupou (*Lightfoot*), Barry Kelley
P: Edward Lewis D: John Frankenheimer SCR: Philip Rock & Hal Dresner PHOTOG: Lionel Lindon MUSIC: Maurice Jarre
Minor fantasy: Ghostly ship captain

Extraordinary Stories
see *Spirits of the Dead*

The Extraordinary Waiter
1902, (GB), R.W. Paul, b&w, 108 ft. (32.9m)
D: W.R. Booth
A.k.a. The Mysterious Heads
Standard comedy-fantasy short: Swiss tourist knocks off head of Negro waiter

Extreme Measures
1996, (USA), Castle Rock/Col, color, 117 mins.
W: Hugh Grant (*Dr. Guy Luthan*), Gene Hackman (*Dr. Lawrence Myrick*), Sarah Jessica Parker (*Jodie Trammel*), David Morse (*Frank Hare*), Bill Nunn (*Burke*), David Cronenberg (*The Lawyer*), John Toles-Bey (*Bobby*), Paul Guilfoyle, Debra Monk
P: Elizabeth Hurley D: Michael Apted SCR: Tony Gilroy from Michael Palmer's novel PHOTOG: John Bailey MUSIC: Danny Elfman
"...stylish and taut with a taste for macabre little surprises"—Janet Maslin
Unusual thriller: Doctor uncovers gruesome conspiracy involving abduction of homeless

Eyeball
1978, (It), Brenner, color, 91 mins
W: John Richardson, Martine Brochard, Ines Pellegrini, Silvia Solar, George Rigaud
D: Umberto Lenzi SCR: Felix Tusell
Minor thriller: Killer cuts out victims' eyes

The Eye Creatures
1965, (USA), Azalea/AIP-TV, color, 80 mins
W: John Ashley, Cynthia Hull, Chet Davis, Warren Hammack, Bob Cowan
D: Larry Buchanan PHOTOG: Ralph K. Johnson
Minor SF-thriller, remake of 'Invasion of the Saucer Men': Space aliens frighten rubes

An Eye for an Eye
see *The Psychopath* (1973)

Eye of the Alien
1965, (Uruguay), Artus, color
W: Brian Weakley, Patricia Flood, Brooks Read, Alexander Morrison
Minor SF-thriller

Eye of the Beholder
1999, (USA), color
W: Ashley Judd, Ewan McGregor, Jason Priestley, k.d. lang, Patrick Bergin
Standard thriller

Eye of the Cat
1969, (USA), Univ, color, 102 mins.
W: Michael Sarrazin, Gayle Hunnicutt, Eleanor Parker, Tim Henry, Laurence Naismith, Jennifer Leak, Mark Herron
P: Bernard Schwartz & Philip Hazelton D: David Lowell Rich SCR: Joseph Stefano PHOTOG: Russell Metty MUSIC: Lalo Schifrin
Standard thriller: Wastrel who fears cats is lured into murder plot

Eye of the Devil
1965, (GB), Filmways-MGM, b&w, 90 mins.
W: Deborah Kerr (*Catherine de Montfaucon*), David Niven (*Philippe de Montfaucon*), Donald Pleasence (*Pere Dominic*), Edward Mulhare (*Jean-Claude Ibert*), Flora Robson (*Countess Estelle*), Emlyn Williams (*Alain de Montfaucon*), Sharon Tate (*Odile*), David Hemmings (*Christian de Caray*), John LeMesurier (*Dr. Monnet*), Suky Appleby (*Antoinette*), Donald Bissett (*Rennard*), Richard Hurndall
P: John Calley & Martin Ransohoff D: J. Lee Thompson SCR: Robin Estridge & Dennis Murphy, from Philip Lorraine's novel *Day of the Arrow* PHOTOG: Erwin Hillier MUSIC: Garry McFarland
Standard thriller: Vineyard owner sacrifices himself in pre-Christian rite. A.k.a. 13

Eye of the Evil Dead
1984, (It), 21st Century, color
D: Lucio Fulci
Minor horror-thriller

The Eye of the Idol
1912, (GB), Clarendon, b&w, 1,285 ft. (391.7m)
D: Wilfred Noy
Standard thriller: Explorer steals jewel from god, is pursued by high priest

Eye of the Needle
1981, (GB), Kings Road/UA, color, 112 mins.
W: Donald Sutherland (*Faber*), Stephen MacKenna (*The Lt.*), Kate Nelligan (*Lucy*), Philip Martin Brown (*Billy Parkin*), Christopher Cazenove (*David*), Barbara Graley (*A Constable*), George Belbin (*Lucy's Father*), Faith Brook (*Lucy's Mother*), Arthur Lovegrove (*Peterson*), Colin Rix (*Oliphant*), Barbara Ewing (*Mrs. Gordon*), Patrick Connor (*Insp. Harris*), David Hayman (*Canter*), Ian Bannen (*Godliman*), William Merrow (*The German Radio Operator*), Rupert Frazer (*Muller*), Jonathan Nicholas Haley (*Joe*), Alex McCrindle (*Tom*), John Bennett (*Kleinmann*), Alan Surtees (*Col. Terry*), Bill Fraser (*Mr. Porter*), Chris Jenkinson (*The German SS Officer*), George Lee (*A Constable*), Sam Kydd (*The Keeper*), John Grieve (*Insp. Kincaid*), Bill Nagy
D: Richard Marquand SCR: Stanley Mann, from Ken Follett's novel PHOTOG: Alan Hume MUSIC: Milos Rozsa
Standard thriller: Nazi spy undercover in Britain

Eye of the Storm
1992, (USA-Ger), Style/Eurofilm, color, 90 mins.
W: Dennis Hopper (*Marvin*), Lara Flynn Boyle (*Sandra*), Craig Sheffer (*Ray*), Bradley Gregg (*Steven*), Adrian Arnold (*Young Steven*), Leon Rippy (*The Sheriff*), Bruce Gray (*Father*), Barbara lindsay (*Mother*), Wilhelm von Homburg (*The Killer*), Ally Walker (*The Killer Girl*), John Storey (*The Deputy*)
D: Yuri Zeltser SCR: Michael Stewart & Yuri Zeltser PHOTOG: Karl Walter Lindenlaub MUSIC: Christopher Franke SONG: *In the Name of Love*
Standard thriller

The Eyes Behind the Stars
1972, (It), Midia Cinematografica, color, 92 mins.
W: Robert Hoffmann, Nathalie Delon, Martin Balsam, Tom Felleghy, Sherry Buchanan, Victor Valente, Giovanna De Luca, Sergio Rossi, Anthony Freeman, Franco Garofalo, Carlo Hintermann, Bruno Di Luia, Cesare Nizzica, Franco Beltramme, George Ardisson
WRIT & D: Roy Garrett PHOTOG: Enrico Menczer MUSIC: Marcello Giombini
Minor SF-thriller: Reporter detects extraterrestrials

The Eyes Have It
1974, (GB), Made for TV, color
W: Sinead Cusack, Dennis Waterman, Peter Vaughan, Alun Armstrong
TVM, minor thriller: Blind students involved in assasination plot

Eyes in the Night
1942, (USA), MGM, b&w, 80 mins
W: Edward Arnold (*Duncan Maclain*), Ann Harding (*Norma Lawry*), Donna Reed (*Barbara Lawry*), Stanley C. Ridges (*Hansen*), Katherine Emery (*Cheli Scott*), Horace (Steven) McNally (*Gabriel Hoffman*), Allen Jenkins (*Marty*), Reginald Denny (*Stephen Lawry*), John Emery (*Paul Gerente*), Erik Rolf (*Boyd*), Rosemary De Camp (*Vera Hoffman*), Reginald Sheffield (*Victor*), Barry Nelson (*Busch*), Steve Geray (*Anderson*), Mantan Moreland (*Alistair*), Friday (*the dog*)
D: Fred Zinnemann SCR: Guy Trosper & Howard Emmett Rogers, from a book by Bayard Kendrick PHOTOG: Robert Planck & Charles Lawton MUSIC SCORE: Lennie Hayton
Standard mystery-thriller: Blind sleuth vs. Nazi spies. cf. The Hidden Eye

The Eyes of Annie Jones

1963, (GB), Parroch-McCallum/20th-Fox, b&w, 71 mins.
W: Richard Conte (*David Wheeler*), Francesca Annis (*Annie Jones*), Joyce Carey (*Aunt Helen*), Myrtle Reed (*Caroline Wheeler*), Shay Gorman (*Lucas*), Mark Dignam (*Frobisher*), Jean Lodge (*Geraldine Wheeler*), Max Bacon (*Hoskins*), Victor Brooks (*Sgt. Henry*)
D: Reginald LeBorg   SCR: Louis Vittes   STORY: Henry Slesar
Minor thriller: Orphaned girl's ESP detects murderer

Eyes of a Stranger

1981, (USA), Georgetown Prods./WB, color, 85 mins.
W: Lauren Tewes (*Jane*), Jennifer Jason Leigh (*Tracy*), Joe DiSanti (*Stanley*), Peter DuPre (*David*), Timothy Hawkins (*Jeff*), Gwen Lewis (*Debbie*), Kitty Lunn (*Annette*), Toni Crabtree (*Mona*), Ted Richert (*Roger*), Stella Rivera (*The Dancer*), Bob Small (*Dr. Bob*), Alan Lee (*The Photographer*), Luke Halpin (*The Tape Editor*), Jose Bahamande (*Jimmy*), Dan Fitzgerald (*The Bartender*), Rhonda Flynn (*The Woman in the Car*), Tony Federico (*The Man in the Car*), Tabbetha Tracey (*Young Tracy*), Amy Krug (*Young Jane*), Pat Warren (*Susan*), Sarah Hutcheson (*The Friend*), Jillian Lindig (*Mother*), George DeVries (*Father*), Robert Goodman (*The Crewman*), Melvin Pape (*The Doctor*), Kathy Suergiu (*Karen*), Madeline Curtis (*The Nurse*), Michael de Silva (*The Technical Director*), Richard Allen (*The News Director*), Herb Goldstein, Sonia Zomina
P: Ronald Zerra   D: Ken Wiederhorn   SCR: Mark Jackson & Eric L. Bloom   PHOTOG: Mini Rojas   MUSIC: Richard Einhorn
Minor thriller: Newswoman tracks sadistic killer

The Eyes of Charles Sand

1972, (USA), WB/NBC-TV, color, 75 mins.
W: Peter Haskell (*Charles Sand*), Barbara Rush, Bradford Dillman, Joan Bennett, Sharon Farrell, Adam West, Ivor Francis, Gary Clarke, Owen Bush
D: Reza S. Badiyi   SCR: Henry Farrell & Stanford Whitmore   PHOTOG: Ben Colman
TVM, minor mystery: Man has visions from beyond grave

Eyes of Evil

see Die Tausend Augen des Dr. Mabuse

Eyes of Fate

1933, (GB), Sound City/Univ, b&w, 67 mins.
W: Allan Jeayes (*Knocker*), Valerie Hobson (*Rene*), Faith Bennett (*Betty*), Terence de Marney (*Edgar*), Nellie Bowman (*Mrs. Knocker*), O.B. Clarence (*Mr. Oliver*), Edwin Ellis (*Jefferson*), Tony Halfpenny (*George*), David Niven (*The Man*)
D: Ivar Campbell   STORY: Holloway Horn
A.k.a All the Winners
Minor fantasy: Bookmaker given tomorrow's newspaper

Eyes of Fire

1983, (USA), Elysian, color, 90 mins.
W: Dennis Lipscomb (*Will Smythe*), Guy Boyd (*Marion Dalton*), Rebecca Stanley (*Eloise Dalton*), Karlene Crockett (*Leah*), Sally Klein (*Fanny Dalton*), Fran Ryan (*Sister*), Rob Paulsen (*Jewell Buchanan*), Kerry Sherman (*Margaret Buchanan*), Caitlin Baldwin (*Cathleen*), Mike Genovese (*The Interrogator*), Erin Buchanan (*Meg*), Will Hare (*Calvin*), Ivy Bethune (*Rachel*), Brett Pearson (*Luther*), Rose Preston (*The Indian Girl*), Mitch Rogers (*The Shawnee*), Bruce Solow (*The Townsman*), Lenard Petit (*The Frenchman*), Russell James Young Jr. (*The Witch*)
WRIT & D: Avery Crouse   PHOTOG: Wade Hanks   IRISH MUSIC: Brad Fiedel
Minor thriller: Sorcery among American settlers

Eyes of Hell

see The Mask (1961)

Eyes of Laura Mars

1978, (USA), Col, color, 103 mins.
W: Faye Dunaway (*Laura Mars*), Tommy Lee Jones (*John Neville*), Brad Dourif (*Tommy Ludlow*), Raul Julia (*Michael Reisler*),Rene Auberjonois (*Donald Phelps*), Frank Adonis (*Sal Volpe*), Lisa Taylor (*Michele*), Darlanne Fluegel (*Lulu*), Marilyn Meyers (*Sheila Weissman*), Rose Gregorio (*Elaine Cassell*), Steve Marachuk (*Robert*), Meg Mundy (*Doris Spenser*), Gary Bayer (*A Reporter*), Mitchell Edmonds (*A Reporter*), Toshi Matsuo (*A Photo Ass't*), Jeff Niki (*A Photo Ass't*), John E. Allen (*Billy T*), Dallas Edward Hayes (*Douglas*), Paula Lawrence (*Aunt Caroline*), Joey R. Mills (*The Make-Up Person*), John Sahag (*The Hairdresser*), Hector Troy (*The Cab Driver*), Bill Boggs, Anna Anderson, Deborah Beck, Jim Devine, Hanny Friedman, Winnie Hollman, Patty Oja, Donna Palmer, Sterling St. Jacques, Rita Tellone, Kari Page, John Randolph Jones, Al Joseph, Gerald Kline, Sal Richards, Tom Degidon
P: Jon Peters   D: Irvin Kershner   SCR: John Carpenter & David Zelag Goodman   SONG: *Prisoner* (sung by Barbra Streisand)
Standard thriller: Woman photographer has visions of murder

The Eyes of Mystery

1918, (USA), Metro, b&w, 5 reels
D: Tod Browning
Minor thriller

Eyes of Terror

1994, (USA), NBC-TV, color, 95 mins.
W: Barbara Eden (*Jesse Newman*), Michael Nouri (*Lt. David Zaccariah*), Ted Marcoux (*Det. Tony Carpelli*), Missy Crider (*Kimberly*), David Marciano (*Kenneth Burch*), Steven Anthony Jones (*Capt. Jim Armstrong*), Joan Pringle (*Gwen Singleton*)
TVM, standard thriller: Female psychologist-clairvoyant aids in search for cop killer. cf. Visions of Murder

Eyes of the Beholder

1992, (USA), color, 89 mins.
W: Joanna Pacula, Matt McCoy
Standard thriller: Escaped psycho terrorizes doctor who drove him mad

Eyes of the Jungle

1953, (USA), Lippert, b&w, 79 mins.
W: Jon Hall, Ray Montgomery, Edgar Barrier, Victor Millan, Frank Fenton, Merrill McCormick, Charles Stevens, Robert Shayne, Leonard Penn, William Tannen, Alyce Lewis
D: Paul Landers   SCR: Barry Shipman & Sherman L. Lowe
Minor adventure-thriller, feature culled from "Ramar of the Jungle" teleseries American doctor's research in India threatened by superstitious natives and villainous traders

The Eyes of the Mummy

see Die Augen der Mumie Ma

Eyes of the Underworld

1942, (USA), Univ, b&w, 61 mins
W: Richard Dix, Wendy Barne, Lon Chaney Jr., Don Porter, Wendy Barrie, Lloyd Corrigan, Don Porter, Marc Lawrence, Billy Lee
D: Roy William Neill
Minor mystery-thriller

Eyes Wide Shut

1999, (GB), WB, color
W: Tom Cruise, Nicole Kidman, Thomas Gibson, Leelee Sobieski, Sydney Pollack
D: Stanley Kubrick, from Arthur Schnitzler's 1926 novella
Long-awaited psychodrama (Kubrick's final film, nearly 3 years in the making): Tale of sexual obsession

Eyes without a Face

see Les Yeux sans Visage

Eye Witness

see Your Witness

Eye Witness

1950, (USA), Eagle Lion, b&w, 104 mins.
W: Robert Montgomery
D: Robert Montgomery   MUSIC: Malcolm Arnold
Standard melodrama

Eyewitness

1956, (GB), Rank/RFD, b&w, 82 mins.
W: Donald Sinden (*Wade*), Muriel Pavlow (*Lucy Church*), David Knight (*Mike*), Belinda Lee (*Penny Mander*), Michael Craig (*Jay Church*), Nigel Stock (*Barney*), Susan Beaumont (*The Nurse*), Ada Reeve (*Mrs. Hudson*), John Stuart (*The Chief Constable*), Leslie Dwyer (*Mr. Cammon*), Allan Cuthbertson (*Insp. Reardon*), Avice Landone (*The Sister*), Nicholas Parsons (*Dr. Bright*), Richard Wattis (*The Anesthetist*), Charles Victor (*The Sgt.*), Godfrey Winn
P: Sydney Box   D: Muriel Box   SCR: Janet Green & Sydney Box   STORY: Janet Green
Standard crime-thriller: Robber and deaf partner try to kill hospitalized witness

Eyewitness

1970, (GB), Irving Allen-ABP/MGM-EMI, color, 91 mins.
W: Mark Lester (*Timothy*), Lionel Jeffries (*The Colonel*), Susan George (*Pippa*), Tony Bonner (*Tom*), Jeremy Kemp (*Galleria*), Pete Vaughan (*Paul*), Betty Marsden (*Mme. Robiac*), Peter Bowle (*Victor*), Antony Stamboulieh (*Tacherie*)
P: Paul Maslansky   D: John Hough   SCR: Ronald Harwood, from a novel by Mark Hebden
Standard crime-thriller: Boy sees assassination

Eyewitness

1981, (USA), 20th-Fox, color, 114 mins.
W: William Hurt (*Daryll Deever*), Sigourney Weaver (*Tony Sokolow*), Christopher Plummer (*Joseph*), James Woods (*Aldo*), Irene Worth (*Mrs. Sokolow*), Kenneth McMillan (*Mr. Deever*), Pamela Ree (*Linda*), Albert Paulsen (*Mr. Sokolow*), Sharon Goldman (*The Israeli Woman*), Morgan Freeman (*Lt. Black*), Steven Hill (*Lt. Jacobs*), Alice Drummond (*Mrs. Deever*), Chao-Li Chi (*Mr. Long*), Keone Young (*Mr. Long's Son*), Mikhail Bogin (*Shlomo*), Moshe Geffen (*The Cantor*), Jo Davidson (*The Man at the Concert*), Bill Mazer (*The Sports Announcer*), John Roland (*The Anchorman*), James Ray Weeks (*The TV Producer*), Dennis Sakamoto (*A Vietnamese*), Henry Yuk (*A Vietnamese*), Milton Zane, Richard Murphy, Don McKeever, Kimmy Wong, Alex Rosa, Mark Burns, Iris Whitney
P & D: Peter Yates   SCR: Steve Tesich   PHOTOG: Matthew F. Leonetti   MUSIC: Stanley Silverman
A.k.a. The Janitor

El Fabricante de Monstruos (The Monster Maker)
1965, (Sp), b&w
D: Pedro Olea
Standard horror-thriller: Scientist creates freaks

The Fabulous Baron Munchausen (1961)
see Baron Prasil

The Fabulous Baron Munchausen
1979, (Fr), color
Animated fantasy: Storyteller given royal mission

Fabulous Joe
1947, (USA), UA, color, 56 mins.
W: Walter Abel, Marie Wilson, Barbara Bates Margot Grahame, Donald Meek
D: Harve Foster
Standard fantasy: Man acquires talking dog. Part of **Hal Roach Comedy Carnival**

The Fabulous World of Jules Verne
see The Diabolical Invention

The Face
see Ansiktet

The Face at the Window
1920, (GB), British Actors/Phillips, b&w, 5,650 ft. (1722.1m)
W: C. Aubrey Smith (*Bentick*), Gladys Jennings (*Marie de Brisson*), Jack Hobbs (*Lucien Cartwright*), Kinsey Peile (*Dr. le Blanc*), Charles Quartermaine (*Lucien Degradoff*), Ben Field (*Peter Pottlebury*), Sir Simeon Stuart (*Henri de Brisson*), Kathleen Vaughan (*Babette*)
P: Gerald Malvern D: Wilfred Noy SCR: Adrian Brunel, from a play by F. Brooke Warren
Standard thriller: Dead detective electrically revived

The Face at the Window
1932, (GB), Real Art/Radio, b&w, 52 mins.
W: Raymond Massey (*Paul le Gros*), Isla Bevan (*Marie de Brisson*), Claude Hulbert (*Peter Pomeroy*), A. Bromley Davenport (*Gaston de Brisson*), Eric Maturin (*Count Fournal*), Henry Mollison (*Lucien Courtier*), Harold Meade (*Dr. Renard*), Dennis Wyndham (*Lafonde*), Charles Groves (*Jacques*), Berenoff & Charlot
D: Leslie Hiscott SCR: H. Fowler Mear, from a play by F. Brooke Warren
Minor thriller: Detective exposes bank robber

The Face at the Window
1939, (GB), Pennant/British Lion, b&w, 65 mins.
W: Tod Slaughter (*Chevalier del Gardo*), Marjorie Taylor (*Cecile de Brisson*), John Warwick (*Lucien Cortier*), Kay Lewis (*Babette*), Leonard Henry (*Gaston*), Robert Adair (*Insp. Guffert*), Aubrey Mallalieu (*de Brisson*), Wallace Evennett (*Prof. le Blanc*), Harry Terry (*The Face*), Margaret Yarde (*Le Pinan*), Dorothy Mackaill
P & D: George King SCR: A.R. Rawlinson & Randall Faye, from a play by F. Brooke Warren
reissued 1942
Standard thriller: Fake revival of corpse exposes bank robbers

The Face Behind the Mask
1941, (USA), Col, b&w, 69 mins.
W: Peter Lorre, Evelyn Keyes, George E. Stone, Don Beddoe
P: Wallace McDonald D: Robert Florey SCR: Allen Vincent & Paul Jarrico, from a radio-play by Tom O'Connell PHOTOG: Franz E. Planer MUSIC: Morris Stoloff
Minor melodrama: Love of blind girl briefly diverts accident-scarred immigrant from life of crime

The Face in the Fog
1922, (USA), Cosmopolitan/Para, b&w, 7 reels (6,095 ft./1857.8m)
W: Lionel Barrymore (*Boston Blackie Dawson*), Seena Owen (*Grand Duchess Tatiana, a Russian Refugee*), Lowell Sherman (*Count Alexis Orloff, a Russian Nobleman*), George Nash (*Huck Kant, a Detective*), Louis Wolheim (*Petrus, a Revolutionist*), Mary MacLaren (*Mary Dawson, Blackie's Wife*), Macey Harlan (*Count Ivan, a Renegade*), Gustav von Seyffertitz (*Michael, a Family Servant*), Joe King (*Det. Wren*), Tom Blake (*Surtep*), Marie Burke (*Olga*), Joseph Smiley (*The Police Captain*), Martin Faust (*Ivan's Valet*), Mario Majeroni (*Grand Duke Alexis*)
D: Alan Crosland SCR: John Lynch & Jack Boyle, from a 1920 story by Jack Boyle PHOTOG: Ira H. Morgan & Harold Wenstrom
Standard "Boston Blackie" thriller: Rogue encounters jewel smugglers, terrorists

Face in the Fog
1936, (USA), Sam Katzman/Victory, b&w, 66 mins.
W: June Collyer, Jack Mulhall, Lloyd Hughes, Al St. John Lawrence Gray, Jack Cowell, John Elliott, Forrest Taylor, Sam Flint, Edward Cassidy
D: Robert F. Hill
Minor thriller: Thespians eliminated by hunchbacked killer

Face in the Night
1957, (GB), Gibraltar/Grand Nat'l/UA, b&w, 78 mins.
W: Griffith Jones (*Rapson*), Lisa Gastoni (*Jean Francis*), Vincent Ball (*Bob Meredith*), Eddie Byrne (*Art*), Victor Maddern (*Ted*), Clifford Evans (*Insp. Ford*), Joan Miller (*Mrs. Victor*), Leslie Dwyer (*Toby*), Leonard Sachs (*Victor*), Barbara Couper (*Mrs. Francis*), Jenny Laird, Angela White, Marie Burke, Andre Van Gysegham
P: Charles Leeds D: Lance Comfort SCR: Norman Hudis & John Sherman, from Bruce Graeme's novel *Suspense* MUSIC: Richard Bennett
USA retitle, Menace in the Night
Standard thriller: Mail-van robbers intimidate girl witness

The Faceless Monster
see Amanti d'Oltretomba

The Face of Another
see Tanin No Kao

The Face of Darkness
1976, (GB), Cromdale/Lloyd, color, 58 mins.
W: Lennard Pearce (*Edward Langdon*), John Bennett (*The Psychiatrist/Inquisitor*), David Allister (*The Undead*), Roger Bizley (*The Peasant/Porter*), Gwyneth Powell (*Eileen*), Jonathan Elsom (*Philip*), Susan Banahan (*Angel*)
WRIT, P & D: Ian Lloyd PHOTOG: Peter Harvey MUSIC: Martin Jacklin
Standard horror-thriller: Politician revives dead inquisition victim

The Face of Eve
1968, (GB-Sp-Germ), Udastex-Hispamer/AA/CUE/W-P, color, 94 mins.
W: Celeste Yarnall (*Eve*), Robert Walker Jr. (*Mike Yates*), Fred Clark (*Lucky Burke*), Herbert Lom (*Diego*), Christopher Lee (*Col. Geoffrey Stuart*), Rosenda Monteros (*Pili*), Maria Rohm (*Anna*), Jean Caffarell (*Jose da Sylva*)
P: Harry Alan Towers D: Jeremy Summers & Robert Lynn SCR: Peter Welbeck [Harry Alan Towers]
USA retitle, Eve
Standard adventure-thriller: Jungle princess leads expedition to Inca treasure

Face of Fear
see Peeping Tom

Face of Fire
1959, (USA-Swed), AA, b&w, 79 mins.
W: James Whitmore (*Monk*), Cameron Mitchell (*Trescott*), Bettye Ackerman (*Grace*), Royal Dano (*Jake*), Miko Oscard (*Jimmie*), Richard Erdman (*Al*), Lois Maxwell (*Ethel*), Robert Simon (*The Judge*), Jill Donahue, Howard Smith
P: Louis Garfinkle & Albert Band D: Albert Band SCR: Louis Garfinkle, based on Stephen Crane's short story "The Monster" PHOTOG: Edward Vorkapich MUSIC: Erik Nordgren
Engrossing melodrama: Popular young man shunned by neighbors after horrible disfigurement

Face of the Frog
see Fellowship of the Frog

The Face of Fu Manchu
1965, (GB), Hallam-7Arts, color, 96 mins.
W: Christopher Lee (*Dr. Fu Manchu*), Nigel Green (*Nayland Smith*), Howard Marion-Crawford (*Dr. Petrie*), Karin Dor (*Maria*), Joachim Fuchsberger (*Jansen*), James Robertson Justice (*Sir Charles*), Tsai Chin (*Lin Tang*), Walter Rilla (*Prof. Ernst Muller*), Harry Brogan (*Prof. Gaskell*), Edwin Richfield (*The Mandarin*), Poulet Tu (*Lotus*), Peter Mossbacher (*Hanumon*), Archie O'Sullivan
WRIT & P: Peter Welbeck [Harry Alan Towers], from a novel by Sax Rohmer
D: Don Sharp PHOTOG: Ernest Steward MUSIC: Christopher Whelen
Minor thriller: Oriental villain kidnaps German chemist

The Face of Marble
1946, (USA), Mono, b&w, 72 mins.
W: John Carradine (*Prof. Randolph*), Veda Ann Borg, Robert Shayne, Claudia Drake, Willie Best, Maris Wrixon
P: Jeffrey Bernard D: William Beaudine SCR: Michel Jacoby
Standard horror-fantasy: Scientist revives dead, zombie beauty prowls the night

Face of a Stranger
1964, (GB), Merton Park/Anglo-Amalgamated, b&w, 56 mins.
W: Jeremy Kemp (*Vince Howard*), Bernard Archard (*Michael Forrest*), Rosemary Leach (*Mary Bell*), Philip Locke (*John Bell*), Elizabeth Begley, Jean Marsh, Mike Pratt, Keith Smith
P: Jack Greenwood D: John Moxey SCR: John Sansom, from Edgar Wallace's novel
Standard crime-thriller: Ex-convict seeks hidden loot

The Face of Terror (1963, Sp)
see La Cara del Terror

The Face of Terror (1963, USA)
see The Sadist

Face of the Screaming Werewolf
see La Casa del Terror

Faces in the Dark
1960, (GB), Penington-Eady/RFD, b&w, 85 mins.
W: John Gregson (*Richard Hammond*), Mai Zetterling (*Christine Hammond*), John Ireland (*Max Hammond*), Michael Denison (*David Merton*), Tony Wright (*Clem*), Nanette Newman (*Janet*), Valerie Taylor (*Miss Hopkins*)
P: Jon Penington D: David Eady SCR: Ephraim Kogan & John Tully, from a novel by Pierre Boileau & Thomas Narcejac
Standard thriller: Man helps mistress drive her blind husband mad

Faces in the Fog
1944, (USA), Rep, b&w, 71 mins.
W: Jane Withers, Paul Kelly
Standard thriller

Face the Music
1954, (GB), Hammer/Exclusive, b&w, 84 mins.
W: Alex Nicol (*James Bradley*), Eleanor Summerfield (*Barbara Quigley*), John Salew (*Max Margulis*), Paul Carpenter (*John Sutherland*), Geoffrey Keen (*Maurice Green*), Ann Hanslip (*Maxine*), Fred Johnson (*Insp. Mackenzie*), Martin Boddey (*Sgt. Mulrooney*), Arthur Lane (*Jeff Colt*), Gordon Crier (*Vic Parsons*)
P: Michael Carreras D: Terence Fisher SCR: Ernest Bornemann, from his novel
USA retitle, **The Black Glove**
Standard crime-thriller: Musician accused of murder

A Face to Die For
1996, (USA), NBC-TV, color, 95 mins.
W: Yasmine Bleeth (*Emily Gilmore/Adrian Corday*), James Wilder (*Alec Dalton*), Robin Givens (*Claudia*), Richard Beymer (*Dr. Matthew Sheridan*), Ricky Paull Goldin (*Paul Mallory*), Mitchell Ryan (*Joe Thomas*), Chandra West, Ian Abercrombie, Mary Ellen Trainor
D: Jack Bender TELEPLAY: Duane Poole, from a book by Marvin & Mark Werlin PHOTOG: Eagle Egilsson MUSIC: Christopher Franke
SONGS: *Dangerous* & *Heaven Knows*
TVM, standard melodrama (similar to **A Stolen Face**): *Plastic surgery lets scarred girl gain revenge*

Face to Face
1916, (GB), Hepworth/Butcher, b&w, 2,725 ft. (830.6m)
W: Stewart Rome (*Geoffrey Cunliffe/Richard Waine*), Chrissie White (*Kathleen Dare*), Lionelle Howard (*Bernard Cunliffe*), William Felton (*Stephen Morel*), Charles Vane (*John Cunliffe*), Frank Wilson (*Henry Dare*)
D: Frank Wilson STORY: Marion Carr
Standard crime-thriller: Millionaire's nephew accused of burglary committed by double

The Faculty
1998, (USA), Dimension, color
W: Robert Patrick, Elijah Wood, Piper Laurie, Usher, Shawn Hatosy, Jon Stewart, Jordana Brewster, Clea DuVall, Bebe Neuwirth, Laura Harris, Josh Hartnett, Famke Janssen, Salma Hayek, Danny Masterson
D: Robert Rodriguez SCR: Kevin Williamson
Unusual SF-thriller: Sinister aliens take over high school

Fade to Black
1980, (USA), Irwin Yablans & Sylvio Tabet/Leisure Investment Co./Movie Venturers Ltd./American Cinema, color, 103 mins.
W: Dennis Christopher (*Eric Binford*), Linda Kerridge (*Marilyn*), Tim Thomerson (*Dr. Moriarty*), Eve Brent Ashe (*Aunt Stella*), Morgan Paull (*Gary*), Hennen Chambers (*Bart*), Marya Small (*Doreen*), Bob Drew (*Rev. Shick*), Gwynn Gilford (*Anne*), John Steadman (*Sam*), Mickey Rourke (*Richie*), Bruce Reed (*Franco*), Melina Fee (*The TV Hostess*), Jane K. Wiley (*The Go-fer*), Al Tafoya (*The Newscaster*), Peter Horton (*Joey*), James Luisi (*Gallagher*), Anita Converse (*Deedee*), Marcie Barkin (*Stacy*), Gilbert Lawrence Kahn (*The Counterman*), Normann Burton, Morgan Paull, Gwynne Gilford, Linda Kerridge.
P: George G. Braunstein & Ron Hamady WRIT & D: Vernon Zimmerman PHOTOG: Alex Phillips Jr. MUSIC: Craig Safan
Unusual thriller: Neurotic movie buff enacts murderous fantasies

Fahrenheit 451
1966, (GB-Fr), Anglo-Enterprise-Vineyard/Univ, color, 113 mins.
W: Oskar Werner (*Montag*), Julie Christie (*Linda/Clarisse*), Cyril Cusack (*The Captain*), Jeremy Spenser (*The Man with the Apple*), Anton Diffring (*Fabian*), Ann Bell (*Doris*), Caroline Hunt (*Helen*), Anna Palk (*Jackie*), Bee Duffell (*The Book Lady*), Alex Scott (*Life of Henry Brulard*), Denis Gilmore (*Martian Chronicles*), Gillian Aldam (*Judoka Woman*), Fred & Frank Cox (*Pride and Prejudice*), Michael Balfour (*Machiavelli's Prince*), John Rae (*Weir of Hermiston*), Judith Drynan (*Plato's Dialogues*), David Glover (*Pickwick Papers*), Yvonne Blake (*Jewish Question*)
P: Louis M. Allen D: Francois Truffaut SCR: Francois Truffaut & Jean-Louis Richard, from Ray Bradbury's novel PHOTOG: Nicolas Roeg MUSIC: Bernard Herrmann
orig. to be titled **Phoenix**
Major SF-thriller: Possession of books is grievous crime in thought-controlled world of future

Fail-Safe
1964, (USA), Col, b&w, 112 mins.
W: Henry Fonda (*The President*), Dan O'Herlihy (*Black*), Frank Overton (*Bogan*), Nancy Berg, Walter Matthau, Dom DeLuise, William Hansen, Edward Binns, Russell Collins, Fritz Weaver, Larry Hagman, Russell Hardy, Sorrell Booke, Robert Gerringer
P: Max Youngstein D: Sidney Lumet SCR: Walter Bernstein, from the best-selling novel by Eugene Burdick & Harvey Wheeler PHOTOG: Gerald Hirschfeld
Major thriller: Nations of world hover on brink of nuclear disaster

The Failure
1917, (GB), Hepworth/Butcher, b&w, 4,275 ft. (1303m)
W: Henry Edwards (*Dick Carson*), Chrissie White (*Margaret Gilder*), Lionelle Howard (*Sidney Carson*), Fred Johnson (*Gustave le Sage*), Charles Vane (*The Police Chief*), W.G. Saunders (*Mr. Gilder*)
D & STORY: Henry Edwards SCR: Blanche McIntosh
A.k.a. **Dick Carson Wins Through**
Standard crime-thriller: Frenchman causes man to drink brother's poison, charges brother with murder

Fair Game
1985, (Austral), color, 83 mins.
W: Cassandra Delaney, Peter Ford, David Sandford, Gary Who
D: Mario Andreacchio
Minor thriller: Outback goons abuse women

Fair Game
1988, (It), color, 85 mins.
W: Gregg Henry, Trudie Styler, Bill Moseley (*Frank*)
Standard thriller: Husband plants venomous snake in estranged wife's apartment

The Fairies' Revenge
1913, (GB), Hepworth, b&w, 750 ft. (228.6m)
W: Percy Manton (*Uncle Alfred*)
D: Hay Plumb
Standard comedy-fantasy: Sprites change scoffer's garb into ballet dress

Fair Wind to Java
1953, (USA), Rep, color, 92 mins.
W: Fred MacMurray, Vera Ralston (*Hruba*), Victor McLaglen (*O'Brien*), Robert Douglas (*Besar*), John Russell, Claude Jarmen Jr., Stephen Bekassy, Buddy Baer, Howard Petrie, Grant Withers, Paul Fix, William Murphy, Sujata, Philip Ahn
P & D: Joseph Kane SCR: Richard Tregaskis, from a novel by Garland Roark PHOTOG: Jack Marta MUSIC: Victor Young
Colorful action-adventure: Search for legendary cache of diamonds complicated by volcanic peril

The Fairy Bottle
1913, (GB), Cricks & Martin, b&w, 790 ft. (240.8m)
W: Una Tristram (*The Fairy*), Bill Haley (*Pat Murphy*)
D: Dave Aylott
Reissued 1916
Standard fantasy: Irishman's magic bottle contains evil spirit.

The Fairy Doll
1912, (GB), B&C/MP, b&w, 718 ft. (218.8m)
W: Alice de Winton (*Mrs. Drayton*), Edward Durrant (*Will Drayton*), Percy Dyer (*Little Will*), Zola Woodruff (*Mary*), Marjorie Manners (*The Fairy*)
D: Laurence Caird
Standard fantasy: Lady's gift doll saves poor girl's life

The Fairy Godmother (1898)
see *Cinderella and the Fairy Godmother*

The Fairy Godmother
1906, (GB), Alpha/Cricks & Sharp, b&w, 140 ft. (42.7m)
D: Arthur Cooper
Minor fantasy short: While maid sleeps, child sees toy Noah's Ark come to life

Fairyland
1916, (GB), Lucoque, b&w, 1,959 ft. (597.1m)
W: Phyllis Bedells (*The Fairy Queen*), Little Alan (*Boykins*), Babs Farren, Wynne St. Clair, Daphne Wynne
D: H. Lisle Lucoque STORY: Pauline Lewis
Standard fantasy: Small boy's dream of Fairyland. Reissued 1925

Fairyland: or, The Kingdom of the Fairies
see *Le Royaume des Fees*

The Fairy's Sword
1908, (GB), Hepworth, b&w, 775 ft. (236.2m)
D: Lewin Fitzhamon
Standard fantasy: Prince uses magic sword to save princess from ogre

Fairy Tale
see *Cuento de Hadas*

Fairy Tale: A True Story
1997, (USA), color, 99 mins.

W: Peter O'Toole, Harvey Keitel, Elizabeth Earl, Florence Hoath

The Faithful Clock
1909, (GB), Hepworth, b&w, 525 ft. (160m)
W: Bob Boucher *(The Clock)*
D: Lewin Fitzhamon
Standard comedy-fantasy: Thieves steal poor couple's grandfather clock; it walks back home

The Faith Healer
1911, (GB), Hepworth, b&w, 425 ft. (129.5m)
D: Bert Haldane
Standard melodrama: Faith healer cures ailing child when doctor gives up hope

A Faithless Friend
1908, (GB), Hepworth, b&w, 500 ft. (152.4m)
D: Lewin Fitzhamon
Standard thriller: Usurper repents after dreaming his ancestors' portraits and skeleton come to life

Fake-Out
1982, (USA), color, 89 mins.
W: Pia Zadora *(Bobbie Warren)*, Telly Savalas *(O.W. Thurston)*, Desi Arnaz Jr. *(Clint Morgan)*, Larry Storch *(Ted)*, George Savalas *(The Pit Boss)*, G. Wesley Stevens *(Michelle)*, Tim Rossovich *(Hit Man #1)*, Matt Cimber *(Hit Man #2)*, Sammy Shore *(The waiter)*, Buck Flower *(Merrick)*, Buddy Lester *(The Blackjack Player)*, Suzanne Buhrer, Betty Bunch, M. Riklis, Paul Ford, Mimi Hines, Nelson Sardelli, Stassia Stakis, Rusty Fever, Diana Jones, Camilla Kath, Noelle Nelson, Lisa McGiveron, Robin Zito, Marie Morris, John Goff, Dan Parker, Kay Wade, Marv Cowan, Fran Dorsey, Bob Mitchell, Frank Romano, Rita Alexander, Abraham Rudnick
D: Matt Cimber   SONG: *Those Eyes*
A.k.a. *Nevada Heat*
Minor thriller: Singer flees mobsters

The Fakers
see *Hell's Bloody Devils*

Fake Spiritualism Exposed
see *Spiritualism Exposed* (1926)

The Fakir
1896, (Fr), Star, b&w, 20m (65.6 ft./1.1 mins.)
D: Georges Melies
Standard fantasy: Hindu mystic performs tricks

Le Fakir de Singapoure (The Fakir of Singapore)
1908, (Fr), Star, b&w, 345m (1,131.9 ft./19.1 mins.)
D: Georges Melies
A.k.a. *Indian Sorcerer*
Standard fantasy

The Fakir of Singapore
see *Le Fakir de Singapoure*

The Fakir's Fan
1911, (GB), Kineto, b&w, 575 ft. (175.3m)
D: Walter R. Booth
reissued (1917) as **The Magic Fan**
Standard fantasy short: Fan makes Hindu fly

The Fakir's Flute
1910, (GB), Hepworth, b&w, 425 ft. (129.5m)
D: Lewin Fitzhamon
Minor fantasy short: Fakir's magic flute makes people dance

The Fakir's Spell
1914, (GB), Dreadnought/Day, b&w, 2,500 ft. (762m)
W: Idleton Newman *(The Child)*
D: Frank Newman
Standard horror-thriller: Hindu's curse turns girl's British lover into gorilla

The Falcon and the Co-Eds
1943, (USA), RKO, b&w, 68 mins.
W: Tom Conway *(Tom Lawrence)*, Jean Brooks *(Vicky Gaines)*, Rita Corday *(Marguerita Serena)*, Amelita Ward *(Jane Harris)*, Isabel Jewell *(Mary Phoebus)*, Edward Gargan *(Bates)*, George Givot *(Dr. Anatole Graelich)*, Barbara Brown *(Miss Keyes)*, Cliff Clark *(Insp. Donovan)*, Juanita Alvarez, Ruth Alvarez, Nancy McCullum, Patti Brill, Dorothy Maloney *(Malone)*
D: William Clemens   SCR: Ardel Wray & Gerald Geraghty, from characters created by Michael Arlen   PHOTOG: Roy Hunt   MUSIC: C. Bakaleinikoff
Standard thriller: Troubleshooter finds murder at girl's school

The Falcon in Danger
1943, (USA), RKO, b&w, 69 mins.
W: Tom Conway *(Tom Lawrence)*, Jean Brooks *(Iris Fairchild)*, Elaine Shepard *(Nancy Palmer)*, Amelita Ward *(Bonnie Caldwell)*, Cliff Clark *(Insp. Donovan)*, Edward Gargan *(Bates)*, Clarence Kolb *(Stanley Harris Palmer)*, Richard Davies *(Ken Gibson)*, Felix Basch *(Morley)*, Richard Martin *(Georgie Morley)*, Erford Gage *(Evan Morley)*, Eddie Dunn *(Grimes)*, Joan Barclay *(The*

Hysterical Girl), Russell Wade *(The Man)*, Jack Mulhall *(The Casino Manager)*, Bruce Edwards *(The Mechanic)*
D: William Clemens   SCR: Fred Niblo Jr. & Craig Rice, from characters created by Michael Arlen   PHOTOG: Frank Redman   MUSIC: C. Bakaleinikoff
Standard thriller: Troubleshooter investigates airplane crash

The Falcon in Hollywood
1944, (USA), RKO, b&w, 67 mins.
W: Tom Conway *(Tom Lawrence)*, Barbara Hale *(Peggy Calahan)*, Veda Ann Borg *(Billie Atkins)*, John Abbott *(Martin S. Dwyer)*, Sheldon Leonard *(Louis Buchanan)*, Konstantin Shayne *(Alex Hoffman)*, Rita Corday *(Lilli D'Allio)*, Emory Parnell *(Insp. McBride)*, Frank Jenks *(Higgins)*, Jean Brooks *(Roxana Miles)*, Walter Soderling *(Ed Johnson)*, Usaf Ali *(Nagari)*, Robert Clarke *(Perc Saunders)*, Carl Kent *(The Art Director)*, Gwen Crawford *(A Secretary)*, Patti Brill *(A Secretary)*, Bryant Washburn *(An Actors' Agent)*, Sammy Blum *(An Actors' Agent)*, Nancy Marlow *(The Mail Clerk)*, George DeNormand *(The Truck Driver)*, Chris Drake *(The Ass't Cameraman)*, Jacques Lory *(The Musician)*, Jimmy Jordan *(The Operator)*, Chester Clute *(The Hotel Manager)*, Perc Launders *(Zoltan)*, Chili Williams *(The Blonde)*, Wheaton Chambers, Bert Moorhouse, Margie Stewart, Greta Christensen
D: Gordon Douglas   SCR: Gerald Geraghty, from characters created by Michael Arlen   PHOTOG: Nicholas Musuraca   MUSIC: C. Bakaleinikoff
Standard thriller: Vacationing troubleshooter becomes involved in former actor's murder

The Falcon in Mexico
1944, (USA), RKO, b&w, 70 mins.
W: Tom Conway *(Tom Lawrence)*, Mona Maris *(Raquel)*, Martha Mac-Vicar *(Vickers) (Barbara Wade)*, Mary Currier *(Paula Dudley)*, Emory Parnell *(James Winthrop Hughes/Lucky Diamond)*, Nestor Paiva *(Manuel Romero)*, Cecilia Callejo *(Dolores Ybarra)*, Joseph Vitale *(Anton)*, Pedro de Cordoba *(Don Carlos Ybarra)*, Fernando Alvarado *(Pancho Romero)*, George Lewis *(The Mexican Detective)*, Bryant Washburn *(Humphrey Wade)*, Julian Rivero *(The Mexican Doctor)*, Juanita Alvarez, Ruth Alvarez
D: William Berke   SCR: George Worthington Yates & Gerald Geraghty, from characters created by Michael Arlen   PHOTOG: Frank Redman   MUSIC: C. Bakaleinikoff
Standard thriller: Troubleshooter trails art collector accused of initiating murders

The Falcon in San Francisco
1945, (USA), RKO, b&w, 65 mins.
W: Tom Conway *(Tom Lawrence)*, Rita Corday *(Joan Marshall)*, Edward S. Brophy *(Goldie Locke)*, Fay Helm *(Doreen Temple)*, Sharyn Moffett *(Annie Marshall)*, Robert Armstrong *(De Forrest Marshall)*, Carl Kent *(Rickey)*, George Holmes *(Dalman)*, John Mylong *(Peter Vantine)*, Edmund Cobb *(The Policeman)*, Myrna Dell *(The Girl)*, Esther Howard *(Mrs. Peabody)*
D: Joseph H. Lewis   SCR: Robert Kent & Ben Markson, from characters created by Michael Arlen   PHOTOG: Virgil Miller & William Sickner   MUSIC: C. Bakaleinikoff
Standard thriller: Sleuth pursues silk thieves

The Falcon Out West
1944, (USA), RKO, b&w, 64 mins.
W: Tom Conway *(Tom Lawrence)*, Carole Gallagher *(Vanessa Drake)*, Barbara Hale *(Marion)*, Joan Barclay *(Mrs. Irwin)*, Cliff Clark *(Insp. Donovan)*, Minor Watson *(Caldwell)*, Edward Gargan *(Bates)*, Don Douglas *(Hayden)*, Perc Launders *(Red)*, Lyle Talbot *(Tex Irwin)*, Lee Trent *(Dusty)*, Wheaton Chambers *(The Sheriff)*, Chief Thundercloud *(Eagle Feather)*, Tom Burton *(The Photographer)*, Steve Winston *(Caldwell Cowboy)*, Harry Clay *(Hall)*, Robert Anderson *(Wally Waldron)*, Edmund Glover *(Frank Daley)*, Mary Halsey *(Cissy)*, Rosemary LaPlanche *(Mary)*, Daun Kennedy *(Gloria)*, Chef Milani *(The Manager)*, Elaine Riley *(The Cigarette Girl)*, Norman Willis *(Callahan)*, Michael St. Angel *(The Man)*, Eddie Clark *(The Coroner)*, Joe Cody *(Toni)*, Bert Roach *(Charlie)*, William Nestell *(The Chef)*, Kernan Cripps *(Murphy)*, Slim Whitaker *(The Cowboy)*, Zedra Conde *(Carlita)*, Norman Mayes *(The Pullman Porter)*, Shirley O'Hara, Patti Brill
D: William Clemens   SCR: Billy Jones & Morton Grant, from characters created by Michael Arlen   PHOTOG: Harry Wilk   MUSIC: C. Bakaleinikoff & Roy Webb
Standard thriller: Playboy cowboy killed in New York City nightclub

The Falcon's Adventure
1946, (USA), RKO, b&w, 61 mins.
W: Tom Conway *(Tom Lawrence)*, Madge Meredith *(Luisa Braganza)*, Edward S. Brophy *(Goldie Locke)*, Robert Warwick *(Kenneth Sutton)*, Myrna Dell *(Doris Blanding)*, Ian Wolfe *(Denison)*, Steve Brodie *(Benny)*, Carol Forman *(Helen)*, Joseph Crehan *(Insp. Cavanaugh)*, Phil Warren *(Mike Geary)*, Tony Barrett *(Paolo)*, Harry Harvey *(Duncan)*, Jason Robards Sr. *(Lt. Evans)*, David Sharpe *(The Crew Member)*
D: William Berke   SCR: Aubrey Wisberg   ADDITIONAL DIALOG: Robert E. Kent, from characters created by Michael Arlen   PHOTOG: Harry Wild & Frank Redman   MUSIC: C. Bakaleinikoff
*Minor thriller, reworking of **A Date with the Falcon**: Sleuth rescues Brazilian beauty, murders ensue*

The Falcon's Alibi
1946, (USA), RKO, b&w, 62 mins.

W: Tom Conway (*Tom Lawrence*), Rita Corday (*Joan Meredith*), Vince Barnett (*Goldie Locke*), Jane Greer (*Lola Carpenter*), Elisha Cook Jr. (*Nick*), Emory Parnell (*Metcalf*), Al Bridge (*Insp. Blake*), Esther Howard (*Gloria Peabody*), Jean Brooks (*Baroness Lena*), Paul Brinkman (*Alex Olmstead*), Jason Robards Sr. (*Harvey Beaumont*), Betty Gillette (*The Elevator Operator*), Morgan Wallace (*Bender*), Edward Clark (*The Coroner*), Lucien Prival (*The Baron*), Forbes Murray (*Thompson*), Edmund Cobb (*Det. Williams*), Bonnie Blair (*The Telephone Operator*), Alphonse Martell (*Louie*), Joe La Barba, Myrna Dell, Nan Leslie, Bob Alden, Eddie Borden, George Holmes, Mike Lally, Jack Stoney, Alf Haugen, Harry Harvey
D: Ray McCarey **SCR:** Paul Yawitz, Dane Lussier & Manny Seff, from characters created by Michael Arlen **PHOTOG:** Frank Redman **MUSIC:** C. Bakaleinikoff
Minor thriller, similar in plot to **The Gay Falcon:** *Sleuth guards socialite's jewels*

The Falcon's Brother
1942, (USA), RKO, b&w, 63 mins.
W: George Sanders (*Gay Lawrence*), Tom Conway (*Tom Lawrence*), Jane Randolph (*Marcia*), Don Barclay (*Goldie Locke*), Amanda Varela (*Carmelita*), George Lewis (*Valdez*), Gwili Andre (*Diane*), Cliff Clark (*Nolan*), Edward Gargan (*Bates*), James Newill (*Paul*), Charlotte Wyn-ters (*Arlette*), Andre Charlot (*Savitski*), Eddie Dunn (*Grimes*), Mary Halsey (*Miss Ross*), Richard Martin (*The Steamship Official*), Kay Aldridge (*The Victory Gown Model/Spanish Girl*), Keye Luke, Charles Arnt
D: Stanley Logan **SCR:** Stuart Palmer & Craig Rice, from characters created by Michael Arlen **PHOTOG:** Russell Metty **MUSIC:** Roy Webb
Standard thriller: Troubleshooter killed by Nazi saboteurs, brother pursues culprits

Falcon's Gold
see **Robbers of the Sacred Mountain**

The Falcon Strikes Back
1943, (USA), RKO, b&w, 66 mins.
W: Tom Conway (*Tom Lawrence*), Harriet Hilliard (*Gwynne Gregory*), Jane Randolph (*Marcia Brooks*), Edgar Kennedy (*Smiley Dugan*), Cliff Edwards (*Goldie Locke*), Rita Corday (*Mia Bruger*), Erford Gage (*Rickey Davis*), Cliff Clark (*Insp. Donovan*), Wynne Gibson (*Mrs. Lipton*), Andre Charlot (*Bruno Steffen*), Edward Gargan (*Bates*), Joan Barclay (*The Girl*), Byron Foulger (*Argyle*), Frank Faylen (*Cecil*), Jack Norton (*The Hobo*)
D: Edward Dmytryk **SCR:** Stuart Palmer, Edward Dein & Gerald Geraghty, from characters created by Michael Arlen **PHOTOG:** Jack McKenzie **MUSIC:** C. Bakaleinikoff
Standard thriller: Troubleshooter uncovers war-bond racket

The Falcon Takes Over
1942, (USA), RKO, b&w, 63 mins.
W: George Sanders (*Gay Lawrence*), Lynn Bari (*Ann Riordan*), James Gleason (*Mike O'Hara*), Allen Jenkins (*Jonathan G. "Goldie" Locke*), Helen Gilbert (*Diana Kenyon*), Ward Bond (*Moose Malloy*), Edward Gargan (*Bates*), Anne Revere (*Jessie Florian*), Hans Conreid (*Lindsey Marriot*), George Cleveland (*Jerry*), Harry Shannon (*Grimes*), Mickey Simpson (*The Bartender*), Turhan Bey (*Jules Amthor*), Selmer Jackson (*Laird Burnett*)
D: Irving Reis **SCR:** Lynn Root & Frank Fenton, based on Raymond Chandler's novel *Farewell, My Lovely* and characters created by Michael Arlen **PHOTOG:** George Robinson **MUSIC:** C. Bakaleinikoff
Polished thriller: Sleuth pursues maniacal killer. Remade as **Farewell My Lovely / Murder My Sweet**

Fallen
1998, (USA), Atlas/Turner/WB, color, 123 mins.
W: Denzel Washington (*John Hobbes*), John Goodman (*Jonesy*), Elias Koteas (*Reese*), Donald Sutherland (*Stanton*), Embeth Davidtz (*Gretta*), James Gandolfini (*Lou*)
D: Gregory Hoblit **SCR:** Nicholas Kazan **MUSIC:** Tan Dun
Unusual fantasy-thriller: Demon possesses human bodies

The Fallen Idol
1948, (GB), London-Reed/British Lion, b&w, 95 mins.
W: Ralph Richardson (*Baines*), Michele Morgan (*Julie*), Sonia Dresdel (*Mrs. Baines*), Bobby Henrey (*Felipe*), Denis O'Dea (*Insp. Crowe*), Jack Hawkins (*Det. Ames*), Dora Bryan (*Rose*), Bernard Lee (*Det. Hart*), Geoffrey Keen (*Det. Davis*), Joan Young (*Mrs. Barrow*), Walter Fitzgerald (*Dr. Fenton*), James Hayter (*Perry*), Karel Stepanek (*The Secretary*), Dandy Nichols (*Mrs. Potterton*), George Woodbridge (*The Sgt.*), John Ruddock (*Dr. Wilson*), Gerard Heinz (*The Ambassador*)
P: David O. Selznick & Carol Reed **D:** Carol Reed **SCR:** Graham Greene, Lesley Storm & William Templeton, from Graham Greene's short story *The Basement Room* **PHOTOG:** Georges Perinal **MUSIC:** William Alwyn
Well-made melodrama: Ambassador's son lies to protect butler suspected of murder

Fall Girl
1961, (USA), Medallion, B7w, 83 mins.
W: John Agar, Greta Chi
Minor melodrama

Falling Fire
1998, (USA), SCI-TV, color, 90 mins.
W: Michael Pare, Heidi Von Palleske (*Marilyn*), Cedric Turner (*Capt. Cyril Jackson*), Christian Vidosa (*Lopez*), Herbie Terry (*Adam*)
TVM, standard SF-thriller: Spaceship crew mysteriously slain

The Fall of a Saint
1920, (GB), Gaumont-British Screencraft, b&w, 6,400 ft. (1925.3m)
W: Josephine Earle (*Countess de la Merthe*), Gerald Lawrence (*Claude Maitland*), W.T. Ellwanger (*Elkin Smith*), Dallas Anderson (*Count de la Merthe*), R. Heaton Grey (*Lord Norten*), Thea Godfrey (*Katie Thimm*), Reginald Culhane (*Sport Kenkinson*)
D: W.P. Kellino, from a novel by Eric Clement Scott
Standard crime-thriller: Detective blackmails nobleman

The Fall of the House of Usher (1927)
see **La Chute de la Maison Usher**

The Fall of the House of Usher
1950, (GB), Vigilant/GIB, b&w, 70 mins.
W: Gwendoline Watford (*Lady Madeleine Usher*), Kay Tendeter (*Lord Roderick Usher*), Irving Steen (*Jonathan*), Lucy Pavey (*The Hag*), Vernon Charles (*Dr. Cordell*), Gavin Lee (*The Butler*)
D & PHOTOG: Ivan Barnett **SCR:** Dorothy Catt & Kenneth Thompson, from Edgar Allan Poe's short story
reissued 1955 & 1961
Unusual cinemadaptation of literary classic: Doomed siblings entertain guest

The Fall of the House of Usher
1958, (USA), NBC-TV, color
W: Marshall Thompson, Tom Tryon (*Roderick Usher*)
ADAPT: Robert Esson, from Edgar Allan Poe's short story
Standard thriller, faithful to source (orig. aired on TV as segment of Albert McCleery's "Matinee Theater"): Decaying mansion linked to lives of inhabitants

The Fall of the House of Usher (1960)
see **House of Usher**

The Fall of the House of Usher
1982, (USA), Schick Sunn/NBC-TV, color, 93 mins.
W: Martin Landau (*Roderick Usher*), Robert Hays (*Jonathan*), Charlene Tilton (*Jennifer*), Ray Walston (*Thaddeus*), Dimitra Arliss (*Madeline Usher*), Peg Stewart, Michael Ruud, H.E.D. Redford
P & D: James L. Conway **TELEPLAY:** Stephen Lord, from Edgar Allan Poe's short story **SPCL-FX:** Harry Woolman
TVM, standard thriller (orig. filmed in 1979): Architect finds mystery in home of childhood friend

The Fall of Troy
see **La Caduta di Troia**

The Falls
1980, (GB), color, 185 mins.
W: Peter Westley, Aad Wirtz, Michael Murray, Lorna Poulter, Patricia Carr
D: Peter Greenaway **MUSIC:** Michael Nyman
Unusual fantasy: Biographies of apocalypse survivors

The False Clue
1913, (GB), Britannia Films/Pathe, b&w, 2,158 ft. (657.8m)
D: A.E. Coleby
Standard crime-thriller: Butler steals money

False Face
see **Scalpel**

False Faces
1919, (USA), Ince/Para-Artcraft, b&w, 7 reels
W: Henry B. Walthall (*Michael Lanyard*), Mary Anderson (*Cecilia Brookes*), Lon Chaney Sr. (*Karl Eckstrom*), Garry McGarry (*The Submarine Lieutenant*), Milton Ross (*Ralph Crane*), Thornton Edwards (*Lt. Thackeray*), William Bowman (*The Submarine Captain*), Ernest Pasque (*Blensop*)
D: Irvin Willate, from Joseph Louis Vance's novel
Standard "Lone Wolf" spy-thriller: Rogue sent to USA on secret mission, meets spy

A False Friend
1911, (GB), Clarendon, b&w, 855 ft. (260.6m)
D: Wilfred Noy
Standard melodrama: Doctor's friend poses as chauffeur to abduct his wife, dies when car crashes

The False Wireless
1914, (GB), Big Ben Films-Union/Pathe, b&w, 3,267 ft. (995.8m)
W: H.O. Martinek (*The Officer*), Ivy Montford (*The Sister*)
D: H.O. Martinek **STORY:** L.C. MacBean
Standard crime-thriller: Ship's officer foils girl jewel thief while sister holds gang at bay

Falsely Accused
1905, (GB), Hepworth, b&w, 850 ft. (259.1m)
D: Lewin Fitzhamon
Standard crime-thriller (in 14 scenes): Framed bank clerk flees prison, is sheltered by vicar

Falsely Accused
1907, (GB), Gaumont, b&w, 555 ft. (169.2m)
Stadard crime-thriller: Framed man flees jail, poses as woman

Fame and the Devil
see *One Night of Fame*

Family Doctor
1958, (GB), Templar/20th-Fox, b&w, 85 mins.
W: Rick Jason (*Jethro Jones*), Marius Goring (*Dr. Henry Dysert*), Lisa Gastoni (*Kitty Mortlock*), Sandu Scott (*Stella Dysert*), Mary Merrall (*Miss Bettyhill*), Vida Hope (*Louise*), Helen Shingler (*Charlotte*), Phyllis Neilson-Terry (*Lady Lacy*), Nicholas Hannen (*The Colonel*), Avice Landon (*Mrs. Mortlock*), Kynaston Reeves (*Mr. Sparrow*), Frederick Leister (*Dr. Alexander*), Patrick Waddington (*Sir George Watson*)
P: John Gossage D & SCR: Derek Twist, from Joan Fleming's novel *The Deeds of Dr. Deadcert*
USA retitle, Rx Murder
Standard thriller: Man proves doctor killed wives

Family Plot
1976, (USA), Univ, color, 126 mins.
W: Bruce Dern (*George Lumley*), Karen Black (*Fran*), William Devane (*Arthur Adamson*), Barbara Harris (*Blanche Tyler*), William Prince (*The Bishop*), Cathleen Nesbitt (*Julia Rainbird*), Marge Redmond (*Vera Hannagan*), Katherine Helmond (*Mrs. Maloney*), Ed Lauter (*Joseph Maloney*), Edith Atwater (*Mrs. Clay*), Nicholas Colasanto (*Constantine*), Warren J. Kemmerling (*Grandison*), John Lehne (*Andy Bush*), Charles Tyner (*Wheeler*), Martin West (*Sanger*), Alexander Lockwood
D: Alfred Hitchcock SCR: Ernest Lehman, from Victor Canning's novel *The Rainbird Pattern* PHOTOG: Leonard J. South MUSIC: John Williams
orig. to be titled Deceit
Standard comedy-thriller: Phony medium and boyfriend become embroiled with professional thieves. Hitchcock's last film.

The Family Solicitor
1914, (GB), Clarendon, b&w, 2,772 ft. (844.9m)
W: Dorothy Bellew (*The Girl*)
D: Wilfred Noy STORY: Marchioness of Townshend
Standard crime-thriller: Lawyer forges earl's will so that his indebted son may inherit

The Famous Box Trick
see *Illusions Phantasmagoriques*

The Famous Illusion of Kolta
1901, (GB), R.W. Paul, b&w, 120 ft. (36.6m)
D: Walter R. Booth
Minor fantasy short: Pierrot's sketch of silkworm becomes girl butterfly

The Fan
1981, (USA), Robert Stigwood/Para, color, 95 mins.
W: Lauren Bacall (*Sally Ross*), Maureen Stapleton (*Belle Goldman*), James Garner (*Jake*), Michael Biehn (*Douglas Breen, the "Fan"*), Hector Elizondo (*Ralph Andrews*), Anna Maria Horsford (*Emily Stolz*), Kurt Johnson (*David Branum*), Feiga Martinez (*Elsa*), Dwight Schultz (*The Director*), Reed Jones (*The Choreographer*), Kauilani Lee (*Douglas' Sister*), Charles Blackwell (*John Vetta*), Dana Delany (*The Saleswoman*), Terence Marinan (*The Young Man in the Bar*), Lesley Rogers (*Heidi*), Parker McCormick (*Hilda*), Robert Weil (*Pop*), Ed Crowley (*The Caretaker*), Themi Sapountzakis (*Markham*), Gail Benedict (*The Ass't Choreographer*), Jean DeBaer (*The Stage Manager*), D. David Lewis (*The Pianist*), Griffin Dunne (*The Production Ass't*), Liz Smith, Haru Aki, Rene Ceballos, Clif DeRaita, Edyie Fleming, Justin Ross, Linda Haberman, Sergio Lopez-Cal, Jamie Patterson, James Ogden, Stephanie Williams, Jim Wolfe, Victoria Vanderkloot, Thomas Saccio, Terri Duhaime, Donna Mitchell, Lionel Pina, Hector Osorio, Miriam Phillips, Jack R. Marks, Leo Schaff, George Peters, Esther Benson, Eric Van Valkenburg, James Bryson, Ann Pearl Gary, Madeline Moroff, J. Nesbit Clark, Tim Elliott, Paul Hummel, Jacob Laufer
D: Edward Bianchi SCR: Priscilla Chapman & John Hartwell, from the novel by Bob Randall PHOTOG: Dick Bush MUSIC SCORE: Pino Donaggio MUSIC: Marvin Hamlisch LYRICS: Tim Rice SONGS: *A Remarkable Woman & Hearts, Not Diamonds*
"...a well-made, quite intelligent piece of popular entertainment, containing a sensibly moral examination of how obsession with a celebrity can lead to mayhem"—Richard Schickel, *Time*
Unusual thriller: Obsessed youth threatens actress

Fanatic
1965, (GB), Hammer/7 Arts/Col, color, 96 mins.
W: Tallulah Bankhead (*Mrs. Trefoile*), Stefanie Powers (*Patricia Carroll*), Peter Vaughan (*Harry*), Yootha Joyce (*Anna*), Maurice Kaufmann (*Alan Glentower*), Donald Sutherland (*Joseph*), Gwendolyn Watts (*Gloria*), Robert Dorning (*Ormsby*), Philip Gilbert (*Oscar*), Diane King (*The Woman Shopper*), Winifred Dennis (*The Shopkeeper*)
P: Anthony Hinds D: Silvio Narrizano SCR: Richard Matheson, from Anne Blaisdell's novel *Nightmare* (orig. to be titled same) PHOTOG: Arthur Ibbetson MUSIC: Wilfred Josephs DESIGN: Peter Proud
USA retitle, Die! Die! My Darling!
Modest thriller (Bankhead's last film): Demented old woman keeps dead son's girlfriend prisoner

Fanatic (1982)
see *The Last Horror Film*

Fangs of the Arctic
1953, (USA), AA, b&w, 63 mins.
W: Kirby Grant
Minor adventure-thriller

Fangs of the Living Dead
1969, (It-Sp), Victory-Cobra/Europix, color, 94 mins.
W: Anita Ekberg, John Hamilton, Diana Lorys, Carlos Casaravilla, Adriana Ambesi
D: Armando De Ossorio
Minor horror-thriller (with unintentional laughs): Castle of vampires

Fangs of the Wild
see *Follow the Hunter*

Fanny by Gaslight
1944, (GB), Gainsborough/GFD/UA, b&w, 108 mins.
W: Phyllis Calvert (*Fanny Hopwood*), James Mason (*Lord Manderstoke*), Wilfrid Lawson (*Chunks*), Stewart Granger (*Harry Somerford*), Margaretta Scott (*Alicia*), Nora Swinburne (*Mrs. Hopwood*), Jean Kent (*Lucy Beckett*), Stuart Lindsell (*Clive Seymour*), John Laurie (*Mr. Hopwood*), Ann Wilton (*Carver*), Amy Veness (*Mrs. Heaviside*), Helen Haye (*Mrs. Somerford*), Cathleen Nesbitt (*Kate Somerford*)
P: Edward Black D: Anthony Asquith SCR: Doreen Montgomery & Aimee Stuart, from a novel by Michael Sadlier
USA retitle, Man of Evil (UA, 1948)
reissued 1945 & 1948 (Eros; cut)
Standard thriller: Minister's bastard son saves secretary from lustful nobleman

Fantasia
1940, (USA), Walt Disney, color, 135 mins.
D: Ben Sharpsteen
Classic animated musical-fantasy: Venerable music given illustration by series of mini-tales

Fantasies
1982, (USA), Mandy Prods./ABC-TV, color, 95 mins.
W: Suzanne Pleshette (*Carla Sherman*), Barry Newman (*Det. Errol Flynn*), Lenora May (*Sandy*), Patrick O'Neal (*John*), Robert Vaughn (*Girard*), Robin Mattson (*April Heffner*), Ben Marley (*Arthur*), Stuart Damon (*Roy*), Peter Bergman (*Larry Walter*), Allyn Ann McLerie (*Shirley*), Madlyn Rhue (*Rebecca*), Barry Corbin (*The Coroner*), John Gabriel (*Quentin Mallory*), Robert S. Woods, Aarika Wells, Rick Gates, J.P. Bumstead, Carole Smith, Terry Alexander, Bob Basso, John Sanderford, Stacey Kuhne, Hap Lawrence, Karen Austin, Laurence Lau, John Gowans, Ruth Cox, Larry Flash Jenkins, Jack Garner, Susan Brecht, Edith Fields, J. Victor Lopez, Robert Nadder, Selma Archerd
D: William Wiard TELEPLAY: David Levinson PHOTOG: Richard L. Rawlings SPCL-FX: Willard G. Ferrier MUSIC: James D. Pasquale
TVM, standard thriller: Soap-opera stars murdered

The Fantasist
1989, (USA), color, 98 mins.
W: Timothy Bottoms, Christopher Cazenove
D: Robin Hardy
Standard thriller: Mad killer makes obscene phone calls to prospective victims

El Fantasma de la Opereta (The Phantom of the Operetta)
1959, (Mex), b&w
W: Tin Tan
Standard comedy-fantasy: Old theater inhabited by ghosts

Fantasmagorie
1908, (Fr), Emile Cohl, b&w
Animated fantasy

The Fantastic Butterfly
see *Le Papillon Fantastique*

The Fantastic Dirigible: or, An Inventor's Nightmare
see *Le Dirigeable Fantastique ou le Cauchemar d'un Inventeur*

The Fantastic Disappearing Man
see *The Return of Dracula*

Fantastic Four
1994, (USA), Concorde, color
Standard SF-adventure: Quartet of futuristic heroes

Fantastic Illusions
see *Creations Spontanees*

Fantastic Invasion of Planet Earth
see *The Bubble*

The Fantastic Meal
see *Le Repas Fantastique*

The Fantastic Night
see *La Nuit Fantastique*

Fantastic Planet
1973, (Fr-Czech), New World, color, 72 mins.
VOICES: Jennifer Drake, Sylvie Renoir, Jean Topart, Jean Valmont & Max Amyi
D: Rene Laloux **SCR:** Roland Topor & Rene Laloux, based on Stefan Wul's novel
Oms en Serie (Oms in Quantity) **MUSIC:** Alain Goraguer
Animated SF-fantasy: Alien giants enslave diminutive race

The Fantastic Puppet People
see *Attack of the Puppet People*

The Fantastic Sketch
see *Le Carton Fantastique*

Fantastic Voyage
1966, (USA), 20th-Fox, color, 100 mins.
W: Stephen Boyd (*Grant*), Raquel Welch (*Miss Peterson*), Donald Pleasence (*Dr. Michaels*), Edmond O'Brien (*Gen. Carter*), Arthur Kennedy (*Dr. Duvall*), William Redfield, Arthur O'Connell, Ken Scott, Jean Del Val, James Brolin, Barry Coe, Shelby Grant, Brendan Fitzgerald
P: Saul David **D:** Richard Fleischer **SCR:** Harry Kleiner **ADAPT:** David Duncan, from a story by Otto Klement & Jay Lewis Bixby (later novelized by Dr. Isaac Asimov) **PHOTOG:** Ernest Laszlo **SPCL-FX:** L.B. Abbott, Art Cruickshank & Emil Kosa Jr (Academy Award Winners). **MUSIC:** Leonard Rosenman
A.k.a. Microscopia and Strange Journey
Superior SF-thriller (over 2 years of research at famous institutes enabled creation of film's "anatomically-correct" sets): To destroy blood clot in brain of important statesman, miniaturized submarine and surgical team are injected into arterial system

The Fantastic Umbrella, or Ten Girls Under a Parasol
see *Le Parapluie Fantastique, ou Dix Femmes Sous une Ombrelle*

Fantasy Illusions
see *Les Illusions Fantaisistes*

Fantasy Island
1977, (USA), ABC-TV, color, 98 mins. **W:** Ricardo Montalban (*Roarke*), Bill Bixby (*Arnold Greenwood*), Eleanor Parker (*Eunice Hollander-Baines*), Sandra Dee (*Franchesca*), Hugh O'Brian (*Paul Henley*), Victoria Principal (*Michelle*), Carol Lynley (*Liz*), Peter Lawford (*Grant Baines*), Christina Sinatra (*Connie*), Dick Sargent (*Charles*), Herve Villechaize (*Tattoo*), Peter MacLean, Cedric Scott

Fantastic Voyage: (IN SHIP) RAQUEL WELCH, ARTHUR KENNEDY, DONALD PLEASENCE, STEPHEN BOYD AND EDMOND O'BRIEN

D: Richard Lang **TELEPLAY:** Gene Levitt **PHOTOG:** Arch Dalzell
Minor romance, pilot TVM for popular teleseries: Master of island retreat makes dreams come true. cf. Return to Fantasy Island

Fantomas
1913, (Fr), b&w
D: Louis Feuillade
series of 5 films based on novels by Pierre Souvestre & Marcel Allain
Standard adventure-fantasy: Exploits of mysterious master criminal

Fantomas (1964)
see *Fantomas Contro Scotland Yard*

Fantomas Contro Scotland Yard (Fantomas vs. Scotland Yard)
1964, (It-Fr), Richard Davis/Lopert/UA, color, 105 mins.
W: Jean Marais, Mylene Demongeot, Louis de Funes, Marie-Helene Arnaud
P & D: Andre Hunebelle **SCR:** Jean Halain & Pierre Foucaud, based on novels by Pierre Souvestre & Marcel Allain
USA retitle, Fantomas
Standard adventure-fantasy: Master criminal baffles the authorities

Fantomas vs. Scotland Yard
see *Fantomas Contro Scotland Yard*

Le Fantome d'Alger (The Phantom of Algiers)
1906, (Fr), Star, b&w, 76m (249.3 ft./4.2 mins.)
D: Georges Melies
A.k.a. A Spiritualistic Meeting
Standard fantasy

Le Fantome du Moulin Rouge (The Phantom of the Moulin Rouge)
1924, (Fr), b&w, 90 mins.
W: Albert Prejean
D: Rene Clair
Standard thriller: Sinister events in Parisian landmark

Faraon (Pharaoh)
1965, (Pol), Film Polski/Atlas/Horizon, color, 183 mins.
W: Jerzy Zelnik (*Ramses*), Barbara Bryl (*Kama*), Krystyna Mikolajewska (*Sara*), Piotr Pawloski (*Herhor*), Leszek Herdegen, Jerzy Buczachi
D: Jerzy Kawalerowicz **SCR:** Tadeusz Konwicki & Jerzy Kawalerowicz, from a novel by Boleslaw Prus
Ambitious melodrama: Life of ancient Egyptian ruler

The Far Chapels of Death (The Long Hair of Death)
see *I Lunghi Capelli della Morte*

Farewell, My Lovely
1975, (USA), Elliott Kastner/Avco Embassy, color, 95 mins.
W: Robert Mitchum, Charlotte Rampling, John Ireland, Anthony Zerbe, Sylvia Miles, Harry Dean Stanton
P: George Pappas & Jerry Bruckheimer **D:** Dick Richards **SCR:** David Zelag Goodman, from Raymond Chandler's novel **PHOTOG:** John A. Alonzo **MUSIC:** David Shire
Standard thriller: Gumshoe seeks missing torch singer. cf. Murder, My Sweet, The Falcon Takes Over

Farewell, Spaceship Yamato
see *Saraba Uchu Senkan Yamato*

Farewell to the Planet of the Apes
1974, (USA), 20th-Fox, Made for TV color, 91 mins.
W: Roddy McDowall (*Galen*), Ron Harper (*Alan*), James Naughton (*Ted*)
from characters created by Pierre Boulle
TVM, minor SF-adventure (culled from teleseries "Planet of the Apes"): Astronauts stranded in simian-controlled future. cf. Back to the Planet of the Apes, Forgotten City of the Planet of the Apes, Treachery and Greed on the Planet of the Apes and Life, Liberty and Pursuit on the Planet of the Apes

Fargo
1996, (USA), Working Title/Polygram, color, 98 mins.
W: Frances McDormand (*Marge*), William H. Macy, Steve Buscemi, Harve Presnell, Peter Stormare, Kristin Rudrud, Larissa Kokernot, Tony Denman, Gary Houston, Sally Wingert, Melissa Peterman, Kurt Schweickhardt, Steven Reevis, Steve Edelman, Warren Keith, Sharon Anderson, Larry Brandenburg, Jessica Shepherd, Michelle Suzanne LeDoux, James Gaulke, Steve Park, John Carroll Lynch, Bruce Bohne, Petra Boden, Cliff Rakerd, Wayne Evenson, Michelle Hutchinson, Peter Schmitz, Robert Ozasky, Steve Shaefer, Don Wescott, David Lomax, Jose Feliciano, Bain Boehlke, Rose Stockton, Don William Skahill, John Bandemer
P: Ethan Coen **D:** Joel Coen **SCR:** Ethan Coen & Joel Coen **PHOTOG:** Roger Deakins **MUSIC:** Carter Burwell **SONG:** Let's Find Each Other Tonight
Acclaimed fact-based thriller: Kidnap-ransom scheme becomes murderous. Academy Award-winning Best Actress and Best Screenplay

The Farm
see *The Curse*

Le Fascinant Capitaine Clegg
see *Captain Clegg*

The Fascinating Captain Clegg
see *Captain Clegg*

Faster, Pussycat! Kill! Kill!
1965, (USA), Russ Meyer Assocs., b&w, 83 mins.
W: Tura Satana, Lori Williams, Haji, Sue Bernard
P: Russ & Eve Meyer **D:** Russ Meyer **SCR:** Jack Moran
A.k.a. Leather Girls, Mankillers and Pussycat
Classic trash-thriller: Three psychotic go-go dancers seek cheap thrills

The Farm: JOHN SCHNEIDER

The Fast Kill
1972, (GB), Shonteff/20th-Fox, color, 88 mins.
W: Tom Adams (*Max Stein*), Susie Hampton (*Angelique Dumas*), Roy Chiarella (*Kevin Klaus*), Patricia Haines (*Victoria Leach*), Peter Halliday (*Fred Chalmers*), Michael Culver (*Jeremy Dryden*), Clive Endersby (*Charles Dumas*), Chris Carbis (*The Aide*), Graham Ashley (*Miller*), Sean Hewitt (*Gamal*), Sheila Dunn (*Karen Dryden*), Harry Shacklock (*Kroll*), John Plume (*The Sadist*)
P & D: Lindsay Shonteff   STORY: Martin Gillman   PHOTOG: Michael Davis   MUSIC: Alan Gorrie
Standard crime-thriller: Crook steals uncut diamonds

The Fatal Appetizer
1909, (GB), Hepworth, b&w, 450 ft. (137.2m)
W: Johnny Butt
D: Lewin Fitzhamon
Standard comedy-fantasy: Hungry thin man eats everything, grows fat

Fatal Attraction
1987, (USA), Para, color, 120 mins.
W: Michael Douglas, Glenn Close, Anne Archer, Ellen Hamilton Latzen, Stuart Pankin, Ellen Foley, Fred Gwynne, Michael Arkin, Meg Mundy, Tom Brennan, Lois Smith, J.J. Johnston, Mike Nussbaum, Sam J. Coppola, Eunice Prewitt, Justine Johnston, Jane Krakowski, Greg Scott
D: Adrian Lyne   SCR: James Dearden   PHOTOG: Howard Atherton   MUSIC: Maurice Jarre
Critically-acclaimed thriller: Psychotic woman lures married man into affair

Fatal Exam
1997, (USA), color
WRIT, P & D: Jack Snyder
Standard horror-thriller: Students visit haunted house

Fatal Exposure
1990, (USA), color
W: Blake Bahner, Ena Henderson, Julie Austin, Dan Schmale, Renee Cline, Gary Wise, Joy Ovington
Standard horror-thriller: Jack the Ripper's grandson makes videotapes of crimes

Fatal Fingers
1916, (GB), B&C/DFSA, b&w, 6,423 ft. (1957.7m)
W: George Bellamy (*The Earl of Ellersdale*), Mary Merrall (*Irene Lambton*), A.V. Bramble (*Rollo Lambton, MP*), Farmer Skein (*The Home Secretary*), Harry Latimer (*Don Mario*), Icilma Rae (*Irene as a Child*)
D: A.V. Bramble & Eliot Stannard   SCR: Eliot Stannard
Standard crime-thriller: Earl fakes suicide to expose murderous Italian don

The Fatal Formula
1915, (GB), Kineto, b&w, 2,000 ft. (609.6m)
WRIT & D: Frank Stather
Standard thriller: Inventor's daughter tracks spies

The Fatal Hand
1907, (GB), R.W. Paul, b&w, 415 ft. (126.5m)
D: J.H. Martin

Minor melodrama short: Escaped lunatic murders

The Fatal Hour
1937, (GB), B&D/Para British, b&w, 66 mins.
W: Edward Rigby (*Cready*), Moira Reed (*Mary Denston*), Dick Hunter (*Peter*), Moore Marriott (*Dixon*), Derek Gorst (*James West*), D.J. Williams (*The Evangelist*), J.H. Lockwood (*Sir George Bell*), Ernest Sefton (*Pat*)
D: George Pearson   SCR: Ralph Neale & Gerald Elliott, from Cicely Frazer-Simpson's novel *The Clock*
Standard thriller: Secret agent vies with spies for antigas formula

The Fatal Hour
1940, (USA), Mono, b&w, 68 mins.
W: Boris Karloff (*James Lee Wong*), Grant Withers (*Capt. Sam Street*), Marjorie Reynolds (*Bobby Logan*), Charles Trowbridge (*Forbes*), John Hamilton (*Belden*), Jack Kennedy (*Mike*), Craig Reynolds (*Francis Belden*), Pauline Drake (*Bessie*), Lita Chevret (*Tanya Serova*), I. Stanford Jolley (*Soapy*), Frank Puglia (*Hardway*), Jason Robards Sr. (*Griswold*)
P: William T. Lackey   D: William Nigh   SCR: Scott Darling & Joseph West, from characters created by Hugh Wiley   PHOTOG: Harry Neumann
GB retitle, **Mr. Wong at Headquarters**
Minor mystery: Chinese sleuth trails diamond smugglers. 'Mr. Wong Series'

Fatal Images
1982, (USA), color, 90 mins.
W: Lane Coyle
D: Dennis Devine
Minor horror-fantasy: Camera causes models to die

Fatal Journey
1954, (GB), Merton Park/Anglo-Amalgamated, b&w, 30 mins.
W: Gordon Bell (*Insp. Durrant*), Edward Forsyth (*The Detective*), Jack Melford (*Mr. Preston*), Jane Welsh (*Mrs. Preston*), Julian Somers (*Goff*)
P: Alec Snowden   D: Paul Gherzo   STORY: James Eastwood
Standard short thriller: Inspector exposes amnesiac as murderous blackmailer

Fatally Yours
1995, (USA), color, 90 mins.
W: Rick Rossovich, George Lazenby, Roddy McDowall, Sarah MacDonnell, Sage Stallone
Standard fantasy-thriller: Man restores mob-massacre house, meets female ghost

The Fatal Night
1948, (GB), Anglofilm/Col, b&w, 50 mins.
W: Lester Ferguson (*Puce*), Jean Short (*Geraldine*), Leslie Armstrong (*Cyril*), Brenda Hogan (*Julia*), Patrick Macnee (*Tony*), Aubrey Mallalieu (*The Yokel*)
P & D: Mario Zampi   SCR: Gerald Butler & Kathleen Connors, from Michael Arlen's story *The Gentleman from America*   PHOTOG: Cedric Williams   MUSIC: Stanley Black
Standard thriller: Man scared to death in haunted house

The Fatal Orchids
see **Black Orchids**

Fatal Passion
1994, (USA), color, 90 mins.
W: Lisa Hayland, Joseph Plato
Standard thriller: Sisters flee murder rap, meet backwoods cultists

Fatal Pulse
1988, (USA), color, 90 mins.
W: Michelle McCormick, Ken Roberts, Joe Phelan, Alex Courtney
Minor horror-thriller: Sorority sisters slain

Fatal Sky
1990, (USA-Austral-Yugo), Sugar, color
W: Michael Nouri, Maxwell Caulfield, Darlanne Fluegel, Derren Nesbitt, Ray Charleson, Charles Durning
D: Frank Shields   MUSIC: Allan Zovia
Standard SF-thriller

The Fatal 30
1921, (USA), Pacific Film, b&w, 5 reels
W: John J. Hayes, Fritzi Ridgeway, Lillian West, Carl Stockdale, Al Fremont
D: John J. Hayes
Standard thriller: Young lovers involved with cult of sunworshippers who perform human sacrifices

The Fatal Witness
1945, (USA), Rep, b&w, 59 mins.
W: Evelyn Ankers, Richard Fraser George Leigh, Barbara Everest, Frederick Worlock
D: Lesley Selander
Standard melodrama: Wealthy matron murdered

The Fate of a King
1913, (GB), Britannia Films/Pathe, b&w, 1,926 ft. (587m)
D: A.E. Coleby
Standard melodrama: King James I ignores witch's warning

Father Brown

1954, (GB), facet/Col, b&w, 91 mins.
W: Alec Guinness (*Father Brown*), Cecil Parker (*The Bishop*), Peter Finch (*Gustave Flambeau*), Joan Greenwood (*Lady Warren*), Bernard Lee (*Insp. Valentine*), Sidney James (*Bert Parkinson*), Gerard Oury (*Insp. Dubois*), Ernest Thesiger (*The Vicomte*), Ernest Clark (*The Sec'y*), Jim Herald (*The Station Master*), Austin Trevor (*The Herald*), Everley Gregg (*The Governess*), John Salew (*The Sgt.*), Eugene Deckers (*The Officer*), Marne Maitland (*The Maharajah*), Noel Howlett (*The Auctioneer*)
P: Paul Finder Moss & Vivian A. Cox   D: Robert Hamer   SCR: Thelma Schnee & Robert Hamer, from stories by G.K. Chesterton
USA retitle, **The Detective**
Stylish comedy-thriller: Catholic priest foils theft of sacred cross

Father Frost

see *Morozko*

Father's Baby Boy

1909, (GB), Clarendon, b&w
D: Percy Stow
Minor fantasy short: Infant grows to gigantic size

Father's Coat to the Rescue

1912, (GB), GS Films/Hepworth, b&w, 425 ft. (129.6m)
D: Gilbert Southwell
Standard crime-thriller: Girl dons father's police uniform, arrests burglar

Father's Forty Winks

1912, (GB), Empire Films/MP Sales, b&w, 370 ft. (112.8m)
P: Frank Butcher
D: Arthur Cooper
Minor fantasy short: Man dreams son's toys come to life

A Father's Vengeance

1902, (GB), New Century Pictures, b&w
Standard melodrama: Squire strangles girl and throws her in river, is shot by her father

A Father's Vengeance

1907, (GB), Hepworth, b&w, 525 ft. (160m)
D: Lewin Fitzhamon
Standard thriller: Tramp rapes foundry owner's daughter

Father Thames' Temperance Cure

1902, (GB), R.W. Paul, b&w, 85 ft. (25.9m)
D: W.R. Booth
Standard fantasy short: Father Thames rises from river, frightens drunk

Fathom

1967, (GB), 20th-Fox, color, 99 mins.
W: Raquel Welch (*Fathom Harvill*), Tony Franciosa (*Peter Merriweather*), Ronald Fraser (*Douglas Campbell*), Richard Briers (*Timothy*), Greta Chi (*JoMay Soon*), Clive Revill (*Serapkin*), Tom Adams (*Mike*), Elizabth Ercy (*Ulla*), Ann Lancaster (*Mrs. Trivers*), Tutte Lemkow (*Mehmed*), Reg Lye (*Mr. Trivers*)
P: John Kohn   D: Leslie H. Martinson   SCR: Lorenzo Semple Jr., from Larry Forrester's novel   PHOTOG: Douglas Slocombe   MUSIC: John Dankworth
Minor thriller: Female sky-diver enlisted for espionage

The Fat Spy

1966, (USA), Phillip Productions/Magna, color, 75 mins
W: Jack E. Leonard, Brian Donlevy, Phyllis Diller, Jayne Mansfield, Jordan Christopher, Johnny Tillotson
P: Everett Rosenthal   D: Joseph Brun   SCR: Matthew Andrews
Standard fantasy-satire: Cosmetics tycoon seeks Fountain of Youth

Faust (1904)

see *Damnation of Doctor Faust*

Faust

1910, (GB), Animatophone, b&w
D: David Barnett
from Gounod's opera
Musical fantasy (several songs synchronized to gramaphone records): Old man makes satanic pact

Faust

1911, (GB), Hepworth, b&w, 15 mins. (4.6m)
W: Hay Plumb (*Faust*), Claire Pridelle (*Marguerite*), Jack Hulcup (*Mephistopheles*), Frank Wilson (*Valentine*)
D: Cecil M. Hepworth, from Charles Gounod's opera
Standard short melodrama (synchronized with gramophone records): Scholar sells soul to Satan. Vivaphone

Faust

1922, (GB), Master Films/Gaumont, b&w, 1,152 ft. (351.1m)
W: Dick Webb (*Faust*), Sylvia Caine (*Marguerite*), Lawford Davidson (*Mephistopheles*), Gordon Hopkirk (*Valentine*), Minnie Rayner (*Martha*)
D: Charles Sanderson   SCR: Frank Miller, from Charles Gounod's opera

Standard fantasy-thriller: Scholar makes satanic pact

Faust

1923, (GB), Bertram Phillips/Butcher, b&w, 1,790 ft. (545.6m)
W: Queenie Thomas, Peter Upcher, Frank Stanmore, Adeline Hayden Coffin, Jeff Barlow, Fatty Phillips
D: Bertram Phillips   STORY: Frank Miller
Standard fantasy-satire (episode from "Syncopated Picture Plays" series): Devil tempts scholar

Faust

1926, (Ger), Ufa/MGM, b&w, 6,500 ft. (1981.2m)
W: Emil Jannings, Gosta Ekman, Yvette Guilbert, Camilla Horn, Hanna Ralph, Frieda Richard, William Dieterle, Eric Barclay, Werner Futter-er
P: Erich Pommer   D: F.W. Murnau   SCR: Hans Kyser based on old German folk sagas   PHOTOG: Carl Hoffmann, film titles composed by Gerhart Hauptmann
Standard fantasy-thriller: Satan rejuvenates old scholar

Faust

1936, (GB), Publicity Picture Prods.-Nat'l Interest/Reunion, b&w, 43 mins.
W: Webster Booth (*Faust*), Anne Ziegler (*Marguerite*), Dennis Hoey (*Mephistopheles*)
D: Albert Hopkins, from Charles Gounod's opera
Standard musical-fantasy: Old man trades soul for youth

Faust

1963, (W. Ger), Devina, color, 133 mins
W: Will Quadflieg, Gustaf Gruendgens, Ella Buchi
from Christopher Marlowe's play *The Tragical History of Doctor Faustus*

Faust and Marguerite

1897, (Fr), Star, b&w, 20m (65.6 ft./1.1 mins.)
P & D: Georges Melies
Minor fantasy short: Old scholar makes deal with Devil

Faust and Marguerite (1904)

see *Damnation of Doctor Faust*

Faust and Mephistopheles

1898, (GB), G.A.S. Films, b&w, 75 ft. (22.9m)
D: George Albert Smith
Standard fantasy short: Old man makes pact with Satan

Faust and the Devil

1948, (It), Col, b&w, 86 mins.
W: Gino Mattera, Nelly Corradi, Mischa Auer, Italo Tajo
P: Gregor Rabinovitch   D: Carmine Gallone   SCR: Leopoldo Marchand, based on Charles Gounod's opera   PHOTOG: V. Vich & A. Gallea
A.k.a. **La Leggenda di Faust (The Legend of Faust)**
Standard fantasy: Old scholar bargains with Devil

Faust aux Enfers (Faust in Hell)

1903, (Fr), Star, b&w, 150m (492.1 ft./8.3 mins.)
D: Georges Melies
A.k.a. **The Condemnation of Faust** and **The Damnation of Faust**
Standard fantasy (in 16 scenes): Journey through infernal world

Faustina

1958, (Sp), Chapalo, color
W: Maria Felix (*Faustina*), Fernando Fernan Gomez, Elisa Montes, Conrado San Martin, Fernando Rey, Tomas Blanco, Xan Das Bolas, Antonio Casal, Juan De Landa, Santiago Ontanon, Jose Isbert, Tony Leblanc, Margot Prieto
WRIT & D: Jose Luis Saenz de Heredia   PHOTOG: Alfredo Fraile
Standard melodrama

Faust in Hell

see *Faust aux Enfers*

Faustine and the Beautiful Summer

see *Faustine et le Bel Ete*

Faustine et le Bel Ete (Faustine and the Beautiful Summer)

1971, (Fr), color
W: Muriel Catala
WRIT & D: Nina Companeez
Standard fantasy

Faust XX

1967, (It), color
Standard fantasy

F.B.I. Code 98

1964, (USA), WB, b&w, 94 mins.
W: Robert P. Cannon, Fred Vitale
Minor melodrama

F.B.I. Girl

1951, (USA), Lippert, b&w, 74 mins.
W: Cesar Romero, Audrey Totter, George Brent, Raymon Burr

Standard thriller

The FBI vs. Dr. Mabuse
see *In the Steel Net of Dr. Mabuse*

Fear
1946, (USA), Mono, b&w, 68 mins.
W: Peter Cookson, Warren William, Anne Gwynne James Cardwell, Nestor Paiva
D: Alfred Zeisler, based on Feodor Dostoevski's novel *Crime and Punishment*
Minor, low-budget adaptation of immortal classic: Young murderer betrayed by conscience

The Fear
1967, (Greece), Trans Lux, b&w, 102 mins.
W: Alexis Damianos, Mary Chronopoulou
Standard melodrama

Fear
1988, (USA), color, 96 mins.
W: Cliff DeYoung, Ken Lenz, Robert Factor, Scott Schwartz, Frank Stallone, Geri Betzler
D: Robert A. Ferretti
Minor thriller: Escaped convicts terrorize family on camping trip

Fear
1990, (USA), SHO-TV, cable, color, 95 mins.
W: Ally Sheedy (*Cayce Bridges*), Lauren Hutton (*Jessica*), Michael O'Keefe (*Jack*), Pruitt Taylor Vince, Stan Shaw, Dina Merrill, John Agar, Keone Young Marta DuBois
D: Rockne S. O'Bannon   MUSIC: Henry Mancini
Made-for-Cable TVM, standard thriller: Psychic stalks criminal with equal mental powers

The Fear
1994, (USA), Devin/A-Pix, video, color, 98 mins.
W: Eddie Bowz (*Richard*), Heather Medway (*Ashley*), Vince Edwards (*Uncle Pete*), Ann Turkel (*Leslie*), Darin Heams (*Troy*), Anna Karin (*Tanya*), Antonio Todd (*Gerald*), Leland Hayward (*Vance*), Monique Mannen (*Mindy*), Erick Weiss ("*Morty*"), Wes Craven (*Dr. Arnold*), Hunter Bedrosian (*Young Richard*), Rebecca Baldwin (*Rose*), Greg Littman (*Claude*), Stacy Edwards (*Becky*), Tom Challis (*Detective #1*), Bill Wallace (*Detective #2*), Daniel Franklin (*Father*), Lisa Iannini (*Mother*), Corey Wilson, Bill Winkler, Ron Ford, Greg "B.D." Roszyk
P: Richard Brandes   D: Vincent Robert   SCR: Ron Ford   PHOTOG: Bernd Heinl   SPCL-FX: Jason Hamer & David Barrett   MUSIC: Robert O. Ragland   SONGS: *Here Come the Gravedigger, Fear, Flesh and Blood, Better Off Dead, Trust No Man & Black Rent*
Made-for-Video, minor horror-fantasy: Collegians probe nature of fear at mountain retreat, supernatural killer prowls

Fear
1996, (USA), Univ, color, 97 mins.
W: William Petersen (*Steve Walker*), Mark Wahlberg (*David McCall*), Reese Witherspoon (*Nicole Walker*), Amy Brenneman (*Laura Walker*), Alyssa Milano, Tracy Fraim, Jason Kristofer, Jed Rees, Gary John Riley, Todd Caldecott, David Fredericks, Christopher Gray, Ravinder Toor, John Oliver, Jo Bates, Andrew Arue, Will Sengotta, L. Harvey Gold
D: James Foley   SCR: Christopher Crowe   PHOTOG: Thomas Kloss   MUSIC: Carter Burwell
"..nasty little potboiler with some darkly amusing situations"—Peter M. Nichols, Times
A.k.a. **No Fear**
Standard thriller: Teen psycho terrorizes girlfriend's family.

Fear and Desire
1953, (USA), Burstyn, b&w, 68 mins.
W: Frank Silvera, Kenneth Harp, Paul Mazursky, Virginia Leith
P,D, SCR, PHOTOG: Stanley Kubrick, his first film.
Standard melodrama

The Fear Chamber
1968, (USA-Mex), Azteca/Col, color, 88 mins.
W: Boris Karloff, Santanon, Carlos East
P: Louis Enrique Vergara   D: Juan Ibanez & Jack Hill
A.k.a. **Torture Zone** and **Chamber of Fear**
Minor horror-thriller: Scientist nurtures intelligent rock

The Fear Inside
1992, (USA), cable, color, 115 mins
W: Christine Lahti, Dylan McDermott
D: Leon Ichaso
Standard thriller: Strangers claiming to be siblings terrorize agoraphobic landlady

Fear in the City of the Living Dead
see *The Gates of Hell*

Fear in the Night
1947, (USA), Para, b&w, 72 mins.
W: Paul Kelly, Ann Doran, DeForest Kelley, Charles Victor, Jeff York, Robert Emmett Keane, Kay Scott

P: William Pine & William Thomas   WRIT & D: Maxwell Shane   based on William Irish's novel *Nightmare*   PHOTOG: Jack Greenhalgh   MUSIC: Rudy Schrager
Standard thriller: Man fears he killed while under hypnosis. cf. **Nightmare** (1956)

Fear in the Night
1972, (GB), Hammer/MGM-EMI, color, 85 mins.
W: Judy Geeson (*Peggy Heller*), Joan Collins (*Molly Carmichael*), Ralph Bates (*Robert Heller*), Peter Cushing (*Michael Carmichael*), Gillian Lind (*Mrs. Beamish*), James Cossins (*The Doctor*), John Bown (*A Policeman*), Brian Grellis (*A Policeman*)
P& D: Jimmy Sangster   SCR: Jimmy Sangster & Michael Syson   PHOTOG: Arthur Grant   MUSIC: John McCabe
A.k.a. **Honeymoon of Fear**
Standard thriller: Faculty wife stalked in deserted school

Fear is the Key
1972, (GB), K.L.K./Anglo-EMI/Para, color, 108 mins.
W: Barry Newman (*John Talbot*), Suzy Kendall (*Sarah Ruthven*), John Vernon (*Vyland*), Dolph Sweet (*Jablonsky*), Ben Kingsley (*Royale*), Ray McAnally (*Ruthven*), Peter Marinker (*Larry*), Elliott Sullivan (*Judge Mollison*), Roland Brand (*The Deputy*), Tony Anholt (*The FBI Agent*)
P: Alan Ladd Jr. & Jay Kanter   D: Michael Tuchner   SCR: Robert Carrington, from a novel by Alistair MacLean   PHOTOG: Alex Thomson   MUSIC: Roy Budd
Standard thriller: Millionaire involves fugitive in scheme to salvage jewels from sunken airplane. Ben Kingsley's film debut

Fearless Frank
1969, (USA), AIP, color, 78 mins, also 83 mins
W: Jon Voight (*Frank*), Monique Van Vooren (*Plethora*), Severn Darden (*The Doctor/Brother/Claude*), Lou Gilbert (*The Boss*), Joan Darling (*Lois*), Ben Carruthers (*Cat*), Anthony Holland (*Alfred*), David Steinberg (*Rat*), David Fisher (*Screwnose*), Nelson Algren (*Needles*), Ken Nordine (*Stranger*)
WRIT, P & D: Philip Kaufman   PHOTOG: Bill Butler   MUSIC: Meyer Kupferman
A.k.a. **Frank's Greatest Adventure**
Bizarre fantasy-satire: Country boy becomes mechanized crime-fighter. Made in 1965, in Chicago. Voight's debut.

The Fearless Vampire Killers or: Pardon Me, But Your Teeth are in My Neck
1967, (GB), Cadre-Filmways/MGM, color, 110 mins.
W: Roman Polanski (*Alfred*), Jack MacGowran (*Prof. Abronsius*), Sharon Tate (*Sarah*), Alfie Bass (*Shagal*), Ferdy Mayne (*Count Von Krolock*), Terry Downes (*Koukol*), Fiona Lewis (*The Maid*), Iain Quarrier (*Herbert Von Krolock*), Jessie Robins (*Mrs. Shagal*), Ronald Lacey (*The Idiot*), Sydney Bromley (*The Driver*), Andreas Malandrinos (*The Woodcutter*)
P: Gene Gutowski   D: Roman Polanski   SCR: Gerard Brach & Roman Polanski   PHOTOG: Douglas Slocombe   MUSIC: Christopher Komeda [Krzysztof Komeda]
orig. to be titled **Your Teeth in My Neck**, *A.k.a.* **The Dance of the Vampires**
Lavish ($5 million budget) horror-spoof: Eccentric professor and his prize pupil try to wipe out nest of vampires

Fearmaker
1989, (Mex), color, 90 mins.
W: Katy Jurado, Paul Picerni, Sonia Amelio, Carlos East
D: Anthony Carras
A.k.a. **House of Fear** and **Violent Rage**
Minor thriller: Treachery entangles heiress

The Fearmakers
1958, (USA), UA, b&w, 83 mins.
W: Dana Andrews, Dick Foran, Mel Torme, Veda Ann Borg, Marilee Earle (*Female lead*)
P: Martin Lancer   D: Jacques Tourneur   SCR: Elliot West & Chris Apple
Standard thriller: Korean War veteran returns home, discovers his ad agency is unknowingly promoting communism

Fear No Evil
1969, (USA), Univ, Made for TV, color, 98 mins.
W: Louis Jourdan (*Dr. David Sorell*), Lynda Day George, Bradford Dillman, Marsha Hunt, Carroll O'Connor, Wilfrid Hyde-White, Ivor Barry, Katharine Woodville, Harry Davis, Susan Brown
P: Paul Wendkos   WRIT & D: Richard Alan Simmons, from a story by Guy Endore   PHOTOG: Andrew J. McIntyre   MUSIC: William Goldenberg
TVM, standard thriller: Shrewd psychic versus satanists, demon in strange mirror. cf. **Ritual of Evil**

Fear No Evil
1981, (USA), Avco Embassy, color, 97 mins.
W: Stefan Arngrim (*Andrew*), Elizabeth Hoffman (*Mikhail/Margaret*), Kathleen Rowe McAllen (*Gabrielle Hulie*), Frank Birney (*Father Daley*), Daniel Eden (*Tony*), Jack Holland (*Rafael/Father Damon*), Barry Cooper (*Mr. Williams*), Paul Haber (*Mark*), Alice Sachs (*Mrs. Williams*), Roslyn Gugino (*Marie*), Richard Jay Silverthorn (*Lucifer*)
P: Frank LaLoggia & Charles LaLoggia   WRIT & D: Frank LaLoggia   PHOTOG: Fred Goodich   SPCL-FX: John Eggett   MUSIC: Frank LaLoggia & David Spear
Standard horror-fantasy: Demonic teen causes havoc

F

Fear of the Hangman
1914, (GB), Solograph, b&w, 1,462 ft. (445.6m)
Standard thriller

Fear Stalk
1989, (USA), color
W: Jill Clayburgh
Standard thriller: Woman TV executive matches wits with psychopath

Feast of Blood
*see **Blood of Dracula's Castle***

The Feathered Serpent
1934, (GB), GS Enterprises/Col, b&w, 72 mins.
W: Enid Stamp-Taylor (*Ella Crewe*), Tom Helmore (*Peter Dewin*), D.A. Clarke-Smith (*Joe Farmer*), Moore Marriott (*Harry Hugg*), Molly Fisher (*Daphne Olroyd*), Iris Baker (*Paula Ricks*), Vincent Holman (*Insp. Clarke*), Evelyn Roberts (*Leicester Crewe*), O.B. Clarence (*George Beale*)
D: Maclean Rogers   SCR: Maclean Rogers & Kathleen Butler, from a novel by Edgar Wallace
Standard crime-thriller: Reporter solves murder

The Feathered Serpent
1948, (USA), Mono, b&w, 68 mins.
W: Roland Winters (*Charlie Chan*), Keye Luke (*Lee Chan*), Victor Sen Yung (*Tommie Chan*), Mantan Moreland (*Birmingham Brown*), Robert Livingston (*John Stanley*), Nils Asther (*Prof. Paul Evans*), Martin Garralaga (*Pedro*), Carol Forman (*Sonia Cabot*), Beverly Jons (*Joan Farnsworth*), Jay Silverheels (*Diego*), George J. Lewis (*Capt. Juan*), Leslie Denison (*Prof. Farnsworth*), Charles Stevens, Frank Leyva, Erville Anderson, Milton Ross, Fred Cordova
D: William Beaudine   SCR: Oliver Drake, from characters created by Earl Derr Biggers   PHOTOG: William Sickner
*Exciting "Charlie Chan" mystery: Oriental sleuth deals with murder on treasure hunt in Mexico. Remake of **Riders of the Whistling Skull** (1937), a Western starring Robert Livingstone*

Federal Agent
1936, (USA), b&w, 53 mins.
W: William Boyd, Charles A. Browne, Irene Ware, Lentia Lace, George Cooper, Dan Alvarado
D: Sam Newfield
Standard thriller: G-man chases spies who seek new explosive

Federal Agent at Large
1950, (USA), Rep, b&w, 60 mins.
W: Robert Rockwell, Dorothy Patrick
Standard thriller

Feet of Clay
1960, (GB), Danziger/UA, b&w, 55 mins.
W: Vincent Ball (*David Kyle*), Wendy Williams (*Fay*), Hilda Fenemore (*Mrs. Clarke*), Robert Cawdron (*Saunders*), Jack Melford (*Soames*), Brian Smith (*Jimmy*), Angela Douglas (*Diana*)
P: Brian Taylor   D: Frank Marshall   STORY: Mark Grantham
Standard crime-thriller: Solicitor exposes probation officer as dope-ring leader

Feet Foremost
1985, (GB), color, 60 mins.
W: Jeremy Kemp
TVM, minor fantasy-thriller: Industrialist haunted by teen girl's spirit

La Feline
*see **Cat People** (1942)*

Les Felins (The Cats)
1964, (Fr), Cipral/Cité/MGM, b&w, 110 mins, also 98 mins.
W: Jane Fonda, Alain Delon, Lola Albright, Sorrell Booke, Carl Studer
D: Rene Clement   PHOTOG: Henri Decae   MUSIC: Lalo Schifrin
*A.k.a. **Joy House** and **The Love Cage***
Unusual comedy-melodrama: Gothic chateau of misfits, in Franscope

Felix the Cat: The Movie
1991, (USA), color, 83 mins.
VOICES: Chris Phillips, Alice Playten, Maureen O'Connell, Peter Neuman, Susan Montanaro
D: Tibor Hernadi
Standard animated fantasy: Feline encounters dimension filled with superheroes

Fellini Satyricon
*see **Satyricon***

Fellowship of the Frog
1960, (W. Ger), b&w 92 mins
W: Joachim Fuchsberger, Carl Lange, Jochen Brockman, Eva Anthes
from the novel by Edgar Wallace
*A.k.a. **Face of the Frog***
Standard thriller: Sinister society

The Female Bunch
1969, (USA), Dalia/Gilbreth/Burbank Int'l, color, 86 mins
W: Russ Tamblyn, Regina Carrol, Lon Chaney Jr., Jennifer Bishop
P: Ralph Nussbaum   D: Al Adamson, John Cardos   SCR: Jale Lockwood & Brent Nimrod
*A.k.a. **A Time to Run***
Minor thriller (filmed on Manson ranch): Man-hating women roam desert

The Female Butcher
*see **Ceremonia Sangrienta***

Female Fiends
1960, (USA), Cinema Assocs., b&w, 71 mins.
W: Lex Barker, Carole Mathews
Minor thriller

The Female Jungle
1956, (USA), ARC/AIP, b&w, 71 mins.
W: Lawrence Tierney, Kathleen Crowley, John Carradine, Jayne Mansfield, Bruno Ve Sota
P: Burt Kaiser   D: Bruno Ve Sota   SCR: Burt Kaiser & Bruno Ve Sota
*A.k.a. **The Hangover***
Standard thriller: Police sergeant found drunk at scene of actress' murder

The Female Swindler
1916, (USA), British Empire, b&w, 5,500 ft. (1676.4m)
W: Henry Lonsdale (*Jack Coulson*), Alice Belmore (*Lu Valroy*), Arthur Poole (*Geoffrey Warden*), Maud Olmar (*May Oliver*), Ralph Forster (*Sir James Oliver*), Ninette de Valois (*The Dancer*), Andrew Emm (*Billy Binks*), Bessie Walters (*Mary*), Newman Maurice (*Mikestein*), Charles Grenville (*Harold Travers*)
D: Albert Ward, from a play by Walter Melville
Standard crime-thriller: Detective loves jewel thief

The Female Trap
*see **The Name of the Game is Kill***

Les Femmes s'en Balancent (Dames Don't Care)
1954, (Fr), CICC/Pathe, b&w, 115 mins.
W: Eddie Constantine (*Lemmy Caution*), Dominique Wilms, Nadia Gray, Jacques Catelot, Dario Moreno, Gil Delamare
D: Bernard Borderie   SCR: Bernard Borderie & Jacques Vilfrid, from Peter Cheyney's novel
3rd "Lemmy Caution" action-thriller: Secret agent tracks currency hijackers

La Femme Nikita (The Girl Nikita)
1990, (It-Fr), Gaumont/Samuel Goldwyn Jr., color, 117 mins.
W: Anne Parillaud, Jean-Hugues Anglade, Tcheky Karyo, Jean Reno, Jeanne Moreau, Roland Blanche, Jean Bouise, Jacques Boudet
D: Luc Besson
*GB retitle, **Nikita***
*Unusual thriller: Gov't turns female sociopath into killing machine. cf. **Point of No Return***

La Femme Volante (The Floating Woman)
1902, (Fr), Star, b&w, 40m (131.2 ft./2.2 mins.)
D: Georges Melies
*A.k.a. **Marvellous Suspension and Evolution***
Standard fantasy: Magician levitates woman

Fencing Contest from 'The Three Musketeers'
1898, (GB), Mutoscope & Biograph, b&w
inspired by Alexander Dumas' novel *The Three Musketeers*
Minor action short: Fencing scene from stage production

Fer-de-Lance
1974, (USA), Leslie Stevens/MGM/CBS-TV, color, 98 mins.
W: David Janssen, Hope Lange, Ivan Dixon, Jason Evers, Charles Knox Robinson, George Pan, Robert Ito, William Mims, Ben Piazza, Shizuko Hoshi, Frank Bonner, Richard Guthrie, Sandra Ego, Richard Le Pore, Elvenn Harvard, Felipe Turich, Alain Patrick, Phillip Montgomery, Bill Catching, Robert Burr
D: Russell Mayberry   STORY: Leslie Stevens   PHOTOG: John M. Stephens   SPCL-FX: Thomas L. Fisher   MUSIC: Dominic Frontiere
*GB theatrical retitle, **Death Dive**, A.k.a. **Death Dive** and **Operation Serpent***
TVM, tense thriller: Submarine stranded on ocean floor, cargo of venomous snakes escapes

Ferngully: The Last Rain Forest
1992, (Austral), color, 76 mins.
VOICES: Samantha Mathis, Christian Slater, Robin Williams, Tim Curry, Jonathan Ward, Grace Zabriskie, Tone Loc, Jim Cox, Richard "Cheech" Marin, Tommy Chong
D: Bill Kroyer   SCR: Jim Cox   MUSIC: Alan Silvestri
Unusual animated eco-musical: Sprites oppose pollution of forest home

Fertilize the Blaspheming Bombshell!
1990, (USA), color
W: Bo Hopkins
Minor fantasy-thriller: Brooklyn beauty chosen to bear Satan's child

Fetters of Fear
1915, (GB), Gaumont, b&w, 1,214 ft. (370m)
W: Peggy Hyland (*Mavis Sinclair*), J.L.V. Leigh (*Roland Stuart*), Clarence Derwent (*Jasper Haynes*)
WRIT & D: Leslie Seldon-Truss
Standard romance: Girl hypnotized by guardian

Fever Lake
1997, (USA), color, 95 mins.
W: Corey Haim, Bo Hopkins, Mario Lopez
Made-for-Video, standard fantasy-thriller: Vacation house is haunted

The Fiancee of the Jungle
see The Bride and the Beast

The Fiance
1997, (USA), color, 95 mins.
W: Lysette Anthony (*Faith*), William R. Moses (*Walter*)
Made-for-Video, standard thriller: Dejected housewife has one-night stand, becomes object of deadly obsession

The Fiction-Makers
1967, (GB), ITC/CBS-TV, color, 102 mins.
W: Roger Moore (*Simon Templar*), Sylvia Syms (*Amos Klein/Darling*), Justine Lord (*Galaxy Rose*), Kenneth J. Warren, Philip Locke
P: Robert S. Baker   D: Roy Baker   TELEPLAY: John Kruse & Harry W. Junkin, from characters created by Leslie Charteris   PHOTOG: Michael Reed   MUSIC: Edwin Astley
TVM, minor thriller culled from "Saint" teleseries: Sleuth hired to protect authoress

Fiddlers Three
1944, (GB), Ealing, b&w, 88 mins.
W: Tommy Trinder (*Tommy*), Frances Day (*Poppaea*), Sonnie Hale (*The Professor*), Francis L. Sullivan (*Nero*), Diana Decker (*Lydia*), Elisabeth Welch (*Thora*), Ernest Milton (*Titus*), Mary Clare (*Volumnia*), James Robertson Justice (*The Centurion*), Frederick Piper (*The Auctioneer*), Russell Thorndike (*The High Priest*), Robert Wyndham (*The LionKeeper*), Danny Green (*The Soldier*), Kay Kendall
D: Harry Watt   STORY: Diana Morgan & Angus Macphail   PHOTOG: Wilkie Cooper   MUSIC: Spike Hughes
reissued 1948
Standard fantasy: Lightning transports sailors to ancient Rome

The Fiend
1972, (GB), World Arts Media/Miracle, color, 87 mins, also 91 mins.
W: Ann Todd (*Birdie Wemyss*), Patrick Magee (*The Minister*), Tony Beckley (*Kenny Wemyss*), Madeleine Hinde (*Brigitte*), Percy Herbert (*The Commissionaire*), David Lodge (*The CID Man*), Suzanna Leigh (*Paddy*), Ronald Allen (*Paul*), Maxine Barrie (*The Singer*), Janet Wild (*The Prostitute*), Diana Chappell (*The Girl*), Susanna East (*The Teenager*)
P & D: Robert Hartford-Davis   STORY: Brian Comfort   PHOTOG: Desmond Dickinson   MUSIC: Tony Osborne
*U.S. release: **Beware of the Brethren** (Cinerama, 1972)*
Minor thriller: Religious fanatic's son kills prostitutes.

Fiend
1980, (USA), Cinema Enterprises, color, 92 mins.
W: Don Leifert (*Eric*), Richard Nelson (*Gary*), Elaine White (*Marsha*), Del Winans (*Jimmy*), George Stover (*Dennis*), Greg Dohler (*Scotty*), Pam Merenda (*Jane*), Anne Frith (*Katie*), Kim Dohler (*Kristy*), Steve Vertlieb (*The Announcer*)
WRIT & D: Don Dohler   PHOTOG: Richard Geiwitz   SPCL-FX: David W. Renwick   MUSIC: Paul Woznicki
Minor horror-thriller: Evil spirit reanimates corpse, goes on senseless murder spree

The Fiendish Ghouls
see The Flesh and the Fiends

The Fiendish Plot of Dr. Fu Manchu
1980, (USA), Orion, color, 98 mins.
W: Peter Sellers (*Fu Manchu/Nyaland Smith*), Helen Mirren (*Alice Rage*), David Tomlinson (*Sir Roger Avery*), John LeMesurier (*Perkins*), Steve Franken (*Pete Williams*), Sid Caesar (*Joe Capone*), Simon Williams (*Robert Townsend*), Stratford Johns (*Ismail*), John Sharp (*Sir Niles Thudd*), Clement Harari (*Dr. Wretch*), Lee Kwan-Young (*Tong*), John Tan, Philip Tan, Serge Julien, Clive Dunn, Lim Bun Song, Burt Kwouk, John Taylor, Katia Chenko, David Powers, Marc Wilkinson, Grace Coyle, Jacqueline Fogt, Iska Khan, George Hilsden, Rene Aranda
D: Piers Haggard   STORY & SCR:: Jim Moloney & Rudy Dochtermann, from characters created by Sax Rohmer   PHOTOG: Jean Tournier   MUSIC: Marc Wilkinson
Modest comedy-thriller (Peter Sellers last film): Archvillain seeks ingredients for life-pro-longing elixir

The Fiends of Hell
see Guarding Britain's Secrets

Fiend without a Face
1958, (GB), Eros/MGM, b&w, 76 mins.
W: Marshall Thompson (*Maj. Jeff Cummings*), Kim Parker (*Barbara Grisselle*), Kynaston Reeves (*Prof. Walgate*), Stanley Maxted (*Col. Butler*), Terence Kilburn (*Capt. Al Chester*), James Dyrenforth (*Mayor Hawkins*), Peter Madden (*Dr. Bradley*), Gilbert Winfield (*Capt. Warren*), Michael Balfour (*Sgt. Kasper*), Shane Cordell, Robert MacKenzie, Kerrigan Prescott, R. Meadows White, Lala Lloyd, Launcc Maraschal
P: John Croydon   D: Arthur Crabtree   SCR: Herbert J. Leder, based on Amelia Reynolds Long's short story *The Thought Monster*   PHOTOG: Leo Rogers   MUSIC: Buxton Orr
Unusual SF-horror (Arthur Crabtree's best film): Scientist's experiments go awry, produce invisible horrors

The Fiend with the Atomic Brain
see Blood of Ghastly Horror

Fiend with the Electronic Brain
see Blood of Ghastly Horror

The Fifth Element
1997, (USA-Fr), Col, color, 127 mins.
W: Bruce Willis (*Korben Dallas*), Gary Oldman (*Zorg*), Milla Jovovich (*Leeloo*), Ian Holm (*Cornelius*), Chris Tucker (*Ruby Rhod*)
D: Luc Besson   SCR: Luc Besson & Robert Mark Kamen   STORY: Luc Besson   PHOTOG: Thierry Arbogast   MUSIC: Eric Serra   EDIT: Sylvie Landra   COSTUMES: Jean-Paul Gaultier
Big-budget ($100 million) SF-action thriller: 23rd-century cab driver and mysterious beauty fight menace to Earth

The Fifth Floor
1980, (USA), Hickmar/Film Ventures, color, 87 mins.
W: Bo Hopkins (*Carl*), Dianne Hull, Patti D'Arbanville, Mel Ferrer, Julie Adams, John David Carson, Robert Englund
P & D: Howard Avedis   SCR: Meyer Dolinsky   STORY: Howard Avedis & Marlene Schmidt   PHOTOG: Daniel Pearl   SONG: *Fly Away*
Minor thriller: Girl trapped in madhouse

The Fifth Horseman is Fear
1967, (Czech), Sigma III-Filmways/Carlo Ponti, b&w, 100 mins
W: Miraslav Machacek, Olga Schenplugova
WRIT & D: Zbynek Brynych
Unusual psychodrama: Terrors of Nazi-occupied Czechoslovakia

The Fifth Missile
1986, (USA), Cinecitta/MGM-UA TV/NBC-TV, color, 180 mins.
W: David Soul (*Kevin Harris*), Robert Conrad (*Cdr. Mark Van Meer*), Richard Roundtree (*The Navy Psychiatrist*), Sam Waterston (*Renslow*), Yvette Mimieux (*Cheryl*), Jonathan Banks (*Olson*), Ed Bishop (*Cullinane*), John Leamer, Dennis Holohan, Art La Fleur, Michael Aronin, Russell Case, Joseph Drago, William Berger
D: Larry Peerce
TVM, standard thriller: Psychosis aboard atom sub

The Fifth Musketeer
1979, (GB), Col, color, 103 mins.
W: Sylvia Kristel (*Marie-Therese*), Beau Bridges (*King Louis*), Ursula Andress (*Mme. de la Valliere*), Cornel Wilde (*D'Artagnan*), Lloyd Bridges (*Aramis*), Ian McShane (*Fourquet*), Alan Hale Jr. (*Porthos*), Olivia de Havilland (*Queen Anne*), Helmut Dantine (*The Ambassador*), Jose Ferrer (*Athos*), Rex Harrison (*Colbert*), Roman Ariznavarreta, Bernard Bresslaw, Stephan Bastian, Victor Couzin, Fritz V. Freidl, Karl Ferth, Christine Glasner, Cissy Kraner, Fritz Goblirsch, Erhart Hartmann, Bill Horrigan, Michael Janisch, Elizabeth Neumann-Viertel, Heinz Nick, Albert Rueprecht, Ingrid Olofson, Stephan Paryla, Tony Smart, Ute Rumm, Robert Werner, Heinz Winter
P: Ted Richmond   D: Ken Annakin   SCR: David Ambrose   based on Alexandre Dumas' novel *The Man in the Iron Mask* and a script by George Bruce   PHOTOG: Jack Cardiff   MUSIC: Riz Ortolani
Standard adventure-comedy: Aging swordsmen find new work

A Fight for Life
1915, (GB), Cricks/DFSA, b&w, 921 ft. (280.7m)
W: Edward Sydney (*Jack*)
D: W.P. Kellino   STORY: Reuben Gillmer
Standard crime-thriller: Sailor saves ex-fiancee from husband who runs counterfeiting den

The Fighting Pimpernel
see The Elusive Pimpernel (1950)

Fighting Wildcats
see West of Suez

La Figlia di Frankenstein (Frankenstein's Daughter)
1971, (It), New World, color, 84 mins.
W: Sarah Bay (*Tanya*), Joseph Cotten (*The Baron*), Mickey Hargitay (*The Captain*), Paul Muller (*Marsh*), Herbert Fux, Peter Whiteman, Renata Cash, Lawrence Tilden, Andrew Ray, Ada Pomeroy, Johnny Loffrey, Peter Martinov, Adam Welles, Richard Beardley

P & D: Mel Welles **STORY & SCR:** Edward Di Lorenzo **ORIG. STORY:** Dick Randall **PHOTOG:** Richard Pallotin **MUSIC:** Alesssandro Alessandrini
*USA retitle, **Lady Frankenstein***
blurb: "Only the monster she made could satisfy her strange desires!"
Minor eroto-horror: Lustful woman scientist creates man

Il Figlio di D'Artgnan (Son of D'Artagnan)
1949, (It), b&w, 86 mins.
D & SCR: Riccardo Freda, from characters created by Alexander Dumas
Standard adventure-thriller

Il Figlio di Spartacus
1962, (It), MGM, color, 110 mins.
W: Steve Reeves (*Randus*), Gianna Maria Canale, Jacques Sernas
D: Sergio Corbucci **SCR:** Adriano Bolzoni, Bruno Corbucci, & Giovanni Grimaldi
*USA retitle, **The Slave***
Standard "Sword & Sandal": Spartacus' son leads slave revolt in 48 B.C.

File It Under Fear
1973, (GB), Made for TV, color
W: Maureen Lipman (*Liz*), Richard O'Callaghan (*George*), James Grout (*Cramer*), Richard Pendrey (*Gerry*), Jerry Quayle (*Betty*), Jan Francis (*Gillian*), John Nightingale (*Steve*), Rose Hill (*Mother*), Colin Fisher (*The Sgt.*)
TVM, standard thriller: Library murders rock rural community

The File of the Golden Goose
1968, (GB), Theme-Caralan-Dador/UA, color, 109 mins.
W: Yul Brynner (*Peter Novak*), Charles Gray (*Nick Harrison*), Edward Woodward (*Peter Thompson*), John Barrie (*Sloane*), Bernard Archard (*Collins*), Ivor Dean (*Reynolds*), Anthony Jacobs (*Firenos*), Adrienne Corri (*Tina Dell*), Walter Gotell (*Leeds*), Karel Stepanek (*Mieller*), Hugh McDermott (*Moss*)
P: David E. Rose **D:** Sam Wanamaker **SCR:** John C. Higgins & James B. Gordon **STORY:** John C. Higgins
Standard crime-thriller: U.S. agent and Scotland Yard man nab counterfeiters

Les Filles du Diable (The Devil's Daughters)
1903, (Fr), Star, b&w, 50m (164 ft./2.8 mins.)
W: Georges Melies
D: Georges Melies
*GB retitle, **The Women of Fire**, USA retitle, **Beelzebub's Daughters***
Standard fantasy: Satan molds flames into three mystic maidens

The Final Conflict
1981, (USA), Harvey Bernhard-Mace Neufeld/20th-Fox, color, 108 mins.
W: Sam Neill (*Damien Thorn*), Rossano Brazzi (*De Carlo*), Don Gordon (*Harvey Dean*), Lisa Harrow (*Kate*), Mason Adams (*The President*), Barnaby Holm (*Peter*), Robert Arden (*The Ambassador*), Tommy Duggan (*Matteus*), Leueen Willoughby (*Barbara*), Marc Boyle (*Benito*), Louis Mahoney (*Paulo*), Richard Oldfield (*Simeon*), Milos Kirek (*Martin*), Norman Bird (*Dr. Philmore*), Tony Vogel (*Antonio*), Eric Richard (*The Astronomer's Technician*), Arwen Holm (*Carol*), Hugh Moxey (*The Manservant*), Marc Smith (*The Press Officer*), Arnold Diamond (*The Astronomer*), Richard Williams (*The Vicar*), Stephen Turner (*Stigwell*), Al Matthews (*The Workman*), William Fox (*The Diplomat*), Larry Martyn (*The Orator*), John Baskcomb, Frank Coda, Harry Littlewood
D: Graham Baker **SCR:** Andrew Birkin, from characters created by David Seltzer **PHOTOG:** Robert Paynter & Phil Meheux **MUSIC:** Jerry Goldsmith
Standard fantasy-thriller, conclusion of 'Omen' trilogy: Anti-Christ faces day of reckoning

The Final Countdown
1980, (USA), color, 105 mins.
W: Kirk Douglas (*Capt. Matthew Yelland*), Katharine Ross (*Laurel Scott*), Martin Sheen (*Warren Lasky*), Ron O'Neal (*Cdr. Dan Thurman*), James Farentino (*Cdr. Richard Owens*), Charles Durning (*Sen. Chapman*), Victor Mohica (*Black Cloud*), James C. lawrence (*Lt. Perry*), Soon-Teck Oh (*Simura*), Joe Lowry (*Cdr. Damon*), Alvin Ing (*Kajima*), Mark Thomas (*Cpl. Kullman*), Harold Bergman (*Bellman*), Dan Fitzgerald (*The Navy Doctor*), Lloyd Kaufman (*Lt. Cdr. Kaufman*), Peter Douglas (*The Quartermaster*), Phil Philbin (*The Admiral*), Ted Richert, George Warren, Gary Morgan, Robert Goodman, Richard Liberty, Neil Ronco, William Couch, Jack McDermott, Masayuki Yamazuki, Orwin Harvey, Colby Smith, George H. Strohsahl Jr., Ronald R. Stoops, Kenneth J. Jaskolski, Sergei M. Kowalchik, Jake Dennis, Jim Toone
D: Don Taylor
Unusual SF-thriller: Aircraft carrier enters time warp

Final Descent
1997, (USA), CBS-TV, color, 95 mins.
W: Robert Urich, Annette O'Toole, Jim Byrnes (*Duke*), Ken Pogue (*Ian Pryce*), Blu Mankuma (*Jack Eberly*), Tom McBeath, Kevin McNulty
D: Mike Robe **TELEPLAY:** Roger Young, from Robert P. Davis' novel *Cockpit*
PHOTOG: Alan Caso **MUSIC:** David Benoit
TVM, standard thriller: Disabled plane cannot land

Final Equinox
1995, (USA), color, 90 mins.
W: Martin Kove, Joe Lara, David Warner
Minor SF-thriller: Space-alien artifact has power to create life

Final Exam
1981, (USA), Bedford Ent. Group/Avco Embassy, color, 90 mins.
W: Cecile Bagdadi (*Courtney*), Joel S. Rice (*Radish*), Ralph Brown (*Wildman*), Deanna Robbins (*Lisa*), Sherry Willis-Burch (*Janet*), John Fallon (*Mark*), Timothy L. Raynor (*The Killer*), Terry W. Farren (*The Pledge*), Sam Kilman (*The Sheriff*), Don Hepner (*Dr. Reynolds*), Jerry Rusing (*The Coach*)
P: John L. Chambliss & Myron Meisel **WRIT & D:** Jimmy Huston
PHOTOG: Darrell Cathcart **MUSIC:** Gary Scott
Standard thriller: Students eliminated by fiendish killer

The Final Executioner
1983, (It), MGM, color, 95 mins.
W: William Mang, Marina Costa, Harrison Muller, Woody Strode
D: Romolo Guerrieri
*A.k.a. **The Last Warrior***
Minor SF-thriller: Innocents slaughtered in post-nuke world

Final Eye
1977, (USA), Culzean-Para/CBS-TV, color, 97 mins.
W: Joseph Cortese (*Michael Stringer*), Susan George (*Lisa Korter*), Tom Clancy (*Hanaran*), David Huddleston (*Chief Sorrenson*), Donald Pleasence (*George Dettler*), Richard Noriega (*The Host*), Elizabeth Wallace (*The Hostess*), Sue Palmer (*The Lady Artist*), Liam Sullivan (*Emery Korter*), Peter Brandon (*Kennison*), Roger Cudney (*Robbins*), Linda Gillin (*The Librarian*), Edgar Justice (*The Store Owner*), Carl Bellanger (*The Security Chief*), William Benedict (*The Elderly Man*), Rod Haase (*Cop #1*), Brian Baker (*Cop #2*), Alan Conrad (*The Gate Guard*), Raye Sheffield (*Reporter #1*), Robert Power (*Reporter #2*), J.D. Hall (*Reporter #3*), Shelley Hoffman (*The Intern*), Joseph Chapman (*The Lab Operator*)
D: Robert Michael Lewis **TELEPLAY:** Robert Foster & Anthony Wilson
PHOTOG: Richard Rawlings **SPCL-FX:** Richard Johnson **MUSIC:** Jack Elliott & Allyn Ferguson
TVM, standard SF: Detective of future finds island retreat conceals cloning center

The Final Mission
1994, (USA), color, 91 mins.
W: Billy Wirth
Standard thriller: Virtual-reality jet tests cause death

Final Notice
1989, (USA), color, 91 mins.
W: Gil Gerard, Melody Anderson, Jackie Burroughs, Louise Fletcher, David Ogden Stiers, Steve Landesburg, Kevin Hicks
D: Steven Hilliard Stern **TELEPLAY:** John Gay, from Jonathan Valin's novel
MUSIC: Tom Scott
Made-for-Cable, standard thriller: Fiend mutilates library books, reduplicates crimes with attractive women

Final Sanction
1989, (USA), color, 90 mins.
W: Robert Z'Dar, Ted Prior
D & SCR: David A. Prior
Standard SF-thriller: Post-nuke battle of one-man armies

The Final Terror
1984, (USA), Samuel Z. Arkoff-Joe Roth/Comworld, color, 83 mins.
W: John Friedrich (*Zorich*), Rachel Ward (*Margaret*), Daryl Hannah (*Windy*), Adrian Zmed (*Marco*), Mark Metcalf, Joe Pantoliano, Akosua Busia, Richard Jacobs, Lori Lee ButlerJoe Pantoliano (*Edgar*), Ernest Harden Jr. (*Hines*), Lewis Smith (*Boone*), Cindy Harrell (*Melanie*), Akosua Busia (*Vanessa*), Irene Sanders (*Sammie*), Donna Pinder (*Mrs. Morgan*), Richard Jacobs (*Morgan*)
D: Andrew Davis **SCR:** Jon George, Neill Hicks & Ronald Shusett **PHOTOG:** Andreas Davidescu **MUSIC:** Susan Justin
*A.k.a. **Carnivore, Bump in the Night, Campsite Massacre** and **The Forest Primeval***
Minor thriller: Forest maniac slaughters campers

The Final War
1960, (Jap), Toei/Medallion/Sam Lake, b&w, scope, 77 mins
W: Tatsuya Umemiya, Yoshiko Mito
D: Shigeaki Hidaka **SCR:** T. Yasumi & Takeshi Kimura
*orig. to be titled **The Last War**, A.k.a. **World War Three Breaks Out**, USA release, 1962*
Standard SF: Nations of Earth engage in last nuclear conflict

La Fin de Don Juan (The End of Don Juan)
1911, (Fr), b&w
WRIT & D: Victorin Jasset
Standard fantasy

Find the Lady
1956, (GB), Major/RFD, b&w, 56 mins.
W: Donald Houston (*Bill*), Beverley Brooks (*June Weston*), Mervyn Johns (*Hurst*), Kay Callard (*Rita*), Edwin Richfield (*Max*), Maurice Kaufmann (*Nicky*), Moray Watson (*Jimmy*), Ferdy Mayne (*Tony Del Roma*), Anne Heywood (*The Receptionist*)
P: John Temple-Smith & Francis Edge **D:** Charles Saunders **SCR:** Kenneth R. Hayton **STORY:** Paul Erickson & Dermot Palmer
Standard crime-thriller: Bank robbers hide in old lady's house, kidnap her niece

La Fin du Monde (The End of the World)
1930, (Fr), Auten, b&w, 90 mins.
<u>W:</u> Abel Gance, Victor Franen
<u>WRIT, D & PHOTOG:</u> Abel Gance, inspired by Edgar Allan Poe's short story
The Conversation of Eiros and Charmion
Classic melodrama: Treatise on possible destruction of Earth by fire

The Finger Man
1955, (USA), AA, b&w, 82 mins.
<u>W:</u> Frank Lovejoy, Peggie Castle, Forrest Timothy Carey, Glenn Gordon, Evelynne
Eaton
<u>D:</u> Harold Schuster
Standard melodrama: Feds capture liquor gang

Finger of Guilt
see The Intimate Stranger

Finger Prints
1923, (USA), Hyperion, b&w
<u>W:</u> Violet Palmer
<u>D:</u> Joseph Levering   <u>STORY:</u> Alton Floyd
Standard melodrama: Pearls inspire murder

Fingerprints Don't Lie
1951, (USA), Lippert, b&w, 67 mins.
<u>W:</u> Richard Travis, Sheila Ryan
Standard thriller

Fingers at the Window
1942, (USA), MGM, b&w, 80 mins.
<u>W:</u> Lew Ayres, Basil Rathbone, Laraine Day
<u>P:</u> Irving Starr   <u>SCR:</u> Charles Lederer   <u>SCR:</u> Rose Caylor & Lawrence P. Bachmann
<u>MUSIC:</u> Bronislau Kaper
blurb: "The Mystery of the Robot Murders!"
*Standard thriller: Magician impersonates head of asylum, hypnotizes inmates so they will
commit axe murders*

Finian's Rainbow
1968, (USA), WB, color, 144 mins.
<u>W:</u> Fred Astaire, Petula Clark, Don Francks, Keenan Wynn, Al Freeman Jr.,
Barbara Hancock, Ronald Colby, Dolph Sweet, Wright King, Tommy Steele
<u>D:</u> Francis Ford Coppola   <u>SCR:</u> E.Y. Harburg & Fred Saidy   <u>PHOTOG:</u> Philip
Lathrop   <u>MUSIC SPRVSR:</u> Ray Heindorf
Standard musical-fantasy

Fiorile
1993, (It), color, 122 mins.
<u>W:</u> Claudio Bigagli Michael Vartan, Galatea Ranzi, Claudio Bigagli, Chiara
Caselli, Lino Capolicchio, Constanze Engelbrecht, Athina Cenci, Giovanni
Guidelli
<u>D:</u> Paolo Taviani & Vittorio Taviani   <u>SCR:</u> Paolo Taviani, Vittorio Taviani &
Sandro Petraglia   <u>MUSIC:</u> Nicola Piovani
A.k.a. Wild Flower
Unusual melodrama: Family journeys to Tuscany, discovers origins of old curse

Fire and Ice
1983, (USA), 20th-Fox, color, 82 mins.
<u>VOICES:</u> Randy Norton (*Larn*), Cynthia Leake (*Princess Teegra*), Steve Sandor
(*Darkwolf*), Sean Hannon (*Nekron*), Leo Gordon (*Jarol*), William Ostrander
(*Taro*), Elizabeth Lloyd Shaw (*Roleil*), Elleen O'Neill (*Juliana*), Mickey
Morton (*Otwa*), Tamarah Park (*The Tutor*), Big Yank (*Monga*), Greg Elam
(*Pako*), Holly Frazetta (*The Subhuman Priestess*), James Bridges, Shane Callan,
Archie Hamilton, Michael Kelloff, Dale Park, Douglas Payton, Susan
Tyrrell, Maggie Roswell, Stephen Mendel, Alan Koss, Clare Nono, Hans
Howes, Nathan Purdee, Ray Oliver
<u>D:</u> Ralph Bakshi   <u>SCR:</u> Roy Thomas & Gerry Conway , from characters created
by Ralph Bakshi & Frank Frazetta   <u>MUSIC:</u> William Kraft
Standard animated "Sword & Sorcery" tale: Blond hero vs dusky subhumans

Fire & Sword
1982, (W. Ger-Irl), color, 84 mins.
<u>W:</u> Christoph Waltz, Antonia Presser, Leigh Lawson, Peter Firth
Standard adventure-romance: Legend of lovers Tristan and Isolde

Fireball Jungle
1969, (USA), Americana, color, 96 mins
<u>W:</u> Lon Chaney Jr., John Russell
A.k.a. Jungle Terror
Minor thriller

Firebird 2015 A.D.
1981, (Can), Maria, color, 95 mins.
<u>W:</u> Darren McGavin, Doug McClure, Robert Charles Wisden, George Touliatos,
Marybeth Rubens, Alex Daikun, Barbara Williams, Bill Berry, Frank
Pellegrino, Lee Broker, Fred Keating, Gary Paller
<u>D:</u> David M. Robertson   <u>SCR:</u> Barry Pearson, Maurice Hurley, & Biff McGuire
<u>PHOTOG:</u> Robert Fresco   <u>MUSIC:</u> Paul Hoffert & Lawrence Shragge
Minor SF-adventure: Illegal hot-rodding in 21st century

The Firechasers
1970, (GB), ITC/RFD, color, 101 mins.
<u>W:</u> Chad Everett (*Quentin Barnaby*), Anjanette Comer (*Toby Collins*), Keith Barron
(*Jim Maxwell*), Joanne Dainton (*Valerie Chrane*), Rupert Davies (*Prentice*),
John Loder (*Routledge*), James Hayter (*Insp. Herman*), Roy Kinnear (*Roscoe*),
Robert Flemyng (*Carlton*), Allan Cuthbertson (*Jarvis*)
<u>P:</u> Julian Wintle   <u>D:</u> Sidney Hayers   <u>STORY:</u> Philip Levine
Standard crime-thriller: Girl reporter helps insurance detective trap arsonist

The Fire Dance
see La Danse de Feu

Firefight
1987, (USA), color, 100 mins.
<u>W:</u> James Pfeiffer, Janice Carraher, Jack Tucker
<u>D:</u> Scott Pfeiffer
Minor SF-thriller: Post-nuke criminals vie for rule of wasteland

Firehead
1990, (USA), color 88 mins.
<u>W:</u> Brett Portern Christopher Plummer, Chris Lemmon, Martin Landau, Gretchen
Becker
<u>D:</u> Peter Yuval
Standard SF-thriller: Telekinetic Russian defector

A Fire in the Sky
1978, (USA), Bill Driskill/Col-TV/NBC-TV, color, 96 mins.
<u>W:</u> Richard Crenna (*Jason Voight*), Elizabeth Ashley (*Sharon Allan*), David Dukes
(*David Allan*), Joanna Miles (*Jennifer Dreiser*), Nicolas Coster (*The Governor*),
Jenny O'Hara (*Ann Webster*), Lloyd Bochner (*Paul Gilliam*), Merlin Olsen
(*Stan Webster*), William Bogert (*Lustus*), Cynthia Eilbacher (*Paula Gilliam*),
Michael Biehn (*Tom Reardon*), Marj Dusay, Andrew Duggan, Diana Douglas,
John Larch, Kip Niven, Al White, Bill Williams, George Petrie
<u>D:</u> Jerry Jameson   <u>PHOTOG:</u> Matthew F. Leonetti   <u>MUSIC:</u> Michael Chihara
TVM, standard thriller: Comet on collision course with Phoenix, Arizona

Fire in the Sky
1993, (USA), Joe Wizan-Todd Black/Para, color, 111 mins.
<u>W:</u> D.B. Sweeney (*Travis Walton*), Robert Patrick (*Mike Rogers*), Craig Sheffer
(*Allan Dallis*), James Garner (*Frank Walters*), Peter Berg (*David Whitlock*),
Henry Thomas (*Greg Hayes*), Bradley Gregg (*Bobby Cogdill*), Noble
Willingham (*Blake Davis*), Kathleen Wilhoite (*Katie Rogers*), Georgia
Emelin (*Dana Rogers*), Wayne Grace (*Cyrus Gilson*), Kenneth White (*Buck*),
Scott MacDonald (*Dan Walton*), Bruce Wright (*Dennis Clay*), Robert
Covarrubias (*Ray Melendez*), Robert Biheller (*Ellis*), Tom McGranahan Sr.
(*Dr. Wilson*), Julie Ariola (*Dr. Cayle*), Peter Mark Vasquez (*Ramon*),
Courtney Esler (*Emily Rogers*), Gordon Scott (*George*), Mical Shannon Lewis
(*Mary Rogers*), Holly Hoffman (*Cathy*), Glen Lee (*The Geiger Counter Man*),
Marcia MacLaine (*The Nurse*), Vernon Barkhurst (*Bill Grant*), Jane Ferguson
(*Lurae Jenkins*), Susan Castillo (*The Anchorwoman*), Nancy Neifert (*Cathy's*

Firestarter: DREW BARRYMORE

Mom), Charley Lang (*Jarvis Powell*), Mari Padron (*Thelma*), Lyn Marie Sager (*Ida*), Frank Chavez (*Orlando*), John Breedlove (*The Balding Man*), Louis A. Lotorto Jr. (*The Paramedic*), Ronald Lee Marriott (*Digger*), Shinichi Mine (*The Japanese Reporter*), Scott M. Seekins (*The Emergency Room Doctor*), Eric Wilsey (*Claude*), Jerry Basham, Teresa Fox, Travis Walton

D: Robert Lieberman   SCR: Tracy Torme, based on Travis Walton's book *The Walton Experience*   PHOTOG: Bill Pope   MUSIC: Mark Isham
Gripping SF-thriller: Fact-based saga of UFO abductee

Fire Maidens of Outer Space
1956, (GB), Criterion/Eros/Topaz/Saturn films, b&w, 80 mins, also 68 mins.
W: Anthony Dexter (*Luther Blair*), Susan Shaw (*Hestia*), Paul Carpenter (*Larson*), Harry Fowler (*Sydney Stanhope*), Jacqueline Curtis (*Duessa*), Sydney Tafler (*Dr. Higgins*), Owen Berry (*Prasus*), Rodney Diak (*Anderson*)
P: George Fowler & Cy Roth   WRIT & D: Cy Roth
Minor SF: Astronauts find Atlantean civilization on moon of Jupiter. Aka **The 13th Moon of Jupiter**

Fire Monsters vs. the Son of Hercules
1962, (It), Embassy, color
W: Reg Lewis (*Hercules*), Margaret Lee
Minor "Sword & Sandal": Muscleman has adventures

Firepower
1979, (GB), Winner/ITC, color, 104 mins.
W: Sophia Loren (*Adele Tasco*), James Coburn (*Jerry Fanon*), O.J. Simpson (*Catlett*), Eli Wallach (*Sal Hyman*), George Grizzard (*Leo Gelborn*), Anthony Franciosa (*Carl Stegner*), Vincent Gardenia (*Frank Hull*), Fred Stuthman (*Haplin*), Richard Caldicot (*Calman*), Frank Sanguineau (*Manley Reckford*), George Touliatos (*Stegner*), Hank Garrett (*Oscar*), Conrad Roberts (*Lestor*), Billy Barty (*Dominic Carbone*), Jack La Motta (*Nickel Sam*), Dominic Chianese (*Dis Orlov*), Vincent Back (*Trilling*), Andrew Duncan (*Cooper*), Paul D'Amato (*Tagua*), Victor Mature (*Harold Everett*)
P & D: Michael Winner   SCR: Gerald Wilson   STORY: Bill Kerby & Michael Winner   PHOTOG: Robert Paynter   MUSIC: Gato Barbieri
Minor thriller: Chemist's widow seeks revenge

The Fire of a Thousand Suns
see **La Brulure de Mille Soleils**

Firestarter
1984, (USA), Dino De Laurentiis/Univ, color, 115 mins.
W: Drew Barrymore, David Keith, Freddie Jones, George C. Scott, Martin Sheen, Art Carney, Heather Locklear, Louise Fletcher, Moses Gunn, Antonio Fargas, Curtis Credel, Jeff Ramsey, Richard Warlock, Keith Colbert, Jack Magner
D: Mark L. Lester   SCR: Stanley Mann, from Stephen King's novel   PHOTOG: Guiseppe Ruzzolini   SPCL-FX: Jeff Jarvis & Michael Wood   MUSIC: Tangerine Dream
Standard SF-thriller: Gov't pursues girl with paranormal powers

Firewalker
1986, (USA), Cannon, color, 104 mins.
W: Chuck Norris (*Max Donigan*), Lou Gossett (*Leo Porter*), Melody Anderson (*Patricia Goodwin*), Will Sampson (*Tall Eagle*), John Rhys-Davies (*Corky Taylor*), Sonny Landham (*El Coyote*), Ian Abercrombie (*Boggs*), Zaide S. Gutierrez (*The Indian Girl*) Richard Lee-Sung, John Hazelwood, Jose Escondon, Miguel Fuentes, Julio Monje, Nicolas Jasso, Alvaro Carcano
P: Menahem Golan & Yorum Globus   D: J. Lee Thompson   SCR: Robert Gosnell   PHOTOG: Alex Phillips   MUSIC: Gary Chang
Minor adventure-thriller: Soldiers-of-fortune seek legendary treasure

The Firm of Girdlestone
1915, (GB), London/Jury, b&w, 5,100 ft. (1554.5m)
W: Edna Flugrath (*Kate Horston*), Fred Groves (*Ezra Girdlestone*), Charles Rock (*John Girdlestone*), Windham Guise (*Maj. Clutterbuck*), Hayford Hobbs (*Tom Dimsdale*), Gwynne Herbert (*Mrs. Scully*), Molly Terraine (*Rebecca*)
D: Harold Shaw   SCR: Bannister Merwin, from a novel by Sir Arthur Conan Doyle
Standard crime-thriller: Old merchant tries to save his firm by killing his ward

The First Deadly Sin
1980, (USA), Filmways, color, 112 mins.
W: Frank Sinatra (*Edward Delaney*), Faye Dunaway (*Barbara Delaney*), David Dukes (*Daniel Blank*), George Coe (*Dr. Bernardi*), Brenda Vaccaro (*Monica Gilbert*), Martin Gabel (*Christopher Langley*), Anthony Zerbe (*Capt. Broughton*), James Whitmore (*Dr. Sanford Ferguson*), Joe Spinell (*The Doorman*), Jeffrey DeMunn (*Sgt. Fernandez*), Fred Fuster (*The Delivery Man*), Richard Backus
D: Brian G. Hutton   SCR: Mann Rubin, from Lawrence Sanders' novel   PHOTOG: Jack Priestley   MUSIC: Gordon Jenkins
Tepid thriller: Cop tracks psychotic killer

First Knight
1995, (USA), Col, color, 134 mins.
W: Richard Gere (*Sir Lancelot*), Sean Connery (*King Arthur*), Julia Ormond (*Guinevere*), Ben Cross (*Malagant*), Sir John Gielgud (*Oswald*), Liam Cunningham (*Sir Agravaine*), Christopher Villiers (*Sir Kay*), Valentine Pelka (*Sir Patrise*), Colin McCormack (*Sir Mador*), Ralph Ineson (*Ralf*), Stuart Bunce (*Peter*), Jane Robbins (*Elise*), Tom Lucy (*Sir Sagramore*), Paul Kynman (*Mark*), Jean Marie Coffey (*Petronella*), John Blakey (*Sir Tor*), Robert Gwyn Davin (*Sir Gawaine*), Sean Blowers (*Sir Carados*), Alexis Denisof (*Sir Gaheris*), Jonathan Cake (*Sir Gareth*), Daniel Naprous (*Sir Amant*), Paul Bentall (*Jacob*), Rose Keegan (*Mark's Wife*), Mark Ryan (*The Challenger*), Jonty Miller (*The Gauntlet Man*), Jeffery Dench (*The 1st Elder*), Neville Phillips (*The 2nd Elder*), Oliver Lewis (*The 1st Marauder*), Wolf Christian (*The 2nd Marauder*), Angus Wright (*The 3rd Marauder*), Jonathan Jaynes (*The 1st Guard*), Eric Stone (*The 2nd Guard*), Ryan Todd (*Young Lancelot*), Albie Woodington (*The Scout*), Richard Claxton (*The Child*), Michael Hodgson (*The Young Man in the Crowd*), Dido Miles (*The Grateful Woman*), Susannah Corbett (*The Young Woman in the Crowd*), Susan Breslau (*The Wedding Guest*), Kate Zucker (*The Flower Girl*), Bob Zucker (*The Little Boy with Birds*), Charlotte Zucker (*A Bread Vendor*), Burt Zucker (*A Bread Vendor*)
P: Jerry Zucker & Hunt Lowry   D: Jerry Zucker   SCR: William Nicholson   STORY: Lorne Cameron, David Hoselton & William Nicholson   PHOTOG: Adam Greenberg   MUSIC: Jerry Goldsmith
Impressive production, standard adventure-romance: Love triangle in fabled Camelot

First Man into Space
1958, (GB), Amalgamated/MGM, b&w, 78 mins.
W: Marshall Thompson (*Chuck Prescott*), Marla Landi (*Tia Francesca*), Bill Edwards (*Dan Prescott*), Robert Ayres (*Ben Richards*), Bill Nagy (*Wilson*), Carl Jaffe (*Dr. von Essen*), Roger Delgado (*The Mexican Consul*), Bill Nick, Richard Shaw, John McLaren, Chuck Keyser, John Fabian
P: John Croydon & Charles F. Vetter Jr.   D: Robert Day   SCR: John C. Cooper & Lance Z. Hargreaves, from a story by Wyott Ordung   PHOTOG: Geoffrey Faithfull   MUSIC: Buxton Orr
orig. to be titled **Satellite of Blood**
Standard SF-horror: Space dust turns astronaut into vampiric monster

First Men in the Moon
1919, (GB), Gaumont, b&w, 5,175 ft. (1577.3m)
W: Bruce Gordon (*Hogben*), Heather Thatcher (*Susan*), Hector Abbas (*Samson Cavor*), Lionel d'Aragon (*Rupert Bedford*), Cecil Morton York (*The Grand Lunar*)
D: J.L.V. Leigh   SCR: R. Byron-Webber, from H.G. Wells' novel
Standard SF: Space-sphere inventor flies to moon, is marooned by crooked financier

First Men in the Moon
1964, (GB), Ameran/Col, color, 105 mins.
W: Edward Judd (*Arnold Bedford*), Martha Hyer (*Kate Callender*), Lionel Jeffries (*Prof. Joseph Cavor*), Norman Bird (*The Workman*), Miles Malleson (*The Registrar*), Hugh McDermott (*Richard Challis*), Gladys Henson (*The Matron*), Betty McDowall (*Maggie Hay*), Erik Chitty (*Gibbs*), Paul Carpenter (*An Announcer*), Marne Maitland (*Dr. Tok*), Huw Thomas (*An Announcer*), Valentine Dyall (*The Commentator*), Peter Finch (*The Bailiff*), Sean Kelly, Lawrence Herder
P: Charles H. Schneer   D: Nathan Juran   SCR: Nigel Kneale & Jan Read, from H.G. Wells' novel   PHOTOG: Wilkie Cooper   SPCL-FX: Ray Harryhausen   MUSIC: Laurie Johnson
Superior SF-adventure: Unsuccessful writer fleeing creditors, proper Boston girl, and eccentric British inventor make daring trip to moon during Queen Victoria's reign

The First Power
1990, (USA), Interscope Communications/Nelson Entertainment/Orion, color, 98 mins.
W: Lou Diamond Phillips (*Russell Logan*), Tracy Griffith (*Tess Seaton*), Jeff Kober (*Patrick Channing*), Mykel T. Williamson (*Det. Oliver Franklin*), Elizabeth Arlen (*Sister Marguerite*), Dennis Lipscomb (*Cmdr. Perkins*), Carmen Argenziano (*Lt. Grimes*), Julianna McCarthy (*Grandmother*), Lisa Specht (*The Anchorwoman*), Sue Giosa (*Carmen*), Clayton Landey (*Mazza*), Nada Despotovich (*The Bag Lady*), Hansford Rowe (*Father Brian*), David Gale (*The Monsignor*), Philip Abbott (*The Cardinal*), J. Patrick McNamara (*The Priest*), Mark Bringelson (*The Driver in the Alley*), William Fair (*Det. #2*), Michael McNab, Dan Tullis Jr., Brian Libby, David Partington, Tiiu Leek, Michael Wise, Andrew Amador, Todd Jeffries, Charles Raymond, Paula McClure, Mitch Carter, Jeff Mooring, Grand L. Bush, David Katims, Lynn Marta, Scott Lawrence, Gokul, Bill Moseley, R. David Stephens, Melanie Shatner, Robert Volaizzi, Oz Tortora, Ron J. Goodman
WRIT & D: Robert Resnikoff   PHOTOG: Theo Van de Sande   MUSIC: Stewart Copeland
Japan retitle (1991), **Pentagram**
Standard horror-fantasy: Occult murderer pursued

First Spaceship on Venus
see **Milczaca Gwiazda**

First Woman into Space
see **Space Monster**

The Fish and the Ring
1913, (GB), Natural Colour Kinematograph Co., color, 2,135 ft. (650.7m)
W: Nancy Barrett (*Joan*), Gerald Royston (*Nicholas*), H. Agar Lyons (*Baron Humphrey*), Harold Barrett, Percy Dyer

D: F. Martin Thornton & R.H. Callum
Standard fantasy: Fairies, swans, and fish save poor girl from magical baron

The Fish Men
1978, (It), Dania-Medusa/New World, color, 90 mins.
W: Barbara Bach (*Amanda*), Claudio Cassinelli (*Claude*), Richard Johnson (*Rackham*), Beryl Cunningham (*Shakira*), Joseph Cotten (*Dr. Ernest Marvin*), Cameron Mitchell (*Capt. Decker*), Mel Ferrer (*Radcliffe*), Eunice Holt (*Samantha*), Tom J. Delaney (*Patterson*), Franco Javarone, Roberto Pogge, Giuseppe Castellano, Francesco Mazzieri, James Alquist
D: Sergio Martino **SCR:** Sergio Donati, Cesare Frugoni, & Sergio Martino **STORY:** Cesare Frugoni & Luciano Martino **PHOTOG:** Giancarlo Ferrando **MUSIC:** Luciano Michelini
released in USA (1981) as **Screamers**
A.k.a. **Isle of the Fishmen** *and* **Something Waits in the Dark**
Minor SF-fantasy: Cad exploits mutant Atlanteans

Fist of the North Star
1991, (Jap), Toei/Streamline, color, 100 mins.
VOICES: John Vickery (*Ken*), Melodee Spivack (*Julia*), Tony Oliver (*Bat*), Wally Burr (*Raoh*), Gregory Snegoff (*Rei*), Michael McConnohie (*Shin*)
D: Toyoo Ashida **SCR:** Susumu Takahisa **PHOTOG:** Tamiyo Hosoda **MUSIC:** Katsuhisa Hattori
Standard animated SF-fantasy: Post-nuke hero vs. giant mutants

Fit to Kill
1993, (USA), color, 94 mins.
W: Dona Speir
Minor thriller: Sexy spies uncover mystery surrounding lost gem

Five
1951, (USA), Col, b&w, 93 mins.
W: William Phipps (*Michael*), Susan Douglas (*Roseanne*), Earl Lee, James Anderson, Charles Lampkin
WRIT, P, & D, Arch Oboler **PHOTOG:** Louis Clyde Stoumen **MUSIC:** Henry Russell
French retitle, **Cinq Survivants (Five Survivors)**
Modest SF-melodrama: Interpersonal conflicts as five people struggle to survive after atomic holocaust

Five Angles on Murder
see **The Woman in Question**

Five Dolls for an August Moon
1970, (It), color
D: Mario Bava, loosely based on Agatha Christie's novel *And Then There Were None*
Minor thriller: Series of mysterious murders

5 Fingers
1952, (USA), 20th-Fox, b&w, 108 mins.
W: James Mason, Danielle Darrieux, Michael Rennie, Walter Hampden, Oscar Karlweis, Herbert Berghof, Michael Pate, John Wengraf
D: Joseph L. Mankiewicz **SCR:** Michael Wilson **PHOTOG:** Norbert Brodine **MUSIC:** Bernard Herrmann
Superior, fact-based espionage thriller: Valet is World War II spy

Five Golden Dragons
1967, (GB-Hong Kong/Ger), Blansfilm/Commonwealth United/W-P/Warner Brothers/7 Arts, color, 93 mins.
W: Robert Cummings (*Bob Mitchell*), Rupert Davies (*Comm. Sanders*), Margaret Lee (*Magda*), Maria Perschy (*Margret*), Klaus Kinski (*Gert*), Maria Rohm (*Ingrid*), Brian Donlevy (*A Dragon*), Dan Duryea (*A Dragon*), George Raft (*A Dragon*), Christopher Lee (*A Dragon*), Yukari Ito
P: Harry Alan Towers **D:** Jeremy Summers **SCR:** Peter Welbeck [Harry Alan Towers] **MUSIC:** Malcolm Lockyer **SONGS:** *Time of Our Lives*
Standard comedy-thriller: Innocent embroiled with secret society

Five Graves to Cairo
1943, (USA), Para, b&w, 96 mins.
W: Franchot Tone, Anne Baxter, Akim Tamiroff, Peter Van Eyck, Erich von Stroheim, Fortunio Bonanova, Konstantin Shayne
D: Billy Wilder **SCR:** Billy Wilder & Charles Brackett, from Lajos Biro's play *Imperial* **PHOTOG:** John Seitz **MUSIC:** Miklos Rozsa
Impressive wartime thriller: British corporal poses as German in North African hotel

Five Millions B.C.
see **One Million B.C.**

Five Million Years to Earth
see **Quatermass and the Pit**

Five to One
1963, (GB), Merton Park/Anglo-Amalgamated, b&w, 56 mins.
W: Lee Montague (*Larry Hart*), Ingrid Haffner (*Pat Dunn*), John Thaw (*Alan Roper*), Brian McDermott (*John Lee*), Ewan Roberts (*Deighton*), Heller Toren (*Mai Hart*), Jack Watson (*Insp. Davis*), Richard Clarke (*Lucas*)
P: Jack Greenwood **D:** Gordon Flemyng **SCR:** Roger Marshall, from Edgar Wallace's story *Thief in the Night*
Standard crime-thriller: Gang's plot to rob bookmaker goes awry

Five Steps to Danger
1957, (USA), UA, b&w, 80 mins.
W: Sterling Hayden, Ruth Roman Werner Klemperer, Richard Gaines
D: Henry S. Kesler
Standard thriller

Five Survivors
see **Five**

The 5000 Fingers of Dr. T
1953, (USA), Col, color, 88 mins.
W: Hans Conried (*Dr. Terwilliker*), Tommy Rettig (*Bart*), Peter Lind Hayes (*Zabladowski*), Mary Healy (*Mrs. Collins*), Noel Cravat (*Sgt. Lunk*), John Heasley (*Uncle Whitney*), Robert Heasley (*Uncle Judson*), Henry Kulky (*Stroogo*)
P: Stanley Kramer **D:** Roy Rowland **SCR:** "Dr. Seuss" & Allan Scott **PHOTOG:** Franz E. Planer **MUSIC:** Morris W. Stoloff
reissued (1958) as **Crazy Music**
Juvenile fantasy classic: Boy dreams piano teacher is merciless ruler of totalitarian state

Five Tombs for a Medium
see **Cinque Tombe per un Medium**

Five Weeks in a Balloon
1962, (USA), 20th-Fox, color, 101 mins.
W: Red Buttons (*Donald O'Shay*), Barbara Eden (*Susan Gale*), Sir Cedric Hardwicke (*Fergusson*), Fabian (*Jacques*), Peter Lorre (*Ahmed*), Richard Haydn (*Sir Henry Vining*), Herbert Marshall (*The Prime Minister*), Barbara Luna (*Makia*), Mike Mazurki (*The Slave Captain*), Reginald Owen (*The Consul*), Billy Gilbert (*The Sultan-Auctioneer*), Ben Astar (*Myanga*), Henry Daniell (*Sheik Ageiba*), Alan Caillou (*The Inspector*), Raymond Bailey (*Randolph*), Chester the Chimp ("*The Duchess*")
P & D: Irwin Allen **SCR:** Irwin Allen, Charles Bennett, & Albert Gail, from Jules Verne's novel **PHOTOG:** Winton C. Hoch **SPCL-FX:** L.B. Abbott & Emil Kosa Jr. **MUSIC:** Paul Sawtell
Standard adventure-romance: Explorers in balloon cross Dark Continent

The Five Wishes
1916, (GB), Clarendon, b&w, 1,035 ft. (315.5m)
D: Wilfred Noy, from a play by Laura Leycester
Standard fantasy: Couple given magic idol that grants wishes literally

The Flame and the Arrow
1950, (USA), Norma-F.R./WB, color, 88 mins.
W: Burt Lancaster, Virginia Mayo, Robert Douglas, Aline MacMahon, Nick Cravat, Frank Allenby, Lynne Baggett, Norman Lloyd, Robin Hughes
D: Jacques Tourneur **SCR:** Waldo Salt **PHOTOG:** Ernest Haller **MUSIC:** Max Steiner
Standard adventure-thriller: Lombardy rescued from wicked oppressors

The Flame Barrier
1958, (USA), Gramercy/UA, b&w, 70 mins.
W: Arthur Franz, Kathleen Crowley, Robert Brown, Vincent Padula, Rodd Redwing, Kaz Oran, Grace Mathews, Pilar Del Rey, Larry Duran, Bernie Gozier, Robert Contreras
P: Arthur Gardner & Jules V. Levy **D:** Paul Landres **SCR:** Pat Fielder & George Worthington Yates **STORY:** George Worthington Yates
orig. co-billed with **The Return of Dracula**
Modest but thought-provoking SF-thriller: Satellite brings rapidly-growing life-form to Earth

Flame of Araby
1951, (USA), Univ, color, 85 mins.
W: Jeff Chandler, Maureen O'Hara, Maxwell Reed, Buddy Baer, Lon Chaney Jr., Richard Egan, Dewey Martin, Royal Dano, Susan Cabot, Henry Brandon
D: Charles Lamont **SCR:** Gerald Drayson Adams **PHOTOG:** Russell Metty **MUSIC DIR:** Joseph Gershenson
Standard adventure-romance: Sheik seeks prize horse, woman

Flames
1917, (GB), Butcher's Film Service, b&w, 5,200 ft. (1585m)
W: Margaret Bannerman (*Cuckoo*), Owen Nares (*Valentine Cresswell*), Edward O'Neill (*Richard Marr*), Douglas Munro (*Dr. Levetier*), Clifford Cobbe (*Julian Addison*)
D: Maurice Elvey **SCR:** Eliot Stannard, from a novel by Robert Hichens
Standard fantasy: Old occultist exchanges souls with young man

Flaming Creatures
1963, (USA), Jonas Mekas-Jack Smith, color
"Underground" film (refused a license, film not in general release): Bizarre "rhapsodic asexuality" as transvestites do their thing

Flaming Ears
1991, (Austria), color, 89 mins.
W: Susanna Heilmayr, Angela Hans Schierl, Ursula Purrer, Margarethe Neumann
D: Angela Hans Schierl, Dietmar Schipek & Ursula Purrer
Bizarre, apocalyptic lesbian fantasy: Decadence in A.D. 2700

The Flaming Urge

1953, (USA), b&w, 67 mins.
W: Harold Lloyd Jr., Cathy Downs
Minor thriller: Mysterious fires plague small town

La Flamme Merveilleuse (The Marvellous Flame)

1903, (Fr), Star, b&w, 37m (121.4 ft./2.1 mins.)
D: Georges Melies
*USA retitle, **The Mystical Flame***
Standard fantasy

The Flanagan Boy

1953, (GB), Hammer/Exclusive, b&w, 81 mins.
W: Barbara Payton (*Lorna Vecchi*), Tony Wright (*Johnny Flanagan*), Frederick Valk (*Giuseppe Vecchi*), Marie Burke (*Mrs. Vecchi*), John Slater (*Charlie*), Sidney James (*Sharkey*), Selma Vaz Dias (*Mrs. Corelli*), George Woodbridge (*The Inspector*)
P: Anthony Hinds   D: Reginald LeBorg   SCR: Richard Landau & Guy Elmes, from a novel by Max Catto
*USA retitle, **Bad Blonde** (Lippert)*
Standard thriller: Wife of old promoter persuades boxing protege to drown him

The Flash

1990, (USA), Pet Fly/WB-TV/CBS-TV, color, 95 mins.
W: John Wesley Shipp (*Barry Allen*), Amanda Pays (*Tina McGee*), Alex Desert (*Julio Mendez*), Paula Marshall (*Iris West*), Michael Nader (*Pike*), Lycia Naff (*Lila*), Priscilla Pointer (*Nora Allen*), Richard Belzer (*Joe Kline*), M. Emmet Walsh (*Henry Allen*), Robert Hooks (*Chief Arthur Cooper*), Tim Thomerson (*Jay Allen*), Patrie-Allen (*Eve Allen*), Biff Manard (*Murphy*), Vito D'Ambrosio (*Bellows*), Wayne Pere (*Rick*), Justin Burnette (*Shawn Allen*), Ricky Dean Logan (*Scott*), Eric Da Re (*Tyrone*), Sam Vlahos (*Dr. Lawrence*), Mariko Tse (*Linda Park*), Virginia Morris (*The Mother*), Josh Cruze (*Petrolli*), David L. Crowley (*The Swat Captain*), Richard Hoyt-Miller (*The Young Father*), Jan Stango (*The Young Mother*), Brad "Cat" Sevy (*The Waiter*)
D: Robert Iscove   TELEPLAY: Danny Bilson & Paul DeMeo, from DC Comics characters   PHOTOG: Sandi Sissel   SPCL-FX COORD: Bill Schirmer   MUSIC: Shirley Walker   THEME: Danny Elfman
TVM, pilot feature for SF-fantasy teleseries: Scientist becomes super-hero

The Flash 2: Revenge of the Trickster

1991, (USA), CBS-TV, color, 92 mins.
W: John Wesley Shipp, Amanda Pays, Mark Hamill, Richard Belzer
TVM, standard SF-fantasy (culled from first two episodes of teleseries "The Flash"): Superhero meets nemesis

Flash Gordon

1980, (GB), Starling/Famous Films/Dino De Laurentiis/Univ, color, 110 mins.
W: Sam J. Jones (*Flash Gordon*), Melody Anderson (*Dale Arden*), Max von Sydow (*Emperor Ming*), Topol (*Dr. Hans Zarkov*), Ornella Muti (*Princess Aura*), Timothy Dalton (*Prince Barin*), Brian Blessed (*Prince Vultan*), Philip Stone (*High Priest Zogi*), Peter Wyngarde (*Klytus*), Ted Carroll (*Biro*), Mariangela Melato (*Kala*), John Hallam (*Luro*), John Osborne (The *Priest*), Suzanne Danielle (The *Servant*), Richard O'Brien (*Fico*), Bobbie Brown (*Hedonia*), William Hootkins (*Munson*), George Harris (*Prince of Ardentia*), Adrienne Kronenberg (*Vultan's Daughter*), Robbie Coltrane (*The Man*), Peter Duncan (*The Treeman*), Tessa Spicer (A *Hawkwoman*), Venetia Spicer (A *Hawkwoman*), Leon Greene (*The Colonel*), Doretta Dunkley (*Queen of Frigia*), Sally Nicholson (*Queen of Azuria*) Stanley Lebor (*The Mongon Doctor*), John Morton (*An Airline Pilot*), Burnell Tucker (An Airline Pilot)
D: Michael Hodges   SCR: Lorenzo Semple Jr., from Alex Raymond's comic strip   PHOTOG: Gilbert Taylor   MUSIC: Howard Blake   SPCL-FX: George Gibbs
Lavish space opera: Hero saves Earth from alien despot

Flatliners

1990, (USA), Stonebridge/Col, colorscope, 111 mins.
W: Kiefer Sutherland (*Nelson*), Julia Roberts (*Rachel*), Kevin Bacon (*Labraccio*), William Baldwin (*Joe*), Oliver Platt (*Steckle*), Kimberly Scott (*Winnie Hicks*), Joshua Rudoy (*Billy Mahoney*), Aeryk Egan (*Young Nelson*), Benjamin Mouton (*Rachel's Father*), Hope Davis (*Anne*), Jim Ortlieb (*Uncle Dave*), Kesha Reed (*Young Winnie*), John Joseph Duda (*Young Labraccio*), Megan Stewart, Elinore O'Connell, Tressa Thomas, Gonzo Gonzalez, Nancy Moran, Afram Bill Williams, Deborah Thompson, Zoaunne LeRoy, Marilyn Dodds Frank, Sanna Vraa, Nicole Niblack, Ilona Margolis, Cynthia Bassham, Sarabeth Tucek, Beth Grant, Julie Warner, Iiliana B'Tiste, Deborah Torchio, Angela Paton, Deborah Goomas, Michelle McKee, Miguel Delgado, Dede Latinopoulos, Patricia Belcher, Jared Milmeister, Susan French, Cage S. Johnson, Patrick Gleeson, Ingrid Oliu, John Benjamin Martin, Lynda Odums, John Fink, Anne James, Evelina Fernandez, Raymond Hanis, Tom Kurlander, Nili Levi, K.K. Dodds, Natsuko Ohama
P: Michael Douglas, Rick Bieber   D: Joel Schumacher   SCR: Peter Filardi   PHOTOG: Jan DeBont   SPCL-FX: Philip Cory & Hans Metz   VS-FX SPRVSR: Peter Donen   MUSIC: James Newton Howard   SONGS: Party Town & The Clapping Song
Modest fantasy-thriller: Medical students sample death experience

Flat No. 3

1934, (GB), British Lion/MGM, b&w, 46 mins.

W: Mary Glynne (*Mrs. Rivington*), D.A. Clarke-Smith (*Kettler*), Betty Astell (*Trixie*), Cecil Parker (*Hilary Maine*), Lewis Shaw (*Harry Rivington*), Dorothy Vernon (*Mrs. Crummitt*), Elizabeth English (*Joan Maine*)
D: Leslie Hiscott   STORY: Michael Barringer
Standard thriller: Lawyer helps widow who believes she killed blackmailer

Flat Two

1962, (GB), Merton Park/Anglo-Amalgamated, b&w, 60 mins.
W: John LeMesurier (*Warden*), Bernard Archard (*Insp. Trainer*), Jack Watling (*Frank Leemington*), Barry Keegan (*Charles Berry*), Ann Bell (*Susan*), Campbell Singer (*Hurley Brown*), Charles Lloyd Pack (*Miller*), David Bauer (*Emil Louba*)
P: Jack Greenwood   D: Alan Cooke   SCR: lindsay Galloway, from an Edgar Wallace novel
Standard crime-thriller: Barrister kills gambler

The Flaw

1933, (GB), Patrick K. Heale/Para, b&w, 67 mins.
W: Henry Kendall (*John Millway*), Eric Maturin (*James Kelver*), Phyllis Clare (*Laura Kelver*), Douglas Payne (*Insp. Barnes*), Eve Gray (*Irene Nelson*), Vera Gerald (*Mrs. Mamby*), Sydney Seaward (*The Sgt.*)
D: Norman Walker   STORY: Brandon Fleming
Standard thriller: Poisoner's victim turns tables

The Flaw

1955, (GB), Cybex/Renown, b&w, 61 mins.
W: John Bentley (*Paul Oliveri*), Rona Anderson (*Monica Oliveri*), Donald Houston (*John Millway*), Tonia Berne (*Vera*), Doris Yorke (*Mrs. Bower*), J. Trevor Davies (*Sir George Bentham*), Cecilia Cavendish (*Lady Bentham*)
P: Geoffrey Goodheart   D: Terence Fisher   STORY: Brandon Fleming
Standard crime-thriller: Solicitor foils racecar driver's murderous plot

Flesh & Blood

1985, (USA-Sp), Riverside/Orion, color, 126 mins.
W: Rutger Hauer (*Martin*), Jennifer Jason Leigh (*Agnes*), Tom Burlinson (*Steven*), Jack Thompson (*Hawkwood*), Susan Tyrrell, Ronald Lacey, Brion James, Bruno Kirby, Marina Saura, John Dennis Johnston, Fernando Hilbeck, Siobhan Hayes, Kitty Courbois, Simon Andreu, Jake Wood, Hector Alterio, Hans Veerman, Blanca Marsillach, Jorge Bosso, Nancy Cartwright, Mario de Barros, Susan Beresford, Ida Bons, Jaime Segura, Bettina Brenner, Monica Luccetti
D: Paul Verhoeven   SCR: Gerard Soeteman & Paul Verhoeven   STORY: Gerard Soeteman   PHOTOG: Jan DeBont   MUSIC: Basil Poledouris
*video title, **The Rose and the Sword***
Standard adventure-thriller: Medieval mercenary rescues maiden

The Flesh and Blood Show

1972, (GB), Pete Walker/Tigon, part 3D, color, 88 mins.
W: Jenny Hanley (*Julia*), Ray Brooks (*Mike*), Luan Peters (*Carol*), Judy Matheson (*June*), Robin Askwith (*Simon*), Candace Glendenning (*Sarah*), Tristan Rogers (*Tony*), Penny Meredith (*Angela*), David Howey (*John*), Patrick Barr (*Maj. Bell/Othello*), Elizabeth Bradley (*Mrs. Saunders*), Raymond Young (*Insp. Walsh*), Brian Tulley (*Willllesden*), Rodney Diak (*Warner*), Sally Lahee (*Iris Voskins*), Alan Curtis (*Jack Phipps*), Michael Knowles (*Insp. Curran*), Tom Mennard (*Fred*), Jane Cardew (*Lady Pamela Downes*), Stuart Bevan (*Harry Mulligan*), Raymond George (*Stephen Brant*), Jess Conrad (*The Actor*), Pete Walker (*Ludovico*), Kent Baker, Carol Allen, John Yule
P & D: Pete Walker   SCR: Alfred Shaughnessy   PHOTOG: Peter Jessop   MUSIC: Cyril Ornadel
*A.k.a. **Asylum of the Insane***
blurb: An appalling amalgam of carnage and carnality
Minor thriller: Deranged killer stalks theater troupe

Flesh and Fantasy

1943, (USA), Univ, b&w, 94 mins.
W: Edward G. Robinson (*Marshall Tyler*), Robert Cummings (*Michael*), Betty Field (*Henrietta*), Barbara Stanwyck (*Joan Stanley*), Anna Lee (*Rowena*), Charles Boyer (*Paul Gaspar*), C. Aubrey Smith (*The Dean of Chichester*), Ian Wolfe (*The Librarian*), Thomas Mitchell (*Septimus Podgers*), Dame May Whitty (*Lady Pamela Hardwick*), Edgar Barrier (*The Stranger*), Charles Winninger (*King Lamarr*), David Hoffman (*Davis*), Leyland Hodgson (*The Cop*), Mary Forbes (*Lady Thomas*), Edward Fielding (*Sir Thomas*), Doris Lloyd (*Mrs. Caxton*), Heather Thatcher (*Lady Flora*), Clarence Muse (*Jeff*), Grace McDonald (*The Equestrienne*), Marjorie Lord (*Justine*), June Lang (*Angel*), Jack Gardner (*The Gunman*), Frank Arnold (*The Clown*), George Lewis (*Harlequin*), Peter Lawford (*Pierrot*), Lane Chandler, Frank Mitchell, Ncara Sanders, Beatrice Barrett, Carl Vernell, Robert Benchley, Sandra Morgan, Phil Warren
P: Charles Boyer & Julien Duvivier   D: Julien Duvivier   SCR: Ernest Pascal, Samuel Hoffenstein & Ellis St. Joseph   based on 3 tales of supernatural by Oscar Wilde (*Lord Saville's Crime*), Ellis St. Joseph & Laszlo Vadnay   PHOTOG: Paul Ivano & Stanley Cortez   MUSIC: Alexander Tansman
*A.k.a. **Obsessions***
*Classic fantasy anthology: Varied tales of suspense and the occult.   cf. **Destiny** (1944)*

The Flesh and the Fiends

1959, (GB), Eros/Pacemaker/Valiant, b&w, 93 mins.
W: Peter Cushing (*Dr. Knox*), June Laverick (*Martha Knox*), Donald Pleasence (*William Hare*), Dermot Walsh (*Dr. Geoffrey Mitchell*), Renee Houston (*Helen*

Burke), George Rose (*William Burke*), Billie Whitelaw (*Mary Patterson*), John Cairney (*Chris Jackson*), Melvyn Hayes (*Daft Jamie*), June Powell (*Maggie O'Hara*), Andrew Faulds (*Insp. McCulloch*), Philip Leaver (*Dr. Elliott*), George Woodbridge (*Dr. Ferguson*), Garard Green (*Dr. Andrews*), Esma Cannon (*Aggie*), Geoffrey Tyrrell (*Old Davey*), George Bishop (*The Blind Man*), Becket Bould (*Old Angus*), George Street (*The Publican*), Michael Balfour (*The Drunken Sailor*), Stephen Scott
D: John Gilling **SCR:** John Gilling & Leon Griffiths **ORIG. STORY:** John Gilling **PHOTOG:** Monty Berman **MUSIC:** Stanley Black
USA retitle, **Mania,** *reissued (1965) as* **The Fiendish Ghouls,** *A.k.a.* **Psycho-Killers**
Modest melodrama: Exploits of grave-robbers Burke & Hare. cf. **The Body Snatcher** *(1945) and* **The Doctor and the Devils**

The Flesh Eaters
1964, (USA), Vulcan/CDA, b&w, 87 mins.
W: Martin Kosleck, Rita Morley, Byron Sanders, Ray Tudor, Barbara Wilkins
P: Jack Curtis & Arnold Drake **D:** Jack Curtis **SCR:** Arnold Drake
Minor SF-horror: Marine biologist conducts sinister experiments on desolate isle

Flesh-Eating Mothers
1988, (USA), Panorama, color, 90 mins.
W: Robert Lee Oliver, Valorie Hubbard, Donatella Hecht, Neal Rosen, Terry Hayes, Katherine Mayfield, Ken Eaton, Michael Feuer, Janice Newman, Suzanne Ehrlich, Carolyn Gratsch, Mickey Ross, Alley Ninestein, Marie Michaels, Grace Gawthrop, Louis Homyak, Tony DeRiso, Allen Rickman, Morty Kliedermacher, Grace Pettijohn, John Daniels, Lori Gustafson, Ginger Anselmo, Scott Lerner, Christian Jones, J.J. Ramirez, Tom Chappelle, Catherine McElhone, C.M. Matticola, Michael Helman, Steve Gladstone, Frank Devlin, Tony Fuentes
D: James Aviles Martin **SCR:** James Aviles Martin & Zev Shlasinger **PHOTOG:** Harry Eisenstein **SPCL-FX:** Carl Sorensen **MUSIC:** Minerva **SONGS:** *Suburbia, Eat Raw Meat, & Monsters*
Minor horror-satire: Disease turns cheating housewives into cannibals

Flesh Feast
1970, (USA), Viking Int'l/Cine World Corp., color, 72 mins.
W: Veronica Lake, Phil Philbin, Heather Hughes, Martha Mischon, Yanka Mann, Dian Wilhite, Chris Martell
P: Veronica Lake & Brad F. Ginter **D:** Brad F. Ginter **SCR:** Brad F. Ginter & Thomas Casey
A.k.a. **Time is Terror**
Minor SF-horror: Woman performs gruesome experiments to restore her youth

Flesh for Frankenstein
see **Frankenstein** *(1974)*

Flesh Gordon
1974, (USA), Graffitti Prods./Mammoth, color, 78 mins.
W: Jason Williams (*Flesh Gordon*), William Hunt (*Wang the Perverted*), Suzanne Fields (*Dale Ardor*), Joseph Hudgins (*Dr. Flexi Jerkoff*), John Hoyt (*Dr. Gordon*), Judy Ziehm, Leonard Goodman, Candy Samples, Lance Larsen, Jack Rowe, Steve Grummette, Mycle Brandy, Nora Wieternik, Patricia Burns, Donald Harris, Mark Fore, Maria Aranoff, Annette Anderson, Rick Lutze, Sally Alt, Linus Gator, Pat Hudson, Susan Moore, Duane Paulsen, Howard Alexander, Mary Gavin, Alan Sinclair, Shannon West, Nancy Ayres, Terri Johnson, Kathy Foster, Linda Shepard, Dee Dee Dailes
P: William Osco & Howard Ziehm **D:** Howard Ziehm & Michael Benveniste **SCR:** Michael Benveniste, from comic-strip characters created by Alex Raymond **PHOTOG:** Howard Ziehm **SPCL-FX:** David Allen & "Mij Htrofnad" [Jim Danforth] **MUSIC:** Ralph Ferraro & Peter Tevis
Raunchy, X-rated satire of "Flash Gordon" serials: Earth hero battles alien tyrant

Flesh Gordon 2: Flesh Gordon Meets the Cosmic Cheerleaders
1990, (Can), color, 98 mins.
W: Vince Murdocco (*Flesh*), Tony Travis (*Dr. Flexi Jerkoff*), Robyn Kelly (*Dale*), William Dennis Hunt (*Emperor Wang*)
D: Howard Ziehm
Minor SF-satire: Space tyrant threatens Earth with impotence ray

The Flesh is Weak
1957, (GB), raystro/Eros, b&w, 88 mins.
W: John Derek (*Tony Giani*), Milly Vitale (*Marissa Cooper*), Freda Jackson (*Trixie*), William Franklyn (*Lloyd Buxton*), Martin Benson (*Angelo Giani*), Vera Day (*Edna*), Shirley Ann Field (*Susan*), Norman Wooland (*Insp. Kingcomb*), Harold Lang (*Harry*), Patricia Jessel (*Millie*), Patricia Plunkett (*Doris Newman*), John Paul (*Sgt. Franks*), Denis Shaw (*Saradine*), Joe Robinson (*Lofty*)
P: Raymond Stross **D:** Don Chaffey **STORY:** Leigh Vance
reissued 1961
Standard crime-thriller: Soho vice king uses brother to lure girls into prostitution

Flick
see **Dr. Frankenstein on Campus**

Flight of Black Angel
1991, (USA), color, 102 mins.
W: Peter Strauss, Wiliam O'Leary, James O'Sullivan, Michael Keys Hall
D: Jon Mostow **WRIT:** Henry Dominick

Made-for-Cable, standard thriller: Psycho pilot decides to nuke Las Vegas

The Flight of Dragons
1986, (USA), WB, color, 98 mins.
VOICES: John Ritter, Victor Buono, James Earl Jones, Larry Storch, Don Messick, James Gregory, Harry Morgan, Ed Peck
D: Arthur Rankin Jr. & Jules Bass **SCR:** Romeo Muller **MUSIC:** Maury Laws
Standard animated fantasy

Flight of the Lost Balloon
1961, (USA), Woolner, color, 91 mins.
W: Marshall Thompson, Mala Powers, Robert Gillette, A.J. Valentine, James Lanphier, Douglas Kennedy, Felippe Birriel
P: Bernard Woolner **WRIT & D:** Nathan Juran **PHOTOG:** Jacques Marquette
Minor adventure-thriller: Woman searches Africa for trace of lost fiance

Flight of the Navigator
1986, (USA), New Star Entertainment/Walt Disney/Buena Vista, color, 89 mins.
W: Joey Cramer (*David Freeman*), Paul Mall (aka Paul Reubens, Pee Wee Herman) (*The Voice of Max*), Veronica Cartwright (*Helen Freeman*), Cliff De Young (*Bill Freeman*), Sarah Jessica Parker (*Carolyn McAdams*), Matt Adler (*Jeff, 16 years*), Howard Hesseman (*Dr. Faraday*), Robert Small (*Troy*), Albie Whitaker (*Jeff, 8 years*), Jonathan Sanger (*Dr. Carr*), Iris Acker (*Mrs. Howard*), Richard Liberty (*Mr. Howard*), Cynthia Caqueli (*The Woman Officer*), Raymond Forchion (*Det. Banks*), Gizelle Elliot, Ted Bartsch, Brigid Cleary, Michael Strano, Tony Tracy, Parris Buckner, Robyn Peterson, Philip Hoelcher, Debbie Casperson, Julio Mechoso, Butch Raymond, Louis Cutolo, Bob Strickland, Michael Brockman, Chase Randolph, Rusty Pough, John Archie, Tony Calvino, Robert Goodman, Peter Lundquist, Ryan Murray, Keri Rogers, Jill Beach, Kenny Davis, Bruce Laks, Courtney Brown, Kevin McGoy, Arnie Ross, Fritz Brauner
D: Randal Kleiser **SCR:** Michael Burton & Matt MacManus, from a story by Mark H. Baker **PHOTOG:** James Glennon **MUSIC:** Alan Silvestri
Modest SF-fantasy: Boy has space-time adventure

The Flight That Disappeared
1961, (USA), Harvard/UA, b&w, 73 mins.
W: Craig Hill, Paula Raymond, Dayton Lummis, Gregory Morton, Addison Richards
P: Robert E. Kent **D:** Reginald LeBorg **SCR:** Ralph Hart, Judith Hart & Owen Harris **PHOTOG:** Gilbert Warrenton **MUSIC:** Richard La Salle
Minor SF-fantasy: Atomic scientists on airliner find themselves in "heaven," being tried by people of future

Flight to a Far Planet
see **Queen of Blood**

Flight to Berlin
1983, (W. Ger), color, 90 mins.
W: Tusse Silberg, Paul Freeman, Lisa Kreuzer, Jean-Francois Stevenin, Ewan Stewart, Eddie Constantine, Tatjane Blacher
D: Christopher Petit
Surreal thriller: Loner suspected in mysterious death

Flight to Fury
1966, (USA), b&w, 73 mins.
W: Jack Nicholson, Dewey Martin, Fay Spain, Jacqueline Hellman, Vic Diaz
P, D & STORY: Monte Hellman **SCR:** Jack Nicholson
Minor thriller: Mercenaries seek diamond hoard, crash in Philippine jungle

Flight to Mars
1951, (USA), Mono, color, 72 mins.
W: Cameron Mitchell (*Steve Abbott*), Marguerite Chapman (*Alita*), Arthur Franz (*Jim Barker*), John Litel (*Dr. Lane*), Carol Stafford, Morris Ankrum, Edwward Earle, Robert Barrat, Lucille Barkley, Richard Gaines, Tris Coffin, Everett Glass
P: Walter Mirisch **D:** Lesley Selander **SCR:** Arthur Strawn **PHOTOG:** Harry Neumann **SPCL-FX:** Milt Rice, Jack Rabin & Irving Block **MUSIC:** Marlin Skiles
Modest space opera: Earthlings rocket to red planet, are menaced by doomed civilization

Flight to Nowhere
1946, (USA), Golden Gate/ Screen Guild, b&w, 72 mins.
W: Alan Curtis, Evelyn Ankers, Micheline Cheirel, Jack Holt, Jerome Cowan, John Craven, Inez Cooper, Michael Visaroff, Roland Varno, Gordon Richards, Hoot Gibson
D: William Rowland **PHOTOG:** Marcel LePicard
Minor thriller: Uranium spies complicate air trip

Flight to Tangier
1953, (USA), Para, color, 3D, 90 mins.
W: Jack Palance, Joan Fontaine, Marcel Dalio
D & SCR: Charles Marquis Warren **PHOTOG:** Ray Rennahan
Standard adventure-thriller

The Flintstones
1994, (USA), Univ, color, 91 mins.
W: John Goodman (*Fred Flintstone*), Elizabeth Perkins (*Wilma Flintstone*), Rick Moranis (*Barney Rubble*), Rosie O'Donnell (*Betty Rubble*), Elaine & Melanie

Silver (*Pebbles*), Hylnur & Marino Sigurdsson (*Bamm-Bamm*), Harvey Korman (*Voice of the Dictabird*), Mel Blanc (*Voice of Dino*), Kyle MacLachlan, Elizabeth Taylor, Halle Berry, Dann Florek, Richard Moll, Jonathan Winters, Sam Raimi, Janice Kent, Jack O'Halloran, Jay Leno, Laraine Newman, Jean Van-derPyl, William Hanna, Joseph Barbera, Sheryl Lee Ralph Irwin Keyes
<u>P</u>: Bruce Cohen <u>D</u>: Brian Levant <u>SCR</u>: Tom S. Parker, Jim Jennewein, & Steven E. De Souza <u>PHOTOG</u>: Dean Cundey <u>SPCL VS-FX</u>: Industrial Light & Magic <u>SPCL-FX SPRVSR</u>: Michael Lantieri <u>MUSIC</u>: David Newman
Standard comedy-fantasy: Life of Stone-Age people

The Floating Dutchman
1953, (GB), Merton Park/Anglo-Amalgamated, b&w, 76 mins.
<u>W</u>: Dermot Walsh (*Alexander James*), Sydney Tafler (*Victor Skinner*), Mary Germaine (*Rose Reid*), Guy Verney (*Snow White*), Hugh Morton (*Insp. Cathie*), James Raglan (*Mr. Wynn*), Nicolas Bentley (*Collis*), Arnold Marle (*Otto*), Derek Blomfield (*Philip Reid*)
<u>P</u>: W.H. Williams <u>D & SCR</u>: Vernon Sewell, from a novel by Nicolas Bentley
reissued 1958
Standard crime-thriller: Gov't man poses as crook, unmasks club owner as jewel thief

Floating Platform 1 Does Not Reply
see **F.P. 1 Antwortet Nicht**

The Floating Woman
see **La Femme Volante**

Flood
1976, (USA), Irwin Allen/WB-TV/NBC-TV, color, 106 mins.
<u>W</u>: Robert Culp (*Steve Brannigan*), Richard Basehart (*John Cutler*), Martin Milner (*Paul Blake*), Cameron Mitchell (*Sam Adams*), Barbara Hershey (*Mary Cutler*), Carol Lynley (*Abbie Adams*), Teresa Wright (*Alice Cutler*), James Griffith (*Charlie Davis*), Francine York (*Daisy*), Whit Bissell (*Dr. Horne*), Eric Olson (*Andy Cutler*), Roddy McDowall (*Franklin*), Gloria Stuart (*Mrs. Parker*)
<u>P</u>: Irwin Allen <u>D</u>: Earl Bellamy <u>TELEPLAY</u>: Don Ingalls <u>PHOTOG</u>: Lamar Boren
TVM, minor thriller: Dam threatens to burst

The Flooded Mine
1912, (GB), Clarendon, b&w, 2,160 ft. (658.4m)
<u>W</u>: Dorothy Bellew (*Lily Smith*)
<u>D</u>: Wilfred Noy
Standard thriller: Dancer learns husband loves her sister, tries to drown both in flooded mine

Floods of Fear
1958, (GB), Rank/Univ, b&w, 84 mins.
<u>W</u>: Howard Keel (*Donovan*), Anne Heywood (*Elizabeth Matthews*), Cyril Cusack (*Peebles*), Harry H. Corbett (*Sharkey*), Eddie Byrne (*The Sheriff*), John Crawford (*Jack Murphy*), James Dyrenforth (*The Mayor*), John Phillips (*Dr. Matthews*), Peter Madden (*The Banker*), Guy Kingsley Poynter (*The Deputy*)
<u>P</u>: Sydney Fox <u>D</u>: Charles Crichton <u>SCR</u>: Charles Crichton & Vivienne Knight, from a novel by John & Ward Hawkins
Standard thriller: Girl trapped in flood with framed convict and moronic thief. Filmed in U.K., set in U.S.

The Floodtide
1913, (GB), Edison, b&w, 1,000 ft. (304.8m)
<u>W</u>: Marc McDermott (*Sidney Brandon*), Miriam Nesbitt (*Connie Lee*), Frederick Annesley (*Joe Muzzey*), Alice Mansfield
<u>D</u>: Charles Brabin <u>STORY</u>: Goring Chalmers
Standard adventure-thriller: Girl climbs Cornwall cliff, saves injured artist from tide

The Florentine Dagger
1935, (USA), WB, b&w, 69 mins.
<u>W</u>: Donald Woods (*Cesare*), Margaret Lindsay (*Florence*), C. Aubrey Smith (*Dr. Lytton*), Henry O'Neill (*Victor Ballau*), Robert Barrat (*The Captain*), Florence Fair, Egon Brecher, Frank Reicher, Charles Judels, Rafaela Ottiano, Paul Porcasi, Eily Malyon, Herman Bing, Henry Kolker
<u>D</u>: Robert Florey <u>SCR</u>: Tom Reed <u>ADDITIONAL DIALOG</u>: Brown Holmes <u>PHOTOG</u>: Arthur L. Todd <u>MUSIC DIR</u>: Leo F. Forbstein
Standard "Crime Club" mystery: Descendant of Borgias encounters murder

A Flowergirl's Romance
1910, (GB), Hepworth, b&w, 650 ft. (198.1m)
<u>W</u>: Flora Morris (*The Flowergirl*)
<u>D</u>: Bert Haldane
Standard crime-thriller: Flowergirl framed for stealing Sailor's purse

The Flower in His Mouth
1976, (It), Carlo Ponti/Zampa Film, color, 104 mins.
<u>W</u>: Jennifer O'Neill, Franco Nero, James Mason, Claudio Gora, Franco Fabrizi, Carla Calo, Gino Pagnani, Gigi Bonos, Aldo Giuffre
<u>D</u>: Luigi Zampa <u>PHOTOG</u>: Ennio Guarnieri <u>MUSIC</u>: Ennio Morricone
Italian title: **Gente Di Rispetto** *(Respectable People)*
Minor thriller: Beautiful schoolteacher comes to Sicilian village, ritual murders ensue

The Flower of Doom
1917, (USA), Univ, b&w
<u>WRIT & D</u>: Rex Ingram

Standard melodrama

Flowers in the Attic
1987, (USA), Fries Entertainment/New World, color, 95 mins.
<u>W</u>: Louise Fletcher (*Grandmother*), Kristy Swanson (*Cathy*), Victoria Tennant (*Mother*), Jeb Stuart Adams (*Chris*), Ben Ganger (*Cory*), Lindsay Parker (*Carrie*), Nathan Davis, Gus Peters, Marshall Colt, Brooke Fries, Alex Koba, Leonard Mann, Bruce Neckels, Clare C. Peck
<u>D & SCR</u>: Jeffrey Bloom, from V.C. Andrews' novel <u>PHOTOG</u>: Frank Byers & Gil Hubbs <u>MUSIC</u>: Christopher Young
Standard thriller: Youngsters secreted and mistreated in grandparents' mysterious home

Flubber
1997, (USA), Hollywood, color
<u>W</u>: Robin Williams, Marcia Gay Harden, Christopher McDonald, Ted Levine, Clancy Brown, Raymond J. Barry
<u>D</u>: Les Mayfield <u>SCR</u>: John Hughes & Bill Walsh <u>PHOTOG</u>: Dean Cundey <u>MUSIC</u>: Danny Elfman
Standard juvenile comedy-fantasy (remake of **The Absent-Minded Professor***): Teacher invents energetic form of matter*

Fluke
1995, (USA), MGM, color, 100 mins.
<u>W</u>: Matthew Modine, Nancy Travis, Eric Stoltz (*Newman*), Max Pomeranc (*Brian*)Ron Perlman, Jon Polito, Bill Cobbs, Frederico Pacifici, Collin Wilcox Paxton, Samuel L. Jackson (*voice*)
<u>D</u>: Carlo Carlei <u>SCR</u>: James Carrington & Carlo Carlei <u>PHOTOG</u>: Raffaele Mertes <u>MUSIC</u>: Carlo Siliotto
Standard fantasy: Slain businessman reincarnated as dog

A Fluke in the 'Fluence
1915, (GB), Martin/DFSA, b&w, 595 ft. (181.4m)
<u>D</u>: Edwin J. Collins
Minor comedy-fantasy short: Mesmerist makes victim act like goat and monkey

The Fly
1958, (USA), 20th-Fox, colorscope, 94 mins.
<u>W</u>: Al [David] Hedison (*Andre DeLambre*), Vincent Price (*Francois DeLambre*), Patricia Owens (*Helene DeLambre*), Herbert Marshall (*Insp. Charas*), Charles Herbert (*Philippe DeLambre*), Betty Lou Gerson (*Nurse Anderson*), Kathleen Freeman (*Emma*), Torben Meyer, Eugene Borden
<u>P & D</u>: Kurt Neumann <u>SCR</u>: James Clavell, from a short story by George Langelaan <u>PHOTOG</u>: Karl Struss <u>SPCL-FX</u>: L.B. Abbott <u>MUSIC</u>: Paul Sawtell
orig. co-billed with **Spacemaster X-7**
Classic SF-thriller: Scientist builds matter-transmitter, gets his atoms mixed with those of common house fly. cf. **Return of the Fly** *and* **Curse of the Fly**

The Fly (1967)
see **Muha**

The Fly (1958): PAT OWENS

The Fly
1986, (Can), Brooksfilms/20th-Fox, color, 95 mins.
W: Jeff Goldblum (*Seth Brundle*), Geena Davis (*Veronica Quaife*), John Getz (*Stathis Borans*), Les Carlson (*Dr. Cheevers*), Joy Boushel (*Taw-ny*), George Chuvalo (*Marky*), Michael Copeman, David Cronenberg, Carol Lazare, Shawn Hewitt
D: David Cronenberg   SCR: Charles Edward Pogue & David Cronenberg, from George Langelaan's short story   PHOTOG: Mark Irwin   MUSIC: Howard Shore
Brilliant semi-remake of 1950's SF-horror classic: Scientist genetically altered by matter-transmission experiment

The Fly II
1989, (USA), Brooksfilms/20th-Fox, color, 105 mins.
W: Eric Stoltz (*Martin Brundle*), Daphne Zuniga (*Beth Logan*), Lee Richardson (*Anton Bartok*), Ann Marie Lee (*Dr. Jainway*), John Getz (*Stathis Borans*), Frank C. Turner (*Dr. Shepard*), Gary Chalk (*Scorby*), Harley Cross
D: Chris Walas   SCR: Mick Garris, Jim Wheat, Ken Wheat, & Frank Darabont   STORY: Mick Garris   PHOTOG: Robin Vidgeon   MUSIC: Christopher Young   SONGS: *Lock, Stock and Teardrops* & *Deep Inside Your Love*
Standard SF-thriller, sequel to The Fly (1986): Son of ill-fated scientist finds his genes are tainted

Fly-Away Baby
1937, (USA), WB, b&w, 60 mins.
W: Glenda Farrell (*Torchy Blane*), Barton MacLane (*Steve McBride*), Gordon Oliver (*Lucien Croy*), Hugh O'Connell (*Hughie Sprague*), Marcia Ralston (*Ila Sayra*), Tom Kennedy (*Gahagan*), Raymond Hatton (*Maxie*), Emmett Vogan (*Clifford Vance*), Gordon Hart (*Sills*), Anderson Lawlor (*Tory*), Harry Davenport (*Col. Higgam*), George Guhl (*The Desk Sgt.*)
D: Frank McDonald   SCR: Don Ryan & Kenneth Gamet, from characters created by Frederick Nebel   PHOTOG: Warren Lynch
Standard thriller, 2nd "Torchy Blane" mystery: Reporter uncovers killer and smuggling racket

Flying Blind
1941, (USA), b&w, 69 mins.
W: Richard Arlen, Jean Parker, Maric Wilson
Minor thriller: Spies seek vital air-defense secret

Flying Disc Man from Mars
1958, (USA), Rep, b&w
W: Walter Reed, Lois Collier, Gregory Gay, James Craven
P: Franklin Adreon   D: Fred C. Brannon   SCR: Ronald Davidson
Minor SF-thriller (feature culled from 1951 serial): Martian attempts conquest of Earth

The Flying Dutchman
1923, (USA), R-C Pictures, b&w, 6 reels (5,800 ft./1767.8m)
W: Lawson Butt (*Philip Vanderdecker*), Nola Luxford (*Melissa*), Ella Hall (*Zoe*), Edward Coxen (*Robert*), Walter Law (*Peter Van Dorn*)
D & ADAPT: Lloyd B. Carleton, from Wagner's opera   PHOTOG: Andre Barltier
Standard romance-fantasy: Dreamer imagines he is cursed mariner

The Flying Eye
see The Trollenberg Terror

Flying from Justice
1913, (GB), Brightonia/Popular, b&w, 2,000 ft. (609.6m)
W: Mark Melford (*Gully*), Nell Emerald (*Mildred Parkes*), H. Agar Lyons (*Charles Baring*), Frank E. Petley (*James Woodruff*)
D: Arthur Charrington   STORY: Mark Melford
Standard crime-thriller: Counterfeiters ensnare cleric's pupil

Flying from Justice
1915, (GB), Neptune, b&w, 4,010 ft. (1222.3m)
W: Gregory Scott (*Charles Baring*), Joan Ritz (*Winnie*), Douglas Payne (*John Gully*), Alice Moseley (*Mildred Parkes*), Fred Morgan (*James Woodruffe*), Cecil Morton York (*Rev. Lacarsey*), Frank Tennant (*John Lacarsey*), Jack Denton (*Pearly Tanner*), Maud Williams (*Mrs. Baring*), Brian Daly (*Maj. Parkes*)
D: Percy Nash, from a play by Mark Melford
Standard crime-thriller: Counterfeiting gang ensnares cleric's pupil

The Flying House
1920, (USA), b&w
D: Winsor McCay
Standard short animated fantasy

The Flying Saucer
1950, (USA), Colonial/Film Classics, b&w, 69 mins.
W: Mikel Conrad, Pat Garrison, Denver Pyle, Lester Sharpe, Virginia Hewitt, Hatz von Teuffen, Russell Hicks, Philip Morris, Frank Darien, Roy Engel, Gerry Owen
WRIT, P, & D: Mikel Conrad   PHOTOG: Philip Tanura
Minor SF-melodrama

The Flying Saucer (1961)
see Il Disco Volante

Flying Saucers
1955, (Mex), b&w
W: Andres Soler, Evangelina Elizondo, Adalberto Martinez
D: Julian Soler
Minor SF-adventure

The Flying Scot
1957, (GB), Insignia/Anglo-Amalgamated, b&w, 69 mins.
W: Lee Patterson (*Ronnie*), Kay Callard (*Jackie*), Margaret Withers (*The Lady*), Alan Gifford (*Phil*), Jeremy Bodkin (*Charlie*), Mark Baker (*Gibbs*), Gerald Case (*The Guard*)
P & D: Compton Bennett   SCR: Norman Hudis   STORY: Ralph Smart & Jan Read
USA retitle, Mailbag Robbery, reissued 1963
Standard crime-thriller: Trio plans to rob express train

The Flying Serpent
1946, (USA), PRC, b&w, 59 mins.
W: George Zucco, Ralph Lewis (*Richard*), Hope Kramer (*Mary*), Eddie Acuff
P: Sigmund Neufeld   D: Sherman Scott [Sam Newfield]   SCR: John T. Neville
Standard horror-thriller (Good Zucco vehicle): Mad archeologist uses murderous bird to guard Aztec treasure. Remake: The Devil Bat

The Flying Sorceror
1975, (GB), Anvil/CFF, color, 52 mins.
W: Kim Burfield (*David Hawkins*), Debbie Russ (*Lady Eleanor*), John Bluthal (*Uncle Charlie*), Tim Barrett (*Astrolabe*), Erik Chitty (*Sir Roger*), Bob Todd (*Crabtree*), Will Stampe (*Sir Griswold*)
P: Hugh Stewart   D: Harry Booth   SCR: Harry Booth & Leo Maguire   STORY: Hazel Swift   PHOTOG: Leslie Dear   MUSIC: Harry Robinson
Standard juvenile fantasy: Boy time-travels to Middle Ages, saves locals from dragon

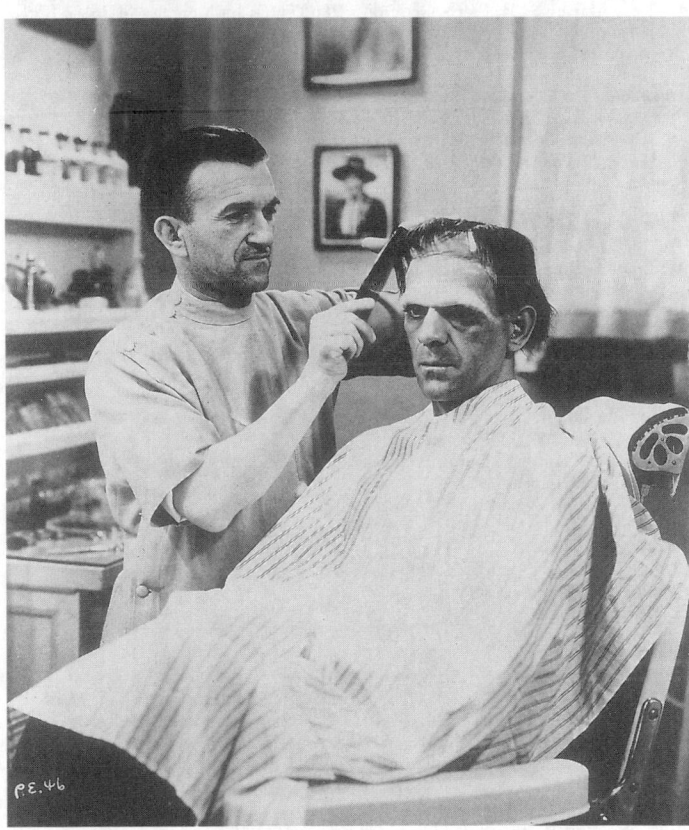

Frankenstein (1931): Jack Pierce working on Boris Karloff

Flying the Foam and Some Fancy Diving
1906, (GB), Williamson, b&w
Standard fantasy: Cyclist rides into sea (then film reverses)

The Flying Torpedo
1916, (USA), Triangle, b&w
W: John Emerson, Spottiswoode Aitken, Bessie Love
WRIT & P: D.W. Griffith   D: Jack O'Brien
Standard SF-thriller: Super-weapon changes power balance

Foiled by a Girl
1912, (GB), Clarendon, b&w, 660 ft. (201.2m)
W: Dorothy Bellew (*The Typist*)
D: Wilfred Noy
Standard crime-thriller: Typist nabs thief, saves framed clerk

Footsteps
1974, (GB), Alan Parker Films/EMI, color, 33 mins.
<u>W:</u> Gemma Jones *(Mollie Blake)*, Rose Hill *(The Landlady)*, Robert Bridges *(The Man)*
<u>WRIT, P & D:</u> Alan Parker
Standard short crime-thriller: Girl hears landlady's "murder"

The Fog
1980, (USA), Entertainment Discoveries Inc./Avco Embassy, color, 87 mins.
<u>W:</u> Adrienne Barbeau *(Stevie Wayne)*, Jamie Lee Curtis *(Elizabeth Solley)*, Janet Leigh *(Kathy Williams)*, Hal Holbrook *(Father Malone)*, Tom Atkins *(Nick Castle)*, John Houseman *(Mr. Machen)*, Nancy Loomis *(Sandy Fadel)*, Charles Cyphers *(Dan O'Bannon)*, John Goff *(Al Williams)*, Ty Mitchell *(Andy Wayne)*, Jim Jacobus *(The Mayor)*, John Vick *(Sheriff Simms)*, George Buck Flower *(Tommy Wallace)*, James Canning *(Dick Baxter)*, Darrow Igus *(Mel Sloan)*, Regina Waldon *(Mrs. Kobritz)*, Jim Haynie *(Hank Jones)*, Bill Taylor *(The Bartender)*, Fred Franklyn *(Ashcroft)*
<u>P:</u> Debra Hill   <u>D:</u> John Carpenter   <u>SCR:</u> John Carpenter & Debra Hill   <u>PHOTOG:</u> Dean Cundey   <u>MUSIC:</u>John Carpenter   <u>ELECTRONIC REALIZATION:</u> Don Wyman
Standard horror-fantasy: Vengeful spirits of dead pirates terrorize seacoast town

Fog for a Killer
see Out of the Fog (1962)

Fog Island
1945, (USA), PRC, b&w, 72 mins.
<u>W:</u> Lionel Atwill *(Alec Ritchfield)*, Sharon Douglas *(Gail)*, George Zucco *(Leo Grainjer)*, Jerome Cowan *(Kavanaugh)*, Veda Ann Borg *(Sylvia)*, Ian Keith *(Dr. Lake)*, Jacqueline de Wit *(Emiline Bronson)*, John Whitney *(Jeff)*, George Lloyd *(Allerton, the Butler)*
<u>D:</u> Terry Morse   <u>SCR:</u> Pierre Gendron   <u>PHOTOG:</u> Ira Morgan   <u>MUSIC:</u> Karl Hajos
Minor thriller: Financier plots demise of shady business associates

La Folie du Docteur Tube (The Madness of Dr. Tube)
1915, (Fr), Louis Nalpas-Les Films d'Art, b&w
<u>W:</u> Albert Dieudonne
<u>WRIT & D:</u> Abel Gance   <u>PHOTOG:</u> Wentzel
Standard thriller

The Folks at Red Wolf Inn
1972, (USA), Far West/Scope III, color, 90 mins.
<u>W:</u> Linda Gillin, Arthur Space, John Neilson, Mary Jackson, Janet Wood, Margaret Avery, Earl Parker, Michael Macready
<u>P:</u> Michael Macready   <u>D:</u> Bud Townsend   <u>SCR:</u> Allen J. Actor   <u>PHOTOG:</u> John McNichol   <u>MUSIC:</u> Bill Marx
A.k.a. Terror at Red Wolf Inn, reissued (1976, Intercontinental) as Terror House
Standard horror-thriller: College girl "wins" free vacation at resort run by cannibals

Follow Me Quietly
1949, (USA), RKO, b&w, 59 mins.
<u>W:</u> William Lundigan, Dorothy Patrick, Edwin Max
<u>D:</u> Richard Fleischer
Minor thriller: Mysterious strangler baffles police

Follow That Woman
1945, (USA), Para, b&w, 70 mins.
<u>W:</u> William Gargan, Nancy Kelly
Standard thriller

Follow the Hunter
1954, (USA), Lippert, b&w, 71 mins.
<u>W:</u> Charles Chaplin Jr. *(Roger)*, Freddy Ridgeway *(Tad)*, Onslow Stevens *(Jim)*, Margia Dean *(Linda)*, Phil Tead *(Mac)*, Robert Stevenson *(The Deputy Sheriff)*, Shep *(Buck, the Wonder Dog)*
<u>P:</u> Robert Lippert, Jr.   <u>D:</u> William Claxton   <u>SCR:</u> Orville H. Hampton   <u>STORY:</u> William Claxton   <u>MUSIC:</u> Paul Dunlap
A.k.a. Fangs of the Wild
Minor adventure-thriller: Wilderness tale of resourceful canine

La Fontaine Merveilleuse (The Marvellous Fountain)
1908, (Fr), Star, b&w, 196m (643 ft./10.9 mins.)
<u>D:</u> Georges Melies
Standard fantasy

La Fontaine Sacre ou la Vengeance de Boudha (The Sacred Fountain: or, The Vengeance of Buddha)
1901, (Fr), Star, b&w, 30m (98.4 ft./1.7 mins.)
<u>D:</u> Georges Melies
USA retitle, The Sacred Fountain
Standard fantasy.

The Food of the Gods
1976, (USA), AIP, color, 88 mins.
<u>W:</u> Marjoe Gortner *(Morgan)*, Pamela Franklin *(Lorna Scott)*, Ida Lupino *(Mrs. Skinner)*, Ralph Meeker *(Bensington)*, Jon Cypher *(Brian)*, Belinda Balaski *(Rita)*, Tom Stovall *(Thomas)*, Chuck Courtney, Reg Tunnicliffe, John McLiam
<u>WRIT, P, D & SPCL-FX:</u> Bert I. Gordon, loosely based on a portion of H.G. Wells' novel   <u>PHOTOG:</u> Reginald Morris   <u>MUSIC:</u> Elliot Kaplan
Standard SF-thriller: Stranded group faces giant rats. cf. Empire of the Ants and Village of the Giants

The Food of the Gods, Part II
1989, (Can), Carolco, color, 90 mins.
<u>W:</u> Paul Coufos *(Dr. Neil Hamilton)*, Jackie Burroughs *(Dr. Kate Trager)*, Lisa Schrage *(Alex)*, Colin Fox *(Edward)*
<u>D:</u> Damian Lee   <u>SCR:</u> Richard Bennett & E. Kim Brewster   <u>STORY:</u> Richard Bennett, inspired by H.G. Wells' novel *The Food of the Gods*   <u>SPCL-FX SPRVSR:</u> David Miller
Standard SF-horror: Hormones create gigantic rats. A.k.a. Gnaw

The Fool
1913, (GB), Big Ben-Union/Pathe, b&w, 3,343 ft. (1018.9m)
<u>W:</u> Godfrey Tearle *(Sterndale)*, Mary Malone *(Mrs. Brockwood)*, James Carew *(Arthur Warde)*, Rex Davis
<u>D & SCR:</u> George Pearson, from Rudyard Kipling's poem *A Fool There Was*
Standard crime-thriller: Man takes blame for girl cardsharp, she saves him from blackmailer

The Foolish Assassin
see Le Fou Assassin

The Fool Killer
1965, (USA), LRO/AA, b&w, 100 mins.
<u>W:</u> Anthony Perkins *(Milo)*, Edward Albert *(George)*, Henry Hull *(Dirty Jim)*, Dana Elcar *(Dodd)*, Salome Jens *(Mrs. Dodd)*, Charlotte Jones *(Ova)*, Arnold Moss *(Rev. Spotts)*, Sindee Ann Richards *(Blessing)*, Wendell Phillips *(The Old Man)*, Frances Garr *(The Old Crab)*
<u>P:</u> David Friedkin   <u>D:</u> Servando Gonzales   <u>SCR:</u> Morton Fine & David Friedkin, from a novel by Helen Eustis   <u>PHOTOG:</u> Alex Phillips Jr.   <u>MUSIC:</u> Gustavo C. Carrean
reissued (1966) as A Violent Journey
Offbeat melodrama: During American Civil War small boy hears fanciful tales of a "fool killer"—then meets one

Footsteps in the Dark
1941, (USA), WB, b&w, 96 mins.
<u>W:</u> Errol Flynn, Brenda Marshall, Ralph Bellamy, Lee Patrick, Alan Hale, Allen Jenkins, Lucille Watson, Roscoe Karns, William Frawley, Grant Mitchell, Maris Wrixon, Turhan Bey, Noel Madison, Jack LaRue
<u>D:</u> Lloyd Bacon & Hugh MacMullen   <u>SCR:</u> lester Cole & John Wexley, based on the play *Blonde* by Ladislaus Fodor, Bernard Merivale & Jeffrey Dell   <u>PHOTOG:</u> Ernest Haller   <u>MUSIC:</u> Frederick Hollander
Standard comedy-mystery: Investment counselor doubles as detective

Footsteps in the Fog
1955, (GB), Film Locations/Col, color, 90 mins.
<u>W:</u> Stewart Granger *(Stephen Lowry)*, Jean Simmons *(Lily Watkins)*, Finlay Currie *(Insp. Peters)*, Bill Travers *(David MacDonald)*, Ronald Squire *(Alfred Travers)*, Belinda Lee *(Elizabeth Travers)*, Peter Bull *(Brasher)*, William Hartnell *(Herbert Moresby)*, Frederick Leister *(Dr. Simpson)*, Percy Marmont *(The Magistrate)*, Margery Rhodes *(Mrs. Park)*, Sheila Manahan *(Mrs. Moresby)*, Norman Macowan *(Grimes)*, Cameron Hall *(Corcoran)*, Victor Maddern *(Jones)*, Arthur Howard *(The Vicar)*, Barry Keegan *(Constable Burke)*, Peter Williams *(Constable Farrow)*
<u>P:</u> M.J. Frankovich & Maxwell Setton   <u>D:</u> Arthur Lubin   <u>SCR:</u> Lenore Coffee & Dorothy Reid, based on W.W. Jacobs' short story "The Interruption"
<u>PHOTOG:</u> Christopher Challis   <u>MUSIC:</u> Benjamin Frankel
Tense thriller: English maid blackmails murderous master

Footsteps in the Night
1957, (USA), AA, b&w, 62 mins.
<u>W:</u> Bill Elliott, Don Haggerty
Standard thriller

For All Eternity
1917, (GB), I.B. Davidson/Ruffells, b&w, 4,500 ft. (1371.6m)
<u>W:</u> Malvine Longfellow *(Ella Morgan)*, A.E. Coleby *(Clifford Morgan)*, Arthur Rooke *(Desmond Leach)*, Janet Alexander *(Nurse Hillyer)*, Richard Buttery, N. Watts-Phillips, Joyce Templeton
<u>D:</u> A.E. Coleby & Arthur Rooke   <u>SCR:</u> A.E. Coleby   <u>STORY:</u> Rowland Talbot
Standard crime-thriller: Framed man saved when nurse confesses to killing her bastard child's father

For All Mankind
1990, (USA), Apollo, color, 87 mins.
<u>NARRATORS:</u> James A. Lovell Jr., Russell L. Schweickart, Eugene A. Cernan, Michael Collins, Charles Conrad Jr., Stuart A. Roosa, Richard F. Gordon Jr., Alan L. Bean, T. Kenneth Mattingly 2nd, John L. Swigert Jr., Charles M. Duke Jr. & Harrison H. Schmitt
<u>P & D:</u> Al Reinert   <u>MUSIC:</u> Brian Eno, Roger Eno & Dan Lanois
Modest documentary: Exploration of outer space

Forbidden
1949, (GB), Pennant/British Lion, b&w, 87 mins.
W: Douglass Montgomery (*Jim Harding*), Hazel Court (*Jane Thompson*), Patricia Burke (*Diana Harding*), Garry Marsh (*Jerry Burns*), Ronald Shiner (*Dan Collins*), Eliot Makeham (*Mr. Thompson*), Kenneth Griffith (*Johnny*), Michael Medwin (*The Cabby*), Frederick Leister (*Dr. Franklin*), Richard Bird (*Jennings*), Andrew Cruickshank (*Baxter*)
P & D: George King   SCR: Katherine Strueby   STORY: Val Valentine
Standard thriller: Chemist tries to poison extravagant wife

Forbidden Games (1952)
see Jeux Interdits

Forbidden Games
1995, (USA), color, 95 mins.
W: Jeff Griggs, Lesli Kay Sterling
Minor thriller: Psychic private eye seeks millionaire's killer

Forbidden Island
1959, (USA), Col, color, 66 mins.
W: Jon Hall, Nan Adams John Farrow, Jonathan Haze, Greigh Phillips
D: Charles B. Griffith
Standard adventure-thriller. Skindiver seeks sunken treasure

Forbidden Jungle
1950, (USA), Eagle Lion, b&w, 67 mins.
W: Don Harvey, Forrest Taylor, Alyce Louis
Minor action-adventure

The Forbidden Land
see Jungle Jim in the Forbidden Land

Forbidden Love
see Freaks

The Forbidden Moon
1953, (USA), Reed, b&w, 78 mins
W: Richard Crane, Robert Lyden
Minor SF-adventure, feature culled from 1950s teleseries "Rocky Jones, Space Ranger"

Forbidden Planet
1956, (USA), MGM, color, 98 mins.
W: Walter Pidgeon (*Dr. Morbius*), Leslie Nielsen (*Cmdr. J.J. Adams*), Anne Francis (*Altaira*), Warren Stevens (*Dr. Ostro*), Richard Anderson (*Lt. Quinn*), Jack Kelly (*Lt. Jerry Farman*), George Wallace (*The Bosun*), Earl Holliman ("*Cookie*"), James Drury (*Strong*), Jimmy Thompson (*Youngersford*), Harry Harvey Jr. (*Randall*), Bob Dix (*Grey*), Peter Miller (*Moran*), Roger McGee (*Lindstrom*), Richard Grant (*Silvers*), Morgan Jones (*Nichols*), Robby the Robot
P: Nicholas Nayfack   D: Fred McLeod Wilcox   SCR: Cyril Hume, from a story by Irving Block & Allen Adler   PHOTOG: George J. Folsey   SPCL-FX: Warren Newcombe, "Id Monster" created by Walt Disney Studios   ELECTRONIC MUSIC: Bebe & Louis Barron
"...justifiably considered one of the most imaginative and innovative genre pieces in that it intelligently employed elements of sci-fi literature instead of the action-adventure basics of competitive entries"—Gary Gerani, "The Space Monster Book—Chapter Seven: Visits to Hostile Planets," Monster Fantasy, Vol. 1, No. 4 (August, 1975), p. 40
Beautifully-produced, futuristic rendering of Shakespeare's play The Tempest: Astronauts travel to far planet, find scientist and daughter are all that remains of colonist party cf. The Invisible Boy

The Forbidden Street
1949, (GB), 20th-Fox, b&w, 91 mins.
W: Dana Andrews, Maureen O'Hara
D: Jean Negulesco
UK title: Britannia Mews A.k.a. The Affairs of Adelaide
Standard thriller

Forbidden World
1982, (USA), New World, color, 82 mins.
W: Jesse Vint (*Mike Colby*), Dawn Dunlap (*Tracy Baxter*), June Chadwick (*Dr. Barbara Glasser*), Linden Chiles (*Dr. Gordon Hauser*), Fox Harris (*Dr. Cal Tinbergen*), Michael Bowen (*Jimmy Swift*), Scott Paulin (*Earl Richards*), Don Olivera (*SAM-104*), Raymond Oliver (*Brian*)
P: Roger Corman   D: Allan Holzman   SCR: Tim Curnen   STORY: Jim Wynorski & R.J. Robertson   PHOTOG: Tim Suhrstedt   MUSIC: Susan Justin
Standard SF-horror, predictable Alien imitation: Escaped mutant prowls space outpost

Forbidden Zone
1980, (USA), color, 75 mins.
W: Herve Villechaize, Susan Tyrrell, Viva   D: Richard Elfman   SCR: Matthew Bright & Richard Elfman   MUSIC: Danny Elfman
Minor fantasy: Midget rules 6th-dimension kingdom

Forbidden Zone: Alien Abduction
1996, (USA), color, 90 mins.
W: Darcy DeMoss, Pia Reyes, Dimitri Bogmaz, Carmen Lacatus, Alina Chivulescu, Florin Chiriac, Meredyth Holmes
D: Lucian S. Diamonde   SCR: Vernon Lumley   PHOTOG: Adolfo Bartoli   MUSIC: Reg Powell
A.k.a. Alien Abduction: Intimate Secrets
Made-for-Video, minor SF-"jiggle": Three girls have sex with space alien

The Forbin Project
see Colossus: The Forbin Project

The Force Beyond
1978, (USA), Film Ventures, color
D: William Sachs
Minor SF-thriller: Humans disappear from Earth

The Forced Confession
1912, (GB), Clarendon, b&w, 1,150 ft. (350.5m)
W: Dorothy Bellew (*Irene Mannering*)
D: Wilfred Noy
Standard thriller: French professor uses hypnosis and filmed reconstruction to force confession from servant

A Force of One
1980, (USA), American Cinema Releasing, color, 91 mins.
W: Chuck Norris, Clu Gulager, Jennifer O'Neill, James Whitmore Jr., Ron O'Neal, Bill Wallace, Clint Ritchie, Eric Laneuville, Pepe Serna, Ray Vitte, Taylor Lacher, Chu Chu Malave, Kevin Geer, Eugene Butler, James Hall, Charles Cyphers
P: Alan Belkin   D: Paul Aaron   SCR: Ernest Tidyman   STORY: Pat Johnson & Ernest Tidyman   PHOTOG: Roger Shearman   MUSIC: Dick Halligan
Minor thriller: Narcotics agents slain by karate killer

The Force on Thunder Mountain
1977, (USA), American Nat'l, color, 93 mins.
W: Christopher Cain (*Father*), Todd Dutson (*Rick*), Borge West, David Fogg, James Lyle Strong
D: Peter B. Good
Minor SF-adventure: Eerie phenomena beset campers

Forces Occultes (Occult Forces)
1943, (Fr), Nova, b&w
W: Maurice Remy, Giselle Parry, Marcel Vibert, Boverio, Henri Valbel, Marcel Raine, Leonce Corne, Darteuil
D: Paul Riche   ORIG. SCR: Jean Marques-Riviere   MUSIC: Jean Martinon
Standard thriller, World War II anti-Masonic propaganda: Frenchman infiltrates sinister brotherhood

For East is East
1913, (GB), Martin Films/Winik, b&w, 3,300 ft. (1005.8m)
W: Wingold Lawrence (*The Captain*)
D: Dave Aylott
USA retitle, In the Python's Den
Standard thriller: Hindu prince captures soldier's wife, throws husband into python pit

Foreign Correspondent
1940, (USA), UA, b&w, 120 mins.
W: Joel McCrea, Laraine Day, George Sanders, Edmund Gwenn, Albert Bassermann, Herbert Marshall, Harry Davenport, Barbara Pepper, Robert Benchley, Eduardo Ciannelli, Martin Kosleck
P: Walter Wanger   D: Alfred Hitchcock, from Vincent Sheean's novel *Personal History*   PHOTOG: Rudolph Maté   MUSIC: Alfred Newman
Classic adventure-thriller: Danger in war-torn Europe

Foreign Intrigue
1956, (USA), UA, color, 106 mins.
W: Robert Mitchum, Genevieve Page, Ingrid Thulin, Frederick O'Brady
WRIT, P & D: Sheldon Reynolds
Standard thriller (inspired by popular teleseries): Man seeks cause of employer's death

The Foreign Spies
see Detective Finn and the Foreign Spies

The Foreign Spy
1911, (GB), Hepworth, b&w, 600 ft. (182.9m)
W: Flora Morris (*Mabel*)
D: Bert Haldane
Standard thriller: Girl escapes from French spies, saves sailor tied in sea

The Foreign Spy
1913, (GB), Cricks & Martin, b&w, 940 ft. (286.5m)
W: Jack Leigh (*Henkel*)
D: Charles Calvert
Standard thriller: Spy poses as artist, seeks gun plans

The Foreman's Treachery
1914, (GB), Edison, b&w

F

W: Marc McDermott (*David Llewellyn*), Miriam Nesbitt (*Anna Lloyd*), Charles Vernon (*Griffith*), Douglas Munro (*Mr. Lloyd*)
D: Charles Brabin   STORY: Anne & Bannister Merwin
Standard crime-thriller: Welsh halfwit sees foreman kill copper mine owner

The Forest
1983, (USA), color, 90 mins.
D: Donald M. Jones
Minor thriller: Spooks and killer-cannibal terrorize campers

Forest of Fear
see Bloodeaters

The Forest Primeval
see The Final Terror

Forever
1993, (USA), color, 93 mins.
W: Sean Young Keith Coogan, Diane Ladd, Sally Kirkland, Terence Knox, Nicholas Guest, Steve Railsback, Renee Taylor
D & SCR: Thomas Palmer Jr.
Standard fantasy: Ghostly seductress inhabits home of music-video director

Forever Evil
1987, (USA), B&S Prods./United Home Video, color, 120 mins.
W: Red Mitchell (*Marc*), Tracey Huffman (*Reggie*), Charles Trotter (*Leo*), Kent Johnson (*Alphie*), Howard Jacobsen (*Nash*), Diane Johnson (*Holly*), Jeffrey Lane (*Jay*), Karen Chatfield (*Jeanne*), David Campbell (*Robert*), Susan Lunt (*Julie*), Marcy Bannor (*Lisa*), Richard Zamecki (*Peter*), Freeman Williams (*Ben*), Kayce Glasse (*Mrs. Weinberger*), Richard Hamner (*Fred*), Polly MacIntyre (*Ms. Cranmeyer*), Natalie Williams (*The Nurse*), James Ebdon (*Policeman #1*), Dana Ryder (*Policeman #2*), Barbara Williams (*The Line Server*), Jon Cox (*The Detective*), Maylon Zerbe, Steven Gore, Paula Marier, Kurt Strans, Daniel Woods, Emmanuel Ikpeama, William Stockham, Kenneth Hamilton, Lois Stover, Itala Azzarelli, Letitia Hunt, Gloria Chubb, Gertrude Maze, William Ford, Ernest Williams, Mildred Clark, Cleofe Santiago, Sandra Chudzinski, Jessy Whittington
Made-for-Video, minor horror-fantasy: Human sacrifices to supernatural being

Forever Young
1992, (USA), WB, color, 104 mins.
W: Mel Gibson (*Daniel*), Jamie Lee Curtis (*Claire*), Elijah Wood (*Nat*), Isabel Glasser (*Helen*), George Wendt (*Harry*), Joe Morton (*Cameron*), Nicolas Surovy (*John*), Robert Hy Gorman (*Felix*), David Marshall Grant (*Wilcox*), Veronica Lauren (*Alice*), Millie Slavin (*Susan Finley*), Eric Pierpoint (*Fred*), Michael Goorjian (*Steven*), Walt Goggins (*The Gate MP*), Art La Fleur (*Alice's Father*), Amanda Foreman (*Debbie*), Karla Tamburrelli (*Blanche*)
D: Steve Miner   SCR: Jeffrey Abrams   PHOTOG: Russell Boyd   MUSIC: Jerry Goldsmith
Standard SF-romance: Man revived after 50 years in suspended ani-mation

Forger of London
1961, (W. Ger.), b&w, 91 mins.
W: Eddi Arent, Viktor de Kowa, Karin Dor, Hellmut Lange, Robert Graf
D: Harald Reinl, from an Edgar Wallace story
Standard thriller: Scotland Yard vs. counterfeiting gang

Forging Ahead
1933, (GB), Harry Cohen/Fox, b&w, 49 mins.
W: Margot Grahame (*Crystal Grey*), Antony Holles (*Percival Custard*), Garry Marsh (*Hon. Horace Slimminger*), Clifford Heatherley (*Prof. Bowe*), Eliot Makeham (*Abraham Lombard*), Melville Cooper (*Smedley*), Edgar Norfolk (*Lt.-Col. Fair*), Edith Saville (*Lady Lev-erton*), George Turner (*Hamilton Fortescue*), Arthur Chesney (*Shutley*), Wallace Lupino (*The Furniture Man*), Gus Sharland (*Insp. Green*)
D: Norman Walker   SCR: Brandon Fleming, from K.R.G. Browne's novel *Easy Money*
Minor comedy-thriller: "Haunted house" is forgers' den

Forgotten
see Rip Van Winkle (1914)

Forgotten City of the Planet of the Apes
1974, (USA), 20th-Fox, Made for TV, color
W: Roddy McDowall (*Galen*), Ron Harper (*Alan*), James Naughton (*Ted*), William Smith (*Tolar*), Zina Bethune (*Arn*), John Hoyt (*Barlow*), Marc Singer (*Dalton*), Mark Lenard (*Urko*), Jackie Earle Haley (*Kraik*), Booth Colman (*Zaius*), Robert Phillips (*The Gorilla Captain*), Andy Albin, Eddie Fontaine, Nick Dimitri, Ron Stein, Jim Stader, Jon Lormer, Wayne Foster, Victor Kilian
D: Don McDougall & Bernard McEveety   SCR: Art Wallace & Robert Hamner, from characters created by Pierre Boulle   PHOTOG: Gerald Perry Finnerman   MUSIC: Lalo Schifrin & Earle Hagen   MUSIC SPRVSR: Lionel Newman
TVM, minor SF-adventure culled from 2 episodes of teleseries Planet of the Apes: Astronauts trapped in world of simian tyrants. cf. Back to the Planet of the Apes, Farewell to the Planet of the Apes, Treachery and Greed on the Planet of the Apes and Life, Liberty and Pursuit on the Planet of the Apes

For Heaven's Sake
1950, (USA), 20th-Fox, b&w, 92 mins.
W: Clifton Webb (*Charles*), Robert Cummings (*Jeff Bolton*), Joan Bennett (*Lydia*), Joan Blondell (*Daphne*), Harry von Zell (*Tex*), Edmund Gwenn (*Arthur*), Gigi Perreau (*Item*), Whit Bissell (*A Doctor*), Jack LaRue (*Tony*), Tommy Rettig (*Joe*), Dick Ryan (*Michael*), Charles Lane (*The Tax Agent*), Robert Kent (*Joe's Father*), Dorothy Neumann (*The Western Union Woman*), Ashmead Scott (*A Doctor*), Perc Launders (*The Doorman*), Albert Pollett (*A Waiter*), Sid Fields (*A Waiter*), Jack Daly, Bob Harlow, Richard Thorne
P: William Perlberg   WRIT & D: George Seaton, based on Harry Segall's stage play   PHOTOG: Lloyd Aherne   MUSIC: Alfred Newman
Sentimental fantasy: Angels visit Earth, rescue marriage

For Love and the Crown
1914, (GB), Anchor Films, b&w, 2,674 ft. (815m)
W: Lillian Hallows (*Queen Irene*)
Standard Ruritanian romance: Prince saves queen and crown jewels from rival prince

For Love...For Magic
see Per Amore...Per Magia

For Mother's Sake
1914, (GB), St. George and Dragon/Anglo-Spanish, b&w, 1,500 ft. (457.2m)
W: Harry Moss (*The Convict*), Evadne Moore (*The Mother*)
D: A. Ray
Standard crime-thriller: Convict escapes

Formula C-12/Beirut
1966, (W. Ger.), color
W: Frederick Stafford, Genevieve Cluny, Chris Howland
Minor thriller: Interpol agents must prevent destruction of Beirut

The Formula
1980, (USA), UA, color, 118 mins.
W: George C. Scott (*Barney Caine*), Marthe Keller (*Lisa*), Sir John Gielgud (*Dr. Esau*), Marlon Brando (*Adam Steiffel*), G.D. Spradlin (*Clements*), Beatrice Straight (*Kay Neeley*), John Van Dreelen (*Hans Lehman*), Ike Eisenmann (*Tony*), Robin Clarke (*Maj. Neeley*), Marshall Thompson (*The Geologist*), Dieter Schidor (*The Assassin*), Jan Niklas (*The Gestapo Captain*), Werner Kreindl (*Schellenberg*), Wolfgang Preiss (*Franz Tauber*), Calvin Jung (*Sgt. Yosuta*), Gerry Murphy (*The Chauffeur*), Alan North (*Nolan*), Ferdy Mayne (*Siebold*), David Byrd (*Obermann*), Francisco Prado (*Mendosa*)
WRIT & P: Steve Shagan, from his novel   D: John G. Avildsen   PHOTOG: James Crabe   MUSIC: Bill Conti
Standard thriller: Formula for synthetic fuel involves Nazi past and contemporary terrorism

Formula for a Murder
1985, (It), color, 89 mins.
W: Christina Nagy, David Warbeck, Rossano Brazzi
Minor thriller: Con artist weds paralyzed rich woman

The Forsaken
1913, (GB), Hepworth, b&w, 1,800 ft. (548.6m)
W: Flora Morris (*Mrs. Roberts*), Harry Royston (*Bill Roberts*), Harry Gilbey (*Mr. Gilbey*), Ruby Belasco (*Mrs. Gilbey*), Eric Desmond (*Jack*)
D: Warwick Buckland   STORY: Muriel Alleyne
Standard crime-thriller: Ex-convict robs house of man who adopted his son

For the Crown of Asia
see Die Spinnen

For the Hand of a Princess
1904, (GB), Hepworth, b&w, 125 ft. (38.1m)
D: Lewin Fitzhamon
Minor adventure short: Knight battles baron, saves kidnapped princess

For Them That Trespass
1949, (GB), Stratford/ABPC, b&w, 95 mins.
W: Richard Todd (*Herb Logan*), Patricia Plunkett (*Rosie*), Stephen Murray (*Christopher Drew*), Rosalyn Boulter (*Frankie*), Michael Laurence (*Jim Heal*), Joan Dowling (*Gracie*), Mary Merrall (*Mrs. Drew*), Frederick Leister (*Mr. Drew*), Helen Cherry (*Mary Drew*), Michael Medwin (*Len Stevens*), Vida Hope (*Olive Mockson*), Harry Fowler (*Dave*), Valentine Dyall (*Sir Archibald*), Irene Handl (*Mrs. Sams*), James Hayter (*Jocko*), George Curzon (*Clark Hall*), Harcourt Williams (*The Judge*)
P: Victor Skatezky   D: Cavalcanti   SCR: J. Lee Thompson & William Douglas Home, from a novel by Ernest Raymond
Standard thriller: Ex-convict proves he did not kill tart

Fortress
1993, (USA-Austral), Davis Entertainment, color, 95 mins.
W: Christopher Lambert, Kurtwood Smith, Loryn Locklin, Clifton Gonzalez Gonzalez, Lincoln Kilpatrick, Jeffrey Combs, Tom Towles, Vernon Wells, Carolyn Purdy-Gordon, Alan Zitner, Denni Gordon, Eric Briant Wells, Dragicia Debert, Heidi Stein, Harry Nurmi, Peter Lamb, Sam Copping, Troy Hunter, Peter Marshall, Annika Thomas, Tracy Martin, Michael Simpson, Kiralee

P: John Davis & John Flock **D:** Stuart Gordon **SCR:** Troy Neighbors, Steven Feinberg, David Venable & Terry Curtis Fox **STORY:** Troy Neighbors & Steven Feinberg **PHOTOG:** David Eggby **SPCL VS-FX:** Praxis Film Works **SPCL-FX SPRVSR:** Tad Pride **MUSIC:** Frederic Talgorn
Standard SF-thriller: Couple trapped in prison of future

Fortess of Amerika
1989, (USA), color
W: Gene Le Brock, Kellee Bradley
Minor SF-thriller: Future mercenaries seek super-weapon

Fortunes of Captain Blood
1950, (USA), Col, b&w, 91 mins.
W: Louis Hayward, Patricia Medina
Standard adventure-thriller

Fortune is a Woman
1957, (GB), John Harvel/Col, b&w, 95 mins.
W: Jack Hawkins (*Oliver Branwell*), Arlene Dahl (*Sarah Morton*), Dennis Price (*Tracey Morton*), Greta Gynt (*Vera Lychen*), Ian Hunter (*Clive Fisher*), Violet Farebrother (*Mrs. Morton*), Bernard Miles (*Jerome*), Patrick Holt (*Fred Connor*), Malcolm Keen (*Abercrombie*), Geoffrey Keen (*Michael Abercrombie*), John Robinson (*Berkeley Reckitt*), Michael Goodliffe (*Sgt. Barnes*), Christopher Lee (*Charles Highbury*)
P: Frank Launder & Sidney Gilliat **D:** Sidney Gilliat **SCR:** Frank Launder, Sidney Gilliat & Val Valentine, from a novel by Winston Graham **MUSIC:** William Alwyn
*USA retitle, **She Played with Fire***
Standard crime-thriller: Insurance investigator probes arson

Fortunes of Captain Blood
W: George Macready, Terry Kilburn
D: Gordon Douglas, from a novel by Raphael Sabatini
Standard adventure-thriller: Irish doctor becomes pirate to avenge wrongdoing

48 Hours to Live
1959, (Swed), Cinema Associates/AIP, b&w, 86 mins.
W: Lewis Charles, Ingemar Johannsen, Anthony Steele, Ina Anders, Marlies Behrens
Minor thriller: Mankind faces last chance for survival

Forty Naughty Girls
1937, (USA), RKO, b&w, 63 mins.
W: James Gleason (*Oscar Piper*), ZaSu Pitts (*Hildegarde Withers*), Marjorie Lord (*June*), George Shelley (*Bert*), Joan Woodbury (*Rita*), Frank M. Thomas (*Jeff*), Barbara Pepper (*Alice*), Tom Kennedy (*Casey*), Ada Leonard (*Lil*), Alan Edwards (*Ricky*), Alden (*Stephen*) Chase (*Tommy*), Edward Marr (*Windy*)
D: Edward Cline **SCR:** John Gray, from characters created by Stuart Palmer **PHOTOG:** Russell Metty **MUSIC:** Roy Webb
Standard "Hildegarde Withers" mystery: Woman sleuth seeks press agent's killer

The 49th Man
1953, (USA), b&w, 73 mins.
W: John Ireland, Richard Denning, Suzanne Dalbert, Peter Marshall, Michael Connors
D: Fred F. Sears
Suspenseful programmer: Feds track spies smuggling A-bomb parts

49th Parallel
1941, (GB), Ortus Films/GFD/Col, b&w, 123 mins.
W: Leslie Howard (*Philip A. Scott*), Raymond Massey (*Andy Brock*), Laurence Olivier (*Johnnie*), Glynis Johns (*Anna*), Anton Walbrook (*Peter*), Eric Portman (*Lt. Hirth*), Niall MacGinnis (*Vogel*), Finlay Currie (*Factor*), John Chandos (*Lohrmann*), Raymond Lovell (*Lt. Kuhnecke*), Eric Clavering (*Art*), Basil Appleby (*Jahner*), Ley On (*Nick the Eskimo*), Charles Victor (*Andreas*), Richard George (*Bernsdorff*)
P: John Sutro & Michael Powell **D:** Michael Powell **SCR:** Emeric Pressburger & Rodney Ackland **STORY:** Emeric Pressburger (Academy Award winner) **PHOTOG:** Frederick A. Young **MUSIC:** Robert Vaughan Williams
*USA retitle, **The Invaders***
Superior thriller: U-boat crew tries to escape to USA from Canada

Forty Winks
1920, (GB), Thespian Prods., b&w, 2,000 ft. (609.6m)
W: Albert Rebla (*The Tramp*), Maud Lofting (*The Girl*), J. Edwards Barber (*The Policeman*), Fred Read (*A Chinaman*), Charles Leoville (*A Chinaman*), Pip Powell
D: Arthur Finn **STORY:** Robert Hargreaves
Standard comedy-fantasy: Hobo dreams of saving drowning girl

For You I Die
1947, (USA), Film Classics, b&w, 77 mins.
W: Cathy Downs, Paul Langton, Mischa Auer
Standard thriller

For Your Eyes Only
1981, (GB), Eon/UA, color, 127 mins.
W: Roger Moore (*James Bond*), Carole Bouquet (*Melina*), Topol (*Columbo*), Lynn-

Holly Johnson (*Bibi*), Julian Glover (*Kristatos*), Cassandra Harris (*Lisl*), Lois Maxwell (*Miss Moneypenny*), Desmond Llewelyn ("*Q*"), Jill Bennett (*Brink*), James Villiers (*Tanner*), Jack Hedley (*Havelock*), Geoffrey Keen (*Minister of Defense*), Toby Robins (*Iona Havelock*), Walter Gotell (*Gen. Gogol*), Michael Gothard (*Locque*), John Wyman (*Kriegler*), Janet Brown (*The Prime Minister*), John Wells (*Denis*), John Moreno (*Ferrara*), Charles Dance (*Claus*), Paul Angelis (*Karageorge*), Jack Klaff (*Apostis*), Alkis Kritikos (*Santos*), Stag Theodore (*Nikos*), Stefan Kalipha (*Gonzales*), Robin Young (*The Girl in the Flower Shop*), Graham Crowden (*First Sea Lord*), Eva Rueber-Staier (*Rublevich*), Noel Johnson (*The Vice Admiral*), William Hoyland (*McGregor*), Fred Bryant (*The Vicar*), Paul Brooke (*Bunky*), Graham Hawkes (*The Mantis Man*), Max Vesterhalt, Lalla Dean, Evelyn Drogue, Kim Mills, Laoura Hadzivageli, Koko, Chai Lee, Tula, Vanya, Viva, Lizzie Warville, Alison Worth
P: Albert R. Broccoli **D:** John Glen **SCR:** Richard Maibaum & Michael G. Wilson, from characters created by Ian Fleming **PHOTOG:** Alan Hume **SPCL-FX:** Paul Wilson **MUSIC:** Bill Conti, title song performed by Sheena Easton
Colorful thriller: British agent tracks top-secret sub

Le Fou Assassin (The Foolish Assassin)
1900, (Fr), Star, b&w, 25m (82 ft./1.4 mins.)
D: Georges Melies
*USA retitle, **The Dangerous Lunatic***
Standard thriller

Found Alive
1934, (USA), b&w, 65 mins.
W: Barbara Bedford, Maurice Murphy, Robert Frazer, Edwin Cross
D: Charles Hutchinson
Minor thriller: Divorced woman kidnaps son, flees to Mexican jungle

The Foundling
1913, (GB), All-British Films/Cosmo, b&w, 775 ft. (236.2m)
D: Ernest G. Batley **STORY:** Ethyle Batley
Standard crime-thriller: Usurper hires poachers to kill squire step-brother

4D Man
1959, (USA), Fairview/Univ, color, 85 mins.
W: Robert Lansing, Lee Meriwether, James Congdon, Robert Strauss, Guy Raymond, Jasper Deeter, Edgar Stehli, Dean Newman, Elbert Smith, Patty Duke, George Kayara, Chick James, Jack Tinsley
P: Jack H. Harris **D:** Irvin Shortess Yeaworth Jr. **SCR:** Theodore Simonson & Cy Chermak, from an orig. idea by Jack H. Harris **SPCL-FX:** Bart Sloane **MUSIC:** Ralph Carmichael
*reissued (1965) as **Master of Terror**, A.k.a. **The Evil Force***
Standard SF-thriller: Scientist electronically alters his body, is able to pass through solid matter

Four Flies on Grey Velvet
see Quatro Mosche di Velluto Gris

Four Frightened People
1934, (USA), Para, b&w, 78 mins.
W: Claudette Colbert, Herbert Marshall, William Gargan, Leo Carrillo, Mary Boland, Chris-Pin Martin, Tetsu Komai, Nella Walker, Ethel Griffies
P&D: Cecil B. DeMille **SCR:** Bartlett Cormack & Lenore Coffee, from a story by E. Arnot Robertson **PHOTOG:** Karl Struss **MUSIC:** Karl Hajos, et al. **ART DIR:** Roland Anderson
Unusual melodrama: Fleeing bubonic plague and cholera, four people stranded in Malaya jungle

Les 400 Farces du Diable (The Devil's 400 Farces)
1906, (Fr), Star, b&w, 323m (1,059.7 ft./17.9 mins.)
D: Georges Melies
*A.k.a. **The Merry Frolics of Satan***
Standard fantasy

Four Hours to Kill
1935, (USA), b&w, 71 mins.
W: Richard Barthelmess, Joe Morrison, Helen Mack, Gertrude Michael, Dorothy Tree, Ray Milland, Roscoe Karns, John Howard, Noel Madison, Charles Wilson, Mitchell Leisen
D: Mitchell Leisen **SCR:** Norman Krasna, from his play *Miracle*
Ingenious thriller: Escaped killer stalks stoolie in old vaudeville theater

The Four Nights of the Full Moon
see Las Cuatro Noches de la Luna Llena

Four Sided Triangle
1953, (GB), Assoc. Artists/Astor, b&w, 81 mins.
W: Barbara Payton (*Lena/Helen*), James Hayter (*Dr. Harvey*), Stephen Murray (*Bill*), John Van Eyssen (*Robin*), Jennifer Dearman (*Young Lena*), Glyn Dearman (*Young Bill*), Sean Barrett (*Young Robin*), Percy Marmont (*Sir Walter*), Kynaston Reeves (*Lord Grant*), John Stuart (*The Solicitor*), Leona Gage
P: Alexander Paal **D:** Terence Fisher **SCR:** Paul Tabori & Terence Fisher, from William F. Temple's novel **PHOTOG:** Reginald Wyer **MUSIC:** Malcolm Arnold

TV retitle, *The Monster and the Woman*
SF classic: Two scientists build duplicating machine, create double of girl they both love

The Four Skulls of Jonathan Drake
1959, (USA), Vogue/UA, b&w, 70 mins.
<u>W:</u> Eduard Franz, Valerie French, Henry Daniell, Grant Richards, Paul Cavanagh, Howard Wendell, Lumsden Hare
<u>P:</u> Robert E. Kent   <u>D:</u> Edward L. Cahn   <u>SCR:</u> Orville H. Hampton   <u>PHOTOG:</u> Maury Gertsman   <u>MUSIC:</u> Paul Dunlap
Standard horror-thriller: Doctor meets head-shrinker

14 Going on 30
1988, (USA), Disney-TV, color, 86 mins.
<u>W:</u> Steve Eckholdt, Patrick Duffy
TVM, standard SF-comedy: Aging machine enables teen to pursue teacher's affections

Fourteen Hours
1951, (USA), 20th-Fox, b&w, 92 mins.
<u>W:</u> Paul Douglas, Richard Basehart, Grace Kelly, Jeffrey Hunter, Agnes Moorehead
<u>D:</u> Henry Hathaway   <u>SCR:</u> John Paxton   <u>PHOTOG:</u> Joe MacDonald   <u>MUSIC:</u> Alfred Newman
Modest thriller: Disturbed man sways on hotel ledge

The Fourth Man
1984, (Belg), De Verenigde Nederlandsche Filmcompagnie/Spectrafilm/Mainline color, 104 mins.
<u>W:</u> Jeroen Krabbe, Rene Soutendijk Thom Hoffman, Dolf De Vries, Geert De Jong, Hans Veerman, Hero Muller, Caroline De Beus, Reinout Bussemaker, Erik J. Meijer, Ursul De Geer, Filip Bolluyt, Hedda Lornie, Paul Nygaard, Guus van der Made, Pamela Teves, Hella Faassen, Helen Hedy
<u>D:</u> Paul Verhoeven   <u>SCR:</u> Gerard Soeteman, from Gerard Reve's novel   <u>PHOTOG:</u> Jan De Bont   <u>MUSIC:</u> Loek Dikker
Unusual thriller: Bisexual involved with female Bluebeard

The Fourth Musketeer
1923, (USA), b&w, 5,800 ft. (1,767.8m)
<u>D:</u> William K. Howard, from characters created by Alexander Dumas
<u>PHOTOG:</u> L. William O'Connell
Standard adventure-thriller

The Fourth Protocol
1987, (GB), Lorimar, color, 110 mins.
<u>W:</u> Michael Caine, Pierce Brosnan, Joanna Cassidy, Julian Glover, Michael Gough, Ned Beatty, Betsy Brantley, Peter Cartwright, David Conville, Matt Frewer, Ray McAnally, Ian Richardson, Anton Rodgers
<u>D:</u> John MacKenzie   <u>SCR:</u> Frederick Forsythe, from his novel   <u>PHOTOG:</u> Phil Meheux   <u>MUSIC:</u> Lalo Schifrin

Standard thriller: Soviet agent sent to detonate A-bomb in Britain

The Fourth Square
1961, (GB), Merton Park/Anglo-Amalgamated, b&w, 57 mins.
<u>W:</u> Conrad Phillips (*Bill Lawrence*), Natasha Parry (*Sandra Martin*), Delphi Lawrence (*Nina Stewart*), Paul Daneman (*Henry Adams*), Miriam Karlin (*Josetta Alvarez*), Jacqueline Jones (*Marie Labonne*), Anthony Newlands (*Tom Alvarez*), Harold Kasket (*Philippe*)
<u>P:</u> Jack Greenwood   <u>D:</u> Allan Davis   <u>SCR:</u> James Eastwood, from Edgar Wallace's novel *Square*
Standard crime-thriller: Lawyer unmasks playboy's ex-wife as murderous gem thief

The Four Troublesome Heads
1898, (Fr), Star, b&w, 20m (65.6 ft./1.1 mins.)
<u>D:</u> Georges Melies
Standard fantasy: Magician removes his head

The Fox and the Hound
1981, (USA), Walt Disney, color, 83 mins.
<u>VOICES:</u> Mickey Rooney, Kurt Russell, Pearl Bailey, Sandy Duncan, Jack Albertson, Jeanette Nolan, Pat Buttram John Fiedler, John McIntire, Paul Winchell, Dick Bakalyan, Keith Mitchell, Corey Feldman
<u>D:</u> Art Stevens, Ted Berman & Richard Rich   <u>SCR:</u> Art Stevens, Peter Young, Steve Hulett, Earl Kress, Vance Gerry, Larry Clemmons, Dave Michener & Burny Mattinson   <u>MUSIC:</u> Buddy Baker
Standard animated fantasy: Puppy and orphaned fox become friends

F.P. 1 Antwortet Nicht (F.P. 1 Does Not Reply)
1933, (GB-Ger), Ufa, b&w, 93 mins.
<u>W:</u> Conrad Veidt (*Elissen*), Leslie Fenton (*Droste*), Jill Esmond (*Claire Lennartz*), George Merritt, Donald Calthrop (*The Photographer*), Nicholas Hannen (*Matthias*), William Freshman (*Conrad*), Alexander Field (*A Sailor*), Warwick Ward (*The Officer*), Francis L. Sullivan (*A Sailor*), Peter Lorre, Hans Albers, Sybille Schmitz, Herman Speelmans, Paul Hartmann
<u>P:</u> Erich Pommer   <u>D:</u> Karl Hartl   <u>SCR:</u> Curt Siodmak, Walter Reisch, Robert Stevenson, & Peter Macfarlane, from Curt Siodmak's novel   <u>PHOTOG:</u> Gunther Rittau & Konstantin Tschetwerikoff
reissued (1938) as Secrets of F.P. 1
Futuristic classic: Dire events on floating oceanic platform

Fragment of Fear
1969, (GB), Col, color, 96 mins.
<u>W:</u> David Hemmings (*Tom Brett*), Gayle Hunnicutt (*Juliet*), Wilfrid Hyde-White (*Mr. Copsey*), Flora Robson (*Lucy Dawson*), Adolfo Celi (*Bardoni*), Daniel Massey (*Maj. Ricketts*), Mona Washbourne (*Mrs. Gray*), Roland Culver (*Mr. Vellacot*), Mary Wimbush ("*Bunface*"), Bernard Archard (*The Priest*), Glynn Edwards (*The C.I.D. Superintendent*), Derek Newark (*Sgt. Matthews*), Arthur Lowe (*Mr. Nugent*), Yootha Joyce (*Mrs. Ward-Cadbury*), Patricia Hayes (*Mrs.*

Frankenstein (1931): BORIS KARLOFF AND MAE CLARKE

Baird), Massimo Sarchielli (Mario), John Rae (Uncle Stanley), Angelo Infanti (Bruno), Hilda Barry (Miss Dacey), Philip Stone (The C.I.D. Sgt.), Edward Kemp (Kenny), Kenneth Cranham (Joe), Michael Rothwell (Rocky), Kurt Christian (Nino), Richard Kerr (The Pop Singer), Jessica Dublin, Louise Cambert, Georgina Moon, Petra Markham, Lois Hyett
D: Richard Sarafian   SCR: Paul Dehn, from a novel by John Bingham
   PHOTOG: Oswald Morris   MUSIC: Johnny Harris
Standard mystery-melodrama: Ex-drug addict investigates aunt's murder in Italy

Framed
1947, (USA), Col, b&w, 82 mins.
W: Glenn Ford, Janis Carter, Barry Sullivan Edgar Buchanan, Karen Morley
D: Richard Wallace   SCR: Ben Maddow
Standard thriller: Innocent man mistaken for robber

Francis
1950, (USA), Univ, b&w, 90 mins.
W: Donald O'Connor (Peter Stirling), Patricia Medina (Maureen Gelder), ZaSu Pitts (Valerie Humpert), Robert Warwick (Col. Carmichael), Ray Collins (Col. Hooker), John McIntire (Gen. Stevens), Eduard Franz (Col. Plepper), Tony Curtis (Capt. Jones), Howland Chamberlin (Maj. Nadel), James Todd (Col. Saunders), Frank Faylen (Sgt. Chillingbacker), Mikel Conrad (Maj. Garber), Loren Tindall (Maj. Richards), Charles Meredith (Banker Munroe). Chill Wills (Voice of Francis)
P: Robert Arthur   D: Arthur Lubin   SCR: David Stern, from his novel
   PHOTOG: Irving Glassberg   MUSIC: Frank Skinner
Modest comedy-fantasy: Talking mule discovered

Francis Covers the Big Town
1953, (USA), Univ, b&w, 86 mins.
W: Donald O'Connor (Peter Stirling), Nancy Guild (Alberta Ames), William Harrigan (Chief Hansen), Gene Lockhart (Tom Henderson), Yvette Dugay (Maria Scola), Silvio Minciotti (Salvatore Scola), Gale Gordon (Evans), Lowell Gilmore (Evans), Larry Gates, Chill Wills (Voice of Francis)
P: Leonard Goldstein   D: Arthur Lubin   SCR: Oscar Brodney, from characters created by David Stern   PHOTOG: Carl Guthrie   MUSIC: Joseph Gershenson
Standard comedy-fantasy: Talking mule meets gangsters

Francis Goes to the Races
1951, (USA), Univ, b&w, 88 mins.
W: Donald O'Connor (Peter Stirling), Piper Laurie (Frances), Cecil Kellaway (Travers), Jesse White (Damer), Barry Kelley (Mallory), Hayden Rorke, Larry Keating, Vaughn Taylor
P: Leonard Goldstein   D: Arthur Lubin   SCR: David Stern & Oscar Brodney, from characters created by David Stern   PHOTOG: Irving Glassberg   MUSIC: Frank Skinner
Standard comedy-fantasy: Talking mule gets racing tips from equine relatives

Francis Goes to West Point
1952, (USA), Univ, b&w, 81 mins.
W: Donald O'Connor (Peter Stirling), Lori Nelson (Barbara Atwood), William Reynolds (Wilbur Van Allen), Alice Kelley (Cynthia Daniels), Les Tremayne (Col. Daniels), Palmer Lee (Greg Palmer) (William Norton), James Best (Cpl. Ransom), Otto Hulett, Paul Burke, Chill Wills (Voice of Francis)
P: Leonard Goldstein   D: Arthur Lubin   SCR: Oscar Brodney, from characters created by David Stern   PHOTOG: Carl Guthrie   MUSIC: Joseph Gershenson
Standard comedy-fantasy: Talking mule and master become heroes in sabotage plot, end up at West Point

Francis in the Haunted House
1956, (USA), Univ, b&w, 80 mins.
W: Mickey Rooney (David Prescott), Paul Cavanagh (Neil Frazer), Virginia Welles (Lorna), James Flavin (Chief Martin), Mary Ellen Kaye (Lorna Ann), Richard Deacon (Jason), Dick Winslow (Sgt. Arnold), David Janssen (Lt. Hopkins), Charles Horvath (Malcolm), Richard Gaines (D.A. Reynolds), Helen Wallace (Mrs. MacPherson), Ralph Dumke (Mayor Hargrove), Timothy Carey (Hugo), Paul Trees (Voice of Francis)
P: Robert Arthur   D: Charles Lamont   SCR: Herbert Margolis & William Raynor, from characters created by David Stern   PHOTOG: George Robinson
Standard comedy-fantasy (mercifully, last film in "Francis" series): Talking mule and friend find murder and mystery in old Scottish castle

Francis in the Navy
1955, (USA), Univ, b&w, 80 mins.
W: Donald O'Connor (Peter Stirling), Martha Hyer (Betsy Donevan), Jim Backus (Cmdr. Hutch), Myrna Hansen (Helen), Leigh Snowden (Appleby), Richard Erdman (Murph), Martin Milner (Rick), David Janssen (Lt. Anders), Phil Garris (Stover), Clint Eastwood (Jonesy), Betty Jane Howarth (Standish), Paul Burke (Tate), Chill Wills (Voice of Francis)
P: Stanley Rubin   D: Arthur Lubin   SCR: Devery Freeman, from characters created by David Stern   PHOTOG: Carl Guthrie   MUSIC: Joseph Gershenson
Standard comedy-fantasy: Talking mule causes nautical confusion

Francis Joins the Wacs
1954, (USA), Univ, b&w, 94 mins.

W: Donald O'Connor (Peter Stirling), Julia Adams (Capt. Parker), Mamie Van Doren (Bunky), Chill Wills (Gen. Kaye/Voice of Francis), ZaSu Pitts (Lt. Humpert), Lynn Bari (Maj. Simpson), Karen Kadler (Marge), Allison Hayes (Lt. Dickson), Elsie Holmes (Bessie), Mara Corday (Kate), Joan Shawlee
P: Ted Richmond   D: Arthur Lubin   SCR: Devery Freeman & James B. Allardice, from characters created by David Stern   PHOTOG: Irving Glassberg   MUSIC: Joseph Gershenson
Standard comedy-fantasy: Talking mule's master mistakenly sent back into armed service— as WAC recruit

Frankenhooker
1990, (USA), Shapiro Glickenhaus, color, 86 mins.
W: James Lorinz (Jeffrey Franken), Patty Mullen (Elizabeth/Frankenhooker), Louise Lasser (Jeffrey's Mother), Lia Chang (Crystal), Charlotte Helmkamp (Honey), Vicki Darnell (Sugar), Sandy Colosimo (Monkey), Jennifer DeLora (Angel), Gittan Goding (Snow), Heather Hunter (Chartreuse), Shirley Stoler (Spike the Bartender), Stephanie Ryan (Anise), Kimberly Taylor (Amber), Joanne Ritchie (Mrs. Shelley), J.J. Clark (Mr. Shelley), Carissa Channing (Dolores), Tom Hair (Motormouth), Shirl Bernheim (Elizabeth's Grandmother), Judy Grafe (The Newscaster), Helmar Cooper (Det. Anderson), John Zacherle (The Weatherman), Joseph Gonzalez (Zorro), Ari Roussimoff (Zorro's Customer), Beverly Bonner (Casey), Max Brandt (The Desk Clerk), James Smythe (The Times Square Businessman), Gregory Gilbert (Times Square Victim #2), David Lipman (Frankenhooker's Trick), Eivind Harum, Thomas Crognale, Kathi Gati, Sonya Hensley, Dominic Marcus, Alan Pratt, Paul-Felix Montez, Jan Saint
P: Edgar Ievins   D: Frank Henenlotter   SCR: Robert Martin & Frank Henenlotter   PHOTOG: Robert M. Baldwin   SPCL VS-FX: Al Magliochetti   MUSIC: Joe Renzetti   SONGS:, Never Say No, Pandora's Box, & Love Handgrenade
Standard horror-satire: Scientist creates immoral woman

The Franken Project
see Doctor Franken

Frankenstein
1910, (USA), Edison, b&w, 975 ft. (297.2m/1 reel) 16 mins.
W: Charles Ogle (The Monster)
D: J. Searle Dawley, based on Mary W. Shelley's novel
Standard horror-fantasy: Man-made human is mirror of scientist's baser nature

Frankenstein
1931, (USA), Univ, b&w, 71 mins.
W: Colin Clive (Henry Frankenstein), Boris Karloff (The Monster), Mae Clarke (Elizabeth), John Boles (Victor), Edward Van Sloan (Dr. Waldmann), Dwight Frye (Fritz), Frederick Kerr (The Old Baron Frankenstein), Lionel Belmore (The Burgomeister), Marilyn Harris (Little Maria), Otis Harlan
P: Carl Laemmle Jr.   D: James Whale   SCR: Garrett Fort, Francis Edwards Faragoh & Robert Florey, from a story by Peggy Webling, based on Mary W. Shelley's novel   PHOTOG: Arthur Edeson
"From its opening sequence in a graveyard, the film carefully builds up to the first appearance of the Monster; never was Karloff more impressive than in this his first entrance"—Carlos Clarens, An Illustrated History of the Horror Film
Classic horror-fantasy: Scientist creates life from dead

Frankenstein
1972, (It-W. Ger), color, 88 mins.
W: John Richardson, Gordon Mitchell, Leila Parker, Dado Galloti, Marisa Travers
D: Mario Mancini
Minor horror-thriller: Man-made monster goes on gory killing spree

Frankenstein
1973, (USA), Dan Curtis, color, 130 mins.
W: Robert Foxworth, Bo Svenson, Susan Strasberg, Willie Aames
D: Glenn Jordan, from Mary W. Shelley's novel
TVM, well-made horror-thriller: Scientist unleashes monster

Frankenstein
1974, (It-W. Ger-USA), Carlo Ponti-Braunsberg-Rassam/Bryanston/Paul Morrissey/Andy Warhol, 3D, color, 95 mins.
W: Joe Dallesandro (The Field Hand), Monique Van Vooren (The Baroness), Udo Keir (Baron Frankenstein), Dalila Di Lazzaro (The Girl Zombie), Arno Juerging (The Baron's Assistant), Srdjan Zelenovic (The Farmer), Carla Mancini (The Daughter), Marco Liofredi (The Son), Liu Bozizio (The Maid)
WRIT & D: Paul Morrissey, from Mary W. Shelley's novel   PHOTOG: Luigi Kuveiller   MUSIC: Claudio Gizzi
A.k.a. Flesh for Frankenstein
"The goriest and sexiest 'Frankenstein' ever filmed" Kevin Sanders, ABC-TV
"Instantly achieves top rank as the most outrageously gruesome epic ever unleashed upon a public always hungry for fashionable kicks... Incurable horror addicts can get a fix from Morrissey"—Playboy
Erotic horror-satire: Venal scientist creates life

Frankenstein
1984, (GB), Elm-Group W Cable-Wester World TV/Yorkshire TV Ltd., color, 81 mins.
W: Robert Powell (Victor Frankenstein), David Warner (The Creature), Carrie Fisher (Elizabeth), Terence Alexander (Alphonse Frankenstein), John Gielgud (De Lacey), Susan Wooldridge (Justine), Michael Cochrane (Henry Clerval), Graham McGrath (William Frankenstein), Edward Judd (Metz), James Coyle (Scholz), Arnold Peters (Busch), Roberta Taylor (Gerta)

D: James Ormerod **TELEPLAY:** Victor Gialanella, from Mary W. Shelley's novel **PHOTOG:** Stuart Hinchliffe **MUSIC:** Alan Parker
Made-for-Cable, minor horror-fantasy: Scientist creates man

Frankenstein
1993, (USA-GB), TNT-TV, color 117 mins.
W: Patrick Bergin, Randy Quaid, John Mills, Lambert Wilson, Fiona Gillies, Alan Bates, Jacinta Mulcahy, Ronald Leigh Hunt, Timothy Stark, Michael Gothard
D & TELEPLAY: David Wickes, from Mary W. Shelley's novel **SPCL-FX SPRVSR:** Graham Longhurst
TVM, opulent horror-fantasy: Nobleman creates life

Frankenstein (1994)
see Mary Shelley's Frankenstein

Frankenstein and Me
1996, (Can), color, 95 mins.
W: Jamieson Boulanger, Burt Reynolds (*Les Williams*), Louise Fletcher (*Mrs. Perdue*)
D: Robert Tinnell
Standard fantasy: Boy attempts to reanimate dummy of Frankenstein's monster

Frankenstein and the Monster from Hell
1974, (GB), Hammer/Para, color, 93 mins.
W: Peter Cushing ("*Dr. Karl Victor*"/*Baron Frankenstein*), Shane Briant (*Dr. Simon Helder*), Madeline Smith (*Sarah*), Dave Prowse (*The Monster*), John Stratton (*The Asylum Director*), Elsie Wagstaff (*The Wild One*), Michael Ward (*Transvest*), Norman Mitchell (*The Sergeant*), Lucy Griffiths (*The Hag*), Clifford Mollison (*The Judge*), Patrick Troughton (*The Body Snatcher*), Chris Cunningham (*Hans*), Philip Voss (*Ernst*), Charles Lloyd-Pack (*Prof. Durendel*), Bernard Lee (*Tarmut*), Jerold Wells (*The Landlord*), Sydney Bromley (*Muller*), Janet Hargreaves (*Chatter*), Sheila D'Union (*Gerda*), Mischa de la Motte (*Twitch*), Winifred Sabine (*Mouse*), Norman Atkyns (*Smiler*), Andrea Lawrence, Victor Woolf, Peter Madden
P: Roy Skeggs **D:** Terence Fisher **SCR:** John Elder [Anthony Hinds] **PHOTOG:** Brian Probyn **SPL-FX:** Les Bowie **MUSIC:** James Bernard **MUSIC SPRVSR:** Philip Martell
Standard horror-thriller: Good Doctor creates new monster while in prison for criminally insane

Frankenstein Conquers the World
see Frankenstein vs. the Giant Devil Fish

Frankenstein Created Woman
1966, (GB), Hammer-7Arts/20th-Fox, color, 86 mins.
W: Peter Cushing (*Baron Frankenstein*), Susan Denberg (*Christina Kleve*), Robert Morris (*Hans Werner*), Thorley Walters (*Dr. Hertz*), Barry Warren (*Karl*), John Maxim (*The Police Sgt.*), Derek Fowlds (*Johann*), Peter Blythe (*Anton*), Kevin Flood (*The Gaoler*), Philip Ray (*The Mayor*), Duncan Lamont (*The Prisoner*), Peter Madden (*The Police Chief*), Alan MacNaughton (*Kleve*), Bartlett Mullins
P: Anthony Nelson Keys **D:** Terence Fisher **SCR:** John Elder [Anthony Hinds] **PHOTOG:** Arthur Grant **SPCL-FX:** Les Bowie **MUSIC:** James Bernard
Standard horror-fantasy: Doctor transforms ugly, crippled girl into raving beauty with homicidal tendencies

Frankenstein '88
see The Vindicator

Frankenstein is Escaping
see The Curse of Frankenstein

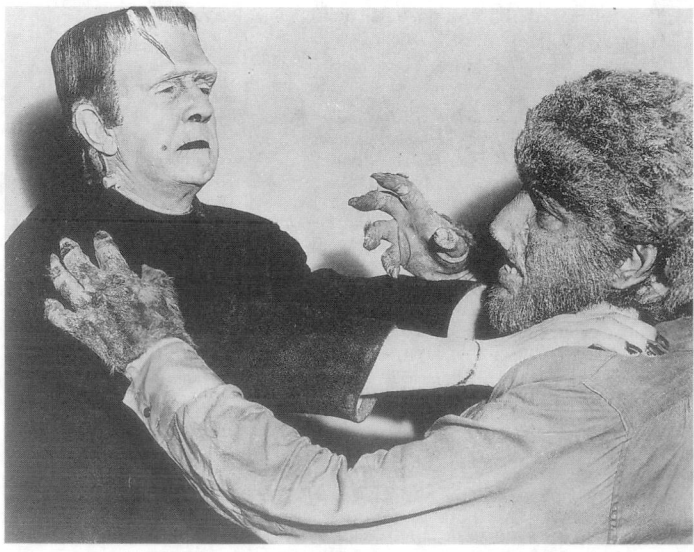

Frankenstein Meets the Wolf Man: BELA LUGOSI and LON CHANEY Jr.

Frankenstein General Hospital
1988, (USA), color, 90 mins.
W: Mark Blankfield, Kathy Shower, Leslie Jordan, Irwin Keyes
D: Deborah Roberts
Minor horror-spoof: Infamous scientist's 12th grandson conducts unorthodox experiments

Frankenstein Island
1981, (USA), Chriswar/Jerry Warren, color, 96 mins.
W: Robert Clarke, Steve Brodie, Cameron Mitchell (*Jayson*), John Carradine (*Dr. Frankenstein*), Andrew Duggn (*The Colonel*), Robert Christopher, Tain Bodkin, George Mitchell, Patrick O'Neil, Kathrin Victor, Dana Norbeck, James Webb, Laurel Johnson, Richard Banks, Marla Conner, Donna Green, Vic Schneider
P & D: Jerry Warren **SCR:** Jacques Lacouter **PHOTOG:** Murray De Ately **MUSIC DIR:** Erich Bromberg
Minor horror-hokum: Balloonists wrecked on remote isle—find nature girls, zombie slaves and mad scientists

Frankenstein Meets the Space Monster
1965, (USA), Futuramic/AA, b&w, 78 mins.
W: Jim Karen, David Kerman, Nancy Marshall, Robert Reilly, Marilyn Hanold, Lou Cutell
D: Robert Gaffney **SCR:** George Garret **SONGS:** That's the Way It's Got to Be
*GB retitle, **Duel of the Space Monsters**, A.k.a. **Mars Invades Puerto Rico***
Minor SF-fantasy: Android saves his inventors from invading space creatures

Frankenstein Meets the Wolf Man
1943, (USA), Univ, b&w, 73 mins.
W: Ilona Massey (*Baroness Elsa von Frankenstein*), Patric Knowles (*Dr. Frank Mannering*), Lon Chaney Jr. (*Larry Talbot, the Wolfman*), Bela Lugosi (*The Frankenstein Monster*), Maria Ouspenskaya (*Maleva*), Lionel Atwill (*The Mayor*), Dennis Hoey (*Insp. Owen*), Dwight Frye (*Rudi*), Doris Lloyd (*The Nurse*), Rex Evans, Don Barclay, Harry Stubbs, Jeff Corey [uncredited], Martha MacVicar (*Vickers*)
P: George Waggner **D:** Roy William Neill **SCR:** Curt Siodmak **PHOTOG:** George Robinson **MUSIC:** Hans Salter
Entertaining horror-fest (sequel to both 'The Wolf Man' {1941} and 'The Ghost of Frankenstein'): Lycanthrope pursues secrets of Dr. Frankenstein so he may end his deathless existence

Frankenstein Must Be Destroyed
1969, (GB), Hammer/WB-7Arts, color, 97 mins.
W: Peter Cushing (*Baron Frankenstein*), Veronica Carlson (*Anna Stengler*), Simon Ward (*Karl*), Thorley Walters (*The Inspector*), Freddie Jones (*Dr. Richter*), Maxine Audley (*Mrs. Brant*), George Pravda (*Dr. Frederick Brant*), Geoffrey Bayldon (*The Police Doctor*), Colette O'Neil (*The Mad Woman*), Harold Goodwin (*The Burglar*), Peter Copley (*The Principal*)
P: Anthony Nelson Keys **D:** Terence Fisher **SCR:** Bret Batt **STORY:** Anthony Nelson Keys & Bret Batt **PHOTOG:** Arthur Grant **MUSIC:** James Bernard **DESIGN:** Bernard Robinson
Literate, low-key horror-thriller: Desiring cryogenic secrets, Baron Frankenstein engineers deranged scientist's escape from asylum

Frankenstein—1970
1958, (USA), AA, b&w, 83 mins.
W: Boris Karloff (*Baron Victor von Frankenstein*), Charlotte Austin, Jana Lund (*Carolyn*), Donald Barry (*Row*), Tom Duggan (*Shaw*), Irwin Berke, John Dennis, Rudolph Anders, Norbert Schiller, Mike Lane (*Hans/The Monster*)
P: Aubrey Schenck **D:** Howard W. Koch **SCR:** Richard Landau & George Worthington Yates **PHOTOG:** Carl Guthrie **MUSIC:** Paul Dunlap
Ger retitle, The Devil's Laboratory of Dr. Rambow
orig. co-billed with Spy in the Sky
Standard horror-thriller: Last member of Frankenstein family tries to reproduce his famous ancestor's experiment in creating life

Frankenstein—1980
1972, (It), color
Minor horror-thriller

Frankenstein's Bloody Horror
see Dracula vs. Frankenstein

Frankenstein's Bloody Terror (1968)
see Dracula vs. Frankenstein

Frankenstein's Bloody Terror (1969)
see La Marca del Hombre Lobo

Frankenstein's Castle of Freaks
see El Castello dell'Orrore

Frankenstein's Daughter
1958, (USA), Layton/Astor, b&w, 85 mins.
W: John Ashley, Sandra Knight, Donald Murphy, Sally Todd, Wolfe Barzell, Harold Lloyd Jr., Robert Dix, Felix Locher, John Zaremba, Harry Wilson, Voltaire Perkins, Bill Coontz (*Foster*), Charlotte Portney, George Barrows, Page Cavanaugh & His Trio

P: Marc Frederic D: Richard Cunha SCR: H.E. Barrie PHOTOG: Meredith Nicholson SPCL-FX: Ira Anderson SONGS:, *Daddy-Bird* & *Special Date*
orig. co-billed with **Missile to the Moon**
Standard horror-fantasy: Infamous monster-maker's grandson creates cantankerous female

Frankenstein's Daughter (1971)
see **La Figlia di Frankenstein**

Frankenstein s'est Echappe
see **The Curse of Frankenstein**

Frankenstein's Great Aunt Tillie
1983, (USA), color, 99 mins.
W: Donald Pleasence, Yvonne Furneaux, Aldo Ray, Zsa Zsa Gabor, June Wilkinson
D & SCR: Myron G. Gold
Minor horror-satire: Scientist threatened with eviction

Frankenstein Sings
1995, (USA), color, 83 mins.
W: Candace Cameron, Ian Bohnen, Jimmie Walker, Anthony Crivello
D: Joel Cohen & Alec Sokolow, from a stage play
Standard horror-musical: Couple spends night with Dracula, the Wolfman, Frankenstein's monster and the corpse of Elvis Presley

Frankenstein's Trestle
1902, (USA), American Mutoscope & Biograph, b&w
Minor melodrama: Trouble at train crossing

Frankenstein: The College Years
1991, (USA), Fox-TV, color, 95 mins.
W: William Ragsdale (*Mark*), Christopher Daniel Barnes (*Jay*), Vincent Hammond (*The Monster*), Patrick Richwood (*Blaine*), Larry Miller
TVM, minor horror-satire: Student completes dead professor's secret experiment

Frankenstein: The True Story
1973, (USA-GB), Univ/NBC-TV, color, 200 mins.
W: Leonard Whiting (*Victor Frankenstein*), Michael Sarrazin (*The Monster*), James Mason (*Dr. Polidori*), Nicola Pagett (*Elizabeth*), Jane Seymour (*Agatha/Prima*), David McCallum (*Dr. Henry Clerval*), Sir Ralph Richardson (*The Blind Hermit*), Sir John Gielgud (*Tanner*), Margaret Leighton (*The Countess*), Agnes Moorehead (*Mrs. Blair*), Yootha Joyce (*Mrs. MacGregor*), Michael Wilding (*Sir Richard Fanshawe*), Julian Barnes (*The Man*), Clarissa Kaye (*Lady Fanshawe*), Tom Baker (*The Captain*), Arnold Diamond (*The Passenger*), Dallas Adams (*Felix*), Peter Sallis
P: Hunt Stromberg Jr. D: John Smight SCR: Christopher Isherwood & Don Bachardy, from Mary W. Shelley's novel *Frankenstein* PHOTOG: Arthur Ibbetson MUSIC: Gil Melle

Frankenstein: The True Story: MICHAEL SARRAZIN

TVM (orig. in 2 parts), opulent horror-fantasy: Scientist creates man and woman, tragedy follows

Frankenstein vs. the Giant Devil Fish
1966, (Jap), Toho/AIP, color, 87 mins.
W: Nick Adams, Tadao Takashima, Kumi Mizuno
P: Tomoyuki Tanaka D: Inoshiro Honda SPCL-FX: Eiji Tsuburaya
USA retitle, **Frankenstein Conquers the World**
Standard horror-fantasy: Old experiments in Nazi Germany culminate in creation of Frankenstein Monster in modern-day Japan

Frankenweenie
1984, (USA), Walt Disney/Buena Vista, color, 27 mins.
W: Shelley Duvall, Daniel Stern, Barret Oliver, Paul Bartel, Joseph Maher, Roz Braverman
D: Tim Burton SCR: Lenny Ripps PHOTOG: Thomas Ackerman
MUSIC: Michael Convertino & David Newman
Unusual short fantasy (launched Tim Burton's career): Dead family pet revived

Frank's Greatest Adventure
see **Fearless Frank**

Frantic
1957, (Fr), Times/Thunderbird-Int'l, b&w, 94 mins.
W: Jeanne Moreau, Maurice Ronet, Yori Bertin, Jean Wall, Elga Andersen
P: Jean Thuillier D: Louis Malle SCR: Louis Malle & Roger Nimier, from Noel Calei's novel JAZZ SCORE: Miles Davis
A.k.a. **Elevator to the Gallows**
Classic thriller: Man commits the perfect crime, but gets trapped in elevator

Fraternity Demon
1991, (USA), color
W: Trixxie Bowie
Minor fantasy: Collegian conjures carnal creature

The Fraudulent Soliciter
1907, (GB), Hepworth, b&w, 350 ft. (166.8m)
D: Lewin Fitzhamon
Standard crime-thriller: Lawyer robs and shoots client

Fraudulent Spiritualism Exposed
see **Spiritualism Exposed (1913)**

Frau im Mond (Woman in the Moon)
1929, (Ger), Fritz Lang Film/GMBH-Ufa, b&w, 14,291 ft. (4356m/115 mins.)
W: Gerda Maurus, Willy Fritsch, Fritz Rasp, Klaus Pohl, Gustav von Wangenheim, Gustl Stark-Gsettenbaur
P&D: Fritz Lang SCR: Fritz Lang & Thea von Harbou PHOTOG: Kurt Kourant, Oskar Fischinger & Otto Kanturek SPCL-FX: Konstantin Tschetwerikoff TECHNICAL ADVISERS: Dr. Willy Ley, Hermann Oberth
US title: **By Rocket to the Moon**, *(UFA, 1931)*
Classic SF-fantasy, prototype of modern space-travel films: Adventurous girl stows away on first spaceship to moon

The Freak Barber
1905, (GB), R.W. Paul, b&w, 168 ft. (51.2m)
D: J.H. Martin
Minor fantasy short: Beheaded customers dismember barber

Freaked
1993, (USA), color, 79 mins.
W: Alex Winter, Megan Ward Michael Stoyanov, Randy Quaid, Mr. T, Brooke Shields, Keanu Reeves, Bob Goldthwaite (voice), William Sadler, Derek McGrath, Alex Zuckerman, Karyn Malchus, Morgan Fairchild, Tom Stern
D: Alex Winter & Tom Stern SCR: Alex Winter, Tom Stern & Tim Burns MUSIC: Kevin Kiner
Standard SF-comedy: Chemical turns industry spokesman into monster

The Freakmaker
see **The Mutations**

Freaks
1932, (USA), Dwain Esper/MGM, b&w, 64 mins.
W: Wallace Ford, Leila Hyams, Olga Baclanova (*Cleopatra*), Roscoe Ates, Rose Dione, Henry Victor, Edward Brophy, Harry & Daisy Earles, Daisy & Violet Hilton, Randian, Martha the Armless Wonder, Matt McHugh, Johnny Eck, Olga Roderick (*The Bearded Lady*), Pete Robinson (*The Living Skeleton*), Schlitzie (*A Pinhead*), Elvira Snow (*A Pinhead*), Jenny Lee Snow (*A Pinhead*), Coo-Koo the Bird Woman
D: Tod Browning SCR: Willis Goldbeck & Leon Gordon, from Tod Robbins' short story *Spurs* (first published in Munsey's Magazine, 1923) DIALOG: Al Boasberg PHOTOG: Merritt B. Gerstad DESIGN: Cedric Gibbons
because of public outrage, MGM made later attempt to release film under title **Nature's Mistakes**
A.k.a. **Barnum, The Monster Show** *and* **Forbidden Love**
"The idea of using real circus freaks to portray the characters in the title was revolting to the cushioned sensibilities of Hollywood. If not for genius studio head Irving Thalberg, the movie might never have been made. Thalberg, then production manager at Metro, backed Browning in the face of opposition from all other sides. But, though the movie did get made, it was not a success by most standards" FREAKS, Monster Fantasy, Vol. I, No. 2 (June, 1975), p. 48
"The difficulty is in telling whether it should be shown at the Rialto Theatre—where it opened yesterday—or in, say, the Medical Center. FREAKS is no normal film, but whether it deserves the title of abnormal is a matter of personal opinion"—N.Y. Times
"...a field day for lovers of the macabre... To some it will be fascinating in its grotesqueries; others will find it revolting"—N.Y. World-Telegram
"As a horror story, it is either too horrible or not horrible enough, according to the viewpoint"—Variety

"...I don't think that everyone on earth should see it. It's certainly not for susceptible young people"—New Yorker
"Mr. Browning has always been an expert in pathological morbidity, but after seeing FREAKS, his other films seem but whimsical nursery tales"—N.Y. Herald Tribune
Morbid classic: Beautiful but greedy trapeze artist weds circus midget, plans to murder him for money. cf. She Freak

Freakshow
1995, (USA), color, 102 mins.
W: Gunnar Hansen, Veronica Carlson, Brian D. Kelly, Shannon Michelle Parsons
D: William Cooke & Paul Talbot
Standard horror-thriller: Two teens find mystery in carnival

Freaky Friday
1976, (USA), Ron Miller/Walt Disney, color, 100 mins.
W: Barbara Harris (*Mrs. Andrews*), Jodie Foster (*Annabel*), John Astin (*Mr. Andrews*), Patsy Kelly, Dick Van Patten, Vicki Schreck, Sorrell Booke, Ruth Buzzi, Fritz Feld, Marie Windsor, Alan Oppenheimer, Kaye Ballard, Laurie Main, Marc McClure, Jack Sheldon, Hank Jones, Sparky Marcus, Ceil Cabot, Karen Smith, Jimmy Van Patten
D: Gary Nelson   SCR: Mary Rodgers   PHOTOG: Charles F. Wheeler   MUSIC: Johnny Mandel   SONG: *I'd Like to Be You for a Day*
Standard comedy-fantasy: Mother and daughter switch places

Freaky Friday
1995, (USA), Walt Disney, color, 90 mins.
W: Shelley Long, Gaby Hoffmann, Catlin Adams, Drew Carey, Carol Kane, Taylor Negron, Alan Rosenberg
D: Melanie Mayron   TELEPLAY: Stu Krieger   PHOTOG: Russ Alsobrook   MUSIC: James McVay
Standard comedy-fantasy (remake)

La Freccia d'Oro (The Golden Arrow)
1962, (It), MGM, color, 91 mins.
W: Tab Hunter, Rossana Podesta, Umberto Meinati
D: Antonio Margheriti
Minor adventure-romance: Prince disguises self as beggar

Freddie as F.R.O.7
1992, (GB), color, 91 mins.
VOICES: Ben Kingsley, Jenny Agutter, Brian Blessed, Nigel Hawthorne, Michael Hordern, Edmund Kingsley, Phyllis Logan, Victor Maddern, Jonathan Pryce, Prunella Scales, Billie Whitelaw
D: Jon Acevski
Bizarre animated fantasy: Magical frog saves Britain

Freddy's Dead: The Final Nightmare
1991, (USA), New Line, color, 3D, 96 mins.
W: Robert Englund (*Freddy Krueger*), Lisa Zane (*Maggie*), Shon Greenblatt (*John*), Lezlie Deane (*Tracy*), Ricky Dean Logan (*Carlos*), Breckin Meyer (*Spencer*), Yaphet Kotto (*Doc*), Tom Arnold, Roseanne, Alice Cooper, Johnny Depp, Einor Donahue
D: Rachel Talalay   SCR: Michael DeLuca   STORY: Rachel Talalay, based on characters created by Wes Craven   PHOTOG: Declan Quinn   MUSIC: Brian May
Standard horror-fantasy: Mad killer meets his match

Freedom to Die
1962, (GB), Bayford/Butcher, b&w, 61 mins.
W: Paul Maxwell (*Craig Owen*), Felicity Young (*Linda*), Kay Callard (*Coral*), Bruce Seton (*Felix*), T.P. McKenna (*Mike*), Laurie Leigh (*Julie*), Charlie Byrne (*Happy Joe*)
P: Charles A. Leeds   D: Francis Searle   STORY: Arthur la Bern
Standard crime-thriller: Robber breaks jail, seeks deposit key to gain loot

Free Fall
1999, (USA), FAM-TV, color, 95 mins.
W: Jaclyn Smith, Bruce Boxleitner, Chad Everett, Hannes Jaenicke, Scott Wentworth, Hayden Christensen, Nigel Bennett
D: Mario Azzopardi   TELEPLAY: Ken & Jim Wheat   STORY: Mark Homer   PHOTOG: Rhett Morita
TVM, standard thriller: Madman causes airplane crashes

Freejack
1992, (USA), WB, color, 110 mins.
W: Emilio Estevez (*Alex Furlong*), Mick Jagger (*Vacendak*), Rene Russo (*Julie Redlund*), Anthony Hopkins (*McCandless*), Jonathan Banks (*Michelette*), David Johansen (Buster Poindexter) (*Brad Hines*), Amanda Plummer (*The Nun*), Grand L. Bush (*Boone*), Frankie Faison (*Eagle Man*), John Shea (*Morgan*), Esai Morales (*Ripper*), Wilbur Fitzgerald (*Earnhart*), Jerry Hall (*The Newswoman*), Glen Trotiner (*Time Travel Technician #1*), Jody Waddell (*Time Travel Technician #2*), J. Don Ferguson (*The Promoter*), Tom Barnes (*Mr. Plugs*), Harsh Nayyar (*The Cab Driver*), James Mayberry (*Bonejacker #1*), Chris Kayser (*Bonejacker #2*), Carl Ciarfalio (*Bonejacker #3*), Jimmy Ortega (*Bonejacker #4*), Danny De La Paz (*Jose*), Johnny Popwell (*The Man in the Apt.*), Myrna White (*The Woman in the Apt.*), Leonard Shinew (*The Old Man*), Bryan Mercer (*The Punk*), Mary Ann Hagen (*The Girl Gangmember*), Daryl Wilcher (*The Youth Gangmember*), Edmund Ikeda (*The Sr. Japanese*

Executive), Tony Epper (*The Hungry Diner*), Patty Mack (*The Waitress*), Jeff Lewis (*The Checkpoint Officer*), Bill McCurdy (*The Checkpoint Guard*), Jon Kohler (*The Pickup Man*), Joshua Lee Patton (*The Bartender*), George Coleman (*The Sax Player*), Jeff Scordino (*The Cameraman*), Mike Starr (*The Shaggy Man*), Alan Burrell (*The Stabbed Shaggy Man*), David Dwyer (*The Squad Leader*), Mert Hatfield (*Tony*), Mark Gordon (*The Switchboard Technician*), Dennis Klein (*McCandless' Chauffeur*)
D: Geoff Murphy   SCR: Steven Pressfield, Ronald Shusett, & Dan Gilroy, based on Robert Sheckley's novel *Immortality, Inc.*   PHOTOG: Amir Mokri   MUSIC: Trevor Jones
Unusual SF-thriller: Future magnate steals body of 20th-century racecar driver

Freelance
1975, (GB), Freelance Films/Butcher, color, 81 mins.
W: Ian McShane (*Robin Mitchell*), Gayle Hunnicutt (*Chris*), Keith Barron (*Gary*), Alan Lake (*Dean*), Peter Gilmore (*The Boss*), Charles Hyatt (*McNair*), John Hollis (*Hartley*), Luan Peters (*Rosemary*), Peter Birrell (*Jeff*), David Graham (*The General*)
P & D: Francis Megahy   STORY: Francis Megahy & Bernie Cooper   PHOTOG: Norman Langley   MUSIC: Basil Kirchin
Modest crime-thriller: Crooked businessman witnesses murderous assault

A Free Pardon
1908, (GB), Hepworth, b&w, 525 ft. (160m)
D: Lewin Fitzhamon
Standard crime-thriller: Starving man involved with murderous burglar

Freeway
1996, (USA), Illusion/Rep, color, 105 mins.
W: Reese Witherspoon (*Vanessa*), Kiefer Sutherland (*Bob Wolverton*), Brooke Shields (*Mimi*), Wolfgang Bodison (*Breer*), Dan Hedaya (*Wallace*), Amanda Plummer (*Ramona*), Michael T. Weiss (*Larry*), Susan Barnes, Bokeem Woodbine, Guillermo Diaz, Brittany Murphy, Julie Araskog, Alanna Ubagh, Conchata Ferrell, Tara Subkoff, Annette Helde, Sydney Lassick
WRIT & D: Matthew Bright   PHOTOG: John Thomas   ORIG. MUSIC: Danny Elfman   ADDITIONAL MUSIC: Tito Larriva   MUSIC SPRVSR: Gerry Gershman
Bizarre thriller (reworking of Little Red Riding Hood): Delinquent girl meets serial killer on way to her grandmother's. cf. The Company of Wolves

Freeway Maniac
1988, (USA), color 94 mins.
W: Loren Winters, James Courtney, Shepard Sanders, Donald Hotton
D: Paul Winters   MUSIC: Robby Krieger
Minor thriller: Mad slasher loose on set of horror movie

The Freaze Bomb
see Death Dimension

The Freezing Mixture
1910, (GB), Kineto, b&w, 600 ft. (182.9m)
D: Walter R. Booth
reissued 1917
Standard comedy-fantasy: Henpeck's nephew freezes wife solid for two hours

Das Fremde Madchen (The Strange Girl)
1913, (Ger), b&w
SCR: Hugo von Hofmannsthal
Standard melodrama

The French Conspiracy
1973, (Fr), Two Worlds/Cine Globe, color, 125 mins.
W: Jean-Louis Trintignant (*Darien*), Michel Piccoli (*Kassar*), Gian Maria Volonte (*Sadiel*), Jean Seberg (*Edith*), Bruno Cremer (*Vigneau*), Francois Perier (*Rouannet*), Philippe Noiret (*Garcin*), Michel Bouquet (*Lempereur*), Daniel Ivernel (*Acconeti*), Roy Scheider (*Howard*)
D: Yves Boisset   SCR: Ben Barzman & Basilio Franchina   ADAPT & DIALOG: Jorge Semprun   PHOTOG: Ricardo Aronovich   MUSIC: Ennio Morricone
Standard crime-thriller

The French Key
1946, (USA), Rep, b&w, 67 mins.
W: Albert Dekker, Evelyn Ankers, Mike Mazurki John Eldredge, Frank Fenton, Richard Arlen, Byron Foulger
D: Walter Colmes
Standard thriller

Frenzy
1972, (GB), Univ, color, 116 mins.
W: Jon Finch (*Richard Blaney*), Barry Foster (*Robert Rusk*), Barbara Leigh-Hunt (*Brenda Blaney*), Alec McCowen (*Chief Inspector Oxford*), Anna Massey (*Babs Milligan*), Michael Bates (*Sgt. Spearman*), Clive Swift (*Johnny Porter*), Billie Whitelaw (*Hetty Porter*), Vivien Merchant (*Mrs. Oxford*), Bernard Cribbins (*Felix Forsythe*), Noel Johnson (*A Customer*), Jimmy Garner (*Porter*), Rita Webb (*Mrs. Rusk*), Jean Marsh (*The Sec'y*), Madge Ryan (*Mrs. Davison*), George Tovey (*Salt*), Gerald Sim (*A Customer*), John Boxer (*Sir George*), Elsie Randolph (*The Wife*), June Ellis (*The Barmaid*), Bunny May (*The Barman*), Robert Keegan (*The Patient*)

P & D: Alfred Hitchcock **SCR:** Anthony Shaffer, from Arthur Labern's novel *Goodbye, Piccadilly; Farewell, Leicester Square* **PHOTOG:** Gil Taylor **MUSIC:** Ron Goodwin

"In the classic Hitchcock tradition... impeccable technique, excellent performances, the perfect script"—Richard Schickel, *Life*

"It's hold your breath, fun and games time again for Alfred Hitchcock has come up with one of his best"—William Wolf, *Cue*

"Hitchcock is in dazzling form. A passionately entertaining film"—Vincent Canby, N.Y. *Times*

Tense thriller: Innocent man flees law when framed for brutal necktie murders

Friday the 13th (1940)
see Black Friday

Friday the 13th
1980, (USA), Georgetown Prods./Para, color, 95 mins.

W: Betsy Palmer, Adrienne King, Robbi Morgan (*Annie*), Mark Nelson (*Ned*), Laurie Bartram (*Brenda*), Jeannine Taylor (*Marcie*), Harry Crosby, Walter Gorney

P & D: Sean S. Cunningham **SCR:** Victor Miller **PHOTOG:** Barry Abrams **MUSIC:** Harry Manfredini

blurb: "They are Doomed"

Standard horror-thriller: Youth counselors at summer camp are viciously murdered

Friday the 13th—Part 2
1981, (USA), Georgetown Prods./Para, color, 81 mins.

W: Adrienne King (*Alice*), Amy Steel (*Ginny*), John Furey (*Paul*), Walter Gorney (*Ralph*), Stu Charno (*Ted*), Marta Kober (*Sandra*), Kirsten Baker (*Terry*), Betsy Palmer (*Mrs. Voorhees*), Bill Randolph (*Jeff*), Warrington Gillette (*Jason*), Tom McBride (*Mark*), Lauren-Marie Taylor (*Vickie*), Russell Todd (*Scott*), Cliff Cudney (*Max*), Jerry Wallace (*The Prowler*), Jack Marks (*The Cop*), Steve Daskawisz (*Jason Stunt Double*), David Brand, China Chen, Jaime Perry, Carolyn Loudon, Tom Shea, Jill Voight

P & D: Steve Miner **SCR:** Ron Kurz, from characters created by Victor Miller **PHOTOG:** Peter Stein **SPCL-FX:** Steve Kirshoff **MUSIC:** Harry Manfredini

Standard horror-thriller: More grisly murders at summer camp

Friday the 13th—Part 3
1982, (USA), Steve Miner/Para, 3D, color, 95 mins.

W: Dana Kimmell (*Chris*), Paul Kratka (*Rick*), Tracie Savage (*Debbie*), Richard Brooker (*Jason*), Jeffrey Rogers

D: Steve Miner **PHOTOG:** Gerald Feil **MUSIC:** Harry Manfredini

Standard horror-thriller: Spectral killer continues to stalk

Friday the 13th—The Final Chapter
1984, (USA), Para, color, 95 mins.

W: Peter Barton, Kimberly Beck (*Trish*), E. Erich Anderson (*Rob*), Crispin Glover (*Jimmy*), Barbara Howard (*Sara*), Corey Feldman

D: Joseph Zito **SCR:** Barney Cohen **MUSIC:** Harry Manfredini

Standard horror-thriller, 4th installment in "Friday 13th" series: More teens slaughtered by ghoulish fiend

Friday the 13th—Part V: A New Beginning
1985, (USA), Para, color, 92 mins.

W: John Shepherd (*Tommy Jarvis*), Shavar Ross (*Reggie*), Melanie Kinnaman (*Pam*), Richard Young (*Dr. Peters*), Juliette Cummins (*Robin*), Vernon Washington (*George*), Jerry Pavlon (*Jake*), Tiffany Helm (*Violet*), Debbisue Voorhees (*Tina*), John Robert Dixon (*Eddie*), Mark Venturini (*Victor*), Marco St. John (*Sheriff Tucker*), Dominic Brascia (*Joey*), Richard Lineback (*Carl Dodd*), Carol Locatell (*Ethel*), Caskey Swain (*Duke Johnson*), Ron Sloan (*Junior*), Dick Wieand (*Roy*), Bob DiSimone (*The Male Nurse*), Sonny Shields (*Raymond*), Curtis Conaway (*Les*), Todd Bryant (*Neil*), Corey Parker (*Pete*), Anthony Barille (*Vinnie*), Rebecca Wood-Sharke (*Lana*), Ric Mancini (*Mayor Cobb*), Miguel A. Nunez Jr. (*Demon*), Corey Feldman (*Tommy, age 12*), Jere Fields (*Anita*), Susanne Bateman (*Nurse Yates*), Tom Morga

D: Danny Steinmann **SCR:** Martin Kitrosser, David Cohen, & Danny Steinmann **PHOTOG:** Stephen L. Posey **MUSIC:** Harry Manfredini

Minor thriller: Camp for disturbed youth is plagued by monstrous killer

Friday the 13th, Part VI: Jason Lives
1986, (USA), Terror Inc./Para, color, 85 mins.

W: Thom Mathews (*Tommy*), Jennifer Cooke (*Megan*), Renee Jones (*Sissy*), Kerry Noonan (*Paula*), Darcy DeMoss (*Nikki*), Tom Fridley (*Cort*), Ron Palillo (*Allen*), David Kagen (*The Sheriff*), Alan Blumenfeld, Ann Ryerson

WRIT & D: Tom McLoughlin **PHOTOG:** Jon R. Kranhouse **SPCL-FX:** Martin Becker **MUSIC:** Harry Manfredini

Modest thriller: Resurrected fiend plagues campers

Friday the 13th, Part VII—The New Blood
1988, (USA), Para, 90 mins.

W: Kane Hodder, Lar Park Lincoln (*Tina*), Kevin Blair (*Nick*), Terry Kiser

D: John Carl Buechler **SCR:** Daryl Haney & Manuel Fidello **MUSIC:** Harry Manfredini & Fred Mollin

Standard horror-thriller: Psychic girl vs. phantom killer

Friday the 13th, Part VIII—Jason Takes Manhattan
1989, (USA), Horror Inc./Para, color, 96 mins.

W: Jensen Daggett (*Rennie*), Scott Reeves (*Sean Robertson*), Barbara Bingham

(*Colleen Van Deusen*), Peter Mark Richman (*Charles McCulloch*), Martin Cummins (*Wayne*), Gordon Currie (*Miles Wolfe*), Alex Diakun (*The Deck Hand*), V.C. DuPree (*Julius Gaw*), Saffron Henderson (*J.J.*), Kelly Hu (*Eva Watanabe*), Sharlene Martin (*Tamara Mason*), Warren Munson (*Adm. Robertson*), Kane Hodder (*Jason*), Todd Shaffer (*Jim*), Fred Henderson (*The Chief Engineer*), Timothy Burr Mirkovich (*Young Jason*), Tiffany Paulsen (*Suzi*), Sam Sarkar (*Gang Banger #1*), Michael Benyaer (*Gang Banger #2*), Roger Barnes (*The Irish Cop*), Amber Pawlick (*Young Rennie*), Vinny Capone (*The Street Urchin*), Peggy Hedden (*The NY Waitress*), David Longworth (*The Sanitation Engineer*), Ace (*Toby the Dog*)

WRIT & D: Rob Hedden **PHOTOG:** Bryan England **MUSIC:** Fred Mollin **SONGS:**, *Darkest Side of the Night, Say This to Me, Tamara's Bio Project, Broken Dream, J.J. Blues, Stalker's Rocker, Living in the City & Strike*

Standard horror-thriller: Maniac stalks teens on cruise ship

Friday the 13th...The Orphan
1980, (USA), World Northal, color

W: Mark Owens, Joanna Miles, Peggy Feury

D & SCR: John Ballard

A.k.a. Killer Orphan

Minor thriller: 10-year-old boy takes gruesome revenge on adult world

The Friend
see Przyjaciel

Fright
1957, (USA), Exploitation Films/Para-TV, b&w

W: Nancy Malone (*Ann Summers*), Eric Fleming (*Dr. Hamilton*), Dean L. Almquist (*Cullen*), Frank Marth (*Morley*), Humphrey Davis (*Prof. Gore*), Elizabeth Watts (*Lady Olive*), Walter Klavun (*The Warden*), Amelia Conley (*Miss Ames*), Norman MacKaye (*The Inspector*), Don Douglas (*Insp. II*), Tom Reynolds (*The City Editor*), Robert Gardett (*The Managing Editor*), Ned Glass (*The Taxi Driver*), Sid Raymond (*The Van Driver*), Philip Kenealy (*The Cop*), Chris Bohn (*The TV Announcer*), Norman Burton (*The Reporter*), Alney Alba (*The Guest*)

P & D: W. Lee Wilder **STORY & SCR:** Myles Wilder **PHOTOG:** J. Burgi Contner **MUSIC:** Lew Davies

A.k.a. Spell of the Hypnotist

blurb: "One murder committed twice—a century apart!"

Minor thriller: Psychiatrist meets girl with split personality

Fright
1972, (GB), Lion-Int'l/AA, color, 87 mins.

W: Susan George (*Amanda*), Honor Blackman (*Helen*), Ian Bannen (*Brian*), John Gregson (*Dr. Cordell*), George Cole (*Jim*), Dennis Waterman (*Chris*), Tara Collinson (*Tara*), Maurice Kaufmann (*The Inspector*), Roger Lloyd-Pack (*The Constable*), Michael Brennan (*The Sergeant*)

P: Harry Fine & Michael Style **D:** Peter Collinson **SCR:** Tudor Gates **PHOTOG:** Ian Wilson **DESIGN:** Disley Jones **SONG:** *Ladybird* (sung by Manette)

A.k.a. Night Legs

Standard thriller: Babysitter terrorized

The Frightened Bride
1952, (GB), Grand Nat'l, b&w, 100 mins.

W: Mai Zetterling (*Doris Richardson*), Michael Denison (*Philip Rackham*), Flora Robson (*Mary Rackham*), Dennis Price (*Maurice Fletcher*), Naunton Wayne (*An Inspector*), Andre Morell (*George Rackham*), Celia Lipton (*Sandra*), Jane Hylton (*Frankie Rackham*), Mervyn Johns (*Uncle Ted*), Hugh Dempster (*An Inspector*), Olive Sloane (*Mrs. Baker*), Barbara Blair (*Nancy Richardson*)

D: Terence Young **SCR:** Audrey Erskine Lindop & Dudley Leslie, from a novel by Audrey Erskine Lindop

reissued 1954

Minor melodrama: Family affected when son hanged for murder

The Frightened City
1961, (GB), Zodiac/Anglo-Amalgamated, b&w, 97 mins.

W: Herbert Lom (*Waldo Zhernikov*), John Gregson (*Insp. Sayers*), Sean Connery (*Paddy Damion*), Yvonne Romain (*Anya*), Alfred Marks (*Harry Foulcher*), David Davies (*Alf Peters*), Olive McFarland (*Sadie*), Kenneth Griffith (*Wally*), George Pastell (*Sanchietti*), Frederick Piper (*Sgt. Ogle*), Bruce Seton (*The Commissioner*), Patrick Holt (*Supt. Carter*), Norrie Paramor (*The Pianist*)

P & STORY: John Lemont & Leigh Vance **D:** John Lemont **SCR:** Leigh Vance

reissued (1964) with 11 mins. cut

Standard melodrama: Accountant unites six gangs, forms protection racket

The Frightened Island
see Island of Terror

The Frightened Lady
1932, (GB), Gainsborough-British Lion/Ideal, b&w, 87 mins.

W: Norman McKinnel (*Insp. Tanner*), Cathleen Nesbitt (*Lady Lebanon*), Emlyn Williams (*Lord Lebanon*), Belle Chrystal (*Aisla Crane*), Gordon Harker (*Sgt. Totty*), Finlay Currie (*Brooks*), Cyril Raymond (*Sgt. Ferraby*), D.A. Clarke-Smith (*Dr. Amersham*), Percy Parsons (*Gilder*), Julian Royce (*Kelver*)

D: T. Hayes Hunter **SCR:** Angus Macphail & Bryan Edgar Wallace, from Edgar Wallace's play *The Case of the Frightened Lady*

USA retitle, Criminal at Large

Standard thriller: Mad lord tries to kill fiancee

F

The Frightened Lady (1940)
see The Case of the Frightened Lady

The Frightened Man
1952, (GB), Tempean/Eros, b&w, 69 mins.
W: Dermot Walsh (*Julius Roselli*), Barbara Murray (*Amanda*), Charles Victor (*Mr. Roselli*), John Blythe (*Maxie*), John Horsley (*Harry*), Michael Ward (*Cornelius*), Thora Hird (*Vera*), Annette Simmonds (*Marcella*)
P: Robert Baker & Monty Berman   **D & STORY:** John Gilling
Standard crime-thriller: Junk dealer's son joins gang, robs diamond merchant

The Frighteners
1996, (USA/New Zealand), Wingnut/Univ, color, 106 mins.
W: Michael J. Fox (*Frank Bannister*), Trini Alvarado (*Dr. Lucy Linskey*), Peter Dobson (*Ray Linskey*), John Astin (*The Judge*), Jeffrey Combs (*Milton Dammers*), R. Lee Ermey (*Hiles*), Dee Wallace Stone (*Patricia Bradley*), Jake Busey (*Johnny Bartlett*), Julianna McCarthy (*Old Lady Bradley*), Troy Evans (*The Sheriff*), Chi McBride (*Cyrus*), Elizabeth Hawthorne (*Magda Rees-Jones*), Jim Fyfe (*Stuart*), Angela Bloomfield (*Debra Bannister*), Desmond Kelly (*Harry Sinclair*), Todd Rippon, Michael Robinson, Jonathan Blick, John Sumner, Paul Yates, Nicola Cliff, Jim McLarty, Anthony Ray Parker, Stuart Devenie, John Leigh, Melanie Linskey, Ken Blackburn, Alan O'Leary, Leslie Wing, Genevieve Westcott, K.C. Kelly, William Pomeroy, Frank Edwards, Danny Lineham, Billy Jackson, Charlie McClellan, George Port, Tony Hopkins, Sophie Watkins, Max Grover, Taea Hartwell, George Grover, Lewis Martin, Clay Nelson, Robert McNeill, Matthew Chamberlain, Vivienne Kaplan, Liz Mullane
P: Peter Jackson & Jamie Selkirk   **D:** Peter Jackson   **SCR:** Peter Jackson & Fran Walsh   **PHOTOG:** Alun Bollinger & John Blick   **VS-FX:** Wes Ford Takahashi   **MUSIC:** Danny Elfman   **SONGS:,** *Don't Fear the Reaper* & *Superstar*
"Drop-dead thrills. A wonderfully insane horror film...dazzling special effects"—Anthony C. Ferrante, Antioch Ledger-Dispatch
"Funny, horrific, and highly entertaining. Michael J. Fox, Peter Jackson and Robert Zemeckis have come up with a winner"—Paul Wunder, WBAI Radio
"A perfect mix of chills and thrills"—Kyle Osborne, WDCA
Entertaining horror-fantasy-comedy: "Ghostbuster" meets dangerous spooks

The Frightening Secret of Dr. Hichcock
see Raptus

Fright House
1989, (USA), color, 110 mins.
W: Al Lewis, Duane Jones
D: Len Anthony
Minor 2-tale thriller: (1) "Fright House" - Witches fix old mansion for visit from Devil, & (2) "Abandon" - Teacher prolongs her youth

Frightmare
1974, (GB), Peter Walker/Tony Tenser/Heritage, color, 86 mins.
W: Rupert Davies (*Edmund Yates*), Sheila Keith (*Dorothy Yates*), Deborah Fairfax (*Jackie*), Paul Greenwood (*Graham*), Kim Butcher (*Debbie*), Fiona Curzon (*Merle*), John Yule (*Robin*), Tricia Mortimer (*Lillian*), Noel Johnson (*The Judge*), Pamela Farbrother (*Delia*), Edward Kalinski (*Alec*), Victor Winding (*The Inspector*), Anthony Hennessey (*The Sgt.*), Michael Sharvell-Martin (*The Barman*), Andrew Sachs (*Barry Nichols*), David McGillivray (*The Doctor*)
P & D: Pete Walker   **STORY:** David McGillivray   **PHOTOG:** Peter Jessop   **MUSIC:** Stanley Myers
A.k.a. **Once Upon a Frightmare** *and* **Cover Up**
Standard thriller: Girl finds parents are cannibals

Frightmare
1983, (USA), Screenwriter Prods./Vestron//Atlantic TV/Saturn International, color, 86 mins
W: Ferdinand Mayne (*Conrad Ragzoff*), Nita Talbot (*Mrs. Rohmer*), Luca Bercovici (*Saint*), Leon Askin (*Wolfgang*), Jennifer Starrett (*Meg*), Barbara Oilavin (*Etta*), Donna McDaniel (*Donna*), Carlene Olson (*Eve*), Jeffrey Combs (*Stu*), Scott Thomson (*Bobo*), Alan Stock, Joe Witherell, Twyla Littleton, Janet Lee Orcutt, Peter Kastner, Chuck Mitchell, Jesse Ehrlich, Ancel Cook, Tallie Cochrane, Michael Linder, Patrick Wright, Jack Marston
D & SCR: Norman Thaddeus Vane   **PHOTOG:** Joel King   **MUSIC:** Jerry Moseley
orig. to be titled **The Horror Star**
Minor horror-fantasy: Fright flick actor returns from dead

Fright Night
1985, (USA), Vistar/Col, color, 106 mins.
W: Chris Sarandon (*Jerry Dandrige*), William Ragsdale (*Charley Brewster*), Amanda Bearse (*Amy Peterson*), Roddy McDowall (*Peter Vincent*), Stephen Geoffreys (*Evil Ed*), Jonathan Stark (*Billy Cole*), Art J. Evans (*Det. Lennox*), Dorothy Fielding (*Judy Brewster*), Stewart Stern (*The Cook*), Nick Savage (*Bouncer #1*), Ernie Holmes (*Bouncer #2*), Heidi Sorenson (*The Hooker*), Irina Irvine (*The Teenage Girl*), Robert Corff (*Jonathan*), Pamela Brown (*Miss Nina*), Chris Hendrie (*The Newscaster*), Prince A. Hughes (*Bouncer #3*)

WRIT & D: Tom Holland   **PHOTOG:** Jan Kieser   **VS-FX:** Richard Edlund   **MUSIC:** Brad Fiedel   **SONGS:,** *Save Me Tonight, Rock Myself to Sleep, You Can't Hide from the Beast Inside, Let's Talk, Give It Up, Armies of the Night* & *Boppin' Tonight*
Wry horror-spoof: Teen learns suave neighbor is vampire

Fright Night II
1989, (USA), Vista/New Century, color, 108 mins.
W: Roddy McDowall (*Peter Vincent*), William Ragsdale (*Charley Brewster*), Traci Lin (*Alex*), Julie Carmen (*Regine*), Jonathan Gries (*Louis*), Russell Clark, Brian Thompson, Merrit Butrick, Ernie Sabella, Matt Landers, Gary Allen, Josh Richman, Karen Anders, Rochelle Ashana, Ed Quinlan, Blair Tafkin, Alexander Polk, Scanlon Gail, Grant Owens, John Lafayette, Brad Kepnick, Neith Hunter, Jennifer Joan Taylor, Jill Augustine, Gar Campbell, Ed Corbett, Robert Jenkins, David Efron
D: Tommy Lee Wallace   **SCR:** Tim Metcalfe, Miguel Tejada-Flores, & Tommy Lee Wallace, from characters created by Tom Holland   **PHOTOG:** Mark Irwin   **SPCL VS-FX:** Gene Warren Jr.   **MUSIC:** Brad Fiedel   **SONG:** *Come to Me*
Standard horror-comedy: Vampiress seeks revenge

Frightshow
1984, (USA), color, 60 mins.
Standard anthology of 4 independent short horror films: **Nightfright, Thing in the Basement, Dr. Dobermind** & **Illegal Alien**

Fritz the Cat
1972, (USA), color, 77 mins.
VOICES: Skip Hinnant, Rosetta Le Noire, John McCurry, Judy Engles
D & SCR: Ralph Bakshi, from an underground comics character by Robert Crumb   **MUSIC:** Ed Bogas
Unusual animated satire: Feline's raunchy 1960's adventures cf. **The Nine Lives of Fritz the Cat**

The Frog
1937, (GB), Wilcox/General Film Distributors, b&w, 75 mins.
W: Gordon Harker (*Sgt. Elk*), Carol Goodner (*Lola Bassano*), Noah Beery (*Joshua Broad*), Jack Hawkins (*Capt. Gordon*), Richard Ainley (*Ray Bennett*), Felix Aylmer (*John Bennett*), Vivian Gaye (*Stella Bennett*), Esme Percy (*Philo Johnson*), Cyril Smith (*PC Balder*), Gordon McLeod (*The Commissioner*), Julien Mitchell (*John Maitland*)
D: Jack Raymond   **SCR:** Ian Hay & Gerald Elliott, from a play by Ian Hay, based on Edgar Wallace's novel *The Fellowship of the Frog*
Standard thriller: Detective exposes criminal organization

The Frog Pond
1938, (USA), Col, color, 1 reel
D: Ub Iwerks
Standard animated fantasy

The Frog Prince
1954, (GB), b&w, 10 mins.
D: Lotte Reiniger
from a story by the Brothers Grimm, color version 1961
Standard short animated fantasy

The Frog Prince
1988, (USA), color, 86 mins.
W: Aileen Quinn
Standard fantasy-musical: Spell on prince broken by princess' kiss

Frogs
1972, (USA), AIP, color, 91 mins.
W: Ray Milland (*Jason Crockett*), Joan Van Ark (*Karen*), Sam Elliott (*Pickett Smith*), Adam Roarke (*Clint*), Judy Pace (*Bella*), George Skaff (*Stuart*), Nicholas Cortland (*Kenneth*), Lynn Borden (*Jenny*), David Gilliam (*Michael*), Mae Mercer (*Maybelle*), Hal Hodges (*Jay*), Lance Taylor Sr. (*Charles*), Dale Willingham (*Tina*), Robert Sanders (*The Young Boy in the Car*), Carolyn Fitzsimmons (*The Lady in the Car*), Holly Irving (*Iris*)
P: George Edwards & Peter Thomas   **D:** George McCowan   **SCR:** Robert Hutchison   **PHOTOG:** Mario Tosi   **MUSIC:** Les Baxter
blurb: "Millions of slimy bodies squirming everywhere—millions of gaping mouths!"
Minor SF-thriller: Nature turns against unsavory family

Frogtown II
1993, (USA), color, 86 mins.
W: Robert Z'dar
Minor SF-adventure: Heroes rescue Flying Texas Rocket Ranger from mutant frogs. cf. **Hell Comes to Frogtown**

Les Fromages Automobiles (The Skipping Cheeses)
1907, (Fr), Star, b&w, 85m (278.9 ft./4.7 mins.)
D: Georges Melies
Standard fantasy: Animated cheeses attack humans

From a Whisper to a Scream
see The Offspring

From Beyond
1986, (USA), Brian Yuzna/Empire, color, 85 mins.
W: Jeffrey Combs (*Crawford Tillinghast*), Barbara Crampton (*Dr. Katherine McMichaels*), Ted Sorel (*Dr. Edward Pretorius*), Ken Foree (*Bubba*), Carolyn Purdy-Gordon (*Dr. Bloch*), Bunny Summers (*The Neighbor Lady*), Bruce McGuire, Regina Bleesz, Del Russel, Dale Wyatt, Karen Christenfeld, Andy Miller, John Leamer
D: Stuart Gordon **SCR:** Dennis Paoli **ADAPT:** Brian Yuzna, Dennis Paoli, & Stuart Gordon, from H.P. Lovecraft's short story **PHOTOG:** Mac Ahlberg **SPCL-FX:** John Buechler, John Naulin, Mark Shostrom & Anthony Doublin **MUSIC:** Richard Band
Modest horror-fantasy: Scientist's device taps unknown dimension where monstrosities lurk

From Beyond the Grave
1973, (GB), Amicus/WB, color, 93 mins.
W: Peter Cushing (*The Antiques Dealer*), Donald Pleasence (*Jim Underwood*), David Warner (*Edward*), Diana Dors (*Mabel Lowe*), Ian Bannen (*Christopher Lowe*), Margaret Leighton (*Mme. Orloff*), Ian Carmichael (*Reginald Warren*), Nyree Dawn Porter (*Susan Warren*), Angela Pleasence (*Emily Underwood*), Ian Ogilvy (*William Seaton*), Lesley-Anne Down (*Rosemary Seaton*), Jack Watson (*Sir Michael Sinclair*), Rosalind Ayres (*The Prostitute*), Marcel Steiner (*The Face*), Tommy Godfrey
P: Max J. Rosenberg & Milton Subotsky **D:** Kevin Connor **SCR:** Robin Clarke & Raymond Christodoulou, from stories by R. Chetwynd-Hayes **PHOTOG:** Alan Hume **MUSIC:** Douglas Gamley
A.k.a. Creatures and The Creatures from Beyond the Grave
Modest anthology of terror-tales: (1) Haunted mirror turns man into murderer, (2) Businessman's life altered by occult, (3) Suburbanite plagued by invisible "elemental," & (4) Antique door leads to "ghost room"

From Dusk Till Dawn
1996, (USA), Band Apart-Los Hooligans/Dimension/Miramax, color, 108 mins.
W: George Clooney (*Seth Gecko*), Quentin Tarantino (*Richard Gecko*), Harvey Keitel (*Jacob Fuller*), Juliette Lewis (*Kate Fuller*), Ernest Liu (*Scott Fuller*), Salma Hayek (*cameo*), Cheech Marin, Tom Savini (*cameo*), Fred Williamson (*cameo*), Brenda Hillhouse, Marc Lawrence, John Saxon, Michael Parks, Kelly Preston, Danny Trejo, John Hawkes, Cristos, Tito Larriva, Danny the Wonder Pony, Pete Atasanoff, Mike Moroff, Johnny Vatos Hernandez, Aimee Graham, Heidi McNeal, Ernest Garcia, Greg Nicotero
D: Roberto Rodriguez **SCR:** Quentin Tarantino **STORY:** Robert Kurtzman **PHOTOG:** Guillermo Navarro **MUSIC:** Graeme Revell **SONGS:** *Dark Night, After Dark, Dengue Woman Blues & Angry Cockroaches*
blurb: "A terrifying evil has been unleashed. Now, four strangers are our only hope to stop it"
Unusual horror-fantasy (adult themes): Murderous bank-robbers meet Undead

From Ear to Ear
see Les Cousines

From Hell It Came
1957, (USA), Milner Bros./AA, b&w, 71 mins.
W: Tod Andrews, Tina Carver, Robert Swan, Gregg Palmer, John McNamara, Baynes Barron, Linda Watkins, Lee Rhodes, Suzanne Ridgway, Mark Sheeler, Grace Mathews, Chester Hayes, Tani Marsh, Lenmana Guerin
P: Jack Milner **D:** Dan Milner **SCR:** Richard Bernstein **STORY:** Richard Bernstein & Jack Milner **MUSIC:** Darrell Calker
*orig. co-billed with **The Disembodied***
Minor fantasy-thriller: Murdered islander returns as vengeful tree-monster

From Russia with Love
1963, (GB), Eon/UA, color, 116 mins.
W: Sean Connery (*James Bond*), Daniela Bianchi (*Tatiana Romanova*), Pedro Armendariz (*Kerim Bey*), Lotte Lenya (*Rosa Klebb*), Robert Shaw (*Red Grant*), Bernard Lee ("*M*"), Vladek Sheybal (*Kronsky*), Lois Maxwell (*Miss Moneypenny*), Desmond Llewelyn (*Q*), George Pastell (*The Train Conductor*), Eunice Gayson (*Sylvia*), Francis De Wolff (*Vavra*), Walter Gotell (*Morzeny*), Peter Madden, Nadja Regin, Martine Beswick, Fred Haggerty, Peter Bayliss, Leila Giraut, Aliza Gur
P: Harry Saltzman & Albert R. Broccoli **D:** Terence Young **SCR:** Richard Maibaum & Johanna Harwood, from Ian Fleming's *James Bond* novel **PHOTOG:** Ted Moore **MUSIC:** John Barry, title sung by Matt Monro
*reissued (1965) with **Dr. No***
2nd "Bond" film, superior thriller: Super-agent covets secret decoder, finds intrigue and romance in Istanbul

From Scotland Yard
1915, (GB), Vernon Films/YCC, b&w
W: Harold A. Crawford (*The Man*)
D: Charles Vernon
Standard crime-thriller

From Servant Girl to Duchess
1909, (GB), Gaumont, b&w, 366 ft. (111.6m)
D: Alf Collins
Standard fantasy short: Maid dreams she is heroine of novelette, is wooed by duke

From the Dead of Night
1989, (USA), NBC-TV, color
W: Lindsay Wagner (*Joanna Darby*), Robin Thomas (*Glen*), Bruce Boxleitner (*Peter*), Diahann Carroll (*Maggie*), Joanne Linville (*Dr. Morgan*), Robert Prosky (*Dr. Walter Hovde*), Merritt Butrick (*Rick*), Peter Jason (*Hank*), Rita Zohar (*The Spiritualist*), Richard Fancy (*Stanley*)
TVM (orig. in 2 parts), standard horror-fantasy: Woman has near-death experience, finds herself pursued by dark forces

From Dusk Till Dawn: JULIETTE LEWIS

From the Depths

1913, (GB), Cricks & Martin, b&w, 1,145 ft. (349m)
D: Edwin J. Collins
Standard crime-thriller: Man saved from suicide, steals benefactor's plans

From the Earth to the Moon

1958, (USA), RKO/WB, color, 100 mins.
W: Joseph Cotten (*Victor Barbicane*), George Sanders (*Stuyvesant Nicholl*), Debra Paget (*Virginia Nicholl*), Melville Cooper (*Bancroft*), Don Dubbins (*Ben Sharpe*), Patric Knowles (*Cartier*), Henry Daniell (*Morgana*), Carl Esmond (*J.V.*), Ludwig Stossel (*Von Metz*), Morris Ankrum (*Pres. Ulysses S. Grant*)
P: Benedict Bogeaus **D:** Byron Haskin **SCR:** Robert Blees, based on Jules Verne's novel **PHOTOG:** Edwin B. DuPar **SPCL-FX:** Lee Zavitz **MUSIC:** Louis Forbes
Superior SF-fantasy: 19th-century inventor desires to use surface of moon as testing site for super-explosive

Frostbiter: Wrath of the Wendigo

1990, (USA), color, 90 mins.
W: Ron Asheton Lori Baker, Patrick Butler, Devlin Burton
D & SCR: Tom Chaney
Minor horror-fantasy: Reckless hunters awaken legendary beast

Frozen Alive

1964, (GB-W. Ger), Alfa-Creole/United Pic/Magna, b&w, 80 mins.
W: Mark Stevens (*Frank*), Marianne Koch (*Helen*), Delphi Lawrence (*Joan*), Joachim Hansen (*Tony*), Walter Rilla (*Sir Keith*), Wolfgang Lukschy (*Insp. Prentow*), Helmuth Weiss (*The Chairman*), John Longden (*Prof. Hubbard*)
P: Artur Brauner & Ronald Rietti **D:** Bernard Knowles **STORY:** Evelyn Frazer
A.k.a. **Der Fall X701**
Standard SF-thriller: Deep-frozen scientist suspected of murdering wife

The Frozen Dead

1966, (GB), Gold Star/WB-7Arts, color, 95 mins.
W: Dana Andrews (*Dr. Norberg*), Anna Palk (*Jean*), Philip Gilbert (*Dr. Ted Roberts*), Karel Stepanek (*Gen. Lubeck*), Kathleen Breck (*Elsa*), Alan Tilvern (*Karl Essen*), Basil Henson (*Capt. Tirpitz*), Tom Chatto (*Insp. Witt*)
WRIT, P, & D: Herbert J. Leder **PHOTOG:** David Boulton **MUSIC:** Don Banks **MUSIC DIR:** Philip Martell
Modest SF-thriller: Scientist conducts cryogenic experiments, tries to revive 1500 Nazis

The Frozen Ghost

1944, (USA), Univ, b&w, 61 mins.
W: Lon Chaney Jr. (*Alex Gregor*), Evelyn Ankers (*Maura Daniel*), Douglass Dumbrille (*Insp. Brant*), Elena Verdugo (*Nina Coudreau*), Milburn Stone (*George Keene*), Martin Kosleck (*Rudi Poldan*), Tala Birell (*Mme. Monet*), Arthur Hohl

ASSOC-P: Will Cowan **D:** Harold Young **SCR:** Bernard Schubert & Luci Ward **ORIG. STORY:** Harrison Carter & Henry Sucher **ADAPT:** Henry Sucher **PHOTOG:** Paul Ivano **MUSIC:** H.J. Salter
Standard "Inner Sanctum" mystery: Hypnotist uncovers murder plot

Frozen Terror

1980, (It), color, 93 mins.
W: Bernice Stegers
D: Lamberto Bava
Minor thriller: Murderous madman resembles Jack Frost and Jack the Ripper

La Frusta e il Corpo (The Whip and the Body)

1963, (It-Fr), Vox/Leone/Futuramic, color, 90 mins.
W: Daliah Lavi, Christopher Lee, Tony Kendall, Harriet White, Jacques Herlin, Isli Oberon
D: John M. Old [Mario Bava] **SCR:** Julian Berry, Robert Hugo, & Martin Hardy **PHOTOG:** David Hamilton [Ubaldo Terzano]
GB retitle, **Night is the Phantom,** *USA retitle,* **What!** *A.k.a.* **Son of Satan**
Unusual, erotic sado-horror: Woman haunted by "ghost" of evil lover

Fuego

see **Pyro**

The Fugitive

1947, (USA), RKO, b&w, 104 mins.
W: Henry Fonda, Dolores Del Rio Pedro Armendariz, J. Carrol Naish, Leo Carrillo, Robert Armstrong, John Qualen, Ward Bond, Mel Ferrer
D: John Ford **SCR:** Dudley Nichols, from Graham Greene's novel **PHOTOG:** Gabriel Figueroa
Standard thriller: Priest pursued by police and informers

The Fugitive

1993, (USA), WB, color, 130 mins.
W: Harrison Ford (*Dr. Richard Kimble*), Tommy Lee Jones (*Deputy Samuel Gerard*), Sela Ward (*Helen Kimble*), Julianne Moore (*Dr. Anne Eastman*), Joe Pantoliano (*Cosmo Renfro*), Andreas Katsulas (*Sykes*), Jeroen Krabbe, Daniel Roebuck, Ron Dean, Joseph Kosala, Tom Wood, Dick Cusack, Richard Riehle, Andy Romano, Nick Searcy, L. Scott Caldwell, John Drummond, Tony Fosco, Joseph F. Fisher, Gene Barge, Danny Goldring, Thomas C. Simmons, Joan Kohn, Eddie "Ed" Smith Jr., Kevin Crowley, Frank Ray Perilli, Michael James, Cynthia Baker, Johnny Lee, Bill Cusack, David Hodges, Lillie Richardson, Tighe Barry, Roxanne Roberts, Alex Hernandez, Cheryl Lynn Bruce, Joel Robinson, Marie Ware, Bernard McGee, Maurice Person, Ana Maria Alvarez, Brent Shaphren, Manny Lopez, Stephen A. Landsman, B.J. Jones, Juan A. Ramirez, Allen Hamilton, Lester Holt, Jay Levine, Kevin LaRosa, Bruce Webb, Criss Horne

Fugitive From the Empire: GEORGE KENNEDY AND IVAN RADO

234

D: Andrew Davis **SCR:** Jeb Stuart & David Twohy, from characters created by Roy Huggins **PHOTOG:** Michael Chapman **MUSIC:** James Newton Howard
Well-made thriller (inspired by popular 1960's teleseries): Surgeon accused of killing wife cf. U.S. Marshalls

Fugitive Alien
1986, (Jap), color, 103 mins.
W: Tatsuya Azuma
Minor SF: Planetary war embroils space-alien statesman

The Fugitive Apparitions
see Les Apparitions Fugitives

Fugitive from the Empire
1981, (USA), Mad-Dog/Univ/NBC-TV, color, 95 mins.
W: Lane Caudell (*Toran*), Belinda Bauer (*Estra*), George Kennedy (*Brakus*), Kabir Bedi (*Gar*), Richard Dix (*Rak*), Marc Alaimo (*Sandros*), Robert Feero (*Capt. Ria*), Ivan J. Rado (*Vors*), Sharon Barr (*Mandras the Horse Chief*), Tony Swartz (*Riis*), Richard Moll (*The Bovum Ferryman*), Andrew Bloch (*Rega*), Fred Pinkard (*The Merchant*), Dee Croxton (*The Woman Scholar*), Chao-Lichi (*The Astrologer*), Ivan Saric (*The 1st Draikian Trooper*), Skip Riley (*The 2nd Draikian Trooper*), Larry Douglas (*Lazar-Sa*), Victor Campos, George Innes, Allan Rich, John Hancock, Priscilla Pointer
WRIT, P, & D, Nicholas Corea **PHOTOG:** John McPherson **SPCL-FX:** Bill Schirmer **MUSIC:** Ian Underwood
Aka The Archer-Fugitive From the Empire
re-televised (1982) as The Archer
TVM, minor "Sword & Sorcer": Prince seeks father's murderers.

The Fugitive Kind
1960, (USA), UA, b&w, 121 mins.
W: Marlon Brando, Anna Magnani, Joanne Woodward, Victor Jory, R.G. Armstrong, Maureen Stapleton, Virgilia Chew, Lucille Benson, Spivy
P: Martin Jurow & Richard J. Shepherd **D:** Sidney Lumet, from Tennessee Williams' play *Orpheus Descending* **PHOTOG:** Boris Kaufman **MUSIC:** Kenyon Hopkins
Classic melodrama, reworking of Greek legend of Orpheus & Eurydice: Moody drifter precipitates tragedy in small Southern town

Full Circle
1978, (GB-Can), Fetter/Classic Film Industries/Discovery, color, 97 mins.
W: Mia Farrow (*Julia Lofting*), Keir Dullea (*Magnus Lofting*), Tom Conti (*Mark*), Jill Bennett (*Lily*), Robin Gammell (*David Swift*), Cathleen Nesbitt (*Mrs. Rudge*), Anna Wing (*Rose Flood*), Edward Hardwicke (*Capt. Paul Wintor*), Mary Morris (*Greta Braden*), Pauline Jameson (*Claudia Branscombe*), Peter Sallis (*Geoffrey Branscombe*), Sophie Ward (*Katie Lofting*), Arthur Howard (*Piggott*), Damaris Hayman (*Miss Pinner*), Hilda Fennemore (*Katherine*), Nigel Havers (*The Agent*), Samantha Gates (*Olivia Rudge*), Ann Mitchell
P: Peter Fetterman & Alfred Pariser **D:** Richard Loncraine **SCR:** Dave Humphries **ADAPT:** Harry Bromley Davenport, from Peter Straub's novel *Julia* **PHOTOG:** Peter Hannan **SPCL-FX:** Thomas Clark **MUSIC:** Colin Towns
USA retitle, The Haunting of Julia
Standard horror-thriller: Spectral girl plagues murderess

Full Confession
1939, (USA), RKO, b&w, 75 mins.
W: Victor McLaglen, Joseph Calleia, Sally Eilers, Elizabeth Risdon, Barry Fitzgerald
D: John Farrow
Standard melodrama: Killer hounded by conscience

Full Eclipse
1993, (USA), Citadel/HBO-TV, color, 105 mins.
W: Mario Van Peebles (*Max Dire*), Patsy Kensit (*Casey Spencer*), Bruce Payne (*Adam Garou*), Anthony John Denison (*Jim Sheldon*), Jason Beghe (*Doug Crane*), Paula Marshall (*Liza*), John Verea (*Ramon Perez*), Dean Norris (*Fleming*), Willie C. Carpenter (*Ron Edmunds*), Victoria Rowell (*Anna Dire*), Scott Paulin (*Teague*), Mel Winkler (*Stratton*), Joseph Culp (*Det. Tom Davies*), Joey De Pinto (*Silvano*), John Apicella (*The Club Mgr.*), Brent Bolthouse, Kelly Brennan, Eric Fiedler, David Gail, Ruben Garfias, Jeff Russell, Vincent Hammond, Howard Himmelstein, Jennifer Rubin, Guy J. Louthan, Larry Mortorff, Piers Plowden, Frederick Ponzlov, Robin Pearson Rose, Ahmad Stoner
D: Anthony Hickox **SCR:,** Richard Christian Matheson & Michael Reaves **PHOTOG:** Sandi Sissel **MUSIC:** Gary Chang
Made-for-Cable, unusual horror-fantasy: Cops become werewolves

Full Moon
see Moonchild

Full Moon High
1982, (USA), Filmways, color, 94 mins
W: Adam Arkin, Ed McMahon, Alan Arkin, Demond Wilson, Elizabeth Hartman, Louis Nye, Kenneth Mars Roz Kelly, Bill Kirchenbauer, Joanne Nail
P D, & SCR: Larry Cohen
Standard horror-comedy: Teen becomes werewolf

The Full Treatment
1961, (GB), Hammer/HilaryFalcon/Col, b&w, 109 mins.
W: Ronald Lewis (*Alan Colby*), Diane Cilento (*Denise*), Claude Dauphin (*Dr. Prade*), Francoise Rosay, Ann Tirard, Bernard Braden, Katya Douglas, Barbara Chilcott, Edwin Styles, George Merritt
D: Val Guest **SCR:** Val Guest & Ronald Scott Thorn, from a novel by Ronald Scott Thorn **PHOTOG:** Gilbert Taylor **MUSIC:** Stanley Black
USA retitle, Stop Me Before I Kill
Standard melodrama: Race-car driver recovers from crash, finds himself trying to murder wife

Fu Manchu
1956, (USA), b&w, 60 mins.
W: Glenn Gordon, Laurette Luez, Clark Howat, Lee Matthews
from characters created by Sax Rohmer
Minor thriller culled from 2 episodes ("The Golden God" & "The Master Plan") of teleseries: Fiend plots to enslave world

Fun and Fancy Free
1947, (USA), Walt Disney, color
W: Edgar Bergen, Luana Patten
2 short animated fantasies: "Bongo" (runaway circus bear) & "Mickey and the Beanstalk"

Funeral Home
1982, (Can), Barry Allen/Wescom/MPM, color, 92 mins.
W: Kay Hawtrey (*Grandma*), Lesleh Donaldson (*Heather*), Barry Morse (*Mr. Davis*), Dean Garbett (*Rick*), Stephen Miller (*Billy Hibbs*), Alfred Humphreys (*Joe*), Harvey Atkin (*Harry*), Peggy Mahon (*Florie*), Bob Warner (*The Sheriff*), Jack Van Evera (*James Chalmers*), Les Rubie (*Sam*), Doris Petrie (*Ruby*), Bill Lake (*Frank*), Brett Davidson (*Young Rick*), Chris Crabb (*Teddy*), Barbara Wheeldon (*Helena Davis*), Robert Craig (*Barry Oaks*), Linda Dalby (*Linda*), Gerard Jordan (*Pete*), Barry Allen (*The Restaurant Proprietor*), Eleanor Beecroft (*Shirley*), James Crammond (*The Reporter*), Ronald Reece (*The Developer*), Peter Sturgess (*Ed*), Allison Fruet (*Georgia*), Paul Hubbard, Terry Harford, Billy Kishonti, Kenneth Garland, Bob Meneray, Carlo Sgussro, Robert Gatrell, Brett McAdams, Janice Pinke, Edith Bolsover, Donald Saunders, Kate McDonald, Don Brennan, William Roth
P & D: William Fruet **SCR:** Ida Nelson **PHOTOG:** Mark Irwin **MUSIC:** Jerry Fielding
A.k.a. 2 Cries in the Night
Standard thriller: Mortuary masks madness & murder

Funeral in Berlin
1966, (GB), Lowndes/Para, color, 102 mins.
W: Michael Caine (*Harry Palmer*), Paul (Christian) Hubschmid (*Johnny Vulkan*), Oscar Homolka (*Col. Stok*), Eva Renzi (*Samantha Steel*), Guy Doleman (*Ross*), Hugh Burden (*Hallam*), Heinz Schubert (*Aaron Levine*), Wolfgang Volz (*Werner*), Thomas Holtzmann (*Reinhart*), Gunter Meisner (*Kreutzman*), Herbert Fux (*Artur*), Rachel Gurney (*Mrs. Ross*), Rainer Brandt (*Benjamin*), Ira Hagen
P: Harry Saltzman & Charles Kasher **D:** Guy Hamilton & Peter Medak **SCR:** Evan Jones, from Len Deighton's novel *The Berlin Memorandum* **PHOTOG:** Otto Heller **MUSIC:** Konrad Elfers
Mature spy-thriller: Secret agent becomes embroiled with defecting Bolshevik. cf. The Ipcress File

The Fun House (1977)
see Last House on Dead End Street

The Funhouse
1981, (USA), Mace Neufeld/Univ, color, 94 mins.
W: Elizabeth Berridge (*Amy*), Shawn Carson (*Joey*), Jack McDermott (*Harper*), Jeanne Austin (*Mrs. Harper*), Cooper Huckabee (*Buzz*), Largo Woodruff (*Liz*), Sylvia Miles (*Mme. Zena*), Miles Chapin (*Richie*), David Carson (*The Geek*), Sonia Zomina (*The Bag Lady*), Kevin Conway (*The Barker*), Ralph Marino (*The Truck Driver*), Herb Robins (*The Carnival Manager*), Mona Agar (*The Stripper*), Wayne Doba (*The Monster*), William Finley (*Marco*), Sid Raymond (*The M.C.*), Susie Malnik (*Carmella*), Larry Ross (*The Heckler*), Frank Grimes (*The Voyeur*), Frank Schuller (*The Poker Player*), Peter Conrad (*The Midget*), Mildred Hughes (*The Tall Lady*), Glen Lawrence, Mike Montalvo, Sandy Mielke, Shawn McAllister
D: Tobe Hooper **SCR:** Larry Block **PHOTOG:** Andrew Laszlo **MUSIC:** John Beal
Standard horror-thriller: Teens regret spending night in carnival funhouse

Funny Games
1997, (Austria), Attitude Films, color
W: Ulrich Muhe (*Georg*), Arno Frisch (*Paul*), Susanne Lothar (*Anna*), Stefan Clapczynski (*Georgie*), Frank Giering
D: Michael Haneke **PHOTOG:** Jurgen Jurges **MUSIC:** John Zorn
Bizarre thriller: Sociopaths terrorize

Funny Man
1994, (GB), color, 93 mins.
W: Tim James, Christopher Lee, Ingrid Lacey, Pauline Black, Matthew Devitt, Benny Young
D: Simon Sprackling
Minor horror-thriller: Mansion harbors evil jester who slays unwelcome guests

F

The Fur Collar

1962, (GB), Albatross/RFD, b&w, 71 mins.
W: John Bentley (*Mike Andrews*), Nadja Regin (*Marie Lejeune*), Martin Benson (*Insp. Legrain*), Philip Friend (*Eddie Morgan*), Balbina (*Jacqueline Legrain*), Hector Ross (*Roger Harding*), Gordon Sterne (*Duclos*), Guy Middleton (*The Resident*), Brian Nissen (*Carl Jorgensen*)
WRIT, P & D: Lawrence Huntington
Standard crime-thriller: Reporter feigns death, exposes spies

Further Exploits of Sexton Blake—The Mystery of the S.S. Olympic

1919, (GB), Atlantic Films/Gaumont, b&w, 4,529 ft. (1380.4m)
W: Douglas Payne (*Sexton Blake*), Marjorie Villis (*Gwenda Howard*), Jeff Barlow (*Mr. Reece*), Frank Dane (*Hamilton*), Neil Warrington (*Tinker*), William Brandon
P & D: Harry Lorraine, from characters created by Harry Blyth
Standard thriller: Inventor murdered for formula

The Fury

1978, (USA), Frank Yablans-Brian De Palma/20th-Fox, color, 117 mins.
W: Kirk Douglas (*Peter*), Andrew Stevens (*Robin Sandza*), John Cassavetes (*Childress*), Carrie Snodgress (*Hester*), Charles Durning (*Dr. Jim McKeever*), Amy Irving (*Gillian Bellaver*), Fiona Lewis (*Susan Charles*), Carol Rossen (*Dr. Ellen Lindstrom*), William Finley (*Raymond*), Joyce Easton (*Katherine Bellaver*), J. Patrick McNamara (*Robertson*), Bernie Kuby (*Nuckles*), Jane Lambert (*Vivian Nuckles*), Rutanya Alda (*Kristen*), Melody Thomas (*Larue*), Alice Nunn (*Mrs. Callahan*), Hilary Thomas (*Cheryl*), Sam Laws (*Blackfish*), Jim Belushi (*extra*), Dennis Franz, Daryl Hannah, Frank Yablans
P: Frank Yablans **D:** Brian De Palma **SCR:** John Farris—from his novel
PHOTOG: Richard H. Kline **MUSIC:** John Williams
Superior SF-horror: Young psychic becomes gov't pawn. film debut of Daryl Hannah

Fury at Smugglers' Bay

1961, (GB), Regal Films International/Mijo/Embassy, colorscope, 92 mins.
W: Peter Cushing (*Squire Trevenyan*), John Fraser (*Christopher Trevenyan*), Bernard Lee (*Black John*), Michele Mercier (*Louise Lejeune*), June Thorburn (*Jenny. Trevenyan*), William Franklyn (*The Captain*), Liz Fraser (*Betty*), Miles Malleson (*The Duke of Avon*), George Coulouris (*Lejeune*), Katherine Kath (*Maman*), Juma (*Juma*), Thomas Duggan (*Red Friars*), Christopher Carlos (*The Tiger*), Maitland Moss (*Tom*), Humphrey Heathcote (*Roger Treherne*), Bob Simmons (*Carlos*), James Liggatt (*The Sergeant*), Alan Browning (*The 2nd Highwayman*), Patrick Desmond (*The Watchman*), Alfred Pim (*Jasper*), Ken Buckle (*The Fox*)
WRIT & D: John Gilling **PHOTOG:** Harry Waxman **MUSIC:** Harold Geller
Standard swashbuckler: Cornish cads loot shipwrecks. Original: **The Wreckers**

Fury of Achilles

1962, (It), AIP-TV, color, 116 mins
W: Jacques Bergerac, Gordon Mitchell
Minor "Sword & Sandal": Hero leads Greeks against Trojans

The Fury of Hercules

see **Samson**

Fury of the Congo

1951, (USA), Col, b&w, 69 mins.
W: Johnny Weissmuller (*Jungle Jim*), Sherry Moreland, Lyle Talbot
P: Sam Katzman **D:** William Berke **SCR:** Carroll Young
blurb: "Barbaric beauties in fierce jungle war!"
Standard adventure-thriller: White native tribe saved from clutches of narcotics gang. 'Jungle Jim' series

Fury of the Pagans

1963, (It), b&w, 86 mins.
W: Edmund Purdom, Rossana Podesta, Livio Lorenzon, Carlo Calo
D: Guido Malatesta
Standard "Sword & Sandal": Savage tribe vs. ancient Rome

Fury of the Succubus

see **Satan's Mistress**

Fury of the Vikings

see **Gli Invasori**

The Fury of the Wolfman

1970, (Sp), Plata Films/Avco Embassy, color, 82 mins.
W: Paul Naschy, Perla Cristal, Michael Rivers
D: Jose Maria Zabala **SCR:** Jacinto Molina
Minor horror-thriller: Lady scientist conducts unethical experiments

The Fury Within

1998, (USA), USA-TV, color, 95 mins.
W: Costas Mandylor (*Mike*), Ally Sheedy (*Jo*), Vincent Berry (*Jimmy*), Steve Bastoni
D: Noel Nosseck **TELEPLAY:** William Bast & Paul Huson **PHOTOG:** John Stokes
TVM, standard fantasy-thriller: Psychic phenomena plague woman

Future Cop

1978, (USA), Para/ABC-TV, color, 74 mins.
W: Ernest Borgnine (*Cleaver*), Michael Shannon (*Haven*), John Amos (*Bundy*), John Larch (*Forman*), Herbert Nelson (*Klausmeier*), James Luisi (*Paterson*), James Daughton (*The Young Rookie*), Ronnie Claire Edwards (*Avery*), Stephen Perlman (*Dorfman*)
WRIT & P: Anthony Wilson **D:** Jud Taylor **PHOTOG:** Terry Meade
MUSIC: Billy Goldenberg
A.k.a. **Cleaver and Haven**
TVM, standard SF-adventure: World's first robot policeman

Future Force

1989, (USA), AIP, color, 90 mins.
W: David Carradine, Robert Tessier, Anna Rapagna, William Zipp
Minor SF-thriller: Future civilian mercenaries attack crime

Future Hunters

1989, (USA), video, color 96 mins
W: Robert Patrick, Linda Carol, Ed Crick, Bob Schott
D: Cirio H. Santiago
Made-for-Video, minor SF-thriller: Hunter from future finds magic sword, is transported to 1989 Los Angeles

Futurekick

1991, (USA), color, 80 mins.
W: Don "The Dragon" Wilson, Meg Foster, Christopher Penn, Eb Lottimer
D & SCR: Damian Klaus
Minor action-SF: Kickboxer with cyborg capabilities opposes evil

Future Kill

1985, (USA), color, 83 mins.
W: Edwin Neal, Marilyn Burns, Doug Davis
D & SCR: Ronald W. Moore
Minor SF-thriller: Future fraternity brothers vs. anti-nuke activists

Future Shock

1993, (USA), color, 93 mins, also 97 mins.
W: Vivian Schilling, Martin Kove Scott Thompson, Sam Clay, Bill Paxton, Brion James, Tim Doyle, Sidney Lassick, James Karen, Amanda Foreman
D: Eric Parkinson, Francis "Oley" Sassone & Matt Reeves
Standard SF-thriller: Psychiatrist's virtual reality therapy goes awry

Futuresport

1998, (USA), ABC-TV, color
W: Wesley Snipes (*Obike Fixxe*), Dean Cain (*Tre Ramzey*), Bill Smitrovich (*Coach*), Vanessa L. Williams (*Alex*)
TVM, standard SF-thriller: High-tech battle for security of world

Future Women

1978, (Sp-Brz), Lonnie Kaufmann, color, 81 mins.
W: Shirley Eaton (*Sumitra*), Richard Wyler (*Jeff Sutton*), Maria Rohm (*Lesley*), Herbert Fleischmann (*Carl*), Marta Reves (*Ulla*), Eliza Montes (*Irene*), Benny Cardoso (*Yana*)
SCR: Peter Welbeck **PHOTOG:** Manuel Merino **MUSIC:** Daniel White
SONG: *The Girl from Rio*
Minor thriller: All-female army plots world conquest

Futureworld

1976, (USA), AIP, color, 107 mins.
W: Peter Fonda (*Chuck Browning*), Yul Brynner (*The Gunslinger*), Blythe Danner (*Tracy Ballard*), Stuart Margolin (*Harry*), Arthur Hill (*Duffy*), Jim Antonio (*Ron*), Robert Cornthwaite (*Mr. Reed*), Angela Greene (*Mrs. Reed*), Allen Ludden (*The Game Show M.C.*), Darrell Larson (*Eric*), John Fujioka (*Mr. Takaguchi*), Nancy Bell (*Erica*), Alex Rodine (*The KGB Man*), Dana Lee (*Takaguchi's Aide*), Burt Conroy (*Gen. Karnovski*), Dorothy Konrad (*Mrs. Karnovski*), Joanna Hall (*The Maiden Fair*)
D: Richard T. Heffron **SCR:** Mayo Simon & George Schenck **PHOTOG:** Howard Schwartz & Gene Polito **MUSIC:** Fred Karlin
Standard SF-thriller, sequel to **Westworld***: Reporters uncover plot to replace world leaders with robot lookalikes*

Future Zone

1990, (USA), color 88 mins.
W: David Carradine, Ted Prior, Patrick Culliton (*Hoffman*), Charles Napier (*Mickland*), Gail Jensen (*Marion*)
D: David A. Prior
Minor SF-thriller: Future law enforcement

Futurisme

see **L'Inhumaine**

FX 18, Secret Agent

1964, (Fr), Gold Key TV, color, 95 mins
W: Ken Clark, Jany Clair
Minor spy-thriller: Agent investigates espionage ring

Gabbeth
1997, (Iran), color
D: Mohsen Makhmalbaf
Standard melodrama

The Gables Mystery (1931)
see *The Man at Six*

The Gables Mystery
1938, (GB), Welwyn/MGM, b&w, 66 mins.
W: Francis L. Sullivan (*Power*), Leslie Perrins (*Insp. Lloyd*), Antoinette Cellier (*Helen Vane*), Derek Gorst (*Frank Rider*), Jerry Verno (*Potts*), Aubrey Mallalieu (*Sir James Rider*), Laura Wright (Mrs. *Mullins*), Sidney King (*Mortimer*)
D: Harry Hughes   SCR: Victor Kendall & Harry Hughes, from the play *The Man at Six* by Jack Celestin & Jack De Leon
Standard thriller: Girl detective unmasks killer thief

Gabriel Grubb the Surly Sexton
1904, (GB), Williamson/Urban, b&w, 400 ft. (121.9m)
D: James Williamson, based on a portion of Charles Dickens' novel *The Pickwick Papers*
Minor fantasy short: Sexton reforms after dreaming of abduction by goblins

Gabriel over the White House
1933, (USA), Cosmopolitan/MGM, b&w, 87 mins.
W: Walter Huston, Karen Morley, Franchot Tone, Samuel S. Hinds, Arthur Byron, Jean Parker, David Landau, C. Henry Gordon, Dickie Moore, William Pawley, Claire DuBrey, Akim Tamiroff
P: Walter Wanger   D: Gregory LaCava   SCR: Carey Wilson, from Frederic Tweed's novel   PHOTOG: Bert Glennon   MUSIC: William Axt
Superior philosophical fantasy: Benign spirit takes over body of U.S. president

Galactic Gigolo
1988, (USA), Titan/Urban Classics, color 82 mins
W: Carmine Capobianco, Debi Thibeault, Ruth Collins, Angela Nicholas, Frank Stewart
D: Gorman Bechard
Minor SF-satire: "An Extra-Terrestrial Sexual Comedy"

Galactic Odyssey
1998, (USA), color, 95 mins.
W: Adam Baldwin, Robert Englund
Standard SF-thriller: Post-nuke spaceship's crew members methodically killed

Galatea
see *Galathee*

Galathee (Galatea)
1910, (Fr), Star, b&w
D: Georges Melies
Standard fantasy: Beautiful statue comes to life

Galaxie
1966, (USA), Gregory Markopoulos, 16mm "underground" film, color, 90 mins.
W: Shirley Clarke, Jonas Mekas
WRIT, D & PHOTOG: Gregory Markopoulos
Standard fantasy

Galaxina
1980, (USA), Marimark/Crown-Int'l, color, 96 mins.
W: Dorothy R. Stratten (*Galaxina*), Stephen Macht (*Thor*), Avery Schreiber (*Capt. Cornelius Butt*), James David Hinton (*Buzz*), Tad Horino (*Sam Wo*), Lionel Mark Smith (*Maurice*), Ronald Knight (*Ordric*), Percy Rodrigues (*Herbert Kaplowitz* (*Kitty*)), Stephen Morrell, Angelo Rossitto, Fred D. Scott (*The Commander*), David A. Cox, Nancy Macauley, (*Elexia*), Marilyn Joi, Pete Schrum, Bartine Zane, Rhonda Shear, Mike Castle, Heather O'Connell, Hugh Warden, George Mather (*Horn Man*), Frank Ferro, Daniel Vincent Audet, Darwin Lee Benjamin, Robert L. Brossman, Michael Margaral, Michael Denis Brox, Keith C. Durkin, Jacqueline Jacobs, Frederick C. Gazelle, Chuck McAmish, Teri Powers, Jeffrey McGrail, Stan Partin, Robin Torell
WRIT & D: William Sachs   PHOTOG: Dean Cundey   SPCL-FX SPRVSR: Chuck Colwell
Uneven SF-comedy: Beautiful robotrix accompanies crew of space-police cruiser

Galaxis
1995, (USA), Interlight/Osmosis, color, 91 mins.
W: Brigitte Nielsen (*Ladera*), Richard Moll (*Kyla*), John H. Brennan (*Jed Sanders*), Roger Aaron Brown (*Carter*), Fred Asparagus (*Victor*), Michael Paul Chan (*Manny*), Alan Fudge (*The Chief*), Cindy Morgan (*Kelly*), Sam Raimi (*The Nervous Official*), Craig Fairbrass (*Tarkin*), Russ Fega (*The Official*), John Romauldi (*Soldier #1*), Arthur Mesa (*The Robot Child*), Kristin Bauer (*The Commander*), Steve Garrett (*The Soldier*), Louisa Moritz (*The Bar Lady*), Nathan Jung (*The Doorman*), Jeff Rector (*Tray*), Jane Clark (*The Rape Victim*), Joey Gaynor (*Stravos*), Richard Narita (*Raymond*), George Kee Cheung (*Eddie*), Chris Doyle (*Seth*), Brent Pfaff (*The Policeman*)
D: William Mesa   SCR: Nick Davis   PHOTOG: Robert C. New   MUSIC:

Christopher L. Stone
Minor SF-adventure: Female warrior seeks power source to save her world from intergalactic tyrant

The Galaxy Criminals
see *I Criminali della Galassia*

The Galaxy Invader
1985, (USA), Moviecraft, color, 80 mins.
W: Richard Ruxton (*Joe*), Faye Tilles (*Carol*), Anne Frith (*Ethel*), George Stover (*J.J.*), Greg Dohler (*David*), Don Leifert (*Frank*), Richard Dyszel (*Dr. William Tracy*), Kim Dohler (*Annie*), Theresa Harold (*Vickie*), Glenn Barnes (*The Alien*)
WRIT & D: Don Dohler   PHOTOG: Paul E. Loeschke   SPCL-FX: David Donoho   MUSIC: Norman Naplock and Led & Silver
Minor SF-thriller: Space creature prowls

Galaxy of Terror
1981, (USA), New World, color, 85 mins.
W: Edward Albert (*Cabren*), Erin Moran (*Aluma*), Bernard Behrens (*Ilvar*), Ray Walston (*Kore*), Zalman King (*Baelon*), Robert Englund (*Ranger*), Taafe O'Connell (*Dameia*), Grace Zabriskie (*Capt. Trantor*), Sid Haig (*Quuhod*), Mary Ellen O'Neill (*Mitre*), Jack Blessing (*Cos*)
D: Bruce Clark   SCR: Marc Siegler & Bruce Clark   PHOTOG: Jacques Haitkin   MUSIC: Barry Schrader
A.k.a. *Planet of Horrors* and *An Infinity of Terror*
Minor SF-horror: Astronauts discover remains of alien civilization

The Gallery Murders
see *L'Uccello delle Piume di Cristallo*

Gallery of Horror
1966, (USA), Borealis-Dorad/American General, color, 80 mins.
W: John Carradine, Lon Chaney Jr., Rochelle Hudson, Roger Gentry, Vic McGee, Karen Joy, Mitch Evans, Gray Daniels, Margaret Moore, Ron Brogan, Joey Benson, Ron Doyle
P: David L. Hewitt & Ray Dorn   D: David L. Hewitt   SCR: David Prentiss & Gary R. Heacock   PHOTOG: Austin McKinney
A.k.a. *Dr. Terror's Gallery of Horror* and *Alien Massacre* reissued (1970) as *The Blood Suckers*, televised as *Return from the Past*
Minor quintet of terror-tales (much stock footage from AIP films—e.g., *House of Usher*, *The Pit and the Pendulum* {1961}, *The Raven* {1963}, *The Ghost in the Invisible Bikini*, *The Premature Burial*, et al): (1) *The Witch's Clock* Young couple finds old clock that summons up ancient warlock, (2) *King Vampire*—London police hunt Undead, (3) *Monster Raid*—Rotting corpse of murdered scientist is revived, (4) *Spark of Life*—Two Scottish medical students restore mad murderer to life, & (5) "*Count Dracula*" Real estate agent helps villagers root out nest of vampires

Gall Force: Eternal Story
1993, (Jap), color
Standard animated SF-fantasy: Story of 'Genesis'

Gambit
1966, (USA), Univ, color, 109 mins.
W: Shirley McLaine, Michael Caine, Herbert Lom, Roger C. Carmel, John Abbott, Arnold Moss
D: Ronald Neame   SCR: Alvin Sargent & Jack Davies   MUSIC: Maurice Jarre
Sly thriller (Michael Caine's first Hollywood film) with unexpected twists: Plot to steal priceless statue

The Gambler
see *Doctor Mabuse*

The Gambler's Nightmare
1906, (GB), Warwick Trading Co., b&w, 255 ft. (77.7m)
D: Charles Raymond
Minor melodrama short: Drunken gambler reforms after dreaming he killed policeman

The Game
1997, (USA), Polygram, color, 128 mins.
W: Michael Douglas, Sean Penn, Deborah Kara Unger, Carroll Baker, Peter Donat, Armin Mueller-Stahl, James Rebhorn
D: David Fincher

Game for Three Losers
1965, (GB), Merton Park/Anglo-Amalgamated, b&w, 55 mins.
W: Michael Gough (*Robert Hilary*), Toby Robins (*Frances Challinor*), Mark Eden (*Oliver Marchant*), Rachel Gurney (*Adele*), Allan Cuthbertson (*Garsden*), Roger Hammond (*Peter Fletcher*), Al Mulock (*Nick*), Lockwood West (*Justice Tree*), Mark Dignam (*The Attorney General*), Catherine Wilmer (*Miss Stewart*), Anne Pichon (*Miss Fawcett*), Leslie Sarony (*Harley*)
P: Jack Greenwood   D: Gerry O'Hara   SCR: Roger Marshall, from a novel by Edgar Lustgarten
Standard crime-thriller: Blackmailer's prosecutor accused of seducing secretary

Game of Danger
see *Bang! You're Dead*

A Game of Death

1945, (USA), RKO, b&w, 72 mins.
W: John Loder (*Rainsford*), Audrey Long, Edgar Barrier (*Kreiger, Zarofftype*), Noble Johnson, Russell Wade, Jason Robards Sr., Russell Hicks, Gene Stutenroth, Robert Clarke
P: Herman Schlom **D:** Robert Wise **SCR:** Norman Houston, from Richard Connell's novella *The Most Dangerous Game* **PHOTOG:** J. Roy Hunt
MUSIC: Paul Sawtell
Standard thriller: Madman hunts humans

The Game of Liberty

1916, (GB), London/Jury, b&w, 5,725 ft. (1745m)
W: Gerald Ames (*Hon. Paul Walmsley*), Douglas Munro (*Joseph H. Parker*), Laura Cowie (*Eve Parker*), Sydney Fairbrother (*Mrs. Bundercombe*), Bert Wynne (*Insp. Cullen*), Hugh Croise (*Bert Johnson*)
D: George Loane Tucker, from a novel by E. Phillips Oppenheim
USA retitle, **Under Suspicion**
Standard crime-thriller: British lord's son loves counterfeiter's daughter

Gamera: Guardian of the Universe

1995, (Jap), color, 98 mins.
W: Tsuyoshi Ihara, Akira Onodera, Ayoko Fujitani
D: Shusuke Kaneko
Entertaining SF-fantasy: Giant flying turtle saves Tokyo from monstrous invader

Games

1967, (USA), Univ, color, 100 mins.
W: James Caan (*Paul Montgomery*), Simone Signoret (*Lisa Schindler*), Katharine Ross (*Jennifer Montgomery*), Estelle Winwood (*Miss Beattie*), Don Stroud (*Norman*), Kent Smith (*Harry*), Marjorie Bennett (*Nora*), Peter Brocco, Florence Marly, Ian Wolfe
P: George Edwards **D:** Curtis Harrington **SCR:** Gene Kearney **PHOTOG:** William A. Fraker **MUSIC:** Samuel Matlovsky
"...director Curtis Harrington, who wrote the original story, knows how to hold your interest with the suspenseful and crazy goings-on. The cast is good throughout; the house is entertaining; and so, in their way, are all the diabolical shenanigans"—Philip T. Hartung, Commonweal
Strong touches of **Diabolique** *in tidy thriller: Wealthy and fun-loving young couple introduced to bizarre and sophisticated games after making acquaintance of mysterious woman*

The Games of the Countess Dolingen of Gratz

1981, (Fr), color, 110 mins.
W: Carol Kane, Marina Vlady
D: Catherine Binet
Unusual fantasy-drama: Strange crossing of paths for woman with remembrances of childhood fears, man plotting to trap burglar, and mysterious noblewoman who rises from tomb

The Gamma People

1956, (GB), Warwick/Col, b&w, 79 mins.
W: Paul Douglas (*Mike Wilson*), Eva Bartok (*Paula Wendt*), Walter Rilla (*Boronski*), Leslie Phillips (*Howard Meade*), Michael Caridia (*Hugo*), Jackie Lane (*Anna*), Martin Miller (*Lochner*), Philip Leaver (*Koerner*), Paul Hardtmuth (*Hans*), Pauline Drewett (*Hedda*), Olaf Pooley (*Bikstein*), Rosalie Crutchley (*Frau Bikstein*), Leonard Sachs (*The Telegraph Clerk*), Cyril Chamberlain (*Graf*), St. John Stuart (*Goon*)
P: John Gossage **D:** John Gilling **SCR:** John Gilling & John Gossage, from an orig. story by Louis Pollock **PHOTOG:** Ted Moore **MUSIC:** George Melachrino
Standard SF-thriller: Two reporters discover experiments in intelligence alteration

Gamma 693

see **Night of the Zombies** *(1981)*

Gammera, the Invincible

1965, (USA-Jap), Daiei/Harris Assocs./World Entertainment, b&w, scope, 88 mins.
W: Brian Donlevy (*Arnold*), Albert Dekker, Diane Findley, Dick O'Neill, John Baragrey, Eiji Funakoshi
P: Masaichi Nagata **D:** Noriaki Yuasa, US sequences by Sandy Howard **SCR:** Fumi Takahashi
Minor SF-fantasy: A-bomb blast revives prehistoric flying turtle

Gammera vs. Barugon

1966, (Jap), Daiei, color, 101 mins.
W: Kojiro Hongo (*Keisuke*), Kyoko Enami (*Karen*), Akira Natsuki
D: Shigeo Tanaka **SCR:** Fumi Takahashi
Minor SF-thriller: Treasure-seekers encounter horror

Gammera vs. Guiron

1969, (Jap), Daiei/AIP, color, 82 mins.
W: Nobuhiro Kashima, Christopher Murphy
P: Hidemasa Nagata **D:** Noriaki Yuasa **SCR:** Fumi Takahashi
A.k.a. **Attack of the Monsters**
Minor SF-fantasy: Prehistoric monsters battle

Gammera vs. Gyaos

1967, (Jap), Daiei, color, 87 mins.

W: Kojiro Hongo, K. Ueda
D: Noriaki Yuasa **SCR:** Fumi Takahashi
Minor SF-fantasy: Giant monsters wage war

Gammera vs. Jiger

1970, (Jap), Daiei, color, 83 mins.
W: Kelly Varis, T. Takakuwa
D: Noriaki Yuasa **SCR:** Fumi Takahashi
Minor SF-fantasy: Revived monsters pillage

Gammera vs. Monster X

1969, (Jap), Daiei, color
W: Tsutomo Takakuwa (*Hiroshi*)
Minor SF-fantasy: Prehistoric horror faces alien threat

Gammera vs. Viras

1968, (Jap), Daiei/AIP, color, 75 mins.
W: Kojiro Hongo, Carl Clay, Peter Williams
P: Hidemasa Nagata **D:** Noriaki Yuasa **SCR:** Fumi Takahashi
A.k.a. **Destroy All Planets**
Minor SF-fantasy: Monsters battle

Gammera vs. Zigra

1971, (Jap), Daiei/Sandy Frank, color
W: Ken Utsui, Yusuke Kawazu, Koji Fujiyama
D: Noriaki Yuasa **SCR:** Fumi Takahashi **PHOTOG:** Akira Uehara **SPCL-FX:** Kazuo Fijii **MUSIC:** Shunsuke Kikuchi
Standard SF-fantasy: Monsters vie for world domination

Der Gang in der Nacht

see **Der Januskopf**

Gang Wars

see **Devil's Express**

Gang War

1962, (GB), Danziger/UA, b&w, 65 mins.
W: Sean Kelly (*Insp. Bob Craig*), Eira Heath (*Maria Alexis*), David Davies (*Jim Alexis*), Sean Sullivan (*Al Hodges*), John Gabriel (*Doc Tobin*), Mark Singleton (*Tony Danton*), Colin Tapley (*Paul Alexis*), Leon Cortez (*Grimes*)
P: Brian Langslow **D:** Frank Marshall **STORY:** Mark Grantham
Standard crime-thriller: Club owner and Chicago crook vie to control jukebox racket

Ganjasauras Rex

1987, (USA), color, 100 mins.
W: Paul Bassis, Dave Fresh, Rosie Jones
D: Ursi Reynolds
Minor SF-spoof: Giant monster emerges from marijuana-laden California hills

Ganja and Hess

1973, (USA), Kelly-Jordan Enterprises, color, 110 mins.
W: Duane Jones (*Dr. Hess Green*), Marlene Clark (*Ganja*), Leonard Jackson (*Archie*), Bill Gunn (*George*), Mabel King (*Queen of Myrthia*), Sam Raymon (*Rev. Williams*), Candace Tarpley (*The Girl in the Bar*), Richard Harrow (*The Dinner Guest*), John Hoffmeister (*Jack*), Enrico Fales (*Green's Son*), Betty Barney (*The Singer*), Tommy Lane (*The Pimp*), Betsy Thurman (*The Poetess*), Tara Fields (*The Woman with the Baby*)
P: Chiz Schultz **D & SCR:** Bill Gunn **PHOTOG:** James E. Hinton **MUSIC:** Sam Waymon
A.k.a. **Double Possession** *and* **Blood Couple**
Standard horror-fantasy: Black vampire has visions of Africa

Gaolbreak

1962, (GB), Butcher's Films, b&w, 61 mins.
W: Peter Reynolds (*Eddie Wallis*), Avice Landone (*Mrs. Wallis*), David Kernan (*Len Rogerson*), Carol White (*Carol Marshall*), David Gregory (*Ron Wallis*), John Blythe (*Slim*), Geoffrey Hibbert (*Dr. Cambus*), Robert Desmond (*Page*)
P: Francis Searle & Ronald Liles **D:** Francis Searle **STORY:** A.R. Rawlinson
Standard crime-thriller: Newsagent's fugitive son robs auctioneer's safe

Gappa, the Triphibian Monster

1965, (Jap), Toho/AIP, color, 90 mins
W: Yoko Yamamoto, Tatsuya Fuji, Yuji Odaka, Tamio Kawaji
D: Haruyasu Noguchi **SCR:** Iwao Yamazaki & Ryuko Nakanishi
USA retitle (1967), **Monster from a Prehistoric Planet**
Minor SF-fantasy: Giant reptilian bird taken to Tokyo

The Garbage Pail Kids

1987, (USA), Topps Chewing Gum/Atlantic, color, 100 mins.
W: Anthony Newley (*Capt. Manzini*), Mackenzie Astin (*Dodger*), Katie Barberi (*Tangerine*), Ron MacLachlan (*Juice*)
P & D: Rod Amateau **SCR:** Melinda Palmer & Rod Amateau **PHOTOG:** Harvey Genkins
Minor fantasy: Sleazoid creatures foment havoc

The Gardener

see **Seeds of Evil**

The Garden Murder Case
1936, (USA), MGM, b&w, 62 mins.
W: Edmund Lowe (*Philo Vance*), Gene Lockhart (*Lowe Hammle*), Virginia Bruce (*Zalia Graem*), Benita Hume (*Nurse Beeton*), Nat Pendleton (*Sgt. Ernest Heath*), H.B. Warner (*Maj. Ralston*), Kent Smith (*Woode Swift*), Grant Mitchell (*D.A. John F.X. Markham*), Frieda Inescort (*Mrs. Ralston*), Henry B. Walthall (*Dr. Garden*), Douglas Walton (*Floyd Garden*), Jessie Ralph (*Mrs. Hammle*), Charles Trowbridge (*Insp. Colby*), Etienne Girardot (*Doremus*), William Austin (*Sneed*), Rosalind Ivan (*Jepson*)
D: Edwin L. Marin   SCR: Bertram Millhauser, from characters created by S.S. Van Dine   PHOTOG: Charles Clarke
Standard "Philo Vance" mystery-thriller: Suave detective tackles triple murder. Film debut of Kent Smith and Rosalind Ivan

Garden of the Dead
1972, (USA), Millenium/Ent.-Pyramid, color, 60 mins.
W: John Kenneally, Joe Pronto, Marland Proctor, Susan Charney, John Dennis, Duncan McCloud, Eric Stern Lee Frost
P: H.A. Milton   D: John Hayes   SCR: John Jones
A.k.a. Tomb of the Undead
Minor horror-thriller: Formaldehyde-drinking zombies

Garganuta
1998, (USA), Fox-TV, color, 95 mins.
W: Adam Baldwin (*Jack*), Emile Hirsch (*Brandon*), Julie Carmen (*Alyson*), Bobby Hosea (*Col. Wayne*), Doug Penty (*Paul Bateman*), Peter Adams, Peter Kent, Cassandra Hyde
D: Bradford May   TELEPLAY: Ronald Parker   PHOTOG: John Stokes   MUSIC: J. Peter Robinson
TVM standard SF-thriller: Monster rises from deep

Gargoyles
1972, (USA), Tomorrow/CBS-TV, color, 74 mins.
W: Cornel Wilde (*Mercer Boley*), Jennifer Salt (*Diana Boley*), Grayson Hall (*Mrs. Parks*), Bernie Casey (*The Head Gargoyle*), Scott Glenn (*James Reeger*), John Gruber (*Jesse*), William Stevens (*The Police Chief*), Tim Burns (*Ray*), Woody Chambliss (*Uncle Willie*), Jim Connell (*Buddy*), Mickey Alzola, Greg Walker, Rock Walker
D: B.W.L. Norton   TELEPLAY: Stephen Karpf & Elinor Karpf   PHOTOG: Earl Rath   SPCL-FX: Milt Rice & George Peckham   MUSIC: Robert Prince
TVM, standard fantasy-thriller: Ancient creatures reside in caves, plot world conquest

Gargoyles the Movie: The Heros Awaken
1994, (USA), coor, 80 mins.
VOICES: Ed Asner, Keith David, Jonathan Frakes, Marina Sirtis, Frank Welker, Bill Fagerbakke, Jeff Bennett, Salli Richardson, Thom Adcox
Standard animated fantasy (culled from 5 episodes of teleseries "Gargoyles"): Crime-fighting grotesques prowl night

A Garret in Bohemia
1915, (GB), London/Jury, b&w, 2,795 ft. (851.9m)
W: Edna Flugrath (*Sarah*), Ben Webster (*Kenneth Douglas*), Christine Rayner (*Miriam West*), Gwynne Herbert (*The Landlady*), Jeff Barlow (*The Blind Fiddler*)
D: Harold Shaw, from a novel by G.E.R. Mayne
Standard fantasy-romance: Blind fiddler's ghost inspires impoverished composer

Garu, the Mad Monk
see **Guru, the Mad Monk**

Gaslight
1940, (GB), British Nat'l, b&w, 88 mins.
W: Anton Walbrook (*Paul Mallen*), Diana Wynyard (*Bella Mallen*), Frank Pettingell (*Rough*), Cathleen Cordell (*Nancy*), Robert Newton (*Vincent Ullswater*), Jimmy Hanley (*Cobb*), Minnie Rayner (*Elizabeth*), Mary Hinton (*Lady Winterbourne*), Marie Wright (*Alice Barlow*), Jack Barty (*The Chairman*), The Darmora Ballet
P: John Corfield   D: Thorold Dickinson   SCR: A.R. Rawlinson & Bridget Boland, from Patrick Hamilton's play *Angel Street*   PHOTOG: Bernard Knowles
USA retitle, Angel Street
Standard thriller: Murderous bigamist tries to drive wife insane

Gaslight
1944, (USA), MGM, b&w, 114 mins.
W: Ingrid Bergman (*Paula Alquist*), Charles Boyer (*Gregory Anton*), Joseph Cotten (*Brian Cameron*), Dame May Whitty (*Miss Thwaites*), Edmund Breon (*Gen. Huddleston*), Angela Lansbury (*Nancy*), Barbara Everest (*Elizabeth*), Heather Thatcher (*Lady Dalroy*), Halliwell Hobbes (*Mr. Mufflin*), Tom Stevenson (*Williams*), Jakob Gimpel (*The Pianist*), Lawrence Grossmith (*Lord Dalroy*), Emil Rameau (*Maestro Guardi*)
D: George Cukor, from Patrick Hamilton's play *Angel Street*   PHOTOG: Joseph Ruttenberg   SPCL-FX: Warren Newcombe   MUSIC: Bronislau Kaper
A.k.a. The Murder in Thornton Square
Classic psychodrama (Oscar-winning performance by Ingrid Bergman): Man tries to drive wife mad

Gas-s-s-s!
1970, (USA), AIP, color, 79 mins.
W: Robert Corff, Elaine Giftos, Bud Cort, Talia Coppola (Shire), Ben Vereen, Cindy Williams, Marshall McLuhan
P & D: Roger Corman   SCR: George Armitage
A.k.a. Gas, or: How It Became Necessary to Destroy the World in Order to Save It
Minor SF-satire (Roger Corman's last film for AIP): Nerve-gas leak kills everyone over 25

The Gate
1987, (Can), Vista/New Century, color, 86 mins.
W: Stephen Dorff (*Glen*), Louis Tripp (*Terry*), Christa Denton (*Al*), Jennifer Irwin (*Linda Lee*), Kelly Rowan (*Lori Lee*), Deborah Grover (*Mom*), Linda Goranson (*Terry's Mom*), Scot Denton (*Dad*), Ingrid Veninger (*Paula*), Andrew Gunn (*Brad*), Sean Fagan (*Eric*), Carl Kraines (*The Workman*)
P: John Kemeny   D: Tibor Takacs   SCR: Michael Nankin   PHOTOG: Thomas Vamos   SPCL-FX: Frank Carere   VS-FX SPRVSR: Randall William Cook   MUSIC: Michael Hoenig & J. Peter Robinson
Standard fantasy-thriller: Teens meet demons

Gate II
1992, (Can), Vision/Triumph, color 95 mins.
W: Louis Tripp, Pamela Segall Simon Reynolds, James Villemaire, Neil Munro, Andrea Ladanyi, James Kidnie
P: Andras Hamori   D: Tobor Takacs   SCR: Michael Nankin   PHOTOG: Bryan England   SPCL VS-FX: Randall William Cook   MUSIC: George Blondheim
Standard fantasy-thriller: Demons return from other dimension

The Gates of Hell
1983, (It), Jerry Zimmerman-Michael Franzese/MPM, color, 93 mins.
W: Christopher George, Katherine MacColl, Robert Sampson, Daniela Doria, Janet Agren
D: Lucio Fulci   STORY & SCR: Lucio Fulci & Danny Sacchetti   PHOTOG: Sergio Salvati   MUSIC: Fabio Frizzi
A.k.a. City of the Living Dead, The Fear, Paura Nella Citta dei Morti Viveti (Fear in the City of the Living Dead), and Twilight of the Dead
Minor horror-fantasy: Priest's suicide causes dead to rise

Gattaca
1997, (USA), Col, color, 107 mins.
W: Ethan Hawke, Uma Thurman, Loren Dean, Gore Vidal, Jude Law
WRIT & D: Andrew Niccol
Standard SF-thriller: Average youth crashes society of genetic elite

The Gaunt Stranger
1938, (GB), Ealing/ABFD, b&w, 73 mins.
W: Sonnie Hale (*Sam Hackett*), Wilfrid Lawson (*Maurice Meister*), Louise Henry (*Cora Ann Milton*), Patrick Barr (*Insp. Alan Wembury*), Alexander Knox (*Dr. Anthony Lomond*), John Longden (*Insp. Bliss*), Patricia Roc (*Mary Lenley*), Peter Croft (*John Lenley*), George Merritt (*Sgt. Carter*), Arthur Hambling (*Sgt. Richards*), Charles Eaton (*Col. Walford*), John Turnbull (*The Governor*)
P: Michael Balcon   D: Walter Forde   SCR: Sidney Gilliat, from Edgar Wallace's play *The Ringer*   PHOTOG: Ronald Neame
USA retitle, The Phantom Strikes (Monogram, 1939), reissued 1945
Standard thriller: Disguised crook kills ex-partner

Gawain and the Green Knight
1973, (GB), Sancrest/UA, color, 93 mins.
W: Murray Head (*Gawain*), Ciaran Madden (*Linet*), Nigel Green (*The Green Knight*), Anthony Sharpe (*The King*), Robert Hardy (*Sir Bertilak*), David Leland (*Humphrey*), Murray Melvin (*The Seneschal*), Tony Steedman (*Fortinbras*), Ronald Lacey (*Oswald*), Willoughby Goddard (*A Knight*), Peter Forbes-Robertson (*A Knight*), George Merritt (*A Knight*), Pauline Letts (*The Lady of Lyoness*), Richard Hurndall (*The Bearded Man*), Peter Copley (*Vosper*), Geoffrey Bayldon (*The Wise Man*), Jerold Wells (*The Sergeant*), Michael Crane (*The Giant*), Jack Woolgar (*The Porter*)
P: Philip Breen   D: Stephen Weeks   SCR: Philip Breen, Stephen Weeks & Rosemary Sutcliff, from a poem by an anonymous author   PHOTOG: Ian Wilson   MUSIC: Ron Goodwin
Standard adventure-fantasy: Knight uses magic ring to save captive maiden

The Gay Falcon
1941, (USA), RKO, b&w, 67 mins.
W: George Sanders (*Gay Lawrence*), Wendy Barrie (*Helen Reed*), Allen Jenkins (*Jonathan G. "Goldy" Locke*), Anne Hunter (*Elinor*), Gladys Cooper (*Maxine*), Turhan Bey (*Retana*), Edward S. Brophy (*Bates*), Eddie Dunn (*Grimes*), Arthur Shields (*Waldeck*), Damian O'Flynn (*Weber*), Hans Conreid (*Herman*), Lucile Gleason (*Mrs. Gardiner*), Willie Fung (*Jerry*), Virginia Dale (*The Girl*)
D: Irving Reis   SCR: Lynn Root & Frank Fenton, from characters created by Michael Arlen   PHOTOG: Nicholas Musuraca   MUSIC: Paul Sawtell
Initial "Falcon" mystery-thriller: Troubleshooter seeks socialite's killer

The Gazebo
1959, (USA), Avon/MGM, b&w, 102 mins.
W: Glenn Ford, Debbie Reynolds, Carl Reiner, ZaSu Pitts, Mabel Albertson, John McGiver, Martin Landau, Bert Freed, Doro Merande
P: Lawrence Weingarten   D: George Marshall   SCR: George Wells, from Alex Coppel's stage play   PHOTOG: Paul C. Vogel   MUSIC: Jeff Alexander

SONG: *Something Called Love*
Cute comedy-thriller: TV writer plots to kill blackmailer

Gebroken Spiegels (Broken Mirrors)
1984, (Neth), Sigma/EMI, color, 116 mins.
W: Lineke Rijxman, Henriette Tol, Edda Barends, Carla Hardy, Coby
    Stunnenberg, Marijke Veugelers, Arline Renfurm, Anke Van't Hoff, Hedda
    Tabet, Elja Pelgrom, Wim Wama, Matthias Maat, Johan Leyssen, Rolf
    Leendeerts, Eddy Brugman, Truus Dekker, Elsje De Wijn, Mara Peelen,
    Beppie Melissen
D & SCR: Marleen Gorris   PHOTOG: Frans Bromet   MUSIC: Lodewijk De
    Boer & Franz Joseph Haydn
Unusual thriller: Killer chains and starves victims

Das Geheiminis des Abbe X (Secret of Abbe X)
1927, (Ger), b&w, 2205m (7,234.2 ft.)
W: William Dieterle
WRIT & D: William Dieterle
Standard melodrama

Geheimnisse einer Seele (Secrets of a Soul)
1926, (Ger), Ufa, b&w, 95 mins.
W: Werner Krauss, Ruth Weyher, Jack Trevor
D: G.W. Pabst   PHOTOG: Guido Seeber & Curt Oertel
Unusual psychodrama, first genuinely Freudian film: Dreams visually externalized

The Gelignite Gang
1956, (GB), Cybex/Renown, b&w, 75 mins.
W: Wayne Morris (*Jimmy Baxter*), James Kenney (*Chapman*), Patrick Holt
    (*Rutherford*), Sandra Dorne (*Sally Morton*), Simone Silva (*Simone*), Arthur
    Young (*Scobie*), Lloyd Lamble (*Insp. Felby*), Eric Pohlmann (*Popoulos*), Hugh
    Miller (*Crosby*)
P: Geoffrey Goodheart   D: Terence Fisher   STORY: Brandon Fleming
Standard crime-thriller: Private detective and secretary expose jewel thieves

Gemini Man
see *Code Name: Minus One*

Generation X
1996, (USA), New World/Fox-TV, color, 95 mins.
W: Matt Frewer (*Russell Tresh*), Heather McComb (*Jubilee*), Finola Hughes (*Emma
    Frost/White Queen*), Agustin Rodriguez (*Skin*), Jeremy Ratchford
    (*Sean/Banshee*), Bumper Robinson (*Mondo*), Suzanne Davis (*Buff*), Amarilis
    (*Monet*), Randall Slavin (*Refrax*), Kevin McNulty
D: Jack Sholder   TELEPLAY: Eric Blakeney, based on Marvel Comics' X-Men
    MUSIC: Peter J. Robinson
TVM, standard SF-fantasy: Mutant youths enlisted to oppose mad genius

Genesis II
1973, (USA), WB/CBS-TV, color, 74 mins.
W: Alex Cord (*Dylan*), Mariette Hartley, Harvey Jason, Ted Cassidy, Percy
    Rodrigues
WRIT & P: Gene Roddenberry   D: John Llewellyn Moxey   PHOTOG: Gerald
    Perry Finnerman
TVM, minor SF: Scientist revived from suspended animation

La Genie de Feu (The Genie of Fire)
1908, (Fr), Star, b&w, 95m (311.7 ft./5.3 mins.)
D: Georges Melies
Standard fantasy

The Genie of Fire
see *La Genie de Feu*

Genii
1969, (Czech), color
Minor fantasy

Genii of Darkness
see *Nostradamus y el Genio de la Tinieblas*

Genius at Work
1946, (USA), RKO, b&w, 61 mins.
W: Alan Carney, Wally Brown, Anne Jeffreys (*Ellen Brent*), Lionel Atwill
    (*Vladimir Marsh*), Bela Lugosi (*Stone*), Marc Cramer, Ralph Dunn
P: Herman Schlom   D: Leslie Goodwins   ORIG. SCR: Robert E. Kent & Monte
    Brice   PHOTOG: Robert De Grasse   SPCL-FX: Vernon L. Walker
    MUSIC DIR: C. Bakaleinikoff
*Minor comedy-thriller: Radio-detectives match wits with notorious killer. Remake of Super
    Sleuth (1937)*

The Gentle Art of Murder
1962, (Fr), Embassy, b&w, 159 mins
W: Michele Morgan, Richard Todd, Edwige Feuillere, Annie Girardot, Raymond
    Loyer, Danielle Darrieux, Jean Servais, Gabriele Ferzetti, Pierre Brasseur,
    Christian Marquand
D: Gerard Oury
A.k.a. Crime Does Not Pay
Standard homicide anthology, 4 tales: (1) The Mask, (2) The Spider's Web, (3) The

Fenayrou Case, & (4) The Man on the Avenue. Original title: **Crime Does
Not Pay**

The Gentleman from Nowhere
1948, (USA), Col, b&w, 66 mins.
W: Warner Baxter, Fay Baker, Noel Madison, Luis Van Rooten
D: William Castle
Standard melodrama

Gentlemen, I Have Killed Einstein
1971, (Czech), color
W: Jana Brejchova, Petr Cepek
D: Oldrich Lipsky
Minor SF-comedy

The Gentle Trap
1960, (GB), Butcher's Films, b&w, 59 mins.
W: Spencer Teakle (*Johnny Ryan*), Felicity Young (*Jean*), Dorinda Stevens (*Mary*),
    Martin Benson (*Ricky Barnes*), Dawn Brooks (*Sylvia*), Alan Edwards (*Al
    Jenkins*), Hugh Latimer (*Vic Carter*)
P: Jack Parsons   D: Charles Saunders   SCR: Brock Williams & Alan Osborne
STORY: Guido Coen
Standard crime-thriller: Girl helps thief elude police and nightclub owner

Genuine
1920, (Ger), Decla-Bioscop, b&w, 7,500 ft. (2286m)
W: Fern Andra, Harald Paulsen, Hans Heinz von Twardowski, Ernst Gronau,
    John Gottowt
D: Robert Wiene   SCR: Carl Mayer   PHOTOG: Willy Hameister
Pretentious fantasy-thriller (tried to mimic revolutionary sets of **Das Kabinett des Dr.
    Caligari***): Kept prisoner in a glass cage, exotic temptress lures young barber into cut-
    ting elderly captor's throat*

George Barnwell, The London Apprentice
1913, (GB), Hepworth, b&w, 2,500 ft. (762m)
W: Alec Worcester (*George Barnwell*), Flora Morris (*Sarah Millwood*)
D: Hay Plumb   SCR: Ivan Patrick Gore, from a play by George Lillo
USA retitle, **In the Toils of the Temptress**
Standard crime-thriller: Woman gets laborer to kill her rich uncle

George of the Jungle
1997, (USA), Mandeville/Walt Disney/Hollywood, color 92 mins.
W: Brendan Fraser (*George*), Leslie Mann (*Ursula*), Thomas Haden Church (*Lyle*),
    Richard Roundtree (*Kwame*), Greg Cruttwell (*Max*), Holland Taylor, Keith
    Scott, Rodney Johnson, Abraham Benrubi, Kelly Miller, John Bennett Perry
D: Sam Weisman   SCR: Dana Olsen & Audrey Wells, from characters created for
    the 1960s cartoon teleseries by Jay Ward   PHOTOG: Thomas Ackerman
    VS-FX SPRVSR: Tim Landry   MUSIC: Marc Shaiman
*Amiable comedy-adventure (inspired by 1960's cartoon teleseries): Jungle man brought to
    San Francisco*

The Ghost and the Darkness: MICHAEL DOUGLAS

Georgette Meunier
1989, (W. Ger), color, 82 mins.
W: Tiziana Jelmini, Dina Leipzig, Thomas Schunke, Manfred Hulverschiedt
D: Tania Stocklin & Cyrille Rey-Coquais
Unusual black comedy: "Black widow" poisons male citizens of turn-of-century German town

The German Chainsaw Massacre
1990, (Ger), color, 63 mins.
W: Udo Keir, Karina Fallenstein
Standard horror-thriller: Refugees from reunification of Germany fall prey to crazed family of human butchers

The German Spy Peril
1914, (GB), Barker/Award, b&w, 1,160 ft. (353.6m)
W: J. Hastings Batson
D: Bert Haldane **STORY:** Rowland Talbot
Standard thriller: Carpenter trails spies through secret tunnel

Germicide
1974, (USA), color, 90 mins.
W: Rod Taylor, Bibi Andersson
Minor thriller: Horrifying bacterial weapon threatens world

Gertie the Dinosaur
1909, (USA), Winsor McCay, b&w
Animated cartoon

Gesom E Kako Shipta (To the Starry Island)
1993, (S. Korea), color, 102 mins.
W: Ahn Song-Gi, Moon Sung-Kuen, Shim Hae-Jin
D: Park Kwang-Su
Unusual melodrama: Supernatural elements infuse flashbacks to Korean Conflict's effect on rural village

Get Carter
1970, (GB), MGM British/EMG-EMI, color, 112 mins.
W: Michael Caine (*Jack Carter*), Ian Hendry (*Eric Paice*), John Osborne (*Cyril Kinnear*), George Sewell (*Con McCarty*), Britt Ekland (*Anna Fletcher*), Geraldine Moffatt (*Glenda*), Tony Beckley (*Peter*), Rosemarie Dunham (*Edna Garfoot*), Dorothy White (*Margaret*), Petra Markham (*Doreen*), Glynn Edwards (*Albert Swift*), Alun Armstrong (*Keith*), Bryan Mosley (*Cliff Brumby*)
P: Michael Klinger **D & SCR:** Mike Hodges, from Ted Lewis' novel *Jack's Return*
Standard crime-thriller: Racketeer takes revenge on those involved in his brother's death

Getting His Own Back
see The Joker's Mistake

Getting Lucky
1990, (USA), Vista Street Entertainment, color
W: Steven Cooke (*Bill*), Lezlie Z. McCraw (*Krissi*), Rick McDowell (*Tony*), Jean Stewart (*Babette*), Dick Monda (*The Teacher*), Garry Kluger (*Lepkey*), C.J. Merrill (*Tim*), Paul G. Kenner (*Dad*), Millie Quinn (*Mom*), Pattie Gordon (*Mrs. Shacker*), Devon Kenner (*Brother*), Dawn Kenner (*Sister*), James Zoppe (*The Horseman*), Julie Dole, Bronwyn St. John, Marshall Hilliard, Wendell Stroup Sr., Russell Coletti, Elliot Tonna, Steven B. McMillin, George Constantin, Jon Philon, Clondell Williams, David Eason, Melisa Sanchez, Brian Moehl, Mark Adams, Jerry Lenz, Diane Block, Luci Monda
WRIT & D: Michael Paul Girard **PHOTOG:** Gerald M. Williams
MUSIC: Miriam Cutler & Michael Paul Girard **SONGS:** *Boy Are U Ready, Hole in One, Can't Get Much Closer, Fits Like a Glove & Love Changes Everything*
Minor comedy-fantasy: Leprechaun grants teen three wishes

The Ghastly Ones
1969, (USA), JER, color, 81 mins.
W: Veronica Radburn, Don Williams Maggie Rogers, Hal Belsoe
P,D & PHOTOG: Andy Milligan **SCR:** Andy Milligan & Hal Sherwood
Minor thriller: Heirs murdered in eerie Maine mansion. cf. Legacy of Horror (1978)

Ghidrah, the Three-Headed Monster
1965, (Jap), Toho/Walter Reade-Sterling/Continental, color, 85 mins.
W: Yosuke Natsuki, Yuriko Hoshi, Takashi Shimura, Kenji Sahara, The Peanuts, Hiroshi Koizumi
P: Tomoyuki Tanaka **D:** Inoshiro Honda **SCR:** Shinichi Sekizawa **PHOTOG:** Hajime Koizumi **SPCL-FX:** Eiji Tsuburaya
Standard SF-fantasy: Godzilla, Rodan and Mothra oppose horror from space

The Ghost (1962)
see Lo Spettro

Ghost
1990, (USA), Howard Koch/Para, color, 122 mins.
W: Patrick Swayze (*Sam Wheat*), Demi Moore (*Molly Jensen*), Whoopi Goldberg (*Oda Mae Brown*), Tony Goldwyn (*Carl Bruner*), Rick Aviles (*Willie Lopez*), Armelia McQueen (*Oda Mae's Sister #1*), Gail Boggs (*Oda Mae's Sister #2*), Phil Leeds (*The Emergency Room Ghost*), Vincent Schiavelli (*The Subway Ghost*), Stanley Lawrence, Christopher J. Keene, John Hugh, Susan Breslau, Martina Degnan, Richard Kleber, Said Faraj, Macka Foley, Sam Troutsouvas, Sharon Breslau Cornell, Thom Curley, Angelina Estrada, Stephen Root, Laura Drake, Augie Blunt, Alma Beltran, Vivian Bonnell, Derek Thompson, Mabel Lockridge, J. Christopher Sullivan, Charlotte Zucker, Sondra Rubin, Tom Finnegan, Bruce Jarchow, Faye Brenner, Minnie Lindsey, William Cort
D: Jerry Zucker **SCR:** Bruce Joel Rubin **PHOTOG:** Adam Greenberg **MUSIC:** Maurice Jarre
Superior comedy-fantasy-thriller: Murdered man's spirit hunts killers. Best Supporting Actress Academy Award for Whoopi Goldberg

The Ghost and Mrs. Muir
1947, (USA), 20th-Fox, b&w, 104 mins.
W: Gene Tierney (*Lucy Muir*), Rex Harrison (*Capt. Daniel Gregg*), George Sanders (*Miles Fairlie*), Natalie Wood (*Anna Muir*), Edna Best (*Martha*), Anna Lee (*Mrs. Fairlie*), Vanessa Brown, Whitford Kane, Robert Coote, Victoria Horne
P: Fred Kohlmar **D:** Joseph L. Mankiewicz **SCR:** Philip Dunne, from R.A. Dick's novel **PHOTOG:** Charles Lang **MUSIC:** Bernard Herrmann
Classic fantasy: Young widow buys house on English coast, discovers haunt of hard-living sea captain. Later a TV series

Ghost of Frankenstein: Bela Lugosi, Lon Chaney Jr., Sir Cedric Hardwicke, Lionel Atwill

The Ghost and Mr. Chicken

1966, (USA), Univ, color, 90 mins.
W: Don Knotts, Joan Staley *(Alma)*, Skip Homeier *(Ollie)*, Liam Redmond *(Kelsey)*, Reta Shaw *(Mrs. Maxwell)*, Lurene Tuttle *(Mrs. Miller)*, Dick Sargent *(George)*, Hal Smith, George Chandler, Philip Ober, Harry Hickox, James Begg, Hope Summers, Eddie Quillan
P: Edward Montagne   **D:** Alan Raskin   **SCR:** Jim Fritzell & Everett Greenbaum   **PHOTOG:** William Margulies   **MUSIC:** Vic Mizzy
Juvenile comedy-thriller: Timid reporter spends night in "haunted" murder mansion

The Ghost and the Candle

see Le Revenant

The Ghost and the Darkness

1996, (USA), Constellation/Para, color, 105 mins.
W: Michael Douglas *(Remington)*, Val Kilmer *(Lt. Col. John Patterson)*, John Kani *(Samuel)*, Om Puri *(Abdullah)*, Brian McCardie *(Starling)*, Bernard Hill *(Dr. Hawthorne)*, Tom Wilkinson *(Beaumont)*, Emily Mortimer *(Helena Patterson)*, Henry Cele, Kurt Egelhof, Teddy Reddy, Jack Devnarain, George Middlekoop
D: Stephen Hopkins   **SCR:** William Goldman   **PHOTOG:** Vilmos Zsigmond   **MUSIC:** Jerry Goldsmith
"...the rare Hollywood action-adventure that becomes more surprising and exotic as it moves along"—Janet Maslin, New York Times
Gripping, fact-based thriller: 19th-century hunters seek to destroy man-killing lions. Remake of **Bwana Devil**

The Ghost and the Guest

1943, (USA), PRC, b&w, 59 mins.
W: James Dunn, Florence Rice, Mabel Todd
D: William Nigh   **SCR:** Morey Amsterdam
Minor mystery-thriller: Gangsters make newlyweds think honeymoon mansion is haunted

The Ghost at St. Michael's

1941, (GB), Ealing/ABFD, b&w, 82 mins.
W: Will Hay *(William Lamb)*, Claude Hulbert *(Hilary Teasdale)*, Ray-mond Huntley *(Mr. Humphries)*, Charles Hawtrey *(Percy Thorne)*, Felix Aylmer *(Dr. Winter)*, Elliot Mason *(Mrs. Wigmore)*, John Laurie *(Jamie)*, Hay Petrie *(Procurator Fiscal)*, Roddy Hughes *(Amberley)*, Derek Blomfield *(Sunshine)*, Manning Whiley *(Stock)*, Brefni O'Rorke *(Sgt. MacFarlane)*
D: Marcel Varnel   **SCR:** Angus Macphail & John Dighton   **PHOTOG:** Derek Williams
reissued 1944, 1947 & 1955
Standard comedy-thriller: Spy poses as ghost

The Ghost Breakers

1940, (USA), Para, b&w, 85 mins.
W: Bob Hope, Paulette Goddard, Richard Carlson *(Geoff)*, Paul Lukas *(Parada)*, Anthony Quinn, Willie Best, Pedro de Cordoba, Virginia Brissac, Noble Johnson, Tom Dugan, Paul Fix, Lloyd Corrigan
P: Arthur Hornblow Jr.   **D:** George Marshall   **SCR:** Walter DeLeon   **PHOTOG:** Charles Lang   **MUSIC:** Ernst Toch
"...one of Hope's best vehicles... The sets and glistening photography would do credit to a major horror film of the earlier 30s, the encounter with a Zombie and a real ghost, genuinely frightening"—William K. Everson, Classics of the Horror Film
Humorous thriller: Murder and zombies on Caribbean isle. cf. **Scared Stiff** *(1953)*

Ghost Brigade

see Grey Knight

Ghostbusters

1984, (USA), Black Rhino-Bernie Brillstein/Col, color, 107 mins.
W: Bill Murray, Dan Aykroyd, Sigourney Weaver, Harold Ramis, Rick Moranis, Annie Potts, Ernie Hudson, William Atherton, David Margulies, Steven Tash, Michael Ensign, Jennifer Runyon, Slavitza Jovan, Alice Drummond
P & D: Ivan Reitman   **SCR:** Dan Aykroyd & Harold Ramis   **PHOTOG:** Laszlo Kovacs   **VS-FX:** Richard Edlund   **MUSIC:** Elmer Bernstein
Standard comedy-fantasy: Bumbling trio captures spooks

Ghostbusters II

1989, (USA), Col, color, 102 mins.
W: Bill Murray *(Dr. Peter Venkman)*, Dan Aykroyd *(Dr. Raymond Stantz)*, Sigourney Weaver *(Dana Barrett)*, Harold Ramis *(Dr. Egon Spengler)*, Rick Moranis *(Louis Tully)*, Ernie Hudson *(Winston Zeddemore)*, Annie Potts *(Janine Melnitz)*, Peter MacNicol *(Janosz Poha)*, Wilhelm von Homburg *(Viga)*, Kurt Fuller, David Margulies, Harris Yulin, Janet Margolin, Will Deutschendorf, Hank Deutschendorf, Michael P. Moran, Olivia Ward, Susan Boehm, Page Leong, Mordecai Lawner, Mary Ellen Trainor, Aaron Lustig, Dave Florek, Jason Reitman, Christopher Villasenor, Richard Foronjy, Mark Schneider, Valery Pappas, Ray Glanzmann, Catherine Reitman, George Wilbur, Sharon Kramer, Walter Flanagan, Bobby Baresford Brown, Christopher Neame, Ron Cummins, Judy Ovitz, Tom Dugan, Angelo Di Mascio, Ralph Monaco, Robert Alan Beuth, Cheech Marin, Yvette Cruise, John Hammil, Alex Zimmerman, Brian Doyle Murray, Louise Troy, Ben Stein, Douglas Seale, Erik Holland, Phillip Baker Hall
P & D: Ivan Reitman   **SCR:** Harold Ramis & Dan Aykroyd   **PHOTOG:** Michael Chapman   **VS-FX SPRVSR:** Dennis Muren   **MUSIC:** Randy

Edelman
Standard comedy-fantasy: Ectoplasm threatens Big Apple

The Ghost Camera

1933, (GB), Real Art/Radio, b&w, 68 mins.
W: Henry Kendall *(John Grey)*, Ida Lupino *(Mary Elton)*, John Mills *(Ernest Elton)*, George Merritt *(The Inspector)*, S. Victor Stanley *(Albert Sims)*, Felix Aylmer *(The Coroner)*
D: Bernard Vorhaus   **SCR:** H. Fowler Mear, from a story by J. Jefferson Farjeon
Standard thriller: Chemist accidentally photographs murder

Ghost Catchers

1944, (USA), Univ, b&w, 68 mins.
W: Ole Olsen, Chic Johnson, Martha O'Driscoll, Gloria Jean, Andy De-vine, Leo Carrillo, Lon Chaney Jr., Kirby Grant, Jack Norton, Tor Johnson, Mel Tormé, Morton Downey (Sr.), Ella Mae Morse
P & SCR: Edmund L. Hartmann   **D:** Edward Cline
Minor comedy-thriller: Spooks infest nightclub

Ghost Chasers

1951, (USA), Mono, b&w, 67 mins.
W: Leo Gorcey, Huntz Hall, Lela Bliss, Philip Van Zandt, Lloyd Corri-gan, Bernard Gorcey, David Gorcey, Jan Kayne, William Benedict, Buddy Gorman, Robert Coogan, Argentina Brunetti, Marshall Bradford, Michael Ross, Hal Gerard
P: Jan Grippo   **D:** William Beaudine   **SCR:** Charles R. Marion   **PHOTOG:** Marcel LePicard   **MUSIC DIR:** Edward J. Kay
Standard comedy-thriller-musical: Bowery Boys break up seance racket

Ghost Crazy

1944, (USA), Mono, b&w, 63 mins.
W: Billy Gilbert, Shemp Howard, Maxie Rosenbloom, Minerva Urecal, Tim Ryan
P: Sam Katzman   **D:** William Beaudine   **SCR:** Tim Ryan
A.k.a. Crazy Knights
Minor comedy-thriller: Bumblers in "haunted" house

The Ghost Creeps

1940, (USA), Mono, b&w 63 mins.
W: Leo Gorcey, Bobby Jordan
P: Sam Katzman   **D:** Joseph Lewis   **SCR:** William Lively
A.k.a. Boys of the City
Minor comedy-thriller: East Side Kids meet phony spooks

Ghost Dad

1990, (USA), SAH Enterprises/Univ, color, 90 mins.
W: Bill Cosby *(Elliot)*, Kimberly Russell *(Diane)*, Denise Nicholas *(Joan)*, Ian Bannen *(Sir Edith Moser)*, Christine Ebersole *(Carol)*, Barry Corbin *(Mr. Collins)*, Salim Grant *(Danny)*, Brooke Fontaine *(Amanda)* Dakin Matthews, Dana Ashbrook, Arnold Stang
P: Terry Nelson   **D:** Sidney Poitier   **SCR:** Chris Reese, Brent Maddock & S.S. Wilson   **STORY:** Brent Maddock & S.S. Wilson   **PHOTOG:** Andrew Laszlo   **MUSIC:** Henry Mancini
Minor comedy-fantasy: Father bemused by his spectral state

Ghost Dance

1983, (USA), color, 93 mins.
W: Sherman Hemsley, Henry Ball, Julie Amato
D: Peter Bufa
Minor thriller: Grim results when Indian burial ground is violated

Ghost Diver

1957, (USA), Regal/20th-Fox, b&w, 76 mins.
W: James Craig, Audrey Totter, Nico Minardos, Rodolfo Hoyos, Pira Louis, Lowell Brown, George Trevino, Paul Stader, Elena Da Vinci, Diane Webber, Robert Lorenz, Tom Garland, Richard Geary, Michael Dugan
P: Richard Einfeld   **WRIT & D:** Richard Einfeld & Merrill G. White   **PHOTOG:** John M. Nickolaus   **MUSIC:** Paul Sawtell & Bert Shefter
Minor melodrama: Island treasure hunt

Ghost Fever

1987, (USA), Miramax, color, 86 mins.
W: Sherman Hemsley, Luis Avalos, Jennifer Rhodes *(Mme. St. Esprit)*, Pepper Martin *(Beauregard)*, Deborah Benson *(Linda)*
Minor comedy-fantasy: Cops meet spooks

A Ghost for Sale

1952, (GB), Bushey/Famous, b&w, 31 mins.
W: Tod Slaughter *(The Caretaker)*, Patrick Barr *(The Man)*, Tucker McGuire *(The Wife)*
P: Gilbert Church   **D:** Victor M. Gover   **STORY:** John Gilling
Standard short fantasy: Manor caretaker relates tale of mad squire, then vanishes. Footage from **The Curse of the Wraydons** *(1946)*

The Ghost Goes West

1935, (GB), London/UA, b&w, 100 mins.
W: Robert Donat *(Murdoch/Donald Glourie)*, Jean Parker *(Peggy Martin)*, Eugene Pallette *(Joe Martin)*, Elsa Lanchester *(Lady Shepperton)*, Ralph Bunker *(Ed Bigelow)*, Patricia Hilliard *(The Shepherdess)*, Elliot Mason *(Mrs. McNiff)*, Everley Gregg *(Gladys Martin)*, Morton Selten *(Gavin Glourie)*, Chili Bouchier *(Cleopatra)*, Mark Daly *(The Groom)*, Herbert Lomas *(Fergus)*, Jack

Lambert, Hay Petrie Colin Leslie, Richard Mackie, J. Neil More, Neil Lester, Quentin McPherson, Arthur Seaton, David Keir
P: Alexander Korda   **D:** Rene Clair   **SCR:** Robert E. Sherwood & Geoffrey Kerr, based on Eric Keown's *Sir Tristram Goes West*   **PHOTOG:** Harold Rosson
reissued 1941 & 1947
Classic comedy-fantasy: Scottish rogue's spirit aids modern member of family

The Ghost Goes Wild
1947, (USA), PRC, b&w, 66 mins.
W: Anne Gwynne, Edward Everett Horton, James Ellison, Stephanie Bachelor
Minor comedy-fantasy

Ghosthouse
1988, (It), color, 91 mins.
D: Umberto Lenzi Lara Wendell, Gregg Scott
Minor horror-thriller: Girl's ghost signals approach of evil powers

A Ghost in Monte Carlo
1990, (GB), Gainsborough/Grade, Made For TV, color, 95 mins.
W: Sarah Miles (*Emilie*), Oliver Reed (*The Rajah*), Lysette Anthony (*Mistral*), Christopher Plummer (*Grand Duke Ivan*), Samantha Eggar (*Jeanne*), Fiona Fullerton (*Lady Violet*), Marcus Gilbert (*Lord Robert Stanford*), Joanna Lumley (*Lady Drayton*), Lewis Collins (*Lord Drayton*), Gareth Hunt (*Dulton*), Jolyon Baker (*Prince Nicholas*), Elizabeth Sellars (*Countess Kisselev*), Ron Moody (*Alphonse*), Carolyn Jones (*Countess Lombard*), Helen Cherry (*Mother Superior*), Neil Dickson (*Dupuis*), Maxine Audley (*Lady Stanford*), Aharon Ipale (*Gopal*), Bernard Kay (*Police Chief Gutier*), Francesca Gonshaw (*Senorita Rodrigues*), Stephan Chase (*The Dealer*), John Carlin (*The Concierge*), Emma Amos (*Alice, 20 yrs.*), Sadie Frost (*Alice, 20 yrs.*), George Cooper (*Aziz*), Angie Wells (*Emilie, 20 yrs.*), Peter Brace (*Potok*), Angela Forry (*Alice Syrs*)
P & D: John Hough   **TELEPLAY:** Terence Feely, from Barbara Cartland's novel   **PHOTOG:** Terence Cole   **MUSIC:** Laurie Johnson
TVM, standard romance-melodrama: Innocent girl trapped by intrigue

The Ghost in the Invisible Bikini
1966, (USA), AIP, color, 82 mins.
W: Tommy Kirk (*Chuck Phillips*), Deborah Walley (*Lillie*), Basil Rath-bone (*Reginald Ripper*), Boris Karloff (*Hiram Stokely*), Patsy Kelly (*Myrtle Forbush*), Susan Hart (*The Ghost*), Nancy Sinatra (*Vicky*), Aron Kincaid (*Bobby*), Harvey Lembeck (*Erich von Zipper*), Quinn O'Hara (*Sinistra*), Bobbi Shaw (*The Princess*), Francis X. Bushman (*Malcolm*), Benny Rubin (*Chief Chicken Feather*), Piccola Pupa, Jesse White, Claudia Martin, George Barrows, Ed Garner, Salli Sachse
D: Don Weis, Ronald Sinclair (Additional scenes)   **SCR:** Louis M. Heyward & Elwood Ullman   **PHOTOG:** Stanley Cortez   **MUSIC:** Les Baxter
SONGS: *Geronimo, Stand Up and Fight & Make the Music Pretty*
*orig. to be titled **Pajama Party in a Haunted House***
Standard comedy-fantasy: Pert heiress, creepy manse, teen hijinks and a meddling she-ghost.
***Last Beach Party** comedy-musical*

Ghost in the Machine
1993, (USA), 20th-Fox, color, 95 mins
W: Karen Allen (*Terry Monroe*), Chris Mulkey (*Bram*), Ted Marcoux (*Karl*), Wil Horneff (*Josh Monroe*), Jessica Walter (*Elaine*), Brandon Quintin Adams (*Frazer*), Rick Ducommun (*Phil*), Nancy Fish (*Karl's Landlord*), Jack Laufer (*Elliott*), Shevonne Durkin (*Carol*), Richard McKenzie (*Frank Mallory*), Mimi Lieber (*Marta*), Mickey Gilbert (*Mickey the Driver*), Ken Thorley (*The Salesman*), Carel Gabriel Yorke (*The Safety Technician*), Richard Schiff (*The Scanner Technician*), Clayton Landey (*Mel*), Walter Addison (*The Veteran Cop*), Matthew Glave (*The Rookie Cop*), Carlease Burke (*The Woman Cop*), Chris Ellis (*The Lieutenant*), Robert Lamar Kemp (*The Yuppie*), Dom Magwili (*The Doctor*), Haunani Minn (*The Nurse*), Charles Stransky (*The Cop at the Police Station*), Alix Koromzay (*The Punk Girl*), Helen Greenberg (*The Customer*), Nigel Gibbs (*The Detective*), Andrew Woodworth (*The Home Security Man*), Zack Phifer (*The Priest*), Don Keith Opper (*The Man in the Office*), Mitchell R. Parnes (*The Bartender*), Edwina Moore (*The Newswoman*), Rick Scarry (*The Newsman*), Michael Laguardia (*A Cop*), Charles Haugk (*A Cop*)
P: Paul Schiff   **D:** Rachel Talalay   **SCR:** William Davies & William Osborne   **PHOTOG:** Phil Meheux   **MUSIC:** Graeme Revell
Unusual SF-thriller: Serial killer transformed into murderous computer virus

Ghost in the Shell
1996, (Jap), Manga, color
D: Mamoru Oshii, from a series of comic books by Masamune Shirow
Unusual animated SF-thriller: Cyber-space secret agent seeks true existence

Ghost Keeper
1980, (USA), color, 87 mins.
W: Riva Spier, Murray Ord, Georgie Collins
D: Vernon Sewell
Minor horror-thriller: Three girls trapped in manse of supernatural happenings

A Ghostly Affair
1914, (GB), Hepworth, b&w, 400 ft. (121.9m)
W: Harry Buss (*The Man*)
D: Hay Plumb
Minor comedy short: Men dress as ghosts, scare each other

A Ghost of a Chance
1968, (GB), Fanfare/CFF, color, 51 mins.
W: Jimmy Edwards (*Sir Jocelyn*), Patricia Hayes (*Miss Woollie*), Graham Stark (*Thomas Dogood*), Terry Scott (*Mr. Perry*), Bernard Cribbins (*Ron*), Ronnie Barker (*Mr. Prendergast*), Stephen Brown (*Mike*), Mark Ward (*John*), Cheryl Vigden (*Jane*), John Bluthal (*The Assistant*)
P: George H. Brown   **D:** Jan Darnley-Smith   **SCR:** Patricia Latham   **STORY:** Ed Harper
Standard juvenile fantasy: Ghosts of Roundhead and Cavalier help children save old manor from destruction

Ghost of a Chance
1987, (USA), CBS-TV, color, 95 mins.
W: Redd Foxx (*Ivory Clay*), Dick Van Dyke (*Bill Nolan*), Richard Romanus (*Julio Mendez*), Geoffrey Holder (*Johnson*), Kimble Joyner (*Jessie*), Brynn Thayer (*Kathleen*), Sean McCann (*Shields*), Timothy Webber (*Fein*), Barbara Harris (*Gladys*), Tom Butler (*Rose*), Jack Jessop (*Goody*)
D: Don Taylor   **TELEPLAY:** Hank Bradford   **PHOTOG:** David Herrington   **MUSIC:** Charles Bernstein
TVM, minor fantasy: Departed spirit returns to Earth

The Ghost of Dragstrip Hollow
1959, (USA), AIP, b&w, 65 mins.
W: Jody Fair (*Lois*), Martin Braddock (*Stan*), Leon Tyler (*Bonzo*), Russ Bender, Jean Tatum, Elaine Dupont, Dorothy Neumann, Jack Ging, Henry McCann, Bill St. John, Beverly Scott, Sanita Pelky, Nancy Anderson, Judy Howard, Tom Ivo, Paul Blaisdell (*The "Ghost"*)
WRIT & P: Lou Rusoff   **D:** William Hole Jr.   **PHOTOG:** Gil Warrenton   **MUSIC:** Ronald Stein
*orig. co-billed with **Diary of a High School Bride***
Minor comedy-thriller: Teens use infamous old house as club headquarters

The Ghost of Elisha Doom
1963, (Yugo), color
Standard fantasy-thriller

The Ghost of Flight 401
1978, (USA), NBC-TV, color
W: Ernest Borgnine (*Don Cimoli*), Gary Lockwood (*Jordan*), Kim Bas-inger (*Prissy*), Allan Miller (*Garrick*), Tina Chen (*Val*), Carol Rossen (*Maria Cimoli*), Beverly Todd (*Dana*), Robert F. Lyons (*Bowdish*), Byron Morrow (*Bailey*), Howard Hesseman (*Stockwell*), Russell Johnson, Luis Avalos, Tom Clancy, Angela Clarke
D: Steven Hilliard Stern   **TELEPLAY:** Robert Malcolm Young, from a novel by John G. Fuller
TVM, standard thriller: Hauntings in aftermath of jetliner crash

The Ghost of Frankenstein
1942, (USA), Univ, b&w, 68 mins.
W: Sir Cedric Hardwicke (*Baron Ludwig von Frankenstein*), Lon Chaney Jr. (*The Monster*), Lionel Atwill (*Dr. Bohmer*), Bela Lugosi (*Ygor*), Ralph Bellamy (*Erik*), Evelyn Ankers (*Elsa von Frankenstein*), Janet Ann Gallow, Doris Lloyd, Leyland Hodgson, Barton Yarborough, Olaf Hytten, Dwight Frye, Holmes Herbert
P: George Waggner   **D:** Erle C. Kenton   **SCR:** W. Scott Darling, from an orig. story by Eric Taylor   **PHOTOG:** Milton Krasner & Woody Bredell
*Standard horror-thriller, sequel to **Son of Frankenstein**: Doctor unwittingly puts brain of mad shepherd into body of immortal monster. cf. **Frankenstein Meets the Wolf Man***

The Ghost of Frankenstein: SIR CEDRIC HARDWICKE AND LON CHANEY JR.

The Ghost of Joan Holling
*see **Mystery Liner***

The Ghost of Professor Hichcock
see ***Raptus***

The Ghost of Rashmon Hall
see ***Night Comes Too Soon***

The Ghost of Slumber Mountain
1918, (USA), World, b&w
<u>P:</u> Herbert M. Dawley   <u>SPCL-FX:</u> Willis O'Brien
Animated thriller: Dinosaur prowls

Ghost of the Strangler
1965, (Mex), color
<u>W:</u> Santo
Minor thriller

The Ghost of Tolston's Manor
1923, (USA), Micheaux Film Corp., b&w
Minor comedy-melodrama. All Black Cast

The Ghost of Yatsuya
1958, (Jap), color, 100 mins.
Unusual fantasy-thriller: Man betrays wife to gain power; horrifying revenge follows

Ghost of Zorro
1959, (USA), Rep, b&w, 69 mins.
<u>W:</u> Clayton Moore, Pamela Blake, Roy Barcroft, George J. Lewis, Gene Roth
<u>D:</u> Fred C. Brannon
Minor action-thriller (feature version of 1949 serial): Descendant of masked hero vs. out-laws who are destroying telegraph lines

Ghost Patrol
1936, (USA), b&w, 57 mins.
<u>W:</u> Tim McCoy, Walter Miller, Wheeler Oakman
<u>D:</u> Sam Newfield
Minor SF-western: Cowboys kidnap ray-gun inventor, seek to rob mail airplanes

Ghost Rider
1935, (USA), b&w, 58 mins.
<u>W:</u> Rex Lease, Bobby Nelson, Franklyn Farnum, Lloyd Ingraham, Ed Parker, Lafe McKee
<u>D:</u> Jack Levine
Minor fantasy-western: Gunfighter's ghost aids lawman

Ghost Rider
1943, (USA), b&w, 58 mins.
<u>W:</u> Johnny Mack Brown, Raymond Hatton, Tim Seidel, Beverly Boyd, Milburn Morante
<u>D:</u> Wallace Fox
Standard fantasy-western: Supernatural dogs cowboy

Ghostriders
1988, (USA), Alan L. Stewart Prods., color, 85 mins.
<u>W:</u> Bill Shaw, Jim Peters, Ricky Long, Mike Ammons, Cari Powell, Arland Bishop
<u>D:</u> Alan Stewart   <u>PHOTOG:</u> Thomas L. Callaway
Minor fantasy-thriller: Spectral outlaws haunt preacher's family

Ghosts
1914, (GB), Ivy Close Films/Hepworth, b&w, 1,125 ft. (342.9m)
<u>W:</u> Ivy Close (*The Girl*), Pope Stamper (*The Man*)
<u>D:</u> Elwin Neame
Standard comedy: Girl investigates "haunted" house

Ghosts Before Breakfast
see ***Vormittagsspuk***

Ghosts Can't Do It
1990, (USA), Epic/Triumph, color, 95 mins.
<u>W:</u> Bo Derek (*Katie*), Anthony Quinn (*Scott*), Don Murray (*Winston*), Leo Damian (*Fausto*), Donald Trump, Julie Newmar, Dee Krainz
<u>WRIT, P, & D:</u> John Derek   <u>MUSIC:</u> Junior Homrich & Randy Tico
Minor eroto-fantasy: Woman seeks sexual fulfillment with shade of deceased husband

The Ghost Ship
1943, (USA), RKO, b&w, 69 mins
<u>W:</u> Richard Dix, Russell Wade, Edith Barrett, Skelton Knaggs, Law-rence Tierney, Sir Lancelot
<u>P:</u> Val Lewton   <u>D:</u> Mark Robson   <u>SCR:</u> Donald Henderson Clarke
Unusual thriller (least known of Val Lewton's classic atmospheric films): Admired sea captain revealed to be psychopathic killer

Ghost Ship
1952, (GB), Anglo-Amalgamated/Lippert, b&w, 74 mins.
<u>W:</u> Dermot Walsh (*Guy*), Hazel Court (*Margaret*), Hugh Burden (*Dr. Fawcett*), John Robinson (*Dr. Martineau*), Hugh Latimer (*Peter*), Pat Owens (*Joyce*), Joan Carol (*Mrs. Martineau*), Joss Ambler (*The Manager*), Mignon O'Doherty (*Mrs. Manley*), Laidman Browne, Meadows White, Pat McGrath, Joss Ackland, John King-Kelly, Colin Douglas

<u>WRIT, P, & D,</u> Vernon Sewell   <u>MUSIC:</u> Eric Spear
Modest thriller: Couple purchases haunted yacht

The Ghosts' Holiday
1907, (GB), Hepworth, b&w, 550 ft. (167.6m)
<u>W:</u> Gertie Potter, Thurston Harris
<u>D:</u> Lewin Fitzhamon
Standard fantasy short: Ghosts rise from churchyard, hold ball in hotel

Ghosts in the Morning
see ***Vormittagsspuk***

Ghosts—Italian Style
1967, (It), MGM, color, 120 mins.
<u>W:</u> Marcello Mastroianni, Sophia Loren (*Maria*), Vittorio Gassman (*Pasquale*), Mario Adorf (*Alfredo*), Margaret Lee (*Sayonara*), Aldo Giuffre (*Raffaele*), Francesco Tensi (*Santanna*)
<u>P:</u> Carlo Ponti   <u>D:</u> Renato Castellani   <u>SCR:</u> Tonio Guerra, based on Eduardo De Flippo's play *Questi Fantasmi*   <u>PHOTOG:</u> Tonino Delli Colli   <u>MUSIC:</u> Luis Enriquez Bacalov
A.k.a. ***Three Ghosts***
Wry fantasy: Amorous spirits cause consternation.

The Ghosts of Berkeley Square
1947, (GB), British Nat'l/Pathe, b&w, 89 mins.
<u>W:</u> Robert Morley (*Gen. Burlap*), Felix Aylmer (*Col. Kelsoe*), Yvonne Arnaud (*Millie*), Abraham Sofaer (*Disraeli*), Claude Hulbert (*Merryweather*), Martita Hunt (*Lady Mary*), Ernest Thesiger (*The Investigator*), Marie Lohr (*Lottie*), A.E. Matthews (*Gen. Bristow*), Ronald Frankau (*Tex Farnham*), John Longden (*Mortimer Digby*), Wilfrid Hyde-White (*The Captain*), Martin Miller (*The Professor*), Edward Lexy (*The Officer*), Wally Patch (*The Foreman*), James Hayter (*Capt. Dodds*), Esme Percy (*The Vizier*), J.H. Roberts (*The Doctor*), Mary Jerrold (*Lettie*)
<u>P:</u> Louis H. Jackson   <u>D:</u> Vernon Sewell   <u>SCR:</u> James Seymour, from the novel *No Nightingales* by S.J. Simon & Caryl Brahms
Sentimental fantasy: Two 18th-century spirits doomed to haunt house until royalty visits

The Ghosts of Hanely House
1968, (USA), color, 80 mins.
<u>W:</u> Barbara Chase, Wilkie De Martel, Elsie Baker, Cliff Scott
Minor thriller (filmed in Texas): Benighted guests spend evening in creepy mansion

Ghosts on the Loose
1943, (USA), Banner/Mono, b&w, 65 mins.
<u>W:</u> Leo Gorcey, Huntz Hall, Ava Gardner, Bela Lugosi, Rick Vallin, Minerva Urecal, Bobby Jordan, Frank Moran, Billy Benedict, Sunshine Sammy Morrison
<u>P:</u> Sam Katzman   <u>D:</u> William Beaudine   <u>SCR:</u> Kenneth Higgins
A.k.a. ***The East Side Kids Meet Bela Lugosi***
Standard "Bowery Boys" comedy-thriller: Nazi propagandists use "haunted house" as base

The Ghost Steps Out
see ***The Time of Their Lives***

Ghosts that Still Walk
1977, (USA), color, 92 mins.
<u>W:</u> Ann Nelson, Matt Boston, Jerry Jenson, Caroline Howe, Rita Crafts
<u>D:</u> James T. Flocker
Minor fantasy-thriller: Demons possess young woman's soul

Ghost Story (1964)
see ***Kwaidan***

Ghost Story
1975, (GB), Weeks Co., color, 89 mins.
<u>W:</u> Larry Dann (*Talbot*), Murray Melvin (*McFayden*), Vivian Mackerall (*Duller*), Marianne Faithfull (*Sophie Quickworth*), Anthony Bate (*Dr. Borden*), Penelope Keith (*Rennie*), Leigh Lawson (*Robert Quick-worth*), Sally Grace (*The Girl*), Barbara Shelley (*The Matron*)
<u>P & D:</u> Stephen Weeks   <u>STORY:</u> Rosemary Sutcliffe & Stephen Weeks   <u>PHO-TOG:</u> Peter Hurst   <u>MUSIC:</u> Ron Geesin
USA retitle, ***Mad House Mansion***
Standard horror-fantasy: Doll strangles visitors to haunted house

Ghost Story
1981, (USA), Burt Weissbourd/Univ, color, 108 mins.
<u>W:</u> Fred Astaire (*Ricky Hawthorne*), Melvyn Douglas (*John Jaffrey*), John Houseman (*Sears James*), Douglas Fairbanks Jr. (*Edward Wanderley*), Alice Krige (*Alma/Eva*), Craig Wasson (*Don/David*), Patricia Neal (*Stella*), Jacqueline Brookes (*Millie*), Miguel Fernandes (*Gregory Bate*), Tim Choate (*Young Hawthorne*), Lance Holcomb (*Fenny Bate*), Mark Chamberlin (*Young Jaffrey*), Ken Olin (*Young James*), Kurt Johnson (*Young Wanderley*), Brad Sullivan (*The Sheriff*)
<u>D:</u> John Irvin   <u>SCR:</u> Lawrence D. Cohen, from Peter Straub's novel   <u>PHOTOG:</u> Jack Cardiff   <u>SPCL-FX:</u> Albert Whitlock   <u>MUSIC:</u> Phillipe Sarde
Well-made spooker: Four elderly men pay dearly for crime of their youth

The Ghost Talks
1929, (USA), Fox, b&w, 9 reels (6,482 ft./1975.7m)

W: Helen Twelvetrees (*Miriam Holt*), Charles Easton (*Franklyn Green*), Earle Fox (*Heimie Heimrath*), Carmel Myers (*Marie Haley*), Stepin Fetchit (*Christopher Lee*), Joe Brown (*Peter Accardi*), Baby Mack (*Isobel Lee*), Clifford Dempsey (*John Keegan*), Arnold Lucy (*Julius Bowser*), Bess Flowers (*Sylvia*), Dorothy McGowan (*Miss Eva*), Mickey Bennett (*The Bellboy*), Henry Sedley (*Joe Talles*)
D: Lew Seiler   SCR: Frederick H. Brennan & Harlan Thompson, from a story by Max Marcin & Edward Hammond   PHOTOG: George Meehan
Standard comedy-thriller: Aspiring detective aids girl in hunt for stolen bonds

The Ghost That Walks Alone
1944, (USA), Col, b&w, 64 mins.
W: Arthur Lake, Janis Carter, Lynne Roberts, Frank Sully
Minor thriller-comedy

Ghost Town
1988, (USA), Charles Band/Empire/New World, color, 85 mins.
W: Frank Luz, Jimmie F. Skaggs, Catherine Hickland, Bruce Glover, Michael Alldredge, Penelope Windust, Laura Schaefer
D: Richard Governor   SCR: Dale Sandefur   STORY: David Schmoeller   PHOTOG: Mac Ahlberg
Minor fantasy-thriller: Outlaw's ghost abducts female traveler

The Ghost Train
1927, (GB), Gainsborough, b&w, 6,500 ft. (1981.2m)
W: Guy Newall (*Teddy Deakin*), Ilse Bois (*Miss Bourne*), Louis Ralph (*Saul Hodgkin*), Anna Jennings (*Peggy Murdock*), John Manners (*Charles Murdock*), Agnes Korolenko (*Elsie Winthrop*), Ernest Verebes (*Richard Winthrop*), Rosa Walter (*Julia Price*)
D: Geza M. Bolvary, from Arnold Ridley's play
Standard comedy-thriller: Detective tracks gun-runners

The Ghost Train
1931, (GB), Gainsborough/W&F, b&w, 72 mins.
W: Jack Hulbert (*Teddy Deakin*), Cicely Courtneidge (*Miss Bourne*), Donald Calthrop (*Saul Hodgkin*), Ann Todd (*Peggy Murdock*), Cyril Raymond (*Richard Winthrop*), Tracy Holmes (*Charles Bryant*), Angela Baddeley (*Julia Price*), Allan Jeayes (*Dr. Sterling*), Carol Coombe (*Elsie Bryant*), Henry Caine (*Herbert Price*)
D: Walter Forde   SCR: Angus Macphail & Lajos Biro, from Arnold Ridley's play
Standard comedy-thriller: Detective poses as fool, nabs smugglers

The Ghost Train
1941, (GB), Gainsborough/GFD, b&w, 85 mins.
W: Arthur Askey (*Tommy Gander*), Richard Murdoch (*Teddy Deakin*), Kathleen Harrison (*Miss Bourne*), Carole Lynn (*Jackie Winthrop*), Morland Graham (*Dr. Sterling*), D.J. Williams (*Ben Isaacs*), Linden Travers (*Julie Price*), Peter Murray-Hill (*Richard Winthrop*), Raymond Huntley (*John Price*), Herbert Lomas (*Saul Hodgkin*), Betty Jardine (*Edna*), Stuart Latham (*Herbert*), George Merritt (*The Inspector*)
P: Edward Black   D: Walter Forde   SCR: Marriott Edgar, Val Guest & J.O.C. Orton, from a play by Arnold Ridley
reissued 1947
Standard comedy-thriller: Detective pursues spies

The Ghost Train Murder
1959, (GB), Merton Park/Anglo-Amalgamated, b&w, 32 mins.
W: Russell Napier (*Supt. Duggan*), Jill Ireland (*Nora*), Mary Laura Wood (*Mrs. Williams*), Gordon Needham (*Sgt. Wallace*)
P: Jack Greenwood   D: Peter Maxwell   STORY: James Eastwood
Standard short thriller: Inspector unmasks shoplifters behind stabbing of Hungarian girl

The Ghost Walks
1934, (USA), Chesterfield/SG/Invincible, b&w, 69 mins.
W: John Miljan, June Collyer, Richard Carle Spencer Charters, Johnny Arthur, Henry Kolker
D: Frank Strayer
Minor thriller: Arrival of real killer complicates playwright's staged murder mystery

The Ghost Walks
1935, (GB), Central/Zenifilms, b&w, 22 mins.
W: George Bass, Barbara Gott
P & D: Walter Tennyson
Minor comedy-fantasy short: Couple has haunting experience

Ghost Warrior
1984, (USA), Charles Band/Harkham/Empire, color, 85 mins.
W: Hiroshi Fujioka (*Yoshimitsu*), John Calvin (*Dr. Alan Richards*), Janet Julian (*Chris Welles*), Frank Schuller (*Det. Berger*), Charles Lampkin (*Willie Walsh*), Robert Kino (*Prof. Takagi*), Andy Wood (*Dr. Pete Denza*), Bill Morey (*Dr. Carl Anderson*), Joan Foley (*Ellie West*), Toshiji Obata (*The Japanese Officer*), Rob Narita (*The Boy Skier*), Lynn Kuratomi (*The Girl Skier*), Peter Liapis (*Johnny Tooth*), Mieko Kobayashi (*Chidori*), Chris Caputo (*Tom Jenks*), Simmy Bow (*Volker*), Alan Lachaumette (*The Police Officer*), J. Bill Jones (*Officer Jones*), Casey Brown (*The Prostitute*), Phil Rubenstein (*Det. Carlysle*), Jerry Tondo (*The Sushi Chef*), Miko Ishikawa (*The Sushi Waitress*), Leslie Wing (*Sushi Bar Customer #1*), Michael Brox (*Sushi Bar Customer #2*), Al Berry (*The Helicopter Pilot*), Larry Cedar (*The Helicopter Observer*), Melvin Jones (*A Gang Member*), Rock A. Walker (*A Gang Member*), Tony Travis (*A Gang Member*),

Charles Ringa (*A Gang Member*), Anthony Leonardi (*A Gang Member*)
D: Larry Carroll   SCR: Tim Curnen   PHOTOG: Mac Ahlberg   MUSIC: Richard Band
Standard SF-thriller: Samurai awakes from suspended animation

Ghost Writer
1990, (USA), Rumar, Made for TV, color, 95 mins.
W: Audrey Landers, Judy Landers, Jeff Conaway, David Doyle, Joey Travolta, John Matuszak, Dick Miller, Ken Tobey, Nels Van Patten, Anthony Franciosa, The Barbarian Brothers
WRIT & D: Kenneth J. Hall   PHOTOG: Nicholas Von Sternberg   MUSIC: Reg Powell & Sam Winans
TVM, minor fantasy: Spirit of '60's actress seeks vindication

The Ghoul
1933, (GB), Gaumont/W&F, b&w, 79 mins.
W: Boris Karloff (*Prof. Morlant*), Sir Cedric Hardwicke (*Broughton*), Ernest Thesiger (*Laing*), Anthony Bushell (*Ralph Morlant*), Dorothy Hyson (*Betty Harlow*), Harold Huth (*Ali Ben Drage*), Kathleen Harrison (*Kaney*), D.A. Clarke-Smith (*Mahmoud*), Ralph Richardson (*Nigel Hartley*), Jack Raine (*The Chauffeur*)
D: T. Hayes Hunter   SCR: Frank King, Leonard Hines, L. DuGarde Peach, Roland Pertwee, John Hastings Turner, & Rupert Downing, from a novel by Frank King & Leonard Hines   PHOTOG: Gunther Krampf
Fr retitle, The Living Ghost
Standard horror-thriller: Egyptologist leaves grave to recover stolen gems

The Ghoul
1974, (GB), Tyburn/Fox-Rank, color, 87 mins.
W: Peter Cushing (*Dr. Lawrence*), John Hurt (*Tom*), Gwen Watford (*Ayah*), Alexandra Bastedo (*Angela*), Veronica Carlson (*Daphne*), Stewart Bevan (*Billy*), Don Henderson (*The Ghoul*), Ian McCulloch (*Geoffrey*), John D. Collins (*The Man*), Dan Meaden (*The Sgt.*)
P: Kevin Francis   D: Freddie Francis   SCR: John Elder [Anthony Hinds]   PHOTOG: John Wilcox   MUSIC: Harry Robinson
Minor thriller: Clergyman's cursed son kills stranded travelers

Ghoulies
1985, (USA), Charles Band/Empire, color, 85 mins.
W: Peter Liapis (*Jonathan Graves*), Lisa Pelikan (*Rebecca*), Michael Des Barres (*Malcolm Graves*), Scott Thomson (*Mike*), Jack Nance (*Wolfgang*), Peter Risch (*Grizzel*), David Dayan (*Eddie*), Tamara De Treaux (*Greedigut*), Charlene Cathleen (*Robin*), Ralph Seymour (*Mark*), Mariska Hargitay (*Donna*), Keith Joe Dick (*Dick*), Victoria Catlin (*Anastasia*), Bobbi Bresee (*The Temptress*)
D: Luca Bercovici   SCR: Luca Bercovici & Jefery Levy   PHOTOG: Mac Ahlberg   MUSIC: Richard Band & Shirley Walker
Minor horror-fantasy: Satanist's son conjures monsters

Ghoulies II
1988, (USA-It), Empire/Vestron, video, color, 90 mins.
W: Damon Martin, Royal Dano, Phil Fondacaro, J. Downing, Kerry Remsen, Dale Wyatt, Jon Maynard Pennell, William Butler, Sasha Jenson, Starr Andreeff, Donnie Jeffcoat, Christopher Burton, Mickey Knox, Michael Deak, Ettore Martini
P & D: Albert Band   SCR: Dennis Paoli   STORY: Charlie Dolan   PHOTOG: Sergio Salvati   MUSIC COMPOSER: Fuzzbee Morse   MUSIC SPRVSR: Jonathan Scott Bogner
Made-for-Video, minor horror-fantasy: Gremlins disrupt carnival

Ghoulies 3: Ghoulies Go to College
1991, (USA), color, 94 mins.
W: Kevin MCarthy, Griffin O'Neal, Evan Mackenzie
D: John Carl Buechler
Minor comedy-fantasy: Beasties beset coeds

The Ghost Walks: JOHN MILJAN AND JUNE COLLYER

Ghoulies IV
1994, (USA), color, 84 mins.
W: Peter Liapis
Minor fantasy-thriller: California policeman vs. devilish dominatrix

Ghoul School
1975, (USA), color, 88 mins.
W: Joe Franklin, Nancy Siriani, William Friedman
Minor horror-spoof: Mayhem in college

The Giant Behemoth
see Behemoth, the Sea Monster

The Giant Claw
1957, (USA), Clover/Col, b&w, 76 mins.
W: Jeff Morrow (*Mitch McAffee*), Mara Corday (*Sally Caldwell*), Robert Shayne (*Gen. Buskirk*), Morris Ankrum (*Gen. Considine*), Louis D. Merrill, Ruell Shayne (Aka Frank Griffin), Clark Howat, Edgar Barrier, Morgan Jones
P: Sam Katzman **D:** Fred F. Sears **SCR:** Samuel Newman & Paul Gangelin **PHOTOG:** Benjamin H. Kline
Minor SF: Anti-matter bird threatens Earth

Giant from the Unknown
1958, (USA), Screencraft/Astor, b&w, 77 mins.
W: Edward Kemmer, Sally Fraser, Bob Steele, Buddy Baer, Morris Ankrum, Billy Dix, Joline Brand, Ned Davenport, Oliver Blake, Gary Crutcher, Ewing Miles
P: Arthur P. Jacobs **D & PHOTOG:** Richard E. Cunha **STORY & SCR:** Frank Hart Taussig & Ralph Brooke **SPCL-FX:** Harold Banks **MUSIC:** Albert Glasser
Minor fantasy-thriller: Evil conquistador returns to life

Giant From the Unknown: MORRIS ANKRUM AND EDWARD KEMMER

The Giant Gila Monster
1959, (USA), McLendon, b&w, 74 mins.
W: Don Sullivan, Lisa Simone, Janice Stone, Shug Fisher, Ken Knox, Jerry Cortwright, Anne Sonka, Fred Graham, Don Flourney, Beverly Thurman, Gay McLendon, Clarke Browne, Pat Simmons, Bob Thompson, Pat Reeves, Cecil Hunt, Grady Vaughn, Stormy Meadows, Howard Ware, Desmond Doogh
P: Ken Curtis **D:** Ray Kellogg **STORY & SCR:** Ray Kellogg & Jay Simms **PHOTOG:** Wilfrid M. Cline **SPCL-FX:** Ralph Hammeras & Wee Risser **MUSIC:** Jack Marshall
orig. co-billed with The Killer Shrews
Minor SF-thriller: Big beastie preys on country folk

The Giant Leeches
see Attack of the Giant Leeches

Giant of Evil Island
1964, (It), color
W: Rock Stevens, Dina De Santis
Minor action-thriller

The Giant of Marathon
see La Battaglia di Maratona

Giant of Metropolis
see Il Gigante di Metropolis

Giants of Thessaly
1960, (It), Medallion, color, 87 mins.

W: Roland Carey, Ziva Rodann, Cathia Caro, Alberto Farnese, Missimo Girotti
D: Riccardo Freda
A.k.a. The Argonauts
Minor "Sword & Sandal" fantasy: Adventurers seek treasure

Giants of Rome
1963, (It), color, 87 mins.
W: Richard Harrison, Ettore Manni
Minor "Sword & Sandal": Eternal City imperiled by secret weapon (giant catapult)
A.k.a. Three Ghosts

The Giant Spider Invasion
1976, (USA), Transcentury/Group 1, color
W: Steve Brodie, Barbara Hale, Leslie Parrish, Alan Hale Jr., Robert Easton, Christina Schmidtmer, Bill Williams
D: Bill Rebane **SCR:** William L. Huff & Robert Easton **ORIG. STORY:** Robert Easton
Minor SF-thriller: "Black Hole" allows alien horrors to invade Earth

The Giant's Three Golden Hairs
1968, (W. Ger), color
Juvenile fantasy

Gideon of Scotland Yard
see Gideon's Day

Gideon's Day
1958, (GB), Col, color, 91 mins.
W: Jack Hawkins (*Insp. George Gideon*), Dianne Foster (*Joanna Delafield*), Cyril Cusack (*Birdy Sparrow*), Andrew Ray (*Simon Farnaby-Green*), James Hayter (*Mason*), Ronald Howard (*Paul Delafield*), Miles Malleson (*The Judge*), Anna Massey (*Sally Gideon*), Grizelda Hervey (*Mrs. Kirby*), Derek Bond (*Sgt. Kirby*), Frank Lawton (*Sgt. Liggott*), Howard Marion-Crawford (*The Chief*), Laurence Naismith (*Arthur Sayer*), Marjorie Rhodes (*Mrs. Saporelli*), Anna Lee (*Kate Gideon*), John Loder (*Ponsford*), Doreen Madden (*Miss Courtney*), Michael Shepley (*Sir Rupert Bellamy*), Michael Trubshawe (*Sgt. Golightly*), Jack Watling (*Rev. Julian Small*)
P&D: John Ford **SCR:** T.E.B. Clarke, from a novel by John Creasey **PHOTOG:** Frederick A. Young **MUSIC:** Douglas Gamley
USA retitle, Gideon of Scotland Yard. Released in b&w.
Polished melodrama: Typically hectic day in life of London detective

The Gifted One
1989, (USA), NBC-TV, color, 96 mins.
W: Pete Kowanko (*Michael Grant*), Brandon Call (*Michael, age 10*), Wendy Phillips (*Sarah Grant*), G.W. Bailey (*Dr. Winslow*), Gregg Henry (*Jack*), John Rhys-Davies (*Carl Boardman*), Khrystyne Haje (*Mary Joe*), Kristopher Kent Hill (*Billy Farady*), James Eric (*Tom Farady*), Kenneth Bridges (*Dr. Helfen*), Shano Palovich (*Beth Farady*), Lucky Hayes (*Mrs. Williams*), Charles Benton (*Mr. Williams*), Dey Young (*Susan Martin*), Dale Swann (*Gordon Thomas*), Rose Weaver (*Dr. Claire Henry*), Jim Newcomer (*Dr. James*), Stephen Hastings (*Dr. Hart*), Tami French (*Hannah*), Spensley Schroder (*Dr. Solomon*), Doug Cotner (*Dr. Richards*), Anthony Holden (*The Technician*), Arell Blanton (*The Guard*), Mark Manning (*The Principal*), Norm McBride (*The Coach*), Michael Mancini (*The Umpire*), Cole Coxon (*Baby Michael*), Jackson Douglas Fisher (*The Doctor*), Emily Y. Ragsdale (*The Nurse*), Christina Herczeg (*The Little Girl*), Mason Arnold (*Tommy*), Steven Suggs (*Jeffrey*), Chris Balcerzak (*Johnny*), Hank Lawrence (*Big Lou*), Christopher Michael (*Bobby*), Sandy Gibbons (*Policeman #1*), Jonathan Voyce (*Policeman #2*), Joe Elrady, Thomas Callaway
D: Stephen Herek **TELEPLAY:** Richard Rothstein & Lisa James **PHOTOG:** Kees Van Ostrum **MUSIC:** J. Peter Robinson
TVM-pilot for unsold teleseries, standard SF: Paranormal youth seeks birth mother

The Gift of Gab
1934, (USA), Univ, b&w, 70 mins.
W: Edmund Lowe, Gloria Stuart, Boris Karloff, Bela Lugosi, Chester Morris, Andy Devine, Alexander Woollcott, Sterling Holloway, Alice White, Winifred Shaw, Paul Lukas
P: Carl Laemmle Jr. **D:** Karl Freund **SCR:** Rian James & Lou Breslow
Standard music-comedy-thriller: Involvements of a radio show

Il Gigante di Metropolis (Giant of Metropolis)
1961, (It), Pan-World, color, 82 mins.
W: Gordon Mitchell (*Obro*), Bella Cortez, Rolando Lupi
P: Emimmo Salvi **D:** Umberto Scarpelli **SCR:** Sabatino Ciuffino, Oreste Palella, Ambrogio Molteni, Gino Stafford, & Emimmo Salvi **MUSIC:** Armando Trovajoli
orig. to be titled Metropolis
Odd mix of SF and "Sword & Sandal": Bizarre experiments on fabled isle of Atlantis

The Gigantic Devil
see Le Diable Geant ou le Miracle de la Madonne

The Gigantic Devil: or, The Miracle of the Madonna
see Le Diable Geant ou le Miracle de la Madonne

Gigantic Marionettes
1913, (GB), Clarendon, b&w, 370 ft. (112.8m)

D: Percy Stow
Minor fantasy short: Performance by huge marionettes

Gigantis, the Fire Monster
see Godzilla Raids Again

Gilda
1946, (USA), Col, b&w, 110 mins.
W: Rita Hayworth (*Gilda*), Glenn Ford (*Johnny Farrell*), George Macready (*Ballin*), Joseph Calleia, Steven Geray, Gerald Mohr, Ludwig Donath, Joe Sawyer
P: Virginia Van Upp   **D:** Charles Vidor   **SCR:** E.A. Ellington   **PHOTOG:** Rudolph Maté   **MUSIC:** Morris Stoloff & Marlin Skiles   **SONGS:** *Amado Mio* & *Put the Blame on Mame*
Classic film noir: Sinister husband of tempestuous beauty conspires with neo-Nazis

Gilda: RITA HAYWORTH

The Gilded Cage
1955, (GB), Tempean/Eros, b&w, 77 mins.
W: Alex Nicol (*Steve Anderson*), Veronica Hurst (*Marcia Farrell*), Clifford Evans (*Ken Aimes*), Ursula Howells (*Brenda Lucas*), Elwyn Brook-Jones (*Bruno*), Michael Alexander (*Harry Anderson*), John Stuart (*Harding*), Trevor Reid (*Insp. Brace*)
P: Robert Baker & Monty Berman   **D:** John Gilling   **SCR:** Brock Williams   **STORY:** Paul Erickson
Standard crime-thriller: USAAF security man proves brother framed by art smuggler

Gildersleeve's Ghost
1944, (USA), RKO, b&w, 64 mins.
W: Harold Peary (*Gildersleeve*), Richard LeGrand, Marion Martin, Amelita Ward, Lillian Randolph, Marie Blake, Emory Parnell, Freddie Mercer, Frank Reicher, Margie Stewart, Joseph Vitale, Nicodemus (Nick) Stewart
D: Gordon M. Douglas   **SCR:** Robert E. Kent   **PHOTOG:** Vernon L. Walker   **MUSIC:** Paul Sawtell   **MUSIC DIR:** C. Bakaleinikoff
Minor comedy-fantasy. 'The Great Gildersleeve' series

Giles has His Fortune Told
1911, (GB), Urban, b&w, 770 ft. (104.5m)

D: Walter R. Booth
Standard fantasy: Yokel dreams Devil shrinks him

Gill-Woman
1969, (It), AIP, color
W: Basil Rathbone
Minor SF-thriller

Giulietta Degli Spiriti
1967, (Swed), Crown Int'l, b&w, 90 mins.
W: Valentina Cortese (*Valentina*), Sylva Koscina (*Sylva*), Lou Gilbert (*Grandfather*), Luisa della Noce (*Adele*), Silvana Jachino (*Dolores*), Alba Cancellieri (*Juliet as a Child*), Mario Pisu (*Giorgio*), Caterina Boratto (*The Mother*), Dany Paris (*The Desperate Friend*), Elena Fondra (*Elena*), Irina Alexeieva (*Grandmother*), Gilberto Galvan (*The Chauffeur*), Seyna Seyn (*Massageuse*), Edoardo Torricella (*The Russian Teacher*), Raffaele Guida (*The Oriental Lover*), Frederick Ledebur (*The Headmaster*), Alberto Plebani (*Lynx-Eyes*), Fred Williams (*The Arabian Prince*), Felice Fulchignoni (*Don Raffaele*), Anne Francine (*The Psychoanalyst*), Mario Conocchia (*The Family Lawyer*), Waleska Gert (*Bhisma*), Genius (*The Medium*), Massimo Sarchielli (*Valentina's Lover*), Alessandra Mannoukine. Jose de Villalonga, Dina de Santis, Cesarino Miceli Picardi, Bob Edwards, Milena Vucotich, Elisabetta Gray, Yvonne Casadei, Nadir Moretti, Hildegarde Golez, Giorgio Ardisson Sven-Bertil Taube, Helena Brodin.
Standard melodrama

The Gingerbread Cottage
see Pernikova Chaloupka

The Gingerbread House
see Who Slew Auntie Roo?

Gipsy Blood
1931, (GB), BIP/Wardour, b&w, 79 mins.
W: Marguerite Namara (*Carmen*), Thomas Burke (*Don Jose*), Lance Fairfax (*Escamillo*), Lester Matthews (*Zuniga*), Mary Clare (*The Factory Girl*), Dennis Wyndham (*Doncairo*), D. Hay Petrie (*Remenado*), Lewin Mannering (*The Innkeeper*)
D: Cecil Lewis   **SCR:** Cecil Lewis & Walter C. Mycroft, from Georges Bizet's opera *Carmen*
Standard melodrama: Soldier deserts and kills for love of wicked gypsy

Gipsy Hate
1913, (GB), Urban Trading Co., b&w, 1,050 ft. (320m)
W: Constance Somers-Clarke (*Norma*)
WRIT & D: Lewin Fitzhamon
Standard melodrama: Gypsy loves fisherman, tries to drown rival

Gipsy Nan
1911, (GB), Hepworth, b&w, 425 ft. (129.5m)
W: Marie de Solla (*The Gypsy*), Chrissie White (*Nan*)
D: Lewin Fitzhamon
Standard melodrama: Farmer rides to save abducted gypsy from being whipped

Girl and the Gorilla
see Nabonga

Girlfriend from Hell
1989, (USA), Live, video, color 95 mins.
W: Liane Curtis (*Maggie*), Dana Ashbrook, James Daughton, James Karen Lezlie Deane, Anthony Barrile, Brad Zutaut, Ken Abraham, Hilary Morse
WRIT & D: Daniel M. Peterson   **PHOTOG:** Gerry Lively   **MUSIC:** Michael Rapp
Made-for-Video, minor horror-comedy: Wallflower possessed by female devil

The Girl from Downing Street
1918, (GB), Int'l Exclusives/Butcher, b&w, 4,832 ft. (1472.8m)
W: Ena Beaumont (*Peggy Marsden*), Sydney Paxton (*Capt. Paul Muller*), William Stack (*Cyril Godfrey*)
D & SCR: Geoffrey H. Malins, from a story by Garth Grayson
Standard thriller: Female spy steals dirigible plans

Girl from 5,000 A.D.
see Terror from the Year 5,000

The Girl from Scotland Yard
1937, (USA), Para, b&w, 61 mins
W: Karen Morley, Eduardo Ciannelli, Robert Baldwin, Lloyd Crane (*John Hall*), Bud Flanagan (*Dennis O'Keefe*)
Standard thriller

The Girl Hunters
1963, (GB), Present Day-Fellane/Colorama/Zodiac International/ B&W, scope, color, 103 mins.
W: Mickey Spillane (*Mike Hammer*), Shirley Eaton (*Laura Knapp*), Lloyd Nolan (*Art Rickaby*), Scott Peters (*Capt. Pat Chambers*), Hy Gardner (*himself*), James Dyrenforth (*Bayliss Henry*), Guy Kingsley Poynter (*Dr. Larry Snyder*), Charles Farrell (*Joe Grissi*), Kim Tracy (*The Nurse*), Bill Nagy (*Georgie*), Benny Lee (*Nat Drutman*), Larry Cross (*Red Markham*), Murray Kash (*Richie*

Cole)
P: Robert Fellows & Charles Reynolds   **D:** Roy Rowland   **SCR:** Mickey Spillane, Row Rowland, & Robert Fellows, from a novel by Mickey Spillane
    PHOTOG: Ken Talbot   **MUSIC:** Philip Green
Standard thriller: Spy network nabs detective's secretary. Spillane plays his own creation. 'Mike Hammer' feature.

The Girl in a Swing
1989, (GB), Millimeter, color, 119 mins.
W: Meg Tilly, Rupert Fraser, Lynsey Baxter, Sophie Thursfield, Jean Boht, Nicholas Le Prevost, Elspet Gray, Claire Shepherd, Lorna Heilbron
WRIT & D: Gordon Hessler   **PHOTOG:** Claus Loof   **MUSIC:** Carl Davis
Unusual thriller: Mysterious bride conceals past

The Girl in Black Stockings
1957, (USA), UA, b&w, 73 mins.
W: Lex Barker, Anne Bancroft, Mamie Van Doren, Marie Windsor, Ron Randell, Stuart Whitman John Dehner, John Holland, Diana Van Der Vlis
D: Howard W. Koch   **SCR:** Richard Landau   **MUSIC:** Les Baxter
Standard thriller: Murder at Utah resort

Girl in His Pocket
see Un Amour de Poche

The Girl in Lover's Lane
1960, (USA), b&w, 78 mins.
W: Brett Halsey, Joyce Meadows, Lowell Brown, Jack Elam
D: Charles R. Rondeau
Standard thriller: Drifter blamed for girl's murder

The Girl in Room 2A
1976, (It), color 90 mins.
W: Raf Vallone, Daniela Giordano
Standard thriller

The Girl in the Case
1944, (USA), Col, b&w, 64 mins.
W: Edmund Lowe, Janis Carter
Standard thriller

The Girl in the Flat
1934, (GB), B&D/Para-British, b&w, 65 mins.
W: Stewart Rome (*Sir John Waterton*), Belle Chrystal (*Mavis Tremayne*), Vera Boggetti (*Girda Long*), Jane Millican (*Kitty Fellows*), John Turnbull (*Insp. Grice*), Noel Shannon (*Maj. Crull*)
D: Redd Davis   **SCR:** Violet Powell, from a story by Evelyn Winch
Standard thriller: Barrister's fiancee blackmailed

Girl in the Headlines
1963, (GB), Viewfinder/Bry, b&w, 93 mins.
W: Ian Hendry (*Insp. Birkett*), Ronald Fraser (*Sgt. Saunders*), Margaret Johnston (*Mrs. Gray*), Kieron Moore (*Herter*), Jeremy Brett (*Jordan Barker*), Peter Arne (*Hammond Barker*), Natasha Parry (*Perlita Barker*), Rosalie Crutchley (*Maud Klein*), Jane Asher (*Lindy Birkett*), Robert Harris (William Lamotte), Duncan Macrae (*Barney*), Zena Walker (*Mildred Birkett*), Marie Burke (*Mme. Lavalle*), James Villiers (*David Dane*), Patrick Holt (*Warbrook*)
P: John Davis   **D:** Michael Truman   **SCR:** Vivienne Knight & Patrick Campbell, from Laurence Payne's novel
Standard crime-thriller: Inspector probes model's death

The Girl in the Kremlin
1957, (USA), Univ, b&w, 81 mins.
W: Zsa Zsa Gabor, Maurice Manson, Lex Barker, William Schallert, Jeffrey Stone
P: Albert Zugsmith   **D:** Russell Birdwell   **SCR:** Harry Ruskin & DeWitt Bodeen
orig. co-billed with **The Deadly Mantis**
Standard satire-thriller: Stalin has plastic surgery, hides out in Greece

The Girl in the Moon
see Die Frau im Mond

The Girl in the News
1940, (GB), 20th Century Prods./MGM, b&w, 78 mins.
W: Margaret Lockwood (*Anne Graham*), Barry K. Barnes (*Stephen Farringdon*), Emlyn Williams (*Tracy*), Roger Livesey (*Bill Mather*), Margaretta Scott (*Judith Bentley*), Basil Radford (*Dr. Treadgrove*), Wyndham Goldie (*Edward Bentley*), Irene Handl (*Miss Blaker*), Mervyn Johns (*James Fetherwood*), Kathleen Harrison (*The Cook*), Felix Aylmer (*The Prosecution*)
P: Edward Black   **D:** Carol Reed   **SCR:** Frank Launder & Sidney Gilliat, from a novel by Roy Vickers
Standard thriller: Butler poisons employer, frames nurse, reissued 1948

The Girl in the Painting
see Portrait from Life

Girl Missing
1933, (USA), WB, b&w, 69 mins.
D: Robert Florey   **STORY:** Jules Furthman   **PHOTOG:** Karl Struss
Minor melodrama

Girl on a Broom
1974, (Czech), color
W: Petra Cernocka
Standard fantasy

The Girl on the Bridge
1951, (USA), 20th-Fox, b&w, 77 mins.
W: Hugo Haas, Beverly Michaels, Robert Dane, Johnny Close
WRIT, P, & D: Hugo Haas
Minor melodrama: Unwed mother obsesses middle-aged watchmaker

The Girl on the Pier
1953, (GB), Major/Apex, b&w, 65 mins.
W: Veronica Hurst (*Rita Hammond*), Ron Randell (*Nick Lane*), Charles Victor (*Insp. Chubb*), Marjorie Rhodes (*Mrs. Chubb*), Campbell Singer (*Joe Hammond*), Eileen Moore (*Cathy Chubb*), Brian Roper (*Ronnie Hall*), Anthony Valentine (*Charlie Chubb*)
P: Lance Comfort & John Temple-Smith   **D:** Lance Comfort   **STORY:** Guy Morgan
Standard crime-thriller: Brighton waxworks exhibitor kills blackmailer

The Girl Rosemarie
see Das Madchen Rosemarie

Girls for Rent
see I Spit On Your Corpse

Girls in Chains
1943, (USA), b&w, 72 mins.
W: Arline Judge, Roger Clark, Robin Raymond, Barbara Pepper, Dorothy Burgess, Clancy Cooper
D: Edgar G. Ulmer
Minor thriller: Corruption in reformatory for girls

Girls in Prison
1956, (USA), Golden State/AIP, b&w, 87 mins.
W: Joan Taylor, Richard Denning, Adele Jergens, Jane Darwell, Helen Gilbert, Diana Darrin, Mae Marsh, Lance Fuller, Raymond Hatton, Luana Walters, Laurie Mitchell, Edmund Cobb, Kermit Maynard
P: Alex Gordon   **D:** Edward L. Cahn   **SCR:** Lou Rusoff
Standard thriller: Earthquake frees female prisoners

Girl's Nite Out
1984, (USA), color
W: Hal Holbrook
Minor thriller: Slasher haunts college campus

Girls School Screamers
1986, (USA), color, 85 mins.
W: Mollie O'Mara, Sharon Christopher, Vera Gallagher
D: John P. Finegan
Minor thriller: Psychotic killer lurks in old mansion

A Girl to Kill For
1990, (USA), color, 85 mins.
W: Sasha Jensen, Karen Austin, Alex Cord, Rod McCary, Karen Medak
D: Richard Oliver
Minor thriller: Temptress lures college boy into murder scheme

The Girl was Young
see Young and Innocent

The Girl Who Didn't Care
1916, (GB), Barker-Neptune-Volcano/Cross, b&w, 3,900 ft. (1188.7m)
W: Agnes Paulton (*Eve Latimer*), Mercy Hatton (*Kitty*), Tom Coventry, Jerrold Robertshaw
D: Fred W. Durrant   **STORY:** Rowland Talbot
Standard crime-thriller: Girl robs father to pay for wedding, becomes morphine maniac's mistress

The Girl Who Knew Too Much
see La Ragazza Che Sapeva Troppo

The Girl Who Took the Wrong Turning
1915, (GB), British Empire, b&w, 5,000 ft. (1524m)
W: Henry Lonsdale (*James Harcourt*), Alice Belmore (*Sophie Coventry*), Nina Lynn (*Vesta le Clere*), Ronald Adair (*Willie Mason*), Mercy Hatton (*Lucy Coventry*), Andrew Emm (*Johnny Walker*), Wingold Lawrence (*Jack Fenton*), Sidney Sarl (*Bill Slater*), Eva Dare (*Poppy Slater*), C.F. Collings (*Richard Fenton*)
D: Leedham Bantock, from a play by Walter Melville
Standard crime-thriller: Squire's nephew frames disowned cousin for murder

The Girl Who Wrecked His Home
1916, (GB), British Empire Films, b&w, 5,000 ft. (1524m)
W: Henry Lonsdale (*Lord Lynton*), Alice Belmore (*Bertha Marshall*), Arthur Poole (*Leonard Kenyon*), Maud Olmar (*Winnie*), Andrew Emm (*Josh*), Cyril Bennell (*William as a Child*), Frances Davies (*Winnie as a Child*)
D & SCR: Albert Ward, from a play by Walter Melville
Standard crime-thriller: Cardsharp frames neglected wife for murder

Girly
1969, (GB), Brigitte-Fitzroy-Francis/CIRO/Cinerama, color, 102 mins.
W: Michael Bryant (*The New Friend*), Vanessa Howard (*Girly*), Howard Trever (*Sonny*), Ursula Howells (*Mumsy*), Pat Heywood (*Nanny*), Robert Swann (*The Soldier*), Imogen Hassall (*The Girlfriend*), Michael Ripper (*The Attendant*)
P: Ronald J. Kahn   D: Freddie Francis   SCR: Brian Comfort, from a play by Maisie Mosco
A.k.a. **Mumsy, Nanny, Sonny and Girly**
Standard thriller: Psychopathic family kills

Giulietta degli Spiriti (Juliet of the Spirits)
1965, (It), Federiz/Francoriz/Rizzoli, color, 148 mins.
W: Giulietta Masina (*Giulietta*), Mario Pisu (*The Husband*), Sandra Milo (*Susy/Iris/Fanny*), Valentina Cortese, Sylva Koscina, Lou Gilbert, Jose de Villalonga, Frederick Ledebur, Caterina Boratto
D: Federico Fellini   SCR: Federico Fellini, Tullio Pinelli, Ennio Flaiano & Bruno Rondi   PHOTOG: Gianni Di Venanzo   MUSIC: Nino Rota
Unusual fantasy: Neglected wife has daydreams

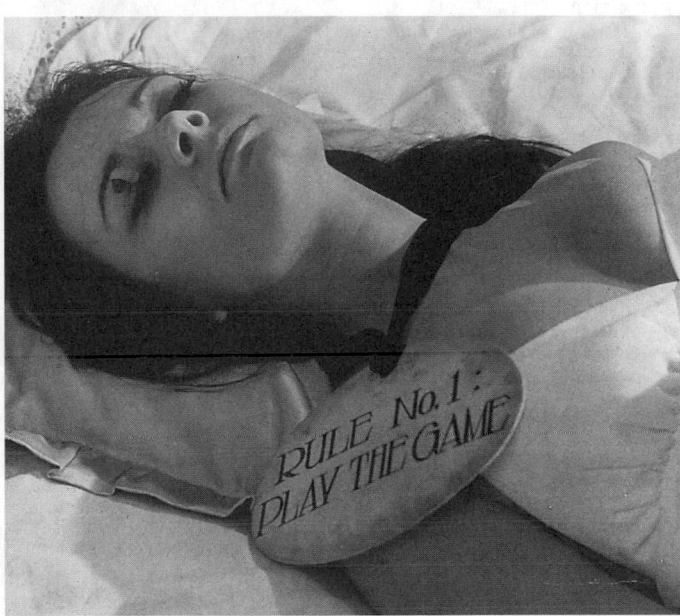

Girly: IMOGEN HASSALL

Giving up the Ghost
1998, (USA), Lifetime, color, 90 mins.
W: Marg Helgenberger, Alan Rosenberg, Brian Kerwin, Kate Lynch, Richard Romanus, Ron Lea, Bob Balaban
D: Claudia Weill   TELEPLAY: Anthea Sylbert & Richard Romanus   PHOTOG: John Holosko   MUSIC: Mader
TVM, standard fantasy: Woman haunted by husband's ghost

Give Us Tomorrow
1979, (GB), Donwin/Col-EMI-WB, color, 94 mins.
W: Sylvia Syms (*Wendy Hammond*), Derren Nesbitt (*Ron*), James Kerry (*Martin Hammond*), Donna Evans (*Nicola Hammond*), Matthew Haslett (*Jamie Hammond*), Chris Holroyd (*Contable McLaren*), Victor Brooks (*The Supt.*), Alan Guy (*The Boy*), Derek Anders (*The Insp.*), Ken Barker (*The Sgt.*), Mark Elwes (*Tom*), Derek Ware (*Raider*)
WRIT, P & D: Donovan Winter   PHOTOG: Austin Parkinson   MUSIC: John Fox
Standard thriller: Gunmen hold bank manager's family captive

La Glace a Trois Faces (The Mirror Has Three Faces)
1927, (Fr), b&w
P & D: Jean Epstein
Standard fantasy

The Gladiator
1938, (USA), Col, b&w
W: Joe E. Brown, June Travis, Man Mountain Dean Dickie Moore, Lucien Littlefield, Robert Kent, Ethel Wales
D: Edward Sedgwick
Minor comedy-fantasy: College student takes experimental pills, becomes super sports star. Reworked as Bowery Boys comedy **Hold That Line,** *1952*

Gladiator Cop: The Swordsman 2
1995, (USA), color, 92 mins.
W: Lorenzo Lamas, George Touliatos
Minor SF-fantasy: Legendary sword stolen

The Gladiators
1970, (USA), color, 90 mins.
W: Arthur Pentelow, Frederick Danner
D: Peter Watkins
A.k.a. **The Peace Game**
Minor SF-thriller: Future gladiatorial bouts televised

The Gladiator's Affianced Bride
1908, (GB), Walter Tyler, b&w, 410 ft. (125m)
Standard "Sword & Sandal": Gladiators vie for beauty's love

Gladiators Seven
1967, (It-Sp), MGM color, 92 mins
W: Richard Harrison (*Darius*) Lordana Nusciak, Livio Lorenzon, Gerard Tichy, Edoardo Toniolo, Joseph Marco, Barta Barry
D: Pedro Lazaga
Minor "Sword & Sandal": Spartan heroes fight tyrannical ruler. US release: 1964

The Glass Alibi
1946, (USA), Rep, b&w, 68 mins.
W: Paul Kelly, Anne Gwynne, Douglas Fowley
D: W. Lee Wilder
Minor thriller. Remade by same director as **The Big Bluff,** *1955*

The Glass-Bottom Boat
1966, (USA), MGM, color, 110 mins.
W: Doris Day, Rod Taylor, Arthur Godfrey, Paul Lynde, Eric Fleming, Alice Pearce, Ellen Corby, John McGiver, Dick Martin, Edward Andrews, Dom DeLuise
D: Frank Tashlin   PHOTOG: Leon Shamroy
Amusing comedy-thriller: Woman suspected of spying

The Glass Cage
1964, (USA), Futuramic, b&w, 78 mins.
W: John Hoyt, Arline Sax, Elisha Cook Jr., Robert Kelljan
D: Antonio Santean   STORY: John Hoyt
TV retitle, **Den of Doom,** *A.k.a.* **Don't Touch My Sister**
Standard thriller

The Glass Cage
1996, (USA), color, 100 mins.
W: Eric Roberts, Lisa Marie Scott, Richard Tyson, Maria Ford, Joseph Nichols
Made-for-Cable, standard thriller: Dancer involved with smugglers

The Glass Cell
1981, (W. Ger), Roxy/Solaris, color, 100 mins.
W: Helmut Griem (*Philip*), Brigitte Fossey (*Lisa*), Dieter Laser (*David*), Walter Kohut (*Lasky*), Bernhard Wicky (*The Commissioner*), Claudius Kracht, Guenther Stack, Klaus Muenster, Jans Guenther Martens, Christa-Maria Netsch, Gerlinde Egger
D: Hans C. Geissendoerfer   SCR: Hans C. Geissendoerfer & Klaus Baedekerl, from Patricia Highsmith's novel   PHOTOG: Robby Mueller   MUSIC: Niels Walen
Standard thriller

A Glass of Goat's Milk
1909, (GB), Clarendon, b&w, 446 ft. (135.9m)
D: Percy Stow
reissued 1913
Standard comedy-fantasy: Bearded man drinks goat's milk, butts people

The Glass Slipper
1955, (USA), MGM, color, 94 mins.
W: Leslie Caron (*Ella*), Michael Wilding (*Prince Charles*), Estelle Winwood (*Mrs. Toquet*), Amanda Blake (*Birdena*), Keenan Wynn (*Kovin*), Elsa Lanchester (*Widow Sonder*), Lisa Daniels (*Serafina*), Barry Jones (*The Duke*), Lurene Tuttle (*Cousin Loulou*), Liliane Montevecchi (*Tehara*)
D: Charles Walters   SCR: Helen Deutsch   PHOTOG: Arthur E. Arling   SPCL-FX: Warren Newcombe   MUSIC: Bronislau Kaper
TV retitle, **Cinderella's Glass Slipper**
Lavish musical-fantasy (with ballet sequences): Scullery maid meets prince

The Glass Sphinx
1967, (Egypt-It-Sp), color, 91 mins.
W: Robert Taylor, Anita Ekberg Gianna Serra, Jack Stuart, Angel Del Pozo, Jose Truchado
D: Luigi Scattini
Minor thriller: Egyptian tomb excavated

The Glass Tomb
1955, (GB), Hammer/Lippert, b&w, 59 mins.
W: John Ireland (*Pel*), Honor Blackman (*Jenny*), Geoffrey Keen (*Stanton*), Eric Pohlmann (*Sapolio*), Valerie Vernon (*Bella*), Sidney James (*Tony Lewis*), Sydney Tafler (*Rorke*), Liam Redmond (*Lindley*), Arnold Marle (*Pop Manoni*), Stanley Little (*Mickelwitz*), Nora Gordon, Ferdy Mayne, Tonia Bern, Sam Kydd, Arthur Howard
P: Anthony Hinds   D: Montgomery Tully   SCR: Richard Landau, from A.E. Martin's novel *The Outsiders*   MUSIC: Leonard Salzedo
Standard thriller: Murder in a carnival

The Glass Tower
1957, (W. Ger), Filmkunst/Ellis Films, b&w, 93 mins.
<u>W</u>: Lilli Palmer, Peter Van Eyck, O.E. Hasse
<u>D</u>: Harold Braun
Standard thriller: Former actress imprisoned by husband

The Glass Web
1953, (USA), Univ, 3D, b&w, 81 mins.
<u>W</u>: Edward G. Robinson (*Henry Hayes*), John Forsythe (*Don Newell*), Richard Denning (*Dave Markson*), Kathleen Hughes (*Paula Ranier*), Marcia Henderson (*Louise Newell*), Clark Howat (*Bob Warren*), Hugh Sanders (*Lt. Stevens*), Duncan Richardson (*Jimmy Newell*), Dick Stewart (*Everett*), Jeri Lou James (*Barbara Newell*), Harry Tyler (*Jake*), Herbert Lytton, James Stone, Beverly Garland, Kathleen Freeman, Eve McVeagh, Lance Fuller, Brett Halsey
<u>D</u>: Jack Arnold   <u>SCR</u>: Robert Blees & Leonard Lee, from a novel by Max Simon Ehrlich   <u>PHOTOG</u>: Maury Gertsman   <u>MUSIC</u>: Joseph Gershenson

Standard thriller: Blackmailing television actress is murdered

Glen and Randa
1971, (USA), UMC, color, 94 mins.
<u>W</u>: Steven Curry (*Glen*), Shelley Plimpton (*Randa*), Woodrow Chambliss (*Sidney*), Garry Goodrow, Roy Rox, Robert Holmer, Hubert Powers, William Fratis, Alice Huffman, Ortega Sangster, Barbara Spiegel, Richard Frazier, Charles Huffman, Martha Furey, Leonard Johnson, Jack Tatarsky, Bud Thompson, Laura Hawbecker, Lucille Johnson, Matthew Levine, Talmadge Holiday, James Nankerius, Winona Tomanoczy, David Woeller
<u>D</u>: Jim McBride   <u>SCR</u>: Lorenzo Mans, Rudolph Wurlitzer & Jim McBride   <u>PHOTOG</u>: Alan Raymond
Unusual SF thriller (cult classic): Young couple struggles to survive after World War III. Rated X

Glen or Glenda?
1953, (USA), George Weiss/Screen Classics?Par., b&w, 67 mins.
<u>W</u>: Bela Lugosi (*The Scientist*), Lyle Talbot (*The Policeman*), Daniel Davis, (Edward D. Wood Jr.) (*Glen/Glenda*), Timmy Haynes (*Alan/Ann*), Dolores Fuller (*Barbara*), Timothy Farrell (*The Psychiatrist*), Charles Crofts, Conrad Brooks,

Edward D. Wood Jr.
<u>WRIT & D</u>: Edward D. Wood Jr.   <u>PHOTOG</u>: William C. Thompson
A.k.a. I Led Two Lives, He or She?, I Changed My Sex and The Transvestite
reissued by Paramount (1981)
Cult-classic hoot: Maudlin tale of troubled transvestite

The Glitterball
1977, (GB), Forstater/CFF, color, 56 mins.
<u>W</u>: Ben Buckton (*Max Fielding*), Keith Jayne (*Peter*), Ron Pember (*George Potter*), Marjorie Yates (*Mrs. Fielding*), Barry Jackson (*Sgt. Fielding*), Andrew Jackson (*The Cpl.*)
<u>P</u>: Mark Forstater   <u>D</u>: Harley Cokliss   <u>SCR</u>: Howard Thompson & Michael Abrams   <u>STORY</u>: Howard Thompson & Harley Cokliss   <u>PHOTOG</u>: Alan Hall   <u>MUSIC</u>: Harry Robinson
Standard juvenile SF-fantasy: Children find UFO

The Glittering Sword
1929, (GB), Altrincham School, b&w, 1,800 ft. (548.6m)
<u>W</u>: T. Hampson (*The Boy King*), L. Galloway (*The Chancellor*), H. Mitchell (*Death*), A. Gregory (*The Devil*)
<u>WRIT & D</u>: Ronald Gow
Standard fantasy (not shown theatrically): Allegory of existence

The Glory of Love
see While Paris Sleeps

The Gloves of Ptames
1914, (GB), Martin Films/DFSA, b&w, 568 ft. (173.1m)
<u>D</u>: Dave Aylott
Standard fantasy: Egyptian gloves make objects vanish

Glump
see Please Don't Eat My Mother

The Glutton's Nightmare
1901, (GB), Hepworth, b&w, 150 ft. (45.7m)
<u>D</u>: Percy Stow
Standard fantasy: Glutton dreams of cats in rabbit pie, dogs in sausages

Gnaw
see The Food of the Gods, Part II

The Gnome-Mobile
1967, (USA), Walt Disney/Buena Vista, color, 84 mins.
<u>W</u>: Walter Brennan, Tom Lowell, Ed Wynn, Matthew Garber, Karen Dotrice, Sean McClory, Norman Grabowski, Richard Deacon, Byron Foulger, Charles Lane, Ellen Corby
<u>D</u>: Robert Stevenson   <u>SCR</u>: Ellis Kadison, from Upton Sinclair's book *The Gnomobile*   <u>PHOTOG</u>: Edward Colman   <u>MUSIC</u>: Buddy Baker
Juvenile fantasy: Adventures of diminutive forest folk

A Gnome Named Gnorm
1989, (USA), HBO-TV, color, 84 mins.
<u>W</u>: Anthony Michael Hall Claudia Christian, Eli Danker, Mark Harelik, Joseph R. Sicari, Robert Z'Dar, Greg Kean
<u>D</u>: Stan Winston   <u>SCR</u>: Pat Densham & John Watson   <u>PHOTOG</u>: Bojan Bazelli   <u>MUSIC</u>: Richard Gibbs
Made-for-Cable, minor fantasy: Young detective acquires subterranean partner

Goaded to Anarchy
1905, (GB), R.W. Paul, b&w, 480 ft. (146.3m)
Standard short thriller: Anarchist blows up general who sent his wife to Siberia

Goblin
1993, (USA), color, 75 mins.
<u>W</u>: Bobby Westrick, Jenny Admire
Minor horror-fantasy: Evil creature inhabits newlyweds' home

Gobots: Battle of the Rock Lords
1986, (USA), Hanna-Barbera, color, 75 mins.
<u>VOICES</u>: Margot Kidder, Roddy McDowall, Michael Nouri, Telly Savalas
Minor animated SF-fantasy: Renegades wage war

The Goddess
see Devi

The Goddess of Love
1988, (USA), Phoenix, Made for TV, color, 95 mins.
<u>W</u>: Vanna White, David Naughton, David Leisure, John Rhys-Davies, Betsy Palmer, Amanda Bearse, Little Richard, Ray O'Connor, Philip Baker Hall, Michael Goldfinger, Lindsey Fields, Jennifer Bassey, Marty Davis, David Donham, John Moskott, James Edgcomb, Stephanie Hershey, Robin Krieger, Mitch Kreindel, Vincent Lucchesi, Stuart Mabray, Florence Schauffler, Philip Reeves, Phil Margo, Don Segall, Shari Shattuck, Paul Tinder, Jordana Capra, Kay E. Kuter, Sid Haig, Ben Schick
<u>D</u>: Jim Drake   <u>TELEPLAY</u>: Don Segall & Phil Margo   <u>PHOTOG</u>: Gil Hubbs   <u>SPCL-FX</u>: Greg Landerer   <u>MUSIC</u>: Mitch Margo, Dennis Dreith & A.S. Dimond
TVM, minor fantasy (rehash of One Touch of Venus): Statue of Venus comes to life

The God King

1974, (GB-India), Dimitri De Grunald/Raymond Torin/Tiger, color, 96 mins.
W: Leigh Lawson (*Kassapa*), Oliver Tobias (*Migara*), Anne Loos (*Leila*), Geoffrey Russell (*Dhatusena*), Wijaya Kumaratunga (*Lalith*), Mano Breckenridge (*The Leader*), Menik (*Somitra*), Joe Abeywick-rema (*The Swami*), Irangani Serasinghe (*Varuni*), Ravindra Randeniya (*Mogollana*), Douglas Wickremasinghe
D: Lester James Peries   **ORIG. SCR:** Anthony Greville-Bell   **PHOTOG:** Willie Blake   **MUSIC:** Nimal Mendis
Static adventure-romance: Cousins vie for throne in 5th-century Ceylon

The Gods and the Dead

see *Os Deuses e os Mortos*

God's Bloody Acre

1975, (USA), color, 90 mins.
W: Scott Lawrence, Jennifer Gregory, Sam Moree, Shiang Hwa Chyang
D: Harry Kerwin
Minor thriller: Mountain-dwelling brothers kill construction workers, prey on vacationers

The Glass Cage: ARLINE SAX

God's Clay

1919, (GB), Arthur Rooke, b&w, 4,500 ft. (1371.6m)
W: Janet Alexander (*Angela Clifford*), Humbertson Wright (*Geoffrey Vance*), Arthur Rooke (*Horace Newton*), Maud Yates (*Poppy Stone*), Adeline Hayden Coffin, John Hastings Batson
D & SCR: Arthur Rooke, from a novel by Claude & Alice Askew
Standard crime-thriller: Paralyzed woman kills seducer, frames his mistress

The Godsend

1979, (Can), Cannon, color, 85 mins.
W: Malcolm Stoddard (*Alan Marlowe*), Cyd Hayman (*Kate Marlowe*), Angela Pleasence (*The Stranger*), Patrick Barr (*Dr. Collins*), Wilhelmina Green (*Bonnie*), Joanne Boorman (*Bonnie*), Angela Deamer (*Lucy*), Clarissa Young (*Lucy*), Piers Eady (*Sam*), Lee Gregory (*Davie*), Anna Wing (*Mrs. Taverner*), Artro Morris (*Taverner*), Hilary Minster (*The Reporter*), Corinne Skinner-Garter (*The Doctor*), James Snell
P & D: Gabrielle Beaumont   **SCR:** Olaf Pooley, from a novel by Bernard Taylor
PHOTOG: Norman Warwick   **MUSIC:** Roger Webb
Unusual thriller: Mystery woman leaves newborn child with unsuspecting couple

God Told Me To

see *Demon (1976)*

Godzilla

1998, (USA), Centropolis/TriStar, color, 139 mins.
W: Matthew Broderick, Maria Pitillo, Hank Azaria, Jean Reno, Harry Shearer, Michael Lerner, Kevin Dunn, Arabella Field, Doug Savant
D: Roland Emmerich   **SCR:** Roland Emmerich & Dean Devlin   **SONG:** *Come With Me*
Lavish remake of SF-fantasy classic: Mighty marine monster menaces

Godzilla, King of the Monsters

see *Gojira*

Godzilla 1985

1985, (Jap), New World, color, 91 mins.
W: Raymond Burr (*Steve Martin*), Keiju Kobayashi (*Prime Minister Mitamura*), Ken Tanaka (*Goro Maki*), Yasuko Sawaguchi (*Naoko Okumura*), Shin Takuma (*Hiroshi Okumura*), Eitaro Ozawa (*Kanzaki*), Taketoshi Naito (*Takegami*), Nobuo Kaneko (*Isomura*), Takeshi Katoh (*Kasaoka*), Mizuho Suzuki (*Kanzaki*), Junkichi Orimoto (*Mohri*), Shinsuke Mikimoto (*Kakurai*), Mikita

Mori (*Ohkochi*), Yoshifumi Tajime (*Hidaka*), Kiyoshi Tamamoto (*Kajita*), Hiroshi Koizumi (*Minami*), Kunio Murai (*Henmi*), Kei Sato (*Gondo*), Takenori Emoto (*Kitagawa*), Shinpei Hayashiya (*Kamijo*), Yosuke Natsuki (*Hayashida*), Takeo Morimoto, Koji Ishizaka, Tetsuya Takeda, James Hess, Warren Kemmerling, Travis Swords
P: Tomoyuki Tanaka & Anthony Randel   **D:** Kohji Hashimoto & R.J. Kizer
SCR: Shuichi Nagahara & Lisa Tomei   **STORY:** Tomoyuki Tanaka
PHOTOG: Kazutami Hara   **SPCL-FX:** Teruyoshi Nakano   **MUSIC:** Reijiro Koroku
Minor SF-fantasy: Prehistoric monster returns to terrorize Japan

Godzilla on Monster Island

1977, (Jap), Toho, color 89 mins.
W: Hiroshi Ichikawa, Tomoko Umeda, Yuriko Hishimi, Minoru Takashima, Zan Fujita
D: Jun Fukuda
Minor SF-fantasy: Prehistoric monsters battle space-alien threat

Godzilla Raids Again

1955, (Jap), Toho/WB, b&w, 78 mins.
W: Horoshi Koizumi, Setsuko Wakayama, Mindru Chiaki
P: Paul Schreibman & Tomoyuki Tanaka   **D:** Motoyoshi & Hugo Grimaldi
SCR: Takeo Murata & Shigeaki Hidaka, from a story by Shigem Kayama
SPCL-FX: Eiji Tsuburaya   **SOUND-FX:** Al Sarno
orig. to be titled **The Volcano Monsters**, *A.k.a.* **Godzilla's Counterattack**, *distrib. in USA (1959) as* **Gigantis, the Fire Monster**
Standard SF-fantasy: Monstrous reptile returns from watery grave

Godzilla's Counterattack

see *Godzilla Raids Again*

Godzilla's Revenge

1967, (Jap), Toho/UPA, color 70 mins.
W: Kenji Sahara, Machiko Naka Tomonori Yazaki, Sachio Sakai, Chotaro Togin, Yoshibumi Tajima
P: Tomoyuki Tanaka   **D:** Inoshiro Honda   **SCR:** Shinichi Sekizawa   **SPCL-FX:** Eiji Tsuburaya   **SONG:** *March of the Monsters*
Juvenile SF-fantasy: Small boy fixated on prehistoric monsters

Godzilla vs. Biollante

1992, (Jap), Toho, color, 104 mins.
W: Kunihiko Mitamura Kazuki Ohmori
D: Kazuki Ohmori
Minor SF-fantasy: Hybrid machine-monster challenges giant reptile

Godzilla vs. the Bionic Monster

1974, (Jap), Toho, color 80 mins.
W: Masaaki Daimon, Kazuya Aoyama, Akihiko Hirata, Hiroshi Koizumi Reiko Tajima, Barbara Lynn
D: Jun Fukuda
A.k.a. **Godzilla vs. the Cosmic Monster** *and* **Godzilla vs. MechaGodzilla**
Minor SF-fantasy: Alien invaders control electronic Godzilla double

Godzilla vs. the Cosmic Monster

see *Godzilla vs. the Bionic Monster*

Godzilla vs. Destroyer

1995, (Jap), Toho, color, 89 mins.
W: Momoko Kochi
D: Takao Okawara
Standard SF-fantasy (final "Godzilla" film): Reptilian behemoth battles winged horror

Godzilla vs. Gigan

1974, (Jap), Toho, color
A.k.a. **War of the Monsters**
Standard SF-fantasy: Alien invaders disguise themselves as amusement-park builders

Godzilla vs. Hedora

see *Godzilla vs. the Smog Monster*

Godzilla vs. King Ghidora

1991, (Jap), Toho, color
Standard SF-fantasy

Godzilla vs. Mechagodzilla

see *Godzilla vs. the Bionic Monster*

Godzilla vs. Megalon

1973, (Jap), Toho/Eizo/Cinema Shares, color, 85 mins.
W: Katsuhiko Sasaki, Hiroyuki Kawase, Yutaka Hayashi, Mori Mikita Robert Dunham
D & SCR: Jun Fukuda
Minor SF-fantasy: Giant reptile defends Earth against clawed terror

Godzilla vs. Monster Zero

see *Monster Zero*

Godzilla vs. Mothra
1964, (Jap), Toho/AIP, color, scope 98 mins.
W: Hiroshi Koizumi, Yu Fujiki, Yuriko Hoshi, Emi Ito, Yumi Ito, Eiji Okada, Kenji Sahara, Akira Takarada
D: Inoshiro Honda　SCR: Shinichi Sekizawa　PHOTOG: Hajime Koizumi
SPCL-FX: Eiji Tsuburaya　MUSIC: Akira Ifukube
Standard SF-fantasy: Giant reptile faces off with giant insect. Original title: Gojira Tai Mosura, US: Godzilla vs. The Thing

Godzilla vs. the Sea Monster
see Ebirah, Horror of the Deep

Glen and Randa: SHELLEY PLIMPTON AND STEVEN CURRY

Godzilla vs. the Smog Monster
1971, (Jap), Toho/AIP, color, 85 mins.
W: Hiroyuki Kawase (*Ken*), Akira Yamaguchi (*Dr. Yano*), Toshie Kimura (*Mrs. Yano*), Keiko Mari (*Miki*), Toshio Shibaki (*Yukio*)
P: Tomoyuki Tanaka　D: Yoshimitsu Banno　SCR: Kaoru Mabuchi & Yoshimitsu Banno　PHOTOG: Yoichi Manoda　MUSIC: Riichiro Manabe
SONG: Save the Earth
A.k.a. Godzilla vs. Hedora
Standard SF-fantasy: Pollution-monster threatens Japan

Godzilla vs. the Thing
see Godzilla vs. Mothra

Gog
1954, (USA), Independent/UA, 3D, color, 85 mins.
W: Richard Egan (*David*), Constance Dowling (*Joanna Merritt*), Herbert Marshall (*Dr. Van Ness*), John Wengraf (*Dr. Zeitman*), Valerie Vernon, Philip Van Zandt, Michael Fox, Steve Roberts, Byron Kane, David Alpert, William Schallert, Marian Richman, Jeanne Dean, Tom Daly, Aline Towne, Patti Taylor, Al Bayer, Andy Andrews, Julian Ludwig
P: Ivan Tors　D: Herbert L. Strock　SCR: Tom Taggart, from a story by Ivan Tors　PHOTOG: Lothrop B. Worth　SPCL-FX: Harry Redmond Jr.
MUSIC: Harry Sukman
orig. to be titled Space Station, U.S.A.
Unusual SF-thriller: Robots suspected of sabotage

Going to Bed Under Difficulties
see Le Deshabillage Impossible

Gojira
1954, (Jap), Toho/Trans-World/Jewel/Embassy, b&w, 98 mins.
W: Raymond Burr [extra footage added him to cast of USA release], Momoko Kochi, Akihiko Hirata, Akira Takarada, Sachio Sakai, Ta-kashi Shimura, Ren Yamamoto, Toranosuke Ogawa, Fuyuki Mura-kami, Toyoaki Suzuki, Tadashi Okabe, Frank Iwanaga
P: Tomoyuki Tanaka　D: Inoshiro Honda & Terry Morse (USA dir)　SCR: Takeo Murata & Inoshiro Honda, from an orig. story by Shigeru Kayama　PHO-TOG: Masao Tamai & Guy Roe (USA photog)　SPCL-FX: Eiji Tsuburaya
USA retitle, Godzilla, King of the Monsters
Classic SF-fantasy (Joseph E. Levine paid $10,000 for USA distrib. rights): Monstrous reptile ravages Japan

Goke, the Body Snatcher from Hell
see Body Snatcher from Hell

Gold
1934, (Ger {Ger-speaking}), Ufa, b&w, 80 mins.
W: Brigitte Helm, Hans Albers, Lien Dyers, Michael Bohnen, Frederick Kayssler
D: Karl Hartl　SCR: Rolf E. Vanloo　PHOTOG: Gunther Rittau, Otto Becker, & Werner Bohne　MUSIC: Hans-Otto Borgmann
Standard SF-thriller. cf. The Magnetic Monster

Gold
1934, (Ger {Fr-speaking}), Ufa, b&w
W: Brigitte Helm, Pierre Blanchar, Line Noro, Jacques Dumesnil
D: Serge de Poligny　SCR: Rolf E. Vanloo
Standard SF-thriller

The Golden Age
see L'Age d'Or

The Golden Arrow
see La Freccia d'Oro

The Golden Blade
1953, (USA), Univ, color, 81 mins.
W: Rock Hudson (*Harun*), Piper Laurie (*Princess Khairuzan*), Gene Evans (*Hadi*), Kathleen Hughes (*Bakhamra*), George Macready (*Jafar*), Steven Geray (*Barcus*), Edgar Barrier (*The Caliph*), Vic Romito (*Sherkan*), Alice Kelley, Erika Norden, Valerie Jackson, Anita Ekberg
D: Nathan Juran　SCR: William R. Cox　PHOTOG: Maury Gertsman
MUSIC: Joseph Gershenson
Standard adventure-fantasy: Magic sword helps youth gain vengeance

The Golden Child
1986, (USA), Feldman-Meeker/Para, color, 93 mins.
W: Eddie Murphy (*Chandler Jarrell*), Charles Dance (*Sardo Numspa*), Charlotte Lewis (*Kee Nang*), J.L. Reate (*The Golden Child*), Victor Wong (*The Old Man*), Randall "Tex" Cobb (*Til*), James Hong (*Dr. Hong*), Shakti (*Kala*), Tau Logo (*Yu*), Tiger Chung Lee (*Khan*), Pons Maar (*Fu*), Eric Douglas (*Yellow Dragon*), Peter Kwong (*Tommy Tong*), Wally Taylor (*Det. Boggs*), Charles Levin (*The TV Host*), Kinko Tsubouchi (*The Old Chinese Woman*), Kenneth "Fruitty" Frith Jr. (*The Friend at Pink's*), Bennett Ohta (*The Herb Shop Clerk*), Govind Chipalu (*The Jabbering Old Man*), Chantara Nop (*Security Man #1*), Phok Ok (*Security Man #2*), Rob Tzudiker (*The Businessman Customer*), Jeff Soo Hoo (*The Waiter*), Cliffy Magee (*Russell*), Bindra Joshi (*The Chicken Lady on the Plane*), Judy Hudson (*The Tortoise Lady*), Ron Packham (*Buttonman*), Marilyn Schreffler (*The Voice of Kala*), Frank Welker (*The Voice of the Thing*)
D: Michael Ritchie　SCR: Dennis Feldman　SPCL-FX SPRVSR: Cliff Wenger
VS-FX SPRVSR: Ken Ralston　MUSIC: Michael Colombier　VS-FX: Industrial Light & Magic　SONGS: The Best Man in the World, Body Talk, Wisdom of the Ages, The Chosen One & Another Day's Life
Standard comedy-fantasy: Streetwise Los Angelino seeks kidnapped Oriental messiah

The Golden Dawn
1921, (GB), Ralph Dewsbury/Pathe, b&w, 5,910 ft. (1801.4m)
W: Gertrude McCoy (*Nancy Brett*), Warwick Ward (*Dick Landon*), Frank Petley (*Henry Warville*), Charles Vane (*Jim Briggs*), Sydney Fairbrother (*Mrs. Briggs*), Mary Brough (*Mrs. Powers*), Philip Hewland (*Insp. Martin*), Charles Pelly (*Charles Proctor*)
D: Ralph Dewsbury　STORY: Bannister Merwin
Standard crime-thriller: Actress accused of shooting ex-husband

The Golden Demon
1956, (Jap), Daiei/Harrison, color, 95 mins.
W: Jun Negami
Standard adventure-thriller

Golden Earrings
1947, (USA), Para, b&w, 95 mins.
W: Ray Milland (*Col. Ralph Denistoun*), Marlene Dietrich (*Lydia*), Murvyn Vye (*Zoltan*), Bruce Lester (*Byrd*), Ivan Triesault (*Maj. Reimann*), Dennis Hoey (*Hoff*), Reinhold Schunzel (*Prof. Otto Krosigk*), Hermine Sterler, Quentin Reynolds
P: Harry Tugend　D: Mitchell Leisen　SCR: Abraham Polonsky, Frank Butler, & Helen Deutsch, from Yolanda Foldes' novel　PHOTOG: Daniel L. Fapp
SPCL-FX: Gordon Jennings　MUSIC: Victor Young
Classic adventure-romance: World War II Allied agent disguises self as gypsy

Die Goldene Gans (The Golden Goose)
1944, (GB), b&w
D: Lotte Reiniger, from a story by the Brothers Grimm
Standard animated fantasy (unfinished)

Der Goldene See
see Die Spinnen

The Golden Eye
1948, (USA), Mono, b&w, 69 mins.
W: Roland Winters (*Charlie Chan*), Wanda McKay (*Evelyn Manning*), Mantan Moreland (*Birmingham Brown*), Victor Sen Yung (*Tommie Chan*), Bruce Kellogg (*Bartlett*), Tim Ryan (*Lt. Mark Ruark*), Evelyn Brent (*Sister Teresa*), Edmund Cobb (*The Miner*), Ralph Dunn (*Driscoll*), Lee "Lasses" White (*Pete*), Lois Austin (*Mrs. Margaret Driscoll*), Forrest Taylor (*Manning*), Tom Tyler, Lee Tung Foo, George L. Spaulding, Barbara Jean Wong, Richard Loo, Herman Cantor, Bill Walker, John Merton
D: William Beaudine　SCR: Scott Darling, from characters created by Earl Derr Biggers　PHOTOG: William Sickner　MUSIC: Edward J. Kay
A.k.a. The Mystery of the Golden Eye
Standard "Charlie Chan" mystery: Oriental sleuth finds smugglers at Arizona ranch

Goldeneye
1995, (USA-GB), MGM-UA, color, 131 mins.
W: Pierce Brosnan (*James Bond*), Sean Bean (*Alec*), Izabella Scorupco (*Natalya*), Famke Janssen (*Xenia Onatop*), Judi Dench ("*M*"), Desmond Llewelyn ("*Q*"), Gottfried John, Joe Don Baker, Robbie Coltrane, Alan Cumming, Michael Kitchen, Samantha Bond, Serena Gordon, Minnie Driver, Simon Kunz, Pavel Douglas, Billy J. Mitchell, Michelle Arthur, Constantine Gregory, Ravil Isyanov, Peter Majer, Vladimir Milanovich, Trevor Byfield
P: Michael G. Wilson & Barbara Broccoli D: Martin Campbell SCR: Jeffrey Caine & Bruce Feirstein STORY: Michael France, from characters created by Ian Fleming PHOTOG: Phil Meheux MUSIC: Eric Serra THEME WRIT BY: Bono and The Edge (sung by Tina Turner)
Fast-moving adventure-thriller: Soviet subversives threaten world with ray from satellites

The Golden Falcon
1960, (It), color
W: Frank Latimore, Nadia Gray
Minor adventure-thriller

The Golden Goose
see Die Goldene Gans

Goldfinger: SEAN CONNERY

The Golden Idol
1954, (USA), AA, b&w, 71 mins.
W: Johnny Sheffield (*Bomba*), Anne Kimbell (*Karen Marsh*), Smoki Whitfield (*Eli*), Paul Guilfoyle (*Ali Ben Mamoud*), Rick Vallin (*Abdullah*), Leonard Mudie (*Barnes*), William Tannen (*Reed*), Lane Bradford (*Joe Hawkins*), Don Harvey (*Graves*), James Adamson (*Ezekial*), Roy Glenn (*Gomo*)
WRIT, P & D: Ford Beebe, from characters created by Roy Rockwood PHOTOG: Harry Neumann SPCL-FX: Ray Mercer
Minor adventure: Arab chief steals Watusi idol, jungle boy retrieves it

Golden Ivory
1954, (GB), Summit/ABP/AIP, color, 86 mins.
W: Robert Urquhart (*Jim Dobson*), John Bentley (*Paul Dobson*), Susan Stephen (*Ruth Meecham*), Alan Tarlton (*Seth*), Howarth Wood (*Meecham*), Maureen Connell (*Elizabeth Johnson*), Tom Lithgow (*Peter Johnson*), Kip Kamoi (*Kip*)
P: John Croydon, Peter Crane, George Breakston & Ray Stahl D: George Breakston STORY: Dermot Quinn
USA retitle (1957, 69 mins.), **White Huntress**
Standard adventure-thriller: Rival brothers seek elephants' burial ground

The Golden Lady
1979, (GB-Hong Kong), Elcotglade/Continental/Target, color, 94 mins.

W: Christina World (*Julia Hemmingway*), June Chadwick (*Luxy*), Suzanne Danielle (*Dahlia*), Anika Pavel (*Carol*), Stephen Chase (*Max Rowlands*), Edward De Souza (*Yorgo Praxis*), David King (*Dietmar Schuster*), Patrick Newell (*Charles Whitlock*), Richard Oldfield (*Wayne Bentley*), Ava Cadell (*Anita*), Terry Downes (*Trainer*), Desmond Llewelyn (*Prof. Nixon*), Michael Stock (*Visyris*), Seymour Green (*Levin*), Andreas Markos (*Victor*)
P: Paul Cowan D: Jose Larraz STORY: Joshua Sinclair PHOTOG: David Griffiths MUSIC: Georges Garvarentz
Standard thriller: Women agents foil assassination plot

The Golden Lake (1919)
see Die Spinnen

The Golden Lake (1935)
see Zolotoye Ozero

The Golden Link
1954, (GB), Parkside/Archway, b&w, 83 mins.
W: Andre Morell (*Supt. Blake*), Patrick Holt (*Terry Maguire*), Thea Gregory (*Joan Blake*), Jack Watling (*Bill Howard*), Arnold Bell (*Insp. Harris*), Olive Sloane (*Mrs. Pullman*), Bruce Beeby (*Sgt. Fred Baker*), Ellen Pollock (*Mme. Sonia*), Alexander Gauge (*Arnold Debenham*), Dorinda Stevens (*Norma Sheridan*), Charlie Drake (*Joe*)
P: Guido Coen D: Charles Saunders STORY: Allan Mackinnon
Standard thriller: Inspector's daughter framed for killing lover's wife

The Golden Mask
1954, (GB), Mayflower/Assoc. British/UA, color, 88 mins.
W: Van Heflin (*Nicholas Chapman*), Wanda Hendrix (*Anne Burnet*), Eric Portman (*Dr. Burnet*), Alec Mango (*Mahmoud*), Charles Goldner (*Petris*), George Pastell (*Hassan*), Marne Maitland (*Thankyou*), Jacques Francois (*Jacques Farnod*), Aubrey Mather (*Prof. Sir Arthur Young*), Simone Silva (*Zara*), Jacques Brunius (*Kress*), Rene Leplat (*Dr. Farnod*), Alec Finter (*The Workman*), Noelle Middleton (*The Stewardess*), Pierre Chaminade (*The Concierge*), Michael Mellinger (*The Spahi NCO*), Arnold Diamond (*The Spahi Officer*), Marie-France (*Yasmin*), Messaoud (*Abdel*)
P: Aubrey Baring & Maxwell Setton D: Jack Lee SCR: Robert Westerby PHOTOG: Oswald Morris MUSIC: Robert Gill
A.k.a. South of Algiers
Standard melodrama: Search for archeological treasure in North African desert

The Golden Mistress
1954, (USA), UA, color, 80 mins.
W: John Agar, Rosemarie Bowe, Abner Biberman, Jacques Molant, Andre Narcisse, Kiki, Pierre Blain, Napoleon Bernard, Andre Germain, National Folklore Theatre of Haiti
P: Richard Kay & Harry Rybnick D: Joel Judge (Abner Bibermen) SCR: Lee Hewitt & Joel Judge (Abner Bibermen) STORY: Lee Hewitt PHOTOG: William C. Thompson MUSIC: Raoul Kraushaar
Standard adventure-thriller: Americans seek forbidden treasure of Haitian tribe

The Golden Nymphs
see Honeymoon of Horror

The Golden Rabbit
1962, (GB), Argo/RFD, b&w, 64 mins.
W: Timothy Bateson (*Henry Tucker*), Maureen Beck (*Sally*), Willoughby Goddard (*Clitheroe*), Dick Bentley (*Insp. Jackson*), John Sharp (*Peebles*), Kenneth Fortescue (*Det. Wilson*), Raymond Rollett (*The Manager*), Humphrey Lestocq, Ronald Adam
P: Jack Lamont & Barry Delmaine D: David MacDonald STORY: Dick Sharples & Gerald Kelsey
Standard SF-comedy: Business men kidnap girl to obtain bank clerk's formula for making gold

The Golden Voyage of Sinbad
1974, (GB), Morningside/Col, color, 105 mins.
W: John Phillip Law (*Sinbad*), Tom Baker (*Koura*), Caroline Munro (*Margiana*), Douglas Wilmer (*The Vizier*), Gregoire Aslan (*Hakim*), Martin Shaw (*Rachid*), Aldo Sambrell (*Omar*), Kurt Christian (*Haroun*), Takis Emmanuel (*Achmed*), John D. Garfield (*Abdul*)
P: Charles H. Schneer D: Gordon Hessler SCR: Brian Clemens PHOTOG: Ted Moore SPCL-FX: Ray Harryhausen MUSIC: Miklos Rozsa
Standard adventure-fantasy: Hero battles wicked magician who has secret of restoring youth

The Golden Web
1920, (GB), Garrick/Anchor, b&w, 5,000 ft. (1524m)
W: Milton Rosmer (*Sterling Deans*), Ena Beaumont (*Winifred Rowan*), Victor Robson (*Sinclair*), Nina Munro (*Rosalie*)
D: Geoffrey H. Malins SCR: Milton Rosmer, from a novel by E. Phillips Oppenheim
Standard crime-thriller: Dead crook's sister weds heir to gold mine

The Gold Express
1955, (GB), Gaumont/RFD, b&w, 58 mins.
W: Vernon Gray (*Bob Wright*), Ann Walford (*Mary Wright*), May Hallatt (*Agatha Merton*), Ivy St. Helier (*Emma Merton*), Patrick Boxill (*Mr. Rover*), John Serrett (*Luke Dubois*), Delphi Lawrence (*Pearl*)
P: Frank Wells D: Guy Fergusson STORY: Jackson Budd
Standard crime-thriller: Reporter and wife thwart gold thieves

Goldfinger

1964, (GB), Eon/UA, color, 109 mins.
W: Sean Connery (*James Bond*), Shirley Eaton (*Jill Masterson*), Honor Blackman (*Pussy Galore*), Gert Frobe (*Auric Goldfinger*), Harold Sakata (*Oddjob*), Tania Mallett (*Tilly Masterson*), Bernard Lee ("M"), Cec Linder (*Felix Leiter*), Desmond Llewelyn ("Q"), Lois Maxwell (*Miss Moneypenny*), Margaret Nolan (*Dink*), Martin Benson (*Solo*), Nadja Regin (*Bonita*), Austin Willis (*Simmons*), Bill Nagy, Alf Joint, Mai Ling, Gerry Duggan, Richard Vernon
P: Harry Saltzman & Albert R. Broccoli **D:** Guy Hamilton **SCR:** Richard Maibaum & Paul Dehn, from Ian Fleming's novel **PHOTOG:** Ted Moore **SPCL-FX:** John Stears **MUSIC:** John Barry **TITLE:** Shirley Bassey
Exciting thriller, 3rd James Bond film: Master criminal plans to upset Western economy by irradiating gold reserves at Fort Knox

Gold for the Caesars

1962, (It), Adelphi Campagnia/MGM, color, 86 mins.
W: Jeffrey Hunter, Mylene Demongeot, Massimo Girotti, Ron Randell
D: Andre de Toth & Riccardo Freda
Minor action-thriller: Romans vs. Celts in Spain, A.D. 96

The Gold of Cristobal

see L'Or du Cristobal

Gold of the Amazon Women

1979, (USA), NBC-TV, color, 100 mins.
W: Bo Svenson (*Tom Jensen*), Anita Ekberg (*Queen Na-Eela*), Donald Pleasence (*Clarence Blasko*), Richard Romanus (*Luis Rodrigues*), Robert Minor (*Noboro*), Bond Gideon (*Taimi*), Maggie Jean Smith (*Reina*), John Sarno, Robert Ross, Ian Edwards
P: Alfred Leone **D:** Mark L. Lester **TELEPLAY:** Sue Donen **PHOTOG:** David Quaid **MUSIC:** Gil Melle
TVM, minor thriller: Ancient warrior caste clashes with modern fortune-hunters

The Gold of the Duke

see L'Or du Duc

Goldstein

1963, (USA), Montrose, b&w, 85 mins.
W: Lou Gilbert, Ellen Madison, Nelson Algren, Severn Darden, Anthony Holland, Thomas Erhart
WRIT, P & D: Philip Kaufman & Benjamin Manaster, inspired by Martin Buber's *Tales of the Hasidim*
Allegorical fantasy: Bedraggled prophet rises from lake

Der Golem (The Golem)

1914, (Ger), Bioscop, b&w, 4,100 ft. (1250m)
W: Paul Wegener (*The Golem*), Lyda Salmonova, Henrik Galeen, Carl Ebert
D: Paul Wegener & Henrik Galeen **PHOTOG:** Guido Seeber
USA retitle, **The Monster of Fate**
Venerable horror-fantasy (once thought to be "lost film"): Workmen digging well in old synagogue discover strange "statue"—the legendary golem of Medieval Jewry. cf. **The Golem: How He Came into the World** *and* **The Curse of the Golem**

Le Golem (The Golem)

1936, (Fr), Metropolis, b&w, 83 mins.
W: Harry Baur, Gaston Jacquet, Germaine Aussey, Jany Holt, Roger Karl, Ferdinand Hart, Roger Duchesne, Charles Dorat, Aimos
D: Julien Duvivier **SCR:** Andre-Paul Antoine **PHOTOG:** V. Vich & Jan Stalich
A.k.a. **The Legend of Prague**.
Interesting horror-fantasy: Gallic rehash of golem saga. cf. **Dr. Terror's House of Horrors** *(1943)*

Le Golem (The Golem)

1966, (Fr), ORTF, color
W: Andre Reybaz
D: Jean Kerchbron
Standard horror-fantasy: Clay automaton amazes

The Golem

1997, (USA), color, 90 mins.
Standard horror-fantasy

The Golem and the Dancing Girl

see Der Golem und die Tanzerin

The Golem and the Emperor's Baker

see Cisaruv Pekar, Pekaruv Cisar

The Golem: How He Came into the World

1920, (Ger), Union-Ufa, b&w, 6,306 ft. (1922m/75 mins.)
W: Paul Wegener (*The Golem*), Albert Steinruck (*Rabbi Loew*), Lyda Salmonova (*Miriam*), Lothar Meuthel (*Florian*), Ernst Deutsch (*The Disciple*), Grete Schroeder, Otto Gebuhr, Hans Sturm, Dore Paetzold, Max Kronert
D: Paul Wegener & Carl Boese **SCR:** Paul Wegener & Henrik Galeen, from the writings of Gustav Meyrink **PHOTOG:** Karl Freund **DESIGN:** Hans Poelzig & Rochus Gleise
Classic horror-fantasy ("prequel" to 1914's 'Der Golem'): Medieval rabbi creates living man of clay to champion cause of oppressed Jewry

Der Golem und die Tanzerin (The Golem and the Dancing Girl)

1917, (Ger), Bioscop, b&w
W: Paul Wegener (*The Golem*)
D: Paul Wegener & Rochus Gleise **STORY & SCR:** Paul Wegener
Minor horror-fantasy

Goliath Against the Giants

1961, (It-Sp), Cine-Produzioni-Procusa/Medallion, color, 79 mins.
W: Brad Harris, Gloria Milland, Fernando Rey, Carmen De Lirio, Barbara Carroll, Fernando Sancho, Rufino Inoles, Ray Martino, Luigi Marturano, Manuel Arbo, Lina Rosales, Nello Pazzafini, Jose Rubio, Ignazio Dolce, Angel Ortiz, Gianfranco Gasparri, Francisco Bernal, Luis Marco
D: Guido Malatesta **SCR:** Gianfranco Parolini, Giovanni Simonelli, Cesare Seccia, Arpad De Riso, & Sergio Sollima **STORY:** Cesare Seccia **PHOTOG:** Alessandro Ulloa **SPCL-FX:** Vittorio Galliano & Beppe Domenici **MUSIC:** Carlo Innocenzi
Standard "Sword & Sandal": Muscleman fights usurper

Goliath and the Barbarians

see Il Terror dei Barberi

Goliath and the Dragon

see La Vendetta di Ercole

Goliath and the Sins of Babylon

see Maciste, l'Eroe Piu Grande del Mondo

Goliath and the Vampires

see Maciste Contre il Vampiro

Goliath at the Conquest of Damascus

1964, (It), Filmways/AIP, color, 86 mins
W: Rock Stevens, Helga Line (*Fatma*), Mario Petri (*Yssur*)
Minor "Sword & Sandal": Hero helps king regain throne

Goliath Awaits

1981, (USA), Larry White-Gay-Jay/Col, Made for TV, color, 179 mins.(edited, 110 mins.)
W: Mark Harmon, Christopher Lee, Eddie Albert, Alex Cord, Robert Forster, John Carradine, Duncan Regehr, Peter von Zerneck, Emma Samms, Jeanette Nolan, Frank Gorshin, Jean Marsh, John McIntire, Alan Fudge, John Ratzenberger, Tom Dunstan, George Innes, Julie Bennett, Colin Drake, Bruce Heighley, John Berwick, Kirk Cameron, Hedley Mattingly, Michael Evans, Belinda Mayne, Michael White, Christina Nigra, Sandy Simpson, Warwick Sims
D: Kevin Connor **TELEPLAY:** Richard Bluel & Pat Fielder **STORY:** Richard Bluel, Pat Fielder, & Hugh Benson **PHOTOG:** Al Francis **SPCL-FX:** Joe Unsinn **MUSIC:** George Duning
TVM (in 2 parts), standard SF-adventure: Sunken luxury liner harbors survivors

Goliathon

1977, (Hong Kong), Shaw Bros./World Northal, color 83 mins.
W: Lee Hassen, Evelyne Kraft
D: Homer Gaugh **SCR:** Li Chen **SPCL-FX:** Andrew Ryan
A.k.a. **The Mighty Peking Man**
Standard SF-thriller: Giant ape-man discovered

Goliath Awaits: CHRISTOPHER LEE AND EMMA SAMMS

Goliath, the Rebel Slave
1963, (It), color
W: Gordon Scott, Massimo Serato
Minor "Sword & Sandal"

Gollywog's Motor Accident
see In Gollywog Land

Gomar the Human Gorilla
see Night of the Bloody Apes

Good Against Evil
1977, (USA), 20th-Fox/ABC-TV, color, 79 mins.
W: Dack Rambo (*Andy Stuart*), Richard Lynch (*Rimmin*), Dan O'Herlihy (*Father Kemschler*), Elyssa Davalos (*Jessica Gordon*), John Harkins (*Father Wheatley*), Jenny O'Hara, Leila Goldoni, Peggy McCay, Peter Brandon, Kim Cattrall, Natasha Ryan, Richard Sanders, Lillian Adams, Erica Yohn, Richard Stahl
D: Paul Wendkos **TELEPLAY:**, Jimmy Sangster **PHOTOG:** Jack Woolf **MUSIC:** Lalo Schifrin **MUSIC SPRVSR:** Lionel Newman
TVM, minor fantasy-thriller: Satanic cult selects writer's sweetheart to bear devil's child

Goodbye Charlie
1964, (USA), Venice/20th-Fox, color, 117 mins.
W: Debbie Reynolds, Tony Curtis, Walter Matthau, Pat Boone, Joanna Barnes, Laura Devon, Roger C. Carmel, Martin Gabel, Harry Madden, Ellen McRae (*Burstyn*), Donna Michelle, Myrna Hansen
P: David Weisbart **D:** Vincente Minnelli **SCR:** Harry Kurnitz, from George Axelrod's play **PHOTOG:** Milton Krasner **MUSIC:** Andre Previn **SONG:** Seven at Once
Standard fantasy: Murdered playboy reborn in girl's body. cf. Switch

Goodbye Gemini
see Twinsanity

Goodbye, Spaceship Yamato
see Saraba Uchu Senkan Yamato

Good for Evil
1913, (GB), Cricks/C&M, b&w, 1,600 ft. (487.7m)
D: Charles Calvert **STORY:** Frederick H-U. Bowman
Standard thriller: Drunkard sets fire to cleric's house

The Good Son
1993, (USA), 20th-Fox, color, 88 mins.
W: Macaulay Culkin (*Henry*), Elijah Wood (*Mark*), Wendy Crewson (*Susan*), David Morse (*Jack*), Jacqueline Brookes (*Alice*), Daniel Hugh-Kelly (*Wallace*), Quinn Culkin (*Connie*), Ashley Crow (*Janice*), Guy Strauss (*The Arizona Doctor*), Keith Braya (*The Doctor in Blackport*), Andria Hall (*The Woman Reporter*), Jerem Goodwin (*The Factory Worker*), Bobby Huber (*The Axe Man*), Mark Stefanich (*The Ice Man*), Susan Hopper, Rory Culkin
P: Mary Anne Page & Joseph Ruben **D:** Joseph Ruben **SCR:** Ian McEwan **PHOTOG:** John Lindley **MUSIC:** Elmer Bernstein
Standard thriller: Male "bad seed" spreads havoc

The Goonies
1985, (USA), WB, color, 111 mins.
W: Sean Astin (*Mickey*), Josh Brolin (*Brand*), Jeff Cohen (*Chunk*), Corey Feldman (*Mouth*), Kerri Green (*Andy*), Ke Huy Quan (*Data*), John Matuszak (*Sloth*), Joe Pantoliano (*Francis*), Robert Davi (*Jake*), Anne Ramsey (*Mama Fratelli*), Lupe Ontiveros (*Rosalita*), Mary Ellen Trainor (*Mrs. Walsh*), Keith Walker (*Mr. Walsh*), Curtis Hanson (*Mr. Perkins*), Steve Antin (*Troy*), Paul Tuerpe, George Robotham, Charles McDaniel, Elaine Cohen McMahon, Bill Bradley, Michael Paul Chan, Jeb Adams, George Nicholas McLean, Eric Briant Wells, Gene Ross, Patrick Cameron, Max Segar, Hewton Dennis Arnold, Jack O'Leary, Erwin Harvey, Ted Grossman
D: Richard Donner **SCR:** Chris Columbus **STORY:** Steven Spielberg **PHOTOG:** Nick McLean **SPCL-FX:** Matt Sweeney **MUSIC:** Dave Grusin **VS-FX:** Industrial Light & Magic **SONGS:** Love Is Alive, I Got Nothing, Eight Arms to Hold You, Save the Night, Red Hot & What a Thrill
Modest comedy-thriller: Youngsters seek pirate treasure

Gor
1988, (It), Cannon International, color, 95 mins.
W: Oliver Reed, Jack Palance, Urbano Barbieri

GORGO

255

from novels by John Norman (*Tarnsman of Gor*)
*Standard SF-fantasy: Professor mystically transported to medieval land. cf. **Outlaw of Gor***

Gorath
1962, (Jap), Toho/Col, color, 89 mins.
W: Ryo Ikebe, Jun Tazaki, Akihiko Hirata
D: Inoshiro Honda **SCR:** Takeshi Kimura **SPCL-FX:** Eiji Tsuburaya
Minor SF-fantasy: Polar prehistoric horror arises

The Gore-Gore Girls
1971, (USA), Boxoffice Spectaculars, color, 90 mins.
W: Frank Kress, Amy Farrell, Russ Badger, Hedda Lubin, Nora Alexis, Frank Rice, Henny Youngman
P&D: Herschell Gordon Lewis **SCR:** Alan J. Dachman **PHOTOG:** Eskandar Ameripoor **MUSIC:** Sheldon Seymour [Herschell Gordon Lewis]
*A.k.a. **Blood Orgy***
Minor horror-satire: Disco owners slaughter dancers

Gore-Met Zombie Chef from Hell
1987, (USA), color, 90 mins.
W: Theo Depuay, Kelley Kunicki, C.W. Casey, Michael O'Neill, Alan Marx
D: Don Swan
Minor horror-satire: Demon-vampire opens restaurant, slays customers

Gorgo
1961, (GB), King Bros./MGM, color, 78 mins.
W: Bill Travers (*Joe Ryan*), William Sylvester (*Sam Slade*), Vincent Winter (*Sean*), Christopher Rhodes (*McCartin*), Martin Benson (*Dorkin*), Bruce Seton (*Prof. Flaherty*), Joseph O'Conor (*Prof. Hendricks*), Barry Keegan (*The Mate*), Dervis Ward (*The Bosun*), Basil Dignam, Maurice Kaufmann
P: Frank & Maurice King **D:** Eugene Lourie & Daniel Hyatt (uncredited direction) **SCR:** John Loring & Daniel Hyatt **PHOTOG:** Frederick A. Young **SPCL-FX:** Tom Howard **MUSIC:** Angelo Francisco Lavagnino
Standard SF-thriller: Giant reptile attacks London

The Gorgon
1964, (GB), Hammer/Col, color, 83 mins.
W: Peter Cushing (*Dr. Namaroff*), Christopher Lee (*Prof. Carl Meister*), Barbara Shelley (*Carla Hoffman*), Richard Pasco (*Paul Heitz*), Patrick Troughton (*Kanof*), Michael Goodliffe (*Prof. Heitz*), Joseph O'Conor (*The Coroner*), Prudence Hyman (*Megira*), Jack Watson (*Ratoff*), Redmond Phillips (*Hans*), Jeremy Longhurst (*Bruno Heitz*), Joyce Hemson, Toni Gilpin, Sally Nesbitt, Michael Peake
P: Anthony Nelson Keys **D:** Terence Fisher **SCR:** John Gilling, from a story by J. Llewellyn Devine **PHOTOG:** Michael Reed **MUSIC:** Angelo Lavagnino
*orig. to be titled **Supernatural***
Standard horror-fantasy: Amnesiac young woman becomes receptacle for reincarnation of legendary horror

The Gorilla
1927, (USA), First Nat'l, b&w, 8 reels
W: Charlie Murray (*Garrity*), Frank Kelsey (*Mulligan*), Tully Marshall (*William Townsend*), Alice Day (*Alice Townsend*), Claude Gillingwater (*Cyrus Townsend*), Walter Pidgeon (*Stevens*), Gaston Glass (*Marsden*), Aggie Herring (*The Cook*), Brooks Benedict (*The Reporter*), Syd Crossley (*The Butler*), John Gough (*The Sailor*)
D: Alfred Santell **SCR:** Alfred A. Cohn, James T. O'Donahue & Henry McCarthy, from Ralph Spence's play **PHOTOG:** Arthur Edeson
Standard comedy-mystery: Simian blamed for murders

The Gorilla
1931, (USA), First Nat'l, b&w, 7 reels
W: Lila Lee (*Alice Denby*), Joe Frisco (*Garrity*), Walter Pidgeon (*Arthur Marsden*), Purnell Pratt (*The Stranger*), Harry Gribbon (*Mulligan*), Edwin Maxwell (*Cyrus Stevens*), Landers Stevens (*The Inspector*), Roscoe Karns (*Simmons*), William H. Philbrick (*Jeff*)
D: Bryan Foy **SCR & DIALOG:** Ralph Spence (from his story) **ADAPT:** B. Harrison Orkow & Herman Ruby **PHOTOG:** Sid Hickox
Standard comedy-mystery: Ape suspected of killings

The Gorilla
1939, (USA), 20th-Fox, b&w, 66 mins.
W: The Ritz Brothers, Lionel Atwill (*Walter Stevens*), Anita Louise (*Norma Denby*), Patsy Kelly (*Kitty*), Bela Lugosi (*Peters*), Edward Norris (*Jack Marsden*), Joseph Calleia (*The Stranger*), Wally Vernon, Paul Harvey, Art Miles
D: Allan Dwan **SCR:** Rian James & Sid Silvers, from Ralph Spence's play **PHOTOG:** Edward Cronjager **MUSIC:** David Buttolph
Standard comedy-mystery

Gorilla (1944)
*see **Nabonga***

Gorilla at Large
1954, (USA), Panoramic-Leonard Goldstein/20th-Fox, 3D, color, 93 mins.
W: Cameron Mitchell (*Joey Matthews*), Anne Bancroft (*Laverne*), Raymond Burr (*Miller*), Charlotte Austin (*Audrey Baxter*), Lee J. Cobb (*Garrison*), Lee Marvin (*Shaughnessy*), Peter Whitney (*Kovacs*), Warren Stevens, John G.

Kellogg, Charles Tannen
P: Robert L. Jacks **D:** Harmon Jones **SCR:** Leonard Praskins & Barney Slater **PHOTOG:** Lloyd Aherne **MUSIC:** Lionel Newman
Standard thriller: Brutal carnival slayings attributed to escaped gorilla

Gorky Park
1983, (GB), Eagle/Orion/Koch/Kirkwood/Rank, color, 130 mins.
W: William Hurt (*Arkady Renko*), Lee Marvin (*Jack Osborne*), Brian Dennehy (*William Kirwill*), Ian Bannen (*Iamskoy*), Joanna Pacula (*Irina Asanova*), Michael Elphick (*Pasha Pavlovich*), Richard Griffiths (*Anton*), Rikki Fulton (*Maj. Pribluda*), Alexander Knox (*The General*), Alexei Sayle (*Golodkin*), Ian McDiarmid (*Prof. Andreev*), Niall O'Brien (*Rurik*), Henry Woolf (*Levin*), Tusse Silberg (*Natasha*), Jukka Hirvikangas (*James Kirwill*), Patrick Field (*Fet*), Marjatta Nissinen (*Valerya Davidova*), Hekki Leppanen, Lauri Torhonen, Elsa Salamaa, Lasse Lindberg, Jussi Parvianen
D: Michael Apted **SCR:** Dennis Potter, from Martin Cruz Smith's novel **PHOTOG:** Ralf D. Bode **MUSIC:** James Horner
Standard thriller: Murders in Moscow

Gosta Berling's Saga
*see **The Story of Gosta Berling***

Gotham
1988, (Can), Phoenix Entertainment-Keith Addis & Assocs./SHO, color, 93 mins.
W: Tommy Lee Jones, Virginia Madsen, Colin Bruce, Denise Stephen-son, Kevin Jarre, Frederic Forrest (*Father George*), J.B. White (*Jimbo*), Michael Chapman (*The Landlord*), Alec Willows (*The Bartender*), Jack Creley (*Grandfather*), Peter Jobin (*The Doorman*), David Cryer (*The Waiter*), Michael Villela (*The Cop*), Hugh McCarten (*The Piano Player*), Holly Johnson (*The Female Singer*)
WRIT & D: Lloyd Fonvielle **PHOTOG:** Michael Chapman **SPCL-FX:** Michael Kavanagh **MUSIC:** George Clinton **SONG:** *Every Step of the Way*
*GB retitle, **The Dead Can't Lie***
Standard mystery-fantasy: Ghost seduces gumshoe

Gothic
1987, (GB), Virgin Vision/Vestron, color, 87 mins.
W: Gabriel Byrne (*Lord Byron*), Natasha Richardson (*Mary Godwin*), Julian Sands (*Percy Bysshe Shelley*), Myriam Cyr (*Claire Clairmont*), Timothy Spall (*Dr. John William Polidori*), Andreas Wisniewski (*Fletcher*), Dexter Fletcher (*Rushton*), Alec Mango (*Murray*), Pascal King (*Justice*), Tom Hickey (*The Tour Guide*), Linda Coggin (*The Mechanical Doll*), Kristine Landon-Smith (*The Mechanical Woman*)
D: Ken Russell **SCR:** Stephen Volk **PHOTOG:** Mike Southon **MUSIC:** Thomas Dolby
*Opulent melodrama: Dark and stormy night for 19th-century literati. cf. **Haunted Summer***

The Gouty Patient
*see **Le Malade Hydrophobe***

The Governess's Love Affair
*see **The New Governess***

The Gracie Allen Murder Case
1939, (USA), Para, b&w, 74 mins.
W: Gracie Allen (*Gracie Allen*), Warren William (*Philo Vance*), Ellen Drew (*Ann Wilson*), Jerome Cowan (*Daniel Mirche*), Kent Taylor (*Bill Brown*), Jed Prouty (*Uncle Ambrose*), Donald MacBride (*D.A. John F.X. Markham*), H.B. Warner (*Richard Lawrence*), William Demarest (*Sgt. Ernest Heath*), Judith Barrett (*Dixie Del Marr*), Horace McMahon (*Gus*), Edgar Dearing (*Officer Corrigan*), Helen MacKellar (*The Secretary*), Richard Denning (*Fred*), Lee Moore (*Benny "The Buzzard" Nelson*), Lillian Yarbo (*The Maid*), Willie Fung (*The Butler*), Walter Sod-erling (*Dr. Doremus*), James Kelso (*The Photographer*), James Flavin (*The Turnkey*), Harry Tyler (*The Police Photographer*), Rube Demerest (*The Reporter*), Jack Baxley (*The 2nd Reporter*), Florence Wix (*The Lady*), Sam Harris (*The Man*), Al Shaw, Sam Lee, Paul Newlan, George Hickman, Addison Richards, Billy Daniels, Norman Phillips Jr., Oscar G. Hendrian, Ben Taggart, Sue Moore, James B. Carson, Ted Oliver, Irving Bacon, Monty Collins, Janet Waldo, Mike Tellegen, Max Wagner, Henry Roquemore, Frank Meredith, William Haade, Philip Warren, Esther Howard, Philip Morris
D: Alfred E. Green **SCR:** Nat Perrin, C. Gardner Sullivan & Eddie Welch, from a story by S.S. Van Dine **PHOTOG:** Charles Lang **MUSIC:** Frank Loesser & Matty Malneck
Amusing "Philo Vance" comedy-mystery: Confused search for murderer

Graduation Day
1981, (USA), Scope III/IFI, color, 85 mins.
W: Christopher George (*Coach Michaels*), Patch Mackenzie (*Anne Ramstead*), E. Danny Murphy (*Kevin*), Michael Pataki (*Guglione*), E.J. Peaker (*Blondie*), Billy Hufsey (*Tony*), Richard Balin (*Roberts*), Carmen Argenziano (*Halliday*), Beverly Dixon (*Elaine Ramstead*), Virgil Frye (*MacGregor*), Hal Bokar (*Ronald Corliss*), Denise Cheshire (*Sally*), Tom Hintnaus (*Pete*), Linnea Quigley (*Dolores*), Aaron Butler (*The Photographer*), Karen Abbott (*Joanne*), Vanna White (*Doris*), Ruth Ann Llorens (*Lara*), Patrick Wright (*The Truck Driver*), Carl Rey (*Ralph*), Grant Loud (*The Singer*), Viola Kate Stimpson (*Mrs. Badger*), Erica Hope (*Diane*), Felony
D: Herb Freed **MUSIC:** Felony **SONGS:** *Gangster Rock, The Killer, Lucky Strike, Graduation Day Blues* & *The Winner*
Minor thriller: Killer stalks high-school athletes

A Grain of Sand
1917, (GB), Hepworth/UK, b&w, 2,900 ft. (883.9m)
W: Stewart Rome (*Dennis Grayle*), Chrissie White (*Doris Kestevan*), Lionelle Howard (*Howard Langton*), William Felton (*James Fordyce*), Ivy Millais (*Liza*), John MacAndrews (*Liza's Father*)
D: Frank Wilson   STORY: Victor Montefiore
Standard crime-thriller: Kitchen maid clears lady's gambling son when he is framed for forgery

Gran Amore del Conde Dracula (Count Dracula's Great Love)
1972, (Sp), Janus/Int'l Amusements, color, USA release, 96 mins
W: Paul Naschy (*Wendell*), Rosanna Yanni (*Senta*), Haydee Politoff (*Karin*), Vic Winner (*Imre*), Ingrid Garbo (*Marlene*), Mirta Miller, Jose Manuel Martin, Alvaro De Luna, Julia Pena, Susana Latur, Benito Pavon Charo Soriano
P: F. Laura Polop   D: Javier Aguirre   ORIG. STORY: Jacinto Molina   MUSIC: Carmelo Bernaolo
USA retitle: **Dracula's Great Love** *A.k.a.* **Cemetery Girls** *and* **Vampire Playgirls**
Minor horror-fantasy: Vampiric nobleman tries to revive dead daughter

The Grand Babylon Hotel
1916, (GB), Hepworth/Shaftesbury, b&w, 5,275 ft. (1607.8m)
W: Fred Wright (*Theodore Racksole*), Margaret Blanche (*Nella Racksole*), Gerald Lawrence (*Jules*), Lionelle Howard (*Prince Eugen*), Stewart Rome (*Prince Aribert*), Violet Hopson (*Miss Spencer*), Alma Taylor (*Princess Anna*), Charles Vane (*Rocco*), Henry Vibart (*King of Ragatz*), Johnny Butt (*Sampson Levi*)
D: Frank Wilson, from a novel by Arnold Bennett
Standard crime-thriller: Daughter of American millionaire saves Ruritanian prince from kidnappers

Le Grande Monde des Petits Enfants
see **Wielka, Wielka I Najwieksza**

The Grand Junction Case
1961, (GB), Merton Park/Anglo-Amalgamated, b&w, 30 mins.
W: Russell Napier (*Supt, Duggan*), Howard Pays (*Sgt. Adams*), Tommy Godfrey (*William Smaller*), Wilfred Brambell (*Dr. Stanton*), Diana Lambert (*Sgt. Barnes*), Kenneth J. Warren (*Brown*)
P: Jack Greenwood   D: Peter Duffell   STORY: James Eastwood, from a novel by Edgar Lustgarten
Standard short crime-thriller: Woman butchered

Grandma's House
1988, (USA), color, 90 mins.
W: Eric Foster, Kim Valentine, Brinke Stevens, Ida Lee
D: Peter Rader
Minor thriller: Siblings encounter, madness, incest and murder

Grandmother's Story
1908, (Fr), Star, b&w, 243m (797.2 ft./13.5 mins.)
D: Georges Melies
Standard fantasy: Girl dreams of visit to Toyland

Grand National Night
1953, (GB), Talisman/Renown, b&w, 81 mins.
W: Nigel Patrick (*Gerald Coates*), Moira Lister (*Babs Coates*), Beatrice Campbell (*Joyce Penrose*), Betty Ann Davies (*Pinkie Collins*), Michael Hordern (*Insp. Ayling*), Colin Gordon (*Buns Darling*), Noel Purcell (*Philip Balfour*), Barry Mackay (*Sgt. Gibson*), Gibb McLaughlin (*Morton*), Leslie Mitchell (*Jack Donovan*), Maria Mercedes (*Maria*)
P: Phil C. Samuel   D: Bob McNaught   SCR: Dorothy & Campbell Christie, from their play
USA retitle: **'Wicked Wife'**
Standard crime-thriller: Inspector tries to convict stable owner for accidental death of faithless wife

Grandpa's Forty Winks
see **In the Land of Nod**

The Grand Tour
see **Disaster in Time**

The Granny
1995, (USA), color, 85 mins.
W: Stella Stevens, Shannon Whirry, Sandy Helberg, Brant Hoffman
D & SCR: Luca Bercovici
Standard horror-thriller: Grandmother returns from grave, seeks revenge on greedy relatives

The Grasshopper and the Ant
see **La Cigale et la Fourmi**

The Grave
1996, (USA), HBO-TV, color, 87 mins.
W: Craig Sheffer, Josh Charles, Gabrielle Anwar, John Doehl, Donal Logue, Eric Roberts
Made-for-Cable, standard thriller: Two convicts seek treasure buried with dead millionaire

Grave Desires
see **Brides of Blood**

Grave of the Vampire
1974, (USA), Millenium/Entertainment Pyramid, color, 95 mins.
W: William Smith, Michael Pataki, Lyn Peters, Jay Adler, Diane Holden, Kitty Vallacher, Jay Scott, William Guhl, Lieux Dressler, Margaret Fairchild, Carmen Argenziano, Frank Winterman, Abbi Henderson, Inga Neilsen, Lindus Guinness
P: Daniel Cady   D: John Hayes   SCR: David Chase   PHOTOG: Paul Hipp   SPCL-FX: Cliff Wingren   MUSIC: Jaime Mendoza-Nava
A.k.a. 'Seed of Terror'
Minor horror-thriller: Young man hunts vampire-father

Grave Robbers
1966, (Mex), color
W: Santo
Minor horror-thriller

Grave-Robbers from Outer Space
see **Plan 9 from Outer Space**

Grave Secrets
1990, (USA), Planet, color, 90 mins.
W: Rene Soutendijk (*Iris Norwood*), Paul LeMat (*David Shaw*), David Warner (*Dr. Carl Farnsworth*), Bob Herron (*Kurt Norwood*), Lee Ving (*Zack*), Olivia Barash (*Darla*), John Crawford (*Homer*), Gilbert Lewis (*Dean Andrews*), Ruth Manning (*Dr. Kathleen Thorpe*), Allison Roth (*The Female Student*), Anthony Rapp (*Jamie*)
D: Donald P. Borchers   SCR: Jeffrey Polman & Lenore Wright   story: Jeffrey Polman   PHOTOG: Jamie Thompson   VS-FX SPRVSR: Chris Nibley   MUSIC: Jonathan Elias
Standard fantasy-thriller: Apparition torments woman

The Graveside Story
see **The Comedy of Terrors**

The Graveyard
see **Persecution**

Graveyard of Horror
see **Necrophagus**

Graveyard of Horror
1971, (Sp), color, 105 mins.
W: Bill Curran, Francisco Brana, Beatriz Lacy
D: Miguel Madrid
Minor horror-thriller: Doctor steals heads from corpses

Graveyard Shift
1987, (Can), Cannon, color, 89 mins.
W: Silvio Oliveiro (*Stephen Tsepes*), Helen Papas (*Michelle*), Cliff Stoker
SONGS: *Contact & Alone in Love*
film shown in Paris, France as **Central Park Driver**
Minor horror-thriller: Vampire cabbie

Graveyard Shift
1990, (USA), Larry Sugar/Para, color, 89 mins.
W: David Andrews (*John*), Kelly Wolf (*Jane*), Stephen Macht (*Warwick*), Andrew Divoff (*Danson*), Vic Polizos (*Brogan*), Brad Dourif (*The Exterminator*), Robert Alan Beuth, Ilona Margolis, Jimmy Woodard, Jonathan Emerson, Dana Packard, Minor Rootes, Kelly L. Goodman, Susan Lowden, Emmet Kane, Joe Perham, Skip Wheeler, Richard France, Anne Rooney, Raissa Danilova Robert Alan Beuth, Ilona Margolis, Jimmy Woodard, Jonathan Emerson,, Susan Lowden, Joe Perham, Dana Packard,
P & D: Ralph S. Singleton   SCR: John Esposito, from Stephen King's short story   PHOTOG: Peter Stein   MUSIC: Anthony Marinelli & Brian Banks
Standard horror-thriller: Monsrosity lurks beneath old textile mill

Graveyard Tramps
see **Invasion of the Bee Girls**

The Gray House
see **The Old Dark House (1932)**

Gray Lady Down
1978, (USA), Mirisch/Univ, color, 111 mins.
W: Charlton Heston (*Capt. Paul Blanchard*), David Carradine (*Capt. Gates*), Stacy Keach (*Capt. Bennett*), Ned Beatty (*Mickey*), Stephen McHattie (*Murphy*), Dorian Harewood (*Fowler*), Ronny Cox (*Comm. Samuelson*), Rosemary Forsyth (*Vickie*), Hilly Hicks (*Page*), William Jordan (*Waters*), Charles Cioffi (*Adm. Barnes*), Jack Rader (*Harkness*), Antony Ponzini (*Caruso*), Charlie Robinson (*McAllister*), Michael O'Keefe (*Harris*), Christopher Reeve (*Phillips*) Melendy Britt (*Liz*), Lawrason Driscoll (*Bloome*), David Wilson (*Hanson*), Robert Symonds (*Sec'y of Navy*), James Davidson, Ted Gehring, Charles Cyphers, William Bryant, Jeff Druce, David Clennon
D: David Greene   SCR: James Whittaker & Howard Sackler   ADAPT: Frank P. Rosenberg, from David Lavalle's novel   PHOTOG: Stevan Larner   MUSIC: Jerry Fielding
Tepid thriller: Submarine stranded 1450 feet down

The Great Alligator

1981, (It), Dania Film, color

W: Barbara Bach, Claudio Cassinelli, Mel Ferrer, Richard Johnson, Romano Puppo, Fabrizia Castagnoli, Peter Boom, Enzo Fisichella, Lory Del Santo, Anny Papa, Clara Colosimo, Bobby Rhodes, Giulia D'Angelo, Geneve Hutton, Marco Mastantuono, Piero Jossa, Marco Giannoni, Silvia Collatina
D: Sergio Martino   **SCR:** Ernesto Gastaldi, Luigi Montefiori, Maria Chianetta & Sergio Martino   **STORY:** Cesare Frugoni, Sergio Martino & Ernesto Gastaldi   **PHOTOG:** Giancarlo Ferrando   **MUSIC:** Stelvio Cipriani
Minor horror-thriller: Stranded tourists face ghastly embodiment of tribal god

The Great Anarchist Mystery

1912, (GB), B&C/MP, b&w, 2,040 ft. (621.8m)

W: Percy Moran (*Jack Logan*), Dorothy Foster (*Betty Lyndhurst*), Derek Powell (*Peter Nickoloff*), Charles Seymour (*Insp. Keen*)
D: Charles Raymond   **STORY:** Silas K. Hocking
Standard thriller: Lighthouse keeper stops foreign agent from sinking duke's ship

The Gorgon: PETER CUSHING AND DIRECTOR TERENCE FISHER

The Great Bullion Robbery

1913, (GB), Barker/Bendon, b&w, 2,110 ft. (643.1m)

W: Fred Paul (*Stephen Crasp*), Will Asher (*The Chauffeur*)
D: Alexander Butler   **STORY:** Rowland Talbot
Standard crime-thriller: Gang uses shop to break into vault

The Great Cheque Fraud

1915, (GB), I.B. Davidson/Walturdaw, b&w, 3,000 ft. (914.4m)

W: Harry Lorraine (*Sexton Blake*), Douglas Payne (*George Marsden Plummer*), Bert Rex (*Tinker*)
D & SCR: Charles Raymond, from characters created by Harry Blyth
Standard crime-thriller: Detective saves boy assistant from murderous swindler

Great Expectations

1934, (USA), Carl Laemmle/Univ, b&w, 97 mins.

W: Henry Hull (*Magwitch*), Phillips Holmes (*Pip*), Jane Wyatt (*Estella*), Florence Reed (*Miss Havisham*), Alan Hale (*Joe Gargery*), Rafaela Ottiano (*Mrs. Joe*), Francis L. Sullivan (*Jaggers*), George Barraud (*Compeyson*), Douglas Wood (*Wopsle*), Forrester Harvey (*Pumble-chook*), Eily Malyon (*Sarah Pocket*), Georgie Breakston (*Pip as a Child*), Harry Cording (*Orlick*), Anne Howard (*Estella as a Child*), Walter Armitage (*Herbert*), Jackie Searle (*Herbert as a Child*), Philip Dakin (*Drummle*), Valerie Hobson (*Biddy*)
D: Stuart Walker   **SCR:** Gladys Unger, from Charles Dickens' novel   **PHOTOG:** George Robinson   **SPCL-FX:** John P. Fulton   **MUSIC SCORE:** Edward Ward
Well-made but softened version of classic romance: 19th-century orphan has unknown bene-factor

Great Expectations

1946, (GB), Cineguild/Univ, b&w, 118 mins.

W: John Mills (*Pip as an Adult*), Valerie Hobson (*Estella as an Adult*), Martita Hunt (*Miss Havisham*), Francis L. Sullivan (*Jaggers*), Finlay Currie (*Magwitch*), Bernard Miles (*Joe Gargery*), Jean Simmons (*Estella as a Child*), Anthony Wager (*Pip as a Child*), Freda Jackson (*Mrs. Joe*), Alec Guinness (*Herbert Pocket*), Eileen Erskine (*Biddy*), Ivor Bernard (*Mr. Wemmick*), Torin Thatcher (*Bentley Drummle*), O.B. Clarence (*The Aged Parent*), George Hayes,

John Forrest, Hay Petric, John Burch, Everley Gregg, Richard George, Frank Atkinson, Anne Holland, Walford Hyden, Eddie Martin, Gordon Begg, Roy Arthur, Grace Denbeigh-Russell
P: Ronald Neame   **D:** David Lean   **SCR:** David Lean, Ronald Neame, Anthony Havelock-Allan, Kay Walsh & Cecil McGivern, from Charles Dickens' novel   **PHOTOG:** Guy Green
Classic melodrama: Poor boy mysteriously elevated in 19th-century England

Great Expectations

1974, (USA-GB), ITC/ABC-TV, color, 116 mins.

W: Michael York (*Pip*), Sarah Miles (*Estella*), James Mason (*Magwitch*), Margaret Leighton (*Miss Havisham*), Joss Ackland (*Joe Gargery*), Anthony Quayle (*Jaggers*), Rachel Roberts (*Mrs. Joe*), Heather Sears (*Biddy*), Peter Bull (*Mr. Wemmick*), Robert Morley (*Pumplechook*), Sam Kydd (*The Convict*), James Faulkner (*Bentley Drummle*), Andrew Ray (*Herbert Pocket*), Simon Gipps-Kent (*Pip as a Boy*), John Clive (*Wopsle*), Patsy Smart (*Mrs. Wopsle*), Dudley Sutton (*The Criminal*), Erik Chitty (*The Old Man*), Noel Trevarthen
P: Robert Fryer   **D:** Joseph Hardy   **SCR:** Sherman Yellen, from Charles Dickens'
novel   **PHOTOG:** Freddie Young   **MUSIC:** Maurice Jarre
TVM, standard melodrama: Working-class youth rises in 19th-century England

Great Expectations

1998, (USA), 20th-Fox, color, 101 mins.

W: Gwyneth Paltrow, Ethan Hawke, Robert De Niro, Anne Bancroft, Chris Cooper, Hank Azaria
D: Alfonso Cuaron   **SCR:** Mitch Glazer , from Charles Dickens' novel   **PHOTOG:** Emmanuel Lubezki   **MUSIC:** Patrick Doyle

The Great Gabbo

1929, (USA), Sono Art/World Wide, b&w, 10 reels (8,049 ft./2453.3m/96 mins.)

W: Erich von Stroheim, Betty Compson, Edna Gregory
D: James Cruze   **SCR:** Hugh Herbert, from Ben Hecht's short story "The Rival Dummy"   **PHOTOG:** Ira Morgan   **SONGS:** *Every Now and Then* & *I'm Laughing*
Classic thriller: Conceited ventriloquist suffers from schizophrenia cf. **Devil Doll** *(1964) and* **Magic**

The Great Gambini

1937, (USA), Schulberg, b&w, 70 mins.

W: John Trent, Marion Marsh, Akim Tamiroff, Reginald Denny, Genevieve Tobin
D: Charles Vidor   **PHOTOG:** Leon Shamroy
Engrossing low-budget melodrama: Magico predicts deaths

The Great Gambler

see **Doctor Mabuse**

The Great German North Sea Tunnel

1914, (GB), Dreadnought, b&w, 3,000 ft. (914.4m)

D: Frank Newman
Standard fantasy-thriller: Germans build tunnel beneath North Sea, invade England

The Great Gold Robbery

1913, (GB), Motograph, b&w, 2,150 ft. (655.3m)

W: Douglas Payne (*Walter Hyde*), Babs Neville (*Dot*), Sydney Smith (*The Diver*)
D: Maurice Elvey

Standard crime-thriller: Detective dives from bridge, nabs gold thieves on barge

The Great Houdinis
1976, (USA), ABC-TV, color, 108 mins.
W: Paul Michael Glaser (*Harry Houdini*), Sally Struthers (*Bess*), Ruth Gordon (*Mrs. Weiss*), Bill Bixby (*Rev. Arthur Ford*), Vivian Vance (*Minnie*), Peter Cushing (*Sir Arthur Conan Doyle*), Adrienne Barbeau (*Daisy*), Clive Revill (*Slater*), Wilfrid Hyde-White (*Melville*), Maureen O'Sullivan (*Lady Doyle*), Barbara Rhoades (*Margery*)
D: Melville Shavelson
TVM, standard bio: Life of master magician

The Great Impersonation
1935, (USA), Univ, b&w, 81 mins.
W: Edmund Lowe, Valerie Hobson, Lumsden Hare, Vera Engels, Spring Byington, Henry Mollison, Charles Waldron, Dwight Frye
D: Alan Crosland   SCR: Frank Wead & Eve Greene, from a novel by E. Phillips Oppenheim   PHOTOG: Milton Krasner   MUSIC: Franz Waxman
Standard melodrama: Man spies

The Great Impersonation
1942, (USA), Univ, b&w, 71 mins.
W: Ralph Bellamy (*Sir Edward Dominey/Baron von Ragenstein*), Evelyn Ankers (*Muriel*), Aubrey Mather (*Sir Ronald*), Edward Norris (*Bardinet*), Kaaren Verne (*Baroness Stephanie*), Mary Forbes (*Lady Leslie*), Henry Daniell (*Seamon*), Ludwig Stossel (*Dr. Schmidt*), Rex Evans (*Sir Tristram*), Charles Irwin (*Yardly*), Charles Coleman (*Mangan*), Victor Zimmerman (*The Nazi Soldier*), Robert O. Davis (*Hofmann*), Fred Vogeding (*Stengel*)
D: John Rawlins   SCR: W. Scott Darling, from a novel by E. Phillips Oppenheim   PHOTOG: George Robinson   MUSIC: H.J. Salter
Standard thriller: Englishman poses as German, hunts Nazi spies

The Great Land of Small
1986, (USA), color, 94 mins.
W: Kim Elkin, Michael Blouin, Michael Anderson Jr., Ken Roberts
D: Vojtech Jasny
Standard juvenile fantasy: Two children enter bizarre world

The Great Manhunt (1950)
see State Secret

The Great Manhunt
1974, (It), color
W: Lino Ventura, Lea Massari
Minor thriller: Russian delegate involved in suspicious London accident

The Great Mouse Detective
1986, (USA), Walt Disney, color, 74 mins.
VOICES: Vincent Price, Barrie Ingham, Basil Rathbone, Val Bettin, Susanne Pollatschek, Candy Candido, Eve Brenner, Alan Young, Melissa Manchester
D: John Musker, Ron Clements, Dave Michener & Burny Mattinson   SCR: Ron Clements & Dave Michener , from Eve Titus' book *Street*   MUSIC: Henry Mancini
*reissued (1992) as **The Adventures of the Great Mouse Detective***
Standard animated fantasy: Victorian mouse-sleuth vs. rat super-criminal

The Great Muppet Caper
1981, (GB), Downshire/ITC, color, 97 mins.
W: Charles Grodin (*Nicky Holiday*), Diana Rigg (*Lady Holiday*), John Cleese (*Neville*), Robert Morley (*The Gentleman*), Jack Warden (*The Editor*), Peter Ustinov (*The Trucker*), Erica Creer (*Marla*), Kate Howard (*Carla*), Della Finch (*Darla*), Michael Robbins (*The Guard*), Joan Sanderson (*Dorcas*), Tommy Godfrey (*The Conductor*), Katia Borg (*A Model*), Valli Kemp (*A Model*), Michele Ivan-Zadeh (*A Model*), Peter Falk (*The Tramp*)
P: David Lazer & Frank Oz   D: Jim Henson   SCR: Tom Patchett, Jay Tarses, Jerry Juhl & Jack Rose, from The Muppet Show teleseries by Jim Henson & Frank Oz   PHOTOG: Oswald Morris   MUSIC: Joe Raposo
Standard juvenile fantasy: Frog and bear foil diamond thieves

The Great Office Mystery
1928, (GB), British Filmcraft/Para, b&w, 2,060 ft. (627.9m)
W: Langhorne Burton (*Sexton Blake*), Fred Raynham (*Gordon Wincliffe*), Mickey Brantford (*Tinker*), Gabrielle Morton (*Sadie*), Ronald Curtis (*Kestrel*)
STORY: Lewis Jackson
Standard "Sexton Blake" mystery: Detective probes corporate crime

The Great Poison Mystery
see The Tragedy of Basil Grieve

The Great Python Robbery
1914, (GB), Regent/Gaumont, b&w, 2,800 ft. (853.5m)
W: Arthur Finn (*Det. Finn*)
D: Arthur Finn
Standard crime-thriller: Detective saved from snakepit, stops crooks using airship to rob train

The Great Rupert
1950, (USA), Eagle Lion, b&w, 86 mins.

W: Jimmy Durante (*Mr. Amendola*), Terry Moore (*Rosalinda*), Tom Drake (*Peter Dingle*), Frank Orth (*Mr. Dingle*), Queenie Smith (*Mrs. Amendola*), Sara Haden (*Mrs. Dingle*), Donald T. Beddoe (*Mr. Haggerty*), Chick Chandler (*Phil Davis*), Jimmy Conlin (*Joe Mahoney*), Hugh Sanders (*Mulligan*), Frank Cady (*The Tax Investigator*), Candy Candido (*Molineri*), Clancy Cooper (*The Policeman*), Harold Goodwin (*The FBI Man*) Queenie Smith, Frank Orth, Jimy Conlin, Chick Chandler, Irving Pichel Frank Orth, Sara Haden.
P: George Pal   D: Irving Pichel   SCR: Laslo Vadnay, from a story by Ted Allen   PHOTOG: Lionel Lindon
Amiable comedy-fantasy (George Pal's first feature production): Dancing squirrel uncovers hidden money

The Great Salome Dance
1908, (GB), Walter Tyler, b&w, 300 ft. (91.4m)
Minor melodrama short: Dancer kisses severed head, swoons

The Great Spy Chase
1966, (Fr), AIP, b&w
W: Lino Ventura, Bernard Blair, Francis Blanche, Mireille Darc, Jess Hahn, Charles Millot, Jacques Balutin, Andre Weber
Minor melodrama

The Great Spy Mission
see Operation Crossbow

The Great Spy Raid
1914, (GB), P&M Films/Feature Supply, b&w, 2,300 ft. (701m)
W: Harry Lorraine (*George England*), Eva Norman (*Mrs. England*), Joan Morgan (*Joan England*)
P: John M. Payne   WRIT & D: Sidney Morgan
Standard crime-thriller: Spies fail to blow up railway line, are caught in Soho

The Great Tiger Ruby
1912, (GB), Cricks & Martin, b&w, 1,090 ft. (332.2m)
D: Charles Calvert
Standard thriller: Detective poses as old woman, catches gem thief posing as sailor

The Great Van Robbery
1959, (GB), Danziger/UA, b&w, 70 mins.
W: Denis Shaw (*Caesar Smith*), Kay Callard (*Ellen*), Philip Saville (*Carter*), Tony Quinn (*Mercer*), Geoffrey Hibbert (*Venner*), Tony Doonan (*Wally*), Vera Fusek (*Mara*), Carl Duering (*Delganu*)
P: Edward J. & Harry Lee Danziger   D: Max Varnel   STORY: Brian Clemens & Eldon Howard
Standard crime-thriller: Interpol agent nabs larcenous coffee importer

Great White
1982, (It), Film Ventures, color
W: James Franciscus, Vic Morrow
P: Maurizio Amati & Ugo Tucci   D: Enzo G. Castellari   SCR: Mark Princi
*Minor thriller (**Jaws** imitation): Monstrous shark pursued*

The Greed of William Hart
1948, (GB), Ambassador/PSI, b&w, 78 mins.
W: Tod Slaughter (*William Hart*), Henry Oscar (*Mr. Moore*), Aubrey Woods (*Daft Jamie*), Jenny Lynn (*Helen Moore*), Mary Love (*Mary Patterson*), Arnold Bell (*Dr. Cox*), Winifred Melville (*Meg Hart*), Patrick Addison (*Hugh Alston*), Ann Trego (*Janet Brown*)
P: Gilbert Church   D: Oswald Mitchell   STORY: John Gilling
Standard thriller: Evil graverobber commits murder

The Greedy Girl
1908, (GB), Hepworth, b&w, 250 ft. (76.2m)
D: Lewin Fitzhamon
Minor fantasy short: Sleepwalking girl dreams knights chop her up

Greedy Terror
1978, (USA), color, 90 mins.
W: Michael MacRae, Perry Lang
Minor thriller: Bloodthirsty maniac stalks two motorcyclists

The Green Archer
1961, (W. Ger), b&w 95 mins.
W: Gert Frobe, Klausjuergen Wussow, Karin Dor Edith Teichman
D: Jurgen Roland
Minor melodrama: Socialite in isolated castle is prime suspect in strange murder of prison guard

The Green Buddha
1954, (GB), Rep, b&w, 62 mins.
W: Wayne Morris (*Gary Holden*), Mary Germaine (*Vivien Blake*), Walter Rilla (*Frank Olsen*), Mary Merrall (*Mrs. Rydon-Smith*), Arnold Marle (*Vittorio Miranda*), Lloyd Lamble (*Insp. Flynn*), Kenneth Griffith (*Nobby*), Leslie Linder (*Harry Marsh*), Percy Herbert (*Casey O'Rourke*), George Woodbridge (*Farmer*)
P: William N. Boyle   D: John Lemont   STORY: Paul Erickson
Standard thriller: American pilot saves nightclub singer from international jewel thieves

The Green Dragon
1907, (GB), Hepworth, b&w, 250 ft. (76.2m)
<u>D:</u> Lewin Fitzhamon
Minor comedy-fantasy short: Drunk chased by dragon

The Greene Murder Case
1929, (USA), Para, b&w, 71 mins.
<u>W:</u> William Powell (*Philo Vance*), Florence Eldridge (*Sibella Greene*), Ullrich Haupt (*Dr. Arthur von Blon*), Gertrude Norman (*Mrs. Tobias Greene*), Jean Arthur (*Ada Greene*), E.H. Calvert (*D.A. John F.X. Markham*), Brandon Hurst (*Sproot*), Eugene Pallette (*Sgt. Ernest Heath*), Lowell Drew (*Chester Greene*), Morgan Farley (*Rex Greene*), Mrs. Wilfred Buckland (*Mrs. Greene's Nurse*), Augusta Burmeister (*Gertrude Mannheim*), Marcia Harris (*Hemming*), Mildred Golden (*Barton*), Helena Phillips (*Miss O'Brien*), Charles E. Evans (*Lawyer Canon*), Shep Camp (*The Medical Examiner*), Harry Strang (*The Cop*)
<u>D:</u> Frank Tuttle <u>SCR:</u> Louise Long & Bartlett Cormack, from characters created by S.S. Van Dine <u>PHOTOG:</u> Henry Gerrard
Superior "Philo Vance" mystery-thriller: Suave sleuth investigates murders in old mansion. cf. A Night of Mystery (1937)

Green Eyes
1934, (USA), Chesterfield, b&w
<u>W:</u> Charles Starrett, Shirley Grey, Claude Gillingwater
Standard thriller: Mystery writer probes masquerade-party murder

Green for Danger
1946, (GB), Individual/Rank, b&w, 91 mins.
<u>W:</u> Sally Gray (*Freddie Linley*), Trevor Howard (*Dr. Barney Barnes*), Rosamund John (*Esther Sanson*), Alastair Sim (*Insp. Cockrill*), Leo Genn (*Mr. Eden*), Henry Edwards (*Mr. Purdy*), Judy Campbell (*Marian Bates*), Megs Jenkins (*Nurse Woods*), Moore Marriott (*Joe Higgins*), George Woodbridge (*Sgt. Hendricks*), Ronald Adam (*Dr. White*)
<u>D:</u> Sidney Gilliat <u>SCR:</u> Sidney Gilliat & Claude Guerney, from a novel by Christianna Brand <u>PHOTOG:</u> Wilkie Cooper
reissued 1948 & 1956
Classic thriller: Inspector solves murders at emergency hospital

The Green Ghost (1927)
see Le Spectre Vert

The Green Ghost (1929)
see The Unholy Night

The Green Glove
1952, (USA), UA, b&w, 88 mins.
<u>W:</u> Glenn Ford, Geraldine Brooks, George Macready, Roger Treville, Sir Cedric Hardwicke, Gaby Andre, Jany Holt, Georges Tabet, Meg Lemonnier, Juliette Greco, Jean Bretonniers, Paul Bonifas, George Macready, Gaby Andre, Roger Treville, Juliette Greco, Jean Bretonniere
<u>D:</u> Rudolph Maté <u>STORY & SCR:</u> Charles Bennett <u>PHOTOG:</u> Claude Renoir <u>MUSIC:</u> Joseph Kosma
Standard melodrama: Fabulous jeweled gauntlet sought

The Green Goddess
1923, (USA), Goldwyn, b&w, 8 reels (8,000 ft./2438.4m)
<u>W:</u> George Arliss (*Rajah of Rukh*), Alice Joyce (*Lucilla Crespin*), David Powell (*Dr. Traherne*), Harry T. Morey (*Maj. Crespin*), Jetta Goudal (*Ayah*), Ivan Simpson (*Watkins*), William Worthington (*The High Priest*)
<u>D:</u> Sidney Olcott <u>ADAPT:</u> Forrest Halsey, from William Archer's play <u>PHOTOG:</u> Harry A. Fischbeck <u>MUSIC SCORE:</u> Joseph Carl Breil
Standard melodrama: Hindu makes Britishers prisoner-guests

The Green Goddess
1929, (USA), WB, b&w, 7 reels (6,653 ft./2027.8m/74 mins.)
<u>W:</u> George Arliss (*The Raja*), Alice Joyce (*Lucilla Crespin*), Ralph Forbes (*Dr. Traherne*), H.B. Warner (*Crespin*), David Tearle (*The Temple High Priest*), Betty Boyd (*Ayah*), Ivan Simpson (*Hawkins*)
<u>D:</u> Alfred E. Green <u>SCR:</u> Julian Josephson, from William Archer's play <u>PHOTOG:</u> James Van Trees
Standard melodrama: Rajah detains fleeing Britons

Green Hell
1940, (USA), Famous Prods./Univ, b&w
<u>W:</u> Douglas Fairbanks Jr., Joan Bennett, George Sanders, Vincent Price, Alan Hale, Noble Johnson, Iron Eyes Cody John Howard, Ray Mala, Gene Garrick, Francis McDonald, Peter Bronte, George Bancroft, Lupita Tovar
<u>P:</u> Harry Edington <u>D:</u> James Whale <u>STORY & SCR:</u> Frances Marion <u>PHOTOG:</u> Karl Freund <u>MUSIC DIR:</u> Charles Previn
Standard adventure-thriller: Expedition finds cannibals, Inca temples. cf. The Mummy's Hand

The Green Hornet
1974, (USA), Aquarius, color
<u>W:</u> Van Williams, Bruce Lee
<u>P:</u> William Dozier <u>D:</u> Norman Foster & Jerry Thomas
Minor adventure-thriller (comprised of 3 episodes from the 1966 teleseries): (1) Rich game hunters kill gangsters, (2) Phony aliens with bomb, & (3) Tong war

The Green Man
1956, (GB), British Lion/DCA, b&w, 80 mins.
<u>W:</u> Alastair Sim (*Hawkins*), Terry-Thomas (*Boughtflower*), Raymond Huntley (*Sir Gregory*), Jill Adams (*Ann Vincent*), Avril Angers (*Marigold*), Colin Gordon (*Reginald*), George Cole (*William Blake*), Dora Bryan (*Lily*), Eileen Moore (*Joan Wood*), John Chandos (*McKecknie*), Richard Wattis, Arthur Brough, Alexander Gauge
<u>D:</u> Robert Day <u>SCR:</u> Frank Launder & Sidney Gilliat, from their play *Meet a Body* <u>PHOTOG:</u> Gerald Gibbs <u>MUSIC:</u> Cedric Thorpe Davie
Wry comedy-melodrama: Assassin uses time bombs

Green Mansions
1959, (USA), MGM, color, 101 mins.
<u>W:</u> Audrey Hepburn (*Rima*), Anthony Perkins (*Abel*), Lee J. Cobb (*Nuflo*), Henry Silva (*Kua-ko*), Sessue Hayakawa (*Runi*), Michael Pate (*The Priest*), Estelle Hemsley (*Clacla*), Nehemiah Persoff
<u>P:</u> Edmund Grainger <u>D:</u> Mel Ferrer <u>SCR:</u> Dorothy Kingsley, from W.H. Hudson's classic novel <u>PHOTOG:</u> Joseph Ruttenberg <u>MUSIC:</u> Bronislau Kaper
Mystical melodrama: Girl raised in South American jungle has deep rapport with nature

The Green Mile
1999, (USA), color
<u>W:</u> Tom Hanks, Garth Brooks
from stories by Stephen King
TVM, standard thriller

Green Pastures
1936, (USA), WB, b&w, 93 mins.
<u>W:</u> Rex Ingram (*de Lawd/Adam/Hezdrel*), Oscar Polk (*Gabriel*), Eddie Anderson (*Noah*), Frank Wilson (*Moses*), George Reed (*Mr. Deshee/Isaac*), Abraham Gleaves (*Archangel*), Myrtle Anderson (*Eve*), Al Stokes (*Cain*), Edna M. Harris (*Zeba*), James Fuller (*Cain the Sixth*), George Randol (*The High Priest*), Ida Forsyne (*Noah's Wife*), Dudley Dickerson (*Ham*), Ray Martin (*Shem*), Jimmy Burress (*Japeth*), Charles Andrews (*Flatfoot*), William Cumby (*Abraham/Head Magician/King of Babylon*), David Bethea (*Aaron*), Ivory Williams (*Jacob*), Slim Thompson (*The M.C.*), Ernest Whitman (*Pharaoh*), Reginald Fenderson (*Joshua*), Clinton Rosamond (*The Prophet*)
<u>P:</u> Henry Blanke <u>D:</u> William Keighley & Marc Connelly <u>SCR:</u> Marc Connelly, from his play & stories by Roark Bradford <u>PHOTOG:</u> Hal Mohr <u>MUSIC:</u> Erich Wolfgang Korngold
Classic comedy-fantasy: Negro interpretation of Scripture

The Green Scarf
1954, (GB), B&A Prods./British Lion, b&w, 96 mins.
<u>W:</u> Michael Redgrave (*Maitre Deloit*), Leo Genn (*Brother Redolec*), Ann Todd (*Solande Vauthier*), Kieron Moore (*Jacques Vauthier*), Michael Medwin (*Henru Teral*), Jane Griffiths (*Daniele*), Anthony Nicholls (*Maitre Goirin*), Phil Brown (*John Bell*), Evelyn Roberts (*The President*), George Merritt (*The Advocate General*), Ella Milne (*Louise*), Jane Henderson (*Mme. Vauthier*), Richard O'Sullivan (*Jacques as a Child*)
<u>P:</u> Bertram Ostrer & Albert Fennell <u>D:</u> George More O'Ferrall <u>SCR:</u> Gordon Wellesley, from Guy des Cars' novel *The Brute*
Standard thriller: Aged lawyer proves deaf, dumb and blind man innocent

The Green Shoes
1968, (GB),Isleworth/Para, color, 27 mins.
<u>W:</u> George Cole (*Braine*), Donald Webster (*Mackie*), Fred Davis (*The Man*), Tom Macaulay (*The Supt.*)
<u>P:</u> Ralph Solomons <u>D:</u> Ian Brims <u>STORY:</u> Ivor Jay
Standard short crime-thriller: Police track girl's killer

The Green Slime
1968, (USA-Jap), Ram-Toei/MGM, color, 110 mins.
<u>W:</u> Robert Horton (*Jack Rankin*), Luciana Paluzzi (*Lisa*), Richard Jaeckel (*Vince Elliott*), Bud Widom (*Jonathan Thompson*), Ted Gunther (*Dr. Halvorsen*), Gary Randolf (*Cordier*), David Yorston (*Lt. Curtis*), Robert Dunham (*Capt. Martin*), William Ross (*Ferguson*), Richard Hylland (*Michael*), Strong Ilimait (*The Doctor*), Clarence Howard (*The Patient*), Arthur Stark (*Barnett*), Tom Conrad (*The Sgt.*), Lynne Frederickson (*The Secretary*), David Sentman (*The Officer*), Bob Morris, Jack Morris, Hans Jorgseeberger, Carl Bengs, Tom Scott, Don Plante, Enver Altenbay, Gunther Greve, Eugene Vince, Patricia Elliot, George Uruf, Linda Hardisty, Kathy Horan, Ann Ault, Susan Skersick, Linda Miller, Helen Kirkpatrick, Linda Malson
<u>P:</u> Ivan Reiner & Walter Manley <u>D:</u> Kinji Fukasaku <u>SCR:</u> Charles Sinclair, William Finger & Tom Rowe <u>STORY:</u> Ivan Reiner <u>PHOTOG:</u> Yoshikazu Yamasawa <u>SPCL-FX:</u> Akira Watanabe & Yukio Manoda <u>MUSIC:</u> Toshiaki Tsushima
orig. to be titled Battle Beyond the Stars
Standard SF-horror: Alien life-form invades space station

The Green Terror
1919, (GB), Gaumont, b&w, 6,524 ft. (1988.5m)
<u>W:</u> Aurele Sydney (*Beale*), Heather Thatcher (*Olivia Cresswell*), W.T. Ellwanger (*Dr. Harden*), Arthur Poole (*Kitson*), Cecil du Gue (*Punsunby*), Maud Yates (*Hilda Glaum*)
<u>D:</u> W.P. Kellino <u>SCR:</u> G.W. Clifford, from a novel by Edgar Wallace
Minor SF-thriller: Evil doctor plans to destroy world's wheat

Gregorio and His Angel
1966, (Mex), color
<u>W</u>: Broderick Crawford, Tin Tan, Connie Carol
Standard fantasy: Bum becomes church custodian, experiences miracle

Gremlins
1984, (USA), Steven Spielberg/WB, color, 105 mins.
<u>W</u>: Zach Galligan (*Billy Peltzer*), Phoebe Cates (*Kate Beringer*), Hoyt Axton, Polly
   Holliday, Frances Lee McCain, Dick Miller, Scott Brady, Judge Reinhold,
   Glynn Turman, Keye Luke, Edward Andrews, Kenneth Tobey, Jackie
   Joseph, Don Elson, Chuck Jones, Belinda Balaski, Corey Feldman, Jonathan
   Banks, John Louie, Harry Carey Jr., John C. Becher, Joe Brooks, Lois
   Foraker, Rudy Doucette
<u>D</u>: Joe Dante   <u>SCR</u>: Chris Columbus   <u>PHOTOG</u>: John Hora   music: Jerry
   Goldsmith   <u>SONG</u>: *Make It Shine*
Major comedy-fantasy: Cute critter spawns demonic imps

Gremlins 2: The New Batch
1990, (USA), Amblin/WB, color, 106 mins.
<u>W</u>: Zach Galligan (*Billy Peltzer*), John Glover (*Daniel Clamp*),
   Robert Prosky (*Grandpa Fred*), Robert Picardo (*Forster*),
   Haviland Morris (*Maria Bloodstone*), Christopher Lee (*Dr. Catheter*), Dick
   Miller (*Murray Futterman*), Jackie Joseph (*Sheila Futterman*), Don Stanton
   (*Martin*), Dan Stanton (*Lewis*), Keye Luke (*Mr. Wing*), Gedde Watanabe
   (*Katsuji*), Shawn Nelson (*Wally*), Kathleen Freeman (*Microwave Marge*),
   Archie Hahn (*A Technician*), Ron Fassler (*A Technician*), Leslie Neale (*A
   Technician*), Time Winters (*A Technician*), Heather Haase (*A Yogurt Jerk*),
   Jason Presson (*A Yogurt Jerk*), Lisa Mende (*A Yogurt Customer*), Patrika Sarbo
   (*A Yogurt Customer*), Jerry Goldsmith (*A Yogurt Customer*), Rick Ducommun
   (*The Security Guard*), John Capodice (*The Fire Chief*), Nicky Rose (*The Movie
   Theatre Kid*), Belinda Balaski (*The Movie Theatre Mom*), Paul Bartel (*The
   Theatre Manager*), Kenneth Tobey (*The Projectionist*), Heidi Kemp (*A TV
   Reporter*), Eric Shawn (*A TV Reporter*), Michael Salort (*A TV Reporter*), Frank
   P. Ryan (*The Cop*), Diane Sainte-Marie (*The TV Reporter at Wing's*), Kristi
   Witker (*The TV Anchor in the Bar*), Sarah Lilly (*The Reporter in the Lobby*),
   Vladimir Bibic (*The Taxi Driver*), Page Hannah (*Tour Guide #1*), Liz Pryor
   (*Tour Guide #2*), Raymond Cruz (*The Messenger*), Julia Sweeney (*The Lab
   Receptionist*), Jeff Swanson (*Forster's Ass't*), Dale Swann (*The Surveillance
   Supervisor*), Charlie Haas (*Casper*), Gray Daniels (*The TV Cameraman*), Jacque
   Lynn Colton (*The Lady at the Elevator*), Stephanie Menuez (*Clamp's Secretary*),
   May Quigley (*A Hallway Employee*), Anthony Winters (*A Hallway Employee*),
   Isiah Whitlock Jr. (*The Fireman*), Saachiko (*The Newsstand Lady*), Dean
   Norris (*The Swat Team Leader*), John Astin (*The Janitor*), Henry Gibson (*The
   Fired Employee*), Tony Randall (*Voice of "Brain" Gremlin*), Howie Mandel
   (*Voice of Gizmo*), Leonard Maltin, Hulk Hogan, Bubba Smith, Dick Butkus
<u>D</u>: Joe Dante   <u>SCR</u>: Charlie Haas   <u>PHOTOG</u>: John Hora   <u>SPCL-FX</u>: Larz
   Anderson, Robert Henderson, Tom Homsher, Dan Lester & Wayne Rose
   <u>SPCL-FX SPRVSR</u>: Ken Pepiot   <u>VS-FX SPRVSR</u>: Dennis Michelson
   <u>MUSIC</u>: Jerry Goldsmith   <u>SONGS</u>: *I'm Ready, Sling Shot, Situation, & Angel
   of Death*
Expensive comedy-fantasy: Beasties terrorize office building

Grendel, Grendel, Grendel
1980, (Austral), color, 90 mins.
<u>VOICES</u>: Peter Ustinov, Keith Michell, Arthur Dignam, Ed Rosser, Bobby
   Bright, Ric Stone
<u>D</u>: Alexander Stitt, from a novel by John Gardner
Standard animated fantasy: Monster reflects on cruel humans

Grey Knight
1993, (USA), Notion, color
<u>W</u>: Corbin Bernsen, Martin Sheen, Adrian Pasdar, Cynda Williams, Ray Wise
<u>D</u>: George Hickenlooper
A.k.a. **The Killing Box**, *video-cassette retitle:* **Ghost Brigade**
Unusual fantasy-thriller: Weird force kills soldiers at height of American Civil War

Grey Matter
see **Mind Warp** *(1972)*

Greystoke: The Legend of Tarzan, Lord of the Apes
1984, (GB), WB, color, 131 mins.
<u>W</u>: Christopher Lambert (*John Clayton, Lord of the Apes*), Sir Ralph Richardson
   (*The 6th Earl of Greystoke*), Andie MacDowell (*Jane Porter*), Ian Holm
   (*Capitaine Phillippe D'Arnot*), James Fox (*Lord Esker*), Cheryl Campbell (*Lady
   Alice*), Ian Charleson (*Jefferson Brown*), Nigel Davenport (*Maj. Downing*),
   Paul Geoffrey (*John Clayton*), David Suchet (*Baller*), Eric Langlois (*Tarzan as
   a Boy*), John Wells (*Sir Evelyn Blount*), Nicholas Farrell (*Sir Hugh Belcher*),
   David Enden (*The Captain*), Tristram Jellineck (*White*), Roddy Maude-
   Roxby (*Olivestone*), Richard Griffiths (*Capt. Billings*), Paul Brooke (*Rev.
   Stimson*), Elliot Cane (*Silverbeard*), Ailsa Berk (*Kala*), John Alexander (*White
   Eyes*), Colin Charles (*Olly*), Daniel Potts, Rona Brown, Ravinder,
   Christopher Beck
<u>P</u>: Hugh Hudson & Stanley Canter   <u>D</u>: Hugh Hudson   <u>SCR</u>: P.H. Vazak &
   Michael Austin, from Edgar Rice Burroughs' novel *Tarzan of the Apes*
   <u>PHOTOG</u>: John Alcott   <u>SPCL-FX</u>: Albert Whitlock   <u>SPCL-FX
   SPRVSR</u>: Peter Hutchinson   <u>MUSIC</u>: John Scott
Lavish, superior version of Burroughs' classic: Youth raised by apes returns to civilization

Grimm's Fairy Tales for Adults
1970, (W. Ger), Cinemation, color
<u>W</u>: Marie Liljedahl
<u>D</u>: Rolf Thiele & Helen Gray (USA version)   <u>SCR</u>: Rolf Thiele
A.k.a. **The Erotic Adventures of Snow White**
Standard eroto-fantasy

Grim Prairie Tales
1990, (USA), Coe Hahn, color, 87 mins.
<u>W</u>: James Earl Jones (*Morrison*), Brad Dourif (*Farley*), Will Hare (*Lee*), William
   Atherton (*Arthur*), Marc McClure (*Tom*), Michelle Joyner (*Jenny*), Lisa
   Eichhorn (*Maureen*), Jennifer Barlow (*Sarah*), Wendy Cooke (*Eva*), Scott
   Paulin (*Martin*), Dan Leegant (*Dr. Leaderman*), William M. Brennan (*Bluey*),
   Tom Simcox (*Horn*), Bruce Fischer (*Colochez*), James Glick (*The Dying Chief*),
   Hannah Fixico, Joan Lemmo, Mony Bass, Joel Shoptesse, Oscar Fragosa,
   Darice Sampson, Jessica Vega Vasquez, Michael Rettew, Timmy Herzer,
   Geoffrey Herzer, Elena Lopez, Erica Vega Vasquez, Terisa Plaza, Bob
   Terhune, Samso-chi Sampson, Lummi Sampson, Amanda Tapia, Shann
   Costello, Jesse Tapia, Mecedes Tapia, Steve Reevis, Robert Kent Ball, Justin
   Lundin, Ray Sanager
<u>WRIT & D</u>: Wayne Coe   <u>PHOTOG</u>: Janusz Kaminski   <u>MUSIC</u>: Steve Dancz
*Quartet of minor terror-tales: (1) Indian curse, (2) Supernatural seduction, (3) Bigoted
   homesteader, & (4) Haunted gunfighter*

The Grim Reaper
1981, (It), Film Ventures, color, 81 mins.
<u>W</u>: Tisa Farrow (*Julie*), Saverio Vallone, Vanessa Steiger, George Eastman, Zora
   Kerova, Mark Bodin, Bob Larsen, Mark Logan, Rubina Rey
<u>P</u>: Oscar Santaniello   <u>D</u>: Joe D'Amato   <u>SCR</u>: Aristide Massaccesi & Lewis
   Montefiore   <u>PHOTOG</u>: Enrico Birbichi
A.k.a. **Anthropophagus**
Minor horror-thriller: Ghoul depopulates Greek isle

The Grip
1913, (GB), Britannic Film Producing Syndicate, b&w, 4,000 ft. (1219.2m)
<u>W</u>: Louis Bouwmeester (*John Strong*), Annesley Healy
<u>D & SCR</u>: A.E. Coleby, from Jean Sartene's play
Standard crime-thriller: Paralyzed farmer regains voice, stops second wife from killing son

The Grip of Ambition
1914, (GB), Hepworth, b&w, 2,025 ft. (617.2m)
<u>W</u>: Stewart Rome (*Rev. Basil Hunt*), Lionelle Howard (*John Bannister*)
<u>D</u>: Frank Wilson
Standard melodrama: Author's ejected wife becomes slum worker

Grip of Fear
see **Experiment in Terror**

The Grip of Iron
1913, (GB), Brightonia/Andrews, b&w, 3,250 ft. (990.6m)
<u>W</u>: Fred Powell (*Jagon/Simmonet*), Nell Emerald (*Cora Jagon*), H. Agar Lyons
   (*Lorenz de Rifas*), Frank E. Petley (*Smiler*), Gertrude Price, Stanley Bedwell
<u>D</u>: Arthur Charrington   <u>STORY</u>: Arthur Shirley
Standard crime-thriller: Parisian lawyer's clerk strangles and steals

The Grip of Iron
1920, (GB), Famous Pictures/General, b&w, 5,000 ft. (1524m)
<u>W</u>: George Foley (*Jagon/Simonnet*), Malvina Longfellow (*Cora Jagon*), James
   Lindsay (*Lorenz de Rifas*), Laurence Tessier (*Paul Blanchard*), Ronald Power
   (*Capt. Guerin*), Ivy King (*Marie Guerin*), Warwick Buckland (*Rolf de Belfort*),
   John Power (*Coucou*), Moore Marriott (*Smiler*)
<u>D</u>: Bert Haldane   <u>SCR</u>: Arthur Shirley & Bert Haldane, from a play by Arthur
   Shirley, based on Belot's novel *Les Etrangleurs de Paris (The Stranglers of Paris)*
Standard thriller: Lawyer's clerk is secret strangler

Grip of the Strangler
1957, (GB), Amalgamated/MGM, b&w, 81 mins.
<u>W</u>: Boris Karloff (*Rankin/Tenant*), Elizabeth Allan (*Mrs. Rankin*), Vera Day
   (*Pearl*), Anthony Dawson (*Insp. Burke*), Jean Kent, Diane Aubrey, Derek
   Birch, Tim Turner, John Fabian, Dorothy Gordon, Max Brimmell, Desmond
   Roberts, Leslie Perrins, Jessica Cairns
<u>P</u>: John Croydon   <u>D</u>: Robert Day   <u>SCR</u>: Jan Read & John C. Cooper, from an
   orig. story by Jan Read   <u>PHOTOG</u>: Leo Rogers   <u>MUSIC</u>: Buxton Orr
orig. to be titled **The Judas Hole**, *USA retitle:* **The Haunted Strangler**
Impressive thriller: Amnesiac doctor discovers he was once murderous fiend

The Grit of a Dandy
1914, (GB), Herkomer Films/Tyler, b&w, 2,520 ft. (768.1m)
<u>W</u>: Sybil Sparkes (*Gladys*), Leonard Ceily (*Clifford Maythorne*), Clarissa Selwyn,
   Archibald Forbes
<u>D</u>: Hubert von Herkomer   <u>STORY</u>: Siegfried von Herkomer
Standard crime-thriller: Rejected dandy saves doctor's daughter from kidnapping burglars

Grizzly
1976, (USA), Edward L. Montoro/Film Ventures, color, 91 mins.
<u>W</u>: Christopher George (*Kelly*), Andrew Prine (*Don*), Richard Jaeckel (*Scott*), Joan
   McCall (*Allison*), Charles Kissinger (*Dr. Hallitt*), Joe Dorsey (*Kittridge*),

Kermit Echols (*Corwin*), Tom Arcuragi (*Tom*), Vicki Johnson (*Gail*), Mike Clifford (*Pat*), Catherine Rickman (*June*), Maryann Hearn (*Margaret*), Sandra Dorsey (*Sally*), Gene Witham (*Harry*), David Holt (*The Lone Hunter*), Susan Orpin (*Mother*), Mike Gerschefski (*George*), Brian Robinson (*Bobby*), David Newton (*Mike*), Harvey Flaxman (*The Reporter*), Amos Gillespie
WRIT & P: David Sheldon & Harvey Flaxman   **D:** William Girdler   **SCR:** Harvey Flaxman & David Sheldon   **PHOTOG:** William Asman   **SPCL-FX:** Phil Corey   **MUSIC:** Robert O. Ragland
A.k.a. *Killer Grizzly*
blurb: "18 feet of gut-crunching, man-eating terror!"
Standard thriller: Huge bear attacks humans

Grizzly Mountain
1995, (USA), color, 97 mins.
W: Dan Haggerty, Dylan Haggerty
Standard adventure-fantasy: Two children are mysteriously transported to 1880s

Grotesque
1988, (USA), Joe Tornatore/United Filmmakers, color, 91 mins.
W: Linda Blair (*Lisa*), Tab Hunter, Donna Wilkes, Nels Van Patten, Brad Wilson, Sharon Hughes, Michelle Bensoussan, Charles Dierkop, Guy Stockwell, Chuck Morrell, John Goff, Lincoln Tate, Luana Patten, Bob Leon, Mike Lane, Holly Morrell
D: Joe Tornatore   **SCR:** Mike Angel   **PHOTOG:** Bill Dickson   **MUSIC:** Bill Loose & Jack Cookerly
Minor thriller: Punks slay family, plastic surgeon enacts gruesome revenge

La Grotte aux Surprises (The Grotto of Surprises)
1905, (Fr), Star, b&w, 38m (124.7 ft./2.1 mins.)
D: Georges Melies
Standard fantasy

The Grotto of Surprises
see *La Grotte aux Surprises*

Groundhog Day
1993, (USA), Col, color, 101 mins.
W: Bill Murray (*Phil Connors*), Andie MacDowell (*Rita*), Chris Elliott (*Larry*), Stephen Tobolowsky (*Ned*), Brian Doyle Murray (*Buster*), Marita Geraghty, Angela Paton
D: Harold Ramis   **SCR:** Danny Rubin & Harold Ramis   **PHOTOG:** John Bailey   **MUSIC:** George Fenton
Amusing comedy-fantasy: Obnoxious TV weatherman finds he is reliving same day

The Groundstar Conspiracy
1972, (USA), Univ, color, 96 mins.
W: George Peppard (*Tuxan*), Christine Belford (*Nicole*), Tim O'Connor (*Gossage*), Michael Sarrazin (*Welles*), Cliff Potts (*Mosely*), James Olson (*Stanton*), Alan Oppenheimer (*Hackett*), James McEachin (*Bender*), Roger Dressler (*Kitchen*), Ty Haller (*Henshaw*), Anna Hagen (*Dr. Plover*), Robin Coller (*The Secretary*), Hagan Beggs (*Dr. Hager*), John Destry Adams (*Zabrinski*), Milos Zatovic (*Dr. Zahl*), Bob Meneray (*Nicole's Doctor*), Martin Moore, John Mitchell, Richard Sargent, Don Vance, William Nunn, Peter Lavender, Barry Cahill
P: Trevor Wallace   **D:** Lamont Johnson   **SCR:** Matthew Howard, based on L.P. Davies' novel *The Alien*   **PHOTOG:** Michael Reed   **MUSIC:** Paul Hoffert   **DESIGN:** Cam Porteous
Standard action-thriller: Security chief of U.S. space center ferrets out saboteurs

Ground Zero
1988, (USA), color, 90 mins.
W: Ron Casteel, Melvin Belli, Yvonne D'Angiers
D: James T. Flocker
Minor thriller: Atom bomb planted on Golden Gate Bridge

Growing Pains
see *The House that Bled to Death/Growing Pains*

The Gruesome Twosome
1966, (USA), Boxoffice Spectaculars, color, 81 mins.
W: Elizabeth David, Chris Martell, Rodney Bedell, Gretchen Welles, Ray Sager
D & PHOTOG: Herschell Gordon Lewis   **SCR:** Allison Louise Downe   **MUSIC:** Larry Wellington
Minor horror-satire: Moron slays to provide wig-maker mother with human hair

The Guardian
1990, (USA), Joe Wizan/Univ, color, 95 mins.
W: Jenny Seagrove (*Camilla*), Dwier Brown (*Phil*), Carey Lowell (*Kate*), Brad Hall (*Ned Runcie*), Miguel Ferrer (*Ralph Hess*), Natalia Nogulich (*Molly Sheridan*), Pamela Brull (*Gail Krasno*), Gary Swanson (*Allan Sheridan*), Josh Fischman, Chris Nemeth, Craig Nemeth, Aaron Fischman, Jack David Walker, Willy Parsons, Frank Noon, Ray Reinhardt Pamela Brull, Frank Noon, Gary Swanson, Willy Parsons
D: William Friedkin   **SCR:** Stephen Volk, Dan Greenburg, & William Friedkin, from Dan Greenburg's novel *The Nanny*   **PHOTOG:** John A. Alonzo   **MUSIC:** Jack Hues
Standard fantasy-thriller: Modern druid priestess revives ancient horror

Guardian of Hell
1980, (It), Cinemec, color, 92 mins.
USA release: 1985
Minor thriller: Nuns slain, priest investigates

Guardian of the Abyss
1982, (GB), color, 90 mins.
W: Ray Lonnen, Rosalyn Landor, Paul Darrow, Barbara Ewing
D: Don Sharp
Minor fantasy-thriller: Antique mirror is gateway to Hell

Guarding Britain's Secrets
1914, (GB), Cricks/Walturdaw, b&w, 3,300 ft. (1005.8m)
W: Douglas Payne (*Rex Omar*), Dr. Nikola Hamilton, Norman Howard
D: Charles Calvert   **STORY:** Dr. Nikola Hamilton
USA retitle: **The Fiends of Hell**
Standard thriller: Detective and hypnotized girl save inventor's plans from Chinese secret society

Guess What Happened to Count Dracula
1970, (USA), Merrick-Int'l, color
W: Des Roberts (*Count Adrian*)
P: Leo Rivers   **D & SCR:** Laurence Merrick
Minor "sexploitation" thriller, made 3 times on same set: (1) under orig. title with actors wearing clothes, (2) actors in buff as 'Does Dracula Suck?,' & (3) degenerate romp as 'Does Dracula Really...?'

Guess Who's Coming for Christmas?
1990, (USA), NBC-TV, color, 95 mins.
W: Richard Mulligan, Beau Bridges, Barbara Barrie, Paul Dooley, James McEachin, John Furey, Michael Patrick Carter, Betsy Randle
TVM, standard SF-fantasy: Eccentric befriends alien

Guest in the House
1944, (USA), UA, b&w, 121 mins.
W: Anne Baxter, Ralph Bellamy, Ruth Warrick, Margaret Hamilton, Marie MacDonald, Cornel Wilde, Scott McKay, Jerome Cowan, Aline MacMahon, Percy Kilbride
D: John Brahm   **SCR:** Ketti Frings, from play *Dear Evelyn* by Dale Eunson & Hagar Wilde   **PHOTOG:** Lee Garmes   **MUSIC:** Werner Janssen
Standard melodrama: Girl taken into household poisons minds

The Guest of the Evening
1914, (GB), Hepworth, b&w, 1,100 ft. (335.3m)
W: Stewart Rome (*Harry Vane*), Alice de Winton (*Mrs. Vane*), Cyril Morton (*Philip Orgill*)
D: Frank Wilson
Standard crime-thriller: Earl poses as bankrupt, exposes friend as thief

Guguste et Belzebuth
1901, (Fr), Star, b&w, 40m (131.2 ft./2.2 mins.)
D: Georges Melies
USA retitle: **The Clown versus Satan**
Standard fantasy: Harlequin confounds Devil

Guillaume Tell (William Tell)
1896, (Fr), b&w
D: Emile Reynaud
Standard adventure-romance: Saga of Swiss hero

La Guirlande Merveilleuse (The Marvellous Wreath)
1903, (Fr), Star, b&w, 80m (262.5 ft./4.4 mins.)
D: Georges Melies
A.k.a. **The Marvellous Hoop**
Standard fantasy

Guilt is My Shadow
1950, (GB), Stratford/ABPC, b&w, 86 mins.
W: Patrick Holt (*Kit*), Peter Reynolds (*Jamie*), Elizabeth Sellars (*Linda*), Lana Morris (*Betty*), Laurence O'Madden (*Tom*), Avice Landon (*Eva*), Esma Cannon (*Peggy*), Wensley Pithey (*Tillingham*)
P: Ivan Foxwell   **D:** Roy Kellino   **SCR:** Ivan Foxwell, Roy Kellino, & John Gilling, from Peter Curtis' novel *You're Best Alone*
USA release: 1954
Standard crime-thriller: Devon farmer helps girl who killed her crooked husband

The Guilty
1947, (USA), Mono, b&w, 71 mins.
W: Bonita Granville, Don Castle
Standard thriller

Guilty?
1956, (GB), Gibraltar/Grand Nat'l, b&w, 93 mins.
W: John Justin (*Nap Rumbold*), Barbara Laage (*Jacqueline Delbois*), Donald Wolfit (*The Judge*), Stephen Murray (*Summers*), Norman Wooland (*Pelton*), Betty Stockfeld (*Mrs. Roper*), Frank Villard (*Pierre Lemaire*), Andree Debar (*Vicki Martin*), Sydney Tafler (*Camino*), Leslie Perrins (*Poynter*), Kynaston Reeves (*Col. Wright*), Russell Napier (*Insp. Hobson*)

P: Charles A. Leeds **D:** Edmond T. Greville **SCR:** Maurice J. Wilson & Ernest Dudley, from Michael Gilbert's novel
Standard crime-thriller: French Policewoman helps lawyer prove forgers framed resistance heroine

Guilty as Sin
1993, color, 120 mins.
W: Don Johnson, Rebecca DeMornay, Jack Warden, Dana Ivey, Stephen Lang, Ron White, Sean McCann, Luis Guzman
D: Sidney Lumet **SCR:** Larry Cohen
Standard thriller: Suave sociopath menaces woman lawyer

Guilty Bystander
1950, (USA), Film Classics, b&w, 92 mins.
W: Zachary Scott, Faye Emerson Mary Boland, Sam Levene, Kay Medford
D: Joseph Lerner
Standard thriller: Detective's child kidnapped

Guinevere
1994, (USA), color, 96 mins.
W: Sheryl Lee, Sean Patrick Flanery
Standard adventure-romance: Camelot queen forsakes true love to unite her country

Gulliver's Travels
1939, (USA), Max Fleischer/Para, color, 74 mins.
VOICES: Lanny Ross, Jessica Dragonette
based on Jonathan Swift's satire
SONGS: *Faithful Forever*
Animated feature: Adventurer visits strange lands

Gulliver's Travels
1977, (GB), Valeness-Belvision/Sunn Classic, color, 81 mins.
W: Richard Harris (*Lemuel Gulliver*), Catherine Schell (*Mary Gulliver*), Norman Shelley (*Father*), Meredith Edwards (*Uncle*)
VOICES: Michael Bates, Denise Bryer, Julian Glover, Bessie Love, Stephen Jack, Murray Melvin, Nancy Nevinson, Roger Snowden, Robert Rietty, Vladek Sheybal, Bernard Spear, Graham Stark
P: Raymond Leblanc & Derek Horne **D:** Peter Hunt **SCR:** Don Black, from Jonathan Swift's classic satire **PHOTOG:** Alan Hume **MUSIC:** Michel Legrand
Standard fantasy, combination of live-action & animation: Sailor shipwrecked on isle of tiny people

Gulliver's Travels
1996, (USA), NBC-TV, color, 187 mins.
W: Ted Danson (*Lemuel Gulliver*), Mary Steenburgen, Peter O'Toole, James Fox, Geraldine Chaplin, Omar Sharif, Sir John Gielgud, Thomas Sturridge, Graham Crowden, Robert Hardy, Shashi Kapoor, Kristin Scott Thomas, Ned Beatty, Richard Wilson, Edward Woodward, Nicholas Lyndhurst, Phoebe Nicholls, Kate Maberly, Warwick Davis, John Standing, Karyn Parsons, Edward Petherbridge
D: Charles Sturridge **TELEPLAY:** Simon Moore, from Jonathan Swift's novel **PHOTOG:** Howard Atherton **MUSIC:** Trevor Jones
TVM, standard fantasy Man visits bizarre lands

Gulliver's Travels Beyond the Moon
1966, (Jap),Continental, color, 85 mins.
D: Yoshio Kuroda, inspired by Jonathan Swift's *Gulliver's Travels*
MUSIC: Milton DeLugg
Standard SF-fantasy, animated feature: Hero has new adventures in outer space

Gun Moll
see *La Mome Vert-de-Gris*

The Gunpowder Plot
1900, (GB), Hepworth, b&w, 50 ft. (15.2m)
W: Cecil Hepworth (*The Father*)
D: Cecil M. Hepworth
Standard fantasy short: Boy puts firework under father's chair and blows him to pieces

Gunhed
1989, (Jap), color, 100 mins.
W: Landy Leyes, Masahiro Takashima, Brenda Bakke, James B. Thompson, Aya Eniyoji
D: Masato Harada
Standard SF-thriller: Robot saves world

Guns Don't Argue
1957, (USA), Visual Drama, b&w, 90 mins.
W: Myron Healey, Jean Harvey
Standard melodrama

Guru, the Mad Monk
1971, (USA), Nova Int'l, color
P, D, & SCR: Andy Milligan
A.k.a. **Garu, the Mad Monk**
Minor horror-thriller: Prisoners tortured on isolated isle

Guyana, Cult of the Damned
1980, (USA), Conacine-Izaro-Care/Univ, color, 90 mins.
W: Stuart Whitman, Bradford Dillman, John Ireland, Gene Barry, Joseph Cotten, Yvonne DeCarlo, Jennifer Ashley
WRIT, P, & D: Rene Cardona Jr. **STORY & SCR:** Carlos Valdemar & Rene Cardona Jr. **PHOTOG:** Leopoldo Villasenor **MUSIC:** Nelson Riddle, Bob Summers & George S. Price
Sleazy exploitation thriller: Charismatic leader directs mass suicide

A Guy Called Caeser
1962, (GB), Bill & Michael Luckwell/Col, b&w, 62 mins.
W: Conrad Phillips (*Tony*), George Moon (*Maurice*), Phillip O'Flynn (*Tex*), Maureen Toal (*Lena*), Peter Maycock (*Ron*), Desmond Perry (*Harry*)
P: Bill Luckwell & Umesh Mallik **D:** Frank Marshall **SCR:** Umesh Mallik & Tom Burdon **STORY:** Umesh Mallik
Standard crime-thriller: Policeman poses as crook, unmasks leader of jewel thieves

Guy Fawkes and the Gunpowder Plot
1913, (GB), B&C/Royal, b&w, 2,000 ft. (609.6m)
W: Caleb Porter (*Guy Fawkes*), Ernest G. Batley (*The Traitor*)
D: Ernest G. Batley
Standard historical melodrama: Catholic conspirator foiled in at-tempt to blow up parliament

A Guy Named Joe
1943, (USA), MGM, b&w, 120 mins.
W: Spencer Tracy, Irene Dunne, Van Johnson, James Gleason, Ward Bond, Lionel Barrymore, Barry Nelson, Esther Williams
D: Victor Fleming **STORY:** Dalton Trumbo **PHOTOG:** George Folsey & Karl Freund **MUSIC:** Herbert Stothart
Sentimental fantasy: Spirit of dead fighter pilot guides young officer. cf. **Always**

The Guyver
1992, (USA-Jap), color, 92 mins.
W: Mark Hamill, Vivian Wu, Jack Armstrong, David Gale, Jimmie Walker, Michael Berryman, Peter Spollos, Spice Williams, Willard Pugh, Jeffrey Combs, David Wells, Linnea Quigley
D: Screaming Mad George & Steve Wang
Minor SF-fantasy: Man infected by alien gadget, becomes armored superhero

Guyver 2: Dark Hero
1994, (USA), color 127 mins.
W: David Hayter Cathy Christopherson, Christopher Michael
D: Steve Wang **SCR:** Nathan Long
Minor SF adventure: Man seeks link between powerful alien armor and spaceship excavated in desert

Gwangi
1942, (USA), RKO, b&w
Production abandoned after 6 months of filming
Spcl-Fx scenes (by Willis O'Brien & team) later used in *Mighty Joe Young* and *The Black Scorpion*
*Standard SF-adventure: Cowboys find prehistoric life on lost mesa. cf. **The Valley of Gwangi***

Gypsy Blood
see **Carmen**(1918)

Gypsy Fury
1951, (USA), Mono, b&w, 63 mins.
W: Viveca Lindfors, Christopher Kent
Standard melodrama

The Gypsy Moon
1953, (USA), Reed, b&w
W: Richard Crane
Feature film culled from "Rocky Jones, Space Ranger" teleseries

The Gypsy Romance
1926, (USA), Prime Pictures, b&w, 6 reels
W: Thur Fairfax (*Jaime*), Shannon Day (*Maya*)
Standard melodrama: Gypsy lovers sentenced to be burned alive

The Gypsy's Curse
1914, (GB), Vaudefilms/A&C, b&w, 412 ft. (125.6m)
D: W.P. Kellino
Minor fantasy short: Curse bedevils gambler

Gypsy Wildcat
1944, (USA), Univ, color, 77 mins.
W: Maria Montez (*Carla*), Jon Hall (*Michael*), Nigel Bruce (*The High Sheriff*), Peter Coe (*Tonio*), Gale Sondergaard (*Rhoda*), Leo Carrillo (*Anube*), Douglass Dumbrille (*Baron Tovar*), Curt Bois (*Valdi*), Harry Cording (*Capt. Marver*)
P: George Waggner **D:** Roy William Neill **SCR:** James Hogan, Gene Lewis, & James M. Cain **ORIG. STORY:** James Hogan & Ralph Stock **PHOTOG:** George Robinson & W. Howard Greene **SPCL-FX:** John P. Fulton **MUSIC:** Edward Ward

Habitat

1997, (USA), color

W: Tcheky Karyo, Alice Krige, Balthazar Getty
Standard SF-thriller: Ozone layer disintegrates; scientist tinkers with "accelerated evolution"

Half-Human

70 mins.

W: Russ Thorson, Robert Karns
D: Inoshiro Honda & Kenneth Crane

Halloween: H2O

1998, (USA), Nightfall/Dimension, color, 87 mins.

W: Jamie Lee Curtis, Adam Arkin, Janet Leigh, Josh Hartnett, Michelle Williams, Jodi Lyn O'Keefe, Adam Hahn-Byrd
D: Steve Miner   SCR: Robert Zappia & Matt Greenberg   MUSIC: John Ottman
"Sensational, Smart And Non-Stop Scary!" —UPN-TV
Gripping thriller: Terror returns to plague former victim

Halloween Night

1990, (USA), color, 90 mins.

W: Hy Pyke, Katrina Garner
D: Emilio P. Miraglio
Standard horror-fantasy: Ancient evil threatens small town

Halloween Party

see Night of the Demons

Halloween: The Curse of Michael Myers

1995, (USA), color

W: Donald Pleasence, George P. Wilbur, Mitchell Ryan, Susan Swift, Devin Gardner, Kim Darby, J.C. Brandy

Halloweentown

1998, (USA), Walt Disney, color, 95 mins.

W: Debbie Reynolds, Judith Hoag (*Gwen*), Kimberly J. Brown (*Mamie*), Robin Thomas (*Calabar*), Joey Zimmerman (*Dylan*), Emily Roeske
D: Duwayne Dunham   STORY: Paul Bernbaum   PHOTOG: Michael Slovis
TVM, standard juvenile fantasy: Benevolent witch aids menaced town

An Hallucinated Alchemist

see L'Hallucination de l'Alchemiste

L'Hallucination de l'Alchemiste (The Alchemist's Hallucination)

1897, (Fr), Star, b&w, 20m (65.6 ft./1.1 mins.)

D: Georges Melies
USA retitle, An Hallucinated Alchemist
Standard fantasy

Les Hallucinations du Baron de Munchausen (The Hallucinations of Baron Munchausen)

1911, (Fr), Star, b&w, 771 ft. (235m)

P & D: Georges Melies
USA retitle, Baron Munchausen A.k.a. Les Aventures du Baron de Munchausen (The Adventures of Baron Munchausen)

The Hallucinators

see The Naked Zoo

Hamlet

1907, (Fr), Star, b&w, 175m (574.1 ft./9.7 mins.)

D: Georges Melies, from Shakespeare's play
A.k.a. Hamlet, Prince of Denmark
Standard melodrama: Prince seeks revenge

Hamlet

1912, (GB), Barker, b&w, 1,525 ft. (464.8m)

W: Charles Raymond (*Hamlet*), Dorothy Foster (*Ophelia*), Constance Backner (*Gertrude*)
D: Charles Raymond, from Shakespeare's play
Standard melodrama: Prince meets father's ghost

Hamlet

1913, (GB), Hepworth/Gaumont, b&w, 5,800 ft. (1767.8m)

W: Johnston Forbes-Robertson (*Hamlet*), Gertrude Elliot (*Ophelia*), Walter Ringham (*Claudius*), J.H. Barnes (*Polonius*), Adeleine Bourne (*Gertrude*), S.A. Cookson (*Horatio*), Alex Scott-Gatty (*Laertes*), Grendon Bentley (*Fortinbras*), Montagu Rutherford (*Rosencrantz*), J.H. Ryley (*The Gravedigger*), Percy Rhodes (The *Ghost*), Robert Atkins (*The First Player*)
D: Hay Plumb, from Shakespeare's play
Standard melodrama: Prince seeks vengeance

Hamlet

1914, (GB), Eric Williams Speaking Pictures, b&w

W: Eric Williams (*Hamlet*), from Shakespeare's play
Standard melodrama: Royal Dane gets revenge

Hamlet

1915, (GB), Cricks/DFSA, b&w, 882 ft. (268.8m)

D: W.P. Kellino   STORY: Reuben Gillmer, inspired by Shakespeare's play
Standard comedy: Burlesque of tale about vengeful prince

Hamlet

1920, (Ger), Ufa, b&w

W: Bela Lugosi, Asta Nielsen
D: Sven Gade, from Shakespeare's play   PHOTOG: Curtis Courant
Standard melodrama: Danish prince urged to vengeance

Hamlet

1948, (GB), Two Cities/Univ, b&w, 155 mins.

W: Sir Laurence Olivier (*Prince Hamlet*), Jean Simmons (*Ophelia*), Eileen Herlie (*Queen Gertrude*), Basil Sydney (*The King*), Norman Wooland (*Horatio*), Stanley Holloway (*The Gravedigger*), Esmond Knight (*Bernardo*), John Laurie (*Francisco*), Peter Cushing (*Osric*), Anthony Quayle (*Marcellus*), Felix Aylmer (*Polonius*), Harcourt Williams (*The First Player*), Terence Morgan (*Laertes*), Christopher Lee, Tony Tarver, Niall MacGinnis, Patrick Troughton, Googie Withers, Patrick Macnee
D: Sir Laurence Olivier, from Shakespeare's play   PHOTOG: Desmond Dickinson, filmed in Elsinore, Denmark   MUSIC: Sir William Walton
Classic psychodrama: Prince plots to avenge father's murder. Oscars: Best Picture; Best Actor- Olivier; Art Direction; Costumes

Hamlet

1960, (W. Ger), Emerson Films/Edward Dmytryk/ Sam Weiler/NTA, Made for TV, b&w, 128 mins

W: Maximilian Schell (*Prince Hamlet*), Wanda Rotha (*Queen Gertrude*), Dunja Movar (*Ophelia*)
D & SPEC: Franz Peter Wirth, from Shakespeare's play
TVM, standard melodrama: Danish prince seeks revenge

Hamlet

1964, (Russ), Lenfilm/Lopert/ b&w, 150 mins.

W: Mikhail Nazvanov (*King*), Inokkenti Smoktunovsky (*Hamlet*)
D: Grigori Kozintsev, from Shakespeare's play
Standard melodrama: Prince avenges father's death

Hamlet

1969, (GB), Woodfall/Col, color, 117 mins.

W: Nicol Williamson (*Hamlet*), Gordon Jackson (*Horatio*), Anthony Hopkins (*Claudius*), Judy Parfitt (*Gertrude*), Ben Aris (*Rosencrantz*), Mark Dignam (*Polonius*), Clive Graham (*Guildenstern*), Michael Pennington (*Laertes*), Marianne Faithfull (*Ophelia*), Peter Gale (*Osric*), John Carney (*The Player King*), Richard Everett (*The Player Queen*), Roger Livesey (*Lucianus/The Gravedigger*), Michael Elphick (*The Captain*), Robin Chadwick (*Francisco*), Mark Griffith (*The Messenger*), Ian Collier (*The Priest*), Anjelica Huston (*A Court Lady*), Bill Jarvis (*The Courtier*), Roger Lloyd-Pack (*Reynaldo*), John Railton (*The First Sailor*), John Trenaman (*Bernardo*), Jennifer Tudor (*A Court Lady*)
D: Tony Richardson, from Shakespeare's play   PHOTOG: Gerry Fisher
MUSIC: Patrick Gowers
Standard melodrama: Ghost spurs prince to vengeance

Hamlet

1990, (It), Icon/Nelson/WB, color, 135 mins.

W: Mel Gibson (*Hamlet*), Glenn Close (*Queen Gertrude*), Alan Bates (*Claudius*), Ian Holm (*Polonius*), Helena Bonham-Carter (*Ophelia*), Paul Scofield (*The Ghost*), Stephen Dillane (*Horatio*), Nathaniel Parker (*Laertes*), Dave Duffy (*Francisco*), Sean Murray (*Guildenstern*), Michael Maloney (*Rosencrantz*), Trevor Peacock (*The Gravedigger*), Richard Warwick (*Bernardo*), John McEnery (*Osric*), Pete Postlethwaite (*The Player King*), Christien Anholt (*Marcellus*), Christopher Fairbank (*The Player Queen*), Vernon Dobtcheff (*Reynaldo*), Roy York, Sarah Phillips, Ned Mendez, Marjorie Bell, Pamela Sinclair, Justin Case, Roger Low, Roy Evans, Baby Simon Sinclair
D: Franco Zeffirelli   SCR: Christopher De Vore & Franco Zeffirelli, from Shakespeare's play   PHOTOG: David Watkin   MUSIC: Ennio Morricone
Well-made melodrama: Prince must decide on course of vengeance

Hamlet

1996, (USA), Castle Rock/Col, color, 3 hrs & 58 mins.

W: Kenneth Branagh (*Hamlet*), Julie Christie (*Queen Gertrude*), Robin Williams (*Osric*), Kate Winslet (*Ophelia*), Billy Crystal (*The Gravedigger*), Jack Lemmon (*Marcellus*), Richard Briers (*Polonius*), Charlton Heston (*The Player King*), Sir John Gielgud, Gerard Depardieu, Derek Jacobi, Rufus Sewell
D & ADAPT: Kenneth Branagh, from Shakespeare's play   PHOTOG: Alex Thomson   MUSIC: Patrick Doyle   SONG: *In Pace* (sung by Placido Domingo)
"A Once-In-A-Century Screen Event"—Bob Campbell Newhouse Newspapers
Faithful film-version of timeless classic

Hamlet, Prince of Denmark

see Hamlet (1907)

Hamlet's Duel

see Le Duel d'Hamlet

Hammerhead

1968, (GB), Irving Allen/Col, color, 99 mins.

W: Vince Edwards (*Charles Hood*), Judy Geeson (*Sue Trenton*), Peter Vaughan

(*Hammerhead*), Diana Dors (*Kit*), Michael Bates (*Andreas/Sir Richard*), Patrick Cargill (*Condor*), Beverly Adams (*Ivory*), Patrick Holt (*Huntzinger*), Tracy Reed (*Miss Hull*), William Mervyn (*Perrin*), Kenneth Cope (*The Motorcyclist*), Douglas Wilmer (*Vendriani*), Jack Woolgar (*Tookey Tate*), Kathleen Byron (*Lady Calvert*), Veronica Carlson (*Ulla*)
D: David Miller   **SCR:** William Bast, Herbert Baker & John Briley, from a novel by James Briley
Standard crime-thriller: U.S. agent foils criminal's plan to kidnap NATO delegate

Hammersmith is Out
1972, (USA), J. Cornelius Crean/CRC, color, 108 mins.
W: Richard Burton (*Hammersmith*), Elizabeth Taylor (*Jimmie Jean Jackson*), Beau Bridges (*Billy Breedlove*), Peter Ustinov (*The Doctor*), Leon Askin (*Dr. Krodt*), Leon Ames (*Gen. Sam Pembroke*), John Schuck (*Henry Joe*), Linda Gaye Scott (*Miss Quim*), George Raft (*Guido Scartucci*), Marjorie Eaton (*Princess*), Anthony Holland (*Oldham*), Mal Berger (*The Fat Man*), Lisa Jak (*Kiddo*), Brook Williams (*Pete Rutter*), Carl Don, Jose Espinoza
P: Alex Lucas   **D:** Peter Ustinov   **SCR:** Stanford Whitmore   **PHOTOG:** Richard H. Kline   **MUSIC:** Dominic Frontiere   **LYRICS:** Dominic Frontiere & Sally Stevens
Bizarre reworking of Faust legend: Madman gains aid of asylum employee

Hammersmith is Out: BEAU BRIDGES, RICHARD BURTON AND ELIZABETH TAYLOR

Hammet
1983, (USA), Orion/WB, color, 97 mins.
W: Frederic Forrest, Peter Boyle, Marilu Hunner, Richard Bradford, Roy Kinnear, Elisha Cook Jr., R.G. Armstrong, Lydia Lei, Sylvia Sidney, Samuel Fuller
D: Wim Wenders   **SCR:** Ross Thomas, Dennis O'Flaherty & Thomas Pope, from Joe Gores' novel   **PHOTOG:** Philip Lathrop, Joseph Biroc & Randy Roberts
Flawed homage to "film noir" (Wenders' first American-made movie): Novelist hunts for missing friend

The Hammond Mystery
see *The Undying Monster*

The Hand
1960, (GB), Butcher/AIP, b&w, 61 mins.
W: Derek Bond (*Roberts/Crawshaw*), Ronald Leigh Hunt (*Insp. Munyard*), Reed de Rouen (*Michael Brodie*), Bryan Coleman (*Adams*), Ray Cooney (*Pollitt*), Tony Hilton (*Foster*), Harold Scott (*Charlie Taplow*), Walter Randall
D: Henry Cass   **STORY:** Ray Cooney & Tony Hilton
Minor thriller: One-arm murders chill London

The Hand
1966, (Czech), color
W: Trnka Puppets
Jiri Trnka short subject

The Hand
1981, (USA), Edward R. Presman-Ixtlan/Orion/WB, color, 108 mins.
W: Michael Caine (*Jon Lansdale*), Viveca Lindfors (*The Doctress*), Andrea Marcovicci (*Anne*), Nicholas Hormann (*Bill Richman*), Mara Hobel (*Lizzie*), Bruce McGill (*Brian Ferguson*), Annie McEnroe (*Stella Roche*), Rosemary Murphy (*Karen Wagner*), Pat Corley (*The Sheriff*), Tracey Walter (*The Cop*), Ed Marshall (*The Doctor*), Charles Fleischer (*David Maddow*), John Stinson (*The Therapist*), Richard Altman (*Hammond*), Sparky Watt (*The Sgt.*), Brian Kenneth Hume (*The Boy in the Classroom*), Lora Pearson (*The Girl in the Classroom*), Oliver Stone (*The Bum*), Jack Evans, Scott Evans, Randy Evans, Patrick Evans
D & SCR: Oliver Stone, from Marc Brandel's novel *The Lizard's Tail*   **PHOTOG:** King Baggott   **MUSIC:** James Horner
*Standard thriller: Man haunted by his severed hand. cf. **The Beast With Five Fingers***

The Hand at the Window
1915, (GB), Regent/MP, b&w, 4,000 ft. (1219.2m)
P: Charles Weston & Arthur Finn
D: Charles Weston
Standard crime-thriller: "Features a despicable hero, drugs, the eternal triangle, revolvers and a murderess"

The Handmaid's Tale
1990, (USA), Cinecom, color, 109 mins.
W: Natasha Richardson (*Kate*), Faye Dunaway (*Serena Joy*), Aidan Quinn (*Nick*), Elizabeth McGovern (*Moira*), Victoria Tennant (*Aunt Lydia*), Robert Duvall (*The Commander*), David Dukes (*The Doctor*), Traci Lind (*Ofwarren/Janine*), Blanche Baker (*Ofglen*), Zoey Wilson, Kathryn Doby, Karma Ibsen Riley, Reiner Schoene, Lucia Hartpeng, J. Michael Hunter, Lucile McIntyre, Gary Bullock, Julian E. Bell, Allison Holmes, Robert Raiford, Mirjam Bohnet, James A. Carleo III, David Barnes, Jim Grimshaw, Ivan Migel, Mil Nicholson, Doris Boggs, Annemarie Fenske, Linda Pierce, Nina Lynn Blanton, Rhesa Reagan Stone, Sara Seidman, Ed L. Grady, Muse Watson, Janell McLeod, Robert Pentz, Tom McGovern, Elke Ritschel, Jane Learned, James G. Martin Jr., Randall Haynes, Rhonda Bond, Danny Simpkins, Molly Sandick, Stefanie J. Chen, Blair Nicole Struble, Bill Owen
D: Volker Schlondorff   **SCR:** Harold Pinter, from Margaret Atwood's novel   **PHOTOG:** Igor Luther   **MUSIC:** Ryuichi Sakamoto
Major SF-thriller: Intrigue in sterility-ridden future

Hand of Death
1962, (USA), Assoc. Producers/20th-Fox, b&w, 60 mins.
W: John Agar, Paula Raymond, Steve Dunne, John Alonzo, Roy Gordon, Jack Younger, Butch Patrick, Fred Krone, Normann Burton, Joe Besser, Kevin Enright, Jack Donner, Ruth Terry, Chuck Niles, Bob Whitney
WRIT & P: Eugene Ling   **D:** Gene Nelson   **PHOTOG:** Floyd Crosby   **MUSIC:** Sonny Burke
*Original title: **Five Fingers of Death**.*
Standard horror-thriller: Scientist turns into monster

The Hand of Fate
1975, (GB), Willis World Wide/EMI, color, 28 mins.
W: John Laurie
D: David Eady   **STORY:** Percy Hoskins
*reissued (1977) as **Crime Casebook***
Standard short crime-thriller: Newspaper vendor kills wife

The Hand of Night
1966, (GB), Assoc. Brit/Pathe, color, 73 mins.
W: William Sylvester (*Paul Carver*), Diane Clare (*Chantal*), Aliza Gur (*Marisa*), Edward Underdown (*Gunther*), Terence de Marney (*Omar*), William Dexter (*Leclerc*), Sylvia Marriott (*Mrs. Petty*), Avril Sadler (*Mrs. Carver*), The Boscoe Holder Dancers
P: Harry Field   **D:** Frederic Goode   **STORY:** Bruce Stewart
*USA retitle, **The Beast of Morocco***
Standard horror-thriller: Vampiress ensnares explorer. Filmed in North Africa

The Hand of the Artist
1906, (GB), Urban, b&w, 200 ft. (60.1m)
D: Walter R. Booth
Minor fantasy short: Artist draws couple; they come to life and dance cakewalk

The Hand of the Devil
see *La Main du Diable*

The Hand of the Gallows
1960, (W. Ger), RB/Constantin/Exportfilm, b&w, 95 mins.
W: Joachim Fuchsberger, Karin Dor, Fritz Rasp, Elisabeth Flickenschildt, Eddie Arent
D: Harald Reinl, from a story by Edgar Wallace
*A.k.a. **The Terrible People** & **Die Bande Des Schreckens***
Minor thriller

Hands of a Killer
see *Planets Against Us*

Hands of a Murderer
1990, (GB), Green Pond-Storke/Yorkshire/Tradewinds, Made for TV, color, 90 mins.
W: Edward Woodward (*Sherlock Holmes*), John Hillerman (*Dr. John Watson*), Anthony Andrews (*Prof. Edward Moriarty*), Kim Thomson (*Angela/Sophie DeVere*), Peter Jeffrey (*Mycroft Holmes*), Warren Clarke (*Col. Boothe*), Terence Lodge (*Insp. Lestrade*)
D: Stuart Orme   **TELEPLAY:** Charles Edward Pogue, from characters created by Sir Arthur Conan Doyle   **PHOTOG:** Ken Westbury   **SPCL-FX:** John Evans   **MUSIC** Colin Towns
*A.k.a. **Sherlock Holmes, Hands of a Murderer** and **Sherlock Holmes and the Prince of Crime***
TVM, standard thriller: Famed sleuth and nemesis vie for British military secrets

Hands of a Stranger
1962, (USA), Glenwood-Neve/AA, b&w, 86 mins.
W: Paul Lukather, Joan Harvey, Michael Du Pont, Ted Otis, James Stapleton, David Kramer, Larry Haddon, Michael Rye, George Sawaya, Sally

Kellerman, Elaine Martone, Irish McCalla, Barry Gordon
P: Newton Arnold & Michael duPont **WRIT & DIR:** Newton Arnold, inspired by Maurice Renard's novel *The Hands of Orlac* **PHOTOG:** Henry Cronjager **MUSIC:** Richard LaSalle
Standard horror-thriller: Murderer's hands transplanted

Hands of a Stranger: SALLY KELLERMAN AND MICHAEL DU PONT

Hands of a Strangler
*see **The Hands of Orlac** (1959)*

The Hands of a Wizard
1908, (GB), Urban, b&w, 365 ft. (111.3m)
D: Walter R. Booth
Minor fantasy short: Conjuror's hands change eggs into chickens, dice, cards

Hands of Death
*see **Beyond the Living***

The Hands of Orlac (1924)
*see **Orlacs Haende***

The Hands of Orlac (1935)
*see **Mad Love***

The Hands of Orlac
1959, (GB-Fr), Britannia-British Lion/Continental, b&w, 105 mins.
W: Mel Ferrer (*Stephen Orlac*), Christopher Lee (*Neron*), Dany Carrel (*Li-Lang*), Felix Aylmer (*Cochrane*), Lucile Saint Simon (*Louise*), Donald Wolfit (*Volcheff*), Yanilou (*Emilie*), Donald Pleasence (*Coates*), Basil Sydney (*Siedelman*), Peter Reynolds, Campbell Singer, Edouard Hemme, David Peel, Anita Sharp Bolster, Mireille Perrey, Arnold Diamond, Janina Faye, Manning Wilson, Walter Randall, Gertan Klauber
P: Steven Pallos & Donald Taylor **D:** Edmond T. Greville **SCR:** John Baines & Edmond T. Greville, from Maurice Renard's novel **PHOTOG:** Desmond Dickinson **MUSIC:** Claude Bolling
*USA retitle, **Hands of a Strangler***
*Standard horror-thriller: Pianist's hands are replaced by those from strangler's corpse. cf. **Mad Love** and **Orlacs Haende***

Hands of the Ripper
1971, (GB), Hammer/Univ, color, 85 mins.
W: Eric Porter (*Pritchard*), Jane Merrow (*Laura*), Angharad Rees (*Anna*), Dora Bryan (*Mrs. Golding*), Marjorie Rhodes (*Mrs. Bryant*), Derek Godfrey (*Dysart*), Norman Bird (*The Inspector*), Keith Bell (*Michael*), Marjie Lawrence (*Dolly*), Lynda Baron (*Long Liz*), April Wilding (*Catherine*), Molly Weir (*The Maid*), Margaret Rawlings (*Mme. Bullard*), A.J. Brown (*Rev. Anderson*), Elizabeth MacLennan (*Mrs. Wilson*), Peter Munt (*Pleasants*), Charles Lamb (*The Guard*), Philip Ryan (*The Policeman*), Katya Wyeth (*The Whore*), Barry Lowe (*Wilson*), Anne Clune, Beulah Hughes, Tallulah Miller, Vicki Woolf
P: Aida Young **D:** Peter Sasdy **SCR:** L.W. Davidson **STORY:** Edward Spencer Shew **PHOTOG:** Kenneth Talbot **MUSIC:** Christopher Gunning
Standard thriller: Young woman possessed by evil spirit of dead father, Jack the Ripper

The Hand that Rocks the Cradle
1992, (USA), Interscope/Hollywood Pictures/Buena Vista, color, 110 mins.
W: Rebecca De Mornay (*Peyton*), Annabella Sciorra (*Claire*), Matt McCoy (*Michael*), Ernie Hudson (*Solomon*), Julianne Moore (*Marlene*), Madeline Zima (*Emma*), John de Lancie (*Dr. Mott*), Kevin Skousen (*Marty*), Mitchell Laurance (*The Lawyer*), Justin Zaremby (*The Schoolyard Bully*), Todd Jamieson (*The Surgeon*), Eric, Jennifer & Ashley Melander (*Baby Joe*), Cliff Lenz & Penny LeGate ("*Seattle Today*" *Hosts*), Therese Xavier Tinling (*The Receptionist*), Mary Anne Owen (*Dr. Mott's Nurse*), Laura Ferri, Dee Dee Van Zyl, Susan Chin, Cristine McMurdo-Wallis, Sara Jennifer Sharp, Jane Jones, Kimberly Hill, Ericka Matson, Robert James, Aimee Kanemori, Elaine Micklesen, Brian Finney, Stephen West, David Scully, Julie Clemmons,

Joseph Franklin, Tom Francis, Jeff Conkel, Patrick Ryals, Chip Lucia
P: David Madden **D:** Curtis Hanson **SCR:** Amanda Silver **PHOTOG:** Robert Elswit **MUSIC:** Graeme Revell
Major thriller: Vengeful nanny disrupts family

Hangar 18
1980, (USA), Taft Int'l/Sunn Classics, color, 93 mins.
W: Darren McGavin (*Harry Forbes*), Robert Vaughn (*Gordon*), Gary Collins (*Steve*), James Hampton (*Lew*), Philip Abbott (*Frank*), Pamela Bellwood (*Sarah*), Tom Hallick (*Phil*), Steven Keats (*Paul*), William Schallert (*Mills*), Cliff Osmond (*The Sheriff*), Andrew Bloch (*Neal*), Stuart Pankin (*Sam*), Betty Ann Carr (*Flo*), H.M. Wynant, Bill Zuckert, Jesse Bennett, Robert Bristol, Ed E. Carroll, J.R. Clark, Craig Clyde, John William Galt, Anne Galvan, Ken Hapner, Michael Irving, Bruce Katzman, Peter Liakakis, Debra MacFarlane, Chet Norris, H.E.D. Redford, Max Robinson, Ocie Robinson, Michael Ruud, Joseph Campanella, Gary Collins, Pamela Bellwood, Robert Vaughn, Cliff Osmond, Tom Hallick, James Hampton, Philip Abbott, Steven Keats, H.M. Wynant, William Schallert, Andrew Bloch, Betty Ann Carr, Stuart Pankin, Bill Zuckert
P: Charles E. Sellier Jr. **D:** James L. Conway **SCR:** Steven Thornley **STORY:** Tom Chapman & James L. Conway **PHOTOG:** Paul Hipp **MUSIC:** John Cacavas
*TV-retitle, **Invasion Force***
Minor SF-thriller: UFO supposedly captured by gov't

The Hanged Man
1964, (USA), Univ/NBC-TV, color, 87 mins.
W: Edmond O'Brien, Vera Miles, Robert Culp, Brenda Scott, J. Carrol Naish, Norman Fell, Gene Raymond, Pat Buttram, Archie Moore, Edgar Bergen
D: Don Siegel **TELEPLAY:** Jack Laird & Stanford Whitmore, from Dorothy B. Hughes' novel *Ride the Pink Horse*
*TVM (orig. for NBC's "Project 190" series), minor thriller: Thief fakes own death, goes undercover. cf. **Ride the Pink Horse***

Hanging Stockings on a Christmas Tree
*see **The Night Before Christmas***

The Hanging Woman
*see **La Orgia de los Muertos***

The Hangman Waits
1947, (GB), Five Star/PSI, b&w, 63 mins.
W: John Turnbull (*The Inspector*), Beatrice Campbell (*The Usherette*), Anthony Baird (*Sinclair*), Kenneth Warrington, Michael Balzagette, Edwin Ellis, Leonard Sharp
P: A. Barr-Smith & Roger Proudlock **WRIT & D:** A. Barr-Smith
Standard thriller: Inspector and reporter track down murdering organist

The Hangover
*see **The Female Jungle***

Hangover Square
1945, (USA), 20th-Fox, b&w, 77 mins.
W: Laird Cregar, Linda Darnell, George Sanders, Frederick Worlock, Alan Napier, Glenn Langan, Faye Marlowe, Francis Ford
P: Robert Bassler **D:** John Brahm **SCR:** Barre Lyndon, from Patrick Hamilton's novel **PHOTOG:** Joseph La Shelle **MUSIC:** Bernard Herrmann
Classic thriller: Composer kills during mental blackouts. Cregar's last film (posthumous)

Hangover Square: LINDA DARNELL

Hanky Panky Cards
1907, (GB), Urban, b&w, 225 ft. (68.6m)
D: Walter R. Booth
Minor fantasy short: Playing cards become animated

Hans Christain Andersen
1952, (USA), RKO, color, 120 mins.
W: Danny Kaye, Zizi Jeanmarie, Farley Granger, Roland Petit, John Qualen, Joey Walsh
D: Charles Vidor   **SCR:** Moss Hart   **PHOTOG:** Harry Stradling   **MUSIC:** Frank Loesser   **SONGS:** *Wonderful, Wonderful Copenhagen & The Ugly Duckling*
Juvenile film-bio with fantasy segments: Life of Danish children's writer

Hans Christian Andersen's Magic Adventure
1973, (Sp), color, 75 mins.
Juvenile animated fantasy

Hansel and Gretel
1987, (USA), color, 90 mins.
W: Hugh Pollard, Nicola Stapleton
Standard fantasy: Witch locks children in gingerbread house

Happy Birthday, Love George
1973, (USA), Cinema 5, color, 90 mins
W: Ron Howard, Cloris Leachman, Bobby Darin, Thayer David, Simon Oakland, Patricia Neal
P & D: Darren McGavin   **SCR:** Robert Clouse
A.k.a. **Run, Stranger, Run**
Standard thriller: Religious-fanatic couple befriends abused youth, gory murders ensue. Bobby Darin's last film

Happy Birthday to Me
1981, (Can), John Dunning-Andre Link/Col, color, 108 mins.
W: Glenn Ford (*Dr. Faraday*), Melissa Sue Anderson (*Virginia*), Lawrence Dane (*Hal*), Tracy Bregman (*Ann*), Jack Blum (*Alfred*), Sharon Acker (*Estelle*), Frances Hyland (*Mrs. Patterson*), Matt Craven (*Steve*), Richard Rabiere (*Greg*), Lenore Zann (*Maggie*), Lisa Langlois (*Amelia*), David Eisner (*Rudi*), Earl Pennington (*Lt. Tracy*), Lesleh Donaldson (*Bernadette*), Vlasta Vrana (*The Bartender*), Michel Rene LaBelle (*Etienne*), Jerome Tiberghien (*Prof. Heregard*), Murray Westgate (*The Gatekeeper*), Alan Katz (*Ann's Date*), Maurice Pedbrey (*Dr. Feinblum*), Griffith Brewer (*Verger*), Walter Massey (*The Conventioneer*), Ron Lea (*Amelia's Date*), Karen Stephen (*Mrs. Calhoun*), Nick Kilbertus (*The Anesthetist*), Louis Del Grande (*The Surgeon*), Terry Haig (*Feinhlum's Ass't*), Damir Andrei (*The Jr. Surgeon*), Gina Dick (*The Waitress*), Stephanie Miller (*The Nurse*), Steven Mayoff (*The Police*), Len Wyatt, Aram Barkev, Alan Barnett, Paul Board, Marc Degagne, Victor Knight, Bruce Gooding, Rollie Nincheri, Joe Wertheimer, Keith Sutherland, Herbert Vool, Nancy Allan, Debbie McGellin, Karen Hynes, Tracy-Marie Langdon, Lori Timmons, Kathy Reid, Debbie Tull, Lynn Wilson
D: J. Lee Thompson   **SCR:** John Saxton, Peter Jobin, & Timothy Bond   **STORY:** John Saxton   **PHOTOG:** Miklos Lente   **MUSIC:** Bo Harwood & Lance Rubin
Standard thriller: Girl has homicidal twin

The Happy Land
1943, (USA), 20th-Fox, b&w, 75 mins.
W: Don Ameche, Frances Dee, Harry Carey, Richard Crane, Henry (Harry) Morgan, Natasha Gurdin [Natalie Wood], Minor Watson, Cara Williams, Dickie Moore, Ann Rutherford
D: Irving Pichel, from MacKinlay Kantor's novel   **PHOTOG:** Joseph La Shelle   **MUSIC:** Cyril Mockridge
Standard fantasy: Grandfather's ghost comforts bereaved family

Harakiri
1962, (Jap), Unijapan/Atlas, b&w, 139 mins.
W: Akira Ishihama, Yoshio Inaba, Rentaro Mikuni, Tatsuya Nakadai, Shima Iwashita, Masao Mishima, Tetsuro Tamba
D: Masaki Kobayashi
Standard melodrama

The Harbour Lights
1914, (GB), Neptune/Globe, b&w, 3,275 ft. (998.2m)
W: Gerald Lawrence (*Lt. David Kingsley*), Mercy Hatton (*Dora Vane*), Daisy Cordell (*Lina Nelson*), Fred Morgan (*Nicholas Morland*), Gregory Scott (*Frank Morland*), Douglas Payne (*Mark Helstone*), Joan Ritz (*Peggy Chudleigh*), Bryan Powley (*Capt. Hardy*), John East (*Capt. Nelson*), May Lynn (*Mrs. Helstone*), Brian Daly (*Tom Dossiter*), Helen Lainsbury (*Polly*)
D: Percy Nash   **SCR:** John M. East & Brian Daly, from a play by George R. Sims & Henry Pettitt
Standard crime-thriller: Lieutenant accused of shooting squire to save heiress is cleared by dying confession

Hard Hunted
1992, (USA), color, 98 mins.
W: Dona Speir, Roberta Vasquez
Minor thriller: Female agents track madman intent on detonating nuclear device

Hard Rock Zombies
1985, (USA), Cannon, color, 90 mins.
W: E.J. Curcio, Geno Andrews, Sam Mann, Mick McMains, Ted Wells, Lisa Toothman, Jennifer Coe, Jack Bliesener, Crystal Shaw
P & D: Krishna Shas   **SCR:** Krishna Shas & David Ball   **PHOTOG:** Tom Richmond   **SPCL-FX:** John Buechler   **MUSIC:** Paul Sabu
Minor horror-fantasy: Undead encounter heavy metal music

Hard Times for Vampires
see **Tempi Duri per i Vampiri**

Hard to Die
1993, (USA), color, 85 mins.
W: Robyn Harris, Melissa Moore, Debra dare, Lindsay Taylor, Forrest J. Ackerman, Bridget Carney
D: Jim Wynorski
Minor fantasy-thriller: Women battle demon in high-rise office building

Hardware
1990, (GB), Wicked Films/Millimeter, color, 91 mins.
W: Dylan McDermott (*Mo*), Stacey Travis (*Jill*), John Lynch (*Shades*), Carl McCoy (*Nomad*), Iggy Pop (*Angry Bob*), Lemmy (*The Taxi Driver*), William Hootkins (*Lincoln*), Mark Northover (*Alvy*), Paul McKenzie (*Vernon*), Mac MacDonald (*The Newscaster*), Chris McHallem, Barbara Yu Ling, Oscar James, Arnold Lee, Susie Ng, Fred Leeown, Mimi Chinn, Sebastian Chee
WRIT & D: Richard Stanley   **PHOTOG:** Steve Chivers   **SPCL-FX COORD:** Barney Jeffrey   **ORIG MUSIC:** Simon Boswell
Standard SF-thriller: Robot stalks post-nuke survivors

Harlequin
1980, (Austral), Hemdale, color, 93 mins.
W: Robert Powell, David Hemmings, Carmen Duncan, Broderick Crawford
P: Tony Ginnane   **D:** Simon Powell   **SCR:** Everett DeRoche   **MUSIC:** Brian May
Standard thriller: Mysterious healer cures boy with leukemia

The Harlequinade
1910, (GB), Acme Films/C&M, b&w, 290 ft. (88.4m)
W: Fred Rains
D: Fred Rains
Minor fantasy short: Clown cuts off barber's head, fools suffragettes

The Harlequinade (1913)
see **Here We are Again**

The Harlequinade
1915, (GB), Union Jack/DFSA, b&w, 518 ft. (157.9m)
Standard comedy-fantasy

Harlequinade—What They Found in the Laundry Basket
1901, (GB), Williamson/Gaumont, b&w, 240 ft. (73.2m)
D: James Williamson
Minor fantasy short: Clown's basket makes people vanish

The Hanged Man: VERA MILES

Harlequins at the Midnight Hour
1995, (USA), color, 95 mins.
<u>W</u>: Patsy Kensit, Simon MacCorkindale, Keegan MacIntosh
TVM, standard thriller: Young widow becomes governess at scientist's eerie mansion

The Harmless Lunatic's Escape
1908, (GB), Hepworth, b&w
<u>D</u>: Lewin Fitzhamon
Standard thriller: Madman escapes in doctor's car, crashes into wall

The H.A.R.M. Machine
see Agent for H.A.R.M.

The Harper Mystery
1913, (GB), Turner Films/Gaumont, b&w, 3,100 ft. (944.9m)
<u>W</u>: Florence Turner (*Margaret Kent*), Coley Goodman (*Joe Miller*), Frank Tennant (*Steve Bright*), Mr. Sefton (*The Inspector*), Mr. Lewellyn, Mr. Wrighton, Miss Sibley
<u>WRIT & DIR</u>: Larry Trimble
Standard crime-thriller: Girl detective poses as ex-convict, saves old woman from kidnappers

Harry and the Hendersons
1987, (USA), Amblin/Univ, color, 111 mins.
<u>W</u>: John Lithgow, Melinda Dillon, Don Ameche, Kevin Peter Hall (*Harry*), David Suchet, Joshua Ruddy, M. Emmet Walsh, Margaret Langrick, John F. Bloom, Lainie Kazan
<u>D</u>: William Dear   <u>SCR</u>: William Dear, William E. Martin, & Ezra D. Rappaport   <u>PHOTOG</u>: Allen Daviau   <u>MUSIC</u>: Bruce Broughton   <u>SONG</u>: *Love Lives On*
Modest comedy-fantasy: Family befriends bigfoot

Harvest Home
see The Dark Secret of Harvest Home

The Harvest of Sin
1912, (GB), Cricks & Martin, b&w, 1,250 ft. (381m)
<u>D</u>: Edwin J. Collins
Standard thriller: Detective exposes bank cashier who framed clerk for theft

Harvey
1950, (USA), Univ, b&w, 104 mins.
<u>W</u>: James Stewart (*Elwood P. Dowd*), Josephine Hull, Charles Drake, Wallace Ford, Cecil Kellaway, Peggy Dow, Jesse White, Nana Bryant, Victoria Horne
<u>P</u>: John Beck   <u>D</u>: Henry Koster   <u>SCR</u>: Mary C. Chase & Oscar Brodney, from the play by Mary C. Chase   <u>PHOTOG</u>: William Daniels   <u>MUSIC</u>: Frank Skinner
Classic comedy: Eccentric has invisible rabbit friend

The Hat Box Mystery
1947, (USA), SG, b&w, 44 mins.
<u>W</u>: Tom Neal, Pamela Blake
Minor thriller

Hatchet for a Honeymoon
1971, (It-Sp), Pan Latina-Mercury/Avco-Embassy TV, color, 83 mins.
<u>W</u>: Stephen Forsyth (*John Harrington*), Dagmar Lassander (*Helen*), Laura Betti, Jesus Puente, Femi Benussi, Alan Collins, Antonia Mas, Gerard Tichy, Fortunato Pascuale, Veroniva Llimera, Jose Ignacio Abadaz, Monserrat Riba, Silvia Lienas
<u>D & PHOTOG</u>: Mario Bava   <u>SCR</u>: Santiago Moncada   <u>MUSIC</u>: Sante Romitelli
Stylish horror-thriller: Psycopathic designer kills. US release by GGP, 1974

Hatchet Murders
see Profundo Rosso

A Hateful Bondage
1914, (GB), Britannia Films/Pathe, b&w, 2,300 ft. (701m)
<u>W</u>: Enid Groome (*Margaret Spencer*)
<u>D</u>: Lewin Fitzhamon
Standard crime-thriller: Children's entertainer stops sister from robbing host

The Hat of Surprises
see Le Chapeau a Surprises

The Hatton Garden Robbery
1915, (GB), British Oak, b&w, 1,130 ft. (344.4m)
<u>W</u>: James Russell (*The Man*)
<u>D</u>: Ethyle Batley
Standard crime-thriller: Stolen diamond hidden in coat

The Hatter's Ghost
1982, (Fr), color, 120 mins.
<u>W</u>: Michel Serrault, Charles Aznavour, Monique Chaumette, Aurore Clement
<u>D</u>: Claude Chabrol, from a novel by Georges Simenon
Minor thriller: Tailor learns nephew is mass killer

The Hat with Many Surprises
see Le Chapeau a Surprises

The Haunted
1991, (USA), Fox-TV, color, 95 mins.
<u>W</u>: Sally Kirkland (*Janet Smurl*), Jeffrey DeMunn (*Jack Smurl*), Louise Latham (*Mary Smurl*), George D. Wallace (*John Smurl*), Joyce Van Patten (*Cora Miller*), Stephen Markle (*Ed Warren*), Diane Baker (*Lorraine Warren*), Allison Barron, William O'Connell, Cassie Yates, Michelle Collins, Krista Murphy, Ashley Bank, John O'Leary, Jake Jacobs, Parker Whitman, Hope Garber, Benj Thall, Sharon Conely, Freyda Thomas, Julie Payne, Mark Chaet, Michael Prince, Gibby Brand, Claudette Roach, Tim Rich, Anthony Delan, John Mallory Asher, Julie Hickman
<u>D</u>: Robert Mandel   <u>TELEPLAY</u>: Darrah Cloud, from the book by Robert Curran, Jack Smurl, Janet Smurl, Ed Warren & Lorraine Warren   <u>PHOTOG</u>: Michael Margulies   <u>MUSIC</u>: Richard Bellis
Fact-based TVM, standard thriller: Spooks scare family

Haunted (1996)
<u>W</u>: Jennifer Tilly, Ed Asner, Shawn Alex Thompson, Nancy Drake
<u>D</u>: Paul Shapiro   <u>SCR</u>: Jay Stapleton, from James Herbert's novel   <u>PHOTOG</u>: Alan Kivilo   <u>MUSIC</u>: Jonathan Goldsmith

Haunted
1996, (GB), color, 110 mins.
<u>W</u>: Aidan Quinn (*David Ash*), Kate Beckinsale (*Christina Mariell*), Jennifer Tilly, Ed Asner, Shawn Alex Thompson, Nancy Drake
<u>D</u>: Paul Shapiro   <u>SCR</u>: Jay Stapleton, from James Herbert's novel   <u>PHOTOG</u>: Alan Kivilo   <u>MUSIC</u>: Jonathan Goldsmith
Modest horror-thriller: Skeptical psychology professor driven mad by apparitions

The Haunted and the Hunted
see Dementia 13

The Haunted Bedroom
1907, (GB), Urban, b&w, 250 ft. (76.2m)
<u>D</u>: Walter R. Booth
Minor fantasy short: Weird happenings perplex

Haunted by Her Past
1987, (USA), Norton Wright/ITC/NBC-TV, color, 95 mins.
<u>W</u>: Susan Lucci, John James (*Eric Beckett*), Robin Thomas (*Charles Kamen*), Marcia Strassman (*Rita Kamen*), Douglas Seale (*Innkeeper MacVey*), Madeleine Sherwood (*Goode*), Kay Hawtrey, Finola Hughes, Page Fletcher, Bernard Behrens, Chris Owens, Susan Douglas Rubes, Deborah Taylor, Brian Taylor, John Stoneham, Victor Ertmanis, Avery Saltzman, Jimmy Loftus, Jim Bearden, Karen Woolridge, Dwayne McLean, Catherine Disher
<u>D</u>: Michael Pressman   <u>PHOTOG</u>: Bert Dunk   <u>MUSIC</u>: Paul Chihara
TVM, minor fantasy-thriller: Modern woman possessed by spirit of 18th-century murderess

The Haunted Castle (1896)
see Le Manoir du Diable

A Hatchet for the Honeymoon: STEPHEN FORSYTH

The Haunted Castle (1897, Fr)
see Le Chateau Hante

The Haunted Castle
1897, (GB), G.A. Smith, b&w, 50 ft. (15.2m)
<u>D</u>: George Albert Smith
Minor fantasy short: Spooks romp

The Haunted Castle (1921)
see Schloss Vogelod

The Haunted Castle (1947)
see Just William's Luck

The Haunted Cave
1898, (Fr), Star, b&w
D: Georges Melies
Minor thriller

The Haunted Curiosity Shop
1901, (GB), R.W. Paul, b&w, 140 ft. (42.7m)
D: W.R. Booth
Standard fantasy short: Egyptian mummy revives, scares curio dealer

Haunted Honeymoon (1940)
see Busman's Honeymoon

Haunted Honeymoon
1986, (USA), Orion, color, 82 mins.
W: Gene Wilder (*Larry Abot*), Gilda Radner (*Vickie Pearle*), Dom DeLuise (*Aunt Kate*), Peter Vaughan (*Francis*), Jonathan Pryce, Paul L. Smith, Bryan Pringle, Ann Way, Don Fellows, Jim Carter, Eve Ferret, Roger Ashton-Griffiths, R.J. Bell, Jo Koss, Will Kenton
D: Gene Wilder **SCR:** Gene Wilder & Terence Marsh **PHOTOG:** Fred Schuler **SPCL-FX CONSULT:** John Stears **MUSIC:** John Morris
Minor comedy-thriller: Radio stars spend night in creepy castle

The Haunted House
1921, (USA), Comique/Metro, b&w, 2 reels
W: Buster Keaton, Eddie Cline, Virginia Fox
WRIT & D:, Buster Keaton, Eddie Cline
Standard comedy-thriller

The Haunted House
1928, (USA), First Nat'l, b&w, 7 reels (5,755 ft./1754.1m)
W: Larry Kent (*Billy*), Thelma Todd (*The Nurse*), Flora Finch (*Mrs. Rackham*), William V. Mong (*The Caretaker*), Eve Southern (*The Sleepwalking Girl*), Edmund Breese (*James Herbert*), Barbara Bedford (*Nancy*), Montagu Love (*The Mad Doctor*), Chester Conklin (*Mr. Rackham*), Sidney Bracy (*Tully*), Johnnie Gough (*Jack, the Chauffeur*)
D: Benjamin Christensen **SCR:** Richard Bee & Lajos Biro, from Owen Davis' play **PHOTOG:** Sol Polito
Standard comedy-thriller: Greedy heirs seek hidden bonds

The Haunting: JULIE HARRIS AND CLAIRE BLOOM

Haunted House (1947)
see Just William's Luck

The Haunted House of Horror
1969, (GB), Tigon/AIP, color, 92 mins.
W: Frankie Avalon (*Chris*), Jill Haworth (*Sheila*), Dennis Price (*The Inspector*), Mark Wynter (*Gary*), Gina Warwick (*Sylvia*), George Sewell (*Bob Kellett*), Richard O'Sullivan (*Peter*), Carol Dilworth (*Dorothy*), Veronica Doran (*Madge*), Julian Barnes (*Richard*), Robin Stewart (*Henry*), Clifford Earl (*The Police Sgt.*), Jan Holden (*Peggy*), Robert Raglan (*Insp. Bradley*)
P: Tony Tenser **D:** Michael Armstrong **STORY:** Michael Armstrong & Peter Marcus **PHOTOG:** Jack Atchelor **MUSIC:** Reg Tilsely
*USA retitle, **Horror House**, (AIP, 1970), A.k.a. **The Dark***
Standard thriller: Grisly murders at haunted house party

The Haunted Man
1966, (GB), Merton Park/Anglo-Amalgamated, color, 26 mins.
W: Keith Barron (*Mark Godfrey*), James Ellis (*Bill Kenton*), Alexandra Bastedo (*Laura*), Isobel Black (*Bridget*), John Gabriel (*The Defense*), Tenniel Evans (*The Prosecution*), John Boxer (*The Jeweler*)
P: Jack Greenwood **D:** Stanley Willis **STORY:** James Eastwood, from characters created by Edgar Lustgarten
Standard short crime-thriller: Injured actor hunts thieves

The Haunted Monte Bravo
see The Beast of Hollow Mountain

Haunted Palace
1949, (GB), Gwynne/Premier, b&w, 34 mins.
W: Shaw Desmond, Ian Russell, John Warren, John Singer, Helene Cooney, Anne Wrigg, Hilary Pritchard, William Holloway
WRIT & D: Richard Fisher
reissued 1952
Standard fantasy short: Ghost expert reconstructs legends of phantom monk, St. James Palace, Hampton Court Palace, etc.

The Haunted Palace
1963, (USA), AIP, color, 85 mins.
W: Vincent Price, Debra Paget, Lon Chaney Jr., Leo Gordon, Frank Maxwell, Elisha Cook Jr., John Dierkes, Cathy Merchant, Barboura Morris, Bruno Ve Sota, Darlene Lucht, Guy Wilkerson, Milton Par-sons, Harry Ellerbe
P & D: Roger Corman **SCR:** Charles Beaumont, from H.P. Lovecraft's short story *The Case of Charles Dexter Ward* **PHOTOG:** Floyd Crosby **MUSIC:** Ronald Stein **DESIGN:** Daniel Haller
*orig. to be titled **The Haunted Village***
Standard horror-fantasy: Soul of dead warlock takes possession of descendant

The Haunted Picture Gallery
1899, (GB), G.A.S. Films, b&w, 75 ft. (22.9m)
D: George Albert Smith
Standard fantasy short: Gainsborough painting comes alive, dances minuet

The Haunted Scene Painter
1904, (GB), R.W. Paul, b&w, 180 ft. (54.9m)
D: Walter R. Booth
Minor fantasy short: Theatre properties (dragon, ghost, moon, etc.) become animated

The Haunted School
1986, (Austral), color, 100 mins.
W: Carol Drinkwater, James Laurie (*Joseph*), Emil Minty (*Patrick*), Grant Navin (*Richard*)
Minor fantasy: Schoolteacher opposes ghost

The Haunted Sea
1998, (USA), color, 75 mins.
W: James Brolin, Joanna Pacula (*Mary*), Krista Allen (*Medina*)
Made-for-Video, standard fantasy-thriller: Steamer crew beset by spooks

Haunted Spooks
1920, (USA), Hal Roach/Rolin, b&w, 2 reels
W: Harold Lloyd, Mildred Davis
Standard comedy-thriller

Haunted Summer
1988, (USA), Cannon, color, 115 mins.
W: Eric Stoltz (*Percy Shelley*), Alice Krige (*Mary Godwin*), Philip Anglim (*Lord Byron*), Laura Dern (*Calire Clairmont*), Alex Winter (*John Polidori*)
P: Martin Bell **D:** Ivan Passer **SCR:** Lewis John Carlino, from Anne Edwards' novel **PHOTOG:** Giuseppe Rotunno
*Standard melodrama: 19th-century intellectuals have bizarre vacation... cf. **Gothic***

Haunted Symphony
1994, (USA), color, 85 mins.
W: Jennifer Burns (*Gabrielle*), Ben Cross (*Marius*), Doug Wert, Beverly Garland
D: David Tausik
Standard fantasy-thriller: Satanic symphony causes mayhem

The Haunted Village
see The Haunted Palace (1963)

Hauntedween
1991, (USA), color
W: Brien Blakely, Blake Pickett, Brad Hanks, Bart White, Leslee Lacey, Ethan Adler
D: Doug Robertson
Minor thriller: Frat-house prank victim returns for revenge

Haunted World
see **Terrore Nello Spazio**

Haunters of the Deep
1985, (GB), Longbow Films/CFF, color, 61 mins.
<u>W</u>: Andrew Keir (*Capt. Tregellis*), Barbara Ewing (*Mrs. Holman*), Bob Sherman (*Roche*), Brian Osborne (*Holman*), Peter Lovstrom (*Daniel*), Tom Watson (*Frank Lacey*), Sean Arnold (*Shannon*), Patrick Murray (*Jack*), Gary Simmons (*Josh*), Barry Craine (*The Leader*), Philip Mar-tin (*Billy Bray*), Amy Taylor (*Becky Roche*)
<u>P</u>: Gordon Scott <u>D</u>: Andrew Bogle <u>SCR</u>: Andrew Bogle, Terry Barbour, & Tony Attard <u>STORY</u>: Terry Barbour <u>PHOTOG</u>: Ronald Maasz <u>MUSIC</u>: Ed Welch
Standard juvenile fantasy: Ghost warns boy that tin mine will cave in

The Haunting
1963, (GB), Argyle/MGM, b&w, 112 mins.
<u>W</u>: Julie Harris (*Eleanor Vance*), Richard Johnson (*Dr. John Markway*), Claire Bloom (*Theodora*), Russ Tamblyn (*Luke Sanderson*), Lois Maxwell (*Grace Markway*), Rosalie Crutchley (*Mrs. Dudley*), Valentine Dyall (*Mr. Dudley*), Ronald Adam (*Eldridge Harper*), Fay Compton (*Mrs. Sanderson*), Freda Knorr (*Mrs. Crain*) Diane Clare (*Carrie Fredericks*), Janet Mansell, Amy Dalby, Pamela Buckley, Howard Lang, Paul Maxwell, Mavis Villiers, Verina Greenlaw, Rosemary Dorken, Claud Jones, Connie Tilton, Susan Richards
<u>P & D</u>: Robert Wise <u>SCR</u>: Nelson Gidding, from Shirley Jackson's novel *The Haunting of Hill House* <u>PHOTOG</u>: David Boulton <u>SPCL-FX</u>: Tom Howard <u>MUSIC</u>: Humphrey Searle
Fr retitle, **La Maison du Diable (The Devil's House)**
Superior fantasy-thriller: Mixed group investigates old mansion with grim history

Haunting Fear
1991, (USA), color, 88 mins.
<u>W</u>: Brinke Stevens, Karen Black, Robert Quarry, Jan-Michael Vincent, Delia Sheppard, Michael Berryman, Jay Richardson, Robert Clarke
<u>D</u>: Fred Olen Ray <u>SCR</u>: Sherman Scott, based on Edgar Allan Poe's short story *The Premature Burial*
Standard horror-thriller: Man fears untimely entombment

The Haunting of Hamilton High
1987, (Can), Simcom Int'l/Samuel Goldwyn, color, 96 mins.
<u>W</u>: Michael Ironside, Wendy Lyon, Justin Louis, Richard Monette, Lisa Schrage, Terri Hawkes, Brock Simpson, Jay Smith, Beverly Hendry, Beth Gondek, Wendell Smith, John Olsen, Steve Atkinson, Robert Lewis, Michael Evans, Loretta Bailey, Dennis Robinson, John Ferguson
<u>D</u>: Bruce Pittman <u>SCR</u>: Ron Oliver <u>PHOTOG</u>: John Herzog <u>SPCL-FX</u>: Jim Doyle <u>MUSIC</u>: Paul Zaz
USA retitle, **Hello Mary Lou: Prom Night II**
Entertaining horror-fantasy: Spirit of slain '50's prom queen possesses girl, gains revenge

The Haunting of Helen Walker
1995, (USA),Made for TV, color
<u>W</u>: Valerie Bertinelli, Diana Rigg
based on Henry James' *The Turn of the Screw*
TVM, standard fantasy-thriller: Evil spirits of two former servants invade English estate cf. **The Innocents**

The Haunting of Julia
see **Full Circle**

The Haunting of Lisa
1996, (USA), Lifetime, cable, color, 95 mins.
<u>W</u>: Cheryl Ladd, Duncan Regehr, Aemilia Robinson
TVM, standard thriller: Girl has visions of child murders

The Haunting of Morella
1990, (USA), Aquarius/Concorde, color, 82 mins.
<u>W</u>: David McCallum (*Gideon*), Nicole Eggert (*Morella/Lenora*), Christopher Halsted (*Guy*), Lana Clarkson (*Coel*), Maria Ford (*Diane*), Jonathan Farwell (*Dr. Gault*), John O'Leary (*Quintis*), Brewster Gould (*Miles Archer*), Gail Harris (*Ilsa*), Clement von Frankenstein (*Judge Brock*), Debbie Dutch (*The Serving Girl*), R.J. Robertson (*Rev. Ward*)
<u>P</u>: Roger Corman <u>D</u>: Jim Wynorski <u>SCR</u>: R.J. Robertson. based on Edgar Allan Poe's short story *Morella* <u>PHOTOG</u>: Zoran Hochstatter <u>MUSIC</u>: Frederic Teetsel & Chuck Cirino <u>DESIGN</u>:Gary Randall
Standard eroto-fantasy (nudity, "jiggle," mild lesbianism): Venal witch seeks rebirth in daughter's body. cf. **Tales of Terror**

The Haunting of Sarah Hardy
1989, (USA), Millennium-Jerry London/Wilshire Court/USA-TV, color, 95 mins.
<u>W</u>: Sela Ward, Michael Woods, Morgan Fairchild, Joe Cronin, Polly Bergen, Roscoe Born, Charles Bernard, Janet Penner, Vana O'Brien, Steven Clark Pachosa, Bethany Ward, Nicholas Leland, Dawn Prociv, Jeff Williams, Richard Wiltshire, Al Taylor, Mitzi Ellis, Rod Pilloud, Tom Enyart, Peggy West, Russ Fast, Todd Tolces, Don Alder, Jane Geeseman, Joanna Goff, Beth Harper, Tracy Conklin, Teddy Deane, Bernard Szymanski, Ross Huffman-Kerr
<u>D</u>: Jerry London <u>TELEPLAY</u>: Thomas Baum, from Jim Flanagan's novel *The Crossing* <u>PHOTOG</u>: Bojan Bazelli <u>SPCL-FX SPRVSR</u>: Gary D'Amico

<u>MUSIC</u>: Michel Rubini
TVM, minor mystery-thriller: Newlywed fears ghostly return of dead mother

The Haunting of Seacliff Inn
1994, (USA), color, 95 mins.
<u>W</u>: William Moses, Ally Sheedy
TVM, standard thriller: Supernatural events when couple buys old home

The Haunting of Silas P. Gould
1915, (GB), Ivy Close Films/Hepworth, b&w, 1,000 ft. (304.8m)
<u>W</u>: Ivy Close (*The Heiress*)
<u>D</u>: Elwin Neame
Standard comedy: Heiress poses as ghost

The Haunting Passion
1983, (USA), BSR-ITC/NBC-TV, color, 97 mins.
<u>W</u>: Jane Seymour (*Julie Evans*), Gerald McRaney (*Dan Evans*), Millie Perkins (*Lois O'Connor*), Ruth Nelson (*Judith Granville*), Paul Rossilli (*Jonathan Kane*), Ivan Bonar (*Thorne Abbott*), Lisa Britt (*Karen Hill*), Ocean Hellman (*Tracy*), Terry David Mulligan (*Steve Roye*), Ted Stidder (*Dr. Corsay*), Tom Heaton (*The TV Director*), Bill Reiter (*Det. Alden*), Lee Taylor (*Coach Richter*), Phil Savath (*Dr. Mosher*)
<u>D</u>: John Korty <u>TELEPLAY</u>: Michael Berk & Douglas Schwartz <u>PHOTOG</u>: Hiro Narita <u>MUSIC</u>: Paul Chihara
TVM, standard fantasy-thriller: Woman seduced by ghost

Haunts
1975, (USA), Nachson/American General/Intercontinental Releasing Corp., color, 98 mins.
<u>W</u>: May Britt (*Ingrid Svenson*), Cameron Mitchell (*Carl*), Aldo Ray (*Sheriff Peterson*), Ben Hammer (*The Vicar*), E.J. Andre (*Doc*), William Gray Espy (*Frankie*), Kendall Jackson (*Loretta*), Susan Nohr (*Nel*), Robert Hippard (*Bill Spry*), Don Dolan (*Hellman*), Lette Rehnolds (*Margaret*), Warren Peters (*Howard Porter*), Jim McKeny (*The Bartender*), Judy Franks (*Mrs. Peterson*), Bob Avery (*The TV Inter-viewer*), Brian Frankish (*The Newscaster*), Margot Lowell (*Brigette*), Larry Finnegan (*Mr. Lewis*), Elmer Adams (*Frank Olsen*), Toni Lemos (*Margaret's Mother*), Norm Rubinfeld, Michele Rubinfeld, Sandy Rubinfeld, Eddie Rubinfeld
<u>D</u>: Herb Freed <u>SCR</u>: Anne Marisse & Herb Freed <u>PHOTOG</u>: Larry Secrist <u>MUSIC</u>: Pino Donaggio
A.k.a. **The Veil**
Minor thriller: Maniacal killer in rural community

Haunts of the Very Rich
1972, (USA), ABC Circle/ABC-TV, color, 73 mins.
<u>W</u>: Lloyd Bridges, Cloris Leachman, Anne Francis, Edward Asner, Tony Bill (*Lyle*), Donna Mills (*Laurie*), Robert Reed (*Fellows*), Moses Gunn (*Seacrist*), Michael Lembeck, Beverly Gill, Todd Martin, Susan Foster, Phyllis Hill
<u>P</u>: Lillian Gallo <u>D</u>: Paul Wendkos <u>TELEPLAY</u>: William Wood, from a story by T.K. Brown <u>PHOTOG</u>: Ben Colman <u>MUSIC</u>: Dominic Frontiere
TVM, standard thriller: Bemused vacationers stranded in eerie resort

Haunts of the Very Rich: LLOYD BRIDGES AND CLORIS LEACHMAN

Hauser's Memory
1970, (USA), Univ/CBS-TV, color, 96 mins.
W: David McCallum (*Hillel*), Susan Strasberg (*Karen*), Leslie Nielsen (*Slaughter*), Helmut Kautner (*Kramer*), Robert Webber (*Dorsey*), Lilli Palmer (*Anna*), Herbert Fleischmann (*Renner*), Hans Elwenspoek (*van Kungen*), Manfred Reddemann (*Borsen*), Peter Capell (*Shepilov*), Peter Ehrlich (*Kucera*), Barbara Lass (*Angelika*), Otto Stern (*Gessler*), Art Brauss (*Bak*), Jochen Busse (*Dieter*), Barbara Capell (*Young Anna*)
D: Boris Sagal   TELEPLAY:, Adrian Spies, loosely based on Curt Siodmak's novel *Donovan's Brain*   PHOTOG: Petrus Schloemp   MUSIC: Bill Byers
TVM, standard SF-thriller: Scientist infused with dead man's memories

Have It Out, My Boy, Have It Out!
1911, (GB), Cricks & Martin, b&w, 475 ft. (144.8m)
D: A.E. Coleby
Standard comedy-fantasy: Patient under gas dreams of imps pulling teeth

Have Rocket, Will Travel
1959, (USA), Col, b&w, 76 mins.
W: Moe Howard, Larry Fine, Joe De Rita, Anna-Lisa, Robert Colbert, Jerome Cowan
P: Harry Romm   D: David Lowell Rich   SCR: Raphael Hayes   PHOTOG: Ray Cory   MUSIC: Mischa Bakaleinikoff
Standard "3 Stooges" SF-comedy: Bumblers have adventure in space

The Hawk
1993, (GB), color, 84 mins.
W: Helen Mirren, George Costigan, Owen Teale, Rosemary Leech
D: David Hayman   SCR: Peter Ransley   MUSIC: Nick Bicat
Unusual thriller: Housewife fears husband is serial killer

Hawkeye, King of the Castle
1915, (GB), Hepworth, b&w, 375 ft. (114.3m)
W: Hay Plumb (*Hawkeye*)
WRIT & D: Hay Plumb
Minor comedy-fantasy short: Castle caretaker deams of fighting knight for hand of maiden

Hawk the Slayer
1980, (GB), Chips/ITC, color, 94 mins.
W: Jack Palance (*Voltan*), John Terry (*Hawk*), Ray Charleson (*Crow*), Bernard Bresslaw (*Gort*), Peter O'Farrell (*Baldin*), Patricia Quinn (*The Woman*), Shane Briant (*Drogo*), Catriona MacColl (*Elaine*), Morgan Sheppard (*Ranulf*), Patrick Magee (*The Priest*), Christopher Benjamin (*Fitzwalter*), Harry Andrews (*The High Abbot*), Roy Kinnear (*The Innkeeper*), Ferdy Mayne (*The Old Man*), Annette Crosbie (*The Abbess*), Cheryl Campbell (*Sister Monica*), Graham Stark (*Sparrow*), Warren Clarke (*Scar*), Declan Mulholland (*Sped*), Derrick O'Connor (*Ralf*), Peter Benson (*The Black Wizard*), Maurice Colbourne (*Axe Man #1*), Barry Stokes (*Axe Man #2*), Robert Putt (*1st Rough in the Tavern*), Anthony Milner (*Ferret*), Ken Parry (*Thomas*), John J. Carney (*The Soldier*), Lindsey Brook (*The Little Nun*), Stephen Rayne (*Brother Peter*), Eddie Stacey (*Chak*), Jo England (*The 1st Nun*), Frankie Cosgrave (*The 2nd Nun*), Melissa Wiltsie (*The 3rd Nun*), Mark Cooper (*2nd Rough in the Tavern*)
P: Harry Robertson   D: Terry Marcel   ORIG STORY & SCR: Terry Marcel & Harry Robertson   PHOTOG: Paul Beeson   SPCL-FX: Effects Associates   MUSIC: Harry Robertson
Standard adventure-fantasy: Brothers vie for possession of magic sword

Hawthorne's Twice-Told Tales
see Twice-Told Tales

Haxan (Witchcraft)
1920, (Swed), Svenska, b&w, 82 mins. (6,840 ft./2084.8m)
W: Maren Pedersen, Elith Pio, Tora Teje, Oscar Stribolt, Clara Pontoppidan, John Andersen, Astrid Holm, Poul Reumert, Alice O'Fredericks, Karen Winther, Benjamin Christensen
WRIT & D: Benjamin Christensen   PHOTOG: John Ankerstjerne
USA retitle, Witchcraft Through the Ages (Ernst Mattsson, 1929)
Classic fantasy: Examination of satanism

He Knows You're Alone
W: Dana Barron (*Diana*), James Rebhorn (*The Professor*), Paul Gleason (*Daley*), Joseph Leon (*Ralph the Tailor*), James Carroll (*Phil*), Brian Byers (*Bernie*), Curtis Hostetter (*Tommy*), Robin Lamont (*Ruthie*), Robin Tilghman (*Marie*), Peter Gumeny (*Thompson*), John Bottoms (*Father McKenna*), Debbie Novak, Russell Todd, Dorian Lopinto, Jamie Haskins, Barbara Quinn, Laurie Faso, Anthony Shaw, Ron Englehardt, Michael Fiorillo, Steve W. James
MUSIC: Alexander & Mark Peskanov

The Head
see The Naked Woman and Satan

Head Above Water
1997, (USA), HBO-TV, color
W: Harvey Keitel, Cameron Diaz
Made-for-Cable (later released to theaters), unusual comedy-thriller: Couple tries to hide body of wife's ex-lover

Headhunter
1990, (USA), color, 92 mins.
W: Kay Lenz, Wayne Crawford, John Fatooh, Steve Kanaly, June Chadwick, Sam Williams
D: Francis Schaeffer
Minor horror-thriller: Murderous beast comes to Boston

The Headless Eyes
1983, (USA), color, 78 mins.
W: Bo Brundin, Gordon Raman, Mary Jane Early
D & SCR: Kent Bateman
Minor horror-thriller: Mad artist mutilates women

The Headless Ghost
1959, (GB), Anglo-Amalgamated/AIP, b&w, 63 mins.
W: Richard Lyon (*Bill*), Liliane Sottane (*Ingrid*), David Rose (*Ronnie*), Clive Revill (*The Fourth Earl*), Jack Ellen (*The Earl of Ambrose*), Alexander Archdale (*Randolph*), Carl Bernard (*Sgt. Grayson*), Patrick Connor, Josephine Blake, John Stacy, Donald Bissett, Trevor Barnett, Mary M. Barclay
P: Herman Cohen   D: Peter Graham Scott   SCR: Herman Cohen & Kenneth Langtry
reissued 1961
orig, co-billed (USA) with Horrors of the Black Museum
Minor fantasy-thriller: Students spend night in haunted castle

The Headless Horseman
1922, (USA), W.W. Hodkinson Corp., b&w, 7 reels (6,145 ft./1873m)
W: Will Rogers (*Ichabod Crane*), Lois Meredith (*Katrina Van Tassel*), Ben Hendricks Jr. ("*Brom*" *Bones*), Mary Foy (*Dame Martling*), Charles Graham (*Hans Van Ripper*)
D: Edward Venturini   ADAPT: Carl Stearns Clancy, from Washington Irving's *The Legend of Sleepy Hollow*   PHOTOG: Ned Van Buren
Standard comedy-melodrama: Schoolteacher has trouble being accepted by community

The Head of Janus
see Der Januskopf

Head of the Family
1996, (USA), color, 85 mins.
W: Blake Bailey (*Lance*), Jacqueline Lovell
Made-for-Video, standard horror-comedy: Teen finds neighbors controlled by disembodied head

Heads
1994, (USA), color, 105 mins.
W: Jon Cryer
Standard thriller: Small-time reporter tracks serial decapitator

The Hearse
1980, (USA), Marimark/Crown Int'l, color, 95 mins.
W: Trish Van Devere (*Jane Hardy*), Joseph Cotten (*Walter Pritchard*), David Gautreaux (*Tom Sullivan*), Donald Hotton (*Rev. Winston*), Med Flory (*Sheriff Denton*), Donald Petrie (*Luke*), Christopher McDonald (*Pete*), Fredric Franklyn (*Mr. Gordon*), Perry Lang (*Paul Gordon*), Olive Dunbar (*Mrs. Gordon*), Al Hansen (*Bo Rehnquist*), Nicholas Shields (*Dr. Greenwalt*), Dominic Barto (*The Driver*), Allison Balson (*Alice*), Chuck Mitchell (*The Counterman*), Jimmy Gatherum (*Boy #1*), Victoria Eubank (*Lois*), Tanya Bowers (*The Schoolgirl*)
D: George Bowers   SCR: Bill Bleich, from a story by Mark Tensor   PHOTOG: Mori Kawa   MUSIC: Webster Lewis
Minor spooker: Evil ghosts torment divorcee

Heart and Souls
1993, (USA), Alphaville-Stampede/Univ, color, 103 mins.
W: Robert Downey Jr. (*Thomas Reilly*), Charles Grodin (*Harrison Winslow*), Kyra Sedgwick (*Julia*), Tom Sizemore (*Milo Peck*), Elizabeth Shue (*Anne*), Alfre Woodward (*Penny Washington*), David Paymer (*Hal the Bus Driver*), Bill Calvert (*Frank Reilly*), Lisa Lucas (*Eva Reilly*), Shannon Orrock (*The Woman at the Audition*), Michael Zebulon (*The Singer at the Audition*), Chasiti Hampton, Wanya Green, Janet MacLachlan, Javar David Levingston, Robert William Newhart, Eric Lloyd, Sean O'Bryan, Steven Clawson, Joan Stuart Morris, Richard Portnow, George Maguire, Marc Shaiman, Jacob Kenner, Janet Rotblatt, Janette Caldwell, Bill Caoizzi, Will Nye, Robert Parnell, Eric Poppick, Susan Kellermann, Ed Hooks, Michael Halton, Wren T. Brown, Lorinne Dills-Vozoff, Richard Roat, Bob Amaral, Luana Anders, John Goodwin, John Durbin, B.B. King, Kymberly Newberry, Jamilah Adams Mapp, Tony Genaro
D: Ron Underwood   SCR: Brent Maddock, S.S. Wilson, Gregory Hansen & Erik Hansen   PHOTOG: Michael Watkins   VS-FX SPRVSR: Jamie Dixon   MUSIC: Marc Shaiman
Entertaining comedy-fantasy: Ghosts beset young executive

Heartbeeps
1981, (USA), Univ, color, 89 mins.
W: Andy Kaufman (*ValCom-17485*), Bernadette Peters (*AquaCom89045*), Randy Quaid (*Charlie*), Kenneth McMillan (*Max*), Melanie Mayron (*Susan*), Christopher Guest (*Calvin*), Richard B. Shull (*The Factory Boss*), Dick Miller (*The Watchman*), Mary Woronov (*The Party House Owner*), Kathleen Freeman

(*The Helicopter Pilot*), Paul Bartel, Anne Wharton, Barry Diamond, Stephanie Faulkner, Jeffrey Kramer, Irene Forrest, Karsen Lee Gould, David Gene LeBell
D: Alan Arkush   **SCR:** John Hill   **PHOTOG:** Charles Rosher Jr.   **SPCL-FX:** Albert Whitlock   **MUSIC:** John Williams
Modest SF-comedy: Runaway robots fall in love

Heart Condition
1990, (USA), New Line, color, 100 mins.
W: Bob Hoskins (*Jack Moony*), Denzel Washington (*Napoleon Stone*), Chloe Webb (*Crystal Gerrity*), Ray Baker (*Harry Zara*), Jeffrey Meek (*Graham*), Roger E. Mosley (*Capt. Wendt*), Alan Rachins (*Dr. Posner*), Lisa Stahl (*Annie*), Eva La Rue (*Peisha*), Frank R. Roach (*Sen. Marquand*), Robert Apisa (*The Teller*), Kieran Mulroney (*Dillnick*), Clayton Landey (*Posner's Ass't*), Julie Silverman (*The Staff Member*), Phyllis Hamlin (*The TV Announcer*), Jeff MacGregor (*The Dating Game Host*), Mary Catherine Wright (*The Nurse*), Ron Taylor (*Bubba*), Ja'net Dubois (*Mrs. Stone*), George Kyle, Bill Applebaum, Johnny Walker, Kenneth J. Martinez, Diane Civita, Monte Landis, Deidre Harris, Anthony "Wink" Atkinson, Kendall McCarthy, Mark Lowenthal, Theresa Randle, Billy Oscar, Chick Hearn, Dasanea Johnson, Johouache Johnson, Shauntae Johnson, Leontine Guilliard, Johnnie Johnson, Rick Marzan, Dean Wein, Bobby Bass, Greg Barnett, Tom Huff, Gary Sax
WRIT & D: James D. Parriott   **PHOTOG:** Arthur Albert   **MUSIC:** Patrick Leonard   **SPCL-FX:** Court Wizard Special Effects   **SONG:** *Have a Heart* (performed by Bonnie Raitt)
Standard comedy-fantasy: Haunted heart-transplant recipient

Heartless
1997, (USA), Amco/USA-TV, color, 95 mins.
W: Madchen Amick, David Packer, Monique Parent, Tom Schanley, Louise Fletcher, Pamela Bellwood, Rusty Schwimmer, Emily Kuroda, Bo Svenson, Quinn Beswick, Antony Sandoval, J.J. Boone, Elizabeth Landis, Scott Alan Larson, Liron Artzi
D: Judith Vogelsang   **TELEPLAY:** Leslie Lehr Spirson   **PHOTOG:** Stevan Larner   **MUSIC:** Mike De Martino
TVM, standard thriller: Heart-transplant recipient adopts personality of donor, a murdered socialite

The Heart of a Woman
1912, (GB), Hepworth, b&w, 625 ft. (190.5m)
W: Flora Morris (*The Spy*)
D: Warwick Buckland
Standard thriller: Woman spy falls for victim, returns stolen treaty

The Heart of Justice
1993, (USA), TNT-TV, color, 95 mins.
W: Eric Stoltz, Dennis Hopper, Jennifer Connelly
TVM, standard thriller: Reporter covers writer's murder

Heartstopper
1992, (USA), color, 96 mins.
W: Moon Zappa, Tom Savini, Kevin Kindlan
Minor fantasy-thriller: 18th-century physician returns from dead

The Heart Within
1957, (GB), Pennington-Eady/RFD, b&w, 61 mins.
W: James Hayter (*Mr. Willard*), Earl Cameron (*Conway*), David Hemmings (*Danny Willard*), Betty Cooper (*Miss Trevor*), Clifford Evans (*Matthew Johnson*), Jack Stewart (*Insp. Matheson*), Dan Jackson (*Joe Martell*), Frank Sanguineau (*Bobo*)
P: Jon Pennington   **D:** David Eady   **SCR:** Geoffrey Orme   **STORY:** John Baxter
Standard crime-thriller: West Indian accused of smuggling drugs

Heathers
1988, (USA), color, 103 mins.
W: Winona Ryder, Christian Slater, Shannen Doherty, Glenn Shadix, Lisanne Falk, Kim Walker, Penelope Milford, Lance Fenton, Patrick Laborteaux
D: Michael Lehmann   **SCR:** Daniel Waters   **MUSIC:** David Newman
Bizarre black comedy: High-school girls' snobbish clique inspires mayhem and death

Heatseeker
W: Gary Daniels
D: Albert Pyun

Heatseeker
1995, (USA), color, 90 mins.
W: Keith H. Cooke, Thom Matthews, Tim Thomerson, Norbert Weisser, Gary Daniels
D: Albert Pyun
Minor action-SF: Kickboxer opposes cyborgs to free kidnapped fiancee

The Heat Wave
1911, (GB), Hepworth, b&w, 400 ft. (121.9m)
W: Hay Plumb (*Smith*)
D: Frank Wilson
Standard comedy-fantasy: Hot man tries to get cool, explodes into vapor

Heatwave
see *The House Across the Lake*

Heaven Can Wait
1943, (USA), 20th-Fox, color, 112 mins.
W: Gene Tierney (*Martha*), Don Ameche (*Henry Van Cleve*), Charles Coburn (*Grandpa Van Cleve*), Laird Cregar (*Satan*), Eugene Pallette (*E.F. Strabel*), Louis Calhern (*Randolph Van Cleve*), Signe Hasso (*Yvette*), Spring Byington (*Bertha Van Cleve*), Marjorie Main (*Mrs. Strabel*), Florence Bates (*Edna Craig*), Helene Reynolds (*Peggy Nash*), Allyn Joslyn (*Albert Van Cleve*), Aubrey Mather (*James*), Michael Ames (*Jack Van Cleve*), Clarence Muse (*Jasper*), Dickie Moore (*Henry Van Cleve, Age 15*), Dickie Jones (*Albert Van Cleve, Age 15*)
P & D: Ernst Lubitsch   **SCR:** Samson Raphaelson, based on Lazlo Bus-Fekete's play *Birthday*   **PHOTOG:** Edward Cronjager   **SPCL-FX:** Fred Sersen   **MUSIC:** Alfred Newman
Sentimental fantasy: Roue recounts life in presence of Satan

Heaven Can Wait
1978, (USA), Para, color, 101 mins.
W: Warren Beatty (*Joe Pendleton*), Julie Christie (*Betty Logan*), James Mason (*Mr. Jordan*), Jack Warden (*Max Corkle*), Charles Grodin (*Tony Abbott*), Dyan Cannon (*Julia Farnsworth*), Buck Henry (The *Escort*), Vincent Gardenia (*Krim*), Joseph Maher (*Sik*), Hamilton Camp (*Bentley*), Arthur Malet (*Everett*), Stephanie Faracy (*Corinne*), Jeannie Linero (*Lavinia*), Harry D.K. Wong (*The Gardener*), Frank Campanella (*Conway*), George J. Manos (*The Security Guard*), Larry Block (*Peters*), Bill Sorrells (*Tomarken*), Dick Enberg (*The TV Interviewer*), Dolph Sweet (*The Head Coach*), R.G. Armstrong (*The General Manager*), Ed V. Peck (*The Trainer*), John Randolph (*The Former Owner*), Keene Curtis (*Oppenheim*), William Larsen (*Renfield*), William Sylvester (*The Nuclear Reporter*), Morgan Farley (*Middleton*), William Bogert (*Lawson*), Robert E. Leonard, Joel Marston, Earl Montgomery, Bernie Massa, Robert C. Stevens, Peter Tomarken, Richard O'Brien, Charlie Charles, Lisa Blake Richards, Nick Outin, Jim Boeke, Jerry Scanlan, Marvin Fleming, Les Josephson, Deacon Jones, Jack T. Snow, Curt Gowdy, Al DeRogatis, Joseph F. Makel, Will Hare, Lee Weaver, Roger Bowen
D: Warren Beatty & Buck Henry   **SCR:** Warren Beatty & Elaine May, from Henry Segall's play   **PHOTOG:** William A. Fraker   **SPCL-FX:** Robert MacDonald   **MUSIC:** Dave Grusin
remake of Here Comes Mr. Jordan
Standard comedy-fantasy: Dead playboy reincarnated

The Heavenly Kid
1985, (USA), Orion, color, 95 mins.
W: Lewis Smith, Richard Mulligan, Jason Gedrick, Jane Kaczmarek (*Emily*), Mark Metcalf (*Joe*)
D: Cary Medoway   **SCR:** Cary Medoway & Martin Copeland
Standard fantasy: Deceased teen aids high-school nerd

Heaven Only Knows
1947, (USA), UA, b&w, 98 mins.
W: Robert Cummings, Marjorie Reynolds, Brian Donlevy, Bill Goodwin, Edgar Kennedy, John Litel, Stuart Erwin, Jorja Curtwright
D: Albert S. Rogell   **SCR:** Art Arthur & Rowland Leigh   **PHOTOG:** Karl Struss   **MUSIC:** Heinz Roemheld
Standard fantasy: Angel sent to old West, reforms bad man. A.k.a. **Montana Mike**

Heaven Over Berlin
see *Wings of Desire*

The Heavens Call
1959, (Russ), Dovzhenko, color, 90 mins.
W: Ivan Pereverzev, L. Lobanov, A. Shvorin
D: Alexander Kozyr & M. Karinkov   **SCR:** V. Pomiesczykov & A. Sazanov
75-min. version released in USA (1963) as **Battle Beyond the Sun** *(with adapt & spcl-fx by Francis Ford Coppola), by AIP*
Standard SF: Two countries compete to reach Mars

Heaven Sent
1994, (USA), color, 95 mins.
W: Vincent Kartheiser, Mary McDonough, William Christopher
Standard fantasy: Near-death experience puts man in touch with friendly angel

Heaven Ship
see Himmelskibet

Heavy Metal
1981, (USA), Ivan Reitman/Col, color, 90 mins.
VOICES: Roger Bumpass, Jackie Burroughs, John Candy, Joe Flaherty, Don
    Francks, Martin Lavut, Eugene Levy, Alice Playten, Marilyn Lightstone,
    Harold Ramis, Susan Roman, Richard Romanus, August Schellenberg, John
    Vernon & Zal Yanovsky
D: Gerald Potterton   SCR: Dan Goldberg & Len Blum, based on orig. art & sto-
    ries by Richard Corben, Angus McKie, Dan O'Bannon, Thomas Warkentin
    & Berni Wrightson   MUSIC: Elmer Bernstein   SONGS BY: Black
    Sabbath, Blue Oyster Cult, Cheap Trick, Devo, Donald Fagen, Don Felder,
    Sammy Hagar, Grand Funk Railroad, Journey, Nazareth, Stevie Nicks,
    Riggs & Trust
Episodic, animated SF-musical: Futuristic comic-strip adventures

Heavy Traffic
1973, (USA), AIP, color, 77 mins.
W: Joseph Kaufman (*Michael*), Beverly Hope Atkinson (*Carole*), Frank DeKova
    (*Angie*), Terri Haven (*Ida*), Mary Dean Lauria (*Molly*), Jacqueline Mills
    (*Rosalyn*), Lillian Adams (*Rosa*)
VOICES: Jim Bates, Jamie Farr, Robert Easton, Morton Lewis, Charles Gordone,
    Bill Strigolis, Jay Lawrence, Phyllis Thopson, Lee Weaver, Kim Hamilton,
    Carol Graham, Candy Candido, Helene Winston, William Keene, John
    Bleifer, Peter Hobbs
P: Steve Krantz   D & SCR: Ralph Bakshi   PHOTOG: Ted C. Bemiller & Gregg
    Heschong   MUSIC: Ray Shanklin & Ed Bogas
Minor adventure-fantasy (live action & animation): Pinball wizard's X-rated exploits

Heba the Snake Woman
1915, (GB), Excel/YCC, b&w, 1,000 ft. (304.8m)
Standard horror-fantasy: Aztec princess changes into reptile, kills doctor

Hector Servadac's Ark
see Na Komete

He Died with His Eyes Open
1985, (Fr), color, 106 mins.
W: Michel Serrault, Charlotte Rampling, Xavier Deluc, Jean Leuvrais, Elisabeth
    Depardieu, Jean-Paul Roussillon
D: Jacques Deray, from a novel by "Derek Raymond" (Robin Cook)
Modest thriller: Concert pianist murdered

He Kills Night After Night After Night
see Night After Night After Night

He Knows You're Alone
1980, (USA), Lansbury-Beruh/MGM, color, 92 mins.
W: Don Scardino (*Marvin*), Caitlin O'Heaney (*Amy*), Elizabeth Kemp (*Nancy*),
    Tom Rolfing (*The Killer*), Tom Hanks (*Elliott*), Lewis Arit (*Gamble*), Patsy
    Pease (*Joyce*), Dana Barron, James Rebhorn, Joseph Leon, Paul Gleason,
    Dana Barron (*Diana*), James Rebhorn (*The Professor*), Paul Gleason (*Daley*),
    Joseph Leon (*Ralph the Tailor*), James Carroll (*Phil*), Brian Byers (*Bernie*),
    Curtis Hostetter (*Tommy*), Robin Lamont (*Ruthie*), Robin Tilghman (*Marie*),
    Peter Gumeny (*Thompson*), John Bottoms (*Father McKenna*), Debbie Novak,
    Russell Todd, Dorian Lopinto, Jamie Haskins, Barbara Quinn, Laurie Faso,
    Anthony Shaw, Ron Englehardt, Michael Fiorillo, Steve W. James
MUSIC: Alexander & Mark Peskanov   D: Armand Mastroianni   SCR: Scott
    Parker   PHOTOG: Gerald Feil   SPCL-FX: Taso N. Stavrakis   SONGS:
    Mystery Lover, I'll Never Tie You Down & It's the Night Again
A.k.a. Blood Wedding
Standard thriller (Tom Hanks' film debut): Psycho stalks brides-to-be

Held For Murder
1932, (USA), b&w, 67 mins.
W: Irene Rich, Conway Tearle, Mary Carlisle, Kenneth Thomson, William B.
    Davidson
D: E. Mason Hopper
A.k.a. Her Mad Night
Standard melodrama: Mother takes blame when daughter accused of murder

Held for Questioning
1983, (E. Ger), color, 102 mins.
W: Sylvester Groth, Fred Duren, Klaus Piontek, Horst Hiemer, Matthias Gunther
D: Frank Beyer
Standard melodrama: Soldier imprisoned for suspected war crimes

Held for Ransom
1913, (GB), Hepworth, b&w, 1,025 ft. (312.4m)
W: Chrissie White (*The Daughter*), Harry Royston (*The Tramp*)
D: Frank Wilson
Standard crime-thriller: Tramp's daughter saves farmer's kidnapped child

Held to Ransom
1906, (GB), Alpha Trading Co., b&w, 560 ft. (170.7m)
D: Arthur Cooper
Standard crime-thriller (in 9 scenes): Blackmailers kidnap girl

Helen of Troy
see The Private Life of Helen of Troy

Helen of Troy
1955, (USA), WB, color, 118 mins.
W: Rossana Podesta (*Helen*), Jacques Sernas (*Paris*), Sir Cedric Hardwicke (*Priam*),
    Brigitte Bardot (*Andraste*), Stanley Baker (*Achilles*), Niall McGinni
    (*Menelaus*), Robert Douglas (*Agamemnon*), Torin Thatcher (*Ulysses*), Ronald
    Lewis (*Aeneas*), Harry Andrews (*Hector*), Janette Scott (*Cassandra*), Nora
    Swinburne (*Hecuba*), Maxwell Reed, Eduardo Ciannelli, Robert Brown,
    Terence Longden, Barbara Cavan
D: Robert Wise   SCR: John Twist & Hugh Gray   PHOTOG: Harry Stradling
    SPCL-FX: Louis Lichtenfield   MUSIC: Max Steiner
Superior "Sword & Sandal": Ill-fated romance breeds war

The Helicopter Spies
1968, (USA), MGM, color, 93 mins.
W: Robert Vaughn (*Napoleon Solo*), David McCallum, John Carradine, Kathleen
    Freeman, Carol Lynley, Bradford Dillman, Lola Albright, Julie London, Sid
    Haig, Leo G. Carroll
P: Anthony Spinner   D: Boris Sagal   SCR: Dean Hargrove
*Standard thriller (culled from 2 episodes of teleseries "The Man from U.N.C.L.E.", from
    'The Prince of Darkness Affair,' NBC-TV, Oct 2 & 9, 1967: Secret agents go to
    Greece, pursue new weapon*

The Helicopter Spies: LOLA ALBRIGHT AND BRADFORD DILLMAN

He Lived to Kill
see Night of Terror (1933)

Hellbent
1988, (USA), color
D: Richard Casey
Minor thriller: Decadent musician meets vengeance-seeking housewife

Hellborn
see The Sinister Urge

Hellbound
W: Chuck Norris, Christopher Neame, Calvin Levels, Sheree J. Wilson
D: Aaron Norris
Standard action-fantasy: Wizard seeks sceptre of power

Hellbound: Hellraiser II
1988, (GB), New World, color, 98 mins.
W: Claire Higgins (*Julia*), Ashley Laurence (*Kirsty*), Sean Chapman (*Frank*),
    Kenneth Cranham (*Channard*), William Hope (*Kyle*), Imogen Boorman
    (*Tiffany*), Barbie Wilde (*The Female Cenobite*), Doug Bradley (*The Pinhead*),
    Simon Bamford (*The Butterball*), Nicholas Vince (*The Chatterer*), Oliver
    Smith (*Browning*), Angus McInnes (*Ronson*), James Tillitt (*Officer Cortez*),
    Deborah Joel ("*Skinless*" *Julia*), Bradley Lavelle (*Officer Kucich*), Edwin Craig
    (*The Wheelchair Patient*), Ron Travis (*Workman #1*), Oliver Parker (*Workman
    #2*), Catherine Chevalier (*Tiffany's Mother*)
D: Tony Randel   SCR: Peter Atkins, from a story by Clive Barker   PHOTOG:
    Robin Vidgeon   MUSIC: Christopher Young
Standard horror-fantasy: Girl tries to rescue father from hell

Hell Comes to Frogtown
1988, (USA), New World, color, 88 mins.

W: Roddy Piper, Sandahl Bergman, William Smith, Nicholas Worth, Rory Calhoun, Kristi Somers, Cec Verrell, Cliff Bemis, Brian Frank
D: R.J. Kizer & Donald G. Jackson   **SCR:** Randall Frakes   **STORY:** Donald G. Jackson & Randall Frakes   **MUSIC:** David Shapiro
Minor SF-adventure: Post-nuke hero opposes mutants

Hellfire
1995, (USA), color, 100 mins.
W: Ben Cross, Jennifer Burns
Made-for-Cable, standard fantasy-thriller: Heiress hires choirmaster to finish uncle's satanic symphony

Hellfire
see **Primal Scream**

The Hell-Fire Club
1961, (GB), Midcentury/Embassy, color, 93 mins.
W: Keith Michell (*Jason*), Adrienne Corri (*Lady Isobel*), Peter Arne (*Thomas*), Kai Fischer (*Yvonne*), David Lodge (*Timothy*), Peter Cushing (*Merryweather*), Miles Malleson (*The Judge*), Bill Owen (*Martin*), Martin Stephens (*Young Jason*), Andrew Faulds (*Lord Netherden*), Jean Lodge (*Lady Netherden*), Francis Matthews (*Sir Hugh*), Desmond Walter Ellis (*Lord Chorley*)
D & PHOTOG: Robert S. Baker & Monty Berman   **SCR:** Leon Griffiths & Jimmy Sangster   **MUSIC:** Clifton Parker
Fr retitle, **Les Chevaliers du Demon (Demon Cavaliers)** *US release, b&w.*
Standard adventure-romance: Circus acrobat ousts usurper

Hellgate
1989, (USA), color, 96 mins.
W: Abigail Wolcott, Ron Palillo
D: William A. levey
Minor horror-fantasy: Hitchhiking woman revealed as living dead

Hellhole
1985, (USA), Arkoff Int'l, color, 92 mins.
W: Ray Sharkey (*Silk*), Judy Landers (*Susan*), Edy Williams (*Vera*), Marjoe Gortner (*Dr. Dane*), Richard Cox (*Ron*), Mae Campbell (*Daisy*), Terry Moore (*Sidnee Hammond*), Mary Woronov (*Dr. Fletcher*), Robert Darcy (*Brad*), Cliff Emmich (*Dr. Blume*), Martin Beck (*Monroe*), Dyanne Thorne (*Crysta*), Lynn Borden (*Mom*), Martin West (*Rollins*), Curtis Taylor (*Jim*), Pamela Ward (*Tina*), Sammy Thurston (*Beat Woman*), Jan Stratton (*Nurse Soto*), Carole Ita White (*Nurse Turner*), Rochelle Firestone (*Darla*), Marneen Fields, Natalie Main, Lamya Derval, Marie LaMarre, Judith Geller, Ingrid Oliu, Ann-Leizabeth Chatterton, Loyda Ramos, Lynne Bell, Charley M. Morgan, Tanya Russell, Juliet Rohde, Annette Claudier, Larraine Blanc Rosner, Joel Bennett, Tony Lopez, Kristina Kirstin, DeVera Marcus, Renee Vicary, Margarita Nosalt, Lauri Creach, Sherry Peterson, Dan Bradley, James Paola, Michele Laurent
D: Pierre De Moro   **SCR:** Vincent Mongol   **PHOTOG:** Steven Posey   **MUSIC:** Jeff Sturges
Minor thriller: Asylum doctors experiment on inmates

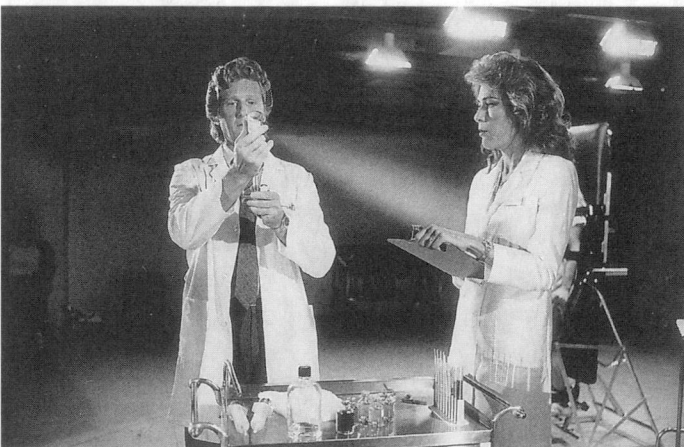

Hellhole: Marjoe Gortner and Mary Woronov

Hell is a City
1960, (GB), Hammer/WPD, b&w, 98 mins.
W: Stanley Baker (*Insp. Martineau*), John Crawford (*Don Starling*), Donald Pleasence (*Gus Hawkins*), Maxine Audley (*Julia Martineau*), Billie Whitelaw (*Chloe Hawkins*), Joseph Tomelty (*Furnisher Steele*), George A. Cooper (*Doug Savage*), Geoffrey Frederick (*Devery*), Charles Houston (*Clogger Roach*), Vanda Godsell (*Lucky Lusk*), Sarah Branch (*Silver Steele*), Russell Napier (*The Supt.*)
P: Michael Carreras   **D & SCR:** Val Guest, from a novel by Maurice Procter
Standard crime-thriller: Inspector tracks escaped convict

Hellmaster
1993, (USA), color, 92 mins.
W: John Saxon, David Emge, Amy Raasch
D & SCR: Douglas Schulze
Minor SF-horror: Mad doctor experiments on collegians

Hell Mountain
1998, (USA), color
W: Bentley Mitchum, Nicole Nieth
Minor thriller

Hell Night
1981, (USA), Compass Int'l, color, 99 mins.
W: Linda Blair (*Marti*), Vincent Van Patten (*Seth*), Kevin Brophy (*Peter*), Peter Barton (*Jeff*), Jenny Neumann (*May*), Suki Goodwin (*Denise*), Jimmy Sturtevant (*Scott*), Ronald Gans (*The Driver*), Hal Ralston (*The Older Cop*), Cary Fox (*The Younger Cop*), Gloria Heilman (*The Party Girl*)
D: Tom De Simone   **SCR:** Randolph Feldman   **PHOTOG:** Mac Ahlberg   **SPCL-FX:** Court Wizard Productions   **MUSIC:** Dan Wyman
Minor thriller: Collegians spend night in murder mansion

Hello Again
1987, (USA), Touchstone-Silver Screen Partners III/Buena Vista, color, 96 mins.
W: Shelley Long (*Lucy Chadman*), Judith Ivey (*Zelda*), Gabriel Byrne (*Kevin Scanlon*), Sela Ward (*Kim Lacey*), Corbin Bernsen (*Jason Chadman*), Austin Pendleton (*Junior Lacey*), Carrie Nye (*Regina Holt*), Robert Lewis (*Phineas Devereux*), Madeleine Potter (*Felicity*), Thor Fields (*Danny Chadman*), John Cunningham (*Bruce Holt*), I.M. Hobson, Mary Fogarty, Kauilani Lee, Shirley Rich, John Rothman, Lynne Thigpen, Chip Zien, Royce Rich, Susan Isaacs, Everett Quinton, John Tillinger, Patricia Gage, Mary Armstrong, Colin R. Fox, Karen Shallo, Ross Indri, Suzanne Barnes, Paul Royce, Illeana Douglas, Esther Gordon, John J. Healey, Jo Jones, Anna Marie Wieder
P & D: Frank Perry   **SCR:** Susan Isaacs   **PHOTOG:** Jan Weincke   **MUSIC:** William Goldstein
Standard comedy-fantasy: Man haunted by first wife's ghost

Hello Down There
1968, (USA), Ivan Tors/Para, color, 90 mins
W: Tony Randall, Janet Leigh, Jim Backus, Merv Griffin, Roddy McDowall, Ken Berry, Richard Dreyfuss, Harvey Lembeck, Bruce Gordon, Arnold Stang
P: George Sherman   **D:** Jack Arnold, Ricou Browning   **SCR:** Frank Telford & John McGreevey   **SONGS:** include *Glub* & *Hey Little Goldfish*
Reissued as **Sub-a-Dub-Dub**
Standard SF-comedy: Family lives in undersea house. Underwater scenes filmed in Florida

Hello Mary Lou: Prom Night II
see **The Haunting of Hamilton High**

Hell on Devil's Island
1957, (USA), 20th-Fox, b&w, 74 mins.
W: Helmut Dantine, William Talman Donna Martell, Rex Ingram, Alan Lee
D: Christian Nyby
Minor melodrama: Unsavory conditions in prison mines

Hellraiser
1987, (GB), Film Futures/Cinemarque Entertainment B.V./New World, color, 93 mins.
W: Andrew Robinson (*Larry Cotton*), Claire Higgins (*Julia Cotton*), Ashley Laurence (*Kirsty Cotton*), Sean Chapman, Oliver Smith, Robert Hines, Antony Allen, Leon Davis, Michael Cassidy, Frank Baker, Kenneth Nelson, Gay Barnes, Niall Buggy, Dave Atkins, Oliver Parker, Pamela Sholto, Nicholas Vince, Simon Bradford, Grace Kirby, Sharon Bower, Raul Newney
P: Christopher Figg   **WRIT & D:** Clive Barker   **MUSIC:** Christopher Young
Unusual horror-fantasy: Man gains entrance to Hades. cf. **Hellbound: Hellraiser II**

Hellraiser: Bloodline
1995, (GB), Trans Atlantic/Dimension, color, 85 mins
W: Bruce Ramsay, Valentina Vargas, Doug Bradley (*Pinhead*)
D: Alan Smithee   **SCR:** Peter Atkins, from characters created by Clive Barker   **PHOTOG:** Gerry Lively   **MUSIC:** Daniel Licht
Standard horror-fantasy

Hellraiser III: Hell on Earth
1992, (GB), Dimension, color, 96 mins.
W: Terry Farrell (*Joey Summerskill*), Doug Bradley (*Pinhead/Elliott*), Paula Marshall (*Terri*), Kevin Bernhardt (*J.P. Monroe*), Ken Carpenter (*Doc/Camerahead*), Ashley Laurence (*Kirsty*), Peter Boynton (*Joey's Father*)
D: Anthony Hickox   **SCR:** Peter Atkins, from characters created by Clive Barker   **PHOTOG:** Gerry Lively   **SPCL-FX:** Bob Keen   **MUSIC:** Randy Miller
Standard horror-fantasy, sequel to **Hellbound: Hellraiser II**: *Satanic forces summoned*

Hellraiser 4: Bloodline
1995, (GB), color, 101 mins.
W: Bruce Ramsay, Valentina Vargas, Doug Bradley (*Pinhead*), Kim Myers, Christina Harnos, Charlotte Chatton, Mickey Cotrell, Paul Perri
D: "Alan Smithee" (Kevin Yeagher)   **SCR:** Peter Atkins   **PHOTOG:** Gerry Lively   **MUSIC:** Daniel Licht
Minor horror-fantasy: Origin of infernal device is explored

Hell's Bloody Devils
1970, (USA), Independent-Int'l, color, 92 mins
W: John Gabriel, Broderick Crawford, Scott Brady, Keith Andes, Kent Taylor, John Carradine, Robert Dix, Vicki Volante, Bambi Allen, Anne Randall, Emily Banks
P & D: Al Adamson   **SCR:** Jerry Evans   **PHOTOG:** Laszlo Kovacs   **MUSIC:**

H

Nelson Riddle
A.k.a. **The Fakers** and **Operation M**, *Smashing the Crime Syndicate*
Minor thriller: Nazi war criminal seeks to distribute counterfeit money

Hell's Bloody Devils: EMILY BANKS AND SCOTT BRADY

Hell's Headquarters
1932, (USA), b&w, 59 mins.
W: Jack Mulhall, Barbara Weeks, Frank Mayo
D: Andrew L. Stone
Minor adventure-thriller: Murder and greed complicate ivory hunt

Hell's Island
1955, (USA), Para, color, 84 mins.
W: John Payne, Mary Murphy, Francis L. Sullivan
D: Phil Karlson
Reissued as **Love's Savage Fury**, *A.k.a.* **Love is a Weapon**
Standard thriller

Hell Ship Mutiny
1957, (USA), Rep, b&w, 66 mins.
W: Jon Hall, Roberta Haynes, Peter Lorre, John Carradine, Peter Coe, Mike Mazurki, Stanley Adams
D: Lee Sholem & Elmo Williams   **SCR:** DeVallon Scott
Standard adventure-thriller: Sea captain helps South Seas princess rid her island of thieves

The Hellstrom Chronicle
1971, (USA), Wolper/Cinema 5, color, 90 mins.
W: Lawrence Pressman (*Dr. Nils Hellstrom*)
D: Wallace Green   **SCR:** David Seltzer   **PHOTOG:** Ken Middleham, Helmut Barth & Walon Green   **MUSIC:** Lalo Schifrin
Standard docu-melodrama: Examination of how insects will inherit Earth

Hellzapoppin
1941, (USA), Mayfair/Univ, b&w, 84 mins.
W: Ole Olsen, Chic Johnson, Martha Raye, Robert Paige, Mischa Auer, Jane Frazee, Hugh Herbert, Clarence Kolb, Elisha Cook Jr., Richard Lane, Shemp Howard
D: Henry C. Potter   **SCR:** Nat Perrin & Warren Wilson   **PHOTOG:** Woody Bredell   **MUSIC DIR:** Charles Previn
Cinemadaptation of popular Broadway show: Burlesque skits

Det Hemmelighedsfulde X (The Mysterious X)
1913, (Den), b&w
W: Benjamin Christensen
WRIT & D: Benjamin Christensen
Standard thriller

The Henderson Monster
1980, (USA), Herbert Brodkin/Titus/CBS-TV, color, 95 mins.
W: Jason Miller (*Dr. Thomas Debs Henderson*), Christine Lahti (*Louise Casimir*), Stephen Collins (*Pete Casimir*), David Spielberg (*Mayor Frank Bellona*), Nehemiah Persoff (*Leo Tedeschi*), Larry Gates (*Pres. Doby*), Josef Sommer (*Dr. Martin Grossman*), Kenneth Kimmins (*Dr. Halloran*), Peter Evans (*Brother Harold*), Anne Goodwyn (*Irene Forster Dodd*), David Kilgore (*Nelson Chase*), Beatrice Bush (*Phoebe Dennison*), Steve Boschen (*The Student Waiter*), Glenn Crone (*Prof. #1*), Lalla Rolfe (*Prof. #2*), Andrew Earley, Carl Lester, Mark Hulcher, Deborah Nunamaker, Cherie Scheer
D: Waris Hussein   **TELEPLAY:** Ernest Kinoy   **PHOTOG:** Edward R. Brown   **MUSIC:** Dick Hyman   **SONG:** *I Saw a Light*
TVM, marginal SF: Social comment on dangers of genetic engineering

Der Henker von London (The Strangler of London)
1963, (W. Ger), CCC-Omnia/Para, b&w, 95 mins.
W: Hansjorg Felmy, Maria Perschy, Dieter Borsche, Wolfgang Preiss
P: Artur Brauner   **D:** Edwin Zbonek   **SCR:** Robert A. Stemmle, from Edgar

Wallace's novel *White Carpet*
USA retitle, **The Mad Executioners**
Standard thriller: Scotland Yard probes beheadings

Henpeck's Nightmare
1914, (GB), Waterwheel/Tyler, b&w, 440 ft. (134.1m)
Minor fantasy short: Drunk dreams of pursuing apparitions

Henry Aldrich Haunts a House
1943, (USA), Para, b&w, 73 mins.
W: James Lydon, Charles Smith, John Litel, Mike Mazurki, Olive Blakeney, Joan Mortimer, Vaughan Glaser, Jackie Moran, Lucien Littlefield
D: Hugh Bennett
Minor comedy-thriller

He or She?
see **Glen or Glenda?**

The Hephaestus Plague
see **Bug**

Her Awakening
1916, (GB), Speed/DFSA, b&w, 1,180 ft. (359.7m)
Standard melodrama: Neglected wife dreams of elopement, murder of lover

Herbie Goes Bananas
1980, (USA), Walt Disney, color, 100 mins.
W: Cloris Leachman (*Aunt Louise*), Charles Martin Smith (*D.J.*), John Vernon (*Prindle*), Stephan W. Burns (*Pete*), Elyssa Davalos (*Melissa*), Joaquin Garay III (*Paco*), Alex Rocco (*Quinn*), Harvey Korman (*Capt. Blythe*), Richard Jaeckel (*Shepard*), Fritz Feld (*The Steward*), Vito Scotti (*Armando*), Jose Gonzalez Gonzalez, Rubin Moreno, Tina Menard, Jorge Moreno, Allan Hunt, Tom Scott, Hector Morales, Iris Adrian, Ceil Cabot, Patricia Van Patten, Jack Perkins, Henry Slate
D: Vincent McEveety   **SCR:** Don Tait, from characters created by Gordon Buford   **PHOTOG:** Frank Phillips   **MUSIC:** Frank De Vol
Standard comedy-fantasy: Sentient Volkswagen involved with South-American art smugglers

Herbie Goes to Monte Carlo
1977, (USA), Disney/Buena Vista, color, 105 mins.
W: Dean Jones, Don Knotts, Julie Sommars
Standard comedy-fantasy: Intelligent Volkswagen finds love and larceny in Europe

Herbie Rides Again
1974, (USA), Walt Disney/Buena Vista, color, 88 mins.
W: Helen Hayes, Ken Berry, Stefanie Powers, John McIntire, Keenan Wynn, Huntz Hall, Dan Tobin, Elaine Devry, Liam Dunn, Vito Scotti, Don Pedro Colley, Fritz Feld, Chuck McCann, John Zaremba, Ivor Barry, Rod McCary
D: Robert Stevenson   **SCR:** Bill Walsh, from a story by Gordon Buford   **PHOTOG:** Frank Phillips   **MUSIC:** George Bruns
Standard comedy-fantasy (1st sequel to **The Love Bug**): *Intelligent car thwarts property speculator*

Hercules
1957, (It), Titanus/Joseph E. Levine/WB, color, 105 mins.
W: Steve Reeves (*Hercules*), Sylva Koscina (*Iole*), Gianna Maria Canale, Mimmo Palmara, Fabrizio Mioni, Ivo Garrani
P: Riccardo Freda   **D:** Pietro Francisci   **PHOTOG:** Mario Bava
Energetic "Sword & Sandal:" Adventurers seek Golden Fleece. cf. **Ercole e la Regina di Lidia**

Hercules
1983, (It), Golan-Globus/Cannon/MGM-UA, color, 100 mins.
W: Lou Ferrigno (*Hercules*), Ingrid Anderson (*Cassiopea*), Sybil Danning (*Princess Arianna*), William Berger (*Minos*), Rossana Podesta (*Hera*), Claudio Cassinelli (*Zeus*), Mirella D'Angelo (*Circe*), Brad Harris, John Garko, Eva Robbins, Bobby Rhodes, Delia Boccardo, Frank Garland
WRIT & D: Lewis Coates   **PHOTOG:** Alberto Spagnoli   **SPCL OPTL-FX:**, Armando Valcauda   **MUSIC:** Pino Donaggio
Confused mythology in minor "Sword & Sandal": Legendary strong-man strives to rescue beloved

Hercules
1997, (USA), Walt Disney/Buena Vista, color, 87 mins.
VOICES: Tate Donovan (*Hercules*), James Woods (*Hades*), Danny DeVito, Rip Torn
D: John Musker & Ron Clements   **SCR:** Ron Clements, John Musker, Donald McEnery & Irene Mecchi   **MUSIC:** Alan Menken   **LYRICS:** David Zippel
Standard animated myth-adventure: Exploits of young Greek hero

Hercules Against Moloch
see **The Conquest of Mycenae**

Hercules Against Rome
see **Ercole Contro Roma**

Hercules Against the Barbarians
1962, (It), AIP/Filmways, color, 91 mins

W: Mark Forest *(Hercules)*, Jose Greci, Ken Clark
A.k.a. Hercules Against the Mongols
Minor "Sword & Sandal": Muscleman fights Asian invaders

Hercules Against the Mongols
see Hercules Against the Barbarian

Hercules Against the Moon Men
see Maciste e la Regina di Samar

Hercules Against the Sons of the Sun
see Ercole Contro i Figli del Sole

The Hellstrom Chronicle: LAWRENCE PRESSMAN

Hercules Against the Tyrants of Babylon
see Ercole Contro i Tiranni di Babilonia

Hercules and the Captive Women
see Ercole alla Conquista della Atlantide

Hercules and the Conquest of Atlantis
see Ercole alla Conquista della Atlantide

Hercules and the Haunted Women
see Ercole alla Conquista della Atlantide

Hercules and the Masked Rider
1960, (It), AIP/Filmways, color
W: Alan Steel *(Hercules)*, Ettore Manni
Minor "Sword & Sandal": Soldier becomes leader of gypsies

Hercules and the Princess of Troy
1965, (USA), Made for TV, color, 75 mins.
W: Gordon Scott, Diana Muldaur
TVM, standard "Sword & Sandal": Strongman vs. sea beast

Hercules and the Queen of Lydia
see Ercole e la Regina di Lidia

Hercules and the Ten Avengers
1964, (It-Fr), color
W: Dan Vadis *(Hercules)*, Marilu Tolo
Aka Hercules vs. The Giant Warriors
Minor "Sword & Sandal": Muscleman champions Greeks, must battle ten giant warriors

Hercules and the Treasure of the Incas
1960, (It), AIP/Filmways, color, 87 mins
W: Alan Steel *(Hercules)*
Minor "Sword & Sandal": Muscleman seeks fabled treasure, fights hostile tribe
Aka Lost Treasure of the Aztecs

Hercules and the Tyrants of Babylon
see Ercole Contri i Tiranni di Babilonia

Hercules and Xena—The Animated Movie: The Battle for Mount Olympus
1997, (USA), MCA/Univ, video, color
Made-for-Video, standard animated myth-adventure

Hercules at the Center of the Earth
see Ercole al Centro della Terra

Hercules at the Conquest of Atlantis
see Ercole alla Conquista della Atlantide

Hercules Goes Bananas
see Hercules in New York

Hercules in New York
1970, (USA), Filmpartners, color, 90 mins.
W: Arnold Schwarzenegger *(Hercules)*, Arnold Stang, Deborah Loomis, James Karen, Taina Elg, Rudy Bond, Lane Carroll, Ernest Graves, Tanny McDonald
WRIT & P: Aubrey Wisberg   **D:** Arthur A. Seidelman   **PHOTOG:** Leo Lebowitz   **MUSIC:** John Balamos
reissued as Hercules-The Movie (82 mins.) and Hercules Goes Bananas (75 mins.)
Minor fantasy-satire (dubbed-in voice for Schwarzenegger): Zeus' son becomes modern wrestler

Hercules in the Haunted World
see Ercole al Centro della Terra

Hercules in the Vale of Woe
1962, (It), Avco Embassy-TV, color, 95 mins
W: Kirk Morris *(Hercules)*, Frank Gordon, Bice Valori
P: Ignacio Luceri   **SCR:** Vittorio Metz & Marcello Marchesi
A.k.a. Maciste Against Hercules in the Vale of Woe
Minor "Sword & Sandal": Two conmen transported to time of Caesar, must do battle with Hercules and Maciste

Hercules of the Desert
1963, (It), Filmways, color, 80 mins
W: Kirk Morris *(Hercules)*, Helene Chanel
A.k.a. Desert Raiders
Standard "Sword & Sandal": Muscleman aids nomads oppressed by ruthless princess

Hercules—Prisoner of Evil
1963, (It), AIP-TV, Filmways, color, 90 mins
W: Reg Park *(Hercules)*, Ettore Manni, Maria Teresa Orsini
P: Adelpho Ambrosiano   **D:** Antonio Margheriti
Minor "Sword & Sandal": Hero meets witch who turns men into werewolves

Hercules, Samson and Ulysses
1963, (It), ICS/MGM, color, 85 mins
W: Kirk Morris, Enzo Cerusico, Liana Orfei, Richard Lloyd, Aldo Giuffre
P: Joseph Fryd   **D & SCR:** Pietro Francisci
Minor myth-adventure

Hercules, the Avenger
1964, (It), color, 90 mins
W: Reg Park *(Hercules)*, Giovanni Cianfriglia, Gya Sandri
Minor "Sword & Sandal"

Hercules-The Movie
see Hercules in New York

Hercules II
see The Adventures of Hercules

Hercules Unchained
see Ercole e la Regina di Lidia

Hercules vs. the Giant Warriors
see Il Trionfo di Ercole

Hercules vs. the Hydra
see Gli Amori di Ercole

Hercules vs. the Vampires
see Ercole al Centro della Terra

Hercules vs. Ulysses
see Ulysses Against the Son of Hercules

Her Deadly Rival
1995, (USA), Rysher, color, 95 mins.
W: Harry Hamlin *(Jim)*, Annie Potts *(Kris)*, Lisa Zane *(Lynne)*, Tommy Hinkley, Susan Diol, Robert Treveiller, Roma Maffia, William Blair
D: James Hayman   **TELEPLAY:** Dan Vining   **PHOTOG:** Michael E. Tershman   **MUSIC:** George S. Clinton
TVM, standard fact-based thriller: Husband stalked by "secret admirer"

Here Comes Mr. Jordan
1941, (USA), Col, b&w, 93 mins.
W: Robert Montgomery, Evelyn Keyes *(Bette)*, Claude Rains *(Mr Jordan)*, Rita Johnson *(Julia)*, James Gleason, John Emery, Edward Everett Horton, Halliwell Hobbes, Don Costello, Donald MacBride
D: Alexander Hall   **SCR:** Seton I. Miller & Sidney Buchman (Academy Award), from a play by Harry Segall (Academy Award, Original Story)   **PHOTOG:** Joseph Walker   **MUSIC:** Morris Stoloff
Classic fantasy: Dead boxer's spirit reborn in body of murdered millionaire. cf. Heaven Can Wait (1978)

Here Come the Littles
1985, (Fr-Jap), Atlantic, color, 75 mins.
VOICES: Jimmy E. Keegan, Bettina Bush, Dobovan Freberg, Hal Smith
D: Bernard Deyries
Juvenile fantasy: Adventures of mouse-like creatures. Animated

Here Come the Munsters
1995, (USA), color
W: Edward Herrmann
Minor horror-comedy: Weird family essays California lifestyle

Here is a Man
see All That Money Can Buy

The Heretic
see Exorcist II: The Heretic

Here We Are Again
1913, (GB), Cricks/C&M, b&w, 495 ft. (150.9m)
D: Edwin J. Collins
reissued (1916) as **The Harlequinade**
Standard comedy-fantasy: Cop dreams tramps and lovers turn into harlequinade

Her Fatal Hand
1915, (GB), Martin/DFSA, b&w, 543 ft. (165.5m)
D: Dave Aylott
Minor fantasy short: Poet's rival blows girl's father to Milky Way

Her Greatest Performance
1916, (GB), Ideal, b&w, 6,000 ft. (1828.8m)
W: Ellen Terry (*Julia Lovelace*), Dennis Neilson-Terry (*Gerald Lovelace*), Joan Morgan (*Barbara Lovelace*), Edith Craig (*The Dresser*), James Lindsay (*Jim Douglas*), Gladys Mason (*Mary Scott*), Nelson Ramsay, Barbara Hannay, Harry Lofting, E. Vivian Reynolds, Fred Rains
D: Fred Paul **SCR:** Benedict James **STORY:** Enid Lorimer
reissued 1918
Unusual crime-thriller: Retired actress poses as dresser to scare confession out of murderer who framed her son

Her Heritage
1919, (GB), Ward's Films, b&w, 5,000 ft. (1524m)
W: Jack Buchanan (*Bob Hales*), Phyllis Monkman (*Lady Mary Strode*), E. Holman Clark (*Gerald Pridling*), Edward O'Neill (*Lord Heston*), Winifred Dennis (*Mrs. Wilter*)
D: Bannister Merwin **STORY:** Arthur Weigell
Standard crime-thriller: Artist helps lady posing as maid to steal her letters from blackmailing cousin

Her Life in London
1915, (GB), Martin/DFSA, b&w, 4,100 ft. (1249.7m)
W: Alesia Leon (*The Girl*), Fred Morgan (*The Man*), Nina Lynn
D: R. Harley West, from a play by Arthur Shirley
Standard crime-thriller: Detective's daughter poses as soldier, helps cleric save vicar's daughter from blind crook's gang

Her Lover's Honour
1909, (GB), B&C/Cosmo, b&w, 645 ft. (196.6m)
W: H.O. Martinek (*The Messenger*), Ivy Martinek (*Annette*)
D & STORY: H.O. Martinek
Standard melodrama: Girl saves king's messenger from Richelieu's agent

Her Luck In London
1914, (GB), B&C/Ashley, b&w, 3,900 ft. (1188.7m)
W: Elizabeth Risdon (*Nellie Harbourne*), Fred Groves (*Richard Lenowen*), A.V. Bramble (*Hon. Gerald O'Connor*), M. Gray Murray (*Stephen Harbourne*)
D: Maurice Elvey **SCR:** Eliot Stannard, from a play by Charles Darrell
Standard crime-thriller: Gambler blackmails nobleman's wife

Her Mad Night
see Held for Murder

The Herncrake Witch
1912, (GB), Heron Films, b&w, 710 ft. (216.4m)
W: Jakidawdra Melford (*Jakidawdra*), Mark Melford (*The Father*)
WRIT & D: Mark Melford
Standard fantasy: Witch helps grandchild's romance

The Heroic Trio
1992, (Hong Kong), color, 82 mins.
W: Maggie Cheung, Michelle Yeoh, Anita Mui, Anthony Wong, Damian Lau
D: Johnny To
Unusual horror-fantasy: Superheroines vs. ancestral evils

Hero of Babylon
see Beast of Babylon Against the Son of Hercules

Her Panelled Door
see The Woman with No Name

Herr Arnes Pengar (Sir Arne's Treasure)
1919, (Swed), Svenska, b&w, 7,280.2 ft. (2219m)
D: Mauritz Stiller **SCR:** Mauritz Stiller & Gustav Molander, from a novel by Selma Lagerlof
Standard fantasy-melodrama

Herr Arnes Pengar (Sir Arne's Treasure)
1954, (Swed), Svensk Filmindustri, color, 91 mins.
W: Ulla Jacobsson, Bibi Andersson
D: Gustav Molander, from a novel by Selma Lagerlof
Standard fantasy-melodrama

Here Comes Mr. Jordan: ROBERT MONTGOMERY

Die Herrin der Welt (The Mistress of the World)
1919, (Ger), b&w
D: Joe May
serial in 8 parts
Standard adventure-thriller: Valiant German girl travels from unexplored interior of China to legendary country of Ophir, finds Queen of Sheba's treasure

Die Herrin von Atlantis (The Mistress of Atlantis)
1932, (Ger), Nero, b&w, 90 mins.
W: Brigitte Helm
D: G.W. Pabst **SCR:** Herbert Rappoport, Laszlo Vajda, & Pierre Ichac, from a novel by Pierre Benoit
Fr retitle L'Atlantide
Classic fantasy: Ageless girl rules lost civilization

Her Rival's Necklace
1907, (GB), Warwick Trading Co., b&w, 625 ft. (190.5m)
D: Charles Raymond
Standard melodrama: Actress, suspected of stabbing rival for necklace, escapes to cottage where she discovers real thief

Her Sister's Secret
1946, (USA), PRC, b&w, 85 mins.
W: Nancy Coleman, Philip Reed, Margaret Lindsay
D: Edgar G. Ulmer
Standard melodrama

He, She or It
see La Poupee

Hets (Torment)
1944, (Swed), b&w, 101 mins.
W: Stig Jarrell, Alf Kjellin, Gunnar Bjornstrand, Mai Zetterling
D: Alf Sjoberg **SCR:** Ingmar Bergman
Intense psychodrama: Sadistic schoolmaster terrifies pupils

He Walked By Night
1948, (USA), Eagle Lion, b&w, 80 mins.
W: Scott Brady, Roy Roberts, Whit Bissell, Jack Webb
D: Alfred Werker (partially directed by Anthony Mann) **PHOTOG:** John Alton
Minor melodrama

He Who Gets Slapped
1924, (USA), Metro-Goldwyn, b&w, 7 reels (6,953 ft./2119.3m)
W: Lon Chaney Sr. ("*He Who Gets Slapped*"), Norma Shearer (*Consuelo*), John Gilbert (*Bezano*), Tully Marshall (*Count Mancini*), Marc MacDermott (*Baron Regnard*), Ford Sterling (*Tricaud*), Harvey Clark (*Briquet*), Paulette Duval (*Zinida*), Ruth King, Clyde Cook, Brandon Hurst, George Davis
D: Victor Seastrom **ADAPT:** Carey Wilson & Victor Seastrom, from a play by Leonid Andreiev **PHOTOG:** Milton Moore
Standard melodrama: Wronged scientist disguises himself as clown

He Who Rides a Tiger

1965, (GB), David Newman/British Lion, b&w, 103 mins.
<u>W:</u> Tom Bell (*Peter Rayston*), Judi Dench (*Joanne*), Jeremy Spenser (*The Panda*), Paul Rogers (*Supt. Taylor*), Kay Walsh (*Mrs. Woodley*), Peter Madden (*Peepers Woodley*), Ray McAnally (*The Orphanage Supt.*), Inigo Jackson (*Sgt. Scott*), Annette Andre (*Julie*), Edina Ronay (*Anna*), Ralph Michael (*Carter*), Naomi Chance (*Lady Cleveland*)
<u>P:</u> David Newman   <u>D:</u> Charles Crichton   <u>STORY:</u> Trevor Peacock
Modest crime-thriller: Woman finds man she loves is burglar

Her Sister's Secret

Hex

1973, (USA), 20th-Fox, color, 90 mins.
<u>W:</u> Keith Carradine, Scott Glenn, Robert Walker Jr., Gary Busey, John Carradine, Hilarie Thompson, Tina Herazo (*Christina Raines*), Mike Combs
<u>P:</u> Clark Paylow   <u>D:</u> Leo Garen   <u>SCR:</u> Leo Garen & Steve Katz   <u>STORY:</u> Doran William Cannon & Vernon Zimmerman
released to video as **The Shrieking**
Minor fantasy-thriller: Biker meets murderous witch

Hexed

1993, (USA), Price Entertainment/Brillstein-Grey/Col, color, 93 mins.
<u>W:</u> Arye Gross, Claudia Christian, Adrienne Shelly (*Gloria*)
Standard thriller-spoof: Hotel clerk involved with homicidal model

Hey There, It's Yogi Bear

1964, (USA), Col, color, 90 mins.
Standard animated fantasy

H.G. Wells' The New Invisible Man

1960, (Mex), Calderon, b&w, 95 mins.
<u>W:</u> Arturo de Cordova, Augusto Benedico, Ana Luisa Peluffo
<u>P:</u> Paul Castelain   <u>D:</u> Alfredo Crevenna   <u>SCR:</u> Julio Alejandro de Castro   <u>STORY:</u> Alfredo Salazar
Minor SF-thriller: Prisoner obtains invisibility formula

Hiawatha

1903, (GB), Urban Trading Co., b&w, 800 ft. (243.8m)
<u>D:</u> Joe Rosenthal, from Henry Wadsworth Longfellow's poem *The Song of Hiawatha*
Standard adventure-romance (filmed in Canada): Amerindian's birth, life, marriage and death (told in 20 scenes)

Hiawatha

1952, (USA), Mon/AA, color, 80 mins.
<u>W:</u> Vince Edwards, Yvette Dugay, Keith Larson, Michael Tolan
<u>D:</u> Kurt Neumann, based on Longfellow's epic poem
Standard adventure-thriller

The Hidden

1987, (USA), Robert Shaye/Heron/New Line, color, 98 mins.
<u>W:</u> Kyle MacLachlan (*Lloyd Gallagher*), Michael Nouri (*Tom Beck*), Ed O'Ross (*Cliff Willis*), Clu Gulager (*Flynn*), Lin Shaye, Clarence Felder, William Boyett, Katherine Cannon, Larry Cedar, James Luisi, Richard Brooks, Frank Renzulli, John McCann, Duane Davis, Kristin Clayton, Jill Friedman, Whitney Reis, Joey Sagal, Jeff Levine, Joseph Whipp, Mark Edward Morante, Rick Lieberman, Donald Willis, Joe Perce, Beau Gibson, Jason Edwards, J.N. Houck, Mary Petrie, Joey Aresco, Judy Kerr, Luce Morgan, Richard Whitaker, Michael Yama, Charlene White, Mark Siegler, Steve Eastin, Buckley Morris, Jack McGee, Ted White, Loren Haynes, Rachel Todd, Lenna Robinson, Cate Caplin, Joe Gilbride, Deke Anderson, Wren Brown, Alan Marcus, Mark Phelan, Danny Trejo, Alonzo Brown Jr., Branscombe Richmond, Charles Edward Smith, Lew Hopson, Doug Collins, Bob Cummings, Rick Diamond, Charlie Skeen, Robert Brown, Chris

Wentzel, Jake
<u>D:</u> Jack Sholder   <u>SCR:</u> Bob Hunt   <u>PHOTOG:</u> Jacques Haitkin   <u>SPCL-FX:</u> Marty Bresin, Eric Rylander & Steve Wolke   <u>MUSIC:</u> Michael Convertino
Exciting SF-thriller: Cops stalk vicious space-alien

The Hidden II

1993, (USA), color, 95 mins
<u>W:</u> Raphael Sbarge
Standard SF-horror: Detective's daughter teams with alien cop to destroy host-hopping monster

The Hidden City

see **Bomba and the Hidden City**

Hidden Enemy

1940, (USA), b&w, 63 mins.
<u>W:</u> Warren Hull, Kay Linaker, William von Brinken, George Cleveland
<u>D:</u> Howard Bretherton
Standard thriller: Spies seek formula for super-metal

The Hidden Eye

1945, (USA), MGM, b&w, 69 mins.
<u>W:</u> Edward Arnold (*Capt. Duncan Maclain*), Frances Rafferty (*Jean Hampton*), Paul Langton (*Barry Gifford*), Ray Collins (*Phillip Treadway*), William "Bill" Phipps (*Marty Corbett*), Thomas Jackson (*Insp. Delaney*), Robert Lewis (*Stormvig*), Morris Ankrum (*Ferris*), Francis Pierlot (*Kossovsky*), Ray Largay (*Arthur Hampton*), Sondra Rodgers (*Helen Roberts*), Theodore Newton (*Gibbs the Chaffeur*), Leigh Whipper (*Alistair*), Jack Lambert (*Louie*), Lee Phelps (*Polasky*), Byron Foulger (*Burton Lorrison*), Eddie Acuff (*Whitey*), Bob Pepper (*Sgt. Kramer*), Clyde Fillmore (*Rodney Hampton*), Friday the dog
<u>D:</u> Richard Whorf   <u>SCR:</u> George Harmon Coxe & Harry Ruskin, from a story by George Harmon Coxe, based on characters created by Bayard Kendrick   <u>PHOTOG:</u> Lester White   <u>MUSIC SCORE:</u> David Snell
Standard mystery-thriller: Blind sleuth hunts unknown killer. cf. **Eyes in the Night**

The Hidden Face

1965, (GB), Merton Park/Anglo-Amalgamated, b&w, 28 mins.
<u>W:</u> Christine Finn (*Jane Penshurst*), Richard Butler (*William Milsom*), Alex Macintosh (*Crispin*), Robert James (*Durrant*), Vernon Dobtcheff (*Strang*), Jill Dixon (*Anne Milsom*), Gretchen Franklin (*Rose Jenkins*)
<u>P:</u> Jack Greenwood   <u>D:</u> Patrick Dromgoole   <u>STORY:</u> James Eastwood
Standard short thriller: Authoress exposes evildoer

Hidden Fear

1957, (USA), UA, b&w, 83 mins.
<u>W:</u> John Payne, Conrad Nagel, Alexander Knox, Natalie Norwick
<u>D:</u> Andre de Toth
Standard thriller: Killer hunted in Copenhagen

Hidden Fears

1993, (USA), color, 90 mins.
<u>W:</u> Meg Foster, Frederic Forrest
Standard thriller: Years after husband's brutal murder, woman confronts killers and exposes horrifying secret

Hiawatha: YVETTE DUGAY, STEPHEN CHAASE, VINCENT EDWARDS

The Hidden Hand

1942, (USA), WB, b&w, 67 mins
<u>W:</u> Craig Stevens, Milton Parsons, Julie Bishop, Elizabeth Fraser, Willie Best, Creighton Hale, Monte Blue
<u>P:</u> William Jacobs   <u>D:</u> Ben Stoloff   <u>SCR:</u> Anthony Coldeway & Raymond Schrock, based on the play *Invitation to a Marder*, by Rufus King
Standard thriller: Asylum escapee involved with suspended animation

Hidden Homicide
1959, (GB), Bill & Michael Luckwell/RFDI/Rep, b&w, 72 mins.
<u>W</u>: Griffith Jones (*Michael Cornforth*), James Kenney (*Oswald/Mrs. Dodge/Kate*), Patricia Laffan (*Jean*), Bruce Seton (*Bill Dodd*), Maya Koumani (*Marian*), Richard Shaw (*Wright*), Robert Raglan (*Ashbury*), Charles Farrell (*Mungo Peddey*)
<u>P</u>: Derek Winn <u>D</u>: Tony Young <u>SCR</u>: Tony Young & Bill Luckwell, from Paul Capon's novel *Murder at Shinglestrand*
Standard thriller: Girl hiker proves female impersonator killed author's uncle

The Hidden Eye: FRANCES RAFFERTY AND EDWARD ARNOLD

The Hidden Menace
1925, (USA), William Steiner Prods., b&w, 5 reels
<u>W</u>: Charles Hutchison
<u>D</u>: Charles Hutchison <u>SCR</u>: J.F. Natteford
Standard thriller: Demented sculptor abducts girl

Hidden Mysteries
see **Cumbres Borrascosas**

Hidden Obsession
1993, (USA), HBO-TV, color, 92 mins.
<u>W</u>: Heather Thomas, Jan-Michael Vincent
Made-for-Cable, standard thriller: Killer stalks investigative reporter on backwoods vacation

The Hidden Room
see **Obsession (1949)**

The Hidden Witness
1914, (GB), Big Ben Films-Union/Pathe, b&w, 2,790 ft. (850.4m)
<u>W</u>: H.O. Martinek (*John Evans*), Ivy Montford (*Eleanor*)
<u>D</u>: H.O. Martinek <u>STORY</u>: L.C. MacBean
Standard crime-thriller: Girl's photograph proves secretary killed her uncle, framed cousin

Hide and Go Shriek
1987, (USA), color, 90 mins.
<u>W</u>: Annette Sinclair, Brittain Frye, Rebunkah Jones
<u>D</u>: Skip Schoolnik
Minor thriller: High-school seniors slain at graduation

Hide and Seek
1963, (GB), Spectrum/Albion/Univ, b&w, 90 mins.
<u>W</u>: Ian Carmichael (*David Garrett*), Janet Munro (*Maggie*), Hugh Griffith (*Wilkins*), Curt Jurgens (*Hubert Marek*), Edward Chapman (*McPherson*), Kieron Moore (*Paul*), Frederick Peisley (*Cottrell*), George Pravda (*Melnicker*), Kynaston Reeves (*Hunter*), Esma Cannon (*The Tea Lady*), Derek Tansley (*Charles*), Lance Percival (*The Idiot*)
<u>P</u>: Hal E. Chester <u>D</u>: Cy Endfield <u>SCR</u>: Robert Foshko & David Stone, from a novel by Harold Greene
Standard thriller: Professor becomes target for kidnap

Hideaway
1995, (USA), Trimark, color, 112 mins.
<u>W</u>: Jeff Goldblum (*Hatch*), Christine Lahti (*Lindsey*), Alfred Molina (*Dr. Jonas*), Alicia Silverstone (*Regina*), Jeremy Sisto (*Vassago*), Rae Dawn Chong (*Rose Orwetto*), Kenneth Welsh (*Det. Breech*), Suzy Joachim (*Dr. Kari Dovell*), Tom McBeath (*Morton Redlow*), Shirley Broderick (*Miss Dockridge*), Roger R. Cross (*Harry*), Joely Collins (*Linda*), Michael McDonald (*The Young Cop*), Don S. Davis (*Dr. Martin*), Hiro Kanagawa (*Nurse Nakamura*), Rebecca Toolan (*The Female Doctor*), Jayme Knox, Norma Wick, Michelle Skalnik, Gaetana Korbin, Sarah Strange, Tiffany Foster, Mara Duronslet, Iris Quinn Bernard, Natasha Morley
<u>D</u>: Brett Leonard <u>SCR</u>: Andrew Kevin Walker & Neal Jimenez, from Dean R.

Koontz' novel <u>PHOTOG</u>: Gale Tattersall <u>VS-FX SPRVSR</u>: Tim McGovern <u>MUSIC</u>: Trevor Jones
Superior horror-thriller: Drowned man revived, discovers psychic link with mad killer

Hideous!
1997, (USA), color, 85 mins.
<u>W</u>: Michael Citriniti, Rhonda Griffin
Made-for-Video, standard horror-fantasy: Four-eyed baby goes on killing spree

The Hideous Sun Demon
1959, (USA), Pacific-Int'l, b&w, 74 mins.
<u>W</u>: Robert Clarke (*Dr. Gilbert McKenna*), Patricia Manning (*Ann Lan-sing*), Nan Peterson (*Trudy Osborne*), Bill Hampton (*The Police Lt.*), Patrick Whyte (*Dr. Frederick Buckell*), Fred La Porta (*Dr. Jacob Hoff-man*), Peter Similuk (*George*), Robert Garry (*Dr. Stern*), Xandra Conkling (*Susie*), Donna King Conkling (*Susie's Mother*), Pearl Driggs (*The Lady on the Hospital Roof*), Del Courtney (*The Radio Announcer*), Richard Cassarino (*The Policeman*), Cass Richards, Darryl Westbrook, Helen Joseph, Bill Currie, Fran Leighton, Bob Hafner, John Murphy, Tony Hilder, Chuck Newell, David Sloan
<u>P & D</u>: Robert Clarke <u>SCR</u>: E.S. Seeley Jr., from an orig. idea by Robert Clarke & Phil Hiner <u>MUSIC</u>: John Seeley <u>SONG</u>: *Strange Pursuit*
orig. to be titled **Saurus** *or* **'Terror from the Sun**, *GB retitle,* **Blood on His Lips**
Standard SF-horror: Astronaut becomes scabrous horror when exposed to sunlight

The Hideout
1956, (GB), Major/RFD, b&w, 57 mins.
<u>W</u>: Dermot Walsh (*Steve Curry*), Rona Anderson (*Helen Grant*), Ronald Howard (*Robert Grant*), Sam Kydd (*Tim Bowers*), Howard Lang (*Greeko*), Edwin Richfield (*The Teacher*), Trevor Reid (*Fraser*), Frank Hawkins (*Insp. Ryan*)
<u>P</u>: John Temple-Smith & Francis Edge <u>D</u>: Peter Graham Scott <u>STORY</u>: Kenneth R. Hayles
Modest crime-thriller: Broker buys stolen furs, finds them diseased with anthrax

Hider in the House
1990, (USA), USA-TV, color, 109 mins.
<u>W</u>: Gary Busey, Michael McKean, Mimi Rogers, Candy Hutson, Kurt Christopher Kinder, Elizabeth Ruscio, Bruce Glover
<u>D</u>: Michael Patrick
TVM, unusual thriller: Madman lurks in attic's secret room

High and Low
1963, (Jap), Toho/Sterling, b&w, 143 mins.
<u>W</u>: Toshiro Mifune, Tatsuya Nakadai, Tsutomu Yamazaki, Yutaka Sada, Kenjiro Ishiyama, Kyoko Kagawa, Takashi Shimura
<u>D</u>: Akira Kurosawa, based on novel *King's Ransom* by "Ed McBain" [Evan Hunter]
Classic Nipponese socio-thriller: Kidnapper pursued, contemporary society revealed

High Desert Kill
1989, (USA), color, 100 mins.
<u>W</u>: Chuck Connors, Anthony Geary, Marc Singer, Micah Grant
<u>D</u>: Harry Falk <u>TELEPLAY</u>: T.S. Cook
TVM, unusual SF-thriller: Alien force invades hunters' bodies

The Highest Bidder
see **Woman Hunt**

High Frequency
1988, (It), color, 105 mins.
<u>W</u>: Oliver Benny, Vincent Spano, Isabelle Pasco, Anne Canovos
<u>D</u>: Faliero Rosati
Minor thriller: Woman's murder witnessed on satellite monitor

High Jump
1959, (GB), Danziger/UA, b&w, 66 mins.
<u>W</u>: Richard Wyler (*Bill Ryan*), Lisa Daniely (*Jackie Field*), Leigh Madison (*Kitty*), Michael Peake (*Ray Shaw*), Arnold Bell (*Tom Rowton*), Nora Gordon (*Mrs. Barlow*), Robert Raglan (*The Inspector*), Tony Doonan (*Frank*)
<u>P</u>: Edward J. & Harry Lee Danziger <u>D</u>: Godfrey Grayson <u>STORY</u>: Brian Clemens & Eldon Howard
Standard crime-thriller: Widow feigns love for ex-trapeze artist, gets him to assist gem thieves

Highlander
1986, (GB-USA), Highlander Prods./20th-Fox, color, 111 mins.
<u>W</u>: Christopher Lambert (*Connor MacLeod*), Sean Connery (*Ramirez*), Roxanne Hart (*Brenda Wyatt*), Clancy Brown (*Kurgan*), Beatie Edney (*Heather*), Alan North (*Lt. Frank Moran*), Hugh Quarshie (*Sunda Kastagir*), Jon Polito (*Det. Walter Bedsoe*), Sheila Gish (*Rachel Ellenstein*), Christopher Malcolm (*Kirk Matunas*), Peter Diamond (*Fasil*), Billy Hartman (*Dugal MacLeod*), James Cosmo (*Angus MacLeod*), Alistair Findlay (*Chief Murdoch*), Celia Imrie (*Kate*), Edward Wiley (*Garfield*), Ron Berglas (*Eric Powell*), James McKenna (*Father Rainey*), John Cassady (*Kenny*), Ian Reddington (*Bassett*), Sion Tudor Owen (*Hotchkiss*), Damien Leake (*Tony*), Louis Guss (*The Newsvendor*), Gordon Sterne (*Dr. Willis Kenderly*), Peter Banks (*The Priest*), Ted Maynard (*The Newscaster*), Helena Stevens (*The Old Woman in Car*), Anthony Mannino (*The Boisterous Drunk*), Frank Dux (*The Old Man in Car*), Prince Howell (*The Drunk in Hotel*), Anthony Fusco (*The Barman*), Corrinne Russell (*Candy*), Ian Tyler (*The Lab Technician*), Buckley Norris (*The Derelict*)
<u>D</u>: Russell Mulcahy <u>SCR</u>: Gregory Widen, Peter Bellwood, & Larry Ferguson

STORY: Gregory Widen **PHOTOG:** Gerry Fisher **SPCL-FX SPRVSR:** Martin Gutteridge **MUSIC SCORE:** Michael Kamen, additional music & songs by Queen
Bizarre fantasy-thriller (directed by rock-video vet): Immortals battle through centuries

Highlander 2: The Quickening
1991, (USA), InterStar, color, 100 mins.
W: Christopher Lambert, Sean Connery, Virginia Madsen, Michael Ironside, John C. McGinley, Allan Rich
D: Russell Mulcahy **SCR:** Peter Bellwood **STORY:** Brian Clemens & William Panzer, from characters created by Gregory Widen **PHOTOG:** Phil Meheux **MUSIC:** Stewart Copeland
Standard SF-fantasy: Immortals face greatest challenge

Highlander: The Final Dimension
1995, (Can-Fr-GB), Dimension, color, 98 mins.
W: Christopher Lambert, Mario Van Peebles, Deborah Unger, Mako, Raoul Trujillo, Jean-Pierre Perusse
D: Andy Morahan, from characters created by Gregory Widen
orig. to be titled Highlander 3: The Magician
Standard SF-fantasy

Highlander: The Gathering
1993, (USA), color, 98 mins.
W: Christopher Lambert, Adrian Paul, Richard Moll, Vanity, Alexandra Vandernoot, Stan Kirsh
D: Thomas J. Wright & Ray Austin **TELEPLAY:** Lorain Despres & Dan Gordon
TVM standard action-fantasy (reedited from teleseries): Immortals battle

Highlander 3: The Magician
see **Highlander: The Final Dimension**

Highly Dangerous
1950, (GB), Two Cities/GFD/Liffert, b&w, 88 mins.
W: Margaret Lockwood (*Frances Gray*), Dane Clark (*Bill Casey*), Marius Goring (*Anton Razinski*), Naunton Wayne (*Hedgerley*), Wilfrid Hyde-White (*Luke*), Eugene Deckers (*Alf*), Olaf Pooley (*The Ass't*), Gladys Henson (*The Attendant*), Paul Hardtmuth (*The Priest*), Michael Hordern (*Rawlings*), George Benson (*The Customer*), Eric Pohlmann (*Joe*), Joan Haythorne (*Judy*), Patric Doonan (*The Customs Man*), Anthony Newley (*The Operator*), Noel Johnson (*Frank Conway's Voice*)
P: Anthony Darnborough **D:** Roy Ward Baker, from a story by Eric Ambler
Standard thriller: American journalist and lady scientist risk lives to obtain secret information from behind Iron Curtain

High Priestess of Sexual Witchcraft
1973, (USA), Triumvirate, color, 90 mins.
W: Georgina Spelvin, Rick Livermore, Jean Palmer, Harding Harrison, Marc Stevens
D & SCR: Beau Buchanan
Minor eroto-fantasy

High Season for Spies
1967, (W. Ger), ITC, color, 92 mins
W: Peter Van Eyck, Letitia Roman
Minor thriller: Undercover men covet secret formula

High Spirits
1988, (USA), Palace/Vision/Tri-Star, color, 99 mins.
W: Daryl Hannah (*Mary Plunkett*), Peter O'Toole (*Peter Plunkett*), Steve Guttenberg (*Jack*), Beverly D'Angelo (*Sharon*), Jennifer Tilly (*Miranda*), Liam Neesom (*Martin Brogan*), Peter Gallagher (*Brother Tony*), Martin Ferrero (*Malcolm*), Connie Booth (*Marge*), Donal McCann (*Eamon*), Mary Coughlan (*Katie*), Liz Smith (*Mrs. Plunkett*), Tony Rohr (*Christy*), Hilary Reynolds (*Patricia*), Tom Hickey (*Sampson*), Isolde Cazelet (*Julia*), Krista Hornish (*Wendy*), Little John (*The Gateman*), Paul O'Sullivan (*Graham*), Matthew Wright (*Woody*), Ray McAnally, Aimee Delamain, Ruby Buchanan, Preston Lockwood
WRIT & D: Neil Jordan **PHOTOG:** Alex Thomson **SPCL VS-FX:** Derek Meddings **MUSIC:** George Fenton
Standard comedy-fantasy: Tourists meet spooks in Irish castle

The High Terrace
1956, (GB), Cipa/RKO, b&w, 82 mins.
W: Dale Robertson (*Bill Lang*), Lois Maxwell (*Stephanie Blake*), Derek Bond (*John Mansfield*), Eric Pohlmann (*Otto Kellner*), Mary Laura Wood (*Moll Kellner*), Carl Bernard (*Jock Dunmow*), Lionel Jeffries (*Monckton*), Jameson Clark (*Insp. Mackay*)
P: Robert Baker & Monty Berman **D:** Henry Cass **SCR:** Brock Williams, Alfred Shaughnessy & Norman Hudis **STORY:** A.T. Weisman
Modest crime-thriller: Playwright takes blame for homicidal actress

High Treason
1929, (GB), Gaumont, b&w, 90 mins.
W: Jameson Thomas (*Michael Deane*), Benita Hume (*Evelyn Seymour*), Basil Gill (*Pres. Stephen Deane*), Humberston Wright (*Vicar-General Seymour*), Henry Vibart (*Lord Sycamore*), James Carew (*Lord Rowleigh*), Alf Goddard (*The Teleradiographer*), Milton Rosmer (*Ernest Stratton*), Hayford Hobbs (*Charles Falloway*), Judd Green (*James Groves*), Irene Rooke (*The Senator*), Clifford

Heatherley (*The Delegate*), Wally Patch (*The Commissioner*), Raymond Massey (*The Man*)
P & SCR: L'Estrange Fawcett **D:** Maurice Elvey, from Noel Pemberton-Billing's play
Standard fantasy-thriller: Women unite to prevent financiers from engineering world war. Raymond Massey's debut

High Treason
1951, (GB), Conqueror/Gaumont/GFD/Pacemaker/Mayer-Kingsley, b&w, 93 mins.
W: Andre Morell (*Supt. Folland*), Liam Redmond (*Cdr. Brennan*), Mary Morris (*Ann Braun*), Kenneth Griffith (*Jimmy Ellis*), Patric Doonan (*George Ellis*), Joan Hickson (*Mrs. Ellis*), Anthony Bushell (*Maj.Elliott*), Anthony Nicholls (*Grant Mansfield*), Geoffrey Keen (*Morgan Williams*), John Bailey (*Stringer*), Dora Bryan (*Mrs. Bowers*), Laurence Naismith (*Gordon Wells*), Charles Lloyd-Pack (*Percy Ward*)
P: Paul Soskin **D:** Roy Boulting **SCR:** Frank Harvey & Roy Boulting, from Noel Pemberton-Billing's play **PHOTOG:** Gilbert Taylor **MUSIC:** John Addison
Standard thriller: Saboteurs plot to rule Britain

Highwayman Hal
1913, (GB), Hepworth, b&w, 1,000 ft. (304.8m)
W: Harry Buss (*Hal Harkaway*)
D: Hay Plumb
Standard adventure-comedy: Girl brings pardon from King, saves highwayman from hanging

Highways By Night
1942, (USA), RKO, b&w, 62 mins.
W: Richard Carlson, Jane Randolph, Jane Darwell, Ray Collins, Barton MacLane, Gordon Jones
D: Peter Godfrey **STORY:** Clarence Buddington Kelland
Standard melodrama: Millionaire framed for racketeer's murder

Highway 13
1949, (USA), Screen Guild/Lippert, b&w, 58 mins.
W: Robert Lowery, Pamela Blake, Lyle Talbot, Michael Whalen, Maris Wrixon, Clem Bevans
D: William Berke
Minor melodrama: Trucker witnesses "accident," falls under suspicion

Highway to Hell
1992, Made in 1989 (USA), Hemdale, color, 94 mins.
W: Patrick Bergin, Chad Lowe, Adam Storke, Kristy Swanson, Richard Farnsworth, Kevin Peter hall, C.J. Graham, Lita Ford, Pamela Gidley, Brian Helgeland, Gilbert Gottfried
D: Ate De Jong
Standard horror-spoof: Teen has 24 hours to rescue fiancee from Satan's domain

A High Wind in Jamaica
1965, (GB), 20th-Fox, color, 104 mins.
W: Anthony Quinn (*Capt. Chavez*), James Coburn (*Zac*), Lila Kedrova (*Rosa*), Dennis Price (*Mathias*), Benito Carruthers (*Alberto*), Gert Frobe (*Capt. Vandervort*), Nigel Davenport (*Mr. Thornton*), Isabel Dean (*Mrs. Thornton*), Kenneth J. Warren (*Capt. Marpole*), Deborah Baxter (*Emily Thornton*), Viviane Ventura (*Margaret Fernandez*), Martin Amis (*John Thornton*), Roberta Tovey (*Rachel Thornton*), Dan Jackson (*Big One*), Jeffrey Chandler (*Edward Thornton*), Karen Flack (*Laura Thornton*), Brian Phelan (*Curtis*)
P: John Croydon **D:** Alexander Mackendrick **SCR:** Stanley Mann, Ronald Harwood & Debnis Cannan, from Richard Hughes' novel *The Innocent Voyage* **PHOTOG:** Douglas Slocombe **MUSIC:** Larry Adler
Standard adventure-thriller: Pirates kidnap children

Hi, Here's Eddie
1958, (W. Ger), WB-TV, b&w, 92 mins
W: Eddie Constantine, Maria Sebaldt, Margit Saad, Silvia Solar, Guther Luders
Minor thriller: Heiresses disappear, pursuit ensues

Hi-Jack
1957, (GB), Aqua Films/New Realm, b&w, 50 mins.
W: Paul Carpenter (*Bob Reynolds*), Mary Martin (*Anna Braun*), Joe Robinson (*Pete Archer*), Ronald Leigh Hunt (*Kleivar*)
WRIT, P & D: Cecil H. Williamson
A.k.a. Action Stations
Standard crime-thriller: Counterfeiters threaten engraver's daughter

The Hi-Jackers
1963, (GB), Butcher's Films, b&w, 69 mins.
W: Anthony Booth (*Terry McKinley*), Derek Francis (*Jack Carter*), Jacqueline Ellis (*Shirley*), Patrick Cargill (*Insp. Grayson*), Glynn Edwards (*Bluey*), David Gregory (*Pete*), Harold Goodwin (*Scouse*), Arthur English (*Bert*), Anthony Wager (*Smithy*)
P: John I. Phillips **D & STORY:** Jim O'Connolly
Standard crime-thriller: Haulage contractor finds partner is crooked

Hillbillys in a Haunted House
1967, (USA), Woolner Bros., color, 88 mins.
W: Ferlin Husky, Joi Lansing, Don Bowman, John Carradine, Lon Chaney Jr., Basil Rathbone, Linda Ho, George Barrows, Sonny James, Molly Bee, Merle Haggard

P: Bernard Woolner   **D:** Jean Yarbrough   **SCR:** Duke Yelton
Minor comedy-thriller: Country singers meet "spooks." (Basil Rathbone's last film)

The Hills Have Eyes
1977, (USA), Blood Relations Co./Vanguard, color, 89 mins.
W: Susan Lanier (*Brenda Carter*), Robert Houston (*Bobby Carter*), Martin Speer (*Doug Wood*), Dee Wallace (*Lynne Wood*), Russ Grieve (*Big Bob Carter*), John Steadman (*Fred*), James Whitworth (*Jupiter*), Virginia Vincent (*Ethel Carter*), Michael Berryman (*Pluto*), Lance Gordon (*Mars*), Janus Blythe (*Ruby*), Cordy Clark (*Mama*), Brenda Marinoff (*Katy*), Arthur King (*Mercury*)
WRIT & D: Wes Craven   **PHOTOG:** Eric Saarinen   **SPCL-FX:** John Frazier & Greg Auer   **MUSIC:** Don Peake
Cult-classic thriller: Subhuman family preys on tourists

The Hills Have Eyes II
1986, (USA), Castle Hill/New Realm, color, 89 mins.
W: Kevin Blair (*Roy*), Michael Berryman (*Pluto*), Tamara Stafford (*Cass*), Janus Blythe (*Ruby*), Peter Frechette (*Harry*), Robert Houston (*Bobby*), John Bloom (*The Reaper*), Penny Johnson, John Laughlin, Willard Pugh, Lance Gordon, Susan Lanier, David Nichols, Virginia Vincent
WRIT & D: Wes Craven   **PHOTOG:** David Lewis   **SPCL-FX:** Richard Brownfield   **MUSIC:** Harry Manfredini
Standard thriller: Detoured racers meet remnants of cannibal family

The Hills of Donegal
1947, (GB), Argyle/Butcher, b&w, 85 mins.
W: Dinah Sheridan (*Eileen Hannay*), James Etherington (*Michael O'Keefe*), Moore Marriott (*Old Jake*), Brendan Clegg (*Paddy Hannay*), Irene Handl (*Mrs. McTavish*), John Bentley (*Terry O'Keefe*), Marie O'Neill (*Hannah*), Tamara Desni (*Carole Wells*)
P & D: John Argyle   **STORY:** John Dryden
reissued 1951
Standard musical-romance: Opera star weds cousin when caddish husband dies

Himmelskibet (Heaven Ship)
1917, (Den), b&w
W: Nicolai Neiiendam, Zanny Petersen, Gunnar Tolnas, Nils Asther
D: Forest Holger-Madsen   **SCR:** Sophus Michaelis & Ole Olsen   **PHOTOG:** Louis Larsen & Frederik Fuglsang
Standard SF-fantasy: Expedition to Mars finds a utopia

Der Himmel Uber Berlin
see Wings of Desire

The Hindoo's Treachery
1910, (GB), Cricks & Martin, b&w, 780 ft. (237.7m)
D: Dave Aylott
Standard thriller: British troops save captain's daughter from abduction by discharged servant

The Hindu
see Sabaka

The Hindu Tomb
see Journey to the Lost City

Hipnosis (Hypnosis)
1963, (Sp-W. Ger-It), Procusa/Int'l Germania/Domiziana Int'l Cinematografica/United Film Enterprises, b&w, 86 mins.
W: Eleonora Rossi-Drago, Gotz George, Jean Sorel, Massimo Serato, Margot Trooper, Heinz Drache, Mara Cruz, Michael Cramer, Hildegarde Kneff, Ana Maria Montaner, Jose Maria Cafarell, Werner Peters, Guido Celano, Diana Rabito
P: Alfons Carcasina   **D:** Eugenio Martin   **SCR:** Giuseppe Mangione, Eugenio Martin, G. Moreno Burgos, Gerhard Schmidt & Francis Niewel   **PHOTOG:** Francisco Sempere   **MUSIC:** Roman Vlad
Ger. retitle, **Nur Tote Zeugen Schweigen (Only a Dead Witness Keeps Quiet)**
A.k.a. **Dummy of Death**
Standard thriller: Ventriloquist's assistant becomes killer

His Brother's Ghost
1945, (USA), PRC, b&w, 54 mins.
W: Buster Crabbe, Al St. John, Charles King, Bud Osborne, Karl Hackett, Archie Hall
D: Sam Newfield
Standard western

His Burglar Brother
1912, (GB), Britannia Films/Pathe, b&w, 939 ft. (286.2m)
D: A.E. Coleby
Standard crime-thriller: Ex-convict takes blame for robber brother

His Conscience
1911, (GB), Natural Colour Kinematograph Co., color, 635 ft. (193.5m).
D: Theo Bouwmeester
Standard melodrama: Jealous officer frames rival for cheating at cards

His Country's Honour
1914, (GB), Cricks/Gaumot, b&w, 3,000 ft. (916.9m)
W: Douglas Payne (*Paul Koffman*), Norman Howard

D: Charles Calvert
USA retitle, **The Aviator Spy**
Standard crime-thriller: Spy saves foreign secretary's daughter from drowning, photographs secret treaty

His Duty
1912, (GB), British Anglo-American/Tyler, b&w, 650 ft. (198.1m)
W: George Bellay (*Father*)
D: Fred Rains
Standard crime-thriller: Detective finds fiancee's father is crook

His Evil Genius
1913, (GB), Hepworth, b&w, 2,025 ft. (617.2m)
W: Alec Worcester (*Jim Dowling*), Flora Morris (*Alice*), Harry Royston (*Harry Beecham*), Frank Wilson (*The Baker*)
D: Frank Wilson
A.k.a. **At the Prompting of the Devil**
Standard crime-thriller: Drunkard robs house

His Honour at Stake
1912, (GB), Barker, b&w, 1,070 ft. (326.1m)
D: Bert Haldane   **STORY:** Rowland Talbot
Standard melodrama: Army surgeon blamed when burglar kills doctor's wife

His Great Opportunity
1914, (GB), Hepworth, b&w, 1,600 ft. (495.3m)
W: Tom Powers (*The Understudy*), Alma Taylor (*The Acress*), Edward Lingard (*The Actor*)
D: Warwick Buckland
Standard crime-thriller: Fired actor tries to kill understudy

His Just Desserts
1914, (GB), Neptune/Browne, b&w, 1,160 ft. (353.6m)
W: Frank Collins (*The Spy*), Daisy Cordell (*The Spy's Wife*), Gregory Scott (*The Manager*)
WRIT & D: Gerald Lawrence
Standard crime-thriller: Spy fakes own death, poses as his barber brother-in-law

His Last 12 Hours
1950, (It), Vinti, b&w, 98 mins.
W: Jean Gabin, Antonella Lualdi, Mariella Lotti
D: Luigi Zampa   **SCR:** Cesare Zavattini
A.k.a. **Twelve Hours to Live**
Minor melodrama

His Majesty, The Scarecrow of Oz
1914, (USA), b&w
WRIT, P & D: Frank L. Baum

His Mother's Necklace
1910, (GB), Kineto, b&w, 575 ft. (178m)
D: Walter R. Booth
Standard crime-thriller: Artist steals mother's necklace

His Other Woman
see Desk Set

His Phantom Burglar
1915, (GB), Martin/DFSA, b&w, 517 ft. (157.6m)
D: Dave Aylott
Minor fantasy short: Police recruit chases magical thief

His Prehistoric Past
1914, (USA), Keystone, b&w, 2 reels
W: Charles Chaplin, Mack Swain, Gene Marsh
WRIT & D: Charles Chaplin
A.k.a. **A Dream**
Standard fantasy: Vision of improbable prehistory

His Reformation
1914, (GB), London, b&w, 1,270 ft. (387.1m)
W: Edna Flugrath (*Ruth Sumner*), Gregory Scott (*Hubert Morton*), Frank Stanmore (*Jim Bowkett*), Arthur Cullin
D: Arthur Holmes-Gore   **STORY:** William J. Elliott
Standard crime-thriller: Disowned man weds cleric's daughter, takes blame for theft

His Sister's Honour
1914, (GB), Barker/Walturdaw, b&w, 1,250 ft. (381m)
W: Blanche Forsythe (*Beatrice*), Moore Marriott
D: Bert Haldane   **STORY:** Rowland Talbot
Standard crime-thriller: Nurse's dying confession clears soldier-brother of stealing necklace

Histoire d'un Crime
see Les Incendiaires

Histoires Extraordinaires (Unusual Tales)
1948, (Fr), b&w
Unusual trilogy (including Edgar Allan Poe's "The Cask of Amontillado" & Thomas DeQuincey's "Ecce Homo")

His Wife's Habit
see Women and Bloody Terror

His Wondeful Lamp
1913, (GB), Cricks & Martin, b&w, 463 ft. (141.1m)
W: Jack Leigh *(Prof. Leigh)*
D: Edwin J. Collins
Minor fantasy: Tramp steals lamp that causes invisibility

The Hitcher
1986, (USA), HBO-Silver Screen Partners/Tri-Star, color, 98 mins.
W: Rutger Hauer *(John Ryder)*, C. Thomas Howell *(Jim Halsey)*, Jennifer Jason Leigh *(Nash)*, John Jackson *(Esteridge)*, Jack Thibeau *(Prestone)*, Eugene Davis *(Dodge)*, Armin Shimerman *(The Interrogation Sgt.)*, Billy Green Bush, Henry Darrow
D: Robert Harmon **SCR:** Eric Red **PHOTOG:** John Seale **MUSIC:** Mark Isham
Taut thriller: Youth gives ride to psychopath

The Hitch-Hiker
1953, (USA), RKO, b&w, 71 mins.
W: Edmond O'Brien, Frank Lovejoy, William Talman, Sam Hayes, Jose Torvay, Jean Del Val
P & D: Ida Lupino **PHOTOG:** Nicholas Musuraca **MUSIC:** Leith Stevens
Unusual thriller: Two men on fishing trip give ride to mass murderer

A Hitch in Time
1979, (GB), Eyeline/CFF, color, 57 mins.
W: Michael McVey *(Paul Gibson)*, Pheona McLellan *(Fiona Hatton-Jones)*, Patrick Troughton *(Prof. Wagstaff)*, Jeff Rawle *(Sniffy Kemp)*, Sorcha Cusack *(Miss Campbell)*, Jo Maxwell Muller *(Mrs. Carter/Ma Kemp/The Witch)*, Ronnie Brody *(Grandpa)*, Norman Mitchell *(The Sgt.)*, Ted Burnett *(The Executioner)*, Ken McDonald *(The Constable)*
P: Harold Orton **D:** Jan Darnley-Smith **STORY:** T.E.B. Clarke **PHOTOG:** Tommy Fletcher **MUSIC:** Harry Robinson
Standard juvenile fantasy: Professor's time machine takes children to 1953, 1816, & 1741

Hitler: The Last Ten Days
1973, (GB-It), Westfilm-Wolfgang Reinhardt/MGM-EMI.Par., color, 106 mins.
W: Alec Guinness *(Adolf Hitler)*, Simon Ward *(Hoffmann)*, Adolfo Celi *(Krebs)*, Diane Cilento *(Hanna)*, Eric Porter *(Von Grei)*, Gabriele Ferzetti *(Keitel)*, Doris Kunstmann *(Eva Braun)*, Joss Ackland *(Burgdorf)*, John Barron *(Dr. Stumpfegger)*, John Bennett *(Goebbels)*, Sheila Gish *(Frau Christian)*, Julian Glover *(Fegelein)*, Barbara Jefford *(Magda Goebbels)*, Michael Goodliffe *(Weidling)*, Angela Pleasence *(Trude)*, John Hallam *(Guensche)*, Philip Stone *(Jodl)*, Mark Kingston *(Bormann)*, Phyllida Law *(Fraulein Manzialy)*, Ann Lynn *(Fraulein Junge)*, Andrew Sachs *(Wagner)*, Timothy West *(Gebhardt)*, Kenneth Colley *(Boldt)*, William Abney *(Voss)*, James Cossins *(The German Officer)*, Philip Locke *(Hanske)*, Richard Fescud *(Von Below)*, John Savident *(Hewel)*
D: Ennio De Concini **SCR:** Ennio De Concini, Maria Pia Fusco, Wolfgang Reinhardt & Ivan Moffat **PHOTOG:** Ennio Guarnieri **MUSIC:** Mischa Spoliansky
Standard melodrama: Study of doomed Nazi dictator

Hitler's Children
1942, (USA), RKO, b&w
W: Tim Holt *(Karl)*, Bonita Granville *(Anna)*, Kent Smith *(Nicky)*, Otto Kruger, H.B. Warner, Lloyd Corrigan, Hans Conried, Erford Gage
D: Edward Dmytryk **PHOTOG:** Russell Metty **MUSIC:** Roy Webb
Modest wartime propaganda-thriller: Nazi youth indoctrinated

Hitler's Daughter
1990, (USA-Can), Wilshire Court/USA-TV, color, 95 mins.
W: Patrick Cassidy, Melody Anderson, Veronica Cartwright, Kay Lenz, Carolyn Dunn, Lindsay Merrithew, George R. Robertson, Gary Reineke *(Holland)*, Donald Davis *(Dr. Bauman)*, Jonathan Welsh *(Zimmerman)*, Cec Linder *(Trautman)*, Clayton Ed McGibbon *(Rutledge)*, Nigel Bennett *(Berger)*, Tom Butler *(Dolan)*, Frank Adamson *(Mitchell)*, Chris Mann *(Dr. Wolt)*, John Stoneham Jr. *(Taylor)*, Deborah Mann *(The Nurse)*, Rex Hagon *(The News Producer)*, Abraham Falconer *(The Pizza Delivery Driver)*, James Mainprize *(Melvin O'Neill)*
D: James A. Contner **TELEPLAY:** Sherman Gray & Christopher Canaan, from Timothy B. Benford's novel **PHOTOG:** Frank Tidy **MUSIC:** Joel McNeely
TVM, standard thriller: Woman heads neo-Nazi conspiracy

Hitler's Son
1978, (W. Ger), Gerd Goering, color
W: Bud Cort, Peter Cushing
D: Rod Amateau **SCR:** Lukas Heller & Burkhard Driest
Standard comedy-satire

The H-Man
1959, (Jap), Toho/Col, color, 79mins.
W: Yumi Shirakawa, Kenji Sahara, Koreya Senda, Akihiko Hirata, Eitaro Ozawa, Mitsuru Sato

P: Tomoyuki Tanaka **D:** Inoshiro Honda **SCR:** Takeshi Kimura, from a story by Hideo Kaijo **PHOTOG:** Hajime Koizumi **MUSIC:** Masaru Sato
Standard SF-horror: Radioactive fallout creates gelatinous, once-human creatures in Tokyo's sewers

The Hobbit
1977, (USA-Jap), Rankin-Bass, Made for TV, color, 78 mins.
VOICES: Orson Bean *(Bilbo Baggins)*, John Huston *(Gandalf)*, Richard Boone *(Smaug)*, Theodore *(Gollum)*, Hans Conried *(Thorin)*, Otto Preminger, Cyril Ritchard, Don Messick, Jack De Leon, Paul Frees & John Stephenson
P & D: Arthur Rankin Jr. & Jules Bass **TELEPLAY:** Romeo Muller, from J.R.R. Tolkien's novel **MUSIC:** Maury Laws **LYRICS:** Jules Bass **SONG:** *The Greatest Adventure* (sung by Glenn Yarbrough)
TVM, animated fantasy: Tiny race journeys to slay dragon

Hocus Pocus
1993, (USA), Disney/Buena Vista, color, 95 mins.
W: Bette Midler, Sarah Jessica Parker, Kathy Najimy, Omri Katz, Vinessa Shaw, Thora Birch, Vinessa Shaw, Amanda Shepherd, Doug Jones, Sean Murray, Karen Getz, Larry Bagby III, Tobias Jelinek, Don Yesso, Stephanie Faracy, Charlie Rocket, Kathleen Freeman
D: Kenny Ortega **SPCL-FX SPRVSR:** Peter Montgomery **SCR:** Neil Cuthbert & Mick Garris **VS-FX SPRVSR:** Peter Montgomery **MUSIC:** John Debney **SONG:** *I Put a Spell on You*
Standard comedy-fantasy: Witches vow to eat children

Hold Back Tomorrow
1955, (USA), Univ, b&w, 75 mins.
W: John Agar, Cleo Moore, Frank de Kova, Harry Guardino
WRIT, P & D: Hugo Haas
Minor melodrama: Man awaits execution

Hold On!
1966, (USA), MGM, color, 85 mins.
W: Peter Noone, Shelley Fabares, Sue Ane Langdon, Herman's Hermits
P: Sam Katzman **D:** Arthur Lubin **SONG:** *A Must to Avoid & Leaning on a Lamppost*
orig. to be titled **There's No Place Like Space**
Standard musical-comedy: Singers have bizarre adventures

Hold That Ghost
1941, (USA), Univ, b&w, 86 mins.
W: Bud Abbott *(Chuck Murray)*, Lou Costello *(Ferdinand Jones)*, Richard Carlson *(Dr. Jackson)*, Evelyn Ankers *(Norma Lind)* Joan Davis *(Camille)*, Mischa Auer *(Gregory)*, Marc Lawrence *(Charlie Smith)*, Shemp Howard *(The Soda Jerk)*, Russell Hicks , William Davidson (Moose Matson), Paul Fix, Ted Lewis and His Orchestra, The Andrews Sisters (singing *Aurora*)
D: Arthur Lubin **SCR:** Robert Lees, Frederic Rinaldo & John Grant **PHOTOG:** Elwood Bredell & Joseph Valentine **MUSIC:** H.J. Salter
A.k.a. **Oh, Charlie**
Standard comedy-thriller: Boobs inherit gangster's counry hideout, said to be haunted

Hold That Hypnotist
1957, (USA), AA, b&w, 61 mins.
W: Huntz Hall, Jane Nigh, Robert Foulk, Stanley Clements, James Fla-vin, Queenie Smith, David Condon, Dick Elliott, Mel Welles *(Black-beard)*, Jimmy Murphy, Murray Alper
P: Ben Schwalb **D:** Austen Jewell **SCR:** Dan Pepper **PHOTOG:** Harry Neumann **MUSIC:** Marlin Skiles
Minor comedy-fantasy: Under hypnotic spell, one of Bowery Boys meets Blackbeard the Pirate. Partial remake of Joe E. Brown's **The Gladiator**

Hold That Hypnotist: ROBERT FOULK, HUNTZ HALL AND STANLEY CLEMENTS

Hold That Line
1952, (USA), Mono, b&w, 64 mins.
<u>W:</u> Leo Gorcey, Huntz Hall, John Bromfield, Veda Ann Borg
<u>P:</u> Jerry Thomas <u>D:</u> William Beaudine <u>SCR:</u> Tim Ryan & Charles F. Marion
Minor comedy-fantasy: Bowery Boys go to college, superstrength formula helps them win big game

The Hole (1959)
see Le Trou

Hold That Ghost: MARC LAWRENCE, FRANK PENNY and LOU COSTELLO

The Hole (1964)
see Onibaba

The Hollow Man
1999, (USA), color
<u>W:</u> Jennifer Lopez
<u>D:</u> Paul Verhoeven
Standard SF-thriller: Man rendered invisible

Hollywood Chainsaw Hookers
1988, (USA), Savage Cinema/Camp Motion Pictures/AmericanIndependent, color, 74 mins.
<u>W:</u> Gunnar Hansen, Linnea Quigley, Jay Richardson, Michelle Bauer, Dawn Wildsmith, Dennis Mooney, Jerry Fox, Esther Alyse, Tricia Brown
<u>P & D:</u> Fred Olen Ray <u>PHOTOG:</u> Scott Ressler <u>MUSIC:</u> Michael Perlsten
A.k.a. Chainsaw Hookers
Minor horror-spoof: Detective probes gruesome cult

The Hollywood Meat Cleaver Massacre
see Meat Cleaver Massacre

The Hollywood Strangler Meets the Skid Row Slasher
1979, (USA), color, 72 mins.
<u>W:</u> Pierre Agostino, Carolyn Brandt, Forrest Duke, Chuck Alford
<u>D:</u> Ray Dennis Steckler
A.k.a. The Model Killer
Minor horror-thriller: Photographer slays models

Holocaust 2000
1978, (GB-It), Aston/Embassy/AIP, color, 102 mins.
<u>W:</u> Kirk Douglas (*Robert Caine*), Simon Ward (*Angel Caine*), Agostina Belli (*Sara Golan*), Anthony Quayle (*Prof. Griffith*), Virginia McKenna (*Eva Caine*), Adolfo Celi (*Dr. Kerouac*), Spiros Focas (*Harbin*), Alexander Knox (*Meyer*), Ivo Garrani (*The Prime Minister*), Geoffrey Keen (*The Gynecologist*), Romolo Valli (*Monsignor Charrier*), Massimo Foschi (*The Assassin*), Penelope Horner (*The Sec'y*), Peter Cellier, John Carlin, Gerald Hely, Jenny Twigg, Caroline Horner, Richard Cornish, Joanne Dainton, Denis Lawson, John Bancroft, Alan Hendricks
<u>P:</u> Edmondo Amati <u>D:</u> Alberto DeMartino <u>SCR:</u> Michael Robson <u>STORY:</u> Sergio Donati & Alberto DeMartino <u>PHOTOG:</u> Enrico Menczer <u>MUSIC:</u> Ennio Morricone
A.k.a. The Chosen
Standard fantasy-thriller: Industrialist's son is reborn Anti-Christ

Holy Terror
see Alice, Sweet Alice

Holy Wednesday
1975, (USA), World Wide, color
Standard thriller

El Hombre y el Monstruo (The Man and the Monster)
1958, (Mex), Azteca/K. Gordon Murray, b&w, 75 mins.

<u>W:</u> Abel Salazar, Enrique Rambal, Martha Roth, Ofelia Guilmain
<u>D:</u> Raphael Baledon <u>SCR:</u> Alfred Salazar <u>STORY:</u> Raul Centeno <u>PHOTOG:</u> Raoul Martinez Solares <u>MUSIC-DIR:</u> Gustavo C. Carrion
USA release, 1962
Minor "Jekyll-Hyde" horror-thriller: Satanic pact turns maestro into monster

Home at Seven
see Murder on Monday

Homebodies
1974, (USA), Avco Embassy, color, 96 mins.
<u>W:</u> Frances Fuller, Ian Wolfe, Ruth McDevitt, Kenneth Tobey
<u>P:</u> Marshal Blackar <u>D:</u> Peter Brocco <u>SCR:</u> Larry Yost
Excellent satire-thriller: Demented senior citizens are threatened with eviction, take drastic steps

Home for the Holidays
1972, (USA), Aaron Spelling-Leonard Goldberg/20th-Fox/ABC-TV, color, 74 mins.
<u>W:</u> Eleanor Parker, Sally Field, Jessica Walter, Jill Haworth, Julie Harris, John Fink, Walter Brennan, Med Flory
<u>P:</u> Paul Junger Witt <u>D:</u> John Llewellyn Moxey <u>SCR:</u> Joseph Stefano
TVM, unusual thriller: Daughters of dying man return for Christmas, encounter murder and mystery

Home Sweet Home
1980, (USA), color, 84 mins.
<u>W:</u> Jake Steinfeld, Sallee Elyse, Peter de Paula
<u>D:</u> Nettie Pena
A.k.a. Slasher in the House
Minor thriller: Escaped psycho disrupts family's Thanksgiving

Home Sweet Homicide
1946, (USA), 20th-Fox, b&w, 90 mins.
<u>W:</u> Lynn Bari, Randolph Scott, Peggy Ann Garner, Dean Stockwell
<u>D:</u> Lloyd Bacon
Standard comedy-thriller. Mystery writer's children solve local murder

Home to Danger
1951, (GB), New World/Eros, b&w, 66 mins.
<u>W:</u> Guy Rolfe (*Robert*), Rona Anderson (*Barbara*), Francis Lister (*Wainwright*), Alan Wheatley (*Hughes*), Stanley Baker (*Willie Dougan*), Bruce Belfrage (*The Solicitor*), Dennis Harkin (*Jimmy the One*), Peter Jones (*Lips Leonard*)
<u>P:</u> Lance Comfort <u>D:</u> Terence Fisher <u>STORY:</u> John Temple-Smith & Francis Edge
Standard crime-thriller: Dope peddler menaces dead partner's daughter

Homewrecker
1992, (USA), cable, color, 88 mins.
<u>W:</u> Robby Benson, Sydney Walsh, Sarah Rose Karr, Kate Jackson (voice)
<u>D:</u> Fred Walton <u>SCR:</u> Eric Harlacher
Made-for-Cable, standard SF-thriller: Scientist programs nuclear-weapons computer with female personality

Homicidal
1961, (USA), Col, b&w, 87 mins.
<u>W:</u> Jean Arless, Glenn Corbett, Patricia Breslin, Alan Bunce, Richard Rust, Eugenie Leontovich, Gilbert Green, James Westerfield, Hope Summers, Wolfe Barzell, Ralph Moody, Joe Forte, Teri Brooks
<u>P & D:</u> William Castle <u>SCR:</u> Robb White <u>PHOTOG:</u> Burnett Guffey <u>MUSIC:</u> Hugo Friedhofer
Bizarre thriller (Castle's answer to Hitchcock's Psycho): Cryptic young woman commits "senseless" murders

Homicide
1949, (USA), WB, b&w, 77 mins.
<u>W:</u> Robert Douglas, Helen Westcott, Robert Alda
Minor thriller

Homicide for Three
1948, (USA), Rep, b&w, 60 mins.
<u>W:</u> Warren Douglas, Audrey Long, Grant Withers
Minor thriller

L'Homme aux Cent Trucs (The Man with 100 Tricks)
1901, (Fr), Star, b&w, 50m (164 ft./2.8 mins.)
<u>D:</u> Georges Melies
USA retitle, The Conjurer with a Hundred Tricks
Standard fantasy

L'Homme aux Mille Inventions (The Man with a Thousand Inventions)
1910, (Fr), Star, b&w
<u>D:</u> Georges Melies
Standard fantasy

L'Homme dans la Lune (The Man in the Moon)
1898, (Fr), Star, b&w, 60m (196.9 ft./3.3 mins.)
<u>D:</u> Georges Melies
A.k.a. The Astronomer's Dream: or, The Man in the Moon
Standard SF-fantasy-comedy

L'Homme-Mouche (The Human Fly)
1902, (Fr), Star, b&w, 40m (131.2 ft./2.2 mins.)
<u>D</u>: Georges Melies
Standard fantasy: Man walks on ceiling

Homicide For Three: GRANT WITHERS, AUDREY LONG AND WARREN DOUGLAS

Un Homme Perdu
see Der Verlorene

Homunculus
1916, (Ger), Bioscop, b&w
<u>W</u>: Olaf Fonss, Frederick Kohn, Maria Carmi, Theodor Loos, Mechtild Their, Gustav Kohne, Egede Nissen
<u>D</u>: Otto Rippert   <u>SCR</u>: Otto Rippert & Robert Neuss   <u>PHOTOG</u>: Carl Hoffmann
A.k.a. **Die Rache des Homunculus (The Revenge of Homunculus)**
Standard fantasy-thriller, 6-chapter serial

Honeycomb
1969, (Sp), Cine Globe/Gold Key, color, 96 mins.
<u>W</u>: Geraldine Chaplin, Per Oscarsson, Teresa Del Rio, Julio Pena
<u>D</u>: Carlos Saura
Stylish psychodrama: Well-to-do couple becomes submerged in fantasy world of games

Honey, I Blew Up the Kid
1992, (USA), Walt Disney/Buena Vista, color, 89 mins.
<u>W</u>: Rick Moranis, Marcia Strassman, Robert Oliveri, Lloyd Bridges, John Shea, Daniel Shalikar, Joshua Shalikar, Keri Russell, Gregory Sierra, Julia Sweeney, Kenneth Tobey, Peter Elbling
<u>P</u>: Dawn Steel & Edward S. Feldman   <u>D</u>: Randal Kleiser   <u>SCR</u>: Thom Eberhardt, Peter Elbling & Garry Goodrow   <u>STORY</u>: Garry Goodrow, from characters created by Stuart Gordon, Brian Yuzna & Ed Naha   <u>MUSIC</u>: Bruce Broughton
Standard comedy-fantasy: Inventor turns infant into giant

Honey, I Shrunk the Kids
1989, (USA), Amblin/Walt Disney/Buena Vista, color, 93 mins.
<u>W</u>: Rick Moranis (*Wayne Szalinski*), Marcia Strassman (*Diane Szalinski*), Matt Frewer (*Big Russ Thompson*), Thomas Brown (*Little Russ Thompson*), Jared Rushton (*Ron Thompson*), Amy O'Neill (*Amy Szalinski*), Kristine Sutherland (*Mae Thompson*), Robert Oliveri (*Nick Szalinski*), Carl Steven (*Tommy Pervis*), Mark L. Taylor (*Don Forrester*), Kimmy Robertson (*Gloria Forrester*), Lou

The Honeymoon Killers: TONY LOBIANCO AND SHIRLEY STOLER

Cutell (*Dr. Brainard*), Laura Waterbury (*The Female Cop*), Trevor Galtress (*The Male Cop*), Martin Aylett (*Harold Boorstein*), Janet Sunderland (*Lauren Boorstein*)
<u>D</u>: Joe Johnston   <u>SCR</u>: Ed Naha & Tom Schulman   <u>STORY</u>: Stuart Gordon, Brian Yuzna & Ed Naha   <u>PHOTOG</u>: Hiro Narita   <u>MUSIC</u>: James Horner
Modest SF-comedy: Tinkerer's invention reduces children

Honey, We Shrunk Ourselves
1997, (USA), Walt Disney/Buena Vista, video, color, 76 mins.
<u>W</u>: Rick Moranis, Eve Gordon
Made-for-Video (first live-action Disney film made expressly for Video), standard SF-comedy: Accident shrinks teens' parents

The Honeymoon Killers
1969, (USA), Cinerama, b&w, 108 mins.
<u>W</u>: Tony LoBianco, Shirley Stoler, Mary Jane Higby, Doris Roberts, Kip McArdle, Marilyn Chris, Dortha Duckworth
<u>P</u>: Warren Steibel   <u>D & SCR</u>: Leonard Kastle   <u>PHOTOG</u>: Oliver Wood   <u>MUSIC</u>: Gustav Mahler
A.k.a. **The Lonely Hearts Killers**
Classic fact-based thriller: Immigrant gigolo and overweight nurse commit atrocities

Honeymoon of Fear
see Fear in the Night (1972)

Honeymoon of Horror
1964, (USA), Manson, color
<u>W</u>: Robert Parsons (*Emile*), Abbey Heller (*Lilli*)
<u>P</u>: Herb Meyer   <u>D</u>: Irwin Meyer   <u>SCR</u>: Alexander Panas
A.k.a. **The Deadly Circle, The Golden Nymphs** *and* **Orgy of the Golden Nudes**
Minor thriller: Sculptor's wife plagued by threatening phone calls, bizarre accidents

Honour Among Thieves
1915, (GB), Burlingham Standard, b&w, 1,270 ft. (387.1m)
<u>W</u>: Ernest G. Batley
<u>D</u>: Ernest G. Batley
Standard crime-thriller: Ex-crook becomes butler, finds adopted son is thief

Honour in Pawn
1916, (GB), Broadwest, b&w, 4,800 ft. (1463m)
<u>W</u>: Manora Thew (*Nancy Raeburn*), Julian Royce (*Sir Roger Singleton*), George Bellamy (*Harvey Denman*), Ivan Berlyn (*Giovanni Leracca*), Helen Haye (*Mrs. Fortescue*), Hetta Bartlett, Marjorie Compton
<u>P</u>: Walter West   <u>D & SCR</u>: Harold Weston, from a novel by W.B. Maxwell
Standard crime-thriller: Crooked dealer adopts girl thief, forces her to steal knight's plate

Hoppity Goes to Town
1941, (USA), color, 77 mins.
<u>D</u>: Dave Fleischer   <u>MUSIC</u>: Frank Loesser & Hoagy Carmichael
A.k.a. **Bug Goes to Town**
Standard animated fantasy: Grasshopper visits big city

Le Horla (The Horla)
1967, (Fr), color, 38 mins.
<u>D & SCR</u>: Jean-Daniel Pollet, from Guy de Maupassant's short story   <u>MUSIC</u>: Ravel
Standard fantasy short: Man possessed by evil spirit

The Horla (1962)
see Diary of a Madman

The Horn Blows at Midnight
1945, (USA), WB, b&w, 80 mins.
<u>W</u>: Jack Benny, Alexis Smith, Dolores Moran, Guy Kibbee, Allyn Joslyn, Reginald Gardiner, Franklin Pangborn, Mike Mazurki, Bobbie Blake, Margaret Dumont, Truman Bradley, Ethel Griffies, John Alexander
<u>P</u>: Mark Hellinger   <u>D</u>: Raoul Walsh   <u>SCR</u>: Sam Hellman & James V. Kern   <u>PHOTOG</u>: Sid Hickox   <u>SPCL-FX</u>: Lawrence Butler   <u>MUSIC</u>: Franz Waxman
Classic comedy-fantasy: Musician dreams he is angel sent to herald end of world

The Horrible Dr. Hichcock
see Raptus

The Horrible House on the Hill
1975, (USA), Barrister/Cinemation/Seymour Borde, color, 90 mins.
<u>W</u>: Gene Evans, Taylor Lacher, Sorrell Booke, Joan McCall, Shelley Morrison, Carolyn Stellar, Tierre Turner, Leif Garrett, John Durren, Gail Smale, Tia Thompson, Dawn Lyn
<u>P</u>: Dylan Jones & Michael Blowitz   <u>D</u>: Sean MacGregor   <u>SCR</u>: John Durren, from a story by Dylan Jones   <u>PHOTOG</u>: Paul Hipp & Mike Shea   <u>MUSIC</u>: William Loose
A.k.a. **People Toys.** *redistributed (1977) as* **Devil Times Five**
Unusual thriller: Escaped band of mentally-ill children enacts ghastly murders

Horrible Hyde
1915, (USA), Lubin, b&w
<u>W</u>: Jerold T. Hevner
Spoof of Robert Louis Stevenson's Dr. Jekyll and Mr. Hyde

The Horrible Sexy Vampire
see *El Vampiro de la Utopista*

Horror
1963, (It-Sp), Films Columbus-Llama Films/AIP-TV/Filmways, b&w, 89 mins
W: Gerard Tichy, Joan Hills, Leo Anchoriz, Iran Eory, Emily Wolko-vicz, Francisco Moran, Richard Davis
D: Martin Herbert [Alberto DeMartino]   SCR: Grimaud & Gordon Wilson Jr., from stories by Edgar Allan Poe   PHOTOG: Alessandro Ulloa   MUSIC: Francis Clark
USA retitle, The Blancheville Monster
Minor thriller: Girl's life must be sacrificed to fulfill ancient family legend

Horror and Sex
see *Night of the Bloody Apes*

The Horror at 37,000 Feet
1973, (USA), CBS-TV, color, 73 mins.
W: William Shatner, Roy Thinnes, Chuck Connors, Tammy Grimes, Buddy Ebsen, Jane Merrow, Lyn Loring, France Nuyen, Paul Win-field, Russell Johnson, Will Hutchins
P: Anthony Wilson   D: David Lowell Rich   TELEPLAY: Ron Austin & Jim Buchanan, from a story by V.X. Appleton
TVM, superior horror-fantasy: Demonic forces terrify passengers on trans-Atlantic airplane

Horror Castle
see *La Vergine di Norimberga*

Horror Chamber of Dr. Faustus
see *Les Yeux sans Visage*

The Horror Chamber of Dr. Thosti
see *The Black Sleep*

Horror Convention
see *Nightmare in Blood*

Horror Creatures of the Prehistoric Planet
see *Horror of the Blood Monsters*

Horror Express
1974, (GB-Sp), Benmar-Granada/Scotia-Int'l/Gala, color, 95 mins.
W: Peter Cushing (*Dr. Wells*), Christopher Lee (*Sir Alexander Caxton*), Telly Savalas (*Capt. Kazan*), Alberto De Mendoza (*Insp. Pujardov*), Silvia Tortosa (*Countess Irina*), Julio Peña (*Mirov*), Jorge Rigaud (*Count Petrovski*), Alice Reinhart (*Miss Jones*), Helga Line (*Natasha*)
P: Bernard Gordon   D & STORY: Eugenio Martin   SCR: Armand d'Usseau & Julian Halevy   PHOTOG: Alejandro Ulloa   MUSIC: John Cacavas
known in Spain as Panico en el Transiberiano (Panic on the Transiberian)
Grim, unusual horror-thriller: Revived corpse of alien creature menaces passengers on Russian train

Horror Express: PETER CUSHING, CHRISTOPHER LEE AND TELLY SAVALAS

The Horror from Beyond
1965, (USA), Journey, b&w
W: Robert Winston, Judy Dennis, Willie Sottelo, Vicente Liwanage
D: Newt Arnold
Minor horror-fantasy. A.k.a. Blood Thirst, Blood Seekers

Horror High
1974, (USA), Jameson/Crown-Int'l, color, 85 mins.
W: Pat Cardi (*Vernon*), Austin Stoker (*Lt. Bozeman*), Rosie Holotik (*The Girlfriend*), Joy Hash (*Miss Grinstaf*), Chuck Beatty, Abner Haynes, Bill Truax, Jeff Alexander, John Niland
P: Tom Moore   D: Larry N. Stouffer   SCR: Jake Fowler   SONG: *Vernon's Theme*
TV retitle, Twisted Brain
Minor horror-fantasy: High-school student concocts potion, turns into monster

Horror Hospital
1973, (GB), Noteworthy Films/Hallmark, color, 91 mins.
W: Michael Gough (*Dr. Storm*), Robin Askwith (*Jason Jones*), Vanessa Shaw (*Judy Peters*), Ellen Pollock (*Aunt Harris*), Skip Martin (*Frederick*), Dennis Price (*Pollack*), Kenneth Benda (*Carter*), Kurt Christian (*Abraham Warren*), Barbara Wendy (*Millie*), George Herbert (*The Ass't*)
P: Richard Gordon   D: Antony Balch   STORY: Antony Balch & Alan Watson   PHOTOG: David McDonald   MUSIC: DeWolfe
A.k.a. Computer Killers
Standard horror-comedy: Songwriter saves girl from mad doctor's experimental lobotomy

Horror Hotel
see *City of the Dead*

Horror Hotel Massacre
see *Eaten Alive (1976)*

Horror House
see *The Haunted House of Horror*

Horror House on Highway 5
1986, (USA), color, 90 mins.
D & SCR: Richard Casey
Minor thriller: Killer wears Nixon mask

The Horror is Among Us
see *The Creature Walks Among Us*

Horror Island
1941, (USA), Univ, b&w, 61 mins
W: Dick Foran (*Bill*), Peggy Moran (*Wendy*), Foy Van Dolsen, Hobart Cavanaugh, Leo Carrillo, Ralf Harolde, Iris Adrian, John Eldredge, Fuzzy Knight, Lewis Howard, Walter Catlett
D: George Waggner   SCR: Maurice Tombragel & Victor McLeod   PHOTOG: Elwood Bredell
Minor thriller: Treasure-seekers find murder on deserted Florida key

The Horror of Death
see *The Asphyx*

Horror of Dracula
1958, (GB), Hammer/Univ, color, 82 mins.
W: Peter Cushing (*Dr. Van Helsing*), Christopher Lee (*Count Dracula*), Michael Gough (*Arthur Holmwood*), Melissa Stribling (*Mina Holm-wood*), John Van Eyssen (*Jonathan Harker*), Janine Faye (*Tanya*), Carol Marsh (*Lucy Holmwood*), Valerie Gaunt (*The Vampire Woman*), Olga Dickie (*Gerda*), Paul Cole (*The Lad*), Charles Lloyd-Pack (*Dr. Seward*), Miles Malleson (*Marx*), George Benson (*The Official*), George Merritt (*The Policeman*), Geoffrey Bayldon (*The Porter*), Barbara Archer (*Inga*), George Woodbridge (*The Landlord*), Guy Mills, Dick Morgan, Judith Nelmes, Humphrey Kent, John Mossman, Stedwell Fulcher, William Sherwood
P: Anthony Hinds   D: Terence Fisher   SCR: Jimmy Sangster, based on Bram Stoker's novel *Dracula: A Tale.*   PHOTOG: Jack Asher   MUSIC: James Bernard   DESIGN: Bernard Robinson
Fr retitle, Le Cauchemar de Dracula (Dracula's Nightmare) GB title: Dracula
"Quite possibly the most horrendous and fearful of all the Dracula vampire-bat tales ever unreeled in film!"—Cue
"The most ghastly, horrifying scare film ever made!"—Daily Mirror
"Christopher Lee enacted his finest role as Count Dracula—a part that assured him of everlasting fame. His fantastic success in the film came from instilling not only horror in the viewer, but also a sort of respect for the monster. Lee's Dracula was cool, calculating—deadly; something to be feared, yet something to be admired for its cunning"—Chris Fellner, "The Intriguing World of Hammer Films," Monster Mania, No. 2 (Jan., 1967), p. 22
"...one of the best horror movies ever made...took the Dracula characterization out of mothballs, made it dynamic and vigorous... emphasized the important underlying sexual quality of vampires"—Gary Gerani, "The Vampire Book—Chapter Seven: A New Classic," Monster Fantasy, Vol. I, No. 1 (April, 1975), p. 30
Classic horror-fantasy: Vampirologist hunts ancient fiend. cf. The Bad Flower

Horror of Frankenstein
1970, (GB), Hammer/Anglo-EMI/American Continental, color, 95 mins.
W: Ralph Bates (*Dr. Frankenstein*), Veronica Carlson (*Elizabeth*), Dave Prowse (*The Monster*), Bernard Archard (*The Father*), Dennis Price (*The Grave-robber*), Joan Rice (*The Grave-robber's Wife*), Graham James (*Wilhelm*)
D: Jimmy Sangster   SCR: Jimmy Sangster & Jeremy Burnham, based on Mary W. Shelley's novel *Frankenstein*   PHOTOG: Murray Grant   MUSIC: James Bernard
Standard horror-thriller: Science student creates life

The Horror of It All
1964, (GB), Lippert/20th-Fox, b&w, 75 mins.

W: Pat Boone (*Jack Robinson*), Erica Rogers (*Cynthia*), Dennis Price (*Cornwallis*), Andree Melly (*Natalia*), Valentine Dyall (*Reginald*), Erik Chitty (*Grandpapa*), Archie Duncan (*Muldoon*), Jack Bligh (*Percival*)
P: Robert L. Lippert & Margia Dean   **D:** Terence Fisher   **SCR:** Ray Russell
Amusing horror-comedy: American discovers his British fiancee's family are maniacs and zombies

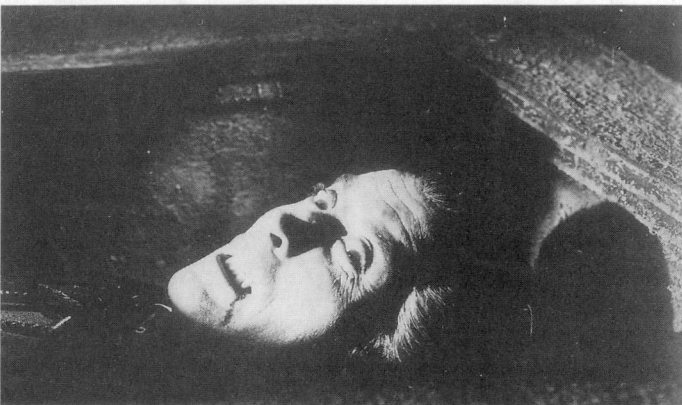

Horror of Dracula: CHRISTOPHER LEE

The Horror of Party Beach
1963, (USA), Iselin-Tenney/20th-Fox, b&w, 78 mins.
W: Alice Lyon (*Elaine*), John Scott (*Hank*), Marilyn Clarke (*Tina*), Allan Laurel (*Gavin*), Eulabelle Moore, Dina Harris, Damon Klebroyd, Sharon Murphy, Carol Grubman, Emily Laurel, Monroe Wade, Diane Prizio with the DelAires
P & D: Del Tenney   **WRIT & PHOTOG:** Richard L. Hilliard   **MUSIC:** Bill Holmes   **SONG:** *Do the Zombie Stomp*
orig. co-billed with **The Curse of the Living Corpse**
Minor horror-fantasy: Pollution monsters vs. teenagers

Horror of the Blood Monsters
1969, (USA-Phil), TAL/Independent-Int'l, color, 85 mins.
W: John Carradine (*Dr. Rynning*), Robert Dix (*Col. Manning*), Vicki Volante (*Valerie*), Joey Benson (*Willy*), Bruce Powers (*Bryce*), Jennifer Bishop (*Lian*), Fred Meyers (*Bob*), Britt Semand (*Linda*)
P & D: Al Adamson   **SCR:** Sue McNair   **PHOTOG:** William Zsigmond & William G. Troiano   **SPCL-FX:** David L. Hewitt   **MUSIC:** Mike Velarde
TV retitle, **Vampire Men of the Lost Planet** *A.k.a.* **Creatures of the Prehistoric Planet, Horror Creatures of the Prehistoric Planet** *and* **Space Mission of the Lost Planet**
Minor Filipino space-opera (with added USA scenes): Astronauts find vampiric tribe on ruined world

Horror of the Werewolf
see **La Maldicion de la Besti**a

Horror of the Zombies
1974, (Sp), Independent Int'l, color, 85 mins
W: Jack Taylor, Maria Perschy, Carl Leonard, Barbara Rey
D & SCR: Armando De Ossorio
A.k.a. **Ship of Zombies**
Standard horror-fantasy (2nd sequel to **Tombs of the Blind Dead**): *Eyeless ghouls menace fashion models at sea. cf.* **Night of the Seagulls**

Horror on Snape Island
see **Tower of Evil**

Horror Planet
see **Inseminoid**

Horror Rises from the Tomb
1970, (Sp), Profilms/Avco Embassy, color, 89 mins.
W: Paul Naschy, Cristina Suriani, Emma Cohen, Helga Line, Vic Winner, Luis Ciges
D: Carlos Aured   **SCR:** Jacinto Molina   **PHOTOG:** Manuel Merino
Minor horror-fantasy: Decapitated French knight's descendants pursued by supernatural terrors

The Horror Show
1989, (USA), Sean S. Cunningham/UA, color, 95 mins.
W: Lance Henriksen (*McCarthy*), Rita Taggart (*Donna*), Brion James (*Max*), Dedee Pfeiffer, Matt Clark, Lawrence Tierney, Thom Bray, Alvy Moore
D: James Isaac   **SCR:** Alan Smithee & Leslie Bohem,
distributed outside USA as **House III**
Minor horror-thriller: Killer immune to electric chair

The Horrors of Burke and Hare
see **Burke and Hare**

The Horrors of Drink
see **The Drunkard's Conversion**

Horrors of Nuremberg Castle
see **Gli Orrori del Castello di Nuremberga**

Horrors of Spider Island
1960, (W. Ger-Yugo), Hakim/Pacemaker/Intercontinental/Rapid, b&w, 77 mins
W: Alex D'Arcy, Barbara Valentine
A.k.a. **It's Hot in Paradise** *and* **Ein Toter Hing Im Netz** (*A Corpse Hangs in the Web*)
Minor horror-thriller

Horrors of the Black Museum
1959, (GB), Anglo-Amalgamated/AIP, color, 94 mins.
W: Michael Gough (*Edmond Bancroft*), June Cunningham (*Joan Berkeley*), Shirley Anne Field (*Angela*), Beatrice Varley (*Aggie*), Austin Trevor (*Commissioner Wayne*), Geoffrey Keen (*Supt. Graham*), Gerald Andersen (*Dr. Ballan*), John Warrick (*Insp. Lodge*), Howard Greene (*Tom Rivers*), Graham Curnow (*Rick*), Malou Pantera (*Peggy*), Dorinda Stevens (*Gail*), Nora Gordon, Hilda Barry, Stuart Saunders
P: Herman Cohen   **D:** Arthur Crabtree   **SCR:** Aben Kandel & Herman Cohen   **PHOTOG:** Desmond Dickinson   **MUSIC:** Gerard Schurmann
Fr retitle, **Les Crimes au Musee des Horreurs** (*Crimes in the Museum of Horrors*)
orig. co-billed with **The Headless Ghost**
Standard horror-thriller: Egotistical crime historian master minds shocking murders

Horrors of the Red Planet
see **The Wizard of Mars**

The Horror Star
see **Frightmare (1983)**

Horror y Sexo
see **Night of the Bloody Apes**

The Horse's Mouth
see **The Oracle (1952)**

The Horse That Ate the Baby
1906, (GB), Clarendon/Gaumont, b&w, 275 ft. (83.8m)
D: Percy Stow
Standard fantasy short: Horse eats baby, is cut open by vet who finds baby alive

Hospital Massacre
1982, (USA), Cannon, color, 89 mins.
W: Barbi Benton, Jon Van Ness, Chip Lucio
P: Menahem Golan & Yoram Globus   **D:** Boaz Davidson   **SCR:** Marc Behm
A.k.a. **Ward 13, X-Ray** *and* **Be My Valentine, Or Else**
Minor thriller: Nurse menaced

Hospital of Terror
see **Beyond the Living**

The Hostage
1956, (GB), Douglas Fairbanks-Westridge/Eros, b&w, 80 mins.
W: Ron Randell (*Bill Trailer*), Mary Parker (*Rosa Gonzalo*), John Bailey (*Dr. Main*), Carl Jaffe (*Dr. Pablo Gonzuelo*), Anne Blake (*Mrs. Steen*), Cyril Luckham (*Hugh Ferguson*), Margaret Diamond (*Mme. Gonzuelo*), Victor Brooks (*Insp. Clifford*)
P: Thomas Clyde   **D:** Harold Huth   **STORY:** Alfred Shaughnessy
Standard crime-thriller: Pilot saves president's daughter from revolutionary

The Horror Of It All: PAT BOONE

The Hostage
1966, (USA), Crown Int'l, color, 84 mins.
<u>W:</u> Harry Dean Stanton (*Eddie*), Don O'Kelly (*Bull*), John Carradine (*Otis Lovelace*), Danny Martins (*Davey*), Danny Martins
<u>P & D:</u> Russell S. Doughton Jr. <u>SCR:</u> Robert Laning <u>PHOTOG:</u> Ted V. Mikels
Standard thriller: Young boy locked in moving van driven by two murderers

Hostile Intent
1997, (USA), color, 90 mins.
<u>W:</u> Rob Lowe
Made-for-Video, standard thriller: Gov't assassins seek computer chip

Hostile Witness
1968, (GB), Caralan-Dador/UA, color, 101 mins.
<u>W:</u> Ray Milland (*Simon Crawford*), Sylvia Sims (*Sheila Larkin*), Felix Aylmer (*Mr. Justice Osborne*), Raymond Huntley (*John Naylor*), Geoffrey Lumsden (*Maj. Hugh Maitland*), Norman Barrs (*Charles Milburn*), Percy Marmont (*Sir Matthew Gregory*), Dulcie Bowman (*Lady Gregory*), Ewan Roberts (*Hamish Gillespie*), Richard Hurndall (*Insp. Elsy*), Ronald Leigh-Hunt (*Dr. Winbourne*)
<u>P:</u> David E. Rose <u>D:</u> Ray Milland <u>SCR:</u> Jack Roffey, from his play
Standard crime-thriller: Barrister framed for murder

The Hotel Manor Inn
1997, (USA), Manor Films, color, 92 mins.
<u>W:</u> John Randolph (*Gus*), Sam Trammell (*Nolan*), Jennifer Corby (*Kathy*), Fred Norris (*Pete*), Lawrence Vincent (*Ed*)
<u>WRIT, P & D:</u> Wayne Chesler <u>PHOTOG:</u> Michael McCurry <u>MUSIC:</u> Alan Schwartz
Standard satire-thriller: Murders in hotel on Massachusetts isle

The Hotel Mystery
1902, (GB), R.W. Paul, b&w, 85 ft. (25.9m)
Standard short melodrama: "Don't blow out the gas, or what happened to a visitor"

Hot Enough for June
1963, (GB), Rank/Walter Reade-Sterling, color, 98 mins.
<u>W:</u> Dirk Bogarde (*Nicholas Whistler*), Sylva Koscina (*Vlasta Simenova*), Robert Morley (*Col. Cunliffe*), Leo McKern (*Simenova*), Roger Delgado (*Josef*), Richard Pasco (*Plakov*), John LeMesurier (*Roger Allsop*), Eric Pohlmann (*Galushka*), Richard Vernon (*Roddinghead*), Amanda Grinling (*The Sec'y*), Noel Harrison (*Johnnie*), Derek Nimmo (*Fred*), George Pravda (*Pavelko*), Frank Finlay (*The Janitor*), Norman Bird (*The Clerk*)
<u>P:</u> Betty E. Box <u>D:</u> Ralph Thomas <u>SCR:</u> Lukas Heller, from Lionel Davidson's novel *Night of Wenceslas* <u>PHOTOG:</u> Ernest Steward <u>MUSIC:</u> Angelo Lavagnino
*USA retitle, **Agent 8 3/4***
Standard satire of "James Bond" genre: Unemployed man becomes spy

Hot Key
1952, (GB), Present Day-SWH Piccadilly/Apex, b&w, 65 mins.
<u>W:</u> John Justin (*Jim Henderson*), Barbara Murray (*Mary*), Ivor Barnard (*Edwin Carson*), John Penrose (*Freddie Usher*), Michael Balfour (*Jacobson*), Gabrielle Brune (*Marcella*), Anthony Pendrell (*Burroughs*), Bill Shine (*Henry*)
<u>D & SCR:</u> Kenneth Hume, from Alan Melville's play *Weekend Thrackley*
Standard crime-thriller: Jewel thief disrupts house party

Hot Money Girl
*see **Long Distance***

Hot Pickles
1910, (GB), Hepworth, b&w, 650 ft. (198.1m)
<u>W:</u> Johnny Butt (*The Colonel*)
<u>D:</u> Lewin Fitzhamon
Minor comedy-fantasy: Colonel's home-made pickles make diners belch flames

Houdini
1953, (USA), Para, color, 106 mins.
<u>W:</u> Tony Curtis (*Houdini*), Janet Leigh (*Bess*), Sig Rumann (*Schultz*), Angela Clarke (*Mrs. Weiss*), Stefan Schnabel (*The Prosecuting Att'y*), Torin Thatcher (*Otto*), Michael Pate (*Dooley*), Ian Wolfe (*Fante*), Connie Gilchrist (*Mrs. Schultz*), Mary Murphy (*Girl #1*), Joanne Gilbert (*Girl #2*), Mabel Paige (*The Medium*), Malcolm Lee Beggs (*The Warden*), Frank Orth, Barry Bernard, Douglas Spencer, Peter Baldwin, Elsie Ames, Richard Shannon, Nick Arno, Tudor Owen, Esther Garber, Lewis Martin, Fred Essler, Alex Harford, Lawrence Ryle, Arthur Gould Porter, Oliver Blake, Harry Hinds, Harold Neiman, Erno Verebes, Anthony Warde, Grace Hayle
<u>P:</u> George Pal <u>D:</u> George Marshall <u>SCR:</u> Philip Yordan <u>PHOTOG:</u> Ernest Laszlo <u>MUSIC:</u> Roy Webb
*Entertaining, but highly-fictionalized film-bio: Life of master magician. cf. **The Great Houdinis***

Houdini
1998, (USA), Trilogy/TNT-TV, color, 95 mins.
<u>W:</u> Johnathon Schaech (*Ehrich Weiss/Harry Houdini*), Stacy Edwards (*Bess*), George Segal (*Beck*), Rhea Perlman (*Esther*), Paul Sorvino (*Blackburn*), David Warner, Mark Ruffalo, Curt Lowens, Emile Hirsch, Grace Zabriskie, Michael Gallagher, Ron Perlman, Judy Geeson, Frank McRae, Karl

Makinen, Jack McGee, David Moreland, Jack Knight, Laura Pallas, Jack Marston, Karen Hartman, Endre Hules, Joshua Breslow
<u>D & TELEPLAY:</u> Pen Densham <u>PHOTOG:</u> Gordon C. Lonsdale <u>SPCL-FX COORD:</u> Dan Lester <u>MUSIC:</u> Don Harper
TVM, well-made bio: Escape artist tempts death

The Hound of London
1993, (Can), color, 72 mins.
<u>W:</u> Patrick Macnee, John Scott-Paget, Colin Skinner, Carolyn Wilkinson, Jack McCreath, Sophia Thornley, Craig Bowlsby, Drew Kemp, Ned Lemley
<u>D:</u> Gil Letourneau & Peter Reynolds-Long <u>SCR:</u> Craig Bowlsby, from his play, based on characters created by Sir Arthur Conan Doyle
Standard thriller: Sleuth probes double murder

The Hound Of The Baskervilles
1917, (Ger), b&w
from Sir Arthur Conan Doyle's Sherlock Holmes story
Standard thriller: Murder blamed on legendary beast

The Hound Of The Baskervilles
1921, (GB), SFC/Stoll, b&w, 5,500 ft. (1676.4m)
<u>W:</u> Eille Norwood (*Sherlock Holmes*), Betty Campbell (*Beryl Stapleton*), Rex McDougall (*Sir Henry Baskerville*), Hubert Willis (*Dr. John Watson*), Lewis Gilbert (*Roger Stapleton*), Robert English (*Dr. Mortimer*), Fred Raynham (*the Butler*), Miss Walker (*Mrs. Barrymore*), Mme. D'Esterre (*Mrs. Hudson*), Allan Jeayes (*Dr. James Mortimer*) Robert Vallis (*The Convict-Barrymore*)
<u>D:</u> Maurice Elvey <u>SCR:</u> William J. Elliott & Dorothy Westlake, from Sir Arthur Conan Doyle's Sherlock Holmes story
US release: R-C/FBO, 1922. note: correct credits from existing British print.
Standard thriller: "Ghost dog" imperils heir

The Hound Of The Baskervilles
1929, (Ger), b&w
<u>W:</u> Carlyle Blackwell (*Sherlock Holmes*)
from Sir Arthur Conan Doyle's Sherlock Holmes story

The Hound Of The Baskervilles
1931, (GB), Gaumont, b&w, 75 mins.
<u>W:</u> John Stuart (*Sir Henry Baskerville*), Robert Rendel (*Sherlock Holmes*), Reginald Bach (*Stapleton*), Heather Angel (*Beryl Stapleton*), Wilfred Shine (*Dr. Mortimer*), Frederick Lloyd (*Dr. John Watson*), Sam Livesey (*Sir Hugo Baskerville*), Henry Hallett (*Barrymore*), Sybil Jane (*Mrs. Barrymore*)
<u>D:</u> V. Gareth Gundrey <u>SCR:</u> Edgar Wallace & V. Gareth Gundrey, from Sir Arthur Conan Doyle's Sherlock Holmes story
Modest thriller: Estate heir menaced by legendary beast

Hound Of The Baskervilles (1972): WILLIAM SHATNER

The Hound Of The Baskervilles
1939, (USA), 20th-Fox, b&w, 80 mins.
<u>W:</u> Basil Rathbone (*Sherlock Holmes*), Nigel Bruce (*Dr. John Watson*), Richard Greene (*Sir Henry Baskerville*), John Carradine (*Barrymore*), Wendy Barrie (*Miss Stapleton*), Lionel Atwill (*Dr. James Mortimer*), Mary Gordon (*Mrs. Hudson*), Beryl Mercer, Nigel de Brulier, Barlowe Borland, Morton Lowry, Ralph Forbes, Eily Malyon, Ivan Simpson, Dennis Green, E.E. Clive, John Burton, Peter Willes, Ivan MacLaren, Evan Thomas
<u>D:</u> Sidney Lanfield <u>SCR:</u> Ernest Pascal, from Sir Arthur Conan Doyle's Sherlock Holmes story <u>PHOTOG:</u> J. Peverell Marley <u>MUSIC:</u> Cyril Mockridge
Classic Rathbone-Holmes thriller, in fact the first: Master detective delves into legend of "Hound of Hell"

The Hound Of The Baskervilles

1959, (GB), Hammer/UA, color, 87 mins.
W: Peter Cushing (*Sherlock Holmes*), Andre Morell (*Dr. John Watson*), Christopher Lee (*Sir Henry Baskerville*), Marla Landi (*Cecile Stapleton*), Ewen Solon (*Stapleton*), Francis De Wolff (*Dr. Mortimer*), Miles Malleson (*Bishop Franklin*), David Oxley (*Sir Hugo Baskerville*), Michael Mulcaster (*The Convict*), John LeMesurier (*Barrymore*), Helen Goss (*Mrs. Barrymore*), Sam Kydd (*Perkins*), Judi Moyens (*The Servant Girl*), David Birks (*The Servant*)
P: Anthony Hinds D: Terence Fisher SCR: Peter Bryan, from Sir Arthur Conan Doyle's *Sherlock Holmes* story PHOTOG: Jack Asher MUSIC: James Bernard
Well-made thriller (Best film-version of classic tale): Detective aids imperiled heir

The Hound Of The Baskervilles

1972, (USA-GB), Univ, color, 73 mins.
W: Stewart Granger (*Sherlock Holmes*), Bernard Fox (*Dr. John Watson*), William Shatner (*Stapleton*), Ian Ireland, Jane Merrow, Anthony Zerbe, Sally Ann Howes, Arthur Malet, Brendan Dillon, John Williams, Chuck Hicks, Arline Anderson, Billy Bowles, Jenifer Shaw, Alan Caillou
D: Barry Crane SCR: Robert E. Thompson, from Sir Arthur Conan Doyle's *Sherlock Holmes* story
TVM, standard thriller: Legendary beast threatens

The Hound Of The Baskervilles

1978, (GB), Michael White Ltd., color, 85 mins.
W: Peter Cook (*Sherlock Holmes*), Dudley Moore (*Dr. John Watson/ Ada Holmes/Spiggot*), Kenneth Williams (*Sir Henry Baskerville*), Terry-Thomas (*Dr. Mortimer*), Denholm Elliott (*Stapleton*), Hugh Griffith (*Frankland*), Irene Handl (*Mrs. Barrymore*), Max Wall (*Barrymore*), Joan Greenwood (*Beryl*), Roy Kinnear (*Selden*), Dana Gillespie (*Mary*), Lucy Griffiths (*Iris*), Spike Milligan (*The PC*), Prunella Scales (*Glynis*), Josephine Tewson (*The Nun*), Geoffrey Moon (*Perkins*), Anna Wing (*Daphne*), Pearl Hackney (*The Passenger*), Penelope Keith (*The Receptionist*), Rita Webb (*The Masseuse*), Jessie Matthews (*Mrs. Tindale*), Henry Woolf (*The Shopkeeper*), Molly Maureen, Helena McCarthy, Vivien Neve, Jacques Stevens, Ava Cadell, Sidney Johnson
P: John Goldstone D: Paul Morrissey SCR: Peter Cook, Dudley Moore & Paul Morrissey, from Sir Arthur Conan Doyle's story PHOTOG: Dick Bush MUSIC: Dudley Moore
Minor spoof: Sleuth probes murderous curse

The Hound Of The Baskervilles

1982, (GB), BBC-TV, color, 78 mins.
W: Ian Richardson (*Sherlock Holmes*), Donald Churchill (*Dr. John Watson*), Denholm Elliott (*Dr. Mortimer*), Nicholas Clay (*Jack*), Brian Blessed
from Sir Arthur Conan Doyle's *Sherlock Holmes* story
TVM, standard thriller: Old curse plagues heir

The Hounds of Zaroff

see *The Most Dangerous Game*

Hour of Decision

1957, (GB), Eros/Tempean, b&w, 81 mins.
W: Jeff Morrow (*Joe Anders*), Hazel Court (*Peggy Sanders*), Lionel Jeffries (*Elvin Main*), Anthony Dawson (*Garry Bax*), Mary Laura Wood (*Olive Bax*), Carl Bernard (*Insp. Gower*), Vanda Godsell (*Eileen Chadwick*), Alan Gifford (*J. Foster Green*), Anthony Snell, Robert Sansom, Garard Green, Marne Maitland, Arthur Lowe, Margaret Allworthy
P: Robert Baker & Monty Berman D: C. Pennington-Richards SCR: Norman Hudis, from Frederic Goldsmith's novel *Murder in Mayfair* PHOTOG: Stanley Pavey MUSIC: Stanley Black
Standard thriller: Writer involved in gossip columnist's murder

Hour of the Wolf

see *Vargtimmen*

The Hour of 13

1952, (GB), MGM, b&w, 79 mins.
W: Peter Lawford (*Nicholas Revel*), Dawn Addams (*Jane Frensham*), Roland Culver (*Connor*), Derek Bond (*Sir Christopher Lenhurst*), Leslie Dwyer (*Ernie Perker*), Michael Hordern (*Sir Herbert Frensham*), Colin Gordon (*MacStreet*), Heather Thatcher (*Mrs. Chumley Orr*), Jack McNaughton (*Ford*), Fabia Drake (*Lady Elmbridge*), Campbell Cotts (*Mr. Chumley Orr*), Michael Goodliffe (*Anderson*), Moultrie Kelsall (*The Magistrate*), Peter Copley (*Cummings*), Richard Shaw (*The Terror*)
P: Hayes Goetz D: Harold French SCR: Leon Gordon & Howard Emmett Rogers, from Philip MacDonald's novel *Mystery of the Dead Police* PHOTOG: Guy Green MUSIC: John Addison
Standard thriller: Gentleman thief hunts mad killer. Remake: The Mystery of Mr. X

The Hour When Dracula Came

see *La Maschera del Demonio*

House

1986, (USA), New World, color, 93 mins.
W: William Katt (*Roger Cobb*), George Wendt (*Harold Gorton*), Richard Moll (*Big Ben*), Kay Lenz (*Sandy*), Michael Ensign (*Chet Parker*), Mary Stavin (*Tanya*), Susan French (*Aunt Elizabeth*), Erik Silver, Mark Silver, Alan Autry, Jim Calvert, Steven Williams, Peter Pitofsky
D: Steve Miner SCR: Ethan Wiley STORY: Fred Dekker PHOTOG: Mac Ahlberg MUSIC: Harry Manfredini
Modest horror-fantasy: Writer inherits spooky mansion

House II: The Second Story

1987, (USA), New World, color, 88 mins.
W: Arye Gross (*Jesse*), Jonathan Stark (*Charlie*), Royal Dano (*Gramps*), Bill Maher (*John*), Lar Park Lincoln (*Kate*), John Ratzenberger (*Bill*), Amy Yasbeck (*Lana*), Dwier Brown (*Clarence*), Gregory Walcott (*The Sheriff*), Ronn Carroll (*The Deputy*), Lenora May (*Judith*), Devin Devasquez (*The Virgin*), Jayne Modean (*Rochelle*), Dean Cleverdon (*Slim*), Doug MacHugh (*The High Priest*), Mitzi Kapture (*The Cowgirl*), David Arnott (*The Banana*), Susan Isaac (*The Cat*), Kane Hodder (*The Gorilla*), Gus Rethwisch (*Arnold the Barbarian*), Gil Birmingham
P: Sean S. Cunningham WRIT & D: Ethan Wiley PHOTOG: Mac Ahlberg MUSIC: Harry Manfredini
Standard comedy-fantasy: Youth inherits sinister family estate

House IV

1992, (USA), color, 95 mins.
W: Terri Treas, William Katt (*Roger*), Scott Burkholder (*Burke*), Melissa Clayton (*Laurel*), Denny Dillon (*Verna*)
Minor fantasy-thriller: Young widow moves into rundown mansion, encounters horrors

The House Across the Lake

1954, (GB), Hammer/ABP, b&w, 69 mins.
W: Alex Nicol (*Mark Kendrick*), Hilary Brooke (*Carol Forrest*), Sidney James (*Beverley Forrest*), Susan Stephen (*Andrea Forrest*), Paul Carpenter (*Vincent Gordon*), Alan Wheatley (*Insp. MacLennan*), Cleo Rose (*Abigail*), Peter Illing (*Harry Stevens*), Hugh Dempster (*Frank*)
P: Anthony Hinds D & SCR: Ken Hughes, from Ken Hughes' novel *High Wray*
USA retitle, Heatwave (Lippert)
Standard thriller: Rich woman drowns husband for love of novelist

House by the River

1950, (USA), Rep, b&w, 88 mins.
W: Louis Hayward, Jane Wyatt, Lee Bowman, Dorothy Patrick, Ann Shoemaker, Kathleen Freeman, Peter Brocco, Jody Gilbert
D: Fritz Lang, from a novel by A.P. Herbert PHOTOG: Edward Cronjager MUSIC: George Antheil
Standard melodrama: Author implicates brother in crime

The House at the End of the World

see *Monster of Terror*

The Houseboat Mystery

1914, (GB), Cygnet Films, b&w, 2,450 ft. (746.8m)
W: Percy Moran, Arola Brereton, Douglas Payne, Eddie Willey
P: Henry P. Smither WRIT & D: B. Harold Brett
Standard crime-thriller

The House by the Cemetery

1983, (It), Almi, color, 84 mins.
W: Katherine MacColl, Paolo Malco, Ania Pieroni, Dagmar Lassander, Giovanni de Nava, Daniela Doria
D: Lucio Fulci SCR: Elisa Briganti PHOTOG: Sergio Salvati
Minor horror-thriller: Evil curse unleashed

The House by the Lake

1977, (Can), Orion/AIP, color, 89 mins.
W: Don Stroud, Brenda Vaccaro, Chuck Shamata, Richard Ayres, Kyle Edwards, Don Granbery
P: Ivan Reitman WRIT & D: William Fruet
A.k.a. Death Weekend
Minor suspense-thriller: Hoodlums terrorize couple

The House in Marsh Road

1960, (GB), Eternal/Grand Nat'l/AIP, b&w, 70 mins.
W: Tony Wright (*David Linton*), Patricia Dainton (*Jean Linton*), Sandra Dorne (*Valerie Stockley*), Sam Kydd (*Lumley*), Derek Aylward (*Richard Foster*), Llewellyn Rees (*Webster*), Anita Sharp Bolster (*Mrs. O'Brien*), Roddy Hughes (*Daniels*), Olive Sloane (*Mrs. Morris*)
P: Maurice J. Wilson D: Montgomery Tully SCR: Maurice J. Wilson, from a novel by Laurence Meynell
USA retitle, The Invisible Creature
Standard fantasy-thriller: Poltergeist stops book critic from murdering wife

The House in Nightmare Park

1973, (GB), Assoc. London/EMI, color, 95 mins.
W: Frankie Howerd (*Foster Twelvetrees*), Ray Milland (*Stewart Henderson*), Hugh Burden (*Maj. Reginald Henderson*), Kenneth Griffith (*Ernest Henderson*), John Bennett (*Patel*), Rosalie Crutchley (*Jessica Henderson*), Ruth Dunning (*Agnes Henderson*), Elizabeth MacLennan (*Verity*), Peter Munt (*The Cabbie*), Aimee Delamain (*Mother*)
D: Peter Sykes SCR: Clive Exton & Terry Nation PHOTOG: Ian Wilson MUSIC: Harry Robinson
USA retitle, The Night of the Laughing Dead & a Crazy House
Standard horror-comedy: Ham actor menaced at eerie Gothic estate

A House in the Hills
1993, (USA), color, 89 mins.
W: Michael Madsen
Minor thriller: Ex-con terrorizes housesitter

The House in the Square
1951, (GB), 20th-Fox, color, b&w, 91 mins.
W: Tyrone Power (*Peter Standish*), Ann Blyth (*Helen Pettigrew*), Michael Rennie (*Roger Forsyth*), Dennis Price (*Tom Pettigrew*), Beatrice Campbell (*Kate Pettigrew*), Raymond Huntley (*Mr. Throsle*), Kathleen Byron (*The Duchess of Devonshire*), Irene Browne (*Lady Ann Pettigrew*), Robert Atkins (*Samuel Johnson*), Alex McCrindle (*James Boswell*), Felix Aylmer (*The Physician*), Gibb McLaughlin (*Jacob*)
P: Sol C. Siegel   **D:** Roy Baker   **SCR:** Ranald MacDougall, from John L. Balderston's play *Berkeley Square*. Remake of 1933 film   **PHOTOG:** Georges Perinal   **MUSIC:** Muir Mathieson
USA retitle, **I'll Never Forget You**
Superior fantasy-romance: American scientist time-travels, becomes own ancestor in 1784 London

The House in the Woods
1957, (GB), Eclat/Archway, b&w, 60 mins.
W: Ronald Howard (*Spencer Rowland*), Patricia Roc (*Carol Carter*), Michael Gough (*Geoffrey Carter*), Norah Hammond (*Mrs. Bletchley*), Andrea Trowbridge (*Mrs. Shellaby*), Bill Shine (*Col. Shellaby*)
P: Geoffrey Goodhart   **D & SCR:** Maxwell Munden, from Walter C. Brown's story "Prelude to Murder"
Standard thriller: Author learns landlord plans to kill his wife

The Housekeeper
1986, (Can), Rawfilm/Schulz Prods/Castle Hill., color, 97 mins.
W: Rita Tushingham (*Eunice Parchman*), Ross Petty (*George Coverdale*), Shelley Peterson (*Jackie*), Jonathan Crombie (*Bobby*), Jessica Steen (*Melinda*), Jackie Burroughs (*Joan Smith*), Tom Kneebone (*Norman Smith*), Peter MacNeill (*William*), Donald Ewer (*Mr. Parchman*), Gary Krawford (*Larry*), Joyce Gordon (*The Aunt*), Aisha Tushingham (*Young Eunice*), Wanda Cannon (*Bernice*), Layne Coleman (*The Pastor*), Betty Harris (*The Teacher*), Sean Collins, Julian Coutts, Eileen Williams, Diane Fabian, Sandra Scott, Andy Knott, Gordon Kliner
D: Ousama Rawi   **SCR:** Elaine Waisglass, from Ruth Rendell's novel *A Judgment in Stone*   **PHOTOG:** David Herrington   **MUSIC:** Paul Zaza
Echoes of Polanski's **Repulsion** *in modest, unusual psychodrama: Dyslexic servant becomes demented, murderous*

House of Crazies
see **Asylum**

House of 1,000 Dolls
1967, (GB-W. Ger-Sp), Harry Alan Towers-Constantin-P.S. Hispamer/ AIP, color, 81 mins.
W: Vincent Price (*Felix Mandeville*), Martha Hyer (*Rebecca*), George Nader (*Stephen Armstrong*), Wolfgang Kieling (*Insp. Emil*), Anne Smyrner (*Marie*), Maria Rohm (*Diane*), Herbert Fux (*Abdu*), Sancho Gracia (*Fernando*), Louis Rivera (*Paul*), Jose Jaspe (*Ahmed*), Juan Olaguivel (*Salim*), Yelena Samarina (*Mme. Viera*), Diane Bond (*Liza*), Andrea Lascelles, Ursula Janis, Karin Skarreso, Jill Echols, Kitty Swan, Francoise Fontages, Loli Munoz, Monique Aime, Lara Lenti, Caroline Coon, Marisol Anon, Sandra Petrelli
D: Jeremy Summers   **SCR:** Peter Welbeck [Harry Alan Towers]   **PHOTOG:** Manuel Merino   **MUSIC:** Charles Camilleri
Standard melodrama: Stage magician involved with Tangier white-slavers

House of Blackmail
1953, (GB), ACT Films/Monarch, b&w, 72 mins.
W: Mary Germaine (*Carol Blane*), William Sylvester (*Jimmy*), Alexander Gauge (*John Markham*), John Arnatt (*Pete Carter*), Denis Shaw (*Bassett*), Ingeborg Wells (*Emma*), C. Denier Warren (*Jock*), Patricia Owens (*Joan*)
P: Phil Brandon   **D:** Maurice Elvey   **STORY:** Allan Mackinnon
Standard mystery-thriller: Blackmailer murdered in house surrounded by high-tension wires

House of Darkness
1948, (GB), Int'l Motion Pictures/British Lion/Broder, b&w, 77 mins.
W: Laurence Harvey (*Francis Merivale*), Lesley Brook (*Lucy*), John Stuart (*The Lawyer*), George Melachrino (*himself*), Alexander Archdale (*John*), Lesley Osmond (*Elaine Merivale*), Henry Oscar (*The Film Director*)
P: Harry Reynolds   **D:** Oswald Mitchell   **SCR:** John Gilling & Ribin Estridge, from Batty Davies' play *Duet*
US release: **Realart** *(1952)*
Standard fantasy: Murdered man's ghost seeks vengeance on step-brother. Lawrence Harvey's film debut

House of Dark Shadows
1970, (USA), MGM, color, 98 mins.
W: Jonathan Frid (*Barnabas Collins*), Grayson Hall (*Dr. Julia Hoffman*), Kathryn Leigh Scott (*Maggie*), Nancy Barrett (*Carolyn*), Roger Davis (*Jeff*), Thayer David (*Prof. Stokes*), Donald Briscoe (*Todd*), Louis Edmonds (*Roger*), David Henesy (*David*), John Karlen (*Willie*), Joan Bennett (*Elizabeth*), Dennis Patrick (*The Sheriff*)
P & D: Dan Curtis   **SCR:** Sam Hall & Gordon Russell   **PHOTOG:** Arthur

---

Ornitz   **MUSIC:** Robert Cobert
Standard horror-fantasy (inspired by TV's first "Gothic soap opera," Dark Shadows {1966-1971}): Vampire at Maine estate. cf. **Night of Dark Shadows**

The House of Death (1932)
see **The Old Dark House** *(1932)*

House of Death
1981, (USA), color, 90 mins.
W: Susan Kiger
Standard thriller: Machete-wielding maniac stalks coeds

The House of Doom (1934)
see **The Black Cat** *(1934)*

House of Doom
1973, (Sp), Independent-Int'l, color, 87 mins
W: Paul Naschy, Diana Lorys, Eduardo Calvo, Maria Perschy, Eva Leon, Ines Morales, Tony Pica
P: Modesto Perez Redondo   **D:** Carlos Aured   **SCR:** Jacinto Molina & Carlos Aured   **STORY:** Jacinto Molina   **PHOTOG:** Francisco Sanchez   **MUSIC:** Juan Carlos Calderon
USA retitle (1975), **House of Psychotic Women**
Standard thriller: Drifter meets maniacal sisters

House of Dracula
1945, (USA), Univ, b&w, 67 mins.
W: Lon Chaney Jr. (*Larry Talbot, the Wolf Man*), John Carradine (*Count Dracula*), Onslow Stevens, Martha O'Driscoll, Lionel Atwill, Jane Adams, Glenn Strange (*The Monster*), Ludwig Stossel, Harry Lamont, Joseph E. Bernard, Skelton Knaggs, Beatrice Gray
P: Paul Malvern   **D:** Erle C. Kenton   **ORIG SCR:** Edward T. Lowe   **PHOTOG:** George Robinson   **MUSIC:** Edgar Fairchild
It retitle, **House of Horror**
"...a fairly taut and sober little film"—William K. Everson, Classics of the Horror Film
Gripping horror-fantasy, sequel to **House of Frankenstein:** *Doctor attempts to cure lycanthrope, is accidentally infected by vampire's blood*

House of Dracula: ONSLOW STEVENS AND JOHN CARRADINE

House of Evil
1968, (USA-Mex), Azteca/Col, color, 90 mins.
W: Boris Karloff, Julissa, Andres Garcia, Anthony Espinosa, Beatriz Baz
P: Luis Enrique Veraga   **D:** Juan Ibanez & Jack Hill   **SCR:** Jack Hill
A.k.a. **Macabre Serenade,** *and* **Dance of Death**
Minor thriller: Mechanical toys become monsters

House of Evil (1978)
see **The Evil**

House of Evil (1983)
see **The House On Sorority Row**

House of Exorcism
1975, (It), Leone Int'l/Peppercorn-Wormser, color, 93 mins.
W: Telly Savalas, Elke Sommer, Sylva Koscina, Alessio Orano, Gabriele Tinti, Kathy Leone, Eduardo Fajardo, Carmen Silva, Alida Valli, Robert Alda, Franz Von Treuberg, Espartaco Santoni
P: Alfred Leone   **D:** Mario Bava   **SCR:** Alberto Cittini & Alfred Leone   **MUSIC:** Carlo Savina
A.k.a. **Lisa and the Devil**
Minor, confused horror-fantasy: Tourist possessed by spirit of deceased lookalike

House of Fear
1939, (USA), Univ, b&w, 65 mins

W: William Gargan, Irene Hervey, El Brendel, Robert Coote, Walter Woolf King, Dorothy Arnold
D: Joe May   SCR: Peter Milne
*Minor thriller (remake of **The Last Warning** {1929}): Theater beset by murderous "ghost"*

The House of Fear
1945, (USA), Univ, b&w, 69 mins.
W: Basil Rathbone (*Sherlock Holmes*), Nigel Bruce (*Dr. John Watson*), Dennis Hoey (*Insp. Lestrade*), Paul Cavanagh (*Dr. Simon Merivale*), Doris Lloyd (*The Innkeeper*), Aubrey Mather (*Bruce Alastair*), Gavin Muir (*Chalmers*), Sally Shepherd (*Mrs. Montieth*), Holmes Herbert (*Alan Cosgrave*), Harry Cording (*Capt. Simpson*), David Clyde (*Alex MacGregor*)
P & D: Roy William Neill   SCR: Roy Chanslor, based on Sir Arthur Conan Doyle's short story "The Adventure of the Five Orange Pips"   PHOTOG: Virgil Miller   MUSIC DIR: Don E. George
Standard thriller: Master detective investigates select club whose members are being murdered

House of Frankenstein
1944, (USA), Univ, b&w, 71 mins.
W: Boris Karloff (*Dr. Niemann*), Lon Chaney Jr. (*Larry Talbot, the Wolf Man*), John Carradine (*Count Dracula*), J. Carrol Naish (*Daniel*), Elena Verdugo (*Ilonka*), Anne Gwynne (*Rita*), Peter Coe (*Carl Hussman*), Glenn Strange (*The Frankenstein Monster*), Lionel Atwill (*Arnz*), Hans Herbert (*Meier*), Sig Rumann (*Hussman*), William Edmunds (*Fejos*), George Zucco (*Prof. Lampini*), Philip Van Zandt (*Muller*), Charles Miller (*Toberman*), Olaf Hytten (*Hoffman*), Julius Tannen (*Hertz*), Frank Reicher (*Ullmann*), Dick Dickinson (*Born*), George Lynn (*Gerlach*), Michael Mark (*Strauss*), Brandon Hurst (*Dr. Geissler*)
P: Paul Malvern   D: Erle C. Kenton   SCR: Edward T. Lowe, from a story by Curt Siodmak   PHOTOG: George Robinson   SPCL-FX: John P. Fulton   MUSIC: H.J. Salter
*Standard horror-fantasy, sequel to **Frankenstein Meets the Wolf Man**: Mad scientist revives Dracula, the Wolf Man, and Frankenstein's monster cf. **House of Dracula***

House of Frankenstein
1997, (USA), NBC-TV, color
W: Adrian Pasdar, Teri Polo, Greg Wise, Peter Crombie
2-part TVM, minor horror-fantasy

House of Freaks
see El Castello dell'Orrore

House of Fright
see The Two Faces of Dr. Jekyll

The House of Horror
1929, (USA), First Nat'l, b&w, 7 reels (5,919 ft./1804.1m)
W: Louise Fazenda (*Louise*), Chester Conklin (*Chester*), Thelma Todd (*Thelma*), James Ford (*Joe*), William V. Mong (*The Mystery Man*), Emile Chautard (*The Old Miser*), Dale Fuller (*Gladys*), William Orlamond (*Miller*), Tenen Holtz (*Brown*), Michael Visaroff (*The Chauffeur*)
D: Benjamin Christensen   STORY & SCR: Richard Bee   DIALOG: William Irish   PHOTOG: Ernest Haller & Sol Polito   MUSIC SCORE: Louis Silvers
Standard comedy-thriller: Brother and sister summoned to uncle's old mansion

House of Horror (1945)
see House of Dracula

House of Horrors
1946, (USA), Univ, b&w, 66 mins.
W: Robert Lowery (*Steve Morrow*), Virginia Grey (*Joan Medford*), Martin Kosleck (*Marcel DeLange*), Bill Goodwin (*Lt. Larry Brooks*), Alan Napier (*F. Holmes Harmon*), Joan Fulton (*Shawlee*) (*Stella McNally*), Rondo Hatton ("*The Creeper*"), Virginia Christine (*The Streetwalker*), Howard Freeman (*Ormiston*), Joan Shawlee
P: Ben Pivar   D: Jean Yarbrough   SCR: George Bricker   ORIG SCR: Dwight V. Babcock   PHOTOG: Maury Gertsman   MUSIC DIR: H.J. Salter
A.k.a. JOAN Medford is Missing
Minor thriller: Disgruntled sculptor enlists "services" of fugitive murderer

House of Insane Women
see Exorcism's Daughter

The House of Lurking Death
1984, (GB), color, 60 mins.
W: James Warwick, Francesca Annis
from an Agatha Christie story
TVM, standard thriller: Chocolates laced with arsenic

House of Madness
1971, (Mex), color
Minor thriller

House of Menace
1935, (USA), MGM, b&w, 77 mins.
W: Basil Rathbone, Aline MacMahon, Frank Reicher, Dudley Digges, Mary Carlisle, Frank Albertson, Doris Lloyd

D: George B. Seitz   SCR: Bernard Schubert, based on a play by Edward Chodorov, from Hugh Walpole's short story *The Silver Mask* (contained in book *All Soul's Night*)   PHOTOG: George Folsey   MUSIC: Edward Ward
A.k.a. Kind Lady
*Standard thriller: Criminals terrorize woman socialite. cf. **Kind Lady** (1951)*

House of Monsters
see La Villa dei Mostri

House of Mortal Sin
1975, (GB), Walker/Heritage/Atlas, color, 104 mins.
W: Anthony Sharp (*Father Xavier Meldrum*), Susan Penhaligon (*Jenny Welch*), Stephanie Beacham (*Vanessa Welch*), Norman Eshley (*Father Bernard Cutler*), Sheila Keith (*Miss Brabazon*), Hilda Barry (*Mrs. Meldrum*), Stuart Bevan (*Terry*), Julia McCarthy (*Mrs. Davey*), John Yule (*Robert*), Mervyn Johns (*Father Duggan*), Victor Winding (*Dr. Gaudio*), Kim Butcher (*Valerie Davey*), Bill Kerr (*Davey*), Jack Allen (*The Doctor*), Andrew Sachs (*The Man*)
P, D & STORY: Pete Walker   SCR: David McGillivray   PHOTOG: Peter Jessop   MUSIC: Stanley Myers
*USA retitle, **The Confessional***
Standard horror-thriller: Mad priest blackmails Catholic girl

The House of Mystery (1901)
see The Magician's Cavern

The House of Mystery
1913, (GB), Clarendon, b&w, 2,090 ft. (637m)
W: Dorothy Bellew (*The Girl*)
D: Wilfred Noy   STORY: Marchioness of Townshend
Standard thriller: Police stalk counterfeiters

The House of Mystery
1934, (USA), Mono, b&w, 62 mins
W: Edward Lowry, Verna Hillie
D: Paul Malvern   SCR: Albert E. DeMond, from Adam Hull Shirk's stage play
*Minor thriller: Heirs spend week in mysterious mansion. Remake: **The Ape** (1940)*

House of Mystery (1939)
see At the Villa Rose (1939)

House of Mystery (1942)
see Night Monster

House of Mystery
1961, (GB), Independent Artists/AA, b&w, 56 mins.
W: Jane Hylton (*Stella Lemming*), Peter Dyneley (*Mark Lemming*), Nanette Newman (*Joan Trevor*), Maurice Kaufmann (*Henry Trevor*), Colin Gordon (*Burdon*), Molly Urquhart (*Mrs. Bucknall*), John Merivale (*Clive*), Colette Wilde (*The Wife*)
P: Julian Wintle & Leslie Parkyn   D & SCR: Vernon Sewell, from a play by Pierre Mills & C. Vylars
Standard fantasy: Ghost tells couple how medium uncovered murder of previous tenants

The House of Peril
1922, (GB), Astra Films, b&w, 5,000 ft. (1524m)
W: Fay Compton (*Sylvia Bailey*), Roy Travers (*Bill Chester*), A.B. Imeson (*Comte de Virieu*), Madeleine Seymour (*Anna Wolsky*), J. Nelson Ramsey (*Herr Wachner*), Irene Tripod (*Frau Wachner*), Wallace Bosco (*Polperro*), Flora Le Breton (*The French Maid*), Blanche Walker (*The Maid*), George Bellamy (*A Gambler*), Hubert Carter (*A Gambler*), Lewis Gilbert (*A Gambler*), Jeff Barlow (*A Gambler*), Tom Coventry (*A Gambler*), Madge Tree (*A Gambler*)
P: H.W. Thompson   D & SCR: Kenelm Foss, from Horace Annesley Vachell's play, based on Marie Belloc Lowndes' novel *Chink in the Armour*
Standard thriller: Girl gamblers lured to "haunted house"

House of Psychotic Women
see House of Doom (1973)

The House of Secrets
1929, (USA), Chesterfield, b&w, 7 reels (6,400 ft./1950.7m)
W: Joseph Striker (*Barry Wilding*), Marcia Manning (*Margery Gordon*), Elmer Grandin (*Dr. Gordon*), Herbert Warren (*Det. Blake*), Francis M. Verdi (*Sir Hubert Harcourt*), Richard Stevenson (*Bill*), Harry Southard (*Warton*), Edward Roseman (*Wu Chang*), Walter Ringham (*Home Sec'y Forbes*)
D: Edmund Lawrence   SCR & DIALOG: Adeline Leitzbach, from a story by Sydney Horler   PHOTOG: George Webber, Irving Browning, George Peters & Lester Lang
Standard mystery-thriller: Inherited mansion harbors danger

The House of Secrets
1937, (USA), b&w, 70 mins.
W: Leslie Fenton, Muriel Evans, Noel Madison, Sidney Blackmer, Morgan Wallace, Holmes Herbert
D: Roland D. Reed
Standard thriller: Inheritance draws Yank to Britain

House of Secrets
1956, (GB), Rank/RFD, color, 97 mins.
W: Michael Craig (*Larry Ellis*), Julia Arnall (*Diane*), David Kossoff (*Van de*

H

Heide), Brenda de Banzie (*Mme. Ballu*), Barbara Bates (*Judy*), Gerard Oury (*Pindar*), Carl Jaffe (*Dorffman*), Geoffrey Keen (*Burleigh*), Jacques Brunius (*Lessage*), Anton Diffring (*Lauderbach*), Eric Pohlmann (*Gratz*), Eugene Deckers (*Vidal*), Balbina (*The Maid*)
P: Julian Wintle & Vivian A. Cox   **D:** Guy Green   **SCR:** Robert Buckner & Bryan Forbes, from a novel by Sterling Noel
USA retitle, **Triple Deception,** *reissued 1960*
Modest crime-thriller: Naval officer poses as dead double, catches forgers

House of Secrets
1993, Lifetime, (USA), color, 95 mins.
W: Melissa Gilbert, Bruce Boxleitner, Kate Vernon, Michael Boatman, Cicely Tyson, Kris Shaw
D: Mimi Leder   **TELEPLAY:** Andrew Laskos, from a novel by Pierre Boileau & Thomas Narcejac   **PHOTOG:** Tom Del Ruth   **MUSIC:** Anthony Marinelli
TVM, Standard thriller: Woman and cohort meet "murdered" husband

The House of Seven Corpses
1973, (USA), TCA/Int'l Amusements, color, 90 mins.
W: John Ireland, Faith Domergue, John Carradine, Carole Wells, Jerry Stricklen
WRIT, P & D:, Paul Harrison
Minor thriller: Murders during a film shoot

House of Seven Corpses: JOHN CARRADINE

The House of the Seven Gables
W: Gilbert Emery, Charles Trowbridge
MUSIC DIR: Charles Previn

The House of the Seven Hawks
1959, (GB), Coronado/MGM, b&w, 92 mins.
W: Robert Taylor (*John Nordley*), Nicole Maurey (*Constanta*), Linda Christian (*Elsa*), Donald Wolfit (*Van Der Stoor*), David Kossoff (*Wilhelm Dekker*), Eric Pohlmann (*Capt. Rohner*), Philo Hauser (*Charlie Ponz*), Gerard Heinz (*Insp. Sluiter*)
P: David E. Rose   **D:** Richard Thorpe   **SCR:** Jo Eisinger, from Victor Canning's novel
Modest crime-thriller: Charterboat skipper seeks Nazi loot

House of Terror (1960)
see **La Casa del Terror**

House of Terror (1963)
see **La Ragazza Che Sapeva Troppo**

House of Terror
1987, (USA), color, 91 mins.
W: Jennifer Bishop, Arell Blanton, Jacquelyn Hyde
Minor thriller: Woman plots boss' murder

The House of the Arrow
1930, (GB), Twickenham/WB, b&w, 76 mins.
W: Dennis Neilson-Terry (*Insp. Hanaud*), Benita Hume (*Betty Harlow*), Richard Cooper (*Jim Frobisher*), Wilfred Fletcher (*Wabersky*), Stella Freeman (*Ann Upcott*), Betty de Malero (*Francine*), Toni de Lungo (*Maurice Thevent*), Barbara Gott (*Mrs. Harlow*)
D: Leslie Hiscott   **SCR:** Cyril Twyford, from a novel by A.E.W. Mason
Standard thriller: Inspector solves poisoning of rich aunt

The House of the Arrow
1940, (GB), ABPC, b&w, 66 mins.
W: Keneth Kent (*Insp. Hanaud*), Diana Churchill (*Betty Harlowe*), Belle Chrystal (*Ann Upcott*), Peter Murray-Hill (*Jim Frobisher*), Clifford Evans (*Maurice Thevent*), Catherine Lacey (*Francine Rollard*), James Harcourt (*Boris Raviart*),

Louise Hampton (*Mme. Harlowe*)
D: Harold French   **SCR:** Doreen Montgomery, from a novel by A.E.W. Mason
USA retitle, **Castle of Crimes** *(PRC1944)*
Standard thriller: Blackmailing girl poisons rich widow, frames companion

The House of the Arrow
1953, (GB), ABPC, b&w, 73 mins.
W: Oscar Homolka (*Insp. Hanaud*), Yvonne Furneaux (*Betty Harlowe*), Robert Urquhart (*Jim Frobisher*), Harold Kasket (*Boris Wabersky*), Anthony Nicholls (*Jeremy Haslett*), Josephine Griffin (*Ann Upcott*), Pierre le Fevre (*Thevenet*), Andrea Lea (*Francine*), Jeanne Pali (*Mme. Harlowe*)
P: Vaughan N. Dean   **D:** Michael Anderson   **SCR:** Edward Dryhurst, from a novel by A.E.W. Mason
Standard thriller: Inspector proves English girl did not poison rich aunt

House of the Black Death
1965, (USA), Medallion/Taurus, color, 80 mins
W: Lon Chaney Jr., John Carradine, Katherine Victor, Andrea King, Tom Drake
P: William White & Richard Shotwell   **D:** Harold Daniels & Reginald LeBorg
   SCR: Richard Mahoney
A.k.a. **Night of the Beast**
never released (once scheduled for release in 1972 as **Blood of the Devil Man**)
Minor horror-thriller: Tale of satanic brothers

House of the Damned
1962, (USA), Assoc. Prods./20th-Fox, b&w, 63 mins.
W: Ronald Foster, Richard Crane, Merry Anders, Richard Kiel, Erica Peters
P & D: Maury Dexter   **SCR:** Harry Spalding   **PHOTOG:** John Nickolaus Jr.
   MUSIC: Henry Vars
Minor thriller: Freaks hide in old mansion, try to scare off visiting couple

The House of the Damned
1974, (GB-Sp), color, 89 mins.
W: Donald Pleasence, Michael Dunn
Minor thriller: Adventurers seek gold statue

House of the Damned
1996, (USA), SHO-TV, color, cable, 90 mins.
W: Alexandra Paul (*Maura*), Greg Evigan (*Will*)
Made-for-Cable, standard fantasy-thriller: California couple moves to Ireland, finds inherited estate possessed by demons

House of the Dark Stairway
see **A Blade in the Dark**

The House of the Dead
1980, (USA), Myriad Cinema Int'l/Zison Int'l, color, 82 mins.
W: John Ericson (*Talmudge*), Ivor Francis (*The Mortician*), Charles Aidman (*Det. Tilivar*), Bernard Fox (*Insp. McDowal*), Judith Novgrod (*Miss Sibiler*), Richard Gates (*Cantwell*), Elizabeth MacRae (*Miss Lumquist*), Burr DeBenning (*Growski*), Bo Byers (*Growski Det. #1*), David O'Malley (*Growski Det. #2*), Kathie Gibboney (*Julie*), Leslie Paxton (*Marie*), John King (*Marie's Husband*), Robert Telford (*The Maitre'd*), Ben Smalley (*The Hanging Man*), Michael Colley (*Stan*), Robert J. Mildfelt (*The Cantwell Businessman*), Gary Willis *The Magazine Store Owner*), Evan Tonsing (*The Newsstand Attendant*)
D: Sharron Miller   **SCR:** David O'Malley   **PHOTOG:** Ken Gibb   **MUSIC:** Stan V. Worth   **SONG:** *The Sound of 'Goodbye'*
Minor horror anthology: Undertaker tells 4 tales of bizarre death

The House of the Devil
see **The Haunting**

House of the Living Dead
1973, (S. Afr), Philip N. Krasne/John B.Kelly/AFP, color, 88 mins.
W: Mark Burns, Shirley Anne Field, David Oxley, Margaret Inglis, Dia Sydow, Lynne Maree, Bill Flynn, Ronald France, William Baird Clark, Don Furnival, Peter Geldenhuys, Amina Gool, Ben Dekker, Limpie Basson
D: Ray Austin   **SCR:** Marc de V Marais, from orig. story by John Brason   **PHOTOG:** Robin Browne, Lionel Friedberg   **SPCL-FX:** Protea Holdings   **MUSIC:** Peter Elliot
Minor thriller: Fiancee finds murder, madness. A.k.a. **Doctor Maniac**

House of the Long Shadows
1983, (GB), Golan-Globus/Cannon, color, 102 mins.
W: Vincent Price (*Lionel Grisbane*), Christopher Lee (*Corrigan*), Peter Cushing (*Sebastian*), John Carradine (*Lord Grisbane*), Sheila Keith (*Victoria*), Desi Arnaz Jr. (*Kenneth Magee*), Julie Peasgood (*Mary Norton*), Louise English (*Diana*), Richard Todd (*Sam Allyson*), Richard Hunter (*Andrew*), Norman Rossington (*The Station Master*)
D: Pete Walker   **SCR:** Michael Armstrong, suggested by the novel *Seven Keys to Baldpate* by Earl Derr Biggers and the dramatization by George M. Cohan. Remake of other versions   **PHOTOG:** Norman Langley   **MUSIC:** Richard Harvey
Modest thriller: Young novelist finds mystery in Welsh manor house

The House of the Seven Gables
1940, (USA), Univ., b&w, 89 mins.
W: Vincent Price, Dick Foran, Margaret Lindsay, George Sanders, Alan Napier, Cecil Kellaway, Nan Grey, Miles Mander

D: Joe May   **SCR:** Lester Cole, from Nathaniel Hawthorne's novel   **PHOTOG:** Milton Krasner
Modest thriller: Curse haunts New England family. cf. Twice-Told Tales

House of Usher
1960, (USA), Alta-Vista/AIP, color, 85 mins.
W: Vincent Price *(Roderick Usher)*, Mark Damon *(Philip Winthrop)*, Myrna Fahey *(Madeleine Usher)*, Harry Ellerbe *(Bristol)*, Bill Borzage, Mike Jordon, Nadajan, George Paul, Ruth Oklander, Eleanor Le Faber, David Andar, John Zimeas, Phil Sylvestre, Geraldine Paulette
P & D: Roger Corman   **SCR:** Richard Matheson, from Edgar Allan Poe's short story *The Fall of the House of Usher* (film known as such in France)   **PHOTOG:** Floyd Crosby   **SPCL-FX:** Ray Mercer & Pat Dinga   **MUSIC:** Les Baxter
*orig. to be titled **The Mysterious House of Usher**, reissued 1964*
Superior thriller (AIP's first million-dollar budget film): Benighted siblings metaphysically linked to ancient mansion

The House of Usher
1988, (GB), color, 90 mins.
W: Oliver Reed, Donald Pleasence, Romy Windsor, Rufus Swart, Norman Coombes, Anne Stradi
D: Alan Birkinshaw, from Edgar Allan Poe's short story *The Fall of the House of Usher*
Minor thriller (filmed in S. Africa): Man seeks mate to continue family line

House of Wax
1953, (USA), WB, 3D, color, 90 mins.
W: Vincent Price *(Henry Jarrod)*, Frank Lovejoy *(Det. Tom Brennan)*, Phyllis Kirk *(Sue Allen)*, Carolyn Jones *(Cathy)*, Paul Picerni *(Scott Andrews)*, Roy Roberts *(Matthew Burke)*, Paul Cavanagh *(Sidney Wallace)*, Charles Buchinsky (Bronson) *(Igor)*, Dabbs Greer *(Sgt. Jim Shane)*, Angela Clarke *(Mrs. Andrews)*, Philip Tonge *(Bruce Allison)*, Reggie Rymal, Stanley Kalish
P: Bryan Foy   **D:** Andre de Toth   **SCR:** Crane Wilbur, from a story by Charles Belden   **PHOTOG:** Bert Glennon   **MUSIC:** David Buttolph
*Classic horror-thriller (most successful of 3D epics—gross $5 million), remake of **Mystery of the Wax Museum**: Mad sculptor turns humans into waxworks*

House of Whipcord
1974, (GB), Pete Walker/Heritage, color, 102 mins.
W: Barbara Markham *(Mrs. Wakehurst)*, Patrick Barr *(Desmond)*, Sheila Keith *(Walker)*, Ray Brooks *(Tony)*, Penny Irving *(Anne Marie de Vernay)*, Ann Michele *(Julia)*, Ivor Salter *(Jack)*, Dorothy Gordon *(Bates)*, Robert Tayman *(Mark Dessart)*, Judy Robinson *(Claire)*, Ka-ren David *(Karen)*, David McGillivray *(Cavan)*, Tony Sympson *(Henry)*, Rose Hill *(The Wife)*, Pete Walker *(The Cyclist)*, Jane Hayward *(Estelle)*, Celia Imrie, Ron Smerczak, Dave Butler, Barry Martin
P & D: Pete Walker   **SCR:** David McGillivray   **ORIG STORY:** Pete Walker   **PHOTOG:** Peter Jessop   **MUSIC:** Stanley Myers
Unusual thriller: French model tries to escape from mad judge's private prison

House on Bare Mountain
1962, (USA), Olympic-Int'l, color, 62 mins
W: Bob Cresse *(Granny Good)*, Warren Ames *(Frankenstein)* Jeffrey Smithers *(Dracula)*, Hugh Cannon *(Wolfman)*
P: Bob Cresse, David Andrew & Wesdon Bishop   **D:** R.L. Frost   **SCR:** Denver Scott
Minor "sexploitation" thriller: Meeting between Dracula, the Wolf Man and the Frankenstein monster

House on Haunted Hill
1958, (USA), AA, b&w, 75 mins.
W: Vincent Price *(Frederick Loren)*, Carol Ohmart *(Annabelle Loren)*, Richard Long *(Lance Schroeder)*, Carolyn Craig *(Nora Manning)*, Alan Marshal *(Dr. David Trent)*, Julie Mitchum *(Ruth Bridges)*, Leona Anderson *(Mrs. Slydes)*, Howard Hoffman *(Jonas Slydes)*, Elisha Cook Jr. *(Watson Pritchard)*
P & D: William Castle   **SCR:** Robb White   **PHOTOG:** Carl E. Guthrie   **SPCL-FX:** Herman Townsley   **MUSIC:** Von Dexter
*Fr retitle, **La Nuit de Tous les Mysteres** (The Night of All the Mysteries)*
Standard horror-thriller: Wealthy eccentric hosts party in notorious murder mansion

The House on Skull Mountain
1974, (USA), Chocolate Chip-Pinto/20th Fox, color, 89 mins.
W: Jean Durand, Victor French, Janee Michelle, Mike Evans, Sen. Leroy Johnson, Xerona Clayton
P: Ray Storey   **D:** Ron Honthaner   **SCR:** Mildred Pares   **PHOTOG:** Monroe Askins   **MUSIC:** Jerrold Immel
Minor fantasy-thriller: Mysteries of voodoo

The House on Sorority Row
1983, (USA), VAE Prods./ARC/Edward L. Montoro, color, 90 mins.
W: Kathryn McNeil, Eileen Davidson, Lois Kelso Hunt, Janis Zido, Christopher Lawrence, Robin Meloy, Michael Kuhn
WRIT & D: Mark Rosman   **MUSIC:** Richard H. Band
*A.k.a. **House of Evil** and **Seven Sisters***
Minor thriller: Mysterious killer disrupts college girls' graduation party

The House on Straw Hill
1976, (GB), color, 86 mins.
W: Udo Keir, Linda Hayden, Fiona Richmond
D: James Kenelm Clarke
Standard thriller: Mysterious farm woman attracts novelist

The House on the Marsh
1920, (GB), London/Jury, b&w, 5,250 ft. (1600.2m)
W: Cecil Humphreys *(Gervas Rayner)*, Peggy Patterson *(Violet Christie)*, Harry Welchman *(Laurence Reed)*, Frank Stanmore *(Rev. Golightly)*, Madge Tree *(Sarah Gooch)*, Mary Godfrey *(Miss Rayner)*
D: Fred Paul, from a novel by Florence Warden
Standard thriller: Governess unmasks employer as leader of gang of thieves

The House Opposite
1917, (GB), Broadwest, b&w, 4,072 ft. (1241.1m)
W: Matheson Lang *(Henry Rivers)*, Violet Hopson *(Mrs. Anstruther)*, Ivy Close *(Mrs. Rivers)*, Gregory Scott *(Richard Cardyne)*, Terence O'Brien *(The Thief)*, Dora de Winton, J. Hastings Batson, Dora Barton
D: Frank Wilson   **SCR:** Reuben Gillmer & Enid Lorimer, from a play by Percival Landon
Standard thriller: Jealous wife witnesses murder

The House Opposite
1931, (GB), BIP/Pathe, b&w, 66 mins.
W: Henry Kendall *(Hobart)*, Frank Stanmore *(Ben)*, Celia Glyn *(Nadine)*, Arthur Macrae *(Randall)*, Wallace Geoffrey *(Clitheroe)*, Rene Macready *(Jessica)*, Charles Farrell *(Wharton)*, Abraham Sofaer *(Fahmy)*, Molly Lamont *(Doris)*
D & SCR: Walter Summers, from a play by J. Jefferson Farjeon
Standard thriller: Girl detective and blackmail victim catch mad scientist's gang

The House That Bled to Death/Growing Pains
1980, (GB), BBC-TV, color
W: Rachel Davis *(Emma)*, Milton Johns *(A.J. Powers)*, Gary Bond *(Terence Morton)*
*TVM, minor thriller: 2 episodes from teleseries **House of Horror***

The House That Cried Murder
*see **The Bride** (1973)*

The House That Dripped Blood
1970, (GB), Amicus/CRC, color, 101 mins.
W: Peter Cushing *(Philip Grayson)*, Christopher Lee *(John Reid)*, Jon Pertwee *(Paul Henderson)*, Ingrid Pitt *(Carla)*, John Bryans *(Stoker)*, Nyree Dawn Porter *(Ann)*, Tom Adams *(Dominick)*, Denholm Elliott *(Charles)*, Geoffrey Bayldon *(Von Hartmann)*, Chloe Franks *(Jane)*, Joss Ackland *(Rogers)*, John Bennett *(Insp. Holloway)*, Wolfe Morris *(The Waxworks Owner)*, Robert Lang *(The Psychiatrist)*, Joanna Dunham *(Alice Hillyer)*, Richard Coe, John Malcolm, Carleton Hobbs, Hugh Manning, Jonathan Lynn
P: Max J. Rosenberg & Milton Subotsky   **D:** Peter Duffell   **SCR:** Robert Bloch—from his short stories *Method for Murder, Sweet to the Sweet, Waxworks & The Cloak*   **PHOTOG:** Robert Parslow   **MUSIC:** Michael Dress
"This spooky carnival from England is a witty, literate, campy, and most of all, paralyzingly scary film—a work of art in the horror movie genre"—Donald J. Mayerson, Cue
Standard horror-satire anthology

The House That Screamed
1970, (Sp), Anabel/AIP, color, 99 mins.
W: Lilli Palmer *(Mme. Fourneau)*, John Moulder-Brown *(Luis)*, Cristina Galbo *(Theresa)*, Mary Maude *(Irenee)*, Tomas Blanco *(M. Baldie)*, Candida Losada *(Mlle. Desprez)*, Pauline Challenor *(Catherine)*, Maribel Martin *(Isabelle)*, Victor Israel *(Brechard)*, Conchita Paredes *(Suzanne)*
D: Narciso Serrador   **SCR:** Luis Verna Penafiel, from a story by Juan Tebar   **PHOTOG:** Manuel Berenguer   **MUSIC:** Waldo de Los Rios
"...a thoroughly convincing, even elegant exercise in evil"—Los Angeles Times
Unusual horror-thriller: Repressed youth "engineers" his concept of perfect woman

The House That Vanished
*see **Scream and Die!***

The House That Wouldn't Die
1970, (USA), Aaron Spelling/ABC-TV, color, 73 mins.
W: Barbara Stanwyck *(Ruth Bennett)*, Richard Egan *(Pat McDougal)*, Michael Anderson Jr. *(Stan Whitman)*, Kitty Winn *(Sara Dunning)*, Doreen Lang *(Sylvia Wall)*, Mabel Albertson *(Delia McDougal)*
P: Aaron Spelling   **D:** John Llewellyn Moxey   **TELEPLAY:** Henry Farrell, from Barbara Michaels' (Aka Elizabeth Peters) novel *Ammie, Come Home*   **PHOTOG:** Fleet Southcott   **MUSIC:** Laurence Rosenthal
TVM, standard thriller: Woman inherits eerie mansion

House III
*see **The Horror Show***

The House Under the Trees
*see **The Deadly Trap***

The House Where Death Lives
*see **Delusion***

The House Where Evil Dwells
1982, (GB-Jap), Martin B. Cohen/UA, color, 88 mins.

W: Edward Albert, Susan George, Doug McClure, Amy Barrett, Mako Hattori, Toshiyuki Sasaki, Toshiya Maruyama
D: Kevin Connor   SCR: Robert Suhosky   STORY: James Hardiman   PHOTOG: Jacques Haitkin   MUSIC: Ken Thorne
Minor horror-fantasy: Samurai ghosts possess family

The House Where Hell Froze Over
see Keep My Grave Open

The House without a Key
1926, (USA), Pathe, b&w
W: Allene Ray, Walter Miller, Frank Lackteen, Charles West, John Webb Dillon, Natalie Warfield, George Kuwa (*Charlie Chan*), William N. Bailey
D: Spencer Gordon Bennet   SCR: Frank Leon Smith, from Earl Derr Biggers' novel
*Standard thriller, 10-chapter serial (progenitor of the "Charlie Chan" series): Sleuth deals with estranged brothers, missing treasure chest. Remake: **Charlie Chan's Greatest Case***

The House with the Dark Staircase
1982, (It), color
D: Lamberto Bava
Standard thriller

Houston, We've Got a Problem
1974, (USA), ABC-TV/Univ-TV, color, 74 mins.
W: Robert Culp, Sandra Dee, Ed Nelson, Gary Collins, Clu Gulager, Sheila Sullivan, Steve Franken, Jack Hogan, Robert Corff
D: Lawrence Doheny   TELEPLAY: Richard Nelson
*TVM, standard thriller: Fictionalized account of ill-fated Apollo space mission. cf. **Apollo 13***

How a Mosquito Operates
1911, (USA), Winsor McCay, b&w
Animated cartoon: Huge mosquito feeds on sleeping man

The Howard Case
1936, (GB), Sovereign/Univ, b&w, 62 mins.
W: Jack Livesey (*Jerry*), Olive Melville (*Pat*), David Keir (*Barnes*), Arthur Seaton (*Howard/Phillips*), Olive Sloane (*Lena Maxwell*), Jack Vyvyan (*Sgt. Halliday*)
D: Frank Richardson, from H.F. Maltby's play *Fraud*
Standard thriller: Lawyer kills twin cousin, frames partner

Howard the Duck
1986, (USA), George Lucas/Univ, color, 111 mins.
W: Lea Thompson, Jeffrey Jones, Tim Robbins, Ed Gale, Tim Rose, Chip Zien, Steve Sleap, Peter Baird, Mary Wells, Ed Holmes, Lisa Sturz, Jordan Prentice, Paul Guilfoyle, Holly Robinson, Liz Sagal, Dominique Davalos, Miles Chapin, Lee Anthony, Tommy Swerdlow, Richard Edson, Michael Sandoval, Richard McGonagle, Virginia Capers, Jorli McLain, Maureen Coyne, Debbie Carrington, Sheldon Feldner, Paul Comi, Tom Rayhall, James Lashly, Tom Parker, Denny Delk, David Paymer, William Hall, Martin Ganapoler, Gary Littlejohn, Ted Kurtz, Gary Littlejohn, Thomas Dolby, Reed Kirk Rahlmann, Kristopher Logan, John Fleck, William McCoy, James Brady, Steve Karvitz, Anne Tofflemire, Marcia Banks, Nancy Fish, Morty Hoffman, Wood Moy, Wanda McCaddon, Carol McElheney, Jeanne Lauren, Margarita Fernandez, Richard Kiley (*Voice of the Cosmos*)
D: Willard Huyck   SCR: Willard Huyck & Gloria Katz, from Marvel Comics character created by Steve Gerber   PHOTOG: Richard H. Kline   SPCL VS-FX: Industrial Light & Magic   MUSIC: John Barry   SONGS: Hunger City, Don't Turn Away, It Don't Come Cheap & I'm On My Way
Modest SF-fantasy: Alien duck stranded on Earth

How Awful About Allan
1970, (USA), Aaron Spelling/ABC-TV, color, 72 mins.
W: Anthony Perkins (*Allan*), Julie Harris (*Katherine*), Joan Hackett (*Olive*), Kent Smith (*Raymond*), Molly Dodd (*The Inmate*), Robert H. Harris (*Dr. Ellins*), Trent Dolan (*Eric*), Billy Bowles (*Harold Dennis*), Jeannette Howe (*Katherine as a Child*), Kenneth Lawrence (*Allan as a Child*), William Erwin (*Dr. Ames*)
D: Curtis Harrington   TELEPLAY: Henry Farrell—from his novel   PHOTOG: Fleet Southcott   SPCL-FX: Joe Lombardi   MUSIC COMPOSER: Laurence Rosenthal   MUSIC SPRVSR: George Duning
TVM, standard thriller: Near-blind man menaced by killer

How Awful About Allan: JULIE HARRIS AND ANTHONY PERKINS

How Billy Kept His Word
1914, (GB), Hepworth, b&w, 1,125 ft. (342.9m)
W: Eric Desmond (*Billy*)
D: Frank Wilson
Standard crime-thriller: Wronged inventor kidnaps daughter of capitalist

How I Cooked Peary's Record
1909, (GB), Urban, b&w, 380 ft. (115.8m)
D: Walter R. Booth
Minor fantasy short: Baron Munchausen's fantastic conquest of Pole

How it Feels to be Run Over
1900, (GB), Cecil M. Hepworth, b&w, 50 ft. (15.2m)
Standard short comedy-fantasy

The Howling
1981, (USA), Daniel H. Blatt/Avco Embassy, color, 89 mins.
W: Dee Wallace (*Karen White*), Patrick Macnee (*Dr. George Waggner*), Dennis Dugan (*Christopher*), Christopher Stone (*William "Bill" Neill*), Belinda Balaski (*Terry Fisher*), John Carradine (*Erle Kenton*), Slim Pickens (*Sam Newfield*), Kevin McCarthy (*Fred W. Francis*), Elisabeth Brooks (*Marsha Quist*), Robert Picardo (*Eddie Quist*), Dick Miller (*Walter Paisley*), Don McLeod (*T.C. Quist*), Margie Impert (*Donna*), Noble Willingham (*Charles Barton*), James Murtaugh (*Jerry Warren*), Jim McKrell (*Lew Landers*), Kenneth Tobey (*The Old Cop*), Steve Nevil (*The Young Cop*), Joe Bratcher (*The Radio Man*), Bill Sorrells (*Kline*), Herb Braha (*The Porno Cashier*), Meshach Taylor, Ivan Saric, Sarina Grant, Forrest J. Ackerman, Chico Martinez, Daniel Nunez, Michael O'Dwyer, Wendell Wright, Roger Corman
P: Michael Finnell & Jack Conrad   D: Joe Dante   SCR: John Sayles & Terence H. Winkless, from Gary Brandner's novel
PHOTOG: John Hora   SPCL-FX: Roger George   SPCL MAKEUP FX: Rob Bottin   MUSIC: Pino Donaggio   SONGS: Howling Chicken (by Rick & Joyce Fienhage) & Rocky Mountain Waltz (by Chris Carney)
"One of the best werewolf movies ever made. The special effects are brilliant beyond all description"—Los Angeles Magazine
"The special makeup effects mark a technical milestone by which all future monster films will be judged"—Michael Blowen, Boston Globe
"A rare treat in horror films... the most realistic and frightening special effects to ever shake up an audience"—Associated Press
Superior horror-fantasy: TV newswoman uncovers lycanthrope nest

Howling II
1984, (GB-USA), Euro Film Fund-Greenberg Bros./Hemdale/Thorn EM, color, 88 mins.
W: Christopher Lee (*Stefan*), Annie McEnroe (*Jenny*), Marsha A. Hunt (*Mariana*), Reb Brown (*Ben*), Sybil Danning (*Stirba*), Judd Omen (*Vlad*), Ferdinand Mayne (*Erle*), Jimmy Nail (*Dom*), Patrick Field (*The Deacon*), James M. Crawford (*The American Priest*), Steven Bronowski (*The Moon Devil*), Jan Kraus (*Tondo*), Jiri Krytinar (*Vasile*), Peter Skarke (*Konstantin*), Ivo Niederle (*Gregore*), Ladislav Krecmer (*Father Florin*), Igor Smrzik (*Luca*), Ed Kleynen, Miro Sustr, Anna Maria Kolarova, Jitka Asterova, Hana Ludvikova, Shirley Hanson, John Brown, Ludmila Safarova, Valerie Kaplanova, Miriam Lugerova, Terry Coppersmith, Alex Kleynen, Jill Sinclair, Ismael Cruz, Paul Leonard, Ron Leonard, Courtney Leonard, Michelle Leonard, John Leonard, Carolyn Doyle, Joyce Walker, Srance Leclerc
D: Philippe Mora, from characters created by Gary Brandner   PHOTOG: Geoffrey Stephenson   MUSIC: Steve Parsons and "punk" group, Babel
A.k.a. Howling II. . . Your Sister is a Werewolf
Standard horror-fantasy: Lycanthrope slayers seek werewolf queen.

Howling III
1987, (Austral), Bancannia, color, 94 mins.
W: Barry Otto (*Prof. Harry Beckmeyer*), Imogen Annesley (*Jerboa*), Max Fairchild (*Thylo*), Michael Pate (*The President*), Dasha Blahova (*Olga Gorki*), Leigh Biolos (*Donny*), Jon Ewing (*Gen. Forster*), Ralph Cotterill (*Prof. Sharp*), Frank Thring (*Jack Citron*), William Yang (*The Siberian Peasant*), Barry Humphries (*The Academy Award Presenter*), Deby Wightman (*The Wolf Woman*), Christopher Pate (*Agent #1*), Jerome Patillo (*Agent #2*), Carole Skinner (*Yara*), Jenny Vuletic (*Goolah*), Glenda Linscott (*Bahloo*), Roger Eagle (*The Priest*), Steve Shaw (*The Horror Movie Actor*), Megan Shapcott (*The Horror Movie Starlet*), Ric Carter (*The 1st Drunk*), Lionel Curtin (*The 2nd Drunk*), Bob McCarron (*The Werewolf in the Park*), Mary Acres (*The Paper Seller*), Bob Barrett (*Policeman #1*), Bill Collins (*Doctor #1*), David Cahill (*Doctor #2*), Pieter Van Der Stolk (*Mikhail*), Mary Haire (*The Nurse*), Alec Maksimovich (*Policeman #9*), Penny Linden (*Police-woman #10*), Fred Welsh (*Dan Ruggle*), Brian Adams (*Gen. Miller*), Rodney Francis (*The Male Dancer*), Sam Toomey (*Policeman #4*), Alan Penny (*Spud McCormack*), Burnham Burnham (*Kendi*), Aminatta Joy Abraham (*The UCLA Girl Student*), Gerry Skilton (*Hunter #1*), Steve Rackman (*Hunter #2*), Gary McGuire (*Hunter #3*), Peter Armstrong (*Hunter #4*), Robert Simper (*Hunter #5*), Wayne Pleace (*Hunter #6*), Tony Deary (*Max*), Alan Dargin (*The Tracker*), Patrick Rowe (*Policeman #6*), Max Aspin (*Policeman #7*), Paul Lennon (*Policeman #8*), Peter Baird (*Omega #1*), Lee Rice (*Omega #2*), Max Skipper (*Zac, 4 yrs.*), Andreas Bayonas (*Zac, 23 yrs.*), Maia Horniak (*Gracie, 5 yrs.*), Danielle Sharp (*Gracie, 15 yrs.*)
WRIT & D: Philippe Mora, from Gary Brandner's novel   PHOTOG: Louis Irving   MUSIC: Allan Zavod
A.k.a. The Marsupials: Howling III
Standard horror-fantasy: Tribulations of werewolves in modern Australia

Howling IV

1988, (Austral), Allied Entertainment, color, 94 mins.

<u>W</u>: Romy Windsor *(Marie)*, Michael T. Weiss *(Richard)*, Lamya Derval *(Eleanor)*, Antony Hamilton *(Tom)*, Susanne Severeid *(Janice)*, Nor-man Anstey *(The Sheriff)*, Kate Edwards *(Mrs. Ormstead)*, Dennis Folbigge *(Dr. Coombes)*, Clive Turner *(The Tow Truck Driver)*, An-thony James *(Father Camefron)*, Dennis Smith *(Mr. Ormstead)*, Dale Cutts *(Dr. Heinemann)*, Maxine John *(Paula)*, Megan Kruskal *(Sister Ruth)*, Bull Forsche *(A Werewolf)*, Peter Ware *(A Werewolf)*, Diana Tilldon-Davis *(The Municipal Clerk)*, Gregg Latler *(John)*, Hugh Jobling *(Mr. Duncan)*, Megan Davies *(Mrs. Duncan)*, Tullio Moneta *(Villager #1)*, Ralph Draper *(Villager #2)*, Beryl Gresak *(Villager #3)*

<u>D</u>: John Hough   **SCR**: Clive Turner & Freddie Rowe   **STORY**: Clive Turner, based on the novels *The Howling (I), II & III* by Gary Brandner   **PHOTOG**: Godfrey Godar   **MUSIC**: David George   **SONGS**: *Something Evil, Something Dangerous & Winter Rain*

Standard horror-fantasy: Woman finds lycanthropy in Australian outback

Howling V: The Rebirth

1989, (GB-Hung), Allied Vision-Lane Pringle Prods., color, 99 mins.

<u>W</u>: Philip Davis *(The Count)*, Victoria Catlin *(Catherine)*, Elizabeth She *(Marylou)*, Ben Cole *(David)*, Nigel Truffitt *(The Professor)*, William Shockley *(Richard)*, Clive Turner *(Ray)*, Mark Sivertsen *(Jonathan)*, Joszef Madaras *(Peter)*, Stephanie Faulkner *(Gail)*, Mary Stavin *(Anna)*, Jill Pearson *(Eleanor)*, Renata Szatler *(Susan)*

<u>D</u>: Neal Sundstrom   **SCR**: Clive Turner & Freddie Rowe   **ORIG STORY**: Clive Turner, from novels by Gary Brandner   **PHOTOG**: Arledge Armenaki   **MUSIC**: The Factory

Minor horror-fantasy: Castle guests fall prey to werewolf

Howling VI: The Freaks

1991, (USA), Allied Lane Pringle, color, 102 mins.

<u>W</u>: Brendan Hughes, Michele Matheson, Bruce Martyn Payne, Jered Barclay, Sean Gregory Sullivan, Antonio Fargas, Carlos Cervantes, Christopher Morley, Deep Roy, Randy Pelish, Ben Kronen, Jeremy West, Joe Gieb, Sheila Lane, Jack Stevens

<u>D</u>: Hope Perello   **SCR**: Kevin Rock, from novels by Gary Brandner   **PHOTOG**: Edward Pei   **SPCL-FX COORD**: John P. Cazin   **MUSIC**: Patrick Gleeson

Standard horror-fantasy: Drifter encounters sinister carnival

A Howling in the Woods

1971, (USA), Univ/CBS-TV, color, 96 mins.

<u>W</u>: Barbara Eden *(Liza)*, Larry Hagman *(Eddie)*, Vera Miles *(Rose)*, John Rubinstein *(Justin)*, Tyne Daly *(Sally)*, Ruta Lee *(Sharon)*, Bill Vint *(Lonnie)*, Ford Rainey, Karl Swenson, George Murdock, Lisa Gerritsen

<u>D</u>: Daniel Petrie   **TELEPLAY**: Richard DeRoy, from Velda Johnston's novel   **PHOTOG**: Jack Marta   **MUSIC**: Dave Grusin

TVM, modest thriller: Child's murder obsesses small Nevada town

The Howling: New Moon Rising

1995, (Austral), color, 90 mins.

<u>W</u>: John Ramsden, Ernest Kester

<u>D & SCR</u>: Clive Turnerfrom novels by Gary Brandner

Standard horror-fantasy: Drifter suspected of being werewolf

How the Artful Dodger Secured a Meal

1908, (GB), Cricks & Martin, b&w, 320 ft. (97.5m)

<u>D</u>: A.E. Coleby

Minor fantasy short: Tramp hypnotizes farmer

How to Destroy the Reputation of the Greatest Secret Agent

1973, (It-Fr), color, 94 mins.

<u>W</u>: Jean-Paul Belmondo *(Bob Saint-Clair)*, Jacqueline Bisset *(Christina/Tatiana)*, Vittorio Caprioli, Monique Tarbes, Raymond Gerome

<u>D</u>: Philippe de Broca

A.k.a. **Le Magnifique** *(The Magnificent)*

Standard spy-spoof: Writer enters fantasy world of his pulp thrillers

How to Make a Doll

1968, (USA), Unusual Films, color

<u>W</u>: Robert Wood

P & D: Herschell Gordon Lewis   **SCR**: Bert Ray & Herschell Gordon Lewis

Minor SF-nudie-comedy: Computer creates beautiful women

How to Make a Monster

1958, (USA), Sunset/AIP, b&w (last seconds in color), 74 mins.

<u>W</u>: Robert H. Harris *(Drummond)*, Gary Conway *(Tony Martell)*, Gary Clarke *(Larry Drake)*, Paul Brinegar, Joan Chandler, Morris Ankrum, John Ashley, Malcolm Atterbury, Rod Dana, Dennis Cross, Heather Ames, Walter Reed, Eddie Marr, Paul Maxwell, Pauline Myers, Jacqueline Ebeier, Robert Shayne, John Phillips, Thomas B. Henry, Voltaire Perkins, Herman Cohen

<u>P</u>: Herman Cohen   <u>D</u>: Herbert L. Strock   **SCR**: Kenneth Langtry & Herman Cohen   **PHOTOG**: Maury Gertsman   **MUSIC**: Paul Dunlap

orig. co-billed with **Teenage Caveman***, reissued 1961*

Standard horror-thriller: Dismissed makeup man gains weird revenge on film studio

How to Make It

see **Target: Harry**

How to Make Time Fly

1906, (GB), R.W. Paul, b&w, 300 ft. (91.4m)

<u>D</u>: J.H. Martin

Minor fantasy short: Girl reverses clock's hands, life speeds up

How to Murder a Rich Uncle

1957, (GB), Warwick/Col, b&w, 80 mins.

<u>W</u>: Charles Coburn *(Uncle George)*, Wendy Hiller *(Edith)*, Nigel Patrick *(Henry)*, Katie Johnson *(Alice)*, Athene Seyler *(Grannie)*, Anthony Newley *(Edward)*, Patricia Webster *(Constance)*, Michael Caine *(Gilrony)*, Trevor Reid *(Insp. Harris)*, Noel Hood *(Aunt Marjorie)*, Kevin Stoney *(The Bar Steward)*, Cyril Luckham *(The Coroner)*, Johnson Bayly *(The Radio Officer)*, Martin Boddey *(The Police Sgt.)*, Anthony Shaw *(The Coloniel Type)*, Ian Wilson *(The Postman)*, Kenneth Fortescue *(Albert)*

P & SCR: John Paxton, from Didier Daix's play *Il Faut Tuer Julie*   <u>D</u>: Nigel Patrick   **PHOTOG**: Ted Moore   **MUSIC**: Muir Mathieson

Amusing comedy-thriller: Heir plots homicide

How to Steal the World

1968, (USA), MGM, color

<u>W</u>: Robert Vaughn *(Napoleon Solo)*, David McCallum, Leo G. Carroll, Barry Sullivan, Eleanor Parker, Leslie Nielsen, Tony Bill, Dan O'Herlihy, Hugh Marlowe

<u>P</u>: Anthony Spinner   <u>D</u>: Sutton Roley   **SCR**: Norman Hudis

Standard espionage thriller (culled from episodes of teleseries "The Man from U.N.C.L.E."): "Obedience gas" threatens world freedom

How to Stuff a Wild Bikini

1965, (USA), AIP, color, 90 mins.

<u>W</u>: Annette Funicello *(Dee Dee)*, Brian Donlevy *(B.D.)*, Dwayne Hickman *(Ricky)*, Beverly Adams *(Cassandra)*, Harvey Lembeck *(Eric Von Zipper)*, Mickey Rooney *(Peachy Keane)*, John Ashley *(Johnny)*, Irene Tsu *(The Native Girl)*, Buster Keaton *(Bwana, the Witch Doctor)*, Bobbi Shaw *(Khola Koku)*, Jody McCrea *(Bonehead)*, Marianne Gaba *(Animal)*, Len Lesser *(North Dakota Pete)*, Arthur Julian *(Dr. Melamed)*, Alberta Nelson *(Puss)*, Andy Romano *(J.D.)*, John Macchia, Jerry Brutsche, Bob Harvey, Myrna Ross, Alan Fife, Tom Quine, Sig Frohlich, Hollis Morrison, Guy Hemric, George Boyce, Charlie Reed, Patti Chandler, Mike Nader, John Fain, Ed Garner, Mickey Dora, Brian Wilson, Bruce Baker, Ned Wynn, Kerry Berry, Rick Jones, Ray Atkinson, Ron Dayton, Toni Harper, Marianne Gordon, Sheila Stephenson, Uta Stone, Rosemary Williams, Sue Hamilton, Tonia Van Deter, Luree Holmes, Michele Barton, Victoria Carroll

<u>D</u>: William Asher   **SCR**: William Asher & Leo Townsend   **PHOTOG**: Floyd Crosby   **MUSIC**: Les Baxter

Standard "beach party" comedy-fantasy: Island witch doctor conjures up mysterious beach beauty

How to Stuff a Wild Bikini: BOBBI SHAW AND BUSTER KEATON

Hugo The Hippo
1975, (USA), color, 90 mins.
VOICES: Robert Morley, Paul Lynde, Ronny Cox, Percy Rodriguez   D: William Feigenbaum
Standard animated fantasy: Kids aid endangered hippo

The Human Duplicators
1964, (USA), Woolner Bros., color, 82 mins.
W: George Nader (*Glenn Martin*), Barbara Nichols (*Gail Wilson*), Hugh Beaumont (*Director of Nat'l Intelligence Agency*), George Macready (*Prof. Dornheimer*), Dolores Faith (*Lisa*), Richard Kiel (*Kolos*), Richard Arlen (*Lt. Shaw*), Lori Lyons, Margot Teele, Tommy Leonetti, Bill Hampton, Walter Maslow, Larry Barton, Andrew Johnson, Kim Satana, Richard Schuyler, John Daston
P: Hugo Grimaldi & Arthur C. Pierce   D: Hugo Grimaldi   SCR: Arthur C. Pierce   PHOTOG: Monroe Askins   SPCL-FX: Roger W. George
Standard SF-thriller: Robots in human form commit sabotage

Human Experiments
1979, (USA), Summer & Edwin Brown/Essex, color, 81 mins.
W: Linda Haynes, Ellen Travolta, Lurene Tuttle, Marie O'Henry
D: Gregory Goodell   SCR: Richard Rothstein   MUSIC: Marc Bucci   SONG: Country Rain
A.k.a. Beyond the Gate
Minor thriller: Young woman railroaded into prison, behavior alteration follows

The Human Factor
1975, (GB-It), Lactifer/Eton/Bryanston, color, 96 mins.
W: George Kennedy (*John Kinsdale*), John Mills (*Mike McAllister*), Raf Vallone (*Dr. Lupo*), Rita Tushingham (*Janice*), Barry Sullivan (*Edmonds*), Arthur Franz (*Gen. Fuller*), Shane Rimmer (*Carter*), Haydee Politoff (*Pidgeon*), Frank Avianca (*Kamal*), Tom Hunter (*Taylor*), Danny Houston (*Mark Kinsdale*), Flamma Verges (*Anne Kinsdale*), Hillary Leaf (*Linda Kinsdale*), Robert Lowell (*Eddy Fonseca*), Sharon Kellogg (*Alice Gerardi*), Anne Ferguson (*Mrs. Simpson*), Conchita Airoldi (*Sandra Pallavicini*)
P: Frank Avianca   D: Edward Dmytryk   ORIG SCR: Peter Powell & Thomas Hunter   PHOTOG: Ousama Rawi   MUSIC: Ennio Morricone
Minor melodrama: Computer expert hunts family's killers

Human Feelings
1978, (USA), Crestview/Charles Fries/Worldvision/NBC-TV, color, 90 mins.
W: Nancy Walker (*God*), Billy Crystal, Armand Assante, Pat Morita, Squire Fridell, Donna Pescow, Richard Dimitri, Tom Pedi, Jack Carter, John Fiedler, Pamela Sue Martin, Scott Walker, Anthony Charnota, James Whitmore Jr., Albert Cole, Barry Hamilton, Rozsika Halmos, Tony Cristino, Biff Yeager, Adele Claire, Pamela Miller, Liberty Godshall, Joe Ross, Charles Bracy, Abigail Shelton
D: Ernest Pintoff   TELEPLAY: Henry Bloomstein   PHOTOG: William J. Jurgensen   MUSIC: John Cacavas
TVM, minor comedy-fantasy: Angel seeks Las Vegas righteous

The Human Fly
see L'Homme-Mouche

Human Gorilla
see Behind Locked Doors

The Human Monster
see Dark Eyes of London

The Humanoid
1979, (It), Col, color, 100 mins
W: Richard Kiel, Barbara Bach, Corinne Clery, Arthur Kennedy, Ivan Rassimov, Leonard Mann
P: Giorgio Venturini   D: George B. Lewis   SCR: Adriano Bolzoni & Aldo Lado   MUSIC: Ennio Morricone
Minor SF-thriller ('Star Wars' imitation): Space-age heroes battle villains

Humanoids from the Deep
1980, (USA), Roger Corman/New World, color, 77 mins.
W: Doug McClure, Ann Turkel, Vic Morrow, Cindy Weintraub, Denise Galik, Anthony Penya, Lynn Theel, Hoke Howell, Don Maxwell, Linda Shayne
P: Martin B. Cohen   D: Barbara Peeters   SCR: Frederick James   PHOTOG: Daniel Lacambre   SPCL-FX: Roger George   MUSIC: James Horner
Minor SF-horror: Sea monsters seek human mates

Humanoid Woman
1981, (Russ), Color, 100 mins.
W: Helen Metelkine, Mady Sementsov
Standard SF-thriller: Earthlings aid space-alien female

Human Timebomb
1996, (USA), color, 100 mins.
W: Bryan Genesse, Joe Lara, J. Cynthia Brooks
A.k.a. Live Wire: Human Timebomb
Standard SF-thriller: Cuban general puts microchips into FBI agent, forces him to become killing machine

The Human Torches
see Les Torches Humaines

The Human Vapor
1960, (Jap), Toho/Col, color, 79 mins.
W: Tatsuya Mihashi, Kaoru Yachigusa, Yoshio Tsuchiya
D: Inoshiro Honda   SCR: Takeshi Kimura
Minor SF-thriller: Scientist enables thief to become mist

Humongous
1981, (Can), Stevenson-Kramreither/Manesco, color, 93 mins.
W: Janet Julian (*Sandy Ralston*), David Wallace (*Eric Simmons*), John Wildman (*Nick Simmons*), Janit Baldwin (*Carla Simmons*), Joy Boushel (*Donna Blake*), Lane Coleman (*Bert Defoe*), Shay Garner (*Ida Parsons*), John McFayden (*Ed Parsons*), Page Fletcher (*Tom Rice*), Mary Sullivan (*Teenage Ida*), Garry Robbins (*Ida's Son*)
P: Anthony Kramreither   D: Paul Lynch   SCR: William Gray   PHOTOG: Brian R.R. Hebb   MUSIC: John Mills Cockrell
Minor thriller: Stranded on island, teens meet human monster

Humpty Dumpty R.A.
1915, (GB), Humpty Dumpty Films/Prieur, b&w, 525 ft. (160m)
Minor fantasy short: Doll draws caricatures

The Humpty Dumpty's Circus
1914, (GB), Humpty Dumpty Films/Prieur, b&w, 448 ft. (136.6m)
Minor fantasy short: Animated dolls perform

The Hunchback
1911, (GB), Cricks & Martin, b&w, 790 ft. (240.8m)
W: Edwin J. Collins (*The Hunchback*)
D: A.E. Coleby
Standard crime-thriller: Hunchback framed for theft, sets fire to farmhand's house

The Hunchback
1914, (GB), Hepworth, b&w, 2,075 ft. (632.5m)
W: Tom Powers (*Tom*), Violet Hopson (*The Girl*), Harry Royston (*Badger*), Ruby Belasco (*The Mother*), Eric Desmond (*The Child*)
D: Frank Wilson
Standard crime-thriller: Crippled boy raised by thieves

The Hunchback
1997, (USA), Alliance Communications/TNT-TV, color
W: Mandy Patinkin (*Quasimodo*), Richard Harris (*Frollo*), Salma Hayek (*Esmeralda*), Edward Atherton (*Gringoire*), Jim Dale (*Clopin*), Nigel Terry (*King Louis*), Benedick Blythe
D: Peter Medak   TELEPLAY: John Fasano, from Victor Hugo's novel *Notre Dame de Paris*   PHOTOG: Elemer Ragalyi   MUSIC: Ed Shearmur
Made-for-Cable, mature melodrama: Gypsy beauty entrances deformed bellringer

The Hunchback of Notre Dame
1923, (USA), Univ, b&w, 99 mins.
W: Lon Chaney Sr. (*Quasimodo*), Patsy Ruth Miller (*Esmeralda*), Norman Kerry (*Phoebus*), Brandon Hurst (*Jehan*), Tully Marshall (*Louis XI*), Ernest Torrence (*Clopin*), Kate Lester (*Mme. de Gondelaurier*), Raymond Hatton (*Gringoire*), Edwin Wallack (*The King's Chamberlain*), Harry L. Van Meter (*Monsieur Neufchatel*), Nigel de Brulier (*Dom Claude*), Winifred Bryson (*Fleur de Lys*), Nick de Ruiz (*Monsieur le Torteru*), John Cossar (*The Justice of the Court*), Gladys Brockwell (*Godule*), W. Ray Meyers (*Charmolu's Ass't*), Eulalie Jensen (*Marie*), William Parke Sr. (*Josephus*)
D: Wallace Worsley   SCR: Percy Poore Sheehan & Edward T. Lowe Jr., from Victor Hugo's novel *Notre Dame de Paris*   PHOTOG: Robert S. Newhard & Tony Kornmann
"Chaney's pathetic, dog-like performance as the hapless Quasimodo was a masterpiece of pantomimic tour de force, and must certainly rank among the great screen portrayals of all time"—Joe Franklin, Classics of the Silent Screen
"His (Chaney's) makeup...was faithful to Hugo's description of the deformed bellringer: bristly hair, collapsed eye, uneven teeth, and an indefinable mixture of malice, bewilderment, and sadness. He also wore a heavy rubber hump and harness-like contraption that prevented him from standing erect. For his pains, the film was selected as one of the ten best of the year (1923), and his performance is regarded as a masterpiece"—Carlos Clarens, An Illustrated History of the Horror Film
Classic melodrama (Notre Dame set reused in 1925 Phantom of the Opera): Ugly bellringer loves gypsy beauty

The Hunchback of Notre Dame
1939, (USA), RKO, b&w, 117 mins.
W: Charles Laughton (*Quasimodo*), Maureen O'Hara (*Esmeralda*), Sir Cedric Hardwicke (*Jehan*), Thomas Mitchell (*Clopin*), Edmond O'Brien (*Gringoire*), Alan Marshal (*Phoebus*), Harry Davenport (*Louis XI*), Richard Clayton, Minna Gombell, Katharine Alexander, Arthur Hohl, Rod La Rocque, Walter Hampden, Fritz Leiber, George Zucco, Spencer Charters, Curt Bois
P: Pandro S. Berman   D: William Dieterle   SCR: Sonya Levien & Bruno Frank, from Victor Hugo's novel *Notre Dame de Paris*   PHOTOG: Joseph August   SPCL-FX: Van Nest Polglase
Definitive "Hunchback" melodrama: Deformed bellringer loves persecuted gypsy girl. US film debut of O'Hara, film debut of O'Brien

The Hunchback of Notre Dame
1957, (It-Fr), Paris/AA, color, 107 mins.
<u>W</u>: Anthony Quinn (*Quasimodo*), Gina Lollobrigida (*Esmeralda*), Jean Tissier (*Louis XI*), Alain Cuny (*Claude Frollo*), Robert Hirsch (*Gringoire*), Maurice Sarfati (*Jehan Frollo*), Jacques Hilling (*Charmolue*), Jean Danet (*Phoebus*), Danielle Dumont (*Fleur de Lys*), Philippe Clay (*Clopin*), Roger Blin (*Mathis Hungadi*), Marianne Oswald (*La Falourdel*), Pieral (*Le Nabot*), Duphilo (*Guillaume Rousseau*)
<u>P</u>: Robert & Raymond Hakim   <u>D</u>: Jean Delannoy   <u>SCR</u>: Jean Aurenche & Jacques Prevert, from Victor Hugo's novel *Notre Dame de Paris*   <u>PHOTOG</u>: Michel Kelber   <u>MUSIC</u>: Georges Auric
A.k.a. **Notre Dame de Paris**
Standard melodrama, most faithful to literary source: No happy ending in classic tale of misshapen bellringer's doomed love for gypsy beauty

The Hunchback of Notre Dame
1965, (GB), BBC-TV, color
<u>W</u>: Peter Woodthorpe (*Quasimodo*), Gay Hamilton (*Esmeralda*), Gary Raymond, Alex Davion, Norman Mitchell, Suzanne Neve, James Maxwell, Beatrix Lehmann, Jeffrey Isaac
<u>P</u>: Douglas Allen   <u>D</u>: James Cellan Jones   <u>ADAPT</u>: Vincent Tilsey, from Victor Hugo's novel *Notre Dame de Paris*   <u>MAKEUP</u>: Sylvia Hurll
TVM, minor melodrama: Bellringer loves gypsy

The Hunchback of Notre Dame
1977, (GB), BBC-TV/NBC-TV, color, 120 mins
<u>W</u>: Warren Clarke (*Quasimodo*), Michelle Newell (*Esmeralda*), Kenneth Haigh (*Archdeacon Frollo*), Christopher Gable (*Pierre*), Richard Morant (*Phoebus*), David Rintoul (*Jehan*)
<u>P</u>: George Messina   <u>D</u>: Alan Cooke   <u>TELEPLAY</u>: Robert Muller, from Victor Hugo's novel *Notre Dame de Paris*
TVM, minor melodrama: Deformed bellringer defies authority, aids persecuted gypsy beauty

The Hunchback of Notre Dame
1982, (GB), CBS-TV/Col-TV, color, 102 mins.
<u>W</u>: Anthony Hopkins (*Quasimodo*), Lesley-Anne Down (*Esmeralda*), Derek Jacobi (*Dom Claude Frollo*), Sir John Gielgud (*Charmolue*), Robert Powell (*Phoebus*), Gerry Sundquist (*Pierre*), David Suchet (*Trouillefou*), Nigel Hawthorne (*The Magistrate at Esmeralda's Trial*), Alan Webb (*The Judge at Quasimodo's Trial*), Tim Pigott-Smith (*Philippe*), Rosalie Crutchley (*Simone*), Roland Culver (*The Bishop of Paris*)
<u>D</u>: Michael Tuchner   <u>TELEPLAY</u>: John Gay, from Victor Hugo's novel *Notre Dame de Paris*   <u>PHOTOG</u>: Alan Hume   <u>MUSIC</u>: Kenneth Thorne
TVM, standard melodrama: Ugly bellringer aids gypsy

The Hunchback of Notre Dame
1996, (USA), Walt Disney/Buena Vista, color, 86 mins.
<u>VOICES</u>: Tom Hulce (*Quasimodo*), Demi Moore (*Esmeralda*), Kevin Kline (*Phoebus*), Jason Alexander (*Hugo*), Tony Jay (*Frollo*), Paul Kandel (*Clopin*), Charles Kimbrough, David Ogden Stiers, Mary Wickes   <u>D</u>: Kirk Wise & Gary Trousdale   <u>SCR</u>: Tab Murphy, Irene Mecchi, Bob Tzudiker, Noni White & Jonathan Roberts, from Victor Hugo's novel *Notre Dame de Paris*   <u>MUSIC</u>: Alan Menken   <u>LYRICS</u>: Stephen Schwartz
Animated musical-adventure: Bellringer loves gypsy girl

The Hunchback of Paris
see **The King's Avenger**

Hunchback of Rome
1963, (It-Fr), Royal, b&w, 84 mins.
<u>W</u>: Gerard Blain, Anna Maria Ferrero
Minor thriller

The Hunchback of Soho
1967, (W. Ger), ITC, color, 87 mins
<u>W</u>: Siegfried Schurenberg, Monika Peitch, Pinkas Braun, Gunther Stoll (*The Inspector*), Eddi Arent
Minor thriller: Vile creature stalks beauties

The Hunchback of the Morgue
see **El Jorobado de la Morgue**

Hundra
1983, (It-Sp), Eric Bruckner-John Ghaffari, color, 105 mins.
<u>W</u>: Laurene Landon (*Hundra*), John Ghaffari, Maria Casal, Ramiro Oliveros, Luis Lorenzo, Tamara, Cristina Torres, Victor Gans, Bettina Brenner, Maria Vico, Elena Segovia, Fernando Bilbao, Jorge Bosso, Hilda Fuchs, Elsa Zabala, Fernando Martinez, Lola Peno, Julio Castellanos, Adolfo Heredia, Mario de Barros, Larri, Arrate Zubizarreta, Ana Gervasone, Alicia Fernandez Cavada, Maria Luisa Crespo, Conchita de Grado, Azucena Hernandez, Eva Lyberten, Elke Stolzemberg, Sally O'Neill, Margarita Herrera, Catherine Bassetti, Juana Gracia, Pat Izquierdo, Paola Matos, Berengueia Parres, Maria Jesus Visedo, Devora Howle, Roxane Kingsley, Angel Gracia, Pedro Fournier, Guillermo Anton, Frank Brana, Eduardo Falardo
<u>D</u>: Matt Cimber   <u>SCR</u>: John Goff & Matt Cimber   <u>ORIG STORY</u>: Matt Cimber   <u>PHOTOG</u>: John Cabrera   <u>MUSIC</u>: Ennio Morricone
Standard "Sword & Sandal": Barbarian beauty seeks stud service

The Hunger
1983, (USA), MGM-UA, color, 94 mins.
<u>W</u>: Catherine Deneuve (*Miriam Blaylock*), David Bowie (*John Blaylock*), Susan Sarandon (*Sarah Roberts*), Cliff De Young (*Tom Haver*), Dan Hedaya, Beth Ehlers, Rufus Collins, James Aubrey, Bessie Love
<u>D</u>: Tony Scott   <u>SCR</u>: Ivan Davis & Michael Thomas, from Whitley Strieber's novel   <u>PHOTOG</u>: Stephen Goldblatt   <u>MUSIC</u>: Michel Rubini & Denny Jaeger   <u>SONG</u>: *Bela Lugosi's Dead*
Stylish horror-fantasy: Vampiress has many lovers through ages

The Hunger Strike
1913, (GB), B&C/MP, b&w, 495 ft. (150.9m)
A.k.a. **'Twas Only a Dream**
Standard comedy-fantasy: Hungry convict dreams of feast

Hunger's Curse
1910, (GB), Hepworth, b&w, 550 ft. (167.6m)
<u>D</u>: Bert Haldane
Standard crime-thriller: Discharged workman robs house, repents after saving girl

Hungry for You
1996, (USA), color, 95 mins.
<u>W</u>: Michael Phenicie, Rochelle Swanson, Gary Wood
Made-for-Cable, standard thriller: Murders during virtual-reality sessions

Hungry Pets
see **Please Don't Eat My Mother**

Hungry Wives
see **Jack's Wife**

The Hunted
1948, (USA), AA, b&w, 85 mins.
<u>W</u>: Belita, Preston Foster, Pierre Watkin, Edna Holland
<u>D</u>: Jack Bernhard
Standard thriller: Cop tries to reform girlfriend

Hunted
1952, (GB), BFM-Independent Artists/GFD/Rank/Janus-TV/Univ, b&w, 84 mins.
<u>W</u>: Dirk Bogarde (*Chris Lloyd*), Kay Walsh (*Mrs. Sykes*), Elizabeth Sellars (*Magda Lloyd*), Jon Whiteley (*Robbie*), Frederick Piper (*Mr. Sykes*), Julian Somers (*Jack Lloyd*), Jane Aird (*Mrs. Campbell*), Jack Stewart (*Mr. Campbell*), Geoffrey Keen (*Insp. Deakin*), Joe Linnane (*The Pawnbroker*)
<u>P</u>: Julian Wintle   <u>D</u>: Charles Crichton   <u>SCR</u>: Jack Whittingham   <u>STORY</u>: Michael McCarthy
USA retitle, **The Stranger in Between**, *reissued 1961*
Unusual thriller: Runaway finds corpse, is taken captive by murderer

Hunted
1973, (GB), Pemini/Col-WB, color, 41 mins.
<u>W</u>: Edward Woodward (*John Drummond*), June Ritchie (*Margaret Lord*)
<u>P</u>: Peter Crane & Richard Sloane   <u>D</u>: Peter Crane   <u>STORY</u>: Michael Sloane   <u>PHOTOG</u>: Brian Jonson   <u>MUSIC</u>: Graham Dee
Standard short crime-thriller: Firearms fanatic holds estate agent captive

The Hunted
1998, (USA), USA-TV, color, 95 mins.
<u>W</u>: Harry Hamlin, Madchen Amick, Hannes Jaenicke, Enuka Okuma, Peter Lacroix, Terence Kelly
<u>D</u>: Stuart Cooper   <u>TELEPLAY</u>: Bennett Cohen & David Ives   <u>PHOTOG</u>: Curtis Petersen   <u>MUSIC</u>: Charles Bernstein
TVM, standard thriller: maniacal woodsman stalks female insurance-fraud agent

Hunted in Holland
1961, (GB), Wessex/CFF, color, 61 mins.
<u>W</u>: Sean Scully (*Tim*), Jacques Verbrugge (*Piet*), Sandra Spurr (*Aanike*), Thom Kelling (*Van Kelling*)
<u>P</u>: Ian Dalrymple   <u>D</u>: Derek Williams   <u>STORY</u>: Ian Dalrymple & Derek Williams
Standard juvenile thriller: Children nab diamond thieves

Hunter's Blood
1987, (USA), Concorde, color, 102 mins
<u>W</u>: Sam Bottoms, Kim Delaney, Clu Gulager, Mayf Nutter
<u>D</u>: Robert C. Hughes   <u>SCR</u>: Emmett Alston
Standard thriller: Hunting party stalked by murderous poachers

Hunters of the Golden Cobra
1982, (It), Gico Cinematografica-Regal/World Wide, color, 95 mins.
<u>W</u>: David Warbeck (*Bob Jackson*), Almanta Suska, Protacio Dee, Alan Collins, Rene Abadesa, John Steiner
<u>D</u>: Anthony M. Dawson   <u>SCR</u>: Tito Carpi   <u>ORIG STORY</u>: Gianfranco Couyoumdjian   <u>PHOTOG</u>: Sandro Mancori   <u>MUSIC</u>: Carlo Savina
Minor action-thriller, **Raiders of the Lost Ark** *imitation: Soldier-of-fortune seeks stolen idol*

The Hunt for Red October
1990, (USA), Para, color, 135 mins.

W: Sean Connery, Alec Baldwin, Scott Glenn, Sam Neill, James Earl Jones, Joss Ackland, Richard Jordan, Peter Firth, Tim Curry, Jeffrey Jones, Stellan Skarsgard, Timothy Carhart, Fred Dalton Thompson, Courtney B. Vance, Tomas Arana, Ned Vaughn, Daniel Davis, Anatoly Davydov, Ronald Guttman, Rick Ducommun, Larry Ferguson, Christopher Janczar, Anthony Peck
D: John McTiernan   SCR: Larry Ferguson & Donald Stewart, from Tom Clancy's novel   PHOTOG: Jan de Bont   MUSIC: Basil Poledouris
Engrossing thriller: Soviet commander heads supersub for U.S. coast

Hunt the Man Down
1950, (USA), b&w, 68 mins.
W: Gig Young, Lynne Roberts, Willard Parker, Gerald Mohr, Paul Frees
D: George Archainbaud
Standard whodunit: Public defender tackles murder case

Hurricane Island
1951, (USA), Col, color, 70 mins.
W: Jon Hall (*Ponce de Leon*), Marie Windsor, Edgar Barrier, Jo Gilbert, Romo Vincent
P: Sam Katzman   D: Lew Landers   STORY & SCR: David Mathews
Standard action-thriller: Ponce de Leon seeks Fountain of Youth

Hush...Hush, Sweet Charlotte
1964, (USA), Associates & Aldrich/20th-Fox, b&w, 133 mins.
W: Bette Davis (*Charlotte Hollis*), Olivia de Havilland (*Miriam Dearing*), Joseph Cotten (*Dr. Drew Bayliss*), Mary Astor (*Jewel Mayhew*), Agnes Moorehead (*Velma Cruther*), Bruce Dern (*John Mayhew*), Cecil Kellaway (*Harry Willis*), William Campbell (*Paul Marchand*), Victor Buono (*Big Sam Hollis*), Dave Willock (*The Taxi Driver*), George Kennedy (*The Foreman*), Wesley Addy (*Sheriff Luke Standish*), John Megna (*The Boy*), Frank Ferguson (*The Newspaper Editor*), Ellen Corby (*A Town Gossip*), Helen Kleeb (*A Town Gossip*), Marianne Stewart (*A Town Gossip*), Michael Petit (*The Gang Leader*), Alida Aldrich (*The Young Girl*), Kelly Flynn (*The 2nd Boy*), Kelly Aldrich (*The 3rd Boy*), Percy Helton (*The Funeral Director*), Carol Delay (*Geraldine*), Lillian Randolph (*A Cleaning Woman*), Geraldine West (*A Cleaning Woman*), Mary Henderson (*A Cleaning Woman*), William Walker (*The Chauffeur*), Idell James (*Ginny Mae*)
P & D: Robert Aldrich   SCR: Henry Farrell & Lukas Heller   STORY: Henry Farrell   PHOTOG: Joseph Biroc   MUSIC: De Vol, title sung by Al Martino
orig. *to be titled* Cross of Iron *or* What Ever Happened to Cousin Charlotte?
Well-made 'Grand Guignol' thriller: Unsolved murder case revived on Southern plantation

Hush. . . Hush, Sweet Charlotte: OLIVIA DE HAVILLAND AND BETTE DAVIS

Hustler Squad
see The Doll Squad

Hutch Stirs 'em Up
1923, (GB), Ideal, b&w, 5,200 ft. (1585m)
W: Charles Hutchison (*Hurricane Hutch*), Joan Barry (*Joan*), Malcolm Tod (*Tom Grey*), Gibson Gowland (*Sir Arthur Blackross*), Aubrey Fitzgerald (*Cruddas*), Violet Forbes (*Mrs. Cruddas*), Sunday Wilshin (*Mrs. Grey*)
D: Frank H. Crane   SCR: Eliot Stannard, from Harry Harding's novel *The Hawk of Rede*
Standard thriller: Cowboy saves village girl from mad squire's torture chamber

Hydra
see La Isla de la Muerte

The Hydrophobic Patient
see Le Malade Hydrophobe

Hypernauts
1997, (USA), color
W: Marc Brandon Daniel, Glenn Herman, Heidi Lucas, Carrie Dobro, Ron Campbell
created by Ron Thornton
Standard juvenile SF

The Hyena of London
1964, (It), Geos, b&w
W: Bernard Price, Diana Martin, Tony Randall
Minor thriller: Victorians hunt killer

Hyper Sapien: People from Another Star
1986, (USA), Tri-Star, color, 95 mins.
W: Sydney Penny (*Robyn*), Ricky Paull Goldin (*Dirt*), Keenan Wynn, Gail Strickland, Peter Jason, Talia Shire
D: Peter Hunt   SCR: Richard Adcock & Christopher Blue
Minor SF-fantasy: Three runaway extraterrestrials take refuge on Wyoming farm

Hypnosis
see Hipnosis

The Hypnotic Eye
1960, (USA), Penguin/AA, b&w, 77 mins.
W: Jacques Bergerac, Allison Hayes, Marcia Henderson, Joe Patridge, Merry Anders, Guy Prescott, James Lydon, Carol Thurston, Holly Harris, Phyllis Cole, Mary Foran, Lawrence Lipton, Fred "The Great Impostor" Demara, Eric "Big Daddy" Nord
P: Charles B. Bloch   D: George Blair   SCR: Gitta & William Read Woodfield, from a story by Charles B. Bloch   PHOTOG: Archie Dalzell   MUSIC: Marlin Skiles
Modest thriller: Police baffled by beautiful women disfiguring themselves. In Hypomagic

The Hypnotic Eye: FRED "THE GREAT IMPOSTER' DEMARA

Hypnotic Suggestion
1909, (GB), Cricks & Martin, b&w, 480 ft. (146.3m)
W: Bill Hewson (*The Victim*)
D: Dave Aylott
Standard fantasy short: Mesmerist makes man think he is horse

The Hypnotist (1897)
see Le Magnetiseur

The Hypnotist (1926)
see London After Midnight

The Hypnotist
1957, (GB), Merton Park/Anglo-Amalgamated, b&w, 88 mins.
W: Roland Culver (*Dr. Francis Pelham*), Patricia Roc (*Mary Foster*), Paul Carpenter (*Val Neal*), William Hartnell (*Insp. Rose*), Kay Callard (*Susie*), Ellen Pollock (*Barbara Barton*), Gordon Needham (*Sgt. Davies*), Martin Wyldeck (*Dr. Bradford*), Oliver Johnston (*Dr. Kenyon*), Edgar Driver (*Atkins*)
P: Alec Snowden   WRIT & D: Montgomery Tully, from a play by Falkland Cary
USA retitle, *Scotland Yard Dragnet* (Republic, 1958)
Standard thriller: Psychiatrist hypnotizes pilot into killing secret wife

A Hypnotist at Work
see Le Magnetiseur

The Hypnotist's Revenge
1909, (Fr), Star, b&w, 107m (351 ft./5.9 mins.)
D: Georges Melies
Standard fantasy

Hysteria!
1964, (GB), Hammer/MGM, b&w, 85 mins.
W: Robert Webber (*Christopher Smith*), Jennifer Jayne (*Gina*), Leila Goldoni (*Denise James*), Maurice Denham (*Hemmings*), Anthony Newlands (*Dr. Keller*), Peter Woodthorpe (*Marcus Allan*), Sandra Boize (*The English Girl*), Sue Lloyd (*The French Girl*)
D: Freddie Francis   P & SCR: Jimmy Sangster   PHOTOG: John Wilcox   MUSIC: Don Banks
Standard thriller: Amnesiac stumbles into murder plot

Hysterical
1983, (USA), color, 87 mins.
W: William Hudson, Mark Hudson, Brett Hudson, Cindy Pickett, Richard Kiel, Julie Newmar, Bud Cort, Murray Hamilton, Robert Donner, Clint Walker, Franklin Ajaye, Charlie Callas, Keenan Wynn, Garry Owens
D: Chris Bearde
Minor comedy-thriller: Parody of Amityville *&* Exorcist *films*

I Accuse (1918 & 1937)
see J'Accuse

I Accuse
1958, (GB), MGM, b&w, 99 mins.
W: Jose Ferrer (*Alfred Dreyfus*), Emlyn Williams (*Emile Zola*), Anton Walbrook (*Maj. Ferdinand Walsin Esterhazy*), Viveca Lindfors (*Lucie Dreyfus*), David Farrar (*Mathieu Dreyfus*), Leo Genn (*Maj. Picquart*), Donald Wolfit (*Gen. Mercier*), Herbert Lom (*Maj. DuPaty de Clam*), Felix Aylmer (*Edgar Demange*), Harry Andrews (*Maj. Henry*), George Coulouris (*Col. Sandherr*), Eric Pohlmann (*Bertillon*), Peter Illing (*Georges Clemenceau*), Carl Jaffe (*Col. Von Schwarzkoppen*), John Chandos (*Drumont*), Anthony Ireland (*The Judge*), Ernest Clark (*The Prosecutor*), Keith Pyott, John Phillips, Laurence Naismith, Michael Hordern, Ronald Howard, Charles Gray, Michael Anthony, Michael Trubshawe, Arthur Howard
P: Sam Zimbalist   **D:** Jose Ferrer   **SCR:** Gore Vidal   **PHOTOG:** Frederick A. Young   **MUSIC:** William Alwyn
Unusual thriller: Faithful dramatization of Dreyfus treason case

I Aim at the Stars
1960, (USA), Morningside-Worldwide/Col, b&w, 106 mins.
W: Curt Jurgens (*Dr. Wernher von Braun*), Gia Scala (*Elizabeth*), Herbert Lom (*Reger*), James Daly (*Taggert*), Gunther Mruwka, Victoria Shaw, Lea Seidel, Helmo Kindermann, Hans Schumm, Adrian Hoven, Austin Willis, Arpad Diener, Gerard Heinz, Karel Stepanek, Peter Capell, Eric Zuckmann
P: Charles H. Schneer   **D:** J. Lee Thompson   **SCR:** Jay Dratler, from a story by George Froeschel, H.W. John & U. Wolter   **PHOTOG:** Wilkie Cooper   **MUSIC:** Laurie Johnson
Standard thriller: Film-bio of rocketry pioneer Wernher von Braun

I'm an Explosive
1933, (GB), George Smith/Fox, b&w, 50 mins.
W: Billy Hartnell (*Edward Whimperley*), Gladys Jennings (*Anne Pannell*), Eliot Makeham (*Prof. Whimperley*), D.A. Clarke-Smith (*Lord Ferndale*), Sybil Grove (*Miss Harriman*), Harry Terry (*Mould*), Blanche Adele (*The French Girl*), George Dillon (*Shilling*)
D & SCR: Adrian Brunel, from a novel by Gordon Phillips
Minor comedy-fantasy: Youth drinks liquid explosive

I am Curious (Yellow)
1967, (Swed), Sandrews/Evergreen/Grove, b&w, 124 mins.
W: Lena Nyman (*Lena*), Borje Ahlstedt (*Borje*), Peter Lindgren (*Rune*), Marie Goranzon (*Marie*), Ulla Lyttkens (*Ulla*), Magnus Nillson (*Magnus*), Chris Wahlstrom (*Chris*), Holger Lowenadler, Gunnel Brostrom
IDEA & D: Vilgot Sjoman   **PHOTOG:** Peter Webster   **MUSIC:** Bengt Ernryd
Classic eroto-surrealistic epic: Young woman awakens to the sensual life

I'm Dangerous Tonight
1990, (USA), BBK Prods./USA-TV, cable, color, 95 mins.
W: Madchen Amick, Corey Parker, Daisy Hall, R. Lee Ermey, Anthony Perkins (*Prof. Buchanan*), Natalie Schafer, Jason Brooks, Dee Wallace Stone, William Berger, Lew Horn, Mary Frann, Stewart Fratkin, Dan Leegant, Jack McGee, Felicia Lansbury, Edward Trotta, David Carlile, Ellen Gerstein, Henry C. Brown, Ivan Gueron, Juan Garcia, Frank DiElsi, Richard Penn, Xavier Barquet, Matthew Walker, Robert H. Harvey, Bill Madden
D: Tobe Hooper   **TELEPLAY:** Bruce Lansbury & Philip John Taylor, from Cornell Woolrich's short story   **PHOTOG:** Levie Isaacks   **MUSIC:** Nicholas Pike
TVM, above-average horror-fantasy: Aztec cloak inspires evil

Ib and Little Christina
1908, (GB), Clarendon, b&w, 590 ft. (180m)
D: Percy Stow   **SCR:** Langford Reed, from a story by Hans Christian Andersen
Standard fantasy

I Became a Criminal
see They Made Me a Fugitive

I Believe
see The Man without a Soul

I Bury the Living
1958, (USA), Maxim/UA, b&w, 90 mins.
W: Richard Boone, Peggy Maurer, Theodore Bikel, Herb Anderson, Howard Smith, Glenn Vernon, Russ Bender, Lynne Bernay, Robert Osterloh
P: Albert Band & Louis Garfinkle   **D:** Albert Band   **SCR:** Louis Garfinkle   **PHOTOG:** Frederick Gately   **MUSIC:** Gerald Fried
Standard fantasy-thriller: Man possesses supernatural power over life and death

Icarus XB1
see Ikaria XB1

Ice
1969, (USA), b&w, 132 Mins.
W: Robert Kramer, Tom Griffin
D: Robert Kramer
Unusual ideological thriller: Insurrection among youth of America

Ice Cream Man
1995, (USA), Showcase/A-Pix, color
W: Clint Howard (*The Ice Cream Man*), Sandahl Bergman, Lee Majors II, Olivia Hussey, Steve Garvey, David Naughton, Jan Michael Vincent, David Warner, Jojo Adams, Justin Isfeld, Mikey Lebeau, Anndi McAlee
P & D: Norman Apstein   **ORIG. STORY:** David Dobkin & Sven Davidson   **PHOTOG:** Garett Griffen
Standard satire-thriller

The Ice House
1969, (USA), C-B, Hollywood Cinemart, color, 85 mins
W: Robert Story, David Story, Scott Brady, Sabrina, Jim Davis
P: Dorrell McGowan   **D:** Stuart E. McGowan
A.k.a. **Cold Blood, The Passion Pit,** *and* **Love in Cold Blood**
Minor thriller: Psycho murders women, assumes twin brother's identity

Iceman
1984, (USA), Univ, color, 100 mins.
W: Timothy Hutton (*Stanley Shephard*), John Lone (*The Iceman*), Lindsay Crouse, Josef Sommer, James Tolkan, Danny Glover, Amelia Hall, David Strathairn, Philip Akin, Blair Anderson
D: Fred Schepisi   **SCR:** John Drimmer & Chip Proser   **PHOTOG:** Ian Baker   **MUSIC:** Bruce Sweaton
Dignified SF-thriller: Neanderthal is revived

The Ice Pirates
1984, (USA), JF/MGM-UA, color, 93 mins.
W: Robert Urich (*Jason*), Mary Crosby (*Princess Karina*), Michael D. Roberts (*Roscoe*), Anjelica Huton (*Maida*), Ron Perlman (*Zeno*), John Matuszak (*Killjoy*), John Carradine (*Supreme Commander*), Marcia Lewis (*The Frog Lady*), Bruce Vilanch (*Weird Wendon*), Natalie Core, Jeremy West, Alan Caillou
P: John Foreman   **D:** Stewart Raffill   **SCR:** Stewart Raffill & Stanford Sherman   **PHOTOG:** Matthew F. Leonetti   **SPCL-FX:** Max W. Anderson   **MUSIC:** Bruce Broughton
Modest SF-adventure-comedy: Space buccaneer meets princess

I Cheated the Law
1949, (USA), Belsam, 20th-Fox, b&w, 64 mins.
W: Tom Conway, Steve Brodie, Chet Huntley
Minor melodrama

I Come in Peace
1990, (USA), Vision Int'l/Triumph, color, 98 mins.
W: Dolph Lundgren (*Caine*), Brian Benben (*Smith*), Matthias Hues (*The Bad Alien*), Betsy Brantley (*Diane*), Jay Bilas (*The Good Alien*), Jim Haynie (*Malone*), Michael J. Pollard (*Boner*), David Ackroyd (*Switzer*), Sherman Howard (*Victor Manning*), Sam Anderson (*Warren*), Mark Lowenthal (*Bruce the Scientist*), Jesse Vint (*The Man in the Mercedes*), Matthew Posey (*Psycho #1*), Alexander Johnston (*Psycho #2*), Kevin Page (*White Boy #1*), Robert Prentiss (*White Boy #2*), Alex Morris (*Ray Turner*), Nik Hagler (*The Bail Bondsman*), Tony Brubaker (*The Garage Sweeper*), Mimi Cochran (*The Female Mechanic*), Jack Willis (*The Liquor Store Owner*), Brandon Smith (*The Market Clerk*), Wayne DeHart (*The Market Customer*), Albert Leong (*The Luggage Salesman*), Kevin Howard (*The Security Guard*), Woody Watson (*The Federal Agent*), Luis Lemus (*Sgt. Hawkins*), Chris Kinkade (*The Detective*), Steve Chizmadia (*White Boy #3*), Sebastian White (*White Boy #4*), Dean Kinkel (*White Boy #5*), David Poynter (*White Boy #6*), Folkert Schmidt (*White Boy #7*), Gary Baxley (*White Boy #8*), Tom Campitelli (*The Patrolman*), Kristin Baxley (*The Girl on the Phone*), Suzanne Savoy (*The Patrolwoman*), Howard French (*The Federal Clerk*), Willie Minor (*The Pool Hustler*), Arienne Battiste (*Malone's Sec'y*), Jack Verbois (*The Man Hostage*), Stacey Cortez (*The Lady Hostage*), Nino Candido (*Frank*)
P: Jeff Young   **D:** Craig R. Baxley   **SCR:** Jonathan Tydor & Leonard Maas Jr.   **PHOTOG:** Mark Irwin   **MUSIC:** Jan Hammer   **SONGS:** *Maggy, Thumbs Up, Ugly & Touch Me Tonight*
GB retitle, **Dark Angel**
Standard SF-action-horror: Space alien seeks human hormones

I Confess
1953, (USA), WB, b&w, 95 mins.
W: Montgomery Clift (*Michael*), Anne Baxter (*Ruth*), Karl Malden (*Larrue*), Brian Aherne (*Robertson*), Charles Andre (*Father Millais*), O.E. Haase (*Keller*), Dolly Haas (*Mrs. Keller*), Roger Dann (*Grandfort*), Judson Pratt (*Murphy*), Ovila Legare (*Villette*), Gilles Pelletier (*Father Benoit*)
D: Alfred Hitchcock   **SCR:** George Tabori & William Archibald, from Paul Anthelme's play *Nos Deux Consciences (Our Two Consciences)*   **PHOTOG:** Robert Burks   **MUSIC:** Ray Heindorf
Gripping thriller: Complications when priest is murdered. Filmed in Quebec

I Cover the Underworld
1955, (USA), Rep, b&w, 70 mins.
D: R.G. Springsteen
W: Sean McClory, Joanne Jordan
Minor thriller

Icy Breasts
1975, (Fr), color, 105 mins.
W: Alain Delon, Mireille Darc

D: Georges Lautner
Standard thriller: Psychiatrist has beautiful but murderous patient

I Deal in Danger
1966, (USA), 20th-Fox, color, 89 mins.
W: Robert Goulet, Christine Carere, Horst Frank, Werner Peters, Don-ald Harron
P: Buck Houghton **D:** Walter Grauman **SCR:** Larry Cohen **PHOTOG:** Sam Leavitt **MUSIC:** Lalo Schifrin
Minor thriller, feature culled from several episodes of short-lived teleseries "Blue Light": Secret agent's adventures

Identity Unknown
1945, (USA), Rep, b&w, 71 mins.
W: Richard Arlen, Cheryl Walker, Bobby Driscoll, Roger Pryor, Bobby Driscoll, Lola Lane, Ian Keith, John Forrest, Sara Padden
D: Walter Colmes
Standard drama, amnesiac war veteran seeks his identity

I, Desire
1982, (USA), Col/ABC-TV, color, 95 mins.
W: David Naughton (*David*), Dorian Harewood (*Det. Jerry Van Ness*), Marilyn Jones (*Cheryl*), Brad Dourif (*Paul*), Barbara Stock (*Mona*), Anne Bloom (*Marge*), Linda Lawrence (*The Undercover Cop*), Timothy Stack (*Daryl*), Marc Silver (*Larry*), Adele Rosse (*The Head Nurse*), James Oliver, Ann Blessing, John Berwick, Nigel Bullard, Cathy Green, Stacy MacGregor, Gary A. McMillan, Holly McCarver, Herb L. Mitchell, Bruce Wright
D: John Llewellyn Moxey **TELEPLAY:** Bob Foster **PHOTOG:** Robert L. Morrison **SPCL-FX:** Al Lorimer **MUSIC:** Don Peake
A.k.a. Desire: The Vampire
TVM, modest horror-fantasy: Vampiress poses as prostitute

The Idiot of the Mountains
1909, (GB), Hepworth, b&w, 450 ft. (137.2m)
D: Theo Bouwmeester
Standard crime-thriller: Idiot helps save kidnapped girl, is cured

I Dismember Mama
1973, (USA), Romal/Pacific/Europix, color, 87 mins
W: Zooey Hall, Joanne Moore Jordan, Marlene Tracy, Geri Reischl, Greg Mullavey, Frank Whiteman
D: Paul Leder **SCR:** William Norton **PHOTOG:** William Swenning **MUSIC:** Herschel Burke Gilbert **SONG:** *Poor Albert*
A.k.a. Poor Albert and Little Annie
Minor thriller: Mad killer flees asylum, terrorizes little girl

Idle Hands
1999, (USA), Col, color
W: Seth Green
Standard horror-comedy: Youth develops monstrous hand

I Don't Want to be Born
1975, (GB), Unicapital/AIP, color, 94 mins.
W: Joan Collins (*Lucy*), Caroline Munro (*Mandy*), Ralph Bates (*Gino*), Donald Pleasence (*Dr. Finch*), Eileen Atkins (*Sister Albana*), Hilary Mason (*Mrs. Hyde*), Janet Key (*Jill*), George Claydon (*Hercules*), John Steiner (*Tommy*), Phyllis McMahon (*The Nun*), John Moore (*The Priest*), Derek Benfield (*The Police Inspector*), Stanley Lebor (*The Police Sgt.*), Andrew Secombe (*The Delivery Boy*), Judy Buxton (*Sheila*), Susan Richards (*The Old Lady*), Janet Key (*Jill*), Floella Benjamin (*The Nurse*), Suzie Lightning (*The Stripper*), Lopez
P: Norma Corney **D:** Peter Sasdy **SCR:** Stanley Price **PHOTOG:** Ken Talbot **MUSIC:** Ron Grainer
*USA retitle, **The Devil Within Her**, reissued (1982) as **The Monster***
Standard horror-thriller: Ex-stripper gives birth to monstrous child

I Drink Your Blood: BHASKAR

I Dream of Jeannie: Fifteen Years Later
1985, (USA), Fries Entertainment/Col-TV, Made for Television, color
W: Barbara Eden (*Jeannie II*), Bill Daily (*Capt. Healey*), Wayne Rogers (*Tony Nelson*), Hayden Rorke (*Dr. Bellows*), Mackenzie Astin, Dori Brenner, Andre DeShields, John Bennett Perry, Dody Goodman
D: William Asher **TELEPLAY:** Irma Kalish **STORY:** Dinah Kirgo, Julie Kirgo & Irma Kalish, from characters created by Sidney Sheldon **PHOTOG:** Jack Whitman **MUSIC:** Mark Snow
TVM, standard comedy-fantasy

I Drink Your Blood
1971, (USA), Jerry Gross/Cinemation, color, 72 mins
W: Bhaskar (*Horace*), Jadine Wong (*Sue*), Ronda Fultz (*Molly*), Elizabeth Marner-Brooks, George Patterson, Riley Mills, John Damon, Iris Brooks, Richard Bowler, Tyde Kierney, Alex Mann, Lynn Lowry, Bruno Damon, Mike Gentry
P: Jerry Gross **WRIT & D:** David Durston **MUSIC:** Clay Pitts
Minor horror-thriller: Rabies infects small community

I Eat Your Skin
*see **Voodoo Blood Bath***

I Escaped from Devil's Island
1973, (USA), UA, color, 87 mins.
W: Jim Brown (*Le Bras*), Christopher George (*Davert*), Rick Ely (*JoJo*), Richard Rust (*Zamorra*)
D: William Witney **SCR:** Richard L. Adams **PHOTOG:** Rosalio Solano **MUSIC:** Les Baxter
Minor thriller

If It's a Man, Hang Up
1975, (GB), color, 71 mins.
W: Carol Lynley, Paul Angelis, Tom Conti, Gerald Harper, John Cater
TVM, minor thriller: Anonymous phone caller terrorizes fashion model

Igor and the Lunatics
1985, (USA), Troma, color, 84 mins.
W: Joseph Ecro, Joe Niola, T.J. Michaels, Mary Ann Schacht
D: Billy Parolini **SCR:** Jocelyn Beard & Billy Parolini **STORY:** Jocelyn Beard **PHOTOG:** John Raugalis **MUSIC:** Sonia Rutstein
Minor horror-satire: Maniacs inspire mayhem

I've Lived Before
1956, (USA), Univ, b&w, 82 mins.
W: Jock Mahoney, Leigh Snowden, Raymond Bailey, John McIntire, Ann Harding, Simon Scott, Jerry Paris, April Kent, Vernon Rich, Phil Harvey, Brad Morrow
P: Howard Christie **D:** Richard Bartlett **SCR:** Norman Jolley & William Talman **PHOTOG:** Maury Gertsman **MUSIC:** Joseph Gershenson **SPCL-FX:** Clifford Stine **MUSIC:** Herbert Stein & Joseph Gershenson
Standard thriller: Pilot finds he is reincarnated

I Hear You Calling Me
1919, (GB), I.B. Davidson/Ruffells, b&w, 5,000 ft. (1524m)
W: Janet Alexander (*Jean*), Richard Buttery (*John Maskman*), Baby Shepherd (*Paul*), Eve Marchew
D: A.E. Coleby **STORY:** Andrew Soutar
Standard crime-thriller: Employer frames clerk, steals invention, and seduces his wife

I Hired a Contract Killer
1990, (Fin-Swed), Finnish Film Foundation/Villealfa Filmproductions/ Christa Saredi, color, 79 mins.
W: Jean-Pierre Leaud (*Henri*), Margi Clarke (*Margaret*), Kenneth Colley, Trevor Bowen, Nicky Tesco, Charles Cork, Serge Reggiani, Peter Graves
D: Aki Kaurismaki **PHOTOG:** Timo Salminen
Droll thriller: French emigre in London hires hit man to put him out of his misery

Ikaria XB1 (Icarus XB1)
1963, (Czech), Barrandov/AIP, color, scope, 90 mins
W: Zdenek Stepanek, Radevan Lukavsky, Dana Medricka, Jiri Vrstala, Irena Kacirkova, Emilie Vasayova, Ludek Munzar
D: Jindrich Polak **SCR:** Pavel Juracek & Jindrich Polak **PHOTOG:** Van Kalis
*Mutilated version shown in USA as **Voyage to the End of the Universe** (81 mins)*

I Killed Rasputin
1967, (Fr), color, 95 mins.
W: Gert Frobe (*Rasputin*), Peter McEnery (*Prince Felix*), Geraldine Chaplin, Robert Hossein, Ivan Desny, Ira Furstenberg
D: Robert Hossein
Superficial bio-thriller: Mad monk wields power

I Killed the Count
1939, (GB), Grafton/Grand Nat'l, b&w, 89 mins.
W: Syd Walker (*Insp. Davidson*), Ben Lyon (*Det.-Sgt. Raines*), Antoinette Cellier (*Louise Rogers*), Barbara Blair (*Renee la Lune*), Athole Stewart (*Lord Sorrington*), Leslie Perrins (*Count Mattoni*), Ronald Shiner (*Mullet*), David Burns (*Diamond*), Kathleen Harrison (*Polly*), Gus McNaughton (*Martin*), Aubrey Mallalieu (*Johnson*)
D: Fred Zelnik **SCR:** Alec Coppel & Lawrence Huntington, from a play by Alec

Coppel
USA retitle, **Who is Guilty?** *(Monogram, 1940), reissued 1942 & 1948*
Standard thriller: Four people confess to killing philandering nobleman

I Know What You Did Last Summer
1997, (USA), TriStar, color, 101 mins.
<u>W:</u> Sarah Michelle Gellar, Jennifer Love Hewitt, Anne Heche, Johnny Galecki,
Freddie Prinze Jr., Bridgette Wilson, Phillippe Ryan
<u>D:</u> Jim Gillespie   <u>SCR:</u> Kevin Williamson, from a story by Lois Duncan
<u>MUSIC:</u> John Debney   <u>SONG:</u> *Hush*

I Hired A Contract Killer: Margi Clarke and Jean-Pierre Leaud

L'Ile de Calypso: Ulysse et Polypheme (The Isle of Calypso: Ulysses and Polyphemus)
1905, (Fr), Star, b&w, 69m (226.4 ft./18.6 mins.)
<u>D:</u> Georges Melies, inspired by Homer's *The Odyssey*
A.k.a. **The Mysterious Island**
Minor fantasy: Greek hero vs. one-eyed giant

I Led Two Lives
see **Glen or Glenda?**

I Like Bats
1985, (Pol), color, 90 mins.
<u>D:</u> Grzegorz Warchol
Unusual fantasy: Vampire wants to be human

I Live in Fear
1967, (Jap), Brandon, b&w, 105 mins.
<u>W:</u> Toshiro Mifune, Eiko Miyoshi
Standard melodrama

L'Ile du Dr. Moreau
see **Island of Lost Souls**

I'll Get You
1953, (GB), Lippert, b&w, 79 mins.
<u>W:</u> George Raft, Sally Gray
Standard thriller

I'll Never Forget You
see **The House in the Square**

The Iliac Passion
1968, (USA), Gregory Markapoulos, color, 90 mins.
<u>W:</u> Jack Smith *(Orpheus)*, Andy Warhol *(Poseidon)*, Gerard Malanga *(Ganymede)*,
Richard Beauvais *(Prometheus)*, David Beauvais *(Prometheus' Conscience)*, Taylor
Mead *(Demon/Sprite)*, Tally Brown
<u>WRIT, D, & PHOTOG:</u> Gregory Markapoulos (also actor, narrator), garbled
adaptation of Aeschylus' play *Prometheus Bound*
"Underground" erotic fantasy (16mm): Desire stirs Greek dieties

Illegal
1955, (USA), b&w, 88 mins.
<u>W:</u> Edward G. Robinson, Nina Foch, Jayne Mansfield, Albert Dekker, Hugh
Marlowe, Ellen Corby, DeForest Kelley, Howard St. John
<u>D:</u> Lewis Allen
Standard melodrama: Former D.A. puts life on line to defend woman homicide suspect

Illegal Entry
1949, (USA), Univ, b&w, 84 mins.
<u>W:</u> Howard Duff, Marta Toren, George Brent, Gar Moore
<u>D:</u> Frederick de Cordova
Standard thriller: Federal agent uncovers smugglers

L'Illusioniste Double et la Tete Vivante (The Double Illusionist and the Living Head)
1900, (Fr), Star, b&w, 26m (85.3 ft./1.4 mins.)

<u>D:</u> Georges Melies
USA retitle, **The Triple Conjurer and the Living Head**
Standard fantasy

Illusions
1992, (USA), color, 95 mins.
<u>W:</u> Heather Locklear
Standard thriller: Woman recovering from nervous breakdown suspects husband and his sister of concealing terrible secret

Les Illusions Fantaisistes (Fantasy Illusions)
1910, (Fr), Star, b&w, 100m (328.1 ft./5.5 mins.)
<u>D:</u> Georges Melies
Standard fantasy

Illusions Fantasmagoriques (Phantasmagoric Illusions)
1898, (Fr), Star, b&w, 20m (65.6 ft./1.1 mins.)
<u>D:</u> Georges Melies
USA retitle, **The Famous Box Trick**
Standard fantasy

Illusions Fantastiques
see **Creations Spontanees**

The Illustrated Man
1969, (USA), SKM/WB-7Arts, color, 103 mins.
<u>W:</u> Rod Steiger *(Carl)*, Claire Bloom *(Felicia)*, Don Dubbins *(Pickard)*, Robert
Drivas *(Willie)*, Jason Evers *(Simmons)*, Chris Matchett *(Anna)*, Tim Weldon
(John)
<u>P & SCR:</u> Howard B. Kreitsek   <u>D:</u> Jack Smight   3 tales from Ray Bradbury's
1951 anthology **The Illustrated Man**; "The Veldt", "The Long Rain", &
"The Last Night of the World"   <u>PHOTOG:</u> Philip H. Lathrop   <u>MUSIC:</u>
Jerry Goldsmith
Uneven SF-fantasy: Young drifter glimpses future terrors in vagabond's tattoos

Illustrious Corpses
see **Cadaveri Eccellenti**

I Love a Mystery
1945, (USA), Col, b&w, 70 mins.
<u>W:</u> Jim Bannon *(Jack)*, Barton Yarborough *(Doc)*, Nina Foch *(Ellen)*, George
Macready *(Monk)*, Carole Matthews *(Jean)*, Gregory Gay *(Han)*
<u>P:</u> Wallace MacDonald   <u>D:</u> Henry Levin   <u>SCR:</u> Charles O'Neal   <u>PHOTOG:</u>
Burnett Guffey
Minor action-thriller: Three detectives track Oriental mystic who drives people to suicide (First of brief series)

I Love a Mystery
1966, (USA), Univ-TV/NBC-TV, color, 98 mins.
<u>W:</u> Ida Lupino, David Hartman *(Doc)*, Hagan Beggs *(Reggie)*, Les Crane *(Jack)*,
Jack Weston *(Job)*, Terry Thomas *(Elliott)*, Don Knotts *(Archer)*, Deanna
Lund, Melodie Johnson, Karen Jensen, Francine York, Peter Mamakos,
Andre Phillippe, Lewis Charles
<u>P:</u> Frank Price   <u>D & TELEPLAY:</u> Leslie Stevens   <u>CREATED BY:</u> Carlton E.
Morse   <u>PHOTOG:</u> Ray Rennahan   <u>MUSIC:</u> Oliver Nelson
TVM, minor satire-thriller: Eccentric woman traps three private eyes. Not shown until 1973

I Love to Kill
see **Impulse!** *(1974)*

I Love You, I Kill You
1972, (W. Ger), New Yorker, b&w, 94 mins.
<u>W:</u> Rolf Becker *(The Hunter)*, Hannes Fuchs *(The Teacher)*, Helmut Basch *(The
Mayor)*, Nikolaus Dutsch *(A Policeman)*, Thomas Eckelmann *(A Policeman)*,
Monika Hansen *(A Village Girl)*, Marianne Blomquist *(A Village Girl)*
<u>WRIT, P, & D:</u> Uwe Brandner   <u>PHOTOG:</u> Andre Debreuil   <u>MUSIC:</u> Mozart,
Uwe Brandner, Heinz Hetter & Kid Olanf
Minor thriller

Ils Appellent Ca un Accident (They Call that an Accident)
1981, (Fr), Island, color, 90 mins.
<u>W:</u> Nathalie Delon, Patrick Norbert, Gilles Segal, Jean-Pierre Bagot, Robert
Benoit
<u>WRIT & D:</u> Nathalie Delon   <u>SONG:</u> *Guilt*
Standard thriller (Nathalie Delon's directorial debut): Woman seeks revenge when only son is killed by negligent doctor

Ilya Mourometz
1956, (Russ), Mosfilm/Valiant, color, 81 mins.
<u>W:</u> Andrei Abrikosov, Natalia Medvedeva, Boris Andreyev, Ninel Myshkova,
Slukur Burkhanov
<u>P & D:</u> Alexander Ptushko   <u>SCR:</u> V. Kotochnev
USA retitle (1960), **The Sword and the Dragon**
Standard adventure-fantasy: 11th-century farmer defeats legendary creatures

I, Madman
1989, (USA), Sarlui-Diamant/Trans World, color, 90 mins.
<u>W:</u> Randall William Cook *(Malcolm)*, Stephanie Hodge *(Mona)*, Michelle Jordan

(*Colette*), Vance Valencia (*Sgt. Navarro*), Mary Baldwin (*The Librarian*), Rafael Nazaro (*The Hotel Clerk*), Bob Frank (*The Hotel Manager*), Bruce Wagner (*The Pianist*), Kevin Best (*The Black Actor*), Vincent Lucchesi (*Lt. Garber*), Steven Memel (*Lenny*), Murray Rubin (*Sidney Zeit*), Tom Badal (*The Composite Artist*), Roger LaPage (*The Acting Teacher*), Nelson Welch (*The Elderly Customer*), James Quincey Hendrick (*The Bus Driver*), Jeff Yesko (*The Patrolman*), Mary Pat Gleason (*The Policewoman*), David P. Lewis (*The Officer*), Christopher Kriesa (*Sarge*), Marty Levy (*Det. Fisk*), Stan Roth (*The Forensic Expert*)
<u>D</u>: Tibor Takacs <u>SCR</u>: David Chaskin <u>PHOTOG</u>: Bryan England <u>MUSIC</u>: Michael Hoenig
Minor thriller: Horror novel becomes reality

The Image
1969, (GB), Border Films, b&w, 14 mins.
<u>W</u>: David Bowie (*The Artist*), Michael Byrne (*The Boy*)
<u>P</u>: O. Negus-Fancey <u>WRIT & D</u>: Michael Armstrong
Standard short fantasy: Artist haunted by face of boy he paints

Images
1972, (GB), Lion's Gate-Hemdale Group/Col, color, 101 mins.
<u>W</u>: Susannah York (*Cathryn*), Rene Auberjonois (*Hugh*), Marcel Buzzofi (*Rene*), Hugh Millais (*Marcel*), Cathryn Harrison (*Susannah*), John Morley (*The Old Man*)
<u>P</u>: Tommy Thompson <u>D & SCR</u>: Robert Altman <u>PHOTOG</u>: Vilmos Zsigmond <u>MUSIC</u>: John Williams
"A stunning job all around"—Independent Film Journal
"The super-puzzle drama of the year. A breath-bating suspense story of lust and blood"—Judith Crist, New York Magazine
Unusual thriller: Young woman hallucinates

The Imaginary Voyage (1924)
see **Le Voyage Imaginaire**

Imaginary Voyage (1963)
see **Viaggio Immaginario**

I Married a Communist
1949, (USA), RKO, b&w, 73 mins.
<u>W</u>: Robert Ryan, Laraine Day, John Agar, Thomas Gomez, Janis Carter, Richard Rober, William Talman, Paul Guilfoyle
<u>D</u>: Robert Stevenson <u>PHOTOG</u>: Nicholas Musuraca
A.k.a. **The Woman on Pier 13**
Well-made thriller: Communists blackmail former party member

I Married a Monster from Outer Space
1958, (USA), Para, b&w, 78 mins.
<u>W</u>: Tom Tryon, Gloria Talbott, Ken Lynch, John Eldredge, Maxie Rosenbloom, Peter Baldwin, Chuck Wassil, Robert Ivers, Valerie Allen, Jean Carson, Alan Dexter, James Anderson, Jack Orrison, Mary Treen, Steve London, Ty Hungerford (*Hardin*)
<u>P & D</u>: Gene Fowler Jr. <u>SCR</u>: Louis Vittes <u>PHOTOG</u>: Haskell Boggs <u>SPCL-FX</u>: John P. Fulton
Fr retitle, **Les Monstres sur Notre Planete** *(The Monsters on Our Planet)*
Modest SF-thriller: Bride finds husband is hideous space alien

I Married an Angel
1942, (USA), MGM, b&w, 84 mins.
<u>W</u>: Jeanette MacDonald, Nelson Eddy, Edward Everett Horton, Regi-nald Owen, Binnie Barnes, Anne Jeffreys, Douglass Dumbrille
<u>D</u>: W.S. Van Dyke II <u>SCR</u>: Anita Loos, from a play by Vasary Janos <u>PHO-TOG</u>: Ray June <u>MUSIC & LYRICS</u>: Richard Rodgers & Lorenz Hart
Engaging musical-fantasy: Ruritanian dreams he weds divine beauty. Last MacDonald-Eddy musical

I Married a Monster
1998, (USA), UPN-TV, color, 95 mins.
<u>W</u>: Susan Walters, Richard Burgi
TVM, standard SF-thriller (remake of mini-classic **I Married a Monster From Outer Space***): Bride finds bridegroom is possessed by alien forces*

I Married a Shadow
1982, (Fr), Spectrafilms, color, 110 mins.
<u>W</u>: Nathalie Baye, Francis Huster, Richard Bohringer, Maurice Jacquemont, Madeleine Robinson, Guy Trejean, Veronique Genest, Victoria Abril, Solenn Jarniou, Humbert Balsan, Marcel Roche
<u>D</u>: Robin Davis <u>SCR</u>: Robin Davis & Patrick Laurent, from Cornell Woolrich's novel <u>PHOTOG</u>: Bernard Zitzermann <u>MUSIC</u>: Philippe Sarde
Well-made thriller: Abused wife assumes dead woman's identity

I Married a Spy
see **Secret Lives**

I Married a Vampire
1987, (USA), Troma, color, 85 mins.
<u>W</u>: Brendan Hickey, Rachel Golden
<u>D</u>: Jay Raskin
Minor horror-comedy: Bride finds groom is Undead

I Married a Werewolf
see **Lycanthropus**

I Married a Witch
1942, (USA), Rene Clair/Cinema Guild/Paramount/UA, b&w, 82 mins.
<u>W</u>: Fredric March, Veronica Lake, Cecil Kellaway, Susan Hayward, Robert Benchley, Elizabeth Patterson, Robert Warwick, Emma Dunn, Emory Parnell
<u>P & D</u>: Rene Clair <u>SCR</u>: Robert Pirosh & Marc Connelly, from a story by Thorne Smith <u>PHOTOG</u>: Ted Tetzlaff <u>MUSIC</u>: Roy Webb
Fr retitle, **My Wife is a Witch**
Classic comedy-fantasy: Beautiful witch and her warlock father cause mayhem in modern society

I'm a Stranger
1952, (GB), Corsair/Apex, b&w, 60 mins.
<u>W</u>: Greta Gynt (*herself*), James Hayter (*Horatio Flowerdew*), Hector Ross (*Insp. Craddock*), Patric Doonan (*George Westcott*), Jean Cadell (*Hannah Mackenzie*), Charles Lloyd-Pack (*Mr. Cringle*), Martina Mayne (*Mary*), Fulton Mackay (*Alastair Campbell*)
<u>D & STORY</u>: Brock Williams
Standard crime-thriller: Actress and window cleaner help heir find missing will

I Met a Murderer
1939, (GB), Gamma/Grand Nat'l/York, b&w, 78 mins., also 70 mins.
<u>W</u>: James Mason (*Mark Warrow*), Pamela Kellino (*Jo*), William Devlin (*Warrow*), Sylvia Coleridge (*Martha Warrow*), James Harcourt (*The Cart-driver*), Esma Cannon (*The Hiker*), Peter Coke (*The Horseman*)
<u>D & PHOTOG</u>: Roy Kellino <u>SCR</u>: Pamela Kellino & James Mason <u>MUSIC</u>: Eric Ansell
reissued 1947
Standard thriller: Farmer kills shrewish wife, is sheltered by authoress

Immediate Disaster
see **Stranger from Venus**

Immoral Tales
see **Contes Immoraux**

The Immortal
1970, (USA), Douglas S. Cramer/Para-TV, color, 74 mins.
<u>W</u>: Christopher George (*Benjamin Richards*), Carol Lynley (*Sylvia*), Ralph Bellamy (*Dr. Pierce*), Martin Silbersher (*The Doctor*), Barry Sullivan (*Jordan Braddock*), Jessica Walter (*Janet Braddock*), Vincent Beck (*Locke*), William Sargent (*The Pilot*), Joseph Bernard (*The Mechanic*), Garry Walberg (*The Detective*), Claudia Bryar (*A Nurse*), Lillian Adams (*A Nurse*), Mimi Dillard (*A Nurse*)
<u>D</u>: Joe Sargent <u>SCR</u>: Robert Specht, from James Gunn's novel *The Immortals* <u>PHOTOG</u>: Howard Schwartz <u>PHOTO-FX</u>: Cinema Research <u>MUSIC</u>:

The Immortal: CAROL LYNLEY AND CHRIS GEORGE

Dominic Frontiere
TVM, unusual SF-thriller: Technocrat pursues man whose blood pre-vents disease and aging

Immortal Combat
1994, (USA), color, 109 mins.
<u>W</u>: Roddy Piper, Sonny "J.J." Chiba, Meg Foster (*Quinn*)
Minor SF-thriller: Madwoman turns martial artists into super-killers

The Immortalizer
1989, (USA), color, 85 mins.
<u>W</u>: Ron Kay, Chris Crone, Melody Patterson, Clarke Lindsley, Bekki Armstrong
<u>D</u>: Joel Bender

Minor SF-horror: Mad doctor transfers brains

Immortal Sins
1992, (USA), color, 76 mins.
<u>W:</u> Maryam D'Abo
<u>SCR:</u> Thomas McKelvey Cleaver
Minor fantasy-thriller: Evil seductress casts spell on heirs to cursed Spanish castle

I, Monster
1970, (GB), Amicus/Cannon, color, 75 mins.
<u>W:</u> Peter Cushing (*Utterson*), Christopher Lee (*Dr. Marlowe/Mr. Blake*), Richard Hurndall (*Lanyon*), Kenneth J. Warren (*Deane*), Mike Raven (*Enfield*), Susan Jameson (*Diane Thomas*), George Merritt (*Poole*), Marjie Lawrence (*Annie*), Aimee Delamain (*The Landlady*)
<u>P:</u> Max J. Rosenberg & Milton Subotsky   <u>D:</u> Stephen Weeks   <u>SCR:</u> Milton Subotsky, loosely based on Robert Louis Stevenson's *Dr. Jekyll and Mr. Hyde*   <u>PHOTOG:</u> Murray Grant   <u>MUSIC:</u> Carl Davis
orig. to be titled **I, Werewolf** *or* **I, Vampire**
Minor horror-thriller: Doctor becomes fiend

Imperceptible Transmutations
see **Les Transmutations Imperceptibles**

The Impersonator
1961, (GB), Herald/Bry, b&w, 64 mins.
<u>W:</u> John Crawford (*Jimmy Bradford*), Jane Griffiths (*Ann Loring*), Patricia Burke (*Mrs. Lloyd*), John Salew (*Harry Walker*), John Dare (*Tommy Lloyd*), Yvonne Ball (*Principal Boy*)
<u>P:</u> Anthony Perry   <u>D:</u> Alfred Shaughnessy   <u>STORY:</u> Alfred Shaughnessy & Kenneth Cavender
Standard crime-thriller: Schoolmistress unmasks widow's killer

Impact
1963, (GB), Butcher's Films, b&w, 61 mins.
<u>W:</u> Conrad Phillips (*Jack Moir*), George Pastell (*The Duke*), Ballard Berkeley (*Bill Mackenzie*), Linda Marlowe (*Diana*), Richard Klee (*Wally*), Anita West (*Melanie*), John Rees (*Charlie*)
<u>P:</u> John I. Phillips   <u>D:</u> Peter Maxwell   <u>STORY:</u> Peter Maxwell & Conrad Philips
Standard crime-thriller: Reporter traps traitorous club owner

The Impossible Balancing Feat
see **L'Equilibre Impossible**

The Impossible Dinner
see **Le Diner Impossible**

The Impossible Lovers
1906, (GB), Sheffield Photo Co., b&w, 130 ft. (39.6m)
<u>D:</u> Frank Mottershaw
Minor fantasy short: Cook's lovers become dancing dolls

Impossible Undressing
see **Le Deshabillage Impossible**

An Impossible Voyage
see **Le Voyage a Travers l'Impossible**

Imposter
1999, (USA), Dimension, color
<u>W:</u> Gary Sinise
from a novel by Philip K. Dick
Standard SF-thriller

L'Impressioniste Fin de Siecle (The End-of-the-Century Impressionist)
1899, (Fr), Star, b&w, 20m (65.6 ft./1.1 mins.)
<u>D:</u> Georges Melies
A.k.a. **An Up-to-Date Conjurer**
Standard fantasy

Impulse
1955, (GB), Tempean/Eros, b&w, 80 mins.
<u>W:</u> Arthur Kennedy (*Alan* Constance Smith (*Lila*), Joy Shelton (*Elizabeth Curtis*), Jack Allen (*Freddie*), James Carney (*Jack Forrester*), Cyril Chamberlain (*Gray*), Cameron Hall (*Joe*)
<u>P:</u> Robert Baker & Monty Berman   <u>D:</u> Charles de la Tour & Cy Endfield   <u>SCR:</u> Lawrence Huntington & Jonathan Roach   <u>STORY:</u> Carl Nystrom & Robert Baker
Standard crime-thriller: American estate agent made to believe he killed jewel thief

Impulse!
1974, (Can), Camelot, color, 91 mins
<u>W:</u> William Shatner, Ruth Roman, Jennifer Bishop, Harold Sakata, James Dobson, Kim Nicholas
<u>D:</u> William Grefe
blurb: "When the demons of evil take over all powers of reason only impulse remains!"
Original title: **Want a Ride Little Girl** *A.k.a.* **I Love to Kill**
Florida-filmed child molester story

Impulse
1984, (USA), ABC Motion Pictures/ 20th- Fox, color, 91 mins.
<u>W:</u> Tim Matheson (*Stuart*), Meg Tilly (*Jennifer*), Hume Cronyn (*Dr. Carr*), John Karlen (*Bob Russell*), Bill Paxton (*Eddie*), Amy Stryker (*Margo*), Claude Earl Jones (*The Sheriff*), Robert Wightman (*Howard*), Lorinne Vozoff (*Mrs. Russell*), Peter Jason, Adam Baumgarten, Mary Celio, Abigail Booraen, Leonard Burns, Jack T. Collis, Christian Crane, Dan Danforth, Chuck Dorsett, Allan Graf, Richard E. Norlie, Holgie Forrester, Christian Giannini, Anne Haney, Gary Kirk, Bernard Kuby, Darren Muir, Thomas J. Sauber, Svi Peters, Dawn Eisler Smith, Hugo L. Stanger, Sherri Stoner
<u>D:</u> Graham Baker   <u>SCR:</u> Bart Davis & Don Carlos Dunaway   <u>PHOTOG:</u> Thomas Del Ruth   <u>SPCL-FX:</u> Tom Fisher & Greg Curtis   <u>MUSIC:</u> Paul Chihara
Modest SF-thriller: Pollution destroys human inhibitions

Inadmissable Evidence
1968, (GB), Para, b&w, 96 mins.
<u>W:</u> Nicol Williamson, Eleanor Fazan, Jill Bennett
Minor thriller

In an Old Manor House
1984, (Pol), color, 90 mins.
<u>D:</u> Jerzy Kotkowski from the play by Stanislaw Witkiewicz
Standard fantasy-thriller: Spirit of murdered adulteress torments husband

In a Sinister House
see **The Old Dark House (1932)**

In a Stranger's Hand
1991, (USA), color
<u>W:</u> Robert Urich, Megan Gallagher
Minor melodrama

The Inauguration of the Pleasure Dome
1966, (USA), Kenneth Anger, b&w
"Underground" film, minor SF-fantasy

In-Between
1992, (USA), color, 92 mins.
<u>W:</u> Alexandra Paul, Wings Hauser, Robert Forster, Robin Mattson
Standard fantasy: Revelations by otherworldly visitor disturb three strangers

Les Incendiaires (The Arsonists)
1906, (Fr), Star, b&w, 307m (1,007.2 ft./17 mins.)
<u>D:</u> Georges Melies
A.k.a. **Histoire d'un Crime (Story of a Crime)** *and* **A Desperate Crime**
Standard melodrama: Murderer guillotined

Incense for the Damned
see **Doctors Wear Scarlet**

Incident: JANE FRAZEE

Incident
1948, (USA), Mono, b&w, 68 mins.
<u>W:</u> Warren Douglas, Jane Frazee, Robert Osterloh, Joyce Compton, Anthony Caruso, Pierre Watkin
Standard melodrama

Incident at Midnight
1963, (GB), Merton Park/Anglo-Amalgamated, b&w, 58 mins.
<u>W:</u> Anton Diffring (*Dr. Erik Leichner*), William Sylvester (*Vince Warren*), Justine Lord (*Diane Graydon*), Martin Miller (*Dr. Schroeder*), Tony Garnett (*Brennan*),

Philip Locke *(Foster)*, Sylva Langova *(Vivienne Leichner)*, Jacqueline Jones *(Vanessa Palmer)*, Warren Mitchell *(The Chemist)*
P: Jack Greenwood   D: Norman Harrison   SCR: Arthur Labern, from a story by Edgar Wallace
Standard thriller: Undercover narcotics agent spots former Nazi

Incident at Victoria Falls
see Sherlock Holmes and the Incident at Victoria Falls

Incident from Don Quixote
see Les Aventures de Don Quichotte

Les Inconnus dans la Maison (Strangers in the House)
1942, (Fr), Continental Films, b&w, 90 mins.
W: Raimu, Raymond Cordy
D: Henri Decoin   ADAPT. & DIALOG: Henri-Georges Clouzot, from a novel by Georges Simenon
*Standard thriller. US release: Lopert, 1949. Remake: **Stranger in the House**, 1967*

The Incorruptible Crown
1915, (GB), Hepworth, b&w, 3,075 ft. (937.3m)
W: Stewart Rome *(Philip)*, Chrissie White *(Mary)*, Lionelle Howard *(Bruce)*, Henry Vibart *(John Milton)*, Harry Gilbey *(The Minister)*
D: Frank Wilson
Standard crime-thriller: Escaped convict hides aboard liner, which sinks

An Increasing Wardrobe
see Le Deshabillage Impossible

The Incredible Face of Dr. B
1961, (Mex), TEC, b&w
W: Elsa Cardenas, Erick del Castillo
Minor thriller: Woman doctor target of kidnapping

The Incredible Genie
1997, (USA), color, 95 mins.
W: Matt Koruba *(Simon)*, George Miserlis *(Peter)*
Standard fantasy: Boy genius finds ancient Egyptian lamp containing genie

The Incredible Hulk
1977, (USA), Univ/CBS-TV, color, 87 mins.
W: Bill Bixby *(Dr. David Bruce Banner)*, Lou Ferrigno *(The Creature)*, Susan Sullivan *(Dr. Elaina Marks)*, Jack Colvin *(McGee)*, Charles Siebert *(Ben)*, Mario Gallo, Terrence Locke
WRIT, P, & D: Kenneth Johnson   PHOTOG: Howard Schwartz
TVM, standard feature-film pilot for teleseries: Scientist releases violent alter ego

The Incredible Hulk, Part 2
1977, (USA), Univ/CBS-TV, color
W: Bill Bixby *(Dr. David Bruce Banner)*, Lou Ferrigno *(The Creature)*, Laurie Prange *(Julie)*, John McLiam *(Michael)*, Dorothy Tristan *(Margaret)*, Jack Colvin *(McGee)*, William Daniels *(Dr. Bonifant)*, Gerald McRaney *(Denny)*, Mills Watson, Robert Phillips, Victor Mohica, Ann Weldon, Linda Wiser
D: Alan Levi
*A.k.a. **The Return of the Incredible Hulk***
TVM, standard SF-thriller: Scientist's imposing alter ego aids crippled heiress

The Incredible Hulk Returns
1988, (USA), NBC-TV, color, 93 mins.
W: Bill Bixby *(David Banner)*, Lou Ferrigno *(The Creature)*, Jack Colvin *(Jack McGee)*, Steve Levitt *(Donald Blake)*, Eric Kramer *(Thor)*, Lee Purcell *(Dr. Margaret Shaw)*, Tim Thomerson *(Jack LeBeau)*, Charles Napier, John Gabriel, Jay Baker, William Riley, Tom Finnegan, Donald Willis, William Malone, Carl Nick Giafalio, Bobby Travis McLaughlin, Joanie Allen, Burke Denis, Nick Costa, Peisha McPhee
WRIT & D: Nicholas Corea   PHOTOG: Chuck Colwell   MUSIC: Lance Rubin
TVM, standard SF-fantasy: Benighted scientist meets incarnate Viking hero

The Incredible Invasion
see Invasion Sinitestra

The Incredible Jerry
see It's Only Money

The Incredible Melting Man
1977, (USA), Rosenberg-Gelfman/AIP, color, 85 mins.
W: Alex Rebar *(The Incredible Melting Man)*, Myron Healey *(Gen. Perry)*, Burr DeBenning *(Dr. Ted Nelson)*, Ann Sweeny *(Judy Nelson)*, Michael Alldredge *(Sheriff Blake)*, Stuart Edmond Rogers *(A Little Boy)*, Julie Drazen *(Carol)*, Chris Whitney *(A Little Boy)*, Lisle Wilson *(Dr. Loring)*, Rainbeaux Smith *(The Model)*, Edwin Max *(Harold)*, Dorothy Love *(Helen)*, Janus Blythe *(Nell)*, Jonathan Demme *(Matt)*, DeForest Covan *(The Janitor)*, Westbrook Claridge *(The 2nd Security Guard)*, Sam Gelfman *(The Fisherman)*, Bonnie Inch *(The Nurse)*, Mickey Lolich *(The 1st Security Guard)*, Don Walters *(The Photographer)*, Keith Michl *(The Maintenance Man)*, Leigh Mitchell *(Carol's Mother)*
WRIT & D: Wiliam Sachs   PHOTOG: Willy Curtis   SPCL-FX: Harry Woolman   MUSIC: Arlon Ober
Minor SF-horror: Astronaut becomes monster

The Incredible Mr. Limpet
1964, (USA), WB, color, 102 mins.
W: Don Knotts *(Mr. Limpet)*, Carole Cook, Jack Weston, Andrew Dug-gan, Larry Keating, Oscar Beregi, Charles Meredith
P: John C. Rose   D: Arthur Lubin   SCR: Jameson Brewer, & John C. Rose, from a story by Theodore Pratt   PHOTOG: Harold Stine   MUSIC: Frank Perkins
animated portions incorporated
Juvenile fantasy: Man becomes a talking fish

The Incredible Petrified World
1959, (USA), Governor, b&w, 78 mins.
W: John Carradine, Robert Clarke, Phyllis Coates, Sheila Noonan, Allen Windsor, George Skaff, Maurice Bernard, Joe Maierhouser, Harry Raven, Lloyd Nelson, Jack Haffner
P & D: Jerry Warren
Minor SF-thriller: Scientists trapped beneath sea

The Incredible Praying Mantis
see The Deadly Mantis

The Incredible Shrinking Man
1957, (USA), Univ, b&w, 94 mins.
W: Grant Williams *(Robert Scott Carey)*, April Kent, Randy Stuart, Paul Langton, Raymond Bailey, Diana Darrin, Frank Scannell, William Schallert, Helene Marshall, Billy Curtis
P: Albert Zugsmith   D: Jack Arnold   SCR: Richard Matheson, from his novel *The Shrinking Man*   PHOTOG: Ellis W. Carter   MUSIC: Joseph Gershenson   DESIGN: Alexander Golitzen
"The film introduced a new kind of fear—not instant annihilation, but rather gradual and irreversible descent into nothingness...the final effect and curtain speech is still hauntingly thoughtful, and successfully lifts the film's ending into the realm of philosophy, making it one of the most stirring closings in science fiction films" Christopher J. Warren, "Monsters: Earthly and Unearthly The Incredible Shrinking Man" (Notes), Wadsworth Atheneum—The American Cinema: A Survey 1896-1976 (Hartford, CN; 1976)
"The fantastic story of an infected man who slowly dwindles in size to an invisible atom is worked out with complete logic from its original premise. Disbelief remains completely suspended, and the terror of the victim's changing situations is maintained throughout ... His panic stricken flight in a doll's house from a clawing cat, his efforts to obtain the cheese from a mousetrap for food without being crushed by the spring, his frightful battle with a spider his own size—all these and other details, aided by excellent trick photography, carry complete conviction, assuming, indeed, an epic quality of man's struggle for survival. The ending is uncompromising. A horror film with the courage of its conclusions"—Ivan Butler, The Horror Film
Classic SF-thriller: Man loses body mass after exposure to radioactive cloud

The Incredible Shrinking Woman
1981, (USA), Lija/Univ, color, 88 mins.
W: Lily Tomlin *(Pat Kramer/Judith Beasley)*, Charles Grodin *(Vance Kramer)*, Ned Beatty *(Dan Beame)*, Henry Gibson *(Dr. Eugene Nortz)*, Elizabeth Wilson *(Dr. Ruth Ruth)*, Nicholas Hormann *(Logan Carver)*, Mark Blankfield *(Rob)*, Maria Smith *(Concepcion)*, Pamela Bellwood *(Sandra Dyson)*, John Glover *(Tom Keller)*, James McMullen *(Lyle Parks)*, Richard A. Baker *(Sidney)*, Shelby Balik *(Beth Kramer)*, Justin Dana *(Jeff Kramer)*
P: Hank Moonjean   D: Joel Schumacher   SCR: Jane Wagner, inspired by Richard Matheson's novel *The Shrinking Man*   PHOTOG: Bruce Logan   MUSIC: Suzanne Ciani   SONG: *Galaxy Glue*
Standard SF-satire: Pollutants make housewife diminish

The Incredible Torture Show
1978, (USA), Rochelle/Troma, 87 mins., color
W: Niles McMaster, Seamus O'Brien Lynette Sheldon, Karen Fraser, Michelle Craig, The Caged Sexoids
P, D, & SCR: Joel M. Reed
*A.k.a. **Blood Sucking Freaks***
Minor horror-thriller: Terror in a Soho "Grand Guignol" theater

The Incredible 2-Headed Transplant
1971, (USA), AIP, color, 88 mins.
W: Bruce Dern *(Roger)*, Pat Priest *(Linda)*, Albert Cole *(Cass)*, Casey Kasem *(Ken)*, John Bloom *(Danny)*, Larry Vincent *(Andrew)*, Berry Kroeger *(Max)*, Darlene Duralia *(Miss Pierce)*, Jack Lester *(The Sheriff)*, Jerry Patterson *(The Deputy)*, Robert Miller *(The Station Attendant)*, Leslie Cole *(Young Danny)*, Ray Thorn, Donald Brody, Bill Collins, Mary Ellen Clawsen, Janice Gelman, Mike Espe, Laura Lanza, Andrew Schneider, Eva Sorensen, Jack English, Carolyn Gilbert, Gary Kent
P: John Lawrence   D & ED: Anthony M. Lanza   SCR: James Gordon White & John Lawrence   PHOTOG: Jack Steely, Glen Gano & Paul Hipp   MUSIC: John Barber   SONG: *It's Incredible* by Baranlous & John Hill
Standard SF-thriller: Deranged scientist grafts killer's head onto body of another

The Incredible Voyage of Stingray
1980, (GB), color, 93 mins.
animated puppets
Standard juvenile SF-fantasy: Undersea ruler battles world defenders

The Incredibly Strange Creatures Who Stopped Living and Became Mixed-Up Zombies

1964, (USA), George J. Morgan-Ray Dennis Steckler/FairwayInt'l/Hollywood Star, color, 81 mins.

W: Cash Flagg (*Ray Dennis Stackler*), Carolyn Brandt, Brett O'Hara, Sharon Walsh, Toni Camel, Erina Enyo, Robert Silliphant, Dan Russe, Jill Carson, Don Marquis, Atlas King, Madison Clarke, Jack Brady, Don Smiley, George Morgan

D: Ray Dennis Steckler **SCR:** Gene Pollock & Robert Silliphant, from an orig. story by E.M. Kevke

*A.k.a. **The Teenage Psycho Meets Bloody Mary***

Standard horror-satire: Monsters create mayhem in carnival setting

L'Increvable Jerry

see It's Only Money

Incubus (1962)

see La Ragazza Che Sapeva Troppo

Incubus

1965, (USA), Daystar, b&w

W: William Shatner

P: Anthony M. Taylor **D & SCR:** Leslie Stevens **PHOTOG:** Conrad Hall

Unusual fantasy-thriller (dialog in Esperanto): Man encounters demons

Incubus

1982, (Can), Marc Boyman/Film Ventures, color, 92 mins.

W: John Cassavetes (*Dr. Samuel M. Cordell*), Kerrie Keane (*Laura Kincaid*), John Ireland (*Police Chief Hank Walden*), Erin Flannery (*Jennifer Cordell*), Helen Hughes (*Mrs. Galen*), Tim McIntosh, Harvey Atkin, Harry Ditson

D: John Hough, from a story by Ray Russell **PHOTOG:** Albert J. Dunk **SPCL-FX:** Colin Chilvers **MUSIC:** Stanley Myers

Standard horror-fantasy: Rape-murders have occult origin

In Dark Places

1997, (USA), color, 100 mins.

W: Joan Severance, Bryan Kestner

Made-for-Video, standard melodrama: Secrets cloud reunion of woman painter and half-brother

Independence Day

1996, (USA), 20th-Fox, color, 145 mins.

W: Jeff Goldblum, Will Smith, Bill Pullman, Mary McDonnell, Harry Connick Jr., Vivica Fox, Robert Loggia, Randy Quaid, Judd Hirsch, Harvey Fierstein, Margaret Colin, James Rebhorn, Brent Spiner Leland Orser

D: Roland Emmerich **SCR:** Roland Emmerich & Dean Devlin **PHOTOG:** Karl Walter Lindenlaub **VS-FX:** Volker Engel & Douglas Smith **MUSIC:** David Arnold

Unusual SF-thriller: Space aliens infiltrate Earth

Indestructible Man

1956, (USA), AA, b&w, 70 mins.

W: Lon Chaney Jr., Casey Adams (*Max Showalter*), Marion Carr, Ross Elliott, Stuart Randall, Kenneth Terrell, Marjorie Stapp, Roy Engel, Robert Shayne, Peggy Maley, Robert Foulk, Rita Green, Joe Flynn, Madge Cleveland, Marvin Ellis

P & D: Jack Pollexfen **SCR:** Vy Russell, Sue Bradford & Jack Pollexfen (uncredited) **PHOTOG:** John Russell Jr. **MUSIC:** Albert Glasser

*orig. co-billed with **World Without End***

blurb: "300,000 volts of horror!"

Minor SF-thriller: Revived brute goes on rampage

Indiana Jones and the Last Crusade

1989, (USA), Lucasfilm/Para, color, 127 mins.

W: Harrison Ford (*Indiana Jones*), Sean Connery (*Dr. Jones*), Denholm Elliott, Alison Doody, John Rhys-Davies, Michael Byrne, Julian Glover, River Phoenix, Richard Young, Kevork Malikyan, Robert Eddison

D: Steven Spielberg **SCR:** Jeffrey Boam **STORY:** George Lucas & Menno Meyjes **PHOTOG:** Douglas Slocombe **MUSIC:** John Williams

Exciting action-adventure: Nazis seek Holy Grail

Indiana Jones and the Temple of Doom

1984, (USA), Lucasfilm/Para, color, 115 mins.

W: Harrison Ford (*Indiana Jones*), Kate Capshaw (*Willie Scott*), Ke Huy Quan (*Short Round*), Amrish Puri (*The High Priest*), Roshan Seth (*Chattar Lai*), Philip Stone (*Capt. Blumburtt*), David Yip (*Wu Han*), Raj Singh (*The Little Maharajah*), Ric Young (*Kao Kan*), Chua Kah Joo (*Chen*), D.R. Nanayakkara (*The Shaman*), Rex Ngui (*The Maitre d'*), Roy Chiao (*Lao Che*), Pat Roach

D: Steven Spielberg **SCR:** Willard Huyck & Gloria Katz **STORY:** George Lucas **PHOTOG:** Douglas Slocombe **MUSIC:** John Williams

*Rousing "prequel" to **Raiders of the Lost Ark**: Two-fisted archeologist seeks sacred stone snatched by Kali cult*

The Indian Chief and the Seidlitz

1901, (GB), Hepworth, b&w, 90 ft. (27.4m)

D: Cecil Hepworth

Minor fantasy short: Red Indian takes powders in wrong order, swells and bursts

The Indian in the Cupboard

1995, (USA), Kennedy-Marshall/Scholastic/Para, color, 97 mins.

W: Hal Scardino (*Omri*), Litefoot (*Little Bear*), David Keith, Rishi Bhat, Lindsay Crouse, Richard Jenkins, Steve Coogan, Vincent Kartheiser

D: Frank Oz **SCR:** Melissa Mathison, from Lynne Reid Banks' 1980 novel **PHOTOG:** Russell Carpenter **SPCL VS-FX:** Industrial Light & Magic **MUSIC:** Randy Edelman

Standard juvenile fantasy: Boy acquires magical, diminutive friend

The Indian Scarf

1963, (W. Ger), Constantin, b&w, 85 mins.

W: Heinz Drache, Klaus Kinski, Gisela Uhlen

D: Albert Vohrer, from Edgar Wallace's story, "The Frightened Lady"

*Minor thriller: Strangler slays heirs. Remake: **The Case of the Frightened Lady***

Indian Sorcerer

see Le Fakir de Singapoure

Une Indigestion (An Indigestion)

1902, (Fr), Star, b&w, 85m (278.9 ft./4.7 mins.)

D: Georges Melies

*A.k.a. **Up-to-Date Surgery and Sure Cure for Indigestion***

Standard fantasy: Surgeon dissects patient, reassembles him in wrong order

In Dreams

1999, (USA), Dreamworks, color

W: Annette Bening, Robert Downey Jr., Aidan Quinn, Stephen Rea

D: Neil Jordan **SCR:** Bruce Robinson & Neil Jordan

Standard thriller

The Inexhaustible Cab

1899, (GB), G.A.S. Films, b&w, 75 ft. (22.9m)

D: George Albert Smith

Minor fantasy short: Clown puts dozen people into taxi that vanishes

In Fairyland

1912, (GB), Natural Colour Kinematograph Co., color

D: Walter R. Booth

Minor fantasy: Child dreams of fairies, Mephistopheles

Infamous Conduct

1966, (GB), Merton Park/Anglo-Amalgamated, color, 30 mins.

W: Dermot Walsh (*Anthony Searle*), Bridget Armstrong (*Janet Davis*), Richard Warner (*The Prosecution*), Ewen Solon (*Dixon*), Terry Wale (*Riki*), Norman Scace (*The Defense*), Nancy Nevinson (*Maggie Searle*)

P: Jack Greenwood **D:** Richard Martin **STORY:** James Eastwood, from characters created by Edgar Lustgarten

Standard short crime-thriller: Surgeon becomes involved with criminals

Infamous Crimes

see Philo Vance Returns

Infernal Affairs

1996, (USA), Touchstone, color

W: Ellen DeGeneres

from Jane Heller's novel

Unusual satire: Woman real-estate agent makes satanic pact

The Infernal Cakewalk

1903, (Fr), Star, b&w, 100m (328.1 ft./5.5 mins.)

W: Georges Melies (*Satan*)

D: Georges Melies

Standard fantasy: Prince of Darkness frolics

The Infernal Cauldron

see Le Chaudron Infernal

The Infernal Cauldron and the Phantasmal Vapours

see Le Chaudron Infernal

The Infernal Trio

see Le Trio Infernal

Inferno (1922)

see Doctor Mabuse

Inferno

1953, (USA), 20th-Fox, 3D, color, 83 mins.

W: Robert Ryan, Rhonda Fleming, William Lundigan, Carl Betz, He ry Hull, Larry Keating

D: Roy Baker **PHOTOG:** Lucien Ballard **MUSIC:** Lionel Newman

Grim suspense thriller: Millionaire left to die in desert

Inferno

1979, (It), Salvatore Argento/20th-Fox, color, 83 mins.

W: Leigh McCloskey (*Mark*), Irene Miracle (*Rose*), Eleonora Giorgi (*Sara*), Daria Nicolodi (*Elise*), Sacha Pitoeff (*Kazanian*), Alida Valli (*Carol*), Veronica Lanro (*The Nurse*), Gabriele Lavia (*Carlo*), Feodor Chaliapin (*Varelli*), James

Fleetwood (*The Cook*), Rosario Rigutini (*The Man*), Leopoldo Mastelloni (*The Butler*), Ania Pieroni (*The Music Student*), Luigi Lodoli (*The Bookbinder*), Ryan Hilliard (*The Shadow*), Rodolfo Lodi (*The Old Man*), Paolo Paoloni (*The Music Teacher*), Fulvio Mingozzi (*The Cabdriver*)
P: Claudio Argento   **D, STORY, & SCR:** Dario Argento   **PHOTOG:** Romano Albani   **SPCL-FX:** Germano Natali   **MUSIC:** Keith Emerson
Unusual horror-fantasy: Youth meets Death trinity

Inferno
1998, (USA), UPN-TV, color, 95 mins.
W: Jonathan LaPaglia, Kathryn Morris, Stephanie Niznick, James Remar, Daniel Von Bargen, Anthony Starke, Fredric Lane
D: Jan Baray   **TELEPLAY:** Bruce W. Taylor & Roderick Taylor   **PHOTOG:** Jacques Haitkin   **MUSIC:** Joel Goldsmith
TVM, standard SF-thriller: Solar flare threatens Los Angeles

An Infinity of Terror
see Galaxy of Terror

Information Received
1961, (GB), United Co-Production/RFD/Univ, b&w, 77 mins.
W: William Sylvester (*Rick Hogan*), Sabina Sesselman (*Sabina Farlow*), Hermione Baddeley (*Maudie*), Edward Underdown (*Drake*), Walter Brown (*Farlow*), David Ensor (*The Judge*), Robert Raglan (*Supt. Jeffcote*), David Courtney (*Mark*), Tim Brinton (*The TV Announcer*)
P: John Clein & George Maynard   **D:** Robert Lynn   **SCR:** Paul Ryder   **STORY:** Berkeley Mather
Standard crime-thriller: American poses as safecracker, helps police catch gang

The Informers
1963, (GB), Rank/RFD, b&w, 105 mins.
W: Nigel Patrick (*Insp. Johnnoe*), Margaret Whiting (*Maisie*), Harry Andrews (*Supt. Bestwick*), Colin Blakeley (*Charlie Ruskin*), Catherine Woodville (*Mary Johnnoe*), Roy Kinnear (*Shorty*), Derren Nesbitt (*Bertie Hoyle*), Frank Finlay (*Leon Sale*), Allan Cuthbertson (*Smythe*), Michael Coles (*Ben*), John Cowley (*Jim Ruskin*), Kenneth J. Warren (*Lou Walters*)
P: William MacQuitty   **D:** Ken Annakin   **SCR:** Alun Falconer & Paul Durst, from Douglas Warner's novel
Standard crime-thriller: Inspector tracks bank robber who framed him for taking bribe

Infra-Man
1975, (Hong Kong), Shaw Bros./Joseph Brenner, color, 89 mins.
W: Terry Liu, Li Hsiu-Hsien, Wang Hsieh, Yuan Man-tzu, Ysen Shu-yi, Lu Sheng
P: Runme Shaw   **D:** Hua-Shan   **SCR:** Peter Fernandez
A.k.a. The Super Inframan
Standard SF fantasy: Man becomes super-hero.

In Gollywog Land
1912, (GB), Natural Colour Kinematograph Co., color, 590 ft. (180m)
D: F. Martin Thornton & W.R. Booth
reissued 1916, USA retitle, Gollywog's Motor Accident
Standard fantasy: Fanciful creature has motor mishap.

Inhabited Planet
see Bezludna Planeta

The Inheritance
see Uncle Silas

In His Father's Shoes
1997, (USA), SHO-TV, color, 95 mins.
W: Robert Richard, Lou Gossett Jr.
Made-for-Cable, standard fantasy: Magic shoes allow bereaved boy to relive events in deceased father's past

L'Inhumaine (The Inhuman One)
1923, (Fr), Cinegraphic, b&w, 5,906 ft. (1800m)
W: Georgette Leblanc, Philippe Heriat
D: Marcel L'Herbier   **SCR:** Georgette Leblanc & Marcel L'Herbier   **PHOTOG:** Specht & Roche
A.k.a. Futurisme
Bizarre fantasy: Man-killing opera star brought back from death

Inhumanoid
1996, (USA), SHO-TV, color, 90 mins.
W: Richard Grieco, Corbin Bernsen (*Foster*), Lara Harris (*Katrina*), Brittany Ashton Holmes (*Amy*)
Made-for-Cable, standard SF-thriller: Lone survivor of space disaster lusts after rescuer's wife

The Inhuman One
see L'Inhumaine

In London's Toils
1913, (GB), Barker, b&w, 2,395 ft. (730m)
W: Thomas H. MacDonald (*Gilbert Mowbray*), Maud Yates (*Stella*), Fred Paul (*John Eames*), Roy Travers (*Spider*)
D: Alexander Butler   **STORY:** Rowland Talbot
Standard crime-thriller: Farmer's gambler son robs uncle, is framed for murder

The Initiation
1984, (USA), Bruce Lansbury-Jock Gaynor/New World, color, 90 mins.
W: Vera Miles (*Frances Fairchild*), Clu Gulager (*Dwight Fairchild*), Daphne Zuniga (*Kelly/Terry Fairchild*), James Read (*Peter*), Marilyn Kagan (*Marcia*), Peter Malof (*Andy*), Robert Dowdell (*Jason Randall*), Frances Peterson (*Megan*), Deborah Morehart (*Alison*), Trey Stroud (*Ralph*), Joy Jones (*Heidi*), Patti Heider (*Nurse Higgins*), Christopher Bradley (*Chad*), Paula Knowles (*Beth*), Mary Davis Duncan (*Gwen*), Rusty Meyers (*The Nightwatchman*), Christi Michelle Allen (*Kelly, age 9*), Cheryl Foster (*A Sorority Girl*), Melissa Toomin (*A Sorority Girl*), Diane Page (*A Sorority Girl*), Traci Odom (*A Sorority Girl*), Jennifer Suttles (*A Sorority Girl*), Dan Dickerson (*The Detective*), Jerry L. Clark (*The Orderly*), Ronald M. Hubner (*The Motorcycle Cop*), Kathy Lee Kennedy (*The Nurse*), Lance Funston (*A Student*), Andrea Vaccarello (*A Student*)
P: Scott Winant   **D:** Larry Stewart   **SCR:** Charles Pratt Jr.   **PHOTOG:** George Tirl   **SPCL-FX:** Jack Bennett   **MUSIC COMPOSED & PERFORMED:** Gabriel Black & Lance Ong   **SONGS:** *Not Me, Stop Following Me, Makin' Up for Lost Time* & *Texas Flash*
Standard thriller: Killer stalks college girls

The Initiation of Sarah
1978, (USA), ABC-TV, color, 95 mins.
W: Shelley Winters, Morgan Brittany (*Patti*), Kay Lenz (*Sarah*), Tony Bill (*Paul Yates*), Morgan Fairchild (*Jennifer*), Tisa Farrow (*Mouse*), Kathryn Crosby (*Mrs. Goodwin*), Robert Hays (*Scott*), Elizabeth Stack (*Laura*), Nora Heflin (*Barbara*), Deborah Ryan (*Bobbie*), Talia Balsam (*Allison*)
P: Jay Benson   **D:** Robert Day   **PHOTOG:** Ric Waite
TVM, minor thriller: Eerie events surround psychic coed

In Like Flint
1966, (USA), 20th-Fox, color, 114 mins.
W: James Coburn (*Derek Flint*), Jean Hale (*Lisa*), Andrew Duggan (*The President*), Lee J. Cobb (*Cramden*), Anna Lee (*Helena*), Yvonne Craig, Diane Bond, Steve Ihnat
P: Saul David   **D:** Gordon Douglas   **SCR:** Hal Fimberg   **PHOTOG:** William Daniels   **MUSIC:** Jerry Goldsmith   **SONG:** *Your Zowie Face*
Standard action-thriller-satire, sequel to Our Man Flint: Secret agent tackles female cabal

The Inner Circle
1946, (USA), Rep, b&w, 57 mins.
W: Warren Douglas, Lynne Roberts, Adele Mara, William Frawley, Virginia Christine, Ricardo Cortez
D: Philip Ford
Standard thriller: Detective framed for murder

Inner Sanctum
1949, (USA), Film Classics, b&w, 62 mins.
W: Charles Russell, Billy House, Mary Beth Hughes, Fritz Leiber, Lee Patrick, Nana Bryant Lee Patrick, Nana Bryant
D: Lew Landers
Minor melodrama, inspired by radio-series: Fortune-teller predicts tragedy for young girl on train

Inner Sanctum
1991, (USA), color 87 mins.
W: Tanya Roberts, Margaux Hemingway, Joseph Bottoms, Valerie Wildman, William Butler, Brett Clark
D: Fred Olen Ray
Minor thriller: Intrigue arises when businessman hires nurse for invalid wife

Inner Sanctum 2
1994, (USA), TriStar/Col, color, 90 mins.
W: Tracy Brooks Swope, David Warner, Jennifer Ciesar, Margaux Hemingway, Michael Nouri, Sandahl Bergman
D: Fred Olen Ray   **SCR:** Sherman Scott   **MUSIC:** Chuck Cirino
Standard thriller: Beautiful heiress kills husband, is terrorized by stalker

Innerspace
1987, (USA), Steven Spielberg/WB, color, 118 mins.
W: Dennis Quaid (*Tuck Pendleton*), Martin Short (*Jack Putter*), Meg Ryan (*Lydia Maxwell*), Fiona Lewis (*Dr. Canker*), Kevin McCarthy (*Victor Scrimshaw*), Vernon Wells (*Mr. Igoe*), Robert Picardo (*The Cowboy*), Wendy Schaal (*Wendy*), William Schallert, Henry Gibson, John Hora, Kathleen Freeman, Dick Miller, Kenneth Tobey, Orson Bean, Archie Hahn, Joe Flaherty, Andrea Martin
D: Joe Dante   **SCR:** Jeffrey Boam & Chip Proser   **STORY:** Chip Proser   **PHOTOG:** Andrew Laszlo   **SPCL-FX SPRVSR:** Michael Wood   **MUSIC:** Jerry Goldsmith
Modest SF-comedy: Miniaturized argonaut injected into supermarket checker's body. Best Visual Effects Academy Award winner

Innocent Blood
1992, (USA), Lee Rich-Leslie Belzberg/WB, color, 115 mins.
W: Anne Parillaud (*Marie*), David Proval (*Lenny*), Robert Loggia (*Sal "The Shark" Macelli*), Rocco Sisto (*Gilly*), Chazz Palminteri (*Tony*), Anthony LaPaglia (*Joe Gennaro*), Don Rickles (*Emmanuel Bergman*), Christopher Lee (*Count Dracula*)
D: John Landis   **SCR:** Michael Wolk   **PHOTOG:** Mac Ahlberg   **MUSIC:** Ira

Newborn, <u>SONGS:</u> *I Wanna Make Love to You*
Erotic horror-fantasy: Vampiress preys on Mafia

Innocent Bystanders
1972, (GB), Sagittarius/Scotia-Barber, color, 111 mins.
<u>W:</u> Stanley Baker (*John Craig*), Geraldine Chaplin (*Miriam Loman*), Dana Andrews (*Blake*), Donald Pleasence (*Loomis*), Sue Lloyd (*Joanna Benson*), Warren Mitchell (*Omar*), John Collin (*Asimov*), Vladek Sheybal (*Aaron Kaplan*), Derren Nesbitt (*Andrew Royce*), Ferdy Mayne (*Marcus Kaplan*), Frank Maher (*Daniel*)
<u>P:</u> George H. Brown   <u>D:</u> Peter Collinson   <u>SCR:</u> James Mitchell from a novel by James Munro   <u>PHOTOG:</u> Brian Probyn   <u>MUSIC:</u> John Keating
Standard crime-thriller: Agents hunt treacherous Russian scientist

Innocent Meeting
1959, (GB), Danziger/UA, v&w, 62 mins.
<u>W:</u> Sean Lynch (*Johnny Brent*), Beth Rogan (*Connie*), Raymond Huntley (*Harold*), Ian Flemyng (*Garside*), Howard Lang (*Macey*), Arnold Bell (*Fry*), Colin Tapley (*Stannard*), Robert Raglan (*Martin*), Denis Shaw (*Uncle*)
<u>P:</u> Edward J. & Harry Lee Danziger   <u>D:</u> Godfrey Grayson   <u>STORY:</u> Brian Clemens & Eldon Howard
Standard crime-thriller: Teen turns gunman

The Innocents
1961, (GB), 20th-Fox, b&w, 99 mins.
<u>W:</u> Deborah Kerr (*Miss Giddens*), Pamela Franklin (*Flora*), Martin Stephens (*Miles*), Megs Jenkins (*Mrs. Grose*), Peter Wyngarde (*Quint*), Michael Redgrave (*The Uncle*), Isla Cameron (*Anna*), Clytie Jessop (*Miss Jessel*), Eric Woodburn
<u>P & D:</u> Jack Clayton   <u>SCR:</u> William Archibald & Truman Capote, based on Henry James' *The Turn of the Screw*   <u>PHOTOG:</u> Freddie Francis   <u>MUSIC:</u> Georges Auric   <u>DESIGN:</u> Wilfrid Shingleton
Superior fantasy-thriller: Governess meets evil ghosts. cf. **The Nightcomers**

Inn of Evil
1971, (Jap), Toho, b&w, 121 mins.
<u>W:</u> Ganemon Nakamura (*Ikuzo*), Komaki Kurihara (*Omitsu*), Kei Sato (*Yohei*), Tatsuya Nakadai (*Sadahichi*), Shintaro Katsu (*The Man Without a Name*), Wakako Sakai (*Okiwa*), Ichido Nakaya (*A Detective*), Shigeru Koyama (*A Detective*), Kei Yamamoto (*Tomijiro*)
<u>D:</u> Masaki Kobayashi   <u>SCR:</u> Tomoe Ryu   <u>STORY:</u> Shugoro Yamamoto   <u>PHOTOG:</u> Kozo Okazaki   <u>MUSIC:</u> Toru Takemitsu
Standard thriller: Murders investigated

Inn of the Damned
1974, (Austral), Terryrod/Medich/Roadshow, color, 89 mins, also 125 mins
<u>W:</u> Dame Judith Anderson (*Carolina Straulle*), Joseph Furst (*Jason Straulle*), Alex Cord (*Cal Kincaid*), Michael Craig (*Paul Melford*), John Meillon (*George Parr*), John Morris (*Martin Cummings*), Robert Quilter (*Biscayne*), Diana Dangerfield (*Mrs. Millington*), Carla Hoogeveen (*Beverly*), Don Barkham (*Sgt. Malone*), John Nash (*Col. Lowe*), Tony Bonner (*Trooper Moore*), Phil Avalon (*Alfred*), Jack Allan (*Gypsy Jake*), Lionel Long (*The Search Horseman*), Louis Wishart (*Arnold*), Colin Drake (*Franz Heller*), Gordon Glenwright (*Squire Grimstead*), Graham Corry (*Andrew Millington*), Josie MacKay (*The Cummings' Girl*), George Pollak ("*Mad Mich*" *Marriott*), Nat Levison (*The Undertaker*), Reg Gorman (*The Coach Co-driver*), Geoffrey Burton (*The Urchin Boy*), Linda Brown ("*Peaches*"), Anna King (*The Coach Passenger*), Carmel Cullen (*The Housekeeper*), Hilary Bamberger (*Mrs. Bennett*), James Moss, Graham Ware, Elaine Wong, Kuki Kaa, Melissa Chappel, Dave Proudman, Roy Harries-Jones, Jim Clifford, Reg Midway, Dave Chard, Terry Bourke Jr.
<u>WRIT & D:</u> Terry Bourke   <u>PHOTOG:</u> Brian Probyn   <u>MUSIC:</u> Bob Young
Minor thriller: Hostel guests murdered

Inn of the Frightened People
see **Revenge** *(1971, GB)*

The Inn on Dartmoor
1964, (W. Ger), b&w
<u>W:</u> Heinz Drache, Paul Klinger
from a story by Edgar Wallace
Minor thriller: Artist and policeman uncover criminality

The Inn on the River
1962, (W. Ger), b&w, 95 mins.
<u>W:</u> Joachim Fuchsberger, Klaus Kinski, Brigitte Grothum, Richard Much
<u>D:</u> Alfred Vohrer   from a story by Edgar Wallace
Standard thriller (remake of **The Return of the Frog**)

In Possession
1985, (GB), color
<u>W:</u> Carol Lynley, Christopher Cazenove
Minor thriller: Visions haunt couple

In Prehistoric Days
1913, (USA), Biograph, b&w, 1 reel
<u>D:</u> D.W. Griffith
Standard melodrama: Life of ancient humans

Inquisition

1976, (Sp), color, 85 mins.
<u>W:</u> Paul Naschy, Daniela Giordano, Juan Gallardo
<u>D & SCR:</u> Paul Naschy
Minor horror-thriller: Witch-hunter accused of demonic deeds

The Inquisitor
1981, (Fr), color, 88 mins.
<u>W:</u> Lino Ventura, Michel Serrault, Guy Marchand, Patrick Depeyrat, Romy Schneider, Didier Agostini
<u>D:</u> Claude Miller, from John Wainwright's novel *Brainwash*
Modest psychological thriller: New Year's Eve interrogation in pronvincial police station

In Search of Dracula
1972, (Swed), Aspekt/Independent International, color, 86 mins
<u>W:</u> Christopher Lee (*Prince Vland and Narrator*)
<u>P, MUSIC & D:</u> Calvin Floyd   <u>SCR:</u> Yvonne Floyd
A.k.a **Dracula's Transylvania**,
Standard docu: Fictional & historical Count Dracula. Filmed in Rumania, footage from Nosferatu, 1922. Made for Swedish and British TV. US theatrical release, 1975

In Search of Dracula

In Search of the Castaways
1962, (GB), Walt Disney/Buena Vista, color, 100 mins.
<u>W:</u> Hayley Mills (*Mary Grant*), Maurice Chevalier (*Jacques Paganel*), George Sanders (*Thomas Ayrton*), Michael Anderson Jr. (*John Glenarvon*), Wilfrid Hyde-White (*Lord Glenarvon*), Jack Gwillim (*Capt. Grant*), Ronald Fraser (*The Guard*), Keith Hamshere (*Robert Grant*), Wilfrid Brambell (*Bill Gaye*), Antonio Cifariello (*Thalcave*), Inia Te Wiata (*The Maori Chief*), Norman Bird, Roger Delgado
<u>D:</u> Robert Stevenson   <u>SCR:</u> Lowell S. Hawley, based on Jules Verne's novels *Captain Grant's Children* and *In Search of the Castaways*   <u>PHOTOG:</u> Paul Beeson   <u>MUSIC:</u> William Alwyn
A.k.a **The Castaways**
Modest adventure-thriller: Two children seek lost father

Insect
see **Blue Monkey**

The Insect Play
1960, (GB), BBC-TV, b&w
<u>W:</u> Patrick McAlinney, Patrick Troughton
Standard thriller

In Self Defense
1987, (USA), Leonard Hill/ACI, color, 95 mins.
<u>W:</u> Linda Purl, Yaphet Kotto, Terry Lester, Billy Drago, Gail Edwards, Rick Lenz, Peter Crook, Andrew Bloch, Lenora May, Richard Green, Whitby Hertford, Tom Fuccello, John M. Jackson, Phillip Richard Allen, James McIntire, Josh Cruze, Harry Basch, Sam Dalton, Jim Doughan, Bill Kohne, Alan David Gelman, Roger Hampton, Darrell Kunitomi, Ken Smolka
<u>D:</u> Bruce Seth Green   <u>TELEPLAY:</u> Robert Crais & David Peckinpah   <u>STORY:</u> David Peckinpah   <u>PHOTOG:</u> Paul Onorato   <u>MUSIC:</u> Patrick Gleeson
TVM, standard thriller: Killer terrorizes witness

In Self Defense
see **Perilous Waters**

Inseminoid
1981, (GB), Brent Walker/Jupiter/Sir Run Run Shaw/Almi, color, 92 mins.
<u>W:</u> Robin Clarke (*Mark*), Jennifer Ashley (*Capt. Holly Mackey*), Ste-phanie Beacham (*Kate*), Judy Geeson (*Sandy*), Steven Grives (*Gary*), Barry Houghton (*Karl*), Trevor Thomas (*Mitch*), Rosalind Lloyd (*Gail*), Victoria Tennant (*Barbra*), Heather Wright (*Sharon*), David Baxt (*Ricky*), Kevin O'Shea (*Corin*), Dominic Jephcott (*Dean*), Robert Pugh (*Roy*), John Segal (*Jeff*)

P: Richard Gordon & David Speechley **D:** Norman J. Warren **STORY:** Nick Maley, & Gloria Maley **PHOTOG:** John Metcalfe **SPCL-FX:** Oxford Scientific Films & Camera Effects **MUSIC:** John Scott
USA retitle, **Horror Planet**
Standard SF-horror: Girl raped by space alien, gives birth to twin monsters

Inside Information
1957, (GB), Merton Park/Anglo-Amalgamated, b&w, 32 mins.
W: Ronald Adam (*Insp. Duggan*), Basil Henson (*Tony Neilson*), Colette Wilde (*Ellie*)
P: Alec Snowden **D:** Montgomery Tully **STORY:** James Eastwood, from a novel by Edgar Lustgarten
Standard short crime-thriller: Inspector tracks crook's killer

The Inside Man
1980, (GB), Dragonfly/ITC, color, 26 mins.
W: Kevin McNally (*Tony Morris*), Nat Jackley (*Frank Morris*), Brian Croucher (*Meecham*), P.H. Moriarty (*Plummer*), Jack Corrish (*Harris*), A.J. Clark (*The Barman*), Barry Craine (*The Foreman*)
P: Tony Grisoni **D:** Andrew Bogle **STORY:** Andrew Bogle & Tony Grisoni **PHOTOG:** Clive Tickner
Standard short crime-thriller: Son of injured nightwatchman seeks revenge

Inside the Room
1935, (GB), Twickenham/Univ, b&w, 66 mins.
W: Austin Trevor (*Pierre Santos*), Dorothy Boyd (*Dorothy Ayres*), Garry Marsh (*Geoffrey Lucas*), George Hayes (*Henry Otisse*), Brian Buchel (*Adam Steele*), Marjorie Chard (*Lady Groombridge*), Frederick Burtwell (*Insp. Grant*), Robert Horton (*Sir George Frame*), Vera Boggetti (*Agnes Judd*), Dorothy Minto (*Lilian Hope*)
D: Leslie Hiscott **SCR:** H. Fowler Mear, from a play by Marten Cumberland
Standard thriller: French detective unmasks murderous singer

Insomnia
1965, (Fr), color (with b&w sequences), 17 mins.
D: Pierre Etaix
Fantasy short: Unable to sleep, man reads vampire tale

Insomnia
1998, (Nor), color
W: Stellan Skarsgard, Sverre Anker Ousdal
D: Erik Skjoldbjaerg **SCR:** Nikolaj Frobenius
Unusual psychodrama: Detective tracks girl's killer

An Inspector Calls
1954, (GB), Watergate/British Lion, b&w, 79 mins.
W: Alastair Sim (*Insp. Poole*), Olga Lindo (*Sybil Birling*), Arthur Young (*Arthur Birling*), Brian Worth (*Gerald Croft*), Eileen Moore (*Sheila Birling*), Jane Wenham (*Eva Smith*), Bryan Forbes (*Eric Birling*), George Woodbridge (*The Shopman*), Barbara Everest (*The Committee Member*), John Welsh (*The Shopwalker*), Norman Bird (*The Foreman*), George Cole (*The Conductor*), Pat Neal (*The Maid*), Catherine Willmer, Amy Green, Olwen Brookes
D: Guy Hamilton **SCR:** Desmond Davis, from a play by J.B. Priestley **PHOTOG:** Ted Scaife **MUSIC:** Francis Chagrin
Standard melodrama: Odd police inspector interviews family responsible for girl's suicide

Inspector Gadget
1999, (USA), Caravan/Walt Disney, color
W: Matthew Broderick, Rupert Everett, Joely Fisher
Amusing comedy-fantasy: Mechanically-rebuilt man fights crime

In Spite of it All
1912, (GB), Diamond Films/Cosmo, b&w, 1,450 ft. (442m)
Standard crime-thriller: Heir tries to thwart cousin's marriage

Insurance Investigator
1951, (USA), Rep, b&w, 60 mins.
W: Richard Denning, Audrey Long
Standard thriller

Intensity
1997, (USA), Fox-TV, color, approx. 190 mins.
W: John C. McGinley, Molly Parker, Piper Laurie, Deanna Milligan, Blu Mankuma, Lori Triolo, Tori Paul, Brent Stait, Kathie Stuart
D: Yves Simoneau **TELEPLAY:** Stephen Tolkin from Dean R. Koontz' novel **PHOTOG:** David Franco **MUSIC:** George S. Clinton
2-part TVM, adequate thriller: Girl shadows serial killer

Intent to Kill
1958, (USA), Zonic/20th-Fox, b&w, 89 mins.
W: Richard Todd (*Bob McLaurin*), Betsy Drake (*Nancy Ferguson*), Herbert Lom (*Juan Menda*), Warren Stevens (*Finch*), Carlo Justini (*Francisco Flores*), Paul Carpenter (*O'Brien*), Alexander Knox (*Mr. McNeil*), Lisa Gastoni (*Carla Menda*), Peter Arne (*Kral*), Catherine Boyle (*Margaret McLaurin*), John Crawford (*Boyd*), Jackie Collins (*Carol Freeman*), Kay Callard (*The Friend*)
P: Adrian Worker **D:** Jack Cardiff **SCR:** Jimmy Sangster, from a novel by Michael Bryan
Standard crime-thriller: Assassins menace South American president

An Interesting Story
1904, (GB), Williamson/Urban, b&w, 235 ft. (71.6m)
D: James Williamson
Minor fantasy short (in 6 scenes): Man absorbed in reading, is flattened by steamroller

Interface
1984, (USA), color, 88 mins.
W: John Davies, Laura Lane, Matthew Sacks
Minor SF-thriller: Computer game turns university campus into battleground

International Crime
1937, (USA), b&w, 62 mins.
W: Rod La Rocque, Astrid Allwyn, William von Brinken
D: Charles Lamont
Standard thriller: Sleuth "The Shadow" tackles tough mystery

International House
1933, (USA), Para, b&w, 73 mins.
W: Peggy Hopkins Joyce, Rudy Vallee, W.C. Fields (*Prof. Quail*), Stuart Erwin (*Tommy Nash*), Sari Maritza (*Carol Fortescue*), George Burns (*Dr. Burns*), Gracie Allen (*Nurse Allen*), Bela Lugosi (*Gen. Petronovich*), Franklin Pangborn (*The Hotel Manager*), Edmund Breese (*Dr. Wong*), Harrison Greene (*Herr Von Baden*), Lumsden Hare (*Sir Mortimer Fortescue*), Baby Rose Marie, Sterling Holloway, Lona Andre, Cab Calloway
D: Edward Sutherland **SCR:** Francis Martin & Walter DeLeon **STORY:** Neil Brant & Louis E. Heifetz **PHOTOG:** Ernest Haller **MUSIC & LYRICS:** Ralph Rainger & Leo Robin **SONG:** *Reefer Man*
Amusing semi-SF: Magnates vie for rights to super-TV

The International Spies
see **Lieutenant Daring and the Plans of the Minefields**

International Spy
see **The Spy Ring**

The Internecine Project
1974, (GB), Maclean & Co./Lion Int'l/Hemisphere/British Lion, color, 89 mins.
W: James Coburn (*Robert Elliot*), Lee Grant (*Jean Robertson*), Harry Andrews (*Albert Parsons*), Michael Jayston (*David Barker*), Ian Hendry (*Alex Hellman*), Keenan Wynn (*E.J. Farnsworth*), Christiane Kruger (*Christina Larson*), Ray Callaghan (*The Producer*), Terence Alexander (*The Tycoon*), Philip Anthony (*The Sec'y*), David Swift (*Chester Drake*), Julian Glover (*Arnold Pryce Jones*), Richard Marner (*The Delegate*), Kevin Scott (*Maxwell*), Ewan Roberts (*The Technician*)
D: Ken Hughes **SCR:** Barry Levinson & Jonathan Lynn from Mort Elkind's novel *Internecine* **PHOTOG:** Geoffrey Unsworth **MUSIC:** Roy Budd
Modest crime-thriller: Tycoon arranges murders of associates

Interplanetary Revolution
see **Mezhplanetnaya Revolutsiya**

Interpol Code 8
1965, (Jap), color
Minor thriller: Undercover agent battles Saigon spy ring

Interpol
1957, (GB), Warwick/Col, b&w, 92 mins.
W: Victor Mature (*Charles Sturgis*), Anita Ekberg (*Gina Broger*), Trevor Howard (*Frank McNally*), Bonar Colleano (*Amalio*), Martin Benson (*Varolli*), Peter Illing (*Capt. Baris*), Dorothy Alison (*Helen*), Andre Morell (*Breckner*), Eric Pohlmann (*Fayala*), Sydney Tafler (*Curtis*), Lionel Murton (*Murphy*), Danny Green (*The Bartender*), Yana (*The Singer*), Sidney James (*Joe*)
D: John Gilling **SCR:** John Paxton, from a book by A.J. Forrest
USA retitle, **Pickup Alley,** *reissued 1961*
Modest crime-thriller: Detective pursues dope smuggler

Interrogation
see **Przesluchanie**

The Interrupted Journey
1949, (GB), Valiant/British Lion, b&w, 80 mins.
W: Valerie Hobson (*Carol North*), Richard Todd (*John North*), Christine Norden (*Susan Wilding*), Tom Walls (*Mr. Clayton*), Ralph Truman (*Insp. Waterson*), Vida Hope (*Miss Marchmont*), Alexander Gauge (*Jerves Wilding*), Arnold Ridley (*Saunders*), Cyril Smith (*George*), Dora Bryan (*The Waitress*)
P: Anthony Havelock-Allan **D:** Dan Birt **SCR:** Michael Pertwee
Standard thriller: Writer becomes involved in murder

Interview with the Vampire
1994, (USA), Geffen/WB, color, 115 mins.
W: Tom Cruise (*Lestat*), Brad Pitt (*Louis*), Antonio Banderas (*Armand*), Kirsten Dunst (*Claudia*), Christian Slater (*The Interviewer*), Stephen Rea, Domiziana Giordano, Indra Ove, Thandie Newton, Laure Marsac
P: Stephen Woolley & David Geffen **D:** Neil Jordan **SCR:** Anne Rice, from her 1976 novel **PHOTOG:** Philippe Rousselot **MUSIC:** Elliot Goldenthal
blurb: "Drink From Me And Live Forever"
"Powerful. One of the best films of the year"—Caryn James, New York Times
"Two thumbs up!"—Siskel & Ebert

"Hypnotic, scary, sexy and perversely funny. An audacious, riveting Tom Cruise performance"—Peter Travers, Rolling Stone
Superior horror-fantasy: New Orleans aristocrat becomes Undead

Interzone
1988, (USA), color, 97 mins.
<u>W:</u> Bruce Abbott
<u>D:</u> Deran Sarafian
Minor SF-thriller: Post-nuke humans vs. mutants

In the Bogie Man's Cave
see La Cuisine de l'Ogre

In the Company of Darkness
1993, (USA), Don Johnson/Univ, color, 95 mins.
<u>W:</u> Helen Hunt, Steven Weber, Jeff Fahey, Juan Ramirez, Dan Conway, Margaret Travolta, Annabel Armour, Julian Brams, Michael Bacarella, Marilyn Dodds Frank, Danny Goldring, Irma Hall, Don James, Kim Klutznick, Peggy Roeder, Tony Mockus Jr., Mitch Rouse, Rudy Ruettiger, Thom Simmons, Michael Sassone, Jennifer Joan Taylor, Tom White
<u>D:</u> David Anspaugh **TELEPLAY:** John Leekley **PHOTOG:** Sandi Sissel
SPCL-FX COORD: Sam Barkan **MUSIC:** Tim Truman
TVM, standard fact-based thriller: Policewoman nabs child-killer

In the Days of Robin Hood
1913, (GB), Natural Colour Kinematograph Co., color, 1,950 ft. (594.4m)
<u>W:</u> H. Agar Lyons (*Robin Hood*), John M. East (*Little John*), Mercy Hatton (*Lady Christobel*), Cecil Dereham (*Will Scarlet*), Harry Ashton (*Friar Tuck*)
<u>D:</u> F. Martin Thornton
Standard adventure-thriller: Outlaw poses as monk, saves man from sheriff

In the Days of Saint Patrick
1920, (GB), General Film Supply/Janion, b&w, 4,200 ft. (1280.2m)
<u>W:</u> Ira Allen (*St. Patrick*), Vernon Whitten (*St. Patrick as a Child*), Alice Cardinall (*Conchessa*), Dermot McCarthy (*Calpurnius*), J.B. Carrickford (*St. Martin*), George Brame (*Pope Celestin*), George Griffin (*King Laoghaire*), Ernest Matthewson (*Bishop Tassach*), Maude Hume (*The Queen*), Mary Murnane (*The Foster Mother*), Herbert Mayne (*Gornias*), Eddie Lawless (*Milcho*), O'Carroll Reynolds (*Niall*), Jack McDermott (*Victor*)
<u>P & D:</u> Norma Whitten **STORY:** Mr. McGuinness
Standard historical melodrama: Bishop opposes paganism

In the Dead Man's Room
1913, (GB), Cricks & Martin, b&w, 1,860 ft. (566.9m)
<u>D:</u> Charles Calvert
Standard crime-thriller: 'Dead' heir exposes crook

In the Devil's Garden
1971, (GB), Peter Rogers/Hemisphere, color, 91 mins.
<u>W:</u> Suzy Kendall (*Julie West*), Frank Finlay (*Supt. John Velyan*), James Laurenson (*Greg Lomas*), Lesley-Anne Down (*Tessa Hurst*), Freddie Jones (*Denning*), Anthony Ainley (*Bartell*), Tony Beckley (*Leslie Sanford*), Dilys Hamlett (*Mrs. Sanford*), James Cosmo (*Sgt. Jim Beale*), Tom Chatto (*The Doctor*), Patrick Jordan (*Sgt. Milton*), Allan Cuthbertson (*The Coroner*), Anabel Littledale (*Susan Miller*), David Essex (*The Man*), John Stone (*The Fire Chief*), Marianne Stone (*The Matron*), Kit Taylor, Jan Butlin, William Hoyland, John Swindells, Jill Cary, Valerie Shute, Janet Lynn, Siobhan Quinlan
<u>D:</u> Sidney Hayers **SCR:** John Kruse, from Kendal Young's novel *The Ravine*
PHOTOG: Ken Hodges **MUSIC:** Eric Rogers
A.k.a. Assault
Standard thriller: Rapist-killer terrorizes schoolgirls

In the Grip of Death
1913, (GB), B&C/MP, b&w, 1,070 ft. (326.1m)
<u>W:</u> Norman Yates (*Dennis McLeod*), Marie d'Albert (*Kitty*), M. Gray Murray (*Lord Verula*), S.P. Goodyer Kettley (*Garston*), Wilfred Ellis (*The Officer*)
<u>D:</u> H.O. Martinek
Standard adventure-thriller: Lord's daughter elopes

In the Grip of Spies
1914, (GB), Big Ben Union/Pathe, b&w, 3,480 ft. (1060.7m)
<u>W:</u> H.O. Martinek (*Dick Steele*), Ivy Montford (*Kate Halifax*)
<u>D:</u> H.O. Martinek **SCR:** L.C. MacBean
Standard thriller: Detective poses as lascar, saves naval code from Chinese crook

In the Grip of the Spider
see Web of the Spider

In the Hands of the London Crooks
1913, (GB), Barker/City, b&w, 4,896 ft. (1492.3m)
<u>W:</u> Thomas H. MacDonald (*Frank Linley*), Blanche Forsythe (*Hilda Linley*), Fred Paul (*Capt. Bland*), Dora de Winton (*Delilah*), Roy Travers (*Harry Norman*), J. Hastings Batson (*Sir James Linley*)
<u>D:</u> Alexander Butler **STORY:** Rowland Talbot
Standard crime-thriller: Disowned gambler, framed for forgery, becomes hero in Afghanistan

In the Hands of the Spoilers
1916, (GB), Baker-Neptune/Renters, b&w, 4,000 ft. (1219.2m)
<u>D:</u> Leon Bary, from a novel by Sydney Paternoster

Standard crime-thriller: Gambling lieutenant fakes suicide, steals rival's child and trains him to steal father's secrets

In the Land of Nod
1908, (GB), Alpha Trading Co./Walturdaw, b&w, 365 ft. (111.3m)
<u>WRIT & D:</u> Arthur Cooper
reissued (1910) as **Grandpa's Forty Winks**
Standard fantasy short: Man dreams toy fire engine saves burning doll's house

In the Midst of Life
see Au Coeur de la Vie

In the Mouth of Madness
1995, (USA), New Line, color, 95 mins.
<u>W:</u> Sam Neill, Julie Carmen, Jurgen Prochnow, John Glover, Charlton Heston, David Warner, Bernie Casey, Peter Jason
<u>D:</u> John Carpenter **WRIT:** Michael De Luca **PHOTOG:** Gary B. Kibbe
MUSIC: John Carpenter & Jim Lang
Unusual horror-fantasy with Lovecraftian elements (touted as John Carpenter's best film): Missing author's nightmare creations become reality

In the Next Room
1930, (USA), First Nat'l, b&w, 7 reels (6,336 ft./1931.2m)
<u>W:</u> Jack Mulhall (*James Godfrey*), Alice Day (*Lorna*), John St. Polis (*Philip Vantine*), Robert E. O'Connor (*Tim Morel*), Jane Winton (*The Lady*), Crauford Kent (*The Lover*), Edward Earle (*The Husband*), Claude Allister (*Parks, the Butler*), Aggie Herring (*Mrs. O'Connor*), Lucien Prival (*The French Exporter*), DeWitt Jennings (*Insp. Grady*), Webster Campbell (*Snitzer*)
<u>D:</u> Edward Cline **SCR:** Harvey Gates **DIALOG:** James A. Starr, from a play by Eleanor Robson Belmont & Harriet Ford, based on a story by Burton Egbert Stevenson **PHOTOG:** John Seitz
Standard mystery-thriller: Diamond smugglers weave web of deceit

In the Nick of Time
1991, (USA), Walt Disney, color, 95 mins.
<u>W:</u> Lloyd Bridges (*Santa Claus*), Michael Tucker (*Ben Talbot*), Alison La Placa, A Martinez, Cleavon Little, Jessie di Cicco
<u>D:</u> George Miller **STORY:** Jon S. Denny **PHOTOG:** Brian R.R. Hebb
MUSIC: Steve Dorff
TVM, standard fantasy: Santa Claus faces retirement, seeks successor

In the Palace of the King
1923, (USA), Goldwyn, b&w, 9 reels (8,657 ft./2638.7m)
<u>W:</u> Edmund Lowe (*Don John*), Blanche Sweet (*Dolores Mendoza*), Hobart Bosworth (*Mendoza*), Pauline Starke (*Inez Mendoza*), Sam de Grasse (*King Philip II*), William V. Mong (*Perez*), Aileen Pringle (*Princess Eboli*), Lucien Littlefield (*Adonis*), Charles Clary (*Gomez*), Harvey Clark (*Alphonso*), Tom Bates (*Eudaldo*), D.N. Clugston (*The Chamberlain*), Charles Gorham (*A Guard*), Jack Pitcairn (*Capt. of the Guard*), Ena Gregory (*The Queen*), David Kirby (*A Guard*), Bruce Sterling (*Gaston*), Charles Newton (*The Aide to Don John*)
<u>D:</u> Emmett Flynn **ADAPT:** June Mathis, from a story by Francis Marion Crawford **PHOTOG:** Lucien Andriot
Spectacular romance: Discord between King Philip of Spain and his popular brother

In the Python's Den
see For East is East

In the Ranks
1914, (GB), Neptune/Jury, b&w, 3,945 ft. (120.2m)
<u>W:</u> Gregory Scott (*Ned/John Drayton*), Daisy Cordell (*Jocelyn Hare*), James Lindsay (*Capt. Holcroft*), Jack Denton (*Joe Buzzard*), Peggy Hyland (*Barbara Herrick*), Douglas Payne (*Richard Belton*), Frank Tennant (*Capt. Wynter*), Edward Sass (*Gidgeon Blake*), Joan Ritz (*Ruth Herrick*), Douglas Cox (*Sgt. Searle*), John East (*Farmer Herrick*), Ruby Wyndham (*Mrs. Buzzard*)
<u>D:</u> Percy Nash **SCR:** John East & Brian Daly from a play by George R. Sims & Henry Pettitt
Standard crime-thriller: Steward frames captain's adopted son for shooting of colonel

In the Shadow of Big Ben
1914, (GB), Hepworth, b&w, 3,000 ft. (914.4m)
<u>W:</u> Tom Powers (*Harry Forrest*), Alma Taylor (*Clara Maitland*), Jack Raymond (*Richard Nash*), Henry Vibart (*Mr. Hamel*), Ruby Belasco (*Mrs. Hamel*)
<u>D:</u> Frank Wilson **SCR:** Frank Howel Evans
Standard crime-thriller: Crook seeks to marry girl, frames her for forgery

In the Shadow of the Rope
1912, (GB), London/Cosmo, b&w, 1,000 ft. (304.8m)
<u>D:</u> Percy Nash
Standard crime-thriller: Corrupt judge frees highwayman in exchange for rival's assassination

In the Shadow of Kilimanjaro
1986, (USA), Intermedia, color, 94 mins.
<u>W:</u> John Rhys-Davies (*Chris Tucker*), Timothy Bottoms (*Jack Ringtree*), Michele Carey (*Ginny Hansen*), Calvin Jung (*Mitsuki Uto*), Irene Miracle (*Lee Ringtree*), Leonard Trolley (*Col. Emerson Maitland*), Don Blakely (*Julius X. Odom*), Jim Boeke (*Claud Gagnon*), Patty Foley (*Lucille Gagnon*), Patrick Gorman (*Eugene Kurtz*), Mark Watters (*Carlysle Bandy*), Ka Vundla
<u>D:</u> Raju Patel **SCR:** Jeffrey Sneller & Michael Harry **PHOTOG:** Jesus Elizondo
MUSIC: Arlon Ober

Standard thriller: Drought-maddened baboons attack humans

In the Spirit
1990, (USA), color, 94 mins.
W: Jeannie Berlin, Olympia Dukakis, Peter Falk, Elaine May, Marlo Thomas, Melanie Griffith, Michael Emil, Christopher Durang, Chad Burto, Thurn Hoffman, Laurie Jones
D: Sandra Seacat **SCR:** Jeannie Berlin & Laurie Jones **MUSIC:** Patrick Williams
Bizarre comedy-thriller: Two women summon supernatural powers to trap prostitute's killer

In the Steel Net of Dr. Mabuse
1961, (W. Ger-It-Fr), CCC-Omnia/Criterion-S.P.A. Cinematgrafica/ 20th-Fox, b&w, 91 mins.
W: Gert Frobe *(Insp. Lohmann)*, Wolfgang Preiss *(Dr. Mabuse)*, Lex Barker, Daliah Lavi, Werner Peters, Fausto Tozzi
P: Artur Brauner **D:** Harald Reinl **SCR:** Ladislas Fodor & Marc Boehm
*released in USA (1962) as **The Return of Dr. Mabuse**, A.k.a. **Phantom Fiend** and **The FBI vs. Dr. Mabuse***
Standard thriller: Criminal genius engineers mayhem

In the Toils of the Blackmailer
1913, (GB), Barker, b&w, 1,170 ft. (356.6m)
W: Peter Gale *(Dick)*, Blanche Forsythe *(Lydia)*, Rolf Leslie *(Mr. Morton)*, May Morton *(Miss Morton)*, Rachel de Solla *(Mrs. Morton)*, Edward Burnham *(Harry)*
D: Alexander Butler **STORY:** Rowland Talbot
Standard crime-thriller: Reformed crook saves rich man from blackmailing woman

In the Toils of the Temptress
see George Barnwell, the London Apprentice

In the Wake of a Stranger
1959, (GB), Crest/Butcher, b&w, 64 mins.
W: Tony Wright *(Tom Cassidy)*, Shirley Eaton *(Joyce Edwards)*, Danny Green *(Barnes)*, Willoughby Goddard *(Shafto)*, Peter Sinclair *(The Captain)*, Harry H. Corbett *(McCabe)*, Alun Owen *(Ferris)*, Tom Bowman *(Spike)*
P: Jacques de Lane Lea & Jon Pennington **D:** David Eady **SCR:** John Tully, from a novel by Ian Stuart Black
Standard crime-thriller: Liverpool schoolmistress helps framed sailor escape murder charge

In the Year 2889
1968, (USA), Azalea/AIP, color, 69 mins.

W: Paul Petersen *(Steve)*, Charla Doherty *(Joanna)*, Quinn O'Hara *(Jada)*, Neil Fletcher *(The Captain)*, Max Anderson, Hugh Feagin, Billy Thurman, Byron Lord
P & D: Larry Buchanan **SCR:** Harold Hoffman **PHOTOG:** Robert C. Jessup **SPCL-FX:** Jack Bennett
*TV retitle, **Year 2889***
*Minor SF-thriller, remake of **Day the World Ended** (1955): After nuke war, mixed group stranded in mountain haven*

Intimate Relations
1953, (GB), Advance/Adelphi, b&w, 86 mins.
W: Harold Warrender *(George)*, Elsy Albiin *(Madeleine)*, Marian Spencer *(Yvonne)*, Ruth Dunning *(Leonie)*, Russell Enoch *(Michael)*
P: David Dent **D & SCR:** Charles Frank, from Jean Cocteau's play *Les Parents Terribles*
reissued (Grand Nat'l) 1956
Standard thriller: Invalid's husband learns his son loves his own ex-mistress

The Intimate Stranger
1956, (GB), Merton Park/Anglo-Amalgamated, b&w, 95 mins.
W: Richard Basehart *(Reggie Wilson)*, Mary Murphy *(Evelyn Stewart)*, Constance Cummings *(Kay Wallace)*, Roger Livesey *(Ben Case)*, Mervyn Johns *(Ernest Chapple)*, Vernon Greeves *(George Mearns)*, Faith Brook *(Lesley Wilson)*, David Lodge *(Sgt. Brown)*, Andre Mikhelson *(Steve Vadney)*, Basil Dignam *(Dr. Gray)*, David Hurst, Grace Denbeigh-Russell, Joseph Losey [unbilled]
P: Alec C. Snowden *(Joseph Losey)* **D:** Joseph Walton [Joseph Losey] **SCR:** Peter Howard [Howard Koch], from his novel *Pay the Piper* **PHOTOG:** Gerald Gibbs **MUSIC:** Richard Taylor
*USA retitle, **Finger of Guilt***
Off-beat thriller: Movie producer victimized by mysterious young woman

Into the Badlands
1991, (USA), Ogiens-Kane/USA-TV, cable, color, 95 mins.
W: Bruce Dern, Mariel Hemingway, Helen Hunt, Lisa Pelikan, Dylan McDermott, Andrew Robinson, Adan Sanchez, Michael J. Metzger, Jerry Gardner, Glen Burns, Steve Tyler, Reynaldo Cantu, Oryan Walsky, Loren Haynes, Steven Schwartz-Hartley, Royce O'Donnell, Dick Beebe
D: Sam Pillsbury **TELEPLAY:** Dick Beebe, Marjorie David, & Gordon Dawson **PHOTOG:** Johnny E. Jensen **MUSIC:** John Debney
TVM, standard thriller: Gothic trilogy of Old West tales

Into the Fire
1987, (Can), color, 93 mins.

Invasion of the Body Snatchers: KEVIN MCCARTHY

W: Susan Anspach, Olivia d'Abo, Art Hindle
D: Graeme Campbell
A.k.a. *Legend of Wolf Lodge*
Standard thriller: Murder-sex triangle in Canadian wilds

Into the Light
1916, (GB), British Oak/New Agency, b&w, 1,120 ft. (341.4m)
D: Ethyle Batley
Standard crime-thriller: Lieutenant's wife develops amnesia when she is attacked while returning jewels stolen by her brother

Into the Darkness
1986, (USA), color, 90 mins.
W: Donald Pleasence, Ronald Lacey
Minor thriller: Mad killer stalks fashion models

L'Intrigo (Intrigue)
1964, (It/Fr/US), Univ, color, 97 mins.
W: Shirley Jones, Rossano Brazzi, George Sanders
D: Vittorio Sala & George Marshall
A.k.a. *Dark Purpose*
Standard thriller

Intrigue
1947, (USA), UA, b&w, 90 mins.
W: George Raft, June Havoc Helena Carter, Tom Tully, Marvin Miller, Dan Seymour, Philip Ahn
D: Edwin L. Marin
Standard thriller: Ex-military man exposes Shanghai crime ring

Intrigue (1964)
see *L'Intrigo*

Introductions Extraordinary
1906, (GB), R.W. Paul, b&w, 300 ft. (91.4m)
D: J.H. Martin
Standard fantasy short: Hotel guests get bags mixed, clothes come to life

The Intruder
1981, (Can), Hazelton, color
W: Pita Oliver (*Chandler*), Gerard Jordan (*Charles*), Trudy Weiss (*Jill*), Jimmy Douglas, Tony Fletcher, John Bayliss, Rocco Bellusci, Gordon Thompson, Robert Galbraith, Nancy Kerr, Kay Hawtrey, Bob Lem
D: David F. Eustace   SCR: Norman Fox   MUSIC: FM
Minor SF: Space alien gives boy strange power

Intruder
1988, (USA), color, 90 mins.
W: Elizabeth Cox, Renee Estevez, Alvy Moore
D: Scott Spiegel   SCR: Lawrence Bender
Standard thriller: Psycho stalks all-night convenience store

The Intruder Within
1981, (USA), ABC-TV, color, 94 mins.
W: Chad Everett (*Jake*), Jennifer Warren (*Colette*), Joseph Bottoms (*Scott*), James Hayden (*Harry*), Mary Ann McDonald (*Wilma*), Lynda Mason Green (*Robyn*), Michael Hogan (*Chili*), Rockne Tarkington (*Mark*), Matt Craven (*Phil*), Ed LaPlante (*Ed*), Paul Larson, Mickey Gilbert, Joe Finnegan
D: Peter Carter   TELEPLAY: Ed Waters   PHOTOG: James Pergola   SPCL-FX: Don Powers   MUSIC: Gil Melle
A.k.a. *Panic Offshore*
TVM, standard SF-horror: Oil rig workers find prehistoric monsters

Invader
1991, (USA), color, 95 mins.
W: Hans Bachman, A. Thomas Smith, Rich Foucheux, John Cooke, Robert Diedermann, Allison Sheehy, Ralph Bluemke
D: Phillip Cook
Standard SF-horror: Reporter meets bloodthirsty space aliens

The Invader
1996, (USA), color, 97 mins.
W: Sean Young, Ben Cross, Daniel Baldwin Ben Cross, Sean Young, Daniel Baldwin, Nick Mancuso
Made-for-Video, standard SF-horror: Pregnant woman carries space-alien spawn

The Invaders
see *49th Parallel*

Invaders from Mars
1953, (USA), Edward L. Alperson/20th-Fox, color, 82 mins.
W: Jimmy Hunt, Arthur Franz (*Kelston*), Helena Carter (*Pat*), Hillary Brooke, Leif Erickson, Bill Phipps, Morris Ankrum, Douglas Kennedy, Max Wagner, Walter Sande, Janine Perreau, Milburn Stone
D: William Cameron Menzies   SCR: Richard Blake   PHOTOG: John F. Seitz   MUSIC: Raoul Kraushaar
"...an absolutely terrifying experience, and one of the few fantasy works this author does not recommend for younger viewers. Using the frightening images and sounds that populate a nightmare, director William Cameron

Menzies turns a child's parents against him and strikes an immediate chord...'Invaders from Mars' stands as one of the few genuine 'horror' films ever made"—Gary Gerani, "The Space Monster Book—Chapter Five: Dehumanization," Monster Fantasy, Vol. 1, No. 4 (August, 1975), p. 35
Classic SF-horror: Boy detects evil space aliens

Invaders from Mars
1986, (USA), Golan-Globus/Cannon, color, 94 mins.
W: Karen Black (*Linda*), Louise Fletcher (*Mrs. McKelch*), Hunter Carson (*David Gardner*), Timothy Bottoms (*George Gardner*), Laraine Newman (*Ellen Gardner*), James Karen (*Gen. Wilson*), Bud Cort, Jim (*Jimmy*) Hunt, Christopher Allport, Eric Pierpoint, Ken Bates, Donald Hotton, Steve Lambert
D: Tobe Hooper   SCR: Dan O'Bannon & Don Jakoby, from a screenplay by Richard Blake   PHOTOG: Daniel Pearl   SPCL VS-FX: John Dykstra   MUSIC: Christopher Young
Elaborate but tepid remake of SF-horror classic: Boy detects alien invasion

Invasion (1963)
see *Invasione*

Invasion
1965, (GB), Anglo-Amalgamated/AIP, b&w, 82 mins.
W: Edward Judd (*Dr. Vernon*), Valerie Gearon (*Dr. Claire Harlan*), Yoko Tani (*The Lystrian Leader*), Lyndon Brook (*Brian Carter*), Tsai Chin (*Nurse Lim*), Eric Young (*The Lystrian Man*), Barrie Ingham (*Maj. Muncaster*), Anthony Sharp (*Lawrence Blackburn*), Glyn Houston (*Sgt. Draycott*), Jean Lodge (*Barbara Gough*), Peter Sinclair (*Old Joe*), Diane Aubrey, Cali Raia
P: Jack Greenwood   D: Alan Bridges   SCR: Roger Marshall   STORY: Robert Holmes   PHOTOG: James Wilson   MUSIC: Bernard Ebbinghouse
Unusual SF-thriller: Hospital workers meet space aliens

Invasion
1969, (Argent), color
Minor SF-thriller

Invasion (1997)
see *Robin Cook's Invasion*

La Invasion de los Vampiros (The Invasion of the Vampires)
1962, (Mex), Azteca/Int'l Sono-Film/AIP, b&w, 93 mins.
W: Carlos Agosti (*Count Frankenhausen*), Erna Martha Bauman, Tito Junco, Rafael Del Rio, Fernando Soto
P: Raphael Grovas   WRIT & D: Miguel Morayta   PHOTOG: Raul Martinez Solares   MUSIC: Luis Hernandez Breton
Standard horror-thriller: Vampire plots Undead plague

Invasione (Invasion)
1963, (It), color
D: Camillo Bazzoni
Minor SF-thriller

Invasion Earth: The Aliens are Here
1987, (USA), color, 84 mins.
W: Janice Fabian, Christian Lee
D: George Maitland
Minor monster-movie spoof: Insectoid projectionist controls minds of movie audience

Invasion Earth 2150 A.D.
see *Daleks' Invasion Earth 2150 A.D.*

Invasion Force
see *Hangar 18*

Invasion from Inner Earth
1974, (Can), color
W: Nick Holt, Paul Bentzen, Debbie Pick
Minor SF-thriller: Scientists seek source of death ray

Invasion of the Animal People
see *Rymdinvasion I Lappland*

Invasion of the Astro-Monster
see *Monster Zero*

Invasion of the Bee Girls
1973, (USA), Dimension, color, 85 mins.
W: William Smith, Anitra Ford, Victoria Vetri, Anna Aries, Cliff Os-mond, Wright King, Ben Hammer, Sid Kaiser, Beverly Powers, Andre Phillippe, Katie A. Saylor, William Keller, Tom Pittman, Cliff Emmich, Susie Player, Steve Lefkowitz, Don Hall, Lloyd McLinn, Danielle Dupont, Amanda Jefferies, Mickey Caruso, Herb Robbins, Gregg White, John Nelson, F. Stewart Wilson, Dick Murphy, Mary Sweeney, Sharon Madigan, Renee Bond, Cathy Hilton, Al Bordiggi, Jack Perkins
D: Denis Sanders   SCR: Nicholas Meyer   PHOTOG: Gary Graver   SPCL-FX: Joe Lombardi   MUSIC: Charles Bernstein
A.k.a. *Graveyard Tramps*
Standard eroto-SF spoof: Mutated human females cause sex exertion deaths

Invasion of the Blood Farmers

1971, (USA), Cinemation, color, 84 mins

W: Cynthia Fleming (*Onhorrid*), Norman Kelly (*Roy*), Tanna Hunter (*Jenny*), Bruce Detrick (*Don*), Frank Iovieno (*The Chief*), Jack Neubeck, Paul Craig Jennings

P & D: Ed Adlum **SCR:** Ed Kelleher & Ed Adlum

Minor horror-satire: Druid cult seeks rare blood type to keep queen alive

Invasion of the Body Snatchers

1956, (USA), AA, b&w, 80 mins.

W: Kevin McCarthy (*Dr. Miles Bennell*), Dana Wynter (*Becky Driscoll*), King Donovan (*Jack Belicec*), Carolyn Jones (*Theodora Belicec*), Larry Gates (*Dr. Daniel Kaufman*), Virginia Christine (*Aunt Wilma*), Jean Willes (*Sally*), Sam Peckinpah (*The Meter Reader*), Bobby Clark (*Jimmy Grimaldi*), Tom Fadden (*Uncle Ira*), Ralph Dumke (*The Sheriff*), Whit Bissell (*The Psychiatrist*), Beatrice Maude, Dabbs Greer, Guy Way, Kenneth Patterson, Eileen Stevens, Richard Deacon, J. Pat O'Malley, Jean Andren, Everett Glass, Marie Selland, Harry Vejar, Guy Rennie

P: Walter Wanger **D:** Don Siegel **SCR:** Daniel Mainwaring, Sam Peckinpah (uncredited), from Jack Finney's novel *The Body Snatchers* **PHOTOG:** Ellsworth Fredericks **SPCL-FX:** Milt Rice **MUSIC:** Carmen Dragon

orig. to be titled Sleep No More, A.k.a. They Came from Another World

"Loss of individuality is the ultimate horror...Siegel captures a sense of subtle terror more devastating than a thousand flying saucer attacks. He assaults the viewer directly on everyday ground, using emotion to create a personal terror. It is not so important that people are being 'taken over' by grotesque seed pods from outer space; what lingers in the viewer's mind is the terrible fear of abandoning our humanity and capacity to love and be loved. Human beings can afford the loss of property, possessions, even essential pride, but they cannot survive without their souls"—Gary Gerani, "The Space Monster Book—Chapter Five: Dehumanization," Monster Fantasy, Vol. 1, No. 4 (August, 1975), pp. 33-34

Classic SF-horror: Earthlings supplanted by space aliens

Invasion of the Body Snatchers

1978, (USA), Solofilm/UA, color, 114 mins.

W: Donald Sutherland (*Matthew Bennell*), Brooke Adams (*Elizabeth Driscoll*), Jeff Goldblum (*Jack Bellicec*), Veronica Cartwright (*Nancy Bellicec*), Art Hindle (*Geoffrey*), Leonard Nimoy (*Dr. David Kibner*), Lelia Goldoni (*Katherine*), Kevin McCarthy (*The Running Man*), Don Siegel (*The Taxi Driver*), Tom Luddy (*Ted Hendley*), Stan Ritchie (*Stan*), David Fisher (*Mr. Gianni*), Tom Dahlgren (*The Detective*), Maurice Argent (*The Chef*), Garry Goodrow (*Boccardo*), Jerry Walter (*The Restaurant Owner*), Sam Conti (*The Street Barker*), Joe Bellan (*The Beggar*), Wood Moy (*Mr. Tong*), R. Wong (*Mrs. Tong*), Sam Hiona (*Policeman #1*), Lee McVeigh (*Policeman #2*), Lee Mines (*The School Teacher*), Albert Nalbandian (*The Rodent Man*), Robert Duvall

P: Robert H. Solo **D:** Philip Kaufman **SCR:** W.D. Richter, from Jack Finney's novel *The Body Snatchers* **PHOTOG:** Michael Chapman **SPCL-FX:** Dell Rheaume & Russ Hessey **MUSIC:** Denny Zeitlin

Standard SF-horror, graphic remake of 1956 classic: San Franciscans supplanted by space aliens. cf. The Body Snatchers

Invasion of the Body Stealers

see The Body Stealers

Invasion of the Flesh Hunters

see Cannibal in the Streets

Invasion of the Girl Snatchers

1973, (USA), L&L Co.-Atlantis/Jeffrey C. Hogue/Majestic Int'l, color, 94 mins.

W: Elizabeth Rush, Ele Grigsby, David Roster, Paul Lenzi, Charles Rubin, Hugh Smith, Harlo Cayse, Ruth Horn, Harold Thom, Dodd Harris III, Paul Urbahns, James DeWitt, Pepper Thurston, Ellen Tripp, James Rueckert, McCain Jeeves, Lee Boylan, Barbara Jones

D & PHOTOG: Lee Jones **SCR:** Phineas T. Pinkham & Carla Rueckert **SPCL-FX:** James Barnhouse

Minor SF-sleaze: Yokels meet body-snatching space aliens

Invasion of the Hell Creatures

see Invasion of the Saucer Men

Invasion of the Neptune Men

1962, (Jap), Toei/Medallion/Manley-TV, b&w

W: Shinjiro Ebara, Shinichi "Sonny" Chiba

P: Hiroshi Okawa **D:** Koji Ota **SCR:** Shin Morita

Minor SF-thriller: Youngsters attacked by space creatures. Original title: Uchu Kaisoku-Sen

Invasion of Planet X

see Monster Zero

Invasion of the Saucer Men

1957, (USA), Malibu/AIP, b&w, 69 mins.

W: Gloria Castillo (*Joan Hayden*), Steve Terrell (*Johnny Carter*), Frank Gorshin, Raymond Hatton, Lyn Osborn, Russ Bender, Jimmy Pickford, Douglas Henderson, Ed Nelson, Sam Buffington, Jason Johnson, Don Shelton, Scott Peters, Jan Englund, Kelly Thordsen, Patti Lawler, Bob Einer, Calvin Booth, Roy Darmour, Orv Mohler, Audrey Conti, Jim Bridges, Joan Dupuis, Buddy Mason, Dean Neville, Angelo Rossitto, Edward Peter

---

Gibbons, Floyd Dixon

P: Robert J. Gurney Jr. & James H. Nicholson **D:** Edward L. Cahn **SCR:** Robert J. Gurney Jr. & Al Martin, from orig. story by Paul Fairman **PHOTOG:** Fred West **SPCL-FX:** Howard Anderson & Alex Weldon **MUSIC:** Ronald Stein

orig. to be titled Spacemen Saturday Night, GB retitle, Invasion of the Hell Creatures, orig. co-billed with I Was a Teenage Werewolf, reissued 1961

blurb: "CREEPING HORROR...From the depths of time and space!"

Standard SF-thriller-comedy: Space aliens invade Lover's Lane. cf. The Eye Creatures

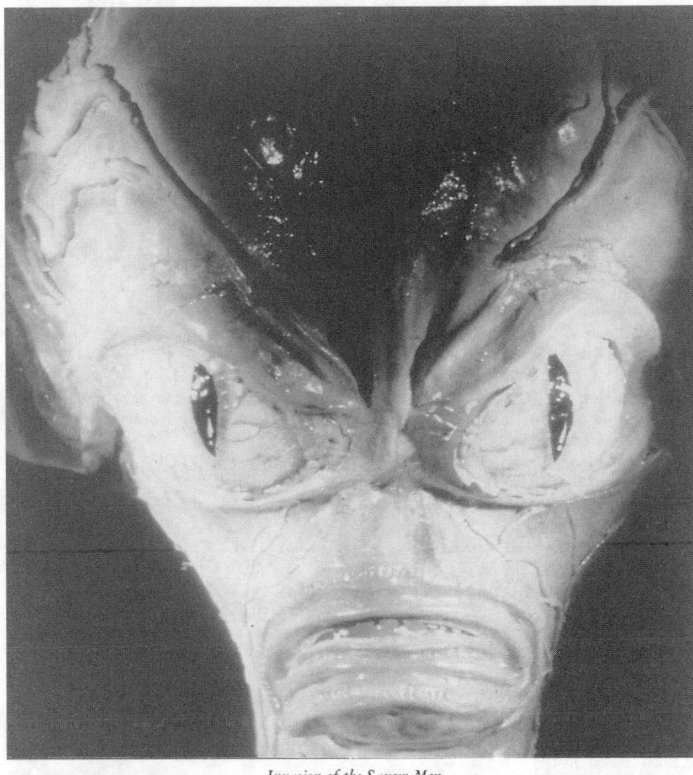

Invasion of the Saucer Men

Invasion of the Star Creatures

1962, (USA), Alta Vista/AIP, b&w, 70 mins

W: Bob Ball, Frankie Ray, Gloria Victor, Dolores Reed, Mark Ferris, Bruno Ve Sota

P: Berj Hagopian **D:** Bruno Ve Sota **SCR:** Jonathan Haze - based on his original 'Monsters from Nicholson Mesa

Released with The Brain that Wouldn't Die A.k.a. The Star Creatures

Minor SF-comedy: Intelligent vegetables invade Earth

The Invasion of the Vampires

see La Invasion de los Vampiros

Invasion of the Zombies

see The Saint vs. the Zombies

Invasion Sinitestra (Sinister Invasion)

1968, (USA-Mex), Azteca/Col, color, 90 mins.

W: Boris Karloff, Maura Monti, Enrique Guzman

P: Luis Enrique Vergara **D:** Juan Ibanez & Jack Hill **SCR:** Karl Schanzer & Luis Enrique Vergara

USA retitle, The Incredible Invasion video title, The Torture Zone, A.k.a. Alien Terror

Minor SF-horror (Karloff's last film): Invisible space aliens take possession of human bodies

Invasion U.S.A.

1952, (USA), American/Col, b&w, 74 mins.

W: Gerald Mohr, Peggie Castle, Robert Bice, Dan O'Herlihy, Wade Crosby, Tom Kennedy, Erik Blythe, Aram Katcher, Phyllis Coates, Edward G. Robinson Jr., Noel Neill

P: Albert Zugsmith & Robert Smith **D:** Alfred E. Green **SCR:** Robert Smith **PHOTOG:** John L. Russell **SPCL-FX:** Jack Rabin **MUSIC:** Albert Glasser

blurb: "...see the mutant horror of the H-bomb!"

Standard SF-thriller: Hypnotist shows barroom patrons horrendous future

Gli Invasori (The Invaders)

1961, (It-Fr), AIP, color, 81 mins.

W: Cameron Mitchell, Alice Kessler, Ellen Kessler, Francoise Christophe, Giorgio Giovannini

D: Mario Bava **SCR:** Oreste Biancoli, Mario Bava & Piero Pierotti

A.k.a. **Fury of the Vikings** and **Erik the Conqueror**
Minor adventure-thriller: Viking avenges massacre

El Invencible Hombre Invisible (The Invincible Invisible Man)

1964, (It-Sp-W. Ger), K-tel, color, 90 mins
<u>W:</u> Dean Jones
<u>D:</u> Antonio Margheriti (Anthony Dawson) <u>SCR:</u> M. Eller & Luis Marquina
USA retitle, **Mr. Superinvisible**
Minor SF-adventure: Invisibility formula causes confusion

Inventing Trouble

1915, (GB), Cricks/DFSA, b&w, 589 ft. (179.5m)
<u>D:</u> W.P. Kellino
<u>STORY:</u> Reuben Gillmer
Standard comedy-fantasy: Inventor of labor-saving devices eaten by prehistoric monster

An Invention for Destruction

see **The Diabolical Invention**

The Inventor Crazybrains and His Wonderful Airship

see **Le Dirigeable Fantastique ou le Cauchemar d'un Inventeur**

Invigorating Electricity

1910, (GB), Hepworth, b&w, 300 ft. (91.4m)
<u>D:</u> Lewin Fitzhamon
Standard comedy-fantasy: Electrified workman shocks spinster, cyclist, cook

The Invincible Barbarian

1985, (USA-It), Leader/American Nat'l, color, 92 mins.
<u>W:</u> David Jenkins (*Gunan*), Diana Roy, Peter McCoy, Marion Lang, Sabrina Siani, Emile Messina, Philip Caradine, Rita Silva, Howard Landsdowna, Herald Fry, Henry Mason
<u>D:</u> Frank Shannon <u>STORY & SCR:</u> Peter Lombard <u>PHOTOG:</u> Atherton Rawnsley <u>MUSIC:</u> Roberto Pregadio
Minor "Sword & Sandal": Boys rescued by Amazons

The Invincible Brothers Maciste

1964, (It), color, 87 mins.
<u>W:</u> Richard Lloyd, Claudia Lange, Tony Freeman
<u>D:</u> Robert Mauri
A.k.a. **Invincible Gladiators**. *Minor "Sword & Sandal": Hercules' sons rescue prince's bride from evil queen*

The Invincible Gladiator

1963, (It-Sp), color, 96 mins.
<u>W:</u> Richard Harrison, Isabel Corey, Livio Lorenzon
<u>D:</u> Frank Gregory
Minor "Sword & Sandal": Warrior aids boy-king

Invincible Gladiators

see **The Invincible Brothers Maciste**

Invisible: The Chronicles of Benjamin Knight

1993, (USA), color, 80 mins.
<u>W:</u> Jennifer Nash, Michael DellaFemina, Curt Lowens, Aharon Ipale, David Kaufman, Alan Oppenheimer
<u>D:</u> Jack Ersgard <u>SCR:</u> Earl Kenton
Standard SF: Lab mishap renders scientist invisible

Invisibility

1909, (GB), Hepworth, b&w, 650 ft. (198.1m)
<u>W:</u> Lewin Fitzhamon
<u>D:</u> Cecil Hepworth & Lewin Fitzhamon
Standard fantasy short: Magic powder makes man invisible

Invisible Adversaries

1977, (W. Ger), color, 112 mins.
<u>W:</u> Suanne Widl, Peter Weibel, Dr. Josef Plavee, Monika Helfer-Friedrich
<u>D:</u> Valie Export
Minor SF-thriller: Woman photographer uncovers space-alien plot

Invisible Agent

1942, (USA), Frank Lloyd Prods./Univ, b&w, 79 mins
<u>W:</u> Jon Hall (*Frank Raymond*), Ilona Massey (*Maria Sorenson*), Peter Lorre (*Baron Ikito*), J. Edward Bromberg (*Karl Heiser*), Sir Cedric Hardwicke (*Conrad Stauffer*), Holmes Herbert, Matt Willis, Albert Bassermann, Keye Luke, John Litel, Philip Van Zandt
<u>D:</u> Edwin L. Marin <u>SCR:</u> Curt Siodmak, suggested by H.G. Wells' novel *The Invisible Man* <u>PHOTOG:</u> Les White <u>SPCL-FX:</u> John P. Fulton <u>MUSIC DIR:</u> H.J. Salter
Standard thriller: Grandson of **Invisible Man** *aids Allies in World War II*

The Invisible Asset

1963, (GB), Merton Park/Anglo-Amalgamated, b&w, 31 mins.
<u>W:</u> Kenneth J. Warren (*Sam Warren*), Ronald Leigh-Hunt (*Jimmy Donovan*), Annette Carrell (*Joyce Warren*), Philip Latham (*The Official Receiver*), Gabriella Licudi (*Beryl*), John Wentworth (*The Registrar*)
<u>P:</u> Jack Greenwood <u>D:</u> Norman Harrison <u>STORY:</u> James Eastwood, from a novel by Edgar Lustgarten
Standard short crime-thriller: Bankrupt restaurant owner embezzles

The Invisible Avenger

1957, (USA), Rep, b&w, 60 mins.
<u>W:</u> Richard Derr (*Lamont Cranston*), Mark Daniels, Helen Westcott
<u>D:</u> John Sledge & James Wong Howe <u>SCR:</u> George Bellak & Betty Jeffries
reissued (1962, with additional footage) as **Bourbon St. Shadows**
Standard "Shadow" thriller: Sleuth probes jazzman's murder

The Invisible Boy

1956, (USA), MGM, b&w, 90 mins.
<u>W:</u> Richard Eyer, Philip Abbott, Diane Brewster, Dennis McCarthy, Harold J. Stone, Robert H. Harris, Than Wyenn, Gage Clarke, Alexander Lockwood, John O'Malley, Michael Miller, Jefferson Dudley Searles, Alfred Linder, Ralph Votrian, Robby the Robot
<u>P:</u> Nicholas Nayfack <u>D:</u> Herman Hoffman <u>SCR:</u> Cyril Hume, from a story by Edmund Cooper <u>PHOTOG:</u> Harold Wellman <u>MUSIC:</u> Les Baxter
Juvenile SF-thriller: Computer seeks world domination

The Invisible Button

1908, (GB), Walturdaw, b&w, 265 ft. (80.1m)
<u>D:</u> Dave Aylott
Minor fantasy short: Quarrelsome man vanishes by touching magic button

The Invisible Creature

see **The House on Marsh Road**

The Invisible Dead

1970, (It-Sp), color, 90 mins.
<u>W:</u> Howard Vernon, Britt Carva
<u>D:</u> Jesus Franco
A.k.a. **Orloff Against the Invisible Man**.
Minor thriller: Scientist creates invisible man

The Invisible Dr. Mabuse

1961, (W. Ger), CCC-Omnia/Thunder Pictures, b&w, 89 mins.
<u>W:</u> Lex Barker, Karin Dor, Siegfried Lowitz, Alain Dijon, Wolfgang Preiss, Rudolf Fernau
<u>P:</u> Artur Brauner <u>D:</u> Harald Reinl <u>SCR:</u> Ladislas Fodor
A.k.a. **The Invisible Horror**
Standard thriller: Master criminal returns to terrorize

The Invisible Dog

1909, (GB), Urban, b&w, 355 ft. (108.2m)
<u>D:</u> Walter R. Booth
Minor fantasy short: Invisible dog steals sausages

The Invisible Fear

1921, (USA), Anita Stewart Prods./First Nat'l, b&w, 6 reels (5,800 ft./1767.8m); later cut to 5 reels (4,900 ft./1493.5m)
<u>W:</u> Anita Stewart (*Sylvia Langdon*), Walter McGrail (*Arthur Comstock*), Allan Forrest (*Bentley Arnold*), Hamilton Morse (*Marshall Arnold*), Estelle Evans (*Mrs. Marshall Arnold*), George Kuwa (*Nagi*), Edward Hunt (*The Butler*), Ogden Crane (*John Randall*)
<u>D:</u> Edwin Carewe <u>SCR:</u> Madge Power <u>STORY:</u> Hampton Del Ruth <u>PHOTOG:</u> Robert B. Kurrle
Standard melodrama: Woman believes she has murdered

The Invisible Ghost

1941, (USA), Banner/Mono/Astor, b&w, 62 mins.
<u>W:</u> Bela Lugosi (*Kessler*), Polly Ann Young (*Virginia Kessler*), John McGuire (*Ralph Dickson/Paul Dickson*), Clarence Muse (*Evans*), Terry Walker (*Cecile Mannix*), Jack Mulhall (*Tim*), Betty Compson (*Mrs. Kessler*), Ernie Adams (*Jules Mason*), George Pembroke (*Williams*), Ottola Nesmith (*Mrs. Mason*), Fred Kelsey (*Ryan*)
<u>P:</u> Sam Katzman <u>D:</u> Joseph H. Lewis <u>STORY & SCR:</u> Helen Martin & Al Martin <u>PHOTOG:</u> Marcel LePicard & Harvey Gould
Minor thriller: Doctor has trances, commits murders

The Invisible Horror

see **The Invisible Dr. Mabuse**

Invisible Informer

1946, (USA), Rep, b&w, 57 mins
<u>W:</u> Linda Stirling, William Henry, Adele Mara, Gerald Mohr
Standard thriller

Invisible Invaders

1959, (USA), Premium/UA, b&w, 67 mins.
<u>W:</u> John Agar (*Maj. Bruce Jay*), Jean Byron (*Phyllis Penner*), Philip Tonge (*Dr. Adam Penner*), Robert Hutton (*Dr. John Lamont*), John Carradine (*Carl Noymans*), Hal Torey (*The Farmer*), Paul Langton (*Gen. Stone*), Eden Hartford (*The WAAF Sec'y*)
<u>D:</u> Edward L. Cahn <u>SCR:</u> Samuel Newman <u>PHOTOG:</u> Maury Gertsman <u>SPCL-FX:</u> Roger George <u>MUSIC:</u> Paul Dunlap
Standard SF-thriller: Alien oppressors inhabit corpses

The Invisible Kid

1988, (USA), Elysian Pictures/Taurus, color, 98 mins.
<u>W:</u> Jay Underwood (*Grover Dunn*), Chynna Phillips (*Cindy Moore*), Wally Ward

(Milton McClane), Brother Theodore (Dr. Theodore), Mike Genovese (Officer Chuck Malone), Nicholas deToth (Donny Zanders), Thomas Cross (Officer Terell), Karen Black (Mom), John Madden Towey (Principal Baxter) Jan King
WRIT & D: Avery Crouse **PHOTOG:** Michael Barnard **MUSIC:** Steve Hunter & Jan King
Minor comedy-fantasy: Nerd vanishes

Invisible Killer
1940, (USA), PRC, b&w, 61 mins.
W: Grace Bradley, Roland Drew, William Newell
D: Sherman Scott [Sam Newfield] **SCR:** Joseph O'Donnell
Minor thriller: Unknown murderer uses sound to kill

The Invisible Man
1933, (USA), Univ, b&w, 80 mins.
W: Claude Rains (Jack Griffin, the Invisible Man), Gloria Stuart (Flora Cranley), William Harrigan (Dr. Kemp), Una O'Connor (Mrs. Hall), Henry Travers (Dr. Cranley), Holmes Herbert (The Chief of Police), Forrester Harvey (Mr. Hall), E.E. Clive (Jaffers), Dudley Digges (The Chief of Detectives), Harry Stubbs (Insp. Bird), Merle Tottenham (Milly), Donald Stuart (Insp. Lane)
P: Carl Laemmle Jr. **D:** James Whale **SCR:** R.C. Sherriff, from H.G. Wells' novel **PHOTOG:** Arthur Edeson & John Mescall **SPCL-FX:** John P. Fulton
"The Invisible Man lent itself particularly well to film treatment; the special trick effects of John P. Fulton would have dazzled pioneer trickster Melies"—Carlos Clarens, An Illustrated History of the Horror Film
"...the moment when the Man (Claude Rains) unwraps his bandaged face and reveals—nothing, is a genuine touch of the macabre"—Ivan Butler, The Horror Film
Classic SF-thriller: Scientist's invisibility drug causes madness

The Invisible Man: CLAUDE RAINS AND GLORIA STUART

The Invisible Man
1975, (USA), Univ/NBC-TV, color, 74 mins.
W: David McCallum (Daniel Weston), Jackie Cooper (Carlson), Melinda Fee (Kate Weston), Alex Henteloff (Steiner), Henry Darrow (Dr. Nick Maggio), Arch Johnson (Gen.Turner), John McLiam (The Blind Man), Jane Goodnow Gillett (Janet), Paul Kent (The Security Chief), Ted Gehring (The Gate Guard)
D: Robert Michael Lewis **TELEPLAY:** Steve Bochco **STORY:** Steve Bochco & Harve Bennett, based on H.G. Wells' novel
TVM, standard SF-thriller: Scientist struggles to protect invisibility formula

An Invisible Man Goes on the Town
1933, (Ger), b&w
W: Harry Piel
D: Harry Piel
Standard SF-comedy: Scientist creates invisibility device

The Invisible Maniac
1990, (USA), color, 87 mins.
W: Noel Peters, Melissa Moore, Robert R. Ross Jr., Shannon Wilsey, Rod Sweiter
D: Rif Coogan
Minor SF-comedy: Teen becomes invisible

The Invisible Man Returns
1940, (USA), Univ, b&w, 81 mins.
W: Vincent Price (Geoffrey Radcliffe), Sir Cedric Hardwicke (Richard Cobb), John Sutton (Dr. Frank Griffin), Nan Grey (Helen Manson), Cecil Kellaway, Forrester Harvey, Frances Robinson, Alan Napier, Ivan Simpson, Edward Fielding, Harry Stubbs
D: Joe May **SCR:** Chester Cole & Curt Siodmak, from an orig. story by Joe May & Curt Siodmak **PHOTOG:** Milton Krasner **SPCL-FX:** John P. Fulton
"...briskly directed by Joe May with a characteristic German edge"—John Baxter, Science Fiction in the Cinema
Standard SF-thriller: Invisibility drug helps innocent man escape prison

The Invisible Man's Revenge
1944, (USA), Univ, b&w, 77 mins.
W: Jon Hall (Robert Griffin), John Carradine (Dr. Drury), Evelyn Ankers (Julie Herrick), Alan Curtis (Mark Foster), Gale Sondergaard (Irene, Lady Herrick), Lester Matthews (Sir Jasper Herrick), Leon Errol (Herbert), Doris Lloyd (Maud), Ian Wolfe (Feeney), Halliwell Hobbes (Cleghorn), Leyland Hodgson (Sir Frederick Travers), Billy Bevan (The Sergeant), Skelton Knaggs, Grey Shadow
D: Ford Beebe **SCR:** Bertram Millhauser, suggested by H.G. Wells' novel The Invisible Man **PHOTOG:** Milton Krasner **SPCL-FX:** John P. Fulton **MUSIC DIR & SCR:** H.J. Salter
Standard SF-thriller: Man falls victim to experiment

The Invisible Man Returns: CEDRIC HARDWICKE

The Invisible Maniac
1990, (USA), color, 87 mins.
W: Noel Peters, Shannon Wilsey, Melissa Moore, Robert Ross, Rod Sweitzer, Eric Champnella, Kalei Shellabarger, Gail Lyon, Debra Lamb
D & SCR: Rif Coogan
Minor thriller: Voyeur perfects invisibility serum

The Invisible Menace
1938, (USA), WB, b&w, 55 mins.
W: Boris Karloff (Jevries), Marie Wilson (Sally), Eddie Craven (Eddie Pratt), Regis Toomey (Lt. Matthews), Henry Kolker (Col. Hackett), Cy Kendall (Col. Rogers), Charles Trowbridge (Dr. Brooks), Eddie Acuff (Cpl. Sanger), Harland Tucker (Reilly), Phyllis Barry (Aline Dolman), Frank Faylen (Private of the Guard), William Haade, Jack Mower, John Ridgely, Anderson Lawlor, John Harron
D: John Farrow **SCR:** Crane Wilbur, from a play by Ralph Spencer Zink **PHOTOG:** L. William O'Connell
A.k.a. **Without Warning**
Minor thriller: Murder on military base

Invisible Mom
1996, (USA), color, 95 mins.
W: Dee Wallace Stone, Trenton Knight (Josh), Barry Livingston (Prof. Griffin), Russ Tamblyn (Dr. Woorter)
Made-for-Video, minor juvenile SF-comedy: Boy accidentally doses mother with father's invisibility formula

The Invisible Monster
see Beach Girls and the Monster

Invisible Opponent
see Schuss im Morgengrauen

The Invisible Ray
1936, (USA), Univ, b&w, 80 mins.
W: Boris Karloff, Bela Lugosi, Frances Drake, Frank Lawton, Walter Kingsford, Beulah Bondi, Paul Weigel, Daniel Haines, Winter Hall, Inez Seabury, Violet Kemble Cooper, Nydia Westman, Adele St. Maur, George Renavent, Lawrence Stewart, Frank Reicher, Etta McDaniel
P: Edmund Grainger **D:** Lambert Hillyer **SCR:** John Colton **PHOTOG:** George Robinson **SPCL-FX:** John P. Fulton **MUSIC:** Franz Waxman
"More than any other horror film in the Thirties, The Invisible Ray is concerned with the uses and misuses of science, uncannily anticipating the post-World War II science fiction thrillers"—Carlos Clarens, An Illustrated History of the Horror Film
Classic SF-horror: Strange radioactive element contaminates scientist

The Invisble Strangler
1984, (USA), color, 85 mins.
W: Robert Foxworth, Stefanie Powers, Elke Sommer, Marianna Hill, Sue Lyon,

Leslie Parrish
D: John Florea
Standard thriller (filmed in 1976): Deathrow inmate becomes invisible, seeks revenge

The Invisible Terror
1963, (W. Ger), Ben Barry, & Assocs./R&B, color, 91 mins.
W: Ellen Schwiers, Hans von Borsody, Christiane Nielsen, Charles Regnier, Ilse Steppat, Heinrich Gretter, Herbert Stass, Ema Damia, Harry Fuss, Hannes Schmidhauser, Erwin Strahl, Egon Peschka, Bert Klaus, Herta Freund, Herbert Fux, Raul Retzer, Ena Valduga, Josef Menschik, Ivan Desny
D: Raphael Nussbaum **SCR:** Raphael Nussbaum & Wladimir Semitjof, from an Edgar Wallace thriller
Standard mystery: Scientist works on invisibility formula, disappears

The Invisible Wall
1947, (USA), 20th-Fox, b&w, 78 mins.
W: Don Castle, Virginia Christine, Jeff Chandler
Standard thriller

The Invisible Wall: EDWARD KEENE, DON CASTLE, JEFF CHANDLER

The Invisible Web
1921, (USA), Fidelity, b&w
WRIT & D: Beverly C. Rule
Standard thriller: Murder committed; finger of suspicion points at four different people

The Invisible Woman
1940, (USA), Univ, b&w, 72 mins.
W: Virginia Bruce, John Barrymore, Oscar Homolka, John Howard, Charles Ruggles, Margaret Hamilton, Edward S. Brophy, Thurston Hall, Donald MacBride, Shemp Howard, Anne Nagel, Maria Montez
D: A. Edward Sutherland **SCR:** Robert Lees, Fred Rinaldo & Gertrude Purcell, from a story by Curt Siodmak & Joe May **PHOTOG:** Elwood Bredell
SPCL-FX: John P. Fulton
"...polished script scores a variety of points, mainly sexual, with Miss Bruce living in a permanent state of embarrassment as her status changes from visible to invisible and back again"—John Baxter, Science Fiction in the Cinema
Standard SF-comedy: Scientist makes disgruntled model invisible. Original title: **Out of Sight Pilot on Tape**

The Invisible Woman
1983, (USA), NBC-TV/Univ-TV, color, 95 mins.
W: Alexa Hamilton, Bob Denver (*Dr. Dudley Plunkett*), David Doyle (*Neil Gillmore*), Harvey Korman (*Carlisle Edwards*), Jacques Tate (*Dan Williams*), Garrett Morris (*Greg Larkin*), Ron Pallilo (*Spike Mitchell*), George Gobel (*Dr. Farrington*), Jonathan Drake, Patricia Hardy, Anne Haney, Art La Fleur, Mel Stewart
D: Alan J. Levi **PHOTOG:** Dean Cundey
TVM, standard SF-comedy: Cub reporter becomes invisible

Invitation to Hell
1984, (USA), Moonlight/ABC-TV, color, 97 mins.
W: Robert Urich (*Winslow*), Joanna Cassidy (*Patricia Winslow*), Susan Lucci (*Jessica Jones*), Barret Oliver (*Robbie Winslow*), Soleil Moon Frye (*Chrissy Winslow*), Joe Regalbuto (*Tom Peterson*), Patricia (Patty) McCormack (*Mary Peterson*), Kevin McCarthy (*Harry Thompson*), Greg Monaghan (*Pete*), Nicholas Worth (*The Sheriff*), Michael Berryman (*The Valet*), Virginia Vincent (*Grace Henderson*), Lois Hamilton (*Miss Winter*), Bill Erwin, Cal Bartlett, Annemarie McEvoy, Gino DeMauro, Bruce Gray, Jason Presson, John Zenda, Frank Von Zerneck Jr., Billy Beck
D: Wes Craven **TELEPLAY:** Richard Rothstein **PHOTOG:** Dean Cundey
MUSIC: Sylvester LeVay
orig. to be titled **The Club**
TVM, standard fantasy-thriller: Family becomes involved with diabolic country club

The Ipcress File
1965, (GB), Lowndes-Steven/Univ, color, 109 mins.
W: Michael Caine (*Harry Palmer*), Nigel Green (*Dalby*), Guy Doleman (*Maj. Ross*), Sue Lloyd (*Jean*), Aubrey Richards (*Radcliffe*), Gordon Jackson (*Jock Carswell*), Frank Gatliff (*Bluejay*), Freda Bamford (*Alice*), Peter Ashmore (*Sir Robert*), Thomas Baptiste (*Barney*), Oliver MacGreevy (*Housemartin*)Pauline Winter (*The Charlady*), Anthony Blackshaw (*Edwards*), Barry Raymond (*Gray*), David Glover (*Chilcott-Oakes*), Tony Caunter (*The O.N.I. Man*), Anthony Baird (*The Raid Sgt.*), Michael Murray (*The Raid Inspector*), Stanley Meadows (*Insp. Keightley*), Charles Rea (*Taylor*), Richard Burrell (*The Operator*), Douglas Blackwell (*Murray*), Ric Hutton (*The Records Officer*), Glynn Edwards (*The Police Station Sgt.*), Zsolt Vadaszffy (*The Prison Doctor*), Joseph Behrmann, Max Faulkner, Paul S. Chapman, Barbara Roscoe
P: Harry Saltzman **D:** Sidney J. Furie **SCR:** Bill Canaway & James Doran, from Len Deighton's novel **PHOTOG:** Otto Heller **MUSIC:** John Barry
Superior thriller: Prisoner assigned to British Army Intelligence is commissioned to retrieve defected scientist. cf. **Funeral in Berlin**

Iphigenia
1977, (Greece),Greek Film Center/Cinema 5, color, 127 mins
W: Tatiana Papamoskou (*Iphigenia*), Irene Papas (*Clytemnestra*), Costa Kazakos (*Agamemnon*) Costa Carras, Christos Tsangas
D & SCR: Michael Cacoyannis
Well-made tragedy: Greek king must sacrifice daughter

I Remember
see Amarcord

Irish Cinderella
1922, (USA), b&w, 72 mins.
W: Pattie MacNamara
Standard fantasy: Socio-political take on famed fairytale

Iron Justice
1915, (GB), Renaissance/KTC, b&w, 4,000 ft. (1219.2m)
W: Fanny Tittell-Brune (*Margaret Brand*), Sydney Fairbrother (*Mrs. O'Connor*), Julian Royce (*Martin Brand*), Alfred Drayton (*Frank Deakin*), Cecil Fletcher (*Ronald O'Connor*), Marguerita Jesson (*Phyllis Brand*), A. Harding Steerman (*Jabez Cole*), Joan Morgan (*Phyllis as a Child*), John M. Payne (*The Footman*)
P: John M. Payne **D & STORY:**, Sidney Morgan
Standard crime-thriller: Clerk jailed for fraud, employer's wife makes his daughter into a whore

The Iron Knight
see Il Conte Ugolino

Iron Man
1992, (Jap), color, 67 mins.
W: Tomoroh Taguchi, Kei Fujiwara, Nobu Kanaoko, Shinya Tsukamoto
WRIT & D: Shinya Tsukamoto
Bizarre SF-fantasy: Man mutates into metal monstrosity

The Iron Mask
1929, (USA), Elton Corp./UA, b&w; silent: 8,659 ft. (2639.3m), with spoken prologue, & epilogue: 8,855 ft. (2699m)
W: Douglas Fairbanks Sr. (*D'Artagnan*), Belle Bennett (*The Queen Mother*), William Bakewell (*Louis XIV/Louis XIV's Twin*), Marguerite De La Motte (*Constance*), Vera Lewis (*Mme. Peronne*), Nigel de Brulier (*Cardinal Richelieu*), Dorothy Revier (*Milady de Winter*), Rolfe Sedan (*Louis XIII*), Gino Corrado (*Aramis*), Gordon Thorpe (*The Young Prince/The Young Prince's Twin*), Ullrich Haupt (*Rochefort*), Lon Poff (*Father Joseph*), Charles Stevens (*Planchet, D'Artagnan's Servant*), Henry Otto (*The King's Valet*), Leon Bary (*Athos*), Stanley J. Sandford (*Porthos*), Robert Parrish
P: Douglas Fairbanks Sr. **D:** Allan Dwan **SCR:** Lotta Woods **STORY:** Elton Thomas [Douglas Fairbanks Sr.], based on Alexandre Dumas' novels *The Three Musketeers*, *The Man in the Iron Mask* and *Twenty Years After* **PHOTOG:** Henry Sharp **MUSIC:** Hugo Riesenfeld **SONG:** One for All, All for One
Standard action-thriller: Struggle for justice in 18th-century France

Ironmaster
1983, (It-Fr-USA), Medusa-Luciano Martino/American Nat'l, color, 96 mins.
W: Sam Pasco, Elvire Audray, George Eastman, Pamela Field, Jacques Herlin, Brian Redford, Benito Stefanelli, Walter Lucchini, Areno D'Adderio, Giovanni Cianfriglia, William Berger, Nello Pazzafini, Nico La Macchi
D: Umberto Lenzi **SCR:** Alberto Cavallone, Dardano Sacchetti, Lea Martino & Gabriel Rossini, from a story by Luciano Martino & Alberto Cavallone **PHOTOG:** Giancarlo Ferrando **SPCL-FX:** Paolo Ricci **MUSIC:** Guido & Maurizio De Angelis
Standard action-adventure: Prehistoric tribes war

The Iron Stair
1920, (GB), Stoll, b&w,5,972 ft. (1820.5m)
W: Reginald Fox (*Geoffrey/George Gale*), Madge Stuart (*Renee Jessup*), Frank Petley (*Andrew Jessup*), H. Agar Lyons (*Mortimer Peacham*), J. Edwards Barber (*Warden Donkin*)
D & SCR: F. Martin Thornton from a novel by "Rita"
USA retitle, **The Branded Soul**
Standard crime-thriller: Man poses as clerical twin to cash forged check

Iron Warrior...The Legend!

1987, (It), Trans World, color, 82 mins.
W: Miles O'Keeffe, Savina Gersak, Tim Lane, Elizabeth Kaza, Frank Daddi
D: Al Bradley STORY & SCR: Steven Luotto & Al Bradley PHOTOG: Wally Gentleman MUSIC: Charles Scott
Standard fantasy-thriller: Hero defies sorceress usurper

The Irony of Fate

1912, (GB), Barker, b&w
D: Bert Haldane
Standard melodrama: 'Drowned' man returns to find sweetheart married to cousin

Isabel

1968, (Can), color, 108 mins.
W: Genevieve Bujold, Mark Strange, Elton Hayes
WRIT, P, & D: Paul Almond PHOTOG: Georges Dufaux MUSIC: Harry Freedman
Modest thriller: Girl returns home, finds fear and mystery

Isabell, A Dream

1968, (It), color
Short fantasy by Luigi Cozzi

I Saw What You Did

1965, (USA), Univ, b&w, 82 mins.
W: Joan Crawford (Amy), John Ireland (Steve Marak), Sarah Lane (Kit Austin), Andi Garrett (Libby), Leif Erickson (David Mannering), Sharyl Locke (Tess), John Archer (John Austin), Patricia Breslin (Ellie Mannering), Joyce Meadows (Judith), Douglas Evans (Tom Ward), Barbara Wilkins (Mary Ward), John Crawford (Trooper)
P & D: William Castle SCR: William McGivern, from Ursula Curtiss' novel Out of the Dark PHOTOG: Joseph Biroc MUSIC: Joseph Gershenson
orig. co-billed with Dark Intruder
Standard thriller: Killer menaces teenaged girls

I Saw What You Did

1988, (USA), Univ/CBS-TV, color, 93 mins.
W: Shawnee Smith (Kim Fielding), Tammy Lauren (Lisa Harris), Candace Cameron, Robert Carradine, David Carradine, Rosanna Huffman, Jo Anderson, Bo Brundin, Dana Gladstone, Patrick O'Bryan, Alan Fudge, Susan Kellermann, James McKrell, Michael Ross, Stack Pierce, Robert Winley, Laura Kamins, Thom Adcox
D: Fred Walton TELEPLAY: Cynthia Cidre, from Ursula Curtiss' novel Out of the Dark PHOTOG: Woody Omens MUSIC: Dana Kaproff
TVM, tepid remake of 1965 thriller: Phone pranks produce peril

La Isla de la Muerte (The Isle of the Dead)

1966, (Sp-W. Ger), Orbita-Tefi/AA, color, 85 mins.
W: Cameron Mitchell (Baron Von Weser), Elisa Montes, Ralph Naukoff, George Martin, Kay Fischer, Richard Valle, Herman Nelsen
P: George Ferrer D: Mel Welles SCR: Stephen Schmidt
USA retitle, Maneater of Hydra, A.k.a. Island of the Doomed, orig. to be titled Hydra
Minor horror-thriller: Man nurtures carnivorous plant

The Island

1980, (USA), Univ, color, 135 mins.
W: Michael Caine (Maynard), David Warner (Nau), Angela Punch McGregor (Beth), Frank Middlemass (Windsor), Don Henderson (Rollo), Dudley Sutton (Dr. Brazil), Colin Jeavons (Hizzoner), Jeffrey Frank (Justin), Zakes Mokae (Wescott), Brad Sullivan (Stark), John O'Leary (A Doctor), Jimmy Casino (A Doctor), Bruce McLaughlin (A Doctor), Suzanne Astor (Mrs. Burgess), Reg Evans (Jack the Bat), William Schilling (Baxter), Stewart Steinberg (Hiller), Susan Bredhoff (Kate), Cary Hoffman (Mr. Burgess), Bob Westmoreland (The Charter Boat Captain), Steve Gladstone, Robert Hirschfield
P: Richard D. Zanuck & David Brown D: Michael Ritchie SCR: Peter Benchley, from his novel MUSIC: Ennio Morricone PHOTOG: Henri Decae SPCL-FX: Cliff Wenger SPCL VS-FX: Albert Whitlock
Standard thriller: Man and son traumatized by modern pirates

The Island at the Top of the World

1974, (USA), Walt Disney/Buena Vista, color, 93 mins.
W: David Hartman (Prof. Ivarsson), Donald Sinden (Sir Anthony Ross), David Gwillim (Donald Ross), Agneta Eckemyr (Freyja), Jacques Marin (Capt. Brieux), Brendan Dillon (The Factor), Mako (Oomiak), Gunnar Ohlund (The Godi), Ivor Barry (The Butler), Lasse Kolstad (Erik), Torsten Wahlund (Sven), Erik Silju (Torvald), Niels Hinrichsen (Sigurd), Rolf Soder (The Lawspeaker), Denny Miller (The Town Guard), Sverre Ousdal (Gunnar), James Almanzar (The French Engineer), Lee Paul (Chief of Boat Archers)
P: Winston Hibler D: Robert Stevenson SCR: John Whedon, from Ian Cameron's novel The Lost Ones PHOTOG: Frank Phillips SPCL-FX: Art Cruickshank & Danny Lee MUSIC: Maurice Jarre
Standard adventure-thriller: Scientist seeks missing son, finds Arctic isle inhabited by Viking descendants

The Island of Dr. Moreau: MICHAEL YORK, DOING PUBLICITY

Island City

1994, (USA), Made for TV, color
W: Kevin Conroy, Brenda Strong, Eric McCormack
TVM, standard SF-thriller: Violent mutants created in 21st century

Island Claws

see The Night of the Claw

The Island Monster

see Il Mostro dell'Isola

Island of Blood

1986, (USA), color, 84 mins.
W: Jim Williams, Dean Richards
Minor thriller: Berserk butcher besets film crew

Island of Desire

see Saturday Island

Island of Despair

1968, (Sp-It-W.Germ), CUE, Hesperia-Corona-Towers of London-Cineproduzione/CUE, 90 mins. color, 86 mins
W: Mercedes McCambridge, Maria Schell, Mercedes McCambridge (Thelma), Maria Schell (Leonie), Herbert Lom (The Governor), Maria Rohm (Marie), Rosalba Neri (76), Valentine Godoy (81), Elisa Montes (99), Luciana Paluzzi (Natalie)
P: Harry Alan Towers D: Jesus Franco STORY: Peter Welbeck, Carlo Fadda, Millo Cuccia & Jesus Franco
A.k.a. 99 Women, and Isle of Lost Women
Minor, lurid thriller: Injustice in women's prison

The Island of Dr. Moreau (1932)

see Island of Lost Souls

The Island of Dr. Moreau

1977, (USA), AIP, color, 104 mins.
W: Burt Lancaster (Dr. Moreau), Michael York (Braddock), Barbara Carrera (Maria), Nigel Davenport (Montgomery), Richard Basehart ("The Sayer of the Law"), Nick Cravat (M'Ling)
D: Don Taylor SCR: John Herman Shaner & Al Ramrus, from H.G. Wells' novel PHOTOG: Gerry Fisher MUSIC: Laurence Rosenthal
Standard SF-horror: Scientist creates humans from animals

The Island Earth: FAITH DOMERGUE, REX REASON AND JEFF MORROW

The Island of Dr. Moreau
1996, (USA), Edward R. Pressman/New Line, color, 114 mins.
<u>W</u>: Marlon Brando (*Dr. Moreau*), Val Kilmer (*Montgomery*), David Thewlis (*Douglas*), Fairuza Balk (*Aissa*), Ron Perlman (*The Sayer of the Law*), Nelson de la Rosa (*Majai*), Daniel Rigney (*Hyena-Swine*), Temeura Morrison, Marco Hofschneider, Peter Elliott, Fiona Mahl, Mark Dacascos, Miguel Lopez, David Hudson, Niel Young, William Hootkins, Clare Grant, Kitty Silver, Ron Vreeken, Lou Horvath
<u>D</u>: John Frankenheimer   <u>SCR</u>: Richard Stanley & Ron Hutchinson, from H.G. Wells' novel   <u>PHOTOG</u>: William Fraker   <u>MUSIC</u>: Gary Chang   <u>SPCL MAKEUP</u>: Stan Winston
"...giddily entertaining, a tropical-horror potboiler with a wry sense of its own absurdity"—David Ansen, Newsweek
Standard SF-horror: Mad scientist dabbles in genetic engineering

The Island of Lost Souls: CHARLES LAUGHTON AND KATHLEEN BURKE

Island of Doomed Men
1940, (USA), Col, b&w, 67 mins
<u>W</u>: Peter Lorre, Rochelle Hudson, Robert Wilcox, Charles Middleton, Don Beddoe George E. Stone, Kenneth MacDonald
<u>P</u>: Wallace MacDonald   <u>D</u>: Charles Barton
Standard thriller: Sadist enslaves island populace

The Island of Living Horror
see **Brides of Blood**

The Island of Lost Men
1939, (USA), Para, b&w, 63 mins
<u>W</u>: J. Carrol Naish, Anna May Wong, Anthony Quinn, Broderick Craw-ford
<u>D</u>: Kurt Neumann
Standard melodrama (remake of **White Woman***): Tyrant rules tropic isle*

Island of Lost Souls
1932, (USA), Para, b&w, 74 mins.
<u>W</u>: Charles Laughton (*Dr. Moreau*), Richard Arlen, Leila Hyams, Kathleen Burke (*Lota, the "Panther Woman"*), Bela Lugosi ("*The Sayer of the Law*"), Arthur Hohl, Rosemary Grimes, Stanley Fields, George Irving, Tetsu Komai, Joe Bonomo, Paul Hurst, Duke York, Hans Steinke, John George
<u>D</u>: Erle C. Kenton   <u>SCR</u>: Waldemar Young & Philip Wylie, from H.G. Wells' novel *The Island of Dr. Moreau*   <u>PHOTOG</u>: Karl Struss
Fr retitle, **L'Ile du Dr.Moreau** *(The Island of Dr. Moreau)*
Classic SF-horror: Mad scientist speeds up evolution. cf. **Terror is a Man**

Island of Lost Women
1959, (USA), Jaguar/WB, b&w, 71 mins.
<u>W</u>: Jeff Richards, John Smith, Venetia Stevenson, Alan Napier, Diane Jergens, June Blair, George Brand, Gavin Muir
<u>P</u>: Albert J. Cohen   <u>D</u>: Frank W. Tuttle   <u>SCR</u>: Ray Buffum, from a story by Prescott Chaplin   <u>PHOTOG</u>: John F. Seitz   <u>MUSIC</u>: Raoul Kraushaar
blurb: "They turned a forbidden paradise into a raging hell!"
Standard SF-thriller: Embittered scientist and his lovely daughters dwell on lonely isle

Island of Terror
1966, (GB), Planet/Univ, color, 89 mins.
<u>W</u>: Peter Cushing (*Dr. Brian Stanley*), Edward Judd (*Dr. David West*), Carole Gray (*Toni Merrill*), Eddie Byrne (*Dr. Reginald Landers*), Sam Kydd (*Constable John Harris*), Liam Gaffney (*Bellows*), James Caffrey (*Argyle*), Roger Heathcote (*Dunley*), Peter Forbes-Robertson (*Dr. Phillips*), Niall MacGinnis (*Mr. Campbell*), Shay Gorman (*Morton*), Keith Bell, Richard Bidlake, Joyce Hemson, Edward Ogden
<u>P</u>: Tom Blakley   <u>D</u>: Terence Fisher   <u>ORIG STORY & SCR</u>: Edward Andrew Mann & Allan Ramsen   <u>PHOTOG</u>: Reg Wyer   <u>SPCL-FX</u>: John St. John Earl   <u>MUSIC</u>: Malcolm Lockyer
A.k.a. **The Frightened Island,** *orig. to have been titled* **The Creepers, The Night of the Silicates** *or* **The Night the Silicates Came**
Standard SF-horror: Cancer-control research creates species of creeping monstrosities

Island of the Burning Doomed
see **The Night of the Big Heat**

Island of the Damned
1976, (Sp), AIP, color, 112 mins.
<u>W</u>: Lewis Fiander, Prunella Ransome
<u>P</u>: Manuel Perez   <u>D</u>: Narciso Ibanez Serrador   <u>SCR</u>: Luis Penafiel, based on novel *El Juego* by J.J. Plans
Unusual, critically-acclaimed thriller: Couple faces killer children on vacation isle

Island of the Doomed
see **La Isla de la Muerte**

Island Women
1958, (USA), UA, b&w, 72 mins.
<u>W</u>: Marie Windsor, Vince Edwards
Standard melodrama

The Isle of Calypso: Ulysses and Polyphemus
see **L'Ile de Calypso: Ulysse et Polypheme**

Isle of Destiny
1940, (USA), RKO, Cosmocolor (2-color process)
<u>W</u>: William Gargan
Minor melodrama

Isle of the Dead
1913, (Den), b&w
<u>D</u>: Gluckstadt
Minor melodrama

Isle of the Dead
1945, (USA), RKO, b&w, 72 mins.
<u>W</u>: Boris Karloff, Ellen Drew, Jason Robards Sr., Helene Thimig, Katherine Emery, Marc Cramer, Skelton Knaggs, Alan Napier, Ernst Dorian, Sherry Hall
<u>P</u>: Val Lewton   <u>D</u>: Mark Robson   <u>SCR</u>: Ardel Wray   <u>PHOTOG</u>: Jack MacKenzie   <u>MUSIC</u>: Leigh Harline
blurb: "201 blood-curdling scenes you'll never tear out of your mind!"
Modest thriller: Plague outbreak strands archeologists on Greek island

Isle of the Dead (1966)
see **La Isla de la Muerte**

Isle of the Fishmen
see **The Fish Men**

Isle of the Snake People
1968, (USA-Mex), Horror Int'l/Col, color, 91 mins.
<u>W</u>: Boris Karloff (*Van Molder/Damballah*), Julissa (*Anabella*), Charles East (*Wilhelm*), Ralph Bertrand (*Capt. Labiche*), Tongolele (*Kalea*), Quintin Bulnes (*Klinsor*), Santanon (*The Midget*), Martinique, July Marichal
<u>P</u>: Luis Enrique Vergara & Juan Ibanez   <u>D</u>: Juan Ibanez   <u>SCR</u>: Jack Hill   <u>PHOTOG</u>: Austin McKinney   <u>SPCL-FX</u>: Ross Hahn   <u>MUSIC</u>: Alice Urreta
USA TV-retitle, **Snake People** *A.k.a.* **Cult of the Dead** *and* **La Muerte Viviente (The Living Dead)**
Minor horror-thriller: Snake cult and zombies on voodoo-dominated island. US release: 1971

Isn't It Shocking?
1973, (USA), ABC-TV, color, 73 mins.
<u>W</u>: Alan Alda, Louise Lasser, Edmond O'Brien, Will Geer, Ruth Gordon, Dorothy Tristan, Lloyd Nolan
<u>P</u>: Ron Bernstein & Howard Rosenman   <u>D</u>: John Badham   <u>SCR</u>: Lane Slate, Ron Bernstein & Howard Roseman
TVM, standard thriller: Strange murders in small town

I Spit on Your Corpse
1974, (USA), color, 90 mins.
<u>W</u>: Georgina Spelvin, Susan McIver, Kent Taylor
<u>D</u>: Al Adamson
A.k.a. **Girls for Rent**
Minor thriller: Female assassin terrorizes

I Spit on Your Grave
1977, (USA), Jerry Gross/Cinemagic, color, 90 mins
<u>W</u>: Camille Keaton, Eron Tabor, Richard Pace, Gunter Kleemann, Anthony Nichols
<u>P</u>: Joseph Zbeda & Meir Zarchi   <u>D, SCR & ED</u>: Meir Zarchi
A.k.a. **Day of the Woman**
Classic exploitation thriller: Rape victim gains gruesome revenge

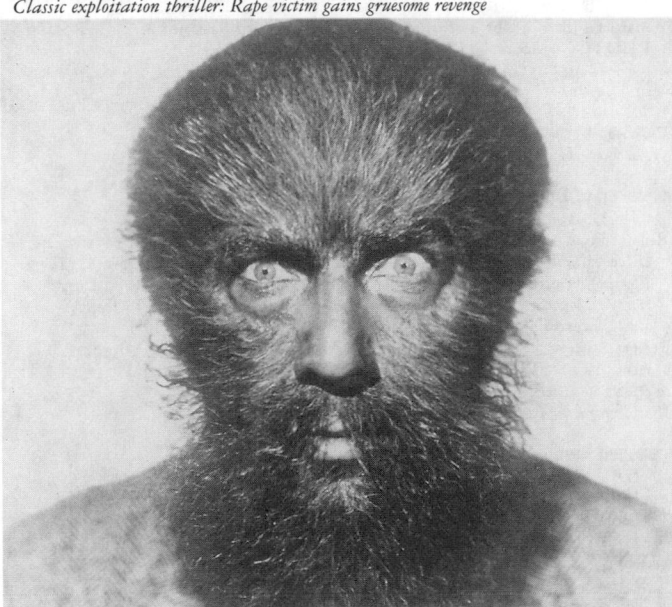

The Island of Lost Souls: BELA LUGOSI

I Spy, You Spy
see **Our Man in Marrakesh**

Istanbul
1957, (USA), Univ, color, 84 mins.
<u>W</u>: Errol Flynn, Cornell Borchers, John Bentley, Nat King Cole, Torin Thatcher, Leif Erickson, Martin Benson, Jan Arvan, Vladimir Sokoloff
<u>D</u>: Joseph Pevney   <u>STORY</u>: Seton I. Miller   <u>PHOTOG</u>: William Daniels   <u>MUSIC</u>: Joseph Gershenson   <u>SONGS.</u>: *I Was a Little Too Lonely* & *When I Fall In Love*
Standard melodrama: Adventurer seeks stolen gems, finds "dead" wife

I Start Counting
1969, (GB), Triumvirate/UA, color, 105 mins.
<u>W</u>: Jenny Agutter (*Wynne*), Bryan Marshall (*George*), Clare Sutcliffe (*Corinne*), Simon Ward (*The Conductor*), Gregory Phillips (*Len*), Lana Morris (*Leonie*), Madge Ryan (*Mrs. Kinch*), Billy Russell (*Grandad*), Michael Feast (*Jim*), Fay Compton (*Mrs. Bennett*)
<u>P</u>: Stanley Jaffe & David Greene   <u>D</u>: David Greene   <u>SCR</u>: Richard Harris, from a novel by Audrey Erskine Lindop
Standard thriller: Teen suspects foster brother is sex killer

Is This Trip Really Necessary?
1970, (USA), Dorn-Thor/Hollywood Star Pictures, color, 84 mins
<u>W</u>: John Carradine, Marvin Miller, Peter Duryea, Carol Kane, Barbara Mallory
<u>P & D</u>: Ben Benoit   <u>SCR</u>: Lee Kalcheim
Minor horror-satire: Mad sex-film director kills actresses. Original title: **Trip to Terror**

I Still Dream of Jeannie
1991, (USA), Bar-Gene TV/Col-TV, color, 95 mins.
<u>W</u>: Barbara Eden (*Jeannie*), Christopher Bolton (*Tony Nelson Jr.*), Bill Daily (*Roger Healey*), Al Waxman (*Gen. Wescott*), Peter Breck (*Sham-Ir*), Brent Stait (*Eddie*), Ken Kercheval (*Simpson*), Jason Scott Schombing (*Guzer*), Garry Chalk, J.J. McColl, Robert Metcalfe, Jackson Davies, Victor Young, Neil D. Mark, Bette Linde, Robert Thurston, D.J. Jackson, Paul McLean, Brigitta Dau, Jano Frandsen, Dale Wilson, Delores Drake, Marcy Goldberg, Peter Chapek, Douglas Newell, Roger Barnes, Sandra Grant, Henry Crowell Jr.
<u>D</u>: Joseph Scanlan   <u>TELEPLAY</u>: April Kelly, from characters created by Sidney Sheldon   <u>PHOTOG</u>: Bert Dunk   <u>SPCL-FX</u>: Tom Storvick   <u>MUSIC</u>: Ken Harrison
TVM, standard comedy-fantasy

I Still Know What You Did Last Summer
1998, (USA), Mandalay/Col, color
<u>W</u>: Jennifer Love Hewitt (*Julie*), Brandy (*Karla*), Freddie Prinze Jr. (*Ray*), Mekhi Phifer (*Tyrell*), Matthew Settle (*Will*), Muse Watson
<u>D</u>: Danny Gannon   <u>SONG</u>: *How Do I Feel*
Standard thriller: Vengeful spectre slays young people

It! (1967)
see **The Curse of the Golem**

It
1990, (USA), Lorimar/ABC-TV, color 193 mins.
<u>W</u>: Richard Thomas (*Bill Denbrough*), Annette O'Toole (*Beverly Marsh*), John Ritter (*Ben Hanscom*), Dennis Christopher (*Eddie Kasprbak*), Tim Reid (*Mike Hanlon*), Harry Anderson (*Richie Tozier*), Tim Curry (*Pennywise/"It"*), Richard Masur (*Stan*), Jonathan Brandis (*Young Bill*), Brandon Crane (*Young Ben*), Emily Perkins (*Young Bev*), Seth Green (*Young Richie*), Adam Faraizl (*Young Eddie*), Marlon Taylor (*Young Mike*), Ben Heller (*Young Stan*), Olivia Hussey (*Audra*), Kim Kondrashoff (*Joey*), Jarred Blancard (*Henry Bowers*), Sheila Moore (*Mrs. Kasprbak*), Drum Garrett (*Belch*), Ryan Michael (*Tom Rogan*), Gabe Khouth (*Patrick*), Charles Siegel (*Nat*), Venus Terzo (*Cyndi*), Frank C. Turner (*Al Marsh*), Caitlin Hicks (*Patti Uris*), Tony Dakota (*Georgie Denbrough*), Noel Geer (*Bradley*), Steven Hilton (*Mr. Denbrough*), Sheelah Megill (*Sharon Denbrough*), Chelan Simmons (*Laurie Anne*), Merrilyn Gann (*Mrs. Winterbarger*), William B. Davis (*Mr. Gedreau*), Susan Astley (*Aunt Jean*), Claire Brown (*Arlene Hanscom*), Garry Chalk (*The Coach*), Donna Peerless (*Miss Douglas*), Terence Kelly (*Officer Neil*), Scott Swanson (*Rademacher*), Stephen Makaj (*Bev's Father*)
<u>D</u>: Tommy Lee Wallace   <u>SCR</u>: Lawrence D. Cohen & Tommy Lee Wallace, from Stephen King's novel   <u>MUSIC</u>: Richard Bellis   <u>PHOTOG</u>: Richard Letterman
TVM (in 2 parts), modest horror-fantasy: Evil force kills children in small Maine town

Italian Secret Service
1967, (It), color, 105 mins.
<u>W</u>: Nino Manfredi
<u>D</u>: Luigi Comencini
Minor comedy-thriller

It Came from Beneath the Sea
1955, (USA), Clover/Col, b&w, 80 mins.
<u>W</u>: Kenneth Tobey, Faith Domergue, Donald Curtis, Harry Lauter, Del Courtney, Dean Maddox Jr., John Hoyt, Rudy Puteska, Ed Fisher, Ian Keith, Tol Avery, Ray Storey, Jack Littlefield, Jules Irving
<u>P</u>: Charles H. Schneer   <u>D</u>: Robert Gordon   <u>SCR</u>: George Worthington Yates & Hal Smith   <u>STORY</u>: George Worthington Yates   <u>PHOTOG</u>: Henry Freulich   <u>TECH-FX</u>: Ray Harryhausen   <u>MUSIC</u>: Mischa Bakaleinikoff
Modest SF-thriller: Atomic waste creates giant octopus

It Came from Outer Space
1953, (USA), Univ, 3D, b&w, 80 mins.
<u>W</u>: Richard Carlson (*John Putnam*), Barbara Rush (*Ellen Fields*), Joe Sawyer (*Frank*), Russell Johnson (*George*), Charles Drake (*Sheriff Matt Warren*), Kathleen Hughes (*Jane*), Dave Willock (*Pete*), Alan Dexter
<u>P</u>: William Alland   <u>D</u>: Jack Arnold   <u>SCR</u>: Harry Essex, from a story by Ray Bradbury   <u>PHOTOG</u>: Clifford Stine   <u>SPCL-FX</u>: David Horsley   <u>MUSIC</u>: Joseph Gershenson
Fr retitle, **Le Meteore de la Nuit (Night Meteor)**
"...Arnold's first brilliant exercise with the elements of fantasy film" —John Baxter, Science Fiction in the Cinema
Classic SF-thriller: Marooned space-aliens frighten inhabitants of Southwest town

It Came From Outer Space: RICHARD CARLSON AND BARBARA RUSH

It Came from Outer Space II
1996, (USA), SciFi-TV, color, 95 mins.
<u>W</u>: Brian Kerwin, Elizabeth Pena
Made-for-Cable, standard SF-thriller: Alien spaceship crashlands

It Came Up from the Bermuda Depths
see **The Bermuda Depths**

It Came Upon the Midnight Clear

1984, (USA), Col-TV, color, 91 mins.

W: Mickey Rooney, Scott Grimes, Barrie Youngfellow, Gary Bayer, George Gaynes, William Griffis, Christina Pickles, Hamilton Camp, Elisha Cook Jr., Nicholas Hormann, Hector Elias, Wynn Irwin, Barbette Tweed, Lew Horn, Annie Potts, Lloyd Nolan, Alyson Kirk, Lurene Tuttle, Jan Chamberlin, George Pentecost, Garry Goodrow, Dan Barrows, Billy Curtis, Ollie O'Toole, Buddy Douglas, Jerry Maren, Michael Laskin, Paddi Edwards, Seth Wagerman, Benny Baker, Irwin Keyes, Gary Imhoff, Eve Smith, Eric Uhler, Jimmy Bridges, Richard Paxton, Joe Van Endres, Edgar Justice, James Fry, Eddie Pisano, John Welsh, Nick De Marinis, Roger Scott, Ellen Gerstein, Chino Williams, Eric Stacey, Ernie Banks, Erwin Fuller, Ray Bengston

D: Peter H. Hunt **P & TELEPLAY:** George Schenck & Frank Cardea **PHOTOG:** Dean Cundey **SPCL-FX:** John Frazier **MUSIC:** Arthur B. Rubinstein

TVM, modest fantasy: Deceased mortal strikes deal with archangel

It Conquered the World

1956, (USA), Sunset/AIP, b&w, 71 mins.

W: Peter Graves (*Dr. Paul Nelson*), Sally Fraser (*Joan Nelson*), Lee Van Cleef (*Tom Anderson*), Beverly Garland (*Claire Anderson*), Charles B. Griffith (*Pete Shelton*), Pamela Duncan, Russ Bender, Karen Kadler, Dick Miller, Jonathan Haze, Paul Harbor, Taggart Casey, Tom Jackson, Marshall Bradford, Paul Blaisdell (*Monster*)

P & D: Roger Corman **STORY & SCR:** Lou Rusoff **PHOTOG:** Frederick E. West **MUSIC:** Ronald Stein **SPCL-FX:** Paul Blaisdell

orig. co-billed with **The She-Creature**
reissued 1961

"...fast-paced screen entertainment. Aided by the scoring of Ronald Stein, and the snappy film editing of Charles Gross, it delighted the young in heart all over the country"—Bradford Knight, "It Conquered the World," Fantastic Monsters of the Films, Vol. 1, No. 4 (1962), p. 7

Classic low-budget SF-thriller: Malevolent creature from Venus makes contact with misguided Earth scientist cf. **Zontar: The Thing from Venus**

It Conquered The World

It Fell from the Sky

1980, (USA), Firebird Int'l, color, 87 mins

W: Buster Crabbe (*Sheriff Kowalski,*) Linda Lewis, Ray Roberts

P & D: Fred Olen Ray **SCR:** Fred Olen Ray & Allan Nicholas

A.k.a. **Alien Dead**

Minor SF-thriller: Meteor turns teens into flesh-eating zombies

It Grows on Trees

1952, (USA), Univ, b&w, 84 mins.

W: Irene Dunne (*Polly Baxter*), Dean Jagger (*Phil Baxter*), Joan Evans (*Diane Baxter*), Richard Crenna (*Ralph Bowen*), Les Tremayne (*Finlay Murchison*), Forrest Lewis (*Dr. Harold Burrows*), Edith Meiser (*Mrs. Pryor*), Frank Ferguson (*John Letherby*), Bob Sweeney (*McGurie*), Dee Pollock (*Flip Baxter*), Sandy Descher (*Midge Baxter*), Malcolm Lee Beggs (*Henry Carrollman*)

P: Leonard Goldstein **D:** Arthur Lubin **SCR:** Leonard Praskins & Barney Slater **PHOTOG:** Maury Gertsman **MUSIC:** Frank Skinner

Modest comedy-fantasy: Complications sprout when woman discovers "money tree" growing in backyard

It Happened at Nightmare Inn

see **Nightmare Hotel**

It Happened at Lake Wood Manor

1977, (USA), Alan Landsburg/ABC-TV, color, 96 mins.

W: Robert Foxworth (*Mike Carr*), Lynda Day George (*Valerie Adams*), Myrna Loy (*Ethel Adams*), Suzanne Somers (*Gloria Henderson*), Gerald M. Gordon (*Tony Fleming*), Bernie Casey (*Vince*), Anita Gillette (*Peggy Kenter*), Karen Lamm (*Linda Howard*), Barry Van Dyke (*Richard Cyril*), Moosie Drier (*Tommy West*), Steve Franken, Brian Dennehy, Bruce French

D: Robert Scheerer **TELEPLAY:** Guerdon Trueblood **PHOTOG:** Bernie Abramson **SPCL-FX:** Roy Downey **MUSIC:** Ken Richmond

A.k.a. **Ants** *and* **Panic at Lake Wood Manor**

TVM, standard thriller: Murderous insects plague resort

It Happened Here

1964, (GB), Rath/UA/Lopert, b&w, 99 mins.

W: Pauline Murray (*Pauline Murray*), Sebastian Shaw (*Dr. Richard Fletcher*), Nicolette Bernard (*The IA Commandant*), Bart Allison (*Skipworth*), Stella Kemball (*Nurse Drayton*), Fiona Leland (*Mrs. Fletcher*), Frank Bennett (*The Group Leader*), John Herrington (*Dr. Westerman*), Reginald Marsh (*MO*), Bertha Russell (*The Matron*), Honor Fehrson (*Honor Hutton*), Ralph Wilson (*Dr. Walton*), Col. Percy Binns, Barrie Pattison

P, D, & STORY: Kevin Brownlow & Andrew Mollo **SCR:** Kevin Brownlow, Andrew Mollo, Dinah Brooke & Jonathan Ingram **PHOTOG:** Peter Suschitsky **MUSIC:** Jack Beaver

Absorbing fantasy-thriller: Nazis win World War II, occupy England

It Happened in Broad Daylight

1960, (Switz-Germ.), Sterling/CCC/Continental, b&w, 97 mins

W: Gert Frobe, Michel Simon, Heinz Ruhmann, Roger Livesey

Standard thriller: Inspector tracks psychotic killer

It Happened in Soho

1948, (GB), FC Films/ABFD, b&w, 55 mins.

W: Richard Murdoch (*Bill Scott*), Patricia Raine (*Susan Marsh*), John Bailey (*Paul Sayers*), Henry Oscar (*Insp. Carp*), Eunice Gayson (*The Girl*)

P & D: Frank Chisnell **STORY:** Terry Sanford

Standard thriller: Reporter unmasks Soho Strangler

It Happened One Christmas

1977, (USA), ABC-TV, color, 112 mins

W: Marlo Thomas (*Mary Bailey*), Cloris Leachman (*The Angel*), Wayne Rogers (*George Hatch*), Orson Welles (*Potter*), Barney Martin (*Uncle Willy*), Richard Dysart (*Bailey*), Doris Roberts (*Mrs. Bailey*), Ceil Cabot (*Cousin Tillie*), Christopher Guest (*Harry Bailey*), Karen Carlson (*Violet*), Archie Hahn (*Ernie*), Morgan Upton (*Bert*), Dick O'Neill (*Gower*), Jim Lovelett (*Sam Wainwright*)

D: Donald Wrye

TVM, minor distaff remake of **It's a Wonderful Life**: *Angel teaches woman the joy of existence*

It Happened Tomorrow

1944, (USA), UA, b&w, 85 mins.

W: Dick Powell, Linda Darnell, Edgar Kennedy, Jack Oakie, George Cleveland, Sig Rumann, Paul Guilfoyle, Ed Brophy, John Philliber

P: Arnold Pressburger **D:** Rene Clair **SCR:** Dudley Nichols & Rene Clair, from a one-act play by Lord Dunsany **PHOTOG:** Archie Stout **MUSIC:** Robert Stolz

Modest fantasy: Mysterious stranger gives journalist tomorrow's newspaper. Inspiration for TV series of late 90's, **Early Edition**

It Happens Every Spring

1949, (USA), 20th-Fox, b&w, 89 mins.

W: Ray Milland, Paul Douglas, Jean Peters, Ted de Corsia, Ed Begley, Ray Collins, Jessie Royce Landis, Bill Murphy, Alan Hale Jr., William E. Green, Edward Keane

P: William Perlberg **D:** Lloyd Bacon **SCR:** Valentine Davies, from a story by Valentine Davies & Shirley W. Smith **PHOTOG:** Joe MacDonald **SPCL-FX:** Fred Sersen **MUSIC:** Leigh Harline

Modest SF-comedy: Chemistry prof discovers wood-repelling substance

I Thank a Fool

1962, (GB), MGM British, color, 100 mins.

W: Susan Hayward (*Christine Allison*), Peter Finch (*Stephen Dane*), Diane Cilento (*Liane Dane*), Cyril Cusack (*Capt. Ferris*), Kieron Moore (*Roscoe*), Brenda de

Banzie (*Nurse Drew*), Athene Seyler (*Aunt Heather*), Richard Wattis (*Ebbligton*), J.G. Devlin (*The Coroner*), Clive Morton (*The Judge*), Laurence Naismith (*O'Grady*), Miriam Karlin (*The Woman*)
P: Anatole de Grunwald   **D:** Robert Stevens   **SCR:** Karl Tunberg, from a novel by Audrey Erskine Lindop
Standard melodrama: Ex-doctor suspects foul play in death of insane wife

I, the Jury
1953, (USA), UA, 3D, b&w, 87 mins.
W: Biff Elliott (*Mike Hammer*), Peggie Castle, Preston Foster, Elisha Cook Jr.
P: Victor Saville   **D & SCR:** Harry Essex, from Mickey Spillane's 1946 novel
Classic thriller: Detective tracks friend's killer

I, the Jury
1982, (USA), 20th-Fox, color, 111 mins.
W: Armand Assante (*Mike Hammer*), Barbara Carrera, Judson Scott, Laurene Landon, Alan King, Paul Sorvino

It Happened Tomorrow: DICK POWELL AND JOHN PHILIBER

P: Robert Solo   **D:** Richard Heffron   **SCR:** Larry Cohen, from Mickey Spillane's novel
Tepid remake of classic thriller: Detective pursues psychotic slasher

I, the Justice
1968, (Czech), color
Standard melodrama

It's a Dog's Life
1955, (USA), MGM, color, 88 mins.
W: Edmund Gwenn (*Jeremiah Nolan*), Jeff Richards (*Patch McGill*), Dean Jagger (*Mr. Wyndham*), Jarma Lewis (*Mabel Maycroft*), Richard Anderson (*George Oakley*), J.M. Kerrigan (*Paddy Corbin*), Sally Fraser (*Dorothy Wyndham*), Willard Sage (*Tom Tattle*)
P: Henry Berman   **D:** Herman Hoffman   **SCR:** John Michael Hayes, from a story by Richard Harding Davis   **PHOTOG:** Paul C. Vogel   **MUSIC:** Elmer Bernstein
A.k.a. **Bar Sinister** *and* **Wildfire**
Standard comedy-melodrama: Adventures of Bowery pooch

It's Alive!
1968, (USA), Azalea/AIP, color, 80 mins.
W: Tommy Kirk, Shirley Bonne, Annabelle Macadams, Billy Thurman, Corveth Ousterhouse
P, D SCR: Larry Buchanan   **PHOTOG:** Robert Alcott   **SPCL-FX:** Jack Bennett
Minor thriller: Wayfarers trapped in madman's cave

It's Alive
1974, (USA), Larco/WB, color, 91 mins.
W: John Ryan (*Frank Davis*), Sharon Farrell (*Lenore*), Guy Stockwell (*Bob Clayton*), Andrew Duggan (*The Professor*), Michael Ansara (*The Captain*), James Dixon (*Lt. Perkins*), Robert Emhardt (*The Executive*), Shamus Locks (*The Doctor*), William Wellman Jr. (*Charlie*), Mary-Nancy Burnett (*The Nurse*), Diana Hale (*The Sec'y*), Daniel Holzman (*The Boy*), Patrick Macallister, Gerald York, Jerry Taft, W. Allen York, Gwil Richards
WRIT, P, & D: Larry Cohen   **PHOTOG:** Fenton Hamilton   **MUSIC:** Bernard Herrmann
Standard horror-fantasy: Monster-baby spreads havoc. cf. **It Lives Again** *and* **It's Alive III: Island of the Alive**

It's Alive III: Island of the Alive
1986, (USA), Larco/WB, color, 95 mins.
W: Michael Moriarty (*Jarvis*), Karen Black (*Ellen*), James Dixon (*Lt. Perkins*), Laurene Landon (*Sally*), Gerrit Graham (*Ralston*), Macdon-ald Carey (*Judge Watson*), Ann Dane (*Dr. Morrell*), Neal Isreal (*Dr. Brewster*), Art Lund (*Dr. Swenson*), Patch Mackenzie (*Robbins*), Rick Garia (*Tony*), William Watson (*Cabot*), Bobby Ramsen (*The TV Host*), C.L. Sussex (*Hunter*), Carlos Palomino (*The 1st Cuban*), Tony Abatemarco (*The 2nd Cuban*), Jill Gatsby (*The Girl in the Cab*), Gladys Portugese (*The Waitress*), Joann Lara (*The 2nd Waitress*), Kevin O'Conner (*The Cab Driver*), Mitchell Edmonds (*Stewart*),

John Woehrle (*The 1st Cop*), Elizabeth Sanders (*The Autograph Seeker*), Lauri Riley (*The Medic*), Marilyn Staley (*Miss Garson*), Richard Duggan (*A Cop*), Steven Alan Green (*The Comic*), Kathleen Kickta (*The Girl on the Beach*), Lynda Clark (*The 2nd Woman*), Dan Rycerz (*The Court Officer*), Edward Shils (*The Medical Examiner*), Charles Vandergrift III (*The Driver*), Jackie Swanson (*The Tenant*), Katja Crosby (*The Girl in Court*), Paul Stader Jr. (*The Ship's Officer*)
WRIT & D: Larry Cohen   **PHOTOG:** Daniel Pearl   **MUSIC:** Laurie Johnson, **THEME:** Bernard Herrmann
Modest horror-satire: Mutant children are isolated

It's Hot in Paradise
see Horrors of Spider Island

It's Not the Size that Counts
1975, (GB), Joseph Brenner, color, 90 mins
W: Denholm Elliott, Elke Sommer, Vincent Price, Judy Geeson, Milo O'Shea, Julie Ege, George Coulouris
P: Betty E. Box   **D:** Ralph Thomas   **SCR:** Sid Colin
A.k.a. **Percy's Progress**
Minor satire (sequel to **Percy***): Chemical in water supply causes male impotence*

It Lives Again
1978, (USA), Larco/WB, color, 91 mins.
W: Frederic Forrest (*Eugene Scott*), Kathleen Lloyd (*Judy Scott*), Andrew Duggan (*Dr. Perry*), John Ryan (*Frank Davis*), Eddie Constantine (*Dr. Forest*), James Dixon (*Det. Perkins*) Dennis O'Flaherty, Melissa Inger
WRIT, P, & D: Larry Cohen   **PHOTOG:** Fenton Hamilton   **MUSIC:** Bernard Herrmann songs, *Dreaming* & *All Time Loser*
Standard horror-fantasy, sequel to **It's Alive** *(1974): Monstrous infant returns to terrorize cf.* **It's Alive III: Island of the Alive**

It's Always Fair Weather
1955, (USA), MGM, color, 101 mins.
W: Gene Kelly (*Ted Riley*), Cyd Charisse (*Jackie Leighton*), Dan Dailey (*Doug Hallerton*), Dolores Gray (*Madeline Bradville*), Michael Kidd (*Augie Valentine*), David Burns (*Tim*), Jay C. Flippen (*Charles Z. Culloran*)
P: Arthur Freed   **D:** Gene Kelly & Stanley Donen   **SCR:** Betty Comden & Adolph Green   **PHOTOG:** Robert Bronner   **MUSIC:** Andre Previn, Betty Comden & Adolph Green
Standard comedy-romance (with Daliesque dance fantasy): Ex-soldiers have reunion

It's a Wonderful Life
1946, (USA), RKO, b&w, 129 mins.
W: James Stewart, Donna Reed, Thomas Mitchell, Lionel Barrymore, H.B. Warner, Beulah Bondi, Frank Faylen
P & D: Frank Capra   **SCR:** Frank Capra, Frances Goodrich, Albert Hackett, Jo Swerling & Michael Wilson, based on Philip Van Doren Stern's short story "The Greatest Gift"   **PHOTOG:** Joseph Walker & Joseph Biroc   **MUSIC:** Dimitri Tiomkin
Classic fantasy: Man wishes he was never born, angel grants wish. cf. **It Happened One Christmas**

It's Love that Makes the World Go Round
1913, (GB), Clarendon, b&w, 520 ft. (158.5m)
D: Percy Stow
Minor fantasy: Cupid's magic arrows stop quarrel

It's Only Money
1962, (USA), Para, b&w, 84 mins.
W: Jerry Lewis (*Lester March*), Joan O'Brien (*Wanda Paxton*), Zachary Scott (*Gregory DeWitt*), Jack Weston (*Leopold*), Mae Questel (*Cecilia Albright*), Jesse White, Pat Dahl, Barbara Pepper
P: Paul Jones   **D:** Frank Tashlin   **SCR:** John Fenton Murray   **PHOTOG:** W. Wallace Kelley   **MUSIC:** Walter Scharf
Fr retitle, **L'Increvable Jerry** *(The Incredible Jerry)*
Modest comedy: Fantastic elements in tale of lost heir. Zachary Scott's last film

Its Name was Robert
1968, (Russ), color
Standard SF-thriller: Robot's adventures

It Stalked The Ocean Floor
see Monster from the Ocean Floor

It!—The Terror from Beyond Space
1958, (USA), Vogue/UA, b&w, 68 mins.
W: Marshall Thompson (*Col. Edward Carruthers*), Shawn Smith (formerly Shirley Paterson) (*Ann*), Kim Spalding (*Van*), Dabbs Greer (*Eric Royce*), Ray "Crash" Corrigan ("*It*"), Paul Langton (*Jim*), Ann Doran (*Mary Royce*), Robert Bice, Richard Benedict, Richard Hervey, Thom Carney
D: Edward L. Cahn   **SCR:** Jerome Bixby   **PHOTOG:** Kenneth Peach
orig. to be titled **It!—The Vampire from Outer Space**
Modest SF-horror (model for **Alien***): Spaceship returning from Mars has vampiric stow-away*

It!—The Vampire from Outer Space
see It!—The Terror from Beyond Space

I, Vampire
see *I, Monster*

Ivan's Childhood
see *My Name is Ivan*

I've Been Waiting for You
1998, (USA), NBC-TV, color, 95 mins.
<u>W:</u> Sarah Chalke, Markie Post (*Rosemary Zoltanne*), Christian Campbell (*Eric*), Soleil Moon Frye (*Kyra*), Ben Foster (*Charlie*), Tom Dugan (*Ted Rankin*), Maggie Lawson, Chad Cox
<u>D:</u> Christopher Leitch **TELEPLAY:** Duane Poole from Lois Duncan's novel *Gallows* **PHOTOG:** Jon Joffin
TVM, standard fantasy-thriller: Teen linked to witchcraft, clique imperiled

The Ivory Ape
1980, (USA), Arthur Rankin Jr.-Jules Bass/ABC-TV, color, 95 mins.
<u>W:</u> Jack Palance (*Marc Kazarian*), Steven Keats (*Baxter Mapes*), Cindy Pickett (*Lil Tyler*), Earle Hyman (*Insp. St. George*), Derek Partridge (*Aubrey Range*), Lou David (*Roomie Pope*), Tricia Sembera (*Vita Havermyer*), William Horrigan (*The Captain*), Celine Lomez (*Valerie Lamont*), David Mann (*Dr. Cole*), Leonard Daniels (*Smith*), George Rushe (*Wilkinson*), John Truscott (*Collins*), John Lough (*Trot Toomer*), Jane Bainridge, Charles Jeffers, Grace Rawlins, Kevin Dill, Marlene Butterfield, Eston Rawlins, Barbara Adams, Courtney Floyd, Irving Wilkinson, Daniel Thomas
<u>D:</u> Tom Kotani **TELEPLAY:** Arthur Rankin Jr. & William Overgard **PHOTOG:** Yozo Inagaki **MUSIC:** Maury Laws & Bernard Hoffer
TVM, standard action-melodrama: Hunt for albino gorilla

The Ivory Hand
1915, (GB), Clarendon, b&w, 3,106 ft. (946.7m)
<u>D:</u> Wilfred Noy
Standard thriller: Chinese priest gains revenge on man who stole idol's jewelled hand

I Wake Up Screaming
1941, (USA), 20th-Fox, b&w, 82 mins.
<u>W:</u> Betty Grable (*Jill Lynn*), Victor Mature (*Frankie Christopher*), Carole Landis (*Vicky Lynn*), Laird Cregar (*Ed Cornell*), William Gargan (*Jerry MacDonald*), Elisha Cook Jr. (*Harry Williams*), Alan Mowbray (*Robin Ray*), Allyn Joslyn (*Larry Evans*), Chick Chandler (*A Reporter*), Cyril Ring (*A Reporter*), Morris Ankrum (*The Ass't D.A.*), Charles Lane (*The Florist*), Frank Orth (*The Caretaker*), Gregory Gay (*The Headwaiter*), May Beatty (*Mrs. Handel*)
<u>P:</u> Milton Sperling **D:** H. Bruce Humberstone **SCR:** Dwight Taylor, from a novel by Steve Fisher **PHOTOG:** Edward Cronjager **MUSIC:** Cyril Mockridge
A.k.a. **Hot Spot.** *Remake:* **Vicki** *1953*
Bizarre melodrama: Entertainer's murderer sought

I Walked with a Zombie
1943, (USA), RKO, b&w, 68 mins.
<u>W:</u> Frances Dee, Tom Conway, James Ellison, Edith Barrett, Christine Gordon, James Bell, Jeni LeGon, Theresa Harris, Darby Jones, Sir Lancelot
<u>P:</u> Val Lewton **D:** Jacques Tourneur **SCR:** Curt Siodmak & Ardel Wray, from an orig. story by Inez Wallace **PHOTOG:** J. Roy Hunt **MUSIC:** Roy Webb
blurb: "She's alive...yet dead! She's dead...yet alive!"
Classic thriller: Nurse finds superstition and zombies on West Indies plantation

I Want Her Dead
see *W*

I Was a Communist for the F.B.I.
1951, (USA), WB, b&w, 83 mins.
<u>W:</u> Frank Lovejoy, Dorothy Hart Philip Carey, James Millican
Standard melodrama

I Was a Spy
1933, (GB), Gaumont/W&F, b&w, 89 mins.
<u>W:</u> Madeleine Carroll (*Marthe Cnockhaert*), Conrad Veidt (*Cmdr. Oberaertz*), Herbert Marshall (*Stephan*), Gerald du Maurier (*The Doctor*), Edmund Gwenn (*The Burgomaster*), Donald Calthrop (*Cnockhaert*), May Agate (*Mme. Cnockhaert*), Eva Moore (*Canteen Ma*), Martita Hunt (*Aunt Lucille*), Nigel Bruce (*Scotty*), George Merritt (*Reichmann*), Anthony Bushell (*Otto*), Cyril Smith (*The Officer*), Eliot Makeham (*The Pharmacist*), Henry Oscar
<u>D:</u> Victor Saville **SCR:** W.P. Lipscomb & Ian Hay, from a book by Marthe Cnockhaert McKenna
Standard thriller: True story of World War I nurse who became espionage agent, reissued 1939

I Was a Teenage Frankenstein
1957, (USA), Santa Rosa/AIP, b&w (last seconds in color), 72 mins.
<u>W:</u> Whit Bissell (*Prof. Frankenstein*), Gary Conway (*The Teenage Monster*), Phyllis Coates (*Margaret*), Robert Burton (*Dr. Karlton*), George Lynn (*Sgt. Burns*), John Cliff (*Sgt. McAfee*), Marshall Bradford (*Dr. Randolph*), Claudia Bryar (*Arlene's Mother*), Russ Whiteman (*Dr. Elwood*), Angela Blake (*The Beautiful Girl*), Larry Carr, Joy Stoner, Charles Seel, Paul Keast, Pat Miller, Gretchen Thomas

<u>P:</u> Herman Cohen **D:** Herbert L. Strock **SCR:** Kenneth Langtry **PHOTOG:** Lothrop B. Worth **MUSIC:** Paul Dunlap
blurb: "Body of a Boy...Mind of a Monster...Soul of an Unearthly Thing!"
orig. co-billed with **Blood of Dracula**
Standard horror-thriller: Doctor creates monstrous youth

I Was a Teen-Age Mummy
1963, (USA), Jerall, color
<u>W:</u> Michael Harris, Jayne Walker, Scott Mullin, Jeff Mullin, Allen Skinner, Steve Emmett
<u>P:</u> Allen Skinner & Jeff Mullin **D:** Ralph Bluemke
16mm amateur production, not in general release. Minor horror-fantasy

I Was a Teenage Sex Mutant
1989, (USA), Phantom Prods., color
<u>W:</u> Billy Jacoby, Olivia Barash, Troy Donahue, Edy Williams, Stuart Fratkin, Bobby Jacoby, Arlene Golonka, Julie Gray, Tom DeFranco, Raymond O'Connor, Jim Hackett, Scott Morris, Judy Landers
<u>D:</u> Dave DeCoteau **SCR:** Kenneth J. Hall **PHOTOG:** Nicholas Von Sternberg **MUSIC:** Reg Powell & Sam Winans
Minor SF-farce: Serum turns nerd into stud

I Was a Teenage Werewolf
1957, (USA), AIP, b&w, 76 mins.
<u>W:</u> Michael Landon (*Tony*), Yvonne Lime (*Arlene*), Whit Bissell (*Dr. Alfred Brandon*), Tony Marshall (*Jimmy*), Barney Phillips (*Det. Donovan*), Dawn Richard (*Teresa*), Vladimir Sokoloff (*Pepe*), Guy Williams (*Chris*), Louise Lewis (*Miss Dawson*), Malcolm Atterbury (*Tony's Father*), Robert Griffin (*Chief Baker*), Michael Rougas (*Frank*), Cindy Robbins, Ken Miller, Joseph Mell, Eddie Marr, Dorothy Crehan, John Launer
<u>P:</u> Herman Cohen **D:** Gene Fowler Jr. **ORIG. STORY & SCR:** Ralph Thornton **PHOTOG:** Joseph La Shelle **MUSIC:** Paul Dunlap **SONG:** Eeny, Meeny, Miney, M
orig. co-billed with **Invasion of the Saucer Men**
blurb: "The most amazing motion picture of our time!"
Semi-classic horror-thriller: Doctor hypnotizes unruly youth, regresses him to primitive state of evolution

I Was a Teenage Zombie
1987, (USA), Horizon, color, 92 mins.
<u>W:</u> Steve McCoy (*Mussolini*), Michael Ruben (*Dan Wake*), Cassie Madden (*Cindy*), George Seminara (*Gordy*) Allen Rickman
<u>D:</u> John Elias Michalakias **PHOTOG:** Peter Lewnes **MUSIC:** Los Lobos, The Fleshtones, The Waitresses, Dream Syndicate, & Violent Femmes
Modest SF-satire: Polluted drug turns high-schoolers into horrors

I Was a Zombie for the F.B.I.
1984, (USA), Ardent Teleproductions, b&w, 108 mins.
<u>W:</u> James Raspberry (*Rex Armstrong*), Larry Raspberry (*Ace Evans*), John Gillick (*Bart Brazzo*), Christina Wellford (*Penny Carson*), Anthony Isbell, Laurence Hall, Jennifer Malolepsy, Rick Crowe, Alan Zellner, Ken Zimmerman, Jim Ostrander, David Mayo, Chris Schadrack, Paul Malolepsy, Jeff Bailey, Rick Clodfelter, Chuck Cooper, D.M. Coger, Allen French, Estelle Helm, Glenda Mace, William Adler, George Larrimore, Nichols Wall, Steve Watermeier, Cindy Bingham, Ken Wilburn, Bob Friedstand, Michael J. Vails, Rick Owings, Tom Clark, John DeCleux, Walter Hamby, Tom McCrory, Jo Lynn Palmer, Lisa Dean Jones, Robert Bruce, Max Maxwell, Debi Barham, Jeff Posson, Carl Eaves, Paul Yates, Richard Ranta, Greg Le May, Thomas Bailey, Trina Carter, Hugh Berry, Kim Burton, Raymond Bursi, Virginia Donelson, David Brown, Ricky Brown, Teresa Brown, Angee Cockroft, Morgan Caer-Myrddin, Hugh Brooks, Max Cheney, George Borg, Glen P. Campbell, Cosette Collier, Jane R. Conway, Michael Conway, Preston Davis, Colonius Davis, Quitman DeLoach, Andrew Diggs, Tom Disney, Lea Fisher, Sue Donelson, Roger Fonseca, Alan Frazier, Billy Grace, Tre Grace, Alan Goodwin, Tracy Gossett, Randle Hopkins, Bill Haines, Reggie Hamilton, John Hampton, Linda Lamb, Bart Mallard, Gill Herren, David S. Hyde, John Kelley, Kathy Kitabachi, Steve Malwee, Eric Melkent, Ken Carter, June Middleton, Danny Bursi, Balerie Miller, Olga Page, Connie Neighbors, Neal Newman, David Nunn, Robert Page, Ashley Pickle, Barbara Pickle, Teresa Roberts, Jolanda Penczner, Mike Farrish, Noel Price, Hal Prewitt, Sandra Seago, Dale Pearce, Paul Penczner, Ira Pylant, Deborah Simpkins, Mike Berry, Phil Herring, Bab Quackenboss, Jim Stelter, Mark Ruleman, Betty Roberts, Julie Wage, Evelyn Stanford, Susan Taylor, Terry Allen Weeks, Glenni Wilson, Tom Zynda
<u>P:</u> Marius Penczner & Nancy Donelson **D:** Marius Penczner **SCR:** Marius Penczner & John Gillick **PHOTOG:** Rick Dupree **SPCL-FX:** Bob Friedstand
Minor SF-satire, B-movie spoof: Aliens tamper with formula for popular soft drink, turn humans into automatons

I, Werewolf
see *I, Monster*

I Worship his Shadow
1997, (USA), color
<u>W:</u> Barry Bostwick, Eva Haberman, Brian Downey, Michael McManus
<u>D:</u> Paul Donovan **PHOTOG:** Les Krizsan **MUSIC:** Marty Simon

Jabberwocky
1977, (GB), Umbrella/Cinema 5, color, 101 mins.
<u>W</u>: Michael Palin (*Dennis Cooper*), Max Wall (*King Bruno the Questionable*), Deborah Fallender (*The Princess*), Annette Badland (*Griselda Fishfinger*), John LeMesurier (*Passelewe*), Warren Mitchell (*Fishfinger*), Brenda Cowling (*Mrs. Fishfinger*), Harry H. Corbett (*The Squire*), Rodney Bewes (*The Other Squire*), Bernard Bresslaw (*The Landlord*), Dave Prowse (*The Good Knight/Bad Knight*), Derek Francis (*The Bishop*), Alexandra Dane (*Betsy*), Frank Williams (*The Merchant*), John Bird (*The Herald*), Neil Innes (*The Herald/Drummer*), Graham Crowden (*The Leader*), Christopher Logue (*The Fanatic*), Peggy Ann Clifford (*The Nurse*), Terry Jones (*The Poacher*), Bryan Pringle (*The Guard*), Gordon Rollings (*Sister Jessica*), Brian Glover (*The Armourer*), Erik Chitty (*The Servant*), Harold Goodwin (*A Peasant*), Tony Sympson (*A Peasant*), Willoughby Goddard (*The Eggman*), Simon Williams (*The Prince*), Anita Sharp Bolster (*The Crone*), Peter Salmon (*The Monster*), Mollie Maureen (*The Nun*), Paul Curran
<u>P</u>: Sandy Lieberson   <u>D</u>: Terry Gilliam   <u>SCR</u>: Terry Gilliam & Charles Alverson, from Lewis Carroll's poem   <u>PHOTOG</u>: Terry Bedford   <u>MUSIC</u>: DeWolfe
Amusing fantasy-farce: Medieval cooper's apprentice slays dragon, wins princess

J'Accuse (I Accuse)
1918, (Fr), Pathe, b&w, 7,000 ft. (2133.6m)
<u>W</u>: Blaise Cendrars
<u>D & SCR</u>: Abel Gance   <u>PHOTOG</u>: Abel Gance & Leonce-Henri Burel
Classic fantasy-thriller: War dead rise. cf. **I Accuse** *(1958)*

J'Accuse (I Accuse)
1937, (Fr), b&w, 104 mins.
<u>W</u>: Victor Francen, Jean Max
<u>D & SCR</u>: Abel Gance
A.k.a. **That They Might Live**
Unusual horror-fantasy: War dead rise from grave

Jack
1996, (USA), American Zoetrope-Great Oaks/Hollywood, color, 113 mins.
<u>W</u>: Robin Williams, Diane Lane, Fran Drescher, Jennifer Lopez, Brian Kerwin, Bill Cosby, Adam Zolotin
<u>D</u>: Francis Ford Coppola   <u>SCR</u>: James DeMonaco & Gary Nadeau   <u>PHOTOG</u>: John Toll   <u>MUSIC</u>: Michael Kamen
Bizarre fantasy: 10-year-old boy trapped in body of 40-year-old man

Jack and Jill
1905, (GB), Graphic/Gaumont, b&w
<u>D</u>: Harold Jeapes
Standard comedy-fantasy short: Burlesque nursery rhymes

Jack and the Beanstalk
1917, (USA), Fox, b&w
<u>W</u>: Francis Carpenter, Virginia Lee Corbin, Arthur Lake, J.G. Traver
Standard fantasy: Yokel meets giant

Jack and the Beanstalk
1924, (USA), Univ, b&w, 2 reels
<u>W</u>: Baby Peggy, Albert Williams, Jack Earle
<u>D & SCR</u>: Alf Goulding
Juvenile fantasy: Tot tempers titan

Jack and the Beanstalk
1952, (USA), Exclusive/WB, color, 78 mins.
<u>W</u>: Bud Abbott (*Dinkelpuss*), Lou Costello (*Jack*), Dorothy Ford (*Polly*), Buddy Baer (*The Giant*), James Alexander (*The Prince*), William Farnum (*The King*), Shaye Cogan (*Eloise Larkin/The Princess*), Barbara Brown (*Mother*), David Stollery (*Donald*)
<u>P</u>: Alex Gottlieb   <u>D</u>: Jean Yarbrough   <u>SCR</u>: Nat Curtis   <u>PHOTOG</u>: George Robinson   <u>MUSIC</u>: Raoul Kraushaar
Juvenile comedy-fantasy: Rube encounters giant

Jack and the Beanstalk: Lou Costello, Bud Abbot and Hank Mann

Jack and the Beanstalk
1976, (Jap), color, 90 mins.
Animated feature, juvenile fantasy: Farm boy obtains magic beans

Jack and the Fairies
1912, (GB), Urban, b&w, 895 ft. (272.8m)
<u>D</u>: Stuart Kinder
Standard fantasy: Boy sweep escapes cruel mother, is taken to Fairyland

Jack et Jim
1903, (Fr), Star, b&w, 58m (190.3 ft./3.2 mins.)
<u>D</u>: Georges Melies
Standard fantasy. A.k.a. **Comical Conjuring**

Jack Frost
1965, (Russ), Corinth, color, 82 mins.
<u>W</u>: Natalya Sedykh, V. Altaskaya, I. Churikova, E. Izotov
<u>D</u>: Alexander Rowe   <u>SCR</u>: M. Volpin & N. Erdman   <u>PHOTOG</u>: D. Surensky   <u>MUSIC</u>: N. Budashkin
Modest fantasy: Magician aids abandoned girl

Jack Jaggs and Dum Dum
see **Tom Tight et Dum Dum**

Jack O'Lantern
1995, (USA), color, 90 mins.
<u>W</u>: Linnea Quigley, Rebecca Wicks
Minor horror-fantasy: Trick-or-Treaters free demon

Jack O'Lantern Murders
see **Condemned to Death**

Jack's Back
1988, (USA), Cinema Group/Palisades, color, 95 mins.
<u>W</u>: James Spader (*John/Rick*), Cynthia Gibb (*Christine*), Rod Loomis (*Sidney*), Rex Ryon (*Jack*), Jim Haynie (*Sgt. Gabriel*), Rod Picardo (*Dr. Carlos Battera*), Chris Mulkey, Wendell Wright, John Wesley, Bobby Hosea, Danitza Kingsley, Daniela Petr, Anne Betancourt, Diane Erikson, Sis Greenspon, Graham Timbes, Mario Machado, Paul Du Pratt, Rana Ford, Pola Del Mar, Shawne Rowe, Kevin Glover, John Sutherland, Cassian Elwes, Spencer Clarke, Kathryn O'Reilly, Richard Parker, Brian "Fats" Bender, Cindy Guyer, Frances Fleming
<u>WRIT & D</u>: Rowdy Herrington   <u>PHOTOG</u>: Shelly Johnson   <u>MUSIC</u>: Daniel Di Paolo
Standard thriller: Cops hunt modern "Jack the Ripper"

Jack's Wife
1972, (USA), Jack H. Harris, color, 130 mins. (some versions minus 40 mins.)
<u>W</u>: Jan White, Ray Laine, Anne Muffly, Joedda McClain, Bill Thunhurst, Neil Fisher, Esther Lapidus, Dan Mallinger, Ken Peters, Daryl Montgomery, Shirlee Strasser, Jean Wechsler, Bob Trow, Linda Creagan, Bill Hinzman, Marvin Lieber, Paul McCollough, Sue Michaels, Hal Priore, Virginia Greenwald
<u>P</u>: Nancy M. Romero   <u>D, SCR, & PHOTOG</u>: George A. Romero   <u>SPCL-FX</u>: Rege Survinski   <u>ORIG. ELECTRONIC MUSIC</u>: Steve Gorn   <u>SONG</u>: *Season of the Witch* sung by Donovan,
A.k.a. **Hungry Wives**, *reissued (1981) as* **Season of the Witch**
Minor horror-thriller: Suburban housewife kills husband, joins satanic cult

Jack the Chimney Sweep
see **Jack le Ramoneur**

Jack the Giant Killer
1962, (USA), Zenith/UA, color, 94 mins.
<u>W</u>: Kerwin Mathews (*Jack*), Judi Meredith (*Princess Elaine*), Torin Thatcher (*Pendragon*), Don Beddoe (*The Imp*), Anna Lee (*Maid Constance*), Roger Mobley (*Peter*), Barry Kelley (*Sigurd*), Dayton Lummis (*King Mark*), Tudor Owen (*The Chancellor*), Helen Wallace (*Jack's Mother*), Walter Burke (*Garna*), Robert Gist (*Capt. McFadden*), Ken Mayer (*The Boatswain*)
<u>P</u>: Edward Small   <u>D</u>: Nathan Juran   <u>SCR</u>: Orville H. Hampton & Nathan Juran from a story by Orville H. Hampton   <u>PHOTOG</u>: David Horsley   <u>SPCL-FX</u>: Howard Anderson   <u>MUSIC</u>: Paul Sawtell
Standard fantasy (UA's answer to Columbia's **7th Voyage of Sinbad**): *Stalwart youth in medieval Britain battles power-hungry magician*

Jack le Ramoneur (Jack the Chimney Sweep)
1906, (Fr), Star, b&w, 307m (1,007.2 ft./17 mins.)
<u>W</u>: Bluette Bernon
<u>D</u>: Georges Melies
A.k.a. **The Chimney Sweep**
Standard fantasy (in 25 scenes): Chimney sweep dreams of visit to Utopia

Jack the Ripper
1959, (GB), Midcentury/Rank/RegalPara, b&w, 84 mins.
<u>W</u>: Lee Patterson (*Sam Lowry*), Eddie Byrne (*Insp. O'Neill*), Betty Mc-Dowall (*Anne Ford*), Ewen Solon (*Sir David Rodgers*), John LeMesurier (*Dr. Tranter*), George Rose (*Clarke*), Philip Leaver (*The Manager*), Barbara Burke (*Kitty Knowles*), Denis Shaw (*Simes*), Endre Muller (*Louis Benz*), Bill Shine, The

Montparnasse Ballet
P, D, & PHOTOG: Robert S. Baker & Monty Berman   **SCR:** Jimmy Sangster
   ORIG. STORY: Colin Craig & Peter Hammond   **MUSIC:** Stanley Black
Standard thriller: Detective pursues murderous fiend

Jack the Ripper
1979, (W. Ger-Switz), Erwin C. Dietrich/Cineshowcase, color, 82 mins.
W: Klaus Kinski, Josephine Chaplin (*Cynthia*), Herbert Fux (*Insp. Anthony Selby*),
   Lina Romay, Nikola Weisse, Ursula V. Weise
P: Peter Baumgartner   **D & SCR:** Jess Franco
Minor thriller: Fictional exploits of infamous fiend

Jack the Ripper: EDDIE BYRNE

Jacob's Ladder
1990, (USA), Carolco/Tri-Star, color, 116 mins.
W: Tim Robbins (*Jacob Singer*), Elizabeth Pena (*Jezzie*), Danny Aiello (*Louis*), Matt
   Craven (*Michael*), Pruitt Taylor Vince (*Paul*), Jason Alexander (*Geary*), Ving
   Rhames (*George*), Patricia Kalember (*Sarah*), Anthony Alessandro (*Rod*),
   Eriq La Salle (*Frank*), Brian Tarantina (*Doug*), S. Epatha Merkerson (*Elsa*),
   Brent Hinkley (*Jerry*), Suzanne Shepherd (*The Hospital Receptionist*), Doug
   Barron (*The Group Leader*), Jan Saint (*Santa*), Kisha Skinner, Patty
   Rosborough, Dion Simmons, Sam Coppola, Gloria Irizarry, Evan O'Meara,
   Kyle Hass, Lewis Black, Christopher Fields, Raymond Anthony Thomas,
   Jaime Perry, Michael Tomlinson, A.M. Marxuach, Antonia Rey, John
   Capodice, Bellina Logan, John Patrick McLaughlin, Scott Cohen, Davidson
   Thomson, Bryan Larkin, B.J. Donaldson, Thomas A. Carlin, Becky Ann
   Baker, Carol Schneider, Diane Kagan, Billie Neal, Dennis Green, Mike
   Stokie, James Ellis Reynolds, Stephanie Berry, Brad Hamler, Byron Keith
   Minns, Reggie McFadden, Arleigh Richards, Chris Murphy, John-Martin
   Green, Barbara Gruen, Ann Pearl Gary, Joe Quintero, John Louis Fischer,
   Alison Gordy, Alva Williams, Elizabeth Abassi, Nora Burns, Perry Lang,
   Jessica Roberts, Holly Kennedy, Blanche Irwin Stuart, Macaulay Culkin
D: Adrian Lyne   **SCR:** Bruce Joel Rubin   **PHOTOG:** Jeffrey L. Kimball   **SPCL-
FX:** Conrad Brink   **MUSIC:** Maurice Jarre
Unusual thriller: Eerie hallucinations plague war veteran

Jacob Two-Two Meets the Hooded Fang
1977, (Can), Gulkin/Cinema Shares, color, 90 mins.
W: Alex Karras
D & SCR: Theodore J. Flicker, from a story by Mordecai Richier
Juvenile fantasy: Nightmare adventures of small boy

Jade
1995, (USA), Para, color
W: David Caruso, Linda Fiorentino, Michael Biehn, Chazz Palminteri, Richard
   Crenna
D: William Friedkin   **SCR:** Joe Eszterhas
Standard thriller: Socialite's wife moonlights as prostitute, becomes involved in murder mystery

The Jade Mask
1945, (USA), Mono, b&w, 66 mins.
W: Sidney Toler (*Charlie Chan*), Mantan Moreland (*Birmingham Brown*), Edwin
   Luke (*Eddie Chan*), Janet Warren (*Jean*), Edith Evanson (*Louise*), Hardie
   Albright (*Meeker*), Cyril Delevanti (*Roth*), Frank Reicher (*Harper*), Alan
   Bridge (*Mack*), Dorothy Granger (*Stella*), Joe Whitehead (*Peabody*), Ralph
   Lewis, Lester Dorr, Jack Ingram, Henry Hall
D: Phil Rosen   **SCR:** George Callahan, from characters created by Earl Derr
   Biggers   **PHOTOG:** Harry Neumann
Minor "Charlie Chan" mystery: Scientist is murdered

Jaguar
1956, (USA), Rep, b&w, 66 mins.
W: Sabu, Chiquita
Minor adventure-thriller

The Jailbird: or, The Bishop and the Convict
1905, (GB), Warwick Trading Co., b&w, 475 ft. (144.8m)
D: Charles Raymond
Standard crime-thriller: Convict steals bishop's clothes, kills girl, flees in boat

Jake Speed
1986, (USA), Force Ten Prods.-Balcor Film Investors/New World, color, 93 mins.
W: Wayne Crawford, Dennis Christopher, Karen Kopins, John Hurt
D: Andrew Lane   **SCR:** Wayne Crawford & Andrew Lane   **PHOTOG:** Brian
   Loftus   **MUSIC:** Mark Snow
*Standard adventure-thriller (**Raiders of the lost Ark** imitation): Superhero battles white
   slavers*

Jalopy
1953, (USA), AA, b&w, 62 mins.
W: Leo Gorcey, Huntz Hall, Robert Lowery, Richard Benedict, Leon Belasco,
   Bernard Gorcey, Jane Easton, David Condon, Murray Alper, Mona Knox,
   Bennie Bartlett, Bernard Gorcey, Tom Hanlon
P: Ben Schwalb   **D:** William Beaudine   **SCR:** Tim Ryan, Jack Crutcher & Bert
   Lawrence
Marginal SF in standard comedy: Bowery Boys obtain secret formula for racing-car fuel

Jamaica Inn
1939, (GB), Mayflower/ABPC/Para, b&w, 107 mins.
W: Charles Laughton (*Sir Humphrey Pengallan*), Maureen O'Hara (*Mary Yelland*),
   Leslie Banks (*Joss Merlyn*), Emlyn Williams (*Harry Pedlar*), Robert Newton
   (*Jem Trehearne*), Wylie Watson (*Salvation Watkins*), Marie Ney (*Patience
   Merlyn*), Morland Graham (*Sealawyer Sydney*), Stephen Haggard (*The Boy*),
   John Longden (*Capt. Johnson*), Mervyn Johns (*Thomas*), Jeanne de Casalis
   (*The Guest*), Edwin Greenwood (*The Dandy*), Frederick Piper (*Davis*),
   Horace Hodges (*Chadwick*), Hay Petrie (*Sam*), George Curzon (*Capt.
   Murray*), Basil Radford (*Lord George*), Herbert Lomas (*The Tenant*), Mabel
   Terry-Lewis (*Lady Beston*), Aubrey Mather (*The Coachman*)
D: Alfred Hitchcock   **SCR:** Sidney Gilliat, Joan Harrison & J.B. Priestley, from
   Daphne du Maurier's novel   **PHOTOG:** Harry Stradling   **MUSIC:** Eric
   Fenby
reissued 1944 & 1948
Vintage adventure-thriller: Cornish shipwreckers exposed

Jamaica Inn
1985, (GB), HTV/Metromedia, color, 188 mins.
W: Jane Seymour (*Mary Yellan*), Patrick McGoohan (*Joss Merlyn*), Trevor Eve
   (*Jem*), Billie Whitelaw (*Aunt Patience*), John McEnery (*Rev. Davey*), Peter
   Vaughan (*Squire Bassett*), Vivian Pickles (*Martha Yellan*), Christopher
   Douglas (*Walter*), Norman Bowker (*The Captain*), Michael Goldie (*Harry*),
   John Abineri (*Richards*), Hubert Tucker (*Dr. Rawlings*), Nick Brimble (*The
   Hussar*), Howard Goorney (*The Coachdriver*), Ian Brimble (*The Customs
   Officer*), Rex Holdsworth (*The Lighthouse Keeper*), Adrian Cairns (*Preacher*),
   Tim Hooper (*Tinker*), Paul Cresswell (*The Helmsman*), Tony Rohr (*The
   Guard*), Susan Dury (*Maria Bassett*), Jo Anderson (*The Prisoner's Woman*),
   Chris Colyer (*The 2nd Guard*), Edwina Ford (*Hannah*), Pavel Douglas
   (*James*), Paul Nicholson (*The Manservant*), Dennis Patten (*The Punch & Judy
   Man*), Bill Wallis (*The Blacksmith*)
D: Lawrence Gordon Clark   **TELEPLAY:** Derek Marlowe, from Daphne du
   Maurier's novel
*TVM (in 2 parts), leisurely adventure-romance: 19th-century cutthroats wreck ships on
   Cornish coast*

Jamaica Run
1953, (USA), Clarion/Para, color, 92 mins.
W: Ray Milland (*Patrick Fairlie*), Arlene Dahl (*Ena Dacey*), Wendell Corey (*Todd
   Dacey*), Patric Knowles (*Montague*), Carroll McComas (*Mrs. Dacey*), Laura
   Eliot (*Janice Clayton*), Michael Moore (*Robert Clayton*), Murray Matheson
   (*Insp. Mole*), William Walker, Lester Matthews, Rex Evans, Robert Warwick
WRIT & D: Lewis R. Foster, from Max Murray's novel   **PHOTOG:** Lionel
   Lindon   **MUSIC:** Lucien Calliet
Standard adventure-melodrama: Lost treasure inspires evil

James and the Giant Peach
1996, (USA), Walt Disney/Allied Filmakers/Buena Vista, color, 79 mins.
W: Paul Terry (*James*), Joanna Lumley, Miriam Margolyes, Pete Postlethwaite
VOICES: Richard Dreyfuss (*Centipede*), Susan Sarandon (*Spider*), Simon
   Callow(*Centipede*) Jane Leeves (*Ladybug*), David Thewlis (*Earthworm*)
D: Henry Selick, from a story by Roald Dahl   **MUSIC:** Randy Newman
*"..boldly beautiful sights unlike anything else on screen"—Janet Maslin, New
   York Times*
Fantasy with live action, stop-motion animation. Boy in giant peach heads for NYC

James Tont: Operation Goldsinger
1966, (W. Ger), color
W: Larry Beach, Eve Moran, Louis Gibbs
Minor spy-satire

Jane and the Lost City
1987, (GB), color, 95 mins.
__W:__ Kirsten Hughes (*Jane*), Sam Jones (*Jack*), Maud Adams (*Lola*)
Minor adventure-thriller: Brits vs. Nazis in African diamond hunt

Jane Eyre
1921, (USA), Hugo Ballin Prods./W.W. Hodkinson Corp., b&w, 7 reels (6,550 ft./1996.4m)
__W:__ Norman Trevor (*Mr. Rochester*), Mabel Ballin (*Jane Eyre*), Crauford Kent (*St. John Rivers*), Stephen Carr (*John Reed*), John Webb Dillon (*Mr. Rochester's Brother*), Emily Fitzroy (*Grace Poole*), Louis Grisel (*John Eyre, Jane's Uncle*), Harlan Knight (*Mr. Brocklehurst*), Vernie Atherton (*Miss Fairfax*), Elizabeth Aeriens (*Mrs. Rochester*), June Ellen Terry (*Adele, Mr. Rochester's Ward*), Helen Miles (*Burns*), Julia Hurley (*Rivers' Maid*), Sadie Mullen (*Miss Ingram*), Bertha Kent (*Mr. Rochester's Maid*), Florence Flagler (*Miss Mason*), Marie Shaffer (*Mrs. Reed*)
__P, D, & SCR:__ Hugo Ballin, from Charlotte Bronte's novel   __PHOTOG:__ James Diamond
Standard melodrama: Woman finds tragic love

Jane Eyre
1934, (USA), Mono, b&w, 62 mins.
__W:__ Colin Clive (*Rochester*), Virginia Bruce (*Jane Eyre*), Beryl Mercer, Jameson Thomas, Edith Fellows, Aileen Pringle
from Charlotte Bronte's novel
First sound version of literary classic, standard melodrama: Governess encounters mystery

Jane Eyre
1944, (USA), 20th-Fox, b&w, 96 mins.
__W:__ Joan Fontaine (*Jane Eyre*), Orson Welles (*Rochester*), Margaret O'Brien, Agnes Moorehead, Peggy Ann Garner, Sara Allgood, Hillary Brooke, Barbara Everest, Edith Barrett, Elizabeth Taylor, John Sutton, Aubrey Mather, Mae Marsh, Henry Daniell, Ethel Griffies
__D:__ Robert Stevenson   __ADAPT:__ Aldous Huxley, from Charlotte Bronte's novel
__PHOTOG:__ George Barnes   __MUSIC:__ Bernard Herrmann   __SPCL-FX:__ Fred Sersen
Classic melodrama: Governess falls in love with brooding aristocrat

Jane Eyre
1957, (USA), Albert McCleery/NBC-TV/NTA, color, 54 mins
__W:__ Joan Elan (*Jane Eyre*), Patrick Macnee (*Rochester*), Tita Purdom
__P:__ Ethel Frank & Winston O'Keefe, from Charlotte Bronte's novel
TVM (orig. an episode of teleseries "Matinee Theater"): Governess unearths secret

Jane Eyre
1970, (GB), Omnibus/Sagittarius/British Lion/NBC-TV, color, 110 mins.
__W:__ George C. Scott (*Rochester*), Susannah York (*Jane Eyre*), Jack Hawkins (*Mr. Brocklehurst*), Rachel Kempson (*Mrs. Fairfax*), Kenneth Griffith (*Mason*), Constance Cummings (*Mrs. Reed*), Ian Bannen (*Rev. St. John Rivers*), Nyree Dawn Porter (*Blanche Ingram*), Jean Marsh (*Mrs. Rochester*), Hugh Latimer (*Col. Dent*), Peter Copley (*John*), Clive Morton (*Mr. Eshton*), Michele Dotrice (*Mary Rivers*), Kara Wilson (*Diana Rivers*), Stella Tanner (*Grace Poole*), Sarah Gibson (*Jane as a Child*), Helen Goss
__P:__ Frederick Brogger   __D:__ Delbert Mann   __SCR:__ Jack Pulman, from Charlotte Bronte's novel   __MUSIC:__ John Williams
Standard melodrama: Governess discovers tragedy

Jane Eyre
1995, (GB-It-Fr-USA), Miramax, color, 117
__W:__ William Hurt (*Mr. Rochester*), Charlotte Gainsbourg (*Jane Eyre*), Anna Paquin (*Young Jane*), Joan Plowright (*Mrs. Fairfax*), Geraldine Chaplin (*Miss Scratcherd*), Elle Macpherson (*Blanche Ingram*), John Wood (*Mr. Brocklehurst*), Leanne Rowe (*Helen Burns*), Josephine Serre (*Adele*), Fiona Shaw, Billie Whitelaw, Maria Schneider
__D:__ Franco Zeffirelli   __SCR:__ Franco Zeffirelli & Hugh Whitemore, from Charlotte Bronte's novel   __PHOTOG:__ David Watkin   __MUSIC:__ Alessio Vlad & Claudio Capponi
Impressive melodrama: Governess loves nobleman

Jane Shore
1908, (GB), Gaumont, b&w, 695 ft. (211.8m)
from a play by Nicholas Rowe
Standard historical melodrama: 15th-century married woman becomes King's mistress, is stoned

Jane Shore
1911, (GB), Britannia Films/Pathe, b&w, 1,238 ft. (377.3m)
__W:__ Florence Barker (*Jane Shore*)
__D:__ Frank Powell, from a play by Nicholas Rowe
Standard historical melodrama: 1480's goldsmith's wife becomes King's mistress, is stoned for witchcraft

Jane Shore
1915, (GB), Barker/Walturdaw, b&w, 6,300 ft. (1920.2m)
__W:__ Blanche Forsythe (*Jane Winstead*), Roy Travers (*Edward IV*), Robert Purdie (*Matthew Shore*), Dora de Winton (*Margaret*), Thomas H. MacDonald (*Lord Hastings*), Nelson Phillips (*William Shore*), Maud Yates (*Queen Elizabeth*), Rolfe Leslie (*The Duke of Gloucester*), Tom Coventry (*Master Winstead*), Rachel

de Solla (*Dame Winstead*), Frank Melrose (*Garth the Bard*), Fred Pitt (*Warwick*)
__D:__ Bert Haldane & F. Martin Thornton   __SCR:__ Rowland Talbot, from a play by Nicholas Rowe & W.G. Willis
USA retitle, __The Strife Eternal__
Standard historical melodrama: Goldsmith's wife becomes king's mistress to save husband's life

The Janus-Faced
see Der Januskopf

Der Januskopf (The Janus-Faced)
1920, (Ger), Lippow/Decla-Bioscop, b&w, 7,546 ft. (2300m)
__W:__ Conrad Veidt, Margarete Schlegel, Willy Keyser-Heyl, Margarete Kupfer, Gustav Botz, Jaro Furth, Magnus Stifter, Danny Gurtler, Marga Reuter, Bela Lugosi, Hans Lanser-Ludolff
__D:__ F.W. Murnau   __SCR:__ Hans Janowitz, from Robert Louis Stevenson's *Dr. Jekyll and Mr. Hyde*   __PHOTOG:__ Carl Hoffmann & Karl Freund
Standard thriller: Doctor becomes fiend

Japanese Magic
1912, (GB), Urban, b&w, 465 ft. (141.7m)
__WRIT & D:__ Stuart Kinder
Standard fantasy short: Mandarin and geisha perform tricks

Jap the Giant Killer
1904, (GB), Cricks & Sharp, b&w, 140 ft. (42.7m)
Standard fantasy short: Japanese soldier dreams he beheads Russian giant, wakes to find war ended

Jason and the Argonauts
1963, (GB), Morningside-World Wide/Col, color, 104 mins.
__W:__ Todd Andrews (*Jason*), Nancy Kovack (*Medea*), Gary Raymond (*Acastus*), Honor Blackman (*Hera*), Niall MacGinnis (*Zeus*), Laurence Naismith (*Argus*), Nigel Green (*Hercules*), Michael Gwynn (*Hermes*), Andrew Faulds (*Phalerus*), Douglas Wilmer (*Pelias*), Jack Gwillim (*Aeetes*), John Crawford (*Polydeuces*), Douglas Robinson, John Cairney, Patrick Troughton, Fernando Poggi
__P:__ Charles H. Schneer   __D:__ Don Chaffey   __SCR:__ Jan Read & Beverly Cross
__PHOTOG:__ Wilkie Cooper   __SPCL-FX:__ Ray Harryhausen   __MUSIC:__ Bernard Herrmann
orig. to be titled __Jason and the Golden Fleece__
Superior myth-adventure: To gain throne, hero must retrieve fabled treasure

Jason and the Golden Fleece
see Jason and the Argonauts

Jason Goes to Hell: The Final Friday
1993, (USA), New Line, color, 91 mins.
__W:__ John D. LeMay (*Steven Freeman*), Kari Keegan (*Jessica Kimble*), Kane Hodder (*Jason Voorhees*), Steven Williams (*Creighton Duke*), Steven Culp (*Robert Campbell*), Richard Gant (*The Coroner*), Erin Gray (*Diana Kimble*), Billy Green Bush (*Sheriff Landis*), Rusty Schwimmer (*Joey B.*), Leslie Jordan (*Shelby*), Kipp Marcus (*Randy*), Andrew Bloch (*Josh*), Adam Cranner (*Ward*), Allison Smith (*Vicki*), Julie Michaels (*Elizabeth Marcus, F.B.I.*), James Gleason (*Agent Abernathy*), Dean Lorey (*The Ass't Coroner*), Tony Ervolina (*The F.B.I. Agent*), Diana Georger (*Edna, Josh's Girlfriend*), Adam Marcus (*Officer Bish*), Mark Thompson (*Officer Mark*), Brian Phelps (*Officer Brian*), Blake Conway (*Officer Andell*), Medelon Curtis (*Officer Ryan*), Michelle Clunie (*Deborah, the Dark-haired Camper*), Michael Silver (*Luke, the Boy Camper*), Kathryn Atwood (*Alexis, the Blonde Camper*)
__P:__ Sean S. Cunningham   __D:__ Adam Marcus   __SCR:__ Dean Lorey & Jay Huguely
__STORY:__ Jay Huguely & Adam Marcus   __PHOTOG:__ William Dill   __SPCL VS-FX:__ Al Magliochetti   __MUSIC:__ Harry Manfredini
Standard horror-fantasy: Murderous fiend possesses new bodies

Jaws
1975, (USA), Zanuck-Brown/Univ, color, 125 mins.
__W:__ Roy Scheider (*Martin Brody*), Robert Shaw (*Quint*), Lorraine Gary (*Ellen Brody*), Richard Dreyfuss (*Matt Hooper*), Murray Hamilton (*Mayor Vaughn*), Carl Gottlieb (*Meadows*), Lee Fierro (*Kintner*), Peter Benchley (*The Interviewer*), Jeffrey C. Kramer (*Hendricks*), Susan Backlinie (*Chrissie*)
__P:__ Richard D. Zanuck & David Brown   __D:__ Steven Spielberg   __SCR:__ Peter Benchley & Carl Gottlieb, from Peter Benchley's best-selling novel   __PHOTOG:__ Bill Butler   __MUSIC:__ John Williams
"...a fast-paced, straight-line thriller that moves without pause toward the climactic contest at sea"—Judith Crist, TV Guide
Gripping thriller: Hunt for man-eating shark

Jaws 2
1978, (USA), Zanuck-Brown/Univ, color, 123 mins.
__W:__ Roy Scheider (*Martin Brody*), Murray Hamilton (*Mayor Vaughn*), Lorraine Gary (*Ellen Brody*), Collin Wilcox (*Dr. Elkins*), Joseph Mascolo (*Peterson*), Barry Coe (*Andrews*), Ann Dusenberry (*Tina*), Jeffrey Kramer (*Hendricks*), Mark Gruner (*Mike*), Marc Gilpin (*Sean*), Susan French (*The Old Lady*), Keith Gordon (*Doug*), Gary Springer (*Andy*), Donna Wilkes (*Jackie*), Gary Dubin (*Ed*), David Elliott (*Larry*), G. Thomas Dunlop (*Timmy*), Cynthia Grover (*Lucy*), Martha Swatek (*Marge*), Ben Marley (*Patrick*), Gigi Vorgan (*Brook*), Billy Van Zandt (*Bob*), Jerry M. Baxter (*The Pilot*), Jean Coulter (*The Boat Driver*), Christine Freeman (*The Skier*), April Gilpin (*Renee*), William

Griffith (*The Lifeguard*), Coll Red McLean (*Red*), Allan L. Paddack (*Crosby*), Oneida Rollins (*The Ambulance Driver*), Kathy Wilson (*Mrs. Bryant*), John Dukakis, Daphne Dibble, David Tintle, Frank Sparks, Greg Harris, Susan O. McMillan, David Owsley
D: Jeannot Szwarc **SCR:** Carl Gottlieb & Howard Sackler, from characters created by Peter Benchley **PHOTOG:** Michael Butler **MUSIC:** John Williams
"...the most expensive film that AIP never made"—*Variety*
Standard thriller: Obnoxious teens jeopardized by shark

Jaws 3-D
1983, (USA), Alan Landsburg/Univ, 3D, color, 99 mins.
W: Dennis Quaid (*Mike Brody*), Bess Armstrong (*Kathy*), Lou Gossett Jr. (*Calvin Bouchard*), John Putch (*Sean*), Simon MacCorkindale (*Philip*), Lea Thompson (*Kelly*), Dan Blasko (*Dan*), P.H. Moriarty (*Jack*)
D: Joe Alves **SCR:** Richard Matheson & Carl Gottlieb **STORY:** Guerdon Trueblood, from characters created by Peter Benchley **PHOTOG:** James A. Contner **MUSIC:** Alan Parker
Standard thriller: Monster shark terrorizes Florida tourist trap

Jaws '87
see Jaws: The Revenge

Jaws 4
see Jaws: The Revenge

Jaws: The Return
see Jaws: The Revenge

Jaws: The Revenge
1987, (USA), Univ, color, 90 mins.
W: Lorraine Gary (*Ellen Brody*), Michael Caine, Mario Van Peebles, Lance Guest, Karen Young, Judith Barsi, Mitchell Anderson, Lynn Whitfield, Jay Mello, Lee Fierro
P & D: Joseph Sargent **SCR:** Michael de Guzman, from characters created by Peter Benchley **PHOTOG:** John McPherson **MUSIC:** Michael Small
orig. to be titled Jaws 4, Jaws '87 *or* Jaws: The Return
blurb: "This Time It's Personal"
Standard thriller: Shark pursues benighted family

Jaws of Satan
1981, (USA), UA, color, 92 mins.
W: Fritz Weaver, Gretchen Corbett, Jon Korkes, Nancy Priddy, Diana Douglas, Norman Lloyd, Bob Hannah, Jack Gordan, Christina Applegate, Larry Jordan, Jane Berman
D: Bob Claver **SCR:** Gerry Holland **PHOTOG:** Dean Cundey **MUSIC:** Roger Kellaway
Standard thriller: Demonic snake plagues priest

J.D.'s Revenge
1976, (USA), AIP, color, 95 mins
W: Glynn Turman, Lou Gossett Jr., Joan Pringle
P & D: Arthur Marks **SCR:** Jaison Starkes
Standard horror-thriller (all-black cast): Law student possessed by spirit of 1930s gangster

The Jealous Doll: or, The Frustrated Elopement
1909, (GB), Clarendon, b&w, 535 ft. (163.1m)
D: Percy Stow
Standard fantasy short: Doll fetches nurse when children elope

Jeanne d'Arc (Joan of Arc)
1900, (Fr), Star, b&w, 247.8m (813 ft./13.7 mins.)
D: Georges Melies
Standard melodrama: Saint persecuted and executed

Jekyll and Hyde
1990, (USA-GB), King Phoenix/London Weedend Television/Wickes/ABC-TV, color, 95 mins.
W: Michael Caine (*Dr. Henry Jekyll/Mr. Hyde*), Cheryl Ladd (*Sara*), Joss Ackland (*Dr. Lanyon*), Ronald Pickup (*Jeffrey Utterson*), Kevin McNally (*Sgt. Hornby*), David Schofield (*Edward Snape*), Kim Thomson (*Lucy*), Frank Barrie (*Poole*), Lee Montague (*Insp. Palmer*), Miriam Karlin (*Mrs. Hackett*), Joan Heal (*Mrs. Clark*), Lionel Jeffries (*Jekyll's Father*), Margaret Rawlings (*Jekyll's Mother*), Diane Keen, Samantha Janus, Lance Percival, Martyn Jacobs, Duncan Gould, Harvey Ashby, John Scarborough, Ray Armstrong, Kiran Shah, Peter Gale, Nina Kennedy, Andrew Castell, Gary Shail, Frederick Bateman, David Michaels, Simon Adams, Richard Dixon, Eric Dodson, Jill Pearson, Michael Stainton, Jazzer Jeyes, Tim Diggle, Terry Walsh, Eric Mason, Philip Locke, Charlotte Howard, Terry Plummer, Ross McCall, Peter Geeves, Antony Brown, Craig Crosbie, Nigel Betts, Daniel Perry, Prentis Hancock, Wendy Pollock, Justin Degan
D & TELEPLAY: David Wickes, from Robert Louis Stevenson's *Dr. Jekyll and Mr. Hyde* **PHOTOG:** Norman Langley **MUSIC:** John Cameron
TVM, standard thriller: Doctor uses drugs to alter mind and body

Jekyll and Hyde...Together Again
1982, (USA), Titan/Para, color, 86 mins.
W: Mark Blankfield (*Dr. Daniel Jekyll/Hyde*), Bess Armstrong (*Mary Carew*), Krista Errickson (*Ivy Venus*), Michael McGuire (*Dr. Carew*), Tim Thomerson

(*Dr. Knute Lanyon*), Peter Brocco, Neil Hunt, Cassandra Peterson (*Elvira*), Jessica Nelson, Noelle North, Michael Klingher, David Murphy, Mary McCusker, Liz Sheridan, Alison Hong, Walter Janowitz, Ann M. Nelson, Belita Moreno, Leland Sun, George Wendt, Glen Chin, Dan Barrows, Tony Cox, Virginia Wing, Jesse Goins, Peter Ivers, Jack Collins, John Dennis Johnston, Michael Ensign, David Ruprecht, Bernadette Birkett, Clarke Coleman, Sam Whipple, Nancy Lenehan, Barret Oliver, Selwyn Emerson Miller, Art La Fleur, Sheila Rogers, Lin Shaye, Gerald Saunderson Peters, Madelyn Cates, Paulette K. Brown, Bud Davis, Jose Borcia, George Chakiris, Petsye Powell, Veda Jackson, Maher Boutros, Kate Fitzmaurice, Howard George
D: Jerry Belson **SCR:** Monica Johnson, Harvey Miller, Jerry Belson, & Michael Leeson, inspired by Robert Louis Stevenson's *Dr. Jekyll and Mr. Hyde* **PHOTOG:** Philip Lathrop **SPCL-FX:** Dewey G.Grigg **MUSIC:** Barry DeVorzon **SONG:** *Hyde's Got Nothing to Hide*
Frenetic horror-comedy-spoof: Doctor turns into sex-crazed cocaine fiend

Jekyll's Inferno
see The Two faces of Dr. Jekyll

Jennie
see Portrait of Jennie

Jennifer
1953, (USA), AA, b&w, 73 mins.
W: Ida Lupino (*Agnes*), Howard Duff (*Jim*), Kitty McHugh (*The Land-lady*), Mary Shipp (*Lorna*), Ned Glass, Russ Conway, Matt Dennis, Lorna Thayer
P: Bernard Swarrtz **D:** Joel Newton, from a story by Virginia Myers **PHOTOG:** James Wong Howe **MUSIC:** Matt Dennis (conduct, Ernest Gold) **SONG:** *Angel Eyes*
Standard thriller: Woman becomes caretaker of lonely estate

Jennifer
1978, (USA), AIP, color, 90 mins
W: Jeff Corey, Lisa Pelikan, Nina Foch, John Gavin, Bert Convy
P: Steve Krantz **D:** Brice Mack **SCR:** Kay Cousins
Minor fantasy-thriller: Religious fanatic's schoolgirl daughter conjures horrors

Jennifer 8
1992, (USA), Para, color, 127 mins.
W: Andy Garcia, Uma Thurman, Lance Henriksen, Kathy Baker, John Malkovich, Kevin Conway, Graham Beckel, Bob Gunton, Lenny Von Dohlen, Paul Bates, Perry Lang, Bryan Larkin
D & SCR: Bruce Robinson **PHOTOG:** Conrad L. Hall **MUSIC:** Christopher Young
Standard thriller: L.A. cop hunts serial killer of women

The Jerusalem File
1972, (USA-Israeli), Sparta-Leisure Media/MGM, color, 96 mins.
W: Bruce Davison (*David*), Nicol Williamson (*Lang*), Daria Halprin (*Nurit*), Donald Pleasence (*Samuels*), Ian Hendry (*Mayers*), Zeev Revan (*Raschid*), Koya Yair Rubin (*Barak*), Itzik Weiss (*Barak's Brother*), David Smader (*Herzen*), Jack Cohen (*Altouli*), Isaac Neeman (*Yussof*), Arie Elias (*The Informer*), Yossi Werzanski (*Alex*), Ori Levy (*Capt. Ori*), Yona Elian (*Raschel*)
P: Ram Ben Effriam **D:** John Flynn **SCR:** Troy Kennedy Martin **PHOTOG:** Raoul Coutard & Brian Probyn **MUSIC:** John Scott
Standard thriller: Archeology student involved in Middle East turmoil

Jesse James Meets Frankenstein's Daughter
1966, (USA), Embassy, color, 88 mins.
W: John Lupton (*Jesse James*), Cal Bolder (*Hank*), Narda Onyx (*Maria Frankenstein*), Estelita Rodrigues (*Juanita*), Jim Davis (*Marshall McFee*), Steven Geray (*Rudolph Frankenstein*), William Fawcett (*Jensen*), Felipe Turich (*Manuel*), Rayford Barnes (*Lonny*), Rosa Turich (*Nina*)
D: William Beaudine
Minor horror-western: Woman scientist makes monster out of outlaw's wounded buddy

The Jester's Joke
1912, (GB), Urban, b&w, 365 ft. (111.3m)
D: Walter R. Booth
reissued (1916) as The Merry Jester
Standard fantasy short: Jester causes pierrots to merge, fade, reappear

La Jetee (The Pier)
1962, (Fr), Argos, b&w
W: Helene Chatelain, Jacques Ledoux, Davos Hanich, Pierre Joffray, Jacques Branchu, Andre Heinrich
D & SCR: Chris Marker **PHOTOG:** Jean Ravel **MUSIC:** Trevor Duncan
Standard fantasy: Symbolism and mysticism merge. cf. 12 Monkeys

The Jetsons: The Movie
1990, (USA), Univ, color, 81 mins.
VOICES: George O'Hanlon, Penny Singleton, Mel Blanc, Tiffany
D: William Hanna & Joseph Barbera
Standard animated SF-fantasy: Life of future family

Jeux Interdits (Forbidden Games)
1952, (Fr), Times, b&w, 102 mins.

W: Georges Poujouly (*Michel*), Brigitte Fossey (*Paulette*), Lucien Hubert (*M. Dolle*), Amedee (*Francis*), Laurence Badie (*Berthe*), Suzanne Courtal (*Mme. Dolle*), Louis Sainteve (*The Priest*), Jacques Marin (*Georges*), Denise Peronne (*Jeanne*)
D: Rene Clement   SCR: Jean Aurenche, Pierre Bost & Rene Clement, from a story by Francois Boyer
Oscar-winning anti-war film: Two French youngsters enact secret games reflecting adult cruelty during 1940 German occupation

The Jewel of the Nile
1985, (USA), 20th-Fox, color, 105 mins.
W: Michael Douglas (*Jack Colton*), Kathleen Turner (*Joan Wilder*), Danny DeVito (*Ralph*), Spiros Focas (*Omar*), Guy Cuevas (*Le Vasseur*), Paul David Magid (*Tarak*), Avner Eisenberg (*The Holy Man*), Hamid Fillali (*Rachid*), Randall Edwin Nelson (*Karak*), Howard Jay Petterson (*Barak*), Samuel Ross Williams (*Arak*), Timothy Daniel Furst (*Sarak*), Holland Taylor (*Gloria*), Peter De Palma (*The Missionary*), Mark Daly Richards (*The Pirate*), Sadeke Colobanane (*The Nubian Chief*), Hyacinthe N'Iaye (*The Nubian Wrestler*), Daniel Peacock (*The Rock Promoter*), Benyahim Ahmed (*The Omar Officer*), Alaoui Hassen (*The Station Master*), Zaouis Abdelmajid (*The F-16 Pilot*), Makoula Ahmed (*The Ticket Seller*), Ted Buffington (*The Fire Walker*), Akasby Mohamed (*The Old Man in Sug*), Flora Alberti, Patience Poullair, Ziraoui Mustapha, Baji Abdelmajid, Kachela Mohammed, Ben Abadi, Attif Mohammed, Hilal Abdellatif, Mohammed Fillali, National Dance Company of Senegal
D: Lewis Teague   SCR: Mark Rosenthal & Lawrence Konner, from characters created by Diane Thomas   PHOTOG: Jan DeBont   SPCL-FX SPRVSR: Nick Allder   MUSIC: Jack Nitzsche   SONG: *When the Going Gets Tough, the Tough Get Going*
Standard adventure, sequel to Romancing the Stone: *Americans tangle with ruthless Arab potentate*

The Jewel Thieves
1909, (GB), Hepworth, b&w, 625 ft. (190.5m)
W: Chrissie White (*The Cyclist*)
D: Lewin Fitzhamon
Standard crime-thriller: Crooks pose as police, are chased by girl cyclist

The Jewel Thieves Run to Earth by Sexton Blake
1910, (GB), Gaumont, b&w, 810 ft. (246.9m)
from characters created by Harry Blyth
Standard thriller: Detective rescues clerk from gang

The Jewel Thieves Outwitted
1913, (GB), Hepworth, b&w, 850 ft. (259.1m)
W: Jack Hulcup (*The Thief*), Violet Hopson (*The Maid*), Rachel de Solla (*The Lady*)
D: Frank Wilson
Standard crime-thriller

Jigsaw
1962, (GB), Figaro/Britania, b&w, 108 mins.
W: Jack Warner (*Insp. Fellows*), Ronald Lewis (*Sgt. Wilks*), Yolande Donlan (*Jean Sherman*), Michael Goodliffe (*Clive Burchard*), John LeMesurier (*Mr. Simpson*), Moira Redmond (*Joan Simpson*), Brian Oulton (*Frank Restlin*), John Barron (*Ray Tenby*), Graham Payn (*Mr. Blake*), Norman Chappell (*Ady Roach*)
P: Val Guest & Frank Sherwin Green   D & SCR: Val Guest, from Hilary Waugh's novel
Minor crime-thriller: Police pursue married man who killed his mistress

Jim of the Mounted Police
1911, (GB), Hepworth, b&w, 650 ft. (198.1m)
W: Gladys Sylvani (*The Gypsy*)
D: Lewin Fitzhamon
Standard thriller: Gypsy girl betrays horse thieves to mounted police

Jim the Scorpion
1915, (GB), Big Ben-Union/L&P, b&w, 3,000 ft. (914.4m)
W: Ivy Martinek (*The Girl*)
D: H.O. Martinek
Standard crime-thriller

Jim the Signalman
1906, (GB), R.W. Paul, b&w, 354 ft. (107.9m)
D: J.H. Martin
Standard crime-thriller: Signalman's crippled son foils train wreckers

Jivaro
1954, (USA), Para, color, 91 mins.
W: Fernando Lamas, Rhonda Fleming, Lon Chaney Jr., Brian Keith, Rita Moreno
P: William H. Pine & William C. Thomas   D: Edward Ludwig   SCR: Winston Miller, from David Duncan's story *The Lost Treasure of the Andes*
GB title: **Lost Treasure of the Amazon**
Standard adventure-thriller: Gold seekers meet headhunters

Joan of Arc
see **Jeanne d'Arc**

Joan of the Angels
see **Matka Joanna od Aniolow**

J.O.E. & the Colonel
1985, (USA), Mad-Dog/Univ-TV, color, 95 mins.
W: Gary Kasper (*J.O.E., a cyborg*), Terence Knox, Bill Lucking, Gail Edwards, Allan Miller, Aimee Eccles, Mike Preston, Marie Windsor, Allan Rich, Christie Houser, Michael Swain, Bruce Cervi, Don Swayze
D: Ron Satlof   TELEPLAY: Nicholas Corea   PHOTOG: William Cronjager   MUSIC: Joseph Conlan
TVM, standard SF-thriller: Gov't hunts cyborg. Pilot for unproduced series

Joe's Apartment
1996, (USA), MTV/Geffen/WB, color, 80 mins
W: Jerry O'Connell, Megan Ward, Robert Vaughn, Don Ho
D & SCR: John Payson   PHOTOG: Peter Deming   MUSIC: Carter Burwell
Amusing SF-fantasy: Youth's life complicated by intelligent cockroaches

Joey's Dream
1916, (GB), Piccadilly/Browne, b&w, 570 ft. (173.7m)
W: Joe Evans (*Joey*)
WRIT & D: Joe Evans
Standard comedy-fantasy short: Man repulses hobo, dreams Satan turns him into tramp

Johnny Cool
1963, (USA), Chrislaw/UA, b&w, 101 mins.
W: Henry Silva, Elizabeth Montgomery, Wanda Hendrix, Jim Backus, Richard Anderson, Joey Bishop, Brad Dexter, John McGiver, Gregory Morton, Elisha Cook Jr., Marc Lawrence, Hank Henry, Joan Staley, Telly Savalas, Sammy Davis Jr., Mort Sahl
P & D: William Asher   SCR: Joseph Landon, from John McPartland's novel *The Kingdom of Johnny Cool*   PHOTOG: Sam Leavitt   MUSIC: Billy May   TITLE SONG: Sammy Cahn & James van Heusen
Fr retitle, **La Revanche du Sicilien** *(The Revenge of the Sicilian)*
Sadistic melodrama: Sicilian bandit on mission of vengeance in USA

Johnny Hamlet
1972, (It), Transvue, color, 91 mins.
W: Chip Gorman (*Johnny*), Gilbert Roland (*Horace*), Gabrielle Grimaldi (*Ophelia*), Horst Frank (*Claude*), Francoise Prevost (*Gertrude*), Pedro Sanchez (*Gil*), Enio Girolami (*Ross*), Stefania Careddu (*The Player Queen*)
D: Enzo G. Castellari   SCR: Tito Carpi, Francesco Scardamaglia & Enzo G. Castellari   STORY: Sergio Corbucci, loosely based on Shakespeare's play *Hamlet*
Standard Western-thriller: Youth seeks vengeance

Johnny Mnemonic
1995, (USA), Alliance/TriStar, color, 98 mins.
W: Keanu Reeves, Dolph Lundgren, Takeshi, Dina Meyer, Ice-T, Udo Keir, Henry Rollins, Denis Akiyama
D: Robert Longo   SCR: William Gibson, from his short story   MUSIC: Brad Fiedel
"A Pulse Pounding Cyber-Slam!"—Mike McKay, WBTV (CBS), Charlotte
Unusual SF-thriller: Gangsters pursue data courier who has "wet-wired brain"

Johnny the Giant Killer
1953, (Fr), Lippert, color, 74 mins.
D: Charles Frank & Jean Image   WRIT: Paul Collins, Nesta Macdonald & Charles Frank   PHOTOG: Kostia Tchikine   MUSIC: Rene Cloerc   ANIMATORS: Albert Champeaux, Denis Boutin O'Klein & Marcel Breuil
Animated feature, juvenile fantasy: Boys find treasure cave guarded by greedy giant

The Joker's Mistake
1912, (GB), Urban, b&w, 385 ft. (117.3m)
WRIT & D: Walter R. Booth
reissued (1916) as **Getting His Own Back**
Standard fantasy short: Conjurer's flowers blacken man's face in revenge for exploding cigarette

Jollyboy's Dream
1914, (GB), Martin/DFSA, b&w, 569 ft. (173.4m)
D: Dave Aylott
Standard fantasy short: Drunkard dreams bed transports him to savage island

The Jonah Man: or, The Traveller Bewitched
1904, (GB), Hepworth, b&w, 250 ft. (76.2m)
D: Lewis Fitzhamon & Cecil Hepworth
USA retitle, **The Bewitched Traveller**
Standard fantasy short: Man's coat, breakfast, bus and train vanish; he does too

Jonathan
1970, (W. Ger), Iduna/New Yorker, color, 103 mins.
W: Jurgen Jung (*Jonathan*), Hans Dieter Jendreyko (*Josef*), Paul Albert Krumm (*The Count*), Eleonore Schminke (*Lena*), Thomas Astan (*Thomas*), Ilse Kunkele (*Lena's Mother*), Oskar Von Schab (*The Professor*), Ilone Grubel

J

(Eleonore)
WRIT & D: Hans W. Geissendorfer   **PHOTOG:** Robby Muller   **MUSIC:** Roland Kovac
distrib. in USA, 1973
Unusual reworking of Dracula legend: University student spies on vampiric nobleman

Jones' Nightmare
1911, (GB), Acme Films/Cricks & Martin, b&w, 435 ft. (132.6m)
W: Fred Rains *(Jones)*
D: Fred Rains
Standard fantasy short: Man dreams of demons, big lobsters, being blown to moon

Jonny's Golden Quest
1993, (USA), color, 87 mins.
Standard animated SF-fantasy: Boy hero joins secret mission to stop mad scientist

El Jorobado de la Morgue (The Hunchback of the Morgue)
1972, (Sp), Evan/Janus/Cinemation, color, 88 mins
W: Paul Naschy, Rosanna Yanni, Alberto Dalves, Maria Elena Arpon, Maria Perschy, Vic Winner
P: F. Lara Polop   **D:** Javier Aguirre   **SCR:** Jacinto Molina, Alberto Insua & Javier Aguirre
*USA video-retitle, **The Rue Morgue Massacres***
Minor horror-thriller: Scientist feeds human entrails to living head; hunchback supplies corpses

Josef Kilian
*see **Order and Disorder***

Jo the Crossing Sweeper
1910, (GB), Walturdaw, b&w, 450 ft. (137.2m)
based on Charles Dickens' novel
Standard crime-thriller: Lawyer blackmails noblewoman over child by previous marriage

Journey Back to Oz
1974, (USA), color, 90 mins.
VOICES: Liza Minnelli, Milton Berle, Margaret Hamilton, Jack E. Leonard, Paul Lynde, Ethel Merman, Mickey Rooney, Rise Stevens, Danny Thomas, Mel Blanc
D: Hal Sutherland
Standard animated fantasy

Journey Beneath the Desert
*see **Antinea, L'Amante della Citta Sepolta***

Journey into Beyond
1977, (USA), Burbank Int'l, color, & b&w
W: John Carradine *(Host/Narrator)*
P: Rudolph Kalmowicz   **D:** Rolf Olsen   **SCR:** Paul Ross
Standard docu: Bizarre phenomena explored (e.g., bloodless surgery, levitation, crying statues)

Journey into Darkness
1968, (GB), 20th-Fox-TV, color, 107
W: Patrick McGoohan, Robert Reed *(Hank)*, Jennifer Hilary *(Anne)*, Patrick Allen *(Luther)*, Milo O'Shea *(Matt)*, Nanette Newman *(Jill Collins)*, Melissa Stribling *(Helen)*, Adrienne Corri *(Terry)*, Michael Ripper
P: Anthony Hinds   **PHOTOG:** Ken Talbot & Arthur Lavis
*Standard thriller, comprised of 2 TV episodes: Paper Dolls (**D:** James Hill; **SCR:** Oscar Millard, from a story by L.P. Davies) & The New People (**D:** Peter Sasdy; **SCR:** Oscar Millard & John Gould, from a story by Charles Beaumont)*

Journey into Fear
1942, (USA), Mercury/RKO, b&w, 71 mins.
W: Joseph Cotten, Orson Welles, Dolores Del Rio *(Josette)*, Ruth Warick *(Stephanie)*, Agnes Moorehead, Everett Sloane, Jack Durant, Edgar Barrier, Hans Conried, Richard Bennett, Eustace Wyatt, Jack Moss
P: Orson Welles   **D:** Norman Foster   **SCR:** Joseph Cotten & Orson Welles, from Eric Ambler's novel   **PHOTOG:** Karl Struss   **MUSIC:** C. Bakaleinikoff
Superior thriller: American armaments expert sought by Axis agents

Journey into Fear
1975, (Can), Stirling Gold, color, 97 mins.
W: Sam Waterston *(Graham)*, Zero Mostel *(Kopelkin)*, Yvette Mimieux *(Josette)*, Vincent Price *(Dervos)*, Scott Marlowe *(Jose)*, Ian McShane *(Banat)*, Joseph Wiseman *(Col. Haki)*, Shelley Winters *(Mrs. Mathews)*, Stanley Holloway *(Mathews)*, Donald Pleasence *(Kuvetlin)*, Alicia Amman *(The Old Lady)*
D: Daniel Mann   **SCR:** Trevor Wallace, from Eric Ambler's novel   **PHOTOG:** Harry Waxman   **MUSIC:** Alex North   **LYRICS:** Hal David
*A.k.a. **Burn Out***
Pedestrian remake of minor classic: Research geologist caught up in international intrigue

Journey into Primeval Times
*see **Cesta do Praveku***

Journey That Shook the World
*see **Those Fantastic Flying Fools***

Journey to a Primeval Age
*see **Cesta do Praveku***

Journey Into Midnight
1969, (GB), 20th-Fox-TV, color, 100 mins
W: Julie Harris *(Leona Gillings)*, Chad Everett *(Steven Miller)*, Tom Adams *(Jerry Crown)*, Susan Brodrick *(Rose)*, Tracy Reed *(Joyce)*, Bernard Lee *(Ben Loker)*, Edward Fox *(Sir Robert Sawyer)*, Marne Maitland, Fay Compton, Sebastian Cabot, Susan Richards, Catherine Lacey
PHOTOG: Ken Talbot & Arthur Lavis
*Standard thriller, comprised of 2 TV episodes: Poor Butterfly (**D:** Alan Gibson; **TELE-PLAY:** Jeremy Paul) & The Indian Spirit Guide (**D:** Roy Ward Baker; **TELE-PLAY:** Robert Bloch)*

Journey to the Beginning of Time
*see **Cesta do Praveku***

Journey to the Center of the Earth
1959, (USA), 20th-Fox, color, 132 mins.
W: James Mason *(Prof. Oliver Lindenbrook)*, Pat Boone *(Alec McKuen)*, Arlene Dahl *(Carla Gotteborg)*, Diane Baker *(Jennie)*, Thayer David *(The Count)*, Peter Ronson, Alan Napier, Robert Adler
P: Charles Brackett   **D:** Henry Levin   **SCR:** Walter Reisch & Charles Brackett, from Jules Verne's novel   **PHOTOG:** Leo Tover   **SPCL-FX:** Emil Kosa Jr. & James B. Gordon   **MUSIC:** Bernard Herrmann   **SONG:** *My Love is Like a Red, Red Rose (from Robert Burns' poem)*
*Classic SF-adventure: Scottish geology prof and star pupil follow ancient route to Earth's core. Remake: **Where Time Began***

Journey to the Center of the Earth (1977)
*see **Viaje al Centro de la Tierra***

Journey to the Center of the Earth
1989, (GB), color, 83 mins.
W: Nicola Cowper, Ilan-Michael Smith
from Jules Verne's novel
Standard SF-adventure: Earth's interior explored

Journey to the Center of Time
1967, (USA), Borealis-Dorad/American General, color, 82 mins.
W: Scott Brady *(Stanton)*, Gigi Perreau *(Karen White)*, Anthony Eisley *(Mark Manning)*, Austin Green *(Mr. Denning)*, Abraham Sofaer *("Doc" Gordon)*, Poupee Gamin *(Vina)*, Andy Davis *(Dave)*, Tracy Olsen *(Susan)*, Jody Millhouse, Larry Evans, Lyle Waggoner, Monica Stevens
P: Ray Dorn & David L. Hewitt   **D:** David L. Hewitt   **SCR:** David Prentiss   **PHOTOG:** Robert Caramico
*Standard SF-thriller (much stock-footage from **The Animal World, The Angry Red Planet**, others): Scientists trapped in baffling time warp*

Journey to the Far Side of the Sun
*see **Doppelganger***

Journey to the Lost City
1959, (It-Fr-W. Ger), Rizzoli/Regina/Criterion/AIP, color, 95 mins.
W: Debra Paget, Paul Christian, Claus Holm, Walter Reyer, Luciana Paluzzi, Inkiginoff, Sabina Bethman, Rene Deltgen
D: Fritz Lang   **SCR:** Werner Joerg Luedecke, from a story by Thea von Harbou
*GB retitle, **Tiger of Bengal***
*Standard adventure-thriller, created by editing & merging of 2 1950's films (**The Tiger of Eschanapur and The Hindu Tomb**) plus new footage: Fabled treasure sought cf. **Beyond the Time Barrier***

Journey to the Seventh Planet
1961, (USA-Swed), Cinemagic/AIP, color, 83 mins.
W: John Agar *(Don)*, Greta Thyssen *(Greta)*, Ann Smyrner *(Ingrid)*, Ove Sprogoe *(Barry)*, Mimi Heinrich *(Ursula)*, Carl Ottosen *(Eric)*, Louis Miehe Renard *(Svend)*, Peter Monch *(Karl)*, Ulla Moritz *(Lise)*, Bente Juel *(Colleen)*, Annie Birgit Garde *(Ellen)*
P & D: Sidney Pink   **SCR:** Ib Melchior & Sidney Pink   **PHOTOG:** Aage Wiltrup   **SPCL-FX:** Bent Barford Films   **MUSIC:** Ib Glindemann
*Standard SF-horror (with tinted stock-footage from **The Spider** {1958}): Uranian brain-creature causes astronauts to hallucinate*

Journey to the Unknown
1969, (GB), Hammer/20th-Fox TV, color, 86 mins.
W: Joan Crawford, Vera Miles *(June Wiley)*, Kay Walsh *(Mrs. Walker)*, Patty Duke *(Barbara King)*, Gay Hamilton *(Sylvia Ann)*, Leon Lissek *(Matakitis)*, Lyn Pinkney *(Tracy)*, John Junkin *(Robert)*, Dermot Walsh *(Ken)*, Geoffrey Bayldon *(Mr. Plimmer)*, Joan Newell *(Mrs. Plimmer)*, John Bailey *(Mitchell)*, Blake Butler *(Butler)*, Michael Craze *(Fred)*, Sally James *(Peggy)*
PHOTOG: Arthur Lavis & Ken Talbot   **MUSIC:** Norman Kaye & David Lindup   **MUSIC DIR:** Philip Martell
Minor thriller, Joan Crawford introduces 2 TV chillers: (1) Killer traps woman in library & (2) American girl terrorized at English inn

The Jovial Fluid
1913, (GB), EcKo, b&w, 432 ft. (131.7m)
W: Sam T. Poluski *(The Boy)*

D: W.P. Kellino
Standard comedy-fantasy short: Boy fills scent-spray with prof's "Laughter Liquid"

The Joyful Skeleton
1897, (Fr), Lumiere, b&w
Standard fantasy short: Bones dance

Joy House
see Les Felins

The Judas Hole
see Grip of the Strangler

The Judas Project
1993, (USA), RS Entertainment, color
W: John O'Banion, Ramy Zada, Richard Herd, Gerald Gordon, Jeff Corey
P: James Nelson & Ervin Melton   **WRIT, D, & MUSIC:** James H. Barden
   PHOTOG: Bryan England
Standard SF-thriller

Judex
1963, (It-Fr), C.F.F.P. Paris-Filmes Rome/Continental, b&w, 103 mins.
W: Channing Pollock, Francine Berge, Theo Sarapo, Edith Scob, Sylva Koscina,
   Benjamin Boda, Rene Genin, Jacques Jouanneau, Michel Vitold, Jean
   Degrave, Suzanne Gossen, Philippe Mareuil, Roger Fradet, Ketty France,
   Luigi Cortese
D: Georges Franju   **SCR:** Jacques Champreux & Francis Lacassin, from the novel
   by Arthur Bernede & Louis Feuillade   **PHOTOG:** Marcel Fradetal
   MUSIC COMP. & DIR: Maurice Jarre
Standard romance-thriller: Master criminal vs. mystery woman

Judge Dee and the Monastery Murder
1974, (USA), color, 100 mins.
W: Khigh Dhiegh, Mako, Soon-Taik Oh, Miiko Taka, Irene Tsu, James Hong,
   Keye Luke
D: Jeremy Kagan   **TELEPLAY:** Nicholas Meyer , from a character created by
   Robert Van Gulick
TVM, unusual thriller: Murder probed by 7th-century Chinese sleuth

Judge Dredd
1995, (USA), Edward R. Pressman-Cinergi/Hollywood/Buena Vista, color, 96 mins.
W: Sylvester Stallone (*Judge Joseph Dredd*), Armand Assante (*Rico*), Diane Lane
   (*Judge Hershey*), Jurgen Prochnow (*Judge Griffin*), Joan Chen (*Dr. Ilsa
   Hayden*), Rob Schneider (*Herman "Fergie" Ferguson*), Max von Sydow (*Judge
   Fargo*), Joanna Miles (*Judge Evelyne McGruder*), Mitchell Ryan (*Hammond*),
   Ian Dury (*Geiger*), Balthazar Getty (*Nathan Olmeyer*), Peter Marinker (*Judge
   Esposito*), Chris Adamson (*Mean Machine*), Angus MacInnes (*Judge Silver*),
   Maurice Roeyes (*Warden Miller*), Ewen Bremner, Ed Stobart, Huggy Lever,
   Bradley Savelle, Dig Wayne, Louise Delamere, Phil Smeeton, Alexis Daniel,
   Steve Toussaint, Mark Morghan, Howard Grace, Christopher Glover, Phil
   Kingston, Martin McDougall, Pat Starr, Brendan Fleming, Stuart Mullen,
   Ewan Bailey, Adam Henderson, John Blakely, Stephen Lord, Ashley Artus,
   James Earl Jones
P: Charles M. Lippincott & Beau E.L. Marks   **D:** Danny Cannon   **SCR:** William
   Wisher & Steven E. deSouza   **STORY:** Michael DeLuca & William Wisher,
   from underground British comic book   **SPCL VS-FX:** Mass Illusion   **VS-
   FX SPRVSR:** Joel Hynek   **COSTUME DESIGNER:** Gianni Versace
   (Judge Dredd Armour)   **MUSIC:** Alan Silvestri   **SONGS:** *The Dredd Song,
   Darkness Falls, Need Fire, Release the Pressure, Supercharger Heaven, Time & You
   Come Closer*
Major SF-thriller: 3rd-millennium law enforcer maligned by sinister cabal

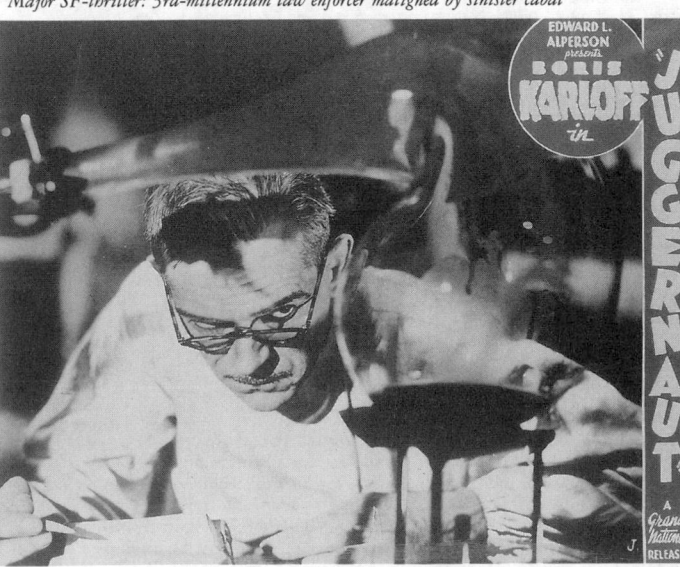

Juggernaut: Boris Karloff

Judgement
1916, (GB), British Oak/New Agency, b&w, 1,090 ft. (332.2m)
D: Ernest G. Batley
Standard crime-thriller: Gambling clerk frames employer's nephew for forgery

Juggernaut
1936, (GB), J.H. Prods./Wardour/Grand Nat'l, b&w, 74 mins.
W: Boris Karloff (*Dr. Sartorius*), Mona Goya (*Lady Yvonne Clifford*), Arthur
   Margetson (*Roger Clifford*), Joan Wyndham (*Eve Rowe*), Morton Selten (*Sir
   Charles Clifford*), Anthony Ireland (*Arthur Halliday*), Nina Boucicault (*Mary
   Clifford*), J.H. Roberts (*Chalmers*)
P: Julius Hagen   **D:** Henry Edwards   **SCR:** Heinrich Fraenkel, Cyril Campion &
   H. Fowler Mear, from a novel by Alice Campbell   **PHOTOG:** Sydney
   Blythe
USA retitle, **The Demon Doctor**, *Belg retitle,* **Crime on the Riviera**
Standard thriller: To obtain research funds, doctor kills lady's aged husband

Le Juif Errant (The Wandering Jew)
1904, (Fr), Star, b&w, 60m (196.9 ft./3.3 mins.)
W: Georges Melies (*Isaac Laquedem*)
D: Georges Melies
Standard fantasy: Jew denies water to Christ, is doomed to roam Earth for eternity

Jules Verne's Extraordinary Adventures
see Les Aventures Extraordinaires de Jules Verne

Jules Verne's Mystery on Monster Island
see Mystery on Monster Island

Jules Verne's Rocket to the Moon
see Those Fantastic Flying Fools

Julie
1956, (USA), MGM, b&w, 99 mins.
W: Doris Day, Louis Jourdan, Frank Lovejoy, Jack Kelly, Barry Sullivan, John
   Gallaudet, Mae Marsh
WRIT & D: Andrew Stone   **PHOTOG:** Fred Jackman Jr.   **MUSIC:** Leith
   Stevens
Standard melodrama: Woman realizes second husband is psychopathic killer

Julie Darling
1982, (Can-W. Ger), Tat/Cinequity, color, 100 mins
W: Anthony Franciosa (*Harold*), Sybil Danning, Isabelle Mejias (*Julie*)
Minor thriller: Teen plots stepmother's murder

Juliet of the Spirits
see Giulietta degli Spiriti

Jumanji
1995, (USA), TriStar, color, 104 mins.
W: Robin Williams (*Alan Parrish*), Kirsten Dunst (*Judy*), David Alan Grier (*The
   Policeman*), Bradley Pierce (*Peter*), Bonnie Hunt (*Sarah*), Jonathan Hyde (*Van
   Pelt*), Bebe Neuwirth (*Aunt Nora*)
D: Joe Johnston   **SCR:** Jonathan Hensleigh, Greg Taylor & Jim Strain, from
   Chris Van Allsburg's book   **PHOTOG:** Thomas Ackerman   **SPCL VS-FX:**
   Industrial Light & Magic   **MUSIC:** James Horner
"A Fantastic Adventure For The Whole Family!"—George Pennacchio, KFMB-TV
Unusual comedy-fantasy: Board game sucks players into perilous jungle

Der Junge Torless (Young Torless)
1966, (Fr-W. Ger), Kanawha, b&w, 90 mins
W: Barbara Steele
P: Frank Seitz   **WRIT & D:** Volker Schlondorff, from Robert Musil's novel
*Unusual psychodrama (critically acclaimed look at seeds of Nazism): Austro-Hungarian
   student visits prostitute*

The Jungle
1952, (USA), Lippert, b&w, 74 mins.
W: Rod Cameron (*Bentley*), Marie Windsor (*Princess Sita*), Cesar Romero (*Rama
   Singh*), Sulochana (*Samira*), M.N. Nambiar (*Nahaji*), David Abraham (*The
   Prime Minister*), Ramakrishna (*Babu*), Chitra Devi (*The Dancer*)
P & D: William Berke   **SCR:** Carroll Young   **PHOTOG:** Clyde DeVinna
   MUSIC: Dakshinamoorthy & G. Ramanathan
Minor adventure-fantasy: Mammoths threaten Hindu princess' kingdom

The Jungle Book
1942, (USA), UA, color, 109 mins.
W: Sabu (*Mowgli*), Ralph Byrd, John Qualen, Joseph Calleia, Rosemary De Camp,
   Frank Puglia, John Mather, Noble Johnson, Faith Brook, Patricia O'Rourke
P: Alexander Korda   **D:** Zoltan Korda   **ADAPT:** Laurence Stallings, from
   Rudyard Kipling's stories   **PHOTOG:** Lee Garmes & W. Howard Greene
   SPCL-FX: Lawrence Butler   **MUSIC:** Mikios Rozsa
Classic adventure-fantasy: Boy raised by wolves

The Jungle Book
1994, (USA), Sharad Patel/Walt Disney/Buena Vista, color, 111 mins.
W: Jason Scott Lee (*Mowgli*), Cary Elwes, Lena Headey, Sam Neill, John Cleese
P: Edward S. Feldman & Raju Patel   **D:** Stephen Sommers   **SCR:** Stephen

Sommers, Ronald Yanover & Mark D. Geldman   **STORY:** Ronald Yanover & Mark D. Geldman, from Rudyard Kipling's stories   **PHOTOG:** Juan Ruiz-Anchia   **MUSIC:** Basil Poledouris
A.k.a. Rudyard Kipling's The Jungle Book
Superior adventure-thriller: Boy raised by jungle wolves.

The Jungle Boy
see Bomba, the Jungle Boy

Jungle Captive
1945, (USA), Univ, b&w, 63 mins.
W: Otto Kruger (*Dr. Stendahl*), Vicky Lane (*Paula Dupree*), Amelita Ward, Robert Shayne, Phil Brown, Jerome Cowan, Rondo Hatton, Eddie Acuff, Ernie Adams
D: Harold Young   **SCR:** M. Coates Webster & Dwight V. Babcock   **PHOTOG:** Maury Gertsman
A.k.a. Wild Jungle Captive
Minor SF-horror, 3rd, & last installment in Universal's "Ape Woman" series: Scientist revives corpse of hybrid simian woman cf. Captive Wild Woman and The Jungle Woman

Jungle Captive: RONDO HATTON

Jungle Gents
1954, (USA), AA, b&w, 64 mins.
W: Leo Gorcey, Huntz Hall, Patrick O'Moore, Laurette Luez, Bernard Gorcey, Rudolph Anders, Bennie Bartlett, David Condon, Harry Cording, Eric Snowden, Roy Glenn, Joel Fluellen, Clint Walker (*Tarzan*), Emil Sitka Woody Strode
P: Ben Schwalb   **D:** Edward Bernds   **SCR:** Elwood Ullman & Edward Bernds   **PHOTOG:** Harry Neumann
Minor adventure-comedy: Bowery Boy finds he can locate diamonds by smell

The Jungle Girl
1952, (USA), Mono, b&w, 70 mins.
W: Johnny Sheffield, Karen Sharpe, Walter Sande, Leonard Mudie, Suzette Harbin
A.k.a. Bomba and the Jungle Girl
blurb: "Savage darts and white man's bullets split the Congo..."
Minor adventure-thriller: Jungle ruler seeks parents' identity

Jungle Goddess
1948, (USA), Lippert/Screen Guild, b&w, 61 mins.
W: George Reeves (*Mike*), Wanda McKay (*Greta*), Ralph Byrd (*Bob*), Armida, Smoki Whitfield, Dolores Castle, Helena Grant, Rudy Robles, Linda Johnson, Zach Williams, Fred Coby
D: Lewis D. Collins   **ORIG SCR:** Jo Pagano, from an idea by William Stephens   **PHOTOG:** Carl Berger   **MUSIC:** Irving Gertz   **SONG:** There's No One in My Heart But You
Minor adventure-thriller: Pilots liberate "white goddess"

Jungle Gold
1966, (USA), Rep, b&w, 100 mins.
W: Linda Stirling, Allan Lane, Duncan Renaldo
D: Spencer G. Bennet & Wallace Grissell
Standard thriller (edited-down feature version of 1944 serial Tiger Woman {A.ka. Perils of the Darkest Jungle}): Jungle girl vs. wicked oil seekers

Jungle Headhunters
1951, (USA), RKO, color, 66 mins.
Standard docu: Amazon expedition

Jungle Heat
1957, (USA), UA, b&w, 75 mins.
W: Lex Barker, Mari Blanchard
Minor adventure-thriller

Jungle Heat (1983)
see Dance of the Dwarfs

Jungle Hell
1956, (USA), Medallion, b&w, 78 mins
W: Sabu, K.T. Stevens, David Bruce, George E. Stone
P, D, & SCR: Norman A. Cerf
Minor SF-adventure: Flying saucers invade jungle

Jungle Jim
1948, (USA), Sam Katzman-Col, b&w, 75 mins.
W: Johnny Weissmuller, Virginia Grey, George Reeves, William Tannen
Standard adventure-thriller (1st Jungle Jim film): Rare drug sought

Jungle Jim in the Forbidden Land
1952, (USA), Col, b&w, 65 mins.
W: Johnny Weissmuller, Angela Greene, Lester Matthews, Jean Willes, William Tannen, George Eldredge, Frederic Berest, Clem Erickson, William Fawcett, Frank Jacquet
P: Sam Katzman   **D:** Lew Landers   **SCR:** Samuel Newman
Standard adventure-thriller

Jungle Man
1941, (USA), PRC, b&w, 63 mins
W: Buster Crabbe, Sheila D'Arcy, Charles Middleton, Vince Barnett
P: T.H. Richmond   **D:** Harry Fraser   **SCR:** Rita Douglas
blurb: "1000 savage thrills"
Minor adventure-thriller: Doctor seeks cure for jungle fever

Jungle Man-Eaters
1954, (USA), Col, b&w, 68 mins.
W: Johnny Weissmuller (*Jungle Jim*), Karin Booth (*Bonnie*), Richard Stapley (*Bernard*), Gregory Gay (*Latour*), Bernard (Bernie) Hamilton (*Zuwaba*), Lester Matthews (*Kingston*), Vince M. Townsend Jr. (*Chief Boganda*), Louise Franklin (*N'Gala*), Paul Thompson (*Zulu*)
P: Sam Katzman   **D:** Lee Sholem   **STORY & SCR:** Samuel Newman
Minor adventure-thriller: Jungle hero vs. diamond smugglers and cannibal tribe

Jungle Manhunt
1951, (USA), Col, b&w, 66 mins.
W: Johnny Weissmuller (*Jungle Jim*), Sheila Ryan, Bill Henry, Jean Byron, Bob Waterfield, Lyle Talbot Rick Vallin
P: Sam Katzman   **D:** Lew Landers   **SCR:** Samuel Newman
Minor adventure-thriller: Jungle hero rescues lost football player

Jungle Moon Men
1955, (USA), Col, b&w, 70 mins.
W: Johnny Weissmuller (*Himself*), Jean Byron, Helene Stanton, Bill Henry, Myron Healey, Billy Curtis, Frank Sully, Michael Granger, Kenneth L. Smith, Ed Hinton, Benjamin F. Chapman Jr., Angelo Rossitto
P: Sam Katzman   **D:** Charles S. Gould   **SCR:** Dwight V. Babcock & Jo Pagano   **STORY:** Jo Pagano
Standard adventure-thriller: Natives worship space aliens. Continuation of 'Jungle Jim' series

Jungle of Chang
1951, (USA), RKO, b&w, 67 mins.
Standard docu: Wildlife in Siam

Jungle Siren
1942, (USA), PRC, b&w, 68 mins.
W: Buster Crabbe, Ann Corio
Minor adventure-romance: Nature girl discovered

Jungle Stampede
1950,(USA), Rep, b&w, 60 mins.
W: George Breakston, Yorke Coplen
Minor adventure-thriller

Jungle Terror
see Fireball Jungle

Jungle Trail of the Son of Tarzan
1923, (USA), Nat'l Film Corp./Howells Sales Co., b&w, 6 reels (6,345 ft./1934m)
W: Dempsey Tabler (*Tarzan/Lord Greystoke*), Karla Schramm (*Jane/ Lady Greystoke*), Gordon Griffith (*Jack, Son of Tarzan*), Kamuela C. Searle (*Jack as a Young Man*), Manilla Martans (*Meriem*), Frank Morrell (*The Sheik*), Eugene Burr (*Ivan Paulvitch*), Ray Thompson (*Malbihn*), May Giraci (*Meriem as a Child*), Lucille Rubey, De Sacia Saville, Kathleen May, Frank Earle
P: David P. Howells   **D:** Harry Revier & Arthur Flaven   **SCR:** Roy Somerville,

from characters created by Edgar Rice Burroughs
Standard adventure-thriller (culled from 1920-21 serial Son of Tarzan): Jungle man's son returns to Africa

Jungle Treasure
see Old Mother Riley's Jungle Treasure

Jungle Witch
see Nabonga

The Jungle Woman
1944, (USA), Univ, b&w, 60 mins.
<u>W</u>: J. Carrol Naish (*Dr. Fletcher*), Evelyn Ankers, Samuel S. Hinds, Lois Collier, Acquanetta, Milburn Stone, Nana Bryant, Richard Powers (*Tom Keene*), Douglass Dumbrille, Alec Craig, Pierre Watkin, Christian Rub
<u>P</u>: Will Cowan   <u>D</u>: Reginald LeBorg   <u>SCR</u>: Bernard Schubert, Henry Sucher & Edward Dein   <u>PHOTOG</u>: Jack MacKenzie
Standard SF-horror, 2nd installment in Universal's "Ape Woman" series: Hybrid simian woman runs amok in sanitorium cf. Captive Wild Woman and Jungle Captive

Burson, Adrian Escober
<u>P</u>: Kathleen Kennedy & Gerald R. Molen   <u>D</u>: Steven Spielberg   <u>SCR</u>: Michael Crichton & David Koepp, from Michael Crichton's novel   <u>PHOTOG</u>: Dean Cundey   <u>SPCL DINOSAUR FX</u>: Michael Lantieri   <u>MUSIC</u>: John Williams
Lavish SF-thriller: Cloned dinosaurs run amok at modern theme park cf. **The Lost World: Jurassic Park**

Jurassic Park 2: The Lost World
see The Lost World: Jurassic Park

Jurassic Women
1995, (USA), color, 95 mins.
<u>W</u>: Jan-Michael Vincent (*Zepp*), Grace Renn (*Koo*)
Minor SF-adventure: Two astronauts crashland on prehistoric world

The Jury of Fate
1917, (USA), Metro, b&w, 5 reels
<u>W</u>: Mabel Taliaferro (*Jeanne/Jacques- Twins*)
<u>D</u>: Tod Browning
Standard melodrama

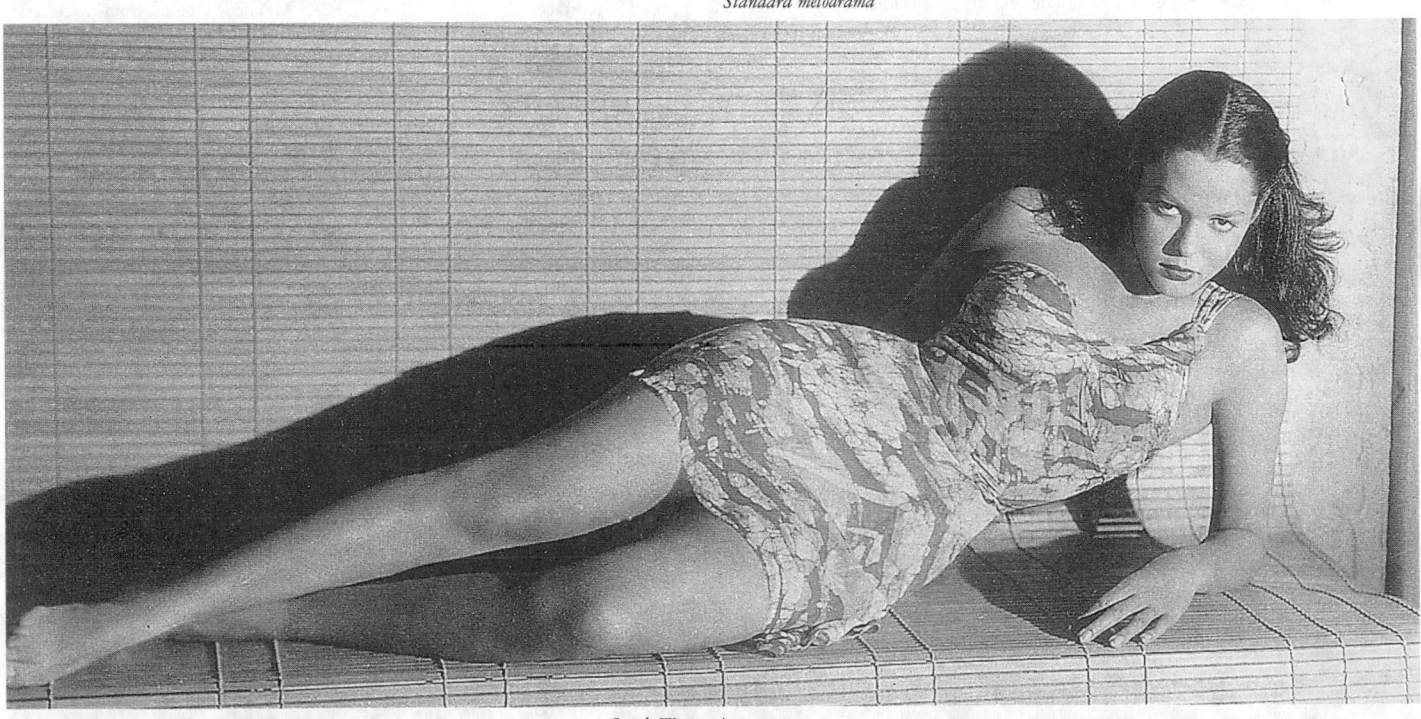

Jungle Woman: ACQUANETTA

Junior
1994, (USA), Northern Lights/Univ, color, 110 mins.
<u>W</u>: Arnold Schwarzenegger, Danny DeVito, Emma Thompson, Frank Langella, Pamela Reed
<u>P & D</u>: Ivan Reitman   <u>SCR</u>: Kevin Wade & Chris Conrad   <u>MUSIC</u>: James Newton Howard
Standard SF-comedy: Male scientist becomes pregnant

Jungle Street
1961, (GB), Theatrecraft/RFI, b&w, 82 mins.
<u>W</u>: David McCallum (*Terry Collins*), Kenneth Cope (*Johnny*), Jill Ireland (*Sue*), Brian Weske (*Joe Lucas*), Thomas Gallagher (*Collins*), Vanda Hudson (*Lucy Bell*), Edna Dore (*Mrs. Collins*), Howard Pays (*Sgt. Pelling*), Joy Webster (*Rene*), Martin Sterndale (*Insp. Bowden*), John Chandos (*Jacko Fielding*), Meier Tzelniker (*Rose*)
<u>P & STORY</u>: Guido Coen   <u>D</u>: Charles Saunders   <u>SCR</u>: Alexander Dore
Standard crime-thriller: Fugitive killer and ex-convict rob strip club

Jupiter's Thunder
see Le Tonnerre de Jupiter

Jupiter's Thunderbolts: or, The Home of the Muses
see Le Tonnerre de Jupiter

Jurassic Park
1993, (USA), Amblin/Univ, color, 127 mins.
<u>W</u>: Sir Richard Attenborough (*John Hammond*), Laura Dern (*Ellie*), Sam Neill (*Grant*), Jeff Goldblum (*Malcolm*), Bob Peck (*Muldoon*), Ariana Richards (*Lex*), Joseph Mazzello (*Tim*), Martin Ferrero (*Gennaro*), Samuel L. Jackson (*Arnold*), Richard Kiley (*Jurassic Park Tour Voice*), Wayne Knight, B.D. Wong, Jerry Molen, Miguel Sandoval, Cameron Thor, Christopher John Fields, Whit Hertford, Jophery Brown, Dean Cundey, Tom Mishler, Greg

Just Before Dawn
1946, (USA), Col, b&w, 65 mins.
<u>W</u>: Warner Baxter (*Dr. Robert Ordway*), Martin Kosleck (*Karl Ganss*), Adelle Roberts (*Claire Foster*), Mona Barrie (*Harriett Travers*), Marvin Miller (*Casper/Whistler*), Charles D. Brown (*Insp. Burns*), Craig Reynolds (*Jack Swain*), Robert Barrat (*Clyde Travers*), Wilton Graff (*Alexander Gerard*), Charles Lane (*Dr. Steiner*), Charles Arnt (*Allan S. Tobin*), Peggy Converse (*Connie Day*), Ted Hecht (*Armand Morcel*), Thomas Jackson (*Walter Cummings*), Irene Tedrow (*Florence White*)
<u>D</u>: William Castle   <u>SCR</u>: Eric Taylor & Aubrey Wisberg, from characters created by Max Marcin   <u>PHOTOG</u>: Philip Tanura
Original title: **Exposed by the Crime Doctor**
Standard "Crime Doctor" thriller: Crime-psychiatrist trails psychopathic killer.

Just Before Dawn
1980, (USA), Doro Vlado Hreljanovic/Oakland Prods., color, 71 mins.
<u>W</u>: George Kennedy (*Roy*), Mike Kellin (*Ty*), Chris Lemmon (*Jonathan*), Gregg Henry (*Warren*), Ralph Seymour (*Daniel*), Deborah Benson (*Constance*), Kati Powell (*Merry Cat*), John Hunsaker (*The Mountain Twins*), Charles Bartlett (*Vachel*), Jamie Rose (*Megan*), Hap Oslund (*Pa Logan*), Barbara Spencer (*Ma Logan*)
<u>D</u>: Jeff Lieberman   <u>SCR</u>: Mark Arywitz & Gregg Irving, based on a story by Joseph Middleton   <u>PHOTOG</u>: Joel King & Dean King   <u>SPCL-FX</u>: John Morello   <u>MUSIC</u>: Brad Fiedel
Minor thriller: Twin "demons" stalk campers

Justice
1914, (GB), Hepworth/Renters, b&w, 3,400 ft. (1036.3m)
<u>W</u>: Alec Worcester (*Jack Raynor*), Alma Taylor (*Nan Prescott*), Stewart Rome (*Paul Meredith*), Harry Royston (*Joe Prescott*), Ruby Belasco (*Mrs. Prescott*), Jamie Darling (*John Meredith*), Marie de Solla (*Mrs. Meredith*)

D: Frank Wilson

Standard crime-thriller: Man hires crook to kill his father, then betrays him and abducts crook's daughter

Just Imagine

1930, (USA), Fox, b&w, 12 reels (10,200 ft./3109m/102 mins.)

W: El Brendel *(Single 0)*, Maureen O'Sullivan *(LN-18)*, John Garrick *(J-21)*, Mischa Auer *(B-36)*, Frank Albertson *(RT42)*, Marjorie White *(D-6)*, Hobart Bosworth *(Z-4)*, Kenneth Thomson *(MT-3)*, Sydney De Grey *(AK-44)*, Wilfred Lucas *(X10)*, Ivan Linow *(Loko/Bobo)*, J.W. Girard *(The Commander)*, Joyzelle *(Loo Loo/Boo Boo)*, Bee Stephens, Kathryn Brown, Lucille Miller, Frances Hopkins, Raymonda Brown, Catherine NaVarre, Bonnie Winslow, Bernice Snell, Carol Miller, Rose Lee, Peggy Beck, Adele Cutler, Mary Lansing, Theo De Voe, Helen Mann, Mary Carr, Beverly Royde, Thelma Perriguey, Margaret La Marr, Joan NaVarre, Bo Beep Karlin, Lorraine Bond, Mildred Laube, Betty Halsey, Miriam Hellman, Paula Langlen, Peggy Cunningham, Mary Carlton, Edna Callahan, Jane Dunlap, Janet De Vine, Gloria Fayth, Adele Fergus, Betty Gordon, Kay Gordon, Dot Humphries, Lee Kenny, Betty Mitchell, Dot Palmer, Emily Renard, Elizabeth Turner, Marbeth Wright, Charles Alexander, George Yeretzian, Murray Smith, Austin Grout, William Brandt, J.L. Riddick, Robert Keith, Fred Silver, Nate Barrager, Armond Jannssen, Gordon Orme, Louis Yaeckel, Roy Strohm, Clarence Simmons, Kenneth Allen, Jack Frost, Roy Tobin, Robert Lake, Ted Sharp, Jack Barrett, Ernest Smith, Ed Rockwell, Don Prosser, Arthur McCullock, Myron Sunde, Bob Knickerbocker, George Gramlich, Clarence Smith, Enrico Cucinelli, J. Harold Reeves, Fifi D'Orsay

WRIT & D: David Butler **ORIG STORY & SONGS:** DeSylva, Brown & Henderson **DANCE DIRECTOR:** Seymour Felix **PHOTOG:** Ernest Palmer **SPCL-FX:** Ralph Hammeras **MUSIC DIR:** Arthur Kay **SONGS:** *The Drinking Song, The Romance of Elmer Stremingway, Never, Never Wed, There's Something About an Old-Fashioned Girl, Mothers Ought to Tell Their Daughters, I Am the Words, You Are the Melody, Dance of Victory, & Never Swat a Fly*

Standard SF-musical-comedy: Fanciful look at life in future

Justin Case

1988, (USA), color, Made for TV, 90 mins.

W: George Carlin, Molly Hagan Douglas Sill, Gordon Jump, Timothy Stack, Paul Sand

D: Blake Edwards

TVM, minor fantasy: Private eye's ghost seeks to solve own murder

Justine

see Marquis de Sade: Justine

Justinian's Human Torches

see Les Torches Humaines

Just in Time

1906, (GB), Hepworth, b&w, 300 ft. (91.4m)

D: Lewin Fitzhamon

Standard comedy-fantasy short: Fortune teller shows client a vision of eloping husband

Just Off Broadway

1942, (USA), 20th-Fox, b&w, 66 mins.

W: Lloyd Nolan *(Michael Shayne)*, Marjorie Weaver *(Judy Taylor)*, Phil Silvers *(Roy Higgins)*, Janis Carter *(Lillian Hubbard)*, Joan Valerie *(Rita Darling)*, Richard Derr *(John Logan)*, Don Costello *(George Dolphin)*, Alexander Lockwood *(Count Telmachio)*, Francis Pierlot *(Arno)*, Leyland Hodgson *(The Butler)*, George Carleton *(The Judge)*, Grant Richards *(The D.A.)*, William Haade *(The Watchman)*, Oscar O'Shea *(The Stage Doorman)*

P: Sol M. Wurtzel **D:** Herbert I. Leeds **SCR:** Arnaud d'Usseau, from characters created by Brett Halliday **PHOTOG:** Lucien Andriot **MUSIC:** Emil Newman

Standard "Michael Shayne" thriller: Detective on jury duty tries to prove girl's innocence

Just William's Luck

1947, (GB), Diadem-Alliance/UA, b&w, 92 mins.

W: William Graham *(William Brown)*, Leslie Bradley *(The Boss)*, A.E. Matthews *(The Tramp)*, Kathleen Stuart *(Ethel Brown)*, Hugh Cross *(Robert Brown)*, Jack Raine *(The Policeman)*, Garry Marsh *(Mr. Brown)*, Jane Welsh *(Mrs. Brown)*, Muriel Aked *(Emily)*, Hy Hazell *(Gloria Gail)*, Brian Roper *(Ginger)*, James Crabbe *(Douglas)*, Brian Weske *(Henry)*, Michael Medwin *(Spiv)*

P: David Coplan & James Carter **D & SCR:** Val Guest, from stories by Richmal Crompton

A.k.a. **The Haunted Castle** *and* **Haunted House**

Minor comedy-thriller: Village boys nab fur thieves in "haunted house"

A Juvenile Hypnotist

1911, (GB), Kineto, b&w, 450 ft. (137.2m)

D: Walter R. Booth

reissued (1918) as **Juvenile Pranks**

Standard comedy: Boy hypnotizes photographer, dude, constable

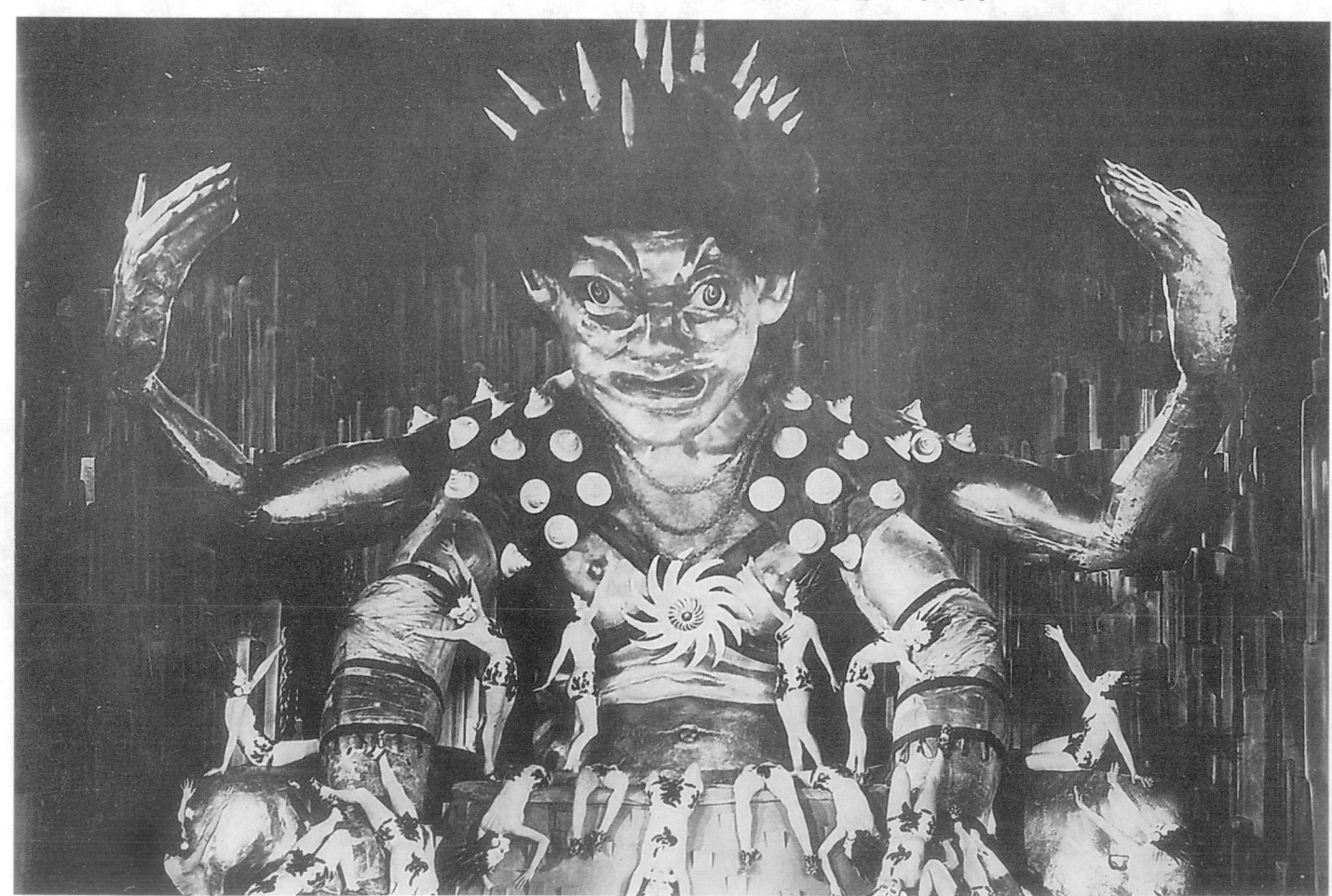

Just Imagine

Das Kabinett des Dr. Caligari (The Cabinet of Dr. Caligari)

1919, (Ger), Decla-Bioscop/Goldwyn, b&w, 5,249 ft. (1600m/6 reels)
W: Werner Krauss (*Dr. Caligari*), Lil Dagover (*Jane*), Conrad Veidt (*Cesare, the Somnambulist*), Hans Heinz von Twardowski (*The Thief*), Fredrich Feyer, Rudolf Littinger
P: Erich Pommer **D:** Robert Wiene **SCR:** Carl Mayer & Hans Janowitz
PHOTOG: Willy Hameister **DESIGN:** Walter Reimann, Hermann Warm & Walter Rohrig
USA release, 1921
"...the most complete essay in the decor of delirium" —Pauline Kael, Kiss Kiss Bang Bang
"...a tour-de-force, of unease perhaps rather than of horror, but a film whose effect can never be forgotten"—Ivan Butler, The Horror Film
Classic expressionist horror-thriller: Malevolent mountebank and eerie sleepwalker terrorize

Das Kabinett Des Dr. Caligari: Werner Krauss, Conrad Veidt and Lil Dagover

German town. cf. Genuine

Kadoyng

1972, (GB), Shand Pictures/CFF, color, 60 mins.
W: Teresa Codling (*Lucy Balfour*), Adrian Hall (*Billy Balfour*), David Williams (*Barney Balfour*), Andrew Mussell (*Williams*), Stephen Bone (*McGrath*), Leo Maguire (*Kadoyng*), Jean Dallas (*Lady Elspeth*), Jack Haig (*Robbo*), Bill Owen (*Jack Flitton*), Ian Piggot (*Eric Flitton*), Frieda Knorr (*Mrs. Balfour*), Dennis Ramsden (*The Minister*), Michael Sharvell-Martin (*Pander-Willoughby*), Gerald Sim (*Prof. Balfour*), Stephen Thorne (*PC Palfrey*)
P: Roy Simpson **D:** Ian Shand **STORY:** Leo Maguire **PHOTOG:** Mark McDonald **MUSIC:** Edwin Astley
Standard juvenile fantasy: Space alien helps children foil motorway plan

The Kaiser's Dream

1914, (GB), Captain Kettle/Imperial, b&w, 300 ft. (91.4m)
STORY: C.J. Cutcliffe-Hyne
Standard fantasy

The Kaiser's Spies

1914, (GB), I.B. Davidson/KTC, b&w, 3,000 ft. (914.4m)
W: Philip Kay (*Sexton Blake*), Lewis Carlton (*Tinker*)
D & SCR: Charles Raymond, from characters created by Harry Blyth
Standard crime-thriller: Entymologist runs bus-driver spy ring from tower in Epping Forest

Kaleidoscope

1966, (GB), Winkast/WPD, color, 103 mins.
W: Warren Beatty (*Barney Lincoln*), Susannah York (*Angel McGinnis*), Clive Revill (*Insp. Manny McGinnis*), Eric Porter (*Harry Dominion*), Murray Melvin (*Aimes*), John Junkin (*Evelyn*), George Sewell (*Billy*), Yootha Joyce (*The Receptionist*), Stanley Meadows (*The Captain*), George Murcell (*Johnny*), Jane Birkin (*Exquisite Thing*)
P: Elliott Kastner & Jerry Gershwin **D:** Jack Smight **STORY:** Robert & Jane Howard-Carrington **PHOTOG:** Christopher Challis
A.k.a. The Bank Breaker
Modest thriller: Playboy gambler pulls caper

Kali-Yug, La Dea della Vendetta (Kali-Yug, Goddess of Vengeance)

1963, (It), color
W: Sergio Fantoni
D: Mario Camerini **PHOTOG:** Aldo Tonti
Minor thriller: Cultists spread misery

Das Kalte Herz (The Cold Heart)

1955, (E. Ger), Gala, color
W: Hanna Rucker, Lutz Molk, Paul Bildt, Erwin Oschonneck, Paul Esser, Georg Laubenthal, Karl Hellmer, Lotte Lobinger, Alexander Engel
D: Paul Verhoeven

Standard fantasy, never released in USA

The Karate Killers

1967, (USA), MGM, color, 92 mins.
W: Robert Vaughn (*Napoleon Solo*), David McCallum, Kim Darby, Telly Savalas, Leo G. Carroll, Joan Crawford, Herbert Lom, Curt Jurgens, Diane McBain, Jill Ireland
P: Boris Ingster **D:** Barry Shear **SCR:** Norman Hudis
Standard thriller (culled from 2 part The Five Daughters Affair episodes of teleseries The Man from U.N.C.L.E.): Enemy agent seeks formula for turning sea water into gold

Karate, the Hand of Death

1961, (USA), Brenner/AA, b&w, 80 mins
W: Joel Holt, Frank Blaine, Reiko Okada
P & D: Joel Hott
Minor thriller: Japanese-raised American framed for international platinum theft. Filmed in Japan

Karnstein

see La Maldicion de los Karnsteins

Katharsis (Catharsis)

1963, (It), Belotti, color
W: Christopher Lee(*Faust/Mephistopholes*)
D: Joseph Vegh
A.k.a. Faust
Standard horror-thriller

Katy Meets the Aliens

1989, (USA), color, 75 mins.
Standard animated fantasy: Space creature threatens caterpillars

Kazaam

1996, (USA), Touchstone/Interscope/Poly-Gram/ Buena Vista, color, 93 mins
W: Shaquille O'Neal (*Kazaam*), Francis Capra (*Max*), Marshall Manesh (*Malik*), Ally Walker, John Costelloe, Jake Glaser James Acheson
D & CO-P: Paul M. Glaser **SCR:** Christian Ford & Roger Soffer **PHOTOG:** Charles Minsky **VS-FX SPRVSR:** Charles Gibson **MUSIC:** Christopher Tyng
Standard fantasy: Genie dwells in boombox

The Keep

1983, (USA), Howard W. Koch Jr.-Gene Kirkwood/Para, color, 96 mins.
W: Scott Glenn (*Glaeken Trismegustus*), Jurgen Prochnow (*Capt. Woermann*), Ian McKellen (*Dr. Theodore Cuza*), Robert Prosky (*Father Fonescu*), Gabriel Byrne, Alberta Watson, Morgan Sheppard, Michael Carter
D & SCR: Michael Mann, from F. Paul Wilson's novel **PHOTOG:** Alex Thomson **SPCL FX SPRVSRS:** Wally Veevers & Robin Browne **MUSIC:** Tangerine Dream
Unusual horror-fantasy: Nazis unleash ancient force in deserted castle

The Keeper

1976, (Can), Lionsgate, color, 96 mins.
W: Christopher Lee, Tell Schreiber, Sally Gray, Malcolm Britton, Ross Vezarian, Ian Tracey, Bing Jensen, Michael Meade, Jack Leavy, Leo Leavy, Burke Lundy, Vikki Vogel, David Engleman, Wendy Who, Victor Mallia, Edith Powell, Laura Thaw, Alex Kliner, Paddy White, Christian Bruyere, Denton Coates, Rod Padmus, Tom Jesse, Jeanie McKinnon, Anthony Roy McKinley, Margee Bruyere, Ian Newby, Linda Grabler White, Joyce Williams, Peggy Hart, Bob Hetherington, Phillipa Malczewska, Richard Keymer
WRIT & D: T.Y. Drake **STORY:** David Curnick & Donald Wilson **PHO-TOG:** Doug McKay **SPCL-FX:** Al Razutis **MUSIC:** Erich Hoyt
Minor horror-spoof: Sinister doctor runs asylum for heirs to great fortunes

Keeper of the Flame

1942, (USA), MGM, b&w, 100 mins.
W: Spencer Tracy, Katherine Hepburn, Richard Whorf, Frank Craven, Forrest Tucker, Margaret Wycherly, Howard da Silva, Audrey Christie, Horace McNally, Darryl Hickman, Donald Meek, Percy Kilbride
D: George Cukor **SCR:** Donald Ogden Stewart **PHOTOG:** William H. Daniels **MUSIC:** Bronislau Keeper
Unusual melodrama: Reporter probes politician's life

Kemek

1970, (It), GHM Prods., color
W: David Hedison (*Nick*), Alexandra Stewart (*Marisa*), Helmut Snider (*Paul*), Mary Woronov, Cal Haynes, Alfonso de Luise, Charles Mitchell, Suzanne Wolders, Paula Stewart, Bruno B. Solitari, Peter Boileau, Dorothy Streisin, Liza de Goya, Lilian S. Laurent, Peter Thompson, Tania Davidson, Michele Cinque, Carolina Sdruscia, Kary McCallum, Sherry McCallum
D: Theodore Gershuny & Don Rene Patterson **SCR:** Harry Millard, Theodore Gershuny & Don Rene Patterson **PHOTOG:** Enzo Barboni **MUSIC:** John Lewis
Minor thriller: Supernatural control and search for mystery drug

The Kennel Murder Case

1933, (USA), WB, b&w, 73 mins.
W: William Powell (*Philo Vance*), Mary Astor (*Hilda Lake*), Eugene Pallette (*Sgt.*

Ernest Heath), Helen Vinson *(Doris Delafield)*, Ralph Morgan *(Raymond Wrede)*, Paul Cavanagh *(Sir Bruce MacDonald)*, Jack LaRue *(Eduardo Grassi)*, Wade Boteler *(The Sgt.)*, Robert Barrat *(Archer Coe)*, Etienne Girardot *(Dr. Doremus)*, Arthur Hohl *(Gamble)*, James Lee *(Liang)*, Henry O'Neill *(Dubois)*, Robert McWade *(Markham)*, Frank Conroy *(Brisbane Coe)*, Spencer Charters *(Snitkin)*, Charles Wilson *(Hennessey)*, Harry Allen *(The Dog Trainer)*, George Chandler *(The Reporter)*, Milton Kibbee *(Charlie Adler)*, Leo White *(The Desk Clerk)*, Monte Vandergrift *(The Detective)*, Don Brodie *(The Photographer)*, James Burke *(The Policeman)*
D: Michael Curtiz   **SCR:** Robert N. Lee & Peter Milne, from characters created by S.S. Van Dine   **PHOTOG:** William Reese
working title, **The Return of Philo Vance***, reissued 1942*
Superior mystery-thriller: Murder in bolted room, suave sleuth investigates. Remake: **Calling Philo Vance**

The Key
1958, (GB), Highroad/Col, b&w, 134 mins.
W: William Holden *(David Ross)*, Sophia Loren *(Stella)*, Trevor Howard *(Chris Ford)*, Kieron Moore *(Kane)*, Oscar Homolka *(Capt. Van Dam)*, Bernard Lee *(Wadlow)*, Beatrix Lehmann *(The Housekeeper)*, Bryan Forbes *(Weaver)*, Noel Purcell *(The Hotel Porter)*, Irene Handl *(The Clerk)*, Sidney Vivian *(Grogan)*, Rupert Davies *(Baker)*, Russell Waters *(Sparks)*, John Crawford *(The American Captain)*, Jameson Clark *(The English Captain)*, Carl Mohner
WRIT & P: Carl Foreman   **D:** Carol Reed, from Jan de Hartog's novel *Stella*   **PHOTOG:** Oswald Morris   **MUSIC:** Malcolm Arnold
Unusual psychodrama: Two men have relationship with same woman

Key Largo
1948, (USA), WB, b&w, 101 mins.
W: Humphrey Bogart, Edward G. Robinson, Lauren Bacall, Dan Seymour, Claire Trevor, Lionel Barrymore, Thomas Gomez
D: John Huston   **SCR:** John Huston & Richard Brooks, from a play by Maxwell Anderson   **PHOTOG:** Karl Freund   **MUSIC:** Max Steiner
Classic crime-thriller: Gangster takes hostages as hurricane approaches

The Key Man
1957, (GB), Insignia/AA, b&w, 63 mins.
W: Lee Patterson *(Lionel Hulme)*, Hy Hazell *(Gaby/Eva)*, Colin Gordon *(Larry Parr)*, Philip Leaver *(Smithers)*, Henry Vidon *(Hallow)*, Paula Byrne *(Pauline)*, Harold Kasket *(Dimitriadi)*, Maudie Edwards *(Mrs. Glass)*
P: Alex Snowden   **D:** Montgomery Tully   **SCR:** J. McLaren Ross, from his play
Standard thriller: Radio reporter tracks robbery loot

Key Witness
1947, (USA), Col, b&w, 67 mins.
W: John Beal, Trudy Marshall
Standard thriller

Khorda
see **The Deathmaster**

A Kid for Two Farthings
1955, (GB), Big Ben-London/Lopert, color, 96 mins.
W: Celia Johnson *(Joanna)*, Diana Dors *(Sonia)*, David Kossoff *(Kandinsky)*, Joe Robinson *(Sam)*, Jonathan Ashmore *(Joe)*, Brenda de Banzie *(Ruby)*, Vera Day *(Mimi)*, Primo Carnera *(Python Macklin)*, Sydney Tafler *(Madam Rita)*, Sidney James *(Ice Berg)*, Daphne Anderson *(Dora)*, Lou Jacobi *(Blackie Isaacs)*, Harold Berens *(Oliver)*, Danny Green *(Bason)*, Irene Handl *(Mrs. Abramowitz)*, Alfie Bass *(Alf)*, Eddie Byrne *(Sylvester)*, Joseph Tomelty *(The Vagrant)*, Lily Kann
D: Carol Reed   **SCR:** Wolf Mankowitz   **PHOTOG:** Ted Scaife   **MUSIC:** Benjamin Frankel
Unusual fantasy-drama: Boy thinks one-horned goat is unicorn

Kid Glove Killwe
1942, (USA), MGM, b&w, 74 mins.
W: Van Heflin, Lee Bowman, Marsha Hunt, Samuel S. Hinds, Cliff Clark, Eddie Quillan, Ava Gardner
D: Fred Zinnemann
Taut "B" thriller: Police chemist uncovers mayor's killer

A Kid in King Arthur's Court
1995, (USA), Walt Disney/Buena Vista, color, 89 mins
W: Thomas Ian Nicholas, Art Malik, Joss Ackland
D: Michael Gottlieb, inspired by Mark Twain's novel *A Connecticut Yankee in King Arthur's Court*
Minor juvenile fantasy: Modern California teen transported to Camelot

The Kidnapped Child
1904, (GB), Autoscope/WTC, b&w, 300 ft. (91.4m)
W: Kenneth Barker *(The Child)*
P: Will Barker   **D:** Charles Raymond
Standard crime-thriller (in 10 scenes): Hag kidnaps rich woman's son, forces him to beg

Kidnapped Co-Ed
1978, (USA), Boxoffice Int'l, color
W: Jack Canon, Leslie Ann Rivers, Gladys Lavitan, Larry Lambeth, Jim Blankinship
WRIT, P & D: Frederick R. Friedel   **MUSIC:** George Newman Shaw & John Willhelm

Minor crime-thriller

The Kidnapped King
1909, (GB), Manufacturer's Film Agency, b&w, 820 ft. (249.9m)
W: Carlotta de Yonson *(Princess Thyra)*, C. Douglas Carlile *(Kit Karson)*, Lee Gilbert *(Patch)*, C.A. Carlile *(Prince Stephen)*, J. Duncan *(Clovis)*, J. Lowe *(Baron Votman)*, Fred Lewes *(King Otto of Merslen)*
from a play by C. Douglas Carlile
Standard melodrama: Detective dons disguises to save boy king from kidnap

Kidnappers from Space
see **The 27th Day**

The Kidnapping of the President
1980, (Can), Sefel/Crown international, color, 113 mins.
W: William Shatner *(Jerry)*, Hal Holbrook *(Pres. Adam Scott)*, Van Johnson *(V.P. Richards)*, Ava Gardner *(Beth Richards)*, Cindy Girling *(Linda)*, Miguel Fernandes *(Assanti)*, Michael J. Reynolds *(MacKenzie)*, Elizabeth Shepherd *(Joan)*, Gary Reineke *(Deitrich)*, Maury Chaykin *(Harvey)*, Murray Westgate *(Archie)*, Michael Kane *(Herb)*, Jackie Burroughs, Aubert Pallascio, Virginia Podesser, Elias Zarov, Larry Duran, Patrick Brymar, Gershon Resnik, John Stocker, Chappelle Jaffe, John Romaine
D: George Mendeluk   **SCR:** Richard Murphy, from a book by Charles Templeton   **PHOTOG:** Michael Molloy
Standard thriller: South American radicals plot extortion

Kids of the Round Table
1995, (USA), Walt Disney, Made for TV, color, 90 mins.
W: Johnny Morina, Malcolm McDowell Jamison Boulanger, Justin Horntraeger, Maggie Castle
TVM, standard juvenile fantasy: 20th-century boy acquires magic sword Excalibur

The Kid with the Broken Halo
1982, (USA), Satellite/NBC-TV, color, 96 mins.
W: Gary Coleman *(Andy)*, Robert Guillaume *(Blake)*, June Allyson *(Dorothea)*, Mason Adams *(Harry Tannenbaum)*, Ray Walston *(Michael)*, Georg Stanford Brown *(Rudy)*, John Pleshette *(Jeff McNulty)*, Lani O'Grady *(Julie McNulty)*, Kim Fields, Telma Hopkins, Tammy Lauren, Keith Mitchell, Don Diamond
D: Leslie Martinson   **TELEPLAY:** George Kirgo   **PHOTOG:** Gary Graver   **SPCL-FX:** Roger George   **MUSIC:** Tommy Vig
TVM, minor fantasy: Young angel must perform good deeds

Kill and Go Hide!
see **The Child**

Kill and Kill Again
1981, (USA), Film Ventures, color, 100 mins.
W: James Ryan *(Steve)*, Anneline Kriel *(Kandy)*, Stan Schmidt *(Fly)*, Norman Robinson *(Gypsy Billy)*, Ken Gampu *(Gorilla)*, Bill Flynn *(Hotdog)*, Michael Mayer *(Marduk)*, Eddie Dorie *(Optimus)*, Marloe Scott-Wilson *(Minerva)*, John Ramsbottom *(Dr. Kane)*, Mervyn John *(The President)*
D: Ivan Hall   **SCR:** John Crowther   **PHOTOG:** Tai Krige
Minor melodrama

Kill, Baby, Kill!
see **Operazione Paura**

Killbots
see **Chopping Mall**

Killdozer
1974, (USA), Univ/ABC-TV, color, 74 mins.
W: Clint Walker, Carl Betz, James Wainwright, Neville Brand, James Watson Robert Urich
D: Jerry London   **TELEPLAY:** Theodore Sturgeon & Ed MacKillop

Killdozer: CARL BETZ AND CLINT WALKER

TVM, minor SF-thriller: Alien being takes possession of construction equipment

Killer Ape
1953, (USA), Col, b&w, 68 mins.
W: Johnny Weissmuller *(Jungle Jim)*, Carol Thurston, Ray "Crash" Corrigan, Max
Palmer, Burt Wenland, Rory Mallinson, Nestor Paiva, Paul Marion, Eddie
Foster, Nick Stuart
P: Sam Katzman   D: Spencer G. Bennet   SCR: Carroll Young & Arthur Hoerl
Standard adventure-thriller: Jungle hero thwarts poachers

Killer at Large
1947, (USA), PRC/Eagle Lion, b&w, 63 mins.
W: Robert Lowery, Anabel Shaw
Standard thriller

Killer Bats
see The Devil Bat

Killer Bees
1974, (USA), RSO/ABC-TV, color, 74 mins.
W: Gloria Swanson, Edward Albert, Kate Jackson, Craig Stevens, Roger Davis,
Don McGovern, John Getz
D: Curtis Harrington   TELEPLAY: Joyce Corrington & John William
Corrington   PHOTOG: Jack Woolf   MUSIC: David Shite
*TVM, standard fantasy-thriller: Matriarch of California wine-grape family has strange
rapport with bees*

The Killer Behind the Mask
see Savage Weekend

The Killer Condom
see Kondom des Grauens

Killer Fish
1979, (It-Brz), Fawcett-Majors/Carlo Ponti/Sir Lew GradeAssociated Films, color, 101 mins.
W: Lee Majors *(Bob Lasky)*, Karen Black *(Kate Neville)*, James Franciscus *(Paul
Diller)*, Margaux Hemingway *(Gabrielle)*, Marisa Berenson *(Ann)*, Gary
Collins *(Tom)*, Anthony Steffen *(Max)*, Ray Brocksmith *(Ollie)*, Fabio Sabag
(Quintin), Frank Pesce *(Warren)*, Dan Pastorini *(Hans)*, George Cherques
(The Inspector), Chico Arago *(Ben)*, Celso Faria *(The Airline Passenger)*, Sonia
Citicica *(The Nurse)*, Herbert V. Theiss *(underwater scenes)*
D: Anthony M. Dawson [Antonio Margheriti]   SCR: Michael Rogers
PHOTOG: Alberto Spagnoli   MUSIC: Guido & Maurizio De Angelis
SONG: *The Winner Takes It All*
*TV retitle, **Deadly Treasure of the Piranha***
Standard thriller: Piranhas prevent emerald thieves from recovering loot

Killer Grizzly
see Grizzly

The Killer Inside Me
1976, (USA), Devi/WB, color, 99 mins
W: Stacy Keach, John Carradine, Susan Tyrrell, Don Stroud, Tisha Sterling,
Keenan Wynn, Royal Dano, Julie Adams John Dehner
P: Michael W. Leighton   D: Burt Kennedy   SCR: Edward Mann & Robert
Chamblee, from the novel by Jim Thompson
Unusual thriller: Saga of psychotic deputy sheriff

Killer in the Mirror
1986, (USA), Litke-Grossbart/WB/NBC-TV, color, 96 mins.
W: Ann Jillian *(Karen/Samantha)*, Len Cariou *(Jason Howell)*, Jessica Walter
(Francesca), Max Gail *(Jim Armbruster)*, Allen Garfield *(The D.A.)*, Eileen
Barnett *(Alison Moreland)*, Christopher Noth *(Johnny)*, Andra Akers, Parley
Baer, David Ursin, Joseph Chapman, Barney Martin, Robin Pearson Rose,
James Louis Watkins, Bill Zuckert, Janice Carroll, Angela Clarke, Ralph M.
Clift, Howard George, Tom McGreevey, Ken Hill, Julie Inouye, Jeff
O'Haco, Richard Partlow, Father George J. Venetos, Nelson Welch
D & TELEPLAY: Frank De Felitta, from characters created by Rian James
PHOTOG: Robert Seaman   MUSIC: Gil Melle
*TVM, standard thriller (semi-remake of **Dead Ringer**): Twin sister framed for murder*

The Killer is Loose
1956, (USA), Crown/UA, b&w, 73 mins.
W: Joseph Cotten, Rhonda Fleming, Wendell Corey Alan Hale, Michael Pate
D: Oscar "Budd" Boetticher Jr.   PHOTOG: Lucien Ballard
Standard thriller

Killer Klowns from Outer Space
1987, (USA), Chiodo Bros./Trans World, color, 90 mins.
W: Grant Cramer *(Mike Tobacco)*, Suzanne Snyder *(Debbie Stone)*, John Allen
Nelson *(Dave Hanson)*, Michael Siegel *(Rich Terenzi)*, John Vernon *(Curtis
Mooney)*, Royal Dano *(Farmer Gene Green)*, Peter Licassi *(Paul Terenzi)*, Chris
Titus *(Bob McReed)*, Irene Michaels *(Stacy)*, Karla Sue Krull *(Tracy)*, Brian
Degan Scott *(Punk #1)*, Danny Kovacs *(Punk #2)*, Adele Proom *(Mrs.
Franco)*, Howard Malpas *(Mr. Myers)*, Karen Raff *(Mom #1)*, Kathleen
Stefano *(Mom #2)*, Claire Bartle *(The Little Girl)*, Sharon O'Mahoney *(The
Waitress)*, Michael Thompson *(The Black Biker)*,
Lucinda Burgess *(Sheila)*, David Piel *(The Security Guard)*, Steven Jones *(A
State Trooper)*, Armon Stover *(A State Trooper)*, Jeff Yesko *(A State Trooper)*,

---

Steve Rockhold, Michael Harington Burris, Scott Beatty, Geno Ponza, Paul
Haley, Dennis C. Walsh, Genie Houdini, Charles Chiodo, Harrod Blank,
Karl Shaeffer, Greg Sykes, Paul Parsons, Jimmy Locust, Mitch Bryan
D: Stephen Chiodo   SCR: Charles Chiodo & Stephen Chiodo   PHOTOG: Alfred
Taylor   SPCL-FX: Fantasy II Film Effects   MUSIC: John Massari
Modest SF-comedy: Bizarre space aliens invade small town

Killer Leopard
1954, (USA), AA, b&w, 70 mins.
W: Johnny Sheffield *(Bomba)*, Beverly Garland *(Linda)*, Donald Murphy *(Fred)*,
Barry Bernard *(Pulham)*, Leonard Mudie *(Barnes)*, Smoki Whitfield *(Eli)*,
Rory Mallinson *(Deevers)*, Russ Conway *(Maitland)*, Roy Glenn *(Daniel)*,
Harry Cording *(Saunders)*, Charles Stevens *(Gonzales)*, Bill Walker *(Jonas)*
WRIT, P, & D: Ford Beebe, from characters created by Roy Rockwood
Standard adventure-thriller: Jungle boy helps actress search for missing husband

Killer Orphan
see Friday the 13th...The Orphan

Killer Party
1986, (USA), color
W: Martin Hewitt *(Blake)*, Ralph Seymour *(Martin)*, Elaine Wilkes *(Phoebe)*, Paul
Bartel *(Zito)* Sherry Willis-Burch, Joanna Johnson
Minor thriller: Psycho plagues college campus

Killers Are Challenged
1965, (It), color, 91 mins.
W: Richard Harrison, Wandisa Guida
D: Martin Donan
Minor thriller: Undercover agent retrieves secret plans

Killers are Challenged
see Secret Agent Fireball

Killer's Curse
see Beyond the Living

Killer's Delight
1978, (USA), Intercontinental, color
W: James Luisi, Susan Sullivan, John Karlan, Martin Speer
P & D: Jeremy Hoenack   SCR: Maralyn Thoma
Minor crime-thriller

Killers from Space
1954, (USA), Planet Filmways/RKO, b&w, 71 mins.
W: Peter Graves *(Doug)*, Barbara Bestar, Jack Daly, Shep Menken, Burt Wenland,
John Merrick, James Seay, Robert Roark, Mark Scott *(Narrator)*, Frank
Gerstle, Steve Pendleton, Ron Kennedy, Lester Dorr, Ben Welden, Ruth
Bennett
P & D: W. Lee Wilder   SCR: Bill Raynor   STORY: Myles Wilder   PHOTOG:

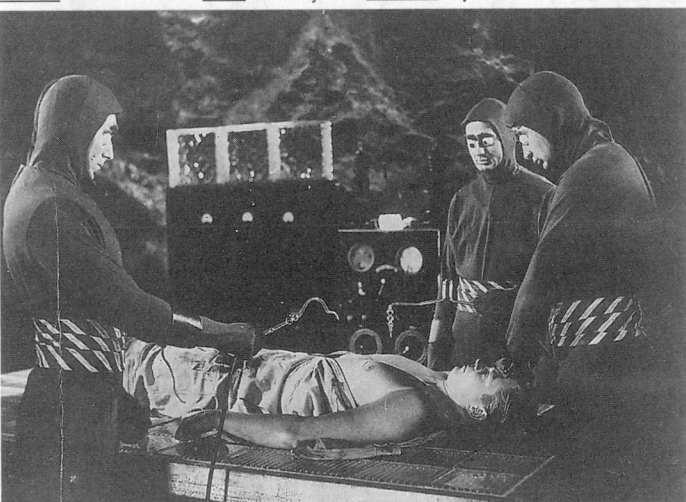

Killers From Space: PETER GRAVES

William Clothier   MUSIC: Manuel Compinsky
*Minor SF-thriller (with much stock-footage from **One Million B.C.**): Evil space aliens
revive dead jet pilot*

Killer Shark
1950, (USA), Mono, b&w, 76 mins.
W: Roddy McDowall, Laurette Luez, Roland Winters
D: Oscar (Budd) Boetticher
Standard thriller

The Killer Shrews
1959, (USA), McLendon/Hollywood, b&w, 70 mins.
W: James Best *(Capt. Thorne Sherman)*, Ingrid Goude *(Ann)*, Ken Curtis *(Jerry)*,

Baruch Lumet (*Dr. Craigis*), Gordon McLendon, J.H. Dupree, Alfredo DeSoto
P: Ken Curtis **D:** Ray Kellogg **STORY & SCR:** Jay Simms **PHOTOG:** Wilfrid M. Cline **MUSIC:** Harry Bluestone & Emil Cadkin
*orig. co-billed with **The Giant Gila Monster***
Standard SF-horror: Giant shrews menace scientists on remote island

Killer's Kiss
1955, (USA), MinotaurUA, b&w, 64 mins.
W: Frank Silvera, Jamie Smith, Irene Kane (Later Chris Chase), Ruth Sobotka, Alec Rubin, Jerry Jarret, Mike Dana, Ralph Roberts, Phil Stevenson, Felice Orlandi, Julius Adelman, David Vaughan
WRIT, D, & PHOTOG: Stanley Kubrick **MUSIC:** Gerald Fried
Unusual melodrama (arty, early Kubrick): Pug saves girl from lecherous dance hall owner

Killer's Moon
1978, (GB), Rothernorth, color, 90 mins.
W: Anthony Forrest (*Pete*), Tom Marshall (*Mike*), Georgina Kean (*Agatha*), Nigel Gregory (*Smith*), David Jackson (*Trubshaw*), Paul Rattee (*Muldoon*), Peter Spraggon (*Jones*), Jane Hayden (*Julie*), Alison Elliott (*Sandy*), Lisa Vanderpump (*Anne*), JoAnne Good (*Mary*), Jane Lester (*Elizabeth*), Debbie Martyn (*Deirdre*), Christina Jones (*Carol*), Elisabeth Counsell (*Miss Lilac*), Lynne Morgan (*Sue*), Chubby Oates (*The Driver*)
P: Alan Birkinshaw & Gordon Keymer **WRIT & D:** Alan Birkinshaw **PHOTOG:** Arthur Lavis **MUSIC:** John Shakespeare
Standard thriller: Four escaped maniacs terrorize stranded schoolgirls

Killer Spy
1963, (Fr), color, 82 mins.
W: Jean Marais, Nadja Tiller
D: Georges Lampin
Minor thriller

A Killer Walks
1952, (GB), Leontine Entertainment/Grand Nat'l, b&w, 57 mins.
W: Laurence Harvey (*Ned*), Susan Shaw (*Joan Gray*), Trader Faulkner (*Frankie*), Laurence Naismith (*The Doctor*), Ethel Edwards (*Gran*), Sheila Shand Gibbs (*Brenda*)
P, D & SCR: Ronald Drake, from Gordon Glennon's play *Gathering*, based on Rayner Barton's novel *Simplicity*
Standard crime-thriller: Man kills grandmother to get farm, frames brother

Killer with a Silk Scarf
1967, (W. Ger), b&w
W: Susanne Uhlen, Carl Mohner
Minor thriller: Child flees mother's murderer

Killer with Two Faces
1974, (GB), Made for TV, color, 70 mins.
W: Donna Mills, Ian Hendry, David Lodge
TVM, standard thriller: American woman falls for Englishman, discovers he has deranged twin

Kill Factor
see Death Dimension

Kill Her Gently
1957, (GB), Fortress/Col, b&w, 73 mins.
W: Griffith Jones (*Jeff Martin*), Maureen Connell (*Kay Martin*), Marc Lawrence (*William Connors*), Shay Gorman (*Dr. Landers*), George Mikell (*Lars Svenson*), Marianne Brauns (*Raina*), Frank Hawkins (*The Inspector*), Elaine Wells, John Gayford, Roger Avon, Patrick Connor, Jonathan Meddings, Peter Stephens, David Lawton, Susan Neil
D: Charles Saunders **SCR:** Paul Erickson **PHOTOG:** Walter J. Harvey **MUSIC:** Edwin Astley
Routine thriller: Escaped convict enlisted to murder wife of ex-mental patient

The Killing
1956, (USA), UA, b&w, 83 mins.
W: Sterling Hayden (*Johnny Clay*), Coleen Gray (*Fay*), Vince Edwards (*Val Cannon*), Joe Sawyer (*Mike O'Reilly*), Jay C. Flippen (*Marvin Unger*), Marie Windsor (*Sherry Peatty*), Elisha Cook Jr. (*George Peatty*), Timothy Carey (*Nikki Arane*), Ted de Corsia (*Randy Kennan*), Jay Adler (*Leo*), Joseph Turkel (*Tiny*), Maurice Oboukhoff (*Kola Kwarian*)
P: James B. Harris **D & SCR:** Stanley Kubrick, based on Lionel White's novel *Clean Break* **PHOTOG:** Lucien Ballard **MUSIC:** Gerald Fried
Taut melodrama: Five men plot big racetrack robbery

The Killing Box
see Grey Knight

The Killing Game
1967, (Fr), Regional, color, 94 mins.
W: Claudine Auger, Jean-Pierre Cassel, Michel Duchaussoy Eleanore Hirt
P: Rene Thevenet **D & SCR:** Alain Jessua **PHOTOG:** Jacques Robin, Bandes Dessinees & Guy Peelaert **MUSIC:** Jacques Loussier
A.k.a. Jeu de Massacre
Bizarre psychodrama: Comic-strip writer and wife become caught up in playboy's fantasy world.

The Killing Jar
1997, (USA), color, 105 mins.
W: Brett Cullen, Tamlyn Tomita, Wes Studi
Made-for-Video, unusual thriller: Murder witness undergoes hypnosis, becomes prime suspect

The Killing Kind
1973, (USA), Media Cinema, color, 95 mins
W: John Savage, Ruth Roman, Ann Sothern, Cindy Williams, Luana Anders
P: George Edwards **D:** Curtis Harrington **SCR:** Lenny Crechalon
Standard thriller: Ex-convict seeks revenge for unjust imprisonment

Killing Mrs. Tingle
1999, (USA), color
W: Katie Holmes, Barry Watson
D & SCR: Kevin Williamson
Standard thriller

Killing Obsession
1994, (USA), color, 95 mins.
W: John Savage, Kimberly Chase, John Saxon, Bernie White
D & SCR: Paul Leder
Minor thriller: Murderous psycho released from asylum

A Killing Success
1963, (Fr), MGM/Gaumont/Gold Key, b&w, 91 mins
W: Jean-Claude Brialy, Sophie Daumier, Louis de Funes, Alfred Adam
Minor melodrama: Ambitious man's efforts to reach top

Kill, Kill, Overkill
1991, (USA), color
W: Bill Black, Susan Deemer
Minor thriller: Madman slays wanton women

Kill Me Again
1989, (USA), color, 96 mins.
W: Val Kilmer, Joanne Whalley-Kilmer, Michael Madsen, Nick Dimitri, Jonathan Gries, Pat Mulligan
WRIT & D: John R. Dahl
Standard thriller: Woman flees psychotic partner-in-crime

Kill Me Tomorrow
1957, (GB), Delta/Renown/Tudor, b&w, 80 mins.
W: Pat O'Brien (*Bart Crosbie*), George Coulouris (*Heinz Webber*), Lois Maxwell (*Jill Brook*), Ronald Adam (*Brook*), Wensley Pithey (*Insp. Lane*), Freddie Mills (*Waxy*), Robert Brown (*Steve*), Richard Pasco (*Dr. Fisher*), April Olrich (*Bella Braganza*), Tommy Steele
P: Francis Searle **D:** Terence Fisher **STORY:** Robert Falconer & Manning O'Brine
Routine melodrama: To gain cash for son's operation, sacked reporter confesses to killing editor

The Kill-Off
1989, (USA), color, 97 mins.
W: Loretta Gross, Andrew Lee Barrett, Jackson Sims, William Russell, Steve Monroe, Cathy Haase, Jorjan Fox, Ralph Graff, Sean O'Sullivan, Ellen Kelly
D: Maggie Greenwald **PHOTOG:** Declan Quinn
Standard thriller: Malicious old woman inspires murder

Kill or Be Killed
1950, (USA), Eagle Lion, b&w, 68 mins.
W: Lawrence Tierney, George Coulouris
Standard thriller

Kill or Be Killed
1980, (USA), Film Ventures, color, 90 mins.
W: James Ryan, Charlotte Michelle, Norman Combes, Daniel Du Plessis
D: Ivan Hall **SCR:** C.F. Beyers-Boshoff **PHOTOG:** Mane Rotha
Standard thriller

Kill or Cure
1962, (GB), MGM, b&w, 88 mins.
W: Terry-Thomas (*Barker-Rynde*), Eric Sykes (*Rumbelow*), Dennis Price (*Dr. Crossley*), Moira Redmond (*Frances Reitman*), Lionel Jeffries (*Insp. Hook*), Katya Douglas (*Rita Fallows*), David Lodge (*Richards*), Ronnie Barker (*Burton*), Hazel Terry (*Mrs. Crossley*), Harry Locke (*Fred Higgins*), Derren Nesbitt (*Roger*), Arthur Howard (*The Clerk*), Peter Butterworth (*The Barman*), Anna Russell (*Margaret Clifford*), Mandy Miller, Julian Orchard
P: George Brown & Lawrence Bachmann **D:** George Pollock **STORY:** David Pursall & Jack Seddon
Standard comedy-mystery: Rich widow poisoned at spa

Kindar the Invulnerable
1964, (It), color
W: Mark Forest, Rosalba Neri
Minor "Sword & Sandal": Muscleman protects countrymen

Kind Hearts and Coronets
1949, (GB), Ealing/Janus/GFD/Eagle-Lion, b&w, 106 mins.
W: Alec Guinness (*The Duke/The Banker/The Parson/The General/ The*

Admiral/Young Ascoyne/Young Henry/Lady Agatha), Dennis Price (*Louis Mazzini*), Joan Greenwood (*Sibella*), Valerie Hobson (*Edith*), Audrey Fildes (*Mama*), Miles Malleson (*The Hangman*), Peggy Ann Clifford (*Maud*), Clive Morton (*The Governor*), Arthur Lowe (*The Reporter*), Hugh Griffith (*Lord High Steward*), Barbara Leakey (*The Schoolmistress*), John Penrose (*Lionel*), John Salew (*Mr. Perkins*), Anne Valery (*The Girl in the Punt*), Cecil Ramage (*The Counsel*), Lyn Evans

Kind Hearts and Coronets: DENNIS RICE AND JOAN GREENWOOD

P: Michael Balcon **D:** Robert Hamer **SCR:** Robert Hamer & John Dighton, from a novel by Roy Horniman, *Noblesse Oblige* **PHOTOG:** Douglas Slocombe **MUSIC:** Mozart
Fr retitle, **Noblesse Oblige**
Classic black comedy: Outcast tries to kill relatives

Kind Hearts are More than Coronets
1913, (GB), Clarendon, b&w, 725 ft. (221m)
D: Wilfred Noy **STORY:** W. Saville
Standard crime-thriller: Policeman and old soldier's daughter battle burglars

Kind Lady (1935)
see House of Menace

Kind Lady
1951, (USA), MGM, b&w, 78 mins.
W: Ethel Barrymore, Maurice Evans, Keenan Wynn, Angela Lansbury, Betsy Blair, Doris Lloyd, John Williams, John O'Malley
P: Armand Deutsch **D:** John Sturges **SCR:** Jerry Davis, Edward Chodorov & Charles Bennett, from Edward Chodorov's play, based on Hugh Walpole's short story *The Silver Mask*, contained in book *All Soul's Night* **PHOTOG:** Joseph Ruttenberg **MUSIC:** David Raksin
Superior thriller: Elderly woman held prisoner by evil street people

The Kindred
1987, (USA), F/M Entertainment, color, 91 mins.
W: David Allen Brooks (*John Hollins*), Rod Steiger (*Dr. Phillip Lloyd*), Amanda Pays (*Melissa Leftridge*), Talia Balsam (*Sharon Raymond*), Kim Hunter (*Amanda Hollins*), Timothy Gibbs (*Hart Phillips*), Julia Montgomery (*Cindy Russell*), Peter Frechette (*Brad Baxter*), Charles Grueber (*Harry*), Bunki Z (*Nell Valentine*), Edgar Small, Ben Perry, Steve Conte
D: Jeffrey Obrow & Stephen Carpenter **SCR:** Stephen Carpenter, Jeffrey Obrow, John Penney, Earl Ghaffari & Joseph Stefano **PHOTOG:** Stephen Carpenter **MUSIC:** David Newman
Standard SF-horror: Genetic engineering produces mutant

King Ape
see King Kong (1933)

King Arthur, The Young Warlord
1975, (GB), color, 97 mins.
W: Oliver Tobias, Michael Gothard, Jack Watson, Peter Firth, Brian Blessed
D: Sidney Hayers, Pat Jackson & Peter Sasdy
A.k.a. **Young Werlord**
Standard adventure-thriller: Young Celtic ruler vs. Saxon hordes

King Arthur was a Gentleman
1942, (GB), Gainsborough/GFD b&w, 99 mins.
W: Arthur Askey (*Arthur King*), Evelyn Dall (*Susan Ashley*), Anne Shelton (*Gwen Duncarron*), Max Bacon (*Maxie*), Brefni O'Rorke (*Col. Duncarron*), Jack Train (*Jack*), Peter Graves (*Lance*), Vera Frances (*Vera*), Al Burnett (*Slim*), Ronald Shiner (*The Sgt.*)
P: Edward Black **D:** Marcel Varnel **STORY:** Val Guest & Marriott Edgar
Standard comedy-fantasy: Soldier thinks he owns King Arthur's magic sword

King Dinosaur
1955, (USA), Zimgor/Lippert, b&w, 58 mins, also 63 mins
W: Bill (later William) Bryant, Wanda Curtis, Douglas Henderson, Patti Gallagher
D: Bert I. Gordon **SCR:** Tom Gries, based on orig. story *Beast from Outer Space* by Bert I. Gordon & Al Zimbalist **PHOTOG:** Gordon Avil **SPCL-FX:** Howard A. Anderson Co. **MUSIC SCORE:** Louis Palange **MUSIC DIR:** Mischa Terr
Minor SF-adventure: Astronauts probe prehistoric planet

The Kingdom
1995, (Den),October Films, TV Miniseries, color, 279 mins- shown in 2 parts
W: Udo Keir, Ernst-Hugo Jaregard (*Helmer*), Kirsten Rolffes (*Mrs. Drusse*), Ghita Norby (*Rigmor*), Annevig Schedle Ebbe, Soren Pilmark, Baard Owe Holger Juul Hansen, Birgitte Raabjerg, Peter Mygind
D: Lars von Trier **SCR:** Lars von Trier & Tomas Gislason **PHOTOG:** Eric Kress **MUSIC:** Joachim Holbek
Unusual gothic allegory (orig. TV miniseries): Events in a haunted hospital

The King of Criminals
see Superargo e i Giganti Senzo Volto

The Kingdom of the Fairies
see Le Royaume des Fees

Kingdom of the Spiders
1977, (USA), Arachnid/Dimension, color, 90 mins.
W: William Shatner (*Dr. Robert "Rack" Hansen*), Tiffany Bolling (*Dr. Diane Ashley*), Woody Strode (*Walter Colby*), Altovise Davis (*Birch Colby*), Lieux Dressler (*Emma Washburn*), David McLean (*Gene Smith*), Natasha Ryan (*Linda Hansen*), Joe Ross (*Vern Johnson*), Marcy Lafferty (*Terry Hansen*), Adele Malis (*Betty Johnson*), Roy Engel (*Mayor Connors*), Hoke Howell (*Earl Forbes*), Whitey Hughes (*The Baron*), Bill Foster (*Clyde*), Jay Lawrence, Valla Rae McDade, Bettie Bolling, Juanita Merritt, Nadia Caillou

King Dinosaur: BILL BRYANT AND WANDA CURTIS

D: John "Bud" Cardos **SCR:** Richard Robinson & Alan Caillou, from a story by Jeffrey M. Sneller & Stephen Lodge **PHOTOG:** John Morrill **SPCL-FX:** Greg Auer **MUSIC SPRVSR:** Igo Kantor **SONGS:** (writ & sung by Dorsey Burnette), *Peaceful Verde Valley, Things I Treasure, Green Side of the Mountain & XKE*
Standard SF-thriller: Tarantulas mass against humans

King Kong
1933, (USA), RKO, b&w, 100 mins.
W: Fay Wray (*Ann Darrow*), Robert Armstrong (*Carl Denham*), Bruce Cabot (*John "Jack" Driscoll*), Frank Reicher (*Capt. Engelhorn*), Noble Johnson (*The Native Chief*), Sam Hardy (*Weston*), Steve Clemento (*The Witch Doctor*), James Flavin (*2nd Mate*), Victor Wong (*Charlie, the Ship's Cook*)
P & D: Ernest B. Schoedsack & Merian C. Cooper **SCR:** James Creelman & Ruth Rose from an orig. story by Edgar Wallace & Merian C. Cooper **PHOTOG:** Edward Linden, Verne Walker & J.O. Taylor **ANIMATION:** Willis O'Brien **MUSIC:** Max Steiner **SOUND-FX:** Murray Spivak
orig. to be titled **The Beast, The Eighth Wonder** *or* **King Ape** *Ger retitle,* **King Kong and the White Woman**
Classic horror-fantasy: Movie-makers find giant gorilla. cf. **Creation**

King Kong
1976, (USA), Dino De Laurentiis-Para, color, 134 mins.
W: Jeff Bridges (*Jack Prescott*), Jessica Lange (*Dwan*), Charles Grodin (*Fred Wilson*), John Agar (*The Mayor*), John Randolph (*Capt. Ross*), Dennis Fimple (*Sunfish*), Rene Auberjonois (*Bagley*), Julius Harris (*Boan*), Jack O'Halloran (*Joe Perko*), Ed Lauter (*Carnahan*), George Whiteman (*The Army Helicopter Pilot*), John Lone (*The Chinese Cook*), Mario Gallo (*Timmons*), Sid Conrad (*The*

King Kong (1933)

Petrox *Chairman*), Jorge Moreno (*Garcia*), Garry Halberg (*The Army General*), Wayne Heffley (*The Air Force Colonel*), Keny Long (*The Ape-Masked Man*) Joe Piscopo, Corbin Bernsen

P: Dino De Laurentiis   **D:** John Guillermin   **SCR:** Lorenzo Semple Jr.   **PHOTOG:** Richard H. Kline   **MUSIC:** John Barry

Standard thriller, expensive remake ($20 million): Petroleum hunters find lost island and giant ape. Jessica Lange's film debut

King Kong and the White Woman
see King Kong (1933)

King Kong Escapes
1968, (Jap), Toho/Univ, color, 96 mins.

W: Rhodes Reason (*Nelson*), Linda Miller (*Susan*), Mie Hama (*Mme. Piranha*), Akira Takarada, Eisei Anamoto

P: Tomoyuki Tanaka   **D:** Inoshiro Honda   **SCR:** William J. Keenan   **PHOTOG:** Eiji Tsuburaya

Standard horror-fantasy: Giant ape meets robot replica

King Kong Lives
1986, (USA), DEG, color, 105 mins.

W: Brian Kerwin (*Hank Mitchell*), Linda Hamilton (*Amy Franklin*), John Ashton (*Col. Nevitt*), Frank Maraden (*Dr. Benson Hughes*), Peter Elliot (*King Kong*), Peter Michael Goetz (*Dr. Ingersoll*), George Yiasomi (*Lady Kong*), Alan Sader (*Faculty Dr. #1*), Lou Criscuolo (*Faculty Dr. #2*), Marc Clement (*The Crew Chief*), Richard Rhodes (*A Reporter*), Larry Souder (*A Reporter*), Ted Prichard (*A Reporter*), Jayne Linday-Gray (*A Reporter*), Debbie McLeod (*A Reporter*), Elizabeth Hayes (*A Reporter*), Natt Christian (*Surgeon #1*), Mac Pirkle (*Surgeon #2*), Larry Sprinkle (*The Journalist*), Rod Davis (*The TV Reporter*), Jimmie Ray Weeks (*Maj. Peete*), David DeVries (*Technician #1*), Bonnie Cook (*Technician #2*), J. Michael Hunter (*Technician #3*), Robin Cahall (*Mazlansky*), Jeff Benninghofen (*Radioman #1*), Don Law (*The Security Chief*), Jack Maloney (*Wrangler #1*), Jim Grimshaw (*The Sgt.*), Bernard Addison (*Capt. #1*), Michael McLendon (*Capt. #2*), Michael Forest (*Vance*), Jimmy Wiggins (*The Boyfriend*), Mary Swafford (*The Girlfriend*), Leon Rippy (*A Hunter*), Wallace Merck (*A Hunter*), Dean Whitworth (*A Hunter*), Hershel Sparber (*A Hunter*), Dandy Stevenson (*Mom #1*), Lydia Smith (*Mom #2*), Margaret Freeman (*The Native Woman*), Hope Nunnery (*The Lady in the Phone Booth*), Buck Ford, Winston Hemingway, Tom Parkhill, Derek Perason, Shannon Rowell, Gary Kaikaka, Duke Ernsberger, Mike Starr

D: John Guillermin   **SCR:** Ronald Shusett & Steven Pressfield, based on "King Kong" character created by Edgar Wallace & Merian C. Cooper   **PHOTOG:** Alec Mills   **SPCL VS-FX SPRVSR:** Barry Nolan   **MUSIC:** John Scott

Modest SF-fantasy: Artificial heart revives giant ape

King Kong vs. Godzilla
1962, (Jap), Toho/Univ, color, 90 mins.

W: James Yagi (*Omura*), Harry Holcombe (*Dr. Arnold Johnson*), Michael Keith

(*Eric Carter*), Mie Hama, Yu Fujiki, Tadao Takashima, Tatsuo Matsumura, Kenji Sahara, Ichiro Arishima, Senkichi Omura

D: Thomas Montgomery & Inoshiro Honda   **SCR:** Paul Mason & Bruce Howard   **SPCL-FX:** Eiji Tsuburaya   **MUSIC:** Peter Zinner

English-speaking version produced by John Beck

Standard SF-fantasy: Monster titans battle

King Lear
1970, (GB-Den), Filmways-Lanterna-Athena/Col, color, 137 mins.

W: Paul Scofield (*King Lear*), Irene Worth (*Goneril*), Tom Fleming (*Earl of Kent*), Alan Webb (*Duke of Gloucester*), Cyril Cusack (*Duke of Albany*), Jack MacGowran (*The Fool*), Susan Engel (*Regan*), Patrick Magee (*Duke of Cornwall*), Robert Lloyd (*Edgar*), Soeren Elung-Jensen (*Duke of Burgundy*), Barry Stanton (*Oswald*), Anne-Lise Gabold (*Cordelia*) Ian Hogg (*Edmund*)

P: Michael Birkett, Sam Lomberg & Mogens Skot-Hansen   **D & SCR:** Peter Brook, from Shakespeare's play   **PHOTOG:** Henning Kristiansen

Modest melodrama: Mad king's conflict with daughters

King Lear (1971)
see Korol Lir

King Lear
1987, (USA-Switz), Cannon, color, 90 mins.

W: Burgess Meredith (*Lear*), Molly Ringwald (*Cordelia*), Peter Sellars, Jean-Luc Godard, Woody Allen, Leos Carax, Norman Mailer, Kate Miller, Quentin Tarantino

D & SCR: Jean-Luc Godard, from Shakespeare's play   **PHOTOG:** Sophie Maintigneux

Bizarre interpretation of classic tragedy: King's folly equals his wisdom

King Lear
1998, (USA), PBS-TV, color

W: Sir Ian Holm (*Lear*)

from Shakespeare's play

TVM, well-made psychodrama: King proves fallible

King of Coins
1903, (GB), Gaumont, b&w, 75 ft. (22.9m)

D: Alf Collins

Standard fantasy short: Conjuror makes coins appear from air

The King of Crime
1914, (GB), Magnet, b&w, 3,600 ft. (1097.3m)

W: John Lawson (*Roujarre*), Claudia Guillot

D: Sidney Northcote, from a play by Arthur Shirley

Standard crime-thriller: Stolen heiress secretly wed to man framed for killing her miserly guardian

King of Kong Island

1978, (Sp), color, 92 mins.
W: Brad Harris, Esmeralda Barros, Marc Lawrence, Adrianna Alben, Mark Farran
D: Robert Morris
A.k.a. Kong Island

King Kong (1976): JESSICA LANGE

Minor SF-thriller: Scientist alters apes' brains

The King of Seven Dials

1914, (GB), Regent/Gaumont, b&w, 2,800 ft. (853.4m)
W: Arthur Finn (*Jim*), Alice Inward (*Mary Fuller*), Charles Weston (*Bill*)
P: Charles Weston & Arthur Finn   D: Charles Weston
Standard crime-thriller: Jealous crook tries to depose boss

King of the Damned

1935, (GB), b&w, 76 mins.
W: Conrad Veidt, Helen Vinson, Noah Beery, Cecil Ramage, Edmund Willard,
    Raymond Lovell, Percy Parsons
D: Walter Forde   PHOTOG: Bernard Knowles
Standard melodrama: Cruel penal colony on Caribbean isle

King of the Jungle

1933, (USA), Para, b&w, 72 mins
W: Buster Crabbe, Irving Pichel, Frances Dee, Nydia Westman, Douglass
    Dumbrille Sidney Toler, Robert Barrat
D: H. Bruce Humberstone & Max Marcin   SCR: Philip Wylie & Fred Niblo Jr.
Standard adventure-thriller: White man raised in jungle becomes circus attraction

King of the Jungleland

see *Darkest Africa*

King of the Mediums

see *Le Roi des Mediums*

King of the Zombies

1941, (USA), Mono, b&w, 67 mins.
W: Dick Purcell, Joan Woodbury, Mantan Moreland, Henry Victor, John Archer
P: Lindsley Parsons   D: Jean Yarbrough   SCR: Edmond Kelso
Minor horror-thriller: Mad doctor creates Nazi-controlled automatons

King Robert of Sicily

1912, (GB), Hepworth, b&w, 1,100 ft. (335.3m)
W: Alec Worcester (*King Robert/The Jester*), Alma Taylor (*The Princess*)
D: Hay Plumb, from a poem by Longfellow
Standard fantasy: Jester changes places with arrogant king, is revealed as angel

King Robot

see *Mother Riley Meets the Vampire*

The King's Avenger

1961, (Fr), color
W: Jean Marais, Sabrina Steelman
USA retitle, **The Hunchback of Paris**
Minor adventure-thriller

Kings and Desperate Men

1981, (Can), color, 118 mins.
W: Patrick McGoohan, Alexis Kanner, Andrea Marcovicci, Margaret Trudeau,
    Jean-Pierre Brown, Robin Spry
D: Alexis Kanner
*Minor psychological thriller (loosely related to last episode of teleseries The Prisoner): Radio
    phone-in host held hostage*

The King's Daughter

1916, (GB), London/Jury, b&w, 4,414 ft. (1345.4m)
W: Gerald Ames (*Montrose*), Janet Ross (*Helene*), Edward O'Neill (*The King*),
    Hayford Hobbs (*Dubois*), Hubert Willis (*The Chief of Police*)
D: Maurice Elvey, from Alexandre Dumas' novel
Standard melodrama: Assassin's daughter learns she is King's bastard; dies to save his life

The King's Minister

1914, (GB), London/Globe, b&w, 2,922 ft. (890.6m)
W: Edna Flugrath (*Lady Muriel Delissa*), Arthur Holmes-Gore (*Braun*), Langhorne
    Burton (*Lord Lincoln*), Charles Rock (*Lord Draconsmere*), George Bellamy
    (*Carl Wagner*), Gerald Ames (*Aubrey Tremayne*)
D: Harold Shaw   SCR: Bannister Merwin, from a play by Cecil Raleigh
*Standard crime-thriller: German frames Prime Minister for murder, forces his daughter to
    steal treaty*

King Solomon's Mines

1937, (GB), Gaumont, b&w, 80 mins.
W: Paul Robeson (*Umbopa*), Roland Young (*Cdr. Good*), Anna Lee (*Kathy O'Brien*),
    Cedric Hardwicke (*Allan Quartermaine*), John Loder (*Henry Curtis*), Sydney
    Fairbrother (*Gagool*), Majabalo Hlubi (*Kapsie*), Ecce Homo Toto (*Infadoos*),
    Robert Adams (*Twala*), Frederick Leister (*The Wholesaler*), Arthur Sinclair
    (*O'Brien*), Alf Goddard (*Red*)
D: Robert Stevenson & Geoffrey Barkas   SCR: Michael Hogan, Roland Pertwee,
    A.R. Rawlinson, Charles Bennett & Ralph Spence, from H. Rider Haggard's
    novel   PHOTOG: Cyril J. Knowles   MUSIC: Mischa Spoliansky
    SONGS: *Kukuana* & *Climbing Up*
Standard adventure: Exiled African king helps explorers find diamond mine

King Solomon's Mines

1950, (USA), MGM, color, 102 mins.
W: Stewart Granger (*Allan Quartermaine*), Deborah Kerr (*Elizabeth Curtis*),
    Richard Carlson (*John Goode*), Hugo Haas (*Smith*), Lowell Gilmore (*Eric
    Masters*), Siriaque (*Umbopa*), Kimursi (*Khiva*), Sekaryongo (*Chief Gagool*),
    Baziga (*King Twala*)
P: Sam Zimbalist   D: Compton Bennett & Andrew Marton   SCR: Helen
    Deutsch from H. Rider Haggard's novel   PHOTOG: Robert L. Surtees
Classic adventure-thriller: Explorers seek missing man, find fabulous treasure. cf. **Watusi**

King Solomon's Mines

1985, (USA), Golan-Globus/Cannon, color, 100 mins.
W: Richard Chamberlain (*Allan Quartermaine*), Sharon Stone (*Jessie*), Herbert Lom
    (*Col. Bockner*), John Rhys-Davies (*Dogati*), Ken Gampu (*Umbopa*), Sam
    Williams (*Scragga*), June Buthelezi (*Gagoola*), Shai K. Ophir (*Kassam*), Mick
    Lesley (*Dorfman*), Fidelis Che A (*The Mapaki Chief*), Vincent Van Der Byl
    (*Shack*), Bob Greer (*Hamid*), Neville Thomas (*The German Pilot*), Oliver
    Tengende (*Bushiri*), Isiah Murert (*The Rug Carrier*), Bishop McThuzen
    (*Dari*), Rocky Green, Calvin Johns, Isaac Mabhikwa, Innocent Choga, Brian
    Kagure, Stanley Norris, Anna Ditano, Andrew Whaley
D: J. Lee Thompson   SCR: Gene Quintano & James R. Silke, from H. Rider
    Haggard's novel   PHOTOG: Alex Phillips   MUSIC: Jerry Goldsmith
Minor adventure-thriller: White hunter aids girl in search for fabled treasure

King Solomon's Treasure

1976, (Can), Canafox, color, 90 mins.
W: David McCallum (*Sir Henry Curtis*), Britt Ekland (*Queen Nypeptha*), John
    Colicos (*Allan Quartermain*), Patrick Macnee (*Capt. Good*), Ken Gampu
    (*Umpslopogas*), Veronique Beliveau (*Neva*), Yvon Dufour (*Alphonse*), Wilfrid
    Hyde-White (*The Oldest Club Member*), John Quentin (*Stetopatris*), Sam
    Williams (*Matawani*), Hugh Rowse (*Rev. McKenzie*), Fiona Fraser (*Mrs.
    McKenzie*), Camilla Hutton (*Flossie McKenzie*)
P: Alvin Rakoff & Susan Lewis   D: Alvin Rakoff   SCR: Colin Turner & Allan
    Prior, based on H. Rider Haggard's novel *Allan Quartermain*   PHOTOG:
    Paul van der Linden   MUSIC: Lew Lehman
Modest adventure: Explorers meet queen of lost civilization

The King's Outcast

1915, (GB), London/Jury, b&w, 3,500 ft. (106.7m)
W: Gerald Ames (*Edward Farley*), Blanche Bryan (*Marjorie*), Charles Rock (*The
    Squire*), W. Kershaw (*Farley*), Philip Hewland (*Capt. Hatherley*), Douglas
    Munro (*The Innkeeper*), Chappel Dossett
D: Ralph Dewsbury   SCR: Bannister Merwin, from a play by W. Gayer MacKay
    & Robert Ord
Standard crime-thriller: Framed man poses as old violinist, saves son from murderous gambler

The King's Peril

1911, (GB), B&C/Cosmo, b&w, 795 ft. (242.3m)
D: H.O. Martinek   STORY:, Harold Brett
Standard thriller: King saved from anarchists who try to blow him up during coronation

The King's Pirate

1967, (USA), Univ, color, 100 mins.
W: Doug McClure, Jill St. John
D: Don Weis
Minor adventure-thriller

The King's Romance

1914, (GB), B&C/KTC, b&w, 4,074 ft. (1241.8m)

W: Fred Morgan (*The Baron*), Ethel Bracewell (*Vera*), Henry Victor (*Prince Andreas*), George Foley (*The Anarchist*), Dick Webb (*Dick*), Ethyle Batley (*The Queen*)
D: Ernest G. Batley, from a play by Mary Austin & E.V. Edmonds
A.k.a. **Revolution,** USA retitle, ***The Revolutionist***
Standard crime-thriller: Ruritanian baron poses as prince to elope with anarchist's sister

King Tut-Ankh-Amen's Eighth Wife
1923, (USA), Max Cohen, b&w, 5 reels (4,100 ft./1249.7m)
D & STORY: Andrew Remo   **SCR:** George M. Merrick & Max Cohen
   PHOTOG: John Bitzer
A.k.a. ***The Mystery of Tut-Ankh-Amen's Eighth Wife***
Standard thriller: Tragedy pursues tomb violators

A King Without Diversion
see La Poursuite

The Kirlian Witness
1978, (USA), Sampson & Cranor Inc., color
W: Nancy Snyder, Joel Colodner, Nancy Boykin, Ted Leplat
P & D: Jonathan Sarno   **SCR:** Jonathan Sarno & Lamar Sanders   **MUSIC:** Harry Manfredini
A.k.a. ***The Plants Are Watching***
Standard thriller: Woman with telepathic sensitivity to plants tries to track sister's killer

Kismet
1914, (GB), Zenith, b&w, 4,000 ft. (1219.2m)
W: Oscar Asche (*Hajj*), Lily Brayton (*Marsinah*), Herbert Grimwood (*Wasir Mansur*), Frederick Worlock (*The Caliph*), Caleb Porter (*The White Sheik*), Bessie Major (*The Nurse*), Suzanne Sheldon (*Kutal-Kulub*)
D: Leedham Bantock, from Edward Knoblock's play
Standard romance: Beggar poses as prince, caliph poses as gardener

Kismet
1920, (USA), b&w, 98 mins.
W: Otis Skinner, Elinor Fair, Herschel Mayall
D: Louis Gasnier   **PHOTOG:** Gaetano Antonio "Tony" Gaudio
Lavish adventure-romance: Beggar drawn into court intrigue

Kismet
1930, (USA), First Nat'l, b&w, 10 reels (8,253 ft./2515.5m)
W: Otis Skinner (*Hajj*), Loretta Young (*Marsinah*), David Manners (*Caliph Abdallah*), Sidney Blackmer (*Wazir Mansur*), Mary Duncan (*Zeleekha*), Montagu Love (*The Jailer*), Edmund Breese (*Jawan*), Ford Sterling (*Amru*), Theodore von Eltz (*The Guide Nazir*), John St. Polis (*The Imam Mahmud*), John Sheehan (*Kazim*), Blanche Frederici (*Narjis*), Otto Hoffman (*Azaf*), Richard Carlyle (*The Muezzin*), Noble Johnson, Olin Francis, Charles Clary, Carol Wines, Sidney Jarvis, Lorris Baker, Will Walling
P: Robert North   **D:** John Francis Dillon   **SCR:** Howard Estabrook, from a play by Edward Knoblock   **PHOTOG:** John Seitz
Standard adventure-romance: Beggar outwits thief

Kismet
1944, (USA), MGM, color, 100 mins.
W: Ronald Colman, Marlene Dietrich, Edward Arnold, James Craig, Hugh Herbert, Joy Ann Page, Yvonne DeCarlo, Jack Cole, Florence Bates, Harry Davenport, Hobart Cavanaugh, Robert Warwick
D: William Dieterle   **SCR:** John Meehan from Edward Knoblock's play   **PHOTOG:** Charles Rosher   **SPCL-FX:** Warren Newcombe   **MUSIC:** Herbert P. Stothart
A.k.a. ***Oriental Dream***
Standard romance-fantasy: Beggar impersonates prince

The Kiss
1896, (USA), b&w
W: May Irwin [first stage actress to appear on film], John C. Rice
First film "shocker" (denounced by Churches): Osculation sequence from popular stage play

The Kiss
1988, (Can), Trilogy/Astral Film Enterprises/Tri-Star, color, 100 mins.
W: Joanna Pacula (*Felice*), Meredith Salenger (*Amy*), Mimi Kuzyk (*Brenda*), Nicholas Kilbertus (*Jack*), Sabrina Boudot (*Heather*), Pamela Collyer (*Hilary*), Peter Dvorsky (*Father Joe*), Shawn Levy (*Terry*), Jan Rubes (*Tobin*), Dorian Joe Clark (*T.C.*), Celine Lomez (*Aunt Irene*), Richard Dumont (*Abe*), Talya Rubin (*Young Hilary*), Johanne Herelle (*The Old African Woman*), Philip Pretten (*Father*), Tyrone Benskin (*The Train Station Conductor*), Norris Domingue (*The Security Guard*), Shannon McDonough (*Eileen*), Vlasta Vrana (*The Bishop*), Claire Rodgers (*The Nurse*), Marty Finkelstein (*The Boy in the Classroom*), Nevin Densham (*The Boy in the Pool*), Robin Bronfman (*The Stewardess*), Andrew Johnson (*The Gunshop Owner*), Priscilla Mouzakiotis
D: Pat Densham   **SCR:** Stephen Volk & Tom Ropelewski   **STORY:** Stephen Volk   **PHOTOG:** Francois Protat   **MUSIC:** J. Peter Robinson
Unusual horror-fantasy: Supernatural aunt spreads grief

Kiss and Kill
see The Blood of Fu Manchu

A Kiss Before Dying
1956, (USA), UA, color, 99 mins.
W: Robert Wagner, Joanne Woodward, Jeffrey Hunter, Mary Astor, George Macready, Virginia Leith
D: Gerd Oswald   **STORY:** Ira Levin   **PHOTOG:** Lucien Ballard

A Kiss Before Dying
1991, (USA), Initial-Robert Lawrence/Univ, color, 93 mins.
W: Matt Dillon, Diane Ladd, Sean Young, Max von Sydow, James Russo, Jim Fyfe, Martha Gehman, Ben Browder, Joy Lee, Shane Rimmer, Adam Horovitz, Sarah Keller, Lia Chang
D & SCR: James Dearden   **STORY:** Ira Levin   **PHOTOG:** Mike Southon   **MUSIC:** Howard Shore

Kiss Daddy Goodbye
1982, (USA), Pendragon, color, 92 mins.
W: Fabian, Marilyn Burns, Jon Cedar, Marvin Miller, Jed Mills, Chester Grimes, Gay French, Robert Dryer, Patrick Reagan III, Nell Reagan
D: Patrick Reagan   **PHOTOG:** George Bakken   **MUSIC:** David Spear
video title, **Revenge of the Zombie**
Minor horror-fantasy: Sheriff meets telekinetic children, grubby bikers, walking corpse

Kissed
1997, (Can), Boneyard-British Columbia/Goldwyn, color, 78 mins.
W: Molly Parker (*Sandra Larson*), Peter Outerbridge (*Matt*), NatashaMorley (*Young Sandra*)
D: Lynne Stopkewich   **SCR:** Angus Fraser & Lynne Stopkewich, based on Barbara Gowdy's story *We So Seldom Look on Love*   **PHOTOG:** Gregory Middleton   **MUSIC:** Don MacDonald
"...a remarkable achievement, offering an understanding of matters unthinkable that will haunt you for a good long time"—Peter Travers, *Rolling Stone*
"Eerily gripping"—John Powers, *Vogue*
Bizarre, poetic melodrama: Erotic exploits of necrophiliac beauty

Kisses for My President
1964, (USA), WB, b&w, 113 mins.
W: Polly Bergen, Fred MacMurray, Edward Andrews (*Walsh*), Arlene Dahl (*Doris*), Eli Wallach (*Valdez*), Donald May
P & D: Curtis Bernhardt   **SCR:** Robert G. Kane & Claude Binyon   **PHOTOG:** Robert L. Surtees   **MUSIC:** Bronislau Kaper
Standard comedy-fantasy: USA gets first woman president

A Kiss for Cinderella
1926, (USA), Para, b&w, 9,686 ft. (2952.3m)
W: Betty Bronson (*Cinderella*), Tom Moore (*The Policeman/Prince Charming*), Esther Ralston (*The Fairy Godmother*), Henry Vibart (*Richard Bodie*), Dorothy Cumming (*The Queen*), Ivan Simpson (*Mr. Cutaway*), Dorothy Walters (*Mrs. Maloney*), Flora Finch (*The 2nd Customer*), Juliet Brenon (*The 3rd Customer*), Marilyn McLaine (*Gladys*), Mary Christian (*Sally*), Patty Coakley (*Marie-Therese*), Edna Hagen (*Gretchen*)
D: Herbert Brenon   **SCR:** Willis Goldbeck & Townsend Martin, based on Charles Perrault's *Cinderella*   **PHOTOG:** J. Roy Hunt
"Pictorially alone...a masterpiece; but by any standards direction, adaptation, performance—it is a film of lasting greatness. Certainly it was the best film that Herbert Brenon ever directed"—Joe Franklin, Classics of the Silent Screen
Classic fantasy: Scullery maid dreams she is Cinderella

A Kiss from Eddie
see Sweet Kill

Kiss Kiss, Kill Kill
1966, (W. Ger), ITC, color, 86 mins
W: Tony Kendall, Brad Harris, Maria Perschy, Pino Mattei, Christa Linder
D: Frank Kramer, from Bert F. Island's novel *Commissioner X*
Minor thriller: Spy shenanigans

Kiss Me Deadly
1955, (USA), UA, b&w, 105 mins.
W: Ralph Meeker (*Mike Hammer*), Cloris Leachman, Albert Dekker, Gaby Rodgers, Maxine Cooper, Leigh Snowden, Jack Elam, Strother Martin Paul Stewart, Wesley Addy, Marjorie Bennett Paul Stewart, Jack Lambert
P & D: Robert Aldrich   **SCR:** I.A. Bezzerides, from Mickey Spillane's novel   **PHOTOG:** Ernest Laszlo
Classic atom-age film noir: Detective aids asylum escapee, becomes embroiled in sinister intrigue

Kiss Meets the Phantom of the Park
1978, (USA), Hanna-Barbera/NBC-TV, color, 95 mins.
W: Peter Criss, Ace Frehley, Gene Simmons, Paul Stanley, Anthony Zerbe (*Abner Devereaux*), Deborah Ryan (*Melissa*), Terry Lester (*Sam*), Carmine Caridi (*Calvin*), John Dennis Johnston (*Chopper*), John Lisbon Wood, Lisa Jane Persky, John Chappell, Don Steele, Richard Hein, Mary Kay Morse, Brion James, Sandra Pann, Bill Hudson, Leon Delaney
P: Terry Morse Jr.   **D:** Gordon Hessler   **TELEPLAY:** Jan-Michael Sherman & Don Buday   **PHOTOG:** Robert Caramico   **SPCL-FX:** Don Courtney   **MUSIC:** Hoyt Curtain
A.k.a. ***Attack of the Phantoms***
TVM, standard SF-fantasy with music: Automaton maker seeks revenge, involves showbiz quartet

Kiss Me, Monster
1968, (Sp-Ger), Aquila Films/Films Montana/Joseph Green, color, 80 mins
__W:__ Janine Reynaud Rosanna Yanni, Adrian Hoven
__D:__ Jess Franco
Standard SF-horror: Mad prof tries to create super-humans

Kiss Me Quick
1964, (USA), G&S Prods/Rossmore/Boxoffice International., color, 67 mins
__W:__ Frank Coe (*Sterilox/Frankenstein*)
__P, D & SCR:__ Russ Meyer   __PHOTOG:__ Laszlo Kovacs
A.k.a. **Dr. Breedlove: or, How I Learned to Stop Worrying and Love**
Standard SF-nudie-comedy: Space alien visits mad scientist who manufactures women

The Kiss of Clay
1914, (GB), Climax/ACL, b&w, 1,078 ft. (328.6m)
__D:__ Stuart Kinder
Standard thriller: Parisian sculptor's wife goes mad when he stuffs her lover's mouth with clay

Kiss of Evil
see Kiss of the Vampire

Kiss of the Beast
*see **Meridian***

Kiss of the Tarantula
1972, (USA), Ben Barry & Assocs./Cinema-Vu/Omni, color, 85 mins.
__W:__ Eric Mason, Suzanne Ling, Rita French, Herman Wallner, Patricia Landon, Beverly Eddins, Rebecca Eddins, Ronald Prather, Linda Spatz, Jay Scott Neal, W. James Eddins, Jared Davis, Stratton Leopold, Mark Smith, Mary Tyree, Art Lane, John Burrows, George Gingell, Susan Eddins
__D:__ Chris Munger   __SCR:__ Warren Hamilton Jr.   __STORY:__, Daniel B. Cady
   __PHOTOG:__ Henning Schellerup   __MUSIC:__ Phillan Bishop
Minor thriller: Undertaker's vengeful daughter raises spiders

Kiss of the Vampire
1962, (GB), Hammer/Univ, color, 88 mins.
__W:__ Clifford Evans (*Prof. Zimmer*), Noel Willman (*Dr. Ravna*), Edward De Souza (*Gerald Harcourt*), Jennifer Daniel (*Marianne Harcourt*), Barry Warren (*Carl Ravna*), Jacquie Wallis (*Sabena Ravna*), Brian Oulton (*The Disciple*), Isobel Black (*Tanya*), Noel Howlett (*Father Xavier*), Peter Madden (*Bruno*), Vera Cook, John Harvey, Margaret Read Olga Dickie, Stan Simmons, Elizabeth Valentine
__P:__ Anthony Hinds   __D:__ Don Sharp   __SCR:__ John Elder [Anthony Hinds]
   __PHOTOG:__ Alan Hume   __SPCL-FX:__ Les Bowie   __MUSIC:__ James Bernard
USA TV retitlo, **Kiss of Evil**
"Hammer's best vampire film...concentrating on mystery and atmo-sphere, until its tastefully savage finale. It exploited the sensual aspects of vampirism far more than the same studio's Dracula films had done"—William E. Everson, Classics of the Horror Film
"...intellectual horror offering, examining the philosophical and spiritual aspect of vampirism while at the same time providing the viewers with a graphically brutal and sexually atuned plot"—Gary Gerani, The Vampire Book Chapter Eight: Horror from Hammer, Monster Fantasy, Vol. I, No. 1 (April, 1975), p. 34
Superior horror-fantasy: Newlyweds meet vampire cult

Kiss the Blood Off My Hands
1948, (USA), Univ, b&w, 79 mins.
__W:__ Burt Lancaster, Joan Fontaine
Standard melodrama

Kiss the Girls
1997, (USA), color, 118 mins.
__W:__ Morgan Freeman, Ashley Judd, Cary Elwes, Tony Goldwyn, Jay O. Sanders, Bill Nunn, Jeremy Piven, Alex McArthur, Brian Cox
__D:__ Gary Fleder   __STORY:__ James Patterson
Taut thriller: Serial killer hunted

Kiss the Girls and Make Them Die
1967, (USA-It), Col, color, 106 mins.
__W:__ Mike Connors, Dorothy Provine, Raf Vallone, Margaret Lee, Terry-Thomas, Beverly Adams
__P:__ Dino De Laurentiis   __D:__ Henry Levin   __SCR:__ Jack Pulman & Dino Maiuri
   __PHOTOG:__ Aldo Tonti
Standard comedy-thriller: Secret agent's adventures

A Kiss to Die For
1993, (USA), Polone Co./NBC-TV, color, 95 mins.
__W:__ Tim Matheson, Mimi Rogers, William Forsythe, Carroll Baker, Car-los Gomez, Roy Tatum, Chris Boyd
__D:__ Leon Ichaso   __TELEPLAY:__ Deborah Dalton   __MUSIC:__ George S. Clinton
TVM, standard thriller: Psych prof meets alluring murderess

Kiss Tomorrow Goodbye
1950, (USA), WB, b&w, 102 mins.
__W:__ James Cagney, Barbara Payton, Luther Adler, Ward Bond, Helena Carter, Barton MacLane, Steve Brodie, Neville Brand, Rhys Williams
__D:__ Gordon Douglas, from a novel by Horace McCoy
Excellent crime-thriller: Vicious ex-con betrays partner, plans ambitious robbery

Kitty in Dreamland
1911, (GB), Urban, b&w, 570 ft. (173.7m)
__D:__ Walter R. Booth
Standard fantasy short: Girl dreams of witches, fairies, ogre

The Kleptomaniac
1914, (GB), Hepworth, b&w, 1,075 ft. (327.9m)
__W:__ Alma Taylor (*Helen*), Violet Hopson (*Lady Cynthia*)
__D:__ Warwick Buckland
Standard crime-thriller: Lady robs shop, companion blamed

Kleptomania Tablets
1912, (GB), HB Films/Cosmopolitan, b&w, 575 ft. (175.3m)
__W:__ Dorothy Batley (*The Girl*), Ernest G. Batley (*The Misogynist*)
__WRIT & D:__ Ernest G. Batley
Standard comedy-fantasy short: Girl gives grandfather's magic pills to curate, soldier, policeman

A Knight Errant
1907, (GB), R.W. Paul, b&w, 480 ft. (146.3m)
__W:__ Langford Reed (*The Knight*)
__D:__ J.H. Martin   __STORY:__ Langford Reed
Standard fantasy short: Fairy helps knight save princess from ogre, witch, and dwarf

A Knight in Camelot
1998, (USA), ABC-TV, color, 95 mins.
__W:__ Whoopi Goldberg (*Vivien Morgan*), Michael York (*King Arthur*), Amanda Donohoe (*Guinevere*), Ian Richardson (*Merlin*), Robert Addie (*Sir Sagramour*), Simon Fenton, Paloma Baeza, James Coombes
__D:__ Roger Young   __TELEPLAY:__ Joe Wiesenfeld, inspired by Mark Twains novel *Connecticut Yankee in King Arthur's Court*   __PHOTOG:__ Elemer Ragalyi
   __MUSIC:__ Patrick Williams
TVM, standard comedy-fantasy: Woman scientist transported to Arthurian times

Knight Moves
1992, (USA), color, 115 mins.
__W:__ Christopher Lambert
Unusual thriller: Chess champion suspect in rash of sinister murders

The Knight of Black Art
1908, (Fr), Star, b&w, 114m (374 ft./6.3 mins.)
__D:__ Georges Melies
Standard fantasy

The Knight of the Dragon
1986, (Sp), color, 90 mins.
__W:__ Klaus Kinski, Harvey Keitel, Fernando Rey, Maria Lamor, Miguel Bose
__D:__ Fernando Colomo
USA retitle, **Star Knight**
Minor SF-fantasy: Spaceship lands in medieval Spain, is mistaken for dragon

Knightriders
1981, (USA), Laurel/UFD color, 145 mins.
__W:__ Ken Foree, Ed Harris (*Billy*), Gary Lahti (*Alan*), Tom Savini (*Morgan*), Amy Ingersoll (*Linet*), Patricia Tallman (*Julie*), Christine Forrest (*Angie*), Warner Shook (*Pippin*), John Hostetter (*Tuck*), Cynthia Adler (*Rocky*), John Amplas (*Whiteface*), Brother Blue (*Merlin*), Ken Hixon (*Steve*), Albert Amerson (*Indian*), Don Berry (*Bagman*), Amanda Davies (*Sheila*), Ken Foree (*Little John*), Martin Ferrero (*Bontempi*), Michael Moran (*Cook*), Harold Wayne Jones (*Bors*), Maureen Sadusk (*Judy*), Randy Kovitz (*Punch*), Scott Reiniger (*Marhalt*), Ronald Carrier (*Hector*), Tom DiLeo (*Corncook*), David Early (*Bleoboris*), John Harrison (*Pellinore*)
__D:__ George A. Romero   __WRIT & D:__ George A. Romero   __PHOTOG:__ Michael Gornick   __MUSIC:__ Donald Rubinstein
Unusual SF-fantasy: Motorbiking King Arthur and noble knights

Knights
1993, (USA), Kings Road color, 89 mins.
__W:__ Kris Kristofferson, Kathy Long, Lance Henriksen, Scott Paulin, Gary Daniels, Nicholas Guest, Vince Klyn, Ben McReady
__D & SCR:__ Albert Pyun   __PHOTOG:__ George Mooradian   __MUSIC:__ Tony Riparetti
Minor SF-thriller: Cyborgs fueled by human blood

Knights of Terror
1962, (It), color
__W:__ Tony Russel, Scilla Gabel
Minor adventure-thriller: Masked bandits plunder, nobleman opposes them

Knights of the Round Table
1954, (USA-GB), MGM, color, 115 mins.
__W:__ Robert Taylor (*Sir Lancelot*), Ava Gardner (*Queen Guinevere*), Mel Ferrer (*King Arthur*), Anne Crawford (*Morgan Le Fay*), Stanley Baker (*Mordred*), Niall MacGinnis (*The Green Knight*), Robert Urquhart (*Gawaine*), Felix Aylmer (*Merlin*), Maureen Swanson (*Elaine*), Gabriel Woolf (*Percival*), Jill Clifford (*Bronwyn*), Anthony Forwood (*Gareth*), Ann Hanslip (*Nan*), Stephen Vercoe (*Agravaine*)
__P:__ Pandro S. Berman   __D:__ Richard Thorpe   __SCR:__ Talbot Jennings, Jan Lustig, &

Noel Langley, based on Sir Thomas Malory's *Le Mort D'Arthur* **PHOTOG:** Frederick A. Young **MUSIC:** Miklos Rozsa
Standard adventure-romance: Love affair threatens Celtic unity. MGM's first widescreen film

Knights of the Teutonic Order
1960, (Pol), color, 180 mins.
<u>W:</u> Aleksander Ford
Standard action-thriller: Medieval strife

Knight without Armour
1937, (GB), London/UA, b&w, 108 mins.
<u>W:</u> Marlene Dietrich (*Alexandra Vladinoff*), Robert Donat (*Ainsley Fothergill*), Irene Vanbrugh (*Duchess of Zorin*), Herbert Lomas (*Gen. Gregor Vladinoff*), Hay Petrie (*The Station Master*), Austin Trevor (*Count Adraxine*), Basil Gill (*Axelstein*), John Clements (*Poushkoff*), David Tree (*Alexis Maronin*), Miles Malleson (*The Drunken Soldier*), Lyn Harding (*The Bargee*), Frederick Culley (*Stanfield*), Lawrence Hanray (*Forrester*), Lisa d'Esterre (*The Czarina*)
<u>D:</u> Jacques Feyder **SCR:** Frances Marion, Lajos Biro & Arthur Wimperis, from James Hilton's novel *Without Armour*
Standard adventure: British spy saves countess from revolutionaries

Knives of the Avenger
1965, (It), World Entertainment, color, 86 mins.
<u>W:</u> Cameron Mitchell (*Rurik*), Luciana Polletin, Fausto Tozzi, Giacomo Rossi-Stuart
<u>D:</u> Mario Bava **SCR:** Alberto Liberati
A.k.a. **Viking Massacre**
Minor action-thriller: Woman awaits Viking husband's return from sea

Kondom des Grauleins (Condom of Terror)
1996, (Ger-Switz), Troma, color, 110 mins.
<u>W:</u> Udo Samel (*Luigi*), Peter Lohmeyer (*Sam Hanks*)
*USA retitle, **The Killer Condom***
Bizarre horror-satire: Killer condoms spread woe in Hotel Sleazy, NY

Konga
1961, (GB), Merton Park/AIP color, 90 mins.
<u>W:</u> Michael Gough (*Dr. Charles Decker*), Margo Johns (*Margaret*), Jess Conrad (*Bob Kenton*), Claire Gordon (*Sandra Banks*), Austin Trevor (*Dean Foster*), Jack Watson (*Supt. Brown*), George Pastell (*Prof. Ta-gore*), Stanley Morgan (*Insp. Lawson*), Leonard Sachs (*Father*), Vanda Godsell (*Mrs. Kenton*), Grace Arnold, John Welsh, Waveney Lee, Kim Tracy, Nicolas Bennett, Rupert Osborn
<u>P:</u> Herman Cohen <u>D:</u> John Lemont **STORY & SCR:** Aben Kandel & Herman Cohen **PHOTOG:** Desmond Dickinson **MUSIC:** Gerard Schurmann
Standard SF-thriller: Botany teacher creates giant ape

Kong Island
see King of Kong Island

Kongo
1932, (USA), MGM, b&w, 86 mins.

<u>W:</u> Walter Huston (*Flint*), Lupe Velez (*Tula*), Virginia Bruce (*Ann*), Conrad Nagel (*Kingsland*), C. Henry Gordon (*Gregg*), Mitchell Lewis (*Hogan*), Curtis Nero (*Fuzzy*), Forrester Harvey (*Cookie*)
<u>D:</u> William Cowen **SCR:** Leon Gordon, from a play by Chester de Vonde & Kilbourn Gordon **PHOTOG:** Harold Rosson
*Unusual melodrama, sound remake of **West of Zanzibar**: Crippled charlatan dominates jungle natives*

Korol Lir (King Lear)
1971, (Russ), Lenfilm, color, 140 mins.
<u>W:</u> Yuri Jarvet, Valentina Shendrikova, Galina Volchek, Elza Radzins, Donatis Banionis, Oleg Dal, Eduard Merzin, Regimantis Adomaitis, V. Yemelianov
<u>D & SCR:</u> Grigori Kozintsev, from Shakespeare's play **PHOTOG:** Jonas Gricius **MUSIC:** Dimitri Shostakovich
Standard melodrama: Celtic king unwisely divides his realm

Koroshi
1967, (GB), ITC, color, 93 mins.
<u>W:</u> Patrick McGoohan (*John Drake*), Yoko Tani (*Ako*), George Coulouris (*The Controller*), Ronald Howard (*Sanders*), John Garrie (*The Old Japanese Man*), Amanda Barrie (*Rosemary*), Kenneth Griffith (*Richards*), Maxine Audley (*Pauline*), Edward Ogden (*Edward Sharp*), Burt Kwouk (*Tanaka*), Jeremy Longhurst (*Fortune*), David Toguri (*Cdr. Yamada*), Tommy Yapp (*The Contact Man*), Christopher Benjamin (*Potter*), Mona Chong (*The 1st Girl Islander*), Paula Li Shiu (*The 2nd Girl Islander*), Robert Lee (*Manager of "Two-Tailed Dragon"*), Lilani Young (*The Japanese Grand-Daughter*), Kristopher Kum (*The Passport Official*), Anna Mai (*The Airline Clerk*), Tudor Davis, Clive Marshall, Kit Williams, Vernon Morris, Daniel Nicolaides, Graham Payne, Stewart Rose, Kenneth Shanley, Richard Wilson
<u>D:</u> Peter Yates & Michael Truman **SCR:** Norman Hudis **PHOTOG:** Brendan J. Stafford **UNDERWATER PHOTOG:** Egil Woxholt **MUSIC DIR:** Edwin Astley
Standard thriller: British agent tackles murderous Japanese brotherhood

Krakatoa--East of Java
1968, (USA), color, 132 mins.
<u>W:</u> Maximilian Schell, Diane Baker, Brian Keith, Sal Mineo, Barbara Werle, John Leyton, Rossano Brazzi
<u>D:</u> Bernard Kowalski
*Modest disaster-thriller: Pacific volcanic isle erupts. cf. **Fair Wind to Java***

Krava Na Mjesecu (The Cow on the Moon)
1959, (Czech), color, 310m (1,017.1 ft.)
<u>WRIT & D:</u> Dusan Vukotic
Standard animated fantasy

The Kremlin Letter
1970, (USA), 20th-Fox, color, 121 mins.
<u>W:</u> Patrick O'Neal (*Rone*), Barbara Parkins (*B.A.*), Nigel Green (*"The Whore"*), Richard Boone (*Ward*), Max von Sydow (*Kosnov*), George Sanders (*"The Warlock"*), Bibi Andersson (*Erika*), John Huston (*The Admiral*), Orson

Welles (*Bresnavitch*), Dean Jagger (*"The Highwayman"*), Lila Kedrova (*Sophie*), Ronald Radd (*Potkin*), Raf Vallone (*"Puppetmaker"*), Sandor Eles (*Grodin*), Michael McLiammoir (*"Sweet Alice"*), Niall MacGinnis (*"The Erector Set"*), Guy Deghy (*The Professor*), Anthony Chinn (*Kitai*), Vonetta McGee (*The Negress*), Fulvia Ketoff (*Sonia*), Marc Lawrence (*The Priest*), Cyril Shaps (*The Police Doctor*), George Pravda (*Kazar*), Christopher Sanford (*Rudolph*), Hana-Maria Pravda (*Mrs. Kazar*), Ludmilla Dudarova (*Mrs. Potkin*), Pehr-Olof Siren (*The Receptionist*), Dimitri Tamarov (*Ilya*), Daniel Smid (*The Waiter*), Victor Beaumont (*The Dentist*), Steve Zacharias (*Dittomachine*), Laura Forin (*Elena*), Sacha Carafa (*Mrs. Grodin*), Saara Ranin (*Mikhail's Mother*)
D: John Huston   SCR: John Huston & Gladys Hill, from Noel Behn's novel
   PHOTOG: Ted Scaife   MUSIC: Robert Drasnin
Clever thriller: Spies pursue dangerous missive

The Kremlin Letter: BIBI ANDERSSON AND PATRICK O'NEAL

Kriemhild's Rache
see *Die Nibelungen*

Kriemhild's Revenge
see *Die Nibelungen*

Kronos
1957, (USA), Regal/20th-Fox, b&w, 78 mins.
W: Jeff Morrow (*Les*), John Emery (*Eliot*), Barbara Lawrence (*Vera*), George O'Hanlon (*Culver*), Morris Ankrum (*Stern*), John Parrish (*Perry*), Kenneth Alton, Marjorie Stapp, Jose Gonzales, Richard Harrison, Robert Shayne, Donald Eitner, Gordon Mills, John Halloran
P & D: Kurt Neumann   SCR: Lawrence Louis Goldman   PHOTOG: Karl Struss
   MUSIC: Paul Sawtell & Bert Shefter
Standard SF-thriller: Space aliens plant giant device on Earth, tap planet's energy

Kronos (1974)
see *Captain Kronos: Vampire Hunter*

Krotki Film o Zabijaniu (A Short Film About Killing)
1987, (Pol), color, 85 mins.
W: Miroslaw Baka, Krzysztof Globisz, Jan Tesarz
D: Krzysztof Kieslowski
Unusual thriller: Ghastly murder, hideous execution

Krug and Company
see *The Last House on the Left*

Krugers Dream of Empire
1900, (GB), R.W. Paul, b&w, 65 ft. (19.8m)
D: Walter Booth
Standard fantasy: German dreams he's offered England's crown; soldier turns him into Britannia

Krull
1983, (GB), Ted Mann-Ron Silverman/Col, color, 121 mins.
W: Ken Marshall (*Prince Colwyn*), Lysette Anthony (*Princess Lyssa*), Francesca Annis (*Widow of the Web*), Alun Armstrong (*Torquil*), Bernard Bresslaw (*Rell*), Freddie Jones (*Ynyr*), David Battley (*Ergo*), Liam Neeson (*Kegan*), John Welsh (*The Seer*), Graham McGrath (*Titch*), Bernard Archard (*Eirig*), Tony Church (*Turold*), Belinda Mayne (*Vella*), Dicken Ashworth (*Bardolph*), Robbie Coltrane (*Rhum*), Todd Carty (*Oswyn*), Clare McIntyre (*Merith*), Bronco McLoughlin (*Nennog*), Gerard Naprous (*Quain*), Andy Bradford (*Darro*)
D: Peter Yates   SCR: Stanford Sherman   PHOTOG: Peter Suschitzky   SPCL-FX: Derek Meddings   MUSIC: James Horner
Standard SF-fantasy: Monstrous tyrant enslaves planet

Kull the Conqueror
1997, (USA), Univ, color, 100 mins.
W: Kevin Sorbo, Tia Carrere, Litefoot, Harvey Fierstein Thomas Ian Griffith, Karina Lomb Roy Brocksmith
D: John Nicolella   SCR: Charles Edward Pigue, from characters created by Robert E. Howard   MUSIC: Joel Goldsmith
Standard "Sword & Sorcery"

Kuroneko
1968, (Jap), Toho, color, 108 mins.
W: Kichiemon Nakamura (*The Son*), Kiwako Taichi (*The Wife*), Nobuko Otowa (*The Mother*)
WRIT & D: Kaneto Shindo
A.k.a. *Black Cat*
Unusual fantasy-thriller: Ghosts of two murdered women obtain revenge.

Kurt Vonnegut's Harrison Bergeron
1995, (USA), SHO-TV, color, 100 mins.
W: Sean Astin (*Harrison*), Miranda de Pencier (*Phillipa*) Christopher Plummer, Nigel Bennett, Buck Henry, Eugene Levy, Howie Mandel, Andrea Martin
D: Bruce Pittman   WRIT: Arthur Crimm
Made-for-Cable, standard SF-satire: 21st-century youth rebels against oppressive government

Kwaidan (Ghost Story)
1964, (Jap), Ninjin Club/Toho, color, 164 mins.
W: Michiyo Aratama, Misako Watanabe, Rentaro Mikuni, Kenjiro Ishiyama, Ranko Akagi, Fumie Kitahara, Keiko Kishi, Katsuhei Matsumoto, Yoshiko Ieda, Otomie Tsukimiya, Kenzo Tanaka, Kiyoshi Nakano, Tatsuya Nakadai, Yuko Mochizuki, Kin Sugai, Noriko Sengoku, Akiko Momura, Torahiko Hamada, Jun Hamamura, Kazuo Nakamura, Tetsuro Tamba, Kunie Tanaka, Takashi Shimura, Yoichi Hayashi, Hideko Muramatsu, Ichiro Nakatani, Kazuo Kitamura, Masanori Tomotake, Tokue Hanazawa, Shizue Natsukawa, Shin Ryuoka, Makiko Hojo, Shoichi Kuwayama, Mutsuhiko Tsurumaru, Akira Tani, Noboru Nakaya, Kan-Emon Nakamura, Osamu Takizawa, Haruko Sugimura, Kei Sato, Ganjiro Nakamura, Seiji Miyaguchi, Tomoko Naraoka, Shigeru Kamiyama, Jun Tazaki
D: Masaki Kobayashi   SCR: Yoko Mizuki   ORIG. STORY: Lafcadio Hearn
   PHOTOG: Yishio Miyajima   MUSIC: Toru Takemitsu
Classic fantasy: Quartet of spook tales

The Kweer Kuss
1915, (GB), Martin/DFSA, b&w, 555 ft. (169.2m)
D: Dave Aylott
Standard fantasy short: Man cursed by beggar

Kyberneticka Babicka (Cybernetic Grandma)
1963, (Yugo), color, 2,634.5 ft. (803m)
WRIT & D: Jiri Trnka
Animated short

Kyle
see *The Love War*

Labirynt (Labyrinth)
1962, (Pol), Film Polski, color, 15 mins.
<u>WRIT & D:</u> Jan Lenica <u>PHOTOG:</u> Antoni Murzynski <u>MUSIC:</u> Wlodzimierz
Kotonski
Animated fantasy short

Laboratory
1980, (USA), color, 93 mins.
<u>W:</u> Camille Mitchell, Corinne Michaels, Garnett Smith
Minor SF-thriller: Space aliens experiment on Earthlings

The Laboratory of Mephistopheles
1897, (Fr), Star, b&w
<u>D:</u> Georges Melies
Standard fantasy short

Labyrinth (1962)
see Labirynt

Labyrinth (1971)
see The Reflection of Fear

Labyrinth
1986, (USA-GB), TriStar, color, 101 mins.
<u>W:</u> David Bowie, Jennifer Connelly, David Goelz, Karen Prell, Ron Mueck, Kevin
Clash, Frank Oz, Toby Froud, Rob Mills, Steve Whitmire, Anthony Asbury,
Kenny Baker, Moira Grant, Jim Henson's Muppets
<u>D:</u> Jim Henson <u>SCR:</u> Terry Jones <u>SPCL-FX SPRVSR:</u> George Gibbs <u>MUSIC
SCORE:</u> Trevor Jones <u>SONGS:</u> *Underground & Dance Magic*
Modest fantasy: Girl meets goblins

Labyrinth: JENNIFER CONNELLY AND JIM HENSON'S MUPPETS

Labyrinth des Grauens (Labyrinth of Terrors)
1920, (Ger), b&w
<u>D:</u> Michael Curtiz
Standard thriller

Labyrinth of Terrors
see Labyrinth des Grauens

Ladies in Retirement
1941, (USA), Col, b&w, 92 mins.
<u>W:</u> Ida Lupino, Louis Hayward, Evelyn Keyes, Edith Barrett, Elsa Lanchester,
Isobel Elsom, Emma Dunn
<u>P:</u> Lester Cowan <u>D:</u> Charles Vidor <u>SCR:</u> Garrett Fort & Reginald Denham,
from the play by Reginald Denham & Edward Percy <u>PHOTOG:</u> George
Barnes <u>MUSIC:</u> Ernst Toch
"First-rate terror melodrama; set in bleak English moors, housekeeper kills her
employer to protect her two mentally retarded sisters. Oscar nominations for
music and sets...Excellent performances"—Anon., Frankenstein TV Movieguide, Castle of Frankenstein, Vol. IV, No. 1 (Spring, 1969), p. 60
Moody thriller: Housekeeper conceals employer's murder cf. **The Mad Room**

Ladies' Man
see Lemmy pour les Dames

Il Ladro di Venezia (The Thief of Venice)
1951, (It), 20th-Fox, b&w, 87 mins.
<u>W:</u> Maria Montez, Paul Christian (*Hubschmid*), Massimo Serato, Faye Marlowe,
Aldo Silvani, Louis Saltamerenda, Maria Tosi, Guido Celano, Humbert
Sacripanti, Paul Stoppa, Camillo Pilotto, Liana Del Balzo, Ferdinand
Tamberlani, Vinicio Sofia, Leon Renoir
<u>D:</u> John Brahm <u>SCR:</u> Jesse L. Lasky Jr. <u>STORY:</u> Michael Pertwee <u>MUSIC:</u>

Alessandro Cicognini
Standard melodrama (Maria Montez' last film)

El Ladron de Cadaveres (The Body Snatcher)
1956, (Mex), Int'l Cinematografica, b&w
<u>W:</u> Columba Dominguez, Wolf Rubinskis, Carlos Riquelme, Arturo Martinez,
Guillermo Hernandez, Crox Alvaredo, Yerye Beirute, Eduardo Alcaraz,
Alejandro Cruz
<u>D:</u> Fernando Mendez <u>SCR:</u> Fernando Mendez & Alejandro Verbitzky <u>PHO-
TOG:</u> Victor Herrera
Grisly horror-thriller (Mexican answer to **Invasion of the Body Snatchers***): Alien force
controls human bodies*

The Lady and the Doctor
see The Lady and the Monster

The Lady and the Monster
1944, (USA), Rep, b&w, 86 mins.
<u>W:</u> Erich von Stroheim, Vera Ralston, Richard Arlen, Mary Nash, Sidney
Blackmer, Helen Vinson, Billy Benedict
<u>D:</u> George Sherman <u>SCR:</u> Dane Lussier & Frederick Kohner, loosely based on
Curt Siodmak's novel *Donovan's Brain* <u>PHOTOG:</u> John Alton <u>MUSIC:</u>
Walter Scharf
TV retitle, **Tiger Man***, GB retitle,* **The Lady and the Doctor**
Standard horror-thriller: Salvaged brain of dead tycoon begins to control surgeon. Remake:
Donovan's Brain

Lady and the Tramp
1955, (USA), Walt Disney, color, 76 mins.
<u>VOICES:</u> Peggy Lee, Barbara Luddy, Larry Roberts, Alan Reed, Stan Freberg, Bill
Thompson, Bill Baucon, Verna Felton, George Givot, Dallas McKennon,
Lee Millar
<u>D:</u> Hamilton Luske, Clyde Geronimi & Wilfred Jackson <u>SONGS:</u> *He's a Tramp
& We Are Siamese*
Classic animated fantasy: Pampered pooch meets carefree cur

Lady at Midnight
1948, (USA), Eagle Lion, b&w, 61 mins.
<u>W:</u> Richard Denning, Frances Rafferty
Standard thriller

Lady Audley's Secret
1906, (GB), Walturdaw, b&w
from a novel by Dorothy Braddon
Minor melodrama: Bigamous woman drowns returned first husband, tries to burn second

Lady Audley's Secret
1920, (GB), Ideal, b&w, 5,150 ft. (1569.7m)
<u>W:</u> Margaret Bannerman (*Lady Audley*), H. Manning Haynes (*Robert Audley*),
Betty Farquhar (*Alysia Audley*), Berenice Melford (*Phoebe*), Randolph
McLeod (*Capt. George Talboys*), Wallace Bosco (*Luke Marks*), William
Burchill (*Capt. Malden*), Hubert Willis (*Sir Michael Audley*), Ida Millais
(*Mrs. Plowson*)
<u>D:</u> Jack Denton <u>SCR:</u> Eliot Stannard, from a novel by Dorothy Braddon
Standard thriller: Old knight's new wife becomes a murderess

Lady Beaulay's Necklace
1911, (GB), Natural Colour Kinematograph Co., color, 620 ft. (189m)
<u>D:</u> Theo Bouwmeester
Standard crime-thriller: Detective poses as pedlar, nabs necklace thief

Lady Beware
1987, (USA), Scotti Bros., color, 108 mins.
<u>W:</u> Diane Lane (*Katya Yarno*), Michael Woods (*Jack Price*), Cotter Smith (*Mac
Odell*), Peter Nevargic (*Lionel*), Tyra Ferrell (*Nan*), Edward Penn (*Thayer*),
Zack Mott, Chelsea Benedict, Don Brockett, David Crawford, Clayton D.
Hill, Maria Barney, Angela Rosignalo Jones, Kathleen Murray, Raymond
Laine, Bingo O'Malley, Trish Simmons, Lawrence Woshner, Audrey Roth,
Lou Spenser
<u>D:</u> Karen Arthur <u>SCR:</u> Susan Miller & Charles Zev Cohen <u>PHOTOG:</u> Tom
Neuwirth <u>MUSIC:</u> Craig Safan
Modest thriller: Psycho stalks beautiful window dresser

Ladybug, Ladybug
1963, (USA), UA, b&w, 84 mins.
<u>W:</u> Christopher Howard, Marilyn Rogers, Doug Chapin, Estelle Parsons, Judith
Lowry, Nancy Marchand (*The Teacher*), Jane Connell (*The Dietician*), William
Daniels (*The Principal*)
<u>P & D:</u> Frank Perry <u>PHOTOG:</u> Gerald Hirschfeld
Modest thriller: Children face doomsday

Lady Candale's Diamonds
1910, (GB), London Cinematograph Co., b&w, 584 ft. (175.5m)
<u>D:</u> S. Wormald
Standard crime-thriller: Detective tracks jewel thieves

The Lady Confesses
1945, (USA), PRC, b&w, 64 mins.
<u>W:</u> Hugh Beaumont, Mary Beth Hughes, Edmund MacDonald, Claudia Drake,
Emmett Vogan

D: Sam Newfield
Standard thriller

Lady Death
see La Senora Muerte

Lady Frankenstein
see La Figlia di Frankenstein

The Lady from Shanghai
1948, (USA), Col, b&w, 86 mins.
W: Rita Hayworth (*Elsa Bannister*), Orson Welles (*Michael O'Hara*), Everett Sloane (*Arthur Bannister*), Erskine Sanford (*The Judge*), Ted de Corsia (*Sidney Broome*), Gus Schilling (*Goldie*), Glenn Anders (*George Grisby*), Carl Frank (*The D.A.*), Louis Merrill (*Jake*), Evelyn Ellis (*Bessie*), Harry Shannon (*The Cab Driver*), Wong Show Chong (*Li*), Sam Nelson (*The Yacht Captain*)
WRIT, P & D: Orson Welles, from Sherwood King's novel *If I Should Die Before I Wake* **PHOTOG:** Charles Lawton Jr. **MUSIC:** Heinz Roemheld
Classic thriller: Temptress lures Irish adventurer into web of violence and murder

The Lady From Shanghai: ORSON WELLES, RITA HAYWORTH AND GLENN ANDERS

Lady Godiva
1951, (USA), Univ, color
W: Maureen O'Hara (*Godiva*), George Nader (*Leofric*), Victor McLaglen (*Grimald*), Rex Reason (*Harold*), Torin Thatcher (*Godwin*), Eduard Franz (*Edward the Confessor*), Arthur Shields, Henry Brandon, Robert Warwick, Leslie Bradley, Grant Withers, Gene Roth
D: Arthur Lubin **SCR:** Oscar Brodney & Harry Ruskin **PHOTOG:** Carl Guthrie **MUSIC:** Joseph Gershenson
Standard historical melodrama: Saxon wife opposes Norman husband, rides naked for cause of downtrodden

Ladyhawke
1985, (GB-It), Richard Donner/WB & 20th-Fox, color, 124 mins.
W: Matthew Broderick (*Phillipe*), Rutger Hauer (*Navarre*), Michelle Pfeiffer (*Isabeau*), Leo McKern (*Imperius*), John Wood (*The Bishop*), Ken Hutchison (*Marquet*), Loris Loddi (*Jehan*), Alfred Molina (*Cezar*), Giancarlo Prete (*Fornac*), Alessandro Serra (*Mr. Pitou*), Nicolina Papetti (*Mrs. Pitou*), Charles Borromel (*The Insane Prisoner*), Massimo Sarchielli (*The Innkeeper*), Russell Kase (*The Lieutenant*), Don Hudson, Gregory Snegoff, Gaetano Russo, Paul Tuerpe, Rod Dand, Stefano Horowitzo, Venantino Venantini, Marcus Berensford Valerie O'Brien, Nana Cecchi
D: Richard Donner **SCR:** Edward Khmara, Michael Thomas & Tom Mankiewicz **STORY:** Edward Khmara **PHOTOG:** Vittorio Storaro **SPCL-FX:** John Richardson **MUSIC:** Andrew Powell
Superior adventure-fantasy: Medieval thief aids cursed lovers

Lady Ice
1973, (USA), color, 93 mins.
W: Donald Sutherland, Jennifer O'Neill, Robert Duvall, Eric Braeden, Patrick Magee, John Cypher, Buffy Dee
D: Tom Gries **SCR:** Alan R. Trustman **MUSIC:** Perry Botkin
Standard thriller: Insurance investigator trails jewel thieves

Lady In a Cage
1964, (USA), Luther Davis/Para, b&w, 100 mins.
W: Olivia de Havilland (*Mrs. Hilyard*), James Caan (*Randall*), Ann Sothern (*Sade*), Jennifer Billingsley (*Elaine*), Rafael Campos (*Essie*), Jeff Corey (*The Wino*), William Swan (*Malcolm Hilyard*), Charles Seel (*The Junkyard Proprietor*), Scatman Crothers (*The Junkyard Proprietor's Ass't*)
WRIT & P: Luther Davis **D:** Walter Grauman **PHOTOG:** Lee Garmes
Standard thriller: Punks terrorize woman trapped in elevator

Lady in the Dark
1944, (USA), Para, color, 100 mins.
W: Ginger Rogers (*Liza Elliott*), Ray Milland (*Charley Johnson*), Warner Baxter (*Kendall Nesbitt*), Jon Hall (*Randy Curtis*), Barry Sullivan (*Dr. Brooks*), Gail Russell (*Barbara, Aged 17*), Mischa Auer (*Russell Paxton*), Mary Phillips (*Maggy Grant*), Marietta Canty (*Martha*), Phyllis Brooks (*Allison DuBois*), Edward Fielding (*Dr. Carlton*), Don Loper (*Adams*), Mary Parker (*Miss Parker*), Catherine Craig (*Miss Foster*), Harvey Stephens (*Liza's Father*), Kay Linaker (*Liza's Mother*), Virginia Farmer (*Miss Edwards*), Fay Helm (*Miss Bowers*), Rand Brooks (*Ben*)
D: Mitchell Leisen **SCR:** Frances Goodrich & Albert Hackett, from Moss Hart's play **PHOTOG:** Ray Rennahan **MUSIC:** Kurt Weill **LYRICS:** Ira Gershwin **SONGS:** *Jenny & Suddenly It's Spring*
Bizarre semi-musical: Neurotic lady executive daydreams

Lady in the Death House
1944, (USA), PRC, b&w, 64 mins.
W: Jean Parker, Lionel Atwill Marcia Mae Jones
Standard melodrama: Innocent woman flees execution

Lady in the Fog
1952, (GB), Hammer/Lippert, b&w, 82 mins.
W: Cesar Romero (*Philip Odell*), Lois Maxwell (*Peggy*), Bernadette O'Farrell (*Heather*), Geoffrey Keen (*Hampden*), Campbell Singer (*Insp. Rigby*), Lloyd Lamble (*Sorroway*), Mary Mackenzie (*Marilyn*), Alastair Hunter (*Sgt. Reilly*), Frank Birch (*Boswell*), Lisa Lee (*Donna Devore*), Wensley Pithey, Reed de Rouen, Peter Swanwick, Bill Fraser, Lionel Harris, Betty Cooper, Clare James, Katie Johnson, Jacques Cey, Jean Bayliss, Richard Johnson, Stuart Nichol, Marguerite Brennan, Robert Adair
P: Anthony Hinds **D:** Sam Newfield **SCR:** Orville H. Hampton, from a radio-serial by Lester Powell **PHOTOG:** Walter Harvey **MUSIC:** Ivor Slaney
USA retitle, Scotland Yard Inspector
Standard thriller: American reporter trails London murderer

The Lady in the Iron Mask
1952, (USA), 20th-Fox, color, 78 mins.
W: Patricia Medina, Louis Hayward, John Sutton, Lester Matthews, Steve Brodie, Alan Hale Jr., Judd Holdren, Hal Gerard, Tor Johnson
P: Walter Wanger & Eugene Frenke **D:** Ralph Murphy **SCR:** Jack Pollexfen & Aubrey Wisberg, loosely based on Alexandre Dumas' novel *The Three Musketeers* **PHOTOG:** Ernest Laszlo **MUSIC:** Dmitri Tiomkin
Standard adventure-thriller: Princess kept prisoner so her twin can inherit throne

Lady in the Lake
1946, (USA), MGM, b&w, 103 mins.
W: Robert Montgomery, Audrey Totter, Lloyd Nolan, Jayne Meadows, Leon Ames, Tom Tully, Dick Simmons, Kathleen Lockhart, Morris Ankrum, Lila Leeds
D: Robert Montgomery **SCR:** Steve Fisher, from Raymond Chandler's novel **PHOTOG:** Paul C. Vogel **MUSIC:** David Snell
Complex thriller: Gumshoe hired to find missing wife, told from the point of view of detective Philip Marlowe (Montgomery)

Lady in the Morgue
1938, (USA), Univ, b&w, 67 mins.
W: Preston Foster, Patricia Ellis, Frank Jenks, Barbara Pepper, Thomas Jackson, Gordon (Bill) Elliott, James Robbins, Morgan Wallace, Rollo Lloyd, Roland Drew, Joseph Downing, Don Brodie, Al Hill, James Robbins, Brian Burke, Donald Kerr, Gordon Hart
D: Otis Garrett **SCR:** Eric Taylor & Robertson White, from Jonathan Latimer's novel **PHOTOG:** Stanley Cortez **MUSIC:** Charles Previn
GB retitle, The Case of the Missing Blonde
Standard Crime Club thriller (2nd Bill Crane mystery): Private eye probes suicide, finds three murders

Lady in White
1988, (USA), New Sky Communications/Virgin Vision, color, 112 mins.
W: Lukas Haas (*Frankie*), Len Cariou (*Phil*), Alex Rocco (*Angelo*), Katherine Helmond (*Amanda*), Angelo Bertolini (*Papa Charlie*), Renata Vanni (*Mama Assunta*), Jason Presson (*Geno*), Joelle Jacobi (*Melissa*), Jared Rushton (*Donald*), Gregory Levinson (*Louie*), Lucy Lee Flippin (*Mrs. La Delia*), Tom Bower (*Sheriff Saunders*), Sydney Lassick (*Mr. Lowry*), Jack Andreozzi (*Tony*), Rita Zohar (*Mrs. Chilak*), Hal Bokar (*Mr. Chilak*), Henry Harris (*Harold Williams*), Rose Weaver (*Matty Williams*), Bruce Kirby (*The Cabbie*), Emily Tracy (*Marianna*), Karen Powell (*The Lady in White*), Lisa Taylor (*Mary Ellen*), Jack Holland (*Father Brennan*), Daniel Rojo (*The Reporter*), Gregory L. Everage (*The Cameraman*)
WRIT, P, D & MUS: Frank LaLoggia **PHOTOG:** Russell Carpenter **VS-FX SPRVSRS:** Ernest D. Farino & Gene Warren Jr.
Unusual fantasy-thriller: Boy meets slayer and spooks

The Lady Killers
1955, (GB), Ealing/Janus, color, 97 mins.
W: Alec Guinness (*Prof. Marcus*), Katie Johnson (*Mrs. Wilberforce*), Peter Sellers (*Harry*), Herbert Lom (*Louis*), Cecil Parker (*The Major*), Jack Warner (*The Police Supt.*), Kenneth Connor (*The Cab Driver*), Danny Green (*One-Round*), Edie Martin, Frankie Howerd, Philip Stainton, Sam Kydd, Fred Griffiths, Phoebe Hodgson, Helene Burls, Jack Melford, Evelyn Kerry, Ewan Roberts,

Neil Wilson, Michael Corcoran, Harold Goodwin, Robert Moore, Madge Brindley, John Rudling, Lucy Griffiths, Leonard Sharp
P: Michael Balcon **D:** Alexander Mackendrick **STORY & SCR:** William Rose **PHOTOG:** Otto Heller **MUSIC:** Tristam Cary
Classic comedy-thriller: Thieves thwarted by old lady

Ladykillers
1988, (USA), Made for TV, color, 92 mins.
W: Marilu Henner, Susan Blakely, Lesley-Anne Down, Thomas Calabro, William Lucking
D: Robert Lewis **TELEPLAY:** Greg Dinallo
TVM, standard thriller: Female cop seeks killer of male strippers

Lady Letmere's Jewelery
1908, (GB), Gaumont, b&w, 1,105 ft. (336.8m)
W: Masie Ellis (*Lady Letmere*)
D & STORY: George R. Sims
Standard crime-thriller: Lady steals countess' pearls

The Lady Luna(tic)'s Hat
1908, (GB), R.W. Paul, b&w, 185 ft. (56.4m)
D: Jack Smith
Standard fantasy short: Lady wearing large hat is blown to moon

A Lady Mislaid
1958, (GB), Welwyn/ABP, b&w, 59 mins.
W: Phyllis Calvert (*Esther Williams*), Alan White (*Sgt. Bullock*), Thorley Walters (*Smith*), Gillian Owen (*Jennifer Williams*), Richard Leech (*George*), Constance Fraser (*Mrs. Small*), Sheila Shand Gibbs (*Betty*)
P: Robert Hall **D:** David Macdonald **SCR:** Frederick Gotfurt, from a play by Kenneth Horne
Standard comedy-thriller: Sisters rent cottage, suspect former tenant killed his wife

Lady of Burlesque
1943, (USA), UA, b&w, 91 mins.
W: Barbara Stanwyck (*Dixie Daisy*), Michael O'Shea (*Biff Brannigan*), Iris Adrian (*Gee Gee Graham*), J. Edward Bromberg (*S.B. Foss*), Stephanie Bachelor (*Princess Nirvena*), Marion Martin (*Alice Angel*), Gloria Dickson (*Polly Baxter*), Victoria Faust (*Lolita La Verne*), Charles Dingle (*Insp. Harrigan*), Eddie Gordon (*Officer Pat Kelly*), Frank Fenton (*Russell Rogers*), Pinky Lee (*Mandy*), Frank Conroy (*Stacchi*)
P: Hunt Stromberg **D:** William A. Wellman **SCR:** James Gunn, from Gypsy Rose Lee's novel *The G-String Murders* **PHOTOG:** Robert De Grasse **MUSIC:** Arthur Lange **LYRICS:** Sammy Cahn & Harry Akst
GB retitle, Striptease Lady
Snappy thriller: Mad killer stalks old opera house

The Lady of Shallot
1912, (GB), Ivy Close/Hepworth, b&w, 800 ft. (243.8m)
W: Ivy Close (*The Lady*)
D & SCR: Elwin Neame, from Tennyson's poem
Standard fantasy: Cursed mirror takes maiden's life

The Lady of the Shadows
see *The Terror* (1963)

Ladt Stay Dead
1983, (Austral), color, 100 mins.
Minor thriller: Knife-wielding psycho pursues girl

Lady Terminator
1989, (USA), color, 83 mins.
W: Barbara Costable, Christopher Hart, Claudia Rademaker, Joseph McGlynn
D: Jalil Jackson
Minor fantasy-thriller: Evil spirit possesses anthropology student

Lady of Vengeance
1957, (GB), Rich & Rich/Princess/UA, b&w, 74 mins.
W: Dennis O'Keefe (*William T. Marshall*), Patrick Barr (*Insp. Madden*), Anton Diffring (*Karnak*), Ann Sears (*Katie Whiteside*), Vernon Greeves (*Larry Shaw*), Eileen Elton (*Melissa*), Frederick Schiller (*Schtegel*), G.H. Mulcaster (*Bennett*)
P: William N. Boyle, Burt Balaban, & Bernard Donnenfield **D:** Burt Balaban **STORY:** Irve Tunick
Standard thriller: Philatelist plots to kill man responsible for his ward's suicide

The Lady Vanishes
1938, (GB), Gainsborough/Gaumont/MGM, b&w, 95 mins.
W: Margaret Lockwood (*Iris Henderson*), Michael Redgrave (*Gilbert Redman*), Paul Lukas (*Dr. Hartz*), Cecil Parker (*Eric Todhunter*), Dame May Whitty (*Miss Froy*), Naunton Wayne (*Caldicott*), Linden Travers (*Margaret*), Mary Clare (*The Baroness*), Basil Radford (*Charters*), Philip Leaver (*Doppo*), Emile Boreo (*The Manager*), Catherine Lacey (*The Nun*), Googie Withers (*Blanche*), Charles Oliver (*The Officer*), Sally Stewart, Thelma Vas Dias
P: Edward Black **D:** Alfred Hitchcock **SCR:** Frank Launder, Sidney Gilliat & Alma Reville, from Ethel Lina White's novel *The Wheel Spins* **PHOTOG:** Jack Cox **MUSIC:** Louis Levy
reissued 1942 & 1948
Classic thriller: Dowager disappears on train

The Lady Vanishes
1979, (GB), Hammer/Rank, color, 97 mins.
W: Elliott Gould (*Robert Condon*), Cybill Shepherd (*Amanda Kelly*), Angela Lansbury (*Miss Froy*), Arthur Lowe (*Charters*), Herbert Lom (*Dr. Hartz*), Ian Carmichael (*Caldicott*), Jean Anderson (*Baroness Kisling*), Gerald Harper (*Todhunter*), Jenny Runacre (*Mrs. Todhunter*), Madlena Nedeva (*Jenny the Nun*), Vladek Sheybal (*The Trainmaster*), Wolf Kahler (*Helmut*), Barbara Markham (*Frau Kummer*), Madge Ryan (*Rose Flood-Porter*), Rosalind Knight (*Evelyn Barnes*), Jeremy Bulloch (*The Guest*), Jonathan Hackett (*The Waiter*)
P: Tom Sachs **D:** Anthony Page **SCR:** George Axelrod, Frank Launder & Sidney Gilliat, from Ethel Lina White's novel *The Wheel Spins* **PHOTOG:** Douglas Slocombe **MUSIC:** Richard Hartley
Standard thriller, inferior remake: American tourists in 1939 Bavaria help lady agent get information to England

The Lair of the White Worm
1988, (GB), Vestron, color, 93 mins.
W: Amanda Donohoe (*Lady Sylvia Marsh*), Hugh Grant (*Lord James D'Ampton*), Catherine Oxenberg (*Eve Trent*), Peter Capaldi (*Angus Flint*), Sammi Davis (*Mary Trent*), Stratford Johns (*Peters*), Paul Brooke, Imogen Claire, Miranda Coe, Chris Pitt, Gina McKee, Christopher Gable, Lloyd Peters, Linzi Drew, Caron Anne Kelly, Fiona O'Conner, Tina Shaw, Caroline Pope, Elisha Scott, Paul Easom, Jackie Russell, James Hicks, David Kiernan, Matthew King, Bob Smith, Ross Murray, Andy Norman
WRIT, P & D: Ken Russell, from Bram Stoker's novel **PHOTOG:** Dick Bush **MUSIC:** Stanislas Syrewicz
Bizarre horror-fantasy: Reptilian vampiress sacrifices to ancient snake-god

The Lake
1978, (GB), Sierra/Relfhurst/Enterprise, color, 33 mins.
W: Julie Peasgood (*The Girl*), Gene Foad (*The Man*)
P & D: Lindsay Vickers
Standard short fantasy: Couple picnics by house haunted by man who killed his family

The Lake
1998, (USA), NBC-TV, color, 95 mins.
W: Yasmine Bleeth
TVM, standard thriller: Woman returns to small-town home, finds local lake has transformed inhabitants' personalities

Lake of Dracula
1971, (Jap), Toho, color, 82 mins.
W: Midori Fujita (*Akiko*), Choei Takahashi (*Sacki*), Sanae Emi (*Natsuoke*), Mori Kishida, Osahide Takahashi, Kaku Takashima
D: Michio Yamamoto **SCR:** Ei Ogawa **PHOTOG:** Rokuro Nishigaki
A.k.a. Bloodthirsty Eyes and Dracula's Lust for Blood
Standard horror-fantasy: Heroine troubled by memories of vampiric visitations

The Lamp
1987, (USA), H.I.T. Films, color
Minor fantasy

Lancelot and Guinevere
1962, (GB), Emblem/Univ, color, 117 mins.
W: Cornel Wilde (*Sir Lancelot*), Jean Wallace (*Queen Guinevere*), Brian Aherne (*King Arthur*), Mark Dignam (*Merlin*), George Baker (*Sir Gawaine*), Michael Meacham (*Mordred*), John Barrie (*Sir Bedivere*), Adrienne Corri (*Lady Vivian*), Iain Gregory (*Sir Tors*), Archie Duncan (*Sir Lamorak*), Joseph Tomelty (*Sir Kaye*), Richard Thorp (*Sir Gareth*), John Longden (*King Leodogran*), Reginald Beckwith (*Sir Dagonet*), Walter Gotell (*Sir Cedric*), Graham Stark (*Rian*)
D: Cornel Wilde **SCR:** Richard Schayer & Jefferson Pascal **PHOTOG:** Harry Waxman **MUSIC:** Ron Goodwin
USA retitle, Sword of Lancelot
Lush, well-made Arthurian romance: Knight has forbidden love for Celtic queen

Lancelot du Lac (Lancelot of the Lake)
1974, (Fr), ORTF/CFDC/New Yorker, color, 84 mins.
W: Vladimir Antolek-Oresek, Humbert Balsan, Patrick Bernard
D: Robert Bresson **PHOTOG:** Pasqualino de Santis **MUSIC:** Philippe Sarde
Standard romance: Life of noble knight

Lancelot Du Lac: HUMBERT BALSAN

Lancer Spy
1937, (USA), 20th-Fox, b&w, 84 mins.
W: George Sanders, Dolores Del Rio, Peter Lorre, Joseph Schildkraut, Lionel
Atwill *(Fenwick)*, Fritz Feld *(Mueller)*, Virginia Field *(Joan)*, Maurice
Moscovich *(Von Meinhardt)*, Luther Adler *(Schratt)*, Sig Rumann, Frank
Reicher
WRIT & P: Philip Dunne   D: Gregory Ratoff, from a novel by Marthe
McKenna   PHOTOG: Barney McGill   MUSIC: Arthur Lange
Standard thriller: Britisher impersonates German officer

The Land Before Time
1988, (USA), Univ, color, 69 mins.
VOICES: Gabriel Damon, Helen Shaver, Bill Erwin, Candace Hutson, Pat
Hingle, Judith Barsi, Burke Barnes, Will Ryan
D: Don Bluth   SCR: Stu Krieger, from characters created by Judy Freudberg &
Tony Geiss   MUSIC: James Horner
Standard animated fantasy: Young dinosaur learns about life

The Land Before Time II: The Great Valley Adventure
1994, (USA), Univ-MCA, color, 75 mins.
VOICES: Scott McAfee, Rob Paulsen, Linda Gary, John Ingle
P & D: Roy Allen Smith   SCR: Dev Ross, John Loy & John Lundin, from char-
acters created by Judy Freudberg & Tony Geiss   MUSIC: Michael Tavera
SONGS: *If We Hold On Together* (by James Horner)
Made-for-Video, standard animated fantasy: Life of juvenile brontosaurus

The Land Before Time III: The Time of the Great Giving
1995, (USA), Univ-MCA, color, 70 mins.
VOICES: Jeff Bennett, Linda Gary, Heather Hogan, John Ingle, Tress MacNeille,
Scott McAfee, Rob Paulsen, Frank Welker, Nicholas Guest, Kenneth Mars,
Candace Hutson, Whitby Hertford
D: Roy Allen Smith   SCR: Dev Ross, from characters created by Judy Freudberg
& Tony Geiss   MUSIC: Michael Tavera   SONGS: *When You're Big, If We
Hold On Together & Kids Like Us*
Made-for-Video, standard animated fantasy: Dinosaurs battle for scarce water supplies

The Land Before Time IV: Journey Through the Mists
1996, (USA), Univ-MCA, color, 75 mins.
VOICES: Scott McAfee, Jeff Bennett, Heather Hogan, Kenneth Mars, Carol
Bruce, Linda Gary, Charles Durning, Candace Hutson
P & D: Roy Allen Smith   SCR: Dev Ross, from characters created by Judy
Freudberg & Tony Geiss   MUSIC: Michael Tavera   SONGS: *If We Hold On
Together, Grandma's Lullaby & Who Needs You?*
*Made-for-Video, standard animated fantasy: Legendary flowers sought to save dinosaur's
dying grandfather*

The Land Before Time V: The Mysterious Island
1997, (USA), Univ, color, 74 mins.
VOICES: John Ingle, Miriam Flynn, Candace Hudson
P & D: Charles Grosvenor   SCR: John Loy   MUSIC: Michael Tavera   SONGS:
If We Hold On Together, Always There & Big Water
Made-for-Video, standard animated fantasy: Dinosaurs seek new home

The Land Before Time VI: The Secret of Saurus Rock
1998, (USA), color
Made-for-Video, standard animated fantasy

Land in Trance
see *Terra em Transe*

Land of Doom
1984, (USA), color, 87 mins.
W: Deborah Rennard, Garrick Dowhen
D: Peter Maris
Minor SF-thriller: Amazon and post-nuke warrior struggle to survive

Land of the Minotaur
see *The Devil's Men*

The Land of the Nursery Rhymes
1912, (GB), Heron Films, b&w, 436 ft. (132.9m)
W: Mark Melford, Jakidawdra Melford
WRIT & D: Mark Melford
reissued 1914
Standard fantasy short: Girl dreams of nursery-rhyme characters

Land of the Pharaohs
1955, (USA), Continental/WB, color, 106 mins.
W: Jack Hawkins *(Pharaoh Khufu)*, Joan Collins *(Princess Nellifer)*, James
Robertson Justice *(Vashtar)*, Sydney Chaplin *(Treneh)*, Dewey Martin *(Senta)*,
Alexis Minotis *(Hamar)*, Luisa Boni *(Kyra)*, James Hayter *(Vashtar's Servant)*,
Kerima *(Queen Nailla)*, Piero Giagnoni *(Pharaoh's Son)*
P & D: Howard Hawks   SCR: William Faulkner, Harry Kurnitz & Harold Jack
Bloom   PHOTOG: Lee Garmes & Russell Harlan   SPCL-FX: Don
Steward   MUSIC: Dimitri Tiomkin
*Opulent, engrossing melodrama: Ruthless Mediterranean princess covets Pharaoh's tomb-
treasure*

Landru
1962, (Fr), Embassy, color, 118 mins.
W: Charles Denner *(Landru)*, Hildegarde Neff, Michele Morgan, Danielle
Darrieux, Francoise Lugagne, Mary Marquet, Robert Burnier, Catherine
Rouvel, Stephane Audran
P & D: Claude Chabrol   SCR & DIALOG: Francoise Sagan   PHOTOG: Jean
Rabier
USA retitle, Bluebeard
Toned-down, under-played bio-thriller: Infamous Frenchman kills wives

Landslide
1992, (USA), HBO-TV, color, 95 mins.
W: Anthony Edwards, Tom Burlinson, Melody Anderson, Ronald Lacey, Ken
James, William Colgate, Lloyd Bochner, Joanna Cassidy
D: Jean-Claude Lord
*Made-for-Cable, standard thriller: Amnesiac geologist finds danger in search for his true
identity*

The Land that Time Forgot
1975, (GB), Amicus/AIP, color, 91 mins.
W: Doug McClure *(Bowen Tyler)*, Susan Penhaligon *(Lisa Clayton)*, John McEnery
(Capt. Schoenvorts), Keith Barron *(Bradley)*, Anthony Ainley *(Dietz)*, Godfrey
James *(Borg)*, Bobby Parr *(Ahm)*, Colin Farrell *(Whiteley)*, Declan
Mulholland *(Olson)*, Ben Howard *(Benson)*, Roy Holder *(Pleaser)*, Andrew
McCulloch *(Sinclair)*, Ron Pember *(Jones)*, Steve James *(Bo-Lu)*, Andrew
Lodge, Brian Hall
P: Max J. Rosenberg & Milton Subotsky   D: Kevin Connor   SCR: James
Cawthorn & Michael Moorcock, from Edgar Rice Burroughs' novel
PHOTOG: Alan Hume   SPCL-FX: Derek Meddings & Roger Dicken
MUSIC: Douglas Gamley
*Standard SF-adventure: Survivors of U-boat attack find prehistoric world cf. **The People
that Time Forgot***

The Land Unknown
1957, (USA), Univ, b&w, 78 mins.
W: Jock Mahoney *(Hal)*, William Reynolds *(Jack)*, Shawn Smith (formerly Shirly
Patterson), Phil Harvey, Henry Brandon, Douglas R. Kennedy
P: William Alland   D: Virgil Vogel   SCR: W. Robson & Laszlo Gorog, from a
story by Charles Palmer, based on an idea (uncredited) by Willis O'Brien
PHOTOG: Ellis W. Carter   SPCL-FX: Roswell A. Hoffman, Jack Kevan,
Orent Ernest & Fred Knorh   MUSIC: Joseph Gershenson
Standard SF-thriller: Prehistoric life found in Antarctic valley

La Lanterne Magique (The Magic Lantern)
1903, (Fr), Star, b&w, 97m (318.2 ft./5.4 mins.)
D: Georges Melies
Standard fantasy

Laputa: Castle in the Sky
1989, (Jap), Streamline, color, 124 mins.
WRIT, D & EDIT: Hayao Miyazaki, from Jonathan Swift's writings   MUSIC:
Joh Hisaishi
Standard animated SF-fantasy: Girl pursued by evil minions

Larceny
1948, (USA), Univ, b&w, 89 mins.
W: John Payne, Joan Caulfield, Dan Duryea, Shelley Winters, Dorothy Hart
D: George Sherman
Standard thriller

Larceny in Her Heart
1946, (USA), PRC, b&w, 68 mins.
W: Hugh Beaumont *(Michael Shayne)*, Cheryl Walker *(Phyllis Hamilton)*, Ralph
Dunn *(Rafferty)*, Paul Bryar, Henry Hall, Charles Wilson, Douglas Fowley,
Gordon Richards, Charles Quigley, Julia McMillan, Marie Harmon, Milton
Kibbee, Lee Bennett
D: Sam Newfield   SCR: Raymond L. Schrock, from characters created by Brett
Halliday   PHOTOG: Jack Greenhalgh   MUSIC: Leo Erdody
Standard "Michael Shayne" thriller: Detective aids beset heiress

The Large Rope
1953, (GB), Insignia/UA, b&w, 72 mins.
W: Donald Houston *(Tom Penney)*, Susan Shaw *(Susan Hamble)*, Robert Brown
(Mick Jordan), Vanda Godsell *(Amy Jordan)*, Peter Byrne *(Jeff Stribling)*,
Christine Finn *(May)*, Richard Warner *(Insp. Harmer)*, Thomas Heathcote
(James Gore), Carl Bernard *(Alfred Hamble)*, Douglas Herald *(Sion Penney)*
P: Victor Hanbury   D: Wolf Rilla   STORY: Ted Willis
Standard crime-thriller: Ex-convict suspected of murder

Larks in Toyland
1913, (GB), Empire Films/DFSA, b&w, 496 ft. (151.2m)
WRIT & D: Arthur Cooper
Standard fantasy short: Animated playthings

Laserblast
1978, (USA), Irvin Yablans/Selected, color, 85 mins.
W: Kim Milford *(Billy)*, Cheryl Smith *(Kathy)*, Gianni Russo *(Tony)*, Ron Masak
(The Sheriff), Roddy McDowall *(Dr. Melon)*, Dennis Burkley *(Pete)*, Barry

Cutler (*Jesse*), Keenan Wynn (*Col. Farley*), Eddie Deezen (*Froggy*), Mike Bobenko (*Chuck*), Rock Walters, Simmy Bow, Joanna Lipari, Melinda Wunderlich, Wendy Wernli, Michael Bryar, Franne Schacht, Eric Jenkins, Janet Dey
P: Charles Band   **D:** Michael Rae   **SCR:** Franne Schacht & Frank Ray Perilli   **PHOTOG:** Terry Bowen   **SPCL-FX:** Dave Allen   **MUSIC:** Joel Goldsmith & Richard Band
Minor SF-thriller: Persecuted teen takes revenge

Laser Moon
1992, (USA), color, 90 mins.
W: Traci Lords, Crystal Shaw, Harrison Leduke, Bruce Carter
D: Bruce Carter
Standard thriller: Serial killer slays with laser beam

The Lash
1931, (USA), WB, b&w, 75 mins.
W: Richard Barthelmess, Mary Astor, Marian Nixon, James Rennie
P & D: Frank Lloyd   **PHOTOG:** Ernest Haller
Standard action-adventure: Don Francisco, alias "El Puma," turns desperado for cause of Justice in Old California. Vitascope

Last Bride of Salem
1974, (USA), R.L. Square/20th-Fox-TV, color, 71 mins.
W: Lois Nettleton, Bradford Dillman, Joni Bick (*Kelly*), Murray Westgate (*Rev. Hiram Fletcher*), Paul Harding (*Sebastian Mayhew*), Susan Rubes (*Grace Fletcher*), Rex Hagon (*The Master*), James Douglas (*Dr. Glover*), Robert Hawkins (*Thomas*), Patricia Hamilton (*Rebecca Glover*), Ed McNamara (*Seth*), Moya Fenwick (*Elsbeth*)
D: Tom Donovan   **TELEPLAY:** Rita Lakin, from a story by Ken Johnson, Justin Edgerton & Rita Lakin
TVM, minor fantasy thriller: Demonic possession threatens family

The Last Chase
1981, (Can.), Crown Int'l, color, 101 mins
W: Lee Majors, Chris Makepeace, Burgess Meredith
P: Martyn Burke & Fran Rosati   **D:** Martyn Burke   **SCR:** C.R. O'Christopher, Roy Moore & Martyn Burke
Minor SF-adventure: Renegade driver pursued by gov't of gasless future

The Last Child
1971, (USA), Aaron Spelling/ABC-TV, color, 73 mins.
W: Van Heflin, Michael Cole, Janet Margolin, Edward Asner, Harry Guardino, Kent Smith, Phyllis Avery
P: William Allyn   **D:** John Moxey   **TELEPLAY:** Peter S. Fischer
TVM, standard SF-thriller (Van Heflin's last film): Young couple of overpopulated future finds birth control rigidly enforced

The Last Days of Man on Earth
1974, (GB), Gladiole/Good Times/New World, color, 89 mins.
W: Jon Finch (*Jerry*), Jenny Runacre (*Miss Brunner*), Sterling Hayden (*Maj. Lindbergh*), Patrick Magee (*Dr. Baxter*), George Coulouris (*Dr. Powys*), Hugh Griffith (*Prof. Hira*), Julie Ege (*Miss Dazzle*), Graham Crowden (*Dr. Smiles*), Sarah Douglas (*Catherine*), Harry Andrews (*John*), Basil Henson (*Dr. Lucas*), Derrick O'Connor (*Frank*), Gilles Milinaire (*Dimitri*), Sandy Ratcliff (*Jenny*), Ronald Lacey (*Shades*), Dolores Del Mar (*The Fortune Teller*), Mary McLeod (*The Nurse*), Sandra Dickinson (*The Waitress*)
P: John Goldstone & Sandy Lieberson   **D & SCR:** Robert Fuest, from Michael Moorcock's novel *The Final Programme*   **PHOTOG:** Norman Warwick   **MUSIC:** Paul Beaver & Bernard Krause
Odd SF-thriller: World's violent demise

Last Days of Planet Earth
see Catastrophe 1999: The Prophecies of Nostradamus

The Last Days of Pompeii
1900, (GB), R.W. Paul, b&w, 80 ft. (24.4m)
D: Walter Booth, inspired by Bulwer-Lytton's novel
Standard action short: Vesuvius erupts, people escape room as ceiling falls

The Last Days of Pompeii (1908)
see Gli Ultimi Giorni di Pompei

The Last Days of Pompeii
1935, (USA), RKO, b&w, 96 mins.
W: Preston Foster (*Marcus*), Basil Rathbone (*Pontius Pilate*), Alan Hale (*Burbix*), John Wood (*Flavius, as a Man*), Dorothy Wilson (*Clodia*), Louis Calhern (*The Prefect*), Gloria Shea (*Julia*), David Holt (*Flavius, as a Boy*), William V. Mong (*Cleon*), Wyrley Birch (*Leaster*), Frank Conroy (*Gaius*), Edward Van Sloan (*Calvus*), Zeffie Tilbury (*The Wise Woman*), Murray Kinnell (*The Judean Peasant*), John Davidson (*The Slave*), Henry Kolker (*The Warden*)
P: Merian C. Cooper   **D:** Ernest B. Schoedsack   **SCR:** Ruth Rose, based on an orig. story by James Ashmore Creelman & Melville Baker   **PHOTOG:** Ray June & Eddie Linden Jr.   **SPCL-FX:** Vernon Walker & Harry Redmond   **MUSIC:** Roy Webb
Classic adventure-romance: Roman blacksmith becomes famed gladiator, but tragedy awaits

The Last Days of Pompeii (1948)
see Les Derniers Jours de Pompeii

The Last Days of Pompeii
1959, (It-Sp), Cineproduzioni-Procusa-Transocean/UA, color, 103 mins.
W: Steve Reeves, Cristina Kauffman, Barbara Carroll, Anne Marie Baumann, Mimmo Palmara, Fernando Rey, Angel Aranda, Carlo Tamberlani, Mino Doro, Mario Morales, Mario Berroatua, Guglielmo Marin, Angel Ortiz, Lola Torres
D: Mario Bonnard   **SCR:** Ennio De Concini, Sergio Leone, Duccio Tessari, & Sergio Corbucci, from Bulwer-Lytton's novel   **PHOTOG:** Antonio Ballesteros   **SPCL-FX:** Magasoli Erasmo Bacci   **MUSIC:** Angelo Francisco Lavagnino
Standard action-thriller: Hero finds intrigue, disaster

The Last Dinosaur
1977, (USA), Rankin-Bass/ABC-TV, color, 100 mins.
W: Richard Boone, Joan Van Ark (*Frankie Banks*), Steven Keats (*Chuck Wade*), Luther Rackley (*Bunta*), Carl Hansen (*Barney*), Tatsu Nakamura (*Dr. Kawamoto*), Mamiya Sekia (*The Prehistoric Girl*), William Ross (*The Expedition Captain*)
D: Alex Grasshoff & Tom Kotani   **TELEPLAY:** William Overgard   **SPCL-FX:** Kaziro Sagawa   **MUSIC:** Maury Laws
TVM, standard SF-adventure: Tyrannosaur found under polar icecap

Last Embrace
1979, (USA), UA, color, 101 mins.
W: Roy Scheider, Janet Margolin, John Glover, Sam Levene, Charles Napier, Christopher Walken, Jacqueline Brookes Mandy Patinkin
D: Jonathan Demme   **PHOTOG:** Tak Fujimoto   **MUSIC:** Miklos Rosza
Unusual 'Hitchcockian' thriller: Former assassin menaced

Last Exit to Earth
1996, (USA), SHO-TV, color, 90 mins.
W: Costas Mandylor (*Jaid*)
Made-for-Cable, standard SF: Space women seek mates to repopulate their world, cf. **Terror from the Year 5,000**

Last Gasp
1995, (USA), color, 91 mins.
W: Robert Patrick, Joanna Pacula, Vyto Ruginis (*Ray*), Mimi Craven (*Goldie*), Alexander Enberg (*Duane*)
Minor fantasy-thriller: Spirit of dead Mexican Indian possesses greedy real-estate developer

The Last Generation
1971, (USA), R&S Films, color
W: Stuart Whitman, Vera Miles, Lew Ayres, Mercedes McCambridge, Pearl Bailey, Lee Grant, Michael Rennie, Connie Stevens, Phil Harris, Cesar Romero
P: Luther Davis   **D:** William Graham   **SCR:** Earl Hammer Jr.
Standard SF-thriller: Overpopulation in 21st century

The Last Glory of Troy
see La Leggendi di Enea

Last Holiday
1950, (GB), Watergate/Assoc. Brit, b&w, 88 mins.
W: Alec Guinness (*George Bird*), Beatrice Campbell (*Sheila Rockingham*), Kay Walsh (*Mrs. Poole*), Bernard Lee (*Insp. Wilton*), Wilfrid Hyde-White (*Chalfont*), Sidney James (*Joe Clarence*), Muriel George (*Lady Oswington*), Ronald Simpson (*The Doctor*), Helen Cherry (*Miss Mellows*), Meier Tzelniker (*The Tailor*), Jean Colin (*Daisy Clarence*), David McCallum (*The Blind Fiddler*), Brian Worth (*Derek Rockingham*), Esma Cannon (*Miss Fox*), Gregoire Aslan (*Gambini*), Peter Jones (*The Agent*), Ernest Thesiger (*Sir Trevor Lampington*), Brian Oulton
D: Henry Cass, from a story by J.B. Priestley   **PHOTOG:** Ray Elton   **MUSIC:** Francis Chagrin
Amusing comedy-melodrama: Man thinks he is dying, goes on spree

The Last Horror Film
1982, (USA), color, 87 mins.
W: Caroline Munro, Joe Spinell, Judd Hamilton
D: David Winters
A.k.a. **The Fanatic**
Minor thriller: Killer stalks horror-movie queen

The Last Hour
1930, (GB), Nettlefold/Butcher, b&w, 75 mins.
W: Stewart Rome (*Prince Nicola*), Kathleen Vaughan (*Mary Tregellis*), Wilfred Shine (*Tregellis*), Richard Cooper (*Byron*), Alexander Field (*Smarty Walker*), Billy Shine (*Ben*), James Raglan (*Charles Lister*), George Bealby (*Blumfeldt*), Frank Arlton (*George*)
D: Walter Forde   **SCR:** H. Fowler Mear, from a play by Charles Bennett
Standard thriller: Evil prince uses death ray, commits air piracy

Last House on Dead End Street
1977, (USA), Cinematic, color
P: Norman F. Kaiser   **D:** Victor Janos   **SCR:** Brian Lawrence
A.k.a. **The Fun House**
Minor thriller: Gory "snuff" murders

The Last House on the Left

1972, (USA), Hallmark, color, 85 mins.
W: David Hess, Lucy Grantham, Sandra Cassel, Marc Sheffler, Ada Washington, Fred Lincoln, Jeramie Rain, Cynthia Carr, Martin Kove
P: Sean S. Cunningham **WRIT & D:** Wes Craven **PHOTOG:** Victor Hurwitz **MUSIC:** David Alexander Hess **SONG:** *The Road Leads to Nowhere*
orig. to be titled Krug and Company or Sex Crime of the Century reissued 1981.
Gruesome thriller (cult classic), inspired by Ingmar Bergman's The Virgin Spring: Two girls tortured by sociopaths

Last House on the Left, Part II
see Twitch of the Death Nerve

The Last Hunt

1956, (USA), MGM, color, 103 mins.
W: Robert Taylor (*Charles Gilson*), Stewart Granger (*Sandy McKenzie*), Debra Paget (*Indian Girl*), Lloyd Nolan (*Woodfoot*), Russ Tamblyn (*Jimmy*), Constance Ford (*Peg*), Ralph Moody (*The Indian Agent*), Joe DeSantis (*Ed Black*), Ainslie Pryor (*The Buffalo Hunter*), Ed Lonehill (*Spotted Hand*), Fred Graham (*The Bartender*) Dan White, Bill Phillips, Roy Barcroft
P: Dore Schary **WRIT & D:** Richard Brooks, from Milton Lott's novel **PHOTOG:** Russell Harlan **MUSIC:** Amfitheatrof
"...Robert Taylor in unusual, almost fiendish villain role—and the bizarre sequence of his retribution in the wilderness is certainly a most exquisite touch of guignol" —Anon., Frankenstein TV Movie-guide, Castle of Frankenstein, Vol. IV, No. 1 (Spring, 1969), p. 58
Gripping melodrama-western: Buffalo butcher gets comeuppance

The Last Laugh
see Der Letzte Mann

The Last Man on Earth

1964, (USA-It), Assoc. Prod./AIP, b&w, 88 mins.
W: Vincent Price, Franca Bettoia, Emma Danieli, Umberto Rau, Gia-como Rossi-Stuart
P: Robert L. Lippert **D:** Sidney Salkow **SCR:** Logan Swanson & William F. Leicester, from Richard Matheson's novel *I Am Legend*
orig. to be titled Naked Fear
Standard SF-horror: Solitary man struggles to live after strange plague turns rest of humanity into vampire-like creatures. cf. The Omega Man

The Last Man to Hang?

1956, (GB), ACT Films-Warwick/Col, b&w, 75 mins.
W: Tom Conway (*Sir Roderick Strood*), Eunice Gayson (*Elizabeth Anders*), Elizabeth Sellars (*Daphne Strood*), Raymond Huntley (*The Attorney-General*), Freda Jackson (*Mrs. Tucker*), David Horne (*Anthony Harcombe*), Victor Maddern (*Bonaker*), Margaretta Scott (*Mrs. Cranshaw*), Walter Hudd (*The Judge*), Anthony Newley (*Cyril Gaskin*), Anna Turner (*Lucy Prynne*), Hugh Latimer (*Mark Perryman*), Russell Napier (*Sgt. Bolton*), Olive Sloane (*Mrs. Bayfield*)
P: John W. Gossage **D:** Terence Fisher **SCR:** Gerald Bullett, Maurice Elvey, Ivor Montagu & Max Trell, from Gerald Bullett's novel *The Jury*
Standard thriller: Knight accused of poisoning wife

The Last Musketeer

1955, (Fr), color, 95 mins.
W: Georges Marchal, Dawn Addams W: Jacques Dumesnil
D: Fernando Cerchio, from characters created by Alexandre Dumas
A.k.a. The Count of Bragelonne
Standard action-adventure: Corruption at court of Louis XIV

The Last of Sheila

1973, (USA), WB, color, 120 mins.
W: Richard Benjamin (*Tom*), Dyan Cannon (*Christine*), James Coburn (*Clinton*), Raquel Welch (*Alice*), Joan Hackett (*Lee*), Ian McShane (*Antony*), Yvonne Romain (*Sheila*), James Mason (*Philip*), Pierro Rosso (*Vittorio*), Serge Citon, Robert Rossi, Jack Pugeat, Elaine Geisinger, Maurice Crosnier, Elliot Geisinger
P & D: Herbert Ross **SCR:** Anthony Perkins & Stephen Sondheim **PHOTOG:** Gerry Turpin **MUSIC:** Billy Goldenberg
Standard comedy-thriller: Widowed nabob plays mind games

Last of the Buccaneers

1950, (USA), Col, color, 79 mins.
W: Paul Henreid (*Jean Lafitte*), Jack Oakie
Standard adventure-thriller

The Last of the Lone Wolf

1930, (USA), Col, b&w, 7 reels, 70 mins
W: Bert Lytell (*Michael Lanyard*), Patsy Ruth Miller (*Stephanie*), Lucien Prival (*Varril*), Otto Matieson (*The Prime Minister*), Alfred Hickman (*The King*), Maryland Morne (*The Queen*), Haley Sullivan (*Camilla*), Pietro Sosso (*The Master of Ceremonies*), Henry Daniell (*Count von Rimpeu*), James Liddy (*Hoffman*)
D: Richard Boleslawsky **SCR:** Dorothy Howell **DIALOG:** James Whittaker **ADAPT:** John Thomas Neville **PHOTOG:** Ben Kline
Standard thriller: Rogue retrieves queen's ring. 'Lone Wolf' series

The Last of the Secret Agents

1966, (USA), Para, color, 90 mins.

W: Steve Rossi, Marty Allen, Nancy Sinatra, Edy Williams, Lou Jacobi, Sig Ruman, Harvey Korman, Ed Sullivan
P & D: Norman Abbott **SCR:** Mel Tolkin
Standard spy-comedy: American tourists in France vs. international art thieves

Last of the Vikings

1962, (It), Galatea/Medallion, color, 102 mins.
W: Edmund Purdom, Helene Remy, Cameron Mitchell, Isabelle Corey, Aldo Bufi Landi, Andrea Aureli, Giorgio Ardisson, Carla Calo, Nando Tamberlani
D: Giacomo Gentilomo
Minor adventure-thriller: Murdered Viking's disguised son seeks vengeance

The Last Page

1952, (GB), Hammer-Lippert/Exclusive, b&w, 84 mins.
W: George Brent (*John Harman*), Marguerite Chapman (*Stella*), Raymond Huntley (*Clive*), Peter Reynolds (*Jeff*), Diana Dors (*Ruby*), Eleanor Summerfield (*Vi*), Harry Fowler (*Joe*), Meredith Edwards (*Dave*), Conrad Phillips (*Todd*), Isabel Dean (*May*)
P: Anthony Hinds **D:** Terence Fisher **SCR:** Frederick Knott, from a play by James Hadley Chase
USA retitle, Manbait
Standard crime-thriller: Bookseller framed for death of blackmailing blonde

The Last Prey of the Vampire
see L'Ultima Preda del Vampiro

Last Rites

1980, (USA), New Empire/Cannon, color, 81 mins.
W: Patricia Lee Hammond, Mimi Weddell, Victor Jorge, Gerald Field-ing, Michael Lally
D & PHOTOG: Domonic Paris **SCR:** Ben Donnelly & Domonic Paris **MUSIC:** Paul Jost & George Small
A.k.a. Dracula's Last Rites
Minor horror-fantasy: Vampirism spreads

*The Last Starfighter:*LANCE GUEST AND DAN O'HERLIHY

Last Rites

1998, (USA), color, 100 mins.
W: Embeth Davidtz, Randy Quaid, A Martinez (*Matt Santos*), Clarence Williams III (*Warden Pierce*), Jack Coleman (*Blake*), Tracy Ellis (*Lydia*)
Made-for-Cable, standard thriller: Serial killer survives execution

The Last Shot You Hear

1970, (GB), Lippert/20th-Fox, b&w, 91 mins.
W: Hugh Marlowe (*Charles Nordeck*), Zena Walker (*Eileen*), Patricia Haines (*Anne Nordeck*), William Dysart (*Peter Marriott*), Thorley Walters (*Gen. Jowett*), Lionel Murton (*Rubens*), Helen Horton (*Dodie Rubens*), John Nettleton (*Nash*), John Wentworth (*Chambers*)
P: Robert L. Lippert & Jack Parsons **D:** Gordon Hessler **SCR:** Tim Shields, from William Fairchild's play *Murder*
Standard crime-thriller: Lovers plot to murder marriage counselor

The Last Slumber Party

1987, (USA), color, 80 mins.
W: Jan Jensen, Nancy Meyer
D: Stephen Tyler
Minor thriller: Asylum escapee crashes teen sleepover

The Last Starfighter

1984, (USA), Lorimar/Univ, color, 101 mins.
W: Lance Guest (*Alex Rogan*), Robert Preston (*Centauri*), Dan O'Herlihy (*Grig*),

Catherine Mary Stewart (*Maggie Gordon*), Barbara Bosson (*Jane*), Dan Mason, Kay E. Kuter, John Maio, Chris Herbert, John O'Leary, George McDaniel, Charlene Nelson, Robert Starr, Al Berry, Scott Dunlop, Vernon Washington, Cameron Dye, Kimberly Ross, Wil Wheaton
D: Nick Castle **SCR:** Jonathan Betuel **PHOTOG:** King Baggott **MUSIC:** Craig Safan
Standard SF-adventure: Earth youth enlisted by aliens to battle stellar invaders

The Last Ten Days
see *The Last Ten Days of Adolf Hitler*

The Last Ten Days of Adolf Hitler
1955, (Austria), Col, b&w, 108 mins.
W: Oskar Werner (*Adolf Hitler*), Albin Skoda, Kurt Eilers, Lotte Tobisch, Erich Suckmann, Helga Kennedy-Dohrn, Willy Krause
P: Carl Szokoll **D:** G.W. Pabst **SCR:** Erich Maria Remarque, from M.A. Musmanno's book *Ten Days to Die* **PHOTOG:** Gunther Anders
A.k.a. The Last Ten Days
Standard semi-historical melodrama: Deranged dictator's deterioration

The Last Tomb of Ligeia
see *The Tomb of Ligeia*

The Last Train
1960, (GB), Merton Park/Anglo-Amalgamated, b&w, 31 mins.
W: Russell Napier (*Sgt. Duggan*), Lisa Daniely (*Mrs. Hunt*), John Sloane (*Sgt. Davy*)
P: Jack Greenwood **D:** Geoffrey Muller **STORY:** James Eastwood
Standard short thriller: Police probe murder in Underground, catch smugglers

Last Train from Bombay
1952, (USA), Col, b&w, 72 mins.
W: Jon Hall, Lisa Ferraday
Standard adventure-thriller

Last Video and Testament
1985, (GB), Made for TV, color
W: David Langton, Deborah Rafferty, Oliver Tobias
TVM, standard thriller: Cuckold plots revenge on wife and her lover

The Last Unicorn
1982, (USA), color, 95 mins.
VOICES: Alan Arkin, Jeff Bridges, Tammy Grimes, Mia Farrow, Angela Lansbury, Robert Klein, Christopher Lee, Keenan Wynn
D: Jules Bass **SCR:** Peter S. Beagle **MUSIC:** Jim Webb
Standard animated fantasy

The Last Voyage
1960, (USA), MGM, color, 91 mins.
W: Robert Stack, Dorothy Malone, George Sanders, Edmond O'Brien, Woody Strode, Jack Kruschen
D & SCR: Andrew L. Stone **PHOTOG:** Hal Mohr
Tense melodrama: Ship sinks

The Last Voyage of Gulliver
see *Le Dernier Voyage de Gulliver*

The Last War
see *The Final War*

The Last Warning
1929, (USA), Univ, b&w, 8 reels (7,980 ft./2432.3m)
W: Laura La Plante (*Doris*), Montagu Love (*McHugh*), John Boles (*Qualie*), Bert Roach (*Mike*), Carrie Daumery (*Barbara*), Roy D'Arcy (*Carlton*), Margaret Livingston (*Evalinda*), Charles K. French (*The Doctor*), Mack Swain (*Robert*), Torben Meyer (*Gene*), Burr McIntosh (*Josiah*), Slim Summerville (*Tommy*), D'Arcy Corrigan (*Woodford*), Bud Phelps (*Sammy*), Harry Northrup (*The Coroner*), Francisco Moran (*Jeffries*), Ella McKenzie (*Ann*), Fred Kelsey (*An*

The Last Wave: RICHARD CHAMBERLAIN

Inspector), Tom O'Brien (*An Inspector*)
D: Paul Leni **SCR:** Alfred A. Cohn **ADAPT:** Alfred A. Cohn, Robert F. Hill & J.G. Hawks, from a play by Thomas F. Fallon **PHOTOG:** Hal Mohr
MUSIC SCORE: Joseph Cherniavsky
Standard thriller: Killer prowls theater. cf. **House of Fear** *(1939)*

The Last Warning
1938, (USA), Univ, b&w, 63 mins.
W: Preston Foster (*Bill Crane*), Kay Linaker, Frank Jenks, E.E. Clive, Joyce Compton, Frances Robinson, Roland Drew, Raymond Parker, Albert Dekker, Robert Paige, Richard Lane, Orville Caldwell, Clem Wilenchick (*Crane Whitley*)
D: Albert Rogell **SCR:** Edmund L.Hartmann, from Jonathan Latimer's novel *The Dead Don't Care*
Standard thriller (3rd & last "Bill Crane" mystery): Detective encounters mysterious killer called "The Eye"

The Last Wave
1977, (Austral), UA/World Northal, color, 104 mins.
W: Richard Chamberlain (*David Burton*), Olivia Hammett (*Anne Bur-ton*), Gulpilil (*Chris Lee*), Vivean Gray (*Dr. Whitburn*), Frederick Parselow (*Rev. Burton*), Nanjiwarra Amagula (*Charlie*), Walter Amagula (*Gerry Lee*), Roy Bara (*Larry*), Cedric Lalara (*Lindsey*), Morris Lalara (*Jacko*), Jo England (*The Babysitter*), Peter Carroll (*Michael Zeadler*), Hedley Cullen (*The Judge*), Athol Compton (*Billy Corman*), Jennifer de Greenlaw (*Zeadler's Sec'y*), Michael Duffield (*Andrew Potter*), Wallas Eaton (*The Morgue Doctor*), John Frawley (*The Policeman*), Richard Henderson (*The Prosecutor*), Greg Rowe (*Carl*), Merv Lilley (*The Publican*), Malcolm Robertson (*Don Fishburn*), John Meagher (*The Morgue Clerk*), Guido Rametta (*Guido*), Katrina Sedgwick (*Sophie Burton*), Ingrid Weir (*Grace Burton*)
D: Peter Weir **SCR:** Peter Weir, Tony Morphett & Peter Popescu **ORIG. IDEA:** Peter Weir **PHOTOG:** Russell Boyd **SPCL-FX:** Neil Angwin **MUSIC:** Charles Wain
Unusual, critically-acclaimed thriller: Lawyer's life is eerily changed by contact with Australian aborigines

The Last Will of Dr. Mabuse
see *Das Testament des Dr. Mabuse*

Last Woman on Earth
1960, (USA), Filmgroup/AIP, color, 71 mins.
W: Antony Carbone (*Harold*), Betsy Jones-Moreland (*Evelyn*), Edward Wain (*Robert Towne*) (*Martin*)
P & D: Roger Corman **SCR:** Robert Towne **PHOTOG:** Jack Marquette
Standard SF-thriller ("She Was The Ultimate Prize!"): Predictable conflict when two men and lone woman find they are only survivors of World War III

Last Year at Marienbad
see *L'Annee Derniere a Marienbad*

Las Vegas Serial Killer
1986, (USA), color, 90 mins.
W: Pierre Agostino, Ron Jason, Tara MacGowran, Kathryn Downey
Made-for-Video, minor thriller: Killer released from prison

The Late Edwina Black
1951, (GB), Elvey-Gartside/IFD, b&w, 78 mins.
W: David Farrar (*Gregory Black*), Geraldine Fitzgerald (*Elizabeth*), Roland Culver (*The Inspector*), Jean Cadell (*Ellen*), Mary Merrall (*Lady Southdale*), Charles Heslop (*The Vicar*), Harcourt Williams (*Dr. Prendergast*), Ronald Adam (*The Schoolmaster*), Sydney Monckton (*Horace*)
D: Maurice Elvey **SCR:** Charles Frank & David Evans, from a play by William Dinner & William Morum **PHOTOG:** Stephen Dade **MUSIC:** Allan Gray
USA retitle, Obsessed
Standard thriller: Victorian schoolteacher's wife found dead; police have three suspects

Late for Dinner
1991, (USA), Castle Rock/New Line/Col, color, 89 mins.
W: Brian Wimmer (*Willie Husband*), Peter Berg (*Frank Lovegren*), Marcia Gay Harden (*Joy Husband*), Peter Gallagher (*Bob Freeman*), Colleen Flynn (*Jessica Husband*), Michael Beach (*Dr. David Arrington*), Kyle Secor (*Leland Shakes*), Cassy Friel (*Little Jessica Husband*), Ross Malinger (*Little Donald Freeman*), Janeane Garofalo
D: W.D. Richter **SCR:** Mark Andrus **PHOTOG:** Peter Sova **MUSIC:** David Mansfield
Unusual SF-melodrama: Men return from suspended animation

Late Night Final
1954, (GB), Merton Park/Anglo-Amalgamated, b&w, 29 mins.
W: Stanley Van Beers (*Burrage/Crawford*), Colin Tapley (*Insp. Turner*), John Wynn (*Sgt. Conway*), Richard Shaw (*Wooland*)
P: Alec Snowden **D & SCR:** Montgomery Tully **STORY:** Gaston Charpentier, from a novel by Edgar Lustgarten
Stadard short crime-thriller: Drug smuggler disguised as cripple

The Lathe of Heaven
1980, (USA), PBS-TV, color, 120 mins
W: Bruce Davison (*George Orr*), Kevin Conway (*Dr. William Haber*), Margaret

Avery (*Heather*), Peyton Park (*Mannie*), Niki Flacks (*Miss Crouch*)
D: David R. Loxton & Fred Barzyk   **TELEPLAY:** Roger E. Swaybill & Diane English, from Ursula K. Le Guin's novel   **MUSIC:** Michael Small
TVM, engrossing SF-fantasy: Young man finds his dreams become reality

Latitude Zero
1969, (USA-Jap), Toho/Nat'l General, color, 106 mins.
W: Joseph Cotten (*The Captain*), Patricia Medina (*Lucretia*), Richard Jaeckel (*Perry*), Cesar Romero (*Malic*), Akira Takarada (*Ken*), Linda Haynes (*Anne*), Masumi Okada (*Masson*), Hikaru Kuroki (*Kroiga*)
D: Inoshiro Honda   **SCR:** Ted Sherdeman & Shinichi Sekizawa   **SPCL-FX:** Eiji Tsuburaya   **MUSIC:** Akira Ifukube
A.k.a. Ido Zero Daisakusen
Standard SF-thriller

Laugh, Clown, Laugh
1928, (USA), MGM, b&w, 8 reels (7,045 ft./2147.3m)
W: Lon Chaney Sr. (*Tito*), Loretta Young (*Simonetta*), Nils Asther (*Luigi*), Bernard Siegel (*Simon*), Cissy Fitzgerald (*Giancinta*), Gwen Lee (*Lucretia*)
P & D: Herbert Brenon   **SCR:** Elizabeth Meehan, from a play by David Belasco & Tom Cushing   **PHOTOG:** James Wong Howe
Standard melodrama: Circus clown has doomed love for adopted waif

Laughing at Danger
1924, (USA), b&w, 45 mins.
W: Richard Talmadge, Joseph Girard, Eva Novak, Joe Harrington, Stanhope Wheatcroft
D: James W. Horne
Standard comedy-thriller: "Playboy" aids death-ray inventor

The Laughing Girl Murder
1973, (GB), Willis World Wide/MGM-EMI, color, 26 mins.
W: George Baker (*Supt. Keegan*), Anthony Baird (*Insp. Adams*), Mark Colleano (*Martin*), Jo Rowbottom (*Mrs. Forbes*), Ronald Hines (*Mr. Forbes*), Richard Leech (*Lemaire*), Graham Stark (*Harker*), John Barrie (*Percy Hoskins*)
D: David Eady   **STORY:** Percy Hoskins
Standard short thriller: Girls strangled

The Laughing Lady
1946, (GB), British Nat'l, color, 93 mins.
W: Anne Ziegler (*Denise Tremayne*), Webster Booth (*Andre*), Peter Graves (*The Prince of Wales*), Francis L. Sullivan (*Sir William Tremayne*), Paul Dupuis (*Pierre*), Felix Aylmer (*Sir Felix Mountroyal*), Chili Bouchier (*Louise*), Ralph Truman (*Lord Mandeville*), Charles Goldner (*Robespierre*), John Ruddock (*Gilliatt*), Jack Melford (*Lord Barrymore*), Hay Petrie (*Tom*), Frederick Burtwell (*Jenkins*), Anthony Nicholls (*Jenkins*)
D: Paul Stein   **SCR:** Jack Whittingham, from a play by Ingram d'Abbes
Standard musical-adventure: Duchess' son turns highwayman

Laura
1944, (USA), 20th-Fox, b&w, 88 mins.
W: Gene Tierney (*Laura Hunt*), Dana Andrews (*Lt. Mark McPherson*), Clifton Webb (*Waldo Lydecker*), Judith Anderson (*Ann Treadwell*), Vincent Price (*Shelby Carpenter*), Dorothy Adams (*Bessie*), James Flavin, Ralph Dunn, Clyde Fillmore, Kathleen Howard
P & D: Otto Preminger (Rouben Mamoulian began directing)   **SCR:** Jay Dratler, Samuel Hoffenstein & Betty Reinhardt, from Vera Caspary's novel   **PHOTOG:** Joseph La Shelle (Academy Award)   **MUSIC:** David Raksin (including 'Laura' theme)
*Classic mystery-romance: Socialite's "murder" causes complications. Remake: **Laura**, 1955 TV movie with Dan Wynter*

Laurel and Hardy in Toyland
see Babes in Toyland (1934)

The Lavender Hill Mob
1951, (GB), Ealing/Univ, b&w, 78 mins.
W: Alec Guinness (*Henry Holland*), Stanley Holloway (*Alfred Pendlebury*), Alfie Bass (*Shorty*), Sidney James (*Lackery*), Marjorie Fielding (*Mrs. Chalk*), Audrey Hepburn (*Chiquita*), Edie Martin (*Miss Evesham*), John Gregson (*Farrow*), Ronald Adam (*The Bank Official*), Clive Morton (*The Police Sgt.*), Sydney Tafler (*The Stallholder*), Patrick Barr (*The Inspector*), Meredith Edwards (*PC Edwards*), Michael Trubshawe (*The British Ambassador*), Robert Shaw (*The Police Scientist*), Moultrie Kelsall
P: Michael Balcon   **D:** Charles Crichton   **STORY & SCR:** T.E.B. Clarke (Oscar winner)   **PHOTOG:** Douglas Slocombe   **MUSIC:** Georges Auric
Classic comedy-thriller: Timid clerk plans Bank of England robbery

Law and Disorder
1940, (GB), British Consolidated/RKO, b&w, 73 mins.
W: Barry K. Barnes (*Larry Preston*), Diana Churchill (*Janet Preston*), Alastair Sim (*Samuel Blight*), Austin Trevor (*Heinrichs*), Edward Chapman (*Insp. Bray*), Ruby Miller, Geoffrey Sumner, Leo Genn, Glen Alyn, Torin Thatcher, Cyril Smith, Carl Jaffe, Cathleen Nesbitt
D: David MacDonald   **STORY:** Roger Macdonald
reissued 1943 & 1952
Standard thriller: Solicitor's partner unmasks saboteurs

The Lawnmower Man
1992, (USA), Allied Vision-Lane Pringle/New Line, color, 105 mins, also 135 mins
W: Pierce Brosnan (*Lawrence Angelo*), Jeff Fahey (*Jobe Smith*), Jenny Wright (*Marnie Burke*), Geoffrey Lewis (*Terry McKeen*), Mark Bringleson (*Sebastian Timms*), Colleen Coffey (*Carline Angelo*), Jeremy Slate (*Father McKeen*), Dean Norris (*The Director*), Troy Evans (*Lt. Goodwin*), John Laughlin (*Jake*), Rosalee Mayeux, Austin O'Brien, Michael Gregory, Joe Hart, Ray Lykins, Jim Landis, Mike Valverde, Dale Paoul, Frank Collison, Jonathan Smart, Steffen Gregory Foster, Doug Hutchison, Denney Pierce, Roger Rook, Craig Benton, Randall Fontana, Duane Byrne, Mara Duronslet
D: Brett Leonard   **SCR:** Brett Leonard & Gimel Everett, from Stephen King's short story   **PHOTOG:** Russell Carpenter   **SPCL-FX:** Paul Haines & Tom Ceglia   **MUSIC:** Dan Wyman
Major SF-thriller: Scientist alters handyman's I.Q.

Lawnmower Man 2: Beyond Cyberspace
1996, (USA-GB-Jap), Fuji Eight-August/New Line, color, 93 mins
W: Patrick Bergin, Matt Frewer, Austin O'Brien, Kevin Conway, Ely Pouget, Camille Cooper Sean Parhm, Mathew Valencia
D & SCR: Farhad Mann   **STORY:** Farhad mann & Michael Miner   **PHOTOG:** Ward Russell   **SPCL VS-FX:** Cinesite   **MUSIC:** Robert Folk
Standard SF-thriller: Megalomaniac rules cyberspace

Law of the Jungle
1942, (USA), b&w, 61 mins.
W: Arline Judge, John "Dusty" King, Mantan Moreland, Martin Wilkins, Arthur O'Connell
D: Jean Yarbrough
Minor thriller: Lady scientist and fugitive oppose Nazis

League of Frightened Men
1937, (USA), Col, b&w, 65 mins
W: Walter Conolly (*Nero Wolfe*), Lionel Stander (*Archie Goodwin*), Eduardo Ciannelli, Irene Hervey, Victor Kilian, Nana Bryant, Kenneth Hunter, Allen Brook (*Joseph Allen, Jr.*), Walter Kingsford, Ian Wolfe, Leonard Mudie, Charles Irwin, Rafaela Ottiano, Jonathan Hale, Edward McNamara, Jameson Thomas, Herbert Ashley, James Flavin
D: Alfred E. Green   **SCR:** Eugene Solow & Guy Endore, from Rex Stout's novel
Standard thriller (2nd & last "Nero Wolfe" mystery): Harvard alumni being murdered, sleuth investigates

The League of Gentlemen
1960, (GB), Allied Film Makers/RFD, b&w, 113 mins.
W: Jack Hawkins (*Norman Hyde*), Nigel Patrick (*Peter Graham Race*), Roger Livesey (*Mycroft*), Richard Attenborough (*Edward Lexy*), Bryan Forbes (*Martin Porthill*), Kieron Moore (*Stevens*), Robert Coote (*Bunny Warren*), Terence Alexander (*Rupert Rutland-Smith*), Melissa Stribling (*Peggy*), Norman Bird (*Frank Weaver*), Nanette Newman (*Elizabeth*), David Lodge (*CSM*), Doris Hare (*Molly Weaver*)
P: Michael Relph   **D:** Basil Dearden   **SCR:** Bryan Forbes, from a novel by John Boland
Entertaining crime-thriller: Ex-colonel plots bank robbery

Leapin' Leprechauns!
1997, (USA), color, 85 mins.
W: John Bluthal, Grant Cramer, Godfrey James (*King Kevin*) Sharon Lee Jones, Gregory Edward Smith, Sylvester McCoy, James Ellis, Tina Martin, Eric Nicole Hess
D: Ted Nicolaou   **SCR:** Ted Nicolaou & Michael McGann
Standard fantasy: Wee folk oppose creation of theme park

Leatherface: Texas Chainsaw Massacre III
1990, (USA), New Line, color, 82 mins.
W: Kate Hodge (*Michelle*), William Butler (*Ryan*), Ken Foree (*Benny*), R.A. Mihailoff (*Leatherface*), Tom Everett (*Alfredo*), Viggo Mortensen, Joe Unger, Toni Hudson, David Cloud, Miriam Byrd-Nethery, Ron Brooks, Beth DePatie, Michael Shamus Wiles, Dwayne Whitaker
D: Jeff Burr   **SCR:** David J. Schow, based on characters created by Kim Henkel & Tobe Hooper   **PHOTOG:** James L. Carter   **MUSIC:** Jim Manzie & Patrick Regan
Standard horror-thriller: Cannibal yahoos continue reign of terror

Leather Girls
see Faster, Pussycat! Kill! Kill!

Leave Her to Heaven
1945, (USA), Darryl F. Zanuck/20th-Fox, color, 110 mins.
W: Gene Tierney, Cornel Wilde, Jeanne Crain, Vincent Price, Mary Phillips, Ray Collins, Gene Lockhart, Darryl Hickman, Reed Hadley, Chill Wills
P: William A. Bacher   **D:** John M. Stahl   **SCR:** Jo Swerling, from Ben Ames Williams' best-selling novel   **PHOTOG:** Leon Shamroy (Academy Award)   **MUSIC:** Alfred Newman
*Standard thriller: Neurotic wife foments tragedy. cf. **Too Good to Be True***

Leaves from Satan's Book
see Blade of Satans Bog

The Lebanese Mission
1956, (Fr), color, 90 mins.
__W:__ Gianna Maria Canale, Jean Servais, Jean Claude Pascal
Minor thriller: Intrigue surrounds uranium find

Lebewohl Fremde (Farewell, Stranger)
1991, (Ger), color, 98 mins.
__W:__ Grazyna Szapoloska, Musfik Kenter
__D:__ Tevfik Baser
Unusual melodrama: Young photographer seeks mysterious woman

Leda
1959, (Fr), Hakim/Times/Janus-TV, color, 101 mins.
__W:__ Jean-Paul Belmondo, Antonella Lualdi, Madeleine Robinson, Jacques
    Dacqmine
__D:__ Claude Chabrol   __PHOTOG:__ Henri Decae   __MUSIC:__ Paul Misraki
USA TV-retitle, __Web of Passion,__ A.k.a. __A Double Tour__
Unusual thriller: Neighbor-girl murdered

The Leech Woman
1960, (USA), Univ, b&w, 77 mins.
__W:__ Coleen Gray, Grant Williams, Gloria Talbott, Phillip Terry, John Van Dreelen,
    Estelle Hemsley, Kim Hamilton, Arthur Batanides
__P:__ Joseph Gershenson   __D:__ Edward Dein   __SCR:__ David Duncan, from a story by
    Ben Pivar & Francis Rosenwald   __PHOTOG:__ Ellis W. Carter   __MUSIC:__
    Irving Gertz
Minor but engrossing SF-horror: Doctor's alcoholic wife finds African elixir of youth

Left in Trust
1911, (GB), Cricks & Martin, b&w, 565 ft. (172.2m)
__D:__ A.E. Coleby
USA retitle, __Saved by a Child__
Standard crime-thriller: Doctor's child thwarts jewel thief and nurse accomplice

The Legacy
1978, (GB), Pethurst/Turman-Foster/Univ, color, 102 mins.
__W:__ Katharine Ross (*Maggie Walsh*), Sam Elliott (*Peter Danner*), Charles Gray (*Karl
    Liebknecht*), John Standing (*Jason Mountolive*), Ian Hogg (*Harry*), Roger
    Daltrey (*Clive*), Margaret Tyzack (*Nurse Adams*), Marianne Broome (*Maria*),
    Patsy Smart (*The Cook*), Hildegard Neil (*Barbara*), William Abney (*The
    Butler*), Lee Montague (*Jacques*), Mathias Kilroy (*The Stable Lad*), Reg
    Harding (*The Gardener*)
__P:__ David Foster   __D:__ Richard Marquand   __SCR:__ Jimmy Sangster, Patrick Tilley &
    Paul Wheeler, from a story by Jimmy Sangster   __PHOTOG:__ Dick Bush &
    Alan Hume   __MUSIC:__ Michael J. Lewis   __SONG:__ Another Side of Me
TV-retitle, __The Legacy of Maggie Walsh__
Bizarre horror-fantasy: Murders cloud supernatural inheritance

Legacy of Blood
1973, (USA), Universal Entertainment, color, 90 mins
__W:__ John Carradine, Faith Domergue, Jeff Morrow, Merry Anders, Buck Kartalian
    John Russell, Richard Davalos
__P & D:__ Carl Monson   __SCR:__ Eric Norden
A.k.a. __Blood Legacy__
Standard thriller: Millionaire's heirs murdered

Legacy of Horror
1964, (W. Ger), b&w 83 mins.
__W:__ Hansjorg Felmy, Ann Smyrner, Hans Nielsen W: Elaine Boies, Chris
    Broderick, Marilee Troncone, Jeannie Cusik
from, a story by Edgar Wallace
Standard thriller

Legacy of Horror
1978, (USA), Ken Lane Films/Take One/Cinema Shares, color, 82 mins
__P, D, SCR & PHOTOG:__ Andy Milligan
Minor horror-thriller (remake of __The Ghastly Ones__): Killer eliminates heirs

The Legacy of Maggie Walsh
see __The Legacy__

Legacy of Satan
1973, (USA), Damiano Films, color
__P, D & SCR:__ Gerard Damiano
Minor horror-thriller: Innocents meet satanic cult

Legend
1986, (USA), Arnon Milchan/Univ, color, 89 mins.
__W:__ Tom Cruise (*Jack*), Mia Sara (*Lili*), Tim Curry (*Darkness*), David Bennent
    (*Gump*), Alice Playten (*Blix*), Billy Barty (*Screwball*), Cork Hubbert (*Brown
    Tom*), Kiran Shah (*Blunder*), Peter O'Farrell (*Pox*), Annabelle Lanyon (*Oona*),
    Robert Picardo (*Meg Mucklebones*), Tina Martın
__D:__ Ridley Scott   __SCR:__ William Hjortsberg   __PHOTOG:__ Alex Thomson   __SPCL-
    FX:__ Nick Adler   __MUSIC:__ Tangerine Dream
Big-budget but standard fantasy: Forest youth opposes Lord of Darkness

The Legendary Case of Lemora, Lady Dracula
see __Lemora, the Lady Dracula__

La Legende de Rip Van Winkle (The Legend of Rip Van Winkle)
1905, (Fr), Star, b&w, 335m (1,099 ft./18.6 mins.)
__D:__ Georges Melies, from Washington Irving's story, "Rip Van Winkle"
A.k.a. __Rip's Dream__
Standard fantasy (in 10 scenes): Sleeper meets grotesques

La Leggendi di Enea (The Legend of Aeneas)
1961, (It-Fr), Medallion, color, 108 mins.
__W:__ Steve Reeves (*Aeneas*), Giacomo Rossi-Stuart, Carla Marlier
__P:__ Albert Band & Giorgio Venturini   __D:__ Giorgio Rivalta   __SCR:__ Ugo Liberatore
A.k.a. __The Avenger__
Standard action-thriller: Trojan hero opposes beseigers

Legend in Leotards
see __The Return of Captain Invincible__

The Legend of Aeneas
see __La Leggendi di Enea__

Legend of Blood Castle
see __Ceremonia Sangrienta__

The Legend of Blood Mountain
1965, (USA), Craddock, color, 61 mins
__W:__ George Ellis, Zenas Sears, Glenda Brunson, Erin Fleming, Sheila Stringer
__P:__ Don Hadley   __D:__ Massey Cramer   __SCR:__ Massey Cramer, Don Hadley & Bob
    Corley
*Minor horror-thriller: Small-town reporter meets pretty girls, bizarre monster. Filmed in
    Georgia*

The Legend of Boggy Creek
1972, (USA), Pierce-Ledwell/Howco-Int'l, color, 90 mins.
__W:__ Willie E. Smith, John P. Nixon, John W. Gates, Buddy Crabtree, Jeff Crabtree
__WRIT, P, D & PHOTOG:__ Charles Pierce   __SCR:__ Earl E. Smith   __MUSIC:__ Jaime
    Mendoza-Nava
*Minor thriller: Hairy monster plagues Arkansas hamlet cf. __Return to Boggy Creek__ and
    __Boggy Creek—The Legend Continues__*

The Legend of Faust
see __Faust and the Devil__

Legend of Gosta Berling
see __The Story of Gosta Berling__

The Legend of Hell House
1973, (GB), Academy/James H. Nicholson/20th-Fox, color, 94 mins.
__W:__ Pamela Franklin (*Florence Tanner*), Roddy McDowall (*Ben Fischer*), Clive Revill
    (*Dr. Chris Barrett*), Gayle Hunnicutt (*Ann Barrett*), Peter Bowles (*Hanley*),
    Roland Culver (*Rudolph Deutsch*), Michael Gough (*Emeric Belasco*)
__P:__ Albert Fennell & Norman T. Herman   __D:__ John Hough   __SCR:__ Richard
    Matheson, from his novel __Hell House__   __PHOTOG:__ Alan Hume   __MUSIC:__
    Brian Hodgson & Delia Derbyshire
Standard horror-fantasy: Spirit hunters probe eerie mansion

The Legend of Hillbilly John
see __Who Fears the Devil?__

The Legend of King Cophetua
1912, (GB), Ivy Close Films/Hepworth, b&w, 625 ft. (190.5m)
__W:__ Ivy Close (*The Beggarmaid*), Alec Worcester (*King Cophetua*)
__WRIT & D:__ Elwin Neame
Standard romance: King weds beggarmaid

The Legend of Lizzie Borden
1975, (USA), Para/ABC-TV, color, 100 mins.
__W:__ Elizabeth Montgomery (*Lizzie Borden*), Fritz Weaver (*Andrew*), Katherine

The Legend of Lizzie Borden: ELIZABETH MONTGOMERY AND FRITZ WEAVER

Helmond (*Emma*), Fionnula Flanagan, Bonnie Bartlett, Ed Flanders, Hayden Rorke, Don Porter, Gail Kobe, John Zaremba, Helen Craig, John Beal, Alan Hewitt
P: George LeMaire   D: Paul Wendkos   **TELEPLAY:** William Bast   **PHOTOG:** Robert B. Hauser
TVM, unusual bio-thriller: New England spinster accused of axe-murders

The Legend of Prague
see Le Golem (1936)

The Legend of Rip Van Winkle
see La Legende de Rip Van Winkle

The Legend of Sleepy Hollow
1979, (USA), Sunn Classics/NBC-TV, color, 97 mins.
W: Jeff Goldblum (*Ichabod Crane*), Dick Butkus (*Brom Bones*), Meg Foster (*Katrina Van Tassel*), Paul Sand (*Frederic*), John Sylvester White (*Vanderhoof*), Laura Campbell (*Thelma*), Michael Ruud (*Palmer*), James Griffith (*Squire Van Tassel*), Karin Isaacson, H.E.D. Redford, "Tiger" Thompson, Michael Witt
D: Henning Schellerup   **TELEPLAY:** Malvin Wald, Jack Jacobs & Tom Chapman, from Washington Irving's story   **PHOTOG:** Paul Hipp   **MUSIC:** Bob Summers
TVM, minor comedy-melodrama: Schoolmaster sees spook

The Legend of Spider Forest
1974, (GB), Cupid-Action Plus, color, 91 mins.
W: Simon Brent (*Paul Greville*), Neda Arneric (*Anna Lutgermann*), Sheila Allen (*Ellen Huber*), Derek Newark (*Johann*), Terence Soall (*Dr. Lutgermann*), Gerard Heinz (*Huber*), Gertan Klauber (*Kurt*), Bette Vivian (*Frau Kessler*), Sean Gerrard (*Rudi*), Nosher Powell (*The Thug*), Ray Barron
P: Michael Pearson & Kenneth Rowles   D: Peter Sykes   **SCR:** Donald & Derek Ford   **ORIG. STORY:** Stephen Collins   **ADDITIONAL DIALOG:** Christopher Wicking   **PHOTOG:** Peter Jessop   **SPCL-FX:** Roy Whybrow   **MUSIC:** John Simco Harrison
orig. filmed (1971) as **Venom**
Minor horror-thriller: Painter meets mysterious woman

The Legend of Tarzan, Lord of the Apes
see Greystoke: The Legend of Tarzan, Lord of the Apes

Leghend of Wolf Lodge
see Into the Fire

Legend of the Bayou
see Eaten Alive! (1976)

Legend of the Dinosaurs
1983, (Jap), color, 92 mins.
Minor SF: Ancient beast found in Mt. Fuji cave

The Legend of the Lone Ranger
1981, (USA), Lord Grade-Jack Wrather/Martin Starger/Univ, color, 98 mins.
W: Klinton Spilsbury (*John Reid/"The Lone Ranger"*), Michael Horse (*Tonto*), Christopher Lloyd (*Cavendish*), Jason Robards Jr. (*Pres. Grant*), Matt Clark (*Sheriff Wiatt*), Juanin Clay (*Amy Striker*), John Bennett Perry (*Dan Reid*)
P: Walter Coblenz   D: William A. Fraker   **SCR:** Ivan Goff, Ben Roberts, Michael Kane & William Roberts   **ADAPT:** Jerry Derloshon   **PHOTOG:** Laszlo Kovacs   **ORIG. MUSIC:** John Barry   **SONG:** (sung by Merle Haggard), *The Man in the Mask*
Minor melodrama-western: Ranger becomes masked crime-fighter

Legend of the Lost
1957, (USA), UA, color, 109 mins.
W: John Wayne, Sophia Loren, Rossano Brazzi, Kurt Kasznar Sonia Moser
D: Henry Hathaway   **PHOTOG:** Jack Cardiff
Engrossing adventure-thriller: Three people seek treasure in ancient ruins of North African city

Legend of the Lost Tomb
1997, (USA), color
W: Stacy Keach, Rick Rossovich, Brock Pierce, Kimberlee Peterson
Juvenile adventure-thriller

Legend of the Seven Golden Vampires
1974, (GB-Hong Kong), Hammer/Shaw Bros., color, 89 mins.
W: Peter Cushing (*Prof. Lawrence Van Helsing*), Julie Ege (*Vanessa Buren*), David Chiang (*Hsi Ching*), Robin Stewart (*Leyland Van Helsing*), John Forbes-Robertson (*Dracula*), Robert Hanna (*The Consul*), Chan Shen (*Kah*), James Ma (*Hsi Ta*), Liu Chia Yung (*Hsi Kwei*), Feng Ko An (*Hsi Sung*), Wong Han Chan (*Leung Hon*), Shih Szu (*Mai Kwei*)
WRIT & P: Don Houghton   D: Roy Ward Baker   **PHOTOG:** John Wilcox & Roy Ford   **SPCL-FX:** Les Bowie   **MUSIC:** James Bernard
released in Hong Kong as **Dracula and the Seven Golden Vampires**. *A.k.a.* **The Seven Brothers Meet Dracula**
Standard horror-fantasy: Master vampire moves to China

Legend of the Werewolf
1975, (GB), Tyburn, color, 90 mins.
W: Peter Cushing (*Paul Cataflanque*), Ron Moody (*The Zoo Keeper*), Hugh Griffith (*Maestro Pamponi*), Roy Castle (*The Photographer*), David Rintoul (*Etoile*),

Stefan Gryff (*Max Gerard*), Lynn Dalby (*Christine*), David Bailie (*Boulon*), Renee Houston (*Chou Chou*), Majorie Yates (*Mme. Tellier*), Norman Mitchell (*Tiny*), Mark Weavers (*Etoile as a Boy*), Michael Ripper (*The Sewerman*), Patrick Holt (*The Dignitary*), John Harvey (*The Prefect*), Pamela Green (*Anne-Marie*)
P: Kevin Francis   D: Freddie Francis   **SCR:** John Elder [Anthony Hinds]   **PHOTOG:** John Wilcox   **MUSIC:** Harry Robinson
Modest horror-thriller: Parisian zoo keeper unmasked as lycanthrope

Legend of the White Horse
1985, (USA-Pol), color, 91 mins.
W: Janusz Morgenstern, Christopher Lloyd, Dee Wallace Stone, Allison Balson, Soon-Teck Oh, Luke Askew
D: Jerzy Domaradzki
Minor fantasy-thriller: Scientist and son visit mythical land, encounter villains and the supernatural

Legend of the Witches
1970, (GB), Negus-Fancey/Border, b&w, 87 mins.
P: Olive Negus-Fancey   **WRIT & D:** Malcolm Leigh   **PHOTOG:** Robert Webb
Standard horror-docu: History of witchcraft

The Legend of the Wolf Woman
1977, (Sp), Dimension, color, 84 mins
W: Frederick Stafford, Dagmar Lassander Anne Borel, fred Stafford, Tino Carey, Elliot Zamuto, Ollie Reynolds, Andrea Scotti, Karen Carter
P: Diego Alchimede   **D & SCR:** Rino Di Silvestro
video title, **Werewolf Woman**
Minor horror-thriller: Woman possessed by lycanthrope's spirit. A.k.a. **La Lupa Monnura**

Legend of Witch Hollow
see The Witchmaker

The Legend of Young Dick Turpin
1965, (GB), Walt Disney, color, 83 mins.
D: James Neilson
Standard adventure-thriller: Exploits of youthful highwayman

La Leggenda di Faust
see Faust and the Devil

La Leggendi di Enea
W: Gianni Garko, Liana Orfei
A.k.a. **The Avenger** *and* **The Last Glory of Troy**

Legion
1998, (USA), SCI-TV, color
W: Terry Farrell
TVM, standard SF-thriller: Enemy base infiltrated

Legion of Fire: Killer Ants
1998, (USA), Fox-TV, color, 95 mins.
W: Eric Lutes (*Dr. Conrad*), Julia Campbell (*Laura Sills*), Mitch Pileggi (*Sheriff Croy*), Jeremy Foley (*Chad*), Bill Osborn (*Officer Blount*), Dallen Gettling (*Bob Hazzard*), Patrick Fugit (*Scott Blount*)
D: James Charleston   **TELEPLAY:** Linda Palmer & Wink Roberts   **PHOTOG:** Don E. Fauntleroy   **SPCL-FX:** Craig Weiss   **MUSIC:** Daniel Licht
orig. to be titled **Marabunta**
TVM, standard SF-thriller: Volcanic activity stirs army ants in Alaska

Lemmy pour les Dames (Lemmy for the Ladies)
1962, (Fr), Films Borderie, b&w, 97 mins.
W: Eddie Constantine (*Lemmy Caution*), Elaine d'Almeida, Jacques Berthier, Francoise Brion, Yvonne Monlaur, Claudine Coster, Robert Berri, Lionel Roc
D: Bernard Borderie   **SCR:** Bernard Borderie & Marc-Gilbert Sauvajon, from an unpublished novel by Peter Cheyney
USA TV-retitle, **Ladies' Man**
Standard action-thriller (6th "Lemmy Caution" film): FBI agent vacations on Riviera, finds espionage and murder

The Lemon Grove Kids Meet the Monsters
1966, (USA), Steckler, color
W: Cash Flagg, Carolyn Brandt
P & D: Ray Dennis Steckler   **SCR:** Ron Haydock & Jim Harmon
Minor comedy-fantasy: Gang has race, meets assorted bizarre creatures

Lemora, the Lady Dracula
1974, (USA), Media Cinema, color, 80 mins
W: Leslie Gilb, Cheryl Smith, Richard Blackburn William Whitton, Steve Johnson, Monty Pyke, Parker West, Maxine Ballantyne
P: Robert Fern   D: Richard Blackburn   **SCR:** Richard Blackburn & Robert Fern
A.k.a. **The Legendary Case of Lemora** & **Lady Dracula**
Standard eroto-horror (condemned by Catholic Film Board): Vampiress lures young church singer to home in woods

Leonor
1975, (It-Fr-Sp), color, 90 mins.
W: Michel Piccoli, Liv Ullmann, Ornella Muti, Jorge Rigaud, Antonio Ferrandis

L

D: Juan Bunuel
Minor fantasy-thriller: Woman rises from tomb

The Leopard Lady
1928, (USA), DeMille/Pathe, b&w, 7 reels (6,650 ft./2026.9m)
W: Jacqueline Logan (*Paula*), Alan Hale Sr. (*Caesar*), Dick Alexander (*Hector, the Lion Tamer*), Hedwig Reicher (*Fran Holweg*), Robert Armstrong (*Chris*), James Bradbury Sr. (*Herman Berlitz*), William Burt (*Presner*), Sylvia Ashton (*Mama Lolita*), Kay Deslys (*An Austrian Maid*), Willie May Carson (*An Austrian Maid*)
P: Bertram Millhauser   **D:** Rupert Julian   **ADAPT:** Beulah Marie Dix, from a play by Edward Childs Carpenter   **PHOTOG:** John Mescall
Standard thriller: Woman leopard trainer probes murders

The Leopard Man
1943, (USA), RKO, b&w, 66 mins.
W: Dennis O'Keefe, Margo, Jean Brooks, Richard Martin, James Bell, Isabel Jewell, Abner Biberman, Tula Parma, Margaret Landry, Ariel Heath, Ben Bard, Fely Franquelli
P: Val Lewton   **D:** Jacques Tourneur   **SCR:** Ardel Wray & Edward Dein, from Cornell Woolrich's novel *Black Alibi*   **PHOTOG:** Robert De Grasse
MUSIC: Roy Webb
blurb: "The blood-racing story of a maniac who kills like a cat!"
Modest thriller: Escaped leopard blamed for grisly murders

Leprechaun
1993, (USA), Trimark, color, 92 mins.
W: Warwick Davis (*The Leprechaun*), Jennifer Aniston (*Tory*), Ken Olandt (*Nathan*), Mark Holton (*Ozzie*), Robert Gorman (*Alex*)
P: Jeffrey B. Mallian   **WRIT & D:** Mark Jones   **PHOTOG:** Levie Isaacks
MUSIC: Kevin Kiner
Standard fantasy-thriller: Demonic imp seeks missing gold

Leprechaun 2
1994, (USA), Trimark, color, 85 mins.
W: Warwick Davis (*The Leprechaun*), Charlie Heath (*Cody*), Shevonne Durkin (*Bridget/William's Daughter*), Sandy Baron (*Morty*), Adam Biesk (*Ian*), James Lancaster (*William O'Day*), Linda Hopkins (*The Housewife*), Arturo Gil (*The Drunk at the Pub*), Kimmy Robertson (*The Tourist's Girlfriend*), Clint Howard (*The Tourist*), Andrew Craig (*The Midwestern Dad*), Dave Powledge (*Frank*), Billy Beck (*The Homeless Man*), Martha Hackett (*The Detective*), Jonathan P. Perkins (*The Partner*), Tony Cox (*The Afro-American Leprechaun*), Mark Keily (*The Talent Agent*), Michael James McDonald (*The Waiter*), Warren A. Stevens (*Wiggins*), Matthew Anderson (*Mat*)
P: Donald P. Borchers   **D:** Rodman Flender   **SCR:** Turi Meyer & Al Septien, from characters created by Mark Jones   **PHOTOG:** Jane Castle   **MUSIC:** Jonathan Elias
Standard fantasy-thriller: Leprechaun seeks human bride

Leprechaun 3
1995, (USA), Trimark, video, color, 93 mins.
W: Warwick Davis, John Gatins, Lee Armstrong, John DeMita, Michael Callan Caroline Williams, Marcelo Tubert
D: Brian Trenchard-Smith   **SCR:** David Dubos, from characters created by Mark Jones   **PHOTOG:** David Lewis   **MUSIC:** Dennis Michael Tenney
Made-for-Video, standard fantasy-thriller: Murderous imp pursues college student

Leprechaun 4: In Space
1997, (USA), color, 95 mins.
W: Warwick Davis, Brent Jasmer
Minor fantasy-thriller: Sadistic gnome tries to conquer universe

Lesbian Twins
see Virgin Witch

The Lesser Evil
1912, (USA), Biograph, b&w
W: Alfred Paget, Blanche Sweet, Mae Marsh (*as an extra*)
D: D.W. Griffith
Standard thriller: Girl captured by smugglers

Let Me Call You Sweetheart
1997, (USA), FAM-TV, color, 95 mins.
W: Meredith Baxter, Victor Garber, Nick Mancuso, Colin Fox, Joe List, Elizabeth Shepherd, Art Hindle, Sophie Lang, Louis Del Grande, Tony Lo Bianco
D: Bill Corcoran   **TELEPLAY:** Christopher Lofton, from Mary Higgins Clark's novel   **PHOTOG:** Laszlo George   **MUSIC:** Domenic Troiano
TVM, standard thriller: Woman D.A. probes 11-year-old murder

Let's Kill Uncle
1966, (USA), Univ, color, 92 mins.
W: Nigel Green, Mary Badham, Pat Cardi, Robert Pickering, Linda Lawson, Nestor Paiva
P & D: William Castle   **SCR:** Mark Rodgers. Based on Rohan O'Grady's novel
PHOTOG: Harold Lipstein   **MUSIC:** Herman Stein
Standard thriller: Man covets inheritance, tries to kill nephew

Let's Live Again
1948, (USA), 20th-Fox, b&w

W: John Emery, Diana Douglas, Hillary Brooke, James Millican
Standard comedy, man reincarnated as dog

Let's Scare Jessica to Death
1971, (USA), Jessica Co./Para, color, 89 mins.
W: Zohra Lampert (*Jessica*), Barton Heyman (*Duncan*), Kevin O'Connor (*Woody*), Gretchen Corbett (*The Girl*), Mariclare Costello (*Emily*), Alan Manson (*Dorker*)
P: Charles B. Moss Jr.   **D:** John Hancock   **SCR:** Norman Jonas & Ralph Rose
PHOTOG: Bob Baldwin   **MUSIC:** Orville Stoeber
Unusual horror-thriller: Woman suspects drifter is vampiric ghost

A Letter to the Princess
1912, (GB), Edison, b&w, 1,000 ft. (304.8m)
W: Mary Fuller (*Mary*), Marc McDermott (*Lt. Straker*), Miriam Nesbitt (*The Spy*), Stewart Dyer (*Rev. W. Cooper*)
D: Ashley Miller   **STORY:** Bannister Merwin
Standard thriller: Spy seeks secret letter

Letters to an Unknown Lover
1985, (GB-Fr), color, 101 mins.
W: Cherie Lunghi, Yves Beneyton, Mathilda May, Ralph Bates, Andrea Ferreol
D: Peter Duffell, from a story by Pierre Boileau & Thomas Narcejac
Standard thriller: Escaped POW poses as dead friend, meets two enigmatic sisters

Der Letzte Mann (The Last Laugh)
1924, (Ger), Ufa/Univ, b&w, 6,680 ft. (2036m/74 mins.)
W: Emil Jannings, Maly Delschaft Kurt Hiller, Emilie Kurz, Hans Unterkircher, Georg John
P: Erich Pommer   **D:** F.W. Murnau   **SCR:** Carl Mayers   **PHOTOG:** Karl Freund
Classic melodrama: Angst of belittled men's-room attendant

Die Leuchter des Kaisers (The Emperor's Candlesticks)
1936, (Austria), b&w
W: Heinz Ruhmann
Standard melodrama

Leviathan
1989, (USA), Gordon Co./MGM, color, 103 mins.
W: Peter Weller (*Beck*), Richard Crenna (*Doc*), Amanda Pays (*Willie*), Ernie Hudson (*Jones*), Hector Elizondo, Daniel Stern, Meg Foster, Michael Carmine, Lisa Eilbacher
D: George Cosmatos   **SCR:** David Peoples & Jeb Stuart   **PHOTOG:** Alex Thomson   **DESIGN:** Ron Cobb
Standard SF-horror: Underwater mining crew meets botched genetic experiment

Liane, das Madchen aus dem Urwald (Liane, the Jungle Girl)
1958, (W. Ger), DCA, b&w, 85 mins.
W: Marion Michael (*Liane*), Hardy Kruger
D: Eduard Borsody
A.k.a. Liane, Jungle Goddess
Standard adventure-thriller

Liane, Jungle Goddess
see Liane, das Madchen aus dem Urwald

Liar Liar
1997, (USA), Imagine Entertainment/Univ, color, 86 mins.
W: Jim Carrey (*Fletcher Reede*), Maura Tierney (*Audrey Reede*), Jennifer Tilly (*Samantha Cole*), Swoosie Kurtz, (*Dana Appleton*), Jason Bernard (*Judge Marshall Stevens*), Ann Haney (*Greta*), Justin Cooper (*Max Reede*), Amanda Donohoe, Cary Elwes, Mitchell Ryan, Justin Cooper, Chip Mayer, Ed Trotta
P: Brian Grazer   **D:** Tom Shadyac   **SCR:** Paul Guay & Stephen Mazur   **PHOTOG:** Russell Boyd   **SCORE COMPOSED & CONDUCT:** John Debney
Amusing comedy-fantasy: Spell makes man tell truth for 24 hours. Inspired by Nothing but the Truth

Licence Revoked
see Licence to Kill (1989)

Licence to Kill
1989, (GB), MGM-UA, color, 135 mins.
W: Timothy Dalton (*James Bond*), Carey Lowell (*Pam Bouvier*), Robert Davi (*Franz Sanchez*), Talisa Soto (*Lupe Lamora*), Anthony Zerbe (*Milton Krest*), Wayne Newton (*Prof. Joe Butcher*), David Hedison (*Felix Leiter*), Desmond Llewelyn ("*Q*"), Robert Brown ("*M*"), Priscilla Barnes, Don Stroud, Pedro Armendariz Jr.
D: John Glen   **SCR:** Michael G. Wilson & Richard Maibaum, from characters created by Ian Fleming   **PHOTOG:** Alec Mills   **MUSIC:** Michael Kamen
orig. to be titled Licence Revoked
Standard adventure-melodrama: Secret agent opposes drug czar

Licensed to Kill
1965, (GB), Alistair/Ward, Embassy, color, 97 mins.
W: Tom Adams (*Charles Vine*), Karel Stepanek (*Henrik Jacobsen*), Veronica Hurst (*Julia Lindberg*), Francis De Wolff (*Walter Pickering*), Peter Bull (*Masterman*), John Arnatt (*Rockwell*), Felix Felton (*Tetchkinov*), George Pastell (*The Commissar*), Judy Huxtable (*The Computer Girl*), Tony Wall (*Sadistikov*), Billy

Milton (*Wilson*), Stuart Saunders (*The Inspector*), Claire Gordon
D: Lindsay Shonteff   **SCR:** Howard Griffiths & Lindsay Shonteff   **PHOTOG:** Terry Maher   **MUSIC:** Bertram Chappell
USA retitle, **The 2nd Best Secret Agent in the Whole Wide World**
Standard comedy-thriller: British agent protects inventor of anti-gravity device

Licensed to Love and Kill
1979, (GB), Shonteff/Palm Springs/Firebird, color, 94 mins.
W: Gareth Hunt (*Charles Bind*), Nick Tate (*Jensen Fury*), Fiona Curzon (*Carlotta Muff Dangerfield*), Geoffrey Keen (*Stockwell*), Gary Hope (*Sen. Orchid*), Jay Benedict (*The Professor*), Don Fellows (*The Vice-President*), Me Me Lai (*Madam Wang*), Eiji Kusuhara (*Madam Wang {male}*), John Arnatt (*Merlin*), Toby Robins (*Scarlet Star*), Noel Johnson (*Lord Dangerfield*), John Junkin (*The Mechanic*), Imogen Hassall (*Miss Martin*), Douglas Robinson (*The Giant*), Deep Roy (*The Midget*)
P: Elizabeth Gray & Lindsay Shonteff   **D:** Lindsay Shonteff   **STORY:** Jeremy Lee Francis   **PHOTOG:** Bill Paterson   **MUSIC:** Simon Bell
Standard thriller: Secret agent foils plot to replace US president with duplicate created by mad scientist

License to Kill (1964)
see Nick Carter va Tout Casser

Lieutenant Daring, Aerial Scout
1914, (GB), B&C/DFSA, b&w, 1,760 ft. (536.4m)
W: Harry Lorraine (*Lt. Daring*)
D: Ernest G. Batley
Standard crime-thriller: Spy wrecks lieut's airplane, hangs him upside down in straitjacket

Lieutenant Daring and the Dancing Girl
1913, (GB), B&C/MP, b&w, 1,742 ft. (531m)
W: Percy Moran (*Lt. Daring*), Dorothy Foster (*The Dancing Girl*)
D: Charles Raymond
Standard crime-thriller: Lieutenant in Jamaica saves dancer from jealous lover's mob

Lieutenant Daring and the International Jewl Thieves
see Lieutenant Daring and the Mystery of Room 41

Lieutenant Daring and the Labour Riots
1913, (GB), B&C/MP, b&w, 1,242 ft. (378.6m)
W: Percy Moran (*Lt. Daring*), Dorothy Foster (*Edith Carr*), J. O'Neil Farrell (*Oswald Carr*), Charles Raymond (*The Agitator*)
D: Charles Raymond
Standard crime-thriller: Rioting workers set plantation afire

Lieutenant Daring and the Mystery of Room 41
1913, (GB), B&C/DFSA, b&w, 2,270 ft. (691.9m)
W: Harry Lorraine (*Lt. Daring*), George Foley (*The Thief*)
D: Charles Weston
USA retitle, **Lieutenant Daring and the International Jewel Thieves**
Standard adventure-thriller: Lieutenant trails American hotel-robber

Lieutenant Daring and the Photographing Pigeon
1912, (GB), B&C/MP, 1,245 ft. (379.5m)
W: Percy Moran (*Lt. Daring*), Ivy Martinek (*The Girl*), W. Gladstone Haley (*The Spy*)
D: H.O. Martinek   **STORY:** Harold Brett
Standard adventure-thriller: Lieutenant saves spy's daughter from fire

Lieutenant Daring and the Plans of the Minefields
1912, (GB), B&C/MP, b&w, 1,425 ft. (434.3m)
W: Percy Moran (*Lt. Daring*), Dickie Thorpe (*Marcella*), Charles Raymond (*Leon Scumwasser*), Lt. E.H. Hotchkiss, Charles Austin
D: H.O. Martinek   **STORY:** Harold Brett
USA retitle, **The International Spies**
Standard adventure-thriller: Spy pursued in France

Lieutenant Daring and the Ship's Mascot
1912, (GB), B&C/MP, b&w, 1,120 ft. (341.1m)
W: Percy Moran (*Lt. Daring*), Dorothy Foster (*Margherita*), Fred Rains (*Miguel*), Sam Jones (*Jumbo*)
D: Dave Aylott   **STORY:** Harold Brett
Standard adventure-thriller: Lieutenant menaced by Algerian brigands

Lieutenant Daring and the Stolen Invention
1914, (GB), B&C/DFSA, b&w, 1,864 ft. (568.1m)
W: James Russell (*Lt. Daring*), George Foley (*The Officer*)
D: Ernest G. Batley
Standard crime-thriller: Lieut. escapes spies, swims to recover model submarine

Lieutenant Daring Avenges an Insult to the Union Jack
1912, (GB), B&C/MP, b&w, 625 ft. (190.5m)
W: Percy Moran (*Lt. Daring*), Fred Paul (*Paulo*)
D: Dave Aylott   **STORY:** Harold Brett
Standard crime-thriller: Lieutenant tracks Corsican brigands

Lieutenant Pimple and the Stolen Submarine
1914, (GB), Folly Films/Phoenix, b&w, 950 ft. (289.6m)
W: Fred Evans (*Pimple*)

WRIT & D: Fred Evans & Joe Evans
Standard comedy-thriller: Lt. poses as diver, saves submarine from Soho spies

Lieutenant Rose and the Boxers
1911, (GB), Clarendon, b&w, 905 ft. (275.8m)
W: P.G. Norgate (*Lt. Rose*)
D: Percy Stow
Standard adventure-thriller: Chinese rob embassy, disguised lieutenant summons help

Lieutenant Rose and the Chinese Pirates
1910, (GB), Clarendon, b&w, 800 ft. (243.8m)
W: P.G. Norgate (*Lt. Rose*)
D: Percy Stow
Standard adventure-thriller: Laundryman imprisons lieutenant and girls in sea cave

Lieutenant Rose and the Foreign Spy
1910, (GB), Clarendon, b&w, 990 ft. (301.8m)
W: P.G. Norgate (*Lt. Rose*)
D: Percy Stow
Standard thriller: Lieutenant escapes capture, unmasks Moor posing as sailor

Lieutenant Rose and the Gun-Runners
1910, (GB), Clarendon, b&w, 810 ft. (246.9m)
W: P.G. Norgate (*Lt. Rose*)
D: Percy Stow
Standard thriller: Lieutenant poses as woman, saves governor's daughter from rebels

Lieutenant Rose and the Hidden Treasure
1912, (GB), Clarendon, b&w, 1,420 ft. (432.8m)
W: P.G. Norgate (*Lt. Rose*)
D: Percy Stow
Standard adventure-thriller: Lieutenant finds treasure in underground cave, Portugese don interfers

Lieutenant Rose and the Moorish Raiders
1912, (GB), Clarendon, b&w, 840 ft. (256m)
W: P.G. Norgate (*Lt. Rose*)
D: Percy Stow
Standard adventure-thriller: Lieutenant poses as Moor, escapes besieged embassy

Lieutenant Rose and the Patent Aeroplane
1912, (GB), Clarendon, b&w, 1,075 ft. (327.7m)
W: P.G. Norgate (*Lt. Rose*), Dorothy Bellew (*The Girl*)
D: Percy Stow
Standard adventure-thriller: Lieutenant escapes from spy's schooner

Lieutenant Rose and the Royal Visit
1911, (GB), Clarendon, b&w, 1,090 ft. (332.2m)
D: Percy Stow
Standard adventure-thriller: Lieutenant battles anarchist intent on blowing up King's ship

Lieutenant Rose and the Sealed Orders
1914, (GB), Clarendon, b&w, 2,335 ft. (711.7m)
W: Harry Lorraine (*Lt. Rose*)
D: Percy Stow   **STORY:** Jack W. Bobin
Standard crime-thriller: Lieutenant pursues criminal count

Lieutenant Rose and the Stolen Code
1911, (GB), Clarendon, b&w, 915 ft. (278m)
W: P.G. Norgate (*Lt. Rose*)
D: Percy Stow
Standard adventure-thriller: Foreign agent poses as woman, tries to steal code

Lieutenant Rose and the Stolen Ship
1912, (GB), Clarendon, b&w
W: P.G. Norgate (*Lt. Rose*)
D: Percy Stow
Standard thriller: Spy poses as captured lieutenant, steals ship

Lieutenant Rose and the Train Wreckers
1912, (GB), Clarendon, b&w, 955 ft. (291.1m)
W: Harry Lorraine (*Lt. Rose*)
D: Percy Stow
Standard crime-thriller: Lieutenant fights train wreckers in tunnel

A Life at Stake
1955, (USA), Filmakers/Gibraltar, b&w, 78 mins.
W: Angela Lansbury, Keith Andes, Jane Darwell
D: Paul Guilfoyle
Standard thriller

Lifeboat
1944, (USA), 20th-Fox, b&w, 96 mins.
W: Tallulah Bankhead (*Constance Porter*), John Hodiak (*Kovac*), William Bendix (*Gus Smith*), Walter Slezak (*Willie*), Hume Cronyn (*Sparks*), Henry Hull (*C.J. Rittenhouse*), Canada Lee (*Joe*), Mary Anderson, Heather Angel
D: Alfred Hitchcock   **SCR:** Jo Swerling, from John Steinbeck's novel   **PHOTOG:** Glen MacWilliams   **MUSIC DIR:** Emil Newman
Classic melodrama: Tension in lifeboat holding survivors of Nazi torpedo attack. Remake: **Lifepod**

L

A Life for a Life

1913, (GB), Cricks/C&M, b&w, 964 ft. (293.8m)
D: Charles Calvert
Standard crime-thriller: Escaped convict strangles doctor

Lifeforce

1985, (GB), Golan-Globus/Cannon/Tri-Star, color, 99 mins, also 116 mins
W: Steve Railsback (*Carlsen*), Peter Firth (*Caine*), Frank Finlay (*Fallada*), Mathilda May (*The Space Girl*), Patrick Stewart (*Dr. Armstrong*), Michael Gothard (*Bukovsky*), Aubrey Morris (*Sir Percy*), Nicholas Ball (*Derebridge*), John Hallam (*Lamson*), Nancy Paul (*Ellen*), John Keegan, Jerome Willis, Christopher Jagger, Bill Malin, Derek Benfield, John Woodnutt, James Forbes-Robertson, Russell Sommers, Peter Porteous, Katherine Schofield, Owen Holder, Jamie Roberts, Patrick Connor, Sidney Kean, Paul Cooper, Chris Sullivan, Milton Cadman, Rupert Baker, Gary Hildreth, Edward Evans, Nicholas Donnelly, Peter Lovstrom, Carl Rigg, Julian Firth, Elizabeth Morton, Geoffrey Frederick, David English, Emma Jacobs, Michael John Paliotti, Christopher Barr, Brian Carroll, Richard Oldfield, Burnell Tucker, Ken Parry, Thom Booker, Michael Fitzpatrick, Richard Sharpe, John Golightly, William Lindsay, David Beckett, Sydney Livingstone, John Edmunds, Haydn Wood
D: Tobe Hooper **SCR:** Dan O'Bannon & Don Jakoby, from a novel by Colin Wilson **PHOTOG:** Alan Hume **SPCL-FX:** John Gant **VS-FX:** John Dykstra **MUSIC:** Henry Mancini
orig. to be titled **Space Vampires**
Lavish but uneven SF-horror: Energy vampires invade Earth

Lifeforce: PETER FIRTH

The Lifeforce Experiment

1994, (Can-GB), color
W: Donald Sutherland, Mimi Kuzyk, Corin Nemec
Standard SF-thriller: Scientist tries to capture human "life force". cf. **The Asphyx**

Lifeform

1996, (USA), color, 90 mins.
W: Cotter Smith (*Case Montgomery*)
*Standard SF-thriller (***Alien** *imitation): Mars Mission returns with blood-thirsty guest*

Life for Ruth

1962, (GB), AFM/Continental, b&w, 91 mins.
W: Michael Craig (*John Harris*), Patrick McGoohan (*Dr. Jim Brown*), Janet Munro (*Pat Harris*), Paul Rogers (*Hart Davis*), Malcolm Keen (*Mr. Harris*), Norman Wooland (*The Crown Counsel*), Megs Jenkins (*Mrs. Gordon*), John Barrie (*Mr. Gordon*), Walter Hudd (*The Judge*), Leslie Sands (*Clyde*), Lynne Taylor (*Ruth Harris*), Michael Aldridge (*Howard*), Basil Dignam (*Mapleton*), Frank Finlay (*Father*), Maureen Pryor (*Mother*)
P: Michael Relph **D:** Basil Dearden **STORY:** Janet Green & John McCormack
USA retitle (1966), **Walk in the Shadow**
Standard melodrama: Religious miner refuses blood transfusion for his dying daughter

The Lifeguardsman

1916, (GB), British Actors/Int-Ex, b&w, 4,279 ft. (1304.2m)
W: Annie Saker (*Princess Dorine*), Alfred Paumier (*Prince Max*), Leslie Carter (*Prince Hugo*), Frederick Volpe (*Lord Chamberlain*), Alfred Bishop (*Gen. Rosenburg*), Cecil Ward (*Baron Strelzer*), Sam Livesey (*Capt. Salzburg*), Fred Kerr (*The Premier*), A.E. Matthews (*Lt. Tosh*), Spencer Trevor (*Lt. Dinkie*), Leslie Henson (*Lt. Spiff*), Cecil Humphreys (*The Valet*), Eva Rowland (*Sylva*), Ninon Dudley (*Nora*)
D: Frank G. Bayly **SCR:** Arthur Shirley & William Deveraux, from a play by Walter Howard
Standard ruritanian adventure: Idiot heir helps wounded prince save princess from forced marriage to usurper

Life is a Circus

1958, (GB), Vale/British Lion, b&w, 84 mins.
W: Bud Flanagan (*Bud*), Jimmy Nervo (*Cecil*), Teddy Knox (*Sebastian*), Charlie

Naughton (*Charlie*), Jimmy Gold (*Goldie*), Eddie Gray (*Eddie*), Shirley Eaton (*Shirley Winter*), Michael Holliday (*Carl Rickenback*), Lionel Jeffries (*Ali*), Joseph Tomelty (*Joe Winter*), Chesney Allen (*Ches*), Eric Pohlmann (*Rickenback*), Maureen Moore (*Rose of Bagdad*)
P: E.M. Smedley Aston **D & SCR:** Val Guest **STORY:** Val Guest, John Warren & Len Heath
Standard comedy-fantasy: Aladdin's lamp helps bankrupt circus thwart rivals

Life, Liberty and Pursuit on the Planet of the Apes

1974, (USA), 20th-Fox, color, 91 mins.
W: Roddy McDowall (*Galen*), Ron Harper (*Alan*), James Naughton (*Ted*), Jacqueline Scott, Michael Strong, Beverly Garland, Normann Burton
D: Arnold Laven & Alf Kjellin from characters created by Pierre Boulle **PHOTOG:** Gerald Perry Finnerman
TVM, minor SF-adventure (culled from 2 episodes of **Planet of the Apes** *teleseries): Astronauts cope on simian-ruled Earth cf.* **Back to the Planet of the Apes**, **Farewell to the Planet of the Apes**, **Forgotten City of the Planet of the Apes** *and* **Treachery and Greed on the Planet of the Apes**

The Life of Moses

1909, (USA), Vitagraph, b&w
D: J. Stuart Blackton
Standard biblical melodrama

Life on a String

1991, (China-GB-Ger), color, 108 mins.
W: Liu Zhongyuan, Huang Lei, Xu Qing, Ma Ling, Zhang Jinzhan, Zhong Ling, Yao Erga
D: Chen Kaige
Unusual mystical fable: Blind master conflicts with pupil

Lifepod

1993, (USA), Trilogy Entertainment/Fox West-TV, color, 120 mins
W: Robert Loggia (*Director Banks*), Ron Silver (*Terman*), Jessica Tuck (*Claire*), Adam Storke (*Kane*), CCH Pounder (*Mayvene*), Kelli Williams (*Rena*), Stan Shaw, Ed Gale, Lisa Waltz, Cork Hubbert
D: Ron Silver. Directing debut **STORY:** Pen Densham, from Jean-Pierre Andrevan's novel *Robots Against Gondohar* **PHOTOG:** Robert Steadman **MUSIC:** Gabriel Yared
TVM, standard SF-thriller (inspired by Hitchcock's **Lifeboat***): Saboteur threatens stranded space travelers*

Life-Saving Up-to-Date

see Le Systeme du Docteur Sonflamort

The Lifetaker

1979, (GB), Onyx/Premier, color, 103 mins.
W: Terence Morgan (*James*), Lea Dregorn (*Lisa*), Peter Duncan (*Richard*), Dimitris Andreas, Leon Silver, Anna Mottram, Paul Beech
WRIT, P & D: Michael Papas **PHOTOG:** Peter Jessop **MUSIC:** Nico Mamangakis
Standard crime-thriller (filmed in 1975): Married woman's young lover framed for her murder

Life without Soul

1915, (USA), Ocean Film Corp., b&w
W: Percy Darrell Standing, Pauline Curley, Jack Hopkins, Lucy Cotton, William W. Cohill, George DeCarlton
D: Joseph W. Smiley, loosely based on Mary W. Shelley's novel *Frankenstein*
Standard fantasy-thriller: Scientist creates life

The Lift

1983, (Belg), Sigma, color, 99 mins.
W: Huub Stapel (*Felix Adelaar*), Willeke van Ammelrooy, Piet Romer, Josine van Dalsum, Gerard Thoolen, Manfred de Graaf, Hans Veerman, Onno Molenkamp, Siem Vroom, Carola Gijsbers van Wijk, Pieter Lutz, Huib Broos, Dick Scheffer, Michiel Kerbosch, Serge-Henri Valcke, Peer Mascini, Cor Witschge, Ab Abspoel, Liz Snoijink, Wiske Sterringa, Isabelle Brok, Arnica Elsendoorn, Ad Noyons, Hans Dagelet, Theo Pont, Aat Ceelen, Kees Prins, Paul Gieske, Emma Onrust, Johan Hobo, Coby Timp, Guus Hoes, Luk van Mello, Matthias Maat, Agnes Schuch, Gervan Groningen, Sydney Kuyer, Jan Anne Drenth
D, SCR & MUS: Dick Maas **PHOTOG:** Marc Felperlaan **SPCL-FX:** Leo Cahn
Unusual thriller: Malevolent elevator kills humans

The Light at the Edge of the World

1971, (USA-Sp-Lichten), Bryna/Jet/Triumfilm/Nat'l General, color, 101 mins.
W: Kirk Douglas (*Will Denton*), Samantha Eggar (*Arabella*), Yul Brynner (*Jonathan Kongre*), Fernando Rey (*Capt. Moriz*), Jean-Claude Drouot (*Virgilio*), Renato Salvatori (*Montefiore*), Massimo Ranieri (*Felipe*), Aldo Sambrell (*Tarcante*), Tito Garcia (*Emilio*)
P: Kirk Douglas **D:** Kevin Billington **SCR:** Tom Rowe, from Jules Verne's novel **PHOTOG:** Henri Decae **MUSIC:** Piero Piccioni
Standard adventure-thriller: Pirates menace lighthouse keeper

Light Blast

1985, (USA), color, 89 mins.
W: Erik Estrada, Michael Pritchard
D: Enzo G. Castellari

Standard SF-thriller: Mad scientist plans to blow up San Francisco

The Lighthouse Keeper
1909, (GB), Walturdaw, b&w, 590 ft. (179.7m)
Standard crime-thriller: Coastguards and lighthouse keeper's daughter nab robbers

Light At The Edge Of The World: KIRK DOUGLAS

Lightning Bolt
1966, (It-Sp), Woolner Bros., color, 96 mins
W: Anthony Eisley (Sennet), Wandisa Leigh (Kary), Diana Lorys, Ursula Parker
P: Alfonso Balcazar   D: Antonio Margheriti   SCR: Alfonso Balcazar & Jose Antonio de la Loma
A.k.a. Operazione Goldman (Operation Goldman)
Minor spy-thriller: Sabotage at Cape Kennedy leads to confrontation in underwater city

The Lightning Change Artist
1899, (Fr), Star, b&w, 40m (131.2 ft./2.2 mins.)
W: Leopoldo Fregoli
D: Georges Melies
A.k.a. The Chameleon Man
Standard fantasy: Illusionist makes 20 character changes

Lightning Field
see The Lightning Incident

The Lightning Incident
1991, (USA), Wilshire Court/USA-TV, color, 95 mins.
W: Nancy McKeon (Martha), Polly Bergen (Carol), Elpidia Carrillo, Tantoo Cardinal, Miriam Colon, Tim Ryan, Gary Clarke, Joaquin Martinez, George Salazar, Sheree Spargo, Dave Adams, George Pompa, Kathleen Erickson, Barbara Glover, Bob Sorenson, Lillie Richardson, Danny O'Haco, Melissa Michaelsen, Brad Michaelson, Jonathan Mincks, George Aguilar, Amanda Rogers
D: Michael Switzer   TELEPLAY: Michael Murray   PHOTOG: Victor Goss   SPCL-FX: Greg Curtis   MUSIC: J. Peter Robinson
orig. to be titled Lightning Field
TVM, standard fantasy-thriller: Woman's infant abducted by American Indian cult

The Lightning Postcard Artist
1908, (GB), Urban, b&w, 325 ft. (99.1m)
D: Walter R. Booth
Standard fantasy short: Drawings come to life

Lightning Strikes Twice
1951, (USA), WB, b&w, 91 mins.
W: Ruth Roman, Richard Todd, Zachary Scott, Mercedes McCambridge, Rhys Williams, Darryl Hickman, Frank Conroy, Byron Foulger, Kathryn Giveney, Jonathan Hale
P: Henry Blanke   D: King Vidor   SCR: Lenore Coffee, from a story by Margaret Echard   PHOTOG: Sid Hickox   MUSIC: Max Steiner
Modest thriller: Actress vacations in Southwest, falls in love with acquitted wife-murderer

The Light of Faith
1922, (USA), b&w, 33 mins.
W: Lon Chaney Sr., Hope Hampton
D: Clarence Brown
Unusual melodrama: Ill woman cured by touching Holy Grail

The Lights O' London
1914, (GB), Barker/Magnet, b&w, 4,000 ft. (1219.2m)
W: Arthur Chesney (Harold Armytage), Phyllis Relph (Hetty Preene), Fred Paul

(Clifford Armytage), Tom H. MacDonald, J. Hastings Batson, Roy Travers, Rolf Leslie
D: Bert Haldane   SCR: Harry Engholm, from a play by George R. Sims
Standard crime-thriller: Framed man escapes jail, saves sweetheart's father from being drowned by cousin

The Light Within
see Der Mude Tod

Light Years
1988, (Fr), Miramax, color, 86 mins.
VOICES: Glenn Close (Ambisextra), Christopher Plummer (Metamorphis), John Shea (Sylvain), Earle Hyman (Maxum), Terrence Mann (The Collective Voice), Jill Haworth, Jennifer Grey
D & ORIG. SCR: Rene Laloux   ADAPT: Isaac Asimov
Animated SF-fantasy: Peaceful planet imperiled

Like Father, Like Santa
1998, (USA), FAM-TV, color, 95 mins.
W: Harry Hamlin, Megan Gallagher, Curtis Black, Roy Dotrice, Stuart Pankin, Gary Coleman, William Hootkins, Michael Munoz
D: Michael Scott   TELEPLAY: Mark Valenti   PHOTOG: John Fleckenstein   MUSIC: Philip Giffin
TVM, standard fantasy: Man substitutes for Saint Nick

Lila
see Mantis in Lace

Li'l Abner
1940, (USA), Astor/Vogue Pictures/RKO Radio, b&w, 78 mins.
W: Granville Owen (Li'l Abner), Martha O'Driscoll (Daisy Mae), Buster Keaton (Lonesome Polecat), Mona Ray (Mammy Yokum), Johnnie Morris (Pappy Yokum), Kay Sutton (Wendy Wilecat), Billie Seward (Cousin Delightful), Edgar Kennedy (Cornelius Cornpone), Maude Eburne (Granny Scraggs), Johnny Arthur (Montague), Lucien Littlefield (The Sheriff/Mr. Oldtimer), Walter Catlett (The Barber), Bud Jamison (Hairless Joe), Charles A. Post (Earthquake McGoon), Joan Standing (Kitty Hoops), Frank Wilder (Abliah Gooch), Dick Elliott (Marryin' Sam), Chester Conklin (Mayor Gurgle), Mickey Daniels (Cicero Grunts), Doodles Weaver (Hannibal Hoops), Marie Blake (Miss Lulubell), Renie Riano (Sarah Jones), Al St. John (Joe Smithpan), Eddie Gribbon (Barney Bargrease), Heinie Conklin (A Bachelor), Hank Mann (A Bachelor), Eddie Borden (A Bachelor), Vic Potel (Fantastic Brown), Salomey (herself)
P: Milton Berle   D: Albert S. Rogell   SCR: Charles Kerr & Tyler Johnson, from Al Capp's comic strip   PHOTOG: Harry Jackson   MUSIC: Lud Gluskin
Minor comedy-fantasy: Exaggerated adventures of hill people

Li'l Abner
1959, (USA), Para, color, 114 mins.
W: Peter Palmer (Li'l Abner), Leslie Parrish (Daisy Mae), Stubby Kaye (Marryin' Sam), Stella Stevens (Apassionata von Climax), Julie Newmar (Stupefyin' Jones), Jerry Lewis ("Dogpatch Boy"-Itchy), Howard St. John, Robert Strauss, Billie Hayes, Joe E. Marks
P: Norman Panama   D: Melvin Frank   SCR: Melvin Frank & Norman Panama, from their stage play, based on characters created by Al Capp   PHOTOG: Daniel L. Fapp   MUSIC: Gene De Paul & Johnny Mercer   SONG: Jubilation T. Cornpone
Tuneful comedy-fantasy: Hillbilly family goes to D.C.

Liliom
1930, (USA), Fox, b&w, 11 reels (8,472 ft./2582.3m/94 mins.)
W: Charles Farrell (Liliom), Rose Hobart (Julie), Estelle Taylor (Mme. Muskat), Walter Abel (The Carpenter), Lee Tracy (Buzzard), H.B. Warner (The Chief Magistrate), James A. Marcus (Linzman), Mildred Van Dorn (Marie), Bert Roach (Wolf), Guinn Williams (Hollinger), Lillian Elliot (Aunt Hulda), Dawn O'Day (Louise)
D: Frank Borzage   SCR: S.N. Behrman & Sonya Levien, from Ferenc Molnar's play   PHOTOG: Chester Lyons   MUSIC: Richard Fall   LYRICS: Richard Fall & Marcella Gardner   SONGS: Dream of Romance, & Thief Song
Classic fantasy: Spirit of Budapest carnival man checks up on family cf. Carousel

Liliom
1933, (Fr), S.A.F/Fox, b&w, 120 mins.
W: Charles Boyer, Madeleine Ozeray, Robert Arnoux, Antonin Artaud, Florelle, Viviane Romance, Mila Parely
P: Erich Pommer   D: Fritz Lang   SCR: Fritz Lang & Robert Liebmann, from Ferenc Molnar's play   PHOTOG: Rudolph Mate & Louis Nee
Standard fantasy: Spirit visits world of living

Lilith
1964, (USA), Centaur/Col, b&w, 126 mins.
W: Jean Seberg (Lilith), Warren Beatty, Kim Hunter, Peter Fonda, Anne Meacham, James Patterson, Gene Hackman, Jessica Walter
P & D: Robert Rossen (Last film)   SCR: Robert Rossen & Robert Alan Aurthur, from J.R. Salamanca's novel   PHOTOG: Eugen Schufftan   MUSIC: Kenyon Hopkins
Celebrated psychodrama: Schizophrenic girl draws hospital attendant into sensual fantasy-world

L

The Lilliputian Minuet
see *Le Menuet Lilliputien*

The Limbic Region
1996, (USA), SHO-TV, color, 90 mins.
W: Edward James Olmos (*Jon Lucca*), George Dzundza
Made-for-Cable, standard thriller: Ailing detective tracks San Francisco serial killer

Limbo Line
1968, (GB), Trio-Group W, color, 99 mins.
W: Craig Stevens (*Manston*), Kate O'Mara (*Irina*), Vladek Sheybal (*Oleg*), Eugene Deckers (*Cadillet*), Moira Redmond (*Ludmilla*), Yolande Turner (*Pauline*), Jean Marsh (*Dilys*), Rosemary Rogers (*Joan Halst*), Norman Bird (*Chivers*), Joan Benham (*Lady Faraday*), Robert Urquhart (*Hardwick*), Ferdy Mayne (*Sutcliffe*)
P: William Gell & Howard Barnes   **D:** Samuel Gallu   **SCR:** Donald James, from a novel by Victor Canning
Standard spy-thriller: Intelligence agent rescues Russian ballerina from kidnappers

Limit Up
1989, (USA), color, 88 mins.
W: Nancy Allen, Dean Stockwell, Brad Hall, Danitra Vance, Ray Charles, Rance Howard, Luana Anders, Sally Kellerman
D: Richard Martini
Standard fantasy: Businesswoman makes satanic pact

The Limping Man (1931)
see *Creeping Shadows*

The Limping Man
1936, (GB), Welwyn/Pathe, b&w, 72 mins.
W: Francis L. Sullivan (*Theodore Disher*), Hugh Wakefield (*Col. Paget*), Patricia Hilliard (*Gloria Paget*), Iris Hoey (*Mrs. Paget*), Robert Cochran (*Philip Nash*), George Pughe (*Chicago Joe*), Leslie Perrins (*Paul Hoyt*), Frank Atkinson (*Insp. Cable*), Judy Kelly (*Olga Hoyt*), John Turnbull (*Insp. Potts*)
D & SCR: Walter Summers, from a play by Will Scott
Standard thriller: Three people plot retired traitor's demise

The Limping Man
1953, (GB), Banner/Eros, b&w, 74 mins.
W: Lloyd Bridges (*Frank Prior*), Moira Lister (*Pauline French*), Helene Cordet (*Helene Castle*), Alan Wheatley (*Insp. Braddock*), Leslie Phillips (*Cameron*), Andre Van Gysegham (*The Stagedoorman*), Bruce Beeby (*Kendal Brown*), Rachel Roberts (*The Barmaid*), Robert Harben, Lionel Blair
P: Donald Ginsberg   **D:** Charles de la Tour & Cy Endfield   **SCR:** Ian Stuart Black & Reginald Long, from a story by Anthony Verney
Standard thriller: Actress accused of killing blackmailing smuggler

The Lineup
1958, (USA), Col, b&w, 86 mins.
W: Warner Anderson, William Leslie, Richard Jaeckel, Robert Keith, Mary La Roche, Eli Wallach, Emile Meyer
D: Don Siegel   **SCR:** Stirling Silliphant   **PHOTOG:** Hal Mohr
Classic melodrama: Psycho killers hired to recover heroin haul

Link
1986, (GB), Link/Cannon, color, 103 mins.
W: Elisabeth Shue (*Jane Chase*), Terence Stamp (*Dr. Steven Phillip*), Steven Pinner (*David*), Richard Garnett (*Dennis*), David O'Hara (*Tom*), Kevin Lloyd (*Bailey*), Joe Belcher (*The Taxi Driver*)
P & D: Richard Franklin   **SCR:** Everett DeRoche, from a story by Lee Zlotoff & Tom Ackerman   **PHOTOG:** Mike Molloy   **SPCL-FX SPRVSR:** John Gant   **MUSIC:** Jerry Goldsmith
Modest SF-thriller: Experiments with simians lead to terror

Links of Justice
1958, (GB), Danziger/Para, b&w, 68 mins.
W: Jack Watling (*Edgar Mills*), Sarah Lawson (*Clare Mills*), Robert Raikes (*Averill*), Denis Shaw (*Heath*), Michael Kelly (*Robert Lane*), Kay Callard (*Stella*), Jacques Cey (*Dr. Zelderman*), Jan Holden (*Elsie*), Geoffrey Hibbert (*Edward Manning*)
P: Edward J. & Harry Lee Danziger   **D:** Max Varnel   **STORY:**, Brian Clemens & Eldon Howard
Standard thriller: Burglar-witness proves girl killed husband in self-defense

The Lion's Cubs
1915, (GB), London/Jury, b&w, 2,890 ft. (880.9m)
W: Hubert Willis (*Karl Kampf*), Wally Bosco (*Jules Schoenberg*)
D: Ralph Dewsbury
Standard crime-thriller: German spies gas French generals to gain secret plans, are caught by scouts

The Lion Hunters
1951, (USA), Mono, b&w, 75 mins.
W: Johnny Sheffield (*Bomba*), Ann Todd (*Jean*), Smoki Whitfield (*Jonan*), Morris Ankrum, Douglas Kennedy
from characters created by Roy Rockwood
A.k.a. Bomba and the Lion Hunters

Minor adventure-thriller: Jungle boy battles evil animal trappers

The Lion King
1994, (USA), Walt Disney, color, 88 mins.
VOICES: Matthew Broderick, Rowan Atkinson, Whoopi Goldberg, Jeremy Irons, James Earl Jones, Cheech Marin, Jonathan Taylor Thomas, Moira Kelly, Niketa Calame, Nathan Lane, Ernie Sabella, Robert Guillaume, Madge Sinclair, Jim Cummings
D: Roger Allers & Ron Minkoff   **SCR:** Jonathan Roberts & Irene Mecchi   **MUSIC:** Tim Rice, Hans Zimmer & Elton John   **SONG:** *The Circle of Life*
Superb animated nature-fantasy: Lion cub's adventures

The Lion King II: Simba's Pride
1998, (USA), Walt Disney, color
VOICES: Nathan Lane, Neve Campbell, Jason Marsden, Ernie Sabella
SONGS: *We Are One* & *He Lives in You*
Made-for-Video, standard animated fantasy: Lion grows into adulthood

Lion Man
1936, (USA), Alexander/Normandy, b&w, 63 mins.
W: Jon Hall (*Charles Locher*), Ted Adams, Kathleen Burke
Minor adventure-thriller: White boy raised by African natives, becomes "King of Lions" Based on Edgar Rice Burroughs' story "The Lad and the Lion", made in 1917

The Lion Man (1964)
see *Curse of Simba*

The Lion of Thebes
1964, (It-Fr), Filmes Rome-Société des Films Sirius/Teleworld, color, 87 mins
W: Yvonne Furneaux (*Helen*), Mark Forest (*Arien*), Alberto Lupo, Massimo Serato, Pierre Cressoy, Rosalba Neri, Nerio Bernardi, Carlo Tamberlani, Enzo Fiermonte, Pietro Campannini, Giovanni Messina, Nello Pazzafini
D: Giorgio Ferroni   **STORY:** Andrey De Coligny   **PHOTOG:** Angelo Lotti   **MUSIC:** Francesco De Masi
Engrossing "Sword & Sandal": After Troy's fall, Helen seeks refuge in Egypt—where her beauty again foments revolt

Lipstick
1960, (It), b&w
W: Georgia Moll, Pierre Brice, Bella Darvi, Laura Vivaldi
Minor thriller: Young girl witnesses murder

The Liquidator
1966, (GB), Leslie Elliot/MGM, color, 104 mins.
W: Rod Taylor (*Boysie Oakes*), Trevor Howard (*Mustyn*), Jill St. John (*Iris*), Wilfrid Hyde-White (*The Chief*), Akim Tamiroff (*Sheriek*), David Tomlinson (*Quadrant*), Jeremy Lloyd (*The Young Man*), Eric Sykes (*Griffen*), Derek Nimmo (*Fly*), Gabriella Licudi (*Corale*), John LeMesurier (*Chekhov*), Betty McDowall (*Frances Anne*), Jennifer Jayne (*Janice Benedict*), Heller Toren (*The Ass't*), Jo Rowbottom (*Betty*), Louise Dunn (*Jessie*), Colin Gordon (*The Vicar*), Henri Cogan (*Yakov*), Daniel Emilfork (*Gregory*), Ronald Leigh-Hunt (*Mac*), Scott Finch (*The Operations Officer*), Richard Wattis (*The Flying Instructor*), David Langton (*The Station Commander*), Tony Wright (*Flying Control*), Suzy Kendall (*Judith*)
P: Jon Pennington   **D:** Jack Cardiff   **SCR:** Peter Yeldham, from John Gardner's novel   **PHOTOG:** Ted Scaife   **MUSIC:** Lalo Schifrin & Shirley Bassey
Modest spy-comedy: Innocent hired as gov't assassin

Liquid Dreams
1992, (USA), Northern Arts Entertainment, color, 89 mins, also 92 mins
W: Candice Daly, Mink Stole
Standard SF-mystery: Woman seeks sister's murderer, finds exotic satellite TV station in future Los Angeles

Liquid Love
1913, (GB), Cricks & Martin, b&w, 425 ft. (129.5m)
*reissued (1915) as **Little Grains of Love***
Standard fantasy short: Prof's son squirts people with love-inducing fluid

Liquid Sky
1982, (USA), Z Films, color, 112 mins., also 118 mins.
W: Anne Carlisle, Bob Brady, Paula E. Sheppard, Stanley Knap, Susan Doukas, Alan Preston, Otto Von Wernherr Elaine Grove, Jack Adalist
D: Slava Tsukerman   **PHOTOG & SPCL-FX:** Yuri Neyman   **MUSIC:** Slava Tsukerman, Brenda I. Hutchinson & Clive Smith   **SONG:** *Me and My Rhythm Box*
Bizarre, R-rated, punk-rocker SF: Alien entity kills sex & drugs freaks

Lisa and the Devil
see *House of Exorcism*

The List of Adrian Messenger
1963, (USA-GB), Joel/Univ, b&w, 98 mins.
W: George C. Scott, Dana Wynter, Kirk Douglas, Clive Brook, Jacques Roux, Herbert Marshall, Tony Curtis, Gladys Cooper, John Merivale, Robert Mitchum, Bernard Archard, Frank Sinatra, Burt Lancaster
D: John Huston   **SCR:** Anthony Veiller   **PHOTOG:** Joe MacDonald   **MUSIC:** Jerry Goldsmith   **MAKEUP:** Bud Westmore
Unusual thriller: Murderer dons disguises

Liszt O' Mania

1975, (GB), Goodtimes Enterprises/WB, color, 104 mins.
W: Roger Daltrey (*Franz Liszt*), Sara Kestelman (*Princess Caroline*), Paul Nicholas (*Richard Wagner*), Nell Campbell (*Olga Janine*), Fiona Lewis (*Marie d'Agoult*), John Justin (*Count d'Agoult*), Veronica Quilligan (*Cosima*), Ken Parry (*Rossini*), Ringo Starr (*The Pope*), Imogen Claire (*George Sand*), Andrew Reilly (*Hans von Bulow*), Anulka Dziubinska (*Lola Montez*), Rick Wakeman (*Thor/Siegfried*), Ken Colley (*Frederic Chopin*), Rikki Howard (*The Countess*), Felicity Devonshire (*The Governess*), Aubrey Morris (*The Manager*), Otto Diamant (*Mendelssohn*), Murray Melvin (*Berlioz*), Andrew Faulds (*Richard Strauss*), Oliver Reed (*The Servant*)
P: Roy Baird & David Putnam   D & SCR: Ken Russell   PHOTOG: Peter Suschitsky   MUSIC: Rick Wakeman
Outre semi-bio: Erotic adventures of famed musician

Little Bigfoot

1996, (USA), color, 100 mins.
W: P.J. Soles
Made-for-Video, minor fantasy: Woman fights to save baby sasquatch from lumber chief

Little Bigfoot 2: The Journey Home

1997, (USA), color, 95 mins.
W: Stephen Furst, Tom Bosley, Steve Eastin, Taran Noah Smith
Made-for-Video, standard juvenile fantasy: Family saves baby sasquatch from circus

The Little Blue Cap

1910, (GB), Hepworth, b&w, 600 ft. (182.9m)
D: Lewin Fitzhamon
Standard crime-thriller: Boy rescues little girl kidnapped by gypsies

The Little Conjurer

1906, (GB), Walturdaw, b&w, 312 ft. (95.1m)
Standard fantasy short: Boy performs tricks, entertains friends

The Little Death

1995, (USA), color, 95 mins.
W: Pamela Gidley, J.T. Walsh
Made-for-Video, modest thriller: Photographer involved with elderly millionaire's young wife

A Little Devil

see Un Petit Diable

The Little Drummer Girl

1984, (USA), pan Arts/WB, color, 130 mins.
W: Diane Keaton, Yorgo Voyagis, Klaus Kinski, Sami Frey, Michael Cristofer, David Suchet, Eli Danker, Thorley Walters, Kerstin De Ahna, Anna Massey, Robert Pereno, Dana Wheeler-Nicholson, Moti Shirin
D: George Roy Hill   SCR: Loring Mandel, from John Le Carre's novel   PHOTOG: Wolfgang Treu   MUSIC: Dave Grusin
Tepid thriller: Actress involved with Palestinian terrorists

A Little Fire, If You Please

see Un Peu de Feu, S.V.P.

The Little Girl Who Lives Down the Lane

1977, (USA), Zev Braun/AIP, color, 94 mins.
W: Jodie Foster (*Rynn*), Martin Sheen (*Frank Hallet*), Scott Jacoby (*Mario Podesta*), Alexis Smith (*Mrs. Hallet*), Mort Shuman (*Officer Miglioriti*), Dorothy Davis (*The Town Hall Clerk*), Hubert Noel
P: Zev Braun   D: Nicolas Gessner   SCR: Laird Koenig, from his novel   PHOTOG: Rene Verzier   MUSIC: Christian Gaubert & Frederic Chopin
Modest thriller: Orphaned girl preserves her life style by unusual means

Little Ghost

1997, (USA), color, 85 mins.
W: James Fitzpatrick, Trishalee Hardy
Made-for-Video, minor juvenile fantasy: Boy and girl's ghost disrupt movie set in old Italian home

Little Grains of Love

see Liquid Love

The Little Housekeeper

1910, (GB), Hepworth, b&w, 425 ft. (129.5m)
D: Lewin Fitzhamon
Standard crime-thriller: Child hides money in doll, sister gets father to summon cops and nab burglars

Little Jim

1909, (GB), Cricks & Martin, b&w, 375 ft. (114.3m)
D: A.E. Coleby
STORY: based on popular song
Standard fantasy: Miner's son dies, angels waft his soul to Heaven

Little Jim: or, The Cottage was a Thatched One

1902, (GB), Harrison, b&w, 170 ft. (51.8m)
WRIT & D: Dicky Winslow

Standard fantasy short: Angel takes child's spirit to heaven

Little Lady Lafayette

1911, (GB), Natural Colour Kinematograph Co., color, 485 ft. (147.8m)
D: Walter R. Booth & Theo Bouwmeester
Standard fantasy short: Girl transmutes flowers

The Little Match Girl

1914, (GB), Neptune/Browne, b&w, 500 ft. (152.4m)
W: John East (*The Warder*)
D: Percy Nash   from Hans Christian Andersen's story
Standard fantasy: Beggar girl dies in snow

The Little Match Girl

1987, (USA), NBC-TV, color, 95 mins.
W: Keshia Knight Pulliam, William Daniels, William Youmans, John Rhys-Davies, Jim Metzler, Hallie Foote, Robyn Stevan, Maryedith Burrell, Rue McClanahan, Stephen Dimopoulos, Ric Reid, Bernard Cuffling, Charles Andre, Norma MacMillan, Kim Kondrashoff, Nikki Sharp, Tamsin Kelsey, Bill Mankuma, Joy Coghill, Stephen E. Miller, Howard Storey, Franklin Johnson, Bill Davis, David Porayko, Chris Porayko, Scott Porayko, Ted Cole, Tosca Baggoo, Imbert Orchard
D: Michael Lindsay-Hogg   TELEPLAY: Maryedith Burrell   PHOTOG: Kenneth MacMillan   SPCL-FX: Dave Gauthier   MUSIC: John Morris
TVM, standard fantasy: Angel reunites family

The Little Match Seller

1902, (GB), Williamson/Gaumont, b&w, 210 ft. (64m)
D: James Williamson, from Hans Christian Andersen's story *The Little Match Girl*
Standard fantasy short: Waif strikes matches for warmth, angel takes her spirit

The Little Mermaid

1989, (USA), Walt Disney, color, 82 mins.
VOICES: Jodi Benson (*Ariel*), Rene Auberjonois, Christopher Daniel Barnes, Pat Carroll, Buddy Hackett, Kenneth Mars, Samuel E. Wright, Ben Wright, Jason Marin, Edie McClurg, Nancy Cartwright
D & SCR: John Musker & Ron Clements, from Hans Christian Andersen's fairy-tale   MUSIC: Alan Menken & Howard Ashman   SONGS: *Under the Sea, Kiss the Girl & Part of Your World*
Entertaining animated fantasy: Mermaid princess loves mortal

Little Micky the Mesmerist

1913, (GB), Kineto, b&w, 525 ft. (160m)
D: Walter R. Booth
Standard comedy short: Precocious child hypnotizes people

Little Miss Magic

1997, (USA), color, 90 mins.
W: Vanessa Koman (*Deirdre*)
Made-for-Video, minor fantasy: Adventures of teen witch

Little Monsters

1989, (USA), Vestron/UA, color, 100 mins.
W: Fred Savage, Howie Mandel (*Maurice*), Daniel Stern (*Glen Stevenson*), Margaret Whitton (*Holly Stevenson*), Frank Whaley (*Boy*), Rick Ducommun (*Snik*), Ben Savage (*Eric Stevenson*), William Murray Weiss, Devin Ratray, Amber Barretto
D: Richard Alan Greenberg   SCR: Terry Rossio & Ted Elliott   PHOTOG: Dick Bush   MUSIC: David Newman
Standard comedy-fantasy: Creature lures boy into surreal world

Little Nemo

1909, (USA), Winsor McCay, b&w
from a comic strip by Winsor McCay
Animated cartoon: Boy visits dreamland

Little Nemo: Adventures in Slumberland

1992, (Jap), Hemdale, color, 85 mins.
VOICES: Gabriel Damon (*Nemo*), Mickey Rooney (*Flip*), Rene Auberjonois (*Prof. Genius*), Danny Mann (*Icarus*), Bernard Erhard (*King Morpheus*), Laura Mooney (*Princess Camille*), William E. Martin (*The Nightmare King*)   Michael Gough, June Foray, Bert Kramer
P: Yutaka Fujioka   D: Masami Hata & William T. Hurtz   SCR: Chris Columbus & Richard Outten   STORY: Jean Mobius Giraud & Yutaka Fujioka   SCREEN CONCEPT: Ray Bradbury, from a comic strip by Winsor McCay   PHOTOG: Hajime Hasegawa   MUSIC: Thomas Chase & Steve Rucker
Standard animated fantasy: Boy chosen as playmate of King Morpheus' daughter

A Little of Your Blood

see Un Peu de Votre Sang

The Little Prince

1974, (GB), Para, color, 88 mins.
W: Richard Kiley (*The Pilot*), Steven Warner (*The Little Prince*), Bob Fosse (*The Snake*), Donna McKechnie (*The Rose*), Gene Wilder (*The Fox*), Joss Ackland (*The King*), Clive Revill (*The Businessman*), Graham Crowden (*The General*), Victor Spinetti
P & D: Stanley Donen   SCR & LYRICS: Alan Jay Lerner, loosely based on the story by Antoine de Saint-Exupery   PHOTOG: Christopher Challis

MUSIC: Frederick Loewe
Unusual musical fantasy: Child from another world seeks meaning of life

Little Red Monkey
1955, (GB), Merton Park/Anglo-Amalgamated, b&w, 74 mins.
<u>W</u>: Richard Conte *(Bill Locklin)*, Rona Anderson *(Julia)*, Russell Napier *(Insp. Harrington)*, Colin Gordon *(Martin)*, Arnold Marle *(Dushenko)*, Sylvia Langova *(Hilde)*, Bernard Rebel *(Vinson)*, Noel Johnson *(Sgt. Hawkins)*, John Horsley *(Sgt. Gibson)*, Colin Tapley *(Sir Clive Raglan)*
<u>P</u>: Alec Snowden <u>D</u>: Ken Hughes <u>SCR</u>: Ken Hughes & James Eastwood, from a TV serial by Eric Maschwitz
USA retitle, **The Case of the Red Monkey**
Standard thriller: Spy ring assassinates scientists

Little Red Riding Hood (1901)
see Le Petit Chaperon Rouge

Little Red Riding Hood
1911, (GB), Cricks & Martin, b&w, 460 ft. (140.2m).
<u>W</u>: Edwin J. Collins *(The Woodman)*
<u>D</u>: A.E. Coleby
reissued 1916
Standard fantasy: Woodman saves girl from wolf

Little Red Riding Hood vs. the Monsters
1960, (Mex), Calderon/AIP/K. Gordon Murray, color, 82 mins.
<u>P & D</u>: Roberto Rodriguez <u>SCR</u>: Fernando Morales Ortiz & Adolfo Torres Portillo
Juvenile fantasy: Aided by Tom Thumb, girl fights vampire and witch in haunted forest

The Little Savage
1959, (USA), 20th-Fox, color, 72 mins.
<u>W</u>: Pedro Armendariz, Terry Rangno, Christiane Martel
<u>D</u>: Byron Haskin <u>SCR</u>: Eric Norden, from Frederick Marryat's novel <u>PHO-TOG</u>: George Stahl Jr. <u>MUSIC</u>: Raul Lavista
Sentimental adventure: Man marooned by pirates, lives with boy and pet seal

The Little Shop of Horrors
1960, (USA), Filmgroup/AIP, b&w, 71 mins.
<u>W</u>: Jonathan Haze *(Seymour)*, Jackie Joseph *(Audrey)*, Mel Welles *(Mushnick)*, Dick Miller, Myrtle Vail, Lynn Storey, Jack Nicholson, Leola Wendorff, Tammy Windsor, Jack Warford, Toby Michaels, Merri Welles, John Shaner, Wally Campo, Dodie Drake
<u>P & D</u>: Roger Corman <u>SCR</u>: Charles B. Griffith <u>PHOTOG</u>: Archie Dalzell
<u>MUSIC</u>: Fred Katz
Minor but classic SF-fantasy: Moronic florist's apprentice nurtures blood-drinking plant cf. **Please Don't Eat My Mother**

Little Shop Of Horrors (1960): JACK NICHOLSON AND JONATHAN HAZE

Little Shop of Horrors
1986, (USA-GB), Frank Oz/Geffen/WB, color, 93 mins.
<u>W</u>: Rick Moranis *(Seymour Krelborn)*, Ellen Greene *(Audrey)*, Vincent Gardenia *(Mushnik)*, Steve Martin *(Orin Scrivello)*, Tichina Arnold *(Crystal)*, Tisha Campbell *(Chiffon)*, Michelle Weeks *(Ronette)*, James Belushi *(Patrick Martin)*, John Candy *(Wink)*, Bill Murray *(Arthur Denton)*, Christopher Guest *(The First Customer)*, Stanley Jones *(The Narrator)*, Levi Stubbs *(Voice of Audrey II)*, Bertice Reading *("Downtown" Old Woman)*, Ed Wiley *("Downtown" Bum #1)*, Alan Tilvern *("Downtown" Bum #2)*, John Scott Martin *("Downtown" Bum #3)*, Vincent Wong *(The Chinese Florist)*, Mak Wilson, Danny Cunningham, Danny John-Jules, Gary Palmer, Paul Swaby, Mildred Shay, Melissa Wiltsie, Kevin Scott, Barbara Rosenblat, Adeen Fogle, Paul Reynolds, Kelly Huntley, Miriam Margolyes, Peter Whitman, Abbie Dabner, Frank Dux, Heather Henson, Doreen Hermitage, Judith Morse, Bob Sherman, Kerry Shale, Robert Arden, Bob Sessions, Stephen Hoye, Michael J. Shannon
<u>D</u>: Frank Oz <u>SCR</u>: Howard Ashman, from an orig. scr by Charles B. Griffith
<u>LYRICS</u>: Howard Ashman <u>PHOTOG</u>: Robert Paynter <u>MUSIC</u>: Alan Menken <u>ORIG. MOTION PICTURE SCORE</u>: Miles Goodman <u>MUSIC</u>

<u>P</u>: Bob Gaudio
Major comedy-fantasy musical: Intelligent plant alters life of nerdy florist

The Littlest Angel
1960, (Mex), K. Gordon Murray, color
<u>W</u>: Maria Gracia, Jorge Martinez de Havos
<u>NARRATOR</u>: Hugh Downs
Minor fantasy

The Littlest Angel
1969, (USA), ABC-TV, color, 77 mins.
<u>W</u>: Johnny Whitaker *(Michael)*, Fred Gwynne, E.G. Marshall, Cab Calloway, Tony Randall, Connie Stevens, James Coco
from Charles Tazewell's story
TVM, minor fantasy: Youngster has difficulty adapting to life in heaven

The Littlest Warrior
1962, (Jap), Signal, color
Minor animated fantasy

Little Witches
1997, (USA), color, 95 mins.
<u>W</u>: Sheeri Rappaport, Jennifer Rubin, Mimi Reichmeister, Jack Nance, Zelda Rubenstein
Made-for-Video, minor fantasy-thriller: Teen sorceresses conjure up demon

The Little Wire-Walker
1910, (GB), Walturdaw, b&w, 595 ft. (181.4m)
Standard crime-thriller: Girl traverses telephone wires, brings police when burglar stabs mother

A Little Town in France
see Le Corbeau

Live Again, Die Again
1974, (USA), Univ/ABC-TV, color, 74 mins.
<u>W</u>: Donna Mills, Cliff Potts, Vera Miles, Geraldine Page, Walter Pid-geon, Mike Farrell, Peter Bromilow, Irene Tedrow, Stewart Moss, Lurene Tuttle
<u>D</u>: Richard A. Colla <u>TELEPLAY</u>: Joseph Stefano, from novel *Come to Mother*
TVM, unusual SF-thriller: Woman revived after 34 years in suspended animation

Live and Let Die
1973, (GB), Eon/UA, color, 121 mins.
<u>W</u>: Roger Moore *(James Bond)*, Jane Seymour *(Solitaire)*, Yaphet Kotto *(Dr. Kananga)*, Geoffrey Holder *(Baron Samedi)*, Clifton James *(Sheriff Pepper)*, Bernard Lee *("M")*, Julius W. Harris *(Tee Hee)*, David Hedison *(Felix Leiter)*, Gloria Hendry *(Rosie)*, Lois Maxwell *(Miss Moneypenny)*, Tommy Lane *(Adam)*, Earl Jolly Brown *(Whisper)*, Roy Stewart *(Quarrel)*, Lon Satton *(Strutter)*, Arnold Williams *(The Cab Driver)*, Ruth Kempf *(Mrs. Bell)*, Joie Chitwood *(Charlie)*, Madeline Smith *(The Beautiful Girl)*, Michael Ebbin *(Dambala)*, Kubi Chaza *(The Sales Girl)*, B.J. Arnau *(The Singer)*
<u>P</u>: Albert R. Broccoli & Harry Saltzman <u>D</u>: Guy Hamilton <u>SCR</u>: Tom Mankiewicz, from Ian Fleming's novel <u>PHOTOG</u>: Ted Moore <u>MUSIC</u>: George Martin <u>TITLE</u>: Paul McCartney & Wings
Exciting spy-thriller: Secret agent encounters voodoo and narcotics smuggling

A Lively Quarter Day
1906, (GB), R.W. Paul, b&w, 332 ft. (101.2m)
<u>D</u>: J.H. Martin
Standard fantasy short: Conjurer makes furniture return from bailiff's

A Lively Skeleton
1910, (GB), London Cinematograph Co., b&w, 270 ft. (82.3m)
<u>D</u>: S. Wormald
Standard office-comedy short: Girl's suitor uses skeleton to scare away father's patients

The Live Mummy
1915, (GB), Britannia/Pathe, b&w, 924 ft. (281.6m)
Standard comedy: Man poses as Egyptian mummy, fools scientist

The Liver Eaters
see Spider Baby

Live Today, Die Tomorrow
1972, (Jap), Toho, color, 120 mins.
<u>W</u>: Daijiro Harada *(Michio)*, Kei Sato *(The Detective)*, Nobuko Otowa *(Take)*, Kiwako Daichi *(Tomoka)*, Daigo Kusano *(Hanijiro)*, Rokuhiro Toura *(Gondo)*
<u>P</u>: Kindai Elga Kyokai <u>D</u>: Kaneto Shindo <u>SCR</u>: Kaneto Shindo, Shozo Matsuda & Isao Seki <u>PHOTOG</u>: Kuyomi Kurado <u>MUSIC</u>: Hikaru Kayashi
Standard melodrama

Live Today for Tomorrow
see An Act of Murder (1948)

Live to Love
see The Devil's Hand (1961)

The Live Wire
1914, (GB), Big Ben Films-Union/Pathe, b&w, 2,542 ft. (774.8m)

W: Percy Moran (*Blake*), Jack Clair (*The Rival*)
D: George Pearson   **STORY:**, L.C. MacBean
Standard thriller: Jealous engineer tries to electrocute rival

The Living Beheaded
see The Thing That Could Not Die

The Living Coffin
1958, (Mex), K. Gordon Murray, b&w, 79 mins.
W: Maria Duval, Gaston Santos
P: Cesar Santos Galindo   **D:** Fernando Mendez   **SCR:** Ramon Obon, inspired by
   Edgar Allan Poe's short story *The Premature Burial*
Standard horror-thriller: Woman fears being buried alive

The Living Costumes
see Les Costumes Animes

The Living Daylights
1987, (GB), MGM-UA, color, 130 mins.
W: Timothy Dalton (*James Bond*), Maryam d'Abo (*Kara Milovy*), Joe Don Baker
   (*Brad Whitaker*), Jeroen Krabbe (*Gen. Koskov*), John Rhys-Davies (*Gen.
   Pushkin*), Art Malik (*Kamran Shah*), Andreas Wisniewski (*Necros*), Desmond
   Llewelyn ("*Q*"), Robert Brown ("*M*"), Thomas Wheatley (*Saunders*), Walter
   Gotell, Julie T. Wallace
D: John Glen   **SCR:** Richard Maibaum & Michael G. Wilson, from a story by Ian
   Fleming   **SPCL-FX:** John Richardson   **MUSIC:** John Barry
Superior thriller: Soviet defection leads to intrigue in Afghanistan

Live Again, Die Again: PETER BROMILOW, DONNA MILLS AND STEWART MOSS

Living Dead
1932, (Ger), Hoffberg, b&w, 89 mins.
W: Paul Wegener
D & SCR: Richard Oswald
US Title: Extraordinary Tales
*Standard trilogy of tales: (1) Edgar Allan Poe's "The Black Cat" (2) Poe's "The System
   of Dr. Tarr and Professor Fether" & (3) Robert Louis Stevenson's "The Suicide
   Club." cf. **Dr. Terror's House of Horrors** (1943)*

The Living Dead (1934)
see The Scotland Yard Mystery

The Living Dead (1968)
see Isle of the Snake People

Living Dead (1983)
see The Gates of Hell

The Living Dead at Manchester Morgue
1974, (Fr-Sp-It), Hallmark, color, 88 mins.
W: Arthur Kennedy (*The Inspector*), Ray Lovelock (*George*), Cristina Galbo (*Edna*),
   Fernando Hilbeck, Aldo Massasso, Anita Colby
D: Jorge Grau   **SPCL-FX:** Gianetto DeRossi
*USA retitle, **Don't Open the Window***
*Standard SF-horror, Euro-answer to **Night of the Living Dead**: Electronic experiment
   in insect control causes dead to walk*

The Living Doll
see La Poupee Vivante

The Living Ghost (1933)
see The Ghoul (1933)

The Living Ghost
1942, (USA), Mono, b&w, 61 mins.
W: James Dunn (*Nick Trayne*), Joan Woodbury (*Billie Hilton*), Paul McVey (*Ed
   Moline*), Vera Gordon (*Sister Lapidus*), J. Farrell MacDonald (*Lt. Peterson*),
   Norman Willis (*Cedric*), Minerva Urecal (*Delia Phillips*), Jan Wiley (*Tina
   Craig*), George Eldredge (*Tony Weldon*), Edna Johnson (*Helen Craig*), Danny

Beck (*Double-Talker*), Gus Glassmire (*Walter Craig*), Lawrence Grant (*Dr.
   Bruhling*), J. Arthur Young (*George Phillips*), Howard Banks (*Arthur
   Wallace*), Frances Richards (*Dr. Bruhling's Nurse*), Harry Depp (*Homer
   Hawkins*)
P: A.W. Hackel   **D:** William Beaudine   **SCR:** Joseph Hoffman   **ORIG.
   STORY:** Howard Dimsdale   **PHOTOG:** Mack Stengler   **MUSIC DIR:**
   Frank Sanucci
video title, A Walking Nightmare
Minor thriller: Man becomes "scientific killer" (a zombie)

The Living Head
see La Cabeza Viviente

The Living Idol
1957, (USA-Mex), MGM, color, 101 mins.
W: Steve Forrest (*Terry Matthews*), James Robertson Justice (*Dr. Alfred Stoner*),
   Sara Garcia (*Elena*), Liliane Montevecchi (*Juanita*), Eduardo Noriega
   (*Manuel*)
P: Albert Lewin & Gregorio Walerstein   **WRIT & D:** Albert Lewin   **PHOTOG:**
   Jack Hildyard   **MUSIC:** Manuel Esperon & Rudolfo Halffter
Standard horror-fantasy: Girl possessed by evil spirit of jaguar-god idol

The Living Playing Cards
see Les Cartes Vivantes

The Living Statue
see La Statue Animee

Living Statues
1900, (GB), Gibbons' Bio-Tableaux, b&w, 120 ft. (36.6m)
D: Jack Smith
Standard fantasy short: Gallery attendant breaks statue and film reverses

Le Livre Magique (The Magic Book)
1900, (Fr), Star, b&w, 60m (196.9 ft./3.3 mins.)
D: Georges Melies
Standard fantasy

A Lizard in a Woman's Skin
1971, (It-Fr-Sp), Apollo/AIP, color, 96 mins.
W: Florinda Bolkan (*Carol*), Stanley Baker (*Corvin*), Leo Genn (*Edmund*), Jean
   Sorel (*Frank*), Alberto De Mendoza (*The Detective*), Silvia Monti (*Julia*),
   Renny Brown (*The Hippy*), Georges Rigaud
D: Lucio Fulci   **SCR:** Lucio Fulci, Roberto Gianviti, Jose Luis Martinez Molla &
   Andre Tranche   **PHOTOG:** Luigi Kuveiller   **MUSIC:** Ennio Morricone
USA retitle, Schizoid
Standard thriller

Lizzie
1957, (USA), MGM, b&w, 81 mins.
W: Eleanor Parker (*Elizabeth Richmond*), Richard Boone (*Dr. Neal Wright*), Joan
   Blondell (*Aunt Morgan*), Hugo Haas (*Walter Brenner*), Ric Roman (*Johnny
   Valenzo*), Dorothy Arnold (*Elizabeth's Mother*), Marion Ross (*Ruth Seaton*), Jan
   Englund (*Helen Jameson*), John Reach (*Robin*), Gene Walker (*The Guard*),
   Johnny Mathis (*The Nightclub Singer*), Carol Wells (*Elizabeth, age 13*), Karen
   Green (*Elizabeth, age 9*), Dick Paxton (*The Waiter*), Michael Mark (*The
   Bartender*), Pat Gordon (*The Man in the Bar*)
P: Jerry Bresler   **D:** Hugo Haas   **SCR:** Mel Dinelli, based on Shirley Jackson's
   novel *The Bird's Nest*   **PHOTOG:** Paul Ivano   **MUSIC:** Leith Stevens
   SONGS: Hal David & Burt Bacharach
Unusual thriller (overlooked "sleeper"): Woman has three personalities

La Loba (The She-Wolf)
1965, (Mex), Sotomayor, b&w
W: Kitty de Hoyos
Standard horror-fantasy: Woman becomes lycanthropic

Lobster Man from Mars
1989, (USA), Electric Pictures/Filmrullen, color, 84 mins.
W: Tony Curtis, Deborah Foreman Patrick Macnee, Tommy Sledge, Billy Barty,
   Phil Proctor
D: Stanley Shiff
Standard SF-satire: Carnivorous beast runs amok in desert

The Lobster Nightmare
1911, (GB), Walturdaw, b&w, 495 ft. (150.9m)
Standard fantasy short: Diner dreams of hell, Africa, and undersea

Le Locataire Diabolique (The Diabolical Place)
1910, (Fr), Star, b&w, 120m (393./ ft./6.7 mins.)
D: Georges Melies
Standard fantasy

Loch Ness
1996, (GB), Working Title/Polygram, Made for TV, color, 95 mins.
W: Ted Danson (*Dempsey*), Joely Richardson (*Laura MacFeteridge*), Ian Holm (*The
   Water Bailiff*), Kirsty Graham (*Isabel MacFeteridge*), James Frain (*Adrian
   Foote*), Keith Allen (*Gordon Shoals*), Harris Yulin, Nick Brimble
P: Steve Ujlaki   **D:** John Henderson   **SCR:** John Fusco   **PHOTOG:** Clive

L

Tickner **MUSIC:** Trevor Jones
TVM, standard SF-thriller: Adventurer hunts legendary beast

The Loch Ness Horror
1982, (USA), Clan Buchanan/Omni-Leisure Int'l, color, 88 mins.
<u>W</u>: Sandy Kenyon, Miki McKenzie, Barry Buchanan, Eric Scott, Karey-Louis Scott, Doc Livingston, Stuart Lancaster, Garth Pillsbury, Preston Hanson, David Clover, Kort Falkenberg, Pat Musik, Don Myshrall, Dee Buchanan
<u>P & D</u>: Larry Buchanan **SCR:** Larry Buchanan & Lynn Shubert **PHOTOG:** Robert Ebinger Jr. **SPCL-FX:** Image Engineering **MUSIC:** Richard H. Theiss
Minor SF-thriller: Researcher seeks fabled beastie

L

Live and Let Die: ROGER MOORE AND GLORIA HENDRY

Locker 69
1962, (GB), Merton Park/Anglo-Amalgamated, b&w, 56 mins.
<u>W</u>: Eddie Byrne (*Simon York*), Paul Daneman (*Frank Griffiths*), Walter Brown (*Craig*), Edward Underdown (*Bennett Sanders*), Penelope Horner (*Julie Denver*), Clarissa Stolz (*Eva Terila*), John Carson (*Miguel Terila*), John Glyn-Jones (*Insp. Roon*)
<u>P</u>: Jack Greenwood <u>D</u>: Norman Harrison **SCR:** Richard Harris, from a story by Edgar Wallace
Standard thriller: Detective seeks employer's killer

The Locket
1946, (USA), RKO, b&w, 86 mins.
<u>W</u>: Laraine Day (*Nancy*), Brian Aherne (*Dr. Harry Blair*), Robert Mitchum (*Norman Clyde*), Gene Raymond (*John Willis*), Sharyn Moffett (*Nancy, age 10*), Katherine Emery (*Mrs. Willis*), Ricardo Cortez (*Andrew Bonner*), Reginald Denny (*Mr. Wendell*), Henry Stephenson (*Lord Wyndham*), Nella Walker (*Mrs. Wendell*), Fay Helm (*Martha Bonner*), Queenie Leonard (*The Woman Singer*), Helene Thimig (*Mrs. Monks*), Myrna Dell (*Thelma*), Lilian Fontaine (*Lady Wyndham*), Johnny Clark (*Donald*), Ellen Corby, Martha Hyer (film debut)
<u>P</u>: Bert Granet <u>D</u>: John Brahm **SCR:** Sheridan Gibney **PHOTOG:** Nicholas Musuraca **SPCL-FX:** Russell A. Cully **MUSIC:** Roy Webb **MUSIC DIR:** C. Bakaleinikoff
Complex psychodrama: Schizophrenic beauty causes torment

Lock Up Your Daughters
1956, (USA), New Realm, b&w
<u>W</u>: Bela Lugosi
<u>P</u>: Sam Katzman
Minor horror-film compilation: Scenes from 6 of Lugosi's Monogram programmers (including **The Ape Man** *and* **Voodoo Man***)*

Lock Your Doors
see **The Ape Man**

The Lodger
1926, (GB), Gainsborough/Para, b&w, 7,500 ft. (2286m)
<u>W</u>: Ivor Novello (*Jonathan Drew*), June (*Daisy Bunting*), Malcolm Keen (*Joe Chandler*), Marie Ault (*Mrs. Bunting*), Arthur Chesney (*Mr. Bunting*)
<u>D</u>: Alfred Hitchcock **SCR:** Eliot Stannard & Alfred Hitchcock, from Marie Belloc Lowndes' novel
USA retitle, **The Case of Jonathan Drew** *(Artlee, 1928)*
Standard thriller: Girl loves suspected murderer

The Lodger
1932, (GB), Twickenham/W&F, b&w, 85 mins.
<u>W</u>: Ivor Novello (*Angeloff*), Elizabeth Allan (*Daisy Bunting*), Jack Hawkins (*Joe Martin*), A.W. Baskcomb (*Mr. Bunting*), P. Kynaston Reeves (*Bob Mitchell*),

Barbara Everest (*Mrs. Bunting*), Peter Gawthorne (*Lord Southcliffe*), George Merritt (*The Commissioner*), Shayle Gardner (*Snell*), Drusilla Wills (*Mrs.Coles*), Antony Holles (*Sylvano*)
<u>D</u>: Maurice Elvey **SCR:** Ivor Novello, Miles Mander, Paul Rotha & H. Fowler Mear, from Marie Belloc Lowndes' novel
USA retitle, **The Phantom Fiend** *(Olympic, 1935)*
Standard thriller: Girl loves roomer suspected of murder

The Lodger
1944, (USA), 20th-Fox, b&w, 84 mins.
<u>W</u>: Merle Oberon, George Sanders, Laird Cregar, Sir Cedric Hardwicke, Aubrey Mather, Sara Allgood, David Clyde, Olaf Hytten, Queenie Leonard, Billy Bevan, Doris Lloyd, Helena Pickard, Lumsden Hare, Anita Bolster, Edmund Breon, Frederick Worlock, Skelton Knaggs, Forrester Harvey
<u>P</u>: Robert Bassler <u>D</u>: John Brahm **SCR:** Barre Lyndon, from Marie Belloc Lowndes' novel **PHOTOG:** Lucien Ballard **MUSIC:** Hugo Friedhofer **SPCL-FX:** Fred Sersen
Classic thriller: "Jack the Ripper" holds London in grip of fear

Logan's Run
1976, (USA), MGM, color, 118 mins.
<u>W</u>: Michael York (*Logan 5*), Jenny Agutter (*Jessica 6*), Peter Ustinov (*Old Man*), Richard Jordan (*Francis*), Michael Anderson Jr. (*Doc*), Farrah Fawcett-Majors (*Holly*), Roscoe Lee Browne (*Box*), Gary Morgan (*Billy*), Denny Arnold (*Runner #1*), Glen Wilder (*Runner #2*), Lara Lindsay (*The Woman Runner*), Bob Neil (*The 1st Sanctuary Man*), Randolph Roberts (*The 2nd Sanctuary Man*), Camilla Carr (*The Sanctuary Woman*), Roger Borden (*Daniel*), Greg Michaels (*The Ambush Man*), Ann Ford (*The Woman on Lastday*), Michelle Stacy (*Mary Two*), Laura Hippe (*The New You Shop Customer*)
<u>P</u>: Saul David <u>D</u>: Michael Anderson **SCR:** Stanley Greenberg, based on the novel by William F. Nolan & George Clayton Johnson **PHOTOG:** Ernest Laszlo **SPCL-FX:** Glen Robinson **MUSIC:** Jerry Goldsmith
Engrossing SF-thriller: Young man of future flees closed utopian society

Lola Montes
1955, (Fr.-Germ.), color, 140 mins, also 110 mins
<u>W</u>: Martine Carol (*Lola Montes*), Oskar Werner (*The Student*), Peter Ustinov (*The Circus Master*), Anton Walbrook (*The King of Bavaria*), Ivan Desny (*James*), Will Quadflieg (*Liszt*), Lise Delamare (*Mrs. Craigie*), Henri Guisol (*Maurice*), Willy Eichberger A.k.a. Carl Esmond (*The Doctor*), Paulette Dubost (*Josephine*)
<u>D</u>: Max Ophuls **PHOTOG:** Christian Matras **MUSIC:** Georges Auric
"Not so much the story...but the directorial genius of the late Max Ophuls that makes this an unusual, engrossing filmic achievement"—Anon., Frankenstein TV Movieguide, Castle of Frankenstein, Vol. IV, No. 1 (Spring, 1969), p. 60
A.k.a. Sins of Lola Montes
Classic film-bio: Legendary beauty becomes little more than side-show freak

London After Midnight
1927, (USA), MGM, b&w, 7 reels (5,687 ft./1733.4m)
<u>W</u>: Lon Chaney Sr. (*Burke*), Marceline Day (*Lucille Balfour*), Henry B. Walthall (*Sir James Hamlin*), Edna Tichenor (*The Bat Girl*), Conrad Nagel (*Arthur Hibbs*), Percy Williams (*The Butler*), Claude King (*The Stranger*), Polly Moran (*Miss Smithson*)
<u>D</u>: Tod Browning **SCR:** Tod Browning & Waldemar Young, from Tod Browning's novel *The Hypnotist* **PHOTOG:** Merritt B. Gerstad
Unusual thriller: Detective probes old "suicide." cf. **The Mark of the Vampire** *(1935)*

London Blackout Murders
1942, (USA), Rep, b&w, 56 mins.
<u>W</u>: John Abbott, Mary McCleod
Standard thriller: Murderer runs rooming house in war-time London

London by Night
1913, (GB), Barker/Walturdaw, b&w, 3,250 ft. (990.6m)
<u>W</u>: Thomas H. MacDonald (*Dick Ralston*), Doreen O'Connor (*Mary Lucas*), Roy Travers (*Sly Ned*), Joan Scaddan (*Estelle*), J. Hastings Batson (*Sir John Ralston*)
<u>D</u>: Alexander Butler **SCR:** Harry Engholm & Rowland Talbot, from a play by Charles Selby
Standard crime-thriller: Disowned lawyer cleared of killing girl thief

London by Night
1937, (USA), MGM, b&w, 69 mins.
<u>W</u>: George Murphy, Leo G. Carroll, George Zucco, Rita Johnson
Minor thriller

The London Connection
1979, (GB), Walt Disney, color, 84 mins.
<u>W</u>: Jeffrey Byron (*Luther Sterling*), Larry Cedar (*Roger Pike*), Roy Kinnear (*Bidley*), Lee Montague (*Vorg*), Mona Washbourne (*Aunt Lydia*), David Kossoff (*Prof. Buchinski*), Frank Windsor (*McGuffin*), Walter Gotell (*Simmons*), Nigel Davenport (*Minton*), Dudley Sutton (*Goetz*), David Battley (*Peters*), Julian Orchard (*Driscoll*), Kathleen Harrison (*The Lady*), Percy Herbert (*The Captain*), Wolfe Morris (*Dr. Krause*), Don Fellows (*The General*), Bruce Boa (*The Colonel*), Rita Webb (*The Cockney*)
<u>P</u>: Jan Williams <u>D & SP</u>: Robert Clouse **SCR:** Gail Morgan Hickman & David Boston **STORY:** Gail Morgan Hickman, David Boston, David Assael, Joshua Bran <u>D</u>: & Martha Coolidge **PHOTOG:** Godfrey Godar

MUSIC: John Cameron
USA retitle, **The Omega Connection**
Standard thriller: American agent saves kidnapped prof

London After Midnight: LON CHANEY AND HENRY B. WALTHALL

A London Flat Mystery
see The Mystery of a London Flat

A London Mystery
1914, (GB), B&C/Century, b&w, 2,993 ft. (912.3m)
D: Charles Calvert
Standard crime-thriller

London Nighthawks
1915, (GB), H. Ambrose, b&w, 3,000 ft. (914.4m)
W: Percy Moran (*The Man*)
D: Percy Moran
Standard crime-thriller: Artist's brother becomes criminal drug addict

London's Enemies
1916, (GB), Phoenix-Couragio/Phillips, b&w, 4,500 ft. (1371.6m)
W: Percy Moran (*Lt. Jack Moran*), Marietta de Leyse (*Zareda*), Lionel d'Aragon (*The Butler*)
Standard crime-thriller: Lieutenant rescues sister from spies, destroys U-Boat

The London Strangler
see Der Henker von London

London's Underworld
1914, (GB), Daring/Anderson, b&w, 3,800 ft. (1158.2m)
W: Harry Lorraine (*Det. Daring*)
Standard crime-thriller: Detective pursues pearl thieves, saves girl from warehouse fire

London's Yellow Peril
1915, (GB), B&C/Standard b&w, 2,172 ft. (662m)
W: Elizabeth Risdon (*Ruth Graham*), Fred Groves (*Gilbert*), A.V. Bramble (*The Negro*), M. Gray Murray (*Rev. Graham*)
D: Maurice Elvey **SCR:** Eliot Stannard
Standard crime-thriller: Missionary's daughter saved from Chinese opium den

The Lonely House
1957, (GB), Merton Park/Anglo-Amalgamated, b&w, 35 mins.
W: Russell Napier (*Insp. Duggan*), Gordon Needham (*Sgt. Conway*), Frank Forsythe (*Insp. Parry*), Bettina Dickson (*Miss Williams*), Dorothy Bramhall (*Miss Hilton*), Felix Felton (*Gen. Urquhart*), Ludovic Kennedy (*The TV Newsreader*)
P: Alec Snowden **D:** Montgomery Tully **STORY:** James Eastwood, from a novel by Edgar Lustgarten
Standard short crime-thriller: Couple runs bogus marriage bureau

The Lonely Hearts Killers
see The Honeymoon Killers

The Lonely Inn
1912, (GB), Cricks & Martin, b&w, 880 ft. (268.2m)
D: A.E. Coleby
Standard thriller: Innkeeper dies of shock after killing convict son in mistake for rich guest

The Lonely Sex
1959, (USA), Brenner, b&w
W: Jean Evans, Karl Light, Mary Gonzales
P, D, & SCR: Richard Hilliard
Minor thriller: Mad killer kidnaps psychiatrist's daughter

The Lone Ranger
1956, (USA), Jack Wrather/WB, color, 86 mins.
W: Clayton Moore (*The Lone Ranger*), Jay Silverheels (*Tonto*), Bonita Granville (*Welcome*), Lyle Bettger (*Kilgore*), Michael Ansara (*Angry Horse*), Perry Lopez (*Ramirez*), Mickey Simpson (*Powder*), Robert Wilke (*Cassidy*), Beverly Washburn (*Lila*), John Pickard (*Sheriff Kimberly*), Frank de Kova (*Red Hawk*), Charles Meredith (*The Governor*), Zon Murray (*Goss*), Lane Chandler (*Whitebeard*)
P: Willis Goldbeck **D:** Stuart Heisler **SCR:** Herb Meadow **MUSIC:** David Buttolph
A.k.a. **Red Hawk Trail**
Standard adventure-thriller: Masked hero defends Indians against depredations of ranchers

The Lone Ranger (1981)
see The Legend of the Lone Ranger

The Lone Ranger and the Lost City of Gold
1958, (USA), Jack Wrather/UA, color, 80 mins.
W: Clayton Moore (*The Lone Ranger*), Jay Silverheels (*Tonto*), Noreen Nash, Douglass Kennedy, Charles Watts, William Henry, Lisa Montell, Ralph Moody, Norman Fredric, Lane Bradford, John Miljan, Maurice Jara, Belle Mitchell
P: Sherman A. Harris **D:** Lesley Selander **SCR:** Robert Schaefer & Eric Freiwald **PHOTOG:** Kenneth Peach **MUSIC:** Les Baxter
Standard adventure-western: Hunt for talisman portions revealing location of fabled Indian metropolis

The Lone Wolf
1917, (USA), Selznick, b&w, 8 reels
W: Bert Lytell (*Michael Lanyard*), Hazel Dawn (*The Detective*), Cornish Beck (*The Waif*), Stephen Grattan (*Burke*), Alfred Hickman (*Eckstrom*), Ben Graham (*Thibault*), Robert Fisher (*Bannon*), William Riley Hatch (*DeMoriban*), Joseph Chailles (*Popinot*), William E. Shay (*Wertheimer*), Florence Ashbrooke (*Mme. Troyon*)
D: Herbert Brenon **SCR:** George Edwards Hall, from Louis Joseph Vance's novel **PHOTOG:** J. Roy Hunt
Standard thriller: Rogue steals plans for stopping German warfare

The Lone Wolf
1924, (USA), Associated Exhibitors, b&w, 6 reels
W: Jack Holt (*Michael Lanyard*), Dorothy Dalton (*Lucy Shannon*), Wilton Lackaye (*William Burroughs*), Tyrone Power Sr. (*Bannon*), Charlotte Walker (*Clare Henshaw*), Lucy Fox (*Annette Dupre*), Edouard Durand (*Popinot*), Robert E. Haines (*Solon*), Gustav von Seyffertitz (*Wertheimer*), Paul McAllister (*Count de Moriban*), Alphonse Ethier (*Eckstrom*), William Tooker (*The Ambassador*)
D & SCR: S.E.V. Taylor, from Louis Joseph Vance's novel **PHOTOG:** Jack Brown, Albert Wilson & Dal Clauson
Standard thriller: Rogue seeks asylum in USA, agrees to find stolen plans for defense weapon

London Blackout Murders: LLOYD CORRIGAN, FREDERICK WORLOCK, PAX WALKER AND PETER LAWFORD

Lone Wolf
1988, (USA), color, 97 mins.
W: Dyann Brown, Kevin Hart, Jamie Newcomb, Ann Douglas
D: John Calas
Minor horror-thriller: Werewolf terrorizes high school

The Lone Wolf and His Lady
1949, (USA), Col, b&w, 60 mins.
W: Ron Randell (*Michael Lanyard*), June Vincent (*Grace Duffy*), Alan Mowbray (*Jamison*), William Frawley (*Insp. Crane*), Collette Lyons (*Marta Frishbie*), Douglass Dumbrille (*John J. Murdock*), James Todd (*Tanner*), Steven Geray (*Van Groot*), Arthur Space (*Fisher*), Robert Barrat (*Steve Taylor*), Philip Van Zandt (*Joe Brewster*), Jack Over-man (*Bill Slovak*), Fred Sears (*Tex Talbot*), Lee Phelps (*Sgt. Henderson*), Robert B. Williams (*Lt. Martin*), William Newell (*Rockling*), George Tyne (*Paul Braud*), Lane Chandler (*The Policeman*)

D: John Hoffman   **SCR:** Malcolm Stuart Boylan & Edward Dein, from characters created by Louis Joseph Vance   **PHOTOG:** Philip Tannura   **MUSIC:** Mischa Bakaleinikoff
Standard thriller: Rogue suspected of diamond theft

The Lone Wolf in London
1947, (USA), *Col, b&w, 68 mins.*
W: Gerald Mohr *(Michael Lanyard)*, Eric Blore *(Jamison)*, Nancy Saunders *(Ann Kelmscott)*, Evelyn Ankers *(Iris Chatham)*, Richard Fraser *(David Woolerton)*, Queenie Leonard *(Lily)*, Alan Napier *(Monty Beresford)*, Frederick Worlock *(Insp. Broome)*, Denis Green *(Garvey)*, Vernon Steele *(Sir John Kelmscott)*, Tom Stevenson *(Henry Robards)*, Paul Fung *(Bruce Tang)*, Guy Kingsford *(Mitchum)*
D: Leslie Goodwins   **SCR:** Brenda Weisberg & Arthur E. Orloff, from characters created by Louis Joseph Vance   **PHOTOG:** Henry Freulich   **MUSIC:** Mischa Bakaleinikoff
Standard thriller: Rogue blamed for jewel robbery

The Lone Wolf in Mexico
1947, (USA), *Col, b&w, 69 mins.*
W: Gerald Mohr *(Michael Lanyard)*, Sheila Ryan *(Sharon Montgomery)*, Eric Blore *(Jamison)*, Jacqueline de Wit *(Liliane Dumont)*, Nestor Paiva *(Carlos Rodriguez)*, Winifred Harris *(Mrs. Van Weir)*, John Gallaudet *(Henderson)*, Peter Brocco *(Emil)*, Bernard Nedell *(Leon Dumont)*, Alan Edwards *(Charles Montgomery)*, Fred Godoy *(Capt. Mendez)*, Theodore Gottlieb (Brother Theodore) *(The Watchman)*
D: Ross Lederman   **SCR:** Maurice Tombragel & Martin Goldsmith, from characters created by Louis Joseph Vance   **PHOTOG:** Allen Siegler   **MUSIC:** Mischa Bakaleinikoff
Standard thriller: Crooks rope gentleman rogue into conspiracy to steal securities

The Lone Wolf in Paris
1938, (USA), *Col, b&w, 66 mins.*
W: Francis Lederer *(Michael Lanyard)*, Frances Drake *(Princess Thania)*, Olaf Hytten *(Jenkins)*, Albert Dekker *(Marquis de Meyervon)*, Walter Kingsford *(Grand Duke Gregor)*, Maurice Cass *(M. Fromont)*, Leona Maricle *(Baroness Cambrell)*, Eddie Fetherston *(Mace)*, Bess Flowers *(Davna)*, Pio Peretti *(The King)*, Ruth Robinson *(Queen Regent)*, Al Herman *(Otto)*, Dick Curtis *(The Guard)*
D: Albert S. Rogell   **SCR:** Arthur T. Horman   from characters created by Joseph Louis Vance   **PHOTOG:** Lucien Ballard
Standard thriller: Rogue helps princess regain jewels

The Lone Wolf Keeps a Date
1941, (USA), *Col, b&w, 65 mins.*
W: Warren William *(Michael Lanyard)*, Frances Robinson *(Patricia Lawrence)*, Bruce Bennett *(Scotty)*, Eric Blore *(Jamison)*, Thurston Hall *(Insp. Crane)*, Jed Prouty *(Capt. Moon)*, Lester Matthews *(Lee)*, Fred Kelsey *(Dickens)*, Don Beddoe *(Big Joe Brady)*, Edward Gargan *(Chimp)*, Mary Servoss *(Mrs. Colby)*, Eddie Laughton *(Measles)*, Francis McDonald *(Santos)*
D: Sidney Salkow   **SCR:** Sidney Salkow & Earl Fenton   from characters created by Louis Joseph Vance   **PHOTOG:** Barney McGill   **MUSIC:** Morris Stoloff
Standard thriller: Suave rogue rescues girl from gangsters

The Lone Wolf Meets a Lady
1940, (USA), *Col, b&w, 71 mins.*
W: Warren William *(Michael Lanyard)*, Eric Blore *(Jamison)*, Jean Muir *(Joan Bradley)*, Victor Jory *(Clay Beaudine)*, Fred Kelsey *(Dickens)*, Roger Pryor *(Pete Rennick)*, Thurston Hall *(Insp. Crane)*, Warren Hull *(Bob Pennion)*, Robert E. Keane *(Peter Van Wyck)*, Georgia Caine *(Mrs. Pennion)*, William Forrest *(Arthur Trent)*, Marla Shelton *(Rose Waverly)*, Bruce Bennett *(McManus)*, Luis Alberni *(Pappakontus)*
D: Sidney Salkow   **SCR:** John Larkin, from characters created by Louis Joseph Vance   **PHOTOG:** Henry Freulich
Standard thriller: Gentleman rogue helps socialite recover stolen gems

The Lone Wolf Returns
1926, (USA), *Col, b&w, 6 reels*
W: Bert Lytell *(Michael Lanyard)*, Billie Dove *(Marcia Mayfair)*, Freeman Wood *(Mallison)*, Gwen Lee *(Liane De Lorme)*, Gustav von Seyffertitz *(Morpheu)*, Alphonse Ethier *(Insp. Crane)*
D: Ralph Ince   **SCR:** J. Grubb Alexander, from a novel by Louis Joseph Vance   **PHOTOG:** J.O. Taylor
A.k.a. Return of the Lone Wolf
Standard thriller: Rogue involved with socialite and necklace theft

The Lone Wolf Returns
1935, (USA), *Col, b&w, 69 mins.*
W: Melvyn Douglas *(Michael Lanyard)*, Gail Patrick *(Marcia Stewart)*, Tala Birell *(Liane)*, Henry Mollison *(Mollison)*, Thurston Hall *(Crane)*, Raymond Walburn *(Jenkins)*, Robert Middlemass *(McGowan)*, Douglas Dumbrille *(Morphew)*, Frank Reicher *(Coleman)*, Nana Bryant *(Aunt Julie)*, Robert Emmet O'Connor *(Benson)*, Wyrley Birch *(Mr. Cole)*, George McKay *(The Maestro)*, Harry Holman, Eddy Chandler, William Howard Gould, Arthur Rankin, Harry Depp, Arthur Loft, Pat Somerset, John Thomas, Olaf Hytten, Lloyd Whitlock, Harry Harvey, Jack Clifford, Roger Gray, Hal Price, Lee Shumway, Jack Gray, Kernan Cripps
D: Roy William Neill   **SCR:** Joseph Krumgold, Bruce Manning, Lionel Houser

& Robert O'Connell, from characters created by Louis Joseph Vance   **PHOTOG:** Henry Freulich
Standard thriller: Reforming rogue blackmailed by crooks

The Lone Wolf's Daughter
1919, (USA), *W.W. Hodkinson Corp., b&w, 6,800 ft. (2072.6m)*
W: Louise Glaum *(Sonia)*, Edwin Stevens *(Prince Victor)*, Thomas Holding *(Roger Karslake)*, Bertram Grassby *(Michael Lanyard)*
D: J. Parker Read Jr., from Joseph Louis Vance's novel
Complicated thriller: Princess divorces husband: hires gentleman rogue to help conceal incriminating letters

The Lone Wolf's Daughter
1929, (USA), *Col, b&w, 7 reels*
W: Bert Lytell *(Michael Lanyard)*, Gertrude Olmstead *(Helen Fairchild)*, Charles Gerrard *(Count Polinac)*, Lilyan Tashman *(Vilma)*, Donald Keith *(Bobby Crenshaw)*, Ruth Cherrington *(Mrs. Crenshaw)*, Florence Allen *(Adrienne)*, Robert Elliott *(Ethier)*
D: Albert S. Rogell   **SCR:** Sig Herzig   **DIALOG:** Harry Reiver, from characters created by Louis Joseph Vance   **PHOTOG:** James Van Trees
Standard thriller: Reformed rogue encounters jewel thieves

The Lone Wolf Spy Hunt
1939, (USA), *Col, b&w, 67 mins.*
W: Warren William *(Michael Lanyard)*, Ida Lupino *(Val Carson)*, Rita Hayworth *(Karen)*, Virginia Weidler *(Patricia Lanyard)*, Ralph Morgan *(Spiro)*, Tom Dugan *(Sgt. Devan)*, Leonard Carey *(Jamison)*, Don Beddoe *(Insp. Thomas)*, Jack Norton *(Charlie Fenton)*, Ben Welden *(Jenks)*, Helen Lynd *(Marie Templeton)*, Brendon Tynan *(Sen. Carson)*, Irving Bacon *(The Sergeant)*, Marek Windheim *(The Waiter)*, Alec Craig *(The License Clerk)*, Tony (J. Anthony) Hughes *(The Bartender)*, Eddie Laughton *(The Footman)*, Forbes Murray *(Palmer)*, James Blaine *(The Policeman)*, Eddie Fetherston *(The Man)*, Russ Clark *(Evans)*, Landers Stevens *(Thatcher)*, Lee Phelps *(The Police Broadcaster)*, Vernon Dent *(The Fat Man)*, Bud Jamison *(The 2nd Bartender)*, Frank Baker *(The Doorman)*, James Millican *(The Cab Driver)*, Edward Hearn *(The Police Sergeant)*, Edmund Cobb *(The Police Clerk)*, James Craig, Marc Lawrence, Dick Curtis, Lou Davis, Dick Elliott, John Tyrrell, Stanley Brown (late Brad Taylor), Beatrice Curtis, Lola Jensen, Lorna Gray *(Adrian Booth)*
D: Peter Godfrey   **SCR:** Jonathan Latimer, from Louis Joseph Vance's novel *The Lone Wolf's Daughter*   **PHOTOG:** Allen G. Siegler   **MUSIC:** Morris Stoloff
Standard thriller: Gentleman rogue vs. spy ring

The Lone Wolf Strikes
1940, (USA), *Col, b&w, 57 mins.*
W: Warren William *(Michael Lanyard)*, Eric Blore *(Jamison)*, Joan Perry *(Delia Jordan)*, Alan Baxter *(Jim Ryder)*, Astrid Allwyn *(Binnie Weldon)*, Montagu Love *(Emil Garlick)*, Peter Lynn *(Dorgan)*, Robert Wilcox *(Ralph Bolton)*, Harland Tucker *(Alberts)*, Don Beddoe *(Conroy)*, Fred Kelsey *(Dickens)*, Roy Gordon *(Philip Jordan)*, Addison Richards *(Stanley Young)*, Murray Alper *(Pete the Bartender)*, Edmund Cobb *(The 3rd Policeman)*
D: Sidney Salkow   **SCR:** Harry Segall, Albert Duffy & Dalton Trumbo, from characters created by Louis Joseph Vance   **PHOTOG:** Henry Freulich
Standard thriller: Gentleman rogue recovers stolen necklace

The Lone Wolf Takes a Chance
1941, (USA), *Col, b&w, 76 mins.*
W: Warren William *(Michael Lanyard)*, June Storey *(Gloria Foster)*, Henry Wilcoxon *(Frank Jordan)*, Eric Blore *(Jamison)*, Thurston Hall *(Insp. Crane)*, Evelyn Knapp *(Evelyn Jordan)*, Don Beddoe *(Sheriff Haggerty)*, William Forrest *(Vic Hilton)*, Fred Kelsey *(Dickens)*, Walter Kingsford *(Dr. Hopper Tupman)*, Lloyd Bridges *(Johnny Baker)*, Ben Taggart *(The Conductor)*, Richard Fiske *(The Brakeman)*, Tom London *(The Policeman)*, Regis Toomey *(Wallace)*, Irving Bacon *(The Projectionist)*
D: Sidney Salkow   **SCR:** Sidney Salkow & Earl Fenton, from characters created by Joseph Louis Vance   **PHOTOG:** John Stumar
Standard thriller: Gentleman rogue blamed for fiery death of private detective

The Lone Wolf on Broadway
see The Notorious Lone Wolf

The Long Ago
1913, (USA), *Selig, b&w*
W: Wheeler Oakman, Bessie Eyton
Standard thriller: Pitfalls of prehistoric mankind

The Long and Short of It
see The Dwarf and the Giant

The Long Arm
1956, (GB), *Ealing/RFD, b&w, 96 mins.*
W: Jack Hawkins *(Supt. Tom Halliday)*, John Stratton *(Sgt. Ward)*, Dorothy Alison *(Mary Halliday)*, Geoffrey Keen *(Supt. Jim Malcolm)*, Ursula Howells *(Mrs. Gilson)*, Newton Blick *(Cdr. Harris)*, Sydney Tafler *(Stone)*, Ralph Truman *(Col. Blenkinsop)*, Maureen Delany *(Mrs. Stevens)*, Richard Leech *(Gilson)*, Meredith Edwards *(Thomas)*, George Rose *(Slob)*, Ian Bannen *(Stanley James)*, Alec McCowen *(The Surgeon)*, John Warwick *(The Inspector)*, Michael Brooke *(Tony Halliday)*, Arthur Rigby *(The Manager)*, Vincent Ball *(A Constable)*, Nicholas Parsons *(A Constable)*, Stratford Johns *(A Constable)*
D: Charles Frend   **SCR:** Robert Barr, Janet Green, Dorothy Christie & Campbell

Christie   **STORY:** Robert Barr
*USA retitle, **The Third Key***
Modest crime-thriller: Safecracker pursued

The Long, Dark Night
1977, (USA), color, 99 mins.
<u>W</u>: Joe Don Baker, Hope Alexander-Willis
*A.k.a. **The Pack***
Standard thriller: Abandoned dogs attack vacationers

Long Distance
1959, (GB-W. Ger), British Lion/United Producers/Alan Enterprises, b&w, 84 mins
<u>W</u>: Eddie Constantine, Dawn Addams, Christopher Lee, Tsai Chin
<u>D</u>: Alvin Rakoff
*A.k.a. **Hot Money Girl** and **The Treasure of San Teresa***
Standard thriller: OSS man hides jewels in Czech monastery during World War II

Long-Distance Wireless Photography
1908, (Fr), Star, b&w 113m (370.7 ft./6.3 mins)
<u>D</u>: Georges Melies
featuring girls from the Folies-Bergere
Standard SF-fantasy: Predictions of age of television

The Long Hair of Death
see La Sanglante Sorciere

Long John Silver
1954, (Austral), DCA, color, 109 mins.
<u>W</u>: Robert Newton (*Long John Silver*), Kit Taylor (*Jim Hawkins*), Connie Gilchrist (*Purity Pinker*), Rod Taylor (*Israel Hands*), Lloyd Berrell (*Mendoza*), Grant Taylor (*Patch*), John Brunskill (*Old Stingley*), Harvey Adams (*Gov. Strong*), Muriel Steinbeck (*Lady Strong*), Henry Gilbert (*Billy Bowlegs*), Harry Hambleton (*Big Eric*), Ned Shill (*Syd*), Eric Reiman (*Trip Fenner*)
<u>D</u>: Byron Haskin   **STORY: & SCR:** Martin Rackin, inspired by Robert Louis Stevenson's novel *Treasure Island*   **PHOTOG:** Carl Guthrie   **MUSIC:** David Buttolph
Standard adventure-thriller (spawned popular teleseries): Exploits of rascally pirate

The Long Kiss Goodnight
1996, (USA), New Line, color, 103 mins.
<u>W</u>: Geena Davis (*Samantha Caine/Charly Baltimore*), Samuel L. Jackson (*Mitch Hennessey*), Patrick Malahide (*Perkins*), Craig Bierko (*Timothy*), Brian Cox (*Nathan*), David Morse (*Luke/Daedalus*), TomAmandes (*Hal*), Yvonne Zima (*Caitlin*), Joseph McKenna, Rex Linn, Melina Kanakaredes, Dan Warry-Smith, Kristen Bone, Alan North, Jennifer Pisana, Edwin Hodge, Bill MacDonald, G.D. Spradlin, Gladys O'Connor, Frank Moore, Graham McPherson, Sharon Washington, Robert Thomas, John Stead, Marc Cohen, Chad Donella, Shawn Doyle, Debra Kirshenbaum, Ken Ryan, Susan Henley, Craig Eldridge, Chuck Tamburro, Larry King
<u>D</u>: Renny Harlin   **SCR:** Shane Black   **PHOTOG:** Guillermo Navarro   **SPCL VS-FX:** Jeffrey A. Okun   **MUSIC:** Alan Silvestri
Unusual action-thriller: Woman amnesiac discovers she was gov't assassin

The Long Knife
1958, (GB), Merton Park/Anglo-Amalgamated, b&w, 57 mins.
<u>W</u>: Joan Rice (*Jill Holden*), Sheldon Lawrence (*Ross Waters*), Dorothy Brewster (*Angela/The Boy*), Ellen Pollock (*Mrs. Cheam*), Victor Brooks (*Supt. Leigh*), Alan Keith (*Dr. Ian Probus*), Arthur Gomez (*Sgt. Bowles*)
<u>P</u>: Jack Greenwood   <u>D</u>: Montgomery Tully   **SCR:** Ian Stuart Black, from Seldon Truss' novel
Standard crime-thriller: Nurse suspected of stabbing rich patient

The Lookalike: MELISSA GILBERT

The Long Wait
1954, (USA), UA, b&w, 93 mins.
<u>W</u>: Anthony Quinn, Peggie Castle, Charles Coburn, Gene Evans Dolores Donlan, Mary Ellen Kay

<u>P</u>: Lesser Samuel   <u>D</u>: Victor Saville   **SCR:** Alan Green & Lesser Samuels, from a story by Mickey Spillane
Standard thriller: Hitchhiker loses memory and face in fiery high-way smash

The Lookalike
1990, (USA), color, 88 mins.
<u>W</u>: Melissa Gilbert, Diane Ladd, Frances Lee McCain, Jason Scott Lee, Thaao Penghlis
<u>D</u>: Gary Nelson   **WRIT:** Linda J. Bergamn, from a novel by Kate Wilhelm
Made-for-Cable, minor thriller: Mother sees dead daughter's double

Look Back in Darkness
1975, (GB), ATV/ITC, video, color, 74 mins
<u>W</u>: Bradford Dillman, Catherine Schell, Ray Smith, Geoffrey Chater
*A.k.a. **The Next Voice You See***
TVM, standard thriller: Blind pianist recognizes voice of man responsible for his sight loss.

Looker
1981, (USA), Ladd Co./WB, color, 92 mins.
<u>W</u>: Albert Finney (*Dr. Larry Roberts*), Susan Dey (*Cindy*), James Coburn (*John Reston*), Leigh Taylor-Young (*Jennifer Long*), Terri Welles (*Lisa*), Dorian Harewood (*Masters*), Tim Rossovich (*Moustache Man*), Kathryn Witt (*Tina*), Ashley Cox (*Candy*), Darryl Hickman (*Dr. Jim Belfield*), Michael Gainsborough (*Sen. Harrison*), Donna Benz (*Ellen*), Barry Jenner (*The Commercial Producer*), Catherine Parks (*Jan*), Richard Venture (*Cindy's Father*), Terry Kiser (*The Commercial Director*), Georgann Johnson (*Cindy's Mother*), Anthony Charnota (*Master's Ass't*), Terrence McNally (*The Scanning Room Technician*), David Adams (*The Guard*), Jeana Tomasino (*Suzy*), John Sanderford, Scott Mulhern, Arthur Taxier, Paul Jasmin, Richard Milholland, Darrel Maury, Eloise Hardt, Gary Combs, Melissa Prophet, Lila Christianson, Lorna Christianson, Joe Medalis, Kelly Black, Jerry Douglas, Randi Brooks, Estelle Omens, Jesse Logan, Steve Strong, Tawny Moyer, Adam Starr, Dick Christie, Katherine DeHetre, Allison Balson
<u>P</u>: Howard Jeffrey   **WRIT & D:** Michael Crichton   **PHOTOG:** Paul Lohmann   **MUSIC:** Barry DeVorzon
Standard SF-thriller: Plastic surgeon investigates strange deaths of beautiful models

Look What's Happened to Rosemary's Baby
1976, (USA), ABC-TV, color, 91 mins.
<u>W</u>: Stephen McHattie (*Andrew/Adrian*), Ruth Gordon (*Minnie Castavet*), Ray Milland (*Roman Castavet*), George Maharis (*Guy Woodhouse*), David Huffman (*Peter Simon*), Donna Mills (*Dr. Ellen Davison*), Patty Duke Astin (*Rosemary Woodhouse*), Philip Boyer (*Young Andrew/Adrian*), Tina Louise (*Marjean*), Broderick Crawford (*Sheriff Holtzman*), Lloyd Haines (*Laykin*), Beverly Sanders, Calvin Rose, D.J. Sullivan, Brian Richards, Buck Young, Andy Stone
WRIT & P: John Wilson   <u>D</u>: Sam O'Steen, from characters created by Ira Levin   **PHOTOG:** John A. Alonzo   **SPCL-FX:** Joe Mercurio   **MUSIC:** Charles Bernstein
*A.k.a. **Rosemary's Baby II***
TVM, standard horror-fantasy: Satan's son comes of age

Loophole
1981, (GB), Brent Walker, color, 105 mins.
<u>W</u>: Albert Finney (*Mike Daniels*), Susannah York (*Dinah Booker*), Martin Sheen (*Stephen Booker*), Colin Blakely (*Gardner*), Jonathan Pryce (*Taylor*), Robert Morley (*Godfrey*), Alfred Lynch (*Harry*), Tony Doyle (*Nolan*), Christopher Guard (*Cliff*), Gwyneth Powell (*Doreen*), Jerry Harte (*Maxwell*), James Grout (*Fairbrother*), Terence Hardiman (*David*), Ian Howarth (*Matthew*), Bridget Brice (*Emily*), Harriet Collins (*Sarah*), Clive Graham (*The Inspector*), James Cossins (*An Interviewer*), Timothy Bateson (*An Interviewer*), Fanny Carby (*The Cleaner*)
<u>P</u>: Julian Holloway & David Korda   <u>D</u>: John Queste   **SCR:** Jonathan Hales, from a novel by Robert Pollock   **PHOTOG:** Michael Reed   **MUSIC:** Lalo Schifrin
Standard crime-thriller: Architect abets bank robbery

Lorca and the Outlaws
see Starship

Lord Blend's Love Story
1910, (GB), Hepworth, b&w, 1,050 ft. (320m)
<u>D</u>: Theo Bouwmeester
Standard crime-thriller: Rich woman has nobleman certified for rejecting her daughter

Lord of Illusions
1995, (USA), Seraphim/UA/MGM, color, 108 mins
<u>W</u>: Scott Bakula, Famke Janssen, Kevin J. O'Connor, Daniel von Bar-gen, Vincent Schiavelli, Susan Traylor
WRIT & D: Clive Barker (also co-producer), Based on Clive Barker's short story *The Last Illusion*   **PHOTOG:** Ronn Schmidt   **MUSIC:** Simon Boswell
Standard horror-fantasy: Detective meets revived demonic cultist

Lord of the Flies
1963, (GB), Allen Hodgdon-Two Arts/British Lion/Continental, b&w, 91 mins.
<u>W</u>: James Aubrey (*Ralph*), Tom Chapin (*Jack*), Hugh Edwards (*Piggy*), Roger Elwin (*Roger*), Tom Gaman (*Simon*), Nicholas Hammond, David Brunjes, Peter Davy, Roger Allan, Jonathan Heape, Kent Fletcher, David St. Clair, Andrew Horne

P: Lewis Allen   **D & ADAPT:** Peter Brook, from William Golding's novel
   PHOTOG: Tom Hollyman & Gerald Feil   **MUSIC:** Raymond Leppard
Gripping thriller: Marooned schoolboys revert to barbarism

Lord of the Flies
1990, (USA), Castle Rock/Col, color, 87 mins.
W: Balthazar Getty (*Ralph*), Chris Furrh (*Jack*), Gary Rule (*Roger*), Danuel Pipoly
   (*Piggy*), Badgett Dale (*Simon*), Zane Rockenbaugh (*Tex*), Edward & Andrew
   Taft (*The Twins*), Angus Burgin (*Greg*), Terry Wells (*Andy*), Martin Zentz
   (*Sheraton*), Braden MacDonald (*Larry*), Brian Jacobs (*Peter*), Chuck Bell
   (*Steve*), Vincent Amabile (*Patterson*), Gordon Elder (*Rusty*), David Weinstein
   (*Mikey*), Everado Elizondo (*Pablo*), Charles Newmark (*Will*), James Hamm
   (*John*), Brian Matthews (*Tony*), Shawn Skie (*Rapper*), Judson McCune (*Luke*),
   Bob Peck (*The Marine Officer*), Bill Schoppert (*The Marine Petty Officer*),
   Robert Shea (*Billy*)
D & ED: Harry Hook   **SCR:** Sara Schiff, from Sir William Golding's novel
   PHOTOG: Martin Fuhrer   **MUSIC:** Philippe Sarde
Standard adventure-thriller remake: Stranded boys espouse savagery

Lord of the Jungle
1955, (USA), AA, b&w, 69 mins.
W: Johnny Sheffield, Wayne Morris, Nancy Hale Paul Picerni, William Phipps,
   Leonard Mudie, Harry Lauter, Joe Fluellen, Juanita Moore
P, D & SCR: Ford Beebe, from characters created by Roy Rockwood
Minor adventure (last "Bomba" film): Jungle boy tries to stop elephant slaughter

The Lord of the Rings
1978, (USA), Saul Zaentz-Ralph Bakshi/Fantasy/UA, color, 131 mins.
P: Saul Zaentz   D: Ralph Bakshi   SCR: Chris Conkling & Peter S. Beagle, based
   on the novels of J.R.R. Tolkien   **PHOTOG:** Timothy Galfas   **MUSIC:**
   Leonard Rosenman
*Animated fantasy (1st half of Tolkien's epic trilogy): Dwarf-like heroes go on desperate
   quest. cf. **The Hobbit***

Lord Shango
1975, (USA), Bryanston, color, 91 mins
W: Lawrence Cook (*Shango*), Marlene Clark, Avis McCarthur
P: Steve Bono & Ronald Hobbs   D: Raymond Marsh   SCR: Paul Carter Harrison
Standard horror-fantasy: Black mother and daughter face voodoo

Lord Shango: PRODUCER STEVE BONO AND MARLENE CLARK

Lords of the Deep
1989, (USA), Concorde, color, 80 mins.
W: Bradford Dillman, Priscilla Barnes, Roger Corman (*Cameo*)
Minor SF-thriller: Strange fish haunts undersea station

Lords of Magick
1988, (USA), color, 98 mins.
W: Jarrett Parker, Matt Gauthier, Brendan Dillon Jr.
D: David Marsh
Minor fantasy-thriller: Warriors time-travel in pursuit of evil sorcerer

Lorna Doone
1912, (GB), Clarendon/Gaumont, b&w, 4,300 ft. (1310.6m)
W: Dorothy Bellew (*Lorna Doone*)
D: Wilfred Noy, from R.D. Blackmore's novel
Standard melodrama (first 5-reel British feature): Yeoman loves outlaw's adopted daughter

Lorna Doone
1920, (GB), Butcher, b&w, 5,150 ft. (1569.7m)
W: Dennis Wyndham (*John Ridd*), Bertie Gordon (*Lorna Doone*), Roy Raymond
   (*Carver Doone*), George Bellamy (*John Fry*), Joan Cockram (*Annie Ridd*),
   Cecil Morton York (*Sir Ensor Doone*), Frank Dane (*Tom Faggus*), Tom Ronald
   (*Jeremy Stickles*), Gertrude Sterroll (*Mistress Ridd*), Bessie Herbert (*Betty
   Muxworthy*)
D: H. Lisle Lucoque   SCR: Nellie E. Lucoque, from R.D. Blackmore's novel
Standard melodrama: Yeoman helps stolen girl escape bandits

Lorna Doone
1922, (USA), First Nat'l, b&w, 7 reels/6,200 ft.
W: Madge Bellamy (*Lorna Doone*), John Bowers (*John Ridd*), Frank Keenan (*Sir
   Charles Ensor*), Jack McDonald ("*The Counsellor*"), Donald MacDonald
   (*Carver Doone*), Norris Johnson (*Ruth*), May Giraci (*Lorna as a Child*),
   Charles Hatton (*John as a Child*)
P & D: Maurice Tourneur   SCR: Katherine Reed, Cecil G. Mumford, Wyndham
   Gittens, & Maurice Tourneur, from R.D. Blackmore's novel   **PHOTOG:**
   Henry Sharp
Standard melodrama: Kidnapped girl raised by outlaw band

Lorna Doone
1934, (GB), ATP/ABFD, b&w, 90 ins.
W: Victoria Hopper (*Lorna Doone*), John Loder (*John Ridd*), Margaret Lockwood
   (*Annie Ridd*), Frank Cellier (*Jeremy Stickles*), Roy Emerton (*Carver Doone*),
   George Curzon (*King James II*), Herbert Lomas (*Sir Ensor Doone*), D.A.
   Clarke-Smith (*Counsellor Doone*), Mary Clare (*Mistress Ridd*), Roger Livesey
   (*Tom Faggus*), Edward Rigby (*Reuben Huckaback*), Lawrence Hanray (*Parson
   Bowden*), Amy Veness (*Betty Muxworthy*), Eliot Makeham (*John Fry*),
   Wyndham Goldie (*Judge Jeffries*)
P & D: Basil Dean   SCR: Dorothy Farnum, Miles Malleson & Gordon Wellesley,
   from R.D. Blackmore's novel
Definitive film-version of classic romance: Girl rescued from clutches of outlaw family

Lorna Doone
1951, (USA), Col, color, 88 mins.
W: Barbara Hale, Richard Greene, Carl Benton Reid, William Bishop
D: Phil Karlson   from R.D. Blackmore's novel   **MUSIC:** George Duning
Standard melodrama: Farmers vs. oppressive landlords

Lorna Doone
1990, (GB), color, 90 mins.
W: Clive Owen, Sean Bean, Polly Walker, Billie Whitelaw, Miles Anderson,
   Rachel Kempson
D: Andrew Grieve   **TELEPLAY:** Matthew Jacobs, from R.D. Blackmore's novel
TVM, standard melodrama: Outlaws and revenge in 17th-century England

L.A. 2017
1971, (USA), color
W: Gene Barry, Sharon Farrell, Barry Sullivan, Edmond O'Brien
P: Dean Hargrove   D: Steven Spielberg   **TELEPLAY:** Philip Wylie
*TVM, standard SF-thriller (feature-length episode from The Name of the Game teleseries):
   Newspaper publisher dreams of future Los Angeles*

Lost and Found on a South Sea Island
1923, (USA), b&w, 7 reels
D: Raoul Walsh
*A.k.a. **Passions of the Sea***
Standard melodrama

The Lost Boys
1987, (USA), WB, color, 98 mins.
W: Jason Patric (*Michael*), Corey Haim (*Sam*), Dianne Wiest (*Lucy*), Barnard
   Hughes (*Grandpa*), Ed Herrmann (*Max*), Jami Gertz (*Star*), Kiefer
   Sutherland (*David*), Corey Feldman (*Edgar Frog*), Jamison Newlander (*Alan
   Frog*), Brooke McCarter, Billy Wirth, Alexander Winter, Chance Michael
   Corbitt, J. Dinan Myrtetus, Alexander Bacon Chapman, Nori Morgan, Todd
   Feder, Christopher Peters, Keith Butterfield, Eric Graves, Gerald
   Younggren, Kelly Jo Minter, Timmy Cappello, Melanie Bishop, Jim Turner,
   Tony Cain, Sandra E. Garcia, Jane Bare, Ian Guindon, B. Lowenberg,
   Captain Colourz, Inez Pandalfi, Cody (*Nanook*), Folsom (*Thor*)
D: Joel Schumacher   SCR: Janice Fischer, James Jeremias, & Jeffrey Boam
   STORY: Janice Fischer & James Jeremias   **PHOTOG:** Michael Chapman
   MUSIC: Thomas Newman   **SONGS:** Lost in the Shadows, Laying Down the
   Law & Cry Little Sister
Modest horror-satire: Boy's older brother snared by vampire cult

The Lost City
1935, (USA), Krellberg/Regal, b&w, 51 mins, also 75 mins.
W: William (Stage) Boyd (*Zolok*), Kane Richmond (*Bruce Gordon*), Sam Baker
   (*Hugo*), Josef Swickard (*Dr. Maneus*), George F. (later Gabby) Hayes, Jerry
   Frank, Ralph Lewis, Milburn Moranti, Claudia Dell, William Bletcher
D: Harry Revier   SCR: Percy Poore Sheehan, Eddy Graneman & Leon d'Usseau,
   from a story by Zelma Carroll, George W. Merrick & Robert Dillon   **PHO-
   TOG:** Roland Price & Edward Linden
Standard SF-thriller (edited-down serial): Mad scientist creates zombies

Lost Continent
1951, (USA), Lippert, b&w (with green tint), 83 mins.
W: Cesar Romero (*Nolan*), Hillary Brooke (*Maria*), John Hoyt (*Rostov*), Hugh
   Beaumont (*Phillips*), Chick Chandler, Murray Alper, Sid Melton,
   Acquanetta, Whit Bissell
P: Sigmund Neufeld   D: Sam Newfield   SCR: Richard Landau   **STORY:**,
   Carroll Young   **PHOTOG:** Jack Greenhalgh   **SPCL-FX:** Augie Lohman
   MUSIC: Paul Dunlap
Minor SF-thriller: Scientists seek downed rocket, find prehistoric life on eerie plateau

The Lost Continent (1968)

1968, (GB), Hammer-7Arts/20th-Fox, color, 89 mins.
W: Eric Porter (*Capt. Lansen*), Hildegarde Knef (*Eva*), Tony Beckley (*Harry Tyler*), Suzanna Leigh (*Unita*), Nigel Stock (*Webster*), Neil McCallum (*Hemmings*), Dana Gillespie (*Sarah*), Benito Carruthers (*Ricaldi*), Jimmy Hanley (*Pat*), James Cossins (*The Chief*), Victor Maddern (*The Mate*), Michael Ripper (*The Sea Lawyer*), Darryl Read (*El Diabolo*), Norman Eshley, Reg Lye, Alf Joint
P & D: Michael Carreras   SCR: Michael Nash, from Dennis Wheatley's novel   PHOTOG: Paul Beeson   MUSIC: Philip Martell
USA retitle, The Lost Continent
Standard SF-thriller: Ship stranded in menacing sea of vegetation

The Lost Continent: SUZANNA LEIGH

The Lost Empire

1985, (USA), Manson Int'l/Harwood/JGM color, 86 mins, also 83 mins
W: Melanie Vincz (*Angel Wolfe*), Raven de la Croix (*Whitestar*), Angela Aames (*Heather*), Paul Coufos (*Rick*), Angus Scrimm (*Dr. Sin Do*), Bob Tessier (*Koro*), Blackie Dammett (*Krager*), Angelique Pettyjohn (*Whiplash*), Kenneth Tobey (*The Cop*), Linda Shayne (*Cindy*), Garry Goodrow (*The Doctor*), Art Hern, Annie Gaybis, Gary Don Cox, Jason Stuart, Tom Rettig
WRIT, P & D: Jim Wynorski   PHOTOG: Jacques Haitkin   MUSIC: Alan Howarth
Minor SF-adventure: Action in anachronistic civilization

The Lost Face

1964, (Czech), Czech State Film, color, 85 mins
D: Pavel Hobl
A.k.a. The Borrowed Face
Standard thriller

The Lost Handkerchief

1908, (GB), Walter Tyler, b&w, 420 ft. (128m)
Standard comedy short: Man seeks stolen handkerchief, is boiled by laundress

Lost Highway

1997, (USA), CIBY 2000-Asymmetrical/October Films, color, 135 mins.
W: Bill Pullman (*Fred Madison*), Patricia Arquette (*Renee Madison/ Alice Wakefield*), Robert Blake (*Mystery Man*), Balthazar Getty (*Pete Dayton*), Robert Loggia (*Mr. Eddy/Dick Laurent*), Marilyn Manson (*Porno Star #1*), Jack Nance, Natasha Gregson Wagner, Gary Busey, Henry Rollins
D: David Lynch   SCR: David Lynch & Barry Gifford   PHOTOG: Peter Deming   MUSIC: Angelo Badalamenti
Bizarre thriller: Man falsely accused of murder, acquires new persona

Lost Horizon

1937, (USA), Col, b&w, 132 mins.
W: Ronald Colman (*Robert Conway*), Jane Wyatt (*Sondra*), Sam Jaffe (*The High Lama*), Thomas Mitchell (*Barnard*), Isabel Jewell (*Gloria*), H.B. Warner (*Chang*), Margo (*Maria*), John Howard (*George Conway*), Edward Everett Horton (*Lovett*)
P & D: Frank Capra   SCR: Robert Riskin, from James Hilton's novel   PHOTOG: Joseph Walker   MUSIC: Dmitri Tiomkin   MUSIC DIR: Max Steiner
TV-retitle, Lost Horizon of Shangri-La
Classic romance: Mixed group skyjacked to secret valley in Himalayas. cf. Bridge of Time

Lost Horizon

1973, (USA), Col, color, 143 mins.
W: Peter Finch (*Richard Conway*), Liv Ullmann (*Catherine*), George Kennedy (*Sam Cornelius*), Michael York (*George Conway*), Olivia Hussey (*Maria*), Sally Kellerman (*Sally Hughes*), Charles Boyer (*The High Lama*), Bobby Van (*Harry Lovett*), Sir John Gielgud (*Chang*), Kent Smith (*Bill Ferguson*), John Van Dreelen (*The Doctor*), James Shigeta (*Brother ToLenn*), Larry Duran (*The Oriental Pilot*), Miiko Taka
P: Ross Hunter   D: Charles Jarrott   SCR: Larry Kramer, from James Hilton's novel   PHOTOG: Robert Surtees   MUSIC: Burt Bacharach   LYRICS: Hal David   SONGS: *I Give It All to You, Question Me an Answer & The World is a Circle*   CHOREOGRAPHY: Hermes Pan
Lavish remake, standard musical-romance: Skyjacked strangers find fulfillment in secret Himalayan utopia. cf. Bridge of Time

Lost Horizon of Shangri-La

see Lost Horizon (1937)

The Lost Hours

1952, (GB), Tempean/Eros, b&w, 72 mins.
W: Mark Stevens (*Paul Smith*), Jean Kent (*Louise Parker*), Garry Marsh (*Foster*), John Bentley (*Clark Sutton*), Dianne Foster (*Dianne Wrigley*), Jack Lambert (*John Parker*), Leslie Perrins (*Dr. Morrison*), Brian Coleman (*Tom Wrigley*), Duncan Lamont (*Bristow*), Cyril Smith (*Roper*), Thora Hird (*The Maid*)
P: Robert Baker & Monty Berman   D: David Macdonald   SCR: John Gilling   STORY: Steve Fisher
USA retitle, The Big Frame (RKO, 1953)
Standard thriller: Yank pilot proves he was framed for killing wartime comrade

Lost in a Harem

1944, (USA), MGM, b&w, 89 mins.
W: Bud Abbott, Lou Costello, Marilyn Maxwell, John Conte, Douglass Dumbrille, Lottie Harrison, Jimmy Dorsey & His Orchestra
D: Charles Reisner   SCR: Harry Ruskin, John Grant & Harry Crane   PHOTOG: Lester White   MUSIC: David Snell
Standard comedy: Magicians have Arabian adventure

Lost in Space

1998, (GB-USA), New Line Cinema, color, 121 mins
W: William Hurt (*John Robinson*), Matt LeBlanc (*Don West*), Gary Oldman (*Dr. Smith/Spider Smith*), Mimi Rogers (*Maureen Robinson*), Lacey Chabert (*Penny Robinson*), Heather Graham (*Judy Robinson*), Jack Johnson (*Will Robinson*), Jared Harris (*Older Will*), Dick Tufeld (*Voice of the Robot*)
D: Stephen Hopkins   SCR: Akiva Goldsman   PHOTOG: Peter Levy   MUSIC: Bruce Broughton
Energetic SF-adventure (inspired by 1960's teleseries)

Lost in the Stratosphere

1934, (USA), Mono, b&w, 65 mins
W: William Cagney, Eddie Nugent, June Collyer
Standard thriller

Lost in Time

1977, (USA), color
W: Scott Thomas, Susan Howard

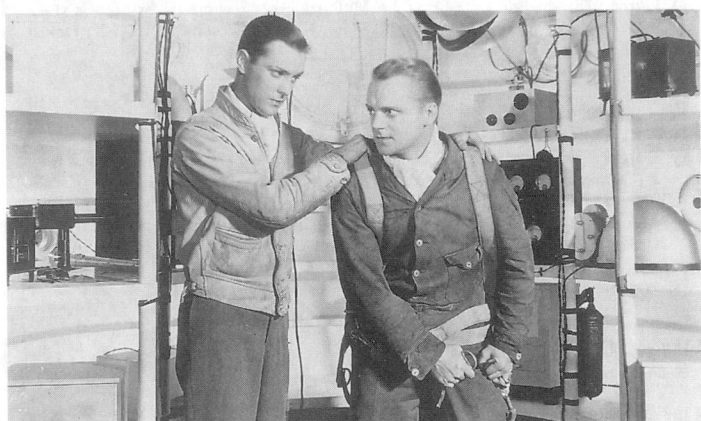

Lost in the Stratosphere: EDDIE NUGENT AND WILLIAM CAGNEY

Minor fantasy-thriller: Archeologists in Bermuda Triangle transported to bizarre island

Lost Island of Kioga

1966, (USA), Rep b&w, 100 mins.
W: Herman Brix (later Bruce Bennet), Mala Monte Blue, Jill Martin, Noble Johnson
D: William Witney & John English
Standard thriller (culled from 1938 serial 'Hawk of the Wilderness'): Shipwreck survivors meet ruler of uncharted isle

The Lost Jungle

1934, (USA), Mascot, b&w, 69 mins.
W: Clyde Beatty (*Clyde*), Cecelia Parker (*Ruth Robinson*), Edward Le Saint (*Ruth's Father*), Syd Saylor (*Larry Henderson*), Warner Richmond (*Sharkey*), Wheeler Oakman (*Kirby*), Lew Meehan (*Flynn*), Max Wagner (*Slade*), Mickey Rooney,

J. Crauford Kent, Lloyd Ingraham, Maston Williams, Lloyd Whitlock
D: Armand Schaefer & David Howard   **SCR:** Colbert Clark & John Rathmell
   STORY: Sherman Lowe & Al Martin   **PHOTOG:** Alvin Wyckoff &
William Nobles

Lost Horizon

Minor adventure-thriller (edited-down serial): Lion tamer aids scientist seeking "cradle of civilization"

The Lost Kingdom
see Antinea, l'Amante della Citta Sepolta

A Lost Man
see Der Verlorene

The Lost Memory
1909, (GB), Hepworth, b&w, 225 ft. (68.6m)
D: Lewin Fitzhamon
Standard comedy: Old butcher hit on head by pickpocket, develops amnesia

The Lost Missile
1958, (USA-Can), William Berke/UA, b&w, 70 mins.
W: Robert Loggia (*David Lorring*), Ellen Parker (*Joan Wood*), Phillip Pine (*Joe*),
Larry Kerr, Marilee Earle, Kitty Kelly, Fred Engleberg, Selmer Jackson, Hari
Rhodes, Shirley Shawn, J. Anthony Hughes, Robert Busch, Jack Holland,
Mike Steele, John McNamara, Cecil Elliott, Nola Harris, Joe Hyams, Myron
Cook, Don Pethley, Mark Dunhill, Bill Bradley
D: Lester William Berke   **SCR:** John McPartland & Jerome Bixby, from a story
by Lester William Berke   **PHOTOG:** Kenneth Peach   **SPCL-FX:** Jack R.
Glass   **MUSIC:** Gerald Fried
Minor SF-thriller: Radioactive missile threatens Earth

The Lost Moment
1947, (USA), Walter Wanger/Univ, b&w, 89 mins.
W: Robert Cummings (*Lewis Venable*), Susan Hayward (*Tina*), Agnes Moorehead
(*Julianna*), John Archer (*Charles Russell*), Eduardo Ciannelli (*Father Rinaldo*),
Joan Lorring, William Edmunds, Minerva Urecal, Frank Puglia
P: Walter Wanger   **D:** Martin Gabel (only film as director)   **SCR:** Leonardo
Bercovici, based on Henry James' novel *The Aspern Papers*   **PHOTOG:** Hal
Mohr   **MUSIC:** Daniele Amfitheatrof
Superior romance-thriller: Young woman has amnesiac spells in which she relives youth of 105-year-old aunt. cf. Aspern

The Lost One
see Der Verlorene

The Lost Patrol
1929, (GB), British Instructional/Fox, b&w, 7,250 ft. (2209.8m)
W: Cyril McLaglen (*The Sergeant*), Sam Wilkinson (*Sanders*), Terence Collier (*Cpl.
Bell*), Hamilton Keene (*Morelli*), Fred Dyer (*Abelson*), Charles Emerald
(*Hale*), James Watts (*Cook*), Anew McMaster (*Brown*), John Valentine
(*Mackay*), Frederick Long (*Pearson*)
D & SCR: Walter Summers, from Philip MacDonald's novel *Patrol*
Standard thriller: Lost desert patrol eliminated by Arab snipers

The Lost Patrol
1934, (USA), RKO, b&w, 74 mins.
W: Victor McLaglen, Boris Karloff (*Sanders*), J.M. Kerrigan (*Quincannon*),
Reginald Denny (*Brown*), Wallace Ford (*Morelli*), Billy Bevan (*Hale*),
Douglas Walton (*Pearson*), Alan Hale (*Cook*), Brandon Hurst, Sammy Stein,
Howard Wilson, Paul Hanson
D: John Ford   **SCR:** Dudley Nichols   **ADAPT:** Garrett Fort, from Philip
MacDonald's novel *Patrol*   **PHOTOG:** Harold Wendstrom   **MUSIC:** Max
Steiner
Classic melodrama: Arabs eliminate desert patrol

Lost Planet Airmen
1951, (USA), Rep b&w, 65 mins.
W: Mae Clarke, Don Haggerty, Tristram Coffin, I. Stanford Jolley Dale Van
Sickel, Tom Steele, Buddy Roosevelt, House Peters Jr.
D: Fred C. Brannon   **SCR:** Royal Cole, William Lively, & Sol Shor
Minor SF-thriller (feature culled from 1949 serial King of the Rocket Men): Flying hero opposes evil scientist

The Lost Platoon
1989, (USA), color, 120 mins.
W: David Parry, William Knight, Sean Heyman
D: David A. Prior
Minor SF-horror: Soldiers transformed into vampires

Lost Prophet
1992, (USA), Rockville Pictures, b&w, 75 mins.
W: Jim Burton (*Jim*), Zandra Huston (*Kym*), Drew Morone (*Mick Prophet/The Real
Estate Agent*), James Tucker (*Kid*), Steven Tucker (*Kid's Brother*), Shannon
Goldman (*The Park Patrolman*), Larry O'Neil (*Punk #1*), Christian Urich
(*Punk #2*), Sophia Ramos (*Punk #3*)
D & PHOTOG: Michael de Avila   **SCR:** Michael de Avila, Drew Morone, Larry
O'Neil & Shannon Gold-man   **MUSIC:** TRF Music Libraries
Unusual horror-fantasy: Drifter meets bizarre characters

The Lost Shoe
see Der Verlorene Schuh

The Lost Squadron
1932, (USA), RKO, b&w, 72 mins.
W: Erich von Stroheim (*Von Furst*), Mary Astor (*Follette*), Robert Armstrong
(*Woody*), Richard Dix (*Gibson*), Joel McCrea (*Red*), Dorothy Jordan, Hugh
Herbert
D: George Archainbaud   **SCR:** Herman J. Mankiewicz & Wallace Smith
   PHOTOG: Leo Tover & Edward Cronjager
Unusual thriller: Mad movie director tyrannizes cast

Lost Souls
1998, (USA), Alliance Atlantis Communications/UPN-TV, color, 95 mins.
W: John Savage (*Victor Robinson*), Barbara Sukowa (*Sandra Robinson*), Richard
Lintern, Laura Harling, Robert Sherman
D: Jeff Woolnough   **TELEPLAY:** Scott Peters   **PHOTOG:** Jon Joffin   **MUSIC:**
Jonathan Goldsmith
TVM, standard fantasy-thriller: Family moves into sinister house

Lost Souls
1999, (USA), color
W: Winona Ryder, Ben Chaplin, Elias Koteas
Unusual fantasy-thriller: Satan threatens takeover of world

Lost Treasure of the Aztecs
1959, (It), AIP/Filmways, color, 79 mins, also 87 mins.
W: Alan Steel, Mario Petri
*A.k.a. **Hercules and the Treasure of the Incas***
Minor adventure-thriller: Man seeks fabled treasure trove.

The Lost Tribe
1949, (USA), Col, b&w, 72 mins.
W: Johnny Weissmuller (*Jungle Jim*), Elena Verdugo (*Li Wanna*), Myrna Dell
(*Norina*), Paul Marion (*Chot*), Ralph Dunn (*Rawling*), Joseph Vitale
(*Calhoun*)Nelson Leigh
P: Sam Katzman   **D:** William Berke   **SCR:** Arthur Hoerl & Don Martin
   PHOTOG: Ira Morgan
blurb: "Africa's most savage diamond hunt!"
Minor adventure-thriller: Jungle hero battles croooks who covet native treasure

Lost Valley
see The Valley of Gwangi

The Lost Volcano
1950, (USA), Mono, b&w, 72 mins.
W: Johnny Sheffield (*Bomba*), Donald Woods (*Paul*), Marjorie Lord (*Ruth*), Elena
Verdugo (*Nona*), John Ridgely, Tommy Ivo, Don Harvey, Grandon Rhodes,
Robert Lewis
P: Walter Mirisch   **D & STORY:** Ford Beebe   **SCR:** Jack DeWitt, from charac-
ters created by Roy Rockwood   **PHOTOG:** Marcel LePicard   **MUSIC:**
Ozzie Caswell
Standard adventure-thriller: Criminals covet ancient treasure, Jungle Boy opposes

The Lost Weekend
1945, (USA), Para, b&w, 101 mins.
W: Ray Milland Jane Wyman, Phillip Terry, Howard Da Silva, Doris Dowling,
Frank Faylen, Lilian Fontaine, Frank Orth, Mary Young, Anita Bolster,
Lewis J. Russell
P: Charles Brackett   **D:** Billy Wilder, from Charles Jackson's novel   **PHOTOG:**
John F. Seitz   **MUSIC SCORE:** Miklos Rozsa
Oscar-winning (Actor, Director & Picture) melodrama: Man succumbs to alcoholism

Lost Women (1950)
see *Prehistoric Women (1950)*

Lost Women (1952)
see *Mesa of Lost Women*

Lost Women of Zarpa
see *Mesa of Lost Women*

The Lost Will
1912, (GB), Hepworth, b&w, 700 ft. (213.4m)
<u>D:</u> Lewin Fitzhamon
Standard crime-thriller: Dead earl's daughter saves father's will from disowned nephew

The Lost World
1925, (USA), First Nat'l-Watterson R. Rothacker, b&w, 52 mins, also 108 mins
<u>W:</u> Wallace Beery (*Prof. Challenger*), Bessie Love (*Paula White*), Lewis Stone (*Sir John Roxton*), Lloyd Hughes (*Edward Malone*), Arthur Hoyt (*Prof. Summerlee*), Alma Bennett (*Gladys Hungerford*), Finch Smiles (*Austin*), Bull Montana (*The Ape Man*), Virginia Brown Faire (*Marquette*), Margaret McWade (*Mrs. Challenger*), Jules Cowles (*Zambo*), Charles Wellesley (*Maj. Hibbard*), George Bunny (*Colin McArdle*)
<u>D:</u> Harry Hoyt   <u>SCR:</u> Marion Fairfax, from Sir Arthur Conan Doyle's novel   <u>PHOTOG:</u> Arthur Edeson   <u>ANIMATION:</u> Willis O'Brien
"...one of the...biggest stunt attractions. The reviews were all raves; nothing quite like it had ever been seen before, and in many ways it still hasn't been equalled... the grand daddy of all the 'monster' thrillers"—Joe Franklin, Classics of the Silent Screen
Classic SF-thriller: Scientists find prehistoric life

The Lost World

The Lost World
1960, (USA), 20th-Fox, color, 98 mins.
<u>W:</u> Claude Rains (*Prof. Challenger*), Jill St. John (*Jennifer Holmes*), Michael Rennie (*Sir John Roxton*), David Hedison (*Malone*), Fernando Lamas (*Gomez*), Jay Novello (*Costa*), Richard Haydn, Ray Stricklyn, Vitina Marcus, Ian Wolfe, John Graham, Colin Campbell
<u>P & D:</u> Irwin Allen   <u>SCR:</u> Irwin Allen & Charles Bennett, from Sir Arthur Conan Doyle's novel   <u>PHOTOG:</u> Winton C. Hoch   <u>SPCL-FX:</u> L.B. Abbott, James B. Gordon & Emil Kosa Jr.   <u>FX TECHNICIAN:</u> Willis O'Brien   <u>MUSIC:</u> Paul Sawtell
Standard SF-adventure: Scientists probe South American mesa, find prehistoric life

The Lost World
1993, (Can), color, 99 mins.
<u>W:</u> John Rhys-Davies, David Warner, Eric McCormack, Nathania Stanford, Darren Peter Mercer, Tamara Gorski, Innocent Chosa, Kate Egan
<u>D:</u> Timothy Bond, based on Sir Arthur Conan Doyle's novel
*Minor SF-thriller: Scientists find dinosaurs. cf. **Return to the Lost World***

The Lost World: Jurassic Park
1997, (USA), Amblin/Univ, color, 134 mins.
<u>W:</u> Jeff Goldblum (*Ian Malcolm*), Julianne Moore (*Sarah Harding*), Pete Postlethwaite (*Roland Tembo*), Arliss Howard (*Peter Ludlow*), Vince Vaughn (*Nick Van Owen*), Sir Richard Attenborough (*John Hammond*), Richard Schiff, Vanessa Lee Chester Peter Stormare, Harvey Jason, Thomas F. Duffy, Camilla Belle
<u>D:</u> Steven Spielberg   <u>SCR:</u> David Koepp, from Michael Crichton's novel   <u>SPCL VS-FX:</u> Industrial Light & Magic   <u>MUSIC:</u> John Williams   <u>PHOTOG:</u> Janusz Kaminski   <u>SPCL DINOSAUR FX:</u> Michael Lantieri
*Exciting SF-thriller (sequel to **Jurassic Park**): Prehistoric monsters threaten San Diego*

The Lost World of Sinbad
see *Samurai Pirate*

The Lost Zeppelin
1929, (USA), Tiffany, b&w, 8 reels/6,882 ft.
<u>W:</u> Conway Tearle (*Cmdr. Hall*), Virginia Valli (*Mrs. Hall*), Ricardo Cortez (*Tom Armstrong*), Duke Martin (*Lt. Wallace*), Kathryn McGuire (*Nancy*), Winter Hall (*Mr. Wilson*)
<u>D:</u> Edward Sloman   <u>SCR:</u> Frances Hyland   <u>STORY:</u> Frances Hyland & John F. Natteford   <u>DIALOG:</u> Charles Kenyon   <u>PHOTOG:</u> Jackson Rose
Standard adventure-melodrama: Dirigible flight to South Pole

The Lottery
1996, (USA), NBC-TV, color, 95 mins.
<u>W:</u> Dan Cortese (*Jason Smith*), Keri Russell (*Felice Dunbar*), Veronica Cartwright (*Mrs. Dunbar*), Stephen Root (*Mr. Dunbar*), Salome Jens (*Faith Lloyd*), William Daniels (*The Reverend*), M. Emmet Walsh (*The Police Chief*), Sean Murray, Michael Burgess
<u>P:</u> Linda Otto   <u>D:</u> Daniel Sackheim   <u>TELEPLAY:</u> Anthony Spinner, based on Shirley Jackson's classic short story   <u>PHOTOG:</u> Rick Maguire   <u>MUSIC:</u> David Michael Frank
TVM, standard thriller: Man finds parents' hometown obsessed by strange ritual

The Loudwater Mystery
1921, (GB), Broadwest/Walturdaw, b&w, 4,800 ft. (1463m)
<u>W:</u> Gregory Scott (*Hubert Manley*), Pauline Peters (*Lady Loudwater*), Clive Brook (*Lord Loudwater*), Cameron Carr (*Insp. Flexen*), C. Tilson-Chowne (*Col. Grey*), Arthur Walcott (*Carrington*), Nan Heriot (*Miss Truslove*), Charles Poulton (*Roper*)
<u>P:</u> Norman Macdonald   <u>D & SCR:</u> Walter West, from a novel by Edgar Jepson
Standard crime-thriller: Detective proves lord was stabbed by secretary

Le Loup-Garou (The Werewolf)
1923, (Fr), b&w, Standard horror-fantasy

Love and Human Remains
1993, (Can), color, 100 mins.
<u>W:</u> Thomas Gibson, Ruth Marshall, Cameron Bancroft, Matthew Ferguson, Mia Kirshner, Joanne Vannicola, Rick Roberts
<u>D:</u> Denys Arcand   <u>SCR:</u> Brad Fraser   <u>PHOTOG:</u> Paul Sarossy
Unusual melodrama: Serial killer terrorizes Montreal

Love and Magic
1914, (GB), Kineto, b&w, 470 ft. (143.3m)
<u>D:</u> Walter R. Booth
Standard fantasy short: Suitor conjures imp to annoy girl's father

Love and Poison
1950, (It), b&w, 73 mins.
<u>W:</u> Lois Maxwell, Amedeo Nazzari
Standard thriller: Woman poisons brother so idiot son can acquire throne

Love and War in Toyland
1913, (GB), Natural Colour Kinematograph Co., color, 3,000 ft. (914.4m)
<u>D:</u> F. Martin Thornton & Edgar Rodgers
Standard fantasy: Animated toys battle

Love at First Bite
1979, (USA), George Hamilton-Robert Kaufman/Melvin Simon/AIP, color, 96 mins.
<u>W:</u> George Hamilton (*Count Dracula*), Susan Saint James (*Cindy Sondheim*), Richard Benjamin (*Dr. Jeff Rosenberg*), Arte Johnson (*Renfield*), Dick Shawn (*Lt. Ferguson*), Isabel Sanford (*The Judge*), Ronnie Schell (*The Gay in the Elevator*), Sherman Hemsley (*Rev. Mike*), Bryan O'Byrne (*The Priest*), Barry Gordon (*The Flashlight Vendor*), Bob Basso (*The TV Repairman*), Stanley Brock (*The Cab Driver*), Michael Pataki (*The Mobster*), Beverly Sanders (*The Lady in the Elevator*), Basil Hoffman (*The Desk Clerk*), Danny Dayton (*Billy*), Robert Ellenstein (*The W.V. Man*), David Ketchum (*The Customs Inspector*)
<u>P:</u> Joel Freeman   <u>D:</u> Stan Dragoti   <u>SCR:</u> Robert Kaufman   <u>PHOTOG:</u> Edward Rosson   <u>MUSIC:</u> Charles Bernstein   <u>SONG:</u> (sung by Alicia Bridges), I Love the Night Life
Amusing horror-farce: Vampire pursues New York model

Love at Stake
1987, (USA), Hemdale/TriStar, color, 88 mins.
<u>W:</u> Patrick Cassidy (*Miles*), Kelly Preston (*Sara*), Bud Cort (*The Parson*), David Graf (*Nathaniel*), Stuart Pankin, Anne Ramsey, Dave Thomas, Barbara Carrera Georgia Brown, Annie Golden, Dr. Joyce Brothers
<u>D:</u> John Moffitt   <u>SCR:</u> Terry Sweeney & Lanier Laney   <u>MUSIC:</u> Charles Fox
*A.k.a. **Burnin' Love***
Standard comedy-fantasy: Beautiful witch entrances Puritans

Love Bites: The Reluctant Vampire
1993, (USA), color
<u>W:</u> Adam Ant, Michelle Forbes
Standard horror-comedy: Vampire seeks to "re-humanize"

The Love Bug
1968, (USA), Walt Disney/Buena Vista, color, 107 mins.

W: David Tomlinson, Dean Jones, Michele Lee, Buddy Hackett, Joe Flynn, Benson Fong, Joe E. Ross
D: Robert Stevenson SCR: Bill Walsh & Don DaGradi PHOTOG: Edward Colman SPCL-FX: Eustace Lycett MUSIC: George Bruns
Standard juvenile fantasy: Volkswagen has mind of its own

Love Butcher
1982, (USA), Desert/Mirror, color, 84 mins
W: Erik Stern (*Caleb/Lester*) Kay Neer, Robin Sherwood
P: Gary Williams & Micky Belski D: Mikel Angel & Don Jones SCR: Don Jones & James Evergreen
Minor thriller: Vengeful gardener kills

The Love Cage
see Les Felins

Love Can Be Murder
1992, (USA), ABC-TV, color
W: Jaclyn Smith, Corbin Bernsen, Anne Francis (*Maggie*), Cliff De Young (*Brad Donaldson*), Tom Bower (*Mike Riordan*), Nicholas Pryor (*Phillip Carlyle*), Elaine Kagan (*Dr. Wilde*)
TVM, standard mystery-fantasy: Female detective teams with spirited ghost

Lovecraft's Necronomicon
see Necronomicon: Book of the Dead

The Loved One
1965, (USA), Filmways/MGM, b&w, 117 mins.
W: Robert Morse (*Dennis Barlow*), Jonathan Winters (*Wilbur Glenworthy/Harry Glenworthy*), Anjanette Comer (*Aimee Thanatogenos*), Sir John Gielgud (*Sir Francis Hinsley*), Robert Morley (*Sir Ambrose Abercrombie*), Rod Steiger (*Mr. Joyboy*), Roddy McDowall (*D.J. Jr.*), Liberace (*Mr. Starker*), Margaret Leighton (*Mrs. Kenton*), Dana Andrews (*Gen. Buck Brinkman*), Milton Berle (*Mr. Kenton*), Paul Williams (*Gunther*), Ayllene Gibbons (*Joyboy's Mother*), Robert Easton (*Dusty*), Tab Hunter (*The Guide*), Lionel Stander (*The Guru Brahmin*), Alan Napier (*The English Club Official*), Bernie Kopell (*The Ass't to the Guru Brahmin*), Joy Harmon (*Miss Benson*), James Coburn (*The Immigration Officer*), Barbara Nichols (*Sadie Blodgett*), Asa Maynor (*The Sec'y to D.J. Jr.*), Roxanne Arlen, Claire Kelly
P: John Calley & Haskell Wexler D: Tony Richardson SCR: Christopher Isherwood & Terry Southern, from Evelyn Waugh's novel PHOTOG: Haskell Wexler MUSIC: John Addison
Uneven, disturbing satire: Young Englishman encounters bizarre Southern California cemeteries

The Love Factor
see Zeta One

The Love Flower
1920, (USA), b&w, 70 mins.
W: Carol Dempster, Richard Barthelmess, George McQuarrie, Anders Randolf, Florence Short
D & SCR: D.W. Griffith
Standard melodrama: Man kills second wife's lover, flees with daughter to tropic isle

Love from a Stranger
1937, (GB), Trafalgar/UA, b&w, 90 mins.
W: Ann Harding (*Carol Howard*), Basil Rathbone (*Gerald Lovell*), Binnie Hale (*Kate Meadows*), Bruce Seton (*Ronald Bruce*), Jean Cadell (*Aunt Lou*), Bryan Powley (*Dr. Gribble*), Donald Calthrop (*Hobson*), Joan Hickson (*Emmy*)
D: Rowland V. Lee SCR: Frances Marion, from a play by Frank Vosper, based on a novel by Agatha Christie
Standard thriller: Lottery winner weds wife-killing maniac

Love from a Stranger
1947, (USA), Eagle Lion, b&w, 81 mins.
W: John Hodiak, Sylvia Sidney, John Howard, Ann Richards, Isobel Elsom, Frederick Worlock Ernest Cossart
D: Richard Whorf SCR: Philip MacDonald, from a story by Agatha Christie PHOTOG: Tony Gaudio MUSIC: Irving Friedman
GB retitle, A Stranger Walked In
Standard thriller: Notorious wife-killer weds innocent

Love in the Welsh Hills
1921, (GB), Harma-Assoc. Exhibitors/Regent, b&w, 6,057 ft. (1846.2m)
W: James Knight (*Bob Lloyd*), Marjorie Villis (*Nan Price*), R. Heaton-Grey (*Owen Hughes*), Roy Raymond (*Morgan Briggs*), Constance Worth, Florence Nelson, J. Edwards Barber, Ernest Spalding
D: Bernard Dudley
Standard crime-thriller: Farmer frames petty officer for theft

Love in the Year 2000
see Le Plus Vieux Metier du Monde

Love Kills
1991, (USA), color, 92 mins.
W: Virginia Madsen, Lenny Von Dohlen, Erich Anderson, Kate Hodge, Jim Metzler
D: Brian Grant
Steamy thriller: Heiress fears lover is assassin

The Love Letter
1998, (USA), CBS-TV, color, 95 mins.
W: Campbell Scott, Jennifer Jason Leigh, Estelle Parsons, David Dukes
TVM, unusual fantasy: Man answers 130-year-old love letter, gets reply

Love Letters
1945, (USA), Para, b&w, 101 mins.
W: Joseph Cotten, Jennifer Jones, Cecil Kellaway, Gladys Cooper, Ann Richards (*Dilly*), Anita Louise (*Helen*), Robert Sully (*Morland*), Ernest Cossart, Lumsden Hare, Reginald Denny, Byron Barr
P: Hal Wallis D: William Dieterle SCR: Ayn Rand, from Chris Massie's novel *Pity My Simplicity* PHOTOG: Lee Garmes MUSIC SCORE: Victor Young
Superior, Oscar-winning melodrama (Oscar nomination for Jones): World War II officer pens love letters for friend; torment and death result

Love Lies Bleeding
1999, (USA), color
W: Faye Dunaway, Malcolm McDowell
Standard thriller: Romance in time of Jack the Ripper

The Love Maniac
see Blood of Ghastly Horror

Love Me Deadly
1972, (USA), Cinema Nat'l, color, 95 mins
W: Mary Wilcox, Lyle Waggoner Christopher Stone, Timothy Scott
P: Buck Edwards D & SCR: Jacques Lacerte
Minor thriller: Woman tries to interest husband in necrophilia

Love Me Tonight
1932, (USA), Para, b&w, 104 mins.
W: Jeanette MacDonald, Maurice Chevalier, Elizabeth Patterson, Charles Ruggles, Myrna Loy, C. Aubrey Smith, Charles Butterworth, Blanche Frederici, Ethel Griffies, Robert Greig
P & D: Rouben Mamoulian SCR: Samuel Hoffenstein, Waldemar Young & George Marion Jr., from a play by Leopold Marchand & Paul Armont PHOTOG: Victor Milner MUSIC: Rodgers & Hart SONG: *Mimi Lover & Isn't It Romantic?*
Classic musical-romance: Ruritanians find love

The Love of a Gypsy
1908, (GB), Warwick Trading Co., b&w
D: Charles Raymond
Standard melodrama

The Love of a Hunchback
1909, (GB), Empire Films/Butcher, b&w, 540 ft. (164.6m)
Standard melodrama: Hunchback saves beloved from evil baron

The Love of a Romany Lass
1909, (GB), Rosie Films, b&w, 767 ft. (233.8m)
D: Joe Rosenthal
Standard crime-thriller: Gypsy girl ordered to stab lover

The Love of Three Queens
1953, (It-Fr), color, 90 mins, originally 180 mins.
W: Hedy Lamarr, Terence Morgan, Cesare Danova, Cathy O'Donnell
Standard melodrama: Hedy Lamarr portrays Helen of Troy, Genevieve of Brabant and Empress Josephine

Love Patches
1912, (GB), Cosmopolitan, b&w, 598 ft. (182.3m)
Standard comedy-fantasy: After woman mends husband's coat with professor's patent patch, he kisses everyone he meets

Love Potion No. 9
1992, (USA), 20th-Fox, color, 97 mins.
W: Tate Donovan, Sandra Bullock, Mary Mara, Dale Midkiff, Anne Bancroft (*The Gypsy*), Hillary Bailey Smith, Dylan Baker, Adrian Paul, Blake Clark
WRIT, P & D: Dale Launer, based on the song PHOTOG: William Wages MUSIC: Jed Leiber
Standard SF-fantasy: Two nerdy scientists become popular after drinking palm reader's formula. cf. An Overdose of Love Potion, 1907

Lovers from Beyond the Grave
see Amanti d'Oltretomba

The Lover's Crime
1904, (GB), Hepworth, b&w, 300 ft. (91.4m)
D: Lewin Fitzhamon
Standard crime-thriller: Man shoots girl, hides body in haystack

Lovers in Limbo
see The Name of the Game is Kill

Love's Mockery
see Der Januskopf

Love Slaves of the Amazon
1957, (USA), Univ, color, 81 mins.
__W:__ Don Taylor, Gianna Segale, Eduardo Ciannelli, Tom Payne, Harvey Chalk, John Herbert, Eugenio Carlos, Wilson Vianna, Anne Marie Nabuco, Gilda Nery, Louis Serrano
__WRIT, P: & D:__ Curt Siodmak
Fr retitle, L'Esclave des Amazones (Slave of the Amazons)
Standard adventure-thriller: Archeologists seek lost tribe

Love Slaves of the Amazons: GIANNA SEGALE AND DON TAYLOR

Loves of Carmen
1927, (USA), Fox, b&w (tinted lavender), 9 reels (8,538 ft./2602.4m)
__W:__ Dolores Del Rio (*Carmen*), Victor McLaglen (*Escamillo*), Don Alvarado (*Jose*), Nancy Nash (*Michaela*), Rafael Valverda (*Miguel*), Mathilde Comont (*Emilia*), Jack Baston (*Morales*), Carmen Costello (*Teresa*), Fred Kohler (*The Gypsy Chief*)
__D:__ Raoul Walsh __SCR:__ Gertrude Orr, from a story by Prosper Merimee __PHOTOG:__ Lucien Andriot & John Marta
Standard melodrama: Gypsy beauty foments tragedy

The Loves of Carmen
1948, (USA), Col, color, 98 mins.
__W:__ Rita Hayworth, Glenn Ford, Ron Randell, Victor Jory, Luther Adler, Arnold Moss, Joseph Buloff
__P & D:__ Charles Vidor, from a story by Prosper Merimee
Standard melodrama: Beautiful gypsy lures soldier

Loves of Count Yorga
see Count Yorga, Vampire

The Loves of Dracula
1979, (USA), Univ, color, 98 mins.
__W:__ Michael Nouri (*Count Dracula*), Carol Baxter, Bever-Leigh Banfield Stephen Johnson, Louise Sorel, Antoinette Stella, Mark Montgomery
__D:__ Richard Milton, Sutton Roley, & Kenneth Johnson __WRIT:__ Myla Lichtman, Craig Buck & Kenneth Johnson, created by Kenneth Johnson __PHOTOG:__ Mario DiLeo, Robert F. Liu, & Howard Schwartz __MUSIC SCORE:__ Les Baxter & Ira Hearshen __THEME:__ Joe Harnell
TVM, standard horror-thriller (culled from episodes of teleseries "Cliffhangers"): Urbane vampire pursues girl. cf. World of Dracula

The Loves of Edgar Allan Poe
1942, (USA), 20th-Fox, b&w, 67 mins.
__W:__ Linda Darnell, John Shepperd (later Shepperd Strudwick), Virginia Gilmore, Jane Darwell, Mary Howard Frank Conroy, Henry (Harry) Morgan
__D:__ Harry Lachman
Standard melodrama: Life of American literary genius

The Loves of Hercules
see Gli Amori di Ercole

The Loves of Omar Khayyam
see Omar Khayyam

The Loves of Pharaoh
see Das Weib des Pharao

Lovespell
1983, (Irl), Clar/Castle Hill, color, 95 mins.
__W:__ Richard Burton (*Mark of Cornwall*), Kate Mulgrew (*Isolt*), Nicholas Clay (*Tristan*), Cyril Cusack (*Gormond of Ireland*), Geraldine Fitzgerald (*Bronwyn*), Niall Tobin (*Andred*), Diana van der Vlis (*Alix*), Niall O'Brien (*Gorvenal*), John Scanlon (*The Bishop*), Kathryn Dowling (*Yseult of the White Hand*), John Jo Brooks (*Father Colm*), John Labine (*Eoghanin*), Trudy Hayes (*Anne*), Bobby Johnson (*William the Guard*)
__D:__ Tom Donovan __SCR:__ Claire Labine __PHOTOG:__ Richard H. Kline

A.k.a. Tristan and Iseult
Modest romance (filmed in 1979): 6th-century Celtic legend of doomed lovers.

Love Spots
1914, (GB), Planet Films/DFSA, b&w, 557 ft. (169.8m)
Standard comedy-fantasy: Magic tonic causes love at first sight

The Love Statue
1964, (USA), Vansan, b&w
__W:__ Peter Ratray, Ondine Use
Minor thriller

Lovestruck
1997, (USA), Irish/FAM-TV, color, 95 mins.
__W:__ Suzanne Somers (*Venus*), Costas Mandylor (*Cupid*), Cynthia Gibb, Annabelle Gurwitch, Mark Joy, Amy Parrish
__D:__ Larry Peerce __TELEPLAY:__ Stephen Witkin & Lindsay Harrison __STORY:__ Stephen Witkin __PHOTOG:__ Tom Priestley __MUSIC:__ Joseph Conlan
TVM, standard comedy-drama-fantasy: Goddess of love sends Cupid to aid lonely woman

Love, the Magician
see El Amor Brujo (1972 & 1986)

Love Trap
see Curse of the Black Widow

Love Versus Science
1909, (GB), R.W. Paul, b&w, 500 ft. (152.4m)
__D:__ Jack Smith
Standard thriller: Professor drugs wife's lover, ties him to time bomb

The Love War
1970, (USA), Aaron Spelling, Made for TV, color, 74 mins.
__W:__ Lloyd Bridges, Angie Dickinson, Harry Basch, Dan (Daniel J.) Travanti, Bill McLean, Allen Jaffe, Byron Foulger
__D:__ George McCowan __SCR:__ David Kidd & Guerdon Trueblood __PHOTOG:__ Paul Uhl
A.k.a. The Sixth Column, orig. to be titled Kyle
TVM, standard SF-thriller: Warring space-aliens use Earth as private battleground

The Loving Touch
see The Psycho Lover

The Loyal 47 Ronin
see Chusingura (1932)

Luch Smerti (The Death Ray)
1925, (Russ), Goskino, b&w, 9,826.1 ft. (2995m)
__W:__ Porfiri Podobed, Alexandra Khokhlova, Sergei Komarov, Vladimir Fogel, Vsevolod Pudovkin, Leonid Obolensky, Pyotr Galadzhev
__D:__ Lev Kuleshov __SCR:__ Vsevolod Pudovkin __PHOTOG:__ Alexander Levitsky

The Lucifer Complex
1979, (USA), Vista/Gold Key, color, 91 mins.
__W:__ Robert Vaughn (*Daniel Manning*), Aldo Ray (*Krauss*), Merrie Lynn Ross, Keenan Wynn, William Lanning, Ross Durfee, Gustof Unger, Victoria Carroll, Glen Ranson, Kieu Chinh, Corinne Cole, Lynn Cartwright, Colin Eliot Brown, Chellio Campbell, Bertil Unger, Carol Terry
__D & SCR:__ David L. Hewitt & Kenneth Hartford __PHOTOG:__ David E. Jackson __SPCL-FX:__ Ray Mercer & Co. __MUSIC:__ William Loose __SONG:__ *Livin' on the Brink* (composed & performed by The Edgar Kelly Band)
Minor SF-thriller: G-man uncovers neo-Nazi cloning

The Lucifer Project
see Barracuda

The Luck of the Irish
1948, (USA), 20th-Fox, b&w, 99 mins.
__W:__ Tyrone Power, Anne Baxter, Lee J. Cobb, Cecil Kellaway, James Todd, Jayne Meadows, J.M. Kerrigan, Dorothy Neumann, Phil Brown
__P:__ Fred Kohlmar __D:__ Henry Koster __SCR:__ Philip Dunne, from novel *There Was a Little Man* by Constance Jones & Guy Jones __PHOTOG:__ Joseph La Shelle __MUSIC:__ Cyril Mockridge
Standard fantasy: Leprechaun attaches himself to American

Lucrezia Borgia
1910, (It), b&w
__D:__ Mario Caserini
Standard melodrama

Lucrezia Borgia
1919, (It), b&w
__D:__ Augusto Genina
Standard melodrama

Lucrezia Borgia
1922, (Ger), b&w, 10,780.8 ft. (3286m)
__W:__ Conrad Veidt, Paul Wegener, William Dieterle
__WRIT, P & D:__ Richard Oswald

L

Standard melodrama

Lucrezia Borgia
1952, (Fr-It), Ariane/Rizzoli/Cinedis, color, 120 mins.
<u>W</u>: Martine Carol, Pedro Armendariz, Maurice Ronet, Christian Mar-quand
<u>D</u>: Christian-Jaque   <u>PHOTOG</u>: Christian Matras
Standard melodrama

Lucrezia Borgia: or, Plaything of Power
1923, (GB), B&C/Regent, b&w, 2,000 ft. (609.6m)
<u>W</u>: Nina Vanna (*Lucrezia Borgia*), Russell Thorndike (*Cesare Borgia*)
<u>P</u>: Edward Godal   <u>D</u>: Edwin Greenwood   <u>STORY:</u>, Eliot Stannard
Standard melodrama (episode from "Wonder Women of the World" series): Beauty faces corrupt court

Luminous Procuress
1972, (USA), Paramour/New Line, color, 77 mins.
<u>W</u>: Pandora, Steven Solberg, Ronald Farrell, Doro Franco, Cherel Fitz-patrick
<u>WRIT, D & PHOTOG</u>: Steven Arnold   <u>MUSIC</u>: Warner Jepson   <u>COSTUMES</u>: Scott Runyon
Standard melodrama

Lunar Cop
1995, (USA), color, 90 mins.
<u>W</u>: Michael Pare, Billy Drago (*Kay*), Robin Smith (*Thora*), Walker Brandt (*Xena*)
Minor SF-thriller: Space cop tries to save Earth from annihilation

Lunatic
1991, (USA), color, 90 mins.
<u>W</u>: Rocky Tucker, Ondrea Tucker, Brian D'Lawrence, Bronwyn St. John, Keith Vallot, Cameron Derrick, Susan Spain, Ernest Jackson, Rookie Macpherson
<u>D & SCR</u>: James Tucker
Minor thriller: Escaped madman stalks teens in forest

The Lunatic at Liberty
1911, (GB), Hepworth, b&w, 475 ft. (144.8m)
<u>D</u>: Frank Wilson
Standard comedy-thriller: Escaped madman poses as policeman

A Lunatic Expected
1910, (GB), Hepworth, b&w, 400 ft. (121.9m)
<u>D</u>: Frank Wilson
Standard comedy-thriller: Railwayman and yokels receive telegram telling them to detain escaped madman

Lunatics in Power
1908, (USA), Edison, b&w
based on Edgar Allan Poe's short story "The System of Dr. Tarr and Professor Fether"
Standard melodrama

I Lunghi Capelli della Morte (The Long Hair of Death)
1965, (It), Felice Testa-Gay-SPA/Unidis, b&w, 100 mins
<u>W</u>: Barbara Steele (*Mary*), Jean Rafferty (*Humbold*), George Ardisson (*Kurt*), Halina Zalewska (*Lizabeth*), Laureen Nuyen (*Grumalda*), Robert Rains (*Von Klage*), John Carey (*Frate*), Jeffrey Darcey (*Messo*)
<u>D</u>: Anthony Dawson [Antonio Margheriti]   <u>SCR</u>: Robert Bohr & Anthony Dawson   <u>PHOTOG</u>: Richard Thierry   <u>MUSIC</u>: Evirust
Standard horror-thriller

Lunnyi Kamen (The Moonstone)
1935, (Russ), b&w
<u>D</u>: Minkin & I. Sirokhtin
<u>SCR</u>: V. Nedobrovo
Standard melodrama

The Lure
1933, (GB), Maude Prods./Para, b&w, 65 mins.
<u>W</u>: Anne Grey (*Julia Waring*), Cyril Raymond (*Paul Dane*), Alec Fraser (*John Baxter*), Billy (*Wilson*) Hartnell (*Billy*), Philip Clarke (*Peter Waring*), P.G. Clark (*Merritt*), Doris Long (*Dorothy*)
<u>D</u>: Arthur Maude, from a play by J.W. Sabben-Clare
Standard thriller: Murderous diamond thief hunted

Lured
1947, (USA), Hunt Stromberg/UA, b&w, 102 mins.
<u>W</u>: Lucille Ball, George Sanders, Boris Karloff, George Zucco, Charles Coburn, Sir Cedric Hardwicke, Joseph Calleia, Robert Coote, Alan Napier, Tanis Chandler, Alan Mowbray
<u>P</u>: James Nasser   <u>D</u>: Douglas Sirk   <u>SCR</u>: Leo Rosten   <u>PHOTOG</u>: William Daniels   <u>MUSIC</u>: Michel Michelet   <u>SONG</u>: *All for Love*
*GB retitle, **Personal Column***
Standard thriller: Dancer helps Scotland Yard find murderer

Lure of the Islands
1942, (USA), b&w, 61 mins.
<u>W</u>: Robert Lowery, Guinn Williams, Warren Hymer, Gale Storm
<u>D</u>: Jean Yarbrough
Minor thriller: Federal agents track criminals to island retreat

Lurkers
1987, (USA), color 90 mins.
<u>W</u>: Christine Moore, Gary Warner, Marina Taylor, Tom Billett, Carissa Channing
<u>D</u>: Roberta Findlay
Minor horror-fantasy: Woman's childhood nightmares start coming true

Lurking Fear
1994, (GB), color, 78 mins.
<u>W</u>: Jon Finch, Blake Bailey, Ashley Lauren Jeffrey Combs, Paul Mantee, Allison Mackie, Vincent Schiavelli, Joe Leavengood
<u>D & SCR</u>: C. Courtney Joyner, from a story by H.P. Lovecraft   <u>MUSIC</u>: Jim Manzie
Minor horror-thriller: Townspeople eradicate graveyard nest of ghouls

The Lurking Vampire
see El Vampiro Acecha

Lust for a Vampire
1970, (GB), MGM-EMI/Hammer/American Continental, color, 95 mins.
<u>W</u>: Ralph Bates (*Giles Barton*), Barbara Jefford (*The Countess*), Suzanna Leigh (*Janet*), Yutte Stensgaard (*Mircalla*), Michael Johnson (*Richard Lestrange*), Helen Christie (*Miss Simpson*), Mike Raven (*Count Karnstein*), Michael Brennan (*The Landlord*), David Healy (*Pelley*), Pippa Steele (*Susan*), Jack Melford (*The Bishop*), Erik Chitty (*Prof. Hertz*)
<u>P</u>: Harry Fine & Michael Style   <u>D</u>: Jimmy Sangster   <u>SCR</u>: Tudor Gates, from Sheridan LeFanu's novel *Carmilla*   <u>PHOTOG</u>: David Muir   <u>MUSIC</u>: Harry Robinson   <u>SONG</u>: *Strange Love*
*USA TV-retitle, **To Love a Vampire***
Standard horror-thriller: Vampirism in 19th-century Austrian girls' school

Lust For A Vampire: MICHAEL JOHNSON AND YUTTE STENSGAARD

Lust for Gold
1910, (GB), Hepworth, b&w, 625 ft. (190.5m)
<u>D</u>: Bert Haldane
Standard crime-thriller: Miner drugs partner, steals gold

Lust of the Vampire
see I Vampiri

Luther the Geek
1990, (USA), color, 90 mins.
<u>W</u>: Edward Terry, Joan Roth, J. Jerome Clarke, Tom Mills
<u>D</u>: Carlton J. Albright
Minor thriller: Boy adversely affected by visit to sideshow

Lycanthropus
1963, (It Austria), Altura/MGM, b&w, 84 mins.
<u>W</u>: Barbara Lass, Carl Schell, Maurice Marsac, Curt Lowens, Mary McNeeran, Grace Neame, Alan Collins, Anni Steinert
<u>P</u>: Jack Forrest   <u>D</u>: Richard Benson   <u>STORY: & SCR</u>: Julian Berry   <u>SONG</u>: *The Ghoul in School*
*GB retitle, **I Married a Werewolf**, USA retitle, **Werewolf in a Girl's Dormitory***
Unusual horror-thriller: Girl's reform school rocked by bestial murders

The Lyons Mail
1916, (GB), Ideal, b&w, 5,200 ft. (1585m)
<u>W</u>: H.B. Irving (*Lesurques/Dubosc*), Nancy Price (*Janette*), Harry Welchman (*Andre*), James Lindsay (*Courriol*), Windham Guise (*Choppard*), Tom Reynolds (*Founiard*), Nelson Ramsey (*Durochat*), Violet Campbell (*Julie*), Alfred Brydone (*Jerome Lesurques*), Charles Vane, Edward Arundell
<u>D</u>: Fred Paul   <u>SCR</u>: Benedict James, from a play by Charles Reade
Standard adventure-thriller: Wealthy Frenchman mistaken for highwayman double

M

1931, (Ger), Nero/Par, b&w, 120 mins.
<u>W</u>: Peter Lorre *(Franz Becker)*, Inge Landgut *(The Child)*, Ellen Widmann *(The Mother)*, Gustaf Gruendgens *(Schraenker)*, Paul Kemp *(The Pickpocket)*, Theodor Loos *(Commissioner Groeber)*, Theo Lingen *(Bauernfaenger)*, Fritz Gnass *(The Burglar)*, Georg John *(The Peddler)*, Franz Stein *(The Minister)*, Ernst Stahl Nachbaur *(The Chief of Police)*, Gerhard Bienert *(The Police Sec'y)*, Rudolf Blumner *(The Defense Lawyer)*, Karl Platen *(The Watchman)*, Rosa Veletti *(The Owner of the Crocodile Club)*, Hertha von Walter *(The Prostitute)*, Fritz Odemar *(The Safe-Breaker)*
<u>P</u>: Seymour Nebenzal   <u>D</u>: Fritz Lang   <u>SCR</u>: Fritz Lang & Thea von Harbou   <u>PHOTOG</u>: Fritz Arno Wagner, Gustav Rathje & Karl Vash
orig. to be titled **Morder Unter Uns (Murderer Among Us)**, *Fr retitle,* **M. Le Maudit (Mr. Curse)**
Classic thriller: German underworld hunts mad child-killer

M: PETER LORRE

M

1951, (USA), Col, b&w, 88 mins.
<u>W</u>: David Wayne, Howard Da Silva, Luther Adler, Martin Gabel, Raymond Burr, Steve Brodie, Glenn Anders, Norman Lloyd, Karen Morley
<u>P</u>: Seymour Nebenzal   <u>D</u>: Joseph Losey   <u>SCR</u>: Norman Reilly Raine & Leo Katcher   <u>ADDITIONAL DIALOG</u>: Waldo Salt   <u>PHOTOG</u>: Ernest Laszlo   <u>MUSIC</u>: Michel Michelet
Standard thriller, minor remake (banned in Ohio): Musician stalks children

Mabuse, the Demon of Crime
see Doctor Mabuse

Macabra
see Demonoid

Macabre
1958, (USA), AA, b&w, 73 mins.
<u>W</u>: William Prince *(Barrett)*, Jacqueline Scott, Jim Backus, Ellen Corby, Christine White, Philip Tonge, Jonathan Kidd Voltaire Perkins, Dorothy Morris, Howard Hoffman, Susan Morrow, Linda Guderman
<u>P & D</u>: William Castle   <u>SCR</u>: Robb White   <u>PHOTOG</u>: Carl Guthrie   <u>MUSIC</u>: Les Baxter
blurb: "We insure you for $1,000 against death by fright!"
Standard thriller (film that launched William Castle's horror-fantasy career): Doctor's daughter kidnapped

Macabre (1980)
1980, (It), color, 89 mins.
<u>W</u>: Larry Ward, Teresa Gimpera, Giacomo Rossi-Stuart
<u>D</u>: Lamberto Bava
Standard thriller: Beauty slays husband

The Macabre Path
1962, (Mex), color
Minor thriller

Macabre Serenade
see House of Evil

Mac and Me
1988, (USA), R.J. Louis/Orion, color, 99 mins.
<u>W</u>: Jade Calegory *(Eric Cruise)*, Christine Ebersole *(Janet Cruise)*, Jonathan Ward *(Michael Cruise)*, Katrina Caspary *(Courtney)*, Lauren Stanley
<u>D</u>: Stewart Raffill   <u>WRIT BY</u>: Stewart Raffill & Steve Feke   <u>PHOTOG</u>: Nick McLean   <u>MUSIC</u>: Alan Silvestri
Minor SF-fantasy: Boy befriends space alien

Macario
1961, (Mex), Clasa Films Mundiales/Azteca, b&w, 91 mins.
<u>W</u>: Ignacio Lopez Tarso, Enrique Lucero, Pina Pellicer, Jose Galvez, Jose Luis Jimenez, Mario Alberto Rodriguez
<u>P</u>: Armando Orive Alba   <u>D</u>: Roberto Gavaldon   <u>SCR</u>: Emilio Carballido & Roberto Gavaldon   <u>STORY</u>: Bruno Traven   <u>PHOTOG</u>: Gabriel Figueroa
Classic fantasy: Death grants peasant power to heal

Macbeth
1909, (It), b&w
<u>D</u>: Mario Caserini, from Shakespeare's play
Standard melodrama: Scottish thane seeks power

Macbeth
1911, (GB), Cooperative Cinematograph Co., b&w, 1,360 ft. (414.5m)
<u>W</u>: Frank Benson *(Macbeth)*, Constance Benson *(Lady Macbeth)*
from Shakespeare's play
Standard melodrama: Scottish scoundrel seeks kingdom

Macbeth
1916, (USA), b&w
<u>W</u>: Sir Henry Beerbohm Tree *(Macbeth)*, Constance Collier *(Lady Macbeth)*
From Shakespeare's play.
Standard melodrama (a "lost" film): Thane conspires

Macbeth
1922, (GB), Master Films/BEF, b&w, 1,175 ft. (358.1m)
<u>W</u>: Russell Thorndike *(Macbeth)*, Sybil Thorndike *(Lady Macbeth)*
<u>D</u>: H.B. Parkinson   <u>SCR</u>: Frank Miller, from Shakespeare's play
Standard melodrama: Scot murders to obtain throne

Macbeth
1948, (USA), Mercury/Rep, b&w, 89 mins, originallly 106 mins
<u>W</u>: Orson Welles *(Macbeth)*, Jeanette Nolan *(Lady Macbeth)*, Roddy McDowall *(Malcolm)*, Dan O'Herlihy *(Macduff)*, Peggy Webber *(Lady Macduff)*, Alan Napier *(A Holy Father)*, Edgar Barrier *(Banquo)*, John Dierkes *(Ross)*, Keene Curtis *(Lennox)*, Erskine Sanford *(Duncan)*, Lionel Braham *(Siward)*, Archie Heugly *(Young Siward)*, Christopher Welles *(The Macduff Child)*, Morgan Farley *(The Doctor)*, Lurene Tuttle *(The Gentlewoman)*, Brainerd Duffield *(The First Murderer)*, William Alland *(The Second Murderer)*, George Chirello *(Seyton)*, Gus Schilling *(A Porter)*
<u>WRIT, P. & D</u>: Orson Welles, from Shakespeare's play   <u>PHOTOG</u>: John L. Russell   <u>MUSIC</u>: Jacques Ibert
Classic melodrama ("archeologically correct" but marred by sloppy, last-minute re-editing): Scot kills to gain crown

Macbeth
1971, (GB), Playboy Prods./Caliban/Col, color, 140 mins.
<u>W</u>: Jon Finch *(Macbeth)*, Francesca Annis *(Lady Macbeth)*, Martin Shaw *(Banquo)*, Terence Bayler *(Macduff)*, Nicholas Selby *(Duncan)*, John Stride *(Ross)*, Stephen Chase *(Malcolm)*, Noel Davis *(Seyton)*, Andrew Laurence *(Lennox)*, Bernard Archard *(Angus)*, Frank Wylie *(Mentieth)*, Bruce Purchase *(Caithness)*, Keith Chegwin *(Fleance)*, Vic Abbott *(Cawdor)*, Noelle Rimmington *(The Young Witch)*, Maisie MacFarquhar *(The Blind Witch)*, Elsie Taylor *(The First Witch)*, Patricia Mason *(The Gentlewoman)*, Bill Drysdale *(King's Groom #1)*, Roy Jones *(King's Groom #2)*, Ian Hogg *(The 1st Minor Thane)*, Geoffrey Reed *(The 2nd Minor Thane)*, Nigel Ashton *(The 3rd Minor Thane)*, Mark Dightman *(Macduff's Son)*, Diane Fletcher *(Lady Macduff)*, Richard Pearson *(The Doctor)*, Sydney Bromley *(The Porter)*, William Hobbs *(Young Seyward)*, Alf Joint *(Old Seyward)*, Michael Balfour *(The 1st Murderer)*, Andrew McCulloch *(The 2nd Murderer)*, Howard Lang *(The 1st Old Soldier)*, David Ellison *(The 2nd Old Soldier)*, Paul Hennen *(The Boy Apprentice)*, Terence Mountain, Beth Owen, Maxine Skelton, Janie Kells, Olga Anthony, Roy Desmond, Pam Foster, Dickie Martyn, John Gordon, Barbara Grimes, Aud Johansen, Anna Willoughby, Christina Paul, Don Vernon
<u>P</u>: Roman Polanski & Andrew Braunsberg   <u>D</u>: Roman Polanski   <u>SCR</u>: Roman Polanski & Kenneth Tynan, from Shakespeare's play   <u>PHOTOG</u>: Gilbert Taylor   <u>MUSIC</u>: The Third Ear Band
Standard eroto-melodrama: Libidinous thane seeks crown

The Machine
1996, (USA), Polygram, color
<u>W</u>: Gerard Depardieu
Made-for-Video, unusual SF-thriller: Psychiatrist invents brain transfer device, joins his psyche to that of killer

Machiste Against the Vampire
see Maciste Contre il Vampiro

Machiste in Hell
1926, (It), b&w, color, 90 mins
US Release: 1931
Standard adventure-fantasy: Hero enters Hades

Machiste in King Solomon's Mines
1964, (It-Fr), Embassy, color, 92 mins
<u>W</u>: Reg Park, Wandisa Guida, Dan Harrison
Minor "Sword & Sandal": Talisman enslaves hero

Machiste, Strongest Man in the World
see *Maciste, l'Eroe Piu Grande del Mondo*

Maciste
1915, (It), b&w, 6,594.5 ft. (2010m)
W: Maciste
D: Giovanni Pastrone
Standard fantasy: Adventures of mythic hero

Maciste Against Hercules in the Vale of Woe
see *Hercules in the Vale of Woe*

Maciste a l'Inferno (Maciste in Hell)
1962, (It), Palisade-Int'l/Medallion, color, 78 mins.
W: Kirk Morris *(Maciste)*, Helene Chanel, Vira Silenti, Andrea Bosic, Angelo
  Zanolli, John Karlsen
P: Ermano Donati & Luigi Carpentieri   **D:** Riccardo Freda   **SCR:** Eddy H.
  Given, Oreste Biancoli, Piero Pierotti, Enniole Concini
USA retitle, **The Witch's Curse** *(Medallion, 1963)*
Standard myth-adventure: Legendary hero enters Hades in attempt to lift curse

Maciste alla Corte del Gran Khan (Maciste at the Court of the Great Khan)
1961, (It-Fr), AIP, color, 95 mins, also 80 mins.
W: Gordon Scott, Yoko Tani
P: Ermanno Donati & Luigi Carpentieri   **D:** Riccardo Freda   **SCR:** Oreste
  Biancoli & Duccio Tessari
USA retitle, **Samson and the Seven Miracles of the World**
Standard "Sword & Sandal": Legendary hero rescues Chinese princess

Maciste alla Corte della Zar (Maciste at the Court of the Czar)
1964, (It), Alexander Films, color (USA: b&w), 91 mins.
W: Kirk Morris
P: Luigi Rovere   **D:** Amerigo Anton   **SCR:** Mario Moroni, Alberto de Rossi &
  Tanio Boccia (Amerigo Anton)
USA retitle, **Samson vs. the Giant King**
*Standard adventure-fantasy: Russian anthropologists revive ancient hero found beneath
  frozen tundra*

Maciste at the Court of the Czar
see *Maciste alla Corte della Zar*

Maciste at the Court of the Great Khan
see *Maciste alla Corte del Gran Khan*

Maciste Contro il Vampiro (Machiste Against the Vampire)
1961, (It), Ambrosiana Cinematografica/Dino De Laurentiis/AIP, color, 91 mins.
W: Gordon Scott, Jacques Sernas, Gianna Maria Canale
P: Paolo Moffa   **D:** Giacomo Gentilomo & Sergio Corbucci   **SCR:** Sergio
  Corbucci & Duccio Tessari
USA retitle, **Goliath and the Vampires** *(AIP, 1964), A.k.a.* **The Vampires**
Standard adventure-fantasy: Muscleman meets Undead

Maciste e la Regina di Samar (Maciste and the Queen of Samaria)
1964, (It-Fr), Nike-Comptoir Francais/Governor, color, 88 mins.
W: Alan Steel *(Sergio Ciani)*, Jany Clair, Anna Maria Polani, Nando Tamberlani,
  Della D'Alberti
P: Luigi Mondello   **D:** Giacomo Gentilomo   **SCR:** Arpad De Riso, Nino Scolaro,
  Giacomo Gentilomo & Angelo Sangarmano   **MUSIC:** Carlo Franci
USA retitle, **Hercules Against the Moon Men**
Standard "Sword & Sandal": Hero opposes alien cultists

Maciste, Gladiatore di Sparta
see *Terror of Rome Against the Son of Hercules*

Maciste, Gladiator of Sparta
see *Terror of Rome Against the Son of Hercules*

Maciste in Hell (1960)
see *Maciste a l'Inferno*

Maciste, l'Eroe Piu Grande del Mondo (Maciste, the World's Greatest Hero)
1963, (It), Leone Film/AIP color, 80 mins.
W: Mark Forest, Eleanora Bianchi
P: Elio Scardamaglia   **D:** Michele Lupo   **SCR:** Roberto Gianviti, Francesco
  Scardamaglia & Lionello De Felice
USA retitle, **Goliath and the Sins of Babylon,** *A.k.a.* **Maciste, Strongest Man in
  the World**
Standard "Sword & Sandal"

Maciste: The Mighty
1960, (It), color, 87 mins.
W: Mark Forest, Chelo Alonso, Angelo Zanolli, Federica Ranchi
D: Carlo Campogalliani
Standard "Sword & Sandal": Egyptians vs. Persians

Mackenna's Gold
1969, (USA), Col, color, 136 mins.
W: Gregory Peck, Omar Sharif, Telly Savalas, Camilla Sparv, Keenan Wynn, Julie
Newmar, Eli Wallach, Raymond Massey, Edward G. Robinson, Burgess
Meredith, Anthony Quayle, Lee J. Cobb, Eduardo Ciannelli, Ted Cassidy,
Rudy Diaz, Dick Peabody, John Garfield Jr.
D: J. Lee Thompson   **SCR:** Carl Foreman   **PHOTOG:** Joe Macdonald   **MUSIC:**
  Dmitri Tiomkin
Bizarre Western-melodrama: Mixed group seeks hidden valley of Apache gold

Macumba
1956, (USA), Banner, b&w
orig. co-billed with **Bride of the Monster**
Minor fantasy-thriller: Voodoo terrifies

Macumba Love
1960, (USA), UA, color, 86 mins.
W: Walter Reed, Ziva Rodann, William Wellman Jr., June Wilkinson, Ruth de
  Souza
P & D: Douglas Fowley   **STORY & SCR:** Norman Graham   **PHOTOG:**
  Rudolfo Icsey   **MUSIC:** Enrico Simonetti
blurb: "Blood lust of the voodoo queen!"
Standard thriller: Innocents encounter voodoo

Macunaima
1970, (Brz), color, 95 mins.
W: Grande Otelo, Paulo Jose
D: Joaquim Pedro De Andrade
*Bizarre fantasy-allegory: Black, born 45 years old, turns white during adventures between
  jungle and city*

Mad About Men
1954, (GB), Group/Eagle Lion, color, 90 mins.
W: Glynis Johns *(Miranda/Caroline)*, Donald Sinden *(Jeff Saunders)*, Anne
  Crawford *(Barbara)*, Margaret Rutherford *(Nurse Carey)*, Dora Bryan
  (Berengaria), Noel Purcell *(Old Salt)*, Peter Martyn *(Ronald)*, Joan Hickson
  (Mrs. Forster), Nicholas Phipps *(Barclay Sutton)*, Judith Furse *(Viola)*, Irene
  Handl *(Mme. Blanche)*, David Hurst *(Mantalini)*, Martin Miller *(Dr. Fergus)*,
  Harry Welchman *(Symes)*, Meredith Edwards *(The Policeman)*
P: Betty Box   **D:** Ralph Thomas   **STORY:**, Peter Blackmore
Standard comedy-fantasy, sequel to **Miranda:** *Mermaid changes places with sportswoman
  double*

Madame DuBarry
1919, (Ger), Ufa, b&w, 135 mins.
W: Pola Negri, Emil Jannings
D: Ernst Lubitsch   **PHOTOG:** Theodor Sparkuhl
USA retitle, **Passion** *(First National, 1920)*
Ornate melodrama: Intrigue involves French-Court beauty

Madame DuBarry
1934, (USA), WB, b&w, 79 mins.
W: Dolores Del Rio
D: William Dieterle   **PHOTOG:** Sol Polito
Standard melodrama

Madame DuBarry
1954, (Fr), color, 106 mins.
W: Martine Carol
D: Christian-Jaque   **SCR:** Henri Jeanson & Christian-Jaque   **PHOTOG:**
  Christian Matras   **MUSIC:** Georges Van Parys
Standard melodrama

Madame Sin
1972, (USA-GB), Robert Wagner/ITC, Made for TV, color, 76 mins.
W: Bette Davis *(Mme. Sin)*, Robert Wagner *(Anthony Lawrence)*, Catherine Schell
  (Barbara), Gordon Jackson *(Cmdr. Cavendish)*, Denholm Elliott *(Malcolm De
  Vere)*, Dudley Sutton *(Monk)*, Al Mancini *(The Fisherman)*, Piksen Lim
  (Nikko), Paul Maxwell *(Connors)*, Charles Lloyd-Pack *(Mr. Willoughby)*,
  Frank Middlemass *(Dr. Henriques)*, Roy Kinnear *(Holidaymaker)*, Alan Dobie
  (White), David Healy *(Braden)*, Arnold Diamond *(Lengett)*
P: Julian Wintle & Lou Morheim   **D:** David Greene   **TELPLAY:** David Greene
  & Barry Oringer, from a story by Lou Morheim & Barry Shear   **PHOTOG:**
  Ted Richmond   **MUSIC:** Michael Gibbs
TVM, standard thriller: Inscrutable villainess bedevils British Isles

Madame Sin: BETTE DAVIS AND ROBERT WAGNER

Madame Spy
1934, (USA), Univ, b&w, 70 mins.
W: Fay Wray, Nils Asther, Edward Arnold
D: Karl Freund
Standard thriller

Madame White Snake
1966, (Nat'list China), Frank Lee Int'l, color, 105 mins.
W: Lin Dai, Chao Lei
Standard thriller

Mad at the Moon
1992, (USA), color, 98 mins.
W: Mary Stuart Masterson, Hart Bochner, Fionnula Flanagan, Cec Verrell
D: Martin Donovan   **SCR:** Martin Donovan & Richard Pelusi
Unusual Western-horror: Bride on American plains suspects husband is lycanthrope

The Mad Bomber
1973, (USA), Cinemation, color, 95 mins.
W: Chuck Connors (*William*), Neville Brand (*Fromley*), Vince Edwards (*Geronimo*), Hank Brandt (*Blake*), Christina Hart (*Fromley's Victim*), Faith Quabius (*Martha*), Ilona Wilson (*Mrs. Fromley*), Nancy Honnold (*Anne*)
WRIT, P & D: Bert I. Gordon   **STORY:** Marc Behm   **MUSIC:** Michel Mention
A.k.a. **Detective Geronimo** *and* **Police Connection**
Standard thriller: L.A. cop seeks link between rapist and mad bomber

The Mad Butcher
1972, (It), Ellman, color, 90 mins.
W: Victor Buono, Karin Field, Brad Harris, John Ireland
D: Guido Zurli   **SCR:** Charles Ross
A.k.a. **Meat is Meat** *and* **Strangler of Vienna**
Minor thriller: Cops seek missing girl, meat seller prospers

Das Madchen Rosemarie (The Girl Rosemarie)
1958, (W. Ger), b&w, 100 mins.
W: Nadja Tiller, Peter Van Eyck, Carl Raddatz, Gert Frobe, Mario Adorf, Horst Frank
D: Rolf Thiele
Unusual fact-based thriller: Callgirl murdered

Mad Death
1985, (GB), color, 120 mins.
Standard SF-horror (culled from teleseries): Virus produces zombies

The Maddening
1994, (USA), color, 97 mins
W: Burt Reynolds, Angie Dickinson, Mia Sara
Standard thriller

The Maddening
1995, (USA), Trimark, color, 97 mins.
W: Mia Sara, Brian Wimmer, Josh Mostel, William Hickey
D: Danny Huston   **SCR:** Henry Slesar & Leslie Greif, from Andrew Neiderman's novel *Playmates*   **PHOTOG:** Nick McLean   **MUSIC:** Peter Manning Robinson   **SONGS:** *Last Chance & Midnight Blues*

The Mad Doctor
1941, (USA), Para, b&w, 90 mins.
W: Basil Rathbone, Ellen Drew, John Howard, Martin Kosleck, Ralph Morgan, Barbara Allen [A.k.a. Vera Vague]
P: George Arthur   **D:** Tim Whelan   **SCR:** Howard J. Green   **PHOTOG:** Ted Tetzlaff
GB retitle, **A Date with Destiny**
Standard thriller: Psychiatrist weds and murders rich women

Mad Doctor of Blood Island
1969, (USA-Phil), Hemisphere, color, 110 mins.
W: John Ashley (*Dr. Bill Foster*), Ronald Remy, Angelique Pettyjohn, Alicia Alonzo, Alfonso Carvajal
P: Eddie Romero   **D:** Gerry (Gerardo) de Leon & Eddie Romero   **SCR:** Reuben Canoy
A.k.a. **Blood Doctor** *and* **Tomb of the Living Dead**
blurb: "In blood-dripping color"
Minor horror-thriller: Scientist's unorthodox experiments

The Mad Doctor of Market Street
1941, (USA), Univ, b&w, 61 mins.
W: Lionel Atwill, Nat Pendleton, Anne Nagel, Una Merkel, Hardie Albright, Claire Dodd, Richard Davies, Ray Mala
D: Joseph H. Lewis   **ORIG. SCR:** Al Martin   **PHOTOG:** Jerome Ash
Production title: **The Terror of the Islands**
Minor thriller: Gruesome experiments on tropic isle

Made in Heaven
1987, (USA), Lorimar, color, 102 mins.
W: Timothy Hutton (*Mike Shea/Elmo Barnett*), Kelly McGillis (*Annie Packert/Alley Chandler*), Ann Wedgeworth (*Annette Shea*), Maureen Stapleton (*Aunt Lisa*), Debra Winger (*Emmett*), James Gammon (*Steve Shea*), Mare Winningham

(*Brenda Carlucci*), Don Murray (*Ben Chandler*), Timothy Daly (*Tom Donnelly*), Amanda Plummer (*Wiley Foxx*), Neil Young (*The Truck Driver*), Tom Petty (*Stanky*), Ric Ocasek (*Shark*), Tom Robbins (*Mario the Toymaker*)
D: Alan Rudolph   **SCR:** Bruce A. Evans   **PHOTOG:** Jan Kiesser   **MUSIC:** Mark Isham
Standard fantasy-romance: Lovers in heaven reborn on Earth

Mademoiselle
1966, (GB-Fr), UA, b&w, 103 mins.
W: Jeanne Moreau, Ettore Manni, Keith Skinner, Umberto Orsini, Jane Berretta
D: Tony Richardson   **STORY & SCR:** Jean Genet   **PHOTOG:** David Watkin
Uneven melodrama: Schoolteacher lusts after woodcutter, commits atrocities

The Mad Executioners
see **Der Henker von London**

The Mad Genius
1931, (USA), WB, b&w, 81 mins.
W: John Barrymore, Marion Marsh, Carmel Myers, Charles Butter-worth, Andre Lugut, Donald Cook, Boris Karloff, Frankie Darro, Mae Madison, Luis Alberni
D: Michael Curtiz   **SCR:** J. Grubb Alexander & Harvey Thew   **PH:** Barney McGill, from Martin Brown's play *The Idol*
Unusual melodrama: Svengali-like balletmaster turns waif into fabulous dancer

The Mad Ghoul
1943, (USA), Univ, b&w, 65 mins.
W: George Zucco, David Bruce, Evelyn Ankers, Milburn Stone, Turhan Bey, Robert Armstrong, Rose Hobart
D: James Hogan   **SCR:** Brenda Weisberg & Paul Gangelin
Bizarre horror-thriller: Doctor finds Aztec anesthetic that turns people into zombies

The Mad Ghoul: DAVID BRUCE AND GEORGE ZUCCO

Madhouse
1974, (GB), Amicus/AIP color, 92 mins.
W: Vincent Price (*Paul Toombes*), Natasha Pyne (*Julia*), Robert Quarry (*Oliver Quayle*), Linda Hayden (*Elizabeth Peters*), Peter Cushing (*Herbert Flay*), Barry Dennen (*Blount*), Jenny Lee Wright (*Carol*), John Garrie (*Insp. Harper*), Adrienne Corri (*Faye*), Julie Crosthwaite (*Ellen*), Michael Parkinson (*The TV Interviewer*), Ellis Dayle (*Alfred*), Peter Halliday (*The Psychiatrist*), Catherine Willmer (*Louise Peters*), Ian Thompson (*Bradshaw*)
P: Max J. Rosenberg & Milton Subotsky   **D:** James Clark   **SCR:** Greg Morrison, from Angus Hall's novel *Devilday*   **PHOTOG:** Ray Parslow   **MUSIC:** Douglas Gamley
orig. to be titled **Dr. Death**
Standard horror-thriller: Fright-film star framed for murders

Madhouse Mansion
see **Ghost Story** (1975)

Mad Love
1935, (USA), MGM, b&w, 83 mins.
W: Peter Lorre, Frances Drake, Colin Clive, Valerie Hobson, Isabel Jewell, Ted Healy, Sara Haden, Edward Brophy, Harold Huber, Cora Sue Collins, Charles Trowbridge, Henry Kolker, Keye Luke, Rollo Lloyd, Murray Kinnell, Ian Wolfe, Michael Mark, May Beatty
D: Karl Freund   **SCR:** Guy Endore, P.J. Wolfson & John L. Balderston   **BASED ON:** Maurice Renard's novel *The Hands of Orlac*   **PHOTOG:** Chester Lyons & Gregg Toland   **MUSIC:** Oscar Radin
GB retitle, **The Hands of Orlac**
Classic thriller: Mad surgeon pursues pianist's wife

The Mad Magician
1954, (USA), Col, 3D b&w, 72 mins.
W: Vincent Price (*Gallico*), Mary Murphy (*Karen*), Patrick O'Neal (*Bruce*), Eva Gabor (*Claire*), John Emery (*Rinaldi*), Donald Randolph (*Ormond*), Lenita Lane (*Alice Prentiss*), Jay Novello (*Mr. Prentiss*), Corey Allen
P: Bryan Foy   **D:** John Brahm   **STORY & SCR:** Crane Wilbur   **PHOTOG:** Bert Glennon   **MUSIC:** Emil Newman & Arthur Lange
Standard thriller: Stage magician seeks revenge

Mad Love: PETER LORRE

Madman

1982, (USA), Jensen Farley Pictures, color, 89 mins.

W: Alexis Dubin, Tony Fish, Harriet Bass, Michael Sullivan, Seth Jones, Jan Claire, Alex Murphy, Carl Fredericks, Jimmy Steele, Gaylen Ross, Paul Ehlers *(Madman Marz)*

P: Gary Sales **D & SCR:** Joe Giannone **STORY:** Joe Giannone & Gary Sales **PHOTOG:** James Momel **ELECTRONIC MUSIC:** Stephen Horelick

Minor thriller: Axe-murderer slays campers

The Madman's Bride

1907, (GB), Hepworth, b&w, 400 ft. (121.9m)

D: Lewin Fitzhamon

Standard melodrama: Demented lord buys girl from father, kills her during night

The Madman's Fate

1906, (GB), R.W. Paul, b&w, 576 ft. (175.6m)

W: Leah Marlborough *(The Wife)*

D: J.H. Martin

Standard thriller: Man kills escaped lunatic

Mad Max

1979, (Austral), AIP, color, 89 mins.

W: Mel Gibson *(Max)*, Hugh Keays-Byrne *(Toecutter)*, Joanne Samuel *(Jessie)*, Steve Bisley *(Jim)*, Mathew Constantine, Roger Ward, Tim Burns, Stephan Clark, Jerry Day, Reg Evans, Howard Eynon, Max Fairchild, John Farndale, Jonathon Hardy, Peter Felmingham, Sheila Florence, Nic Gazzana, Vince Gil, Hunter Gibb, Andrew Gilmore, Brendan Heath, Nick Lathouris, Paul Johnstone, John Ley, Steve Millichamp, Neil Thompson, Phil Motherwell, George Novak, Geoff Parry, Kristine Kaman, Lulu Pinkus, Billy Tisdall, Gil Tucker, Kim Sullivan, Peter Ford, Tom Broadbridge, John Arnold Telford Jackson, Clive Hearne, Joan Letch, Kerry Miller, Janine Ogden, Paul Young, Di Trelour, Vernon Weaver, Brendan Young

D: George Miller **SCR:** James McCausland & George Miller **STORY:** George Miller, Byron Kennedy **PHOTOG:** David Eggby **SPCL-FX:** Chris Murray **MUSIC:** Brian May

Standard thriller: Post-nuke struggle for survival. cf. **Mad Max Beyond Thunderdome** *and* **The Road Warrior**

Mad Max II

see **The Road Warrior**

Mad Max Beyond Thunderdome

1985, (Austral), WB, color, 108 mins.

W: Mel Gibson *(Max)*, Bruce Spence *(Jedediah)*, Adam Cockburn *(Jedediah Jr.)*, Tina Turner *(Aunty Entity)*, Angelo Rossitto *(The Master)*, Frank Thring *(The Collector)*, Angry Anderson *(Ironbar)*, Paul Larsson *(The Blaster)*, Edwin Hodgeman *(Dr. Dealgood)*, Robert Grubb *(Pigkiller)*, Helen Buday *(Savannah Nix)*, George Spartels *(Blackfinger)*, Mark Kounnas *(Gekko)*, Bob Hornery *(Waterseller)*, Andrew Oh *(Ton Ton Tattoo)*, Mark Spain *(Mr. Skyfish)*, Rod Zuanic *(Scrooloose)*, Adam Willits *(Mr. Scratch)*, Justine Clarke *(Anna Goanna)*, Shane Tickner *(Eddie)*, Toni Allaylis *(Cusha)*, Adam Scougall *(Finn McCoo)*, James Wingrove *(Tubba Tintye)*, Tom Jennings *(Slake)*, Ollie Hall, Susan Leonard, Ray Turnbull, Lee Rice, Robert Simper, Brian Ellison, Gerard Armstrong, Max Worrall, Marion Sands, Virginia Wark, Geeling, Gerry D'Angelo, Travis Latter, Paul Daniel, Miguel Lopez, Tushka Hose,

Emily Sbocker, Charlie Kenney, Sandie Lillingston, Ben Chesterman, Dan Chesterman, Liam Nikkinen, Christopher Norton, Katharine Cullen, Heilan Robertson, Gabriel Dilworth, Hugh Sands, Rebekah Elmaloglou, Shari Flood, Kate Tatar, Rachael Graham, Pega Williams, Emma Howard, Tarah Williams, Joanna McCarroll, Tonya Wright, Toby Messiter, Daniel Willits, Amanda Nikkinen, William Manning, Flynn Kenney, Luke Panic, James Robertson, Adan McCreadie, Sally Morton

D: George Miller & George Ogilvie **SCR:** Terry Hayes & George Miller **PHOTOG:** Dean Semler **SPCL-FX:** Mike Wood, Steve Courtley & Brian Cox **MUSIC:** Maurice Jarré **SONG:** *We Don't Need Another Hero*

Standard SF-adventure: Drifter meets dominatrix of postnuclear society

Madmen of Mandoras

1963, (USA), Crown Int'l, b&w, 70 mins.

W: Walter Stocker *(Phil)*, Audrey Caire *(Kathy)*, Dani Lynn *(Suzanne)*, Carlos Rivas *(Camine)*, Nestor Paiva *(Alaniz)*, John Holland *(John)*, Scott Peters, Keith Dahle, Marshall Reed, Pedro Regas, Jerry Riggio, Bill Freed *(Mr. H)*

D: David Bradley **SCR:** Richard Miles, Steve Bennett **ORIG. STORY:** Steve Bennett **PHOTOG:** Stanley Cortez

TV retitle, **They Saved Hitler's Brain***, A.k.a.* **The Return of Mr. H**

Standard thriller (with soundtrack music from 'Creature from the Black Lagoon'): Hoping for a Fourth Reich, scientists keep dictator's head alive

The Mad Monkey

see **A Bag of Monkey Nuts**

The Mad Monster

1942, (USA), PRC, b&w, 77 mins.

W: Johnny Downs *(Tom Gregory)*, George Zucco *(Dr. Lorenzo Cameron)*, Anne Nagel *(Leonora)*, Glenn Strange, Sarah Padden, Gordon DeMain, Mae Busch, Reginald Barlow, Charles (Slim) Whitaker, Robert Strange, Henry Hall, Edward Cassidy, Eddie Holden, John Elliott, Gil Patrick

P: Sigmund Neufield **D:** Sam Newfield **ORIG. SCR:** Fred Myton **PHOTOG:** Jack Greenhalgh **SPCL-FX:** George Stone **MUSIC:** David Chudnow

Standard horror-thriller: Scientist plans army of wolfmen

Mad Monster Party

1968, (USA), Videocraft Int'l/Avco Embassy/Joseph E. Levine, color, 94 mins.

VOICES: Boris Karloff & Phyllis Diller

P: Arthur Rankin Jr. **D:** Jules Bass **SCR:** Len Korobkin & Harvey Kurtzman

Juvenile comedy-fantasy (enacted by animated puppets): Monsters hold frenetic celebration

The Madness of Doctor Tube

see **La Folie du Docteur Tube**

The Madonna's Secret

1946, (USA), b&w, 79 mins.

W: Francis Lederer, Gail Patrick, Ann Rutherford, Linda Stirling, John Litel

D: William Thiele

Standard whodunit: Search for model's killer

The Mad Room

1968, (USA), Col, color, 92 mins.

W: Stella Stevens *(Ellen Hardy)*, Shelley Winters *(Mrs. Armstrong)*, Skip Ward *(Sam Aller)*, Severn Darden *(Nate)*, Carol Cole *(Chris)*, Beverly Garland *(Mrs. Racine)*, Michael Burns *(George)*, Barbara Sammeth *(Mandy)*, Lloyd Haynes *(Dr. Marion Kincaid)*, Jennifer Bishop *(Mrs. Ericson)*, Lou Kane *(Armand Racine)*, Gloria Manon *(Edna)*

P: Norman Maurer **D:** Bernard Girard **SCR:** Bernard Girard & A.Z. Martin, loosely based on Reginald Denham & Edward Percy's play *Ladies in Retirement* (remake) **PHOTOG:** Harry Stradling Jr. **MUSIC:** David Grusin **SONGS:** *Open My Eyes & Wildwood Blues*

Standard thriller: Children thought to have committed gory atrocities

The Mafu Cage

1979, (USA), American General, color, 101 mins.

W: Carol Kane, Lee Grant, James Olson, Will Geer

P: Diana Young **D:** Karen Arthur **SCR:** Don Christian

A.k.a. **My Sister, My Love**

Standard thriller: Madwoman tortures, kills

Magic

1978, (USA), 20th-Fox, color, 106 mins.

W: Anthony Hopkins *(Corky)*, Ann-Margret *(Peggy Ann)*, Burgess Meredith *(Ben Greene 'Gangrene')*, Ed Lauter *(Duke)*, Jerry Houser *(The Cab Driver)*, E.J. Andre *(Merlin)*, David Ogden Stiers *(Todson)*, Joe Lowry *(The Club M.C.)*, Lillian Randolph *(Sadie)*, Beverly Sanders *(The Laughing Lady)*, I.W. Klein *(The Maitre d')*, Stephen Hart *(The Captain)*, Bob Hackman *(The Father)*, Patrick McCullough *(The Doorman)*, Mary Munday *(The Mother)*, Scott Garrett *(Corky's Brother)*, Brad Beesley *(Young Corky)*, Michael Harte *(The Minister)*

D: Richard Attenborough **SCR:** William Goldman—from his novel **PHOTOG:** Victor J. Kemper **MUSIC:** Jerry Goldsmith

Unusual thriller: Ventriloquist controlled by evil alter ego

The Magical Box

1903, (Fr), Star, b&w

W: Georges Melies

WRIT, P & D: Georges Melies

Standard fantasy

Magic: Joseph E. Levine, Richard P. Levine, Anthony Hopkins, Burgess Meredith and Fats the Dummy

Magical Mysteries
1914, (GB), Kineto, b&w, 500 ft. (152.4m)
D: Walter R. Booth
Standard fantasy

The Magic Book
see Le Livre Magique

The Magic Bottle
1906, (GB), Urban, b&w, 200 ft. (60.1m)
D: Walter R. Booth
Standard fantasy short: Mysterious bottle produces magical effects

The Magic Box
1908, (GB), R.W. Paul, b&w
D: Jack Smith
Standard fantasy short: When man's magic box produces girl, wife uses it to produce man

The Magic Boy
1960, (Jap), color, 85 mins.
Standard animated fantasy: Young hero vs. evil witch

The Magic Bubble
1992, (USA), Amazing Films, color, 95 mins.
W: Diane Salinger, John Calvin (*Charles*), Priscilla Pointer (*Grandma*), George Clooney (*Mac*), Wallace Shawn, Colleen Camp, Nicholas Guest, Anthony Peck, Michael Greene, Dayle Haddon, Lyndsay Riddell, Michael Boatman
D: Alfredo Ringell & Deborah Taper Ringell   **SCR:** Meredith Baer & Geof Pryssir   **PHOTOG:** Harry Mathias   **MUSIC:** Jeff Lass
orig tilte **Unbecoming Age**
Standard fantasy: Depressed housewife finds Magic bubbles that give her the mentality of an 8-year-old

The Magic Carpet
1909, (GB), Urban, b&w, 350 ft. (106.7m)
D: Walter R. Booth
Standard fantasy short (14 scenes): Tramp steals sorcerer's flying carpet

The Magic Carpet
1951, (USA), Col, color, 84 mins.
W: Lucille Ball, John Agar, Raymond Burr, Patricia Medina, George Tobias
P: Sam Katzman   **D:** Lew Landers   **SCR:** David Mathews
Standard adventure-fantasy

The Magic Christian
1969, (GB), Commonwealth United/Grand Films, color, 95 mins.
W: Peter Sellers (*Sir Guy Grand*), Ringo Starr (*Youngman Grand*), Laurence Harvey (*Hamlet*), Raquel Welch (*The Slave Priestess*), Richard Attenborough (*The Oxford Coach*), Wilfrid Hyde White (*Klaus*), Christopher Lee (*The Vampire*), Spike Milligan (*The Warden*), Isabel Jeans (*Aunt Agnes*), Leonard Frey (*The Psychiatrist*), Roman Polanski (*The Listener*), Patrick Cargill (*The Auctioneer*), John LeMesurier (*Sir John*), Fred Emney (*Fitzgibbon*), Dennis Price (*Winthrop*), John Cleese (*Dugdale*), Yul Brynner (*Lady Singer*), Michael Trubshawe (*A Man*), Caroline Blakiston (*Esther Gerard*), Roland Culver (*Sir Herbert*), Terence Alexander (*Maj. Trubshawe*), Clive Dunn (*The Sommelier*), Peter Graves (*The Lord*), Patrick Holt (*The Duke*), Hattie Jacques (*Ginger*

Horton), Ferdy Mayne (*Edouard*), Guy Middleton (*Duke of Mantisbriar*), Graham Stark (*A Waiter*), Edward Underdown (*Prince Henry*), David Hutcheson (*A Man*), Harold Berens (*A Waiter*), Harry Carpenter, Graham Chapman, Michael Aspel, W. Barrington Dalby, Michael Barratt, John Snagge, Alan Whicker
P: Henry Weinstein & Anthony Unger   **D:** Joseph McGrath   **SCR:** Terry Southern, Joseph McGrath & Peter Sellers, based on Terry Southern's iconoclastic novel   **PHOTOG:** Geoffrey Unsworth   **MUSIC:** Ken Thorne
Bizarre comedy: Mad adventures of world's richest eccentric

The Magic Cloak of Oz
1914, (USA), b&w
WRIT, P & D: Frank L. Baum

The Magic Extinguisher
1901, (GB), Williamson, b&w, 110 ft. (33.5m)
W: Sam Dalton
D: James Williamson
Standard fantasy short: Conjuror makes animals disappear, then vanishes himself

The Magic Garden
1908, (GB), R.W. Paul, b&w
Standard fantasy short: Drunken gardener sees giant frog, snake, etc.

The Magic Glass
1914, (GB), Hepworth, b&w, 825 ft. (251.5m)
W: Eric Desmond (*Tommy*)
D: Hay Plumb   **STORY:** S.A. Screech
Standard fantasy: Boy uses professor's liquid to make objects disappear

The Magic Horse
1953, (GB), b&w, 10 mins.
D: Lotte Reiniger
Standard short animated fantasy

Magic Hunter
1996, (GB-Hung), color
W: Gary Kemp, Sadie Frost
Bizarre fantasy-thriller: Policeman makes supernatural pact

The Magician (1898)
see Le Magicien

The Magician
1926, (USA), MGM, b&w, 7 reels (6,960 ft./2121.4m)
W: Paul Wegener (*Oliver Haddo*), Alice Terry (*Margaret Dauncey*), Ivan Petrovich (*Dr. Arthur Burdon*), Firmin Gemier (*Dr. Porhoet*), Gladys Hamer (*Susie Bond*), Stowitts
D & SCR: Rex Ingram, from Somerset Maugham's novel   **PHOTOG:** John F. Seitz
Standard thriller: Beauty hypnotized by student of occult

The Magician (1958)
see Ansiktet

The Magician
1973, (USA), Para-B&B Prods./CBS-TV, color, 73 mins.
W: Bill Bixby (*Anthony Dorian*), Kim Hunter (*Nora*), Barry Sullivan (*Baker*), Elizabeth Ashley (*Sallie*), Keene Curtis (*Max*), Signe Hasso (*Mme. Parga*), Joan Caulfield, Don Brit Reid, Jim Watkins, Todd Crespi, Allen Case, Jeff Morris, Robert Mandan, Richard Van Vleet, Anne Lockhart, Michael Clark, Tol Avery, Bill Quinn, Holly Irving, David Moses, Arline Anderson, Dale Tarter, Johnny Haymer, Bruce Watson, Nancy Stephens, Edward Knight
D: Marvin Chomsky   **TELEPLAY:** Laurence Heath   **STORY:** Joseph Stefano
PHOTOG: Robert Hoffman   **SPCL-FX:** Jonnie Burke   **MUSIC:** Pat Williams
TVM-pilot, standard thriller: Stage magician aids people

The Magician's Cavern
1901, (Fr), Star, b&w, 60m (196.9 ft./3.3 mins.)
D: Georges Melies
A.k.a. **The House of Mystery**
Standard fantasy

Le Magicien (The Magician)
1898, (Fr), Star, b&w, 20m (65.6 ft./1.1 mins.)
D: Georges Melies
GB retitle, **Black Magic**
Standard fantasy

Magic in the Water
1995, (Can), TriStar, color, 98 mins.
W: Mark Harmon, Joshua Jackson, Sarah Wayne, Willie Nark-Orn, Frank S. Salsedo
D: Rick Stevenson   **SCR:** Icel Dobell Massey & Rick Stevenson   **PHOTOG:** Thomas Burstyn   **MUSIC:** David Schwartz
Standard fantasy: Psychiatrist finds monstrous creature at lakeside community

Magic Island
1995, (USA), Moobeam/Para, color, 90 mins.
W: Zachery Ty Bryan, Edward Kerr, Lee Armstrong, French Stewart, Jessie-Ann Friend, Oscar Dillon, Abraham Benrubi, Sean O'Kane, Schae Harrison, Andrew Divoff, Ja'net DuBois
D: Sam Irvin **SCR:** Neil Ruttenberg & Brent Friedman **PHOTOG:** James Lawrence Spencer **VS-FX SPRVSR:** Joseph Grossberg **MUSIC:** Richard Band
Standard fantasy: Book transports boy to enchanted world

The Magic Lantern
see La Lanterne Magique

Magic Lotus Lantern
1966, (Red China), color
W: Experimental Opera Company
Unusual fantasy: Fairytale told solely through mime and ballet

The Magic Riddle
1991, (USA), color, 92 mins.
VOICES: Robyn Moore
Standard animated fantasy: Grandmother relates tangled fairy tales

The Magic Ring
1906, (GB), Hepworth, b&w, 500 ft. (152.4m)
W: Dolly Lupone (*The Maiden*)
D: Lewin Fitzhamon
Standard fantasy: Youth rescues maiden from witch's castle

The Magic Ring
1911, (GB), Natural Colour Kinematograph Co., color, 525 ft. (160m)
D: Theo Bouwmeester
Standard fantasy: Archeologist finds ring that induces love

The Magic Serpent
1966, (Jap), Toei/AIP, color, 85 mins
W: Hiroki Matsukata, Tomoko Ogawa, Ryutaro Otomo, Bin Amatsu
D: Tetsuya Yamaguchi **SCR:** Masaru Igami
Standard fantasy: Youth avenges father's murder, battles monsters

The Magic Shop
1982, (GB), Sunley-Centrespur/Col-EMI-Warner, color, 23 mins.
W: William Rushton, Peter Bull, Karl Johnson, Paul Erangey
D: Ian Eames, from a story by H.G. Wells
Standard short fantasy: Magic-shop proprietor performs amazing tricks on boy and father

The Magic Snowman
1987, (USA-Yugo), Miramaxcolor, 84 mins.
W: Justin Fried, Dragana Marjanovic (*Mandy*), Roger Moore (*The Voice of Mr. Ukko*)
Minor juvenile fantasy: Youth gets advice from snowman

Magic Spectacles
1961, (USA), Fairway Int'l, color, 74 mins
W: Tommy Holden, June Parr, Kay Cramer, Cindy Tyler, Jean Cartwright, Danice Daniels, Carla Olson
P & SCR: Arch Hall Jr. **D:** Bob Wehling
A.k.a. **Tickled Pink**
Minor nudie-comedy: Unusual glasses allow man to see through women's clothes

Magic Squares
1914, (GB), B&C/DFSA, b&w, 498 ft. (151.8m)
WRIT & D: Louis Nikola
Standard fantasy: Paper squares form people, monsters, etc.

The Magic Sword: or, A Mediaeval Mystery
1901, (GB), R.W. Paul, b&w, 180 ft. (54.9m)
D & STORY: Walter R. Booth
Standard fantasy short: Knight saves lady from ogre and witch

The Magic Sword
1962, (USA), UA, color, 80 mins.
W: Gary Lockwood (*St. George*), Basil Rathbone (*Lodac*), Anne Helm (*Princess Helene*), Estelle Winwood (*Sybil*), Danielle De Metz (*The French Girl*), David Cross (*Sir Pedro*), Jacques Gallo (*Sir Dennis*), Liam Sullivan (*Sir Branton*), Anne Graves (*Princess Laura*), Leroy Johnson (*Sir Ulrich*), John Mauldin (*Sir Patrick*), Angus Duncan (*Sir James*), Vampira (A.k.a. Maila Nurmi) (*The Hag*), Merritt Stone (*The King*), Taldo Kenyon (*Sir Anthony*), Jack Kosslyn (*The Ogre*), Lorrie Richards (*Anne*), Marlene Callahan (*Princess Grace*)
P & D: Bert I. Gordon **SCR:** Bernard Schoenfeld, from a story: by Bert I. Gordon **PHOTOG:** Paul C. Vogel **SPCL-FX:** Milt Rice **MUSIC:** Richard Markowitz
A.k.a. **Saint George and the Seven Curses**
Standard fantasy: Knight raised by amiable witch rescues princess from wicked sorcerer

Magic Through the Ages
see La Magie a Travers les Ages

The Magic Toyshop
1986, (GB), Palace/Skouras, color, 107 mins.
W: Tom Bell, Caroline Milmoe, Kilian McKenna, Patricia Kerrigan, Lorcan Cranitch, Gareth Bushill, Georgina Hulme, Marlene Sidaway, Marguerite Porter, Lloyd Newson
D: David Wheatley **SCR:** Angela Carter, from her novel **PHOTOG:** Ken Morgan **MUSIC:** Bill Connor
Standard psychodrama: Orphans go to live with dour toymaker uncle

The Magic Christian: RAQUEL WELCH

The Magic Voyage
1994, (USA-Ger), color, 80 mins.
VOICES: Dom DeLuise (*Columbus*), Corey Feldman (*Pico*)
Standard animated fantasy: Worm accompanies Columbus on trip to New World

The Magic Voyage of Sinbad
1953, (Russ.), Mosfilm/Filmgroup, color, 79 mins.
W: Edward Stolar (*Sinbad*), Anna Larion, Lucille Vertisya, Arnold Kaylor, Maurice Troyan, Robert Surow, William Leon, Irving Perev
D: Alfred Posco **SCR:** Karl Isar **PHOTOG:** Frank Provor **SPCL-FX:** Sidney Mulin **MUSIC:** Rimsky-Korsakov **LYRICS:** John Smich
Originally **Sadko**. *US release: 1962, adapted by Francis Ford Coppola, directed by John Landis*
Minor fantasy: Fabled sailor seeks bird of happiness

The Magic Weaver
1965, (Russ), color
Minor fantasy: Returning soldier tells improbable tales

La Magie a Travers les Ages (Magic Through the Ages)
1906, (Fr), Star, b&w, 74m (242.8 ft./4.1 mins.)
D: Georges Melies
A.k.a. **Old and New Style Conjurers**
Standard fantasy

Magie Diabolique (Diabolic Magic)
1898, (Fr), Star, b&w, 40m (131.2 ft./2.2 mins.)
D: Georges Melies
GB retitle, **Devilish Magic**, *USA retitle,* **Black Art**
Standard fantasy

The Magnetic Monster
1953, (USA), A-Men/UA, b&w, 75 mins.
W: Richard Carlson (*Dr. Jeff Stewart*), King Donovan (*Dr. Dan Forbes*), Jean Byron (*Connie Stewart*), Harry Ellerbe (*Dr. Allard*), Michael Fox (*Dr. Cerni*), Leonard Mudie (*Dr. Howard Denker*), Byron Foulger (*Simon Hart*), Kathleen Freeman (*Nellie*), Leo Britt, Lee Phelps, Jarma Lewis, Michael Granger, John

Zaremba, Frank Gerstle, John Vosper, Watson Downs, Roy Engel, Billy Benedict, Strother Martin
P: Ivan Tors   D: Curt Siodmak   SCR: Curt Siodmak & Ivan Tors   PHOTOG: Charles Van Enger   SPCL-FX: Jack Glass   MUSIC: Blaine Sanford
blurb: "Cosmic Frankenstein terrorizes Earth!"
Engrossing SF-thriller (with stock-footage from 1934 film **Gold***): Scientist creates dangerous new element; polarity of Earth threatened*

Le Magnetiseur (The Hypnotist)
1897, (Fr), Star, b&w, 20m (65.6 ft./1.1 mins.)
D: Georges Melies
GB retitle, **While Under a Hypnotist's Influence***, USA retitle,* **A Hypnotist at Work**
Standard fantasy: Hypnotist magically undresses woman

The Magnificent
see **How to Destroy the Reputation of the Greatest Secret Agent**

Le Magnifique
see **How to Destroy the Reputation of the Greatest Secret Agent**

The Magus
1968, (GB), Blazer/20th-Fox, color, 116 mins.
W: Michael Caine (*Nicholas Urfe*), Anthony Quinn (*Maurice Conchis*), Candice Bergen (*Lily/Julie Holmes*), Anna Karina (*Anne*), Paul Stassino (*Meli*), Julian Glover (*Anton*), Takis Emmanuel (*Kapetan*), Daniele Noel (*Soula*), George Pastell (*The Priest*), Andreas Malandrinos (*Goathead*), Corin Redgrave (*Capt. Wimmel*), Anthony Newlands, Roger Lloyd-Pack, Jerome Willis
P: John Kohn & Jud Kinberg   D: Guy Green   SCR: John Fowles, from his novel   PHOTOG: Billy Williams   MUSIC: John Dankworth
Standard thriller: British schoolteacher swept into perplexing nightmare amid Greek islands

The Maid and the Martian
see **Pajama Party**

Maid for Pleasure
1974, (Fr), color, 91 mins.
W: Brigitte de Borghers, Olivier Mathot, Valerie Boisgel, Marcel Charvey, Bob Askloff
D: Guy Maria
Minor thriller: Nurse menaced in creepy mansion

The Maid of CEFN YDFA
1914, (GB), Haggar, b&w, 3,000 ft. (916.9m)
W: William Haggar Jr. (*Will Hopkins*), Jenny Haggar (*Ann Thomas*)
D & SCR: William Haggar Jr., from a play by James Haggar
Standard crime-thriller: Lawyer tries to drown thatcher to prevent marriage to heiress

Maid of Salem
1937, (USA), Para, b&w, 86 mins.
W: Claudette Colbert, Fred MacMurray, Louise Dresser, Gale Sondergaard, Beulah Bondi, Bonita Granville, Virginia Weidler, Donald Meek, Harvey Stephens, Edward Ellis, Mme. Sulte-Wan, E.E. Clive, Halliwell Hobbes, Sterling Holloway, Lucy Beaumont, Mary Treen
P & D: Frank Lloyd   MUSIC: Victor Young
Well-made melodrama: Puritans accused of witchcraft

A Maid of the Alps
1912, (GB), Terrier/Cooperative, b&w, 1,330 ft. (405.4m)
W: George Moore Marriott
D: Alf Collins   SCR: George Moore Marriott
Standard melodrama: Knight finds innkeeper's daughter is stolen heiress

The Maids
1976, (GB-Can), Mantis/Landau/Cinevision/Cine Films, color, 95 mins.
W: Glenda Jackson (*Solange*), Susannah York (*Claire*), Vivien Merchant (*Madame*), Mark Burns (*Monsieur*)
P: Ely Landau & Robert Enders   D: Christopher Miles   SCR: Robert Enders & Christopher Miles, from a play by Jean Genet   PHOTOG: Douglas Slocombe   MUSIC: Laurie Johnson
Unusual thriller: Sisters plot to kill employer

Maid to Order
1987, (USA), Vista, color, 93 mins.
W: Ally Sheedy (*Jessie Montgomery*), Michael Ontkean (*Nick McGuire*), Beverly D'Angelo (*Stella*), Dick Shawn (*Stan Starkey*), Valerie Perrine (*Georgette Starkey*), Merry Clayton (*Audrey James*), Tom Skerritt (*Charles Montgomery*), Begona Plaza (*Maria*), Rainbow Phoenix (*Brie Starkey*), Theodore Wilson (*Woodrow*), Leland Crooke (*Dude*), Jason Beghe, Diana Bellamy, Vince Monroe Townsend Jr., Kimberly Beck, Khandi Alexander, Katey Sagal, Perla Walter, Rita Gomez, Theresa Randle, Robert Jaffe, Keith Joe Dick, Harry Woolf, Alyson Croft, Rigg Kennedy, Alexander Folk, Vance Colvig, Bennett Guillory, Kim Sylver, Reina King, Kevin Clayton, Victoria Catlin, Raymond Garcia, Tony Simotes, Carmine Iannaccone, Brett Hadley, Ed Quinlan, Lorne Black, Steven Ross, Julianna McCarthy, Jack Russell, Audie Desbrow, Michael Lardie, Mark Kendall
D: Amy Jones   SCR: Amy Jones, Perry Howze & Randy Howze   PHOTOG: Shelly Johnson   SPCL-FX: Roger George Inc.   MUSIC: Georges Delerue   SONG: *I Can Still Shine*
Standard comedy-fantasy: Fairy godmother reforms spoiled girl

Maigret
1988, (GB), color, 100 mins.
W: Richard Harris, Patrick O'Neal, Victoria Tennant, Barbara Shelley, Ian Ogilvy, Eric Deacon, Caroline Munro, Andrew McCulloch
D: Paul Lynch
TVM (teleseries pilot), standard mystery-thriller: French sleuth seeks friend's killer

Mailbag Robbery
see **The Flying Scot**

The Mail Van Murder
1957, (GB), Merton Park/Anglo-Amalgamated, b&w, 29 mins.
W: Hy Hazell (*Carla Craig*), Denis Castle (*Insp. Hammond*), Gordon Needham (*Sgt. Wilson*), Robert Reardon (*Jack Tanner*), Derek Sydney (*Charlie Sparks*)
P: Alec Snowden   D: John Knight   STORY: James Eastwood, from a novel by Edgar Lustgarten
Minor short crime-thriller: Inspector tracks mail thieves

The Main Chance
1964, (GB), Merton Park/Anglo-Amalgamated, b&w, 61 mins.
W: Gregoire Aslan (*Potter*), Edward de Souza (*Michael Blake*), Tracy Reed (*Christine*), Stanley Meadows (*Joe Hayes*), Jack Smethurst (*Ross*), Bernard Stone (*Miller*), Joyce Barbour (*Mme. Rozanne*), Will Stampe (*Carter*)
P: Jack Greenwood   D: John Knight   SCR: Ricahrd Harris, from an Edgar Wallace novel
Modest crime-thriller: Pilot tries to steal crook's diamonds

La Main du Diable (The Devil's Hand)
1943, (Fr), Tobis-Continental, b&w, 82 mins.
W: Pierre Fresnay, Josseline Gael, Palau, Pierre Larquey, Guillaume de Sax, Noel Roquevert, Andre Varennes
D: Maurice Tourneur   SCR: Jean-Paul Le Chanois   PHOTOG: Armand Thirard
USA retitle, **Carnival of Sinners/ The Devil's Hand** *(Distinguished,1946)*
Standard thriller

Main Street After Dark
1944, (USA), MGM, b&w, 56 mins.
W: Edward Arnold, Selena Royle, Audrey Totter, Hume Cronyn, Dan Duryea,
D: Edward L. Cahn
Standard thriller: Family of pickpockets routed

La Maison du Diable
see **The Haunting**

La Maison Sous Les Arbres
see **The Deadly Trap**

Majin, Monster of Terror
1964, (Jap), Daiei/AIP-TV, color, 68 mins.
W: Yoshihiko Aoyama (*Tadafumi*), Miwa Takada (*Kozasa*), Jun Fujimaki, Ryutaro Gomi
D: Kimiyoski Yasuda   SCR: Tetsuo Yoshida   PHOTOG: Yoshiyuki Kuroda   MUSIC: Akira Ifukube
A.k.a. **Majin, the Hideous Idol**
Standard fantasy-thriller: Petrified war-god revives in medieval Japan. cf. **The Return of Giant Majin**

Majin, the Hideous Idol
see **Majin, Monster of Terror**

Majstori I Margarita (The Master and Margarita)
1972, (It-Yugo), color, 101 mins.
W: Ugo Tognazzi, Mimsy Farmer, Alain Cuny, Bata Zivojinovic, Pavle Vujisic
D: Aleksandar Petrovic, from a novel by Mikhail Bulgakov
Unusual fantasy-thriller: Satanic gent aids stage production

The Majorettes
1986, (USA), Joe Ross, color, 93 mins.
W: Terry Godfrey, Sueanne Seamens, Sana Maiello, Kevin Kindlin, Colin Martin, Russ Streiner, Tom Madden, Mark V. Jevicky
D: Bill Hinzman   SCR: John Russo   PHOTOG & MUS: Paul McCollough
Standard thriller: Killer stalks cheerleaders

Make Haste to Live
1954, (USA), Rep, b&w, 90 mins.
W: Dorothy McGuire, Stephen McNally, Mary Murphy, Edgar Barrier, John Howard, Carolyn Jones, Edgar Buchanan
D: William A. Seiter   MUSIC: Elmer Bernstein
Standard thriller: Woman pursued

Maker of Monsters
see **El Fabricante de Monstruos**

Make Them Die Slowly
see **Cannibal Ferox**

Making Contact
1985, (W. Ger), Centropolis/New World, color, 85 mins.

W: Joshua Morrell, Eva Kryll, Tammy Shields, Jan Zierold, Barbara Klein, Jerry Hall, Sean Johnson, Axel Berg, Berit Morrell, Mathias Kraus, Ray Kaselonis, Christine Goebbels, Joel Kleinman, Christoph Lindert, Sandra Freeding, Gunther Zorn, Myres, James Baumgartner, James Hefferman, Christian Behrens, Peter Kosma, Sheila Behrens, John Caruso, Michael Goebbels, Joe Azzato, Kevin Peck, Ralph Nordenhold, Carrie Shields, Joshua Ellis, Charly Dere, Allison Koblik, Daniel Bayer, Tim Edwards, Elliot Smith, Ann Katrin Behrens, Fred Ambrosio, Fabian Muliawan, Tanja Hartmann, Ann Paris, Ruth Poklekowski, Myriam Thiele, Guido Seitz, Stefania Sabucci, Miguel Ninaus, Daniel Markwald, Volker Konrad, Dan Porter, Holger Schweizer, Joe Brown, Rainer Pietschmann, Sebastian Riehm, Ina Bohnsch, Monic Wintermaier, Thilo Scheuermann, Bruce Burney, Charly Hack, Reid Morrell, Volker Hamp, John Curthan, Frank Loomis, Antje Hilbert, Frank Leather, Simon Stone, Choanne Anderson, Bebby Dalton, Dr. Hollis, Michael Gregory, Peter W. Kleg, Dr. Hobkins, Birgit Stutz, Liesel Luft, Caplan Brown, Sacha Luft, Elisabeth Chambers, Renata Bechner, Lynnea Minger
D: Roland Emmerich **SCR:** Roland Emmerich, Hans J. Haller & Thomas Lechner **PHOTOG:** Egon Werdin **SPCL-FX SPRVSR:** Hubert Bartholomae **MUSIC:** Paul Gilreath
Juvenile fantasy-adventure: Demonic puppet menaces boy

Making Mr. Right
1987, (USA), Orion, color, 100 mins.
W: John Malkovich (*Jeff/Ulysses*), Ann Magnuson (*Frankie Stone*), Glenne Headly (*Trish*), Ben Masters (*Steve Marcus*), Laurie Metcalf (*Sandy*), Polly Bergen (*Estelle Stone*), Hart Bochner (*Don*), Harsh Nayyar (*Dr. Ramdas*), Susan Berman (*Ivy Stone*), Polly Draper (*Suzy Duncan*), Robert Trebor (*The Tux Salesman*), Christian Clemenson (*Bruce*), Merwin Goldsmith, Sid Raymond, Sidney Armus, John Hambrick, Michael Seidelman, Susan Lichtman, Steve Rondinaro, Sherry Diamont, Ruthe Geier, Mike Hanly, Eve Marsh, P.R. Floyd, Trip Hamilton, Ronnie Rosado, Ruth Mullen, Stephen McFarland, Ralph Gunderman, Tom Schwartz, James F. Murtaugh, Harry Chase, Janice Frank, Bob Cruz, Stanley Kirk, Kevin Williams, Jose Ramirez, Clayton Ludovitch, Gerald Owens
D: Susan Seidelman **SCR:** Floyd Byars & Laurie Frank **PHOTOG:** Edward Lachman **SPCL VS-FX:** Bran Ferren **MUSIC:** Chaz Jankel
Standard feminist SF-comedy: Girl meets android

Making Sausages
1897, (GB), G.A. Smith, b&w, 75 ft. (22.9m)
D: George Albert Smith
A.k.a. **The End of All Things**
Standard fantasy short: Four cooks make sausages from cats, dogs, ducks and old boots

Le Malade Hydrophobe (The Hydrophobic Patient)
1900, (Fr), Star, b&w, 20m (65.6 ft./1.1 mins.)
D: Georges Melies
GB retitle, **The Gouty Patient***, USA retitle,* **The Man with Wheels in His Head**
Standard comedy-fantasy

Malaga
see **Moment of Danger**

Malatesta's Carnival
1973, (USA), Windmill Films, color, 74 mins
W: Herve Villechaize
P:&D: Richard Grosser & Walker Stuart **SCR:** Christopher Speeth
Standard horror-comedy: Monsters devour fright-film buffs

La Maldicion de la Bestia (Curse of the Beast)
1976, (Sp), Profilms/Independent Int'l, color, 80 mins.
W: Paul Naschy (*Valdemar*), Grace Mills, Silvia Solar, Gil Vidal, Luis Induni, Victor Israel
D: Miguel Iglesias Bonns **SCR:** Jacinto Molina
USA retitle, **Night of the Howling Beast***, A.k.a.* **Horror of the Werewolf** *and* **The Werewolf and the Yeti**
Minor horror-fantasy: Lycanthrope travels to Tibet

La Maldicion de la Llorona (The Curse of the Crying Woman)
1962, (Mex), Azteca/AIP b&w, 74 mins.
W: Rosita Arenas, Domingo Soler, Rita Macedo, Abel Salazar
P: Abel Salazar **D & SCR:** Rafael Baledon
A.k.a. **The Witch House**
Standard fantasy-thriller: Girl finds curse hanging over aunt's house.

La Maledicion de los Karnsteins (The Curse of the Karnsteins)
1963, (It-Sp), Hispamer Films-NEC Cinematografica/AIP, b&w
W: Christopher Lee, Adriana Ambesi, Jose Campos, Pier Ana Quaglia, Nela Conjiu, Jose Villasante, Vera Valmont, Ursula Davis, Angela Minervini
P: William Mulligan **D:** Camillo Mastrocinque, Aka Thomas Miller, loosely based on J. Sheridan LeFanu's novel *Carmilla*
A.k.a. **Karnstein** *and* **Crypt of Horror***, USA retitle,* **Terror in the Crypt**
Standard horror-fantasy: Count suspects his daughter is reincarnated witch

La Maledicion de Nostradamus (The Curse of Nostradamus)
1960, (Mex), Azteca/AIP, b&w, 77 mins
W: German Robles, Julio Aleman, Domingo Soler, Aurora Alvarado
D: Frederick Curiel **STORY & SCR:** Charles E. Taboada & Alfred Ruanova

PHOTOG: Ferdinand Colin
Minor horror-fantasy (culled from 3 episodes {The Finger of Destiny, The Book of the Centuries, & Night Victims} of 1959 serial): Vampire tries to establish cult of Undead cf. Nostradamus y el Destructor de Monstruos, Nostradamus y el Genio de la Tinieblas and Blood of Nostradamus

Male and Female
1919, (USA), Para-Artcraft, b&w, 9 reels (110 mins.)
W: Lila Lee, Raymond Hatton, Gloria Swanson, Theodore Roberts, Julia Faye, Thomas Meighan, Mildred Reardon, Bebe Daniels, Edna Mae Cooper, Sam Searle
P & D: Cecil B. DeMille, from J.M. Barrie's *The Admirable Crichton*
Standard melodrama: Fantasies are imagined

Les Malefices de la Momie
see **The Curse of the Mummy's Tomb**

Malenka the Vampire
see **Fangs of the Living Dead**

Male Vampire
see **Onna Kyuketsuki**

The Malibu Beach Vampires
1991, (USA), color, 90 mins.
W: Angelyne, Becky Le Beau, John Rudelstein, Rod Sweitzer, Marcus A. Frishman, Francis Creighton, Anet Anatelle, Yvette Buchanan, Cherie Romaors, Kelly Galindo
D: Francis Creighton
Minor horror-comedy: Yuppies lured by beautiful vampires

Malice
1993, (USA), color, 107 mins.
W: Alec Baldwin, Nicole Kidman, Bill Pullman, Bebe Neuwirth, Anne Vancroft, George C. Scott, Peter Gallagher, Josef Sommer
D: Harold Becker **SCR:** Aaron Sorkin & Scott Frank **PHOTOG:** Gordon Willis **MUSIC:** Jerry Gldsmith
Complicated thriller: Malpractice suit involved in insurance scam

The Malpas Mystery
1960, (GB), Independent Artists-Langton/AA, b&w, 69 mins.
W: Maureen Swanson (*Audrey Bedford*), Allan Cuthbertson (*Lacy Marshalt*), Geoffrey Keen (*Torrington*), Sandra Dorne (*Dora*), Ronald Howard (*Insp. Dick Shannon*), Alan Tilvern (*Gordon Seager*), Leslie French (*Wilkins*), Catherine Feller (*Ginette*)
P: Julian Wintle & Leslie Parkyn **D:** Sidney Hayers **SCR:** Paul Tabori & Gordon Wellesley, from Edgar Wallace's novel *Face in the Night*
Standard thriller: Girl uncovers crime ring

The Maltese Bippy
1969, (USA), MGM, color
W: Dan Rowan, Dick Martin, Julie Newmar, Carol Lynley, Fritz Weaver
P: Everett Freeman & Robert Enders **D:** Norman Panama **SCR:** Everett Freeman & Ray Singer
Standard comedy-thriller: Murders in Long Island mansion

The Maltese Bippy: DAN ROWAN AND DICK MARTIN

The Maltese Falcon
1931, (USA), WB, b&w, 75 mins.
W: Ricardo Cortez (*Sam Spade*), Bebe Daniels (*Ruth Wonderly*), Dudley Digges (*Kaspar Gutman*), Thelma Todd (*Iva Archer*), Una Merkel (*Effie Perine*), J. Farrell MacDonald (*Polhouse*), Robert Elliott (*Det. Dundy*), Dwight Frye (*Wilmer Cook*), Morgan Wallace (*The D.A.*), Otto Matieson (*Joel Cairo*), Walter Long (*Miles Archer*), Augustino Borgato (*Capt. Jacoby*), Oscar Apfel
D: Roy Del Ruth **SCR:** Maude Fulton, Lucien Hubbard & Brown Holmes, loosely based on: Dashiell Hammett's novel **PHOTOG:** William Reese
working title: **Woman of the World***, TV-retitle,* **Dangerous Female**
Standard thriller: Priceless treasure inspires murder

The Maltese Falcon
1941, (USA), WB, b&w, 100 mins.
__W:__ Humphrey Bogart (*Sam Spade*), Peter Lorre (*Joel Cairo*), Mary Astor (*Brigid O'Shaughnessy*), Sydney Greenstreet (*Kasper "The Fat Man" Gutman*), Gladys George (*Iva Archer*), Lee Patrick (*Effie Perine*), Elisha Cook Jr. (*Wilmer Cook*), Ward Bond (*Det. Tom Polhaus*), Barton MacLane (*Det. Lt. Dundy*), James Burke (*Luke*), Walter Huston (*Jacoby*), Murray Alper (*Frank Richmond*), John Hamilton (*Bryan*), Emory Parnell (*The Ship's Mate*), Jack Mower (*The Announcer*), Hank Mann, William Hopper, Charles Drake, Creighton Hale
__P:__ Hal B. Wallis   __D & SCR:__ John Huston, from Dashiell Hammett's novel   __PHOTOG:__ Arthur Edeson   __MUSIC:__ Adolph Deutsch
Classic thriller: Shady characters seek precious statue

Mamma Dracula
1980, (Fr-Belg), Limelight/UGC, color, 90 mins
__W:__ Louise Fletcher, Maria Schneider, Marc-Henri Wajnberg, Alexander Wajnberg, Jess Hahn
__P & D:__ Boris Szulzinger   __SCR:__ Boris Szulzinger, Pierre Sterckx & Marc-Henri Wajnberg
Minor horror-comedy: Countess bathes in virgins' blood

A Man About the House
1947, (GB), British Lion, b&w, 99 mins.
__W:__ Margaret Johnston (*Agnes Isit*), Dulcie Gray (*Ellen Isit*), Kieron Moore (*Salvatore*), Felix Aylmer (*Richard Sanctuary*), Guy Middleton (*Sir Benjamin Dench*), Jone Salinas (*Maria*), Lilian Braithwaite (*Mrs. Armitage*), Maria Fimiani (*Assunta*), Reginald Purdell (*Higgs*)
__P:__ Edward Black   __D:__ Leslie Arliss   __SCR:__ Leslie Arliss & J.B. Williams, from a play by John Perry, based on a novel by Francis Brett Young
Standard thriller: Spinsters imperiled by butler

Man Accused
1959, (GB), danziger/UA, b&w, 58 mins.
__W:__ Ronald Howard (*Bob Jenson*), Carol Marsh (*Kathy Riddle*), Ian Fleming (*Sir Thomas*), Catherine Ferraz (*Anna*), Brian Nissen (*Derek*), Robert Dorning (*Beckett*), Colin Tapley (*The Inspector*), Stuart Saunders (*Curran*)
__P:__ Edward J. & Harry Lee Danziger   __D:__ Montgomery Tully   __STORY:__ Mark Grantham
Standard crime-thriller: Rich widow's fiance accused of murders

Man Afraid
1957, (USA), Univ, b&w
__W:__ George Nader (*Rev. David Collins*), Phyllis Thaxter (*Lisa Collins*), Tim Hovey (*Michael Collins*), Harold J. Stone (*Lt. Martin*), Eduard Franz (*Simmons*), Reta Shaw, Judson Pratt, Mabel Albertson, Butch Bernard, Martin Milner, Kevin Corcoran
__D:__ Harry Keller   __SCR:__ Herb Meadow   __STORY:__ Dan Ullman   __PHOTOG:__ Russell Metty   __MUSIC:__ Henry Mancini   __MUSIC DIR:__ Joseph Gershenson
Standard thriller: Minister's young son menaced by vengeful father of slain burglar

The Man and His Bottle
1908, (GB), Hepworth, b&w, 350 ft. (106.7m)
__W:__ Thurston Harris (*The Drunkard*)
__D:__ Lewin Fitzhamon
Standard fantasy short: Drunkard has visions of everything turning into bottles

Man and His Mate
see One Million B.C.

The Man and the Beast
1972, (Mex), color
based on Robert Louis Stevenson's *Dr. Jekyll and Mr. Hyde*
Standard horror-fantasy

The Man and the Latchkey
1908, (GB), Hepworth, b&w, 200 ft. (61m)
__W:__ Thurston Harris
__D:__ Lewin Fitzhamon
Standard fantasy: Drunkard pursues an enlarged, mobile keyhole

The Man and the Monster
see El Hombre y el Monstruo

The Man at Six
1931, (GB), BIP/Wardour, b&w, 70 mins.
__W:__ Anne Grey (*Sybil Vane*), Lester Matthews (*Campbell Edwards*), Gerald Rawlinson (*Frank Pine*), Arthur Stratton (*Sgt. Hogan*), John Turnbull (*Insp. Dawford*), Kenneth Kove (*Joshua Atkinson*), Charles Farrell (*George Wollmer*), Herbert Ross (*Sir Joseph Pine*), Minnie Rayner (*Mrs. Cummerpatch*)
__D:__ Harry Hughes   __SCR:__ Harry Hughes & Victor Kendall, from a play by Jack De Leon & Jack Celestin
USA retitle, __The Gables Mystery__ (Powers Pictures, 1932)
Standard thriller: Girl detective unmasks murderous colleague

Man at the Carlton Tower
1961, (GB), Merton Park/Anglo-Amalgamated, b&w, 57 mins.
__W:__ Maxine Audley (*Lydia Daney*), Lee Montague (*Tim Jordan*), Allan Cuthbertson (*Supt. Cowley*), Nigel Green (*Lew Daney*), Terence Alexander (*Johnny Time*), Nyree Dawn Porter (*Mary Greer*), Alfred Burke (*Harry Stone*), Geoffrey Frederick (*Sgt. Pepper*)
__P:__ Jack Greenwood   __D:__ Robert Tronson   __SCR:__ Philip Mackie, from Edgar Wallace's novel *The Man at the Carlton*
Standard thriller: Sleuth tracks murderous jewel thief

Man Bait
see The Last Page

Man Beast
1956, (USA), Jerry Warren/Medallion, b&w, 65 mins.
__W:__ Rock Madison, Virginia Maynor, George Skaff, Tom Maruzzi, Lloyd Cameron, Wong Sing
__P & D:__ Jerry Warren   __SCR:__ Arthur Cassidy   __PHOTOG:__ Victor Fisher
blurb: "See: women stalked and captured for breeding by Yeti monsters!"
Minor SF-thriller: Search for Abominable Snowman

The Man Behind the Mask
1914, (GB), Hepworth, b&w, 1,075 ft. (327.7m)
__W:__ Flora Morris (*Dorothy Oliver*), Alec Worcester (*Harry Lowremer*)
__D:__ Warwick Buckland
Standard adventure-thriller: Girl hides highwayman

The Man Behind the Mask
1936, (GB), Joe Rock/MGM, b&w, 79 mins.
__W:__ Hugh Williams (*Nick Barclay*), Jane Baxter (*June Slade*), Maurice Schwartz (*The Master*), Henry Oscar (*The Officer*), Donald Calthrop (*Dr. Walpole*), Peter Gawthorne (*Lord Slade*), Ronald Ward (*Jimmy Slade*), Kitty Kelly (*Miss Weeks*), George Merritt (*Mallory*), Reginald Tate (*Hayden*), Hal Gordon (*The Sgt.*), Ivor Barnard (*Hewitt*)
__D:__ Michael Powell   __SCR:__ Ian Hay, Syd Courtenay, Jack Byrd & Stanley Haynes   __BASED ON:__ Jacques Futrelle's novel *The Chase of the Golden Plate*
Standard thriller: Mad astronomer kidnaps Lord's daughter to obtain oriental shield

The Man Behind "The Times"
1917, (GB), Hepworth/Harma, b&w, 3,725 ft. (1135.4m)
__W:__ Stewart Rome (*Aaron Moss*), Chrissie White (*Jet Overbury*), Lionelle Howard (*Alan Garth*), Harry Gilbey (*John Overbury*), Charles Vane (*John Walcott*), Mrs. Bedells (*Mrs. Overbury*), John MacAndrews (*The Doctor*), Johnny Butt (*The Clerk*)
__D:__ Frank Wilson   __STORY:__ Percy Manton
Standard crime-thriller: Usurer weds girl whose lover is blamed for her father's murder

Man Bites Dog
1991, (Belg), color, 95 mins.
__W:__ Benoit Poelvoorde, Remy Belvaux, Andre Bonzel
__D:__ Benoit Poelvoorde, Remy Belvaux & Andre Bonzel   __SCR:__ Benoit Poelvoorde, Remy Belvaux, Andre Bonzel & Vincent Tavier
Unusual thriller: Serial killer films his crimes

A Man Called Dagger
1968, (USA), Global Screen Assocs./MGM, color, 86 mins.
__W:__ Paul Mantee, Jan Murray, Terry Moore, Eileen O'Neil, Sue Ane Langdon, Maureen Arthur, Bruno Ve Sota, Richard Kiel, Leonard Stone
__P:__ Lewis M. Horwitz   __D:__ Richard Rush   __PHOTOG:__ Leslie Kovacs
Minor thriller: Secret agent vs. neo-Nazis

The Man Called Flintstone
1966, (USA), Hanna-Barbera/Col, color, 87 mins.
__VOICES:__ Alan Reed, Mel Blanc
Standard animated fantasy: Caveman becomes spy

The Manchurian Candidate
1962, (USA), M.C./UA, b&w, 126 mins.
__W:__ Laurence Harvey (*Raymond Shaw*), Frank Sinatra (*Bennett Marco*), Angela Lansbury (*Raymond's Mother*), Janet Leigh (*Rosie*), James Gregory (*Sen. John Iselin*), John McGiver (*Sen. Thomas Jordon*), Leslie Parrish (*Jocie Jordon*), Henry Silva (*Chunjin*), Khigh Dhiegh (*Yen Lo*), Douglas Henderson (*The Colonel*), James Edwards (*Cpl. Melvin*), Albert Paulsen (*Zilkov*), Barry Kelley (*The Sec'y of Defense*), Lloyd Corrigan (*Holborn Gaines*), Madame Spivy (*Berezovo*), Reggie Nalder, Whit Bissell
__P:__ George Axelrod & John Frankenheimer   __D:__ John Frankenheimer   __SCR:__ George Axelrod, based on Richard Condon's novel   __PHOTOG:__ Lionel Lindon   __MUSIC:__ David Amram
Superior thriller: Red Chinese brainwash American soldier, turn him into murderous robot

The Mandarin Mystery
1936, (USA), Rep, b&w, 63 mins.
__W:__ Eddie Quillan (*Ellery Queen*), Charlotte Henry (*Josephine Temple*), Rita La Roy (*Martha Kirk*), Wade Boteler (*The Inspector*), Franklin Pangborn (*Mellish*), George Irving (*Dr. Alexander Kirk*), Kay Hughes (*Irene Kirk*), William Newell (*Guffy*), George Walcott (*Donald Trent*), Monte Vandergrift (*The First Detective*), Edwin Stanley (*Bronson*), Edgar Allen (*A Reporter*), Richard Beach (*A Reporter*), Anthony Merrill (*Craig*)
__D:__ Ralph Staub   __SCR:__ John F. Larkin, Rex Taylor, Gertrude Orr & Cortland Fitzsimmons, from Ellery Queen's novel *The Chinese Orange Mystery*   __PHOTOG:__ Jack Marta   __MUSIC:__ Harry Gray
Standard thriller: Rare Chinese postage stamp stolen

Man Detained

1961, (GB), Merton Park/Anglo-Amalgamated, b&w, 59 mins.
W: Bernard Archard *(Insp. Verity)*, Elvi Hale *(Kay Simpson)*, Paul Stassino *(James Helder)*, Michael Coles *(Frank Murray)*, Ann Sears *(Stella Maple)*, Victor Platt

Once Unbelievable
Now Unthinkable
The Chilling Classic

**Frank Sinatra
Laurence Harvey
Janet Leigh

The Manchurian Candidate**

(Thomas Maple), Patrick Jordan *(Brand)*, Jean Aubrey *(Gillian Murray)*
P: Jack Greenwood **D:** Robert Tronson **SCR:** Richard Harris, from Edgar Wallace's novel *A Debt Discharged*
Standard thriller: Burglar accused of robbery and murder

Mandragore

see **Alraune (1928)**

Mandrake

1979, (USA), NBC-TV, color, 100 mins.
W: Anthony Herrera *(Mandrake)*, Ji-Tu Cumbuka *(Lothar)*, Simone Griffeth *(Stacy)*, Gretchen Corbett *(Jennifer)*, Robert Reed *(Arkadian)*, Hank Brandt *(Gordon)*, Peter Haskell
D: Harry Falk **TELEPLAY:** Rick Husky
TVM, standard thriller: Magician foils madman controlling robot army

Mandroid

1993, (USA), color, 81 mins.
W: Brian Cousins, Jane Caldwell, Michael DellaFemina, Curt Lowens, Patrick Ersgard, Robert Symonds
D: Joakim Ersgard **SCR:** Jackson Barr & Earl Kenton
Minor SF-thriller: Dangerous android fuel developed

Maneater of Hydra

see **La Isla de la Muerte**

Man-Eater of Kumaon

1948, (USA), Univ, b&w, 79 mins.
W: Sabu *(Narain)*, Wendell Corey *(Dr. John Collins)*, Joanne Page *(Lali)*, Morris Carnovsky *(Ganga Ram)*, James Moss, Ted Hecht, Argentina Brunetti, John Mansfield, Eddie Das, Alan Foster, Charles Wagenheim, Estelle Dodge, Lal Chand Mehra, Phiroze Nazir, Virginia Wave, Frank Lackteen, Ralph Moody, Jerry Riggio, Neyle Morrow
D: Byron Haskin **SCR:** Jeanne Bartlett & Lewis Meltzer, from Jim Corbett's book **PHOTOG:** William C. Mellor **MUSIC:** Hans J. Salter
Minor adventure-thriller: Society doctor stalks tiger

A Man Escaped

1957, (Fr), Continental, b&w, 94 mins, also 102 mins
D & SP: Robert Bresson
Standard thriller

Man Facing Southeast

1987, (Argent), Filmdallas, color, 105 mins.
W: Hugo Soto, Lorenzo Quinteros, Ines Vernengo, Chrustina Scarmuzza
D, SP & SCR: Eliseo Subiela **PHOTOG:** Ricardo De Angelus **MUSIC:** Pedro Aznar
Unusual melodrama: Mental patient claims to be space alien

Manfish

1956, (USA), UA, color, 78 mins.
W: John Bromfield *(Brannigan)*, Lon Chaney Jr. *("Swede")*, Victor Jory *("Professor")*, Barbara Nichols *(Mimi)*, Tessa Prendergast *(Alita)*, Eric Coverly *(Chavez)*, Vincent Chang *(Domingo)*, Theodore Purcell *("Big Boy")*, Vere Johns *(Bianco)*, Jack Lewis *(Warren)*, Arnold Shanks *(Aleppo)*, Clyde Hoyte *(Calypso)*
D: W. Lee Wilder **SCR:** Joel Murcott **STORY:** Myles Wilder, loosely based on Edgar Allan Poe's short stories "The Goldbug" & "The Tell-Tale Heart" **PHOTOG:** Charles S. Welbourne **MUSIC:** Albert Elms **SONGS:** *Beware the Caribbean, Big Fish & Goodbye*
GB retitle, **Calypso**
Minor thriller: Scoundrels seek pirate treasure

The Man from Atlantis

1977, (USA), NBC-TV, color, 96 mins.
W: Patrick Duffy *(Mark)*, Victor Buono *(Mr. Schubert)*, Art Lund *(Adm. Pierce)*, Belinda J. Montgomery *(Dr. Merrill)*, Dean Santoro *(Ernie)*, Mark Jenkins *(Ainsley)*, Allen Case *(Johnson)*, Lawrence Pressman *(Cmdr. Roth)*
TELEPLAY: Mayo Simon
TVM, standard SF-adventure: Youth from lost civilization meets modern world

The Man from Beyond

1922, (USA), Houdini Picture Corp., b&w, 7 reels (6,500 ft./1981.2m)
W: Harry Houdini *(The Man from Beyond)*, Arthur Maude *(Dr. Gilbert Trent)*, Albert Tavernier *(Dr. Crawford Strange)*, Erwin Connelly *(Dr. Gregory Sinclair)*, Frank Montgomery *(Francois Duval)*, Luis Alberni *(Capt. of the Barkentine)*, Yale Benner *(Milt Norcross)*, Nita Naldi *(Marie Le Grande)*
D: Burton King **STORY:** Harry Houdini **ADAPT:** Coolidge Streeter **PHOTOG:** Frank Zucker, Irving B. Ruby, Harry A. Fischbeck, A.G. Penrod, Louis Dunmyre & L.D. Littlefield
Standard thriller: Arctic expedition finds man in suspended animation

The Man from Downing Street

1922, (USA), Vitagraph, b&w, 5 reels (4,950 ft./1508.8m)
W: Earle Williams *(Capt. Robert Kent)*, Charles Hill Mailes *(Col. Wentworth)*, Boris Karloff *(Maharajah Jehan)*, Betsy Ross Clarke *(Doris Burnham)*, Kathryn Adams *(Norma Graves)*, Herbert Prior *(Capt. Graves)*, Eugenia Gilbert *(Sarissa)*, James Butler *(Lt. Wyndham)*, George Stanley *(Sir Edward Craig)*
D: Edward Jose **SCR:** Bradley J. Smollen **STORY:** Clyde C. Westove, Lottie Horner & Florine Williams **PHOTOG:** Ernest Smith
Standard melodrama: British agent in India seeks to unmask spy

The Man From Hong Kong

1975, (Austral-Hong Kong), color, 103 mins.
W: Jimmy Wang Yu, George Lazenby, Ros Spiers, Frank Thring, Rebecca Gilling, Hugh Keays-Byrne, Roger Ward
D: Brian Trenchard-Smith
Minor action-thriller: Hong Kong super-cop arrives in Sydney

The Man from Nowhere

1976, (GB), Charles Barker/CFF, color, 59 mins.
W: Sarah Hollis-Andrews *(Alice Harvey)*, Ronald Adam *(George Harvey)*, Anthony McCaffery *(Spikey)*, Shane Franklin *(William)*, Reginald Winch *(Nobby)*, Robin Keston *(Jim)*, John Forbes-Robertson *(Freeman)*, Gabrielle Hamilton *(Mrs. Smee)*
P: Jean Wadlow **D:** James Hill **STORY:** John Tully **PHOTOG:** Desmond Dickinson **MUSIC:** John Cameron
Standard juvenile thriller: Mysterious man warns orphan girl to leave her uncle's house

The Man from Planet X

1951, (USA), UA, b&w, 70 mins.
W: Robert Clarke, Raymond Bond, Margaret Field (later Maggie Mahoney), Roy Engel, William Schallert, Gilbert Fallman, David Ormont, Charles Davis
P: Aubrey Wisberg & Jack Pollexfen **D:** Edgar G. Ulmer **ORIG. STORY & SCR:** Aubrey Wisberg & Jack Pollexfen **PHOTOG:** John L. Russell **SPCL-FX:** Andy Anderson & Howard Weeks
Minor SF-thriller: Scientists meet space alien

The Man from Scotland Yard

1944, (GB), British Foundation, b&w, 36 mins.
W: Franklyn Scott *(Sir Richard Pellis)*, Walter Piers *(Col. Dewsbury)*, Muriel George *(Agatha Dewsbury)*, Geoffrey Heathcote *(Insp. Maclean)*, Elizabeth Wilson *(Ethel Dewsbury)*
WRIT, P & D: Ronald Haines
Standard crime-thriller short: Man plots jewel theft

Man From Tangier
1957, (GB), Butcher's Films, b&w, 67 mins.
<u>W</u>: Robert Hutton (*Chuck Collins*), Lisa Gastoni (*Michele*), Martin Benson (*Voss*), Derek Sydney (*Darracq*), Jack Allen (*Rex*), Leonard Sachs (*Heinrich*), Robert Raglan (*Insp. Meredith*), Harold Berens (*Sammy*)
<u>P</u>: W.G. Chalmers <u>D</u>: Lance Comfort <u>STORY</u>: Manning O'Brine
*USA retitle, **Thunder Over Tangier***
Standard crime-thriller: Crooks seek plates for forging passports

The Mangler
1995, (USA), New Line, color, 105 mins.
<u>W</u>: Robert Englund, Ted Levine, Vanessa Pike, Jeremy Crutchley (*Pictureman*), Daniel Matmor (*Jackson*), Demetre Phillips, Lisa Morris, Ashley Hayden, Vera Blacker
<u>D</u>: Tobe Hooper <u>SCR</u>: Tobe Hooper, Peter Welbeck & Stephen Brooks
  <u>PHOTOG</u>: Amnon Salomon <u>MUSIC</u>: Barrington Pheloung, from Stephen King's short story
Standard horror-fantasy: Laundering establishment possessed by evil entity

The Mangler: LISA MORRIS AND ROBERT ENGLUND

Manhattan Baby
1972, (It), Fabrizio De Angelis/Fulvia, color, 89 mins.
<u>W</u>: Christopher Connelly, Martha Taylor, Brigitta Boccoli, Giovanni Frezza, Cinzia De Ponti, Laurence Welles, Andrea Bosic, Carlo De Mejo, Vincenzo Bellanich, Mario Moretti, Lucio Fulci, Antonio Pulci
<u>D</u>: Lucio Fulci <u>SCR</u>: Elisa Livia Briganti & Dardano Sacchetti <u>PHOTOG</u>: Guglielmo Mancori <u>MUSIC</u>: Fabio Frizzi
Minor horror-thriller: Egyptian curse plagues archeologist's daughter

The Manhattan Project
1986, (USA), Gladden/20th-Fox, color, 116 mins.
<u>W</u>: John Lithgow (*John Mathewson*), Christopher Collet (*Paul Stephens*), Jill Eikenberry (*Mrs. Stephens*), Cynthia Nixon (*Jenny*), Richard Jenkins, Sully Boyar, John Mahoney
<u>D</u>: Marshall Brickman <u>SCR</u>: Marshall Brickman & Thomas Baum <u>PHOTOG</u>: Billy Williams <u>SPCL VS-FX</u>: Bran Ferren <u>MUSIC</u>: Philippe Sarde
Standard thriller: Youth pilfers plutonium

Manhunt in Milan
1972, (It-W. Ger), color, 92 mins.
<u>W</u>: Mario Adorf, Henry Silva, Woody Strode, Luciana Paluzzi, Adolfo Celi, Sylva Koscina, Cyril Cusack
<u>D</u>: Fernando Di Leo
Standard crime-thriller: Mafia inter-gang feuding

Manhunt in Space
1954, (USA), Reed, b&w, 78 mins.
<u>W</u>: Richard Crane, Sally Mansfield
Minor SF-adventure, re-edited from teleseries "Rocky Jones, Space Ranger"

Mania
*see **The Flesh and the Fiends***

Maniac
1934, (USA), b&w, 67 mins.
<u>W</u>: Bill Woods, Horace Carpenter, Ted Edwards, Thea Ramsey, Jennie Dark, Marcel Andre, Celia McGann
<u>D</u>: Dwain Esper
Minor horror-thriller: Scientist tries to raise dead

Maniac
1962, (GB), Hammer/Col, b&w, 86 mins.
<u>W</u>: Kerwin Mathews (*Geoff Farrell*), Nadia Gray (*Eve Beynat*), Donald Houston (*Georges Beynat*), Liliane Brousse (*Annette Beynat*), George Pastell (*Insp. Etienne*), Norman Bird (*Salon*), Arnold Diamond (*Janiello*), Justine Lord (*Grace*), Jerold Wells (*Giles*)

<u>WRIT & P</u>: Jimmy Sangster <u>D</u>: Michael Carreras <u>PHOTOG</u>: Wilkie Cooper
Unusual thriller: Mad criminal takes fiendish revenge upon faithless wife and her lover

Maniac
1980, (USA), Magnum, color, 88 mins.
<u>W</u>: Joe Spinell (*Frank Zito*), Caroline Munro (*Anna D'Antoni*), Kelly Piper (*The Nurse*), Gail Lawrence (*Rita*), Rita Montone (*The Hooker*), James Brewster (*The Beach Boy*), Linda Lee Walter (*The Beach Girl*), Tom Savini (*The Disco Boy*), Hyla Marrow (*The Disco Girl*), Sharon Mitchell (*The 2nd Nurse*), Tracie Evans (*The Street Hooker*), Carol Henry (*The Deadbeat*), Nelia Bacmeister (*Carmen Zito*), Louis Jawitz (*The Art Director*), Denise Spagnuolo (*Denise*), Billy Spagnuolo (*Billy*), Frank Pesco (*The TV Reporter*), Kim Hudson (*The Lobby Hooker*), Candace Clements (*The 1st Park Mother*), Diana Spagnuolo (*The 2nd Park Mother*), Terry Gagnon (*The Woman in the Alley*), Joan Baldwin (*The 1st Model*), Jeni Paz (*The 2nd Model*), Janelle Winston (*The Waitress*), Randy Jurgensen (*The 1st Cop*), Jimmy Aurichio (*The 2nd Cop*)
<u>D</u>: William Lustig <u>SCR</u>: C.A. Rosenberg & Joe Spinell <u>STORY</u>: Joe Spinell
  <u>PHOTOG</u>: Robert Lindsay <u>MUSIC</u>: Jay Chattaway
Minor thriller: Psycho slays beauties

Maniac Cop
1988, (USA), Schapiro Glickenhaus Entertainment, color, 85 mins, also 92 mins
<u>W</u>: Tom Atkins (*Det. McCrae*), Bruce Campbell, Laurene Landon, Robert Z'Dar, Richard Roundtree, William Smith, Sheree North, Erik Holland
<u>D</u>: William Lustig <u>SCR</u>: Larry Cohen
Standard thriller: Psycho killer terrorizes New York City

Maniac Cop 2
1990, (USA), color, 88 mins.
<u>W</u>: Robert Davi, Claudia Christian, Michael Lerner, Robert Z'Dar, Leo Rossi, Laurene Landon, Bruce Campbell, Clarence Williams III
<u>D</u>: William Lustig <u>SCR</u>: Larry Cohen
Standard thriller: Killer psycho returns from dead

Maniac Cop 3: Badge of Silence
1993, (USA), color, 85 mins.
<u>W</u>: Robert Davi, Robert Z'Dar, Gretchen Becker, Paul Gleason, Doug Savant, Caitlin Dulany
<u>D</u>: William Lustig & Joel Soisson <u>SCR</u>: Larry Cohen <u>MUSIC</u>: Jerry Goldsmith
Standard crime-thriller

Maniac Mansion
*see **Amuck***

The Maniac's Guillotine
1902, (GB), Haggar & Sons/WTC, b&w, 125 ft. (38.1m)
<u>D</u>: William Haggar
Standard crime-thriller

Maniacs on the Loose
*see **The Thrill Killers***

The Man in Black
1950, (GB), Hammer/Exclusive, b&w, 75 mins.
<u>W</u>: Betty Ann Davies (*Bertha Clavering*), Sidney James (*Henry Clavering*), Anthony Forwood (*Victor Harrington*), Courtney Hope (*Mrs. Carter*), Sheila Burrell (*Janice*), Hazel Penwarden (*Joan*), Lawrence Baskcomb (*Sandford*), Valentine Dyall (*The Storyteller*)
<u>P</u>: Anthony Hinds <u>D</u>: Francis Searle <u>SCR</u>: John Gilling, from John Dickson Carr's radio-series *Appointment with Fear*
Standard thriller: Yoga expert fakes death, poses as gardener to expose scheming wife

The Man in Grey
1943, (GB), Gainsborough/GFD/Univ, b&w, 116 mins.
<u>W</u>: Margaret Lockwood (*Hesther Shaw*), James Mason (*Marquis of Rohan*), Phyllis Calvert (*Clarissa Richmond*), Stewart Granger (*Peter Rokeby*), Harry Smith (*Toby*), Martita Hunt (*Miss Patchett*), Helen Haye (*Lady Rohan*), Beatrice Varley (*The Gypsy*), Raymond Lovell (*Prince Regent*), Diana King (*Jane Seymour*), Nora Swinburne (*Mrs. Fitzherbert*), Amy Veness (*Mrs. Armstrong*), Roy Emerton (*The Gamekeeper*), A.E. Matthews (*The Auctioneer*)
<u>P</u>: Edward Black <u>D</u>: Leslie Arliss <u>SCR</u>: Margaret Kennedy, Leslie Arliss & Doreen Montgomery, from a novel by Lady Eleanor Smith
reissued 1946 & 1950
Standard thriller: Love triangle involves evil marquis

The Man in Half Moon Street
1944, (USA), Para, b&w, 91 mins.
<u>W</u>: Nils Asther, Helen Walker, Paul Cavanagh, Edmund Breon, Reinhold Schunzel, Brandon Hurst
<u>P</u>: Walter MacEwen <u>D</u>: Ralph Murphy <u>SCR</u>: Charles Kenyon <u>ADAPT</u>: Garrett Fort, from Barre Lyndon's play <u>PHOTOG</u>: Henry Sharp <u>MUSIC</u>: Miklos Rozsa
*Standard thriller: Doctor commits crimes to prolong his unnatural youth. cf. **The Man Who Could Cheat Death***

Man in Hiding
1953, (GB), UA, b&w, 79 mins.
<u>W</u>: Paul Henreid, Lois Maxwell, Kay Kendall
<u>D</u>: Terence Fisher

Standard thriller

The Man in Motley
1916, (GB), London/Jury, b&w, 4,757 ft. (1449.9m)
W: Fred Morgan, Hayford Hobbs, Winifred Sadler, John East, Philip Hewland, Hubert Willis, Jeff Barlow, Judd Green
D: Ralph Dewsbury, from a novel by Tom Gallon
Standard crime-thriller: Framed juggler breaks jail, poses as ghost to force killer's confession

Man in Outer Space
see The Man of the First Century

The Man Inside
1958, (GB), Warwick/Col, b&w, 97 mins.
W: Jack Palance (*Milo March*), Anita Ekberg (*Trudie Hall*), Nigel Patrick (*Sam Carter*), Gerard Heinz (*Stone*), Anthony Newley (*Ernesto*), Bonar Colleano (*Martin Lomar*), Josephine Brown (*Mrs. Frazur*), Sean Kelly (*Rizzio*), Donald Pleasence (*The Organ Grinder*), Sidney James (*Franklin*), Alec Mango (*Lopez*), Eric Pohlmann (*Tristao*), Anne Aubrey (*The Girl*), Naomi Chance (*Jane Leyton*), Mary Laura Wood, Angela White, Alfred Burke, Bill Shine, Joan Ingram, Mark Baker, Richard Golding, Alex Gallier, Walter Gotell, Maxwell Shaw
D: John Gilling **SCR:** Richard Maibaum, John Gilling & David Shaw, from M.E. Chaber's novel **PHOTOG:** Ted Moore **MUSIC:** Muir Mathieson
Standard thriller: Private eye seeks missing diamond

The Man in the Attic
1915, (GB), London/Jury, b&w, 3,478 ft. (1060.1m)
W: Blanche Bryan (*Maggie Holmes*), Charles Rock (*Jacob Clay*), Philip Hewland (*Paul Prior*), Hubert Willis (*Jarvis*), Gwynne Herbert (*Mrs. Holmes*)
D: Ralph Dewsbury, from a play by Charles McEvoy
Standard crime-thriller: Reporter proves girl's drunken mother did not strangle her miserly benefactor

Man in the Attic
1953, (USA), Panoramic/20th-Fox, b&w, 82 mins.
W: Jack Palance (*Slade*), Constance Smith (*Lily*), Rhys Williams (*Harley*), Frances Bavier (*Helen Harvey*), Byron Palmer (*Paul*), Isabel Jewell, Lillian Bond
P: Robert L. Jacks **D & PHOTOG:** Hugo Fregonese **SCR:** Barre Lyndon & Robert Presnell Jr., based on Marie Belloc Lowndes' novel *The Lodger* (remake) **MUSIC:** Lionel Newman
Standard thriller: Lodger proves to be "Jack the Ripper"

The Man in the Attic
1995, (USA), SHO-TV, color, 103 mins.
W: Anne Archer, Neil Patrick Harris, Len Cariou
Made-for-Cable, standard thriller: Woman hides lover in attic

Man in the Dark
1953, (USA), Col, 3D, b&w, 70 mins.
W: Edmond O'Brien, Audrey Totter, Ted de Corsia, Horace McMahon
P: Wallace MacDonald **D:** Lew Landers **SCR:** George Bricker & Jack Leonard
Standard thriller (remake of The Man Who Lived Twice & Crime Doctor): Criminal's face and memory are altered

Man in the Dark
1965, (GB), Univ, b&w, 80 mins.
W: William Sylvester, Barbara Shelley, Elizabeth Shepherd, Alex Davion, Mark Eden, Edward Evans, Ronnie Carroll, Frank Forsythe, Joy Allen, Wendy Martin, Unity Grimwood
D: Lance Comfort **SCR:** James Kelly & Peter Miller **STORY:** Vivian Kemble **PHOTOG:** Basil Emmott **MAIN THEME:** ("Concerto") by Peter Hart **SONGS:** Stan Butcher & Syd Cordell
A.k.a. Blind Corner
Standard thriller

The Man in the Iron Mask
1939, (USA), Edward Small/UA, b&w, 119 mins.

The Man In The Iron Mask (1939): DIRECTOR JAMES WHALE AND LOUIS HAYWARD

W: Louis Hayward, Joan Bennett, Warren William, Alan Hale, Joseph Schildkraut, Edward Brooks, Walter Kingsford, Doris Kenyon, Bert Roach, Miles Mander, Marion Martin, Montagu Love, Albert Dekker, Peter Cushing ("double" for Louis Hayward)
D: James Whale **SCR:** George Bruce, from Alexandre Dumas' novel **PHOTOG:** Robert Planck **MUSIC:** Lucien Moraweck
Classic melodrama: Louis XIV's twin brother kept prisoner

The Man in the Iron Mask
1962, (Fr), MGM/UAcolor, 132 mins.
W: Jean Marais, Claudine Auger, Enrico Salerno, Jean Lara, Giselle Pascal
from Alexander Dumas' novel
Standard melodrama: King's brother imprisoned

The Man in the Iron Mask
1998, (USA), color
W: Leonardo DiCaprio, John Malkovich (*Athos*), Gerard Depardieu (*Porthos*), Jeremy Irons (*Aramis*), Gabriel Byrne, Gerard Depardieu, Anne Parillaud, Judith Godreche
D & SCR:: Randall Wallace, from Alexandre Dumas' novel **PHOTOG:** Peter Suschitzky **MUSIC:** Nick Glennie-Smith
Well-made adventure-melodrama: Intrigue in French court

The Man in the Mirror
1936, (GB), J.H. Prods./Wardour/Grand Nat'l, b&w, 82 mins.
W: Edward Everett Horton (*Jeremy Dilke*), Genevieve Tobin (*Helen Dilke*), Ursula Jeans (*Veronica Tarkington*), Garry Marsh (*Charlie Tarkington*), Aubrey Mather (*Bogus of Bokhara*), Alastair Sim (*The Interpreter*), Renee Gadd (*Miss Blake*), Viola Compton (*Mrs. Massiter*), Stafford Hilliard (*Dr. Graves*), Felix Aylmer (*The Earl of Wigan*), Syd Crossley (*The Janitor*)
D: Maurice Elvey **SCR:** F. McGrew Willis & Hugh Mills, from a novel by William Garrett **PHOTOG:** Curtis Courant
Unusual fantasy: Timid businessman supplanted by his reflection

The Man in the Moon (1898)
see L'Homme dans la Lune

Man in the Moon
1960, (GB), Excalibur/Rank/Trans-Lux, b&w, 99 mins.

Man In The Moon (1960): KENNETH MORE

W: Kenneth More (*William Blood*), Shirley Anne Field (*Polly*), Michael Hordern (*Dr. Davidson*), Charles Gray (*Leo*), Norman Bird (*Herbert*), John Glyn-Jones (*Dr. Wilmot*), John Phillips (*Prof. Stephens*), Noel Purcell (*The Prospector*), Bernard Horsfall (*Rex*), Newton Blick (*Dr. Hollis*), Lionel Gamlin (*The Doctor*), Russell Waters (*The Director*), Danny Green (*The Driver*), Bruce Boa
P: Michael Relph **D:** Basil Dearden **SCR:** Michael Relph & Bryan Forbes **PHOTOG:** Harry Waxman **MUSIC:** Philip Green
Amusing SF-comedy: Man trained to be astronaut lands in Australia

The Man in the Moonlight Mask
1963, (Jap), color
Minor SF-fantasy

The Man in the Net
1959, (USA), UA, b&w, 97 mins.
W: Alan Ladd, Carolyn Jones, Diane Brewster, John Lupton
P: Walter Mirisch **D:** Michael Curtiz **SCR:** Reginald Rose **PHOTOG:** John F. Seitz **MUSIC:** Hans J. Salter
Confused thriller: Man falsely accused of killing neurotic wife

The Man in the Road
1956, (GB), Gibraltar/Grand Nat'l/Rep, b&w, 84 mins.
W: Derek Farr (*Ivan Mason*), Ella Raines (*Rhona Ellison*), Donald Wolfit (*Prof. Cattrell*), Lisa Daniely (*Mitzi*), Karel Stepanek (*Dmitri Balenkov*), Cyril

Cusack (*Dr. Kelly*), Olive Sloane (*Mrs. Lemming*), Bruce Beeby (*Dr. Manning*), Frederick Piper (*Insp. Hayman*), Russell Napier (*Supt. Davidson*), John Welsh, Alfred Maron
<u>P</u>: Charles A. Leeds   <u>D</u>: Lance Comfort   <u>SCR</u>: Guy Morgan, from Anthony Armstrong's novel *He Was Found in the Road*   <u>MUSIC</u>: Bruce Campbell
Standard thriller: Amnesiac scientist becomes target of foreign spies

The Man in the Santa Claus Suit
1979, (USA), Dick Clark/NBC-TV, color, 100 mins.
<u>W</u>: Fred Astaire, Bert Convy (*Gil Travis*), Gary Burghoff (*Bob Willis*), Tara Buckman (*Polly*), Nanette Fabray (*Dora Dayton*), John Byner (*Stan*), Harold Gould (*Dickie Dayton*), Ed Barth (*Babyskin*), Brooke Bundy (*Linda*), Ronald Feinberg (*Bruno*), David E. Greenan (*Ron*), Ray Vitte (*Eddie*), Debbie Lytton (*Melissa*), Pat Petersen (*Lance*), Majel Barrett (*Ms. Forsythe*), Danny Wells (*Chandler*), Tony La Torre (*Angelo*), Andre Gower (*Terry*), Eddie Ryder (*Hans*), Ted Thurston (*The Clerk*), Sasha Von Scherler (*The Shopper*)
<u>D</u>: Corey Allen   <u>TELEPLAY</u>: George Kirgo   <u>PHOTOG</u>: Woody Omens   <u>MUSIC</u>: Peter Matz   <u>SONG</u>: (lyrics, Norman Gimbel), *Once a Year Night*
TVM, standard fantasy: Wanderer teaches meaning of Xmas

Man in the Shadow
1957, (GB), Merton Park/Anglo-Amalgamated, b&w, 84 mins.
<u>W</u>: Zachary Scott (*John Sullivan*), Faith Domergue (*Barbara Peters*), Faith Brook (*Joan Lennox*), Peter Illing (*Carl Raffone*), Gordon Jackson (*Jimmy Norris*), Kay Callard (*Pamela Norris*), John Welsh (*Insp. Hunt*), John Horsley (*Alan Peters*), Fabia Drake (*Sister Veronica*)
<u>P</u>: Alec Snowden   <u>D</u>: Montgomery Tully   <u>STORY</u>: Stratford Davis
Standard thriller: Blackmailed woman proves convicted husband innocent of murder

The Man in the White Suit
1951, (GB), Ealing/Janus/Univ, b&w, 85 mins.
<u>W</u>: Alec Guinness (*Sidney Stratton*), Joan Greenwood (*Daphne Birnley*), Michael Gough (*Michael Corland*), Ernest Thesiger (*Sir John Kierlaw*), Vida Hope (*Bertha*), Cecil Parker (*Alan Birnley*), Miles Malleson (*The Tailor*), Joan Harben (*Miss Johnson*), Howard Marion-Crawford (*Cranford*), Patric Doonan (*Frank*), Duncan Lamont (*Harry*), Colin Gordon (*Bill*), Henry Mollison (*Hoskins*), Harold Goodwin (*Wilkins*), Mandy Miller (*Gladdie*), Frank Atkinson (*The Baker*), Russell Waters (*Davidson*), Ewan Roberts, George Benson, Judith Furse, Stuart Latham, Edie Martin, Olaf Olsen, Billy Russell, John Rudling
<u>P</u>: Michael Balcon   <u>D</u>: Alexander Mackendrick   <u>SCR</u>: Alexander Mackendrick, Roger MacDougall & John Dighton   <u>PHOTOG</u>: Douglas Slocombe   <u>MUSIC</u>: Benjamin Frankel
Classic SF-satire: Panic in British textile industry when benighted chemist invents indestructible fabric

The Manipulator
see Effects

The Manitou
1978, (USA), Avco Embassy, color, 104 mins.
<u>W</u>: Tony Curtis (*Harry Erskine*), Susan Strasberg (*Karen Tandy*), Michael Ansara (*John Singing Rock*), Ann Sothern (*Mrs. Karmann*), Stella Stevens (*Amelia Crusoe*), Burgess Meredith (*Dr. Ernest Snow*), Jon Cedar (*Dr. Jack Hughes*), Paul Mantee (*Dr. Robert McEvoy*), Hugh Corcoran (*MacArthur*), Jeanette Nolan (*Mrs. Winconis*), Lurene Tuttle (*Mrs. Heaz*), Michael Laren (*Michael*), Ann Mantee (*The Floor Nurse*), Carole Hemingway (*The Prostitute*), Tenaya (*Singing Rock's Wife*), Jan Heininger (*Wolf*), Beverly Kushida (*The 2nd Floor Nurse*)
<u>P & D</u>: William Girdler   <u>SCR</u>: William Girdler, Jon Cedar & Tim Pope, from Graham Masterton's novel   <u>PHOTOG</u>: Michel Hugo   <u>SPCL-FX</u>: Tom Burman   <u>MUSIC</u>: Lalo Schifrin
Standard horror-fantasy: Diabolic possession and the reincarnation of an Indian medicine man

The Manitou: SUSAN STRASBERG

Mankillers
see Faster, Pussycat! Kill! Kill!

Man-Made Monster
1941, (USA), Univ, b&w, 59 mins.
<u>W</u>: Lon Chaney Jr. (*Dan McCormick*), Lionel Atwill (*Dr. Paul Regas*), Anne Nagel (*June Lawrence*), Samuel S. Hinds (*Dr. John Lawrence*), Frank Albertson (*Mark Adams*), Ben Taggart, William Davidson, Russell Hicks, Connie Bergen, Ivan Miller, Chester Gan, George Meader, Frank O'Connor, Byron Foulger, John Dilson
<u>D</u>: George Waggner   <u>SCR</u>: Joseph West   <u>PHOTOG</u>: Elwood Bredell   <u>SPCL-FX</u>: John P. Fulton   <u>MUSIC</u>: Charles Previn
GB retitle, **The Electric Man,** *orig. to be titled* **The Mysterious Dr. R,** *reissued as*

MAN-MADE MONSTER: LON CHANEY JR. AND LIONEL ATWILL

The Atomic Monster
"...an expert little made-to-measure horror vehicle...Chaney, fresh from *Of Mice and Men*, and still considered essentially a character actor, played his fairly well written role for pathos and tragedy as much as menace, and came as close as he ever would to Karloff's genius for making an audience feel sorry for him even while they feared him...The laboratory scenes were spectacular and exciting"—William K. Everson, Classics of the Horror Film
Unusual SF-horror: Dead criminal revived and electrified

The Man Monkey
1907, (GB), Walturdaw, b&w, 170 ft. (51.8m)
Standard short thriller: Ape steals baby, is chased by soldiers

Mannequin
1987, (USA), 20th-Fox, color, 90 mins.
<u>W</u>: Andrew McCarthy (*Jonathan*), Kim Cattrall (*Emmy*), James Spader (*Richards*), Estelle Getty (*Mrs. Timkin*), Meshach Taylor (*Hollywood*), G.W. Bailey (*The Watchman*), Carole Davis (*Roxie*), Steve Vinovich (*B.J. Wert*), Christopher Maher, Phyllis Newman
<u>D</u>: Michael Gottlieb   <u>SCR</u>: Michael Gottlieb & Edward Rugoff   <u>PHOTOG</u>: Tim Suhrstedt   <u>SONG</u>: *Nothing's Gonna Stop Us Now*
Standard comedy-fantasy: Ancient Egyptian girl reborn as living mannequin

Mannequin Two: On the Move
1991, (USA), 20th-Fox, color, 95 mins.
<u>W</u>: Kristy Swanson (*Jessie*), William Ragsdale (*Jason Williamson/ Prince William*), Meshach Taylor (*Hollywood/The Doorman*), Terry Kiser (*Count Spretzle/The Sorcerer*), Stuart Pankin (*Mr. James*), Cynthia Harris (*Mom/The Queen*), Julie Foreman, Andrew Hill Newman, Jackye Roberts, John Edmondson, Phil Latella, Sherry Wallen, Ellen Sabino, Matt Myers
<u>D</u>: Stewart Raffill   <u>SCR</u>: Edward Rugoff, David Isaacs, Ken Levine & Betsy Israel   <u>PHOTOG</u>: Larry Pizer   <u>MUSIC</u>: David McHugh
Minor comedy-fantasy: Medieval statue comes to life

The Man of a Hundred Tricks
see L'Homme aux Cent Trucs

Man of a Thousand Faces
1957, (USA), Univ, b&w, 122 mins.
<u>W</u>: James Cagney (*Lon Chaney Sr.*), Jane Greer (*Hazel Bennet*), Dorothy Malone (*Cleva Creighton Chaney*), Jim Backus (*Clarence Logan*), Marjorie Rambeau (*Gert*), Robert J. Evans (*Irving Thalberg*), Celia Lovsky (*Mrs. Chaney*), Jack Albertson (*Dr. J. Wilson Shields*), Roger Smith (*Creighton Chaney, Age 21*), Robert Lyden (*Creighton Chaney, Age 13*), Rickie Sorenson (*Creighton Chaney, Age 8*), Jeanne Cagney (*Carrie Chaney*), Nolan Leary (*Pa Chaney*), Dennis Rush (*Creighton Chaney, Age 4*), Simon Scott (*Carl Hastings*), Philip Van Zandt (*George Loane Tucker*), Danny Beck (*Max Dill*), Hank Mann, Clarence Kolb, Snub Pollard
<u>P</u>: Robert Arthur   <u>D</u>: Joseph Pevney   <u>SCR</u>: R. Wright Campbell, Ivan Goff &

Man of a Thousand Faces: ROBERT EVANS AND JAMES CAGNEY

Ben Roberts   **PHOTOG:** Russell Metty   **MUSIC:** Joseph Gershenson
Superior film-bio: Life of 1920's cinema horror-great

The Man of a Thousand Inventions
see L'Homme aux Mille Inventions

Man of Evil
see Fanny by Gaslight

A Man of Mystery
1912, (GB), Hepworth, b&w, 400 ft. (121.9m)
D: Frank Wilson
Standard fantasy short: Disappearing clown covers audience with soot

The Man of the First Century
1961, (Czech), AIP, color, 85 mins.
W: Milos Kopecky, Anita Kajlicheva, Radevan Lukavsky
D: Oldrich Lipsky
*USA retitle, **Man in Outer Space***
Standard SF-adventure

Man of Violence
1970, (GB), Peter Walker/Miracle, color, 107 mins.
W: Michael Latimer *(Moon)*, Luan Peters *(Angel)*, Derek Aylward *(Nixon)*,
   Maurice Kaufmann *(Charles Grayson)*, Derek Francis *(Sam Bryant)*, Kenneth
   Hendel *(Hunt)*, Virginia Wetherell *(Gale)*, George Belbin *(Burgess)*, Andreas
   Malandrinos *(Pergolesi)*, Erika Raffael *(Goose)*
P & D: Peter Walker   **SCR:** Peter Walker & Brian Comfort
*A.k.a. **The Sex Racketeers***
Standard crime-thriller: Loan operator involved in theft of Arab bullion

Le Manoir du Diable (The Devil's Mansion)
1896, (Fr), Star, b&w, 60m (196.9 ft./3.3 mins.)
D: Georges Melies
*GB retitle, **The Haunted Castle***
Standard fantasy: Satan conjures occult creatures

Le Manoir Maudit (The Cursed Mansion)
1964, (Fr), b&w
W: Marc Marian, Anne Albert
Minor thriller

Man on a Swing
1974, (USA), Para, color, 108 mins.
W: Cliff Robertson *(Lee Tucker)*, Dorothy Tristan *(Janet Tucker)*, Joel Grey
   (Franklin Wills), Elizabeth Wilson *(Dr. Anna Wilson)*, George Voskovec *(Dr.
   Nicholas Holnar)*, Peter Masterson *(Willie Younger)*, Ron Weyand *(Dr. Philip
   Fusco)*, Lane Smith *(Ted Ronan)*, Joe Ponazecki *(Dan Lloyd)*, Richard Venture
   (The Man in the Motel), Gil Gerard *(Donald Forbes)*, Christopher Allport
   (Richie Tom Keating), Patricia Hawkins *(Diana Spenser)*, Dianne Hull *(Maggie
   Dawson)*, Brendan Fay *(Father Connally)*, Richard Dryden *(Mr. Dawson)*, Roy
   Mason *(The Plant Manager)*, Alice Drummond *(Mrs. Dawson)*, Richard
   McKenzie *(Sam Gallagher)*, Clarice Blackburn *(Mrs. Brennan)*, Nicholas
   Pryor *(Paul Kearney)*, Josef Sommer *(Peter Russell)*, Shawn Campbell *(Steve
   Barron)*, Clarence Felder *(The Coach)*, Benjamin Slack *(Ronnie)*, Penelope
   Milford *(Evelyn Moore)*, Bruce French *(The Checkout Man)*, James Galvin *(The
   Man in the Plant)*, Loretta Fury *(Mrs. Segretta)*
P: Howard B. Jaffe   **D:** Frank Perry   **SCR:** David Zelag Goodman, from William
   Clark's novel *The Girl on the Volkswagen Floor*   **PHOTOG:** Adam Holender
   MUSIC: Lalo Schifrin
Standard thriller: Clairvoyant aids police chief in search for strangler

A Man on the Beach
1956, (GB), Hammer/Exclusive, color, 29 mins.
W: Donald Wolfit *(Carter)*, Michael Medwin *(Max)*, Michael Ripper *(The
   Chauffeur)*, Edward Forsyth *(Insp. Clement)*, Alex de Gallier *(The Casino
   Manager)*, Corinne Grey *(The Blonde)*, Barry Shawzin *(The American)*
P: Anthony Hinds   **D:** Joseph Losey   **SCR:** Jimmy Sangster, from Victor

Mannequin Two: On The Move: KRISTY SWANSON

Canning's story "Chance at the Wheel"
Standard short crime-thriller: Man poses as woman, tries to rob casino

The Man on the Cliff
1955, (GB), E.J. Fancey/New Realm, b&w, 23 mins.
W: Ronald Leigh-Hunt, Adrienne Scott, Billie Lane, Russell Carr
D: Robert Hartford-Davis   **STORY:** Maxwell Munden
Standard short crime-thriller: Amnesiac assumes identity of dead atomic scientist

Man on the Prowl
1957, (USA), UA, b&w, 86 mins.
W: Mala Powers, James Best
Standard thriller

Man on the Roof
1976, (Swed), Cinema 5/Svensk Filmindustri, color, 109 mins.
W: Carl-Gustaf Lindstedt *(Beck)*, Sven Wollter *(Kollberg)*
D: Bo Widerberg
Unusual thriller: Sniper kills police

Man on the Run
1949, (GB), ABPC/Stratford, b&w, 82 mins.
W: Derek Farr *(Peter Burdon)*, Joan Hopkins *(Jean Adams)*, Edward Chapman *(Insp.
   Mitchell)*, Laurence Harvey *(Sgt. Lawson)*, John Bailey *(Dan Underwood)*, John
   Stuart *(Insp. McBain)*, Edward Underdown *(Slim)*, Leslie Perrins *(Charlie)*,
   Kenneth More *(Cpl. Newman)*, Martyn Miller *(The Proprietor)*, Eleanor
   Summerfield *(May Baker)*, Anthony Nicholls *(The Inspector)*
WRIT, P & D: Lawrence Huntington
Standard thriller: Deserter involved in jewel robbery

Man on the Staircase
1970, (GB), Ralco/London Screen, color, 27 mins.
W: John Cazabon *(The Man)*
D: Roy Cannon
Standard short crime-thriller: Man kills intruder

Manos, the Hands of Fate
1966, (USA), Sun City/Emerson, color, 74 mins
W: Tom Neyman, John Reynolds, Diane Mahree, Hal P. Warren
P, D, & SCR: Hal P. Warren
*Minor fantasy-thriller: Vacationers trapped in phantasmagoric house; filmed in El Paso,
   Texas*

The Man Outside
1933, (GB), Real Art/Radio, b&w, 51 mins.
W: Henry Kendall *(Harry Wainwright)*, Gillian Lind *(Ann)*, Joan Gardner *(Peggy
   Fordyce)*, John Turnbull *(Insp. Jukes)*, Michael Hogan *(Shiner Talbot)*, Cyril
   Raymond *(Capt. Fordyce)*, Louis Hayward *(Frank Elford)*, Ethel Warwick
   (Georgina Yapp)
D: George A. Cooper   **SCR:** H. Fowler Mear, from a story by Donald Stuart

Standard thriller: Detective unmasks jewel-thief murderer

The Man Outside
1967, (GB), Trio-Group W/London Independent Producers/AA, color, 98 mins.
<u>W</u>: Van Heflin (*Bill Maclean*), Heidelinde Weis (*Kay Sebastian*), Pinkas Braun (*Rafe Machek*), Peter Vaughan (*Nicolai Volkov*), Charles Gray (*Charles Griddon*), Willoughby Gray (*The Inspector*), Paul Maxwell (*Judson Murphy*), Bill Nagy (*Morehouse*), Ronnie Barker (*George Venaxas*), Larry Cross (*Austen*), Linda Marlowe (*Dorothy*), Gary Cockrell (*Brune Parry*), Carole Ann Ford (*Cindy*)
<u>P</u>: William Gell   <u>D</u>: Samuel Gallu   <u>SCR</u>: Samuel Gallu, Julian Bond & Roger Marshall, from Gene Stackleborg's novel *Double Agent*
Standard thriller: Ex-CIA agent framed for murder

Man's Best Friend
1993, (USA), New Line, color, 87 mins.
<u>W</u>: Ally Sheedy (*Lori Tanner*), Lance Henriksen (*Dr. Jarret*), Robert Costanzo (*Det. Kovacs*), Fredric Lehne (*Perry*), John Cassini (*Det. Bendetti*), J.F. Daniels (*Rudy*), Heidi, Max
<u>D & SCR</u>: John Lafia   <u>PHOTOG</u>: Mark Irwin   <u>MUSIC</u>: Joel Goldsmith
Standard SF-thriller: Genetically-altered canine proves deadly

Man's Genesis
1912, (USA), Biograph, b&w, 15 mins
<u>W</u>: Robert Harron, Mae Marsh
<u>D & SP</u>: D.W. Griffith
Standard melodrama: Caveman intellect triumphs over brawn

The Mansion of the Devil
see Le Manoir du Diable

Mansion of the Doomed
1976, (USA), Group 1, color, 89 mins.
<u>W</u>: Richard Basehart (*Dr. Chaney*), Gloria Grahame (*Katherine*), Trish Stewart (*Nancy*), Lance Henriksen (*Dr. Bryan*), Libbie Chase (*The Girl*), Vic Tayback (*The Detective*), Arthur Space
<u>P</u>: Charles Band   <u>D</u>: Michael Pataki   <u>SCR</u>: Frank Ray Perilli   <u>PHOTOG</u>: Andrew Davis   <u>MUSIC</u>: Robert O. Raglan
A.k.a. **The Terror of Dr. Chaney**
*Minor thriller: Doctor commits crimes in attempt to restore daughter's eyesight. Remake: **Les Yeus Sans Visage***

A Man's Shadow
1912, (GB), Cricks & Martin, b&w, 910 ft. (277.4m)
<u>D</u>: Edwin J. Collins
Standard crime-thriller: Ex-convict poses as amnesiac's double

A Man's Shadow
1920, (GB), Progress/Butcher, b&w, 5,500 ft. (1676.4m)
<u>W</u>: Langhorne Burton (*Peter Beresford/Julian Grey*), Violet Graham (*Vivian Beresford*), Gladys Mason (*Yolande Hampden*), Arthur Lennard (*Robert Hampden*), J. Denton-Thompson (*Williams*), Sydney Paxton (*Billings*), Babs Ronald (*Helen Beresford*), Warris Linden (*Simon Oppenheim*)
<u>P</u>: Frank E. Spring   <u>D & SCR</u>: Sidney Morgan, from a play by Robert Buchanan
Standard crime-thriller: Poor man's double murders Jewish usurer, is betrayed by ex-mistress

The Manster
1962, (GB-Jap), Lopert/UA, b&w, 72 mins.
<u>W</u>: Peter Dyneley (*Larry*), Jane Hylton (*Linda*), Satoshi Nakamura (*Dr. Suzuki*), Terri Zimmern (*Tara*), Jerry Ito, Toyoko Tackechi, Norman Van Hawley
<u>P</u>: George Breakston   <u>D</u>: George Breakston & Kenneth G. Crane   <u>SCR</u>: Walter J. Sheldon   <u>STORY</u>: George P. Breakston
orig. to be titled **The Split** *A.k.a.* **The Monster, Half Man, Half Monster**
Standard horror-thriller: Man falls victim to hideous Oriental curse

The Man They Could Not Arrest
1931, (GB), Gainsborough/W&F, b&w, 74 mins.
<u>W</u>: Hugh Wakefield (*Dain*), Gordon Harker (*Tansey*), Renee Clama (*Mercia*), Nicholas Hannen (*Lyall*), Dennis Wyndham (*Shaughnessy*), Garry Marsh (*Delbury*), Robert Farquharson (*Count Lazard*)
<u>D</u>: T. Hayes Hunter   <u>SCR</u>: Arthur Wimperis, Angus Macphail & T. Hayes Hunter, from a novel by Edgar Wallace
Standard thriller: Scientist's "eavesdrop wireless" exposes crime

The Man They Could Not Hang
1939, (USA), Col, b&w, 65 mins.
<u>W</u>: Boris Karloff, Robert Wilcox, Lorna Gray (Adrian Booth), Roger Pryor, Ann Doran, Don Beddoe, Byron Foulger, John Tyrrell, James Craig, Joseph de Steffani, Charles Trowbridge, Dick Curtis
<u>P</u>: Wallace MacDonald   <u>D</u>: Nick Grinde   <u>SCR</u>: Karl Brown, from a story by Leslie T. White & George W. Sayre   <u>PHOTOG</u>: Benjamin Kline
Standard horror-thriller: Executed scientist returned to life

Mantis
1994, (USA), Fox-TV, color
<u>W</u>: Carl Lumbly, Bobby Hosea, Gina Torres, Steve James, Alan Fudge, Marcia Cross, Yvonne Farrow
<u>D</u>: Sam Raimi   <u>TELEPLAY</u>: Sam Hamm   <u>PHOTOG</u>: William Dill   <u>MUSIC</u>:

Joseph Lo Duca
TVM (feature-pilot for teleseries), standard SF-thriller: Paraplegic becomes crime-fighting superhero

Mantis in Lace
1968, (USA), Boxoffice Int'l, color, 80 mins
<u>W</u>: Susan Stewart (*Lila*)
<u>P & SCR</u>: Sanford White   <u>D</u>: William Rotsler   <u>PHOTOG</u>: Laszlo Kovacs
A.k.a. **Lila**
Minor thriller: Topless dancer takes LSD, kills lovers while hallucinating

Mantrap
1953, (GB), Hammer, b&w, 78 mins.
<u>W</u>: Paul Henreid (*Hugo Bishop*), Lois Maxwell, Kieron Moore (*Mervyn Speight*), Hugo Sinclair (*Maurice Jerrard*), Lloyd Lamble (*Frisnay*), Anthony Forwood (*Rex*), Bill Travers (*Victor Tasman*), Mary Laura Wood (*Susie*), Kay Kendall (*Vera*), John Penrose (*du Vancet*)
<u>P</u>: Michael Carreras & Alexander Paal   <u>D</u>: Terence Fisher   <u>SCR</u>: Paul Tabori & Terence Fisher, from Elleston Trevor's novel *Danger*
Standard crime-thriller: Detective aids escaped madman

The Man Upstairs
1958, (GB), ACT/British Lion/Kingsley-Union, b&w, 88 mins.

The Man Upstairs: RICHARD ATTENBOROUGH AND VIRGINIA MASKELL

<u>W</u>: Richard Attenborough (*Peter Watson*), Bernard Lee (*Thompson*), Donald Houston (*Sanderson*), Virginia Maskell (*Helen Grey*), Dorothy Alison (*Mrs. Barnes*), Patricia Jessel (*Mrs. Lawrence*), Kenneth Griffith (*Pollen*), Charles Houston (*Nicholas*), Maureen Connell (*Eunice Blair*), Walter Hudd (*The Supt.*), Edward Judd (*PC Stevens*), Alfred Burke (*George Barnes*)
<u>P</u>: Robert Dunbar   <u>D</u>: Don Chaffey   <u>SCR</u>: Robert Dunbar & Don Chaffey   <u>STORY</u>: Alun Falconer   <u>PHOTOG</u>: Gerald Gibbs
Standard thriller: Police try to persuade neurotic scientist to leave locked room

The Manuscript Found in the Sargasso
see Rekopis Znaleziony w Saragossie

The Man Who Changed His Mind
1936, (GB), Gainsborough/Gaumont, b&w, 66 mins.
<u>W</u>: Boris Karloff (*Dr. Laurience*), Anna Lee (*Claire Wyatt*), John Loder (*Dick Haslewood*), Frank Cellier (*Lord Haslewood*), Donald Calthrop (*Clayton*), Cecil Parker (*Dr. Gratton*), Lyn Harding (*Prof. Holloway*)
<u>D</u>: Robert Stevenson   <u>SCR</u>: John L. Balderston, L. DuGarde Peach & Sidney Gilliat   <u>PHOTOG</u>: Jack Cox
reissued 1949, Fr retitle, **Switched Brains** *USA retitles,* **The Brainiac, The Brainsnatcher, Dr. Maniac** *and* **The Man Who Lived Again**
Standard horror-thriller: Exchange of brains between nobleman and cripple

The Man Who Changed His Name
1934, (GB), Real Art, b&w, 80 mins.
<u>W</u>: Lyn Harding (*Selby Clive*), Betty Stockfeld (*Nita Clive*), Leslie Perrins (*Frank Ryan*), Ben Welden (*Jerry Muller*), Aubrey Mather (*Sir Ralph Whitcomb*), Richard Dolman (*John Boscombe*)
<u>D</u>: Henry Edwards   <u>SCR</u>: H. Fowler Mear, from a play by Edgar Wallace
Standard thriller: To prevent wife's elopement, husband poses as murderer

The Man Who Could Cheat Death
1959, (GB), Hammer/Para, color, 83 mins.
<u>W</u>: Anton Diffring (*Dr. Georges Bonner*), Hazel Court (*Janine Dubois*), Christopher Lee (*Dr. Pierre Gerard*), Arnold Marle (*Dr. Ludwig Weisz*), Delphi Lawrence (*Margo Philippe*), Francis De Wolff (*Insp. Legris*), Gerda Larsen (*The Street Girl*), Michael Ripper
<u>P</u>: Michael Carreras   <u>D</u>: Terence Fisher   <u>SCR</u>: Jimmy Sangster, based on Barre Lyndon's play *The Man in Half Moon Street* (remake)   <u>PHOTOG</u>: Jack Asher   <u>MUSIC</u>: John Hollingsworth
Standard horror-thriller: Doctor commits murder to maintain his unnatural youth, reissued 1965

The Man Who Could Cheat Death: ARNOLD MARLE AND ANTON DIFFRING

The Man Who Couldn't Walk
1960, (GB), Bill & Michael Luckwell/Butcher, b&w, 63 mins.
W: Peter Reynolds (*Keefe Brand*), Eric Pohlmann (*The Consul*), Pat Clavin (*Carol*), Reed de Rouen (*Luigi*), Bernadette Milnes (*Cora*), Richard Shaw (*Enrico*), Martin Cass (*Beppo*)
P: Jock MacGregor & Umesh Mallik   D: Henry Cass   STORY: Umesh Mallik
Standard crime-thriller: Crippled diplomat commits murder

The Man Who Could Work Miracles
1936, (GB), London/UA, b&w, 82 mins.
W: Roland Young (*George McWhirter Fotheringay*), Ralph Richardson (*Col. Winstanley*), Edward Chapman (*Maj. Grigsby*), Ernest Thesiger (*Maydig*), Joan Gardner (*Ada Price*), Sophie Stewart (*Maggie Hooper*), Robert Cochran (*Bill Stoker*), Lady Tree (*Grigsby's Housekeeper*), George Zucco (*The Colonel's Butler*), Lawrence Hanray (*Mr. Bamfylde*), Wally Lupino (*Constable Which*), Joan Hickson (*Effie*), Torin Thatcher (*The Observer*), Wally Patch (*Supt. Smithells*), Mark Daly (*Toddy Beamish*), George Sanders (*Indifference*), Ivan Brandt (*The Player*)
P: Alexander Korda   D: Lothar Mendes   SCR: Lajos Biros, from H.G. Wells' short story   PHOTOG: Harold Rosson   SPCL-FX: Ned Mann   MUSIC: Michael Spolianski   MUSIC DIR: Muir Mathieson
Classic fantasy: Ordinary man acquires supernatural powers

The Man Who Died Twice
1958, (USA), Rep, b&w, 70 mins.
W: Rod Cameron, Vera Ralston, Mike Mazurki, Gerald Milton
D: Joseph Kane
Standard thriller (Vera Ralston's last film): Chanteuse involved in murder

The Man Who Fell to Earth
1976, (GB), British Lion/Cinema 5, color, 138 mins.
W: David Bowie (*Thomas Jerome Newton*), Buck Henry (*Oliver Farnsworth*), Candy Clark (*Mary-Lou*), Bernie Casey (*Peters*), Rip Torn (*Nathan Bryce*), Jackson D. Kane (*Prof. Canutti*), Rick Riccardo (*Trevor*), Tony Mascia (*Arthur*), Linda Hutton (*Elaine*), Hilary Holland (*Jill*), Adrienne Larussa (*Helen*), Lilybelle Crawford (*The Jewelry Store Owner*), Albert Nelson (*The Waiter*), Richard Breeding (*The Receptionist*), Peter Prouse (*Peters' Associate*), Capt. James Lovell
P: Michael Deeley & Barry Spikings   D: Nicolas Roeg   SCR: Paul Mayersberg, from Walter Tevis' novel *Icarus Drowning*   PHOTOG: Anthony Richmond   SPCL-FX: P.S. Ellenshaw   MUSIC DIR: John Phillips
Superior SF-thriller: Alien refugee from dying world is corrupted by Earth existence

The Man Who Fell To Earth: DAVID BOWIE AND CANDY CLARK

The Man Who Fell to Earth
1987, (USA), David Gerber/MGM-TV, color, 95 mins.
W: Lewis Smith (*John*), Beverly D'Angelo (*Eva*), Wil Wheaton (*Billy*), James Laurenson (*Felix Hawthorne*), Robert Picardo (*Morse*), Bruce McGill (*Gage*), Annie Potts (*Louise*), Henry G. Sanders, Bobbi Jo Lathan, Carmen Argenziano, Amy Sawaya, Chris DeRose, Ritch Shydner, Rob Neilson, Michael Fontaine, Steve Natole, Albert Owens, Annie O'Neill, Hank Stratton, Scott Fouser, Diana Wolfe, Carl Parker
D: Robert J. Roth   TELEPLAY: Richard Kletter, from Walter Tevis' novel *Icarus Drowning*   PHOTOG: Frederick Moore   SPCL-FX: Charles E. Dolan   MUSIC: Doug Timm
TVM remake, standard SF: Alien arrives from doomed world

The Man Who Finally Died
1962, (GB), White Cross/Magna/British Lion/Goldstone, b&w, 100 mins.
W: Stanley Baker (*Joe Newman*), Peter Cushing (*Dr. Peter von Brecht*), Mai Zetterling (*Lisa von Deutsch*), Eric Portman (*Insp. Hoffmeister*), Nigel Green (*Sgt. Hirsch*), Barbara Everest (*Martha*), Niall MacGinnis (*Brenner*), Harold Scott (*The Professor*), Georgina Ward (*Maria*)
D: Quentin Lawrence   SCR: Lewis Greifer & Louis Marks, from an orig. story by Lewis Greifer   PHOTOG: Stephen Dade   MUSIC: Philip Green
Standard thriller: Man probes father's mysterious death

The Man Who Forgot
1916, (GB), British Oak/New Agency, b&w, 1,095 ft. (333.8m)
W: James Russell
D: Ernest G. Batley
Standard crime-thriller: Girl crook saves millionaire's son from kidnapper's bullet

The Man Who Haunted Himself
1970, (GB), Anglo-EMI/Nat Cohen/Associated British/Levitt-Pickman, color, 94 mins.
W: Roger Moore (*Harold Pelham*), Hildegard Neil (*Eve Pelham*), Freddie Jones (*Dr. Harris*), Thorley Walters (*Bellamy*), Anton Rodgers (*Tony Alexander*), John Welsh (*Sir Charles Freeman*), Edward Chapman (*Barton*), Olga Georges-Picot (*Julie*), Kevork Malikyan (*Luigi*), Hugh Mackenzie (*James*), Alastair Mackenzie (*Michael*), Laurence Hardy (*Mason*), Charles Lloyd-Pack (*Jameson*), Anthony Nicholls (*Sir Arthur Richardson*), John Carson (*Ashton*), Aubrey Richards
P: Michael Relph   D: Basil Dearden   SCR: Michael Relph & Basil Dearden, from Anthony Armstrong's novel *The Case of Mr. Pelham*   PHOTOG: Tony Spratling   SPCL-FX: Tommy Howard & Charles Staffell   MUSIC: Michael Lewis
Unusual fantasy-thriller: Executive contends with dangerous alter ego

The Man Who Haunted Himself: ROGER MOORE

The Man Who Kept Silent
1911, (GB), Hepworth, b&w, 725 ft. (221m)
D: Bert Haldane
Standard thriller: Clerk takes blame when girl robs safe to help her gambling brother

The Man Who Knew Too Much
1934, (GB), Gaumont, b&w, 75 mins.
W: Leslie Banks (*Bob Lawrence*), Edna Best (*Jill Lawrence*), Peter Lorre (*Abbott*), Nova Pilbeam (*Betty Lawrence*), Frank Vosper (*Levine*), Hugh Wakefield (*Clive*), D.A. Clarke-Smith (*Insp. Binstead*), Pierre Fresnay (*Louis Bernard*), Cicely Oates (*Nurse Agnes*), George Curzon (*Gibson*), Henry Oscar (*George Barbor*)
D: Alfred Hitchcock   SCR: A.R. Rawlinson, Edwin Greenwood & Emlyn Williams, from a story by Charles Bennett & D.B. Wyndham-Lewis   PHOTOG: Curtis Courant   MUSIC: Arthur Benjamin
Classic thriller: Couple's daughter kidnapped by political assassins

The Man Who Knew Too Much
1956, (USA), Para, color, 119 mins.
W: James Stewart (*Ben McKenna*), Doris Day (*Jo McKenna*), Reggie Nalder (*Rien-*

Assassin), Bernard Miles (*Mr. Drayton*), Brenda de Banzie (*Mrs. Drayton*), Daniel Gelin (*Louis Bernard*), Alan Mowbray (*Val Parnell*), Carolyn Jones (*Cindy Fontaine*), Chris Olsen (*Hank McKenna*), Ralph Truman (*Buchanan*), Leo Gordon (*The Chauffeur*), Mogens Wieth (*The Ambassador*), Hillary Brooke (*Jan Peterson*), Noel Willman (*Woburn*), Alix Talton (*Helen Parnell*), Richard Wattis (*The Ass't Manager*), Yves Brainville (*The Police Inspector*), Louis Mercier, Betty Baskcomb, Abdelhaq Chraibi, Patrick Aherne, Anthony Warde, Lewis Martin
P & D: Alfred Hitchcock   **SCR:** John Michael Hayes & Angus Macphail, from a story by Charles Bennett & D.B. Wyndham-Lewis   **PHOTOG:** Robert Burks   **SPCL-FX:** John P. Fulton   **MUSIC:** Bernard Herrmann   **SONG:** *Que Sera Sera*, Oscar winner
Superior thriller: Doctor's son abducted by assassins

The Man Who Knew Too Much: FRANK VOSPER, LESLIE BANKS, NOVA PILBEAM AND PETER LORRE

The Man Who Laughs
1928, (USA), Univ, b&w, 10 reels (10,195 ft./3107.4m/124 mins.)
W: Conrad Veidt (*Gwynplaine*), Mary Philbin (*Dea*), Brandon Hurst (*Barkilphedro, the Jester*), Olga Baclanova (*Duchess Josiana*), George Siegmann (*Dr. Hardquannone*), Josephine Crowell (*Queen Anne*), Cesare Gravina (*Ursus*), Sam de Grasse (*King James*), Stuart Holmes (*Lord Dirry-Noir*), Torben Meyer (*The Spy*), Nick de Ruiz (*The Wapentake*), Julius Molnar Jr. (*Gwynplaine, as a Child*), Charles Puffy (*The Innkeeper*), Frank Puglia (*A Clown*), Jack Goodrich (*A Clown*), Carmen Costello (*Dea's Mother*), Zimbo (*Homo, the Wolf*)
D: Paul Leni   **SCR:** J. Grubb Alexander   **ADAPT:** Charles E. Whittaker, Marion Ward & May McLean, from Victor Hugo's novel   **PHOTOG:** Gilbert Warrenton   **SONG:** *When Love Comes Stealing*
Classic romance-thriller: Disfigured man gains social prominence in 18th-century France

The Man Who Laughs
1965, (It), Gold Key, color, 101 mins
W: Edmund Purdom, Ilaria Occhini, Lisa Gastoni, Jean Sorel
from Victor Hugo's novel
Minor thriller: Love and terror under Italy's Borgias

The Man Who Learned to Fly
1908, (GB), Hepworth, b&w, 300 ft. (91.4m)
D: Lewin Fitzhamon
Minor fantasy short: Inventor dreams he is flattened by roller, flown as kite

The Man Who Lived Again
see *The Man Who Changed His Mind*

The Man Who Lived Twice
1936, (USA), Col, b&w
W: Ralph Bellamy, Marian Marsh, Thurston Hall, Ward Bond
P: Ben Pivar   **D:** Harry Lachman   **SCR:** Tom Van Dycke, Fred Niblo Jr. & Arthur Strawn
Standard thriller: Operation gives horribly-scarred gangster handsome face, but he develops amnesia. cf. **Man in the Dark** *(1953),* **Crime Doctor** *(1943)*

The Man Who Made Diamonds
1937, (GB), First Nat'l/WB, b&w, 73 mins.
W: Noel Madison (*Joseph*), James Stephenson (*Ben*), Lesley Brook (*Helen Calthrop*), George Galleon (*Tony*), Renee Gadd (*Marianne*), Philip Ray (*Tompkins*), J. Fisher White (*Prof. Calthrop*), Wilfrid Lawson (*Gahanie*), Hector Abbas (*Nichols*)
D: Ralph Ince   **SCR:** Michael Barringer & Anthony Hankey, from a story by Frank A. Richardson
Standard thriller: Assistant kills inventor of manufactured diamonds

The Man Who Reclaimed His Head
1935, (USA), Univ, b&w, 81 mins.
W: Claude Rains, Lionel Atwill, Joan Bennett, Henry O'Neill, Lawrence Grant, Henry Armetta, Wallace Ford, Juanita Quigley
P: Carl Laemmle Jr.   **D:** Edward Ludwig   **SCR:** Jean Bart & Samuel Ornitz, from a play by Jean Bart   **PHOTOG:** Merritt B. Gerstad
Unusual thriller: Abused author gains revenge. cf. **Strange Confession**

The Man Who Saw Tomorrow
1981, (USA), WB, color, 88 mins
W: Orson Welles (*host/narrator*), Philip L. Clarke (*The Voice of Nostradamus*), Bob Ruggiero, Roy Edmonds, Ray Chubb, Ray Laska, Richard Butler, Jason Nesmith, Howard Ackerman, Brass Adams, Terry Clotiaux, David Burke, Bob Bigelow, Marji Martin, Ross Evans, Thor Nielsen, Paul Valentine, Harry Bugin, Emile Hamaty, Dante Rochetti, Howard David, Charles Castilla
P: Robert Guenette, Lee Kramer & Paul Drane   **D:** Robert Guenette   **SCR:** Robert Guenette & Alan Hopgood   **MUSIC:** William Loose & Jack Tillar
Standard speculation-docu: Exploration of Nostradamus' predictions

The Man Who Stayed at Home
1915, (GB), Hepworth/Central, b&w, 3,575 ft. (1089.7m)
W: Dennis Eadie (*Christophr Brent*), Violet Hopson (*Miriam Leigh*), Alma Taylor (*Molly Preston*), Lionelle Howard (*Carl Sanderson*), Chrissie White (*Daphne Kidlington*), Dorothy Rowan (*Mrs. Sanderson*), Henry Edwards (*Fritz*), William G. Saunders (*Col. Preston*), Jean Cadell (*Miss Myrtle*)
D: Cecil M. Hepworth, from a play by Letchmere Worrall & Harold Grey
Standard crime-thriller: Detective poses as wartime shirker to unmask spies at East Coast boarding house

The Man Who Turned to Stone
1957, (USA), Clover/Col, b&w, 71 mins.
W: Victor Jory (*Dr. Murdock*), Charlotte Austin (*Carol Adams*), Ann Doran (*Mrs. Ford*), William Hudson (*Dr. Jess Rogers*), Tina Carver (*Big Marge*), Paul Cavanagh (*Cooper*), Jean Willes (*Tracy*), Victor Varconi (*Myers*), George Lynn (*Freneau*), Barbara Wilson (*Anna*), Frederick Ledebur (*Eric*)
P: Sam Katzman   **D:** Leslie Kardos   **SCR:** Raymond T. Marcus   **PHOTOG:** Benjamin H. Kline   **MUSIC:** Ross Di Maggio
Belg retitle: Le Penitencier de la Peur (The Penitentiary of Fear)
Minor SF-thriller: Fiendish scientists seek immortality, experiment on reform-school girls

The Man Who Wagged His Tail
1957, (It-Sp), Chamartin-Falco, b&w, 91 mins.
W: Peter Ustinov, Pablito Calvo, Silvia Marco, Isabel de Pomes, Maurizio Arena, Arnoldo Tieri
D: Ladislas Vajda
A.k.a. **An Angel Passed over Brooklyn**
Standard fantasy: Cruel slumlord turned into dog

Man Who Walked Through the Wall
1959, (W. Ger), Shawn-Int'l, b&w, 99 mins
W: Heinz Ruhmann
Standard fantasy. US release: 1964

The Man Who Wanted to Live Forever
see *The Only Way Out is Dead*

The Man Who Was Nobody
1960, (GB), Merton Park/Anglo-Amalgamated, b&w, 58 mins.
W: Hazel Court (*Marjorie Stedman*), John Crawford (*South Africa Smith*), Lisa Daniely (*Alma Weston*), Paul Eddington (*Franz Reuter*), Robert Dorning (*Vance*), Kevin Stoney (*Joe*), Jack Watson (*The Inspector*), Vanda Godsell (*Mrs. Ferber*)
P: Jack Greenwood   **D:** Montgomery Tully   **SCR:** James Eastwood, from a novel by Edgar Wallace
Minor thriller: Girl sleuth exposes killer

The Man Who Wasn't
1915, (GB), Hepworth, b&w, 550 ft. (167.6m)
W: Lionelle Howard (*The Husband*)
D: Hay Plumb   **STORY:** Lionelle Howard
Standard fantasy: Drunk dreams he becomes invisible

The Man Who Wasn't There
1983, (USA), Frank Mancuso Jr./Para, color, 111 mins.
W: Steve Guttenberg (*Sam Cooper*), Lisa Langlois (*Cindy Worth*), Jeffrey Tambor (*Boris Potemkin*), Art Hindle, Morgan Hart, Bill Forsythe, Vincent Bagetta, Charlie Brill, Joseph Ruskin, Val Bettin
D: Bruce Malmuth   **SCR:** Stanford Sherman   **PHOTOG:** Frederick Moore   **MUSIC:** Miles Goodman
Standard SF-comedy: Gov't employee becomes invisible

The Man Who Watched Trains Go By
see *Paris Express*

The Man Who Would Be King
1975, (USA-GB), Emanuel L. Wolf/AA/Col, color, 129 mins.
W: Sean Connery (*Daniel Dravet*), Michael Caine (*Peachey Carnehan*), Christopher Plummer (*Rudyard Kipling*), Shakira Caine (*Roxanne*), Saeed Jaffrey (*Billy Fish*), Jack May (*The District Commissioner*), Karroum Ben Bouih (*Kafu-Selim*), Doghmi Larbi (*Ootah*), Mohammed Shamsi (*Babu*), Paul Antrim (*Mulvaney*), Yvonne Ocampo (*The Dancer*)
P: Carl Foreman   **D:** John Huston   **SCR:** John Huston & Gladys Hill, from Rudyard Kipling's novella   **PHOTOG:** Oswald Morris   **MUSIC:** Maurice Jarre
"...a classic romance-of-exploration story of the type that Haggard brought to full

flower. Here, two British soldiers of the Empire find a hidden kingdom beyond the Hindu Kush in the 19th century; it's a sort of a "lost race" since it dates from the time of the Alexandrian conquests, and is portrayed as a peculiar mixture of Hellenistic, Afghan, Tibetan, and Moroccan"—Baird

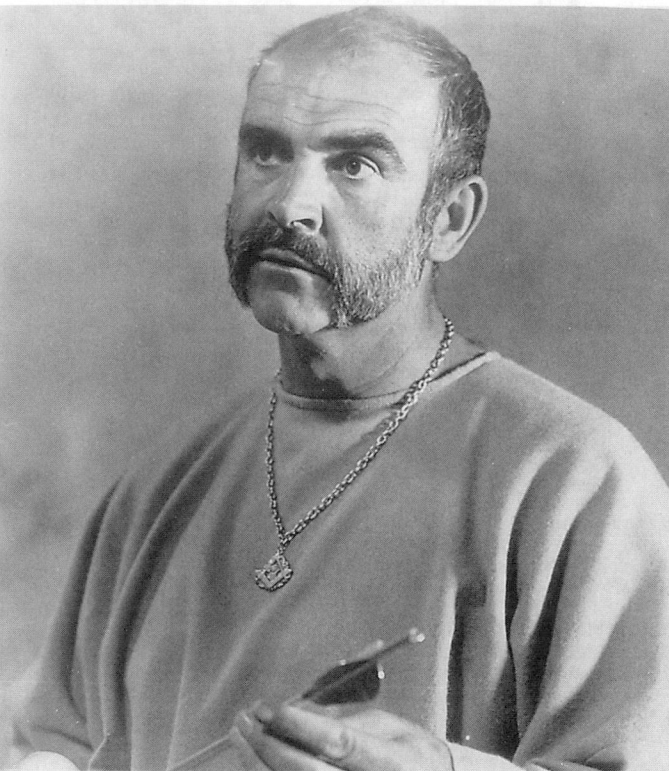

The Man Who Would Be King: SEAN CONNERY

Searles, "Films," The Magazine of Fantasy and Science Fiction, Vol. 50, No. 5 (May, 1976), p. 96
Major adventure-thriller: Soldiers find lost civilization

The Man Who Wouldn't Die
1942, (USA), 20th-Fox, b&w, 65 mins.
W: Lloyd Nolan (*Michael Shayne*), Marjorie Weaver (*Catherine Wolff*), Helene Reynolds (*Anne Wolff*), Henry Wilcoxon (*Dr. Haggard*), Paul Harvey (*Dudley Wolff*), Richard Derr (*Roger Blake*), Billy Bevan (*Phillips*), Olin Howland (*Chief Meeks*), Robert Emmett Keane (*Alfred Dunning*), Francis Ford (*The Caretaker*), LeRoy Mason (*Zorah Bey*), Jeff Corey (*Coroner Larsen*)
D: Herbert I. Leeds **SCR:** Arnaud d'Usseau, based on Clayton Rawson's novel *No Coffin for the Corpse* and characters created by Brett Halliday **PHOTOG:** Joseph P. MacDonald **MUSIC:** Emil Newman
Standard thriller: Detective seeks killer, becomes involved with mysterious yogi

The Man Who Wouldn't Talk
1958, (GB), Everest/British Lion, b&w, 97 mins.
W: Anna Neagle (*Mary Randall*), Anthony Quayle (*Dr. Frank Smith*), Zsa Zsa Gabor (*Eve Trent*), Katherine Kath (*Yvonne Delbeau*), Dora Bryan (*The Telephonist*), Patrick Allen (*Jim Kennedy*), Lloyd Lamble (*Bellamy*), Hugh McDermott (*Bernie*), John Welsh (*George Fraser*), John Paul (*John Castle*), Leonard Sachs (*Prof. Horvard*), John LeMesurier (*The Judge*), Edward Lexy (*Hobbs*)
P & D: Herbert Wilcox **SCR:** Edgar Lustgarten, from a novel by Stanley Jackson
Standard crime-thriller: Virologist charged with killing secret agent

The Man with a Cloak
1951, (USA), MGM, b&w, 81 mins.
W: Joseph Cotten (*Dupin*), Barbara Stanwyck (*Lorna Bounty*), Louis Calhern (*Thevenet*), Leslie Caron (*Madeline Minot*), Jim Backus (*Flaherty*), Roy Roberts (*The Policeman*), Francis Pierlot (*The Pharmacist*), Margaret Wycherly (*Mrs. Flynn*), Joe DeSantis (*Martin*), Richard Hale (*Durand*), Jean Inness (*The Landlady*), Nicholas Joy (*Dr. Roland*), Mitchell Lewis (*Walter*), Hank Worden (*The Driver*), Charles Watts, Cameron Grant, Phil Dunham, James Logan, Helyn Eby-Rock
P: Stephen Ames **D:** Fletcher Markle **SCR:** Frank Fenton, from John Dickson Carr's short story *Gentleman from Paris* **PHOTOG:** George J. Folsey **MUSIC:** David Raksin
Standard thriller: Edgar Allan Poe aids French immigrant, foils murder plot

Man With a Gun
1958, (GB), Merton Park/Anglo-Amalgamated, b&w, 60 mins.
W: Lee Patterson (*Mike Davies*), Rona Anderson (*Stella*), John LeMesurier (*Harry Drayton*), Warren Mitchell (*Joe Harris*), Glen Mason (*Steve Riley*), Harold

Lang (*John Drayson*), Carlo Borelli (*Carlo*), Cyril Chamberlain (*Supt. Wood*)
P: Jack Greenwood **D:** Montgomery Tully **STORY:** Michael Winner
Standard crime-thriller: Insurance investigator exposes arsonists

The Man with a Scar
1914, (GB), Captain Kettle, b&w, 1,135 ft. (345.9m)
STORY: C.J. Cutcliffe-Hyne
Standard crime-thriller: Roue stabs himself trying to kill rival

Man with Icy Eyes
1971, (It), Gold Key, color, 97 mins
W: Antonio Sabato, Barbara Bouchet, Victor Buono, Keenan Wynn, Faith Domergue
Minor thriller: Young Mexican falsely accused of senator's murder

The Man with My Face
1951, (USA), UA, b&w, 865 mins.
W: Barry Nelson, Carole Mathews
Standard thriller

The Man with Nine Lives
1940, (USA), Col, b&w, 73 mins.
W: Boris Karloff, Jo Ann Sayers, Roger Pryor, Ernie Adams, Charles Trowbridge, Stanley Brown (later Brad Taylor) John Dilson, Hal Taliaferro, Byron Foulger
D: Nick Grinde **SCR:** Karl Brown **PHOTOG:** Benjamin H. Kline
*GB retitle, **Behind the Door***
Standard thriller: Suspended-animation experiments go awry

The Man without a Body
1957, (GB), British Filmplays/Eros, b&w, 79 mins.
W: Robert Hutton (*Dr. Phil Merritt*), George Coulouris (*Karl Brussard*), Julia Arnall (*Jean*), Nadja Regin (*Odette*), Peter Copley (*Leslie*), Sheldon Lawrence (*Lew*), Norman Shelley (*Dr. Alexander*), Michael Golden (*Nostradamus*), William Sherwood (*Dr. Charot*), Stanley van Beers (*The Mme. Tussaud's Guide*), Tony Quinn (*Dr. Brandon*), Maurice Kaufmann (*The Chauffeur*), Edwin Ellis (*The Publican*), Frank Forsyth (*The Detective*), Donald Morley (*The Stock Broker*), Ernest Bale (*The Customs Officer*), Kim Parker (*The Maid*)
P: Guido Coen **D:** W. Lee Wilder **SCR:** William Grote & Charles Saunders **PHOTOG:** Brendan Stafford **MUSIC:** Albert Elms
blurb: "A diabolical dream come true!"
Standard thriller: Tycoon seeks brain transplant, steals Nostradamus' head

Man without a Face
*see **Who?***

The Man without a Name
*see **Mensch ohne Namen***

The Man without a Soul
1916, (GB), London/Jury, b&w, 7,200 ft. (2194.6m)
W: Milton Rosmer (*Stephen Ferrier*), Edna Flugarth (*Lucy*), Edward O'Neill (*The Atheist*), Charles Rock (*Rev. John Ferrier*), Barbara Everest, Frank Stanmore, Hubert Willis, Kitty Cavendish
D & SCR: George L. Tucker, from a story by Kenelm Foss
*USA retitle, **I Believe** Tucker-Cosmofotofilm-Sherman, 1917*
Standard fantasy: Church student loses soul after scientist revives his dead body

The Man without Desire
1923, (GB), Atlas-Biograph, b&w, 7,000 ft. (2133.6m)
W: Ivor Novello (*Vittorio Dandolo*), Nina Vanna (*Leonora/Genevia*), Sergio Mari (*Almoro/Gordi*), Jane Dryden (*Luigia*), Chris Walker (*Roger/Mawdesley*), Dorothy Warren (*Foscolnia*), Adrian Brunel (*The Reporter*)
P: Ivor Novello **D:** Adrian Brunel **SCR:** Frank Fowell, from a story by Monckton Hoffe
Standard fantasy: Mourning lover awakes after 200-year suspended animation

The Man with the Golden Gun
1974, (GB), Eon/UA, color, 125 mins.
W: Roger Moore (*James Bond*), Christopher Lee (*Scaramanga*), Britt Ekland (*Mary Goodnight*), Maud Adams (*Andrea*), Herve Villechaize (*Nick Nack*), Richard Loo (*Hai Fat*), Clifton James (*Sheriff J.W. Pepper*), Bernard Lee ("M"), Lois Maxwell (*Miss Moneypenny*), Marc Lawrence (*Rodney*), Desmond Llewelyn ("Q"), Marne Maitland (*Lazar*), James Cossins (*Colthorpe*), Gerald James (*Frazier*), Michael Osborne (*The Naval Lieutenant*), Chan Yiu Lam (*Chula*), Carmen Sautoy (*Saida*), Michael Fleming (*The Communications Officer*)
P: Harry Saltzman & Albert R. Broccoli **D:** Guy Hamilton **SCR:** Richard Maibaum & Tom Mankiewicz, from Ian Fleming's novel **PHOTOG:** Ted Moore & Oswald Morris **MUSIC:** John Barry
Standard thriller: Int'l assassin plots to monopolize solar energy

The Man with the Power
1977, (USA), Univ/NBC-TV, color, 106 mins.
W: Bob Neill (*Eric Smith*), Tim O'Connor (*Walter Bloom*), Vic Morrow (*Paul*), Persis Khambatta (*Princess Siri*), Rene Assa (*Sajid*), Noel de Souza (*Shanda*), James Ingersoll, Regis J. Cordic, Bill Fletcher, Austin Stoker, John de Lancie, Judd Laurance, Sheldon Allman, Jason Wingreen, Jonathan Segal, Jim Raymond

M

WRIT & P: Allan Balter **D:** Nicholas Sgarro **PHOTOG:** J.J. Jones **MUSIC:** Patrick Williams
TVM, standard SF: Gov't uses psychokinetic man

The Man with the Rubber Head
1902, (Fr), Star, b&w, 50m (164 ft./2.8 mins.)
W: Georges Melies
D: Georges Melies
A.k.a. A Swelled Head
Standard fantasy: Apothecary enlarges severed human head

The Man with the Scar
1915, (GB), Hepworth, b&w, 1,575 ft. (480.1m)
W: Stewart Rome (*The Doctor*), Chrissie White (*The Girl*), Lionelle Howard (*The Crook*), Harry Gilbey (*The Father*)
D: Frank Wilson
Standard thriller: Girl exposes murderer

Man with the Synthetic Brain
see Blood of Ghastly Horror

The Man with the Twisted Lip
1921, (GB), Stoll, b&w, 2,412 ft. (735.2m)
W: Eille Norwood (*Sherlock Holmes*), Hubert Willis (*Dr. John Watson*), Robert Vallis (*Neville St. Clair*), Paulette del Baye (*Mrs. St. Clair*), Mme. d'Esterre (*Mrs. Hudson*)
D: Maurice Elvey **SCR:** William J. Elliott, from the writings of Sir Arthur Conan Doyle
Standard crime-thriller (episode in "Adventures of Sherlock Holmes" series)

The Man with the Twisted Lip
1951, (GB), Telecine Films/Grand Nat'l, b&w, 35 mins.
W: John Longden (*Sherlock Holmes*), Campbell Singer (*Dr. Watson*), Hector Ross (*Neville St. Clair*), Beryl Baxter (*Doreen*), Walter Gotell (*Luzatto*)
P: Rudolph Cartier **D:** Richard M. Grey, from Sir Arthur Conan Doyle's short story
Standard thriller short: Detective tracks missing husband to opium den

The Man with the Yellow Eyes
see Planets Against Us

The Man with Three Coffins
1988, (S. Korea), color, 105 mins.
W: Lee Bo-Hee
D: Lee Chang-Ho
Unusual fantasy: Man makes mystical pilgrimage

The Man with Two Brains
1983, (USA), Aspen/WB, color, 79 mins.
W: Steve Martin, Kathleen Turner, David Warner, Paul Benedict, James Cromwell, Merv Griffin (*The Elevator Killer*), Sissy Spacek (*The Voice of the Brain*), Steve Martin (*Dr. Michael Hfuhruhurr*), Kathleen Turner (*Dolores Benedict*), David Warner (*Dr. Necessiter*), Paul Benedict (*The Butler*), Richard Brestof, (*Dr. Pasteur*), James Cromwell (*The Realtor*), George Furth (*Timon*), Peter Hobbs (*Dr. Brandon*), Earl Boen (*Dr. Conrad*), Bernie Hern (*The Gun Seller*),Frank McCarthy (*Olsen*), William Traylor (*The Inspector*), Randi Brooks (*Fran*), Bernard Behrens (*Gladstone*), Russell Orozco (*Juan*), Natividad Vacio (*Ramon*), David Byrd (*The Desk Clerk*), Adrian Ricard (*The Nurse in the Room*), Sparky Marcus (*The Bellboy*), Perla Walter (*The Housekeeper*), Mya Akerling (*The Little Girl*), Don McLeod (*Schlermie Beckerman/The Gorilla*), Peter Elbling (*The Morgue Attendant*), Diane Peterson (*Hooker #1*), Kate Sarchet (*Hooker #2*), Wendy Sherman (*Hooker #3*), Warwick Sims (*The Drunk Test Policeman*), Breck Costin (*The Handsome Waiter*), Tom Spratley (*The Minister*), Art Holliday (*The O.R. Attendant*), Estelle Reiner (*The Tourist in the Elevator*), Jeffrey Combs (*Dr. Jones*), Jenny Gago (*Nurse #1*), Elma V. Jackson (*Nurse #2*), Oceana Marr (*The Older Nurse*), John "Easton" Stuart (*The Doorman*), Haunani Minn (*Nurse Breen*), Mel Gold (*The Cab Driver*), Stephanie Kramer (*The Beautiful Girl*), George Fisher (*The Patrol Car Officer*), Carl Reiner
D: Carl Reiner **PHOTOG:** Michael Chapman **MUSIC:** Joel Goldsmith
Standard SF-comedy: Brain surgeon seeks female body to house beloved's gray matter

The Man with Two Faces
see Dilemma

The Man with Two Heads
1972, (USA-GB), William Mishkin, color, 80 mins
W: Denis DeMarne, Julia Stratton, Gay Feld
D, SCR & PHOTOG: Andy Milligan
Minor thriller: Jekyll-Hyde yarn, set in 1835 London

The Man with Two Lives
see Troubled Waters (1964)

The Man with Wheels in His Head
see Le Malade Hydrophobe

The Many Adventures of Winnie the Pooh
1977, (USA), Walt Disney, color
Standard animated fantasy

Marabunta
see Legion of Fire: Killer Ants

Mara of the Wilderness
1964, (USA), Unicorn/AA, color, 90 mins.
W: Linda Saunders (*Mara*), Adam West, Theo Marcuse, Denver Pyle, Roberto Contreras, Eve Brent, Ed Kemmer, Sean McClory, Stuart Walsh, Lelia Walsh
P: Brice Mack **D:** Frank McDonald **SCR:** Tom Blackburn **STORY:** Ewing Scott **PHOTOG:** Robert Wyckoff **MUSIC:** Harry Bluestone
Standard adventure-thriller: Girl raised in Nature

Marathon Man
1976, (USA), Para, color, 125 mins.
W: Dustin Hoffman (*Babe Levy*), Laurence Olivier (*Szell*), Marthe Keller (*Elsa*), Roy Scheider (*Doc Levy*), Tito Goya (*Melendez*), Fritz Weaver (*Prof. Biesenthal*), Lou Gilbert (*Rosenbaum*), Richard Bright (*Karl*), William Devane (*Janeway*), Marc Lawrence (*Erhard*), Ben Dova (*Szell's Brother*), Jacques Marin (*LeClerc*), Allen Joseph (*Mr. Levy*), James Wing Woo (*Chen*), Nicole Deslauriers (*Nicole*), Lotta Andor Palfi (*The Old Lady in the Street*)
D: John Schlesinger **SCR:** William Goldman, from his novel **PHOTOG:** Conrad Hall **MUSIC:** Michael Small
Major thriller: Runner crosses path of Nazi war-criminal

Marat/Sade
see The Persecution and Assassination of Jean-Paul Marat as Performed by the Inmates of the Asylum of Charenton Under the Direction of the Marquis de Sade

La Marca del Hombre Lobo (The Mark of the Wolf Man)
1968, (Sp), Maxper/Independent Int'l, 3D, color, 133 mins
W: Paul Naschy
D: Enrique L. Equiluz **SCR:** Jacinto Molina
USA retitle, Frankenstein's Bloody Terror
Extravagant horror-fantasy (approx. 45 mins. cut from USA release): Werewolf seeks cure, cf. Las Noches del Hombre Lobo

La Marca del Muerto
see Creature of the Walking Dead

The March Hare
1956, (GB), Achilles/British Lion, color, 85 mins.
W: Peggy Cummins (*Pat Maguire*), Terence Morgan (*Sir Charles Hare*), Wilfrid Hyde-White (*Col. Keene*), Martita Hunt (*Lady Anne*), Cyril Cusack (*Lazy Mangan*), Derrick de Marney (*Capt. Marlow*), Charles Hawtrey (*Fisher*), Maureen Delany (*Bridget*), Ivan Samson (*Hardwicke*), Macdonald Parke (*Maguire*), Reginald Beckwith (*The Broker*)
P: Bertram Ostrer & Albert Fennell **D:** George More O'Ferrall **SCR:** Gordon Wellesley, Allan Mackinnon & Paul Vincent Carroll, from T.H. Bird's novel *Gamblers Sometimes Win*
Standard fantasy: Fairy gives trainer magic word that makes horse win Derby

The March of the Amazons
see The Amazons' March and Evolutions

March of the Wooden Soldiers
see Babes in Toyland (1934)

Mardi Gras for the Devil
1993, (USA), color, 95 mins.
W: Robert Davi, Michael Ironside, Lesley-Anne Down, Lydie Denier, Mike Starr, Margaret Avery, John Amos
D & SCR: David A. Prior
Standard thriller: New Orleans' festivities disrupted by demonic killer

Mardi Gras Massacre
1978, (USA), color, 92 mins.
W: Curt Dawson, Gwen Arment, Wayne Mack, Laura Misch
D: Jack Weis
Minor horror-thriller: Aztec priest performs ritual murders in New Orleans

Margin for Murder
1981, (USA), color, 98 mins.
W: Kevin Dobson, Cindy Pickett, Donna Dixon, Charles Hallahan
D: Daniel Haller, from characters created by Mickey Spillane
A.k.a. Mickey Spillane's Margin for Murder
TVM, standard thriller: Detective's best friend murdered

Maria Marten
1928, (GB), QTS/Ideal, b&w, 7,430 ft. (2264.7m)
W: Trilby Clark (*Maria Marten*), Warwick Ward (*William Corder*), James Knight (*Carlos*), Charles Ashton (*Sam Giles*), Vesta Sylva (*Ann Marten*), Frank Perfitt (*John Marten*), Tom Morriss (*Ishmael*), Margot Armand (*Lady Maude Derringham*), Judd Green (*William Giles*), Dora Barton
D: Walter West
Standard thriller: Squire kills pregnant mistress

Maria Marten (1935)
see Maria Marten: or, The Murder in the Red Barn (1935)

Maria Marten: or, The Murder at the Red Barn
1902, (GB), Harrison, b&w, 400 ft. (121.9m)
W: A.W. Fitzgerald *(William Corder)*, Mrs. Fitzgerald *(Maria Martin)*
D & SCR: Dicky Winslow, based on a play (author unknown)
Standard thriller (in 5 scenes): Maria's disguise; The murder; The dream; The arrest; The condemned cell

Maria Marten: or, The Murder in the Red Barn
1913, (GB), Motograph, b&w, 2,850 ft. (868.7m)
W: Elizabeth Risdon *(Maria Marten)*, Fred Groves *(William Corder)*, Douglas Payne *(Roger Deaves)*, Nessie Blackford *(Mary Marten)*, A.G. Ogden *(Tom Marten)*, Mary Mackenzie *(Mary Moore)*, Maurice Elvey *(Capt. Matthews)*
D & SCR: Maurice Elvey
Standard thriller: Squire's mistress murdered

Maria Marten: or, The Murder in the Red Barn
1935, (GB), George King/MGM/Olympic, b&w, 67 mins.
W: Tod Slaughter *(William Corder)*, Sophie Stewart *(Maria Marten)*, Eric Portman *(Carlos)*, D.J. Williams *(Thomas Marten)*, Clare Greet *(Mrs. Marten)*, Ann Trevor *(Nan)*, Stella Rho *(The Gypsy)*, Gerrard Tyrrell *(Tim Winterbottom)*, Dennis Hoey *(Sir John)*, Antonia Brough *(Maud Sennett)*, Quinton McPherson *(Matthew Sennett)*, Leonard Sharp *(Withey)*
D: George King   **SCR:** Randall Faye
*reissued 1940, A.k.a. **Maria Marten** and **Murder in the Old Red Barn***
*Standard thriller: Nobleman kills pregnant mistress.cf. **The Red Barn Crime***

Marie Antoinette
1938, (USA), MGM, b&w, 149 mins.
W: Norma Shearer, Tyrone Power, John Barrymore, Robert Morley, Anita Louise, Gladys Cooper, Joseph Calleia, Reginald Gardiner, Henry Stephenson, Joseph Schildkraut, Peter Bull, Albert Dekker, Barnett Parker, George Zucco, Henry Daniell, Cora Witherspoon, Henry Kolker, Harry Davenport, Mae Busch, Robert Barrat, Barry Fitzgerald
D: W.S. Van Dyke   **SCR:** Claudine West, Donald Ogden Stewart & Ernest Vajda   **PHOTOG:** William H. Daniels   **MUSIC:** Herbert P. Stothart
Major melodrama: Life of doomed French queen

Marie Antoinette
1953, (Fr-It), Gaumont, color, 125 mins.
W: Michele Morgan, Richard Todd, Michel Piccoli
D: Jean Delannoy
*A.k.a. **Shadow of the Guillotine***
Standard melodrama: French nobility deposed

La Mariee etait en Noir (The Bride Wore Black)
1968, (Fr-It), Lopert/Dino De Laurentiis, color, 107 mins.
W: Jeanne Moreau, Jean-Claude Brialy, Charles Denner, Alexandra Stewart, Claude Rich, Renaud Fontanarosa, Frederique Fontanarosa, Michel Bouquet, Daniel Boulanger, Michel Lonsdale, Christophe Brunot
D: Francois Truffaut   **SCR:** Francois Truffaut & Jean-Louis Richard, from a 1940 novel by William Irish [Cornell Woolrich]   **PHOTOG:** Raoul Coutard   **MUSIC:** Bernard Herrmann
Classic thriller: Woman avenges her bridegroom's death

Marjory's Goldfish
1914, (GB), Urban, b&w, 490 ft. (149.4m)
WRIT & D: Stuart Kinder
Standard fantasy short: Magic goldfish takes small girl on undersea adventure

The Mark
1961, (GB), Stross/20th-Fox, b&w, 127 mins.
W: Maria Schell *(Ruth)*, Stuart Whitman *(Jim Fuller)*, Rod Steiger *(Dr. McNally)*, Maurice Denham *(Arnold)*, Brenda de Banzie *(Mrs. Cartwright)*, Donald Wolfit *(Clive)*, Paul Rogers *(Milne)*, Donald Houston *(Austin)*, Amanda Black *(Janie)*, Russell Napier *(The Inspector)*, Marie Devereux *(Ellen)*
P: Sidney Buchman & Raymond Stross   **D:** Guy Green   **SCR:** Sidney Buchman & Stanley Mann, from a novel by Charles Israel   **PHOTOG:** Douglas Slocombe
Standard crime-thriller: Widow's lover exposed as child molester

The Marked One
1963, (GB), Planet, b&w, 65 mins.
W: William Lucas *(Don Mason)*, Zena Walker *(Kay Mason)*, Patrick Jordan *(Insp. Mayne)*, Laurie Leigh *(Maisie)*, David Gregory *(Ed Jones)*, Edward Ogden *(Nevil)*, Brian Nissen *(Charles Warren)*, Arthur Lovegrove *(Benson)*
P: Tom Blakeley   **D:** Francis Searle   **STORY:** Paul Erickson
Standard crime-thriller: Ex-convict truck driver traces counterfeit plates, saves kidnapped child

The Mark of Cain
1948, (GB), Two Cities/GFD, b&w, 88 mins.
W: Eric Portman *(Richard Howard)*, Sally Gray *(Sarah Bonheur)*, Patrick Holt *(John Howard)*, Dermot Walsh *(Jerome Thorne)*, Denis O'Dea *(Sir William Godfrey)*, Edward Lexy *(Lord Rochford)*, Therese Giehse *(Sister Seraphine)*, Vida Hope *(Jennie)*, Maureen Delany *(Daisy Cobb)*, Helen Cherry *(Mary)*, James Hayter *(Dr. White)*, Andrew Cruickshank *(Sir Jonathan)*, Miles Malleson *(Mr. [...])*
P: W.P. Lipscomb   **D:** Brian Desmond Hurst   **SCR:** W.P. Lipscomb, Francis

Crowdy, & Christianna Brand, from Joseph Shearing's novel *Airing in a Closed Carriage*
Standard thriller: Crime of passion stuns Victorian society

Mark of Terror
*see **Drums of Jeopardy** (1931)*

Mark of the Claw
*see **Dick Tracy's Dilemma***

Mark of the Dead
*see **Creature of the Walking Dead***

Mark of the Devil
1972, (W. Ger-GB), Hallmark, b&w, 90 mins.
W: Herbert Lom *(The Count)*, Udo Keir *(Christian)*, Reggie Nalder *(Albino)*, Olivera Vuco *(Vanessa)*, Herbert Fux, Gaby Fuchs, Michael Maien, Ingeborg Schoener, Gunter Clemens
D: Michael Armstrong   **SCR:** Sergio Cassner   **MUSIC:** Michael Holin
*A.k.a. **Brenn, Hexe, Brenn (Burn, Witch, Burn)***
Semi-classic horror-thriller: Witchfinder's gruesome tactics

Mark of the Devil
1985, (GB), Hammer/Fox Mystery Theatre, Made for TV, color, 69 mins.
W: Dirk Benedict *(Frank Rowlett)*, Jenny Seagrove *(Sara Helston)*, George Sewell *(Det.-Insp. Grant)*, James Ellis *(Father Dowd)*, John Paul *(Matt Helston)*, Tom Adams *(Westcott)*, Peter Settelen *(Det.-Sgt. Kirby)*, Burt Kwouk *(Lee)*, Maggie Rennie *(Ma Perkins)*, Reginald Marsh *(Dr. Melford)*, Hugh Morton *(The Butler)*, Michael Cronin *(Pymar)*, Robert Oates *(Hara)*, Alibe Parsons *(Momma Rose)*, Nicholas Field *(Billy)*, Marianne Sherman *(The Butch Girl)*, Robert Lee *(Chong Woy)*, Hilary Crane *(Carla)*, Tony Sibbald *(Wilson)*, Anthony Chinn *(Soo)*, Dinah May *(The Sexy Blonde)*, Roger Milner *(The Registrar)*, William Derrick *(Hatfield)*, Vernon Nesbeth *(The Sick Man)*
D: Val Guest   **TELEPLAY:** Brian Clemens   **PHOTOG:** Frank Watts   **MUSIC:** David Bedford   **MUSIC SPRVSR:** Philip Martell
TVM, minor thriller: Man's tattoo predicts violent acts

Mark of the Devil II
1974, (W. Ger-GB), Hallmark/Atlas-Int'l, color, 90 mins.
W: Anton Diffring, Erika Blanc, Reggie Nalder
D: Adrian Hoven   **SCR:** Adrian Hoven & Fred Denger
Minor horror-thriller: Sex-crazed withchfinder persecutes beautiful countess

Mark of the Gorilla
1950, (USA), Col, b&w, 68 mins.
W: Johnny Weissmuller, Trudy Marshall, Suzanne Dalbert, Onslow Stevens, Robert Purcell, Pierce Lyden, Selmer Jackson, Neyle Morrow
P: Sam Katzman   **D:** William Berke   **SCR:** Carroll Young   **PHOTOG:** Ira Morgan   **MUSIC DIR:** Mischa Bakaleinokoff
Standard "Jungle Jim" adventure-thriller: Crooks disguised as gorillas seek buried Nazi loot

Mark of the Phoenix
1958, (GB), Butcher's Films, b&w, 64 mins.
W: Julia Arnall *(Petra)*, Sheldon Lawrence *(Chuck Martin)*, Anton Diffring *(Insp. Schell)*, Eric Pohlmann *(Duser)*, Martin Miller *(Brunet)*, George Margo *(Emilson)*, Bernard Rebel *(Vachek)*, Michael Peake *(Koos)*, Jennifer Jayne *(The Clerk)*
P: W.G. Chalmers   **D:** Maclean Rogers   **SCR:** Norman Hudis   **STORY:** Desmond Cory
Standard thriller: Jewel thief foils art collector seeking rare alloy

Mark Of The Vampire: CAROL BORLAND AND BELA LUGOSI

The Mark of the Vampire
1935, (USA), MGM, b&w, 61 mins.
W: Lionel Barrymore, Elizabeth Allan, Lionel Atwill, Bela Lugosi, Jean Hersholt, Henry Wadsworth, Donald Meek, Carol Borland ("Luna"), Jessie Ralph, Leila Bennett, Ivan Simpson, Holmes Herbert, Michael Visaroff, June Gittelson
D: Tod Browning **SCR:** Guy Endore & Bernard Schubert **STORY:** Tod Browning **PHOTOG:** James Wong Howe
orig. to be titled Vampires of Prague
Classic thriller (remake of London After Midnight): Bizarre phenomena investigated

Mark of the Vampire (1957)
see The Vampire (1957)

Mark of the Werewolf
see The Werewolf (1955)

Mark of the Whistler
1944, (USA), Col, b&w, 61 mins.
W: Richard Dix, Janis Carter, Porter Hall, Paul Guilfoyle, John Calvert
D: William Castle
Minor thriller: Swindler seeks cash in dormant bank account

The Mark of the Wolf Man
see La Marca del Hombre Lobo

The Mark of Zorro
1920, (USA), UA, b&w, 90 mins.
W: Douglas Fairbanks Sr. (*Don Diego/Senor Zorro*), Noah Beery (*Sgt. Pedro*), Charles H. Mailes (*Don Carlos*), Marguerite de la Motte (*Lolita*), Claire McDowell (*Don Carlos' Wife*), Walt Whitman (*Frey Felipe*), Robert McKim (*Capt. Ramon*), George Periolat (*Gov. Alvarado*), Sydney De Grey (*Don Alejandro*), Charles Stevens (*A Peon*)
D: Fred Niblo, from Johnston McCulley's novel *The Curse of Capistrano*
PHOTOG: Tony Gaudio
Standard adventure-thriller: Mysterious masked man fights to restore law and order

The Mark of Zorro
1940, (USA), 20th-Fox, b&w, 94 mins.
W: Tyrone Power, Linda Darnell, Basil Rathbone (*Esteban*), Gale Sondergaard (*Inez*), Eugene Pallette (*Felipe*), Montagu Love (*Vega*), J. Edward Bromberg, Janet Beecher, Robert Lowery
D: Rouben Mamoulian **SCR:** John Taintor Foote, Garrett Fort, & Bess Meredyth, from Johnston McCulley's novel *The Curse of Capistrano*
PHOTOG: Arthur C. Miller **MUSIC:** Alfred Newman
Classic adventure-thriller: Masked hero aids Justice

The Mark of Zorro
1974, (USA), 20th-Fox/ABC-TV, color, 74 mins.
W: Frank Langella (*Don Diego/Senor Zorro*), Gilbert Roland, Ricardo Montalban, Louise Sorel, Robert Middleton, Yvonne DeCarlo, Tom Lacy, Anne Archer
D: Don McDougall **TELEPLAY:** Brian Taggart, from Johnston McCulley's novel *The Curse of Capistrano* **PHOTOG:** Jack Woolf
TVM, standard adventure-thriller: Champion of Justice aids early Californians

Markus 4
1996, (USA), color
W: John Savage, Bentley Mitchum
Minor SF-thriller

Marnie
1964, (USA), Univ, color, 130 mins.
W: Sean Connery, Tippi Hedren, Diane Baker, Martin Gabel, Bob Sweeney, Louise Latham, Alan Napier, Emmaline Henry, Milton Parsons, Bruce Dern
P & D: Alfred Hitchcock **SCR:** Jay Presson Allen, from Winston Graham's novel **PHOTOG:** Robert Burks **MUSIC:** Bernard Herrmann
Unusual thriller: Socialite probes kleptomaniac wife's past

Maroc 7
1967, (GB), John Gale-Leslie Phillips/Cyclone/Rank/Par, color, 91 mins.
W: Gene Barry (*Simon Grant*), Cyd Charisse (*Louise Henderson*), Elsa Martinelli (*Claudia*), Leslie Phillips (*Raymond Lowe*), Denholm Elliott (*Insp. Barrada*), Alexandra Stewart (*Michele Craig*), Angela Douglas (*Freddie*), Maggie London (*Suzie*), Eric Barker (*Prof. Bannen*), Tracy Reed (*Vivienne*), Ann Norman (*Alexa*), Penny Riley (*Penny*), Lionel Blair (*The Hotel Receptionist*), Anthony Bygraves (*The Young Photographer*), Paul Danquah (*The Police Officer*), Richard Montez (*Pablo*), Tom Lee (*Abdullah*), Robert Mill (*Tony*), Colette Wilde (*The 1st Woman*), Diane Bester (*The 2nd Woman*), Anne Padwick (*Consuela*), George Selway (*The Police Patrolman*), Michael Mundell (*The Man*), Vivienne Burgess (*The Woman*), Michael Haynes (*Another Man*), Jonathan Hanson (*The 1st Dice Player*), John Wreford (*The 2nd Dice Player*), Mark Elwes (*The 3rd Dice Player*), Pamela Abbott (*The Busy Woman*)
D: Gerry O'Hara **ORIG. STORY & SCR:** David Osborn **PHOTOG:** Kenneth Talbot **MUSIC:** Kenneth V. Jones
Minor thriller: Secret agent stalks jewel thieves

Marooned
1969, (USA), Frankovich-Sturges/Col, color, 133 mins.
W: Gregory Peck, Lee Grant, David Janssen, Richard Crenna, James Franciscus, Nancy Kovack, Gene Hackman, John Carter, Mariette Hartley, Scott Brady, Craig Huebing, Tom Stewart, Walter Brooke, Frank Martin
P: M.J. Frankovich **D:** John Sturges **SCR:** Mayo Simon, from Martin Caidin's novel **PHOTOG:** Daniel Fapp
Standard SF-thriller: Astronauts stranded in space

Marriage of Convenience
1960, (GB), Merton Park/Anglo-Amalgamated, b&w, 58 mins.
W: John Cairney (*Larry Wilson*), Harry H. Corbett (*Insp. Jock Bruce*), Jennifer Daniel (*Barbara Blair*), Russell Waters (*Sam Spencer*), Trevor Maskell (*Sgt. Collins*), Trevor Reid (*Supt. Carver*), John Van Eyssen (*John Mandle*), Motra Redmond (*Tina*), Patricia Burke (*The Woman*)
P: Jack Greenwood **D:** Clive Donner **SCR:** Robert Stewart, from Edgar Wallace's novel *Mystery*
Standard crime-thriller: Robber breaks jail, finds his ex-partner wed to inspector who arrested him

Marquis de Sade
1996, (USA), cable, color, 90 mins.
W: Nick Mancuso (*De Sade*), John Rhys-Davies (*Insp.Marais*), Janet Gunn (*Justine*)
Made-for-Cable, standard thriller: 18th-century French nobleman suspected in series of murders

Marquis de Sade: Justine
1969, (It-Sp), AIP, color
W: Jack Palance, Mercedes McCambridge, Klaus Kinski, Sylva Koscina, Maria Rohm, Akim Tamiroff
D: Jesus Franco **SCR:** Arpad De Riso & Erich Krohnke
USA retitle, Justine
Standard horror-thriller: Necromancer sacrifices women

Mars Attacks!
1996, (USA), WB, color, 103 mins.
W: Jack Nicholson (*Pres. James Dale/Art Land*), Glenn Close (*Marsha Dale*), Michael J. Fox (*Jason Stone*), Pierce Brosnan (*Prof. Donald Kessler*), Sarah Jessica Parker (*Nathalie Lake*), Rod Steiger (*Gen. Decker*), Annette Bening (*Barbara Land*), Danny DeVito (*The Low Roller*), Jim Brown (*Byron Williams*), Pam Grier (*Louise Williams*), Natalie Portman (*Taffy Dale*), Martin Short (*Jerry Ross*), Lisa Marie (*The Martian Girl*), Sylvia Sidney (*Grandma*), Paul Winfield (*Gen. Casey*), Lukas Haas, Tom Jones, Jack Black, Janice Rivera, Ray J, OLan Jones, Joe Don Baker, Brandon Hammond, Christina Applegate, Brian Haley, Jerzy Skolimowski, Barbet Schroeder, Tommy Bush, Joseph Maher, Betty Bunch, Gloria Hoffmann, Willie Garson, Michael Reilly Burke, Vinny Argiro, Valerie Wildman, Richard Irving, Jonathan Emerson, Coco Leigh, Rebecca Broussard, Steve Valentine, Jeffrey King, Enrique Castillo, Don LaMoth, C. Wayne Owens, Kevin Mangan, Joseph Patrick Moynihan, Velletta Carlson, Roger Peterson, John Finnegan, Ed Lambert, Gregg Daniel, John Gray, J. Kenneth Campbell, Jeanne Mori, Rance Howard, Richard Assad, Ken Thomas
D: Tim Burton **SCR:** Jonathan Gems **PHOTOG:** Peter Suschitzky **MUSIC:** Danny Elfman
Entertaining SF-satire: Bubble-headed aliens invade Earth

Mars Attacks the World
1938, (USA), Univ, b&w, 87 mins
W: Buster Crabbe (*Flash Gordon*), Jean Rogers (*Dale Arden*), Charles Middleton (*Ming the Merciless*), Frank Shannon (*Dr. Zarkov*), Beatrice Roberts
Standard SF-adventure, feature-version of serial Flash Gordon's Trip to Mars

Mars, God of War
see Marte, Dio della Guerra

Mars Invades Puerto Rico
see Frankenstein Meets the Space Monster

Mars Needs Women
1968, (USA), Azalea/AIP, color, 80 mins.
W: Tommy Kirk, Yvonne Craig, Byron Lord, Warren Hammack, Anthony Houston, Roger Ready, Barnett Shaw, Neil Fletcher, Chet Davis, Ron Scott, Cal Duggan, Pat Delany, Ann Palmer, Larry Tanner, George Edgley, Dick Simpson, David England, Don Campbell, Bob Hazlett, Sherry Roberts, Donna Lindberg, "Bubbles" Cash, Gordon Bulow, Bill Thurman, Pat Cranshaw, Claude Earls, Sally Casey, Bob Lorenz, Terry Davis, Sylvia Rundell
WRIT & D: Larry Buchanan **PHOTOG:** Robert C. Jessup
Minor SF: Martian race dying, new genes required

The Marsupials: Howling III
see Howling III

Marta
1971, (It-Sp), Atlantida-Cinemar/Avco Embassy, color, 95 mins.
W: Marisa Mell (*Marta*), Stephen Boyd (*Miguel*), Jesus Puente, Nelida Quiroga, George Rigaud, Isa Miranda, Howard Ross
D: Jose Antonio Nieves-Conde **SCR:** Ricardo Lopez Aranda, Juan Jose Alonso

Millan, Tito Carpi, & Jose Antonio Nieves-Conde, from orig. story by Juan Jose Alonso Millan **PHOTOG:** Ennio Guarnieri **SPCL-FX:** Pablo Perez **MUSIC:** Piero Piccioni **SONG:** *Right or Wrong*
Minor thriller: Socialite harbors beauty who resembles "missing" wife

Marte, Dio della Guerra (Mars, God of War)
1962, (It), SPA Cinematografica-Incei Film/Embassy, color, 92 mins.
W: Roger Browne, Jackie Lane, Dante Di Paolo, Michele Baly, Renato Speziali, Mossimo Serato
D: Marcello Baldi **SCR:** Continenza & Baldi
A.k.a. **Venus Against the Son of Hercules**
Minor "Sword & Sandal".

Martians Go Home
1990, (USA), Taurus, color, 87 mins.
W: Randy Quaid (*Mark Devereaux*), Anita Morris (*Dr. Jane Buchanan*), Margaret Colin (*Sara Brody*), John Philbin (*Donny*), Barry Sobel, Vic Dunlop
D: David Odell **SCR:** Charlie Haas, from a novel by Frederic Brown **PHOTOG:** Peter Deming **MUSIC:** Allan Zavod
Standard SF-comedy: TV jingle writer meets obnoxious aliens

Martin
1976, (USA), Laurel, color, 95 mins.
W: John Amplas (*Martin*), Lincoln Maazel (*Cuda*), Christine Forrest (*Christina*), Elyane Nadeau (*Mrs. Santini*), George A. Romero (*Father Howard*), Tom Savini (*Arthur*), James Roy (*The Deacon*), Sara Venable (*The Housewife Victim*), Robert Ogden (*The Businessman*), Al Levitsky (*Lewis*), J. Clifford Forrest Jr. (*Father Zulemas*), Fran Middleton (*The Train Victim*), Donaldo Soviero (*The Flashback Priest*), Donna Siegal (*The Woman*), Albert J. Schmaus, Frances Mazzoni, Tony Buba, Vincent D. Survinski, Pasquale Buba, Robert Barner, Clayton McKinnon, Regis J. Survinski, Tony Pantanella, Tom Weber, Harvey Eger, Stephen Fergelic, Douglas Serene, Nick Mastandrea, John Sozansky, Ingeborg Forrest, Carol McCloskey
WRIT & D: George A. Romero **PHOTOG:** Michael Gornick **SPCL-FX & MAKEUP:** Tom Savini **MUSIC:** Donald Rubinstein
Modest horror-thriller: Modern vampire preys

The Martyrdom of Thomas A Becket
1908, (GB), Clarendon, b&w, 450 ft. (137.2m)
D: Percy Stow **STORY:** Langford Reed
Standard historical melodrama: King has archbishop murdered

Marvellous Egg Producing with Surprise Developments
see La Danseuse Microscopique

The Marvellous Flame
see La Flamme Merveilleuse

The Marvellous Fountain
see La Fontaine Merveilleuse

The Marvellous Hair Restorer
1901, (GB), Williamson, b&w, 105 ft. (32m)
W: Sam Dalton
D: James Williamson
Standard fantasy short: Bald man grows hair, so does splashed table

The Marvellous Hoop
see La Guirlande Merveilleuse

The Marvellous Living Fan
see Le Merveilleux Eventail Vivant

Marvellous Suspension and Evolution
see La Femme Volante

The Marvellous Syringe
1903, (GB), Gaumont, b&w, 65 ft. (19.8m)
D: Alf Collins
Standard fantasy short: Boy squirts mud on couple's clothing, film reverses

The Marvellous Wreath
see La Guirlande Merveilleuse

Mary Jane's Mishap: or, Don't Fool with the Paraffin
1903, (GB), G.A.S. Films/WTC, b&w, 250 ft. (76.2m)
D: George Albert Smith
Standard comedy-fantasy short: Maid pours paraffin on fire, is blown to pieces up chimney

Mary, Mary, Bloody Mary
1975, (Mex), Proa/Continental, color, 95 mins.
W: Cristina Ferrare (*Mary*), John Carradine, Helena Rojo, David Young
D: Juan Moctezuma **SCR:** Malcolm Marmorstein
Minor thriller: Woman artist terrorized

Mary Poppins
1964, (USA), Walt Disney/Buena Vista, color, 139 mins.
W: Julie Andrews (*Mary Poppins*), Dick Van Dyke (*Bert/The Bank President*), David Tomlinson (*Mr. Banks*), Glynis Johns (*Winifred Banks*), Matthew Garber

(*Michael Banks*), Karen Dotrice (*Jane Banks*), Arthur Treacher (*Constable Jones*), Jane Darwell (*The Bird Lady*), Hermione Baddeley (*Ellen*), Reta Shaw (*Mrs. Brill*), Reginald Owen (*Adm. Boom*), Ed Wynn (*Uncle Albert*), Cyril Delevanti, Elsa Lanchester, Arthur Malet
D: Robert Stevenson **SCR:** Bill Walsh & Don DaGradi **BASED ON:** P.L. Travers' books for children **PHOTOG:** Edward Colman **SPCL-FX:** Eustace Lycett, Peter Ellenshaw & Robert A. Mattey **MUSIC & LYRICS:** Richard M. Sherman & Robert B. Sherman
Oscar-winning fantasy: Magical nanny transforms family

Mary Ryan, Detective: PAUL BRYAR, MARSHA HUNT, BEN WELDEN AND BILL PHILLIPS

Mary, Queen of Scots
see The Execution of Mary, Queen of Scots

Mary Reilly
1996, (GB), TriStar, color, 108 mins.
W: Julia Roberts (*Mary Reilly*), John Malkovich (*Dr. Henry Jekyll/Edward Hyde*), Michael Gambon (*Mr. Reilly*), Glenn Close (*Mrs. Farraday*), George Cole (*Mr. Poole*), Michael Sheen (*Bradshaw*), Bronagh Gallager (*Annie*), Kathy Stuff (*Mrs. Kent*), Henry Goodman (*Haffinger*), Linda Bassett (*Mary's Mother*), Sasha Hanau (*Young Mary*), Ciaran Hinds (*Sir Arthur Carewe*), Moya Brady (*The Young Woman*), Emma Griffiths Malin (*The Young Whore*), David Ross (*The Doctor*), Tim Barlow (*The Vicar*), Stephen Boxer (*The Inspector*), Isabella Marsh (*The Screaming Girl*), Wendy Nottingham (*The Screaming Girl's Mother*), Richard Leaf (*The Screaming Girl's Father*), Bob Mason (*The Policeman*), Ellie Crockett, Piu Fan Lee, Robbie Stevens, Mimi Potworowska, Evelyn Doggart, Julia Hagen, Samantha Hones
D: Stephen Frears **SCR:** Christopher Hampton, from Valerie Martin's novel **PHOTOG:** Philippe Rousselot **MUSIC:** George Fenton
"Solemn, portentous and curiously dull..."—David Ansen, Newsweek
Unusual thriller: Impoverished Irish girl becomes maid in home of Dr. Jekyll

Mary Ryan, Detective
1950, (USA), Col, b&w, 68 mins.
W: Marsha Hunt, John Litel
Minor thriller

Mary Shelley's 'Frankenstein'
1994, (GB), TriStar, color, 128 mins.
W: Kenneth Branagh (*Victor Frankenstein*), Robert De Niro (*The Creature/The Sharp-Featured Man*), Helena Bonham-Carter (*Elizabeth*), Tom Hulce (*Henry Clerval*), John Cleese (*Prof. Waldman*), Aidan Quinn (*Walton*), Ian Holm (*Victor's Father*), Richard Briers (*Grandfather*), Robert Hardy (*Prof. Krempe*), Cherie Lunghi (*Victor's Mother*), Celia Imrie (*Mrs. Moritz*), Trevyn McDowell (*Justine*), Ger-ard Horan (*Claude*), Richard Clifford (*The Minister*), Mark Hadfield (*Felix*), Alfred Bell (*The Landlord*), Joanna Roth (*Marie*), Sasha Hanau (*Maggie*), Joseph England (*Thomas*), Richard Bonneville (*Schiller*), George Asprey (*The Policeman*), Ryan Smith (*William*), Rory Jennings (*Young Victor*), Christina Cuttall (*Young Justine*), Charles Wyn-Davies (*Young William*), Hannah Taylor-Gordon (*Young Elizabeth*), Susan Field (*Frau Brach*), Jimmy Yuill, Chris Barnes, Shaun Prendergast, Tommy Wright, Alex Lowe, David Kennedy, Paul Gregory, Chris Hollis, Robin Lloyd, Simon Cox, Graham Loughridge, Robert Hines, Lonnie James, Jenny Galloway, Peter Jonfield, Edward Jewesbury, Sue Long, Siobhan Redmond, Francine Morgan, Angus Wright, Max Gold, Michael Gould, Abigail Reynolds, Theresa Fresson, Meriel Schofield, Mark Inman, Dudi Appleton
D: Kenneth Branagh, from Mary Shelley's novel *Frankenstein* **PHOTOG:** Roger Pratt **MUSIC:** Patrick Doyle
Opulent, fast-moving retread of horror classic: Scientist's obsessive desire to create life leads to tragedy for all he loves

Marzipan of the Shapes
1920, (GB), Alliance Film Corp., b&w
W: Ray Forrest, Irene Tripod, Frank Stanmore
D: A.C. Hunter
Standard comedy: Burlesque of Tarzan of the Apes

Mas alla de la Aventura (On the Far Side of Adventure)
1980, (Argent), CCN, color, 95 mins.
W: Catherine Alric, Andy Pruna
D: Oscar Barney Finn
Standard SF-thriller: Naturalist and woman journalist hunt UFOs in South American jungle

Mascara
1987, (Belg-Neth-Fr-USA), color, 98 mins.
W: Charlotte Rampling *(Gaby)*, Michael Sarrazin *(Sanders)*, Derek De Lint, Jappe Claes, Herbert Flack, Harry Cleven, Eva Robbins
D: Patrick Conrad
Minor eroto-thriller: Perverse police chief embraces lurid lifestyle

La Maschera del Demonio (The Mask of the Demon)
1960, (It), Galatea-Jolly/AIP, b&w, 88 mins.
W: Barbara Steele *(Princess Asa/Princess Katia)*, John Richardson *(Dr. Andreas Gorobec)*, Ivo Garrani *(Prince Vaida)*, Clara Bindi *(The Innkeeper)*, Arturo Dominici *(Javuto)*, Andrea Checchi *(Dr. Thomas Kruvajan)*, Tino Bianchi *(Ivan)*, Germana Dominici *(The Innkeeper's Daughter)*, Enrico Olivieri, Antonio Pierfederici
D: Mario Bava **SCR:** Ennio De Concini & Mario Serandrei, based on Gogol's short story *The Vij* **PHOTOG:** Ubaldo Terzano
GB retitle, **Revenge of the Vampire,** *Ger retitle,* **The Hour When Dracula Came** *USA retitle,* **Black Sunday**
Major horror-fantasy (Mario Bava's most ambitious film): Vampire-witch returns from death to wreak vengeance

The Mask
1953, (GB), Vandyke/Archway, b&w, 28 mins.
W: Robert Ayres *(The Miller)*, Cecile Chevreau *(The Wife)*
P: Roger Proudlock **D:** Don Chaffey
Standard short crime-thriller: Cornwall miller's wife and her lover plot to murder her disfigured husband

The Mask (1959)
see **The Bat (1959)**

The Mask
1961, (Can), Taylor-Roffman/Beaver-Champion/WB, portions in "Depth Dimension" (3D), b&w, 83 mins.
W: Paul Stevens *(Barnes)*, Claudette Nevins *(Pamela)*, Anne Collings *(Jill)*, Bill Walker, Eleanor Beecroft, William Bryden, Leo Leyden, Martin Lavut, Ray Lawlor, Jim Moran, Nancy Island, Rudi Linschoten
P & D: Julian Roffman **SCR:** Frank Taubes & Sandy Haber **PHOTOG:** Herbert S. Alpert **SPCL-FX:** Herman S. Townsley **3D-FX:** James B. Gordon **MUSIC:** Louis Applebaum
reissued (1968) as **Eyes of Hell,** *A.k.a.* **The Spooky Movie Show**
Standard horror-fantasy: Mayan mask reveals hellish world

The Mask
1994, (USA), New Line Cinema, color, 101 mins.
W: Jim Carrey *(Stanley Ipkiss/The Mask)*, Cameron Diaz *(Tina Carlyle)*, Peter Riegert *(Lt. Mitch Kellaway)*, Amy Yasbeck *(Peggy Brandt)*, Peter Greene *(Dorian Tyrel)*, Richard Jeni *(Charlie Schumaker)*, Orestes Matacena *(Niko)*, Tim Bagley *(Irv)*, Nancy Fish *(Mrs. Peenman)*, Johnny Williams *(Burt)*, Reginald E. Cathey *(Freeze)*, Jim Doughan *(Doyle)*, Denis Forest *(Sweet Eddy)*, Joseph Alfieri, B.J. Barie, Krista Buonauro, Catherine Berge, Phil Boardman, Suzanne Dunn, Debra Casey, Blake Clark, Christopher Darga, Benjamin J. Stein, Joely Fisher, Kevin Grevioux, Peter Jazwinski, Howard Kay, Robert Keith, Beau Lotterman, Ivory Ocean, Scott McElroy, Richard Montes, Robert O'Reilly, Daniel James Peterson, Louie Ortiz, Jeremy Roberts, Nils Allen Stewart, Eamonn Roche, Randi Ruimy, Chris Taylor, Wendy Walsh, Bullet Valmont, Meadows Williams Max *(Milo the Dog)*
D: Charles Russell **SCR:** Mike Werb **PHOTOG:** John R. Leonetti **STORY:** Michael Fallon & Mark Verheiden **SPCL-FX COORD:** Thomas L. Bellissimo **SPCL VS-FX:** Industrial Light & Magic **MUSIC:** Randy Edelman **SONGS:** (I Could Only) Whisper Your Name, This Business of Love & Gee Baby, Ain't I Good to You
Amusing comedy-fantasy: Ancient mask turns bank clerk into bizarre superhero

The Masked Conqueror
1960, (It), AIP/Filmways, color, 94 mins
W: Alberto Lupo, Giorgio Ardisson
Minor adventure-thriller

The Masked Man Against the Pirates
1962, (Sp), Rio Films/Art Greenfield, color, 105 mins
W: George Hilton, Claude Dantes
Minor adventure-thriller

The Masked Pirate
see **I Pirati di Capri**

The Masked Smuggler
1912, (GB), Cricks & Martin, b&w, 1,000 ft. (304.8m)
W: Una Tristram *(The Girl)*
D: Edwin J. Collins

Standard thriller: 1770's lieutenant unmasks girl's father as chief smuggler

Mask of Death
1996, (USA), HBO-TV, color, 89 mins.
W: Lorenzo Lamas, Rae Dawn Chong, Billy Dee Williams
Made-for-Cable, standard thriller: Detective goes undercover, poses as lookalike pathological killer

The Mask of Dijon
1946, (USA), PRC, b&w, 74 mins.
W: Erich von Stroheim, Jeanne Bates, Edward Van Sloan, Denise Vernac, William Wright
P: Max Alexander & Alfred Stern **D:** Lew Landers **SCR:** Arthur St. Clair & Griffin Jay
Standard thriller: Magician hypnotizes enemies, makes them kill and commit suicide

The Mask of Dimitrios
1944, (USA), WB, b&w, 99 mins.
W: Sydney Greenstreet *(Mr. Peters)*, Peter Lorre *(Leyden)*, Zachary Scott *(Dimitrios)*, Faye Emerson *(Irana)*, Eduardo Ciannelli *(Murakakis)*, John Abbott *(Pappas)*, Kurt Katch *(Col. Haki)*, Victor Francen *(Grodek)*, Monte Blue *(Abdul)*, Steven Geray *(Buclic)*, Marjorie Hoshelle *(Mrs. Buclic)*, Florence Bates *(Mme. Chavez)*, Georges Metaxa *(Werner)*, David Hoffman *(Konrad)*
P: Henry Blanke **D:** Jean Negulesco **SCR:** Frank Gruber, from Eric Ambler's novel *A Coffin for Dimitrios* **PHOTOG:** Arthur Edeson **MUSIC:** Adolph Deutsch
Standard thriller: Writer probes life of master criminal. Zachary Scott's film debut

The Mask of Fu Manchu
1932, (USA), MGM, b&w, 70 mins.
W: Boris Karloff *(Dr. Fu Manchu)*, Lewis Stone, Jean Hersholt, Myrna Loy, Charles Starrett, Karen Morley, Lawrence Grant, David Torrence
D: Charles Brabin & Charles Vidor **SCR:** Irene Kuhn, Edgar Woolf & John Willard, from Sax Rohmer's novel **PHOTOG:** Tony Gaudio
Fr retitle, **Le Masque d'Or (The Mask of Gold)**
"...the movies found its best Fu Manchu in Boris Karloff...Physically an ideal choice, Karloff was able to make the doctor an intelligent as well as a sinister villain, and to suggest something of the ageless quality of the Fu Manchu of the books. However, grand and glorious hokum though it was, the film reduced Fu's international omnipotence to a mere serial-like procession of lurid thrills and fantastically elaborate torture devices"—William K. Everson, The Bad Guys
Unusual thriller: Oriental villain seeks ancient artifact

The Mask of Gold
see **The Mask of Fu Manchu**

The Mask of Sheba
1970, (USA), MGM-TV, color, 100 mins.
W: Walter Pidgeon *(Dr. Max Van Condon)*, Eric Braeden *(Dr. Roan Morgan)*, Stephen Young *(Travis Comanche)*, Corinne Camacho *(Dr. Joanna Glenville)*, Inger Stevens *(Sarah Kramer)*, Joseph Wiseman *(Fahdil Bondalok)*, William Marshall *(Capt. Condor Sekallie)*, Christopher Cary *(Peter Drake)*, Lincoln Kilpatrick *(Ben Takahene)*
WRIT & P: Sam Rolfe **D:** David Lowell Rich **PHOTOG:** Gabriel Torres & Harold Wellman **MUSIC:** Lalo Schifrin
TVM, standard adventure-thriller: Scholars seek priceless heirloom in Ethiopia

Mask of the Avenger
1951, (USA), Col, color, 83 mins.
W: John Derek, Anthony Quinn, Jody Lawrance, Arnold Moss
D: Phil Karlson **SCR:** Jesse Lasky Jr. from a story by George Bruce **PHOTOG:** Charles Lawton Jr. **MUSIC:** George Duning
Standard adventure-thriller: Man poses as Count of Monte Cristo, routs traitors

The Mask of the Demon
see **La Maschera del Demonio**

Mask of the Dragon
1951, (USA), Lippert, b&w, 55 mins.
W: Richard Travis, Sheila Ryan
Minor thriller

The Mask of the Gorilla
1964, (Fr), Astral, b&w, 100 mins
W: Lino Ventura, Bella Darvi, Charles Vanel
Minor thriller: Secret agent exposes spy network

Mask of the Musketeers
1960, (It), AIP, color, 101 mins
W: Gordon Scott
Minor adventure-thriller

The Mask of the Red Death
see **The Masque of the Red Death**

The Mask of Zorro
1998, (USA), Amblin/TriStar, color, 138 mins.
W: Antonio Banderas, Anthony Hopkins, Catherine Zeta Jones

D: Martin Campbell **MUSIC:** James Horner, from Johnston McCulley's
   novel *The Curse of Capistrano*
orig. to be titled **Zorro**
Elaborate adventure-thriller: Masked hero champions oppressed

Masks of Death
1984, (GB), Made for TV, color, 90 mins. also 75 mins.
W: Peter Cushing (*Sherlock Holmes*), John Mills (*Doctor Watson*), Anne Baxter, Ray
   Milland

D: Roy Ward Baker, from characters created by Sir Arthur Conan Doyle
Minor thriller: Sleuth investigates mysterious deaths. A.k.a. **Sherlock Holmes and the**
   Mask of Death

Le Masque
see **The Bat (1959)**

Le Masque d'Or
see **The Mask of Fu Manchu**

The Masque of the Red Death
1964, (USA-GB), Alta-Vista/AIP, color, 89 mins.
W: Vincent Price (*Prince Prospero*), Hazel Court (*Juliana*), Jane Asher (*Francesca*),
   David Weston (*Gino*), Patrick Magee (*Alfredo*), Nigel Green (*Ludovico*), Paul
   Whitsun-Jones (*Scarlatti*), Julian Burton (*Senor Veronese*), John Westbrook
   (*The Man in Red*), Skip Martin (*Hoptoad*), Gaye Brown (*Senora Escobar*),
   Verina Greenlaw (*Esmeralda*), Doreen Dawne (*Anna-Marie*), Harvey Hall,
   Sarah Brackett, Jean Lodge, Robert Brown, David Davies
P & D: Roger Corman **SCR:** Charles Beaumont & R. Wright Campbell, from
   Edgar Allan Poe's short stories *The Masque of the Red Death* & *Hop-Frog*
   PHOTOG: Nicolas Roeg **SPCL-FX:** George Blackwell **MUSIC:** David
   Lee **DESIGN:** Robert Jones
Elegant horror-fantasy: Plague ravishes countryside, wicked nobleman entertains

Masque of the Red Death
1989, (USA), Roger Corman/New World, color, 83 mins
W: Adrian Paul, Clare Hoak, Jeff Osterhage, Patrick Macnee, Tracy Reiner
D: Larry Brand, from Edgar Allan Poe's short story
Minor horror-fantasy

Masque of the Red Death
1989, (USA), 21st Century, color
W: Herbert Lom, Brenda Vaccaro, Frank Stallone
from Edgar Allan Poe's short story
Minor horror-fantasy

Masquerade
1964, (GB), Novus/UA, color, 102 mins.
W: Cliff Robertson (*David Frazer*), Marisa Mell (*Sophie*), Jack Hawkins (*Col.
   Drexel*), Michel Piccoli (*Sarrassin*), Bill Fraser (*Dunwoody*), Charles Gray
   (*Benson*), Jose Burgos (*El Mono*), John LeMesurier (*Sir Robert*), Ernest Clark
   (*The Minister*), Felix Aylmer (*Henrickson*), Christopher Witty (*Prince Jamil*),
   Tutte Lemkow (*Paviot*), Keith Pyott (*Gustave*), Roger Delgado (*Ahmid Ben
   Faid*), Jerold Wells (*Brindle*), Denis Bernard (*King Ahmed*), James Mossman
P: Michael Relph & Basil Dearden **D:** Basil Dearden **SCR:** Michael Relph &
   William Goldman, from Victor Canning's novel *Castle Minerva* **PHOTOG:**
   Otto Heller **MUSIC:** Philip Green
Standard thriller: Int'l plot to kidnap young ruler of Near Eastern country

Massacre Game
see **The Killing Game**

The Masses
see **Modern Times**

The Master and Margarita
see **Majstori i Margarita**

The Master Crook
1913, (GB), B&C/DFSA, b&w, 3,169 ft. (965.9m)
W: Arthur Finn (*The Master Crook*), Marie Pickering (*The Blind Girl*), Harry
   Lorraine (*A Crook*), Jack Jarman (*A Crook*), Bert Berry (*A Crook*)
D: Charles Weston
Standard crime-thriller: Crook reforms, returns stolen gems

The Master Crook Outwitted by a Child
1914, (GB), B&C/DFSA, b&w, 2,489 ft. (758.6m)
W: Ernest G. Batley (*The Master Crook*), Dorothy Batley (*The Child*), Ethel
   Bracewell (*The Girl*)
D: Ernest G. Batley
Standard crime-thriller: Crook plants stolen diamond on orphan fruit-seller

The Master Minds
1949, (USA), RKO, b&w
W: Bela Lugosi, Glenn Strange
Minor horror-thriller

Master Minds
1949, (USA), Jan Grippo/Mono, b&w, 64 mins

W: Leo Gorcey, Huntz Hall, Gabriel Dell, Alan Napier, William Benedict, Bennie
   Bartlett, Glenn Strange, David Gorcey, Minerva Urecal, Skelton Knaggs
D: Jean Yarbrough **SCR:** Charles R. Marion
Standard horror-comedy: Bowery Boys meet mad scientist

Master of Horror
1960, (Argent), Gates-Torres/Jack H. Harris/ US Films, color, 115 mins
W: Narciso Menta, Inez Moreno, Carlos Estrada
P: Nicolas Carreras **D:** Enrique Carreras **SCR:** Luis Penafiel **BASED ON:**
   Edgar Allan Poe's short stories "The Facts in the Case of M. Valdemar" &
   "The Cask of Amontillado" & "The Tell-Tale Heart"
USA release, 1964 (in b&w, 61 mins, third tale eliminated)
Minor horror-thriller

The Master of Merripit
1915, (GB), Clarendon/Renters, b&w, 3,445 ft. (1050m)
W: Dorothy Bellew (*Sarah Dennis*)
D: Wilfred Noy, from a novel by E. Phillips Oppenheim
Standard adventure-thriller: 18th-century squire must capture highwayman to win girl

Master of Terror
see **4D Man**

Master of the World
1961, (USA), AIP, color, 104 mins.
W: Vincent Price (*Robur*), Charles Bronson (*John Strock*), Henry Hull (*Prudent*),
   Mary Webster (*Dorothy Prudent*), David Frankham (*Phillip Evans*), Richard
   Harrison (*Alistair*), Vito Scotti (*Topage*), Wally Campo (*Turner*), Steve
   Masino, Ken Terrell, Peter Besbas
P: James H. Nicholson **D:** William Witney **SCR:** Richard Matheson, based on
   Jules Verne's novels *Master of the World* and *Robur, the Conqueror* **PHOTOG:**
   Gilbert Warrenton **MUSIC:** Les Baxter
Standard SF-adventure: Genius declares war on all feuding nations of Earth

Masters of the Universe
1987, (USA), Golan-Globus/Cannon, color, 106 mins.
W: Dolph Lundgren (*He-Man*), Frank Langella (*Skeletor*), Meg Foster (*Evil-Lyn*),
   Courteney Cox (*Julie Winston*), Robert Duncan McNeill (*Kevin*), Billy Barty
   (*Gwildor*), Jon Cypher (*The Man-at-Arms*), James Tolkan (*Det. Lubic*),
   Christina Pickles (*The Sorceress*), Chelsea Field (*Teela*), Jessica Nelson, Tony
   Carroll, Pons Maar, Anthony DeLongis, Barry Livingston, Robert Towers
D: Gary Goddard **SCR:** David Odell **PHOTOG:** Hanania Baer & William
   Neil **VS-FX:** Richard Edlund **MUSIC:** Bill Conti
Standard SF-fantasy: Space war comes to Earth

The Master Plan
1954, (GB), Gibraltar/Grand Nat'l, b&w, 78 mins.
W: Wayne Morris (*Maj. Brent*), Tilda Thamar (*Helen*), Mary Mackenzie (*Miss
   Gray*), Norman Woland (*Col. Cleaver*), Arnold Bell (*Gen. Goulding*), Marjorie
   Stewart (*Yvonne*), Laurie Main (*Johnny Orwell*), Frederick Schrecker (*Dr.
   Morgan Stern*)
P: Steven Pallos & Charles A. Leeds **D:** Hugh Raker (Cy Endfield) **SCR:** Hugh
   Raker (Cy Endfield) & Donald Bull, from Harold Bratt's teleplay *Operation*
Standard crime-thriller: Spy drugs U.S. major, makes him photograph secret files

The Master Spy
1914, (GB), Regent/MP, b&w, 3,000 ft. (916.9m)
W: Rowland Moore, Gordon Begg
D: Charles Weston
Standard crime-thriller: Detective foils German spy

Master Spy
1963, (GB), Eternal/Grand Nat'l/AA, b&w, 74 mins.
W: Stephen Murray (*Boris Turgenev*), June Thorburn (*Leila*), Alan Wheatley (*Paul
   Skelton*), John Carson (*Richard Colman*), John Brown (*John Baxter*), Jack
   Watson (*Capt. Foster*), Marne Maitland (*Dr. Asafu*), Ernest Clark (*Dr.
   Pembury*), Ellen Pollock (*Dr. Morrell*)
P: Maurice J. Nelson **D:** Montgomery Tully **SCR:** Maurice J. Wilson &
   Montgomery Tully, based on story "They Also Serve" by Gerald Anstruther
   & Paul White
Standard thriller: Russian scientist seeks political asylum in England

Master Stroke
1967, (It), color
W: Richard Harrison, Adolfo Celi, Margaret Lee, Mary Arden, Alan Collins,
   Gerard Tichy
P: Edmondo Amati **D:** Michele Lupo **PHOTOG:** Francisco Sanchez
Standard thriller: Actor becomes pawn in fantastic plot to steal gems

Mata Hari
1931, (USA), MGM, b&w, 92 mins.
W: Greta Garbo (*Mata Hari*), Ramon Novarro (*Lt. Alexis Rosanoff*), Lionel
   Barrymore (*Gen. Shubin*), Lewis Stone (*Andriani*), C. Henry Gordon
   (*Dubois*), Helen Jerome Eddy (*Sister Genevieve*), Karen Morley (*Carlotta*),
   Blanche Frederici (*Sister Angelica*), Alec B. Francis (*Caron*), Frank Reicher
   (*The Cook-Spy*), Edmund Breese (*The Warden*), Mischa Auer (*Condemned
   Prisoner*)
D: George Fitzmaurice **ORIG. STORY & SCR:** Benjamin Glazer & Leo
   Birinski **PHOTOG:** William Daniels

Mata Hari: GRETA GARBO AND RAMON NOVARRO

Lavish melodrama: Intrigues of World War I's infamous double agent

Mata Hari
1985, (GB), Cannon, color, 108 mins.
W: Sylvia Kristel (*Mata Hari*), Christopher Cazenove (*Karl von Beyerling*), Oliver Tobias (*Capt. Ladoux*), Gaye Brown (*Fraulein Doktor*), Gottfried John (*Wolff*), William Fox (*Clunet*), Michael Anthony (*Duke Montorency*), Brian Badcoe (*Gen. Messigny*), Vernon Dobtcheff (*The Prosecutor*), Tutte Lemkow (*Ybarra*), Anthony Newlands (*Baron Joubert*), Taylor Ryan (*The Contessa*), Tobias Rolt (*Jean Prevost*), Carlos Sutton (*Capt. Schlesser*), Victor Langley (*Col. Michaud*), Malcolm Terris (*Von Krohn*), Nicholas Selby (*Von Jagow*), Ferenc Bencze (*Col. Heissig*), Odon Gyalog (*Gen. Carriere*), Gabor Nagy (*Lt. Bouchette*), Lajos Mezey (*Von Fahlenberg*), Emese Balogh (*Marquesa Casa Funta*), Geza Laczkovich (*The President*)

Mata Hari: GRETA GARBO AND JEAN HERSHOLT

P: Rony Yacov   **D:** Curtis Harrington   **STORY:** Joel Ziskin   **PHOTOG:** David Gurfinkel   **MUSIC:** Wilfred Josephs
Standard melodrama: Dancer becomes spy

Mata Hari, Agent H21
1964, (Fr-It), Films du Carosse/ Simar/Fida Cinematografica/Magna, color, 93 mins.
W: Jeanne Moreau (*Mata Hari*), Jean-Louis Trintignant, Frank Villard
D: Jean-Louis Richard   **SCR:** Jean-Louis Richard & Francois Truffaut   **MUSIC:** Georges Delerue
Tongue-in-cheek thriller: Beautiful spy's loves and larcenies

Mata Hari's Daughter
1954, (Fr-It), Regent, color, 102 mins.
W: Ludmilla Tcherina, Frank Latimore, Erno Crisa
D: Renzo Merusi, Carmine Gallone
A.k.a. **Daughter of Mata Hari**
Standard thriller: Offspring of notorious spy operates in World War II Java

Matango
1963, (Jap), Daiei/AIP, color, 89 mins.
W: Akiro Kubo, Niki Wyashiro, Kumi Mizuno
D: Inoshiro Honda   **SCR:** Takeshi Kimura   **SPCL-FX:** Eiji Tsuburaya
USA retitle, **Attack of the Mushroom People**, *A.k.a.* **Curse of the Mushroom People**
Minor SF-horror: Fungus turns humans into monstrosities

Matchless
1967, (It), De Laurentiis/UA, color, 104 mins.
W: Patrick O'Neal, Ira Furstenberg, Donald Pleasence, Henry Silva
D: Alberto Lattuada
Standard thriller: Secret agent gains invisibility formula

The Material Witness
1965, (GB), Merton Park/Anglo-Amalgamated, b&w, 30 mins.
W: Reginald Marsh (*Harry Turner*), Noel Trevarthen (*Lewis Carter*), Sally Nesbitt (*Pat Turner*), Harry Locke (*Sam*), Hector Ross (*George Lennox*), Sheila Manahan (*Jean Turner*), John Horsley (*Nelson*)
P: Jack Greenwood   **D:** Geoffrey Nethercott   **STORY:** James Eastwood, from a novel by Edgar Lustgarten
Standard short crime-thriller: Ass't gets executive jailed, takes over his job

Matinee
1993, (USA), Renfield/Univ, color, 99 mins.
W: John Goodman (*Lawrence Woolsey*), Cathy Moriarty (*Ruth Corday*), Simon Fenton (*Gene Loomis*), Omri Katz (*Stan*), Kellie Martin (*Sherry*), Lisa Jakub (*Sandra*), Dick Miller (*Herb*), Robert Picardo (*Howard, the Theater Manager*), Lucinda Jenney (*Anne Loomis*), Jesse Lee (*Dennis Loomis*), James Villemaire (*Harvey Starkweather*), John Sayles (*Bob*), Charlie Haas (*Mr. Elroy*), Mark McCracken (*The Mant/Bill*), David Clennon, Kevin McCarthy, Robert Cornthwaite, Georgie Cranford, Lucy Butler, Joe Gonzalez, Belinda Balaski, Luke Halpin, Archie Hahn, Naomi Watts, Chris Stacy, Allison McKay, Glenda Chism, Aaron Stormer, Lana Bucciarelli, Dennis Neal, Richard Rossomme, D. Christian Gottshall, Elizabeth Dimon, Bernard Blanding, Eulan Middlebrooks, Summer-Healy Chapin, Shane Obedzinski, James Scott Hess, Jesse Zeigler, Shawn Edward Watkins, Danny Hanemann, Andy Isaacs, Steve Zurk, Joe Candelora, Mary Moriarty, John Paul Lehman, Ike Pappas, Jacob Witkin, Tracy Roberts, Marc Macaulay, Peggy O'Neal, Timothy Bass, Jeff Breslauer, Molly Condle, Steve Dumouchel, Colette Piceau, Kurt Smildsin, Michael T. Kelly, Brett Rice, Jeff Smolek, William Schillert, Jesse White, Dick Miller
D: Joe Dante   **SCR:** Charlie Haas   **STORY:** Jerrico Haas & Charlie Haas   **PHOTOG:** John Hora   **MUSIC:** Jerry Goldsmith
Amusing comedy-satire: Schlockmeister (patterned on William Castle) holds sneak preview of new SF epic on eve of Cuban Missile Crisis

Matka Joanna od Aniolow (Mother Joan of the Angels)
1961, (Pol), Kadar Unit of Film Polski/Telepix, b&w, 108 mins, also 125 mins.
W: Lucyna Winnicka, Mieczyslaw Voit, Anna Ciepielewska, Maria Chwalibog, Kazimierz Fabisiak, Zygmunt Zintel, Stanislaw Jasiukiewicz
D: Jerzy Kawalerowicz   **SCR:** Jerzy Kawalerowicz & Tadeusz Konwicki   **STORY:** Jaroslav Iwaskiewicz
A.k.a. **The Devil and the Nun & Joan of the Angels**
Unusual, mystical thriller: 17th-century tale of nuns possessed by devils

The Matrix
1999, (USA), color
W: Keanu Reeves, Laurence Fishburne, Carrie-Anne Moss
Shot in Sidney, Australia
Unusual SF-thriller: Youth finds alternate existence, returns to Earth with super powers

The Mattei Affair
1973, (It), Cinema Int'l/Para, color, 118 mins.
W: Gian Maria Volonte (*Enrico Mattei*), Luigi Equarzina (*The Journalist*), Franco Graziosi (*The Minister*), Gianfranco Ombuen (*The Engineer*), Elio Jotta (*The Official of the Inquiry Commission*), Edda Ferronao (*Mrs. Mattei*), Luciano Colitti (*Bertuzzi*)
D: Francesco Rosi   **SCR:** Francesco Rosi, Tonino Guerra, Nerio Minuzzo & Tito de Stafano   **MUSIC:** Piero Piccioni
Standard thriller

A Matter of Choice
1963, (GB), Holmwood/Bry, b&w, 79 mins.
W: Anthony Steel (*John Crighton*), Jeanne Moody (*Lisa Grant*), Ballard Berkeley (*Charles Grant*), Malcolm Gerard (*Mike*), Michael Davis (*Tony*), Penny Morell (*Jackie*), Lisa Peake (*Jane*), James Bree (*Alfred*), George Moon (*Spiek*)
P: George Maynard   **D:** Vernon Sewell   **SCR:** Paul Ryder   **STORY:** Vernon Sewell & Derren Nesbitt
Standard crime-thriller: Youths accidentally kill married woman's lover

A Matter of Life and Death
1946, (GB), Archers/Univ, color, 104 mins.
W: David Niven (*Peter Carter*), Kim Hunter (*June*), Raymond Massey (*Abraham Farlan*), Roger Livesey (*Dr. Reeves*), Joan Maude (*The Recorder*), Marius Goring (*Conductor 71*), Edwin Max (*Dr. McEwan*), Abraham Sofaer (*The Judge*), Robert Atkins (*The Vicar*), Robert Coote (*Bob Trubshawe*), Kathleen Byron (*The Angel*), Bonar Colleano Jr. (*A Pilot*), Richard Attenborough (*A Pilot*)
WRIT, P & D: Michael Powell & Emeric Pressburger   **PHOTOG:** Jack Cardiff   **SPCL-FX:** Henry Harris, Percy Day & Douglas Woolsey   **MUSIC:** Allan Gray
USA retitle, **Stairway to Heaven**
Standard fantasy: Dead pilot given second chance at life

Matt Helm
1975, (USA), Col/ABC-TV, color, 74 mins.
W: Tony Franciosa (*Matt Helm*), Ann Turkel (*Maggie*), Gene Evans (*Hanrahan*),

A Matter of Life and Death: KIM HUNTER

Laraine Stephens (*Kronski*), John Vernon (*Paine*), Val Bisoglio (*James*), Patrick Macnee (*Shawcross*), Michael C. Gwynne, James Shigeta, Frank Marc Alaimo, Hari Rhodes
D: Buzz Kulik   **SCR:** Sam Rolfe, from novels by Donald Hamilton
TVM, standard thriller: Roguish private eye probes death of actress' father

Matt Riker
see *Mutant Hunt*

Mausoleum
1983, (USA), Western-Int'l/MPM, color, 96 mins.
W: Marjoe Gortner (*Oliver Farrell*), Bobbie Bresee (*Susan Farrell*), Norman Burton (*Dr. Simon Andrews*), LaWanda Page (*Elsie*), Maurice Sherbanee (*Ben*), Laura Hippe (*Aunt Cora*), Sheri Mann (*Dr. Logan*), Julie Christy Murray (*Young Susan*)
P: Robert Madero   **D:** Michael Dugan   **SCR:** Robert Barich & Robert Madero   **PHOTOG:** Robert Barich   **MUSIC:** Jaime Mendoza-Nava
Minor eroto-horror: Demon possesses young wife's body

Maximum Overdrive
1986, (USA), DEG, color, 97 mins.
W: Emilio Estevez, Pat Hingle, Laura Harrington, Holter Graham, Christopher Murney, John Short, Yeardley Smith, Ellen McElduff, J.C. Quinn, Pat Miller, Barry Bell, Bob Gunter, Stephen King, Marla Maples
WRIT & D: Stephen King   **PHOTOG:** Armando Nabbuzzi   **MUSIC:** AC/DC
Standard SF-thriller: Energy beings from comet animate machines

Maximum Thrust
1988, (USA), color, 80 mins.
W: Rick Gianasi, Joe Derrig, Jennifer Kanter, Mizan Nunes
D: Tim Kincaid
A.k.a. **Waldo Warren: Private Dick without a Brain**
Minor thriller: White men confront Caribbean voodoo tribe

Maxim Xul
1991, (USA), color, 90 mins.
W: Adam West, Jefferson Leinberger, Hal Strieb, Mary Schaeffer
D: Arthur Egeli
Minor horror-fantasy: Professor of occult meets demonic beast

Max Q: Emergency Landing
1998, (USA), ABC-TV, color, 95 mins.
W: Bill Campbell (*Clay Jarvis*), Ned Vaughn (*Scott Hines*), Paget Brewster (*Rena Bartlett*), Geoffrey Blake (*Jonah Randall*), Tasha Smith (*Karen Daniels*), Christopher John Fields (*Elliot Henschel*), Denis Arndt, Kevin McNulty, Leslie Moran, Chris Ellis
P: Jerry Bruckheimer   **D:** Michael Shapiro   **TELEPLAY:** Marty Kaylen & Robert J. Avrech   **PHOTOG:** Glen MacPherson
TVM, standard SF-thriller: Malfunctioning satellite plagues space shuttle

The Maze
1953, (USA), AA, 3D, b&w, 81 mins.
W: Richard Carlson (*Gerald*), Veronica Hurst (*Kitty*), Michael Pate (*William*), Katherine Emery, Hillary Brooke, Lillian Bond, John Dodsworth, Stanley Fraser, Owen McGiveney, Robin Hughes
P: Richard Heermance   **D:** William Cameron Menzies   **SCR:** Dan Ullman   **STORY:** Maurice Sandoz   **PHOTOG:** Harry Neumann   **MUSIC:** Marlin Skiles
Standard horror-thriller: Scottish castle conceals human freak. cf. **Castle Freak**

Mazeppa
1908, (GB), Walturdaw, b&w, 500 ft. (152.4m)
D: Frank Dudley, from a poem by Lord Byron
Standard melodrama: Polish nobleman ties wife's lover to back of wild horse

Mazes and Monsters
see *Rona Jaffe's Mazes and Monsters*

The McGuffin
1985, (GB), WW Entertainment, color, 104 mins.
W: Charles Dance (*Paul Hatcher*), Brian Glover (*The Man in Brown*), Mark Rylance (*Gavin*), Ritza Brown (*Celestia*), Ann Todd (*Mrs. Forbes-Duthie*), Phyllis Logan (*Anne*), Francis Matthews (*The Silver-Haired Gent*), Giovanni Samaritani (*Franco*), Anna Massey (*Nina*), Bill Shine, Jerry Stiller, Ray Shell, Neville Phillips, Paul MacKenzie, Ashok Kumar, Stephen Ruff, Roger Lloyd-Pack, Sue Peacock, Mark Burdis, Chris Langham, Michael Aitkin, Kenny Andrews, Simona De Laurentis, Natasha Gomperts, Massimo Sarchielli, Stephen Lewis, Issam El-Nasrawi, Mario Angelucci, Caliban
D: Colin Bucksey   **SCR:** Michael Thomas, from John Bowen's novel   **MUSIC:** Richard Hartley
Standard thriller, homage to Hitchcock: Film reviewer embroiled in mystery

Me and Him
1989, (USA-W. Ger), color, 95 mins.
W: Griffin Dunne, Ellen Greene (*Annette*), Kelly Bishop, Carey Lowell, Craig T. Nelson, Mark Linn-Baker (*Voice of "Him"*)
D: Doris Dorrie   **MUSIC:** Klaus Doldinger
Unusual fantasy: Architect's lower half develops its own persona

Meanwhile on a Distant Planet
1983, (GB), Sunflower Films, color, 4 mins.
Standard short fantasy

Meat Cleaver Massacre
1977, (USA), Group 1, color, 82 mins.
W: Christopher Lee, (*Narrator*)
D: Evan Lee
A.k.a. **The Hollywood Meat Cleaver Massacre**
Minor thriller: Professor of occult gains revenge on thugs who slew his family

The Meateater
1979, (USA), color, 84 mins.
W: Arch Jaboulian, Diane Davis, Emily Spendler
D: Derek Savage
Minor horror-thriller: Disfigured hermit terrorizes movie house

Meat is Meat
see *The Mad Butcher*

A Mechanical Husband
1910, (GB), London Cinematograph Co., b&w, 415 ft. (126.5m)
D: S. Wormald
Standard comedy-fantasy short: Girl loves automaton

Mechanical Legs
1908, (GB), Gaumont, b&w, 415 ft. (126.5m)
D: Alf Collins
Standard fantasy short: Mechanical legs run off with amputee

The Mechanical Mary Anne
1910, (GB), Hepworth, b&w, 560 ft. (170.7m)
D: Lewin Fitzhamon
Standard fantasy short: Clockwork maid wrecks house

Mechanics of the Brain
see *Mekhanikha Golovnovo Mozga*

The Medium
1934, (GB), Film Tests/MGM, b&w, 38 mins.
W: Nancy O'Neil (*Carol*), Shayle Gardner (*Dr. Petrov*), Barbara Gott (*Maria*), Richard Littledale (*Martin*), Ben Welden (*Deval*), Sandra Lawson (*Annette*)
D & SCR: Vernon Sewell, from a play by Pierre Mills & Celia de Vylars
Standard thriller: Psychic model reveals mad sculptor's crime

The Medium
1951, (It), Transfilm/Lopert, b&w, 84 mins.
W: Marie Powers, Anna Maria Alberghetti, Beverly Dame, Leo Coleman, Belwa Kibler, Donald Morgan
P: Walter Lowendahl   **D:** Gian-Carlo Menotti   **PHOTOG:** Enzo Serafin
Standard opera-spooker: Occult fraud begins to suspect she has conjured up real ghost

The Medium Exposed
1906, (GB), R.W. Paul, b&w, 385 ft. (117.3m)
D: J.H. Martin
Standard comedy short: Men expose fake medium, take revenge

The Medusa Against the Son of Hercules
see *Perseus the Invincible*

The Medusa Touch
1978, (GB-Fr), Coatesgold/Sir Lew Grade/ITC, color, 110 mins.
W: Richard Burton (*John Morlar*), Lee Remick (*Dr. Zonfeld*), Lino Ventura (*Insp. Brunel*), Harry Andrews (*The Ass't Commissioner*), Alan Badel (*The Barrister*),

Gordon Jackson (*Dr. Johnson*), Marie-Christine Barrault (*Patricia*), Jeremy Brett (*Parrish*), Michael Hordern (*The Palmist*), Derek Jacobi (*The Publisher*), Robert Lang (*Pennington*), Jennifer Jayne (*Morlar's Mother*), Avril Elgar (*Mrs. Pennington*), Michael Byrne (*Duff*), Norman Bird (*Morlar's Father*), Philip Stone (*The Dean*), John Normington (*The Schoolmaster*), Robert Flemyng (*Judge McKinley*), Malcolm Tierney (*The Deacon*), Mark Jones (*Sgt. Hughes*), James Hazeldine (*Loveless*), Brooke Williams (*The Male Nurse*), Wendy Gifford (*The Receptionist*), Gordon Honeycombe (*The TV Newscaster*), Shaw Taylor (*The TV Space Reporter*), Maurice O'Connell (*Sgt. Robbins*), Victor Winding (*The Senior Police Officer*), Frances Tomelty (*The Nanny*), Anthony Blackett (*The Mounted Police Officer*), Ian Master (*The Detective in the Street*), Denyse Alex-ander (*The Hospital Doctor*), John Flanagan (*The Police Constable*), Stanley Lebor (*The Police Doctor*), George Innes (*The Van Driver*), Cornelius Bowe (*Young Morlar*), Adam Bridge (*Morlar, age 10*), Joseph Clark (*Morlar, age 14*), Earl Rhodes (*Parsons*), Colin Rix (*The Engineer*), Christopher Burgess (*The Pilot*), Matthew Long (*The Co-Pilot*)
P: Jack Gold & Anne V. Coates   **D:** Jack Gold   **SCR:** John Briley, from Peter Greenaway's novel   **PHOTOG:** Arthur Ibbetson   **SPCL-FX:** Brian Johnson   **MUSIC:** Michael J. Lewis
Standard fantasy-thriller: Writer can destroy with his mind

Meet Boston Blackie
1941, (USA), Col, b&w, 58 mins.
W: Chester Morris (*Boston Blackie*), Rochelle Hudson (*Cecelia Bradley*), Richard Lane (*Insp. Farraday*), Jack O'Malley (*Monk*), Charles Wagenheim (*Runt*), Constance Worth (*Marilyn Howard*), George Magrill (*Georgie*), Michael Rand (*Mechanical Man*), Eddie Laughton (*The Freak Show Barker*), John Tyrrell (*The Freak Show Doorman*), Harry Anderson (*The Dart Game Barker*), Byron Foulger (*The Blind Man*)
D: Robert Florey   **SCR:** Jay Dratler, from characters created by Jack Boyle   **PHOTOG:** Franz E. Planer
Standard thriller: Rogue finds spy ring in amusement park

Meeting at Midnight
see *Black Magic (1944)*

Meet Mr. Lucifer
1953, (GB), Ealing/GFD, b&w, 83 mins.
W: Stanley Holloway (*Sam Hollingsworth/Lucifer*), Peggy Cummins (*Kitty Norton*), Jack Watling (*Jim Norton*), Kay Kendall (*The Lonely Hearts Singer*), Joseph Tomelty (*Mr. Pedelty*), Barbara Murray (*Patricia Pedelty*), Gordon Jackson (*Hector McPhee*), Charles Victor (*Mr. Elder*), Raymond Huntley (*Mr. Patterson*), Humphrey Lestocq (*Arthur Simmonds*), Jean Cadell (*Mrs. Macdonald*), Ernest Thesiger (*Eun Macdonald*), Frank Pettingell (*Mr. Roberts*), Joan Sims (*The Fairy Queen*), Olive Sloane (*Mrs. Stannard*), Ian Carmichael (*Man Friday*), Philip Harben, Gilbert Harding, McDonald Hobley, David Miller
D: Anthony Pelissier   **SCR:** Monja Danischewsky, Peter Myers & Alec Graham, from Arthur Ridley's play *Beggar My Neighbour*   **PHOTOG:** Desmond Dickinson   **MUSIC:** Eric Rogers
Standard fantasy: Has-been comic plots with Satan to discredit television

Meet Nero Wolfe
1936, (USA), Col, b&w, 73 mins.
W: Edward Arnold (*Nero Wolfe*), Lionel Stander (*Archie Goodwin*), Joan Perry, Victor Jory, Nana Bryant, Dennis Moore, Walter Kingsford, Boyd Irwin Jr., Russell Hardie, William Benedict, John Qualen, Gene Morgan, Rita Hayworth, Raymond Borzage, Frank Conroy, Juan Toreno, Martha Tibbetts, David Worth, Eddy Waller, George Offerman Jr., William Anderson, Eric Wilton, Al Matthews, Roy Bliss, Arthur Stewart Hull, Jay Owen, Henry Roquemore, Arthur Rankin
D: Abner Biberman   **SCR:** Howard J. Green, Bruce Manning & Joseph Anthony, from Rex Stout's novel *Fer de Lance*
Standard thriller (first "Nero Wolfe" mystery): Professor murdered on golf course, detective seeks killer

Meet Joe Black
1998, (USA), Univ, color, 170 mins.
W: Brad Pitt (*Death/Joe Black*), Anthony Hopkins (*Bill Parrish*), Claire Forlani (*Susan Parrish*), Jake Weber (*Drew*), Marcia Gay Harden (*Allison*), Jeffrey Tambor (*Quince*), Lois Kelly-Miller
P & D: Martin Brest   **SCR:** Ron Osborn, Jeff Reno, Kevin Wade & Bo Goldman   **MUSIC:** Thomas Newman
Well-made but overlong fantasy: Incarnation of Death falls in love with mortal girl

Meet Mr. Callaghan
1954, (GB), Pinnacle/Eros, b&w, 88 mins.
W: Derrick de Marney (*Slim Callaghan*), Harriette Johns (*Cynthia Meraulton*), Peter Neil (*William Meraulton*), Adrienne Corri (*Mayola*), Delphi Lawrence (*Effie*), Belinda Lee (*Jenny Appleby*), Larry Burns (*Darkey*), Trevor Reid (*Insp. Gringall*), John Longden (*Jeremy Meraulton*), Roger Williams (*Bellamy Meraulton*)
P: Guido Coen & Derrick de Marney   **D:** Charles Saunders   **SCR:** Brock Williams, from a play by Gerald Verner, based on Peter Cheyney's novel *UrgentHangman*
Standard crime-thriller: Private detective unmasks wealthy man's killer

Meet Mr. Malcolm
1954, (GB), Corsair/APB, b&w, 65 mins.

W: Adrianne Allen (*Mrs. Durant*), Sarah Lawson (*Louise Knowles*), Richard Gale (*Colin Knowles*), Duncan Lamont (*Supt. Simmons*), Meredith Edwards (*Whistler Grant*), Pamela Galloway (*Andria Durant*), John Horsley (*Tony Barlow*), John Blythe (*Carrington-Phelps*), Claude Dampier (*Joe Tutt*)
P: Theo Lageard   **D:** Daniel Birt   **STORY:** Brock Williams
Standard crime-thriller: Producer kills ex-wife's husband

Meet Sexton Blake
1944, (GB), British Nat'l/Strand, b&w, 80 mins.
W: David Farrar (*Sexton Blake*), John Varley (*Tinker*), Magda Kun (*Yvonne*), Gordon McLeod (*Insp. Venner*), Manning Whiley (*Raoul Sudd*), Kathleen Harrison (*Mrs. Bardell*), Cyril Smith (*Belford*), Dennis Arundell (*Johann Sudd*), Jean Simmons (*Eva Watkins*), Ferdi Mayne (*Slanteyes*), Betty Huntley-Wright (*Nobby*)
D & SCR: John Harlow, from Anthony Parsons' novel *The Case of the Stolen Dispatches*
Standard thriller: Crook steals brother's formula for airplane alloy

Meet the Applegates
1991, (USA), New World Int'l-Cinemarque Entertainment/Heron/Triton, color, 90 mins.
W: Ed Begley Jr. (*Dick Applegate*), Stockard Channing (*Jane Applegate*), Dabney Coleman (*Aunt Bea*), Bobby Jacoby (*Johnny Applegate*), Cami Cooper (*Sally Applegate*), Glenn Shadix (*Greg Samson*), Susan Barnes (*Opal Withers*), Savannah Smith Boucher (*Dottie*), Adam Biesk (*Vince Samson*)
D: Michael Lehmann   **SCR:** Redbeard Simmons & Michael Lehmann   **PHOTOG:** Mitchell Dubin   **MUSIC:** David Newman
Standard SF-comedy: Mutated bugs become humans

Meet the Feebles
1989, (New Zeal), color & b&w, 97 mins.
VOICES: Danny Mulheron, Donna Akersten, Stuart Devenie, Mark Hadlow, Ross Jolly, Frances Walsh   **D:** Peter Jackson   **SCR:** Peter Jackson & Danny Mulheron   **PHOTOG:** Murray Milne
Bizarre fantasy: Puppets seek show-biz fame

Megaforce
1982, (USA), Golden Harvest/20th-Fox, color, 99 mins.
W: Barry Bostwick (*Ace Hunter*), Michael Beck (*Dallas*), Persis Khambatta (*Maj.Zara Benhbutto*), Henry Silva (*Maj. Guerrera*), Edward Mulhare (*Sir Edward Byrne-White*), George Furth (*Prof. Eggstrum*)
P: Albert S. Ruddy   **D:** Hal Needham   **SCR:** James Whittaker, Albert S. Ruddy, Hal Needham & Andre Morgan, from a story by Robert S. Kachler   **PHOTOG:** Michael Butler   **MUSIC:** Jerrold Immel
Standard SF: Special agents fight terrorists of future

Megaville
1990, (USA), color, 100 mins.
W: Billy Zane, J.C. Quinn, Grace Zabriskie (*Mrs. Panilov*), Daniel J. Travanti
D & SCR: Peter Lehner
Standard SF-thriller: Undercover cop in city of future

Meg the Lady
1916, (GB), London-Diploma/Jury, b&w, 4,740 ft. (1444.8m)
W: Elizabeth Risdon (*Lady Brisby*), Eric Stuart (*Teddy*), Fred Groves (*Giles Curwen*)
D: Maurice Elvey, from a novel by Tom Gallon
Standard crime-thriller: Lord's wife kills robber, then is blackmailed by lover

Mekhanikha Golovnovo Mozga (Mechanics of the Brain)
1926, (Russ), Mezhrabpom-Russ, b&w, 6,070 ft. (1850m)
WRIT & D: Vsevolod Pudovkin   **PHOTOG:** Anatoli Golovnya   **CONSULTANTS:** D. Fursikov & L. Voskresensky
Unusual science docu: Pavlovian methods & principles

Melody of Death
1922, (GB), Stoll, b&w, 4,771 ft. (1454.2m)
W: Philip Anthony (*Gilbert Standerton*), Enid R. Reed (*Enid Cathcart*), Dick Sutherd (*George Wallis*), H. Agar Lyons (*Sir John Standerton*), Frank E. Petley, Hetta Bartlett, Bob Vallis
D: F. Martin Thornton   **SCR:** Leslie Howard Gordon, from a novel by Edgar Wallace
Standard thriller: Man retrieves stolen jewels

Melody of Hate
1975, (GB), Made for TV, color
W: Susan Flannery, Keith Baxter, Stuart Damon, Sydney Tafler, Ronald Leigh-Hunt
TVM, standard thriller: "Dead" husband complicates opera singer's remarriage plans

Melody Time
1948, (USA), Walt Disney, color
Standard animated musical-fantasy

Le Melomane (The Melomaniac)
1903, (Fr), Star, b&w, 51m (167.3 ft./2.8 mins.)
D: Georges Melies
Standard fantasy: Teacher uses human heads for musical instruments

M

The Melomaniac
see *Le Melomane*

Memoirs of an Invisible Man
1992, (USA), WB, color, 99 mins.
W: Chevy Chase (*Nick Halloway*), Daryl Hannah (*Alice Monroe*), Sam Neill (*David Jenkins*), Michael McKean (*George Talbot*), Stephen Tobolowsky (*Warren Singleton*), Jim Norton (*Dr. Bernard Wachs*)
D: John Carpenter **SCR:** Robert Collector, Dana Olsen & William Goldman from H.F. Saint's book **PHOTOG:** William A. Fraker **MUSIC:** Shirley Walker **VS-FX SPRVSR:** Bruce Nicholson
Standard SF-thriller: Man becomes victim of gov't experiment

Memoirs of a Survivor
1981, (GB), Memorial Films/EMI, color, 115 mins.
W: Julie Christie (*D*), Christopher Guard (*Gerald*), Leonie Mellinger (*Emily*), Debbie Hutchings (*June*), Pat Keen (*The Victorian Mother*), Nigel Hawthorne (*The Victorian Father*), Georgina Griffiths (*Victorian Emily*), Christopher Tsangarides (*The Victorian Son*), Mark Dignam (*The Newsvendor/The Gardener*), Alison Dowling (*Janet White*), Rowena Cooper (*Mrs. White*), John Franklyn-Robbins (*Prof. White*), Barbara Hicks, John Comer, Adrienne Byrne, Marion Owen Smith, Mark Farmer, Tara MacGowran, John Altman, David Squire, Pamela Cundell, Jeanne Watts, Bryan Matheson, Ann Tirard, Jeillo Edwards, Arthur Lovegrove, John Rutland
D: David Gladwell **SCR:** Kerry Crabbe & David Gladwell, from Doris Lessing's novel **PHOTOG:** Walter Lassally **MUSIC:** Mike Thorne
Unusual SF-fantasy: Future woman explores decaying urban civilization

Memorial Valley Massacre
1988, (USA), color, 93 mins.
W: Cameron Mitchell, William Smith, John Kerry, Lesa Lee, Mark Mears, John Caso
D: Robert C. Hughes
Minor thriller: Nutty hermit slays campers

Memories of Murder
1990, (USA), Lifetime (cable), color, 95 mins.
W: Nancy Allen, Robin Thomas, Vanity, Olivia Brown, Linda Darlow, Don Davis, Veena Sood, Robyn Simons, Peter Yunker, Helena Yea, Tasha Simms, John Destry, Michael Sicoly, Ian Black, Pedro Salvin, Sherry Bie, Ed Harrington, Pam Howard-Jones
P & D: Robert Lewis **TELEPLAY:** John Harrison & Nevin Schreiner **STORY:** John Harrison **PHOTOG:** Richard Leiterman **MUSIC:** Joseph Conlan
TVM, standard thriller: Mystery woman stalks amnesiac

The Memory of Eva Ryker
1980, (USA), Irwin Allen/CBS-TV, color, 180 mins.
W: Natalie Wood (*Eva Ryker*), Robert Foxworth (*Norman Hall*), Ralph Bellamy (*Ryker*), Bradford Dillman (*Eddington*), Peter Graves (*Rogers*), Morgan Fairchild (*Lisa*), Roddy McDowall (*MacFarland*), Jean-Pierre Aumont (*Insp. Laurier*), Robert Hogan (*J.H. Martin*), Mel Ferrer (*Dr. Stanford*)
D: Walter E. Grauman **TELEPLAY:** Laurence Heath, from a novel by Donald A. Stanwood
TVM, standard thriller

The Menace
1932, (USA), Col, b&w, 64 mins.
W: H.B. Warner (*Tracy*), Bette Davis (*Peggy*), Walter Byron (*Ronald*), William B. Davidson (*Utterson*), Natalie Moorhead (*Caroline*), Crauford Kent (*Lewis*), Halliwell Hobbes (*Phillips*), Charles Gerrard (*The Bailiff*), Murray Kinnell (*Carr*)

Men In Black: TOMMY LEE JONES AND WILL SMITH

P: Sam Nelson **D:** Roy William Neill **SCR:** Dorothy Howell & Charles Logue, from Edgar Wallace's novel *The Feathered Serpent* **PHOTOG:** L. William O'Connell
Standard thriller

Menace in the Night
see *Face in the Night*

Menaces

Men In Black: WILL SMITH AND TOMMY LEE JONES

1939, (Fr), b&w
W: Erich Von Stroheim
D: Edmond T. Greville
Standard melodrama

Menilmontant
1924, (Fr), b&w, 50 mins. (2,854 ft./869.9m)
W: Nadia Sibirskaia, Yoland Beaulieu, Guy Belmont
D: Dimitri Kirsanoff
Unusual impressionistic thriller: Tale of suburban axe-muderer

Men in Black
1997, (USA), Sony/Col, color, 98 mins.
W: Tommy Lee Jones, Will Smith, Linda Fiorentino, Rip Torn, Vincent D'Onofrio
D: Barry Sonnenfeld
Standard SF-comedy-thriller: Space-alien invaders hunted

Menno's Mind
1997, (USA), color, 100 mins.
W: Bill Campbell, Corbin Bernsen
Made-for-Cable, standard SF-thriller: Virtual-reality technician becomes involved with political cabal

Men of Action Meet the Women of Drakula
1969, (Phil), color
Minor horror-adventure

Men of Sherwood Forest
1954, (GB), Hammer/Astor, color, 77 mins.
W: Don Taylor (*Robin Hood*), Eileen Moore (*Lady Alys*), Reginald Beckwith (*Friar Tuck*), Patrick Holt (*King Richard*), David King-Wood (*Sir Guy Belton*), Douglas Wilmer (*Sir Nigel Saltire*), John Van Eyssen (*Will Scarlett*), Harold Lang (*Hubert*), Leslie Linder (*Little John*), Vera Pearce (*Elvira*), John Kerr (*Brian of Eskdale*), John Stuart (*Moraine*), Bernard Bresslaw (*The Outlaw*), Raymond Rollett (*Abbot St. Jude*), Leonard Sachs (*The Sheriff of Nottingham*), Ballard Berkeley (*Walter*), Wensley Pithey (*Hugo*), Toke Townley, Howard Lang, Jackie Lane, Tom Bowman, Edward Hardwicke, Michael Godfrey, Robert Hunter, Peter Arne, Dennis Wyndham, Jack McNaughton
P: Michael Carreras **D:** Val Guest **SCR:** Alan Mackinnon
reissued 1961
Standard adventure-thriller: Outlaw seeks lost plan to rescue King

Men of Time
see *Doctor Mabuse*

Menschen der Zeit
see *Doctor Mabuse*

Mensch ohne Namen (The Man without a Name)
1932, (Ger), Ufa, b&w
W: Werner Krauss
Standard melodrama: Amnesiac war veteran returns home to find no one recognizes him

Le Menuet Lilliputien (The Lilliputian Minuet)
1905, (Fr), Star, b&w, 60m (196.9 ft./3.3 mins.)

D: Georges Melies
Standard fantasy

Mephisto
1912, (GB), Natural Colour Kinematograph Co., color, 2,000 ft. (609.6m)
W: Alfred de Many (*Mephisto*)
D: Alfred de Manby & F. Martin Thornton   **STORY:** Alfred de Manby &
   Leedham Bantock
Standard fantasy: Devil tempts

The Mephisto Waltz
1971, (USA), 20th-Fox, color, 108 mins.
W: Alan Alda (*Myles Clarkson*), Jacqueline Bisset (*Paula Clarkson*), Barbara
   Parkins (*Roxanne*), Curt Jurgens (*Duncan Ely*), Bradford Dillman (*William*

The Mephisto Waltz: JAQUELINE BISSET, ALAN ALDA, BARBARA PARKINS

Delancey), William Windom (*Dr. Roger West*), Kathleen Widdoes (*Maggie*),
   Khigh Dhiegh (*Zanc Theun*), Pamelyn Ferdin (*Abby Clarkson*), Gregory
   Morton (*The Conductor*), Lilyan Chauvin (*The Woman Writer*), Janee Michelle
   (*The Agency Head's Girl*), Terence Scammell (*Richard*), Alberto Morin
   (*Bennet*), Berry Kroeger (*Raymont*), Curt Lowens (*The Agency Head*)
P: Quinn Martin   **D:** Paul Wendkos   **SCR:** Ben Maddow, from Fred Mustard
   Stewart's novel   **PHOTOG:** William W. Spencer   **MUSIC:** Jerry
   Goldsmith
Engrossing fantasy-thriller: Transmigration of souls among Southern California's elite

Le Mepris (Contempt)
1963, (It-Fr), Embassy, color, 103 mins.
W: Brigitte Bardot, Michel Piccoli, Jack Palance, Georgia Moll, Fritz Lang, Jean
   Luc Godard
D & SCR: Jean-Luc Godard, from Albert Moravia's novel   **PHOTOG:** Raoul
   Coutard   **MUSIC:** Georges Delerue
Unusual melodrama: Young woman comes to detest her script-writer husband

Mercia the Flower Girl
1913, (GB), Brightonia/MP, b&w, 1,560 ft. (475.5m)
W: Nell Emerald (*Mercia*), H. Agar Lyons (*Capt. Jack*), Frank Petley (*Sir Harry
   Fielding*), Eily Adair, Monnie Mine
D: Arthur Charrington
Standard crime-thriller: Lord weds flowergirl, save her from blackmailing nephew

Meridian
1990, (USA), Full Moon, color, 85 mins
W: Sherilyn Fenn, Malcolm Jamieson, Hilary Mason, Charlie, Alex Daniels, Phil
   Fondacaro
D: Charles Band   **SCR:** Dennis Paoli   **STORY:** Charles Band   **PHOTOG:** Mac
   Ahlberg   **MUSIC:** Pino Donaggio
A.k.a. **Kiss of the Beast**
Minor horror-fantasy: Werewolf seduces girl

Merlin
1993, (USA), color, 112 mins.
W: Nadia Cameron, Richard Lynch, Peter Phelps (*Pope*), James Hong (*Leong Tao*),
   Desmond Llewelyn (*Myercroft*), Ted Markland
D: Paul Hunt   **SCR:** Nick McCarty
Minor fantasy-thriller: Mythical magician's reincarnated daughter vs. evil sorcerer

Merlin
1998, (USA), Hallmark/NBC-TV, color
W: Sam Neill (*Merlin*), Isabella Rossellini (*Nimue*), Miranda Richardson (*Lady of
   the lake/Queen Mab*), Rutger Hauer (*King Vortigern*), Martin Short (*Frik*),
   James Earl Jones (*Voice of the Mountain King*), Helena Bonham Carter
   (*Morgan Le Fay*), Paul Curran (*King Arthur*), Billie Whitelaw (*Ambrosia*),
   Jason Done (*Mordred*), Sir John Gielgud, Emma Lewis, Lena Heady, Robert
   Addie, Timothy Bateson

D: Steve Barron   **PHOTOG:** Sergei Kozlov   **VS-FX SPRVSR:** Tim Webber
   MUSIC: Trevor Jones
2-part TVM, lavish fantasy: Life of legendary magician

Merlin and the Knights of King Arthur
see **Excalibur**

Merlin of the Crystal Cave
1991, (GB), color, 159 mins.
TVM, standard fantasy: Adventures of boy magician

Merlin's Shop of Mystical Wonders
1996, (USA), color, 95 mins.
W: Ernest Borgnine, George Milian, Bunny Summers
Standard fantasy: Ancient wizard finds trouble in 20th century

Merlin: The Magic Beans
1998, (GB), color
W: Jason Connery
TVM, standard adventure-fantasy (edited from teleseries): Magician battles blackmagic

The Mermaid
see **La Sirene**

Mermaids of Tiburon
1962, (USA), Filmgroup, color, 77 mins
W: Diane Webber, Timothy Carey, George Rowe, John Mylong, Jose Gonzales,
   Vicki Kantenwine, Nani Morissey, Judy Edwards, Gil Baretto, Jean Carroll,
   Karen Goodman, Diana Cook, Nancy Burns
WRIT, P & D: John Lamb   **MUSIC:** Richard LaSalle
A.k.a. **The Aqua Sex**
Standard semi-fantasy: Mermaid aids imperiled pearl expedition

The Merry Frolics of Satan
see **Les 400 Farces du Diable**

The Merry Men of Sherwood
1932, (GB), Delta/Filmphone, b&w, 36 mins.
W: John Thompson (*Robin Hood*), Aileen Marson (*Maid Marian*), Eric Adeney
   (*The Sheriff of Nottingham*), Terence de Marney, John Milton, Patrick Barr
D: Widgey R. Newman
Standard adventure short: Outlaw rescues captive cousin

A Merry Night
1914, (GB), Martin Films/DFSA, b&w, 680 ft. (207.3m)
D: Dave Aylott
reissued (1915) as **Some Evening**
Standard fantasy: Drunkard beset by animated objects

Le Merveilleux Eventail Vivant (The Marvellous Living Fan)
1904, (Fr), Star, b&w, 90m (295.7 ft./3.9 mins.)
D: Georges Melies
A.k.a. **The Wonderful Living Fan**
Standard fantasy

Mesa of Lost Women
1953, (USA), Howco, b&w, 70 mins.
W: Jackie Coogan, Allan Nixon, Tandra Quinn, Mary Hill, Katena Vea
   [*Katherine Victor*], Mona McKinnon, Robert Knapp, Lyle Talbot, Angelo
   Rossitto
P: G. William Perkins & Melvin Gale   **D:** Herbert Tevos & Ron Ormond   **SCR:**
   Herbert Tevos   **PHOTOG:** Gilbert Warrenton & Karl Struss
A.k.a. **Lost Women** *and* **Lost Women of Zarpa**
Minor SF-thriller: Mad scientist creates superwomen and giant tarantula

Mesaventures D'Un Aeronaute (Misadventures of an Aeronaut)
1901, (Fr), Star, b&w, 20m (65.6 ft.)
D: Georges Melies
Standard short fantasy-thriller

A Mesmerian Experiment
1905, (Fr), Star, b&w, 60m (196.9 ft./3.3 mins.)
D: Georges Melies
Standard fantasy: Hypnotism examined

The Mesmerist
1898, (GB), G.A.S. Films, b&w, 75 ft. (22.9m)
D: George Albert Smith
Standard fantasy short: Prof draws spirit from girl's body

The Mesmerist
1915, (GB), Neptune/Browne, b&w, 1,250 ft. (381m)
W: Douglas Payne (*The Mesmerist*)
D: Percy Nash
Standard thriller: Hypnotist forces victims to steal

A Message from Mars
1913, (GB), United Kingdom Films, b&w, 4,000 ft. (1219.2m)
W: Charles Hawtrey Sr. (*Horace Parker*), Frank Hector (*Arthur Dicey*), E. Holman

Clark (*Ramiel*), Hubert Willis (*The Tramp*), Crissie Bell (*Minnie*), Kate Tyndale (*Aunt Martha*), Evelyn Beaumont (*Bella*), Eileen Temple (*Mrs. Clarence*), R. Crompton (*The God of Mars*), B. Stanmore (*The Wounded Man*), Tonie Reith (*The Wounded Man's Wife*)
<u>D & SCR:</u> J. Wallett Waller, from a play by Richard Ganthony
Standard SF-fantasy: Martian sent to Earth to cure selfish man

A Message from Mars
1921, (USA), Metro, b&w, 6 reels (5,187 ft./1581m)
<u>W:</u> Bert Lytell (*Horace Parker*), Raye Dean (*Minnie Talbot*), Maude Milton (*Martha Parker*), Alphonz Ethier (*The Messenger*), Gordon Ash (*Arthur Dicey*), Mary Louise Beaton (*Mrs. Jones*), Leonard Mudie (*Fred Jones*), Frank Currier (*Sir Edwards*), George Spink (*The Butler*)
<u>D:</u> Maxwell Karger   <u>SCR:</u> Arthur J. Zellner & Arthur Maude   <u>PHOTOG:</u> Arthur Martinelli
Standard comedy-fantasy: Man dreams of Martian envoy

Message from Space
1978, (Jap), Toei/UA, color, 105 mins.
<u>W:</u> Vic Morrow, Hiroyuki Sanada (*Shiro*), Philip Casnoff (*Aaron*), Makata Sato (*Urocco*), Sonny Chiba (*Prince Hans*), Peggy Lee Brennan (*Meia*), Sue Shiomi (*Esmeralda*), Tetsuro Tamba (*Noguchi*), Mikio Narita (*Rockseia XII*)
<u>D:</u> Kinji Fukasaku   <u>SCR:</u> Hiroo Matsuda   <u>PHOTOG:</u> Toro Nakajima   <u>MUSIC:</u> Ken-Ichiro Morioka
Standard SF-adventure: Earthlings aid alien world

Messalina Against the Son of Hercules
1964, (It-Fr), Avco/color, 105 mins, also 98 mins.
<u>W:</u> Richard Harrison (*Glaucus*), Lisa Gastoni, Marilu' Tolo
Standard "Sword & Sandal": Warrior leads Romans against oppressive ruler

Messiah of Evil
see Dead People

Metallica
1985, (USA), color, 90 mins.
<u>W:</u> Anthony Newcastle, Sharon Baker
<u>D:</u> Al Bradley
Minor SF-thriller: Space-alien warmongers beset Earth

Metalstorm: The Destruction of Jared-Syn
1983, (USA), Univ, 3D, color, 84 mins.
<u>W:</u> Mike Preston (*Jared-Syn*), Jeffrey Byron (*Dogen*), Tim Thomerson (*Rhodes*), Richard Moll (*Hurok*), Kelly Preston (*Dhyana*), R. David Smith (*Baal*), Larry Pennell (*Alx*), Marty Zagon (*Zax*), Mickey Fox (*Poker Annie*), J. Bill Jones (*Baal's Lt.*), Winston Jones (*Chimera*), Mike Jones, Mike Walter, Rick Militi, Speed Stearns, Lou Joseph, Rush Adams, Kelly Palzis
<u>P & D:</u> Charles Band   <u>SCR:</u> Alan J. Adler   <u>PHOTOG:</u> Mac Ahlberg   <u>SPCL-FX:</u> Joe Quinlan & Gregory Van Der Veer   <u>MUSIC:</u> Richard Band
Minor space-opera: Ranger pursues space-alien villain

Metaluna Does Not Answer
see This Island Earth

Metamorphoses
1978, (Jap), Sanrio, color, 89 mins.
<u>P, WRIT & D:</u> Takashi, from Ovid's classic   <u>PHOTOG:</u> Bill Millar   <u>MUSIC:</u> Bob Randles
Standard animated fantasy: Recreation of Greek myths

Metamorphosis
1990, (USA), color, 96 mins.
<u>W:</u> Gene LeBrock, Catherine Baranov, Harry Cason, Stephen Brown, David Wicker, Jason Arnold
<u>D:</u> G.L. Eastman
Minor SF-horror: Professor takes immortality drug, begins to devolve

Metamorphosis: The Alien Factor
1990, (USA), Vidmark, video, color, 98 mins.
<u>W:</u> Tara Leigh, Tony Gigante, Dianna Flaherty, Katherine Romaine, George Gerard, Allen Lewis Rickman, Greg Sullivan, Patrick Barnes, Marcus Powell (*Dr. Viallini*)
<u>D, STORY & SCR:</u> Glenn Takajian   <u>PHOTOG:</u> John A. Corso   <u>VS-FX DIR:</u> Dan Taylor   <u>MUSIC:</u> John Gray
Made-for-Video, standard SF-thriller: Contaminated scientist becomes monster

Meteor
1979, (USA), Sandy Howard-Gabriel Katzka-Sir Run Run Shaw/Film-ways/AIP, color, 103 mins.
<u>W:</u> Sean Connery (*Bradley*), Natalie Wood (*Tatiana*), Trevor Howard (*Sir Michael Hughes*), Karl Malden (*Sherwood*), Brian Keith (*Dubov*), Henry Fonda (*The President*), Martin Landau (*Adlon*), Joseph Campanella (*Easton*), Richard Dysart (*The Sec'y of Defense*), Clyde Kusatsu (*Yamashiro*), Gregory Gay (*The Russian Premier*), Roger Robinson (*Hunter*), Katherine DeHetre (*Jan*), Bo Brundin (*Manheim*), Michael Zaslow (*Mason*), James Richardson (*Alan*), John McKinney (*Watson*), John Findlater (*Tom Easton*), Paul Tulley (*Bill Frager*), Bibi Besch (*Mrs. Bradley*), Allen Williams (*Michael McKendrick*), Zitto Kazann (*The Hawk-faced Party Member*), Burke Byrnes (*The Coast Guard Officer*)

<u>P:</u> Arnold Orgolini & Theodore Parvin   <u>D:</u> Ronald Neame   <u>SCR:</u> Stanley Mann & Edmund H. North, from a story by Edmund H. North   <u>PHOTOG:</u> Paul Lohmann   <u>MUSIC:</u> Laurence Rosenthal
Standard SF-thriller: Meteor on collision course with Earth

La Meteore de la Nuit
see It Came from Outer Space

The Meteor Man
1993, (USA), Tinel Townsend/MGM, color, 99 mins.
<u>W:</u> Robert Townsend, Marla Gibbs (*Mrs. Reed*), Eddie Griffin (*Michael*), Robert Guillaume (*Mr. Reed*), James Earl Jones (*Mr. Moses*), Ray Fegan (*Simon*), Big Daddy Kane, Luther Vandross, Sinbad, Bill Cosby, Cynthia Belgrave, Marilyn Coleman, Don Cheadle, Jennifer Lewis, Frank Gorshin, LaWanda Page, Beverly Johnson, Nancy Wilson
<u>WRIT & D:</u> Robert Townsend   <u>PHOTOG:</u> John A. Alonzo   <u>MUSIC:</u> Cliff Edelman
Standard SF-comedy: Meteor fragment transforms timid school-teacher into superhero

Meteorites!
1998, (USA), USA-TV, color, 95 mins.
<u>W:</u> Tom Wopat, Roxanne Hart, Pato Hoffmann, Leo Taylor, Amiel Daemion
<u>D:</u> Chris Thomson   <u>TELEPLAY:</u> Bart Baker   <u>PHOTOG:</u> John Stokes   <u>MUSIC:</u> Peter Bernstein
TVM, standard SF-thriller: Meteor shower menaces Southwest town

Meteor Monster
see Teenage Monster

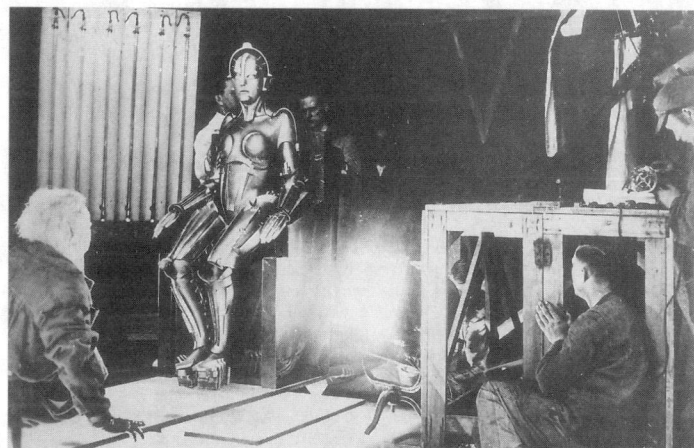

Metropolis: Rudolf Klein-Rogge

Meteor of the Night
see It Came from Outer Space

Metropolis
1926, (Ger), Ufa/Para, b&w, 131 mins.
<u>W:</u> Brigitte Helm (*Maria/The Robotrix*), Rudolf Klein-Rogge (*Rotwang*), Gustav Froelich (*Eric Masterman*), Alfred Abel (*John Masterman*), Heinrich George, Theodor Loos, Heinrich Gotho, Erwin Biswanger, Olaf Strom, Hans Leo Reich, Georg John, Margarete Lanner, Max Dietze, Walter Kuhle, Arthur Reinhard, Erwin Vater, Fritz Rasp, Curt Siodmak (*unbilled extra*)
<u>P:</u> Erich Pommer   <u>D:</u> Fritz Lang   <u>STORY & SCR:</u> Thea von Harbou   <u>PHO-TOG:</u> Karl Freund & Gunther Rittau   <u>DESIGN:</u> Erich Kettlehut, Otto

Metropolis: Rudolf Klein-Rogge

Hunte & Karl Vollbrecht

"METROPOLIS: the film that goes beyond the 5 senses into the mos-kowitzian realm of the 6th, into the Sense of Wonder"—Forrest J. Ackerman, "Metropolis," Spacemen, Vol. II, No. 2 (January, 1962), p. 36

"...a film of immense fantasy, a sensuous voyage into a manufactured universe happily alien both to Lang's time and our own... The clever special effects still represent one of the finest combinations of reality and fantasy in the cinema"—John Baxter, Science Fiction in the Cinema

Classic SF-fantasy (considered greatest SF film epic until 2001: A Space Odyssey)*: Future scientist supplants girl with amazing robot double Footage used on TV's 'Working'*

Metropolis (1961)
see Il Gigante di Metropolis

Meurtre par Procuration
see Nightmare (1963)

Mexican Spitfire Sees a Ghost
1942, (USA), RKO, b&w, 70 mins.
W: Lupe Velez, Leon Errol, Charles "Buddy" Rogers, Elisabeth Risdon, Donald MacBride, Minna Gombell, Mantan Moreland
D: Leslie Goodwins
Minor comedy-thriller

Mezhplanetnaya Revolutsiya (Interplanetary Revolution)
1924, (Russ), Animation Workshop, b&w
PHOTOG: V. Alexeyev
Standard SF-adventure

Mi Adorable Esclava (My Adorable Slave)
1962, (Sp), b&w
W: Antonio Casal, Ethel Rojo, Jose Maria Cafarell, Licia Calderon, Cesar Gonzalez Ruano
D: Jose Maria Elorrietta   **SCR:** Augustin Navarro & Jose Maria Elorrietta   **PHOTOG:** Alessandro Ulloa
Standard comedy-fantasy

Miami Golem
1987, (It), color, 85 mins.
W: David Warbeck, John Ireland, Laura Trotter, Alessandra Camale
D: Alberto DeMartino   **SCR:** Martin Herbert [Alberto DeMartino]   **PHOTOG:** Lorenzo Battaglia
A.k.a. **Cosmic Killer** *and* **Miami Horror**
Standard SF-horror: Scientists clone monstrous creature

Miami Horror
see Miami Golem

Michael
1996, (USA), New Line, color, 105 mins.
W: John Travolta (*Michael*), William Hurt, Andie MacDowell, Robert Pastorelli, Bob Hoskins, Jean Stapleton
D: Nora Ephron   **SCR:** Nora Ephron, Delia Ephron, Peter Dexter & Jim Quinlan   **PHOTOG:** John Lindley   **MUSIC:** Randy Newman
blurb: "He's an angel. Not a saint"
Superior comedy-fantasy: Angel helps skeptical reporter find love

Micheal Dwyer
1912, (GB), Irish Films/Cosmo, b&w, 850 ft. (259.1m)
Standard crime-thriller: Outlaw thwarts informer, escapes capture

Michael Shayne, Private Detective
1940, (USA), 20th-Fox, b&w, 77 mins.
W: Lloyd Nolan (*Michael Shayne*), Marjorie Weaver (*Phyllis Brighton*), Joan Valerie (*Marsha Gordon*), Walter Abel (*Elliott Thomas*), Elizabeth Patterson (*Aunt Olivia*), Donald MacBride (*Chief Painter*), Adrian Morris (*The Policeman*), Douglass Dumbrille (*Gordon*), George Meeker (*Harry Grange*), Clarence Kolb (*Brighton*), Charles Coleman (*Ponsley the Butler*)
D: Eugene Forde   **SCR:** Stanley Rauh & Manning O'Connor based on, Brett Halliday's novel *Dividend on Death*   **MUSIC:** Emil Newman
Standard thriller: Businessman hires private eye to protect heiress daughter

Mickey One
1965, Col, b&w, 93 mins.
W: Warren Beatty, Alexandra Stewart, Hurd Hatfield, Franchot Tone, Jeff Corey
P & D: Arthur Penn   **PHOTOG:** Ghislain Cloquet
Unusual melodrama (Arthur Penn's most "European" film): Nightclub comic assumes dead man's identity

Mickey Spillane's Margin for Murder
see Margin for Murder

The Microscopic Dancer
see La Danseuse Microscopique

Microwave Massacre
1983, (USA), color, 80 mins.
W: Jackie Vernon, Loren Schein, Al Troupe

D: Wayne Berwick
Minor thriller: Lounge comic goes on murder spree

The Midas Touch
1939, (GB), WB, b&w, 68 mins.
W: Barry K. Barnes (*Evan Jones*), Judy Kelly (*Lydia Brenton*), Frank Cellier (*Corris Morgan*), Bertha Belmore (*Mrs. Carter Blake*), Iris Hoey (*Ellie Morgan*), Eileen Erskine (*Rosalie*), Philip Friend (*David Morgan*), Anna Konstam (*Mamie*), Evelyn Roberts (*Maj. Arnold*)
D: David MacDonald, from a novel by Margaret Kennedy
Standard thriller: Medium predicts fatal auto crash

Midnight
1931, (GB), George King/Fox, b&w, 44 mins.
W: John Stuart (*Larry Byrne*), Eve Gray (*Dorothy Harding*), George Bellamy (*Max Strubel*), Ellen Pollock (*Sonia Strubel*), Kyoshi Takase (*Ching*)
D: George King   **SCR:** Charles Bennett & Billie Bristow, from a play by Charles Bennett
Standard thriller: Spies covet secret plans

Midnight
1980, (USA), Independent-Int'l, color, 88 mins.
W: Lawrence Tierney (*Bert Johnson*), Melanie Verlin (*Nancy Johnson*), John Amplas (*Abraham*), Greg Besnak (*Luke*), John Hall (*Tom*), Charles Jackson (*Hank*), Robin Walsh (*Cynthia*), David Marchick (*Cyrus*), Doris Hackney (*Harriet Johnson*), Bob Johnson (*Rev. Carrington*), Jackie Nicoll (*Mama*), Amy Brinton (*The Girl in the Trap*), Ellie Wyler (*Gwen Davis*), Debra Smith (*Young Cynthia*), Daniel Costello (*Young Abraham*), Chris Riblett (*Young Luke*), Billy Green (*Young Cyrus*), Maura Minteer (*Sharon*), Doug Mertz (*Billy*), Bud Mellot (*The Sheriff*), Lucian White (*The Man in the Car*), Dan Kamerer (*The Gas Station Attendant*), David McCollough (*The Man at the Station*), Jim Grippo, Lou Grippo, Glenn Shannon, John Blaho, Connie Gori, Raymond Russo, Ann Kambes, Tom Milas, Kenneth Croyle, Armand Martin, Frank Pryzbylski, John Rice, Eugene Ratkiewicz, Jack Ruffing
WRIT & D: John Russo, from his novel   **PHOTOG:** Paul McCollough   **SONG:** *Midnight Again*
A.k.a. **Backwoods Massacre**
Minor horror-thriller: Satanists sacrifice girls

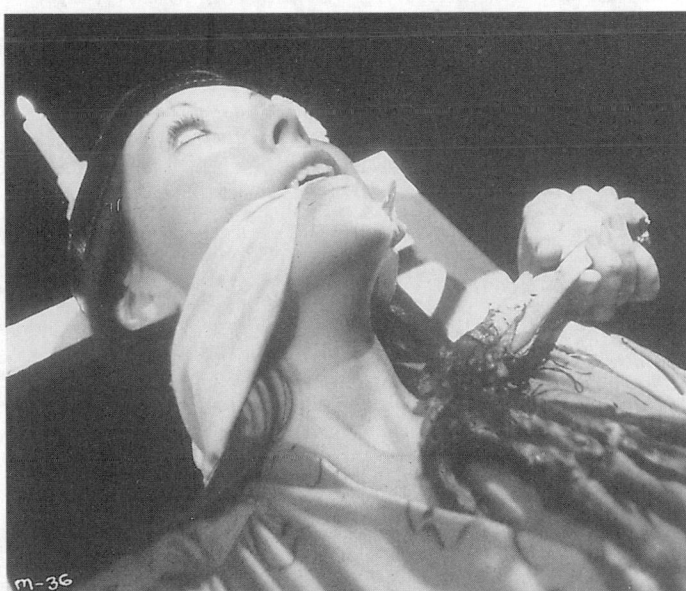
Midnight: MAURA MINTEER

Midnight
1989, (USA), SVS, color, 90 mins.
W: Lynn Redgrave, Tony Curtis, Steve Parrish, Rita Gam, Gustav Vintas, Karen Witter, Frank Gorshin, Wolfman Jack
WRIT & D: Norman Thaddeus Vane   **PHOTOG:** David Golia   **MUSIC:** Michael Wetherwax
Standard horror-comedy: Horror-show hostess has adventures

Midnight 2: Sex, Death and Videotape
1993, (USA), color, 70 mins.
W: Matthew Jason Walsh, Joe Norcia
D: John Russo
Minor thriller (sequel to 1980's **Midnight**)*: Only surviving memeber of crazed family stalks girl*

Midnight at Madame Tussaud's
1936, (GB), Premier Sound Films/Para, b&w, 66 mins.
W: Lucille Lisle (*Carol Cheyne*), James Carew (*Sir Clive Cheyne*), Charles Oliver (*Harry Newton*), Kim Peacock (*Nick Frome*), Patrick Barr (*Gerry Melville*),

Bernard Miles (*The Modeller*), Billy (*William*) Hartnell (*Stubbs*), Lydia Sherwood (*Brenda*)
D: George Pearson **SCR:** Roger MacDougall & Kim Peacock, from a story by James Edwards & Roger MacDougall
USA retitle, **Midnight at the Wax Museum**
Standard thriller: Attempted murder in Chamber of Horrors

Midnight Cabaret
1990, (USA), color, 94 mins.
W: Michael Des Barres, Thom Mathews, Carolyn Seymour, Lydie Denier, Leonard Termo, Norbert Weisser
D & SCR: Pece Dingo **MUSIC:** Michel Colombier
Minor horror-thriller: Satanic cult selects child actress to bear Devil's child

Midnight Faces
1926, (USA), b&w, 72 mins.
W: Francis X. Bushman, Jack Perrin, Kathryn McGuire
Standard thriller: Mystery in Florida bayou house

Midnight Fear
1990, (USA), color, 90 mins.
W: David Carradine, Craig Wasson, John Carradine
D: William Crain
Minor thriller: Killer skins woman alive

Midnight Girl
1925, (USA), Chadwick, b&w, 7 reels (6,300 ft./1920.2m)
W: Lila Lee (*Anna*), Gareth Hughes (*Don Harmon*), Dolores Cassinelli (*Nina*), Charlotte Walker (*Mrs. Schuyler*), Bela Lugosi (*Nicholas Schuyler*), John D. Walsh (*Victor*), William Harvey (*Nifty Louis*), Sidney Paxton (*Joe*), Signor N. Salerno (*The Manager*)
D: Wilfred Noy **STORY:** Garrett Fort **ADAPT:** Wilfred Noy & Jean Conover **PHOTOG:** G.W. Bitzer & Frank Zukor
Standard melodrama: Beautiful Russian singer involved in American intrigue

The Midnight Hour
1985, (USA), Ervin Zavada/ABC Circle-TV, color, 92 mins.
W: Shari Belafonte-Harper (*Melissa Cavender*), LeVar Burton, Jonelle Allen, Peter DeLuise, Jonna Lee, Deedee Pfeiffer, Kevin McCarthy, Lee Montgomery, Cindy Morgan, Bill DeLand, Dick Van Patten, Mark Blankfield, Sheila Larken, Dennis Redfield, Wolfman Jack (*voice*)
D: Jack Bender **TELEPLAY:** Bill Bleich **PHOTOG:** Rexford Metz **SPCL-FX:** Jack Monroe **MUSIC:** Brad Fiedel **SONG:** *Get Dead*
TVM, minor horror-comedy: Halloween revelers unknowingly revive dead

Midnight in Saint Petersburg
1998, (GB), Harry Alan Towers, color
W: Michael Caine (*Harry Palmer*), Jason Connery (*Nick*), Tanya Jackson (*Tatiana*), Michelle Rene Thomas (*Brandy*), Michael Gambon (*Alex*), Michael Sarrazin, Serge Houde, Vlasta Vrana
D: Doug Jackson **SCR:** Peter Welbeck, from a novel by Len Deighton **PHOTOG:** Peter Benison **MUSIC:** Rick Wakeman
Standard thriller: Agent seeks stolen plutonium

Midnight Kiss
1993, (USA), color, 85 mins.
W: Michelle Owens, Gregory A. Greer
D: Joel Bender **SCR:** John Weidner & Ken Lamplugh
Standard horror-fantasy, Made-for-Video: Policewoman sets trap for vampire

Midnight Lace
1960, (USA), Ross Hunter-Arwin/Univ, color, 108 mins.
W: Doris Day (*Kit Preston*), Rex Harrison (*Anthony Preston*), Myrna Loy (*Aunt Bea*), John Gavin (*Brian Younger*), Herbert Marshall (*Charles Manning*), Roddy McDowall (*Malcolm*), John Williams (*Insp. Byrnes*), Doris Lloyd (*Nora*), Natasha Parry (*Peggy*), Anthony Dawson (*Roy Ash*), Hermione Baddeley (*Dora*), Richard Ney (*Daniel*), Richard Lupino (*Foster*), Rhys Williams (*Victor Elliott*), Hayden Rorke, Elspeth March, Peter Adams, Rex Evans
P: Ross Hunter & Martin Melcher **D:** David Miller **SCR:** Ben Roberts & Ivan Goff, from Janet Green's play *Mathilda Shouted Fire* **PHOTOG:** Russell Metty **MUSIC:** Frank Skinner
Well-produced thriller: American heiress in London threatened by assassin

Midnight Lace
1981, (USA), Four R./Univ/NBC-TV, color, 97 mins.
W: Mary Crosby (*Cathy Preston*), Gary Frank (*Brian Preston*), Celeste Holm (*Sylvia Randall*), Robin Clarke (*Craig Clinton*), Shecky Greene (*Lt. Sam Ackerman*), Susan Tyrrell (*Ann Galvan*), Carolyn Jones (*Dr. Bernadette Chase*), Missy Francis (*Young Cathy*), Marlena Amey (*Leslie Noonan*), Chris Caputo (*Artie Coleman*), David Castle (*The Engineer*), Brian Collins (*Vinnie DeNiseo*), DeForest Covan (*Fred*), Blackie Dammett (*Herman Laird*), Jim Haynie (*The S.W.A.T. Commander*), Sonny LaRocca (*The Technical Director*), Tony Lorea (*The M.C.*), William Marquez (*Det. Al Sanchez*), Michael Prince (*Dr. Irving Berman*), Joanne Nail (*Luana Smiley*), Charles Rowe (*The Anchorman*), Joseph Whipp (*The Detective*)
D: Ivan Nagy **TELEPLAY:** Jerry Ludwig, from Janet Green's play *Mathilda Shouted Fire* **PHOTOG:** Isidore Mankofsky **MUSIC:** Stu Phillips
TVM, standard thriller: Young heiress terrorized

The Midnight Mail
1915, (GB), Hepworth, b&w, 825 ft. (251.5m)
D: Warwick Buckland
Standard crime-thriller: Maid foils burglar

Midnight Movie Massacre
1990, (USA), color, 86 mins.
W: Robert Clarke, Ann Robinson
D: Mark Stock
Standard satirical thriller: Space alien vs. theater patrons

Midnight Mystery
1930, (USA), RKO, b&w, 7 reels (6,463 ft./1969.9m)
W: Betty Compson (*Sally Wayne*), Lowell Sherman (*Tom Austen*), Hugh Trevor (*Gregory Sloane*), Rita La Roy (*Madeline Austen*), Ivan Lebedeff (*Mischa Kawelin*), Raymond Hatton (*Paul Cooper*), Marcelle Corday (*Harriet Cooper*), June Clyde (*Louise Hollister*), Sidney D'Albrook (*Barker*), William P. Burt (*Rogers*)
D: George B. Seitz **ADAPT & DIALOG:** Beulah Marie Dix, from Howard Irving Young's 1929 play *Hawk Island* **PHOTOG:** Joseph Walker
Standard thriller: Murders in castle on Maine island

Midnight Offerings
1981, (USA), Stephen J. Cannell/Para-TV/ABC-TV, color, 95 mins.
W: Melissa Sue Anderson (*Vivian*), Mary McDonough (*Robin*), Patrick Cassidy (*Dave*), Marion Ross (*Emily Moore*), Gordon Jump (*Sherm*), Cathryn Damon (*Diane*), Ray Girardin (*Clausen*), Peter MacLean, Jack Garner, Dana Kimmell, Jeff MacKay, Kym Karath, Curt Ayers, Jack Bridges, Gary Dubin, Robin Klein, Loren Lister, Michael Morgan, Terry Wagner, Dean Wein, Dino Shorte, Vanna White
D: Rod Holcomb **TELEPLAY:** Juanita Bartlett **PHOTOG:** Hector Figueroa **SPCL-FX:** John Coles **MUSIC:** Walter Scharf
TVM, above-average fantasy-thriller: Schoolgirl witches in opposition

The Midnight Phantom
1935, (USA), b&w
W: Reginald Denny
Standard thriller: Bizarre murder at midnight lecture

Midnight Ride
1992, (USA), Ovidio G. Assonitis/Cannon, color, 95 mins.
W: Michael Dudikoff, Mark Hamill, Savina Gersak, Robert Mitchum, Pamela Ludwig, Timothy Brown, Kent Gregory
D: Robert Bralver **PHOTOG:** Roberto D'Ettore Piazzoli
Made-for-Video, standard thriller: Runaway wife meets psycho

Midnight's Child
1992, (USA), Lifetime, color, 95 mins.

A Midsummer Night's Dream: JAMES CAGNEY

W: Marcy Walker, Olivia D'Abo, Cotter Smith, Judy Parfitt, Elissabeth Moss, Jim Norton, Roxann Biggs, Mary Larkin
D: Colin Bucksey   **TELEPLAY:** David Chaskin   **PHOTOG:** Anthony B. Richmond   **MUSIC:** Richard Hartley
TVM, standard thriller: Au pair suspected of links to the netherworld

Midnight Confessions
1995, (USA), color, 98 mins.
W: David Millbern, Carol Hoyt, Julie Strain, Monique Parent, Richard Lynch
Standard thriller: Woman D.J. involved with serial killer

Midnight Tease
1994, (USA), color, 87 mins.
W: Cassandra Leigh, Rachel Reed, Edmund Halley, Ashlie Rhey, Todd Joseph
D: Scott Levy
Minor thriller: Killer slays strippers

Midnight Warning
1932, (USA), b&w, 63 mins.
W: William Boyd, Claudia Dell, Henry Hall, Hooper Atchley, John Harron
D: Spencer G. Bennet
*remade (1952) as **Son Long at the Fair***
Standard thriller: Woman's brother disappears at 1893 World's Fair

A Midsummer Night's Dream
1935, (USA), WB, b&w, 132 mins, also 117 mins.
W: James Cagney (*Bottom*), Anita Louise (*Titania*), Victor Jory (*Oberon*), Hugh Herbert (*Snout*), Frank McHugh (*Quince*), Joe E. Brown (*Flute*), Olivia de Havilland (*Hermia*), Dick Powell (*Lysander*), Ross Alexander (*Demetrius*), Jean Muir (*Helena*), Verree Teasdale (*Hippolyta, the Queen of the Amazons*), Mickey Rooney (*Puck*), Otis Harlan (*Starveling*), Ian Hunter (*Theseus*), Grant Mitchell (*Egeus*), Arthur Treacher (*Ninny's Tomb*), Nini Theilade (*The Prima Ballerina Fairy*), Dewey Robinson (*Snug*), Hobart Cavanaugh (*Philostrate*), Helen Westcott (*Cobweb*), Fred Sale (*Moth*), Billy Barty (*Mustard Seed*), Katherine Frey (*Peace-Blossom*), Kenneth Anger (*Boy*)
D: Max Reinhardt & William Dieterle   **SCR:** Charles Kenyon & Mary C. McCall Jr. , from Shakespeare's play   **PHOTOG:** Hal Mohr   **MUSIC:** Jakob Ludwig Felix Mendelssohn, arranged by Erich Wolfgang Korngold
ballet trained by Bronislava Nijinska
Opulent fantasy: Mortals mix with fairies. De Havilland's debut

A Midsummer Night's Dream
1959, (Czech), Showcorporation, color, 77 mins.
CREATED & DESIGNED: Jiri Trinka   **ADAPT & DIR:** Howard Sackler   **NARRATOR:** Richard Burton
Unusual fantasy (winner, Cannes Festival Grand Prix): King and Queen of fairies involved in lives of mortals

A Midsummer Night's Dream
1985, (GB-Sp), Cabochon/Television Espanola/Channel 4/Mainline, color, 78 mins.
W: Lindsay Kemp (*Puck*), Manuela Vargas (*Hippolyta*), Incredible Orlando (*Titania*), Michael Matou (*Oberon*), Neil Caplan (*Theseus/ Beast*), Francois Testory (*Snout/Tree/Changeling*), David Meyer (*Lysander*), Annie Huckle (*Hermia*), David Haughton (*Demetrius*), Christian Michaelson (*Flute/Juliet*), Jose Luis Aguirre (*Quince*), Javier Sanz (*Starveling/Moon*), Cheryl Hazelwood (*Helena*), Douglas McNicol (*The Fairy*), Atlio Lopez (*Bottom/Romeo*), Kevin L'Anglaise (*Snug/ Lion*), Carlos Miranda (*The Accordionist*)
P: Miguel Campos   **D:** Celestino Coronado, Lindsay Kemp & David Haughton, from William Shakespeare's play   **PHOTOG:** Peter Middleton   **MUSIC:** Carlos Miranda
TVM (also shown theatrically), standard fantasy: Fairy king's mischievous sprite mixes up affections of two couples

Mifanwy—A Tragedy
1913, (GB), Ivy Close Films/Hepworth, b&w, 675 ft. (205.7m)
W: Ivy Close (*Mifanwy*)
WRIT & D: Elwin Neame
Standard romance: Girl dreams dead fisherman calls her

Mighty Colossus
*see **Colossus: The Forbin Project***

The Mighty Gorga
1969, (USA), American General, color, 83 mins
W: Anthony Eisley, Scott Brady, Kent Taylor
P: Robert O'Neil & David Hewitt   **D:** David L. Hewitt   **SCR:** Joan Hewitt & David Prentiss
Minor adventure-thriller: Researchers find 50-ton gorilla

Mighty Joe Young
1949, (USA), RKO, b&w, 94 mins.
W: Terry Moore (*Jill Young*), Ben Johnson (*Gregg Johnson*), Robert Armstrong (*Max O'Hara*), Frank McHugh (*Windy*), Regis Toomey, Douglas Fowley, Nestor Paiva, James Flavin, Denis Green, Irene Ryan, Lora Lee Michel, Paul Guilfoyle, Primo Carnera, Ellen Corby
P: John Ford & Merian C. Cooper   **D:** Ernest B. Schoedsack   **SCR:** Ruth Rose   **PHOTOG:** J. Roy Hunt   **SPCL-FX:** Harold Stine   **TECH-FX:** Willis O'Brien (assisted by Ray Harryhausen)   **MUSIC:** Roy Webb
*A.k.a. **Mr. Joseph Young of Africa***

*Well-made fantasy-thriller: Giant gorilla exploited by show-biz mogul, Remade 1998. cf. **The Black Scorpion, Gwangi** and **The Valley of Gwangi***

Mighty Joe Young
1998, (USA), Walt Disney, color, 114 mins.
W: Bill Paxton, Charlize Theron, David Paymer, Regina King, Rade Serbegia, Jill Puri, Terry Moore
D: Ron Underwood   **MUSIC:** James Horner
Standard juvenile thriller (remake of classic): Big ape brought to USA

Mighty Morphin Power Rangers
1995, (USA), Saban Entertainment-Toei/20th-Fox, color, 88 mins.
W: Karan Ashley, Johnny Yong Bosch, Steve Cardenas, Jason David Frank, Amy Jo Johnson, David Yost, Jason Narvy, Paul Schrier, Paul Freeman, Stephen Antonio Cardenas
P: Haim Saban, Shuki Levy & Suzanne Todd   **D:** Bryan Spicer   **SCR:** Arne Olsen   **STORY:** John Kamps & Arne Olsen   **PHOTOG:** Paul Murphy   **MUSIC:** Graeme Revell   **MUSIC SPRVSR:** Happy Walters
Standard SF-fantasy: Six teens become superheroes

The Mighty Peking Man
*see **Goliathon***

Mighty Ursus
1961, (It-Sp), UA, color, 92 mins.
W: Ed Fury (*Ursus*), Moira Orfei, Cristina Gajoni, Soledad Miranda, Luis Prendes
D: Carlo Campogalliani
Minor "Sword & Sandal": Muscleman seeks abducted mate

Mike and the Miser
1916, (GB), Martin/DFSA, b&w, 569 ft. (173.4m)
W: Tom Morriss (*Mike Murphy*)
D: Dave Aylott
Standard comedy-fantasy: Tramp robs miser and is chased by barrel, fairy, policeman, etc.

Mike and the Zeppelin Raid
1915, (GB), Martin/DFSA, b&w, 593 ft. (180.7m)
D: Dave Aylott
Stadard fantasy: Tramp dreams of destroying airship fleet

Mike Murphy's Dream of Love and Riches
1914, (GB), Martin Films/DFSA, b&w, 593 ft. (180.7m)
W: Ernie Westo (*Mike Murphy*)
D: Dave Aylott
*reissued (1915) as **Murphy's Millions***
Standard comedy-fantasy: Tramp dreams he is duke and saves rich girl from ruffians

Mike Murphy's Dream of the Wild West
1914, (GB), Martin Films/DFSA, b&w, 539 ft. (164.3m)
W: Ernie Westo (*Mike Murphy*)
D: Dave Aylott
Standard comedy-fantasy: Tramp dreams he rescues girl from Indians

Milczaca Gwiazda (The Silent Star)
1959, (Pol-E. Ger), Film Polski-DEFA/Crown-Int'l, color, 109 mins. (USA release, 78 mins.)
W: Yoko Tani, Oldrich Lukes, Ignacy Machowski, Michail N. Postnikov, Lucina Winnicka, Julius Ongewe, Gunther Simon, Tang-Hua-Ta, Eva-Maria Hagen, Omega the Robot
D: Kurt Maetzig   **SCR:** J. Barckhausen, J. Fethke, W. Kohlaase, Kurt Maetzig, G. Reisch, G. Rucker & A. Stenbock-Fermor, based on Stanislaw Lem's novel *Astronauci* (published in Germany as *Planet of the Dead*)   **PHOTOG:** Joachim Hasler   **SPCL-FX:** Ernst Kunstmann, Vera Kunstmann, Jan Olejiniczak & Helmut Grewald   **MUSIC:** Andrzej Markowski
*USA retitle, **First Spaceship on Venus**, A.k.a. **(Europe) Spaceship Venus Does Not Reply**, USA release, 1962*
Ambitious Euro-SF: First manned Venus probe finds chaos

Les Mille et une Filles de Bagdad
*see **Babes in Bagdad***

Millennium
1989, (Can), Gladden/20th-Fox, color, 108 mins.
W: Kris Kristofferson (*Bill Smith*), Cheryl Ladd (*Louise Baltimore*), Daniel J. Travanti (*Arnold Mayer*), Robert Joy (*Sherman*), Lloyd Bochner (*Walters*), Brent Carver (*Coventry*), David McIlwraith (*Tom Stanley*), Lawrence Dane (*Vern Rockwell*), Maury Chaykin (*Roger Keane*), Thomas Hauff (*Ron Kennedy*), Al Waxman (*Dr. Brindle*), Peter Dvorsky (*Janz*), Raymond O'Neill (*Harold Davis*), Philip Akin (*Briley*), David Calderisi (*Leacock*), Gary Reineke (*Carpenter*), Eugene Clark (*Craig Ashby*), Cedric Smith (*Eli Seibel*), Michael J. Reynolds (*Jerry Bannister*), Victoria Snow (*Pinky Djakarta*), Susannah Hoffman (*Susan Melbourne*), Claudette Roach (*Inez Manila*), Barry Meier (*The Helicopter Pilot*), James Kirchner (*The Foreman*), Bill MacDon-ald, Jamie Shannon, Leonard Chow, Timothy Webber, Chapelle Jaffe, Christopher Britton, Gerry Quigley, Scott Thompson, John Kozak, James Mainprize, Daryl Shuttleworth, Bob Bainborough, Gerard Theoret, Edward Roy, Debbie Kirby, John Stoneham, Linda Goranson, Mark Terene, Syd Libman, Patrick Young, Paula Barrett, Cordelia Strube, Richard Fitzpatrick, Reg Dreger, Marvin Caron, David Bolt, Maida Rogerson, Jank Azman, Kevin

Fullam
D: Michael Anderson   **SCR:** John Varley, from his short story "Air Raid"
   PHOTOG: Rene Ohashi   **MUSIC:** Eric N. Robertson
Engrossing SF-adventure: Time-travelers try to mend glitch in continuum

The Millerson Case
1947, (USA), Col, b&w, 72 mins.
W: Warner Baxter (*Dr. Robert Ordway*), Nancy Saunders (*Belle Englehart*), Clem
   Bevans (*Sheriff Akers*), Griff Barnett (*Dr. Sam Millerson*), Paul Guilfoyle (*Jud
   Rookstool*), James Bell (*Ezra Minnich*), Addison Richards (*Dr. Wickersham*),
   Russell Simpson (*Squire Tuttle*), Mark Dennis (*Bye Minnich*), Robert Stevens
   (*Dr. Prescott*), Eddie Parker (*Lt. Callahan*), Sarah Padden (*Emma Millerson*),
   Victor Potel (*Hank Nixon*), Barbara Pepper (*Eadie Rookstool*), Frances Morris
   (*Ella Min-nich*), Eddy Waller (*Jeremiah Dobbs*)
D: George Archainbaud   **SCR:** Gordon Rigby, Carlton Sand & Raymond L.
   Schrock   from characters created by Max Marcin   **PHOTOG:** Philip
   Tannura   **MUSIC:** Mischa Bakaleinikoff
working title, **Crime Doctor's Vacation**
Standard "Crime Doctor" thriller: Psychiatrist finds typhoid epidemic used to mask murder

The Mill Girl
1913, (GB), Hepworth, b&w, 845 ft. (283m)
W: Alma Taylor (*Lizzie*), Harry Royston (*The Foreman*), Jack Hulcup (*Softy*)
D: Warwick Buckland
Standard crime-thriller: Foreman frames millgirl for theft

Million B.C.
1918, (USA), Manikin/Edison, b&w, 5 mins.
CONCEIVED & EXECUTED: Willis O'Brien
Standard fantasy short: Life in prehistoric times

The $1,000,000 Duck
1971, (USA), Walt Disney, color, 92 mins.
W: Dean Jones (*Prof. Albert Dooley*), Sandy Duncan (*Katie Dooley*), Joe Flynn
   (*Finley Hooper*), Tony Roberts (*Fred Hines*), James Gregory (*Rutledge*), Lee
   Harcourt Montgomery (*Jimmy Dooley*), Jack Kruschen (*Dr. Gottlieb*), Virginia
   Vincent (*Eunice Hooper*), Jack Bender (*Arvin Wadlow*), Ted Jordan (*Mr.
   Forbes*), Billy Bowles (*Orlo Wadlow*), Sammy Jackson (*Frisby*), Arthur
   Hunnicutt (*Mr. Purdham*), Frank Wilcox (*The Bank Manager*), Pete
   Renoudet (*Mr. Beckert*), Neil Russell (*Mr. Smith*), Bryan O'Byrne (*The Bank
   Teller*), Frank Cady (*The Assayer*), George O'Hanlon (*The Parking Attendant*),
   Jonathan Daly (*The Purchasing Agent*), Hal Smith (*The Courthouse Guard*),
   Edward Andrews (*Morgan*)
SCR: Roswell Rogers, from a story by Ted Key   **PHOTOG:** William Snyder
   MUSIC: Buddy Baker

Million Dollar Mystery
1927, (USA), b&w
Minor thriller: Old house, secret society, missing money

The Million Eyes of Sumuru
1966, (GB), Anglo-Amalgamated/AIP, color, 95 mins.
W: Frankie Avalon (*Tommy Carter*), George Nader (*Nick West*), Shirley Eaton
   (*Sumuru*), Wilfrid Hyde-White (*Col. Baisbrook*), Klaus Kinski (*Pres. Boong*),
   Maria Rohm (*Helga*), Krista Nell (*Zoe*), Patti Chandler (*Louise*), Ursula
   Rank (*Erna*), Salli Sachse (*Mikki*), Paul Chang (*Insp. Koo*), Essie Huang
   (*Kitty*), Jon Fong (*Col. Medika*), Denise Davreux, Mary Cheng, Margaret
   Cheung, Jill Hamilton, Lisa Gray, Christine Lok, Louise Lee
P: Harry Alan Towers   **D:** Lindsay Shonteff   **SCR:** Kevin Kavanagh   **ORIG.
   STORY:** Peter Welbeck [Harry Alan Towers], from Sax Rohmer's stories
   PHOTOG: Norman Williams   **MUSIC:** John Scott
A.k.a. **Sumuru**
Standard action-thriller: American agents uncover society of sinister females. cf. **Rio 70**

Mill of the Stone Women
see **Il Mullino della Donne di Pietra**

The Milpitas Monster
1975, (USA), color, 80 mins.
W: Doug Hagdahl, Scott A. Henderson, Scott Parker
D: Robert L. Burrill
Minor SF-horror: Waste dump spawns weird creature

The Mind Benders
1963, (GB), Novus/AIP, b&w, 113 mins.
W: Dirk Bogarde (*Dr. Henry Longman*), Mary Ure (*Oonagh Longman*), John
   Clements (*Maj. Hall*), Michael Bryant (*Dr. Tate*), Wendy Craig (*Annabelle*),
   Harold Goldblatt (*Prof. Sharpey*), Geoffrey Keen (*Calder*), Terry Palmer
   (*Norman*), Norman Bird (*Aubrey*), Edward Fox, Roger Delgado, Terence
   Alexander
P: Michael Relph   **D:** Basil Dearden   **SCR:** James Kennaway   **PHOTOG:**
   Denys Coop   **MUSIC:** Georges Auric
orig. to be titled **The Pit**
Unusual thriller: Sensory-deprivation experiments go awry

Mind Benders (1987)
see **Alien High**

Mindfield

1989, (Can), color, 91 mins.
W: Michael Ironside, Lisa Langlois, Christopher Plummer, Stefan Wodoslowsky,
   Sean McCann
D: Jean-Claude Lord
Minor SF-thriller: CIA conducts mind-control experiments on innocent man

Mind Games (1981)
see **Agency**

Mind Games
1989, (USA), color, 93 mins.
W: Edward Albert Jr., Shawn Weatherly, Matt Norero, Maxwell Caulfield
D: Bob Yari
Standard thriller: Young couple picks up hitchhiker, a deranged psychology student

Mind Games
1998, (USA), ABC-TV, color, 95 mins.
W: Jayne Brook, Lindsay Frost, Kyle Secor, William Greenblatt (*Luke Berrick*),
   Hayley Lochner (*Amy Berrick*), Marnie McPhail (*Cora*)
TVM, minor thriller

Mind Killer
1987, (USA), color, 86 mins.
W: Joe McDonald, Christopher Wade, Shirley Ross, Kevin Hart
D: Michael Krueger
Minor horror-satire: Strange manuscript affects nerdy librarian

The Mind of Mr. Reeder
1939, (GB), Grand Nat'l, b&w, 75 mins.
W: Will Fyffe (*J.G. Reeder*), Kay Walsh (*Peggy Gillette*), George Curzon (*Welford*),
   Chili Bouchier (*Elsa Welford*), John Warwick (*Ted Bracher*), Lesley Wareing
   (*Mrs. Gaylor*), Romilly Lunge (*Insp. Gaylor*), Derek Gorst (*Langdon*), Ronald
   Shiner (*Sam Hackett*), George Hayes (*Brady*), Wally Patch (*Lomer*), Betty
   Astell (*The Barmaid*)
D: Jack Raymond   **SCR:** Bryan Edgar Wallace, Marjorie Gaffney & Michael
   Hogan, from Edgar Wallace's novel
released in USA (1940) as **The Mysterious Mr. Reeder** *(Monogram), reissued 1943*
Standard thriller (3rd "J.G. Reeder" mystery): Inspector cleans up gang of counterfeiters

The Mind of Mr. Soames
1970, (GB), Amicus/Col, color, 98 mins.
W: Terence Stamp (*John Soames*), Robert Vaughn (*Dr. Michael Bergen*), Nigel
   Davenport (*Dr. Maitland*), Donal Donnelly (*Dr. Joe Allan*), Christian
   Roberts (*Thomas Fleming*), Scott Forbes (*Richard Bannerman*), Norman Jones
   (*Davis*), Dan Jackson (*Nicholls*), Vickery Turner (*Naomi*), Judy Parfitt (*Jenny
   Bannerman*), Joe McPartland (*Insp. Moore*), Pamela Moseiwitsch (*The Girl on
   the Train*), Billy Cornelius (*Sgt. Clifford*), Esmond Webb (*The Ticket Seller*),
   Jon Croft (*The Guard*), Bill Pilkington (*The Pub Owner*), Kate Bimchy (*The
   Barmaid*), Tony Caunter (*The Schoolteacher*), Joe Gladwin (*The Old Man in
   Car*), Eric Brooks (*The TV Floor Manager*)
P: Max Rosenberg & Milton Subotsky   **D:** Alan Cooke   **SCR:** John Hale &
   Edward Simpson, from a novel by Charles Eric Maine   **PHOTOG:** Billy
   Williams   **MUSIC:** Michael Dress
Unusual thriller: 30-year-old man revives after spending entire life in coma

Mind Over Murder
1979, (USA), CBS-TV, color, 95 mins.
W: Deborah Raffin (*Suzy*), David Ackroyd (*Ben*), Bruce Davison (*Jason*), Andrew
   Prine (*The Bald Man*), Christopher Cary (*John Povey*), Robert Englund (*Ted*),
   Carl Anderson (*Baker*), Penelope Willis (*Pierce*), Wayne Heffley (*Lt. Wales*),
   Paul Reid Roman (*Arnold*), Jan Burrell (*Mrs. Winterspoon*), Jack Griffin (*The
   Cameraman*), Paul Lukather (*Capt. Moran*), Don Ray Hall (*The Reporter*), Rex
   Riley (*Anderson*), Lanny Duncan (*The Cab Driver*), Clint Young (*Mr.
   Glazier*), Michael Horsley (*The Rookie*), Linda Ryan (*The Young Woman*),
   Amy Allen Karr (*The Receptionist*), Craig Baxley (*Bobby*), Lenny Geer (*The
   Derelict*), Natalija Nogulich (*The Girl*), Richard Winterstein (*The Bus
   Driver*)
D: Ivan Nagy   **TELEPLAY:** Robert Carrington   **PHOTOG:** Dennis Dalzell
   MUSIC: Paul Chihara
TVM, standard thriller: Psychic woman detects mad killer

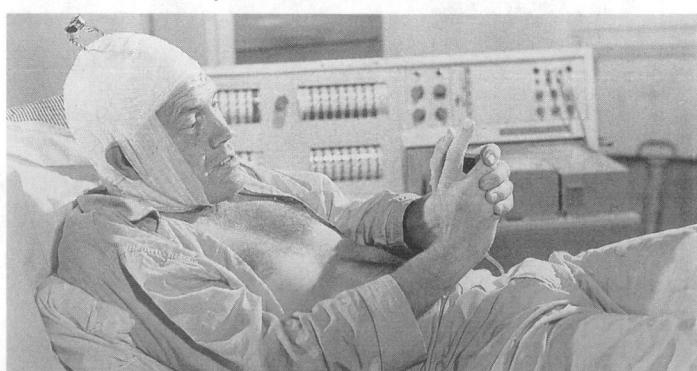
The Mind Snatchers: RONNY COX

The Mind Reader

1933, (USA), WB, b&w, 69 mins.
W: Warren William (*Chandra*), Constance Cummings (*Sylvia*), Allen Jenkins (*Frank*), Natalie Moorhead (*Mrs. Austin*), Mayo Methot (*Jenny*), Earle Fox (*Don*), Clarence Muse (*Sam*)
D: Roy Del Ruth   SCR: Robert Lord & Wilson Mizner   BASED ON: a play by Vivian Cosby   PHOTOG: Sol Polito
Standard melodrama: Fake clairvoyant distresses

Mind Ripper

see Wes Craven Presents Mind Ripper

The Mind Snatchers

1972, (GB-W. Ger), Int'l Film Ventures/CRC, color, 94 mins.
W: Ronny Cox (*Miles*), Christopher Walken (*Reese*), Ralph Meeker (*The Major*), Joss Ackland (*Dr. Frederick*), Marco St. John (*The Orderly*), Bette Henritze (*Anna Kraus*), Tom Aldredge (*The Medic*), Susan Travers (*Nurse Schroeder*), Claus Nissen (*The Psychiatrist*), Birthe Newmann (*Lisa*)
P: George Goodman   D: Bernard Girard   SCR: Ron Whyte, from Dennis Reardon's play *The Happiness Cage* (original title)   PHOTOG: Manny Wynn   MUSIC: Phil Ramone
Standard thriller: Military hospital's unorthodox sense stimulation experiments

Mind Twister

1993, (USA), color, 87 mins.(unrated, 94 mins.)
W: Telly Savalas, Gary Hudson, Richard Roundtree, Suzanne Slater, Erica Nann
D: Fred Olen Ray
Minor eroto-thriller: Police detective trails sadistic killer

Mind Warp

1972, (USA), color, 92 mins.
W: James Best, Barbara Burgess, Gil Peterson, Gerald McRaney, Marcus J. Grapes, Doug Collins, Anne Latham
D: Joy Houck Jr.
A.k.a. **Grey Mateer** *and* **The Brain Machine**
Minor SF-thriller: Future society controls minds of citizens

Mindwarp

1990, (USA), Fangoria, color, 92 mins.
W: Bruce Campbell (*Stover*), Angus Scrimm (*The Seer*), Marta Alicia (*Judy*)
D: Steve Barnett
Standard SF-thriller: Post-nuke girl flees underground city

Ministry of Fear

1944, (USA), Para, b&w, 84 mins.
W: Ray Milland, Marjorie Reynolds, Carl Esmond, Dan Duryea, Hillary Brooke, Alan Napier, Erskine Sanford, Percy Waram
D: Fritz Lang   SCR: Seton I. Miller, from Graham Greene's novel   PHOTOG: Henry Sharp   MUSIC: Victor Young
Standard thriller: Man accidentally involved with Nazis

Mini Weekend

1967, (GB), Global/Tigon, b&w, 79 mins.
W: Anthony Trent (*Tom*), Veronica Lang (*Jenny*), Anna Palk (*The Girl in Tiles*), Liza Rogers (*Sandra*), Karen Leslie (*The Girl in the Pub*), Connie Fraser (*Mother*), Nina Dwyer (*The Girl on the Bus*), Valerie Stanton (*The Girl in the Shop*), Eve Aubrey (*The Hag*), Vicky Hodge (*The Girl in the Dream*)
P: Tony Tenser   D: Georges Robin   STORY: Georges Robin & Tony Tenser
Minor eroto-fantasy: Man lives dream existence with girls he sees in street

Minority Report

2000, (USA), Amblin/Univ, color
W: Tom Cruise
D: Steven Spielberg
Unusual thriller

The Minotaur

1961, (It), UA, color, 92 mins.
W: Bob Mathias (*Theseus*), Rosanna Schiaffino (*Ariadne*), Alberto Lupo, Rick Battaglia, Nerio Bernardi, Nico Pepe, Tiziana Casetti, Paul Muller, Carlo Tamberlani, Susanne Loret, Tina Lattanzi, Alberto Plebani
P: Giorgio Agliani, Dino Mordini & Rudolphe Solmsen   D: Silvio Amadio   SCR: S. Continenza, J.P. Callegari & Daniel Mainwaring   PHOTOG: Aldo Giordani   MUSIC: Carlo Rustichelli
A.k.a. The Wild Beast of Crete and Teseo Contro il Minotauro (Theseus vs. the Minotaur)
Standard myth-adventure: Greek hero battles Cretan monster

The Miracle (1948)

see Il Miracolo

The Miracle

1959, (USA), WB, color, 121 mins.
W: Carroll Baker, Roger Moore, Walter Slezak, Dennis King, Vittorio Gassman, Katina Paxinou, Torin Thatcher, Gustavo Rojo, Carlos Rivas, Isobel Elsom, Eduard Franz, Lester Matthews, Daria Massey
P: Henry Blanke   D: Irving Rapper   SCR: Frank Butler, from Karl Vollmoeller's play, based on, Max Reinhardt's stage spectacle   PHOTOG: Ernest Haller

MUSIC: Elmer Bernstein
Lavish romance-fantasy: Statue of Virgin comes to life, takes place of renegade postulant

Miracle Beach

1992, (USA), color, 87 mins.
W: Ami Dolenz, Martin Mull, Pat Morita, Felicity Waterman, Dean Cameron
Standard fantasy: Genie falls in love with new master

Miracle in Milan

1951, (It), Joseph Burstyn, b&w, 96 mins.
W: Branduani Gianni (*Little Toto, age 11*), Paolo Stoppa (*The Bad Rappi*), Francesco Golisano (*The Good Toto*), Emma Gramatica (*The Old Lolatta*), Guglielmo Barnabo (*The Rich Man*), Brunella Bovo (*The Little Edvige*), Alba Arnova (*The Statue*), Anna Carena (*Signora Altezzosa*), Virgilio Riento (*The Sergeant*), Flora Cambi (*The Unhappy Sweetheart*), Arturo Bragaglia (*Alfredo*), Ermino Spalla (*Gaetano*), Angelo Prioli (*The 1st Commander*), Francesco Rissone (*The 2nd Commander*), Riccardo Bertazzolo (*The Wrestler*)
D: Vittorio De Sica   SCR: Cesare Zavattini   PHOTOG: G.R. Aldo   MUSIC: Alessandro Cicognini
Classic fantasy

The Miracle Man

1919, (USA), Para-Artcraft, b&w, 9 reels
W: Lon Chaney Sr., Thomas Meighan, Betty Compson, Joseph Dowling, Ruby Lafayette, Lucille Hutton, Frankie Lee, W. Lawson Butt, J.M. Dumont
D: George Tucker
Unusual melodrama (Chaney Sr.'s first great film role): Contortionist fakes amazing cures for phony faith healer

The Miracle Man

1932, (USA), Para, b&w, 85 mins
W: Chester Morris, Sylvia Sidney, Irving Pichel, Boris Karloff
D: Norman Z. McLeod   SCR: Waldemar Young & Samuel Hoffenstein
Standard thriller (remake of Chaney film): Crooks employ "faith healer," witness real miracle

Miracle Mile

1988, (USA), Ilemdale, color, 88 mins.
W: Anthony Edwards (*Harry Washello*), Mare Winningham (*Julie Peters*), John Agar (*Ivan Peters*), Mykel T. Williamson (*Wilson*), Lou Hancock (*Lucy Peters*), Kelly Minter (*Charlotta*), Kurt Fuller, Denise Crosby, Robert DoQui, O-Lan Jones, Earl Boen, Claude Earl Jones, Alan Rosenberg, Diane Delano, Jose Mercado, Danny De La Paz, Alan Berger, Howard Swain, Edward Bunker, Raphael Sbarge, Lucille Bliss, Chad Taylor, Herbert Fair, Cynthia Phillips, Brian Thompson, Tina Webster, Kirby Tepper, Jenette Goldstein, Victoria Powells, Alan Dillard, Jordana Capra, Bruce Hayes, Rickie Diggs, Peter Berg, Chloe Amateau
WRIT & D: Steve DeJarnatt   PHOTOG: Theo Van de Sande   SPCL-FX COORD: Robbie Knott   MUSIC: Tangerine Dream
Engrossing SF-thriller: Los Angeles faces nuclear holocaust

Miracle on 34th Street

1947, (USA), 20th-Fox, b&w, 96 mins.
W: Maureen O'Hara, John Payne, Edmund Gwenn ("*Santa Claus*"), Natalie Wood, Gene Lockhart, Jerome Cowan, William Frawley, Thelma Ritter, Porter Hall, Philip Tonge, Jack Albertson, Shirley O'Hara
P: William Perlberg   WRIT & D: George Seaton, from a story by Valentine Davies   PHOTOG: Charles G. Clarke & Lloyd Aherne   MUSIC: Cyril J. Mockridge
A.k.a. The Big Heart Oscar winner, Edmund Gwenn, Best Supporting Actor
Classic Xmas fantasy: Department-store Santa claims to be real article

Miracle on 34th Street

1973, (USA), CBS-TV, color, 100 mins.
W: Jane Alexander, Sebastian Cabot ("*Santa Claus*"), David Hartman, Suzanne Davidson, Roddy McDowall, James Gregory, Tom Bosley, David Doyle, Jim Backus, Roland Winters, Liam Dunn, Ellen Weston
P: Norman Rosemont   D: Fielder Cook   TELEPLAY: Jeb Rosebrook, from a story by Valentine Davies   PHOTOG: Earl Rath   MUSIC: Sid Ramin   SONGS: Miracles & Open Your Eyes and Dream
TVM, minor fantasy: Little girl meets real Santa

Miracle on 34th Street

1994, (USA), John Hughes/20th-Fox, color, 114 mins
W: Sir Richard Attenborough, Elizabeth Perkins, Dylan McDermott, Mara Wilson, James Remar, J.T. Walsh, Robert Prosky
D: Les Mayfield   SCR: George Seaton & John Hughes, from a story by Valentine Davies   PHOTOG: Julio Macat   MUSIC: Bruce Broughton
Standard fantasy: Reality of Santa Claus debated

Miracles Do Happen

1938, (GB), George Smith Enterprises/Univ, b&w, 59 mins.
W: Jack Hobbs (*Barry Strangeways*), Marjorie Taylor (*Peggy*), Bruce Seton (*Rodney*), George Carney (*Greenlaw*), Aubrey Mallalieu (*Prof. Gilmore*), Antony Holles (*The Proctor*), Molly Hamley-Clifford (*Mrs. Greenlaw*)
D: Maclean Rogers   SCR: Kathleen Butler, from a story by Con West & Jack Marks
Standard SF-comedy: Professor's nephew seeks backing for artificial milk

M

Les Miracles du Brahmane (Miracles of the Brahmin)
1900, (Fr), Star, b&w, 80m (262.5 ft./4.4 mins.)
D: Georges Melies
Standard fantasy

Miracles for Sale
1939, (USA), MGM, b&w, 71 mins.
W: Robert Young, Florence Rice, Astrid Allwyn, Henry Hull, Gloria Holden,
   Frank Craven, Lee Bowman, William Demarest, Cliff Clark, Frederick
   Worlock
D: Tod Browning   SCR: Harry Ruskin, James E. Grant & Marion Parsonnet
PHOTOG: Charles Lawton Jr.
*Standard thriller (Tod Browning's last feature film): Murder and fake seances investigated
by magician-detective*

Miracles of Creation
see Wunder der Schopfung

Miracles of the Brahmin
see Les Miracles du Brahmane

Un Miracle Sous l'Inquisition (A Miracle Under the Inquisition)
1904, (Fr), Star, b&w, 44m (144.4 ft./2.4 mins.)
D: Georges Melies
Standard thriller: Chaste woman burned at stake

A Miracle Under the Inquisition
see Un Miracle Sous l'Inquisition

Il Miracolo (The Miracle)
1948, (It-Fr), Joseph Burstyrt, b&w
W: Anna Magnani (*Nanni*), Federico Fellini (*The Stranger*)
D: Roberto Rossellini   SCR: Roberto Rossellini & Tullio Pinelli, from a story by
   Federico Fellini
Standard fantasy. Episodes of Ways of Love, 121 mins.

The Miraculous Rose-Tree
see Le Rosier Miraculeux

Miranda
1948, (GB), Gainsborough/GFD/Eagle Lion, b&w, 80 mins.
W: Glynis Johns (*Miranda*), Googie Withers (*Clare Marten*), Griffith Jones (*Paul
   Marten*), John McCallum (*Nigel Hood*), David Tomlinson (*Charles*), Margaret
   Rutherford (*Nurse Cary*), Yvonne Owen (*Betty*), Sonia Holm (*Isobel*), Maurice
   Denham (*The Cockle Man*), Brian Oulton (*Manell*), Zena Marshall (*The
   Secretary*), Charles Penrose (*The Stage Manager*)
P: Betty Box   D: Ken Annakin   SCR: Peter Blackmore & Denis Waldock, from
   a play by Peter Blackmore   PHOTOG: Ray Elton   MUSIC: Temple
   Abady
Amusing fantasy: Mermaid exposed to world of humans. cf. **Mad About Men**

Mirage
1965, (USA), Univ, b&w, 109 mins.
W: Gregory Peck (*David*), Diane Baker (*Shela*), Walter Matthau (*Ted Caselle*),
   Kevin McCarthy (*Josephson*), Leif Erickson (*Maj. Crawford*), Jack Weston
   (*Lester*), George Kennedy (*Willard*), Walter Abel (*Calvin*), Robert H. Harris
   (*Dr. Broden*), Anne Seymour (*Frances*), House B. Jameson (*Bo*), Hari Rhodes
   (*Lt. Franken*), Syl Lamont (*Benny*), Eileen Baral (*Irene*), Neil Fitzgerald (*Joe
   Turtle*), Franklin E. Cover (*The Group Leader*)
D: Edward Dmytryk   SCR: Peter Stone, from a story by Walter Ericson
   PHOTOG: Joseph Macdonald   MUSIC: Quincy Jones
Engrossig melodrama: Amnesiac caught in vortex of crime

Mirage
1995, (USA), color, 90 mins.
W: Edward James Olmos, Sean Young (*Jennifer/Shannon*)
*Made-for-Video, standard thriller (*Vertigo *redux): Ex-cop hired to protect man's wife*

Le Miroir de Cagliostro (Cagliostro's Mirror)
1899, (Fr), Star, b&w, 20m (65.6 ft./1.1 mins.)
D: Georges Melies
Standard fantasy

La Miroir de Venise, Ou le Mesaventures de Shylock (The Venetian Mirror, or the Misadventures of Shylock
1905, (Fr), Star, b&w, 66m (198.2 ft.)
D: Georges Melies
Standard fantasy

Miroir de la Vie
see Astrologie

The Mirror and Markheim
1954, (GB), Motley/Exclusive, b&w, 28 mins.
W: Philip Saville (*Markheim*), Arthur Lowe (*Arthur Henry*), Christopher Lee
   (*Visitant*), Lloyd Lamble (*Kelly*), Ruth Sheil (*The Maid*)
P: Norman Williams   D & SCR: John Lamont, from a story by Robert Louis
   Stevenson

*Standard short fantasy: Mirror figure shows man what would happen if he stabbed antique
dealer*

The Mirror Crack'd
1980, (GB), John Brabourne-Richard Goodwin/EMI/AFD, color, 105 mins.
W: Elizabeth Taylor (*Marina*), Angela Lansbury (*Miss Marple*), Rock Hudson
   (*Jason Rudd*), Kim Novak (*Lola Webster*), Edward Fox (*Dermot*), Tony Curtis
   (*The Producer*), Charles Gray (*Edwards*), Margaret Courtenay (*Mrs. Bantry*),
   Wendy Morgan (*Cherry*), Geraldine Chaplin (*Ella Zielinsky*), Maureen
   Bennett (*Heather Babcock*), Carolyn Pickles (*Miss Giles*), Charles Lloyd-Pack
   (*The Vicar*), Richard Pearson (*Dr. Haydock*), Anthony Steel (*Sir Derek
   Ridgeley*), Peter Woodthorpe (*The Scoutmaster*), Dinah Sheridan (*Lady
   Amanda*), Oriane Grieve (*Kate Ridgeley*), Kenneth Fortescue (*Charles
   Foxwell*), Hildegard Neil (*Lady Foxcroft*), Allan Cuthbertson (*Peter Montrose*),
   Nigel Stock (*Insp. Gates*), Eric Dodson (*The Major*), Pat Nye (*The Mayoress*),
   Marella Oppenheim (*Margot Bence*), George Silver (*DaSilva*), John Bennett
   (*Barnsby*)
D: Guy Hamilton   SCR: Jonathan Hales & Barry Sandler, from Agatha Christie's
   novel   PHOTOG: Christopher Challis   MUSIC: John Cameron
Standard thriller: Murder at English estate

The Mirror Has Three faces
see La Glace a Trois Faces

Mirror Images
1991, (USA), color, 95 mins.
W: Delia Sheppard, Jeff Conaway
Standard thriller: Twin sisters switch identities

Mirror Images II
1994, (USA), color
W: Shannon Whirry
Standard thriller: Opposed twin sisters involved in conflict over family fortune

Mirror, Mirror
1990, (USA), Orphans Entertainment, color, 105 mins.
W: Rainbow Harvest, Karen Black, Kristin Dattilo (*Nikki*), Ricky Paull Goldin,
   Yvonne DeCarlo, William Sanderson
D: Marina Sargenti
Standard fantasy-thriller: Demon aids unpopular teen

Mirror, Mirror 2: Raven Dance
1993, (USA), color, 91 mins.
W: Roddy McDowall, Sally Kellerman, Tracy Wells, Veronica Cartwright,
   William Sanderson, Lois Nettleton
D: Jimmy Lifton   SCR: Jimmy Lifton & Virginia Perlifi
Standard fantasy-thriller: Evil force escapes enchanted mirror, bedevils religious community

The Mirror of Cagliostro
see Le Miroir de Cagliostro

Mirror of Death
see Dead of Night (1987)

Mirror of Deception
1975, (GB), Made for TV, color
W: Kim Darby, James Maxwell, Julian Glover, Keith Barron
TVM, minor thriller: Woman's roommates disappear

Mirror of Life
see Astrologie

Mirrors
1976, (USA), Southern Cinema Ventures/Cinema Systems, color, 89 mins.
W: Kitty Winn (*Marianne*), Peter Donat (*Dr. Philip Godard*), William Swetland
   (*Charbonnet*), Lou Wagner (*Chet*), Barbara Coleman (*The Art Tour Guide*),
   Mary-Robin Redd (*Helene*), Tom Alden (*Bob*), Becki Davis (*Betty*), Don
   Keefer (*Peter*), William Burns (*Gary Whitman*), Charles Keel (*The
   Pharmacist*), Gin Taylor (*The Bus Tour Guide*), Carol Sutton (*The Perfume
   Lady*), Vanessa Hutchinson (*Marie Laveau*), Warren Kenner (*The Surrey
   Driver*), Kuumba Williams (*Nurse Spence*), Elizabeth Sosa (*The Seamstress*),
   Wille Tee & The Wild Magnolias (*The Party Musicians*)
D: Noel Black   SCR: Sidney L. Stebel, based on an orig. screen story by Noel
   Black & Sidney L. Stebel   PHOTOG: Michael D. Murphy   MUSIC:
   Stephen Lawrence
Minor thriller: Woman meets New Orleans' voodoo

Mirth and Mystery
1912, (GB), Urban, b&w, 445 ft. (135.6m)
WRIT & D: Stuart Kinder
Minor fantasy short: Conjuror and assistant enlarge and reduce their heads

Misadventures of an Aeronaut
see Mesaventures d'un Aeronaute

The Misadventures of Merlin Jones
1964, (USA), Walt Disney/Buena Vista, color, 88 mins.
W: Tommy Kirk (*Merlin Jones*), Annette Funicello, Leon Ames, Kelly Thordsen,
   Stuart Erwin, Alan Hewitt, Connie Gilchrist, Norman Grabowski

D: Robert Stevenson **SCR:** Tom & Helen August **STORY:** Bill Walsh **PHOTOG:** Edward Colman **MUSIC:** Buddy Baker
Standard comedy-fantasy

The Misadventures of Mike Murphy
1913, (GB), Cricks & Martin, b&w, 530 ft. (161.5m)
W: Ernie Westo (*Mike Murphy*)
D: Dave Aylott
reissued (1914) as Murphy and the Magic Cap
Standard fantasy short: Irish laborer finds cap that makes people and objects vanish

Mischievous Puck
1911, (GB), Natural Colour Kinematograph Co., color, 425 ft. (129.5m)
D: Walter R. Booth & Theo Bouwmeester
Standard fantasy short: Fairy plays tricks on haymaker, gardener & motorcar

A Mischievous Sketch
see Le Carton Fantastique

Les Miserables
1918, (USA), Fox, b&w, 10 reels
W: William Farnum
D: Frank Lloyd, from Victor Hugo's novel
Standard melodrama: Detective pursues petty thief

Les Miserables
1922, (GB), Master Films/BEF, b&w, 1,195 ft. (364.2m)
W: Lyn Harding (*Jean Valjean*)
SCR: W.C. Rowden, from Victor Hugo's novel
Standard melodrama

Les Miserables
1925, (Fr), Ste des Cineromans-Films de France, b&w
D: Henri Fescourt, from Victor Hugo's novel
Standard melodrama (in 4 episodes)

Les Miserables
1935, (USA), UA/20th-Fox, b&w, 110 mins.
W: Fredric March (*Jean Valjean*), Charles Laughton (*Javert*), Rochelle Hudson (*Cosette*), Sir Cedric Hardwicke (*Bienvenue*), John Beal (*Marius*), Florence Eldridge (*Fantine*), John Carradine, Frances Drake, Jessie Ralph, Mary Forbes, Jane Kerr, Florence Roberts, John Bleifer, Eily Malyon
D: Richard Boleslawsky **SCR:** W.P. Lipscomb, from Victor Hugo's novel **PHOTOG:** Gregg Toland **MUSIC:** Alfred Newman
Classic melodrama: Petty thief pursued

Les Miserables
1943, (It), IFE, b&w, 122 mins.
W: Gino Cervi, Valentina Cortese
From Victor Hugo's novel
Standard melodrama. US release, 1952.

Les Miserables
1952, (USA), 20th-Fox, b&w, 106 mins.
W: Michael Rennie (*Jean Valjean*), Robert Newton (*Javert*), Debra Paget (*Cosette*), Edmund Gwenn (*The Bishop*), Cameron Mitchell (*Marius*), Sylvia Sidney (*Fantine*), Rhys Williams (*Brevet*), Elsa Lanchester (*Mme. Magloire*), James Robertson Justice (*Robert*), Joseph Wiseman (*Genflou*), Florence Bates (*Mme. Bonnet*), Merry Anders (*Cicely*), John Rogers (*Bonnet*), Charles Keane (*The Corporal*), John Dierkes (*The Bosun*), Sean McClory, John Costello, Norma Varden, Bobby Hyatt, William Cottrell, Queenie Leonard, Sanders Clark
P: Fred Kohlmar **D:** Lewis Milestone **SCR:** Richard Murphy, from Victor Hugo's novel **PHOTOG:** Joseph La Shelle **MUSIC:** Lionel Newman
Standard melodrama: Detective pursues French peasant

Les Miserables
1957, (It-Fr), Pathe/Para, color, 2 parts (97 mins.& 120 mins.)
W: Jean Gabin (*Jean Valjean*), Bernard Blier (*Javert*), Beatrice Altariba (*Cosette*), Bourvil (*Thenardier*), Danielle Delorme (*Fantine*), Gianni Esposito (*Marius*), Martine Havet, Serge Reggiani
D: Jean-Paul Le Chanois **SCR:** Michel Audiard, Rene Barjavel & Jean-Paul Le Chanois, from Victor Hugo's novel **PHOTOG:** Jacques Natteau
Standard melodrama

Les Miserables
1978, (USA), color, 150 mins.
W: Richard Jordan (*Jean Valjean*), Anthony Perkins (*Javert*), Cyril Cusack, Claude Dauphin, Sir John Gielgud, Joyce Redman, Flora Robson, Celia Johnson
D: Glenn Jordan, from Victor Hugo's novel
TVM, standard melodrama: Pety thief relentlessly pursued

Les Miserables
1979, (Jap), color
Based on Victor Hugo's novel
Animated feature, rendered for children: Man flees heartless Justice

Les Miserables
1995, (Fr), WB, color, 174 mins.
W: Jean-Paul Belmondo, Salome Lelouch, Alessandra Martines, Michel Boujenah,

Annie Girardot, Clementine Celarie, Philippe Leotard, Philippe Khorsand
D, SCR & PHOTOG: Claude Lelouch **MUSIC:** Francis Lai, based on Victor Hugo's novel
Intriguing, updated version of classic: Nazi agent pursues Frenchman during World War II

Les Miserables
1998, (USA), color, 134 mins.
W: Liam Neeson, Geoffrey Rush, Uma Thurman, Claire Danes
D: Bille August, from Victor Hugo's novel
Lavish melodrama: Petty criminal hounded

The Miser's Doom
1899, (GB), R.W. Paul, b&w, 45 ft. (13.7m)
D: Walter Booth
Standard thriller short: Miser dies of shock when ghost of poor woman appears

The Miser's Fate
1909, (GB), Anglo-American Films, b&w, 460 ft. (140.2m)
Standard melodrama: Mother makes son strangle rich woman, denounces him for reward

Misery
1990, (USA), Castle Rock/Nelson Entertainment/Col, color, 120 mins.
W: James Caan (*Paul Sheldon*), Kathy Bates (*Annie Wilkes*), Frances Sternhagen (*Virginia*), Richard Farnsworth (*Buster*), Lauren Bacall (*Marcia Sindell*), Graham Jarvis (*Libby*), Tom Brunelle (*The Anchorman*), Jerry Potter (*Pete*), June Christopher (*The Anchorwoman*), Julie Payne (*Reporter #1*), Archie Hahn III (*Reporter #2*), Gregory Snegoff (*Reporter #3*), Wendy Bowers (*The Waitress*), Misery the Pig
D: Rob Reiner **SCR:** William Goldman, from Stephen King's novel **PHOTOG:** Barry Sonnenfeld **SPCL-FX:** Hans Metz & Ray Svedin **MUSIC:** Marc Shaiman
Major thriller (Best Actress Oscar for Kathy Bates): Madwoman holds writer captive

Misfits of Science
1985, (USA), color, 96 mins.
W: Dean Paul Martin, Kevin Peter Hall, Mark Thomas Miller, Kenneth Mars, Courteney Cox
D: Philip DeGuere
TVM, minor SF-fantasy (pilot for failed teleseries): Teens with superpowers fight to save Earth

Miss Death
see The Diabolical Dr. Z

Missile Monsters
1958, (USA), Rep, b&w, 75 mins.
W: Walter Reed (*Kent Fowler*), Gregory Gay (*Mota*), Lois Collier (*Helen*), James Craven, Harry Lauter, Tom Steele, Richard Irving, Sandy Sanders, Michael Carr, Lester Dorr, Dale Van Sickel, George Sherwood, Jimmy O'Gatty, John DeSimone, Dick Cogan
D: Fred C. Brannon **SCR:** Ronald Davidson **MUSIC:** Stanley Wilson
Standard SF-thriller, feature-version of 1950 serial Flying Disc Man from Mars

Missile to the Moon
1958, (USA), Layton/Astor, b&w, 79 mins.
W: Richard Travis, Cathy Downs, Tommy Cook, Gary Clarke, Michael Whalen, K.T. Stevens, Nina Bara, Laurie Mitchell, Lee Roberts, Henry Hunter, Marjorie Hellen, Leslie Parrish, Sandra Wirth, Pat Mowry, Tania Velia, Sanita Pelky, Lisa Simone, Renate Hoy, Marianne Gaba, Mary Ford
P: Marc Frederic **D:** Richard Cunha **SCR:** H.E. Barrie & Vincent Fotre **SPCL-FX:** Ira Anderson & Harold Banks **MUSIC:** Nicholas Carras
orig. co-billed with Frankenstein's Daughter (1958)
Standard SF-thriller (semi-remake of low-budget "classic" Cat Women of the Moon): Delinquents visit Luna

The Missing Corpse
1945, (USA), PRC, b&w, 62 mins.
W: J. Edward Bromberg, Frank Jenks, Eric Siclair, Isabel Randolph, Paul Guilfoyle, Lorell Sheldon, John Shay
D: Albert Herman
Minor thriller: Newspaperman involved in murder mystery

The Missing Guest
1938, (USA), Univ, b&w, 67 mins.
W: Paul Kelly ("*Scoop*" *Hanlon*), Constance Moore (*Stephanie Kirkland*), William Lundigan (*Larry Dearden*), Edwin Stanley (*Dr. Carroll*), Selmer Jackson (*Frank Baldrich*), Patrick J. Kelly (*Edwards*), Billy Wayne ("*Vic*"), Florence Wix (*Linda Baldrich*), George Cooper ("*Jake*"), Harlan Briggs (*Kendall*), Pat C. Flick (*The Inventor*)
D: John Rawlins **SCR:** Charles Martin & Paul Perez, based on a story by Erich Philippi **PHOTOG:** Milton Krasner **MUSIC DIR:** Charles Previn
Minor thriller. cf. Murders in the Blue Room and The Secret of the Blue Room

The Missing Head
see Strange Confession

The Missing Juror
1944, (USA), Col, b&w, 66 mins.
W: Jim Bannon, Janis Carter, George Macready, Jean Stevens, Joseph Crehan,

M

The Missing Juror: JIM BANNON AND JANIS CARTER

Carole Mathews
D: Budd Boetticher, Oscar "Budd" Boetticher Jr.
Minor thriller: Unknown killer takes revenge on jury

The Missing Lady
1946, (USA), Mono, b&w, 60 mins.
W: Kane Richmond, Barbara Reed
Minor thriller. 'The Shadow' series

Missing Link
1988, (USA), Univ, color, 95 mins.
W: Peter Elliot, Brian Abrahams, Dave Holland
D: David & Carol Hughes   **WRIT, D & PHOTOG:** David & Carol Hughes   **NARRATION:** Michael Gambon
Standard action-thriller: Adventures of last ape-man

Missing Millions
1922, (USA), Para, b&w, 6 reels
W: Alice Brady (*May Dawson*), David Powell (*Boston Blackie*), Frank Losee (*Jim Franklin*), Riley Hatch (*John Webb*), George Le Guere (*Daniel Regan*), H. Cooper Cliffe (*Sir Arthur Cumberland*), John B. Cooke (*Handsome Harry Hawks*), Beverly Travers (*Claire Dupont*), Sydney Deane (*Donald Gordon*), Sidney Herbert (*Frank Garber*)
D: Joseph Henaberry   **SCR:** Albert Shelby Le Vino, from Jack Boyle's short stories "A Problem in Larceny" & "An Answer in Grand Larceny"   **PHOTOG:** Gilbert Warrenton
Standard "Boston Blackie" thriller: Woman seeks revenge for father's incarceration

The Missing People
1939, (GB), Jack Raymond/Grand Nat'l, b&w, 71 mins.
W: Will Fyffe (*J.G. Reeder*), Lyn Harding (*Joseph Branstone*), Kay Walsh (*Peggy Gillette*), Ronald Shiner (*Sam Hackett*), Antony Holles (*Ernest Branstone*), Patricia Roc (*Doris Bevan*), Ronald Adam (*Surtees*), Reginald Purdell (*Harry Morgan*), Maire O'Neill (*The Housekeeper*)
D: Jack Raymond   **SCR:** Lydia Hayward, from Edgar Wallace's novel *The Mind of Mr. Reeder*
released in USA (1940) by Monogram Pictures, reissued 1943
Standard thriller (4th & last "J.G. Reeder" mystery): Inspector nabs mass-murderer

The Missing Rembrandt
1932, (GB), Twickenham/Producers Distributing Corp./First Division, b&w, 84 mins.
W: Arthur Wontner (*Sherlock Holmes*), Ian Fleming (*Dr. John Watson*), Jane Welsh (*Lady Violet Lumsden*), Miles Mander (*Claude Holford*), Francis L. Sullivan (*Baron von Guntermann*), Dino Galvani (*Carlo Ravelli*), Philip Hewland (*Insp. Lestrade*), Ben Welden (*The Pinkerton Man*), Minnie Rayner (*Mrs. Hudson*), Antony Holles (*Marquess de Chaminade*)
D: Leslie Hiscott   **SCR:** Cyril Twyford & H. Fowler Mear, from Sir Arthur Conan Doyle's story "Charles August Milverton"
Standard thriller: Drug-addict artist steals painting

The Missing Tiara
1912, (GB), Cricks & Martin, b&w, 840 ft. (256m)
D: Charles Calvert
Standard thriller: Hypnotist forces man to steal fiancee's tiara

Missing Women
1951, (USA), Rep, b&w, 60 mins.
W: Penny Edwards, James Millican
Standard melodrama

Mission a Tangiers (Mission to Tangiers)
1949, (It-Fr), b&w, 100 mins.
D: Andre Hunebelle   **SCR:** Michel Audiard
Standard adventure-thriller

Mission Galactica: The Cyclon Attack
see **Battlestar Galactica**

Mission: Impossible
1996, (USA), Para, color, 110 mins.
W: Tom Cruise (*Ethan Hunt*), Jon Voight (*Jim Phelps*), Emmanuelle Beart (*Claire Phelps*), Vanessa Redgrave (*Max*), Jean Reno, Henry Czerny, Kristin Scott-Thomas, Ving Rhames, Emilio Estevez, Andreas Wisniewski, Ingeborga Dapkunaite, Valentina Yakunina, Rolf Saxon, Marek Vasut, Nathan Osgood, John McLaughlin, Karel Dobry, David Shaeffer, Mark Houghton, Sam Douglas, Rudolf Pechan, Ricco Ross, Gaston Subert, Annabel Mullion, Bob Friend, Garrick Hagon, Jirina Trebicka, Maya Dokic, Andrzei Borkowski, Oleg Federov, Pat Starr, Carmela Marner, Mimi Potworowska, David Schneider, Tony Vogel, Helen Lindsay, Randall Paul, Richard D. Sharp, Suzanne Doucette, Graydon Gould, Laura Brook, Michael Rogers, David Phelan, Morgan Deare, Melissa Knatchbull
D: Brian De Palma   **CO-P:** Tom Cruise   **SCR:** Robert Towne & David Koepp   **STORY:** David Koepp & Steven Zallian, from the teleseries created by Bruce Geller   **PHOTOG:** Stephen H. Burum   **SPCL VS-FX:** Industrial Light & Magic   **MUSIC:** Danny Elfman
Engrossing thriller: US agents must wrest spy list from enemy hands

Mission Mars
1968, (USA), Red Ram/Sagittarius/AA, color, 95 mins.
W: Darren McGavin (*Mike Blaiswick*), Nick Adams (*Nick Grant*), Heather Hewitt (*Edith Blaiswick*), George DeVries (*Duncan*), Shirley Parker (*Alice Grant*), Bill Kelly (*The Russian Astronaut*), Michael DeBeausset (*Cliff Lawson*), Chuck Zink (*The Radio Technician*), Ralph Miller (*Simpson*), Art Barker (*The Doctor*), Monroe Myers (*Lawson's Aide*)
D: Nick Webster   **SCR:** Mike St. Clair   **STORY:** Aubrey Wisberg   **PHOTOG:** Cliff Poland   **SPCL-FX:** Haberstroh Studios   **MUSIC:** Berje Kalajian, Gus Pardalis & The Forum Quorum   **SONG:** *No More Tears*
Minor SF-adventure: Astronauts have problems in space

Mission Stardust: ESSY PERSSON

Mission Stardust
1968, (W. Ger-It-Sp), Times, color, 95 mins.
W: Lang Jeffries (*Perry Rodan*), Essy Persson (*Thora*), Luis Davila (*Capt. Bull*), Pinkas Braun (*Rotkin*), John Karlsen (*Kress*), Ann Smyrner, Tom Felleghy, Gianni Rizzo
D: Primo Zeglio   **SCR:** Karl H. Volgeman & Frederico d'Urrutia   **PHOTOG:** Riccardo Pallottini   **MUSIC:** Anton G. Abril   **SONG:** *Seli*
Standard SF-adventure: Superhuman beings from far galaxy detour Earth expedition to moon

Mission to Tangiers
see **Mission a Tangiers**

Mission to Venice
1963, (Fr), color
W: Sean Flynn, Madeleine Robinson
Minor thriller: Sleuth uncovers spy ring

Miss Meurtre
see **The Diabolical Dr. Z**

Miss Morison's Ghosts
1981, (GB), Made for TV, color

W: Wendy Hiller, Hannah Gordon
TVM, standard fantasy: Two professors meet Marie Antoinette's ghost

Miss Pinkerton
1932, (USA), WB, b&w, 66 mins.
W: Joan Blondell, George Brent, John Wray, Ruth Hall, Elizabeth Patterson, Holmes Herbert, C. Henry Gordon
D: Lloyd Bacon
Standard thriller: Nurse imperiled in old dark house

Mrs. Cassell's Profession
see The Striped Stocking Gang

Mrs. Munck
1995, (USA), SHO-TV, color, 100 mins.
W: Diane Ladd, Bruce Dern, Kelly Preston, Shelley Winters
D: Diane Ladd   WRIT: Diane Ladd   PHOTOG: James Glennon   MUSIC: Leonard Rosenman
Made-for-Cable, standard melodrama: Abused widow tortures her wheelchair-bound father-in-law

Mrs. Pym of Scotland Yard
1939, (GB), Hurley/Grand Nat'l, b&w, 65 mins.
W: Mary Clare (*Mrs. Pym*), Edward Lexy (*Insp. Shott*), Nigel Patrick (*Richard Loddon*), Janet Johnson (*Maraday Wood*), Anthony Ireland (*Henry Menchen*), Vernon Kelso (*Frank Wood*), Irene Handl (*Miss Bell*), Robert English (*The Commissioner*)
D: Fred Elles   SCR: Fred Elles, Nigel Morland & Peggy Barwell, from a novel by Nigel Morland
reissued 1942
Minor thriller: Woman detective unmasks fake medium

Mrs. Santa Claus
1996, (USA), Hallmark/CBS-TV, color, 95 mins.
W: Angela Lansbury, Lynsey Bartilson, Charles Durning, Michael Jeter, Terrence Mann, Bryan Murray, David Norona
D: Terry Hughes   TELEPLAY: David Saltzman   PHOTOG: Stephen M. Katz
MUSIC & LYRICS: Jerry Herman   SONGS: include *Avenue A*
TVM, standard musical-fantasy: Santa's wife aids 1910 sweat-shop worker

Mistaken Identity
1909, (GB), Hepworth, b&w, 400 ft. (121.9m)
D: Theo Bouwmeester
Standard comedy-thriller: Strong girl saves man from being framed for murder

Mr. and Mrs. Bulldog Drummond
see Bulldog Drummond's Bride

Mr. Arkadin
1955, (GB-Sp), Mercury/WB, b&w, 99 mins.
W: Orson Welles, Patricia Medina, Katina Paxinou, Gregoire Aslan, Jack Watling, Akim Tamiroff, Mischa Auer, Peter Van Eyck, Paola Mori, Michael Redgrave, Suzanne Flon, Terrence Langdon, Tamara Shane, Robert Arden, Annabel
ORIG. STORY, SCR & D: Orson Welles   PHOTOG: Jean Bourgoin   MUSIC: Paul Misraki
A.k.a. Confidential Report
Unusual, rarely-seen melodrama: Wealthy financier seeks to unravel his forgotten past

Mr. Atlas
1997, (USA), color, 100 mins.
W: T.J. Lowther, Laura Johnson
Standard fantasy: Greek hero rescues boy

Mr. Curse
see M (1931)

Mr. Denning Drives North
1951, (GB), London/British Lion, b&w, 93 mins.
W: John Mills (*Tom Denning*), Phyllis Calvert (*Kay Denning*), Sam Wanamaker (*Chick Eddowes*), Herbert Lom (*Mados*), Eileen Moore (*Liz Denning*), Raymond Huntley (*Wright*), Bernard Lee (*Insp. Dodds*), Russell Waters (*Harry Stokes*), Freda Jackson (*Ma Smith*), Wilfrid Hyde-White (*Woods*), Sheila Shand Gibbs (*Matilda*), Michael Shepley (*The Chairman*), Trader Faulkner (*Ted Smith*), John Stuart (*Wilson*)
P: Anthony Kimmins & Stephen Mitchell   D: Anthony Kimmins   SCR: Alec Coppel   PHOTOG: John Wilcox   MUSIC: Benjamin Frankel
reissued 1960. US Release: Carroll Pictures, 1953
Engrossing thriller: Man accidentally kills daughter's lover, loses corpse

Mr. Destiny
1990, (USA), Touchstone/Buena Vista, color, 110 mins.
W: James Belushi (*Larry Burrows*), Michael Caine (*Mike*), Linda Hamilton (*Ellen Burrows*), Jon Lovitz (*Clip Burrows*), Bill McCutcheon (*Leo Hansen*), Rene Russo (*Cindy Jo*), Jay O. Sanders (*Jackie Earle*), Pat Corley (*Harry Burrows*), Maury Chaykin (*Guzelman*), Douglas Seale (*Boswell*), Courteney Cox (*Jewel Jagger*), Doug Barron (*Lewis Flick*), Jeff Weiss (*Ludwig*), Tony Longo (*The Huge Guy*), Kathy Ireland (*Gina*), Andrew Stahl (*Jerry Haskins*), Bryan Buffinton (*The Boy*), Sari Caine (*The Girl*),

Martin Thompson (*The Guest Stilton*), Michael Genevie (*Guest #1*), Osamu Sakabe (*Nakamura*), Howard Kingkade (*Guest #2*), Eddita Hill (*Juanita*), Collin Bernsen (*Tom Robertson*), William Griffis (*The Maitre D'*), John Garver (*The Waiter*), Terry Loughlin (*The Wine Steward*), Adam Eichhorst (*The Teenager*), Jeffrey Pillars (*The Truck Driver*), Richie Devaney (*Young Larry*), Bruce Evers (*The Team Coach*), Raymond L. Anderson (*The Umpire*), Whit Edwards (*Young Jerry*), Sky Berdahl (*Young Clip*), Heather Lynch (*Young Ellen*), James Douglas (*Mr. Ripley*), Chris Stacy (*The Teammate*), Jesse J. Donnelly (*The Cop*)
WRIT & P: James Orr & Jim Cruickshank   D: James Orr   PHOTOG: Alex Thomson   MUSIC: David Newman
Minor fantasy: Man makes dreams come true

Mr. District Attorney
1941, (USA), Rep, b&w, 81 mins.
W: Dennis O'Keefe, Peter Lorre, Florence Rice, Marguerite Chapman, Stanley Ridges
D: William Morgan   SCR: Karl Brown
Standard thriller (based on popular radio-series): D.A. vs. corrupt officials

Mr. Drake's Duck
1950, (GB), Angel Prods./Eros/UA, b&w, 85 mins.
W: Douglas Fairbanks Jr. (*Don Drake*), Yolande Donlan (*Penny Drake*), A.E. Matthews (*The Brigadier*), Jon Pertwee (*Reuben*), Reginald Beckwith (*Mr. Boothby*), Wilfrid Hyde-White (*Mr. May*), Howard Marion-Crawford (*Maj. Travers*), Peter Butterworth (*Higgins*), Tom Gill (*Capt. White*)
P: Daniel Angel & Douglas Fairbanks Jr.   D & SCR: Val Guest, from Ian Messiter's radio-play   PHOTOG: Jack Cox   MUSIC: Bruce Campbell
Standard SF-comedy: Duck lays uranium eggs. Remake: Million Dollar Duck, 1971

Mister Freedom
1969, (Fr), O.P.E.R.A., Grove Press, color, 110 mins.
W: John Abbey, Donald Pleasence, Delphine Seyrig, Simone Signoret, Yves Montand, Philippe Noiret, Serge Gainsbourg
D & SCR: William Klein
Standard political fantasy-satire: Superhero saves France from communism

Mr. Frost
1990, (GB-Fr), color, 95 mins.
W: Jeff Goldblum, Alan Bates, Kathy Baker (*Sarah*), Roland Giraud (*Dr. Reynhardt*), Jean-Pierre Cassel, Daniel Gelin, Charley Boorman, Henri Serre, Francois Negret, Maxine Leroux, Vincent Schiavelli, Catherine Allegret
D: Philippe Setbon
Standard thriller: Psychopath claims to be Satan

Mr. Griggs Returns
see The Cockeyed Miracle

Mr. H.C. Andersen
1950, (GB), British Foundation, b&w, 62 mins.
W: Ashley Glynne (*Hans Andersen*), Constance Lewis (*Mrs. Andersen*), Terence Noble (*Mr. Andersen*), Stuart Sanders (*The Bailiff*), June Elvin (*Jenny Lind*), Edward Sullivan (*Charles Dickens*), Victor Rietty (*King Frederick*)
P & D: Ronald Haines   SCR: Ronald & Jean Haines, from Hans Christian Andersen's book *The True Story of My Life*
Standard bio: Life of Danish author (with fairytales in animation)

Mr. Hate
see M (1931)

Mr. Hex
1946, (USA), Jan Grippo/Mono, b&w, 63 mins.
W: Leo Gorcey, Huntz Hall, Bobby Jordan, Gabriel Dell, Ben Welden, William Benedict, Gale Robbins, Ian Keith, David Gorcey
D: William Beaudine   SCR: Cyril Endfield   PHOTOG: James Brown   MUSIC: Edward J. Kay
Standard comedy: Bowery Boys encounter hypnosis

Mr. Horatio Knibbles
1971, (GB), Anvil/CFF, color, 60 mins.
W: Lesley Roach (*Mary Bunting*), Gary Smith (*Tom*), Rachel Brennock (*Nancy*), John Ash (*Bob*), Nigel Chivers (*Derek*), David Richards (*Billy*), Bernard Horsfall (*Mr. Bunting*), Anthony Sheppard (*Horatio Knibbles*), Jane Jordan Rogers (*Mrs. Bunting*), Fred Evans (*PC Briggs*), David Lodge (*The Sgt.*), Freddie Jones (*The Gamekeeper*)
P: Hugh Stewart   D: Robert Hird   SCR: Peter Blackmore   STORY: Wally Bosco   PHOTOG: Adrian Jeakins   MUSIC: Muir Matheson
Standard juvenile fantasy: Girl has invisible 6-foot rabbit for companion

Misterios del Ultratumba (Mysteries from Beyond the Grave)
1958, (Mex), Alameda/UPRO/Pan-World/Joseph Brenner, b&w, 71 mins.
W: Gaston Santos, Ralph Bertrand, Mapita Cortes
P: Alfred Ripstein Jr.   D: Fernando Mendez   SCR: Ramon Obon
Minor horror-thriller. released in USA (1962) as The Black Pit of Dr. M

Mr. Joseph Young of Africa
see Mighty Joe Young

Mr. Lyndon at Liberty

W: Jacques Lerner *(Jocko/Fano)*, Olive Borden *(Olivette)*, Don Alva-rado *(Sam Wick/Pierre)*, Malcolm Waite *(Bergerin)*, Raymond Hitchcock *(Lorenzo)*, Ted McNamara *(Firmin)*, Jane Winton *(Maisie)*, August Tollaire *(Mata)*
D: Raoul Walsh **SCR:** L.G. Rigby **FROM:** a story by Rene Fauchois **PHOTOG:** L. William O'Connell
Standard melodrama: Members of traveling French circus disguise man as talking monkey

The Monocle
1964, (Fr), Cocinor/Laetitia/Four Star/ WB-TV, color, 100 mins.
W: Paul Meurisse, Barbara Steele, Marcel Dalio
D: Georges Lautner
Minor thriller: Secret agent vs. Hong Kong terrorists

Monolith
1993, (USA), EGM Film Int'l/Shapiro Glickenhaus Entertainment, color, 96 mins.
W: Bill Paxton *(Tucker)*, Lindsay Frost *(Flynn)*, John Hurt *(Villano)*, Lou Gossett Jr. *("Mac")*, Paul Ganus *(Connor)*, Musetta Vander *(Katya Pavlova)*, Andrew Lamond *(Schaefer)*, Mark Phelan *(Rickman)*, Alex Gaona *(The Boy)*, Angela Gordon *(Jorjivik)*, Boris Krutonog *(Rourke)*, Steve Barbro *(Officer Jenkins)*, Jennifer Naud *(The Rookie Cop)*, Bill Woodbridge *(Jacobs)*, Todd Jeffries *(LaRue)*, Red Horton *(Rovello)*, David St. James *(The Attendant)*, Steve Blackwood *(Bio-Team Member #1)*, Edward Paul Allen *(Bio-Team Member #2)*, Craig Diffenderfer *(Bio-Team Member #3)*, Michael Halsey *(The Tired Cop)*, Kevin E. West *(The Locker Room Cop)*, Frank G. Davis *(The Tramp)*, Stan Yale *(The Bum)*, Jefferson Wagner *(The Gunman)*, Debb Lee Phillips *(The Flashback Wife)*
D: John Eyres **SCR:** Stephen Lister **PHOTOG:** Alan M. Trow **SPCL VS-FX:** Introvision **ORIG. MUSIC:** Frank Becker **SONGS:** Sweet Innocence, Misery, Flesh & Fire, Desert Rain, & Falling
Standard SF-thriller: Cops detect space-alien coverup

The Monolith Monsters
1957, (USA), Univ, b&w, 77 mins.
W: Grant Williams, Lola Albright, Les Tremayne, Phil Harvey, Trevor Bardette, William Flaherty, Dean Cromer, Richard Cutting, Harry Jackson, Steve Darrell, Linda Scheley
P: Howard Christie **D:** John Sherwood **SCR:** Norman Jolley & Robert M. Fresco from a story by Jack Arnold **PHOTOG:** Ellis W. Carter **SPCL-FX:** Clifford Stine **MUSIC:** Joseph Gershenson
Standard SF-thriller: Earth threatened by giant towers of silicon crystals

El Mono Loco (The Mad Monkey)
1990, (Sp), color, 108 mins.
W: Jeff Goldblum, Miranda Richardson, Anemone, Liza Walker, Dexter Fletcher, Daniel Ceccaldi, Arielle Dombasle
D: Luchino Visconti
Unusual psychological thriller: Scriptwriter drawn into web of sexual fantasy

M. Le Maudit
see M (1931)

M. Moto Court sa Chance
see Mr. Moto Takes a Chance

M. Moto dans les Bas-Fonds
see The Mysterious Mr. Moto

M. Moto sur le Ring
see Mr. Moto's Gamble

Monsieur Verdoux
1947, (USA), UA, b&w, 123 mins.
W: Charles Chaplin *(Henri Verdoux/alias Varnay/alias Bonheur/alias Floray)*, Martha Raye *(Annabella Bonheur)*, Mady Correll *(Mona Verdoux)*, Allison Roddan *(Peter)*, Isobel Elsom *(Marie Grosnay)*, Robert Lewis *(Maurice Bottello)*, Audrey Betz *(Mme. Bottello)*, Helene Heigh *(Yvonne)*, Margaret Hoffman *(Lydia Floray)*, Edwin Mills *(Jean)*, Ada-May *(Annette)*, Marjorie Bennett *(The Maid)*, Irving Bacon *(Pierre)*, Virginia Brissac *(Carlotta)*, Almira Sessions *(Lena)*, Eula Morgan *(Phoebe)*, Bernard J. Nedell *(The Prefect of Police)*, Charles Evans *(Det. Morrow)*, Cyril Delevanti
D, SCR & MUSIC: Charles Chaplin **IDEA:** Orson Welles **PHOTOG:** Roland Totheroh
Classic comedy-melodrama: Frenchman kills wives

The Monster (1903)
see Le Monstre (1903)

The Monster
1925, (USA), Metro-Goldwyn, b&w, 7 reels (6,425 ft./1958.3m)
W: Lon Chaney Sr. *(Dr. Ziska)*, Gertrude Olmstead *(Betty Watson)*, Hallam Cooley *(The Head Clerk)*, Johnny Arthur *(The Under Clerk)*, Charles A. Sellon *(The Constable)*, Walter James *(Caliban)*, Knute Erickson *(Daffy Dan)*, George Austin *(Rigo)*, Edward McWade *(Luke Watson)*, Ethel Wales *(Mrs. Watson)*
D: Roland West **SCR:** Willard Mack & Albert Kenyon **BASED ON:** "the famous stage success by Crane Wilbur" **PHOTOG:** Hal Mohr
Standard horror-thriller: Mad scientist seeks to revive dead

The Monster (1955)
see The Quatermass Experiment

Monster (1978)
see Monstroid

The Monster (1982)
see I Don't Want to Be Born

Monster
1994, (It-Fr), color, 115 mins.
W: Roberto Benigni, Nicoletta Braschi, Dominique Lavanant *(Jolanda)*, Michel Blanc *(Taccone)*
Amusing farce: Con man targeted as serial killer

The Monster (1998)
see Stephen Crane's "The Monster"

Monster A-Go-Go
1965, (USA), Boxoffice Spectaculars, b&w, 70 mins.
W: Phil Morton, June Travis, Lois Brooke, George Perry, Henry Hite, Bill Rebane, Sheldon Seymour
D: Herschell Gordon Lewis & Bill Rebane **SCR:** Jeff Smith, Bill Rebane, & Don Stanford **PHOTOG:** Frank Pfieffer **MUSIC:** Other Three
a.k.a. Terror at Halfday
blurb: "You've never seen a picture like this"
Minor SF-horror (compiled from unsold excerpts culled by Herschell Gordon Lewis): Beatnik beauties vs. space beast

The Monster and the Girl
1941, (USA), Para, b&w, 65 mins.
W: Rod Cameron *(Sam)*, Paul Lukas *(Bruhl)*, Ellen Drew, Marc Lawrence, Robert Paige, George Zucco, Joseph Calleia, Onslow Stevens, Phillip Terry, Gerald Mohr, Cliff Edwards
P: Jack Moss **D:** Stuart Heisler **SCR:** Stuart Anthony **PHOTOG:** Victor Milner
Standard horror-thriller: Executed man's brain put into body of gorilla

The Monster and the Stripper
1973, (USA), color, 90 mins.
Minor horror-thriller: Gangster pursues bayou creature

The Monster and the Woman
see Four Sided Triangle

The Monster Baran
see Varan the Unbelievable

The Monster Club
1980, (GB), Sword & Sorcery/Chips/ITC, color, 99 mins.
W: Vincent Price *(Eramus)*, Richard Johnson *(Father)*, John Carradine *(R. Chetwynd-Hayes)*, Britt Ekland *(Mother)*, Donald Pleasence *(Pick-ering)*, Stuart Whitman *(Sam)*, Simon Ward *(George)*, Lesley Dunlop *(Luna)*, James Laurenson *(Raven)*, Roger Sloman *(The Club Sec'y)*, Barbara Kellermann *(Angela)*, Patrick Magee *(The Innkeeper)*, Geoffrey Bayldon *(The Psychiatrist)*, Warren Saire *(Linlom)*, Neil McCarthy *(Watson)*, Anthony Valentine *(Mooney)*, Anthony Steel *(Lintom Busotsky)*, Suzanna Willis *(The Stripper)*, Fran Fullenwider
P: Milton Subotsky **D:** Roy Ward Baker **SCR:** Edward & Valerie Abraham **FROM:** stories by R. Chetwynd-Hayes **PHOTOG:** Peter Jessop **MUSIC:** Douglas Gamley
Standard trio of terror tales: (1) Con-woman targets unhuman, (2) Boy finds father is vampire, & (3) Filmmaker encounters ghouls

The Monster Demolisher
see Nostradamus y el Destructor de Monstruos

Monster Dog
1982, (USA), color, 88 mins.
W: Alice Cooper, Victoria Vera
D: Clyde Anderson
Minor horror-thriller: Mutant canine menaces rock band

Monster from a Prehistoric Planet
see Gappa, the Triphibian Monster

The Monster from Green Hell
1957, (USA), Gross-Krasne/DCA, b&w, 71 mins.
W: Jim Davis, Barbara Turner, Robert E. Griffin, Eduardo Ciannelli, Vladimir Sokoloff, Joel Fluellen
P: Al Zimbalist **D:** Kenneth G. Crane
Minor SF-thriller: Scientists battle giant wasps

Monster from Mars
see Robot Monster

Monster from the Ocean Floor
1954, (USA), Palo Alto/Lippert, b&w, 66 mins.
W: Stuart Wade, Anne Kimbell, Dick Pinner, Inez Palange, Jack Hayes, Wyott Ordung, David Garcia
P: Roger Corman **D:** Wyott Ordung **SCR:** William Danch **PHOTOG:** Floyd Crosby **MUSIC:** Andre Brummer
A.k.a. It Staked the Ocean Floor and Monster Maker

1915, (GB), London/Jury, b&w, 5,130 ft. (1563.6m)
<u>W</u>: Edna Flugrath (*Joyce Aylmer*), Fred Groves (*Tom Morrison*), Harry Welchman (*Neil Lyndon*), Charles Rock (*Dr. McMurtie*), Manora Thew (*Sonia Savaroff*), S. Jensen (*George Marwood*)
<u>D</u>: Harold Shaw, from a novel by Victor Bridges
Standard crime-thriller: Escaped convict unmasks doctor as spy

Mr. Meek's Nightmare
1914, (GB), Hepworth, b&w, 50 ft. (137.2m)
<u>W</u>: Arthur Staples (*Mr. Meek*), Ruby Belasco (*Mrs. Meek*)
<u>D</u>: Hay Plumb
Standard fantasy short: Henpeck dreams he is everybody

Mr. Mosenstein
1904, (GB), Gaumont, b&w, 158 ft. (48.2m)
<u>D</u>: Alf Collins
Standard comedy-fantasy: Vanishing boys play tricks on old Jew

Mr. Moto in Egypt
see *Mr. Moto's Last Warning*

Mr. Moto in the Underworld
see *The Mysterious Mr. Moto*

Mr. Moto in Danger Island
1939, (USA), 20th-Fox, b&w, 69 mins.
<u>W</u>: Peter Lorre (*Mr. Moto*), Jean Hersholt (*Sutter*), Amanda Duff (*Joan Castle*), Warren Hymer (*Twister McGurk*), Richard Lane (*Commissioner Gordon*), Leon Ames (*Commissioner Madero*), Douglass Dumbrille (*Cmdr. La Costa*), Paul Harvey (*Gov. John Bentley*), Charles D. Brown (*Col. Tom Castle*), Robert Lowery (*Lt. George Bentley*), Eddie Marr (*Capt. Dahlen*), Harry Woods (*Grant*), Neely Edwards (*Moore*), Harry Strang (*The Henchman*), George Magrill (*The Officer*), Grace Hayle (*Mrs. Brown*), Tony Martelli (*The Servant*), Edwin Stanley (*The Doctor*), Gloria Roy (*The Nurse*), Jimmie Dundee (*The Driver*), Jack Stoney (*The Guard*), Al Kikume (*The Sgt.*), Ralph Dunn (*The Policeman*), Lester Dorr, Ray Walker, Don Douglas, Max Wagner, Oscar Hendrian, Ward Bond, Willie Best, Edward Keane, Lee Shumway, Al Ferguson, Juan Duval, Renie Riano, W.R. Deming
<u>D</u>: Herbert I. Leeds   <u>SCR</u>: John W. Vandercook, John Reinhardt, George Bricker & Peter Milne, from characters created by John P. Marquand   <u>PHOTOG</u>: Lucien Andriot
A.k.a. Danger Island
Standard thriller: Japanese sleuth foils diamond smugglers. Remake: **Murder in Trinidad**, *1934, remade as* **The Caribbean Mystery**, *1945.*

Mr. Moto's Gamble
1938, (USA), 20th-Fox, b&w, 71 mins.
<u>W</u>: Peter Lorre (*Mr. Moto*), Keye Luke (*Lee Chan*), Lynn Bari (*Penny Kendall*), Dick Baldwin (*Bill Steele*), Jayne Regan (*Linda Benton*), Douglas Fowley (*Nick Crowder*), Harold Huber (*Lt. Riggs*), Maxie Rosenbloom (*Wellington*), George E. Stone (*Connors*), John Hamilton (*Philip Benton*), Ward Bond (*Big Moran*), Bernard Nedell (*Clipper McCoy*), Cliff Clark (*McGuire*), Charles Williams (*Gabby Marden*), Edward Marr (*Sammy*), Lon Chaney Jr. (*Joey*), Russ Clark (*Frankie Stanton*), Addison Richards (*The D.A.*), Charles D. Brown (*The Editor*), Fred Kelsey, Chester Clute, Ralph Dunn, Irving Bacon, Syd Saylor, Paul Fix, Edwin Stanley, Edward Earle, Olin Howland, Harrison Greene, Dick Elliott
<u>D</u>: James Tinling   <u>SCR</u>: Charles Belden & Jerry Cady, from characters created by John P. Marquand   <u>PHOTOG</u>: Lucien Andriot
Standard thriller: Japanese sleuth aids boxer accused of murder. Started as a Charlie Chan film Warner Oland.

Mr. Moto's Last Warning
1939, (USA), 20th-Fox, b&w, 71 mins.
<u>W</u>: Peter Lorre (*Mr. Moto*), Ricardo Cortez (*Fabian*), Virginia Field (*Connie*), John Carradine (*Danforth*), George Sanders (*Eric Norvel*), Joan Carol (*Mary Delacour*), Margaret Irving (*Mme. Delacour*), Robert Coote (*Rollo*), Leyland Hodgson (*Hawkins*), John Davidson (*Hakim*), Teru Shimada (*The Mr. Moto Impersonator*), George Renavent (*Adm. Delacour*), E.E. Clive (*The Commandant*), Holmes Herbert (*Bentham*), George Humbert (*The Stage Manager*), C. Montague Shaw (*First Lord of the Admiralty*), Jacques Lory (*The Juggler*), Denis d'Auburn (*The Deck Officer*), Eric Wilton (*The Deck Steward*), Jimmie Aubrey (*The Waiter*), Lal Chand Mehra (*The Customs Officer*), Wayne Rivers (*The Cable Man*), Bert Roach (*The Hotel Clerk*), A.R. Bogard (*The Hoist Man*), Jack Perry, Daniel Boone, Robert F. Owens, Al Weaslen, H.W. Stroele, Neil Fitzgerald
<u>D</u>: Norman Foster   <u>SCR</u>: Philip MacDonald & Norman Foster, from characters created by John P. Marquand   <u>PHOTOG</u>: Virgil Miller   <u>MUSIC</u>: Samuel Kaylin
A.k.a. Mr. Moto in Egypt
Standard thriller: Japanese sleuth counters saboteurs

Mr. Moto's Promise
see *Thank You, Mr. Moto*

Mr. Moto Takes a Chance
1938, (USA), 20th-Fox, b&w, 63 mins.
<u>W</u>: Peter Lorre (*Mr. Moto*), Rochelle Hudson (*Vicki*), Robert Kent (*Marty Weston*), J. Edward Bromberg (*Hajah Ali*), Chick Chandler (*Chick Davis*), George

Regas (*Boker*), Frederick Vogeding (*Zimmerman*), Al Kikume (*Yan*), Gloria Roy (*The Wife*), C.J. Thunderbolt (*The Fire Eater*), Tetsu Komai (*The Officer*), Julie Carter, James B. Leong
<u>D</u>: Norman Foster   <u>SCR</u>: Willis Cooper, Norman Foster, Lou Breslow & John Patrick, from characters created by John P. Marquand   <u>PHOTOG</u>: Virgil Miller
Standard thriller: Japanese sleuth poses as archaeologist, braves danger in Indochina

Mr. Moto Takes a Vacation
1939, (USA), 20th-Fox, b&w, 61 mins.
<u>W</u>: Peter Lorre (*Mr. Moto*), Joseph Schildkraut (*Bayard Manderson*), Lionel Atwill (*Prof. Hildebrand*), Virginia Field (*Eleanor Kirke*), John King (*Howard Stevens*), Victor Varconi (*Paul*), George P. Huntley Jr. (*Rollo*), John Bleifer (*Wendling*), Honorable Wu (*Wong*), Morgan Wallace (*Perez*), Willie Best (*The Driver*), Anthony Warde (*Rubla*), Tom O'Grady (*The Husband*), Harry Strang (*O'Hara*), Stanley Blystone (*Ship's Officer*), John Davidson (*Prince Suleid*), Isabelle La Mal (*The Older Woman*), Robert Winckler (*The Boy*), Bobby Hale (*The Steward*), Maj. Sam Harris (*The Professor*), Iris Wong (*The Waitress*), Jadine Wong (*Lander*), Victor Wong (*The Proprietor*), Jimmie Aubrey (*The Bum*), Brooks Benedict (*The Gangster*), Jack Clifford (*The Motorcycle Sergeant*), Chick Collins (*The Armored Car Driver*), George Chandler (*The Cameraman*), Ralph Dunn, Pat O'Malley, Lee Phelps
<u>D</u>: Norman Foster   <u>SCR</u>: Philip MacDonald & Norman Foster, from characters created by John P. Marquand   <u>PHOTOG</u>: Charles G. Clarke
Standard thriller: Thieves covet Queen of Sheba's crown

Il Mistero del Templo Indiano (Mystery of the Indian Temple)
1963, (It), color
<u>D</u>: Mario Camerini   <u>PHOTOG</u>: Aldo Tonti
Standard adventure-thriller

Mr. Peabody and the Mermaid
1948, (USA), Inter-John/Univ, b&w, 89 mins.
<u>W</u>: William Powell (*Mr. Peabody*), Ann Blyth (*The Mermaid*), Irene Hervey, Andrea King, Clinton Sundberg, Hugh French, Fred Clark, Art Smith, Lumsden Hare
<u>P & SCR</u>: Nunnally Johnson, based on novel *Peabody's Mermaid* by Guy & Constance Jones   <u>D</u>: Irving Pichel   <u>PHOTOG</u>: Russell Metty   <u>MUSIC</u>: Robert Emmett Dolan
Amusing fantasy: Middle-aged man enchanted by young mermaid. Original: **Le Passe-Muraille**; *also an English version.*

Mr. Peek-a-Boo
1951, (Fr), Cité Films/UA, b&w, 74 mins.
<u>W</u>: Bourvil, Joan Greenwood, Marcel Arnold, Roger Treville
<u>D</u>: Jean Boyer   <u>SCR</u>: Jean Boyer & Michel Audiard, from Marcel Ayme's novel   <u>PHOTOG</u>: Charles Suin   <u>MUSIC</u>: Georges Van Parys
Standard fantasy: Man has power to walk through walls

Mr. Poorluck's Dream
1910, (GB), Hepworth, b&w, 300 ft. (91.4m)
<u>W</u>: Harry Buss (*Mr. Poorluck*)
<u>D</u>: Lewin Fitzhamon
Standard fantasy: Husband returns drunk, dreams of ride in bed

Mr. Potts Goes to Moscow
see *Top Secret (1952)*

Mr. Reeder in Room 13
1938, (GB), British Nat'l/ABPC, b&w, 78 mins.
<u>W</u>: Gibb McLaughlin (*J.G. Reeder*), Peter Murray-Hill (*Johnnie Gray*), Sara Seegar (*Lila*), Sally Gray (*Claire Kane*), Malcolm Keen (*Peter Kane*), Leslie Perrins (*Jeff Legge*), D.J. Williams (*Emmanuel Legge*), Robert Cochran (*Barker*), George Merritt (*Stevens*), Phil Ray, Rex Cravel, Florence Graves
<u>D</u>: Norman Lee   <u>SCR</u>: Doreen Montgomery, Victor Kendall & Elizabeth Meehan, from Edgar Wallace's novel *Room 13*
USA retitle, **Mystery of Room** 13 (Alliance, 1941)
Standard thriller: Detective nabs counterfeiters

Mr. Sardonicus
1961, (USA), Col, b&w, 89 mins.
<u>W</u>: Guy Rolfe (*Sardonicus*), Ronald Lewis (*Sir Robert*), Oscar Homolka (*Krull*), Audrey Dalton, Lorna Hanson, Vladimir Sokoloff, Constance Cavendish, Erika Peters, James Forrest, Tina Woodward
<u>P & D</u>: William Castle   <u>SCR</u>: Ray Russell, from his novel *Sardonicus*   <u>PHOTOG</u>: Burnett Guffey   <u>MUSIC</u>: Von Dexter
Standard horror-thriller: Nobleman seeks cure for his disfigured face

Mr. Selkie
1979, (GB), Wadlow/Grosvenor/CFF, color, 52 mins.
<u>W</u>: Samantha Weyson (*Eileen Ross*), Clark Flanagan (*Jimmy Ross*), Michael Mannion (*Roger Craine*), Peter Bayliss (*Mr. Selkie*), Noel Howlett (*Grandpa Ross*), Mollie Weir (*Grannie Ross*), Zara Nutley (*Mrs. Craine*), Derek Tansey (*PC Fletcher*), Christine Ozanne (*Susan*), Donald Currie (*The Householder*)
<u>P</u>: Jean Wadlow   <u>D</u>: Anthony Squire   <u>SCR</u>: Anthony Squire, John Tully & James Hill   <u>STORY</u>: Janet Eckford   <u>PHOTOG</u>: Norman Jones   <u>MUSIC</u>: John Gale
Standard juvenile fantasy: Seal takes human form, protests pollution

Mr. Stitch

1996, (USA), SCI-TV, color, 98 mins.
<u>W:</u> Wil Wheaton, Rutger Hauer, Nia Peeples, Ron Perlman, Taylor Negron, Michael Harris, Tom Savini
<u>D:</u> Roger Roberts Avary
TVM, standard SF-thriller: Scientist creates man

Mr. Superinvisible
see El Invencible Hombre Invisible

Mr. Sycamore
1975, (USA), Capricorn, color, 89 mins.
<u>W:</u> Jason Robards Jr. (*John*), Sandy Dennis (*Jane*), Jean Simmons (*Estelle Benbow*), Robert Easton (*Fred*), Brenda Smith (*Daisy*), Mark Miller (*Fletcher*), Richard Bull (*The Doctor*), Ian Wolfe (*Abner & Arnie*), David Osterhout (*Officer Kelly*), Lou Picetti (*Humphrey*), Jerome Thor (*Higgins*), Sydna Scott (*The Clubwoman*), Curtis Taylor (*Harry*), Ron D'Ippolito (*An Attendant*), Richard Redd (*An Attendant*), Hall Brock (*Albert*), Tawna Nugent (*Albert's Sister*), Paul Berini (*A Milkman*), Eddie Lewis (*A Milkman*), Darby Hinton (*Frank*), Lance Cremer, Janine Johnson, Walter Scott, Evert Smith, Wayne Smith, Don Specter
<u>P & D:</u> Pancho Kohner <u>SCR:</u> Ketti Frings & Pancho Kohner, from Ketti Frings' play & the story by Robert Ayre <u>PHOTOG:</u> John A. Morrill <u>MUSIC:</u> Maurice Jarre <u>SONG:</u> *Time Goes By*
Minor fantasy: Postman yearns to become a tree

Mr. Tubby's Triumph
1910, (GB), Cricks & Martin, b&w, 470 ft. (143.3m)
<u>D:</u> Dave Aylott
Standard comedy-fantasy: Meek fat man finds hat which causes persecutors to vanish

Mister V
see Pimpernel Smith

Mr. Vampire
1986, (Hong Kong), color, 99 mins.
<u>W:</u> Ricky Hui
<u>D:</u> Lau Koon Wai
Standard horror-comedy: Undead has adventures

Mr. Vampire II
1986, (Hong Kong), color, 91 mins.
<u>W:</u> Yuen Biao
<u>D:</u> Lau Koon Wai
Standard horror-comedy: More adventures of Oriental Undead

Mr. Vampire III
1987, (Hong Kong), color, 95 mins.
<u>W:</u> Richard Ng
<u>D:</u> Lau Koon Wai
Standard horror-comedy: Undead meets witches

Mr. Vampire IV
1988, (Hong Kong), color, 90 mins.
<u>D:</u> Lau Koon Wai
Standard horror-comedy: Cantonese bloodsucker has fun

Mr. Wong at Headquarters
see The Fatal Hour (1940)

Mr. Wong, Detective
1938, (USA), Mono, b&w, 67 mins.
<u>W:</u> Boris Karloff (*James Lee Wong*), Grant Withers (*Capt. Sam Street*), Maxine Jennings (*Myra*), Evelyn Brent (*Olga*), John St. Polis (*Roemer*), Lucien Prival (*Mohl*), William Gould (*Meisel*), Hooper Atchley (*Wilk*), Frank Bruno (*Lascari*), John Hamilton (*Dayton*), George Lloyd (*Devlin*), Lee Tung Foo (*Tchuin*), Wilbur Mack, Grace Wood, Lynton Brent
<u>D:</u> William Nigh <u>SCR:</u> Houston Branch, from characters created by Hugh Wiley <u>PHOTOG:</u> Harry Neumann <u>MUSIC:</u> Art Meyer
Minor thriller: Chinese sleuth probes murder. cf. **The Docks of New Orleans**

Mr. Wong in Chinatown
1939, (USA), Mono, b&w, 70 mins.
<u>W:</u> Boris Karloff (*James Lee Wong*), Marjorie Reynolds (*Bobby Logan*), Grant Withers (*Insp. Sam Street*), Huntley Gordon (*Davidson*), Peter George Lynn (*Capt. Jackson*), Lotus Long (*Princess Lin Hwa*), William Royle (*Capt. Jalme*), Richard Loo (*The Aged Chinese*), James Flavin (*Sgt. Jerry*), Bessie Loo (*Lilly May*), Lee Tung Foo (*Willie*), Guy Usher (*The Commissioner*), "Little" Angelo Rossitto (*The Dwarf*), Ernie Stanton
<u>P:</u> Scott R. Dunlap <u>D:</u> William Nigh <u>SCR:</u> Scott Darling, from characters created by Hugh Wiley <u>PHOTOG:</u> Harry Neumann <u>MUSIC DIR:</u> Edward Kay
Minor thriller: Chinese princess killed by poison dart. cf. **The Chinese Ring**

Mr. Wu
1919, (GB), Stoll, b&w, 5,170 ft. (1575.8m)
<u>W:</u> Matheson Lang (*Mr. Wu*), Lillah McCarthy (*Mrs. Gregory*), Meggie Albanesi (*Nang Ping*), Roy Royston (*Basil Gregory*), Teddy Arundell (*Mr. Gregory*)
<u>D:</u> Maurice Elvey <u>SCR:</u> Frederick Blatchford, from a play by Harry Vernon & Harold Owen

reissued 1922
Standard thriller: Evil Chinese merchant masterminds crimes

Mr. Wu
1927, (USA), MGM, b&w, 8 reels (7,603 ft./2317.4m)
<u>W:</u> Lon Chaney Sr. (*Mr. Wu/Mr. Wu's Grandfather*), Louise Dresser (*Mrs. Gregory*), Renee Adoree (*Nang Ping*), Ralph Forbes (*Basil Gregory*), Holmes Herbert (*Mr. Gregory*), Gertrude Olmstead (*Hilda Gregory*), Mrs. Wong Wing (*Ah*

Mr. Wu: Lon Chaney

Wong), Claude King (*Mr. Muir*), Sonny Loy (*Little Wu*), Anna May Wong (*Loo Song*)
<u>D:</u> William Nigh <u>ADAPT:</u> Lorna Moon, from the 1914 play by Harry Vernon & Harold Owen <u>PHOTOG:</u> John Arnold
Standard thriller: Chinaman compelled to kill daughter, seeks revenge on English family

Mister, You Are a Widower
1972, (Czech), color
Minor fantasy

The Mistletoe Bough
1904, (GB), Clarendon/Gaumont, b&w, 500 ft. (152.4m)
<u>D:</u> Percy Stow, from a poem by E.T. Bayley
Standard melodrama (15 scenes): Bride hides in chest, is found 15 years later

The Mistress of Atlantis
see Die Herrin von Atlantis

Mistress of Paradise
1981, (USA), ABC-TV, color, 100 mins.
<u>W:</u> Chad Everett (*Charles*), Genevieve Bujold (*Elizabeth/Marie*), Anthony Andrews (*Buckley*), Olivia Cole (*Victorine*), Myron Natwick (*Dr. Slocum*), Carolyn Seymour (*Adele*), Tonea Stewart (*Sister Sarah*), Fred D. Scott (*Franklin*), Lelia Goldoni (*Peg*), John McLiam, Bill Wiley, Valarian Smith
<u>D:</u> Peter Medak <u>TELEPLAY:</u> Bennett Foster & William Bast <u>PHOTOG:</u> Ken Lamkin <u>MUSIC:</u> John Addison
orig. to be titled **The Dark Secret of Black Bayou**
TVM, minor thriller (partly a rehash of **Rebecca***): Rich Yankee gal weds dashing Creole, faces voodoo and murder intrigue*

Mistress of the Apes
1980, (USA), Cineworld, color, 88 mins.
<u>W:</u> Barbara Leigh, Garth Pillsbury, Jenny Neumann, Walt Robin, Stuart Lancaster, Suzy Mandel Mark Thomas Miller, Art Evans, Mary McDonough, Claudia Christian, Brion James, Stella Stevens
<u>D:</u> Patrick Rand <u>WRIT & D:</u> Larry Buchanan
blurb: "Liberated at last!"
Minor adventure-thriller: Woman seeks lost husband, finds "missing link" race

The Mistress of the World (1919)
see *Die Herrin der Welt*

Mistress of the World
1959, (It-Fr-W. Ger), CCC, color, 190 mins, 2 parts.
<u>W</u>: Martha Hyer, Carlos Thompson, Sabu, Gino Cervi, Lino Ventura, Wolfgang Preiss
<u>D</u>: William Dieterle   <u>SCR</u>: Jo Eisinger & M.G. Petersson
Standard SF-adventure: Chinese agents pursue professor with invention for controlling Earth's gravity

Ms. 45
1981, (USA), Navaron Films/Rochelle, color, 84 mins.
<u>W</u>: Zoe Tamerlis, Bogey, Albert Sinkys, Darlene Stuto, Helen McGara, Nike Zachmanoglou, Jimmy Laine, Peter Yellen, Editta Sherman, Vincent Gruppi, S. Edward Singer, Stanley Timms, Faith Peters, Lawrence Zavaglia, Alex Jachino, Jack Thibeau, Jane Kennedy, Steve Singer, Jack Thibeau, Editta Sherman
<u>D</u>: Abel Ferrera   <u>SCR</u>: Nicholas St. John   <u>PHOTOG</u>: James Momel   <u>MUSIC</u>: Joe Delia
Unusual thriller: Mute girl goes on killing spree after being raped twice in one day

Ms. Scrooge
1997, (USA), Power/Wilshire Court/USA-TV, color, 95 mins.
<u>W</u>: Cicely Tyson (*Ebenita*), Michael Beach, Katherine Helmond, John Bourgeois, Karen Glave, Ken James, Allegra Fulton, Sandi Ross
<u>D</u>: John Korty   <u>TELEPLAY</u>: John McGreevey, inspired by: Charles Dickens' *Christmas Carol*   <u>PHOTOG</u>: Elemer Ragalyi   <u>MUSIC</u>: David Shire
TVM, standard fantasy: Black female skinflint reformed by spirits

Mix Me a Person
1962, (GB), Wessex/British Lion, b&w, 116 mins.
<u>W</u>: Anne Baxter (*Dr. Anne Dyson*), Adam Faith (*Harry Jukes*), Donald Sinden (*Philip Bellamy*), Topsy Jane (*Mona*), Jack MacGowran (*Terence*), Walter Brown (*Max Taplow*), Carol Ann Ford (*Jenny*), Glyn Houston (*Sam*), Meredith Edwards (*Johnson*), Dilys Hamlett (*Doris*), Alfred Burke (*Lumley*), David Kerran (*Socko*)
<u>P</u>: Victor Saville & Sergei Nolbandov   <u>D</u>: Leslie Norman   <u>SCR</u>: Ian Dalrymple & Roy Kerridge, from a novel by Jack Trevor Story
Standard crime-thriller: Barrister's psychiatrist wife proves convicted teen did not kill policeman

Mizpah: or, Love's Sacrifice
1915, (GB), Magnet, b&w, 4,000 ft. (1219.2m)
<u>W</u>: Kahli Ru (*Princess Zaga*)
<u>D</u>: Stuart Kinder, from a play by Wood Lawrence
Standard adventure-thriller: Egyptian princess loves soldier who beats prince in combat

M.M.M. 83
1965, (It), Franco Fanfani/Filmways, color
<u>W</u>: Pier Angeli, Fred Beir, Gerard Blain
Minor thriller: Scientist murdered

Moby Dick
1930, (USA), WB, b&w, 75 mins.
<u>W</u>: John Barrymore (*Ahab*), Joan Bennett (*Faith*), Nigel de Brulier (*Elijah*), Lloyd Hughes (*Derek*), May Boley (*Whale Oil Rosie*), Tom O'Brien (*Starbuck*), Noble Johnson (*Queequeg*), Walter Long (*Stubbs*), Virginia Sale (*The Old Maid*), John Ince (*Rev. Mapple*)
<u>D</u>: Lloyd Bacon   <u>SCR & DIALOG</u>: J. Grubb Alexander   <u>ADAPT</u>: Oliver H.P. Garrett, from Herman Melville's novel   <u>PHOTOG</u>: Robert Kurrle
*Standard adventure-thriller: Sea captain seeks leviathan. cf. **The Sea Beast***

Moby Dick
1956, (GB), Moulin/WB, color, 115 mins.
<u>W</u>: Gregory Peck (*Capt. Ahab*), Richard Basehart (*Ishmael*), Leo Genn (*Starbuck*), Orson Welles (*Father Mapple*), Harry Andrews (*Stubb*), Bernard Miles (*Manxman*), James Robertson Justice (*Capt. Boomer*), Royal Dano (*Elijah*), Mervyn Johns (*Peleg*), Noel Purcell (*The Carpenter*), Francis De Wolff (*Capt. Gardiner*), Edric Connor (*Daggoo*), Joseph Tomelty (*Peter Coffin*), Philip Stainton (*Bildad*), Seamus Kelly (*Flask*), Friedrich Ledebur (*Queequeg*), Ted Howard (*The Blacksmith*), Tamba Alleney (*Pip*), Tom Clegg (*Tashtego*)
<u>P & D</u>: John Huston   <u>SCR</u>: Ray Bradbury & John Huston, from Herman Melville's novel   <u>PHOTOG</u>: Oswald Morris   <u>MUSIC</u>: Louis Levy
Major adventure-thriller: Maniacal sea captain pursues legendary white whale

Moby Dick
1998, (USA-Austral-GB), USA-TV, color
<u>W</u>: Patrick Stewart (*Capt. Ahab*), Henry Thomas (*Ishmael*), Gregory Peck (*Father Mapple*), Ted Levine (*Starbuck*), Piripi Waretini (*Queequeg*), Norman Golden II, Kee Chan, Hugh Keays-Byrne, Matthew Montoya, Bill Hunter, Bruce Spence, Michael Edward Stevens, Warren Owens
<u>D</u>: Franc Roddam   <u>TELEPLAY</u>: Anton Diether & Franc Roddam, from Herman Melville's novel   <u>PHOTOG</u>: David Connell   <u>VS-FX</u>: David Duguid   <u>MUSIC</u>: Christopher Gordon
2-part TVM, standard adventure thriller: White whale pursued

Mockery
1927, (USA), MGM, b&w, 7 reels (5,957 ft./1815.7m)
<u>W</u>: Lon Chaney Sr. (*Serge*), Ricardo Cortez (*Dimitri*), Barbara Bedford (*Tatiana*), Mack Swain (*Mr. Gaidaroff*), Emily Fitzroy (*Mrs. Gaidar-off*), Charles Puffy (*Ivan*), Kai Schmidt (*The Butler*)
<u>D & SCR</u>: Benjamin Christensen, from a story by Stig Esbern   <u>PHOTOG</u>: Merritt B. Gerstad
*working title, **Terror***
Standard melodrama: Passion and vengeance during Russian Revolution

Model for Murder
1959, (GB), Parroch/Criterion, b&w, 75 mins.
<u>W</u>: Keith Andes (*David Martens*), Hazel Court (*Sally Meadows*), Jean Aubrey (*Annabel Meadows*), Michael Gough (*Kingsley Beauchamp*), Julia Arnall (*Diane Leigh*), Patricia Jessel (*Mme. Dupont*), Edwin Richfield (*Costard*), Howard Marion-Crawford (*Insp. Duncan*), Alfred Burke (*Podd*), Peter Hammond (*George*), George Benson (*Freddie*), Richard Pearson (*Bullock*), Barbara Archer (*Betty Costard*), Diane Bester (*Tessa*), Neil Hallett (*Sgt. Anderson*), Charles Lamb (*The Lock-Keeper*), Annabel Maule (*The Hospital Sister*)
<u>D</u>: Terry Bishop   <u>SCR</u>: Terry Bishop & Robert Dunbar, from an orig. story by Peter Fraser   <u>MUSIC</u>: William Davies
Standard thriller: American in England seeks dead brother's girl friend, finds intrigue

Modelling Extraordinary
1912, (GB), Natural Colour Film Co., color, 1,000 ft. (304.8m)
<u>D</u>: Walter R. Booth
Standard fantasy: Animated putty forms shapes

The Model Killer
see *The Hollywood Strangler Meets the Skid Row Slasher*

The Model Murder Case
1964, (GB), Cinema V, b&w, 90 mins.
<u>W</u>: Ian Hendry, Ronald Fraser
Standard thriller

A Modern Dick Whittington
1913, (GB), Clarendon, b&w, 655 ft. (199.6m)
<u>D</u>: Percy Stow   <u>STORY</u>: H.S. Middleton
Standard crime-thriller: Boy leads police to thieves' lair

A Modern Galatea
1907, (GB), Urban, b&w, 305 ft. (93m)
<u>D</u>: Walter R. Booth
Standard comedy short: Girl breaks artist's statue, takes its place

A Modern Love Potion
1910, (GB), Hepworth, b&w, 475 ft. (144.8m)
<u>D</u>: Lewin Fitzhamon
Standard comedy short: Man gives love potion to girl

A Modern Mystery
1912, (GB), Urban, b&w, 290 ft. (88.4m)
<u>WRIT & D</u>: Walter R. Booth
Standard fantasy short: Animated clay models of conjurer, skeleton, lady

Modern Problems
1981, (USA), Shamberg-Greisman/20th-Fox, color, 92 mins.
<u>W</u>: Chevy Chase (*Max*), Patti D'Arbanville (*Darcy*), Mary Kay Place (*Lorraine*), Dabney Coleman (*Mark*), Nell Carter (*Dorita*), Mitch Kreindel (*Barry*), Brian Doyle-Murray (*Brian*), Arthur Sellers (*The Mobile Supervisor*), Ron House (*The Vendor*), Sandy Helberg (*Pete*), Henry Corden (*Dubrovnik*), Buzzy Linhart (*The Tile Man*), Christine Nazareth (*The Redhead*), Luke Andreas (*The Tough Guy*), Jan Speck (*The Brunette*), Vincenzo Gagliardi (*The Singer*), Francois Cartier (*The Pianist*), Pat Proft (*The Maitre d'*), Tom Sherohman (*The Waiter*), Jim Hudson (*The Doctor*), Frank Birney (*The Man in the Lobby*), Reid Olson (*The Principal Dancer*), Neil Thompson, Carl Irwin
<u>P</u>: Alan Geisman & Michael Shamberg   <u>D</u>: Ken Shapiro   <u>SCR</u>: Ken Shapiro, Tom Sherohman & Arthur Sellers   <u>PHOTOG</u>: Edmund Koons   <u>MUSIC</u>: Dominic Frontiere
Minor SF-comedy: Man exposed to nuclear waste develops telekinetic powers

The Modern Pygmalion and Galatea
1911, (GB), Natural Colour Kinematograph Co., color, 335 ft. (102.1m)
<u>D</u>: Walter R. Booth & Theo Bouwmeester
Standard fantasy short: Artist's drawings of girl and children come to life

A Modern Salome
1919, (USA), Pathe, b&w
<u>D & SCR</u>: Leonce Perret, from Oscar Wilde's play *Salome*
Standard melodrama

Modern Times
1936, (USA), UA, b&w, 87 mins.
<u>W</u>: Charles Chaplin (*The Tramp*), Paulette Goddard ("*The Gamin*"), Allan Garcia (*The Steel Corp. Pres.*), Chester Conklin (*A Mechanic*), Wilfred Lucas, Hank Mann (*A Burglar*), Louis Natheux (*A Burglar*), Stanley "Tiny" Sandford (*A Burglar*), Henry Bergman (*The Cafe Proprietor*)

WRIT, D & MUSIC: Charlie Chaplin **PHOTOG:** Rollie Totteroh & Ira Morgan
orig. to be titled The Masses
Classic comedy: Humorous swipe at Industrial Revolution

Modesty Blaise
1966, (GB), 20th-Fox, color, 119 mins.
W: Monica Vitti *(Modesty Blaise)*, Terence Stamp *(Willie Garvin)*, Dirk Bogarde *(Gabriel)*, Harry Andrews *(Sir Gerald Tarrant)*, Michael Craig *(Paul Hagan)*, Scilla Gabel *(Melina)*, Clive Revill *(McWhirter/ Sheikh Abu Tahir)*, Rossella Falk *(Mrs. Fothergill)*, Tina Marquand *(Nicole)*, Joe Melia *(Crevier)*, Lex Schoorel *(Walter)*, Alexander Knox *(The Minister)*, Jack Lambert
P: Norman Priggen, Michael Birkett & Joseph Janni **D:** Joseph Losey **SCR:** Evan Jones, based on the comic-strip character by Peter O'Donnell **PHOTOG:** Jack Hildyard (Amsterdam exteriors photographed by David Boulton) **MUSIC:** John Dankworth **ART DIRECTION:** Jack Shampan
Standard adventure-satire: Superheroine battles shrewd villain

Moebius
1997, (Arg), Universidad del Cine (Buenos Aires), color, 88 mins.
W: Guillermo Angelelli *(Daniel Prat)*, Roberto Carnaghi *(Marcos Blasi)*, Annabella Levy *(Abril)*
D: Gustavo Mosquera **SCR:** Gustavo Mosqura, Arturo Onativia, Natalia Urruty, Gabriel Lifschitz, Pedro Cristiani & Maria Angeles Mira, based on a story by A.J. Deutsch **PHOTOG:** Abel Penalba **MUSIC:** Mariano Nunez West
"Mystery, mysticism, science fiction, religion and the politics of dictatorship are combined to intriguing effect..."—Lawrence Van Gelder, New York Times
Bizarre thriller: Subway train vanishes

Molemen Against the Son of Hercules
1962, (It), Interfilm/Leone, color, 97 mins.
W: Mark Forest, Moira Orfei, Paul Wynter
Standard "Sword & Sandal": Maciste battles hideous race of subterranean albinos

The Mole People
1956, (USA), Univ, b&w, 78 mins.
W: John Agar *(Dr. Roger Bentley)*, Cynthia Patrick *(Adad)*, Hugh Beaumont *(Dr. Jud Bellamin)*, Nestor Paiva *(Dr. LaFarge)*, Alan Napier *(Elinu, the High Priest)*, Phil Chambers, Robin Hughes, Rodd Redwing
P: William Alland **D:** Virgil Vogel **SCR:** Laszlo Gorog **PHOTOG:** Ellis Carter **SPCL-PHOTOG:** Clifford Stine **MUSIC:** Joseph Gershenson
reissued 1965, orig. co-billed with Curucu, Beast of the Amazon
Standard SF-adventure: Archeologists find Sumerian culture in cavern beneath Himalayas

Mom
1990, (USA), color, 100 mins.
W: Jeanne Bates
Minor horror-thriller: TV reporter's mother becomes flesh-eating monster

Mom and Dad Save the World
1992, (USA), WB, color, 87 mins.
W: Teri Garr *(Marge Nelson)*, Jeffrey Jones *(Dick Nelson)*, Jon Lovitz *(Tod Spengo)*, Eric Idle *(Raff)*, Wallace Shawn *(Sibor)*, Dwier Brown *(Sirk)*, Kathy Ireland *(Semage)*, Thalmus Rasulala *(Gen. Afir)*
D: Greg Beeman **SCR:** Chris Matheson & Ed Solomon **PHOTOG:** Jacques Haitkin **MUSIC:** Jerry Goldsmith
Standard SF-fantasy

Moment of Danger
1960, (GB), Cavalcade/WPD, b&w, 96 mins.
W: Trevor Howard *(John Bain)*, Dorothy Dandridge *(Gianna)*, Edmund Purdom *(Peter Carran)*, Michael Hordern *(Insp. Farrell)*, Paul Stassino *(Juan Montoya)*, Alfred Burke *(Shapley)*, John Bailey *(Cecil)*, Peter Illing *(The Pawnbroker)*, Barry Keegan *(Corrigan)*, Brian Worth *(The Guard)*
P: Thomas Clyde **D:** Laslo Benedek **SCR:** David Osborn & Donald Ogden Stewart, from a novel by Donald Mackenzie
USA retitle: Malaga
Tense crime-thriller: Cheated crook pursues jewel thief to Spain

A Moment of Darkness
1915, (GB), Hepworth, b&w, 1,625 ft. (495.3m)
W: Alma Taylor *(The Girl)*, Violet Hopson *(The Woman)*, Stewart Rome, Lionelle Howard
D: Cecil M. Hepworth
Standard crime-thriller: Father trains daughter to be jewel thief

Moment of Decision
1962, (GB), Merton Park/Aglo-Amalgamated, b&w, 30 mins.
W: Ray Barrett *(Bert West)*, Pat Healy *(Mary West)*, Marjy Lawrence *(Sally Mason)*, Viola Keats *(Mrs. Davies)*, Tim Hudson *(Dudley Chelsham)*, Norman Claridge *(The Judge)*, Mike Sarne *(The Boyfriend)*, Michael Aspel *(The Newsreader)*
P: Jack Greenwood **D:** John Kight **STORY:** James Eastwood, from a novel by Edgar Lustgarten
Standard short crime-thriller: Childless wife steals baby; husband holds it for ransom

Moment of Indescretion
1958, (GB), Danziger/UA, b&w, 71 mins.

W: Ronald Howard *(John Miller)*, Lana Morris *(Janet Miller)*, John Van Eyssen *(Corby)*, John Witty *(Bryan)*, Denis Shaw *(Insp. Marsh)*, Ann Lynn *(Pauline)*, John Stone *(Eric)*, Arnold Bell *(The Surgeon)*
P: Edward J. & Harry Lee Danziger **D:** Max Varnel **STORY:** Brian Clemens & Eldon Howard
Modest crime-thriller: Woman accused of stabbing ex-fiance's mistress

Moments
1974, (GB), Pemini Org./Col, color, 92 mins.
W: Keith Michell *(Peter Samuelson)*, Angharad Rees *(Chrissy)*, Bill Fraser, Jeannette Sterke, Donald Hewlett, Keith Bell, Val Minifie, Paul Michell, Helena Michell
P: Brian J. Bilgorri **D:** Peter Crane **STORY:** Michael Sloan **PHOTOG:** Wolfgang Suschitzky **MUSIC:** John Cameron
Standard thriller: Accountant's relationship with fugitive girl is suicidal fantasy

Moment to Moment
1965, (USA), Univ, color, 108 mins.
W: Jean Seberg, Honor Blackman, Arthur Hill *(Neil)*, Sean Garrison *(Mark)*, Peter Robbins *(Tim)*, Gregoire Aslan
P & D: Mervyn LeRoy **SCR:** John Lee Mahin, from an orig. story by Alec Coppel **PHOTOG:** Harry Stradling **MUSIC:** Henry Mancini
Standard soap-opera: Wayward wife fears she has murdered lover

La Mome Vert-de-Gris (Poison Ivy)
1953, (Fr), Pathe,. b&w, 89 mins.
W: Eddie Constantine *(Lemmy Caution)*, Dominique Wilms, Howard Vernon, Philippe Ernest, Dario Moreno, Gaston Modot
D: Bernard Borderie **SCR:** Bernard Borderie & Jacques Berland, from Peter Cheyney's novel *Poison Ivy*
A.k.a. Gun Moll
Standard thriller (1st "Lemmy Caution" adventure): Gangster seeks gold hijackers

A Mom for Christmas
1990, (USA), color, 95 mins.
W: Olivia Newton-John
Standard fantasy: Mannequin comes to life, fulfills yuletide dreams of motherless girl

La Momia (The Mummy)
1957, (Mex), Azteca, b&w, 67 mins.
W: Ramon Gay, Rosita Arenas, Steve Grant
P: William Calderon Stell **D:** Rafael Lopez Portillo
A.k.a. The Aztec Mummy and Curse of the Aztec Mummy
Minor horror-fantasy: Tomb-robbers disturb vengeful mummy

La Momia Contra el Robot Humano (The Mummy vs. the Human Robot)
1959, (Mex), C.L.A.S.A./AIP-TV, b&w, English-dubbed version, 63 mins.
W: Rosita Arenas *(Flora)*, Ramon Gay, Crox Alvaredo, Jorge Mondragon, Luis Aceves Castaneda, Emma Rolden
P: William C. Stell **D:** Rafael Portillo **SCR:** Alfred Salazar **PHOTOG:** Enrique Wallace
USA retitle, The Robot vs. the Aztec Mummy
Minor horror-fantasy: Scientist employs robot in search for Aztec treasure

Mondo Balordo
1964, (It), Ivanhoe/Crown Int'l, color, 93 mins, also 87 mins.
W: Boris Karloff (host/narrator)
D: Roberto Bianchi Montero
Standard docu: Bizarre customs explored

Money Madness
1948, (USA), Film Classics, b&w, 73 mins
W: Hugh Beaumont, Frances Rafferty
Minor thriller: Girl finds husband is larcenous killer

Mongrel
1983, (USA), color, 90 mins.
W: Aldo Ray, Terry Evans
D: Robert Burns
Minor horror-thriller: Man dreams he is murderous beast

Monica's Journey
1993, (Austria), 3D, color
D: Klaus Schroeder
Intense, controversial horror-fantasy: Woman travels through Hell to retrieve kidnapped daughter

The Monitors
1969, (USA), Wilding-Second City/Commonwealth United, color, 90 mins.
W: Guy Stockwell *(Harry)*, Susan Oliver *(Barbara)*, Keenan Wynn *(The General)*, Ed Begley *(The President)*, Sherry Jackson *(Mona)*, Shepperd Strudwick *(Tersh)*, Avery Schreiber *(Max)*, Larry Storch *(Col. Stutz)*, Alan Arkin, Adam Arkin, Xavier Cugat, Barbara Dana, Everett Dirksen, Stubby Kaye, Lynn Lipton, Jackie Vernon
P: Bernard Samlins **D:** Jack Shea **SCR:** Myron J. Gold, from a novel by Keith Laumer **PHOTOG:** William Zsigmond **MUSIC:** Fred Katz **SONGS:** Odetta & Sandy Holt
Standard SF-thriller: Space aliens conquer Earth to impose peace and goodwill

Monkey Business
1952, (USA), 20th-Fox, b&w, 97 mins.
W: Cary Grant (*Dr. Barnaby Fuller*), Ginger Rogers (*Edwina Fuller*), Charles Coburn (*Oxley*), Hugh Marlowe (*Hank*), Roger Moore, Kathleen Freeman, Dabbs Greer, Marilyn Monroe, Robert Cornthwaite, Esther Dale, George Winslow, Larry Keating, Douglas Spencer, Jerry Paris
P: Sol C. Siegel   D: Howard Hawks   SCR: Ben Hecht, Charles Lederer & I.A.L. Diamond   PHOTOG: Milton Krasner   MUSIC: Lionel Newman   SPCL-FX: Ray Kellogg
Standard comedy: Confusion about "rejuvenation" formula

Monkey Shines
1988, (USA), Orion, color, 113 mins.
W: Jason Beghe, John Pankow, Kate McNeil, Joyce Van Patten, Janine Turner, Christine Forrest, Stephen Root, Stanley Tucci, Ella the Monkey
D: George A. Romero
Unusual thriller: Monkey forms psychic link with vengeful, crippled master

The Monkey's Paw
1915, (GB), Magnet, b&w, 2,800 ft. (853.4m)
W: John Lawson (*John White*)
D: Sidney Northcote, from W.W. Jacobs' story
Standard fantasy: Mummified paw grants three wishes

The Monkey's Paw
1923, (GB), Artistic, b&w, 5,700 ft. (1737.4m)
W: Moore Marriott (*John White*), Marie Ault (*Mrs. White*), Charles Ashton (*Herbert White*), Johnny Butt (*Sgt. Tom Morris*), A.B. Imeson, George Wynn, Tom Coventry
P: George Redman   D: Manning Haynes   SCR: Lydia Hayward, from W.W. Jacobs' story
Standard horror-fantasy: Couple dreams magic paw returns dead son

The Monkey's Uncle
1964, (USA), Walt Disney/Buena Vista, color, 87 mins.
W: Tommy Kirk (*Merlin Jones*), Annette Funicello (*Jennifer*), Leon Ames (*Judge Holmsby*), Arthur O'Connell (*Darius Green III*), Frank Faylen (*Dearborn*), Leon Tyler (*Leon*), Connie Gilchrist, Norman Grabowski, Cheryl Miller, Gage Clarke, The Beach Boys, Connie Gilchrist (*The Housekeeper*), Norman Grabowski (*Norman*), Cheryl Miller (*Lisa*), Alan Hewitt (*Prof. Shattuck*), Gage Clarke (*The College President*), Mark Goddard (*Haywood*), Harry Holcombe, Alexander Lockwood, Harry Antrim
D: Robert Stevenson   SCR: Tom & Helen August   PHOTOG: Edward Colman   MUSIC: Buddy Baker   TITLE SONG: by Richard & Robert Sherman, sung by the Beach Boys
Standard SF-comedy. Sequel to Misadventures of Merlin Jones

The Monkey Talks
1927, (USA), Fox, b&w, 6 reels (5,500 ft./1676.4m)
W: Jacques Lerner (*Jocko/Fano*), Olive Borden (*Olivette*), Don Alvarado (*Sam Wick/Pierre*), Malcolm Waite (*Bergerin*), Raymond Hitchcock (*Lorenzo*), Ted McNamara (*Firmin*), Jane Winton (*Maisie*), August Tollaire (*Mata*)
D: Raoul Walsh   SCR: L.G. Rigby, from a story by Rene Fauchois   PHOTOG: L. William O'Connell
Standard melodrama: Members of traveling French circus disguise man as talking monkey

The Monocle
1964, (Fr), Cocinor/Laetitia/Four Star/ WB-TV, color, 100 mins.
W: Paul Meurisse, Barbara Steele, Marcel Dalio
D: Georges Lautner
Minor thriller: Secret agent vs. Hong Kong terrorists

Monolith
1993, (USA), EGM Film Int'l/Shapiro Glickenhaus Entertainment, color, 96 mins.
W: Bill Paxton (*Tucker*), Lindsay Frost (*Flynn*), John Hurt (*Villano*), Lou Gossett Jr. ("*Mac*"), Paul Ganus (*Connor*), Musetta Vander (*Katya Pavlova*), Andrew Lamond (*Schaefer*), Mark Phelan (*Rickman*), Alex Gaona (*The Boy*), Angela Gordon (*Jorjivik*), Boris Krutonog (*Rourke*), Steve Barbro (*Officer Jenkins*), Jennifer Naud (*The Rookie Cop*), Bill Woodbridge (*Jacobs*), Todd Jeffries (*LaRue*), Red Horton (*Rovello*), David St. James (*The Attendant*), Steve Blackwood (*Bio-Team Member #1*), Edward Paul Allen (*Bio-Team Member #2*), Craig Diffenderfer (*Bio-Team Member #3*), Michael Halsey (*The Tired Cop*), Kevin E. West (*The Locker Room Cop*), Frank G. Davis (*The Tramp*), Stan Yale (*The Bum*), Jefferson Wagner (*The Gunman*), Debb Lee Phillips (*The Flashback Wife*)
D: John Eyres   SCR: Stephen Lister   PHOTOG: Alan M. Trow   SPCL VS-FX: Introvision   ORIG. MUSIC: Frank Becker   SONGS: *Sweet Innocence, Misery, Flesh & Fire, Desert Rain, & Falling*
Standard SF-thriller: Cops detect space-alien coverup

The Monolith Monsters
1957, (USA), Univ, b&w, 77 mins.
W: Grant Williams, Lola Albright, Les Tremayne, Phil Harvey, Trevor Bardette, William Flaherty, Dean Cromer, Richard Cutting, Harry Jackson, Steve Darrell, Linda Scheley
P: Howard Christie   D: John Sherwood   SCR: Norman Jolley & Robert M. Fresco, from a story by Jack Arnold   PHOTOG: Ellis W. Carter   SPCL-FX: Clifford Stine   MUSIC: Joseph Gershenson

Standard SF-thriller: Earth threatened by giant towers of silicon crystals

El Mono Loco (The Mad Monkey)
1990, (Sp), color, 108 mins.
W: Jeff Goldblum, Miranda Richardson, Anemone, Liza Walker, Dexter Fletcher, Daniel Ceccaldi, Arielle Dombasle
D: Luchino Visconti
Unusual psychological thriller: Scriptwriter drawn into web of sexual fantasy

M. Le Maudit
see M (1931)

M. Moto Court sa Chance
see Mr. Moto Takes a Chance

M. Moto dans les Bas-Fonds
see The Mysterious Mr. Moto

M. Moto sur le Ring
see Mr. Moto's Gamble

Monsieur Verdoux
1947, (USA), UA, b&w, 123 mins.
W: Charles Chaplin (*Henri Verdoux/alias Varnay/alias Bonheur/alias Floray*), Martha Raye (*Annabella Bonheur*), Mady Correll (*Mona Verdoux*), Allison Roddan (*Peter*), Isobel Elsom (*Marie Grosnay*), Robert Lewis (*Maurice Bottello*), Audrey Betz (*Mme. Bottello*), Helene Heigh (*Yvonne*), Margaret Hoffman (*Lydia Floray*), Edwin Mills (*Jean*), Ada-May (*Annette*), Marjorie Bennett (*The Maid*), Irving Bacon (*Pierre*), Virginia Brissac (*Carlotta*), Almira Sessions (*Lena*), Eula Morgan (*Phoebe*), Bernard J. Nedell (*The Prefect of Police*), Charles Evans (*Det. Morrow*), Cyril Delevanti
D, SCR & MUSIC: Charles Chaplin   IDEA: Orson Welles   PHOTOG: Roland Totheroh
Classic comedy-melodrama: Frenchman kills wives

The Monster (1903)
see Le Monstre (1903)

The Monster
1925, (USA), Metro-Goldwyn, b&w, 7 reels (6,425 ft./1958.3m)
W: Lon Chaney Sr. (*Dr. Ziska*), Gertrude Olmstead (*Betty Watson*), Hallam Cooley (*The Head Clerk*), Johnny Arthur (*The Under Clerk*), Charles A. Sellon (*The Constable*), Walter James (*Caliban*), Knute Erickson (*Daffy Dan*), George Austin (*Rigo*), Edward McWade (*Luke Watson*), Ethel Wales (*Mrs. Watson*)
D: Roland West   SCR: Willard Mack & Albert Kenyon, based on, "the famous stage success by Crane Wilbur"   PHOTOG: Hal Mohr
Standard horror-thriller: Mad scientist seeks to revive dead

The Monster (1955)
see The Quatermass Experiment

Monster (1978)
see Monstroid

The Monster (1982)
see I Don't Want to Be Born

Monster
1994, (It-Fr), color, 115 mins.
W: Roberto Benigni, Nicoletta Braschi, Dominique Lavanant (*Jolanda*), Michel Blanc (*Taccone*)
Amusing farce: Con man targeted as serial killer

The Monster (1998)
see Stephen Crane's "The Monster"

Monster A-Go-Go
1965, (USA), Boxoffice Spectaculars, b&w, 70 mins.
W: Phil Morton, June Travis, Lois Brooke, George Perry, Henry Hite, Bill Rebane, Sheldon Seymour
D: Herschell Gordon Lewis & Bill Rebane   SCR: Jeff Smith, Bill Rebane, & Don Stanford   PHOTOG: Frank Pfieffer   MUSIC: Other Three
A.k.a. Terror at Halfday
blurb: "You've never seen a picture like this"
Minor SF-horror (compiled from unsold excerpts culled by Herschell Gordon Lewis): Beatnik beauties vs. space beast

The Monster and the Girl
1941, (USA), Para, b&w, 65 mins.
W: Rod Cameron (*Sam*), Paul Lukas (*Bruhl*), Ellen Drew, Marc Lawrence, Robert Paige, George Zucco, Joseph Calleia, Onslow Stevens, Phillip Terry, Gerald Mohr, Cliff Edwards
P: Jack Moss   D: Stuart Heisler   SCR: Stuart Anthony   PHOTOG: Victor Milner
Standard horror-thriller: Executed man's brain put into body of gorilla

The Monster and the Stripper
1973, (USA), color, 90 mins.
Minor horror-thriller: Gangster pursues bayou creature

The Monster and the Woman
see *Four Sided Triangle*

The Monster Baran
see *Varan the Unbelievable*

The Monster Club
1980, (GB), Sword & Sorcery/Chips/ITC, color, 99 mins.
W: Vincent Price (*Eramus*), Richard Johnson (*Father*), John Carradine (*R. Chetwynd-Hayes*), Britt Ekland (*Mother*), Donald Pleasence (*Pickering*), Stuart Whitman (*Sam*), Simon Ward (*George*), Lesley Dunlop (*Luna*), James Laurenson (*Raven*), Roger Sloman (*The Club Sec'y*), Barbara Kellermann (*Angela*), Patrick Magee (*The Innkeeper*), Geoffrey Bayldon (*The Psychiatrist*), Warren Saire (*Linlom*), Neil McCarthy (*Watson*), Anthony Valentine (*Mooney*), Anthony Steel (*Lintom Busotsky*), Suzanna Willis (*The Stripper*), Fran Fullenwider
P: Milton Subotsky **D:** Roy Ward Baker **SCR:** Edward & Valerie Abraham, from stories by R. Chetwynd-Hayes **PHOTOG:** Peter Jessop **MUSIC:** Douglas Gamley
Standard trio of terror tales: (1) Con-woman targets unhuman, (2) Boy finds father is vampire, & (3) Filmmaker encounters ghouls

The Monster Demolisher
see *Nostradamus y el Destructor de Monstruos*

Monster Dog
1982, (USA), color, 88 mins.
W: Alice Cooper, Victoria Vera
D: Clyde Anderson
Minor horror-thriller: Mutant canine menaces rock band

Monster from a Prehistoric Planet
see *Gappa, the Triphibian Monster*

The Monster from Green Hell
1957, (USA), Gross-Krasne/DCA, b&w, 71 mins.
W: Jim Davis, Barbara Turner, Robert E. Griffin, Eduardo Ciannelli, Vladimir Sokoloff, Joel Fluellen
P: Al Zimbalist **D:** Kenneth G. Crane
Minor SF-thriller: Scientists battle giant wasps

Monster from Mars
see *Robot Monster*

Monster from the Ocean Floor
1954, (USA), Palo Alto/Lippert, b&w, 66 mins.
W: Stuart Wade, Anne Kimbell, Dick Pinner, Inez Palange, Jack Hayes, Wyott Ordung, David Garcia

Monster From The Ocean Floor: Anne Kimbell

P: Roger Corman **D:** Wyott Ordung **SCR:** William Danch **PHOTOG:** Floyd Crosby **MUSIC:** Andre Brummer
A.k.a. **It Staked the Ocean Floor** *and* **Monster Maker**
Minor SF-thriller: Aquatic horror stalks oceanographer

The Monster from the Past
see *The Beast from 20,000 Fathoms*

Monster from the Surf
see *Beach Girls and the Monster*

Monster High
1989, (USA), Col, color, 89 mins.
W: Dean Iandoli, David Marriott, Diana Frank, D.J. Kerzner
D: Rudger Poe
Minor fantasy-thriller: High-school students oppose demon

The Monster in the Basement
1962, (USA), Robert Kraus, b&w

W: Lee Lorenz, Lenore Ross
WRIT, P & D: Robert Kraus **PHOTOG:** Jerry Cohen & Arthur Blumenfeld
Minor horror-thriller (amateur 16mm production, not in general release)

Monster in the Closet
1986, (USA), Troma, color, 92 mins.
W: Donald Grant (*Richard Clark*), Denise DuBarry (*Diane Bennett*), Henry Gibson (*Dr. Pennyworth*), Howard Duff (*Father Finnegan*), Donald Moffat (*Gen. Turnbull*), Paul Walker (*The Professor*), Claude Akins (*Sheriff Ketchum*), Frank Ashmore (*Scoop Johnson*), John Carradine (*Old Joe*), Stella Stevens (*Margo Crane*), Kevin Peter Hall (*The Monster*), Jesse White, Paul Dooley
D & SCR: Bob Dahlin **STORY:** Bob Dahlin & Peter L. Bergquist **PHOTOG:** Ronald W. McLeish **MUSIC:** Barrie Guard
Modest horror-satire: Reporter tracks weird creature

Monster in the Night
see *Monster on the Campus*

The Monster Maker
1944, (USA), PRC, b&w, 62 mins.
W: J. Carrol Naish (*Dr. Igor Markoff*), Ralph Morgan (*Lawrence*), Tala Birell (*Maxine*), Glenn Strange (*Steve*), Wanda McKay (*Patricia*), Terry Frost (*Bob Blake*), Alexander Pollard, Sam Flint
P: Sigmund Neufeld **D:** Sam Newfield **SCR:** Pierre Gendron & Martin Mooney **MUSIC SCORE:** Albert Glasser
Minor horror-thriller: Evil doctor infects pianist with acromegaly

Monster Maker (1954)
see *Monster from the Ocean Floor*

The Monster Maker (1965)
see *El Fabricante de Monstruos*

Monster Meets the Gorilla
see *The Boys from Brooklyn*

The Monster of Fate
see *Der Golem (1914)*

The Monster of Highgate Ponds
1961, (GB), Halas & Batchelor/CFF, b&w, 59 mins.
W: Roy Vincente (*The Monster*), Ronald Howard (*Uncle Dick*), Rachel Clay (*Sophie*), Michael Wade (*David*), Terry Raven (*Chris*), Frederick Piper (*Sam*), Michael Balfour (*Bert*), Beryl Cooke (*Miss Haggerty*)
P: John Halas **D:** Alberto Cavalcanti **SCR:** Mary Cathcart Borer **STORY:** Joy Batchelor
Standard juvenile fantasy: Children hatch Malayan monster, save it from circus showmen

The Monster of London (1935)
see *Werewolf of London*

The Monster of London City
1964, (W. Ger), PRO/CCC-Omnia-Gloria-Manley, b&w, 87 mins
W: Hansjorg Felmy, Marianne Koch, Hans Nielsen, Dietmar Schoenherr
Minor thriller

The Monster of Piedras Blancas
1959, (USA), Vanwick, Film Service Distributing, b&w, 71 mins.
W: Les Tremayne, Jeanne Carmen, Don Sullivan, John Harmon, Forrest Lewis, Frank Arvidson
P: Jack Kevan **D:** Irvin Berwick **SCR:** H. Haile Chace **PHOTOG:** Philip H. Lathrop
Standard SF-horror: Lighthouse keeper unwisely befriends aquatic beast

The Monster of Piedras Blancas: Jeanne Carmen

Monster of Terror

1965, (GB), Alta Vista/AIP, color, 78 mins.
W: Boris Karloff (*Nahum Witley*), Nick Adams (*Steve Reinhart*), Suzan Farmer (*Susan Witley*), Freda Jackson (*Letitia Witley*), Terence de Marney (*Merwin*), Paul Farrell (*Jason*), Patrick Magee (*Dr. Henderson*), Leslie Dwyer (*The Villager*), Harold Goodwin (*The Taximan*), Sydney Bromley (*The Old Man*), Billy Milton (*Henry*), Gretchen Franklin (*Miss Bailey*), Sheila Raynor
P: Pat Green **D:** Daniel Haller **SCR:** Jerry Sohl, from H.P. Lovecraft's short story "The Colour Out of Space" **PHOTOG:** Paul Beeson **MUSIC:** Don Banks
*USA retitle, **Die, Monster, Die!***
orig. to be titled 'The House at the End of the World'
*Standard horror-thriller: Meteorite radiation produces grotesques. cf. **The Curse***

The Monster of the Island
see Il Mostro dell'Isola

The Monster of London (1964)
D: Edwin Zbonek
Minor thriller: Murders plague stage production about Jack the Ripper

The Monster of Venice
see Il Mostro di Venezia

Monster on the Campus
1958, (USA), Univ, b&w, 76 mins.
W: Arthur Franz, Joanna Moore, Troy Donahue, Helen Westcott, Phil Harvey, Judson Pratt, Nancy Walters, Whit Bissell, Ross Elliott, Alexander Lockwood
D: Jack Arnold **SCR:** David Duncan **PHOTOG:** Russell Metty
*orig. to be titled **Monster in the Night***
"...certain scenes are grimly horrific. Searching through a wrecked house for the monster that has been menacing the town, scientist Arthur Franz moves into the dark back garden, unaware that, slightly out of focus behind him, the corpse of a girl is transfixed to a tree"—John Baxter, Science Fiction in the Cinema
Effective SF-horror: College professor accidentally turns himself into savage ape-man

Monster on the Hill
see Teenage Monster

The Monsters are Loose
see The Thrill Killers

The Monsters are Attacking the Town
see Them! (1954)

The Monsters Christmas
1981, (New Zeal), color, 50 mins.
W: Lucy McGrath, Paul Farrell, Michael Wilson
Juvenile fantasy: Girl tries to save friendly monsters from clutches of witch

Monsters Crash the Pajama Party
1965, (USA), color
W: Peter J. D'Noto
D: David L. Hewitt
Minor horror-thriller: Teens meet mad scientist

Monsters from the Moon
see Robot Monster

Monsters from the Unknown Planet
see Terror of Mechagodzilla

The Monster Show
see Freaks

Monsters of Dr. Frankenstein
see El Castello dell'Orrore

The Monsters on Our Planet
see I Married a Monster from Outer Space

The Monster Squad
1987, (USA), Taft Entertainment-Keith Barish/Tri-Star, color, 82 mins.
W: Andre Gower (*Sean*), Robby Kiger (*Patrick*), Stephen Macht (*Del*), Duncan Regehr (*Count Dracula*), Tom Noonan (*Frankenstein*), Brent Chalem (*Horace*), Ryan Lambert (*Rudy*), Ashley Bank (*Phoebe*), Michael Faustino (*Eugene*), Mary Ellen Trainor (*Emily*), Leonardo Cimino (*The Scary German Guy*), Jonathan Gries (*The Desperate Man*), Stan Shaw (*Det. Sapir*), Michael MacKay (*The Mummy*), Lisa Fuller (*Patrick's Sister*), Carl Thibault (*The Wolfman*), Jason Hervey (*E.J.*), Adam Carl (*Derek*), Tom Woodruff Jr. (*The Gillman*), Jack Gwillim (*Van Helsing*), David Proval (*The Pilot*), Daryl Anderson (*The Co-Pilot*), Robert Lesser (*Eugene's Dad*), Geill Richards (*Mr. Metzger*), Ernie Brown (*The Night Watchman*), Sonia Curtis (*The Peasant Girl*), Paul Barringer (*Squad Room Cop #1*), Julius LeFlore (*Squad Room Cop #2*), Jim Stephen (*Squad Room Cop #3*), Bryan Kestner (*The Rookie Cop*), Denver Mattson (*The Beefy Cop*), Diana Lewis (*The TV Anchorwoman*), Gary

Rebstock (*The TV Anchorman*), David Wendel (*The Army General*), Charly Morgan, Phil Culotta, Mary Albee, Joan-Carrol Baron, Julie Merrill, Marianne De Camp, Paul Van Camp, Riad
D: Fred Dekker **SCR:** Shane Black & Fred Dekker **PHOTOG:** Bradford May
VS-FX: Richard Edlund **MUSIC:** Bruce Broughton **SONGS:** include *Rock Until You Drop*
Juvenile horror-comedy: Kids oppose revived fiends

The Monster That Challenged the World
1957, (USA), UA, b&w, 83 mins.
W: Tim Holt, Audrey Dalton, Casey Adams (*Max Showalter*), Hans Conried, Mimi Gibson, Gordon Jones, Marjorie Stapp, Barbara Darrow, Byron Kane, Hal Taggert, Jody McCrea, William Swan, Ralph Moody, Charles Tannen, Milton Parsons, Harlan Wade, Michael Dugan, Dennis McCarthy, Bob Beneveds, Mack Williams, Eileen Harley, Gil Frye, Dan Gachman
P: Jules V. Levy & Arthur Gardner **D:** Arnold Laven **SCR:** Pat Fielder, from a story by David Duncan **PHOTOG:** Lester White **UNDERWATER PHOTOG:** Scotty Welbourne **MUSIC:** Heinz Roemheld
Standard SF-thriller: Monstrous slug threatens humanity

Monster: The Legend That Became a Terror
see Monstroid

The Monster Walks
1932, (USA), Mayfair, b&w, 69 mins.
W: Rex Lease, Vera Reynolds, Sheldon Lewis, Mischa Auer, Martha Mattox, Sidney Bracy, Sleep'n'Eat [later Willie Best]
P: Cliff Broughton **D:** Frank Strayer **SCR:** Robert Ellis **PHOTOG:** Jules Cronjager
Minor thriller: Evil paraplegic plots heiress-niece's demise

Monster Zero
1967, (Jap), Toho/Maron, color, 93 mins.
W: Nick Adams, Akira Takarada, Kumi Mizuno, Akira Kubo
D: Inoshiro Honda **SCR:** Shinichi Sekizawa **SPCL-FX:** Eiji Tsuburaya **MUSIC:** Akira Ifukube
*A.k.a. **Invasion of Astro-Monster, Godzilla vs. Monster Zero, Battle of the Astros**, and **Invasion of Planet X***
Standard SF-fantasy: New Planet discovered behind Jupiter

Le Monstre (The Monster)
1903, (Fr), Star, b&w, 51m (167.3 ft./2.8 mins.)
D: Georges Melies
Standard fantasy

Le Monstre (1955)
see The Quatermass Experiment

Le Monstre de Londres
see Werewolf of London

Les Monstres sur Notre Planete
see I Married a Monster from Outer Space

Monstroid
1978, (USA), Academy, color
W: Jim Mitchum, John Carradine, Phil Carey, Tony Eisley, Maria Rubio, Luis Suarez, Coral Kassel, Leslie Meigs, John Lamarr, Andrea Hartford, Glen Hartford, Connie Moore, Aldo Sambrell, Emanuel Smith, Roberto Martinez
D: Herbert L. Strock (uncredited) & Kenneth Hartford **SCR:** Kenneth Hartford, Walter Roeber Schmidt, Herbert L. Strock & Garland Scott **PHOTOG:** John Wilder Mincey & Arthur Fitzsimmons **SPCL-FX:** Kenneth Hartford, Steve Czerkas & Marc Wolf **MUSIC:** Gene Kauer
*A.k.a. **Monster** and **Monster: The Legend That Became a Terror***
*Minor SF-horror (features music lifted from **The Astounding She-Monster**): Problems with Colombian swamp-monster*

Monstrosity
1963, (USA), Emerson, b&w, 72 mins.
W: Marjorie Eaton, Frank Gerstle, Frank Fowler, Erica Peters
P: Jack Pollexfen & Dean Dillman Jr. **D:** Joseph V. Mascelli **SCR:** Vy Russell, Sue Bradford Dwiggins, Dean Dillman Jr. & Jack Pollexfen (uncredited) **NARRATOR:** Bradford Dillman
*A.k.a. **The Atomic Brain**, orig. to be titled **The Brain Snatchers***
Minor horror-thriller: Wealthy woman seeks brain transplant

Il Montagna di Dio Cannibale (Mountain of the Cannibal God)
1979, (It), Dania/Medusa/New Line, color, 86 mins.
W: Ursula Andress (*Susan*), Stacy Keach (*Edward Foster*), Claudio Cassinelli, Antonio Marsina, Lanfranco Spinola, Franco Fantasia, Akushla Sellajaah, Carlo Longhi, T.M. Munna, Luigina Rocchi, Dudley Wanaguru, M. Suki
P: Luciano Martino **D:** Sergio Martino **SCR:** Cesare Frugoni & Sergio Martino **PHOTOG:** Giancarlo Ferrando **MUSIC:** Guido & Maurizio De Angelis
*USA retitle, **Slave of the Cannibal God***
Minor adult (full nudity) thriller: Woman seeks lost husband in New Guinea wilds

Montana Mike
see Heaven Only Knows

Monte Cristo
1922, (USA), Fox, b&w, 10 reels (9,828 ft./2995.6m)
<u>W</u>: John Gilbert *(Edmond Dantes)*, Estelle Taylor *(Mercedes, Countess de Morcerf)*, Robert McKim *(De Villefort)*, William V. Mong *(Caderousse, the Innkeeper)*, Virginia Brown Faire *(Haidee, an Arabian Princess)*, George Siegmann *(Luigi Vampa, an Ex-Pirate)*, Spottiswoode Aitken *(Abbe Faria)*, Ralph Cloninger *(Fernand, Count de Morcerf)*, Albert Prisco *(Baron Danglars)*, Gaston Glass *(Albert de Morcerf)*, Al Filson *(Morrel, the Shipowner)*, Harry Lonsdale *(Dantes, Father of Edmond)*, Francis McDonald *(Benedetto, Son of De Villefort)*, Jack Cosgrove *(Gov. of Chateau d'If)*, Maude George *(Baroness Danglars)*, Renee Adoree *(Eugenie Danglars)*, George Campbell *(Napoleon)*, Willard Koch *(The Tailor at Chateau d'If)*, Howard Kendall *(The Surgeon)*
<u>D</u>: Emmett J. Flynn   <u>SCR</u>: Bernard McConville   <u>STORY</u>: Alexander Salvini, from Alexandre Dumas' novel *The Count of Monte Cristo*   <u>PHOTOG</u>: Lucien Andriot
reissued 1927
Standard adventure-thriller: Persecuted man gains revenge

Monty Learns to Swim
1909, (GB), Urban, b&w, 355 ft. (108.2m)
<u>D</u>: Walter R. Booth
Standard fantasy short: Amateur swimmer dreams of diving from moon, etc.

Monty Python and the Holy Grail
1975, (GB), EMI/Col, color, 90 mins.
<u>W</u>: Graham Chapman *(King Arthur/A Guard)*, John Cleese *(The Black Knight/Sir Lancelot/The French Knight/Tim)*, Michael Palin *(Sir Galahad/The King/A Knight)*, Terry Gilliam *(Patsy/The Soothsayer)*, Eric Idle *(Sir Robin/Concorde/Roger/Maynard/A Guard)*, Terry Jones *(Bedevere/Herbert)*, John Young *(The Historian)*, Carol Cleveland *(Zoot/Dingo)*, Neil Innes, Connie Booth, Bee Duffell, Rita Davies, Sally Kinghorn
<u>D</u>: Terry Gilliam & Terry Jones   <u>SCR</u>: Graham Chapman, Eric Idle, Terry Jones, John Cleese, Terry Gil-liam & Michael Palin   <u>PHOTOG</u>: Terry Bedford   <u>MUSIC</u>: Neil Innes
"...Lewis Carroll type of non-sequitur humor... There are moments which are liter-al evocations of Tolkien, Garner, and other of the magic English writers"— Baird Searles, "Films," The Magazine of Fantasy and Science Fiction, Vol. 49, No. 4 (October, 1975), p. 105
Amusing comedy-satire: Bumbling knights seek Silver Chalice

Monty's Monocle
1915, (GB), Bamforth/YCC, b&w, 755 ft. (230.1m)
<u>D</u>: Cecil Birch
Standard comedy-fantasy: Eyeglasses reveal the invisible

The Moon
1965, (Russ), color
Impressive Soviet short (won Gold Seal for Best Documentary in sci-fi field at Trieste's 4th International Science-Fiction Festival)

Moonbeam Magic
1924, (GB), Spectrum Films, color
<u>W</u>: Arthur Pusey, Margot Greville, Tom Heslewood, Roy Travers, Mabel Poulton, Kitty Foster, Joan Carr
<u>WRIT & D</u>: Felix Orman
Standard fantasy: Legend of how color came into world

Moonbeams
*see **An Eclipse of the Moon***

Moonchild
1974, (USA), American Films/Cinemation, color, 90 mins.
<u>W</u>: Victor Buono, John Carradine, Mark Travis, Marie Dunn, Janet Landgard, Pat Renella, William Challee, Frank Corsentino
<u>P</u>: Dick Alexander   <u>D & SCR</u>: Alan Gadney
*Standard fantasy: Young man visits inn whose residents have been repeating same experi-ences since the 1700's. A.k.a. **Full Moon***

Moon 44
1990, (USA-W. Ger), Centropolis, color, 102 mins.
<u>W</u>: Michael Pare *(Felix Stone)*, Lisa Eichhorn *(Terry Morgan)*, Dean Devlin *(Tyler)*, Brian Thompson *(Jake O'Neal)*, Malcolm McDowell *(Maj. Lee)*, Stephen Geoffreys *(Cookie)*, Leon Rippy *(Sgt. Sykes)*, Jochen Nickel *(Scooter Bailey)*, David Williamson *(Gallagher)*, John March *(Moose Haggerty)*, Mechmed Yilmaz *(Marc)*, Alec Murdock, Kat Sawyer-Young, Carol Rippy, Charles Haigh, Drew Lucas, Roscoe Lee Browne, Calvin Burke, Bernhard Bolden, Andy Howarth, William Begatte, Frederic Mills, Lloyd Fields, Michael Antoniou, Bernhard Nickel, Thomas Nickel, James Herdig, Ingo Eberle
<u>D</u>: Roland Emmerich   <u>SCR</u>: Dean Heyde & Oliver Eberle   <u>STORY</u>: Roland Emmerich, Oliver Eberle, Dean Heyde & P.J. Mitchell   <u>PHOTOG</u>: Karl Walter Lindenlaub   <u>SPCL-FX SPRVSR</u>: Volker Engel   <u>MUSIC</u>: Joel Goldsmith
Standard SF-adventure: Sabotage at space mining station

Moon in Scorpio
1987, (USA), video, color, 90 mins.
<u>W</u>: Britt Ekland *(Linda)*
Made-for-Video, minor fantasy-thriller: Supernatural beings terrorize vacationing Vietnam vets

Moonlight Becomes You
1998, (USA), FAM-TV, color, 95 mins.
<u>W</u>: Donna Mills, Winston Rekert, Frances Hyland, Helen Hughes *(Greta)*, David Beecroft *(Liam)*
from Mary Higgins Clark's novel
TVM, standard thriller: Fashion photographer probes step-mother's death, becomes killer's new target

Moon Madness
1982, (Fr), color
Standard animated fantasy: Balloon expedition to moon

Moon of the Wolf
1972, (USA), Filmways, Made for TV, color, 74 mins.
<u>W</u>: David Janssen, Barbara Rush, Bradford Dillman, Claudia MacNeil, John Beradino, Royal Dano, Bernardo Segall, John Chandler, Geoffrey Lewis, Dan Priest, George Sawaya, Dick Crockett, Paul R. DeVille, Robert Phillips
<u>P</u>: Everett Chambers & Peter Thomas   <u>D</u>: Daniel Petrie   <u>TELEPLAY</u>: Alvin Sapinsley, from Leslie H. Whitten's novel   <u>MAKEUP</u>: William & Tom Tuttle
TVM, standard horror-thriller: Murders in Louisiana bayou

Moon Pilot
1962, (USA), Walt Disney/Buena Vista, color, 98 mins.
<u>W</u>: Tom Tryon *(Capt. Richmond Talbot)*, Dany Saval *(Lyrae)*, Brian Keith *(Maj.-Gen. John Vanneman)*, Edmond O'Brien *(McClosky)*, Tommy Kirk *(Walter Talbot)*, Sarah Selby *(Celia Talbot)*, Bob Sweeney *(Sen. Henry McGuire)*, Dick Whittinghill *(Col. Briggs)*, Simon Scott *(The Medical Officer)*, Kent Smith *(Sec'y of the Air Force)*, Bert Remsen *(Agent Brown)*, Nancy Kulp
<u>D</u>: James Neilson   <u>SCR</u>: Maurice Tombragel   from a story by Robert Buckner   <u>PHOTOG</u>: William Snyder   <u>MUSIC</u>: Paul Smith
Standard SF-romance: Astronaut meets girl from another world

Moonraker
1979, (GB), Eon/UA, color, 126 mins.
<u>W</u>: Roger Moore *(James Bond)*, Lois Chiles *(Holly Goodhead)*, Richard Kiel *("Jaws")*, Michael Lonsdale *(Hugo Drax)*, Emily Bolton *(Manuela)*, Corinne Clery *(Miss Dufour)*, Bernard Lee *("M")*, Lois Maxwell *(Miss Moneypenny)*, Toshiro Suga *(Chang)*, Blanche Ravalec *(Dolly)*, Desmond Llewelyn *("Q")*, Walter Gotell *(Gen. Gogol)*, Geoffrey Keen *(Frederick Gray)*, Michael Marshall *(Col. Scott)*, Irka Bochenko *(The Blonde Beauty)*, Leila Shenna *(The Private Jet Hostess)*, Anne Lonnberg *(The Museum Guide)*, Jean-Pierre Castaldi *(The Private Jet Pilot)*, Douglas Lambert *(Mission Control Director)*, Alfie Bass *(The Consumptive Italian)*, Arthur Howard *(Cavandish)*, Brian Keith *(The U.S. Shuttle Captain)*, Kim Fortune, Nicholas Arbez, Chris Dillinger, Georges Beller, Catherine Serre, Denis Seurat, Beatrice Libert
<u>P</u>: Albert R. Broccoli   <u>D</u>: Lewis Gilbert   <u>SCR</u>: Christopher Wood, from charac-ters created by Ian Fleming   <u>PHOTOG</u>: Jean Tournier   <u>VS-FX SPRVSR</u>: Derek Meddings   <u>MUSIC</u>: John Barry   <u>LYRICS</u>: Hal David   <u>TITLE</u>: Shirley Bassey
Major SF-thriller: Entrepreneur plans race of supermen

The Moon-Spinners
1964, (GB), Walt Disney/Buena Vista, color, 119 mins.
<u>W</u>: Hayley Mills *(Nikky Ferris)*, Eli Wallach *(Stratos)*, Peter McEnery *(Mark Canford)*, Joan Greenwood *(Frances Ferris)*, Irene Papas *(Sophia)*, Pola Negri *(Mme. Habib)*, Paul Stassino *(Lambis)*, John LeMesurier *(Anthony Gamble)*, Sheila Hancock *(Cynthia Gamble)*, Michael Davis *(Alexis)*, Andre Morell *(The Captain)*, George Pastell *(The Lieutenant)*
<u>P</u>: Bill Anderson & Hugh Attwooll   <u>D</u>: James Neilson   <u>SCR</u>: Michael Dyne from Mary Stewart's novel   <u>PHOTOG</u>: Paul Beeson   <u>MUSIC</u>: Ron Grainer
Standard thriller: Girl vacationing on Crete runs afoul of jewel thieves

The Moonstone
1915, (USA), Shubert/World, b&w, 5 reels
<u>W</u>: Eugene O'Brien, Ellaine Hammerstein
<u>D</u>: Frank Crane, from Wilkie Collins' novel
Standard thriller: Sacred jewel stolen, grief follows

The Moonstone (1935)
*see **Lunnyi Kamen***

Moontrap
1989, (USA), Magic Films/Shapiro Glickenhaus, color, 92 mins.
<u>W</u>: Walter Koenig *(Jason Grant)*, Bruce Campbell *(Ray Tanner)*, Leigh Lombardi *(Mera)*, John L. Saunders *(Barnes)*, Reavis Graham *(Haskell)*, Tom Case *(Beck)*, Robert Kurcz, Reuben Yabuku, Judy Levitt, Doug Childs, Mariafae Mytnyk, James Courtney, Tony Abruzzo, Tom Whalen, Pat Carozzo
<u>P & D</u>: Robert Dyke   <u>SCR</u>: Tex Ragsdale   <u>PHOTOG</u>: Peter Klein   <u>SPCL-FX</u>: Acme Special Effects Co.   <u>SPCL-FX SPRVSR</u>: Gary Jones   <u>MUSIC</u>: Joseph LoDuca
Standard SF-thriller: Lunar robots menace astronauts

Moonwalk One
1972, (USA), color
<u>NARRATOR</u>: Laurence Luckinbill
Standard docu: Account of historic walk on moon

Moon Zero Two
1969, (GB), Hammer/WB, color, 100 mins.
W: James Olson (*Bill Kemp*), Catherina von Schell (*Clementine Taplin*), Neil McCallum (*The Captain*), Ori Levy (*Karminski*), Adrienne Corri (*Liz Murphy*), Warren Mitchell (*J.J. Hubbard*), Dudley Foster (*Whitsun*), Bernard Bresslaw (*Harry*), Joby Blanhard (*Smith*), Michael Ripper (*Player*), Sam Kydd (*The Barman*), Robert Tayman
P & SCR: Michael Carreras, from a story by Gavin Lyall, Frank Hardman & Martin Davidson D: Roy Ward Baker PHOTOG: Paul Beeson SPCL-FX: Les Bowie, Nick Allder & Kit West MUSIC: Don Ellis
Standard SF-thriller (reminiscent of 'Satellite in the Sky'): Magnate covets sapphire-asteroid

Morbidity of the Soul
2000, (USA), color
W: Jodie Foster, Anthony Hopkins
Sequel to **The Silence of the Lambs**

Morder Unter Uns
see M (1931)

More Deadly than the Male
1959, (GB), U.N.A./Cross Channel, color, 60 mins.
W: Jeremy White (*Saul Coe*), Ann Davy (*Estelle le Fol*), Edna Dore (*Ruth*), Lorraine Peters (*Rita*), John Mahoney (*Godfrey le Fol*)
D: Robert Bucknell, from a novel by Paul Chavalier
Standard crime-thriller: Tourist covets fruitgrower's wife, commits murder

More Than a Miracle
see C'Era Una Volta

Morgan the Pirate
1960, (It-Fr), Lux-Adelphia/MGM, color, 93 mins.
W: Steve Reeves (*Morgan*), Valerie Lagrange, Ivo Garrani, Lydia Alfonsi, Giulio Bosetti, Angelo Zanolli, Giorgio Ardisson, Dino Malacrida, Anita Todesco, Armand Mestral, Chelo Alonso (*Consuela*)
WRIT & D: Andre de Toth PHOTOG: Tonino & Franco Delli Colli MUSIC: Franco Mannino
Standard adventure-thriller: Buccaneer prowls seas

Morgen Grauen (Morning Terror)
1989, (Austria), color, 90 mins.
W: Albert Fortell, Hannelore Elsner
D: L.E. Neiman
USA retitle, **Time Troopers**
Minor SF thriller: Post nuke police perform executions

Morianna
1965, (Swed), Sebricon, b&w, 100 mins.
W: Anders Henriksson, Lotte Tarp, Tor Isedal, Eva Dahlbeck, Valter Norman, Ella Henriksson, Elisabet Oden, Erik Hell, Ove Tjernberg
D: Arne Mattsson SCR: Arne Mattsson & Per Wahloo from Jan Ekstrom's novel
Standard thriller

Moriarty
see Sherlock Holmes (1922)

Morning Call
1957, (GB), Winwell/Astral, b&w, 75 mins.
W: Ron Randell (*Nick Logan*), Greta Gynt (*Annette Manning*), Bruce Seton (*Insp. Brown*), Charles Farrell (*Karver*), Virginia Kelly (*Vera Clark*), Garard Green (*Stevens*), Wally Patch (*Wally*)
P: Bill Luckwell & Derek Winn D: Arthur Crabtree SCR: Paul Tabori, Bill Luckwell & Tom Waldron STORY: Leo Townsend
Standard crime-thriller: Doctor's wife tries to ransom kidnapped husband

Morning Terror
see Morgen Grauen

Morons from Outer Space
1985, (GB), Thorn-EMI/Univ, color, 87 mins.
W: Jimmy Nail (*Desmond Brock*), Mel Smith (*Bernard*), Joanne Pearce (*Sandra Brock*), Paul Bown (*Julian Tope*), Griff Rhys Jones (*Graham Sweetley*), Robert Austin (*The Newscaster*), John Barcroft (*McKenzie*), Bill Stewart (*Walters*), R.J. Bell (*Klutz*), Olivier Pierre (*Jablowski*), Peter Whitman (*Friborg*), Billy J. Mitchell (*The Commander*), Joanna Dickens (*The Lady Farmer*), Leonard Fenton (*The Commissionaire*), George Innes (*Stanley Benson*), John Joyce (*Insp. Miller*), Dinsdale Landen (*Cdr. Matteson*), James B. Sikking (*Col. Laribee*), Mark Jones (*Godfrey*), Andre Maranne (*Trousseaux*), Tristram Jellinek (*Simpson*), Shane Rimmer (*The Redneck*), Miriam Margolyes (*The Scientist*), Edward Arthur (*The Host*), Ronnie Stevens (*The Manager*), Peter Straker (*The Choir Singer*), Angela Crow, Jo Ross, Jimmy Mulville, Lesley Grantham, James Taylor, Edward Wiley, Christopher Northey, Joss Buckley, Tim Barker, Roger Hammond, Karen Lancaster, Barbara Hicks
P: Barry Hanson SCR: Mel Smith & Griff Rhys Jones
PHOTOG: Phil Meheux MUSIC: Peter Brewis
Minor SF-comedy: Space aliens become Earth celebrities

Moro Witch Doctor
1964, (USA-Phil), Assoc. Producers-Hemisphere/20th-Fox, b&w, 61 mins
W: Jock Mahoney (*Jefferson Stark*), Margia Dean, Reed Hadley
WRIT, P & D: Eddie Romero PHOTOG: Felipe Sacdalan MUSIC: Ariston Avelino
Standard melodrama: Drug smuggling, opium plantations, religious fanatics and death in Manila. Original title: Amok

Morozko (Father Frost)
1924, (Russ), b&w
D: Yuri Zheliabuzhsky, from a story by Pushkin
Juvenile fantasy: Children meet winter spirit

Morphia, the Death Drug
1914, (GB), Hepworth, b&w, 1,950 ft. (594.4m)
W: Tom Powers (*The Boy*), Alma Taylor (*The Girl*), William Felton (*The Doctor*)
D: Cecil M. Hepworth SCR: Blanche McIntosh, from a story by Tom Powers
Standard thriller: Doctor forces secretary to become morphine addict

Mortal Kombat
1995, (USA), New Line, color, 102 mins
W: Christopher Lambert (*Lord Rayden*), Robin Shou (*Liu Kang*), Linden Ashby (*Johnny Cage*), Bridgette Wilson (*Sonya Blade*), Cary-Hiroyuki Tagawa (*Shang Tsung*), Talisa Soto, Trevor Goddard
D: Paul Anderson SCR: Kevin Droney PHOTOG: John R. Leonetti MUSIC: George S. Clinton
Standard action-fantasy: Legion of superheroes battles villains

Mortal Kombat: Annihilation
1997, (USA), New Line, color, 91 mins.
W: Brian Thompson, Talisa Soto, Robin Shou
Standard SF-fantasy-action: Superheroes battle evil

Mortal Passions
1990, (USA), color, 96 mins.
W: Zach Galligan, Krista Erickson, Michael Bowen, Sheila Kelley, Luca Bercovici, David Warner
D: Andrew Lane
Minor thriller (Double Idemnity imitation): Scheming woman manipulates men

Mortal Sins
1992, (USA), ITC, cable, color, 95 mins.
W: Christopher Reeve, Roxann Biggs, Francis Guinan, Phillip R. Allen, Lisa Vultaggio, George Touliatos, Mavor Moore, Karen Kondazian, Thomas Peacocke, Blu Mankuma
D: Bradford May TELEPLAY: Greg Martinelli & Dennis Paoli PHOTOG: Peter F. Woeste MUSIC: Joseph Conlan
Made-for-cable, standard thriller: Priest tracks serial killer

Mortal Thoughts
1991, (USA), New Visions/Polar/Col, color, 103 mins.
W: Demi Moore, Glenne Headly, Bruce Willis, Harvey Keitel, Billie Neal, John Pankow, Frank Vincent, Karen Shallo
D: Alan Rudolph SCR: Wiliam Reilly & Claude Kerven PHOTOG: Elliot Davis MUSIC: Mark Isham
Unusual, well-acted thriller: Woman defended in complex murder trial

Le Mort du Soleil (The Death of the Sun)
1920, (Fr), Germaine Dulac, b&w
Standard SF-fantasy

La Mort en Ce Jardin (Death in This Garden)
1956, (Fr-Mex), Dismage/Oscar Dancigers/Cinediscolor, 97 mins, also 110 mins.
W: Simone Signoret, Michel Piccoli, Charles Vanel, Tito Junco
D: Luis Bunuel SCR: Luis Bunuel, Luis Alcoriza & Raymond Queneau, from a novel by José-André Lacour MUSIC: Paul Misraki
A.k.a. **Evil Eden**, **Diamond Hunters** *and* **Gina**
Standard thriller

La Morte Risale a ieri Sera (Death Occurred Last Night)
1970, (It- Germ), Filmes/Lombard/CCC/Titanus, color, 96 mins.
W: Raf Vallone
D: Duccio Tessari
Standard thriller

Mortuary
1983, (USA), Hickman/Artists Releasing Corp., color, 92 mins.
W: Mary McDonough, David Wallace, Bill Paxton, Christopher George, Lynda Day George, Curt Ayers, Alvy Moore
D: Howard Avedis SCR: Howard Avedis & Marlene Schmidt PHOTOG: Gary Graver MUSIC: John Cacavas
Minor horror-thriller: Mortician's son amasses corpses

The Mosaic Project
1995, (USA), color, 89 mins.
W: Jon Tabler, Ben Marley, Joe Estevez
D: John Sjogren
Minor action-SF: Two friends victimized by mad scientist

I Moschettiere del Mare (Musketeer of the Sea)

1962, (It), color, 115 mins.
W: Aldo Ray
D: Steno
Standard adventure-thriller

Mosquito

1995, (USA), Acme-Excalibur, color, 92 mins.
W: Gunnar Hansen, Ron Asheton, Steve Dixon, Rachel Loiselle, Tim Loveface
D: Gary Jones **SCR:** Gary Jones, Steve Hidge & Tom Chaney **PHOTOG:** Tom Chaney **MUSIC:** Allen Lynch & Randall Lynch **SONG:**, *Stinger Up Yours*
Minor SF-thriller: Campers meet mutant bugs

Moss Rose

1947, (USA), 20th-Fox, b&w, 82 mins.
W: Victor Mature, Peggy Cummins, Vincent Price, Patricia Medina, Ethel Barrymore, George Zucco
P: Gene Markey **D:** Gregory Ratoff **SCR:** Jules Furthman & Tom Reed
Standard thriller: Cockney girl blackmails killer nobleman

The Most Dangerous Game

1932, (USA), RKO, b&w, 65 mins.
W: Leslie Banks (*Count Zaroff*), Joel McCrea (*Bob*), Fay Wray (*Eve*), Robert Armstrong (*Martin*), Steve Clemento (*The Tartar*), Noble Johnson (*Ivan*), William Davidson (*The Captain*), Hale Hamilton, Dutch Hendrian, Lon Chaney Jr. [edited out of release print]
P: Merian C. Cooper **D:** Irving Pichel & Ernest B. Schoedsack **SCR:** James A. Creelman, based on Richard Connell's novella **PHOTOG:** Henry Gerrard **MUSIC:** Max Steiner **DESIGN:** Carroll Clark
GB retitle: The Hounds of Zaroff
Classic thriller: Mad count hunts humans. cf. Bloodlust!, Run for the Sun and A Game of Death

Most Dangerous Man Alive

1961, (USA), Col, b&w, 82 mins.
W: Ron Randell, Elaine Stewart (*Carla*), Anthony Caruso (*Damon*), Debra Paget, Gregg Palmer, Morris Ankrum, Joel Donte, Tudor Owen, Steve Mitchell
P: Benedict Bogeaus **D:** Allan Dwan **SCR:** James Leicester & Phillip Rock, based on story *The Steel Monster* by Phillip Rock & Michael Pate **PHOTOG:** Carl Carvahal **MUSIC:** Louis Forbes
Minor SF-thriller: Criminal imbued with superhuman fortitude

The Most Dangerous Sin

see Crime and Punishment (1958)

Il Mostro dell'Isola (The Island Monster)

1953, (It), Romano, b&w, 85 mins.
W: Boris Karloff, Franca Marzi, Renato Vicario, Carlo Duse, Patricia Remiddi
D: Roberto Montero **SCR:** Roberto Montero & Alberto Vecchietti
Minor melodrama: Drug smuggling on Italian isle

Il Mostro di Venezia (The Monster of Venice)

1965, (It), Europix, b&w, 76 mins.
W: Maureen Brown, Gin Mart
D & STORY: Dino Tavella **SCR:** Dino Tavella & G. Muretta
*USA retitle, **The Embalmer***
Minor thriller: Venice journalist probes murders by insane embalmer

A Most Unusual Woman

see La Donna Scimmia

Motel Hell

1980, (USA), UA, color, 106 mins.
W: Nina Axelrod (*Terry*), Wolfman Jack (*The Rev. Billy*), Elaine Joyce (*Edith*), Dick Curtis (*Guy*), Monique St. Pierre (*Debbie*), Rosanne Katon (*Suzi*), E. Hampton Beagle (*Bob*), Everett Creach (*Bo*), Michael Melvin (*Ivan*), John Ratzenberger, Marc Silver, Victoria Hartman, Gwil Richards, Toni Gillman, Shaylin Hendrixson, Margot Hope, Barbara Goodson, Kim Fowler
WRIT & P: Steven-Charles Jaffe & Robert Jaffe **D:** Kevin Connor **SCR:** S.C. Jaffe & Robert Jaffe **PHOTOG:** Thomas Del Ruth **MUSIC:** Lance Rubin
Standard thriller: Motel's check-out time leads to slaughterhouse

Mother Gets the Wrong Tonic

1913, (GB), Cricks & Martin, b&w, 431 ft. (131.4m)
D: Charles Calvert
Standard comedy-fantasy short: Neuralgic woman drinks horse tonic, acts equine

Mother Goose A Go-Go

1966, (USA), Jack H. Harris, color, 82 mins
W: Tommy Kirk, Anne Helm, Jacques Bergerac, Henny Youngman, Joe Pyne
WRIT, P & D: Jack H. Harris
Aka Unkissed Bride.
Minor comedy-fantasy: Impotent young husband visits psychiatrist, discovers he has "Mother Goose Complex"

Mother Goose Nursery Rhymes

1902, (GB), G.A.S. Films, b&w, 600 ft. (182.9m)
W: Tom Green

D: George Albert Smith
Standard comedy-fantasy (in 8 scenes): Tales of Old Mother Hubbard, Goosey Gander, Little Miss Muffet, Jack & Jill, others

Mother Goose Rock 'N' Rhyme

1990, (USA), color, 87 mins.
W: Shelley Duvall, Dan Gilroy
Standard musical fantasy: Fairy-tale characters search for Mother Goose

Mother Joan of the Angels

see Matka Joanna od Aniolow

Mother, May I Sleep with Danger?

1996, (USA), NBC-TV, color, 95 mins.
W: Tori Spelling, Ivan Sergei, Lisa Banes, Todd Caldecott (*Jackson*), Lochlyn Munro (*Kevin Shane*), Bryn-Erin Libman (*Erin*), Gabrielle Miller, Kevin McNulty
D: Jorge Montesi **TELEPLAY:** Edmond Stevens, from Claire Rainwater Jacobs' novel **PHOTOG:** Philip Linzey **MUSIC:** Irwin Fisch
TVM, standard thriller: Coed acquires psychotic boyfriend

Mother Riley Meets the Vampire

1951, (GB), Fernwood/Renown, b&w, 74 mins.
W: Arthur Lucan (*Mrs. Riley*), Bela Lugosi (*Von Housen*), Dora Bryan (*Tillie*), Richard Wattis (*PC Freddie*), Judith Furse (*Freda*), Philip Leaver (*Anton*), Maria Mercedes (*Julia Loretti*), Roderick Lovell (*Douglas*), David Hurst (*Mugsy*), Hattie Jacques (*Mrs. Jenks*), Graham Moffatt (*The Yokel*), Cyril Smith
P & D: John Gilling **SCR:** Val Valentine **PHOTOG:** Stan Pavey
*USA retitles, **Vampire Over London** and **My Son, the Vampire**, reissued 1964. Also **King Robot***

Mother Riley Meets The Vampire: BELA LUGOSI

Standard horror-comedy: Country crone meets Undead

Mother's Day

1980, (USA), Duty/Saga Films A.B./United Film, color, 98 mins.
W: Holden McGuire (*Ike*), Billy Ray McQuade (*Addley*), Rose Ross (*Mother*), Nancy Hendrickson (*Abbey*), Robert Collins (*Ernie*), Deborah Luce (*Jackie*), Tiana Pierce (*Trina*), Karl Sandys (*The "Dobber"*), Marsella Davidson (*Terry*), Robert Carnegie (*Tex*), Kevin Lowe (*Ted*), Scott Lucas (*The Storekeeper*), Ed Battle (*The Doorman*), Stanley Knapp (*Charlie*), Silas Davis, John Radom, Sondra Fortunato, Marshall Auerbach, John Castellano, John Fanelli, Steve Sturm, Joe Stanton, Vince Piccolo, Lawrence Mayer, Bill Smith, Stanley Kaufman, Louie Cogie, Leilani Gorre, Sheldon Reide, Timmie Leight, Suzy Fried, Gwen Van Highland, Katya, Josh Smilowitz, Doreen Richardson, Joel Greenberg, Sture Sjostedt
D: Charles Kaufman **SCR:** Charles Kaufman & Warren Leight **PHOTOG:** Joe Mangine **MUSIC:** Phil Gallo & Clem Vicari **SONG:** *I Think We're Alone Now*
Modest horror-satire: Backwoods cretins terrorize former coeds

Mothra

1961, (Jap), Toho/Col, color, 99 mins.
W: Jelly Ito, Ken Uehara, Yumi Ito, Emi Ito, Kenji Sahara, Takashi Shimura, Seizaburo Kawazu, Akihiko Harata, Yoshio Kosugi, Yoshibumi Tajima, Yasushi Yamamoto, Koro Sakurai, Haruya Kato, Ko Mishima, Tetsu Nakamura, Hiroshi Iwamoto, Shoichi Hirose, Hiroshi Takagi, Yasuhisa Tsutsumi, Teruko Mita, Mitsuo Tsuda, Masamitsu Tayma, Toshio Miura, Yutara Nakayama, Tadashi Okabe, Akira Wakamatsu, Johnny Yuseph, Obel Wyatt, Harold Conway, Robert Dunham, Koji Uno, Akira Yamada, Wataru Ohmae, Toshihiko Furuta, Keisuke Matsuyama, Yoshiyuki Kamimura, Katsumi Tezuka, Takeo Nagashima, Arai Hayamizu, Matsuo Matsumoto, Shinpei Mitsui, Kazuo Higata, Shigeo Kato, Rinsaku Ogata, Yutaka Okada, Yoshio Hattori, Hiroyuki Satake, Kazuo Imai, Hiroshi Akitsu, Akio Kusama, Haruo Nakajima
D: Inoshiro Honda **SCR:** Shinichi Sekizawa **ORIG. STORY:** Shinichiro

Nakamura, Takehiko Fukunaga & Yoshie Hotta PHOTOG: Hajime Koizumi SPCL-FX: Hiroshi Mikouyama SPCL-PHOTOG: Eiji Tsuburaya MUSIC: Yuji Koseki
Superior SF-fantasy: Giant moth attacks Japan

The Motor Bandits
1912, (GB), Brighton & County Films, b&w, 1,370 ft. (417.6m)
D: Walter Speer
Standard crime-thriller: Pursued bank robbers kidnap cadets

Motor Psycho
1965, (USA), Eve Prods., b&w, 73 mins.
W: Stephen Oliver, Haji, Alex Rocco, Holle K. Winters, Joseph Cellini, Thomas Scott, Coleman Francis, Steve Masters, Sharron Lee, Arshalouis Alvasian, F. Rufus Owens, E.E. Meyer, George Costello, Richard Brummer
P, D & PHOTOG: Russ Meyer SCR: Russ Meyer & W.E. Sprague MUSIC: Igo Kanter THEME: Paul Sawtell & Bert Shefter
Standard exploitation thriller

The Motor Valet
1906, (GB), Alpha Trading Co., b&w, 200 ft. (60.1m)
D: Arthur Cooper
A.k.a. The New Moto Valet
Standard fantasy short: Robot servant smashes furniture and explodes

Mountain of the Cannibal God
see Il Montagna di Dio Cannibale

Mountaintop Motel Massacre
1986, (USA), New World, color, 96 mins.
W: Bill Thurman (*Rev. Bill McWilley*), Anna Chappell (*Evelyn*), Will Mitchell (*Al*), Virginia Loridans (*Tanya*), Greg Brazzel (*Vernon*), Major Brock (*Crenshaw*), James Bradford (*The Sheriff*), Jill King (*Lorie*), Marian Jones (*Mary*), Amy Hill (*Prissy*), Rhonda Atwood (*The Barowner*), Foster Litton (*The Sheriff Dispatcher*), Linda Blankenship (*Al's Sec'y*), Angela Christine (*The Singing Voice*)
P & D: Jim McCullough Sr. SCR: Jim McCullough Jr. PHOTOG: Joseph Wilcots MUSIC: Don Dilullio
Minor thriller (filmed in 1983): Madwoman runs motel, commits atrocities

The Mouse and his Child
1978, (USA-Jap), Sanrio/Col, color, 83 mins.
VOICES: Peter Ustinov, Cloris Leachman, Andy Devine, Sally Kellerman, Neville Brand
D: Fred Wolf & Charles Swenson, from a story by Russell Hoban
Standard animated fantasy: Malevolent rat foments trouble

The Mouse on the Moon
1963, (GB), Walter Shenson/Lopert/UA, color, 85 mins.
W: Margaret Rutherford (*Grand Duchess Gloriana*), Bernard Cribbins (*Vincent Mountjoy*), Ron Moody (*Mountjoy*), David Kossoff (*Prof. Kokintz*), Terry Thomas (*Spender*), John LeMesurier (*The British Delegate*), June Ritchie (*Cynthia*), John Phillips (*Bracewell*), Eric Barker (*A Member*), Roddy McMillan (*Benter*), Tom Aldredge (*Wendover*), Peter Sallis (*The Russian Delegate*), Hugh Lloyd (*The Plumber*), Clive Dunn (*The Bandleader*), Michael Trubshawe (*The Aide*), John Bluthal (*Max Von Neidel*), Robin Bailey (*A Member*), Mario Fabrizi (*Mario*), Graham Stark (*The Guardsman*), Frankie Howerd (*A Fenwickian*), Allan Cuthbertson (*Simon*)
P: Walter Shenson D: Richard Lester SCR: Michael Pertwee, from characters created by Leonard Wibberley PHOTOG: Wilkie Cooper MUSIC: Ron Grainer
orig. to be titled A Rocket from Fenwick
Standard comedy (sequel to The Mouse That Roared): Bankrupt duchy lands first rocket on moon

The Mouse That Roared
1959, (GB), Highroad/Col, color, 90 mins.
W: Peter Sellers (*Tully Bascombe/Gloriana/Count Mountjoy*), Jean Seberg (*Helen*

The Mouse That Roared: WILLIAM HARTNELL, PETER SELLERS AND JEAN SEBERG

Kokintz), William Hartnell (*Will*), Leo McKern (*Benter*), David Kossoff (*Kokintz*), Macdonald Parke (*Snippet*), Austin Willis (*Sec'y of Defense*), Monty Landis (*Cobbley*), Timothy Bateson (*Roger*), Robin Gatehouse (*Mulligan*), Colin Gordon (*The Announcer*), Larry Cross (*Chester Beston*), George Margo (*O'Hara*), Harold Kasket
P: Carl Foreman & Walter Shenson D: Jack Arnold SCR: Stanley Mann & Roger MacDougall, from Leonard Wibberley's novel *The Wrath of the Grapes* PHOTOG: John Wilcox MUSIC: Edwin Astley
Classic satire: Impoverished duchy declares war on USA, hopes to reap post-war largesse cf. **The Mouse on the Moon**

Le Mousquetaire de la Reine (The Queen's Musketeer)
1910, (Fr), Star, b&w
D: Georges Melies
Standard adventure-thriller

Les Mousquetaires de la Reine (The Queen's Musketeers)
1903, (Fr), Star, b&w, 50m (164 ft./2.8 mins.)
D: Georges Melies
Standard adventure-thriller

Moveite, a New Hustling Powder
1910, (GB), Walturdaw, b&w, 310 ft. (94.5m)
Standard comedy-fantasy: Prof's powder gyrates burglar, policeman, sailors, sheep

The Movie House Massacre
1978, (USA), color, 80 mins.
W: Mary Woronov
Minor thriller: Psycho terrorizes theater

M3: The Gemini Strain
see Plague

Muchachas de Bagdad
see Babes in Bagdad

Der Mude Tod (The Weary Death)
1921, (Ger), Decla-Bioscop, b&w, 80 mins. (7,565.6 ft./2306m)
W: Rudolf Klein-Rogge, Lil Dagover, Bernhard Goetzke, Walter Janssen
P: Erich Pommer D: Fritz Lang SCR: Fritz Lang & Thea von Harbou PHOTOG: Erich Nietzchmann, Herman Salfrank & Fritz Arno Wagner SETS: Hermann Warm, Robert Herlth & Walter Rohrig
Fr retitle, **Les Trois Lumieres (The Three Lights),** *GB retitle,* **Destiny** *(Also US title, Artclass, 1922), USA retitles,* **Between Two Worlds and The Light Within**
Classic fantasy: Personification of Death allows girl to live three lives in doomed attempt to restore lover to land of the living

La Muerte Viviente
see Isle of the Snake People

Los Muertos No Perdonan (The Dead Do Not Forgive)
1963, (Sp), Juro Films-P.C., b&w
W: Javier Escriva, Luis Prendes, Francisco Moran, Antonio Molino, Iran Eory, May Heatherly, Alberto Dalbes, Antonio Casas
D: Julio Coll PHOTOG: Julio Rojas
Standard thriller

The Mugger
1958, (USA), UA, b&w, 74 mins.
W: Kent Smith, Nan Martin
Standard thriller

Muha (The Fly)
1967, (Yugo), color
Minor fantasy short

Las Mujeres Vampiras
see El Santo Contra las Vampiras

Il Mulino delle Donne di Pietra (Mill of the Stone Women)
1960, (It-Fr), Galatea/Parade, color, 94 mins.
W: Wolfgang Preiss, Scilla Gabel, Pierre Brice, Dany Carrel, Herbert Boehme
P: Gianpaolo Bigazzi D: Giorgio Ferroni SCR: Remigio Del Grosso, Ugo Liberatore, Giorgio Stegani & Giorgio Ferroni
Standard horror-thriller: Doctor's weird experiments cause beauties to become petrified

Multiple Maniacs
1970, (USA), b&w, 90 mins.
W: Divine, David Lochary, Mary Vivian Pearce, Edith Massey, Mink Stole
D: John Waters
Bizarre minor thriller: Spectators killed at freak show

Multiplicity
1996, (USA), Col, color, 117 mins.
W: Michael Keaton, Andie MacDowell, Harris Yulin, Richard Masur, Eugene Levy
D: Harold Ramis SCR: Chris Miller, Mary Hale, Lowell Ganz & Babaloo Mandel, from Chris Miller's short story PHOTOG: Laszlo Kovacs VS-

FX SPRVSR: Richard Edlund **MUSIC:** George Fenton
Unusual SF-comedy: Busy construction worker has himself cloned

The Mummy
1911, (USA), b&w
Standard melodrama

The Mummy
1912, (GB), Britannia Films/Pathe, b&w, 528 ft. (160.9m)
D: A.E. Coleby
Standard comedy short: Man poses as revived mummy to fool sweetheart's father

The Mummy
1932, (USA), Univ, b&w, 72 mins.
W: Boris Karloff (*Imhotep/Ardath Bey*), Edward Van Sloan (*Prof. Muller*), Zita Johann (*Auck-es-en-Amon/Helen Grosvenor*), David Manners (*Frank Whemple*), Arthur Byron (*Sir Joseph Whemple*), Noble Johnson (*The Nubian*), Bramwell Fletcher (*Norton*), Katherine Byron (*Mrs. Muller*), Tony Marlow (*The Inspector*), Leonard Mudie (*Prof. Pearson*), James Crane (*The Pharaoh*), Eddie Kane (*The Doctor*), Arnold Grey (*The Horseman*), Henry Victor (*Marion*)
P: Carl Laemmle Jr. **D:** Karl Freund **SCR:** John L. Balderston & Richard Schayer, from a story by Nina Wilcox Putnam **PHOTOG:** Charles Stumar **MAKEUP:** Jack Pierce
"...as much a love story as it is a horror film. The theme of passionate desire enduring constants of time and death pervades most of the tale, and it is precisely this premise that lends a soft delicate poetry to a genre dominated by thrills, violence and horror... It is a brooding, slow-moving romantic myth, as ageless and eternal as its ancient source"—Gary Gerani, "The Book of the Mummy—Chapter Three: A Classic Tale," Monster Fantasy, Vol. I, No. 2 (June, 1975), p. 21
"Editing (Milton Carruth) very much in the Germanic style, magnificent lighting credited to Charles Stumar (but pure Freund) and a superb performance by Karloff makes this a fantasy almost without equal"—John Baxter, Hollywood in the Thirties
"THE MUMMY is the best film of its genre because of the quality of its performances and the very high quality of its effects, especially Karloff's makeup, both as mummy and as Ardath Bey... Karloff's ever so slowly opening eye is the essence of THE MUMMY"—R.H.W. Dillard, "Even a Man who is Pure of Heart," Man and the Movies
"...the closest that Hollywood ever came to creating a poem out of horror"—William K. Everson, Classics of the Horror Film
Classic horror-fantasy: Egyptologist accidentally revives mummy

The Mummy (1957)
see La Momia

The Mummy
1959, (GB), Hammer/Univ, color, 88 mins.
W: Peter Cushing (*John Banning*), Christopher Lee (*Kharis, the Mummy*), Yvonne Furneaux (*Isobel Banning*), Felix Aylmer (*Stephen Banning*), Raymond Huntley (*Joseph Whemple*), Eddie Byrne (*Insp. Mulrooney*), George Pastell (*Mehemet Bey*), John Stuart (*The Coroner*), Michael Ripper (*The Poacher*), Harold Goodwin, Gerald Lawson, Denis Shaw
P: Michael Carreras **D:** Terence Fisher **SCR:** Jimmy Sangster **PHOTOG:** Jack Asher **MUSIC:** Franz Reizenstein
Fr retitle, **Curse of the Pharaohs**
"Britain's ghoulish, gaunt and gruesome Christopher (*Dracula*) Lee spends most of his time all wrapped up (*he's the Mummy*) in this remake of a famous horror classic. Chris does get out of wraps long enough to play his former self, a handsome Egyptian High Priest, in a flashback—Way back, to 2,000 B.C.! It's the archeologists who spring him after 4,000 uncomfortable years, when

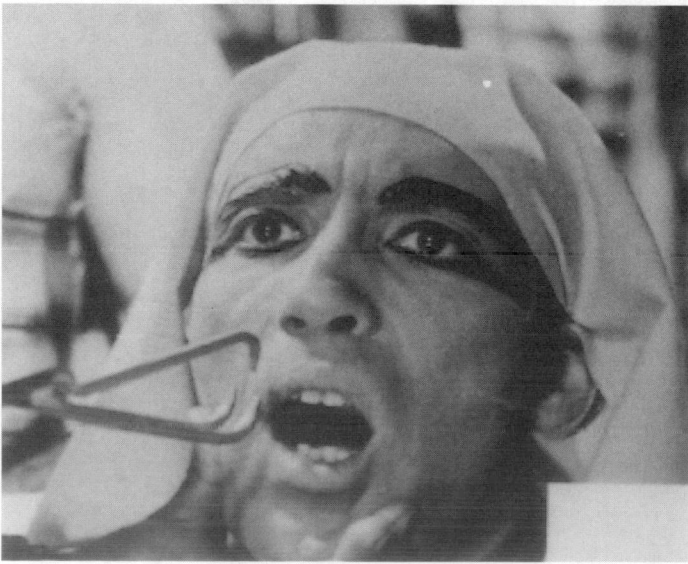

The Mummy (1959): CHRISTOPHER LEE

they flout an ancient curse and untomb his princess (lucky Yvonne Furneaux)"—Photoplay
"Christopher Lee innovates the genre as a tall, muscular, streamlined '59 model mummy, fast on his feet and violently cruel in his punishments. Marvelous sets, excellent use of the Technicolor process and a beautiful music score also contribute to the overall success of Hammer's first foray into the tomb-and-temple genre"—Gary Gerani, "The Book of the Mummy—Chapter Five: Hammer and Beyond," Monster Fantasy, Vol. I, No. 2 (June, 1975), pp. 26-27
Well-made horror-fantasy: Living mummy seeks revenge

The Mummy

The Mummy (1932): NOBLE JOHNSON, BORIS KARLOFF AND ZITA JOHANN

1999, (USA), Univ, color
W: Brendan Fraser, Rachel Weisz
D: Stephen Sommers
Exciting horror-fantasy: Archeologist meets immortal foe

The Mummy and King Rameses
1909, (Fr), Lux, b&w
D: Gerard Bourgeois
Standard horror-fantasy

The Mummy and the Curse of the Jackals
1969, (USA), Vega Int'l, color, 86 mins.
W: Anthony Eisley, John Carradine, Robert Allen Brown, Saul Goldsmith (*The Mummy*), Maurine Dawson, Marliza Pons, Burke Reynolds, William Whitton, Drake Michaels, Nancy Sheldon, Rebecca Rothchild, Frankie Dee, Judy Cassel
WRIT & P: William C. Edwards **D:** Oliver Drake **PHOTOG:** William Troiano **SPCL-FX:** Harry Woolman
Minor horror-fantasy: Egyptian princess revives, antiquarian becomes lycanthrope

The Mummy Lives
1995, (USA), Cannon, video, color
W: Tony Curtis
Standard horror-satire

The Mummy's Curse
1945, (USA), Univ, b&w, 62 mins.
W: Lon Chaney Jr. (*Kharis, the Mummy*), Virginia Christine (*Ananka*), Peter Coe, Martin Kosleck, William Farnum, Kurt Katch, Kay Harding, Holmes Herbert, Dennis Moore, Charles Stevens, Addison Richards, Napoleon ·Simpson
D: Leslie Goodwins **SCR:** Bernard Schubert **PHOTOG:** Virgil Miller
Standard horror-fantasy (sequel to **The Mummy's Ghost***, finale to* **Kharis, the Mummy** *series): Reincarnated Egyptian princess revived*

The Mummy's Eyes
see Die Augen der Mumie Ma

The Mummy's Ghost
1944, (USA), Univ, b&w, 61 mins.
W: Lon Chaney Jr. (*Kharis, the Mummy*), Ramsay Ames (*Amina Mansori*), John Carradine (*Ahmed Bey*), Robert Lowery (*Harvey*), George Zucco (*Andoheb*), Frank Reicher (*Prof. Norman*), Oscar O'Shea, Barton MacLane, Lester Sharpe, Emmett Vogan, Claire Whitney, Harry Shannon
D: Reginald LeBorg **SCR:** Griffin Jay, Henry Sucher & Brenda Weisberg **PHOTOG:** William Sickner
Standard horror-fantasy (sequel to 'The Mummy's Tomb'): Living mummy seeks reincarnated love. cf. **The Mummy's Curse**

The Mummy's Hand
1940, (USA), Univ, b&w, 67 mins.

W: Dick Foran (*Stephen Banning*), Peggy Moran (*Marta*), Wallace Ford (*Babe Hanson*), George Zucco (*Andoheb*), Eduardo Ciannelli, Cecil Kellaway, Charles Trowbridge, Tom Tyler (*Kharis, the Mummy*), Michael Mark, Siegfried (Sig) Arno, Eddie Foster, Mara Tartar, Harry Stubbs, Leon Belasco
P: Ben Pivar   **D:** Christy Cabanne   **SCR:** Griffin Jay & Maxwell Shane   **PHOTOG:** Elwood Bredell
Standard horror-fantasy (1st film in "Kharis, the Mummy" series): Soldiers-of-fortune seek ancient tomb, meet living mummy. cf. **The Mummy's Tomb**

The Mummy Lives
W: Greg Wrangler, Jack Cohen, Leslie Hardy
P: Harry Alan Towers   **D:** Gerry O'Hara   **SCR:** Nelson Gidding, suggested by Edgar Allan Poe's short story "Some Words With a Mummy"   **PHOTOG:** Avi Koren   **MUSIC:** Dov Seltzer

The Mummy's Revenge
1973, (Sp), Lotus/Avco Embassy TV, color, 85 mins.
W: Paul Naschy (*Assad Bey*), Jack Taylor (*Nathan*), Rina Ottolina (*Amarna/Helen*), Luis Davila (*Insp. Taylor*), Eduardo Calvo, Maria Silva, Helga Line, Fernando S. Polack, Celia Cruz, Luis Gaspar, Jose Yepes, Juan A. Soler, Jose Monne, Pilar Bardem, Ann Mary Pool, M. Cruz Fernandez
P: Luis Mendez   **D:** Carlos Aured   **STORY, SCR & DIALOG:** Jacinto Molina   **PHOTOG:** Francisco Sanchez   **MUSIC:** Alfonso Santisteban
Minor horror-fantasy: Revived pharaoh seeks body to house wife's soul

The Mummy's Shroud
1966, (GB), Hammer-7Arts/20th-Fox, color, 90 mins.
W: Andre Morell (*Sir Basil Walden*), David Buck (*Paul Preston*), Maggie Kimberley (*Claire*), John Phillips (*Stanley Preston*), Elizabeth Sellars (*Barbara Preston*), Tim Barrett (*Harry Newton*), Michael Ripper (*Longbarrow*), Dickie Owen (*Prem*), Richard Warner (*Insp. Barrani*), Roger Delgado (*Hasmid*), Catherine Lacey (*Haiti*), Bruno Barnabe (*The Pharaoh*), Toni Gilpin (*Pharaoh's Wife*), Toolsie Persaud (*Kah-to-Bey*), Eddie Powell (*The Mummy*), Andreas Malandrinos (*The Curator*)
P: Anthony Nelson Keys   **D & SCR:** John Gilling   **ORIG. STORY:** John Elder [Anthony Hinds]   **PHOTOG:** Arthur Grant   **SPCL-FX:** Bowie Films Ltd.   **MUSIC:** Don Banks
Standard horror-fantasy: Egyptian curse plagues archeologists

The Mummy's Tomb
1942, (USA), Univ, b&w, 67 mins.
W: Lon Chaney Jr. (*Kharis, the Mummy*), Turhan Bey (*Mehemet Bey*), Dick Foran (*Stephen Banning*), George Zucco (*Andoheb*), Elyse Knox (*Isobel Evans*), John Hubbard (*John Banning*), Wallace Ford (*Babe Hanson*), Cliff Clark (*The Sheriff*), Mary Gordon (*Jane*), Virginia Brissac (*Mrs. Evans*), Paul Burns (*Jim*), Frank Reicher (*Prof. Norman*), Emmett Vogan (*The Coroner*)
D: Harold Young   **SCR:** Griffin Jay & Henry Sucher   **ORIG. STORY:** Neil T. Varnick   **PHOTOG:** George Robinson
Standard horror-fantasy (sequel to **The Mummy's Hand**): *Young Egyptian priest forsakes vows of vengeance. cf.* **The Mummy's Ghost**

The Mummy's Tomb: TURHAN BEY AND LON CHANEY JR.

The Mummy vs. the Human Robot
see *La Momia Contra el Robot Humano*

Mumsy, Nanny, Sonny and Girly
see *Girly*

Munchie
1992, (USA), color, 80 mins.
W: Loni Anderson, Andrew Stevens, Arte Johnson, Dom DeLuise (voice), Jamie McEnnan
D: Jim Wynorski
Standard SF-fantasy (sequel to **Munchies**): *Deseted space alien aids boy*

Munchies
1987, (USA), Concorde/Reger Corman, color, 83 mins.
W: Harvey Korman, Charles Stratton, Nadine Van Der Velde
D: Bettina Hirsch
Minor SF-comedy: Archeologist finds mischievous alien creature that craves junk food

Munchie Strikes Back
1994, (USA), color, 80 mins.
W: Lesley-Anne Down, Andrew Stevens
Minor SF-fantasy: Mischievous space alien given chance to do good deed

El Mundo de los Vampiros (The World of the Vampires)
1960, (Mex), AIP-TV, b&w, 83 mins.
W: Mauricio Garces, Silvia Fournier
P: Abel Salazar   **D:** Alfonso Corona Blake   **SCR:** Ramon Obon
Minor horror-fantasy: Undead count controls coven

Munster Go Home!
1966, (USA), Univ, color, 96 mins.
W: Fred Gwynne (*Herman Munster*), Yvonne DeCarlo (*Lily Munster*), Butch Patrick (*Eddie Munster*), Terry Thomas (*Freddy*), Debbie Watson (*Marilyn*), Al Lewis (*Grandpa*), John Carradine (*Cruickshank*), Hermione Gingold (*Lady Munster*), Jeanne Arnold (*Grace*), Richard Dawson, Bernard Fox, Robert Pine
D: Earl Bellamy   **SCR:** Joe Connelly, George Tibbles & Bob Mosher   **PHOTOG:** Benjamin H. Kline   **MUSIC:** Jack Marshall
Standard horror-comedy: Ghoulish family visits Britain

The Munsters' Revenge
1981, (USA), NBC-TV/Univ, Made for TV, color, 95 mins.
W: Fred Gwynne (*Herman Munster*), Yvonne DeCarlo (*Lilly Munster*), Al Lewis (*Grandpa*), K.C. Martel, Jo McDonnell, Bob Hastings, Peter Fox, Herbert Voland, Colby Chester, Charles Macaulay, Joseph Ruskin, Ezra Stone, Sid Caesar, Howard Morris, Michael McManus, Gary Vinson, Read Morgan, Tom Newman, Sandy-Alexander Champion, Anita Dangler, Hillary Horan, Dolores Mann, Billy Sands, Barry Pearl, Kenny Rhodes, Mickey Deems
D: Don Weis   **TELEPLAY:** Arthur Alsberg & Don Nelson   **PHOTOG:** Harry L. Wolf   **MUSIC:** Vic Mizzy
TVM, minor horror-comedy: Ghoulish family runs afoul of law

The Munsters' Scary Little Christmas
1996, (USA), Fox-TV, color, 95 mins.
W: Sam McMurray (*Herman Munster*), Ann Magnuson (*Lily Munster*), Bug Hall (*Eddie Munster*), Sandy Baron (*Grandpa*), Elaine Hendrix (*Marilyn*), Mark Mitchell (*Santa*), Ed Gale, Mary Woronov, Arturo Gil
D: Ian Eames   **TELEPLAY:** Ed Ferrara & Kevin Murphy   **PHOTOG:** Roger Lanser   **MUSIC:** Christopher Stone
TVM, standard juvenile comedy-fantasy: Ghoulish family has yuletide problems

The Muppet Christmas Carol
1992, (USA), color, 86 mins.
W: Michael Caine (*Scrooge*)
VOICES: Steven Mackintosh, Meredith Braun, Donald Austen, Robin Weaver
D: Brian Henson, inspired by Charles Dickens' *Christmas Carol*

The Muppet Movie
1979, (GB-USA), ITC, color, 97 mins.
W: Charles Durning (*Doc Hopper*), Austin Pendleton (*Max*), Scott Walker (*Snake Walker*), Tommy Madden (*The Midget*), Lawrence Gabriel (*The Sailor*), Milton Berle (*Mad Man Mooney*), Ira Grubman (*The Bartender*), James Frawley (*A Waiter*), Edgar Bergen (*himself*), Mel Brooks (*Prof. Max Krassman*), James Coburn (*The Owner*), Elliott Gould (*The Compere*), Dom DeLuise (*Bernie*), Carol Kane (*Myth*), Bob Hope (*The Ice Cream Man*), Madeline Kahn (*The Patron*), Cloris Leachman (*The Sec'y*), Steve Martin (*A Waiter*), Richard Pryor (*The Balloon Man*), Telly Savalas (*The Tough*), Orson Welles (*Lew Lord*), Paul Williams (*The Pianist*)
P: Jim Henson & David Lazer   **D:** James Frawley   **SCR:** Jerry Juhl & Jack Burns from "The Muppet Show" teleseries by Jim Henson & Frank Oz   **PHOTOG:** Isidore Mankofsky   **MUSIC:** Paul Williams   **SONGS:** *The Rainbow Connection & Movin' Right Along*
Standard juvenile fantasy: Starstruck female pig saves frog from killers

The Muppets Take Manhattan
1984, (USA), Delphi II/TriStar, color, 94 mins.
W: Art Carney, James Coco, Dabney Coleman, Gregory Hines, Linda Lavin, Joan Rivers, Juliana Donald
VOICE: Frank Oz (*Miss Piggy*)   **D:** Frank Oz   **SCR:** Frank Oz & Jay Tarses   **PHOTOG:** Robert Paynter   **MUSIC:** Ralph Burns
Standard comedy-fantasy: Pig weds frog in New York City

Murder
1930, (GB), BIP/Wardour, b&w, 108 mins.
W: Herbert Marshall (*Sir John Menier*), Norah Baring (*Diana*), Phyllis Konstam (*Dulcie Markham*), Edward Chapman (*Ted Markham*), Miles Mander (*Gordon Druce*), Esme Percy (*Handel Fane*), Donald Calthrop (*Ion Stewart*), Amy Brandon Thomas (*The Defense*), Marie Wright (*Miss Mitcham*), Hannah Jones (*Mrs. Didsome*), Una O'Connor (*Mrs. Grogram*), Kenneth Kove (*Matthews*), R.E. Jeffrey (*The Foreman*), Violet Farebrother (*Mrs. Ward*), Gus McNaughton (*Tom Trewitt*)

The Munsters (1960's)

D: Alfred Hitchcock SCR: Alfred Hitchcock, Alma Reville & Walter C.
    Mycroft, from the play *Enter, Sir John* by Clemence Dane & Helen Simpson
Standard thriller: Actress accused of homicide

The Munster's Revenge: FRED GWYNNE AND YVONNE DECARLO

Murder Ahoy
1964, (GB), MGM British, b&w, 93 mins.
W: Margaret Rutherford (*Miss Marple*), Lionel Jeffries (*Capt. Sidney Rhumstone*),
    Charles Tingwell (*Insp. Craddock*), William Mervyn (*Cdr. Breeze
    Connington*), Joan Benham (*Alice Fanbraid*), Stringer Davis (*Mr. Stringer*),
    Miles Malleson (*The Bishop*), Nicholas Parsons (*Dr. Crump*), Henry Oscar
    (*Lord Rudkin*), Derek Nimmo (*Lt. Humbert*), Francis Matthews (*Compton*)
P: Lawrence P. Bachmann D: George Pollock SCR: David Pursall & Jack
    Seddon, from characters created by Agatha Christie
Modest crime-thriller: Lady detective probes deaths of trustees on cadet-training ship

Murder Anonymous
1955, (GB), Merton Park/Anglo-Amalgamated, b&w, 31 mins.
W: Peter Arne (*Douglas Sheldon*), Jill Bennett (*Mrs. Sheldon*), Ewen Solon (*Insp.
    Conway*)
P: Alec Snowden D: Ken Hughes STORY: James Eastwood & Roy H. Lewis,
    from a novel by Edgar Lustgarten
Standard short crime-thriller: Blind man kills wife's lover

Murder at Covent Garden
1932, (GB), Twickenham/W&F, b&w, 68 mins.
W: Dennis Neilson-Terry (*Jack Trencham*), Anne Grey (*Helen Osmond*), Walter
    Fitzgerald (*Donald Walpace*), George Curzon (*Belmont*), Henri de Vries (*Van
    Blond*), Binnie Barnes (*The Girl*), Fred Pease (*Snowball*)
D: Michael Barringer & Leslie Hiscott SCR: Michael Barringer & H. Fowler
    Mear, from a novel by W.J. Makin
Standard thriller: Detective seeks smuggled gems, poses as crook

Murder at 45 R.P.M.
1960, (Fr), MGM, b&w, 105 mins.
W: Danielle Darrieux, Michel Auclair
Minor thriller

Murder at Midnight
1931, (USA), b&w, 69 mins.

M

424

W: Alice White, Leslie Fenton, Aileen Pringle, Hale Hamilton, Robert Elliott, Clara Blandick, Brandon Hurst
D: Frank Strayer
Standard thriller: Partying socialites slain

Murder at Monte Carlo
1935, (GB), First Nat'l/WB, b&w, 70 mins.
W: Errol Flynn (*Dyter*), Eve Gray (*Gillian*), Paul Graetz (*Dr. Heinrich Becker*), Molly Lamont (*Margaret Becker*), Ellis Irving (*Marc Orton*), Henry Victor (*The Major*), Lawrence Hanray (*Collum*), Peter Gawthorne (*Duprez*), Brian Buchel (*Yates*)
D: Ralph Ince   SCR: John Hastings Turner & Michael Barringer, from a novel by Tom Van Dyke
Standard thriller: Reporter solves professor's murder

Murder at Scotland Yard
1952, (GB), Bushey/Ambassador, b&w, 75 mins.
W: Tod Slaughter (*Terence Riley*), Patrick Barr (*Insp. Morley*), Tucker McGuire (*Eileen Trotter*), Dorothy Bramhall (*Maria Flame*), Tom Macauley (*Insp. Grant*)
P: Gilbert Church   D: Victor M. Gover   STORY: John Gilling
reissued (1962) as 2 films
Standard thriller: Trilogy of crime tales

Murder at Site Three
1959, (GB), Exclusive, b&w, 67 mins.
W: Geoffrey Toone (*Sexton Blake*), Barbara Shelley (*Susan*), Jill Melford (*Paula Dane*), John Warwick (*Cdr. Chambers*), Richard Burrell (*Tinker*), Reed de Rouen (*McGill*), Harry Towb (*Kenney*)
P: Charles Leeds   D: Francis Searle   SCR: Manning O'Brine, from W. Howard Baker's novel *Crime is My Business*
reissued 1961
Standard thriller: Detective uses truth drug to expose missile security chief as spy

Murder at the Baskervilles
see Silver Blaze (1937)

Murder at the Burlesque
see Murder at the Windmill

Murder at the Gallop
1963, (GB), MGM, b&w, 81 mins.
W: Margaret Rutherford (*Miss Marple*), Robert Morley (*Hector Enderby*), Flora Robson (*Miss Gilchrist*), Charles Tingwell (*Insp. Craddock*), Katya Douglas (*Rosamund Shane*), Stringer Davis (*Mr. Stringer*), Duncan Lamont (*Hillman*), James Villiers (*Michael Shane*), Robert Urquhart (*George Crossfield*), Finlay Currie (*Enderby*)
P: Lawrence P. Bachmann & George Brown   D: George Pollock   SCR: James P. Cavanagh, from Agatha Christie's novel *After the Funeral*
Amusing crime-thriller: Spinster sleuth solves murder of cat-hating recluse and his sister

Murder at the Grange
1952, (GB), Bushey/Famous, b&w, 31 mins.
W: Tod Slaughter (*The Butler*), Patrick Barr (*Insp. Morley*), Margaret Boyd (*Agatha Quelch*)
P: Gilbert Church   D: Victor M. Gover   STORY: John Gilling
Standard short thriller: Cripple persuades butler to strangle her sister

Murder at the Inn
1934, (GB), First Nat'l/WB, b&w, 56 mins.
W: Wendy Barrie (*Angela Worthing*), Harold French (*Tony*), Jane Carr (*Fifi*), Davy Burnaby (*Col. Worthing*), Nicholas Hannen (*Dedreet*), H. Saxon-Snell (*The Inspector*), Minnie Rayner (*The Aunt*)
D: George King   STORY: Randall Faye
Standard thriller: Elopers involved in murder of blackmailing landlord

Murder at the Vanities
1934, (USA), Para, b&w, 89 mins.
W: Victor McLaglen, Kitty Carlisle, Jack Oakie, Dorothy Stickney, Carl Brisson, Gertrude Michael, Jessie Ralph, Gail Patrick, Clara Lou Sheridan [Ann Sheridan]
D: Mitchell Leisen   SCR: Carey Wilson, Sam Hellman & Joseph Gollomb   PHOTOG: Leo Tover
Standard thriller: Killer plagues musical show

Murder at the Windmill
1949, (GB), Daniel Angel/Nat Cohen/Mono, b&w, 70 mins.
W: Garry Marsh (*The Inspector*), Jack Livesey (*Vivian Van Damm*), Jon Pertwee (*The Sgt.*), Diana Decker (*Frankie*), Jill Anstey (*Patsy*), Donald Clive (*Donald*), Margot Johns (*The Box Office Girl*), Eliot Makeham (*Gimpy*), Genine Graham (*The Usherette*), Peter Butterworth (*The PC*), Constance Smith (*The Cloakroom Girl*), Jimmy Edwards, Robin Richmond, Ron Perriam, Christine Welsford, Johnnie Gale, Anita d'Ray, Johnnie McGregor, The Windmill Girls
WRIT & D: Val Guest
USA retitle, Murder at the Burlesque
Standard musical-thriller: Revue patron slain

Murder at 3 AM
1953, (GB), David Henley/Renown, b&w, 60 mins.
W: Dennis Price (*Insp. Peter Lawton*), Peggy Evans (*Joan Lawton*), Philip Saville (*Edward/Jim King*), Arnold Bell (*McMann*), Greta Mayaro (*Lena*), Rex Garner (*Sgt. Bill Todd*), Leonard Sharp (*Old Skip*), Nora Gordon (*Nanna*)
D: Francis Searle   STORY: John Ainsworth
Standard crime-thriller: Inspector traps villainous half-brother of sister's fiancee

Murder by Confession
see Absolution

Murder by Contract
1958, (USA), Col, b&w, 81 mins.
W: Vince Edwards, Michael Granger, Philip Pine, Herschel Bernardi, Caprice Toriel
D: Irving Lerner   PHOTOG: Lucien Ballard
Standard thriller

Murder by Death
1976, (USA), Rastar/Col, color, 94 mins.
W: Peter Sellers (*Insp. Sidney Wang*), David Niven (*Dick Charleston*), Peter Falk (*Sam Diamond*), James Coco (*Milo Perrier*), Elsa Lanchester (*Jessica Marbles*), Truman Capote (*Lionel Twain*), Eileen Brennan (*Tess Skeffington*), Alec Guinness (*Bensonmum, the Butler*), Estelle Winwood (*Miss Withers*), Maggie Smith (*Dora Charleston*), Richard Narita (*Willie Wang*), Nancy Walker (*Yetta*), James Cromwell (*Marcel*)
P: Ray Stark   D: Robert Moore   SCR: Neil Simon, from his play   PHOTOG: David M. Walsh   MUSIC: David Grusin   PRODUCTION DESIGN: Stephen Grimes
Standard comedy-thriller: World's greatest detectives invited to dinner at mansion

Murder by Decree
1979, (GB-Can), Canadian Film Development Corp.-Famous Players Ltd./Avco Embassy, color, 121 mins.
W: Christopher Plummer (*Sherlock Holmes*), James Mason (*Dr. John Watson*), Genevieve Bujold (*Annie Crook*), Susan Clark (*Mary*), Donald Sutherland ("*The Psychic*," *Robert Lees*), David Hemmings (*Foxborough*), Anthony Quayle (*Sir Charles*), John Gielgud (*Salisbury*), Frank Finlay (*Insp. Lestrade*), Chris Wiggins (*Dr. Harding*), Teddi Moore (*Mrs. Lees*), Peter Jonfield (*William Slade*), Hilary Sesta (*Catherine Eddowes*), Roy Lansford (*Sir Thomas Spivey*), June Brown (*Annie Chapman*), Catherine Kessler (*Carrie*), Ron Pember (*Makins*), Terry Duggan (*Dannie*), Betty Woolfe (*Mrs. Hudson*), Iris Fry (*Elizabeth Stride*), Geoffrey Russell (*The Home Secretary*), Victor Langley (*The Prince of Wales*), Pamela Abbot (*Princess Alexandra*), Robin Marchall (*The Duke of Clarence*), Danny Long (*PC Long*)

Murder By Decree: PETER JENFIELD AND DAVID HEMMINGS

P: Rene Dupont & Bob Clark   D: Bob Clark   SCR: John Hopkins   PHOTOG: Reg Morris   MUSIC: Carl Zittrer & Paul Zaza
Well-made thriller: Sherlock Holmes stalks "Jack the Ripper"

Murder by Mail
see Schizoid (1980)

Murder by Moonlight
1989, (GB), NBC-TV, color, 95 mins.
W: Brigitte Nielsen, Julian Sands, Gerald McRaney (*Dennis Huff*), Jane Lapotaire (*Louise Mackey*), Michael J. Shannon (*Vince Ivanov*), Brian Cox (*Voronov*), Alphonsia Emmanuel (*Isabelle Klein*), Tomeck Bork (*Sorokin*), Celia Imrie (*Patsy Diehl*)
D: Michael Lindsay-Hogg   TELEPLAY: Carla Jean Wagner   MUSIC: Trevor Jones
TVM, minor SF-thriller: Killer sought at lunar base

Murder by Night
1989, (USA), color, 95 mins.
W: Robert Urich, Kay Lenz, Jim Metzler, Michael Ironside, Richard Monette,

Michael Williams
D: Paul Lynch
Made-for-Cable, standard thriller: Amnesia victim suspected of murder

Murder by Proxy
1954, (GB), Exclusive/Lippert, b&w, 87 mins.
W: Dane Clark *(Casey Morrow)*, Belinda Lee *(Phyllis Brunner)*, Betty Ann Davies *(Alicia Brunner)*, Michael Golden *(Insp. Johnson)*, Eleanor Summerfield *(Maggie Doone)*, Jill Melford *(Miss Nardis)*, Andrew Osborn *(Lance Gorden)*, Cleo Laine *(The Singer)*, Harold Lang *(Travis)*, Delphi Lawrence *(Linda)*, Alfie Bass *(Ernie)*
P: Michael Carreras **D:** Terence Fisher **SCR:** Richard Landau, from Helen Nielsen's novel **PHOTOG:** Jimmy Harvey **MUSIC:** Ivor Slaney
*USA retitle, **Blackout***
Confused thriller: Man involved with murder and amnesia

Murder by Proxy (1963)
*see **Nightmare** (1963)*

Murder by Rope
1936, (GB), B&D/Para British, b&w, 64 mins.
W: Constance Godridge *(Daphne Farrow)*, D.A. Clarke-Smith *(Hanson)*, Sunday Wilshin *(Lucille Davine)*, Philip Hewland *(Judge Paxton)*, Wilfrid Hyde-White *(Alastair Dane)*, Donald Read *(Peter Paxton)*, Daphne Courtney *(Flora)*, Guy Belmore *(Simpson)*, Dorothy Hamilton *(Mrs. Mulcaire)*
D: George Pearson, from a story by Ralph Neale
reissued 1948
Standard thriller: Hanged man seems to return for revenge

Murder by Television
1935, (USA), William M. Pizor/Cameo/Imperial, b&w, 55 mins.
W: Bela Lugosi, June Collyer, Huntley Gordon, Allan Jung, George Meeker, Henry Mowbray, Charles Hill Mailes, Claire McDowell, Hattie McDaniel, Charles K. French, Henry Hall, Larry Francis, William (Billy) Sullivan, William Tooker
P & D: Clifford Sanforth **SCR:** Joseph O'Donnell **PHOTOG:** James Brown & Arthur Freed
Minor thriller: TV cameras emit death rays

Murder by the Book
1987, (USA), color, 100 mins.
W: Robert Hays, Catherine Mary Stewart, Celeste Holm, Fred Gwynne, Christopher Murney
D: Mel Damski, from Mel Arrighi's novel
*A.k.a. **Alter Ego***
TVM, standard thriller: Mystery writer solves crime

Murder by the Clock
1931, (USA), Para, b&w, 76 mins.
W: Lilyan Tashman, William ("stage") Boyd, Irving Pichel, Regis Toomey, Blanche Frederici, Walter McGrail, Lester Vail
D: Edward Sloman **SCR:** Henry Myers, Rufus King & Charles Beahan, from a play by Charles Beahan, based on a novel by Rufus King
Standard thriller: Man seems to return from death

The Murder Clinic
1966, (It-Fr), Europix/Ben Barry & Assocs., color, 82 mins.
W: William Berger *(Dr. Robert Vance)*, Barbara Wilson *(Mary)*, Mary Young *(Lizabeth)*, Francoise Prevost, Philippe Hersent, Grant Laramy, Harriet White, Max Dean, Delphine Maurin, Ann Sherman, Patricia Carr, William Gold
P & D: Michael Hamilton [Elio Scardamaglia] **SCR:** Julian Berry [Ernesto Gastaldi] & Martin Hardy [Sergio Martino] **PHOTOG:** Marc Lane **MUSIC:** Frank Mason
*A.k.a. **The Murder Society** and **Revenge of the Living Dead***
Minor thriller: Surgeon tries to restore woman's disfigured face

Murder Czech Style
1968, (Czech), Royal, b&w, 90 mins.
W: Rudolf Hrusinsky, Kveta Fialova, Vaclac Voska
Minor comedy-thriller

Murder Elite
1986, (GB), color, 98 mins.
W: Ali MacGraw, Billie Whitelaw, Hywel Bennett
D: Claude Whatham
Minor thriller: Murderous maniac in English countryside

Murderer Among Us
*see **M** (1931)*

Murderer's Keep
1988, (USA), color, 89 mins.
W: Vic Tayback, Talia Shire, Robert Walden
D: Paul-Michel Miekhe
Minor horror-thriller: Deaf girl finds meat market's wares are suspect

Murderers' Row
1966, (USA), Col, color, 108 mins.

W: Dean Martin, Karl Malden, Ann-Margret *(Suzie)*, Camilla Sparv *(Coco)*, Richard Eastham *(Dr. Solaris)*, Duke Howard, Beverly Adams, Ted Hartley, James Gregory, Patrick Holt, Tom Reese
P: Irving Allen **D:** Henry Levin **SCR:** Herbert Baker, from Donald Hamilton's novel **PHOTOG:** Sam Leavitt **SPCL-FX:** Danny Lee **MUSIC:** Lalo Schifrin
*Standard satire-thriller ("Matt Helm" adventure): Secret agent rescues scientist from scheming villain.   cf. **The Ambushers** and **The Wrecking Crew***

The Murder Game
1965, (GB), Robert L. Lippert/20th-Fox, b&w, 76 mins.
W: Ken Scott *(Steve Baldwin)*, Marla Landi *(Marie Aldrich)*, Trader Faulkner *(Chris Aldrich)*, Conrad Phillips *(Peter Shanley)*, Gerald Sim *(Larry Landstrom)*, Duncan Lamont *(Insp. Telford)*, Rosamund Greenwood *(Mrs. Potter)*, Ballard Berkeley *(Sir Colin Chalmers)*, Victor Brooks *(Rev. Francis Hood)*, Clement Freud (The Croupier), Jimmy Gardner, Peter Bathurst, Jennifer White, Frank Thornton, Derek Partridge, Gretchen Franklyn, John Dunbar
D: Sidney Salkow **SCR:** Harry Spalding **STORY:** Irving Yergin **PHOTOG:** Geoffrey Faithful **MUSIC:** Carlo Martelli
Standard thriller: Man frames conspirators for his own death

Murder in a Small Town
1999, (USA), Granada/A&E, color, 95 mins.
W: Gene Wilder, Mike Starr, Cherry Jones, Frances Conroy, Deirdre O'Connell, Terry O'Quinn, Elisabeth Rosen, Ben Bass, Carlo Rota, David Fox
D: Joyce Chopra **TELEPLAY:** Gilbert Pearlman & Gene Wilder **PHOTOG:** Bruce Surtees **MUSIC:** John Morris
TVM, standard thriller: Widowed theater director involved in homicide case

Murder in Eden
1961, (GB), Bill & Michael Luckwell/Colorama/Schoenfeld, b&w, 64 mins.
W: Ray McAnally *(Insp. Sharkey)*, Catherine Feller *(Genevieve Beaujean)*, Yvonne Buckingham *(Vicky Woolf)*, Mark Singleton *(Arnold Woolf)*, Norman Rodway *(Michael Lucas)*, Jack Aranson *(Bill Robson)*, Robert Lepler *(Max Aaronson)*
P: Bill Luckwell & John Macgregor **D:** Max Varnel **SCR:** H.E. Burden **STORY:** John Haggarty
Standard crime-thriller: Inspector unmasks killer involved in counterfeit paintings

The Murdering Mite
1957, (Jap), Daiei, color
Minor SF-thriller

Murder-In-Law
1992, (USA), color, 97 mins.
W: Marilyn Adams, Joe Estevez, Sandy Snyder, Darrel Guilbeau
D: Tony Jiti Gill
Minor thriller: Murderous mother-in-law escapes asylum

Murder in Mind
1973, (GB), Cecil Clarke/ITC, Made for TV, color, 71 mins.
W: Richard Johnson *(George Drew)*, Zena Walker *(Betty Drew)*, Donald Gee *(Tom Paterson)*, Ronald Radd *(Supt. Terson)*, Anthony Boden *(Sgt. Frost)*, David Lampson *(Police Constable Peters)*, Robert Dorning *(Dr. Sammers)*, Christina Greatorex *(Jill Pembury)*
D: Alan Gibson **TELEPLAY:** Brian Clemens **PHOTOG:** Dai Higgon **MUSIC:** Laurie Johnson
TVM, minor thriller: Writer plots wife's demise

Murder in Reverse
1945, (GB), British Nat'l/Anglo/Four Continents, b&w, 88 mins.
W: William Hartnell *(Tom Masterick)*, Jimmy Hanley *(Peter Rogers)*, Chili Bouchier *(Doris Masterick)*, Dinah Sheridan *(Jill Masterick)*, John Slater *(Fred Smith)*, Wylie Watson *(The Tailor)*, Edward Rigby *(Spike)*, Brefni O'Rorke *(Sullivan)*, Maire O'Neill *(Mrs. Moore)*, Ellis Irving *(Sgt. Howell)*, Petula Clark *(Jill as a Child)*, Scott Sanders *(The Landlord)*, Kynaston Reeves *(Crossley KC)*, John Salew *(Blake KC)*, Aubrey Mallalieu *(The Judge)*, Maudie Edwards *(The Customer)*
P: Louis H. Jackson **D & SCR:** Montgomery Tully, from the novel *Query* by Seamark
USA release, 1947
Standard thriller: Ex-convict tracks man he was supposed to have killed

Murder in Space
1985, (USA), color, 95 mins.
W: Wilford Brimley, Martin Balsam, Michael Ironside
D: Steven Hilliard Stern
TVM standard SF-thriller: Killer on space station

Murder in the Air
1940, (USA), WB, b&w, 55 mins.
W: Ronald Reagan, John Litel, Lya Lys, James Stephenson, Eddie Foy Jr.
D: Lewis Seiler
Standard thriller: Dirigible armed with death-ray. Breass Bancroft series.

Murder in the Air (1949)
*see **The Sky Dragon***

Murder in the Blue Room
1944, (USA), Univ, b&w, 61 mins.

W: John Litel (*Baldrich*), Anne Gwynne (*Nan*), Donald Cook (*Steve*), Grace McDonald, June Preisser, Betty Kean, Bill MacWilliams [Bill Williams], Regis Toomey
D: Leslie Goodwins
Minor thriller: Deaths in "haunted" house investigated. cf. **The Missing Guest** *and* **The Secret of the Blue Room**

Murder in the Doll House
1979, (Jap), color, 92 mins.
W: Yusaka Matsuda, Hiroko Shino, Yoko Nosaki
Standard thriller: Detective seeks link between doll-maker and three puzzling murders

Murder in the Music Hall
1946, (USA), Rep, b&w, 84 mins.
W: Vera Ralston, William Marshall
Standard thriller. Reissued as **Midnight Melody**

Murder in the Old Red Barn
see **Maria Marten: or, Murder in the Red Barn** *(1935)*

The Murder in Thornton Square
see **Gaslight** *(1944)*

Murder is a One-Act Play
1974, (GB), Made for TV, color, 74 mins.
W: George Maharis, Jennie Linden
A.k.a. **Death to Sister Mary**
TVM, standard thriller: TV-serial actors become stalked by crazed fan

Murder is Easy
1982, (GB), WB/CBS-TV, color, 95 mins.
W: Bill Bixby (*Luke Williams*), Lesley-Anne Down (*Bridget*), Olivia de Havilland (*Miss Waynflete*), Helen Hayes (*Lavinia Fullerton*), Patrick Allen (*Maj. Horton*), Shane Briant (*Dr. Thomas*), Freddie Jones (*Reed*), Leigh Lawson (*Jimmy*), Ivor Roberts (*The Vicar*), Timothy West (*Easterfield*), Jonathan Pryce (*Ellsworthy*), Anthony Valentine
P: Stan Margulies **D:** Claude Whatham **TELEPLAY:** Carmen Culver, from a novel by Agatha Christie **PHOTOG:** Brian Tufano **MUSIC:** Gerald Fried
A.k.a. **Agatha Christie's Murder is Easy**
TVM, standard thriller: Homicide among British elite

Murder is My Beat
1955, (USA), AA, b&w, 77 mins.
W: Barbara Payton, Paul Langton
D: Edgar J. Ulmer
Standard thriller

Murder is My Business
1946, (USA), PRC, b&w, 63 mins.
W: Hugh Beaumont (*Michael Shayne*), Cheryl Walker (*Phyllis Hamilton*), Lyle Talbot, George Meeker, Ralph Dunn, Pierre Watkin, Richard Keene, David Reed, Carol Andrews, Virginia Christine, Julia McMillan, Helene Heigh, Parker Garvie, Donald Kerr, Jack Collins, Broderick O'Farrell, Jack Ford, Jack Chefe
D: Sam Newfield **SCR:** Fred Myton, from the novel by Brett Halliday **PHOTOG:** Jack Greenhalgh **MUSIC:** Leo Erdody
Standard thriller ("Michael Shayne" mystery): Detective protects wealthy woman from blackmailers

Murderlust
1986, (USA), color, 90 mins.
W: Eli Rich, Rochelle Taylor, Dennis Gannon, Lisa Nichols, Bonnie Schneider
D: Donald M. Jones
Minor thriller: Security guard kills prostitutes

Murder Mansion
1970, (Sp), Avco Embassy, color, 85 mins.
W: Analia Gade (*Elsie*), Evelyn Stewart (*Marta*), Anna Lisa Nardi, Andres Resino, Franco Fantasia, Alberto Dalbes
D: Francisco Lara Polop **SCR:** Luis G. De Blain & Antonio Trosio **STORY:** Luis G. De Blain **PHOTOG:** Guglielmo Mancori **MUSIC:** Marcello Giombini
Minor thriller: Stranded travelers meet "ghosts"

Murder Most Foul
1964, (GB), MGM, b&w, 90 mins.
W: Margaret Rutherford (*Miss Marple*), Ron Moody (*H. Driffold Cosgood*), Dennis Price (*Harris Tumbrill*), Terry Scott (*PC Wells*), Charles Tingwell (*Insp. Craddock*), Francesca Annis (*Sheila Howard*), Andrew Cruickshank (*Justice Crosby*), Megs Jenkins (*Mrs. Thomas*), James Bolam (*Bill Hanson*), Stringer Davis (*Mr. Stringer*), Ralph Michael (*Ralph Summers*)
P: Lawrence P. Bachmann & Ben Arbeid **D:** George Pollock **SCR:** David Pursall & Jack Seddon, from Agatha Christie's novel *Mrs. McGinty's Dead*
Amusing crime-thriller: Spinster juror joins repertory company, exposes actress' murderer

Murder Motel
1974, (GB), Cecil Clarke/ITC, Made for TV, color, 72 mins.
W: Robyn Millan (*Kathy*), Derek Francis (*Sam*), Ralph Bates (*Michael Spencer*), Edward Judd (*Charles Burns*), John Hallam (*Roscoe*), Allan McClelland (*Lee*),

Anne Rutter (*Helen Spencer*), June Watson (*Petra*), Patrick Jordan (*Insp. Turner*), Gillian McCutcheon (*Janice Freeman*), Patrick Tull (*Terry*), Paul Humpoletz (*Osgood*), Keith Anderson (*The Auditor*), Peter MacKriel (*Mr. Taylor*), Lynn Miller, Adrian Shergood
D: Malcolm Taylor **TELEPLAY:** Brian Clemens **MUSIC:** Laurie Johnson
TVM, minor thriller: Larcenous siblings on lam, find dubious refuge

Murder, My Sweet
1944, (USA), RKO, b&w, 95 mins.
W: Dick Powell, Claire Trevor, Anne Shirley, Miles Mander, Otto Kruger, Douglas Walton, Mike Mazurki, Ralf Harolde, Don Douglas
D: Edward Dmytryk **SCR:** John Paxton, from Raymond Chandler's novel *Farewell, My Lovely* **PHOTOG:** Harry J. Wild **SPCL-FX:** Vernon L. Walker **MUSIC:** Roy Webb
Semi-classic thriller: Private eye seeks murderer

Murder of Innocence
1993, (USA), Marquee VII/Hearst, color, 93 mins.
W: Valerie Bertinelli, Stephen Caffrey, Graham Beckel, Jerry Hardin, Millie Perkins, Anne Ramsay, Steven Banks, Justin Whalin, Megan Cavanagh, John Scott Clough, Frank Novak, Juanita Jennings, Nancy McLoughlin, Trishalee Hardy, Ron Joseph, Charles Carroll, Albert Ash, Tony Reitano, Joyce Meadows, Whitney Rydbeck, Jill Ito, Jim Phelan, Robert Harvey, Kevin Lowe, Cynthia Kania, Shane Sweet, Jay W. MacIntosh, Taylor Nix, Zachary Freeman, Cassandra Friel, Jessica Frank, Sandee Van Dyke, J.D. Stone, Victoria Fairbrother, Natalie Zimmerman
D: Tom McLoughlin **TELEPLAY:** Philip Rosenberg, from the book by Joel Kaplan, George Papajohn & Eric Zorn **PHOTOG:** Shelly Johnson **MUSIC:** Don Davis
TVM, modest fact-based thriller: Newlywed woman proves demented, shoots schoolchildren

The Murder of Squire Jeffrey
1913, (GB), Cricks & Martin, b&w, 950 ft. (289.6m)
W: Charles Vane (*Paul Sleuth*)
D: Dave Aylott **STORY:** Stanhope Sprigg
Standard crime-thriller: Detective poses as murdered squire, traps burglar

Murder on a Bridle Path
1936, (USA), RKO, b&w, 65 mins.
W: Helen Broderick (*Hildegarde Withers*), James Gleason (*Oscar Piper*), Louise Latimer (*Barbara Foley*), Owen Davis Jr. (*Eddie Fry*), John Arledge (*Joey*), Leslie Fenton (*Don Gregg*), John Carroll (*Latigo Wells*), Christian Rub (*Thomas*), Sheila Terry (*Violet*), John Miltern (*Pat Gregg*), Willie Best (*High Pockets*), Harry Jans (*Addie*), James Donlan (*Kane*), Gustav von Seyffertitz (*Dr. Bloom*), Spencer Charters (*Mahoney*), Frank Reicher (*Dr. Peters*), Lucille Ball (*Drunk*), Tony Martin (*Pete*)
D: Edward Killy & William Hamilton **SCR:** Dorothy Yost, Thomas Lennon, Edmund North & James Gow, from characters created by Stuart Palmer **PHOTOG:** Nick Musuraca
Standard thriller ("Hildegarde Withers" mystery): Female sleuth pursues woman's murderer

Murder on a Honeymoon
1935, (USA), RKO, b&w, 74 mins.
W: Edna May Oliver (*Hildegarde Withers*), James Gleason (*Oscar Piper*), Lola Lane (*Phyllis La Font*), Spencer Charters (*Chief Britt*), Chick Chandler (*Pilot French*), George Meeker (*Kelsey*), Dorothy Libaire (*Kay Deving*), Harry Ellerbe (*Marvin Deving*), DeWitt Jennings (*Capt. Beegle*), Leo G. Carroll (*Joseph B. Tate*), Arthur Hoyt (*Dr. O'Rourke*), Morgan Wallace (*Arthur J. Mack*), Matt McHugh (*Pilot Madden*), Willie Best (*The Porter*), Brooks Benedict (*Forrest*), Rollo Lloyd (*The Hotel Clerk*)
D: Lloyd Corrigan **SCR:** Seton I. Miller & Robert Benchley from characters created by Stuart Palmer **MUSIC:** Albert Columbo
Standard thriller ("Hildegarde Withers" mystery): Vacationing school teacher investigates murder on Catalina Island

Murder on Approval
see **Barbados Quest**

Murder Once Removed
1971, (USA), color, 74 mins.
W: John Forsythe, Richard Kiley, Barbara Bain, Joseph Campanella
D: Charles S. Dubin
TVM, standard thriller: Doctor's bedside manner suspected

Murder on Diamond Row
see **The Squeaker** *(1937)*

Murder on Flight 502
1975, (USA), Spelling-Goldberg/ABC-TV, color, 100 mins.
W: Robert Stack, Polly Bergen, Ralph Bellamy, Hugh O'Brian, Theodore Bikel, Walter Pidgeon, Molly Picon, Laraine Day, Sonny Bono, Fernando Lamas, George Maharis, Danny Bonaduce, Dane Clark, Elizabeth Stack, Farrah Fawcett-Majors
D: George McGowan **TELEPLAY:** David P. Harmon
TVM, minor thriller: Unknown killer strikes on 747 flight to London

Murder on Monday
1951, (GB), British Lion, b&w, 85 mins.
W: Ralph Richardson (*David Preston*), Margaret Leighton (*Janet Preston*), Jack

Hawkins (*Dr. Sparling*), Campbell Singer (*Insp. Hemmingway*), Meriel Forbes (*Peggy Dobson*), Michael Shepley (*Maj. Watson*), Frederick Piper (*Petherbridge*), Gerald Case (*Sgt. Evans*), Margaret Withers (*Mrs. Watson*), Diana Beaumont (*Ellen*), Johnnie Schofield (*Joe Dobson*)
P & SCR: Anatole de Grunwald, from a play by R.C. Sherriff **D:** Ralph Richardson **PHOTOG:** Jack Hildyard & Edward Scaife
A.k.a. **Home at Seven**, US release: **Mayer-Kingsley**, 1953
Standard thriller: Crimes committed, bank clerk with lapses of memory suspected

Murder on the Air
see The Twenty Questions Murder

Murder on the Bayou
see Eaten Alive (1976)

Murder on the Blackboard
1934, (USA), RKO, b&w, 71 mins.
W: Edna May Oliver (*Hildegarde Withers*), James Gleason (*Oscar Piper*), Bruce Cabot (*Addison Stevens*), Gertrude Michael (*Janey Davis*), Regis Toomey (*Smiley*), Edgar Kennedy (*Det. Donahue*), Tully Marshall (*Mr. MacFarland*), Jackie Searle (*Leland Jones*), Fredrik Vogeding (*The School Janitor*), Barbara Fritchie (*Louise Halloran*), Gustav von Seyffertitz (*Max*)
D: George Archainbaud **SCR:** Willis Goldbeck, from characters created by Stuart Palmer **PHOTOG:** Nick Musuraca
Standard thriller ("Hildegarde Withers" mystery): Woman sleuth seeks teacher's killer

Murder on the Campus
1963, (GB), Colorama, color, 61 mins.
W: Terence Longden, Donald Gray
Standard thriller

Murder on the Last Night Train
1975, (It), European Inc., color
W: Flavio Bucci
Minor thriller

Murder on the Midnight Express
1975, (GB), Cecil Clarke/ITC, Made for TV, color, 71 mins.
W: Judy Geeson, Charles Gray, Jim Smilie, Edward Burnham, Jeffrey Wickham, Anthony Nash, Alister Williamson
P & D: John Cooper **TELEPLAY:** Brian Clemens **MUSIC:** Laurie Johnson
TVM, minor thriller: Girl encounters spy plot

Murder on the Orient Express
1974, (GB), John Brabourne-Richard Goodwin/Nat Cohen/Para, color, 131 mins.
W: Albert Finney (*Hercule Poirot*), Lauren Bacall (*Mrs. Hubbard*), Vanessa Redgrave (*Mary Debenham*), Sean Connery (*Col. Arbuthnot*), Ingrid Bergman (*Greta Ohlsson*), Richard Widmark (*Ratchett*), Martin Balsam (*Bianchi*), Wendy Hiller (*Princess Dragomiroff*), Sir John Gielgud (*Beddoes*), Jean-Pierre Cassel (*Pierre Paul Michel*), Jacqueline Bisset (*Countess Andrenyi*), Michael York (*Count Andrenyi*), Anthony Perkins (*Hector McQueen*), Rachel Roberts (*Hildegarde Schmidt*), Denis Quilley (*Foscarelli*), George Couloris (*Dr. Constantine*), John Moffatt (*The Chief Attendant*), Colin Blakely (*Hardman*), Vernon Dobtcheff (*The Concierge*), Jeremy Lloyd (*A.D.C.*)
D: Sidney Lumet **SCR:** Paul Dehn, from Agatha Christie's novel (novel known in USA as *Murder on the Calais Coach*) **PHOTOG:** Geoffrey Unsworth **MUSIC:** Richard Rodney Bennett
Classic mystery-thriller: 12 murder suspects on train. Academy Award. Ingrid Bergman-Best supporting Actress

Murderous Vision
1991, (USA), color, 95 mins.
W: Bruce Boxleitner, Laura Johnson, Joseph d'Angerio
TVM, standard thriller: Cop and psychic hunt killer

Murder Over New York: SIDNEY TOLER, VICTOR SEN YUNG, DONALD MCBRIDE, LEYLAND HODGESON AND JOHN SUTTON

Murder over New York
1940, (USA), 20th-Fox, b&w, 65 mins.
W: Sidney Toler (*Charlie Chan*), Marjorie Weaver (*Patricia Shaw*), Robert Lowery (*David Elliott*), Ricardo Cortez (*George Kirby*), Donald MacBride (*Insp. Vance*), Melville Cooper (*Herbert Fenton*), Joan Valerie (*June Preston*), Victor Sen Yung (*Jimmy Chan*), Kane Richmond (*Ralph Percy*), Leyland Hodgson (*Boggs*), John Sutton (*Richard Jeffrey*), Clarence Muse (*The Butler*), Frederick Worlock (*Hugh Drake*), Frank Coghlan Jr. (*Gilroy*), Lal Chand Mehra (*Ramullah*), Trevor Bardette (*The Suspect*), Shemp Howard (*Shorty McCoy*)
D: Harry Lachman **SCR:** Lester Ziffren, from characters created by Earl Derr Biggers **PHOTOG:** Virgil Miller
Standard thriller ("Charlie Chan" mystery): Oriental sleuth pursues saboteurs

Murder Reported
1957, (GB), Fortress/Col, b&w, 58 mins.
W: Paul Carpenter (*Jeff Holly*), Melissa Stribling (*Amanda North*), Patrick Holt (*Bill Stevens*), John Laurie (*Mac*), Peter Swanwick (*Hatter*), Maurice Durant (*Carmady*), Trevor Reid (*Insp. Palisay*), Georgia Brown (*Myra*), Hal Osmonde, David Coote, Gaylord Cavallaro, Ann Blake, Yvonne Warren, Edna Kove, Robert Vossler, Gladys Boot, The Reg Wale Four
D: Charles Saunders **SCR:** Doreen Montgomery **BASED ON:** Robert Chapman's novel *Murder for the Millions*
Standard thriller: Reporter and boss' daughter solve mysterious death

Murder She Said
1961, (GB), MGM British, b&w, 86 mins.
W: Margaret Rutherford (*Jane Marple*), Arthur Kennedy (*Dr. Quimper*), Muriel Pavlow (*Emma Ackenthorpe*), James Robertson Justice (*Ackenthorpe*), Thorley Walters (*Cedric Ackenthorpe*), Charles Tingwell (*Insp. Craddock*), Joan Hickson (*Mrs. Kidder*), Conrad Phillips (*Harold*), Ronald Howard (*Brian Eastley*), Stringer Davis (*Mr. Stringer*), Ronnie Raymond (*Alexander Eastley*), Peter Butterworth (*The Conductor*), Richard Briers ("*Mrs. Binster*")
P: George H. Brown **D:** George Pollock **SCR:** David Pursall, Jack Seddons & David Osborn, from Agatha Christie's novel *4.50 from Paddington*
Amusing crime-thriller: Spinster poses as maidservant, unmasks killer of French girl

Murders in the Rue Morgue
1932, (USA), Carl Laemmle/Univ, b&w, 62 mins.
W: Bela Lugosi (*Dr. Mirakle*), Betsy Ross Clarke (*Camille*), Sidney Fox, Leon Waycoff [Leon Ames], Brandon Hurst, Noble Johnson, Bert Roach, Arlene Francis, D'Arcy Corrigan
P: Carl Laemmle Jr. **D:** Robert Florey **SCR:** Tom Reed & Dale Van Avery based on Edgar Allan Poe's short story **PHOTOG:** Karl Freund **SPCL-FX:** John P. Fulton
1948 reissue by Realart/Film Classics
Standard horror-thriller: Mad scientist experiments with evolution, injects ape with blood of murdered girls. Film debut of Leon Ames

Murders In The Rue Morgue: LEON WAYCOFF

Murders in the Rue Morgue
1971, (USA-Sp), AIP, color, 87 mins.
W: Jason Robards Jr. (*Cesar Charron*), Christine Kaufmann (*Madeleine*), Maria Perschy (*Genevre*), Herbert Lom (*Marot*), Adolfo Celi (*Vidocq*), Michael Dunn (*Pierre*), Lilli Palmer (*Madeleine's Mother*), Peter Arne (*Aubert*), Jose Calvo (*The Hunchback*), Werner Umburg (*The Theatre Manager*), Virginia Stach (*Lucie*), Luis Rivera (*The Actor*), Marshall Jones (*Orsini*), Dean Selmier (*Jacques*), Ruth Platt (*Orsini's Ass't*), Rosalind Elliot (*Gabrielle*)
D: Gordon Hessler **SCR:** Christopher Wicking & Henry Slesar, from Edgar Allan Poe's short story **PHOTOG:** Manuel Berenguer **MUSIC:** Waldo de Los Rios
Standard horror-thriller: Bizarre killings confound

The Murders in the Rue Morgue
1986, (USA-GB-Fr), Robert Halmi-Int'l Film Prods./CBS-TV, color, 93 mins.
W: George C. Scott (*Auguste Dupin*), Rebecca De Mornay (*Claire Dupin*), Val Kilmer (*Phillipe Huron*), Neil Dickson (*Adolphe Le Bon*), Ian McShane (*Prefect*

of Police), Maud Rayer (*Melle L'Espanaye*), Maxence Mailfort (*Insp. Alphonse*), Fernand Guiot (*Dupar*), Patrick Floersheim (*The Sailor*), Roger Lumont (*Sgt. Marcel*), Erick Desmarestz (*Insp. Bec*), Yvette Petit (*The Laundress*), Serge Ridoux (*The Prison Guard*)
D: Jeannot Szwarc TELEPLAY: David Epstein, from Edgar Allan Poe's short story PHOTOG: Bruno de Keyzer MUSIC: Charles Gross
TVM, standard thriller: Detective comes out of retirement to solve grisly slayings

Murders in the Zoo
1933, (USA), Para, b&w, 64 mins.
W: Lionel Atwill, Randolph Scott, Kathleen Burke, Charles Ruggles, Gail Patrick, John Lodge, Harry Beresford
D: Edward Sutherland SCR: Philip Wylie & Seton I. Miller
"Atwill gets matters off to a colorful start...in the opening sequence, he is seen in the jungle, just concluding a neat job of sewing up his victim's lips after the manner of headshrinkers and leaving him trussed up in the jungle at the mercy of marauding wildlife. Later, when his unsuspecting wife asks if her erstwhile lover left her any message before 'leaving,' Atwill replies with honesty, nonchalance and a superbly timed, pregnant pause, 'He didn't say anything'"—William K. Everson, Classics of the Horror Film
Standard thriller

The Murder Society
see The Murder Clinic

Murder Will Out (1899)
see Le Spectre (1899)

Murder Will Out
1930, (USA), First Nat'l, b&w, 7 reels (6,200 ft./1889.8m)
W: Jack Mulhall (*Leonard Staunton*), Lila Lee (*Jeanne Baldwin*), Noah Beery Sr. (*Lt. Condon*), Malcolm McGregor (*Jack Baldwin*), Tully Marshall (*Dr. Mansfield*), Alec B. Francis (*Sen. Baldwin*), Hedda Hopper (*Aunt Pat*), Claud Allister (*Alan Fitzhugh*)
D: Clarence Badger ADAPT & DIALOG: J. Grubb Alexander, from Will F. Jenkins' 1920 story "The Purple Hieroglyph" PHOTOG: John Seitz
Standard thriller: Blackmail and murder cloud lovers' engagement. Remade as **Torchy Blane in Chinatown, Murder Will Out** WB, British, 1939

Murder Will Out (1952)
see The Voice of Merrill

Murder with Mirrors
1985, (GB), Hajeno/WB/CBS-TV, color, 95 mins.
W: Helen Hayes (*Miss Jane Marple*), Bette Davis (*Carrie Louise Serrocold*), John Mills (*Serrocold*), John Woodvine (*Christian*), Leo McKern (*Insp. Curry*), Liane Langland (*Gina*), John Laughlin (*Wally*), Dorothy Tutin (*Mildred*), James Coombes (*Steven*), Anton Rodgers (*Dr. Hargrove*), Tim Roth (*Edgar*), Frances de la Tour (*Miss Belever*), Christopher Fairbank (*Sgt. Lake*), Amanda Maynard
D: Dick Lowry TELEPLAY: George Eckstein, from Agatha Christie's novel PHOTOG: Brian West MUSIC: Richard Rodney Bennett
TVM, standard thriller: Woman sleuth delves into murder of society matron's stepson

Murder With Mirrors: HELEN HAYES, BETTE DAVIS AND LIANE LANGLAND

Murder without Crime
1950, (GB), ABPC, b&w, 76 mins.
W: Dennis Price (*Matthew*), Derek Farr (*Stephen*), Patricia Plunkett (*Jan*), Joan Dowling (*Grena*)
P: Victor Skutezky D & SCR: J. Lee Thompson—from his play Double Error
Standard crime-thriller: Landlord suspects author killed nightclub girl, blackmails him

Murder without Tears
1953, (USA), AA, b&w, 64 mins.
W: Craig Stevens, Joyce Holden
Minor thriller

The Murdock Trial
1914, (GB), Turner Films/Hepworth, b&w, 3,425 ft. (1043.9m)
W: Florence Turner (*Helen Story*), Frank Tennant (*Lionel Mann*), Richard Norton (*Henry Murdock*), G.C. Colonna (*The Nephew*), William Felton (*The Butler*), Lucy Sibley (*The Housekeeper*), Eric Forbes-Robertson (*The Prosecution*), Alfred Phillips (*The Defense*), Larry Trimble
D: Larry Trimble
Standard crime-thriller: Heiress takes blame for uncle's stabbing, thinking her lover guilty

Murphy's Millions
see Mike Murphy's Dream of Love and Riches

Museum Mystery
1937, (GB), B&D/Para British, b&w, 69 mins.
W: Jock McKay (*Jock*), Elizabeth Inglis (*Ruth Carter*), Tony Wylde (*Mr. Varleigh*), Gerald Case (*Peter Redding*), Charles Paton (*Clutters*), Alfred Wellesley (*The Mayor*), Sebastian Smith (*Dr. Trapnell*), Roy Byford (*Prof. Wicksteed*)
D: Clifford Gulliver STORY: Gerald Elliott
Standard thriller: Student and curator's daughter prevent theft of Burmese idol

The Musgrave Ritual
1912, (GB-Fr), Franco-British Film Co.-Eclair/Fenning, b&w, 1,290 ft. (393.2m)
W: Georges Treville (*Sherlock Holmes*), Mr. Moyse (*Dr. John Watson*)
D: Georges Treville, from a story by Sir Arthur Conan Doyle
Standard thriller

The Music Hall Manager's Dilemma
1904, (GB), R.W. Paul, b&w, 260 ft. (79.2m)
D: Walter R. Booth
Standard fantasy short: When unpaid artistes refuse to perform, posters come to life

The Music of the Spheres
1984, (Can), Lightscape, color, 80 mins.
W: Anne Dansereau (*Melody*), Peter Brikmanis (*Andrew*), Ken Lemaire (*The Bureaucrat*), Jacques Couture (*Paul*), Kenneth Gordon (*Einstein*), Grant Roll (*The Guard*), Denis Pelletier, Sandra Kaizer, Cory Siddall
D: G. Philip Jackson SCR: G. Philip Jackson & Gabrielle deMontmollin PHOTOG: Nadine Humenick SPCL-FX: James Stuart Allan MUSIC: Claude Boux
Minor SF: Alien force invades computer

Musketeer of the Sea
see I Moschettiere del Mare

The Mutagen
1988, (Can), Emmeritus, Made for TV, color, 95 mins.
W: Jackie Samuda (*Chris Hansen*), Les Williams (*Derek Kane*), Marianna Pascal (*Julie Kane*), Casey Leigh (*Frieda*), Robbie Fox (*Lt. Grover*), Steve Behal (*Davis*), Patrick Myles (*Prescott*), Michael Kopsa (*Doug*), Kenneth Foster (*Ralph Dexter*), Austin Schatz (*Felton*), Richard Headwelles (*Val Simpson*), James Knapp (*Jonas*), Heather Lee Mills (*Sue*), Michael King (*Jeff*), Margaret Innes (*Angela*), Anthony Crumb (*Waite*), Tom Elwell (*Jimmy*), Mike Ward (*Talbot*), Peter Read (*Cronin*), Jennifer Scott (*Nurse #1*), Leslie Kelly (*Nurse #2*), Silvan Alexander (*The Drug Suspect*), Gabrielle Desbarates (*The Street Walker*)
D & TELEPLAY: Eli Necakov STORY: Terence Gadsden MUSIC: Steven Sauve
TVM, minor SF-thriller: Killer mutant flees bio-lab

Mutant
1983, (USA), Laurelwood/Film Ventures, color, 100 mins.
W: Wings Hauser (*Josh Cameron*), Bo Hopkins (*Sheriff Will Stewart*), Jody Medford (*Holly Pierce*), Marc Clement (*Albert*), Lee Montgomery (*Mike Cameron*), Jennifer Warren (*Dr. Myra Tate*), Cary Guffey (*Billy*), Danny Nelson (*Jack*), Mary Nell Santacroce (*Mrs. Mapes*), Stuart Culpepper (*Mel*), Tina Kincaide (*Judy Ann*), Johnny Popwell Sr. (*Dawson*), Wallace Wilkinson (*Mr. Mitchell*), Ralph Redpath (*Vic*), Ralph Pace (*Art*), Larry Quackenbush (*Harve*), Charles Franzen (*The E.P.A. Man*), Lit Connah (*Mrs. Miller*), Pat Moss (*Penelope*), Jerry Rushing, Chester Clark, Joshua Lee Patton
D: John "Bud" Cardos SCR: Peter Z. Orton, Michael Jones, & John C. Kruize STORY: Michael Jones & John C. Kruize PHOTOG: Al Taylor SPCL-FX: Paul Stewart MUSIC: Richard Band
A.k.a. **Forbidden World,** *orig. to be titled* **Pestilence** *or* **Night Shadows**
Standard SF-horror, Night of the Living Dead imitation: Illegal chemical dumping spawns horrors

Mutant Hunt

1987, (USA), Empire, color

W: Rick Gianasi *(Matt Riker)*, Bill Peterson *(Z)*, Marc Umile, Taunie VreNon, Mary-Anne Fahey
WRIT & D: Tim Kincaid
A.k.a. **Matt Riker**
Minor SF-thriller: Cyborgs roam Manhattan

Mutants in Paradise

1988, (USA), Blue Ridge Cinema, color, 78 mins.

W: Brad Greenquist *(Steve Awesome)*, Anna Nicholas *(Alice Durchfall)*, Robert Ingham *(Oscar Tinman)*, Skipp Suddeth *(Bob)*, Ray "Boom Boom" Mancini *(Steve's Trainer)*, Richard Jones *(John Thompson)*, Edith Massey *(Dr. Durchfall)*, Tim Shutt *(Ivan)*, Amy Greenison *(Sonya)*, Ron Benson *(Tom Johnson)*, John Manolukas *(Vladimir)*, Colin Granpree *(Wayne)*, David Cupp *(The TV Announcer)*, John Dean *(Dwayne)*, Elaine Brown *(The Fairy Godmother)*, Darden Towe *(The Mad Bomber)*, Ray Buckland, Rod Dew, Fred Schmitt, James Shore, David Seitz, Steve Fafard, Danita Roundtree, William Moses Jr., Tom Evans, George Cushner, Barbara Gibney, Peter Wirth, Renee Means, William Massie Smith Jr., Jim Dumbrowski, G. Neal Means, Lynn McCune, Scott Apostolou, Bette Collins, Lisa Winsor, J.R. Getcher, Houston Reid, John Gilliland, Kevin Lynch, John Suttles, James Sprinkle, Marty Hampford, Tomasina Keremes, Tiffany Terranova, Anne Hampford, Lynne Tillach, John Gamble, Allison Tillach, Mike Clarke, Frank Harris, Syte the Fool
WRIT & D: Scott Apostolou   **PHOTOG:** G. Neal Means   **MUSIC:** Jep Epstein & William Moses Jr.   **SONGS:** *Pass Away, Red Hot, Try to Run, Little Lucille, Shock Value, Blackout & Atmospheric Fragments*
Minor SF-spoof: Scientist tries to create radiation-proof man

Mutant Species

see **Bio-Force I**

The Mutations

1973, (GB), Getty/Col, color, 92 mins.

W: Donald Pleasence *(Nolter)*, Julie Ege *(Hedi)*, Michael Dunn *(Burns)*, Brad Harris *(Brian)*, Jill Haworth *(Lauren)*, Tom Baker *(Lynch)*, Lisa Collings *(The Prostitute)*, Scott Anthony *(Tony)*, Olga Anthony *(Bridget)*, Esther Blackmon *(The Alligator Girl)*, Joan Scott *(The Landlady)*, Richard Davies *(The Doctor)*, Toby Lennon *(The Tramp)*, Ethne Dunn *(The Nurse)*, John Wreford *(The Policeman)*, Kathy Kitchen *(The Midget)*, Tony Mayne *(Dwarf Tony)*, Molly Tweedlie *(Dwarf Molly)*, Fran Fullenwider *(The Fat Lady)*, Lesley Roose *(The Skinny Lady)*, Fay Bura *(The Bearded Lady)*, Dee Bura *(The Fire-Eater)*, Madge Barnett *(The Monkey Woman)*, Willie Ingram *(Popeye)*, Hugh Baily *(The Pretzel Boy)*, Felix Duarte *(The Frog Boy)*
P: Robert Weinbach   **D:** Jack Cardiff   **SCR:** Robert D. Weinbach & Edward Mann   **PHOTOG:** Paul Beeson   **MUSIC:** Basil Kirchin
released on video-cassette as **The Freakmaker**
Minor SF-horror: Professor creates human mutants

Mutator

1990, (S. Africa), color, 91 mins.

W: Embeth Davidtz, Brion James, Cardyn Ann Clark, Milton Raphiel Murrill
D: John R. Bowey   **SCR:** Lynn Rose Higgins
A.k.a. **Time of the Beast**
Minor SF-horror: Animal activists meet mutant

Mute Witness

1995, (USA-Russ), color, 100 mins.

W: Marina Sudina, Fay Ripley, Evan Richards *(Andy)*
Unusual thriller: Speech-impaired American in Moscow sees murder

The Mutilator (1979)

see **The Dark** *(1979)*

The Mutilator

1985, (USA), Buddy Cooper/O.K. Prods., color, 85 mins.

W: Matt Mitler, Ruth Martinez, Connie Rogers, Ben Moore, Bill Hitchcock, Morey Lampley, Frances Raines, Pamela Weddle Cooper, Trace Cooper, Jack Chatham
WRIT & D: Buddy Cooper   **PHOTOG:** Peter Schnall   **MUSIC:** Michael Minard   **SONG:** *Fall Break*
Minor thriller: Killer stalks vacationing college students

The Mutineers

1949, (USA), Col, b&w, 60 mins.

W: Jon Hall, Adele Jergens, George Reeves, Noel Cravat, Tom Kennedy, Lyle Talbot
D: Jean Yarbrough
A.k.a. **Pirate Ship**.
Standard adventure-thriller

Mutiny

1952, (USA), UA, color, 77 mins.

W: Mark Stevens, Patric Knowles, Angela Lansbury
D: Edward Dmytryk
Standard adventure-thriller

Mutiny in Outer Space

1965, (USA), Woolner Bros., color, 81 mins.

W: William Leslie, Dolores Faith, Richard Garland, Pamela Curran, James Dobson, Harold Lloyd Jr., Glenn Langan
P: Hugo Grimaldi & Arthur C. Pierce   **D:** Hugh Grimaldi   **SCR:** Arthur C. Pierce   **SPCL-FX:** Roger George
orig. to be titled **Space Station X**
Standard SF-thriller: Lunar fungus attacks astronauts

My Adorable Slave

see **Mi Adorable Esclava**

My Best Friend is a Vampire

1988, (USA), Kings Road, color, 84 mins, also 90 mins.

W: Robert Sean Leonard *(Jeremy Capello)*, Evan Mirand *(Ralph)*, Cheryl Pollak *(Darla Blake)*, Rene Auberjonois *(Modoc)*, Fannie Flagg *(Mrs. Capello)*, Kenneth Kimmins *(Mr. Capello)*, Cecilia Peck *(Nora)*, David Warner *(Prof. McCarthy)*, Lee Anne Locken *(Candy Andrews)*, Erica Zeitlin *(Gloria)*, Michelle La Vigne *(Flo)*, Harvey Christiansen *(George)*, Paul Willson *(Grimsdyke)*, Gary Chason, Kathy D. Bates, John Chappell, J.R. Conroy, Staness Caroll, Mimi Kincaide, Jill Bianchine, Linda Moore, Ronald R. Rondell, Chris Wycliff, Coy Sevier
D: Jimmy Huston   **SCR:** Tab Murphy   **PHOTOG:** James Bartle   **MUSIC:** Steve Dorff   **SONGS:** *Heartbeat Getting Stronger, One Way or Another, Sex is a Weapon, Don't Follow Me, When It Comes to Me and You, Coming Back for More, Same Man I Was Before, The Future's So Bright, I Gotta Wear Shades, Power of Your Suggestion, Scream Machine & Bad Blood Slam Dance*
Minor horror-comedy: Teen becomes Undead

My Blood Runs Cold

1965, (USA), WB, b&w, 108 mins.

W: Troy Donahue *(Ben Gunther)*, Joey Heatherton *(Julie Merriday)*, Barry Sullivan *(Julian Merriday)*, Jeanette Nolan *(Aunt Sarah)*, Nicolas Coster *(Harry Lindsay)*, John Holland *(Mr. Courtland)*, Russell Thorson *(The Sheriff)*, Ben Wright *(Lansbury)*, Shirley Mitchell *(Mrs. Courtland)*, Howard McNear *(Henry)*, Howard Wendell *(The Mayor)*, John McCook *(Owen)*
P & D: William Conrad   **SCR:** John Mantley   **PHOTOG:** Sam Leavitt   **MUSIC:** George Duning
Standard thriller: Fortune-hunter entrances wealthy girl

My Bloody Valentine

1980, (Can), Para, color, 91 mins.

W: Paul Kelman *(T.J.)*, Lori Hallier *(Sarah)*, Neil Affleck *(Axel)*, Keith Knight *(Hollis)*, Alf Humphreys *(Howard)*, Rob Stein *(John)*, Cynthia Dale *(Patty)*, Helene Udy *(Sylvia)*, Tom Kovacs *(Mike)*, Terry Waterland *(Harriet)*, Carl Marotte *(Dave)*, Jim Murchison *(Tommy)*, Gina Dick *(Gretchen)*, Peter Cowper *(The Miner/Harry Warden)*, Don Francks *(Newby)*, Jack Van Evera *(Happy)*, Patricia Hamilton *(Mabel)*, Jeff Danks *(Young Axel)*, Larry Reynolds *(The Mayor)*, Graham Whitehead *(Mac)*, Pat Hemingway *(The Woman)*, Pat Walsh *(Harvey)*, John MacDonald *(The Rescuer)*, Marguerite McNeil *(Mrs. Raleigh)*, Sandy Leim *(Ben)*, Fred Watters, Jeff Fulton
D: George Mihalka   **SCR:** John Beaird   **STORY:** Stephen Miller   **PHOTOG:** Rodney Gibbons   **MUSIC:** Paul Zaza
Standard thriller: Ghastly murders in mining town

My Boyfriend's Back

1993, (USA), color, 84 mins.

W: Andrew Lowery, Edward Herrmann, Mary Beth Hurt, Philip Hoffman, Matthew Fox, Austin Pendleton, Cloris Leachman, Jay O. Sanders, Paul Dooley, Bob Dishy, Paxton Whitehead
D: Bob Balaban   **SCR:** Dean Lorey
A.k.a. **Johnny Zombie**
Minor horror-comedy: Love-struck teen returns from grave

My Bride is Supernatural

see **Bell, Book and Candle**

My Brother Has Bad Dreams

1977, (USA), American Pictures, color, 91 mins

Mutiny In Outer Space: JAMES DOBSON AND DOLORES FAITH

W: Nick Kleinholtz
P & D: Robert Emery
Minor thriller: Jealousy drives man to murder

My Cousin Rachel
1952, (USA), 20th-Fox, b&w, 98 mins.
W: Olivia de Havilland (*Rachel*), Richard Burton (*Philip*), John Sutton (*Ambrose*),

My Cousin Rachel: RICHARD BURTON

Audrey Dalton (*Louise*), Tudor Owen (*Seecombe*), Ronald Squire (*Kendall*), George Dolenz (*Rinaldi*), J.M. Kerrigan (*Rev. Pascoe*), Margaret Brewster (*Mrs. Pascoe*), Alma Lawton (*Mary Pascoe*), Earl Robie (*Philip, age 5*), Robin Camp (*Philip, age 15*), Argentina Brunetti (*The Signora*), Mario Siletti (*The Caretaker*), Victor Wood (*The Foreman*), Lumsden Hare (*Tamblyn*), George Plues (*The Coachman*), Trevor Ward (*Lewin*), Bruce Payne, Oreste Seragnoli, James Fairfax, Ola Lorraine, Kathleen Mason
WRIT & P: Nunnally Johnson, from Daphne du Maurier's novel **D:** Henry Koster **PHOTOG:** Joseph La Shelle **MUSIC:** Franz Waxman
Classic thriller: Young heir tries to prove his beautiful cousin is treacherous murderess. US debut of Richard Burton, Oscar nominee, Best Supporting Actor.

My Daughter Joy
1950, (GB), London-BLPA/British Lion/Col, b&w, 81 mins.
W: Edward G. Robinson (*George Constantin*), Peggy Cummins (*Georgette Constantin*), Richard Greene (*Larry*), Nora Swinburne (*Ava Constantin*), Walter Rilla (*Andrews*), Finlay Currie (*Sir Thomas MacTavish*), James Robertson Justice (*Prof. Keval*), Ronald Adam (*Col. Fogarty*), Peter Illing (*The Sultan*), David Hutcheson (*Annix*), Ronald Ward (*Dr. Schindler*), Gregory Ratoff (*Marcus*)
P & D: Gregory Ratoff **SCR:** Robert Thoeren & William Rose, from Irene Nemirowsky's novel *David Golder*
USA retitle, **Operation X**
Standard melodrama: Financier plans to wed sultan's daughter, start dynasty

My Demon Lover
1987, (USA), Robert Shaye/New Line, color, 86 mins.
W: Scott Valentine (*Kaz*), Michelle Little (*Denny*), Arnold Johnson (*Fixer*), Robert Trebor (*Charles*), Alan Fudge (*Capt. Phil Janus*), Gina Gallego (*Sonia*), Calvert DeForest (Aka Larry 'Bud' Melman). (*The Man in the Healthfood Store*), Eva Charney (*Grady*), Dan Patrick Brady (*Chip*)
D: Charles Loventhal **SCR:** Leslie Ray **PHOTOG:** Jacques Haitkin **MUSIC SPRVSR:** Kevin Benson
Standard comedy-fantasy: Libido turns cursed youth into monster

My Favorite Martian
1999, (USA), Walt Disney, color
W: Christopher Lloyd, Elizabeth Hurley, Jeff Daniels, Ray Walston, Wallace Shawn
Standard SF-comedy (inspired by 1960's teleseries): Earthling befriends space alien

My Friend, Dr. Jekyll
1961, (It), Union/Prime TV, b&w, 104 mins
W: Ugo Tognazzi, Abbe Lane
D: Mario Girolami
Minor comedy: Spoof of Robert Louis Stevenson's Dr. Jekyll and Mr. Hyde

My Gun is Quick
1957, (USA), UA, b&w, 88 mins.
W: Robert Bray (*Mike Hammer*), Whitney Blake, Pat O'Donahue, Richard Garland, Pamela Duncan
P: George White & Phil Victor **D:** George White **SCR:** Richard Collins & Richard Powell, from Mickey Spillane's novel
Standard thriller: Private eye involved with girl who is murdered

My Lady's Revenge
1907, (GB), R.W. Paul, b&w, 520 ft. (158.5m)
D: J.H. Martin
Standard melodrama: Man kills rival in duel for girl, who then poses as man and kills him

My Little Pony
1986, (USA), color, 89 mins.
VOICES: Danny DeVito, Madeline Kahn, Tony Randall, Cloris Leachman, Rhea Perlman **D:** Michael Joens
Standard animated fantasy: Good ponies vs. evil witch

My Lord Conceit
1921, (GB), Stoll, b&w, 6,034 ft. (1839.2m)
W: Evelyn Boucher (*Beryl Foster*), Maresco Marisini (*Count Savona*), Rowland Myles (*Ivor Grant*), E.L. Frewen (*Sir Hector Grant*), Frank E. Petley (*John Marsden*), Emilie Nichol (*Mrs. Grant*), J. Edwards Barber (*Dr. Clark*), Eric George (*Cyril*), Edward Thornton (*Jackie*), Coomarie Gawthorne (*Matabia*)
D & SCR: F. Martin Thornton, from a novel by "Rita"
Standard crime-thriller: Count frames runaway wife for killing husband

My Magic Dog
1998, (USA), color, 95 mins.
W: Bryan Mendez (*Toby*), Leo Milbrook (*Chet*)
Made-for-Video, minor fantasy: Invisible talking dog saves boy from evil aunt

My Name is Ivan
1962, (Russ), Shore, b&w, 94 mins.
W: Kolya Burlaiev (*Ivan*), Valentin Zubkov (*Capt. Kholin*), Ye Zharikov, Nikolai Grinko, E. Zharikov, S. Krylov, N. Grinko, D. Miliutenko
D: Andrei Tarkovsky **SCR:** Vladimir Bogomolov
A.k.a. **The Youngest Spy** *and* **Ivan's Childhood**
Prize-winning melodrama: Russian boy spies on Nazis

My Name is Julia Ross
1945, (USA), Col, b&w, 64 mins.
W: Nina Foch, George Macready, Dame May Whitty, Roland Varno, Anita Bolster
D: Joseph H. Lewis **PHOTOG:** Burnett Guffey
Taut thriller: Secretary menaced in Cornish manse. cf. **Dead of Winter**

My Neighbor Tortoro
1988, (Jap), color, 86 mins.
VOICES: Lisa Michaelson, Cheryl Chase, Greg Snegoff, Natalie Core, Kenneth Hartman **D:** Hayao Miyazaki
Standard animated fantasy: Two sisters have adventures with giant forest spirit

My Nights with Susan, Sandra, Olga and Julie
1975, (Neth), color, 100 mins.
W: Willeke Van Ammelrooy, Hans Van der Gragt, Nelly Frijda, Franulka Heyermans, Marya de Heer, Jerry Brouwer
D: Pim de la Parra **SCR:** Harry Kumel, et al.
Minor eroto-thriller: Blond biker stays at farmhouse full of weirdos

Myra Breckinridge
1970, (USA), 20th-Fox, color, 94 mins.
W: Raquel Welch (*Myra*), Mae West (*Leticia*), John Huston (*Buck Loner*), Rex Reed (*Myron*), Farrah Fawcett (*Mary Ann*), John Carradine (*The Surgeon*), Jim Backus (*The Doctor*), Tom Selleck (*The Stud*), Andy Devine (*Coyote Bill*), Roger Herren (*Rusty*), Kathleen Freeman (*Bobby Dean Loner*), George Furth (*Charlie Flagler Jr.*), Roger C. Carmel (*Dr. Montag*), Grady Sutton (*Kid Barlow*), Calvin Lockhart (*Irving Amadeus*), Skip Ward (*Chance*), Robert Lieb (*Charlie Flagler Sr.*), B.S. Pully (*Tex*), Buck Kartalian (*Jeff*), Nelson Sardelli (*Mario*), Monty Landis (*Vince*), Peter Ireland (*The Student*), William Hopper
D: Michael Sarne **SCR:** Michael Sarne & Gore Vidal, from Gore Vidal's best-selling novel **PHOTOG:** Richard Moore **MUSIC:** Lionel Newman

Myra Breckinridge: REX REED AND RAQUEL WELCH

Bizarre comedy: Sex-change tries to reform men in general and Hollywood in particular

My Science Project
1985, (USA), SilverScreen Partners II/Touchstone, color, 94 mins.
W: John Stockwell (*Michael Harlan*), Danielle Von Zerneck (*Ellie Sawyer*), Fisher Stevens (*Vince Latello*), Raphael Sbarge (*Sherman*), Richard Masur (*Det. Isadore Nulty*), Ann Wedgeworth (*Dolores*), Barry Corbin (*Lew Harlan*), Dennis Hopper (*Bob Roberts*), Candace Silvers (*Irene*), Beau Dremann (*Matusky*), Pat Simmons (*Crystal*), John Vidor (*Jock #1*), Vincent Barbour (*Jock #2*), Jaime Alba (*Jock #3*), Elven Havard (*The Fireman*), Robert Beer (*Pres. Eisenhower*), John Carter (*The General*), Cameron Young (*The General's Aide*), Noel Conlon (*The Secret Service Man*), Linda Hoy (*The Librarian*), Jackson Bostwick (*The Sentry*), Robert DoQui (*The Desk Sergeant*), Robin Allyn (*Ellie's Friend*), Michael Berryman (*The Mutant*), Chuck Hemingway (*Coy*), Ann Culotta, Pamela Springsteen, Matt Hoelscher, Jack O'Leary, Clare Peck, Joel Harrison, Scott Bailey Spangler, Hank Calia
WRIT & D: Jonathan R. Betuel   PHOTOG: David M. Walsh   VS-FX SPRVSR: John Scheele   MUSIC: Peter Bernstein
songs include Hit and Run, Hard to Believe & My Mind's Made Up
Standard SF-adventure: Teens find alien device, warp time and space

My Sister, My Love
see The Mafu Cage

My Son
1914, (GB), Piccadilly/MP, b&w, 1,151 ft. (352.9m)
D: Charles Weston
Standard crime-thriller: Bank manager shoots drunken son, mistaking him for new wife's lover

My Son, the Hero
see Les Titans

My Son, the Vampire
see Mother Riley Meets the Vampire

My Stepmother is an Alien
1988, (USA), Weintraub Entertainment, color, 108 mins.
W: Dan Aykroyd (*Dr. Steve Mills*), Kim Basinger (*Celeste*), Jon Lovitz (*Ron Mills*), Alyson Hannigan (*Jessie Mills*), Joseph Maher (*Dr. Lucas Budlong*), Seth

My Stepmother Is An Alien: KIM BASINGER AND DAN AYKROYD

Green (*Fred Glass*), Wesley Mann (*Grady*), Ann Prentiss (*The Voice of Bag*), Harry Shearer (*The Voice of Carl Sagan*)
D: Richard Benjamin   SCR: Jerico Weingrod, Herschel Weingrod, Timothy Harris & Jonathan Reynolds   PHOTOG: Richard H. Kline   MUSIC: Alan Silvestri
Standard SF-comedy: Alien beauty bemuses scientist

Le Mystere de la Chambre Jaune (Mystery of the Yellow Room)
1931, (Fr), Films Osso, b&w, 108 mins
D: Marcel L'Herbier
Standard thriller

The Mysterians
1957, (Jap), Toho/MGM, color, 85 mins.
W: Kenji Sahara, Momoko Kochi, Akihiko Hirata, Takashi Shimura, Yumi Shirakawa, Susumu Fujita, Yoshio Kosugi, Fuyuki Murakami, Kisaya Ito, Minosuke Yamada
P: Tomoyuki Tanaka   D: Inoshiro Honda   SCR: Takeshi Kimura, from a story by Jotaro Okami   PHOTOG: Hajime Koizumi   SPCL-FX: Eiji Tsuburaya   MUSIC: Akira Ifukube
blurb: "See! See! See! A daring attempt by love-starved men of another planet to steal our women!"
Standard SF-thriller: Space-aliens seek Earth women for breeding purposes

Mysteries from Beyond Earth
1977, (USA), color, 95 mins
Standard speculation docu: Scientists probe paranormal (e.g., UFOs, telekinesis, ESP)

Mysteries from Beyond the Grave
see Misterios de Ultratumba

The Mysteries of London
1915, (GB), Martin's Exclusives, b&w, 4,000 ft. (1219.2m)
W: Wingold Lawrence (*Bob Willis*), Flora Morris (*Louise Willis*)
D & STORY: A.E. Coleby
reissued (1917) by Albion Pictures
Standard crime-thriller: Framed clerk freed in time to save daughter from being murdered for inheritance

The Mysterious Bullet
1955, (GB), Merton Park/Anglo-Amalgamated, b&w, 31 mins.
W: Robert Raglan (*Insp. Dexter*), Christine Adrian (*Emily Thatcher*), John Warwick (*Robert Churchill*), Carol Marsh (*Julie Thatcher*), Howard Lang (*Patterson*)
P: Alec Snowden   D: Paul Gherzo   STORY: James Eastwood
Standard short crime-thriller: Ballistic expert pursues killer of widow's fiance

The Mysterious Cabinet
see L'Armoire des Freres Davenport

Mysterious Dislocation
see Dislocation Mysterieuse

The Mysterious Doctor
1943, (USA), WB, b&w, 57 mins.
W: John Loder, Eleanor Parker, Lester Matthews, Forrester Harvey, Bruce Lester, Matt Willis
D: Ben Stoloff   ORIG. SCR: Richard Weil   PHOTOG: Henry Sharp
Minor thriller: Legendary headless ghost deters Cornish miners

The Mysterious Dr. Fu Manchu
1929, (USA), Para, b&w, 7,663 ft./2335.7m/86 mins.; (also silent, 7,965 ft./2427.7m)
W: Warner Oland (*Dr. Fu Manchu*), Jean Arthur (*Lia Eltham*), Neil Hamilton (*Dr. Jack Petrie*), O.P. Heggie (*Nayland Smith*), William Austin (*Sylvester Wadsworth*), Claude King (*Sir John Petrie*), Charles Stevenson (*Gen. Petrie*), Noble Johnson (*Li Po*), Evelyn Selbie (*Fai Lu*), Charles Giblyn (*Weymouth*), Donald MacKenzie (*Trent*), Lawford Davidson (*Clarkson*), Laska Winter (*Fu Mela*), Chappell Dossett (*Rev. Mr. Eltham*), Charles Stevens (*Singh*), Tully Marshall (*The Ambassador*), Tetsu Komai
D: Rowland V. Lee   SCR & DIALOG: Florence Ryerson & Lloyd Corrigan   COMEDY DIALOG: George Marion Jr.   PHOTOG: Harry A. Fischbeck
"Warner Oland made his Fu Manchu films in that unfortunate period of the change-over to sound. Rohmer's lightning-paced stories required a tempo and steadily building tension that the static adaptations of 1929 lacked quite deplorably. In any case, Oland, although an excellent actor, had been too steeped in Oriental villainy for years for his new role to be anything more than an extension of his earlier performances"—William K. Everson, The Bad Guys
Standard thriller: Chinese criminal plots mayhem. cf. Daughter of the Dragon

The Mysterious Dr. R
see Man-Made Monster

The Mysterious Heads
see The Extraordinary Waiter

The Mysterious Horror
see Caltiki, il Mostro Immortale

The Mysterious House of Usher
see House of Usher (1962)

Mysterious Intruder
1946, (USA), Col, b&w, 62 mins.
<u>W</u>: Richard Dix
<u>D</u>: William Castle
Minor thriller. 'Whistler' mystery

Mysterious Invader
see The Astounding She-Monster

The Mysterious Island (1905)
see L'Ile de Calypso: Ulysse et Polypheme

The Mysterious Island
1929, (USA), MGM, color, 8,569 ft. (2611.8m)
<u>W</u>: Lionel Barrymore (*Dakkar*), Lloyd Hughes (*Nikolai*), Jane Daly (*Sonia*),
    Montagu Love (*Falon*), Snitz Edwards (*Anton*), Harry Gribbon (*Mikhail*),
    Gibson Gowland (*Dmitry*), Dolores Brinkman (*Teresa*)
<u>D</u>: Lucien Hubbard, Maurice Tourneur, & Benjamin Christensen   <u>SCR</u>: Lucien
    Hubbard & Carl L. Pierson, from Jules Verne's novel   <u>PHOTOG</u>: Percy
    Hilburn   <u>MUSIC SCORE</u>: Martin Broones & Arthur Lange
Standard fantasy-adventure: Scientist finds underwater civilization

Mysterious Island
1961, (GB), Col, color, 101 mins.
<u>W</u>: Michael Craig (*Capt. Cyrus Harding*), Herbert Lom (*Capt. Nemo*), Joan
    Greenwood (*Lady Mary Fairchild*), Michael Callan (*Herbert Brown*), Gary
    Merrill (*Gideon Spillett*), Beth Rogan (*Elena*), Percy Herbert (*Sgt. Pencroft*),
    Dan Jackson (*Neb*), Nigel Green (*Tom*), Andre Morell
<u>P</u>: Charles H. Schneer   <u>D</u>: Cy Endfield   <u>SCR</u>: John Prebble, Daniel Ullman &
    Crane Wilbur, from Jules Verne's novel   <u>PHOTOG</u>: Wilkie Cooper
    <u>SPCL-FX</u>: Ray Harryhausen   <u>MUSIC</u>: Bernard Herrmann
*Superior SF-adventure: Prison camp escapees in American Civil War find island refuge of
    embittered genius*

Mysterious Island of Beautiful Women
1979, (USA), color, 100 mins.
<u>W</u>: Jamie Lyn Bauer, Jayne Kennedy, Kathryn Davis, Deborah Shelton, Susie
    Coelho, Peter Lawford, Steven Keats, Clint Walker
<u>D</u>: Joseph Pevney
TVM, minor thriller: Men stranded amid tribe of angry females

The Mysterious Island of Captain Nemo
1974, (Sp-Fr), Citu/CRC, color, 96 mins.
<u>W</u>: Omar Sharif (*Nemo*), Philippe Nicaud (*Spillett*), Gerard Tichy (*Smith*), Jess
    Hahn (*Pencroft*), Rafael Bardem (*Herbert*), Gabriele Tinti (*Ayrton*), Vidal
    Molina (*Harvey*), Rick Battaglia (*Finch*), Ambroise M'Bia
<u>D</u>: Juan Antonio Bardem & Henri Colpi   <u>SCR</u>: Jacques Champreux & Juan
    Antonio Bardem   <u>PHOTOG</u>: Enzo Serafin, Guy Delecluze & Julio Ortaz
    <u>MUSIC</u>: Gianni Ferrio
Minor SF-adventure

The Mysterious Knight
see Le Chevalier Mystere

The Mysterious Magician
1965, (W. Ger), Gold Key, b&w, 95 mins.
<u>W</u>: Joachim Fuchsberger, Siegfried Lowitz, Sophie Hardy, Heinz Drache, Margot
    Trooper, Carl Lange, Eddie Arent, Karl John
<u>D</u>: Alfred Vohrer, from a story by Edgar Wallace, *The Ringer*
Standard thriller: Phantom figure avenges death

The Mysterious Mechanical Toy
1903, (GB), Gaumont, b&w, 120 ft. (36.6m)
<u>W</u>: M. Trevallion (*Phroso*), Mr. Webster (*The Manager*), Alf Collins (*The Man from
    the Audience*)
<u>D</u>: Alf Collins
A.k.a. Phroso the Mysterious Mechanical Doll
*Standard fantasy short: Tivoli manager demonstrates "mechanical man" who causes trouble
    for audience*

The Mysterious Mr. Moto
1938, (USA), 20th-Fox, b&w, 62 mins.
<u>W</u>: Peter Lorre (*Mr. Moto*), Henry Wilcoxon (*Anton Darvak*), Mary Maguire (*Ann
    Richman*), Harold Huber (*Ernst Litmar*), Erik Rhodes (*David Scott-Frensham*),
    Leon Ames (*Paul Brissac*), Forrester Harvey (*George Higgins*), Lester
    Matthews (*Sir Charles Murchison*), Frederick Vogeding (*Gottfried Brujo*), John
    Rogers (*Sniffy*), Karen Sorrell (*Lotus Liu*), Mitchell Lewis (*The Bartender*),
    Billy Bevan (*The Customs Inspector*), Herbert Evans (*The Constable*), Jimmie
    Aubrey (*The News Peddler*), Maj. Sam Harris (*Lord Gilford*), Frank Hagney
    (*The Bouncer*), Leonard Mudie (*The Art Gallery Ass't*), Paul McVey (*The
    Bystander*)
<u>D</u>: Norman Foster   <u>SCR</u>: Philip MacDonald & Norman Foster   <u>BASED ON</u>:
    John P. Marquand's novel *Mr. Moto's Last Warning*   <u>PHOTOG</u>: Bernard
    Herzbrun & Lewis Creber
Fr retitle, M. Moto dans les Bas-Fonds (Mr. Moto in the Under-world) A.k.a.
    Mysterious Mr. Moto on Devil's Island
Standard thriller: Japanese sleuth vs. league of assassins

Mysterious Mr. Moto on Devil's Island
see The Mysterious Mr. Moto

The Mysterious Mr. Reeder
see The Mind of Mr. Reeder

The Mysterious Mr. Wong
1935, (USA), George Yohalem/Mono, b&w, 58 mins.
<u>W</u>: Bela Lugosi (*Mr. Wong*), Wallace Ford (*Jay*), Arline Judge (*Peg*), Fred Warren,
    Lotus Long, Robert Emmet O'Connor, Etta Lee, Edward Piel, Lee Shumway,
    Luke Chan, Ernest F. Young
<u>D</u>: William Nigh   <u>SCR</u>: Nina Howatt   <u>ADAPT</u>: Lew Levenson   <u>SUGGESTED</u>
    <u>BY</u>: Harry Stephen Keeler's story "The Twelve Coins of Confucius"   <u>PHO-
    TOG</u>: Harry Neumann
Minor thriller: Newshound battles Oriental fiend

The Mysterious Mr. Nicholson
1947, (GB), Bushey/Ambassador, b&w, 78 mins.
<u>W</u>: Anthony Hulme (*Nicholson/Raeburn*), Lesley Osmond (*Peggy Dundas*), Frank
    Hawkins (*Insp. Morley*), Andrew Laurence (*Waring*), Douglas Stewart
    (*Seymour*), George Bishop (*Mr. Browne*), Josie Bradley (*Frieda*)
<u>P</u>: Gilbert Church   <u>D</u>: Oswald Mitchell   <u>SCR</u>: Francis Miller & Oswald
    Mitchell, from a story by Francis Miller
reissued 1949
Standard thriller: Gentleman thief tracks down murderous double

Mysterious Mr. Valentine
1946, (USA), Rep, b&w, 56 mins.
<u>W</u>: William Henry, Linda Stirling
Standard thriller

The Mysterious Monsters
1976, (USA), Sunn Classics/Viacom, color, 93 mins
<u>W</u>: Peter Hurkos, William Stenberg, Dr. Sidney Walter, Jerilou Whelchel
<u>D & SCR</u>: Robert Guenette   <u>NARRATOR</u>: Peter Graves   <u>PHOTOG</u>: David
    Myers, Eric Daarstadt & Tony Coggans
Standard docu-thriller: Unexplained phenomena probed

The Mysterious Paper
1896, (Fr), Star, b&w, 20m (65.6 ft./1.1 mins.)
<u>D</u>: Georges Melies
Standard comedy-thriller

Mysterious Planet
1984, (USA), color, 90 mins.
Minor SF-thriller: Humans vs. space-alien hordes

The Mysterious Portrait
see Le Portarit Mysterieux

The Mysterious Rabbit
1896, (GB), R.W. Paul, b&w, 40 ft. (12.2m)
<u>W</u>: David Devant
Standard fantasy short: Conjurer produces rabbit from hat, duplicates it

The Mysterious Retort
1906, (Fr), Star, b&w, 60m (196.9 ft./3.3 mins.)
<u>D</u>: Georges Melies
Standard comedy-fantasy: Alchemist's experiments

Mysterious Satellite
see Uchujin Tokyo No Arawaru

The Mysterious Stranger
1982, (W. Ger), Made for TV, color, 89 mins.
<u>W</u>: Fred Gwynne, Christopher Makepeace, Lance Kerwin
from a story by Mark Twain
TVM, standard fantasy-adventure: 10th-century printer has dream of life in medieval castle

The Mysterious Two
1982, (USA), NBC-TV, color, 97 mins.
<u>W</u>: John Forsythe (*He*), Priscilla Pointer (*She*), Robert Pine (*Arnold Brown*), James
    Stephens (*Tim Armstrong*), Noah Beery Jr. (*Virgil Molloy*), Vic Tayback (*Ted
    Randall*), Karen Werner (*Natalie*), Bruce French (*Bob Lahey*), E.J. Andre
<u>D & TELEPLAY</u>: Gary Sherman   <u>PHOTOG</u>: Steve Poster
TVM, standard SF: Alien humanoids mesmerize Earthlings in New Mexico desert

The Mysterious X
see Det Hemmelighedsfulde X

Mystery Circle Murder
1939, (USA), b&w, 69 mins.
<u>W</u>: Betty Compson, Robert Fiske, Helene Le Berthon, Arthur Gardner
<u>D & STORY</u>: Frank O'Connor
A.k.a. Religious Racketeers
Minor thriller: Reporter exposes phony mediums

The Mystery Film
1924, (GB), Int'l Cine Corp., b&w, 1,253 ft. (381.9m)
<u>W</u>: Ah-Ben-Aza

reissued (1926) as Where-U-Seer?
Standard fantasy: Bagdad magician reads minds

Mystery House
1938, (USA), b&w, 60 mins.
W: Dick Purcell, Ann Sheridan, Anne Nagel
Minor thriller: Banker murdered

Mystery in Mexico
1948, (USA), RKO, b&w, 66 mins.
W: William Lundigan, Jacqueline White, Ricardo Cortez, Tony Barrett, Jacqueline Dalya, Walter Reed, Jaime Jimeniz, Jose Torvay
D: Robert Wise   SCR: Lawrence Kimble   PHOTOG: Jack Draper   MUSIC DIR: C. Bakaleinokoff
Standard thriller

Mystery in Room 13
see Mr. Reeder in Room 13

Mystery Island
1980, (Austral), color, 75 mins.
W: Jayson Duncan, Nicklas Juhlin, Allan Penny
Minor adventure-thriller: Children marooned on isle with criminals

Mystery Junction
1951, (GB), Merton Park/Anglo-Amalgamated, b&w, 67 mins.
W: Sydney Tafler (*Larry Gordon*), Barbara Murray (*Pat Dawn*), Pat (Patricia)Owens (*Mabel Dawn*), Martin Benson (*Steve Harding*), John Salew (*John Martin*), Christine Silver (*Miss Owens*), Philip Dale (*Elliot Fisher*), Pearl Cameron (*Helen Mason*), Denis Webb (*Insp. Clarke*), Joan Young (*The Cashier*)
P: William H. Williams   WRIT & D: Michael McCarthy
Standard thriller: Novelist solves murders in snowbound railway station

Mystery Liner
1934, (USA), b&w, 62 mins.
W: Noah Beery, Astrid Allwyn, Cornelius Keefe, Ralph Lewis, Gustav von Seyffertitz, Edwin Maxwell, Zeffie Tilbury, Gabby Hayes, Boothe Howard
D: William Nigh
A.k.a. The Ghost of Joan Holling
Standard thriller: Secret weapon developed aboard cruise ship

Mystery Monsters!
1997, (USA), color, 90 mins.
W: Ashley Lyn Cafagna (*Susie*), Timothy Redwine (*Tommy*)
Made-for-Video, juvenile SF-fantasy: Evil space queen threatens children

The Mystery of a Hansom Cab
1915, (GB), B&C/Ideal, b&w, 5,500 ft. (1676.4m)
W: Milton Rosmer (*Mark Frettleby*), Fay Temple (*Madge Frettleby*), A.V. Bramble (*Moreland*), James Dale (*Brian Fitzgerald*), Arthur Walcott (*Oliver White*)
D: Harold Weston   SCR: Eliot Stannard, from a novel by Fergus Hume
Standard crime-thriller: Heiress helps counsel prove fiance did not kill cabby's passenger

The Mystery of a London Flat
1915, (GB), Broadwest/Gerrard, b&w, 3,000 ft. (914.4m)
W: Vera Cornish (*Margaret Foster*), George Foley (*Bentley*), Reginald Stevens (*Bob Pritchard*), Constance Backner (*Mrs. Hooper*), Richard Norton (*Will Hooper*), Andrew Jackson (*Leo Scott*), Hugh Croise (*The Inspector*)
P & D: Walter West
A.k.a. A London Flat Mystery
Standard crime-thriller: Shot girl recovers in time to save framed fiance

The Mystery of Boscombe Vale
1912, (GB-Fr), Franco-British Film Co.-Eclair/Fenning, b&w, 1,700 ft. (518.2m)
W: Georges Treville (*Sherlock Holmes*), Mr. Moyse (*Dr. John Watson*)
D: Georges Treville, from a story by Sir Arthur Conan Doyle
Standard thriller

The Mystery of Edwin Drood
1909, (GB), Gaumont, b&w, 1,030 ft. (313.9m)
W: Cooper Willis (*Edwin Drood*), Nancy Bevington (*Rosa Budd*), James Annand (*Neville Landless*)
D: Arthur Gilbert, from Charles Dickens' unfinished novel
Standard thriller (in 13 scenes): Cleric involved in crime

The Mystery of Edwin Drood
1935, (USA), Univ, b&w, 85 mins.
W: Claude Rains (*John Jasper*), Valerie Hobson (*Helen Landess*), David Manners (*Edwin Drood*), Heather Angel (*Rosa Bud*), Douglass Montgomery (*Neville Landless*), E.E. Clive, Francis L. Sullivan, Louise Carter, Zeffie Tilbury, George Ernest, Veda Buckland, Walter Kingsford
P: Carl Laemmle Jr.   D: Stuart Walker   SCR: John L. Balderston & Bradley King, from Charles Dickens' unfinished novel
Standard thriller: Cleric possessed by dark passion

The Mystery of Edwin Drood
1993, (GB), color, 98 mins.
W: Robert Powell, Michelle Evans, Jonathan Phillips, Finty Williams, Rupert Rainsford, Nanette Newman, Rosemary Leach, Freddie Jones, Ronald Fraser

D & SCR: Timothy Forder, from Charles Dickens' unfinished novel
Standard melodrama

Mystery of Los Hermanos Valley
see Rekopis Znaleziony w Saragossie

The Mystery of Marie Roget
1942, (USA), Univ, b&w, 61 mins.
W: Maria Montez, Patric Knowles, John Litel, Edward Norris, Maria Ouspenskaya, Lloyd Corrigan, Frank Reicher, Nell O'Day
D: George Waggner   SCR: Michael Jacoby, from Edgar Allan Poe's short story   PHOTOG: Elwood Bredell
A.k.a. Phantom of Paris
Standard thriller: 19th-century Parisian dance-hall star disappears

The Mystery of Mr. Bernard Brown
1921, (GB), Stoll, b&w, 5,558 ft. (1694.1m)
W: Ruby Miller (*Helen Thirwell*), Pardoe Woodman (*Bernard Brown*), Clifford Heatherley (*Sir Alan Beaumerville*), Ivy King (*Rachel Kynaston*), Annie Esmond (*Lady Thirwell*), Lewis Dayton (*Sir Geoffrey Kynaston*), Frank E. Petley (*Benjamin Levy*), Teddy Arundell (*Guy Thirwell*), Norma Whalley (*Mrs. Martival*)
D: Sinclair Hill   SCR: Mrs. Sydney Groome, from a novel by E. Phillips Oppenheim
Standard crime-thriller: Novelist blamed for stabbing fiance of squire's daughter

The Mystery of Mr. Marks
1914, (GB), Hepworth, b&w, 2,275 ft. (693.4m)
W: Alma Taylor (*Isobel Denton*), Lionelle Howard (*Gerald Lee*)
D: Warwick Buckland
A.k.a. By Whose Hand?
Standard thriller: Socialite proves father killed usurer while sleepwalking

The Mystery of Mr. Wong
1939, (USA), Mono, b&w, 69 mins.
W: Boris Karloff (*James Lee Wong*), Grant Withers (*Capt. Sam Street*), Dorothy Tree (*Valerie Edwards*), Lotus Long (*Drina*), Craig Reynolds (*Harrison*), Morgan Wallace (*Edwards*), Holmes Herbert (*Prof. Janney*), Ivan Lebedeff (*Strongonoff*), Bruce Wong (*The Man*), Lee Tung Foo (*Willie*), Hooper Atchley (*Carslake*), Chester Gan (*Sing*)
D: William Nigh   SCR: Scott Darling, from characters created by Hugh Wiley   PHOTOG: Harry Neumann
Minor thriller: Precious jewel inspires murder. 'Mr. Wong' Series

The Mystery of Mr. X
1934, (USA), MGM, b&w, 84 mins.
W: Robert Montgomery (*Nick Revel*), Elizabeth Allan (*Jane*), Lewis Stone (*Connor*), Ralph Forbes (*Marche*), Ivan Simpson (*Hutchinson*), Henry Stephenson (*Frensham*), Forrester Harvey (*Palmer*), Leonard Mudie (*Mr. X*), Alec B. Francis (*Judge Malpas*), Charles Irwin (*Willis*)
D: Edgar Selwyn   SCR: Howard Emmett Rogers, from Philip MacDonald's novel   PHOTOG: Oliver T. Marsh
Standard thriller: Gentleman crook tracks mad killer. Remake: The Hour of 13, 1952.

The Mystery of Professor Zazul
see Profesor Zazul

The Mystery of Rampo
1994, (Jap), color, 96 mins.
W: Naoto Takenaka, Michiko Hada, Masahiro Motoki, Teruyuki Kagawa, Mikijiro Hira
D: Kazuyoshi Okuyama   SCR: Kazuyoshi Okuyama & Yuhei Enoki   PHOTOG: Yasushi Sasakibara   MUSIC: Akira Senju
Unusual fantasy-thriller: Mystery writer enters his own stories

The Mystery of the Black Castle
see The Black Castle

Mystery of the Black Jungle
see Black Devils of Kali

The Mystery of the Diamond Belt
1914, (GB), I.B. Davidson/KTC, b&w, 3,500 ft. (1066.8m)
W: Philip Kay (*Sexton Blake*), Lewis Carlton (*Tinker*), Eve Balfour (*Kitty the Moth*), Douglas Payne (*George Marsden Plummer*), Percy Moran (*Flash Harry*), Austin Camp (*Jack Braham*), Lily Maxwell (*Nora Plummer*), Harry Graham (*Maurice Braham*)
D & SCR: Charles Raymond, from characters created by Harry Blyth
Standard crime-thriller: Crook poses as lord to rob merchant, holds detective captive in cellar

The Mystery of the Golden Eye
see The Golden Eye

Mystery of the Indian Temple
see Il Mistero del Tempio Indiano

The Mystery of the Mary Celeste
1935, (GB), Hammer/GFD, b&w, 80 mins.
W: Bela Lugosi (*Anton Lorenzen*), Arthur Margetson (*Capt. Briggs*), Shirley Grey (*Sarah Briggs*), Edmund Willard (*Toby Bilson*), George Mozart (*Tommy*

Duggan), Ben Welden (*Boas Hoffman*), Dennis Hoey (*Tom Goodschard*), Clifford McLaglen (*Capt. Marchant*), Gibson Gowland (*Andy Gillings*), Terence de Marney (*Charlie Kaye*), James Carew (*James Winchester*), Ben Soutten (*Jack Samson*), Gunner Moir (*Ponta Katz*)
<u>WRIT & D:</u> Denison Clift
*USA retitle, **The Phantom Ship***
Standard thriller: Mad sailor kills crew

The Mystery of the Old Mill
1914, (GB), Big Ben Films-Union/Pathe, b&w, 3,000 ft. (914.4m)
<u>W:</u> H.O. Martinek (*Dick Steele*), Ivy Montford (*Kate Halifax*), Irene Vernon (*Daphne Morrison*)
<u>D:</u> H.O. Martinek   <u>STORY</u>: L.C. MacBean
Standard thriller: Detectives unmask blackmailer

The Mystery of the Silent Death
1928, (GB), British Filmcraft/Para, b&w, 1,965 ft. (598.9m)
<u>W:</u> Langhorne Burton (*Sexton Blake*), Roy Travers (*Mr. Reece*), Mickey Brantford (*Tinker*), Thelma Murray (*Peggy*), Mrs. Fred Emney (*Mrs. Bardell*), Roy Raymond (*Ross*)
<u>D:</u> Leslie Eveleigh
Standard thriller ("Sexton Blake" mystery): Detective and young assistant solve murder

The Mystery of the 13th Guest
1943, (USA), Mono, b&w, 61 mins
<u>W:</u> Dick Purcell, Helen Parrish, Addison Richards, Tim Ryan, Herbert Heyes

The Mystery of the 13th Guest: ADDISON RICHARDS, TIM RYAN, HERBERT HEYES, CHARLES MURPHY AND DICK PURCELL

<u>D:</u> William Beaudine   <u>SCR:</u> Charles Marion & Tim Ryan
*Standard thriller (remake of **The Thirteenth Guest**): Hunt for fiendish killer*

Mystery of the Wax Museum
1933, (USA), WB, color, 77 mins.
<u>W:</u> Lionel Atwill, Fay Wray, Glenda Farrell, Gavin Gordon, Allen Vincent, Monica Bannister, DeWitt Jennings, Edwin Maxwell, Frank McHugh, Arthur Edmund Carewe, Mathew Betz, Pat O'Malley, Holmes Herbert
<u>D:</u> Michael Curtiz   <u>SCR:</u> Don Mullany & Carl Erickson   <u>PHOTOG:</u> Ray Rennahan
*Classic horror-thriller: Murderous mad sculptor turns his victims into waxworks cf. **House of Wax***

The Mystery of the Wentworth Castle
*see **Doomed to Die***

Mystery of the White Room
1939, (USA), Univ., b&w, 58 mins.
<u>W:</u> Bruce Cabot, Helen Mack
Minor thriller: Surgeon and nurse are suspects in operating room stabbing. 'Crime Club' series.

The Mystery of Thug Island
1964, (It-Germ.), Liber/Eichberg/Col., color, 88 mins.
<u>W:</u> Guy Madison, Inge Schoner, Ivan Desny
*Minor thriller: Snake cultists cause upheaval in India. Remake: **Black Devils of Kali***

The Mystery of Tut-Ankh-Amen's Eighth Wife
*see **King Tut-Ankh-Amen's Eighth Wife***

Mystery on Monster Island
1981, (USA-Sp), Almena Films-Fort Films/20th-Fox, color, 96 mins.
<u>W:</u> Ian Sera, Terence Stamp, Peter Cushing, David Hatton, Gasphar Ipua, Bianca Estrada, Ana Obregon, Frank Brana, Manuel Pereiro, George Bosso, Ioshio Murakami, Paul Naschy, Daniel Martin
<u>D:</u> J. Piquer Simon   <u>INSPIRED BY:</u> Jules Verne's writings   <u>PHOTOG:</u> Andres

Berenguer   <u>SPCL-FX:</u> Basilio Cortijo   <u>MUSIC:</u> Alfonso Agullo, Carlos Villa & Alejandro Monroy
*A.k.a. **Jules Verne's Mystery on Monster Island***
Juvenile adventure-romance: Boy and tutor shipwrecked on treasure-laden volcanic isle

Mystery Plane
1939, (USA), Mono, b&w, 60 mins.
<u>W:</u> John Trent, Marjorie Reynolds, Milburn Stone, Jason Robards Sr., Tommy Bupp, Polly Ann Young
<u>D:</u> George Waggner   <u>PHOTOG:</u> Archie Stout
Minor adventure-thriller (from comic-strip character "Tailspin Tommy"): Youth vs. spy ring

Mystery Science Theater 3000: The Movie
1996, (USA), Gramercy/Univ, color, 73 mins.
<u>W:</u> Mike J. Nelson (*Mike*), Trace Beaulieu (*Dr. Clayton Forrester*), Mary Jo Pehl, Paul Chaplin, Bridget Jones
<u>ROBOT VOICES:</u> Kevin Murphy, Jim Mallon
<u>D:</u> Jim Mallon   <u>SCR:</u> Trace Beaulieu, Kevin Murphy, Paul Chaplin, Mary Jo Pehl & Mike J. Nelson
Amusing SF-comedy (from popular teleseries): Robots criticize film 'This Island Earth'

Mystery Sea Raider
1940, (USA), Para, b&w, 75 mins.
<u>W:</u> Henry Wilcoxon, Carole Landis
<u>D:</u> Edward Dmytryk
Minor adventure-thriller

Mystery Street
1950, (USA), MGM, b&w, 93 mins.
<u>W:</u> Ricardo Montalban (*Peter Moralas*), Sally Forrest (*Grace Shanway*), Elsa Lanchester (*Mrs. Smerrling*), Jan Sterling (*Vivian Heldon*), Bruce Bennett (*Dr. McAdoo*), Betsy Blair (*Jackie Elcott*), Marshall Thompson (*Henry Shanway*), Edmon Ryan (*James Joshua Harkley*), Wally Maher (*Tim Sharkey*), Ralph Dumke (*A Tattooist*), Willard Waterman (*A Mortician*), Walter Burke (*An Ornithologist*), Don Shelton (*A District Attorney*), King Donovan
<u>D:</u> John Sturges   <u>SCR:</u> Sydney Boehm & Richard Brooks, from a story by Leonard Spigelgass   <u>PHOTOG:</u> John Alton   <u>MUSIC:</u> Rudolph Kopp
Engrossing docu-style thriller: Playgirl's murder probed

Mystery Submarine
1950, (USA), Univ, b&w, 78 mins.
<u>W:</u> Macdonald Carey, Marta Toren, Carl Esmond, Ludwig Donath
<u>D:</u> Douglas Sirk
Standard melodrama

The Mystic
1925, (USA), MGM, b&w, 7 reels (6,147 ft./1873.6m)
<u>W:</u> Aileen Pringle (*Zara*), Conway Tearle (*Michael Nash*), Mitchell Lewis (*Zazarack*), Robert Ober (*Anton*), Stanton Heck (*Carlo*), David Torrence (*Bradshaw*), Gladys Hulette (*Doris Merrick*), DeWitt Jennings (*The Police Inspector*)
<u>D & STORY:</u> Tod Browning   <u>SCR:</u> Waldemar Young   <u>PHOTOG:</u> Ira Morgan
Standard thriller: Crook defrauds heiress

The Mystical Flame
*see **La Flamme Merveilleuse***

Mystic Manipulations
1911, (GB), Natural Colour Kinematograph Co., color, 495 ft. (150.9m)
<u>D:</u> Walter R. Booth & Theo Bouwmeester
Standard fantasy short: Conjurer turns milk into claret

The Mystic Mat
1913, (GB), Cricks & Martin, b&w, 430 ft. (131.1m)
<u>D:</u> Dave Aylott   <u>STORY:</u> W. Saville
Standard fantasy short: Magician's carpet makes people disappear

The Mystic Moonstone
1913, (GB), Cricks & Martin, b&w, 325 ft. (99.1m)
<u>D:</u> Dave Aylott
reissued 1916
Standard fantasy short: Farmer finds magic ring that causes objects to vanish

The Mystic Ring
1912, (GB), Cricks & Martin, b&w, 610 ft. (186m)
<u>D:</u> Dave Aylott
Standard fantasy short: Tramp dreams Satan gives him ring that causes invisibility

My Uncle the Alien
1996, (USA), color, 90 mins.
<u>W:</u> Hailey Foster, Joshua Paddock, Dink O'Neal
Made-for-Video, minor SF-comedy: President's daughter helps children's shelter

My Wife is a Witch
*see **I Married a Witch***

My World Dies Screaming
*see **Terror in the Haunted House***

Nabonga

1944, (USA), PRC, b&w, 71 mins.
<u>W</u>: Buster Crabbe (*Ray Gorman*), Fifi D'Orsay (*Marie*), Barton MacLane (*Carl Hurst*), Julie London (*Doreen Stockwell*), Bryant Washburn, Herbert Rawlinson, Prince Modupe, Jackie Newfield
<u>P</u>: Sigmund Neufeld   <u>D</u>: Sam Newfield   <u>ORIG. STORY & SCR</u>: Fred Myton   <u>PHOTOG</u>: Robert Cline   <u>SPCL-FX</u>: Gene Stone   <u>MUSIC SCORE</u>: Willy Stahl   <u>MUSIC SPRVSR</u>: David Chudnow
A.k.a. **Gorilla, Girl and the Gorilla** *and* **Jungle Witch**
Minor adventure-thriller: Tracer of stolen loot finds absconder's daughter gone native, film debut of Julie London

Nadja

1995, (USA), October Films, color, 92 mins.
<u>W</u>: Elina Lowensohn, Peter Fonda (*Dracula/ Dr. Van Helsing*), David Lynch
<u>P</u>: David Lynch   <u>D</u>: Michael Almereyda
Unusual avant-garde horror-fantasy: Vampire family moves to New York City

Nagana

1933, (USA), Univ, b&w
<u>W</u>: Melvyn Douglas, Tala Birell
Standard thriller: Adventurers seek priceless relic. cf. **Zanzibar**

Nail Gun Massacre

1986, (USA), color, 90 mins.
<u>W</u>: Rocky Patterson, Ron Queen, Beau Leland, Michelle Meyer
<u>D</u>: Bill Lesley
Minor horror-thriller: Crazed killer goes on hammering spree

Naked Alibi

1954, (USA), Univ, b&w, 86 mins.
<u>W</u>: Sterling Hayden, Gloria Grahame Gene Barry, Marcia Henderson, Casey Adams, Chuck Connors
<u>D</u>: Jerry Hopper
Standard thriller: Dismissed policeman stalks cop-killer

The Naked Ape

1973, (USA), Univ, color, 85 mins
<u>W</u>: Johnny Crawford, Victoria Principal, Marvin Miller
<u>P</u>: Zev Bufman   <u>D & SCR</u>: Donald Driver, from Desmond Morris' book   <u>PHOTOG</u>: John Alonzo   <u>MUSIC</u>: Jimmy Webb
Unusual docu-fantasy: Live action & animation used to explore human evolution

Naked Cage

1986, (USA), color, 97 mins.
<u>W</u>: Shari Shattuck, Angel Tompkins, Lucinda Crosby, Christina Whitaker
<u>D</u>: Paul Nicholas
Minor thriller: Predictable discord in women's prison

The Naked Cell

1987, (GB), color, 90 mins.
<u>W</u>: Vicky Jeffrey, Richard Fallon, May Jacquetta, Yvonne Bonnamy, Jill Spurrier
<u>D</u>: John Crome
Minor eroto-thriller: Nymphomaniac reveals her past

The Naked Detective

1996, (USA), color, 85 mins.
<u>W</u>: Jim Gardiner, Julia Parton, Taylor St. Claire
Minor thriller: Private eye has misadventures

The Naked Edge

1961, (GB), UA, b&w, 99 mins.
<u>W</u>: Gary Cooper, Deborah Kerr, Eric Portman, Diane Cilento, Hermione Gingold, Peter Cushing, Michael Wilding, Wilfrid Lawson, Sandor Eles, Diane Clare, Ronald Howard
<u>P</u>: Walter Seltzer & George Glass   <u>D</u>: Michael Anderson   <u>SCR</u>: Joseph Stefano, from Max Ehrlich's novel *First Train to Babylon*   <u>PHOTOG</u>: Erwin Hillier   <u>MUSIC</u>: William Alwyn
Taut thriller (Gary Cooper's last film): Woman suspects husband is calculating murderer

Naked Evil

1966, (GB), Gibraltar/Col, b&w, 79 mins.
<u>W</u>: Anthony Ainley (*Dick Alderson*), Basil Dignam (*Benson*), Suzanne Neve (*Janet*), Richard Coleman (*Hollis*), Ronald Bridges (*Wilkins*), George A. Saunders (*Danny*), Dan Jackson (*Lloyd*), Pearl Prescod (*The Landlady*), Carmen Munroe (*Beverley*), Brylo Ford, Addison Greene, Olaf Pooley, Bari Jonson, Oscar James
<u>P</u>: Steven Pallos   <u>D & SCR</u>: Stanley Goulder, from Jon Manchip White's play *The Obi*   <u>PHOTOG</u>: Geoffrey Faithfull   <u>MUSIC</u>: Bernard Ebbinghouse
released in USA (1979, Independent-Int'l, 89 mins.) as **Exorcism at Midnight** *(with added footage featuring Lawrence Tierney, Bob Allen, Catharine Erhardt & Nuba Stuart)*
Standard fantasy: Murdered voodoo practitioner takes over body of student hostel's secretary

Naked Fear

see **The Last Man on Earth**

Naked Fury

1959, (GB), Coenda/Butcher, b&w, 60 mins.
<u>W</u>: Reed de Rousen (*Eddy*), Kenneth Cope (*Johnny*), Ann Lynn (*Judy*), Leigh Madison (*Carol*), Arthur Lovegrove (*Syd*), Thomas Eytle (*Steve*), Alexander Field (*Vic*), Marianne Brauns (*Joy*), Katy Cashfield (*Commere*)
<u>P</u>: Guido Coen   <u>D</u>: Charles Saunders   <u>SCR</u>: Brock Williams   <u>STORY</u>: Guido Coen
Minor crime-thriller: Safe robbers hold watchman's daughter captive in old warehouse

The Naked Goddess

see **The Devil's Hand** (1961)

The Naked Gun

1956, (USA), Assoc. Film, b&w, 69 mins.
<u>W</u>: Mara Corday, Jody McCrea, Barton MacLane, Tom Brown, Veda Ann Borg, Morris Ankrum, Willard Parker
<u>P</u>: Ron Ormond   <u>D</u>: Edward Dew   <u>SCR</u>: Ron Ormond & Jack Lewis
Standard Western thriller: Insurance man searches for heiress to cursed Aztec fortune

The Naked Jungle

1954, (USA), Para, color, 95 mins.
<u>W</u>: Charlton Heston (*Leiningen*), Eleanor Parker (*Joanne*), William Conrad (*The Commissioner*), Abraham Sofaer (*Incacha*), Romo Vincent (*The Boat Captain*), Douglas Fowley (*The Medicine Man*), John Dierkes (*Gruber*), Leonard Strong (*Kutina*), Norma Calderon (*Zala*), John Mansfield (*The Foreman*), Pilar Del Rey, Ronald Alan Numkena, Bernie Gozier, Leon Lontoc, Jack Reitzen, Rodd Redwing, John E. Wood, Carlos Rivero, Jerry Groves
<u>P</u>: George Pal   <u>D</u>: Byron Haskin   <u>SCR</u>: Philip Yordan & Ranald MacDougall, based on Carl Stephenson's short story "Leiningen Versus the Ants" (published in Esquire, 1938)   <u>PHOTOG</u>: Ernest Laszlo   <u>MUSIC</u>: Daniele Amfitheatrof
Tense adventure-thriller: South-American plantation owner and mail-order bride face terror of army ants

The Naked Runner

1967, (GB), Artanis-Sinatra Enterprises/WB, color, 102 mins.
<u>W</u>: Frank Sinatra (*Sam Laker*), Nadia Gray (*Karen Gisevius*), Derren Nesbitt (*Col. Hartmann*), Peter Vaughan (*Martin Slattery*), Toby Robins (*Ruth*), Inger Stratton (*Anna*), Cyril Luckham (*The Minister*), Michael Newport (*Patrick Laker*), Edward Fox (*Ritchie Jackson*)
<u>P</u>: Brad Dexter   <u>D</u>: Sidney J. Furie   <u>SCR</u>: Stanley Mann, from a novel by Francis Clifford
Standard crime-thriller: Ex-intelligence agent forced to kill fugitive spy

Naked Souls

1996, (USA), HBO-TV, color, 85 mins.
<u>W</u>: Brian Krause, David Warner, Pamela Anderson Lee (*Britt*), Dean Stockwell (*Duncan*), Clayton Rohner (*Jerry*), Justina Vail (*Amelia*)
<u>D</u>: Lyndon Chubbuck   <u>SCR</u>: Frank Dietz   <u>PHOTOG</u>: Eric Goldstein   <u>MUSIC</u>: Nigel Holton
Made-for-Cable, standard SF-thriller: Thought-transference experiment goes awry

The Naked Temptress

see **The Naked Witch**

Naked Terror

1961, (USA), Joseph Brenner Asocs., color, 74 mins.
<u>W</u>: Vincent Price (*host/narrator*)

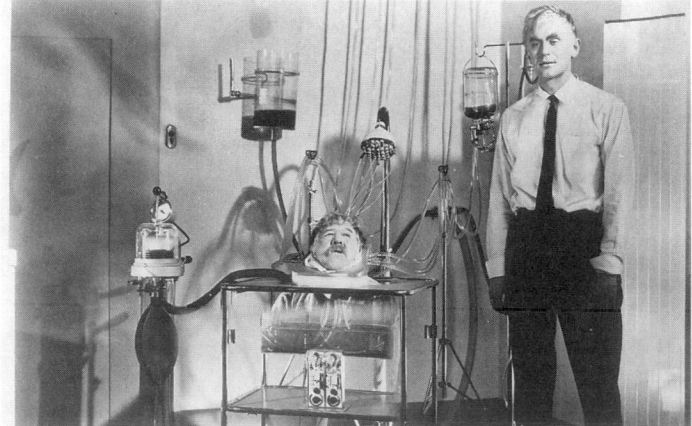

The Naked Woman and Satan: MICHAEL SIMON AND HORST FRANK

Standard docu: Zulu practices (e.g., initiation of virgins into tribe, murder by witchcraft)

The Naked Witch

1964, (USA), color, 60 mins.
<u>W</u>: Beth Porter, Robert Burgos, Bryarly Lee, Lee Forbes
<u>D</u>: Andy Milligan
A.k.a. **The Naked Temptress**
Minor horror-fantasy: College students revive long-dead witch

The Naked Woman and Satan

1959, (W. Ger), Prisma Wolfgang Hartwig Rapid-Film/TransLux, b&w, 92 mins.

W: Horst Frank, Michel Simon, Paul Dahlke, Kurt Muller-Graf, Christiane Maybach, Helmut Schmid, Karin Kernke, Dieter Eppler, Otto Storr, Maria Stadler

P: Wolfgang Hartwig   **WRIT & D:** Victor Trivas, loosely based on Curt Siodmak's novel *Donovan's Brain*

USA retitle, **The Head,** *Trans-Lux, 1961*

Standard SF-horror ("The body is gone...but the head lives on!:" "It just won't lay down and stay dead!;" "This is Irene who wears her own face and the body of a dead stripteaser!"): Scientist experiments in transplants

The Naked Zoo

1970, (USA), R&S Films, color, 91 mins.

W: Stephen Oliver, Rita Hayworth, Fay Spain, Ford Rainey, Willie Pastrano

P & D: William Grefe   **SCR:** Roy Preston

A.k.a. **The Hallucinators**

Standard thriller: Love and crime in Miami's Coconut Grove artist's colony

Na Komete (Off on a Comet)

1970, (Czech), Barrandov, color, 85 mins.

W: Emil Horvath, Frantisek Filipovsky Magda Vasarykova

D & SCR: Karel Zeman, loosely based on Jules Verne's novel *Off on a Comet*

  MUSIC: Lubos Fiser

A.k.a. **Hector Servgadac's Ark**

Minor SF-adventure: Men torn from Earth by passing comet. cf. **Valley of the Dragons**

A Name for Evil

1970, (USA), color, 74 mins.

W: Robert Culp, Samantha Eggar, Sheila Sullivan, Mike Lane

D: Bernard Girard

Standard thriller: Couple moves into old house near Great Lakes; weirdness ensues

The Nameless Terror

see **The Blob** (1958)

The Name of the Game is Kill

1968, (USA), Poore & Todd/Fanfare, color, 88 mins.

W: Jack Lord, Susan Strasberg, Collin Wilcox, T.C. Jones, Tisha Sterling

D: Gunnar Hellstrom   **SONG:** *Shadows*

TV retitle, **The Female Trap,** *A.k.a.* **Lovers in Limbo**

Weird thriller: Drifter becomes involved with strange family

The Name of the Rose

1986, (W. Ger-It-Fr), Bernd Eichinger-Bernd Schaefers/20th Fox, color, 128 mins.

W: Sean Connery (*William of Baskerville*), F. Murray Abraham (*Bernardo Gui*), Christian Slater (*Adso of Melk*), Elya Baskin (*Severinus*), Feodor Chaliapin Jr. (*Jorge de Burgos*), William Hickey (*Ubertino de Casale*), Michael Lonsdale (*The Abbot*), Ron Perlman (*Salvatore*), Volker Prechtel (*Malachia*), Helmut Qualtinger (*Remigio de Varagine*), Valentina Vargas (*The Girl*), Pete Lancaster

P: Bernd Eichinger   **D:** Jean-Jacques Annaud   **SCR:** Andrew Birkin, Gerard Brach, Howard Franklin & Alain Godard   **PHOTOG:** Tonino Delli Colli   **MUSIC:** James Horner

Elegant mystery-thriller (a palimpsest of Eco's novel): 14th-century monastic detective probes murders

Nancy Drew and the Hidden Staircase

1939, (USA), WB, b&w, 60 mins.

W: Bonita Granville (*Nancy Drew*), John Litel (*Carson Drew*), Frankie Thomas, Frank Orth, Renie Riano, Vera Lewis, Louise Carter, William Gould, George Guhl, John Ridgely, William Hopper, Frank Mayo, Fred Tozere, Creighton Hale, Don Rowan, Dick Elliott

D: William Clemens   **SCR:** Kenneth Gamet, from characters created by Carolyn Keene

Standard thriller (4th & last "Nancy Drew" mystery): Girl sleuth aids two elderly sisters,

Nancy Drew and the Hidden Staircase: RENIE RIANO, BONTIA GRANVILLE AND CLIFF SAUM

solves murder

Nancy Drew, Detective

1938, (USA), WB, b&w, 60 mins.

W: Bonita Granville (*Nancy Drew*), John Litel (*Carson Drew*), James Stephenson, Frankie Thomas, Frank Orth, Dick Purcell, Renie Riano, Helena P. Evans, Charles Trowbridge, Ed Keane, Brandon Tynan, Vera Lewis, Mae Busch, Lottie Williams, Tommy Bupp

D: William Clemens   **SCR:** Kenneth Gamet, from Carolyn Keene's novel *The Password to Larkspur Lane*

Standard thriller (1st "Nancy Drew" mystery): Girl sleuth searches for kidnapped philanthropist

Nancy Drew, Reporter

1939, (USA), WB, b&w, 68 mins.

W: Bonita Granville (*Nancy Drew*), John Litel (*Carson Drew*), Frankie Thomas, Mary Lee, Sheila Bromley, Frank Orth, Larry Williams, Betty Amann, Thomas Jackson, Dickie Lee, Charles Halton, Olin Howland, Joan Leslie, Florence Halop, Charles Smith, Lois Verner, Jack Wagner

D: William Clemens   **SCR:** Kenneth Gamet, from characters created by Carolyn Keene

Standard thriller (2nd "Nancy Drew" mystery): Girl sleuth aids young man accused of killing elderly guardian

Nancy Drew, Troubleshooter

1939, (USA), WB, b&w, 69 mins.

W: Bonita Granville (*Nancy Drew*), John Litel (*Carson Drew*), Frankie Thomas, Aldrich Bowker, Charlotte Wynters, Erville Alderson, Edgar Edwards, Renie Riano, Roger Imhoff, Willie Best

D: William Clemens   **SCR:** Kenneth Gamut, from characters created by Carolyn Keene

Standard thriller (3rd "Nancy Drew" mystery): Girl sleuth aids lawyer father, helps clear client falsely accused of crime

Nan in Fairyland

1912, (GB), Cricks & Martin, b&w, 1,250 ft. (381m)

W: Edwin J. Collins (*The Policeman*)

D: Edwin J. Collins

reissued 1916

Standard fantasy: Orphan dreams Puck saves her from ogre

The Nanny

1965, (GB), Jimmy Sangster/Hammer/WB, b&w, 93 mins.

W: Bette Davis (*Nanny*), Wendy Craig (*Virgie*), William Dix (*Joey*), James Villiers (*Bill*), Jill Bennett (*Pen*), Pamela Franklin (*Bobby*), Alfred Burke (*Dr. Wills*), Jack Watling (*Dr. Medman*), Maurice Denham (*Dr. Beamaster*), Nora Gordon (*Mrs. Griggs*), Harry Fowler (*The Milkman*), Angharad Aubrey (*Susy*), Sandra Power (*Sarah*)

D: Seth Holt   **SCR:** Jimmy Sangster, from Evelyn Piper's novel   **PHOTOG:** Harry Waxman   **MUSIC:** Richard Rodney Bennett

Superior thriller: Boy accuses his nanny of murder

The Narrow Margin

1952, (USA), RKO, b&w, 71 mins.

W: Charles McGraw, Marie Windsor, Jacqueline White, Queenie Leonard, Jack Maxey, Don Beddoe, Gordon Gebert, Harry Harvey

D: Richard Fleischer   **SCR:** Earl Fenton, from a story by Martin Goldsmith & Jack Leonard   **PHOTOG:** George E. Diskant

Semi-classic melodrama: Cops escort hoodlum's widow

Narrow Margin

1990, (USA), Carolco, color, 97 mins.

W: Gene Hackman, Anne Archer, James B. Sikking, J.T. Walsh, M. Emmet Walsh, Susan Hogan, Harris Yulin, Nigel Bennett, B.A. Smith, J.A. Preston

WRIT, DIR & PHOTOG: Peter Hyams, from a story by Martin Goldsmith & Jack Leonard   **MUSIC:** Bruce Broughton

Modest thriller: Gangsters try to prevent mobster's widow from testifying. Remake of 1952 film.

Die Nashorner (The Rhinoceros)

1963, (W. Ger), color, 11 mins.

D: Jan Lenica, from Eugene Ionesco's play *Rhinoceros*

Animated short, philosophical fantasy: Moral decay turns humans into animals

The Nasty Rabbit

1964, (USA), Fairway-Int'l, color, 85 mins.

W: Mischa Terr, Arch Hall Jr., Melissa Morgan, Little Jack Little, Laszlo Kovacs, Arch Hall Sr.

P: Nicholas Merriwether (Arch Hall, Sr.)   **D:** James Landis   **SCR:** Arch Hall Sr. & Jim Crutchfield   **PHOTOG:** Vilmos Zsigmond & Laszlo Kovacs   **SONGS.:** *The Jackrabbit Shuffle, The Robot Walk & Jackie*

A.k.a. **Spies-A-Go-Go**

Minor comedy-thriller: Soviet saboteur seeks to release contaminated bunny on Continental Divide

Nata's...The Reflection

1983, (USA), color, 90 mins.

W: Randy Mulkey, Pat Bolt, Craig Hensley, Kelli Kuhn

Minor fantasy-thriller: Reporter probes Indian demon myth

Nathalie, Agent Secret
1959, (Fr), Sirius-SFC/CFDC, b&w, 95 mins.
W: Martine Carol
D: Henri Decoin **DIALOG:** Henri Jeanson **MUSIC:** Georges Van Parys
Minor thriller: Woman becomes involved in espionage

Nathaniel Hawthorne's Twice-Told Tales
see Twice-Told Tales

National Lampoon's Men in White
1998, (USA), Saban/Fox-TV, color, 95 mins.
W: Tom Wilson, Karim Prince, Barry Bostwick, Donna D'Errico, M. Emmet Walsh, Wigald Boning (*Strangemeister*), George Kennedy, Don Stroud, Brion James, Ben Stein
D: Scott Levy **PHOTOG:** Brad Rushing **MUSIC:** Kenneth Burgomaster
TVM, standard SF-satire: Space aliens target Earthlings as pet food

Nattmara (Nightmare)
1966, (Swed), b&w, 88 mins.
W: Ulla Jacobsson
D: Arne Mattsson
Standard thriller

Natural Laws Reversed
1905, (GB), Urban, b&w, 75 ft. (22.9m)
D: Tom Green
Standard fantasy short: Log cabin dweller finds everything goes in reverse

The Nature of the Beast
1995, (USA), Itasca Pictures, color, 90 mins.
W: Eric Roberts (*Adrian*), Lance Henriksen (*Jack Powell*), Sasha Jenson (*Gerald*), Ana Gabriel (*Dahlia*), Eloy Casados (*Sheriff #1*), Brion James (*Sheriff Gordon*), Frank Novak (*Manfred Holliday*), Eliza Roberts (*Patsy*), William A. Temple (*The Elderly Gentleman*), Hollace Colburn (*The Counter Waitress*), Earl Theroux (*Mr. Winneman*), Lila Garrett (*Mrs. Winneman*), Bob May (*The Trooper in the Diner*), Sara Young (*The Lady in the Diner*), Zachary Bogatz (*The Young Man at the Motel*), John Toles-Bey (*The Trooper at the Roadblock*), Curt Darling, Virgil Frye, Mark Johnson, Ava Lazar, Tom Tarantini, Marc Daniel, Lin Shaye, Phil Fondacaro
WRIT & D: Victor Salva **PHOTOG:** Levie Isaacks **MUSIC:** Bennett Salvay
Standard thriller: Serial killer prowls desert

Nature's Mistakes
see Freaks

La Nave de los Monstruos (The Ship of the Monsters)
1959, (Mex), Col, b&w
W: Ana Bertha Lepe, Piporro, Lorena Velazquez
Standard SF-fantasy: Space aliens visit Earth

The Navigator: An Odyssey Across Time
1989, (New Zeal), Circle Releasing Corp., color, 92 mins.
W: Bruce Lyons (*Connor*), Chris Haywood (*Arno*), Hamish McFarlane (*Griffin*), Marshall Napier (*Searle*), Sarah Pierse (*Linnet*), Noel Appleby (*Ulf*), Paul Livingston (*Martin*)
D: Vincent Ward **SCR:** Vincent Ward, Kely Lyons & Geoff Chapple, from an orig. idea by Vincent Ward **PHOTOG:** Geoffrey Simpson **MUSIC:** Davood A. Tabrizi
Unusual fantasy-adventure: Medieval villagers flee Black Death, travel through time

The Navy vs. the Night Monsters
1966, (USA), Jack Broder/Realart, color, 87 mins.
W: Anthony Eisley, Mamie Van Doren, Bill Gray, Bobby Van, Pamela Mason, Del West, Phillip Terry, Walter Sande, Russ Bender, Edward Faulkner, David Brandon
P: George Edwards **D & SCR:** Michael A. Hoey, from a story by Murray Leinster **PHOTOG:** Stanley Cortez
orig. to be titled The Night Crawlers
Standard SF-horror: Monstrous nocturnal plants produce flesh-destroying enzyme

Nazi Agent
1942, (USA), MGM, b&w, 84 mins.
W: Conrad Veidt, Ann Ayars, Frank Reicher, Martin Kosleck, Dorothy Tree Sidney Blackmer, Marc Lawrence, William Tannen
D: Jules Dassin **SCR:** Paul Gangelin & John Meehan Jr. **PHOTOG:** Harry Stradling
Standard thriller: War-time spies conspire

The Neanderthal Man
1953, (USA), Global/UA, b&w, 78 mins.
W: Robert Shayne (*Prof. Groves*), Joy Terry (*Jan Groves*), Doris Merrick (*Ruth Marshall*), Richard Crane (*Dr. Ross Harkness*), Beverly Garland (*Nola Mason*), Robert Long (*Jim*), Dick Rich (*The Sheriff*), Jeanette Quinn, Lee Morgan, Eric Colmar, Anthony Jochim, Robert Easton, Marshall Bradford
WRIT & P: Aubrey Wisberg & Jack Pollexfen **D:** E.A. Dupont **PHOTOG:** Stanley Cortez **SPCL-FX:** Jack Rabin & David Commons **MUSIC:** Albert Glasser
Standard SF-thriller: Scientist regresses animals and humans to primitive states of evolution

Near Dark
1987, (USA), F/M/De Laurentiis, color, 95 mins.
W: Adrian Pasdar (*Caleb*), Jenny Wright (*Mae*), Joshua Miller (*Homer*), Lance Henriksen (*Jesse*), Tim Thomerson (*Loy*), Bill Paxton, Jenette Goldstein, Marcie Leeds, Kenny Call, Troy Evans
D: Kathryn Bigelow **SCR:** Eric Red & Kathryn Bigelow **PHOTOG:** Adam Greenberg **MUSIC:** Tangerine Dream
Unusual horror-fantasy: Youth drawn into vampire nest

Near Death

The Necklace of Death
1919, (Ger), Eichberg, b&w
W: Bela Lugosi
Standard thriller

Necromancer: Satan's Servant
1989, (USA), color, 88 mins.
W: Elizabeth Kaitan, Russ Tamblyn Rhonda Dorton
D: Dusty Nelson
Minor fantasy-thriller: Assaulted by classmates, student hires Gypsy sorceress

Necromancy
1972, (USA), Zenith-Int'l/CRC, color, 82 mins.
W: Orson Welles (*Cato*), Pamela Franklin (*Lori*), Lee Purcell (*Priscilla*), Michael Ontkean (*Frank*), Lisa James (*Georgette*), Harvey Jason (*Jay*), Sue Bernard (*Nancy*), Teddy Quinn (*Cato's Son*)
WRIT, P, & D: Bert I. Gordon **PHOTOG:** Winton C. Hoch **MUSIC:** Fred Karger
A.k.a. Toy Factory video-title The Witching (Video Treasures, 1990)
Minor horror-fantasy: Sinister toy manufacturer tries to raise son from dead

Necronomicon
1968, (W. Ger), Aquila/Trans-American, color, 93 mins.
W: Janine Reynaud (*Lorna*), Jack Taylor (*Bill*), Nathalie Nord (*Bella*), Eva Brauner (*Olga*), Pier A. Caminneci (*Hermann*), Adrian Hoven (*The Psychiatrist*), Howard Vernon, Michel Lemoine
P: Adrian Hoven **D:** Jesus Franco **SCR:** Pier A. Caminneci
USA retitle, Succubus
"...perversely funny and incredibly pretentious"—Castle of Frankenstein
Standard eroto-horror: Nightclub performer believes herself controlled by demon

Necronomicon: Book of the Dead
1993, (USA), color
W: Bruce Payne, Jeffrey Combs, Tony Azito, Richard Lynch, Belinda Bauer, David Warner, Bess Myer, Millie Perkins, Signy Coleman, Obba Babatunde, Don Calfa
D: Brian Yuzna, Christophe Gans & Shu Kaneko, from a story by H.P. Lovecraft
A.k.a. Lovecrafts Necronomicon
Unusual horror trilogy: The Drowned, The Cold & Whispers

Necrophagus
1971, (Sp), Int'l Films, color
D & SCR: Miguel Madrid
USA retitle, Graveyard of Horror
Minor horror-thriller: Man tends ghoul brother

Necropolis
1987, (USA), color, 77 mins.
W: Leeanne Baker, Michael Conte, Jacquie Fritz, Paul Ruben, William Reed
D: Tim Kincaid
Minor fantasy-thriller: Ancient witch returns to life as motorcycle punkette

Needful Things
1993, (USA), Castle Rock-New Line/Col, color, 120 mins.(director's cut, 188 mins.)
W: Ed Harris, Max Von Sydow, Bonnie Bedelia, J.T. Walsh, Amanda Plummer Lisa Blount, Shane Meier, Valri Bromfield, Ray McKinnon, Duncan Fraser, W. Morgan Sheppard
P: Jack Cummins   D: Fraser C. Heston   SCR: W.D. Richter, from Stephen King's book   PHOTOG: Tony Westman   MUSIC: Patrick Doyle
Standard horror-thriller: Satanic gentleman wreaks havoc in small Maine town

Nefertiti, Queen of the Nile (Nefertite, Regina del Nilo)
1962, (It), Colorama, color, 106 mins.
W: Jeanne Crain, Vincent Price, Edmund Purdom
P: Ottavio Poggi   D: Fernando Cerchio   SCR: John Byrne & Ottavio Poggi
USA retitles, Nefertiti and Queen of the Nile
Standard melodrama: Greatest beauty of Antiquity (c. 1350 B.C.) forced to wed mad pharaoh

Nefertiti
see Nefertite, Regina del Nilo

Negatives
1968, (GB), Continental/Para, color, 98 mins.
W: Peter McEnery (*Theo*), Diane Cilento (*Reingard*), Glenda Jackson (*Vivien*), Maurice Denham (*Father*), Norman Rossington (*The Auctioneer*), Steven Lewis (*The Dealer*), Billy Russell (*The Old Man*)
P: Judd Bernard   D: Peter Medak   SCR: Peter Everett & Roger Lowry, from a novel by Peter Everett   PHOTOG: Ken Hodges   MUSIC: Basil Kirchin
Unusual thriller: Antique store owner and wife play strange games

The Neighbor
1993, (USA), color, 95 mins.
W: Rod Steiger, Linda Kozlowski, Ron Lea, Francis Bay, Jane Wheeler, Bruce Boa
D: Rodney Gibbons   SCR: Kurt Wimmer
Made-for-Video, standard thriller: Psychotic doctor meets pregnant woman

Neighbors
1981, (USA), Zanuck-Brown/Col, color, 95 mins.
W: John Belushi (*Earl Keese*), Dan Aykroyd (*Vic*), Cathy Moriarty (*Ramona*), Kathryn Walker (*Enid Keese*), Lauren-Marie Taylor (*Elaine Keese*), Igors Gavon (*Chic*), Dru-Ann Chukron (*Chic's Wife*), Tim Kazurinsky (*Pa Greavy*), Dale Two Eagle (*Thundersky*), Tino Insana (*Perry*), P.L. Brown, Bert Kittel, Henry Judd Baker, Sherman Lloyd, J.B. Friend, Bernie Friedman, Edward Kotkin, Michael Manoogian
D: John G. Avildsen   SCR: Larry Gelbart, from a novel by Thomas Berger
PHOTOG: Gerald Hirschfeld   MUSIC: Bill Conti
Bizarre comedy: Neighbors turn couple's life into nightmare

Neither the Sea Nor the Sand
1972, (GB), L.M.G. Portland/Tigon, color, 94 mins.
W: Susan Hampshire (*Anna Robinson*), Michael Petrovitch (*Hugh Dabernon*), Frank Finlay (*George Dabernon*), Michael Craze (*Collie*), Jack Lambert (*Dr. Irving*), David Garth (*Mr. MacKay*), Betty Duncan (*Mrs. MacKay*), Anthony Booth (*Delamere*)
P: Jack Smith & Peter Fetterman   D: Fred Burnley   SCR: Gordon Honeycombe & Rosemary Davies, from a novel by Gordon Honeycombe   PHOTOG: David Muri   MUSIC: Nahum Heiman
US Release: International Amusements Corp., 1974
Standard horror-thriller: Married woman's lover returns from death

Neither the Sea Nor the Sand: MICHAEL PETROVICH AND SUSAN HAMPSHIRE

Nemesis
1992, (USA), Shah-Jensen/Imperial Entertainment, color, 95 mins.
W: Olivier Gruner (*Alex*), Tim Thomerson (*Farnsworth*), Cary-Hiroyuki Tagawa (*Angie-Liv*), Merle Kennedy (*Max Impact*), Yuji Okumoto (*Yoshiro Han*),

Marjorie Monaghan (*Jared*), Nicholas Guest (*Germaine*), Vince Klyn (*Michelle*), Brion James (*Maritz*), Marjean Holden (*Sam*), Borovnisa Blervaque (*The 1st Woman*), Jennifer Gatti (*The 2nd Woman/Rosaria*), Thom Mathews (*Marion*), Deborah Shelton (*Julian*), Jackie Earl Haley (*Einstein*), Tom Janes (*Billy*), Adriana Milles (*The German National*), Rhino Michaels (*The Bar Patron*), Robert Carlton (*The Waiter*), Mabel Falls (*The Old Woman*), Jack Thomerson (*The Technician*), Branscombe Richmond (*The Mexican Man*), Thunderwolf (*The Columbian Man*), Barbara C. Adside
D: Albert Pyun   SCR: Rebecca Charles   PHOTOG: George Mooradian   VS-FX SPRVSR: Gene Warren Jr.   MUSIC: Michel Rubini
Standard SF-thriller: L.A. cop vs. aggressive cyborgs

Nemesis 2
1994, (USA), color
W: Sue Price, Tina Cote, Earl White, Jahi J.J. Zuri, Chad Stahelski
A.k.a. Nemesis 2: Nebula
Minor SF: Superhuman flees cyborg, time-travels to 20th century

Nemesis 3: Time Lapse
1995, (USA), color 90 mins.
W: Sue Price, Tim Thomerson, Norbert Weisser, Xavier DeClie, Sharon Bruneau, Debbie Muggli
D & SCR: Albert Pyun   PHOTOG: George Mooradian   MUSIC: Tony Riparetti
Made-for-Video, standard SF-thriller: Woman's DNA holds humanity's hope in conflict against evil cyborgs

Neon City
1991, (Can), color 99 mins.
W: Michael Ironside Vanity, Lyle Alzado, Valerie Wildman, Nick Klar, Juliet Landau, Arsenio "Sonny" Trinidad, Richard Sanders
D: Monte Markham
Standard SF-thriller: Environmental hazards and vicious bikers threaten transport crossing post-nuke wastelands

Neon Maniacs
1986, (USA), Cimarron/Steven Mackler, color, 90 mins.
W: Allan Hayes (*Steven*), Leilani Sarelle (*Natalie*), Victor Elliot Brandt (*Devin*), Donna Locke (*Paula*), P.R. Paul (*Eugene*), David Muir (*Wylie*), Marta Kober (*Lorraine*), Jessie Lawrence Ferguson (*Carson*), Jeff Tyler (*Wally*), Amber Austin (*Lisa*), James Atcheson (*Ray*), Chuck Hemingway (*Gary*), John LaFayette (*Thomas*), Bo Sabato (*Manello*), Gene Bicknell (*Cozzie*), Katherine Heard (*Sue*), Frank Baleno (*Joe*), Elizabeth Lauren (*The Waiting Girlfriend*), Trish Doolan (*Donna*), Teri Ralston (*Marilyn Peterson*), Dick Frattali (*Alex Peterson*), Cynthia Sprink (*Angela*), Anthony Henderson (*The Rookie*), Shari Moskau (*The Drunk Girl*), Lydia Weiss (*Mother #1*), Betty Vaughan (*Mother #2*), Cooper Neal (*The Irate Father*), T.J. Snell, Matthew Asner, Clarke Coleman, Susan Mierisch, Shawn Lieber, Tom Noble, Alfred Boyer, Solly Mark, Michael Walter, John Michael Stewart, Mark Allen, Joseph Shirley, Barry Buchanan, Scott McKenna, Douglas Markell, James H. Smith, Mark Twogood, Andrew Divoff, Scott Guetzkow, David Wellington, Robert E. Veilliux, Chuck Cohen, Michael Todd, Zac Baldwin, Doyle McCurley, Mario Valdes, Daniel Burrell, Jerome L. Dennae, Kathy Hooker, Chuck Secor, Joel Steven Hammond, Allan Aperlo
D: Joseph Mangine   SCR: Mark Patrick Carducci   PHOTOG: Oliver Wood & Joseph Mangine   SPCL-FX: Image Engineering   MUSIC: Kendall Schmidt   SONGS: Baby Lied, The Choice You Made, We Had Enough, Treat Me, I Don't Want to Be Alone Tonight & Rock Me All Night
Minor horror-thriller: Zombies in San Francisco

The Neptune Disaster
see The Neptune Factor

Neptune et Amphitrite
1899, (Fr), Star, b&w, 20m (65.6 ft./1.1 mins.)
D: Georges Melies
Standard fantasy: Sea sprites cavort

The Neptune Factor
1973, (Can), Conquest of the Deeps Ltd./20th-Fox, color, 98 mins.
W: Ben Gazzara (*Blake*), Walter Pidgeon (*Andrews*), Yvette Mimieux (*Leah*), Ernest Borgnine (*Mack*), Donnelly Rhodes (*Bob*), David Yorston (*Stephens*), Chris Wiggins (*The Captain*), Ed McGibbon (*Norton*), Michael J. Reynolds (*Hal*), Stuart Gillard (*Bradley*), Mark Walker (*Mounton*), Kenneth Pogue (*Thomas*), Frank Perry (*The Sub Captain*), Dave Mann (*Hawkes*), Dan MacDonald (*Hobbs*), Leslie Carlson (*Briggs*), David Renton (*The Warrant Officer*), Joan Gregson (*Dobson*), Kay Fujiwara (*Anita*), Richard Whelan (*The Radio Officer*)
P: Sanford Howard   D: Daniel Petrie   SCR: Jack de Witt   PHOTOG: Harry Makin   MUSIC: Lalo Schifrin
A.k.a. An Underwater Odyssey, TV retitle, The Neptune Disaster
Minor SF-thriller: Standard undersea adventures

Neptune's Daughter
1914, (USA), Univ, b&w, 7 reels
W: Annette Kellermann
D, Herbert Brenon
Standard aquatic fantasy: Magic seashell turns woman into mermaid

THE MOST FANTASTIC UNDERSEA ODYSSEY EVER FILMED

THE NEPTUNE FACTOR

20th Century-Fox presents SANFORD HOWARD'S PRODUCTION of "THE NEPTUNE FACTOR" Starring BEN GAZZARA YVETTE MIMIEUX · WALTER PIDGEON · and ERNEST BORGNINE as the Aquanaut. Directed by DANIEL PETRIE
Written by JACK DE WITT Music LALO SCHIFRIN PANAVISION® PRINTS BY DE LUXE®

Nero Wolfe
1977, (Austral), ABC-TV, color, 100 mins.
W: Thayer David (*Nero Wolfe*), Anne Baxter (*Mrs. Bruner*), Tom Mason (*Archie*), Brooke Adams (*Sarah Dacos*), Biff McGuire (*Insp. Cramer*), John Randolph (*Cohen*), Sarah Cunningham (*Mrs. Althaus*)
based on Rex Stout's novel *The Doorbell Rang*
TVM, minor thriller: Cultured detective tangles with FBI while solving murder mystery

The Nest
1988, (USA), Julie Corman/Concorde, color, 89 mins.
W: Robert Lansing (*Elias Johnson*), Lisa Langlois (*Elizabeth Johnson*), Franc Luz (*Richard Turbell*), Terri Treas (*Dr. Morgan Hubbard*), Stephen Davies (*Homer*), Jack Collins (*Shakey Jake*), Diana Bellamy (*Mrs. Penington*), Nancy Morgan (*Lillian*), Jeff Winkless (*Church*), Steve Tannen (*Mr. Perkins*), Heidi Helmer (*Jenny*), Karen Smythe (*The Diner*), Noel Steven Geray
D: Terence H. Winkless   SCR: Robert King, from Eli Cantor's novel   PHOTOG: Ricardo Jacques Gale   MUSIC: Rick Conrad
Standard SF-thriller: Cockroach-control experiments go awry

The Nesting
1981, (USA), Feature Films, color, 104 mins.
W: Robin Groves (*Lauren*), Christopher Loomis (*Mark*), Michael David Lally (*Daniel*), John Carradine (*Col. LeBrun*), Gloria Grahame (*Florinda Costello*), Bill Rowley (*Frank*), David Tabor (*Abner*), Patrick Farrelly (*Dr. Webb*), Bobo Lewis, June Berry, Ann Varley, Cecile Liebman, Ron Levine, James Saxon, Bruce Kronenberg, Jim Nixon, Jery Hewitt, Jeffrey McLaughlin, James Hayden, Cliff Cudney, Lee Steele
P & D: Armand Weston   SCR: Daria Price & Armand Weston   PHOTOG: Joao Fernandes   MUSIC: Jack Malken & Kim Scholes
Minor horror-thriller: Gothic novelist rents haunted mansion. A.k.a. **Phobia**

Nestasni Robot (The Playful Robot)
1956, (Yugo), color
D: Dusan Vukotic
Animated SF-fantasy

The Nest of the Cuckoo Birds
1965, (USA), Williams, b&w, 88 mins
W: Bert Williams, Chuck Frankle, Ann Long, Jack Scalso, Larry Wright
P, D, & SCR: Bert Williams
Minor thriller: Revenue agent meets Everglades woman who keeps human trophies

The Net
1952, (GB), Two Cities/British Lion/Univ, b&w, 86 mins.
W: Phyllis Calvert (*Lydia Heathley*), James Donald (*Michael Heathley*), Robert Beatty (*Sam Seagram*), Herbert Lom (*Alex Leon*), Muriel Pavlow (*Caroline Cartier*), Noel Willman (*Dr. Dennis Bord*), Walter Fitzgerald (*Sir Charles Craddock*), Patric Doonan (*Brian Jackson*), Maurice Denham (*Carrington*), Marjorie Fielding (*Mama*), Cavan Watson (*Ferguson*), Herbert Lomas (*George Jackson*), Cyril Chamberlain (*Insp. Carter*), Tucker McGuire (*Myrna*)
P: Anthony Darnsborough   D: Anthony Asquith   SCR: William Fairchild, from a novel by John Pudney   PHOTOG: Desmond Dickinson   MUSIC: Benjamin Frankel
USA retitle, **Project M-7**
Modest thriller: Jet-plane inventor thwarts spy

Netforce
1999, (USA), ABC-TV, color, approx. 190 mins.
W: Kris Kristofferson (*Steve*), Scott Bakula (*Alex Michaels*), Joanna Going (*Toni*), Brian Dennehy (*Lowell Davidson*), Judge Reinhold (*Will Stiles*), C.C.H. Pounder (*Sandra Knight*), Cary-Hiroyuki Tagawa (*Leong Chen*), Chelsea Field, Xander Berkeley, Sterling Macer, Paul Hewitt, Alexa Vega, Frank Vincent, Kirk Baltz, Odile Broulard, Ingo Neuhaus, Lynn Filusch, Richard Fullerton, David Jung, Tony Cosby, Rick Warner, Dale Raoul, Anjul Nigam, Rhoda Gemignoni, Victor Raider-Wexler, Gemma Parry, James McBride, Lance Lewman
D: Robert Lieberman   TELEPLAY: Lionel Chetwynd, from a story by Tom Clancy   PHOTOG: David Hennings   MUSIC: Jeff Rona
2-part TVM, standard thriller: Internet menaces world peace

Netherworld
1992, (USA), color
W: Michael Bendetti, Denise Gentile Anjanette Comer, Holly Floria, Robert Burr
D: David Schmoeller   SCR: Billy Chicago   MUSIC: Edgar Winter
Minor fantasy-thriller: Young man embroiled in black magic

Neutron Battles the Karate Assassins
1962, (Mex), TEC, b&w, 72 mins.
W: Wolf Rubinskis, Carlos Lopez
Minor action-thriller

Neutron, el Enmascarado Negro (Neutron, the Black-Masked)
1963, (Mex), TEC, b&w, 89 mins.
W: Wolf Rubinskis, Armando Silvestre
D: Frederick Curiel
Minor action-thriller

Neutron, the Black-Masked
see *Neutron, el Enmascarado Negro*

Neutron Traps the Invisible Killers
1964, (Mex), TEC, b&w, 78 mins
W: Wolf Rubinskis, Guillermo Murray
Minor action-thriller

Neutron vs. the Amazing Dr. Caronte
1963, (Mex), TEC, b&w, 83 mins.
W: Wolf Rubinskis
Minor action-thriller

Neutron vs. the Death Robots
see *Los Automatas de la Muerte*

Neutron vs. the Maniac
1961, (Mex), TEC, b&w, 81 mins.
W: Wolf Rubinskis, Rodolfo Landa, Ruben Rojo
Minor action-thriller

Nevada Heat
see *Fake-Out*

Never Again, Never!
1912, (GB), Hepworth, b&w, 325 ft. (99.1m)
D: Lewin Fitzhamon
Standard fantasy short: Man steals cask of beer, dreams he is chased by it

Never Back Losers
1961, (GB), Merton Park/Anglo-Amalgamated, b&w, 61 mins.
W: Jack Hedley (*Jim Matthews*), Jacqueline Ellis (*Marion Palmer*), Patrick Magee (*Ben Black*), Derek Francis (*R.R. Harris*), Richard Warner (*Crabtree*), Austin Trevor (*Col. Warburton*), Harry Locke (*Burnside*), Larry Martyn (*Clive Parker*)
P: Jack Greenwood   D: Robert Tronson   SCR: Lukas Heller, from Edgar Wallace's novel *Ribbon*
Minor crime-thriller: Insurance investigator probes jockey's death

Never Complain to Your Laundress
1907, (GB), Hepworth, b&w
D: Lewin Fitzhamon
Standard comedy-fantasy short: Customer complains about washing and is scrubbed, mangled, and parcelled

The Neverending Story
1984, (W. Ger), Producers Sales Org./WB, color, 93 mins.
W: Noah Hathaway (*Atreyu*), Barret Oliver (*Bastian*), Tami Stronach (*The Childlike Empress*), Patricia Hayes, Sydney Bromley, Gerald McRaney, Moses Gunn, Alan Oppenheimer
D: Wolfgang Petersen   SCR: Wolfgang Petersen & Herman Weigel   PHOTOG: Jost Vacano   SPCL-FX: Brian Johnson   MUSIC: Klaus Doldinger & Giorgio Moroder
Standard juvenile fantasy: Mysterious book transports boy's mind into world of imagination

The Neverending Story II: The Next Chapter
1991, (Ger), WB, color, 89 mins.
W: Jonathan Brandis (*Bastian Balthazar Bux*), Alexandra Johnes (*The Childlike Empress*), Kenny Morrison (*Atreyu*), Clarissa Burt (*Xayide*), John Wesley Shipp (*The Father*), Chris Burton (*Tri-Face*), Martin Umbach (*Nimbly*)
D: George Miller   SCR: Karin Howard   PHOTOG: David Connell   SPCL-FX: Derek Meddings   MUSIC: Robert Folk   SONG: *Dreams We Dream*
Minor juvenile fantasy: Boy has magical adventures

Never Let Go
1960, (GB), Independent Artists/RFD, b&w, 91 mins.
W: Richard Todd (*John Cummings*), Peter Sellers (*Lionel Meadows*), Elizabeth Sellars (*Anne Cummings*), Adam Faith (*Tommy Towers*), Carol White (*Jackie*), Mervyn Johns (*Alfie Barnes*), Noel Willman (*Insp. Thomas*), David Lodge (*Cliff*), Peter Jones (*Alec Berger*), John Bailey (*Mackinnon*), Nigel Stock (*Regan*), John LeMesurier (*Pennington*)

P: Peter de Sarigny **D:** John Guillermin **SCR:** Alun Falconer **STORY:** John Guillermin & Peter de Sarigny **PHOTOG:** Christopher Challis **MUSIC:** John Barry
Standard crime-thriller: Salesman opposes sadistic boss of car-theft ring

Never Look Back
1952, (GB), Hammer/Exclusive, b&w, 73 mins.
W: Rosamund John (*Anne Maitland*), Hugh Sinclair (*Nigel Stuart*), Guy Middleton (*Guy Ransome*), Henry Edwards (*Whitcomb*), Terence Longdon (*Alan Whitcomb*), Brenda de Banzie (*Molly Wheeler*), Bruce Belfrage (*The Judge*), Arthur Howard (*Charles Vaughan*), John Warwick (*Insp. Raynor*), Frances Rowe (*Liz*), Bill Shine (*Willie*)
P: Michael Carreras & James Brennan **D:** Francis Searle **STORY:** John Hunter, Guy Morgan & Francis Searle
Standard crime-thriller: Woman forced to provide alibi when ex-fiance kills his mistress

Never Mention Murder
1964, (GB), Merton Park/Anglo-Amalgamated, b&w, 56 mins.
W: Maxine Audley (*Liz Teasdale*), Dudley Foster (*Philip Teasdale*), Michael Coles (*Tony Sorbo*), Pauline Yates (*Zita Sorbo*), Brian Haines (*Felix Carstairs*), Philip Stone (*The Inspector*), Peter Butterworth
P: Jack Greenwood **D:** John Nelson Burton **SCR:** Robert Banks Stewart, from a story by Edgar Wallace
Standard thriller: Surgeon poisons and tries to operate on wife's lover

Never-Never Land
1981, (GB), Artemis/American Nat'l, color, 86 mins.
W: Petula Clark, Cathleen Nesbitt, John Castle, Michael Jay Shannon, Anne Seymour, Evelyn Laye, Roland Culver, Heather Miller, Christian Henson, Lucy Durham-Mathews, James Marcus, Ruby Head, Toby Rushton, Virginia Snyders, Nicholas Leahey, Michael Hadley, Noel Collins, Suzanne Storer, Kamal Murari, Susan Tully, Brendan Quinn, Mark Burdis, Paul Charles, Ian Land, Sheldon Nichols, Charmain Falode, David Smith
D: Paul Annett **ORIG. STORY & SCR,** Marjorie L. Sigley **PHOTOG**: Brian West **MUSIC:** Ron Grainer
Minor melodrama: Girl fears growing up

The Never Never Murder
1961, (GB), Merton Park/Anglo-Amalgamated, b&w, 30 mins.
W: Russell Napier (*Supt. Duggan*), Genine Graham (*Alice Bennett*), Maurice Good (*Sgt. Harper*), Harriette Johns (*Molly Davis*)
P: Jack Greenwood **D:** Peter Duffell **STORY:** James Eastwood, from a novel by Edgar Lustgarten
Standard short crime-thriller: Woman's corpse discovered in demolished building

Never Say Never Again
1983, (GB), Jack Schwartzman-Kevin McClory/Taliafilm-Irvin Kershner/WB, color, 131 mins.
W: Sean Connery (*James Bond*), Klaus Maria Brandauer (*Largo*), Max von Sydow (*Ernst Stavro Blofeld*), Kim Basinger (*Domino*), Barbara Carrera (*Fatima Blush*), Alec McCowen ("Q"), Edward Fox ("M"), Bernie Casey (*Felix Leiter*), Pamela Salem (*Miss Moneypenny*), Rowan Atkinson (*Small-Fawcett*), Anthony Sharp (*Lord Ambrose*), Milow Kirck (*Kovacs*), Gavan O'Herlihy (*Petuchi*), Pat Roach (*Lippe*), Prunella Gee (*Patricia*), Valerie Leon (*The Lady*), Ronald Pickup (*Elliott*), Robert Rietty (*The Minister*), Vincent Marzello (*Culpepper*), Billy J. Mitchell (*Capt. Pedersen*), Michael Medwin (*The Doctor*)
P: Jack Schwartzman **D:** Irvin Kershner **SCR:** Lorenzo Semple Jr., based on an orig. story by Kevin McClory, Jack Whittingham & Ian Fleming **PHOTOG:** Douglas Slocombe **MUSIC:** Michel Legrand **TITLE:** Lani Hall (music by Michel Legrand, lyrics by Alan & Marilyn Bergman)
*Standard thriller (remake of **Thunderball**): Sinister organization uses stolen atomic devices to blackmail superpowers*

Never Talk to Strangers
1995, (USA), Alliance/TriStar, color, 86 mins.
W: Rebecca De Mornay (*Dr. Sarah Taylor*), Antonio Banderas (*Tony Ramirez*), Dennis Miller (*Cliff*), Harry Dean Stanton (*Max Cheski*), Beau Starr (*Grogan*), Len Cariou (*Henry Taylor*), Tim Kelleher, John Bourgeois, Eugene Lipinski, Phillip Jarrett, Reg Dreger, Susan Coyne, Martha Burns, Emma Corosky, Joseph R. Gannascoli, Bret Pearson, Frances Hyland, Kevin Rushton, Kelley Grando, Bruce Beaton, Nolan Jennings, Tony Meyler, Rodger Barton, Teresa Hergert
D: Peter Hall **SCR:** Lewis Green & Jordan Rush **PHOTOG:** Elemer Ragalyi **MUSIC:** Pino Donaggio **SONGS:** *Her Body Makes Vows, A Girl Like You & Paranoia*
Standard thriller: Stalker torments woman psychiatrist

The New Adventures of Baron Munchausen
1915, (GB), Kent Films, b&w, 995 ft. (303.3m)
D: F. Martin Thornton
Standard comedy-fantasy: Liar's unlikely war exploits

The New Adventures of Don Juan
see The Adventures of Don Juan

A New Aladdin
1912, (GB), Hepworth, b&w, 500 ft. (152.4m)
D: Frank Wilson
Standard fantasy short: Tramp finds lamp, dreams it is Aladdin's

New Crime City: Los Angeles 2020
1994, (USA), color, 95 mins.
W: Rick Rossovich Stacy Keach, Sherrie Rose
SCR: Rick Rossovich
Standard SF-thriller: Future cop vs. criminal who threatens to release deadly virus

The New Death Penalty
see La Nouvelle Peine du Mort

New Eden
1994, (USA), SciFi-TV, color, 89 mins.
W: Stephen Baldwin, Lisa Bonet, Tobin Bell (*Ares*), Michael Bowen, Jant Hubert-Whitten
D: Alan Metzger **SCR:** Dan Gordon
Standard SF-adventure: Engineer on prison planet aids nomadic tribe

The New Gladiators
1987, (It), color, 90 mins.
W: Jared Martin, Fred Williamson, Eleanor Gold, Claudio Cassinelli, Howard Ross
D: Lucio Fulci
Minor SF-thriller: Criminals fight to death on future TV

The New Governess
1915, (GB), Horseshoe/YCC, b&w, 471 ft. (143.6m)
*A.k.a. **The Governess's Love Affair***
Standard comedy-fantasy short: Professor's love powder causes marital strife

A New Gulliver
see Novyi Gulliver

The New House on the Left
1977, (It), Hallmark, color, 94 mins.
W: Kay Beal, Patty Edwards Norma Knight, Delbert Moss, Richard Davis
P & D: Aldo Ladd & Evans Isle
*A.k.a. **Second House from the Left***
Minor thriller: Murdering rapist attacks women on train

New Invisible Man
see H.G. Wells' New Invisible Man

The Newlydeads
1987, (USA), color, 84 mins.
W: Scott Kaske, Jim Williams, Jean Levine, Jay Richardson
D: Joseph Merhi
Minor fantasy-thriller: Murdered transvestite enacts revenge on honeymoon resort

The New, Original Wonder Woman
1975, (USA), WB/ABC-TV, color, 74 mins.
W: Lynda Carter (*Diana Prince/Wonder Woman*), Lyle Waggoner (*Steve Trevor*), Cloris Leachman (*The Queen Mother*), Kenneth Mars, Red Buttons, Stella Stevens, Eric Braeden, Henry Gibson, John Randolph, Fannie Flagg, Severn Darden, Helen Verbit
P: Douglas S. Cramer **D:** Leonard Horn **TELEPLAY:** Stanley Ralph Ross, from Charles Moulton's comic-book characters **MUSIC:** Charles Fox
TVM, standard adventure-thriller: Amazon princess comes to USA to fight crime and injustice

A Newsboy's Christmas Dream
1913, (GB), Cricks & Martin, b&w, 1,940 ft. (591.3m)
W: Eileen Daybell, Leo Cauty, R. Howard Cricks
D: Edwin J. Collins
reissued 1916
Standard fantasy: Orphan newboy adpoted after dreaming of wiz-ards and dragons

New Wave
see Nouvelle Vague

New Year's Evil
1980, (USA), Golan-Globus/Cannon, color, 86 mins.
W: Roz Kelly, Kip Niven, Chris Wallace, Grant Cramer, Jed Mills, Louisa Moritz, Anita Crane, Taafe O'Connell, Teri Copley, Jon Greene, John Alderman, Bob Jarvis
D: Emmett Alston **SCR:** Leonard Neubauer **PHOTOG:** Edward Thomas **MUSIC SPRVSR:** Rex Devereaux **MUSIC COMPOSED & CONDUCT:** W. Michael Lewis & Laurin Rinder **MUSIC:** Shadow **SONGS:** *When I Wake Up, Simon Bar Sinister & Temper Tantrum*
Minor thriller: Killer psycho phones progress reports to lady disc jockey

New York Ripper
1987, (It), color, 88 mins.
W: Jack Hedley, Almanta Keller Fred Williamson
D: Lucio Fulci
blurb: "Someone's taking a big slice out of the Big Apple"
Minor thriller: Killer terrorizes Big Apple

Next!
see Lo Strano Caso della Signora Ward

The Next Corner
1924, (USA), Famous Players-Lasky/Para, b&w, 7,081 ft. (2155.6m)
W: Lon Chaney Sr.
D: Sam Wood
Standard melodrama

The Next of Kin
1908, (GB), London Cinematograph Co., b&w, 655 ft. (199.6m)
D: S. Wormald
Standard crime-thriller: Miner strangles uncle

Next of Kin
1983, (GB), SIS/Filmco/Miracle, color, 86 mins.
W: Jackie Kerin, Alex Scott, John Jarratt, Charles McCallum, Gerda Nicholson
D: Tony Williams   **SCR:** Michael Heath & Tony Williams   **PHOTOG:** Gary Hansen   **MUSIC:** Klaus Schulze
Standard thriller: Demented old lady kills rest-home inmates

The Next One
1981, (USA-Greece), Allstar/American Nat'l, color, 94 mins.
W: Keir Dullea, Adrienne Barbeau, Peter Hobbs, Betty Arvanitis, Phaedon Georgitsis, Michael Yannatos, Danos Lygizos, Jeremy Licht
WRIT & D: Nico Mastorakis   **PHOTOG:** Ari Stavrou
Minor SF: Amnesiac suspected of being extraterrestrial

Next Victim *(1970)*
see *Lo Strano Caso della Signora Ward*

The Next Victim
1975, (GB), ATV/ITC, Made for TV, color, 80 mins.
W: Carroll Baker, Max Mason
TVM, minor thriller: Wheelchair-bound woman fears psychopath's attack

The Next Voice You Hear
1950, (USA), MGM, b&w, 83 mins.
W: James Whitmore (*Joe Smith, American*), Nancy Davis (*Mrs. Joe Smith*), Gary Gray (*Johnny Smith*), Jeff Corey (*Freddie*), Lillian Bronson (*Aunt Ethel*), Douglas Kennedy (*The Man in the Bar*), Tom D'Andrea (*Hap Magee*), Art Smith (*Mr. Brannan*)
P: Dore Schary   **D:** William A. Wellman   **SCR:** Charles Schnee, suggested by George Sumner Albee's short story of same name (Cosmopolitan, 8/1948) and George Loveridge's short story *So Early in the Morning* (New Yorker, 1/13/1945)   **PHOTOG:** William C. Mellor   **MUSIC:** David Raksin
Unusual fantasy: Voice of God heard on radio

Niagara
1953, (USA), 20th-Fox, color, 87 mins.
W: Marilyn Monroe (*Rose Loomis*), Jean Peters (*Polly Cutler*), Joseph Cotten (*George Loomis*), Casey Adams (Max Showalter) (*Ray Cutler*), Don Wilson (*Jess Kettering*), Lurene Tuttle, Denis O'Dea, Russell Collins, Will Wright, Sean McClory, Richard Allan (*Patrick*)
P: Charles Brackett   **D:** Henry Hathaway   **SCR:** Charles Brackett & Richard L. Breen   **PHOTOG:** Joe MacDonald   **SPCL-FX:** Ray Kellogg   **MUSIC:** Sol Kaplan   **SONG:** *Kiss*
Semi-classic thriller: Faithless wife drives man to murder. Filmed on location.

Die Nibelungen (The Nibelungs)
1924, (Ger), Ufa, b&w, 195 mins. (22,283.4 ft./6792m)
W: Paul Richter (*Siegfried*), Bernhard Goetzke, Hanna Ralph, Margarete Schon, Theodor Loos, Rudolf Klein-Rogge, Hans Adalbert von Schlettow, George John, Gertrud Arnold
P: Erich Pommer   **D:** Fritz Lang   **SCR:** Fritz Lang & Thea von Harbou, adapted from Germanic saga   **PHOTOG:** Carl Hoffmann, Gunther Rittau & Walter Ruttmann   **SETS:** Otto Hunte, Eric Kettelhut & Karl Vollbrecht, inspired by Arnold Bocklin's paintings in 2 parts; *Siegfried's Tod (Siegfried's Death)* and *Kriemhild's Rache (Kriemhild's Revenge)*
Classic fantasy: Mythic heroes vie for mastery

The Nibelungs
1966, (W. Ger-Yugo), CCC/Constantin, color, 91 mins.
W: Karin Dor, Rolf Henniger, Mario Girotti, Uwe Beyer, Fred Williams, Siegfried Wischnewski
D: Harald Reinl   **SCR:** Ladislas Fodor, Harald Petersson, Harald Reinl
Standard fantasy: Teutonic demi-gods battle. Part 1: Siegfried

Nice Girls Don't Explode
1987, (USA), color, 92 mins.
W: Barbara Harris, Michelle Meyrink, William O'Leary, James Nardini, Wallace Shawn
D: Chuck Martiez   **MUSIC:** Brian Banks
Minor comedy-fantasy

Nick Carter
1908, (USA), Itala, b&w
from characters created by John R. Coryell
Standard thriller

Nick Carter
1921, (GB), Int'l Cine Corp., b&w
W: Tom Carrigan (*Nick Carter*)
from characters created by John R. Coryell
Standard thriller (15-chapter serial)

Nick Carter and the Black-Coated Thieves
1915, (USA), Eclair, b&w
from characters created by John R. Coryell
Standard thriller

Nick Carter as an Acrobat
1910, (USA), Eclair, b&w
from characters created by John R. Coryell
Standard thriller

Nick Carter—Bandits in Evening Dress
1908, (USA), Itala, b&w
from characters created by John R. Coryell
Standard thriller

Nick Carter et le Trefle Rouge (Nick Carter and the Red Club)
1965, (Fr), Chaumiane-Parc Films/Col, b&w, 85 mins.
W: Eddie Constantine (*Nick Carter*), Nicole Courcel, Jeanne Valerie, Jo Dassin, Jacques Herden, Jean Ozenne, Santesso Felio, Marcel Pagliero, Roger Rudel, Pierre Rousseau, Gordon Felio, Michel Ruhl, Graziella Galvani
D: Jean-Paul Savignac   **SCR:** Jean-Paul Savignac & Paul Vechialli, from Claude Rank's novel *Bombe sur Table (Bomb on the Table)*, based on characters created by John R. Coryell
Standard thriller: Sleuth trails thieves of poison-gas rockets

Nick Carter Goes into Danger
see *Nick Carter Va Tout Casser*

Nick Carter in Danger
1909, (USA), Itala, b&w
from characters created by John R. Coryell

Nick Carter in Panama
see *Phantom Raiders*

Nick Carter, Master Detective
1939, (USA), MGM, b&w, 59 mins.
W: Walter Pidgeon (*Nick Carter*), Donald Meek (*Bartholomew*), Rita Johnson, Henry Hull, Stanley Ridges, Addison Richards, Henry Victor, Milburn Stone, Frank Faylen, Martin Kosleck, Sterling Holloway, Wally Maher, Edgar Dearing
D: Jacques Tourneur   **SCR:** Bertram Millhauser & Harold Buckley, from characters created by John R. Coryell   **PHOTOG:** Charles Lawton Jr.
Standard thriller: Sleuth investigates copying of plans for new airplane. 'Nick Carter' series.

Nick Carter—Sleeping Pills
1909, (USA), Itala, b&w
from characters created by John R. Coryell

Nick Carter Va Tout Casser (Nick Carter Goes into Danger)
1964, (Fr), Florida Films/4 Star, b&w, 95 mins.
W: Eddie Constantine (*Nick Carter*), Daphne Dayle, Vladimir Injikinoff, Paul Frankeur, Yvonne Monlaur, Charles Belmont
D: Henri Decoin   **SCR:** Jean Marcillac, Andre Haguet & Andre Legrand, from the novel by Jean Marcillac, based on characters created by John R. Coryell
USA TV-retitle, License to Kill
Standard thriller: Sleuth pursues Chinese spies

Nick Fury: Agent of Shield
1998, (USA), Fox-TV, color, 95 mins.
W: David Hasselhoff (*Nick Fury*), Lisa Rinna (*Val*), Sandra Hess (*Viper*), Ron Canada (*Gabe Jones*), Neil Roberts, Tom McBeath, Garry Chalk, Tracey Waterhouse
D: Ron Hardt   **TELEPLAY:** David Goyer   **PHOTOG:** James Bartle   **MUSIC:** Kevin Kiner
TVM, standard SF-adventure: Espionage hero saves world from deadly virus

Nick Knight
1989, (USA), CBS-TV, color, 95 mins.
W: Rick Springfield (*Nick Knight*), Laura Johnson (*Alyce*), John Kapelos (*Schanke*), Robert Harper (*Dr. Brittington*), Michael Nader (*Lacroix*)
TVM, standard horror-fantasy: Vampiric L.A. detective

Niebezpieczenstwo (The Danger)
1963, (Pol), Film Polski-SE-MA-FOR-LODZ, b&w
D: Jerzy Kotowski   **SCR:** Jan Czerny   **PHOTOG:** Eugeniusz Ignaciuk   **MUSIC:** Wlodzimierz Kotonski
Standard thriller

The Night After Halloween
1983, (It), color, 90 mins.

W: Chantel Contouri, Robert Bruning, Sigrid Thornton
Minor thriller: Young woman finds boyfriend is crazed killer

Night After Night After Night
1970, (GB), Dudley Birch/Butcher, color, 88 mins.
W: Jack May (*Judge Charles Lomax*), Justine Lord (*Helena Lomax*), Gilbert Wynne (*Insp. Bill Rowan*), Terry Scully (*Carter*), Linda Marlowe (*Jenny Rowan*), Donald Sumpter (*Pete Laver*), Peter Forbes-Robertson (*Powell*), April Harlow (*The Stripper*), Jacqueline Clark (*Josie Leach*), Jack Smethurst (*The Chief Inspector*)
P: James Mellor **D:** Lewis J. Force **STORY:** Dail Ambler
A.k.a. He Kills Night After Night After Night
Standard crime-thriller: Teen convicted of murder committed by judge

Night Angel
1990, (USA), Fries Entertainment, color, 90 mins.
W: Isa Anderson (*Lilith*), Karen Black (*Rita*), Linden Ashby (*Craig*), Debra Feuer (*Kirstie*), Helen Martin (*Sadie*), Doug Jones (*Ken*), Sam Hennings, Gary Hudson, B.J. Turner
D: Dominique Othenin-Girard **PHOTOG:** David Lewis **MUSIC:** Cory Lerios
blur: "An ancient evil has awakened and lust is her lifeforce..."
Standard thriller: She-devil conspires

Night Beat
1931, (USA), b&w, 61 mins.
D: George Seitz **PHOTOG:** Edward Cronjager
Minor melodrama

Nightbeast
1978, (USA), Amazing Film/Cinemagic, color, 82 mins.
W: Tom Griffith (*Sheriff Cinder*), Karin Kardian (*Lisa Kent*), George Stover (*Steven Price*), Jamie Zemarel (*Jamie Lambert*), Anne Frith (*Ruth Sherman*), Don Leifert (*Drago*), Greg Dohler (*Greg*), Eleanor Herman (*Mary Jane*), Richard Dyszel (*Mayor Bert Wicker*), Kim Dohler (*Kim*), Monica Neff (*Suzie*), Glenn Barnes (*Glenn*), Rose Wolfe (*Glenn's Girl*), Richard Ruxton (*Gov. Embry*), Bump Roberts (*Bill Perkins*), Rick Ernest (*The Governor's Aide*), Don Michaels (*Jimmy Perkins*), David Donoho (*Uncle Dave*), Richard Geiwitz (*Pete*), Chris Gummer (*Clay*), Larry Reichman (*Berkeley*), Dave Parson, Chris Burke, Steve Sandkuhler, Bill Wieman, Richard Nelson, Gary Svehla, Dick Svehla, Chris White, Dave Ellis, Mary Hopkins, Toni Patti, Christine Herman, Phyllis Hammond, Maria Morris, Dennis McGeehan, Martha Brown, Richard Christensen, C.A. Murray, Pam Dohler, John Merenda, Charlotte Merenda, Rick Hammontree, Brenda Blanks, Norman Belbot
WRIT & D: Don Dohler **PHOTOG:** Richard Geiwitz **MUSIC:** Rob Walsh & Jeffrey Abrams
A.k.a. The Alien Factor
Minor SF-horror: Monstrous alien kills humans

The Night Before Christmas
1905, (USA), Edison, b&w, 17 ft. (5.2m)
D: Edwin S. Porter, based on Clement Clarke Moore's poem *A Visit from St. Nicholas*
A.k.a. Hanging Stockings on a Christmas Tree
Standard fantasy short: Santa Claus spreads cheer

The Night Bell
1914, (GB), Hepworth, b&w, 1,075 ft. (327.7m)
W: Jamie Darling (*Bill Woodford*)
D: Frank Wilson
Standard crime-thriller: Burglar robs doctor

The Nightbirds of London
1915, (GB), Hepworth, b&w, 4,150 ft. (1239.5m)
W: Stewart Rome, Chrissie White, Violet Hopson, Lionelle Howard, William Felton, John MacAndrews, Henry Vibart, Arthur Staples
D: Frank Wilsonn **SCR:** Blanche McIntosh, from a play by George R. Sims
Standard crime-thriller

Nightbreed
1990, (USA-GB), Morgan Creek/20th-Fox, color, 101 mins.
W: Craig Sheffer (*Boone*), Anne Bobby (*Lori*), Charles Haid (*Capt. Eigerman*), David Cronenberg (*Decker*), Hugh Quarshie (*Det. Joyce*), Hugh Ross (*Narcisse*), Catherine Chevalier (*Rachel*), Doug Bradley (*Lylesburg*), Malcolm Smith (*Ashberry*), Bob Sessions (*Pettine*), Oliver Parker (*Peloquin*), Nicholas Vince (*Kinski*), Debora Weston (*Sheryl Ann*), Vincent Keene, Simon Bamford, Kim Robertson, Nina Robertson, Tony Bluto, Christine McCorkindale, Bernard Henry, Richard Van Spall, David Young, Valda Aviks, Mac McDonald, John Agar, Richard Bowman, McNally Segal, Daniel Kash, Tom Hunsinger, Bradley Lavelle, Stephen Hoye, George Roth, Peter Marinker, Lindsay Holiday, Kenneth Nelson, Carolyn Jones, Mitch Webb, Ted Maynard, Scott Gilmore, Eric Loren
WRIT & D: Clive Barker, from his novel *Cabal* **PHOTOG:** Robin Vidgeon
MUSIC: Danny Elfman
Modest horror-fantasy: Innocent framed for monstrous serial killings, finds refuge with grotesques

The Night Brings Charlie
1990, (USA), color, 90 mins.
W: Kerry Knight, Joe Fishback, Aimee Tenalia, Monica Simmons

D: Tom Logan
Minor thriller: Disfigured tree surgeon suspected of grisly murders

The Night Caller
1975, (Fr), Col, color, 91 mins.
W: Jean-Paul Belmondo, Charles Denner, Lea Massari
D: Henri Verneuil
"The violence is real and graphic"—Motion Picture Digest
Unusual thriller: Pyschotic killer hunted in Paris

Night Caller from Outer Space
1966, (GB), Armitage/New Art, b&w, 84 mins.
W: John Saxon (*Jack Costain*), Patricia Haines (*Ann Barlow*), Maurice Denham (*Prof. Morley*), Alfred Burke (*Supt. Hartley*), John Carson (*The Major*), Jack Watson (*Sgt. Hawkins*), Warren Mitchell (*Lilburn*), Stanley Meadows (*Grant*), Anthony Wager (*Pte. Higgins*), Ballard Berkeley (*Cdr. Savage*), Robert Crewdson (*Medra*), Diane Clare
P: John Phillips & Ronald Liles **D:** John Gilling **SCR:** Jim O'Connolly, from Frank Crisp's novel *The Night Callers*
USA retitle, Blood Beast from Outer Space
Unusual SF-shocker: Mutated man from space seeks Earth women for breeding stock

The Night Cap
see Secrets of the Night

Night Child
see The Cursed Medallion

The Nightcomers
1971, (GB), Scimitar/Avco Embassy, color, 96 mins.
W: Marlon Brando (*Peter Quint*), Stephanie Beacham (*Miss Jessel*), Thora Hird (*Mrs. Grose*), Verna Harvey (*Flora*), Christopher Ellis (*Miles*), Harry Andrews (*Master of the House*), Anna Palk (*The New Governess*)
P & D: Michael Winner **SCR:** Michael Hastings, based on characters created by Henry James **PHOTOG:** Robert Paynter **MUSIC:** Jerry Fielding
Standard thriller ("prequel" to James' The Turn of the Screw): Evil doings on Victorian estate. cf. The Innocents

Night Comes Too Soon
1948, (GB), Federated/Butcher, b&w, 52 mins.
W: Valentine Dyall (*The Doctor*), Anne Howard, Alec Faversham, Howard Douglas, Beatrice Marsden, Arthur Brander, Anthony Baird, David Keir
P: Harold Baim **D:** Denis Kavanagh **SCR:** Pat Dixon, from Lord Lytton's play *The Haunted and the Haunters*
A.k.a. The Ghost of Rashmon Hall
Standard fantasy: Doctor rids old house of ghosts

The Night Crawlers
see The Navy vs. the Night Monsters

Night Creature
1977, (USA-Thai), Lee Madden Assocs./Dimension, color, 87 mins.
W: Donald Pleasence (*Axel MacGregor*), Nancy Kwan (*Leslie*), Ross Hagen (*Ross*), Jennifer Rhodes (*Georgia*), Lesly Fine (*Peggy*), Prakit Yaungstri (*Tom*), Rachan Kanghanamat (*Nippon*), Claire Hagen
D: Lee Madden **SCR:** Hubert Smith, from orig. story by Lee Madden & Hubert Smith **PHOTOG:** Permphol Cheyaroon **MUSIC:** Jim Helms
A.k.a. Out of the Darkness
Minor thriller (variation on The Most Dangerous Game): White hunter in Thailand stalks killer leopard

Night Creatures
see Captain Clegg

Night Crossing
1957, (GB), Merton Park/Anglo-Amalgamated, b&w, 32 mins.
W: Russell Napier (*Supt. Duggan*), Julian Strange (*Sgt. Jason*), John Serrett (*Jacques Renault*), Andre Maranne (*Det. Nouvel*), Bandana Das Gupta (*Colette*)
P: Alec Snowden **D:** Montgomery Tully **SCR:** James Eastwood, from a novel by Edgar Lustgarten
Standard short crime-thriller: Knife-thrower kills his drug-addicted partner

The Night Digger
1971, (GB), MGM, color, 110 mins.
W: Patricia Neal (*Maura*), Nicholas Clay (*Billy*), Pamela Brown (*Mother*), Jean Anderson (*Mrs. McMurtrey*), Graham Crowden (*Bolton*), Yootha Joyce (*Mrs. Palafox*), Sebastian Breaks (*Dr. Robinson*), Peter Sallis (*Rev. Palafox*), Zoe Alexander (*The Stroke Patient*), Brigit Forsyth (*The Nurse*), Diana Patrick (*Mary*), Jenny McCracken (*The Farmwife*), Bruce Myles (*The Clerk*), Christopher Rey-nalds (*Young Billy*), Sibylla Kay (*The Whore*), Elaine Ives Cameron (*The Gypsy*)
D: Alastair Reid **SCR:** Roald Dahl, from Joy Crowley's novel *Nest in a Falling Tree* **PHOTOG:** Alex Thomson **MUSIC:** Bernard Herrmann
A.k.a. The Road Builder
Standard thriller: Spinster drawn to mysterious young handy man

Night Drum
see Yoru No Tsuzumi

443

Night Duty: or A Policeman's Experiences
1906, (GB), Cricks & Sharp, b&w, 230 ft. (76.2m)
<u>D</u>: Tom Green
Standard crime-thriller (in 7 scenes): Constable captures murderous pickpocket

The Night Evelyn Came Out of the Grave
1972, (It), Phoenix/Phase One, color, 99 mins.
<u>W</u>: Anthony Steffen {Antonio DeTeffe}, Marina Malfatti, Rod Murdock, Giacomo Rossi-Stuart, Umberto Raho, Roberto Maidera, Joan C. Davie, Erika Blanc
<u>D</u>: Emilio P. Miraglia   <u>SCR</u>: Fabio Pittoru, Massimo Felisatti & Emilio P. Miraglia   <u>PHOTOG</u>: Gastone DiGiovanni   <u>MUSIC</u>: Bruno Nicolai
Standard thriller: Playboy entertains women in his torture chamber

Night Eyes...Fatal Passion
1995, (USA), color, 105 mins.
<u>W</u>: Paula Barbieri, Jeff Trachta
Made-for-Video, standard thriller: Woman psychiatrist menaced by dangerous ex-patient

Nightfall
1956, (USA), Copa/Col, b&w, 78 mins.
<u>W</u>: Anne Bancroft (*Marie Gardner*), Aldo Ray (*James Vanning*), Brian Keith (*John*), James Gregory (*Ben Fraser*), Rudy Bond (*Red*), Frank Albertson (*Dr. Edward Gursten*), Jocelyn Brando (*Laura Fraser*), George Cisar (*The Bus Driver*), Eddie McLean (*The Taxi Driver*), Orlando Beltran, Maria Belmar, Lillian Culver, Maya Van Horn
<u>D</u>: Jacques Tourneur   <u>SCR</u>: Stirling Silliphant, from David Goodis' novel *The Dark Chase*   <u>PHOTOG</u>: Burnett Guffey   <u>MUSIC</u>: George Duning
Standard thriller: Robbers pursue artist

Nightfall
1988, (USA), New Horizons/Concorde, color, 83 mins.
<u>W</u>: David Birney, Sarah Douglas, Alexis Kanner, Andra Millian, Starr Andreeff, Charles Hayward, Susie Lindeman, Dan Wells, Jonathan Emerson, Russell Wiggins, Ronald R. Burns, Bernard J. Garsen, Bradley Reid, Beth A. Corell, Stephen D. Nathenson, James Barry Blakeley, Charles E. Carpenter, Derek Penfield, Ilene Cara Zeff
<u>D & SCR</u>: Paul Mayersberg, from Isaac Asimov's short story   <u>PHOTOG</u>: Dariusz Wolski   <u>MUSIC</u>: Frank Serafine
Minor SF: Planet of constant sunlight faces darkness

Night Fiend
1977, (Sp), Emaus Films/Independent-Int'l, color, 90 mins.
<u>W</u>: Fernando Rey (*Oscar Bataille*), Marisa Mell (*Patricia Bataille*), Espartaco Santoni (*Wilson Vargas*), Elisa Laguna (*Laura*), Maximo Valverde, Julian Navarro, Maria Vico, Julio Morales
<u>D</u>: Jorge Grau, from "a theme" (*The Horla*) by Guy de Maupassant   <u>PHOTOG</u>: Fernando Arribas   <u>MUSIC</u>: Antonio Perez Olea
Minor thriller: Judge obsessed by brutal murders. cf. **Diary of a Madman**

Night Flight from Moscow
see **The Serpent**

The Night Flier
1997, (USA), color, 93 mins.
<u>W</u>: Miguel Ferrer, Julie Entwisle, Michael H. Moss
from a story by Stephen King
Made-for-Cable, standard horror-fantasy: Vampire haunts airports

Nightflyers
1987, (USA), New Century/Vista, color, 89 mins.
<u>W</u>: Catherine Mary Stewart (*Miranda*), Michael Praed (*Royd*), John Standing (*D'Branin*), Lisa Blount (*Audrey*), Helene Udy (*Lilly*), Glenn Withrow (*Keelor*), James Avery (*Darryl*), Annabel Brooks (*Eliza*), Michael Des Barres (*Jon Winderman*)
<u>D</u>: T.C. Blake   <u>SCR</u>: Robert Jaffe, from George R.R. Martin's novella   <u>PHOTOG</u>: Shelly Johnson   <u>MUSIC</u>: Doug Timm
Standard SF-adventure: Astronauts contend with "living" spaceship

A Night for Crime
1942, (USA), b&w, 75 mins.
<u>W</u>: Glenda Farrell, Lyle Talbot, Lena Basquette, Donald Kirke, Ralph Sanford
<u>D</u>: Alexis Thurn-Taxis
Minor thriller: Movie star murdered

Night Fright
1968, (USA), Azalea/AIP, color
<u>W</u>: John Agar, Bill Thurman
<u>D</u>: Larry Buchanan
Minor SF-horror: Expedition encounters mutant

Night Gallery
1969, (USA), Univ, Made for TV, color, 100 mins.
<u>W</u>: Joan Crawford (*Miss Menlo*), Barry Sullivan (*Dr. Heatherton*), Tom Bosley (*Resnick*), Byron Morrow (*Packer*), Richard Kiley (*Strobe*), Garry Goodrow (*Louis*), Sam Jaffe (*Bleum*), Roddy McDowall (*Jeremy*), George Macready (*Hendricks*), Ossie Davis (*Portifoy*), Barry Atwater (*Carson*), Richard Hale (*The Doctor*), George Murdock (*The 1st Agent*), Tom Basham (*Gibbons*), Norma Crane (*Gretchen*), Shannon Farnon (*The 1st Nurse*)

<u>P</u>: William Sackheim   <u>D</u>: Boris Sagal, Steven Spielberg & Barry Shear
   <u>TELEPLAY</u>: Rod Serling   <u>PHOTOG</u>: Richard Batcheller & William Margulies   <u>MUSIC</u>: William Goldenberg
TVM, feature-pilot for teleseries, trilogy of terror-tales: (1) Blind tycoon has eye transplant, (2) Nephew is "haunted" by murdered uncle, & (3) Eerie retribution in old concentration camp

The Night God Screamed
1971, (USA), Cinemation, color, 85 mins.
<u>W</u>: Jeanne Crain, Alex Nicol, David Spelling, James B. Sikking
<u>D</u>: Lee Madden   <u>SCR</u>: Gil Lasky
Minor thriller: Woman terrorized by cultists. A.k.a. **Scream**

Night Hair Child
1972, (GB), Leander/Avco Embassy, color, 89 mins.
<u>W</u>: Mark Lester (*Marcus Bezant*), Britt Ekland (*Elsie Bezant*), Hardy Kruger (*Paul Bezant*), Lilli Palmer (*Dr. Viorne*), Harry Andrews (*Dr. Kessie*), Conchita Montez (*Sophie*), Collette Jack (*Sarah*)
<u>P</u>: Graham Harris   <u>D</u>: James Kelly   <u>ORIG. SCR</u>: Trevor Preston   <u>PHOTOG</u>: Harry Waxman & Luis Cuadrado   <u>MUSIC</u>: Stelvio Cipriani
USA retitle, **What the Peeper Saw**
Minor psychodrama: Precocious boy torments stepmother

Night Has a Thousand Eyes
1948, (USA), Para, b&w, 80 mins.
<u>W</u>: Edward G. Robinson, Gail Russell, William Demarest, John Lund, Virginia Bruce, Onslow Stevens, Richard Webb, Jerome Cowan
<u>P</u>: Endre Boehm   <u>D</u>: John Farrow   <u>SCR</u>: Barre Lyndon & Jonathan Latimer, from Cornell Woolrich's novel   <u>PHOTOG</u>: John F. Seitz   <u>MUSIC</u>: Victor Young
Well-made melodrama: Clairvoyant predicts girl's death

The Night Has Eyes
1942, (GB), Assoc. British/Pathe/PRC, b&w, 79 mins.
<u>W</u>: James Mason (*Stephen*), Wilfrid Lawson (*Sturrock*), Mary Clare (*Mrs. Ranger*), Joyce Howard (*Marian*), Tucker McGuire (*Doris*), John Fernald (*Barry*), Amy Dalby (*Miss Miggs*), Dorothy Black (*Miss Fenwick*)
<u>D</u>: Leslie Arliss   <u>SCR</u>: Alan Kennington   <u>PHOTOG</u>: Gunther Krampf   <u>MUSIC</u>: Charles Williams
USA retitle, **Terror House**
Standard thriller: Two schoolteachers lost on moors, take refuge in home of shell-shocked musician

The Night Holds Terror
1955, (USA), Col, b&w, 86 mins.
<u>W</u>: Jack Kelly, Hildy Parks John Cassavetes
<u>WRIT, P & D</u>: Andrew L. Stone
Standard thriller

Night Hunter
1995, (USA), color, 86 mins.
<u>W</u>: Don "The Dragon" Wilson, Melanie Smith, Nicholas Guest, Maria Ford
<u>D</u>: Rick Jacobson
Made-for-Video, standard horror-thriller: Vampire hunter seeks vengeance

A Night in Paradise
1946, (USA), Univ, color, 84 mins.
<u>W</u>: Merle Oberon, Turhan Bey, Thomas Gomez, Gale Sondergaard, Ray Collins, George Dolenz, John Litel, Ernest Truex, Jerome Cowan, Douglass Dumbrille
<u>D</u>: Arthur Lubin   <u>SCR</u>: Ernest Pascal & Emmet Lavery, from George S. Hellman's novel *Peacock's Feather*   <u>PHOTOG</u>: Hal Mohr   <u>MUSIC</u>: Frank Skinner
Standard fantasy-romance: Aesop falls for beauty at court of King Croesus

Night into Morning
1951, (USA), MGM, b&w, 86 mins.
<u>W</u>: Ray Milland, Nancy Davis
Standard melodrama

The Night is Ending
see **Paris After Dark**

Night is the Phantom
see **La Frusta e il Corpo**

Night Key
1937, (USA), Univ, b&w, 67 mins.
<u>W</u>: Boris Karloff, Jean Rogers, Warren Hull, Alan Baxter, Samuel S. Hinds, Ward Bond, Edwin Maxwell
<u>D</u>: Lloyd Corrigan   <u>SCR</u>: Tristam Tupper & John C. Moffit   <u>PHOTOG</u>: George Robinson
Standard thriller: Wronged inventor seeks revenge

Nightland
1993, (USA), Para, color
Standard horror-fantasy: Ex-cop becomes hero vampire

Night Legs
see **Fright** (1972)

Night Life
1989, (USA), color, 89 mins.
W: Scott Grimes (*Archie*), John Astin (*Flanders*), Lisa Fuller (*Joanie*), Cheryl Pollack (*Charly*), Ken Davis (*Rog*)
P: Charles Lippincott   D: David Acomba   SCR: Keith Critchlow
Minor horror-thriller: Teens battle reanimated corpses

Nightlife
1989, (USA-Mex), Cine Enterprises/Univ, color, 95 mins.
W: Ben Cross (*Vlad*), Maryam d'Abo, Keith Szarabajka, Jesse Corti, Camille Saviola, Glenn Shadix, Oliver Clark, Martin LaSalle, Gerardo Mayol, Juan Antonio Llanes, Gerardo Paz, Gilberto Compan, Gerardo Moreno, Carlos Gonzalez, Marta Resnikoff, Paco Pharrez, Bob Skodis
D: Daniel Taplitz   TELEPLAY: Daniel Taplitz & Anne Beatts   STORY: Anne Beatts   PHOTOG: Peter Fernberger   SPCL-FX: Laurencio Cordero   MUSIC: Dana Kaproff
TVM, standard horror-comedy: Vampiress seeks normalacy

Night Life of the Gods
1935, (USA), Univ, b&w, 73 mins.
W: Henry Armetta, Robert Warwick, Ray Corrigan
D: L. Herman, from a novel by Thorne Smith
Standard melodrama

The Nightmare (1897)
see **Le Cauchemar**

Nightmare
1956, (USA), Shane/Pine-Thomas/UA, b&w, 89 mins.
W: Edward G. Robinson, Kevin McCarthy, Virginia Christine, Connie Russell
WRIT & D: Maxwell Shane, from a novel by Cornell Woolrich   PHOTOG: Joseph Biroc   MUSIC: Herschel Burke Gilbert
remake of **Fear in the Night** *(1947)*
Standard thriller: Hypnotized man commits murder

Nightmare
1963, (GB), Hammer/Univ, b&w, 83 mins.
W: David Knight (*Henry Baxter*), Jenny Linden (*Janet*), Moira Redmond (*Grace Maddox*), Brenda Bruce (*Mary Lewis*), George A. Cooper (*John*), Irene Richmond (*Mrs. Gibbs*), John Welsh (*The Doctor*), Timothy Bateson (*The Barman*), Clytie Jessop (*The Woman in White*), Isla Cameron (*Mother*)
WRIT & P: Jimmy Sangster   D: Freddie Francis   PHOTOG: John Wilcox   MUSIC: Don Banks
Fr retitle, **Meurtre par Procuration** *(Murder by Proxy)*
Standard thriller: Guardian and nurse conspire to drive ward insane

Nightmare (1965)
see **Fanatic**

Nightmare (1966)
see **Nattmara**

Nightmare (1973)
see **Voices**

Nightmare
1981, (USA), David Jones/Goldmine/21st Century, color, 97 mins.
W: Sharon Smith (*Susan*), Mik Cribben (*Bob*), Baird Stafford (*George*), Kathleen Ferguson (*Barbara*), Danny Ronan (*The Babysitter*), John Watkins (*The Man with the Cigar*), C.J. Cooke
P: John L. Watkins   WRIT & D: Romano Scavolini   PHOTOG: Gianni Fiore   MUSIC: Jack Eric Williams
Minor thriller: Psycho plots wife's murder

Nightmare (1983)
see **City of the Walking Dead**

Nightmare Alley
1947, (USA), 20th-Fox, b&w, 112 mins.
W: Tyrone Power (*Stan Carlisle*), Coleen Gray (*Molly*), Joan Blondell (*Zeena*), Helen Walker (*Lilith Ritter*), Ian Keith (*Pete*), Mike Mazurki (*Bruno*), Taylor Holmes (*Ezra Grindle*), James Flavin (*Hoatley*), Julia Dean (*Mrs. Peabody*), Marjorie Wood (*Mrs. Prescott*), Roy Roberts (*McGraw*), Maurice Navarro (*The Fire-Eater*), James Burke (*The Town Marshall*), Leo Gray (*The Detective*), Albin Robeling (*The Captain*), Harry Hays Morgan (*The Headwaiter*), George Beranger (*The Geek*), Harry Cheshire (*Mr. Prescott*), Mike Lally (*Charlie*), Edward Clark (*The Farmer*), Nina Gilbert (*A Woman*), Laura Treadwell (*A Woman*), Eddy Waller (*The Old Farmer*), Bill Free (*The Man in Spode Room*), George Davis (*The Waiter*), Hollis Jewell (*The Delivery Boy*), Henry Hall (*A Man*), John Wald (*The Radio Announcer*), Oliver Blake (*A Hobo*), George Chandler (*A Hobo*), Emmett Lynn (*A Hobo*), Jack Raymond (*A Hobo*), George Lloyd (*A Hobo*)
P: George Jessel   D: Edmund Goulding   SCR: Jules Furthman, from William Lindsay Gresham's novel   PHOTOG: Lee Garmes   SPCL-FX: Fred Sersen   MUSIC: Cyril Mockridge   MUSIC DIR: Lionel Newman
Classic thriller: Carnival double-dealer excels in spiritualist racket

Nightmare at Noon
1988, (USA), color
W: Wings Hauser, George Kennedy, Bo Hopkins
Standard SF-thriller: Experiment turns inhabitants of desert community into homicidal maniacs

The Nightmare Before Christmas
1993, (USA), Tim Burton/Touchstone, color, 75 mins.
VOICES: Chris Sarandon (*Jack Skellington*), Catherine O'Hara (*Sally*), Danny Elfman William Hickey, Glenn Shadix, Paul Reubens, Ken Page
D: Henry Selick   SCR: Caroline Thompson   MUSIC: Danny Elfman
Amusing animated fantasy-thriller: Denizens of Halloween muscle in on Christmas holiday action

Nightmare Castle
see **Amanti d'Oltretomba**

Nightmare City
see **City of the Walking Dead**

Nightmare Honeymoon
1973, (USA), MGM, color, 115 mins.
W: Dack Rambo, Rebecca Dianna Smith, John Beck, Pat Hingle, Jeanette Nolan Bob Steele, David Huddleston
P: Hugh Benson   D: Elliott Silverstein   SCR: S. Lee Pogostin   MUSIC: Elmer Bernstein
blurb:"Thank heavens it's only a movie!"
Standard thriller: Killer rapists pursue newlyweds

Nightmare Hotel
1973, (Sp), color 95 mins.
W: Judy Geeson, Aurora Bautista, Victor Alcazar, Esperanza Roy Lone Fleming
D: Eugenio Martin
A.k.a. **It Happened at Nightmare Inn**
Minor thriller: Paranoid sisters run hostelry

Nightmare House
see **Scream, Baby, Scream**

Nightmare in Blood
1978, (USA), PFE, color, 90 mins.
W: Kerwin Mathews (*Prince*), Kathleen Quinlin, Jerry Walter (*Malakai*), Dan Caldwell (*Seabrook*), Barrie Youngfellow (*Cindy*), John J. Cochran (*Scotty*), Ray K. Gorman (*B.B.*), Hy Pyke (*Harris*), Irving Israel (*Ben-Halik*), Drew Eshelman (*Arlington*), Morgan Upton (*George*), Justin Bishop (*Unworth*), Charles Murphy (*Flannery*), Stan Ritchie (*Marsdon*), Yvonne Young (*Barbara*), Mike Hitchcock (*Driscoll*), Erika Stanley (*The Girl*) Jerry Walter, Barrie Youngfellow
P & SCR: John Stanley & Kenn Davis   D: John Stanley   PHOTOG: Charles Rudnick
A.k.a. **Horror Convention**
Minor horror-thriller: Actor portrays vampire, turns out to be real thing

Nightmare in the Sun
1964, (USA), AA/Zodiac Films, color, 81 mins.
W: John Derek, Ursula Andress, Aldo Ray, Richard Jaeckel, Sammy Davis Jr., Arthur O'Connell, Chick Chandler, Keenan Wynn, George Tobias, Lurene Tuttle, Robert Duvall, Allyn Joslyn, John Marley
WRIT, P & D: Marc Lawrence, inspired by Richard Connell's *The Most Dangerous Game*   PHOTOG: Stanley Cortez   MUSIC: Paul Glass
Standard thriller: Crooked sheriff frames drifter for brutal murder

Nightmare in Wax
1969, (USA), Paragon-Int'l/Crown International, color, 95 mins.
W: Cameron Mitchell, Anne Helm (*Marie Morgan*), Scott Brady (*Haskell*), Berry Kroeger (*Max*), John Cardos, James Forrest
D: Bud Townsend   SCR: Rex Carlton   PHOTOG: Glenn Smith
A.k.a. **Crimes in the Wax Museum**
Minor thriller (House of Wax imitation): Celebrities disappear, police mystified

Nightmare Island (1979)
see **Queen of the Cannibals**

Nightmare Island (1982)
see **The Slayer**

Nightmare Maker
see **Butcher, Baker (Nightmare Maker)**

The Nightmare of Dracula
see **Horror of Dracula**

Nightmare of Terror
see **Demons of the Mind**

A Nightmare on Elm Street
1984, (USA), New Line, color, 90 mins.
W: John Saxon, Ronee Blakely, Heather Langenkamp, Johnny Depp, Amanda

Wyss, Nick Corri, Lin Shaye, Robert Englund (*Freddy Krueger*), Jack Shea
WRIT & D: Wes Craven **PHOTOG:** Jacques Haitkin **MUSIC:** Charles Bernstein
Semi-classic horror-fantasy: Teenagers' dreams of monstrous killer become reality

A Nightmare on Elm Street, Part 2: Freddy's Revenge
1985, (USA), Heron/Smart Egg/New Line, color, 88 mins.
W: Mark Patton (*Jesse Walsh*), Kim Myers (*Lisa*), Clu Gulager (*Mr. Walsh*), Robert Rusler (*Grady*), Robert Englund (*Freddy Krueger*), Hope Lange (*Mrs. Walsh*), Marshell Bell, Lyman Ward, Melinda O. Fee, Thom McFadden
P: Robert Shaye **D:** Jack Sholder **SCR:** David Chaskin, from characters created by Wes Craven **PHOTOG:** Jacques Haitkin **MUSIC:** Christopher Young
Standard horror-fantasy: Spirit of monstrous killer torments teens

A Nightmare on Elm Street 3: Dream Warriors
1987, (USA), New Line, color, 96 mins.
W: Craig Wasson (*Dr. Neil Goldman*), Heather Langenkamp (*Nancy Thompson*), Patricia Arquette (*Kristen Parker*), Robert Englund (*Freddy Krueger*), Priscilla Pointer (*Dr. Elizabeth Simms*), Larry (Lawrence) Fishburne (*Max*), John Saxon (*Thompson*), Brooke Bundy (*Elaine Parker*), Ken Sagoes (*Kincaid*), Zsa Zsa Gabor (*herself*), Bradley Gregg (*Phillip*), Dick Cavett (*himself*), Ira Heiden (*Will*), Rodney Eastman (*Joey*), Jennifer Rubin (*Taryn*), Nan Martin (*Pam*), Penelope Sudrow (*Jennifer*), Clayton Landey (*Lorenzo*), Kristen Clayton (*The Little Girl*), Sally Piper (*Nurse #1*), Rozlyn Sorrell (*Nurse #2*), Stacey Alden (*Marcie*), Michael Rougas (*The Priest in the Church*), Jack Shea (*The Priest in the Cemetery*), Paul Kent (*Dr. Carver*), Mary Brown (*The Neurosurgeon*), Melanie Doctors (*The Girl in the Cemetery*), Donna Durham (*The Girl in the Crowd*)
D: Chuck Russell **SCR:** Wes Craven, Bruce Wagner, Chuck Russell & Frank Darabont **PHOTOG:** Roy Wagner **SPCL VS-FX:** Dream Quest Images **MUSIC:** Angelo Badalamenti
Standard horror-fantasy: Disturbed youths unite to combat monstrous terror

A Nightmare on Elm Street 4: The Dream Master
1988, (USA), New Line, color, 93 mins.
W: Robert Englund (*Freddy Krueger*), Rodney Eastman (*Joey*), Danny Hassel (*Danny*), Tuesday Knight (*Kristen*), Lisa Wilcox (*Alice*), Andras Jones (*Rick*), Toy Newkirk (*Sheila*), Brooke Bundy, John Beckman, Nicholas Mele, Jody Montana, Duane Davis
D: Renny Harlin **SCR:** Brian Helgeland & Scott Pierce, from characters created by Wes Craven **PHOTOG:** Steven Pierberg **MUSIC:** Craig Safan
Standard horror-fantasy: Fiend returns to slay teens

A Nightmare on Elm Street 5: The Dream Child
1989, (USA), Smart Egg/Heron/New Line, color, 90 mins.
W: Robert Englund (*Freddy Krueger*), Lisa Wilcox (*Alice*), Danny Hassel (*Dan*), Whitby Hertford (*Jacob*), Erika Anderson, Kelly Jo Muntz, Valorie Armstrong, Burr DeBenning, Nick Mele
P: Robert Shaye & Rupert Harvey **D:** Stephen Hopkins **SCR:** Leslie Bohem, from characters created by Wes Craven **PHOTOG:** Peter Levy **VS-FX SPRVSR:** Alan Munro **MUSIC:** Jay Ferguson
*Standard horror-fantasy: Girl's unborn child menaced by evil spirit. cf. **Freddy's Dead: The Final Nightmare***

The Nightmare of the Glad-Eye Twins
1913, (GB), Kineto, b&w, 770 ft. (234.7m)
D: Edgar Rogers
*reissued (1916) as **Elsie's Nightmare***
Standard fantasy: Girl dreams dolls come to life

Nightmare on the 13th Floor
1990, (USA), Wilshire Court/USA-TV, color, 95 mins.
W: Michele Greene, James Brolin, Louise Fletcher, John Karlen, Alan Fudge, Terri Treas, Alan Haufrect, Juli Donald, Kerry Noonan, Steve Eastin, Norma MacMillan, Jeff Marcus, Harvey Vernon, Molly Morgan, Michael Melvin, Chip Hipkins, David James Alexander, Charles Bazaldua, Tony Auer, Neile (Adams) McQueen, Phyllis Flax, Edwina Moore, Frank Kopvc, Charles R. Penland, Dana Craig, Joe Faust, Ken Kerman, Sharon Conley, Michael McNab, James R. Sweeney
D: Walter Grauman **SCR:** J.D. Feigelson & Dan DiStefano **PHOTOG:** Tom Richmond **SPCL-FX:** Greg Curtis **MUSIC:** Jay Gruska
TVM, standard thriller: Woman journalist probes hotel mystery

Nightmares (1977)
*see **Cauchemares***

Nightmares
1983, (USA), Univ, color, 90 mins.
W: Cristina Raines (*Lisa*), Veronica Cartwright (*Claire*), Albert Hague (*Mel Keefer*), Richard Masur (*Steven*), Lance Henriksen (*Frank*), Emilio Estevez (*J.J. Cooney*), Bridgette Andersen (*Brooke*), Billy Jacoby (*Maxwell*), Joe Lambie (*Lisa's Husband*), Anthony James (*The Clerk*), Clare Nono (*The Newswoman*), Raleigh Bond (*The Newsman*), Robert Phelps (*The Newsman*), Dixie Lynn Royce (*The Little Girl*), Lee James Jude (*The Glazier*), Mariclare Costello (*Mrs. Cooney*), Louis Giambalvo (*Cooney*), Joshua Grenrock (*Willie*), Moon Zappa (*Pamela*), Gary Cervantes (*Mazenza*), C. Stewart Burns (*Root*), Andre Diaz (*Pedro*), Tony Plana (*Del Amo*), Rachel Goslins (*Phyllis*), Christopher Bubetz (*Jeffrey*), Joel Holman (*Z-Man*), Rudy Negretl (*Emiliano*), James Tolkan (*The Bishop's Voice*), Robin Gammell (*The Bishop*)

Timothy Scott (*The Sheriff*), Rose Marie Campos (*The Mother*), Howard F. Flynn (*The Announcer*)
D: Joseph Sargent **PHOTOG:** Gerald Perry Finnerman & Mario DiLeo **MUSIC:** Craig Safan
*Standard fantasy anthology; quartet of terror tales—**Terror in Topanga, The Bishop of Battle, The Benediction** (screenplays by Christopher Crowe) & **Night of the Rat** (screenplay by Jeffrey Bloom)*

Nightmare Sisters
1989, (USA), Dave DeCoteau/Cinema Home Videos, color, 82 mins.
W: Linnea Quigley (*Melody*), Brinke Stevens (*Marci*), C.J. Cox (*Bud*), Michelle McClellan (*Mickey*), William Dristas (*Duane*), Richard Gabai (*Kevin*), Marcus Vaughter (*Freddy*), Timothy Kauffman (*Phil*), Matthew Phelps (*J.J.*), Dukey Flyswatter (*Omar*), Jim Culver, Sandy Brooke, Amanda Detweiler
P & D: Dave DeCoteau **SCR:** Kenneth J. Hall **PHOTOG:** Voya Mikulic **MUSIC:** Del Casher **LYRICS:** Haunted Garage **SONGS:** *Sorority Sister Succubus, Brain in a Jar* & *Yumpin' Yiminy, Suck on My Chimney*
Made-for-Video, minor horror-spoof: Coeds become succubi

Nightmare Street
1998, (USA), Longbow/ABC-TV, color, 95 mins.
W: Sherilyn Fenn, Thomas Gibson, Rena Soter, Steve Harris, Matthew Walker, Lauren Diewold
D: Colin Bucksey, from a book by Margaret Tabor **PHOTOG:** Jan Kiesser **MUSIC:** Dana Kaproff
TVM, standard thriller: Woman has concussion, finds former life has vanished

Nightmare Weekend
1986, (USA), color, 86 mins.
W: Dale Midkiff, Debbie Laster, Debra Hunter, Lori Lewis
D: Henry Sala
Minor horror-thriller: Scientist turns girls and their dates into crazed zombies

The Night Meteor
*see **It Came from Outer Space***

Night Monster
1942, (USA), Univ, b&w, 73 mins.
W: Bela Lugosi, Lionel Atwill, Irene Hervey, Ralph Morgan, Fay Helm, Leif Erickson, Don Porter, Frank Reicher, Nils Asther
P & D: Ford Beebe **SCR:** Clarence Upson Young **PHOTOG:** Charles Van Enger
*GB retitle, **House of Mystery***
Standard thriller: Cripple goes on nocturnal murder sprees

Night Must Fall
1937, (USA), MGM, b&w, 117 mins.
W: Robert Montgomery (*Danny*), Rosalind Russell (*Olivia*), Dame May Whitty (*Mrs. Bransom*), Alan Marshal (*Justin*), Kathleen Harrison (*Mrs. Terrence*), Merle Tottenham (*Dora*), Matthew Boulton (*Belsize*), Eily Malyon (*The Nurse*), E.E. Clive (*The Guide*), Beryl Mercer (*The Saleslady*), Winifred Harris (*Mrs. Laurie*)
D: Richard Thorpe **SCR:** John Van Druten, from Emlyn Williams' play **PHOTOG:** Ray June **MUSIC:** Edward Ward
Classic thriller: Suave psychotic murders women

Night Must Fall
1964, (GB), MGM, b&w, 105 mins.
W: Albert Finney (*Danny*), Susan Hampshire (*Olivia Bramson*), Mona Washbourne (*Mrs. Bramson*), Sheila Hancock (*Dora*), Joe Gladwin (*Dodge*), Michael Medwin (*Derek*), John Gill (*Foster*), Martin Wyldeck (*Insp. Willet*)
P: Albert Finney & Karel Reisz **D:** Karel Reisz **SCR:** Clive Exton, from Emlyn Williams' play **PHOTOG:** Freddie Francis **MUSIC:** Ron Grainer
Standard thriller: Woman suspects handyman is killer

Night of Adventure
1944, (USA), RKO, b&w, 65 mins.
W: Tom Conway, Jean Brooks
Standard thriller

The Night of All the Mysteries
*see **House on Haunted Hill***

Night of Anubis
*see **Night of the Living Dead** (1968)*

The Night of a Thousand Cats
1972, (Mex), Avant Films S.A./Ellman, color, 95 mins.
W: Anjanette Comer, Hugo Stiglitz, Teresa Velazquez, Zulma Faiad, Christa Linder
D: Rene Cardona Jr. **STORY & SCR:** Mario Marzac **PHOTOG:** Alex Phillips Jr.
Minor horror-thriller: Madman feeds beauties to carnivorous kitties

Night of Bloody Horror
1969, (USA), Howco-Int'l, color, 80 mins.
W: Gaye Yellen, Gerald McRaney, Evelyn Hendricks
P & D: Joy N. Houck Jr. **SCR:** Joy N. Houck Jr. & Robert A. Weaver
Minor thriller: Former mental patient suspected of meat-cleaver mutilations

Night of Dark Shadows

1971, (USA), MGM, color, 97 mins.
<u>W</u>: David Selby *(Quentin/Charles)*, Kate Jackson *(Tracy)*, Thayer David *(Rev. Strack)*, Lara Parker *(Angelique)*, John Karlen *(Alex)*, Grayson Hall *(Carlotta)*, Clarice Blackburn *(Mrs. Castle)*, Nancy Barrett *(Claire)*, Monica Rich *(Sarah)*, James Storm *(Gerard)*, Diana Millay *(Laura)*, Christopher Pennock *(Gabriel)*
<u>P & D</u>: Dan Curtis   <u>SCR</u>: Sam Hall   <u>STORY</u>: Sam Hall & Dan Curtis   <u>PHOTOG</u>: Richard Shore   <u>MUSIC</u>: Robert Cobert
Standard fantasy-thriller: Artist's wife discovers husband is reincarnated. cf. House of Dark Shadows

A Night of Horror

1916, (Ger), b&w
<u>W</u>: Werner Krauss, Emil Jannings
<u>D</u>: Arthur Robison
Standard thriller

A Night of Magic

1944, (GB), Premier/Berkeley, b&w, 56 mins.
<u>W</u>: Robert Griffith *(Reggie)*, Billy "Uke" Scott *(Reggie's Pal)*, Marian Olive *(Princess Raviola)*
<u>P</u>: Burt Hyams   <u>D</u>: Herbert Wynne   <u>STORY</u>: Eversley Bracken
Standard musical-fantasy: Playboy dreams 3000-year-old Egyptian princess revives

Night of Mystery

1928, (USA), Para, b&w, 6 reels (5,741 ft./1749.9m)
<u>W</u>: Adolphe Menjou *(Capt. Ferreol)*, Evelyn Brent *(Gilberte Boismartel)*, Nora Lane *(Therese D'Egremont)*, Raoul Paoli *(Marcasse)*, William Collier Jr. *(Jerome D'Egremont)*, Claude Kin *(Marquis Boismartel)*, Frank Leigh *(Rochemore)*, Margaret Burt *(Rochemore's Sec'y)*
<u>D</u>: Lothar Mendes   <u>ADAPT & SCR</u>: Ernest Vajda, from a story by Victorien Sardou   <u>PHOTOG</u>: Harry A. Fischbeck
Standard melodrama: French army captain involved in murder intrigue

Night Of Mystery: ADOLPHE MENJOV

A Night of Mystery

1937, (USA), Para, b&w, 75 mins.
<u>W</u>: Grant Richards *(Philo Vance)*, Roscoe Karns *(Sgt. Ernest Heath)*, Helen Burgess *(Ada Greene)*, Ruth Coleman *(Sibella Greene)*, Elizabeth Patterson *(Mrs. Tobias Greene)*, Harvey Stephens *(Dr. Von Blon)*, June Martel *(Barton)*, Purnell B. Pratt *(D.A. John F.X. Markham)*, Terry Ray *(Ellen Drew)* *(The Secretary)*, Colin Tapley *(Chester Greene)*, James H. Bush *(Rex Greene)*, Ivan F. Simpson *(Sproot)*, Greta Meyer *(Mrs. Mannheim)*, Barlowe Borland *(The Medical Examiner)*, Leonard Carey *(Lister)*, Nora Cecil *(Hemming)*, George Anderson *(Det. Snitkin)*, Myra Marsh *(The Police Nurse)*
<u>D</u>: E.A. Dupont   <u>SCR</u>: Frank Partos & Gladys Unger, from S.S. Van Dine's novel *The Greene Murder Case*   <u>PHOTOG</u>: Harry Fischbeck
Standard thriller ("Philo Vance" mystery): Low-budget remake of 'The Greene Murder Case'

A Night of Peril

1912, (GB), Hepworth, b&w, 550 ft. (167.6m)
<u>W</u>: Harry Royston *(The Man)*, Ruby Belasco *(The Woman)*
<u>D</u>: Bert Haldane
Standard thriller: Sleepwalking girl kidnapped

Night of Revenge

see La Nuit de la Revanche

Night of Terror

1933, (USA), Col, b&w
<u>W</u>: Bela Lugosi, Wallace Ford, Sally Blane, Oscar Smith, Gertrude Michael, Tully Marshall, George Meeker, Bryant Washburn, Edwin Maxwell, Mary Frey, Matt McHugh
<u>D</u>: Benjamin Stoloff   <u>SCR</u>: Beatrice Van, William Jacobs & Lester Nielsen, from a story by Willard Mack   <u>PHOTOG</u>: Joseph Hilton
A.k.a. **He Lived to Kill**
Standard thriller: Mysterious killer hunted

Night of Terror

1972, (USA), Para, Made for TV, color, 73 mins.
<u>W</u>: Donna Mills, Eddie Egan, Martin Balsam, Chuck Connors, Agnes Moorehead
<u>D</u>: Jeannot Szwarc
TVM, standard thriller: Unknown assailant terrorizes woman

Night of Terror

1987, (USA) color, 105 mins.
<u>W</u>: Renee Harmon, Henry Lewis
Standard thriller: Weird family conducts disastrous brain experiments

Night of the Beast

see House of the Black Death

The Night of the Big Heat

1967, (GB), Planet/Maron, color, 94 mins.
<u>W</u>: Christopher Lee *(Hanson)*, Peter Cushing *(Dr. Stone)*, Jane Merrow *(Angela Roberts)*, Sarah Lawson *(Frankie Callum)*, William Lucas *(Ken Stanley)*, Kenneth Cope *(Tinker Mason)*, Jack Bligh *(Ben Siddle)*, Thomas Heathcote *(Bob Hayward)*, Sydney Bromley *(The Tramp)*, Percy Herbert *(Gerald Foster)*
<u>P</u>: Tom Blakeley   <u>D</u>: Terence Fisher   <u>SCR</u>: Ronald Liles, Pip Baker & Jane Baker from John Lymington's novel
A.k.a. **Island of the Burning Doomed**
Standard SF-thriller: Space-aliens cause temperature rise

Night of the Blood-Beast

1958, (USA), Balboa/AIP, b&w, 65 mins.
<u>W</u>: Michael Emmet, Angela Greene, Tyler McVey, John Baer, Ed Nelson, Georgianna Carter, Ross Sturlin
<u>P</u>: Gene Corman   <u>D</u>: Bernard L. Kowalski   <u>SCR</u>: Martin Varno   <u>STORY</u>: Gene Corman   <u>MUSIC</u>: Alexander Laszlo
orig. to be titled **The Creature from Galaxy 27***, orig. co-billed with* **She-Gods of Shark Reef***, reissued 1961*
Semi-classic SF-horror with shuddery music score: Isolated astro-physicists menaced by space alien that ingests human brains. cf. Alien

Night of the Blood Monster

1972, (Sp-W. Ger-It), AIP, color, 82 mins.
<u>W</u>: Christopher Lee, Maria Schell, Leo Genn, Hans Hass, Maria Rohm, Margaret Lee, Peter Martell, Howard Vernon
<u>P</u>: Harry Alan Towers & Anthony Scott Veitch   <u>D</u>: Jess Franco   <u>SCR</u>: Anthony Scott Veitch, from a story by Peter Welbeck
A.k.a. **Bloody Judge** *and* **El Procesco de las Brujas** *(Prosecution of the Witches)*
*Minor thriller (***Witch-Finder General** *imitation): Tale of relentless witch-hunter*

Night of the Bloodsuckers

see The Vampire Girls

Night of the Bloody Apes

1968, (Mex), Calderon/Jerand/Unistar, color, 84 mins.
<u>W</u>: Armando Silvestre
<u>D</u>: Rene Cardona   <u>SCR</u>: Rene Cardona & Rene Cardona Jr.
A.k.a. **Gomar the Human Gorilla** *and* **Horror y Sexo** *(Horror and Sex)*
Minor SF-horror: Gruesome experiments produce ape people

The Night of the Claw

1982, (USA), Island Claws-Joint Venture, color, 91 mins. (TV, 63 mins.)
<u>W</u>: Robert Lansing *(Moody)*, Steve Hanks *(Pete)*, Nita Talbot *(Rosie)*, Barry Nelson *(Prof. McNeal)*, Jo McDonnell, Martina Deignan, Tony Rico, Ray Forchion, Dick Callinan, Mal Jones, Dolores Sandoz, Frank Schuller, John Furey, Ric O'Feldman, Will Knickerbocker, Tom Monahan, Dan Chandler, Dee Dee Deering
<u>D</u>: Hernan Cardenas   <u>SCR</u>:Jack Cowden & Ricou Browning   <u>STORY</u>: Colby Cardenas & Hernan Cardenas   <u>PHOTOG</u>: James Pergola   <u>SPCL-FX</u>: Glen Robinson, Ray Scott, Don Chandler, Sam Dockrey, Robert MacDonald, Ralph Robinson, Wayne Rose, John Sampson, Robert Staples, Gene Stoddard, J.B. Jones & Bill Seckel   <u>MUSIC</u>: Bill Justis
A.k.a. **Island Claws**
Minor SF-thriller: Mutant crab attacks

Night of the Cobra Woman
1972, (USA), New World, color, 85 mins.
W: Joy Bang (*Joanna*), Marlene Clark (*Lena*), Roger Garrett (*Duff*), Slash Marks (*Sgt. Merkle*)
D: Andrew Meyer   **SCR:** Andrew Meyer & Kerry Magness
blurb: "She sucks the life from the bodies of men"

Night of the Comet
1984, (USA), Thomas Coleman-Michael Rosenblatt/Atlantic, color, 95 mins.
W: Robert Beltran (*Hector*), Catherine Mary Stewart (*Regina*), Kelli Maroney (*Samantha*), Sharon Farrell (*Doris*), Peter Fox (*Wilson*), Mary Woronov (*Audrey*), Geoffrey Lewis (*Oscar*), John Achorn (*Oscar*), Michael Bowen (*Larry*), Devon Ericson, Lissa Layng, Ivan E. Roth, Janice Kawaye, Chance Boyer, Andrew Boyer, Stanley Brock, Marc Poppel, Raymond Lynch, John Stuart West, Bob Perlow, Alex Brown, Dick Rude, Wilson Camp, Chris Pedersen, Karl Johnson, Joel Levine, Anna Mathias, Tim Hannon, Bobby Porter, Steve LaBeau, Michael Hanks, Sandra Lee Gimpel, Chris Chesser, Dale House, Debby Lynn Ross
WRIT & D: Thom Eberhardt   **PHOTOG:** Arthur Albert   **VS-FX:** Ted Rae
Modest SF-satire: Comet radiation decimates Earth, Valley Girls cope

Night of the Creeps
1986, (USA), Charles Gordon/Tri-Star, color, 89 mins.
W: Jason Lively (*Chris*), Steve Marshall (*J.C.*), Tom Atkins (*Det. Ray Cameron*), Jill Whitlow (*Cynthia*), Bruce Solomon (*Det. Raimi*), Wally Taylor (*Det. Landis*), Vic Polizos (*The Coroner*), Allan J. Kayser (*Brad*), Dick Miller (*The Police Armorer*), Ken Heron (*Johnny*), Alice Cadogan (*Pam*), Evelyne Smith (*The House Mother*), June Harris (*Karen*), David Paymer (*The Young Scientist*), David Oliver (*Steve*), Ivan E. Roth (*The Psycho Zombie*), Daniel Frishman (*The Alien Zombie*), Kevin Thompson (*Alien Pursuer #1*), Joseph S. Griffo (*Alien Pursuer #2*), Katherine Britton (*The Sorority Girl on the Phone*), Leslie Ryan (*The Sorority Girl with the Hairbrush*), Dave Alan Johnson (*Young Ray Cameron*), Jay Wakeman (*Judy*), Suzanne Snyder (*Lisa*), Elizabeth Cox (*Kathy*), Emily Fiola (*Jennifer*), Russell Moss (*Biff*), John J. York (*Todd*), Jim Townsend (*Chett*), Richard DeHaven (*Dick*), Jay Arlen Jones, Tex Donaldson, Craig Schaefer, Richard Sassin, Robert Kino, Robert Kerman, Jack Lightsy, Elizabeth Alda, Beal Carrotes, Earl Ellis, Robert Kurtzman, Keith Werle, David B. Miller, Arick Stillwagon, Ted Rae, Howard Berger, Todd Bryant, Dawn Schroder, Chris Dekker, Brian MacGregor
WRIT & D: Fred Dekker   **PHOTOG:** Robert C. New   **MUSIC:** Barry DeVorzon
Modest SF-horror satire: Space aliens turn collegians into zombies

Night of the Demon
1957, (GB), Sabre/Hammer/Col, b&w, 83 mins.
W: Dana Andrews (*Dr. John Holden*), Peggy Cummins (*Joanna Harrington*), Niall MacGinnis (*Dr. Karswell*), Ewan Roberts (*Williamson*), Athene Seyler (*Mrs. Karswell*), Liam Redmond (*Prof. Mark O'Brien*), Peter Elliott (*Kumar*), Richard Leech (*Insp. Mottram*), Reginald Beckwith (*Mr. Meek*), Brian Wilde, Janet Barrow, Peter Hobbs, Lynn Tracy, Percy Herbert, Lloyd Lamble, Charles Lloyd-Pack, Rosamund Greenwood
P: Hal E. Chester   **D:** Jacques Tourneur   **SCR:** Charles Bennett & Hal E. Chester, from Montague R. James' story "Casting the Runes"   **PHOTOG:** Ted Scaife   **MUSIC:** Clifton Parker   **DESIGN:** Ken Adam
*USA retitle, **Curse of the Demon**, orig. co-billed with **The Revenge of Frankenstein***
Classic horror-fantasy: Couple jeopardized by attempts to expose satanists

Night of the Demon (1971)
*see **The Touch of Satan***

Night of the Demons
1988, (USA), Paragon Arts Int'l/Meridian, color, 90 mins.
W: William Gallo (*Sal*), Hal Havins (*Steve*), Mimi Kinkade (*Angela*), Cathy Podewell (*Judy*), Linnea Quigley Alvin Alexis, Lance Fenton
WRIT & P: Joe Augustyn   **D:** Kevin S. Tenney   **PHOTOG:** David Lewis   **MUSIC:** Dennis Michael Tenney
*A.k.a. **Halloween Party***
Minor horror-thriller: Party turns ugly

Night of the Demons 2
1994, (USA), color, 96 mins.
W: Amelia Kinkade
Standard horror-fantasy: Demon menaces Halloween revelers

Night of the Demons 3
1997, (USA), color, 85 mins.
W: Amelia Kinkade (*Angela*), Kris Holdenreid (*Vince*)
Standard horror-fantasy: Demoness plagues juveniles in possessed house

Night of the Doomed
*see **Amante D'Otlretomba***

Night of the Eagle
1962, (GB), Julian Wintle-Leslie Parkyn/Independant Artists/AA/AIP, b&w, 87 mins.
W: Janet Blair (*Tansy Taylor*), Peter Wyngarde (*Norman Taylor*), Margaret Johnston (*Flora Carr*), Colin Gordon (*Prof. Lindsay Carr*), Anthony Nicholls (*Harvey Sawtelle*), Kathleen Byron (*Evelyn Sawtelle*), Reginald Beckwith (*Harold Gunnison*), Jessica Dunning (*Hilda Gunnison*), Norman Bird (*The*

Doctor), Judith Stott (*Margaret Abbott*), Bill Mitchell (*Fred Jennings*)
P: Albert Fennell   **D:** Sidney Hayers   **SCR:** Richard Matheson & Charles Beaumont, based on Fritz Leiber's novel *Conjure Wife*   **PHOTOG:** Reginald Wyer   **MUSIC:** William Alwyn
*USA retitle, **Burn, Witch, Burn***
"...successfully captures the essence of Leiber's brilliant novel that concern (sic) the use of witchcraft...The horror lies in the very mundanity of the setting, and Leiber was among the first to bring off this device"—Baird Searles, "Films," The Magazine of Fantasy and Science Fiction, Vol. 51, No. 1 (July, 1976), p. 60
*Classic fantasy-thriller: College professor finds wife practices "white witchcraft." cf. **'Weird Woman'** and **'Witches' Brew'***

Night of the Flesh Eaters
*see **Night of the Living Dead** (1968)*

The Night of the Full Moon
1954, (GB), Hedgerley/UA, b&w, 67 mins.
W: Dermot Walsh (*Robby*), Kathleen Byron (*Jane*), Philip Saville (*Dale Merritt*), Anthony Ireland (*The Watercan Man*), Tim Turner (*George*), Everley Gregg (*Mrs. Jeans*), Elizabeth Wallace (*Helen*), George Merritt (*Charlie*)
P, D & SCR: Donald Taylor   **STORY:** Carl Koch
Standard thriller: Spies trap FBI agent in country farmhouse

The Night of the Generals
1966, (GB-Fr), Horizon-Filmsonor/Col, color, 148 mins.
W: Peter O'Toole (*Gen. Tanz*), Omar Sharif (*Maj. Grau*), Tom Courtenay (*Cpl. Curt Hartmann*), Christopher Plummer (*Field Marshall Rommel*), Donald Pleasence (*Gen. Kahlenberg*), Joanna Pettet (*Ulrike von Seydlitz-Gabler*), Philippe Noiret (*Insp. Morand*), Juliette Greco (*Juliette*), Charles Gray (*Gen. von Seydlitz-Gabler*), Coral Browne (*Eleanor*), John Gregson (*Col. Sandauer*), Nigel Stock (*Otto*), Gerard Buhr (*von Stauffenberg*), Yves Brainville (*Liesowski*), Gordon Jackson (*Capt. Engel*), Patrick Allen (*Col. Mannheim*), Harry Andrews (*The Governor*), Veronique Vendell
P: Sam Spiegel   **D:** Anatole Litvak   **SCR:** Joseph Kessel & Paul Dehn, from a novel by Hans Helmut Kirst   **PHOTOG:** Andre Decae   **MUSIC:** Maurice Jarre
Standard thriller: "Jack the Ripper" murders in Nazi-occupied Paris

Night of the Ghouls
1959, (USA), Atomic/AA, b&w, 77 mins.
W: Kenne Duncan, Lon Chaney Jr., Tor Johnson, Vampira [Maila Nurmi], Valda Hansen, Dr. Tom Mason
D & SCR: Edward D. Wood Jr.
*orig. to be titled **Revenge of the Dead**, not released theatrically (available on video)*
Standard horror-fantasy ("Monsters to be pitied...Monsters to be despised"): Fake mediums must contend with "walking dead"

The Night of the Great Attack
1964, (It), color
W: Fausto Tozzi, Agnes Laurent
Minor adventure-thriller: Cesare Borgia schemes to acquire dukedom

Night of the Howling Beast
*see **La Maldicion de la Bestia***

The Night of the Hunter
1955, (USA), UA, b&w, 93 mins.
W: Robert Mitchum (*Preacher Harry Powell*), Shelley Winters (*Willa Harper*), Lillian Gish (*Rachel*), Billy Chapin (*John*), Sally Jane Bruce (*Pearl*), Peter Graves (*Ben Harper*), Gloria Castillo (*Ruby*), Don Beddoe (*Walt*), Cheryl Callaway (*Mary*), Mary Ellen Clemons (*Clary*), James Gleason (*Birdie*),

The Night of the Hunter: JAMES GLEASON

Evelyn Varden (*Icey*), Corey Allen
D: Charles Laughton & R. Denis Sanders   **SCR:** James Agee, from Davis Grubb's novel   **PHOTOG:** Stanley Cortez   **SPCL-FX:** Jack Rabin & Louis DeWitt   **MUSIC:** Walter Schumann
Classic thriller (Charles Laughton's sole directorial effort): Psychotic "preacher" seeks stolen loot, pursues children

Night of the Hunter
1991, (USA), ACI/ABC-TV, color, 95 mins.
W: Richard Chamberlain, Diana Scarwid, Amy Bebout, Ray McKinnon, Mary Nell, Burgess Meredith, Reid Binion
D: David Greene   **TELEPLAY:** Edmond Stevens, from Davis Grubb's novel   **MUSIC:** Peter Manning Robinson
TVM, standard thriller: Psychotic preacher pursues children

The Night of the Laughing Dead
see **The House in Nightmare Park**

Night of the Lepus
1972, (USA), MGM, color, 88 mins.
W: Stuart Whitman (*Roy*), Janet Leigh (*Gerry*), Rory Calhoun (*Cole*), DeForest Kelley (*Elgin*), Paul Fix (*The Sheriff*), Melanie Fullerton (*Amanda*), Chris Morell (*Jackie*), Chuck Hayward (*Jud*), Francesca Jarvis (*Mildred*), William Elliott (*Dr. Leopold*), Richard Jacome (*Prof. Dirkson*), Henry Wills (*Frank*), Evans Thornton (*Maj. White*), G. Leroy Gaintner (*Walker*), Inez Perez (*The Housekeeper*), I. Stanford Jolley (*The Dispatcher*), Don Starr (*Cutler*), Robert Gooden (*Leslie*), Frank Kennedy (*The Doctor*), Walter Kelley (*The Truckdriver*), Russell Morrell (*The Priest*), Phillip Avenetti (*The Officer*), Jerry Dunphy (*The TV Newscaster*), Peter O'Crotty (*Arlen*), Stephen de France, Donna Gelgur, Sherry Hummer, Rick Hummer
P: A.C. Lyles   **D:** William F. Claxton   **SCR:** Don Holliday & Gene R. Kearney, from Russell Braddon's novel *Year of the Angry Rabbit*   **PHOTOG:** Ted Voigtlander   **MUSIC:** Jimmie Haskell   **DESIGN:** Stan Jolley
orig. to be titled **Rabbits**
Standard SF-thriller: Experimental serum produces monster rabbits

Night of the Living Dead
1968, (USA), Image Ten/Walter Reade/Continental, b&w, 93 mins.
W: Russell Streiner (*Johnny*), Karl Hardman (*Harry Cooper*), Judith O'Dea (*Barbara*), Marilyn Eastman (*Helen Cooper*), Duane Jones (*Ben*), Keith Wayne (*Tom*), Judith Ridley (*Judy*), Kyra Schon (*Karen Cooper*), Bill "Chilly Billy" Cardille (*The Newscaster*), Frank Doak (*Dr. Grimes*), Charles Craig, Bill Heinzman, George Kosana, A.C. McDonald, Lee Hartman, Samuel R. Solito, Mark Ricci, Jack Givens, Paula Richards, R.J. Ricci, William Burchinal, Ross Harris, Steve Hutsko, Al Croft, Jason Richards, Dave James, Sharon Carroll, Joann Michaels, William Mogush, Phillip Smith, Randy Burr, Ella Mae Smith
D & PHOTOG: George A. Romero   **SCR:** John Russo & George A. Romero
orig. to be titled either **Night of Anubis** *or* **Night of the Flesh Eaters**
Low-budget horror classic: Radiation animates cannibal corpses. cf. **Dawn of the Dead**

Night of the Living Dead
1990, (USA), 21st Century/Col, color, 96 mins.
W: Tony Todd (*Ben*), Patricia Tallman (*Barbara*), Tom Towles (*Harry*), McKee Anderson (*Helen*), Bill Mosley (*Johnnie*), Katie Finnerman (*Judy Rose*), Heather Mazur (*Sarah*)
D: Tom Savini   **SCR:** George A. Romero, from an orig. scr by John A. Russo & George A. Romero   **PHOTOG:** Frank Prinzi   **MUSIC:** Paul McCollough
Standard horror-fantasy (tepid remake of 1968 classic): Dead prey on living

Night of the Prowler
1962, (GB), Butcher's Films, b&w, 60 mins.
W: Patrick Holt (*Robert Langton*), Colette Wilde (*Marie Langton*), Bill Nagy (*Paul Conrad*), Mitzi Rogers (*Jacky Reed*), John Horsley (*Insp. Cameron*), Benny Lee (*Benny*), Marianne Stone (*Mrs. Cross*), Mark Singleton (*Anders*), Anthony Wager (*Sgt. Baker*)
P: John I. Phillips   **D:** Francis Searle   **STORY:** Paul Erickson
Standard crime-thriller: Executive seeks control of car company, frames ex-embezzler for murder

Night of the Red Hunter
1989, (New Zeal), TVNZ Ltd., Made for TV, color
W: Toni Driscoll, Toby Lainz, Perry Piercy, Lloyd Scott, Ilona Rodgers, Kate Harcourt, Bernard Kearns, Kerry Fox, Peter Hambleton, Peter Hawes, Henry Vaeoso, Rongo Do Kahu, Oeter Dennett, Peter Sledmere
PHOTOG: Martin Stewart
TVM, minor SF-adventure: Space-aliens attempt to return home

Night of the Scarecrow
1995, (USA), color
W: John Mese, Elizabeth Barondes

Night of the Seagulls
1975, (Sp), Big Apple, color
P: Jose Angel Santos
D & SCR: Armando De Ossorio
blurb: "Seven Nights, Seven Victims, Seven Human Hearts!"
Minor horror-fantasy (3rd sequel to '**Tombs of the Blind Dead**'): Re-animated Templars kill modern Spaniards*

The Night of the Silicates
see **Island of Terror**

Night of the Sorcerers
1970, (Sp), Avco Embassy, color, 75 mins.
W: Simon Andreu (*Rod Carter*), Kali Hansa (*Anika*), Lorena Tower, Maria Kosti, Jack Taylor, Joseph Thelman, Barbara King
D & SCR: Armando De Ossorio   **PHOTOG:** Fernando Sanchez   **MUSIC:** Fernando G. Morcillo
Minor horror-thriller: Voodoo, African vampire cult, "jiggle"

Night of the Spies
see **La Nuit des Espions**

Night of the Twisters
1996, (USA), Atlantis/FAM-TV, color, 95 mins.
W: John Schneider, Devon Sawa, Lori Hallier, Amos Crawley, David Ferry, Helen Hughes
D: Timothy Bond   **TELEPLAY:** Sam Graham & Chris Hubbell   **PHOTOG:** Peter Bennison
TVM, standard thriller: Tornadoes in small town

Night of the Werewolf
see **The Curse of the Werewolf**

Night of the Witches
1970, (USA), Medford, color, 78 mins
W: Keith Larsen
P: Keith Erik Burt & Vincent Forte   **D & SCR:** Keith Eric Burt (Keith Larsen)
Minor eroto-horror: Phony-preacher rapist tries to blackmail witch coven

Night of the Zombies
1981, (USA), Lorin E. Price-Evelyn Waxman/NMD Film Distrib., color, 85 mins.
W: Jamie Gillis (*Nick Monroe*), Ryan Hilliard (*Dr. Clarence Proud*), Ron Armstrong (*Capt. Fleck*), Shoshana Ascher (*The Prostitute*), Dick Carballo (*The Man in the Bar*), Alphonso DeNoble (*The CIA Agent*), Richard De Faut (*The Sgt.*), Lorin E. Price (*The Priest*), Joel M. Reed (*The Neo-Nazi*), Samantha Grey (*Susan*), John Barilla, Michael Casconi, Gordon C. Dixon, Juni Kulis, Bob Laconi, Charlene Matus, Lee Moore, Glen A. Pence, Renate Schlessinger, Kuno Sponholtz, Carl Woerner, Kai Wulff, Donald K. Wallace
WRIT & D: Joel M. Reed   **SPCL-FX:** Peter Kunz   **MUSIC & SOUNDS:** Onomatopoeia Inc., Matt Kaplowitz & Maggie Nolin
A.k.a. **Gamma 693**
Minor fantasy-thriller (with Bavarian locations): Living dead World War II soldiers haunt German mountains

Night of the Zombies
1983, (It-Sp), MPM, color, 95 mins.
W: Margit Evelyn Newton, Frank Garfield, Bernard Seray, Gaby Renom, Selan Karay
D: Vincent Dawn [Bruno Mattei]   **PHOTOG:** John Cabrera   **MUSIC:** Goblin
Minor SF-horror (Euro-answer to 'Dawn of the Dead'): Experiments to control world population result in cannibalistic corpses

Night Owl
1993, (USA), color
W: Jennifer Beals
Standard fantasy-thriller: Woman battles supernatural radio siren

The Night Porter
1974, (It), Robert Gordon Edwards/ESA DeSimone/Lotar/Joseph E. Levine/AVCO Embassy, color, 115 mins.
W: Dirk Bogarde (*Max*), Charlotte Rampling (*Lucia*), Isa Miranda (*Countess Stein*), Gabriele Ferzetti (*Hans*), Philippe Leroy (*Klaus*), Giuseppe Addobbati (*Stumm*), Nino Bignamini (*Adolph*), Marino Mase (*Atherton*), Geoffrey Copleston (*Kurt*), Amedeo Amodio (*Bert*), Piero Vida (*The Day Porter*), Manfred Freiberger (*Dobson*), Ugo Cardea (*Mario*), Piero Mazzinghi (*The Concierge*), Hilda Gunther (*Greta*), Kai S. Seefield (*Jacob*), Nora Ricci (*The Neighbor*)
D: Liliana Cavani   **SCR:** Liliana Cavani & Italo Moscati   **STORY:** Liliana Cavani, Barbara Alberti & Amedeo Pagani   **PHOTOG:** Alfio Contini   **MUSIC:** Daniele Paris
Unusual adult thriller: Former Nazi officer rekindles sado-erotic affair with Jewess

Night Plane to Amsterdam
1955, (GB), Merton Park/Anglo-Amalgamated, b&w, 31 mins.
W: Gerald Case (*Insp. Carron*), Shay Gorman (*The Sgt.*), Selma Vas Diaz (*Mme. Langer*), Andrea Malandrinos (*Pierce*), Guy Deghy (*Capt. Haas*)
P: Alec Snowden   **D:** Ken Hughes   **STORY:** James Eastwood, from a novel by Edgar Lustgarten
Standard short crime-thriller: Diamond robbery traced to woman fence

Night Rhythms
1992, (USA), color, 85 mins.
W: Martin Hewett, Delia Sheppard, David Carradine, Deborah Driggs, Terry Tweed, Sam Jones, Julie Strain
D: Alexander Gregory Hippolyte
Minor thriller: Radio talk-show host suspected of murder

Night Ripper
1986, (USA), color, 88 mins.
<u>W</u>: James Hansen, April Anne, Larry Thomas
<u>D</u>: Jeff Hathcock
Minor thriller: Psycho slays high-fashion models

Night School
1981, (USA), Resource/Lorima/Parr, color, 80 mins.
<u>W</u>: Leonard Mann, Rachel Ward, Drew Snyder Joseph R. Sicari
<u>D</u>: Kenneth Hughes   <u>SCR</u>: Ruth Avergon   <u>PHOTOG</u>: Mark Irwin   <u>MUSIC</u>:
    Brad Fiedel
A.k.a. **Terror Eyes**
Standard thriller: Mysterious killer decapitates women

Nightscream
1997, (USA), NBC-TV, color, 95 mins.
<u>W</u>: Teri Garr (*Julie Ordwell*), Candace Cameron-Bure (*Drew/Laura*), Casper Van
    Dien (*Teddie/Ray Jr.*), Denis Arndt (*Ray Ordwell*), Bobby Hosea (*Sheriff R.J.
    Turnage*), Ned Vaughn (*Charles Pendekton*), Marie Stillin (*Maggie Johnson*)
<u>D</u>: Noel Nosseck
TVM, standard thriller: Woman possessed by spirit of murder victim

Night Screams
1987, (USA), color, 85 mins.
<u>W</u>: Joe Manno, Ron Thomas, Randy Lundsford, Megan Wyss
<u>D</u>: Allen Plone
Minor thriller: Murders of escaped convicts and partying teens

Night Shadow
1990, (USA), color, 90 mins.
<u>W</u>: Brenda Vance, Dana Chan, Tom Boylan
<u>D & SCR</u>: Randolph Cohlan
Minor thriller: Hitchhiker suspected of serial killings

Night Shadows
see **Mutant**

Night Slasher
1984, (GB), color, 87 mins.
<u>W</u>: Jack May, Linda Marlowe
Minor thriller: Madman disembowels London prostitutes

Nights in a Harem
see **Son of Sinbad**

Night Slaves
1970, (USA), Bing Crosby Prods./WB/NBC-TV, color, 74 mins.
<u>W</u>: James Franciscus, Lee Grant, Leslie Nielsen, Scott Marlowe, Tisha Sterling,
    Andrew Prine, Morris Buchanan, John Kellogg, Virginia Vincent, Cliff
    Carnell, Nancy Valentine, Victor Izay, Raymond Mayo, Russell Thorson
<u>P</u>: Everett Chambers   <u>D</u>: Ted Post   <u>TELEPLAY</u>: Robert B. Hauser   <u>SPCL-FX</u>:
    James L. Klinger   <u>MUSIC</u>: Bernardo Segall
TVM, standard SF-thriller: Space aliens use mental powers, force humans to labor for them

The Nights of Dracula
see **Count Dracula**

The Nights of Lucretia Borgia
1961, (It), Col, color, 108 mins.
<u>W</u>: Belinda Lee, Jacques Sernas, Michele Mercier, Arnoldo Foa
<u>D</u>: Sergio Grieco   <u>SCR</u>: Mario Caiano & Aldo Segri   <u>PHOTOG</u>: Massimo
    Dallamano   <u>MUSIC</u>: Alexander Derevitsy
Standard costume-thriller: Intrigue in Italian dukedom

Nights of Rasputin
1960, (It-Fr), Brigadier, color, 95 mins.
<u>W</u>: Edmund Purdom (*Rasputin*), Gianna Maria Canale (*Czarina Alexandra*), John
    Drew Barrymore (*Prince Yousoupoff*)
<u>P</u>: Vincent Forte   <u>D</u>: Pierre Chenal   <u>SCR</u>: Ugo Liberatore, Pierre Chenal &
    Andre Tabet Jany Clair
A.k.a. **The Night They Killed Rasputin**
Standard history-thriller: Aristocrat plots assassination of mad monk

Nights of the Wolf Man
see **Las Noches del Hombre Lobo**

The Night Stalker
1971, (USA), Aaron Spelling/ABC-TV, color, 73 mins.
<u>W</u>: Darren McGavin (*Carl Kolchak*), Claude Akins (*Sheriff Butcher*), Carol Lynley
    (*Gail Foster*), Barry Atwater (*Janos Skorzeny*), Charles McGraw (*Chief
    Masterson*), Simon Oakland (*Vincenzo*), Ralph Meeker (*Bernie Jenks*), Kent
    Smith (*D.A. Paine*), Larry Linville (*Makurji*), Elisha Cook Jr. (*Mickey
    Crawford*), Jordan Rhodes (*Dr. O'Brien*), Stanley Adams (*Fred Hurley*),
    Virginia Gregg
<u>P</u>: Dan Curtis   <u>D</u>: John Llewellyn Moxey   <u>TELEPLAY</u>: Richard Matheson,
    from an unpublished story by Jeff Rice   <u>PHOTOG</u>: Michel Hugo
    <u>MUSIC</u>: Robert Cobert
TVM, standard horror-thriller: Reporter tracks vampire. cf. **Crackle of Death** *and* **The
    Night Strangler**

Nightstalker
1979, (USA), color, 90 mins.
<u>W</u>: Aldo Ray
Minor horror-fantasy: Brother and sister eat virgins to deter ancient death curse

The Nightstalker: DARREN MCGAVIN

The Night Stalker
1987, (USA), Silver Production Corp./Almi, color, 91 mins.
<u>W</u>: Charles Napier, Michelle Reese, Katherine Kelly Lang, Robert Z'dar, Joey
    Gian, Leila Carlin, Gary Crosby, Robert Viharo
<u>D</u>: Max Kleven   <u>SCR</u>: John Goff & Don Edmonds   <u>PHOTOG</u>: Don Burgess
    <u>MUSIC SPRVSR</u>: Steve Tyrell
Minor horror-thriller: Detective hunts supernatural killer

Night Star, Goddess of Electra
see **Roma Contra Roma**

The Night Strangler
1972, (USA), Aaron Spelling/ABC Circle Film, color, 74 mins.
<u>W</u>: Darren McGavin (*Carl Kolchak*), Jo Ann Pflug, Simon Oakland, Scott Brady,
    George Tobias, Wally Cox, Kate Murtagh, Margaret Hamilton, Richard
    Anderson, John Carradine, Nina Wayne, Wilma Peters, Ivor Francis
<u>P & D</u>: Dan Curtis   <u>SCR</u>: Richard Matheson, from characters created by Jeff
    Rice   <u>SPCL-FX</u>: Ira Anderson   <u>MUSIC</u>: Robert Cobert
A.k.a. **The Time Killer**
*TVM, standard fantasy-thriller (semi-sequel to 'The Night Stalker' {1971}): Strange
    murders lead reporter to buried city under Seattle, Washington cf.* **Crackle of Death**

The Night That Panicked America
1975, (USA), ABC-TV, color, 100 mins.
<u>W</u>: Vic Morrow (*Hank Muldoon*), Paul Shenar (*Orson Welles*), Will Geer (*Rev.
    Davis*), Meredith Baxter (*Linda Davis*), Tom Bosley (*Norman Smith*), John
    Ritter (*Walter Wingate*), Cliff De Young (*Stefan Grubowski*), Eileen Brennan
    (*Ann Muldoon*), Michael Constantine (*Jess Wingate*), Walter McGinn (*Paul
    Stewart*), Shelley Morrison
<u>D</u>: Joseph Sargent   <u>TELEPLAY</u>: Nicholas Meyer & Anthony Wilson
orig. to be titled **The Night the Martians Landed**
*TVM, standard thriller: Recreation of events surrounding Orson Welles' 1938 radio-
    broadcast of H.G. Wells'* **The War of the Worlds**

The Night the Martians Landed
see **The Night That Panicked America**

The Night the Silicates Came
see **Island of Terror**

The Night the World Exploded
1957, (USA), Clover/Col, b&w, 65 mins.
<u>W</u>: William Leslie, Kathryn Grant, Tris Coffin, Marshall Reed, Raymond
    Greenleaf, Charles Evans, Frank Scannell, Fred Coby, Paul Savage, Terry
    Frost

P: Sam Katzman   D: Fred F. Sears   SCR: Jack Natteford & Luci Ward
   PHOTOG: Benjamin H. Kline   MUSIC: Ross Di Maggio
blurb: "Nature goes mad!"
Standard SF-thriller: Explosive cave rocks threaten Earth

The Night They Killed Rasputin
see Nights of Rasputin

The Night They Saved Christmas
1984, (USA), Robert Halmi/ABC-TV, color, 95 mins.
W: Art Carney (*Santa Claus*), Jaclyn Smith (*Claudia*), Paul Williams (*Ed*), Paul
   LeMat (*Michael*), Mason Adams (*Sumner*), R.J. Williams (*C.B.*), Scott
   Grimes (*David*), June Lockhart (*Mrs. Claus*), Laura Jacoby (*Marianne*),
   Buddy Douglas (*Dr. Fernando*), James Staley (*Marin*), Anne Haney (*Hedda*),
   Albert Hall (*Loomis*), Billy Curtis (*Jack*), Randy Crosby (*The Pilot*), Michael
   Keys-Hall (*Faulkner*)
D: Jackie Cooper   TELEPLAY: Jim Moloney & David Niven Jr.   STORY: Jim
   Moloney, Rudy Dochtermann & David Niven Jr.   PHOTOG: David Worth
   SPCL-FX: Richard Wood, Peter Chesney & Michael Manzel   MUSIC:
   Charles Gross   LYRICS: Paul Williams
TVM, standard juvenile fantasy: Young wife and her children aid Saint Nick

Night Tide
1961, (USA), Virgo/AIP, b&w, 84 mins, also 95 mins.
W: Dennis Hopper, Linda Lawson, Luana Anders, Gavin Muir, Marjorie Eaton,
   Dave Scott, Tom Dillon, H.E. West, Bruno Ve Sota, Ben Roseman, Cameron
P: Aram Kantarian   WRIT & D: Curtis Harrington   PHOTOG: Vilis
   Lapenieks   SONGS: *The Tell-Tale Harp & Seaweed*
orig. co-billed with The Raven (1963)
Critically-acclaimed fantasy (filmed in 1961): Young sailor drawn to girl who works as
"mermaid" in boardwalk side show

Night Train for Inverness
1959, (GB), Danziger/Para, b&w, 69 mins.
W: Norman Wooland (*Roy Lewis*), Jane Hylton (*Marion*), Denis Waterman (*Ted
   Lewis*), Sylvia Francis (*Ann Lewis*), Valentine Dyall (*Ken*), Irene Arnold (*Mrs.
   Wall*), Colin Tapley (*Jackson*), Howard Lang (*The Sgt.*)
P: Edward J. & Harry Lee Danziger   D: Ernest Morris   STORY: Mark
   Grantham
Standard thriller: Ex-embezzler abducts son without knowing he is diabetic

Night Train to Munich
1940, (GB), 20th Century Prods./MGM, b&w, 95 mins.
W: Margaret Lockwood (*Anna Bomasch*), Rex Harrison (*Gus Bennett*), Paul Von
   Hernried (*Karl Marsen*), Basil Radford (*Charters*), Naunton Wayne
   (*Caldicott*), James Harcourt (*Axel Bomasch*), Felix Aylmer (*John Fredericks*),
   Roland Culver (*Roberts*), Eliot Makeham (*Schwab*), Austin Trevor (*Capt.
   Prada*), Raymond Huntley (*Lt. Kampenfeldt*), Keneth Kent (*Strata*), C.V.
   France (*Adm. Hassinger*), Wally Patch (*The Fisherman*), Frederick Valk (*The
   Officer*), Morland Graham (*The Attendant*), Irene Handl (*The Station-Master*),
   Albert Lieven (*The Guard*), David Horne (*The Minister*), Billy Russell (*Adolf
   Hitler*)
D: Carol Reed   SCR: Frank Launder & Sidney Gilliat, from a novel by Gordon
   Wellesley
USA retitle, Night Train, A.k.a. Gestapo, reissued 1948
Standard thriller: British agent poses as Nazi, rescues Czech inventor

Night Train to Paris
1964, (GB), Lippert/20th-Fox, b&w, 64 mins.
W: Leslie Nielsen (*Alan Holiday*), Aliza Gur (*Catherine Carrel*), Dorinda Stevens
   (*Olive Davies*), Eric Pohlmann (*Krogh*), Edina Ronay (*Julie*), Andre Maranne
   (*Louis Vernay*), Cyril Raymond (*Insp. Fleming*), Hugh Latimer (*Jules Lemoine*)
P: Robert L. Lippert & Jack Parsons   D: Robert Douglas   SCR: Henry Cross
Standard crime-thriller: Ex-OSS agent saves tape recording from spies

Night Unto Night
1947, (USA), WB, b&w, 85mins.
W: Ronald Reagan, Viveca Lindfors, Broderick Crawford, Craig Stevens,
   Rosemary DeCamp Osa Massen, Art Baker
P: Owen Crump   D: Don Siegel   SCR: Kathryn Scola
Unusual melodrama: Doomed epileptic scientist loves mentally-ill woman who sees ghosts

Night Vision
1987, (USA), color, 102 mins.
W: Ellie Martins, Stacy Carson, Shirley Ross, Tony Carpenter
D: Michael Krueger
Minor fantasy-thriller: Writer receives video monitor that reveals future

Night Visions
1990, (USA), MGM-UA/NBC-TV, color, 95 mins.
W: Loryn Locklin (*Dr. Sally Powers*), James Remar (*Tom Mackie*), Jon Tenney
   (*Martin*), Mitch Pileggi (*Keller*), Francis X. McCarthy (*Dowd*), Penny
   Johnson (*Luanne*), Angela Alvarado (*Aura*), Bruce MacVittie (*Stark*), Mark
   Lindsay Chapman (*The Famous Actor*), Daniel Beer (*The Rocker*), Kirsten
   Corbett (*Young Sally*), Jessica Craven (*Woman #1*), Ron Howard George (*The
   Killer Ghost*), Timothy Leary (*The New Age Minister*), John Benjamin Martin
   (*Higgins*), Roxanna Michaels (*Alene*), Eric Rosse (*Ray Burgess*), Michele Roth
   (*The TV Reporter*), Dendrie Taylor (*The Palm Reader*), Bruce Wagner (*The*

Agent)
D: Wes Craven   TELEPLAY: Wes Craven & Thomas Baum   PHOTOG: Peter
   Stein   MUSIC: Brad Fiedel
TVM, standard thriller: Psychic tracks killer

The Night Visitor
1970, (Swed), Hemisphere/UMC, color, 102 mins.
W: Max von Sydow (*Salem*), Trevor Howard (*The Inspector*), Liv Ullmann (*Ester
   Jenks*), Andrew Keir (*Dr. Kemp*), Per Oscarsson (*Dr. Anton Jenks*), Rupert
   Davies (*Clemens*), Arthur Hewlett (*Pop*), Jim Kennedy (*Carl*), Hanne Bork
   (*Emmie*), Bjorn Watt Boolsen (*Tokens*), Lottie Freddie (*Britt*)
P: Mel Ferrer   D: Laslo Benedek   SCR: Guy Elmes   PHOTOG: Henning
   Kristiansen   MUSIC: Henry Mancini
Unusual thriller: Imprisoned man gains revenge

Night Visitors
1996, (USA), NBC-TV, color, 95 mins.
W: Faith Ford, Thomas Gibson, Stephen Tobolowsky, Charles S. Dutton, Todd
   Allen, Eric McCormack, Christopher Gray, Claire Riley, Roman Podhora
D: Jorge Montesi   TELEPLAY: D. Brent Mote   PHOTOG: Philip Linzey
   MUSIC: Irwin Fisch
TVM, minor SF-thriller: Gov't coverup of space aliens

Night Walk
see Deathdream

The Night Walker
1964, (USA), Univ, b&w, 86 mins.
W: Barbara Stanwyck (*Irene Trent*), Robert Taylor (*Barry Morland*), Lloyd Bochner
   ("*The Dream*"), Judith Meredith (*Joyce Holliday*), Hayden Rorke (*Howard
   Trent*), Rochelle Hudson (*Hilda*), Tetsu Komai (*The Gardener*), Jess Barker
   (*Frank Malone*), Marjorie Bennett (*The Manager*), Kathleen Mulqueen (*The
   Customer*), Paulle Clark (*Pat*), Teddy Durant (*The Narrator*)
P & D: William Castle   SCR: Robert Bloch   PHOTOG: Harold E. Stine
   MUSIC: Vic Mizzy   MUSIC DIR: Joseph Gershenson
orig. to be titled The Dream Killer
*Clever thriller (Wry pairing of divorced stars Stanwyck & Taylor): Woman fears haunting
   by dead husband*

Night Warning
see Butcher, Baker (Nightmare Maker)

Night Was Our Friend
1951, (GB), ACT/Monarch, b&w, 61 mins.
W: Elizabeth Sellars (*Sally Raynor*), Michael Gough (*Martin Raynor*), Ronald
   Howard (*Dr. John Harper*), Marie Ney (*Emily Raynor*), Edward Lexy (*Arthur
   Glenville*), John Salew (*Mr. Lloyd*), Nora Gordon (*Kate*), Cyril Smith (*The
   Reporter*), Michael Pertwee (*The Young Man*)
D: Michael Anderson   SCR: Michael Pertwee, from his play
Standard crime-thriller

The Night Watch (1959)
see Le Trou

Night Watch
1973, (GB), Brut/Joseph E. Levine/Avco Embassy, color, 105 mins.
W: Elizabeth Taylor (*Ellen Wheeler*), Laurence Harvey (*John Wheeler*), Billie
   Whitelaw (*Sarah Cooke*), Robert Lang (*Appleby*), Tony Britton (*Tony*), Bill
   Dean (*Insp. Walker*), Michael Danvers-Walker (*Sgt. Norris*), Pauline Jameson
   (*The Sec'y*), Rosario Serrano (*Dolores*), Linda Hayden (*The Girl in the Car*),
   Kevin Colson (*Carl*), Laon Maybanke (*The Florist*)
P: Martin Poll, George W. George & Bernard Straus   D: Brian G. Hutton   SCR:
   Tony Williamson, from a play by Lucille Fletcher   PHOTOG: Billy
   Williams   MUSIC: John Cameron   SONG: *The Night Has Many Eyes*
Standard thriller: Woman thinks she sees murder committed

Nightwatch
1998, (USA), Dimension, color
W: Nick Nolte, Patricia Arquette, Ewan McGregor, Josh Brolin
SCR: Steven Soderbergh
Standard thriller

Nightwing
1979, (USA), Martin Ransohoff-Arthur Hiller/Col, color, 105 mins.
W: Nick Mancuso (*Duran*), Kathryn Harrold (*Anne*), David Warner (*Philip*),
   Stephen Macht (*Chee*), Donald Hotton (*John*), Strother Martin (*Selwyn*),
   George Clutesi (*Abner*), Charles Hallahan (*Henry*), Ben Piazza (*Roger*), Judith
   Novgrod (*Judy*), Alice Hirson (*Claire*), Pat Corley (*The Vet*), Charlie Bird
   (*Beejay*), Danny Zapien (*Joe*), Peter Prouse (*The Doctor*), Jose Toledo
   (*Harold*), Richard Romancito (*Ben*), Flavio Martinez III (*Isla*), Lena Carr,
   Virginia P. Maney, Glynn Rubin, Wade Stevens, Robert Dunbar, John R.
   Leonard Sr., James Arnett, Gary Epper, Craig Baxley
P: Martin Ransohoff   D: Arthur Hiller   SCR: Steve Shagan, Bud Shrake &
   Martin Cruz Smith, from Martin Cruz Smith's novel   PHOTOG: Charles
   Rosher   MUSIC: Henry Mancini
Standard thriller: Rabid vampire bats harass Indian reservation

Nightwish
1989, (USA), color, 96 mins.

<u>W</u>: Alisha Das, Jack Starrett, Elizabeth Kaitan, Clayton Rohner, Arthur Cybulski, Robert Tessier, Brian Thompson
<u>D</u>: Bruce R. Cook
Minor horror-fantasy: Parapsychology professor and students probe old desert house

Night Without Pity
1962, (GB), Parroch/GEF, b&w, 56 mins.
<u>W</u>: Sarah Lawson *(Diana Martin)*, Neil McCallum *(O'Brien)*, Alan Edwards *(Randall)*, Michael Browning *(Philip)*, Dorinda Stevens *(The Girl Friend)*, Patrick Newell *(The Doctor)*, Beatrice Varley *(Mother)*, John Moulder-Brown *(Geoffrey Martin)*, Brian Weske *(Arthur)*, Vanda Godsell
<u>P</u>: Jack Parsons   <u>D</u>: Theodore Zichy   <u>STORY</u>: Aubrey Cash
Standard crime-thriller: Crook holds woman and child hostage

Night without Stars
1951, (GB), Europa/GFD, b&w, 86 mins.
<u>W</u>: David Farrar *(Giles Gordon)*, Nadia Gray *(Alix Delaisse)*, Maurice Teynac *(Louis Malinay)*, Giles Queyant *(Deffond)*, Gerard Landry *(Pierre Cheval)*, June Clyde *(Claire)*, Clive Morton *(Dr. Carlson)*, Robert Ayres *(Walter)*, Martin Benson *(The White Cap)*, Eugene Deckers *(Armand)*
<u>P</u>: Hugh Stewart   <u>D</u>: Anthony Pelissier   <u>SCR</u>: Winston Graham, from his novel
Standard thriller: Blind lawyer solves traitor's death

The Night Won't Talk
1952, (GB), Corsair/ABP, b&w, 60 mins.
<u>W</u>: Hy Hazell *(Theo Castle)*, John Bailey *(Clayton Hawkins)*, Mary Germaine *(Hazel Carr)*, Ballard Berkeley *(Insp. West)*, Elwyn Brook-Jones *(Martin Soames)*, Grey Blake *(Kenneth Wills)*, Duncan Lamont *(Sgt. Robbins)*, Sarah Lawson *(Susan)*
<u>P</u>: Harold Richmond   <u>D</u>: Daniel Birt   <u>SCR</u>: Brock Wiliams   <u>STORY</u>: Roger Burford
Standard crime-thriller: Three suspects in murder of Chelsea model

Nikita
see La Femme Nikita

Nine Days in One Year
see Devyat'dney Odnogo Goda

984: Prisioner of the Future
1984, (USA), color, 70 mins.
<u>W</u>: Don Francks, Stephen Markle
<u>D</u>: Tibor Takacs
A.k.a. The Tomorrow Man
Taut SF-thriller: Futuristic tale of human self-destruction

Nine Lives Are Not Enough
1941, (USA), WB, b&w, 63 mins.
<u>W</u>: Ronald Reagan, Joan Perry, James Gleason, Faye Emerson, Peter Whitney, Howard da Silva, Edward Brophy, Charles Drake
<u>D</u>: A. Edward Sutherland
Fast-paced melodrama: Newspaperman solves murder

The Nine Lives of Fritz the Cat
1974, (USA), AIP, color, 76 mins.
<u>VOICES</u>: Skip Hinnant, Reva Rose, Bob Holt, Robert Ridgely, Pat Harrington
<u>D</u>: Robert Taylor, from characters created by Robert Crumb
Standard animated fantasy (sequel to Fritz the Cat): Stoned cat becomes vagrant

976-Evil
1989, (USA), Cinetel, color, 100 mins.
<u>W</u>: Stephen Geoffreys *(Hoax)*, Patrick O'Bryan *(Spike)*, Sandy Dennis *(Aunt Lucy)*, Jim Metzler *(Marty)*, Maria Rubell *(Angella)*, Lezlie Deane *(Suzie)*, J.J. Cohen *(Marcus)*, Joanna Keyes *(Suzie's Mother)*, Paul Willson *(Mr. Michaels)*, Darren Burrows *(Jeff)*, Greg Collins *(Mr. Selby)*, Jon Slade *(John Doe)*, Gunther Jensen *(Airhead)*, J.J. Johnston *(Virgil)*, Don Bajema *(The Deputy)*, Demetre Phillips *(Sgt. Bell)*, Roxanne Rogers *(The Waitress)*, Jim Thiebaud *(Rags)*, Wendy Cooke *(The Gang Girl)*, Thom McFadden *(The Minister)*, Larry Turk *(Operator #1)*, Cynthia Szigeti *(The Female Operator)*, Christopher Metas *(The Cashier)*, Bert Hinchman *(The Coroner)*, Nan Dorsey *(Paramedic #1)*, Jim Landis *(Paramedic #2)*, Ed Cornett *(Santa Claus)*, Quigley *(Aunt Lucy's Parrot)*, Mindy Seeger
<u>D</u>: Robert Englund   <u>SCR</u>: Rhet Topham & Brian Helgeland   <u>PHOTOG</u>: Paul Elliot   <u>MUSIC</u>: Thomas Chase & Steve Rucker
Standard horror-fantasy: Telephone "horrorscope" inspires mayhem

976-Evil II: The Astral Factor
1991, (USA), color, 93 mins.
<u>W</u>: Patrick O'Bryan, Rene Assa, Debbie James
Minor horror-fantasy: Biker tries to deter murderous phone caller

1984
1955, (GB), A.B.P.C./Holiday/Col, b&w, 91 mins.
<u>W</u>: Edmond O'Brien *(Winston Smith)*, Jan Sterling *(Julia)*, Michael Redgrave *(O'Connor)*, David Kossoff *(Charrington)*, Mervyn Johns *(Jones)*, Donald Pleasence *(Parsons)*, Ernest Clark *(The Announcer)*, Carol Wolveridge *(Selina Parsons)*, Ronan O'Casey *(Rutherford)*, Kenneth Griffith *(The Prisoner)*, Patrick Allen, Ewen Solon, Michael Ripper
<u>P</u>: N. Peter Rathvon   <u>D</u>: Michael Anderson   <u>SCR</u>: William P. Templeton &

Ralph Bettinson, from George Orwell's novel   <u>PHOTOG</u>: C. Pennington-Richards   <u>MUSIC</u>: Louis Levy
Standard thriller: Repression in totalitarian future

1984
1984, (GB), Virgin/Atlantic, color, 110 mins.
<u>W</u>: John Hurt *(Winston Smith)*, Richard Burton *(O'Brien)*, Suzanna Hamilton *(Julia)*, Cyril Cusack *(Charrington)*, Gregor Fisher *(Parsons)*, James Walker *(Syme)*, Andrew Wilde *(Tillotson)*, Pam Gems *(The Washerwoman)*, David Trevena *(Friend)*, David Cann *(Martin)*, Anthony Benson *(Jones)*, Peter Frye *(Rutherford)*, Phyllis Logan *(The Announcer)*, Joscik Barbarossa *(Aaronson)*, John Boswall *(Emmanuel Goldstein)*, Roger Lloyd-Pack *(The Waiter)*, P.J. Nicholas *(William Parsons)*, Lynne Radford *(Susan Parsons)*, Bob Flag *(Big Brother)*, Shirley Stelfox *(The Whore)*
<u>P</u>: Simon Perry, Al Clark & Robert Devereux   <u>D & SCR</u>: Michael Radford, from George Orwell's novel   <u>PHOTOG</u>: Roger Deakins   <u>MUSIC</u>: Eurythmics & Dominic Muldowney
Superior film-version of literary classic (Richard Burton's last theatrical film): Man rebels against future dystopia

99 and 44/100% Dead
1974, (USA), 20th-Fox, color, 98 mins.
<u>W</u>: Richard Harris, Bradford Dillman, Edmond O'Brien, Ann Turkel, Chuck Connors
<u>P</u>: Joe Wizan   <u>D</u>: John Frankenheimer   <u>SCR</u>: Robert Dillon
Standard thriller: Future gangland warfare

99 River Street
1953, (USA), UA, b&w, 83 mins.
<u>W</u>: John Payne
<u>D</u>: Phil Karlson   <u>PHOTOG</u>: Franz Planer
Standard melodrama

99 Women
see Island of Despair

Noah's Ark
1999, (USA), NBC-TV, color
<u>W</u>: Jon Voight, Mary Steenburgen, James Coburn
TVM, standard religious fantasy: Flood destroys world

No Blade of Grass
1970, (GB), Symbol/MGM, color, 97 mins.
<u>W</u>: Nigel Davenport *(John Custance)*, Jean Wallace *(Ann Custance)*, Patrick Holt *(David Custance)*, John Hamill *(Roger Burnham)*, Lynne Frederick *(Mary Custance)*, Wendy Richard *(Clara)*, Anthony May *(Pirrie)*, Nigel Rathbone *(Davey)*, Ruth Kettlewell *(The Fat Woman)*, M.J. Matthews *(George)*, Michael Percival *(The Police Constable)*, Tex Fuller *(Mr. Beaseley)*, Simon Merrick *(The TV Interviewer, Fred Gray)*, John Lewis *(The Corporal)*, Anthony Sharp *(Sir Charles Brenner)*, George Coulouris *(Mr. Sturdevant)*, Max Hartnell *(The Lieutenant)*, Norman Atkyns *(Dr. Cassop)*, Christopher Lofthouse *(Spooks)*, John Avison *(The Yorkshire Sergeant)*, Jimmy Winston *(The 1st Hun)*, Richard Penny *(The 2nd Hun)*, R.C. Driscoll *(The 3rd Hun)*, Geoffrey Hooper *(Tweed Jacket)*, Christopher Wilson *(The Farmer)*, William Duffy *(The Murdered Farmer)*, Mervyn Patrick *(Joe Ashton)*, Denise Mockler *(Emily Ashton)*, Ross Allan *(Alf Parsons)*, Karen Terry *(Parson's Daughter)*, Joan Ward *(Mrs. Parsons)*, Brian Crabtree *(Joe Harris)*, Susan Sydney *(Liz Harris)*, Michael Landy *(Jess Arkwright)*, Louise Kay *(Susan Arkwright)*, Bruce Myers *(Bill Riggs)*, Margaret Chapman *(Prudence Riggs)*, Christopher Neame *(Locke)*, Derek Keller *(Mrs. Scott)*, Suzanne Pinkstone *(Jill Locke)*, Bridget Brice *(Jill Locke)*, Reg Staniford *(Mr. Blennit)*, Maureen Rutter *(Mrs. Blennit)*, Surgit Sood *(Surgit)*, Dick Offord *(Joe)*, Joanna Annin *(Joe's Wife)*, John Buckley *(The Captain)*, Malcolm Toes *(The Sgt. Maj.)*
<u>P & D</u>: Cornel Wilde   <u>SCR</u>: Sean Forestal & Jefferson Pascal, from John Christopher's novel   <u>PHOTOG</u>: H.A.R. Thompson   <u>MUSIC</u>: Burnell Whibley
Standard SF-thriller: Earth's deforestation provides "future shock"

The Noble Bachelor
1921, (GB), Stoll, b&w, 2,100 ft. (640.1m)
<u>W</u>: Eille Norwood *(Sherlock Holmes)*, Hubert Willis *(Dr. John Watson)*, Arthur Bell *(Insp. Lestrade)*, Cyril Percival *(Simon)*, Temple Bell *(Hetty Doran)*, Fred Earle *(Moulton)*, Mme. d'Esterre *(Mrs. Hudson)*
<u>D</u>: Maurice Elvey   <u>SCR</u>: William J. Elliott, from the writings of Sir Arthur Conan Doyle
Standard crime-thriller (episode in "Adventures of Sherlock Holmes" series)

A Noble Outcast
1910, (GB), Cricks & Martin, b&w, 600 ft. (182.9m)
<u>D</u>: A.E. Coleby
Standard crime-thriller: Tramp foils burglars' plans

Noblesse Oblige
see Kind Hearts and Coronets

Nobody Runs Forever
1968, (GB), Selmur-Rank/RFD, color, 101 mins.
<u>W</u>: Rod Taylor *(Scobie Malone)*, Christopher Plummer *(Sir James Quentin)*, Lilli

Palmer (*Sheila Quentin*), Camilla Sparv (*Lisa Pretorius*), Daliah Lavi (*Maria Cholon*), Franchot Tone (*Ambassador Townsend*), Clive Revill (*Joseph*), Calvin Lockhart (*Jamaica*), Leo McKern (*Premier of NSW*), Charles Tingwell (*Jackaroo*), Derren Nesbitt (*Pallain*), Lee Montague (*Denzil*), Russell Napier (*Leeds*), Edric Connor (*Julius*)
P: Selig J. Seligman & Betty E. Box   **D:** Ralph Thomas   **SCR:** Wilfred Greatorex, from Jon Cleary's novel *Commissioner*   **MUSIC:** Georges Delerue
Standard crime-thriller: Australian detective unmasks killer

La Noche de Walpurgis (Walpurgis Night)
1970, (Sp-W. Ger), Plata Films/Ellman Enterprises, color, 82 mins.
W: Paul Naschy, Gaby Fuchs, Patty Shepard, Barbara Capell Valerie Samarine, Julio Pena, Andres Resino
D: Leon Klimovsky   **SCR:** Jacinto Molina & Hans Munkell
USA retitle (1972), **The Werewolf vs. the Vampire Woman.** *A.k.a.* **Blood Moon** *and* **Shadow of the Werewolf**
Standard horror-fantasy: Lycanthrope joins two female students on search for witch's tomb

Las Noches del Hombre Lobo (Nights of the Wolf Man)
1968, (Sp), Plata Films, color
W: Paul Naschy
D: Rene Govar   **SCR:** Jacinto Molina, Rene Govar & C. Belard
Standard horror-fantasy (sequel to **La Marca del Hombre Lobo***): Lycanthrope fights mad scientist*

Nocturna, Granddaughter of Dracula
1979, (USA), Compass Int'l, color, 83 mins.
W: Nai Bonet, John Carradine, Yvonne DeCarlo, Brother Theodore
Minor horror-comedy: Vampire follows runaway granddaughter to Manhattan

Nocturne
1946, (USA), RKO, b&w, 88 mins.
W: George Raft, Lynn Bari, Virginia Huston, Myrna Dell, Joseph Pevney, Edward Ashley, Walter Sande, Mabel Paige
D: Edwin L. Marin   **SCR:** Jonathan Latimer
Taut thriller: Suspended cop probes supposed suicide

Noddy in Toyland
1958, (GB), Luckwell, color, 87 mins.
W: Colin Spaull (*Noddy*), Gloria Johnson (*Silky*), Leslie Sarony (*Mr. Pinkwhistle*), Peter Elliott (*PC Plod*)
P: Kay Luckwell   **D:** Maclean Rogers, from a play by Enid Blyton
Standard juvenile fantasy: Toyland boy blamed for crimes of Red Goblins

No Escape
1934, (GB), First Nat'l/WB, b&w, 70 mins.
W: Binnie Barnes (*Myra Fengler*), Ralph Ince (*Lucky*), Ian Hunter (*Jim Brandon*), Molly Lamont (*Helen Arnold*), Charles Carson (*Mr. Arnold*), Philip Strange (*Kirk Fengler*), George Merritt (*Insp. Matheson*), Madeleine Seymour (*Mrs. Arnold*)
D: Ralph Ince   **STORY:** W. Scott Darling
Standard thriller: Malaya planter framed for poisoning partner

No Escape
1994, (USA), Pacific Western/Savoy, color, 110 mins.
W: Ray Liotta (*Robbins*), Lance Henriksen (*Father*), Stuart Wilson (*Marek*), Michael Lerner, Kevin Dillon, Ernie Hudson, Kevin J. O'Connor, Don Henderson, Ian McNeice, Jack Shepherd, Brian M. Logan
P: Gale Anne Hurd   **D:** Martin Campbell   **SCR:** Michael Gaylin & Joel Gross, based on Richard Herley's novel *The Penal Colony*   **PHOTOG:** Phil Meheux   **MUSIC:** Graeme Revell
Standard SF-thriller: Unrest on future prison island

No Exit
1962, (USA-Arg.), Zenith, b&w, 85 mins.
W: Viveca Lindfors (*Inez*), Rita Gam (*Estelle*), Ben Piazza (*Camarero*), Morgan Sterne (*Garcin*), Susana Mayo (*Florence*), Orlando Sacha (*Gomez*), Manuel Roson (*Capitan*), Elsa Dorian (*Shirley*), Mirtha Miller (*Carmencita*), Miguel A. Irarte (*Robert*), Mario Horna (*Albert*), Carlos Brown (*Roger Delaney III*)
P: Fernando Ayala & Hector Olivera   **D:** Tad Danielewski   **SCR:** George Tabori, from Jean-Paul Sartre's play   **MUSIC:** Vladimir Ussachevsky
Existentialist fantasy-thriller: Five people await Eternity in bleak anteroom to hell

No Haunt for a Gentleman
1952, (GB), Anglo-Scottish/Apex, b&w, 58 mins.
W: Anthony Pendrell (*John Northwick*), Sally Newton (*Miriam Northwick*), Jack McNaughton (*FitzCholmondley*), Patience Rentoul (*Mother*), Dorothy Summers (*Mrs. Mallett*), Peter Swanwick (*Brother Ravioli*), Rufus Cruickshank (*Angus McDingle*), Barbara Shaw (*Lady Madeline de Boudoir*), Hattie Jacques (*Mrs. FitzCholmondley*), Joan Hickson (*Mme. Omskaya*), Joan Sterndale-Bennett (*Mother Skipton*)
P: Charles Reynolds   **D:** Leonard Reeve   **SCR:** Julian Caunter, Gerard Bryant & Leonard Reeve   **STORY:** Frederick Allwood
Standard fantasy: Ghost helps newlyweds frighten away mother-in-law

No Highway in the Sky
1951, (GB), 20th-Fox, b&w, 98 mins.
W: James Stewart (*Theodore Honey*), Marlene Dietrich (*Monica Teasdale*), Glynis Johns (*Marjorie Corder*), Jack Hawkins (*Denis Scott*), Elizabeth Allan (*Shirley*

Scott*), Janette Scott (*Elspeth Honey*), Ronald Squire (*Sir John*), Wilfrid Hyde-White (*Fisher*), Niall MacGinnis (*Capt. Samuelson*), Kenneth More (*Dobson*), Maurice Denham (*Maj. Pearl*), Dora Bryan (*Rosie*), David Hutcheson (*Bill Penworthy*), Donald Stewart (*The Controller*), Peter Murray (*Peter*), John Salew (*The Inspector*), Hugh Wakefield (*The Chairman*)
D: Henry Koster   **SCR:** Oscar Millard, R.C. Sheriff & Alec Coppel, from Nevil Shute's novel *Highway*
Modest thriller: Scientist fears passenger airplane will disintegrate

No Holds Barred
1952, (USA), Mono, b&w, 66 mins.
W: Leo Gorcey, Huntz Hall, Marjorie Reynolds, Henry Kulky, Hombre Montana
P: Jerry Thomas   **D:** William Beaudine   **SCR:** Tim Ryan, Jack Crutcher & Bert Lawrence
Minor comedy-fantasy: Magic turns Bowery Boys into professional wrestlers

Nomads
1985, (USA), Cinema 7/Atlantic, color, 93 mins.
W: Pierce Brosnan, Lesley-Anne Down, Anna-Maria Monticelli, Alan Autry, Frances Bay, Adam Ant, Mary Woronov, Nina Foch, Paul Anselmo, Freddie Duke, Anita Jesse, Tim Wallace
WRIT & D: John McTiernan   **PHOTOG:** Steven Ramsey   **SPCL-FX:** Paul Staples   **MUSIC:** Bill Conti
Modest fantasy-thriller: Anthropologist stalks evil creatures

No Mercy, No Future
1981, (W. Ger), color, 108 mins.
W: Elisabeth Stepanek, Hubertus von Weyrauch, Irmgard Mellinger, Nguyen Chi Danh, Erich Koitzsch-Koltzack
D: Helma Sanders-Brahms
Unusual melodrama: Schizophrenic woman wanders through Berlin

None But the Lonely Spy
1964, (It), color
W: Ken Clark, Bella Cortez
Minor thriller: Secret agent breaks up dope-smuggling ring

The Nonentity
see *Le Paltoquet*

None Shall Escape
1944, (USA), Col, b&w, 85 mins.
W: Alexander Knox, Marsha Hunt, Henry Travers, Richard Crane, Dorothy Morris, Trevor Bardette
D: Andre de Toth   **SCR:** Lester Cole   **PHOTOG:** Lee Garmes
Unusual psychodrama: War criminal's past examined

Der Noorderlingen (The Northeners)
1992, (Neth), color, 107 mins.
W: Leonard Lucieer, Jack Wouterse, Rudolf Lucieer, Alex Van Warmerdam, Annet Malherbe, Loes Wouterson
D: Alex Van Warmerdam
Bizarre comedy: Misfits inhabit remote village

Noose
1948, (GB), Edward Dryhurst/Pathe, b&w, 95 mins.
W: Carole Landis (*Linda Medbury*), Derek Farr (*Capt. Jumbo Hoyle*), Joseph Calleia (*Sugiani*), Stanley Holloway (*Insp. Rendall*), Nigel Patrick (*Bar Gorman*), John Slater (*Puddn Bason*), Ruth Nixon (*Annie Foss*), Edward Rigby (*Slush*), Leslie Bradley (*Basher*), Hay Petrie (*The Barber*), Reginald Tate (*The Editor*), Carol Van Derman (*Mercia Lane*), John Salew (*Greasy Anderson*), Ella Retford (*Nelly*), Ronald Boyer, Jeanne Ravel, Olive Lucius
D: Edmond T. Greville   **SCR:** Richard Llewellyn & Edward Dryhurst, from a play by Richard Llewellyn
USA retitle, **The Silk Noose Monogram,** *1950, reissued (1951) with 12 mins. cut*
Standard crime-thriller: Ex-commando and tough friends help girl reporter smash Soho club-owner's black market

Noose for a Lady
1953, (GB), Insignia/Anglo-Amalgamated, b&w, 73 mins.
W: Dennis Price (*Simon Gale*), Rona Anderson (*Jill Hallam*), Ronald Howard (*Dr. Evershed*), Pamela Allan (*Margaret Allan*), Alison Leggatt (*Mrs. Langdon-Humphries*), Melissa Stribling (*Vanessa Lane*), Charles Lloyd-Pack (*Robert Upcott*), Colin Tapley (*Maj. Fergusson*), George Merritt (*Insp. Frost*)
P: Victor Hanbury   **D:** Wolf Rilla   **SCR:** Rex Rienits, from Gerald Verner's novel *Whispering Woman*
Standard crime-thriller: Detective proves his convicted cousin did not poison her blackmailer husband

No Place Like Homicide
see *What a Carve Up!*

No Place to Hide
1956, (USA), AA, color, 72 mins.
W: David Brian, Marsha Hunt
Standard thriller

No Place to Hide
1981, (USA), CBS-TV, color, 120 mins.

W: Kathleen Beller (*Amy Manning*), Mariette Hartley (*Adele Manning*), Arlen Dean Snyder (*James Stockwood*), Keir Dullea (*Cliff Letterman*), Gary Graham (*David Norlan*), Sandy McPeak (*Sgt. Newman*)
D: John Llewellyn Moxey   TELEPLAY: Jimmy Sangster   PHOTOG: Robert Hauser   MUSIC: John Cacavas
TVM, standard thriller: Girl claims to be menaced by masked figure

Norah's Debt of Honour
1912, (GB), Clarendon, b&w, 1,100 ft. (335.3m)
W: Norah Chaplin (*Norah*)
D: Wilfred Noy
Standard crime-thriller: Gambler forces girl to steal

The Norliss Tapes
1973, (USA), CBS-TV, color, 74 mins.
W: Roy Thinnes, Angie Dickinson, Claude Akins, Nick Dimitri, Hurd Hatfield
P & D: Dan Curtis   TELEPLAY: William F. Nolan
TVM, standard thriller: Writer probes reports of "walking dead man"

Norman's Awesome Experience
1988, (USA), color, 90 mins.
W: Tom McCamus, Laurie Paton, Jacques Lussier
D: Paul Donovan
Minor fantasy: Three adolescents time-travel to ancient Rome

No Road Back
1957, (GB), Gibraltar/RKO, b&w, 83 mins.
W: Skip Homier (*John Railton*), Paul Carpenter (*Clem Hayes*), Patricia Dainton (*Beth*), Norman Wooland (*Insp. Harris*), Margaret Rawlings (*Mrs. Railton*), Eleanor Summerfield (*Marguerite*), Alfie Bass (*Rudge Haven*), Sean Connery (*Spike*)
P: Steven Pallos & Charles Leeds   D: Montgomery Tully   SCR: Charles Leeds & Montgomery Tully, from the play *Madame Tictac* by Philip Weathers & Falkland Cary
Standard crime-thriller: Jewel thieves frame club-owner's son

The Norsemen
1978, (USA), AIP, color, 90 mins.
W: Lee Majors (*Thorvald*), Cornel Wilde (*Ragnar*), Mel Ferrer (*King Eurich*), Christopher Connelly (*Rolf*), Jack Elam (*Death Dreamer*), Kathleen Freeman (*The Indian*), Denny Miller (*Rauric*), Seaman Glass (*Gunnar*), Jimmy Clem (*Olaf*), Susie Coelho (*Winnetta*), Jerry Daniels (*Kiwonga*), Deacon Jones (*Thrall*), Bill Lawler (*Bjorn*), Fred Biletnikoff, David Kent, Frank Anderson, Curtis Jordan, Glen Hollis, John Welsh, Kevin Myers, Anthony Vitale, Cecil Kent, Steve Denny, Mike Kaminsky, Eric Crandall, Sandy Sanders, Ron Britt, Bob Hewlett, Gary Roy, Bill Twofeathers, Cyrus Strongshield, Mike Gallagher, Mike Rivera, Mike Vincent, Greg Rivera, Mark Wiles, Rick Merino, Wayne Harht, Joe Lopez
WRIT, P & D: Charles B. Pierce   PHOTOG: Robert Bethard   MUSIC: Jaime Mendoza-Nava
Bizarre adventure-thriller: Viking seeks missing father

North by Northwest
1959, (USA), MGM, color, 136 mins.
W: Cary Grant (*Roger O. Thornhill*), Eva Marie Saint (*Eve Kendall*), James Mason (*Van Dam*), Leo G. Carroll (*The Professor*), Jessie Royce Landis (*Mrs. Thornhill*), Martin Landau (*Leonard*), Adam Williams (*Valerian*), Philip Ober (*Lester Townsend*), Josephine Hutchinson (*The Handsome Woman*), Edward Binns (*Capt. Junket*), Robert Ellenstein (*Licht*), Edward Platt (*Victor Larrabee*), Les Tremayne (*The Auctioneer*), Philip Coolidge (*Dr. Cross*)
P & D: Alfred Hitchcock   SCR: Ernest Lehman   PHOTOG: Robert Burks   MUSIC: Bernard Herrmann
Classic thriller: Businessman mistaken for spy

The Northerners
see **Der Noorderlingen**

Northstar
1986, (USA), WB/ABC-TV, color, 69 mins.
W: Greg Evigan (*Jack North*), Deborah Wakeham (*Dr. Alison Taylor*), Mitchell Ryan (*Evan Marshall*), Mason Adams (*Dr. Karl Janss*), David Hayward (*Bill Harlow*), Sonny Landham (*Becker*), Robin Curtis, Ken Foree, Richard Garrison, Steven Williams
D, Peter Levin   TELEPLAY: Howard Lakin   PHOTOG: Michael D. Margulies   MUSIC: Brad Fiedel
TVM, standard SF (feature-pilot for unsold teleseries): Solar disturbance turns astronaut into superhero

No Safety Ahead
1959, (GB), Danziger/Para, b&w, 68 mins.
W: James Kenney (*Clem*), Susan Beaumont (*Jean*), Denis Shaw (*The Inspector*), Gordon Needham (*Richardson*), Robert Raglan (*Langton*), Tony Doonan (*Don*), John Charlesworth (*Jeff*), Brian Weske (*Bill*)
P: Edward J. & Harry Lee Danziger   D: Max Varnel   STORY: Robert Hurst
Standard crime-thriller: Poor clerk joins gang of bank robbers

The Nosferatu Diaries: Embrace of the Vampire
1995, (USA), cable, Ministry of Film/General Media, color, 100 mins.
W: Martin Kemp, Alyssa Milano, Harrison Pruett (*Chris*), Charlotte Lewis

(*Sarah*), Jennifer Tilly (*Marika*) Jordan Ladd, Rachel True
D: Anne Goursaud   MUSIC: Joseph Williams
Made-for-Cable, standard horror-fantasy: College girl must choose between boyfriend and nighttime visitor

Nosferatu, eine Symphonie des Grauens (Nosferatu, a Symphony of Terrors)
1922, (Ger), Prana, b&w, 72 mins.
W: Max Schreck (*Count Orlock*), Grete Schroeder (*Nina*), Gustav von Wangenheim (*Hutter*), Alexander Granach (*Renfield*), Ruth Landshoff (*Annie*), Gustav Botz (*Prof. Siwers*), Hardy von Francois (*The Doctor*), Gitt Schnell (*Harding*), John Gottowt (*Prof. Bullwer*), Max Nemetz (*The Captain*), Heinrich Witte, Wolfgang Heinz, Albert Donohr, Herzfeld
D: F.W. Murnau   SCR: Henrik Galeen, loosely based (uncredited) on Bram Stoker's novel *Dracula: A Tale*   PHOTOG: Fritz Arno Wagner   SETS: Albin Grau
US release: *Nosferatu, The Vampire*, Film Arts Guild, 1929
"The imagery is both terrifying and richly romantic by turn, and the film—a remarkable achievement, especially given the prevailing standards in Germany at that time—is still one of the best vampire essays"—William K. Everson, Classics of the Horror Film
Classic horror-fantasy: Vampire spreads death and disease

Nosferatu, Phantom der Nacht
see *Nosferatu, the Vampyre*

Nosferatu, Phantom of the Night
see *Nosferatu, the Vampyre*

Nosferatu, the Vampyre
1979, (W. Ger), Michael Gruskoff/20th-Fox, color, 106 mins.
W: Klaus Kinski (*Count Dracula*), Isabelle Adjani (*Lucy Harker*), Bruno Ganz (*Jonathan Harker*), Roland Topor (*Renfield*), Jan Groth (*The Harbormaster*), Jacques Dufilho (*The Captain*), Walter Ladengast (*Dr. Van Helsing*), Martje Grohmann (*Mina*), Dan Van Husen (*The Warden*), Carsten Bodinus (*Schrader*), Ryk De Gooyer (*The Town Official*), Clemens Scheitz (*The Town Employee*), Lo Van Hartingsveld (*The Councilman*), Tim Beekman (*The Coffinbearer*)
WRIT, P & D: Werner Herzog, loosely based on Bram Stoker's novel *Dracula: A Tale*   PHOTOG: Joerg Schmidt-Reitwein   SPCL-FX: Cornelius Siegel
A.k.a. **Nosferatu, Phantom der Nacht (Nosferatu, Phantom of the Night)**
Opulent remake of horror-fantasy classic: Innocent couple drawn into vampire's evil web

Nostradamus
1994, (GB-Ger), Orion classics, color, 118 mins.
W: Tcheky Karyo (*Nostradamus*), F. Murray Abraham (*Salinger*), Rutger Hauer (*The Mystic Monk*), Julia Ormond (*Marie*), Amanda Plummer (*Catherine de Medici*), Assumpta Serna, Anthony Higgins, Diana Quick, Michael Gough, Magdalena Ritter, Maja Morgenstern, Bruce Meyers, Maria Varsami, Thomas Christian
D: Roger Christian   STORY: Knut Boeser & Piers Ashworth   PHOTOG: Denis Crossan   MUSIC: Barrington Pheloung
Lavish bio-pic: Life of doctor and prognosticator

Nostradamus and the Destroyer of Monsters
see *Nostradamus y el Destructor de Monstruos*

Nostradamus and the Genie of Darkness
see *Nostradamus y el Genio de la Tinieblas*

Nostradamus y el Destructor de Monstruos (Nostradamus and the Destroyer of Monsters)
1962, (Mex), Azteca/AIP, b&w
W: German Robles, Domingo Soler, Julio Aleman, Aurora Alvarado
D & SCR: Frederick Curiel   STORY: Charles Taboada & Alfred Ruanova   PHOTOG: Ferdinand Colin   MUSIC: George Perez
*USA TV-retitle, **The Monster Demolisher***
*Minor horror-fantasy culled from 2 episodes (**The Student and the Gallows & The Empty Coffin**) of 1959 serial: Vampire seeks power cf. **Blood of Nostradamus, Nostradamus y el Genio de la Tinieblas** and **La Maldicion de Nostradamus***

Nostradamus y el Genio de la Tinieblas (Nostradamus and the Genie of Darkness)
1960, (Mex), Azteca/AIP, b&w, 77 mins.
W: German Robles, Domingo Soler, Julio Aleman, Aurora Alvarado
D: Frederick Curiel
*televised (USA) as **Genii of Darkness***
*Minor horror-fantasy culled from 2 episodes (**Beyond Life & Son of Night**) of 1959 serial: Vampire seeks revenge. cf. **Blood of Nostradamus, Nostradamus y el Destructor de Monstruos** and **La Maldicion de Nostradamus***

No Survivors, Please
1963, (W. Ger), Shorcht, b&w, 95 mins.
W: Maria Perschy, Robert Cunningham, Gustavo Rojo
P: Hans Albin   D: Hans Albin & Peter Berneis   SCR: Peter Berneis
Minor SF-thriller: Reporter and secretary investigate alien forces

Not Guilty
1974, (GB), Cecil Clarke/ITC, Made for TV, color, 71 mins.

W: Christopher George (*Bernard Peel*), **Dinsdale Landen** (*Matthew Earp-Tomson*), Richard Todd (*Tulliver*), Edward Hardwicke (*Clifford*), Suzanne Neve (*The Blonde*), Frank Wylie (*Hendry*), Derek Bond (*Maycroft*), Hans Meyer (*Karl Vorster*), Andrew Mann (*Garfield*), Marion Diamond (*Jennifer Peel*), Belinda Mayne (*The Boutique Ass't*), Simon Merrick (*The Doctor*)
D: Robert D. Cardona   **TELEPLAY**: Brian Clemens   **PHOTOG**: Roy S mper   **MUSIC**: Laurie Johnson
TVM, standard thriller: American executive in Britain accused of murdering wife

Nothing But the Night
1972, (GB), Charlemagne/Rank/20th-Fox, color, 90 mins.
W: Christopher Lee (*Col. Bingham*), Peter Cushing (*Sir Mark Ashley*), Diana Dors (*Anna Harb*), Georgia Brown (*Joan Foster*), Gwynneth Strong (*Mary Valley*), John Robinson (*Lord Fawnlee*), Keith Barron (*Dr. Haynes*), Fulton MacKay (*Cameron*), Michael Gambon (*Insp. Grant*), Morris Perry (*Dr. Yeats*), Duncan Lamont (*Dr. Knight*), Shelagh Fraser (*Mrs. Alison*), Kathleen Byron (*Dr. Rose*), Geoffrey Frederick (*The Computer Operator*), Louise Nelson (*The Nurse*), Robin Wentworth (*The Head Porter*), Michael Segal (*The 1st Reporter*), John Kelland (*The 2nd Reporter*), Michael Wynne (*Donald*), Ken Watson (*Jamie*), Andrew McCulloch (*Malcolm*), Paul Humpoletz (*Angus*), Stanley Lebor (*The Policeman*), Stuart Saunders (*The Police Sgt.*), Michael Brennan (*The Deck Hand*), Beatrice Kane (*Helen Van Treylan*), Janet Bruce (*Naureen Stokes*), Geoffrey Denton (*Paul Anderson*)
D: Peter Sasdy   **SCR**: Brian Hayles, from John Blackburn's novel   **PHOTOG**: Ken Talbot   **SPCL-FX**: Les Bowie   **MUSIC**, Malcolm Williamson
distrib. on video-cassette as **The Devil's Undead**. *A.k.a.* **The Resurrection Syndicate**
Standard SF-horror: Experiments in immortality

Nothing But the Truth
1995, (USA), CBS-TV, color, 95 mins.
W: Patricia Wettig, Ken Olin, Bradley Whitford ("*Mack*" *McCarthy*), Tia Carrere (*Simone Gideon*), Harry Lennix (*Det. Vernon Jones*), Katherine LaNasa (*Susie Marsh*), Peggy Rea, Kurt Deutsch
D: Michael Switzer   **TELEPLAY**: Matt Dorff   **PHOTOG**: Robert Draper   **MUSIC**: Joseph Vitarelli
TVM, standard thriller: Woman polygraph examiner becomes involved with murder suspect

Nothing But Trouble
1991, (USA), Applied Action/WB, color, 93 mins.
W: Chevy Chase (*Chris*), Dan Aykroyd (*The J.P./Bobo*), Demi Moore (*Diane*), John Candy (*Eldona/Dennis*), Taylor Negron (*Fausto*), Valri Bromfield, Bertila Damas, Raymond J. Barry, Brian Doyle-Murray, John Wesley, Peter Aykroyd, Deborah Lee Johnson, Daniel Baldwin, James Staskel, Karla Tamburrelli, John Daveikis, Earl Dixon, Danielle Aykroyd, P.H. Aykroyd, Richard Kruk, Robert K. Weiss, Laurence Bilzerian, Isaac Tigrett, Catherine Quinn, Ron Ulstad, Paul LeClair, James Clark, Stan Garner, Jeffrey P. Baggett, Kristina Kochoff, Gary Velasco, Roger Grimsby, Susan Campos
P: Robert K. Weiss   **D & SCR**: Dan Aykroyd   **STORY**: Peter Aykroyd   **PHOTOG**: Dean Cundey   **SPCL-FX**: Tom Pahk, Daniel Ossello, Brian Tipton, Mark Noel, Bruce Minkus, Bryson Gerard, Joss Geiduschek, Louie

Lantieri, Scott Fisher, Ron Goldstein, Jon Porter, Eric Rylander & Kim Derry   **MUSIC**: Michael Kamen
Standard comedy-thriller: Grotesque family traps travelers

Not in These
1912, (GB), Cosmopolitan, b&w, 510 ft. (155.4m)
Standard fantasy short: Clairvoyant puts spell on Jew's trousers

Not of This Earth
1957, (USA), AA, b&w, 72 mins.
W: Paul Birch, Beverly Garland, Morgan Jones, Dick Miller, William Roerick, Jonathan Haze, Anne Carroll, Roy Engel, Pat Flynn, Tamar Cooper, Harold Fong, Gail Ganley, Ralph Reed
P & D: Roger Corman   **SCR**: Charles B. Griffith & Mark Hanna   **PHOTOG**: John D. Mescall   **MUSIC**: Ronald Stein
orig. co-billed with **Attack of the Crab Monsters**
Standard SF-horror: Ruthless space-aliens seek cure for strange blood malady

Not of This Earth
1988, (USA), Roger Corman/Miracle, color, 82 mins.
W: Traci Lords (*Nadine*), Arthur Roberts (*Johnson*), Lenny Juliano (*Jeremy*), Ace Mask (*Dr. Rochelle*), Roger Lodge (*Harry*), Rebecca Perle, Michael DeLano, Becky LeBeau, Monique Gabrielle, Cynthia Thompson, Kelli Maroney, Belinda Grant
D: Jim Wynorski   **SCR**: R.J. Robertson & Jim Wynorski, based on orig. scr by Charles B. Griffith & Mark Hanna   **PHOTOG**: Zoran Hochstatter   **MUSIC**: Chuck Cirino
Minor remake of 1950s mini-classic: Space-alien seeks human blood

Not of This Earth
1995, (USA), SHO-TV, color, 90 mins.
W: Michael York, Mason Adams, Parker Stevenson, Elizabeth Barondes
Made-for-Cable, yet another remake of SF-horror mini-classic: Extraterrestrial seeks human blood

Not of This World
1991, (USA), Barry & Enright Prods., Made for TV, color, 95 mins.
W: Lisa Hartman, A Greene, Pat Hingle, Michael Greene, Luke Edwards, Tracey Walter, Tim Choate, Ivory Ocean, Ian Patrick Williams, Cary-Hiroyuki Tagawa, Xander Berkeley, Richard Grove, Stephen Prutting, Richard Epcar, J.B. Quon, Greg Natale, Elizabeth Gill, Burr Middleton, Nicholas D. Bussey, Lisa Hart Carroll, Michele Palermo, Timothy Davis Reed, Michele Roth, Elizabeth Jee
D: Jon Daniel Hess   **TELEPLAY**: Robert Glass   **STORY**: Les Alexander, Don Enright, Jonathon Brauer & Robert Glass   **PHOTOG**: Mark Irwin   **SPCL-FX**: Bruno Van Zeebroeck   **MUSIC**: Johnny Harris
TVM, standard SF-thriller: Alien life-form loose in small town

Not on Your Life!
1963, (Sp-It), Naga-Zabra/Pathe Contemp b&w, 110 mins.
W: Nino Manfredi (*Jose Luis*), Emma Penella (*Carmen*), Jose Isbert (*Amedeo*), Jose

Nosferatu: Max Schreck

Luis Lopez Vazquez (*Antonio*), Angel Alvarez (*Alvarez*), Maruja Isbert (*Ignacia*), Guido Alberti (*The Prison Warden*), Maria Luisa Ponte (*Estefania*)
D: Luis Garcia Berlanga   **SCR**: Luis Berlanga, Rafael Azcona & Ennio Flaiano   **STORY**: Luis Berlanga   **PHOTOG**: Tonino Delli Colli   **MUSIC**: Miguel Asins Arbo
A.k.a. El Verdugo (The Executioner)
Standard satire: Adventures of executioner

Notorious
1946, (USA), Selznick/RKO, b&w, 102 mins.
W: Cary Grant, Ingrid Bergman, Claude Rains, Louis Calhern, Ivan Triesault, Madame Leopoldine Konstantin, Moroni Olsen, Reinhold Schunzel
P & D: Alfred Hitchcock   **SCR**: Ben Hecht   **PHOTOG**: Ted Tetzlaff   **MUSIC**: Roy Webb
Classic thriller: Daughter of convicted German spy helps American agents root out neo-Nazis

Notorious
1992, (USA), Berger Queen Prods./Lifetime TV, color, 95 mins.
W: John Shea, Jenny Robertson, Jean-Pierre Cassel, Paul Guilfoyle, Marisa Berenson, Ronald Guttman, Jean-Pierre Stewart, Igor de Savitch, Albert Pariente, Marc Samuel, Stephane Meldegg, Bill Bailey, Alan Rossett, Dominique Figaro, Laurence Bouvencourt, Isabelle Lazard, Michael Morris, Jessie Joe Walsh
D: Colin Bucksey   **TELEPLAY**: Douglas Lloyd McIntosh   based on **STORY & SCR**: Ben Hecht   **PHOTOG**: Peter Sinclair   **MUSIC**: Don Davis
TVM, minor remake of suspense classic: Traitor's daughter recruited for espionage

The Notorious Lone Wolf
1946, (USA), Col, b&w, 64 mins.
W: Gerald Mohr (*Michael Lanyard*), Janis Carter (*Carla Winter*), Eric Blore (*Jamison*), John Abbott (*Lal Bara*), William Davidson (*Insp. Crane*), Don Beddoe (*Stanley*), Robert Scott (*Dick Hale*), Adelle Roberts (*Rita Hale*), Peter Whitney (*Harvey Beaumont*), Olaf Hytten (*Prince of Rapur*), Maurice Cass (*The Ass't Hotel Manager*), Ian Wolfe (*Adam Wheelright*), Edith Evanson (*Olga*), Eddie Acuff (*Jones*), Virginia Hunter (*Lili*)
D: D. Ross Lederman   **SCR**: Martin Berkeley, Edward Dein & William J. Bowers, from characters created by Joseph Louis Vance
*working title, **The Lone Wolf on Broadway***
Standard thriller: Gentleman rogue implicated in robbery. 'Lone Wolf' series

Not Quite Human
1987, (USA), color, 97 mins.
W: Joseph Bologna, Jay Underwood, Robyn Lively, Robert Harper
D: Steven Hilliard Stern
Minor SF-fantasy

Not Quite Human II
1989, (USA), color, 91 mins.
W: Alan Thicke, Jay Underwood, Robyn Lively, Greg Mullavey, Mark Arnott, Katie Barberi, Dey Young, Scott Nell, Mike Russell, Ty Miller
WRIT & D: Eric Luke   **PHOTOG**: Jules Brenner   **MUSIC**: Michel Rubini
Minor SF-comedy: Android infected by computer virus

No Trace
1950, (GB), Tempean/Eros, b&w, 76 mins.
W: Hugh Sinclair (*Robert Southley*), Dinah Sheridan (*Linda*), John Laurie (*Insp. McDougall*), Barry Morse (*Harrison*), Dora Bryan (*Maisie*), Michael Brennan (*Fenton*), Michael Ward (*The Salesman*)
P: Robert Baker & Monty Berman   **WRIT & D**: John Gilling
Standard thriller: Crime novelist kills blackmailer, pretends to help police

Notre Dame de Paris
1911, (Fr), b&w, 3 reels
from Victor Hugo's novel
Standard melodrama: Hunchback loves gypsy dancer

Notre Dame de Paris (1957)
see The Hunchback of Notre Dame (1957)

No Trees in the Street
1959, (GB), Allegro/ABP, b&w, 96 mins.
W: Sylvia Syms (*Hetty*), Herbert Lom (*Wilkie*), Joan Miller (*Jess*), Ronald Howard (*Frank*), Stanley Holloway (*Kipper*), Liam Redmond (*Bill*), Carole Lesley (*Lova*), Lana Morris (*Marje*), Melvyn Hayes (*Tommy*), Lily Kann (*Mrs. Jacobson*), Marianne Stone (*Mrs. Jokel*), Edwin Richfield (*Jackie*), Campbell Singer (*The Inspector*), David Hemmings (*Kenny*)
P: Frank Godwin   **D**: J. Lee Thompson   **SCR**: Ted Willis, from his play
Standard crime-thriller: Crooked bookie influences children of 1930s slum mother

La Nouvelle Peine de Mort (The New Death Penalty)
1907, (Fr), Star, b&w, 123m (403.5 ft./6.8 mins.)
D: Georges Melies
Standard comedy-fantasy: Man killed by fumes from old shoes

Nouvelle Vague (New Wave)
1990, (Fr), color, 90 mins.
W: Alain Delon, Domiziana Giordano, Roland Amstutz, Laurence Cote
D: Jean-Luc Godard
Standard thriller: Woman kills lover, meets his double

The November Plan
1976, (USA), color, 103 mins.
W: Wayne Rogers, Elaine Joyce, Philip Sterling, Diane Ladd, Clifton James, Meredith Baxter Birney, Jack Kruschen, Laurence Luckinbill, Dorothy Malone, Lloyd Nolan
D: Don Medford
Standard thriller (cobbled out of 3 episodes of teleseries "City of Angels"): 1930s L.A. detective probes murder of starlet's lover

Novyi Gulliver (A New Gulliver)
1934, (Russ), Mosfilm, b&w
D: Alexander Ptushko   **SCR**: Grigori Roshal & Alexander Ptushko, from Jonathan Swift's classic satire *Gulliver's Travels*   **PHOTOG**: N. Renkov
Standard fantasy: European visits bizarre lands

No Way Out
1987, (USA), Orion, color, 114 mins.
W: Kevin Costner (*Tom Farrell*), Gene Hackman (*David Brice*), Sean Young (*Susan Atwell*), Will Patton (*Scott Pritchard*), Howard Duff (*Sen. Duvall*), Iman (*Nina Beka*), Fred Dalton Thompson (*Marshall*) George Dzundza, Jason Bernard, Leon Russom, Leo Geter, Dennis Burkley, Marshall Bell, Chris D., Peter Bell, Michael Shillo, Nicholas Worth, Matthew Barry, Matthew Evans, John DiAquino, Tony Webster
D: Roger Donaldson   **STORY & SCR**: Robert Garland, from Kenneth Fearing's novel *The Big Clock*   **PHOTOG**: John Alcott   **MUSIC**: Maurice Jarre
*Modest thriller: Intrigue embroils naval officer. cf. **The Big Clock***

No Way to Treat a Lady
1968, (USA),Para, color, 108 mins.
W: Rod Steiger, Lee Remick, George Segal, Eileen Heckart (*Mrs. Brummel*), Murray Hamilton (*Haines*), Michael Dunn (*Kupperman*), Kim August (*Sadie*), Irene Dailey, Barbara Baxley, Martine Bartlett
P: Sol C. Siegel   **D**: Jack Smight   **SCR**: John Gay, from William Goldman's novel   **PHOTOG**: Jack Priestley   **MUSIC**: Stanley Myers
Standard thriller: Psychotic dons disguises, murders women

Nowhere to Go
1958, (GB), Ealing/MGM, b&w, 97 mins.
W: George Nader (*Paul Gregory*), Maggie Smith (*Bridget Howard*), Bernard Lee (*Vic Sloane*), Geoffrey Keen (*Insp. Scott*), Bessie Love (*Harriet Jefferson*), Andree Melly (*Rosa*), Howard Marion Crawford (*Cameron*), Harry Locke (*Bendel*), Arthur Howard (*Dodds*), Lionel Jeffries (*The Pet Shop Man*), Margaret McGrath (*Rosemary*), Harry H. Corbett (*Sullivan*)
P: Eric Williams   **D**: Seth Holt   **SCR**: Seth Holt & Kenneth Tynan, from a novel by Donald Mackenzie
Standard crime-thriller: Socialite aids escaped thief

Now You See Him, Now You Don't
1972, (USA), Walt Disney/Buena Vista, color, 88 mins.
W: Kurt Russell (*Dexter Riley*), Cesar Romero (*A.J. Arno*), Joe Flynn (*Dean Higgins*), Jim Backus (*Timothy Forsythe*), William Windom (*Lufkin*), Joyce Menges (*Debbie Dawson*), Alan Hewitt (*Dean Collingsgood*), Richard Bakalyan (*Cookie*), Neil Russell (*Alfred*), Kelly Thordsen (*Sgt. Cassidy*), Michael McGreevey (*Richard Schuyler*), George O'Hanlon (*Ted*), John Myhers (*The Golfer*), Pat Delany (*The Sec'y*), Dave Willock (*Mr. Burns*), Robert Rothwell (*The Driver*), Frank Aletter (*The TV Announcer*), Ed Begley Jr. (*Druffle*), Edward Andrews (*Mr. Sampson*), Jack Bender (*Slither Roth*), Paul Smith (*The Road Block Officer*), Frank Welker (*Myles*), Mike Evans (*Henry Fathington*), Billy Casper (*A Professional Golfer*), Dave Hill (*A Professional Golfer*)
P: Ron Miller   **D**: Robert Butler   **SCR**: Joseph McEveety, from a story by Robert L. King   **PHOTOG**: Frank Phillips   **MUSIC**: Robert F. Brunner
*Juvenile comedy-fantasy (sequel to **The Computer Wore Tennis Shoes**): Invisibility spray helps save bankrupt college*

The Nude Bomb
1980, (USA), Time-Life/Univ, color, 94 mins
W: Don Adams (*Maxwell Smart*), Sylvia Kristel (*Agent 34*), Dana Elcar (*The Chief*), Rhonda Fleming (*Edith von Secondberg*), Pamela Hensley (*Agent 36*), Andrea Howard (*Agent 22*), Vittorio Gassman (*Nino Sebastiani*), Norman Lloyd (*Carruthers*), Bill Dana (*Seigle*), Gary Imhoff (*Jerry*), Sarah Rush (*Pam*), Walter Brooke (*The Ambassador*), Thomas Hill (*The President*), Ceil Cabot (*The Landlady*), Joey Forman (*Agent 13*), Patrick Gorman (*The French Delegate*), Earl Maynard (*The Jamaican Delegate*), Alex Rodine (*The Russian Delegate*), Richard Sanders (*The German Delegate*), Vito Scotti (*The Italian Delegate*), Byron Webster (*The English Delegate*), Horst Ehrhardt (*The Polish Delegate*), James Gavin, Gary Young
P: Jennings Lang   **D**: Clive Donner   **SCR**: Arne Sultan, Bill Dana & Leonard B. Stern, from characters created by Mel Brooks & Buck Henry   **PHOTOG**: Harry L. Wolf   **MUSIC**: Lalo Schifrin   **SONG**: *You're Always There*
*TV retitle, **The Return of Maxwell Smart***
Standard SF-comedy

Nudist Colony of the Dead
1990, (USA), Artistic License, color
Minor horror-satire

Nude in his Pocket
see Une Amour de Poche

Nude on the Moon
1961, (USA), color, 83 mins.
D: Doris Wishman   **SONG:** *I'm Moonig Over You, My Little Moon Doll*
Minor SF-sleaze: Moon found inhabited by nudists

La Nuit de la Revanche (Night of Revenge)
1924, (Fr), b&w
W: Charles Vanel
WRIT & D: Julien Duvivier
Standard melodrama

La Nuit de Tous les Mysteres
see House on Haunted Hill

La Nuit des Espions (Night of the Spies)
1959, (Fr), Gaumont, b&w, 80 mins.
W: Marina Vlady
WRIT & D: Robert Hossein
Standard melodrama

La Nuit du Loup-Garou
see The Curse of the Werewolf

La Nuit Fantastique (The Fantastic Night)
1942, (Fr), UTC, b&w, 89 mins, also 103 mins.
W: Micheline Presle
D: Marcel L'Herbier   **SCR:** Henri Jeanson
Standard comedy-fantasy

Les Nuits de Dracula
see Count Dracula

Les Nuits Rouges (Red Nights)
1973, (Fr), Terra Films/New Line, color, 88 mins. (USA release)
W: Jacques Champreux, Gayle Hunnicutt, Josephine Chaplin, Gert Frobe
P: Raymond Froment   **D:** Georges Franju   **SCR:** Jacques Champreux
*USA retitle, **Shadowman** (New Line Cinema, 1975)*
Standard thriller: Masked supercriminal seeks missing half of treasure map

Une Nuit Terrible (A Terrible Night)
1896, (Fr), Star, b&w, 20m (65.6 ft./1.1 mins.)
D: Georges Melies
Standard fantasy

Nukie
1993, (GB), color, 99 mins.
W: Glynis Johns, Ronald France, Steve Railsback
Minor SF-thriller: Evil researchers capture space alien

No. 1 of the Secret Service
1978, (GB), Shonteff/Hemdale, color, 93 mins.
W: Nicky Henson (*Charles Bind*), Richard Todd (*Arthur Loveday*), Aimi MacDonald (*Anna Hudson*), Sue Lloyd (*Sister Jane*), Geoffrey Keen (*Rockwell*), Dudley Sutton (*The Leader*), Jon Pertwee (*Rev. Walter Braithwaite*), Milton Reid (*Eyepatch*), The Baker Twins (*Paula & Chrissie Williams*), Fiona Curzon (*The Bar Girl*), Jenny Till (*The Vampire*), Katya Wyeth (*Miss Martin*), Roberta Gibbs (*Stormy Weather*), Oliver MacGreevy (*Simms*)
P: Elizabeth Gray   **D:** Lindsay Shonteff   **STORY:** Howard Craig   **PHOTOG:** Ivan Strasberg   **MUSIC:** Leonard Young
Standard comedy-thriller: Agent thwarts mad millionaire

Number 17
1932, (GB), BIP/Wardour, b&w, 63 mins.
W: Leon M. Lion (*Ben*), Anne Grey (*Nora Brant*), John Stuart (*Gilbert Fordyce*), Donald Calthrop (*Brant*), Barry Jones (*Henry Doyle*), Ann Casson (*Rose Ackroyd*), Henry Caine (*Ackroyd*), Garry Marsh (*Sheldrake*), Herbert Langley (*The Guard*)
D: Alfred Hitchcock   **SCR:** Alfred Hitchcock, Alma Reville & Rodney Ackland, from a play by J. Jefferson Farjeon
Standard thriller: Girl jewel thief reforms, helps detective capture gang

Number Six
1962, (GB), Merton Park/Anglo-Amalgamated, b&w, 59 mins.
W: Ivan Desny (*Charles Valentine*), Nadja Regin (*Nadia Leiven*), Michael Goodliffe (*Supt. Hallett*), Joyce Blair (*Carol Clyde*), Brian Bedford (*Jimmy Gale*), Leonard Sachs (*Welland*), Michael Shaw (*Luigi Pirani*), Harold Goodwin (*Smith*)
P: Jack Greenwood   **D:** Robert Tronson   **SCR:** Philip Mackie, from a novel by Edgar Wallace
Standard thriller: Secret agent foils crook

The Nun
1907, (GB), Hepworth, b&w, 525 ft. (160m)
D: Lewin Fitzhamon
Standard melodrama: Lover poses as artist, saves girl from convent

The Nurse
1997, (USA), color, 90 mins.
W: Lisa Zane, John Stockwell (*Jack*)
Made-for-Video, minor thriller: Nurse seeks revenge on family that drove her father to sucide

The Nursemaid's Dream
1908, (GB), Hepworth, b&w, 450 ft. (137.2m)
W: Gertie Potter (*The Fairy*)
D: Lewin Fitzhamon
Standard fantasy short: Nursemaid dreams fairies save her baby from giants

Nursery Rhymes
1915, (GB), British Oak, b&w, 920 ft. (280.4m)
W: Dorothy Batley (*The Child*)
D: Ethyle Batley
Standard comedy-fantasy: Retelling of "Cat and the Fiddle," "Mother Hubbard," etc.

Nurse Sherri
see Beyond the Living

Nurse Will make It Better
1975, (USA), ABC-TV, color, TVM, minor
Thriller

Nur Tote Zeugen Schweigen
see Hipnosis

The Nutcracker Prince
1990, (Can), WB, color, 75 mins.
VOICES: Kiefer Sutherland, Megan Fellows, Peter O'Toole, Mike McDonald, Peter Boretski, Phyllis Diller
D: Paul Schibli, from a story by E.T.A. Hoffmann
Standard animated fantasy: Girl's Christmas fantasies come to life

The Nutty Professor
1963, (USA), Para, color, 107 mins.
W: Jerry Lewis (*Prof. Julius Kelp/"Buddy Love"*), Stella Stevens (*Stella Purdy*), Howard Morris (*Elwood Kelp*), Del Moore (*Dr. Warfield*), Kathleen Freeman (*Millie*), Elvia Allman (*Edwina Kelp*), Henry Gibson (*Gibson*), Skip Ward, Norman Alden, Med Flory, Les Brown, Milton Frome, Marvin Kaplan, Buddy Lester, David Landfield
P: Ernest D. Glucksman   **D:** Jerry Lewis   **SCR:** Jerry Lewis & Bill Richmond, inspired by Robert Louis Stevenson's *Dr. Jekyll and Mr. Hyde*   **PHOTOG:** W. Wallace Kelley   **MUSIC:** Walter Scharf
*Fr retitle, **Dr. Jerry et Mr. Love***
Classic comedy-fantasy: Potion turns nerdish college professor into amoral swinger

The Nutty Professor
1996, (USA), Imagine/Univ, color, 96 mins.
W: Eddie Murphy (*Sherman Klump/Buddy Love/Papa Klump/Mama Klump/Grandma Klump/Ernie Klump/Richard Simmons*), Jada Pinkett (*Carla Purty*), James Coburn (*Harlan Hartley*), John Ales (*Jason*), Dave Chappelle (*Reggie Warrington*), Larry Miller (*Dean Richmond*), Traci Bingham, Patricia Wilson, Jamal Mixon, Doug Williams, Quinn Duffy, Nichole McAuley, Hamilton Von Watts, Tony Carlin, Chao-Li Chi, David Ramsey, Chaz Lamar Shepherd, Retha Jones, John Prosky, Lisa Halpern, Mark McPherson, Stanley D. Petters III, Greg Natale, Sara Ballantine, Roy Werner, Steve Monroe, Joe Greco, Lisa Boyle, Nick Kokotakis, Julianne Christie, Michael D. Starks, Alexia Robinson, Christie Blanchard-Power, Athena Massey, Judith Woodbury, Mark Bryan Wilson, William Sturgeon
P: Brian Grazer & Russell Simmons   **D:** Tom Shadyac   **SCR:** David Sheffield, Barry W. Blaustein, Tom Shadyac & Steve Oedekerk based on the motion picture written by Jerry Lewis & Bill Richmond   **PHOTOG:** Julio Macat   **MUSIC:** David Newman   **MUSIC SPRVSR:** Danny Bramson
Standard comedy-fantasy (remake of Jerry Lewis classic): Fat chemistry teacher discovers body-altering secret

The Nylon Noose
1963, (W. Ger), Monarchia/Urania/Medallion-TV, b&w, 83 mins.
W: Richard Goodman, Laya Raki
Minor thriller: Strangler plagues stockholders meeting in grim mansion

A Nymphoid Barbarian in Dinosaur Hell
1991, (USA), Troma, color, 85 mins.
W: Linda Corwin, Paul Guzzi, Alex Pirnie, Marc Deshales, K. Alan Hodder, Russ Greene, Rick Stewart, Scott Ferro, Ryan Piper
WRIT & D: Brett Piper   **MUSIC:** The Astral Warriors
Minor SF-adventure: Humans vs. post-nuke mutants

Nyoka and the Lost Secrets of Hippocrates
1966, (USA), Rep, b&w, 100 mins.
W: Kay Aldridge, Clayton Moore, Frank Lackteen, Lorna Gray (*Adrian Booth*), Tristram Coffin, Charles Middleton William Benedict
D: William Witney   **SCR:** Ronald Davidson, Norman S. Hall, William Lively, Joseph O'Donnell & Joseph Poland
Standard adventure-thriller (feature-version of 1942 serial 'Perils of Nyoka'): Jungle girl helps expedition find sacred tablets

Oasis of the Zombies
1982, (Fr-Sp), color, 75 mins.
<u>W</u>: Manuel Gelin, France Jordan, Jeff Montgomery, Miriam Landson, Eric Saint-Just, Caroline Audret, Henry Lambert
<u>D</u>: A.M. Frank
Minor horror-thriller: Students in Sahara find treasure and Nazis

Object of Obsession
1995, (USA), color, 95 mins.
<u>W</u>: Erika Anderson, Scott Valentine
Minor eroto-thriller: Sexual escapades turn dangerous for divorced woman

Oblivion
1994, (USA), color, 94 mins.
<u>W</u>: Richard Joseph Paul, Andrew Divoff, Jackie Swanson, Meg Foster, Isaac Hayes, Julie Newmar, George Takei, Carel Struycken
<u>D</u>: Sam Irvin <u>SCR</u>: Peter David <u>MUSIC</u>: Pino Donaggio
Standard SF-thriller

The Oblong Box
1969, (GB), AIP, color, 95 mins.
<u>W</u>: Vincent Price (*Julian*), Christopher Lee (*Dr. Neuhartt*), Hilary Dwyer (*Elizabeth*), Sally Geeson (*Sally Baxter*), Rupert Davies (*Joshua Kemp*), Carl Rigg (*Mark Norton*), Peter Arne (*Samuel Trench*), Alister Williamson (*Sir Edward Markham*), Maxwell Shaw (*Tom Hackett*), Harry Baird (*N'Galo*), Michael Balfour (*Ruddock*), Godfrey James (*Weller*), Ivor Dean (*Hawthorne*), Uta Levka, Martin Wyldeck
<u>P & D</u>: Gordon Hessler <u>SCR</u>: Lawrence Huntington, suggested by Edgar Allan Poe's short story <u>PHOTOG</u>: John Coquillon <u>MUSIC</u>: Harry Robinson
Standard thriller: African curse estranges brothers

L'Obsede
*see **The Collector***

Obsessed (1951)
*see **The Late Edwina Black***

The Obsessed (1965)
*see **The Collector***

Obsessed
1992, (USA), World Int'l Network, color, 95 mins.
<u>W</u>: Shannen Doherty, William Devane, Clare Carey, Lois Chiles, James Handy, Lisa Ann Poggi
<u>D</u>: Jonathan Sanger <u>TELEPLAY</u>: David Peckinpah <u>PHOTOG</u>: Steven McNutt <u>MUSIC</u>: Lee Holdridge
TVM, standard thriller: Unbalanced woman pursues divorced man

Obsession: PRODUCER GEORGE LITTO AND CLIFF ROBERTSON

Obsession
1949, (GB), British Lion, b&w, 98 mins.
<u>W</u>: Robert Newton (*Riordan*), Sally Gray (*Stella*), Naunton Wayne (*Supt. Finsbury*), Phil Brown (*Bill Kronin*), Ronald Adam (*A Clubman*), Allan Jeayes (*A Clubman*), Olga Lindo (*Mrs. Humphreys*), James Harcourt (*Aitkin*), Russell Waters (*The Detective*), Michael Balfour, Betty Cooper
<u>P</u>: Nat A. Bronsten <u>D</u>: Edward Dmytryk <u>SCR</u>: Alec Coppel, from his novel *A Man about a Dog* <u>PHOTOG</u>: C. Pennington-Richards <u>MUSIC</u>: Nino Rota
*USA retitle: **The Hidden Room**, Eagle-Lion/Astor*
Classic thriller: Man plots demise of wife's lover

Obsession
1954, (Fr), b&w, 89 mins.
<u>W</u>: Michelle Morgan, Raf Vallone
<u>D</u>: Jean Delannoy, from William Irish's novel *Silent as the Grave* <u>MUSIC</u>: Paul Misraki
Standard thriller: Woman learns awful truth about man she loves

Obsession
1976, (USA), Col, color, 98 mins.
<u>W</u>: Cliff Robertson (*Michael Courtland*), Genevieve Bujold (*Elizabeth Courtland/Sandra Portinari*), Wanda Blackman (*Amy Courtland*), John Lithgow (*Robert LaSalle*), Stanley J. Reyes (*Insp. Brie*), Sylvia Williams (*Judy*), Nick Krieger (*Farber*), Patrick McNamara (*The 3rd Kidnapper*), Don Hood (*Ferguson*), Stocker Fontelieu (*Dr. Ellman*), Andrea Esterhazy (*D'Annunzio*), John Creamer
<u>P</u>: George Litto & Harry N. Blum <u>D</u>: Brian De Palma <u>SCR</u>: Paul Schrader <u>PHOTOG</u>: Vilmos Zsigmond <u>MUSIC</u>: Bernard Herrmann
Unusual thriller: Widower meets double of dead wife, is drawn into strange plot

Obsession: A Taste for Fear
1989, (It), color, 90 mins.
<u>W</u>: Virginia Hey (*Diane*), Gerard Darmon (*Georges*), Gioia Scola (*Valerie*), Carlo Mucari (*Paul*)
<u>D</u>: Piccio Raffanini
Standard thriller: Killer stalks fashion models

Obsessions
*see **Flesh and Fantasy***

An Occational Hell
1996, (USA), color, 95 mins.
<u>W</u>: Tom Berenger, Valeria Golino, Kari Wuhrer, Robert Davi
Standard thriller: College instructor probes colleague's murder

The Occultist
1989, (USA), color, 82 mins.
<u>W</u>: Rick Gianasi
<u>D & SCR</u>: Tim Kincaid
Minor horror-thriller: Satanists skin men alive

The Octagon
1980, (USA), American Cinema, color, 103 mins.
<u>W</u>: Chuck Norris (*Scott James*), Karen Carlson (*Justine*), Lee Van Cleef (*McCarn*), Art Hindle (*A.J.*), Carol Bagdasarian (*Aura*), Kim Lankford (*Nancy*), Tadashi Yamashita (*Seikura*), Kurt Grayson (*Doggo*), Larry D. Mann (*Tibor*), Redmond Gleeson (*Duffy*), Yuki Shimoda, John Fujioka, Jack Carter, Alan Chappuis, Richard Norton, Brian Libby, Ken Gibbel, Gerald Okamura, Cheyenne Rivera, Ted Duncan, Alan Marcus, Robert B. Loring, Jo McDonnell, Ernie Hudson, Fenton Jones, Bill Beau, Crane Jackson, Clarke Gordon, Ben Freedman, Shannon Scott David, Elizabeth Carder, Kitty Beau, Enrique Lucero, Ken Lesco, Aaron Norris, John Barrett, Gasper A. Henaine, Eric F. Valdez, Carlos Romano, Mario Valdez, Brian Tochi, Michael Norris, Kevin Brando, Darrin Lee, Thad Geer, John Shields, Haven Earle Haley, Ben Perry, Don Pike, Janette Jiliano, Janell Twomey, J. Ross Imler
<u>D</u>: Eric Karson <u>SCR</u>: Leigh Chapman <u>STORY</u>: Paul Aaron & Leigh Chapman <u>PHOTOG</u>: Michel Hugo <u>SPCL-FX</u>: Gene Griggs <u>MUSIC</u>: Dick Halligan
Standard action-thriller: Master of martial arts opposes secret society

Octaman
1971, (USA), Filmers Guild, color, 70 mins.
<u>W</u>: Pier Angeli, Kerwin Mathews, Jeff Morrow, David Essex, Jerome Guardino, Robert Warner, Norman Fields, Jax Jason Carroll, Wally Rose, Buck Kartalian, Richard Cohen, Samuel Peloso
<u>P</u>: Michael Kraike <u>WRIT & D</u>: Harry Essex <u>PHOTOG</u>: Robert Caramico <u>MUSIC</u>: Post Production Associates
Minor SF-thriller (low-budget reworking of 'Creature from the Black Lagoon'): Expedition runs afoul of aquatic horror

The October Man
1947, (GB), Two Cities/British Lion, b&w, 110 mins. (USA, 89 mins.)
<u>W</u>: John Mills (*Jim Ackland*), Joan Greenwood (*Jenny Carden*), Edward Chapman (*Mr. Peachey*), Joyce Carey (*Mrs. Vinton*), Kay Walsh (*Molly Newman*), Adrianne Allen (*Joyce Carden*), Felix Aylmer (*Dr. Martin*), Catherine Lacey (*Miss Selby*), Frederick Piper (*Godby*), Patrick Holt (*Harry*), Jack Melford (*Wilcox*), George Benson (*Mr. Pope*), John Boxer (*Troth*), Juliet Mills (*The*

Girl), Edward Underdown (*The Official*), James Hayter (*The Garage Man*), Jack Raine (*The Supt.*)
P & SCR: Eric Ambler   **D:** Roy Ward Baker, from a novel by Eric Ambler   **PHOTOG:** Erwin Hillier   **MUSIC SCORE:** William Alwyn   **MUSIC DIR:** Muir Mathieson
reissued 1954
Modest thriller: Mentally-ill chemist suspects he may have murdered

October Moth
1960, (GB), Independent Artists/RFD, b&w, 54 mins.
W: Lee Patterson (*Finlay*), Lana Morris (*Molly*), Peter Dyneley (*Tom*), Robert Cawdron (*The PC*), Sheila Raynor (*The Woman*)
P: Arthur Alcott   **WRIT & D:** John Kruse
Standard thriller: Farm girl tries to convince insane brother that crashed motorist is not their dead mother

The Octopus Gang
1915, (GB), Big Ben-Union/L&P, b&w, 4,000 ft. (1219.2m)
W: Ivy Martinek (*The Girl*)
D, H.O. Martinek
Standard crime-thriller

Octopussy
1983, (GB), Albert R. Broccoli/MGM-UA, color, 131 mins.
W: Roger Moore (*James Bond*), Maud Adams (*Octopussy*), Louis Jourdan (*Kamal*), Kristina Wayborn (*Magda*), Kabir Bedi (*Gobinda*), Steven Berkoff (*Orlov*), Walter Gotell (*Gen. Gogol*), Douglas Wilmer (*Fanning*), Lois Maxwell (*Miss Moneypenny*), Desmond Llewelyn ("*Q*"), Robert Brown ("*M*"), Vijay Armitrij (*Vijay*), Geoffrey Keen (*The Minister*), Bruce Boa (*The US General*), Stuart Saunders (*Maj. Clive*), Patrick Barr (*The Ambassador*), Ken Norris (*Col. Toro*), Gertan Klauber (*Bubi*), David Meyer (*Twin One*), Anthony Meyer (*Twin Two*), Michaela Clavell (*Penelope Smallbone*), Albert Moses (*Sadruddin*), Andy Bradford (*009*), Douglas Wilmer (*Fanning*), Dermot Crowley (*Kamp*), Peter Porteous (*Lenkin*), Tina Hudson (*Bianca*), Eva Rueber-Staier (*Rublevich*), Jeremy Bulloch (*Smithers*), Richard Graydon (*Francisco the Fearless*), Julie Barth, Kathy Davies, Helene Hunt, Tina Robinson, Safira Afzal, Louise King, Alison Worth, Janine Andrews, Lynda Knight, Ravinder Singh Reyett, Gurdial Sira, Michael Moor, Peter Edmund, Gabor Vernon, Sven Surtees, Talib Johnny, Hugo Bower, Tony Arjuna, Joni Flynn, Mary Stavin, Brenda Cowling, Carolyn Seaward, David Grahame, Brian Coburn, Carole Ashby, Gillian De Terville, Cheryl Anne, Julie Martin, Jani-Z, Michael Halphie
D: John Glen   **SCR:** George MacDonald Fraser, Richard Maibaum & Michael G. Wilson, from characters created by Ian Fleming   **PHOTOG:** Alan Hume   **MUSIC:** John Barry   **SONG:** *All Time High* (performed by Rita Coolidge)
Major thriller: Deception and atomic sabotage in Europe and India

Odin: Photon Space Sailor Starlight
1985, (USA), color
VOICES: Edward Glen
Standard animated SF-adventure: Spaceship crew finds birthplace of humanity

O Dwoch Takich Co Ukradli Ksiezyc (About Two Persons Who Stole the Moon)
1962, (Pol), Film Polski-SYRENA, color
W: Lech Kaczynski, Jaroslaw Kaczynski, Tadeusz Wozniak, Ludwik Benait, Helena Grossowna, Waclaw Kowalski, Jadwiga Kuryluk, Janusz Strachocki, Bronislaw Darski, Zbigniew Jozefowicz
D: Jan Batory   **SCR:** Jan Batory & Jan Brzechwa, from the story by K. Makuszynski   **PHOTOG:** Boguslaw Lambach   **MUSIC:** Adam Walacinski
Fr retitle, Les Voleurs de la Lune (Thieves of the Moon)
Juvenile fantasy: Boys have amazing adventure

The Odyssey
1997, (USA), NBC-TV, color, approx. 190 mins.
W: Armand Assante (*Ulysses*), Vanessa Williams (*Calypso*), Isabella Rossellini (*Athena*), Greta Scacchi (*Penelope*), Bernadette Peters (*Circe*), Michael J. Pollard (*Aeolus*), Freddie Douglas (*Hermes*), Reid Asato (*Polyphemus*), Eric Roberts (*Eurymachus*), Christopher Lee (*Tiresias*), Richard Truett (*Achilles*), Nicholas Clay (*Menelaus*), Geraldine Chaplin (*Eurycleia*), Irene Papas (*Odysseus' Mother*), Peter Woodthorpe (*Mentor*), Jeroen Krabbe, Ron Cook, William Houston, Alan Cox, Roger Ashton-Griffiths, Stewart Thompson, Heathcote Williams
D, Andrei Konchalovsky   **TELEPLAY:** Andrei Konchalovsky & Chris Solimine, from Homer's epic   **PHOTOG:** Sergei Kozlov   **VS-FX:** Mike McGee   **MUSIC:** Edward Artemyev
2-part TVM ($40 million), ambitious adventure-fantasy: Adventures of Achaean hero on return from Trojan War

Oedipus Rex
1956, (Can), Motion Pictures, b&w, 90 mins.
W: Douglas Rain, Douglas Campbell, Eric House, Eleanor Stuart
D: Tyrone Guthrie, from Sophocles' play
Classic tragedy: Unknowing incest brings disaster

Oedipus Rex
1967, (It), color, 110 mins.
W: Franco Citti, Silvana Mangano, Alida Valli, Carmelo Bene, Julian Beck, Pier Paolo Pasolini
D: Pier Paolo Pasolini, from Sophocles' play

Oedipus the King
see Edipo Re

0-18: or, A Message from the Sky
see On His Majesty's Service

L'Oeuf du Sorcier (The Sorcerer's Egg)
1902, (Fr), Star, b&w, 40m (131.2 ft./2.2 mins.)
D: Georges Melies
GB retitle, The Egg in Black Art, A.k.a. The Prolific Magical Egg
Standard fantasy

The Of-Course-I-Can Brothers
1913, (GB), Hepworth, b&w, 575 ft. (175.3m)
W: Harry Buss (*The Brothers*)
D: Hay Plumb
Standard satire: Man caught in fight causes pain to sympathetic twin

Offbeat
1961, (GB), Northiam/British Lion, b&w, 72 mins.
W: William Sylvester (*Steve Layton*), Mai Zetterling (*Ruth Lombard*), Anthony Dawson (*James Dawson*), John Meillon (*Johny Remick*), John Phillips (*Supt. Gault*), Victor Brooks (*Insp. Adams*), Joseph Furst (*Paul Varna*), Neil McCarthy (*Leo Farrell*), Ronald Adam (*J.B. Wykeham*)
P: E.M. Smedley Aston   **D:** Cliff Owen   **STORY:** Peter Barnes
Standard crime-thriller: Gov't agent poses as bank robber becomes corrupted

The Offence
1973, (GB), Tantallon/UA, color, 113 mins.
W: Sean Connery (*Sgt. Johnson*), Trevor Howard (*Cartwright*), Vivien Merchant (*Maureen*), Ian Bannen (*Baxter*), Ronald Radd (*Lawson*), Derek Newark (*Jessurd*), Howard Goorney (*Lambeth*), John Hallam (*Panton*), Peter Bowles (*Cameron*), Antony Sagar (*Hill*), Richard Moore (*Garrett*), Maxine Gordon (*Janie*)
P: Denis O'Dell   **D:** Sidney Lumet   **SCR:** John Hopkins, from his play
Standard crime-thriller: Detective assaults man he suspects of child molestation

Offerings
1989, (USA), Arista/Southgate, color, 96 mins.
W: Loretta Leigh Bowman (*Gretchen*), Elizabeth Greene (*Kacy*), G. Michael Smith (*Sheriff Chism*), Jerry Brewer (*Jim Paxton*), Tobe Sexton (*David*), J. Max Burnett (*Tim*), Doobie Potter (*The English Teacher*), Rayette Potts (*John's Mom*), Mark Massey (*The Mortician Intern*), Jackie Shaw (*Nurse Jackie*), Patrick H. Berry (*Greg*), Chase Hampton (*Ben Dover*), Heather Scott (*Linda*), Barry Brown (*Deputy Buddy*), Keri Bechthold (*Little Gretchen*), Richard A. Buswell (*John Radley*), Josh Coffman (*Little John*), Patrick Stratton (*Little Tim*), Jay Ferguson (*Little David*), Soren Myatt (*Little Greg*), Barbie Yocum (*Little Linda*), Amanda Tyner (*Little Kacy*), Lorraine Gray (*Gretchen's Mom*), Gail Tucker (*David's Mom*), John A. Blake (*David's Dad*), Robert Griffis (*Gretchen's Dad*), Jevy Schrock (*Tim's Mom*), Christopher Reynolds (*Dr. Rowland*), Damita Davis (*Nurse #2*), Cindy Frankenfield (*Mrs. Davis*), Steve Rosich (*Mr. Lewis*), Keno Driver (*The Hall Orderly*), Christine Soli (*Sally's Voice*), Stephen Treuting (*The Alarm Orderly*), Leroy (*Bud the Dog*)
WRIT & D: Christopher Reynolds   **PHOTOG:** R.E. Braddock   **MUSIC:** Russell D. Allen
Minor horror-thriller (unabashed Halloween imitation): Psycho returns to butcher child-hood tormentors

Official Denial
1993, (USA), color 86 mins.
W: Parker Stevenson Erin Gray, Dirk Benedict, Chad Everett
D: Brian Trenchard-Smith   **TELEPLAY:** Bruce Zabel   **MUSIC:** Garry McDonald & Laurie Stone
Standard SF-thriller: UFO abductee tries to communicate with captive space aliens

The Office Boy's Dream
1908, (GB), Walturdaw, b&w, 385 ft. (117.3m)
D: Dave Aylott
Standard comedy-fantasy: Office boy dreams he is bandit's prisoner

The Offspring
1987, (USA), Darin Scott-William Burr/Manson International/Conquest Entertainment/TMS, color, 99 mins.
W: Vincent Price (*Julian White*), Martine Beswicke (*Katherine White*), Lawrence Tierney (*The Warden*), Susan Tyrrell (*Beth Chandler*), Rick Cox (*The Doctor*), Nicos Argentiogorgis (*The Priest*), Clu Gulager (*Stanley Burnside*), Bob Hannah (*Harry Essex*), Megan McFarland (*Grace Scott*), Terry Knox (*Burt*), Miriam Byrd-Nethery (*Eileen Burnside*), Terry Kiser (*Jesse Hardwick*), Frank Shaheen (*A Truck Loader*), Paul Barberi (*A Truck Loader*), Katherine Kaden (*Mary Hardwick*), Gene Witham (*Jack McCoy*), Harry Caesar (*Felder Evans*), Whit Davies (*The Physician*), Nancy Shaheen (*The Nurse*), Ron Brooks (*Steven Arden*), Didi Lanier (*Amarrillis*), Angelo Rossitto (*Tinker*), Gordon Paddison (*Leonard*), Barney Burney (*No Face*), Cameron Mitchell (*Gallen*), Rosalind Cash (*Snakewoman*), Tim Wingard (*Bullock*), Leon Edwards (*McBride*), C.J. Cox (*Pike*), George Davies (*A Confederate*), Tony Wright (*A Confederate*), Mark Hannah (*A Confederate*), Tommy Nowell (*Andrew*), Ashli Bare (*Amanda*), Sergio Aguire (*Ambrose*), Jajary Bennett (*Jake*), David Styncromb, Justin Nowell, Christopher Cobb, Chastity Waters, David Ford

D: Jeff Burr **SCR**: Courtney Joyner, Darin Scott, & Jeff Burr **PHOTOG**: Craig Greene **MUSIC**: Jim Manzie
orig. to be titled From a Whisper to a Scream
Minor thriller: Anthology of terror tales linked to small town

Off to Bedlam
see Off to Bloomington Asylum

Off to Bloomington Asylum
1901, (Fr), Star, b&w, 20m (65.6 ft./1.1 mins.)
D: Georges Melies
A.k.a. Echappes de Charenton (Escapees of Charenton) and Off to Bedlam
Standard comedy-fantasy: Bizarre madhouse events

Of Mice and Men
1939, (USA), Hal Roach/UA, b&w, 107 mins.
W: Burgess Meredith (*George Milton*), Lon Chaney Jr. (*Lenny Small*), Betty Field, Charles Bickford, Bob Steele, Roman Bohnen, Noah Beery Jr., Leigh Whipper
P & D: Lewis Milestone **SCR**: Eugene Solow, from John Steinbeck's novel **PHOTOG**: Norbert Brodine **MUSIC**: Aaron Copland
Classic melodrama: Two drifters—one normal, one a moron—engender trouble

Of Mice and Men
1981, (USA), NBC-TV, color, 150 mins.
W: Robert Blake (*George Milton*), Randy Quaid (*Lenny Small*), Lew Ayres (*Candy*), Ted Neeley (*Curley*), Cassie Yates (*Mae*), Mitchell Ryan (*Slim*), Pat Hingle (*Jackson*), Whitman Mayo (*Crooks*), Dennis Fimple (*Whit*), Pat Corley (*Carlson*)
D: Reza Badiyi **TELEPLAY**: E. Nick Alexander, from John Steinbecks's novel
TVM, standard melodrama: Drifter and moron companion find trouble

Of Mice and Men
1992, (USA), MGM, color, 110 mins.
W: John Malkovich (*Lennie*), Gary Sinise (*George*), Ray Walston (*Candy*), John Terry (*Slim*), Casey Siemaszko (*Curley*), Sherilyn Fenn (*Curley's Wife*), Richard Riehle (*Carlson*), Alexis Arquette (*Whitt*), Joe Morton (*Crooks*), Noble Willingham (*The Boss*)
D: Gary Sinise **SCR**: Horton Foote, from John Steinbeck's novel **PHOTOG**: Kenneth MacMillan **MUSIC**: Mark Isham
Superior melodrama: Mismatched drifters find tragedy

Of Unknown Origin
1983, (Can), Pierre David-Lawrence Nesis/WB, color, 89 mins.
W: Peter Weller (*Bart Hughes*), Shannon Tweed (*Meg Hughes*), Jennifer Dale (*Lorrie Wells*), Lawrence Dane (*Eliot Riverton*), Kenneth Welsh (*James Hall*), Louis Del Grande (*Clete*), Maury Chaykin (*Dan Errol*), Leif Anderson (*Peter Hughes*), Keith Knight (*The Hardware Salesman*), Earl Pennington (*Mr. Thompson*), Jimmy Tapp (*Meg's Father*), Bronwen Mantel (*Florence Riverton*), Gayle Garfinkle (*Janis Wycoff*), Jacklin Webb (*The Newspaper Vendor*), Monik Nantel (*The Sec'y*), Aimee Castle, Jesse Grasis, Tara O'Donnell
D: George Cosmatos **SCR**: Brian Taggart, from Chauncey G. Parker III's novel *The Visitor* **PHOTOG**: Rene Verzier **SPCL-FX**: Jacques Godbout & Louis Craig **MUSIC**: Ken Wannberg
Standard horror-thriller: Rodent terrorizes executive

The Ogre of Athens
see Dracos

The Ogre's Cuisine
see La Cuisine de l'Ogre

Oh, Charlie
see Hold That Ghost

Oh Dad Poor Dad, Mamma's Hung You in the Closet and I'm Feelin' So Sad
1965, (USA), 7Arts/Para, color, 86 mins.
W: Rosalind Russell (*Mme. Rosepettle*), Robert Morse (*Jonathan*), Barbara Harris (*Rosalie*), Hugh Griffith (*Commodore Roseabove*), Jonathan Winters (*Dad/Narrator*), Lionel Jeffries (*The Airport Commander*), Cyril Delevanti (*Hawkins*), Hiram Sherman (*Breckenduff*), Janis Hansen (*The Other Woman*), George Kirby (*Moses*)
P: Ray Stark & Stanley Rubin **D**: Richard Quine, reshot by Alexander Mackendrick for 1967 release **SCR**: Ian Bernard, from Arthur Kopit's stage play **PHOTOG**: Geoffrey Unsworth **SPCL-FX**: Charles Spurgeon **MUSIC**: Neal Hefti
Bizarre comedy: Eccentric woman controls son's life

Oh, God!
1977, (USA), WB, color, 104 mins.
W: George Burns (*The Almighty*), John Denver (*Jerry Landers*), Teri Garr (*Bobbie Landers*), Paul Sorvino (*Rev. Williams*), Barnard Hughes (*Judge Baker*), Ralph Bellamy (*Raven*), David Ogden Stiers (*McCarthy*), William Daniels (*Summers*), George Furth (*Briggs*), Carl Reiner, Dinah Shore, Jeff Corey, Barry Sullivan, Donald Pleasence
P: Jerry Weintraub **D**: Carl Reiner **SCR**: Larry Gelbart, from Avery Corman's novel **PHOTOG**: Victor Kemper **MUSIC**: Jack Elliott
Modest comedy-fantasy: Supermarket manager becomes God's emissary

Oh, God! Book II
1980, (USA), Gilbert Gates/WB, color, 94 mins.
W: George Burns (*The Almighty*), Suzanne Pleshette (*Paula*), David Birney (*Don*), Louanne (*Tracy*), John Louie (*Shingo*), Howard Duff (*Dr. Whitley*), Hans Conried (*Dr. Barnes*), Anthony Holland (*Dr. Newell*), Wilfrid Hyde-White (*The Judge*), Hugh Downs, Dr. Joyce Brothers, Rodney Allen Rippy Conrad Janis (*Mr. Benson*), Marian Mercer, Mari Gorman, Bebe Drake Massey, Vernon Weddle, Alma Beltran
P & D: Gilbert Gates **SCR**: Josh Greenfeld, Hal Goldman, Fred S. Fox, Seaman Jacobs & Me-lissa Miller **STORY**: Josh Greenfeld **MUSIC**: Charles Fox
Standard comedy-fantasy: God befriends little girl

Oh, God! You Devil
1984, (USA), WB, color, 95 mins.
W: George Burns (*The Almighty/Harry O. Tophet*), Ted Wass, Ron Silver, Roxanne Hart, Eugene Roche, Robert Desiderio, James Cromwell, Robert Picardo, Belita Moreno, Jason Wingreen, Arthur Malet
D: Paul Bogart **SCR**: Andrew Bergman **PHOTOG**: King Baggott **MUSIC**: David Shire **SONGS**: *If It Was Only Up to Me & Dangerous Eyes*
Standard comedy-fantasy: Satan aids struggling musician

Oh Heavenly Dog
1980, (USA), Mulberry Square Prods./20th-Fox, color, 103 mins.
W: Chevy Chase & Benji (*Benjamin J. Browning*), Omar Sharif (*Malcolm Bart*), Jane Seymour (*Jackie Howard*), Alan Sues (*Freddie*), Robert Morley (*Bernie*), Donnelly Rhodes (*Montanero*), Stuart Germain (*Higgins*), Margaret Courtenay (*Lady Chalmers*), John Stride (*Alistair Becket*), Richard Vernon (*Quimby Charles*), Barbara Leigh-Hunt (*Margaret*), Lorenzo Music (*Carlton*), Frank Williams (*Mr. Easton*), Albin Pahernik (*The Pelican Man*), Susan Kellerman (*The German Clerk*), Marguerite Corriveau (*Patricia Elliot*), Harry Hill (*Jeffrey Edgeware*), David Samain (*Postie #1*), Neil Affleck (*Postie #2*), Gerald Iles (*Patricia's Doorman*), Jennifer Foote (*The Lady with the Dog*), Joe Camp (*Mover #1*), Dan Witt (*Mover #2*), Jerome Tiberghien (*The Taxi Driver*), Norman Tavis (*The Elderly Man*), Doris Malcolm (*The Elderly Lady*), George E. Zeeman (*The Elderly Lady's Driver*), Wendy Dawson (*The Autograph Lady*), Jeannette Casenave (*The Gallery Woman*), Gayle Garfinkle (*The Puzzled Lady*), Mary Rathbone (*The Umbrella Lady*), Steve Michaels (*The Maitre d'*), Henry Hardy, Steven Lanthier, Derek Osborne, John Lefebvre, Kay Tremblay, Tony Angelo, Derek Cracknell, Michaeline Syvret, Monica Zajdman, Una Kay, Eric Laliberte, Derek Copeland, Victoria Kogan, Jean-Guy Beauchard, Natalie Monet, Victor Desy, Carine Fiszauf, Philip Spensley, Debbie Gordon, Garrett Lewis, Peter Cowper, David Maltby, June Ainley
P & D: Joe Camp **SCR**: Rod Browning & Joe Camp **PHOTOG**: Don Reddy **SPCL-FX**: Richie Adee & Michael Bird **MUSIC**: Euel Box **SONGS**: *Return to Paradise*, (performed by Elton John, writ by Elton John & Gary Osborne), *Arrow Through Me* (performed by Wings, writ by Paul McCartney) & *Song for Guy* (writ by Elton John)
Standard comedy-fantasy: Murdered detective returns to Earth as cute pooch

O.H.M.S.
1913, (GB), Barker, b&w, 1,450 ft. (442m)
W: Harry W. Scaddan (*Cdr. Scott-Neville*), Blanche Forsythe (*Mrs. Scott-Neville*), Doreen O'Connor (*Mary*), Fred Paul (*Col. von Harlan*)
D: Alexander Butler **STORY**: Rowland Talbot
Standard crime-thriller: Spy blackmails commander's wife, gets her to steal treaty

Ohms--Our Helpless Millions Saved
1914, (GB), George A. Cooper, b&w, 2,000 ft. (609.6m)
W: Percy Moran (*Lt. JakJack Moran*)
D & STORY: Percy Moran
Standard crime-thriller: Lieutenant stops spies trying to sabotage water reservoir

Oh That Molar!
1907, (GB), Alpha Trading Co./Gaumont, b&w, 215 ft. (65.5m)
D: Arthur Cooper
Standard fantasy short: Man with toothache dreams of demon teeth dancing in head

O.K. Connery
see Operation Kid Brother

OK, Nero!
1951, (It), I.F.E., b&w, 84 mins.
W: Walter Chiari (*Fiorella*), Silvana Pampanini (*Poppea*), Carlo Campanini (*Jimmy*), Gino Cervi (*Nero*), Jackie Frost (*Licia*), Piero Palermini (*Marcus*), Giulio Donnini (*Tigellinus*), Alda Mangini (*Sophonisba*), Rocco D'Assunto (*Pannunzio*), Alba Arnova (*The Dancer*)
D: Mario Soldati **SCR**: Age, Continenza, Monicelli, Scarpelli, Steno & Ciannelli **MUSIC**: Mario Nascimbene
Standard comedy-fantasy: Two modern Italians transported back to ancient Rome

Old and New Style Conjurers
see La Magie a Travers les Ages

Old Bill Through the Ages
1924, (GB), Ideal, b&w, 7,800 ft. (2377.4m)
W: Syd Walker (*Old Bill*), Arthur Cleave (*Bert*), Jack Denton (*Alf*), Gladys Folliott (*Queen Elizabeth I*), Austin Leigh (*William Shakespeare*), Franzi Carlos

(*Ann Hathaway*), William Pardue (*The Redskin*), Douglas Payne, Wally Bosco, Clive Currie, Cecil Morton York, Cyril Dane, Bruce Bairnsfather

D: Thomas Bentley, from cartoons by Bruce Bairnsfather

Standard fantasy: Man dreams he is different historical characters

The Old Dark House

1932, (USA), Univ, b&w, 71 mins.

W: Boris Karloff, Melvyn Douglas, Raymond Massey, Gloria Stuart, Charles Laughton, Lillian Bond, Ernest Thesiger, John (Espeth) Dudgeon, Eva Moore, Brember Wells

D: James Whale   **SCR:** Benn V. Levy, from J.B. Priestley's novel *Benighted*   **DIALOG:** R.C. Sherriff   **PHOTOG:** Arthur Edeson

Belg retitles, **Call of the Flesh** *&* **The Gray House,** *Fr retitles,* **The House of Death** *&* **A Strange Evening,** *Mex retitle,* **In a Sinister House**

Standard thriller: Intrigues of bizarre family

The Old Dark House

1963, (GB), William Castle-Hammer/Col, color, 86 mins.

W: Tom Poston (*Tom Penderel*), Robert Morley (*Roderick Femm*), Mervyn Johns (*Potiphar Femm*), Fenella Fielding (*Morgana Femm*), Janette Scott (*Cecily Femm*), Joyce Grenfell (*Agatha Femm*), Peter Bull (*Casper Femm/Jasper Femm*), Danny Green (*Morgan Femm*), John Harvey

P & D: William Castle   **SCR:** Robert Dillon, from J.B. Priestley's novel *Benighted*   **PHOTOG:** Arthur Grant

Modest comedy-thriller: American car salesman finds murder and madness among eccentric British family

Old Dracula

see **Vampira**

The Oldest Profession on Earth

see **Le Plus Vieux Metier du Monde**

The Old Favourite and the Ugly Golliwog

1908, (GB), Clarendon, b&w, 250 ft. (76.2m)

D: Percy Stow   **STORY:** Langford Reed

Standard fantasy short: Child's doll resents new favorite

The Old Gardener

1912, (GB), B&C/MP, b&w, 960 ft. (267.2m)

W: Harry Raneo (*John Collins*), Ivy Clifford (*Mary Tayling*), George Laundy (*Courtney Mayverne*), Lillie Smead (*Beatrice Mayverne*), S.P. Goodyer Kettley (*Sir John Tayling*)

D: H.O. Martinek

Standard crime-thriller: Fired gardener dies saving knight's daughter from thief

The Old Man

1931, (GB), British Lion, b&w, 77 mins.

W: Maisie Gay (*Mrs. Harris*), Anne Grey (*Lady Arranways*), Lester Matthews (*Keith Keller*), Cecil Humphreys (*Lord Arranways*), D.A. Clarke-Smith (*John Lorney*), Diana Beaumont (*Millie Jeans*), Gerald Rawlinson (*Dick Mayford*), Finlay Currie (*Rennet*), Frank Stanmore (*Charles*)

D: Manning Haynes   **SCR:** Edgar Wallace, from his play

reissued 1939

Standard thriller: Charlady unmasks killer

Old Mother Hubbard

1912, (GB), Empire Films/MP, b&w, 410 ft. (125m)

WRIT & D: Arthur Cooper

Standard fantasy short: Toys enact nursery rhymes

Old Mother Riley Meets the Vampire

see **Mother Riley Meets the Vampire**

Old Mother Riley's Ghosts

1941, (GB), British Nat'l, b&w, 82 mins.

W: Arthur Lucan (*Mrs. Riley/Ned*), Kitty McShane (*Kitty Riley*), John Stuart (*John Cartwright*), A. Bromley Davenport (*Butterick*), Dennis Wyndham (*Jem Hartop*), Henry Longhurst (*Warrender*), John Laurie (*McAdam*), Peter Gawthorne (*Cartwright*), Ben Williams (*Spike*), Charles Paton (*Mason*)

P & D: John Baxter   **STORY:** Con West, Geoffrey Orme & Arthur Lucan

Standard comedy-thriller: Charwoman foils spies in "haunted" castle

Old Mother Riley's Jungle Treasure

1951, (GB), Oakland/Renown, b&w, 75 mins.

W: Arthur Lucan (*Mrs. Riley*), Kitty McShane (*Kitty Riley*), Garry Marsh (*Kim*), Cyril Chamberlain (*Capt. Daincourt*), Roddy Hughes (*Mr. Orders*), Robert Adams (*Chief Stinker*), Anita D'Ray (*Estelle*), Willer Neal (*Harry Benson*), Sebastian Cabot (*Morgan*), Michael Ripper (*Jake*), Bill Shine (*FO Prang*)

P: George Minter   **D:** Maclean Rogers   **STORY:** Val Valentine

Standard adventure-comedy: Charwoman finds treasure map

The Old Solider

1910, (GB), Hepworth, b&w, 625 ft. (190.5m)

D: Theo Bouwmeester

Stadard crime-thriller: Veteran suspected of stealing locket from colonel's daughter

Old St. Paul's

1914, (GB), Clarendon, b&w, 3,077 ft. (937.9m)

W: Lionelle Howard (*Leonard Holt*), R. Juden (*Annabel*), P.G. Ebbutt (*King Charles*), Ivan Cleveland (*The Earl of Rochester*), J. Cooper (*Solomon Eagle*), F.J.J. Hunt (*Chowles*), M. Sinclair (*Nurse Malmayne*), Cyril Smith (*The Boy*)

D: Wilfred Noy   **SCR:** Low Warren, from a novel by Harrison Ainsworth

USA retitle, **When London Burned,** *reissued 1915*

Standard historical melodrama: Couple's adventures during Great Fire and Plague

An Old Toymaker's Dream

1913, (GB), Empire Films/MP, b&w, 311 ft. (94.8m)

WRIT & D: Arthur Cooper

Standard fantasy short: Toymaker dreams toys come to life

The Old Toymaker's Dream

see **The Enchanted Toymaker**

Olga's Girls

1964, (USA), Weiss, b&w

Minor eroto-thriller: Sadism in brothel

O Lita 2000

1997, (USA), color, 85 mins.

W: Jacqueline Lovell, Gabriella Hall

Made-for-Video, minor eroto-fantasy

Oliver & Company

1988, (USA), Walt Disney, color, 74 mins.

VOICES: Joey Lawrence, Billy Joel, Bette Midler, Richard Mulligan, Cheech Marin, Roscoe Lee Browne, Dom DeLuise, Sheryl Lee Ralph, Taurean Blacque, Robert Loggia

D: George Scribner, based on Charles Dickens' *Oliver*

Standard animated fantasy: Animals oppose meanie

Omar Khayyam

1957, (USA), Para, color, 101 mins.

W: Cornel Wilde (*Omar*), John Derek (*Malik*), Debra Paget (*Sharain*), Michael Rennie (*Hassan*), Raymond Massey (*The Shah*), Yma Sumac (*Karina*), Sebastian Cabot (*Nizam*), Joan Taylor (*Yaffa*), Margaret Hayes (*Zarada*), Edward C. Platt (*Jayhan*), Perry Lopez (*Prince Ahmud*), Morris Ankrum (*Imam Mowaffak*), Abraham Sofaer (*Tutush*), James Griffith (*Buzorg*), Peter Adams, Henry Brandon, Paul Picerni, Kem Dibbs

D: William Dieterle   **SCR:** Barre Lyndon   **PHOTOG:** Ernest Laszlo   **SPCL-FX:** John P. Fulton   **MUSIC:** Victor Young   **SONGS:** *The Loves of Omar Khayyam, Take My Heart & Lament*

A.k.a. **The Loves of Omar Khayyam**

Standard adventure romance: Poet battles assassins threatening Persia

L'Ombre dans la Glace (Shadow in the Mirror)

1967, (Fr), b&w

Standard melodrama

The Omega Connection

see **The London Connection**

Omega Cop

1990, (USA), color, 89 mins.

W: Ron Marchini, Adam West, Stuart Whitman, Troy Donahue, Meg Thayer, Jennifer Jostyn, Chrysti Jimenez, Chuck Katzakian, D.W. Landingham

D: Paul Kyriazi

A.k.a. **John Travis, Solar Survivor**

Minor SF-thriller: Post-nuke cop rescues three women

Omega Doom

1995, (USA), color, 85 mins.

W: Rutger Hauer, Shannon Whirry, Norbert Weisser, Tina Cole

Minor SF-adventure: Cyborg warrior roams post-nuke wasteland

The Omega Man

1971, (USA), WB, color, 98 mins.

W: Charlton Heston (*Neville*), Rosalind Cash (*Lisa*), Anthony Zerbe (*Matthias*), Paul Koslo (*Butch*), Lincoln Kilpatrick (*Zachary*), Eric Laneuville (*Richie*), Jill Giraldi Brian Tochi, John Dierkes

P: Walter Seltzer   **D:** Boris Sagal   **SCR:** John William & Joyce H. Corrington, from Richard Matheson's novel *I Am Legend*   **PHOTOG:** Russell Metty   **MUSIC:** Ron Grainer

Standard SF-thriller: Last normal man menaced by vampire-like plague victims. cf. **The Last Man on Earth**

The Omegans

1968, (USA), Merit/Para, color, 86 mins.

W: Keith Larsen (*Chuck*), Ingrid Pitt (*Linda*), Lucien Pan (*Valdemar*), Bruno Punzalan (*Oki*), Joaquin Fajardo (*Tumba*), John Yench (*McAvoy*), Jeorge Santos (*The Clerk*), Joseph de Cordova (*Dr. Balani*), Lina Inigo (*The Singer*)

P & D: W. Lee Wilder   **SCR:** Waldron Wheeland   **PHOTOG:** Herbert V. Theis   **SPCL-FX:** Francis Rooker   **MUSIC:** Albert Elms

Minor SF-thriller: Artist plots demise of wife and her lover

The Omen

1976, (USA), 20th-Fox, color, 111 mins.

W: Gregory Peck (*Robert Thorn*), Lee Remick (*Katherine Thorn*), Billie Whitelaw

(*Mrs. Baylock*), Patrick Troughton (*Father Brennan*), David Warner (*Jennings*), Harvey Stevens (*Damien*), Martin Benson (*Father Spiletto*), Leo McKern (*Bugenhagen*), John Stride (*The Psychiatrist*), Robert Rietty (*The Monk*), Tommy Duggan (*The Priest*), Holly Palance (*The Nanny*), Anthony Nicholls (*Dr. Becker*), Betty McDowall (*The Sec'y*), Sheila Raynor (*Mrs. Horton*), Bruce Boa (*The Aide*), Ronald Leigh-Hunt (*The Gentleman*), Patrick McAlinney
P: Harvey Bernhard **D:** Richard Donner **SCR:** David Seltzer **PHOTOG:** Gilbert Taylor **MUSIC:** Jerry Goldsmith
Classic fantasy-thriller: Socialites adopt satanic child. cf. **Damien—Omen II** *and* **The Final Conflict**

Omen IV: The Awakening
1991, (USA), Fox-TV, color, 95 mins.
W: Michael Woods, Asia Vieria, Faye Grant (*Karen*), Michael Lerner (*Earl Knight*), Madison Mason (*Dr. Hastings*), Don S. Davis (*Jake Madison*), Ann Hearn (*Jo*), Jim Byrnes (*Noah*), Megan Leitch (*Sister Yvonne/Felicity*)
D: Jorge Montesi & Dominique Othenin-Girard **TELEPLAY:** Brian Taggert
TVM, standard fantasy-thriller: Rising politican's adopted daughter develops satanic powers

Omicron
1962, (It), Walter Reade-Sterling, color, 110 mins.
D & SCR: Ugo Gregoretti
PHOTOG: Carlo Di Palma
Standard SF-thriller

Omoo Omoo the Shark God
1949, (USA), b&w, 58 mins.
W: Ron Randell, Devera Burton, Trevor Bardette, Pedro de Cordoba, Richard Benedict, Rudy Robles, Michael Whalen, George Meeker
D: Leo Leonard
Minor adventure-thriller: Sea captain cursed when he steals black pearls from shark idol

On a Clear Day You Can See Forever
1970, (USA), Para, color, 129 mins.
W: Barbra Streisand (*Daisy Gamble/Melinda*), Yves Montand (*Dr. Marc Chabot*), John Richardson (*Robert Tentrees*), Bob Newhart (*Mason Hume*), Jack Nicholson (*Tad*), Pamela Brown (*Mrs. Fitzherbert*), Simon Oakland (*Dr. Conrad Fuller*), Roy Kinnear (*The Prince Regent*), Larry Blyden (*Warren Pratt*), Mabel Albertson (*Mrs. Hatch*), Elaine Giftos (*Muriel*), Leon Ames (*Clews*), Irene Handl (*Winnie Wainwhistle*), Paul Camen (*Millard*), Peter Crowcroft (*The Divorce Attorney*), Byron Webster (*The Prosecuting Attorney*), Kermit Mur-dock (*Hoyt III*), Laurie Main (*Lord Percy*), John LeMesurier (*Pelham*), Angela Pringle (*Diana Smallwood*), George Neise (*Wytelipt*), Tony Colti (*Preston*), Judith Lowry
P: Howard W. Koch **D:** Vincente Minnelli **SCR & LYRICS:** Alan Jay Lerner **PHOTOG:** Harry Stradling **MUSIC:** Burton Lane **SONGS:** *Come Back to Me, Melinda, He Isn't You, Love with All the Trimmings & What Did I Have That I Don't Have?*
Lavish comedy-fantasy-musical: Girl discovers she is reincarnation of psychic Victorian adventuress

On a Runaway Motor Car Through Piccadilly Circus
1899, (GB), R.W. Paul, b&w, 80 ft. (24.4m)
Standard trick-photography fantasy: Whirlwind ride through busy London traffic

On Borrowed Time
1939, (USA), MGM, b&w, 99 mins.
W: Lionel Barrymore (*Julian Northrup*), Bobs Watson (*Pud*), Sir Cedric Hardwicke (*Mr. Brink/Death*), Beulah Bondi (*Nellie Northrup*), Una Merkel (*Marcia*), Henry Travers (*Dr. Evans*), Eily Malyon (*Demetria*), Grant Mitchell (*Mr. Pilbeam*), Philip Terry (*Bill*), Nat Pendleton (*Mr. Grimes*), Charles Waldron, Ian Wolfe, Truman Bradley
P: Sidney Franklin **D:** Harold S. Bucquet **SCR:** Alice Duer Miller, Frank O'Neill & Claudine West, from the stage play by Paul Osborn & Lawrence Watkin **PHOTOG:** Joseph Ruttenberg **MUSIC:** Franz Waxman
Classic fantasy: Old man traps Death up a tree

Once Bitten
1985, (USA), Samuel Goldwyn Jr., color, 94 mins.
W: Lauren Hutton (*The Countess*), Jim Carrey (*Mark Kendall*), Karen Kopins (*Robin Pierce*), Cleavon Little (*Sebastian*), Thomas Ballatore (*Jamie*), Skip Lackey (*Russ*), Robin Klein (*The Flowerchild Vampire*), Jeb Adams (*The World War I Ace Vampire*), Joseph Brutsman (*The Confederate Vampire*), Stuart Charno (*The Cabin Boy Vampire*), Glen Mauro (*Twin Vampire #1*), Gary Mauro (*Twin Vampire #2*), Carey More (*The Moll Flanders Vampire*), Peter Elbling (*The Bookseller*), Richard Schaal (*Mr. Kendall*), Peggy Pope (*Mrs. Kendall*), Anna Mathias (*Daphne*), Kate Zentall (*Tanya*), Dan Barrows (*Harry*), Laura Urstein (*Darlene*), Megan Mullally (*Suzette*), Garry Goodrow (*The Wino*), Alan McRae (*The Man in Drag*), Dee Dee Rescher (*The Laundromat Lady*), Ruth Silveira (*The Instructor*), Ron Vernan (*The Man at the Table*), Opelene Bartley (*The Lunch Counter Lady*), Terry Wills (*The Principal*), Don Richey (*The Bouncer*), Nancy Hunter (*The Woman Shopper in the Unisex Store*), Dominick Brascia (*The Young Man Buying Ice Cream*), Philip Linton (*The Boy in the Shower*), Anthony Storm (*Kid #1*), Casey Storm (*Kid #2*), Maria Vidal, Rainbow Shalom, Kimberlye Gold, Kelly Salloum
D: Howard Storm **SCR:** David Hines, Jeffrey Hause & Jonathan Roberts **STORY:** Dimitri Villard **PHOTOG:** Adam Greenberg **SPCL-FX:** Court Wizard **MUSIC:** John DuPrez **SONGS:** *Hands Off, Just One Kiss, Stop*

Talking About Us, She Makes Me Crazy, Face to Face & Blue Night Shadow
Modest horror-comedy: Vampiress seeks virgin boy's blood

Once in a New Moon
1935, (GB), Fox British, b&w, 63 mins.
W: Eliot Makeham (*Harold Drake*), Rene Ray (*Stella Drake*), Morton Selten (*Lord Bravington*), Wally Patch (*Syd Parrott*), Derrick de Marney (*Hon. Bryan Grant*), John Clements (*Edward Teale*), Mary Hinton (*Lady Bravington*), Gerald Barry (*Col. Fitzgeorge*), Richard Goolden (*Rev. Benjamin Buffett*), John Turnbull (*Capt. Crump*), H. Saxon-Snell (*K. Pilkington-Bigge*)
D: Anthony Kimmins, based on Owen Rutter's novel *Lucky Star*
Standard fantasy: Postmaster thrown into space when moon collides with star

Once the Killing Starts
1974, (GB), ITC, Made for TV, color
W: Patrick O'Neal, Patricia Donahue, Angharad Rees, Gerald Sim, Michael Kitchen, Gary Watson, Terry Wright
D: John Scholz-Conway **TELEPLAY:** Brian Clemens **MUSIC:** Laurie Johnson
TVM, minor thriller: Anonymous letters test alibi of professor who murdered wife

Once Upon a Brothers Grimm
1977, (USA), color, 102 mins.
W: Dean Jones, Paul Sand, Cleavon Little, Ruth Buzzi, Chita Rivera, Teri Garr
Standard musical-fantasy: Famed writers meet their storybook characters

Once Upon a Forest
1993, (USA), Hanna-Barbera, color, 80 mins.
VOICES: Michael Crawford (*Cornelius*), Ben Vereen (*Phineas*), Ellen Blain, Ben Gregory, Paige Gosney, Elizabeth Moss, Janet Waldo, Susan Silo
D: Charles Grosvenor **SCR:** Mark Young & Kelly Ward
Standard animated fantasy: "Furlings" leave forest, protest environmental pollution

Once Upon a Frightmare
see *Frightmare* (1974)

Once Upon a Midnight Scary
1990, (USA), color, 50 mins.
W: Vincent Price (*Narrator*), Rene Auberjonois, Severn Darden
D: Neil Cox
Standard short anthology of juvenile spook tales: "The Ghost Belonged to Me," Washington Irving's "The Legend of Sleepy Hollow" and "The House With a Clock in Its Walls"

Once Upon a Spy
1980, (USA), Col-TV/ABC-TV, color, 100 mins
W: Ted Danson (*Jack Chenault*), Christopher Lee (*Marcus Valorium*), Mary Louise Weller (*Paige Tannehill*), Eleanor Parker (*The Lady*), Leonard Stone (*Dr. Webster*), Jo McDonnell (*Susan*), Terry Lester (*Rudy*)
P: Jay Daniel **D:** Ivan Nagy **TELEPLAY:** Jimmy Sangster
TVM, minor SF-thriller: Superagent vs. mad scientist

Once Upon a Time
1913, (GB), Folly Films/Phoenix, b&w, 700 ft. (213.4m)
W: Fred Evans (*The Yokel*), Joe Evans (*The Tramp*)
WRIT & D: Fred & Joe Evans
Standard comedy-fantasy: Fairy changes yokel, tramp, farmer, and daughter into clowns

Once Upon a Time
1944, (USA), Col, b&w, 89 mins.
W: Cary Grant, Janet Blair, Ted Donaldson, James Gleason, William Demarest, Howard Freeman, Art Baker, John Abbott
D: Alexander Hall **SCR:** Lewis Meltzer & Oscar Saul, from Norman Corwin's radio-play *My Client Curley* **PHOTOG:** Franz Planer **MUSIC:** Frederick Hollander
StandardModest fantasy: Man finds dancing caterpillar

Once Upon a Time (1967)
see *C'era una Volta*

Once Upon a Time
1976, (USA), color, 83 mins.
Standard animated fantasy: Girl and puppy meet prince and grinch

Once Upon a Time
1987, (USA), color, 92 mins.
Standard animated fantasy: Rivalry of ancient tribes spoils love of prince and princess

Once You Kiss a Stranger
1969, (USA), color, 106 mins.
W: Paul Burke, Carol Lynley, Martha Hyer, Peter Lind Hayes, Philip Carey, Stephen McNally, Whit Bissell
D: Robert Sparr
Minor thriller (thinly-disguised remake of **Strangers on a Train**): *Woman involves man in "reciprocal murder" scheme*

Once You Meet a Stranger
1996, (USA), CBS-TV, color, 95 mins.
W: Jacqueline Bisset (*Sheila Gaines*), Theresa Russell (*Margo Anthony*), Robert Desiderio (*Andy*), Peter Haskell (*Capt. Hammond*), Nick Mancuso, Andi Chapman, Celeste Holm, Symba Smith

D: Tommy Lee Wallace, from a novel by Patricia Highsmith PHOTOG: Steven Poster MUSIC: Peter Manning Robinson
TVM, standard thriller (semi-remake of Strangers on a Train*): Chance meeting leads former child star and psychotic socialite into murderous web*

On Dangerous Ground
1952, (USA), RKO, b&w, 82 mins.
W: Ida Lupino, Robert Ryan, Ward Bond, Ed Begley, Charles Kemper, Cleo Moore, Sumner Williams
D: Nicholas Ray PHOTOG: George Diskant MUSIC: Bernard Herrmann
Unusual thriller: Embittered cop tracks sex killer in upstate New York, becomes attracted to blind woman

One Arabian Night (1920)
see Sumurun

One Arabian Night (1923)
see Widow Twan-Kee

One Body Too Many
1944, (USA), Pine-Thomas/Para, b&w, 76 mins.
W: Jack Haley (*Albert Tuttle*), Jean Parker (*Carol Dunlap*), Bela Lugosi (*The Butler*), Blanche Yurka (*Matthews*), Lyle Talbot (*James Davis*), Douglas Fowley, Bernard Nedell, Fay Helm, Lucien Littlefield, Dorothy Granger, Maxine Fife
P: William Pine & William Thomas D: Frank McDonald ORIG. SCR: Winston Miller & Maxwell Shane PHOTOG: Fred Jackman Jr. MUSIC: Alexander Laszlo
Standard mystery-comedy: Insurance salesman involved with heirs, missing corpse

One Dangerous Night
1943, (USA), Col, b&w, 77 mins.
W: Warren William (*Michael Lanyard*), Marguerite Chapman (*Eve Andrews*), Eric Blore (*Jamison*), Mona Barrie (*Jane Merrick*), Tala Birell (*Sonia*), Margaret Hayes (*Patricia*), Ann Savage (*Vivian*), Thurston Hall (*Insp. Crane*), Warren Ashe (*Sidney*), Fred Kelsey (*Dickens*), Frank Sully (*Hertzog*), Eddie Laughton (*The Drunk*), Eddie Marr (*Mac*), Gerald Mohr (*Harry Cooper*), Gregory Gay (*Dr. Eric*)
D: Michael Gordon SCR: Donald Davis, Arnold Phillips & Max Nosseck, from characters created by Joseph Louis Vance PHOTOG: L.W. O'Connell MUSIC: Morris Stoloff
"Lone Wolf" thriller: Gentleman rogue blamed for hood-lum's murder

One Dark Night
1983, (USA), Comworld, color, 88 mins.
W: Meg Tilly (*Julie*), Melissa Newman (*Olivia*), Robin Evans (*Carol*), Leslie Speights (*Kitty*), David Mason Daniels (*Steve*), Elizabeth Daily (*Leslie*), Adam West (*Allan*), Donald Hotton (*Dockstader*), Rhio H. Blair (*The Coroner*), Leo Gorcey Jr. (*Barlow*), Larry Carroll (*The TV Reporter*), Katee McLure (*A Reporter*), Kevin Peter Hall (*Eddie*), Ted Lehman (*The Drunk*), Nancy Mott (*Lucy*), Martin Nosseck (*A Caretaker*), Albert Cirimele (*A Reporter*), Shandor (*The Russian Minister*)
D: Tom McLoughlin SCR: Tom McLoughlin & Michael Hawes PHOTOG: Hal Trussell SPCL-FX: Tom Burman, Ellis Burman & Bob Williams

One Frightened Night: WALLACE FORD AND RAFAELA OTTIANO

MUSIC: Bob Summers
orig. to be titled Rest in Peace
Modest horror-thriller: Girls'-club initiate spends night in creepy mausoleum

One Deadly Owner
1973, (GB), Cecil Clarke/ITC, Made for TV, color, 71 mins.
W: Donna Mills (*Helen Cook*), Jeremy Brett (*Peter Tower*), Robert Morris (*Freddy Green*), Laurence Payne (*John Jacey*), Eric Lander (*Hans*), Michael Beint (*Hawkins*), Anthony Dawes (*The Car Salesman*), Bob Holness (*The Announcer*), Roy Marioni (*The Waiter*)
D: Ian Fordyce TELEPLAY: Brian Clemens PHOTOG: Roy Simper MUSIC: Laurie Johnson
TVM, minor thriller: Woman menaced by "haunted" auto

One Deadly Summer
1983, (Fr), color, 133 mins.
W: Isabelle Adjani, Alain Souchon, Suzanne Flon, Jenny Cleve, Michel Galabru, Francois Cluzet, Manuel Gelin Maria Machado
D: Jean Becker MUSIC: Georges Delerue
Unusual melodrama: Mysterious beauty visits small French town, seeks revenge

One Exciting Night
1922, (USA), UA, b&w, 11 reels (11,500 ft./3505.2m)
W: Carol Dempster (*Agnes Harrington*), Henry Hull (*John Fairfax*), Margaret Dale (*Mrs. Harrington*), Irma Harrison (*The Maid*), Morgan Wallace (*J. Wilson Rockmaine*), Porter Strong (*Romeo Washington*), Grace Griswold (*Auntie Fairfax*), C.H. Crocker-King (*The Neighbor*), Percy Carr (*The Butler*), Frank Wunderlee (*Samuel Jones*), Frank Sheridan (*The Detective*), Herbert Sutch (*Clary Johnson*), Charles E. Mack (*A Guest*)
D & SCR: D.W. Griffith, from a story by Irene Sinclair PHOTOG: Hendrick Sartov MUSIC SCORE: Albert Pesce
Standard comedy-mystery: Murder and hunt for hidden loot

One Frightened Night
1935, (USA), Nat Levine/Mascot, b&w, 65 mins.
W: Charley Grapewin, Mary Carlisle, Wallace Ford, Arthur Hohl, Regis Toomey, Hedda Hopper, Clarence Wilson, Adrian Morris, Fred Kelsey
D: Christy Cabanne SCR: Wellyn Totman STORY: Stuart Palmer PHOTOG: Ernest Miller & William Nobles
Fast-moving thriller: Old millionaire tries to give away his fortune

One Girl's Confession
1953, (USA), Col, b&w, 74 mins.
W: Cleo Moore, Hugo Haas, Glenn Langan, Russ Conway
WRIT, P, & D: Hugo Haas
Minor melodrama: Waitress imprisoned for robbery

One Good Turn Deserves Another
1909, (GB), Hepworth, b&w, 625 ft. (190.5m)
D: Theo Bouwmeester
Standard crime-thriller: Waif rescues kidnapped gir

One Hour Before Dawn
1920, (USA), Pathe, b&w, 5 reels
D: Henry King
Standard melodrama

One Hour Past Midnight
1924, (USA), Jupiter, b&w, 5 reels (4,724 ft./1439.9m)
D & STORY: B.C. Rule
Standard mystery-thriller: Thief menaces inventor

One Hour to Doomsday
see City Beneath the Sea (1970)

101 Dalmatians
1961, (USA), Walt Disney/Buena Vista, color, 79 mins.
VOICES: Rod Taylor, Lisa Davis, Cate Bauer, Ben Wright, Fred Warlock, J. Pat O'Malley, Betty Lou Gerson
D: Wolfgang Reitherman, Hamilton Luske & Clyde Geronimi, from a story by Dodie Smith MUSIC: George Bruns
Classic animated adventure-fantasy: Evil socialite seeks puppies' fur

101 Dalmatians
1996, (USA), Walt Disney, color, 103 mins.
W: Glenn Close, Jeff Daniels, Joely Richardson, Joan Plowright
D: Stephen Herek SCR: John Hughes, from a story by Dodie Smith
Live-action remake of animated classic

100 Cries of Terror
1965, (Mex), Mexico Films/AIP-TV, b&w
W: Ariadne Welter, George Martinez, Joaquim Cordero
Standard thriller, 2 short terror tales: (1) Man plots wife's death & (2) Woman buried alive

One Jump Ahead
1955, (GB), Kenilworth/GFD, b&w, 66 mins.
W: Paul Carpenter (*Paul Banner*), Diane Hart (*Maxine*), Jill Adams (*Judy*), Freddie Mills (*Bert Tarrant*), Arnold Bell (*Supt. Faro*), Peter Sinclair (*Old Tarrant*), David Hannaford (*Brian*), Roddy Hughes (*Mac*)

P: Guido Coen **D:** Charles Saunders **SCR:** Doreen Montgomery, from a novel
by Robert Chapman
Standard crime-thriller: Reporter probes deaths of girl blackmailer and schoolboy witness

One Magic Christmas
1985, (USA-Can), Walt Disney/Buena Vista, color, 100 mins.
W: Harry Dean Stanton, Mary Steenburgen, Gary Basaraba *(Jack)*, Arthur Hill
(Caleb)
Standard fantasy: Guardian angel boosts spirits of unhappy housewife

George McKay *(Sgt. McNulty)*, Robert B. Williams *(Matt Healy)*, Dorothy
Maloney *(Malone)* *(Eileen Daley)*, Robert E. Scott *(George Daley)*, Early
Cantrell *(Margaret Dean)*, Lyle Latell *(Sgt. Matthews)*, John Tyrrell *(Austin)*,
Joseph Crehan *(Jumbo Madigan)*, Ann Loos *(The Newstand Clerk)*, Henry
Jordan *(The 2nd Man)*, Ben Taggart *(The Traffic Officer)*
D: Oscar (Budd) Boetticher Jr. **SCR:** Paul Yawitz, from characters created by
Jack Boyle **PHOTOG:** L.W. O'Connell **MUSIC:** Mischa Bakaleinikoff
*Standard "Boston Blackie" thriller: Search for stolen gem. Originally titled **Boston
Blackie's Appointment with Death***

One Million B.C.: EDGAR EDWARDS, LON CHANEY JR., AND VICTOR MATURE

The One Man Band
1900, (Fr), Star, b&w, 40m (131.2 ft./2.2 mins.)
W: Georges Melies *(enacting 7 roles, via multiple exposure)*
D: Georges Melies
Standard fantasy short

One Million B.C.
1940, (USA), UA, b&w, 80 mins.
W: Victor Mature *(Tumak)*, Carole Landis *(Loana)*, Lon Chaney Jr. *(Akhoba)*,
Jacqueline Dalya *(Ataf)*, John Hubbard *(Odtao)*, Nigel de Brulier *(Peytow)*,
Inez Palange, Mamo Clark, Edgar Edwards, Mary Gale Fisher, Norman
Budd, Ed Coxen, Creighton Hale, Jean Porter, Lorraine Gauguin, Conrad
Nagel
P: Hal Roach Sr. **D:** Hal Roach Jr. & Hal Roach Sr. **SCR:** Mickell Novak,
George Baker & Joseph Frickert **PHOTOG:** Norbert Brodine **SPCL-FX:**
Roy Seawright **MUSIC:** Werner R. Heymann **NARRATION:** Conrad
Nagel
*reissued as **Cave Man**, Fr retitle, **Tumak, Fils de la Jungle (Tumak, Son of the
Jungle)**, A.k.a. **The Cave Dwellers and Man and His Mate**, orig. to be titled
Five Millions B.C.*
blurb: "The most exciting adventure in a million years!"
Classic adventure-fantasy: Struggles of prehistoric humans

One Million Years B.C.
1966, (GB), Hammer-7Arts/20th-Fox, color, 91 mins.
W: Raquel Welch *(Loana, the Fair One)*, John Richardson *(Tumak)*, Percy Herbert
(Sakana), Yvonne Horner *(Ulla)*, Robert Brown
(Akhoba), Lisa Thomas *(Sura)*, Jean Wladon *(Ahot)*, Malya Nappi *(Tohana)*,
William Lyon Brown *(Payto)*
WRIT & P: Michael Carreras **ADAPT FROM ORIG. SCR:** Michell Novak,
George Baker & Joseph Frickert **D:** Don Chaffey **PHOTOG:** Wilkie
Cooper **ANIMATED DINOSAURS:** Ray Harryhausen **MUSIC:** Mario
Nascimbene
Standard adventure-fantasy: Prehistoric man counters nature and opposite sex

One Minute Before Death
1988, (USA), color, 87 mins.
W: Giselle MacKenzie
Minor thriller: Woman buried alive

One Mysterious Night
1944, (USA), Col, b&w, 62 mins.
W: Chester Morris *(Boston Blackie)*, Janis Carter *(Dorothy Anderson)*, Richard Lane
(Insp. Farraday), George E. Stone *(Runt)*, William Wright *(Paul Martens)*,

One Night of Fame
1948, (Fr), Scalera, b&w, 80 mins.
W: Marilyn Buferd, Mischa Auer, Ferruccio Taglavini
D: Mario Monicelli & Steno
*A.k.a. **Fame and the Devil***
Standard fantasy

One of the Bulldog Breed
1909, (GB), Rosie Films, b&w, 523 ft. (159.4m)
D: Joe Rosenthal
Standard crime-thriller: Wounded sailor saves girl from kidnapping thieves

One of Our Dinosaurs is Missing
1975, (GB), Walt Disney/Buena Vista, color, 94 mins.
W: Helen Hayes *(Hettie)*, Peter Ustinov *(Hnup Wan)*, Clive Revill *(Quon)*, Derek
Nimmo *(Lord Southmere)*, Joan Sims *(Emily)*, Bernard Bresslaw *(Fan Choy)*,
Natasha Pyne *(Susan)*, Roy Kinnear *(Supt. Grubbs)*, Deryck Guyler *(Harris)*,
Joss Ackland *(B.J. Spence)*, Andrew Dove *(Lord Castleberry)*, Max Harris
(Truscott), Richard Pearson *(Sir Geoffrey)*, Amanda Barrie *(Mrs. Spence)*, Jon
Pertwee *(The Colonel)*, Max Wall *(The Juggler)*, John Laurie *(Jock)*, Hugh
Burden *(Haines)*, Arthur Howard *(Thumley)*, Joan Hickson *(Mrs. Gibbons)*,
Anthony Sharp *(The Home Secretary)*, Wensley Pithey *(Bromley)*, Frank Wil-
liams *(Dr. Freemo)*, Percy Herbert *(Gibbons)*, Jane Lapotaire *(Miss Prescott)*,
Peter Madden *(Sanders)*, Leslie Dwyer *(The Driver)*, Kathleen Byron *(The
Wife)*, Erik Chitty *(The Guard)*, Molly Weir *(The Nanny)*
P: Bill Walsh **D:** Robert Stevenson & Anthony Squire **SCR:** Bill Walsh, from
Daniel Forrest's novel *The Great Dinosaur Robbery* **PHOTOG:** Paul Beeson
MUSIC: Ron Goodwin
Juvenile adventure: Old lady attempts to retrieve stolen dinosaur skeleton

One of Our Spies is Missing
1966, (USA), MGM, color, 91 mins.
W: Robert Vaughn *(Napoleon Solo)*, David McCallum *(Illya Kuryakin)*, Vera Miles,
Maurice Evans, Leo G. Carroll, Yvonne Craig, James Doohan
P: Boris Ingster **D:** E. Darrel Hallenbeck **SCR:** Howard Rodman
*Standard thriller (culled from episodes of teleseries "The Man from U.N.C.L.E."): Enemy
agents seek rejuvenation serum*

One Plus One
1968, (GB), Cupid/Connoisseur, color, 109 mins.
W: Mick Jagger, The Rolling Stones, Anne Wiazemsky, Frankie Dymon Jr., Iain
Quarrier, Danny Daniels, Illario Pedro, Roy Stewart, Nike Arrighi,
Francoise Pascal, Joanna David
P: Eleni Collard, Michael Pearson & Iain Quarrier **D & STORY:** Jean-Luc

Godard, from a novel by Sean Lynch,   **MUSIC:** The Rolling Stones
Standard fantasy: Melange of diverse episodes (e.g., Bolivian revolutionary in hiding, pop group, Black Power militants, etc.)

One Spy Too Many
1966, (USA), Arena/MGM, color, 100 mins.
W: Robert Vaughn (*Napoleon Solo*), David McCallum (*Illya Kuryakin*), Rip Torn (*Alexander*), Dorothy Provine (*Tracey Alexander*), Leo G. Carroll (*Mr. Waverly*), David Opatoshu (*Kavon*), Yvonne Craig (*Maude Waverly*), Robert Karnes (*Col. Hawks*), Donna Michelle (*Princess Nicole*), Leon Lontoc (*Gen. BonPhouma*), Clarke Gordon, James Hong, Cal Bolder, Arthur Wong, Carole Williams, Teru Shimada
P: David Victor   **D:** Joseph Sargent   **SCR:** Dean Hargrove   **PHOTOG:** Fred Koenekamp   **MUSIC:** Gerald Fried
Standard thriller (culled from episodes of teleseries "The Man from U.N.C.L.E."): Madman plots world conquest

On Her Majesty's Secret Service: GEORGE LAZENBY

1,001 Arabian Nights
1959, (USA), UPA, color, 75 mins.
VOICES: Jim Backus, Kathryn Grant, Dwayne Hickman, Hans Conried, Herschel Bernardi, Alan Reed
D: Jack Kinney
Entertaining animated fantasy: "Mr. Magoo" has Oriental adventures

1,000 Years from Now
see *Captive Women*

One Touch of Venus
1948, (USA), Univ, b&w, 81 mins.
W: Ava Gardner, Robert Walker, Dick Haymes, Eve Arden, Tom Conway, James Flavin, Olga San Juan
P: Lester Cowan   **D:** William Seiter   **SCR:** Harry Kurnitz & Frank Tashlin, from the musical play by Ogden Nash & S.J. Perelman (with lyrics by Ogden Nash) suggested by F. Anstey's *The Tinted Venus*   **PHOTOG:** Franz Planer   **MUSIC:** Kurt Weill   **MUSIC SCORE & NEW LYRICS:** Ann Ronell   **SONG:** *Speak Low When You Speak Love*
Classic comedy-fantasy: Statue of Aphrodite comes to life. cf. **The Goddess of Love, Mannequin** *and* **Xanadu**

One Way Out
1955, (GB), Major/RFD, b&w, 61 mins.
W: Jill Adams (*Shirley Harcourt*), Lyndon Brook (*Leslie Parrish*), Eddie Byrne (*Supt. Harcourt*), John Chandos (*Danvers*), Olive Milbourne (*Mrs. Harcourt*), Arthur Howard (*Marriott*), Ryck Rydon (*Harry*), Anne Valery (*Carol Martin*)
P: John Temple-Smith & Francis Edge   **D:** Francis Searle   **SCR:** Jonathan Roche
STORY: John Temple-Smith & Jean Scott-Rogers
Standard crime-thriller: Jewel thieves blackmail detective

One Wish Too Many
1956, (GB), Realist/British Lion-Children's Film Foundation, b&w, 56 mins.

W: Anthony Richmond (*Peter Brown*), Rosalind Gougey (*Nancy*), Terry Cooke (*Bert*), John Pike (*Ian*), Sam Costa (*Mr. Pomfret*), Arthur Howard (*The Headmaster*), Gladys Young (*Miss Mint*)
P: Basil Wright   **D:** John Durst   **SCR:** John Eldridge & Mary Cathcart Borer   **STORY:** Norah Pulling
Standard juvenile fantasy: Magic marble grants wishes

On Her Bed of Roses
1966, (USA), Famous Players, b&w, 104 mins.
W: Sandra Lynn, Ronald Warren (*Stephen Long*)
P: Robert Caramico   **D & SCR:** Albert Zugsmith
Minor thriller: Girl seeks psychiatric help after disturbed fiance kills his mother, passing motorists, and himself

On Her Majesty's Secret Service
1969, (GB), Eon/UA, color, 140 mins.
W: George Lazenby (*James Bond*), Diana Rigg (*Tracy*), Telly Savalas (*Blofeld*), Bernard Lee ("*M*"), Gabriele Ferzetti (*Draco*), Ilse Steppat (*Irma Bunt*), George Baker (*Sir Hilary Bray*), Yuri Borienko (*Grunther*), Lois Maxwell (*Miss Moneypenny*), Bernard Horsfall (*Campbell*), Catherina von Schell (*Nancy*), Virginia North (*Olympe*), Angela Scoular (*Ruby*), Bessie Love (*The Casino Guest*), Irving Allen (*Che Che*), Les Crawford (*Felsen*), Geoffrey Chesire (*Toussaint*), Bill Morgan (*Klett*), Terry Mountain (*Raphael*), James Bree (*Gumpold*), George Cooper (*Braun*), Brian Worth (*Manuel*), Dani Sheridan, Julie Ege, Joanna Lumley, Mona Chong, Anoushka Hempel, Zara, Ingrit Back, Jenny Hanley, Sylvana Henriques, Helena Ronee, Desmond Llewelyn (*Q*)
P: Harry Saltzman & Albert R. Broccoli   **D:** Peter Hunt   **SCR:** Richard Maibaum, from Ian Fleming's novel   **PHOTOG:** Michael Reed, Egil Woxholt, Roy Ford & John Jordan   **MUSIC:** John Barry   **SONG:** *We Have All the Time in the World* (sung by Louis Armstrong)
Major adventure-thriller: Spy matches wits with nemesis. George Lazenby's only James Bond film

On His Majesty's Service
1914, (GB), London/Globe, b&w, 3,300 ft. (1000.6m)
W: Jane Gail (*0-18*), Douglas Munro (*Otto Bergmann*), Gerald Ames (*The Secret Agent*), Wyndham Guise (*William Bergmann*), Edward O'Neill (*The Spy*), Lewis Gilbert
D: George L. Tucker   **STORY:** Frank Fowell
USA retitle, 0-18: or, A Message from the Sky
Standard crime-thriller: Typist exposes businessmen as spies

Onibaba (The Hole)
1964, (Jap), Tokyo Eiga-Kindai Eiga Kyokai/Toho, b&w, 105 mins.
W: Kei Sato (*Machi*), Nobuko Otowa (*The Old Woman*), Jitsuko Yoshimura (*The Young Girl*), Taiji Tonomura (*Ushi*), Jukichi Uno (*The Samurai in the Mask*), Kentaro Kaji, Hochui Araya
P: Toshio Konya   **WRIT & D:** Kiyomi Kuroda   **PHOTOG:** Kazuo Enoki   **MUSIC:** Hikaru Mitsu Hoyashi
Classic fantasy-thriller: Samurai tale of murder, haunting

Only a Dead Witness Keeps Quiet
see *Hipnosis*

Only a Room-er
1916, (GB), Cricks/DFSA, b&w, 663 ft. (202.1m)
W: Jack Jarman (*The Roomer*), Mrs. Dangerfield (*The Landlady*)
D: Toby Cooper   **STORY:** Ernest Dangerfield
Standard comedy: Men persuade friend to sleep in haunted room, play tricks on him

Only a Scream Away
1974, (GB), Cecil Clarke/ATV/ITC, Made for TV, color, 71 mins.
W: Gary Collins (*Howard Heston*), Hayley Mills (*Samantha Miller*), Joyce Carey (*Liza Meredith*), David Warbeck (*Robert Miller*), Jeremy Bulloch (*Tom Manners*), Jonathan Elsom (*John Stratford*), Ronald Mayer (*Dr. Lambert*), Richard Beaumont (*Heston as a Child*), Candida Brown (*Samantha as a Child*), Barrie Fletcher (*Det. Sgt. Sullivan*)
D: Peter Jefferies   **TELEPLAY:** Terence Feely, from orig. story by Brian Clemens   **PHOTOG:** Mike Whitcutt & Tony Mander   **MUSIC:** Laurie Johnson
TVM, minor thriller: Accidents beset newlywed

Only One Girl: or, A Boom in Sausages
1910, (GB), Clarendon, b&w, 495 ft. (150.9m)
D: Percy Stow
Standard comedy-fantasy short: Bumpkin wins only girl in village by making sausages out of rivals

The Only Way Out is Dead
1970, (Can), Palomer, Made for TV, color, 100 mins.
W: Burl Ives, Sandy Dennis, Stuart Whitman, Ron Hartman, Robert Goodier
D: John Trent   **TELEPLAY:** Henry Denker
A.k.a. **The Man Who Wanted to Live Forever**
TVM (theatrical release in Europe), standard SF-thriller: Billionaire seeks immortality, steals body parts from young men

Onna Kyuketsuki (Male Vampire) (Vampire Man)
1959, (Jap), Shintoho, color, 78 mins.
W: Shigeru Amachi, Yoko Mihara, Junko Ikeuchi, Keinosuke Wada

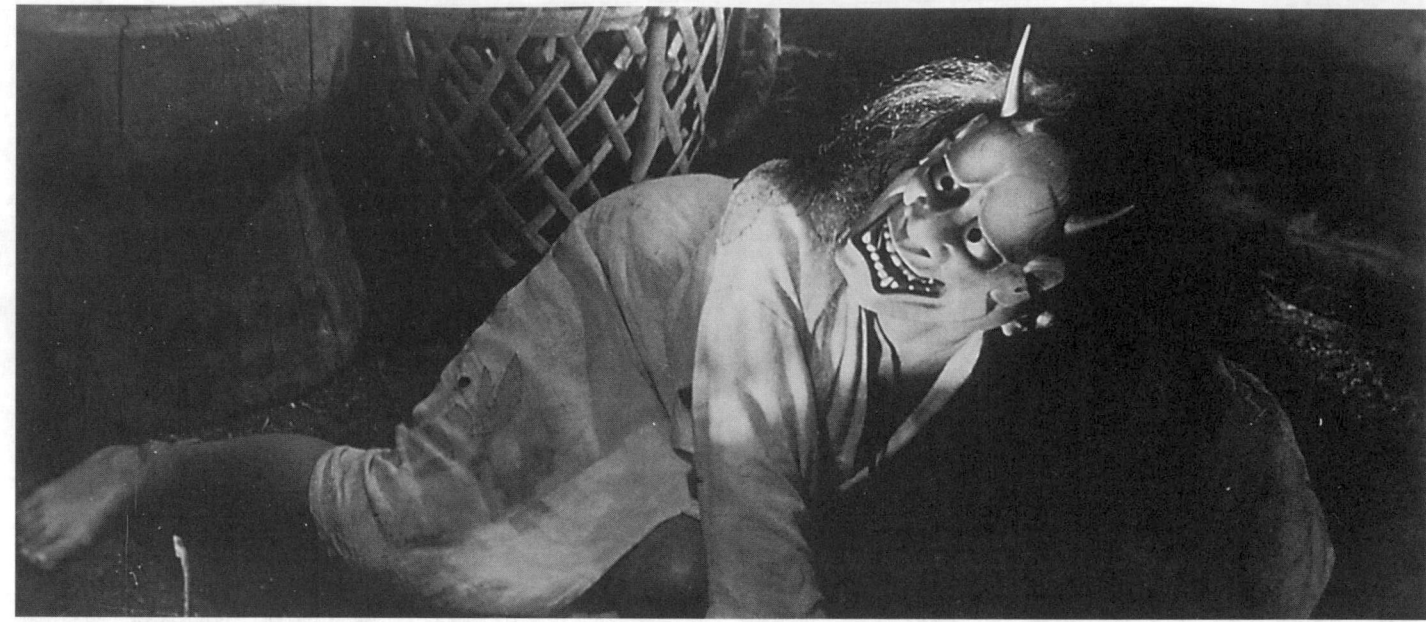

Onibaba: NOBUKO OTOWA

D: Nobuo Nakagawa
Standard horror-fantasy: Oriental Undead preys

On Secret Service
1933, (GB), BIP/Wardour, b&w, 91 mins.
W: Greta Nissen *(Marchesa Marcella)*, Carl Ludwig Diehl *(Hauptmann von Hombergk)*, Don Alvarado *(Valenti)*, Lester Matthews *(Coronello Ramenelli)*, Esme Percy *(Bleuntzli)*, C.M. Hallard *(Waldmuller)*, Austin Trevor *(ADC Larco)*, Cecil Ramage *(Da Villa)*, Wallace Geoffrey *(B18)*, Ernest Jay *(The Patient)*, Andreas Malandrinos *(The Innkeeper)*
D: Arthur Woods   **SCR:** Frank Vosper, Max Kimmich, Herbert Juttke & Arthur Woods, based on novel *Spione am Werk (Spies at Work)* by Georg Kloren & Robert Baberske
USA retitle, Secret Agent Alliance, 1935
Standard thriller: Austrian officer loves Italian girl who is really spy

On the Beach
1959, (USA), UA, b&w, 133 mins.
W: Gregory Peck *(Capt. Dwight Lionel Towers)*, Ava Gardner *(Moira Davidson)*, Fred Astaire *(Julian Osborn)*, Anthony Perkins *(Lt. Peter Holmes)*, Donna Anderson *(Mary Holmes)*, Guy Doleman *(Dr. Fletcher)*, John Tate, Lola Brooks, John Meillon, Richard Meikle, Ken Wayne, Lou Vernon, Harp McGuire, Grant Taylor
P & D: Stanley Kramer   **SCR:** James Lee Barrett & John Paxton, from Nevil Shute's novel   **PHOTOG:** Giuseppe Rotunno   **MUSIC:** Ernest Gold
SONG: *Waltzing Matilda*
Classic SF-thriller: Australians await nuclear doomsday

On the Brink of the Precipice
1913, (GB), Hepworth, b&w, 1,800 ft. (548.6m)
W: Harry Gilbey *(Stephen Veriker)*, Harry Royston *(The Groom)*, John McAndrews *(The Detective)*, Jack Raymond, Johnny Butt
D: Warwick Buckland
Standard crime-thriller: Acrobats save kidnapped child of nobleman's widow

On the Carpet
1916, (GB), Martin/DFSA, b&w, 1,048 ft. (319.4m)
D: Edwin J. Collins
Standard fantasy: Drunken groom dreams he and landlady fly by magic carpet to sultan's harem

On the Far Side of Adventure
*see **Mas alla de la Aventura***

On the Isle of Samoa
1950, (USA), Col, b&w, 65 mins.
W: Jon Hall, Susan Cabot Raymond Greenleaf, Henry Marco
D: William Berke
Standard adventure-thriller

On the Run
1963, (GB), Merton Park/Anglo-Amalgamated, b&w, 59 mins.
W: Emrys Jones *(Frank Stewart)*, Sarah Lawson *(Helen Carr)*, Patrick Barr *(Sgt. Brent)*, Delphi Lawrence *(Yvonne)*, Kevin Stoney *(Wally Lucas)*, Katy Wild *(Jean Stuart)*, William Abney *(Jock McKay)*, Philip Locke *(David Hughes)*
P: Jack Greenwood   **D:** Robert Tronson   **SCR:** Richard Harris, from a story by Edgar Wallace
Standard crime-thriller: Bookie helps convict break jail, uncover hidden bonds

On the Run
1958, (GB), danziger/UA, b&w, 70 mins.
W: Neil McCallum *(Wesley)*, Susan Beaumont *(Kitty Casey)*, William Hartnell *(Tom Casey)*, Philip Saville *(Driscol)*, Gordon Tanner *(Bart Taylor)*, Gilbert Winfield *(Joe)*
P: Edward J. & Harry Lee Danziger   **D:** Ernest Morris   **STORY:** Brian Clemens & Eldon Howard
Standard crime-thriller: Boxer flees crooks

On the Threshold of Space
1956, (USA), 20th-Fox, color, 98 mins.
W: Guy Madison *(Capt. James Hollenbeck)*, John Hodiak *(Maj. Ward Thomas)*, Martin Milner *(Lt. Morton Glenn)*, Virginia Leith *(Pat Lange)*, Dean Jagger *(Dr. Hugh Thornton)*, Warren Stevens *(Capt. Mike Bentley)*, King Calder *(Lee Welch)*, Ken Clark *(Sgt. Ike Forbes)*, Donald Murphy *(Sgt. Zack Deming)*, Rex Lease, Don Freed, Barry Coe, Richard Grant, Joe Locke, Jess Kirkpatrick, Leonard Penn, Carlyle Mitchell, Robert Cornthwaite, Guy Kingsford, Jo Gilbert, Charles Lind, Helen Bennett, David Armstrong
P: William Bloom   **D:** Robert D. Webb   **SCR:** Simon Wincelberg & Francis Cockrell   **PHOTOG:** Joe MacDonald   **MUSIC:** Lionel Newman
Standard semi-docu thriller: Experimental incursions on upper atmosphere

Open Secret
1948, (USA), Marathon/Eagle Lion, b&w, 70 mins.
W: John Ireland, Jane Randolph
Standard thriller

Opera
*see **Terror at the Opera***

Operation Atlantis
1965, (It), AIP-TV/color, 91 mins
W: John Ericson *(George Steel)*, Berna Rock *(Albia)*, Maria Granada *(Fatma)*, Beni Deus *(Ben Ullah)*
D: Paul Fleming
Minor thriller: Secret agent probes sabotage in Africa

Operation C.I.A.
1965, (USA), AA, b&w, 90 mins.
W: Burt Reynolds, John Hoyt, Kieu Chinh, Danielle Aubry, Cyril Collick, Victor Diaz, William Catching, Chaiporn, Marsh Thomson, John Laughinghouse, Frank Estes, Michael Schwiner, Robert Gulbranson, Janet Russcll
D: Christian Nyby   **STORY:** Peer J. Oppenheimer & Bill S. Ballinger
PHOTOG: Paul Dunlap   **MUSIC:** Leonard "Buzz" Blair
Standard melodrama

Operation Conspiracy
*see **Cloak without Dagger***

Operation Counterspy
1966, (Fr-It-Span), color, 111 mins.
W: George Ardisson, Helene Chanel
Minor thriller

Operation Crossbow
1965, (GB), Carlo Ponti/MGM, color, 116 mins.
W: Sophia Loren *(Nora)*, George Peppard *(Lt. John Curtis)*, Trevor Howard *(Prof. Lindemann)*, John Mills *(Gen. Boyd)*, Richard Johnson *(Duncan Sandys)*, Tom

Courtenay (*Robert Henshaw*), Jeremy Kemp (*Phil Bradley*) (*Frieda*), Anthony Quayle (*Bamford*), Paul Henreid (*Gen. Ziemann*), Helmut Dantine (*Gen. Linz*), Richard Todd (*WC Kendall*), Sylvia Syms (*Constance Babington-Smith*), John Fraser (*FL Kenny*), Barbara Rueting (*Hanna Reitsch*), Patrick Wymark (*Winston Churchill*), Richard Wattis (*Charles Sims*), Maurice Denham (*The Officer*), Allan Cuthbertson (*The Examiner*), Karel Stepanek (*Prof. Van Leyden*), Anton Diffring (*The SS Officer*), Ferdy Mayne (*Hauptman*), Carl Jaffe

P: Carlo Ponti   **D:** Michael Anderson   **SCR:** Richard Imrie, Derry Quinn & Ray Rigby   **STORY:** Duilio Coletti & Vittoriano Petrilli   **PHOTOG:** Erwin Hillir   **MUSIC:** Ron Goodwin

USA retitle, **The Great Spy Mission**
Exciting World War II thriller: Allied officers pose as German scientists, seek to sabotage V2 rocket

Operation Double Cross
1965, (Fr), color
W: Jean Marais, Marisa Mell, Howard Vernon
Minor thriller

Operation Fear
see **Operazione Paura**

Operation Goldman
see **Lightning Bolt**

Operation Hong Kong
see **Secret Agent 077—Operation Hong Kong**

Operation Kid Brother
1967, (It), UA, color, 104 mins.
W: Neil Connery, Daniela Bianchi, Bernard Lee, Adolfo Celi, Agata Fiori, Lois Maxwell, Anthony Dawson, Nando Angelini, Yachuco Yama, Mario Soria, Guido Lollobrigida, Anna Maria Noe, Franco Giacobini
D: Alberto DeMartino   **MUSIC:** Ennio Morricone
A.k.a. **O.K. Connery,** *video title,* **Secret Agent 00**
Minor thriller: Intrigue involves James Bond's younger brother

Operation: Lovebirds
1968, (Den), Nordisk/Emerson, color
W: Morten Grunwald, Essy Persson
Minor thriller

Operation M
see **Hell's Bloody Devils**

Operation Manhunt
1954, (USA), UA, b&w, 77 mins.
W: Irja Jensen, Harry Townes, (Igor Gouzenko, who delivers the epilogue)
Minor melodrama. Also done as **The Iron Curtain,** *1998.*

Operation Murder
1957, (GB), Danziger/ABP, b&w, 66 mins.
W: Tom Conway (*Dr. Wayne*), Sandra Dorne (*Pat Wayne*), Robert Ayres (*Larry Winton*), Patrick Holt (*Dr. Bowen*), Rosamund John (*The Head Nurse*), Virginia Kelley (*Julie*), Alastair Hunter (*Williams*), John Stone (*Insp. Price*)
D: Ernest Morris   **STORY:** Brian Clemens
Standard crime-thriller: Surgeon plots rich cousin's murder

Operation Secret
1952, (USA), WB, b&w, 108 mins.
W: Cornel Wilde (*Peter Forrester*), Karl Malden (*Lautrec*), Steve Cochran (*Marcel*), Phyllis Thaxter (*Maria*), Paul Picerni (*Armand*), Lester Matthews, Dan O'Herlihy, Dan Riss, Jay Novello, Wilton Graff, Harlan Warde, Kenneth Patterson, William Leicester (*Lester*), Gayle Kellogg
D: Lewis Seiler   **SCR:** James R. Webb & Harold Medford   **STORY:** Alvin Josephy & John Twist, as suggested by Lt. Col. Peter Ortiz   **PHOTOG:** Ted McCord   **MUSIC:** Roy Webb
Standard thriller: Dangerous doings of French underground

Operation Serpent
see **Fer-de-Lance**

Operation Solo
1965, (W. Ger), color
W: Pierre Brice, Senta Berger
Standard thriller: Secret agent seeks stolen missile-control unit

Operation Third Form
1966, (GB), World Wide/CFF, b&w, 58 mins.
W: John Moulder-Brown (*Dick*), Kevin Bennett (*Tom*), Sidney Bromley (*Paddy*), Derren Nesbitt (*Skinner*), Michael Crockett (*Alan*), Ronnie Caryl (*Brian*), Roberta Tovey (*Jill*), George Roderick (*Boss*)
P: Hindle Edgar   **D:** David Eady   **SCR:** Michael Barnes   **STORY:** Hindle Edgar & David Eady
Standard juvenile thriller: Schoolchildren track thieves

Operation X
see **My Daughter Joy**

Operazione Goldman
see **Lightning Bolt**

Operazione Paura (Operation Fear)
1966, (It), Europix, color, 85 mins.
W: Erika Blanc, Giacomo Rossi-Stuart, Fabienne Dali, Max Lawrence, Franca Dominici, Giana Vivaldi
D: Mario Bava
released in USA (1973) as **Curse of the Living Dead,** *A.k.a.* **Curse of the Dead** *and* **Kill, Baby, Kill!**
Standard horror-fantasy: Revenge murders by girl's ghost

The Oracle: MICHAEL MEDWIN AND JOSEPH TOMELTY

The Opium Cigarettes
1914, (GB), Climax, b&w, 1,000 ft. (304.8m)
WRIT & D: Stuart Kinder
Standard fantasy: Man smokes drugged cigarettes, has weird visions

The Oracle
1952, (GB), Group 3/Eros, b&w, 84 mins.
W: Robert Beatty (*Bob Jefferson*), Joseph Tomelty (*Terry Roche*), Mervyn Johns (*Tom Mitchum*), Michael Medwin (*Timothy Blake*), Virginia McKenna (*Shelagh*), Ursula Howells (*Peggy*), Gillian Lind (*Jane Bond*), Arthur Macrae (*Alan Digby*), John Charlesworth (*Denis*), Louise Hampton (*Miss Turner*), Maire O'Neill (*Mrs. Lenham*), Gilbert Harding (*The Oracle*)
P: John Grierson & Colin Lesslie   **D:** C. Pennington-Richards   **SCR:** Patrick Campbell, from Robert Barr's radio-play *To Tell You the Truth*   **PHOTOG:** Wolfgang Suschitzky   **MUSIC:** Temple Abady
USA retitle, **The Horse's Mouth** *(Mayer-Kingsley, 1953)*
Standard fantasy: Reporter cashes in on predictions of voice from well

The Oracle
1985, (USA), Reeltime, color, 94 mins.
W: Caroline Capers Powers (*Jennifer*), Roger Neil, Dorin Seymour, Victoria Dryden, Pam LaTesta, Chris Maria de Koron
D & PHOTOG: Roberta Findlay   **STORY & SCR:** R. Allen Leider   **MUSIC:** Walter E. Sear
Minor horror-thriller: Coeds become guinea pigs in sadistic experiments

L'Oracle de Delphes (The Oracle of Delphi)
1903, (Fr), Star, b&w, 30m (98.4 ft./1.7 mins.)
D: Georges Melies
Standard fantasy: Ancient Greek seer predicts

The Oracle of Delphi
see **L'Oracle de Delphes**

Ora Pro Nobis
1917, (GB), Windsor/Walturdaw, b&w, 4,400 ft. (1341.1m)
W: Henry Victor (*Lord Osborne*), Harding Thomas (*The Organist*), Elizabeth Calkin (*The Child*)
P: Arrigo Bocchi   **D:** Rex Wilson   **STORY:** Rowland Talbot
Standard thriller: Organist dreams he kills lord who eloped with his adopted daughter

Ora Pro Nobis: or, The Poor Orphan's Last Prayer
1901, (GB), R.W. Paul, b&w, 100 ft. (30.5m)
D: Walter R. Booth
Standard fantasy short: Orphan dies in snow, angels bear spirit to heaven

Orca
1977, (USA), Famous Films, N.V./Dino De Laurentiis/Para, color, 92 mins.
W: Richard Harris (*Capt. Nolan*), Charlotte Rampling (*Rachel Bedford*), Bo Derek (*Annie*), Will Sampson (*Umilak*), Keenan Wynn (*Novak*), Scott Walker (*Swain*), Robert Carradine (*Ken*)
P: Luciano Vincenzoni D: Michael Anderson ORIG. STORY & SCR: Luciano Vincenzoni & Sergio Donati MUSIC: Ennio Morricone
Standard thriller: Killer whale seeks revenge

The Orchard End Murder
1981, (GB), Marnham & Harvey, color, 50 mins.
W: Bill Wallis (*The Gatekeeper*), Tracy Hyde (*Pauline Cox*), Clive Mantle (*Ewen*), Raymond Adamson (*Wickstead*), Jessie Evans (*Mrs. Trowel*), Mark Hardy (*Mike Robins*), Cyril Cross (*The Constable*), Mollie Maureen (*The Old Lady*), Alexander John (*The Newsreader*), Peter Hutchins (*The Detective*)
P: Julian Harvey WRIT & D: Christian Marnham PHOTOG: Peter Jessop MUSIC: Sam Sklair
Standard thriller: Railwayman's assistant strangles girl, buries body

Ordeal
1973, (USA), color, 74 mins.
W: Arthur Hill, Diana Muldaur, James Stacy, Macdonald Carey, Michael Ansara
D: Lee H. Katzin
*TVM, standard thriller (remake of 1953's **Inferno**): Scheming wife deserts injured husband in wilderness*

Ordeal by Innocence
1985, (GB), Cannon, color, 88 mins.
W: Donald Sutherland, Faye Dunaway, Christopher Plummer, Ian McShane, Sarah Miles, Diana Quick, Annette Crosbie, Anita Carey, Michael Elphick, George Innes, Michael Maloney, Phoebe Nichols, Valerie Whittington, Cassie Stuart, Ron Pember, Kevin Stoney, John Bardon, Brian Glover, Billy McColl
D: Desmond Davis SCR: Alexander Stuart, from an Agatha Christie novel PHOTOG: Billy Williams MUSIC: Dave Brubeck
Standard thriller: Murder probed

Order and Disorder
1964, (Czech), Czechs State, b&w, 40 mins.
W: Karel Vasicek, Pavel Bertl
D: Pavel Juracek & Schmidt
GB retitle, Josef Kilian
Standard melodrama

Order of the Black Eagle
1987, (GB), color, 93 mins.
W: Ian Hunter, Charles K. Bibby, William T. Hicks, Jill Donnellan
D: Worth Keeter
Minor thriller: Spy vs. neo-Nazis

L'Or du Cristobal (Cristobal's Gold)
1939, (Fr), Beryl, b&w, 80 mins.
W: Albert Prejean, Charles Vanel, Dita Parlo
D: Jacques Becker [uncredited] & Jean Stelli PHOTOG: Nicholas Hayer
Standard adventure-romance

L'Or du Duc (The Duke's Gold)
1965, (Fr), color, 88 mins.
W: Dorothee Blank
D: Jacques Baratier
Standard melodrama

Orfeo
1971, (USA), Pyramid, color, 11 mins.
Animated short, juvenile fantasy: Legend of Orpheus and Eurydice

Orgasmo
1968, (It-Fr), Titanus/Fanfare, color, 91 mins.
W: Carroll Baker (*Kathryn*), Lou Castel (*Peter*), Collette Descombes (*Eva*), Tino Carraro (*Brian*)
P: Salvatore Alabiso D: Umberto Lenzi SCR: Ugo Moretti, Umberto Lenzi & Marie Clair Solleville
USA retitle, Paranoia
Standard thriller: Bored widow drawn into web of perversion and blackmail

La Orgia de los Muertos (The Orgy of the Dead)
1972, (Sp), color 91 mins
W: Paul Naschy (*Igor*), Stanley Cooper {Stelvio Rosi}, Vickie Nesbitt Marcella Wright, Catherine Gilbert, Gerard Tichy
D: J.L. Merino
released in USA (1974) as Beyond the Living Dead A.k.a. The Hanging Woman and Return of the Zombies
Standard horror-thriller: Weird count creates army of corpses

La Orgia Nocturna de los Vampiros (The Vampires' Night Orgy)
1973, (Sp-It), International Amusements, color, 86 mins.
W: Jack Taylor
P: Jose Frade D: Leon Klimovsky SCR: Gabriel Burgos & Antonio Fos
A.k.a. Orgy of the Vampires

Standard horror-fantasy: Undead infest tourist trap

Orgy of Blood
see *Brides of Blood*

Orgy of the Dead
1965, (USA), Astra/Crest/F.O.G. Distributors, color, 90 mins.
W: Criswell, Pat Barringer, Texas Starr, Bunny Glaser, Fawn Silver, William Bates, Louis Ojena, John Andrews
P & D: Stephen C. Apostoloff (Aka A.C. Stephen) SCR: Edward D. Wood Jr., based on his novel
Standard nudie-horror: Couple meets Prince of Darkness

The Orgy of the Dead (1972)
see *La Orgia de los Muertos*

Orgy of the Golden Nudes
see *Honeymoon of Horror*

Orgy of the Vampires
see *La Orgia Nocturna de los Vampiros*

Oriental Black Art
1908, (Fr), Star, b&w
D: Georges Melies
Standard fantasy short

Oriental Dream
see *Kismet (1944)*

Orient Express
1953, (W. Ger-It), Prime-TV, b&w, 98 mins.
W: Curt Jurgens (*Bate*), Eva Bartok (*Roxanne*), Silvana Pampanini
D: Carlo Ludovico Bragaglia
Standard thriller: Avalanche strands train in Alps

Orion's Key
1997, (USA), color
W: Frank Zagarino, Jennifer MacDonald
Made-for-Video, standard SF-horror (a 'Shadowchaser" sequel): Architects in Africa awaken monster

Orlacs Haende (The Hands of Orlac)
1924, (Austria), Pan-Film, b&w, 100 mins
W: Conrad Veidt, Alexandra Sorina, Fritz Kortner, Carmen Cartellieri Paul Adkonas
D: Robert Wiene SCR: Ludwig Kerzt, from Maurice Renard's novel PHOTOG: Gunther Krampf & Hans Andreschlin
*Standard horror-thriller: Transplanted hands have life of their own cf. **Mad Love**. US Release: **The Mystic Mirror**, Ufa, 1928*

Orlak, el Infierno de Frankenstein (Orlak, Frankenstein's Inferno)
1960, (Mex), Col, b&w, 103 mins.
P & D: Rafael Baledon SCR: Alfredo Ruanova & Carlos E. Taboada
Minor horror-thriller: Scientist creates ultimate man

Orlando
1993, (GB-Russ-Fr-It-Neth), color, 93 mins.
W: Tilde Swinton, Billy Zane, John Wood, Lothaire Bluteau, Charlotte Valandrey, Heathcote Williams, Quentin Crisp (*Queen Elizabeth I*), Dudley Sutton, Peter Eyre, Jimmy Somerville, Thom Hoffman, Kathryn Hunter, Ned Sherrin
D & SCR: Sally Potter, from Virginia Woolf's modernist 1928 novel PHOTOG: Alexei Rodionov
Bizarre fantasy: Immortal spans ages as both man and woman

Orloff Against the Invisible Man
see The Invisible Dead

Orphée (Orpheus)
1950, (Fr), Andre Paulve-Films du Palais Royal/Discina Int'l, b&w, 112 mins.
W: Jean Marais (*Orpheus*), Francoise Perier (*Heurtebise*), Maria Casares (*The Princess*), Maria Dea (*Eurydice*), Roger Blin (*The Writer*), Pierre Bertin (*The Inspector*), Jacques Varennes (*The First Judge*), Henri Cremieux (*The Man*), Edouard Dermithe (*Cegeste*), Juliette Greco (*Aglaonice*), Jean-Pierre Mocky
WRIT & D: Jean Cocteau PHOTOG: Nicholas Hayer MUSIC: Georges Auric SETS: D'Eaubonne
*Classic fantasy: Man enters Netherworld. cf. **Black Orpheus'** and **The Fugitive Kind***

Orpheus
see *Orphee*

Orpheus Descending
1990, (USA), Nederlander/TNT-TV, color, 117 mins.
W: Vanessa Redgrave (*Lady Torrance*), Kevin Anderson (*Val Xavier*), Anne Twomey (*Carol Cutrere*), Brad Sullivan (*Jabe Torrance*), Vee Talbot), Sloane Shelton (*Beulah Binnings*), Patti Allison (*Dolly Hamma*), Peg Small (*Sister Temple*), Marlene Cameron (*Eva Temple*), Manning Redwood (*Sheriff Talbot*), Pat MacNamara (*Peewee Binnings*), Michael McCarty (*Dog*

Hama), Marcia Lewis (*Nurse Porter*), Doyle Richmond (*The Conjure Man*), Lewis Arlt (*David Cutrere*), Donna Lee Betz (*The Woman on the Telephone*), Michael Emerson (*The Clown*)
D & ADAPT: Peter Hall, from Tennessee Williams' play **PHOTOG:** Michael Fash **MUSIC:** Stephen Edwards
TVM, standard melodrama: Drifter disturbs life of small Southern town. cf. **The Fugitive Kind**

Gli Orrori del Castello di Nuremberga (Horrors of Nuremberg Castle)
1972, (It), AIP, color, 90 mins.
W: Joseph Cotten (*Alfred*), Elke Sommer (*Eva*), Massimo Girotti (*Karl*), Antonio Cantafora (*Peter*), Humi Raho (*The Inspector*), Alan Collins (*Fritz*), Rada Rassimov (*Christine*), Dieter Tressler (*Dortmundt*), Nicoletta Elmi (*Gretchen*)
D: Mario Bava **STORY & SCR:** Vincent Fotre **ADAPT:** William A. Bairn **PHOTOG:** Emilio Varriani **MUSIC:** Les Baxter
USA retitle, **Baron Blood,** *A.k.a.* **The Torture Chamber of Baron Blood**
Standard horror-thriller: Sadistic nobleman reincarnated

O.S.S.
1946, (USA), Para, b&w
W: Alan Ladd, Geraldine Fitzgerald, Patric Knowles, John Hoyt
Standard melodrama

OSS 117—Double Agent
1968, (It-Fr), Carlton Films/UPA, color
W: John Gavin, Margaret Lee, Curt Jurgens, Luciana Paluzzi
D: Andre Hunebelle
Minor thriller: Secret agent vs. assassination bureau

OSS 117—Mission for a Killer
1965, (It-Fr), Embassy, color, 84 mins.
W: Frederick Stafford, Mylene Demongeot
P: Paul Cadeac **D:** Andre Hunebelle **SCR:** Jean Halian, Pierre Fouchaud & Andre Hunebelle
Standard thriller: Secret agent uncovers world-domination plot

The Other (1913)
see **Der Andere**

The Other (1947)
see **La Otra**

The Other
1972, (USA), Rem-Benchmark/20th-Fox, color, 100 mins.
W: Uta Hagen (*Ada*), Diana Muldaur (*Alexandra*), Chris Udvarnoky (*Niles Perry*), Martin Udvarnoky (*Holland Perry*), Norma Connolly (*Aunt Vee*), Victor French (*Angelini*), Portia Nelson (*Mrs. Rowe*), Loretta Leversee (*Winnie*), Lou Frizzell (*Uncle George*), Jenny Sullivan (*Torrie*), Jack Collins (*Mr. P.C. Pretty*), John Ritter (*Rider*), Clarence Crow (*Russell*), Ed Bakey (*Chan-Yu*)
P & D: Robert Mulligan **SCR:** Thomas Tryon, from his novel **PHOTOG:** Robert L. Surtees **MUSIC:** Jerry Goldsmith **DESIGN:** Albert Brenner
Superior thriller: Psychic phenomena and brutal murders in New England town

The Other Fu-Manchu
see **El Otro Fu-Manchu**

Other Hell
1985, (It), color, 88 mins.
W: Carlo De Meyo, Francesca Carmeno
D: Stefan Oblowsky
Minor horror-thriller: Devil invades convent

The Other Man
1970, (USA), Univ/ABC-TV, color, 99 mins.
W: Roy Thinnes, Joan Hackett, Tammy Grimes, Arthur Hill
D: Richard A. Colla **TELEPLAY:** Michael Blankfort & Eric Bercovici
TVM, standard thriller: Wealthy woman attracted to mystery man

Other Meni's Gold
1912, (GB), P&B Films/Gerrard, b&w, 570 ft. (173.7m)
Standard crime-thriller: Works manager tempted to rob boss

The Other Person
1921, (GB), Granger-Binger, b&w, 5,319 ft. (1621.2m)
W: Zoe Palmer (*Alice Dene*), Adelqui Migliar (*Andrew Grain*), Arthur Pusey (*Chris Larcher*), E. Story-Gofton (*Dr. Pess*), William Hunter (*Amos Larcher*), Ivo Dawson (*Squire Grain*), Nora Hayden (*Dolly Banks*), Arthur Walcott (*Rev. Augustus Dene*)
D: B.E. Doxat-Pratt **SCR:** Benedict James, from a novel by Fergus Hume
Standard fantasy: Seance ghost reveals murderer

Otley
1968, (GB), Open Road/Col, color, 91 mins.
W: Tom Courtenay (*Gerald Arthur Otley*), Romy Schneider (*Imogen*), Leonard Rossiter (*Johnston*), Alan Badel (*Hadrian*), James Villiers (*Hendrickson*), James Bolam (*Albert*), Freddie Jones (*Proudfoot*), Fiona Lewis (*Lin*), Ronald Lacey (*Curtis*), Geoffrey Bayldon (*Hewett*), James Cossins (*Jeffcock*), James Maxwell (*Rollo*), Edward Hardwicke (*Lambert*), Damian Harris (*Miles*), Phyllida Law (*Jean*), Frank Middlemass (*Bruce*), Bernard Sharpe (*Tony*), Robert Brownjohn (*Paul*), Maureen Toal (*The Landlady*), Barry Fantoni

---

(*Larry*), Paul Angelis (*The Constable*), David Kernan (*The Ground Steward*), Sheila Steafel (*The Ground Stewardess*), Katherine Parr (*The Newsagent*), Kathleen Helm (*The Dietician*), Norman Shelley, Jimmy Young, John Savident, Ken Parry, Jonathan Cecil, Georgina Simpson, Ron Owen, Stella Tanner, Robin Askwith, Kevin Bennett, Pete Murray, Kenneth Cranham, Robert Gillespie, Donald McKillop
P: Bruce Cohn Curtis **D:** Dick Clement **SCR:** Dick Clement & Ian La Frenais **PHOTOG:** Austin Dempster **MUSIC DIR:** Stanley Myers
Standard comedy-thriller: Innocent involved in espionage

La Otra (The Other)
1946, (Mex), Panamerican Films, b&w, 93 mins.
W: Dolores Del Rio
Standard thriller: Dead woman impersonated. cf. **Dead Ringer**

El Otro Fu-Manchu (The Other Fu-Manchu)
1945, (Sp), Genfuegos, b&w
W: Adela Esteban, Alfonso Horna, Jose Jaspe, Rosita Yarza, Alicia Torres, Candida Lopez, Mary Gonzalez, Carlos Munos, Manuel Requena, Manuel Kayser
WRIT & D: Ramon Barreiro, inspired by Sax Rohmer's *Fu Manchu* novels
Standard thriller: Oriental villain conspires

Oubliette
1914, (USA), b&w, 35 mins.
W: Lon Chaney Sr.
Minor melodrama (earliest extant Chaney Sr. film): Misspent life of poet Francois Villon

Our Man Flint
1965, (USA), 20th-Fox, color, 107 mins.
W: James Coburn (*Derek Flint*), Lee J. Cobb (*Cramden*), Gila Golan, Edward Mulhare, Russ Conway, Sigrid Valdis, Benson Fong, Rhys Williams, Peter Brocco, Lewis Charles, Gianna Serra
P: Saul David **D:** Daniel Mann **SCR:** Hal Fimberg & Ben Starr, from a story by Hal Fimberg **PHOTOG:** Daniel L. Fapp **SPCL-FX:** Howard Lydecker & Emil Kosa Jr. **MUSIC:** Jerry Goldsmith
Standard comedy-thriller: Secret agent has Russian adventure. cf. **In Like Flint**

Our Man Flint: Dead on Target
1976, (USA), color, 78 mins.
W: Ray Danton, Sharon Acker, Lawrence Dane, Linda Sorenson, Donnelly Rhodes, Susan Sullivan
D: Joseph L. Scanlon
TVM (pilot for unsold teleseries), minor thriller: Super agent rescues kidnapped oil executive

Our Mother's House: PAMELA FRANKLIN AND DIRK BOGARDE

Our Man in Marrakesh
1966, (GB), Marrakesh-Towers of London/Anglo-Amalgamated, color, 94 mins.
W: Tony Randall (*Andrew Jessel*), Senta Berger (*Kyra Stanovy*), Herbert Lom (*Narim Casimir*), Wilfrid Hyde-White (*Arthur Fairbrother*), Terry-Thomas (*El Caid*), Gregoire Aslan (*Achmed*), John LeMesurier (*George C. Lilleywhite*), Klaus Kinski (*Jonquil*), Margaret Lee (*Samia Voss*), Keith Peacock (*Philippe*)
P: Harry Alan Towers **D:** Don Sharp **SCR:** Peter Yeldham
USA retitle, **Bang, Bang, You're Dead.** *A.k.a.* **I Spy, You Spy**
Standard comedy-thriller: American tourist and girl secret agent are framed for murder

Our Mother's House
1967, (GB), Heron/Filmways-MGM, color, 105 mins.
W: Dirk Bogarde (*Charlie Hook*), Margaret Brooks (*Elsa Hook*), Pamela Franklin (*Diana Hook*), Louis Sheldon Williams (*Hubert Hook*), John Gugolka (*Dunstan Hook*), Mark Lester (*Jiminee Hook*), Sarah Nicholls (*Gerty Hook*),

Anthony Nicholls (*Mr. Halbert*), Gustav Henry (*Willy Hook*), Claire Davidson (*Miss Bailey*), Yootha Joyce (*Mrs. Quayle*), Edina Ronay (*Doreen*), Parnham Wallace

P & D: Jack Clayton   **SCR:** Jeremy Brooks & Haya Harareet, from Julian Gloag's novel   **PHOTOG:** Larry Pizer   **MUSIC:** Georges Delerue

Superior thriller: Frightened of being sent to orphanage, seven children conceal mother's death

L'Ours (The Bear)

1960, (Fr-It), Filmsonor/Intermondia/Titanus/Embassy, b&w, 90 mins.

W: Renato Rascel, Francis Blanche, Cora Camoin, Daniel Lecourtois, Gocha, Yvette Etievant, Hubert DeLapparent, Jean Bellanger, Jeanne Lapin

D & PHOTOG: Edmond Sechan   **STORY:** Roger Mauge   **ADAPT & DIALOG:** Roger Mauge & Edmond Sechan

*US release: **The Bear**, Embassy, 1963*

Modest comedy-fantasy: Discovery of talking bear

Outbreak

1995, (USA), Arnold Kopelson-Punch Prods./WB, color, 127 mins.

W: Dustin Hoffman (*Sam Daniels*), Rene Russo (*Robby Keough*), Morgan Freeman (*Gen. Billy Ford*), Cuba Gooding Jr. (*Maj. Sale*), Patrick Dempsey (*Jimbo*), Donald Sutherland (*Maj. Donald McClintock*), Kevin Spacey (*Casey*), Zakes Mokae, Malick Bowens, Jim Antonio, Leland Hayward III, Susan Lee Hoffman, Bruce Jarchow, Benito Martinez, Daniel Chodos, Dale Dye, Cara Keough, Michelle Joyner, Gina Menza, Donald Forrest, Julie Pierce, Tim Ransom, Michelle M. Miller, Maury Sterling, Per Didrik Fasmer, Lucas Dudley, Michael Emanuel, Joseph Latimore, Ed Beechner, Robert Alan Joseph, Jae Woo Lee, Michael Sottile, Matthew Saks, Lance Kerwin, Diana Bellamy, Brett Oliver, Larry Hine, Douglas Hebron, Nicholas H. Marshall, Derek Kim, Bill Stevenson, Dana Andersen, Buzz Barbee, Kellie Overbey, Traci Odom, Patricia Place, Nicholas Pappone, Herbert Jefferson Jr., Jenna Byrne, Thomas Crawford, Brian Reddy, Ina Romeo, Mimi Doyka, Jack Rader, Teresa Velarde, J.J. Chaback, Carmela Rappazzo, C. Jack Robinson, Albert Owens, Kurt Boesen, Robert Rigamonte, Peter Looney, Cynthia Harrison, Robert Alan Beuth, Gordon Michaels, Conrad Bachmann, Cary J. Pitts, Marilyn Brandt, Marcus Hennessy, David Silverbrand, Julie Araskog, Frank Rositani, George Christy, Bruce Isacson, Philip Handy, Tim Frazee, Moses Williams, Roland Tsui, Mark Drown, Jim Blumenthal, David Lee Phillips, Keith Butler, Ralph Miller, Robert "Bobby Z" Zajonc, David W. Paris, Chuck Tamburro, Rick Wheeler, Alan Purwin, Michael Tamburro, Harry J. Clark, David A. Kunz

P: Arnold Koppelson, Wolfgang Petersen & Gail Katz   **D:** Wolfgang Petersen   **SCR:** Laurence Dworet & Robert Roy Pool   **PHOTOG:** Michael Ballhaus   **SPCL-FX SPRVSR:** John Frazier   **MUSIC:** James Newton Howard

blurb: "Try to remain calm"

Unusual thriller: Virulent disease spreads terror

The Outcasts

1982, (Ire), Cinegate, color, 104 mins.

W: Mary Ryan (*Maura O'Donnell*), Mick Lally (*Scarf Michael*), Don Foley (*Hugh O'Donnell*), Tom Jordan (*Conor Farrell*), Cyril Cusack (*Myles Kennan*), Bairbre ni Chaoimh (*Janey O'Donnell*), Brenda Scallon (*Breda O'Donnell*), Gillian Hackett (*Triona*), Martin O'Flathearta (*Eamon Farrell*), Hilary Reynolds (*Roisin*), Paul Bennett (*Father O'Connolly*)

D & STORY: Robert Wynne-Simmons   **PHOTOG:** Seamus Corcoran   **MUSIC:** Stephen Cooney

Unusual melodrama: Village woman suspected of black magic

Outer and Inner Space

1966, (USA), Andy Warhol/Film-Makers' Cooperative, color, 70 mins.

W: Edie Sedgwick

P & D: Andy Warhol

Standard fantasy (16mm)

Outer Heat

see *Alien Nation*

The Outer Space Connection

1975, (USA), Sunn Classics, color, 93 mins.

W: Rod Serling (*narrator*)

D & SCR: Fred Warshofsky

Minor speculation-docu: Space aliens implicated in historical events

Outer Touch

1979, (GB), Three Six Two/Miracle, color, 78 mins.

W: Barry Stokes (*Oliver*), Tony Maiden (*Willy*), Glory Annen (*Cosia*), Michael Rowlatt (*Cliff*), Ava Cadell (*Partha*), Kate Ferguson (*Skipper*), Lynne Ross (*Prudence*), Bill Mitchell (*Voice of "Wurlitzer"*)

P & STORY: David Speechley   **D:** Norman J. Warren   **SCR:** Andrew Payne   **PHOTOG:** John Metcalfe & Peter Sinclair   **MUSIC:** Alan Brawer & Anna Pepper   **THEME:** The Chance

*USA retitle, **Spaced Out**, Miramax, 1981*

Standard eroto-SF: Three women from far planet take Earthmen aboard spacecraft, learn about sex

The Outing

1987, (USA), H.I.T. Films/TMS, color, 89 mins.

W: Deborah Winters (*Eve Farrell*), James Huston (*Dr. Al Wallace*), Andra St. Ivanyi (*Alex Wallace*), Scott Bankston (*Ted Pinson*), Mark Mitchell (*Mike Daley*), Damon Merrill, Tracye Walker, Andre Chimene, Barry Coffing,

Raan Lewis, Michelle Watkins, Hank Amigo, Brian Floores, Danny D. Daniels, Blue Deckert, Roy Alan Wilson, Coy Sevier, Christopher Wycliff, Warren Chaney, Beverly Wilson, Ron Shotola, William Gilinsky, Alan Stepp, Billy St. John, Roy Morgan, Valerie Padilla, Ron Stone, Mike Gilles, Gary Hourani, Chris Ford, Wendy Parras, Lesley Chaney, Audra Bennett, Laura Staffa, Alayna Bennett, Jason Flintoft, Chris McCauley, Jonathan Yancey, Stephanie Lewis, Tom Smith, Trey Lewis, Dominique Yuro, Jason Chaney

D: Tom Daley   **SCR:** Warren Chaney   **PHOTOG:** Herbert Raditschnig   **MUSIC:** Joel Rosenbaum & Bruce Miller

Standard horror-fantasy: Evil genie menaces teens

Outland

1981, (GB), Ladd Co./Stanley O'Toole/WB, color, 107 mins.

W: Sean Connery (*William O'Neil*), Peter Boyle (*Sheppard*), Frances Sternhagen (*Dr. Lazarus*), James B. Sikking (*Montone*), Kika Markham (*Carol O'Neil*), Clarke Peters (*Deputy Ballard*), Steven Berkoff (*Sagan*), Nicholas Barnes (*Paul O'Neil*), John Ratzenberger (*Tarlow*), Pat Starr (*Mrs. Spector*), Manning Redwood (*Lowell*), Hal Galili (*Nelson*), Anni Domingo (*Morton*), Angus MacInnes (*Hughes*), Stuart Milligan (*Walters*), Eugene Lipinski (*Cane*), Norman Chancer (*Slater*), Ron Travis (*Fanning*), Bill Bailey (*Hill*), Chris Williams (*Caldwell*), Marc Boyle (*Spota*), Richard Hammat (*Yario*), James Berwick (*Rudd*), Gary Olsen (*The Worker*), Isabelle Lucas (*The Nurse*), Sharon Duce (*The Prostitute*), P.H. Moriarty (*Man #1*), Doug Robinson (*Man #2*), Angelique Rockas (*The Maintenance Woman*), Judith Alderson, Rayner Bourton, Julia Depyer, Nina Francoise, Brendan Hughes, Norri Morgan, Philip Johnston

P: Richard A. Roth   **WRIT & D:** Peter Hyams   **PHOTOG:** Stephen Goldblatt   **MUSIC:** Jerry Goldsmith

"...what most people mean when they talk about good escapist entertainment. A movie of unexpected pleasures"—Vincent Canby, New York Times

Unusual SF-thriller (reminiscent of 'High Noon'): Law enforcer deals with corruption on mining colony of moon Io

Outlaw of Gor

1989, (It), color, 89 mins.

W: Urbano Barbieri, Jack Palance, Rebecca Ferratti Donna Denton, Nigel Chipps, Russel Savadier

D: John "Bud" Cardos   from novels by John Norman

Standard SF-fantasy (sequel to 'Gor'): College professor has trials in land of despotic queen

Out of Annie's Past

1995, (USA), USA-TV, color, 95 mins.

W: Catherine Mary Stewart, Scott Valentine, Dennis Farina, Carsten Norgaard

TVM, standard thriller: Woman haunted by secret past and unsolved murder

Out Of The Fog: DAVID SUMNER AND SUSAN TRAVERS

Out of Order

1984, (W. Ger), Sandstar, color, 88 mins.

W: Gotz George, Renee Soutendijk, Wolfgang Kieling, Hannes Jaenicke, Klaus Wennemann

D & SP: Carl Schenkel

Tense thriller: Four people trapped in elevator of empty office high-rise

Out of the Body
1988, (USA), color, 91 mins.
W: Mark Hembrow, Tessa Humphries
D: Brian Trenchard-Smith
Minor horror-thriller: Man possessed by murderous evil spirit

Out of the Dark
1989, (USA), Cinetel Films/New Line, color, 90 mins.
W: Cameron Dye (*Kevin*), Karen Black (*Ruth*), Geoffrey Lewis (*Dennis*), Lynn Danielson (*Kristi*), Bud Cort (*Stringer*), Divine (*Langella*), Paul Bartel, Tracey Walter, Lainie Kazan, Tab Hunter, Hector Morales
D: Michael Schroeder SCR: J. Greg De Felice & Zane W. Levitt PHOTOG: Julio Macat MUSIC: Paul Antonelli
Modest thriller: Phone sex inspires murder

Out of the Darkness (1958)
see Teenage Cave Man

Out of the Darkness (1977)
see Night Creature

Out of the Fog
1941, (USA), WB, b&w, 93 mins.
W: John Garfield, Ida Lupino, Thomas Mitchell, Eddie Albert, John Qualen, George Tobias, Jerome Cowan, Aline MacMahon, Leo Gorcey
P: Hal Wallis D: Anatole Litvak SCR: Jerry Wald & Robert Rossen, from Irwin Shaw's play *The Gentle People* PHOTOG: James Wong Howe
Standard melodrama: Young Racketeer affects community

Out of the Fog
1962, (GB), Eternal Films/Grand Nat'l, b&w, 68 mins.
W: David Sumner (*George Mallon*), Susan Travers (*June Lock*), John Arnatt (*Supt. Chadwick*), James Hayter (*Daniels*), Jack Watson (*Sgt. Tracey*), Olga Lindo (*Mrs. Mallon*), Anthony Oliver (*The Chaplain*), Renee Houston (*Ma*), George Woodbridge (*Chopper*)
P: Maurice J. Wilson WRIT & D: Montgomery Tully
USA retitle, Fog for a Killer, Gold Key TV
Standard thriller: POW decoys ex-convict suspected of killing girls when moon is full

Out of the Mist
see Der Sohn der Hagar

Out of the Night
1945, (USA), PRC, b&w, 85 mins.
W: James Lydon, Warren William, Sally Eilers, Regis Toomey, Charles Arnt, George Reed
D: Edgar G. Ulmer
A.k.a. Strange Illusion
Minor thriller: Teen suspicious of mother's smooth-talking boyfriend

Out of the Past
1947, (USA), RKO, b&w, 96 mins.
W: Robert Mitchum, Jane Greer, Kirk Douglas, Rhonda Fleming, Richard Webb, Steve Brodie, Virginia Huston, Ken Niles, Paul Valentine, Dickie Moore
D: Jacques Tourneur SCR: Daniel Mainwaring PHOTOG: Nicholas Musuraca SPCL-FX: Russell A. Cully MUSIC: Roy Webb MUSIC DIR: C. Bakaleinikoff
A.k.a. Build My Gallows High
Classic: Innocent involved with criminals

Out of the Storm
1948, (USA), Rep, b&w, 61 mins.
W: James Lydon, Lois Collier
Minor melodrama. Remake: The Wrong Road

Out of the Shadow
1961, (GB), Border/New Realm, b&w, 61 mins.
W: Terence Longden (*Mark Kingston*), Donald Gray (*Insp. Wills*), Diane Clare (*Mary Johnson*), Robertson Hare (*Ronald Fortescue*), Felicity Young (*The Waitress*), Dermot Walsh (*Prof. Taylor*)
P: O. Negus-Fancey D & STORY: Michael Winner
Standard crime-thriller: Reporter proves brother's suicide was murder

Outside the Law
1921, (USA), MGM, b&w, 8 reels (8,000 ft./2438.4m/77 mins.)
W: Priscilla Dean (*Molly Madden*), Ralph Lewis ("*Silent*" *Madden*), Lon Chaney Sr. ("*Black Mike*" *Sylva/Ah Wing*), E.A. Warren (*Chang Lo*), Wheeler Oakman ("*Dapper Bill*" *Ballard*), Stanley Goethals ("*That Kid*"), Melbourne MacDowell (*Morgan Spencer*), Wilton Taylor (*The Inspector*)
D & STORY: Tod Browning SCR: Lucien Hubbard & Tod Browning PHOTOG: William Fildew
Standard melodrama: Gang warfare over jewel heist

Out There
1995, (USA), SHO-TV, color, 98 mins.
W: Bill Campbell, Wendy Schaal, Julie Brown, David Rasche, Paul Dooley, Bill Cobbs, Rod Steiger, Bobcat Goldthwait, June Lockhart, Jill St. John, Carel Struycken, Billy Bob Thornton, P.J. Soles
D: Sam Irvin SCR: Thomas Strelich & Alison Nigh PHOTOG: Gary Tieche MUSIC: Deborah Holland & Frankie Blue
Made-for-Cable, standard SF-thriller: Photographer finds snapshots of grounded flying saucer

Outward Bound
1930, (USA), WB, b&w, 10 reels (7,568 ft./2306.7m/88 mins.)
W: Leslie Howard (*Tom Prior*), Helen Chandler (*Ann*), Douglas Fairbanks Jr. (*Henry*), Beryl Mercer (*Mrs. Midget*), Alison Skipworth (*Mrs. Cliveden-Banks*), Dudley Digges (*Thompson, the Examiner*), Alec B. Francis (*Scrubby*), Montagu Love (*Mr. Lingley*), Lionel Watts (*Rev. William Duke*)
D: Robert Milton SCR: J. Grubb Alexander, from Sutton Vane's play PHOTOG: Hal Mohr
Standard fantasy: Passengers on ship headed for Purgatory. cf. Between Two Worlds

Outwitted by a Child
1910, (GB), Walturdaw, b&w, 585 ft. (175.5m)
Standard crime-thriller: Doctor's child drugs burglar's beer

The Oval Portrait
1988, (USA), color, 89 mins.
W: Giselle MacKenzie, Barry Coe
D: Regelio A. Gonzalez Jr., from Edgar Allan Poe's short story
Standard thriller: Maiden's illicit love for Confederate soldier

Overcharged
1912, (GB), Hepworth, b&w, 350 ft. (106.7m)
D: Lewin Fitzhamon
Standard fantasy short: Weak man electrified, becomes magnetic

The Overcoat
1960, (Russ), Lenfilm/Cinemasters Int'l, b&w, 78 mins.
W: Roland Bykov, Y. Tolubeyev
D: Alexei Batalov, from a story by Gogol
Standard fantasy: Dead Jew's spirit retrieves garment. cf. Shinel and The Bespoke Overcoat, US release, 1965

The Overcoat (1952)
see Il Cappotto

An Overdose of Love Potion
1907, (GB), Clarendon/Gaumont, b&w, 300 ft. (91.4m)
D: Percy Stow, from a story by Langford Reed
Standard comedy-fantasy short: Too much love potion makes man kiss everybody. cf. Love Potion No. 9, 1992

An Over-Incubated Baby
1901, (GB), R.W. Paul, b&w, 80 ft. (24.4m)
D: Walter Booth
Standard comedy-fantasy short: Child put into professor's incubator comes out an old man

Overlords of the UFO
1977, (USA), Gold Key, color, 92 mins.
Standard speculation-docu: Investigation of flying saucers

Over My Dead Body
see Vengeance

The Owl and the Lemming
1973, (Can), ACI, color, 7 mins.
Juvenile short (enacted by puppets): Eskimo "trickster tale"

Oxo-Omo-Ono
1970, (USA), Apex, color
WRIT & D: John Wash
Unusual short animated fantasy: Winged creatures battle on far planet

Pacific Heights
1990, (USA), Morgan Creek/20th Century Fox, color, 104 mins.
W: Michael Keaton (*Carter Hayes*), Matthew Modine (*Drake*), Melanie Griffith
(*Patty*), Mako, Nobu McCarthy, Carl Lumbly, Laurie Metcalf, Dorian
Harewood, Luca Bercovici, Sheila McCarthy, Beverly D'Angelo, Tippi
Hedren, Dan Hedaya, Miriam Margolyes, Nicholas Pryor
D: John Schlesinger   **SCR:** Daniel Pyne   **MUSIC:** Hans Zimmer
Taut thriller: Psychotic tenant terrorizes young landlords

The Pack
1977, (USA), WB, color, 99 mins.
W: Joe Don Baker (*Jerry*), Hope Alexander-Willis (*Millie*), Richard B. Shull
(*Hardiman*), R.G. Armstrong (*Cobb*), Ned Wertimer (*Walker*), Bibi Besch
(*Marge*), Delos V. Smith Jr. (*McMinnimee*), Richard O'Brien (*Dodge*), Sherry
Miles (*Lois*), Paul Willson (*Tommy*), Eric Knight (*Guy*), Steve Lytle (*Paul*),
Rob Narke (*The Husband*), Peggy Price (*The Wife*), Steve Butts (*Bobby*)
D & SCR: Robert Clouse, from a play by Dave Fisher   **PHOTOG:** Ralph
Woolsey   **MUSIC:** Lee Holdridge
*A.k.a. **The Long, Dark Night***
Standard thriller: Wild dogs prowl resort

The Package
1989, (USA), Orion, color, 108 mins.
W: Gene Hackman (*Johnny Gallagher*), Joanna Cassidy (*Eileen Gallagher*), Tommy
Lee Jones (*Thomas Boyette*), John Heard (*Col. Glen Whitacre*), Dennis Franz,
Reni Santoni, Pam Grier, Chelcie Ross, Ron Dean, Kevin Crowley, Marco
St. John, Thalmus Rasulala, Nathan Davis, Joe Greco, Miguel Nino, Ike
Pappas, Michael Skewes, Johnny Lee Davenport, Juan Ramirez, Mik Scriba,
Joe Guzaldo, Harry Lennix, Michael Tomlinson, Cody Glenn, Carlos Sanz,
Don James, Diane Timmerman, Charles Mueller, Wilhelm von Homburg,
Anatoly Davydov, William Musyka, Gary Berkovich, Allen Hamilton, Greg
Noonan, Harry Teinowitz, Gary Goldman, Katherine Lynch, Mary Seibel,
Joe D. Lauck, Dick Cusack, Boris Leskin, Danny Goldring, Gregory Alan-
Williams, Jack Kandel, Nick Kusenko, Tina Gloschenko, John Hardy,
Henry Godinez, Kathryn Joosten, Oksana Fedunszyn, Ralph Foody, Michael
Bacarella, Steve Barbo, Eddie Bo Smith Jr., Greg Goossen, Dennis Cockurm,
Ivory Ocean, Michael Gaylord James, Metta Davis, Alex Ross, Will Zahrn,
Dr. Christine Cassel, Nancy Baird, Gene Barge, Ray Allen, Walter Markley,
Otto von Wernherr, Hilda McLean, Leon Samoilovich, Dmitri Polytnsev,
Lana Berkovich, Phillip Prerost, John D'Amico, Billy Bosco, Chad Smith,
Jack Gold
D: Andrew Davis   **SCR:** John Bishop   **PHOTOG:** Frank Tidy   **SPCL-FX:** Tom
Tokunaga & Rodman Kiser   **MUSIC:** James Newton Howard   **SONGS:**
Soul of the Land & I Don't Know
Modest Cold-War thriller: Murderous faction seeks to abort East-West peace accord

Pacto Diabolico (Diabolical Pact)
1968, (Mex), Vergara, color
W: John Carradine, Miguel Angel Alvarez, Regina Thorne
P: Luis Enrique Vergara   **D:** Jaime Salvador   **SCR:** Ramon Obon Jr. & Adolpho
Torres Portillo
*Minor horror-fantasy (reworking of **Jekyll & Hyde**): Extracts from living women turn
old scientist into young murderer*

Pagan Island
1960, (USA), b&w, 67 mins.
W: Eddie Dew, Nani Maka
D: Barry Mahon   **SCR:** Clelle Mahon
Minor adventure-thriller: Treasure hunt in South Seas

The Pagemaster
1994, (USA), Turner Pictures/20th-Fox, color, 75 mins.
W: Macaulay Culkin, Christopher Lloyd, Ed Begley Jr., Mel Harris
VOICES: Whoopi Goldberg, Patrick Stewart, Leonard Nimoy, & Frank Welker
LIVE-ACTION DIR: Joe Johnston   **ANIMATION DIR:** Maurice Hunt   **SCR:**
David Kirschner, David Casci & Ernie Contreras   **STORY:** David Kirschner
& David Casci   **MUSIC:** James Horner
Standard adventure-fantasy (live action & animation): Boy taught vital lessons by books

Pages from Satan's Book
see *Blades af Satans Bog*

Paid to Kill
1954, (GB), Hammer/Exclusive/Lippert, b&w, 70 mins.
W: Dane Clark
*Standard thriller. GB title: **Five Days***

Painted Heart
1992, (USA), color, 90 mins.
W: Will Patton, Bebe Neuwirth, Robert Pastorelli, Casey Siemaszko, Mark Boone
Jr., Jayne Haynes
D: Michael Taav
Bizarre thriller: Lipstick Killer on loose

The Painted Smile
1962, (GB), Blakeley's Films-Doverton/Planet, b&w, 60 mins.
W: Liz Fraser (*Jo Lake*), Kenneth Griffith (*Kleinie*), Craig Douglas (*Singer*), Peter
Reynolds (*Mark*), Nanette Newman (*Mary*), Tony Wickert (*Tom*), Harold

Berens (*Mikhala*)
P: Tom Blakeley   **D:** Lance Comfort   **SCR:** Pip & Jane Baker   **STORY:** Brock
Williams
Standard crime-thriller: Fugitive tracks confidence trickster

Paint it Black
1989, (USA), color, 101 mins.
W: Rick Rossovich, Sally Kirkland, Martin Landau, Julie Carmen, Doug Savant,
Peter Frechette, Jason Bernard
D: Tim Hunter
Minor thriller (never released theatrically): Sculptor betrayed by lover

The Paint Job
1992, (USA), color, 96 mins.
W: Will Patton
Minor thriller: Dull-witted house painter falls in love with boss' murderous wife

Paint Me a Murder
1985, (GB), Hammer/Fox Mystery Theatre, Made for TV, color, 69 mins.
W: Michelle Phillips (*Sandra Lorenz*), James Laurenson (*Luke Lorenz*), David Robb
(*Vincent Rhodes*), Alan Lake (*Darcy*), Morgan Sheppard (*Mahaffy*), Tony
Steedman (*The Chief Inspector*), Mark Heath (*Det. Insp. Robinson*), Michael
Watkins (*Det. Sgt. Harris*), Michael McKevitt (*Soames*), Gerald Sim (*The
Vicar*), Richard Parmentier (*Kates*), Indira Joshi (*Mrs. Patel*), Jeillo Edwards
(*The Landlady*), David Millett (*The Police Sergeant*), Neil Morrissey (*The
Policeman*), Peggy Aitchison (*The Bag Lady*), Lynn Clayton (*The Secretary*)
D: Alan Cooke   **TELEPLAY:** Jesse Lasky Jr. & Pat Silver   **PHOTOG:** Frank
Watts   **MUSIC:** Francis Shaw   **MUSIC SPRVSR:** Philip Martell
TVM, standard thriller: Artist's greedy wife plans homicide

Pajama Party
1964, (USA), AIP, color, 85 mins.
W: Tommy Kirk, Annette Funicello, Donna Loren, Jesse White, Harvey Lembeck,
Elsa Lanchester, Jody McCrea, Susan Hart, Don Rickles, Dorothy Lamour,
Buster Keaton, Bobbi Shaw, Ben Lessy, Candy Johnson
P: James H. Nicholson & Samuel Z. Arkoff   **D:** Don Weis   **SCR:** Louis M.
Heyward   **PHOTOG:** Floyd Crosby   **SONGS:** *Where Did I Go Wrong*
*orig. to be titled **The Maid and the Martian***
Standard SF-comedy: Martian teen studies Earth adolescents

Pajama Party in a Haunted House
see *The Ghost in the Invisible Bikini*

P.A.K.
see *The Automatic Motorist*

Le Palais des Mille et une Nuits (The Palace of a Thousand and One Nights)
*1905, (Fr), Star, b&w, 430m (1,410.8 ft./23.8 mins.); abbrev. version: 338m (1,108.9
ft./18.7 mins.)*
D: Georges Melies
*A.k.a. **Palace of the Arabian Nights***
Standard fantasy: Prince seeks hand of rajah's daughter

The Palace of a Thousand and One Nights
see *Le Palais des Mille et une Nuits*

The Palace of Mystery
1912, (GB), Urban, b&w, 590 ft. (179.8m)
D: Stuart Kinder
Standard fantasy: Devil's tricks reform ill-tempered king

Palace of the Arabian Nights
see *Le Palais des Mille et une Nuits*

Pale Blood
1991, (USA), color
W: George Chakiris
Minor horror-fantasy: Vampire seeks mate, comes to Los Angeles

The Pale Horse
1996, (GB), A&E, color
W: Colin Buchanan, Jayne Ashbourne, Jean Marsh, Hermione Norris, Leslie
Phillips, Michael Byrne
D: Charles Beeson   **TELEPLAY:** Alma Cullen, from an Agatha Christie story
TVM standard thriller: Sculptor accused of murder becomes involved with occult

Le Paltoquet (The Nonentity)
1986, (Fr), color, 93 mins.
W: Fanny Ardant, Daniel Auteil, Richard Bohringer, Philippe Leotard, Jeanne
Moreau, Michel Piccoli, Claude Pieplu, Jean Yanne, An Luu
D: Michel Deville, loosely based on a novel by Franz-Rudolph Falk
Standard mystery: Detective probes murder in flophouse

Panama Menace
1941, (USA), b&w, 68 mins.
W: Roger Pryor, Virginia Vale, Lionel Royce, Lucien Prival, Duncan Renaldo,
Lester Dorr, Hugh Beaumont
D: Jean Yarbrough
*Minor thriller: Spies seek invisibiity-producing paint. A.k.a. **South of Panama***

Pandemonium

1982, (USA), Krost-Chapin/TMC/UA, color, 82 mins.

W: Tom Smothers (*Cooper*), Carol Kane (*Candy*), Miles Chapin (*Andy*), Debralee Scott (*Sandy*), Marc McClure (*Randy*), Teri Landrum (*Mandy*), Judge Reinhold (*Glenn*), Candy Azzara (*Bambi*), David L. Lander (*Pepe*), Paul Reubens (PeeWee Herman) (*Johnson*), Gary Allen (*Dr. Fuller*), Tab Hunter (*Blue Grange*), Kaye Ballard (*Glenn's Mom*), Eve Arden (*Warden June*), Sydney Lassick (*The Man in the Bus Station*), Edie McClurg (*Blue's Mom*), Donald O'Connor (*Glenn's Dad*), Jim McKrell (*Mandy's Dad*), Richard Romanus (*Jarrett*), Lenny Montana (*The Coach*), Alix Elias, Izabella Telezynska, Tammy Alverson, Pamela Harlow, Sallee Sunshine Young, Jan Speck, Lynn Herring, Phil Hartman, Pat Ast, Michael Kless, Bradley Lieberman, Victoria Carroll, Don McLeod, Ebbe Roe Smith, Randy Bennett, David Becker, David McCharen, John Paragon, Richard C. Adams, Nancy Ryan, Jim Boeke, Shirley Prestia, Michael Tucci, Candi Brough, Randi Brough, Daniel Davies, Lynne Marie Stewart, Mae Hi, Mildred T. Ogata, Vern Rowe, Rob Sullivan, Joe Shea

D: Alfred Sole   SCR: Richard Whitley & Jaime Klein   PHOTOG: Herb Pearl   MUSIC: Dana Kaproff

A.k.a. **Thursday the 12th**

Minor thriller-spoof: Mountie seeks cheerleaders' killer

Pandora and the Flying Dutchman

1951, (GB), Romulus/Independent/MGM, color, 112 mins.

W: James Mason (*Hendrick van der Zee*), Ava Gardner (*Pandora Reynolds*), Nigel Patrick (*Stephen Cameron*), Harold Warrender (*Geoffrey Fielding*), Sheila Sim (*Janet Fielding*), Mario Cabre (*Juan Montalvo*), Marius Goring (*Reggie Demarest*), Pamela Kellino (*Jenny Ford*), John Laurie (*Angus*), Margarita d'Alvarez (*Senora Montalvo*), Patricia Raine (*Peggy Ford*), Abraham Sofaer (*The Judge*), La Piillina (*The Dancer*)

P: John Bryan   WRIT & D: Albert Lewin   PHOTOG: Jack Cardiff   MUSIC: Alan Rawsthorne

reissued 1955

Unusual fantasy: Legendary ship captain must wander Earth until finding selfless love

Pandora's Box

see **Die Buchse der Pandora**

Pandora's Clock

1996, (USA), Citadel-Comsky Group/NBC-TV, color

W: Richard Dean Anderson (*Capt. James Holland*), Robert Loggia (*Jonathan Roth*), Daphne Zuniga (*Dr. Roni Sanders*), Jane Leeves (*Rachel Sherwood*), Robert Guillaume (*Amb. Lee Lancaster*), Teru McDonald (*Amanda*), Edward Herrmann (*The President*), Tim Grimm (*Steve Ellis*), Richard Lawson (*Capt. Robb*), Vladimir Kulich (*The Pilot*), Kurt Fuller, Stephen Root, Jerry Hardin, Kate Hodge, Jennifer Savidge, Grant Goodeve, Scott Bryce, Byrne Piven, Michael Winters, Michael David, John Considine, Dick Arnold

P: Michael O. Gallant   D: Eric Laneuville   TELEPLAY: David Israel, from the novel by John J. Nance   PHOTOG: Steven Shaw   SPCL-FX COORD: Robbie Knott   MUSIC: Don Davis

2-part TVM, standard thriller: Virus outbreak on airplane

Panic

1979, (GB), Dearfilm/Para, color, 25 mins.

W: Avis Bunnage, Peter Blake, Julie Neesam, Leonard Fenton

P: James Dearden & Chris Slater   WRIT & D: James Dearden   PHOTOG: Vernon Layton   MUSIC: Geoff Leach

Standard short horror-thriller: Girl motorist gives ride to werewolf

Panic

1983, (It), color, 90 mins.

W: David Warbeck, Janet Agren

Minor SF-horror: Genetic experiment goes awry

Panic at Lake Wood Manor

see **It Happened at Lake Wood Manor**

Panic at Madame Tussaud's

1948, (GB), Vandyke/Exclusive, b&w, 49 mins.

W: Harry Locke (*Gladstone Green*), Harry Fine (*Bugs Maloney*), Patricia Owens (*Phyllis Edwards*), Frances Clare (*Mrs. Ellis*), Ivan Craig (*Anthony Carter*), Brian Oulton (*The Manager*), Sam Lee (*Slugger Bates*), Arthur Brander (*The Inspector*)

P: Roger Proudlock   D: Peter Graham Scott   SCR: Roger Proudlock & Peter Graham Scott, from a story by Sam Lee

Standard comedy-thriller: Crooks seek stolen gems hidden in waxworks chamber of horrors

Panic in New York

see **The Beast from 20,000 Fathoms**

Panic in the City

1968, (USA), Commonwealth United, color, 97 mins.

W: Howard Duff, Linda Cristal, Nehemiah Persoff, Stephen McNally, Anne Jeffreys, Dennis Hopper, John Hoyt, Stanley Clements

P: Earl Lyon   D: Eddie Davis   SCR: Eddie Davis & Charles E. Savage

Standard thriller: Communist conspirators plan to A-bomb Los Angeles

Panic in the Skies!

1996, (USA), Regent/FAM-TV, color, 95 mins.

W: Kate Jackson (*Laurie*), Robert Guillaume (*Barnes*), Ed Marinaro (*Brett*), Erik Estrada, Maureen McCormick, Howard G.H. Dell, Billy Warlock, Robert Maloney, Brandy Ledford

D: Paul Ziller   TELEPLAY: Robert Hamilton   STORY: Rick Rosner & Robert Hamilton   PHOTOG: Rod Parkhurst   MUSIC: Todd Hayen

TVM, standard thriller: Lightning strikes jetliner, cockpit crew found dead

Panic in Year Zero!

1962, (USA), AIP, b&w, 92 mins.

W: Ray Milland (*Harry Baldwin*), Jean Hagen (*Ann Baldwin*), Frankie Avalon (*Rick Baldwin*), Joan Freeman (*Marilyn Hayes*), Mary Mitchel (*Karen Baldwin*), Richard Garland (*Mr. Johnson*), Rex Holman (*Mickey*), Willis Bouchey (*Dr. Strong*), Richard Bakalyan (*Carl*), Neil Nephew (*Andy*), Hugh Sanders (*Becker*), O.Z. Whitehead (*Hogan*), Byron Morrow (*Haenel*), Russ Bender (*Harkness*), Shary Marshall (*Mrs. Johnson*)

P: Lou Rusoff & Arnold Houghland   D: Ray Milland   SCR: Jay Simms & John Morton   STORY: Jay Simms, loosely adapted (uncredited) from Ward Moore's short stories *Lot & Lot's Daughter*   PHOTOG: Gil Warrenton   MUSIC: Les Baxter

reissued (1965) as **The End of the World**

Standard SF-melodrama: Family tries to survive aftermath of atom war

Panico en el Transiberiano

see **Horror Express**

Panic Offshore

see **The Intruder Within**

Panther Island (*aka* Bomba On Panther Island)

1950, (USA), Mono, b&w, 76 mins.

W: Johnny Sheffield, Allene Roberts, Lita Brown, Charles Irwin, Harry Lewis, Smoki Whitfield

D & SCR: Ford Beebe, from characters created by Roy Rockwood   PHOTOG: William Sickner   MUSIC DIR: Edward J. Kay

Standard thriller: Agriculturists seek aid of Jungle Boy when panther kills three workmen. 'Bomba' series

The Panther's Claw

1942, (USA), b&w, 72 mins.

W: Sidney Blackmer, Byron Foulger, Rick Vallin, Herbert Rawlinson

D: William Beaudine

Standard thriller: Murder in opera troupe

Panther's Moon

see **Spy Hunt**

Paper Gallows

see **Torment (1949)**

Paperhouse

1988, (GB), Working Title/Veston, color, 92 mins.

W: Charlotte Burke (*Anna*), Ben Cross (*Dad*), Glenne Headly (*Kate*), Elliott Spiers (*Marc*), Gemma Jones (*Dr. Sarah Nicols*), Jane Bertish (*Miss Vanstone*), Gary Bleasdale (*The Policeman*), Samantha Cahill (*Sharon*), Steven O'Donnell (*The Dustman*), Sarah Newbold (*Karen*), Barbara Keogh (*The Hotel Receptionist*), Karen Gledhill (*The Nurse*)

D: Bernard Rose   SCR: Matthew Jacobs, from Catherine Storr's novel *Marianne Dreams*   PHOTOG: Mike Southon   SPCL-FX SPRVSR: Alan Whibley   MUSIC: Hans Zimmer & Stanley Myers

Standard fantasy-thriller: Young girl creates nightmarish dream world

Paper Mask

1990, (GB), color, 105 mins.

W: Paul McGann (*Matthew Harris*), Amanda Donohoe (*Christine*) Frederick Treves, Tom Wilkinson, Barbara Leigh-Hunt, Jimmy Yuill, Mark Lewis Jones

D: Christopher Morahan   SCR: John Collee

Standard thriller: Hospital porter impersonates dead doctor

Paper Tearing

1908, (GB), Urban, b&w, 400 ft. (121.9m)

D: Walter R. Booth

Standard fantasy short: Paper tears itself into shapes that change

Le Papillon Fantastique (The Fantastic Butterfly)

1910, (Fr), Star, b&w, 80m (262.5 ft./4.4 mins.)

D: Georges Melies

Standard fantasy

The Paradine Case

1947, (USA), Selznick/UA, b&w, 115 mins, original 132 mins.

W: Gregory Peck, Charles Laughton, Ann Todd, Leo G. Carroll, Valli, Louis Jourdan, Ethel Barrymore, Charles Coburn, Joan Tetzel, Patrick Aherne

WRIT & P: David O. Selznick   ADAPT: Alma Reville & James Bridie   D: Alfred Hitchcock   PHOTOG: Lee Garmes   MUSIC: Franz Waxman

Standard thriller: Woman charged with killing husband

P

Paradisio

1962, (GB), Fanfare, 3D, b&w, 82 mins.
W: Arthur Howard, Eva Waegner
P: Jacques Henrici   **SCR:** Lawrence Zeitlin, Henri Haile & Jacques Henrici
Minor nudie-fantasy: Special sunglasses make people appear naked

Parad Planyet (Parade of the Planets)

1984, (Russ), color, 96 mins.
W: Sergei Nikonenko, Oleg Borisov, Sergei Shakurov, Pyotr Zaichenko, Alexei Zharkov
D: Vadim Abdrashitov
Bizarre fantasy: Red Guard veterans unexpectedly "killed," find themselves on strange odyssey

Paranoia

see Orgasmo

Paranoiac

1963, (GB), Hammer/Univ, b&w, 80 mins.
W: Janette Scott (*Eleanor Ashby*), Oliver Reed (*Simon Ashby*), Liliane Brousse (*Francoise*), Sheila Burrell (*Harriet*), John Bonney (*Keith Kos-set*), Alexander Davion (*Tony Ashby*), Colin Tapley (*The Vicar*), John Stuart (*Williams*), Maurice Denham (*John Kosset*), Harold Lang, Laurie Leigh, Marianne Stone, Sydney Bromley, Jack Taylor
P: Anthony Hinds   **D:** Freddie Francis   **SCR:** Jimmy Sangster   **PHOTOG:** Arthur Grant   **SPCL-FX:** Les Bowie   **MUSIC:** Elisabeth Lutyens
Modest thriller: Man poses as dead heir, becomes involved in mystery

Le Parapluie Fantasquie, ou Dix Femmes Sous une Ombrelle (The Fantastic Umbrella, or Ten Girls Under a Parasol)

1903, (Fr), Star, b&w, 55m (180.4 ft.)
D: Georges Melies
Standard short fantasy

Les Parapluies de Cherbourg (The Umbrellas of Cherbourg)

1964, (Fr-Germ), Parc/Madeleine/Beta/20th-Fox/Landau, color, 90 mins.
W: Catherine Deneuve, Nino Castelnuovo, Anne Vernon, Marc Michel, Ellen Farner, Jean Champion, Philippe Dumat, Paul Pavel, Mireille Perrey, Harald Wolff, Pierre Caden, Jean Paul Chizat, Jean-Pierre Dorat, Michel Benoist, Jacques Camelinat, Patrick Bricard, Bernard Garnier, Jane Carat, Roger Perrinoz, Francois Charet, Gisele Grandpre, Dorothee Blank, Bernard Fradet
P: Mag Bodard   **WRIT & D:** Jacques Demy   **PHOTOG:** Jean Rabier   **MUSIC:** Michel Legrand   **THEME:** *I Will Wait for You*
Superior romantic-fantasy (told in song): Young lovers parted

Parasite

1982, (USA), Irwin Yablans-Charles Band/Embassy, 3D, color, 82 mins.
W: Robert Glaudini, Demi Moore, Luca Bercovici, Al Fann, James Davidson, Cherie Currie, Vivian Blaine, Tom Villard, Scott Thomson, James Cavan, Joanelle Romero
P & D: Charles Band   **SCR:** Alan Adler, Michael Shoob & Frank Levering   **PHOTOG:** Mac Ahlberg   **MUSIC:** Richard Band
blurb: "...the first futuristic monster movie in 3-D"
Standard SF-horror: Scientist races clock to destroy monstrous creature he helped gov't create

The Parasite Murders

see Shivers

Paras Pathar (The Philosopher's Stone)

1958, (Ind), b&w, 111 mins.
WRIT & D: Satyajit Ray   **PHOTOG:** Subrata Mitra   **MUSIC:** Ravi Shankar
Moody Hindu fantasy

Parents

1989, (USA), Great American Films/Vestron, color, 83 mins.
W: Randy Quaid (*Nick Laemle*), Mary Beth Hurt (*Lily Laemle*), Sandy Dennis (*Millie Dew*), Bryan Madorsky (*Michael Laemle*), Juno Mills-Cockrell (*Sheila Zellner*), Kathryn Grody (*Miss Baxter*)
D: Bob Balaban   **SCR:** Christopher Hawthorne   **PHOTOG:** Ernest Day & Robin Vidgeon   **MUSIC:** Jonathan Elias
Modest horror-satire: Boy fears parents are cannibals

Les Parents Terribles (The Terrible Parents)

1948, (Fr), Ariane/Discina Int'l, b&w, 98 mins.
W: Jean Marais (*Michel*), Josette Day (*Madeleine*), Yvonne de Bray (*Yvonne*), Marcel Andre (*Georges*), Gabrielle Dorziat (*Leo*)
WRIT & D: Jean Cocteau   **PHOTOG:** Michel Kelber   **MUSIC:** Georges Auric
GB retitle, The Storm Within, US release, 1950
Classic melodrama. cf. Intimate Relations

The Pariah's Dream

see Le Reve du Pariah

Paris After Dark

1943, (USA), b&w, 85 mins.
W: George Sanders, Philip Dorn, Brenda Marshall, Madeleine LeBeau, Marcel Dalio, Robert Lewis, Henry Roland
D: Leonide Moguy   **SCR:** Howard Buchman

A.k.a. The Night is Ending
Standard wartime thriller: Brutality and sabotage in occupied Paris

Paris Asleep

see Paris Qui Dort

Paris Calling

1941, (USA), Univ, b&w, 95 mins.
W: Elisabeth Bergner, Randolph Scott, Gale Sondergaard, Lee J. Cobb, Basil Rathbone, J. Pat O'Malley, Charles Arnt, Eduardo Ciannelli
D: Edwin L. Marin   **SCR:** Benjamin Glazer & Charles Kaufmann   **PHOTOG:** Milton Krasner   **MUSIC:** Richard Hageman
Reissued as Paris Bombshell
Standard wartime melodrama: Woman finds husband is traitor

Paris Express

1952, (GB), Raymond Stross/Eros/George Schaefer, color, 83 mins.
W: Claude Rains (*Kees Popinga*), Marta Toren (*Michele*), Marius Goring (*Insp. Lucas*), Anouk Aimee (*Jeanne*), Herbert Lom (*Julius de Koster*), Lucie Mannheim (*Mme. Popinga*), Felix Aylmer (*Merkemans*), Ferdy Mayne (*Louis*), Gibb McLaughlin (*de Koster*), Eric Pohlmann (*Goin*), Mary Mackenzie (*Mrs. Lucas*), Michael Nightingale, Joan St. Clair, Robin Alalouf, Michael Alain, Macdonald Parke
P: Joseph Shaftel   **D & SC:** Harold French, from a novel by Georges Simenon   **PHOTOG:** Otto Heller   **MUSIC:** Benjamin Frankel
A.k.a. The Man Who Watched Trains Go By, reissued 1962
Standard psychodrama: Old man obsessed with young woman

Paris Playboys

1954, (USA), AA, b&w, 62 mins.
W: Leo Gorcey, Huntz Hall
P: Ben Schwalb   **D:** William Beaudine   **SCR:** Elwood Ullman
Minor SF-comedy: Bowery Boy mistaken for French scientist who discovered atomic sour-cream fuel

Paris Qui Dort (Paris Asleep)

1923, (Fr), Henri Diamant-Berger, b&w, 61 mins.
W: Madeleine Rodrigue, Henri Rolland, Albert Prejean, Marcel Vallee, Martinelli
WRIT & D: Rene Clair   **PHOTOG:** Maurice Desfassiaux & Paul Guichard
A.k.a. The Crazy Ray
Standard SF-satire: Inventor's ray suspends animation

Paris When It Sizzles

1964, (USA), Para, color, 110 mins.
W: William Holden, Audrey Hepburn, Gregoire Aslan, Raymond Bussieres, Noel Coward, Mel Ferrer, Tony Curtis [cameo], Marlene Dietrich [cameo]
P: Noel Coward   **D:** Richard Quine   **SCR:** George Axelrod   **STORY:** Julien Duvivier & Henri Jeanson   **PHOTOG:** Charles B. Lang Jr.   **MUSIC:** Nelson Riddle
Standard comedy (filmed in 1961): Cinematic fantasies as writer and secretary have short time to create screenplay

Paroxysmus

1969, (It-W. Ger-GB), CUE/AIP, color, 90 mins.
W: James Darren, Barbara McNair, Klaus Kinski, Maria Rohm, Dennis Price, Margaret Lee
P: Harry Alan Towers   **D:** Jesus Franco   **SCR:** Jesus Franco & Malvin Wald, Suggested by Sacher-Masoch's story   **MUSIC:** Manfred Mann & Mike Hugg
USA retitle, Venus in Furs
Unusual thriller: Jazz musician meets dead woman's double

Parsifal

1951, (Sp), Huguet, b&w
W: Ludmilla Tcherina, Gustavo Rojo, Felix de Pomes, Carlo Tamberlani, Alfonso Estela, Angel Jordan, Jesus Varela
D: Daniel Mangrane & Carlos Serrano   **SCR:** Daniel Mangrane, from Wagner's opera   **PHOTOG:** Antonio Canovas
Standard fantasy: Arthurian hero seeks Holy Grail

The Partner

1963, (GB), Merton Park/Anglo-Amalgamated, b&w, 58 mins.
W: Yoko Tani (*Lin Siyan*), Guy Doleman (*Wayne Douglas*), Ewan Roberts (*Insp. Simons*), Mark Eden (*Richard Wehh*), Helen Lindsay (*Helen Douglas*), Anthony Booth (*Buddy Forrester*), Noel Johnson (*Charles Briers*), Denis Holmes (*Sgt. Rigby*), Virginia Wetherell (*Karen*)
P: Jack Greenwood   **D:** Gerard Glaister   **SCR:** John Roddick, from Edgar Wallace's story "A Million Dollar Story"
Standard crime-thriller: Film director's accountant murdered

Partners in Crime

1913, (GB), Hepworth, b&w, 2,275 ft. (693.4m)
W: Alma Taylor (*Ruth Merideth*), Harry Royston (*Sam Surridge*), Flora Morris (*The Innkeeper's Daughter*), Harry Gilbey (*Mr. Merideth*)
D: Warwick Buckland
Standard thriller: Sailor blamed when smuggler stabs fiancee's father

Partners in Crime

1961, (GB), Merton Park/Anglo-Amalgamated, b&w, 54 mins.
W: Bernard Lee (*Insp. Mann*), John Van Eyssen (*Merrill*), Moira Redmond (*Freda*

Strickland), Gordon Boyd (*Rex Holland*), Ernest Clark (*Ashton*), Ruth Meyers (*Mary Nuttall*), Stanley Morgan (*Sgt. Rutledge*), Richard Shaw (*Bill Cross*), Victor Platt (*Harold Strickland*)
P: Jack Greenwood   D: Peter Duffell   SCR: Robert Stewart, from Edgar Wallace's novel
Standard crime-thriller: Gun traced to company director

Parts
see *The Clonus Horror*

Party Line
1988, (USA), Westwind, color, 90 mins.
W: Richard Hatch (*Dan*), Shawn Weatherly (*Stacy*), Leif Garrett (*Seth*), Greta Blackburn (*Angelina*), Richard Roundtree (*Capt. Barnes*), James O'Sullivan (*Henry*), Terrence McGovern (*Simmons*), Karen Mayo Chandler (*Sugar Lips*), Patricia Patts (*Jennifer*), Shelli Place (*Mrs. Simmons*), Richard Brandes (*Rick*), Tara Hutchins (*Alice*), Marty Dudek (*Butch*), James Paradise (*The Victim*), Hank Baumert (*Fernando*), Lee Nicholl (*Herk*), Angela Gibbs (*Beth*), June Rowan (*Ruth*), Jim Malinda (*Reporter #1*), Marsha Van Winkle (*Reporter #2*), Ed Corbett (*The Bum*), Bill Reynolds, Pam Byrnes, John T. Olsen, Karen Beck, West Buchanan, Behrooz Afrakhan, Ed Byrnes, Russell Law, Mary Reid, Christopher Webb, Kim Lewis, Steve Love
D: William Webb   SCR: Richard Brandes   STORY: Tom Byrnes   PHOTOG: John Huneck   MUSIC: Sam Sorensen
Minor thriller: Psycho siblings slay phone-date partyers

The Passenger
1975, (It-Fr-Sp), MGM-UA, color, 119 mins.
W: Jack Nicholson, Maria Schneider, Jenny Runacre, Steven Berkoff, Ian Hendry, Ambrose Bia, Jose Maria Cafarel, James Campbell
D: Michelangelo Antonioni   SCR: Peter Wollen, Michelangelo Antonioni & Mark Peploe   PHOTOG: Luciano Tovoli
A.k.a. Profession: Reporter
Modest thriller: Reporter assumes dead man's identity, finds himself hunted

Passenger de la Pluie (Rider on the Rain)
1969, (It-Fr), Avco Embassy, color, 119 mins.
W: Charles Bronson, Marlene Jobert, Jill Ireland, Gabriele Tinti, Annie Cordy, Corinne Marchand, Jean Gaven, Marika Green
D: Rene Clement
Unusual thriller: Rapist's identity sought

Passenger to London
1937, (GB), Fox British, b&w, 57 mins.
W: John Warwick (*Frank Drayton*), Paul Neville (*Vautel*), Jenny Laird (*Barbara Lane*), Ivan Wilmot (*Veinberg*), Aubrey Pollock (*Sir James Garfield*), Victor Hagen (*Carlton*), Nigel Barrie (*Sir Donald Frame*)
D: Lawrence Huntington   STORY: David Evans
Standard thriller: British agent saves secret documents

Passenger to Tokyo
1954, (GB), Merton Park/Anglo-Amalgamated, b&w, 32 mins.
W: Kenneth Henry (*Insp. Ross*), Ken Marshall (*The Sgt.*), Peter Penn (*Geoffrey Craig*), Dorothy Bramhall (*Mrs. Craig*), Genine Graham (*Miss Summers*)
P: Alec Snowden   D: Ken Hughes   STORY: James Eastwood, from a novel by Edgar Lustgarten
Standard short crime-thriller: Killer of rich women goes to Tokyo in a trunk

Passing Clouds
see *Spellbound (1941)*

The Pasisng of a Soul
1915, (GB), Hepworth, b&w, 1,775 ft. (541m)
W: Tom Powers (*The Son*), Alma Taylor (*The Girl*), Henry Vibart (*The Father*)
D & STORY: Cecil M. Hepworth
Standard melodrama: man saves girl from suicide, has her pose as double of murdered girl

The Passing of the Third Floor Back
1918, (GB), b&w
W: Johnston Forbes-Robertson
from a play by Jerome K. Jerome
Standard fantasy: Mystery man in boardinghouse

The Passing of the Third Floor Back
1935, (GB), Gaumont, b&w, 90 mins.
W: Conrad Veidt (*The Stranger*), Anna Lee (*Vivian Tompkin*), Rene Ray (*Stasia*), Frank Cellier (*Mr. Wright*), Mary Clare (*Mrs. Sharpe*), Beatrix Lehmann (*Miss Kite*), John Turnbull (*Maj. Tompkin*), Cathleen Nesbitt (*Mrs. Tompkin*), Barbara Everest (*The Cook*), Ronald Ward (*Chris Penny*), Jack Livesey (*Larkcomb*), Sara Allgood (*Mrs. de Hooley*)
D: Berthold Viertel   SCR: Michael Hogan & Alma Reville, from a play by Jerome K. Jerome
Standard fantasy: Christ-like visitor reforms boardinghouse inhabitants

Passing Shadows
1934, (GB), British Lion/Fox, b&w, 67 mins.
W: Edmund Gwenn (*David Lawrence*), Barry Mackay (*Jim Lawrence*), Aileen Marson (*Mary Willett*), D.A. Clarke-Smith (*The Stranger*), Viola Lyel (*Mrs. Willett*), Wally Patch (*The Sgt.*), John Turnbull (*Insp. Goodall*), Barbara

---

Everest (*Mrs. Lawrence*)
D: Leslie Hiscott   STORY: Michael Barringer
Standard thriller: Burglar tricks chemist into thinking he killed man

Passion
see *Madame DuBarry (1919)*

The Passion of Fr. Hohner
see *The Climax*

The Passion of Joan of Arc
1928, (Fr), b&w, 7,251 ft. (2210.1m)
W: Maria Falconetti, Maurice Schutz, Ravet, Eugene Silvain, Andre Berley, Antonin Artaud, A. Lurville, Jacques Arnna, R. Narlay, Henry Maillard, Michel Simon, Jean Ayme, Jean d'Yd, L. Larive, Henry Gaultier, Paul Jorge
WRIT & D: Carl Dreyer   PHOTOG: Rudolph Mate
Classic melodrama (Dreyer's masterpiece): Saint's trial and execution

The Passion Pit
see *The Ice House*

The Passions of Men
1913, (GB), Barker, b&w, 2,520 ft. (768.1m)
D: Alexander Butler   STORY: Rowland Talbot
Standard thriller: Jealous chemist poisons wife

Passions of the Sea
see *Lost and Found on a South Sea Island*

A Passion to Kill
1994, (USA), Bruce Cohn Curtis/Rysher, color, 95 mins.
W: Scott Bakula, Chelsea Field, Sheila Kelley, John Getz, Rex Smith, Eddie Velez, Michael Warren, France Nuyen, Michael Cavanaugh
D: Rick King   TELEPLAY: William Delligan   PHOTOG: Paul Ryan   MUSIC: Robert Spraysberry
Made-for-Video, standard thriller: Psychiatrist involved with adultery and murder

Passkey to Danger
1946, (USA), Rep, b&w, 56 mins.
W: Kane Richmond, Stephanie Bachelor
Standard thriller

Passport to China
see *Visa to Canton*

Passport to Hell
see *Agent 383/Passport to Hell*

Passport to Shame
1959, (GB), United Co-Prods./British Lion, b&w, 91 mins.
W: Odile Versois (*Malou*), Diana Dors (*Vicki*), Herbert Lom (*Nick*), Eddie Constantine (*Johnny*), Brenda de Banzie (*Aggie*), Robert Brown (*Mike*), Elwyn Brook-Jones (*Heath*), Cyril Shaps (*Willie*), Denis Shaw (*Mac*), Lana Morris (*The Girl*), Joan Sims (*Miriam*), Robert Fabian (*Himself*)
P: John Clein   D: Alvin Rakoff   STORY: Patrick Alexander
USA retitle, Room 43
Standard crime-thriller: Taxi driver weds French girl for money

Passport to Suez
1943, (USA), Col, b&w, 71 mins.
W: Warren William (*Michael Lanyard*), Ann Savage (*Valerie King*), Eric Blore (*Jamison*), Robert Stanford (*Donald Jamison*), Sheldon Leonard (*Johnny Booth*), Gavin Muir (*Karl*), Lloyd Bridges (*Fritz*), Lou Merrill (*Rembrandt*), Jay Novello (*Cezanne*), Frederick Worlock (*Sir Roger Wembley*), Sig Arno, Frank O'Connor
D: Andre de Toth   SCR: John Stone & Alden Nash, from characters created by Joseph Louis Vance   PHOTOG: L.W. O'Connell   MUSIC: Morris Stoloff
Standard "Lone Wolf" thriller: Gentleman rogue aids British Intelligence seeking Nazis in Egypt

Passport to Treason
1956, (GB), Mid-Century/Eros/Astor, b&w, 80 mins.
W: Rod Cameron (*Mike O'Kelly*), Lois Maxwell (*Diane Boyd*), Clifford Evans (*Orlando Sims*), Marianne Stone (*Miss Jones*), Peter Illing (*Giorgio Sacchi*), John Colicos (*Pietro*), Douglas Wilmer (*Dr. Randolph*), Ballard Berkeley (*Insp. Threadgold*), Andrew Faulds (*Barrett*)
P: Robert S. Baker & Monty Berman   D: Robert S. Baker   SCR: Norman Hudis & Kenneth R. Hayles, from a novel by Manning O'Brine
Standard thriller: American detective and British girl expose fascists behind peace league

Paste
1916, (GB), London/Jury, b&w, 5,700 ft. (1737.4m)
W: Henri de Vries (*Richard Waite*), Gerald Ames (*Prince Maletta*)
D: Ralph Dewsbury   STORY: Bannister Merwin
Standard crime-thriller: Jewel setter blackmailed because of kleptomaniac wife

Past Midnight
1992, (USA), CineTel/New Line, color, 100 mins.
W: Natasha Richardson, Rutger Hauer, Clancy Brown, Guy Boyd, Ernie Lively,

Tom Wright
D: Jan Eliasberg   **SCR:** Frank Norwood   **PHOTOG:** Robert Yeoman   **MUSIC:** Steve Bartek
Stadard thriller: Woman social worker involved with murder suspect

Past Perfect
1996, (USA), cable, color, 95 mins.
W: Eric Roberts *(Dylan Cutter)*, Laurie Holden *(Alley Mersey)*, Nick Mancuso *(Stone)*, Mark Hildreth *(Rusty Walker)*
Standard SF-thriller: Terminator cops from future pursue juvenile delinquent

Past Tense
1994, (USA), color, 96 mins.
W: Scott Glenn, Lara Flynn Boyle *(Toby)*, Anthony LaPaglia *(Talbert)*, Ron Marquette, David Ogden Stiers, Sheree J. Wilson, Marita Geraghty, Stephen Graziano
D: Graeme Clifford
Cable TVM, standard thriller: Cop-author involved in murder mystery

The Patchwork Girl of Oz
1914, (USA), L. Frank Baum/OZ Films Co./Par., b&w, 5 reels 80 mins
W: Violet MacMillan *(Ojo)*, Pierre Couderc *(Scraps)*
D & SCR: L. Frank Baum, from his writings
Standard fantasy: Girl has adventures in enchanted land

The Patient Vanishes
1941, (GB), Rialto/Pathe/Film Classics, b&w, 82 mins.
W: James Mason *(Mick Cardby)*, Mary Clare *(The Matron)*, Gordon McLeod *(Insp. Cardby)*, Margaret Vyner *(Mollie Bennett)*, Frederick Valk *(Dr. Moger)*, Barbara Everest *(Mrs. Cardby)*, Barbara James *(Lena Morne)*, G.H. Mulcaster *(Lord Morne)*, Eric Clavering *(Al Meason)*, Brefni O'Rorke *(Dr. Crosbie)*, Michael Rennie *(The Inspector)*
P: John Argyle   **D:** Lawrence Huntington   **SCR:** John Argyle & Edward Dryhurst, from David Hume's novel *They Called Him Death*
A.k.a. **This Man is Dangerous**, *reissued 1945. US Release, 1947. Reissued as* **Death Cell**, *Monogram, 1942*
Standard thriller: Inspector's son saves lord's daughter from fake doctor's nursing home

Patrick
1978, (Austral), Anthony I. Ginnane/Vanguard/Monarch, color, 96 mins.
W: Susan Penhaligon *(Kathy)*, Robert Helpmann *(Dr. Roget)*, Robert Thompson *(Patrick)*, Rod Mullinar, Bruce Barry, Helen Hemingway, Julia Blake, Maria Mercedes, Frank Wilson, Peter Culpan, Marilyn Rodgers, Peggy Nichols, Carole-Ann Aylett, Walter Pym
D: Richard Franklin   **SCR:** Everett DeRoche   **MUSIC:** Brian May
distrib. in USA in 1980
Standard SF-thriller: Human "vegetable", sustained by life support system, exercises psychokinesis

Pattern for Murder
1964, (W. Ger), b&w
W: George Mather, Juli Reding
Minor thriller: Sleuth pursues maniacal killer

Paul Sleuth and the Mystic Seven
1914, (GB), Cricks, b&w, 3,500 ft. (1066.8m)
W: Charles Vane *(Paul Sleuth)*, Lionel d'Aragon *(The Crook)*
D: Charles Calvert   **STORY:** Stanhope Sprigg
USA retitle, **The Secret Seven**, *Apex Film Co., 1914*
Standard crime-thriller: Detective saves kidnapped heiress

Paul Sleuth, Crime Investigator: The Burglary Syndicate
1912, (GB), Cricks & Martin, b&w, 1,140 ft. (347.5m)
W: Charles Vane *(Paul Sleuth)*, Minna Grey *(The Girl)*
D: Dave Aylott   **STORY:** Stanhope Sprigg
Standard thriller: Detective captures gang

Paul Sleuth--The Mystery of the Astotrian Crown Prince
1912, (GB), Cricks & Martin, b&w, 765 ft. (233.2m)
W: Charles Vane (Paul Sleuth)
D: Dave Aylott   **STORY:** Stanhope Sprigg
Standard crime-thriller: Detective poses as king, saves prince from kidnappers

Paul Temple Returns
1952, (GB), Nettlefold/Butcher, b&w, 71 mins.
W: John Bentley *(Paul Temple)*, Patricia Dainton *(Steve Temple)*, Valentine Dyall *(Supt. Bradley)*, Christopher Lee *(Sir Felix Reybourne)*, Ronald Leigh-Hunt *(Insp. Ross)*, Ben Williams *(Roddy Carson)*, Grey Blake *(Storey)*, Peter Gawthorne *(Sir Graham Forbes)*, Dan Jackson *(Sakki)*, Arthur Hill *(Cranmer Guest)*, Robert Urquhart *(Slater)*
P: Ernest G. Roy   **D:** Maclean Rogers   **SCR:** Francis Durbridge, from his radio-serial
Standard thriller: Novelist unmasks criminal "The Marquis." 'Paul Temple' series

Paul Temple's Triumph
1950, (GB), Nettlefold/Butcher, b&w, 80 mins.
W: John Bentley *(Paul Temple)*, Dinah Sheridan *(Steve Temple)*, Jack Livesey *(Sir Graham Forbes)*, Beatrice Varley *(Mrs. Benton)*, Barbara Couper *(Mrs. Morgan)*, Jenny Mathot *(Jacqueline Giraud)*, Andrew Leigh *(Prof. Hardwicke)*,

---

Hugh Dempster *(Oliver Ffollett)*, Bruce Seton *(Bill Bryant)*, Ivan Samson *(Maj. Murray)*
P: Ernest G. Roy   **D:** Maclean Rogers   **SCR:** A.R. Rawlinson, from Francis Durbridge's radio-serial *News of Paul Temple*
reissued 1953 & 1958
Standard thriller: Atomic scientist kidnapped. 'Paul Temple' series

Paura Nella Citta del Morti Viventi
see **The Gates of Hell**

Pauvre Pierrot (Poor Pierrot)
1891, (Fr), b&w
D: Emile Reynaud
Standard "praxinoscope" fantasy: Clown emotes

Pawns of Mars
1915, (USA), Broadway Star/Vitagraph, b&w, 3 reels
W: Charles Kent, James Morrison, Dorothy Kelly
D: Theodore Marston   **SCR:** Donald I. Buchanan
Standard SF: Future city-states war for world dominance

Paying the Penalty
1913, (GB), Hepworth, b&w, 2,000 ft. (609.6m)
W: Alec Worcester *(Alf Smollett)*, Alma Taylor *(Ruby Jenkins)*, Harry Royston *(Mark Jones)*, Harry Gilbey *(The Master)*
D: Warwick Buckland
Standard crime-thriller: Sawmill owner abducts workman's daughter, locks her lover in safe

Payment in Kind
1967, (GB), Merton Park/Anglo-Amalgamated, color, 30 mins.
W: Justine Lord *(Paula Morgan)*, Derrick Sherwin *(Andrews)*, Maxine Audley *(The Counsel)*, Brian Haines *(John Morgan)*, Gwen Cherrill *(Mrs. Ferguson)*, Peter Bathurst *(Ferguson)*, Henry McGee *(The Jeweler)*
P: Jack Greenwood   **D:** Peter Duffell   **STORY:** John Roddick & Peter Duffell, from characters created by Edgar Lustgarten
Standard short crime-thriller: Indebted wife kills lustful blackmailer

Payroll
1961, (GB), Lynx-Independent Artists/Anglo-Amalgamated, b&w, 105 mins.
W: Michael Craig *(Johnny Mellors)*, Francoise Prevost *(Katie Pearson)*, Billie Whitelaw *(Jackie Parker)*, William Lucas *(Dennis Pearson)*, Kenneth Griffith *(Monty)*, Edward Cast *(Sgt. Mark Bradden)*, Tom Bell *(Blackie)*, Andrew Faulds *(Insp. Carberry)*, Barry Keegan *(Bert Langridge)*, Vanda Godsell *(Doll)*, William Peacock *(Harry Parker)*, Joan Rice *(Madge Moore)*
P: Norman Priggen   **D:** Sidney Hayers   **SCR:** George Baxt, from a novel by Derek Bickerton
Standard crime-thriller: Widow of armored-car driver tracks gang

The Peace Game
see **The Gladiators**

Peacemaker
1990, (USA), Gibraltar-Mentone/Fries Entertainment, color, 82 mins.
W: Hilary Shepard, Lance Edwards, Robert Forster, Bert Remsen, Robert Davi, Wally Taylor, Jerry Spicer
WRIT & D: Kevin S. Tenney   **PHOTOG:** Thomas Jewett   **MUSIC:** Dennis Michael Tenney
Standard SF-thriller: Woman doctor meets space-alien rivals

The Peacemaker
1997, (USA), color, 124 mins.
W: George Clooney, Nicole Kidman, Armin Mueller-Stahl, Marcel Jures
D: Mimi Leder   **SCR:** Michael Schiffer   **MUSIC:** Hans Zimmer

The Peacock Fan
1929, (USA), b&w, 50 mins.
W: Lucien Prival
Minor thriller: Fan protected by deadly curse

The Peacock Princess
1966, (Red China), color
animated puppets, based on legend of Tai people of Southwest China
Juvenile fantasy

The Peanut Butter Solution
1985, (USA), color, 96 mins.
W: Matthew Mackay, Siluck Saysanasy, Alison Podbrey, Helen Hughes, Michael Maillot, Griffith Brewer, Michael Hogan
D & SCR: Michael Rubbo   **MUSIC:** Lewis Furey
Standard juvenile fantasy: Boy meets friendly ghosts

The Pearl of Death
1944, (USA), Univ, b&w, 69 mins.
W: Basil Rathbone *(Sherlock Holmes)*, Nigel Bruce *(Dr. John Watson)*, Evelyn Ankers *(Naomi Drake)*, Dennis Hoey *(Insp. Lestrade)*, Miles Mander *(Gilles Conovor)*, Mary Gordon *(Mrs. Hudson)*, Rondo Hatton *("The Creeper")*, Ian Wolfe *(Amos Hodder)*, Charles Francis, Richard Nugent, Holmes Herbert
P & D: Roy William Neill   **SCR:** Bertram Millhauser, from Sir Arthur Conan Doyle's short story "The Six Napoleons"   **PHOTOG:** Virgil Miller

MUSIC DIR: Don E. George
Standard thriller: To protect legendary gem, Sherlock Holmes disguises self as clergyman

Pearl of the South Pacific
1955, (USA), RKO, color, 85 mins.
W: Dennis Morgan (*Dan*), Virginia Mayo (*Rita*), David Farrar (*Bully*), Lisa Montell (*Momu*), Lance Fuller (*George*), Basil Ruysdael (*Mr. Michael*), Murvyn Vye (*Halemano*)
P: Benedict Bogeaus **D:** Allan Dwan **SCR:** Jesse Lasky Jr. **PHOTOG:** John Alton **MUSIC:** Lou Forbes
Standard melodrama: Native utopia disrupted by adventurers seeking black pearls

Pearls of Death
1914, (GB), Phoenix Film Agency, b&w, 3,000 ft. (914.4m)
W: Joe Evans (*Lockwood Beck*), Geraldine Maxwell
WRIT & D: Joe Evans
Standard crime-thriller: Detective foils anarchists who put explosives in necklace of earl's wife

The Peasant Girl's Revenge
1906, (GB), Hepworth, b&w, 300 ft. (91.4m)
W: Lewin Fitzhamon (*The Cossack*), Dolly Lupone (*The Peasant*)
D: Lewin Fitzhamon
Standard thriller: Wife of murdered peasant poisons Cossack's wine

Peau d'Ane (Donkey Skin)
1970, (Fr), Janus, color, 90 mins.
W: Catherine Deneuve, Jean Marais, Jacques Perrin, Delphine Seyrig, Micheline Presle
WRIT & D: Jacques Demy, from a story by Charles Perrault **PHOTOG:** Ghislain Cloquet **MUSIC:** Michel Legrand
Adult fairytale: Beautiful princess flees mandated marriage to own father

The Pebble and the Penguin
1995, (USA), MGM, color, 74 mins.
VOICES: Martin Short, Annie Golden, Tim Curry, James Belushi
SCR: Rachel Koretsky & Steve Whitestone **MUSIC:** Barry Manilow, Bruce Sussman & Mark Watters
Standard animated fantasy: Penguin travels to Antarctica

Peeping Tom
1959, (GB), Anglo-Amalgamated/Archers/Astor, color, 109 mins.
W: Carl Boehm (*Mark Lewis*), Moira Shearer (*Vivian*), Maxine Audley (*Mrs. Stephens*), Anna Massey (*Helen Stephens*), Jack Watson (*Insp. Gregg*), Brenda Bruce (*Dora*), Martin Miller (*Dr. Rosan*), Esmond Knight (*Arthur Baden*), Bartlett Mullins (*Mr. Peters*), Michael Goodliffe (*Don Jarvis*), Shirley Anne Field (*Diane Ashley*), Pamela Green (*Milly*), Michael Powell (*Mr. Lewis*), Nigel Davenport, Brian Worth, Maurice Durant, Susan Travers, Brian Wallace, Veronica Hurst, Alan Rolfe, Miles Malleson
P & D: Michael Powell **SCR:** Leo Marks **PHOTOG:** Otto Heller **MUSIC:** Brian Easdale **DESIGN:** Arthur Lawson
Fr retitle, **Le Voyeur,** *USA TV-retitle,* **Face of Fear,** *reissued 1980*
Controversial thriller: Murderer photographs crimes

Peggy Sue Got Married
1986, (USA), 20th-Fox, color, 103 mins.
W: Kathleen Turner, Nicholas Cage, Don Murray, Barry Miller, Barbara Harris, Kevin O'Connor, Leon Ames, Joan Allen, Maureen O'Sullivan, Helen Hunt, Catherine Hicks, Sofia Coppola, John Carradine, Jim Carrey, Sachi Parker
D: Francis Coppola **SCR:** Arlene Samer & Jerry Leichtling **MUSIC:** John Barry
Entertaining comedy-fantasy: Housewife visits past

Peking Express
1951, (USA), Para, b&w, 95 mins.
W: Joseph Cotten, Corinne Calvet, Edmund Gwenn, Marvin Miller
D: William Dieterle **SCR:** John Meredyth Lucas **ADAPT:** Jules Furthman, from Harry Hervey's novel *Shanghai Express* **PHOTOG:** Charles B. Lang Jr. **MUSIC:** Dimitri Tiomkin
Standard thriller (remake of **Shanghai Express**): *Intrigue on train*

The Peking Blonde
1968, (Fr), color, 80 mins.
W: Mireille Darc, Claudio Brook, Edward G. Robinson, Pascale Roberts
D: Nicolas Gessner **SCR:** Nicolas Gessner & Marc Behm
Minor thriller: Amnesiac thought to hold secrets

The Penalty
1920, (USA), Rex Beach/Goldwyn, b&w, 7 reels.60 mins.
W: Lon Chaney Sr., Claire Adams, Charles Clary, Charles Kenyon
D: Wallace Worsley
Standard thriller

Penetration
1976, (It), Mishkin, color
W: Farley Granger, Kim Pope, Marc Stevens, Sylva Koscina, Harry Reems, Tina Russell
P: William Mishkin **D:** Roberto Montero
USA retitle, **The Slasher is the Sex Maniac**
Minor sex-thriller (with added U.S. footage): Cop trails sex-killer

The Penguin Pool Murder
1932, (USA), RKO, b&w, 69 mins.
W: Edna May Oliver (*Hildegarde Withers*), James Gleason (*Oscar Piper*), Mae Clarke (*Gwen Parker*), Donald Cook (*Philip Seymour*), Robert Armstrong (*Barry Costello*), Edgar Kennedy (*Det. Donahue*), Clarence H. Wilson (*Bertrand B. Hemingway*), Mary Mason (*The Secretary*), Rochelle Hudson (*The Telephone Operator*), Guy Usher (*Gerald Parker*), James Donlan (*Fink*), Joe Hermano (*Chicago Lew*), Gustav von Seyffertitz (*Max*), William Le Maire
D: George Archainbaud **SCR:** Willis Goldbeck, from characters created by Stuart Palmer **PHOTOG:** Enry Gerrard **MUSIC:** Max Steiner
Standard "Hildegarde Withers" mystery (1st in series): Wily woman sleuth witnesses murder at aquarium

Le Penitencier de la Peur
see **The Man Who Turned to Stone**

The Penitentiary of Fear
see **The Man Who Turned to Stone**

Penny Gold
1973, (GB), Fanfare/Scotia-Barber, color, 90 mins.
W: Francesca Annis (*Delphi Emerson*), James Booth (*Insp. Matthews*), Nicky Henson (*Roger*), Una Stubbs (*Anna*), Joseph O'Conor (*Charles Blachford*), Richard Heffer (*Claude Grancourt*), Joss Ackland (*Jones*), Sue Lloyd (*The Model*), George Murcell (*Dr. Merrick*), Marianne Stone (*Mrs. Parsons*)
P: George H. Brown **D:** Jack Cardiff **STORY:** David Osborne & Liz Charles-Williams **PHOTOG:** Ken Hodges **MUSIC:** John Scott
Standard crime-thriller: Rare-stamp swindle involves murder

Pentagram
see **The First Power**

The Penthouse
1967, (GB), Tahiti/Para, color, 96 mins.
W: Suzy Kendall (*Barbara*), Terence Morgan (*Bruce*), Norman Rodway (*Dick*), Tony Beckley (*Tom*), Martine Beswick (*Harry*)
P: Harry Fine **D & SCR:** Peter Collinson, from C. Scott Forbes' play *The Meter Man* **PHOTOG:** Arthur Lavis **MUSIC:** John Hawksworth
Standard thriller: Sadistic hoodlums terrorize couple

The Penthouse
1989, (USA), color
W: Robin Givens, David Hewlett
Minor thriller: Wealthy woman terrorized by insane former classmate

The People
1971, (USA), Metromedia/ABC-TV, color, 74 mins.
W: Kim Darby, William Shatner, Dan O'Herlihy, Diane Varsi, Chris Valentine, Laurie Walters, Stephanie Valentine, Johanna Baer
D: John Korty **TELEPLAY:** James M. Miller, from stories by Zenna Henderson **MUSIC:** Carmine Coppola
TVM, standard SF-thriller: Inhabitants of secluded valley possess strange powers, share secret bond

The People: KIM DARBY AND CHRIS VALENTINE

The People Eater
see **The Woman Eater**

The People of the Rocks
1914, (GB), Captain Kettle, b&w, 1,200 ft. (365.8m)
W: Connie Somers (*The Girl*)

D: Dalton Somers   **STORY:** C.J. Cutcliffe-Hyne
reissued 1917
Standard fantasy: Touring family dreams of druids

People Toys
see **The Horrible House on the Hill**

The People That Time Forgot
1977, (GB), Amicus/AIP, color, 90 mins.
W: Patrick Wayne (*Maj. Ben McBride*), Doug McClure (*Bowen Tyler*), Sarah
   Douglas (*Lady Charlotte*), Thorley Walters (*Dr. Norfolk*), Dana Gillespie
   (*Ajor*), Shane Rimmer (*Hogan*), Dave Prowse (*The Executioner*), Milton Reid
   (*Sabbala*), John Hallam (*Chang-Sha*), Tony Britton (*Capt. Lawton*), Richard
   Parmentier (*Lt. Whitby*), Kiran Shah (*Bolum*)
P: John Dark   **D:** Kevin Connor   **SCR:** Patrick Tilley, from novels by Edgar Rice
   Burroughs   **PHOTOG:** Alan Hume   **SPCL-FX:** Ian Wingrove   **MUSIC:**
   John Scott
Standard SF-fantasy (sequel to **The Land That Time Forgot***): Adventures in prehistoric world*

The People Under the Stairs
1991, (USA), Univ, color, 102 mins.
W: Brandon Adams (*Fool*), Everett McGill (*The Man*), Wendy Robie (*The
   Woman*), A.J. Langer (*Alice*), Ving Rhames (*Leroy*), Bill Cobbs (*Grandpa
   Booker*), Kelly Jo Minter (*Ruby*), Sean Whalen (*Roach*), Jeremy Roberts
   (*Spenser*), Conni Marie Brazelton (*Mary*), Joshua Cox (*The Young Cop*), John
   Hostetter (*The Veteran Cop*), John Mahon (*The Police Sergeant*), Teresa Velarde
   (*The Social Worker*), George R. Parker, Nick Cramer, Yan Birch, Wayne
   Daniels, Michael Kopelow, Robert Michael, Earl Dax, David Robinson,
   Daniel Windtree, Gregory Kavtzer, Burton Pierce
WRIT & D: Wes Craven   **PHOTOG:** Sandi Sissel   **SPCL-FX:** Image
   Engineering Inc.   **MUSIC:** Don Peake   **SONG:** *Do the Right Thing*
Bizarre horror-thriller: Boy trapped in psycho's labyrinthine house

People Who Own the Dark
1975, (Sp), Newcal, color, 87 mins.
W: Paul Naschy, Maria Perschy, Tony Kendall, Terry Kemper, Tom Weyland,
   Anita Brock, Paul Mackey
D & SCR: Armando De Ossorio
Minor SF-horror: End of world

Per Amore...Per Magia (For Love...For Magic)
1967, (It), color
D & SCR: Duccio Tessari, from story *Aladdin's Lamp*
Standard fantasy: Youth meets genie

Perceval
1978, (Fr), Gaumont/New Yorker, color, 137 mins.
W: Fabrice Luchini (*Perceval*), Andre Dussolier (*Gawain*), Arielle Dombasle
   (*Blanchefleur*), Marc Eyraud (*King Arthur*), Michel Etchverry (*The Fisher
   King*), Marie-Christine Barrault (*Queen Guenievre*), Pascale de Boysson
   (*Perceval's Mother*), Clementine Amouroux (*The Damsel in the Tent*), Antoine
   Baud (*The Red Knight*), Jacques le Carpentier (*The Proud Lord of the Heath*),
   Jocelyne Boisseau (*The Damsel Who Laughs*), Gerard Falconnetti (*Kay*), Alain
   Serve (*The Fool*), Daniel Tarrare (*Yvonet*), Raoul Billerey (*Gornemant of
   Gohort*), Sylvain Levignac (*Anguingueron*), Coco Ducados (*The Hideous
   Damsel*), Guy Delorme (*Clamadieu of the Isles*), Jean Boissery (*Guingambresil*),
   Gilles Raab (*Sagremor*), Claude Jaeger (*Thiebaut of Tintaguel*), Frederique
   Cerbonnet (*Thiebaut's Elder Daughter*), Anne-Laure Meury (*The Damsel with
   Small Sleeves*), Frederic Norbert (*King of Escavalon*), Hubert Gignoux (*The
   Hermit*), Christine Lietot
D & SCR: Eric Rohmer from a novel by Chretien de Troyes   **PHOTOG:** Nestor
   Almendros   **MUSIC:** Guy Robert
Modest Arthurian romance: Adventures of virtuous knight

Percy
1971, (GB), Anglo-EMI/MGM, color, 100 mins.
W: Hywel Bennett, Elke Sommer, Britt Ekland, Denholm Elliott, Tracy Reed,
   Ray Davies
P: Betty E. Box   **D:** Ralph Thomas   **SCR:** Hugh Leonard
Minor satire: Man seeks penis implant. cf. **It's Not the Size That Counts**

Percy's Progress
see **It's Not the Size That Counts**

The Perfect Alibi (1930)
see **Birds of Prey**

Perfect Alibi
1994, (USA), Bruce Cohn Curtis/Rysher, color, 95 mins.
W: Teri Garr, Hector Elizondo, Lydie Denier, Anne Ramsay, Kathleen Quinlan,
   Alex McArthur, Gedde Watanabe, Bruce McGill, Rex Linn, Estelle Harris,
   Patrick Thomas, Eric Howe, Charles Martin Smith, Robert Rockwell, Jean-
   Paul Vignon, Max Ornstein
D & STORY: Kevin Meyer   **PHOTOG:** Doyle Smith   **MUSIC:** Amotz
   Plessner
TVM, standard thriller

The Perfect Crime
1937, (GB), First Nat'l/WB, b&w, 69 mins.
W: Hugh Williams (*Charles Brown*), Glen Alyn (*Sylvia Burton*), Ralph Ince (*Jim
   Lanahan*), Iris Hoey (*Mrs. Pennypacker*), John Carol (*Snod-grass*), Philip Ray
   (*Newbold*), James Stephenson (*Parker*), Wilfred Caithness (*Rawhouse*)
D: Ralph Ince, from a story by Basil Woon
Standard thriller: Clerk framed for murder

Perfect Friday
1970, (GB), London Screenplays, color, 95 mins.
W: Ursula Andress (*Lady Britt Dorset*), Stanley Baker (*Mr. Graham*), David
   Warner (*Lord Nicholas Dorset*), Patience Collier (*Nanny*), T.P. McKenna
   (*Smith*), Joan Benham (*Miss Welsh*), David Waller (*Williams*), Trisha
   Mortimer (*Janet*), Carleton Hobbs (*The Peer*), Julian Orchard (*Thompson*),
   Ann Tirard (*Miss Marsh*)
P: Jack Smith   **D:** Peter Hall   **SCR:** C. Scott Forbes & Anthony Greville-Bell
   STORY: C. Scott Forbes
*Standard crime-thriller (enlivened by Ms. Andress' "reverse striptease"): Clerk and Lady
plan bank robbery*

Perfect Little Angels
1998, (USA), TVA Int'l-Shavick/FAM-TV, color, 95 mins.
W: Cheryl Ladd (*Elaine*), Michael York (*Dr. Calvin Lawrence*), Jody Thopson
   (*Justine*), Brendan Fehr (*Mitch*), Jade Pawluck (*Brad*), Tanya Reichert
D: Timothy Bond   **TELEPLAY:** Bart Baker   **PHOTOG:** Peter Benison
   MUSIC: Ken Williams
TVM, standard SF-thriller (echoing **The Stepford Wives***): Community controlled by
radio waves*

A Perfect Murder
1998, (USA), WB, color, 107 mins.
W: Michael Douglas, Gwyneth Paltrow, Viggo Mortensen, David Suchet, Sarita
   Choudhury
D: Andrew Davis   **SCR:** Patrick Smith Kelly, loosely based on Frederick Knott's
   play *Murder*   **PHOTOG:** Dariusz Wolski   **MUSIC:** James Newton Howard
Well-made thriller: Magnate suspects trophy wife's fidelity

Perfect Victims
1987, (USA), color, 100 mins.
W: Deborah Shelton, Clarence Williams III, Lyman Ward
D: Shuki Levy
Minor thriller: Madman stalks beautiful models

The Perfect Woman
1949, (GB), Two Cities/Rank/Eagle-Lion, b&w, 89 mins.
W: Patricia Roc (*Penelope*), Stanley Holloway (*Ramshead*), Nigel Patrick (*Roger
   Cavendish*), Miles Malleson (*Prof. Belmond*), Irene Handl (*Mrs. Butter*), Anita
   Sharp-Bolster (*Lady Diana*), Fred Berger (*Farini*), David Hurst (*Wolfgang
   Winkel*), Pamela Devis (*Olga the Robot*), Contance Smith (*The Receptionist*),
   Bernard Knowles, Jerry Verno, Jerry Desmonde, Johnie Schofield, Jerry
   Desmonde, Dora Bryan, Philippa Gill, Noel Howlett
P: George & Alfred Black   **D:** Bernard Knowles   **ADAPT:** George Black,
   Bernard Knowles & J.B.Boothroyd, from play by Wallace Geoffrey & Basil
   John Mitchell   **PHOTOG:** Jack Hildyard & Russell Thompson   **MUSIC:**
   Arthur Wilkinson   **MUSIC CONDUCT:** John Hollinsworth
Classic SF-fantasy: Scientists create automated female

Performance
1970, (GB), Goodtimes/WB, color, 105 mins.
W: James Fox (*Chas Devlin*), Mick Jagger (*Turner*), Anita Pallenberg (*Pherber*),
   Michele Breton (*Lucy*), Ann Sidney (*Dana*), John Bindon (*Moody*), Stanley
   Meadows (*Rosebloom*), Allan Cuthbertson (*The Lawyer*), Antony Morton
   (*Dennis*), Johny Shannon (*Harry Flowers*), Anthony Valentine (*Joey Maddocks*)
P: Sanford Lieberson   **D:** Donald Cammell & Nicolas Roeg   **STORY:** Donald
   Cammell   **MUSIC:** Jack Nitzsche
Standard crime-thriller: Fugitive killer hides in pop star's house

Peril from the Planet Mongo
1965, (USA), Univ, b&w, 100 mins.
W: Buster Crabbe (*Flash Gordon*), Carol Hughes (*Dale Arden*), Charles Middleton
   (*Ming the Merciless*), Frank Shannon (*Dr. Zarkov*)
D: Ford Beebe & Ray Taylor   **SCR:** George H. Plympton, Basil Dickey & Barry
   Shipman   **PHOTOG:** Jerome Ash & William Sickner
*Standard SF-thriller (culled from 2nd half of 1938 serial 'Flash Gordon's Trip to
Mars'): Hero faces alien menace. cf.* **Purple Death from Space**

A Perilous Journey
1953, (USA), Rep, b&w, 90 mins.
W: Vera Ralston, David Brian
Standard thriller

Perilous Waters
1948, (USA), Mono, b&w, 66 mins.
W: Don Castle, Audrey Long
Originall title **In Self Defense**
Minor melodrama

Perils of Paris
see *Terreur*

The Perils of Pauline
1967, (USA), Univ, color, 99 mins.
W: Pat Boone (*George Stedman*), Pamela Austin (*Pauline*), Hamilton Camp (*Thorpe*), Doris Packer (*Mrs.Carruthers*), Terry Thomas (*Martin*), Edward Everett Horton, Leon Askin, Kurt Kasznar, Aram Katcher
P: Herbert B. Leonard D: Herbert B. Leonard & Joshua Shelley SCR: Albert Beich PHOTOG: Jack A. Marta MUSIC: Vic Mizzy
Standard satire: Cute spoof of "Pearl White" serials, made as a TV pilot, released theatrically

The Perils of the Fleet
1909, (GB), London Cinematograph Co., b&w, 535 ft. (163.1m)
D: S. Wormald
Standard thriller: Spies throw detective over cliff, but he survives and stops fleet's destruction

Perils of the Jungle
1927, (USA), b&w
W: Frank Merrill
Minor adventure-thriller. cf. **The White Gorilla**

Perils of the Jungle
1953, (USA), Lippert, b&w, 63 mins.
W: Clyde Beatty
Standard adventure-thriller

Pernikova Chaloupka (The Gingerbread Cottage)
1951, (Czech), b&w
D: Bretislav Pojar
Standard animated fantasy

Persecution
1974, (GB), Tyburn/Fanfare, color, 92 mins.
W: Lana Turner (*Carrie Masters*), Ralph Bates (*David Masters*), Olga Georges-Picot (*Monique Kalfon*), Suzan Farmer (*Jane Masters*), Patrick Allen (*Robert Masters*), Trevor Howard (*Paul Bellamy*), Catherine Brandon (*Mrs. Deacon*), Shelagh Fraser (*Mrs. Banks*), Jennifer Guy (*The Waitress*), Ronald Howard (*Dr. Ross*), Mark Weavers (*Young David*), John Ryan (*The Gardener*)
P: Kevin Francis D: John Chaffey ORIG. STORY & SCR: Robert B. Hutton & Rosemary Wootten PHOTOG: Kenneth Talbot MUSIC: Paul Ferris
USA retitle, **The Graveyard**, *A.k.a.* **Terror of Sheba**
Standard thriller: Wealthy woman torments son

The Persecution and Assassination of Jean-Paul Marat as Performed by the Inmates of the Asylum of Charenton Under the Direction of the Marquis de Sade
1966, (GB), Marat-Sade/UA, color, 116 mins.
W: Patrick Magee (*Marquis de Sade*), Ian Richardson (*Jean-Paul Marat*), Glenda Jackson (*Charlotte Corday*), Michael Williams (*The Herald*), Clifford Rose (*Coulmier*), Freddie Jones (*Cucuracu*), Hugh Sullivan (*Kokol*), Morgan Sheppard (*Mad Animal*), Jonathan Burn (*Polpoch*), Jeanette Landis (*Rossignol*), John Steiner (*Duperret*), Robert Lloyd (*Jacques Roux*), Mark Jones
P: Michael Birkett D: Peter Brook SCR: Adrian Mitchell, from Peter Weiss' play PHOTOG: David Watkin MUSIC: Richard Peaslee
Unusual psychodrama: Madmen enact famed murder

Perseus the Invincible
1962, (It), Emo Bistolfi-Copercines/Embassy/Teleworld, color, 90 mins
W: Richard Harrison (*Perseus*), Anna Ranalli, Elisa Cegani, Arturo Dominici, Molino Rojo, Armand Jordan, Leo Anchoriz, Roberto Camardiel, Fernando Lijer, Bruno Scipioni
P: Emo Bistolfi D: Alberto DeMartino SCR: Guerra, Martino, Gastaldi & DeMartino, from an idea by Eduardo Giorgio Conti PHOTOG: Dario De Palma & Eloy Mella MUSIC: Carlo Franci
USA retitle, **The Medusa Against the Son of Hercules**
Standard "Sword & Sandal" fantasy: Hero opposes monsters at dawn of civilization

Persona
1966, (Swed), Svensk Filmindustri/Lopert, b&w, 95 mins.
W: Liv Ullmann (*Actress Elisabeth Vogler*), Bibi Andersson (*Nurse Alma*), Gunnar Bjornstrand (*Mr. Vogler*), Margareta Krook (*The Woman Doctor*), Jorgen Lindstrom (*The Boy*)
WRIT & D: Ingmar Bergman PHOTOG: Sven Nykvist MUSIC: Lars Johan Werle
Classic psychodrama: Nurse begins to absorb personality of actress patient

Personal and Confidential
1965, (GB), Merton Park/Anglo-Amalgamated, b&w, 30 mins.
W: Ellen McIntosh (*Marion Corbet*), Robert Cartland (*Ronald Chadwell*), Harry Littlewood (*Gibbs*), Howard Lang (*Abbott*), David Morell (*Wilson*), Geoffrey Toone (*Sir Joseph Kenton*), Billy Milton (*Lane*), Genine Graham (*Betty Hill*)
P: Jack Greenwood D: Geoffrey Nethercott STORY: James Eastwood, from a novel by Edgar Lustgarten
Standard short crime-thriller: Cabinet minister's girl assistant framed for betraying secrets

Personal Column
see *Lured*

Person Unknown
1956, (GB), Merton Park/Anglo-Amalgamated, b&w, 32 mins.
W: Russell Napier (*Insp. Duggan*), Marianne Stone (*Mrs. Cusick*), George Pravda (*Josef Cusick*), Bill Nagy (*Vince*), Edward Cast (*The Sgt.*), Lloyd Lamble (*The Pathologist*)
P: Alec Snowden D: Montgomery Tully STORY: James Eastwood, from a novel by Edgar Lustgarten
Standard short crime-thriller: Polish spy changes places with would-be assassin

The Perverse Countess
1973, (Fr), color, 86 mins.
W: Lina Romay, Robert Woods, Howard Vernon, Alice Arno, Caroline Riviere
D: Jesus Franco
Minor horror-thriller: Tourist meets cannibalistic nobles

Pestilence
see *Mutant*

Peter Benchley's 'Creature'
1998, (USA), ABC-TV, color, approx. 190 mins.
W: Craig T. Nelson (*Simon Chase*), Kim Cattrall (*Amanda*), Matthew Carey (*Max*), Cress Williams (*The Tall Man*), Blu Mankuma (*Rollie*), Giancarlo Esposito (*Werewolf*), Colm Feore (*Richland*), Gary Reineke, Brian Steele, Michael Reilly Burke, John Aylward, Jill Teed
D: Stuart Gillard TELEPLAY: Rockne S. O'Bannon from Peter Benchley's novel PHOTOG: Thomas Burstyn MUSIC: John Van Tongreen
2-part TVM, standard SF-thriller: Gov't-spawned mutant kills

Peter Ibbetson
1935, (USA), Para, b&w, 88 mins.
W: Gary Cooper, Ann Harding, Douglass Dumbrille, Dickie Moore, Ida Lupino, John Halliday, Virginia Weidler, Doris Lloyd, Donald Meek, Elsa Buchanan, Christian Rub, Gilbert Emery, Thomas Monk, Marcelle Corday, Elsa Prescott, Colin Tapley, Theresa Maxwell Conover, Adrienne d'Ambricourt, Ambrose Barker, Clive Morgan, Blanche Craig
D: Henry Hathaway SCR: Vincent Lawrence, Waldemar Young, Constance Collier, John Meehan & Edwin Justus Mayer, from John Nathaniel Raphael's play, based on George du Maurier's novel PHOTOG: Charles Lang & Gordon Jennings SPCL-FX: Gordon Jennings MUSIC: Ernst Toch
Unusual melodrama: Architect and duke's wife share mystical childhood bond

Peter Pan: MARY BRIAN AND BETTY BRONSON

Peter Pan
1924, (USA), Para, b&w, 10 reels (7,568 ft./2306.7m)
W: Betty Bronson (*Peter Pan*), Esther Ralston (*Mrs. Darling*), Cyril Chadwick (*Mr. Darling*), Ernest Torrence (*Capt. Hook*), Mary Brian (*Wendy Darling*), Virginia Brown Faire (*Tinker Bell*), George Ali (*Nana, the Dog*), Anna May Wong (*Tiger Lily*), Phillipe de Lacy (*Michael Darling*), Jack Murphy (*John Darling*)
D: Herbert Brenon SCR: Willis Goldbeck, from James M. Barrie's story PHOTOG: James Wong Howe
Classic fantasy: Children visit magical world

Peter Pan
1953, (USA), Walt Disney/RKO, color, 76 mins.
VOICES: Bobby Driscoll (*Peter Pan*), Hans Conreid (*Capt. Hook*), Stan Freberg, Catherine Beaumont, Tom Conway, Heather Angel, Bill Thompson, Paul Collins, Tommy Luske, Candy Candido
D: Norm Ferguson, Ward Kimball & Eric Larson STORY: Joe Rinaldi & Milt Banta, from James M. Barrie's classic SPCL-FX: Ub Iwerks MUSIC: Oliver Wallace SONGS: *You Can Fly* & *What Makes the Red Man Red*
Classic animated fantasy: Sprite lures children to land of magic

P

Peter Rabbit and the Tales of Beatrix Potter
1971, (GB), EMI/MGM, color, 90 mins.
W: Erin Geraghty (*Beatrix Potter*), Joan Benham (*The Nurse*), Wilfred Babbage (*The Butler*), Frederick Ashton (*Mrs. TiggyWinkle*), Alexander Grant (*Pigling Bland/Peter Rabbit*), Michael Coleman (*Jeremy Fisher*), Carole Ainsworth (*Squirrel/Country Mouse*), Sally Ashby (*Mrs. Pettitoes/Tabitha*), Avril Bergen (*Pig/Town Mouse*), Lesley Collier (*Hunca Munca*), Jill Cooke (*Squirrel/Country Mouse*), Leslie Edwards (*Mr. Brown*), Graham Fletcher (*Pig/Town Mouse*), Bridget Goodricke (*Squirrel/Country Mouse*), Garry Grant (*Alexander/Town Mouse*), Ann Howard (*Jemima Puddleduck*), Brenda Last (*Black Berkshire Pig*), Keith Martin (*Johnny Town Mouse*), Robert Mead (*Fox*), Suzanna Raymond (*Pig/Town Mouse*), Wayne Sleep (*Squirrel Nutkin/Tom Thumb*), Julie Wood (*Mrs. Tittlemouse*), Rosemary Taylor (*Squirrel/Country Mouse*), Anita Young (*Pig*), Royal Ballet Co.
P: Richard Goodwin   D: Reginald Mills   ADAPT: Richard Goodwin & Christine Edzard, from stories by Beatrix Potter   MUSIC: John Lanchbery
Modest fantasy: Animal adventures

Pete's Dragon
1977, (USA), Walt Disney/Buena Vista, color, 127 mins, also 134 mins.
W: Helen Reddy (*Nora*), Jim Dale (*Dr. Terminus*), Mickey Rooney (*Lampie*), Red Buttons (*Hoagy*), Shelley Winters (*Lena Gogan*), Sean Marshall (*Pete*), Jane Kean (*Miss Taylor*), Jim Backus, Charlie Callas, Jeff Conaway
D: Ron Chaffrey
Standard juvenile fantasy (mixing live action and animation)

Le Petit Chaperon Rouge (Little Red Riding Hood)
1901, (Fr), Star, b&w, 160m (524.9 ft./8.9 mins.)
W: Rachel Gillet
D: Georges Melies
Standard fantasy: Innocent meets wolf

Un Petit Diable (A Little Devil)
1896, (Fr), Star, b&w, 20m (65.6 ft./1.1 mins.)
W: Georgette Melies
D: Georges Melies
Standard fantasy short: Imp capers

Pet Sematary
1989, (USA), Para, color, 105 mins.
W: Dale Midkiff (*Dr. Louis Creed*), Fred Gwynne (*Jud Crandall*), Denise Crosby (*Rachel Creed*), Blaze Berdahl (*Ellie Creed*), Miko Hughes (*Gage Creed*), Brad Greenquist (*Victor Pascow*), Susan J. Blommaert (*Missy Dandridge*)
D: Mary Lambert   SCR: Stephen King from his novel   PHOTOG: Peter Stein   MUSIC: Elliot Goldenthal
blurb: "Sometimes dead is better"
Standard horror-fantasy: Indian burial ground ressurects dead

Pet Sematary Two
1992, (USA), Para, color, 102 mins.
W: Edward Furlong (*Jeff Matthews*), Anthony Edwards (*Chase Matthews*), Clancy Brown (*Sheriff Gus Gilbert*), Jared Rushton (*Clyde*), Darlanne Fluegel (*Renee Hallow*), Lisa Waltz (*Amanda Gilbert*), Sarah Trigger (*Marjorie Hargrove*), Jason McGuire (*Drew Gilbert*)
P: Ralph S. Singleton   D: Mary Lambert   SCR: Richard Outten   PHOTOG: Russell Carpenter   MUSIC: Mark Governor   SONGS: *Fading Away, Gush Forth My Tears, I've Got Spies, Love Never Dies, Poison Heart, Reverence, Revolt, Ride On, Shitlist & The Slasher*
Standard horror-fantasy: Teens meet zombies

Pet Shop
1994, (USA), Moonbeam/Para color, 80 mins.
W: Terry Kiser, Lleigh Ann Orsi, Spencer Vrooman, David Wagner, Joanne Baron, Jane Morris, Jeff Michalski, Shashawnee Hall, Sabrina Wiener, Cody Burger, John La Motta, Alfred Dennis
D: Hope Perello   SCR: Mark Goldstein, Greg Suddeth & Brent Friedman   PHOTOG: Karen Grossman   MUSIC: Reg Powell
Minor SF-thriller: Extraterrestrials devise plan to kidnap Earth children

The Pets' Tea Party
1908, (GB), Hepworth, b&w, 275 ft. (83.8m)
W: Gertie Potter (*The Girl*)
D: Lewin Fitzhamon
Standard fantasy: Children's horses and dogs hold celebration

Petticoat Planet
1996, (USA), color, 80 mins.
W: Elizabeth Kaitan
Minor eroto-SF

Un Peu de Feu, S.V.P. (A Little Fire, If You Please)
1904, (Fr), Star, b&w, 22m (72.2 ft./1.2 mins.)
D: Georges Melies
A.k.a. Every Man His Own Cigar Lighter
Standard fantasy: English tourist creates double to light his cigars

Un Peu de Votre Sang (A Little of Your Blood)
1965, (Fr), color

D: Michel Nuridsany
Standard horror-fantasy

Phantasm
1979, (USA), Avco Embassy, color, 87 mins.
W: Michael Baldwin (*Mike*), Bill Thornbury (*Jody*), Reggie Bannister (*Reggie*), Kathy Lester (*Lavender*), Terrie Kalbus (*The Granddaughter*), Ken Jones (*The Caretaker*), Bill Cone (*Tommy*), Susan Harper (*The Girl Friend*), Ralph Richmond (*The Bartender*), Lynn Eastman (*Sally*), David Arntzen (*Toby*), Laura Mann (*Double Lavender*), Mary Ellen Shaw (*The Fortune Teller*), Myrtle Scotton (*The Maid*), Angus Scrimm (*The Tall Man*)
WRIT, D & PHOTOG: Don Coscarelli   MUSIC: Fred Myrow
Unusual horror-fantasy: Boy has fantastic visions

Phantasm: Bill Thornbury

Phantasm II
1988, (USA), Univ, color, 97 mins.
W: James LeGros (*Mike*), Reggie Bannister (*Reggie*), Angus Scrimm (*The Tall Man*), Kenneth Tigar (*Father Meyers*), Paula Irvine (*Liz*), Samantha Phillips (*Alchemy*)
WRIT & D: Don Coscarelli   PHOTOG: Daryn Okada   MUSIC: Fred Myro
Standard horror-fantasy, a higher-tech sequel

Phantasm III: Lord of the Dead
1993, (USA), Starway Int'l/MCA-Univ, color, 91 mins.
W: Reggie Bannister (*Reggie*), A. Michael Baldwin (*Mike*), Bill Thornbury (*Jody*), Gloria Lynne Henry (*Rocky*), Kevin Connors (*Tim*), Angus Scrimm (*The Tall Man*), Cindy Ambuehl (*Edna*), John Chandler (*Henry*), Brooks Gardner (*Rufus*), Irene Roseen (*The Demon Nurse*), Sarah Davis (*Tanesha*), Duane Tucker (*The Motel Owner*), Wendy Way (*The Woman at the Orphanage*), Claire Benedek (*Tim's Mother*), Robert Beecher (*The Gas Station Attendant*), Chuck Bhutto (*The Doctor*), Beau Lotterman (*Tim's Father*), Jennifer Bross (*The Station Nurse*), Paula Irvine (*Liz*), Samantha Phillips (*Alchemy*), Kat Lester (*The Attending Nurse*)
WRIT & D: Don Coscarelli   PHOTOG: Chris Chomyn   SPCL-FX: Kevin McCarthy   MUSIC: Fredric Myrow & Christopher L. Stone
Standard horror-fantasy: Wayfarers flee murderous ghouls

Phantasmagoric Illusions
see Illusions Phantasmagoriques

Phantom
1922, (Ger), Decla-Bioscop, b&w, 9,530.8 ft. (2905m)
W: Lil Dagover
P: Erich Pommer   D: F.W. Murnau   SCR: Thea von Harbou
Standard thriller

The Phantom
1931, (USA), b&w, 62 mins.
W: Guinn Williams, Wilfrid Lucas, Sheldon Lewis, Tom O'Brien, William Gould
D: Alan James
Minor thriller: Hooded killer strikes

The Phantom
1996, (USA), Village Roadshow/Para, color, 100 mins.
W: Billy Zane, Treat Williams, Kristy Swanson, Catherine Zeta Jones, James Remar, Patrick McGoohan, Jon Tenney, Samantha Eggar, Cary-Hiroyuki Tagawa, Robert Coleby, David Proval
P: Robert Evans & Alan Ladd Jr.   D: Simon Wincer   SCR: Jeffrey Boam, from characters created by Lee Falk   PHOTOG: David Burr   MUSIC: David Newman
Standard adventure-thriller: Spectral crime-fighter haunts jungle

Phantom Apparitions
see Le Roi des Mediums

The Phantom Baron
see Le Baron Fantome

The Phantom Broadcast

1933, (USA), b&w, 63 mins.

W: Ralph Forbes, Gail Patrick, Vivienne Osborne, George Hayes, Guinn
    Williams
D: Phil Rosen
A.k.a. Phantom of the Air
Standard thriller: Radio crooner murdered

The Phantom Chariot

1920, (Swed), b&w, 89 mins.

D: Victor Sjostrom
*Standard fantasy (based on Swedish myth): Death's coach driven by last man to die each
    year*

The Phantom Clown-Girl

see La Clownesse Fantome

The Phantom Creeps

1939, (USA), Univ, b&w, 80 mins.

W: Bela Lugosi (*Dr. Alex Zorka*), Robert Kent (*Capt. Bob West*), Dorothy Arnold
    (*Jean Drew*), Edwin Stanley (*Dr. Fred Mallory*), Regis Toomey (*Jim Daly*),
    Jack Smith (*Monk*), Edward Van Sloan (*Jarvis*), Dora Clemant, Monte
    Vandergrift, Anthony Averill, Hugh Huntley, Frank Mayo, James Farley,
    Eddie Acuff, Reed Howes, Edward Wolff
D: Ford Beebe & Saul A. Goodkind **SCR:** George Plympton, Basil Dickey &
    Mildred Barish **ORIG. STORY:** Willis Cooper **PHOTOG:** Jerry Ash &
    William Sickner
Standard thriller (feature version of serial): Mad scientist guards secrets

The Phantom Empire

1986, (USA), American-Independent, color, 85 mins.

W: Ross Hagen (*Cort Eastman*), Jeffrey Combs (*Andrew Paris*), Dawn Wildsmith
    (*Eddy Colchilde*), Russ Tamblyn (*Bill*), Robert Quarry (*Prof. Strock*), Susan
    Stokey (*Denea Chambers*), Sybil Danning (*The Alien Queen*), Michelle Bauer
    (*The Cave Bunny*), Michael D. Sonye (*The Picnic Guy*), Victoria Alexander
    (*The Picnic Girl*), Duffy (*Simon*), Tony Lorea (*Pedro*), Robby the Robot (*him-
    self*), Gary J. Levinson, Dan Malloy, John Gonzales, Jerry Shull, Jon
    Edmunds, Bob Ivy, Nicole Morgan, Tricia Brown, Angela Post, Nicole
    Morgan, Maggie Martin, Liat Mathias, Julie Crow, Cory Kaplan
P & D: Fred Olen Ray **SCR:** Fred Olen Ray & T.L. Lankford **PHOTOG:** Gary
    Graver **SPCL VS-FX:** Mark D. Wolf, Wizard Works & Cory Kaplan
    MUSIC: Robert Garrett
Minor SF-thriller: Adventurers seek legendary treasure

The Phantom Fiend (1932)

see The Lodger (1932)

Phantom Fiend (1961)

see In the Steel Net of Dr. Mabuse

Phantom from Space

1953, (USA), Planet/UA, b&w, 73 mins.

W: Ted Cooper (*Hazen*), Noreen Nash (*Barbara Randall*), James Seay (*Maj.
    Andrews*), Harry Landers (*Lt. Bowers*), Rudolph Anders (*Dr. Wyatt*), Tom
    Daly (*Charlie*), Michael Mark (*The Watchman*), Steve Acton (*The Operator*),
    Burt Wenland (*Joe*), Lela Nelson (*Betty Evans*), Bert Arnold (*Darrow*), Sandy
    Sanders (*The Policeman*), Harry Strang (*The Neighbor*), Steve Clark (*Bill
    Randall*), Jim Bannon (*The Police Sgt.*), Dick Sands (*The Phantom*)
P & D: W. Lee Wilder **SCR:** Bill Ranor & Myles Wilder, from a story by Myles
    Wilder **PHOTOG:** William Clothier **SPCL-FX:** Alex Welden **MUSIC:**
    William Lava
Minor SF-thriller: Murderous space-alien pursued

The Phantom from 10,000 Leagues

1956, (USA), Milner Bros./American, b&w, 80 mins.

W: Cathy Downs, Kent Taylor, Michael Whalen, Rodney Bell, Vivi Janiss, Pierce
    Lyden, Phillip Pine, Helene Stanton, Michael Garth
P: Dan & Jack Milner **D:** Dan Milner **SCR:** Lou Rusoff **ORIG. STORY:**
    Dorys Lukather
Minor SF-horror: Aquatic monster terrorizes

Phantom Killer

1942, (USA), Supreme/Mono, b&w, 61 mins.

W: Dick Purcell, Joan Woodbury, John Hamilton, Warren Hymer
D: William Beaudine
Minor thriller (remake of 'The Sphinx' {1933}): Killer pursued

The Phantom Lady (1904)

see La Dame Fantome

Phantom Lady

1944, (USA), Univ, b&w, 87 mins.

W: Franchot Tone, Ella Raines, Alan Curtis, Thomas Gomez, Elisha Cook Jr., Fay
    Helm, Andrew Tombes, Aurora Miranda, Regis Toomey, Joseph Crehan
    Regis Toomey, Joseph Crehan, Doris Lloyd, Virginia Brissac
D: Robert Siodmak **SCR:** Bernard C. Schoenfeld, from a novel by William Irish
    (Cornell Woodrich) **PHOTOG:** Elwood Bredell **MUSIC DIR:** Don E.
    George

Stylish thriller: Murder suspect's only alibi is mystery woman he met in bar

The Phantom Light

1935, (GB), Gainsborough/Gaumont, b&w, 75 mins.

W: Binnie Hale (*Alice Bright*), Gordon Harker (*Sam Higgins*), Ian Hunter (*Jim
    Pierce*), Donald Calthrop (*David Owen*), Alice O'Day (*Mrs. Owen*), Milton
    Rosmer (*Dr. Carey*), Reginald Tate (*Tom Evans*), Mickey Brantford (*Bob
    Peters*), Herbert Lomas (*Cliff Owen*), Fewlass Llewellyn (*Griffith Owen*)
D: Michael Powell **SCR:** Austin Melford & Ralph Smart, from play *The Haunted
    Light* by Evadne Price & Joan Roy Byford
reissued 1950
Standard thriller: Wreckers pose as ghosts to scare new lighthouse-keeper

The Phantom of Algiers

see Le Fantome d'Alger

Phantom of Chinatown

1941, (USA), Mono, b&w, 61 mins.

W: Keye Luke (*Jimmy Wong*), Grant Withers (*Capt. Sam Street*), Lotus Long (*Win
    Len*), Paul McVey (*Grady*), Charles Miller (*Dr. Benton*), Virginia Carpenter
    (*Louise Benton*), John Dilson (*Charles Fraser*), Dick Terry, John Holland, Lee
    Tung Foo, Robert Kellard, William Castello, Huntley Gordon
D: Phil Rosen **SCR:** Joseph West, from characters created by Hugh Wiley
    PHOTOG: Fred Jackman Jr.
*Final "Mr. Wong" thriller: Murders committed to gain ancient scroll with secret of
    Mongolian oil deposits*

Phantom of Chinatown: PAUL MCVEY, GRANT WITHERS AND LOTUS LONG

The Phantom of Crestwood

1932, (USA), David O. Selznick/RKO, b&w, 77 mins.

W: Ricardo Cortez (*Curtis*), Karen Morley (*Jenny Wren*), H.B. Warner (*Priam
    Andes*), Anita Louise (*Esther Wren*), Pauline Frederick (*Faith Andes*), Mary
    Duncan (*Dorothy Mears*), Sam Hardy (*Pete Harris*), Tom Douglas (*Allen
    Herrick*), Richard "Skeets" Gallagher (*Mack*), Ivan Simpson (*Mr. Vayne*),
    Hilda Vaughn (*Carter*), Aileen Pringle (*Mrs. Walcott*), George E. Stone (*The
    Cat*), Robert McWade (*Herbert Walcott*), Gavin Gordon (*Will Jones*), Matty
    Kemp (*Frank Andes*), Eddie Sturges (*Bright-Eyes*)
D: J. Walter Ruben **SCR:** Bartlett Cormack, from a story by Bartlett Cormack &
    J. Walter Ruben **PHOTOG:** Henry Gerrard **MUSIC DIR:** Max Steiner
Standard thriller: Murders occur when blackmailer assembles her victims

Phantom of Death

1987, (It), color, 95 mins.

W: Michael York, Donald Pleasence, Edwige Fenech
D: Ruggero Deodato **MUSIC:** Pino Donaggio
Minor thriller: Pianist's fatal disease causes rapid aging

The Phantom 42nd Street

1945, (USA), b&w, 58 mins.

W: Dave O'Brien, Kay Aldridge, Alan Mowbray, Frank Jenks
D: Al(bert) Herman
Standard thriller: Actor and cop hunt killer

The Phantom of Hollywood

1974, (USA), MGM/CBS-TV, color, 74 mins.

W: Skye Aubrey, Jack Cassidy, Peter Haskell, John Ireland, Peter Lawford, Jackie
    Coogan, Kent Taylor, Corinne Calvet, John Lupton, Broderick Crawford,
    Bill Williams, Elisha Cook Jr., Fredd Wayne, Regis Toomey
P & D: Gene Levitt **TELEPLAY:** George Schenck **PHOTOG:** Gene Polito
TVM, standard thriller: Disfigured actor haunts movie studio

Phantom of Paris
see *The Mystery of Marie Roget*

The Phantom of Soho
1963, (W. Ger), CCC/Producers Releasing Org., b&w, 92 mins.
W: Dieter Borsche, Barbara Rueting, Hans Sohnker, Elisabeth Flickenschildt, Peter Vogel, Helga Sommerfeld
P: Artur Brauner   D: Franz Josef Gottlieb   SCR: Ladislas Fodor, from a Bryan Wallace novel
Standard thriller: Woman writer unmasks hooded killer

Phantom of Terror
see *L'Uccello delle Piume di Cristallo*

Phantom of the Air
see *The Phantom Broadcast*

The Phantom of the Brain
1914, (GB), Searchlight/Prieur, b&w, 1,120 ft. (341.4m)
Standard thriller: Jealous man dreams of committing murder

The Phantom of the Convent
1934, (Mex), b&w
Standard thriller

Phantom of the Jungle
1955, (USA), Arrow/Lippert, b&w, 75 mins.
W: Jon Hall, Anne Gwynne, Ray Montgomery, Kenneth MacDonald, Carleton Young, James Griffith, Nick Stewart, Milton Wood
D: Spencer G. Bennet   SCR: William Lively & Sherman L. Lowe
Standard "Ramar of the Jungle" adventure: Doctor aids scientists menaced by African tribe

Phantom of the Mall: Eric's Revenge
1988, (USA), Fries Entertainment, color, 91 mins.
W: Derek Rydall, Jonathan Goldsmith, Rob Estes, Pauly Shore, Kimber Sissons, Gregory Scott Cummins, Ken Foree, Tom Fridley, Kari Whitman, Morgan Fairchild, John Walter Davis, Dante D'Andre, Terrence Evans, Kelly Rutherford, Gary McGurk, Sean Reilly, Jake Jacobs, Dick Hancock
D: Richard Friedman   SCR: Scott J. Schneid, Tony Michelman & Robert King   STORY: Scott J. Schneid & Frederick R. Ulrich   PHOTOG: Harry Mathias   MUSIC: Stacy Widelitz   SONGS: *Heart of Darkness, Easy Money, I Need an Alibi, Shame on You, The Sensual One, When the Lights Go Down, Don't Wait, Tonight, Running, You Are the One, Body Heat & Is There a Phantom in the Mall?*
Minor horror-thriller: Disfigured teen seeks vengeance

The Phantom of the Moulin Rouge
see *Le Fantome du Moulin Rouge*

The Phantom of the Opera
1925, (USA), Univ, b&w & color, 90 mins.
W: Lon Chaney Sr. (*Erik, the Phantom*), Mary Philbin (*Christine Daae*), Norman Kerry (*Raoul de Chagny*), Snitz Edwards (*Florine Papillon*), Gibson Gowland (*Simon*), John St. Polis (*Philippe de Chagny*), Arthur Edmund Carewe (*The Persian*), Edith Yorke (*Mamma Valerius*), John Miljan (*Valentine*), Anton Vaverka (*The Prompter*), Edward Cecil (*Faust*), Bernard Siegel (*Joseph Buquet*), Olive Ann Alcorn (*La Sorelli*), George B. William (*M. Richard, the Manager*), Alexander Bevani (*Mephisto*), Ward Crane (*Count Ruboff*), Grace Marvin (*Martha*), Bruce Covington (*M. Monacharmin*), Cesare Gravina (*The Retiring Manager*), Chester Conklin (*The Orderly*), William Tryoler (*The Director of the Opera Orchestra*)
P: Carl Laemmle   D: Rupert Julian   SCR: Raymond Shrock & Elliot Clawson, from Gaston Leroux's novel   PHOTOG: Charles Van Enger, Virgil Miller & Milton Bridenbecker
"...one of Lon Chaney's most successful vehicles. As a piece of expertly contrived hokum, the film couldn't miss. With that plot, those wonderful settings...and the superb performance of Chaney, no director could have turned out a dull picture"—Joe Franklin, Classics of the Silent Screen
"...PHANTOM OF THE OPERA, played to perfection by the late Lon Chaney Sr., was a sensitive character study that needed no sound, for the tortured face of the sufferer was clearly pronounced"—Anon., "The Silent Years," Modern Monsters, No. 2 (June, 1966), p. 63
"Chaney's disguise as the Phantom was perfect. He moved through his scenes with a swiftness which gave the character an element of bizarre terror...The only clues that it was Chaney behind the disfigured face was the unmistakable and characteristic use of his hands. He exaggerated many of his gestures and postures to create an eerie and pitiful man" —Max Miller, "The Phantom of the Opera," Monster Fantasy, Vol. 1, No. 4 (August, 1975), p. 80
"...Chaney's characterization was everything the public had come to expect of him. In a daily, self-imposed ordeal, Chaney's features were distended, pulled apart, and disfigured into a livid, cadaverous face of Death itself. Since familiarity would diminish the effect, Chaney withholds the unmasking scene until the story is well under way"—Carlos Clarens, "An Illustrated History of the Horror Film"
Classic horror-thriller: Grotesque haunts opera house

Phantom of the Opera
1943, (USA), Univ, color, 93 mins.

W: Nelson Eddy (*Anatole Garron*), Susanna Foster (*Christine DuBois*), Claude Rains (*Enrique Claudin/The Phantom*), Edgar Barrier (*Inspector Raul Daubert*), Leo Carrillo (*Signor Ferretti*), Jane Farrar (*Biancarolli*), Fritz Leiber Sr. (*Liszt*), Barbara Everest (*Aunt*), J. Edward Bromberg, Fritz Feld, Frank Puglia, Steven Geray, Hume Cronyn, Nicki Andre, Gladys Blake, Miles Mander, Hans Herbert, Kate Lawson, Rosina Galli, Paul Marion
P: George Waggner   D: Arthur Lubin   SCR: Eric Taylor & Samuel Hoffenstein, from Gaston Leroux's novel   MUSIC SCORE & DIR: Edward Ward
Oscar-winning color photog by Hal Mohr & W. Howard Greene
Lavish horror-thriller: Disfigured musician seeks revenge

The Phantom of the Opera: LON CHANEY

The Phantom of the Opera
1962, (GB), Hammer/Univ, color, 90 mins.
W: Herbert Lom (*Prof. Petrie/The Phantom*), Heather Sears (*Christine Charles*), Edward De Souza (*Harry Hunter*), Ian Wilson (*The Dwarf*), Michael Gough (*Lord Ambrose D'Arcy*), Thorley Walters (*Lattimer*), Martin Miller (*Rossi*), Renee Houston (*Mrs. Tucker*), Michael Ripper (*The Cabbie*), Miles Malleson, Miriam Karlin, Marne Maitland, Harold Goodwin, Sonya Cordeau, Liane Aukin, Leila Forde, Patrick Troughton
P: Anthony Hinds   D: Terence Fisher   SCR: John Elder [Anthony Hinds], from Gaston Leroux's novel   PHOTOG: Arthur Grant   MUSIC: Edwin Astley
Standard horror-thriller: Betrayed composer terrorizes opera house

Phantom of the Opera
1983, (GB-Hung), Robert Halmi/CBS-TV, color, 96 mins.
W: Maximilian Schell (*Sandor Korvin/Orpheus*), Jane Seymour (*Maria Gianelli*), Michael York (*Michael Hartnell*), Jeremy Kemp (*The Baron*), Philip Stone (*Kraus*), Diana Quick (*Brigida Bianchi*), Paul Brooke (*The Inspector*), Andras Miko, Gellert Raksanyi, Laszlo Nemeth, Jeno Kis, Denes Ujlaky, Laszlo Sos, Terez Bod, Agnes David, Sandor Halmagyi, Pal Kovacs, Lajos Mezey, Sandor Deki Lakatos, Ferenc Begalyi, Nora Nemeth
D: Robert Markowitz   TELEPLAY: Sherman Yellen, from Gaston Leroux's novel   PHOTOG: Larry Pizer   SPCL-FX: Janos Kukoricza   MUSIC: Ralph Burns
TVM, modest horror-thriller: Beautiful opera singer pursued by masked terror

The Phantom of the Opera
1989, (USA-GB), 21st Century, color, 95 mins.
W: Robert Englund (*Erik Destler/The Phantom*), Jill Schoelen (*Christine*), Alex Hyde-White (*Richard*), Bill Nighy (*Barton*), Stephanie Lawrence (*Carlotta*), Terence Harvey, Nathan Lewis, Peter Clapham, Molly Shannon
D: Dwight H. Little   SCR: Duke Sandefur, based on a story by Gerry O'Hara, from Gaston Leroux's novel   PHOTOG: Elemer Ragalyi   MUSIC: Misha Segal
Standard horror-thriller: Ancient fiend abducts singer

The Phantom of the Opera
1990, (USA-GB), Saban-Scherick/NBC-TV, color
W: Burt Lancaster (*Gerard Carriere*), Charles Dance (*Erik, the Phantom*), Teri Polo (*Christine Daee*), Ian Richardson (*Cholet*), Adam Storke (*Count Philippe de Chagny*), Andrea Ferreol (*Carlotta*), Jean-Pierre Cassel (*Insp. Ledoux*), Jean Rougerie (*Jean-Claude*), Andre Chauneau (*Buquet*), Anne Roumanoff (*Fleure*), Marie-Therese Orain (*Mme. Giry*), Marie Lenoir (*Florence*), Marie-Christine Robert (*Flora*), Catherine Erhardy (*A Chorus Girl*), Caroline Beaune (*A Chorus Girl*), Francois Lalande, Sebastien Floche, Michel Feder, Philippe De Brugada, Bernard Spiegel, Luc Gentil, Jacques Mars, Jean-Claude Bouillon, Jean Dupouy, Michele Lagrange, Gerard Garino, Helia T'hezan, Anne-Julia Goddet, Frankie Pain, Frederic Durie
P: Ross Milloy   D: Tony Richardson   TELEPLAY: Arthur Kopit, from his play based on Gaston Leroux's novel   PHOTOG: Steve Yaconelli   MUSIC: John Addison

TVM (2-part), standard thriller: Disfigured musician haunts Paris Opera

The Phantom of the Opera
1998, (It), color
<u>W</u>: Julian Sands, Asia Argento
<u>D</u>: Dario Argento, from Gaston Leroux's novel
Standard horror-thriller

The Phantom of the Opera
1999, (USA), color
<u>W</u>: Antonio Banderas
from Andrew Lloyd Webber's musical, based on Gaston Leroux's novel

Phantom of the Paradise
1974, (USA), 20th-Fox, color, 91 mins.
<u>W</u>: Paul Williams (*Swan*), William Finley (*William Leach/The Phantom*), Jessica Harper (*Phoenix*), Gerrit Graham (*Beef*), George Memmoli (*Philbin*), Gene Gross (*Warden*), Henry Calvert (*The Night Watchman*), Jeffrey Comanor, Archie Hahn, Harold Oblong, Ken Carpenter, Sam Forney, Leslie Brewer, Celia Derr, Linda Larimer, Roseanne Romine, Nydia Amagas, Sara Ballantine, Kristi Bird, Cathy Buttner, Linda Cox, Susan Weiser, Jane DeFord, Bibi Hansen, Robin Jeep, Deen Summers, Judy Washington, Janet Savarino, Jean Savarino, Keith Allison, Bobby Birkenfeld, Sandy Catton, William Donovan, Scott Lane, Dennis Olivieri, Adam Wade, Nancy Moses, Diana Walden, Sherri Adeline, Carol O'Leary, Mary Bongfeld, Jim Lovelett, Bridgett Dunn, Coleen Crudden, William Shephard, Andrew Epper, Steven Richmond, James Gambino, Colin Cameron, David Garland, Gary Mallaber, Art Munson, James Bohan, Mary Margaret Amato, Janis Eve Lynn, Rand Bridges, Janit Baldwin, Herb Pacheco, Jennifer Ashley, Patrice Rohmer, Robin Mattson, Katherine Mastellos, Ruthey Ross, Cheryl Smith, April Troy, Walter Foster, Peter Harrell, Troy Haskins, Sandy Catton & Friends
<u>D & SCR</u>: Brian De Palma <u>PHOTOG</u>: Larry Pizer <u>MUSIC</u>: Paul Williams
<u>SONG</u>: *Life at Last* (sung by Ray Kennedy)
Offbeat comedy-thriller: Scarred composer haunts rock palace

The Phantom of Paris
1931, (USA), MGM, b&w, 73 mins.
<u>W</u>: John Gilbert, Leila Hyams, Lewis Stone, Jean Hersholt, C. Aubrey Smith, Natalie Moorhead, Ian Keith
<u>D</u>: John S. Robertson, from a novel by Gaston Leroux
Standard melodrama: Magician-illusionist accused of murder

Phantom of Paris (1942)
see **The Mystery of Marie Roget**

The Phantom of the Red House
1959, (Mex), Chapultepec, b&w
<u>W</u>: Alma Rose Aguirre, Raoul Martinez
Unusual farce-thriller: Man plays dead to test love of heirs

Phantom of the Rue Morgue
1954, (USA), WB, 3D, color, 84 mins.
<u>W</u>: Karl Malden (*Dr. Marais*), Patricia Medina (*Jeannette Rovere*), Steve Forrest (*Prof. Paul Dupin*), Claude Dauphin (*Insp. Bonnard*), Allyn McLerie (*Yvonne*), Dolores Dorn (*Camille*), Veola Vonn (*Arlette*), Paul Richards (*Rene*), Merv Griffin (*Georges Brevert*), Anthony Caruso (*Jacques*), Erin O'Brien-Moore (*The Wardrobe Woman*), Rolfe Sedan (*LeBon*), The Flying Zacchinis
<u>P</u>: Henry Blanke <u>D</u>: Roy Del Ruth <u>SCR</u>: Harold Medford & James Webb, based on Edgar Allan Poe's short story "The Murders in the Rue Morgue"
<u>PHOTOG</u>: J. Peverell Marley <u>MUSIC</u>: David Buttolph
Standard thriller: French detective probes brutal murders

The Phantom Picture
1916, (GB), British Empire Films, b&w, 5,500 ft. (1676.4m)
<u>W</u>: Henry Lonsdale (*John Gordon*), Violet Campbell (*Pauline Mainwaring*), Arthur Poole (*Lionel Carruthers*), Ivan Berlyn (*Isaac Bernstein*)
<u>D & SCR</u>: Albert Ward, from a play by Harold Simpson
Standard crime-thriller: Artist's model poses as painting, shocks Jew into confessing he stabbed connoisseur

The Phantom Planet
1961, (USA), Four Crown/AIP, b&w, 82 mins.
<u>W</u>: Dean Fredericks (*Chapman*), Coleen Gray (*Liara*), Anthony Dexter (*Herron*), Dolores Faith, Francis X. Bushman, Dick Haynes, Michael Marshall, Richard Webber, Richard Kiel (*The Solarite*)
<u>P</u>: Fred Gebhardt <u>D</u>: William Marshall <u>SCR</u>: William Telaak, Fred de Gortner & Fred Gebhardt <u>SPCL-FX</u>: Louis DeWitt
Standard SF-thriller: Astronaut involved with warring planetoids

Phantom Raiders
1940, (USA), MGM, b&w, 70 mins.
<u>W</u>: Walter Pidgeon (*Nick Carter*), Donald Meek (*Batholomew*), Florence Rice, Joseph Schildkraut, John Carroll, Nat Pendleton, Steffi Duna, Cecil Kellaway, Alec Craig, Matthew Boulton, Thomas Ross, Dwight Frye
<u>D</u>: Jacques Tourneur <u>SCR</u>: William P. Lipman & Jonathan Latimer, from characters created by John R. Coryell
working title, **Nick Carter in Panama**
Standard "Nick Carter" mystery: Sleuth probes ship sinkings

Phantoms
1998, (USA), Dimension, color, 96 mins.
<u>W</u>: Peter O'Toole, Ben Affleck, Rose McGowan, Liev Schreiber, Joanna Going, Clifton Powell
from Dean R. Koontz' novel
Unusual SF-horror: Amorphous creature becomes demonic

The Phantom Ship
1908, (GB), Cricks & Martin, b&w, 490 ft. (149.4m)
<u>D</u>: J.H. Martin & A.E. Coleby
Standard melodrama: Bizarre happenings aboard ship

The Phantom Ship (1935)
see **The Mystery of the Mary Celeste**

The Phantom Speaks
1945, (USA), Rep, b&w, 68 mins.
<u>W</u>: Richard Arlen, Lynne Roberts
Minor thriller

The Phantom Thief
1946, (USA), Col, b&w, 65 mins.
<u>W</u>: Chester Morris (*Boston Blackie*), Jeff Donnell (*Anne Duncan*), Richard Lane (*Insp. Farraday*), George E. Stone (*Runt*), Dusty Anderson (*Sandra*), Frank Sully (*Sgt. Matthews*), Marvin Mueller (*Miller*) (*Dr. Nejijo*), Wilton Graff (*Rex Duncan*), Murray Alper (*Eddie Alexander*), Forbes Murray (*Dr. Purchell Nash*), Joseph Crehan (*Jumbo Madigan*), Edward F. Dunn, Edmund Cobb, Eddie Fetherston, George Magrill
<u>D</u>: D. Ross Lederman <u>SCR</u>: Richard Wormser, Richard Weil & G.A. Snow, from characters created by Jack Boyle <u>PHOTOG</u>: George Meehan Jr.
<u>MUSIC</u>: Mischa Bakaleinikoff
Standard "Boston Blackie" mystery: Sleuth encounters spiritualism and murder

The Phantom Tollbooth
1970, (USA), Chuck Jones/MGM, color, 90 mins.
<u>W</u>: Butch Patrick
<u>VOICES</u>: Candy Candido, Hans Conried, Daws Butler, et al.
<u>D</u>: (live action), David Monahan <u>SCR</u>: Chuck Jones & Sam Rosen, from a story by Norman Juster <u>PHOTOG</u>: Maurice Noble <u>MUSIC</u>: Dean Elliott & Lee Pockriss
Juvenile fantasy (combination of live action & animation): Boy visits magical world

Pharaoh
see **Faraon**

Pharaoh's Curse
1957, (USA), Bel-Air/UA, b&w, 66 mins.
<u>W</u>: Mark Dana (*Storm*), Diane Brewster (*Sylvia*), Ziva Rodann (*Simira*), George Neise (*Robert*), Alvaro Guillot, Terence de Marney, Ben Wright, Guy Prescott, Richard Peel, Kurt Katch, Robert Fortin, Ralph Clanton
<u>P</u>: Howard W. Koch <u>D</u>: Lee Sholem <u>ORIG. STORY & SCR</u>: Richard Landau
<u>PHOTOG</u>: William Margulies <u>PHOTO-FX</u>: Jack Rabin & Louis DeWitt
<u>MUSIC</u>: Les Baxter
Standard fantasy-thriller: Archeological expedition unearths ancient horror

Pharos the Wonder Worker
1911, (GB), Tress Films, b&w, 340 ft. (103.6m)
Standard fantasy short: Conjuror does tricks

Phase IV
1974, (GB), Shailinburgh/Alced/PBR/Para, color, 91 mins.
<u>W</u>: Nigel Davenport (*Hubbs*), Lynne Frederick (*Kendra*), Robert Henderson (*Clete*), Michael Murphy (*Lesko*), Alan Gifford (*Eldridge*), Helen Horton (*Mrs. Eldridge*)
<u>P</u>: Paul Radin <u>D</u>: Saul Bass <u>SCR</u>: Mayo Simon <u>PHOTOG</u>: Dick Bush
<u>MUSIC</u>: Brian Gascoyne
"...wonderfully original moviemaking; though most of the film is more or less a shambles, PHASE IV opens up some new potential in the usage of biophotography for dramatic effect which could result in some extraordinary cinema"—Baird Searles, "Films," The Magazine of Fantasy and Science Fiction, Vol. 47, No. 6 (December, 1974), p. 81
Unusual SF-fantasy: Intelligent ants plan world conquest

Le Phenix ou le Coffret de Cristal (The Phoenix: or, The Crystal Casket)
1905, (Fr), Star, b&w, 92m (301.9 ft./5.1 mins.)
<u>D</u>: Georges Melies
A.k.a. **The Crystal Casket**
Standard fantasy

Phenomena
1985, (It), DACFilm-Rome/New Line, color, 83 mins.
<u>W</u>: Jennifer Connelly (*Jennifer*), Donald Pleasence (*John McGregor*), Daria Nicolodi, Fiore Argento, Patrick Bauchau, Federica Mastroianni, Dalila Di Lazzaro, Michele Soavi, Fiorenza Tessari
<u>D</u>: Dario Argento <u>SCR</u>: Dario Argento & Franco Ferrini <u>MUSIC</u>: Bill Wyman, Iron Maiden, Motorhead, et al.
USA retitle, **Creepers**
Stylish thriller: Murders plague Alpine girl's school

Phenomenon

1996, (USA), Touchstone, color, 123 mins.

W: John Travolta *(George Malley)*, Kyra Sedgwick *(Lace Pennamin)*, Forest Whitaker *(Nate Pope)*, Robert Duvall *(Doc)*, Brent Spiner *(Dr. Bob)*, Jeffrey DeMunn *(Prof. Ringold)*, Richard Kiley *(Dr. Wellin)*, Vyto Ruginis *(Ted Rhome)*, Michael Milhoan *(Jimmy)*, Bruce Young *(Jack Hatch)*, Sean O'Bryan *(Banes)*, David Gallagher *(Al)*, Troy Evans *(Roger)*, Ashley Buccille *(Glory)*, Tony Genaro *(Tito)*, James Keane *(Pete the Cop)*, Elisabeth Nunziato *(Ella)*, Ellen Geer *(Bonnie)*, James Cotton *(Cal)*, Susan Merson *(The Nurse)*, Justin DiPego *(The UFO Man)*, Mark Soper *(The Reporter)*, Daniel Zacapa *(The Father at the Book Fair)*, Cab Covay *(The Book Fair Heckler)*, Tony A. Mattos *(Ella's Father)*, Mark Valim *(Alberto)*, Carl Parker *(The Man in the Orchard)*, Beth Kennedy *(The Female FBI Agent)*, Tom Fridley *(The Male FBI Agent)*, Richard Gross *(The Customer at Malley's)*, Jack Chouchanian *(The MRI Technician)*, Michael Forner *(Charlie Shipper)*, Sage Callaway *(The Female Officer)*, Jewel Benedict, Mariann V. Carothers, Betsy Berryhill, Claudia Crespin, Joseph A. Nicosia, Isaac Reiswig, Dan Partain

D: Jon Turteltaub **SCR:** Gerald DiPego **PHOTOG:** Phedon Papamichael **SPCL-FX:** Rod M. Janusch **MUSIC:** Thomas Newman **SONG:** *Change the World* by Eric Clapton

Unusual SF-comedy-drama: Ordinary guy develops extraordinary intellect

The Philadelphia Experiment

1984, (USA), Cinema Group/New World, color, 98 mins.

W: Michael Pare, Bobby DiCicco, Nancy Allen, Louise Latham, Eric Christmas, Kene Holliday, Michael Currie, Joe Dorsey, Jay Bernard, Debra Troyer, Stephen Tobolowsky, Vivian Brown, Garry Brockette, Ralph Manza, Miles McNamara, James Edgcomb, Glenn Morshower, Rodney Saulsberry, Stephenie Faulkner

D: Stewart Raffill **SCR:** William Gray & Michael Janover **STORY:** Wallace Bennett & Don Jakoby, from a book by William I. Moore & Charles Berlitz **PHOTOG:** Dick Bush **VS-FX:** Max W. Anderson **MUSIC:** Ken Wannberg

Entertaining SF-thriller: Secret test in World War II sends two men into 1980's

Philadelphia Experiment II

1993, (USA), Vidmark, video, color, 98 mins.

W: Brad Johnson *(David Herdeg)*, Marjean Holden *(Jess)*, Gerrit Graham *(Mailer/Mahler)*, John Christian Graas *(Benjamin)*, Cyril O'Reilly *(Decker)*, Geoffrey Blake *(Logan)*, Lisa Robins *(Scotch)*, David Wells *(Pinstripes)*, Larry Cedar *(Hank the Controller)*, James Greene *(Longstreet)*, Al Pugilese *(Coach)*, Andrew Steel *(The Lt.)*, Allen Perada *(Mahler's Double)*, Hank Stone, John Rixey Moore, Robert Gould, Alan De Satti, James Jude Courtney, Allan Rust, Craig Branham

D: Stephen Cornwell **SCR:** Kevin Rock & Nick Paine **STORY:** Kim Steven Ketelsen & Kevin Rock, from characters created by Wallace C. Bennett & Don Jakoby **PHOTOG:** Ronn Schmidt **MUSIC:** Gerald Gourift

Made-for-Video, standard SF-thriller: Time traveler thrust into Nazified alternate present

The Philosopher's Stone (1899)

see La Pierre Philosophale

The Philosopher's Stone (1958)

see Paras Pathar

Philosophy in the Boudoir

see Eugenie...The Story of Her Journey into Perversion

Philo Vance Returns

1947, (USA), PRC, b&w, 64 mins.

W: William Wright *(Philo Vance)*, Leon Belasco *(Alexis)*, Terry Austin *(Lorena Simms)*, Clara Blandick *(Stella Blendon)*, Ramsay Ames *(Virginia)*, Iris Adrian *(Choo-Choo Divine)*, Damian O'Flynn *(Larry Blendon)*, Frank Wilcox *(George Hullman)*, Ann Staunton *(Helen)*, Mary Scott *(The Maid)*, Tim Murdock *(The Policeman)*

D: William Beaudine **SCR:** Robert E. Kent, from characters created by S.S. Van Dine **PHOTOG:** Jackson Rose

A.k.a. Infamous Crimes

Standard "Philo Vance" mystery: Playboy's fiancee and ex-wife are murdered

Philo Vance's Gamble

1947, (USA), PRC, b&w, 62 mins.

W: Alan Curtis *(Philo Vance)*, Terry Austin *(Laurian March)*, Frank Jenks *(Ernie Clark)*, Tala Birell *(Tina Cromwell)*, Gavin Gordon *(Oliver Tennant)*, Cliff Clark *(The Inspector)*, Toni Todd *(Geegee Desmond)*, James Burke *(Lt. Burke)*, Garnett Marks *(Charles O'Mara)*, Francis Pierlot *(Robert)*, Joseph Crehan *(The D.A.)*, Grady Sutton *(Mr. Willets)*, Joanne Frank *(Norma Harkness)*, Charles Mitchell *(Guy Harkness)*, Dan Seymour *(Jeff)*

D: Basil Wrangell **SCR:** Eugene Conrad, Arthur St. Clair & Lawrence Edmund Taylor, from characters created by S.S. Van Dine **PHOTOG:** Jackson Rose **MUSIC:** Irving Friedman

Standard "Philo Vance" mystery: Stage-show producer mixes with murderous smugglers

Philo Vance's Secret Mission

1947, (USA), PRC/Eagle Lion, b&w, 58 mins.

W: Alan Curtis *(Philo Vance)*, Sheila Ryan *(Mona Bannister)*, Tala Birell *(Mrs. Philips)*, Frank Jenks *(Ernie Clark)*, Paul Maxey *(Martin Jamison)*, James Bell *(Harry Madison)*, David Leonard *(Carl Wilson)*, Frank Fenton *(Paul Morgan)*,

Toni Todd *(Louise Roberts)*

D: Reginald LeBorg **SCR:** Lawrence Edmund Taylor, from characters created by S.S. Van Dine **PHOTOG:** Jackson Rose

Standard "Philo Vance" mystery: Sleuth helps publisher solve old murder

Phobia

1980, (Can), Borough Park/Para, color, 95 mins.

W: Paul Michael Glaser *(Dr. Peter Ross)*, Susan Hogan *(Jenny St. Clair)*, John Colicos *(Insp. Barnes)*, Alexandra Stewart *(Barbara Grey)*, Robert O'Ree *(Bubba King)*, Patricia Collins *(Dr. Alice Toland)*, David Bolt *(Henry Owen)*, David Eisner *(Johnny Venuti)*, Lisa Langlois *(Laura Adams)*, Neil Vipond *(Dr. Clegg)*, Marian Waldman *(Mrs. Casey)*, Gwen Thomas *(Dr. Clemens)*, Kenneth Welsh *(Sgt. Wheeler)*, Paddy Campanaro *(Newswoman #1)*, Gerry Salsberg *(Newsman #1)*, Peter Hicks *(Newsman #2)*, Joan Fowler *(The Head Nurse)*, John Stoneham *(The Security Guard)*, Terry Martin *(Policeman #1)*, Ken Anderson *(Policeman #2)*, Janine Cole *(The Child)*, Karen Pike *(Girl #1)*, Wendy Jewell *(Girl #2)*, Coleen Embree *(Girl #3)*, Lorne Stepak *(The Teamate)* Diane Lasko

D: John Huston **SCR:** Lew Lehman, Jimmy Sangster & Peter Bellwood **STORY:** Gary Sherman & Ronald Shusett **PHOTOG:** Reginald H. Morris **MUSIC:** Andre Gagnon

Stylish thriller (minor Huston effort): Psychiatrist's patients are murdered

Phoenix (1966)

see Fahrenheit 451

Phoenix

1978, (Jap), color, 137 mins.

W: Tatsuya Nakadai, Tomisaburo Wakayama, Raoru Yumi, Reiko Ohara

Standard fantasy: Aging queen seeks eternal life

Phoenix

1995, (USA), color

W: Stephen Nichols, Billy Drago, William Sanderson, Brad Dourif

Minor SF-thriller: Killing machine prowls deep-space outpost

The Phoenix

1980, (Hong Kong), 21st Century, color

W: Richard Kiel

P: Frank Wong **D:** Richard Caan & Sadamasa Arikawa **SCR:** F. Kenneth Lin

Minor adventure-fantasy: Giant helps fisherman battle evil queen

The Phoenix

1981, (USA), ABC-TV, color, 95 mins.

W: Judson Scott *(Bennu)*, Shelley Smith *(Noel Marshall)*, E.G. Marshall *(Dr. Ward Frazier)*, Fernando Allende *(Diego De Varga)*, Daryl Anderson *(Dr. Cliff Davis)*, Hersha Parady *(Lynn)*, Jimmy Mair *(Tim)*, Lyman Ward *(Howard)*, Angus Duncan, Wayne Storm, Terry Jastrow

WRIT & P: Anthony & Nancy Lawrence **D:** Douglas Hickox

TVM, standard SF-thriller: Revived ancient astronaut has mysterious mission on Earth

The Phoenix (1981)

see War of the Wizards

The Phoenix: or, The Crystal Casket

see Le Phenix ou le Coffret di Cristal

The Pheonix and the Magic Carpet

1995, (USA), color, 80 mins.

W: Dee Wallace Stone, Timothy Hegeman, Nick Klein, Laura Kamrath, Peter Ustinov

D: Zoran Perisic **SCR:** Florence Fox, from a book by Edith Nesbit **MUSIC:** Alan Parker

Standard juvenile fantasy: Mythical bird takes children on adventure

Phoenix the Warrior

1988, (USA), Action Int'l, color, 90 mins.

W: Persis Khambatta *(Cobalt)*, Kathleen Kinmont *(Phoenix)*, Peggy Sands *(Keela)*, James H. Emery *(Guy)*, Sheila Howard *(Rev. Mother Badger)*, Nina Jaffe *(Chainsaw)*, Linda Santo *(Snapper)*, Skyler Corbett *(Skyler)*, Lorie De Nuccio *(Neon)*, Courtney Caldwell *(The Motorcycle Woman/T. Bird)*, Roxanne Kernchan *(Meda)*, B.B. Bowen *(Ginsu)*, Michi *(The Escaping Sister)*, Kathy Armstrong *(The Bartender/ Arena Announcer)*, Pipa Danyon *(Rattail)*, Dusty Woods *(Mohawk)*, Susan Overman *(Blondie)*, Kastle *(The Psycho Chick)*, Veronica Carothers *(Suga)*, Isis Richardson *(Riptide)*, Miranda Fredrick *(Dreadlock)*, Ginger Justin *(Orangehair)*, Barbara Buck *(The Slave)*, Bo Money *(The Snake Dancer)*, Buffy Fletcher *(The Head Rezule)*, Andy Harrington *(The 2nd Rezule)*, Kimberley Casey *(Scratch)*, Mary May *(The Prostitute)*, Cheryl Butner, Dana Crawford, Chantel Anderson, Catherine Vargas, Kim Whitton, Sherreen Burger, Jessica Clark, Corey Ripley, Lorna Atkinstall, Judy Ramirez, Charlene McCloud, Juliana Greene, Lorene Duran

D: Robert Hayes **SCR:** Robert Hayes & Dan Rotblatt **PHOTOG:** Paul Maibaum **SPCL-FX:** Chuck Whitton **MUSIC:** Dan Radlauer

Minor SF-adventure: Post-nuke females battle

A Photographic Episode

1903, (GB), Gaumont, b&w, 65 ft. (19.8m)

D: Alf Collins

Standard fantasy short: Camera shoots inquisitive spinster into wall

Photographing a Ghost
1898, (GB), G.A.S. Films, b&w, 76 ft. (23.2m)
D: George Albert Smith
Standard fantasy short: Photographer pursues elusive spirit

The Phrenological Burlesque
see La Phrenologie Burlesque

La Phrenologie Burlesque (The Phrenological Burlesque)
1901, (Fr), Star, b&w, 30m (98.4 ft./1.7 mins.)
D: Georges Melies
GB retitle, **The Phrenologist and the Lively Skull**
Standard comedy-fantasy

Piccadilly Third Stop
1960, (GB), Ethiro/RFD, b&w, 90 mins.
W: Terence Morgan (*Dominic Colpoys-Owen*), Mai Zetterling (*Christine Preedy*), Yoko Tani (*Seraphina Yokami*), John Crawford (*Joe Preedy*), William Hartnell (*The Colonel*), Dennis Price (*Edward*), Ann Lynn (*Mouse*), Charles Kay (*Toddy*), Douglas Robinson (*Albert*), Gillian Maude (*Mother*)
P: Norman Williams **D:** Wolf Rilla **STORY:** Leigh Vance
Standard crime-thriller: Playboy's gang robs Eastern embassy

Picking Up the Pieces
1991, (USA), Para, color 89 mins.
W: Jake Dengel, Joe Sharkey, Suzanne Fletcher, Pat Logan, Beverly Penberthy, Shawn Elliott, Jane Hamilton
D: Alan Smithee **SCR:** Dean Tschetter **MAKEUP FX:** Tom Savini
released to video as **Bloodsucking Pharaohs in Pittsburgh**
Minor horror-satire: Crazed cannibals seek immortality

Pickup
1951, (USA), Col, b&w, 78 mins.
W: Hugo Haas, Beverly Michaels, Allan Nixon
WRIT, P & D: Hugo Haas
Minor melodrama: Middle-aged widower weds young woman, finds his life threatened

Pickup Alley
see Interpol

Picnic at Hanging Rock
1975, (Austral), B.E.F. Distributors/Atlantic, color, 115 mins.
W: Rachel Roberts (*Mrs. Appleyard*), Dominic Guard (*Michael Fitzhubert*), Helen Morse (*Dianne De Poiters*), Jacki Weaver (*Minnie*), Vivean Gray (*Miss McCraw*), Kirsty Child (*Dora Lumley*), Anne Lambert (*Miranda*), Karen Robson (*Irma*), Jane Vallis (*Marion*), Christine Schuler (*Edith*), John Jarratt (*Albert*), Margaret Nelson (*Sara*), Ingrid Mason (*Rosamund*), Martin Vaughan (*Ben Hussey*), Wyn Roberts (*Sgt. Bumpher*), Jack Fegan (*Doc McKenzie*), Frank Gunnell (*Edward Whitehead*), Garry McDonald (*Jim Jones*)
D: Peter Weir **SCR:** Cliff Green, from Joan Lindsay's novel **PHOTOG:** Russell Boyd **MUSIC:** Bruce Smeaton
Fact-based, critically-acclaimed melodrama: Disappearance of Australian schoolgirls leads to fear and torment

Picnic At Hanging Rock: HAIRDRESSER JOSE PEREZ AND RACHEL ROBERTS

Picture Mommy Dead
1966, (USA), Embassy, color, 88 mins.
W: Don Ameche, Martha Hyer, Susan Gordon, Zsa Zsa Gabor [Ms. Gabor's role orig. intended for Hedy Lamarr], Maxwell Reed, Wendell Corey, Signe Hasso, Anna Lee
P & D: Bert I. Gordon

Standard thriller: Young girl loses memory after mother's tragic death

The Picture of Dorian Gray (1915)
see Portret Doriana Greya

The Picture of Dorian Gray
1916, (GB), Barker-Neptune/Browne, b&w, 5,752 ft. (1753.2m)
W: Henry Victor (*Dorian Gray*), Pat O'Malley (*Sybil Vane*), Jack Jordan (*Lord Henry Wootton*), Sydney Bland (*Basil Hallward*), A.B. Imeson (*Satan*), Douglas Cox (*James Vane*), Dorothy Fane (*Lady Marchmont*), Miriam Ferris
D: Fred W. Durrant **SCR:** Rowland Talbot, from Oscar Wilde's novel
Standard fantasy: Rake remains young while his portrait ages

The Picture of Dorian Gray
1945, (USA), MGM, b&w (some sequences in color), 110 mins.
W: Hurd Hatfield (*Dorian Gray*), George Sanders (*Lord Henry*), Donna Reed (*Gladys*), Angela Lansbury (*Sybil Vane*), Richard Fraser (*James Vane*), Peter Lawford (*David Stone*), Douglas Walton (*Allen Campbell*), Lowell Gilmore (*Basil Hallward*), Mary Forbes (*Lady Agatha*), Morton Lowry (*Adrian Singleton*), Lillian Bond (*Kate*), Miles Mander (*Sir Robert Bentley*), Lydia Bilbrook (*Mrs. Vane*), Robert Greig (*Sir Thomas*), Moyna MacGill (*The Duchess*), Billy Bevan, Renee Carson, Devi Dja & Her Balinese Dancers, Arthur Shields

The Picture of Dorian Gray: BILLY BEVAN, ANGELA LANSBURY AND HURD HATFIELD

NARRATION: Sir Cedric Hardwicke
P: Pandro S. Berman **D & SCR:** Albert Lewin, from Oscar Wilde's novel
PHOTOG: Harry Stradling **MUSIC:** Herbert P. Stothart **SONG:** *Goodbye, Little Yellow Bird*
Superior fantasy-thriller: Victorian fop gains eternal youth

The Picture Thieves
1910, (GB), Hepworth, b&w, 675 ft. (205.7m)
D: Theo Bouwmeester   .
Standard crime-thriller: Art thieves pose as mad count and asylum warders

A Piece of Cake
1948, (GB), Production Facilities/GFD, b&w, 45 mins.
W: Cyril Fletcher (*Cyril Clarke*), Betty Astell (*Betty Clarke*), Laurence Naismith (*Merlin Mound*), Jon Pertwee (*Mr. Short*), Harry Fowler (*Spiv*), Sam Costa (*The Bandleader*), Tamara Lees (*The Guest*)
P: Adrian Worker **D:** John Irwin **SCR:** Bernard McNab, Lyn Lockwood & Dick Pepper, from a story by John Croydon & Betty Astell
Standard fantasy: Conjurer dreams magic tricks cause trouble with authorities

Pieces
1983, (Sp), Almena/Spectacular, color, 89 mins.
W: Christopher George (*Lt. Bracken*), Lynda Day (*Mary Riggs*), Frank Brana (*Sgt. Holden*), Paul Smith (*Willard*), Edmund Purdom (*The Dean*), Ian Sera (*Kendall*), Isabelle Luque (*Sylvia*), Jack Taylor (*Prof. Brown*), Gerard Tichy (*Dr. Jennings*), Hilda Fuchs (*The Secretary*), May Heatherly
D: J. Piquer Simon **SCR:** Dick Randall & John Shadow **PHOTOG:** John Marine **MUSIC:** Cam
Standard thriller: Grisly campus murders

The Pied Piper
1907, (GB), Clarendon, b&w, 755 ft. (230.1m)
D: Percy Stow **SCR:** Langford Reed, from Robert Browning's poem *The Pied Piper of Hamelin*
Standard fantasy: Unpaid piper lures children

The Pied Piper
1972, (GB), Goodtimes/Sagittarius/Scotia Barber/Para, color, 90 mins.

W: Donovan (*The Pied Piper*), Jack Wild (*Gavin*), John Hurt (*Franz*), Donald Pleasence (*The Baron*), Diana Dors (*Frau Poppendick*), Roy Kinnear (*The Burgomeister*), Cathryn Harrison (*Lisa*), Michael Hordern (*Melius*), Peter Vaughan (*The Bishop*), Keith Buckley (*Mattio*), Peter Eyre (*Pilgrim*), Arthur Hewlett (*Otto*), Hamilton Dyce (*The Papal Nuncio*), Andre Van Gyseghem (*The Friar*), Patsy Puttnam (*Helga*), John Falconer (*The Priest*), David Netheim (*Kulik*), John Welsh (*The Chancellor*), Sammie Winmill (*Gretel*), Gertan Klauber (*The Town Crier*)
P: David Putnam **D:** Jacques Demy **SCR:** Andrew Birkin, Jacques Demy & Mark Peploe, from Robert Browning's poem *The Pied Piper of Hamelin*
PHOTOG: Peter Suschitzky **MUSIC:** Donovan
Standard musical fantasy: Piper eliminates rats, steals children when payment unmet

The Pied Piper: DIANA DORS

The Pied Piper of Hamelin
1926, (GB), British Projects, b&w, 2,000 ft. (609.6m)
W: Edward Sorley (*The Pied Piper*), Judd Green (*The Mayor*)
D: Frank Tilley **SCR:** Ralph C. Wells, from Robert Browning's poem
Standard fantasy: Rat remover absconds with children

The Pier
see La Jetee

Pier 5, Havana
1959, (USA), UA, b&w, 67 mins.
W: Cameron Mitchell, Allison Hayes
Minor thriller

Pier 23
1951, (USA), Lippert, b&w, 58 mins.
W: Hugh Beaumont, Richard Travis, David Bruce, Raymond Greenleaf, Joi Lansing
Minor melodrama: Detective hunts ex-convict, finds impostor

La Pierre Philosophale (The Philosopher's Stone)
1899, (Fr), Star, b&w, 20m (65.6 ft./1.1 mins.)
D: Georges Melies
Standard fantasy: Alchemist dabbles in magic

The Pierrot and the Devil's Dice
1905, (GB), R.W. Paul, b&w, 175 ft. (53.3m)
D: J.H. Martin
A.k.a. **The Conjuring Clown**
Standard fantasy short: Tiny Pierrot makes huge dice appear and vanish, etc.

The Pierrot's Romance
1904, (GB), Urban Trading Co., b&w, 550 ft. (167.6m)
W: G.V. Rosi (*The Pierrot*)
from a sketch by G.V. Rosi
Standard melodrama: Jealous pierrot stabs unfaithful milliner, then himself

Pigs
see Blood Pen

Pikovaya Dama (Queen of Spades)
1910, (Russ), Khanzhonkov, b&w
W: P. Biryukov, A. Gromov, A. Goncharova, A. Pozharskaya
D & SCR: Pyotr Chardynin, from Pushkin's story
Standard thriller: Scoundrel seeks noblewoman's mysterious secret for winning at cards

Pikovaya Dama (Queen of Spades)
1916, (Russ), Yermoliev, b&w, 7,545.9 ft. (2300m)
W: Ivan Mozhukhin, Vera Orlova, Y. Shebuyeva
D: Yakov Protazanov **SCR:** Fyodor Otzep, from Pushkin's story **PHOTOG:** Yevgeni Slavinsky
Standard thriller: Russian soldier covets secret of winning at cards

Pillow of Death
1945, (USA), Univ, b&w, 66 mins.
W: Lon Chaney Jr. (*Wayne Fletcher*), Brenda Joyce (*Donna Kincaid*), Rosalind Ivan (*Amelia Kincaid*), J. Edward Bromberg (*Julian*), Clara Blandick (*Belle Kincaid*), Victoria Horne (*Vivian Fletcher*), Wilton Graff (*Capt. McCracken*), George Cleveland (*Sam Kincaid*), J. Farrell MacDonald (*The Sexton*), Bernard B. Thomas (*Bruce Malone*)
D: Wallace Fox **SCR:** George Bricker **ORIG. STORY:** Dwight V. Babcock **PHOTOG:** Jerome Ash **MUSIC DIR:** Frank Skinner
Standard "Inner Sanctum" mystery: Lawyer implicated in murders by smothering.

Pimpernel Smith
1941, (GB), British Nat'l, b&w, 121 mins.
W: Leslie Howard (*Prof. Horatio Smith*), Francis L. Sullivan (*Gen. von Graum*), Mary Morris (*Ludmilla Koslowski*), Raymond Huntley (*Marx*), Hugh McDermott (*David Maxwell*), Allan Jeayes (*Dr. Beckendorf*), Manning Whiley (*Bertie Gregson*), Lawrence Kitchen (*Clarence Elstead*), Peter Gawthorne (*Sidimir Koslowski*), Dennis Arundell (*Hoffman*), David Tomlinson (*Steve*), Joan Kemp-Welch (*The Teacher*), Philip Friend (*Spencer*), Basil Appleby (*Jock McIntyre*), Percy Walsh (*Dvorak*), Charles Paton (*Steinhof*), Roland Pertwee (*Sir George Smith*), A.E. Matthews (*The Earl of Meadowbrook*), George Street (*Schmidt*), Aubrey Mallalieu (*Dean*), Oriel Ross (*Lady Willoughby*), Ernest Butcher (*Weber*), Michael Rennie (*The Officer*), Sebastian Cabot
P & D: Leslie Howard **SCR:** Anatole de Grunwald, Roland Pertwee & Ian Dalrymple, from a story by A.G. MacDonnell & Wolfgang Wilhelm **MUSIC:** John Greenwood
USA retitle, **Mister V** *(UA, 1942)*
Standard thriller: Archeologist helps Polish journalist escape Nazis

Pimple and Galatea
1914, (GB), Folly Films/Phoenix, b&w, 575 ft. (175.3m)
W: Fred Evans (*Pimple*)
WRIT & D: Fred & Joe Evans
Standard comedy-fantasy: Sculptor has marital troubles when statue comes to life

Pimple's Inferno
1913, (GB), Folly Films/Phoenix, b&w, 720 ft. (219.5m)
W: Fred Evans (*Pimple*)
WRIT & D: Fred Evans & Joe Evans
Standard comedy-fantasy: Man reads Dante, dreams hell is full of suffragettes and film comedians

Pimple's Midsummer Night's Dream
1916, (GB), Piccadilly/Browne, b&w, 805 ft. (245.4m)
W: Fred Evans (*Pimple*)
WRIT & D: Fred & Joe Evans
Standard comedy-fantasy: Man eats lobster, has nightmare about cannibals

The Pink Chiquitas
1986, (Can), SC Entertainment, color, 85 mins.
W: Frank Stallone, John Hemphill, Elizabeth Edwards, Bruce Pirrie, Caludia Udy, Don Lake, McKinlay Robinson, Gerald Isaac, Cindy Valentine, Eartha Kitt (*Voice of Betty the Meteor*), Heather Smith, Kevin Frankoff, T.J. Scott, Robert Bredin, Diana Platts, Sharon Dyer, Harold Bachman, Bob Aaron, Marlow Vella, Marcia Bennett, Christopher Tugnett, Andrew Paul Bernard, David Rigby, Alan Fox, Danny Addario, Michael Gerace, Angelo Christou, Brock Jolliffe, Shaun Taylor, Durango Coy, Linda Arbuckle, Michael O'Farrell, Jan Anderson, Anne Sketchley, Valerie Miller, Jason Shout, Chris Shout, Paul Hembruff, Jean Currie, Dorin Ferber, Gloria Wrona, Julian Grant, Marcia Aguiar, Michelle Baker, Brigitte Biller, Susan Booth, Astrid Brandt, Ingrid Bower, Carol Chin, Lisa Chiverton, Lolita David, Tracy Hunt, Nancy Hammond, Topaz Hasfal, Susan Haskell, Jennifer Kent, Lorrie Howe, Cynthia Kereluk, Konnie Krome, Marcia Levine, Sherry Lee, Caroline Neilson, Renata Nobrega, Cynara Pitimac, Jane Sowerby, Rosanna Torres, Danita Tynes, Colin Gleason, Shari Tureck, Nicholas Campbell, Michael Ferguson, Carrie Gleason-Kennedy, Karen Kennedy, Karen Mair, Don Richardson, Elverez Ryan, Mike Simone, Sharolyn Sparrow
WRIT & D: Anthony Currie **ORIG SCRIPT:** Frank Stallone **STORY CONCEPT:** Anthony Currie & Nick Rotundo **PHOTOG:** Nicolas Stiliadis **SPCL VS FX:** David Stipes Prods. Inc. **MUSIC:** Paul J. Zaza

Minor SF-spoof: Meteor turns females into amorous amazons

Pinocchio
1911, (It), b&w
from Carlo Collodi's story
Standard fantasy: Marionette given life

Pinocchio
1940, (USA), Walt Disney/RKO, color, 88 mins.
<u>VOICES:</u> Dickie Jones, Christian Rub, Cliff Edwards, Evelyn Venable, Walter Catlett, Frankie Darro, Charles Judels, Don Brodie
<u>D:</u> Ben Sharpsteen & Hamilton Luske <u>SCR:</u> A. Battaglia, William Cottrell, Otto Englander, Ted Sears, Erdman Penner, Joseph Sabo & Webb Smith, from the story by Carlo Collodi <u>MUSIC:</u> Leigh Harline & Paul Smith **LYRICS:** Ned Washington **SONGS:** *When You Wish Upon a Star & I've Got No Strings*
Classic animated fantasy: Fairy gives life to marionette

Pinocchio
1969, (W. Ger), color
from Carlo Collodi's story
Standard fantasy: Adventures of living marionette

Pinocchio
1971, (USA), color
inspired by Carlo Collodi's story
Minor skin-flick: Large proboscis provokes venality

Pinocchio
1973, (It), color
from Carlo Collodi's story
Standard fantasy: Spirit gives life to marionette

Pinocchio
1976, (USA), Made for TV, color, 80 mins.
<u>W:</u> Danny Kaye (*Gepetto*), Sandy Duncan (*Pinocchio*), Flip Wilson (*The Fox*)
from Carlo Collodi's 1883 fable
TVM, standard musical-fantasy: Marionette wants to be human

Pinocchio and the Emperor of the Night
1987, (USA), Filmation/New Worldcolor, 87 mins.
<u>VOICES:</u> Edward Asner, Tom Bosley, Scott Grimes, James Earl Jones, Don Knotts, Rickie Lee Jones, Lana Beeson, Linda Gary, Jonathan Harris, William Windom, Frank Welker
<u>D:</u> Hal Sutherland <u>SCR:</u> Robby London, Barry O'Brien & Dennis O'Flaherty <u>PHOTOG:</u> Ervin L. Kaplan <u>MUSIC:</u> Anthony Marinelli & Brian Banks
Standard animated fantasy: Marionette transported by magic carnival

Pinocchio in Outer Space
1965, (USA), Swallow-Belvision/Univ, color, 71 mins.
<u>VOICES:</u> Arnold Stang, Comrad Jameson, Cliff Owens, Peter Lazer, Mavis Mims, Kevin Kennedy, Minerva Pious, Jess Cain, Norman Rose
<u>D:</u> Ray Goossens <u>SCR:</u> Fred Laderman, from an orig. idea by Norm Prescott, from characters created by Carlo Collodi
Standard animated fantasy: Marionette has off-world adventures

Pinocchio's Revenge
1996, (USA), color, 85 mins.
<u>W:</u> Rosalind Allen, Brittany Alyse Smith
Minor horror-fantasy: Little girl meets demonic puppet

Pippi Longstocking
1997, (Can-Swed), AB Svensk Filmindustri-Iduna-TFC Trickompany & Nelvana, color
<u>VOICES:</u> Melissa Altro (*Pippi*), Catherine O'Hara, Dave Thomas, Wayne Robson, Gordon Pinsent
<u>D:</u> Clive Smith <u>SCR:</u> Catharina Stackelberg, from stories by Astrid Lindgren <u>MUSIC:</u> Anders Berglund
Standard animated musical-fantasy: Plucky girl has amazing adventures

Piranha
1978, (USA), New World, color, 96 mins.
<u>W:</u> Bradford Dillman (*Paul Grogan*), Heather Menzies (*Maggie McKeown*), Kevin McCarthy (*Dr. Robert Hoak*), Dick Miller (*Buck Gardner*), Keenan Wynn (*Jack*), Barbara Steele (*Dr. Mengers*), Belinda Balaski (*Betsy*), Richard Deacon (*Earl Lyon*), Barry Brown (*The Trooper*), Shannon Collins (*Suzie Grogan*), Melody Thomas (*Laura*), Shawn Nelson (*Whitney*), Bruce Gordon (*Col. Waxman*), Paul Bartel (*Dumont*), Janie Squire (*Barbara*), Roger Richman (*David*), Bill Smillie (*The Jailer*), Guich Koock (*The TV Pitchman*), Jack Pauleson (*The Boy in the Canoe*), Eric Henshaw (*The Father in the Canoe*), Robert Vinson (*The Soldier*), Virginia Dunnam (*The Girl*), Hill Farnsworth (*The Water Skier*), Bruce Barbour (*The Man in the Boat*), Robyn Ray (*The Screaming Woman*), Mike Sullivan (*The Dam Guard*), Jack Cardwell (*Brandy*), Nick Palmisano, Bobby Sargent, Roger Creed
<u>D:</u> Joe Dante <u>SCR:</u> John Sayles **STORY:** Richard Robinson & John Sayles <u>PHOTOG:</u> Jamie Anderson <u>SPCL-FX:</u> Jon Berg <u>MUSIC:</u> Pino Donaggio **MUSIC CONDUCT:** Natale Massara
*Standard SF-horror (minor **Jaws** imitation): Super-piranhas turned loose in US waterway*

Piranha
1995, (USA), SHO-TV, color
<u>W:</u> Alexandra Paul (*Maggie MacNamara*), William Katt (*Paul*), Monte Markham (*J.R.*), Darleen Carr (*Dr. Leticia Baines*), Mila Kunis (*Susie Grogan*), Soleil Moon Frye (*Laura*), Ben Slack, James Karen, Kehli O'Byrne, Leland Orser
<u>D:</u> Scott Levy <u>WRIT:</u> Alex Simon, from an orig. screenplay by John Sayles <u>PHOTOG:</u> Christopher Baffa <u>MUSIC:</u> Christopher Lennertz
Made-for-Cable, standard SF-thriller: Aquatic terrors found

Piranha II: The Spawning
1983, (USA-It), Ovidio G. Assonitis, color, 90 mins.
<u>W:</u> Tricia O'Neil (*Anne*), Steve Marachuk (*Tyler*), Lance Henriksen (*Steve*), Ted Richert, Ricky G. Paull, Leslie Graves, Tracy Berg, Arnie Ross, Ricky G. Paull (*Chris*), Ted Richert (*Raoul*), Leslie Graves (*Allison*), Carole Davis, Connie Lynn Hadden, Albert Sanders, Anne Pollack
<u>D:</u> James Cameron <u>SCR:</u> H.A. Milton <u>PHOTOG:</u> Roberto D'Ettore Piazzoli <u>MUSIC:</u> Steve Powder
Standard SF-horror (sequel to 'Piranha' {1978}): Mutant fish plague vacationers

The Pirate and the Slave Girl
1962, (It-Fr), SNC/Crest, color, 87 mins.
<u>W:</u> Lex Barker, Chelo Alonso Massimo Serato, Michele Malaspina, Enzo Maggio
<u>D:</u> Piero Pierotti
Minor adventure-thriller: Pirate abducts governor's daughter

Pirate of the Black Hawk
1960, (It-Fr), Filmgroup, color, 87 mins.
<u>W:</u> Gerard Landry, Mijanou Bardot
<u>D:</u> Sergio Grieco
Standard adventure-thriller

Les Pirates du Diable
*see **The Devil-Ship Pirates***

The Pirate Ship
1906, (GB), Hepworth, b&w, 450 ft. (137.2m)
<u>W:</u> Hetty Potter (*The Girl*), Lewin Fitzhamon (*The Pirate*)
<u>D:</u> Lewin Fitzhamon
Standard adventure short: Sailors save girl from pirates

Pirate Ship (1949)
*see **The Mutineers***

The Pirates of Blood River
1961, (GB), Hammer/Col, color, 84 mins.
<u>W:</u> Christopher Lee (*Capt. LaRoche*), Kerwin Mathews (*Jonathan Standing*), Marla Landi (*Bess*), Andrew Keir (*Jason Standing*), Glenn Corbett (*Henry*), Oliver Reed (*Brocaire*), David Lodge (*Smith*), Michael Ripper (*Mac*), Marie Devereaux (*Maggie*), Peter Arne, Jack Stewart, Diane Aubrey, Jerold Wells, Dennis Waterman, Lorraine Clewes, John Roden, Keith Pyott, Desmond Llewelyn, Richard Bennett, Michael Mulcaster, Ronald Blackman, Denis Shaw, Michael Peake, John Colin, John Bennett, Don Levy
<u>P:</u> Anthony Nelson Keys <u>D:</u> John Gilling <u>SCR:</u> John Hunter & John Gilling <u>PHOTOG:</u> Arthur Grant <u>MUSIC:</u> Gary Hughes
Standard adventure-thriller: Pirate forces fugitive to help him raid Huguenot settlement

The Pirates of Capri
*see **I Pirati di Capri***

Pirates of Monterey
1947, (USA), Univ, color, 77 mins.
<u>W:</u> Maria Montez, Rod Cameron
Standard adventure-thriller

The Pirates of 1920
1911, (GB), Cricks & Martin, b&w, 945 ft. (288m)
<u>D:</u> Dave Aylott & A.E. Coleby <u>PHOTOG:</u> J.H. Martin
Standard thriller: Aerial pirates kidnap girl, naval officer to the rescue

The Pirates of the Devil
*see **The Devil-Ship Pirates***

Pirates of Tripoli
1955, (USA), Col, color, 72 mins.
<u>W:</u> Paul Henreid, Patricia Medina
Standard adventure-thriller

The Pirate Ship
1908, (GB), Walturdaw, b&w, 350 ft. (106.7m)
<u>D:</u> Dave Aylott
Standard adventure-thriller: Negro servant swims to fetch sailors, saves mistress from pirates

Pirate Submarine
1952, (Fr), Croix du Sud/Lippert, b&w, 69 mins.
Minor adventure-thriller

I Pirati di Capri (The Pirates of Capri)

1949, (It), Film Classics, b&w, 89 mins.
W: Louis Hayward, Binnie Barnes, Manella Lotti
D: Edgar G. Ulmer **MUSIC:** Nino Rota
A.k.a. ***The Masked Pirate*** *&* ***Captain Sirocco***
Standard adventure-thriller

The Pit

1962, (GB), BFI, b&w, 25 mins.
W: Brian Peck *(The Victim)*, Bert Betts *(The Inquisitor)*
P, D & SCR: Edward Abrahams, from Edgar Allan Poe's short story *The Pit and the Pendulum*
Standard short thriller: Spanish inquisitor tortures victim

The Pit (1963)

see ***The Mind Benders*** *(1963)*

The Pit (1967)

see ***Quatermass and the Pit***

The Pit

1983, (Can), New World, color, 96 mins.
W: Sammy Snyders *(Jamie)*, Jeannie Elias *(Sandy)*, Sonja Smits *(Mrs. Lynde)*, Laura Hollingsworth *(Marg Livingstone)*, John Auten *(The Library Janitor)*, Paul Grisham *(Freddy)*, Laura Press *(Mrs. Benjamin)*, Wendy Schmidt *(Christina)*, Lillian Graham *(Miss Oliphant)*, Andrea Swartz *(Abergail)*, Richard Alden *(Mr. Benjamin)*, Edith Bedker *(Louise)*, Gerard Jordan *(Allan)*, Cindy Auten *(The Library Clerk)*, Patrick Patterson *(The Butcher)*, Roger Van Haren *(The Truck Driver)*, Jennifer Lehman *(Caren)*, John Stoneham *(Garth)*, Jack Zimmerman *(Sgt. McNally)*, Sandy Kovack *(Officer Bentley)*, John C. Bassett *(Greg)*, Bill Taylor *(The Farmer)*, Era Keil *(Grandmother)*, Marvin Keil *(Grandfather)*, Allison Tye *(Alicia)*, Harris Kal *(A Trog)*, Alison McCuaig *(A Trog)*, Paul Martin *(A Trog)*, Tom Martin *(A Trog)*
D: Lew Lehman **ORIG SCR:** Ian A. Stuart **PHOTOG:** Fred Guthe **MUSIC:** Victor Davies
Minor SF-horror: Problem child befriends prehistoric monsters

The Pit and the Pendulum

1913, (USA), b&w
D: Alice Guy-Blache, from Edgar Allan Poe's short story
Standard thriller

The Pit and the Pendulum

1961, (USA), Alta Vista/AIP, color, 85 mins.
W: Vincent Price *(Nicholas Medina/Sebastian Medina)*, Barbara Steele *(Elizabeth Medina)*, John Kerr *(Francis Barnard)*, Luana Anders *(Catherine Medina)*, Anthony Carbone *(Dr. Charles Leon)*, Patrick Westwood *(Maximilian)*, Lynne Bernay *(Maria)*, Mary Menzies *(Isabella Medina)*, Charles Victor, Larry Turner
P & D: Roger Corman **SCR:** Richard Matheson, from Edgar Allan Poe's short story **PHOTOG:** Floyd Crosby **MUSIC:** Les Baxter **DESIGN:** Daniel Haller
orig. co-billed with ***Capture That Capsule!***, *reissued 1964*
hailed by Famous Monsters of Filmland magazine as yass's best horror film
Superior horror-thriller (slow start, but nail-biting finish): Son of Spanish inquisitor goes mad, reactivates father's diabolical instruments of torture

The Pit and the Pendulum (1967)

see ***Die Schlangengrube und das Pendel***

The Pit and the Pendulum

1990, (USA), Full Moon, color, 92 mins.
W: Lance Henriksen *(Torquemada)*, Jeffrey Combs *(Francesco)*, Rona De Ricci *(Maria)*, Jonathan Fuller *(Antonio)*, Francis Bay, Tom Towles, Mark Margolis, Oliver Reed
D: Stuart Gordon from Edgar Allan Poe's short story
Standard horror-thriller: Youth tries to rescue lover from torture chamber

Pitfall

1948, (USA), UA, b&w, 86 mins.
W: Dick Powell, Lizabeth Scott, Raymond Burr, Jane Wyatt, Byron Barr, John Litel, Ann Doran
D: Andre de Toth **PHOTOG:** Harry J. Wild
Modest film noir: Siren ensnares insurance claims agent

Pit of Darkness

1961, (GB), Butcher's Films, b&w, 76 mins.
W: William Franklyn *(Richard Logan)*, Moira Redmond *(Julie Logan)*, Bruno Barnabe *(Maxie)*, Leonard Sachs *(Conrad)*, Nigel Green *(Jonathan)*, Bruce Beeby *(Mayhew)*, Humphrey Lestocq *(Bill)*, Anthony Booth *(Ted Mellis)*, Nanette Newman *(Mary)*, Michael Balfour *(Fisher)*, Ronnie Hall *(The Singer)*
WRIT, P & D: Lance Comfort, from Hugh McCutcheon's novel
Standard crime-thriller: Wife helps amnesiac recall how he was manipulated by jewel thieves

A Place of One's Own

1945, (GB), Gainsborough/Eagle Lion, b&w, 92 mins.
W: Margaret Lockwood *(Annette Allenbury)*, James Mason *(Henry Smedhurst)*, Barbara Mullen *(Mrs. Smedhurst)*, Dennis Price *(Dr. Robert Selbie)*, Dulcie

Gray *(Sarah)*, Helen Haye *(Florence Manning-Tuthorne)*, Moore Marriott *(George)*, Michael Shepley *(Maj. Manning-Tuthorne)*, O.B. Clarence *(Perkins)*, Helen Goss *(The Barmaid)*, Edie Martin *(The Cook)*, Muriel George *(The Nurse)*, Gus McNaughton *(PC Hargreaves)*, John Turnbull *(Sir Roland Jarvis)*, Ernest Thesiger *(Dr. Marsham)*, Clarence Wright *(Brighouse)*, Aubrey Mallalieu *(The Vicar)*
D: Bernard Knowles **SCR:** Brock Williams & Osbert Sitwell, from a novel by Osbert Sitwell **PHOTOG:** Stephen Dade **MUSIC:** Louis Levy
reissued 1949
Standard thriller: Retired tradesman buys sinister mansion

A Place to Die

1975, (GB), Cecil Clarke/ITC, Made for TV, color, 71 mins.
W: Alexandra Hay *(Tessa Nelson)*, Bryan Marshall *(Dr. Bruce Nelson)*, John Turner *(Bart)*, Glynn Edwards *(Lob)*, Georgine Anderson *(Jane)*, Lila Kaye *(Bess Tarling)*, Sally Stephens *(Jill)*, Juan Moreno *(Nick)*, Sydney Bromley *(Seth)*, Bill Ward *(Job)*, Jenny Laird *(Nan)*, Peggy Ann Wood *(Belle)*, Graham Weston *(Dan)*, John Flint *(The Police Inspector)*, Arnold Ridley *(The 1st Old Man)*, Harold Bennett *(The 2nd Old Man)*, Elsie Wagstaff *(The Old Woman)*, John Gabriel *(Dr. Sharp)*, Lewis Wilson *(The Policeman)*
D: Peter Jefferies **TELEPLAY:** Terence Feely **ORIG. STORY:** Brian Johnson **PHOTOG:** Roy Simper **MUSIC:** Laurie Johnson
TVM, minor thriller: Brit doctor and American bride encounter devil worship

A Place to Go

1963, (GB), Excalibur/Bry, b&w, 86 mins.
W: Rita Tushingham *(Cat)*, Mike Sarne *(Ricky Flint)*, Bernard Lee *(Matt Flint)*, Doris Hare *(Lil Flint)*, Barbara Ferris *(Betsy)*, John Slater *(Jack Ellerman)*, William Marlowe *(Charlie Batey)*, David Andrews *(Jim)*, Jerry Verno *(Nobby Knowles)*, Roy Kinnear *(Bunting)*, Michael Wynne *(Pug)*
P: Michael Relph **D:** Basil Dearden **SCR:** Michael Relph & Clive Exton, from Michael Fisher's novel *Bethnal*
Standard crime-thriller: Unemployed dock-worker's son steals truck, abets robbery

Plague

1978, (Can), Harmony Ridge/Group I, color, 88 mins.
W: Daniel Pilon *(Dr. Fuller)*, Kate Reid *(Dr. Morgan)*, Celine Lomez *(Margo)*, Michael J. Reynolds, Brenda Donohue, Barbara Gordon
WRIT & P: Ed Hunt & Barry Pearson
A.k.a. ***M3: The Gemini Strain***
Minor thriller

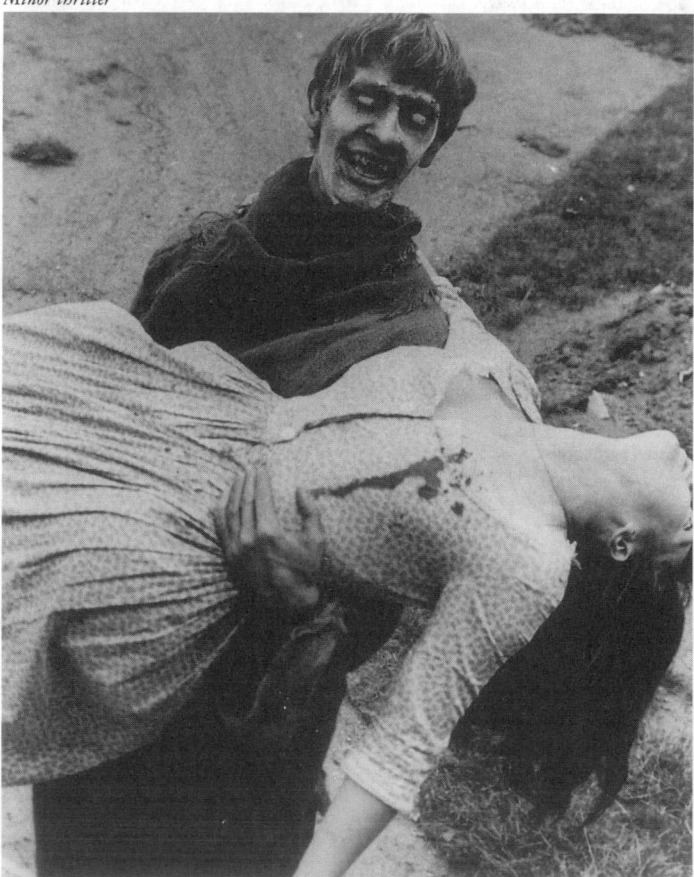

The Plague of the Zombies: TIM CONDRON AND JACQUELINE PEARCE

The Plague of the Zombies

1965, (GB), Hammer-7Arts/20th-Fox, color, 91 mins.
W: Andre Morell *(Sir James Forbes)*, Brook Williams *(Dr. Peter Thompson)*, Diane Clare *(Sylvia Forbes)*, Jacqueline Pearce *(Alice)*, John Carson *(Clive Hamilton)*,

Alex Davion (*Harry Denver*), Dennis Chinnery (*Constable Christian*), Roy Royston (*The Vicar*), Michael Ripper (*Sgt. Swift*), Marcus Hammond (*Martinus*), Louis Mahoney (*The Coloured Servant*), Ben Aris (*John Martinus*), Tim Condron, Bernard Egan, Norman Mann, Francis Wiley
<u>P</u>: Anthony Nelson Keys <u>D</u>: John Gilling <u>SCR</u>: Peter Bryan <u>PHOTOG</u>: Arthur Grant <u>MUSIC</u>: James Bernard <u>DESIGN</u>: Don Mingaye
Standard horror-fantasy: Voodoo in small English village

Planeta Bura (Storm Planet)
1962, (Russ), Leningrad/New Realm, color, 75 mins.
<u>W</u>: Kyunna Ignatova, Georgi Zhonov, Gennadi Vernov, Yurie Sarantsev, Vladimir Yemelianov
<u>D</u>: Pavel Klushantsev <u>SCR</u>: Pavel Klushantsev & Alexander Kazantsev <u>PHOTOG</u>: Arkady Klimov <u>MUSIC</u>: I. Admoni & A. Tschernow
released in USA (1965) by AIP as **Voyage to the Prehistoric Planet** *(with added scenes featuring Faith Domergue & Basil Rathbone). USA version produced by George Edwards, writ & dir by John Sebastian*
Standard SF-thriller: Venusian probe

Il Planeta degli Uomini Spenti (The Planet of Extinguished Men)
1961, (It), Ultra/Topaz, color, 84 mins.
<u>W</u>: Claude Rains, Maya Brent, Bill Carter, Jacqueline Derval, Umberto Orsini, Carol Danell, Renzo Palmer, John Stacy, Jim Dolen, Carlo D'Angelo
<u>D</u>: Anthony Dawson [Antonio Margheriti] <u>SCR</u>: Vassiliz Petrov <u>PHOTOG</u>: Marcello Masciocchi
USA retitle, **Battle of the Worlds**, *1963*
Standard SF-thriller (Claude Rains' last science fiction film): Astronauts probe mysterious planet on collision course with Earth

Planet Busters
1985, (Jap), color, 80 mins.
Standard animated SF-fantasy: Magic sword, bounty hunters, evil robots

Planet Earth
1974, (USA), Norway Prods./WB-TV, color, 75 mins.
<u>W</u>: John Saxon (*Dillon*), Janet Margolin (*Harper*), Ted Cassidy (*Isaiah*), Diana Muldaur (*Marg*), Johana deWinter (*Villar*), Majel Barrett (*Yuloff*), James D. Antonio Jr. (*Dr. Jonathan Connor*), Aron Kincaid (*Gorda*), Claire Brennen (*Delba*), John Quade (*The Kreeg Commandant*), Sally Kemp (*Treece*), Corinne Camacho (*Bronta*), Rai Tasco (*Pater Kimbridge*), Sara Chattin (*Thetis*), Lew Brown (*Merlo*), Raymond Sutton (*The Kreeg Captain*), Joan Crosby (*Kyla*), Craig Hundley (*The Harpsichordist*), Robert McAndrew (*1st Dink*), Bob Golden (*2nd Dink*), Susan Page (*The Little Girl*), James Bacon (*Partha*), Christopher Cary
<u>P</u>: Robert H. Justman <u>D</u>: Marc Daniels <u>SCR</u>: Gene Roddenberry & Juanita Bartlett, created by Gene Roddenberry <u>PHOTOG</u>: Arch Dalzell <u>MUSIC</u>: Harry Sukman
TVM, standard SF-thriller: Humans of 22nd century combat sadistic matriarchy and warlike mutants

Planet of Blood
see Queen of Blood

Planet of Dinosaurs
1978, (USA), Wells/Filmpartners, color 85 mins
<u>W</u>: James Whitworth, Pamela Bottaro, Harvey Shain, Charlotte Speer, Chuck Pennington, Derna Wylde, Michael Thayer, Mary Appleseth, Louie Lawless
<u>P & D</u>: James K. Shea <u>SCR</u>: Ralph Lucas <u>MUSIC</u>: Kelly Lammers & John O'Verlin
Minor space-opera: Survivors of starship explosion trapped on prehistoric world

The Planet of Extinguished Men
see Il Planeta degli Uomini Spenti

Planet of the Apes: RODDY McDOWALL

Planet of Horrors
see Galaxy of Terror

Planet of Storms
see Planeta Bura

Planet of the Apes
1968, (USA), Arthur P. Jacobs/20th-Fox, color, 112 mins.
<u>W</u>: Charlton Heston (*Taylor*), Kim Hunter (*Zira*), Roddy McDowall (*Cornelius*), Maurice Evans (*Dr. Zaius*), James Daly (*Honorius*), Linda Harrison (*Nova*), Lou Wagner (*Lucius*), James Whitmore (*The Assembly President*), Jeff Burton, Bob Lombardo, Paul Lambert, Wright King, Robert Gunner, Diane Stanley
<u>D</u>: Franklin J. Schaffner <u>SCR</u> Michael Wilson & Rod Serling, from Pierre Boulle's novel *Monkey Planet* <u>PHOTOG</u> Leon Shamroy <u>MUSIC</u>: Jerry Goldsmith
Superior SF-thriller: Astronauts break time barrier, find simian-dominated world. cf. **Beneath the Planet of the Apes**

Planet of the Apes: CHARLTON HESTON AND LINDA HARRISON

Planet of the Vampires
see Terrore Nello Spazio

Planet on the Prowl
1966, (It), Mercury-Int'l/Fanfare, color, 80 mins.
<u>W</u>: Giacomo Rossi-Stuart (*Rod*), Ombretta Colli (*Terry Sanchez*)
<u>D</u>: Anthony Dawson [Antonio Margheriti]
A.k.a. **Devil Men from Space** *and* **War Between the Planets**
Minor SF-adventure: Rogue planet causes Earth disruptions

Planet Outlaws
see Destination Saturn

Planets Against Us
1961, (It-Fr), Teleworld, color, 85 mins.
<u>W</u> Jany Clair, Michel Lemoine, Maria Pia Luzi, Marco Guglielmo, Otello Toso
<u>P</u>: Alberto Chimenz & Vico Pavoni <u>D</u>: Romano Ferrara <u>SCR</u> Romano Ferrara & Piero Pierotti
A.k.a. **Hands of a Killer** *and* **The Man with the Yellow Eyes**
Standard SF-thriller: Runaway robot dispenses death

Planet Sigma's 27 Days
see The 27th Day

Plan 9 from Outer Space
1959, (USA), J. Edwards Reynolds/DCA, b&w, 78 mins.
<u>W</u>: Bela Lugosi (*The Ghoul Man*), Tor Johnson (*Insp. Clay*), Vampira (*The Vampire Girl*), Gregory Walcott (*Jeff Trent*), Mona McKinnon (*Paula Trent*), Duke Moore (*Lt. Harper*), Tom Keene (*Col. Edwards*), Dudley Manlove (*Eros*), Lyle Talbot (*The General*), Joanna Lee (*Tanna*), John Breckinridge (*The Ruler*), Carl Anthony (*Patrolman Larry*), Paul Marco (*Patrolman Kelton*), David De Mering (*Danny*), Norma McCarty (*Edith*), Bill Ash (*The Captain*), Rev. Lynn Lemon (*The Reverend*), Ben Frommer (*The Man*), Gloria Dea (*The Girl*), Conrad Brooks (*The Policeman*), Dr. Tom Mason (*Lugosi's double*), Criswell
<u>WRIT, P & D</u>: Edward D. Wood Jr. <u>PHOTOG</u>: William Thompson <u>SPCL-FX</u>: Charles Duncan <u>MUSIC SPRVSR</u>: Gordon Zahler
orig. to be titled **Grave-Robbers from Outer Space**
Minor SF-horror, camp classic hailed as worst movie ever made (filmed in 1956): Space

Plan 10 from Outer Space
1995, (USA), color, 82 mins.
<u>W</u>: Stefene Russell, Pat Collins, Curtis James, Karen Black
<u>D & SCR</u>: Trent Harris <u>PHOTOG</u>: Bryan Duggan <u>MUSIC</u>: Fred Myrow
Standard SF-satire: UFO conspiracy uncovered

The Plants Are Watching
see The Kirlian Witness

Platinum High School
1960, (USA), MGM, b&w, 93 mins.
W: Mickey Rooney, Yvette Mimieux, Dan Duryea, Elisha Cook Jr., Terry Moore, Warren Berlinger, Richard Jaeckel, Mason Alan Dinehart, Conway Twitty, Jimmy Boyd, Harold Lloyd Jr., Cliff Edwards
D: Charles F. Haas   **SCR:** Robert Smith, from a story by Howard Breslin   **PHOTOG:** Russell Metty   **MUSIC:** Van Alexander
*A.k.a. **Trouble at 16** and **Rich, Young and Deadly***
Minor melodrama: Man probes son's death at exclusive school

Plan 9 From Outer Space: VAMPIRA, TOR JOHNSON, DR. TOM MASON AND CRISWELL

Playback
1962, (GB), Merton Park/Anglo-Amalgamated, b&w, 62 mins.
W: Margit Saad *(Lisa Shillack)*, Barry Foster *(Dave Hollis)*, Victor Platt *(Insp. Gorman)*, Dinsdale Landen *(Joe Ross)*, George Pravda *(Simon Shillack)*, Nigel Green *(Ralph Monk)*, Jerold Wells *(Insp. Parkes)*
P: Jack Greenwood   **D:** Quentin Lawrence   **SCR:** Robert Stewart   **STORY:** Edgar Wallace
Standard thriller: Woman persuades indebted policeman to kill her rich husband

The Playbirds
1978, (GB), Roldvale/Tigon, color, 94 mins.
W: Mary Millington *(Lucy Sheridan)*, Glynn Edwards *(Supt. Jack Holbourne)*, Gavin Campbell *(Insp. Morgan)*, Alan Lake *(Harry Dougan)*, Windsor Davies *(The Commissioner)*, Derren Nesbitt *(Jeremy)*, Kenny Lynch *(The Doctor)*, Suzy Mandel *(Lena Cunningham)*, Ballard Berkeley *(The Trainer)*, Sandra Dorne *(The Secretary)*, Alec Mango *(George Ransome)*, Tony Kenyon *(Dolby)*, Penny Spencer *(WPC Andrews)*, Susie Silvey *(Doreen)*, Michael Gradwell *(Terry Day)*, John East *(The Media Man)*, Dudley Sutton *(Hern)*
P & D: Willy Roe   **STORY:** Bud Tobin & Robin O'Connor   **PHOTOG:** Douglas Hill   **MUSIC:** David Whitaker
Standard thriller: Porno-magazine cover girl slain

The Playful Robot
see Nestasni Robot

Playgirl Killer
1965, (Can), Hemisphere/Group IV, color, 90 mins.
W: William Kirwin
P: Max A. Sendel   **D:** Enrick Santamaran   **SONGS:** *If You Don't Wanna, You Don't Hafta & Waterbug,* sung by Neil Sedaka
*Minor thriller: Mad artist kills models. A.k.a. **Decay for Terror***

The Playgirls and the Vampire
see L'Ultima Preda del Vampiro

The Playground
1965, (USA), Jerand, b&w, 95 mins.

W: Rees Vaughan, Inger Stratton, Edmon Ryan, Andrea Blayne, Loretta Leversee, Richard Kilbride, Carol White, Marian Blake, Peter MacLean, Conrad Jameson, Paul Schmidt, Roger Talbot, Stanley Greene, Philip Brown, Sol Schwade, Ethel Shutta
D: Richard Hilliard   **SCR:** George Garrett, inspired by Cyrus L. Sulzberger's story "My Brother Death"
Unusual thriller: Prostitute's bizarre experiences. Filmed in Boston

Play Misty for Me
1971, (USA), Univ, color, 102 mins.
W: Clint Eastwood *(Dave)*, Donna Mills *(Tobie Williams)*, Jessica Walter *(Evelyn Draper)*, John Larch *(Sgt. McCallum)*, Jack Ging *(Dr. Frank Dewan)*, Irene Hervey *(Madge Brenner)*, Donald Siegel *(Murphy)*, Jack Kosslyn *(The Cab Driver)*, Juke Everts *(Jay Jay)*, James McEachin *(Al Monte)*, George Fargo *(The Man)*, Clarice Taylor *(Birdie)*, Mervin W. Frates *(The Locksmith)*, Tim Frawley *(The Deputy Sheriff)*, Otis Kadani *(The Policeman)*, Brit Lind *(Anjelica)*, Paul E. Lippman *(The 2nd Man)*, Ginna Patterson *(Madalyn)*, Malcolm Moran *(The Man in the Window)*
D: Clint Eastwood   **SCR:** Jo Heims & Dean Riesner   **PHOTOG:** Bruce Surtees   **MUSIC:** Dee Barton
"A cliff-hanger...maximum tension"—Cue
"Clint Eastwood's first directorial endeavor...at times brushes the top of cinematic genius...it comes close to being a masterpiece, it's one of the very greatest works of its kind made recently...Eastwood has verified his immense, under-rated talents not only as actor, but as a filmmaker"—Dale Winogura, Cinefantastique
Unusual thriller: Psychotic woman stalks disc jockey

Pleasantville
1998, (USA), New Line, color
W: Jeff Daniels, Tobey Maguire, Reese Witherspoon, William H. Macy, Joan Allen, Don Knotts, J.T. Walsh
D: Gary Ross
Unusual fantasy: Two modern teens pass through dimensional warp, disrupt idyllic '50's-style society

Please Don't Eat My Mother
1973, (USA), Boxoffice Int'l. color 95 mins.
W: Buck Kartalian, Renee Bond   **P & D:** Carl Monson   **SCR:** Jack Beckett
*A.k.a. **Hungry Pets** and **Glump***
Standard comedy-fantasy (soft-core remake of 'The Little Shop of Horrors' {1960}): Middle-aged mama's boy grows man-eating plant

Please, Don't Joke with Martians
1968, (Fr), color
Minor SF-comedy

Please Murder Me
1956, (USA), DCA, b&w, 78 mins.
W: Angela Lansbury, Raymond Burr, Dick Foran, John Dehner, Lamont Johnson, Robert Griffin, Denver Pyle, Alex Sharpe, Lee Miller, Madge Blake, Russ Thorson, Peter Godfrey
D: Peter Godfrey   **SCR:** Al C. Ward & Donald Hyde. Based on *Big Town* TV episode.   **PHOTOG:** Alan Stensvold
Engrossing melodrama: Attorney bends law to gain acquittal for beauty accused of murder

Pledge Night
1990, (USA), color, 90 mins.
W: Will Kempe, Shannon McMahon, Todd Eastland
D: Paul Ziller
Standard horror-thriller: Gory revenge for fraternity hazing

The Pleydell Mystery
1916, (GB), British Empire Films, b&w, 5,000 ft. (1524m)
W: Cecil Humphreys *(John Pleydell)*, Christine Silver *(Felicity Harwood)*, Richard Lindsay *(Tony Masters)*, Mrs. Bennett *(Rosa Latimer)*, Frank Randall
D &SCR: Albert Ward, from the novel *Poison* by Claude & Alice Askew
Standard crime-thriller: Man frames heiress-wife for the poisoning of his mistress

The Plot Thickens
1936, (USA), RKO, b&w, 67 mins.
W: ZaSu Pitts *(Hildegarde Withers)*, James Gleason *(Oscar Piper)*, Owen Davis Jr. *(Robert Wilkins)*, Louise Latimer *(Alice Stevens)*, Arthur Aylesworth *(Kendall)*, Barbara Barondess *(Marie)*, Paul Fix *(Joe)*, Agnes Anderson (Lynn Anders) *(Dagmar)*, Richard Tucker *(John Carter)*, James Donlan *(Jim)*, Oscar Apfel *(Robbins)*
D: Ben Holmes   **SCR:** Clarence Upson Young, from characters created by Stuart Palmer   **PHOTOG:** Nick Musuraca
Standard "Hildegarde Withers" mystery: Woman sleuth probes murder, finds jewel thieves and smugglers

Plucked
1969, (It-Fr), UM, color, 90 mins.
W: Jean-Louis Trintignant, Gina Lollobrigida, Ewa Aulin
D: Giulio Questi
Standard melodrama: Murder scheme in countryside

A Plucky Kiddie
1910, (GB), Hepworth, b&w, 400 ft. (121.9m)

D: Bert Haldane
Standard crime-thriller: Burglar traps butler, is caught by small girl

Plughead Rewired: Circuitry Man II
1994, (USA), color
W: Vernon Wells, Deborah Shelton
Minor SF-thriller

The Plumber
1978, (Austral), Cinema Ventures, Made for TV, color, 76 mins.
W: Ivar Kants (*Max*), Judy Morris (*Jill*), Robert Coleby (*Brian*), Candy Raymond
WRIT & D: Peter Weir
TVM, unusual psychodrama: Unsettling handyman pries into life of young wife

Le Plus Vieux Metier du Monde (The Oldest Profession on Earth)
1967, (Fr-W. Ger-It), Goldstone/VIP, color, 115 mins.
W: Elsa Martinelli, Jeanne Moreau, Jean-Claude Brialy, Anna Karina, Jacques Charrier, Jean-Pierre Leaud, Raquel Welch
Eroto-melodrama in 4 episodes: *Nuits Romaines* (D: Mauro Bolognini), *Mademoiselle Mimi* (D: Philippe De Broca), *Au jourd'hui* (D: Claude Autant-Lara) & *Anticipation, ou L'an 2000* (D & SCR: Jean-Luc Godard; mus, Michel Legrand [this segment shown at 1967 Trieste Science-Fiction Film Festival under title *Love in the Year 2000*])

Plutonium Baby
1987, (USA), color, 85 mins.
W: Patrick Molloy, Danny Guerra
D: Ray Hirschman
Minor thriller: Mutated kid seeks revenge

The Plutonium Incident
1980, (Can), CBS-TV, color, 95 mins.
W: Janet Margolin (*Judith Longden*), Bo Hopkins (*Art Reeves*), Powers Boothe (*Dick Hawkins*), Joseph Campanella (*Harry*), Bibi Besch (*Barbara O'Neill*), Jordan Charney (*Orr*), Margaret Martin (*The Woman with Groceries*), J.A. Preston (*Dr. Samuels*), Nicholas Pryor (*Gildea*), Judy Penrod (*Dr. Montgomery*), Larry Musser (*The N.O.N. Guard*), Blu Kankuma (*Benny*), Don MacKay (*The Head of Personnel*), Stephen Miller (*Haskins*), Christian Bruyere (*Sam*), Robert Silcock (*Art's Father*), Tim Dundom (*The Health Physicist*), David Major (*A Worker*), Fred Galloway (*A Worker*), Lloyd Berry (*The Sheriff*), Fred Latremouille (*The Washington, DC Official*), Bob Robertson (*Phelan*), Jackson Davies (*Walker*)
D: Richard Michaels   TELEPLAY: Dalene Young, from a book by Thomas B. Allen   PHOTOG: Harry May   SPCL-FX: George Erschbamer   MUSIC: Fred Karlin
TVM, standard thriller: Plutonium handlers seek unionization

Plymouth
1991, (USA), ABC-TV, color, 95 mins.
W: Dale Midkiff (*Gil*), Cindy Pickett (*Addy*), Perrey Reeves (*Hannah*), Richard Hamilton (*Wendell*), Matthew Brown (*Jed*), Jerry Hardin (*Lowell*), James R. Rebhorn (*Ezra*), Ron Vawter (*Percy*), Robin Frates (*Donna*), Brent Fraser (*Litchfield*), Anne Haney (*Emily*), John Thornton, Lindsay Price
WRIT & D: Lee David Zlotoff   PHOTOG: Hiro Narita   MUSIC: Brad Fiedel
TVM, standard SF-adventure (feature-pilot for unsold teleseries): Oregon community relocates to lunar mining base

The Poacher
1909, (GB), Walturdaw, b&w, 630 ft. (192m)
Standard crime-thriller: Unemployed mechanic shoots policeman

Pocahontas
1995, (USA), Walt Disney, color, 90 mins.
VOICES: Irene Bedard (*Pocahontas*), Mel Gibson (*Capt. John Smith*), Linda Hunt (*Grandmother Willow*), Judy Kuhn, Joe Baker, Christian Bale, Bill Connolly, James Apaumut Fall, John Kassir, Danny Mann, Bill Cobbs, David Ogden Stiers, Michelle St. John, Gordon Tootoosis, Frank Welker
D: Mike Gabriel & Eric Goldberg   SCR: Carl Binder, Susannah Grant & Philip LaZebnik   MUSIC: Alan Menken & Stephen Schwartz   SONG: *Colors of the Wind*
Standard animated fantasy: American Indian princess meets Europeans

Pocahontas II: Journey to a New World
1998, (USA), Walt Disney, color
VOICES: Irene Bedard (*Pocahontas*), Billy Zane (*John Rolfe*), David Ogden Stiers
SONGS: *Where Do I Go from Here*
Made-for-Video, standard animated adventure-romance: American indian princess goes to Britain

Pocket Boxers
1903, (GB), R.W. Paul, b&w, 80 ft. (24.4m)
D: Walter R. Booth
Standard fantasy short: Sportsmen produce midget boxers from pockets, wager on their fight

A Pocket Love
see *Un Amour de Poche*

Pocomania
1939, (USA), Lenwal, b&w, 65 mins.

W: Nina Mae McKinney, Jack Carter, Ida James, Hamtree Harrington
P & D: Arthur Leonard   SCR: George Terwilliger
A.k.a. *Devil's Daughter*
Standard fantasy: Voodoo priestess curses rival. All black cast

Pod Gwiazda Frygijska (Under the Phrygian Star)
1954, (Pol), b&w
D: Jerzy Kawalerowicz
Standard SF-fantasy

Poe's Tales of Terror
see *Tales of Terror*

The Point
1971, (USA), color, 74 mins.
VOICE: Paul Frees   D: Fred Wolf   MUSIC: Harry Nilsson
TVM, unusual fantasy-allegory: Round-headed child rejected by pointy-headed society

The Pointing Finger
1933, (GB), Real Art/Radio, b&w, 68 mins.
W: John Stuart (*Lord Rollstone*), Viola Keats (*Lady Mary Stuart*), Leslie Perrins (*Hon. James Mallory*), A. Bromley Davenport (*Lord Edensore*), Michael Hogan (*Patrick Lafone*), Henriette Watson (*Lady Anne Rollestone*), Clare Greet (*The Landlady*), D.J. Williams (*Grimes*)
D: George Pearson   SCR: H. Fowler Mear, from novel by Rita
Standard thriller: Heir tries to kill half-brother

Point of No Return
1992, (USA), Art Linson/WB, color, 108 mins.
W: Bridget Fonda (*Maggie*), Gabriel Byrne (*Bob*), Miguel Ferrer (*Kaufman*), Dermot Mulroney (*J.P.*), Anne Bancroft (*Amanda*), Olivia D'Abo (*Angela*), Richard Romanus (*Fahd Bahktiar*), Harvey Keitel (*Victor the Cleaner*), Lorraine Toussaint (*Beth*), Geoffrey Lewis (*The Drugstore Owner*), Ray Oriel (*Burt*), Mic Rodgers (*The Cop*), Michael Rapaport (*Big Stan*), Spike McClure (*Johnny D*), Lieux Dressler (*Johny's Mom*), John Capodice (*The Detective*), Carmen Zapata (*The Judge*), Calvin Levels (*The Computer Instructor*), Michael Runyard (*The Weapons Instructor*), Bill M. Ryusaki (*The Karate Instructor*), Jan Speck (*Kaufman's Ass't*), Lee Dupree (*The Guy with the Gun*), Francesco Messina (*The Waiter in the Restaurant*), Peter Mark Vasquez (*The Guard in the Booth*), Wendy L. Davies (*The Shopping Woman*), James Handy (*The Operative*), David Sosna (*The Operative with the Headset*), Bruce Barnes (*The New Orleans Thug*), Jacqueline Koch (*The VIP Woman*), Kenny Endoso, Gary Kasper, Rosalind Jue, Joe Garcia, Eric Cohen, Francois Chau, Frank Girardeau, Harry Perry, Charles Heathcliffe Brolly, Jodie Markell, Robert Harvey
D: John Badham   SCR: Robert Getchell & Alexander Seros   PHOTOG: Michael Watkins   MUSIC: Hans Zimmer
A.k.a. *The Assasian*
Standard thriller (remake of La Femme Nikita): Girl criminal becomes gov't assassin

Point of Terror
1971, (USA), Crown Int'l, color, 88 mins.
W: Peter Carpenter (*Tony*), Dyanne Thorne (*Andrea*), Leslie Simms (*Fran*), Lory Hansen (*Helayne*), Paula Mitchell (*Sally*), Joel Marston (*Martin*), Roberta Robson (*The First Wife*), Dana Diamond (*The Barmaid*), Ernest Charles (*The Detective*), Al Dunlap (*The Bartender*), Tony Kent (*The Priest*)
P: Chris Marconi & Peter Carpenter   D: Alex Nicol   SCR: Tony Crechales & Ernest A. Charles
Minor horror-fantasy: Man's nightmares prove real

Poison
1951, (Fr), Gaumont, b&w, 96 mins.
W: Michel Simon, Sacha Guitry, Louis de Funes
WRIT & D: Sacha Guitry
Standard thriller: Man and wife plan each other's murder

Poison
1991, (USA), Zeitgeist Films/Bronze Eye, b&w, 85 mins.
W: Edith Meeks, Scott Renderer, James Lyons, Susan Norman, John R. Lombardi, Larry Maxwell
D & SP: Todd Haynes
Unusual trilogy of tales with bizarre themes: (1) "Hero"—Boy disappears after killing his father, (2) "Horror"—Sex-serum turns scientist into mutant, & (3) "Homo"-Obsessive love of imprisoned thief for inmate he first met in reform school

Poison Ivy
see *La Mome Vert-de-Gris*

Poison Ivy
1992, (USA), color, 89 mins.
W: Drew Barrymore, Sara Gilbert, Tom Skerritt, Cheryl Ladd
D: Katt Shea Ruben
Standard melodrama: Nymphet seduces girlfriend's father

Poison Pen
1939, (GB), ABPC, b&w, 79 mins.
W: Flora Robson (*Mary Rider*), Robert Newton (*Sam Hurrin*), Ann Todd (*Ann Rider*), Geoffrey Toone (*David*), Edward Rigby (*Badham*), Reginald Tate (*Rev. Rider*), Belle Chrystal (*Sucal Hurrin*), Edward Chapman (*Len Griffin*),

Athole Stewart (*Col. Cashelton*), Mary Hinton (*Mrs. Cashelton*), Cyril Chamberlain (*Peter Cashelton*), Catherine Lacey (*Connie Fateley*), Wally Patch (*Mr. Suggs*), Ella Retford (*Mrs. Suggs*), Esma Cannon (*Mrs. Warren*), Jean Clyde (*Mrs. Griffin*), Marjorie Rhodes (*Mrs. Scaife*), Wilfrid Hyde-White (*The Postman*), Kenneth Connor (*The Telephonist*)
D: Paul Stein **SCR:** Doreen Montgomery, William Freshman, N.C. Hunter & Esther McCracken, from a play by Richard Llewellyn. US release, *Republic, 1941*
Classic thriller: Malicious letter turns peaceful village into place of chaotic horror. cf. **Le Corbeau**

The Polar Star
1919, (GB), Windsor/Walturdaw, b&w, 5,000 ft. (1524m)
W: Manora Thew, Hayford Hobbs, Peggy Patterson, Bert Wynne, Charles Vane
D: Arrigo Bocchi **STORY:** Leslie Stiles
Standard crime-thriller: Mystery surrounds London solicitor's death and dishonor

Police Connection
see *The Mad Bomber*

Police Dog
1955, (GB) Westridge Fairbanks/Eros, b&w, 70 mins.
W: Joan Rice (*Pat Lewis*), Tim Turner (*Frank Mason*), Sandra Dorne (*The Blonde*), Jimmy Gilbert (*Ken Lade*), Charles Victor (*The Sgt.*), Nora Gordon (*Mrs. Lewis*), Christopher Lee (*The Man*), John LeMesurier (*The Inspector*)
P: Harold Huth **D & STORY:** Derek Twist
Standard crime-thriller: Constable trains stray Alsatian dog, collars friend's killer

Police Nurse
1963, (USA), 20th-Fox, b&w, 64 mins.
W: Ken Scott, Merry Anders
Minor melodrama

A Polish Vampire in Burbank
1984, (USA), Pirrovision, color, 84 mins.
W: Mark Pirro, Lori Sutton, Bobbi Dorsch, Hugh O. Fields, Marya Gant, Eddie Deezen, Steve Dorsch, Catharine Wheatley, Brad Waisbren, Alfie Pearl, Louise Samuels, Jim Bruce, John McCafferty, Rik Martino, Katina Garner, Conrad Brooks, Phil Liskum, Tyrone Dubose, Paul Farbman, Lois Hunter, James Hunter
WRIT, P & D: Mark Pirro **PHOTOG:** CraigBassuk **MUSIC:** Gregg Gross & Sergio Bandera **SONGS:** *All I Ever Need is You & My Baby's Back*
Minor horror-satire: Undead youth eschews vampirism

Polka on the Brain
1908, (GB), Urban Trading Co., b&w, 435 ft. (132.6m)
D: W.R. Booth
Standard comedy-fantasy: Man has polka mania, cannot stop dancing

Polly the Girl Scout and the Jewel Thieves
1913, (GB), Barker, b&w, 780 ft. (237.7m)
W: May Morton (*Polly*)
D: Bert Haldane **STORY:** Rowland Talbot
Standard crime-thriller: Girl chases and captures thieves

Poltergeist
1982, (USA), MGM-UA, color, 112 mins.
W: Craig T. Nelson (*Steve*), JoBeth Williams (*Diane*), Beatrice Straight (*Dr. Lesh*), Dominique Dunne (*Dana*), Zelda Rubinstein, Heather O'Rourke, Oliver Robins
D: Tobe Hooper **SCR:** Steven Spielberg, Michael Grais & Mark Victor **STORY:** Steven Spielberg **PHOTOG:** Matthew F. Leonetti **SPCL-FX:** Jeff Jarvis & Michael Wood **MUSIC:** Jerry Goldsmith
Classic horror-fantasy: Family tormented by vengeful spirits

Poltergeist II: The Other Side
1986, (USA), MGM-UA, color, 89 mins.
W: Craig T. Nelson (*Steve*), JoBeth Williams (*Diane*), Oliver Robins, Heather O'Rourke, Will Sampson, Julian Beck, Zelda Rubinstein, Geraldine Fitzgerald, John P. Whitecloud, Nobel Craig, Helen Boll
WRIT & P: Michael Grais & Mark Victor **D:** Brian Gibson **PHOTOG:** Andrew Laszlo **SPCL VS-FX:** Richard Edlund **MUSIC:** Jerry goldsmith
Standard horror-fantasy: Haunts pursue family

Poltergeist III
1988, (USA), MGM, color, 97 mins.
W: Tom Skerritt (*Bruce Gardner*), Nancy Allen (*Patricia Gardner*), Heather O'Rourke (*Carol Anne*), Zelda Rubinstein (*Tangina Barrons*), Lara Flynn Boyle (*Donna Gardner*), Kip Wentz (*Scott*), Richard Fire (*Dr. Seaton*), Nathan Davis (*Kane*), Roger May (*Burt*), Paul Graham (*Martin*), Stacy Gilchrist (*Melissa*), Meg Weldon (*Sandy*), Joey Garfield (*Jeff*), Roy Hytower (*Nathan*), Chris Murphy (*Dusty*), Catherine Gatz (*Marcie*), Meg Thalken (*Deborah*), Dean Tokuno (*Takamitsu*), Paty Lombard (*Helen*), E.J. Murray (*Mary*), Sherry Narens (*Mrs. Seaton*), Phil Locker (*Bill*), Maureen Steindler (*The Old Woman*), Alan Wilder (*An Observer*), Brent Shaphren (*An Observer*), Mindy Bell (*An Observer*), Conrad Allan (*The Young Boy*), Maureen Mueller (*The Gallery Woman*), Laurie V. Logan (*The Elevator Woman*), John Rusk (*The Gallery Man*), Sam Sanders (*The Security Guard*), Jerry Birn (*The Elevator Man*), Jane Alderman (*Scott's Mother*), Harold Taulbee, Mary Hogan, Laura

Koppel, Chris Montana, Lynn Koppel, Mark Zweigler, Wendy Wolfman, Christy Davis
D: Gary Sherman **SCR:** Gary Sherman & Brian Taggart **PHOTOG:** Alex Nepomniaschy **MUSIC:** Joe Renzetti **SONGS:** *Jungle Music & Night Rider*
Standard horror-fantasy: Occult forces pursue little girl

Polyester
1981, (USA), New Line, color, 86 mins.
W: Divine (*Francine Fishpaw*), Tab Hunter (*Todd Tomorrow*), Edith Massey, Mink Stole, Edith Massey (*Cuddles*), Mink Stole (*Sandra*), David Samson (*Elmer*), Joni Ruth White (*LaRue*), Mary Garlington (*Lulu*), Ken King (*Dexter*), Hans Kramm (*The Chauffeur*), Stiv Bators (*Bo-Bo*), George Stover, Steve Yeager
WRIT, P & D: John Waters **PHOTOG:** David Insley **MUSIC:** Chris Stein & Michael Kamen
Bizarre cult classic (first feature in "Odorama"): Depressed housewife meets man of her dreams

Pooh's Grand Adventure: The Search for Christopher Robin
1997, (USA), Disney, color
from characters created by A.A. Milne
Made-for-Video, standard animated fantasy: Bear hunts boy

Pool of London
1951, (GB), Ealing/Univ, b&w, 85 mins.
W: Bonar Colleano (*Dan MacDonald*), Renee Asherson (*Sally*), Susan Shaw (*Pat*), Earl Cameron (*Johnny*), Max Adrian (*Vernon/George*), Moira Lister (*Maisie*), Joan Dowling (*Pamela*), James Robertson Justice (*Trotter*), Alfie Bass (*Alf*), John Longden (*Insp. Williamson*), Michael Golden (*Andrews*), Leslie Phillips (*Harry*), George Merritt (*The Captain*), George Benson (*George*), Victor Maddern (*The Conductor*), John Warwick (*The Inspector*), Ellis Irving (*The Officer*)
P: Michael Balcon **D:** Basil Dearden **STORY:** Jack Whittingham & John Eldridge
Standard melodrama: Merchant seaman smuggles diamonds

Poor Albert and Little Annie
see *I Dismember Mama*

Poor Devil
1973, (USA), Para-TV, color, 73 mins.
W: Sammy Davis Jr. (*Sammy*), Jack Klugman (*Burnett Emerson*), Emily Yancy (*Chelsea*), Christopher Lee (*Lucifer*), Adam West (*Crawford*), Gino Conforti (*Mr. Bligh*), Madlyn Rhue, Byron Webster, Alan Manson, Ken Lynch, Buddy Lester, Owen Bush, Nick Georgiade, Don Ross, Lila Teigh, Stephen Coit, Clyde Ventura, Jo deWinter, George Kramer, Nancy Reichert, David Young, Tom Vize
D: Robert Scheerer **TELEPLAY:** Arne Sultan, Earl Barret & Richard Baer **PHOTOG:** Howard Schwartz **SPCL-FX:** Richard Webb **MUSIC:** Morton Stevens
TVM, minor comedy-fantasy: Satan's aide seeks bookkeeper's soul

Poor Pierrot
1892, (Fr), Emile Reynaud, b&w, 15 mins.
Animated fantasy short ("praxinoscope" cartoon): Clown cavorts

Popcorn
1991, (USA-Jamaica), Movie Partners-Century/Studio Three, color, 93 mins.
W: Jill Schoelen (*Maggie*), Tom Villard (*Toby*), Dee Wallace Stone (*Suzanne*), Derek Rydall (*Mark*), Malcolm Danare (*Bud*), Elliott Hurst (*Leon*), Ray Walston (*Dr. Mnesyne*), Kelly Jo Minter (*Cheryl*), Tony Roberts (*Mr. Davis*), Ivette Soler (*Joanie*), Freddie Marie Simpson (*Tina*), Karen Witter (*Joy*), Scott Thompson, Will Knickerbocker, Ethan Ormsby, Suzanne Hunt, Ben Stotes, Ken Ryan, Mat Falls, Giana Hardy, Barry Jenner, Cindy Tavares-Finson, Thom Adcox, Robert Dickman, Bruce Glover, Munair Zaza, Bobby Chisays, Lori Creevay, Ed Amatrudo, George Bemuth, Rohan Henry, Maki Fame, Hikonari Washimo, Kimio Satoh, Fumito Noozaki, Adam Ormsby, April Harris, Mike Stephens, Guy Christopher
D: Mark Herrier **SCR:** Tod Hackett **PHOTOG:** Ronnie Taylor **SPCL-FX SPRVSR:** Georgio Gerrari **MUSIC:** Paul J. Zaza
Standard thriller: Maniac slays during fright-film revival

Popdown
1968, (GB), Premar/New Realm, color, 98 mins.
W: Diane Keen (*Miss 1970*), Jane Bates (*Aries*), Zoot Money (*Sagittarius*), Carol Rachell (*Miss Withit*), Nicole Yarna (*The Body*), Debbie Slater (*The Girl*), Bill Aron (*The Host*), Fred Marshall (*The Boy*), Margaret Evans (*The Nude*)
WRIT, P & D: Fred Marshall
Standard SF-musical: Space aliens observe music scene of Earth teens

Popsy Wopsy
1913, (GB), Motograph, b&w, 478 ft. (145.7m)
W: Fred Groves (*The Composer*)
D: Maurice Elvey
Standard comedy-fantasy: Composer gets drunk on song proceeds, sees furniture dance

Port Afrique
1956, (GB), Coronado/Col, color, 92 mins.
W: Pier Angeli (*Ynez*), Phil Carey (*Rip Reardon*), Dennis Price (*Robert Blackton*),

Eugene Deckers (*Col. Moussac*), James Hayter (*Nino*), Rachel Gurney (*Diane Blackton*), Anthony Newley (*Pedro*), Christopher Lee (*Franz Vermes*), Guido Lorraine (*Abdul*)
<u>P</u>: David E. Rose & John R. Sloan   <u>D</u>: Rudolph Mate   <u>SCR</u>: Frank Partos & John Cresswell, from a novel by Bernard Victor Dyer   <u>MUSIC</u>: Malcolm Arnold
Standard crime-thriller: Crippled pilot in Morocco solves wife's shooting

Le Port du Desir (Port of Desire)
1954, (Fr), b&w, 94 mins.
<u>W</u>: Jean Gabin
<u>D</u>: Edmond T. Greville   <u>PHOTOG</u>: Henri Alekan   <u>MUSIC</u>: Joseph Kosma
Standard melodrama

Portnoy's Complaint
1972, (USA), WB, color, 101 mins.
<u>W</u>: Richard Benjamin, Lee Grant, John Carradine (*The Voice of God*), Karen Black, Jill Clayburgh, Kevin Conway
<u>P, D & SCR</u>: Ernest Lehman, from Philip Roth's novel
Unusual comedy-satire: Young modern has sexual hangups

Port of Desire
see Le Port du Desir

Port of Escape
1956, (GB), Wellington/Renown, b&w, 76 mins.
<u>W</u>: Googie Withers (*Anne Stirling*), John McCallum (*Mitchell Gillie*), Bill Kerr (*Dinty Missouri*), Alexander Gauge (*Insp. Levins*), Joan Hickson (*Rosalie Watchett*), Wendy Danielli (*Daphne Stirling*), Hugh Pryse (*Skinner*), Ewan Roberts (*Sgt. Rutherford*), Ingeborg Wells (*Lucy*)
<u>P</u>: Lance Comfort   <u>D</u>: Tony Young   <u>SCR</u>: Barbara Harper, Tony Young & Abby Mann, from Barbara Harper's story *Safe Harbour*
Standard crime-thriller: Girl reporter menaced by fugitive and insane comrade

Port of 40 Thieves
1944, (USA), Rep, b&w, 58 mins.
<u>W</u>: Stephanie Bachelor, Richard Powers (*Tom Keene*)
Minor melodrama

The Port of Missing Girls
1938, (USA), b&w, 56 mins.
<u>W</u>: Harry Carey Sr., Judith Allen, Milburn Stone, Betty Compson
<u>D</u>: Karl Brown
Minor thriller: Young woman implicated in murder, stows away on freighter

The Port of Missing Women
1915, (GB), Weston Feature Films/Clarion, b&w, 3,000 ft. (914.4m)
<u>W</u>: Alice Inward, James Lindsay, Lily Saxby, Gordon Begg
<u>D</u>: Charles Weston
Standard crime-thriller: White slavers run fashion model agency in Piccadilly

Portrait from Life
1948, (GB), Gainsborough/GFD, b&w, 89 mins.
<u>W</u>: Mai Zetterling (*Hildegarde*), Robert Beatty (*Campbell Reid*), Guy Rolfe (*Maj. Lawrence*), Herbert Lom (*Hendlemann*), Patrick Holt (*Ferguson*), Arnold Marle (*Prof. Menzel*), Thora Hird (*Mrs. Skinner*), Sybilla Binder (*Eitel*), Gerard Heinz (*Heine*), Yvonne Owen (*Helen*), Ernest Thesiger (*Bloomfield*), John Blythe (*Johnnie*)
<u>P</u>: Anthony Darnborough   <u>D</u>: Terence Fisher   <u>SCR</u>: Muriel Box, Sydney Box & Frank Harvey   <u>STORY</u>: David Evans
USA retitle, **The Girl in the Painting**, *Universal International, 1949*
Standard thriller: Major aids amnesiac girl, uncovers spy plot

Portrait in Black
1960, (USA), Univ, color, 112 mins.
<u>W</u>: Lana Turner, Anthony Quinn, Lloyd Nolan, John Saxon, Sandra Dee, Anna May Wong
<u>P</u>: Ross Hunter   <u>D</u>: Michael Gordon   <u>SCR</u>: Ivan Goff & Ben Roberts, from their play   <u>PHOTOG</u>: Russell Metty   <u>MUSIC</u>: Frank Skinner
Standard thriller: Woman and her doctor/lover commit murder

Portrait in Terror
1965, (USA), AIP, color, 81 mins.
<u>W</u>: Patrick Magee, William Campbell, Anna Pavane
<u>D</u>: Jack Hill
Modest thriller: Sadistic assassin meets deranged artist. cf. **Blood Bath** *(1966)*

Le Portrait Mysterieux (The Mysterious Portrait)
1899, (Fr), Star, b&w, 20m (65.6 ft./1.1 mins.)
<u>D</u>: Georges Melies
Standard fantasy

Portrait of Allison
see *Postmark for Danger*

The Portrait of Dolly Grey
1916, (GB), Kineto, b&w, 1,960 ft. (597.4m)
<u>D & STORY</u>: Walter R. Booth
Standard fantasy: Lord hypnotizes model into becoming revue star, is thwarted when poster

of Satan comes to life

Portrait of Jennie
1949, (USA), Selznick/SRO, b&w, 86 mins.
<u>W</u>: Jennifer Jones (*Jennie Appleton*), Joseph Cotten (*Eben Adams*), David Wayne (*Gus*), Ethel Barrymore (*Miss Spinney*), Cecil Kellaway (*Matthews*), Lillian Gish (*Sister Mary*), Felix Bressart, Henry Hull, John Farrell, Florence Bates, Esther Somers, Clem Bevans, Maude Simmons, Albert Sharpe, Robert Dudley, Anne Francis
<u>P</u>: David O. Selznick   <u>D</u>: William Dieterle   <u>SCR</u>: Paul Osborn & Peter Berneis   <u>ADAPT</u>: Leonardo Bercovici, from Robert Nathan's novel   <u>PHOTOG</u>: Joseph August   <u>MUSIC</u>: Dimitri Tiomkin
GB retitle, **Jennie**
Engrossing fantasy-romance: Artist meets girl via time warp

Portrait Of Jennie: JENNIFER JONES

Portraits of a Killer
1995, (USA), color, 93 mins.
<u>W</u>: Jennifer Grey, Costas Mandylor, Michael Ironside, Kenneth Welsh, Patricia Charbonneau, M. Emmet Walsh
<u>D</u>: Bill Corcoran
Made-for-Video, standard thriller: Photographer suspected in murders of prostitutes

Le Portrait Spirite (The Spirit Portrait)
1903, (Fr), Star, b&w, 44m (144.4 ft./2.4 mins.)
<u>D</u>: Georges Melies
A.k.a. **A Spiritualistic Photographer**
Standard fantasy: Photograph comes to life

Portret Doriana Greya (The Picture of Dorian Gray)
1915, (Russ), Russian Golden Series, b&w
<u>W</u>: Varvara Yanova, Meyerhold, G. Enriton, Doronin, Alexander Volkov, P. Belova, Y. Uvarova
<u>D</u>: Vsevolod Meyerhold   <u>CO-D</u>: Mikhail Doronin   <u>SCR</u>: Vsevolod Meyerhold, from Oscar Wilde's novel   <u>PHOTOG</u>: Alexander Levitsky
Standard fantasy: Roue achieves eternal youth

Port Said
1948, (USA), Col, b&w, 69 mins.
<u>W</u>: Gloria Henry, William Bishop
Minor melodrama

Port Sinister
1953, (USA), American/RKO, b&w, 65 mins.
<u>W</u>: James Warren, Lynne Roberts, Paul Cavanagh, House Peters Jr., Marjorie Stapp, William Schallert, Helen Winston, Eric Colmar, Norman Budd, Anne Kimbell, Robert Bice, Dayton Lummis, Merritt Stone, Ken Terrell, Charles Victor, E.(Edward), Guy Hearn
<u>WRIT & P</u>: Aubrey Wisberg & Jack Pollexfen   <u>D</u>: Harold Daniels   <u>PHOTOG</u>: William Bradford   <u>SPCL-FX</u>: Jack Rabin   <u>MUSIC</u>: Albert Glasser
reissued as **Beast of Paradise Isle**
blurb: "An Island of Terror in an Ocean of Evil!"
Standard thriller: Adventurers battle giant crabs when sunken city of Port Royal emerges from sea

Port Said: GLORIA HENRY AND WILLIAM BISHOP

Posed for Murder
1989, (USA), color, 90 mins.
W: Charlotte J. Helmkamp, Carl Fury, Rick Gianasi, Michael Merrins
D: Brian Thomas Jones
Standard thriller: Psycho stalks centerfold model

The Poseidon Adventure
1972, (USA), Kent/20th-Fox, color, 117 mins.
W: Gene Hackman (*Rev. Frank Scott*), Ernest Borgnine (*Rogo*), Stella Stevens (*Linda Rogo*), Carol Lynley (*Nonnie*), Shelley Winters (*Belle Rosen*), Jack Albertson (*Manny Rosen*), Roddy McDowall (*Acres*), Red Buttons (*Martin*), Leslie Nielsen (*The Captain*), Arthur O'Connell (*The Chaplain*), Pamela Sue Martin (*Susan*), Fred Sadoff (*Linarcos*), Eric Shea (*Robin*), Sheila Mathews (*The Nurse*), Jan Arvan (*The Doctor*), Byron Webster (*The Purser*), John Crawford (*The Chief Engineer*), Erik Nelson (*Tinkham*), Bob Hastings (*The M.C.*)
P: Irwin Allen **D:** Ronald Neame **SCR:** Stirling Silliphant & Wendell Mayes, from Paul Gallico's novel **PHOTOG:** Harold E. Stine **MUSIC:** John Williams **SONG:** *The Morning After*, sung by Maureen McGovern **DESIGN:** William Creber
Superior thriller: Tidal wave overturns luxury liner. cf. **Beyond the Poseidon Adventure**

Position of Trust
1963, (GB), Merton Park/Anglo-Amalgamated, b&w, 32 mins.
W: Derrick Sherwin (*Simon Derrington*), Imogen Hassall (*Yvonne Purvis*), Edward Atienza (*William Purvis*), Peter Barkworth (*Robbins*), Cyril Luckham (*Lawson*), Geoffrey Chater (*Soames*), Anthea Wyndham (*Julia*)
P: Jack Greenwood **D:** Lionel Harris **SCR:** James Eastwood, from a novel by Edgar Lustgarten
Standard short crime-thriller: Detective blackmails industrialist's adulterous son

Possessed
1947, (USA), WB, b&w, 108 mins.
W: Joan Crawford (*Louise Howell*), Van Heflin (*David Sutton*), Raymond Massey (*Dean Graham*), Geraldine Brooks (*Carol Graham*), Stanley Ridges (*Dr. Harvey Williard*), John Ridgely (*Lt. Harker*), Moroni Olsen (*Dr. Ames*), Erskine Sanford (*Dr. Max Sherman*), Isabel Withers (*Nurse Rosen*), Douglas Kennedy (*The Ass't D.A.*), Lisa Golm (*Elsie, the Maid*), Richard (Peter) Miles (*Wynn Graham*), Monte Blue (*Norris, the Caretaker*), Clifton Young (*The Intern*), Rory Mallinson (*The Coroner's Ass't*), Don McGuire (*Dr. Craig, the Psychiatrist*), Philo McCullough (*Edwards, the Butler*), Griff Barnett (*The Coroner*), Wheaton Chambers (*The Waiter*), Ralph Dunn (*The Motorman on the Trolley*), Creighton Hale (*The Court Reporter*), Sarah Padden (*Mrs. Norris, the Caretaker's Wife*), Max Wagner, Dick Bartell, Rose Plummer, Jeffrey Sayre
P: Jerry Wald **D:** Curtis Bernhardt **SCR:** Silvia Richards & Ranald MacDougall from a story by Rita Weiman **PHOTOG:** Joseph Valentine **SPCL-FX:** William McGann & Robert Burks **MUSIC:** Franz Waxman
Superior melodrama: Woman loses her sanity

The Possessed
1977, (USA), NBC-TV, color, 74 mins.
W: James Farentino (*Kevin Leahy*), Joan Hackett (*Louise Gelson*), Claudette Nevins (*Ellen Sumner*), Eugene Roche (*Sgt. Taplinger*), Harrison Ford (*Paul Winjam*), P.J. Soles (*Marty*), Ann Dusenberry (*Weezie*), Diana Scarwid (*Lane*), Susan Walden (*Sandy*)
D: Jerry Thorpe **TELEPLAY:** John Sacret Young **PHOTOG:** Charles G. Arnold **MUSIC:** Leonard Rosenman
TVM, standard fantasy-thriller: Defrocked cleric battles demonic forces at girl's school

Possessed by the Night
1994, (USA), color 84 mins.

W: Shannon Tweed, Ted Prior, Sandahl Bergman, Chad McQueen, Henry Silva
D: Fred Olen Ray
Standard fantasy-thriller: Mysterious statue casts spell over novelist, his wife, and his secretary

Possession
1973, (GB), Cecil Clarke/ITC, Made for TV, color, 71 mins.
W: John Carson (*Ray Burns*), Joanna Dunham (*Penny Burns*), James Cossins (*Kellet*), Hilary Hardiman (*Cecily Rafting*), Athol Coats (*Mr. Filson*), Richard Aylen (*Insp. Miles*), Jack Galloway (*The Young Man*), Mary Ann Severne (*The Young Woman*)
D: John Cooper **TELEPLAY:** Brian Clemens **PHOTOG:** Roy Simper **MUSIC:** Laurie Johnson
TVM, minor thriller: Unease in former murder mansion

Possession
1981, (Fr-W. Ger), color, 80 mins. (USA release)
W: Sam Neill, Isabelle Adjani, Heinz Bennent
WRIT & D: Andrzej Zulawski **SPCL-FX:** Carlo Rambaldi
Minor horror-fantasy: Mysterious beauty gives birth to own worst fears

The Possession of Joel Delaney
1972, (USA), ITC/Para, color, 105 mins.
W: Shirley MacLaine (*Norah*), Perry King (*Joel*), Michael Hordern (*Dr. Reichman*), Robert Burr (*Ted*), Lovelady Powell (*Erika*), Earle Hyman (*Charles*), Edmundo Rivera Alvarez (*Don Pedro*), Miriam Colon (*Veronica*), Lisa Kohane (*Carrie Benson*), Teodorino Bello (*Mrs. Perez*), Jose Fernandez (*Tonio Perez*), Aukie Herger (*Mr. Perez*), David Elliott (*Peter Benson*), Ernesto Gonzales (*The Handsome Seance Subject*), Peter Turgeon (*Brandy*), Paulita Iglesias (*The Female Bruja*), Martita Lindholm (*Marta*), Barbara Trentham (*Sherry*)
D: Waris Hussein **SCR:** Matt Robinson & Grimes Grice **PHOTOG:** Arthur Ornitz **MUSIC:** Joe Raposo **DESIGN:** Peter Murton
Standard horror-fantasy: Young man possessed by spirit of dead Puerto Rican who beheaded girls

The Postman
1910, (GB), Hepworth, b&w, 575 ft. (178m)
D: Frank Wilson
Standard crime-thriller: Fired postman's son trails thief

The Postman
1997, (USA), color, 177 mins.
W: Kevin Costner, Olivia Williams, Will Patton, Larenz Tate, Tom Petty, James Russo
D: Kevin Costner **SCR:** Brian Helgeland **STORY:** David Brin & Eric Roth **PHOTOG:** Stephen Windom **MUSIC:** James Newton Howard
Unusual SF-thriller: Post-nuke mailman's deliveries are a matter of life and death

Postmark for Danger
1956, (GB), Insignia/Anglo-Amalgamated/RKO, b&w, 84 mins.
W: Terry Moore (*Alison Ford*), Robert Beatty (*Tim Forrester*), William Sylvester (*David Forrester*), Geoffrey Keen (*Insp. Colby*), Josephine Griffin (*Jill Stewart*), Henry Oscar (*Smith*), Allan Cuthbertson (*Henry Carmichael*), William Lucas (*Dorking*), Terence Alexander (*Fenby*), Raymond Francis (*The Superintendent*), Stuart Sanders (*Sgt. Haines*)
P: Frank Godwin **D:** Guy Green **SCR:** Guy Green & Ken Hughes, from a TV serial by Francis Durbridge
GB title: **Portrait of Alison**, *AA, 1955*
Standard crime-thriller: Diamond smuggler kills artist's brother and model

Postmortem
1998, (USA), color, 106 mins.
W: Charlie Sheen, Michael Halsey
Standard thriller: Serial killer stalks small town

Post Office Investigator
1949, (USA), Rep, b&w, 59 mins.
W: Warren Douglas, Audrey Long
Minor melodrama

Pot Luck
see **Woman of Terror**

Potter of the Yard
1952, (GB), Collingwood/New Realm, b&w, 30 mins.
W: John Laurie (*Edward Potter*), Hector Ross (*Insp. Greenaway*), Avis Scott (*Eloise Tremaine*)
P: E.J. Facey **D:** John Wall & Oscar Burn
Standard short crime-thriller: Scotland Yard clerk poses as mechanic, nabs bankrobber

La Poupee (The Doll)
1962, (Fr), Hakim/Lionex, color, 100 mins.
W: Zbigniew Cybulski, Sonne Teal, Claudio Gora, Catherine Milinaire, Daniel Emilfork, Jacques Dufilho, Michel de Re, Sacha Pitoeff, Jean Aron, Gabriel Jabour
P: Gaston Hakim **D & SCR:** Jacques Baratier, from his novel **MUSIC:** Joseph Kosma
orig. to be titled **He, She or It**
Standard fantasy: Automaton causes problems

Les Poupees du Diable
see Devil Doll (1936)

La Poupée Vivante (The Living Doll)
1908, (Fr), Star, b&w, 60m (196.9 ft./3.3 mins.)
<u>D</u>: Georges Melies
Standard fantasy

La Poursuite (The Pursuit)
1963, (Fr), Les Films Jean Giono/Gaumont, color, 85 mins.
<u>W</u>: Claude Giraud, Colette Renard, Charles Vanel, Pierre Repp, Albert Remy, Rene Blancard
<u>D</u>: Francois Leterrier   <u>SCR</u>: Jean Giono, from his story   <u>PHOTOG</u>: Jean Badal   <u>MUSIC</u>: Maurice Jarre
A.k.a. Un Roi sans Divertissement (A King without Diversion)
Standard thriller: Monarch seeks bizarre excitements

Powder
1995, (USA), Caravan/Hollywood, color, 111 mins.
<u>W</u>: Sean Patrick Flanery (*Powder*), Mary Steenburgen (*Jessie Caldwell*), Jeff Goldblum (*Donald Ripley*), Lance Henriksen (*Sheriff Barnum*), Ray Wise (*Stipler*), Bradford Tatum (*John Box*), Brandon Smith (*Duncan*), Susan Tyrrell (*Maxine*), Chad Cox (*Zane*), Missy Crider (*Lindsey*), Esteban Louis Powell (*Mitch*), Reed Fredrichs (*Skye*), Joe Marchman, Philip Maurice Hayes, Dannette McMann, Tom Tarantini, Woody Watson, Brady Coleman, Alex Allen Morris, Barry Berfield, Paula Engel, Meason Wiley, James Houston, Dee Macaluso, Bonnie Gallup, Bill Grant-Minchen
<u>P</u>: Roger Birnbaum & Daniel Grodnik   <u>WRIT & D</u>: Victor Salva   <u>PHOTOG</u>: Jerzy Zielinski   <u>VS-FX SPRVSR</u>: Stephanie Powell   <u>MUSIC</u>: Jerry Goldsmith   <u>SONGS</u>: *Roll Up Waltz* & *Puppet March*
Standard SF-thriller: Albino has strange powers

The Power
1967, (USA), MGM, color, 109 mins, also 104 mins.
<u>W</u>: George Hamilton (*Prof. James Tanner*), Suzanne Pleshette (*Prof. Marge Lansing*), Earl Holliman (*Prof. Talbot Scott*), Aldo Ray (*Bruce*), Michael Rennie (*Prof. Arthur Nordlin*), Richard Carlson (*Prof. Van Zandt*), Yvonne DeCarlo (*Sally Hallson*), Arthur O'Connell (*Prof. Henry Hallson*), Barbara Nichols (*Flora*), Ken Murray (*Fred*), Nehemiah Persoff (*Prof. Carl Melinker*), Gary Merrill (*Corlane*), Miiko Taka (*Mrs. Van Zandt*), Celia Lovsky (*Old Mrs. Hallson*), Vaughn Taylor (*Old Mr. Hallson*), Miss Beverly Hills (*Sylvia*)
<u>P</u>: George Pal   <u>D</u>: Byron Haskin   <u>SCR</u>: John Gay, from Frank M. Robinson's novel   <u>PHOTOG</u>: Ellsworth Fredericks   <u>SPCL-FX</u>: J. McMillan Johnson & Gene Warren   <u>MUSIC</u>: Miklos Rozsa
Superior SF-thriller: Scientists hunt psychic mutant

The Power
1980, (USA), Film Ventures, color, 87 mins.
<u>W</u>: Susan Stokey (*Sandy*), Warren Lincoln (*Jerry*), Ben Gilbert (*Matt*), Lisa Erickson (*Julie*), Chad Christian (*Tommy*), Stan Weston (*Prof. Wilson*), J. Dinan Myrtetus (*Francis Lott*), Rod Mays (*Lee McKennah*), Chris Morrill (*Ron Prince*), Gabe Cohen (*Marty*), Alice Champlin (*Roxanne*), Juan Del Valle (*The Jeep Driver*), Jackie Cowgill (*Mrs. Lawrence*), Ted Novak (*Rick*), James Gilchrist (*Bill Hopkins*), Brian Grayson (*Mark*), Costy Basile (*Jorge*), Jay Fisher (*Raphael*), Milton Robinson (*Jack*), Steve Nagle (*The Driver*), Barbara Murray (*Tommy's Mother*), Richard Cowgill (*The Cemetery Guard*), Jake Jones (*The Janitor*)
<u>D & SCR</u>: Jeffrey Obrow & Stephen Carpenter   <u>STORY</u>: Jeffrey Obrow, Stephen Carpenter, John Penney & John Hopkins   <u>PHOTOG</u>: Stephen Carpenter   <u>MUSIC</u>: Chris Young
Minor horror-fantasy: Aztec idol unleashes evil

Power 98
1995, (USA), color, 85 mins.
<u>W</u>: Eric Roberts, Jason Gedrick (*Jon*)
Minor thriller: Killer contacts radio "shock jock"

The Power of the Whistler
1945, (USA), Col, b&w, 66 mins.
<u>W</u>: Richard Dix, Janis Carter, Loren Tindall (*Kent*), Jeff Donnell (*Frances*)
<u>D</u>: Lew Landers
Minor thriller

The Power Within
1979, (USA), color, 90 mins.
<u>W</u>: Eric Braeden, David Hedison, Susan Howard, Art Hindle
<u>D</u>: John Llewellyn Moxey
Minor thriller: Stuntman gains electric touch

The Power Within
1995, (USA), PM Entertainment Group, video, color, 100 mins.
<u>W</u>: Ted Jan Roberts, Karen Valentine, Keith Coogan, John O'Hurley, Jacob Parker, Ed O'Ross, William Zabka
<u>P</u>: Richard Pepin & Joseph Mehri   <u>D</u>: Art Camach   <u>SCR</u>: Jacobsen Hart   <u>STORY</u>: Scott McAboy & Jacobsen Hart   <u>PHOTOG</u>: Ken Blakey   <u>ORIG. SCORE</u>: Jim Halfpenny
Made-for-Video, standard fantasy-thriller: Magic ring gives teen superpowers

Practical Magic
1998, (USA), WB, color
<u>W</u>: Sandra Bullock, Nicole Kidman, Aidan Quinn, Dianne Wiest, Stockard Channing
<u>D</u>: Griffin Dunne   <u>SCR</u>: Robin Swicord, Akiva Goldsman & Adam Brooks, from Alice Hoffman's novel   <u>PHOTOG</u>: Andrew Dunn   <u>MUSIC</u>: Alan Silvestri
Unusual fantasy: Sisters espouse witchcraft

Pranks
1981, (USA), Jeff Obrow/Wescom/New Image, color, 84 mins.
<u>W</u>: Laurie Lapinski (*Joanne*), Stephen Sachs (*Craig*), David Snow (*Brian*), Pamela Holland (*Patti*), Dennis Ely (*Bobby Lee Tremble*), Woody Roll (*John Hemmit*), Daphne Zuniga (*Debbie*), Jake Jones (*Bill Edgar*), Robert Frederick (*Tim*), Chris Morrill (*Jack*), Chandre (*Alice*), Billy Criswell (*Rick*), Kay Beth (*Debbie's Mother*), Richard Cowgill (*Debbie's Father*), Jimmy Betz (*Officer Lewis*), Thomas Christian (*Officer Dean*), Robert Richardson, Chris Schroeder
<u>D</u>: Jeffrey Obrow & Stephen Carpenter   <u>SCR</u>: Jeffrey Obrow, Stephen Carpenter & Stacey Giachino   <u>PHOTOG</u>: Stephen Carpenter   <u>MAKEUP & SPCL-FX</u>: Matthew Mungle   <u>MUSIC</u>: Chris Young
*orig. to be titled **Death Dorm**, reissued (1983) as **The Dorm That Dripped Blood***
Standard thriller: Psycho-killer stalks coeds

Pray for Death
1985, (GB), Trans World/ADG, color, 92 mins.
<u>W</u>: Sho Kosugi
<u>D</u>: Gordon Hessler
Standard action-thriller: Former ninja wreaks havoc on thugs terrorizing his family

Praying Mantis
1993, (USA), Wilshire Court/Para, color, 95 mins.
<u>W</u>: Jane Seymour (*Linda*), Barry Bostwick (*Don*), Chad Allen (*Bobby*), Frances Fisher (*Betty*), Colby Chester (*Agent Johnson*), Michael MacRae (*Agent Broderick*), John Martin (*Sam*), Anne Schedeen (*Karen*), Sherri Jensen (*Kate*), John Knotts (*Capt. Stringer*), Kathleen Randall (*Pratt*), Karen Johnson-Miller (*Paula*), Barbara Kite (*The Mother*), Mariah Milner (*The Daughter*), Roger Welch (*The Bellboy*), Victor Morris (*Det. Hutchins*), Frank Roberts (*A Minister*), Terry Ward (*A Minister*), Sherry Marens (*Harriet*), Jerry Basham (*Hank*), Amy Stering (*Sally*), Mark Allen (*Prof. Clark*), Barbara Lee (*The Coroner*), Curt Hanson (*George*)
<u>D</u>: James Keach   <u>TELEPLAY</u>: William Delligan & Duane Poole   <u>STORY</u>: William Delligan   <u>PHOTOG</u>: Ross Maehl   <u>MUSIC</u>: John Debney
TVM, standard thriller: Female psychopath marries and murders

The Preacher's Wife
1996, (USA), Parkway-Mundy Lane/Touchstone, color, 124 mins.
<u>W</u>: Denzel Washington (*Dudley*), Whitney Houston (*Julia Biggs*), Courtney B. Vance (*Henry Biggs*), Gregory Hines (*Joe Hamilton*), Jenifer Lewis (*Marguerite Coleman*), Justin Pierre Edmund (*Jeremiah*), Loretta Devine, Darvel Darvis Jr., Lionel Ritchie
<u>D</u>: Penny Marshall   <u>SCR</u>: Nat Mauldin & Allan Scott, from a screenplay by Robert E. Sherwood & Leonardo Bercovici, based on Robert Nathan's novel *The Bishop's Wife*   <u>PHOTOG</u>: Miroslav Ondricek   <u>MUSIC SCORE</u>: Hans Zimmer   <u>MUSIC SPRVSR</u>: Mervyn Warren   <u>SONG</u>: *I Believe in You and Me*
*Entertaining, music-filled fantasy: Natty angel helps preacher build church. cf. **The Bishop's Wife***

Precious Find
1997, (USA), Initial Entertainment/Rep, video, color
<u>W</u>: Rutger Hauer, Joan Chen, Harold Pruett, Brion James
<u>D</u>: Philippe Mora
Standard SF-thriller (made-for-Video): Space Prospectors face alien dangers

Predator
1987, (USA), Gordon-Silver-Davis/20th-Fox, color, 111 mins.
<u>W</u>: Arnold Schwarzenegger (*Dutch*), Carl Weathers (*Dillon*), Bill Duke (*Mac*), Jesse Ventura (*Blain*), Elpidia Carrillo (*Anna*), Kevin Peter Hall (*The Predator*), Sonny Landham, Richard Chaves, Shane Black, R.G. Armstrong
<u>D</u>: John McTiernan   <u>SCR</u>: James E. Thomas & John C. Thomas   <u>PHOTOG</u>: Donald McAlpine   <u>MUSIC</u>: Alan Silvestri
*orig. to be titled **Hunter***
Modest SF-thriller: He-man vs. space alien

Predator 2
1990, (USA), 20th-Fox, color, 102 mins.
<u>W</u>: Danny Glover (*Det. Mike Harrigan*), Gary Busey (*Keyes*), Ruben Blades (*Danny Archuleta*), Maria Conchita Alonso (*Leona Cantrell*), Bill Paxton (*Jerry Lambert*), Robert Davi (*Capt. Heineman*), Kevin Peter Hall (*The Predator*), Morton Downey Jr., Adam Baldwin, Kent McCord, Calvin Lockhart, Steve Kahan, Lilyan Chauvin
<u>D</u>: Stephen Hopkins   <u>SCR</u>: Jim Thomas & John Thomas   <u>PHOTOG</u>: Peter Levy   <u>MUSIC</u>: Alan Silvestri
Standard SF-horror: Space-alien hunter terrorizes city

A Prehistoric Love Story
1915, (GB), Zenith, b&w, 2,000 ft. (609.6m)
<u>W</u>: Seymour Hicks (*The Man*), Isobel Elsom (*The Girl*), Violet Russell, Franklyn Bellamy
<u>D</u>: Leedham Bantock, from a sketch by Seymour Hicks
Standard comedy-fantasy: Burlesque of Stone Age romance

P

The Prehistoric Man
1908, (Fr), b&w
Standard fantasy: Life in Stone Age

The Prehistoric Man
1908, (GB), Urban, b&w, 300 ft. (91.4m)
<u>D:</u> Walter R. Booth
Standard fantasy short: Drawing of cave man comes to life

The Prehistoric Man
1911, (GB), B&C/Cosmo, b&w, 370 ft. (112.8m)
<u>D:</u> H.O. Martinek
Standard comedy short: Man dressed as cave man for pageant is mistaken for real one

The Prehistoric Man
1924, (GB), Stoll, b&w, 4,500 ft. (1371.6m)
<u>W:</u> George Robey (*He-of-the-Beetle-Brow*), Marie Blanche (*She-of-the-Permanent-Wave*), H. Agar Lyons (*He-of-the-Clutching-Hand*), W.G. Saunders (*He-of-the-Knotty-Joints*), Johnny Butt (*He-of-the-O-Cedar-Mop*), Elsie Marriot-Watson (*She-of-the-Tireless-Tongue*), Laurie Leslie (*He-of-the-Matted-Beaver*)
<u>D:</u> A.E. Coleby <u>SCR:</u> Sinclair Hill <u>STORY:</u> George Robey
Standard comedy: Cave man elopes in stolen car

Prehistoric Peeps
1905, (GB), Hepworth, b&w, 375 ft. (114.3m)
<u>W:</u> Sebastian Smith (*Prof. Chump*), Mrs. Smith (*Martha Chump*), Hetty Potter (*Bacteria*), Lottie Martin (*Scrofula*), W. Young (*The Giant*), Rosina White (*Germs*), Harry Weekes (*Boko*), Bob Boucher (*Bucephalus*), Wordsworth Harrison (*The Apeman*)
<u>WRIT & D:</u> Lewin Fitzhamon
Standard comedy-fantasy: Osteologist dreams of Stone-Age adventures

Prehistoric Planet Women
see Women of the Prehistoric Planet

Prehistoric Valley
see Valley of the Dragons

Prehistoric Women
1950, (USA), Alliance/Eagle Lion/UA, color, 74 mins.
<u>W:</u> Laurette Luez, Joan Shawlee, Allan Nixon, Judy Landon, Mara Lynn, Jackie Coogan, Jo Carroll Dennison, Janet Shaw, Kerry Vaughn, Johann Peturrson, Tony Devlin, James Summers, Dennis Dengate
<u>D:</u> Gregg Tallas <u>SCR:</u> Sam X. Abarbanel & Gregg Tallas
TV retitle, Lost Women
blurb: "Savage struggle! Primitive passion!"
Minor SF-thriller: Amazons hunt mates

Prehistoric Women
1966, (GB), Hammer-7Arts/20th-Fox, color, 95 mins.
<u>W:</u> Martine Beswick (*Kari*), Edina Ronay (*Zaria*), Michael Latimer (*David*), Stephanie Randall (*Amyak*), Carol White (*Gido*), Alexandra Stevenson (*Luri*), Yvonne Horner (*The First Amazon*), Sydney Bromley, Frank Hayden,

Prehistoric Women: MARA LYNN, JOHANN PETURRSON AND KERRY VAUGHN

Robert Raglan, Steven Berkoff, Mary Hignett, Louis Mahoney, Bari Jonson, Danny Daniels
<u>P & D:</u> Michael Carreras <u>SCR:</u> Henry Younger <u>PHOTOG:</u> Michael Reed <u>MUSIC:</u> Carlo Martelli
A.k.a. Slave Girls
Standard adventure-fantasy: Hunter time-travels, contends with neolithic matriarchy

Prehistoric World
see Teenage Cave Man

Prehysteria
1993, (USA), color, 86 mins.
<u>W:</u> Austin O'Brien, Samantha Mills, Colleen Morris, Tony Longo, Stephen Lee, Stuart Fratkin
<u>D:</u> Albert & Charles Band <u>SCR:</u> Greg Duddeth & Mark Goldstein
Standard SF-comedy: Five tiny dinosaurs wreak havoc in suburban family's basement

Prehysteria! 2
1994, (USA), color 81 mins
<u>W:</u> Kevin R. Connors, Jennifer Harte, Dean Scofield, Bettye Ackerman, Larry Hankin, Greg Lewis, Alan Palo, Michael Hagiwara, Owen Bush
<u>D:</u> Albert Band <u>SCR:</u> Brent Friedman & Michael Paul Davis <u>MUSIC:</u> Richard Band
Minor SF-comedy: Pygmy dinosaurs aid youth

Prehysteria! 3
1995, (USA), color, 95 mins.
<u>W:</u> Fred Willard, Bruce Weitz, Whitney Anderson, Pam Matteson
<u>D:</u> Julian Breen <u>SCR:</u> Michael Paul Davis & Neil Ruttenberg
Minor SF-comedy: Tiny dinosaurs aid miniature-golf franchise

Prelude
1927, (GB), Castleton Knight, b&w, 600 ft. (182.9m)
<u>W:</u> Castleton Knight (*The Man*)
<u>D &SCR:</u> Castleton Knight, from Edgar Allan Poe's short story *The Premature Burial*
Standard horror-thriller: Man dreams he is victim of premature entombment

Prelude to a Kiss
1992, (USA), 20th-Fox, color, 110 mins.
<u>W:</u> Alec Baldwin (*Peter Hoskins*), Meg Ryan (*Rita Boyle*), Kathy Bates (*Leah Blier*), Ned Beatty (*Dr. Boyle*), Patty Duke (*Mrs. Boyle*), Richard Riehle (*Jerry Blier*), Sydney Walker (*The Old Man*), Stanley Tucci (*Taylor*)
<u>D:</u> Norman Rene <u>SCR:</u> Craig Lucas, from his play <u>PHOTOG:</u> Stefan Czapsky <u>MUSIC:</u> Howard Shore
Standard romance-fantasy: Body switch between young bride and dying old man

The Premature Burial
1962, (USA), AIP, color, 82 mins.
<u>W:</u> Ray Milland (*Guy Carrell*), Hazel Court (*Emily*), Heather Angel (*Kate*), Richard Ney (*Miles*), Alan Napier (*Dr. Gideon Gault*), Brendan Dillon (*The Minister*), Dick Miller (*Mole*), John Dierkes (*Sweeney*), Clive Halliday
<u>P & D:</u> Roger Corman <u>SCR:</u> Charles Beaumont & Ray Russell, from Edgar Allan Poe's short story <u>PHOTOG:</u> Floyd Crosby <u>MUSIC:</u> Ronald Stein
<u>SONG:</u> *Molly Malone* <u>DESIGN:</u> Daniel Haller
Modest horror-thriller: Man entombed by scheming bride. cf. Prelude

Premonition
1972, (USA), Joyce Prod./Transvue, color, 83 mins.
<u>W:</u> Carl Crow (*Neal*), Winfrey Hester Hill (*Baker*), Tim Ray (*Andy*), Victor Izay (*Kilkenny*), Judith Patterson (*Janice*), Michele Fitzsimmons (*Denise*), Cheryl Adams (*Susan*), Barry Brown (*Michael*), Jon Huss (*Jon*), Doug DiGioila (*Norm*), John Holman (*Lotheridge*), Eddie Patterson (*Ralph*), Diana Daves (*Miss Thorsen*), Lee Alpert (*Frat Brother*), Miles Tilton (*The Promoter*), Larry Loveridge (*The Man in the Cabin*), Andy Hare (*Drummer*), Shelley Snell, Joyce Rudolph, Tom Akers, Alex Del Zoppo, Paul Katz
<u>P:</u> Christopher R. Robertson <u>WRIT & D:</u> Alan Rudolph <u>PHOTOG:</u> John Bailey <u>MUSIC:</u> Tim Ray & Alex Del Zoppo
Minor horror-thriller

The Premonition
1975, (USA), Galaxy/Avco Embassy, color, 94 mins.
<u>W:</u> Sharon Farrell (*Sheri Bennett*), Edward Bell (*Miles Bennett*), Jeff Corey (*Lt. Mark Denver*), Richard Lynch (*Jude*), Chitra Neogy (*Dr. Kingsly*), Ellen Barber (*Andrea*), Danielle Brisebois (*Janie Bennett*), Rosemary McNamara (*Lenora*), Roy White (*Dr. Larabee*), Margaret Graham (*The Landlady*), Thomas Williams (*Todd Fletcher*), Wilmuth Cooper (*The Gypsy Lady*), Mark Schneider (*The Patrolman*), Robert Harper (*The Night Watchman*), Stanley W. Winn (*Dean Fuller*), Tamara Bergdall (*The Nurse*), Bonita Chambers (*The Receptionist*), Edward L. Emling Jr. (*The Student*)
<u>P & D:</u> Robert Allen Schnitzer <u>SCR:</u> Anthony Mahon & Robert Allen Schnitzer <u>PHOTOG:</u> Victor C. Milt <u>SPCL-FX:</u> Ken Newman <u>MUSIC:</u> Henry Mollicone <u>ELECTRONIC MUSIC:</u> Pril Smiley
Minor thriller: Psychic phenomena muddles search for kidnapped child

The Presence
1992, (USA), NBC-TV, color, 90 mins.
<u>W:</u> Lisa Banes, Richard Beymer, Maria Celedonio, Joe Lara, Gary Graham, Kathy Ireland, Beth Toussaint, Eddie Velez, Christopher Pettiet, Nikki Cox, June

Lockhart (*Kate*), Ray Bumatai (*Tupac*), Steven Goldsberry (*Frank*), Kimo Hugho (*The Chief*), Gina Malia Aurio (*Linda*), Annie MacLachlan (*Maria*), Ned Van Zandt (*Paul*)
WRIT & P: William Bleich   **D:** Tommy Lee Wallace   **PHOTOG:** Alan Caso   **SPCL-FX:** Peter Knowlton   **MUSIC:** Peter Manning Robinson
TVM (feature-pilot for unsold teleseries), standard SF thriller: Plane-crash survivors on mysterious isle

A Present from India
1911, (GB), Hepworth, b&w, 350 ft. (106.7m)
D: Frank Wilson
Standard fantasy short: Hindu idol changes into magician when touched by white man

The President's Analyst
1967, (USA), Panpiper/Para, color, 104 mins.
W: James Coburn (*Dr. Sidney Schaefer*), Godfrey Cambridge (*Don Masters*), Severn Darden (*Kropotkin*), Pat Harrington (*Arlington Hewes*), Joan Delaney (*Nan Butler*), Eduard Franz (*Ethan Allan Cocket*), Barry McGuire (*The Old Wrangler*), Will Geer (*Dr. Lee-Evans*), Joan Darling (*Jeff Quantrill*), William Daniels (*Wynn Quantrill*), Sheldon Collins (*Bing Quantrill*), Walter Burke (*Henry Lux*), Jill Banner (*Snow White*), Arte Johnson (*Sullivan*), Martin Horsey, Kathleen Hughes, William Beckley, T.C. Jones
P: Howard W. Koch   **WRIT & D:** Theodore J. Flicker   **PHOTOG:** William A. Fraker   **SPCL-FX:** Westheimer Co.   **MUSIC:** Lalo Schifrin   **SONG:** *Inner Manipulations*
Standard spy-comedy: President's psychiatrist targeted by foreign powers, seeks anonymity

Pretty Maids All in a Row
1971, (USA), MGM, color, 95 mins.
W: Rock Hudson (*Tiger*), Angie Dickinson (*Miss Smith*), Telly Savalas (*Surcher*), John David Carson (*Ponce*), Keenan Wynn (*Pooldaski*), Roddy McDowall (*Proffer*), James Doohan (*Follo*), William Campbell (*Grady*), Susan Tolsky (*Miss Craymire*), Barbara Leigh (*Jean*), Amy Eccles (*Hilda*), Joy Bang (*Rita*), Gretchen Burrell (*Marjorie*), JoAnna Cameron (*Yvonne*), Margaret Markov (*Polly*), June Fairchild (*Sonny*), Brenda Sykes (*Pamela*), Diane Sherry (*Sheryl*), Phillip Brown (*Jim*), Mark Malmborg (*Dink*), Kyle Johnson (*Dave*), Warren Seabury (*Harold*), Stephanie Mizrahi (*Tiger's Daughter*), Orville Sherman (*The Pastor*), Gary Tigerman, Tim Ray, Alberto Isaac, Dawn Roddenberry, Judy Michie, Larry Marmorstein, Adriana Bentley, Fredricka Myers, Joyce Williams, Chris Allen Woodley, Linda Morand, Topo Swope, Jomarie Ward, Otis Greene, Guy Remsen, Joe Quinn, Estrellita Rania
D: Roger Vadim   **SCR:** Gene Roddenberry, from a novel by Francis Pollini   **PHOTOG:** Charles Rosher   **MUSIC:** Lalo Schifrin
Minor comedy-thriller (Vadim's first American-made feature): High-school girls murdered

Pretty Poison
1968, (USA), Lawrence Turman/20th-Fox, color, 89 mins.
W: Anthony Perkins, Tuesday Weld, Beverly Garland, Clarice Blackburn, John Randolph, Dick O'Neill, Joseph Bova, Ken Kercheval
P: Marshal Backlar & Noel Black   **D:** Noel Black   **SCR:** Lorenzo Semple Jr., from Stephen Geller's novel *She Let Him Continue* (film orig. to be titled same)   **PHOTOG:** David Quaid   **MUSIC:** Johnny Mandel
Unusual thriller: Unbalanced young man drawn into murder plot

Pretty Poison
1996, (USA), Lawrence Turman/Fox-TV, color, 95 mins.
W: Grant Show (*Dennis*), Wendy Benson (*Sue Anne*), Michelle Phillips (*Mrs. Stepanek*), Lynne Thigpen (*Jane Azenauer*), Doug Lennox (*Bud Munsch*), Jayne Paterson
D: David Burton Morris   **TELEPLAY:** Brian Ross, based on Lorenzo Semple Jr.'s screenplay, from Stephen Geller's novel *She Let Him Continue*   **PHOTOG:** Francis Kenny   **MUSIC:** Pray for Rain
TVM remake, standard thriller: Teen temptress provokes murder

The Preview Murder Mystery
1936, (USA), Par, b&w, 60 mins
D: Robert Florey
Standard melodrama

Prey
1978, (GB), Kevin O'Driscoll/Tymar/Supreme, color, 85 mins.
W: Glory Annen (*Jessica*), Sally Faulkner (*Jo*), Barry Stokes (*Anderson*), Sandy Chinney (*Sandy*), Eddie Stacey, Jerry Crampton
P: Terence Marcel & David Wimbury   **D:** Norman J. Warren   **SCR:** Max Cuff   **STORY:** David Wimbury, Terence Marcel & Quinn Donoghue   **PHOTOG:** Derek V. Browne   **MUSIC:** Ivor Slaney
*released in USA (1984) as **Alien Prey***
Adult SF-horror: Lesbians meet space-being

The Prey
1980, (USA), Summer Brown/Essex/New World, color, 81 mins.
W: Debbie Thureson (*Nancy*), Steve Bond (*Joel*), Lori Lethin (*Bobbie*), Robert Wald (*Skip*), Gayle Gannes (*Gail*), Philip Wenckus (*Greg*), Jackson Bostwick (*Mark O'Brien*), Jackie Coogan (*Lester Tile*), Connie Hunter (*Mary Sylvester*), Ted Hayden (*Frank Sylvester*), Garry Goodrow (*Sgt. Parsons*), Carel Struycken (*The Monster*)
D: Edwin Scott Brown   **SCR:** Summer & Edwin Brown   **PHOTOG:** Teru Hayashi   **MUSIC:** Don Peake
Minor thriller: Human monster stalks campers

Prey for the Hunter
1992, (USA), color, 90 mins.
W: Todd Jensen, Andre Jacobs, Michelle Bestbier, Evan J. Klisser, David Butler, Allan Granville
D: John H. Parr
Minor thriller: Hunters pursue photojournalist

Prey of the Chameleon
1992, (USA), cable, Prism-Saban color, 91 mins.
W: Daphne Zuniga, Alexandra Paul, James Wilder, Red West, Alexander Folk, Mark Carlton, Don Harvey, Bob Larkin, Michele McBride, Kelly Gwinn, Patricia Place, Kenny Call
D: Fleming B. Fuller   **SCR:** April Campbell Jones & Fleming B. Fuller   **PHOTOG:** Randolph Sellars   **MUSIC:** Shuki Levy   **SONG:** *We Can't Lose*
Made-for-Cable, standard thriller: Murderous mental patient assumes victims' characteristics

Prey of the Jaguar
1996, (USA), color 95 mins
W: Maxwell Caulfield, Linda Blair (*Lt. Cody Johnson*), Stacy Keach, Trevor Goddard
Made-for-Video, standard SF-adventure: Cop becomes superhero, battles drug cartel

The Prey of the Vampire
see El Vampiro

The Price He Paid
1916, (GB), Regal Films, b&w, 2,920 ft. (890m)
W: George Keene (*John Clive*), Letty Paxton (*Irene Clive*), George Foley (*Insp. Brill*), Wingold Lawrence (*Capt. Larson*), Lionel d'Aragon (*Blakeson*), Charles Ashwell (*The Priest*)
D & STORY: Dave Aylott
Standard crime-thriller: Tibetan priest kills blackmailer for stealing jewel from idol

The Price of Deception
1913, (GB), Barker, b&w, 1,070 ft. (326.1m)
W: Fred Paul (*Lord Neston*), Blanche Forsythe (*Lady Neston*), Roy Travers (*The Thief*), Tom Coventry (*Aaron*)
D: Bert Haldane   **STORY:** Rowland Talbot
Standard crime-thriller: Lord replaces wife's pearls with paste copy

The Price of Fear
1956, (USA), Univ, b&w, 79 mins.
W: Merle Oberon, Lex Barker, Charles Drake, Gia Scala, Warren Stevens
D: Abner Biberman
Standard thriller: Woman involved in hit-and-run; events snowball into disaster

The Price of her Silence
1914, (GB), B&C/DFSA, b&w, 1,964 ft. (598.6m)
D: Ernest G. Batley
Standard crime-thriller: Married woman's ex-lover kills blackmailer

The Price of Justice
see Beautiful Jim

The Price of Silence
1960, (GB), Eternal/Grand Nat'l, b&w, 73 mins.
W: Gordon Jackson (*Roger Fenton*), June Thorburn (*Audrey Truscott*), Maya Koumani (*Maria Shipley*), Mary Clar (*Mrs. West*), Terence Alexander (*John Braine*), Victor Brooks (*Supt. Wilson*), Joan Heal (*Ethel*), Olive Sloane (*The Landlady*)
D: Montgomery Tully   **P & SCR:** Maurie J. Wilson, from Lawrence Meynell's novel *Murder*
Standard crime-thriller: Ex-convict estate agent accused of rich client's strangling

A Price on His Head
1914, (GB), Hepworth, b&w, 1,900 ft. (579.1m)
W: Eric Desmond (*Eric*)
D: Warwick Buckland
Standard crime-thriller: Kidnappers nab detective, who flashes for help by heliograph

La Prima Donna
1963, (Fr), DOFRA, b&w
W: Nelly Kaplan, Philippe Henry, Jean Hess, Nicole Francois, Eugene Grillet, Philippe Arthuys
WRIT & D: Philippe Lifchitz
Standard melodrama

Primal Fear
1996, (USA), Rysher Entertainment/Para, color, 130 mins.
W: Richard Gere (*Martin Vail*), Laura Linney (*Janet Venable*), John Mahoney (*Shaughnessy*), Edward Norton (*Aaron/Roy*), Alfre Woodard (*The Judge*), Frances McDormand (*Molly*), Tony Plana (*Martinez*), Terry O'Quinn (*Yancy*), Andre Braugher (*Goodman*), Steven Bauer (*Pinero*), Stanley Anderson (*Rushman*), Kenneth Tigar, Joe Spano, Maura Tierney, Jon Seda, Reg Rogers, Brian Reddy, Wendy Cutler, Christopher Carroll, Ron O.J. Parson, Sigrid K. Zahner, Diann Burns, Linda Yu, Mary Ann Childers, Andy Shaw, Lester D. Holt, Joseph R. Ryan, Sylvia Gomez, David Eckert, Jon Duncanson, Robert Jordan, Joanie Lum, Randy Salerno, Kyle Colerider-Krugh, Mike

Bacarella, Joseph Luis Caballero, Turk Muller, Randall Slavin, Joe Kosala, Lenny Wilson, Tony Fitzpatrick, Peter Schreiner, Larry Cook, Dwight Brad Dyer, Azalea Davila, Wayne Wright, Clarence Williams Jr., Rosalie V. Lewis, Bob Kenney

P: Gary Lucchesi   D: Gregory Hoblit   SCR: Steve Shagan & Ann Biderman, from William Diehl's novel   PHOTOG: Michael Chapman   MUSIC: James Newton Howard

"A classic sit-on-the-edge-of-your-seat suspense film with a brilliant double-twist ending"—Paul Wunder, WBAI-FM

"A mesmerizing mystery! An Awesome ending!"—George Pennacchio, CBS-TV

"A tense thriller"—Bruce Williamson, Playboy

Unusual thriller: Publicity-hungry attorney defends youth accused of killing archbishop

Primal Rage
1990, (USA), color, 92 mins.

W: Bo Svenson, Patrick Lowe, Mitch Watson, Sarah Buxton, Cheryl Arutt

D: Vittoria Rambaldi

Minor SF-thriller: Experiment monkey bites student

Primal Scream
1987, (USA), Oakcrest, color, 95 mins.

W: Kenneth J. McGregor (*Corby McHale*), Sharon Mason (*Samantha Keller*), Julie Miller (*Caitlin Foster*), Jon Maurice (*Capt. Frank Gitto*), Joseph White (*Nicky Fingers*), Mickey Shaughnessy (*Charlie Waxman*), Stephan Caldwell (*Olan Robert Foster*), Edward Fallon (*Dr. Charles Kesselman*), Michael Laird (*Karp*), Vivian Nothaft (*Dirty Mary*), Stephen Emhe (*Burman*), Ryn Hodes (*Lisa*), Morton Hodge, Jerry Albert, Steve Langone, Susan Farrell, Lori Hoffman, Herb James, Peter Harp, Gary Hollrah, Anne Horne Foulkrod, Leonard Reino, Vincent Langone, Sven Widecrantz, Kevin Morrissey

WRIT & D: William Murray   PHOTOG: Dennis Peters   MUSIC: Mark Knox

A.k.a. Hellfire

Minor SF-thriller: Detective of future probes corporation's mysterious deeds

Prime Evil
1988, (USA), Crown Int'l, color 87 mins

D: Roberta Findlay, William Beckwith, Christine Moore

Standard horror-fantasy: Satanic monks sacrifice blood relatives to obtain immortality

The Primeval Test
1914, (USA), Univ, b&w

W: Robert Leonard, Margarita Fischer

Standard melodrama: Trials of prehistoric man

The Primatives
1962, (GB), Border/RFD, b&w, 70 mins.

W: Jan Holden (*Cheta*), Bill Edwards (*Peter*), Rio Fanning (*John*), George Mikell (*Claude*), Terence Fallon (*Sgt. Henry*), Derek Ware (*Philip*), Peter Hughes (*Insp. Wills*)

P: O. Negus-Fancey   D: Alfred Travers   STORY: Alfred Travers & Moris Farhi

Standard crime-thriller: Girl dancer and her partners, don disguises, rob jewelers

Primitive Man, or Wars of the Primal Tribes
1913, (USA), Biograph, b&w, 1 reel

W: Mae Marsh

D: D.W. Griffith

Standard melodrama

Prince of Darkness
1987, (USA), Alive/Univ, color, 101 mins.

W: Donald Pleasence (*The Priest*), Jameson Parker (*Brian*), Victor Wong (*Birack*), Lisa Blount (*Catherine*), Dennis Dun (*Walter*), Susan Blanchard (*Kelly*), Anne Howard (*Susan*), Ann Yen (*Lisa*), Dirk Blocker (*Mullins*), Ken Wright (*Lomax*), Peter Jason (*Dr. Leahy*), Jessie Lawrence Ferguson (*Calder*), Robert Grasmere (*Wyndham*), Thom Bray (*Etchinson*), Joanna Merlin (*The Bag Lady*), Alice Cooper (*The Street Schizo*), Betty Ramey (*The Nun*)

P: Larry Franco   D: John Carpenter   SCR: Martin Quatermass   PHOTOG: Gary B. Kibbe   MUSIC: John Carpenter & Alan Howarth

blurb: "Before man walked the earth...It slept for centuries. It is evil. It is real. It is awakening."

Modest horror-fantasy: Scientists examine ancient cylinder containing Absolute Evil

Prince of Egypt
1998, (USA), DreamWorks, color

VOICES: Val Kilmer (*Moses*), Ralph Fiennes (*Ramses*), Sandra Bullock (*Miriam*), Michelle Pfeiffer (*Tzipporah*), Danny Glover (*Jethro*), Jeff Goldblum (*Aaron*), Helen Mirren (*Pharaoh's Wife*), Patrick Stewart (*Seti*), Martin Short (*Huy*), Steve Martin (*Hotep*)

D: Brenda Chapman, Steve Hickner & Simon Wells   MUSIC: Hans Zimmer   SCORE: Stephen Schwartz   SONGS: *I Will Be There for You, When You Believe, Once in a While & The River Lullaby*

Impressive animated fantasy: Life of Hebrew leader

A Prince of Khyber
1909, (GB), Empire Films/Butcher, b&w, 600 ft. (182.9m)

Standard melodrama: Hindu princess helps colonel and his family flee wicked prince

The Prince of Magicians
see Excelsior!

Prince of Pirates
1953, (USA), Col, color, 80 mins.

W: John Derek, Barbara Rush

Standard adventure-thriller

The Prince of Thieves
1948, (USA), Col, color, 72 mins.

W: Jon Hall, Patricia Morison

Standard adventure-thriller

The Princess and the Goblin
1993, (GB-Hung), color, 85 mins.

VOICES: Sally Ann Marsh, Peter Murray, Claire Bloom

from a story by George MacDonald

Standard fantasy: Princess and miner's son vs. evil goblins

The Princess and the Goblin
1991, (Hung-Wales), color, 82 mins.

VOICES: Claire Bloom, Joss Ackland, Sally Ann Marsh, Peter Murray, Rik Mayall, Victor Spinetti, Roy Kinnear

D: Jozsef Gemes, based on George MacDonald's 1872 novel-length fairytale

Standard animated fantasy (USA release, 1994): Princess and miner's son vs. subterranean goblins

The Princess and the Pea
1979, (GB), Boyd's Co./Kendon/Bordeaux Int'l, color, 10 mins.

W: Judy Bowker (*The Princess*), Roy Kinnear, Charles Hawtrey

P: Don Boyd   D: Keith Goddard, from Hans Christian Andersen's fairytale

Standard short fantasy: Princess' validity questioned

The Princess and the Pearls
1973, (Czech), LCA, color, 14 mins.

Juvenile fantasy short (enacted by animated puppets): Tale of Sinbad the Sailor

The Princess and the Swineherd
1960, (W. Ger), b&w, 82 mins.

from a story by the Brothers Grimm

Minor fantasy: Suitor tries to please materialistic princess

The Princess Bride
1987, (USA), Act III Communications/20th-Fox, color, 98 mins.

W: Cary Elwes (*Westley*), Mandy Patinkin (*Inigo Montoya*), Chris Sarandon (*Prince Humperdinck*), Christopher Guest (*Count Rugen*), Wallace Shawn (*Vizzini*), Andre the Giant (*Fezzik*), Robin Wright (*Buttercup*), Carol Kane (*Valerie*), Peter Cook (*The Clergyman*), Billy Crystal (*Miracle Max*), Peter Falk, Fred Savage, Mel Smith, Willoughby Gray, Malcolm Storry, Margery Mason, Betsy Brantley, Anne Dyson, Paul Badger

D: Rob Reiner   SCR: William Goldman   PHOTOG: Adrian Biddle   MUSIC: Mark Knopfler

Modest comedy-adventure-fantasy: Youth champions kidnapped beauty

Princess Clementina
1911, (GB), Barker, b&w, 1,800 ft. (548.6m)

W: H.B. Irving (*Charles Wogan*), Alice Young (*Princess Clementina*), Dorothea Baird (*Jenny*), Eille Norwood (*James Stuart*), Nigel Playfair (*The Prince of Baden*), Arthur Whitby (*Harry Whittington*), Charles Allan (*Cardinal Origo*), Henry Vibart (*Maj. Richard Gaydon*), Frederick Lloyd (*Capt. John Missen*)

D: Will Barker, from a play by George Pleydell Bancroft & A.E.W. Mason

Standard adventure-thriller: King James' agent saves Dutch princess, marries her as King's proxy

Princess Mononoke
1997, (Jap), color

Standard animated fantasy (an enormous money-maker in Nippon)

The Princess of Happy Chance
1916, (GB), London/Jury, b&w, 4,885 ft. (1489m)

W: Elizabeth Risdon (*Princess Felicia/Lucidora Eden*), Gerald Ames (*Harvey Royle*), Hayford Hobbs (*Michael Berland*), Dallas Cairns (*Prince Jocelyn*), Douglas Munro (*Josiah Buckworthy*), Gwynne Herbert, Edna Maude, Cyril Percival, Janet Ross, Beatrix Templeton

D: Maurice Elvey, from a novel by Tom Gallon

Standard romance: Princess evades forced marriage by changing places with double

A Princess of the Blood
1916, (GB), Clarendon, b&w, 3,855 ft. (1175m)

W: Barbara Conrad, Harry Welchman

D: Wilfred Noy

Standard melodrama

Princess Warrior
1989, (USA), Vista Street, color

W: Sharon Lee Jones (*Ovule*), Dana Fredsti (*Curette*), Mark Pacific (*Bob*), Tony Riccardi (*Johnny*), Isibella Peralta (*Bulemia*), Laurie Warren (*Exzema*), Sydney Coale Phillips (*The First Priestess*), Augie Blunt (*Matt*), Cheryl Janecky (*The Queen Mother*), Lee N. Gerovitz (*Vinnie*), Stephen J. Cassarino (*Vito*), Selga Sanders (*The High Priestess*), Diana Karanikas (*Ricketsia*), Cindy Coatman (*Priestess 2*), Christine Bessiere (*Priestess 3*), Lisa Stucky (*Priestess 4*),

Melisa Sanchez (*Priestess 5*), Darrel H. Johnson (*Ruggio*), Kathryn Peterson (*Betty*), Fritz Lopez (*The Driver*), Richard Winston (*The Older Cop*), Tony Cicchetti (*The Rookie Cop*), Jeff Borden (*Drunk #1*), Sonny Chicago (*Drunk #2*), Herman Golightly (*Drunk #3*), Tim Squignoli (*Drunk #4*), Mark Adams (*Concubine #1*), Don Richie (*Concubine #2*), Michael Girard (*Concubine #3*), R.J. Jones, Heather Kennedy, Janie Liszewski, Colleen Aristides, Kim Hannaman, Mark Greenewalt, Mike Blackwolf
D: Lindsay Norgard SCR: John Riley PHOTOG: Robert Duffin MUSIC: Marc Decker SONGS: *Voo Doo Stew, Put on Your Hi-Heels, I Hear the Back Beat* & *Jawbreaker*
Minor SF-adventure: Royal sisters on far planet vie for power

Prince Valiant
1954, (USA), 20th-Fox, color, 100 mins.
W: Robert Wagner (*Prince Valiant*), Janet Leigh (*Aleta*), Sterling Hayden (*Sir Gawain*), Debra Paget (*Ilene*), James Mason (*Sir Brack*), Brian Aherne (*King Arthur*), Victor McLaglen (*Voltar*), Tom Conway (*Sir Kay*), Donald Crisp (*King Aguar*), Barry Jones (*King Luke*), Mary Philips (*The Queen Mother*), Howard Wendell (*Morgan Todd*), Neville Brand (*The Viking Warrior Chief*), Sammy Ogg (*The Small Page*), Jarma Lewis (*Queen Guinevere*), Ben Wright (*The Seneschal*), Ray Spiker (*Gorlock*), Robert Adler (*Sir Brack's Man at Arms*), Primo Carnera (*Sligon*), Basil Ruysdael (*The Old Viking*), Fortune Gordian (*The Strangler*), Percival Vivian (*The Doctor*), Don Megowan (*Sir Launcelot*), Otto Waldis (*Patch Eye*), Richard Webb (*Sir Galahad*), John Dierkes (*Sir Tristram*), Carleton Young (*The Herald*), John Davidson (*The Patriarch*), Lloyd Ahern Jr. (*Valiant, age 12*), Lou Nova (*The Captain of Guards*), Eugene (Gene) Roth (*The Viking*), Hal Baylor, Mickey Simpson
P: Robert L. Jacks D: Henry Hathaway SCR: Dudley Nichols, from Harold Foster's popular comic strip PHOTOG: Lucien Ballard MUSIC: Franz Waxman
Standard adventure-thriller: Daring youth finds romance and danger in Arthurian times

Prince Valiant
1998, (USA), 20th-Fox, color
from Harold Foster's classic comic strip
Minor adventure-thriller: Youth of ancient Britain vs. invaders

El Principe Encadenado (The Ensorcelled Prince)
1961, (Sp), b&w
W: Antonio Vilar, Javier Escriva, Luis Prendes, Maria Mahor, Luis Morris, Katia Loritz, Javier Loyola
P: Miguel A. Martin D: Luis Lucia SCR: Jose R. Boeta & V. Escriva, from Pedro Calderon de la Barca's *Life is a Song* PHOTOG: Alessandro Ulloa MUSIC: Cristobal Halffter
Standard fantasy-melodrama

Print of Death
1958, (GB), Merton Park/Anglo-Amalgamated, b&w, 26 mins.
W: John Warwick (*Supt. Reynolds*), Tim Turner (*Webber*), Phi Brown (*Kovacs*)
P: Jack Greenwood D: Montgomery Tully STORY: James Eastwood, from a novel by Edgar Lustgarten
Standard short crime-thriller: Detectives nail murderous payroll robbers

The Priory School
1921, (GB), Stoll, b&w, 2,100 ft. (640.1m)
W: Eille Norwood (*Sherlock Holmes*), Hubert Willis (*Dr. John Watson*), Leslie English (*Dr. Huxtable*), Irene Rooke (*The Duchess*), C.H. Croker-King (*The Duke of Holderness*), Tom Ronald (*Reuben Hayes*), Patrick Kay (*Lord Saltire*), Cecil Kerr (*Wilder*), Mme. d'Esterre (*Mrs. Hudson*)
D: Maurice Elvey SCR: Charles Barnett, from the writings of Sir Arthur Conan Doyle
Standard crime-thriller (episode in "Adventures of Sherlock Holmes" series)

Prison (1948)
see The Devil's Wanton

Prison
1988, (USA), Irwin Yablans-Charles Band/Eden Ltd./Empire, color, 102 mins.
W: Lane Smith (*Sharpe*), Viggo Mortensen (*Burke*), Chelsea Field (*Katherine*), Andre DeShields (*Sandor*), Ivan Kane (*Lasagna*), Lincoln Kilpatrick (*Cresus*), Tom "Tiny" Lister Jr. (*Big Sam*) Steven E. Little, Mickey Yablans, Larry Flash Jenkins, Arlen Dean Snyder, Hal Landon Jr.
D: Renny Harlin SCR: C. Courtney Joyner ORIG STORY: Irwin Yablans PHOTOG: Mac Ahlberg MUSIC: Richard Band & Christopher L. Stone
Minor horror-thriller: Haunted penetentiary

Prisoner of Mars
1942, (USA), Kenneth Anger, b&w, 11 mins.
W: Kenneth Anger
WRIT, D, & PHOTOG: Kenneth Anger
Experimental SF-fantasy short (unreleased): Adventure on red planet

The Prisioner of Shark Island
1936, (USA), 20th-Fox, b&w, 95 mins.
W: Warner Baxter, Gloria Stuart, John Carradine, Joyce Kay, Claude Gillingwater, Harry Carey, Paul Fix, Robert Parrish
D: John Ford SCR: Nunnally Johnson & Dudley Nichols PHOTOG: Bert Glennon
Well-made melodrama: Innocent physician sent to prison isle

The Prisoner of the Iron Mask
1962, (It), AIP, color, 80 mins.
W: Michel Lemoine, Wandisa Guida, Andrea Bosic, Jany Clair, Giovanni Materassi
D: Francesco DeFeo SCR: Silvio Amadio, Ruggero Jacobbi & Francesco DeFeo
Standard adventure-thriller: Man in 18th-century Italy refuses to aid assassins, is put in fearsome iron mask

The Prisoner of Zenda
1913, (USA), Para, b&w, 4 reels
W: James K. Hackett
D: Edwin S. Porter, from Anthony Hope's novel
Standard adventure-thriller (first American-made feature): Man impersonates royalty

The Prisoner of Zenda
1915, (GB), London/Jury, b&w, 5,500 ft. (1676.4m)
W: Henry Ainley (*Rudolph Rassendyl*), Jane Gail (*Princess Flavia*), Gerald Ames (*Rupert*), Arthur Holmes-Gore (*Duke Michael*), Charles Rock (*Col. Sapt*), George Bellamy (*Capt. Reichenheim*), Norman Yates (*Fritz von Tarlenheim*), Marie Anita Bozzi (*Antoinette*)
D: George Loane Tucker SCR: William Courtenay Rowden, from a play by Edward Rose, based on Anthony Hope's novel
Standard adventure-thriller: Tourist poses as royal double

The Prisoner of Zenda
1922, (USA), MGM, b&w, 10 reels (10,467 ft./3190.3m)
W: Lewis Stone (*Rudolf Rassendyll/King Rudolf*), Alice Terry (*Princess Flavia*), Robert Edeson (*Col. Sapt*), Stuart Holmes (*Duke {Black} Michael*), Ramon Novarro (*Rupert of Hentzau*), Barbara La Marr (*Antoinette de Mauban*), Malcolm McGregor (*Count von Tarlenheim*), Edward Connelly (*Marshall von Strakencz*), Lois Lee (*Countess Helga*)
P & D: Rex Ingram SCR: Mary O'Hara, from Anthony Hope's novel PHOTOG: John F. Seitz
Standard adventure-thriller: Englishman impersonates Ruritanian king

The Prisoner of Zenda
1937, (USA), UA, b&w, 104 mins.
W: Ronald Colman (*Rudolf*), Madeleine Carroll (*Flavia*), Mary Astor (*Antoinette*), Douglas Fairbanks Jr. (*Rupert*), David Niven (*Fritz*), Raymond Massey (*Black Michael*), Montagu Love (*Detchard*), C. Aubrey Smith, Alex D'Arcy, Byron Foulger
P: David O. Selznick D: John Cromwell SCR: John L. Balderston, from Anthony Hope's novel PHOTOG: James Wong Howe SPCL-FX: Jack Cosgrove MUSIC: Alfred Newman
Classic adventure-thriller: Royal impersonation causes complications

The Prisoner of Zenda
1952, (USA), MGM, color, 100 mins.
W: Stewart Granger (*Rudolf*), Deborah Kerr (*Princess Flavia*), James Mason (*Count Rupert*), Robert Douglas (*Prince Michael*), Louis Calhern (*Col. Zandt*), Lewis Stone (*The Cardinal*), Jane Greer (*Antoinette*), Francis Pierlot (*Josef*), Robert Coote (*Fritz von Tarlenheim*), Peter Brocco (*Johann*), Kathleen Freeman
P: Pandro S. Berman D: Richard Thorpe SCR: John L. Balderston and Noel Langley, from Anthony Hope's novel PHOTOG: Joseph Ruttenberg SPCL-FX: Warren Newcombe MUSIC: Alfred Newman
Colorful adventure-thriller: Englishman drawn into complex plot when he impersonates Ruritanian king

The Prisoner of Zenda
1979, (GB), Walter Mirisch/Univ, color, 108 mins.
W: Peter Sellers (*Rudolph/Syd*), Lynne Frederick (*Princess Flavia*), Lionel Jeffries (*Gen. Sapt*), Elke Sommer (*The Countess*), Gregory Sierra (*The Count*), Jeremy Kemp (*Duke Michael*), Catherine Schell (*Antoinette*), Simon Williams (*Fritz*), Stuart Wilson (*Rupert of Hentzau*), John Laurie (*The Archbishop*), Norman Rossington (*Bruno*), Michael Balfour (*Luger*), Graham Stark (*Erik*), Ian Abercrombie (*Johann*), Arthur Howard (*The Deacon*), Michael Segal (*The Conductor*), Eric Cord, Joe Dunne, Dick Geary, Mickey Gilbert, Jaysen Hayes, Orwin Harvey, Larry Holt, John Hudkins, John Moio, Pete Kellet, Victor Paul, Gil Perkins, George Robotham, Joe Yrigoyen
D: Richard Quine SCR: Dick Clement & Ian La Frenais, from Anthony Hope's novel PHOTOG: Arthur Ibbetson SPCL-FX: Albert Whitlock MUSIC: Henry Mancini
Standard adventure-thriller spoof: Man impersonates king

Prisoner of Zenda, Inc.
1996, (USA), SHO-TV, color, 100 mins.
W: Jonathan Jackson, William Shatner, Jay Brazeau (*Prof. Wooley*)
inspired by Anthony Hope's novel *The Prisoner of Zenda*
Made-for-Cable, standard thriller: 14-year-old executive kidnapped by wicked uncle

Prisoners of the Casbah
1953, (USA), Col, color, 78 mins.
W: Gloria Grahame (*Princess Nadja*), Cesar Romero (*Firouz*), Turhan Bey (*Ahmed*), Nestor Paiva (*Marouf*), Lucille Barkley (*Soura*), Philip Van Zandt (*Selim*), Wade Crosby (*Yagoub*), Gloria Saunders (*Zeida*), Eddy Fields (*Abdullah*), Nelson Leigh (*The Emir*), Ray Singer (*Yussef*), John Mansfield (*Mokar*), John Marshall (*Ayub*), Paul Newlan, Frank Richards, John Parrish, Willetta Smith, Mimi Borrel
P: Sam Katzman D: Richard Bare SCR: DeVallon Scott STORY: William

Raynor
Minor adventure-thriller: Intrigue in Arab court

Prisoners of the Lost Universe
1983, (GB), Marcel-Robertson/United Media/Samuel Goldwyn, cable, color, 92 mins.
W: Richard Hatch (*Dan Roebuck*), Kay Lenz (*Carrie Madison*), John Saxon (*Kleel*), Peter O'Farrell (*Malachi*), Philip Van Der Byl (*The Manbeast*), Ray Charleson (*The Greenman*), Kenneth Hendel (*Dr. Hartmann*), Larry Taylor (*Vosk*), Dawn Abraham (*Shareen*), Ron Smerczak (*The Head Trader*), Danie Voges (*Giant Nabu*), Charles Comyn (*Treet*), Ian Steadman (*The 1st Prisoner*), Bill Flynn (*The 2nd Prisoner*), Myles Robertson (*The Waterbeast*)
D: Terry Marcel   ORIG. STORY & SCR: Terry Marcel & Harry Robertson   PHOTOG: Derek Browne   SPCL-FX: Ray Hanson   MUSIC: Harry Robinson
Made-for-Cable, minor SF-adventure: Three people transported to parallel world

Prison Girls
1973, (USA), AIP, color, 3D
W: Robin Whitting, Maria Arnold, Angie Monet, Ushi Diagart, Lisa Ashbury, Tracy Handfuss, Jamie McKenna, Claire Bow, Ilona Lakes, Lois Darst, Carol Peters
D: Thomas DeBurton   SCR: Burton Gershfeld
Minor exploitation thriller: Saga of sleazy slammer sluts

Prison Heat
1996, (USA), color, 90 mins.
W: Rebecca Chambers, Lori Jo Hendrix, Kena Land
Minor exploitation thriller: Four women wrongfully jailed in Turkey

Prison Planet
1992, (USA), color, 90 mins.
W: James Phillips, Jack Willcox, Michael Foley, Deborah Thompson-Carlin
D & SCR: Armand Gazarian
Minor SF-adventure: Future warriors oppose usurper

Privarzaniat Balon (The Attached Balloon)
1967, (Bulgar), color
D: Binka Zheljazkova
Standard allegorical fantasy: Nature of spiritual freedom explored

Private Eyes
1953, (USA), AA, b&w, 64 mins.
W: Leo Gorcey, Huntz Hall, Lee Van Cleef, Myron Healey, Emil Sitka
P: Ben Schwalb   D: Edward Bernds   SCR: Edward Bernds & Elwood Ullman
Minor SF-comedy: After blow to head, Bowery Boy can read minds

The Private Eyes
1980, (USA), New World, color, 92 mins.
W: Tim Conway (*Dr. Tart*), Don Knotts (*Insp. Winship*), Trisha Noble (*Phyllis*), Bernard Fox (*Justin*), Grace Zabriskie (*Nanny*), John Fujioka (*Mr. Uwatsum*), Stan Ross (*Tibet*), Irwin Keyes (*Jock*), Suzy Mandel (*Hilda*), Fred Stuthman (*Lord Morley*), Mary Nell Santacroce (*Lady Morley*), Robert V. Barron (*The Gas Station Attendant*), Patrick Cranshaw (*Roy*)
D: Lang Elliott   SCR: Tim Conway & John Myhers   PHOTOG: Jacques Haitkin   MUSIC: Peter Matz
Standard comedy-thriller: Bumblers solve crime

Private Hell 36
1954, (USA), Filmakers, b&w, 81 mins.
W: Ida Lupino, Howard Duff, Steve Cochran, Dean Jagger, Dorothy Malone
D: Don Siegel   CO-SCR: Ida Lupino   PHOTOG: Burnett Guffey   MUSIC: Leith Stevens
Compact thriller: Two cops corrupted by stolen loot

The Private Life of Don Juan
1934, (GB), London/UA, b&w, 90 mins.
W: Douglas Fairbanks Sr. (*Don Juan*), Merle Oberon (*Antonia*), Benita Hume (*Dolores*), Binnie Barnes (*Rosita*), Joan Gardner (*Carmen*), Melville Cooper (*Leporello*), Athene Seyler (*Theresa*), Owen Nares (*The Actor*), Patricia Hilliard (*The Girl in the Castle*), Gina Malo (*Pepita*), Heather Thatcher (*The Actress*), Claud Allister (*The Duke*), Barry Mackay (*Roderigo*), Lawrence Grossmith (*The Guardian*), Edmund Breon (*The Author*), Clifford Heatherley (*Pedro*), Gibson Gowland (*Don Ascanio*), Diana Napier (*The Would-be Wife*), Hay Petrie (*The Manager*), Natalie Paley (*The Wife*), Elsa Lanchester
P & D: Alexander Korda   SCR: Lajos Biro & Frederick Lonsdale, from a play by Henri Bataille   PHOTOG: Georges Perinal   MUSIC: Mischa Spoliansky
Elaborate comedy-adventure: Aging lover fakes death, tries to stage comeback

The Private Life of Helen of Troy
1927, (USA), First Nat'l, b&w, 8 reels (7,694 ft./2345.1m)
W: Maria Corda (*Helen*), Lewis Stone (*Menelaus*), Ricardo Cortez (*Paris*), George Fawcett (*Eteoneus*), Alice White (*Adraste*), Gordon (Bill) Elliott (*Telemachus*), Tom O'Brien (*Ulysses*), Bert Sprotte (*Achilles*), Mario Carillo (*Ajax*), Constantine Romanoff (*Aeneas*), Charles Puffy (*Malapokitoratoreadetos*), George Kotsonaros (*Hector*), Emilio Borgato (*Sarpedon*), Virginia Thomas (*Hera*), Alice Adair (*Aphrodite*), Helen Fairweather (*Athena*), Gus Partos
P, ADAPT, & SCR: Carey Wilson, from John Erskine's play   D: Alexander Korda   PHOTOG: Lee Garmes & Sidney Hickox
A.k.a. Helen of Troy

Standard romance-farce: Spartan queen abducted

The Private Life of Sherlock Holmes
1970, (GB), Mirisch/UA, color, 125 mins.
W: Robert Stephens (*Sherlock Holmes*), Colin Blakely (*Dr. John Watson*), Christopher Lee (*Mycroft Holmes*), Genevieve Page (*Gabrielle Valladon*), Clive Revill (*Rogozhin*), Tamara Toumanova (*Petrova*), Peter Madden (*Von Tirpitz*), Stanley Holloway (*The 1st Gravedigger*), Catherine Lacey (*The Old Lady*), Michael Balfour (*The Cabby*), George Benson (*Insp. Lestrade*), Irene Handl (*Mrs. Hudson*), Robert Cawdron (*The Hotel Manager*), Mollie Maureen (*Queen Victoria*), Michael Elwyn (*Cassidy*), Frank Thornton (*The Porter*), James Copeland (*The Guide*), Alex McCrindle (*The Baggageman*), Kenneth Benda (*The Minister*), Graham Armitage (*Wiggins*), Ina De La Haye (*Petrova's Maid*), Eric Francis (*The 2nd Gravedigger*), Kynaston Reeves (*The Old Man*), Phillip Ross (*McKellar*), Anne Blake (*The Madam*), Daphne Riggs (*The Lady-in-Waiting*), John Gatrell (*The Equerry*), Philip Anthony (*The Lt. Commander*), Annette Kerr (*The Secretary*), John Garrie, Wendy Lingham, Godfrey James, Marilyn Head, Anna Matisse, Penny Brahms, Sheena Hunter, Tina Spooner, Judy Spooner
P & D: Billy Wilder   SCR: Billy Wilder & I.A.L. Diamond   PHOTOG: Christopher Challis   MUSIC: Miklos Rozsa
Entertaining adventure-comedy: Famed detective tackles case involving espionage, midgets, shipments of canaries and the Loch Ness Monster

The Private Lives of Adam and Eve
1960, (USA), Famous Players-Fryman Entertainment/Univ, color & b&w, 87 mins.
W: Mickey Rooney (*Satan*), Marty Milner (*Adam*), Mamie Van Doren (*Eve*), Fay Spain (*Lilith*), Tuesday Weld (*The Runaway Teen*), Paul Anka (*Pinkie Parker*), Mel Torme (*The Traveling Salesman*), Cecil Kellaway (*Doc*), Ziva Rodann, Sharon Wiley, Phillipa Fallon, June Wilkinson, Theona Bryant, Mieko Kato, Barbara Walden, Toni Cov-ington, Nancy Root, Stella Garcia, Donna Lynne, Andrea Smith, Buni Bacon
P: Red Doff   D: Albert Zugsmith & Mickey Rooney   SCR: Robert Hill, from a story by George Kennett   PHOTOG: Philip H. Lathrop   MUSIC: Van Alexander
Standard comedy-fantasy: Man and woman dream they are Adam and Eve

Private Lives of Adam and Eve: MAMIE VAN DOREN AND MICKEY ROONEY

Private Obsession
1995, (USA), color, 105 mins.
W: Shannon Whirry
Minor thriller: Feminist supermodel held captive by sexist psycho

Private Parts
1972, (USA), MGM, color, 87 mins.
W: Ayn Ruymen, Stanley Livingston, John Venantonio, Lucille Benson
P: Gene Corman   D: Paul Bartel   SCR: Philip Kearney & Les Rendelstein
Unusual thriller (mixture of Peeping Tom and Homicidal): Runaway girl meets bizarre types in seedy L.A. hotel

Private Property
1960, (USA), Citation, b&w, 79 mins.
W: Kate Manx, Corey Allen, Warren Oates
P, D & SCR: Leslie Stevens   PHOTOG: Ted McCord
Unusual thriller (made on $60,000 budget): Two beatnik drifters stalk woman

Privilege
1966, (GB), Memorial/Worldfilm/Univ, color, 103 mins.
W: Paul Jones (*Steve Shorter*), Jean Shrimpton (*Vanessa Ritchie*), Mark London (*Alvin Kirsch*), Max Bacon (*Julie Jordan*), Jeremy Child (*Martin Crossley*), James Cossins (*Tatham*), William Job (*Andrew Butler*), Frederick Danner

Private Property: KATE MANX

(Hooper), Victor Henry (*Freddie K*), Arthur Pentelow (*Stanley*)
<u>P:</u> John Heyman   <u>D:</u> Peter Watkins   <u>SCR:</u> Norman Bogner, from Johnny
Speight's story   <u>PHOTOG:</u> Peter Suschitzky   <u>MUSIC:</u> Mike Leander
<u>SONG:</u> *Free Me*
Standard thriller: Church and gov't use pop singer to control nation's youth

A Prize of Arms
1962, (GB), Inter-State/Bry, b&w, 105 mins.
<u>W:</u> Stanley Baker (*Turpin*), Helmut Schmidt (*Swavek*), Patrick Magee (*RSM
Hicks*), Tom Bell (*Fenner*), John Phillips (*Col. Fowler*), John Westbrook
(*Capt. Stafford*), Frank Gatliff (*Maj. Palmer*), Kenneth Mackintosh (*Capt.
Nicholson*), Jack May (*MO*), Michael Ripper (*Cpl. Freeman*), John Rees (*Sgt.
Jones*)
<u>P:</u> George Maynard   <u>D:</u> Cliff Owen   <u>SCR:</u> Paul Ryder   <u>STORY:</u> Nicolas Roeg
& Kevin Kavanagh
Standard crime-thriller: Crooks pose as soldiers, seek fortune on army base

A Prize of Gold
1955, (GB), Warwick/Col, color, 100 mins.
<u>W:</u> Richard Widmark (*Sgt. Joe Lawrence*), Mai Zetterling (*Maria*), Nigel Patrick
(*Brian Hammell*), George Cole (*Sgt. Roger Morris*), Donald Wolfit (*Alfie
Scratton*), Andrew Ray (*Conrad*), Karel Stepanek (*Dr. Zachman*), Joseph
Tomelty (*Uncle Dan*), Robert Ayres (*Tex*), Eric Pohlmann (*Hans Fischer*),
Olive Sloane (*Mavis*)
<u>D:</u> Mark Robson   <u>SCR:</u> Robert Buckner & John Paxton, from a novel by Max
Catto   <u>PHOTOG:</u> Ted Moore
reissued 1961
Standard crime-thriller: Serviceman steals cargo of gold

The Prize of Peril
1983, (Fr-Yugo), color, 98 mins.
<u>W:</u> Gerard Lanvin, Michel Piccoli, Marie-France Pisier, Jean Rougerie, Bruno
Cremer, Andrea Ferreol
<u>D:</u> Yves Boisset
Standard SF-thriller: TV game show pits individuals against hunters of humans

Probe
1972, (USA), WB-TV, color, 97 mins.
<u>W:</u> Hugh O'Brian (*Hugh Lockwood*), Sir John Gielgud (*Harold L. Streeter*), Burgess
Meredith (*Cameron*), Angel Tompkins (*Gloria Harding*), Kent Smith (*Dr.
Laurent*), Elke Sommer (*Fraulein Ullman*), Lilia Skala (*Frau Ullman*), Ben
Wright, Alfred Ryder, Jaclyn Smith
<u>WRIT & P:</u> Leslie Stevens   <u>D:</u> Russell Mayberry   <u>PHOTOG:</u> John M. Stephens
<u>MUSIC:</u> Dominic Frontiere
re-televised as **Search**
*TVM, standard SF-thriller (feature-pilot for teleseries "Search"): Electronically-modified
sleuth seeks missing gems*

Proces de Jeanne D'Arc (Trial of Joan of Arc)
1962, (Fr), Pathe Contemp, b&w, 65 mins.
<u>W:</u> Florence Carrez (*Joan*), Jean-Claude Fourneau (*Bishop Cauchon*), Roger Honorat
(*Interrogator Beaupere*), Marc Jacquier (*Inquisitor LeMaitre*), Philippe Martin
(*Joan's Confessor*), Jean Gillibert (*Jean de Chatillon*), Michel Herubel (*Brother
Isambart*)
<u>D & SCR:</u> Robert Bresson, from orig. court records   <u>PHOTOG:</u> Leonce-Henri
Burel
Engrossing historical melodrama: Maid of Orleans tried for witchcraft

The Prodigal's Return
1913, (GB), Hepworth, b&w, 875 ft. (266.7m)
<u>W:</u> Alec Worcester (*Arthur Blanchard*)
<u>D:</u> Frank Wilson
Standard crime-thriller: Banker disowns forger son

The Professionals
1960, (GB), Independent Artists/Anglo-Amalgamated, b&w, 61 mins.
<u>W:</u> William Lucas (*Philip Bowman*), Colette Wilde (*Ruth*), Andrew Faulds (*Insp.
Rankin*), Stratford Johns (*Lawson*), Vilma Ann Leslie (*Mabel*), Edward Cast
(*Clayton*), Charles Vince (*Holden*)
<u>P:</u> Norman Priggen   <u>D:</u> Don Sharp   <u>STORY:</u> Peter Barnes
Standard crime-thriller: Gang utilizes sewers, breaks into bank

Profession: Reporter
see **The Passenger**

Professor Zazul
1962, (Pol), SE-MA-FOR-Lodz, b&w
<u>W:</u> Stanislaw Milski, Piotr Kurowski
<u>WRIT, D, & PHOTOG:</u> Marek Nowicki & Jerzy Stawicki, from Stanislaw Lem's
novel   <u>MUSIC:</u> Edward Pallasz
Fr retitle, **The Mystery of Professor Zazul**
Standard thriller

Professor G. and the Bikini Machine
see **Dr. Goldfoot and the Bikini Machine**

Professor Garland the Conjurer
1897, (GB), Prestwich Mfg. Co., b&w, 50 ft. (15.2m)
<u>W:</u> Prof. Garland
Standard fantasy short: Conjurer produces articles from hat

Professor Hoskin's Patent Hustler
1913, (GB), Martin/Thanhouser, b&w, 434 ft. (132.3m)
<u>D:</u> Dave Aylott
Standard fantasy short: Prof's invention makes things accelerate

Professor Piecan's Discovery
1910, (GB), Cricks & Martin, b&w, 580 ft. (176.8m)
<u>D:</u> A.E. Coleby
Standard fantasy short: Boy squirts magic fluid onto weaklings, making them strong

Professor Popper's Problem's
1975, (GB), color, 70 mins., from a six-chapter serial.
<u>W:</u> Charlie Drake, Milo O
Minor fantasy: Eccentric's potion shrinks humans

Professor Potter's Magic Potions
1983, (GB), color
<u>W:</u> Richard Wilson, John Warner, Stephen Brassett
Standard juvenile fantasy: Eccentric teacher's curious concoctions

Prof. Puddenhead's Patents—The Aerocab and Vacuum Provider
1909, (GB), Urban, b&w, 385 ft. (117.3m)
<u>D:</u> Walter R. Booth
Standard fantasy short: Children steal prof's plane, have adventures

Professor Puddenhead's Patents—The Electric Enlarger
1909, (GB), Urban, b&w, 330 ft. (100.6m)
<u>D:</u> Walter R. Booth
Standard fantasy short: Servant steals prof's invention—enlarges dog, caterpillar, and himself

The Professor's Antigravitational Fluid
1908, (GB), Hepworth, b&w, 350 ft. (106.7m)
<u>W:</u> Bertie Potter (*The Boy*)
<u>D:</u> Lewin Fitzhamon
Standard fantasy short: Youth steals prof's fluid, levitates objects

The Professor's Dream
1909, (GB), Urban, b&w, 360 ft. (109.7m)
<u>D:</u> Walter R. Booth
Standard fantasy short: Prof dreams he rejuvenates old friends

The Professor's Great Discovery
1908, (GB), Williamson, b&w, 350 ft. (106.7m)
<u>D:</u> James Williamson
Standard fantasy short: Prof's patent snuff makes people dance

The Professor's Strength Tablets
1909, (GB), Clarendon, b&w, 450 ft. (137.2m)
<u>D:</u> Percy Stow
Standard fantasy short: Prof devises explosive pills

The Professor's Twirly-Whirly Cigarettes
1909, (GB), B&C/Cosmo, b&w, 425 ft. (129.5m)
<u>D:</u> H.O. Martinek
Standard fantasy short: Prof mixes liver powder with tobacco, causes smokers to spin

Profile

1954, (GB), major/Monarch, b&w, 65 mins.
W: John Bentley (*Peter Armstrong*), Kathleen Byron (*Margot Holland*), Thea Gregory (*Susan Holland*), Stuart Lindsell (*Aubrey Holland*), Garard Green (*Charlie Pearson*), Ivan Craig (*Jerry*), Lloyd Lamble (*Michael*), Arnold Bell (*Insp. Crawford*)
P: John Temple-Smith & Francis Edge   **D:** Francis Searle   **STORY:** John & Maurice Temple-Smith
Standard crime-thriller: Editor accused of killing publisher

The Profile of Terror

see The Sadist

The Profound Desire of the Gods

1968, (Jap), East-West Classics, color, 175 mins.
W: Rentaro Mikuni (*Nekichi*), Choichiro Kawarazaki (*Kametaro*), Hideko Okiyama
D: Shohei Imamura   **SCR:** Shohei Imamura & Keiji Hasabe
USA release, 1988
Erotic psychodrama: Tokyo engineer finds lust and superstition on primitive isle

Profundo Rosso (Deep Red)

1976, (It), Salvatore Argento/Rizzoli, color, 101 mins.
W: David Hemmings (*Marcus Daly*), Gabriele Lavia (*Carlo*), Daria Nicolodi (*Gianna Brezzi*), Macha Meril (*Helga Ullman*), Glauco Mauri (*Giordani*), Eros Pagni (*Calcabrini*), Giuliana Calandra (*Amanda Righetti*), Piero Mazzinghi (*Bardi*), Clara Calamai ("*Martha*")
D: Dario Argento   **SCR:** Dario Argento & Bernardino Zapponi   **PHOTOG:** Luigi Kuveiller   **SPCL-FX:** Germano Natali   **MUSIC:** Giorgio Gaslini & The Goblins
A.k.a. Hatchet Murders
Standard thriller: Maniac at large in Rome

Programmed to Kill

1987, (USA), Trans World, color, 91 mins.
W: Robert Ginty, Sandahl Bergman, Louise Caire Clark, James Booth, Paul Walker, Arnon Tzadock
D: Allan Holzman   **SCR:** Robert Short   **PHOTOG:** Nitcho Lion Nissim   **MUSIC:** Immel/Huxley
A.k.a. Retaliator
Standard SF-thriller: Female terrorist revived as cyborg killing machine

Les Proies du Vampire

see El Vampiro

The Project

1981, (GB), Giftone/Point Blank/ITC, color, 42 mins.
W: Peter Howell, Raymond Young, David Daker, Sean Gascoine, Richard Evans, Richard Hunter
P: Anya Slatter   **D:** Chris Slatter
Standard short crime-thriller: Schoolboys plan bank robbery

Project A-KO

1986, (Jap), color, 86 mins.
Unusual animated SF-fantasy: Supernatural teens ecounter space aliens

Project: Alf

1996, (USA), ABC-TV, color, 95 mins.
W: Martin Sheen (*The Colonel*), William O'Leary (*Mullican*), Jensen Daggett (*Hill*), Miguel Ferrer (*Moyers*), Scott Michael Campbell (*Lt. Reese*), Ray Walston (*The Motel Manager*), John Schuck
D: Dick Lowry   **TELEPLAY:** Tom Patchett & Paul Fusco
TVM, standard SF-comedy (based on 1986-1990 teleseries): Scientists aid furry, smart-mouthed space alien

Project: Alien

1989, (USA), color, 92 mins.
W: Michael Nouri, Darlanne Fluegel, Maxwell Caulfield, Charles Durning
D: Frank Shields   **SCR:** Anthony Able
Standard SF-thriller (filmed in Yugoslavia): Biological weapons tested

The Projected Man

1966, (GB), Compton-Camero/Univ, color, 76 mins.
W: Bryant Halliday (*Prof. Steiner*), Mary Peach (*Dr. Pat Hill*), Norman Wooland (*Dr. Blanchard*), Derek Farr (*Insp. Davis*), Ronald Alden (*Christopher Mitchell*), Derrick de Marney (*Latham*), Tracey Crisp (*Sheila Anderson*), Gerard Heinz (*Prof. Lembach*), Sam Kydd (*Harry*)
P: John Croydon & Maurice Foster   **D:** Ian Curteis   **SCR:** John C. Cooper & Peter Bryan
Standard SF-thriller: Scientist projects body via electronic beam

Project: Genesis

1993, (USA), color, 79 mins.
W: David Ferry, Olga Prokhorova
D & SCR: Philip Jackson   **MUSIC:** Andy McNeill
Standard SF-thriller: Earthman and space-alien woman are shipwrecked on desolate planet

The Projectionist

1970, (USA), Maglan/Maron, color, 88 mins.
W: Chuck McCann (*The Projectionist/Captain Flash*), Rodney Dangerfield (*Renaldi/The Bat*), Ina Balin (*The Girl*), Jara Kohout (*Candy Man/Scientist*), Harry Hurwitz (*The Friendly Usher*), Robert Staats (*The TV Pitchman*), Robert King (*The Premiere Announcer*), David Holiday (*Fat Man/Henchman*), Clara Rosenthal (*The Crazy Lady*), Stephen Phillips (*The Minister*), Jacqueline Glenn (*The Nude on Bearskin*), Morocco (*The Belly Dancer*), Mike Gentry, Lucky Kargo, Sam Stewart, Robert Lee, Alex Stevens
WRIT, P & D: Harvey Hurwitz   **PHOTOG:** Victor Petrashevic   **MUSIC:** Igo Kantor & Erma E. Levin
Standard fantasy: Daydreams of bored projectionist

Project: Metalbeast

1994, (USA), color, 92 mins.
W: Kim Delaney
Standard SF-horror: Werewolf given metal skin, becomes almost indestructible

Project: Metalbeast, DNA Overload

1995, (USA), color, 90 mins.
W: Kim Delaney, Barry Bostwick
D: Alessandro DeGaetano   **SCR:** Timothy E. Sabo   **MUSIC:** Conrad Pope
Standard SF-horror: Gov't scientist accidentally revives werewolf

Project Moonbase

1953, (USA), Lippert, b&w, 63 mins.
W: Donna Martell, Hayden Rorke, Ross Ford, James Craven, Larry Johns, Herb Jacobs, Barbara Morrison, John Hedloe, Ernestine Barrier, Peter Adams, Robert Karnes, Charles Keane, John Straub, John Tomecko
P: Jack Seaman   **D:** Richard Talmadge   **SCR:** Robert A. Heinlein & Jack Seaman   **SPCL-FX:** Jacques Fresco   **MUSIC:** Herschel Burke Gilbert
Minor space-opera (culled from episodes of unsold teleseries): Saboteur abooard spaceship headed for moon

Project M-7

see The Net

Project: Nightmare

1985, (USA), color, 75 mins.
W: Elly Koslo, Lance Dickson
D: Donald M. Jones
Standard horror-thriller: Nightmares become reality

Project: Shadowchaser

1992, (USA), color, 95 mins.
W: Martin Kove, Meg Foster, Frank Zagarino, Paul Koslo, Joss Ackland
D: John Eyres
Standard SF-thriller: Android holds hospital hostage

Project Shadowchaser III

1995, (USA), color, 99 mins.
W: Sam Bottoms, Christopher Atkins, Frank Zagarino, Christopher Neame, Musetta Vander
D: John Eyres   **SCR:** Nick Davis   **MUSIC:** Steve Edwards
A.k.a. Project Shadowchaser 3000
Minor SF-thriller: Astronauts meet shape-shifting android

Project Vampire

1993, (USA), color, 90 mins.
W: Brian Knudson, Mary-Louise Gemmill, Christopher Cho, Myron Natwick
D: Peter Flynn
Standard horror-fantasy: Vampire perfects serum to turn humans into Undead

Project X

1949, (USA), Film Classics, b&w, 60 mins.
W: Keith Andes, Rita Colton, Jack lord (film debut)
Standard thriller

Project X

1968, (USA), Hanna-Barbera, Para, color, 97 mins.
W: Christopher George, Greta Baldwin, Henry Jones, Monte Markham, Harold Gould, Phillip E. Pine, Robert Cleaves, Lee Delano, Keye Luke, Charles Irving, Sheila Bartold, Ed Prentiss, Ivan Bonar, Patrick Wright
P & D: William Castle   **SCR:** Edmund Morris   **PHOTOG:** Harold E. Stine   **SPCL-FX:** Paul Lerpae   **MUSIC:** Van Cleave
Complex SF-melodrama: Scientists make man think he is living several decades in past

Project X

1987, (USA), 20th-Fox, color, 107 mins.
W: Matthew Broderick (*Jimmy*), Helen Hunt (*Teri*), Johnny Ray McGhee (*Robertson*), Bill Sadler (*Dr. Carroll*), Robin Gammell (*Col. Niles*), Jonathan Stark (*Sgt. Krieger*), Jean Smart (*Dr. Criswell*), Stephen Lang (*Watts*), Chuck Bennett (*Gen. Claybourne*), Daniel Roebuck (*Hadfield*), Mark Harden (*Airman Lewis*), Duncan Wilmore (*Maj. Duncan*), Dick Miller, Marvin J. McIntyre, Swede Johnson, Michael Eric Kramer, Harry E. Northup, Reed R. McCants, Ward Costello, Lance August, Jackson Sleet, Stan Foster, Gil Mandelik, Shelly Desai, Michael Milgrom, Catherine Paolone, John Chilton, David Raynr, Lynn Eastman, Julian Sylvester, Ken Lerner, Kim Robillard, David Stenstrom, Randal Patrick, Richard Cummings Jr., Sonny Davis, Bob Minor, Raymond Elmendorf, Robert Covarrubias, Dino Shorte, Travis Swords, William Snider, Philip A. Roberson, Michael McGrady, Mady

Kaplan, Lance Nichols, Tee Rodgers, Jackie Kinner, Chevis Cooper, Kenneth Sagoes, Louis A. Perez, Sam Laws
<u>D</u>: Jonathan Kaplan   <u>SCR</u>: Stanley Weiser   <u>STORY</u>: Stanley Weiser & Lawrence Lasker   <u>PHOTOG</u>: Dean Cundey   <u>MUSIC</u>: James Horner
Modest SF-adventure: Air Force experiments on chimps

The Prolific Magical Egg
see L'Oeuf du Sorcier

The Promise
1913, (GB), Hepworth, b&w, 1,450 ft. (442m)
<u>W</u>: Alec Worcester (*Jack*), Chrissie White (*Ivy Morton*), Harry Royston (*Tom Parker*)
<u>D</u>: Warwick Buckland
Standard crime-thriller: Vicar's son saves squire from burglars

The Promise of Mr. Moto
see Thank You, Mr. Moto

Prom Night
1980, (Can), Simcon/Avco Embassy, color, 91 mins.
<u>W</u>: Jamie Lee Curtis (*Kim Hammond*), Leslie Nielsen (*Mr. Hammond*), Casey Stevens (*Nick*), Antoinette Bower (*Mrs. Hammond*), Eddie Benton (*Wendy*), Michael Tough (*Alex*), Robert Silverman (*Sykes*), Pita Oliver (*Vicki*), George Touliatos (*McBride*), David Mucci (*Lou*), Marybeth Rubens (*Kelly*), Melanie Morse MacQuarrie (*Henri-Anne*), Sheldon Rybowski (*Slick*), David Bolt (*Weller*), David Gardner (*Dr. Fairchild*), Jeff Wincott (*Drew*), Joy Thompson (*Jude*), Rob Garrison (*Sayer*), Beth Amos (*The Housekeeper*), Sonia Zimmer (*Melanie*), Pam Henry (*The Car Hop*), Sylvia Martin (*Mrs. Cunningham*), Liz Stalker-Mason (*Adele*), Ardon Bess (*The Teacher*), Lee Wildgen (*The Gang Member*), Joyce Kite (*Young Kelly*), Brock Simpson (*Young Nick*), Leslie Scott (*Young Wendy*), Tammy Bourne (*Young Robin*), Dean Bosacki (*Young Alex*), Debbie Greenfield (*Young Kim*), Karen Forbes (*Young Jude*)
<u>D</u>: Paul Lynch   <u>SCR</u>: William Gray   <u>STORY</u>: Robert Guza Jr.   <u>PHOTOG</u>: Robert New   <u>SPCL-FX</u>: Al Cotter   <u>MUSIC</u>: Carl Zittrer & Paul Zaza   <u>SONGS</u>: *Fade to Black & Love Me Till I Die*
Above-average horror-thriller: Masked murderer stalks high-school grads

Prom Night II
see The Haunting of Hamilton High

Prom Night III
1989, (Can), color, 97 mins.
<u>W</u>: Courtney Taylor (*Mary Lou*), Tim Conlon (*Alex*)
Minor horror-fantasy: Female ghost bedevils teens

Prom Night IV: Deliver Us from Evil
1991, (Can), color, 95 mins.
<u>W</u>: Nikki De Boer, Alden Kane, Joy Tanner (*Laura*), Alle Ghadban Ken McGregor, Brock Simpson, James Carver, Phil Morrison
<u>D</u>: Clay Borris
Minor thriller: Homicidal monk terrorizes teens

Prophecy
1979, (USA), John Frankenheimer-Robert L. Rosen/Para, color, 102 mins.
<u>W</u>: Robert Foxworth (*Rob Vern*), Talia Shire (*Maggie Vern*), Armand Assante (*John Hawks*), Richard Dysart (*Bethel Isley*), Victoria Racimo (*Ramona*), Evans Evans (*The Cellist*), George Clutesi (*M'Rai*), Burke Byrnes (*Father*), Mia Bendixsen (*The Girl*), Johnny Timko (*The Boy*), Everett L. Creach (*Kelso*), Charles H. Gray (*The Sheriff*), Livingston Holms, James H. Burk, Graham Jarvis, Bob Terhune, Lon Katzman, Mel Waters, Steve Shemayme, John A. Shemayme, Jaye Durkus, Roosevelt Smith, Renato Moore, Eric Mansker
<u>P</u>: Robert L. Rosen   <u>D</u>: John Frankenheimer   <u>SCR</u>: David Seltzer   <u>PHOTOG</u>: Harry Stradling Jr.   <u>SPCL-FX</u>: Robert Dawson   <u>MUSIC</u>: Leonard Rosenman
Minor horror-thriller: Pollution-engendered mutations in Maine woods

The Prophecy
1995, (USA), Neo/Dimension, color, 102 mins.
<u>W</u>: Christopher Walken (*Gabriel*), Elias Koteas (*Thomas*), Eric Stoltz (*Simon*), Virginia Madsen, J.C. Quinn, Amanda Plummer, Viggo Mortensen, Adam Goldberg, Steve Hytner, Moriah Shining, Dove Snyder
<u>P</u>: Joel Soisson   <u>WRIT & D</u>: Gregory Widen   <u>PHOTOG</u>: Bruce Douglas Johnson & Richard Clabaugh   <u>MUSIC</u>: David C. Williams   <u>SONG</u>: *Breakin' Down*
Standard horror-fantasy: Angels war on Earth

The Prophecy II
1997, (USA), Dimension, color
<u>W</u>: Jennifer Beals, Christopher Walken, Russell Wong
Made-for-Video, minor horror-fantasy

Prophet
1996, (USA), TriStar, color
based on an Image Comic Books character
Standard SF-thriller: Adventures of superhero

La Prophetesse de Thebes (The Theban Prophetess)
1908, (Fr), Star, b&w, 139m (456 ft./7.7 mins.)
<u>D</u>: Georges Melies
Standard melodrama

The Prophetess of Thebes
see La Prophetesse de Thebes

El Proscesco de las Brujas
see Night of the Blood Monster

Prosecution of the Witches
see Night of the Blood Monster

Prospero's Books
1991, (GB-Dutch), Miramax, color, 129 mins.
<u>W</u>: Sir John Gielgud (*Prospero*), Michael Clark (*Caliban*), Michel Blanc (*Alonso*), Erland Josephson (*Gonzalo*), Isabelle Pasco (*Miranda*), Tom Bell (*Antonio*), Kenneth Cranham (*Sebastian*), Mark Rylance (*Ferdinand*), Gerard Thoolen (*Adrian*)
<u>D & SCR</u>: Peter Greenaway, from Shakespeare's play *The Tempest*   <u>PHOTOG</u>: Sacha Vierny   <u>MUSIC</u>: Michael Nyman
Classic fantasy: Magician summons spirits

Proteus
1995, (USA), color
<u>W</u>: Craig Fairbrass, Toni Barry
Standard SF-horror: Drug smugglers find oil rig occupied by monster

Prototype
1983, (USA), CBS-TV, color, 97 mins.
<u>W</u>: Christopher Plummer, David Morse (*Michael*), Arthur Hill (*Gen. Keating*), Frances Sternhagen (*Dorothy*), James Sutorius (*Dr. Gene Pressman*), Stephen Elliott (*Arthur Jarrett*)
<u>D</u>: David Greene   <u>TELEPLAY</u>: Richard Levinson & William Link   <u>MUSIC</u>: Billy Goldenberg
TVM, standard SF-thriller: Scientist creates android

Prototype X29A
1992, (USA), color, 98 mins.
<u>W</u>: Lane Lenhart, Robert Tossbert, Brenda Swanson
<u>D & SCR</u>: Phillip J. Roth
Minor SF-thriller: Scientist creates half-man/half-robot

Proud Clarissa
1911, (GB), Hepworth, b&w, 550 ft. (167.6m)
<u>D</u>: Bert Haldane
Standard crime-thriller: Boss' daughter robs safe, clerk takes blame

The Prowler
1951, (USA), UA, b&w, 92 mins.
<u>W</u>: Van Heflin, Evelyn Keyes, John Maxwell, Katherine Warren, Emerson Treacy, Madge Blake
<u>D</u>: Joseph Losey   <u>SCR</u>: Dalton Trumbo (uncredited) & Hugo Butler   <u>PHOTOG</u>: Arthur C. Miller
Unusual thriller: Rich man's wife becomes involved with opportunistic cop

The Prowler
1981, (USA), Graduation/Sandhurst, color, 84 mins.
<u>W</u>: Vicky Dawson (*Pam*), Christopher Goutman (*Mark*), Cindy Weintraub (*Lisa*), John Seitz (*Kingsley*), Farley Granger
<u>P</u>: Joseph Zito & David Streit   <u>D</u>: Joseph Zito   <u>SCR</u>: Glenn Leopold & Neal F. Barbera   <u>PHOTOG</u>: Raoul Lomas   <u>MAKEUP & SPCL-FX</u>: Tom Savini   <u>MUSIC</u>: Richard Einhorn
*reissued (1983) as **Rosemary's Killer***
Minor thriller: World War II veteran becomes mad slasher

Przesluchanie (Interrogation)
1982, (Pol), color, 116 mins.
<u>W</u>: Krystyna Janda (*Tonia*), Adama Ferencego, Janusz Gajos, Agnieszka Holland, Anna Romantowska
<u>D</u>: Ryszard Bugajski
Intense melodrama (with touches of Kafka and Orwell): Cafe artiste imprisoned, tormented

Przyjaciel (The Friend)
1963, (Pol), SE-MA-FOR-Lodz, b&w
<u>W</u>: Piotr Kurowski, Josef Pieracki
<u>WRIT & D</u>: Marek Nowicki & Jerzy Stawicki, from Stanislaw Lem's novel   <u>SPCL-FX</u>: Experimental Studio of Polish Radio
Standard SF-fantasy

PSI Factor
1980, (USA), color, 91 mins.
<u>W</u>: Peter Mark Richman, Gretchen Corbett, Tommy Martin
<u>D</u>: Bryan Trizers   <u>SCR</u>: Quentin Masters
Standard SF-thriller: Researcher detects signals from space

Psyche 59
1964, (GB), Schenck/Troy/Col, b&w, 94 mins.
<u>W</u>: Patricia Neal (*Allison Crawford*), Curt Jurgens (*Eric Crawford*), Samantha Eggar (*Robin*), Ian Bannen (*Paul*), Beatrix Lehmann (*Grandmother*), Elspeth March (*Mme. Valadier*), Sandra Lee (*Susan*), Peter Porteous, Gladys Spencer

P

P: Philip Hazelton **D:** Alexander Singer **SCR:** Julian Halevy, from Francois des Ligneris' novel **PHOTOG:** Walter Lassally **MUSIC:** Kenneth V. Jones
Standard thriller: Woman has hysterical blindness

The Psychic
1977, (It), Cinecompany/Rizzoli/Group I, color, 90 mins.
W: Jennifer O'Neill, Marc Porel, Evelyn Stewart, Gabriele Ferzetti, Jenny Tamburi
D: Lucio Fulci
Minor thriller: Woman's visions reveal old murder

Psychic Killer
1975, (USA), Avco Embassy, color, 90 mins.
W: Jim Hutton (*Arnold*), Julie Adams (*Laura*), Paul Burke, Nehemiah Persoff, Aldo Ray, Rod Cameron, Mary Wilcox, Whit Bissell, Judith Brown, Della Reese, Greydon Clark, Joseph Della Sorte, Stack Pierce, John Dennis, Harry Holcombe
D: Raymond (Ray) Danton **SCR:** Greydon Clark, Mike Angel & Raymond Danton **MUSIC:** William Kraft
Standard thriller: Persecuted man uses mental powers to gain revenge

Psychic Killer: NEVILLE BRAND AND DELLA REESE

Psycho
1960, (USA), Shamley/Univ, b&w, 109 mins.
W: Anthony Perkins (*Norman Bates*), Janet Leigh (*Marion*), Vera Miles (*Lila*), John Gavin (*Sam*), Martin Balsam (*Arbogast*), John McIntire (*Sheriff Chambers*), Lurene Tuttle (*Mrs. Chambers*), John Anderson (*The Car Salesman*), Simon Oakland (*The Psychiatrist*), Frank Albertson, Mort Mills, Pat Hitchcock, Vaughn Taylor, TedKnight
P & D: Alfred Hitchcock **SCR:** Joseph Stefano, from Robert Bloch's novel **PHOTOG:** John L. Russell **SPCL-FX:** Clarence Champagne **MUSIC:** Bernard Herrmann
Remade in 1998
erroneously reported to have pre-release "working title" of **Wimpy**
"PSYCHO is the most thrilling of thrillers; even Hitchcock has never bettered some of its shock effects...it is also the most savagely amusing of comedies noires, balancing us, even at its most horrifying on the knife-edge where there is almost no distinction between a laugh and a scream" John Russell Taylor, Cinema Eye, Cinema Ear
Classic thriller: Demented young man runs motel and checks guests out

Psycho II
1983, (USA), Oak/Univ, color, 111 mins.
W: Anthony Perkins (*Norman Bates*), Meg Tilly (*Mary*), Vera Miles (*Lila*), Robert Loggia (*Dr. Raymond*), Dennis Franz (*Toomey*), Hugh Gillin (*Sheriff Hunt*), Claudia Bryar (*Mrs. Spool*), Robert Alan Browne (*Statler*), Ben Hartigan (*The Judge*), Lee Garlington (*Myrna*), Tim Maier (*Josh*), Chris Hendrie (*Deputy Pool*), Jill Carroll (*Kim*), Robert Destri (*The Public Defender*), Tom Holland (*Deputy Morris*), Gene Whittington (*The Diver*), Michael Lomazow (*The D.A.*), Osgood Perkins (*Young Norman*), George Dickerson (*The County Sheriff*), Ben Frommer (*The Sexton*), Robert Traynor (*The Desk Clerk*), Thaddeus Smith (*The Deputy Sheriff*), Sheila K. Adams (*The Deputy Woman*), Victoria Brown (*The Deputy Clerk*)
D: Richard Franklin **SCR:** Tom Holland, from characters created by Robert Bloch **PHOTOG:** Dean Cundey **SPCL-FX:** Melbourne Arnold **MUSIC:** Jerry Goldsmith
Standard thriller: Murderer released from prison asylum

Psycho III
1986, (USA), Univ, color, 91 mins.
W: Anthony Perkins (*Norman Bates*), Diana Scarwid (*Maureen*), Jeff Fahey (*Duane*), Roberta Maxwell (*Tracy Venable*), Hugh Gillin, Robert Alan Browne, Lee

Garlington, Lisa Ives, Gary Bayer
D: Anthony Perkins **SCR:** Charles Edward Pogue, from characters created by Robert Bloch **PHOTOG:** Bruce Surtees **MUSIC:** Carter Burwell
Standard thriller: Schizo meets renegade nun

Psycho IV: The Beginning
1990, (USA), Smart Money Prods./Univ/SHO-TV, color, 96 mins.
W: Anthony Perkins (*Norman Bates*), Henry Thomas (*Young Norman*), Olivia Hussey (*Norma Bates*), Warren Frost (*Dr. Leo Richmond*), C.C.H. Pounder (*Fran Ambrose*), Donna Mitchell (*Connie Bates*), Thomas Schuster (*Chet Rudolph*), Kurt Paul (*Raymond Linette*), Sharen Camille (*Holly*), Cynthia Garris (*Ellen Stevens*), Bobbi Evors (*Gloria*), John Landis (*Mike Calveccio*), Louis Crume (*George Emeric*), Doreen Chalmers (*Mrs. Lane*), Alice Hirson (*The Voice of Mother*), Ryan Finnigan (*Child Norman*), Peggy O'Neal (*The Nurse*), George Zaloom (*The Janitor*), Bob Barnes (*The Salesman*)
D: Mick Garris **SCR:** Joseph Stefano from characters created by Robert Bloch **PHOTOG:** Rodney Charters **SPCL-FX:** Rick Jones **MUSIC:** Graeme Revell **ORIG PSYCHO SCORE:** Bernard Herrmann
Made-for-Cable, standard thriller: Semi-prequel details making of a matricide

Psycho: ANTHONY PERKINS

Psycho
1998, (USA), Univ, color
W: Vince Vaughn, Anne Heche, Viggo Mortensen, William H. Macy, Julianne Moore
D: Gus Van Sant **PHOTOG:** Christopher Doyle

Psycho-A-Go-Go!
see Blood of Ghastly Horror

Psycho Boy and His Killer Dog
see A Boy and His Dog

Psycho-Circus
see Circus of Fear

Psycho Cop
1988, (USA), color, 89 mins.
D: Wallace Potts
Minor thriller

Psycho Cop 2
1994, (USA), color, 80 mins.
W: Bobby Ray Shafer, Barbara Lee Alexander, Julie Strain
D: Rif Coogan

Psycho From Texas
1983, (USA), color, 85 mins.
W: King John III, Candy Dee, Janel King
A.k.a. **The Butcher**
Minor thriller: Random murders in small town

Psycho Girls
1987, (Can), MGM-UA, color 87 mins

W: John Haslett Cuff, Rose Graham (*Diana*), Darlene Mignacco (*Sarah*), Agi Gallus (*Victoria*) Silvio Oliviero, Michael Hoole, Pier Giorgia DiCicco, Fernne Kane
D: Gerard Ciccoritti   **SCR:** Gerard Ciccoritti & Michael Boekner   **PHOTOG:** Robert Bergman
Minor thriller (never released theatrically): Crazed woman disrupts anniversary celebration

Psycho Killer
see The Psycho Lover

Psycho-Killers
see The Flesh and the Fiends

The Psycho Lover
1970, (USA), Medford, color, 75 mins.
W: Lawrence Montaigne, Joanne Meredith, Elizabeth Plumb, Frank Cuva
P, D & SCR: Robert Vincent O'Neil
A.k.a. The Loving Touch and Psycho Killer
Standard thriller: Mad psychiatrist plots wife's murder. Refers to The Manchurian Candidate

Psychomania
1964, (USA), Victoria, b&w, 90 mins.
W: Lee Philips, Jean Hale, Shepperd Strudwick, Lorraine Rogers, James Farentino, Dick Van Patten, Sylvia Miles
P: Del Tenney & Margot Hartman   **D:** Richard L. Hilliard   **SCR:** Robin Miller & Margot Hartman
A.k.a. Violent Midnight & Sezomania
Standard thriller: Tale of psychotic artist

Psychomania
1972, (GB), Scotia-Barber/Benmar, color, 95 mins.
W: George Sanders (*Shadwell*), Beryl Reid (*Mrs. Latham*), Nicky Henson (*Tom Latham*), Mary Larkin (*Abby*), Roy Holder (*Bertram*), Robert Hardy (*Insp. Hesseltine*), Patrick Holt (*The Sergeant*), Denis Gilmore (*Hatchet*), Miles Greenwood (*Chopped Meat*), Ann Michele (*Jane*), Peter Whiting (*Gash*), June Brown (*Mrs. Pettibone*), Lane Meddick (*Pettibone*), Bill Pertwee (*The Publican*), Serretta Wilson (*Stella*), Fiona Kendall (*Monica*), Martin Boddey (*The Coroner*), Roy Evans (*The Farmworker*), Denis Carey (*Bassett*)
D: Don Sharp   **SCR:** Armand d'Usseau   **PHOTOG:** Ted Moore   **MUSIC:** David Whitaker
A.k.a. The Death Wheelers
Curious horror-fantasy: Zombified motorcycle gang

The Psychopath
1965, (GB), Amicus/Para, color, 83 mins.
W: Patrick Wymark (*Insp. Holloway*), Margaret Johnston (*Mrs. von Sturm*), John Standing (*Mark von Sturm*), Judy Huxtable (*Louise Saville*), Alexander Knox (*Frank Saville*), Thorley Walters (*Martin Rolfe*), Don Borisenko (*Donald Loftis*), Robert Crewdson (*Victor Ledoux*), Frank Forsyth (*Tucker*), Colin Gordon (*Dr. Glyn*), John Harvey
P: Max J. Rosenberg & Milton Subotsky   **D:** Freddie Francis   **SCR:** Robert Bloch   **PHOTOG:** John Wilcox   **MUSIC:** Elisabeth Lutyens   **DESIGN:** Bill Constable
A.k.a. Schizo
Standard thriller: Multiple murders and strange German household

The Psychopath
1973, (USA), Brentwood, color, 84 mins.
W: Tom Basham
P, D & SCR: Larry Brown
A.k.a. An Eye for an Eye
Minor thriller: Host of children's TV show kills abusive parents

Psychophobia
1982, (W. Ger), Orbis, color, 77 mins.
W: Mary Saint Peter, Nelson Mentley, Ramsey Oliver
D, STORY & SCR: Seymour Darbowitz
Minor thriller: Mysterious phenomena threaten widow

Psycho Puppet
see Delerium

Psycho Sex Fiend
see Scream and Die!

Psychos in Love
1987, (USA), Wizard Video/Generic Films/ICN Bleecker, color, 87 mins.
W: Debi Thibault, Carmine Capobianco
P, D, ED, & PHOTOG: Gorman Bechard   **SCR:** Gorman Bechard & Carmine Capobianco
Minor thriller: Manicurist and bartender commit atrocities

Psycho Sisters
see So Evil, My Sister

Psychotherapy
see Don't Get Me Started

The Psychotronic Man
1980, (USA), Int'l Harmony, color, 82 mins.

W: Peter Spelson (*Rocky*), Christopher Carbis (*O'Brien*), Curt Colbert (*Jackson*), Robin Newton (*Kathy*), Jeff Caliendo (*Maloney*), Paul Marvel (*Steinberg*), Lindsey Novak (*Mrs. Foscoe*), Irwin Lewin (*The Professor*), Corney Morgan (*Gorman*), Bob McDonald (*The Old Man*) , Paul Marvel, Lindsey Novak, Corney Morgan, Phil Lanier, Shirl Maschinski, Robert Vanni, Tony Campo, James Wirag
P: Peter Spelson   **D & PHOTOG:** Jack M. Sell   **SCR:** Jack M. Sell & Peter Spelson   **ORIG. STOR:** Peter Spelson   **MUSIC:** Tommy Irons
Minor thriller: Man acquires destructive powers

Psycho IV: The Beginning

Psychout for Murder
1971, (It), Times, color, 88 mins.
W: Adrienne La Russa (*Licia*), Rossano Brazzi (*Daddy*), Nino Castelnuovo (*Mario*), Paola Pitagora (*Giovanna*), Alberto De Mendoza (*Francesco*), Idelma Carlo (*Laura*), Renzo Petretto (*Paterlini*), Nestor Garay (*The Politician*)
D: Edward Ross & Ted Kneeland   **MUSIC:** Benedetto Ghiglia
Standard thriller

Psych-Out
1968, (USA), AIP, color, 89 mins.
W: Susan Strasberg, Jack Nicholson, Dean Stockwell, Bruce Dern, Adam Roarke, Robert Kelljan, Max Julien
D: Richard Rush   **SCR:** E. Hunter Willit, Betty Ulius & Betty Tusher   **PHOTOG:** Laszlo Kovacs   **SONG:** *Incense, Peppermint*, by Strawberry Alarm Clock
Unusual thriller: Deaf girl seeks brother in San Francisco's Haight-Ashbury district

Psycosissimo
1962, (It), Flora-Variety/Trans-Lux, b&w, 88 mins.
W: Ugo Tognazzi, Raimondo Vianello, Edy Vessel, Monique Just, Spiros Focas, Francesco Mule, Franca Marzi
D: Steno   **SCR:** Vittorio Metz & Roberto Gianviti
Minor thriller

P.T. Barnum's Rocket to the Moon
see Those Fantastic Flying Fools

Pulp
1972, (GB), Three Michaels/UA, color, 95 mins.
W: Michael Caine (*Mickey King*), Mickey Rooney (*Preston Gilbert*), Lionel Stander (*Ben Dinuccio*), Lizabeth Scott (*Princess Betty*), Nadia Cassini (*Liz Adams*), Al Lettieri (*Miller*), Dennis Price (*The Englishman*), Amerigo Tot (*Sotgio*), Leopoldo Trieste (*Marcovic*), Robert Sacchi (*Jim Norman*), Victor Mercieca (*Prince Cippola*), Joe Z. Cordina (*Santana*), Ave Ninchi (*The Maid*), Janet Agrett (*Silvana*), Maria Quasimodo (*Senora Pavone*), Jeanne Lass (*Marlene Dietrich*), Mary Caruana (*Mae West*), Tondi Barr (*Gloria Swanson*), Jennifer Gauci (*Shirley Temple*), Kate Sullivan (*Joan Crawford*)
P: Michael Klinger, Mike Hodges & Michael Caine   **D & STORY:** Mike Hodges   **PHOTOG:** Ousama Rawi   **MUSIC:** George Martin
Modest thriller: Ghostwriting biographer involved in crime

Pulse
1988, (USA), HBO-TV, color, 92 mins.
W: Joey Lawrence (*David*), Cliff DeYoung (*Bill*), Roxanne Hart (*Ellen*)
TVM, standard SF-thriller: Electrical force possesses home

The Puma Man
1980, (It), color, 100 mins.
W: Donald Pleasence, Walter George Alton
Minor comic-strip adventure: Evil doctor vs. magic-powered paleontologist

Pumpkinhead
1988, (USA), Stan Winston/Lion Films/MGM-UA, color, 87 mins.
W: Lance Henriksen (*Ed Harley*), Jeff East (*Chris*), Kimberly Ross (*Kim*), John DiAquino (*Joel*), Cynthia Bain (*Tracy*), Joel Hoffman (*Steve*), Kerry Remsen (*Maggie*), Florence Schauffler (*Haggis*), Brian Bremer (*Bunt*), Buck Flower (*Mr. Wallace*), Matthew Burley (*Billy Harley*), Peggy Walton Walker (*Ellie Harley*), Lee DeBroux (*Tom Harley*), Chance Corbitt Jr. (*Eddie Harley*), Richard Warlock (*Clayton Heller*), Joseph Piro (*Jimmy Joe*), Devon Odessa (*Hessie*), Mayim Bialik (*A Wallace Kid*), Jandi Swanson (*A Wallace Kid*), Greg Michaels (*The Hill Man*), Robert Fredrickson (*Ethan*), Medeleine Taylor Holmes (*The Old Hill Woman*), Mary Boessow (*The Mountain Girl*), Tom Woodruff Jr. (*Pumpkinhead*), Mushroom (*Gypsy*)
D: Stan Winston **SCR:** Mark Patrick Carducci & Gary Gerani **STORY:** Mark Patrick Carducci, Stan Winston & Richard C. Weinman, inspired by a poem by Ed Justin **PHOTOG:** Bojan Bazelli **ORIG. SCORE:** Richard Stone
Unusual horror-fantasy: Demon conjured for hill-country vengeance

Pumpkinhead II: Blood Wings
1993, (USA), Live Entertainment/Motion Picture Corp. of America, color, 88 mins.
W: Andrew Robinson (*Sean Braddock*), Ami Dolenz (*Jenny Braddock*), Soleil Moon Frye (*Marcie*), J. Trevor Edmond (*Danny Dixon*), Hill Harper (*Peter*), Alexander Polinsky (*Paul*), Mark McCracken (*Pumpkinhead*), Steve Kanaly (*Judge Dixon*), Gloria Hendry (*Delilah Pettibone*), Lilyan Chauvin (*Miss Osie*), Caren Kaye (*Beth Braddock*), Jean-Paul Manoux (*Tommy*), John Gatins (*Young Caspar Dixon*), Joe Unger (*Ernst*), Roger Clinton (*Mayor Bubba*), R.A. Mihailoff (*Red Byers*), Linnea Quigley (*Nadine*), Kane Hodder (*Keith Knox*), Chuck Aronberg (*Fred Knox*), Will Huston (*Brian Knox*), Michael J. Carra (*Cory*), Barry Davis (*Young Sean Braddock*), Nicole Maggio (*The Mute Girl*), Harri James (*The Nurse*), Michael Mandaville (*The Grizzled Man*), Mike Johnson (*The Coroner*), Robert H. Harvey (*Henchman #2*), Jason Sanford (*50's Teen #3*), Ed Anders (*Hunter #3*), Monte R. Perlin (*Hunter #5*), Lon Sunders (*Hunter #6*), Chad Oman (*The Ugly Hunter*), Peter Lupus III (*Cockfighter #1*), Peter Lupus (*Cockfighter #2*), Cecile Krevoy (*Pretty Townswoman #1*), Tracie Graham (*Townswoman #2*)
D: Jeff Burr **WRIT:** Ivan & Constantine Chachornia **PHOTOG:** William Dill **SPCL-FX:** Ultimate Effects **MUSIC:** Jim Manzie **SONGS:** You'll Never See Me Cry, She's a Siren, I Ain't What You Need, Souls Not for Sale, A Taste of Latin, Twila Star, Guantanamera, Go Away, Free Fall, You Might Be the One, The Right Way, It's Still Love, You Don't Want to See (*Pumpkinhead*) & Just Like You (*Theme from Pumpkinhead II*)
Standard horror-fantasy: Murdered freak returns in demonic form

Punch and Judy
1906, (Fr), Star, b&w, 43m (141.1 ft./2.4 mins.)
W: Georges Melies
D: Georges Melies
Standard fantasy: Marionettes become human, attack puppeteer

The Punisher
1989, (Austral), Robert Mark Kamen/New World, color, 92 mins.
W: Dolph Lundgren (*Frank Castle/The Punisher*), Louis Gossett Jr. (*Jake Berkowitz*), Jeroen Krabbe (*Gianni Franco*), Bryan Marshall (*Dino Moretti*), Kim Miyori (*Lady Tanaka*), Nancy Everhard (*Sam Leary*), Barry Otto (*Shake*), Brian Rooney (*Tommy Franco*), Zoshka Mizak (*Tanaka's Daughter*), Kenji Yamaki, Hirofumi Kanayama, Larry McCormick, Todd Boyce, Courtney Keiler, Larney Tupu, John Negroponte, Noga Bernstein, Emma Soloman, Emily Nicol, Cathy Stirk, Dominic Baudish, Robert Fraser, James Klein, Fotis Pelekis, Christian Manon, Brian McDermott, Colin Leong, May Lloyd, Brooke Anderson, Robert Simper, Holly Rogers, Lois Larimore, Lawrence Woodward, Tom Coltraine, Harry Weiss, John Samaha, John Raaen, Ken Wayne, Donal Gibson, David Arnett, Brett Williams, Colin Handley, Al Gockimen, Isao Hirata, David Morris, Ric Carter, Roslyn Gentle, Char Fontaine, Aku Kadogo, Steve Kuhn, Joanna Lambert, Maurice Brimo, Arthur Sherman, Chris Hession
D: Mark Goldblatt **SCR:** Boaz Yakin, from the Marvel Comics character **PHOTOG:** Ian Baker **MUSIC:** Dennis Dreith **SONGS:** Planet of Love, Vicious Minds & Winning Isn't Everything, It's the Only Thing
Standard thriller: Vigilante eliminates criminals

Die Puppe (The Doll)
1919, (Ger), Ufa, b&w, 60 mins.
D: Ernst Lubitsch, from a theme by E.T.A. Hoffmann **PHOTOG:** Theodor Sparkuhl
Anti-clerical & anti-authoritarian sentiments in bizarre fantasy: Girl changed into doll

Puppet Master
1989, (USA), Full Moon, color, 90 mins.
W: Paul LeMat (*Alex Whitaker*), Irene Miracle (*Dana Hadley*), William Hickey (*Andre Toulon*), Matt Roe (*Frank Forrester*), Kathryn O'Reilly (*Carissa Stamford*), Merrya Small (*Theresa*), Jimmie F. Skaggs (*Neil Gallagher*), Robin Frates (*Megan Gallagher*), Barbara Crampton (*The Woman at the Carnival*), David Boyd (*The Man at the Carnival*), Peter Frankland (*Assassin #1*), Andrew Kimbrough (*Assassin #2*)

D: David Schmoeller **SCR:** Joseph G. Collodi **STORY:** Charles Band & Kenneth J. Hall **PHOTOG:** Sergio Salvati **MUSIC:** Richard Band
Standard fantasy-thriller: Psychics vs. living marionettes

Puppet Master II
1990, (USA), Full Moon/Para, color, 90 mins.
W: Elizabeth MacLellan (*Carolyn Bramwell/Elsa*), Collin Bernsen (*Michael Kenney*), Steve Welles (*Andre Toulon/Erique Chanee*), Gregory Webb (*Patrick Bramwell*), Charlie Spradling (*Wanda*), Jeff Weston (*Lance*), Nita Talbot (*Camille Kenney*), Sage Allen (*Martha*), George "Buck" Flower (*Mathew*), Sean B. Ryan (*Billy*), Ivan J. Rado (*The Cairo Merchant*), Julianne Mazziotti (*Puppet Camille/Elsa*), Michael Todd (*Puppet Toulon*), Taryn Band (*A Cairo Child*), Alex Band (*A Cairo Child*)
D: David Allen **SCR:** David Pabian **STORY:** Charles Band **PHOTOG:** Thomas F. Denove **MUSIC:** Richard Band
Standard horror-fantasy: Demonic dolls plague psychic researchers

Puppet Master III: Toulon's Revenge
1991, (USA), Full Moon, color, 90 mins.
W: Guy Rolfe, Ian Abercrombie, Sarah Douglas, Richard Lynch
D: David DeCoteau
Standard fantasy: Nazis acquire deadly dolls

Puppet Master 4
1993, (USA), color, 80 mins.
W: Gordon Currie, Jason Adams, Teresa Hill, Guy Rolfe
D: Jeff Burr **SCR:** Todd Henschell, Steven E. Carr, Jo Duffy, Keith Payson & Dough Aarniokoski **MUSIC:** Richard Band
Standard fantasy-thriller: Evil puppets make war

Puppet Master 5
1994, (USA), color, 81 mins.
W: Gordon Currie, Chandra West, Ian Ogilvy, Teresa Hill, Nicholas Guest, Willard Pugh, Diane McBain, Kaz Garas, Guy Rolfe
D: Jeff Burr **MUSIC:** Richard Band
*A.k.a. **Puppet Master 5: The Final Chapter***
Standard fantasy-thriller: Living puppets vs. monster from another dimension

The Puppet Masters
1994, (USA), Hollywood, color, 109 mins.
W: Donald Sutherland (*Andrew Nivens*), Eric Thal (*Sam Nivens*), Julie Warner (*Dr. Mary Sefton*), Keith David (*Holland*), Will Patton (*Graves*), Richard Belzer (*Jarvis*), Marshall Bell (*Gen. Morgan*), Yaphet Kotto (*Ressler*), Tom Mason (*Pres. Douglas*), Gerry Bamman (*Viscott*), Nicholas Gascone (*Greenberg*), Bruce Jarchow (*Barnes*), Benj Thall (*Jeff*), David Pasquesi (*Vargas*), Benjamin Mouton (*Higgins*), Bo Sharon (*Casey*), Andrew Robinson (*Hawthorne*), Nick Browne (*Mike*), Donna Garrett (*Miss Haines*), William Wellman Jr. (*The Doctor*), Elizabeth Sung (*Technician #1*), Dinah Lenney (*Technician #2*), Tom Dugan (*Operator #1*), Dale Dye (*Brande*), John C. Cooke (*Lt. Abbey*), Fabio Urena (*The Infantryman*), Michael Shamus Wiles (*Capt. Farley*), Dale Harimoto (*The Anchorwoman*), James Pearson (*The Merging Soldier*), Evan C. Morris (*Danny*), K.T. Vogt (*The Slugged Woman*), Alexa Jago (*Wendy Markham*), Eric Briant Wells (*Vince Hayward*), Scott Armstrong (*The Infected Boy*), Marianne Curan (*The Newscaster*), Katy Summerland (*Graves' Ass't*), Todd Bryant (*A Soldier*), Don James (*A Soldier*) C. Marvin Campbell (*A Soldier*)
D: Stuart Orme **SCR:** Ted Elliott, Terry Rossio & David S. Goyer, based on Robert A. Heinlein's novel **PHOTOG:** Clive Tickner **SPCL-FX SPRVSR:** Peter Montgomery **MUSIC:** Colin Towns
*Gripping SF-horror: Alien parasites control human hosts. cf. **The Brain Eaters***

Puppet on a Chain
1970, (GB), Big City/Scotia-Barber, color, 98 mins.
W: Sven Bertil-Taube (*Paul Sherman*), Barbara Parkins (*Maggie*), Alexander Knox (*Col. De Graaf*), Patrick Allen (*Insp. Van Gelder*), Vladek Sheybal (*Meegeren*), Ania Marson (*Astride Lemay*), Penny Casdagli (*Trudi*), Henni Orri (*Herta*), Peter Hutchins (*The Assassin*), Stewart Lane (*George Lemay*)
P: Kurt Unger **D:** Geoffrey Reeve & Don Sharp **SCR:** Alistair MacLean, Don Sharp & Paul Wheeler, from a novel by Alistair MacLean
Minor thriller: Narcotics agent vs. Amsterdam drug ring

Puppets of Fate
1933, (GB), Real Art/UA, b&w, 72 mins.
W: Godfrey Tearle (*Richard Sabine*), Russell Thorndike (*Dr. Munro*), Isla Bevan (*Joan*), Fred Groves (*Arthur Brandon*), John Turnbull (*The Inspector*), Michael Hogan, Ben Welden, Kynaston Reeves, S. Victor Stanley, Roland Culver
D: George A. Cooper **SCR:** H. Fowler Mear, from a story by Arthur Rigby & R.H. Douglas
*USA retitle, **Wolves of the Underworld**, Regal, 1935*
Standard thriller: Escaped convict blackmails murderous doctor

Purgatory
1999, (USA), Rosemont/TNT-TV, color, 95 mins.
W: Eric Roberts, Sam Shepard, Donnie Wahlberg, Randy Quaid, Brad Rowe, Peter Stormare, John David Souther, Richard Edson, Amelia Heinle, John Diehl, R.G. Armstrong, John Dennis Johnston, Michael Shaner, Les Lannom, Shannon Kenny, Gregory Scott Cummins, Saginaw Grant
D: Uli Edel **TELEPLAY:** Gordon Dawson **PHOTOG:** William Wage **SPCL-FX COORD:** Dean Miller **VS-FX SPRVSR:** Craig Weiss **MUSIC:** Brad Fiedel
TVM, unusual fantasy-oater: Robbers take refuge in strange Western town

P

Puritan Passions
1923, (USA), Film Guild-Hodkinson, b&w, 7 reels (6,859 ft./ 2090.6m)
W: Glenn Hunter (*Lord Ravensbane/The Scarecrow*), Mary Astor (*Rachel*), Osgood Perkins (*Dr. Nicholas*), Maude Hill (*Goody Rickby*), Frank Tweed (*Gillead Wingate*), Thomas Chalmers (*The Minister*), Dwight Wiman (*Bugby*)
D: Frank W. Tuttle   SCR: James A. Creelman & Frank W. Tuttle, from Percy MacKaye's 1908 play *The Scarecrow*   PHOTOG: Fred Waller Jr.
Standard fantasy: Puritan woman spurned, makes satanic pact

Purple Death from Outer Space
1965, (USA), Univ, b&w, 100 mins.
W: Buster Crabbe (*Flash Gordon*), Carol Hughes (*Dale Arden*), Frank Shannon (*Dr. Zarkov*), Charles Middleton (*Ming the Merciless*), Anne Gwynne (*Sonja*), Michael Mark, John Hamilton, Shirley Deane, Roland Drew, Herbert Rawlinson, Ben Taggart, Don Rowan, Harry C. Bradley, Lee Powell, Victor Zimmerman, Edgar Edwards, Earl Dwire, Sigurd Nilssen, Byron Foulger, Mimi Taylor, William Royle
D: Ford Beebe & Ray Taylor   SCR: George H. Plympton, Basil Dickey & Barry Shipman   PHOTOG: Jerome Ash & William Sickner
Standard space-opera (feature culled from first half of 1938 serial 'Flash Gordon Conquers the Universe): Earth hero vs. alien menace. cf. **Peril from the Planet Mongo**

The Purple Mask
1955, (USA), Univ, color, 82 mins.
W: Tony Curtis, Colleen Miller, Angela Lansbury Dan O'Herlihy, Gene Barry, John Hoyt, George Dolenz, Donald Randolph, Paul Cavanagh, Everett Glass, Myrna Hansen, Robert Cornthwaite
P: Howard Christie   D: Bruce Humberstone   SCR: Oscar Brodney   PHOTOG: Irving Glassberg   MUSIC: Joseph Gershenson
Standard adventure-thriller

Purple People Eater
1988, (USA), color, 90 mins.
W: Neil Patrick Harris (*Billy*), Ned Beatty (*Grandpa*), Shelley Winters (*Rita*) Peggy Lipton, Chubby Checker, Little Richard, Thora Birch, James Houghton, Molly Cheek, Kareem Abdul-Jabbar, Sheb Wooley
D: Linda Shayne
Standard comedy-fantasy: Bizarre creature starts rock band

The Purple Rose of Cairo
1985, (USA), Orion, color, 84 mins.
W: Mia Farrow, Jeff Daniels, Danny Aiello, Irving Metzman, Stephanie Farrow, Van Johnson, Dianne Wiest, John Wood, Zoe Caldwell, Deborah Rush, Milo O'Shea, Mark Hammond, Edward Herrmann, Tom Degidon, David Kieserman, Victoria Zussin, Elaine Grollman, Wade Barnes, Joseph G. Graham, Don Quigley, Maurice Brenner, Rick Petrucelli, Milton Seaman, Paul Herman, Peter Castellotti, Mimi Weddell, Mary Hedahl
WRIT & D: Woody Allen   PHOTOG: Gordon Willis   MUSIC: Dick Hyman
Classic fantasy: Film hero leaves screen, romances depressed housewife

Pursued
1947, (USA), WB, b&w, 101 mins.
W: Robert Mitchum, Teresa Wright, Judith Anderson, Dean Jagger, Alan Hale, John Rodney, Harry Carey Jr.
D: Raoul Walsh   SCR: Niven Busch   PHOTOG: James Wong Howe   MUSIC: Max Steiner
Standard thriller: Westerner pursues father's killers

The Pursuers
1961, (GB), Danziger/Col, b&w, 63 mins.
W: Cyril Shaps (*Karl Luther*), Susan Denny (*Jenny Walmer*), Francis Matthews (*David Nelson*), Sheldon Lawrence (*Rico*), George Murcell (*Freddy*), John Gabriel (*Wally*), Stev Plytas (*Petersen*), Tony Doonan (*Wilmo*)
P: Philip Elton & Ralph Goddard   D: Godfrey Grayson   STORY: Brian Clemens & David Nicholl
Standard crime-thriller: Investigator tracks concentration camp chief

The Pursuit (1963)
see *La Poursuite*

Pursuit
1972, (USA), NBC-TV, color, 73 mins.
W: Ben Gazzara, E.G. Marshall, Joseph Wiseman (*Dr. Nordman*), William Windom (*Phillips*), Jim McMullen (*Lewis*), Martin Sheen (*Drew*)
D: Michael Crichton   SCR: Robert Dozier, from a novel by Michael Crichton
TVM, standard thriller: Gov't agent tries to stop madman from committing unknown crime

The Pursuit of Venus
1914, (GB), Cricks/DFSA, b&w, 426 ft. (129.8m)
D: Edwin J. Collins
Standard fantasy: Artist dreams statue of goddess comes to life

Pursuit to Algiers
1945, (USA), Univ, b&w, 61 mins.
W: Basil Rathbone (*Sherlock Holmes*), Nigel Bruce (*Dr. John Watson*), Marjorie Riordan (*Sheila*), Martin Kosleck (*Mirko*), John Abbott, Leslie Vincent, Gerald Hamer, Frederick Worlock, Rex Evans, Rosalind Ivan
P & D: Roy William Neill   SCR: Leonard Lee, from characters created by Sir Arthur Conan Doyle   PHOTOG: Paul Ivano   MUSIC DIR: Edgar Fairchild
Standard thriller: Famed detective vs. shipboard thieves and assassins

Puss in Boots
1988, (USA), Cannon, color, 96 mins.
W: Christopher Walken
from Charles Perrault's fairytale
Standard musical-fantasy: Cat transformed into French aristocrat

Pussycat
see *Faster, Pussycat! Kill! Kill!*

Putiat Kam Pleadite (Road to the Pleiades)
1967, (Bulgar), color
Standard SF-fantasy

Puzzle
1978, (Austral), color, 90 mins.
W: James Franciscus, Wendy Hughes, Robert Helpmann, Peter Gwynne, Gerald Kennedy, Kerry McGuire
D: Gordon Hessler
Standard thriller: Hunt for urn containing Buddha's ashes

The Puzzled Bather and His Animated Clothes
1901, (GB), Williamson, b&w, 80 ft. (24.4m)
D: James Williamson
Standard fantasy short: The more clothes bather removes, the more appear

The Puzzle Maniac
1906, (GB), Gaumont, b&w, 295 ft. (89.9m)
D: Alf Collins
Standard comedy short: Absorbing puzzle drives man mad

Pygmalion and Galatea (1898)
see *Pygmalion et Galatee*

Pygmalion and Galatea
1912, (GB), Ivy Close Films/Hepworth, b&w, 625 ft. (190.5m)
W: Ivy Close (*Galatea*)
WRIT & D: Elwin Neame
Standard fantasy: Lydian artist finds statue lives

Pygmalion et Galatee (Pygmalion and Galatea)
1898, (Fr), Star, b&w, 20m (65.6 ft./1.1 mins.)
D: Georges Melies
Standard fantasy short: Sculptor's creation comes to life

Pygmy Island
1950, (USA), Col, b&w, 69 mins.
W: Johnny Weissmuller, Ann Savage, David Bruce, Tris Coffin, Steven Geray, William Tannen, Billy Curtis, Tommy Farrell, Pierce Lyden, Rusty Wescoatt, Billy Barty
P: Sam Katzman   D: William Berke   SCR: Carroll Young   PHOTOG: Ira H. Morgan
Standard "Jungle Jim" adventure-thriller: Jungle hero teams with pygmy tribe to defeat enemy agents seeking war supplies

Pyramid
see *The Awakening*

Pyro
1963, (USA-Sp), SWP-Esamer/AIP, color, 99 mins.
W: Barry Sullivan, Martha Hyer, Sherry Moreland, Luis Prendes, Soledad Miranda, Fernando Hilbeck, Carlos Casaravilla, Hugo Pimental, Marisenka, Francisco Moran, Pilarin Gomez, Eric Chapman
P: Sidney W. Pink & Richard C. Meyer   D: Julio Coll   SCR: Louis de Los Arcos & Sidney W. Pink   STORY: Sidney W. Pink   PHOTOG: Manuel Berenguer   MUSIC: Jose Sola
Sp title, **Fuego***, A.k.a.* **Wheel of Fire**
Standard thriller: Victim of arson seeks vengeance

Q

1982, (USA), Larry Cohen/Larco/United Film, color, 92 mins.
W: Michael Moriarty, Candy Clark, David Carradine, Richard Roundtree, Lee
  Louis, David Snell, John Capodice, Tony Page
WRIT, P & D: Larry Cohen **PHOTOG:** Fred Murphy **MUSIC:** Robert O.
  Raglan **SONGS:** *Let's Fall Apart Together Tonight* & *Evil Dream*
*A.k.a. **The Winged Serpent***
*Modest SF-thriller (with bizarre "method" performance by Michael Moriarty): Ancient
  winged serpent terrorizes metropolis*

Le Quai Des Brumes (Port of Shadows)
1938, (Fr), b&w, 89 mins.
W: Jean Gabin, Michele Morgan, Michel Simon, Marcel Peres, Pierre Brasseur,
  Robert Le Vigan, Aimos
D: Marcel Carne **SCR & DIALOG:** Jacques Prevert
PHOTOG: Eugen Schuftan **MUSIC:** Maurice Jaubert
Classic melodrama: Army deserter protects beauty from criminals

Quand la Terre s'Entrouvrira
*see **Crack in the World***

Quarantine
1989, (Can), Apple Pie, color, 92 mins.
W: Beatrice Boepple (*Ivan Joad*), Garwin Sanford (*Spencer Crown*), Jerry
  Wasserman (*Sen. Ford*), Kah-Erik Eriksen (*The Kid*), Tom McBeath (*Lt.
  Beck*), Susan Chapple (*Sen. Campbell*), Michele Goodger (*Berlin Ford*), Lee
  Taylor, David Brass, Don Mackie, Amy Newman, Frank Ferrucci, Peri Best,
  Kim Kondrashoff, Mark Acheson, Steve Dotto, Roman Podhora, Sheila
  Paterson, Jeremy Mathews, Curt Bonn, Shelly Cheung, Rob Morton, Blaine
  Lamoureux, Robert Cassell, Kelly Yeun, David Soo, Kevin Andruschak,
  Adam Yaranko, Gerry Rousseau, Bryon Lucas, Doreen Ramus, Denise
  Clowater, Bryan Anderson, Winnifred Waterhouse, Mal Beveridge, Keith
  Provost, Whitey Dropko, David Hurry, Geoff Robinson, Ron Martin, Ted
  Conley, Al Waterhouse, Bert Price, Joan O'Donahue, George Lee, Peter
  Smith
WRIT, P & D: Charles Wilkinson **PHOTOG:** Tobias Schliessler
MUSIC: Graeme Coleman
Minor SF-thriller: Future plague causes social disruption

The Quarry Mystery
1914, (GB), Hepworth, b&w, 1,800 ft. (548.6m)
W: Stewart Rome, Violet Hopson, John MacAndrews
D: Cecil M. Hepworth
Standard crime-thriller: Detective proves blacksmith did not kill debtor

Quatermass and the Pit
1967, (GB), Hammer-7Arts/20th-Fox, color, 97 mins.
W: Andrew Keir (*Prof. Bernard Quatermass*), Barbara Shelley (*Barbara Judd*), James
  Donald (*Dr. Matthew Roney*), Julian Glover (*Col. Breen*), Duncan Lamont
  (*Sladden*), Bryan Marshall (*Capt. Potter*), Peter Copley (*Howell*), Maurice
  Good (*Sgt. Cleghorn*), Edwin Richfield (*The Minister*), Grant Taylor (*Sgt.
  Ellis*), Sheila Steafel (*The Journalist*), Thomas Heathcote (*The Vicar*), Brian
  Peck, Noel Howlett, Charles Lamb, Roger Avon, Bee Duffell, Robert Morris
P: Anthony Nelson Keys **D:** Roy Ward Baker **STORY & SCR:** Nigel Kneale,
  based on a GB teleseries **PHOTOG:** Arthur Grant **SPCL-FX:** Bowie
  Films Ltd. **MUSIC COMPOSED:** Tristam Cary
*orig. to be titled **The Pit**, USA retitle, **Five Million Years to Earth***
"...superb example of imaginative sci-fi and the film medium merging to produce
  a work of lasting importance"—Gary Gerani, "The Space Monster Book—
  Chapter Six: England and Prof. Quatermass," Monster Fantasy, Vol. 1, No.
  4 (August, 1975), p. 39
Superior SF-horror: Subway excavators find martian spaceship

The Quatermass Conclusion
1978, (GB), Euston, Made for TV, color, 107mins.
W: John Mills (*Prof. Bernard Quatermass*), Simon MacCorkindale (*Kapp*), Barbara
  Kellermann (*Clare Kapp*), Brewster Mason (*Gurov*), Margaret Tyzack (*Annie
  Morgan*), Jane Bertish (*Bee*), Ralph Arliss (*Kickalong*), Paul Rosebury
  (*Caraway*), Rebecca Saire (*Hettie*), Toyah Willcox (*Sal*), Bruce Purchase,
  Brenda Fricker, David Yip, Annabelle Lanyon, Tony Sibbald, Joanne Joseph,
  Neil Stacy, Sophie Kind, Joy Harrington, Ian Price, Brian Croucher, Kevin
  Stoney, David Ashford, Lennox Milne, Elsie Randolph, Ishaq Bux, John
  Dunbar, Declan Mulholland, John Richmond, Barbara Keogh, Luke
  Hanson, Charles Bolton, James Leith, Chris Driscoll, Stewart Harwood,
  Larry Noble, Trevor Lawrence, Frederick Radley, Gretchen Franklin, James
  Ottaway, Clare Ruane, Donald Eccles, Beatrice Shaw, Kathleen St. John
D: Piers Haggard **SCR:** Nigel Kneale **PHOTOG:** Ian Wilson **SPCL-FX:**
  Effects Associates **MUSIC:** Marc Wilkinson & Nic Rowley
*Standard SF-thriller (final "Quatermass" installment): Earth society crumbles, alien enig-
  ma devours youth*

The Quatermass Experiment
1955, (GB), Hammer/UA, b&w, 82 mins.
W: Brian Donlevy (*Prof. Bernard Quatermass*), Jack Warner (*Insp. Lomax*), Margia
  Dean (*Judith Caroon*), Richard Wordsworth (*Victor Caroon*), David King
  Wood (*Dr. Gordon Briscoe*), Thora Hird (*Rosie*), Gordon Jackson (*The TV
  Producer*), Lionel Jeffries (*Blake*), Harold Lang (*Christie*), Maurice Kaufmann
  (*Marsh*), Frank Phillips (*The BBC Announcer*), Donald Gray (*The TV*

Announcer), Sam Kydd, Gron Davies, Stanley van Beers
D: Val Guest **SCR:** Richard Landau & Val Guest, from a teleseries by Nigel
  Kneale **PHOTOG:** Jimmy Harvey **SPCL-FX:** Leslie Bowie **MUSIC:**
  James Bernard **MUSIC CONDUCT:** John Hollingsworth
*Fr retitle, **Le Monstre (The Monster)**, USA retitle, **The Creeping Unknown***
Classic SF-horror: Astronaut infected by weird space organism

Quatermass II
1956, (GB), Corinth/UA, b&w, 84 mins.
W: Brian Donlevy (*Prof. Bernard Quatermass*), John Longden (*Lomax*), Sidney
  James (*Jimmy Hall*), Bryan Forbes (*Marsh*), William Franklyn (*Brand*), Vera
  Day (*Sheila*), Percy Herbert (*Gorman*), Charles Lloyd-Pack (*Dawson*), Tom
  Chatto (*Broadhead*), John Van Eyssen (*The P.R.O.*), Marianne Stone (*The
  Sec'y*), Michael Ripper (*Ernie*), John Rae (*McLeod*), Ronald Wilson (*The
  Young Man*), Jane Aird (*Mrs. McLeod*), Betty Impey (*Kelly*), Lloyd Lamble
  (*The Inspector*), John Stuart (*The Commissioner*), Gilbert Davis (*The Banker*),
  Joyce Adams (*The Woman M.P.*), Edwin Richfield (*Peterson*), Howard
  Williams (*Michaels*), Philip Baird, Robert Raikes, George Merritt, John
  Fabian, Arthur Blake, Michael Balfour
P: Anthony Hinds **D:** Val Guest **SCR:** Nigel Kneale & Val Guest **PHOTOG:**
  Gerald Gibbs **SPCL-FX:** Bill Warrington, Henry Harris & Frank George
  MUSIC: James Bernard
*USA retitle, **Enemy from Space***
Standard SF-thriller: Space-aliens threaten Earth

Quatro Mosche di Velluto Gris (Four Flies on Grey Velvet)
1972, (It-Fr), INC.I.R. de Paoli-Rome/Para, color, 101 mins.
W: Michael Brandon (*Robert*), Mimsy Farmer (*Nina*), Francine Racette (*Dalia*),
  Jean Pierre Marielle (*Arrosio*), Bud Spencer (*Godfrey*)
P: Salvatore Dargento **WRIT & D:** Dario Argento, from a story by Dario
  Argento, Luigi Cozzi & Mario Foglietti **MUSIC:** Ennio Morricone
*Stylish thriller: Doctors photograph retinas of murder victims but get blurred image of four
  flies*

Queen Bee
1955, (USA), Col, b&w, 95 mins.
W: Joan Crawford, Barry Sullivan, John Ireland, Betsy Drake, Fay Wray, Tim
  Hovey, Lucy Marlow
D & SCR: Ranald MacDougall **PHOTOG:** Charles B. Lang
MUSIC: George Duning
Grim melodrama (classic Crawford): Grasping woman spreads grief

The Queen Mother
1916, (GB), Clarendon, b&w, 4,500 ft. (1371.6m)
W: Owen Roughwood (*Duke of Carola*), Gladys Mason (*Princess of Saxonia*),
  Barbara Rutland (*Duchess Miramar*), Sydney Lewis Ransome (*Prince Ludwig*),
  Ronald Hammond (*Osric*), M. Mills (*King of Montania*)
D: Wilfred Noy, from a play by J.A. Campbell
Standard adventure-romance: Ex-lover of Ruritanian queen destroys threat to throne

The Queen of Babylon
1954, (It), Pantheon/20th Century For, color, 105 mins.
W: Rhonda Fleming (*Semiramis*), Ricardo Montalban (*Amak*), Carlo Ninchi
  (*Sibari*), Rolando Lupi (*Assur*), Tamara Lees (*Lysia*)
D: Carlo Ludovico Bragaglia **SCR:** Ennio De Concini, Giuseppe Mangione &
  Carlo Ludovico Bragaglia **MUSIC:** Renzo Rossellini
*A.k.a. **The Slave Woman***
Standard "Sword & Sandal" thriller: Warrior puts beautiful goatherd on throne of Babylon

Queen of Blood
1966, (USA), AIP, color, 80 mins.
W: John Saxon (*Allan*), Florence Marly (*Velena*), Judi Meredith (*Judi*), Basil
  Rathbone (*Dr. Farraday*), Dennis Hopper (*Paul*), Robert Boon, Virgil Frye,
  Robert Porter, Terry Lee, Don Eitner, Forrest J. Ackerman
P: George Edwards **WRIT & D:** Curtis Harrington **PHOTOG:** Vilis
  Lapenieks **MUSIC:** Leonard Morand
*orig. to be titled **Flight to a Far Planet**, TV retitle, **Planet of Blood***
Standard SF-horror: Astronauts rescue female alien, discover her vampiric nature

Queen of Evil
*see **La Sorella di Satan***

Queen of My Heart
1917, (GB), Clarendon/Globe, b&w, 5,000 ft. (1524m)
W: Hayden Coffin (*The Singer*), Christine Rayner (*Dorothy Lethridge*), Charles Vane
  (*Joseph Hawks*), Alfred Lugg (*Jack Lethridge*), Jack Wilcocks (*Mr. Lethridge*)
D: Albert Ward **SCR:** Reuben Gillmer **STORY:** Hetty Langford Reed
Standard crime-thriller: Crook frames cousin for forgery, lures away his wife

Queen of Outer Space
1958, (USA), AA, color, 80 mins.
W: Zsa Zsa Gabor, Eric Fleming, Paul Birch, Dave Willock, Patrick Waltz, Laurie
  Mitchell (*The Queen*), Barbara Darrow, Lisa Davis, Marilyn Buford, Mary
  Ford, Laura Mason, Kathy Marlowe, Tania Velia, Marjorie Durant, Marya
  Stevens, Lynn Cartwright, Colleen Drake, Gerry Gaylor
P: Ben Schwalb **D:** Edward Bernds **SCR:** Charles Beaumont & Ben Hecht
  SPCL-FX: Milt Rice, Irving Block & Jack Rabin **MUSIC:** Marlin Skiles
Standard SF-thriller: Astronauts investigate destructive rays from Venus, find alien matriarchy

The Queen of Outer Space: ERIC FLEMING AND ZSA ZSA GABOR

Queen of Sheba
1954, (It), Oro Films/Loppert, b&w, 99 mins.
W: Eleonora Ruffo, Gino Cervi
Standard melodrama: Exotic ruler lures Hebrew king

The Queen of Sheba Meets the Atom Man
1963, (USA), Ron Rice, color, 70 mins.
D: Ron Rice
unfinished 16mm "underground" film
Standard SF-fantasy

Queen of Spades
Russian silent
see *Pikovaya Dama (1910 & 1916)*

The Queen of Spades
1937, (Fr), General Production/Hoffberg, b&w, 87 mins.
W: Marguerite Moreno, Pierre Blanchar, Andre Lugut, Madeleine Ozeray
D: Fyodor Ozep, from Pushkin's story.
Originally La Dame de Pique
Standard thriller: Cad seeks noblewoman's secret of winning at cards

The Queen of Spades
1948, (GB), Assoc. British/Stratford, b&w, 95 mins.
W: Anton Walbrook (*Herman Suvorin*), Edith Evans (*Countess Ranevskaya*), Ronald Howard (*Andrei*), Mary Jerrold (*Vavarushka*), Yvonne Mitchell (*Lizavetta Ivanovna*), Anthony Dawson (*Fyodor*), Pauline Tennant (*Countess as a Young Woman*), Miles Malleson (*Tchybukin*), Athene Seyler (*Princess Ivashin*), Michael Medwin (*Ilovaisky*), Valentine Dyall (*The Messenger*), Ivor Barnard (*The Bookseller*), Yusef Ramart (*The Lover*), Gibb McLaughlin (*The Birdseller*), Violetta Elvin, Maroussia Dmitravitch, Aubrey Woods
P: Anatole de Grunwald   D: Thorold Dickinson   SCR: Rodney Ackland & Arthur Boys, from Pushkin's story   PHOTOG: Otto Heller   MUSIC: Georges Auric
Best cinemadaptation of Pushkin classic: Unscrupulous Russian captain plots to learn old countess' card-playing secret

The Queen of Spades
1960, (Russ), Artkino, color, 100 mins.
W: Yelena Polevitskaya, Oleg Strizhenov, Olga Krasina, Tamara Milashkina
D: Roman Tikhomirov
Operatic version of Pushkin classic

The Queen of Spades
1966, (Fr), Paris-Cite, b&w, 92 mins.
W: Dita Parlo, Michel Subor, Simone Bach, Zurab Anzhaparidze
D: Leonard Keigel
from Pushkin's story

Queen of the Amazons
1947, (USA), Lippert/SG, b&w, 61 mins.
W: Robert Lowery (*Gary Lambert*), Patricia Morison (*Jean Preston*), J. Edward Bromberg (*Gabby*), John Miljan (*Col. Jones*), Amira Moustafa (*Zeeda*), Keith Richards, Wilson Benge, Bruce Edwards, Jack George, Cay Forrester, Vida Aldana, Hassam Kayyam
P & D: Edward F. Finney   ORIG. STORY & SCR: Roger Merton   PHOTOG: Robert Pittack   MUSIC DIR: Lee Zahler
Minor adventure-thriller: Expedition seeks missing explorer, finds "white goddess"

Queen of the Amazons (1960)
see *La Regina delle Amazzoni*

Queen of the Cannibals
1979, (It), Aquarius, color, 81 mins.
W: Ian McCulloch, Donald O'Brian (*Dr. Butcher*)
D & SCR: Francesco Martino
USA retitle, Dr. Butcher, M.D. (Medical Deviate). orig. to be titled Cannibal Holocaust, Nightmare Island or Zombie Holocaust
Minor horror-thriller: Corpses stolen from hospital

Queen of the Counterfeiters
see *Queen of the London Counterfeiters*

Queen of the Gorillas
see *The Bride and the Beast*

Queen of the Jungle
1935, (USA), b&w, 87 mins.
W: Mary Kornman, Reed Howes, Dickie Jones, Marilyn Spinner, Lafe McKee
D: Robert F. Hill
Minor adventure-thriller: White girl raised in jungle

Queen Kelly
1928, (USA), UA, b&w, 8 reels/113 mins.
W: Gloria Swanson, Walter Byron, Seena Owen, Tully Marshall, Mme. Sulte-Wan, Wilhelm von Brinken, Florence Gibson, Madge Hunt
WRIT & DIR: Erich von Stroheim   PHOTOG: Ben Reynolds
Classic, partially-finished melodrama: Convent girl inherits South African bordello

Queen of the London Counterfeiters
1914, (GB), B&C/L&Y, b&w, 2,746 ft. (837m)
W: Lillian Wiggins (*Lillian Howard*), Fred Morgan (*Dick Garter*)
D: James Youngdeer
USA retitle, Queen of the Counterfeiters Apex, 1914
Standard crime-thriller: Detective trails girl counterfeiter, is thrown into Thames in sack

The Queen of the May
1910, (GB), Hepworth, b&w, 750 ft. (228.6m)
D: Bert Haldane
Standard thriller: Mad blacksmith fights rival brother with red-hot irons

Queen of the Nile
see *Nefertite, Regina del Nilo*

Queen of the Pirates
cf. *Tiger of the Seven Seas*

Queen of the Pirates
1960, (It-Germ), Col, color, 80 mins.
W: Gianna Maria Canale, Massimo Serato, Scilla Gabel, Paul Muller
D: Mario Costa   SCR: Kurt Nachman & Rolf Olsen   PHOTOG: Raffaele Masciocchi
Standard adventure-thriller

Queen of the Sea
1918, (USA), Fox, b&w, 5350 ft., 6 reels
W: Annette Kellermann, Hugh Thompson, Walter Law, Beth Irvine
D & SP: John G. Adolfi
Standard aquatic fantasy

Queen of the Seas
1960, (It), AIP/Filmways, color, 87 mins.
W: Lisa Gastoni, Jerome Courtland
Standard swashbuckler: Girl poses as man, takes over pirate ship

Queen of the Wicked
1916, (GB), British Empire Films, b&w, 5,500 ft. (1676.4m)
W: Henry Lonsdale (*Lucien la Verne*), Nina Lynn (*Ligeah Dupont*), Janet Alexander (*Lady Doris Manners*)
D & SCR: Albert Ward, from a play by Ronald Grahame
Standard crime-thriller: Dancer drugs husband, robs safe, strangles husband and frames lord for murder

Queenie of the Circus
1914, (GB), Motograph, b&w, 2,850 ft. (868.7m)
W: Lieut. Pommerol (*Julian*), Joan Morgan (*Queenie*), Harry Lorraine (*The Sec'y*), Joan Legge (*The Maid*), Martin Valmour (*The Valet*), Scott Clarke (*Sir Edward Ware*), Hazel Hastings (*The Girl*), Hen Pearce (*The Gypsy*)
P: Joseph Bamberger   D: Charles Raymond
Standard crime-thriller: Usurper kidnaps child heiress, sells her to traveling circus

The Queen's Musketeer
see *Le Mousquetaire de la Reine*

The Queen's Musketeers
see *Les Mousquetaires de la Reine*

The Queen's Swordsman

1960, (Mex), K. Gordon Murray, color, 86 mins.
W: Elmo Michel, Ariadne Welter, Enano Santanon
P & D: Roberto Rodriguez **SCR:** Roberto Rodriguez & Manuel Ojeda
    PHOTOG: Alex Phillips
Standard adventure-thriller

Quelque'un Derriere la Porte (Someone Behind the Door)

1971, (It-Fr), Lira-Medusa/Avco Embassy, color, 97 mins.
W: Charles Bronson (*The Stranger*), Anthony Perkins (*Laurence*), Jill Ireland
    (*Frances*), Henri Garcin (*Paul*), Andre Penvern (*The Intern*), Adriano
    Magestretti (*Andrew*), Agathe Natanson (*Lucy*), Viviane Everly (*The Young*
    Girl on the Beach), Carl J. Studer, Colin Mann, Denise Peronne, Yves Elliot,
    Isabelle Del Rio, Silvana Blasi
D: Nicolas Gessner **SCR:** Marc Behm, Jacques Robert & Nicolas Gessner, from
    Jacques Robert's novel **PHOTOG:** Pierre Lhomme **MUSIC:** Georges
    Garvarentz
Standard thriller: Brain surgeon tries to make amnesiac commit murder

The Quest

1986, (Austral), Miramax, color, 93 mins.
W: Henry Thomas
Standard adventure-thriller

A Question of Silence

1982, (Neth), Sigma/Quartet, color, 96 mins.
W: Edda Barends, Nelly Frijda, Henriette Tol, Hans Croiset, Cox Habbema, Eddy
    Brugman, Dolf de Vries
D & SCR: Marleen Gorris **PHOTOG:** Froms Bromet
Unusual feminist mystery-thriller: Three strangers brutally murder boutique manager

Quest for Camelot

1998, (USA), WB, color, 87 mins.
VOICES: Jane Seymour, Pierce Brosnan, Celine Dion, Sir John Gielgud, Bryan
    White, Don Rickles, Gary Oldman, Gabriel Byrne, Cary Elwes, Andrea
    Carr, Jessalyn Gilsig, Bronson Pinchot, Eric Idle
D: Frederik Du Chau
Standard animated fantasy: Adventure in Arthurian times

Quest for Fire

1981, (Fr-Can), ICC/Michael Gruskoff/20th-Fox, color, 100 mins.
W: Everett McGill (*Naoh*), Rae Dawn Chong (*Ika*), Ron Perlman (*Amou-kar*),
    Nameer El-Kadi (*Gaw*), Yves Langlois
P: John Kemeny & Denis Heroux **D:** Jean-Jacques Annaud **SCR:** Gerard
    Brach, from J.H. Rosny Sr.'s novel, special languages created by Anthony
    Burgess **PHOTOG:** Claude Agostini **MUSIC:** Philippe Sarde
Superior thriller: Cave men seek fire at mankind's dawn

Quest for Love

1971, (GB), Rank, color, 91 mins.
W: Joan Collins (*Ottillie*), Tom Bell (*Colin Trafford*), Denholm Elliott (*Tom Lewis*),
    Lyn Ashley (*Jennifer*), Laurence Naismith (*Sir Henry Lanstein*), Neil
    McCallum (*Jimmy Rand*), Juliet Harmer (*Geraldine Lambert*), Trudy Van
    Doorn (*Sylvia*), Jeremy Child (*Douggie Rayne*), Ray McAnally (*Jack Kahn*),
    Sam Kydd (*The Taximan*), John Hallam (*Jonathan Keene*), Geraldine Moffatt
    (*Stella*), Simon Ward (*Jeremy*), David Weston (*Johnny Prescott*), Drewe Henley
    (*The Man*), Edward Cast (*Jenkins*), Dudley Foster (*Grimshaw*), Angus
    Mackay (*Dr. Rankin*), Philip Stone (*Mason*), Bernard Horsfall (*Telford*)
P: Peter Eton **D:** Ralph Thomas **SCR:** Terence Feely, from John Wyndham's
    novel *Random Quest* **PHOTOG:** Ernest Steward **MUSIC:** Eric Rogers
Intriguing SF-romance: Physicist falls in love with doomed girl in parallel world

Quest for the Mighty Sword

1990, (It), color, 95 mins.
W: Eric Allen Kramer, Margaret Lenzey, Donal O'Brien (*Prince Gunther*), Dina
    Morrone (*Sunn*), Chris Murphy
D: David Hills
Minor fantasy: Hero rescues damsel in distress

A Question of Suspense

1961, (GB), Bill & Michael Luckwell/Col, b&w, 62 mins.
W: Peter Reynolds (*Tellman Drew*), Noelle Middleton (*Rose Marples*),Yvonne
    Buckingham (*Jean Forbes*), Norman Rodway (*Frank Brigstock*), James Neylin
    (*Insp. Hunter*), Pauline Delany (*Mrs. Barlow*), Anne Mulvey (*Sally*)
P: Bill Luckwell & Jock MacGregor **D:** Max Varnel **SCR:** Lawrence
    Huntington, from a novel by Roy Vickers
Standard crime-thriller: Girl takes revenge on tycoon who killed her lover

The ? Motorist

1906, (GB), b&w, 190 ft. (57.9m)
P: R.W. Paul **D:** Walter Booth
A.k.a. P.A.K.
Standard SF-fantasy: Motoring couple exceeds speed limit, has adventures in space

Quest of the Delta Knights

1993, (USA), color, 97 mins.
W: Corbin Allred, David Warner, Olivia Hussey, David Kriegel, Brigid Conley Walsh
D: James Dodson

Standard juvenile fantasy: Young hero vs. evil knight

The Questor Tapes

1974, (USA), Univ-TV, color, 100 mins.
W: Robert Foxworth, Mike Farrell (*Jerry*), Dana Wynter (*Lady Helena*), John
    Vernon (*Darro*), Lew Ayres (*Dr. Vaslovik*), Ellen Weston (*Allison Sample*),
    James Shigeta (*Dr. Chen*), Fred Sadoff (*Dr. Audret*), Majel Barrett (*Dr.*
    Bradley), Reuben Singer (*Dr. Gorlov*), Alan Caillou (*The Immigration Officer*),
    Gerald Saunderson Peters (*Randolph*), Walter Koenig (*The Administration*
    Ass't), Edie Gerard (*The Stewardess*), Robert Douglas
P: Howie Horwitz **D:** Richard A. Colla **TELEPLAY:** Gene Roddenberry &
    Gene Coon, from a story by Gene Roddenberry **PHOTOG:** Michael
    Margulies **SPCL-FX:** Albert Whitlock **MUSIC:** Gil Melle
TVM, above-average SF-thriller: Robot in human form seeks missing creator

A Quick-Change Mesmerist

1908, (GB), Urban, b&w, 315 ft. (96m)
D: Walter R. Booth
Standard fantasy: Hypnotist changes costumes of victims, vanishes

Quicksands of Life

1915, (GB), Gaumont-Victory, b&w, 4,000 ft. (1219.2m)
W: Malcolm Mortimer (*The Man*)
P: George Pearson **D:** J.L.V. Leigh
Standard crime-thriller

The Quiet Earth

1985, (New Zeal), Cinepro-Pillsbury/Skouras, color, 91 mins.
W: Bruno Lawrence (*Zac*), Alison Routledge (*Joanne*), Peter Smith (*Api*)
D: Geoff Murphy **SCR:** Bill Baer, Bruno Lawrence & Sam Pillsbury, from Craig
    Harrison's novel **PHOTOG:** James Bartle **MUSIC:** John Charles
Modest SF: Trio faces post-nuclear world

Quiet Killer

1992, (USA), Made for TV, color
W: Kate Jackson
TVM, standard thriller: Doctor discovers outbreak of new plague virus

A Quiet Place in the Country

see Un Tranquillo Posto di Campagna

A Quiet Place to Kill

1969, (It-Sp), AVCO Embassy, color, 90 mins.
W: Carroll Baker (*Helen*), Jean Sorel (*Maurice*), Anna Proclemer, Alberto Dalbes
D: Umberto Lenzi
Standard thriller: Jealousy complicates murder plots

The Quiller Memorandum

1966, (GB), Rank/20th Century-Fox, color, 103 mins.
W: George Segal (*Quiller*), Alec Guinness (*Pol*), Max von Sydow (*Oktober*), Senta
    Berger (*Inge*), George Sanders (*Gibbs*), Robert Helpmann (*Weng*), Robert
    Flemyng (*Rushington*), Peter Carsten (*Hengel*), Edith Schneider (*The*
    Headmistress), Gunter Meisner (*Hassler*), Ernest Walder, Philip Madoc, John
    Rees
D: Michael Anderson **SCR:** Harold Pinter, from a novel by Adam Hall
    PHOTOG: Erwin Hillier **SPCL-FX:** Les Bowie & Arthur Beavis
    MUSIC: John Barry **SONG:** (music, John Barry; lyric, Mack David; sung
    by Matt Munro), *Wednesday's Child*
Modest thriller: American agent crosses neo-Nazis in modern day Europe

Quiller: Price of Violence

1975, (GB), ABC-TV, color
W: Michael Jayston (*Quiller*), Moray Watson (*Angus*), Sinead Cusack (*Rosalind*),
    Ed Bishop (*Frank*)
from a character created by Adam Hall
TVM, minor thriller: British Intelligence agent marked for death by foreign assassins

The Quilt of Hathor

1988, (USA), Para-TV, color, 95 mins.
W: John D. LeMay, Robey, Chris Wiggins, Jack Marshak, Kate Trotter, Scott
    Paulin, Diego Matamoros (*Matthew*), Rebecca Lamp (*Diana Rowland*), David
    Brown (*Elder Fraser*), Bernard Behrens (*Inquisitor Holmes*), Helen Carscallen
    (*Sarah Good*), Araby Lockhart (*Elder Florence*), Patricia Strelioff (*Jane Spring*),
    James Kirchner (*Penitite Man #1*), Judith Orban (*Penitite Woman*), Ric
    Sarabia (*Penitite Man #2*)
D: Timothy Bond **TELEPLAY:** Janet MacLean **PHOTOG:** Rodney Charters
    SPCL-FX: John Gajdecki, Nicolette Beasley & Bruce Turner **MUSIC:**
    Fred Mollin
TVM, minor fantasy-thriller (culled from teleseries "Friday the 13th"): Satanic coverlet
inspires murder

Quintet

1979, (USA), 20th-Fox, color, 110 mins.
W: Paul Newman, Vittorio Gassman, Bibi Andersson, Fernando Rey, Brigitte
    Fossey
P & D: Robert Altman **SCR:** Frank Barhydt, Robert Altman & Patricia Resnick
    MUSIC: John Williams
Standard SF-thriller: Murder games during end-of-world ice age

Rabbits
see Night of the Lepus

Rabid
1976, (Can), New World, color, 90 mins.
<u>W</u>: Marilyn Chambers (*Rose*), Frank Moore (*Hart Read*), Joe Silver (*Murray Cypher*), Howard Ryshpan (*Dr. Dan Keloid*), Patricia Gage (*Dr. Roxanne Keloid*), Susan Roman (*Mindy Kent*), J. Roger Periard (*Lloyd Walsh*), Lynne Deragon (*Nurse Louise*), Victor Desny (*Claude Lapointe*), Terry Schonblum (*Judy Glasberg*), Julie Anna, Gary McKeehan, Miguel Fernandes, Terrence G. Ross, Greg Van Riel, Robert O'Ree, Jerome Tiberghien, Allan Moyle, Richard Farrell, Carl Wasserman, Jeannette Casenave, John Boylan, Malcolm Nelthorpe, Vlasta Vrana, Kirk McColl, Jack Messinger, Yvon Lecompte, Grant Lowe, John Gilbert, Tony Angelo, Una Kay, Madeline Pageau, Peter McNeill, Mark Walker, Bob Silverman, Terry Donald, Monique Belisle, Ron Mlodzik, Isabelle Lajeunesse, Louis Negin, Bob Girolani, Harry Hill, Kathy Keefler, Riva Spier, Marcel Fournier, Valda Dalton, Murray Smith, Denis LaCroix, Sherman Maness, Basil Fitzgibbon
<u>WRIT & D</u>: David Cronenberg <u>PHOTOG</u>: Rene Verzier <u>MUSIC SPRVSR</u>: Ivan Reitman
Unusual horror-thriller: Woman infected with new strain of rabies

Rabid Grannies
1989, (Belg), Troma, color, 88 mins.
<u>W</u>: Elie Lison, Catherine Aymerie, Caroline Brackman, Anne Marie Fox, Danielle Daven, Raymond Lescot, Patricia Davie, Richard Cotica
<u>D & SCR</u>: Emmanuel Kervyn
Minor horror-fantasy: Elderly aunts possessed by demonic forces

A Race for Life
1954, (GB), Hammer/Lippert, b&w, 69 mins.
<u>W</u>: Richard Conte, Mari Aldon
<u>D</u>: Terence Fisher
Original title, Mask of Dust
Standard thriller

Race with the Devil
1975, (USA), Saber-Maslansky/20th-Fox, color, 88 mins.
<u>W</u>: Peter Fonda, Warren Oates, Loretta Swit, R.G. Armstrong, Lara Parker, Clay Tanner, Carol Blodgett, Phil Hoover
<u>D</u>: Jack Starrett <u>TELEPLAY</u>: Lee Frost & Wes Bishop <u>PHOTOG</u>: Robert Jessup <u>MUSIC</u>: Leonard Rosenman
Standard thriller: Witch coven pursues vacationers

Die Rache der Schwarzen Spinne
see The Spider (1958)

Die Rache des Homunculus
see Homunculus

Rachel's Sin
1911, (GB), Hepworth, b&w, 900 ft. (274.3m)
<u>W</u>: Gladys Sylvani (*Rachel*), Hay Plumb (*Jacob*), Harry Royston (*The Husband*)
<u>D</u>: Lewin Fitzhamon
Standard crime-thriller: Wife kills drunken husband, her ex-fiance is blamed

Radan
see Rodan, the Flying Monster

Radar Secret Service
1950, (USA), Lippert, b&w, 59 mins.
<u>W</u>: John Howard, Adele Jergens, Tom Neal, Myrna Dell, Sid Melton, Ralph Byrd, Pierre Watkin, Robert Kent, Tristram Coffin, Riley Hill, Bob Carson, Marshall Reed, Jan Kayne, John McKee, Holly Bane (*Mike Ragan*), Bob Woodward, Boyd Stockman, Bill Crespinel, Kenne Duncan, Bill Hammond
<u>D</u>: Sam Newfield <u>SCR</u>: Beryl Sachs
Minor thriller: Spies wreak havoc

The Radiance of a Thousand Suns
see La Brulure de Mille Soleils

Radioactive Dreams
1984, (USA), ITM/Hal Roach, color, 94 mins.
<u>W</u>: John Stockwell, Michael Dudikoff, Lisa Blount, Michelle Little, Don Murray, George Kennedy, Norbert Weisser, Demian Slade, Christian Andrews
<u>WRIT & D</u>: Albert F. Pyun <u>PHOTOG</u>: Charles Minsky <u>SPCL-FX</u>: R.J. Hohman <u>MUSIC</u>: Pete Robinson <u>SONGS</u>: *Nightmare, Daddy's Gonna Boogie Tonight, She'll Burn You, All Talk, Young Thing, Tickin' of the Clock, Psychedelic Man, Guilty Pleasures, Eat You Alive, Turn Away, When Lightning Strikes & She's a Fire*
Minor SF-adventure: Two youths seek answers in post-nuke world

Radio Cab Murder
1954, (GB), Insignia/Eros, b&w, 70 mins.
<u>W</u>: Jimmy Hanley (*Fred Martin*), Lana Morris (*Myra*), Sonia Holm (*Jean*), Jack Allen (*Parker*), Sam Kydd (*Spencer*), Pat McGrath (*Henry*), Bruce Beeby (*Insp. Rawlings*), Elizabeth Seal (*Gwen*), Frank Thornton (*Insp. Finch*)
<u>P</u>: George Maynard <u>D & SCR</u>: Vernon Sewell <u>STORY</u>: Pat McGrath, Donald Rawlings & Michael Storm
Standard crime-thriller: Ex-convict taxi-driver poses as crook, nabs bank robbers

Radio Ranch
1935, (USA), Mascot, b&w, 70 mins.
<u>W</u>: Gene Autry, Betsy King Ross, Smiley Burnette, Frankie Darro, Dorothy Christie, Wheeler Oakman, Charles K. French, Edward Piel Sr., Warner Richmond, William Moore (*Peter Potter*)
<u>D</u>: Otto Brower & B. Reeves Eason <u>SCR</u>: John Rathmell & Armand Shaefer <u>PHOTOG</u>: Ernest Miller & William Nobles
Standard SF-adventure (feature culled from 12-chapter serial The Phantom Empire): Singing cowboy outwits denizens of underground world

Der Raecher (The Avenger)
1960, (W. Ger), CCC, b&w, 102 mins.
<u>W</u>: Heinz Drache, Ingrid Van Bergen, Ina Duscha, Maria Litto, Klaus Kinski
<u>P & SCR</u>: Kurt Ulrich <u>D</u>: Karl Anton, from a story by Edgar Wallace
Minor thriller: Terror stalks movie studio

Rag Doll
1961, (GB), Blakeley's Films/Butcher, b&w, 67 mins.
<u>W</u>: Jess Conrad (*Shane*), Hermione Baddeley (*Princess*), Kenneth Griffith (*Wilson*), Christina Gregg (*Carol*), Patrick Magee (*Flynn*), Patrick Jordan (*Wills*), Frank Forsyth (*The Supt.*), Michael Wynne (*Bellamy*)
<u>P</u>: Tom Blakeley <u>D</u>: Lance Comfort <u>SCR</u>: Brock Williams & Derry Quinn <u>STORY</u>: Brock Williams
Standard crime-thriller: Cafe owner's teen stepdaughter falls for singing burglar

La Ragazza Che Sapeva Troppo (The Girl Who Knew Too Much)
1962, (It), Massimo De Rita-Galatea/AIP, b&w, 92 mins.
<u>W</u>: Leticia Roman, John Saxon, Valentina Cortese, Dante Di Paolo, Peggy Nathan, Jim Dolen, Gianni Di Benedetto, Milo Quesada, Robert Buchanan, Marta Melocco, Virginia d'Oro, Lucia Modugno, Franco Morici, Jim Stacy, Titti Tomaino, Dafydd Havard, Pini Lido, Chana Coubert, Luigi Bonos
<u>D</u>: Mario Bava <u>SCR</u>: Enzo Corbucci, Ennio De Concini, Eliana De Sabata, Nino Guerrini, Franco Prosperi & Mario Bava <u>PHOTOG</u>: Ubaldo Terzano <u>MUSIC</u>: Roberto Nicolosi
USA retitle, The Evil Eye (retitle orig. to be Incubus, Schizo or House of Terror)
Standard thriller: Girl uncovers frightening secret

Rage
1972, (USA), WB, color, 104 mins.
<u>W</u>: George C. Scott (*Dan Logan*), Richard Basehart (*Dr. Cardwell*), Barnard Hughes (*Dr. Spencer*), Nicolas Beauvy (*Chris Logan*), Paul Stevens (*Col. Franklin*), Martin Sheen (*Maj. Holliford*), Stephen Young (*Maj. Reintz*), Kenneth Tobey (*Col. Nickerson*), William Jordan (*Maj. Cooper*), Robert Walden (*Dr. Janeway*)
<u>P</u>: Fred Weintraub <u>D</u>: George C. Scott <u>SCR</u>: Philip Friedman & Dan Kelinman <u>PHOTOG</u>: Fred Koenekamp <u>MUSIC</u>: Lalo Schifrin
Standard thriller: Rancher seeks revenge for son's death by army nerve gas

Rage in Heaven
1941, (USA), MGM, b&w, 82 mins.
<u>W</u>: Robert Montgomery, Ingrid Bergman, George Sanders, Lucile Watson, Oscar Homolka
<u>D</u>: W.S. Van Dyke <u>CO-SCR</u>: Christopher Isherwood, from a novel by James Hilton
Standard thriller: Wealthy scion plots revenge

Rage of the Buccaneers
1962, (It), Max/Colorama, color, 88 mins.
<u>W</u>: Ricardo Montalban, Vincent Price, Giulia Rubini
<u>P</u>: Ottavio Poggi <u>D</u>: Mario Costa <u>SCR</u>: John Byrne & Ottavio Poggi
A.k.a. The Black Buccaneer
Minor adventure-thriller: Pirate imprisoned by evil governor's secretary

Raiders from Beneath the Sea
1964, (USA), Lippert/20th-Fox, b&w, 73 mins.
<u>W</u>: Ken Scott, Merry Anders, Russ Bender, Booth Coleman, Garth Benton, Bruce Anson, Walter Maslow, Stacy Winters, Ray Dannis, Larry Barton, Roger Creed
<u>P & D</u>: Maury Dexter
Standard adventure-thriller

Raiders of Atlantis
1983, (USA), color, 100 mins.
<u>W</u>: Christopher Connelly
<u>D</u>: Roger Franklin
A.k.a. The Atlantis Interceptors
Minor SF-thriller: Warfare when lost continent surfaces

Raiders of the Living Dead
1986, (USA), Cineronde-Canada/Independent-Int'l, color, 86 mins.
<u>W</u>: Scott Schwartz (*Jonathan*), Robert Deveau (*Morgan Randall*), Donna Asali (*Shelly Godwin*), Bob Allen (*Dr. Carstairs*), Zita Johann (*The Librarian*), Bob Sacchetti (*The Man in Black*), Leonard Corman (*Dr. Kapek*), Corri Burt (*Michelle*), Christine Farish (*Karen*), Nino Rigali (*Det. Kruger*), Barbara Patterson (*Mrs. Levitt*), Mark Elliot (*Axton*), Kevin Long, Robert Huber, C. Dumas, Mark Kjelle, Tex Tuttle, Robert Fausak, Barry Doe, Jim Morgan,

Kaye Ernst, Mary Lang, Ray Good, Charles Aughenbaugh, George Seavey, Tyler Smith, Richard Abair, Michael Brown, Craig Davis, James Focarille, George E. Hansel, Paul Hersh, Kenneth J. Hart, Marvin Jefferson, Mark LaFave, Kendell Lide, Daniel Lieb, Greg Magoon, Steve Mascutto, Michael McCabe, Calvin A. McLinton, D.J. Queenan, Craig Scott, Greg McGrath, Ron Tassinaro, Duncan Stephens, Glenn Steers, Bruce D. Waugh, Brian Magoon
D: Samuel M. Sherman   **STORY & SCR:** Samuel M. Sherman & Brett Piper   **PHOTOG:** Douglas Meltzer   **SPCL-FX:** Bob LeBar
Minor horror-thriller: Evil doctor creates zombies

Raiders of the Lost Ark
1981, (USA), Lucasfilm Ltd./Para, color, 111 mins.
W: Harrison Ford *(Indiana Jones)*, Karen Allen *(Marion)*, Paul Freeman *(Belloq)*, John Rhys-Davies *(Sallah)*, Denholm Elliott *(Brody)*, Ronald Lacey *(Toht)*, Alfred Molina *(Satipo)*, Tutte Lemkow *(Imam)*, Wolf Kahler *(Dietrich)*, Anthony Higgins *(Gobler)*, Vic Tablian *(Barranca)*, Don Fellows *(Col. Musgrove)*, William Hootkins *(Maj. Eaton)*, Fred Sorenson *(Jock)*, Sonny Caldinez *(The Mean Mongolian)*, Matthew Scurfield *(The 2nd Nazi)*, Bill Reimbold *(The Bureaucrat)*, Patrick Durkin *(The Australian Climber)*, Malcolm Weaver *(The Ratty Nepalese)*, Anthony Chinn *(Mohan)*, Pat Roach *(The Giant Sherpa/The 1st Mechanic)*, Christopher Frederick *(Otto)*, Ishaq Bux *(Omar)*, Kiran Shah *(Abu)*, Souad Messaoudi *(Fayah)*, Terry Richards *(The Swordsman)*, Steve Hanson *(The German Agent)*, John Rees *(The Sergeant)*, Frank Marshall *(The Pilot)*, Martin Kreidt *(The Young Soldier)*, George Harris *(Katanga)*, Eddie Tagoe *(The Messenger Pirate)*, Tony Vogel *(The Tall Captain)*, Ted Grossman *(The Peruvian Porter)*, Jack Dearlove *(The Stand-In)*
P: Frank Marshall   **D:** Steven Spielberg   **SCR:** Lawrence Kasdan   **STORY:** George Lucas & Philip Kaufman   **PHOTOG:** Douglas Slocombe   **MUSIC:** John Williams
Classic thriller: Adventurous professor seeks Ark of the Covenant, battles Nazis. cf. **Indiana Jones and the Temple of Doom**

Raiders of the Seven Seas
1953, (USA), Global/UA, color, 88 mins.
W: John Payne, Donna Reed, Lon Chaney Jr., Gerald Mohr, Anthony Caruso, Henry Brandon, Frank de Kova, William Tannen, Skip Torgerson, Claire DuBrey, Anthony Warde
P & D: Sidney Salkow   **PHOTOG:** W. Howard Greene
Standard adventure-thriller: Pirate captures countess

Raiders of the Sun
1992, (USA), color, 80 mins.
W: Richard Norton, Rick Dean, Blake Boyd, Brigitta Stenberg, William Steis
D: Cirio H. Santiago
Minor SF-thriller: Earth ruined by biological disaster

Rainbow Brite and the Star Stealer
1985, (Jap), Hallmark/WB, color, 97 mins.
Standard animated fantasy: Space princess covets universe's source of light

The Rain Killer
1990, (USA), Califilm/Concorde, color, 94 mins.
W: Ray Sharkey, David Beechcroft
Minor thriller: Serial killer strikes only in stormy weather

Rain Without Thunder
1993, (USA), color, 87 mins.
W: Betty Buckley, Jeff Daniels, Ali Thomas, Frederic Forrest, Carolyn McCormick, Linda Hunt, Robert Earl Jones, Graham Greene, Iona Morris, Austin Pendleton
D & SCR: Gary Bennett   **MUSIC:** Randall Lynch & Allen Lynch
Minor SF-melodrama: Girl tries to obtain forbidden abortion in 2042

Raising Cain
1991, (USA), Univ, color, 95 mins.
W: John Lithgow *(Carter/Cain/Dr. Nix/Josh/Margo)*, Lolita Davidovich *(Jenny)*, Steven Bauer *(Jack)*, Frances Sternhagen *(Dr. Waldheim)*, Gregg Henry *(Lt. Terri)*, Mel Harris *(Sarah)*, Tom Bower *(Sgt. Cally)*, Gabrielle Carteris *(Nan)*, Barton Heyman *(Mack)*, Amanda Pombo *(Amy)*, Kathleen Callan *(Emma)*, Teri Austin
WRIT & D: Brian De Palma   **PHOTOG:** Stephen H. Burum   **MUSIC:** Pino Donaggio
Bizarre thriller: Split-personality causes mayhem

The Rajah's Dream: or, The Enchanted Forest
see Le Reve du Rajah ou la Foret Enchantee

The Rajah's Revenge
1912, (GB), Cricks & Martin, b&w, 1,170 ft. (356.6m)
W: Wingold Lawrence *(The Officer)*, Cicely Gilbert *(The Wife)*, Jack Leigh *(The Rajah)*
D: Dave Aylott
reissued 1916
Standard melodrama: Rajah tortures officer to force wife's submission, dies in own crocodile pool

The Rajah's Tiara
1914, (GB), Big Ben Films-Union/Pathe, b&w, 2,275 ft. (693.4m)

W: James Carew *(Henry Arnold)*, Ivy Montford *(Dolores)*, Mr. Jackson *(Fred Creston)*
D: H.O. Martinek   **STORY:** L.C. MacBean
Standard thriller: Crime gang steals gems

Ramar and the Burning Barrier
1952, (USA), ITC, b&w, 82 mins.
W: Jon Hall
Standard thriller (edited from "Ramar of the Jungle" teleseries)

Ramar and the Deadly Females
1952, (USA), ITC, b&w, 80 mins.
W: Jon Hall
Standard thriller (edited from "Ramar of the Jungle" teleseries)

Ramar and the Jungle Secrets
1952, (USA), ITC, b&w, 81 mins.
W: Jon Hall
Standard thriller (edited from "Ramar of the Jungle" teleseries)

Ramar and the Savage Challengers
1952, (USA), ITC, b&w, 83 mins.
W: Jon Hall
Standard thriller (edited from "Ramar of the Jungle" teleseries)

Ramar and the Unknown Terror
1952, (USA), ITC, b&w, 83 mins.
W: Jon Hall
Standard thriller (edited from "Ramar of the Jungle" teleseries)

Ramar of the Jungle
1952, (USA), ITC, b&w, 77 mins.
W: Jon Hall
Standard thriller (edited from "Ramar of the Jungle" teleseries)

Ramar's Mission to India
1952, (USA), ITC, b&w, 80 mins.
W: Jon Hall
Standard thriller (edited from "Ramar of the Jungle" teleseries)

Rampage
1963, (USA), WB, color, 98 mins.
W: Robert Mitchum, Elsa Martinelli, Jack Hawkins, Sabu, Emile Genest
D: Phil Karlson & Henry Hathaway (uncredited)   **SCR:** Robert Holt & Marguerite Roberts, from a novel by Alan Caillou   **PHOTOG:** Harold Lipstein   **MUSIC:** Elmer Bernstein
Standard thriller: Love triangle complicated by escaped tiger

Ran (Chaos)
1985, (Jap-Fr), Orion Classics, color, 160 mins.
W: Tatsuya Nakadai, Mieko Harada, Akira Terao, Jinpachi Nezu, Daisuke Ryu, Masayuki Yui, Yoshiko Miyazaki, Hisashi Igawa
D: Akira Kurosawa, inspired by Shakespeare's play *King Lear*   **SCR:** Akira Kurosawa, Hideo Oquino & Masato Ide   **PHOTOG:** Takao Saito, Masaharu Ueda & Asaishi Nakai   **MUSIC:** Toru Takemitsu
Epic melodrama: Warfare in feudal Japan

Rana: The Legend of Shadow Lake
1980, (USA), Galaxy One, color, 96 mins.
W: Glenn Scherer *(Kelly Sr.)*, Doreen Moze *(Chris)*, Brad Ellingson *(Kelly Jr.)*, Karen McDiarmid *(Elli)*, Alan Ross *(John)*, Julie Wheaton *(Susan)*, Jerry Gregoris *(Charlie)*, Jim Iaquinta *(Burley)*, Bruno Aclin *(Cal)*, Lorry Getz *(Sorenson)*, Michael J. Skewes *(Mike)*, Paul Callaway, Richard Lange, Angel Rebane
D: Bill Rebane
Minor horror-thriller: Orphan returns to river where parents were killed by monster

Rape of Eden
1994, (USA), color, 90 mins.
W: Francine Lapensee
D & SCR: Sam Auster
A.k.a. **Bounty Hunter 2002**

Rapture
1950, (It), Film Classics, b&w, 79 mins.
W: Glenn Langan *(Pietro Leoni)*, Elsy Albiin *(Francesca Hutton)*, Lorraine Miller *(Marisa Hutton)*, Eduardo Ciannelli *(Arnaldo)*, Douglass Dumbrille *(W.C. Hutton)*, Harriet White *(The Nurse)*, Goffredo Alessandrini *(Renato)*
D: Goffredo Alessandrini   **SCR:** Geza Herczeg, David M. Pelham & John C. Shepridge, from Arpad Herczeg's novel *Invasion on the Lake*
Standard melodrama

Raptus
1962, (It), Panda/Sigma III, color, 88 mins.
W: Barbara Steele, Robert Flemyng, Montgomery Glenn, Maria Teresa Vianello, Harriet White, Spencer William
P: Louis Mann [Luigi Carpentieri & Ermanno Donati]   **D:** Robert Hampton [Riccardo Freda]   **SCR:** Julian Perry [Ernesto Gastaldi]   **PHOTOG:** Donald Green [Raffaele Masciocchi]
Fr retitle, **Le Spectre du Professeur Hichcock** *(The Ghost of Professor Hichcock)*

USA retitle, The Horrible Dr. Hichcock, A.k.a. The Abominable Dr. Hichcock and The Frightening Secret of Dr. Hichcock
blurbs: "His secret was a coffin named desire!"; "The candle of his lust, burnt brightest in the shadow of the grave!"
Standard thriller: Wife of sex-deviant doctor returns from grave

Rapunzel Let Down Your Hair
1978, (GB), color, 78 mins.
W: Margaret Ford, Suzie Hickford, Jessica Swift, Laka Koc, Lydia Blackman
D: Susan Shapiro, Esther Ronay & Francine Winham
Unusual feminist anthology: Various interpretations of the "Rapunzel" fairytale

The Rare Book Murder
1938, (USA), MGM, b&w, 73 mins.
W: George Zucco, Melvyn Douglas, Florence Rice
Minor thriller. Orignally **Fast Company**, *TV title*

Raskolnikov
1923, (Ger), Neumann, b&w, 10,393.7 ft. (3168m)
W: Grigor Chmara
WRIT & D: Robert Wiene, based on Dostoevski's novel *Crime and Punishment*
Standard thriller: Conscience bedevils murderer

Rasputin
1930, (Ger), b&w
W: Conrad Veidt
Standard thriller: Mad monk controls Russian nobles

Rasputin
1938, (Fr), b&w
W: Harry Baur
Standard thriller: Evil monk corrupts Russian court

Rasputin
1985, (Russ), Int'l Film Exchange, color & b&w, 107 mins, orignally 148 mins.
W: Alexi Petrenko *(Rasputin)*, Anatoly Romashin, Velta Linne, Alice Freindikh
D: Elem Klimov   **SCR:** Semyon Lunghin & Ilya Nusinov   **MUSIC:** Alfred Shnitke
Superior historical melodrama (filmed in 1975): Mad monk dominates Russian royal family

Rasputin
1996, (USA), HBO-TV, color, 105 mins.
W: Alan Rickman *(Rasputin)*, Ian McKellen *(Czar Nicholas)*, Greta Scacchi *(Empress Alexandra)*, John Wood *(Stolypin)*, David Warner *(Dr. Botkin)*, Freddie Findley *(Alexei)*
D: Udi Edel   **TELEPLAY:** Peter Pruce   **MUSIC:** Brad Fiedel
Made-for-Cable, modest bio-thriller: Evil monk preys on Romanoff royalty

Rasputin and the Empress
1932, (USA), MGM, b&w, 135 mins.
W: John Barrymore *(Prince Chegodieff)*, Ethel Barrymore *(Czarina Alexandra)*, Lionel Barrymore *(Rasputin)*, Diana Wynyard *(Princess Irina)*, Ralph Morgan *(Czar Nicholas)*, Jean Parker, Nigel de Brulier, C. Henry Gordon, Gustav von Seyffertitz, Edward Arnold, Anne Shirley
D: Richard Boleslavsky   **STORY & SCR:** Charles MacArthur   **PHOTOG:** William H. Daniels   **MUSIC:** Herbert P. Stothart
Lavish melodrama: Intrigue in court of Romanoffs

Rasputin, the Mad Monk
1966, (GB), Hammer-7Arts/20th-Fox, color, 92 mins.
W: Christopher Lee *(Rasputin)*, Barbara Shelley *(Sonia)*, Francis Matthews *(Ivan)*, Richard Pasco *(Dr. Zargo)*, Suzan Farmer *(Vanessa)*, Nicholas Pennell *(Peter)*, Derek Francis *(The Innkeeper)*, Renee Asherson *(The Tsarina)*, John Welsh *(The Abbott)*, Alan Tilvern *(The Patron)*, Joss Ackland *(The Bishop)*, Robert Duncan *(The Tsarevitch)*, John Bailey *(The Court Physician)*, Dinsdale Landen *(Peter)*, Bryan Marshall, Cyril Shaps, Fiona Hartford, Helen Christie, Maggie Wright
P: Anthony Nelson Keys   **D:** Don Sharp   **SCR:** John Elder [Anthony Hinds]
PHOTOG: Michael Reed   **MUSIC:** Don Banks   **DESIGN:** Don Mingaye
"Christopher Lee is indeed a competent actor, having played all manner of parts, most of them of the horrific type, if memory serves. He shows his ability once again by donning the robes of the mad menace of Russian history and doing a very effective job"—Motion Picture Exhibitor
Unusual thriller: Melodramatic look at salad days of infamous Russian charlatan

Ratboy
1986, (USA), Malpaso/WB, color, 104 mins.
W: Sondra Locke, Robert Townsend, Christopher Hewett, Sharon Baird, Gerrit Graham, Louie Anderson
D: Sondra Locke   **SCR:** Rob Thompson   **MUSIC:** Lennie Niehaus
Standard satire-thriller: Woman promoter exploits human freak

Rat Pfink & Boo Boo
1966, (USA), Craddock, b&w, 72 mins.
W: Vin Saxon, Titus Moede, Carolyn Brandt, George Caldwell, Mike Kannon, James Bowie
P & D: Ray Dennis Steckler   **SCR:** Ronald Haydock
Standard adventure-satire: Rock singer and gardener transform selves into superheroes

The Rats are Coming!—The Werewolves are Here!
1972, (USA), William Mishkin, color, 92 mins
W: Hope Stansbury, Jack Skarvellis, Noel Collins, Douglas Phair, Joan Ogden, Bernard Kaler
D & SCR: Andy Milligan   **PHOTOG:** Wiliam Mishkin
Minor horror-thriller: Female werewolf raises man-eating rodents

Rattled
1996, (USA), USA-TV, color, 95 mins.
W: William Katt *(Paul)*, Shanna Reed *(Krista)*, Ed Lauter *(Murray)*, Bibi Besch *(Gail)*, Monica Creel *(Michelle)*
Made-for-Cable, standard thriller: Housing construction awakens his bernating snakes

Rattlers
1984, (USA), Lorimar, color, 80 mins.
W: Sam Chew *(Tom)*, Elisabeth Chauvet *(Ann)*, Dan Priest *(The Colonel)*, Ron Gold *(Delaney)*, Al Dunlap *(The General)*, Dan Balentine *(The Pilot)*, Gary Van Orman *(Woodley)*, Darwin Jostin *(Palmer)*, Cary Pitts *(The Sergeant)*, Eric Lawson *(The Guard)*, Tony Ballen *(The Sheriff)*, Richard Lockmiller *(The Deputy)*, Jo Jordon *(The Mother)*, Scott McCarter *(Rick)*, Tipp McClure *(Plummer)*, Celia Kaye *(The Woman)*, Travis Gold *(Timmy)*, Alan Decker, Bob Merehon, Ancel Cook, Matthew Knox, John Landon
D: John McCauley   **MUSIC:** Miles Goodman
Minor thriller: Snakes attack humans, bio-warfare gas blamed

Ravager
1997, (USA), color
W: Bruce Payne
Minor thriller

Ravagers
1979, (USA), Cinecorp/Col, color, 95 mins.
W: Richard Harris *(Falk)*, Ernest Borgnine *(Rann)*, Ann Turkel *(Faina)*, Art Carney *(The Sergeant)*, Anthony James *(The Ravager Leader)*, Woody Strode *(Brown)*, Seymour Cassel *(The Blind Lawyer)*, Alana Hamilton *(Miriam)*, Brian Carney *(Foy)*, Kurt Grayson *(Coop)*, Arch Archambault *(The First Ravager)*, Robert Westmoreland *(Hank)*, Gordon Hyde, Ph.D. *(Bert)*, Kim Crow *(The Flocker Woman)*, Steve Lashley *(The 2nd Ravager)*, George Stokes *(Bant)*, Cecily Hovanes *(Grace)*, Andre Tayir *(The Prisoner)*, Harvey Evans *(The Prison Guard)*, Olivia Barton *(The Mushroom Woman)*
D: Richard Compton   **SCR:** Donald S. Sanford, from Robert Edmond Alter's novel *Path to Savagery*   **PHOTOG:** Vincent Saizis   **SPCL-FX:** Fred Cramer   **MUSIC:** Fred Karlin
Minor SF-adventure: Post-nuke wanderer encounters opposing factions

The Raven
1915, (USA), Essanay, b&w, 50 mins.
W: Henry B. Walthall, Wanda Howard
D: George C. Hazelton, from Edgar Allan Poe's poem
Standard melodrama

The Raven
1935, (USA), Univ, b&w, 62 mins.
W: Bela Lugosi *(Dr. Richard Vollin)*, Boris Karloff *(Bateman)*, Irene Ware *(Jean Thatcher)*, Lester Matthews *(Jerry Halden)*, Samuel S. Hinds *(Judge Thatcher)*, Inez Courtney *(Mary Burns)*, Spencer Charters *(Col. Grant)*, Maidel Turner, Ian Wolfe, Arthur Hoyt
D: Louis Friedlander [Lew Landers]   **SCR:** David Boehm, inspired by Edgar Allan Poe's poem   **PHOTOG:** Charles Stumar
"With stunning sets and marvelously full-blooded dialogue, *The Raven* gives Karloff and Lugosi their heads, and their delightful collaboration results in a film that is both a sharply-etched lampoon (if one chooses to take it that way) and an excellent Grand Guignol to boot"—William K. Everson, The Bad Guys
Classic thriller: Spurned neurosurgeon goes mad, activates torture chamber

The Raven: IRENE WARE AND LESTER MATTHEWS

The Raven
1948, (Fr.), Westport-Int'l, b&w, 90 mins.
W: Pierre Fresnay
D: Henri-Georges Clouzot, based on Edgar Allan Poe's poem
Standard melodrama

The Raven
1963, (USA), Alta-Vista/AIP, color, 86 mins.
W: Vincent Price (*Dr. Erasmus Craven*), Boris Karloff (*Dr. Scarabus*), Peter Lorre (*Dr. Bedlo*), Hazel Court (*Lenore*), Jack Nicholson (*Rexford*), Olive Sturgess (*Estelle*), Aaron Saxon, Connie Wallace, William Baskin, Jim Jr. (*The Raven*)
P & D: Roger Corman SCR: Richard Matheson, inspired by Edgar Allan Poe's poem PHOTOG: Floyd Crosby SPCL-FX: Pat Dinga MUSIC: Les Baxter DESIGN: Daniel Haller
orig. co-billed with Night Tide
Amusing horror-comedy: Two wizards have duel of magic

Rave Review
1994, (USA),Gnu-Wildebeast Co., color, 90 mins.
W: Jeff Seymour, Carmen Argenziano, Ed Begley Jr.
WRIT & D: Jeff Seymour
Standard dark satire: L.A. director tries to save career by scaring critic to death

Rawhead Rex
1987, (GB), Green Man/Alpine/Empire, color, 89 mins.
W: David Dukes (*Howard Hallenbeck*), Kelly Piper (*Elaine Hallenbeck*), Niall Toibin (*Rev. Coot*), Niall O'Brien (*Det. Insp. Isaac Gissing*), Ronan Wilmot (*Declan O'Brien*), Hugh O'Conor (*Robbie Hallenbeck*), Cora Lunny (*Minty Hallenbeck*), Heinrich Von Schellerdorf (*Rawhead Rex*), Gladys Sheehan, Donal McCann, Eleanor Feely, Gerry Walsh, Madelyn Erskine, Noel O'Donovan, John Olohan, Peter Donovan, Barry Lynch, Bob Carlile, Patrick Dawson, Maeve Germaine, Simon Kelly, Derry Power, Sheila Flitton, Derek Halligan, Dave Carey, Bairbre Ni Chacimh, Tom Lawlor, Vincent Smith, Bob Coyle, Michael Ford, Frank Melia, Lana McDonald, Robert Byrne, David Nolan, Mary Ryan, Julie Hamilton, Liv Clausen
D: George Pavlou SCR: Clive Barker PHOTOG: John Metcalfe SPCL-FX SPRVSR: Gerry Johnston MUSIC: Colin Towns
Standard horror-fantasy: Legendary demon revives

Raw Meat
see Deathline

Raw Nerve
1991, (USA),Pyramid/AIP Studios color, 93 mins.
W: Glenn Ford, Sandahl Bergman, Traci Lords, Randall "Tex" Cobb, Ted Prior, Jan-Michael Vincent
SCR: David A. Prior
Standard thriller: Cops doubt youth who claims visions of serial killer

Raw Wind in Eden
1958, (USA), Univ, color, 93 mins.
W: Jeff Chandler, Esther Williams, Rossana Podesta, Eduardo DeFilippo, Rik Battaglia, Carlos Thompson
D: Richard Wilson SCR: Elizabeth & Richard Wilson PHOTOG: Enzo Serafin MUSIC: Hans J. Salter MUSIC DIR: Joseph Gershenson
Standard melodrama: Plane-crash survivors find mystery and tension on isolated Greek isle

Rays That Erase
1916, (GB), Martin/DFSA, b&w, 567 ft. (172.8m)
D: Edwin J. Collins
Standard fantasy: Rays from prof's lamp make objects disappear

Razorback
1983, (Austral), UAA/WB, color, 95 mins.
W: Gregory Harrison (*Carl Winters*), Arkie Whiteley (*Sarah Cameron*), Bill Kerr (*Jake Cullen*), Chris Haywood (*Benny Baker*), David Argue (*Dicko Baker*), Judy Morris (*Beth Winters*), Jim Howard (*Danny*), John Ewart (*Turner*), Mervyn Drake (*Andy*), Don Smith (*Wallace*), Redmond Phillips (*The Magistrate*), Alan Beecher (*The Counsel*), Peter Schwartz (*The Lawyer*), Beth Child (*Louise Cullen*), Chris Hession (*The TV Cowboy*), Rick Kennedy (*The Farmer*), Brian Adams (*The Male Newscaster*), Jinx Lootens (*The Female Newscaster*), Angus Malone (*Scotty*), Peter Boswell (*Wagstaff*), Don Lane (*himself*)
D: Russell Mulcahy SCR: Everett DeRoche, based on Peter Brennan's novel PHOTOG: Dean Semler SPCL-FX: Mark Canny, Bob McCarron, David Yardley & Jim Morphett MUSIC: Iva Davies
Engrossing thriller: Monster boar plagues Aussie "Outback"

Reactor
1985, (USA), color, 90 mins.
W: Yanti Somer, Melissa Long, James R. Stuart, Nick Jordan, Robert Barnes
Minor SF-thriller: Space aliens, kidnapped Earth scientists, and dangerous nuclear reactor

Really Weird Tales
1986, (USA), color, 85 mins.
W: John Candy, Martin Short, Joe Flaherty, Catherine O'Hara
Standard SF-satire: 3 sci-fi spoofs

Re-Animator
1985, (USA), Brian Yuzna/Empire, color, 86 mins.
W: Jeffrey Combs (*Herbert West*), Bruce Abbott (*Dan Cain*), Barbara Crampton (*Megan Halsey*), David Gale (*Dr. Carl Hill*), Robert Sampson (*Dean Halsey*), Carolyn Purdy-Gordon (*Dr. Harrod*), Peter Kent (*Melvin the Re-Animated*), Ian Patrick Williams (*The Swiss Professor*), Gerry Black (*Mace*), Barbara Pieters (*The Nurse*), Bunny Summers (*The Swiss Woman Doctor*), Al Berry (*Dr. Gruber*), Derek Pendleton, Gene Scherer, James Ellis, James Earl Cathay, Hans Jonnason, Greg Rose, Annyce Holzman, Velvet Debois, Lawrence Lowe, Robert Holcomb, Mike Filloon, Greg Reid, Jack Draheim, Robert Pitzele
D: Stuart Gordon SCR: Dennis Paoli, William J. Norris & Stuart Gordon, from H.P. Lovecraft's short story *Herbert West—The Reanimator* PHOTOG: Mac Ahlberg SPCL-FX & MAKEUP: Anthony Doublin & John Naulin MUSIC: Richard Band
Bizarre horror-fantasy: Med student revives dead. cf. Bride of Re-Animator

Rearview Mirror
1984, (USA), Simon-Asher/Sunn Classic, color, 95 mins.
W: Lee Remick, Michael Beck, Tony Musante, Don Galloway, Jim Antonio, Ned Bridges, Allison Biggers, Stuart Boyd, Kaya carter, Sherry Foster, Pamela Garmon, Don Hann, Edith Ivey, Elmer Davis Javier, Jack Leland, Roy Tatum, Joe Powell, Julie Ridley, Mary Nell santacroce, Andrew Stahl, Lou Walker, William Ashley Ward, Bonnie Jane Willard
D: Lou Antonio TELEPLAY: Lorenzo Semple Jr. PHOTOG: Frank Watts SPCL-FX: Cliff Wenger MUSIC: William Goldstein
Minor thriller: Psycho criminal takes woman hostage

Rear Window
1954, (USA), Patron/Par/Univ, color, 112 mins.
W: James Stewart (*L.B. Jeffries*), Grace Kelly (*Lisa Fremont*), Wendell Corey (*Lt. Tom Doyle*), Raymond Burr (*Lars Thorwald*), Ross Bagdasarian (A.k.a. David Seville) (*The Composer*), Thelma Ritter (*Stella*), Judith Evelyn ("*Miss Lonelyhearts*"), Sara Berner (*The Woman on the Fire Escape*), Frank Cady (*The Fire Escape Man*), Rand Harper (*The Honeymooner*), Georgine Darcy (*Miss Torso*), Jesslyn Fax (*Miss Sculptress*), Irene Winston (*Mrs. Thorwald*), Havis Davenport (*The Newlywed*), Alan Lee (*The Landlord*), Anthony Warde (*The Detective*), Harry Landers (*The Young Man*), Bennie Bartlett (*Miss Torso's Friend*), Iphigenie Castiglioni (*The Bird Woman*), Marla English, Len Hendry, Kathryn Grandstaff (Grand), Fred Graham, Edwin (Eddie) Parker, Dick Simmons, Mike Mahoney
P & D: Alfred Hitchcock SCR: John Michael Hayes, from Cornell Woolrich's story PHOTOG: Robert Burks SPCL-FX: John P. Fulton MUSIC: Franz Waxman SONG: *Lisa*
Classic thriller: Recuperating from broken leg, man observes neighbors. cf. Body Double. *Remade as 1998 TV Movie with Christopher Reeve*

Rear Window
1998, (USA), ABC-TV, color, 95 mins.
W: Christopher Reeve, Daryl Hannah, Robert Forster, Ruben Santiago-Hudson, Anne Twomey, John Rothman, Ali Marsh, Allison Mackie, Peter Giles
TELEPLAY: Eric Overmyer & Larry Gross, from a Cornell Woolrich story PHOTOG: Ken Kelsch MUSIC: David Shire
TVM, standard thriller: Crippled voyeur witnesses murder

Rebecca
1940, (USA), Selznick-UA/20th-Fox, b&w, 130 mins.
W: Joan Fontaine, Laurence Olivier (*Maxim de Winter*), Judith Anderson (*Mrs. Danvers*), George Sanders (*Jack Favell*), Reginald Denny (*Frank Crawley*), Gladys Cooper (*Beatrice*), Nigel Bruce (*Gilies*), C. Aubrey Smith (*Col. Julyan*), Leo G. Carroll (*Dr. Baker*), Melville Cooper (*The Coroner*), Edward Fielding (*Frith*), Lumsden Hare (*Tabb*), Florence Bates (*Mrs. Van Hopper*), Phillip Winter (*Robert*), Leonard Carey (*Ben*), Forrester Harvey (*Chalcroft*)
P: David O. Selznick D: Alfred Hitchcock SCR: Robert E. Sherwood & Joan Harrison, from Daphne du Maurier's novel PHOTOG: George Barnes (Academy Award) MUSIC: Franz Waxman
Academy Award, Best Picture
Classic thriller: Young bride finds her existence overshadowed by haunting memory of husband's first wife. Hitchcock's US debut

Rebellion de las Muertas (Rebellion of the Dead Women)
1972, (Mex), color
Minor horror-fantasy

Rebellion of the Dead Women
see Rebellion de las Muertas

The Reckless Moment
1949, (USA), Col, b&w, 82 mins.
W: James Mason, Joan Bennett, Geraldine Brooks, Henry O'Neill, Shepperd Strudwick
D: Max Ophuls PHOTOG: Burnett Guffey
Superior melodrama: Housewife conceals daughter's accidental killing of seedy older lover

Recluse
1981, (GB), Jarastar/Bentley Films/20th-Fox, color, 28 mins.
W: Maurice Denham, Derek Smith, Ann Tirard
P: Vivian Pottersman D: Bob Bentley STORY: Paddy Fletcher & Bob Bentley

PHOTOG: Nic Knowland
Fact-based short thriller: Family killed on remote farm

Recoil
1953, (GB), Tempean/Eros, b&w, 79 mins.
W: Kieron Moore (*Nicholas Conway*), Elizabeth Sellars (*Jean Talbot*), Edward Underdown (*Michael Conway*), Bill Lowe (*Walters*), Ethel O'Shea (*Mrs. Coway*), John Horsley (*Insp. Turnbridge*), Robert Raglan (*Sgt. Perkins*), Ian Fleming (*Talbot*), Martin Benson (*Farnborough*), Michael Kelly (*Crouch*)
P: Robert Baker & Monty Berman **D & STORY:** John Gilling
Standard crime-thriller: Dead jeweler's daughter poses as crook, nabs burglar

Red Aces
1929, (GB), Beaconsfield, b&w, 7,200 ft. (2194.6m)
W: Geoffrey Gwyther (*J.G. Reeder*), Janice Adair, Muriel Angelus, James Raglan, Nigel Bruce, George Bellamy, Douglas Payne, W. CroninWilson
D & SCR: Edgar Wallace—from his novel
First "J.G. Reeder" mystery-thriller: Banker framed for murder

Red Alert
1977, (USA), Jozak/Para/NBC-TV, color, 106 mins.
W: William Devane (*Frank Brolen*), Adrienne Barbeau (*Judy Wyche*), Ralph Waite (*Cmdr. Stone*), Michael Brandon (*Carl Wyche*), David Hayward (*Cadwell*), Jim Siedow (*Howard Ives*), M. Emmet Walsh (*Sweeney*), Don Wiseman (*Yancy*), Don Rausch (*Dryer*), Jim Danko (*Parkins*), John Martin (*Ajax*), Howard Finch (*Holland*), Dan Ammerman (*Rogers*), Arnie Shayne (*The Business Man*), Charles Krohn (*Parker*), Dixie Taylor (*Mrs. Kerwin*), Charles J. Bailey (*The Airline Clerk*), Lois Fleck (*Marie Ives*), Arnold Lipin, Malcolm Wittman, Mike Scott
D: Billy (William) Hale **TELEPLAY:** Sandor Stern, from Harold King's novel *Paradigm Red* **PHOTOG:** Ric Waite **SPCL-FX:** A.D. Flowers **MUSIC:** George Aliceson Tipton
TVM, standard thriller: Sabotage and computer error cause nuclear crisis

The Red Balloon
1956, (Fr), Lopert, color, 36 mins.
W: Pascal Lamorisse, Sabine Lamorisse
WRIT, P, & D: Albert Lamorisse **PHOTOG:** Edmond Sechan
Critically-acclaimed fantasy short: Drifting balloon leads small boy into adventures

The Red Barn Crime: or, Maria Martin
1908, (GB), Haggar & Sons/Tyler, b&w, 685 ft. (208.8m)
W: Walter Haggar (*William Corder*), Violet Haggar (*Maria Martin*)
Standard melodrama: Squire's murder of pregnant mistress revealed by mother's dream. Cf. Maria Marten

Red Blooded American Girl
1990, (Can), SC Entertainment Int'l-Prism, color, 89 mins.
W: Heather Thomas (*Paula Bukowsky*), Andrew Stevens (*Owen Augustus Urban III*), Christopher Plummer (*Dr. Alcore*), Kim Coates (*Dennis*), Lydie Denier (*Rebecca Murrin*), Andrew Jackson (*Donald*), Anne Hutcheson, Lionel Williams, Dean Richards, Cindy Fidler, Phil Morrison, Shelly Lynn Jardin, Phil Hay, Alan Rose
D: David Blyth **SCR:** Allan Moyle **PHOTOG:** Ludek Bogner **MUSIC:** Jim Manzie
Standard horror-thriller: Experiments produce vampirism

The Red Circle
1929, (Ger), b&w, from a story by Edgar Wallace
Standard thriller

The Red Circle
1960, (W. Ger), Astral, b&w, 94 mins.
W: Karl Georg Saebisch, Renate Ewert, Klausjuergen Wussow, Thomas Alder
D: Jurgen Roland, from a story by Edgar Wallace
A.k.a. The Crimson Circle
Standard thriller: Murderous blackmailer terrorizes London society.

The Red Cloak
1961, (It-Fr), Franca-Centra-Trio/Sefo International-AA, color, 95 mins.
W: Fausto Tozzi, Patricia Medina, Bruce Cabot, Domenico Modugno
Standard thriller: Masked avenger aids downtrodden

Red Dawn
1984, (USA), MGM-UA, color, 114 mins.
W: Patrick Swayze, C. Thomas Howell, Lea Thompson, Charlie Sheen, Darren Dalton, Jennifer Grey, Brad Savage, Doug Toby, Ben Johnson, Harry Dean Stanton, Ron O'Neal, Lane Smith, William Smith, Vladek Sheybal, Powers Boothe, Franke McRae, Roy Jenson, Pepe Serna
D: John Milius **SCR:** Kevin Reynolds & John Milius, from a story by Kevin Reynolds **PHOTOG:** Ric Waite **MUSIC:** Basil Poledouris
Minor thriller: Survivalist teens vs. invading communists

Red Desert
1964, (It-Fr), Rizzoli Films, color, 120 mins.
W: Monica Vitti, Richard Harris, Carlo Chionetti, Xenia Valderi, Rita Renoir, Valero Bartoleschi, Aldo Girotti
D: Michelangelo Antonioni **PHOTOG:** Carlo Di Palma **MUSIC:** Giovanni Fusco, Vittorio Gelmetti
Superior melodrama: Disturbed woman's neurotic world

The Red Dragon
1945, (USA), Mono, b&w, 64 mins.
W: Sidney Toler (*Charlie Chan*), Fortunio Bonanova (*Insp. Luis Carvero*), Benson Fong (*Tommie Chan*), Robert Emmett Keane (*Alfred Wayne*), Willie Best (*Chattanooga Brown*), Carol Hughes (*Marguerite Fontan*), George Meeker (*Edmond Slade*), Marjorie Hoshelle (*Countess Irena*), Barton Yarborough (*Joseph Bradish*), Charles Trowbridge (*Prentiss*), Don Costello (*Charles Massack*), Mildred Boyd (*Josephine*), Jean Wong (*Iris Ling*), Donald Dexter Taylor (*Dorn*)
D: Phil Rosen **SCR:** George Callahan, from characters created by Earl Derr Biggers **PHOTOG:** Vincent Farrar
Standard "Charlie Chan" thriller: Oriental sleuth becomes involved with A-bomb secrets

Red Dragon
1965, (It-W. Germ), Arca/PEA/Woolner Bros., color, 89 mins.
W: Stewart Granger, Rosanna Schiaffino, Harald Juhnke, Horst Frank
D: Ernest Hofbauer
Minor thriller: Secret agent finds intrigue in Hong Kong

The Redeemer
1978, (USA), Dimension, color, 87 mins.
W: T.G. Finkbinder, Damien Knight, Nick Carter, Jeanetta Arnetta
P: Sheldon Tromberg **D:** Constantine S. Gochis
A.k.a. Class Reunion Massacre
Minor horror-fantasy: Sinful collegians killed by angel from hell

The Red Hand
1960, (W. Ger), Gold Key, b&w, 98 mins.
W: Eleonora Rossi-Drago, Paul Hubschmid (*Christian in US*), Hannes Messemer from a story by Edgar Wallace
Standard thriller: Mysterious figure leaves imprint of red hand at scene of crimes

The Red Hangman
see Il Boia Scarlatto

The Red-Headed League
1921, (GB), Stoll, b&w, 2,140 ft. (652.3m)
W: Eille Norwood (*Sherlock Holmes*), Hubert Willis (*Dr. John Watson*), Edward Arundell (*Jabez Wilson*), H. Townsend (*Spalding*)
D: Maurice Elvey **SCR:** William J. Elliott, from the writings of Sir Arthur Conan Doyle
Standard crime-thriller (episode in "Adventures of Sherlock Holmes" series)

Red Hell
see Two Before Zero

The Red Hornet
see The Chinese Ring

The Red House
1947, (USA), Thalia/UA, b&w, 99 mins.
W: Edward G. Robinson, Judith Anderson, Allene Roberts, Lon McCallister, Julie London, Rory Calhoun, Arthur Space, Harry Shannon, Ona Munson
P: Sol Lesser **WRIT & D:** Delmer Daves, from Charles Agnew Chamberlain's novel **PHOTOG:** Bert Glennon **MUSIC:** Miklos Rozsa
Classic thriller (unsettling performance by Robinson): Old murder comes to light when girl finds herself mysteriously drawn to abandoned house in forest

The Red Inn
see L'Auberge Rouge

The Red Light
1913, (GB), Hepworth, b&w, 1,050 (320m)
W: Alec Worcester (*Joe*), Chrissie White (*Mrs. Joe*)
D: Warwick Buckland
Standard crime-thriller: Wounded signalman saves train from wreckers

Redline
1997, (USA), color, 95 mins.
W: Rutger Hauer, Mark Dacascos
Standard SF-thriller: Murdered man resurrected, stalks Moscow to find his killer

The Red Mantle
1967, (Swed-Den-Ice), ASA Film-Movie Art of Europe-AB-Edda Film/Prentoulis, color, 92 mins, originally 105 mins.
W: Eva Dahlbeck, Gunnar Bjornstrand, Oleg Vidov, Johannes Meyer, Gitte Haenning, Lisbeth Movin, Henning Palner
CO-P: Henning Bendtsen **D & SP:** Gabriel Axel, based on Scandinavian legend **PHOTOG:** Henning Bendtsen **MUSIC:** Per Norgaard
USA retitle, Hagbard and Signe
Unusual melodrama: Medieval tale of love and bloodshed

The Red Menace
1949, (USA), Rep, b&w, 87 mins.
W: Robert Rockwell, Hanne Axman, Betty Lou Gerson, Barbara Fuller
D: R.G. Springsteen
Standard thriller: Communists infiltrate USA

R

Redneck Zombies

1988, (USA), Troma, color, 83 mins.
W: Floyd Piranha, Lisa DeHaven, W.E. Benson, James Housely, William W. Decker, Zoofoot, Tyrone Taylor, Pericles Lewnes
Minor horror-satire: Hillbillies become cannibals

Red Nightmare

1962, (USA), WB, b&w, 30 mins.
W: Jack Webb, Jack Kelly, Jeanne Cooper, Peter Brown
Short propaganda-thriller: Communists conspire to take over USA

Red Ocean

1985, (It), color
D: Lamberto Bava
Standard thriller

Red Planet Mars

1952, (USA), Veiller-Hyde/UA, b&w, 87 mins.
W: Peter Graves, Andrea King, Walter Sande, Herbert Berghof, Orley Lindgren, Bayard Veiller, Morris Ankrum, House Peters Jr., Marvin Miller, Willis Bouchey, Lewis Martin, Richard Powers (Tom Keene), Gene Roth, Bill Kennedy, John Topa, Claude Dunkin, Vince Barnett, Grace Leonard
P: Anthony Veiller **D:** Harry Horner **SCR:** John L. Balderston & Anthony Veiller, from the play by John Hoare & John L. Balderston **PHOTOG:** Joseph Biroc **MUSIC:** Mahlon Merrick
Standard SF-thriller: Attempts to communicate with Mars puts Earth in jeopardy

Red Riding Hood

1987, (USA), color, 84 mins.
W: Craig T. Nelson, Rocco Sisto
D: Adam Brooks
Standard fantasy: Evil prince spies on missing king's beautiful wife

Red Signals

1927, (USA), b&w, 70 mins.
W: Wallace MacDonald, Earl Williams, Eva Novak, Frank Rice, J.P. McGowan
D: J.P. McGowan
Standard thriller: Mysterious criminal causes trains to collide

Red Sleep

1993, (USA), Joel Silver, color
Standard horror-fantasy: Man has affair with vampiress

Red Sonja

1985, (GB-It), Dino De Laurentiis/MGM-UA, color, 89 mins.
W: Brigitte Nielsen (*Red Sonja*), Arnold Schwarzenegger (*Kalifor*), Sandahl Bergman (*Queen Gedren*), Paul Smith (*Falkon*), Ernie Reyes Jr. (*Tarn*), Ronald Lacey (*Ikol*), Terry Richards (*Djart*), Pat Roach (*Brytag*), Janet Agren (*Varna*), Donna Osterbuhr (*Kendra*), Lara Maszinsky (*The Handmaid*), Hans Meyer (*The Father*), Francesca Romana Coluzzi (*The Mother*), Tutte Lemkow, Kiyoshi Yamazaki
D: Richard Fleischer **SCR:** Clive Exton & George MacDonald Fraser, from characters created by Robert E. Howard **PHOTOG:** Giuseppe Rotunno **SPCL-X:** John Stirber **MUSIC:** Ennio Morricone
Standard "Sword & Sorcery" adventure: Warrior woman seeks vengeance

The Red Spectre

1907, (Fr), Pathe, b&w & tint
Standard fantasy short: Magician-skeleton performs marvels

The Red Squirrel

see **La Ardilla Roja**

The Red Tent

1969, (Russ-It), Para, color, 121 mins.
W: Sean Connery (*Amundsen*), Claudia Cardinale (*Valeria*), Peter Finch (*Nobile*), Hardy Kruger (*Lundborg*), Mario Adorf (*Biagi, the Radio Operator*), Massimo Girotti (*Romagna*), Luigi Vannucchi (*Zappi*), Edward Marzevuc (*Malmgren*), Juri Solomin (*Troiani*), Boris Kmelnizki (*Viglieri*), Donatis Banionis (*Mariano*), Juri Vizbor (*Behounek*), Otar Koberidze (*Cecioni*), Grigori Gaj (*Samoilovich*), Nikita Mikhalkov (*Chuknovsky*), Nicolai Ivanov (*Kolka*)
D: Mikhail Kalatozov **SCR:** Ennio De Concini & Richard Adams **PHOTOG:** Leonid Kalashnikov **MUSIC SCORE:** Ennio Morricone
Standard adventure-thriller: Sole survivor of arctic expedition agonizes with ghosts of those who perished

The Reflecting Skin

1991, (Can-GB), British Screen BBC Films-Zenith/Miramax/Prestige, color, 98 mins, also 106 mins.
W: Viggo Mortensen (*Cameron Dove*), Lindsay Duncan (*Dolphin Blue*), Jeremy Cooper (*Seth Dove*), Sheila Moore (*Ruth Dove*), Duncan Fraser (*Luke Dove*), David Longworth (*Joshua*), Sherry Bie (*Cassie*), Robert Koous (*Sheriff Ticker*), David Bloom (*The Deputy*), Evan Hall (*Kim*), Codie Lucas Wilbee (*Eben*), Jason Wolfe (*The Cadillac Driver*), Jeff Walker (*Adam Blue*), Dean Hass, Guy Buller, Jason Brownlow, Joyce Robbins, Walt Healy, Jacqueline Robbins, Debi Greenawdt
WRIT & D: Philip Ridley **PHOTOG:** Dick Pope **MUSIC:** Nick Bicat
Standard fantasy-thriller: Boy fears neighbor is vampiress

A Reflection of Fear

1971, (USA), Col, color, 89 mins.
W: Robert Shaw (*Michael*), Mary Ure (*Katherine*), Sally Kellerman (*Anne*), Sondra Locke (*Marguerite*), Liam Dunn (*The Coroner*), Mitch Ryan (*McKenna*), Gordon DeVol (*Hector*), Gordon Anderson (*Voice of Aaron*), Victoria Risk (*Peggy*), Leonard John Crofoot (*Aaron*), Michael St. Clair (*Kevin*), Michelle Marvin (*The Nurse*), Michele Montau (*Mme. Caraquet*), Signe Hasso
D: William Fraker **SCR:** Edward Hume & Lewis John Carlino, from Stanton Forbes' novel *Go to Thy Deathbed* **PHOTOG:** Laszlo Kovacs **MUSIC:** Fred Myrow
orig. to be titled **Labyrinth**
Standard thriller: Girl develops split personality

Reflections in a Golden Eye

1967, (USA), WB-7Arts, color, 109 mins.
W: Marlon Brando, Elizabeth Taylor, Brian Keith, Julie Harris, Robert Forster, Zorro David
P: Ray Stark **D:** John Huston **SCR:** Chapman Mortimer & Gladys Hill, from Carson McCullers' novel **PHOTOG:** Aldo Tonti **MUSIC:** Toshiro Mayuzumi
Unusual psychodrama (released in Italy): Neuroses and sexual aberrations on army base

Reflections in the Dark

1995, (USA), Concorde, color, 95 mins.
W: Mimi Rogers, Billy Zane, John Terry (*James*), Kurt Fuller (*Howard*)
Standard melodrama: Prison guard commiserates with condemned murderess

Reflections of Murder

1974, (USA), ABC Circle/ABC-TV, color, 96 mins.
W: Tuesday Weld (*Vicky*), Joan Hackett (*Claire Elliott*), Sam Waterston (*Michael Elliott*), Lucille Benson (*Mrs. Turner*), Michael Lerner (*Jerry Steele*), Lance Kerwin (*Chip*), Ed Bernard (*The Coroner*), R.G. Armstrong (*Mr. Turner*), John Levin (*Keith*), William Turner (*Mr. Griffiths*), Jesse Vint (*The Cop on the Freeway*), James A. Newcombe, Sam Henriot, Rita Conde, Don Sparks, Sandra Coburn
D: John Badham **TELEPLAY:** Carol Sobieski, from a novel by Pierre Boileau & Thomas Narcejac **PHOTOG:** Mario Tosi **SPCL-FX:** Cliff Wenger **MUSIC:** Billy Goldenberg
TVM, standard thriller (remake of **Diabolique***): Murdered man's body vanishes*

Reflections Of Murder: JOAN HACKETT AND TUESDAY WELD

The Refrigerator

1992, (USA), Avenue D Films Ltd., color, 86 mins.
W: David Simonds (*Steve Bateman*), Julia McNeal (*Eileen Bateman*), Angel Caban (*Juan the Plumber*), Nena Segal (*Eileen's Mother*), Jaime Rojo (*Paolo the Plumber's Ass't*), Michelle DeCosta (*Young Eileen*)
WRIT & D: Nicholas A.E. Jacobs **PHOTOG:** Paul Gibson **MUSIC:** Don Peterkofsky, Chris Burke & Adam Roth
Unusual horror-fantasy: Kitchen appliance develops craving for human flesh

The Regimental Pet

see **The Stolen Airship Plans**

La Regina della Amazzoni (Queen of the Amazons)
1960, (It), Alta-Vista/AIP-TV, color, 94 mins.
W: Rod Taylor, Gianna Maria Canale, Ed Fury, Dorian Gray, Daniela Rocca
D: Vittorio Sala
USA retitle, **Colossus and the Amazon Queen**
Standard "Sword & Sandal": Amazons turn Trojan War survivors into love slaves

Il Rei de Criminali
see *Superargo e i Giganti Senzo Volto*

The Reigate Squires
1912, (GB-Fr), Franco-British Film Co.-Eclair/Fenning, b&w, 1,800 ft. (548.6m)
W: Georges Treville (*Sherlock Holmes*), Mr. Moyse (*Dr. John Watson*)
D: Georges Treville, from a story by Sir Arthur Conan Doyle
Standard thriller

Reign of Terror
see *The Black Book*

The Reincarnate
1971, (Can), IFD/Meridian, color, 89 mins.
W: Jack Creley, Jay Reynolds, Trudy Young, Terry Tweed
P & SCR: Seeleg Lester   **D:** Don Haldane
blurb: "No one ever dies"
Minor fantasy-thriller: Dying lawyer's spirit transferred to body of sculptor

Reincarnation
see *Curse of the Crimson Altar*

The Reincarnation of Peter Proud
1974, (USA), Bing Crosby Prods./CRC, color, 104 mins.
W: Michael Sarrazin (*Peter Proud*), Jennifer O'Neill (*Ann Curtis*), Margot Kidder (*Marcia Curtis*), Cornelia Sharpe (*Nora Hayes*), Normann Burton (*Dr. Spear*), Paul Hecht (*Dr. Goodman*), Tony Stephano (*Jeff Curtis*), Anne Ives
D: J. Lee Thompson   **SCR:** Max Ehrlich, from his novel   **PHOTOG:** Victor J. Kemper   **MUSIC:** Jerry Goldsmith
"...embodies all the thrills of Max Ehrlich's bestseller, plus an outstandingly rich performance from Margot Kidder" —Variety
Unusual thriller: College professor haunted by memories of a past life

The Rejuvenation of Dan
1913, (GB), H&W Films/Prieur, b&w, 465 ft. (141.7m)
D: Stuart Kinder
Standard comedy-fantasy: Old man made young again

The Rejuvenator
1988, (USA), Cinema Group, color, 86 mins.
W: Vivian Lanko, John MacKay
D: Brian Thomas Jones   **SCR:** Simon Nuchtern   **MUSIC:** Larry Juris
A.k.a. **Rejuvenatrix**
blurb: "The Fountain Of Youth For The Living Dead"
Standard horror-thriller: Anti-aging serum turns actress into monster

Rejuvenatrix
see *The Rejuvenator*

Rekopis Znaleziony w Saragossie (The Manuscript Found in the Sargasso)
1964, (Pol), Film Polski-KAMERA, b&w, 124 mins, also 180 mins.
W: Zbigniew Cybulski (*Alfons*), Joanna Jedryka (*The Moorish Princess*), Slawomir Linder (*Alfons' Father*), Kazimierz Opalinski (*The Hermit*), Franciszek Pieczka (*Pascheco*), Gustaw Holoubek, Miroslawa Lombardo, Iga Cembrzynska, Pola Raksa, Leon Niemczyk, Barbara Krafftowna, Adam Pawlikowski, Beata Tyszkiewicz, Bogumil Kobiela, Elzbieta Czyzewska, Zdzislaw Maklakiewicz, Krzysztof Litwin
D: Wojciech Jerzy Has   **SCR:** Tadeusz Kwiatkowski, from Jan Potocki's story   **PHOTOG:** Mieczyslaw Jahoda   **MUSIC:** Krzysztof Penderecki
A.k.a. **Tajemnica Doliny Los Hermanos (Mystery of Los Hermanos Valley)** *US Release:* **The Saragossa Manuscript**, *Amerpol Enterprise Films, 1966, 155 mios.*
Standard mystical thriller

Relative Fear
1995, (Can), color, 95 mins.
W: Matthew Dupuis, Darlanne Fluegel, Martin Neufeld (*Peter*), James Brolin (*Det. Atwater*), Bruce Dinsmore (*Clive*)
D: George Mihalka   **SCR:** Kurt Wimmer
Minor thriller: Multiple deaths point to 4-year-old "bad seed"

Relativity
1966, (USA), Coop, color
Modest film-poem: Exploration of mankind's unity with cosmos

Relax, Freddie
1968, (Den), NTA, color, 91 mins.
W: Morten Grunwald, Hanne Bork
Minor comedy-thriller: Adventures of secret agent

The Relic
1997, (USA), Cloud Nine/Para, color, 110 mins.
W: Penelope Ann Miller (*Dr. Margo Green*), Tom Sizemore (*Lt. Vincent D'Agosta*), Linda Hunt (*Dr. Ann Cuthbert*), James Whitmore (*Dr. Albert Frock*), Audra Lindley (*Dr. Zwiezic*), Clayton Rohner (*Det. Hollingsworth*), Chi Muoi Lo (*Greg Lee*), Thomas Ryan (*Parkinson*), Robert Lesser (*Mayor Owen*), Diane Robin (*The Mayor's Wife*), Lewis Van Bergen (*John Whitney*), Constance Towers (*Mrs. Blaisedale*), Francis X. McCarthy (*Mr. Blaisedale*), John Kapelos (*McNally*), Tico Wells, Mike Bacarella, Gene Davis, John Di Santi, David Proval, Ron Cummins, David Graubart, Ronald Joshua Scott, Jophery C. Brown, Thomas Joseph Carroll, Montrose Hagins, Santos Morales, La Donna Tittle, Ralph Seymour, Edward Jemison, David Hollander, Amanda Ingber, Katharine Mitchell, Candy Coburn, Kurt Naebig, Don Harvey, Don MacLellan, Marc P. Shelton, Ken Magee, Aaron Lustig, Lynn A. Henderson, Kent George, Matthew Daniel Moses Furlin, Dina Bair, Elwood Forbes, Mark Lake, Ned Schmidtke
D & PHOTOG: Peter Hyams   **SCR:** Amy Holden Jones, John Raffo, Rick Jaffa & Amanda Silver, from a novel by Douglas Preston & Lincoln Child   **VS-FX SPRVSR:** Gregory L. McMurry   **MUSIC:** John Debney
"An absolute shocker! White knuckles until the very last minute!"—Doug Moore, Fox-TV
Gripping SF-horror: Brain-sucking mutant from Amazon rain forest prowls Chicago museum

The Relic: TOM SIZEMORE AND PENELOPE ANN MILLER

The Reluctant Astronaut
1966, (USA), Univ, color, 101 mins.
W: Don Knotts, Joan Freeman, Jeanette Nolan (*Mrs. Fleming*), Arthur O'Connell (*Buck*), Leslie Nielsen, Jesse White, Guy Raymond, Joan Shawlee, Frank McGrath, Nydia Westman, Paul Hartman
P & D: Edward J. Montagne   **SCR:** Jim Fritzell & Everett Greenbaum   **PHOTOG:** Rexford Wimpy   **MUSIC:** Vic Mizzy
Juvenile SF-comedy: Vertigo-prone young man enters space program

The Reluctant Saint
1962, (It-USA), Royal, b&w, 105 mins.
W: Maximilian Schell (*Giuseppe Desa*), Lea Padovani (*Francesca Desa*), Akim Tamiroff (*Bishop Durso*), Carlo Croccolo (*Gobbo*), Ricardo Montalban (*Father Raspi*), Giulio Bosetti (*Brother Orlando*), Harold Goldblatt (*Father Giovanni*), Arnoldo Foa (*Felixa Desa*), Elisa Cegani (*Sister Nunziata*)
P & D: Edward Dmytryk   **SCR:** John Fante & Joseph Petracca   **MUSIC:** Nino Rota
Minor comedy-drama: Bio of legendary 17th-century levitating priest

The Reluctant Spy
1963, (Fr), b&w, 93 mins.
W: Jean Marais, Genevieve Page, Maurice Teynac, Jean Gallar
D: Jean-Charles Dudrumet
Standard action-spoof: Secret agent chases around Continent

The Remarkable Andrew
1941, (USA), Para, b&w, 82 mins.
W: William Holden, Ellen Drew, Brian Donlevy, Rod Cameron, Richard Webb, Porter Hall, James Millican, Nydia Westman, Frances Gifford, Montagu Love
D: Stuart Heisler   **SCR:** Dalton Trumbo, from his novel *The Magnificent Andrew*   **PHOTOG:** Theodor Sparkuhl
Standard fantasy: Bookkeeper refuses to juggle books—is aided by ghosts of American founding fathers

The Remarkable Andrew: ELLEN DREW, BRIAN DONLEVY, RICHARD WEBB AND WILLIAM HOLDEN

Remember Me
1995, (USA), CBS-TV, color, 95 mins.
W: Kelly McGillis, Cotter Smith, Michael T. Weiss, Stephen McHattie, Amy Hargreaves, Bernard Behrens, Shanna Reed, Mary Higgins Clark [cameo]
D: Michael Switzer, from Mary Higgins Clark's novel **PHOTOG:** Rob Draper **MUSIC:** Domenic Troiano
TVM, standard thriller: Grieving couple rents "haunted" house

Remember my Name
1978, (USA), Lions Gate/Col, color, 94 mins.
W: Geraldine Chaplin, Anthony Perkins, Moses Gunn, Berry Berenson, Jeff Goldblum, Alfre Woodard, Tim Thomerson, Marilyn Coleman
D & SCR: Alan Rudolph **PHOTOG:** Tak Fujimoto **BLUES SCORE:** Alberta Hunter
Unusual melodrama: Woman released from prison, bedevils husband's new marriage

Remorse
1903, (GB), Williamson, b&w, 450 ft. (137.2m)
W: D. Philippe (*The Blackmailer*)
D: James Wiliamson, from a play by D. Philippe
Standard crime-thriller (in 5 scenes): Killer plants knife on drunk, is blackmailed, and confesses in court after vision of injustice

Remote Control
1930, (USA), MGM, b&w, 5,955 ft. (1815.1m), 62 mins.
W: William Haines
D: Malcolm St. Clair
Standard comedy-thriller

Remote Control
1988, (USA), Vista, video, color, 88 mins.
W: Kevin Dillon (*Cosmo*), Deborah Goodrich (*Belinda*), Frank Beddor (*Victor*), Christopher Wynne (*Georgie*), Kaaren Lee (*Patricia*), Jennifer Tilly (*Allegra*), Bert Remsen (*Bill Denver*), Jaime McEnnan (*Matthew*), Jennifer Buchanan (*Julia Bard*), Jerold Pearson (*Alan Bard*), Deborah Downey (*Eva*), Will Nye (*Milo*), Marilyn Adams (*Neighbor #1*), Richard Warlock (*Mr. James*), Ann Walker (*Mrs. James*), John LaFayette (*Pete*), Michael Pniewski (*Artie*), Al Eisenmann II (*Boyfriend #1*), Allen Michael Lerner (*Manager #1*), Tad Horino (*Controller #1*), Yosh Moriwaki (*1st Q.C. Man*), Gerald Jann (*2nd Q.C. Man*), Ty Kelley (*The Young Hero*), Lisa Aliff (*The Heroine*), Larry Mintz (*Controller #2*), Dick Durock (*Driver #1*), George P. Wilbur (*The Dockman*), Randy Sutter (*The Young Man*), Ina Romeo (*The Clerk*), Jack Slater (*Detective #1*), Joe Beruh (*Detective #2*), Jeffrey Sudzin (*The Fireman*), Janeen Weiss (*Mrs. Watson*)
WRIT & D: Jeff Lieberman **PHOTOG:** Timothy Suhrstedt **MUSIC:** Peter Bernstein
Made-for-Video, standard SF-thriller: Alien-engineered videos prompt human mayhem

Remo Williams: The Adventure Begins
1985, (USA), Orion, color, 120 mins.
W: Fred Ward (*Remo Williams*), Joel Grey (*Chun*), Charles Cioffi (*George S. Groves*), Wilford Brimley (*Harold Smith*), J.A. Preston (*Conn MacCleary*), George Coe (*Gen. Scott Watson*), Kate Mulgrew (*Maj. Rayner Fleming*), Michael Pataki (*Jim Wilson*), Patrick Kilpatrick (*Stone*), Cosie Costa (*Private Damico*), William Hickey, Davenia McFadden, Joel J. Kramer, J.P. Roman, Frank Ferrara, Marv Albert, Webster Whinery, Ray Woodfork, Phil Neilson, Frank Simpson, Dodi Kenan, Reginald Veljohnson, Jon Polito, Gene LeBell, Jeff Allin, Michael M. Ryan, Will Jeffries, Sebastian Ligarde, Roger Chudney, Duane B. Clark, John Christianson, Andrew MacMillan, Phil Culotta, Tom McBride, Wendy Gazelle, Suzy Snyder

---

D: Guy Hamilton **SCR:** Christopher Wood **PHOTOG:** Andrew Laszlo **SPCL-FX:** Andy Evans **MUSIC:** Craig Safan
Standard action-thriller: Gov't trains man for high-level assassinations

Rendezvous at Midnight
1935, (USA), Univ, b&w, 64 mins.
W: Ralph Bellamy, Valerie Hobson, Catherine Doucet, Irene Ware, Helen Jerome Eddy
D: Christy Cabanne
Standard whodunit: City commissioner murdered

Renegade Girls
see Caged Heat!

Renegades
1930, (USA), Fox, b&w
W: Warner Baxter, Myrna Loy, Bela Lugosi
Standard melodrama: High passions in Arabia

Rentadick
1972, (GB), Virgin/David Paradine/RFD, color, 94 mins.
W: James Booth (*Hamilton*), Richard Briers (*Gannet*), Julie Ege (*Utta*), Ronald Fraser (*Upton*), Donald Sinden (*Armitage*), Tsai Chin (*Mme. Greenfly*), Kenneth Cope (*West*), John Wells (*Owltruss*), Richard Beckinsale (*Hobbs*), Leon Sinden (*The Inspector*), Michael Bentine (*Hussein*), Will Stampe (*The Gatekeeper*), Derek Griffiths (*Henson*), Veronica Clifford (*The Attendant*), Kristopher Kum (*The Japanese*), Cheryl Hall (*Maxine*), Penelope Keith (*Madge*), Spike Milligan (*The Official*), David Battley (*The Sgt.*), Winnie Holman (*The Maid*), Michael Segal (*The Picnicker*)
P: Ned Sherrin & Terry Glinwood **D:** Jim Clark & Richard Loncraine **SCR:** John Cleese, Graham Chapman, John Wells & John Fortune **STORY:** John Cleese & Graham Chapman **PHOTOG:** John Coquillon **MUSIC:** Carl Davis
Standard SF-comedy: Nerve gas paralyzes from waist down

Le Repas Fantastique (The Fantastic Meal)
1900, (Fr), Star, b&w, 30m (98.4 ft./1.7 mins.)
D: Georges Melies
Standard fantasy

Repeat Performance
1947, (USA), Eagle Lion, b&w, 93 mins.
W: Louis Hayward (*Barney Page*), Joan Leslie (*Sheila Page*), Richard Basehart (*William*), Tom Conway (*John Friday*), Virginia Field (*Paula Costello*), Natalie Schafer (*Eloise Shaw*)
P: Aubrey Schenck **D:** Alfred Werker **SCR:** Walter Bullock, from William O'Farrell's novel **PHOTOG:** Lew O'Connell **MUSIC:** George Antheil
Modest fantasy-thriller: Murderess given chance to relive previous year—Will she kill again? cf. **Turn Back the Clock**

Replica of a Crime
see Amuck

Replikator: Cloned to Kill
1994, (USA), color, 96 mins.
W: Michael St. Gerard, Brigitte Bako, Ned Beatty
D: G. Phillip Jackson **SCR:** Tony Johnston, Michelle Bellerose & John Dawson
Standard SF-thriller: 21st-century criminal duplicates humans

Repo Man
1984, (USA), City Prods./Univ, color, 92 mins.
W: Harry Dean Stanton, Emilio Estevez, Tracey Walter, Olivia Barash, Sy Richardson, Susan Barnes, Fox Harris, Zander Schloss, Tom Finnegan, Del Zamora, Eddie Velez, Jennifer Balgobin, Dick Rude, Michael Sandoval, Richard Foronjy, Vonetta McGee, Bruce White, Biff Yeager
D & SCR: Alex Cox **PHOTOG:** Robby Muller **MUSIC:** Tito Larriva & Steven Hufsteter
Bizarre cult-classic: Hunted auto holds lethal cargo

Repossessed
1990, (USA), Carolco/New Line Cinema, color, 89 mins.
W: Linda Blair (*Nancy Aglet*), Ned Beatty (*Ernest Weiler*), Leslie Nielsen (*Father Mayii*), Anthony Starke (*Father Luke Brophy*), Thom J. Sharp (*Braydon Aglet*), Lana Schwab (*Fanny Weiler*), Benj Thall (*Ned Aglet*), Dove Dellos (*Frieda Aglet*), Jacquelyn Masche (*Nancy's Mother*), Willie Garson (*The Nerd Student*), Melissa Moore (*The Bimbo Student*), Robert Fuller (*The Doctor*), Jesse "The Body" Ventura, Greg Lewis, Army Archerd, Erna Gregory, Carol Shermer, Linda Brennan, Richard Halpern, Kathy Tapia, Gary Howe Scott, Douglas W. Kelly, Murray Langston, Melissa Shear, Glen Vincent, Jack Hanrahan, Barbara Alyn Wood, Peter Gaulke, Marc Siegler, John Copage, Dani Douthette, Tim D'Arcy, Chuck Kovacic, Peggy Faracy, May Quigley, Annie Waterman, Bryan O'Byrne, Roger Scott, Nancy Kaine, John H. Ingle, Frederick Daniel Scott, Ben Kronen, Doug Draizin, Johnny Dark, Belle Avery, Jake Steinfeld, Aaron Baker, Norman Large, Karen Person, Charlotte Helkamp, Bob Drew, Frazier Smith, Jack LaLanne, Joseph V. Perry, Sheryl Bernstein, Wally George, George A. Simonelli, Floyd Levine, Eugene Greytak, Dawn Mazzella, Bob Zany, Gene Okerlund
WRIT & D: Bob Logan **PHOTOG:** Michael D. Margulies **MUSIC:** Charles Fox
Minor horror-spoof: Young woman requires second exorcism

The Reptile

1966, (GB), Hammer-7Arts/Warner-Pathe/20th-Fox, color, 91 mins.
W: Noel Willman (*Dr. Franklyn*), Jennifer Daniel (*Valerie Spalding*), Jacqueline Pearce (*Anna Franklyn*), Ray Barrett (*Harry Spalding*), Marne Maitland (*The Malay*), David Baron (*Charles Spalding*), Michael Ripper (*Tom Bailey*), Charles Lloyd-Pack (*The Vicar*), John Laurie (*Mad Peter*), George Woodbridge
P: Anthony Nelson Keys   **D:** John Gilling   **SCR:** John Elder [Anthony Hinds]   **PHOTOG:** Arthur Grant   **MUSIC:** Don Banks   **DESIGN:** Don Mingaye
Standard horror-fantasy: Doctor's cursed daughter turns into venomous monster

Repeat Performance: LOUIS HAYWARD, VIRGINIA FIELD AND TOM CONWAY

Reptilicus

1961, (Den), Saga Studio/AIP, color, 90 mins.
W: Carl Ottosen, Ann Smyrner, Bodil Miller, Dirk Passer, Asbjorn Anderson, Mimi Heinrich
D: Poul Bang   **SCR:** Sidney W. Pink & Ib Melchior   **PHOTOG:** Aage Wiltrup
Standard SF-thriller: Revived tissue of prehistoric horror grows into new monster

Repulsion

1965, (GB), Compton-Cameo/Royal, b&w, 104 mins.
W: Catherine Deneuve (*Carol Ledoux*), Yvonne Furneaux (*Helen Ledoux*), Ian Hendry (*Michael*), Patrick Wymark (*The Landlord*), John Fraser (*Colin*), Renee Houston (*Miss Balch*), Mike Pratt (*The Workman*), Valerie Taylor (*Mme. Denise*), James Villiers (*John*), Hugh Futcher (*Reggie*), Helen Fraser (*Bridget*), Wally Bosco (*The Old Man*), Monica Merlin, Imogen Graham
D: Roman Polanski   **SCR:** Roman Polanski & Gerard Brach   **PHOTOG:** Gil Taylor   **MUSIC:** Chico Hamilton   **DESIGN:** Seamus Flannery
Superior psychodrama: Young woman descends into madness, commits ghastly murders

Requiem for a Secret Agent

1965, (It), CPT/Intercontinental/Metheus, color
W: Stewart Granger, Daniela Bianchi, Peter Van Eyck, Georgia Moll
D: Sergio Sollima
Minor thriller: British adventurer fights spy ring

Rescued from an Eagle's Nest

1907, (USA), Edison, b&w, 8 mins. (1 reel)
W: Lawrence Griffith [D.W. Griffith]
D: Edwin S. Porter & J. Searle Dawley
A.k.a. **The Eagle's Nest**
Unusual thriller short: Man vs. bird of prey

The Rescuers

1977, (USA), Walt Disney/Buena Vista, color, 77 mins.
VOICES: Bob Newhart, Eva Gabor, Geraldine Page, Joe Flynn, Jeanette Nolan, John McIntire, Jim Jordan, Bernard Fox, Michelle Stacy, Dub Taylor, Pat Buttram
D: Wolfgang Reitherman, John Lounsbery & Art Stevens, from a story by Margery Sharp   **MUSIC SCORE:** Artie Butler
Standard animated fantasy: Animals save imperiled child

The Rescuers Down Under

1990, (USA), Walt Disney, Color, 77 mins.
VOICES: Bob Newhart, Eva Gabor, John Candy, Tristan Rogers, Adam Ryan, George C. Scott, Frank Welker, Peter Firth
D: Hendel Butoy & Mike Gabriel   **SCR:** Jim Cox, Karey Kirkpatrick, Joe Ranft & Byron Simpson, from characters created by Margery Sharp   **MUSIC:** Bruce Broughton
Standard animated fantasy: Animals aid kidnapped boy in Australian outback

The Resident Patient

1921, (GB), Stoll, b&w, 2,404 ft. (732.7m)

W: Eille Norwood (*Sherlock Holmes*), Hubert Willis (*Dr. John Watson*), C. Pitt-Chatham (*Dr. Percy Trevelyan*), Arthur Bell (*Insp. Lestrade*), Judd Green (*Blessington*), Wally Bosco (*Moffatt*)
D: Maurice Elvey   **SCR:** William J. Elliott, from the writings of Sir Arthur Conan Doyle
Standard crime-thriller (episode in "Adventures of Sherlock Holmes" series)

Rest in Peace
see **One Dark Night**

Rest in Pieces

1987, (USA), color, 90 mins.
W: Scott Thompson Baker, Lorin Jean, Dorothy Malone
D: Joseph Braunstein
Standard thriller: Woman inherits eerie estate

The Resurrected

1992, (USA), Borde-Raich/Scotti Bros., color, 105 mins.
W: Chris Sarandon (*Charles Dexter Ward/Joseph Curwen*), John Terry (*John March*), Jane Sibbett (*Claire Ward*), Robert Romanus (*Lonnie Peck*), Laurie Briscoe (*Holly Tender*), Patrick Pon (*Raymond*), Ken Camroux (*Capt. Ben Szandor*), Bernard Cuffling (*Dr. Waite*), J.B. Bivens (*Station Orderly 1*), Des Smiley (*The Janitor*), Robert Sidley (*The 3rd Orderly*), Tom Shorthouse (*The Gas Man*), Eric Newton (*Lucius Fenner*), Jim Smith (*The Butcher*), Philip Hayes (*The Uniform Cop*), Megan Leitch (*Eliza*), Elizabeth Barclay (*The Lab Technician*), Judith Maxie (*Dr. Lyman*), Charles Kristian (*Ezra Ward*), Paul Jarrett (*Town Father #1*), Serge Houde (*The Physician*), Joan O'Donahue (*Mrs. Bishop*), Scott Ateah (*Orderly Dave*), Deborra Hope (*The News Anchor*), Deep Roy (*The Main Monster*), Keith Hay (*Pitman #1*), Greg Allen (*Pitman #2*), Lee Matheson (*Town Father #2*), Lloyd Tinney (*Town Father #3*), Todd Masters (*The Male Nurse*), Marc Howard, James Grant, Gordie Herron
D: Dan O'Bannon   **SCR:** Brent V. Friedman, inspired by H.P. Lovecraft's short story *The Case of Charles Dexter Ward*   **PHOTOG:** Irv Goodnoff   **SPCL VS-FX:** Todd Masters   **MUSIC:** Richard Band
Standard horror-fantasy: Detective investigates scientist who revives dead cf. **The Haunted Palace** *(1963)*

The Resurrected Monster

1952, (Mex), Internacional Cinematografica, b&w
W: Miroslava
Minor horror-fantasy

The Resurrection of Zachary Wheeler

1971, (USA), Vidtronics/Gold key, color, 100 mins.
W: Bradford Dillman (*Sen. Wheeler*), Leslie Nielsen (*Harry*), Angie Dickinson (*Dr. Johnson*), James Daly (*Dr. Redding*), Don Haggerty (*Jake*), Jack Carter (*Dwight Chiles*), Robert J. Wilke (*Fielding*), Lew Brown (*Collins*), Patrick O'Moore (*Martin*), Richard Schuyler (*Bates*), William Bryant (*Craig Harmon*), Richard Simmons (*Adams*), Peter Mamakos (*Premier Mabulla*), Tris Coffin (*Dr. Keating*), Steve Cory (*Carson*), Ruben Moreno (*Gen. Munoz*), Jim Healy (*TV Commentator #1*), Lee Giroux (*TV Commentator #2*), Jill Jaress (*Ens. Lee*), Tom Peters (*The Shipping Clerk*), Byron Morrow (*Gen. Towns*), Del Murray (*Williams*), Paul Sorensen (*Thompson*), Ray Fine (*Jerry*), Harry Holcombe (*Wilson*), Tyler McVey (*George*), Rodolfo Hoyos (*Medina*), Linda London (*A Nurse*), Dean Stewart (*The Orderly*), John Bill (*Medic #1*), Andy Davis (*Radio Operator #1*), Steve Conte (*Radio Operator #2*), Lois Corey (*The Navy Nurse*), Sue Ann Carpenter (*The Airline Clerk*), Thomas J. Conlan (*The Service Station Attendant*), Samuel Cordova (*Guard Dennis*), Lou DeMenno (*Lou*), Thomas Dycus (*Dr. Rand*), Frederick Dwyer (*The Shore Patrol*), Bill Hicks (*The Truck Driver*), Tony Griego (*The Mexican*), Jim Jimmerson (*Officer Holms*), Philip Mead (*Dr. Marx*), Thomas Mitman (*The Admiral*), A.W. Samuell (*The Cab Driver*), Charles Tansey (*Guard Gates*), Emanuel Smith (*Art*), John VanSickler (*The Ambulance Attendant*), Gene Wilson, Myrna Wood, Aly Yoder
D: Robert Wynn   **TELEPLAY:** Jay Simms & Tom Rolf   **PHOTOG:** Bob Boatman   **MUSIC:** Marlin Skiles
Standard SF-thriller: Auto-crash victim rehabilitated at mysterious New Mexico clinic. Shot on video released theatrically

The Resurrection Syndicate
see **Nothing But the Night**

Retaliator
see **Programmed to Kill**

Retik, the Moon Menace

1966, (USA), Rep, b&w, 100 mins.
W: George Wallace (*Cmdr. Cody*), Clayton Moore, Aline Towne, Roy Barcroft, William Bakewell
D: Fred Brannon   **SCR:** Ronald Davidson
Standard SF-thriller (feature culled from 12-chapter 1952 serial 'Radar Men from the Moon'): Hero battles space-alien invaders

Retribution

1913, (GB), Hepworth, b&w, 1,125 ft. (342.9m)
W: Jack Raymond (*The Clerk*), Harry Royston (*A Robber*), John McAndrews (*A Robber*)
D: Frank Wilson
Standard crime-thriller: Police chase bank robbers, set fire to hideout

Retribution
1916, (GB), British Oak/New Agency, b&w, 1,180 ft. (359.7m)
D: Ernest G. Batley
Standard crime-thriller: Disowned gambler tries to kill cousin's doctor fiance

Retribution
1988, (USA), Renegade/Unicorn/Taurus, color, 107 mins.
W: Dennis Lipscomb (*George Miller*), Leslie Wing (*Jennifer Curtis*), Hoyt Axton (*Lt. Ashley*), Suzanne Snyder (*Angel*), Jeff Pomerantz (*Alan Falconer*), George Murdock (*Dr. Talbot*), Pamela Dunlap (*Sally Benson*), Susan Peretz, Clare Peck, Chris Caputo, Ralph Manza, Mario Roccuzzo, Jeffrey Josephson, Harry Caesar, Danny D. Daniels, Mike Muscat, Ed Berke, Pearl Adell, George Caldwell, David Dunard, Brian Christian, Tony Cox, Trish Fillmore, Kenneth Gray, Steve Lerman, Richard Jamison, Joan-Carol Kent, Muriel Minot, Guy Magar, Matthew Newmark, Diane Robin, Michelle Roth, Miss Holly (*The Hotel Dog*)
P & D: Guy Magar **SCR:** Guy Magar & Lee Wasserman **PHOTOG:** Gary Thieltges **SPCL-FX:** Kevin Yagher **MUSIC:** Alan Howarth
Minor horror-thriller: Murder victim's ghost possesses artist's body

Retroactive
1996, (USA), color
W: James Belushi
Minor SF-comedy

Retroactive
1997, (USA), color, 90 mins.
W: Kylie Travis, James Belushi (*Frank*), Frank Whaley (*Brian*)
Made-for-Cable, standard SF-thriller: Psychiatrist employs time travel to save wife's life

The Return
1973, (Can), color
W: Keir Dullea, Lloyd Bochner, Edward Andrews
Minor SF-thriller (re-edited from "Starlost" teleseries): Problems of Earth's last survivors

The Return
1973, (GB), Jocelyn/MGM-EMI, color, 30 mins.
W: Peter Vaughan (*Stephen Royds*), Rosalie Crutchley (*Mrs. Park*)
P: Elizabeth McKay **D:** Sture Rydman **SCR:** Brian Scobie & Sture Rydman, from Ambrose Bierce's Story "The Middle Toe of the Right Foot", & A.M. Burrage's story "Nobody's House" **PHOTOG:** Douglas Slocombe **MUSIC:** Marc Wilkinson
Standard short thriller: Madman flees asylum to relive night when he shot deformed bride

Return
1985, (USA), Andrew Silver, color, 78 mins.
W: Karlene Crockett (*Diana Stoving*), John Walcutt (*Day Whittaker*), Anne Lloyd Francis (*Eileen Sedgely*), Lenore Zann (*Susan*), Lisa Richards (*Ann Stoving*), Frederic Forrest (*Brian Stoving*), Ariel Aberg-Riger (*Diana at 3*), Lee Stetson (*Daniel Montross*), Thomas Cross Rolapp (*Lucky the Mechanic*), Dennis Hoerter (*The Mechanic's Ass't*), Harry Murphy (*The MDC Policeman*)
WRIT & D: Andrew Silver, from Donald Harington's novel *Some Other Place. The Right Place* **PHOTOG:** Janos Zsombolyai **SPCL-FX:** Tassilo Baur **MUSIC:** Ragnar Grippe & Michael Shrieve **SONGS:** *Transfer Station Blue* & *View from the Window*
Minor thriller: Young man possessed by spirit of girlfriend's grandfather

Return from the Ashes
1965, (GB), Mirisch/UA, b&w, 104 mins.
W: Maximilian Schell (*Stanislaus Pilgrin*), Ingrid Thulin (*Dr. Michele Wolf*), Samantha Eggar (*Fabienne*), Herbert Lom (*Dr. Charles Bovard*), Talitha Pol (*Claudine*), Vladek Sheybal (*The Chess Club Manager*), Jacques Brunius (*A Detective*), Yvonne Andre (*The Woman*), John Serret (*The Man*), Jean Marc, Andre Charise, Daniele Noel, Arnold Diamond, Franco Derosa, Doreen Moore, Harriet Harper, Henry Vidon, Eugene Keeley, Pamela Stirling, Jean Driant, Mischa de la Motte, Rica Fox, Vivienne Ventura, Jacques Cey
P & D: J. Lee Thompson **SCR:** Julius J. Epstein **PHOTOG:** Christopher Challis **MUSIC:** John Dankworth
blurb: "No One May Enter the Theater After Fabi has Entered Her Bath"
Superior melodrama: Woman survives concentration camp, must contend with faithless husband and scheming stepdaughter

Return from the Beyond
1962, (Mex), Medallion TV, b&w, 79 mins.
W: Elsa Cardenas, Jaime Fernandez
Minor fantasy-thriller

Return from the Past
see *Gallery of Horror*

Return from Witch Mountain
1978, (USA), Walt Disney/Buena Vista, color, 93 mins.
W: Bette Davis (*Letha*), Christopher Lee (*Victor*), Kim Richards (*Tia*), Ike Eisenmann (*Tony*), Anthony James (*Sickle*), Jack Soo (*Mr. Yokomoto*), Dick Bakalyan (*Eddie*), Ward Costello (*Mr. Clearcole*), Christian Juttner (*Dazzler*), Brad Savage (*Muscles*), Poindexter (*Crusher*), Jeffrey Jacquet (*Rocky*), Denver Pyle
P: Ron Miller & Jerome Courtland **D:** John Hough **SCR:** Malcolm

Marmorstein, from characters created by Alexander Key **PHOTOG:** Frank Phillips **SPCL-FX:** Hal Bigger **MUSIC:** Lalo Schifrin
*Standard SF-fantasy (sequel to **Escape to Witch Mountain**)*

The Returning
1991, (USA), color
Minor fantasy-thriller: Stone activates supernatural forces

El Returno de la Walpurgis (Return of Walpurgis)
1973, (Sp), color, 73 mins.
W: Paul Naschy, Patty Shepard, Maria Silva, Fay Falcon
D: Carlos Aured **SCR:** Paul Naschy
*USA retitle, **Curse of the Devil***
Minor horror-fantasy: Gypsies turn man into werewolf

Return of a Stranger
1962, (GB), Danziger/WPD, b&w, 63 mins.
W: John Ireland (*Ray Reed*), Susan Stephen (*Pam Reed*), Cyril Shaps (*Homer Trent*), Timothy Beaton (*Tommy Reed*), Patrick McAlinney (*Whittaker*), Kevin Stoney (*Wayne*), Ian Fleming (*Meecham*), Raymond Rollett (*Somerset*), Frederick Piper (*Fred*)
P: Brian Taylor **D:** Max Varnel **STORY:** Brian Clemens
Standard thriller: Ex-convict plans to kill husband of schoolgirl he assaulted

The Return of Boston Blackie
1927, (USA), Chadwick, b&w, 6 reels
W: Raymond Glenn(Bob Custer) (*Boston Blackie*), Corliss Palmer (*The Girl*), Rosemary Cooper (*The Dancer*), Strongheart (*The Dog*), Coit Albertson, William Worthington, Florence Wix, Violet Palmer, J.P. Lockney
D: Harry O. Hoyt **SCR:** Leah Baird, from characters created by Jack Boyle
Standard thriller: Ex-con helps girl thief go straight

The Return of Bulldog Drummond
1934, (GB), BIP-Wardour, b&w, 71 mins.
W: Ralph Richardson (*Hugh "Bulldog" Drummond*), Ann Todd (*Phyllis Drummond*), Joyce Kennedy (*Irma Peterson*), Francis L. Sullivan (*Carl Peterson*), Spencer Trevor (*Sir Bryan Johnstone*), Claud Allister (*Algy Longworth*), Charles Mortimer (*Insp. McIver*), H. Saxon-Snell (*Zadowa*), Pat Aherne (*Jerry Seymour*), Wallace Geoffrey (*Charles Latter*)
D & SCR: Walter Summers, from Sapper's novel *The Black Gang*
distrib. in USA (1936) by Mundus Films
Standard thriller

The Return of Captain Invincible
1983, (USA-Austral), color, 90 mins.
W: Alan Arkin, Christopher Lee, Kate Fitzpatrick, Michael Pate
D: Philippe Mora
*A.k.a. **Legend in Leotards***
Standard spoof

The Return of Captain Marvel
see *The Adventures of Captain Marvel*

The Return of Charlie Chan
see *Charlie Chan: Happiness is a Warm Clue*

The Return of Count Yorga
1971, (USA), AIP, color, 97 mins.
W: Robert Quarry (*Count Yorga*), Roger Perry (*Dr. David Baldwin*), Mariette Hartley (*Cynthia Nelson*), Yvonne Wilder (*Jennifer*), George Macready (*Prof. Rightstat*), Tom Toner (*Rev. Thomas*), Rudy De Luca (*Lt. Madden*), Philip Frame (*Tommy*), Walter Brooke (*Bill Nelson*), Craig Nelson (*Sgt. O'Connor*), Edward Walsh (*Brudah*), David Lampson (*Jason*), Karen Houston (*Ellen*), Helen Baron (*Mrs. Nelson*), Jesse Wells (*Mitzi*), Mike Pataki (*Joe*), Allen Joseph (*Michael Farmer*), Peg Shirley (*Claret Farmer*), Corinne Conley (*The Witch*), Liz Rogers (*Laurie Greggs*), Paul Hansen (*Jonathan Greggs*)
D: Bob Kelljan **SCR:** Bob Kelljan & Yvonne Wilder **MUSIC:** Bill Marx
*Standard horror-fantasy (sequel to **Count Yorga, Vampire**): Undead stalks orphanage*

The Return of Dr. Fu Manchu
1930, (USA), Para, b&w, 8 reels (6,586 ft./2007.4m)
W: Warner Oland (*Dr. Fu Manchu*), Neil Hamilton (*Dr. Jack Petrie*), Jean Arthur (*Lia Eltham*), O.P. Heggie (*Nayland Smith*), William Austin (*Sylvester Wadsworth*), Evelyn Hall (*Lady Agatha Bartley*), Margaret Fealy (*Lady Helen Bartley*), Evelyn Selbie (*Fai Lu*), David Dunbar (*Lawrence*), Shayle Gardner (*Insp. Harding*), Tetsu Komai (*Chang*), Toyo Fujita (*Ah Ling*), Ambrose Barker (*The Reporter*)
D: Rowland V. Lee **SCR & DIALOG:** Florence Ryerson & Lloyd Corrigan, from characters created by Sax Rohmer **PHOTOG:** Archie J. Stout
Standard thriller: Insidious Chinaman seeks revenge

The Return of Dr. Mabuse
see *In the Steel Net of Dr. Mabuse*

The Return of Dr. X
1939, (USA), First Nat'l/WB, b&w, 62 mins.
W: Humphrey Bogart, Rosemary Lane, Wayne Morris, John Litel, Dennis Morgan, Charles Wilson, DeWolf (William) Hopper, Olin Howland, Lya Lys, Huntz Hall, Vera Lewis, Creighton Hale, Jack Mower, Arthur

Aylesworth, Howard Hickman, Joseph Crehan, Glenn Langan
D: Vincent Sherman **SCR:** Lee Katz, from William J. Makin's novel *The Doctor's Secret* **PHOTOG:** Sid Hickox
Standard horror-thriller (not a sequel to 'Doctor X'; Bogart's only "monster" role): Scientist revives dead

The Return of Dracula
1958, (USA), Gramercy/UA, b&w, 77 mins.
W: Francis Lederer (*Count Dracula*), Norma Eberhardt, Ray Stricklyn, Gage Clarke, Greta Granstedt, Virginia Vincent, Ivan Young, Jimmy Baird, John Wengraf, Norbert Schiller, John McNamara, Harry Harvey Sr., Mel Allen, Hope Summers, Dan Gachman, Robert Lynn
P: Arthur Gardner & Jules V. Levy **D:** Paul Landers **SCR:** Pat Fielder **PHOTOG:** Jack MacKenzie **MUSIC:** Gerald Fried
*GB retitle, **The Fantastic Disappearing Man**, USA TV-retitle, **Curse of Dracula***
*orig. co-billed with **The Flame Barrier***
Standard horror-fantasy: Master vampire takes place of traveler to America

The Return of Frankenstein
see Bride of Frankenstein

The Return of Giant Majin
1966, (Jap), Daiei/AIP-TV, color, 80 mins.
W: Kojiro Hongo, Shinji Hori
P: Masaichi Nagata **D:** Kenji Misumi & Yoshiyuki Kuroda **SCR:** Tetsuo Yoshida
*Minor fantasy-thriller (sequel to **Majin, Monster of Terror**): Petrified war-god faces new challenges*

The Return of Jafar
1994, (USA-Jap), Walt Disney, color, 66 mins.
VOICES: Scott Weinger (*Aladin*), Linda Larkin (*Jasmine*), Gilbert Gottfried (*Iago*), Val Bettin, Dan Castellaneta, Jason Alexander, Jonathan Freeman, Liz Callaway, Frank Welker, Brad Kane
D: Toby Shelton, Tad Stones & Alan Zaslove **SCR:** Kevin Campbell & Mirith J.S. Colao **ORIG. MUSIC:** Mark Watters **SONGS:** *Forget About Love* & *You're Only Second Rate*
*Made-for-Video, standard animated fantasy (first sequel to 1992's **Aladin**): Youth and genie vs. escaped sorcerer*

The Return of Maxwell Smart
see The Nude Bomb

The Return of Mr. H
see Madman of Mandoras

The Return of Mr. Moto
1965, (GB), 20th-Fox, b&w, 71 mins.
W: Henry Silva (*Mr. Moto*), Martin Wyldeck (*Dargo*), Terence Longdon (*Jonathan Westering*), Suzanne Lloyd (*Maxine Powell*), Marne Maitland (*Wasir Hussein*), Harold Kasket (*The Shahrdar of Wadi*), Henry Gilbert (*David Lennox*), Brian Coburn (*Magda*), Stanley Morgan (*Insp. Halliday*), Richard Evans (*Chief Insp. Marlow*), Peter Zander (*Ginelli*), Alister Williamson (*The Maitre d'Hotel*), Anthony Booth (*Hovath*), Gordon Tanner (*McAllister*), Denis Holmes (*Chapel*), Ian Fleming (*Rogers*), Tracy Connell (*The Arab*), Sonyia Benjamin (*The Belly Dancer*)
D: Ernest Morris **SCR:** Fred Eggers, from characters created by John P. Marquand **PHOTOG:** Basil Emmett **MUSIC:** Douglas Gamley
Minor thriller: Japanese sleuth vs. oil saboteurs

The Return of Monte Cristo
1946, (USA), Col, b&w, 91 mins.
W: Louis Hayward, Barbara Britton, George Macready, Steven Geray, Una O'Connor, Henry Stephenson, Ray Collins, Ludwig Donath, Ivan Triesault, Jean Del Val
D: Henry Levin **SCR:** Curt Siodmak & Arnold Phillips, from a story by George Bruce & Alfred Neumann **MUSIC SCORE:** Lucien Moraweck **MUSIC DIR:** Lud Gluskin **PHOTOG:** Charles Lawton Jr.
Minor adventure- thriller: Heir to fortune framed for crime

The Return of October
1948, (USA), Col, color, 89 mins.
W: Terry Moore, Glenn Ford, Steve Dunne, James Gleason, Samuel S. Hinds, Roland Winters, Dame May Whitty, Lloyd Corrigan, Henry O'Neill, Nana Bryant, Horace McMahon, Byron Foulger
P: Rudolph Maté **D:** Joseph H. Lewis **SCR:** Norman Panama & Melvin Frank **PHOTOG:** William Snyder **MUSIC SCORE:** George Duning
Standard comedy-whimsy: Girl thinks uncle reincarnated as race horse

The Return of Peter Grimm
1926, (USA), Fox, b&w, 7 reels (6,961 ft./2121.7m)
W: Alec B. Francis (*Peter Grimm*), John Roche (*Frederick Grimm*), Janet Gaynor (*Catherine*), Richard Walling (*James Hartman*), John St. Polis (*Andrew MacPherson*), Lionel Belmore (*Rev. Bartholomey*), Elizabeth Patterson (*Mrs. Bartholomey*), Bodil Rosing (*Marta*), Mickey McBan (*William*), Florence Gilbert (*Annamarie*), Sammy Cohen (*The Clown*)
D: Victor Schertzinger **ADAPT:** Bradley King, from David Belasco's 1911 play **PHOTOG:** Glen MacWilliams
Standard fantasy: Deceased man's ghost rights family's problems

The Return of Peter Grimm
1935, (USA), RKO, b&w, 84 mins.
W: Lionel Barrymore, Helen Mack, Edward Ellis, Donald Meek, George Breakston
D: George Nichols Jr., from David Belasco's play **PHOTOG:** Lucien Andriot
Standard fantasy: Dead man communicates through body of dying child

The Return of Philo Vance
see The Kennel Murder Case

The Return of Sherlock Holmes
1929, (USA), Par, b&w, 71 mins
W: Clive Brook (*Sherlock Holmes*), H. Reeves-Smith (*Dr. John Watson*), Phillips Holmes
D: Basil Dean, from characters created by Sir Arthur Conan Doyle
Standard thriller. First sound Holmes shot in Astoria, NY

The Return of Sherlock Holmes
1986, (USA-GB), CBS-TV, color, 94 mins.
W: Michael Pennington (*Sherlock Holmes*), Margaret Colin (*Jane Watson*), Lila Kaye (*Ms. Houston*), Nicholas Guest (*Toby*), Connie Booth (*Violet*), Barry Morse (*Carter Morstan*), William Hootkins (*Spelman*), Tony Steedman (*The Doctor*), Paul Maxwell (*Hopkins*), Shane Rimmer (*Stark*), Ray Jewers (*Singer*), Olivier Pierre (*Hampton*), Sheila Brand (*Kitty*), Daniel Benzali (*Ross*), John Sterland, Sneh Gupta, Miles Richardson, Ricco Ross, Nancy Paul, Howard Swinson, Debora Weston, Hubert Tucker
D: Kevin Connor **TELEPLAY:** Bob Shayne, from characters created by Sir Arthur Conan Doyle **PHOTOG:** Tony Imi **MUSIC:** Ken Thorne
TVM, standard thriller: Famed detective revived from cryogenic sleep, solves USA murder

The Return of Swamp Thing
1989, (USA), Lightyear/Millimeter Films, color, 88 mins.
W: Louis Jourdan (*Dr. Anton Arcane*), Heather Locklear (*Abigail Arcane*), Sarah Douglas (*Dr. Lana Zurrell*), Dick Durock (*Swamp Thing*)
D: Jim Wynorski **SCR:** Derek Spencer & Grant Morris **PHOTOG:** Zoran Hochstatter **MUSIC:** Chuck Cirino
Minor fantasy-thriller: Mutant faces arch-foe

The Return of Tarzan
1920, (USA), Numa/Goldwyn, b&w, 7 reels
W: Gene Pollar, from characters created by Edgar Rice Burroughs
*orig. to be titled **The Revenge of Tarzan***
Minor adventure-thriller: Jungle lord seeks vengeance

Return of the Ape Man
1944, (USA), Mono, b&w, 60 mins.
W: Bela Lugosi, John Carradine, Judith Gibson, Michael Ames (*Tod Andrews*), Frank Moran, Mary Currier
P: Sam Katzman & Jack Dietz **D:** Philip Rosen **SCR:** Robert Charles
*Minor horror-thriller (sequel to **The Ape Man**): Botched experiment produces hairy monster*

Return of the Blind Dead
see El Ataque de los Muertos sin Ojos

Return of the Fly
1959, (USA), 20th-Fox, b&w, 78 mins.
W: Vincent Price (*Francois Delambre*), Brett Halsey (*Philippe Delambre*), David Frankham (*Alan*), John Sutton (*Insp. Beacham*), Danielle De Metz, Dan Seymour, Richard Flato, Jack Daly, Janine Grandel, Joan Cotton, Florence Strom, Pat O'Hara, Michael Mark, Barry Bernard, Gregg Martell
P: Bernard Glasser **WRIT & D:** Edward Bernds, from a story by George Langelaan **PHOTOG:** Brydon Baker **MUSIC:** Paul Sawtell & Bert Shefter
*orig. co-billed with **The Alligator People***
*Standard SF-thriller (sequel to **The Fly** {1958}): Son of ill-fated scientist runs afoul of spies, falls victim to his father's electronic devices. cf. **Curse of the Fly***

The Return of the Frog
1938, (GB), Imperator/British Lion/Select, b&w, 75 mins.
W: Gordon Harker (*Insp. Elk*), Rene Ray (*Lila*), Una O'Connor (*Mum Oaks*), Hartley Power (*Sandford*), Cyril Smith (*Maggs*), Charles Lefeaux (*Golly Oaks*), Charles Carson (*The Commissioner*), George Hayes (*Lane*), Aubrey Mallalieu (*The Banker*), Meinhart Maur (*Alkman*)
P: Herbert Wilcox **D:** Maurice Elvey **SCR:** Ian Hay & Gerald Elliott, from Edgar Wallace's novel *The India-Rubber Men*
*US TV title: **Nobody Home**, reissued 1944*
Standard thriller: Detective exposes master criminal

Return of the Giant Monsters
1966, (Jap), Daiei/AIP, color, 85 mins.
W: Kojiro Hongo, Reiko Kashara, Kichijiro Ueda, Nayoyuki Abe
P: Hidemasa Nagata **D:** Noriaki Yuasa **SCR:** Fumi Takahashi
Minor fantasy-thriller

The Return of the Incredible Hulk
see The Incredible Hulk, Part 2

Return of the Jedi
1983, (USA), Lucasfilm/20th-Fox, color, 132 mins.
W: Mark Hamill (*Luke Skywalker*), Carrie Fisher (*Princess Leia*), Harrison Ford (*Han Solo*), Billy Dee Williams (*Lando Calrissian*), Anthony Daniels (*C3P0*), Peter Mayhew (*Chewbacca*), Sebastian Shaw (*Anakin Skywalker*), Ian McDiarmid (*The Emperor*), Frank Oz (*Yoda*), David Prowse (*Darth Vader*), James Earl Jones (*Voice of Darth Vader*), Michael Pennington (*Moff Jerjerrod*), Alec Guinness (*Obi Wan "Ben" Kenobi*), Kenny Baker (*R2D2*), Kenneth Colley (*Adm. Piett*), Tim Rose (*Adm. Ackbar*), Michael Carter (*Bib Fortuna*), Denis Lawson (*Wedge*), Dermot Crowley (*Gen. Madine*), Caroline Blakiston (*Mon Mothma*), Warwick Davis (*Wicket*), Jeremy Bulloch (*Boba Fett*), Femi Taylor (*Oola*), Michele Gruska (*Sy Snootles*), Claire Davenport (*The Fat Dancer*), Mike Edmonds (*Logray*), Jack Purvis (*Teebo*), Nicki Reade (*Nicki*), Jane Busby (*Chief Chirpa*), Malcolm Dixon, Mike Cottrell, Adam Bareham, Toby Philpott, Jonathan Oliver, Pip Miller, Tom Mannion, David Barclay, Michael McCormick, Deep Roy, Michael Quinn, Hugh Spirit, Simon Williamson, Swin Lee, Richard Robinson
P: Howard Kazanjian **D:** Richard Marquand **SCR:** Lawrence Kasdan & George Lucas **STORY:** George Lucas **PHOTOG:** Alan Hume **VS-FX:** Richard Edlund, Dennis Muren & Ken Ralston **SPCL-FX:** Roy Arbogast **MUSIC:** John Williams
orig. to be titled **Revenge of the Jedi**
Major SF-fantasy (3rd & last installment in Star Wars trilogy): Young hero battles evil planetary rulers. cf. **Star Wars** *and* **The Empire Strikes Back**

Return of the Killer Tomatoes
1988, (USA), Four Square/New World, color, 90 mins.
W: John Astin (*Prof. Gangreen*), Karen Mistal (*Tara*), George Clooney, Anthony Starke, Steve Lundquist, Rock Peace, Frank Davis, Charlie Jones, Ian Hutton, Harvey Weber, Rick Rockwell, Mike Villani, Gordon Howard, Mark Wenzel, Alice "Easy Squeezin'" Devlin, C.J. "Clark" Dillon, D.J. Sullivan, John Ara Martin, Spike Sorrentino, Deborah Gates, Ron Trim, Teri Weigel, John DeBello, Chad Peace, Brett Peace, Clint Peace, Dave Adams, Debra Fares, Thom Owens, Deirdre Andrews, Bruce Binkowski, Ka'imi Kuha, Mary Egan
D: John DeBello **SCR:** Constantine Dillon, J. Stephen Peace & John DeBello **PHOTOG:** Steven Kent Welch **MUSIC:** Rick Patterson & Neal Fox
Minor SF-satire: Mad scientist turns tomatoes into humans

The Return of the King
1980, (USA), Jules Bass-Arthur Rankin Jr./ABC-TV, color, 97 mins.
VOICES: Orson Bean (*Frodo*), Theodore Bikel (*Aragorn*), Roddy McDowall (*Samwise*), William Conrad (*Denethor*), John Huston (*Gandalf*), Theodore (*Gollum*), Glen Yarborough, Paul Frees, Sonny Melendez, Casey Kasem
TELEPLAY: Romeo Muller, based on last novel in J.R.R. Tolkien's fantasy trilogy *The Lord of the Rings* **MUSIC:** Maury Laws **LYRICS:** Jules Bass **SONGS:** *Frodo of the Nine Fingers, And the Ring of Doom, It's So Easy, Not to Try, Roads, Small Things, Leave Tomorrow 'till It Comes & Where There's a Whip There's a Way*
TVM, standard animated fantasy: Diminuitive beings go on dangerous quest. cf. **The Hobbit**

Return of the Living Dead (1974)
see **Dead People**

The Return of the Living Dead
1985, (USA), Hemdale/Orion, color, 90 mins.
W: Clu Gulager, James Karen, Don Calfa, Thom Mathews, David Bond, Miguel Nunez, Paul Cloud, Beverly Randolph, Jonathon Terry, John Philbin, Jewel Shepard, Derrick Brice, Blair Burrows
P: Tom Fox **D & SCR:** Dan O'Bannon **STORY:** Rudy Ricci, John Russo & Russell Streiner **PHOTOG:** Jules Brenner **MUSIC:** Matt Clifford
Standard horror-satire: Revived corpses eat human brains

Return of the Living Dead, Part II
1988, (USA), Greenfox/Lorimar, color, 89 mins.
W: James Karen (*Ed*), Thom Mathews (*Joey*), Marsha Dietlein (*Lucy Wilson*), Dana Ashbrook (*Tom Essex*), Suzanne Snyder (*Brenda*), Philip Bruns (*Doc Mandel*), Jason Hogan (*Johnny*), Michael Kenworthy (*Jesse Wilson*), Thor Van Lingen (*Billy*), Don Maxwell (*Billy's Dad*), Sally Smythe (*Billy's Mom*), Suzan Stadner (*The Aerobics Instructor*), Jonathon Terry (*The Colonel*), Allan Trautman (*The Tarman*), Mitch Pileggi (*The Sarge*), Reynold Cindrich (*The Soldier*), Terrence Riggins (*Frank*), Arturo Bonilla (*Lee*), James McIntire (*The Officer*), Larry Nicholas, Forrest Ackerman, Douglas Benson, David Eby, Annie Marshall, Nicholas Hernandez, Brian Peck, Steve Neuvenheim, Richard Moore, Derek Loughran
WRIT & D: Ken Wiederhorn **PHOTOG:** Robert Elswit **MUSIC:** J. Peter Robinson **SONGS:** *Flesh to Flesh, Spacehopper, Alone in the Night, Bad Case of Lovin' You, Looking for Clues, I'm the Man & High, Priest of Love*
Standard horror-satire: Toxic waste revives corpses

Return of the Living Dead III
1993, (USA), Trimark, color, 97 mins.
W: Mindy Clarke, J. Trevor Edmond
Minor horror-satire: Scientist's son turns dead girlfriend into ravenous zombie

The Return of the Man from U.N.C.L.E.
1983, (USA), CBS-TV, color, 96 mins.
W: Robert Vaughn (*Napoleon Solo*), David McCallum (*Illya Kuryakin*), Patrick Macnee (*Sir John*), George Lazenby (*James Bond*), Gayle Hunnicutt (*Andrea*), Anthony Zerbe (*Sepheran*), Geoffrey Lewis (*Janus*), Tom Mason (*Kowalski*), Keenan Wynn (*Castillian*), Simon Williams (*Nigel*), Carolyn Seymour, John Harkins
D: Ray Austin **TELEPLAY:** Michael Sloan **PHOTOG:** Fred J. Koenekamp
TVM, standard thriller: World threatened with nuclear war

The Return of the Musketeers
1989, (GB-Fr-Sp), color, 103 mins.
W: Michael York, Oliver Reed, Frank Finlay, Kim Cattrall, Richard Chamberlain, C. Thomas Howell, Christopher Lee, Geraldine Chaplin, Roy Kinnear, Philippe Noiret, Billy Connolly, Jean-Pierre Cassel, Eusebio Lazaro
D: Richard Lester **SCR:** George MacDonald Fraser, from Alexandre Dumas' novel *Twenty*
Standard adventure-thriller

The Return of the Scarlet Pimpernel
1937, (GB), London/UA, b&w, 94 mins.
W: Barry K. Barnes (*Sir Percy Blakeney*), Sophie Stewart (*Marguerite Blakeney*), Margaretta Scott (*Theresa Cabarrus*), James Mason (*Jean Tallien*), Francis Lister (*Chauvelin*), Anthony Bushell (*Sir Andrew Foulkes*), David Tree (*Lord Denning*), Patrick Barr (*Lord Hastings*), George Merritt (*The Chief of Police*), Henry Oscar (*Robespierre*), Hugh Miller (*de Calmet*), Allan Jeayes (*The Judge*), O.B. Clarence (*de Marre*), Evelyn Roberts (*The Prince of Wales*), Esme Percy (*Richard Sheridan*), Edmund Breon (*Col. Winterbottom*)
D: Hans Schwartz **SCR:** Lajos Biro, Arthur Wimperis & Adrian Brunel, from a novel by Baroness Orczy
reissued 1943
Standard adventure-thriller: Fop aids aristocrats in French Revolution

The Return of the Six Million Dollar Man and the Bionic Woman
1987, (USA), Univ/NBC-TV, color, 95 mins.
W: Lee Majors (*Steve Austin*), Lindsay Wagner (*Jamie Sommers*), Richard Anderson (*Oscar Goldman*), Tom Schanley (*Michael Austin*), Martin Landau (*Lyle Stenning*), Lee Majors II (*Jim Castillian*), Gary Lockwood (*John Praiser*), Deborah White (*Sally*), Martin Brooks, Will Bledsoe, Gary Blumsack, Robert F. Hoy, William Campbell, Terry Kiser, Cheryl McMannis, Danil Torppe, Patrick Pankhurst, Bob Seagren, Scott Kraft, Susan Woollen, Bryan Cranston, Keith Farrell, Phil Nordell, Pamela Bryant, Catherine McGoohan, Kawena Charlot, Leonard Kibrick, Sandey Grinn, Michele Minailo, Julie H. Morgan
D: Ray Austin **TELEPLAY:** Michael Sloan **STORY:** Michael Sloan & Bruce Lansbury, based on Martin Caidin's novel *Cyborg* **PHOTOG:** William J. Jurgensen **MUSIC:** Marvin Hamlisch
TVM, standard SF-adventure: Artificially-enhanced humans battle mercenaries

Return of the Terror
1934, (USA), First Nat'l/WB, b&w, 65 mins.
W: Mary Astor, John Halliday, J. Carrol Naish, Lyle Talbot, Frank Reicher, Irving Pichel, Frank McHugh
D: Howard Bretherton
SCR: Eugene Solow & Peter Milne, from a novel by Edgar Wallace
Standard thriller ("talkie" remake of 'The Terror' {1928}): Inventor of super X-ray machine escapes from asylum; murders begin

Return of the Texas Chainsaw Massacre
1995, (USA), CFP, color, 94 mins, also 84 mins.
W: Matthew McConaughey, Renee Zellweger
A.k.a. **The Texas Chainsaw Massacre: The Next Generation**
Minor horror-satire

The Return of the Vampire
1943, (USA), Col, b&w, 69 mins.
W: Bela Lugosi (*Armand Tesla*), Frieda Inescort (*Lady Jane*), Nina Foch (*Nicki*), Matt Willis (*Andreas*), Miles Mander, Ottola Nesmith, Roland Varno, Leslie Denison, Gilbert Emery
P: Sam White **D:** Lew Landers **SCR:** Griffin Jay, Randall Faye., from an idea by Kurt Neumann **PHOTOG:** John Stumar & L. William O'Connell **MUSIC:** M.W. Stoloff
Semi-classic horror-fantasy: Woman doctor fights to save son's fiancee, from clutches of relentless vampire

Return of the Vikings
1945, (GB), b&w, 54 mins.
D: Charles Frend
Minor adventure-thriller

The Return of the Whistler
1948, (USA), Col, b&w, 63 mins.
W: Lenore Aubert, Michael Duane, Richard Lane
Minor thriller

The Return of the World's Greatest Detective
1976, (USA), Univ/NBC-TV, color, 72 mins.
W: Larry Hagman (*Sherman/Sherlock*), Jenny O'Hara (*Dr. Watson*), Ivor Francis (*Spiner*), Ron Silver (*Collins*), Woodrow Parfrey (*Himmel*), Nicholas Colasanto (*Lt. Tinker*), Charles Macaulay (*Judge Harley*), Helen Verbit (*The Landlady*), Sid Haig (*Cooley*)

D: Dean Hargrove **TELEPLAY:** Roland Kibbee & Dean Hargrove **PHOTOG:** William Mendenhall **MUSIC:** Dick de Benedictus

A.k.a. Alias Sherlock Holmes
*TVM, standard thriller (similar to **They Might Be Giants**): Bumbling cop and psychiatric social worker seek killer*

Return of the Zombies
*see **La Orgia de los Muertos***

Return of Walpurgis
*see **El Retorno de la Walpurgis***

The Return of Wonder Woman
1977, (USA), ABC-TV, color, 90 mins.
W: Lynda Carter
TVM, standard fantasy (culled from teleseries)

Return to Boggy Creek
1977, (USA), Pierce-Ledwell/Howco-Int'l, color, 87 mins.
W: Dawn Wells, Dana Plato
P: Bob Gates **D:** Tom Moore **SCR:** Dave Woody
*Minor horror-thriller (sequel to **The Legend of Boggy Creek**): Hairy creature aids lost children*

Return to Fantasy Island
1978, (USA), ABC-TV, color, 97 mins.
W: Horst Buchholz, Karen Valentine, Adrienne Barbeau, Pat Crowley, George Maharis, Joseph Campanella, Ricardo Montalban (*Roarke*), Herve Villechaize (*Tattoo*), George Chakiris (*Pierre*), Laraine Day (*Mrs. Grant*), Joseph Cotten (*Grant*), Cameron Mitchell (*Raoul*), France Nuyen, John Zaremba
D: George McCowan **TELEPLAY:** Marc Brandel **PHOTOG:** Arch Dalzell
TVM, minor adventure-fantasy: Three couples face emotional changes on vacation isle

Return to Horror High
1987, (USA), Greg H. Sims/Froehlich-Lisson/New World, color, 95 mins.
W: Lori Lethin, Brendan Hughes, Alex Rocco, Scott Jacoby, Andy Romano, Richard Brestoff, Al Fann, Maureen McCormick, Pepper Martin, Vince Edwards, Philip McKeon, Remy O'Neill, Panchito Gomez, Michael Eric Kramer, Marvin McIntyre, Will Etra, George Clooney, Darcy DeMoss, Cliff Emmich, George Fisher, Dexter Hamlett, Joy Heston, Frank Kniest, Alison Noble, John Mueller, Kristi Somers, Larry Spinak
D: Bill Froehlich **SCR:** Bill Froehlich, Mark Lisson, Dana Escalante & Greg H. Sims **PHOTOG:** Roy H. Wagner **MUSIC:** Stacy Widelitz **SONGS:** *Greet the Teacher, Man for Me & Scary Movies*
Minor horror satire: Filmmakers try to recreate high school massacre

Return to Oz
1985, (USA-GB), Silver Screen Partners II/Walt Disney/Buena Vista, color, 109 mins.
W: Nicol Williamson (*Dr. Worley/The Nome King*), Jean Marsh (*Nurse Wilson/Princess Mombi*), Fairuza Balk (*Dorothy*), Matt Clark (*Uncle Henry*), Piper Laurie (*Aunt Em*), Michael Sundin & Tim Rose (*Tik Tok*), Mak Wilson (*Billina*), Brian Henson & Stewart Larange (*Jack Pumpkinhead*), Lyle Conway & Steve Norrington (*Gump*), Justin Case (*The Scarecrow*), Deep Roy (*The Tin Man*), John Alexander (*The Cowardly Lion*), Emma Ridley (*Ozma*), Pons Maar (*The Lead Wheeler & Nome Messenger*), Tansy (*Toto*), Sophie Ward (*Mombi II*), Fiona Victory (*Mombi III*), Bruce Boa (*The Policeman*), Susan Dacre, Swee Lim, Geoff Felix, David Greenaway, Rachel Ashton, Robbie Barnett, Ailsa Berk, Peter Elliott, Roger Ennals, Philip Tan, Ken Stevens, Robert Thirtle, Sean Barrett, Nichola Roche, Cheryl Brown, Alison Lynn, Sarah White, Denise Bryer
P: Paul Malansky **D:** Walter Murch **SCR:** Walter Murch & Gill Dennis, based on L. Frank Baum's *The Land of Oz* and *Ozma of Oz* **PHOTOG:** David Watkin **SPCL-FX:** Ian Wingrove **MUSIC:** David Shire
Bizarre fantasy: Girl revisits magical land

A Return to Salem's Lot
1987, (USA), Larco/WB, color, 101 mins.
W: Michael Moriarty (*Joe Weber*), Ricky Addison Reed (*Jeremy*), Samuel Fuller (*Van Meer*), Andrew Duggan (*Judge Axel*), Evelyn Keyes (*Mrs. Axel*), Jill Gatsby (*Sherry*), June Havoc (*Aunt Clara*), Ronee Blakely (*Sally*), James Dixon (*Rains*), David Holbrook (*The Deputy*), Kayja Crosby (*Cathy*), Robert Burr (*Dr. Fenton*), Tara Reid (*Amanda*), Jacqueline Britton (*Mrs. Fenton*), Brad Rijn (*Clarence*), Georgia Janelle Webb (*Sarah*), Gordon Ramsey (*Allen*), Kathleen Kichta (*The Vampire Woman*), David Ardao (*The Car Salesman*), Edward Shils (*A Farmer Vampire*), Richard Duggan (*A Farmer Vampire*), Ron Milkie (*A Townsperson*), Stewart G. Day (*Jeremiah*), Lynda A. Clark (*A Townsperson*), Nancy Duggan (*The Farm Girl*), Ted Noose (*A Hobo*), Jim Gillis (*A Hobo*), Rick Garia (*The Cameraman*), Bobby Ramsen (*The Jungle Guide*), Peter Hock (*The Farmer Drone*)
D & STORY: Larry Cohen **SCR:** Larry Cohen & James Dixon, from characters created by Stephen King **PHOTOG:** Daniel Pearl **MUSIC:** Michael Minard
Minor horror-thriller: Anthropologist ensnared by vampires

Return to Sender
1963, (GB), Merton Park/Anglo-Amalgamated, b&w, 61 mins.
W: Nigel Davenport (*Dino Steffano*), Yvonne Romain (*Lisa*), Geoffrey Keen (*Robert Lindley*), William Russell (*Mike Cochrane*), Jennifer Daniel (*Beth Lindley*), Richard Bird (*Fox*), Paul Williamson (*Tony Shaw*), John Horsley (*Supt.*

Gilchrist)
P: Jack Greenwood **D:** Gordon Hales **SCR:** John Roddick, from an Edgar Wallace story
Standard crime-thriller: Crooked speculator hires man to compromise prosecutor

Return to the Horrors of Blood Island
*see **Beast of Blood***

Return to the Lost World
1993, (Can), color, 99 mins.
W: John Rhys-Davies, David Warner, Darren Peter Mercer, Geza Kovacs
D: Timothy Bond, from characters created by Sir Arthur Conan Doyle
*Minor SF-thriller, sequel to **The Lost World** (1993)*

Return to Treasure Island
1954, (USA), World Films, UA, color, 67 mins.
W: Tab Hunter (*Clive Stone*), Dawn Addams (*Jamesina Hawkins*), Porter Hall (*Maximillian Harris*), James Seay (*Felix Newman*), Harry Lauter (*Parker*), William Cottrell (*Cookie*), Henry Rowland (*Williams*), Lane Chandler (*Cardigan*), Dayton Lummis (*Capt. Flint*), Robert Long (*Long John Silver*), Ken Terrell (*Thompson*)
WRIT & P: Aubrey Wisberg & Jack Pollexfen **D:** E.A. Dupont **PHOTOG:** William Bradford **SPCL-FX:** Pat Dinga **MUSIC:** Paul Sawtell
Minor adventure-thriller: Modern girl seeks pirate treasure. Last, post-humous frilm of Porter Hall

Revak, lo Schiavo di Cartagine (Revak, the Slave of Carthage)
1960, (It), color, 86 mins.
W: Jack Palance
D: Rudolph Mate
*A.k.a. **The Barbarians** and **Revak the Rebel***
Minor "Sword & Sandal"

Revak the Rebel
*see **Revak, lo Schiavo di Cartagine***

Revak, the Slave of Carthage
*see **Revak, lo Schiavo di Cartagine***

La Revanche du Sicilien
*see **Johnny Cool***

Le Reve d'Artiste (The Artist's Dream)
1898, (Fr), Star, b&w, 20m (65.6 ft./1.1 mins.)
D: Georges Melies
Standard comedy-fantasy

Le Reve de l'Horloger (The Clockmaker's Dream)
1904, (Fr), Star, b&w, 51m (167.3 ft./2.8 mins.)
D: Georges Melies
Standard fantasy

Le Reve de Noel (The Christmas Dream)
1900, (Fr), Star, b&w, 160m (525 ft./8.8 mins.)
D: Georges Melies
Standard fantasy

Le Reve de Shakespeare (Shakespeare's Dream)
1907, (Fr), Star, b&w
D: Georges Melies
*USA retitle, **Shakespeare Writing Julius Caesar***
Standard fantasy short

Le Reve du Maitre de Ballet (The Ballet Master's Dream)
1903, (Fr), Star, b&w, 47m (154.2 ft./2.6 mins.)
W: Mlle. Zizi Papillon
D: Georges Melies
Standard fantasy

Le Reve d'un Fumeur d'Opium (The Dream of an Opium Smoker)
1908, (Fr), Star, b&w, 106m (347.8 ft./5.9 mins.)
D: Georges Melies
*A.k.a. **The Dream of an Opium Fiend***
Standard fantasy

Le Reve du Pariah (The Pariah's Dream)
1902, (Fr), Star, b&w, 40m (131.2 ft./2.2 mins.)
D: Georges Melies
*USA retitle, **The Dream of a Hindu Beggar***
Standard fantasy

Le Reve du Pauvre (The Beggar's Dream)
1898, (Fr), Star, b&w, 20m (65.6 ft./1.1 mins.)
D: Georges Melies
Standard comedy-fantasy: Mendicant dreams of riches

Le Reve du Rajah ou la Foret Enchantee (The Rajah's Dream: or, The Enchanted Forest)
1900, (Fr), Star, b&w, 50m (164 ft./2.8 mins.)

D: Georges Melies
Standard fantasy

Le Revenant (The Apparition)
1903, (Fr), Star, b&w, 51m (167.3 ft./2.8 mins.)
D: Georges Melies
A.k.a. **The Apparition: or, Mr. Jones' Comical Experience with a Ghost** *and* **The Ghost and the Candle**
Standard comedy-fantasy

Revenge!
1904, (GB), Gaumont, b&w, 375 ft. (114.3m)
D: Alf Collins
Standard crime-thriller: Mechanic avenges wronged wife by strangling guilty officer

Revenge
1918, (USA), Metro, b&w, 5 reels
W: Wheeler Oakman, Edith Storey
D: Tod Browning
Standard thriller-western

Revenge
1971, (GB), Peter Rogers/RFD/Hemisphere, color, 89 mins.
W: James Booth *(Jim Radford)*, Sinead Cusack *(Rose)*, Joan Collins *(Carol Radford)*, Ray Barrett *(Harry)*, Tom Marshall *(Lee Radford)*, Kenneth Griffith *(Seely)*, Zuleika Robson *(Jill Radford)*, Donald Morley *(The Inspector)*, Geoffrey Hughes *(The Driver)*, Barry Andrews *(The Sgt.)*, Patrick McAlinney *(George)*, Angus Mackay *(The Priest)*, Basil Lord *(The Salesman)*, Martin Carroll *(The Undertaker)*
P: George H. Brown   **D:** Sidney Hayers   **STORY:** John Kruse   **PHOTOG:** Ken Hodges   **MUSIC:** Eric Rogers
A.k.a. **Terror from Under the House**, **After Jenny Died** *and* **Inn of the Frightened People**
Standard thriller: Man seeks daughter's killers

Revenge
1971, (USA), Aaron Spelling/ABC-TV, color, 73 mins.
W: Shelley Winters, Bradford Dillman, Roger Perry, Stuart Whitman, Carol Rossen
P: Mark Carliner   **D:** Jud Taylor   **TELEPLAY:** Joseph Stefano, from a novel by Elizabeth Davis
TVM, standard thriller: Mad woman cages innocent man whom she thinks wronged her daughter

Revenge
1986, (USA), color, 104 mins.
W: Patrick Wayne, John Carradine, Bennie Lee McGowan, Josef Hanet, Stephane Kropke
D: Christopher Lewis
Minor horror-thriller (sequel to **Blood Cult***): Dog worshippers covet tract of land*

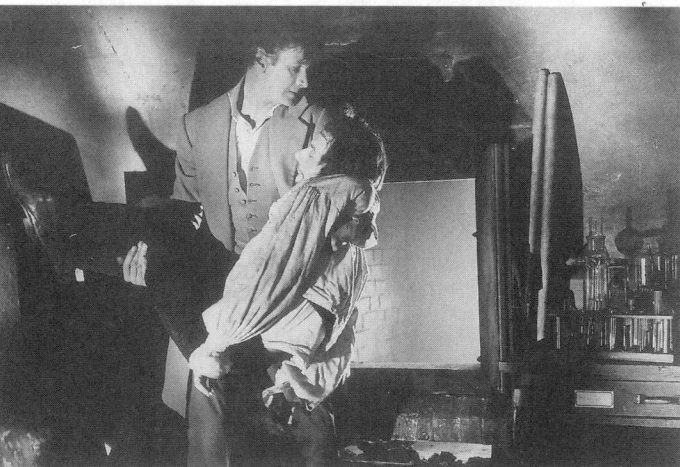

The Revenge of Frankenstein: MICHAEL GWYNN

Revenge in the House of Usher
1985, (Fr-Sp), Eurocine, color, 94 mins.
W: Howard Vernon, Dan Villers, Jean Tolzac, Oliver Mato, Joan Virly, Francoise Blanchard
D: A.M. Franck   **SCR:** H.L. Rostaine, inspired by Edgar Allan Poe's short story *The Fall of the House of Usher*   **PHOTOG:** Allan Hardy   **SPCL-FX:** S.O.I.S. Co.   **MUSIC:** Daniel White
Minor thriller: Mad doctor seeks to revive comatose daughter, drains prostitutes' blood

The Revenge of Dracula
see **Dracula vs. Frankenstein**

The Revenge of Frankenstein
1958, (GB), Hammer/Col, color, 94 mins.
W: Peter Cushing *(Baron Victor Frankenstein)*, Francis Matthews *(Hans Kleeve)*, Eunice Gayson *(Margaret Conrad)*, Michael Gwynn *(Karl)*, John Welsh *(Bergman)*, Lionel Jeffries *(Fritz)*, Oscar Quitak *(Karl, as a Dwarf)*, John Stuart *(The Inspector)*, Richard Wordsworth *(Up Patient)*, Margery Gresley *(Countess Barscynska)*, Charles Lloyd-Pack *(The President)*, Arnold Diamond, Avril Leslie, Ian Whittaker, George Woodbridge, Anna Walmsley
P: Anthony Hinds   **D:** Terence Fisher   **SCR:** Jimmy Sangster   **PHOTOG:** Jack Asher   **MUSIC:** Leonard Salzedo
orig. co-billed (USA) with **Curse of the Demon** *{***Night of the Demon***}*
Muted but superior horror-thriller (sequel to **The Curse of Frankenstein***): Maligned scientist escapes guillotine, returns to continue novel experiments*

Revenge of Homunculus
see **Homunculus**

Revenge of Kriemhild
see **Die Nibelungen**

The Revenge of Tarzan
see **The Return of Tarzan**

Revenge of the Black Eagle
1946, (It), color
W: Rossano Brazzi, Gianna Maria Canale
A.k.a. **L'Aquila Nera**
Minor swashbuckler: Prince seeks vengeance for death of family

The Revenge of the Black Spider
see **The Spider** *(1958)*

The Revenge of the Blood Beast
see **La Sorella di Satan**

Revenge of the Colossal Man
see **War of the Colossal Beast**

Revenge of the Creature
1955, (USA), Univ, 3D, b&w, 82 mins.
W: John Agar *(Clete)*, Lori Nelson *(Helen)*, John Bromfield *(Joe)*, Nestor Paiva *(Lucas)*, Robert B. Williams *(George)*, Grandon Rhodes, Dave Willock, Charles R. Cane, Brett Halsey, Ricou Browning *(The Creature)*, Clint Eastwood (film debut)
P: William Alland   **D:** Jack Arnold   **SCR:** Martin Berkeley   **PHOTOG:** Charles S. Welbourne   **MUSIC:** Joseph Gershenson
"This is Arnold's most assured work outside his masterpiece, The Incredible Shrinking Man, *cynically playing on the audience's sensibilities with a series of ingenious tricks" —John Baxter, Science Fiction in the Cinema*
Classic SF-thriller (sequel to **Creature from the Black Lagoon***; first 3D feature film broadcast on TV {1982}): Amazonian gill-man brought to civilization. cf.* **The Creature Walks Among Us**

Revenge of the Dead (1959)
see **Night of the Ghouls**

Revenge of the Dead
1984, (It), MPM, color, 100 mins.
W: John Stacy, Ann Canovas, Gabriele Lavia
D: Pupi Avati
Standard horror-thriller: Archeologists discover force that revives dead

Revenge of the Gladiators
1965, (It-Fr), Para, color, 100 mins.
W: Roger Browne, Scilla Gabel, Giacomo Rossi-Stuart, Daniele Vargas, Gordon Mitchell, Germano Longo
D: Michele Lupo   **SCR:** Lionello De Felice & Ernesto Guida
Standard "Sword & Sandal"

Revenge of the Humanoids
1981, (Fr), color
Standard animated SF-fantasy: Intergalactic power struggle

Revenge of the Jedi
see **Return of the Jedi**

Revenge of the Living Dead
see **The Murder Clinic**

Revenge of the Living Zombies
1988, (USA), color, 85 mins.
W: Bill Hinzman, John Mowod, Leslie Ann Wick, Kevin Kindlan
D: Bill Hinzman
Minor horror-fantasy: Teens on Halloween hayride meet ghouls

Revenge of the Pirates
1951, (It), b&w, 95 mins.
W: Maria Montez, Jean-Pierre Aumont, Milly Vitale, Robert Risso, Saro Urzi,

Paul Muller
D: Primo Zeglio
Standard swashbuckler: Wicked governor hoards stolen gold

Revenge of the Radioactive Reporter
1991, (USA), color, 90 mins.
W: David Scammell, Kathryn Boese, Randy Pearlstein, Derrick Strange
D: Craig Pryce
Standard SF-horror: Probing journalist becomes monster

Revenge of the Screaming Dead
see Dead People

Revenge of the Sicilian
see Johnny Cool

Revenge of the Stepford Wives
1980, (USA), NBC-TV, color, 95 mins.
W: Sharon Gless (*Kay Foster*), Julie Kavner (*Megan*), Arthur Hill (*Diz*), Don Johnson (*Andy*), Mason Adams (*Wally*), Audra Lindley (*Barbara*), Ellen Weston (*Kitten*), Howard Witt (*The Police Chief*), Tom Hill (*Dr. Trent*), Melissa Newman (*Muffin*), Peter Maloney (*The Druggist*), Millie Slavin (*The Sales Lady*), Sheldon Feldner (*Norman Kahn*), Ed Bell (*Gary Tarshis*), Gay Rowan (*Angelina*), James McKrell (*Bruce Manson*), Lee Bernard (*Sally Tarshis*), Stephanie Blackmore (*The Druggist's Wife*), Joe Medalis (*The Real Estate Agent*), Gayanne Meyers (*The Stepford Wife Attendant*), Dean Wein (*The Ambulance Driver*), David Boyle (*Charlie Gray*), Bonnie Sullivan (*A Stepford Wife*)
P: Scott Rudin **D:** Robert Fuest **TELEPLAY:** David Wiltse, based on characters created by Ira Levin **PHOTOG:** Ric Waite **MUSIC:** Laurence Rosenthal
TVM, standard SF-thriller: Woman reporter finds town where females are turned into automatons

Revenge of the Teenage Vixens from Outer Space
1985, (USA), Malamute Prods., color
W: Lisa Schwedop, Howard Scott, Amy Crumpacker, Sterling Ramberg, Julian Schembri, Peter Guss, Anne Lilly, Jerry Crisman, Lisa McGregor, Kim Wickenburg, Susanne Dailey, Sarah Barnes, Paul Fleming, Katie Green, Bob Yarnall, Katie McGee, Catherine Holmes, Eric Kohl
WRIT & P: Jeff Ferrell & Michelle Lichter **D & PHOTOG:** Jeff Ferrell
Minor SF-satire: Space women seek mates

Revenge of the Vampire
see La Maschera del Demonio

Revenge of the Virgins
1962, (USA), b&w, 53 mins.
W: Jewell Morgan, Charles Veltman, Jodean Russo, Stanton Pritchard, Kenne Duncan (*narrator*)
D: Paul Perri
Standard exploitation thriller: Topless Indian women guard sacred land

Revenge of the Zombie
see Kiss Daddy Goodbye

Revenge of the Zombies
1943, (USA), Mono, b&w, 61 mins.
W: John Carradine, Gale Storm, Robert Lowery, Veda Ann Borg, Mantan Moreland, Bob Steele
P: Lindsley Parsons **D:** Steve Sekely **SCR:** Edmond Kelso & Van Norcross
Standard horror-thriller: Evil scientist creates soulless horde

Revenge of the Zombies
1981, (Hong Kong), World Northal, color
W: Ti Lung, Lily Tu
P: Run Run Shaw **D:** Horace Menga
A.k.a. Black Magic II
Standard horror-fantasy: Evil sorcerer stays young by imbibing human milk

Revenge of Ursus
1960, (It), color
W: Samson Burke
Minor Sword & Sandal

The Revival of Dracula
1960, (It), b&w
Minor horror-fantasy

Revolt of the Dead Women
see Rebellion de las Muertas

Revolt of the Zombies
1936, (USA), Academy, b&w, 68 mins.
W: Dean Jagger, Dorothy Stone, Robert Noland, Roy D'Arcy, George Cleveland, Fred Warren, Carl Stockdale, Teru Shimada, William Crowell
P: Edward Halperin **D:** Victor Halperin **SCR:** Howard Higgin, Rollo Lloyd & Victor Halperin **PHOTOG:** J. Arthur Feindel
Standard horror-thriller: Soldier finds secret of creating zombies

Revolution
see The King's Romance

The Revolutionist
see The King's Romance

The Rhinoceros (1963)
see Die Nashorner

Rhinoceros
1974, (USA), American Express-Ely Landau/American Film Theatre, color, 101 mins.
W: Gene Wilder (*Stanley*), Zero Mostel (*John*), Karen Black (*Daisy*), Robert Weil (*Carl*), Joe Silver (*Norman*), Marilyn Chris (*Mrs. Bingham*), Lou Cutell (*The Cashier*), Don Calfa (*The Waiter*), Lorna Thayer (*The Restaurant Owner*), Robert Fields (*The Logician*), Kathryn Harkin (*The Lady with the Cat*), Melody Santangelo (*The Young Woman*), Howard Morton (*The Doctor*), Percy Rodrigues (*Mr. Nicholson*)
P: Ely Landau **D:** Tom O'Horgan **SCR:** Julian Barry, from Eugene Ionesco's play **PHOTOG:** James Crabe **SPCL-FX:** Robert Dawson **MUSIC:** Galt MacDermot **SONG:** What Did You Do to Yourself?
Standard philosophical grotesquerie: Community must reevaluate its ideas about conformity

Rich and Strange
1931, (GB), BIP/Wardour, b&w, 92 mins.
W: Henry Kendall (*Fred Hill*), Joan Barry (*Emily Hill*), Percy Marmont (*Cdr. Gordon*), Betty Amann (*The Princess*), Elsie Randolph (*Miss Imery*), Hannah Jones (*Miss Porter*), Aubrey Dexter (*The Colonel*)
D: Alfred Hitchcock **SCR:** Val Valentine, Alma Reville, & Alfred Hitchcock, from a novel by Dale Collins **PHOTOG:** John Cox & Charles Martin **MUSIC:** Hal Dolphe
A.k.a. East of Shanghai, US release Powers Pictures, 1932
Standard melodrama: Couple inherits money, troubles follow

Richard III
1911, (GB), Cooperative Cinematograph Co., b&w, 1,385 ft. (422.1m)
W: Frank Benson (*Richard III*), Constance Benson (*Lady Anne*), Eric Maxon (*Earl of Richmond*), Violet Farebrother (*Queen Elizabeth*), Murray Carrington (*Clarence*), Alfred Brydone (*Edward IV*), Harry Caine (*Hastings*), Moffat Johnston (*Buckingham*), Marion Rathbone (*Queen Margaret*), from Shakespeare's play
Standard melodrama: Vicious king plots

Richard III
1955, (GB), Lopert, color, 161 mins.
W: Laurence Olivier (*Richard III*), Claire Bloom (*Lady Anne*), Sir Ralph Richardson (*Buckingham*), Sir John Gielgud (*Clarence*), Sir Cedric Hardwicke (*Edward IV*), Alec Clunes (*Hastings*), Pamela Brown (*Jane Shore*), Stanley Baker (*Henry Tudor*), Andy Shine (*The Young Duke of York*), Laurence Naismith (*Stanley*), Helen Haye (*The Duchess of York*), Clive Morton (*Rivers*), Michael Ripper (*Forrest*), Douglas Wilmer (*Dorset*), Nicholas Hannen (*Archbishop of Canterbury*), Mary Kerridge (*Queen Elizabeth*), Paul Huson (*The Prince of Wales*), Stewart Allen (*Page to Richard III*), Andrew Cruickshank (*Brakenbury*), Terence Greenidge (*The Scrivener*), Norman Wooland (*Catesby*), Michael Gough (*Dighton*), Dan Cunningham (*Grey*), George Woodbridge (*Lord Mayor of London*), Roy Russell (*The Abbot*), Esmond Knight (*Ratcliffe*), John Laurie (*Lovel*), Bill Shine (*Beadle*), Richard Bennett (*George Stanley*), Patrick Troughton (*Tyrrell*), John Phillips (*Norfolk*), Russell Thorndike, Wally Bascoe, Norman Fisher, Peter Williams, Timothy Bateson, Willoughby Gray, Anne Wilton, Derek Prentice, Brian Nissen, Deering Wells, Alexander Davion, Robert Bishop, Lane Meddick
D: Laurence Olivier, from Shakespeare's play **PHOTOG:** Otto Heller **MUSIC:** Sir William Walton
Classic melodrama: Tale of England's infamous ruler

Richard III
1995, (GB), First Look Pictures/UA, color, 105 mins.
W: Ian McKellen (*Richard III*), Annette Bening (*Queen Elizabeth*), Jim Broadbent (*Buckingham*), Robert Downey Jr. (*Rivers*), Maggie Smith (*The Duchess of York*), Nigel Hawthorne (*Clarence*), John Wood (*King Edward*), Kristin Scott-Thomas (*Lady Anne*)
P: Lisa Katselas Pare & Stephen Bayly **D:** Richard Loncraine **SCR:** Ian McKellen & Richard Loncraine, based on a stage production by Richard Eyre, from Shakespeare's play **PHOTOG:** Peter Biziou **EDIT:** Paul Green **MUSIC:** Trevor Jones **PROD. DESIGN:** Tony Burrough
Unusual melodrama: Saga of ruthless egotist, set in fascist Europe of 1930s

Richelieu, or The Cardinal's Conspiracy
1909, (USA), Biograph, b&w, 1 reel
W: Thomas H. Ince
D: D.W. Griffith
Standard historical melodrama

Riches and Rogues
1913, (GB), B&C/MP, b&w, 1,245 ft. (379.5m)
W: Mae Hamilton (*Portia Fielding*), Harold Holland (*Dr. Rogers*), Margot Kelly (*Mrs. Whittingham*), E. Trelawney (*Mr. Whittingham*), R. Peyton (*Ernest Holt*), Cedric Hardwicke

R

D: Charles Weston
Standard crime-thriller: Girl poses as accident victim, robs benefactor

The Rich Man's Wife
1996, (USA), Hollywood, color, 128 mins.
<u>W</u>: Halle Berry (*Josie Potenza*), Christopher McDonald (*Tony Potenza*), Clive Owen (*Jake*), Peter Greene (*Cole Wilson*), Clea Lewis
<u>WRIT & D</u>: Amy Holden   <u>PHOTOG</u>: Haskell Wexler
Standard film noir: Widow becomes suspect in gory murders

Rich, Young and Deadly
*see **Platinum High School***

Ricochet
1963, (GB), Merton Park/Anglo-Amalgamated, b&w, 64 mins.
<u>W</u>: Maxine Audley (*Yvonne Phipps*), Richard Leech (*Alan Phipps*), Alex Scott (*John Brodie*), Dudley Foster (*Peter Dexter*), Patrick Magee (*Insp. Cummins*), Frederick Piper (*Siddall*), June Murphy (*Judy*), Virginia Wetherell (*Brenda*)
<u>P</u>: Jack Greenwood   <u>D</u>: John Moxey   <u>SCR</u>: Roger Marshall, from Edgar Wallace's story *Angel of Terror*
Standard crime-thriller: Solicitor's rich wife shoots lover

Riddler's Moon
1998, (USA), UPN-TV, color, 95 mins.
<u>W</u>: Kate Mulgrew, Daniel Newman, Corbin Bernsen
TVM, unusual fantasy-thriller: Farmwoman's crippled son has visions

The Ride of the Valkyries
1907, (GB), Graphic Cinematograph Co., b&w
<u>D</u>: Harold Jeapes
Standard fantasy (Made for use during Covent Garden opera production)

Riders of the Storm
1988, (GB), Miramax, color, 92 mins.
<u>W</u>: Dennis Hopper (*Captain*), Michael J. Pollard (*Tesla*), Eugene Lipinski (*Ace*), James Aubrey (*Claude*), Al Matthews (*Ben*), William Armstrong (*Jerry*), Michael Ho (*Minh*), Derek Hoxby (*Sam*), Nigel Pegram (*Mrs. Westinghouse*)
<u>D</u>: Maurice Phillips   <u>SCR</u>: Scott Roberts   <u>PHOTOG</u>: John Metcalfe   <u>MUSIC</u>: Brian Bennett
Minor SF-comedy: Post-nuke crusaders

Riders to the Stars
1954, (USA), UA, color, 81 mins.
<u>W</u>: Herbert Marshall, Richard Carlson, Martha Hyer, James Best, William Lundigan, George Eldredge, Robert Karnes, Dawn Addams, King Donovan, Lawrence Dobkin, Michael Fox, Dan Riss, Kem Dibbs, John Hedloe
<u>P</u>: Ivan Tors   <u>D</u>: Richard Carlson   <u>SCR</u>: Curt Siodmak   <u>PHOTOG</u>: Stanley Cortez   <u>SPCL-FX</u>: Harry Redmond Jr.   <u>MUSIC</u>: Harry Sukman   <u>TITLE SUNG BY</u>: Kitty White
Standard SF-thriller: Problems when scientists try to capture meteor

Ride the Pink Horse
1947, (USA), Univ, b&w, 101 mins.
<u>W</u>: Robert Montgomery, Wanda Hendrix, Thomas Gomez, Andrea King, Art Smith, Fred Clark, Richard Gaines, Rita Conde, Iris Flores, Tito Renaldo, John Doucette, Grandon Rhodes, Martin Garralaga, Edward Earle
<u>D</u>: Robert Montgomery   <u>SCR</u>: Ben Hecht & Charles Lederer, from Dorothy B. Hughes' novel   <u>PHOTOG</u>: Russell Metty   <u>MUSIC</u>: Frank Skinner
*Classic thriller: Hoodlum crossed by his employers. cf. **The Hanged Man***

The Right Hand of the Devil
1963, (USA), Cinema-Video Int'l, b&w, 75 mins.
<u>W</u>: Aram Katcher, Lisa McDonald, Brad Trumbull, James V. Christy, Chris Randall
<u>WRIT, P & D</u>: Aram Katcher
Minor thriller: Crook uses acid bath to dispose of accomplices

Right is Might
1911, (GB), Hepworth, b&w, 800 ft. (243.8m)
<u>D</u>: Bert Haldane
Standard thriller: Crook steals jewel, frames best friend

The Ring
1927, (GB), BIP/Wardour, b&w, 8,454 ft. (2576.8m)
<u>W</u>: Carl Brisson (*Jack Sander*), Lilian Hall Davis (*Mabel*), Ian Hunter (*Bob Corby*), Forrester Harvey (*James Ware*), Gordon Harker (*George*), Harry Terry (*Barker*), Bdr. Billy Wells (*The Boxer*), Charles Farrell (*The Second*), Clare Greet (*The Gypsy*)
<u>D & STORY</u>: Alfred Hitchcock   <u>SCR</u>: Alfred Hitchcock & Alma Reville
Standard melodrama: Fairground boxer struggles for success

The Ring and the Rajah
1914, (GB), London, b&w, 1,170 ft. (356.6m)
<u>W</u>: Edna Flugrath (*Edith Blayne*), Arthur Holmes-Gore (*The Rajah*), Vincent Clive (*Capt. Blayne*), Edward O'Neill (*Ferak*)
<u>D</u>: Harold Shaw   <u>STORY</u>: Anne Merwin
Standard thriller: Rajah dies saving captain's wife when plan to poison her husband goes wrong

The Ringer
1928, (GB), British Lion/Ideal, b&w, 7,150 ft. (2179.3m)
<u>W</u>: Leslie Faber (*Dr. Lomond*), Annette Benson (*Cora Ann Milton*), Lawson Butt (*Maurice Meister*), Nigel Barrie (*Insp. Wembury*), Hayford Hobbs (*Insp. Bliss*), John Hamilton (*John Lenley*), Muriel Angelus (*Mary Lenley*), Charles Emerald (*Sam Hackett*), Esther Rhodes (*Gwenda Milton*)
<u>D</u>: Arthur Maude   <u>SCR</u>: Edgar Wallace, from his play
Standard thriller: Police seek murderous disguised crook

The Ringer
1931, (GB), Gainsborough-British Lion/Ideal, b&w, 75 mins.
<u>W</u>: Gordon Harker (*Sam Hackett*), Franklin Dyall (*Maurice Meister*), John Longden (*Insp. Wembury*), Carol Goodner (*Cora Ann Milton*), Patrick Curwen (*Dr. Lomond*), Esmond Knight (*John Lenley*), Dorothy Bartlam (*Mary Lenley*), Arthur Stratton (*Sgt. Carter*), Henry Hallett (*Insp. Bliss*), Kathleen Joyce (*Gwenda Milton*)
<u>D</u>: Walter Forde   <u>SCR</u>: Angus Macphail & Robert Stevenson, from a play by Edgar Wallace
Standard thriller: Disguised crook kills ex-partner

The Ringer
1952, (GB), British Lion, b&w, 78 mins.
<u>W</u>: Herbert Lom (*Maurice Meister*), Donald Wolfit (*Dr. Lomond*), Mai Zetterling (*Lisa*), Greta Gynt (*Cora Ann Milton*), William Hartnell (*Sam Hackett*), Denholm Elliott (*John Lenley*), Norman Wooland (*Insp. Bliss*), Walter Fitzgerald (*The Commissioner*), Dora Bryan (*Mrs. Hackett*), Charles Victor (*Insp. Wembury*), John Stuart (*Gardener*), Edward Chapman (*The Stranger*), John Slater (*Bell*), Campbell Singer
<u>P</u>: Hugh Perceval   <u>D</u>: Guy Hamilton   <u>SCR</u>: Val Valentine & Lesley Storm, from a play by Edgar Wallace   <u>PHOTOG</u>: Ted Scaife   <u>MUSIC</u>: Malcolm Arnold
reissued 1964
Standard thriller: Master of disguise avenges secretary's murder

Ringer
1996, (USA), color, 105 mins.
<u>W</u>: Maud Adams
Standard thriller: Detective and hooker hunt psychopath

Ring of Fear
1954, (USA), WB, color, 88 mins.
<u>W</u>: Clyde Beatty, Mickey Spillane, Pat O'Brien (*Frank Wallace*), Marion Carr (*Valerie St. Denis*), John Bromfield (*Armand St. Denis*), Sean McClory (*Dublin O'Malley*), Jack Stang (*Paul Martin*), Pedro Gonzalez Gonzalez (*Gonzalez*), Emmett Lynn (*Twitchy*), Kenneth Tobey (*Shreveport*), Kathy Cline (*Suzette*)
<u>D</u>: James Edward Grant   <u>SCR</u>: Paul Fix, Philip MacDonald & James Edward Grant   <u>PHOTOG</u>: Edwin B. DuPar   <u>MUSIC</u>: Emil Newman & Arthur Lange
Standard thriller: Homicidal maniac terrorizes circus

Ring of Fire
1961, (USA), MGM, color, 91 mins.
<u>W</u>: David Janssen, Joyce Taylor, Frank Gorshin, Joel Marston, Doodles Weaver
<u>D & SCR</u>: Andrew L. Stone   <u>PHOTOG</u>: William H. Clothier
Engrossing melodrama: Delinquents start forest fire

Ring of Spies
1963, (GB), British Lion/Para, b&w, 90 mins.
<u>W</u>: Bernard Lee (*Henry Houghton*), William Sylvester (*Gordon Lonsdale*), Margaret Tyzack (*Elizabeth Gee*), David Kossoff (*Peter Kroger*), Nancy Nevinson (*Helen Kroger*), Patrick Barr (*Capt. Warner*), Thorley Walters (*Cdr. Winters*), Hector Ross (*Supt. Woods*), Newton Blick (*PO Meadows*), Gillian Lewis (*Marjorie Shaw*), Brian Nissen (*Lt. Downes*)
<u>P</u>: Leslie Gilliat   <u>D</u>: Robert Tronson   <u>STORY</u>: Frank Launder & Peter Barnes
*USA retitle, **Ring of Treason***
Standard thriller: Warrant Officer joins spy ring

Ring of Terror
1960, (USA), Ashcroft, b&w, 71 mins.
<u>W</u>: George Mather, Ernest Furst, Austin Green
<u>D</u>: Clark Paylow
Minor thriller: Student must steal corpse's ring as part of initiation

Ring of the Musketeers
1994, (USA), color, 86 mins.
<u>W</u>: David Hasselhoff, Cheech Marin, Alison Doody, Thomas Gottschalk, Corbin Bernsen, John Rhys-Davies
<u>D</u>: John Paragon   <u>SCR</u>: Joel Surnow
Standard adventure-thriller: Descendants of original Three Musketeers battle crime in modern-day Los Angeles

Ring of Treason
*see **Ring of Spies***

The Ring that Wasn't
1914, (GB), Martin Films/DFSA, b&w, 537 ft. (163.7m)
<u>D</u>: Dave Aylott
Standard fantasy: Convict dreams fairy gives him ring that makes things vanish

Rio 70
1970, (Sp-W. Ger-USA), Ada/Terra/Udastex, color
W: Shirley Eaton, George Sanders, Maria Rohm, Richard Wyler
P & SCR: Harry Allan Towers   D: Jesus Franco
A.k.a. *The Seven Men of Sumuru*
Standard SF-thriller (sequel to The Million Eyes of Sumuru): Females in Amazon jungle plot world conquest

The Riot Squad
see *Scream in the Night*

Rip's Dream
see *La Legende de Rip Van Winkle*

The Ripper
1985, (USA), color, 90 mins.
W: Tom Schreier, Wade Tower, Mona Van Pernis, Andrea Adams, Tom Savini
D: Christopher Lewis
Made-for-Video, minor horror-thriller: Evil power of Jack the Ripper's ring possesses college professor

The Ripper
1997, (USA), color, 100 mins.
W: Patrick Bergin, Gabrielle Anwar
Made-for-Cable, standard thriller: Scotland Yard inspector tracks Jack the Ripper

Rip Van Winkle
1896, (USA), Biograph, b&w
W: Joseph Jefferson (*Rip Van Winkle*), from Washington Irving's story

Rip Van Winkle
1903, (GB), Gaumont, b&w, 450 ft. (137.2m)
W: Alf Collins, William Carrington
D: Alf Collins, from Washington Irving's story
Standard fantasy (in 5 scenes): Henpeck returns home after 20 years' sleep

Rip Van Winkle
1910, (USA), Thanhouser, b&w, from Washington Irving's story
Standard fantasy: Man sleeps 20 years

Rip Van Winkle
1914, (GB), Climax, b&w, 3,000 ft. (914.4m)
W: Fred Storey (*Rip Van Winkle*), Ella Brandon (*Gretchen*), Martin Stuart (*Nick Vedder*), Maitland Stapley (*Derrick Beekman*)
D: Stuart Kinder   SCR: Fred Storey, from Washington Irving's story
A.k.a. *Forgotten*
Standard fantasy: Husband returns home after sleeping 20 years in forest

Rip Van Winkle
1921, (USA), Ward Lascelle Prods./W.W. Hodkinson, b&w, 7 reels (6,700 ft./2042.2m)
W: Thomas Jefferson (*Rip Van Winkle*), Milla Davenport (*Gretchen Van Winkle*), Daisy Robinson (*Meenie Van Winkle*), Gertrude Messinger (*Meenie Van Winkle, 20 years later*), Pietro Sosso (*Derrick Van Beekman*), Max Asher (*Nick Vedder*), Francis Carpenter (*Hendrick Vedder*)
P & D: Ward Lascelle   SCR: Agnes Parsons, from Washington Irving's story   PHOTOG: David Abel & George Larson
Standard fantasy: Strange little people put man into 20 year sleep

Rising Storm
1989, (USA), color, 100 mins.
W: Zack Galligan (*Artie*), Wayne Crawford (*Joe*)
Standard SF-adventure: Future revolution in totalitarian USA

Ritual of Evil
1969, (USA), Univ/ABC-TV, color, 98 mins.
W: Louis Jourdan (*Dr. David Sorell*), Anne Baxter (*Jolene*), Diana Hyland (*Leila*), John McMartin, Wilfrid Hyde-White, Belinda Montgomery, Carla Borelli, Georg Stanford Brown, Rege Cordic, Dehl Berti, Richard Alan Knox, Johnny Williams, Jimmy Joyce, James LaSane
D: Robert Day   TELEPLAY: Robert Presnell Jr., from characters created by Richard Alan Simmons   PHOTOG: Lionel Lindon   MUSIC: William Goldenberg
TVM, standard fantasy-thriller: Psychic investigates death of young heiress. cf. Fear No Evil (1969)

Rituals
1978, (Can), Astral, color, 90 mins.
W: Hal Holbrook (*Harry*), Lawrence Dane (*Mitzi*), Ken James (*Abel*), Robin Gammell (*Martin*), Gary Reineke (*D.J.*), Jack Creley, Murray Westgate, Michael Zenon
P: Lawrence Dane   D: Peter Carter   SCR: Ian Sutherland   PHOTOG: Rene Verzier   MUSIC: Hagood Hardy
distrib. in USA (1982) as The Creeper
Minor thriller: Maniac terrorizes five doctors in Canadian wilderness

The Rival Music Hall Artistes
see *Tom Tight et Dum Dum*

The Rivals
1963, (GB), Merton Park/Anglo-Amalgamated, b&w, 56 mins.
W: Jack Gwillim (*Rolf Neilson*), Erica Rogers (*Kim Harris*), Brian Smith Steve Houston), Tony Garnett (*Jimmy Vosier*), Barry Linehan (*Paul Kenyon*), Murray Hayne (*Alex Nichols*), Howard Greene (*Eddy McQuire*), Philip Latham (*Lawrence*)
P: Jack Greenwood   D: Max Varnel   SCR: John Roddick, from Edgar Wallace's novel *Elegant Edward*
Standard crime-thriller: Car thieves kidnap daughter of Swedish millionaire

The River House Ghost
1932, (GB), First Nat'l, b&w, 52 mins.
W: Florence Desmond (*Flo*), Hal Walters (*Walter*), Joan Marion (*Sally*), Mike Johnson (*Johnson*), Erle Stanley (*Black Mask*), Shayle Gardner (*Skeleton*), Helen Ferrers (*Martha Usher*)
D: Frank Richardson   STORY: W. Scott Darling
Minor comedy-thriller: Cockney girl unmasks crooks posing as ghosts

River of No Return
1954, (USA), 20th-Fox, color, 91 mins.
W: Robert Mitchum (*Matt Caulder*), Marilyn Monroe (*Kay*), Tommy Rettig (*Mark Caulder*), Rory Calhoun (*Harry Weston*), Murvyn Vye (*Colby*), Douglas Spencer (*Sam*), Edmund Cobb
P: Stanley Rubin   D: Otto Preminger   SCR: Frank Fenton, from a story by Louis Lantz   PHOTOG: Joseph La Shelle   SPCL-FX: Ray Kellogg   MUSIC: Cyril Mockridge   SONGS: *Down in the Meadow, One Silver Dollar & I'm Gonna File My Claim*
Superior melodrama: Three people flee Indians, risk lives on dangerous river

River of Souls
1998, (USA), TNT-TV, color, 95 mins.
W: Martin Sheen, Jerry Doyle, Ian McShane, Tracy Scoggins, Jeff Conaway, Richard Biggs, Jeff Doucette
D: Janet Greek   TELEPLAY: J. Michael Straczynski   PHOTOG: Frederick V. Murphy II   MUSIC: Christopher Franke
TVM (feature film augmenting "Babylon 5" teleseries), standard SF-adventure: Ancient repository of souls discovered

The Road Builder
see *The Night Digger*

Road Flower
1993, (USA), color, 86 mins.
W: Christopher Lambert, Craig Sheffer, David Arquette, Noah Fleiss, Adrienne Shelley, Richard Srafian
D: Deran Sarafian   SCR: Tedi Sarafian
Standard thriller: Family terrorized in Midwestern desert

Road Games
1981, (Austral), Essaness/Avco Embassy, color, 100 mins.
W: Stacy Keach (*Pat*), Jamie Lee Curtis (*Hitch/Pamela*), Bill Stacey (*Capt. Careful*), Marion Edward (*Frita*), Grant Page (*Smith or Jones*), Thaddeus Smith (*Abbott*), Stephen Millichamp (*Costello*), Alan Hopgood (*Lester*), John Murphy, Paul Harris, Robert Thompson, Ed Turley, Angela Bozzetta, Tony Bishop, Abbe Holmes
P & D: Richard Franklin   SCR: Everett DeRoche   PHOTOG: Vincent Monton   MUSIC: Brian May
Minor thriller: Truck driver vs. modern Jack the Ripper

The Road Killers
1995, (USA), color, 89 mins.
W: Christopher Lambert, Craig Sheffer, Adrienne Shelly
D: Deran Sarafian   SCR: Tedi Sarafian
Standard thriller: Psycho and gang terrorize family

Road Kill USA
1993, (USA), color, 98 mins.
W: Andrew Porter, Sean Bridges, Deanna Perry
D: Tony Elwood
Standard thriller: Two murderous drifters meet hitchhiking college student

The Road to Bali
1952, (USA), Para, color, 92 mins.
W: Bob Hope (*Harold Gridley*), Bing Crosby (*George Cochran*), Dorothy Lamour (*Lalah*), Murvyn Vye (*Ken Arok*), Leon Askin (*Ramayana*), Peter Coe (*Gung*), Ralph Moody (*Bhoma Da*), Dean Martin [cameo], Jerry Lewis [cameo], Jane Russell [cameo], Bob Crosby [cameo]
D: Hal Walker   SCR: Frank Butler, Hal Kanter & William Morrow   PHOTOG: George Barnes   MUSIC: Joseph J. Lilley
Standard adventure-comedy: Vaudevillians in tropic paradise

The Road to Hong Kong
1962, (GB), Melnor/UA, b&w, 91 mins.
W: Bing Crosby (*Harry Turner*), Bob Hope (*Chester Babcock*), Robert Morley (*The Leader*), Joan Collins (*Diane*), Dorothy Lamour (*herself*), Walter Gotell (*Dr.*

Zorbb), Peter Madden (*The Lama*), Felix Aylmer (*The Grand Lama*), Roger Delgado (*Jhinnah*), Julian Sherrier (*The Doctor*), Guy Standeven (*The Photographer*), Bill Nagy (*The Agent*), John McCarthy (*The Messenger*), Simon Levy (*The Servant*), Mai Ling (*The Chinese Girl*), Katya Douglas (*The Receptionist*), Alan Gifford, Roy Patrick, Robert Ayres, Robin Hughes, Harry Baird, Irving Allen, Jacqueline Jones, Victor Brooks, John Dearth, David Randall, Michael Wynne, Peter Sellers [cameo], Frank Sinatra [cameo], Dean Martin [cameo]
P: Melvin Frank **D:** Norman Panama **SCR:** Melvin Frank & Norman Panama **PHOTOG:** Gerry Fisher **MUSIC:** Robert Farnon **SONG:** *Warmer Than a Whisper* **DESIGN:** Roger Furse
orig. to be titled **The Road to the Moon**
Standard adventure-comedy: Hustlers involved in international intrigue

The Road to Mandalay
1926, (USA), MGM, b&w, 7 reels (6,562 ft./2000.1m)
W: Lon Chaney Sr. (*Singapore Joe*), Lois Moran (*Joe's Daughter*), Henry B. Walthall (*Father James*), Owen Moore (*The Admiral*), Kamiyama Sojin (*English Charlie Wing*), Rose Langdon (*Pansy*), John George (*The Servant*)
D: Tod Browning **SCR:** Elliott Clawson **STORY:** Tod Browning & Herman J. Mankiewicz **PHOTOG:** Merritt Gerstad
Standard melodrama: Former sea captain leads degenerate life

The Road to the Moon
see **The Road to Hong Kong**

Road to the Pleiades
see **Putiat Kam Pleadite**

The Road to Utopia
1945, (USA), Para, b&w, 89 mins.
W: Bing Crosby, Bob Hope, Dorothy Lamour, Hillary Brooke, Douglass Dumbrille, Robert Benchley, Jack LaRue
D: Hal Walker **SCR:** Norman Panama & Melvin Frank **PHOTOG:** Lionel Lindon **MUSIC:** Leigh Harline **SONG:** *Personality*
Amusing adventure-comedy: Vaudeville team seeks Alaskan gold mine

The Road to Yesterday
1925, (USA), DeMille/PDC, b&w, 10 reels (9,980 ft./3041.9m)
W: William Boyd (*Jack Moreland*), Vera Reynolds (*Beth Tyrell*), Trixie Friganza (*Harriett Tyrell {Aunt}*), Joseph Schildkraut (*Kenneth Paulton*), Jetta Goudal (*Malena Paulton*), Julia Faye (*Dolly Foules*), Clarence Burton (*Hugh Armstrong*), Charles West (*Watt Earnshaw*), Casson Ferguson (*Adrian Tompkyns*), Josephine Norman (*Anne Vener*), Junior Coghlan (*The Boy Scout*), Iron Eyes Cody (*The Indian*), Dick Sutherland (*The Torturer*), Charles Clary, Chester Morris, Walter Long, Sally Rand
P & D: Cecil B. DeMille **ADAPT:** Jeanie Macpherson & Beulah Marie Dix, from the 1906 play by Beulah Marie Dix & Evelyn Greenleaf Sutherland **PHOTOG:** J. Peverell Marley **MUSIC SCORE:** Rudolph Berliner
Standard melodrama: Woman in train wreck, dreams of past life in 17th-century England

The Road Warrior
1981, (Austral), Kennedy-Miller/WB, color, 95 mins.
W: Mel Gibson (*Max*), Bruce Spence (*Gyro Captain*), Vernon Wells (*Wez*), Mike Preston (*Pappagallo*), Emil Minty (*The Feral Child*), Kjell Nilsson (*Humungous*), Max Phipps
D: George Miller **SCR:** Terry Hayes, George Miller & Brian Hannant **PHOTOG:** Dean Semler **MUSIC:** Brian May
A.k.a. **Mad Max II**
Standard action-thriller (sequel to **Mad Max***): Roadies war in violent future. cf.* **Mad Max Beyond Thunderdome** *and* **Warriors of the Wasteland**

Robbers of the Sacred Mountain
1982, (Can), cable, color, 97 mins.
W: Simon MacCorkindale, John Marley, Louis Vallance (*Tracey*), Blanca Guerra (*B.G.*), George Touliatos (*Murdoch*), Jorge Reynoso (*Marques*)
D: Bob Schulz, from Sir Arthur Conan Doyle's story *Challenger's Gold*
A.k.a. **Falcon's Gold**
Made-for-Cable, standard adventure-thriller: Treasure hunt in Mexican jungle

Robbery
1967, (GB), Oakhurst/Para, color, 114 mins.
W: Stanley Baker (*Paul Clifto*), James Booth (*Insp. Kangdon*), Frank Finlay (*Robinson*), Joanna Pettet (*Kate Clifton*), Barry Foster (*Frank*), William Marlowe (*Dave*), Clinton Greyn (*Jack*), George Sewell (*Ben*), Michael McStay (*Don*), Patrick Jordan

Robbery with Violence
1959,(GB), GIB Films/RFI, b&w, 67 mins.
W: Ivan Craig (*Peter Frayne*), Sally Day (*Brenda Bailey*), Michael Golden (*Insp. Wilson*), John Martin Lewis (*Derek Bailey*), John Trevor Davis (*Insp. Greenway*)
P & D: George Ivan Barnett **SCR:** David Cumming **STORY:** Edith M. Barnett
Standard crime-thriller: Bank robber shoots mistress' husband

Robbing Cleopatra's Tomb
see **Cleopatre**

Robin and Marian
1976, (USA), Rastar/Col, color, 107 mins.
W: Sean Connery (*Robin Hood*), Audrey Hepburn (*Maid Marian*), Robert Shaw (*The Sheriff of Nottingham*), Nicol Williamson (*Little John*), Ronnie Barker (*Friar Tuck*), Richard Harris (*King Richard*), Denholm Elliott (*Will Scarlett*), Kenneth Haigh (*Sir Ranulf*), Ian Holm (*King John*), Veronica Quilligan (*Sister Mary*), Bill Maynard (*Mercadier*), Esmond Knight (*The Old Defender*), Peter Butterworth (*The Surgeon*), John Barrett (*Jack*), Kenneth Cranham (*Jack's Apprentice*), Victoria Merida Roja (*Queen Isabella*), Montserrat Julio (*The 1st Sister*), Victoria Hernandez Sanguino (*The 2nd Sister*), Margarita Minguillon (*The 3rd Sister*)
D: Richard Lester **SCR:** James Goldman **PHOTOG:** David Watkin **MUSIC:** John Barry
Modest action-melodrama: Middle-aged angst of famous outlaw

Robin Cook's Harmful Intent
1993, (USA), CBS-TV, color
W: Tim Matheson, Emma Samms, Alex Rocco, Robert Pastorelli, from a novel by Robin Cook
TVM, standard thriller: Doctor uncovers insidious plot

Robin Cook's Invasion
1997, (USA), NBC-TV, color, approx. 190 mins.
W: Luke Perry (*Beau Stark*), Rebecca Gayheart (*Cassy Winslow*), Kim Cattrall (*Dr. Sheila Moran*), Christopher Orr (*Pitt Henderson*), Louis Crugnali (*John*), Michael Warren (*Doc McCoy*)
D: Armand Mastroianni **TELEPLAY:** Rockne S. O'Bannon, from a novel by Robin Cook **PHOTOG:** Bryan England **SPCL-FX:** Craig Weiss
2-part miniseries, standard SF-thriller: Alien virus mutates humans

Robin Cook's "Mortal Fear"
1994, (USA), ACI, color, 91 mins.
W: Joanna Kerns (*Dr. Jennifer Kessler*), Gregory Harrison (*Philip Montgomery*), Max Gail (*Det. Curran*), Tobin Bell (*Dr. Alvin Hayes*), Robert Englund (*Ralph*), Amanda Bruce (*Mrs. Harring*), Rebecca Schull (*Dr. Danforth*), Suzanne Barnes (*Holly Boncher*), Leslie Ackerman (*Claudia*), Bus Riley (*The Plainclothesman*), Jerome Butler (*The EMT*), Jeff Olson (*Cedric Harring*), Michael Robert Berger (*The Waiter*), Donre Sampson (*The Janitor*), Katherine LaNasa, Judith Chapman
D: Larry Shaw **TELEPLAY:** Rob Gilmer & Roger Young, from Robin Cook's novel **PHOTOG:** William Wages **SPCL-FX:** Richard C. Welch **MUSIC:** Garry Schyman
TVM, standard thriller: Hospital chief of staff probes mysterious deaths

Robin Hood
1912, (USA), Eclair America, b&w & tint, 45 mins.
W: Robert Frazer (*Robin Hood*), Barbara Tennant (*Maid Marion*), Guy Oliver (*Friar Tuck*)
Standard adventure: Noble outlaw rights wrongs

Robin Hood
1922, (USA), UA, b&w, 11 reels (10,680 ft./3255.3m), 110 mins.
W: Douglas Fairbanks Sr. (*The Earl of Huntingdon/Robin Hood*), Wallace Beery (*Richard the Lion-Hearted*), Sam de Grasse (*Prince John*), Enid Bennett (*Lady Marian Fitzwalter*), Paul Dickey (*Sir Guy of Gisbourne*), William Lowery (*The High Sheriff of Nottingham*), Roy Coulson (*The King's Jester*), Billie Bennett (*Lady Marian's Serving Woman*), Willard Louis (*Friar Tuck*), Alan Hale Sr. (*Little John*), Maine (Bud) Geary (*Will Scarlett*), Lloyd Talman (*Alan-a-Dale*), Wilson Benge (*A Henchman to King John*), Merrill McCormick (*A Henchman to King John*), Mary Pickford [uncredited]
P & STORY: Douglas Fairbanks Sr. **SCR:** Lotta Woods **D:** Allan Dwan **PHOTOG:** Arthur Edeson
A.k.a. **Douglas Fairbanks in Robin Hood**
Classic adventure-thriller: Famed outlaw fights for justice

Robin Hood
1973, (USA), Walt Disney, color, 83 mins.
VOICES: Brian Bedford (*Robin*), Roger Miller (*The Narrator*), Peter Ustinov (*Prince John*), Terry-Thomas (*Sir Hiss*), Monica Evans (*Maid Marian*), Phil Harris (*Little John*), Andy Devine (*Friar Tuck*), Carole Shelley (*Lady Kluck*), Pat Buttram (*The Sheriff of Nottingham*), Ken Curtis (*Nutsy*), George Lindsey (*Trigger*)
P & D: Wolfgang Reitherman **STORY:** Larry Clemmons, based on a story & character conceptions by Ken Anderson **MUSIC:** George Bruns **SONGS:** by Roger Miller, Floyd Huddleston, George Bruns & Johnny Mercer
Standard animated adventure: Animals portray Sherwood Forest crowd

Robin Hood
1991, (USA-GB), Working Title/20th-Fox, color, 116 mins.
W: Patrick Bergin (*Robin Hood*), Uma Thurman (*Maid Marian*), Jurgen Prochnow (*Folcanet*), Jeroen Krabbe (*Daguerre*), Owen Teale (*Will Scarlett*), Edward Fox (*Prince John*), Jeff Nuttal (*Friar Tuck*), David Morrissey (*Little John*)
D: John Irvin **WRIT BY:** Mark Allen Smith & John McGrath **MUSIC:** Geoffrey Burgon
TVM, standard adventure-thriller: Outlaw fights corruption

Robin Hood and His Merrie Men (1952)
see **The Story of Robin Hood**

Robin Hood and His Merry Men
1908, (GB), Clarendon, b&w, 496 ft. (151.2m)
<u>D</u>: Percy Stow   <u>STORY</u>: Langford Reed
Standard adventure-thriller: Outlaw saves captured man from sheriff's gallows

Robin Hood and the Pirates
1960, (It), color, 83 mins.
<u>W</u>: Lex Barker *(Robin Hood)*, Jackie Lane *(Karin)*, Rossana Rory *(Lisbeth)*, Mario Scaccia *(Brooks)*, Giulio Donini *(Goliath)*, Renato Chiantoni *(Gladmore)*, Marco Tulli *(Friar Lawrence)*, Renato Maddalena *(Trinea)*, Giovanni Vari, Bruno Tocci
<u>D</u>: Giorgio Simonelli   <u>SCR</u>: Edoardo Anton, Marcello Ciorciolini, Leo Bomba, Carlo Infascelli & Enrico Spadorcia   <u>STORY</u>: Carlo Infascelli   <u>MUSIC</u>: Gian Stellari & Guido Robusti
Minor action-adventure: Outlaw hero allies with buccaneers

Robin Hood and the Sorcerer
1984, (GB), color, 115 mins.
<u>W</u>: Michael Praed *(Robin Hood)*, Anthony Valentine
Standard action-thriller (feature culled from teleseries): Outlaw herow vs. demonic baron

Robin Hood Jr.
1923, (USA), Export & Import Film Co., b&w, 4 reels
<u>W</u>: Frankie Lee *(The Boy, afterward Robin Hood)*, Peggy Cartwright *(The Girl, afterward Maid Marian)*, Stanley Bingham *(The Father, afterward King Richard)*, Ashley Cooper *(The Doctor, afterward Prince John)*, Harry La Mont *(Sir Guy of Gisbourne)*, Phillip Dunham *(High Sheriff of Nottingham)*
<u>D</u>: Clarence Bricker   <u>DIALOG</u>: Carol Owen   <u>PHOTOG</u>: Vernon Walker
Standard juvenile adventure: Children enact legend

Robin Hood Junior
1975, (GB), Brocket/CFF, color, 60 mins.
<u>W</u>: Keith Chegwin *(Robin)*, Mandy Tulloch *(Marian)*, Keith Jayne *(Will)*, Nicholas Dunn *(John)*, Dean Lawrence *(Edmund)*, Rachel Brennock *(Edith)*, Maurice Kaufmann *(Baron de Malherbe)*, Anthony Bailey *(Tybald)*, Sean Barrett *(The Sgt.)*, Andrew Sachs *(The Friar)*, Sydney Bromley *(Alfric)*, Alexander John *(Lord Gilbert)*
<u>P & D</u>: Matt McCarthy & John Black   <u>SCR</u>: William Smethurst   <u>STORY</u>: Matt McCarthy   <u>PHOTOG</u>: Tony Imi   <u>MUSIC</u>: De Wolfe
Standard juvenile adventure: Young archer and nobleman's daughter thwart usurping baron

Robin Hood: Men in Tights
1993, (USA), Brooksfilms-Gaumont/20th-Fox, color, 102 mins.
<u>W</u>: Cary Elwes *(Robin Hood)*, Richard Lewis *(Prince John)*, Roger Rees *(The Sheriff of Rottingham)*, Amy Yasbeck *(Maid Marian)*, Tracey Ullman *(Latrine)*, Dom DeLuise *(Don Giovanni)*, Mel Brooks *(The Rabbi)*, Matthew Porretta *(Will Scarlet O'Hara)*, Mark Blankfield, Isaac Hayes, Megan Cavanagh, Dave Chappelle, Robert Ridgely
<u>D</u>: Mel Brooks   <u>SCR</u>: Mel Brooks, J. David Shapiro & Evan Chandler   <u>STORY</u>: J. David Shapiro & Evan Chandler   <u>PHOTOG</u>: Michael D. O'Shea   <u>MUSIC</u>: Hummie Mann
Standard comedy-adventure: Farcical situations as forest outlaw champions oppressed

Robin Hood Outlawed
1912, (GB), B&C/MP, b&w, 1,186 ft. (361.5m)
<u>W</u>: A. Brian Plant *(Robin Hood)*, Ivy Martinek *(Maid Marian)*, George Foley *(Friar Tuck)*, Edward Durrant *(Will Scarlett)*, Jack Houghton *(Sir Hybert de Boissy)*, J. Leonard *(The Abbot of Ramsey)*, Harry Lorraine *(Little John)*
<u>D</u>: Charles Raymond   <u>STORY</u>: Harold Brett
Standard adventure-thriller: Outlawed earl forms robber band

Robin Hood: Prince of Thieves
1991, (USA), Morgan Creek/WB, color, 144 mins.
<u>W</u>: Kevin Costner *(Robin Hood)*, Morgan Freeman *(Azeem)*, Mary Elizabeth Mastrantonio *(Maid Marian)*, Alan Rickman *(The Sheriff of Nottingham)*, Christian Slater *(Will Scarlett)*, Nick Brimble *(Little John)*, Michael McShane *(Friar Tuck)*, Michael Wincott *(Guy of Gisborne)*, Geraldine McEwan *(Mortianna)*, Sean Connery *(King Richard)*, Soo Drouet *(Fanny)*, Daniel Newman *(Wolf)*, Daniel Peacock *(Bull)*, Walter Sparrow *(Duncan)*, Harold Innocent *(The Bishop)*, Jack Wild *(Much)*, Michael Goldie, Liam Halligan, Marc Zuber, Imogen Bain, Merelina Kendall, Jimmy Gardner, Bobby Parr, Derek Deadman, John Francis, John Hallam, Howard Lew Lewis, Pat Roach, Andy Hockley, John Dallimore, John Tordoff, Andrew Lawden, Susannah Corbett, Sarah Alexandra, Christopher Adamson, Richard Strange, Paul Weston
<u>D</u>: Kevin Reynolds   <u>SCR</u>: Pen Densham & John Watson   <u>STORY</u>: Pen Densham   <u>PHOTOG</u>: Douglas Milsome   <u>MUSIC</u>: Michael Kamen
Superior adventure-thriller: Medieval hero fights oppression

Robin Hood's Men
1924, (GB), Regent Films, b&w, 1,000 ft. (304.8m)
<u>W</u>: Gerald Ames
Standard adventure-thriller (episode from Fights Through the Ages series): Outlaw champions justice

Robin Hood: The Swords of Wayland
1984, (GB), color, 105 mins.
<u>W</u>: Michael Praed *(Robin Hood)*, Judi Trott *(Maid Marian)*, Rula Lenska

(Morgwyn), Phil Rose *(Friar Tuck)*
Standard adventure-thriller (feature culled from teleseries): Outlaw hero vs. evil priestess

Robinson Crusoe (1902)
see *Les Aventures de Robinson Crusoe*

Robinson Crusoe
1927, (GB), Epic Films, b&w, 6,500 ft. (1981.2m/34 mins.)
<u>W</u>: M.A. Wetherell *(Robinson Crusoe)*, Fay Compton *(Sophie)*, Herbert Waithe *(Man Friday)*, Reginald Fox
<u>D & SCR</u>: M.A. Wetherell, from Daniel Defoe's novel
Standard adventure: Shipwrecked man has prolonged stay on desert isle

Robinson Crusoe and the Tiger
1969, (Mex), Avant Films/Avco Embassy, color, 95 mins.
<u>W</u>: Hugo Stiglitz *(Robinson Crusoe)*, Ahui *(Friday)*
<u>D</u>: Rene Cardona Jr., inspired by Daniel Defoe's novel *Robinson Crusoe*   <u>PHOTOG</u>: Luis Medina   <u>MUSIC</u>: Raul Lavista
Standard adventure: Shipwrecked man investigates Nature

Robinson Crusoeland
see *Atoll K*

Robinson Crusoe on Mars
1964, (USA), Schenck-Zabel/Para, color, 109 mins.
<u>W</u>: Paul Mantee *(Commander Christopher Draper)*, Victor Lundin *("Friday")*, Adam West *(Col. Dan McReady)*, Mona the Woolly Monkey
<u>P</u>: Aubrey Schenck   <u>D</u>: Byron Haskin   <u>SCR</u>: Ib Melchior & John Higgins, based on a story by Daniel Defoe *(Robinson Crusoe)*   <u>PHOTOG</u>: Winton C. Hoch   <u>MUSIC</u>: Van Cleave
Unusual SF-thriller: Stranded astronaut struggles to survive in harsh Martian wastes

RoboCop
1987, (USA), Jon Davison/Orion, color, 103 mins.
<u>W</u>: Peter Weller *(Murphy)*, Nancy Allen *(Lewis)*, Ronny Cox *(Dick Jones)*, Daniel O'Herlihy *(The Old Man)*, Kurtwood Smith *(Clarence Boddicker)*, Miguel Ferrer *(Robert Morton)*, Robert DoQui *(Sgt. Reed)*, Ray Wise *(Leon)*, Felton Perry *(Johnson)*, Paul McCrane *(Emil)*, Jesse Goins *(Joe)*, Calvin Jung, Del Zamora, Rick Lieberman, Lee DeBroux, Mark Carlton, Edward Edwards, Michael Gregory, Fred Hice, Charles Carroll, Neil Summers, Gene Wolande, Gregory Poudevigne, Ken Page, Yolanda Williams, Tygress Allen, Laird Stuart, John Davies, Stephen Berrier, Sage Parker, Jerry Haynes, Karen Radcliffe, Darryl Cox, Bill Schockley, Debra Zach, Donna Keegan, Mike Moroff, Marjorie Rynearson, Adrianne Sachs, Jo Livingston, Joan Pirkle, Diane Robin, Maarten Goslins, Angie Bolling, Jason Levine, S.D. Nemeth, Bill Farmer, Michael Hunter, Spencer Prokop, L.J. King, David Packer, Leeza Gibbons, Mario Machado
<u>D</u>: Paul Verhoeven   <u>SCR</u>: Edward Neumeier & Michael Miner   <u>PHOTOG</u>: Jost Vacano   <u>SPCL-FX</u>: Dale Martin   <u>MUSIC</u>: Basil Poledouris   <u>SONG</u>: *Show Me Your Spine*
Exciting SF-thriller: Android opposes crime syndicate

RoboCop 2
1990, (USA), Orion, color, 117 mins.
<u>W</u>: Peter Weller *(Robocop)*, Nancy Allen *(Anne Lewis)*, Belinda Bauer *(Juliette Faxx)*, Tom Noonan *(Cain)*, Willard Pugh *(Mayor Kuzak)*, Felton Perry *(Donald Johnson)*, Gabriel Damon *(Hob)*, Stephen Lee *(Duffy)*, Galyn Gorg *(Angie)*, Dan O'Herlihy, Robert DoQui, Mario Machado, Leeza Gibbons, Lila Finn, John Glover, Roger Aaron Brown, John Ingle, Tommy Rosales, Mark Rolston, John Hateley, Gage Tarrant, Lily Chen, Martin Casella, Brandon Smith, Wallace Merck, Michael Medeiros, Jo Perkins, Linda Thompson, Ken Lerner, Angie Bolling, Clinton Austin Shirley, Jeff McCarthy, Phil Rubenstein, Erik Cord, John Doolittle, Richard Reyes, Charles Bailey, Yogi Baird, George Cheling, Wanda De Jesus, Tzi Ma, Gary Bullock, David Dwyer, Ed Geldhart, Adam Faraizl, Justin Seidner, Wayne DeHart, Bill Bolender, Fabiana Udenio, Cynthia Mackey, James McQueen, Jerry Nelson, Michael Weller, Woody Watson, Rutherford Cravens, Christopher Quinten
<u>D</u>: Irvin Kershner   <u>SCR</u>: Frank Miller & Walon Green   <u>STORY</u>: Walon Green, based on characters created by Edward Neumeier & Michael Miner   <u>PHOTOG</u>: Mark Irwin   <u>VS-FX</u>: Phil Tippett   <u>MUSIC</u>: Leonard Rosenman
Standard SF-thriller: Android continues fight against crime

RoboCop 3
1992, (USA), Orion, color, 104 mins.
<u>W</u>: Robert John Burke, Rip Torn, Nancy Allen, John Castle, Jill Hennessy, C.C.H. Pounder, Mako, Robert DoQui, Remy Ryan, Bruce Locke, Felton Perry
<u>P</u>: Patrick Crowley   <u>D</u>: Fred Dekker   <u>SCR</u>: Frank Miller & Fred Dekker   <u>STORY</u>: Frank Miller, from characters created by Edward Neumeier & Michael Miner   <u>MUSIC</u>: Basil Poledouris
Standard SF-thriller

Roboman
see *Who?*

Robot Carnival
1991, (Jap), color, 91 mins.

D: Katsuhiro Otomo, Atsuko Fukushima, Kouji Morimoto, Mao Lamdo, Kiroyuki Kitazume, Hidetoshi Ohmori, Yasuomi Umetsu, Hiroyuki Katakubo & Takashi Nakamura
Animated anthology: Automaton antics

Robot Holocaust
1987, (USA), color, 79 mins.
W: Norris Culf, Nadine Hart, Joel von Ornsteiner, Jennifer Delora, Andrew Howarth, Angelika Jager, Rick Gianasi
D & SCR: Tim Kincaid
Standard SF-thriller: Future humans vs. robots society

Robot in the Family
1994, (USA), color, 92 mins.
W: Joe Pantoliano, John Rhys-Davies, Danny Gerard, Matthew Locricchio, Amy Wright, Tom Signorelli, Peter Maloney, John Wylie, David Shuman, Don Peoples *(voice)*
D: Mark Richardson & Jack Shaoul **SCR:** Jack Shaoul **MUSIC:** Papo Gely & Ted Mason
Standard SF-comedy: Youth and robot companion hunt priceless antique

Robot Jox
1990, (USA), Charles Band/Empire, color, 85 mins.
W: Gary Graham, Anne Marie Johnson, Paul Koslo, Robert Sampson, Hilary Mason, Michael Alldredge, Danny Kamekona
D: Stuart Gordon **SCR:** Joe Haldeman **MUSIC:** Frederic Talgorn
Minor SF-thriller: Future war games

Robot Monster
1953, (USA), Astor, 3D, b&w, 63 mins.
W: George Nader, Claudia Barrett, Selena Royle, John Mylong
D: Phil Tucker **MUSIC:** Elmer Bernstein
incorporating stock-footage from *One Million B.C.*
reissued (in 2D) as **Monsters from the Moon**, *A.k.a.* **Monster from Mars**
"'Robor Monster...had the advantage of 3-D photography in its favor, but nothing could reduce the laughable reaction to the title character's ridiculous appearance. This nasty invader calling himself Roman (no insult to Italian-Americans intended) was essentially a gorilla wearing a diving bell helmet surrounded by curious soap bubbles emanating from his 'futuristic' equipment"—Gary Gerani, "The Space Monster Book—Chapter Four: Other Invasions," Monster Fantasy, August, 1975), p. 32
Minor SF-fantasy: Family opposes space-alien

The Robot vs. the Aztec Mummy
see **La Momia Contro el Robot Humano**

Robot Wars
1993, (USA), color, 73 mins.
W: Don Michael Paul, Barbara Crampton, James Staley, Lisa Rinna, Danny Kamekona, Yuji Okumoto, J. Downing, Peter Haskell
D: Albert Band
Standard SF-thriller: Terrorist seizes control of monstrous machine

Rocket and Roll
see **Abbott and Costello Go to Mars**

Rocket Attack U.S.A.
1956, (USA), Exploit, b&w, 68 mins.
W: Monica Davis, John McKay, Edward Czerniuk, Phillip St. George, Daniel Kern, Richard Downs, Herbert Flato, Janice Gilmain, Ray Brewer, Robert Reeh, Arthur (Art) Metrano, William Osborn, Jane Ross, Marco Behar, Ronnie Cooper, John Horner, Nicolai Grushko, Sara Amman, Vladovia Lazareff, James Tura
P & D: Barry Mahon **PHOTOG:** Mike Tubb
Minor SF-thriller: World War III threatened by planned Soviet missile attack

The Rocketeer
1991, (USA), Walt Disney/Buena Vista, color, 108 mins.
W: Bill Campbell *(Cliff)*, Jennifer Connelly *(Jenny)*, Alan Arkin *(Peevy)*, Timothy Dalton *(Neville Sinclair)*, Paul Sorvino *(Eddie Valentine)*, Terry O'Quinn *(Howard Hughes)*, Ed Lauter *(Fitch)*
D: Joe Johnston **SCR:** Danny Bilson & Paul DeMeo **STORY:** Danny Bilson, Paul DeMeo & William Dear, from Dave Stevens' novel **PHOTOG:** Hiro Narita **MUSIC:** James Horner
Juvenile SF-adventure: Amazing invention helps youth battle Nazis

A Rocket from Calabuch
1956, (Sp-It), Film Castellazione/Trans-Lux, b&w, 90 mins.
W: Edmund Gwenn, Valentina Cortese, Jose Isbert, Jose Luis Ozores, Franco Fabrizi, Francisco Bernal, Felix Fernando
D: Luis Berlanga
Standard melodrama: Guilt-ridden atomic scientist goes into retreat disguised as tramp

A Rocket from Fenwick
see **The Mouse on the Moon**

Rocket Man
1954, (USA), 20th-Fox, b&w, 79 mins.
W: George "Foghorn" Winslow, Anne Francis, John Agar, Beverly Garland, Charles Coburn, Spring Byington, Stanley Clements, Emory Parnell, June Clayworth, Don Haggerty
P: Leonard Goldstein **D:** Oscar Rudolph **SCR:** Lenny Bruce & Jack Henley **STORY:** George W. George & George F. Slavin
Standard Sf-fantasy: Space alien gives boy ray gun that reveals truth

Rocketman
1997, (USA), Caravan/Disney, color, 95 mins.
W: Harland Williams, William Sadler, Jessica Lundy, Beau Bridges, Peter Onorati, Jeffrey DeMunn, Shelley Duvall, James Pickens Jr., Don Lake
D: Stuart Gillard **PHOTOG:** Steven Poster
Juvenile SF-comedy: Misfit sent to Mars

Rocket Ship
see **Spaceship to the Unknown**

The Rocky Horror Picture Show: TIM CURRY, BARRY BOSTWICK AND SUSAN SARANDON

Rocketship X-M
1950, (USA), Lippert, b&w, 79 mins.
W: Lloyd Bridges (*Col. Floyd Graham*), Osa Massen (*Dr. Lisa Van Horn*), John Emery (*Dr. Karl Eckstrom*), Noah Beery Jr. (*Maj. William Corrigan*), Hugh O'Brian (*Henry Chamberlain*), Morris Ankrum (*Dr. Robert Fleming*), Patrick Ahern, Sherry Moreland, John Dutra, Katherine Marlowe
WRIT, P & D: Kurt Neumann, from his orig. screenplays *None Came Back* and *Journey into the Unknown* **PHOTOG:** Karl Struss **SPCL-FX:** Jack Rabin & Don Stewart **MUSIC SCORE:** Ferde Grofe **MUSIC DIR:** Albert Glasser
A.k.a. Expedition Moon
Semi-classic SF-thriller: Moon rocket goes off course, lands on Mars

Rocket to Nowhere
1957, (Czech), Brandon, b&w, 79 mins.
W: Jiri Vrstala, Eva Hrabetova, Hanus Bor
D: Jindrich Polak
Juvenile SF-fantasy: Space-alien robot kidnaps clown and three children

Rocket to the Moon
see Those Fantastic Flying Fools

The Rocking Horse Winner
1949, (GB), Rank/Univ, b&w, 91 mins.
W: Valerie Hobson (*Hester*), John Howard Davies (*Paul*), John Mills (*Bassett*), Ronald Squire (*Oscar*), Hugh Sinclair (*Grahame*), Susan Richards (*Nannie*), Cyril Smith (*The Bailiff*), Charles Goldner (*Mr. Tsaldouris*), Anthony Holles ("*Bowler Hat*"), Melanie McKenzie (*Matilda*), Caroline Steer (*Joan*)
P: John Mills **WRIT & D:** Anthony Pelissier, from D.H. Lawrence's short story **PHOTOG:** Desmond Dickinson **MUSIC:** William Alwyn
Gripping fantasy-melodrama: Young boy has power to select winning racehorses

Rodan, The Flying Monster

Rock 'N' Roll Nightmare
see The Edge of Hell

The Rocks of Valpre
1919, (GB), Stoll, b&w, 6,272 ft. (1911.7m)
W: Basil Gill (*Trevor Mordaunt*), Peggy Carlisle (*Christine Wyndham*), Cowley Wright (*Bertrand de Montville*), Humbertson Wright (*Capt. Rodolphe*), Barry Bernard (*Noel Wyndham*), Hugh Dabernon-Stoke (*Rupert Wyndham*), William Saville (*Jack Forrest*), Winifred Sadler (*The Aunt*)
D: Maurice Elvey **SCR:** R. Byron-Webber, from a novel by Ethel M. Dell
Standard crime-thriller: Framed 19th-century captain escapes jail, saves ex-fiancee from blackmail

Rocktober Blood
1985, (USA), color, 88 mins.
W: Donna Scoggins, Tray Loren, Nigel Benjamin, Beverly Sebastian
D: Fred Sebastian
Minor horror-fantasy: Executed rock star returns from grave

Rockula
1990, (USA), Cannon, color, 95 mins.
W: Dean Cameron, Toni Basil (*Phoebe*), Tawny Fere (*Mona*)
Minor horror-comedy: Adventures of teen vampire

Rocky and Bullwinkle
1999, (USA), Univ, color
W: Robert De Niro (*Fearless Leader*), Jason Alexander (*Boris Badenov*)
Amusing fantasy (mix of live action & animation): Moose and flying squirrel vs. inept spies

The Rocky Horror Picture Show
1975, (GB), Gloria/20th-Fox, color, 109 mins.
W: Tim Curry (*Frank N. Furter*), Susan Sarandon (*Janet Weiss*), Barry Bostwick (*Brad Majors*), Richard O'Brien (*Riff Raff*), Jonathan Adams (*Dr. Everett*

Scott*), Nell "Little Nell" Campbell (*Columbia*), Peter Hinwood (*Rocky*), Meatloaf (*Eddie*), Koo Stark (*The Bridesmaid*), Patricia Quinn (*Magenta*), Charles Gray (*The Narrator*), Hilary Labow (*Betty Munroe*), Jeremy Newson (*Ralph Hapschatt*), Christopher Biggins (*The Transylvanian*)
D: James Sharman **SCR:** Richard O'Brien & James Sharman, from a play by Richard O'Brien **PHOTOG:** Peter Suschitzky **MUSIC:** Richard O'Brien **SONGS:** *Creature of the Night*
"...a sort of philosophical analog between obscenity in the 19th century sense (which is what experiments such as Frankenstein's were considered) and obscenity in the 20th century sense, i.e. purely sexual matters"—Baird Searles, "Films," The Magazine of Fantasy and Science Fiction, Vol. 49, No. 2 (August, 1975), p. 109
Bizarre musical-fantasy (cult classic): Newlyweds seek refuge at mansion where space aliens are holding convention

Rodan, the Flying Monster
1956, (Jap), Toho/DCA/King Bros., color, 70 mins.
W: Kenji Sawara, Yumi Shirakawa, Akihiko Hirata, Minosuke Yamada, Akio Kobori, Yasuko Nakata, Yoshibumi Tajima, Kiyoharu Ohnaka
D: Inoshiro Honda **SCR:** Takeshi Kimura & Takeo Murata, from a story by Takashi Kuronuma **PHOTOG:** Isamu Ashida **SPCL-FX:** Eiji Tsuburaya **MUSIC:** Akira Ifukube
Jap title, Radan
Standard SF-thriller: Giant reptile terrorizes Nippon

Roger Corman's Dracula Rising
see Dracula Rising

Roger Corman's Frankenstein Unbound
1990, (USA), Mount Co./20th-Fox, color, 96 mins.
W: John Hurt (*Dr. Joseph Buchanan*), Raul Julia (*Dr. Victor Frankenstein*), Bridget Fonda (*Mary Godwin*), Nick Brimble (*The Monster*), Jason Patric (*Lord Byron*), Michael Hutchence (*Percy Shelley*), Catherine Rabett (*Elizabeth*), William Geiger (*The Lab Technician*), Mickey Knox (*Gen. Reade*), Catherine Corman (*Justine*), Terri Treas (*The Computer Voice*), Myriam Cyr (*The Information Officer*), Cynthia Allison (*The Newswoman*), Isabella Rocchietta (*Dorrie*), Matt Cassidy (*Boy #1*), Hauck Bjorck (*Boy #2*), Olga Angelo (*Girl #2*), Donal Hodson (*The Old Man*), Geoffrey Copleston (*The Innkeeper*), John Karlsen (*The Parson*), Bruce McGuire (*The Prosecutor*), Grady Clarkson (*The Judge*), Andrew Newton (*The Head Juror*), Paul Weston (*The Watchman*), Brian Ames (*Urchin #2*), Peter Goetz (*Man #1*), Nick Gillard (*Man #2 & #3*), Cyrus Elias (*Werner*)
D: Roger Corman **SCR:** Roger Corman, F.X. Feeney & Ed Neumeier, from Brian W. Aldiss' novel *Frankenstein Unbound* **PHOTOG:** Armando Nannuzzi & Michael Scott **VS-FX:** Bill Taylor & Syd Dutton **MUSIC:** Carl Davis
Major production, standard SF-horror tale: Time traveler visits 19th-century scientist

The Rogues of London
1915, (GB), Barker/Ashley, b&w, 4,450 ft. (1356.4m)
W: Blanche Forsythe (*Ruth Davies*), Fred Paul (*Ralph Munt*), Maud Yates (*Vera Verez*), Roy Travers
D: Bert Haldane **STORY:** Rowland Talbot
Standard crime-thriller: Cleric's son saves maid from suicide, she saves him when he is framed for killing crook's mistress

Rogues of Sherwood Forest
1950, (USA), Col, color, 80 mins.
W: John Derek (*Robin, Earl of Huntington*), Diana Lynn (*Lady Marianne*), George Macready (*King John*), Alan Hale (*Little John*), Paul Cavanagh (*Sir Giles*), Lowell Gilmore (*The Count of Flanders*), Billy House (*Friar Tuck*), William (Billy) Bevan (*Will Scarlett*), Lester Matthews (*Alan-a-Dale*), Donald Randolph (*Archbishop Stephen Langton*), Wilton Graff (*Baron Fitzwalter*), John Dehner (*Sir Baldric*), Gavin Muir (*Baron Alfred*), Tim Huntley (*Baron Chandos*), Paul Collins (*Arthur*)
P: Fred M. Packard **D:** Gordon Douglas **SCR:** George Bruce **STORY:** Ralph Bettinson **PHOTOG:** Charles Lawton Jr. **MUSIC:** Morris Stoloff
Standard adventure-thriller: Robin Hood's son battles unfair taxation

A Rogue's Wife
1915, (GB), Neptune/Walturdaw, b&w, 3,500 ft. (1606.7m)
W: Gregory Scott, Daisy Cordell, Joan Ritz, Frank Tennant, Douglas Payne
D: Percy Nash
Standard crime-thriller: Scottish thief steals laird's diamond

Rogue's Yarn
1957, (GB), Cresswell/Eros, b&w, 80 mins.
W: Nicole Maurey (*Michele Cartier*), Elwyn Brook-Jones (*Insp. Walker*), Derek Bond (*John Marsden*), Hugh Latimer (*Sgt. Adams*), John Serrett (*Insp. Lefarge*), John Salew (*Sam Youles*), Joan Carol (*The Nurse*)
P: George Maynard **D:** Vernon Sewell **STORY:** Ernie Bradford & Vernon Sewell
Standard crime-thriller: Yachter accused of killing rich, invalid wife

Le Roi des Mediums (King of the Mediums)
1910, (Fr), Star, b&w, 167m (547.9 ft./9.3 mins.)
D: Georges Melies
A.k.a. Apparitions Fantomatiques (Phantom Apparitions)
Standard fantasy

Un Roi sans Divertissement
see La Poursuite

Roland the Mighty
1961, (It), color, 80 mins.
W: Rik Battaglia
D: Gordon Douglas
Standard action-thriller: Saracens and legions of Charlemagne meet in battle

Rollerball
1975, (GB), UA, color, 123 mins.
W: James Caan (*Jonathan E*), John Houseman (*Bartholomew*), Maud Adams (*Ella*), Pamela Hensley (*Mackie*), Moses Gunn (*Cletus*), John Beck (*Moonpie*), Barbara Trentham (*Daphne*), Ralph Richardson (*The Librarian*), John Normington, Burt Kwouk
P & D: Norman Jewison **SCR:** William Harrison **PHOTOG:** Douglas Slocombe **MUSIC CONDUCT:** Andre Previn
Unusual SF-thriller: Deadly sport amuses future masses

Roller Blade Warriors: Taken by Force
1989, (USA), Golden Circle, color
W: Kathleen Kinmont (*Karin Crosse*), Rory Calhoun (*Old Turkel*), Jack Damon (*Rinaldi*), Norman Alden (*The Bartender*), Elizabeth Kaitan (*Gretchen Hope*), Cleve A. Hall (*Streak*), Kathleen Elizabeth (*Tawny*), Sam Mann (*Marachek*), Suzanne Solari (*Sharon Crosse*), Michael Sonye (*Karp*), Abby Dalton (*Mother Speed*), Leslie Marccella (*Valjean*), Jonnie Saiko (*Kosai*), Susan Henderson (*Sister Slo*), Mina Sanjo (*Miko*), Jeffery Hutchinson (*Lyle the Miner*), Mark Siegler (*Doobie*), Chris Corso (*Smack*), Robert A. Kline (*Hebert*), Chris Roth (*Trader #1*), Greg Miller (*Trader #2*), Erin Michael (*The Boy Sacrifice*), Kelsey (*Johnny Topp*), Lisa Toothman (*Slave Girl #1*), Susan Jones (*Slave Girl #2*), Theresa Bailey (*Slave Girl #3*)
D, STORY & PHOTOG: Donald G. Jackson **SCR:** Lloyd Strathern **SPCL-FX:** Don Power **MUSIC:** Robert Garrett **SONGS:** *Savior, Single Life for Me, Kick Around & Lies*
Minor SF-adventure: Post-nuke female soldiers

Rollercoaster
1977, (USA), Univ, color, 118 mins.
W: George Segal, Richard Widmark, Timothy Bottoms, Henry Fonda, Susan Strasberg, Harry Guardino, Tom Baker
P: Jennings Lang **D:** James Goldstone **SCR:** Richard Levinson & William Link **MUSIC:** Lalo Schifrin **SONG:** (performed by Sparks), *Big Boy*
Standard thriller: Madman sabotages rollercoasters

Rolling Vengeance
1987, (USA), Apollo, color, 91 mins.
W: Don Michael Paul (*Joey Russo*), Lawrence Dane (*Big Joe*), Ned Beatty (*Tiny Doyle*), Lisa Howard (*Misty*)
P & D: Steven H. Stern **SCR:** Michael Montgomery **PHOTOG:** Laszlo George **MUSIC:** Phil Marshall
Minor thriller: Monster truck avenges

Roma Contro Roma (Rome vs. Rome)
1963, (It), Galatea/AIP, color, 85 mins.
W: John Drew Barrymore, Ettore Manni, Susi Andersen, Ida Galli, Matilde Calnan, Philippe Hersent, Mino Doro
D: Giuseppe Vari **SCR:** Piero Pierotti & Marcello Sartarelli
*USA retitles, **War of the Zombies** and **Night Star, Goddess of Electra***
Standard fantasy-thriller: Scheme to conquer world with army of zombies

Romance of Tarzan
1918, (USA), First Nat'l, b&w, 7 reels
W: Elmo Lincoln, Enid Markey
from characters created by Edgar Rice Burroughs
Standard adventure-thriller: Exploits of jungle lord

Romance of the Nile
1924, (USA), Kerman, b&w, 5 reels
Standard melodrama

Romancing the Stone
1984, (USA), 20th-Fox, color, 105 mins.
W: Michael Douglas (*Jack Colton*), Kathleen Turner (*Joan Wilder*), Danny DeVito (*Ralph*), Zack Norman (*Ira*), Holland Taylor (*Gloria*), Mary Ellen Trainor (*Elaine*), Eve Smith, Alfonso Arau, Manuel Ojeda
D: Robert Zemeckis **SCR:** Diane Thomas **PHOTOG:** Dean Cundey **MUSIC:** Alan Silvestri
*Modest adventure-thriller: Authoress seeks kidnapped sister. cf. **The Jewel of the Nile***

Le Roman de Renard (The Tale of the Fox)
1930, (Fr), b&w, 65 mins.
VOICES: Claude Dauphin, Romain Bouquet, Sylvain Itkine
D: Wladyslaw Starewicz, from a fable by Goethe
Unusual stop-motion fantasy: Fox comes into conflict with lion king

Roman Scandals
1933, (USA), Goldwyn/UA, b&w, 95 mins.
W: Eddie Cantor, Gloria Stuart, David Manners, Ruth Etting, Alan Mowbray, Verree Teasdale, Lucille Ball, Jane Darwell, Edward Arnold
D: Frank Tuttle **SCR:** William Anthony McGuire, George Oppenheimer, Nat Perrin & Arthur Sheekman, from a story by George S. Kaufman & Robert E. Sherwood **PHOTOG:** Gregg Toland

Standard comedy-fantasy: Young man daydreams about ancient Rome

The Romany Rye
1915, (GB), Neptune, b&w, 3,030 ft. (923.5m)
W: Gerald Lawrence (*Paul Royston*), Gregory Scott (*Philip Royston*), Daisy Cordell (*Lora Lee*), Frank Tennant (*Ralph Endicott*), Joan Ritz (*Gertie Heckett*), Douglas Payne (*Edward Marsden*), Frank Arlton (*Goliath Lee*), Lindsay Fincham (*Sinfi Lovell*), Douglas Cox (*Boss Knivett*), Evelyn Maude (*Ivy Adrian*), John East (*Black Nathan*), Brian Daly (*Joe Heckett*), Mercy Hatton
D: Percy Nash **SCR:** John East & Brian Daly, from a play by George R. Sims
Standard adventure-thriller: Heir turns gypsy, eludes usurping half-brother

Romeo is Bleeding
1994, (USA), Working Title-Hilary Henkin/Polygram, color, 110 mins.
W: Gary Oldman (*Jack Grimaldi*), Lena Olin (*Mona*), Juliette Lewis (*Sheri*), Annabella Sciorra (*Natalie*), Roy Scheider (*Don Falcone*), David Proval (*Scully*), Gene Canfield (*John*), Will Patton (*Martie*), Wallace Wood (*The Waiter*), William Duff-Griffin (*Paddy*), Larry Joshua (*Joey*), Michael Wincott (*Sal*), James Cromwell (*Cage*), Paul Butler (*Skouras*), Tony Sirico (*Malacci*), Victoria Bastel (*Girl #1*), Katrina Rae (*Girl #2*), Joe Paparone (*Ginny*), Owen Hollander (*Stan*), Neal Jones (*The Clerk*), James Murtaugh (*The Priest*), Gary Hope (*The Driver*), Americo Mongriello (*Man #1*), James Mongriello (*Man #2*), Ron Perlman (*Jack's Att'y*)
D: Peter Medak **SCR:** Hilary Henkin **PHOTOG:** Dariusz Wolski **MUSIC:** Mark Isham
Intense thriller: Crooked cop meets vicious female assassin

Rome vs. Rome
*see **Roma Contro Roma***

Romolo e Remo (Romulus and Remus)
1961, (It), Titanus/Ajace/Para, color, 88 mins.
W: Steve Reeves (*Romulus*), Gordon Scott (*Remus*), Jacques Sernas (*Curtius*), Virna Lisi (*Julie*), Massimo Girotti (*Tatius Titus*), Ornella Vanoni (*Tarpeia*), Franco Volpi (*Amulius*)
D: Sergio Corbucci **SCR:** Sergio Corbucci, Luciano Martino, Sergio Leone, Giorgio Prosperi, Franco Rossetti, Ennio De Concini & Duccio Tessari
*USA retitle, **Duel of the Titans***
Standard "Sword & Sandal": Adventures of Rome's legendary founders

Romulus and Remus
*see **Romolo e Remo***

Romulus and the Sabines
1961, (It), color
W: Roger Moore, Mylene Demongeot
Standard "Sword & Sandal": Early Romans steal women

Rona Jaffe's Mazes and Monsters
1982, (USA), McDermott Prods./CBS-TV, color, 100 mins.
W: Tom Hanks (*Robbie*), Wendy Crewson (*Kate*), David Wallace (*Daniel*), Chris Makepeace (*Jay Jay*), Vera Miles (*Robbie's Mother*), Murray Hamilton (*Lt. John Martini*), Anne Francis, Lloyd Bochner, Louise Sorel, Susan Strasberg, Peter Donat, Jim Bearden
D: Steven H. Stern **TELEPLAY:** Tom Lazarus, from Rona Jaffe's novel *Mazes and Monsters* **PHOTOG:** Laszlo George **MUSIC:** Hagood Hardy **SONG:** *Friends in This World*
TVM, standard thriller: College students become enmeshed in dangerous fantasy game

Roogie's Bump
1954, (USA), Rep, b&w, 71 mins.
W: Robert Marriot, Ruth Warwick, Olive Blakeney, William Harrigan, Roy Campanella, Robert F. Simon, Brooklyn Dodgers
P: John Bash & Elizabeth Dickenson **D:** Harold Young **SCR:** Jack Henley & Dan Totheroh **PHOTOG:** J. Burgi Contner
*Standard juvenile fantasy: Boy magically becomes big league pitcher. Remake: **Rookie of the Year**, 1993*

The Rook
*see **Something for Everyone***

Room 43
*see **Passport to Shame***

Room to Let
1949, (GB), Hammer/Exclusive, b&w, 68 mins.
W: Jimmy Hanley (*Curley Minter*), Valentine Dyall (*Dr. Fell*), Christine Silver (*Mrs. Musgrave*), Merle Tottenham (*Alice*), Charles Hawtrey (*Mike Atkinson*), Constance Smith (*Molly Musgrave*), J. Anthony la Penna (*J.J.*), Reginald Dyson (*Sgt. Cranbourne*)
P: Anthony Hinds **D:** Godfrey Grayson **SCR:** John Gilling & Godfrey Grayson, from a radio-play by Margery Allingham
Standard thriller: Elderly reporter tells of having known Jack the Ripper

Rope
1948, (USA), Transatlantic/WB, color, 80 mins.
W: James Stewart, John Dall, Farley Granger, Douglas Dick, Joan Chandler, Sir Cedric Hardwicke, Constance Collier, Edith Evanson
D: Alfred Hitchcock **SCR:** Arthur Laurents, from a play by Patrick Hamilton **PHOTOG:** Joseph Valentine & William V. Skall **MUSIC:** Leo F. Forbstein

Unusual thriller: Two youths murder, hide body in trunk

Rope Around the Neck
1964, (Fr), color
W: Jean Richard, Dany Robin, Magali Noel
Standard thriller: Man tries to murder wife

Rorret
1989, (It), New Yorker, color, 105 mins.
W: Lou Castel (*Rorret*), Anna Galiena (*Barbara*), Massimo Venturiello (*Carlo*), Enrica Rosso (*Sara*), Rossana Coggiola (*Sheila*), Patrizia Punzo (*Cecilia*)
D: Fulvio Wetzl   **SCR:** Fulvio Wetzl & Enzo Capua   **PHOTOG:** Carlo Cerchio
Standard thriller: Cinephile enacts gruesome fantasies

The Rosary Murders
1987, (USA), Robert G. Laurel-First Take/Samuel Goldwyn, color, 105 mins.
W: Donald Sutherland, Charles Durning, Belinda Bauer, Josef Sommer, James Murtaugh, Kathleen Tolan, Roger Angelini, Anita Barone, Constance Barry, Ed Seamon, Joel Nash, Jo Mullin White, Stefan Gierasch, Mark Margolis
D: Fred Walton   **SCR:** Elmore Leonard & Fred Walton, from a novel by William X. Kienzle   **PHOTOG:** David Golia   **MUSIC:** Bobby Laurel & Don Sebesky   **SONG:** *In Your Eyes*
Standard thriller: Serial killer preys on nuns and priests

The Rose and the Sword
see Flesh & Blood

Rosemary's Baby
1968, (USA), Para, color, 134 mins.
W: Mia Farrow (*Rosemary Woodhouse*), John Cassavetes (*Guy Woodhouse*), Ruth Gordon (*Minnie Castavet*), Sidney Blackmer (*Roman Castavet*), Maurice Evans (*Hutch*), Charles Grodin (*Dr. C.C. Hill*), Ralph Bellamy (*Dr. Abraham Saperstein*), Elisha Cook Jr. (*Mr. Nicklas*), Patsy Kelly (*Laura-Louise*), Hannah Landy (*Grace Cardiff*), Emmaline Henry, Wendy Wagner, Philip Leeds, Angela Dorian [later Victoria Vetri], Hope Summers, Almira Sessions
P: William Castle   **D & SCR:** Roman Polanski, from Ira Levin's novel   **PHOTOG:** William A. Fraker   **MUSIC:** Krzysztof Komeda   **DESIGN:** Joel Schiller
Classic horror-thriller: Housewife becomes satanists' pawn. cf. **Look What's Happened to Rosemary's Baby**

Rosemary's Baby II
see Look What's Happened to Rosemary's Baby

Rosemary's Killer
see The Prowler (1981)

Roses of Picardy
1918, (GB), Union Photoplays, b&w, 4,000 ft. (1219.2m)
P: David Rosenfeld
Standard crime-thriller: Actress loves engineer whose hydroplane is stolen by spies

Le Rosier Miraculeux (The Miraculous Rose-Tree)
1904, (Fr), Star, b&w, 60m (196.9 ft./3.3 mins.)
D: Georges Melies
A.k.a. The Wonderful Rose-Tree
Standard fantasy

Le Rossignol de Empereur de Chine
see Cisaruv Slavik

Roswell
1994, (USA), SHO-TV, color, 91 mins.
W: Kyle MacLachlan, Martin Sheen, Eugene Roche, Kim Greist, Dwight Yoakam, Xander Berkeley, J.D. Daniels, Doug Wert, John M. Jackson, Peter MacNicol, Bob Gunton, Charles Martin Smith
D: Jeremy Paul Kagan   **WRIT:** Jeremy Paul Kagan, Arthur Kopit & Paul Davids, from the book *Roswell* by Kevin D. Randle & Donald R. Schmitt   **PHOTOG:** Steven Poster   **MUSIC:** Elliot Goldenthal   **SONGS:** *Miller's Moonlight, Smokin' Steel Guitar, Tampico Ride & Still There*
Made-for-Cable, standard fact-based thriller: Army intelligence officer investigates alien spacecraft

Roswell: The Aliens Attack
1999, (USA), Para/UPN-TV, color, 95 mins.
W: Steven Flynn, Kate Greenhouse, Heather Hanson, Donelly Rhoses, Brent Stait, Sean McCann
D: Brad Turner   **TELEPLAY:** Jim Makichuk   **PHOTOG:** Robert Steadman   **MUSIC:** Fred Mollin
TVM, standard SF-thriller: Space aliens pose as humans

R.O.T.O.R.
1988, (USA), color, 90 mins.
W: Richard Gesswein, Margaret Trigg, Jayne Smith
D: Cullen Blaine
Minor SF-thriller: "Robotic Officer of Tactical Operations Research" goes berserk

Roujin Z
1991, (Jap), color, 84 mins.
VOICES: Allan Wenger, Toni Barry, Barbara Barnes

D: Hiroyuki Kitakubo
Animated eroto-SF: Widower tests ultra-tech hospital bed, finds it possessed by spirit of dead wife

Royal Flash
1975, (GB), Two Roads/20th-Fox, color, 118 mins.
W: Malcolm McDowell (*Capt. Harry Flashman*), Alan Bates (*Rudi Von Starnberg*), Florinda Bolkan (*Lola Montez*), Tom Bell (*De Gautet*), Britt Ekland (*Duchess Irma*), Oliver Reed (*Otto von Bismarck*), Lionel Jeffries (*Kraftstein*), Christopher Cazenove (*Eric Hansen*), Joss Ackland (*Sapten*), Leon Greene (*Grundwig*), Alastair Sim (*Greig*), Roy Kinnear (*The Roue*), Richard Hurndall (*Detchard*), Michael Hordern (*The Headmaster*), Richard Pearson (*Josef*), Rula Lenska (*Helga*), Margaret Courtenay (*The Soprano*), Noel Johnson (*The Chamberlain*), Elizabeth Larner (*Baroness Pechman*), Henry Cooper (*John Gully*), John Stuart (*The General*), David Jason (*The Mayor*)
P: David V. Picker & Richard Lester   **SCR:** George MacDonald Fraser, based on his "Harry Flashman" novels   **PHOTOG:** Geoffrey Unsworth   **MUSIC:** Ken Thorne
Bizarre comedy-adventure: Exploits of cowardly Hussar

Royal Love
1915, (GB), Transatlantic, b&w, 3,949 ft. (1203.6m)
W: Joan Ritz (*Grand Duchess Thora*), Eve Balfour (*Anita*), Gregory Scott (*The Prince*), Frank Tennant (*Alexis*), Daisy Cordell (*The Queen*), Patrick Noonan (*Capt. Moran*), J. Hastings Batson (*The King*), Charles Vane, Douglas Payne
D: Percy Nash   **STORY:** Rowland Talbot
Standard adventure: Ruritanian prince avenges father's murder

Le Royaume des Fees (The Kingdom of the Fairies)
1903, (Fr), Star, b&w, 320m (1,049.9 ft./17.7 mins.)
D: Georges Melies
A.k.a. Fairyland: or, The Kingdom of the Fairies and Wonders of the Deep
Standard fantasy: Witch abducts princess

Rubezahls Hochzeit (Rubezahl's Marriage)
1916, (Ger), b&w
W: Paul Wegener
WRIT & D: Paul Wegener
Standard melodrama

Rubezahl's Marriage
see Rubezahls Hochzeit

Ruby
1977, (USA), Steve Krantz/Dimension, color, 85 mins.
W: Piper Laurie (*Ruby*), Roger Davis (*Doc*), Stuart Whitman (*Vince*), Janit Baldwin (*Leslie*), Sal Vecchio (*Nicky*), Paul Kent (*Jake*), Crystin Sinclaire (*Lila*), Len Lesser
P: George Edwards   **D:** Curtis Harrington   **SCR:** George Edwards & Barry Schneider   **STORY:** Steve Krantz   **PHOTOG:** Brice Mack   **MUSIC:** Don Ellis
Standard fantasy-thriller: Drive-in theater plagued by supernatural events

The Ruby Ring
1996, (USA), color, 90 mins.
W: Emily Hamilton, Christien Anholt
Made-for-Cable, standard fantasy: Magic ring transports teen girl to castle in past

The Rue Morgue Massacres
see El Jorobado de la Morgue

The Rules of the Game (La Régle Du Jeu)
1939, (Fr), N.E.F./Cine-Classics/Janus, b&w, 113 mins, also 80 mins.
W: Marcel Dalio (*Robert*), Roland Tutain (*Andre*), Paulette Dubost (*Lisette*), Nora Gregor (*Christine*), Mila Parely (*Genevieve*), Jean Renoir (*Octave*), Julien Carette (*Marceau*), Gaston Modot (*Schumacher*)
D: Jean Renoir   **PHOTOG:** Sam Levin
Classic satire-melodrama: French aristocrats gambol on brink of World War II

The Ruling Class
1972, (GB), Keep/UA/Avco Embassy, color, 154 mins.
W: Peter O'Toole (*14th Earl of Gurney*), Coral Browne (*Lady Claire*), Ni-gel Green (*McKyle*), Alastair Sim (*Bishop Lampton*), Arthur Lowe (*Tucker*), Harry Andrews (*13th Earl of Gurney*), James Villiers (*Dinsdale*), Hugh Burden (*Matthew Peake*), Michael Bryant (*Dr. Herder*), William Mervyn (*Sir Charles*), Patsy Byrne (*Mrs. Treadwell*), Carolyn Seymour (*Grace*), Joan Cooper (*Nurse Brice*), Graham Crowden (*Truscott*), James Grout (*The Inspector*), Kay Walsh (*Mrs. Piggot-Jones*), Margaret Lacey (*The Midwife*), James Hazeldine (*Sgt. Fraser*), Hugh Owens (*The Toastmaster*), Henry Woolf (*The Inmate*), Ronald Adam (*The Lord*)
P: Jules Buck & Jack Hawkins   **D:** Peter Medak   **SCR:** Peter Barnes, from his play   **PHOTOG:** Ken Hodges   **MUSIC:** John Cameron
Unusual satire: Nutty nobleman thinks he is God

Rumpelstiltskin
1987, (USA), Cannon, color, 84 mins.
W: Amy Irving, Billy Barty, John Moulder-Brown, Priscilla Pointer, Clive Revill, Robert Symonds
D: David Irving
Standard juvenile fantasy: Evil troll tricks miller's daughter

Rumpelstiltskin
1996, (USA), TransnationalRep, color, 91 mins.
<u>W</u>: Kim Johnston Ulrich *(Shelly)*, Tommy Blaze *(Max)*, Allyce Beasley *(Hildy)*
Minor horror-fantasy: Troll stalks soul of young widow's baby

Runaway
1984, (USA), Tri-Star, color, 99 mins.
<u>W</u>: Tom Selleck *(Ramsay)*, Cynthia Rhodes *(Thompson)*, Gene Simmons *(Luther)*, Kirstie Alley *(Jackie)*, G.W. Bailey *(The Chief)*, Stan Shaw *(Marvin)*, Joey Cramer *(Bobby)*, Michael Paul Chan *(Wilson)*, Chris Mulkey *(Johnson)*, Paul Batten *(Harry)*, Jackson Davies *(The Inspector)*, Anne-Marie Martin *(The Hooker at the Bar)*, Elizabeth Norment *(Miss Shields)*, Carol Teesdale *(Sally)*, Babs Chulla, Marilyn Schreffler, Cec Verrell, Natino Bellantino, Judith Johns, Betty Phillips, Andrew Rhodes, Louise Johan, Stephen Thorne, Steve Wright, Stephen Miller, Bob Metcalfe, David Longworth, Todd Duckworth, Moira Walley, Albert Eggen, Jon Brydon, Rooney Gage, Murray Ord, Daryl Hayes, Keith Gordey, Frank Serio, Wayne York, Lloyd Berry, Dennis Kelli
<u>WRIT & D</u>: Michael Crichton   <u>PHOTOG</u>: John A. Alonzo   <u>MUSIC</u>: Jerry Goldsmith
Standard SF-thriller: Cop tracks killer robots

Runaway Train
1986, (USA), color, 112 mins.
<u>W</u>: Jon Voight, Eric Roberts, Rebecca DeMornay, John P. Ryan, Kyle T. Heffner, T.K. Carter, Kenneth MacMillan, Danny Trejo
<u>D</u>: Andrei Konchalovsky   <u>SCR</u>: Andrei Konchalovsky, Djordje Millicevic & Edward Bunker   <u>MUSIC</u>: Trevor Jones
Exciting thriller: Convicts steal train

The Runestone
1992, (USA), Hyperion, color, 105 mins.
<u>W</u>: Peter Riegert, Joan Severance
Standard fantasy-thriller: Ancient rock turns archeologist into monster

Run for the Hills
1953, (USA), Realart, b&w, 67 mins.
<u>W</u>: Sonny Tufts, Barbara Payton, John Harmon, Byron Foulger
<u>D</u>: Lew Landers
Minor comedy melodrama: Man invests life's savings in A-bomb shelter

Run for the Sun
1956, (USA), Russ-Field/UA, color, 99 mins.
<u>W</u>: Richard Widmark *(Michael Latimer)*, Peter Van Eyck *(Van Anders)*, Trevor Howard *(Browne)*, Jane Greer *(Katie Connors)*, Carlos Henning, Juan Garcia, Jose Antonio Carbajal, Jose Chavez Trowe, Guillermo Calles, Margarita Luna, Enedina Diaz De Leon, Guillermo Bravo Sosa
<u>P</u>: Harry Tatleman   <u>D</u>: Roy Boulting   <u>SCR</u>: Dudley Nichols & Roy Boulting, based on Richard Connell's novella *The Most Dangerous Game* (remake)
<u>PHOTOG</u>: Joseph La Shelle   <u>MUSIC</u>: Fred Steiner
Standard thriller: Author and lady journalist crash in Mexican jungle, become prisoners of fugitive Nazis

Run Lola Run
1998, (Ger), color, 81 mins
<u>W</u>: Franka Potente
<u>D</u>: Tom Tykwer
Innovative techno-thriller: Hip woman has 20 minutes to find 100,000 deutschmarks to save boyfriend from mobster

Running Against Time
1990, (USA), Finnegan-Pinchuk/Coastline/MTE/USA-TV, color, 95 mins.
<u>W</u>: Robert Hays, Catherine Hicks, Sam Wanamaker, Wayne Tippit, James DiStefano, Tracy Fraim, Mark Phelan, Juanita Jennings, Paul Scherrer, Brian Smiar, Milt Tarver, Julie Ariola, Russ Marin, Duncan Gamble, Damion Stevens, Michael Whaley, Dean Hill, Richard Gilbert-Hill, Darlene Kardon, Gerald Berns, Warren Sweeney, J. Lamont Pope, Nike Doukas, Pepper Sweeney, Rusty Schwimmer, Andrew Walker, Ron Troncatty, Thomas Robert Burke, Tim de Zarn, Albert Manquero
<u>D</u>: Bruce Seth Green   <u>TELEPLAY</u>: Stanley Shapiro & Robert Glass, from Stanley Shapiro's novel *A Time to Remember*   <u>PHOTOG</u>: Brian R.R. Hebb   <u>MUSIC</u>: Don Davis
TVM, standard SF-thriller: Teacher time-travels to prevent JFK's assassination

Running Delilah
1994, (USA), color, 85 mins.
<u>W</u>: Kim Cattrall, Francois Guetary, Yorgo Voyagis
Standard SF-thriller: Murdered gov't operative rebuilt with latest technology, sent to nab int'l arms dealer

The Running Man
1963, (GB), Peet Prods./Col, color, 113 mins.
<u>W</u>: Laurence Harvey *(Rex Black)*, Lee Remick *(Stella Black)*, Alan Bates *(Stephen Maddox)*, Felix Aylmer *(The Parson)*, Eleanor Summerfield *(Hilda Tanner)*, Colin Gordon *(The Solicitor)*, Allan Cuthbertson *(Jenkins)*, Noel Purcell *(Miles Bleeker)*, Harold Goldblatt *(Tom Webster)*, Ramsay Ames *(Madge Penderby)*, Fortunio Bonanova *(The Bank Official)*, Fernando Rey *(The Police Official)*, John Meillon *(Jim Jerome)*
<u>P</u>: Carol Reed & John R. Sloan   <u>D</u>: Carol Reed   <u>SCR</u>: John Mortimer, from Shelley Smith's novel *Ballad Running*   <u>PHOTOG</u>: Robert Krasker
<u>MUSIC</u>: William Alwyn
Standard crime-thriller: Insurance agent loves wife of pilot who faked his own death

The Running Man
1987, (USA), Linder-Zinnemann/Taft/Keith Barish/Tri-Star, color, 100 mins.
<u>W</u>: Arnold Schwarzenegger *(Ben Richards)*, Maria Conchita Alonso *(Amber Mendez)*, Richard Dawson *(Damon Killian)*, Yaphet Kotto *(Laughlin)*, Jim Brown *(Fireball)*, Jesse Ventura *(Capt. Freedom)*, Erland Van Lidth, Prof. Toru Tanaka, Gus Rethwisch
<u>D</u>: Paul Michael Glaser   <u>SCR</u>: Steven de Souza, based on novel by Richard Bachman [Stephen King]   <u>PHOTOG</u>: Thomas Del Ruth   <u>MUSIC</u>: Harold Faltermeyer
Modest SF-thriller: Gladiators battle in 21st century

Run, Psycho, Run
1966, (It), b&w
<u>W</u>: Gary Merrill, Elga Andersen
Minor thriller: Judge's wife slain, judge's new fiancee worries

Run, Stranger, Run
see Happy Mother's Day, Love George

Rupert of Hentzau
1915, (GB), London/Jury, b&w, 5,500 ft. (1676.4m)
<u>W</u>: Henry Ainley *(Rudolph Rassendyl)*, Jane Gail *(Queen Flavia)*, Gerald Ames *(Rupert)*, Douglas Munro *(Bauer)*, Charles Rock *(Col. Sapt)*, George Bellamy *(Count Reichenheim)*, Warwick Wellington *(Lt. Berenstein)*, Stella St. Audrie *(The Chancellor's Wife)*, Jeff Barlow, Eva Westlake
<u>D</u>: George Loane Tucker   <u>SCR</u>: William Courtenay Rowden, inspired by Anthony Hope's novel *The Prisoner of Zenda*
Standard adventure-thriller: Ruritanian king killed, English double takes his place

Rupert of Hentzau
1923, (USA), Selznick, b&w, 9 reels (9,646 ft./2940.1m)
<u>W</u>: Elaine Hammerstein *(Queen Flavia)*, Bert Lytell *(King of Ruritania/Rudolph Rassendyll)*, Lew Cody *(Rupert of Hentzau/Countess Helga)*, Claire Windsor *(Countess Helga)*, Hobart Bosworth *(Col. Sapt)*, Bryant Washburn *(Count Fritz)*, Marjorie Daw *(Rosa Holf)*, Mitchell Lewis *(Bauer)*, Adolphe Menjou *(Count Rischenheim)*, Elmo Lincoln *(Simon, the King's Forester)*, Irving Cummings *(Von Bernenstein)*, Josephine Crowell *(Mother Holf)*, Nigel de Brulier *(Herbert)*, Gertrude Astor *(Paula)*
<u>D</u>: Victor Heerman   <u>SCR</u>: Edward J. Montagne, from Anthony Hope's 1898 novel   <u>PHOTOG</u>: Glen MacWilliams & Harry Thorpe
*Standard adventure-thriller (sequel to **The Prisoner of Zenda** {1922}): Conspirator blackmails nobleman*

La Rupture
1970, (It-Fr-Belg), color, 125 mins.
<u>W</u>: Jean-Pierre Cassel, Stephanie Audran, Annie Cordy, Michel Bouquet, Michel Duchaussoy, Marguerite Cassan, Catherine Rouvel, Jean-Claude Drouot, Mario David, Margo Lion, Dominique Zardi
<u>D & SCR</u>: Claude Chabrol, from Charlotte Armstrong's novel *Balloon*   <u>PHOTOG</u>: Jean Rabier
Bizarre thriller: Dysfunctional family beset by drugs, sex and schizophrenia

Rush Week
1988, (USA), color, 93 mins.
<u>W</u>: Dean Hamilton, Gregg Allman, Kathleen Kinmont, Pamela Ludwig, Roy Thinnes
<u>D</u>: Bob Bravler
Minor thriller: Dead coeds during frat week

Russian Roulette
see Two Before Zero

Russicum
1989, (It), color, 113 mins.
<u>W</u>: F. Murray Abraham, Treat Williams, Danny Aiello, Rita Rusic, Robert Balchus, Rossano Brazzi, Nigel Court, Leopoldo Mastelloni
<u>D</u>: Pasquale Squitieri
*A.k.a. **The Third Solution***
Minor spy-thriller: Plot to foil Pope's visit to Soviet Union

Ruthless
1948, (USA), Eagle Lion, b&w, 105 mins.
<u>W</u>: Zachary Scott, Louis Hayward, Diana Lynn, Raymond Burr, Sydney Greenstreet, Lucille Bremer, Martha Vickers
<u>D</u>: Edgar G. Ulmer   <u>PHOTOG</u>: Bert Glennon
Well-made melodrama: Ambitious cad rises to power

Rx Murder
see Family Doctor

Rymdinvasion i Lappland (Space-Invasion of Lappland)
1958, (USA-Swed), Unger/ADP, b&w
<u>W</u>: Barbara Wilson, John Carradine, Robert Burton, Bengt Blomgren, Stan Gester, Jack Haffner
<u>D</u>: Virgil Vogel & Jerry Warren   <u>SCR</u>: Arthur C. Pierce   <u>PHOTOG</u>: Hilding Bladh
*USA retitle (1960), **Invasion of the Animal People**, orig. to be titled **Terror in the Midnight Sun***
Minor SF-thriller: Space-alien giant kidnaps woman

Saadia

1954, (USA), MGM, color, 82 mins.

W: Cornel Wilde (*Si Lahssen*), Mel Ferrer (*Henrik*), Rita Gam (*Saadia*), Marcel Poncin (*Moha*), Cyril Cusack (*Khadir*), Michel Simon (*Bou Rezza*), Wanda Rotha (*Fatima*), Anthony Marlowe (*Capt. Sabert*), Helene Vallier (*Zoubida*), Mahjoub Ben Brahim (*Ahmed*), Jacques Dufilho (*The Bandit Leader*), Bernard Farrel (*Lt. Camuzac*), Richard Johnson (*Lt. Girard*), Peter Bull, Peter Copley, Marne Maitland, Edward Leslie, Harold Kasket, Abdullah Mennebhi
WRIT, P & D: Albert Lewin PHOTOG: Christopher Challis MUSIC: Bronislau Kaper
Standard melodrama: Berber ruler and doctor friend both love girl thought to have "Evil Eye"

Sabaka

1953, (USA), UA, color, 89 mins.

W: Boris Karloff, Nino Marcel, Lisa Howard, Reginald Denny, Victor Jory, Jeanne Bates, Jay Novello, June Foray, Peter Coe, Lou Krugman, Paul Marion, Vito Scotti, Larry Dobkin, Lou Merrill
WRIT, P & D: Frank Ferrin MUSIC: Dokshnimurti
A.k.a. The Hindu
Standard adventure-thriller: Human-sacrifice cult exposed

Sabotage

1936, (GB), Gaumont, b&w, 76 mins.

W: Sylvia Sidney (*Sylvia Verloc*), Oscar Homolka (*Carl Verloc*), John Loder (*Ted Spencer*), Desmond Tester (*Steve*), S.J. Warmington (*Hollingshead*), Joyce Barbour (*Renee*), Matthew Boulton (*Supt. Talbot*), Peter Bull (*Michaelis*), Aubrey Mather (*The Greengrocer*), William Dewhurst (*A.S. Chatman*), Torin Thatcher (*Yunct*), Austin Trevor (*Vladimir*), Charles Hawtrey (*The Youth*), Martita Hunt (*Miss Chatman*), Frederick Piper (*The Conductor/Reporter*), Hal Walters (*The Father*), D.A. Clarke-Smith, Francis L. Sullivan
D: Alfred Hitchcock SCR: Charles Bennett, Ian Hay, Alma Reville, Helen Simpson & E.V.H. Emmett, from Joseph Conrad's novel *The Secret Agent*
PHOTOG: Bernard Knowles MUSIC: Louis Levy
USA retitle, The Woman Alone (GB, 1937)
Standard thriller: Detective unmasks foreign saboteur

Saboteur

1942, (USA), Univ, b&w, 109 mins.

W: Robert Cummings, Priscilla Lane, Otto Kruger, Alan Baxter, Clem Bevans, Alma Kruger, Norman Lloyd, Matt Willis
D: Alfred Hitchcock SCR: Peter Viertel, Joan Harrison & Dorothy Parker, from a story by Alfred Hitchcock PHOTOG: Joseph Valentine MUSIC: Charles Previn & Frank Skinner
Classic thriller: Innocent accused of wartime sabotage

Sabrina Goes to Rome

1998, (USA), ABC-TV, color, 95 mins.

W: Melissa Joan Hart, Eddie Mills, Tara Charendoff (*Gwen*), James Fields (*Travis*), Eric Alexander (*Alberto*)
TVM, standard fantasy: Teen witch loses powers on European vacation

Sabrina the Teenage Witch

1996, (USA), SHO-TV, color, 95 mins.

W: Melissa Joan Hart, Charlene Fernetz, Sherry Miller, Michelle Beaudoin, Ryan Reynolds, Lalainia Lindbjerg, Tobias Mehler
D: Tibor Takacs TELEPLAY: Barney Cohen, Kathryn Wallack & Nicholas Factor, from characters in "Archie" comics
Made-for-Cable, standard comedy-fantasy: New girl in school has odd powers

Sabu and the Magic Ring: SABU AND DARIA MASSEY

Sabu and the Magic Ring

1957, (USA), AA, color, 61 mins.

W: Sabu, Daria Massey, William Marshall, Vladimir Sokoloff, Robert Shafto, Peter Mamakos, John Doucette, George Khoury, Robin Morse, Bernie Rich, Kenneth Terrell, John Lomma
P: Maurice Duke D: George Blair SCR: Sam Roeca, Benedict Freedman & John Fenton Murray MUSIC: Harry Sukman
Minor adventure-fantasy (Feature culled from unsold teleseries): Stable boy gains aid of genie

The Sacred Fountain

see La Fontaine Sacree ou la Vengeance de Boudha

The Sacred Fountain: or, the Vengeance of Buddha

see La Fontaine Sacree ou la Vengeance de Boudha

Sacrifice

see Cage of Gold

Sadique de l'Autoroute

see The Sadist

The Sadist

1963, (USA), Fairway-Int'l, b&w, 95 mins.

W: Arch Hall Jr., Helen Hovey, Richard Alden, Don Russell, Marilyn Manning
P: Nicholas Merriweather & L. Steven Snyder WRIT & D: James Landis PHOTOG: Vilmos Zsigmond
Fr retitle, Sadique de l'Autoroute (Sadist of the Highway) USA TV-retitle, The Face of Terror, A.k.a. The Profile of Terror
Minor thriller: Psycho menaces three teachers

Sadist Erotica

1973, (W. Ger-Sp), color

W: Janine Reynaud, Rosanna Yanni, Adrian Hoven
Minor thriller: Two girls hunt brutal killer

Sadist of the Highway

see The Sadist

Safari

1956, (USA), Col, color, 91 mins.

W: Victor Mature, Janet Leigh
D: Terence Young
Standard adventure-melodrama

Safari Drums

1953, (USA), AA, b&w, 71 mins.

W: Johnny Sheffield, Barbara Bestar, Douglas Kennedy, Paul Marion, Emory Parnell, Leonard Mudie, Smoki Whitfield, Russ Conway, Rory Mallinson
WRIT, P & D: Ford Beebe, from characters created by Roy Rockwood MUSIC: Marlin Skiles
Minor adventure-thriller: Jungle Boy helps moviemakers in Africa solve murder. 'Bomba' series

A Safe Place

1971, (USA), color, 94 mins.

W: Tuesday Weld, Jack Nicholson, Orson Welles, Gwen Welles, Philip Proctor
D: Henry Jaglom
Bizarre fantasy: Girl lives in dream world where she can never grow up

The Saga of the Draculas

1972, (Sp), color, 90 mins.

W: Narciso Ibanez Menta, Tina Sainz, Tony Isbert, Cristina Suriani, Maria Koski, Helga Line
D: Leon Klimovsky
A.k.a. Dracula Saga, Dracula, The Bloodline Continues... and The Saga of Dracula
Minor horror-thriller: Aging vampire seeks heir

The Saga of the Viking Women and Their Voyage to the Waters of the Great Sea Serpent

see The Viking Women and the Sea Serpent

Sail into Danger

1957, (GB), Patria/Grand Nat'l, b&w, 72 mins.

W: Dennis O'Keefe (*Steve Ryman*), Kathleen Ryan (*Lana*), Ana Luisa Peluffo (*Josafina*), James Hayter (*Monty*), Pedro de Cordoba (*Luis*), Barta Barry (*Emil*), Felix de Pommes (*Insp. Gomez*)
P: Steven Pallos D & STORY: Kenneth Hume
Standard crime-thriller: Launch owner foils plot to stea valuable Madonna

The Saint

1997, (USA), Para, color, 118 mins.

W: Val Kilmer (*Simon Templar*), Elisabeth Shue (*Dr. Emma Russell*), Rade Serbedzija (*Ivan*), Valery Nikolaev (*Ilya*), Roger Moore (*Voice on Radio*) Peter Guinness, Alun Armstrong, David Schneider, Barbara Jefford, Roger Moore, Ginny Holder, Tony Armatrading, Irina Apeximova, Akiko, Lucy Akhurst, Michael Byrne, Kate Isitt, Nigel Clauzel, Michael Cochrane, Richard Cubison, Charlotte Cornwell, Verity Dearsley, Tommy Flanagan, Henry Goodman, Stefan Griff, William Hope, Ravil Isyanov, Ronnie Letham, Alexander Kadanyov, Caroline Lee Johnson, Alla A. Kazanskaya, Lorelei

S

King, Melissa Knatchbull, Pat Laffan, Evgeny Lazarev, Agnieszka Liggett, Michael Marquez, Valery Nikolaev, Eric Loren, Emily Mortimer, Sean O'Kane, Etela Pardo, Cliff Parisi, Oxana Popkova, Susan Porrett, Yegor Pozenko, Lev Prigunov, Christopher Rozycki, Tusse Silberg, Lucija Serbedzija, Rade Serbedzija, Adam Smith, Alexander Tutin, Vadim Stepashkin, Malcolm Tierney, Stephen Tiller, Velibor Topic, Nikolai Veselov, Peter Vidovic, Benjamin Whitrow, Lydia Zoykic
D: Phillip Noyce SCR: Jonathan Hensleigh & Wesley Strick, from a story by Jonathan Hensleigh, based on characters created by Leslie Charteris
  SPCL-FX: Robert Grasmere PHOTOG: Phil Meheux MUSIC: Graeme Revell SONGS: *Before Today, Dead Man Walking, A Dream Within a Dream & Setting Sun*
Impressive thriller: Master of disguise aids pursued lady scientist

Saint and the Blue Demon vs. Dracula and the Wolf Man
1972, (Mex), color
W: Santo
Minor fantasy-thriller: Monsters duel

The Saint and the Blue Demon vs. the Monsters
1970, (Mex), color
W: Santo
Minor fantasy-thriller

The Saint and the Brave Goose
1980, (GB), Robert S. Baker/ITC, Made for TV, color, 99 mins.
W: Ian Ogilvy (*Simon Templar*), Gayle Hunnicutt (*Annabel*), Stratford Johns (*Duchamp*), Derren Nesbitt (*Lebec*), Michael Robbins (*Becky*), Joe Lynch (*Finnigan*), John Hallam (*Bernadotti*), Leon Lissek (*Pancho*), Edward Brayshaw (*Oscar West*), Prentis Hancock (*Vic*), Wensley Pithey (*Franklyn*), Michelle Newell (*Genevieve*), Peggy Thorpe-Bates (*Mrs. Cloonan*), Cyril Luckham (*The Coroner*), David English (*The Salesman*), Peter Brace (*The Crewman*)
D: Cyril Frankel SCR: John Kruse, from characters created by Leslie Charteris
  PHOTOG: Frank Watts MUSIC: John Scott
TVM, minor thriller (culled from 2 episodes of teleseries "Return of the Saint"): Rogue-detective aids young widow, seeks missing gold

St. Elmo
1923, (GB), R.W. Syndicate/Capitol, b&w, 5,840 ft. (1780m)
W: Shayle Gardner (*St. Elmo Murray*), Gabrielle Gilroy (*Agnes Powell*) Madge Tree (*Mrs. Murray*), Harding Thomas (*Rev. Hammond*)
D & SCR: Rex Wilson, from a novel by Augusta J. Evans-Wilson
Standard fantasy-thriller: Widow's son kills clerical rival in duel, becomes possessed by devil

The Saint Faces Black Magic
1972, (Mex), color
W: Santo
Minor fantasy-thriller

St. George and the Dragon
1929, (GB), Whitehall Films/Fox, b&w, 1,585 ft. (483.1m)
Minor comedy-fantasy: Modern-dress St. George rescues princess

Saint George and the Seven Curses
see *The Magic Sword* (1962)

The Saint in London
1939, (GB), RKO, b&w, 77 mins.
W: George Sanders (*Simon Templar*), Sally Gray (*Penelope Parker*), David Burns (*Dugan*), Gordon McLeod (*Insp. Claude Teal*), Athene Seyler (*Mrs. Buckley*), Charles Carson (*John Morgan*), Henry Oscar (*Bruno Lang*), John Abbott (*Count Duni*), Ralph Truman (*Count Stengler*), Carl Jaffe (*Paul Stengler*), Ballard Berkeley (*Sir Richard Blake*), Nora Howard (*Mrs. Morgan*), Charles Paton (*The Newsagent*), Charles Oliver (*Dr. Jim*), Hugh McDermott (*Tim*)
D: John Paddy Carstairs SCR: Lynn Root & Frank Fenton, from Leslie Charteris' novel *The Million Pound Day* PHOTOG: Claude Friese-Greene
Standard thriller: Sleuth aids British Intelligence

The Saint in New York
1938, (USA), RKO, b&w, 72 mins.
W: Louis Hayward (*Simon Templar*), Kay Sutton (*Fay Edwards*), Sig Rumann (*Hutch Rellin*), Jonathan Hale (*Insp. Fernack*), Jack Carson (*Red Jenks*), Paul Guilfoyle (*Hymie Farno*), Ben Welden (*Papinoff*), Cliff Bragdon (*Sebastian*), Charles Halton (*Vincent Nather*), Frederick Burton (*William Valcross*)
D: Ben Holmes SCR: Charles Kauffman & Mortimer Offner, from Leslie Charteris' novel PHOTOG: Joseph August & Frank Redman
Standard thriller: Sleuth hired to kill six gangsters. 1st film in 'The Saint' series

The Saint in Palm Springs
1941, (USA), RKO, b&w, 66 mins.
W: George Sanders (*Simon Templar*), Wendy Barrie (*Elna Johnson*), Paul Guilfoyle (*Pearly Gates*), Jonathan Hale (*Insp. Fernack*), Linda Hayes (*Margaret Forbes*), Ferris Taylor (*Mr. Evans*), Harry Shannon (*Chief Graves*), Joey Ray (*The Hoodlum*), Eddie Dunn (*Det. Barker*), Gene Rizzi (*The Bartender*), Richard Crane (*Whitey*), Charles Quigley (*Fletcher*), Vinton Haworth (*The Hotel Clerk*), Robert Carson (*The Mystery Man*), James Harrison (*The Bellhop*), Frank O'Connor (*Brady*), Lee Bonnell (*Tommy*), Norman Mayes (*The Club Car Bartender*), Edmund Elton (*Peter Masson*), Henry Roquemore (*Flannery*)

Ed Thomas (*The Waiter*), Chuck Collins (*Callahan*), Peter Lynn (*Jimmy*), er, Chester Tallman, Gayle Mellot, Betty Farrington, Mary MacLaren
D: Jack Hively SCR: Jerry Cady, from characters created by Leslie Charteris
  PHOTOG: Harry Wild MUSIC: Roy Webb
Standard thriller: Sleuth involved with rare postage stamps

The Saint in the Revenge of the Vampire Women
1968, (Mex), color
W: Santo
Minor fantasy-thriller

The Saint in the Vengeance of the Mummy
1971, (Mex), color
W: Santo
Minor fantasy-thriller

The Saint in the Wax Museum
1961, (Mex), Tele-Cine-Radio Mexico/Filmadora Panamericana, b&w, 92 mins
W: Santo, Norma Mora, Claudio Brook, Ruben Rojo
P: Alberto Lopez D: Alfonso Corona Blake SCR: Fernando Galiana & Julio Porter
USA retitle, Samson in the Wax Museum
Minor fantasy-thriller: Mad doctor remakes people's faces to reflect their true personalities

The Saint Leads the Dance
see *Le Saint Mene la Dance*

The Saint Lies in Wait
see *Le Saint Prend l'Affut*

The Saint Meets the Tiger
1941, (GB), RKO Britsh, b&w, 70 mins.
W: Hugh Sinclair (*Simon Templar*), Jean Gillie (*Pat Holmes*), Gordon McLeod (*Insp. Teal*), Clifford Evans (*Sidmarsh*), Wylie Watson (*Horace*), Dennis Arundell (*Bently*), John Salew (*Merridon*), Charles Victor (*Bittle*), Louise Hampton (*Aunt Agatha*), Arthur Hambling (*The Police Constable*), Amy Veiness (*Mrs. Jones*), Claude Bailey (*Mr. Jones*), Noel Dainton (*Burton*), Eric Clavering (*Frankie*), Alf Goddard (*The Man*), Ben Williams (*Joe*), Tony Quinn (*Paddy*), John Slater (*Eddie*)
D: Paul Stein SCR: Leslie Arliss, James Seymour & Wolfgang Wilhelm, from Leslie Charteris' novel *Meet the Tiger* PHOTOG: Bob Krasker
*Standard thriller: Sleuth pursues gold smugglers. US Release: **Republic**, 1943*

Le Saint Mene la Dance (The Saint Leads the Dance)
1961, (Fr), Films du Cyclope, b&w, 90 mins.
W: Felix Marten (*Simon Templar*), Michele Mercier (*Dany*), Francoise Brion (*Norma*), Jean Desailly (*Freddy Pellman*), Nicole Mirel (*Gina*), Henri Nassiet, Clement Harari, Andre Valmy, Jean-Marie Riviere, Jean-Roger Caussimon
D: Jacques Nahum SCR: Albert Simonin, Jacques Nahum & Yvan Audouard, from Leslie Charteris' novel *The Saint in Miami* PHOTOG: Robert Hubert & Rene G. Vuattoux MUSIC: Paul Durand
Standard thriller: Debonair sleuth encounters murder

Le Saint Prend l'Affut (The Saint Lies in Wait)
1966, (Fr), SNC/Intermondia, color, 90 mins.
W: Jean Marais (*Simon Templar*), Jean Hohn (*Uniatz*), Henri Virlogeux (*Oscar*), Daniele Evanou (*Sophie*), Dario Moreno (*The Fat Man*), Jean Yanse (*The German*)
D: Christian-Jaque SCR: Jean Ferry, Henri Jeanson & Christian-Jaque, from characters created by Leslie Charteris PHOTOG: Pierre Petit
Standard thriller: Sleuth seeks wartime loot

The Saint's Double Trouble
1940, (USA), RKO, b&w, 68 mins.
W: George Sanders (*Simon Templar/Duke Piato*), Helene Whitney (*Anne Bitts*), Jonathan Hale (*Insp. Fernack*), Bela Lugosi (*The Partner*), Donald MacBride (*Boblen*), John F. Hamilton (*Limpy*), Thomas W. Ross (*Prof. Bitts*), Donald Kerr, Elliott Sullivan, Pat O'Malley
D: Jack Hively SCR: Ben Holmes, from characters created by Leslie Charteris
  PHOTOG: J. Roy Hunt
Standard thriller: Sleuth pursues diamond smugglers

The Saint's Girl Friday
see *The Saint's Return*

The Saint's Return
1953, (GB), Hammer-Exclusive/RKO, b&w, 73 mins.
W: Louis Hayward (*Simon Templar*), Sydney Tafler (*Lennar*), Naomi Chance (*Lady Carol Denbigh*), Charles Victor (*Insp. Teal*), Harold Lang (*Jarvis*), Thomas Gallagher (*Hoppy Uniatz*), Jane Carr (*Katie French*), Fred Johnson (*Irish Cassidy*), Russell Enoch (*Keith Merton*), Diana Dors (*Margie*)
P: Julian Lesser & Anthony Hinds D: Seymour Friedman SCR: Allan Mackinnon, from characters created by Leslie Charteris PHOTOG: Walter Harvey MUSIC: Ivor Slaney
USA retitle, The Saint's Girl Friday
Standard thriller: Detective unmasks blackmailer

The Saint Strikes Back
1939, (USA), RKO, b&w, 64 mins.

W: George Sanders (*Simon Templar*), Wendy Barrie (*Val Travers*), Jonathan Hale (*Insp. Fernack*), Neil Hamilton (*Allan Breck*), Jerome Cowan (*Cullis*), Barry Fitzgerald (*Zipper Dyson*), Robert Elliott (*Webster*), Russell Hopton (*Harry Donnell*), Edward Gargan (*Pinky Budd*), Gilbert Emery (*Martin Eastman*), Robert Strange (*The Commissioner*), Nella Walker (*Mrs. Fernack*), James Burke (*The Secretary*)
D: John Farrow   SCR: John Twist, from Leslie Charteris' novel *Angels of Doom*   PHOTOG: Frank Redman
Standard thriller: Sleuth encounters New Year's Eve murder

The Saint's Vacation
1941, (GB), RKO, b&w, 78 mins.
W: Hugh Sinclair (*Simon Templar*), Sally Gray (*Mary Langdon*), Arthur Macrae (*Monty Hayward*), Cecil Parker (*Rudolph*), John Warwick (*Gregory*), Leueen MacGrath (*Valerie*), Gordon McLeod (*Insp. Teal*), Ivor Bernard (*Emil*), Manning Whiley (*Marko*), Felix Aylmer (*Leighton*), Roddy Hughes (*The Valet*)
D: Leslie Fenton   SCR: Jeffrey Dell & Leslie Charteris, from characters created by Leslie Charteris   PHOTOG: Bernard Knowles   MUSIC: Bretton Byrd
Standard thriller: Sleuth encounters espionage

The Saint Takes Over
1940, (USA), RKO, b&w, 69 mins.
W: George Sanders (*Simon Templar*), Wendy Barrie (*Ruth*), Jonathan Hale (*Insp. Fernack*), Paul Guilfoyle (*Pearly Gates*), Morgan Conway (*Sam Reese*), Robert Emmett Keane (*Lex Sloan*), Cy Kendall (*Max Bremer*), James Burke (*Mike*), Nella Walker (*Mrs. Fernack*), Robert Middlemass (*Capt. Wade*), Roland Drew (*Weldon*), Pierre Watkin (*Egan*)
D: Jack Hively   SCR: Lynn Root & Frank Fenton, from characters created by Leslie Charteris   PHOTOG: Frank Redman
Standard thriller: Sleuth involved with racetrack fixers

The St. Valentine's Day Massacre
1967, (USA), 20th-Fox, color, 100 mins.
W: Jason Robards Jr. (*Al Capone*), George Segal, Jean Hale, Ralph Meeker, Frank Silvera, David Canary, Harold J. Stone, Richard Bakalyan, Jan Merlin, Milton Frome, Bruce Dern, Leo Gordon, Celia Lovsky, Alex D'Arcy, Dick Miller, Barboura Morris, Betsy Jones-Moreland, Shelley Berman, Joan Shawlee, Gabriele Ferzetti, Kurt Kreuger, Jack Nicholson
P & D: Roger Corman   SCR: Howard Browne   PHOTOG: Milton Krasner   MUSIC: Lionel Newman
Standard docu-thriller: Al Capone reinforces his gangland power

The Saint vs. Capulina
1971, (Mex), color
W: Santo
Minor fantasy-thriller

The Saint vs. Frankenstein's Daughter
1971, (Mex), color
W: Santo
Minor fantasy-thriller

The Saint vs. the Blue Demon in Atlantis
1968, (Mex), color
W: Santo
*Minor fantasy-thriller (with stock-footage from **Monster Zero**)*

The Saint vs. the Vampire Women
see El Santo Contra las Vampiras

The Saint vs. the Zombies
1962, (Mex), Azteca/AIP, b&w, 85 mins.
W: Santo, Carlos Agosti, Lorena Velazquez
P: Fernando Oses   D: Benito Alazraki
USA retitle, Samson Against the Zombies, A.k.a. Invasion of the Zombies
Minor fantasy-thriller

Sakima and the Masked Marvel
1966, (USA), Rep, b&w, 100 mins.
W: William Forrest, Louise Currie, Johnny Arthur Tom Steele, Rod Bacon, Richard Clarke
D: Spencer G. Bennet
Standard thriller (feature version of 1943 serial "The Masked Marvel")

Le Salaire de la Peur (The Wages of Fear)
1953, (Fr), Filmsonor/International Affiliates, b&w, 155 mins.
W: Charles Vanel (*Jo*), Yves Montand (*Mario*), Peter Van Eyck (*Bimba*), Folco Lulli (*Luigi*), Vera Clouzot (*Linda*), Jo Dest (*Smerloff*), William Tubbs (*O'Brien*), Centa (*Chief of Boss Camps*), Mario Moreno (*Hernandez*)
WRIT, P & D: Henri-Georges Clouzot, from a novel by Georges Arnaud   PHOTOG: Armand Thirard   MUSIC: Georges Auric
Classic thriller: Truckers transport explosives. Remade as Sorcerer, 1977

Salammbo
1914, (It), b&w, 49 mins.
W: Ernesto Pagani
D: Giovanni Pastrone, from a novel by Flaubert
Epic melodrama: Turmoil in ancient Carthage

Salem's Lot
1979, (USA), WB/CBS-TV, color, 175 mins. (edited-down video release, 112 mins.)
W: David Soul (*Ben Mears*), Bonnie Bedelia (*Susan Norton*), James Mason (*Straker*), Lance Kerwin (*Mark Petrie*), Kenneth McMillan (*Constable Gillespie*), Brad Savage (*Danny Glick*), Fred Willard (*Larry Crockett*), Julie Cobb (*Bonnie Sawyer*), Clarissa Kaye (*Marjorie Glick*), Ronnie Scribner (*Ralphie Glick*), Geoffrey Lewis (*Mike Ryerson*), Marie Windsor (*Eva Miller*), Elisha Cook Jr. (*Weasel*), George Dzundza (*Cully Sawyer*), Lew Ayres (*Jason Burke*), Reggie Nalder (*Barlow*), Ed Flanders (*Dr. Norton*), Barney McFadden (*Ned Tebbets*), James Gallery (*Father Callahan*), June Petrie (*Barbara Babcock*), Robert Lussier, Joshua Bryant, Bonnie Bartlett
P: Richard Kobritz   D: Tobe Hooper   TELEPLAY: Paul Monash, from Stephen King's novel   PHOTOG: Jules Brenner   SPCL-FX: Frank Torre   MUSIC: Harry Sukman
TVM, engrossing horror-fantasy: Horrendous vampire spreads evil in small Maine town

Salome
1918, (USA), Fox, b&w, 8 reels
W: Theda Bara (*Salome*)
D: J. Gordon Edwards
Standard melodrama: Princess seeks Baptist's head

Salome
1922, (USA), Nazimova Prods./Allied Producers & Distributors, b&w, 6 reels (5,595 ft./1705.4m)
W: Alla Nazimova (*Salome*), Rose Dione (*Herodias*), Mitchell Lewis (*Herod*), Nigel de Brulier (*Jokaanan*), Earl Schenck (*The Young Syrian*), Arthur Jasmine (*The Page*), Frederic Peters (*Naaman, the Executioner*), Louis Dumar (*Tigellinus*)
D: Charles Bryant   SCR: Peter M. Winters, from Oscar Wilde's 1894 one-act play   PHOTOG: Charles Van Enger
Arty melodrama: Herod's stepdaughter seeks head of holy man

Salome
1923, (USA), Malcolm Strauss Pictures, b&w, 6 reels
W: Diana Allen (*Salome*), Vincent Coleman, Christine Winthrop
D: Malcolm Strauss
Standard melodrama: Princess caught in court intrigue

Salome
1953, (USA), Col, color, 103 mins.
W: Rita Hayworth (*Princess Salome*), Charles Laughton (*King Herod Antipas*), Judith Anderson (*Herodias*), Stewart Granger (*Commander Claudius*), Alan Badel (*John the Baptist*), Basil Sydney (*Pontius*) Rex Reason (*Marcellus Fabius*), Sir Cedric Hardwicke (*Caesar Tiberius*), Maurice Schwartz (*Ezra*), Arnold Moss (*Micha*), Robert Warwick (*The Courier*), Michael Granger (*Capt. Quintus*), Karl Davis (*The Slave Master*), Carmen D'Antonio (*Salome's Servant*) Rex Reason (*Marcellus*), Sujata & Asoka (*The Dancers*), Jay Novello
P: Maurice E. "Buddy" Adlerv   D: William Dieterle   SCR: Harry Kleiner & Jesse Lasky Jr.   PHOTOG: Charles Lange   MUSIC: Daniele Amfitheatrof   MUSIC SCORE: George Duning
Opulent melodrama: Beautiful princess caught in court intrigue

Salome Mad
1909, (GB), Cricks & Martin, b&w, 500 ft. (152.4m)
D: A.E. Coleby
Standard fantasy: Man chases windblown poster of "Salome" under sea

Salo, o Le Centoventi Giornate di Sodom (Salo, or the 120 Days of Sodom)
1975, (It-Fr), Zebra Releasing, color, 117 mins.
W: Paolo Bonicelli, Giorgio Cataldi, Umberto P. Quintavalle
D: Pier Paolo Pasolini   from De Sade's novel   PHOTOG: Tonino Delli Colli   MUSIC: Ennio Morricone
Murky allegory (Pasolini's last film): Sexual atricities in Mussolini's Italy

Salto
1966, (Pol), KADR/Film Polski/Kanawha, b&w, 104 mins.
W: Zbigniew Cybulski
Standard melodrama

Saludos Amigos
1943, (USA), Walt Disney, color, 43 mins.
Standard animated musical-fantasy

Salute of the Jugger
see The Blood of Heroes

Salvage
1979, (USA), ABC-TV, color
W: Andy Griffith (*Harry Broderick*), Joel Higgins (*Skip Carmichael*), Trish Stewart (*Mel Slozar*), Jacqueline Scott (*Lorene*), Richard Jaeckel (*Jack Klinger*), J.J. Saunders (*Mack*), Raleigh Bond (*Fred*)
TVM, standard SF-adventure: Scrap man schemes to build rocketship, salvage NASA equipment on moon

Sammy's Super T-Shirt
1978, (GB), Monument/CFF, color, 58 mins.
W: Reggie Winch (*Sammy Smith*), Lawrie Mark (*Marvin*), David Young (*Big Sid*), Keith Jayne (*Chalky*), Richard Vernon (*Beckett*), Julian Holloway (*Trotter*),

S

Patsy Rowlands (*Mum*), Jack May (*The Sports Master*), Michael Ripper (*The Gateman*), Marianne Stone (*The Neighbor*)
P & SCR: Frank Godwin **D:** Jeremy Summers **STORY:** H. McLeod Robertson
PHOTOG: Norman Jones **MUSIC:** Harry Robinson
Standard juvenile fantasy: Eccentric's invention turns boy into successful runner

Sampo
1959, (Fin-Russ), AIP, color, 99 mins
W: Jon Powers, Nina Anderson, Ingrid Elhardt, Peter Sorenson
P: Julius Strandberg **D:** Gregg Sebelious **SCR:** Elias Lenrot
released in USA (1964) by AIP as **The Day the Earth Froze** *(with narration by Marvin Miller), 67 mins.*
Standard fantasy

Samson
1960, (It), Telewide/Medallion, color, 95 mins.
W: Brad Harris (*Samson*), Brigitte Corey (*Jasmine*), Alan Steel, Serge Gainsbourg, Mara Berni, Walter Reeves, Carlo Tamberlani, Elke Arendt
D: Gianfranco Parloni
USA retitle, **The Fury of Hercules**
Standard "Sword & Sandal": Rebels plot to restore true queen to throne

Samson Against the Sheik
1960, (It), color
W: Ed Fury
Minor "Sword & Sandal"

Samson Against the Zombies
see **The Saint vs. the Zombies**

Samson and Dalila
1922, (Austria), Vita Film-AG, b&w
D: Michael Curtiz
Standard thriller: Temptress betrays muscleman

Samson and Delilah
1949, (USA), Para, color, 131 mins.
W: Victor Mature (*Samson*), Hedy Lamarr (*Delilah*), George Sanders (*The Philistine Leader*), Angela Lansbury (*Semadar*), Henry Wilcoxon (*Ahtur*), Victor Varconi (*Lord of Ashdod*), Pedro de Cordoba (*Bar Simon*), Olive Deering (*Miriam*), Russ Tamblyn (*Saul*), William Farnum (*Tubal*), Fritz Leiber (*Lord Sharif*), Frank Reicher (*The Village Barber*), Moroni Olsen (*Targil*), Fay Holden (*Hazlelponit, Aka Hazel*), John Miljan (*Lesh Lakish*), George Reeves (*The Wounded Messenger*), Julia Faye (*Hisham*), Lane Chandler (*Teresh*), Francis J. McDonald (*The Story Teller*), William Davis (*Garmiskar*), Arthur Q. Bryan (*The Fat Philistine Merchant*), Laura Elliot (*The Spectator*), John Parrish (*Lord of Gath*), Frank Wilcox (*Lord of Ekron*), Russell Hicks (*Lord of Ashkelon*), Mike Mazurki (*Leader of Philistine Soldiers*), Boyd Davis (*The First Priest*), Colin Tapley (*The Prince*), Davison Clark (*The Merchant Prince*)
P & D: Cecil B. DeMille **SCR:** Jesse Lasky Jr. & Frederick M. Frank, from orig. treatments by Harold Lamb & Vladimir Jabotinsky **PHOTOG:** George Barnes **MUSIC:** Victor Young
Lavish biblical melodrama: Beauty betrays strongman

Samson and the Mighty Challenge
1964, (It), color
W: Alan Steel, Red Ross
Standard "Sword & Sandal": Musclemen have slugfest

Samson and the Sea Beasts
1963, (It), AIP/Filmways, color, 84 mins.
W: Kirk Morris, Margaret Lee
Minor "Sword & Sandal"

Samson and the Seven Challenges
1964, (It), color
W: Dan Vadis
Minor "Sword & Sandal": Hero overthrows wicked queen

Samson and the Seven Miracles of the World
see **Maciste alla Corte del Gran Khan**

Samson and the Slave Queen
see **Zorro Contro Maciste**

Samson and the Vampire Women
see **El Santo Contra las Vampiras**

Samson in the Wax Museum
see **The Saint in the Wax Museum**

Samson vs. the Giant King
see **Maciste alla Corte della Zar**

Samurai Pirate
1965, (Jap), Toho/AIP, color, 95 mins.
W: Toshiro Mifune, Makoto Sato, Mie Hama
P: Yuko Tanaka **D:** Senkichi Taniguchi **SCR:** Takeshi Kimura, Shimichi Sekizawa **SPCL-FX:** Eiji Tsuburaya

USA retitle, **The Lost World of Sinbad**
Standard adventure-fantasy

Samurai Reincarnation
1981, (Jap), color, 122 mins.
D: Kinji Fukasaku
Standard action-fantasy: Reborn warrior seeks vengeance

Sanctuary of Fear
1979, (USA), Marble Arch/Martin Strager/ITC-TV, color, 98 mins.
W: Barnard Hughes (*Father Brown*), Michael McGuire, George Hearn, Robert Schenkkan, David Rasche, Fred Gwynne, Elizabeth Wilson, Kay Lenz (*Carol*), Peter Maloney (*Eli*), Saul Rubineck (*Jerry*), Jeffrey DeMunn (*Whitney*), Thomas Hill (*Carl*), Donald Symington (*Heyman*), Alice Drummond (*Grace*), Maureen Silliman (*Beth*), Sydney Hibbert (*The Steeldrummer*), David Ramsey (*An Auction Guest*), Robin Mary Paris (*An Auction Guest*), Gary Bayer (*Mike*), Sudie Bond (*Annie*)
D: John Llewellyn Moxey **WRIT BY:** Don M. Mankiewicz & George Cotler, based on the "Father Brown" character by G.K. Chesterton **PHOTOG:** Ronald Lautore **MUSIC:** Allyn Ferguson & Jack Elliott
TVM, standard thriller: Detective-priest probes strange happenings centering on young actress

The Sandal
1969, (GB), Rosalba/Eagle, color, 29 mins.
W: Anna Matisse (*The Woman*), Lionel Blair
D: Ray Austin
Standard short fantasy: Drugged woman's dream saves her from suicide

The Sand Castle
1961, (USA), Noel/Louis de Rochemont/Barney Pitkin.Contemporary Films, b&w & color, 70 mins.
W: Barry Cardwell, Laurie Cardwell, George Dunham, Alec Wilder, Maybelle Nash, Ghislain Dussart, Allegra Ahern, Erica Speyer, Charles Rydell, Lester Judson, Martin Russ, Mabel Mercer (*Voice of the shell*)
WRIT, P & D: Jerome Hill
Unusual fantasy: Children enter world of sandcastle they constructed

Sandcastles
1972, (USA), CBS-TV, color, 73 mins.
W: Herschel Bernardi, Jan-Michael Vincent, Mariette Hartley, Bonnie Bedelia, Gary Crosby, Lloyd Gough, William Long Jr., Loretta Leversee, S. Frank White, William Hansen, Mimi Davis, Jody Hauber
D: Ted Post
TVM, standard fantasy: Man dies in auto crash, spirit returns to make amends for previous thievery

Sandokan Against the Leopard of Sarawak
1964, (It), Ottavio Poggi/Teleworld, color, 94 mins.
W: Ray Danton, Guy Madison Franca Bettoia, Mario Petri
D: Luigi Capuano
Minor adventure-thriller: Brave ruler battles old enemy

Sandokan Fights Back
1964, (It), Ottavio Poggi/Teleworld, color, 96 mins.
W: Ray Danton, Guy Madison Franca Bettoia, Mino Doro
D: Luigi Capuano
Minor adventure-thriller: Brave ruler vs. evil usurpers

Sandokan the Great
1964, (It-Fr-Sp), MGM, color, 110 mins, also 105 mins.
W: Steve Reeves Genevieve Grad, Rik Battaglia, Maurice Poli
P: Solly V. Bianco, Joseph Fryd **D:** Umberto Lenzi **SCR:** Fulvio Gicca & Umberto Lenzi
Standard adventure-thriller: Hero in 19th-century North Africa leads revolutionaries against British

The Sands of Time
1919, (GB), Harma Photoplays, b&w, 5,899 ft. (1798m)
W: Mercy Hatton (*Esther Conway*), Bertram Burleigh (*Allan Ross*), John Gliddon (*Kenneth Wayne*), Kate Phillips (*Miss Wayne*), Adeline Hayden Coffin (*Mrs. Ross*), Jeff Barlow, Charles Groves, J. Edwards Barber
D: Randle Ayrton **STORY:** Reuben Gillmer
Standard adventure: Squire's son and blacksmith rival seek rare Tibetan orchid

Le Sang d'un Poete (The Blood of a Poet)
1930, (Fr), b&w, 55 mins
W: Enrico Ribero, Lee Miller, Jean Desbordes Pauline Carton, Odette Talazac, Elizabeth Lee Miller
WRIT & D: Jean Cocteau **PHOTOG:** Georges Perinal **MUSIC:** Georges Auric, film financed by Vicomte de Noailles
Classic fantasy, 4 surrealistic segments: **The Wounded Hand, Do Walls Have Ears?, The Battle of the Snowballs** *&* **The Profanation of the Host**

La Sanglante Sorciere (The Bloodstained Witch)
1964, (It-Fr), BIFO/Cinegai, color, 100 mins.
W: Barbara Steele
released in GB & USA (1967) as **The Long Hair of Death**

Santa Claus
1898, (GB), b&w, 75 ft. (22.9m)
D: George Albert Smith
A.k.a. **The Visit of Santa Claus**
Standard fantasy short: Children dream Santa comes down chimney

Santa Claus
1912, (GB), Natural Colour Kinematograph Co., color
W: Leedham Bantock (*Santa Claus*), Margaret Favronova (*Tingaling*)
D: F. Martin Thornton, R.H. Callum & Walter R. Booth   **STORY:** Alfred de
    Manby, Leedham Bantock & Harold Simpson
Standard fantasy: Girl dreams she visits Toyland, helps Santa Claus

Santa Claus
1959, (Mex), Azteca/K. Gordon Murray, color, 94 mins.
W: Jose Elias Moreno, Cesareo Quezada
P: William Calderon   **D:** Rene Cardona   **SCR:** Rene Cardona & Adolpho Portillo
Standard fantasy: Santa teams with Merlin the Magician, opposes red devil

Santa Claus
1985, (USA), Tri-Star, color, 110 mins.
W: David Huddleston (*Santa Claus*), Judy Cornwell (*Mrs. Claus*), John Lithgow
    (*B.Z.*), Dudley Moore (*Patch*), Burgess Meredith (*The Elder Elf*), Carrie Kei
    Heim (*Cornelia*), Tim Stern (*Boog*), Jeffrey Kramer (*Towzer*), John Barrad
    (*Dooley*), Christian Fitzpatrick (*Joe*), Anthony O'Donnell (*Puffy*), Judith
    Morse (*Miss Abruzzi*), Christopher Ryan (*Vout*), Melvyn Hayes (*Goober*),
    Dorothea Phillips (*Miss Tucker*), Aimee Delamain (*The Storyteller*), Don
    Estelle (*Groot*), Peter O'Farrell (*Honka*), Dickie Arnold (*Goober*), John
    Hallam (*Grizzard*)
P: Ilya Salkind & Pierre Spengler   **D:** Jeannot Szwarc   **ORIG. STORY:** David
    Newman   **PHOTOG:** Arthur Ibbetson   **VS-FX:** Derek Meddings
    MUSIC: Henry Mancini   **SONG:** (sung by Sheena Easton), *Christmas All
    Over the World*
Elaborate fantasy: Kindly immortal vs. wicked magnate

Santa Claus and the Children
1898, (GB), R.W. Paul, b&w, 60 ft. (18.3m)
Standard fantasy short: Saint Nicholas comes down chimney, delivers toys to children

Santa Claus Conquers the Martians
1964, (USA), JaLor/Embassy, color, 82 mins.
W: John Call (*Santa Claus*), Leonard Hicks (*Kimar*), Vincent Beck (*Voldar*), Bill
    McCutcheon (*Dropo*), Pia Zadora (*Girmar*), Victor Stiles (*Billy*), Donna
    Conforti (*Betty*), Chris Month (*Bomar*), Leila Martin (*Momar*), Doris Rich
    (*Mrs. Claus*), Carl Don (*Chochem/Von Green*), Al Nesor (*Stobo*), Ivor Bodin
    (*Winky*), Jim Bishop (*Lomas*), Joe Elic, Lin Thurmond, Don Blair, Tony
    Ross, Scott Aronesty, Ronnie Rotholz, Glenn Schaffer
P: Paul L. Jacobson   **D:** Nicholas Webster   **SCR:** Glenville Mareth   **ORIG.**
    STORY: Paul L. Jacobson   **PHOTOG:** David Quaid   **MUSIC:** Milton
    DeLugg   **SONGS:** *Hooray for Santa Claus*
Standard juvenile SF-fantasy: Mars ruler kidnaps St. Nick

The Santa Clause
1994, (USA), Outlaw/Walt Disney-Hollywood Pictures/Buena Vista, color, 95 mins.
W: Tim Allen, Judge Reinhold, Wendy Crewson, David Krumholtz, Peter Boyle,
    Eric Lloyd
P: Brian Reilly, Jeffrey Silver & Robert Newmyer   **D:** John Pasquin   **SCR:** Leo
    Benvenuti & Steve Rudnick
Standard comedy-fantasy: Mortal substitutes for Kris Kringle

Santo and the Hotel of Death
1961, (Mex), b&w
W: Santo
Minor fantasy-thriller

Santo and the Treasure of Dracula
see The Vampire and Sex

Santo Attacks the Witches
1964, (Mex), Vergara, b&w
W: Santo
Minor fantasy-thriller

El Santo Contra las Vampiras (The Saint vs. the Vampire Women)
1960, (Mex), Tele-Cine-Radio Mexico/AIP-TV, b&w, 89 mins.
W: Santo, Lorena Velazquez, Maria Duval, Javier Loyola, Augusto Benedico, Jaime
    Fernandez, Ofelia Montesco, Ray Mendoza, Laura Marqueti, Eduardo
    Bonada, Cavernario Galindo, Lobo Negro, Black Shadow, Boby Bonales
P: Luis Garcia DeLeon   **WRIT & D:** Alfonso Corona Blake   **ORIG. STORY:**
    Antonio Orellana, Fernando Osses & Rafael G. Travesi   **PHOTOG:** Manuel
    Gonzalez   **MUSIC:** Raul Lavista
A.k.a. **Las Mujeres Vampiras (The Vampire Women)** *USA retitle,* **Samson and**
    the Vampire Women
Standard fantasy-thriller: Professor summons superhero to rescue daughter from vampire's
    spell

Santo vs. Baron Brakola
1965, (Mex), b&w

W: Santo
Minor fantasy-thriller

Santo vs. the King of Crime
1962, (Mex), Azteca, b&w
W: Santo
Minor fantasy-thriller

Sapphire
1959, (GB), Artna/Rank/Univ, color, 92 mins.
W: Nigel Patrick (*Hazard*), Yvonne Mitchell (*Mildred*), Michael Craig (*Learoyd*),
    Paul Massie (*David*), Bernard Miles (*Mr. Harris*), Olga Lindo (*Mrs. Harris*),
    Earl Cameron (*Dr. Robbins*), Gordon Heath (*Paul Slade*), Harry Baird
    (*Johnnie Fiddle*), Jocelyn Britton (*Patsy*), Rupert Davies (*Ferris*), Orlando
    Martins (*The Barman*), Freda Bamford (*Sgt. Cook*), Robert Adams (*Horace Big
    Cigar*), Yvonne Buckingham (*Sapphire*), Peter Vaughan, Barbara Steele
P: Michael Relph   **D:** Basil Dearden   **ORIG. SCR:** Janet Green   **PHOTOG:**
    Harry Waxman   **MUSIC:** Philip Green
Modest melodrama: Race relations complicate girl's murder

Saraba Uchu Senkan Yamato (Goodbye, Spaceship Yamato)
1978, (Jap), color
Standard SF-adventure

The Saracen Blade
1954, (USA), Col, color, 77 mins.
W: Ricardo Montalban (*Pietro*), Betta St. John (*Iolanthe*), Rick Jason (*Enzio*),
    Carolyn Jones (*Elaine of Siniscola*), Whitfield Connor (*Frederick II*), Michael
    Ansara (*Count Siniscola*), Edgar Barrier (*Baron Rogliano*), Gene D'Arcy (*The
    Italian Prince*), Nelson Leigh (*Isaac*), Pamela Duncan (*Zenobia*), Frank
    Pulaski (*Donati*), Leonard Penn (*Haroun*), Nyra Monsour (*Maria*), Edward
    Coch (*Guiseppi*), Poppy Deluando (*Gina*)
P: Sam Katzman   **D:** William Castle   **SCR:** DeVallon Scott & George
    Worthington Yates, from Frank Yerby's novel   **PHOTOG:** Henry Freulich
    MUSIC: Mischa Bakaleinikoff
Standard adventure-thriller: Man avenges father's murder in 13th-century Italy

Sarah's House
1984, (Pol), color, 70 mins.
D: Zygmunt Lech
Standard psychodrama: Woman degrades her lovers

Sgt. Kabukiman, N.Y.P.D.
1990, (USA), Troma, color, 105 mins.
W: Rick Gianasi
Standard satire: Cop becomes samurai crime-fighter

Sasquatch, the Legend of Bigfoot
1978, (USA), North American Film Enterprises, color, 102 mins.
W: George Lauris (*Chuck*), Steve Boergadine (*Hank*), William Emmons (*Dr.
    Markham*), Jim Bradford (*Barney*), Joe Morello (*Techka Blackhawk*), Ken
    Kenzle (*Josh*)
D: Ed Ragozzini   **SCR:** Edward H. Hawkins   **STORY:** Ronald B. Olson
    PHOTOG: John Fabian & Bill Farmer
Minor thriller: Hunt for fabled beast

Satan
1913, (GB), b&w
Standard thriller (5-part)

Satanas
1919, (Ger), b&w
W: Conrad Veidt (*Satan*)
D: F.W. Murnau   **PHOTOG:** Karl Freund
Standard thriller

The Satan Bug
1964, (USA), Mirisch-Kappa/UA, color, 114 mins.
W: George Maharis (*Lee Barrett*), Anne Francis (*Ann*), Dana Andrews (*The
    General*), Richard Basehart (*Dr. Hoffman*), Edward Asner (*Veretti*), John
    Larkin (*Michaelson*), James Hong (*Dr. Yang*), Simon Oakland (*Tesserly*),
    Frank Sutton (*Donald*), Richard Bull (*Cavanaugh*), John Anderson (*Reagan*),
    Martin Blaine (*Martin*), John Clarke (*Raskin*), Henry Beckman (*Dr. Baxter*),
    Harry Lauter Russ Bender (*Mason*), Hari Rhodes (*Johnson*), Harold Gould
    (*Dr. Ostrer*)
P & D: John Sturges   **SCR:** James Clavell & Edward Anhalt, from Alistair
    MacLean's novel   **PHOTOG:** Robert L. Surtees   **SPCL-FX:** Paul Pollard
    MUSIC: Jerry Goldsmith
Fr retitle, **Station 3 Ultra-Secret**
Unusual SF-thriller: Deadly germ culture stolen from secret gov't base

Satan en Prison (Satan in Prison)
1907, (Fr), Star, b&w, 92m (301.8 ft./5.1 mins.)
D: Georges Melies
Standard fantasy

The Satanic Rites of Dracula
1973, (GB), Hammer/WB, color, 88 mins.
W: Christopher Lee *(Count Dracula)*, Peter Cushing *(Van Helsing)*, Michael Coles *(Murray)*, William Franklyn *(Torrence)*, Freddie Jones *(Prof. Keeley)*, Joanna Lumley *(Jessica)*, Barbara Yu Ling *(Chin Yang)*, Richard Vernon *(Mathews)*, Patrick Barr *(Lord Carradine)*, Richard Mathews *(Porter)*, Lockwood West *(Freeborne)*, Valerie Van Ost *(Jane)*, Maurice O'Connell *(Hanson)*, Peter Adair *(The Doctor)*, Maggie Fitzgerald, Mia Martin, Pauline Peart, Finnuala O'Shannon, Marc Zuber, Ian Dewar, John Harvey, Paul Weston, Graham Rees
P: Roy Skeggs D: Alan Gibson SCR: Don Houghton PHOTOG: Brian Probyn MUSIC: John Cacavas
orig. to be titled Dracula is Dead and Well and Living in London reissued (1978) as Count Dracula and His Vampire Bride
Standard horror-thriller: Master of Undead plots to turn world into charnel house

Satanik
1969, (It-Sp), Radiocines-Copercines/AA, color, 85 mins.
W: Magda Konopka *(Marnie Bannister)*, Julio Pena, Umi Raho, Luigi Montini, Armando Calvo, Mimma Ippoliti, Isarco Ravioli, Nerio Bernardi, Joe Atlanta, Antonio Pica, Gaetano Quartararo Mirella Pamphili, Giancarlo Prete, Gustavo Simeone, Pedro Fenollar, Luis De Tejadad, Piero Vivarelli
P: Romano Mussolini D: Piero Vivarelli SCR: Eduardo M. Brochero PHOTOG: Enrico Sasso MUSIC: Manuel Parada
Minor SF-melodrama (retread of La Cara del Terror): Miracle drug turns disfigured woman scientist into homicidal beauty

Satan in Prison
see Satan en Prison

The Satanist
1976, (GB), Tyburn, color
W: Peter Cushing, Trevor Howard, Orson Welles, Shirley Bassey, from Dennis Wheatley's novel
Standard thriller

Satan Met a Lady
1936, (USA), WB, b&w, 66 mins.
W: Bette Davis *(Valerie Purvis)*, Warren William *(Ted Shane)*, Alison Skipworth *(Mme. Barabbas)*, Marie Wilson *(Murgatroyd)*, Arthur Treacher *(Anthony Travers)*, Maynard Holmes *(Kenneth)*, Winifred Shaw *(Astrid Ames)*, Porter Hall *(Mr. Ames)*, Charles Wilson *(Pollock)*, Olin Howland *(Dunhill)*, Joseph King *(McElroy)*, Barbara Blane *(Babs)*, John Elliott *(The City Father)*, Alphonse Martell *(The Headwaiter)*, Edward McWade *(Richards)*, Eddie Shubert, Stuart Holmes, Alice La Mont, James Burtis, Francis Sayles, Billy Bletcher
D: William Dieterle SCR: Brown Holmes, based on Dashiell Hammett's novel *The Maltese Falcon* (remake- 2nd version) PHOTOG: Arthur Edeson MUSIC: Leo F. Forbstein
Standard thriller: Machinations of female-led gang

Satan—or, The Drama of Humanity
1911, (It), b&w
partially based on John Milton's epic poem "Paradise Lost"

Satan's Amazon
1915, (GB), Barker/Award, b&w, 2,960 ft. (902.2m)
D: A.E. Coleby STORY: Rowland Talbot
Standard thriller: Female criminal brought to justice

Satan's Black Wedding
1975, (USA), color, 61 mins.
W: Greg Braddock, Ray Miles, Lisa Milano
Minor horror-fantasy: Ghoulish group gathers at Monterey monastery

Satan's Blade
1984, (USA), color, 87 mins.
Minor horror-thriller: Ancient talisman inspires killings

Satan's Blood Freaks
see Dracula vs. Frankenstein

Satan's Cheerleaders
1977, (USA), World Entertainment, color, 90 mins.
W: John Ireland *(The Sheriff)*, Yvonne DeCarlo *(Emmy)*, Jack Kruschen *(Billy)*, John Carradine *(The Bum)*, Sydney Chaplin *(The Monk)*, Jacqulin Cole *(Ms. Johnson)*, Joseph Carlo *(The Coach)*, Kerry Sherman *(Patti)*, Hillary Horan *(Chris)*, Lane Caudell *(Stevie)*, Alisa Powell *(Debbie)*, Robin Greer *(The Baker Girl)*, Sherry Marks *(Sharon)*, Michael Donovan O'Donnell *(The Farmer)*
D: Greydon Clark SCR: Greydon Clark & Alvin Fast PHOTOG: Dean Cundey MUSIC: Gerald Ice SONGS: *One for All and All for One & Who You Gonna Love Tonight*, sung by Sonoma
Minor thriller: Satanists menace high-school girls

Satan's Mistress
1978, (USA), Motion Picture Marketing/Diversified/Manson Int'l, color, 98 mins.
W: Lana Wood, Britt Ekland, John Carradine, Kabir Bedi, Don Galloway, Sherry Scott

P & D: James Polakof
A.k.a. Fury of the Succubus, Demon Rage and Dark Eyes
Minor fantasy-thriller: Woman plagued by invisible spirit

Satan's Sadists
1969, (USA), Independent Int'l, color, 88 mins.
W: Russ Tamblyn, Scott Brady, Kent Taylor, Regina Carrol, John Cardos, Robert Dix, Gary Kent, Bambi Allen, Greydon Clark, Jackie Taylor, Evelyn Frank, Bill Bonner, Bobby Clark, Yvonne Stewart, Cheryl Anne, Breck Warwick, Randee Lynn
P & D: Al Adamson SCR: Dennis Wayne MUSIC: The Nightriders
blurb: "Human garbage—in the sickest love parties!"
"Probably the grossest biker movie of them all"—Michael Weldon, The Psychotronic Encyclopedia of Film
Standard thriller: Vicious bikers taught lesson by Vietnam veteran

Satan's Princess
1990, (USA), color, 90 mins.
W: Robert Forster, Caren Kaye, Lydie Denier
D: Bert I. Gordon
Minor fantasy-thriller: Cult terrorizes

Satan's Satellites
1958, (USA), Rep, b&w, 70 mins.
W: Judd Holdren, Aline Towne, Lane Bradford, Wilson Wood, Leonard Nimoy, John Crawford, Stanley Waxman, Craig Kelly, Ray Boyle, Tom Steele, Dale Van Sickel, Roy Engel, Gayle Kellogg, Jack Harden, Paul Stader, Jack Shea, Robert Garabedian
D: Fred C. Brannon SCR: Ronald Davidson MUSIC: Stanley Wilson
Standard SF-thriller (feature version of 1952 serial Zombies of the Stratosphere): Space aliens threaten Earth

Satan's School for Girls
1973, (USA), Spelling-Goldberg/ABC-TV, color, 74 mins.
W: Pamela Franklin, Kate Jackson, Jo Van Fleet, Roy Thinnes, Cheryl Jean Stoppelmoor [Cheryl Ladd], Lloyd Bochner, Bill Quinn, Jamie Smith Jackson, Terry Lumley, Gwynne Gilford
D: David Lowell Rich TELEPLAY: Arthur A. Ross PHOTOG: Tim Southcott MUSIC: Laurence Rosenthal
TVM, standard fantasy-thriller: Girl probes sister's suicide at private school

Satan's Sister
see La Sorella di Satan

Satan's Skin
see The Blood on Satan's Claw

Satan's Slave
1976, (GB), Monumental/Crown Int'l, color, 86 mins.
W: Michael Gough *(Alexander Yorke)*, Martin Potter *(Stephen Yorke)*, Candace Glendenning *(Catherine Yorke)*, James Bree *(Malcolm Yorke)*, Barbara Kellermann *(Frances)*, Celia Hewitt *(Elizabeth Yorke)*, Michael Craze *(John)*, Gloria Walker *(Janice)*, David McGillivray *(The Priest)*
P: Les Young & Richard Crafter D: Norman J. Warren STORY: David McGillivray PHOTOG: Les Young MUSIC: John Scott
Minor horror-thriller: Accident victim learns she is to be used in ceremony to resurrect witch

Satan's Touch
1984, (USA), color, 86 mins.
W: James Lawless, Shirley Venard
Minor horror-fantasy: Simpleton worships Satan

Satan's Triangle
1975, (USA), ABC-TV, color, 74 mins.
W: Kim Novak *(Eva)*, Doug McClure *(Haig)*, Alejandro Rey *(Martin)*, Jim Davis *(Hal)*, Michael Conrad *(Pagnolini)*, Ed Lauter *(Strickland)*, Titos Vandis *(Salao)*, Hank Stohl *(The Coast Guard Captain)*, Zitto Kazann *(Juano)*, Buck Gee *(DeSoma)* Peter Bourne, Tom Dever
D: Sutton Roley TELEPLAY: William Woodfield
TVM, standard SF-thriller: Lone woman survives bizarre storm at sea

Satellite in the Sky
1956, (GB), Tridelta/WB, color, 84 mins.
W: Kieron Moore *(Michael)*, Lois Maxwell *(Kim)*, Donald Wolfit *(Merrity)*, Bryan Forbes *(Jimmy)*, Jimmy Hanley *(Larry)*, Thea Gregory *(Barbara)*, Barry Keegan *(Lefty)*, Alan Gifford *(Col. Galloway)*, Walter Hudd *(Blandford)*, Donald Gray *(Capt. Ross)*, Carl Jaffe *(Bechstein)*, Trevor Reid, Robert O'Neil, Shirley Lawrence, Peter Neil, Rick Rydon, Charles Richardson, Ronan O'Casey, Alastair Hunter, John Baker
P: Edward J. & Harry Lee Danziger D: Paul Dickson SCR: John C. Mather, J.T. McIntosh & Edith Dell PHOTOG: Denys Coop SPCL-FX: Wally Veevers MUSIC: Albert Elms
Standard SF-thriller: Astronauts attempt to detonate superbomb in outer space

Satellite of Blood
see First Man into Space

Saturday Island
1952, (GB), Coronado/UA, color, 103 mins.

W: Linda Darnell (*Elizabeth Smythe*), Tab Hunter (*Chicken Dugan*), Donald Gray (*William Peck*), John Laurie (*Grimshaw*), Sheila Chong (*Tukua*), Russell Waters (*Dr. Snyder*), Diana Decker (*The Nurse*), Macdonald Parke (*The Captain*), Peter Butterworth (*The Marine*), Michael Newell, Hilda Fenemore, Lloyd Lamble, Harold Ayer, Joan Benham, Katharine Blake, Brenda Hogan
P: David E. Rose   **D:** Stuart Heisler   **SCR:** Stephanie Nordli   **SCREEN STORY:** Stuart Heisler, from Hugh Brooke's novel   **PHOTOG:** Oswald Morris   **SPCL-FX:** George Blackwell   **MUSIC:** William Alwyn   **MUSIC CONDUCT:** Muir Mathieson
USA retitle, **Island of Desire**
Minor melodrama: Nurse and young marine shipwrecked on lonely isle

Saturday the 14th
1982, (USA), Julie Corman/New World, color, 73 mins.
W: Richard Benjamin (*John*), Paula Prentiss (*Mary*), Jeffrey Tambor (*Waldemar*), Severn Darden (*Van Helsing*), Rosemary De Camp (*Aunt Lucille*), Kari Michaelsen (*Debbie*), Nancy Lee Andrews (*Yolanda*), Kevin Brando (*Billy*), Roberta Collins (*Rhonda*), Craig Coulter (*Duane*), Thomas Newman (*Phil*), Annie O'Donnell (*Annette*), Carol Androsky (*Marge*), Michael Miller (*The Cop*), Stacy Keach Sr. (*The Attorney*), Patrick Campbell (*The Mailman*), Paul "Mousie" Garner (*The Major*), Irwin Russo (*The Truck Driver*)
D & SCR: Howard R. Cohen   **STORY:** Tom Begun   **PHOTOG:** Daniel Lacambre   **MUSIC:** Parmer Fuller
Minor horror-comedy

Saturday the 14th Strikes Back
1988, (USA), New World, color, 79 mins.
W: Ray Walston, Avery Schreiber
Minor horror-comedy: Monsters emerge from mansion basement

Saturn 3
1980, (GB), Sir Lew Grade/AFD, color, 88 mins.
W: Kirk Douglas (*Adam*), Farrah Fawcett (*Alex*), Harvey Keitel (*Benson*), Douglas Lambert (*Capt. James*), Ed Bishop (*Harding*), Christopher Muncke (*The Crewman*)
P & D: Stanley Donen   **SCR:** Martin Amis, from a story by John Barry   **PHOTOG:** Billy Williams   **SPCL-FX:** Colin Chilvers   **MUSIC:** Elmer Bernstein
Standard SF-thriller: On Saturnian moonbase, scientist and lovely assistant are menaced by madman with deadly robot

Satyricon (Aka Fellini's Satyricon)
1969, (It-Fr), PEA/UA, color, 120 mins.
W: Martin Potter (*Encolpius*), Hiram Keller (*Ascyltus*), Max Born (*Giton*), Fanfulla (*Vernacchio*), Salvo Randone (*Eumolpus*), Magali Noel (*Fortunata*), Alain Cuny (*Licha*), Joseph Wheeler (*The Suicide*), Lucia Bose (*The Matron*), Tanya Lopert (*The Emperor*), Hylette Adolphe (*The Slave Girl*), Donyale Luna (*Oenothea*), Capucine (*Tryphaena*), Gordon Mitchell (*The Robber*), Mario Romagnoli (*Trimalchio*), Giuseppe Sanvitale (*Habinnas*), Eugenio Mastroianni (*Cinedo*), Danica La Loggia (*Scintilla*), Antonia Pietrosi (*The Widow of Ephesus*), Elio Gigante (*The Owner of the Garden of Delights*), Wolfgang Hillinger (*The Soldier at the Tomb*), Carlo Giordana (*The Ship Captain*), Sibilla Sedat (*The Nymphomaniac*), Lorenzo Piani (*The Nymphomaniac's Husband*), Luigi Zerbinati (*The Nymphomaniac's Slave*), Vittorio Vittori (*The Notary*), Marcello DiFalco (*The Proconsul*), Luigi Montefiori (*The Minotaur*), Elisa Mainardi (*Ariadne*)
P: Alberto Grimaldi   **D:** Federico Fellini   **STORY:** Federico Fellini & Bernardino Zapponi, from Petronius Arbiter's novel   **PHOTOG:** Giuseppe Rotunno   **MUSIC:** Ilhan Mimaroglu, Nino Rota, Ted Dockstader & Andrew Rudin
Bizarre melodrama: Grotesque depravities of Imperial Rome

Saurus
see **The Hideous Sun Demon**

The Savage
1926, (USA), First Nat'l, b&w, 5 reels (6,275 ft./1912.6m)
W: Ben Lyon (*Danny Terry*), May McAvoy (*Ysabel Atwater*), Tom Maguire (*Prof. Atwater*), Philo McCullough (*Howard Kipp*), Sam Hardy (*The Managing Ed.*), Charlotte Walker (*Mrs. Atwater*)
D: Fred Newmeyer   **SCR:** Jane Murfin & Charles E. Whittaker, from a story by Ernest Pascal   **PHOTOG:** George Folsey
Standard comedy: Wild-animal expert poses as "white savage"

Savage
1997, (USA), color, 105 mins.
W: Olivier Gruner, Jennifer Grant, Luke Askew, Kario Salem, Kristin Minter
Made-for-Video, standard SF-thriller: Virtual-reality expert causes deaths

The Savage Bees
1976, (USA), NBC-TV, color, 106 mins.
W: Ben Johnson (*Sheriff McKew*), Paul Hecht (*Rufus*), Michael Parks (*Jeff DuRand*), Horst Buchholz (*Dr. Mueller*), Gretchen Corbett (*Jeannie Devereaux*), James Best (*Pelligrino*), David Gray (*The Coast Guard Lieutenant*), Richard Boyle (*The Coast Guard Chief*), Bruce French (*The Police Lieutenant*), Eliott Keener (*The Freighter Boatswain*), Boardman O'Connor (*The Freighter Captain*), Danny Barker (*The Taxicab Driver*), Don Hood (*Deputy Churn*), Bill Holliday (*Deputy Stilt*), Tiffany Gautier Chase (*Julie Compher*), Lyla Hay Owen (*Mrs. McKew*), Tom Smith Alden (*The Young Priest*), James Bowers

(*The Morgue Technician*), Sylvia "Kuumba" Williams (*The Morgue Receptionist*), Kenneth Lorenzen (*The Pirate*), Christine Ellsworth (*The Pirate Girl*), Wayne "V" Mack (*Councilman Ralston*), Dr. Norman Gary (*Caziot*), Cary Wilmot Alden (*Mrs. Caziot*), Jack L. Morrison (*Councilman Tyne*)
P & D: Bruce Geller   **TELEPLAY:** Guerdon Trueblood   **PHOTOG:** Richard Glouner   **MUSIC:** Walter Murphy
orig. to be titled **Attack of the Killer Bees**
TVM, minor thriller: Killer bees threaten New Orleans' Mardi Gras

The Savage Curse
1974, (GB), CBS-TV, color
W: George Chakiris, Jenny Agutter (*Dominie*), Anton Diffring (*Jonathan*), John Sharp (*Jack*), Stephen Greif (*Croon*), Peggy Sinclair (*Miss Faversham*), John Atkinson (*Hawkes*), Russell Hunter
P & D: John Sichel   **TELEPLAY:** Terence Feely   **ORIG. STORY:** Brian Clemens   **PHOTOG:** Bill Brown   **MUSIC:** Laurie Johnson
TVM, standard thriller: American seeks missing brother in small English village

Savage Drums
1951, (USA), Lippert, b&w, 70 mins.
W: Sabu, Sid Melton, H.B. Warner, Lita Baron
D: William Berke
Minor adventure-thriller: Youth opposes communist takeover of his island paradise

The Savage Hunt of King Stakh
1982, (Russ), Sovexportfilm, color, 129 mins.
W: Boris Plotnikov, Albert Filozov, Yelena Dimitrova, Boris Khmelnitsky, Valentina Chendrikova, Igor Kluss
D: Valery Rubinchink   **SCR:** Vladimir Korotkevich & Valery Rubinchink   **PHOTOG:** Tatyana Logineva   **MUSIC:** Yevgeny Glabov
Minor horror-fantasy: Ethnographer seeks ghosts

Savage Island
1985, (It-Sp), color, 74 mins.
W: Nicholas Beardsley, Linda Blair, Anthony Steffen, Ajita Wilson, Christina Lai, Leon Askin
D: Edward Muller   **SCR:** Nicholas Beardsley
Minor melodrama: Bad conditions in tropical women's prison

Savage Mutiny
1953, (USA), Col, b&w, 73 mins.
W: Johnny Weissmuller, George Robotham, Lester Matthews, Paul Marion, Angela Stevens, Gregory Gay, Leonard Penn, Ted Thorpe, Nelson Leigh, Charles Stevens
P: Sam Katzman   **D:** Spencer G. Bennet   **SCR:** Sol Shor   **PHOTOG:** William Whitley
Standard "Jungle Jim" adventure-thriller: Jungle hero warns natives of A-bomb testing

Savage Princess
1955, (Ind), UA, color, 101 mins.
W: Dilip Kumar, Mimmi
Standard adventure-thriller

Savages
1972, (USA), Angelika, color, 106 mins.
W: Lewis J. Stadlen (*Julian*), Anne Francine (*Carlotta*), Thayer David (*Otto*), Susie Blakely (*Cecily*), Salome Jens (*Emily*), Neil Fitzgerald (*Sir Harry*), Russ Thacker (*Andrew*), Sam Waterston (*James*), Eva Saleh (*Zia*), Margaret Brewster (*Lady Cora*), Ultra Violet (*Iliona*), Martin Kove (*Archie*), Kathleen Widdoes (*Leslie*), Asha Puthili (*The Forest Girl*), Paulita Sedgwick (*Penelope*)
P: Ismail Merchant   **D:** James Ivory   **SCR:** James Ivory, George Swift Trow & Michael O'Donoghue   **PHOTOG:** Walter Lassally   **MUSIC:** Joe Raposo
Offbeat melodrama: Forest wanderers take over deserted mansion, become touched by civilization

The Savage Woman
1918, (USA), Select, b&w, 5 reels
W: Clara Kimball Young, Milton Sills
Standard adventure-thriller: Tale of female "Tarzan"

Savage Weekend
1980, (USA), color, 88 mins.
W: Christopher Allport
A.k.a. **The Killer Behind the Mask** *and* **The Upstate Murders**
Minor thriller: Masked killer prowls boonies

Saved by a Burglar
1909, (GB), Urban Trading Co., b&w, 345 ft. (105.4m)
D: W.R. Booth
Standard crime-thriller (in 13 scenes): Burglar frees girl locked in safe

Saved By a Dream
1909, (GB), Williamson, b&w, 485 ft. (147.8m)
D: James Williamson
Minor fantasy: Gambler reforms after upsetting dream

Saved By a Dream
1914, (GB), B&C/DFSA, b&w, 1,097 ft. (334.4m)
D: Ethyle Batley
Standard fantasy: Rich man dreams he is Satan, flirts with blacksmith's wife

Saved by His Sweetheart
1910, (GB), Hepworth, b&w, 450 ft. (137.2m)
D: Lewin Fitzhamon
Standard crime-thriller: Framed clerk's fiancee nabs thief

Saved by the Telegraph Code
1908, (GB), Clarendon, b&w, 327 ft. (81.9m)
D: Percy Stow   SCR: Langford Reed
Standard crime-thriller: Escaped convict menaces girl on train

Saved from the Spy
1914, (GB), Captain Kettle/A&C, b&w, 1,090 ft. (332.2m)
STORY: C.J. Cutcliffe-Hyne
Standard crime-thriller: Boy scout foils spy's sabotage

Sawbones
1995, (USA), color
W: Adam Baldwin, Barbara Carrera, Don Harvey, Nina Siemaszko
Minor thriller: Sadistic doctor murders patient

Scalawag Bunch
1978, (It), color, 103 mins.
W: Mark Damon, Luis Davila
Minor adventure-thriller: Robin Hood protects England's crown for absent King Richard

Scalpel
1976, (USA), P.J. Prods./Avco Embassy, color, 96 mins.
W: Robert Lansing (*Dr. Phillip Reynolds*), Judith Chapman (*Heather/Jane*), Arlen Dean Snyder (*Uncle Bradley*), David Scarroll (*Dr. Robert Dean*), Sandy Martin (*Sandy*), Muriel Moore (*Cousin Margaret*), Clara Dunn (*The Gossipy Woman*), Bruce Atkins (*The Bartender*), Laura Whyte (*Jennifer Reynolds*), Stanley Wojno (*Donald*), Larry Quackenbush (*Keith Jarvey*), Greg Oliver (*The Killer*), Ellen Heard (*The Woman at the Party*), Mimi Honce (*Maddie Schuster*), Tad Currie (*Mr. Branch*), Warde Q. Butler (*Mr. Clyde*), George Macrenaris (*The Face Smasher*), Lynda Simon, Debbie Ness, Lydia M. Woodhead, Kenneth J. Hodge, Mike Fedack, Tom Pietschner, Valerie L. Strange, Richard H. Brannan, Terrie Bolinger, J. Kermit Echols, John Barbe, Thomas J. Howard Jr., James W. Hudson, Wesley John Jackson, John Thomas Kelly, Walter R. Mays, Ralph E. Mays, Allen Murphy, Julius Wimby
D & SCR: John Grissmer   ORIG. STORY: Joseph Weintraub   PHOTOG: Edward Lachman Jr.   MUSIC: Robert Cobert
A.k.a. *False Face*
Modest psychodrama: Plastic surgeon seeks inheritance, creates double of absent daughter

Scalps
1983, (USA), 21st Century, color
W: Kirk Alyn (*Dr. Machen*), Carol Borland (*Dr. Reynolds*), Jo Ann Robinson (*D.J.*), Richard Hench (*Randy*), Barbara Magnusson (*Ellen*), Roger Maycock (*Kershaw*), Carol Sue Flockhart (*Louise*), Frank McDonald (*Ben*), George Randall (*Billy Iron Wing*), Forrest J. Ackerman (*Prof. Treatwood*)
D & SP: Fred Olen Ray   PHOTOG: Brett Webster & Larry van Loon   MUSIC: Drew Neumann & Eric Rasmussen
Minor thriller

Le Scandale (The Scandal)
1966, (Fr), Univ, color, 105 mins.
W: Anthony Perkins, Yvonne Furneaux, Maurice Ronet, Suzanne Lloyd
D: Claude Chabrol   PHOTOG: Jean Rabier
USA retitle, *The Champagne Murders*
Standard thriller: Corruption and murder among France's "wine country" class

A Scandal in Bohemia
1921, (GB), Stoll, b&w, 2,100 ft. (642.4m)
W: Eille Norwood (*Sherlock Holmes*), Hubert Willis (*Dr. John Watson*), Joan Beverley (*Irene Adler*), Alfred Drayton (*The King of Bohemia*)
D: Maurice Elvey   SCR: William J. Elliott, from the writings of Sir Arthur Conan Doyle
Standard crime-thriller (episode in "Adventures of Sherlock Holmes" series)

Scandalous
1984, (GB), Raleigh/Angeles/Hemdale, color, 92 mins.
W: Robert Hays (*Frank Swedlin*), John Gielgud (*Uncle Willie*), Pamela Stephenson (*Fiona Maxwell Sayle*), M. Emmett Walsh (*Simon Reynolds*), Nancy Wood (*Lindsay Manning*), Conover Ron Travis (*The Porno Director*), Ed Dolan (*The Purser*), Kennard (*Francine Swedlin*), Kevin Elyot (*Matt*), Jim Dale (*Insp. Anthony Crisp*), Alita Kennedy (*The Stewardess*), Duncan Preston (*Hal*), Maureen Bennett (*Patti*), Preston Lockwood (*Leslie*), Peter Dennis (*The Maitre d'*), Stuart Saunders (*Croft*), Jim Magill (*The Constable*), Zoot Money (*The Taxidriver*), Mike Walling (*Scotty*), Peter Whitman (*Sgt. MacWilliams*), Toby Robins (*Pamela Reynolds*)
P: Arlene Sellers & Alex Winitsky   D: Rob Cohen   SCR: Rob Cohen & John Byrum   STORY: Larry Cohen, Rob Cohen & John Byrum   PHOTOG: Jack Cardiff   MUSIC: Dave Grusin
Standard thriller: TV reporter framed for wife's murder

Scanner Cop
1993, (USA), color, 94 mins.
W: Daniel Quinn, Darlanne Fluegel Richard Lynch, Mark Rolston, Hilary Shepard, Gary Hudson, Cyndi Pass, Luca Bercovici, Brion James, Richard Grove
D: Pierce David   SCR: John Bryant & George Saunder
Standard SF-thriller: Telepath cop opposes madman's brainwashed assassins

Scanners
1980, (Can), Pierre David & Victor Solnicki/Filmplan-Int'l/Avco Embassy, color, 103 mins.
W: Jennifer O'Neill (*Kim Obirst*), Stephen Lack (*Cameron Vale*), Patrick McGoohan (*Dr. Paul Ruth*), Michael Ironside (*Darryl Revok*), Lawrence Dane (*Keller*), Adam Ludwig (*Crostic*), Charles Shamata (*Gaudi*), Victor Desny (*Dr. Gafineau*), Mavor Moore (*Trevellyan*), Geza Kovacs, Sonny Forbes, Steve Michaels, Robert Boyd, Lee Broker, Robert Silverman, Jerome Thibergien, Lee Murray, Denis Lacroix, Tony Sherwood, Louis Del Grande, Elizabeth Mudry, Ken Umland, Anne Anglin, Jock Brandis, Jack Messinger, Victor Knight, Margaret Gadbois, Karen Fullerton, Terry Coady, Malcolm Nelthorpe, Nickolas Kilbertus, Rolland Nincheri, Don Buchsbaum, Dean Hagopian, Kimberly McKeever, Graham Batchelor, Alex Stevens, Neil Affleck
P: Claude Heroux   WRIT & D: David Cronenberg   PHOTOG: Mark Irwin   SPCL-FX: Gary Zeller   MUSIC: Howard Shore
"A MIND BLOWER!...'Scanners' is a tense and unusually brainy chiller, conceived by a remarkably keen cinematic mind. David Cronenberg is an authentic and astonishing film making stylist"—Gary Arnold, Washington Post
"For those who like their horror dark, intelligent, artful, yet truly horrifying in its effects, 'SCANNERS' is FIRST CLASS IN ITS FIELD"—Sheila Benson, Los Angeles Times
"MIND-BOGGLING! A movie thriller that will delight. It provides gigantic goose-pimples of horror...the special effects are truly shocking"—Archer Winsten, New York Post
Unusual SF-thriller: Psychic mutants threaten human race

Scanners II: The New Order
1991, (Can), Triton/Malofilm, color, 105 mins.
W: David Hewlett, Yvan Ponton, Deborah Raffin Isabelle Mejias, Tom Butler, Raoul Trujillo, Dorothee Berryman, Vlasta Vrana, Valentin Trujillo
D: Christian Duguay   SCR: B.J. Nelson   MUSIC: Marty Simon
Standard SF-thriller: Politician exploits psychic mutants

Scanners III: The Takeover
1992, (Can), color, 105 mins.
W: Liliana Komorowska, Valerie Valois, Steve Parrish Daniel Pilon, Collin Fox, Claire Cellucci, Michael Copeman
D: Christian Duguay
Standard SF-thriller: Untested migraine drug turns mind reader into murderess

Scanners: The Showdown
1994, (Can), color, 95 mins.
W: Daniel Quinn, Patrick Kilpatrick Khrystyne Haje, Stephen Mendel, Brenda Swanson, Robert Forster, Jewel Shepard
D: Steve Barnett   SCR: Mark Sevi
Standard SF-thriller: Telepathic policeman vs. adversary with life-draining powers

The Scapegoat
1959, (GB), DuMaurier-Guinness/MGM, b&w, 92 mins.
W: Alec Guinness (*John Barratt/Count Jacques*), Bette Davis (*Countess de Gue*), Nicole Maurey (*Bela*), Irene Worth (*Francoise de Gue*), Pamela Browne (*Blanche*), Annabel Bartlett (*Marie-Noel de Gue*), Geoffrey Keen (*Gaston*), Leslie French (*Lacoste*), Noel Howlett (*Dr. Aloin*), Peter Bull (*Aristide*)
P: Michael Balcon   D: Robert Hamer   SCR: Gore Vidal & Robert Hamer, from a novel by Daphne du Maurier
Unusual crime-thriller: French count plots rich wife's murder

The Scarab Murder Case
1936, (GB), B&D/Para British, b&w, 68 mins.
W: Kathleen Kelly (*Angela Hargreaves*), Wilfred Hyde-White (*Philo Vance*), Wally Patch (*Insp. Moor*), Henri de Vries (*Dr. Bliss*), John Robinson (*Donald Scarlett*), Stella Moya (*Meryt Amen*), Wallace Geoffrey (*Salveter*), Rustum Medora (*Hani*), Grahame Chesewright (*Makeham*), Shaun Desmond (*The Detective*)
D: Michael Hankinson   SCR: Selwyn Jepson, from a novel by S.S.Van Dine
Standard thriller: Detective proves archeologist murdered wealthy backer

The Scarecrow
1916, (GB), Bamforth/YCC, b&w, 650 ft. (198.1m)
D: Cecil Birch
Standard comedy-fantasy: Scarecrow comes to life, is mistaken for eccentric Lord

Scared Stiff
1945, (USA), Para, b&w, 65 mins.
W: Jack Haley, Ann Savage Veda Ann Borg, Arthur Aylesworth, George E. Stone
TV title *"Treasure of Fear"*
Minor comedy-mystery

Scared Stiff
1953, (USA), Para, b&w, 108 mins.
W: Dean Martin (*Larry Todd*), Jerry Lewis (*Myron Mertz*), Lizabeth Scott (*Mary Carroll*), George Dolenz (*Mr. Cortega*), Tom Powers (*The Police Lieutenant*),

Carmen Miranda (*Carmelita Castina*), Hugh Sanders (*The Cop on the Pier*), William Ching (*Tony Warren*), Dorothy Malone (*Rosie*), Jack Lambert (*The Zombie*), Frank Fontaine (*The Drunk*), Paul Marion (*The Carriso Twins*), Tony Barr (*Trigger*), Leonard Strong (*Shorty*), Henry Brandon (*Pierre*), Robert Emmett Keane, Danny Arnold, Earl Holliman [unbilled], Bob Hope [cameo], Bing Crosby [cameo]
<u>P</u>: Hal B. Wallis <u>D</u>: George Marshall <u>SCR</u>: Herbert Baker & Walter DeLeon, from a play by Paul Dickey & Charles W. Goddard <u>PHOTOG</u>: Ernest Laszlo <u>MUSIC</u>: Joseph J. Lilley <u>SONGS</u>: *The Bongo Bingo & The Enchilada Man*
Amusing comedy-thriller (remake of 'The Ghost Breakers'): Two performers aid young woman who inherits creepy Caribbean castle. Last film of Carmen Miranda

Scared Stiff
1987, (USA), Fremont/Int'l Film Marketing, color, 87 mins.
<u>W</u>: Andrew Stevens (*David Young*), Mary Page Keller (*Kate Christopher*), Josh Segal (*Jason*)
Minor thriller: Ex-mental patient is "haunted"

Scared to Death
1947, (USA), Golden Gate/Screeen Guild, color, 72 mins.
<u>W</u>: Bela Lugosi, Molly Lamont, George Zucco, Douglas Fowley, Nat Pendleton, Joyce Compton
Minor thriller: Possessive woman found murdered

Scared to Death
1980, (USA), Rand Marlis-Gil Shilton/Lone Star, color, 90 mins.
<u>W</u>: John Stinson (*Ted Lonergan*), Diana Davidson (*Jennifer Stanton*), Jonathan David Moses (*Lou Capell*), Toni Jannotta (*Sherry Carpenter*), Kermit Eller (*The Syngenor*), Walker Edmiston (*Chief Warren*), Pamela Bowman (*Janie Richter*), Michael Muscat (*Howard Tindall*), Freddie Dawson (*Virgil Watson*), Tracy Weddle (*Kathy Sperry*), Joleen Porcaro (*Kelly*), Joseph Daniels (*Michael*), Stephen Fenning (*Scott*), Greer Justin (*Sandy*), Johnny Greer (*Victor Colter*), John Moskel Jr. (*The Lab Man*), Evan Cole (*The Medic*), Michael Griswold (*Dr. Epstein*), Robert Short (*Ed*), William Malone
<u>D & SCR</u>: William Malone <u>STORY</u>: Robert Short & William Malone <u>PHOTOG</u>: Patrick Prince <u>SPCL-FX</u>: Tom Russo <u>MUSIC</u>: Tom Chase & Ardell Hake
A.k.a. **The Terror Factor**
Minor SF-horror: Mutant stalks Los Angeles

The Scarf
1951, (USA), Gloria/UA, b&w, 93 mins.
<u>W</u>: Emlyn Williams (*David Dunbar*), John Ireland (*John Barrington*), Mercedes McCambridge (*Connie Carter*), Lloyd Gough (*Dr. Gordon*), James Barton (*Ezra Thompson*), Basil Ruysdael (*Cyrus Barrington*), David Wolfe (*Level Louie*), Celia Lovsky (*Mrs. Barrington*), Harry Shannon (*The Warden*), Frank Jenks (*Tom*), Dave McMahon (*The State Trooper*), Dick Wessel (*Sid*), Chubby Johnson (*Sam*), Emmett Lynn (*Jack, the Waiter*), John Merrick (*The Deputy*), Frank Jacquet (*The Sheriff*), Lyle Talbot (*The Detective*), King Donovan (*Tiger*), Frank Richards (*Gargantua*), O.Z. Whitehead (*Woopie*), Sue Casey (*The Receptionist*)
<u>WRIT & D</u>: Ewald-Andre Dupont, from a story by I.G. Goldsmith & E.A. Rolfe <u>PHOTOG</u>: Franz Planer <u>MUSIC</u>: Herschel Burke Gilbert
Standard thriller

The Scarlet Blade
1963, (GB), Hammer/Col, color, 82 mins.
<u>W</u>: Lionel Jeffries (*Col. Hudd*), Oliver Reed (*Capt. Sylvester*), Jack Hedley (*Edward Beverley*), June Thorburn (*Clare Judd*), Michael Ripper (*Pablo*), Harold Goldblatt (*Jacob*), Duncan Lamont (*Maj. Bell*), Clifford Elkin (*Philip Beverley*), Suzan Farmer (*Constance Beverley*), Charles Houston (*Drury*), Robert Rietty (*Charles I*), John Stuart (*Col. Beverley*)
<u>P</u>: Anthony Nelson Keys <u>D & SCR</u>: John Gilling <u>PHOTOG</u>: Jack Asher <u>MUSIC</u>: Gary Hughes
Standard action-thriller: Cromwellian colonel plots destruction of royalists

The Scarlet Claw
1944, (USA), Univ, b&w, 74 mins.
<u>W</u>: Basil Rathbone (*Sherlock Holmes*), Nigel Bruce (*Dr. John Watson*), Miles Mander, Gerald Hamer, Paul Cavanagh, David Clyde, Kay Harding, Arthur Hohl, Victoria Horne
<u>P & D</u>: Roy William Neill, from characters created by Sir Arthur Conan Doyle
blurb: "Holmes vs. Monster!"
Standard thriller: Famed sleuth hunts legendary Canadian "marsh monster"

The Scarlet Clue
1945, (USA), Mono, b&w, 65 mins.
<u>W</u>: Sidney Toler (*Charlie Chan*), Benson Fong (*Tommie Chan*), Mantan Moreland (*Birmingham Brown*), Helen Devereaux (*Diane Hall*), Robert Homans (*Capt. Flynn*), Virginia Brissac (*Mrs. Marsh*), I. Stanford Jolley (*Ralph Brett*), Reid Kilpatrick (*Wilbur Chester*), Jack Norton (*Willie Rand*), Charles Sherlock (*Sgt. McGraw*), Janet Shaw (*Gloria Bayne*), Ben Carter (*Ben*), Milton Kibbee (*Herbert Sinclair*), Kernan Cripps (*The Detective*), Victoria Faust (*Hulda Swenson*), Charles Jordan (*Nelson*), Leonard Mudie (*Horace Carlos*)
<u>D</u>: Phil Rosen <u>SCR</u>: George Callahan, from characters created by Earl Derr Biggers <u>PHOTOG</u>: William A. Sickner <u>MUSIC</u>: Edward J. Kay
Minor "Charlie Chan" thriller: Oriental sleuth probes murders at radar plant

The Scarlet Daredevil
see **The Triumph of Sherlock Holmes**

The Scarlet Drop
1918, (USA), Univ, b&w, 5 reels
<u>W</u>: Harry Carey
<u>D & STORY</u>: John Ford <u>PHOTOG</u>: Ben Reynolds
Standard melodrama

The Scarlet Executioner
see **Il Boia Scarlatto**

The Scarlet Hour
1956, (USA), Para, b&w, 95 mins.
<u>W</u>: Carol Ohmart, Tom Tryon, Jody Lawrence, James Gregory, Elaine Stritch, E.G. Marshall, Edward Binns
<u>P & D</u>: Michael Curtiz <u>PHOTOG</u>: Lionel Lindon <u>MUSIC</u>: Leith Stevens
Standard melodrama: Marital discord leads to murder

The Scarlet Letter
1908, (USA), Kalem, b&w, 1 reel
from Nathaniel Hawthorne's novel
Standard melodrama: Colonial adulteress stigmatized

The Scarlet Letter
1911, (USA), IMP, b&w
from Nathaniel Hawthorne's novel
Standard melodrama: Adultery in Colonial America

The Scarlet Letter
1913, (GB), Urban, b&w
from Nathaniel Hawthorne's novel
Standard melodrama: Puritan woman stigmatized by adultery

The Scarlet Letter
1913, (USA), Kinemacolor Co. of America, color
<u>W</u>: Linda Arvidson [Mrs. D.W. Griffith]
from Nathaniel Hawthorne's novel
Standard melodrama: Adulteress shunned by society

The Scarlet Letter
1917, (USA), Fox, b&w, 5 reels
<u>W</u>: Stuart Holmes, Mary Martin, Kittens Reichert
from Nathaniel Hawthorne's novel
Standard melodrama: Woman's adultery foments tragedy

The Scarlet Letter
1920, (USA), Selznick, b&w, 1 reel
from Nathaniel Hawthorne's novel
Standard melodrama: Colonial woman commits adultery

The Scarlet Letter
1922, (GB), Master Films/BEF, b&w, 1,198 ft. (365.2m)
<u>W</u>: Sybil Thorndike (*Hester Prynne*), Tony Fraser (*Pastor Dimmesdale*), Dick Webb (*Roger Chillingsworth*), Rice Cassidy (*The Governor*)
<u>D</u>: Challis Sanderson <u>SCR</u>: Frank Miller, from Nathaniel Hawthorne's novel
Standard melodrama: Puritan branded as adulteress

The Scarlet Letter
1926, (USA), MGM, b&w, 9 reels (8,229 ft./2508.2m/88 mins.)
<u>W</u>: Lillian Gish (*Hester Prynne*), Lars Hanson (*Rev. Dimmesdale*), Henry B. Walthall (*Roger Prynne*), William H. Tooker (*The Governor*), Karl Dane (*Giles*), Marcelle Corday (*Mistress Hibbins*), Fred Herzog (*The Jailer*), James A. Marcus (*The French Sea Captain*), Jules Cowles (*The Beadle*), Joyce Coad (*Pearl*), Chief Yowlachie (*The Indian*), Polly Moran (*The Townswoman*), Mary Hawes (*Patience*)
<u>D</u>: Victor Seastrom <u>SCR</u>: Frances Marion, from Nathaniel Hawthorne's novel
"Made by the noted Swedish director Victor Seastrom, it is perhaps the most un-American film ever put out by Metro...The austere theme and backgrounds, the intermingling of beauty and sensitivity with bigotry and tragedy, these were elements that were second nature to the Scandinavian directors...Lillian Gish's performance...is almost certainly her finest in any film"—Joe Franklin, Classics of the Silent Screen
Classic melodrama: Puritans ostracize adulteress

The Scarlet Letter
1934, (USA), Majestic, b&w, 69 mins.
<u>W</u>: Colleen Moore (*Hester Prynne*), Hardie Albright (*Rev. Dimmesdale*), Henry B. Walthall (*Roger Prynne*), Iron Eyes Cody (*The Indian*), Cora Sue Collins (*Pearl*), Alan Hale, Betty Blythe, William Farnum, Virginia Howell, William Kent
<u>D</u>: Robert Vignola, from Nathaniel Hawthorne's novel
Classic melodrama: Puritan adulteress bears mark of shame

The Scarlet Letter
1972, (W. Ger-Sp), color, 90 mins.
<u>W</u>: Senta Berger, Hans Christian Blech, Lou Castel, Yelena Samarina, Yella Rottlander, William Layton

S

D: Wim Wenders, from Nathaniel Hawthorne's novel   **MUSIC:** Jurgen Knieper
Standard melodrama: Puritan woman commits adultery

The Scarlet Letter
1995, (USA), Andrew G. Vajna/Lightmotive/Allied Stars/Cinergi/Moving Pictures Prods./Hollywood, color, 135 mins.
W: Demi Moore (*Hester Prynne*), Gary Oldman (*Rev. Dimmesdale*), Robert Duvall (*Roger Prynne/ "Chillingworth"*), Robert Prosky, Edward Hardwicke, Joan Plowright, Amy Wright, Roy Dotrice
P & D: Roland Joffe   **SCR:** Douglas Day Stewart, from Nathaniel Hawthorne's novel   **PHOTOG:**, Alex Thomson   **MUSIC:** John Barry   **COSTUME DESIGN:** Gabriella Pescucci
Opulent melodrama (with happy ending Hawthorne never intended): Puritan adulteress gives all for love

The Scarlet Pimpernel
1934, (GB), London/UA, b&w, 98 mins.
W: Leslie Howard (*Sir Percy Blakeney*), Merle Oberon (*Marguerite Blakeney*), Raymond Massey (*Chauvelin*), Nigel Bruce (*The Prince of Wales*), Bramwell Fletcher (*The Priest*), Anthony Bushell (*Sir Andrew Foulkes*), Joan Gardner (*Suzanne de Tournay*), Walter Rilla (*Armand St. Just*), O.B. Clarence (*Count de Tournay*), Mabel Terry-Lewis (*Countess de Tournay*), Ernest Milton (*Robespierre*), Edmund Breon (*Winterbottom*), Melville Cooper (*Romney*), Gibb McLaughlin (*Barber*), Morland Graham (*Treadle*), Allan Jeayes (*Lord Greville*), A. Bromley Davenport (*The Innkeeper*), William Freshman (*Lord Hastings*), John Turnbull (*Jellyband*), Gertrude Musgrove (*The Daughter*), Hindle Edgar (*Lord Wilmot*), Bill Shine
P: Alexander Korda   **D:** Harold Young   **SCR:** Robert E. Sherwood, Sam Berman, Arthur Wimperis & Lajos Biro, from a novel by Baroness Orczy
PHOTOG:, Hal Rosson   **MUSIC:** Arthur Benjamin
reissued 1942 & 1947
Classic adventure-thriller: Nobleman rescues aristocrats from guillotine

The Scarlet Pimpernel (1950)
see The Elusive Pimpernel (1950)

The Scarlet Pimpernel
1982, (USA), CBS-TV, color, 142 mins.
W: Anthony Edwards (*Sir Percy Blakeney*), Jane Seymour (*Marguerite Blakeney*), Ian McKellen (*Chauvelin*), Malcolm Jamieson (*Armand*), James Villers (*DeBatz*), Eleanor David (*Louise*), Richard Morant (*Robespierre*), Dominic Jephcott (*Andrew*), Dennis Lill (*De Tournay*)
TVM, standard adventure-thriller: Englishman helps aristocrats flee Reign of Terror

The Scarlet Pimpernel
1999, (USA), A&E, color, 95 mins.
W: Richard E. Grant, Elizabeth McGovern
D: Patrick Lau, from a novel by Baroness Orczy

The Scarlett Shadow
1919, (USA), Univ, b&w, 6,000 ft. (1828.8m)
D: Robert Z. Leonard
Standard melodrama

The Scarlet Spear
1954, (GB), UA, color, 78 mins.
W: John Bentley, Martha Hyer
Standard adventure-thriller

Scarlet Thread
1951, (GB), Nettlefold-Int'l Realist/Butcher, b&w, 84 mins.
W: Kathleen Byron (*Josephine*), Laurence Harvey (*Freddie*), Sydney Tafler (*Marcon*), Arthur Hill (*Shaw*), Eliot Makeham (*Jason*), Dora Bryan (*Maggie*), Harry Fowler (*Sam*), Cyril Chamberlain (*Mason*), Renee Kelly (*Eleanor*)
P: Ernest G. Roy   **D:** Lewis Gilbert   **SCR:** A.R. Rawlinson, from a play by A.R. Rawlinson & Moie Charles
reissued 1953
Standard thriller: Crooks hide in university, try to steal jewels

The Scarlet Web
1954, (GB), Fortress/Eros, b&w, 63 mins.
W: Griffith Jones (*Jake Winter*), Zena Marshall (*Laura Vane*), Hazel Court (*Susan Honeywell*), Robert Percival (*Charles Dexter*), Molly Raynor (*Miss Riggs*), John Fitzgerald (*Bert*), Ronald Stevens (*Simpson*)
P: Frank Bevis   **D:** Charles Saunders   **STORY:** Doreen Montgomery
Standard crime-thriller: Insurance agent poses as ex-convict accused of stabbing girl

Scars of Dracula
1970, (GB), Hammer/Anglo-EMI/American Continental, color, 91 mins.
W: Christopher Lee (*Dracula*), Jenny Hanley (*Sarah Framsen*), Dennis Waterman (*Simon*), Christopher Matthews (*Paul*), Wendy Hamilton (*Julie*), Patrick Troughton (*Klove*), Michael Gwynn (*The Priest*), Bob Todd (*The Burgomaster*), Delia Lindsay (*Alice*), Anoushka Hempel (*Tania*), Toke Townley (*The Wagonmaster*), Michael Ripper (*The Landlord*), Margot Boht (*The Landlord's Wife*), David Lealand (*The 1st Officer*), Richard Durden (*The 2nd Officer*), Morris Bush (*The Farmer*), Clive Barrie (*The Fat Young Man*)
P: Aida Young   **D:** Roy Ward Baker   **SCR:** John Elder [Anthony Hinds]
PHOTOG:, Murray Grant   **SPCL-FX:** Roger Dicken   **MUSIC:** James Bernard
Standard horror-fantasy: Vampire returns to terrorize

Scary Movie
see Scream

The Scavengers
1959, (USA), Valiant, b&w, 79 mins.
W: Vince Edwards, Carol Ohmart
WRIT & P: Eddie Romero   **D:** John Cromwell
Minor melodrama: Former smuggler finds missing wife in Hong Kong

Lo Sceicco Bianco (The White Sheik)
1952, (It),PDC-OFI/Janus, b&w, 86 mins.
W: Alberto Sordi, Giulietta Masina, Brunella Bovo
D: Federico Fellini, from a story by Federico Fellini & Michelangelo Antonioni
       MUSIC: Nino Rota
Standard adventure-comedy

Scene of the Crime
1949, (USA), MGM, b&w, 95 mins.
W: Van Johnson, Gloria De Haven, Arlene Dahl Tom Drake, Leon Ames
D: Roy Rowland   **MUSIC:** Andre Previn
Standard thriller

Scenes from a Murder
1972, (It), color, 90 mins.
W: Telly savalas, Anne Heywood, Giorgio Piazza, Rossella Falk, Osvaldo Ruggeri
D: Alberto DeMartino
Minor thriller: Killer stalks actress

Schatten, eine Nachtliche Halluzination (Shadows, a Nocturnal Hallucination)
1922, (Ger), Defu, b&w, 70 mins.
W: Fritz Kortner, Ruth Weyher, Fritz Rasp Alexander Granach
D: Arthur Robison, from an idea by Albin Grau   **PHOTOG:**, Fritz Arno Wagner
*USA retitle, **Warning Shadows** (Film Arts, 1928)*
Standard fantasy: Mysterious wizard reveals possible futures of various nobles. cf.
       Invasion U.S.A.

Scheherazade
1963, (It-Fr-Sp), Speva-Cine-Alliance-Filmsonor-Dear-Tecisa/Shawn International, color, 115 mins.
W: Anna Karins (*Scheherazade*), Gerard Barray, Fausto Tozzi
Minor adventure-thriller: Charlemagne's nephew frees princess from Bedouin captors

The Schemers: or, The Jewels of Hate
1914, (GB), Hepworth, b&w, 1,800 ft. (548.6m)
W: Tom Powers (*James Mortimer*), Stewart Rome (*George Kingsley*), Alma Taylor (*Doreen Milford*), Violet Hopson (*Vera Mortimer*), Henry Vibart (*Mr. Milford*), Ruby Belasco (*Mrs. Milford*)
D: Frank Wilson
Standard melodrama

Schizo (1963)
see La Ragazza Che Sapeva Troppo

Schizo (1965)
see The Psychopath (1965)

Schizo
1977, (GB), Walker/Heritage/Niles Int'l, color, 105 mins.
W: Lynne Frederick (*Samantha*), John Leyton (*Alan*), John Fraser (*Leonard*), Stephanie Beacham (*Beth*), Jack Watson (*Haskin*), Victoria Allum (*Samantha as a Child*), Queenie Watts (*Mrs. Wallace*), Paul Alexander (*Peter*), John McEnery (*Stephens*), Trisha Mortimer (*Joy*), Robert Mill (*The Maitre d'*), Colin Jeavons (*The Commissioner*), Diane King (*Mrs. Falconer*), Raymond Bowers (*The Manager*), Lindsay Campbell (*Falconer*), Terry Duggan (*The Editor*), Victor Winding (*The Sergeant*), Pearl Hackney (*The Lady at the Seance*), Primi Townsend (*The Secretary*), Wendy Gilmore (*Samantha's Mother*), David McGillivray (*The Man*)
P & D: Peter Walker   **SCR:** David McGillivray   **PHOTOG:**, Peter Jessop
MUSIC: Stanley Myers
*A.k.a. **Amok** and **Blood of the Undead***
Standard thriller: Woman haunted by mother's murder

Schizoid (1971)
see A Lizard in a Woman's Skin

Schizoid
1980, (USA), Golan-Globus/Cannon, color, 87 mins.
W: Klaus Kinski (*Pieter Fales*), Donna Wilkes (*Allison Fales*), Marianna Hill (*Julie*), Craig Wasson (*Doug*), Richard Herd (*Donahue*), Joe Regalbuto (*Jake*), Christopher Lloyd (*Gilbert*), Flo Gerrish (*Pat*), Kiva Lawrence (*Rosemary*), Claude Duvernoy (*Francoise*), Cindy Donlan (*Sally*), David Assael (*Barney*), Jon Greene (*Archie*), Gracia Lee (*Bruce*), Richard Balin (*Freddy*), Fredric Cook (*Willy*), Tobar Mayo (*Fritz*), Kathy Garrick (*Maxine*), Jonathan Millner (*Fritz' Friend*), Frances Nealy (*The Housekeeper*), Kimberly Jensen (*The Girl on the Motorbike*), Jay May (*The Boy on the Motorbike*)
WRIT & D: David Paulsen   **PHOTOG:** Norman Leigh   **SPCL-FX:** Joe Quinlivan   **MUSIC:** Craig Hundley
*Standard thriller: Members of therapy group are brutally dispatched. A.k.a. **Murder by Mail***

S

Schizopolis
1997, (USA), 406 Ltd., color, 96 mins.
W: Steven Soderbergh (*Fletcher Munson/Dr. Jeffrey Korchek*), Betsy Brantley (*The Wife/Attractive Woman No. 2*), Mike Malone (*T. Azimuth Schwitters*)
WRIT & D: Steven Soderbergh
Bizarre, Kafkaesque satire: Corporate drone assumes dentist's persona

Die Schlangengrube und das Pendel (The Pit and the Pendel)
1967, (W. Ger), Constantin-Film/Hemisphere, color, 85 mins.
W: Christopher Lee, Karin Dor, Lex Barker
P: Wolfgang Kuhnlenz   **D:** Harald Reinl   **SCR:** Manfred R. Kohler, loosely based upon Edgar Allan Poe's short story
USA retitle, **Blood Demon** *(Hemisphere, 1969), 73 mins. A.k.a.* **The Torture Chamber of Dr. Sadism** *orig. to be titled* **The Snake Pit**
Standard horror-thriller: Vampire seeks revenge

Schlock
1972, (USA), Jack H. Harris, color, 77 mins.
W: John Landis, Forrest J. Ackerman, John Chambers, Jack H. Harris Saul Kahan, Joseph Piantadosi, Eliza Garrett Saul Kahan, Joseph Piantadosi, Eliza Garrett, Eric Allison, Enrica Blankey, Charles Villiers
P: James C. O'Rourke   **D & SCR:** John Landis   **PHOTOG:** Bob Collins
MUSIC: David Gibson
A.k.a. **The Banana Monster**
Standard horror-satire (John Landis' first cinematic effort): Prehistoric ape man terrorizes

Das Schloss (The Castle)
1968, (W. Ger), Continental, color, 90 mins.
W: Maximilian Schell ("K"), Cordula Trantow (*Frieda*), Helmut Qualtinger (*Burgel*), Johann Misar (*Jeremiah*), Franz Misar (*Arthur*), Hanns Ernst Jager (*The Landlord*), Georg Lehn (*Barnabas*), Friedrich Maurer (*The Mayor*), Leo Mally (*Gerstaecker*), Else Ehser (*Mizzi*), Iva Janzurova (*Olga*), Martha Wallner (*Amalia*), Karl Hellmer (*The Schoolmaster*), Ilse Kunkele (*The Schoolmistress*), Benno Hoffmann (*The Uniformed Man*), E.O. Fuhrmann (*Momus*), Hans Possnebacher (*The Innkeeper*), Armand Ozory (*Erlanger*)
P: Maximilian Schell   **WRIT & D:** Rudolf Noelte, from Franz Kafka's novel
PHOTOG:, Wolfgang Treu
Allegorical thriller: Man battles suffocating bureaucracy

Schloss Vogelod (Castle Vogelod)
1921, (Ger), Decla-Bioscop, b&w, 75 mins.
W: Paul Hartmann, Olga Tschechowa, Arnold Korff, Paul Bildt
P: Erich Pommer   **D:** F.W. Murnau   **SCR:** Carl Mayer & Berthold Viertel, from Rudolf Stratz' novel   **PHOTOG:,** Fritz Arno Wagner
USA retitle, **The Haunted Castle**
Standard thriller: Strange happenings at elegant country mansion

School Spirit
1985, (USA), Amritraj Chroma III, color, 88 mins.
W: Tom Nolan (*Billy Batson*), Elizabeth Foxx (*Judith Hightower*), John Finnegan (*Pinky*), Daniele Arnaud (*Madeleine*), Larry Linville (*Pres. Grimshaw*), Roberta Collins (*Helen Grimshaw*), Marta Kober (*Ursula*), Nick Segal (*Gregg*), Toni Hudson (*Rita*), Frank Mugavero (*Lasky*), Brian Mann (*Barducci*), David Byrd (*The Boss*), Julie Gray (*Kendall*), Robert Briscoe, Johnny Lee, Jimbo Goodwin, Leslie Bohem, Michael Miller, David Kendrick, Bob Haag, Leslee Bremer, Laurence Haddon, Beach Dickerson, Cynthia Harrison, Karen Smythe, Helen Vick, Liz Sheridan, Pamela Ward, Jay Scorpio, Diane Hoyes, Laura Lee Kasten, Marlene Janssen, Biff Yeager, Jay Cohen, Charles Dayton, Becky LeBeau, Dina Russo, Katherine McBride, Jacki Easton, Jeff Yesko, Daniel Friedman, Sandra Grass, Deke Anderson, Tony Baldrama, Linda Carol, Theresa Mesquita, Kathi Pierce, Leslie Kelly, Susan Schroeder
D: Alan Holleb   **SCR:** Geoffrey Baere   **PHOTOG:** Robert Ebinger   **MUSIC:** Tom Bruner   **SONGS:** *Hot for You Tonight, Bad Hangover Everyday I Stay in Love With You, Dedication, Amor, Here Comes Mr. Fun Hog, String Trio in D, I Want More, A Boy and a Girl, Kiss Me Where It Hurts & Doin' Those Things You Do,* performed by The Gleaming Spires
Minor sex-fantasy: Randy college student becomes ghost

The School That Ate My Brain
see **Zombie High**

Schuss im Morgengrauen (A Shot at Dawn)
1933, (Ger), Sam Spiegel, b&w
W: Peter Lorre, Oscar Homolka
D: Alfred Zeisler
USA retitle, **Invisible Opponent**
Standard thriller

Der Schweigende Stern
see **Milczaca Gwiazda**

Science Crazed
1990, (Can), color, 90 mins.
W: Cameron Klein
D: Ron Switzer
Minor SF-thriller: Scientist creates monster

SCI-Fighters
1996, (USA), color, 95 mins.
W: Roddy Piper, Billy Drago, Jayne Heitmeyer
D: Peter Svatek
Campy SF-thriller: Renegade cop trails escaped rapist

Scissors
1991, (USA), color, 105 mins.
W: Sharon Stone, Steve Railsback, Michelle Phillips, Ronny Cox
D: Frank De Felitta
Minor thriller

Scorned
1994, (USA), color, 100 mins.
W: Andrew Stevens
*Standard thriller (***Hand That Rocks the Cradle*** imitation): Vengeful woman plagues man she holds responsible for her husband's suicide*

Scorpian with Two Tails
1982, (USA), color, 99 mins.
W: John Saxon, Van Johnson
Minor thriller: Woman dreams of grotesque deaths

Scorpio
1972, (USA), color, 114 mins.
W: Burt Lancaster, Alain Delon, Paul Scofield, John Colicos, Gayle Hunnicutt, J.D. Cannon, Joanne Linville, James B. Sikking
D: Michael Winner
Standard thriller: Betrayal and death among spies

The Scorpio Letters
1966, (USA), MGM, Made for TV, color, 97 mins.
W: Alex Cord, Shirley Eaton, Laurence Naismith
P & D: Richard Thorpe   **TELEPLAY:** Adrian Spies & Jo Eisinger   **PHOTOG:** Ellsworth Fredericks
TVM, minor thriller: Secret agents smash blackmailing ring

The Scorpion's Sting
see **The Devil's Bondman**

Scotland Yard
1930, (USA), Fox, b&w, 8 reels (6,750 ft./2057.4m/65 mins.)
W: Edmund Lowe (*Sir John Lasher/Dakin Barrolles*), Joan Bennett (*Xandra, Lady Lasher*), Donald Crisp (*Charles Fox*), Georges Renevant (*Dr. Dean*), David Torrence (*Capt. Graves*), Lumsden Hare (*Sir Clive Heathcote*), Barbara Leonard (*Nurse Cecilia*), Halliwell Hobbes (*Lord St. Arran*), Arnold Lucy (*McKillop*), J. Carrol Naish (*Dr. Remur*)
P: Ralph Block   **D:** William K. Howard   **SCR & DIALOG:** Garrett Fort, from Denison Clift's 1929 play   **PHOTOG:** George Schneiderman
Standard thriller: Thief has plastic surgery, supplants nobleman

Scotland Yard
1941, (USA), 20th-Fox, b&w, 68 mins.
W: Nancy Kelly, Edmund Gwenn, Henry Wilcoxon, John Loder, Melville Cooper, Gilbert Emery, Norma Varden
D: Norman Foster   **SCR:** Samuel G. Engel & John L. Balderston, from a play by Denison Clift   **PHOTOG:,** Virgil Miller
Standard thriller: Nazis kidnap London banker

Scotland Yard Dragnet
see **The Hypnotist**

Scotland Yard Inspector
see **Lady in the Fog**

Scotland Yard Investigator
1945, (USA), Rep, b&w, 68 mins.
W: Erich von Stroheim, C. Aubrey Smith, Stephanie Bachelor, Forrester Harvey, Doris Lloyd, Eva Moore
D: George Blair
Standard thriller: Art theft probed

The Scotland Yard Mystery
1934, (GB), BIP/Wardour, b&w, 76 mins.
W: Gerald du Maurier (*Insp. Stanton*), George Curzon (*Dr. Masters*), Grete Natzler [Della Lind] (*Irene*), Leslie Perrins (*John*), Belle Chrystal (*Mary Stanton*), Paul Graetz (*Paston*), Wally Patch (*Sgt. George*), Henry Victor (*Floyd*)
D: Thomas Bentley   **SCR:** Frank Miller, from a play by Wallace Geoffrey
USA retitle, **The Living Dead** *(Alliance/First Division)*
Standard thriller: Crook injects victims with life-suspending serum, collects insurance

The Scout's Motto
1914, (GB), Martin/DFSA, b&w, 827 ft. (252.1m)
D: Dave Aylott
Standard crime-thriller: Scout trails burglar, is rescued by his troop

Scouts to the Rescue
1909, (GB), Williamson, b&w, 550 ft. (167.6m)

S

W: Frank Sutherland (*The Gypsy Man*), Mrs. Sutherland (*The Gypsy Woman*), Dave Aylott (*Farmer Giles*), Anita March (*Mrs. Giles*)
D & STORY: Dave Aylott
Standard thriller: Scouts track gypsies, save farmer's kidnapped child

Scream

1996, (USA), Woods Entertainment/Dimension, color, 110 mins.
W: Courteney Cox (*Gale Weathers*), Neve Campbell (*Sidney Prescott*), David Arquette (*Deputy Dewey Riley*), Jamie Kennedy (*Randy*), Skeet Ulrich, Matthew Lillard, Rose McGowan, Lisa Beach, Ryan Kennedy, W. Earl Brown, Lisa Canning, Kevin Patrick Walls, Lawrence Hecht, Aurora Draper, David Booth, Troy Bishop, Kurtis Bedford, Carla Hatley, Roger Jackson, Kenny Kwong, Frances Lee McCain, Tony Kilbert, Nancy Ann Ridder, C.W. Morgan, Angela Miller, Lois Saunders, Leonora Scelfo, Bonnie Wood, Justin Sullivan, Joseph Whipp, Joshua Jackson
D: Wes Craven **SCR:** Kevin Williamson **PHOTOG:** Mark Irwin **MUSIC:** Marco Beltrami **SONGS:** *Drop Dead Gorgeous, Artificial World, Better Than Me, Bitter Pill, I Don't Care, Red Right Hand, Whisper & Youth of America*
*orig. to be titled **Scary Movie***
Entertaining horror-satire: Group of youths ponders elements of classic film thrillers, becomes fodder for mad killer

Scream II

1997, (USA), Dimension, color, 120 mins.
W: Neve Campbell (*Sidney Prescott*), Courteney Cox (*Gale Weathers*), David Arquette, Liev Schreiber, Jamie Kennedy, Sarah Michelle Gellar, Duane Martin, Jada Pinkett, Jerry O'Connell Timothy Olyphant, Portia Da Rossi, David Warner, Rebecca Gayheart, Laurie Metcalf, Diane Martin, Elise Neal Lewis Arquette, Heather Graham, Omar Epps, Paulette Patterson, Kevin Williamson
D: Wes Craven **SCR:** Kevin Williamson **PHOTOG:** Peter Deming **MUSIC:** Marco Beltrami
Entertaining horror-satire: New murders terrify

Scream and Die!

1973, (GB), Blackwater/Variety, color, 99 mins.
W: Andrea Allan (*Valerie*), Karl Lanchbury (*Paul*), Maggie Walker (*Aunt Susanna*), Peter Forbes-Robertson (*Hornby*), Judy Matheson (*Lorna*), Annabella Wood (*Stella*), Lawrence Keane (*Mike*), Alex Leppard (*Terry*), Daphne Lea (*The Landlady*), Raymond Young (*The Driver*)
P: Diana Daubeney **D:** Joseph Larraz **STORY:** Derek Ford **PHOTOG:**, Trevor Wrenn **MUSIC:** Terry Warr
*reissued (1977) as **Psycho Sex Fiend** USA retitle, **The House That Vanished** (AIP, 1974, 95 mins)*
Standard thriller: Model finds artist is sex killer

Scream and Scream Again

1970, (GB), AIP, color, 94 mins.
W: Vincent Price (*Dr. Browning*), Christopher Lee (*Fremont*), Peter Cushing (*Maj. Benedek*), Marshall Jones (*Konratz*), Alfred Marks (*Supt. Bellaver*), Christopher Matthews (*David*), Michael Gothard (*Keith*), Uta Levka (*Jane*), Judy Huxtable (*Sylvia*), Kenneth Benda (*Kingsmill*), David Lodge (*Strickland*), Peter Sallis (*Schweitz*), Anthony Newlands (*Ludwig*), Judi Bloom (*Helen*), Clifford Earl (*Det. Joyce*)
P: Max J. Rosenberg & Milton Subotsky **D:** Gordon Hessler **SCR:** Christopher Wicking, from Peter Saxon's novel *The Disoriented Man* **PHOTOG:**, John Coquillon **MUSIC:** David Whitaker
Standard horror-thriller: Mad Scientist assembles "perfect" people

Scream, Baby, Scream

1969, (USA), Westbury, color, 86 mins.
W: Ross Harris **P & D:** Joseph Adler **SCR:** Lawrence Robert Cohen **MUSIC:** Odyssey Eugenie Wingate, Chris Martell, Suzanne Stuart, Larry Swinson, Brad Grinter
D: Joseph Adler
*A.k.a. **Nightmare House***
Standard horror-thriller: Demented artist kidnaps people, disfigures them to provide models for creepy paintings

Scream, Blacula, Scream

1973, (USA), AIP, color, 96 mins.
W: William Marshall (*Mamuwalde*), Pam Grier (*Lisa*), Michael Conrad (*The Sheriff*), Don Mitchell (*Justin*), Richard Lawson (*Willis*), Barbara Rhoades (*Elaine*), Bernie Hamilton (*The Ragman*), Lynn Moody (*Denny*), Beverly Gill (*Maggie*), Janee Michelle (*Gloria*), Don Blackman (*The Doll Man*), Van Kirksey (*Prof. Walston*), Arnold Williams (*Louis*)
P: Joseph T. Narr **D:** Bob Kelljan **SCR:** Joan Torres, Raymond Koenig & Maurice Jules **STORY:** Joan Torres & Raymond Koenig **PHOTOG:** Isidore Mankofsky **MUSIC:** Bill Marx **SONG:** *Torment*
*Standard horror-fantasy (sequel to **Blacula**): Vampire pursues reborn love*

Scream Bloody Murder

1972, (USA), Indepix, color, 90 mins.
W: Paul Vincent, Marlena Lustik Fred Holbert, Leigh Mitchell, Robert Knox, A. Maana Tanelah, Suzette Hamilton Fred Holbert, Leigh Mitchell, Suzanne Hamilton, Robert Knox
P, D & SCR: Robert J. Emery
blurb: "So horrifying you need a blindfold to see it!"
Minor thriller: Killer with hook hand goes on rampage

Scream Dream

1989, (USA), color, 80 mins.
W: Melissa Moore, Carole Carr, Nikki Riggins, Jesse Ray
D & SCR: Donald Farmer
Minor horror-fantasy: Beautiful rock star's supernatural powers turn fans into monsters

Screamer

1974, (GB), Made for TV, color, 71 mins.
W: Pamela Franklin, Frances White (*Virna*), Jim Norton (*The Man*), Donal McCann (*Jeff*), Peter Howell (*Dr. Ward*), Derek Smith (*The Inspector*), George Pravda (*Balsam*)
TVM, minor thriller: Young woman fears rapist is stalking her

Screamers (1978)
*see **The Fish Men***

Screamers

1996, (Can), Allegro/Triumph, color, 108 mins.
W: Peter Weller (*Col. Hendricksson*), Andy Lauer (*Ace*), Roy Dupuis (*Becker*), Charles Powell (*Ross*), Jennifer Rubin (*Jessica*), Ron White, Michael Caloz, Liliana Komorowska, Jason Cavalier, Leni Parker, Sylvain Masso, Bruce Boa, Henry Ramer
D: Christian Duguay **SCR:** Dan O'Bannon & Miguel Tejada-Flores, based on Philip K. Dick's 1952 short story "Second Variety" **PHOTOG:** Rodney Gibbons **VS-FX SPRVSR:** Ernest Farino **MUSIC:** Normand Corbeil
Unusual SF-thriller: Hybrid mining creatures turn murderous

Scream for Help

1985, (GB), Torremodo/Videoform/Lorimar/Miracle, color, 89 mins.
W: Rachael Kelly (*Christie Cromwell*), David Brooks (*Paul Fox*), Marie Masters (*Karen Cromwell Fox*), Rocco Sisto (*Lacey Bohle*), Lolita Lorre (*Brenda Bohle*), Corey Parker (*Josh Dealey*), Tony Sibbald (*Bob Dealey*), Sandra Clark (*Janey Ralston*), Stacey Hughes (*Seudi*), Leslie Lowe (*The Girl*), David Baxt (*Jerry*), Morgan Deare (*Peacock*), Sarah Brackett (*The Sec'y*), Clare Burt (*Patty Sea*), Diane Ricardo (*Mrs. Ralston*), Matthew Peters (*Charlie*), Robyn Mandell (*The Nurse*), Burnell Tucker (*Ralston*), Bruce Boa (*The Surgeon*), Michael Corby, Marlene Marcus
P & D: Michael Winner **STORY:** Tom Holland **PHOTOG:** Robert Paynter & Dick Kratina **MUSIC:** John Paul Jones, Howard Blake & Johnny Pearson
Standard thriller (filmed in USA): Teen suspects stepfather is plotting her mother's murder

A Scream From Silence

1979, (Can), color, 96 mins.
W: Julie Vincent, Germain Houde, Paul Savoie, Monique Miller, Micheline Lanctot
D: Anne Claire Poirier
Harrowing psychodrama: Rape victim's life disintegrates

Screaming Mimi

1958, (USA), Sage/Col, b&w, 79 mins.
W: Anita Ekberg, Phil Carey, Harry Townes, Gypsy Rose Lee, Linda Cherney, Romney Brent, Alan Gifford, Oliver McGowan, Stephen Ellsworth, Vaughn Taylor, Frank Scannell, Red Norvo and Trio
P: Harry Joe Brown **D:** Gerd Oswald **SCR:** Robert Blees, from Frederick Brown's novel **PHOTOG:**, Burnett Guffey **MUSIC:** Mischa Bakaleinikoff
Standard thriller: Striptease artist terrorized

The Screaming Skull

1958, (USA), Madera/AIP, b&w, 68 mins.
W: John Hudson (*Eric*), Peggy Webber (*Jenni*), Alex Nicol, Russ Conway, Tony Johnson
WRIT & P: John Kneubuhl **D:** Alex Nicol **PHOTOG:** Floyd Crosby **MUSIC:** Ernest Gold
Modest horror-thriller: Bride menaced on eerie estate

The Screaming Woman

1972, (USA), Univ/ABC-TV, color, 73 mins.
W: Olivia de Havilland (*Laura Wynant*), Laraine Stephens (*Caroline Wynant*), Joseph Cotten (*George Tresvant*), Gene Andrusco (*David*), Charles Knox Robinson (*Howard Wynant*), Ed Nelson, Alexandra Hay (*Evie Carson*), Walter Pidgeon (*Dr. Amos Larkin*), Jan Arvan (*Martin*), Russell G. Wiggins (*Harry Sands*), Charles Drake (*Ken Bronson*), Joyce Cunning (*Bernice Wilson*), Ray Montgomery (*Ted Wilson*), John Alderman (*Slater*), Jackie Russell, Lonny Chapman, Kay Stewart, Russell Thorson
P: William Frye **D:** Jack Smight **TELEPLAY:** Merwin Gerard, from a story by Ray Bradbury **PHOTOG:** Sam Leavitt **MUSIC:** John Williams
TVM, standard thriller: Woman buried alive

Scream in the Night

1935, (USA), Commodore/Astor, b&w, 58 mins.
W: Lon Chaney Jr.
*orig. to be titled **The Riot Squad**. Reissued in 1943*
Minor melodrama

Scream of Fear
*see **A Taste of Fear***

Scream of the Butterfly

1965, (USA), Emerson, b&w, 76 mins.
W: Nick Novarro, Nelida Lobato, William Turner
P: Ray Dennis Steckler   **D:** Ebar Lobato
*Minor thriller: Nymphomaniac killed by lover. A.k.a. **The Passion Pit.***

Scream of the Demon Lover

1971, (It-Sp), New World, color, 84 mins.
W: Jeffrey Chase *(The Baron)*, Jennifer Hartley *(Ivana)*, Ronald Grey *(The Inspector)*, Agostina Belli, Giancarlo Fantini, Cristiana Galloni, Antonio Gimenez Escribano, Enzo Fisichella, Mariano Vidal Molina, Ezio Sancrotti, Franco Moraldi, Paracchi Renato
P & D: J.L. Merino   **STORY & SCR:** E. Colombo & J.L. Merino   **PHOTOG:** Emanuele Di Cola   **MUSIC:** Luigi Malatesta
Minor horror-thriller: Unknown killer stalks 19th-century village

Scream of the Wolf

1974, (USA), Metromedia/ABC-TV, color, 74 mins.
W: Peter Graves, Clint Walker, Jo Ann Pflug, Philip Carey, Don Megowan, Brian Richards, Lee Paul, Bonnie Van Dyke, Grant Owens, Jim Storm, Dean Smith, Orville Sherman
D: Dan Curtis   **TELEPLAY:** Richard Matheson
*TVM, modest horror-fantasy: **Werewolf** hysteria grips small town*

Screamplay

1987, (USA), Troma, color
W: Rufus Butler Seder *(Edgar Allen)*, George Kuchar *(Martin)*
WRIT & D: Rufus Butler Seder
Minor thriller

Scream, Pretty Peggy

1973, (USA), ABC-TV, color, 74 mins.
W: Bette Davis *(Mrs. Elliott)*, Charles Drake *(George Thornton)*, Ted Bessell *(Jeffrey Elliott)*, Tovah Feldshuh *(Agnes Thornton)*, Sian Barbara Allen *(Peggy Johns)*, Jessica Rains *(Lloyd, the Office Girl)*, Allan Arbus *(Dr. Eugene Saks)*, Johnnie Collins III *(The Student)*, Christiana Schmidtmer *(Jennifer Elliott)*
P: Lou Morheim   **D:** Gordon Hessler   **TELEPLAY:** Jimmy Sangster & Arthur Hoffe   **PHOTOG:** Leonard J. South   **MUSIC:** Bob Prince
TVM, standard thriller: College student becomes part-time housekeeper in creepy mansion

Screams of a Winter Night

1979, (USA), Full Moon/Dimension, color, 91 mins.
W: Matt Borel, Gil Glascow, Mary Agen Cox, Patrick Byers, Robin Bradley, Ray Gaspard, Beverly Allen, Brandy Barrett, Jan Norton, Charles Rucker
P: Richard Wadsack & James Wilson   **D:** James L. Wilson   **SCR:** Richard H. Wadsack   **MUSIC SCORE:** Don Zimmers
Minor thriller: Teenage campers tell several scary tales

Screamtime

1983, (GB), color, 89 mins.
W: Jean Anderson, Robin Bailey Dora Bryan, David Van Day
D: Al Beresford
Minor horror-fantasy: Two friends watch terror tales on stolen video tapes, meet real-life demon

Scroggins Goes in for Chemistry and Discovers a Marvellous Powder

1911, (GB), Cricks & Martin, b&w, 525 ft. (160m)
D: A.E. Coleby
Standard comedy-fantasy: Scroggins shrinks bride, constable, lamp-post

Scroggins Has His Fortune Told

1911, (GB), Cricks & Martin, b&w, 465 ft. (141.7m)
D: A.E. Coleby
*USA retitle, **Scroggins Visits a Palmist***
Standard comedy-fantasy: Palmist's prediction comes true

Scroggins Visits a Palmist

see Scroggins Has His Fortune Told

Scrooge

1913, (GB), Zenith Films, b&w, 2,500 ft. (762m)
W: Seymour Hicks *(Ebenezer Scrooge)*, William Lugg, Leedham Bantock, J.C. Buckstone, Dorothy Buckstone, Osborne Adair, Leonard Calvert, Adela Measor
D: Leedham Bantock   **SCR:** Seymour Hicks, from Charles Dickens' *A Christmas Carol*
Standard fantasy: Miser reformed by ghosts

Scrooge

1922, (GB), Master Films/BEF, b&w, 1,280 ft. (390.1m)
W: H.V. Esmond *(Ebenezer Scrooge)*
D: George Wynn   **SCR:** W.C. Rowden, from Charles Dickens' *A Christmas Carol*
Standard fantasy: Spirits reform skinflint

Scrooge

1923, (GB), B&C/Walturdaw, b&w, 1,600 ft. (487.7m)
W: Russell Thorndike *(Ebenezer Scrooge)*, Jack Denton *(Bob Cratchit)*, Nina Vanna *(Alice)*, Forbes Dawson *(Marley)*

D: Edwin Greenwood   **SCR:** Eliot Stannard, from Charles Dickens' *A Christmas Carol*
*Standard fantasy (episode from **Gems of Literature** series): Yuletide spirits reform miser*

Scrooge

1928, (GB), British Sound Film Prods., b&w, 9 mins.
W: Bransby Williams *(Ebenezer Scrooge)*
D: Hugh Croise   **SCR:** Bransby Williams, from Charles Dickens' *A Christmas Carol*
Fantasy short: Old miser haunted by dead business partner

Scrooge

1935, (GB), Twickenham, b&w, 78 mins.
W: Seymour Hicks *(Ebenezer Scrooge)*, Donald Calthrop *(Bob Cratchit)*, Robert Cochran *(Fred)*, Mary Glynne *(Belle)*, Oscar Asche *(Christmas Present)*, Maurice Evans *(The Poor Man)*, Mary Lawson *(The Poor Man's Wife)*, Athene Seyler *(The Charwoman)*, Garry Marsh *(Belle's Husband)*, Morris Harvey *(The Poulterer)*, Barbara Everest *(Mrs. Cratchit)*, C.V. France *(Christmas Future)*, Eve Gray *(Fred's Wife)*, D.J. Williams *(The Undertaker)*, Philip Frost *(Tiny Tim Cratchit)*, Marie Ney *(Christmas Past)*, Charles Carson *(Middlemark)*, Hugh E. Wright *(Joe)*, Margaret Yarde *(The Laundress)*
D: Henry Edwards   **SCR:** Seymour Hicks & H. Fowler Mear, from Charles Dickens' *A Christmas Carol*   **PHOTOG:** Sydney Blythe & William Luff   **MUSIC:** W.L. Trytel
Standard fantasy: Visions reform miser

Scrooge

1951, (GB), Renown/UA, b&w, 86 mins.
W: Alastair Sim *(Ebenezer Scrooge)*, Kathleen Harrison *(Mrs. Dilber)*, Jack Warner *(Mr. Jorkins)*, Michael Hordern *(Jacob Marley)*, Mervyn Johns *(Bob Cratchit)*, Hermione Baddeley *(Mrs. Cratchit)*, Clifford Mollison *(Mr. Wilkins)*, George Cole *(Young Scrooge)*, Rona Anderson *(Alice)*, Glyn Dearman *(Tiny Tim)*, John Charlesworth *(Peter Cratchit)*, Francis De Wolff *(Christmas Present)*, Carol Marsh *(Fan)*, Brian Worth *(Fred)*, Miles Malleson *(Old Joe)*, Ernest Thesiger *(The Undertaker)*, Michael Dolan *(Christmas Past)*, Roddy Hughes *(Mr. Fezziwig)*, Fred Johnson, Hugh Dempster, Eliot Makeham, Peter Bull
P & D: Brian Desmond Hurst   **ADAPT & SCR:** Noel Langley, from Charles Dickens' *A Christmas Carol*   **PHOTOG:** C. Pennington-Richards   **MUSIC:** Richard Addinsell
*USA retitle, **A Christmas Carol***
reissued 1955
Superior film-version of classic fantasy: Spirits change miser's perspective

Scrooge

1970, (GB), Cinema Center Films/Nat'l General, color, 118 mins.
W: Albert Finney *(Ebenezer Scrooge)*, Alec Guinness *(Marley's Ghost)*, Dame Edith Evans *(Ghost of Christmas Past)*, David Collings *(Bob Cratchit)*, Kenneth More *(Ghost of Christmas Present)*, Laurence Naismith *(Fezziwig)*, Anton Rodgers *(Tom Jenkins)*, Michael Medwin *(Scrooge's Nephew)*, Richard Beaumont *(Tiny Tim)*, Suzanne Neve *(Isabel)*, Geoffrey Bayldon *(The Toy Shop Owner)*, Derek Francis *(A Portly Gentleman)*, Gordon Jackson *(Scrooge's Nephew's Friend)*, Roy Kinnear *(A Portly Gentleman)*, Mary Peach *(The Wife of Scrooge's Nephew)*, Paddy Stone *(Ghost of Christmas Yet to Come)*, Kay Walsh *(Mrs. Fezziwig)*, Molly Weir *(A Woman Debtor)*, Helen Gloag *(A Woman Debtor)*, Reg Lever *(The Punch & Judy Man)*, Keith March *(The Well Wisher)*, Marianne Stone *(A Party Guest)*
D: Ronald Neame   **SCR, MUSIC, & LYRICS:** Leslie Bricusse, from Charles Dickens' *A Christmas Carol*   **PHOTOG:** Oswald Morris   **ADDITIONAL MUSIC:** Ian Fraser   **SONGS:** *Thank You Very Much* & *I Hate People*
Standard musical fantasy: Miser reformed by Yule spirits

Scrooged

1988, (USA), Art Linson-Mirage/Para, color, 115 mins.
W: Bill Murray *(Frank Cross)*, Karen Allen *(Claire Phillips)*, John Forsythe *(Lew Hayward)*, Carol Kane *(Ghost of Christmas Present)*, Robert Mitchum *(Preston Rhinelander)*, John Glover *(Brice Cummings)*, David Johansen *(Ghost of Christmas Past)*, Bobcat Goldthwaite, Michael J. Pollard, Alfre Woodard, John Houseman, Buddy Hackett, Pat McCormick
D: Richard Donner   **SCR:** Mitch Glazer & Michael O'Donoghue, inspired by Charles Dickens' *A Christmas Carol*   **PHOTOG:** Michael Chapman   **MUSIC:** Danny Elfman
Major comedy-fantasy: Ruthless businessman visited by Yule spirits

Scrooge: or, Marley's Ghost

1901, (GB), R.W. Paul, b&w, 620 ft. (189m)
D: Walter R. Booth, from Charles Dickens' *A Christmas Carol*
Standard fantasy (in 13 scenes): Miser reforms after visions of past, present and future

The Sculptor's Dream

1910, (GB), Cricks & Martin, b&w, 480 ft. (146.3m)
D: A.E. Coleby
Standard fantasy: Every time sculptor embraces model she changes shape

The Sculptors' Jealous Model

1904, (GB), R.W. Paul, b&w, 183 ft. (55.1m)
Standard thriller: Model stabs sculptor, commits suicide

S

The Sea Beast

1926, (USA), WB, b&w, 10 reels (10,250 ft./3124.2m)
W: John Barrymore *(Ahab Creeley)*, Dolores Costello *(Esther Harper)*, George O'Hara *(Derek Creeley)*, Mike Donlin *(Flask)*, Sam Baker *(Queequeg)*, George Burrell *(Perth)*, Sam Allen *(The Sea Captain)*, Frank Nelson *(Stubbs)*, Mathilde Comont *(Mula)*, James Barrows *(Rev. Harper)*, Vadim Uraneff *(Pip)*, Sojin *(Fedallah)*, Frank Hagney *(Daggoo)*, Leonora Summers
D: Millard Webb   ADAPT: Bess Meredyth, loosely based on Herman Melville's 1851 novel *Moby Dick*   PHOTOG: Byron Haskin   ADDTL PHOTOG: Frank Kesson
Standard melodrama: Passions on the briney

Sea Creatures
see Beyond Atlantis

Sealed Verdict

1948, (USA), Para, b&w, 83 mins.
W: Ray Milland, Florence Marly [US Debut] , Broderick Crawford John Hoyt, John Ridgely
D: Lewis Allen
Standard thriller: Army lawyer falls in love with woman traitor

Seance de Prestidigitation

1896, (Fr), b&w, 20m (65.6 ft./1.1 mins.)
USA retitle, *Conjuring*
Standard fantasy

Seance on a Wet Afternoon

1964, (GB), Richard Attenborough-Bryan Forbes/Beaver/Allied Film Makers /Artixo/ Artie Shaw-Don Getz, b&w, 111 mins.
W: Kim Stanley *(Myra Savage)*, Richard Attenborough *(Billy Savage)*, Nanette Newman *(Mrs. Clayton)*, Patrick Magee *(Supt. Walsh)*, Mark Eden *(Charles Clayton)*, Marian Spencer *(Mrs. Wintry)*, Gerald Sim *(Sgt. Beedle)*, Lionel Gamlin *(The Man)*, Judith Donner *(Amanda Clayton)*, Arnold Bell *(Mr. Weaver)*, Diana Lambert *(The Secretary)*, Marie Burke *(The Woman)*, Ronald Hines
P: Richard Attenborough   WRIT & D: Bryan Forbes, from Mark McShane's novel   PHOTOG: Gerry Turpin   MUSIC: John Barry
Intense thriller: Demented medium has child kidnapped

Sea People
see Beyond Atlantis

The Sea Pirate

1967, (It), color, 85 mins.
W: Gerald Barray, Antonella Lualdi, Terence Morgan, Genevieve Casile
D: Roy Rowland
Standard adventure-thriller: Buccaneer seeks fortune

The Sea Serpent

1986, (Sp), color, 92 mins.
W: Timothy Bottoms, Taryn Power, Jared Martin, Ray Milland, Gerard Tichy, Carole James
D: Gregory Greens
Minor SF-thriller (filmed in 1984; Ray Milland's last film): Discredited captain hunts marine monster

Search
see Probe

Searchers for Voodoo Mountain
see Warriors of the Apocalypse

The Search for Bridey Murphy

1956, (USA), Para, b&w, 84 mins.
W: Louis Hayward, Teresa Wright, Nancy Gates, Janet Riley, Kenneth Tobey, Richard Anderson, Tom McKee, Charles Boaz, Lawrence Fletcher, Charles Maxwell, Walter Kingsford, Noel Leslie, William J. Bark, Eilene Janssen, Bradford Jackson, James Kirkwood, Hallene Hill, Denise Freeborn, Ruth Robinson
WRIT & D: Noel Langley, from Morey Bernstein's book   PHOTOG: John F. Warren   SPCL-FX: John P. Fulton   MUSIC SPRVSR: Irvin Talbot
Standard thriller: Housewife proves to be reincarnated

Search for Danger

1949, (USA), Film Classics, b&w, 62 mins.
W: John Calvert *(Mike Waring)*, Albert Dekker *(Kirk)*, Myrna Dell *(Wilma)*, Ben Welden *(Gregory)*, Douglas Fowley *(The Inspector)*, Michael Mark *(Perry)*, Anne Cornell *(Elaine)*, Jack Daly *(The Drunk)*, James Griffith *(Cooper)*, Mauritz Hugo *(Larry Andrews)*, Peter Brocco *(Morris Jason)*, Billy Nelson *(The Thug)*, Peter Michael
P & D: Don Martin   SCR: Don Martin & Jerome Epstein, from characters created by Michael Arlen   PHOTOG: Paul Ivano   MUSIC: Karl Hajos
Minor "Falcon" thriller: Murder committed, sleuth trails gamblers

Search for the Gods

1975, (USA), Douglas S. Cramer-WB/ABC-TV, color, 100 mins.
W: Kurt Russell *(Shan)*, Stephen McHattie *(Willie)*, Victoria Racimo, Raymond

St. Jacques, Ralph Bellamy, Albert Paulsen, John War Eagle, Carmen Argenziano, Joe David Marcus
D: Jud Taylor   TELEPLAY: Ken Pettus   STORY: Herman Miller   PHOTOG: Matt Leonetti   SPCL-FX: Marcel Vercoutere   MUSIC: Billy Goldenberg
TVM, standard SF-thriller: Factions seek pieces of space-alien medallion

The Seashell and the Clergyman
see La Coquille et le Clergyman

Season of the Witch
see Jack's Wife

Sebastian Star Bear: First Mission

1991, (USA), color, 87 mins.
VOICES: Peter Banks
Standard animated SF-fantasy: Space-faring bruin vs. evil circus master

The 2nd Best Secret Agent in the Whole Wide World
see Licensed to Kill

Second Breath
see Le Deuxieme Souffle

Second Chance

1953, (USA), Edmund Grainger/RKO, 3D, color, 82 mins.
W: Robert Mitchum, Linda Darnell, Jack Palance, Roy Roberts, Reginald Sheffield, Sandro Giglio, Rodolfo Hoyos Jr., Margaret Brewster, Judy Walsh, Dan Seymour, Milburn Stone, Fortunio Bonanova
D: Rudolph Mate   SCR: Oscar Millard & Sydney Boehm, from a story by D.M. Marshman Jr.   PHOTOG: William Snyder   MUSIC: Roy Webb
Standard melodrama: Professional killer stalks gangster's beautiful moll

The Second Coming
see Dead People

The Second Face of Dr. Jekyll
see The Son of Dr. Jekyll

Second House from the Left
see The New House on the Left

The Second Jungle Book: Mowgli and Baloo

1997, (USA), TriStar, color, 88 mins.
D: Duncan McLachlan, from stories by Rudyard Kipling
*Minor adventure-fantasy (bruited as a "prequel" to **The Jungle Book** {1994}): Jungle boy faces challenges*

The Second Penalty

1914, (GB), Kineto, b&w, 1,900 ft. (579.1m)
D: F. Martin Thornton
Standard crime-thriller: Man gains revenge on convict who swindled his mother and caused her death

Seconds

1966, (USA), Joel/Para, b&w, 106 mins.
W: Rock Hudson *(Antiochus Wilson)*, Salome Jens *(Nora Marcus)*, John Randolph *(Arthur Hamilton)*, Will Geer *(The Old Man)*, Richard Anderson *(Dr. Innes)*, Jeff Corey *(Mr. Ruby)*, Murray Hamilton *(Charlie)*, Frank Campanella *(The Man in the Station)*, Karl Swenson *(Dr. Morris)*, Edgar Stehli *(The Tailor Shop Presser)*, Frances Reid *(Emily Hamilton)*, Aaron Magidow *(The Meat Man)*, Wesley Addy *(John)*, Barbara Werle *(The Sec'y)*, De De Young *(The Nurse)*, Thom Conroy *(The Dayroom Attendant)*, Francoise Ruggieri *(The Girl in the Boudoir)*, Khigh Dhiegh *(Davalo)*, John Lawrence *(The Texan)*, Ned Young *(Henry Bushman)*, Dody Heath *(Sue Bushman)*, Kirk Duncan *(Mr. Filter)*, Elisabeth Fraser *(The Plump Blonde)*, Robert Brubaker *(Mayberry)*, Dorothy Morris *(Mrs. Filter)*, William Richard Wintersole *(The Doctor in the Operating Room)*
P: Edward Lewis   D: John Frankenheimer   SCR: Lewis John Carlino, from David Ely's novel   PHOTOG: James Wong Howe   MUSIC: Jerry Goldsmith
Superior thriller: Faustian tale of secret society that provides wealthy with new faces and identities

Second Sight

1989, (USA), Ursus/Lorimar/WB, color, 83 mins.
W: John Larroquette *(Wills)*, Bronson Pinchot *(Bobby McGee)*, Bess Armstrong *(Sister Elisabeth)*, Stuart Pankin *(Preston Pickett)*
D: Joel Zwick   SCR: Tom Schulman & Patricia Resnick   PHOTOG: Dana Christiansen   MUSIC: John Morris   SPCL VS-FX: Bran Ferren
Standard comedy-fantasy: Psychic aids cop

The Secret

1955, (GB), Laureate-Golden Era/Eros, color, 80 mins.
W: Sam Wanamaker *(Nick Delaney)*, Mandy Miller *(Katie Martin)*, Andre Morell *(Insp. Lake)*, Harold Berens *(Frank Farmer)*, Jan Miller *(Margaret)*, Wyndham Goldie *(Dr. Scott)*, Henry Caine *(The Superintendent)*, Marian Spencer *(Aunt Doris)*, Richard O'Sullivan *(John Martin)*
P: S. Benjamin Fisz   D & SCR: C. Raker Endfield (Cy Endfield), from a play by Robert Brenon
Standard crime-thriller: American thief seeks stolen gems

The Secret Adventures of Tom Thumb
1993, (GB), color, 60 mins.
W: Nick Upton, Deborah Collard, John Schofield, Mike Gifford, Frank Passingham
WRIT & D: DaveBorthwick
Unusual fantasy-thriller (mix of live action & animation): Spawn of artificial-insemination accident is abducted by gov't agents

The Secret Agent
1936, (GB), Gaumont, b&w, 86 mins.
W: Madeleine Carroll (*Elsa*), Peter Lorre (*The General*), Robert Young (*Marvin*), John Gielgud (*Edgar Brodie*), Percy Marmont (*Mr. Caypor*), Florence Kahn (*Mrs. Caypor*), Lilli Palmer (*Lilli*), Charles Carson ("*R*"), Michel Saint-Denis (*The Coachman*), Andreas Malandrinos (*The Manager*), Howard Marion-Crawford (*Carl*), Tom Helmore (*Capt. Anderson*), Dino Galvani (*The Receptionist*), Rene Ray (*The Maid*), Sebastian Cabot, Michael Redgrave
D: Alfred Hitchcock   SCR: Charles Bennett, Ian Hay, Jesse Lasky Jr. & Alma Reville, from a play by Campbell Dixon, based on Somerset Maugham's stories *Ashenden, Triton & The Hairless Mexican*   PHOTOG: Bernard Knowles   MUSIC: Louis Levy
Standard thriller: Author and girl agent hunt murderous spy

Secret Agent
1973, (Fr), CCFC, color, 93 mins.
W: Jean-Paul Belmondo, Jacqueline Bisset, Monique Tarbes, Vittorio Caprioli, Raymond Gerome
D: Phillipe De Broca
Aka Le Magnifique, How to Destroy the Reputation of the Greatest Secret Agent
Minor thriller-spoof: "Walter Mitty" type has spy adventure

The Secret Agent
1996, (GB), Capitol/Fox Searchlight, color, 94 mins.
W: Bob Hoskins (*Verloc*), Patricia Arquette (*Winnie*), Gerard Depardieu (*Ossipon*), Robin Williams (*The Professor*), Eddie Izzard (*Vladimir*), Christian Bale (*Stevie*), Jim Broadbent
D & SCR: Christopher Hampton, from Joseph Conrad's novel   PHOTOG: Denis Lenoir   MUSIC: Philip Glass
A.k.a. Joseph Conrad's The Secret Agent
Unusual thriller: Spy compelled to blow up clock at Greenwich Observatory

Secret Agent Fireball
1965, (It-Fr), AIP, color, 89 mins.
W: Richard Harrison, Dominique Boschero Wandisa Guida
D: Mario Donen
A.k.a. Killers Are Challenged
Standard spy-thriller: Superspy poses as scientist

Secret Agent of Japan
1942, (USA), 20th-Fox, b&w, 72 mins.
W: Preston Foster, Lynn Bari (*Kay*), Noel Madison (*Saito*), Janis Carter (*Doris*), Steven Geray (*Alecsandri*), Trudy Marshall Sen Yung, Addison Richards, Frank Puglia, Ian Wolfe
D: Irving Pichel   PHOTOG: Lucien Andriot
Standard thriller: American tangles with Japanese spies

Secret Agent Superdragon
1966, (Fr-It-W. Ger), United Screen, color, 95 mins.
W: Ray Danton, Marisa Mell, Margaret Lee L Jess Hahn
P: Roberto Amoroso   D: Calvin Jackson Padgett (*Giorgio Ferroni*)   SCR: Bill Coleman, Mike Mitchell, Remigio Del Grosso, Roberto Amoroso & Calvin Jackson Padgett   ORIG STORY: Calvin Jackson Padgett   PHOTOG: Tony Secchi   MUSIC: Benedetto Ghiglia
Minor thriller: Drug pusher attempts conquest of USA

Secret Agent 077—Operation Hong Kong
1964, (W. Ger), color
W: Horst Frank, Brad Harris, Maria Perschy, Dietmar Schoenherr
A.k.a. Operation Hong Kong
Minor thriller

Secret Agent 00
see Operation Kid Brother

The Secretary
1995, (USA), Pierre David/Image/Rep, color, 94 mins.
W: Mel Harris, Sheila Kelley, Barry Bostwick, James Russo, Rayond Baker, Rod McCary, Grainger Hines, Mimi Craven, Ashley Peldon, Richard Herd
D: Andrew Lane   SCR: Graham Flashner   PHOTOG: Steven Bernstein   MUSIC: Louis Febre
Standard thriller: Woman joins brokerage firm, is drawn into plans of psychotic assistant

The Secretary's Crime
1909, (GB), Cricks & Martin, b&w, 700 ft. (213.4m)
D: A.E. Coleby
Standard crime-thriller: Deathbed confession saves clerk from robbery charge

Secret Beyond the Door
1948, (USA), Walter Wanger/Diana/Univ, b&w, 98 mins.
W: Joan Bennett, Michael Redgrave, Anne Revere, Barbara O'Neil, Paul Cavanagh, Natalie Schafer, Anabel Shaw, Rosa Rey, James Seay, Mark Dennis
P & D: Fritz Lang   SCR: Silvia Richards, from a story by Rufus King, *Museum Piece No. 13*   PHOTOG: Stanley Cortez   MUSIC: Miklos Rozsa
Engrossing thriller: Bride finds husband has emotional problems

Secret Ceremony
1968, (GB), World Films/Univ, color, 109 mins.
W: Elizabeth Taylor (*Leonora*), Mia Farrow (*Cenci*), Robert Mitchum (*Albert*), Pamela Brown (*Aunt Hilda*), Dame Peggy Ashcroft (*Aunt Hanna*)
D: Joseph Losey   SCR: George Tabori, from a short story by Marco Denevi   PHOTOG: Gerry Fisher   MUSIC: Richard Rodney Bennett
Off-beat psychodrama: Prostitute mothers disturbed girl

Secret Cinema
1965, (USA), color, 28 mins.
W: Amy Vane, Gordon Felio, Philip Carlson
D: Paul Bartel
Unusual short fantasy: Secret society screens 'cinema verite' films of people going mad

The Secret Door
1964, (GB), AA, b&w, 72 mins.
W: Robert Hutton, Sandra Dorne, Peter Illing
P: Charles Baldour & Robert Hutton   D: Gilbert L. Kay
Minor thriller: World War II spy-adventure

Le Secret du Medecin (The Doctor's Secret)
1910, (Fr), Star, b&w, 229m (751.3 ft./12.7 mins.)
D: Georges Melies
Standard melodrama

The Secret Fury
1950, (USA), b&w, 86 mins.
W: Claudette Colbert, Robert Ryan, Jane Cowl, Vivian Vance, Paul Kelly, Philip Ober
D: Mel Ferrer
Exciting whodunit: Unknown fiend tries to drive woman mad

The Secret Life of Walter Mitty: DANNY KAYE

The Secret Kingdom
1925, (GB), Stoll, b&w, 5,930 ft. (1807.5m)
W: Matheson Lang (*John Quarrain*), Stella Arbenia (*Mary Quarrain*), Eric Bransby Williams (*Philip Darent*), Rudolph de Cordova (*The Protege*), Genevieve Townsend (*The Sec'y*), Robin Irvine (*The Son*), Lillian Oldland (*The Daughter*), Frank Goldsmith (*Henry*)
D: Sinclair Hill   SCR: Alicia Ramsey, from Bertram Atkey's novel *Hidden Fires*

S

The Secret of Dr. Mabuse: VALERY INKIJINOFF, PETER VAN EYCK, LEO GENN AND CLAUDIO GORA (TWICE)

reissued (1929) as **Beyond the Veil**
Standard fantasy: Financier buys mind-reading device

A Secret Life
1914, (GB), Clarendon, b&w, 2,730 ft. (832.1m)
<u>W</u>: Lionelle Howard, Dorothy Bellew
<u>D</u>: Wilfred Noy
Standard crime-thriller: Squire kills captain, impersonates him

The Secret Life of Ian Fleming
1990, (USA-GB), Saban-Scherick/TNT-TV, color
<u>W</u>: Jason Connery (*Ian Fleming*), Kristin Scott Thomas (*Leda*), David Warner, Joss Ackland, Patricia Hodge, Richard Johnson, Colin Welland, Fiona Fullerton, Marsha Fitzalan, Julian Firth, Arkie Whiteley, Tara McGowran, Ingrid Held, Geoffrey Chater, Edita Brychta, Nina Marc, Clive Mantle, Christopher Benjamin, Cathy Underwood, Nicholas Frankau, Victor Baring, Octavia Verdin, Robert Longden, Richard Clifford, Bill Wallis, Sarah Harper, David Quilter, Roger Davidson, Ray Llewellyn, Lauren Heston, Harriet Reynolds, Sylvia Rotter, Arturo Venegas, Pamela Hunter, Leo Fenn, Isabel Dinning, Hugo Bower, Horst Jantschek
<u>D</u>: Ferdinand Fairfax <u>WRIT</u>: Robert J. Avrech <u>PHOTOG</u>: Mike Southon <u>SPCL-FX</u>: Alan Whibley <u>MUSIC</u>: Carl Davis
A.k.a. **Spymaker**
TVM, standard adventure-thriller: Fictionalized bio of "James Bond" creator

The Secret Life of Walter Mitty
1947, (USA), Goldwyn/RKO, color, 105 mins.
<u>W</u>: Danny Kaye, Virginia Mayo, Boris Karloff, Fritz Feld, Florence Bates, Thurston Hall, Doris Lloyd, Frank Reicher, Ann Rutherford
<u>P</u>: Samuel Goldwyn <u>D</u>: Norman Z. McLeod <u>SCR</u>: Ken Englund, from James Thurber's story <u>PHOTOG</u>: Lee Garmes <u>MUSIC</u>: David Raksin
Classic comedy-fantasy: Youth has bizarre daydreams

Secret Lives
1937, (GB), IFP-Phoenix, b&w, 80 mins.
<u>W</u>: Brigitte Horney (*Lena Schmidt*), Neil Hamilton (*Lt. Pierre de Montmalion*), Ivor Barnard (*Baldhead*), Gyles Isham (*Franz Abel*), Charles Carson (*Henri*), Raymond Lovell (*The German SS Chief*), Frederick Lloyd (*The French SS Chief*), Ben Field (*Karl Schmidt*), Hay Petrie (*Robert Pigeon*), Leslie Perrins (*J 14*)
<u>D</u>: Edmond T. Greville <u>SCR</u>: Basil Mason, from a novel by Paul de Saint-Colombe
USA retitle, **I Married a Spy** *(Grand National, 1938) reissued 1953*
Standard thriller: German girl forced to spy for France in World War I

The Secret Man
1958, (GB), Producers Assocs.-Amalgamated/Butcher, b&w, 68 mins.
<u>W</u>: Marshall Thompson (*Dr. Cliff Mitchell*), John Loder (*Maj. Anderson*), Anne Aubrey (*Jill Warren*), John Stuart (*Dr. Warren*), Magda Miller (*Ruth*), Henry Oscar (*John Manning*), Murray Kash (*Waldo*), Michael Mellinger (*Tony*)

<u>P & D</u>: Ronald Kinnoch <u>STORY</u>: Tony O'Grady
Standard thriller: American missile expert poses as runaway idealist to unmask spy

The Secret Mark of D'Artagnan
1960, (It-Fr), Liber-Agiman/Medallion, color, 91 mins.
<u>W</u>: George Nader, Magali Noel
<u>D</u>: Siro Marcellini
Minor adventure-thriller: Swordsman vs. Cardinal Richelieu

El Secreto del Doctor Orlof (The Secret of Doctor Orlof)
1962, (Sp-Fr-Austria), Hispamer/Sigma III/AIP, b&w, 88 mins.
<u>W</u>: Marcelo Arroita-Jauregui, Perla Cristal, Hugo Blanco, Agnes Spaak, Jose Rubio, Luisa Sala, Martha Reves, Pastor Serrador
<u>D</u>: Jesus Franco <u>SCR</u>: Jesus Franco & Nick Frank
GB retitle, **The Demon Doctor** *USA retitle,* **Dr. Orlof's Monster** *&* **The Awful Dr. Orlof** *(Sigma III, 1964)*
Standard horror-thriller: Mad doctor creates zombies

Secret of Abbe X
see **Das Geheimnis des Abbe X**

The Secret of Blood Island
1964, (GB), Hammer/Univ, color, 84 mins.
<u>W</u>: Barbara Shelley (*Elaine*), Jack Hedley (*Sgt. Crewe*), Patrick Wymark (*Maj. Jocomo*), Charles Tingwell (*Maj. Dryden*), Bill Owen (*Bludgin*), Peter Welch (*Richardson*), Edwin Richfield (*O'Reilly*), Lee Montague (*Levy*), Michael Ripper (*Lt. Tojoko*), Philip Latham (*Capt. Drake*), Glyn Houston (*Berry*)
<u>D</u>: Quentin Lawrence <u>SCR</u>: John Gilling <u>PHOTOG</u>: Jack Asher <u>MUSIC</u>: James Bernard
Standard melodrama: Inmates of Japanese POW camp conceal girl secret agent
cf. **The Camp on Blood Island**

Secret of Deep Harbor
1961, (USA), UA, b&w, 70 mins.
<u>W</u>: Ron Foster, Barry Kelly
Minor melodrama

The Secret of Dr. Alucard
see **A Taste of Blood**

The Secret of Dr. Mabuse
1964, (W. Ger-It-Fr), Filmkunst/Telewide/Omnia Filmexsport, b&w, 90 mins.
<u>W</u>: Peter Van Eyck, Wolfgang Preiss, Yvonne Furneaux, Yoko Tani, Leo Genn
<u>D</u>: Fritz Lang <u>SCR</u>: Ladislas Fodor & Bryan Edgar Wallace
A.k.a. **Deathray Mirror of Dr. Mabuse**
Standard thriller: Mad doctor steals death-ray invention

The Secret of Dorian Gray
see **Dorian Gray**

The Secret of Madame Blanche
1933, (USA), MGM, b&w, 83 mins.
W: Lionel Atwill, Irene Dunne, Phillips Holmes.Douglas Walton, Una Merkel, C. Henry Gordon, Jean Parker
D: Charles Brabin
Standard thriller: Estranged mother and son involved in murder

The Secret of Magic Island
1964, (Fr-It), Embassy/Joseph E. Levine, color, 63 mins.
D: Jean Tourane   SCR: Louise de Vilmorin   MUSIC: Richard Cornu   NARRA-TION: Robert Lamoureaux
Standard juvenile fantasy

Secret of Monte Cristo
see The Treasure of Monte Cristo (1961)

The Secret of My Success
1965, (GB), MGM, color, 96 mins.
W: Shirley Jones (*Marigold Marado*), Stella Stevens (*Violet Lawson*), Honor Blackman (*Baroness von Lukenberg*), Lionel Jeffries (*Insp. Hobart/Baron von Lukenberg/Pres. Esteda/Earl of Aldershot*), James Booth (*Arthur Tate*), Amy Dalby (*Mrs. Tate*), Joan Hickson (*Mrs. Pringle*), Robert Barnete (*Col. Armandez*), Richard Vernon, Nicolau Breyner (*Pallazio*)
P: Andrew & Virginia L. Stone   WRIT & D: Andrew L. Stone   PHOTOG: David Boulton   MUSIC: Roland Shaw
Standard comedy-thriller: Upwardly-mobile constable perfects art of murder

The Secret of NIMH
1982, (USA), MGM-UA, color, 82 mins.
VOICES: Derek Jacobi, Elizabeth Hartman, Arthur Malet, Dom DeLuise, John Carradine, Hermione Baddeley, Aldo Ray
D: Don Bluth, from Robert O'Brien's novel *Mrs. Frisby and the Rats of NIMH*
Unusual animated fantasy: Rats flee laboratory

The Secret of Roan Inish
1995, (USA-Irish), TriStar, color, 102 mins.
W: Jeni Courtney, Richard Sheridan, John Lynch Michael Lally, Eileen Colgan, Susan Lynch, Cillian Byrne
D: John Sayles   PHOTOG: Haskell Wexler   MUSIC: Mason Daring
Unusual fantasy-melodrama: Girl seeks lost brother

Secret of St. Ives
1949, (USA), Col, b&w, 75 mins.
W: Richard Ney, Vanessa Brown
STORY: Robert Louis Stevenson
Minor thriller

The Secret of Seagull Island
1981, (GB-It), ITC, color, 95 mins.
W: Jeremy Brett (*David Malcolm*), Prunella Ransome (*Barbara*), Nicky Henson (*Martin Foster*), Pamela Salem (*Carol*), Gabriele Tinti (*Enzo Lombardi*), Fabrizio Iovine (*Insp. Casati*), Marco Mastantuono (*Frederick*), Vassili Karamesinis (*Giulio*), Helen Stirling (*The Director of the Academy*), Walter Williams (*The Optician*), Sherry Buchanan (*Mary Ann*), Peter Boom (*The Hotel Concierge*), Umberto Raho (*The Doctor*), Veronica Wells (*Cynthia*), Chigo Tocci (*Marco*), Mascia Musy (*Consuelo*), Katherine Berg (*Arlene*), Paul Mueller (*Maresciallo*), Stefania Maccarone (*The Girl on the Boat*)
P & D: Nestore Ungaro   SCR: Augusto Caminito, Nestore Ungaro & Jeremy Burnham   ORIG STORY: Nestore Ungaro   PHOTOG: Armando Nannuzzi   SPCL-FX: Germano Natali   MUSIC: Tony Hatch
Modest melodrama: Woman seeks missing sister, finds terror on Mediterranean isle

The Secret of Stamboul
1936, (GB), Wainwright/GFD, b&w, 93 mins.
W: Valerie Hobson (*Tania*), Frank Vosper (*Kazdim*), Kay Walsh (*Diana*), James Mason (*Larry*), Peter Haddon (*Peter*), Robert English (*Sir George*), Laura Cowie (*The Baroness*), Cecil Ramage (*Prince Ali*), Emilio Cargher (*Renouf*), Leonard Sachs (*Arif*)
D: Andrew Marton   SCR: Richard Wainwright, Howard Irving Young & Noel Langley, from novel *The Eunuch of Stamboul* by Dennis Wheatley & George A. Hill
*reissued in GB (1940) as **The Spy in White***
Standard thriller: Englishman foils revolution. US Release: Hoffberg, 1939

The Secret of the Air
1914, (GB), Imp Films/Transatlantic, b&w, 2,567 ft. (782.4m)
W: King Baggott (*Wilbur Norton*), Leah Baird (*Mrs. Norton*), Herbert Brenon (*The Turkish Spy*), Claude Grahame-White (*A Pilot*), Gustav Hamel (*A Pilot*)
D: Herbert Brenon
*USA retitle, **Across the Atlantic***
Standard thriller: Framed inventor flees to England, nabs spy at Epsom

The Secret of the Black Trunk
1962, (W. Ger), b&w, 96 mins.
W: Joachim Hansen, Senta Berger, Hans Reiser, Leonard Steckel, Peter Carsten
D: Werner Klinger, from a novel by Edgar Wallace
*A.k.a. **Das Gehemnis Der Schwartzen Koffer***
Standard thriller: Detective unmasks master criminal

The Secret of the Blue Room
1933, (USA), Univ, b&w
W: Lionel Atwill, Gloria Stuart, Edward Arnold, Onslow Stevens, Paul Lukas
D: Kurt Neumann
blurb: "The 10-star mystery drama!"
Minor thriller: Weird murders in mysterious German castle
*cf. **The Missing Guest** and **Murder in the Blue Room**. Remake of **Geheimnis Des Blauen Zimmers**, (German, 1932)*

Secret of the Chateau
1934, (USA), Univ, b&w, 67 mins.
W: Clark Williams, Claire Dodd, Osgood Perkins, Ferdinand Gottschalk, Frank Reicher, Alice White, Helen Ware, George E. Stone, Alphonse Ethier, Jack LaRue, DeWitt Jennings
D: Richard Thorpe
Standard thriller: Rare bible stolen from French mansion

The Secret of the Forest
1956, (GB), Rayant/British Lion-CFF, b&w, 61 mins.
W: Kit Terrington (*Henry*), Diana Day (*Mary*), Jacqueline Cox (*Caroline*), Barry Knight (*Johnny*), Vincent Ball (*Mr. Lawson*), Michael Balfour (*Len*), Arthur Lovegrove (*Wally*)
P: Anthony Gilkison   D: Darcy Conyers   SCR: Darcy Conyers & Gerard Bryant   STORY: George Ewart Evans
Standard juvenile thriller: Archeologist's niece and nephew catch gold cup thieves

The Secret of the Golden Eagle
1991, (USA), color, 90 mins.
W: Michael Berryman, Brandon McKay
D: Cole McKay
Standard family-fare adventure-fantasy: Quest for statue that causes aging

Secret of the Incas
1954, (USA), Para, color, 101 mins.
W: Charlton Heston (*Harry Steele*), Robert Young (*Dr. Stanley Moorehead*), Nicole Maurey (*Elena Antonescu*), Thomas Mitchell (*Ed Morgan*), Kurt Katch (*The Man with the Rifle*), Yma Sumac (*Kori-Tica*), Glenda Farrell (*Mrs. Winston*), Edward Colmans (*Col. Emilio Cardoza*), Michael Pate (*Pachacutec*), Leon Askin (*Anton Marcu*), William Henry (*Phillip Lang*), Grandon Rhodes (*Mr. Winston*), Geraldine Hall (*Mrs. Richmond*), Harry Stanton (*Mr. Richmond*), Booth Colman (*Juan Fernandez*), Rosa Rey, Robert Tafur, Martin Garralaga, Alvy Moore, Rodolfo Hoyos, Zacharias Yaconelli, John Marshall, Marion Ross, Carlos Rivero, Delmar Costello, Miguel Contreras, Dimas Sotello, Anthony Numkena
D: Jerry Hopper   SCR: Ranald MacDougall & Sydney Boehm   PHOTOG: Lionel Lindon   MUSIC: David Buttolph
Standard adventure-thriller: Man finds map revealing location of priceless artifact. Robert Young's last theatrical film

The Secret of the Loch
1934, (GB), Wyndham/ABFD, b&w, 80 mins.
W: Seymour Hicks (*Prof. Heggie*), Nancy O'Neil (*Angela Heggie*), Gibson Gowland (*Angus*), Eric Hales (*Jack Campbell*), Frederick Peisley (*Jimmy Andrews*), Rosamund John (*Maggie Fraser*), Ben Field (*The Piermaster*), Robert Wilton (*The Reporter*), Hubert Harben (*Prof. Fothergill*), Cyril McLaglen (*The Mate*), Fewlass Llewellyn (*The Professor*), D.J. Williams (*The Judge*), Stafford Hilliard (*Macdonald*)
D: Milton Rosmer   STORY: Charles Bennett & Billie Bristow
Standard fantasy: Divers find prehistoric monster in Loch Ness

The Secret of the Loch
1957, (GB), Eros, color
*from Samuel Crockett's novel **The Raiders***
Standard thriller

The Secret of the Moor
1919, (GB), British Lion/Granger, b&w, 5,095 ft. (1553m)
W: Gwen Williams (*Margaret Marson*), Philip Hewland (*George Marson*), Henry Thompson (*Adam Ducros*), Hazel Jones (*Mildred Morpeth*), Edgar W. Hylton (*Jack Myddleton*), George Goodwin (*Dr. Morpeth*)
P: David Falcke   D: Lewis Willoughby, from a novel by Maurice Gerard
Standard crime-thriller: Boatman smuggles gold for mining expert

The Secret of the Purple Reef
1960, (USA), 20th-Fox, color, 80 mins.
W: Jeff Richards, Margia Dean, Richard Chamberlain, Peter Falk
Minor adventure-thriller: Two brothers probe sinking of father's ship

Secret of the Red Orchid
1962, (W. Ger), Rialto/Export/Bischoffb&w, 94 mins.
W: Christopher Lee, Marisa Mell, Adrian Hoven, Klaus Kinski
D: Helmuth Ashley, from an Edgar Wallace thriller
Standard thriller: Scotland Yard & FBI join forces to nab murderous blackmailer

Secret of the Sphinx
1963, (Fr), ITC, color, 95 mins
W: Tony Russel, Maria Perschy
Minor adventure-thriller: Insurance investigator and archeologists seek stolen gold

S

The Secret of the Sword

1985, (USA), Filmation/Atlantic, color, 91 mins.
VOICE: John Erwin
SCR: Larry Ditillo & Bob Forward
Animated feature, standard SF-fantasy: Adventures of He-Man

The Secret of the Telegian

1960, (Jap), Toho/Herts-Lion, color, 85 mins.
W: Akihiko Hirata, Koji Tsuruta Yumi Shirakawa, Tadao Nakamura
P: Tomoyuki Tanaka   **D:** Jun Fukuda   **SCR:** Shinichi Sekizawa
Standard SF-thriller: Electric man teleports himself, commits crimes

The Secret of the Three Sword Points

see *Il Segreto delle Tre Punte*

The Secret of the Whistler

1946, (USA), Col, b&w, 65 mins.
W: Richard Dix, Leslie Brooks Mary Currier, Michael Duane, Mona Barrie, Ray Walker
D: George Sherman
Minor thriller: Insane artist suspected of murder

Secret of Treasure Mountain

1956, (USA), Col, b&w, 68 mins.
W: Raymond Burr, William Prince, Valeris French
Standard adventure-thriller

The Secret Partner

1961, (GB), MGM British, b&w, 91 mins.
W: Stewart Granger (*John Brett*), Haya Harareet (*Nicole Brett*), Bernard Lee (*Supt. Hanbury*), Lee Montague (*Insp. Henderson*), Hugh Burden (*Charles Standish*), Melissa Stribling (*Helen Standish*), John Lee (*Clive Lang*), Conrad Phillips (*Alan Richford*), Norman Bird (*Ralph Beldon*), Peter Illing (*Strakarios*)
P: Michael Relph   **D:** Basil Dearden   **STORY:** David Pursell & Jack Seddon
Minor crime-thriller: Executive blackmailed, charged with company robbery

Secret People

1952, (GB), Ealing/GFD, b&w, 96 mins.
W: Valentina Cortese (*Maria*), Serge Reggiani (*Louis*), Megs Jenkins (*Penny*), Audrey Hepburn (*Nora Brent*), Charles Goldner (*Anselmo*), Irene Worth (*Miss Jackson*), Reginald Tate (*Insp. Eliot*), Michael Shepley (*The Manager*), John Ruddock (*Daly*), Athene Seyler (*Mrs. Kellick*), Geoffrey Hibbert (*Steenie*), Sydney Tafler (*Syd Burnett*), Michael Allan (*Rodd*), John Field (*Fedor Luki*), Norman Williams (*Sgt. Newcome*), Bob Monkhouse
P: Sidney Cole   **D:** Thorold Dickinson   **SCR:** Thorold Dickinson, Wolfgang Wilhelm & Christianna Brand   **STORY:** Thorold Dickinson & Joyce Cary
Standard crime-thriller: Political exiles plot tyrant's assassination

The Secret Place

1957, (GB), Rank/RFD, b&w, 98 mins.
W: Belinda Lee (*Molly Wilson*), Ronald Lewis (*Gerry Carter*), Michael Brooke (*Freddie Haywood*), Michael Gwynn (*Stephen Waring*), Geoffrey Keen (*PC Haywood*), Favid McCullum (*Mike Wilson*), Maureen Pryor (*Mrs. Haywood*), George A. Cooper (*Harry*), George Selway (*Paddy*)
P: John Bryan & Anthony Perry   **D:** Clive Donner   **STORY:** Linette Perry
Standard crime-thriller: Diamond thieves dupe constable's son

Secret Rites

1972, (GB), Meadway/Butcher, color, 47 mins.
W: Alex Sanders
P: Norton Lewis   **WRIT & D:** Derek Ford   **PHOTOG:** Roy Poynter   **MUSIC:** Bryn Walton
Standard horror-docu: Vagaries of witchcraft

Secret Scrolls—Parts I & II

1968 (year distrib. in USA; actual release 1957-8), (Jap), Toho, color, 106 mins, each part.
W: Toshiro Mifune, Koji Tsuruta, Yoshiko Kuga
D: Hiroshi Inagaki   **SCR:** Hiroshi Inagaki & Takeshi Kimura   **ORIG STORY:** Kosuke Gomi
Celebrated melodrama: Feuding noble families in 17th-century Nippon

Secret Service

1913, (GB), Cricks & Martin, b&w, 1,335 ft. (406.9m)
D: Charles Calvert
Standard crime-thriller: Chinaman impersonates captain, is exposed by detective posing as lascar

Secret Service Investigator

1948, (USA), Rep, b&w, 60 mins.
W: Lloyd Bridges, Lynne Roberts
Standard thriller

The Secret Seven

see *Paul Sleuth and the Mystic Seven*

Secrets in the Attic

1993, (USA), Aims Media/Vidmark, video, color, 89 mins.
W: Amanda Rowse (*Amy*), Lindsay Jackson (*Claire*), Rebekah Baker (*Louann*),

Hillary Brooks (*Ellen*), Lissa Reynolds (*Mother*), Charles Bruce (*Father*), Courtney Campbell (*Young Claire*), J.J. Reardon (*Tom Keaton*), Bob Chaffee (*The Handyman*), Jan Hathaway DeLoe (*Grandmother*), Thomas F. McKnight (*Grandfather*), Harry Alvin (*The Florist*), Nancy Giles (*The Librarian*), Oliver Joslin (*The Boy*), Chrissie Carlson, Ray Moore, Christina Moses, Stephanie Vu, Mark Boothby, Rhonda Kitley, Robaire Nieves, Don Nored, Mara LaValley
D: Dianne Haak   **SCR:** Marion Nelson & Bernard Wilets, from Betty Ren Wright's novel   **PHOTOG:** Tom Evans   **MUSIC:** Firstcom
Made-for-Video, minor thriller: Dollhouse reveals truth about old murders

Secrets of a Sorority Girl

1946, (USA), PRC, b&w, 58 mins.
W: Mary Ware, Rick Vallin
Minor melodrama. GB Title: Secrets of Linda Hamilton

Secrets of a Soul

see *Geheimnisse einer Seele*

The Secrets of Dracula

1964, (Phil), color
Minor horror-fantasy

Secrets of Monte Carlo

1951, (USA), Rep, b&w, 60 mins.
W: Warren Douglas, Lois Hall
Standard thriller

Secrets of Scotland Yard

1944, (USA), Rep, b&w, 68 mins.
W: Edgar Barrier, Stephanie Bachelor, Lionel Atwill, Henry Stephenson, C. Aubrey Smith, John Abbott, Walter Kingsford, Martin Kosleck, Forrester Harvey, Frederick Worlock, Matthew Boulton, Bobby Cooper
D: George Blair   **SCR:** Denison Clift, from his story *Room 40, O.B.*   **PHOTOG:** William Bradford   **MUSIC DIR:** Morton Scott
Standard thriller: Twins try to crack Nazi code, unknown spy opposes

Secrets of Sex

1970, (GB), Noteworthy/Balch, color, 91 mins.
W: Richard Schulman (*The Judge*), Janet Spearman (*The Wife*), Dorothy Grumbar (*The Photographer*), Anthony Rowlands (*The Model*), George Herbert (*The Steward*), Kenneth Benda (*Sacha Seremona*), Yvonne Quenet (*Mary-Clare*), Reid Anderson (*Dr. Rilke*), Cathy Howard (*The Burglar*), Mike Britton (*The Burgled Man*), Maria Frost (*Lindy Leigh*), Peter Carlisle (*Col. X*), Sue Bond (*The Callgirl*), Elliott Stein (*The Strange Man*)
P: Richard Gordon & Anthony Balch   **D:** Anthony Balch   **SCR:** Martin Locke, John Eliot, Maureen Owen, Elliott Stein & Anthony Balch, from a story by Alfred Mazure
Standard eroto-fantasy: Mummified Arabian recounts strange sex stories

Secrets of the Lone Wolf

1941, (USA), Col, b&w, 67 mins.
W: Warren William (*Michael Lanyard*), Ruth Ford (*Helene de Leon*), Roger Clark (*Paul Benoit*), Victor Jory (*Dapper Dan Streever*), Eric Blore (*Jamison*), Fred Kelsey (*Dickens*), Thurston Hall (*Insp. Crane*), Lester Scharpe (*Deputy Duval*), Victor Kilian (*Col. Costals*), Marlo Dwyer (*Bubbles Deegan*), Irving Mitchell (*Benjamin Evans*), John Harmon (*Bernard*), Joe McGuinn (*Bob Garth*)
D: Edward Dmytryk   **SCR:** Stuart Palmer, from characters created by Joseph Louis Vance   **MUSIC:** Morris Stoloff
Standard thriller: Gentleman rogue helps protect jewels. The 'Lone Wolf' Series

Secrets of the Night

1925, (USA), Univ, b&w, 7 reels (6,138 ft./1870.9m)
W: James Kirkwood (*Robert Andrews*), Madge Bellamy (*Anne Maynard*), Rosemary Theby (*Mrs. Lester Knowles*), ZaSu Pitts (*Celia Stebbins*), Tom Wilson (*Old Tom Jefferson White*), Tom Ricketts (*Jerry Hammond*), Tom S. Guise (*Col. James Maynard*), Frederick Cole (*Teddy Hammond*), Joe Singleton (*Charles*), Bull Montana (*The Killer*), Tyrone Brereton (*Anne's Brother*), Otto Hoffman (*The Coroner*), Arthur Thalasso (*Det. Reardon*), Anton Vaverka (*Joshua Brown*), Edward Cecil
P: Carl Laemmle   **D:** Herbert Blache   **ADAPT & SCR:** Edward J. Montagne, from a play by Guy Bolton & Max Marcin   **PHOTOG:** Gilbert Warrenton
working title, **The Night Cap**
Standard comedy-mystery: Banker stages own death

Secrets of the Phantom Caverns

1984, (USA), Sandy Howard/Adam's Apple, color, 90 mins.
W: Robert Powell (*Rupert "Wolf" Wolfson*), Lisa Blount (*Leslie Peterson*), Richard Johnson (*Ben Gannon*), Anne Heywood (*Frieda Shelley*), Timothy Bottoms (*Maj. Elbert Stevens*), A.C. Weary (*Lt. George Barwell*), Jackson Bostwick (*Hunter Prime*), Richard Beauchamp (*Santos Arias*), William Gribble (*Sgt. Neumann*), Carl Spurlock (*Maj. Castillo*), Jason Laskay (*Hunter Second*), Liam Sullivan (*The Lemurian Elder*), Carlos Cervantes (*Hector Lopez*), Tim Powell (*Jim White*), Tom Stubblefield (*The Eastern European Military Advisor*), Heather Hollinghead, George Jessup, Rich Davis, Stephanie Winchester, David Jacko, Steve Lacy, Doug Bishop, Martha Jo King, Chuck McKnight, Emerson Cole, Jim Remick, Tracy McNabb, Edie Winchester, Debbie Shuttleworth, Kyle Weir, Deborah Carter, Kenny Moore, Tracy Clark, Alberta Quinn, Billy Lee, Warren Rutledge, Brent Talley, Joann Carroll,

Susan Flanders, Kathy Brown, B.J. Cooley, Dwayne Allison, Jamie Bodie, John Sandford, Bobby Shuttleworth, Adrianne Talley, Theresa Quinn, Libby Reed, Charles Cruse, Belinda Talley, Mike Delcour, Marie Shuttleworth, Traci Flanders, Heather Rayfield, Anna Mitchell, Mark Cantrell, Dick Curtis, John White, James Mitchell, Bob Montgomery, Charles E. McKnight, David Avery, James W. Swain, Campbell Boyd, Howard E. Farris, Jimmy Kirkland, Cecil E. Moody, Teddy B. Grandey, John B. McGuire, Robert H. Brady, Lee Drew, Janine Porter, Mark Northern, Alan McCormick, Jay Castro, Billy Campbell, Barry Rogers, Denny Abbot, Alton Patton, Danny R. Martin, Stuart J. Lamb, R.K. Lush Jr., Anthony B. Campbell, Roger D. Taylor, Ronald C. Barnes, Joe Nunley, Ned Vaughn, Brian Stevens, Mike Newton, Paul Thomas, Mark Warren, Bruce Howard, Guy McAllister
D: Don Sharp **SCR:** Christy Marx & Robert Vincent O'Neil **STORY:** Ken Barnett **PHOTOG:** Virgil Harper **SPCL-FX:** Rick Josephsen **MUSIC:** Michel Rubini & Denny Jaeger
A.k.a. **What Waits Below**
Standard SF-thriller: Scientists find underground humanoids

Secrets of the Red Bedroom
see Secret Weapons

Secrets of the Sphinx
see Die Spinnen

The Secret Tent
1956, (GB), Forward/British Lion, b&w, 69 mins.
W: Donald Gray (*Chris Martyn*), Andree Melly (*Ruth Martyn*), Jean Anderson (*Mrs. Martyn*), Dinah Ann Rogers (*Sally*), Sonia Dresdel (*Miss Mitchum-Browne*), Andrew Cruickshank (*Insp. Thornton*), Peter Hammond (*Smith*), Conrad Phillips (*The Sgt.*)
P: Nat Miller & Frank Bevis **D:** Don Chaffey **SCR:** Jan Read, from a play by Elizabeth Addeyman
Standard crime-thriller: Man's missing wife helps he burglar brother elude justice

Secret Venture
1955, (GB), Rep, b&w, 68 mins.
W: Kent Taylor (*Ted O'Hara*), Jane Hylton (*Joan Butler*), Kathleen Byron (*Renee l'Epine*), Karel Stepanek (*Zelinsky*), Frederick Valk (*Otto Weber*), Maurice Kaufmann (*Dan Fleming*), Martin Boddey (*Squire Marlowe*), Arthur Lane (*Bob Hendon*), Michael Balfour (*Stevens*), John Boxer (*Insp. Dalton*)
P: William N. Boyle **D:** R.G. Springsteen **STORY:** Paul Erickson & Kenneth R. Hayles
Standard thriller: Bodyguard saves jet-fuel inventor from kidnapping by spies

The Secret Ways
1961, (USA), Heath/Univ, b&w, 112 mins.
W: Richard Widmark, Sonja Ziemann, Charles Regnier, Walter Rilla, Howard Vernon, Senta Berger, Heinz Moog, Stefan Schnabel, Walter Wilz
D: Phil Karlson **SCR:** Jean Hazlewood, from a novel by Alistair MacLean **PHOTOG:** Walter Wilz **MUSIC:** Johnny Williams **MUSIC SPRVSR:** Joseph Gershenson
Standard Cold-War thriller: Journalist tries to smuggle scholar out of communist Hungary

Secret Weapons
1985, (USA), ITC/NBC-TV, color, 97 mins.
W: Linda Hamilton (*Elena/Joanna*), James Franciscus (*Col. Khudenko*), Sally Kellerman (*Maj. Malevich*), Geena Davis (*Tamara/Brenda*), Hunt Block (*Jack Spalding*), Christopher Atkins (*Allen Collier*), Viveca Lindfors (*Aunt Roza*), Barrie Ingham, Donald Pilon, Vlasta Vrana, Kimberley Myles, Catherine Lalonde, Fernanda Tavares, Rona Waddington, Tom Rack, Hamish McEwan, Alan Fawcett, Barbara Reid-Harris, Daniele Schneider, Gavin Patrick, Jerome Tiberghien, Maria Revelins
D: Don Taylor **TELEPLAY:** Thomas Baum & Sandor Stern **STORY:** Thomas Baum **PHOTOG:** Richard Cunha **MUSIC:** Charles Bernstein
re-televised (1987) as **Secrets of the Red Bedroom**
TVM, standard thriller: Soviet females trained by KGB to blackmail Americans

The Secret World of Dr. Lao
see 7 Faces of Dr.Lao

The Secret World of Polly Flynt
1987, (GB), BBC-TV, color, 120 mins.
W: Katie Reynolds (*Polly*), Brenda Bruce (*Granny*)
TVM, standard juvenile fantasy: Lonely girl uses imagination, visits magical world

Security Risk
1954, (USA), AA, b&w, 69 mins.
W: John Ireland, Dorothy Malone Keith Larsen, John Craven, Joe Bassett
D: Harold Schuster
Standard thriller: FBI agents vs. communists

Seddok, Son of Satan
see Atom Age Vampire

Sedmi Kontinent (The Seventh Continent)
1966, (Czech-Yugo), UM/Sidney Glazier, color, 88 mins.
W: Iris Vrus
D: Dusan Vukotic **SCR:** Dusan Vukotic & Andro Lusicic **PHOTOG:** Karol

Krska **MUSIC:** Tomislav Simovic
Standard adventure-fantasy: Children live alone on island

Seduced by Evil
1994, (USA), USA-TV, color 88 mins
W: Suzanne Somers, John Vargas James B. Sikking, Mindy Spence, Nancy Moonves, Julie Carmen, Doug Coleman, Miguel Ortega
D: Tony Wharmby **TELEPLAY:** Bill Svanoe, from Jann Arrington Wolcott's novel **PHOTOG:** Joao Fernandes **MUSIC:** George S. Clinton
TVM, standard fantasy-thriller: Magazine writer falls into clutches of wicked sorcerer

The Seduction
1982, (USA), Avco Embassy, color, 101 mins.
W: Morgan Fairchild (*Jamie Douglas*), Andrew Stevens (*Derek Sanford*), Michael Sarrazin (*Brandon*), Vince Edwards (*Capt. Maxwell*), Colleen Camp (*Robin*), Kevin Brophy (*Bobby*), Joanne Linville, Diana Rose
WRIT & D: David Schmoeller **PHOTOG:** Mac Ahlberg **MUSIC:** Lalo Schifrin **SONG:** (sung by Dionne Warwick), *Love's Hiding Place*
Standard thriller: Obsessed fan terrorizes beautiful TV personality

Seduction: Three Tales from the 'Inner Sanctum'
1992, (USA), Made for TV, color, 95 mins.
W: Victoria Principal, John Terry
TVM, standard thriller (inspired by classic radio-series): Steamy mix of romance and mystery

Seed of Terror
see Grave of the Vampire

Seed People
1992, (USA), color, 87 mins.
W: Sam Hennings, Andrea Roth Dane Witherspoon, David Dunard, Holly Fields, Sonny Carl Davis, Anne Betancourt, Bernard Kates
D: Peter Manoogian **SCR:** Jackson Barr **MUSIC:** Bob Mithoff
Minor SF-thriller: Small-town doctor activates 500-year-old spores from outer space

Seeds of Destruction
1952, (USA), Astor, b&w, 84 mins.
W: Kent Taylor, Gene Lockhart, Gloria Holden, David Bruce
D: Frank Strayer
Minor "Cold War" thriller: Communist spy assumes identity of imprisoned missionary

Seeds of Evil
1974, (USA), KKI Films, color, 97 mins.
W: Joe Dallesandro, Rita Gam, Katharine Houghton, James Congdon
D & SCR: Jim Kay
A.k.a. **The Gardener**
Minor fantasy-thriller: Gardener exercises mysterious powers

Seizure: MARY WORONOV

See No Evil
see Blind Terror

The Seer of Bond Street
see Spiritualism Exposed (1913)

Il Segreto delle Tre Punte (The Secret of the Three Sword Points)
1952, (It), b&w,
W: Massimo Girotti
D: Carlo Ludovico Bragaglia
Minor adventure-thriller

Sei Donne per l'Assassino (Six Women for the Assassin)
1964, (It-Fr-W. Germ), Emmepi-de Beauregard-Monachia/Woolner Bros/AA., color, 90

mins.

W: Cameron Mitchell, Eva Bartok, Francesca Ungaro, Thomas Reiner, Mary Arden, Louis Pigot, Lea Kruger, Heidi Stroh, Mara Carminoso, Arianna Gorini, Claude Dantes, Nadia Anty, Harriet White

P: Alfred Mirabel, Massimo Patrizi **D:** Mario Bava **SCR:** Mario Bava, Marcello Fondata & Giuseppe Barilla **PHOTOG:** Ubaldo Terzano **MUSIC:** Carlo Rustichelli

USA retitle, **Blood and Black Lace**
Standard thriller: Fashion models murdered

Seizure
1974, (Can), Cinerama/AIP, color, 93 mins.

W: Jonathan Frid (*Edmund*), Martine Beswick (*The Queen of Evil*), Troy Donahue (*Mark*), Christina Pickles (*Nicole*), Herve Villechaize (*Spider*), Joe Sirola (*Charlie*), Roger de Kovan (*Serge*), Henry Baker (*Jackal*), Anne Meacham (*Eunice*), Mary Woronov (*Mikki*), Richard Cox, Lucy Bingham, Mike Meola

P: Garrard Glenn & Jeffrey Kapelman **D:** Oliver Stone **SCR:** Ed Mann & Oliver Stone **PHOTOG:** Roger Racine **MUSIC:** Lee Gagnon
Standard horror-fantasy (Oliver Stone's first feature): Writer's vengeful characters come to life

Self-Accused
1914, (GB), Regent/MP, b&w, 3,000 ft. (914.4m)

W: Arthur Finn, Charles Weston

P: Charles Weston & Arthur Finn **WRIT & D:** Charles Weston
Standard crime-thriller: Burglar clears man accused of shooting count's rival

Selina-Ella
1915, (GB), Martin/DFSA, b&w, 734 ft. (223.7m)

D: Dave Aylott
Standard fantasy: Maid dreams she is Cinderella and Kaiser is Demon King

The Sender
1982, (GB), Kingsmere/Para, color, 91 mins.

W: Kathryn Harrold (*Dr. Gail Farmer*), Paul Freeman (*Dr. Denman*), Zeljko Ivanek ("*The Sender*"), Shirley Knight (*Jerolyn*), Sean Hewitt, Tracy Harper, Marsha Hunt, Ron Travis, Harry Ditson, Jana Shelden

D: Roger Christian **SCR:** Thomas Baum **PHOTOG:** Roger Pratt **MUSIC:** Trevor Jones
Standard fantasy-thriller: Amnesiac's nightmares become other people's reality

Send for Paul Temple
1946, (GB), Butcher, b&w, 83 mins.

W: Anthony Hulme (*Paul Temple*), Joy Shelton (*Steve Trent*), Tamara Desni (*Diana Thornley*), Jack Raine (*Sir Graham Forbes*), Beatrice Varley (*Miss Marchmont*), Phil Ray (*Horace Daley*), Hylton Allen (*Dr. Milton*), Maire O'Neill (*Mrs. Neddy*), Olive Sloane (*Ruby*)

P & D: Jhn Argyle **SCR:** Francis Durbridge & John Argyle, from a radio-serial by Francis Durbridge
reissued 1950
Standard crime-thriller: Novelist unmasks master thief

La Senora Muerte (Lady Death)
1968, (Mex), Col, color

W: John Carradine, Regina Thorne, Elsa Cardenas

P: Luis Enrique Vergara **D:** Jaime Salvador **SCR:** Ramon Obon Jr.
Minor horror-thriller: Mad scientist blackmails scarred woman into committing murders
A.k.a. **Mrs. Death**

Sensation
1937, (GB), BIP/ABPC, b&w, 67 mins.

W: John Lodge (*Pat Heaton*), Diana Churchill (*Maisie Turnpit*), Francis Lister (*Richard Grainger*), Joan Marion (*Mrs. Grainger*), Margaret Vyner (*Claire Lindsay*), Athene Seyler (*Mme. Henry*), Richard Bird (*Henry Belcher*), Jerry Vernon (*Spikey*), Martin Walker (*Dimmitt*), Henry Oscar (*Supt. Stainer*), Leslie Perrins (*Strange*), Felix Aylmer (*Lord Bouverie*), James Hayter (*Jock*)

D: Brian Desmond Hurst **SCR:** Dudley Leslie, Marjorie Deans & William Freshman, from the play *Murder* by Basil Dean & George Munro
Standard crime-thriller: Reporter solves waitress' murder

Sensation
1994, (USA), color, 98 mins.

W: Eric Roberts, Ro Perlman, Ed Begley, Jr., Paul LeMat, Claire Stansfield, Kieran Mulroney, Tracey Needham

D: Brian Grant **SCR:** Doug Wallace **MUSIC:** Arthur Kempel
Standard thriller: Student endangered when she assists in psychic phenomena investigation

Senseless
1962, (USA), Ron Rice, color
Standard "underground" film

Senseless
1998, (USA), Mandeville/Dimension, color, 93 mins.

W: Marlon Wayans, David Spade, Rip Torn, Matthew Lillard, Brad Dourif, Tamara Taylor

D: Penelope Spheeris
Standard SF-comedy: Secret formula amplifies youth's senses

Sensuous Vampires
see The Vampire Girls

Sentenced for Life
1960, (GB), Danziger/UA, b&w, 64 mins.

W: Francis Matthews (*Jim Richards*), Jill Williams (*Sue Thompson*), Basil Dignam (*Ralph Thompson*), Jack Gwillim (*John Richards*), Lorraine Clewes (*Mrs. Richards*), Mark Singleton (*Edward Thompson*), Nyree Dawn Porter (*Betty*), Arnold Bell (*Williams*)

P: Edward J. & Harry Lee Danziger **D:** Max Varnel **STORY:** Eldon Howard & Mark Grantham
Standard crime-thriller: Lawyer proves father was framed

The Sentinel
1976, (USA), Michael Winner/Univ, color, 93 mins.

W: Chris Sarandon (*Michael Lerman*), Cristina Raines (*Alison Parker*), Ava Gardner (*Miss Logan*), Sylvia Miles (*Gerde*), John Carradine (*Father Halliran*), Burgess Meredith (*Charles Chazen*), Martin Balsam (*Prof. Ruzinsky*), Deborah Raffin (*Jennifer*), Eli Wallach, Jose Ferrer, Arthur Kennedy, Jerry Orbach, Beverly D'Angelo, Esther Blackmon, Hank Garrett, Christopher Walken, Nana Tucker, Gary Allen, Tom Berenger, William Hickey

WRIT & P: Michael Winner & Jeffrey Konvitz **D:** Michael Winner, based on Jeffrey Konvitz' novel **PHOTOG:** Dick Kratina **SPCL-FX:** Albert Whitlock **MUSIC:** Gil Melle
Standard horror-thriller: Young model rents in house concealing gateway to Hades

Separate Lives
1995, (USA), Interscope/Trimark, color 101 mins

W: James Belushi, Linda Hamilton, Vera Miles (*Dr. Goldin*) Vera Miles, Elisabeth Moss, Drew Snyder, Mark Lindsay Chapman, Marc Poppel, Elizabeth Arlen, Josh Taylor, Ken Kerman

D: David Madden **SCR:** Steven Pressfield **PHOTOG:** Kees Van Oostrum **MUSIC:** William Olvis
Minor thriller: Ex-cop aids woman professor with split personality

Separation
1968, (GB), Bond/London Independent Producers, color, 93 mins.

W: Jane Arden (*Jane*), David De Keyser (*The Husband*), Ann Lynn (*The Woman*), Ian Quarrier (*The Lover*), Terence de Marney (*The Man*)

P & D: Jack Bond **STORY:** Jane Dewar
Standard fantasy: Woman dreams of separation from husband

Les Sept Chateaux de Diable (Seven Castles of the Devil)
1901, (Fr), Pathe, b&w, 50m (164 ft.)

W: Ferdinand Zecca

D: Ferdinand Zecca
Standard short fantasy

September Storm
1960, (USA), 20th-Fox, 3D, color, 99 mins.

W: Joanne Dru, Mark Stevens, Robert Strauss, Asher Dann, M. Jean-Pierre Karien, Vera Valmont
Minor melodrama: Tension on a yacht

Les Sept Peches Capitaux (The Seven Capital Sins)
1900, (Fr), Star, b&w, 60m (196.9 ft./3.3 mins.)

D: Georges Melies
Standard fantasy

Serena
1962, (GB), Butcher's Films, b&w, 62 mins.

W: Patrick Holt (*Insp. Gregory*), Emrys Jones (*Howard Rogers*), Honor Blackman (*An Rogers*), Bruce Beeby (*Sgt. Conway*), John Horsley (*Mr. Fisher*), Vi Stevens (*The Landlady*), Wally Patch (*The Barman*)

P: John I. Phillips **D:** Peter Maxwell **SCR:** Edward Abraham & Reginald Hearne **STORY:** Edward & Valerie Abraham
Standard crime-thriller: Model shoots artist's wife

Sergeant Deadhead the Astronut!
1965, (USA), AIP, color, 90 mins.

W: Frankie Avalon, Deborah Walley, Harvey Lembeck, Buster Keaton, John Ashley, Eve Arden, Cesar Romero, Gale Gordon, Fred Clark, Reginald Gardiner, Donna Loren, Romo Vincent, Mike Nader, Tod Windsor, Norman Grabowski, Ed Faulkner, Pat Buttram, Bobbi Shaw, Patti Chandler, Salli Sachse, Luree Holmes, Sue Hamilton, Jo Collins, Bob Harvey, Jerry Brutsche, Andy Romano, John Macchia, Mary Hughes, Astrid De Brea, Jean Ingram, Peggy Ward, Stephanie Nader, Lyzanne Ladue, Janice Levinson, Alberta Nelson, Sallie Dornan

P: James H. Nicholson & Samuel Z. Arkoff **D:** Norman Taurog **SCR:** Louis M. Heyward **PHOTOG:** Floyd Crosby
A.k.a. **Sergeant Deadhead**
Standard SF-comedy: Astronaut develops aggressive new personality

Serial Killer
1995, (USA), color, 95 mins.

W: Kim Delaney, Gary Hudson
Standard thriller: Sadistic maniac escapes asylum, stalks cop who put him away

Serial Mom

1994, (USA), Savoy, color, 93 mins.

W: Kathleen Turner (*Mom*), Sam Waterston (*Dad*), Ricki Lake (*Misty*), Matthew Lillard (*Chip*), Scott Wesley Morgan (*Det. Pike*), Walt MacPherson (*Det. Gracey*), Justin Whalin (*Scotty*), Patricia Dunnock (*Birdie*), Lonnie Horsey (*Carl*), Mink Stole (*Dottie Hinkle*), Mary Jo Catlett (*Rosemary Ackerman*), Traci Lords (*Carl's Date*), Tim Caggiano (*Marvin Pickles*), Jeff Mandon (*Howell Hawkins*), Colgate Salsbury (*Father Royce*), Patsy Grady Abrams (*Mrs. Jenson*), Richard Pilcher (*Herbie Hebden*), Beau James (*Timothy Nazlerod*), Stan Brandorff (*The Judge*), Alan J. Wendl (*Sloppy*), Bus Howard (*Gus*), Patricia Hearst (*Juror #8*), Suzanne Somers (*herself*), Nancy Robinette (*The Jury Forewoman*), Peter Bucossi (*The Rookie Cop*), Loretta McNally (*The Policewoman*), Wilfred E. Williams (*Press A*), John Calvin Doyle (*Carl's Brother*), Joshua L. Shoemaker (*The Court TV Reporter*), Rosemary Knower (*Court Groupie A*), Susan Lowe (*Court Groupie B*), Mary Vivian Pearce (*The Book Buyer*), Brigid Berlin (*The Mean Lady*), Jordan Brown (*The Police Officer*), Anthony "Chip" Brienza (*The Vendor*), Zachary S. Pete (*The Church Baby*), Teresa K. Pete (*The Baby's Mother*), Jeffrey Pratt Gordon (*The Flea Market Boy*), Shelbi Clarke (*The Flea Market Girl*), Nat Benchley (*The Macho Man*), Kyf Brewer (*The Dealer*), Richard Pelzman (*The Doorman*), Chad Bankerd (*Kid A*), Johnny Alonso (*Kid B*), Robert Roser (*Kid C*), Mike Offenheiser (*Joe Flowers*), Jennifer Mendenhall (*The Reporter*), Michael S. Walter (*Burglar A*), Mojo Gentry (*Burglar B*), Lee Hunsaker (*The Girl*), Joan Rivers (*herself*), Gwendolyn Briley-Strand (*Mrs. Taplotter*), Catherine Anne Hayes (*The TV Serial Hag*), Susan Duvall (*Lady C*), Valerie Yarborough (*The Press*), Jordan Young (*The Kid*), Lyrica Montague (*The Court Clerk*), L7, Jennifer Finch, Suzi Gardner, Demetra Plakas, Donita Sparks, John A. Schneider

WRIT & D: John Waters   PHOTOG: Robert M. Stevens   MUSIC: Basil Poledouris   MUSIC SPRVSR: Bones Howe

Unusual comedy-thriller: Homicidal housewife erases irritating neighbors

Le Serment de M. Moto

see *Thank You, Mr. Moto*

The Serpent

1916, (USA), Fox, b&w, 6 reels

W: Theda Bara (*Vania Lazar*)

WRIT, P & D: Raoul Walsh

Standard melodrama: Serf's daughter dreams she is evil woman

The Serpent

1973, (It-Fr-W. Ger), Avco Embassy, color, 113 mins.

W: Yul Brynner (*Vlassov*), Henry Fonda (*Allan Davies*), Dirk Bogarde (*Philip Boyle*), Philippe Noiret (*Berthon*), Martin Held (*Lepke*), Virna Lisi (*Annabel Lee*), Guy Trejean (*Deval*), Michel Bouquet (*Tavel*), Farley Granger (*The Computer Programming Chief*), Marie Dubois (*Suzanne*), Robert Alda (*The Interrogator*)

D: Henri Verneuil   SCR: Henri Verneuil & Gilles Perrault, from a novel by Pierre Nord   PHOTOG: Claude Renoir   MUSIC: Ennio Morricone

released to USA TV (1975) as **Night Flight from Moscow**

Minor action-thriller: KGB officer defects to West

The Serpent and the Rainbow

1988, (USA), Rob Cohen-David Ladd/Keith Barish/Univ, color, 105 mins.

W: Bill Pullman (*Dennis Alan*), Zakes Mokae (*Peytraud*), Cathy Tyson (*Marielle Celine*), Paul Winfield (*Lucien Celine*), Brent Jennings (*Mozart*), Conrad Roberts (*Christophe*), Badja Djola (*Gaston*), Michael Gough, Theresa Merritt, Dey Young, Aleta Mitchell, Paul Guilfoyle

D: Wes Craven   SCR: Richard Maxwell & A.R. Simoun, inspired by Wade Davis' book   PHOTOG: John Lindley   MUSIC: Brad Fiedel

Unusual fantasy-thriller: American probes Haitian voodoo

Serpent Island

1954, (USA), Medallion-TV, color, 63 mins.

W: Sonny Tufts, Mary Munday

P, D, & SCR: Bert I. Gordon

Minor fantasy-thriller: Voodoo on tropic isle

Serpent of the Nile

1953, (USA), Col, color, 81 mins.

W: Rhonda Fleming, Raymond Burr, William Lundigan, Michael Ansara, Julie Newmar

P: Sam Katzman   D: William Castle

Standard melodrama (using sets from 1953's **Salome***): Queen of Egypt conspires*

Serpent's Lair

1995, (USA), color, 90 mins.

W: Jeff Fahey, Lisa B. (*Lilith*), Heather Meadway (*Alex*), Anthony Palermo (*Mario*)

Standard eroto-horror: Succubus lures married man

The Servant

1963, (GB), Springbok/Elstree/Landau, b&w, 115 mins.

W: Dirk Bogarde (*Barrett*), James Fox (*Tony*), Sarah Miles (*Vera*), Wendy Craig (*Susan*), Catherine Lacey (*Lady Mounset*), Richard Vernon (*Lord Mounset*), Dorothy Bromiley (*The Girl*), Brian Phelan (*The Irishman*), Hazel Terry (*The Woman in the Hat*), Alison Seebohm (*The Girl in the Pub*), Patrick Magee (*The Bishop*), Philippa Hare (*The Girl in the Bedroom*), Alun Owen (*The Curate*), Harold Pinter (*The Society Man*), Ann Firbank, Doris Knox, Jill Melford, Derek Tansley

P: Joseph Losey & Norman Priggen   D: Joseph Losey   SCR: Harold Pinter, from a novel by Robin Maugham   PHOTOG: Douglas Slocombe   MUSIC: John Dankworth   SONG: (sung by Cleo Laine), *All Gone*

Bizarre psychodrama: Sinister manservant caters to master's vices

The Servants of Twilight

1991, (USA), Trimark, color

W: Bruce Greenwood (*Charlie*), Belinda Bauer (*Christine*), Grace Zabriskie (*Grace Spivy*), Jack Kehoe, Jarrett Lennon (*Joey*), Richard Bradford, Carel Struycken

D: Jeffrey Obrow   SCR: Jeffrey Obrow & Stephen Carpenter, from Dean R. Koontz' novel   PHOTOG: Antonio Soriano   MUSIC: Jim Manzie

Standard thriller: Religious fanatic stalks child

La Setta (The Sect)

1991, (It), color, 120 mins.

W: Kelly Leigh Curtis, Herbert Lom, Mariangela Giordano

D: Michele Soave

Standard thriller: Schoolteacher becomes involved with devil-worship

Sette Contro la Morte (Seven Against Death)

1964, (It-W.Germ),Melcher/20th Century-Fox, b&w, 83 mins.

W: John Saxon, Brian Aherne, Rosanna Schiaffino

P & D: Edgar G. Ulmer

USA retitle, **The Cavern**

Standard melodrama

The Set-Up

1949, (USA), RKO, b&w, 72 mins.

W: Robert Ryan, Audrey Totter, George Tobias, Alan Baxter, Wallace Ford, Percy Helton, Darryl Hickman, James Edwards Phillip Pine, Edwin Max

D: Robert Wise   SCR: Art Cohn   PHOTOG: Milton Krasner

Unusual melodrama: Aging boxer prepares for fight he's expected to lose

The Set-Up

1963, (GB), Merton Park/Anglo-Amalgamated, b&w, 58 mins.

W: Maurice Denham (*Theo Gaunt*), John Carson (*Insp. Jackson*) Maria Corvin (*Nicole Romain*), Brian Peck (*Arthur Payne*) Anthony Bate (*Ray Underwood*), John Arnatt (*Supt. Ross*), Manning Wilson (*Sgt. Bates*), Billy Milton (*Simpson*)

P: Jack Greenwood   D: Gerald Glaister   SCR: Roger Marshall, from a story by Edgar Wallace

Standard crime-thriller: Ex-convict hired to steal woman's jewels, is framed for her murder

Seven (Se7en)

1995, (USA), New Line, color, 127 mins.

W: Brad Pitt (*Det. David Mills*), Morgan Freeman (*Det. William Somerset*), Gwyneth Paltrow (*Tracy Mills*), Kevin Spacey (*John Doe*), John C. McGinley, Richard Roundtree, R. Lee Ermey, Julie Araskog, Mark Boone Junior, John Cassini, Reg E. Cathey, Peter Crombie, Hawthorne James, Michael Masee, Leland Orser, Richard Schiff, Richard Portnow, Pamala Tyson, Andy Walker, Endre Hules, Daniel Zacapa, Bob Mack, George Christy, Mario Di Donato, Roscoe Davidson, Bob Collins, Allan Kolman, Charline Su, Jimmy Dale Hartsell, Dominique Jennings, Beverly Burke, Alfonso Freeman, Michael Reid MacKay, Robert Stephenson, Lennie Loftin, Tudor Sherrard, Harrison White, David Correia, Cat Mueller, Sarah Hale Reinhardt, Evan Miranda, Ron Blair, Paul S. Eckstein, Jim Deeth, Harris Savides, Rachel Schadt, Brian Evers, Shannon Wilcox, Heidi Schanz, John Santini, Duffy Gaver, Charles Tamburro, Richmond Arquette

D: David Fincher   SCR: Andrew Kevin Walker   PHOTOG: Darius Khondji   MUSIC: Howard Shore

Gripping thriller: Fiendish killer slays according to Seven Deadly Sins

Seven Against Death

see *Sette Contro la Morte*

The Seven Brothers Meet Dracula

see *Legend of the Seven Golden Vampires*

The Seven Capital Sins

see *Les Sept Peches Capitaux*

Seven Castles of the Devil

see *Les Sept Chateaux du Diable*

Seven Days in May

1964, (USA), Joel/Para, b&w, 118 mins.

W: Burt Lancaster, Fredric March, Kirk Douglas, Ava Gardner, Martin Balsam, Edmond O'Brien, Charles Watts, Hugh Marlowe, Richard Anderson, Andrew Duggan, John Houseman, George Macready, Whit Bissell

P: Edward Lewis   D: John Frankenheimer   SCR: Rod Serling, from the novel by Fletcher Knebel & Charles W. Bailey II   PHOTOG: Ellsworth Fredericks   MUSIC: Jerry Goldsmith

Superior thriller: Politics and problems of survival in nuclear age

Seven Days to Noon

1950, (GB), London/British Lion/Mayer-Kingsley/Disdtinguished, b&w, 94 mins.

S

W: Barry Jones (*Prof. Willingdon*), Andre Morell (*Supt. Folland*), Olive Sloane (*Goldie*), Marie Ney (*Mrs. Willingdon*), Sheila Manahan (*Ann Willingdon*), Hugh Cross (*Stephen Lane*), Joan Hickson (*Mrs. Peckett*), Ronald Adam (*The Prime Minister*), Merrill Mueller (*The American Commentator*), Geoffrey Keen
P: John Boulting   **D:** Roy Boulting   **SCR:** Roy Boulting & Frank Harvey, from a story by Paul Dehn & James Bernard (Academy Award Winner)   **PHOTOG:** Gilbert Taylor   **MUSIC:** John Addison
Standard thriller: Mad professor threatens to A-bomb London

Seven Deadly Sins
1953, (It-Fr), Arlan/Davis, b&w, 120 mins.
W: Gerard Philipe, Michele Morgan, Francoise Rosay
Standard melodrama

Seven Deaths in the Cat's Eye
1972, (It-Fr-W. Ger), color, 90 mins.
W: Jane Birkin, Hiram Keller, Francoise Christophe, Doris Kunstmann, Venantino Venantini, Anton Diffring, Dana Ghia, George Korrado, Serge Gainsbourg
D: Anthony M. Dawson [Antonio Margheriti]   **STORY & SCR:** Antonio Margheriti & Giovanni Simonelli, from a novel by Peter Bryan   **PHOTOG:** Carlo Carlini   **MUSIC:** Riz Ortolani
Minor thriller: Murder and madness in old manse

7 Doors of Death
1981, (It), Aquarius, color, 86 mins.
W: Katherine MacColl, David Warbeck, Sarah Keller, Tony Saint John, Veronica Lazar, Philip Ostrow, Margaret Lund
D: Louis Fuller [Lucio Fulci]   **SCR:** Roy Corchoran   **PHOTOG:** Glenn Kimbell   **MUSIC:** Mitch Yuspeh & Ira Yuspeh
Minor horror-thriller: Woman inherits hotel concealing doorway to hell. CF. The Sentinel

Seven Doors to Death
1944, (USA), PRC, b&w, 64 mins.
W: Chick Chandler, June Clyde, George Meeker, Gregory Gay, Edgar Dearing
D: Elmer Clifton
Minor thriller: Architect tries to solve crime

The Seven Dwarfs to the Rescue
1965, (It), PWT/Childhood/AIP, b&w, 84 mins.
W: Rossana Podesta, Georges Marchal, Roberto Risso Ave Ninchi, Salvatore Furmari, Francesco Gatto, Ulisse Lorenzelli, Mario Mastriantonio, Arturo Tosi, Giovanni Solinas, Domenico Tosi
WRIT, P, & D: P.W. Tamburella
Standard juvenile fantasy: Prince of Darkness threatens magic kingdom

7 Faces of Dr. Lao
1964, (USA), MGM, color, 99 mins.
W: Tony Randall (*Dr. Lao*), Barbara Eden, John Ericson, Arthur O'Connell, Noah Beery Jr., Royal Dano, Minerva Urecal, John Doucette, John Qualen, Lee Patrick
P & D: George Pal   **SCR:** Charles Beaumont, from Charles G. Finney's novel *The Circus of Dr. Lao*   **PHOTOG:** Robert Bronner   **MUSIC:** Leigh Harline
orig. to be titled **The Secret World of Dr. Lao**
Unusual fantasy (with stock-footage from **Quo Vadis?** *{1951} &* **Atlantis, the Lost Continent**): *Oriental's bizzare circus changes lives in small Western town*

Seven Footprints to Satan
1929, (USA), First Nat'l, b&w, 6 reels (5,405 ft./1647.4m/60 mins.)
W: Creighton Hale (*Jim*), William V. Mong (*The Professor*), Thelma Todd (*Eve*), Sheldon Lewis (*The Spider*), Laska Winters (*Satan's Mistress*), Ivan Christy (*Jim's Valet*), DeWitt Jennings (*Uncle Joe*), Nora Cecil (*The Old Witch*), Kalla Pasha (*Prof. Von Viede*), Angelo Rositto (*The Dwarf*), Cissy Fitzgerald (*The Old Lady*), Harry Tenbrook (*Eve's Chauffeur*), Thelma McNeil (*The Tall Girl*)
D: Benjamin Christansen   **SCR:** Richard Bee, from A. Merritt's novel   **PHOTOG:** Sol Polito
Classic fantasy-thriller: Criminal mastermind conspires

Seven Keys
1962, (GB), Independent Artists/Anglo-Amalgamated, b&w, 57 mins.
W: Jeannie Carson (*Shirley Steele*), Alan Dobie (*Russell*), Delphi Lawrence (*Natalie Worth*), John Carson (*Norman*), John Lee (*Jefferson*), Anthony Nicholls (*The Governor*), Alan White (*The Warder*), Robertson Hare (*Mr. Piggott*), Fabia Drake (*Mrs. Piggott*), Colin Gordon (*Mr. Barber*), Peter Barkworth (*The Estate Agent*)
P: Julian Wintle & Leslie Parkyn   **D:** Pat Jackson   **STORY:** Jack Davies & Henry Blyth
Standard crime-thriller: Ex-convict seeks dead cellmate's hidden loot

Seven Keys to Baldpate
1917, (USA), Cohan/Artcraft, b&w, 5 reels 66 mins
W: George M. Cohen, Hugh Ford, Anna Q. Nilsson, George M. Cohan, Elda Furry, Corene Uzzell, Joseph Smiley, Armand Cortes, C. Warren Cook
D: Mae Gaston from Earl Derr Biggers' play
Standard thriller

Seven Keys to Baldpate
1925, (USA), Famous Player-Lasky/Para, b&w, 7 reels (6,648 ft./2026.3m)
W: Douglas MacLean (*William Halowell Magee*), Edith Roberts (*Mary Norton*),

Anders Randolf (*J.K. Norton*), Crauford Kent (*Bentley*), Ned Sparks (*Bland*), William Orlamond (*The Hermit*), Wade Boteler (*Cargan*), Edwin Sturgis (*Lou Max*), Fred Kelsey (*The Sheriff*), Betty Francisco (*Myra Thornhill*), John P. Lockney (*Quimby*), Edith Yorke (*Mrs. Quimby*), Maym Kelso (*Mrs. Rhodes*)
D: Fred Newmeyer, from Earl Derr Biggers' play
Standard thriller: Mystery at isolated mansion. cf. **House of the Long Shadows**

Seven Keys to Baldpate
1929, (USA), RKO, b&w, 8 reels (6,742 ft./2055m)
W: Richard Dix (*William Magee*), Miriam Seegar (*Mary Norton*), Crauford Kent (*Hal Bentley*), Joseph Allen (*Peters*), Margaret Livingston (*Myra Thornhill*), Lucien Littlefield (*Thomas Hayden*), DeWitt Jennings (*Mayor Cargan*), Carleton Macy (*Kennedy*), Nella Walker (*Mrs. Rhodes*), Joe Herbert (*Max*), Harvey Clark (*Elijah Quimby*), Alan Roscoe (*Bland*), Edith York (*Mrs. Quimby*)
D: Reginald Barker   **ADAPT:** Jane Murfin, from Earl Derr Biggers' play   **PHOTOG:** Edward Cronjager
Standard thriller
cf. **House of the Long Shadows**

Seven keys to Baldpate: MIRIAM SEEGER AND RICHARD DIX

Seven Keys to Baldpate
1947, (USA), RKO, b&w, 68 mins.
W: Phillip Terry, Jacqueline White Eduardo Ciannelli, Margaret Lindsay, Arthur Shields
D: Lew Landers
Standard thriller

The Seven-Per-Cent Solution
1976, (GB), CIC/Univ, color, 114 mins.
W: Nicol Williamson (*Sherlock Holmes*), Robert Duvall (*Dr. Watson*), Alan Arkin (*Dr. Sigmund Freud*), Vanessa Redgrave (*Lola Devereaux*), Laurence Olivier (*Prof. Moriarty*), Joel Grey (*Lowenstein*), Samantha Eggar (*Mary Watson*), Charles Gray (*Mycroft Holmes*), Jeremy Kemp (*Baron von Leinsdorf*), Georgia Brown (*Mrs. Freud*), Regine (*The Madame*), John Bird (*Berger*), Anna Quayle (*Freda*), Frederick Jaeger (*Marker*), Jill Townsend (*Mrs. Holmes*), Alison Leggatt (*Mrs. Hudson*), Gertan Klauber (*The Pasha*), Jack May (*Dr. Schultz*), Erik Chitty (*The Butler*), Leon Greene (*Squire Holmes*), Ashley House (*Young Freud*), Sheila Shand Gibbs (*The Nun*), Erich Padalewsky (*The Station Master*), John Hill (*The Train Engineer*), Michael Blagdon (*Young Sherlock*)
P & D: Herbert Ross   **SCR:** Nicholas Meyer, from his novel   **PHOTOG:** Oswald Morris   **MUSIC:** John Addison   **SONG:** (by Stephen Sondheim), *The Madame's Song*
Lavish thriller: Famed detective seeks treatment for cocaine addiction, uncovers dastardly plot

Seven Sinners
1936, (GB), Gaumont, b&w, 70 mins.
W: Edmund Lowe (*John Harwood*), Constance Cummings (*Caryl Fenton*), Thomy Bourdelle (*Paul Turbe*), Henry Oscar (*Axel Hoyt*), Felix Aylmer (*Sir Charles Webber*), Allan Jeayes (*Karl Wagner*), Joyce Kennedy (*Elizabeth Wentworth*), O.B. Clarence (*The Registrar*), David Horne (*The Manager*), Mark Lester (*The Chief Constable*), Edwin Lawrence (*The Guide*), Antony Holles (*The Receptionist*), James Harcourt (*The Vicar*)

S

P: Michael Balcon   **D:** Albert de Courville   **SCR:** Frank Launder, Sidney Gilliat, L. DuGarde Peach & Austin Melford, from the play *Wrecker* by Arnold Ridley & Bernard Merivale
USA retitle, **Doomed Cargo** *reissued 1947*
Standard crime-thriller: American detective in France foils train-wrecking gunrunners

Seven Slaves Against the World
1965, (It), color, 96 mins.
W: Roger Browne, Gordon Mitchell, Scilla Gabel, Germano Longo, Alfredo Rizzo
D: Michle Lupo
Minor "Sword & Sandal": Swordsman ousts tyrant

7 Surprizes
1964, (Can), Quartet-Int'l, color & b&w, 77 mins.
W: Claude Jutra
P: Harvey Chertok   **NARRATION:** William Weintraub & Stanley Jackson
Septet of unusual shorts: **Cars in Your Life, Wrestling, Nahanni, A Chairy Tale, Le Merle, Neighbors** *&* **Corral**

The Seventh Continent
see **Sedmi Kontinent**

The Seventh Floor
1993, (USA), color, 99 mins.
W: Brooke Shields, Masaya Kato, Craig Pearce, Linda Cropper
D: Ian Barry
Minor thriller: Psycho controls woman's computer-operated apartment

The Seventh Juror
1964, (Fr), Orex/Trans Lux, b&w, 90 mins.
W: Daniele Delorme, Bernard Blier
Standard thriller

The Seventh Seal
see **Det Sjunde Inseglet**

The Seventh Sign
1988, (USA), Interscope Communications/Tri-Star, color, 97 mins.
W: Demi Moore *(Abby)*, Michael Biehn *(Russell)*, Jurgen Prochnow *(The Boarder)*, Peter Friedman, Manny Jacobs, Harry W. Basil, John Heard, Lee Garlington, John Taylor, Patricia Allison, Akosua Busia, Arnold Johnson, John Walcutt, Hugo L. Stanger, Michael Laskin, Ian Buchanan, Glenn Edwards, Robin Groth, Dick Spangler, Darwyn Carson
D: Carl Schultz   **SCR:** W.W. Wicket & George Kaplan   **PHOTOG:** Juan Ruiz Anchia   **MUSIC:** Jack Nitzsche
Standard horror-fantasy: Expectant mother involved in apocalyptic mystery

The Seventh Sword
1962, (It-Sp), color, 84 mins.
W: Brett Halsey Beatrice Altariba, Giulio Bosetti, Gabriele Antonini
D: Riccardo Freda
Standard adventure-thriller: Hero thwarts plot to overthrow Philip III of Spain

Seven Thunders
1957, (GB), Dial/Rank, b&w, 100 mins.
W: Stephen Boyd *(Dave)*, James Robertson Justice *(Dr. Martout)*, Kathleen Harrison *(Mme. Abou)*, Tony Wright *(Jim)*, Anna Gaylor *(Lise)*, Eugene Deckers *(Emile Blanchard)*, Rosalie Crutchley *(Therese Blanchard)*, Katherine Kath *(Mme. Parfait)*, James Kenney *(Eric Triebel)*, Anton Diffring *(Col. Trautman)*, Martin Miller *(Schlip)*, Denis Shaw *(The Soldier)*, George Coulouris *(Bourdin)*, Carl Duering *(Maj. Grautner)*, Edric Connor *(Abou)*, Gerard Heinz *(Von Dronitz)*, Leonard Sachs *(The Officer)*, Shirley Anne Field *(The Prostitute)*
P: Daniel M. Angel   **D:** Hugo Fregonese   **SCR:** John Baines, from a novel by Rupert Croft-Cooke
USA retitle, **Beasts of Marseilles,** *(Lopert, 1959)*
Unusual war-time psychodrama: Escaped POWs meet Landru-like killer

The Seventh Victim
1943, (USA), RKO, b&w, 71 mins.
W: Tom Conway, Jean Brooks, Kim Hunter, Ben Bard, Isabel Jewell, Erford Gage, Evelyn Brent, Hugh Beaumont, Wally Brown, Marguerita Sylva, Mary Newton, Feodor Chaliapin, Chef Milani, Elizabeth Russell Barbara Hale
P: Val Lewton   **D:** Mark Robson   **SCR:** DeWitt Bodeen & Charles O'Neal   **PHOTOG:** Nicholas Musuraca   **MUSIC:** Roy Webb
Standard thriller: Woman joins satanic cult, is told to kill herself

The 7th Voyage of Sinbad
1958, (USA), Morningside/Col, color, 89 mins.
W: Kerwin Mathews *(Sinbad)*, Kathryn Crosby *(Princess Parisa)*, Torin Thatcher *(Sokurah)*, Richard Eyer *(The Genie)*, Alec Mango *(The Caliph)*, Harold Kasket *(The Sultan)*, Nana de Herrera *(Sadi)*, Virgilio Teixeira *(Ali)*, Alfred Brown *(Harufa)*, Danny Green *(Karim)*, Luis Guedes *(The Crewman)*, Nino Falanga *(The Gaunt Sailor)*
P: Charles H. Schneer   **D:** Nathan Juran   **SCR:** Kenneth Kolb   **PHOTOG:** Wilkie Cooper   **SPCL-FX:** Ray Harryhausen   **MUSIC:** Bernard Herrmann
Superior fantasy: Legendary sailor vs. evil magician

The Seventh Word
1915, (GB), Clarendon, b&w, 2,835 ft. (864.1m)
W: Dorothy Bellew *(The Girl)*
D: Wilfred Noy
Standard crime-thriller: Girl and Prussian count hold halves of locket revealing hidden fortune

Seven Years in Tibet
1997, (USA),TriStar, color, 131 mins.
W: Brad Pitt, David Thewliss, Mako, B.D. Wong, Jetsun Fema, Lhakpa Tsamchoe
D: Jean-Jacques Annaud   **SCR:** Becky Johnston
Standard adventure: Explorer finds enlightenment in Himalayas

The Severed Arm
1973, (USA), color, 89 mins.
W: Deborah Walley, Marvin Kaplan, Paul Carr, John Crawford, David Cannon
D: Thomas Alderman
Minor thriller

Severed Ties
1992, (USA), color, 95 mins.
W: Billy Morrissette, Elke Sommer, Oliver Reed, Garrett Morris
D: Damon Santostefano
Minor SF-horror: Genetically-altered arm proves deadly

Sex Adventures of the Three Musketeers
see **The Erotic Adventures of the Three Musketeers**

Sex and the Single Alien
1993, (USA), color, 89 mins.
W: Eric Kohner
Minor eroto-SF: Space aliens teach Earth man sex secrets

Sex Crime of the Century
see **The Last House on the Left**

Sex Kittens Go to College
1960, (USA), AA, b&w, 94 mins.
W: Mamie Van Doren, Tuesday Weld, Mijanou Bardot, Mickey Shaughnessy, Louis Nye, Pamela Mason, Martin Milner, John Carradine, Jackie Coogan, Vampira, Conway Twitty, Charles Chaplin Jr., Harold Lloyd Jr.
P & D: Albert Zugsmith   **SCR:** Robert Hill
A.k.a. **Beauty and the Brain** *and* **Beauty and the Robot**
Standard comedy-fantasy: Robot selects stripper to head university science department

Sex Kittens Go To College: MAMIE VAN DOREN

The Sex Machine
1975, (It), color
W: Agostina Belli, Luigi Proietti
Standard eroto-SF: Future energy problem solved by harnessing human libido

Sex Monsters
see **Doctor of Doom**

Sexomania
see **Psychomania** *(1964)*

S

Sex on the Groove Tube
see *Case of the Full Moon Murders*

The Sexorcists
see *The Tormented* (1977)

The Sexplorer
1975, (GB), Meadway/Butcher, color, 85 mins.
<u>W:</u> Monika Ringwald (*The Girl*), Andrew Grant (*Alan*), Mark Jones (*The Lecher*), Tanya Ferova (*The Stripper*), Michael Cronin (*The Doctor*), Albin Pahernik (*The Man*), Maria Ski (*The Usherette*), Tony Kenyon (*The Patron*), Dave Carter (*The Inspector*), Catriona Nurse (*The Policewoman*), Rose Strang (*The Sauna Girl*), Prudence Drage (*Doris*)
<u>P:</u> Morton Lewis   <u>WRIT & D:</u> Derek Ford   <u>PHOTOG:</u> Roy Pointer   <u>MUSIC:</u> John Shakespeare
A.k.a. *Diary of a Space Virgin*
Standard eroto-SF: Space-alien girl investigates Earth sex

The Sex Racketeers
see *Man of Violence*

Sexton Blake
1909, (GB), Melodrama Production Syndicate/Gaumont, b&w, 1,280 ft. (390.1m)
<u>D:</u> C. Douglas Carlile, from a story by W. Murray Graydon
Standard thriller: Detective poses as cleric, saves girl from marrying murderer

Sexton Blake and the Bearded Doctor
1935, (GB), Fox British/MGM, b&w, 64 mins.
<u>W:</u> George Curzon (*Sexton Blake*), Henry Oscar (*Dr. Gibbs*), Tony Sympson (*Tinker*), Gillian Maude (*Janet*), James Knight (*Red*), Phil Ray (*Jim Cameron*), John Turnbull (*Insp. Donnell*), Edward Dignon (*Hawkins*), Donald Wolfit (*Percy*)
<u>D:</u> George A. Cooper, based on Rex Hardinge's novel *The Blazing Launch Murder*
Standard thriller: Doctor kills violinist to defraud insurance company

Sexton Blake and the Hooded Terror
1938, (GB), George King/MGM, b&w, 70 mins.
<u>W:</u> George Curzon (*Sexton Blake*), Tod Slaughter (*Michael Larron*), Greta Gynt (*Mlle. Julie*), Charles Oliver (*Max Fleming*), Tony Sympson (*Tinker*), Marie Wright (*Mrs. Bardell*), David Farrar (*Granite Grant*), Norman Pierce (*Insp. Bramley*)
<u>D:</u> George King   <u>SCR:</u> A.R. Rawlinson, from Pierre Quiroule's novel *Mystery of Caversham Square*
reissued 1942
Standard thriller: Detective unmasks millionaire as leader of hooded gang

Sexton Blake and the Mademoiselle
1935, (GB), Fox British/MGM, b&w, 63 mins.
<u>W:</u> George Curzon (*Sexton Blake*), Lorraine Grey (*Mlle. Roxanne*), Tony Sympson (*Tinker*), Vincent Holman (*Carruthers*), Edgar Norfolk (*Insp. Thomas*), Raymond Lovell (*The Captain*), Ian Fleming (*Henry Norman*), Wilson Coleman (*Pierre*)
<u>D:</u> Alex Bryce   <u>SCR:</u> Michael Barringer, from G.H. Teed's novel *They Shall Repay*
Standard thriller: Girl robs crooked financier

Sexton Blake, Gambler
1928, (GB), British Filmcraft/Para, b&w, 1,962 ft. (598m)
<u>W:</u> Langhorne Burton (*Sexton Blake*), Marjorie Hume (*Joan Fairfield*), Mickey Brantford (*Tinker*), Frank Atherley (*Lord Fairfield*), Adeline Hayden Coffin (*Lady Fairfield*), Oscar Rosander (*Ralph Garvin*)
<u>D:</u> George J. Banfield
Standard thriller: Detective investigates upper crust

Sexton Blake v. Baron Kettler
1912, (GB), Humanity Story Films, b&w, 645 ft. (196.6m)
<u>D:</u> Hugh Moss
Standard thriller: Secret plans stolen

Sexton Pimple
1915, (GB), Folly Films/Phoenix, b&w, 966 ft. (294.4m)
<u>W:</u> Fred Evans (*Sexton Pimple*)
<u>D & STORY:</u> Joe & Fred Evans
Standard comedy-satire (spoof of **Sexton Blake** thrillers): Detective takes over train, saves King of Cork from spies

The Sex Victims
1973, (GB), Border, color, 40 mins.
<u>W:</u> Ben Howard (*Jack Piper*), Alun Armstrong (*George*), Jane Cardew, Felicity Devonshire
<u>WRIT, P & D:</u> Derek Robbins
Standard short eroto-fantasy: Truck driver makes love to ghost of murdered girl

Shades of Gray
1996, (USA), color, 110 mins.
<u>W:</u> Kelly Burns, Doug Jeffrey, Blake Adams
Made-for-Video, minor thriller: Police sketch artist finds she may be dating madman

Shaddey
1985, (GB), color, 106 mins.
<u>W:</u> Anthony Sher, Billie Whitelaw, Patrick Macnee, Lesley Ash Larry Lamb, Bernard Hepton, Katherine Helmond
<u>D:</u> Philip Saville
Uusual comedy-fantasy-thriller: Youth can transfer mental images to film

The Shadow
1933, (GB), Real Art/UA, b&w, 74 mins.
<u>W:</u> Henry Kendall (*The Shadow*), Elizabeth Allan (*Sonia Bryant*), Sam Livesey (*Sir Richard Bryant*), Jeanne Stuart (*Moya Silverton*), Cyril Raymond (*Silverton*), Viola Compton (*Mrs. Bascomb*), John Turnbull (*The Inspector*)
<u>D:</u> George A. Cooper   <u>SCR:</u> H. Fowler Mear & Terence Egan, from a play by Donald Stuart
Standard thriller: Novelist unmasks murderer

The Shadow
1994, (USA), Univ, color, 107 mins.
<u>W:</u> Alec Baldwin, Penelope Ann Miller, John Lone, Jonathan Winters, Peter Boyle, Ian McKellen, Tim Curry, James Hong, Joseph Maher
<u>D:</u> Russell Mulcahy   <u>SCR:</u> David Koepp   <u>MUSIC:</u> Jerry Goldsmith
<u>PHOTOG:</u> Stephen Burum
Opulent fantasy-thriller ($50 million budget): Crimefighter employs psychic powers

The Shadow Between
1920, (GB), Seal/Granger, b&w, 5,000 ft. (1524m)
<u>W:</u> Doris Lloyd (*Marion West*), Lewis Dayton (*Clement Mawgan*), Sir Simeon Stuart (*Lord Grovely*), Cherry Winter (*Esther Mawgan*), Gertrude Sterroll (*Mrs. Mawgan*), Wally Bosco (*Dick West*), Billie Berkeley (*Julia Treven*), Horace Corbyn (*Mr. Jackson*), H. Lane Bayliff (*Mr. Evans*)
<u>D & SCR:</u> George Dewhurst, from a novel by Silas K. Hocking
Standard crime-thriller: Cornish lord steals servant's papers proving she is his dead brother's child

Shadow Conspiracy
1997, (USA), color
<u>W:</u> Charlie Sheen, Linda Hamilton, Donald Sutherland, Nicholas Turturro, Sam Waterston, Dey Young, Gore Vidal, Theodore Bikel, Terry O'Quinn, Paul Gleason, Ben Gazzara, Charles Cioffi, Stephen Lang, Richard Bauer, Casey Biggs, Beverly Brigham, Roy Bordon, Charles Bowen, Karen Braloye, Andreas Brandt, James L. Byrd, Helen Carey, Bob Child, James L. Chory, Karyn V. Cody, Ralph Cosham, Reginald C. Colbert, Michael Cunningham, Reginald Davis, Dominick De Marco, Jonas Elmblad, Ramon Estevez, Penny Fuller, Tom Quinn, John Leisenring, Richard A. Mention III, Walt MacPherson, Lawrence Leonard, J. Williams Midkiff Jr., Johnny Newman, Scott Wesley Morgan, Nick Olcott, Oscar Pitts Jr., Thomas Shelton, Nicholas A. Puccio, F.T. Rea, Vicki Ross-Norris, Stanley Anderson, Brian Smyj, Henry Strozier, Jeffrey Thompson, Harold Surratt, Katrina Tabori, Antonio Todd, Richard Turner, Bobby Zajonc
<u>D:</u> George P. Cosmatos   <u>WRIT:</u> Ric Gibbs & Adi Hasak   <u>PHOTOG:</u> Thomas L. Fisher   <u>SPCL-FX:</u> Buzz Feitshans IV   <u>MUSIC:</u> Bruce Broughton

Shadowed
1946, (USA), Col, b&w, 70 mins.
<u>W:</u> Anita Louise, Lloyd Corrigan, Robert Scott (*Scott Roberts*), Wilton Graff, Helen Koford (*Terry Moore*), Doris Houck
<u>D:</u> John Sturges   <u>SCR:</u> Brenda Weisberg, from a story by Julian Harmon
<u>PHOTOG:</u> Henry Freulich   <u>MUSIC DIR:</u> Mischa Bakaleinikoff
Standard thriller

The Shadow-Girl
see *La Clownesse Fantome*

Shadowhunter
1992, (USA), color, 90 mins.
<u>W:</u> Scott Glenn
Standard fantasy-thriller: Los Angeles detective vs. evil Amerind shaman

The Shadow in the Mirror
see *L'Ombre dans la Glace*

Shadow in the Sky
1952, (USA), MGM, b&w, 78 mins.
<u>W:</u> Ralph Meeker, Nancy Davis, James Whitmore, Eduard Franz, Jean Hagen
<u>P:</u> William H. Wright   <u>D:</u> Fred Wilcox   <u>SCR:</u> Ben Maddow
Standard melodrama: World War II vet returns home a shell-shocked psychopathic wreck

The Shadow Lady
see *La Dame Fantome*

Shadow Man (1953)
see *Street of Shadows*

Shadowman (1973)
see *Les Nuits Rouges*

Shadow Men
1997, (USA), color, 95 mins.

W: Eric Roberts, Sherilyn Fenn, Dean Stockwell, Andrew Prine
Standard SF-thriller: Family sees space aliens, flees from sinister gov't agents

Shadow of a Doubt
1943, (USA), Skirball/Univ, b&w, 108 mins.
W: Joseph Cotten (*Charles Oakley*), Teresa Wright (*Charlotte "Charlie" Newton*),
Macdonald Carey (*Jack Graham*), Patricia Collinge (*Emma Newton*), Wallace
Ford (*Fred Saunders*), Hume Cronyn (*Herb Hawkins*) (Film debut), Henry
Travers (*Joseph Newton*), Edna May Wonacott (*Ann Newton*), Charles Bates
(*Roger Newton*), Irving Bacon (*The Station Master*), Clarence Muse (*The
Pullman Porter*), Janet Shaw (*Louise*), Estelle Jewel (*Katherine*), Minerva
Urecal (*Mrs. Henderson*)
P: Jack H. Skirball **D:** Alfred Hitchcock **SCR:** Thornton Wilder, Sally Benson
& Alma Reville, based on a story by Gordon McDonell **PHOTOG:** Joseph
Valentine **MUSIC:** Dimitri Tiomkin
Classic thriller: Girl suspects visiting uncle is murderer. cf. **Step Down to Terror** *(also a
1991 TV Movie)*

Shadow of a Doubt
1991, (USA), Hallmark Hall of Fame/Rosemont/Univ, Made for TV, color, 95 mins.
W: Mark Harmon (*Charles Spencer*), Margaret Welsh (*Charlie*), Diane Ladd
(*Emma*), Norm Skaggs (*Gary*), William Lanteau (*Henry*), Shirley Knight
(*Mrs. Potter*), Rick Lenz (*Herb*), Tippi Hedren (*Mrs. Mathewson*), Sydney
Walker (*Granville*), Seth Smith (*Bobby*), Bianca Rose, Michael Wisley, John
Gavigan, Fran Lish, Olivia Charles, Romy Rosemont, Richard LaTouche,
Ken Grantham, Jason Kertel
D: Karen Arthur **TELEPLAY:** John Gay, from a screenplay by Thornton Wilder,
Sally Benson & Alma Reville, based on a story by Gordon McDonell
PHOTOG: Thomas Neuwirth **MUSIC:** Allyn Ferguson
TVM, standard thriller: Murderer returns to home town

Shadow of a Man
1955, (GB), E.J. Fancey/New Realm, b&w, 69 mins.
W: Paul Carpenter (*Gene*), Rona Anderson (*Linda*), Ronald Leigh-Hunt (*Norman*),
Jane Griffiths (*Carol*), Tony Quinn (*The Inspector*), Jack Taylor (*Sgt. McBride*),
Rose Alba (*The Singer*), Robert O'Neill (*Max*)
D: Michael McCarthy **SCR:** Paul Erickson & Michael McCarthy, from a play by
Paul Erickson
Standard thriller: Author exposes murderer

Shadow of a Woman
1946, (USA), WB, b&w, 78 mins.
W: Andrea King, Helmut Dantine
Standard thriller

Shadow of Death
1939, (GB), MM Films/ABFD, b&w, 25 mins.
W: Donald Calthrop (*Henry Wilson*), Ellen Pollock (*Mrs. Wilson*), Simon Lack,
Winifred Evans, Avice Astor
D: Harry S. Marks, from a play by John Quin
reissued 1948
Minor thriller: Henpeck poses as murderer

Shadow of Death
1983, (USA), Ulli Lommel/Cineamerica, color, 80 mins.
W: Suzanna Love, Keir Dullea (*Julian Bedford*), Vera Miles (*Marion Noonan*), Tony
Curtis (*Dr. Clavius*), Paul Willson (*Dr. Schroder*), Percy Rodrigues (*Dr.
Robinson*), Eve Brents Ashe (*Miss Simpson*), Ryan Seitz (*Danny Bedford*),
Nicholas Love (*Willy Meiser*), Corinne Alphen (*Lelia Adams*), Jessie Gordon,
Philippe Carr, Roger Burgraff, Michael DeFrancisco, Jason Fong, Diane
Doucette
WRIT, P, & D: Ulli Lommel **PHOTOG:** Jon Kranhouse **MUSIC:** Robert O.
Raglan
Minor SF-melodrama: Experiment to revive comatose woman transfers murder victim's memories. A.k.a. **Brainwaves**

Shadow of Doubt
1935, (USA), MGM, b&w, 75 mins.
W: Virginia Bruce, Ricardo Cortez, Bradley Page
D: George Seitz **PHOTOG:** Charles G. Clarke
Standard thriller: Actress accused of playboy's murder

Shadow of Evil
1921, (GB), British Art/Regent, b&w, 5,694 ft. (1735.5m)
W: Cecil Humphreys, Mary Dibley, Reginald Fox, Gladys Mason
P: Arrigo Bocchi **D:** James Reardon **SCR:** Harry Hughes, from a novel by
Carlton Dawe
Standard crime-thriller: Thief blackmails actress who thinks she killed husband

Shadow of Evil
1964, (It-Fr), PAC/CICC/DA.MA/7Arts, color, 92 mins.
W: Kerwin Mathews, Pier Angeli, Robert Hossein Stuart Nesbitt
P: Paul Cadeac **D:** Andre Hunebelle **SCR:** Pierre Foucaud, Raymond Borel,
Andre Hunebelle, Michel Lebrun, Richard Caron & Patrice Rondard
A.k.a. **Banco a Bangkok.** *US Release: 1967*
*Minor SF-thriller: Superagent foils mad scientist trying to exterminate "inferior races" with
deadly virus*

Shadow of Fear
see **Before I Wake**

Shadow of Suspicion
1944, (USA), Mono, b&w, 68 mins.
W: Peter Cookson, Marjorie Weaver
Minor thriller

Shadow of Terror
1945, (USA), PRC, b&w, 60 mins.
W: Richard Fraser **SCR:** Arthur St. Clair
D: Lew Landers **SCR:** Arthur St. Clair
Minor SF-thriller: Scientist develops A-bomb, dodges spies

The Shadow of the Cat
1961, (GB), BHP/Univ, b&w, 79 mins.
W: Barbara Shelley (*Elizabeth Venable*), Andre Morell (*Walter Venable*), William
Lucas (*Jacob*), Freda Jackson (*Clara*), Conrad Phillips (*Michael Latimer*),
Catherine Lacey (*Ella Venable*), Richard Warner (*Edgar*), Andrew Crawford
(*Andrew*), Henry Kendall (*The Doctor*), Vanda Godsell
P: Jon Pennington **D:** John Gilling **SCR:** George Baxt **PHOTOG:** Arthur
Grant **SPCL-FX:** Les Bowie **MUSIC:** Mikis Theodorakis
Modest thriller: Demonic cat avenges mistress' murder

Shadow of the Eagle
1950, (GB), Valiant-Tuscania/UA/IFD, b&w, 93 mins.
W: Richard Greene (*Count Alexei Orloff*), Valentina Cortese (*Princess Tarakanova*),
Greta Gynt (*Countess Camponiello*), Binnie Barnes (*Empress Catherine*), Charles
Goldner (*Gen. Korsakoff*), Walter Rilla (*Prince Rasiwill*), Hugh French (*Capt.
Nikolsky*), Dennis Vance (*Vaska*)
P: Anthony Havelock-Allan **D:** Sidney Salkow **SCR:** Doreen Montgomery &
Hagar Wilde **STORY:** Jacques Companeez
USA release, 1955
Standard adventure-thriller: Russian envoy ordered to kidnap princess

Shadow of the Guillotine
see **Marie Antoinette (1953)**

Shadow of the Hawk
1976, (Can), Col, color, 92 mins.
W: Jan-Michael Vincent (*Mike*), Marilyn Hassett (*Maureen*), Chief Dan George
(*Old Man Hawk*), Marianne Jones (*Dsonoqua*), Pia Shandel (*Faye*), Jacques
Hubert (*Andak*), Anna Hagen (*The Desk Nurse*), Cindi Griffith (*The
Secretary*), Murray Lowry (*The Intern*)
D: George McCowan **SCR:** Norman Thaddeus Vane & Herbert J Wright
STORY: Peter Jensen, Lynette Cahill & Norman Thaddeus Vane
PHOTOG: Jack Holbrook & Reginald Morris **SPCL-FX:** Dick Albain &
John Thomas **MUSIC:** Robert McMullin
Minor fantasy-thriller: Youth encounters Indian mysteries

Shadow of the Past
1950, (GB), Anglofilm/Col, b&w, 83 mins.
W: Joyce Howard (*The Lady in Black*), Terence Morgan (*John Harding*), Michael
Medwin (*Dick Stevens*), Andrew Osborn (*George Bentley*), Wylie Watson (*The
Caretaker*), Marie Ney (*Mrs. Bentley*), Ella Retford (*The Daily Help*), Ronald
Adam (*The Solicitor*), Louise Gainsborough (*Susie*)
P: Mario Zampi & Mae Murray **D:** Mario Zampi **SCR:** Aldo di Benedetti & Ian
Stuart Black **STORY:** Aldo di Benedetti
Minor thriller: "Ghost" of murderer's wife is her sister seeking revenge

Shadow of the Thin Man
1941, (USA), MGM, b&w, 97 mins.
W: William Powell (*Nick Charles*), Myrna Loy (*Nora Charles*), Barry Nelson (*Paul
Clarke*), Donna Reed (*Molly Ford*), Dickie Hall (*Nick Charles Jr.*), Sam
Levene (*Lt. Abrams*), Alan Baxter (*Whitey Barrow*), Loring Smith (*Link
Stephens*), Joseph Anthony (*Fred Macy*), Henry O'Neill (*Maj. Jason I. Sculley*),
Stella Adler (*Claire Porter*), Louise Beavers (*Stella*), Lou Lubin (*Rainbow
Benny Loomis*), Will Wright (*Maguire*), Oliver Blake (*Fenster*), Noel Cravat
(*Baku*), Tito Vuolo (*Luis*), Joe Oakie (*Spider Webb*), Tor Johnson (*Jack the
Ripper*), Jody Gilbert (*Lana*), Sid Melton (*Fingers*), Robert Kellard, Cliff
Danielson, J. Louis Smith, Edgar Dearing, John Dilson, Inez Cooper, Arthur
Aylesworth, James Flavin, Edward Hearn, Art Belasco, Bob Ireland, Jerry
Jerome, Buddy Roosevelt, Hal Le Sueur, Hardboiled Haggerty, Wee Willie
Davis, Ken Christy, Ray Teal
D: W.S. Van Dyke **SCR:** Harry Kurnitz & Irving Brecher, from characters created by Dashiell Hammett **PHOTOG:** William Daniels
Modest thriller, 4th "Nick & Nora Charles" mystery: Sleuthing couple finds crime at racetrack

Shadow of the Werewolf
see **La Noche de Walpurgis**

The Shadow of Zorro
1962, (Sp), color
W: Frank Latimore (*Don Diego/Zorro*), Maria Luz Galicia Mario Feliciani, Marco
Tulli
D: Joaquin Romero Marchent
Minor adventure-thriller: Villains lure Zorro out of hiding, come to regret it

S

Shadow on the Land
1968, (USA), Col-TV/ABC-TV, color, 97 mins.
W: Gene Hackman, Carol Lynley, Jackie Cooper, John Forsythe, Myron Healey
P: Matthew Rapf **D:** Richard C. Sarafian **TELEPLAY:** Nedrick Young
TVM, standard SF-thriller: Couple opposes fascist gov't

Shadow on the Wall
1950, (USA), MGM, b&w, 84 mins.
W: Nancy Davis, Zachary Scott, Gigi Perreau, Ann Sothern, John McIntire, Jimmy Hunt, Barbara Billingsley
P: Robert Sisk **D:** Patrick Jackson **SCR:** William Ludwig
Standard psychodrama: Girl witnesses stepmother's murder

The Shadow on the Window
1957, (USA), Col, b&w, 78 mins.
W: Phil Carey, Betty Garrett
Standard thriller

The Shadow Returns
1946, (USA), Mono, b&w, 61 mins.
W: Kane Richmond (*Lamont Cranston*), Barbara Reed, Tom Dugan
Minor thriller: Sleuth seeks missing jewels. 'Shadow' series

Shadows, a Nocturnal Hallucination
see Schatten, eine Nachtliche Halluzination

Shadows in the Night
1944, (USA), Col, b&w, 67 mins.
W: Warner Baxter (*Dr. Robert Ordway*), Nina Foch (*Lois Garland*), George Zucco (*Frank Swift*), Minor Watson (*Frederick Gordon*), Lester Matthews (*Stanley Carter*), Ben Welden (*Nick Kallus*), Edward Norris (*Jess Hilton*), Jeanne Bates (*Adele Carter*), Charles Wilson (*The Sheriff*), Charles Halton (*Doc Stacey*), Arthur Hohl (*Riggs*)
D: Eugene Forde **SCR:** Eric Taylor, from characters created by Max Marcin
Standard Crime Doctor thriller: Crime-psychiatrist aids girl stalked by hooded figure

The Shadows of Forgotten Ancestors
1964, (Russ), Artkino, color, 99 mins.
W: Ivan Mikolaitchouk, Larisa Kadotchnikova, T. Bestaeva
D: Sergei Paradjanov **SCR:** Sergei Paradjanov & I. Tchendei **MUSIC:** M. Chorik
Critcially-acclaimed melodrama: Man tries to cope with loss of lover and family, finds himself lost in past

Shadows on the Stairs
1941, (USA), Univ, b&w, 63 mins.
W: Frieda Inescort, Paul Cavanagh, Heather Angel, Lumsden Hare, Bruce Lester, Miles Mander, Turhan Bey
D: David Ross Lederman
Standard thriller: Murders in creepy boarding house

Shadows over Chinatown
1946, (USA), Mono, b&w, 64 mins.
W: Sidney Toler (*Charlie Chan*), Mantan Moreland (*Birmingham Brown*), Victor Sen Yung (*Tommie Chan*), Tanis Chandler (*Mary Conover*), John Gallaudet (*Jeff Hay*), Bruce Kellogg (*Jack Tilford*), Paul Bryar (*Mike Rogan*), Jack Norton (*Cosgrove*), Alan Bridge (*Capt. Allen*), Mary Gordon (*Mrs. Conover*), John Hamilton (*The Bus Passenger*), Charles Jordan (*Jenkins*), Dorothy Granger (*Joan Mercer*), George Eldredge, Lyle Latell, Myra McKinney
D: Terry Morse **SCR:** Raymond Schrock, from characters created by Earl Derr Biggers **PHOTOG:** William A. Sickner
Standard "Charlie Chan" thriller: Oriental sleuth cracks insurance racket

Shadows Run Black
1984, (USA), color, 89 mins.
W: William J. Kulzer, Elizabeth Trosper, Kevin Costner
D: Howard Heard
Minor thriller: Maniac stalks coed

The Shadow Strikes
1937, (USA), b&w, 61 mins.
W: Rod La Rocque, Lynn Anders
Minor thriller: Sleuth pursues killer and gangster

Shadow Warriors
1996, (USA), color, 80 mins.
W: Terry O'Quinn
Standard SF-horror: Evil scientists seeks human corpses to produce line of enhanced cyborgs

Shadowzone
1990, (USA), Full Moon/Para, color, 96 mins.
W: Louise Fletcher (*Dr. Erhart*), David Beecroft (*Capt. Hickock*), James Hong (*Van Fleet*), Shawn Weatherly (*Kidwell*), Miguel Nunez (*Wiley*), Lu Leonard (*Cutter*), David Hicks (*The Pilot*), Frederick Flynn (*Shivers*), Jack Leal (*The Corpse*), Maureen Flaherty (*Jenna*), John Stuart (*Mme. Pip*), Robbie Rives (*James*), Mac (*Bingo*)
WRIT & D: J.S. Cardone **PHOTOG:** Karen Grossman **MUSIC:** Richard Band
Minor SF-thriller: Scientists menaced by beast from another dimension

Shadow Zone: My Teacher Ate My Homework
1997, (USA), color, 95 mins.
W: Shelley Duvall, Gregory Smith
Made-for-Cable, standard thriller: Teen acquires voodoo doll that resembles teacher

Shadow Zone: The Undead Express
1996, (USA), SHO-TV, color, 95 mins.
W: Ron Silver (*Valentine*), Chauncey Leopardi (*Zach*), Tony T. Johnson (*J.T.*), Wes Craven
D: Stephen Williams, from books by J.R. Black
Made-for-Cable, juvenile fantasy-thriller: Boy on subway befriended by vampire

The Shaggy D.A.
1976, (USA), Walt Disney/Buena Vista, color, 91 mins.
W: Dean Jones (*Wilby Daniels*), Suzanne Pleshette (*Betty Daniels*), Tim Conway (*Tim*), Keenan Wynn (*John Slade*), Jo Anne Worley (*Katrinka*), Dick Van Patten (*Raymond*), Vic Tayback (*Eddie Roschak*), Shane Sinutko (*Brian Daniels*), John Myhers (*Adm. Brenner*), Warren Berlinger (*Dip*), Hans Conried (*Prof. Whatley*), John Fiedler (*Howie Clemmings*), Richard Bakalyan (*Freddie*), Ronnie Schell (*The TV Director*), Jonathan Daly (*The TV Interviewer*), Michael McGreevey (*Sheldon*), Richard O'Brien (*The Desk Sergeant*), Dick Lane (*The Roller Rink Announcer*), Benny Rubin (*The Waiter*), Ruth Gillette (*The Song Chairman*), Hank Jones (*The Policeman*), Pat McCormick (*The Bartender*), Iris Adrian (*The Manageress*), Henry Slate, Mary Ann Gibson, Milton Frome, Walt Davis, Albert Able, Helene Winston, Joan Crosby, Sarah Fankboner, Herb Vigran, Danny Wells, Olan Soule, Vern Rowe, Karl Lukas, Christina Anderson, John Hayes, George Kirby (*Canine Character Voices*)
P: Bill Anderson **D:** Robert Stevenson **SCR:** Don Tait, suggested by Felix Salten's *The Hound of Florence* **PHOTOG:** Frank Phillips **MUSIC:** Buddy Baker
Standard comedy-fantasy (sequel to The Shaggy Dog): Weredog curse plagues socialite

The Shaggy Dog
1959, (USA), Walt Disney/Buena Vista, b&w, 104 mins.
W: Tommy Kirk (*Wilby Daniels*), Fred MacMurray (*Wilson Daniels*), Jean Hagen (*Frieda Daniels*), Annette Funicello (*Allison*), Tim Considine (*Buzz Miller*), Roberta Shore (*Francesca*), Kevin Corcoran (*Moochie*), Alexander Scourby, Jack Albertson, Cecil Kellaway, Strother Martin, Forrest Lewis, James Westerfield, Jacques Aubuchon
D: Charles T. Barton **SCR:** Bill Walsh & Lillie Hayward, suggested by Felix Salten's *The Hound of Florence* **PHOTOG:** Edward Colman **MUSIC:** Paul Smith
Amusing comedy-fantasy: Curse of Borgia ring turns youth into canine at inopportune moments. cf. The Shaggy D.A.

The Shaggy Dog
1994, (USA), Walt Disney, color
W: Ed Begley Jr., Scott Weinger Sharon Lawrence, Jeremy Sisto, Jon Polito, James Cromwell, Jordan Blake Warkol, Bobby Slayton, Rick Ducommun
D: Dennis Dugan **TELEPLAY:** Bill Walsh, Lillie Hayward & Tim Doyle **PHOTOG:** Russ Alsobrook
Standard comedy-fantasy (remake of classic)

The Shakedown
1960, (GB), Ethiro/Rank, b&w, 92 mins.
W: Hazel Court (*Mildred Hyde*), Terence Morgan (*Augie Cortona*), Donald Pleasence (*Jessel*), Robert Beatty (*Insp. Jarvis*), Bill Owen (*Spettigue*), Sheila Buxton (*Nadia*), Harry H. Corbett (*Gollar*), Gene Anderson (*Zena*), Dorinda Stevens (*Grace*), Eddie Byrne (*George*), John Salew (*Mr. Arnold*), Edward Judd (*Bernie*), Joan Haythorne (*Miss Ogilvie*), Angela Douglas (*Jennifer*), Jackie Collins (*Rita*)
P: Norman Williams **D:** John Lemont **SCR:** John Lemont & Leigh Vance
Modest thriller: Woman spies on crime boss

Shake Hands with Murder
1944, (USA), American Prods./PRC, b&w, 62 mins.
W: Iris Adrian, Frank Jenks, Douglas Fowley
Minor thriller

Shakespeare's Dream
see Le Reve de Shakespeare

Shakespeare's Tragedy King Lear
1909, (GB), b&w
D: J. Stuart Blackton, based on Shakespeare's play *King Lear*
Standard melodrama: Ruler's foolishness destroys kingdom

Shakespeare Writing Julius Caesar
see Le Reve de Shakespeare

Shakma
1990, (USA), color
W: Christopher Atkins, Amanda Wyss, Roddy McDowall
Standard SF-thriller: Killer baboon traps medical students

The Shaman
1987, (USA), color, 88 mins.

W: Michael Conforti, Elvind Harum, James Farkas, Lynn Weaver
D: Michael Yakub
Minor thriller: Mystic casts hypnotic spell

Shame of the Jungle
see **Jungle Burger**

Shamus
1959, (GB), Border/New Realm, color, 54 mins.
W: John Francis Rooney (*Seamus Rooney*), Tiny Littler (*The Leprechaun*)
P: O. Negus-Fancey **D & STORY:** Eric Marquis
Standard fantasy: Leprechaun aids orphan boy

Shamus O'Brien: or, Saved from the Scaffold
1905, (GB), Cricks & Sharp, b&w, 300 ft. (91.4m)
D: Tom Green, from a poem by Sheridan le Fanu
Standard crime-thriller (in 6 scenes): Man frames rival for stabbing rich uncle

The Shanghai Chest
1948, (USA), Mono, b&w, 65 mins.
W: Roland Winters (*Charlie Chan*), Mantan Moreland (*Birmingham Brown*), Tim Ryan (*Lt. Mike Ruark*), Victor Sen Yung (*Tommie Chan*), Deannie Best (*Phyllis Powers*), John Alvin (*Vic Armstrong*), Tristram Coffin (*Ed Seward*), Philip Van Zandt (*Tony Pindello*), Russell Hicks (*D.A. Bronson*), Bill Woolf (*The Juror*), Pierre Watkin (*Judge Armstrong*), Milton Parsons (*Grail*), Olaf Hytten (*Bates*), Erville Alderson (*Walter Somerville*), Louis Mason (*The Custodian*), George Eldredge (*Finley*), Willie Best (*Willie*), David Hoffman (*Graves*), Edward Coke, Charlie Sullivan, William Ruhl, Paul Scardon, Lois Austin, Chabing, John Shay
D: William Beaudine **SCR:** Scott Darling & Sam Newman, from characters created by Earl Derr Biggers **PHOTOG:** William Sickner
Standard "Charlie Chan" thriller: Young man accused of murdering district attorney

The Shanghai Cobra
1945, (USA), Mono, b&w, 64 mins.
W: Sidney Toler (*Charlie Chan*), Mantan Moreland (*Birmingham Brown*), Benson Fong (*Tommie Chan*), Addison Richards (*John Adams/Jan VanHorn*), Joan Barclay (*Paula Webb*), James Flavin (*Jarvis*), Walter Fenner (*Insp. Harry Davis*), Joe Devlin (*Taylor*), James Cardwell (*Ned Stewart*), Gene Stutenroth (*Morgan*), Arthur Loft (*Bradford Harris/Hume*), Roy Gordon (*Walter Fletcher*), Janet Warren (*Lorraine*)
D: Phil Karlson **SCR:** George Callahan & George Wallace Sayre, from characters created by Earl Derr Biggers **PHOTOG:** Vincent Farrar **MUSIC:** Edward J. Kay
Standard "Charlie Chan" thriller: Oriental sleuth hunts killer who uses cobra venom

Shanghai Express
1932, (USA), Para, b&w, 84 mins.
W: Marlene Dietrich, Clive Brook, Warner Oland, Anna May Wong, Eugene Pallette, Lawrence Grant, Louise Closser Hale, Gustav von Seyffertitz, Forrester Harvey
D: Josef von Sternberg **SCR:** Jules Furthman, from Harry Hervey's novel **PHOTOG:** Lee Garmes
Classic melodrama: British train passengers waylaid by Chinese bandits. cf. **Peking Express** *also* **Night Plane to Chungking**

Shangri-La
see **Lost Horizon** (1937)

Shanks
1974, (USA), Para, color, 93 mins.
W: Marcel Marceau (*Malcolm Shanks/Old Walker*), Philippe Clay (*Barton*), Tsilla Chelton (*Mrs. Barton*), Cindy Eilbacher (*Celia*), Helena Kallianiotes (*Mata Hari*), Larry Bishop (*Napoleon*), Don Calfa (*Einstein*), Biff Manard (*Goliath*), Mondo (*Genghis Khan*), Read Morgan (*The Policeman*), William Castle (*The Grocer*), Phil Adams (*Beethoven*), Lara Wing (*The Little Girl*)
P: Steven North **D:** William Castle **SCR:** Ranald Graham **PHOTOG:** Joe Biroc **MUSIC:** Alex North
Odd, uneven horror-thriller (director William Castle's last film): Mute puppeteer revives dead, uses them against enemies

Shape of Things to Come (1936)
see **Things to Come**

The Shape of Things to Come
1979, (Can), CFI/Film Ventures, color, 93 mins.
W: Jack Palance (*Omus*), Carol Lynley (*Niki*), Barry Morse (*John Caball*), John Ireland (*Sen. Smedley*), Nicholas Campbell (*Jason Caball*), Eddie Benton (*Kim Smedley*), Ardon Bess (*Merrick*), Lynn Green, Bill Lake
P: William Davidson **D:** George McCowan **SCR:** Martin Lager, inspired by H.G. Wells' writings **PHOTOG:** Reginald H. Morris **MUSIC:** Paul Herbert
Minor SF-thriller: Couple opposes dictator of future

Sharad of Atlantis
1966, (USA), Nat Levine/Rep, b&w, 100 mins.
W: Ray "Crash" Corrigan, William Farnum, Monte Blue, Lois Wilde, Lon Chaney Jr., Boothe Howard, Smiley Burnette, Raymond Hatton
P: Barney Sarecky **D:** B. Reeves "Breezy" Eason & Joseph Kane **SCR:** John

Rathmell, Maurice Geraghty & Oliver Drake, from a story by Tracy Knight & John Rathmell **MUSIC SPRVSR:** Harry Grey
Standard SF-adventure (feature version of 1936 serial **Undersea Kingdom**): *Scientists find lost continent*

The Share Out
1962, (GB), Merton Park/Anglo-Amalgamated, b&w, 61 mins.
W: Bernard Lee (*Supt. Meredith*), Alexander Knox (*Col. Calderwood*), Moira Redmond (*Diana Marsh*), William Russell (*Mike Stafford*), Richard Vernon (*John Crewe*), Richard Warner (*Mark Speller*), John Gabriel (*Monet*), Jack Rodney (*Gregory*)
P: Jack Greenwood **D:** Gerald Glaister **SCR:** Philip Mackie, from Edgar Wallace's novel *Judgement*
Minor crime-thriller: Detective unmasks blackmailing colonel

Shark Kill
1976, (USA), D'Antoni-Weitz/NBC-TV, color, 74 mins.
W: Richard Yniguez, Jennifer Warren, Philip Clark
P: Barry Weitz **D:** William A. Graham **TELEPLAY:** Sandor Stern
TVM, minor thriller (**Jaws** *imitation): Man vs. great white shark*

Shark Reef
see **She-Gods of Shark Reef**

The Sharks' Cave
1978, (It-Sp), color, 90 mins.
W: Andres Garcia, Janet Agren, Arthur Kennedy, Pino Colizzi, Maximo Valverde
D: "Anthony Richmond" (*Teodoro Ricci*)
Minor SF-adventure: Toltec aquanauts control killer sharks

Sharks' Treasure
1975, (USA), color, 95 mins.
W: Yaphet Kotto, John Nellson, Cliff Osmond, David Canary, David Gilliam
D & SCR: Cornel Wilde
Minor thriller

Sharon's Secret
1995, (USA), USA-TV, color, 91 mins.
W: Mel Harris, Candace Cameron, Alex McArthur, Paul Regina, James Pickens Jr., Elaine Kagan, Gregg Henry
D: Michael Scott **TELEPLAY:** Mark Homer **PHOTOG:** Stephen M. Katz **MUSIC:** Philip Giffin
TVM, standard thriller

Shatter
see **Call Him Mr. Shatter**

A Shattered Idyll
1916, (GB), British Photoplay Prods., b&w, 5,000 ft. (1524m)
W: Peggy Mills, Peter Lewis, Dorothy Dare, Martin Herbert
P: Edward Godal **D:** Dave Aylott
Standard melodrama: Love, jealousy and hate among gypsy caravans

Shattered Silence
see **When Michael Calls**

She (1899)
see **La Danse de Feu**

She
1911, (USA), Thanhouser, b&w
W: Marguerite Snow (*Ayesha*), James Cruze
from H. Rider Haggard's novel
Standard fantasy: Immortal woman seeks lost love

She
1916, (GB), Barker/Lucoque, b&w, 5,400 ft. (1646m)
W: Alice Delysia (*Ayesha*), Henry Victor (*Leo Vincey*), Sydney Bland (*Horace Holley*), Blanche Forsythe (*Ustane*), Jack Denton (*Job*), J. Hastings Batson (*Bilali*)
D: Will Barker & H. Lisle Lucoque **SCR:** Nellie E. Lucoque, from H. Rider Haggard's novel
Standard adventure-fantasy: Explorer is reincarnated lover of 2000-year-old queen

She
1917, (USA), Fox, b&w, 5 reels
W: Valeska Suratt
D: Kenean Buel, from H. Rider Haggard's novel
Standard adventure-fantasy: Explorers meet immortal queen

She
1925, (GB-Ger), Reciprocity Films/Artlee, b&w, 8,250 ft. (2514.6m)
W: Betty Blythe (*Ayesha*), Carlyle Blackwell (*Leo Vincey/Kallikrates*), Mary Odette (*Ustane*), Tom Reynolds (*Job*), Heinrich George (*Horace Holly*), Jerrold Robertshaw (*Bilali*), Marjorie Statler (*Amenartes*), Alexander Butler (*Mahomet*), Henry Victor
D: Leander de Cordova **SCR:** Walter Summers, from H. Rider Haggard's novel
Standard adventure-fantasy: Explorer is ageless queen's reincarnated lover

S

She

1935, (USA), RKO, b&w, 89 mins.
W: Helen Gahagan *(Ayesha)*, Randolph Scott *(Leo Vincey/Kallikrates)*, Nigel Bruce *(Maj. Holly)*, Helen Mack, Samuel S. Hinds, Lumsden Hare, Gustav von Seyffertitz, Noble Johnson
P: Merian C. Cooper **D:** Irving Pichel & Lansing C. Holden **SCR:** Ruth Rose loosely based on H. Rider Haggard's novel **MUSIC:** Max Steiner
blurb: "Young and beautiful for 500 years...and wicked every one of them!"
Bizarre adventure-fantasy: Explorers find ageless queen in hidden city at North Pole

She

1965, (GB), Hammer-7Arts/MGM, color, 106 mins.
W: Ursula Andress *(Ayesha)*, John Richardson *(Leo Vincey (Kallikrates))*, Peter Cushing *(Maj. Holly)*, Christopher Lee *(Bilali)*, Bernard Cribbins *(Job)*, Rosenda Monteros *(Ustane)*, Andre Morell *(Haumeid)*, John Maxim *(The Captain)*, Soraya, Julie Mendes, Lisa Peake
P: Michael Carreras **D:** Robert Day **SCR:** David Chantler, from H. Rider Haggard's novel **PHOTOG:** Harry Waxman **SPCL-FX:** Bowie Films Ltd. **MUSIC:** James Bernard
Lavish adventure-fantasy: Ageless queen awaits reborn love. cf. **The Vengeance of She**

S*H*E

1980, (USA-W. Ger-It), Martin Bregman/CBS-TV, color, 96 mins.
W: Cornelia Sharpe *(Lavinia Kean)*, Omar Sharif *(Cesare Magnasco)*, William Traylor *(Lacey)*, Anita Ekberg *(Else)*, Robert Lansing *(Owen Hooper)*, Fabio Testi *(Rudolph Caserta)*, Isabella Rye *(Fanya)*, Tom Christopher, Mario Colli
D: Robert Lewis **TELEPLAY:** Richard Maibaum **PHOTOG:** Jules Brenner **MUSIC:** Michael Kamen
TVM, minor thriller: Adventures of female spy

She

1983, (USA-It), Royal Film/American Nat'l, color, 106 mins.
W: Sandahl Bergman *(She)*, David Goss *(Tom)*, Quin Kessler *(Shanda)*, Harrison Muller *(Dick)*, Elena Wiedermann *(Hari)*, Gordon Mitchell *(Hector)*, Laurie Sherman *(Taphir)*, Andrew McLeay *(Tark)*, Cyrus Elias *(Kram)*, David Brandon *(Pretty Boy)*, Susan Adler *(Pretty Girl)*, Gregory Snegoff *(Godan)*, Mary D'Antin *(Eva)*, Mario Pedone *(Rudolph)*, Donald Hodson *(Rabel)*, Maria Quasimodo *(Moona)*, David Traylor *(Xenon)*
WRIT & D: Avi Nesher, inspired by H. Rider Haggard's novel **PHOTOG:** Sandro Mancori **SPCL-FX:** Armando Grilli **MUSIC:** Rick Wakeman **ADDITIONAL MUSIC:** Justin Hayward, Motorhead, & Bastard **SONGS:** *Eternal Woman, Rescue Me, Why?, Scream in the Night & War*
Standard SF-"Sword & Sandal": Amazonian postnuclear "goddess" helps muscleman find kidnapped sister

She and the Fear
see Ella y el Miedo

The She Beast
see La Sorella di Satan

The She-Creature

1956, (USA), Golden State/AIP, b&w, 77 mins.
W: Marla English *(Andrea Talbott)*, Chester Morris *(Dr. Carlo Lombardi)*, Tom Conway *(Timothy Chappel)*, Frieda Inescort *(Mrs. Chappel)*, Lance Fuller *(Ted Erickson)*, Cathy Downs *(Dorothy Chappel)*, Ron Randell *(Lt. Ed James)*, Frank

The She-Creature

Jenks, Flo Burt, El Brendel, Kenneth MacDonald, Bill Hudson, Paul Dubov, Jeanne Evans, Jack Mulhall, Paul Blaisdell, Stuart Holmes, Creighton Hale, Luana Walters, Edward Earle, Franklyn Farnum, Edmund Cobb
P: Alex Gordon **D:** Edward L. Cahn **SCR:** Lou Rusoff, from an orig. idea by Jerry Zigmond **PHOTOG:** Frederick E. West
orig. co-billed with **It Conquered the World**
blurb: "Reincarnated as a monster from Hell!"
Standard horror-fantasy: Hypnotist gives frightening substance to primitive, reincarnated facet of beautiful girl's personality. cf. **Creature of Destruction**

She Demons

1957, (USA), Screencraft/Astor, b&w, 77 mins.
W: Irish McCalla *(Jerrie)*, Tod Griffin *(Fred)*, Rudolph Anders *(Osler)*, Victor Sen Yung *(Sammy)*, Gene Roth *(Igor)*, Leni Tana *(Mona Osler)*, Charles Opunui, Billy Dix, Whitey Hughes, Bill Coontz *(Foster)*, Larry Gelman, Maureen Janzen, Michael Stoycoff, Grace Mathews, George Barrows, The Diana Nellis Dancers
P: Arthur A. Jacobs **D:** Richard Cunha **SCR:** Richard Cunha & H.E. Barrie **PHOTOG:** Meredith Nicholson **SPCL-FX:** David Koehler **MUSIC:** Nicholas Carras
Minor SF-thriller: Nazi-type scientist experiments on jungle girls

She Devil (1934)
see Drums O'Voodoo

She-Devil

1957, (USA), Regal/20th-Fox, b&w, 77 mins.
W: Mari Blanchard, Albert Dekker, Jack Kelly, John Archer, Fay Baker, Blossom Rock (Marie Blake), Paul Cavanagh, George Baxter, Tod Griffin, Helen Jay, Joan Bradshaw
P & D: Kurt Neumann **SCR:** Kurt Neumann & Carroll Young, loosely based on Stanley G. Weinbaum's short story *The Adaptive Ultimate* **MUSIC:** Paul Sawtell & Bert Shefter
Engrossing SF-thriller: Scientists rescue woman from death, find they have created amoral monster

She-Devils on Wheels

1968, (USA), Creative/Mayflower, color,.83 mins.
W: Ruby Tuesday
P & D: Herschell Gordon Lewis **SCR:** A. Louis Downe
Minor thriller: Exploits of vicious female motorcycle gang

Sheena

1984, (USA), Col, color, 115 mins.
W: Tanya Roberts *(Sheena)*, Ted Wass, Donovan Scott, Trevor Thomas, Elizabeth of Toro, Clifton James, John Forgeham, France Zobda
D: John Guillermin **SCR:** David Newman & Lorenzo Semple Jr. **STORY:** David Newman & Leslie Stevens **PHOTOG:** Pasqualino De Santis **MUSIC:** Richard Hartley
Standard adventure-thriller: Jungle girl opposes evil land barons

She Freak

1966, (USA), Sonney-Friedman, color, 87 mins.
W: Claire Brennen, Lynn Courtney, Lee Raymond Madame Lee
P & SCR: David F. Friedman **D:** Byron Mabe
A.k.a. Alley of Nightmares
Minor thriller (Sleazy partial-remake of **Freaks***): Sideshow barker weds venal waitress*

She-Gods of Shark Reef

1958, (USA), AIP, color, 62 mins.
W: Don Durant, Lisa Montell, Bill Cord, Jeanne Gerson, Carol Lindsay
D: Roger Corman **SCR:** Robert Hill & Victor Stoloff **PHOTOG:** Floyd Crosby **SONGS:** *Nearer My Love to You*
GB retitle, **Shark Reef** *orig. co-billed with* **Night of the Blood-Beast**
Standard adventure-thriller (similar to 'Tabu'): Island girl marked for sacrifice

She Let Him Continue
see Pretty Poison (1968)

Shell Shock

1964, (USA), Parade, color, 75 mins.
W: Beech Dickerson, Carl Crow
Minor thriller

She Must Have Swallowed It

1912, (GB), Clarendon, b&w, 450 ft. (137.2m)
D: Percy Stow
Standard comedy-fantasy: Horse eats baby, is cut open by vet

She Played with Fire
see Fortune Is a Woman

The Sheriff and the Satellite Kid

1979, (It), color
W: Cary Guffey, Bud Spencer, Joe Bugner, Raimund Harmstorf
Minor SF-fantasy: Gruff lawman befriends cute extraterrestrial

S

Sherlock and Me
see *Without a Clue*

Sherlock Holmes
1909, (Den), Nordisk, b&w
W: Forrest Holger Madsen
WRIT & D: Forrest Holger Madsen, from characters created by Sir Arthur Conan Doyle

Sherlock Holmes
1922, (USA), Famous Players/Para, b&w, 9 reels (8,200 ft./2499.4m)
W: John Barrymore (*Sherlock Holmes*), Roland Young (*Dr. John Watson*), Gustav von Seyffertitz (*Prof. Moriarty*), William Powell [Film debut] (*Forman Wells*), Carol Dempster (*Alice Faulkner*), Hedda Hopper (*Madge Larrabee*), Louis Wolheim (*Craigin*), Margaret Kemp (*Therese*), Percy Knight (*Sid Jones*), Peggy Bayfield (*Rose Faulkner*), Anders Randolf (*James Larrabee*), Robert Schable (*Alf Bassick*), David Torrence (*Count Von Stalburg*), Reginald Denny (*Prince Alexis*), Lumsden Hare (*Dr. Leighton*), Robert Fischer (*Otto*), Jerry Devine (*Billy*), John Willard (*Insp. Gregson*)
D: Albert Parker   SCR: Marion Fairfax & Earle Browne, from characters created by Sir Arthur Conan Doyle   PHOTOG: J. Roy Hunt
GB retitle, Moriarty
Standard thriller

Sherlock Holmes
1932, (USA), Fox, b&w, 68 mins.
W: Clive Brook (*Sherlock Holmes*), Reginald Owen (*Dr. John Watson*), Ernest Torrence (*Prof. Moriarty*), Miriam Jordan, Herbert Mundin, C. Montague Shaw, Alan Mowbray, Howard Leeds
D: William K. Howard   SCR: Bertram Millhauser, from characters created by Sir Arthur Conan Doyle   PHOTOG: George Barnes
Standard thriller: Master villain plans famed detective's destruction

Sherlock Holmes (1939)
see *The Adventures of Sherlock Holmes (1939)*

Sherlock Holmes and the Deadly Necklace
1964, (W. Ger), Constantin/Screen Gems/CCC, b&w, 84 mins.
W: Christopher Lee (*Sherlock Holmes*), Thorley Walters (*Dr. John Watson*), Senta Berger, from characters created by Sir Arthur Conan Doyle
Standard thriller: Priceless artifact stolen from Egyptian tomb

Sherlock Holmes and the House of Fear
see *The House of Fear*

Sherlock Holmes and the Incident at Victoria Falls
1991, (GB), color, 120 mins.
W: Christopher Lee, Patrick Macnee, Jenny Seagrove
D: Bill Corcoran, from characters created by Sir Arthur Conan Doyle
A.k.a. Incident at Victoria Falls
Standard thriller: Sleuth comes out of retirement, endeavors to transport diamond from Africa to London

Sherlock Holmes and the Scarlet Claw
see *The Scarlet Claw*

Sherlock Holmes and the Secret Code
see *Dressed to Kill (1946)*

Sherlock Holmes and the Voice of Terror: BASIL RATHBONE AND EVELYN ANKERS

Sherlock Holmes and the Secret Weapon
1942, (USA), Univ, b&w, 68 mins.
W: Basil Rathbone (*Sherlock Holmes*), Nigel Bruce (*Dr. John Watson*), Lionel Atwill

(*Prof. Moriarty*), Dennis Hoey (*Insp. Lestrade*), Mary Gordon (*Mrs. Hudson*), Kaaren Verne (*Charlotte Eberli*), William Post Jr. (*Dr. Franz Tobel*), Holmes Herbert (*Sir Reginald*), Henry Daniell
D: Roy William Neill   SCR: Edward T. Lowe Jr., W. Scott Darling & Edmund L. Hartmann, from Sir Arthur Conan Doyle's short story "Dancing Men"   PHOTOG: Les White   MUSIC: Frank Skinner
orig. to be titled Sherlock Holmes Fights Back
Standard thriller: Criminal genius covets bomb-sight plans

Sherlock Holmes and the Voice of Terror
1942, (USA), Univ, b&w, 65 mins.
W: Basil Rathbone (*Sherlock Holmes*), Nigel Bruce (*Dr. John Watson*), Evelyn Ankers (*Kitty*), Reginald Denny (*Sir Evan Barham/Heinrich von Bork*), Thomas Gomez (*Meade*), Hillary Brooke (*Jill*), Montagu Love (*Lawford*), Mary Gordon (*Mrs. Hudson*), Henry Daniell (*Lloyd*), Rudolph Anders (*Schiller*), Olaf Hytten (*Prentiss*), Leyland Hodgson (*Col. Shore*)
D: John Rawlins   SCR: Lynn Riggs & John Bright, from Sir Arthur Conan Doyle's short story "His Last Bow"   PHOTOG: Woody Bredell   MUSIC DIR: Charles Previn
Standard thriller: Nazi broadcast scares English populace

Sherlock Holmes and the Woman in Green
see *The Woman in Green*

Sherlock Holmes Baffled
1900, (USA), Edison, b&w
from characters created by Sir Arthur Conan Doyle
Standard thriller

Sherlock Holmes Faces Death
1943, (USA), Univ, b&w, 68 mins.
W: Basil Rathbone (*Sherlock Holmes*), Nigel Bruce (*Dr. John Watson*), Dennis Hoey (*Insp. Lestrade*), Gavin Muir (*Philip Musgrave*), Hillary Brooke (*Sally Musgrave*), Milburn Stone (*Capt. Pat Vicary*), Gerald Hamer (*Langford*), Mary Gordon (*Mrs. Hudson*), Arthur Margetson, Halliwell Hobbes, Minna Phillips, Frederick Worlock, Olaf Hytten
P & D: Roy William Neill   SCR: Bertram Millhauser, from characters created by Sir Arthur Conan Doyle   PHOTOG: Charles Van Enger   MUSIC DIR: H.J. Salter
Standard thriller: Chessboard provides clue to several puzzling murders

Sherlock Holmes' Fatal Hour
see *The Sleeping Cardinal*

Sherlock Holmes Fights Back
see *Sherlock Holmes and the Secret Weapon*

Sherlock Holmes in New York
1976, (USA), 20th-Fox/NBC-TV, color, 100 mins.
W: Roger Moore (*Sherlock Holmes*), Patrick Macnee (*Dr. John Watson*), John Huston (*Prof. Moriarty*), Charlotte Rampling (*Irene Adler*), Geoffrey Robert Moore (*Scott Adler*), David Huddleston (*Insp. Lafferty*), Gig Young (*Mortimer McGraw*), Jackie Coogan (*The Haymarket Proprietor*), John Abbott (*Heller*), Signe Hasso (*Fraulein Reichenbach*), Leon Ames (*Daniel Furman*), Maria Grimm (*Nicole Romaine*), Paul Sorensen (*The Man in the Checked Suit*), William Benedict (*The Telegraph Office Manager*), Marjorie Bennett (*Mrs. Hudson*), Robert F. Ball (*Nickers*), John Steadman (*The Stage Doorman*), Vince Barbi (*Workman #1*), Roy Goldman (*Workman #2*), Tom Denver (*The Policeman*), Gil Perkins (*The Carriage Driver*), Alvin Sapinsley (*The Engineer*), Shawn Mallory (*The Workman on the Pier*), Meredith Cutts (*The Telegram Boy*)
P: John Cutts   D: Boris Sagal   TELEPLAY: Alvin Sapinsley, from characters created by Sir Arthur Conan Doyle   PHOTOG: Michael Margulies   MUSIC: Richard Rodney Bennett   MUSIC CONDUCT: Leonard Rosenman
TVM, standard thriller: Famed detective opposes criminal genius

Sherlock Holmes in Washington
1942, (USA), Univ, b&w, 71 mins.
W: Basil Rathbone (*Sherlock Holmes*), Nigel Bruce (*Dr. John Watson*), Henry Daniell (*Easter*), John Archer (*Pete*), George Zucco (*Stanley*), Don Terry (*Howe*), Marjorie Lord, Thurston Hall, Holmes Herbert, Edmund MacDonald, Bradley Page, Gerald Hamer
D: Roy William Neill, from characters created by Sir Arthur Conan Doyle   PHOTOG: Les White   MUSIC: Frank Skinner   MUSIC CONDUCT: Charles Previn
Standard thriller: Famed detective trails stolen document and missing secret agent

Sherlock Jr.
1924, (USA), Metro, b&w, 5 reels (4,065 ft./1239m/48 mins.)
W: Buster Keaton (*Sherlock Jr.*), Kathryn McGuire (*The Girl*), Ward Crane (*The Rival*), Joe Keaton (*The Father*), Erwin Connelly, Horace Morgan, Jane Connelly, Ford West, Ruth Holly, George Davis, John Patrick
P, D, & SCR: Buster Keaton   STORY: Clyde Bruckman, Jean Havez & Joseph Mitchell   PHOTOG: Byron Houck & Elgin Lessley
Standard spoof: Youth fantasizes about sleuthing

She's Dressed to Kill
1979, (USA), Barry Weitz/NBC-TV, color, 96 mins.
W: Eleanor Parker (*Regine Danton*), Jessica Walter (*Irene Barton*), Connie Sellecca (*Alix Goodman*), John Rubinstein (*Alan Lenz*), Jim McMullen (*David*),

Gretchen Corbett (*Laura Gooch*), Joanna Cassidy (*Camille*), Barbara Cason (*Deenie*), Clive Revill (*Victor De Salle*), Corinne Calvet, Jonathan Banks, Peter Horton, Marianne McAndrew, Russ Martin, Noah Keen, Grayce Spence
D: Gus Trikonis **TELEPLAY:** George Lefferts **PHOTOG:** Thomas Del Ruth **MUSIC:** George Romanis
re-televised (1983) as *Someone's Killing the World's Greatest Models*
TVM, standard thriller: Couturiere's comeback show complicated by murder

Sherlock Jr.: BUSTER KEATON

She Shall Have Murder
1950, (GB), Concanen Recordings/IFD, b&w, 90 mins.
W: Rosamund John (*Jane Hamish*), Derrick de Marney (*Dagobert Brown*), Mary Jerrold (*Mrs. Robjohn*), Felix Aylmer (*Mr. Playfair*), Joyce Heron (*Rosemary Proctor*), Beatrice Varley (*Mrs. Hawthorne*), Jack Allen (*Maj. Stewart*), John Bentley (*Douglas Robjohn*), Henryetta Edwards (*Sarah Swinburne*), Harry Fowler (*Albert Oates*), June Elvin (*Barbara Jennings*)
P: Derrick de Marney & Guido Coen **D:** Daniel Birt **SCR:** Allan Mackinnon, from a novel by Delano Ames
Standard thriller: Novelist and law clerk solve death of old lady client

She Waits
1972, (USA), Metromedia/CBS-TV, color, 73 mins.
W: Patty Duke, David McCallum, Dorothy McGuire, Lew Ayres, Beulah Bondi, James Callahan, Nelson Olmsted
P & D: Delbert Mann **TELEPLAY:** Art Wallace **PHOTOG:** Charles Wheeler
TVM, standard thriller (similar to **Supernatural** *{1933}): Murder victim's spirit takes possession of young woman's body*

She Was a Hippy Vampire
see **The Wild World of Batwoman**

She Woke Up
1992, (USA), Mandy/ABC-TV, color, 95 mins.
W: Lindsay Wagner (*Claudia Parr*), David Dukes (*Sloan*), Frances Sternhagen (*Noelle*), Maureen Mueller, Ben Savage, Ron Frazier, Patricia Barry, Erika Flores, Jan Stratton, Paul Perri, Bruce A. Young, Christopher Murray
D: Waris Hussein **TELEPLAY:** Claire Labine **PHOTOG:** Robert Steadman **MUSIC:** Christopher Franke
TVM, standard thriller: Victim of attempted murder comes out of coma, suspects relative

The She-Wolf
1954, (It), Ponti-DeLaurentiis/Rep, b&w, 83 mins.
W: Kerima, May Britt
Minor thriller

The She-Wolf (1965)
see **La Loba**

She-Wolf of London
1946, (USA), Univ, b&w, 61 mins.
W: June Lockhart, Don Porter, Sara Haden, Martin Kosleck, Dennis Hoey, Jan Wiley, Lloyd Corrigan, Frederick Worlock, Eily Malyon
P: Ben Pivar **D:** Jean Yarbrough **SCR:** George Bricker **PHOTOG:** Maury Gertsman
Minor thriller: Girl fears she may be werewolf

Shield for Murder
1954, (USA), Camden/UA, b&w, 80 mins.
W: Edmond O'Brien, Marla English, John Agar, Carolyn Jones, Claude Akins
D: Edmond O'Brien, Howard Koch
Standard thriller: Crooked detective involved in theft-murder

The Shimmy Sheik
1923, (GB), Atlas Biograph, b&w, 567 ft. (172.8m)
WRIT & D: Adrian Brunel
Standard fantasy (performed by silhouettes): Prince uses magic pipe to save princess

Shinel (The Cloak)
1926, (Russ), Leningradkino, b&w, 6,302.5 ft. (1921m)
W: Andrei Kostritchkin, A. Kapler, Sergei Gerassimov, Anna Zheimo, A. Eremeeva, V. Plotnikov, Piotr Sobolevski, Emil Gal
D: Grigori Kozintsev & Leonid Trauberg **SCR:** Yuri Tinyanov, based on Gogol's novels *Shinel* and *Nevskii Prospekt* **PHOTOG:** Andrei Moskvin & Yevgeni Mikhailov
Standard melodrama. cf. **The Bespoke Overcoat** *and* **The Overcoat**

Shinel (The Cloak)
1965, (Russ), Lenfilm/Cinemasters Int'l, b&w, 78 mins.
W: Roland Bykov (*Akaky Akakyevich*), Y. Tolubeyev (*Petrovich*), A. Yezhkina (*Petrovich's Wife*), Y. Ponsova (*The Landlady*)
D: Alexei Batalov **SCR:** L. Solovyov, from Gogol's story **PHOTOG:** G. Marandjyan **MUSIC:** N. Sidelnikov
Standard melodrama

The Shining
1980, (USA-GB), Hawk Films/Peregrine/Producer Circle Co./ WB, color, 144 mins.
W: Jack Nicholson (*Jack Torrance*), Shelley Duval (*Wendy Torrance*), Danny Lloyd (*Danny Torrance*), Scatman Crothers (*Dick Halloran*), Barry Nelson (*Stuart Ullman*), Joe Turkel (*Lloyd*), Philip Stone (*Delbert Grady*), Lia Beldam (*The Woman*), Billie Gibson (*The Old Woman*), David Baxt (*The Forest Ranger*), Barry Dennen (*Bill Watson*), (*The Grady Girl*), Alison Coleridge (*Susie*), Kate Phelps (*The Receptionist*), Anne Jackson (*The Doctor*), Tony Burton (*Larry Durkin*) Lisa & Louise Burns (*The Grady Girls*), Jana Sheldon (*The Stewardess*), Robin Pappas (*The Nurse*), Norman Gay (*The Injured Guest*), Burnell Tucker (*The Policeman*), Manning Redwood
P & D: Stanley Kubrick **SCR:** Stanley Kubrick & Diane Johnson, from Stephen King's novel **PHOTOG:** John Alcott **MUSIC:** Bela Bartok
Classic horror-thriller: Hotel caretakers menaced by evil spirits. Remade as TV Movie, 1997

The Ship of the Monsters
see **La Nave de los Monstruos**

Ship of Zombies
see **Horror of the Zombies**

The Shirker's Nightmare
1914, (GB), Cherry Kearton, b&w, 650 ft. (198.1m)
D & STORY: Walter R. Booth
Standard fantasy: Man's dream of Prussians and zeppelins makes him join Guards

Shivers
1975, (Can), Trans-America, color, 88 mins.
W: Paul Hampton (*Roger*), Joe Silver (*Rollo*), Barbara Steele (*Betts*), Lynn Lowry (*Forsythe*), Alan Migicovsky (*Nicholas*), Susan Petrie (*Janine*), Ronald Mlodzik (*Merrick*)
P: Ivan Reitman **WRIT & D:** David Cronenberg **PHOTOG:** Robert Saad
USA retitle, **They Came from Within** *A.k.a.* **The Parasite Murders**
Standard horror-fantasy: Aphrodisiac parasites infest tenants of apartment complex

The Shock
1923, (USA), Univ, b&w, 7 reels (6,738 ft./2053.7m/87 mins.)
W: Lon Chaney Sr. (*Wilse Dilling*), Virginia Valli (*Gertrude Hadley*), Jack Mower (*Jack Cooper*), William Welsh (*Mischa Hadley*), Henry Barrows (*John Cooper Sr.*), Christine Mayo (*Anne Vincent {"Queen Anne"}*), Harry De Vere (*Olaf Wismer*), John Beck (*Bill*), Walter Long (*The Captain*)
D: Lambert Hillyer **PHOTOG:** Dwight Warren
working title, **Bittersweet**
Standard melodrama: Crippled killer works for female crimelord

Shock
1946, (USA), 20th-Fox, b&w, 70 mins.
W: Vincent Price (*Dr. Richard Cross*), Lynn Bari (*Elaine Jordan*), Frank Latimore (*Paul Stewart*), Anabel Shaw (*Janet Stewart*), Reed Hadley (*O'Neill*), Charles Trowbridge (*Dr. Franklin Harvey*), Renee Carson (*Miss Hatfield*), Michael Dunne
P: Aubrey Schenck **D:** Alfred Werker **SCR:** Eugene Ling, from a story by Albert DeMond **PHOTOG:** Glen MacWilliams **SPCL-FX:** Fred Sersen **MUSIC DIR:** Emil Newman
Standard thriller: Woman sees psychiatrist kill wife, becomes murder target

Shock (1972)
see Traitement de Choc

Shock
1978, (It), Film Ventures, color, 92 mins.
W: Daria Nicolodi (*Dora*), John Steiner (*Bruno*), David Conlin Jr. (*Marco*), Ivan Rassimov (*Carlos*)
D: Mario Bava   **SCR:** Lamberto Bava & Franco Barbieri   **PHOTOG:** Mario Bava & Giuseppe Maccari   **MUSIC:** Libra
USA retitle, **Beyond the Door #2**
Standard thriller (Mario Bava's final theatrical film): Son threatens mother's life

Shock Chamber
1984, (Can), Emmeritus, Made for TV, color
W: Doug Stone, Karen Cannata, Jackie Samuda, James Lackie, Russell Ferrier, George T. Cunningham, Robert Perischini, Hadley Sandiford, Silvan Alexander, Karlheinz Theil, Enio Mescherin, Andy Adoch, Frank McNalty, J.D. Philip, Robert Latimer, Bill Zagot, Norm Bornstein, Bill Boyle, Margaret Miniovich, Sue Minor, Bina Dylinsky, Dan Sergent, Eileen Williams, Sue Morrison, Carole MacNeil, Dave Healy, Laura Centeno, Bruce Salatore, Victor P. Farkas
WRIT & D: Steve DiMarco   **PHOTOG:** N. "Kuri" Kuriata   **MUSIC:** Peter Dick
TVM, minor trilogy of terror tales: (1) Teen obtains love potion, (2) Greed and murder divide people of small town, & (3) Brothers plot insurance scam

Shock Corridor
1963, (USA), Leon Fromkess-Sam Firks/AA, b&w, 101 mins.
W: Constance Towers, Peter Breck, Gene Evans, James Best, Larry Tucker, William Zuckert, Philip Ahn, John Mathews, Hari Rhodes, Neyle Morrow, Chuck Roberson, John Craig
WRIT, P, & D: Samuel Fuller   **PHOTOG:** Stanley Cortez
Standard thriller: Man infiltrates madhouse, finds he can't get out

Shock 'em Dead
1990, (USA), color, 94 mins.
W: Traci Lords, Aldo Ray, Troy Donahue, Stephen Quadros
D: Mark Freed   **SCR:** Andrew Cross
Standard fantasy-thriller: Satanist seeks rock 'n' roll fame

Shocker
1989, (USA), Alive/Univ, color, 107 mins.
W: Michael Murphy (*Lt. Parker*), Peter Berg (*Jonathan Parker*), Cami Cooper (*Alison*), Mitch Pileggi (*Horace Pinker*), Richard Brooks, Vincent Guastaferro, Sam Scarber, Theodore Raimi, Dr. Timothy Leary, Kane Roberts, John Tesh, Heather Langenkamp, Jessica Craven, Keith Anthony Lubow-Bellamy, Virginia Morris, Emily Samuel, Peter Tilden, Bingham Ray, Sue Ann Harris, Eugene Chadbourne, Jack Hoar, Stephen Held, Joyce Guy, Joseph Roy O'Flynn, Linda Kaye, Janne K. Peters, Bruce Wagner, Marvin Elkins, Christopher Kriesa, Bobby Lee Swain, Michael Matthews, Ricardo Gutierrez, John Mueller, Jonathan Christian Craven, Lindsay Parker, Dendrie Allyn Taylor, Stephen R. Hudis, Gary Michael Davies, Christopher Keyes, Marji Martin, Ray Bickel, Mark Slama, Karl Vincent, Wes Craven, Holly Kaplan
WRIT & D: Wes Craven   **PHOTOG:** Jacques Haitkin   **MUSIC:** William Goldstein
Standard horror-fantasy: Executed killer returns for revenge

A Shocking Complaint
1912, (GB), Cricks & Martin, b&w, 375 ft. (114.3m)
D: Dave Aylott
reissued 1916
Standard comedy-fantasy short: Electric shock machine overcharges man

Shockproof
1949, Col, b&w, 79 mins.
W: Cornel Wilde, Patricia Knight, John Baragrey, Esther Minicotti, Howard St. John
D: Douglas Sirk   **SP:** Helen Deutsch & Samuel Fuller   **CO-SCR:** Samuel Fuller
Standard melodrama: Parole officer lured into affair with female parolee

Shock! Shock! Shock!
1987, (USA), b&w, 60 mins.
W: Brad Isaac, Cyndy McCrossen, Allen Rickman, Brian Fuorry
D: Todd Rutt & Arn McConnell
Minor SF-slasher-thriller: Space-alien jewel thieves meet homicidal maniac

Shock Treatment
1964, (USA), Arcola/20th-Fox, b&w, 94 mins.
W: Stuart Whitman (*Dale*), Lauren Bacall (*Dr. Beighley*), Roddy McDowall (*Ashley*), Carol Lynley (*Cynthia*), Ossie Davis (*Capshaw*), Olive Deering, Bert Freed, Edward C. Platt, Paul Langton
P: Aaron Rosenberg   **D:** R. Denis Sanders   **SCR:** Sydney Boehm   **PHOTOG:** Sam Leavitt   **MUSIC:** Jerry Goldsmith
Standard thriller: Lady psychiatrist seeks fortune stolen by mental patient

Shock Treatment (1972)
see Traitement de Choc

Shock Treatment!
1981, (GB), Lou Adler-Michael White/20th-Fox, color, 95 mins.
W: Cliff De Young (*Brad Majors/Farley Flavors*), Jessica Harper (*Janet Majors*), Patricia Quinn (*Nation McKinley*), Richard O'Brien (*Cosmo McKinley*), Charles Gray (*Judge Wright*), Ruby Wax (*Betty Hapschatt*), Nell Campbell (*Nurse Ansalong*), Darlene Johnson (*Emily Weiss*), Rik Mayall (*Rest Home Ricky*), Manning Redwood (*Harry Weiss*), Ray Charleson (*The Manager*), Wendy Raebeck (*Macy Struthers*), Jeremy Newson (*Ralph*), Chris Malcolm (*Vance Parker*), Imogen Claire (*The Wardrobe Mistress*), Eugene Lipinski (*Kirk*), Barry Dennen (*Irwin Lapsey*), Betsy Brantley (*Neely*), Gary Shail (*Oscar Drill*), Perry Bedden, Rufus Collins
P: John Goldstone   **D:** Jim Sharman   **SCR:** Richard O'Brien & Jim Sharman (additional ideas by Brian Thomson)   **BOOK & LYRICS:** Richard O'Brien   **PHOTOG:** Mike Molloy   **MUSIC:** Richard Hartley & Richard O'Brien
Standard musical-fantasy: Couple trapped in TV studio that replaces real life

Shock Waves
1976, (USA), Joseph Brenner Assocs./Zopix, color, 96 mins.
W: Peter Cushing (*The SS Commander*), Brooke Adams (*Rose*), Fred Buch (*Chuck*), John Carradine (*The Captain*), Luke Halpin (*Keith*), Jack Davidson (*Norman*), D.J. Sidney (*Beverly*), Don Stout (*Dobbs*), Clarence Thomas (*The Fisherman*), Sammy Graham, Preston White, Reid Finger, Mike Kennedy, Donahue Guillory, Jay Maeder, Talmedge Scott, Gary Levinson, Robert Miller
D: Ken Wiederhorn   **SCR:** John Harrison & Ken Wiederhorn   **PHOTOG:** Reuben Trane & Irving Pare   **MUSIC:** Richard Einhorn
orig. to be titled **Death Corps**
Minor horror-thriller: Shipwrecked tourists meet Nazi zombies

The Shoemaker and the Elves
1971, (W. Ger), Films Inc., color, 15 mins.
Standard fantasy short

Shoot Loud, Louder...I Don't Understand
see Spara Forte, Piu Forte...Non Capisco

Shoot to Kill
1947, (USA), Screen Guild, b&w, 63 mins.
W: Russell Wade, Susan (Luana) Walters Edmund MacDonald, Vince Barnett, Douglas Blackley, Nesto Paiva
D: William Berke
Standard melodrama: Gov't man involved with ruthless escape convict

Shoot to Kill
1961, (GB), Border/New Realm, b&w, 64 mins.
W: Dermot Walsh (*Mike Roberts*), Joy Webster (*Lee Fisher*), John East (*Boris Altovitch*), Frank Hawkins (*Neale Patterson*), Zoreen Ismael (*Anna*), Theodore Wilhelm (*Nicholi*), Victor Beaumont (*Nauman*), Ronald Adam (*Wood*)
P: O. Negus Fancey   **D & SCR:** Michael Winner
Standard thriller: Reporters rescue atomic secrets from clutches of communist agents

The Shop at Sly Corner
1947, (GB), Pennant/British Lion, b&w, 92 mins.
W: Oscar Homolka (*Descius Heiss*), Derek Farr (*Robert Graham*), Muriel Pavlow (*Margaret Heiss*), Kathleen Harrison (*Mrs. Catt*), Manning Whiley (*Morris*), Johnnie Schofield (*Insp. Robson*), Kenneth Griffith (*Archie Fellowes*), Garry Marsh (*Maj. Elliott*), Irene Handl (*Ruby Towser*), Diana Dors (*The Girl*)
P & D: George King   **SCR:** Katherine Strueby, from a play by Edward Percy
USA retitle, **The Code of Scotland Yard** *(republic, 1948)*
Standard thriller: Shop owner murders blackmailer

Short Circuit
1986, (USA), Turman-Foster/Tri-Star, color, 99 mins.
W: Ally Sheedy (*Stephanie Speck*), Steve Guttenberg (*Newton Crosby*), Austin Pendleton (*Howard Marriner*), Fisher Stevens (*Ben Jabituya*), G.W. Bailey (*Skroeder*), John Garber, Tim Blaney, Penny Santon, Howard Krick, Brian McNamara
D: John Badham   **SCR:** S.S. Wilson & Brent Maddock   **PHOTOG:** Nick McLean   **MUSIC:** David Shire   **SONGS:** Who's Johnny
Modest SF-fantasy: Runaway robot has adventures

Short Circuit 2
1988, (USA), Turman-Foster/Tri-Star, color, 112 mins.
W: Fisher Stevens (*Ben Jahrvi*), Michael McKean (*Fred Ritter*), Cynthia Gibb (*Sandy Banatoni*), Jack Weston (*Oscar Baldwin*), Dee McCafferty (*Saunders*), David Hemblen (*Jones*), Don Lake (*Manic Mike*), Damon D'Oliveira (*Bones*), Robert LaSardo (*Spooky*), Tito Nunez (*Zorro*), Jason Kuriloff (*Lil Man*), Lili Francks (*Officer Mendez*), Wayne Best (*Officer O'Malley*), Gerry Parkes (*The Priest*), Adam Ludwig (*Hans de Ruyter*), Rex Hagon (*Dartmoor*), Rummy Bishop (*The News Vendor*), Tony DeSantis (*The Russian Taxi Driver*), Jeremy Ratchford (*Bill*), Richard Comar (*Mr. Slater*), Eric Keenleyside (*Simpson's Truck Driver*), Phil Jarrett (*The Card Hustler*), Kurt Reis (*Mr. Arnold*), Garry Robbins (*Francis*), Ric Sarabia (*The Toy Robot Builder*), Barry Flatman (*The Robotic Company CEO*), James Schoettle (*The Robotic Executive*), Carlton Watson (*The Robotic Engineer*), Eve Crawford (*The Federal Judge*), Tim Blaney, Craig Gardner, Sam Moses, Micki Moore, Norwich Duff, Chris Barker, Patrick Greenwood, Claudette Roach, Frank Adamson, Peter Shanne, James Killeen
D: Kenneth Johnson   **SCR:** S.S. Wilson & Brent Maddock   **PHOTOG:** John

McPherson **MUSIC:** Charles Fox
Amusing SF-comedy: Robot meets big-city criminals

Shortcut to Paradise
see Desvio al Paraiso

Short Walk to Daylight
1972, (USA), Univ/ABC-TV, color, 73 mins.
W: James Brolin, Don Mitchell
P: Edward J. Montagne, Harry Tatelman **D:** Barry Shear **TELEPLAY:** Philip
H. Reisman Jr., Gerald di Pego & Richard Hesse
TVM, standard thriller: Earthquake traps eight people in New York subway

A Shot at Dawn
see Schuss im Morgengrauen

The Shot in the Dark
1933, (GB), Real Art/Radio, b&w, 53 mins.
W: Dorothy Boyd (*Alaris Browne*), O.B. Clarence (*Rev. John Malcolm*), Jack
Hawkins (*Norman Paul*), Russell Thorndike (*Dr. Stuart*), Michael Shepley
(*Vivian Waugh*), Davy Burnaby (*Col. Michael Browne*), A. Bromley Davenport
(*Peter Browne*), Hugh E. Wright (*George Barrow*), Henrietta Watson (*Angela
Browne*)
D: George Pearson **SCR:** H. Fowler Mear, from a novel by Gerard Fairlie
Standard thriller: Several people confess to killing hated recluse

The Shout
1979, (GB), Jeremy Thomas/Rank/Col, color, 87 mins.
W: Alan Bates (*Charles Crossley*), Susannah York (*Rachel Fielding*), John Hurt
(*Anthony Fielding*), Robert Stephens (*CMO*), Tim Curry (*Robert Graves*),
Carol Drinkwater (*The Wife*), Julian Hough (*The Vicar*), Nick Stringer (*The
Cobbler*), John Rees (*The Inspector*), Susan Woolridge (*Harriet*), Colin
Higgins, Jim Broadbent, Peter Benson
D: Jerzy Skolimowski **SCR:** Michael Austin & Jerzy Skolimowski, from a story
by Robert Graves **PHOTOG:** Mike Molloy **MUSIC:** Anthony Banks &
Michael Rutherford
Modest, adult thriller: Mystery man practices Aborigine magic in small English village

Showgirl Murders
1996, (USA), color, 80 mins.
W: Maria Ford
Made-for-Video, minor eroto-thriller: Woman flees narcotics dealers, hides at strip club

The Showman's Dream
1914, (GB), Sunny South/Walturdaw, b&w, 1,150 ft. (350.5m)
W: Will Evans (*The Showman*), Arthur Conquest (*The Artiste*)
D: F.L. Lyndhurst, from a sketch by Will Evans
Standard comedy-fantasy: Showman let down by artists dreams he stages show

The Shrieking
see Hex

A Shriek in the Night
1933, (USA), b&w, 66 mins.
W: Ginger Rogers, Lyle Talbot, Arthur Hoyt, Purnell Pratt, Harvey Clark
D: Albert Ray
Modest whodunit: Rival reporters trail murderer

Shriek of the Mutilated
1974, (USA), AM Films/Film Brokers/Cinemation, color, 84 mins.
W: Alan Brock (*Dr. Ernst Prell*), Jennifer Stock (*Karen Hunter*), Tawm Ellis (*Dr.
Karl Werner*), Michael Harris (*Keith Henshaw*), Darcy Brown (*Lynn Kelly*),
Tom Grail (*Spencer St. Claire*), Jack Neubeck (*Tom Nash*), Luci Brandt (*April
Ste. Claire*), Ivan Agar (*Laughing Crow*), Dwight Marfield (*The Station
Attendant*), Marina Stefan (*The Party Hostess*), Harriet McFaul (*The Girl at the
Party*), Warren D'Oyly-Rhind (*The Waiter*), Jimmy Silva (*The Policeman*)
D: Michael Findlay **SCR:** Ed Kelleher & Ed Adlum **PHOTOG:** Roberta
Findlay **SONGS:** *Popcorn, Love Shriek & Hot Butter*
Minor horror-thriller: College students hunt yeti

Shrunken Heads
1994, (USA), color, 86 mins.
W: Aeryk Egan
Minor horror-satire: Crime boss kills three teens, voodoo witch doctor revives them

Sh! The Octopus
1937, (USA), WB, b&w, 54 mins.
W: Hugh Herbert, Allen Jenkins, Marcia Ralston, John Eldredge
D: William McGann
Standard comedy-thriller: Bumbling sleuths seek master criminal

The Shuttered Room
1967, (GB), Troy Schenck/WB-7Arts, color, 99 mins.
W: Gig Young (*Mike Kelton*), Carol Lynley (*Suzanna Whateley*), Oliver Reed
(*Ethan*), Flora Robson (*Aunt Agatha*), Ann Bell (*Mary Whateley*), Bernard
Kay (*Tait*), Judith Arthy (*Emma*), William Devlin (*Zebulon Whateley*),
Robert Cawdron (*Luther Whateley*), Celia Hewitt (*Aunt Sarah*), Charles
Lloyd-Pack (*Wilkes*), Rick Jones, Murray Evans
P: Philip Hazleton & Bernard Schwartz **D:** David Greene **SCR:** D.B. Ledrov &

Nathaniel Tanchuck, adapted from the story by H.P. Lovecraft & August
Derleth **PHOTOG:** Kenneth Hodges **MUSIC:** Basil Kirchin **MUSIC
DIR:** Jack Nathan
*video title, **Blood Island***
Standard thriller: Young woman uncovers horrible family secret

The Shuttered Room: CAROL LYNLEY

The Shuttle of Life
1920, (GB), British Actors/Phillips, b&w, 4,256 ft. (1297.2m)
W: C. Aubrey Smith (*Rev. John Stone*), Evelyn Brent (*Miriam Grey*), Jack Hobbs
(*Ray Sinclair*), Gladys Jennings (*Audrey Bland*), Bert Darley (*Tom*), Cecil
Ward (*Meeson*), Rachel de Solla (*Mrs. Bland*)
D: D.J. Williams **SCR:** S.H. Herkomer, from a novel by Isobel Bray
Standard crime-thriller: Actress poses as heiress who died, opposes blackmailing detective

The Sibling
see So Evil, My Sister

The Sicilian's Revenge
see Johnny Cool

Siddhartha
1973, (Ind), color
W: Shashi Kapoor (*Siddhartha*), Simi Garewal (*Kamala*), Zul Vellani (*Vasudeva*),
Romesh Sharma (*Govinda*), Pincho Kapoor (*Kamaswami*), Amrik Singh
(*Siddhartha's Father*), Shanti Hiranand (*Siddhartha's Mother*), Kunal Kapoor
(*Siddhartha's Son*)
P, D & ADAPT: Conrad Rooks, from Hermann Hesse's novel **PHOTOG:** Sven
Nykvist **MUSIC:** Hemanta Kumar
Standard melodrama

Sideshow
1950, (USA), Mono, b&w, 67 mins.
W: Don McGuire, Tracey Roberts
Minor melodrama

Siege of Syracuse
1959, (It), Galatea-Glomer-Lyre/Para, color, 97 mins.
W: Rossano Brazzi, Tina Louise, Sylva Koscina, Gino Cervi, Enrico Maria Salerno,
Alberto Farnese, Luciano Marin, Alfredo Varelli
D: Pietro Francisci
*Standard "Sword & Sandal:" Greek genius Archimedes helps defend Carthage when
Romans attack*

Siege of the Saxons
1963, (GB), Ameran/Col, color, 85 mins.
W: Ronald Lewis (*Robert Marshall*), Janette Scott (*Katherine*), Ronald Howard

(*Edmund of Cornwall*), John Laurie (*Merlin*), Mark Dignam (*King Arthur*), Jerome Willis (*The Limping Man*), Francis De Wolff (*The Blacksmith*), Charles Lloyd-Pack (*The Doctor*), Richard Clarke (*The Prince*)
P: Jud Kinberg **D:** John Kohn & Jud Kinberg
  PHOTOG: Wilkie Cooper & Jack Willis
Standard adventure-thriller: Dashing outlaw rescues King Arthur's daughter

Siegfried
see *Die Nibelungen*

Siegfried's Death
see *Die Nibelungen*

Siegfried's Tod
see *Die Nibelungen*

Signals in the Night
1913, (GB), B&C/MP, b&w, 730 ft. (222.5m)
W: Harry Lorraine (*Jack Dennison*), May Hamerton (*Winnie Dennison*), James Russell (*Bill*), Nancy Roberts (*Sarah*), M. Gray Murray (*Mr. Dennison*), E. Romney (*Mrs. Dennison*)
D: H.O. Martinek
Standard crime-thriller: Girl flashes morse code, thwarts burglar

Sign It Death
1973, (GB),Made for TV, color
W: Francesca Annis (*Tracy*), Patrick Allen (*Richard*), Moira Redmond (*Janice*)
TVM, minor thriller: Woman kills love rivals

The Sign of Four
1923, (GB), Stoll, b&w, 6,750 ft. (2057.4m)
W: Eille Norwood (*Sherlock Holmes*), Isobel Elsom (*Mary Marstan*), Fred Raynham (*Prince Andullah Khan*), Arthur Culin (*Dr. John Watson*), Norman Page (*Jonathan Small*), Humberston Wright (*Dr. Sholto*), Henry Wilson (*The Pygmy*), Arthur Bell (*Insp. Athelney Jones*), Mme. D'Esterre (*Mrs. Hudson*)
D & SCR: Maurice Elvey, from Sir Arthur Conan Doyle's story
Standard thriller: Convict gains revenge on cheating partners

The Sign of Four
1932, (GB), ARP/Radio, b&w, 75 mins.
W: Arthur Wontner (*Sherlock Holmes*), Ian Hunter (*Dr. John Watson*), Isla Bevan (*Mary Marstan*), Ben Soutten (*Jonathan Small*), Miles Malleson (*Thaddeus Sholto*), Kynaston Reeves (*Bartholomew Sholto*), Herbert Lomas (*Maj. Sholto*), Clare Greet (*Mrs. Hudson*), Gilbert Davis (*Athelney Jones*), Roy Emerton (*Bailey*), Edgar Norfolk (*Capt. Marstan*), Moore Marriott (*Mordecai Smith*)
D: Rowland V. Lee & Graham Cutts **SCR:** W.P. Lipscomb, from Sir Arthur Conan Doyle's story
Standard thriller: Ex-convict seeks vengeance

The Sign of Four
1983, (GB), color, 97 mins.
W: Ian Richardson (*Sherlock Holmes*), David Healy (*Dr. John Watson*), Joe Melia (*Small*), Thorley Walters (*Sholto*)
from Sir Arthur Conan Doyle's story
Minor thriller: Detective opposes vengeful ex-convict

The Sign of the Cross
1904, (GB), Haggar &Sons/Gaumont, b&w, 700 ft. (213.6m)
W: Will Haggar Jr. (*Marcus Superbus*), Jenny Linden (*Mercia*), James Haggar, Will Desmond, Kate Sylvester
D: William Haggar, from a play by Wilson Barrett
Standard "Sword & Sandal:" Christian maid and converted Roman prefect die in arena

Sign of the Gladiator
1959, (It), AIP, color, 84 mins.
W: Anita Ekberg, Georges Marchal, Folco Lulli, Chelo Alonso, Jacques Sernas
D: Vittorio Musy Glori
Standard "Sword & Sandal": Gladiator tries to win confidence of Syrian queen

Sign of the Pagan
1954, (USA), Univ, color, 92 mins.
W: Jeff Chandler, Jack Palance, Ludmilla Tcherina, Rita Gam, Jeff Morrow, George Dolenz, Eduard Franz, Alexander Scourby, Allison Hayes, Howard Petrie, Leo Gordon, Sara Shane, Moroni Olsen, Michael Ansara, Norbert Schiller, Pat Hogan
D: Douglas Sirk **SCR:** Oscar Brodney & Barre Lyndon **PHOTOG:** Russell Metty **MUSIC:** Frank Skinner & Hans J. Salter **MUSIC DIR:** Joseph Gershenson
Unusual historical melodrama: Attila seeks Rome's destruction

The Sign of Zorro (1951)
see *Il Sogno di Zorro*

The Sign of Zorro
1960, (USA), Walt Disney/Buena Vista,b&w, 91 mins.
W: Guy Williams (*Don Diego/Zorro*), Britt Lomond, Henry Calvin, Gene Sheldon Lisa Gaye, George Lewis
P: William H. Anderson **D:** Norman Foster & Lewis R. Foster **SCR:** Norman Foster, Lowell S. Hawley, Bob Weblin & John Meredyth Lucas, from stories

by Johnston McCulley **PHOTOG:** Gordon Avil **MUSIC:** William Lava
Standard action-thriller: Masked hero champions Justice in Old California

Signpost to Murder
1965, (USA), Marten/MGM, b&w
W: Joanne Woodward (*Molly Thomas*), Stuart Whitman (*Alex Forrester*), Edward Mulhare (*Dr. Mark Fleming*), Leslie Denison (*Supt. Bickley*), Alan Napier (*The Vicar*), Joyce Worsley (*Mrs. Barnes*), Murray Matheson (*Dr. Graham*), Hedley Mattingly (*Officer Rogers*), Carol Veazie (*Auntie*)
D: George Englund **SCR:** Sally Benson, from a play by Monte Doyle
  PHOTOG: Paul C. Vogel **MUSIC:** Lyn Murray
Standard thriller

The Silence
see *Tystnaden*

The Silence of the Hams
1994, (It), color, 85 mins.
W: Ezio Greggio (*Antonio Motel*), Billy Zane (*Jo Dee Fostar*), Dom DeLuise (*Dr. Animal*), Joanna Pacula (*Lily*), Charlene Tilton (*Jane*), Martin Balsam (*Det. Balsam*), Stuart Pankin (*Pete Putrid*), Bubba Smith (*Olaf*), John Astin (*The Ranger*), Nedra Volz (*The Ranger's Wife*), Larry Storch (*The Sgt.*),Rip Taylor (*Mr. Laurel*), Shelley Winters (*Mother*), Phyllis Diller (*The Old Sec'y*), Rosey Brown (*The Motorcycle Cop*), Tony Cox (*The Dwarf Guard*), Henry Silva (*The Police Chief*), Marshall Bell (*The Cross Dresser Agent*), Lee Allan (*The 1st Agent*), Sal Landi (*The 2nd Agent*), John Carpenter, (*The Trench Coat Man*), John Roarke (*George Bush*), Joe Dante (*The Dying Man*), Mel Brooks, Irwin Keyes, Jeff Bright, Pat Rick, Kimber Sissons, Al Ruscio, Eddie Deezen, Kenneth Davitian, Rudy DeLuca, John Landis, Jeff Weston, David DeLuise, John Fadule, Dom Irrera, Lance Kinsey, Shelly Desai, Lonnie Burr, Debra Christofferson, Linda Luiz, Jim Maniaci, Manny Molina, Heather Elizabeth Parkhurst, Raymond Serra, Robert Muse, Lana Schwab, Daniel McVicar, Wilhelm Von Homburg, Matteo Molinari, Rino Piccoli, Seifullah Ziyad II
WRIT & D: Ezio Greggio **PHOTOG:** Jacques Haitkin **MUSIC:** Parmer Fuller
Standard comedy-thriller: Gagfest spoof of numerous melodramas

The Silence of the Lambs
1991, (USA), Orion, color, 118 mins.
W: Jodie Foster (*Clarice Starling*), Anthony Hopkins (*Dr. Hannibal Lecter*), Scott Glenn (*Jack Crawford*), Ted Levine (*Jame Gumb*), Anthony Heald (*Dr. Frederick Chilton*), Diane Baker (*Sen. Ruth Martin*), Kasi Lemmons (*Ardelia Mapp*), Roger Corman (*FBI Director Hayden Burke*), Chris Isaak (*SWAT Commander*), Ron Vawter (*Paul Krendler*), Frankie Faison (*Barney*), Lawrence A. Bonney (*The FBI Instructor*), Don Brockett (*The Friendly Psychopath*), Lawrence T. Wrentz (*Agt. Burroughs*), Frank Seals Jr. (*The Brooding Psychopath*), Stuart Rudin (*Miggs*), Masha Skorobogatov (*Young Clarice*), Lcib Lensky (*Mr. Lang*), James B. Howard (*The Boxing Instructor*), Jeffrie Lane (*Clarice's Father*), Red Schwartz (*Mr. Lang's Driver*), Jim Roche (*The TV Evangelist*), Bill Miller (*Mr. Brigham*), Chuck Aber (*Agt. Terry*), Gene Borkan (*Oscar*), Pat McNamara (*Sheriff Perkins*), Tracey Walter (*Lamar*), Kenneth Utt (*Dr. Akin*), Dan Butler (*Roden*), Paul Lazar (*Pilcher*), Darla ("*Precious*"), Adelle Lutz (*The TV Anchorwoman*), Obba Babatunde (*The TV Anchorman*), George Michael (*The TV Sportscaster*), Charles Napier (*Lt. Boyle*), Jim Dratfield (*Sen. Martin's Aide*), Cynthia Ettinger (*Officer Jacobs*), Stanton-Miranda (*The 1st Reporter*), Rebecca Saxon (*The 2nd Reporter*), Danny Darst (*Sgt. Tate*), Brent Hinkley (*Officer Murray*), Steve Wyatt (*The Airport Flirt*), Alex Coleman (*Sgt. Pembry*), David Early (*The Spooked Memphis Cop*), Andre Blake (*The Tall Memphis Cop*), Bill Dalzell III (*The Distraught Memphis Cop*), Josh Broder (*The EMS Attendant*), Daniel von Bargen (*The SWAT Communicator*), Tommy LaFitte (*The SWAT Shooter*), Lamont Arnold (*The Flower Delivery Man*), Buzz Kilman (*The EMS Driver*), Harry Northup (*Mr. Bimmel*), Lauren Roselli (*Stacy Hubka*)
D: Jonathan Demme **SCR:** Ted Tally, from Thomas Harris' novel **PHOTOG:** Tak Fujimoto **MUSIC:** Howard Shore
Superior thriller: Psychopath aids FBI agent in hunt for serial killer. Sequel to ***Manhunter***, *1986*

The Silence of Richard Wilton
1913, (GB), Hepworth, b&w, 725 ft. (221m)
W: Alec Worcester (*Richard Wilton*), Harry Royston (*Tommy Porson*), Flora Morris (*Mrs. Porson*)
D: Warwick Buckland
Standard crime-thriller: Wife's ex-lover wrongly accused of necklace theft

The Silencers
1966, (USA), Col, color, 104 mins.
W: Dean Martin (*Matt Helm*), Stella Stevens, Victor Buono, Roger C. Carmel, Daliah Lavi, Robert Webber, Nancy Kovack, Beverly Adams, James Gregory, Arthur O'Connell, Richard Devon, Cyd Charisse [cameo]
P: Irving Allen **D:** Phil Karlson **SCR:** Oscar Saul, based on two *Matt Helm* detective novels by Donald Hamilton, *The Silencers & Death of a Citizen* **PHOTOG:** Burnett Guffey **MUSIC:** Elmer Bernstein **TITLE SONGS:** Robert Phillips, Grant Woods
Standard adventure-comedy: Oriental plot to sabotage U.S. missile bases

The Silencers
1995, (USA), PM Entertainment color, 105 mins.
W: Jack Scalia, Dennis Christopher, Carlos Lauchu, Lucinda Weist, Stephen Rowe,

Lance LeGault, Clarence Williams III, Terri Power, Madison Mason, Bill Frenzer, Chris Kriesa, Jeffrey Broadhurst, Steve Mattila, David Parry, Tristan Wolff, Peter Vogt, Jane Higginson, Chuck Winston, Betty Perry, Ken Resnick, Thorsten Kaye, June Chandler, Laure Larkin, Jim Ishida, Charles McDaniel, Steven Ruge, John Fromberg, Brittany Levenbrown, Jim Hatch, Vinny Argiro, Jennifer Chaparro, Douglas Aucoin, Jennifer Washick, Raven DeLumiere, Kevin LoRosa
D: Richard Pepin **SCR:** Joseph John Barmettler **STORY:** Joseph John Barmettler, Richard Preston Jr. & William Applegate Jr. **PHOTOG:** Ken Blakey **VS-FX:** Steve Rundell **MUSIC:** Louis Febre
Standard SF-thriller: Secret Service agent and intergalactic peace officer thwart space-alien plot

Le Silencieux (The Silent One)
1973, (It-Fr), color, 118 mins.
W: Lino Ventura, Leo Genn, Robert Hardy, Suzanne Flon, Lea Massari, Bernard Dheran, Pierre Zimmer
D: Claude Pinoteau
Standard thriller: KGB pursues French nuclear scientist

Silent Death
see *Voodoo Island*

Silent Evidence
1922, (GB), Gaumont/British Screencraft, b&w, 5,700 ft. (1737.4m)
W: David Hawthorne *(Mark Stanton)*, Marjorie Hume *(Rosamund)*, Frank Dane *(Raoul de Merincourt)*, H.R. Hignett *(Charles)*, Cecil du Gue *(Dr. Hickson)*, Winifred Nelson *(The Fiancee)*
D: C.C. Calvert **STORY:** Alicia Ramsey
Standard SF-melodrama: Inventor's wireless-vision device reveals wife's indiscretion

The Silent Flute
see *Circle of Iron*

The Silent House
1929, (GB), Nettlefold/Butcher, b&w, 9,376 ft. (2857.8m)
W: Mabel Poulton *(T'Mala)*, Gibb McLaughlin *(Chang Fu)*, Arthur Pusey *(George Winsford)*, Frank Perfitt *(Richard Winsford)*, Gerald Rawlinson *(Capt. Barty)*, Kiyoshi Takase *(Ho Fang)*, Arthur Stratton *(Benson)*, Albert Brouett *(Peroda)*, Danny Green *(W'Hang)*, Rex Maurice *(Legarde)*
D: Water Forde **SCR:** H. Fowler Mear, from a play by John G. Brandon & George Pickett
Standard thriller: Mandarin hypnotizes partner's daughter, seeks hidden bonds

Silent Madness
1984, (USA), color, 93 mins.
W: Belinda J. Montgomery, Viveca Lindfors, Sydney Lassick
D: Simon Nuchtern
Minor thriller: Psychiatrist tracks deranged killer

Silent Night, Bloody Night
1973, (USA), Cannon, color, 88 mins.
W: Patrick O'Neal *(John Carter)*, James Patterson *(Jeffrey Butler)*, Mary Woronov *(Diane Adams)*, John Carradine *(Towman)*, Walter Abel *(Mayor Adams)*, Astrid Heeren *(Ingrid)*, Fran Stevens *(Tess)*, Jay Garner *(Dr. Robinson)*, Philip Bruns *(Wilfred Butler)*, Walter Klavun *(Sheriff Mason)*, Lisa Richards *(Maggie Daly)*, Alex Stevens *(The Burning Man)*, Candy Darling, Donelda Dunne, Harvey Cohen, Hettie MacLise, Charlotte Fairchild, Michael Pendrey, Barbara Sand, George Strus, Tally Brown, Debbie Parness, George Trakas, Lewis Love, Susan Rothenberg, Cleo Young, Leroy Lessane, Kristin Steen, Ondine, Jack Smith, Bob Darchi, Grant Code, Staats Cotsworth
P: Ami Artzi & Jeffrey Konvitz **D:** Theodore Gershuny **SCR:** Theodore Gershuny, Jeffrey Konvitz & Ira Teller **SPCL-FX:** Louis Antzes **MUSIC:** Gershon Kingsley
A.k.a. Death House and Night of the Dark Full Moon
Minor thriller: Confused tale of madness and forgotten crime

Silent Night, Deadly Night
1984, (USA), Scott J. Schneid-Dennis Whitehead/Tri-Star, color, 81 mins.
W: Lilyan Chauvin, Gilmer McCormick, Toni Nero, Charles Dierkop, Robert Brian Nelson, Leo Geter, Jonathan Best, Will Hare, Britt Leach, Jeff Hansen
D: Charles E. Sellier Jr. **SCR:** Michael Hickey **PHOTOG:** Henning Schellerup **SPCL-FX:** Rick Josephson **MUSIC:** Perry Botkin **SONG:** *The Warm Side of the Door*
Minor thriller: Demented youth dressed as Santa Claus commits brutal murders

Silent Night, Deadly Night, Part II
1987, (USA), TriStar, color, 88 mins.
W: Eric Freeman, Elizabeth Clayton
Minor thriller: Demented killer's brother continues reign of terror

Silent Night, Deadly Night III
1989, (USA), Quiet Films, color, 90 mins.
W: Richard Beymer *(Dr. Newbury)*, Samantha Scully *(Laura)*, Bill Moseley *(Ricky)*, Eric Da Re *(Chris)*, Laura Herring *(Jerri)*, Elizabeth Hoffman *(Granny)*, Robert Culp *(Lt. Connelly)*, Richard C. Adams *(Santa)*, Melissa Hellman, Isabel Cooley, Leonard Mann, Carlos Palomino, Marc Dietrich, Jim Ladd, Richard N. Gladstein, Tamela Song, David Mount, Tom Herod Jr., Michael Ameen, David Umstadter, Corrie Gorson, Joe Torina, Tomczek Bednarek,

Bonnie Gaisford, Ila Dane, Carole Hill, Patty Matlen, Sheri Mount, Suzette Boucher, Stuart Snyder, Cheryl Ventura, Natalie Anderson, Lauren Becker, Alan Benjamin, Adam Friedson, Trissa Gabay, The Weiner Family
D: Monte Hellman **SCR:** Carlos Laszlo, from a story by Carlos Laszlo, Monte Hellman & Arthur H. Gorson **PHOTOG:** Josep M. Civit **MUSIC:** Steven Soles
Minor thriller: Maniac murderer tracks psychic blind girl

Silent Night, Deadly Night 4: Initiation
1990, (USA), Richard N. Gladstein/Silent Films, color
W: Maud Adams *(Fima)*, Neith Hunter *(Kim)*, Tommy Hinkley *(Hank)*, Allyce Beasley *(Janice)*, Clint Howard *(Ricky)*, Marjean Holden *(Jane)*, Jeanne Bates *(Katherine)*, Laurel Lockhart *(Ann)*, Ben Slack *(Gus)*, Conan Yuzna *(Lonnie)*, Hugh Fink *(Jeff)*, Richard N. Gladstein *(Woody)*, Reggie Bannister *(Eli)*, David Wells
D: Brian Yuzna **SCR:** Woody Keith **STORY:** S.J. Smith, Arthur H. Gorson & Brian Yuzna **PHOTOG:** Philip Holahan **MUSIC:** Richard Band
Standard horror-fantasy: Woman encounters female cultists

Silent Night, Deadly Night 5: The Toymaker
1991, (USA), color, 90 mins.
W: Mickey Rooney, Brian Bremer
Minor thriller: Toymaker has homicidal son

Silent Night, Evil Night
1974, (Can), Film Funding-Vision IV/WB, color, 93 mins.
W: Keir Dullea *(Peter)*, Olivia Hussey *(Jess)*, Margot Kidder *(Barb)*, Andrea Martin *(Phyl)*, John Saxon *(Fuller)*, Marian Waldman *(Mrs. Mac)*, Art Hindle *(Chris)*, James Edmonds *(Harrison)*, Lynne Griffin *(Clare)*
P & D: Bob Clark **SCR:** Roy Moore **PHOTOG:** Reg Morris **MUSIC:** Carl Zittrer
orig. to be titled Stop Me A.k.a. Black Christmas USA TV-retitle, Stranger in the House
Standard thriller: Sorority terrorized by mad murderer

The Silent One
see *Le Silencieux*

The Silent Passenger
1935, (GB), Phoenix Films/ABFD, b&w, 75 mins.
W: John Loder *(John Ryder)*, Peter Haddon *(Lord Peter Wimsey)*, Mary Newland *(Mollie Ryder)*, Austin Trevor *(Insp. Parker)*, Donald Wolfit *(Henry Camberley)*, Leslie Perrins *(Maurice Windermere)*, Aubrey Mather *(Bunter)*, Robb Wilton *(Porter)*, Ralph Truman *(Saunders)*
D: Reginald Denham **SCR:** Basil Mason, from a novel by Dorothy L. Sayers
Standard thriller: English lord probes blackmailer's murder

Silent Rage
1982, (USA), Col, color, 105 mins.
W: Chuck Norris, Ron Silver, Steven Keats, Toni Kalem
D: Michael Miller
Standard thriller: SF meets martial arts when twisted science creates indestructible man

Silent Running
1971, (USA), Univ, color, 90 mins.
W: Bruce Dern *(Lowell)*, Cliff Potts *(Wolf)*, Ron Rifkin *(Barker)*, Jesse Vint *(Keenan)*, Steve Brown, Cheryl Sparks, Mark Persons, Larry Whisenhunt
P: Michael Gruskoff **D:** Douglas Trumbull **SCR:** Deric Washburn, Mike Cimino & Steve Bochco **PHOTOG:** Charles F. Wheeler **MUSIC:** Peter Schickele songs performed by Joan Baez
"Silent Running will become the object of cult worship by the young romantics of the Tolkien-Vonnegut generation"— Paul D. Zimmerman, Newsweek
"A first feature by Douglas Trumbull, who was responsible for many of the best special effects in 2001, it retains that film's awe of the beauties of space. But it goes several steps beyond in its witty satire of Space Age technology"— Richard Schickel, Life
Superior SF-thriller: Existence of space-greenhouse is threatened

Silent Scream
1979, (USA), Joan Harris & Denny Harris/American Cinema, color, 87 mins.
W: Rebecca Balding *(Scotty)*, Barbara Steele *(Victoria)*, Cameron Mitchell *(Lt. McGiver)*, Avery Schreiber *(Sgt. Rusin)*, Steve Doubet *(Jack)*, Brad Rearden *(Mason)*, Yvonne DeCarlo *(Mrs. Engels)*, Juli Andelman *(Doris)*, John Widelock *(Peter)*
P: Jim & Ken Wheat **D:** Denny Harris **SCR:** Ken Wheat, Jim Wheat & Wallace C. Bennett
Minor thriller: Maniac kills college students

The Silent Scream (1980)
see *Witching Time/The Silent Scream*

The Silent Star
see *Milczaca Gwiazda*

The Silent Stranger
see *Step Down to Terror*

Silent Trigger
1996, (USA), color, 90 mins.

W: Dolph Lundgren, Gina Bellman, Conrad Dunn
Made-for-Video, standard thriller: Hit man becomes quarry

The Silent Watcher
1924, (USA), First Nat'l, b&w, 8 reels
W: Glenn Hunter, Bessir love, Hobart Bosworth
D: Frank Lloyd   **PHOTOG:** Norbert Brodine
Standard melodrama

The Silent Weapon
1961, (GB), Merton Park/Anglo-Amalgamated, b&w, 28 mins.
W: Geoffrey Keen (*Supt. Duggan*), Stanley Morgan (*Sgt. Dobbs*), Norma Parnell (*Joan Drew*)
P: Jack Greenwood   **D:** Peter Duffell   **STORY:** James Eastwood, from a novel by Edgar Lustgarten
Standard short crime-thriller: Actress involved in greyhound doping

A Silent Witness
1913, (GB), Hepworth, b&w, 1,000 ft. (304.8m)
W: Eric Desmond (*The Boy*)
D: Frank Wilson
Standard crime-thriller: Boy uses film company's camera, clears convicted man of killing fiancee's father

The Silent Witness
1954, (GB), Merton Park/Anglo-Amalgamated, b&w, 32 mins.
W: Ivan Craig (*Stafford*), Kenneth Henry (*Insp. Baker*), Namara Michael (*Ann Stafford*), Jean Lodge (*Mrs. Price*), Molly Weir (*Mum*)
P: Alec Snowden   **D:** Montgomery Tully   **STORY:** James Eastwood, from a novel by Edgar Lustgarten
Standard short crime-thriller: Man must kill again to conceal wife's murder

Silk Degrees
1994, (USA), color, 85 mins.
W: Marc Singer, Mark Hamill, Deborah Shelton, Michael Des Barres, Adrienne Barbeau
Standard thriller: Two Federal marshals guard TV-actress murder witness

Silken Threads
1928, (GB), British Filmcraft/Para, b&w, 1,832 ft. (558.4m)
W: Langhorne Burton (*Sexton Blake*), Mickey Brantford (*Tinker*), Leslie Perrins (*Stormcroft*), Frank Atherley (*The Man*), Marjorie Hume (*Nadia Petrowski*), Mrs. Fred Emney (*Mrs. Bardell*)
D: Leslie Eveleigh
Standard thriller (Sexton Blake mystery): Detective hunts killer

The Silk Noose
see Noose

Silver Blaze
1912, (GB-Fr), Franco-British Film Co.-Eclair/Fenning, b&w, 1,300 ft. (396.2m)
W: Georges Treville (*Sherlock Holmes*), Mr. Moyse (*Dr. John Watson*)
D: Georges Treville, from Sir Arthur Conan Doyle's story
Standard thriller

Silver Blaze
1937, (GB), Twickenham/ABPC, b&w, 70 mins.
W: Arthur Wontner (*Sherlock Holmes*), Lyn Harding (*Prof. Moriarty*), Judy Gunn (*Diana Baskerville*), Ian Fleming (*Dr. John Watson*), Lawrence Grossmith (*Sir Henry Baskerville*), Arthur Macrae (*Jack Trevor*), Eve Gray (*Mrs. Straker*), John Turnbull (*Insp. Lestrade*), Martin Walker (*John Straker*), Robert Horton (*Col. Ross*), Arthur Goullet (*Col. Sebastian Moran*), Minnie Rayner (*Mrs. Hudson*)
D: Thomas Bentley   **SCR:** Arthur Macrae & H. Fowler Mear, from Sir Arthur Conan Doyle's story
USA retitle, **Murder at the Baskervilles** *(Astor, 1941)*
Standard thriller: Famed detective proves racehorse did not kill groom and trainer

The Silver Bridge
1920, (GB), Cairns-Torquay Films, b&w, 5,000 ft. (1524m)
W: Dallas Cairns (*Mordred Baskerville*), Betty Farquhar (*Mystery Destin*), Madeleine Meredith (*Mrs. Baskerville*), Madge Tree (*Eillean Destin*), J. Hastings Batson (*Shepherd*), Stella Wood-Sims (*A Child*), Alan Michaels (*A Child*)
P & D: Dallas Cairns   **SCR:** Eliot Stannard, from a novel by Helen Prothero Lewis
Standard crime-thriller: Squire's new wife tries to poison his son and frame witch's adopted daughter

Silver Bullet
1985, (USA), Dino De Laurentiis/Para, color, 94 mins.
W: Gary Busey (*Uncle Red*), Corey Haim (*Marty Coslaw*), Megan Follows (*Jane Coslaw*), Everett McGill (*Rev. Lowe*), Terry O'Quinn (*Sheriff Joe Chambers*), Robin Groves, Leon Russom, James Gammon, Lawrence Tierney
D: Daniel Attias   **SCR:** Stephen King, from his novelette *Cycle of the Werewolf*
PHOTOG: Armando Nannuzzi   **MUSIC:** Jay Chattaway   **SONGS:** *All Dressed Up With No Place to Go, Joyride* & *Mansion of Misery*
Modest horror-thriller: Crippled boy discovers werewolf's identity

The Silver Greyhound
1919, (GB), Harma Photoplays, b&w, 4,775 ft. (1455.4m)
W: James Knight (*John Vane*), Mary Dibley (*Lady Chalmore*), Marjorie Villis (*Nance Lisle*), Frank E. Petley (*The Master*), Charles Ashley (*Lord Chalmore*), Jeff Barlow, Dallas Cairns, Clifford Pembroke, Hamilton Stewart, Frank Gerrard
P: Harry Maze Jenks   **D:** S. Bannister Merwin
Standard thriller: Girl helps king's messenger regain secret plans

The Silver Greyhound
1932, (GB), First Nat'l/WB, b&w, 47 mins.
W: Percy Marmont (*Norton Fitzwarren*), Janice Adair (*Ira Laennic*), Anthony Bushell (*Gerald Norton*), Eric Stanley (*Sir Wallace Cantripp*), Harry Hutchinson (*Regan*), J.A. O'Rourke (*O'Brien*), Dino Galvani (*Valdez*)
D: William McGann   **SCR:** Roland Pertwee & John Hastings Turner, from a story by John Hastings Turner
Standard thriller: Female spy steals secret papers

The Silver Lining
1911, (GB), Hepworth, b&w, 700 ft. (213.4m)
W: Flora Morris (*The Girl*), Ruby Belasco (*The Woman*), Harry Royston (*The Man*)
D: Bert Haldane
Standard crime-thriller: Couple forces orphan to sell flowers, kidnaps her benefactor

Silver Needle in the Sky
see **Duel in Space**

Silver Top
1938, (GB), Triangle/Para, b&w, 66 mins.
W: Marie Wright (*Mrs. Deeping*), Betty Ann Davies (*Dushka Vernon*), Marjorie Taylor (*Hazel Summers*), David Farrar (*Babe*), Brian

Simon
1980, (USA), Orion/WB, color, 95 mins.
W: Alan Arkin (*Simon*), Madeline Kahn (*Cynthia*), Austin Pendleton (*Becker*), Judy Graubart (*Lisa*), William Finley (*Fichandler*), Jayant (*Barundi*), Adolph Green (*The Commune Leader*), Fred Gwynn (*Korey*), Wallace Shawn (*Von Dongen*), Max Wright (*Hundertwasser*), Keith Szarabajka (*Josh*), Ann Risley (*Pam*), Pierre Epstein (*The Military Aide at the Map*), Roy Cooper (*The General's Aide*), Rex Robbins (*The Army Deserter*), David Warrilow (*Blades*), Hetty Galen (*The Voice of Mother*), David Gideon (*The Security Guard*), Remak Ramsay (*The TV Newscaster*), Hansford Rowe (*The TV Priest*), Yusef Bulos (*The TV Philosopher*), Jerry Mayer (*The TV Scientist*), Sol Frieder (*The TV Rabbi*), Willia Griffis (*The TV Senator*), Frank J. Lucas (*The TV Psychologist*), David Susskind, Dick Cavett
P: Martin Bregman   **D & SCR:** Marshall Brickman   **STORY:** Marshall Brickman & Thomas Baum   **PHOTOG:** Adam Holender   **MUSIC:** Stanley Silverman
Standard SF-comedy: Think-tank scientists convince professor that he is space alien

Simon, King of the Witches
1971, (USA), Fanfare, color, 91 mins.
W: Andrew Prine (*Simon*), Brenda Scott (*Linda*), Norman Burton (*Rackum*), George Paulsin (*Turk*), Gerald York (*Hercules*), Ultra Violet, Michael C. Ford, Lee J. Lambert, Harry Rose, William Martel, Angus Duncan, Richard Shepard, John Yates, Richard Ford Grayling, Allyson Ames, Ray Galvin, Art Hern, Mike Kopcha, Jerry Brooks, Buck Holland, David Vaile, John Hart, Helen Jay, Sharon Berryhill
D: Bruce Kessler   **SCR:** Robert Phippeny   **PHOTOG:** David Butler   **MUSIC:** Stu Phillips
blurb: "He curses the Establishment"
Minor fantasy-thriller: Warlock fights drug traffic

A Simple Wish
1997, (USA), The Bubble Factory/Univ, color, 90 mins.
W: Martin Short, Mara Wilson, Kathleen Turner, Robert Pastorelli
D: Michael Ritchie   **SCR:** Jeff Rothberg   **MUSIC:** Bruce Broughton
Standard comedy-fantasy: Man becomes fairy godfather

Simply Irresistible
1999, (USA), Polar/Regency, color
W: Sarah Michelle Gellar, Sean Patrick Flanery, Patricia Clarkson, Dylan Baker, Christopher Durang, Betty Buckley, Larry Gilliard Jr.
D: Mark Tarlov   **SCR:** Judith Roberts   **MUSIC:** Gil Goldstein
Standard romance-fantasy: Witchcraft complicates love affair

Sinbad
1986, (USA-It), Cannon, color
W: Lou Ferrigno (*Sinbad*)
Minor adventure-fantasy

Sinbad and the Eye of the Tiger
1977, (USA-GB), Col, color, 113 mins.
W: Patrick Wayne (*Sinbad*), Jane Seymour (*Farah*), Margaret Whiting (*Zenobia*), Taryn Power (*Dione*), Patrick Troughton (*Melanthius*), Damien Thomas (*Kassim*), Kurt Christian (*Rafi*), Nadim Sawalha (*Hassan*), Bruno Barnabe (*Balsora*), Bernard Kay (*Zabid*), Samali Coker (*Maroof*), David Sterne (*Aboo Seer*)

S

P: Ray Harryhausen & Charles H. Schneer   **D:** Sam Wanamaker   **SCR:** Beverly Cross   **PHOTOG:** Ted Moore   **SPCL-FX:** Ray Harryhausen   **MUSIC:** Roy Budd
orig. to be titled Sinbad at the World's End
Standard adventure-fantasy: Famed sailor attempts to break sinister spell

Sinbad and the Seven Seas
1990, (It), color, 95 mins.
W: Lou Ferrigno (*Sinbad*), John Steiner, Teagan Clive, Leo Gullotta
D: Enzo Girolami Castellari
Minor adventure-fantasy: Legendary sailor seeks magic gems

Sinbad at the World's End
see Sinbad and the Eye of the Tiger

Sinbad the Sailor
1946, (USA), RKO, color, 117 mins.
W: Douglas Fairbanks Jr. (*Sinbad*), Maureen O'Hara, Walter Slezak, Anthony Quinn, George Tobias, Jane Greer, Sheldon Leonard, Mike Mazurki
D: Richard Wallace   **SCR:** John Twist   **PHOTOG:** George Barnes   **MUSIC:** Roy Webb
Modest adventure-fantasy: Pirate seeks lost treasure of Alexander the Great

Sinful Davey
1969, (GB), Mirisch-Webb/UA, color, 95 mins.
W: John Hurt (*David Haggart*), Pamela Franklin (*Annie*), Nigel Davenport (*Richardson*), Noel Purcell (*Jock*), Ronald Fraser (*MacNab*), Robert Morley (*Duke of Argyll*), Maxine Audley (*Duchess of Argyll*), Fionnuala Flanagan (*The Daughter*), Fidela Murphy (*Jean Carlisle*), Francis De Wolff (*The Friend*), Donal McCann (*Sir James Campbell*), Eddie Byrne (*Yorkshire Bill*), Niall McGinnis
P: Walter Mirisch & William Graf   **D:** John Huston   **SCR:** James Haggart, from David Haggart's book *Haggart*
Modest, fact-based adventure-thriller: 19th-century Scottish deserter turns highwayman

Sinful Intrigue
1995, (USA), color, 90 mins.
W: Bobby Johnston, Beckie Mullen, Griffen Drew, Mark Zuelke
Standard thriller: Masked attacker preys on women in wealthy neighborhood

Singapore Sling
1990, (Greece), b&w, 115 mins.
W: Meredyth Herold, Micele Valley, Panos Thanassoulis
D: Nicos Nicolaidis
Standard film noir: Displaced detective becomes involved with disturbed mother and daughter

Das Singende Ringende Baumchen (The Singing Ringing Tree)
1958, (E. Ger), color, 73 mins.
W: Christel Bodelstein, Charles-Hans Vogt, Richard Kruger, Eckard Dux
D: Francesco Stefani
Modest fantasy: Cruel spell teaches humility to haughty princess

The Singing Musketeer
see The Three Musketeers (1939)

The Singing Princess
1952, (GB), IMA-Film/Trans-National, color, 65 mins.
VOICE: Julie Andrews
Animated feature, standard fantasy: Princess' true love imprisoned by evil caliph GB release of La Rosa Di Bagdad (The Rose of Bagdhad), Italian, 1949

The Singing Ringing Tree
see Das Singende Ringende Baumchen

Single White Female
1992, (USA), Col, color, 107 mins.
W: Bridget Fonda (*Allison Jones*), Jennifer Jason Leigh (*Hedra Carlson*), Steven Weber (*Sam Rawson*), Peter Friedman (*Graham Knox*), Stephen Tobolowsky (*Mitchell Myerson*), Frances Bay (*The Elderly Neighbor*), Michele Farr (*Myerson's Ass't*), Tara Karsian (*The Mannish Applicant*), Rene Estevez (*The Perfect Applicant*), Christiana Capetillo (*The Exotic Applicant*), Jessica Lundy (*The Talkative Applicant*), Tiffany & Krystle Mataras (*The Twins*), Amelia Campbell (*The Check Cashier*), Ken Tobey (*The Desk Clerk*), Eric Poppick (*The Nosy Neighbor*), Kim Sykes (*The TV Reporter*), Michael James Collins (*The Cashier Manager*), Jerry Mayer (*The News Vendor*), George Gerdes (*The Sniper*), Robert Martin Steinberg (*Hedy's Date*), Leslie A. Sank (*The Woman in the Club*), Ron Athey (*The Bartender*), Karen Boothroyd (*The Bookstore Customer*), Jack Wilson (*The Man in the Cage*)
P & D: Barbet Schroeder   **SCR:** Don Roos, from John Lutz' novel *SWF Seeks Same*   **PHOTOG:** Luciano Tovoli   **SPCL-FX:** Eddie Etan Surkin   **MUSIC:** Howard Shore   **SONGS:** *State of Independence*
Unusual thriller: Roommate proves psychotic

The Sinister Invasion
see Invasion Sinitestra

The Sinister Man
1961, (GB), Merton Park/Anglo-Amalgamated, b&w, 60 mins.
W: John Bentley (*Supt. Wills*), Patrick Allen (*Dr. Nelson Pollard*), Jacqueline Ellis

(*Elsa Marlowe*), John Glyn-Jones (*Dr. Maurice Tarn*), Eric Young (*Johnny Choto*), Arnold Lee (*Soyoki*), Brian McDermott (*Sgt. Stillman*), Gerald Andersen (*Maj. Paul Amery*), Yvonne Buckingham (*Miss Russell*)
P: Jack Greenwood   **D:** Clive Donner   **SCR:** Robert Stewart, from a novel by Edgar Wallace
Standard thriller: Archeologist murdered

The Sinister Urge
1961, (USA), Headliner, b&w, 75 mins.
W: Dino Fantini, Kenne Duncan, James Moore, Jean Fontaine, Carl Anthony, Jeanne Willardson, Toni Costello, April Lynn
WRIT, P, & D: Edward D. Wood Jr.
A.k.a. Hellborn and The Young and the Immoral
Minor thriller: Pornography inspires sex-murder

The Sinking of the Lusitania
1918, (USA), Winsor McCay/Jewel, b&w, 1 reel
Animated featurette (first example of animation being used to give serious account of actual event): Ship torpedoed in World War I

The Sin of Adam and Eve
1972, (Mex), color, 72 mins.
W: Jorge Rivero, Candy Wilson
D: Miguel Zacarias
Minor fantasy: Expelled from Eden, the first mortals struggle to find each other again

Sins of Babylon
1963, (It), color
W: Mark Forest, Jose Greci
Standard "Sword & Sandal": Tyrant sacrifices virgins

The Sins of Dorian Gray
1983, (USA), Rankin-Bass/ABC-TV, color, 95 mins.
W: Belinda Bauer (*Dorian Gray*), Anthony Perkins (*Henry Lord*), Olga Karlatos (*Sofia Vane*), Joseph Bottoms (*Stuart Vane*), Michael Ironside (*Campbell*), Caroline Yeager (*Angela Vane*)
D: Tony Maylam   **TELEPLAY:** Ken August & Peter Lawrence   suggested by Oscar Wilde's *The Picture of Dorian Gray*   **PHOTOG:** Zale Magder   **MUSIC:** Bernard Hoffer   **SONGS:** *I Need You*
TVM, standard fantasy-thriller: Beauty acquires immortality

The Sins of Harvey Clare
1914, (GB), Britannia Films/Pathe, b&w, 2,166 ft. (660.2m)
A.k.a. Victims of Blackmail
Standard crime-thriller: Man frames cousin, drowns after fighting mad witness on railway bridge

Sins of Jezebel
1953, (USA), Lippert, color, 74 mins.
W: Paulette Goddard, George Nader John Hoyt, Eduard Franz
D: Reginald LeBorg
Standard melodrama

Sins of Lola Montes
see Lola Montes

Sins of Pompeii
1955, (It), Visual Drama, b&w, 73 mins.
W: Micheline Presle, Georges Marchal
Standard melodrama: Volcanic eruption destroys wicked city

Sins of Rome
1954, (It), RKO, b&w, 75 mins.
W: Massimo Girotti, Ludmilla Tcherina Gianna Maria Canale, Yves Vincent
D: Riccardo Freda
Standard "Sword & Sandal" melodrama

Sinthia: The Devil's Doll
1970, (USA), color
W: Shula Roan, Diane Webber
D: Ray Dennis Steckler
Minor fantasy-thriller: Small girl seems demon-possessed

Sin You Sinners
1963, (USA), b&w, 73 mins.
W: June Colbourne, Dian Lloyd, Derek Murcott, Beverly Nazarow, Charles Clements
D: Anthony Farrar
Minor horror-fantasy: Amulet restores aging stripper's youth

Sir Arne's Treasure
see Herr Arnes Pengar (1919 & 1954)

La Sirene (The Mermaid)
1904, (Fr), Star, b&w, 71m (232.9 ft./3.9 mins.)
D: Georges Melies
Standard fantasy: Sea nymph's saga

Siren of Atlantis
see Atlantis (1948)

Siren of Bagdad
1953, Col, color, 77 mins.
W: Paul Henreid, Patricia Medina, Hans Conried, Charlie Lung
P: Sam Katzman   D: Richard Quine
Standard fantasy: Arabian Nights adventure

Sirens of the Sea
1917, (USA), Univ, b&w, 5 reels
W: Jack Mulhall, Louise Lovely, Carmel Myers Sally Blane
Standard adventure-fantasy

Sister Mary Jane's Top Note
1907, (GB), Hepworth, b&w, 100 ft. (30.5m)
D: Lewin Fitzhamon
Standard comedy-fantasy short: Singing pupil's voice wrecks room

The Sister of Satan
see La Sorella di Satan

Sisters
1973, (USA), Pressman-Williams/AIP, color, 92 mins.
W: Margot Kidder (*Danielle/Dominique*), Jennifer Salt (*Grace Collier*), Charles Durning (*Joseph Larch*), Barnard Hughes (*Editor McLennen*), Bill Finley (*Emil Breton*), Lisle Wilson (*Philip Woode*), Dolph Sweet (*Det. Kelley*), Mary Davenport (*Mrs. Collier*)
P: Edward D. Pressman   D: Brian De Palma   SCR: Brian De Palma & Louisa Rose   PHOTOG: Gregory Sandor   MUSIC: Bernard Herrmann
Standard thriller: Reporter witnesses murder

Sister, Sister
1987, (USA), Odyssey/New World, color, 91 mins.
W: Eric Stoltz, Jennifer Jason Leigh, Judith Ivey, Dennis Lipscomb, Anne Pitoniak, Benjamin Mouton
D: Bill Condon   SCR: Bill Condon, Joel Cohen & Ginny Cerrella   PHOTOG: Stephen M. Katz   MUSIC: Richard Einhorn
Minor thriller: Passion and madness in spooky Southern mansion

Sisters of Death
1978, (USA), Independent-Int'l, color
W: Arthur Franz, Claudia Jennings, Cheri Howell, Paul Carr, Sherry Boucher, Sherry Alberoni, Roxanne Albee, Elizabeth Bergen, Paul Fierro, Vern Mathison
D: Joseph A. Mazzuca   SCR: Peter Arnold & Elwyn Richards   ORIG STORY: Elwyn Richards   PHOTOG: Grady Martin
Minor fantasy-thriller: Satanic sorority brews trouble

The Sitter
1991, (USA), color
W: Kim Myers Susan Barnes, Brett Cullen, Eugene Roche, Susanne Reed, Patricia George, Gregory White, James McDonnell, Chad Power
D & TELEPLAY: Rick Berger, from Charlotte Armstrong's novel *Mischief*   PHOTOG: Edward Pei   MUSIC: Laura Karpman
Standard thriller (remake of Don't Bother to Knock*): Neurotic babysitter threatens young charge*

The Sister-in-Law
1995, (USA), cable, color
W: Kate Vernon, Shanna Reed (*Madeline*), Craig Wasson (*Andy*)
Made-for-Cable, standard thriller: Vengeance-bent woman infiltrates wealthy Southern family

Sitting Target
1972, (GB), Peerford/MGM-EMI, color, 93 mins.
W: Oliver Reed (*Harry Lomart*), Jill St. John (*Pat Lomart*), Ian McShane (*Birdy Williams*), Edward Woodward (*Insp. Milton*), Frank Finlay (*Marty Gold*), Freddie Jones (*MacNeil*), Jill Townsend (*Maureen*), Robert Beatty (*Dealer*), Tony Beckley (*Soapy Tucker*), Robert Ramsey (*The Bodyguard*), Susan Shaw (*The Woman*), Mike Pratt (*A Warder*), Robert Russell (*A Warder*), Joe Cahill (*A Warder*)
P: Barry Kulick   D: Douglas Hickox   SCR: Alexander Jacobs, from a novel by Laurence Henderson   PHOTOG: Edward Scaife   MUSIC: Stanley Myers
Standard crime-thriller: Robber breaks jail to kill pregnant wife

Siva, l'Invisible (Siva, the Invisible)
1904, (Fr), Star, b&w, 29m (95.1 ft./1.6 mins.)
D: Georges Melies
Standard fantasy

Six Hours to Live
1932, (USA), b&w, 78 mins.
W: Warner Baxter, Miriam Jordan, John Boles, George Marion, Beryl Mercer, Irene Ware
D: William Dieterle
Unusual thriller: Murdered diplomat revived

The Six Men
1951, (GB), Planet/Eros, b&w, 65 mins.
W: Harold Warrender (*Supt. Holroyd*), Peter Bull (*Walkeley*), Olga Edwardes (*Christina Frazer*), Desmond Jeans (*The Colonel*), Michael Evans (*Hunter*), Reed de Rouen (*Lewis*), Ivan Craig (*Wainwright*)
D: Michael Law   SCR: Reed de Rouen, Michael Law & Richard Eastham   STORY: E. & M.A. Radford
Standard crime-thriller: Superintendent poses as blind informer, routs jewel thieves

The Six Million Dollar Man
1973, (USA), Univ/ABC-TV, color, 74 mins.
W: Lee Majors, Darren McGavin, Barbara Anderson, Martin Balsam, Dorothy Green, Charles Knox Robinson, Ivor Barry, Anne Whitfield, Maurice Sherbanee
D: Richard Irving   SCR: Henri Simoun, from Martin Caidin's novel *Cyborg* (orig. to be titled same)
TVM, standard SF-thriller (feature pilot for teleseries): Injured astronaut turned into bionic spy

Six Penguins
1971, (Bulgar), McGraw, color, 5 mins.
Standard fantasy short (enacted by animated puppets): Reworking of Aesop's fable of lion and the mouse

16 Fathoms Deep
1948, (USA), Mono, color, 82 mins.
W: Arthur Lake, Lon Chaney Jr., Lloyd Bridges, Tanis Chandler
P: James S. Burkett, Irving Allen & Arthur Lake   D: Irving Allen   SCR: Max Trell
blurb: "Spine-chilling thrills in the monster-ridden world beneath the sea!"
Minor adventure-thriller. Remake of 1934 film with Chaney

The Sixth Column
see The Love War

The Silver Lining
1911, (GB), Hepworth, b&w, 700 ft. (213.4m)
W: Flora Morris (*The Girl*), Ruby Belasco (*The Woman*), Harry Royston (*The Man*)
D: Bert Haldane
Standard crime-thriller: Couple forces orphan to sell flowers, kidnaps her benefactor

The Sister-in-Law
95 mins.
W: Kevin McCarthy
D: Noel Nosseck   WRIT: David Callaway & Megan Marks

Sisters of Satan
1975, (Mex), color, 91 mins.
W: Claudio Brook, David Silva, Tina Romero, Susana Kamini
D: Juan Lopez Moctezuma
Standard thriller: Nuns embrace satanism

Six Hours to Live
1932, (USA), b&w, 78 mins.
W: Warner Baxter, Miriam Jordan, John Boles, George Marion, Beryl Mercer, Irene Ware
D: William Dieterle
Unusual thriller: Murdered diplomat revived

The Sixth Commandment
1912, (GB), Cricks & Martin, b&w, 1,125 ft. (342.9m)
W: Una Tristram (*The Girl*), Fred Paul (*Jack Howard*)
D: Edwin J. Collins
Standard crime-thriller: Heir recovers from gunshot, stops girl from marrying impostor

The 6th Man
1997, (USA), Mandeville/Touchstone, color, 107 mins.
W: Marlon Wayans (*Kenny Tyler*), Kadeem Hardison (*Antoine Tyler*), Michael Michele (*R.C. St. John*), Kevin Dunn, David Paymer
P: David Hoberman   D: Randall Miller   SCR: Christopher Reed & Cynthia Carle   PHOTOG: Michael Ozier   MUSIC: Marcus Miller   MUSIC SPRVSR: Peter Afterman
Standard comedy-fantasy: Ghost helps brother play basketball

Six Women for the Assassin
see Sei Donne per l'Assassino

Det Sjunde Inseglet (The Seventh Seal)
1957, (Swed), Svensk Filmindustri/Janus, b&w, 105 mins.
W: Max von Sydow (*The Knight*), Bibi Andersson (*Mia*), Gunnar Bjornstrand (*The Squire*), Nils Poppe (*Jof*), Gunnel Lindblom (*The Girl*), Ake Fridell (*Plog*), Inga Gill (*Lisa*), Anders Ek (*The Monk*), Bengt Ekerot (*Death*), Maud Hansson (*The Witch*), Inga Landgre (*The Knight's Wife*), Bertil Anderberg (*Raval*), Gunnar Olsson (*The Church Painter*), Erik Strandmakr (*Skat*), Benkt-Ake Benktsson, Gudrun Brost, Ulf Johansson, Lars Lind
P: Allan Ekelund   WRIT & D: Ingmar Bergman   PHOTOG: Gunnar Fischer   MUSIC: Erik Nordgren
Classic fantasy: Weary knight returns from Crusades, finds homeland ravaged by plague. Cannes film festival 'Most Artistic Film' winner

The Seventh Seal: NILS POPPE AND BIBI ANDERSSON

Skeeter
1994, (USA), color, 95 mins.
<u>W:</u> Tracy Griffith Jim Youngs, Charles Napier, Michael J. Pollard
<u>D:</u> Clark Brandon   <u>SCR:</u> Clark Brandon & Lanny Horn   <u>MUSIC:</u> David Lawrence
Standard SF-thriller: Toxic waste spawns ravenous mosquitos

Sketches of a Strangler
1978, (USA), color, 91 mins.
<u>W:</u> Allen Garfield, Meredith MacRae
<u>D:</u> Paul Leder
TVM, minor thriller: Psychotic art student slays prostitutes

Skin of the Donkey
see **Peau d'Ane**

Skipper
see **The Todd Killings**

The Skipping Cheeses
see **Les Fromages Automobiles**

The Skull
1965, (GB), Amicus/Para, color, 83 mins.
<u>W:</u> Peter Cushing (*Prof. Christopher Maitland*), Christopher Lee (*Sir Matthew Phillips*), Patrick Wymark (*Anthony Marco*), Nigel Green (*Insp. Wilson*), Jill Bennett (*Jane Maitland*), Michael Gough (*The Auctioneer*), April Olrich (*The Girl*), George Coulouris (*Dr. Londe*), Peter Woodthorpe (*Bert Travers*), Maurice Good (*Pierre*), Patrick Magee (*The Doctor*), Anna Palk (*The Maid*), Frank Forsyth
<u>P:</u> Max J. Rosenberg & Milton Subotsky   <u>D:</u> Freddie Francis   <u>SCR:</u> Milton Subotsky, from Robert Bloch's short story *The Skull of the Marquis de Sade*   <u>PHOTOG:</u> John Wilcox   <u>MUSIC:</u> Elisabeth Lutyens   <u>DESIGN:</u> Scott Slimon
Standard horror-fantasy: Skull of Marquis de Sade exerts evil influence

The Skull: PETER CUSHING

Skullduggery
1970, (USA), Univ, color, 105 mins.
<u>W:</u> Burt Reynolds (*Douglas*), Susan Clark (*Sybil*), Alexander Knox (*Buffington*), Roger C. Carmel (*Kreps*), Paul Hubschmid A.k.a. Christian Van Cruysen, Pat Suzuki (*Topazia*), Chips Rafferty (*Pop*), Wilfrid Hyde-White (*Eaton*), Edward Fox (*Spofford*), William Marshall (*The Attorney General*), Rhys Williams (*Judge Draper*), Mort Marshall (*Dr. Figgins*), Michael St. Clair (*Tee Hee*), Booker Bradshaw (*Smoot*), John Kimberley (*Epstein*), James Henry Eldridge (*The Officer*), Totty Ames (*The Motel Manager*), James Bacon (*The Commentator*), Clarence Harris (*Siria*), Gilbert Senior (*Kauni*), Newton D. Arnold (*Mimms*), Burnal "Custus" Smith (*The Chief*), Wendell Baggett (*Rev. Holzapple*), John Woodcock (*Spigget*), Mike Preece (*Naylor*), Charles Washburn (*The Papuan*), Saul David (*Berle Tanen*), Cliff Bell Jr. (*The Worker*), Alex Gradussov (*The Russian Delegate*), Jim Alexander (*The Reporter*), Bernard Pike (*The Associate Judge*), Eddie Fuchs (*The Israeli Delegate*)
<u>D:</u> Gordon Douglas   <u>SCR:</u> Nelson Gidding, from Vercors' novel *You Shall Know Them*   <u>PHOTOG:</u> Robert Moreno   <u>MUSIC:</u> Oliver Nelson
Standard SF-thriller: Researchers find half-human race

Sky above Heaven
1965, (It-Fr), Gaumont/Galatea, color, 107 mins
<u>W:</u> Andre Smagghe, Marcel Bozzuffi
Minor SF-thriller

The Sky Bike
1967, (GB), Eyeline/CFF, color, 62 mins.
<u>W:</u> Spencer Shires (*Tom Smith*), Liam Redmond (*Mr. Lovejoy*), Ian Ellis (*Porker*), William Lucas (*Mr. Smith*), Bill Shine (*Wingco*), Ellen McIntosh (*Mrs. Smith*), David Lodge (*The Guard*), Della Rands (*Daphne*), John Howard (*Jack*), Harry Locke (*The Owner*)
<u>P:</u> Harold Orton   <u>D & STORY:</u> Charles Frend
Standard juvenile fantasy: Boy pedals inventor's flying bicycle to win contest

The Sky Dragon
1949, (USA), Mono, b&w, 64 mins.
<u>W:</u> Roland Winters (*Charlie Chan*), Keye Luke (*Lee Chan*), Mantan Moreland (*Birmingham Brown*), Noel Neill (*Jane Marshall*), Tim Ryan (*Lt. Mike Ruark*), Elena Verdugo (*Marie Burke*), Iris Adrian (*Wanda LaFern*), Eddie Parks (*Tibbets*), Milburn Stone (*Tim Norton*), Paul Maxey (*John Anderson*), Lyle Talbot (*Andy Barrett/Smith*), Joel Marston (*Don Blake*), John Eldredge (*William E. French*), Louise Franklin (*Lena*), Lyle Latell (*Ed Davidson*), George Eldredge (*Stacey*), Bob Curtis (*Watkins*), Steve Pendleton, Emmett Vogan, Charles Jordan, Edna Holland, Joe Whitehead, Lee Phelps, Suzette Harbin, Frank Cady
<u>D:</u> Lesley Selander   <u>SCR:</u> Oliver Drake & Clint Johnston, from characters created by Earl Derr Biggers   <u>PHOTOG:</u> William Sickner
working title, **Murder in the Air**
Standard thriller ("Charlie Chan" mystery): Passengers aboard airplane are drugged. Last of series

Sky Murder
1940, (USA), MGM, b&w, 72 mins.
<u>W:</u> Walter Pidgeon (*Nick Carter*), Donald Meek (*Bartholomew*), Kaaren Verne (*Pat*), Edward Ashley, Joyce Compton, Dorothy Tree, Tom Conway, George Lessy, Chill Wills, Byron Foulger, Tom Neal
<u>D:</u> George B. Seitz   <u>SCR:</u> William P. Lipman, from characters created by John R. Coryell   <u>PHOTOG:</u> Charles Lawton Jr.
Standard thriller ("Nick Carter" mystery): Sleuth probes killing on airplane

Sky Pirates
1986, (Austral), color, 86 mins.
<u>W:</u> John Hargreaves, Meredith Phillips, Max Phipps, Simon Chilvers, Bill Hunter, Alex Scott
<u>D:</u> Colin Eggleston
Minor SF-fantasy: Aircraft crashes time barrier

Skyscraper
1996, (USA), color, 95 mins.
<u>W:</u> Anna Nicole Smith, Richard Steinmetz (*Gordon*), Charles Huber (*Fairfax*)
Made-for-Video, minor thriller: Woman helicopter pilot vs. terrorists in corporate high-rise

Sky Ship
see **Himmelskibet**

Slalom
1965, (It), Official Films, color, 97 mins.
<u>W:</u> Vittorio Gassman, Daniela Bianchi
<u>D:</u> Luciano Salce
A.k.a. **Snow Job**
Minor thriller: Vacationing businessman involved with counterfeiters

Slam Dance
1987, (USA), Zenith, color, 101 mins.
<u>W:</u> Tom Hulce (*C.C. Drood*), Mary Elizabeth Mastrantonio (*Helen Drood*), Adam Ant (*Jim*), Virginia Madsen (*Yolanda*), Judith Barsi (*Bean*), Don Opper (*Buddy*), Rosalind Chao (*Mrs. Bell*), Harry Dean Stanton (*Smiley*), Lisa Niemi (*Mrs. Schell*), Millie Perkins (*Bobby Nye*), Herta Ware (*Mrs. Raines*),

Sasha Delgado (*The Girl at the Nursery*), Joshua Caceras (*The Boy at the Nursery*), John Doe (*Gilbert*), Marty Levy (*The Detective*), Jon C. Slade (*The Junkie*), Marc Anthony Thompson (*The Bartender*), Julian Deyer (*The Cop at the Police Station*), Dennis Hayden (*The Mean Drunk*), Robert Beltran (*Frank*), Lin Shaye (*The Librarian*), Jerris L. Poindexter (*The Party Cop*), Michael Ennis (*The Morgue Clerk*), Christopher Keene (*The Cop on the Street*), John Fleck (*The Opera Singer*), Laura Campbell (*Pat Menninger*), Philip Granger (*George*), Buckley Norris (*The Minister*)
<u>D:</u> Wayne Wang   <u>SCR:</u> Don Opper   <u>SONGS:</u> *Bing Can't Walk, Art Life & High Hopes*
Unusual melodrama: Cartoonist suspected of murder

Slam Dunk Ernest
1995, (USA), color, 95 mins.
<u>W:</u> Jim Varney, Cylk Cozart, Miguel A. Nunez Jr.
Made-for-Video, standard juvenile comedy: Magic sneakers turn klutz into basketball star

Slashdance
1989, (USA), color, 83 mins.
<u>W:</u> Cindy Maranne, James Carroll Jordan, Queen Kog, Joel von Ornsteiner, Jay Richardson
<u>D & SCR:</u> James Shyman
Minor thriller: Lady cop seeks killer of dancers

The Slasher
see **Cosh Boy**

The Slasher is the Sex Maniac
see **Penetration**

Slaughter
see **Dogs**

Slaughter High
1985, (USA), Steve Minasian-Dick Randall/Spectacular Trading Co., color, 91 mins.
<u>W:</u> Caroline Munro (*Carol*), Simon Scuddamore (*Marty*), Donna Yaeger (*Stella*), Carmine Iannaccone (*Skip*), Billy Hartman (*Frank*), Kelly Baker (*Nancy*), Gary Martin (*Joe*), Michael Saffran (*Ted*), Josephine Scandi (*Shirley*), Marc Smith (*The Coach*), John Segal (*Carl*), Dick Randall (*Manny*), Jon Clark (*Digby*)
<u>WRIT & D:</u> George Dugdale, Mark Ezra & Peter Litten   <u>PHOTOG:</u> Alan Pudney   <u>MUSIC:</u> Harry Manfredini
Minor thriller: Tormented nerd gains ghoulish revenge

Slaughter Hotel
1972, (It), Hallmark, color, 72 mins.
<u>W:</u> Klaus Kinski, Margaret Lee, Jane Garrett, John Karlsen, Sandro Rossi, Monica Strebel, John Ely, Rosalba Neri
<u>P:</u> Armando Novelli & Tizio Longo   <u>D:</u> Fernando Di Leo   <u>SCR:</u> Fernando Di Leo & Nino Latino   <u>PHOTOG:</u> Franco Villa
A.k.a. **Asylum Erotica**
blurb: "The Slasher Massacre of eight innocent nurses!"
Minor thriller: Inmates meet grisly fates in private asylum

Slaughter Hotel (1976)
see **Eaten Alive! (1976)**

Slaughterhouse-Five
1972, (USA), Vanadas/Univ, color, 104 mins.
<u>W:</u> Michael Sacks (*Billy Pilgrim*), Valerie Perrine (*Montana Wildhack*), Ron Leibman (*Paul Lazzaro*), Eugene Roche (*Derby*), Sharon Gans (*Valencia*), Kevin Conway (*Weary*), Roberts Blossom (*Wild Bob Cody*), Gary Waynesmith (*Stanley*), Sorrell Booke (*Lionel Merble*), Friedrich Ledebur (*The German Leader*), Stan Gottlieb (*Rumford*), John Dehner (*Rumford*), Nick Belle (*The Young German Guard*), Perry King (*Robert*), Henry Bumstead (*Eliot Rosewater*), Tom Wood (*The Englishman*), Lucille Benson (*Billy Pilgrim's Mother*), Holly Near (*Barbara*), Richard Schaal (*Campbell*), Karl Otto Alberty (*The German Guard, Group 2*), Gilmer McCormick (*Lily*)
<u>P:</u> Paul Monash   <u>D:</u> George Roy Hill   <u>SCR:</u> Stephen Geller, from Kurt Vonnegut Jr.'s novel   <u>PHOTOG:</u> Miroslav Ondricek   <u>MUSIC:</u> Glenn Gould
Unusual fantasy-parable: Adventures of American "Everyman"

Slaughterhouse Rock
1987, (USA), First American-Arista Films/Taurus, color, 90 mins.
<u>W:</u> Toni Basil (*Sammy Mitchell*), Nicholas Celozzi (*Alex Gardner*), Tom Reilly (*Richard Gardner*), Hope Marie Carlton (*Krista Halpern*), Donna Denton (*Carolyn Harding*), Tamara Hyler (*Jan Squires*), Steven Brian Smith (*Jack*), Ty Miller (*Marty*), Al Fleming (*The Commandant*), Michal J. Scherlis (*The Tour Guide*), Danny Somrack, Lenka Novak, Charles P. Bernuth, Julie Rhodes, Richard Hench, Mindy Miller, Jeff Speakman, Nathan Holland, Denise Ferrell, Gerard Dinardi, Lorraine Watson, Muna Deriane, Marc Daniels, Ted Landon, Ron E. Dickenson
<u>D:</u> Dimitri Logothetis   <u>WRIT:</u> Sandra Willard & Nora Goodman   <u>STORY:</u> Dimitri Logothetis   <u>PHOTOG:</u> Nicholas Von Sternberg   <u>SPCL-FX COORD:</u> Kenneth McCarthy   <u>MUSIC:</u> Mark Mothersbaugh & Gerald V. Casale   <u>MUSIC PERFORMED BY:</u> Devo   <u>SONGS:</u> *The Only One, Man Turned Inside Out, Set Me Free, & Part of You*
Standard horror-fantasy: Students probe Alcatraz haunting

Slaughter of the Vampires
see **La Strage dei Vampiri**

The Slave
see **Il Figlio di Spartacus**

Slave Girl
1947, (USA), Univ, color, 80 mins.
<u>W:</u> Yvonne DeCarlo, George Brent Broderick Crawford, Albert Dekker, Lois Collier, Arthur Treacher, Andy Devine
<u>D:</u> Charles Lamont
Standard adventure-thriller

Slave Girls
see **Prehistoric Women (1966)**

Slavegirls from Beyond Infinity
1987, (USA), Titan/Urban Classics, color, 80 mins.
<u>W:</u> Elizabeth Cayton, Cindy Beal, Brinke Stevens, Carl Horner, Don Scribner
<u>WRIT, P, & D:</u> Ken Dixon   <u>PHOTOG:</u> Ken Wiatrak & Tom Callaway   <u>MUSIC:</u> Carl Dante
orig. co-billed with **Creepozoids**
Minor SF-satire: Imprisoned females flee spacecraft, land on uncharted planet

Slave Girls of Sheba
1961, (It), AIP-TV, color, 92 mins
<u>W:</u> Linda Cristal, Jose Suarez
Minor "Sword & Sandal": Saracen sultan outwits tyrant

Slave of the Amazons
see **Love Slaves of the Amazons**

Slave of the Cannibal God
see **Il Montagna di Dio Cannibale**

Slave Queen of Babylon
1962, (It), AIP/Globe/Filmways, color, 101 mins.
<u>W:</u> Yvonne Furneaux, John Ericson
Standard Sword & Sandal: Queen loves slave

Slavers of the Thames
1915, (GB), H. Ambrose, b&w, 2,450 ft. (746.8m)
<u>W:</u> Percy Moran (*Hon. Jack Courtney*)
<u>D & STORY:</u> Percy Moran
Standard crime-thriller: Lord's disowned son saves boatman's daughter from white slaver

Slaves of Babylon
1953, (USA), Col, color, 82 mins.
<u>W:</u> Richard Conte, Linda Christian, Terence Kilburn, Maurice Schwartz, Michael Ansara
<u>P:</u> Sam Katzman   <u>D:</u> William Castle   <u>SCR:</u> DeVallon Scott   <u>PHOTOG:</u> Henry Freulich   <u>MUSIC:</u> Mischa Bakaleinikoff
Standard adventure-thriller: Hebrews flee Babylonian captivity

Slaves of the Invisible Monster
1966, (USA), Rep, b&w, 100 mins.
<u>W:</u> Richard Webb, Aline Towne Lane Bradford, Stanley Price, George Meeker
<u>D:</u> Fred C. Brannon
Minor thriller (feature culled from 1950 serial **The Invisible Monster***)*

The Slave Woman
see **The Queen of Babylon**

The Slavey's Dream
1904, (GB), Hepworth, b&w, 100 ft. (30.5m)
<u>W:</u> May Clark (*The Slavey*), Lewin Fitzhamon (*The Villain*)
<u>D:</u> Lewin Fitzhamon
Standard fantasy short: Maid dreams of hero and villain fighting

The Slayer
1982, (USA), 21st Century/International Picture Show, color, 95 mins.
<u>D & SCR:</u> J.S. Cardone   <u>MUSIC:</u> Robert Folk
A.k.a. **Nightmare Island**
Minor thriller: Two young couples terrorized on island retreat

Slayground
1983, (GB), Jennie & Co./Col-EMI-WB, color, 89 mins.
<u>W:</u> Peter Coyote (*Stone*), Billie Whitelaw (*Madge*), Mel Smith (*Terry Abbott*), Philip Sayer (*Costello*), Clarence Felder (*Orzel*), Bill Luhrs (*Sheer*), Marie Masters (*Joni*), David Hayward (*Laufman*), Ned Eisenberg (*Lonzini*), Michael Ryan (*Danard*), Barret Mulligan (*Lucy*), Kelli Maroney (*Jolene*), Margareta Arvidssen (*Grete*), Rosemary Martin (*Dr. King*), Malcolm Terris (*Venner*), Jon Morrison (*Webb*), Bill Dean (*The Compere*), Cassie Stuart (*Fran*), Debby Bishop (*Beth*), Stephen Yardley (*Turner*)
<u>P:</u> John Dark & Gower Frost   <u>D:</u> Terry Bedford   <u>SCR:</u> Trevor Preston, from a novel by Richard Stark   <u>PHOTOG:</u> Stephen Smith   <u>MUSIC:</u> Colin Towns
Standard crime-thriller: Crook flees assassin

S

Sledgehammer
1983, (USA), color, 87 mins.
W: Ted Prior, Doug Matley, Steven Wright
Minor thriller: Madman abuses small town

Sleepaway Camp
1983, (USA), color, 88 mins.
W: Mike Kellin, Jonathan Toersten, Felissa Rose, Christopher Collet
Minor thriller: Crazed killer at peaceful summer camp

Sleepaway Camp 2: Unhappy Campers
1988, (USA), color, 82 mins.
W: Pamela Springsteen, Renee Estevez, Walter Gotell, Brian Patrick Clark
D: Michael A. Simpson
Minor thriller: Camp counselor revealed as bloodthirsty madwoman

Sleepaway Camp 3: Teenage Wasteland
1989, (USA), color, 80 mins.
W: Pamela Springsteen, Tracy Griffith, Michael J. Pollard
D: Michael A. Simpson
Minor thriller: Mad camper dismembers teens

Sleeper
1973, (USA), Jack Rollins-Charles H. Joffe/UA, color, 88 mins.
W: Woody Allen (*Miles Monroe*), Diane Keaton (*Luna*), John Beck (*Erno*), Don Keefer (*Dr. Tryon*), Mary Gregory (*Dr. Melic*), Don McLiam (*Dr. Agon*), Chris Forbes (*Rainer*), Bartlett Robinson (*Dr. Orva*), Peter Hobbs (*Dr. Dean*), Marya Small (*Dr. Nero*), Spencer Milligan (*Jeb*), Stanley Ross (*Sears*), Whitney Rydbeck (*Janus*), Jessica Rains, Brian Avery, Susan Miller, Howard Cosell [cameo]
P: Jack Grossberg   D: Woody Allen   SCR: Woody Allen & Marshall Brickman   PHOTOG: David M. Walsh   SPCL-FX: A.D. Flowers   MUSIC: Woody Allen
Standard SF-comedy: 1970's misfit revived from suspended animation, 200 years in future

Sleepers West
1941, (USA), 20th-Fox, b&w, 74 mins.
W: Lloyd Nolan (*Michael Shayne*), Lynn Bari (*Kay Bentley*), Mary Beth Hughes (*Helen Carlson*), Louis Jean Heydt (*Everett Jason*), Edward Brophy (*George Trautwein*), Don Costello (*Carl Izzard*), Don Douglas (*Tom Linscott*), Harry Hayden (*Lyons*), Oscar O'Shea (*McGowan*), Hamilton MacFadden (*Meyers*), Ferike Boras (*The Old Lady*), Ben Carter
D: Eugene Forde   SCR: Lou Breslow & Stanley Rauh, based on Frederick Nebel's novel *Sleepers East* and characters created, by Brett Halliday   PHOTOG: J. Peverell Marley
*Standard thriller ("Michael Shayne" mystery): Detective protects witness on train journey. Remake of **Sleepers East**, Fox, 1934*

The Sleeping Beauty
1912, (GB), Ivy Close Films/Hepworth, b&w, 1,000 ft. (304.8m)
W: Ivy Close (*Sleeping Beauty*)

The Sleeping Beauty
1954, (GB), b&w, 10 mins,
D: Lotte Reiniger, from a story by the Brothers Grimm
Standard short animated fantasy

Sleeping Beauty
1959, (USA), Walt Disney, color, 75 mins.
VOICES: Mary Costa (*Aurora*), Bill Shirley (*Prince Philip*), Eleanor Audley (*Maleficent*), Taylor Holmes, Pinto Colvig, Marvin Miller
D: Clyde Geronimi, Eric Larson, Wolfgang Reitherman & Les Clark   MUSIC: George Bruns   SONG: *Once Upon a Dream*
Well-made animated fantasy: Cursed princess raised by three fairies in forest

The Sleeping Beauty
1965, (Russ), Lenfilm/Cinemasters-Int'l, color, 90 mins.
W: Yuri Soloviev, Alla Simova, Leningrad Kirov Ballet
D: Appolonari Dudko, Konstantin Sergeyev & Josif Shapiro   SCR: Appolonari Dudko & Konstantin Sergeyev, based on Tchaikovsky's ballet   PHOTOG: Anatoli Nazarov
Standard dance-fantasy: Princess falls under spell

Sleeping Beauty
1965, (W. Ger), Childhood, color, 70 mins.
NARRATION: Paul Tripp
WRIT, P, & D: Fritz Genschow   MUSIC: Anne & Milton DeLugg
Standard fantasy: Evil fairy curses princess

Sleeping Beauty
1986, (USA-Isrl), Cannon, color
W: Tahnee Welch, Morgan Fairchild Nicholas Clay, Sylvia Miles, Kenny Baker, David Holliday
WRIT & D: Elwin Neame
Standard fantasy: Cursed princess awakened by prince's kiss

The Sleeping Car
1990, (USA), color, 90 mins.

W: David Naughton, Judie Aronson, Kevin McCarthy Jeff Conaway, Ernestine Mercer, John Carl Buechler, Dani Minnick
D: Douglas Curtis
Minor fantasy: Spirit bedevils college student

The Sleeping Cardinal
1931, (GB), Twickenham/WB, b&w, 84 mins.
W: Arthur Wontner (*Sherlock Holmes*), Norman McKinnel (*Prof. Moriarty*), Ian Fleming (*Dr. John Watson*), Jane Welsh (*Kathleen Adair*), Louis Goodrich (*Col. Sebastian Moran*), Philip Hewland (*Insp. Lestrade*), Charles Paton (*J.J. Godfrey*), Minnie Rayner (*Mrs. Hudson*)
D: Leslie Hiscott   SCR: Cyril Twyford & H. Fowler Mear, based on Sir Arthur Conan Doyle's short stories "The Empty House" & "The Final Problem"
*USA retitle, **Sherlock Holmes' Fatal Hour**, First Division, 1931*
Standard thriller: Diplomat forced into smuggling

The Sleeping Car Murders
1965, (Fr), PECF/Fox/7 Arts, b&w, 95 mins.
W: Yves Montand, Simone Signoret, Jean-Louis Trintignant, Daniel Gelin, Michel Piccoli, Jacques Perrin
WRIT & D: Costi Costa-Gavras
Superior thriller: Complex tale of multiple murder

Sleeping Car to Trieste
1948, (GB), Two Cities/Eagle Lion, b&w, 95 mins.
W: Jean Kent (*Valya*), Albert Lieven (*Zurta*), Derrick De Marney (*George Grant*), Paul Dupuis (*Insp. Jolif*), Bonar Colleano (*Top-Sgt. West*), Rona Anderson (*Joan Maxted*), David Tomlinson (*Tom Bishop*), Finlay Currie (*Alastair McBain*), Alan Wheatley (*Poole*), Hugh Burden (*Mills*), Coco (*Gregoire*) Aslan (*Poirier*), David Hutcheson (*Denning*), Zena Marshall (*Suzanne*), Eugene Deckers (*The Attendant*), Michael Ward (*Sullivan*)
P: George H. Brown   D: John Paddy Carstairs   SCR: Allan Mackinnon & William Douglas Home, from a story by Clifford Grey
*Standard thriller: Spies seek diary aboard Orient Express. Remake of **Rome Express**, 1933*

Sleeping Dogs
1977, (New Zeal), color, 101 mins.
W: Sam Neill, Warren Oates, Bernard Kearns, Nevan Rowe, Ian Mune
D: Roger Donaldson
Standard thriller: Totalitarian gov't suppresses terrorists

Sleeping Dogs
1998, (USA), color, 95 mins.
W: C. Thomas Howell, Scott McNeil
TVM, standard SF-thriller: Burglar sent to prison spaceship

Sleep, My Love
1948, (USA), Mary Pickford Prods.-Triangle/UA, b&w, 97 mins.
W: Claudette Colbert (*Alison Courtland*), Robert Cummings (*Bruce Alcott*), Don Ameche (*Richard Courtland*), George Coulouris (*Charles Vernay*), Hazel Brooks (*Daphne*), Keye Luke, Rita Johnson, Queenie Smith, Ralph Morgan, Maria San Marco, Raymond Burr, Lillian Bronson
P: Charles Buddy Rogers & Ralph Cohn   D: Douglas Sirk   PHOTOG: Joseph Valentine   MUSIC: Rudy Schrager
Standard "film noir": Man tries to drive wife to madness and suicide

Sleep No More
see **Invasion of the Body Snatchers** (1956)

Sleep of Death
1979, (Swed), color, 90 mins.
W: Per Oscarsson, Patrick Magee, Curt Jurgens, Marilu' Tolo
Minor horror-thriller: Count suspected of vampirism

Sleepstalker
1995, (USA), Osmosis/Prism, video, color, 102 mins.
W: Jay Underwood (*Griffin*), Kathryn Morris (*Megan*), William Lucking (*Det. Bronson Worth*), Kathleen McMartin (*Dana*), A.J. Glassman (*Kenny*), Marc McClure (*Dad*), Caryn Richman (*Mom*), Michael D. Roberts (*The Preacher*), Michael Harris (*The Sandman*), Vincent Berry (*Griffin, Age 7*), Ken Foree (*Det. Rolands*), Angel Ashley (*Cheryl*), David O'Shea (*The Prison Guard*), Barry Lynch (*Pierson*), Gabriel Carrier (*The Witness*), Peter Mark Vasquez (*Dog Sanchez*), Lillian Hurst (*The Homeless Woman*), Lenore Van Camp (*Julia*), Christopher Boyer (*Det. Garcia*), Carmen Mormino (*The Officer*), Michael Faella (*The Sandman's Father*), Brett Gathrid (*The Crack Addict*), Joey Andrews (*The Young Sandman*)
P: Luigi Cingolani   D: Turi Meyer   SCR: Al Septien & Turi Meyer   PHOTOG: Michael G. Wojciechowski   MUSIC: Jim Manzie   SONGS: *Blue to Black, Birth of the Sandman, I Cry* & *Sleep Baby Sleep*
Made-for-Video, minor fantasy-thriller: Youth stalked by supernatural killer

Sleepwalk
1987, (W. Ger), Driver Films Inc./Ottoskop Filmproduktion, color, 78 mins.
W: Suzanne Fletcher (*Nicole*), Ann Magnuson (*Isabelle*), Dexter Lee (*Jimmy*)
D: Sara Driver   PHOTOG: Franz Prinzi & Jim Jarmusch
Unusual fantasy-thriller: Ancient Chinese manuscript wields mysterious power

S

The Sleepwalker

1909, (GB), Hepworth, b&w, 425 ft. (129.5m)
D: Theo Bouwmeester
Standard thriller: Girl sleepwalker captured by couple, saved by waif

Sleepwalker

1975, (GB), Made for TV, color
W: Darleen Carr, Ian Redford, Robert Beatty, Elaine Donnelly, Michael Kitchen
TVM, minor thriller: Somnambulist stumbles across murder, wonders if it was dream

Sleepwalkers

1992, (USA), Col, color, 91 mins.
W: Brian Krause *(Charles Brady)*, Madchen Amick *(Tanya Robertson)*, Alice Krige *(Mary Brady)*, Jim Haynie *(Ira)*, Cindy Pickett *(Mrs. Robertson)*, Ron Perlman *(Capt. Soames)*, Lyman Ward *(Mr. Robertson)*, Dan Martin *(Andy Simpson)*, Cynthia Garris *(Laurie)*, Glenn Shadix *(Mr. Fallows)*, Stephen King *(The Cemetery Caretaker)*
D: Mick Garris **SCR:** Stephen King **PHOTOG:** Rodney Charters **MUSIC:** Nicholas Pike
Standard horror-fantasy: Mother and son feed on human life

Sleepwalkers: BRIAN KRAUSE

Sleepy Sam's Awakening

1910, (GB), Cricks & Martin, b&w, 485 ft. (147.8m)
D: A.E. Coleby
Standard fantasy: Tired man drinks energy restorer, does everything fast

Sleuth

1972, (GB), Palomar/20th-Fox, color, 139 mins.
W: Sir Laurence Olivier *(Andrew Wyke)*, Michael Caine *(Milo Tindle)*, Alec Cawthorne *(Insp. Doppler)*, Margo Channing *(Marguerite)*, John Matthews *(Sgt. Tarrant)*, Teddy Martin *(PC Higgs)*
P: Morton Gottlieb **D:** Joseph L. Mankiewicz **SCR:** Anthony Shaffer, from his stage play **PHOTOG:** Oswald Morris **MUSIC:** John Addison
Unusual thriller: Writer involves hairdresser in murder plot

Slime City

1988, (USA), color 90 mins
W: Robert C. Sabin, Mary Huner, J.J. Merrick, Dick Biel
D: Gregory Lamberson
Minor horror-fantasy: Demonic possession in NYC

The Slime People

1963, (USA), Hansen/AIP, b&w, 76 mins.
W: Robert Hutton *(Tom Gregory)*, Les Tremayne *(Tolliver)*, Robert Burton *(Prof. Galbraith)*, Susan Hart *(Lisa)*, Judee Morton *(Bonnie)*, William Boyce *(Cal)*, John Close
P: Joseph F. Robertson **D:** Robert Hutton **SCR:** Blair Robertson & Vance

Skarstedt **PHOTOG:** William Troiano **SPCL-FX:** Harry Woolman
Minor SF-thriller: Subterranean creatures invade Los Angeles

Sling Blade

1997, (USA), Miramax, color, 134 mins.
W: Billy Bob Thornton, Dwight Yoakam, J.T. Walsh, John Ritter, Natalie Canerday, Lucas Black, Robert Duvall, James Hampton, Jim Jarmusch, Lacey Bailey, Stacy Barrow, Sarah Boss, Natalie Canerday, Brent Briscoe, Kathy Sue Brown, Vic Chestnutt, Rick Dial, Gary Don Fletcher, Bill Glassock, Tim Holder, Betty Lynn Hall, Ret. Col. Bruce Hampton, Mickey Jones, Tom Kagy, Raymond Lewallen, Ian Moore, Wendell Rafferty, D.J. Royston, Jackie Stewart, Jamie Stewart, Scott Stewart, Judy Pryor Trice, Christy Ward
WRIT & D: Billy Bob Thornton **PHOTOG:** Barry Markowitz **ORIG MUSIC:** Daniel Lanois **MUSIC SPRVSR:** Barry Cole **SONGS:** *Darlin', Lonely One, The Maker, The One I Love, Plunger & Soul Dressing*
Critically-acclaimed thriller (Special Jury Prize: 1996 Chicago Int'l Film Festival): Ex-killer returns to hometown

The Slipper and the Rose

1976, (GB), Univ, color, 146 mins.
W: Gemma Craven *(Cinderella)*, Richard Chamberlain *(The Prince)*, Lally Bowers *(The Queen)*, Edith Evans *(The Dowager Queen)*, Michael Hordern *(The King)*, Margaret Lockwood *(The Stepmother)*, Annette Crosbie *(The Fairy Godmother)*, Christopher Gable *(John)*, Sherrie Hewson *(Palatine)*, John Turner *(A Major Domo)*, Rosalind Ayres *(Isobella)*, Julian Orchard *(Montague)*, Kenneth More *(The Chamberlain)*, Norman Bird *(The Dress Shop Proprietor)*, Keith Skinner *(Willoughby)*, Polly Williams *(Lady Caroline)*, Gerald Sim *(First Lord of the Navy)*, Peter Graves *(The General)*, Elizabeth Mansfield *(The Lady in Waiting)*, Roy Barraclough *(The Tailor)*, Andre Morell *(Father)*, Geoffrey Bayldon *(The Archbishop)*, Bryan Forbes *(The Herald)*, Valentine Dyall *(A Major Domo)*, Peter Leeming *(The Singer)*, Jenny Lee Wright *(The Milkmaid)*, Tim Barrett, Vivienne McKee, Myrtle Reed, Marianne Broome, Ludmilla Nova, Tessa Dahl, Lea Dreghorn, Eva Reuber-Staier, Ann Rutherford, Suzette St. Claire, Patrick Jordan, Rocky Taylor, Paul Schmitzburger, Wendy Barry
P: Stuart Lyons **D:** Bryan Forbes **SCR:** Bryan Forbes, Robert Sherman & Richard Sherman **PHOTOG:** Tony Imi **SONGS:** Robert Sherman & Richard Sherman
reissued 1980 (with 19 mins. cut)
Lavish musical-fantasy: Prince romances scullery maid

Slipstream

1989, (GB), Gary Kurtz/Entertainment Film, color, 92 mins.
W: Mark Hamill, Bob Peck, Bill Paxton, Kitty Aldridge, Ben Kingsley, Eleanor David, F. Murray Abraham, Robbie Coltrane, Roshan Seth, Richard Huggett, Rita Wolf, Deborah Leng, Tony Allef, Susan Leong, Alkis Kritikos, Rico Ross, Bruce Boa, George Camiller, Diana Defries, Gay Baynes, Jennifer Hilary, Paul Reynolds, Eris Akman, Maiser Asghar, Roberta Fox, Alan Polonsky, Trevor Laird, Murray Melvin, Judith Hibbert, Heathcote Williams
D: Steven M. Lisberger **SCR:** Tony Kayden, from story material by Bill Bauer **PHOTOG:** Frank Tidy **VS-FX SPRVSR:** Brian Johnson **ORIG MUSIC:** Elmer Bernstein
Minor SF-adventure: Pilot of future finds intrigue

Slithis

see **Spawn of the Slithis**

Sliver

1993, (USA), Para, color, 106 mins.
W: Sharon Stone, William Baldwin, Tom Berenger, Polly Walker, Martin Landau, Nina Foch, Colleen Camp, Keene Curtis, Nicholas Pryor Amanda Forman, C.C.H. Pounder
D: Phillip Noyce, from Ira Levin's novel **SCR:** Joe Eszterhas **PHOTOG:** Vilmos Zsigmond
Standard thriller: Woman finds passion and mystery in high-rise

Slugs

1988, (Sp), Dister/New World, color, 90 mins.
W: Michael Garfield *(Mike Brady)*, Kim Terry *(Kim Brady)*, Philip Machale *(Don Palmer)*, Alicia Moro *(Maureen Watson)*, Santiago Alvarez *(John Foley)*, John Battaglia *(Sheriff Reese)*, Kris Mann *(Bobby Talbot)*, Kari Rose *(Donna Moss)*, Andy Alsup *(Officer Dobbs)*, Stan Schwartz *(Ron Bell)*, Jay R. Ingerson *(Ricky Palmer)*, Concha Cuetos *(Maria Palmer)*, Emilio Linder *(David Watson)*, Miguel De Grandy *(Mr. Riggs)*, Manuel De Blas *(Mayor Eaton)*, Frank Brana *(Frank Phillips)*, Juan Majan *(Harold Morris)*, Lucia Prado *(Jean Morris)*, Tony Gold *(Dino)*, Patty Sheppard *(Sue Channing)*, Glen Greenberg *(Danny Palmer)*, Tammy Reger *(Pam)*, Harriet L. Stark *(Mrs. Fortune)*, Nazareno Natale *(The Chef)*, Carla M. Fox *(Julie)*, Isabel Prinz *(The Mayor's Sec'y)*, Laura Notario *(Mr. Phillips' Sec'y)*, Daniel L. Jones *(Teenager #1)*, Kristin L. Kilian *(Girl #1)*, Edward Trathen *(Teenager #2)*, Erik Swanson *(The Boy in the Boat)*, Karen Landberg *(The Girl in the Boat)*, Anibal Blas Laramie G. Evans *(Mr. Moss)*, Neveda Killips *(Mrs. Moss)*, Larry Bornheimer *(Policeman #1)*, Wally Frazer *(The Ambulance Driver)*
D: J.P. Simon **SCR:** Ron Gantman, from Shaun Hutson's novel **PHOTOG:** Julio Bragado **SPCL-FX SPRVSR:** Emilio Ruiz **MUSIC:** Tim Souster
Standard SF-thriller: Man-eating larvae attack town

S

The Slime People: ROBERT BURNTON, SUSAN HART AND ROBERT HUTTON

The Slumber Party Massacre
1982, (USA), Santa Fe/Embassy, color, 78 mins.
W: Michele Michaels *(Trish)*, Robin Stille *(Valerie)*, Debra Deliso *(Kim)*, Michael Villela *(Russ Thorn)*, Andree Honore *(Jackie)*, Gina Mari *(Diane)*, Jennifer Myers *(Courtney)*, Joe Johnson *(Neil)*, David Millbern *(Jeff)*, Brinke Stevens *(Linda)*, Jim Boyce *(John Minor)*, Pamela Roylance *(Coach Jana)*, Ryan Kennedy *(David Contant)*, Jean Vargas *(The Telephone Repairman)*, Anna Patton *(Mrs. Deveraux)*, Howard Purgason *(Mr. Deveraux)*, Pam Canzano *(The Carpenter)*, Aaron Lipstadt *(The Pizza Boy)*, Francis Menendez *(The Paper Boy)*
P & D: Amy Jones   **SCR:** Rita Mae Brown   **PHOTOG:** Steve Posey   **MUSIC:** Ralph Jones
Standard thriller: Escaped psycho slays teens

Slumber Party Massacre II
1987, (USA), color 75 mins
W: Crystal Bernard Kimberly McArthur, Juliette Cummins, Patrick Lowe
D & SCR: Deborah Brock
Standard thriller

Slumber Party Massacre 3
1990, (USA), MGM-UA, color
W: Keely Christian, Brittain Frye, M.K. Harris, Hope Marie Carlton, David Greenle, Maria Ford
D: Sally Mattison   **SCR:** Catherine Cyran
Minor thriller: More mayhem at girl's sleepover

Small Soldiers
1998, (USA), Dreamworks SKG/Univ, color, 114 mins.
W: Phil Hartman, Gregory Smith, Dick Miller, Frank Langella, Tommy Lee Jones *(Voice of Chip Hazard)*, George Kennedy, Kirsten Dunst
D: Joe Dante
Standard comedy-fantasy: Factory mistake releases bellicose action figures

Small Town Massacre
see *Strange Behavior* (1981)

Smart Blonde
1937, (USA), WB, b&w, 59 mins.
W: Glenda Farrell *(Torchy Blane)*, Barton MacLane *(Steve McBride)*, Winifred Shaw *(Dolly Ireland)*, Craig Reynolds *(Tom Carney)*, Addison Richards *(Fitz Mularkey)*, Charlotte Wynters *(Marcia Friede)*, Jane Wyman *(Dixie)*, Joseph Crehan *(Tiny Torgensen)*, David Carlyle (Robert Paige) *(Friel)*, Tom Kennedy *(Gahagan)*, John Sheehan *(Blyfuss)*, Max Wagner *(Chuck Gannon)*, George Lloyd *(Pickeny Fox)*
D: Frank McDonald   **SCR:** Don Ryan & Kenneth Gamut, from Frederick Nebel's novel *No Hard Feelings*   **PHOTOG:** Warren Lynch
Standard thriller (1st **Torchy Blane** *mystery): Girly reporter searches for killer*

A Smart Set
1919, (GB), British Lion, b&w, 5,000 ft. (1524m)
W: Concordia Merrill *(Pauline)*, Neville Percy *(Neville Temple)*, S.J. Warmington *(Herbert Sterne)*, Doriel Paget *(Fay Trevor)*, Arthur Cullin *(Sir Philip Trevor)*,
Gwen Williams, Iris Mackie, Judd Green, Gordon McLeod, Rex Harold
D: A.V. Bramble   **SCR:** Eliot Stannard   **STORY:** Neville Percy
Standard crime-thriller: Detective poses as opium fiend, saves addicted knight and daughter from abduction by jeweller

Smashing the Crime Syndicate
see *Hell's Bloody Devils*

Smile, Jenny, You're Dead
1974, (USA), WB/CBS-TV, color, 90 mins.
W: David Janssen, Andrea Marcovicci, Zalman King, Howard Da Silva, John Anderson, Jodie Foster, Clu Gulager
D: Jerry Thorpe   **TELEPLAY:** Howard Rodman
TVM, minor thriller: Private eye investigates murder of friend's son-in-law

Smile of the Great Tempter
see *The Tempter* (1973)

The Smiling Ghost
1941, (USA), WB, b&w, 71 mins.
W: Wayne Morris, Alexis Smith, Brenda Marshall, Richard Ainley, Lee Patrick, Helen Westley
D: Lewis Seiler
Standard comedy-thriller: Heiress' fiances meet violent deaths

Smokescreeen
1964, (GB), Butcher's Films, b&w, 66 mins.
W: Peter Vaughan *(Ropey Roper)*, John Carson *(Trevor Baylis)*, Yvonne Romain *(Janet Dexter)*, Glyn Edwards *(Insp. Wright)*, Gerald Flood *(Graham Turner)*, John Glyn-Jones *(Player)*, Sam Kydd *(The Waiter)*, Penny Morell *(Helen)*, Deryck Guyler
P: John I. Phillips   **D & STORY:** Jim O'Connolly
Standard crime-thriller: Insurance investigator finds that accident victim was murdered

A Smoky Story
1912, (GB), Cricks & Martin, b&w, 495 ft. (150.9m)
D: Charles Calvert
Standard comedy-fantasy: Hookah smoker dreams he is in harem

The Smugglers' Cave
1914, (GB), Cunard/George, b&w, 2,100 ft. (640.1m)
W: Harold Weston *(Arthur Morris)*, Charles Cantley *(Ben Lee)*, Mary Manners *(Nell)*
D: Wallett Waller   **STORY:** Harold Weston
Standard thriller: Cornish fishergirl poses as man, saves captured artist from smugglers

Smuggler's Cove
1948, (USA), Mono, b&w, 66 mins.
W: Leo Gorcey, Huntz Hall
Minor comedy-thriller: Bowery Boys vs. gangsters

The Smuggler's Daughter
1913, (GB), Cricks & Martin, b&w, 895 ft. (272.8m)
D: Edwin J. Collins
Standard thriller: Smuggler's daughter saves life of exciseman

Smuggler's Gold
1951, (USA), Col, b&w, 64 mins.
W: Cameron Mitchell, Amanda Blake
Minor thriller

Smuggler's Island
1951, (USA), Univ, color, 75 mins.
W: Jeff Chandler, Evelyn Keyes
Standard adventure-thriller

The Smuggler's Revenge
1912, (GB), Union Films, b&w, 990 ft. (301.8m)
Standard adventure-thriller: Cheated smuggler betrays gang to disguised detective

Smulltronstallet (Wild Strawberries)
1957, (Swed), Svensk Filmindustri, b&w, 95 mins.
W: Victor David Sjostrow, Bibi Andersson, Ingrid Thulin, Gunnar Bjornstrand, Max von Sydow, Gunnel Lindblom
WRIT & D: Ingmar Bergman   **PHOTOG:** Gunnar Fischer
Classic psychodrama: Professor recalls the past

The Smurfs and the Magic Flute
1983, (Belg-Fr), color, 74 mins.
D: John Rust   **MUSIC:** Michel Legrand
Animated feature, juvenile fantasy: Diminutive forest-dwellers seek legendary musical instrument

The Snails
see *Les Escargots*

Snake Eyes
1998, (USA), Para, color
W: Nicholas Cage, Gary Sinise
Standard thriller: Political assassination probed

The Snake Hunter Strangler
1966, (It), color, 65 mins.
<u>W:</u> Guy Madison, Ivan Desny
<u>D:</u> Luigi Capuano
Minor thriller: Girl rescued from evil cult

Snake People
see Isle of the Snake People

The Snake Pit
1948, (USA), Darryl F. Zanuck/20th-Fox, b&w, 108 mins.
<u>W:</u> Olivia de Havilland (*Virginia Cunningham*), Mark Stevens (*Robert Cunningham*), Leo Genn (*Dr. Mark Kik*), Celeste Holm (*Grace*), Glenn Langan (*Dr. Terry*), Leif Erickson (*Gordon*), Helen Craig (*Miss Davis*), Beulah Bondi (*Mrs. Greer*), Minna Gombell (*Miss Hart*), Mae Marsh (*Tommy's Mother*), Ann Doran (*Valerie*), Ruth Donnelly (*Ruth*), Frank Conroy (*Dr. Jonathan Gifford*), Katherine Locke (*Margaret*), Damian O'Flynn (*Mr. Stuart*), June Storey (*Miss Bixby, the Ward Nurse*), Esther Somers (*Miss Vance*), Betsy Blair (*Hester*), Lora Lee Michel (*Virginia, age 6*), Jacqueline de Wit (*Miss Sommerville*), Lela Bliss (*Miss Greene*), Virginia Brissac (*Miss Seiffert*), Queenie Smith (*Lola*), Ashley Cowan, Isabel Jewell, Victoria Horne, Tamara Shayne, Grace Poggi, Sally Shepherd, Theresa Lyon, Geraldine Garrick, Sylvia Andrew, Marie Blake, Ellen Lowe, Jeri Jordan
<u>P:</u> Anatole Litvak & Robert Bassler <u>D:</u> Anatole Litvak <u>SCR:</u> Frank Partos & Millen Brand, from Mary Jane Ward's novel <u>PHOTOG:</u> Leo Tover <u>SPCL-FX:</u> Fred Sersen <u>MUSIC:</u> Alfred Newman
Classic psychodrama: Woman has nervous breakdown, faces graphic horrors of mental hospital

The Snake Pit (1967)
see Die Schlangengrube und das Pendel

The Snake Woman
1960, (GB), Caralan/UA, b&w, 68 mins.
<u>W:</u> John McCarthy (*Charles Prentice*), Susan Travers (*Atheris*), Geoffrey Danton (*Col. Wynborn*), Elsie Wagstaff (*Aggie*), Arnold Marle (*Dr. Murton*), John Cazabon (*Dr. Adderson*), Hugh Moxey (*The Inspector*), Frances Bennett (*Polly*), Michael Logan, Stevenson Lang, Dorothy Frere, Jack Cunningham
<u>P:</u> George Fowler <u>D:</u> Sid J. Furie <u>SCR:</u> Orville H. Hampton <u>PHOTOG:</u> Stephen Dade <u>MUSIC:</u> Buxton Orr
orig. co-billed with **Dr. Blood's Coffin**
Standard horror-thriller: Snake-hormone treatments produce baby girl with reptilian characteristics

Snapdragon
1993, (USA), 96 mins USA-TV, color
<u>W:</u> Steven Bauer, Pamela Anderson Lee, Chelsea Field
<u>D:</u> Worth Keeter <u>TELEPLAY:</u> Gene Church
TVM, standard thriller: Police psychiatrist obsessed with alluring amnesiac

Snapshot
see The Day After Halloween

Snatched from a Terrible Death
1908, (GB), Hepworth, b&w, 550 ft. (167.6m)
<u>W:</u> Gertie Potter (*The Girl*)
<u>D:</u> Lewin Fitzhamon
Standard melodrama: Colonel in India saves daughter from native sacrifice

Snatched from Death
1913, (GB), Cricks/Gaumont, b&w, 2,400 ft. (731.5m)
<u>D:</u> Charles Calvert
Standard crime-thriller: Detective catches crooks after escaping from canal lock

The Sniper
1952, (USA), Kramer/Col, b&w, 87 mins.
<u>W:</u> Adolphe Menjou, Arthur Franz, Marie Windsor, Jay Novello, Richard Kiley, Frank Faylen, Mabel Paige, Max Palmer, Sidney Miller, Geraldine Carr, Marlo Dwyer, Ralph Peters, Danie Sue Nolan, Cliff Clark, Gerald Mohr
<u>P:</u> Stanley Kramer <u>D:</u> Edward Dmytryk <u>SCR:</u> Edward & Edna Anhalt <u>STORY:</u> Harry Brown <u>PHOTOG:</u> Burnett Guffey <u>MUSIC:</u> George Antheil
Standard thriller: Deranged sniper baffles police

The Snorkel
1958, (GB), Hammer/Col, b&w, 80 mins.
<u>W:</u> Peter Van Eyck (*Jacques Duval*), Betta St. John (*Jean Duval*), Mandy Miller (*Candy Duval*), Gregoire Aslan (*The Inspector*), William Franklyn (*Wilson*), Marie Burke (*The Daily Woman*), Irene Prador (*The French Woman*), Henry Vidon
<u>D:</u> Guy Green <u>SCR:</u> Peter Myers & Jimmy Sangster <u>STORY:</u> Anthony Dawson (Antonio Margheriti) <u>PHOTOG:</u> Jack Asher <u>MUSIC:</u> Francis Chagrin
Standard thriller: Girl tries to expose murderous stepfather

Snowbeast
1977, (USA), NBC-TV, color, 106 mins.
<u>W:</u> Bo Svenson (*Gar Seberg*), Yvette Mimieux (*Ellen Seberg*), Robert Logan (*Tony Rill*), Clint Walker (*Sheriff Paraday*), Sylvia Sidney (*Carrie Rill*), Jacquie

Botts (*Betty Jo*), Anne McEnroe (*Heidi*), Thomas W. Babson (*Buster*), Kathy Christopher (*Jennifer*), Michael J. London (*The Snowbeast*)
<u>P:</u> Douglas S. Cramer <u>D:</u> Herb Wallerstein
TVM, minor thriller: Bigfoot terrorizes ski resort

The Snow Creature
1954, (USA), Planet Filmways/UA, b&w, 75 mins.
<u>W:</u> Paul Langton (*Frank Parrish*), Bill Phipps (*Lt. Dunbar*), Leslie Denison (*Peter Wells*), Teru Shimada (*Subra*), Rollin Moriyama (*Leva*), Robert Kino (*Insp. Karma*), Rudolph Anders (*Dr. Dupont*), Robert Hinton (*The Airline Manager*), Darlene Fields (*Joyce Parrish*), George Douglas (*Corey Jr.*), Robert Bice (*Fleet*), Keith Richards (*Harry Bennett*), Rusty Westcoat (*The Warehouse Guard*), Jack Daly (*Edwards*)
<u>P & D:</u> W. Lee Wilder <u>STORY & SCR:</u> Myles Wilder <u>PHOTOG:</u> Floyd D. Crosby <u>SPCL-FX:</u> Lee Zavitz <u>MUSIC:</u> Manuel Compinsky
Minor SF-thriller: Yeti escapes in Los Angeles

Snow Demons
see I Diavoli della Spazio

Snow Devils
see I Diavoli della Spazio

Snow Dog
1950, (USA), Mono, b&w, 64 mins.
<u>W:</u> Kirby Grant, Elena Verdugo
Minor adventure-thriller

Snow Kill
1990, (USA), Wilshire Court/Para, color, 95 mins.
<u>W:</u> Terence Knox, Patti D'Arbanville, Jon Cypher, Clayton Rohner, David Dukes (*Murdoch*), Joey Travolta (*Myles*), Rick Lieberman (*Jerry*), Branscombe Richmond (*Loomis*), Lee Arenberg (*Kolt*), Dennis Saylor (*Geller*), Sam Cosby (*The Cashier*), Dave Jensen (*Dwayne*), Margo Watson (*Beth*)
<u>D:</u> Thomas J. Wright <u>TELEPLAY:</u> Raymond Hartung & Harv Zimmel <u>STORY:</u> Raymond Hartung <u>PHOTOG:</u> Frank Beascoechea <u>SPCL-FX SPRVSR:</u> Rick Josephsen <u>MUSIC:</u> Sylvester Levay
TVM, standard thriller: Corporate executives on mountain exercise menaced by criminals

The Snow Man
see La Statue de Neige

The Snow Queen
1960, (Russ), Univ, color, 70 mins.
<u>VOICES:</u> Sandra Dee, Tommy Kirk, Patty McCormack, Paul Frees, June Foray
<u>D:</u> Lev Atamanov
Well-made animated fantasy: Boy abducted by enigmatic personification of winter

The Snow Was Black
1956, (Fr), Continental, b&w, 104 mins.
<u>W:</u> Daniel Gelin
Standard melodrama

Snow White
1916, (USA), Para-Artcraft, b&w, 6 reels
<u>W:</u> Marguerite Clark
Standard fantasy

Snow White
1965, (W. Ger), Childhood, color, 74 mins.
Standard fantasy

Snow White
1989, (USA), color, 85 mins.
<u>W:</u> Diana Rigg, Sarah Patterson, Billy Barty
<u>D:</u> Michael Berz
Standard fantasy

Snow White and Rose Red
1953, (GB), b&w, 10 mins.
<u>D:</u> Lotte Reiniger, from a story by the Brothers Grimm
Standard short animated fantasy

Snow White and the Seven Dwarfs
1937, (USA), Walt Disney/RKO, color, 83 mins.
<u>VOICES:</u> Adriana Caselotti (*Snow White*), Harry Stockwell, Lucille LaVerne, Scotty Mattraw, Roy Atwell, Otis Harlan, Pinto Colvig, Billy Gilbert, Marion Darlington, Stuart Buchanan, Jim Macdonald, Moroni Olsen
<u>D:</u> Walt Disney <u>SCR:</u> Ted Sears, Otto Englander, Earl Hurd, Dorothy Ann Blank, Richard Creedon, Dick Rickard, Merrill De Maris & Webb Smith <u>MUSIC:</u> Frank Churchill, Leigh Harline & Paul Smith <u>SONGS:</u> *Someday My Prince Will Come, Hi-Ho, One Song & Whistle While You Work*
Classic animated fantasy (Disney's first feature film): Princess flees murderous stepmother

Snow White and the Three Clowns
see Snow White and the Three Stooges

Snow White and the Three Stooges
1961, (USA), Chanford/20th-Fox, color, 107 mins.

S

<u>W</u>: Carol Heiss (*Snow White*), Moe Howard, Larry Fine, Joe De Rita, Patricia Medina, Guy Rolfe, Edson Stroll, Buddy Baer, Michael David, Edgar Barrier, Lisa Mitchell, Peter Coe
<u>P</u>: Charles Wick   <u>D</u>: Walter Lang   <u>SCR</u>: Noel Langley & Elwood Ullman, from a story by Charles Wick   <u>PHOTOG</u>: Leon Shamroy   <u>MUSIC</u>: Harry Harris & Earl Brent
GB retitle, **Snow White and the Three Clowns**
Entertaining comedy-fantasy: Fugitive ice-skating princess given refuge by three bumpkins

Snow White and the Three Stooges: MOE HOWARD, JOE DE RITA AND LARRY FINE

Snow White: A Tale of Terror
1997, (USA), Interscope/Polygram, color, 100 mins.
<u>W</u>: Sigourney Weaver (*Claudia Hoffman*), Sam Neill (*Frederick Hoffman*), Monica Keena (*Lilli Hoffman*), Gil Bellows (*Will*), Taryn Davis (*Little Lilli*), Brian Glover (*Lars*), Anthony Brophy (*Rolf*), David Conrad (*Peter Gutenberg*), Frances Cuka, Christopher Bauer, John Edward Allen, Dale Wyatt, Miroslav Taborsky, Andrew Tiernan, Bryan Pringle, Joanna Roth
<u>D</u>: Michael Cohn   <u>SCR</u>: Tom Szollosi & Deborah Serra   <u>PHOTOG</u>: Mike Southon   <u>MUSIC</u>: John Ottman
Unusual blend of fantasy & gritty realism: Noblewoman has conflict with stepdaughter

Snow White in the Black Forest (Snow White: A Tale of Terror)
1997, (USA-GB), color, 101 mins.
<u>W</u>: Sigourney Weaver, Monica Keena, Sam neill
Unusual dark fantasy. Filmed in Czechoslovakia, debuted in US on cable

Snuff
1975, (It), color
<u>W</u>: Claudine Auger
Minor thriller

Soap Bubbles
1906, (Fr), Star, b&w, 70m (229.7 ft./3.9 mins.)
<u>D</u>: Georges Melies
Standard fantasy: Conjurer blows bubbles that become butterfly-women

Society
1989, (USA), color, 99 mins.
<u>W</u>: Bill Warlock, Devin DeVasquez, Evan Richards, Charles Lucia, Ben Meyerson, Connie Danese, Patrice Jennings, Heidi Kozak, Ben Slack, Tim Bartell
<u>D</u>: Brian Yuzna
Intriguing thriller (Brian Yuzna's first directorial effort): Beverly Hills teen encounters mystery

Society Crooks
see **Strategy**

Society Detective
see **Detective Finn: or, In the Heart of London**

So Dark the Night
1946, (USA), Col, b&w, 70 mins.
<u>W</u>: Micheline Cheirel, Steven Geray Eugene Borden, Ann Codee, Egon Brecher, Helen Freeman
<u>D</u>: Joseph H. Lewis
Standard thriller: Vacationing Parisian detective finds mystery in French countryside

Sodom and Gomorrah
1963 (It-Fr), Titanus/20th-Fox, color, 154 mins.
<u>W</u>: Stewart Granger (*Lot*), Pier Angeli, Anouk Aimee, Stanley Baker Rossana Podesta, Rik Battaglia, Aldo Silvani, Giacomo Rossi-Stuart, Scilla Gabel, Antonio de Taffe, Gabriele Tinti, Enzo Fiermonte, Daniele Vargas, Feodor Chaliapin, Claudia Mori, Mitzuko Takara, Mimmo Palmara, Massimo Pietrobon, Liana Del Balzo, Francesco Tensi, Andrea Tagliabue, Alice & Ellen Kessler, Emilio & Roberto Messina
<u>D</u>: Robert Aldrich & Sergio Leone   <u>ORIG. SCR</u>: Hugo Butler   <u>PHOTOG</u>: Silvan Ippoliti, Mario Motuori & Cyril Knowles   <u>SPCL-FX</u>: Lee Zavitz,

Serse Urbisaglia & Wally Veevers   <u>MUSIC</u>: Miklos Rozsa
A.k.a. **The Last Days of Sodom and Gomorrah**
Standard biblical melodrama: Divine vengeance wreaked on ancient cities of sin

So Evil My Love
1948, (GB), Para, b&w, 109 mins, also 112 mins.
<u>W</u>: Ray Milland, Ann Todd
Standard thriller

So Evil, My Sister
1972, (USA), color, 85 mins.
<u>W</u>: Susan Strasberg, Faith Domergue, Sydney Chaplin, Charles Knox Robinson, Steve Mitchell, Kathleen Freeman, John Howard
<u>D</u>: Reginald LeBorg
A.k.a. **Psycho Sisters** *and* **The Sibling**
Standard thriller: Sisters play cat and mouse with police probing murder

Il Sogno de Zorro (The Mask of Zorro)
1951, (It), b&w, 93 mins.
<u>W</u>: Vittorio Gassman, Sophia Loren
<u>D</u>: Mario Soldati
Standard adventure-thriller

Der Sohn der Hagar (The Son of Hagar)
1927, (Ger), Defu, b&w
<u>D</u>: Fritz Wendhausen
USA retitle, **Out of the Mist**
Standard melodrama

Soho Incident
1956, (GB), Film Locations/Col, b&w, 77 mins.
<u>W</u>: Faith Domergue (*Bella Francesi*), Lee Patterson (*Jim Bankley*), Rona Anderson (*Betty Walker*), Martin Benson (*Ricco Francesi*), Robert Arden (*Buddy*), Joss Ambler (*Tom Walker*), Peter Hammond (*Bill Walker*), Peter Burton (*Insp. Collis*), Sam Kydd (*Sam*), Russell Westwood, Patricia Ryan, Bernard Fox
<u>P</u>: Anthony Gilkison   <u>D</u>: Vernon Sewell   <u>SCR</u>: Ian Stuart Black, from Robert Westerby's novel *Wide Boys Never Work*
USA retitle, **Spin a Dark Web**
Standard thriller: Gang boss' sister tries to stop her lover from quitting crime

Solarbabies
1986, (USA), Brooksfilms/MGM-UA, color, 94 mins.
<u>W</u>: Richard Jordan (*Grock*), Jami Gertz (*Terra*), Jason Patric (*Jason*), Lukas Haas (*Daniel*), Charles Durning (*The Warden*)
<u>D</u>: Alan Johnson   <u>SCR</u>: Walon Green & Douglas Anthony Metrov   <u>PHOTOG</u>: Peter MacDonald   <u>VS-FX</u>: Richard Edlund   <u>MUSIC</u>: Maurice Jarre
Standard SF-thriller: Future youth meet alien entity

Solar Crisis
1990, (USA-Jap), Trimark, color, 118 mins.
<u>W</u>: Tim Matheson, Charlton Heston, Peter Boyle, Annabel Schofield, Tetsuya Bessho, Jack Palance, Dorian Harewood, Paul Koslo, Sandy McPeak, Dan Shor, Frantz Turner, Brenda Bakke, Eric James, David Ursin, Paul Williams, Richard S. Scott, Rhonda Dotson, Roy Jenson, Steve Welles, Richard Eden, Tammy Maples Corin Nemec
<u>D</u>: Alan Smithee (Richard Sarafian)   <u>SCR</u>: Joe Gannon & Crispan Bolt, from a novel by Takeshi Kawata   <u>PHOTOG</u>: Russ Carpenter   <u>SPCL-FX</u>: Craig Smith   <u>VS-FX</u>: Boss Film Corp.   <u>MUSIC</u>: Maurice Jarre   <u>ADDITIONAL MUSIC</u>: Michael Boddicker   <u>SONGS</u>: *Was a Time, Orlop Piano & Freedom Sings*
Standard SF-thriller: Sun phenomenon threatens Earth

Solaris
1972, (Russ), Mosfilm/Magna, color, 165 mins.
<u>W</u>: Donatis Banionis (*Chris Calvin*), Yuri Jarvet (*Sartorius*), Natalie Bondarchuk (*Hari*), Anatoly Solonitsyn (*Dr. Snoutt*), Vladislav Dvorjetski (*Burton*), Sos Sarkissian (*Gibarian*), Nikolai Grinko (*Father*)
<u>D</u>: Andrei Tarkovsky   <u>SCR</u>: Andrei Tarkovsky & F. Gorenchstein, from the novel by Stanislaw Lem   <u>PHOTOG</u>: Vadim Youssov   <u>MUSIC</u>: Eduard Artemiev
Unusual SF-thriller (Soviet answer to 2001: A Space Odyssey*): Cosmic force gives eerie substance to astronaut's memories of lost love*

Soldier
1998, (USA), color
<u>W</u>: Kurt Russell, Gary Busey, Connie Nielsen, Jason Scott Lee
<u>D</u>: Paul Anderson
Standard SF-thriller: Man reared solely for warfare

Sole Survivor
1970, (USA), Cinema Center/CBS-TV/WB-TV, color, 100 mins.
<u>W</u>: Richard Basehart, Vince Edwards, William Shatner, Patrick Wayne
<u>P</u>: Walter Burr   <u>D</u>: Paul Stanley   <u>TELEPLAY</u>: Guerdon Trueblood
TVM, minor fantasy-thriller: Ghosts accuse general of desertion

Sole Survivor
1984, (USA), color, 85 mins.
<u>W</u>: Anita Skinner, Kurt Johnson, Caren Larkey
<u>D</u>: Thom Eberhardt
Minor fantasy-thriller: Zombies pursue plane-crash survivor

So Like a Woman
1911, (GB), Walturdaw, b&w, 700 ft. (213.4m)
Standard crime-thriller: Spy persuades admiral's daughter to steal plans

The Solitary Child
1958, (GB), Beaconsfield/British Lion, b&w, 64 mins.
W: Philip Friend (*James Random*), Barbara Shelley (*Harriet Random*), Rona Anderson (*Jean Dennison*), Jack Watling (*Cyril Sully*), Sarah Lawson (*Ann Random*), Julia Lockwood (*Maggie Random*), Catherine Lacey (*Mrs. Evans*), Violet Farebrother (*Mrs. Dennison*)
P: Peter Rogers   D: Gerald Thomas   SCR: Robert Dunbar, from a novel by Nina Bawden
Standard thriller: Girl weds farmer, suspects him of shooting first wife

The Solitary Cyclist
1921, (GB), Stoll, b&w, 2,140 ft. (652.3m)
W: Eille Norwood (*Sherlock Holmes*), Hubert Willis (*Dr. John Watson*), R.D. Sylvester (*Carruthers*), Violet Hewitt (*Violet Relph*), Allan Jeayes (*Woodley*)
D: Maurice Elvey   SCR: William J. Elliott, from the writings of Sir Arthur Conan Doyle
Standard crime-thriller (episode in "Adventures of Sherlock Holmes" series)

Solo
1996, (USA), Orpheus-John Flock/Triumph, color
W: Mario Van Peebles, William Sadler, Adrien Brody, Barry Corbin
P: Joseph Newton Cohen & John Flock   D: Norberto Barba   SCR: David Corley, from Robert Mason's novel *Weapon*   PHOTOG: Chris Walling   MUSIC: Christopher Franke
Standard SF-action: Bionically-enhanced superhero

Solo for Sparrow
1962, (GB), Merton Park/Anglo-Amalgamated, b&w, 56 mins.
W: Anthony Newlands (*Reynolds*), Glyn Houston (*Insp. Sparrow*), Nadja Regin (*Mrs. Reynolds*), Michael Coles (*Pin Norman*), Allan Cuthbertson (*Supt. Symington*), Ken Wayne (*Baker*), Jerry Stovin (*Lewis*), Jack May (*Insp. Hudson*), Michael Caine (*Puddy Mooney*), Jack May (*Insp. Hudson*), Murray Melvin (*Larkin*), Nancy O'Neil (*Miss Martin*)
P: Jack Greenwood   D: Gordon Flemyng   SCR: Roger Marshall, from Edgar Wallace's novel *Gunner*
Standard crime-thriller: Inspector nails murderous jeweler

So Long at the Fair
1950, (GB), Gainsborough/UA/Eagle-Lion/Rank, b&w, 86 mins.
W: Jean Simmons (*Vicky Barton*), Dirk Bogarde (*George Hathaway*), David Tomlinson (*John Barton*), Honor Blackman (*Rhoda O'Donovan*), Cathleen Nesbitt (*Mme. Herve*), Felix Aylmer (*The Consul*), Betty Warren (*Mrs. O'Donovan*), Marcel Poncin (*Narcisse*), Austin Trevor (*The Commissaire*), Andre Morell (*Dr. Hart*), Zena Marshall (*Nina*)
P: Betty Box   D: Anthony Darnborough & Terence Fisher   SCR: Hugh Mills & Anthony Thorne, from a novel by Anthony Thorne
Engrossing mystery-thriller: Girl's brother vanishes in turn-of-the-century Paris

Solo Se Muere Dos Veces (You Only Die Twice)
1997, (Sp), color
W: Santiago Segura, Alex Angulo
Minor thriller

Solution by Phone
1954, (GB), Pan Prods./ABP, b&w, 60 mins.
W: Clifford Evans (*Richard Hanborough*), Thea Gregory (*Ann Selby*), John Witty (*Peter Wayne*), Georgina Cookson (*Frances Hanborough*), Enid Hewitt (*Mrs. Garner*), Geoffrey Goodhart (*Insp. Kirby*), Max Brimmell (*Sgt. Woods*)
P: Geoffrey Goodhart & Brandon Fleming   D: Alfred Travers   STORY: Brandon Fleming
Standard thriller: Actor kills mistress, frames her novelist husband

Sombra, the Spider Woman
1966, (USA), Rep, b&w, 100 mins.
W: Bruce Edwards, Virginia Lindley, Carol Forman Anthony Warde, (*Brother*) Theodore Gottlieb, Ramsay Ames
D: Spencer G. Bennet & Fred C. Brannon
*Standard action-thriller (feature version of 1947 serial **The Black Widow**)*

Some Call It Loving
1973, (USA), Cine Globe, color, 103 mins.
W: Zalman King (*Robert*), Tisa Farrow (*Jennifer*), Richard Pryor (*Jeff*), Carol White (*Scarlett*), Veronica Anderson (*Angelica*), Logan Ramsey (*The Doctor*), Brandy Herred (*The Cheerleader*), Pat Priest (*The Nurse*), Ed Rue (*The Mortician*), Joseph DeMeo (*The Bartender*)
P, D, & SCR: James B. Harris   PHOTOG: Mario Tosi   MUSIC: Richard Hazard
Unusual fantasy-thriller: Jazz musician buys sleeping beauty from seedy carnival

Some Fish!
1914, (GB), Martin/DFSA, b&w, 662 ft. (201.8m)
D: Dave Aylott
Standard fantasy: Angler dreams of visit to Father Neptune

Some Girls Do
1969, (GB), Ashdown/Rank, color, 93 mins.
W: Richard Johnson (*Hugh "Bulldog" Drummond*), Daliah Lavi (*Helga*), Beba Loncar (*Pandora*), James Villiers (*Carl Peterson*), Vanessa Howard (*Robot #7*), Robert Morley (*Miss Mary*), Maurice Denham (*Dr. Mortimer*), Sydne Rome (*Flicky*), Adrienne Posta (*Drummond's Daily*), Ronnie Stevens (*Carruthers*), Florence Desmond (*Lady Manderley*), Virginia North (*Robot #9*), Nicholas Phipps (*Lord Dunberry*)
P: Betty E. Box   D: Ralph Thomas   SCR: David Osborn & Liz Charles-Williams, from characters created by Sapper   PHOTOG: Ernest Steward   SPCL-FX: Kit West   MUSIC: Charles Blackwell
Standard thriller: Famed sleuth opposes evil genius. 'Bulldog Drummond' feature

Some Girls for a Vampire
*see **L'Ultima Preda del Vampiro***

Some of Your Blood
*see **Un Peu de Votre Sang***

Someone at the Door
1936, (GB), BIP/Wardour, b&w, 74 mins.
W: Billy Milton (*Ronald Martin*), Aileen Marson (*Sally Martin*), Noah Beery (*Harry Hapel*), Lawrence Hanray (*Poole*), Edward Chapman (*Price*), John Irwin (*Bill Reid*), Hermione Gingold (*Mrs. Appleby*), Charles Mortimer (*Sgt. Spedding*), Edward Dignon (*Soames*), Jimmy Godden (*PC O'Brien*)
D: Herbert Brenon   SCR: Jack Davies & Marjorie Deans, from a play by Dorothy & Campbell Christie
Standard comedy-thriller: Reporter inherits house, fakes murder that comes true

Someone at the Top of the Stairs
1973, (GB), ATV-ITC, Made for TV, color, 74 mins.
W: Donna Mills (*Chrissie*), Judy Carne (*Jill*), Francis Wallis, Alethea Charlton
TVM, standard thriller: American girls menaced in Victorian mansion

Someone Behind the Door
*see **Quelqu'un Derriere la Porte***

Someone's Killing the World's Greatest Models
*see **She's Dressed to Kill***

Someone's Watching Me!
1978, (USA), WB/CBS-TV, color, 112 mins.
W: Lauren Hutton (*Lee Michaels*), David Birney (*Paul*), Len Lesser (*The Burly Man*), Adrienne Barbeau (*Sophie*), Charles Cyphers (*Insp. Hunt*), Grainger Hines (*Steve*), George Skaff (*Herbert Stiles*), John Mahon (*Frimsin*), James Murtaugh (*Leone*), J. Jay Saunders (*The Police Inspector*), Michael Laurence (*The TV Announcer*), Robert Phalen (*Wayne*), Jean Le Bouvier (*The Waitress*), Robert Snively (*Groves*), James McAlpine (*The Slick Man*), Edgar Justice (*Charlie*), John Fox (*Eddie*)
WRIT & D: John Carpenter   PHOTOG: Robert Hauser   MUSIC: Harry Sukman
TVM, standard thriller: Voyeur stalks woman journalist

Something Evil
1972, (USA), Bedford/CBS-TV, color, 73 mins.
W: Sandy Dennis (*Marjorie Worden*), Darren McGavin (*Paul Worden*), Ralph Bellamy (*Harry Lincoln*), Johnny Whitaker (*Stevie Worden*), Jeff Corey (*Gehmann*), John Rubinstein (*Ernest*), Laurie Hagan (*Beth*), David Knapp (*John*), Herb Armstrong, Margaret Avery, Norman Bartold, Bella Bruck, Sheila Bartold, Lois Battle, Lynn Cartwright, Margaret Muse, John J. Fox, Alan Frost, Carl Gottlieb, Elizabeth Rogers, John Hudkins, Crane Jackson, Michael Macready, Paul Micale, John Nolan, Connie Hunter Ragaway, Steven Spielberg, Bruno Ve Sota, Debbie Lempert, Sandy Lempert
P: Alan Jay Factor   D: Steven Spielberg   TELEPLAY: Robert Clouse   PHOTOG: Bill Butler   MUSIC: Wladimir Selinsky
TVM, standard fantasy-thriller: Family experiences satanic happenings in old Pennsylvania farmhouse

Something for Everyone
1970, (USA), Nat'l General, color, 113 mins.
W: Angela Lansbury, Michael York, Anthony Corlan, Heidelinde Weis, Eva-Marie Meinke, John Gill Jane Carr
D: Harold Prince, from Harry Kressing's novel   PHOTOG: Walter Lassally
*A.k.a. **Black Flowers for the Bride** and **The Rook***
Superior black comedy: Ruthless social climber employs seduction and murder

Something in the Air
*see **The Disappearance of Flight 412***

Something is Out There
1988, (USA-Austral), Hoysts/NBC-TV, color, 170 mins.
W: Joseph Cortese, Maryam d'Abo, George Dzundza (*Frank Dileo*), Kim Delaney (*Mandy Estabrook*), Robert Webber (*Commissioner Estabrook*), Gregory Sierra (*Victor Maldonaldo*), Joseph Cali (*Roger*), John O'Hurley (*Remar*), Earl Billings (*The Coroner*), Daniel Moriarty (*The Valet*), Hope North (*The Jogger*), Anne Elizabeth Ramsey (*The Limo Driver*), Melanie Jones (*Claire Riggs*), Hank Rolike (*The Doorman*), Christopher Carroll (*The Maitre d'*), Mickey Jones (*Annie McKuen*), Jack Bricker (*The Creature*), Kristoffer Greaves

(*Prisoner X-90*), David Jobling (*Prisoner #2*), Robert Taylor (*The 1st Officer*), Ian Mortimer (*Guard #1*), Michael Cutt (*McCready*), Maitthew Faison (*Ron Cobb*), Ray Reinhardt (*Prof. Dietrich*), Lori Michaels (*Kelly Simon*), Hector Mercado (*Enriquez*), Cal Gibson (*The Cabbie*), Richard Burns (*The Driver*), Dean Scofield (*Andrew Brockhurst*), Roger Eagle (*Harv*), Andi Chapman (*The TV Interviewer*), James Emery (*The Coveralled Man*), Noelle Bou-Sliman (*A Passerby*), Clive Rosengren (*A Passerby*), Doug MacHugh (*A Passerby*), Jack Scalici (*A Passerby*), Tyler Coppin (*The Lab Technician*), John Putch
D: Richard Colla TELEPLAY: Frank Lupo PHOTOG: Laszlo George & Geoff Burton MUSIC: Sylvester LeVay
TVM, standard SF-thriller (in 2 parts): Earth cop and alien beauty pursue space-horror

Something Like a Bag
1915, (GB), Hepworth, b&w, 450 ft. (137.2m)
D: Frank Wilson
Minor fantasy; Drunken burglar's loot bag grows and shrinks

Something to Hide
1973, (GB), Avton Films/Avco Embassy, color, 99 mins.
W: Peter Finch (*Harry Field*), Shelley Winters (*Gabrielle Field*), Colin Blakely (*Blagdon*), John Stride (*Sgt. Tom Winnington*), Linda Hayden (*Lorelei*), Harold Goldblatt (*Dibbick*), Rosemarie Dunham (*Elsie*), Graham Crowden (*The Preacher*), Helen Fraser (*Miss Bunyan*), Jack Shepherd (*Joe Pepper*)
P: Michael Klinger D & SCR: Alastair Reid, from a novel by Nicholas Monsarrat PHOTOG: Wolfgang Suschitzky MUSIC: Roy Budd
Bizarre psychodrama: Middle-aged office worker kills drunken wife, incinerates hitch-hiker's baby

Something Waits in the Dark
see The Fish Men

Something Weird
1968, (USA), Mayflower/Boxoffice Spectaculars, color, 80 mins.
W: Tony McCabe, Elizabeth Lee, William Brooker, Ted Heil, Mudite Arums, Lawrence J. Aberwood, Stan Dale, Ione
P & SCR: James F. Hurley D: Herschell Gordon Lewis
Original title: The Eerie World of Dr. Jordan
Minor thriller: Disfigured man develops ESP

Something Wicked This Way Comes
1983, (USA), Walt Disney/Buena Vista, color, 94 mins.
W: Jason Robards Jr. (*Charles Halloway*), Jonathan Pryce (*Mr. Dark*), Diane Ladd (*Mrs. Nightshade*), Pam Grier (*The Fortuneteller*), Vidal Peterson (*Will Halloway*), Royal Dano (*Tom Fury*), Mary Grace Canfield (*Miss Foley*), James Stacy (*Ed*), Shawn Carson (*Jim Nightshade*), Angelo Rossitto (*Little Person #1*), Peter D. Risch (*Little Person #2*), Tony Christopher (*Young Ed*), Sharan Lea (*Young Miss Foley*), Scott DeRoy (*Cooger as a Young Man*), Sharon Ashe (*The Townswoman*), Arthur Hill (*The Narrator*), Jake Dengel (*Mr. Tetley*), Richard Davalos (*Mr. Crosetti*), Bruce M. Fischer (*Mr. Cooger*), Jack Dodson (*Dr. Douglas*), Ellen Geer (*Mrs. Halloway*), Brendan Klinger (*Cooger as a Child*)
D: Jack Clayton SCR: Ray Bradbury, from his novel PHOTOG: Stephen H. Burum SPCL-FX: Lee Dyer MUSIC: James Horner
Standard fantasy-thriller: Sinister carnival visits small town

Something Wild
1961, (USA), Prometheus/UA, b&w, 112 mins.
W: Carroll Baker, Ralph Meeker, Mildred Dunnock, Martin Kosleck, Jean Stapleton, Charles Watts
P: George Justin D: Jack Garfein SCR: Jack Garfein & Alex Karmel, from Alex Karmel's novel *Mary Ann* PHOTOG: Eugen Shuftan MUSIC: Aaron Copland
Standard psychodrama: Rape victim readjusts to life

Sometimes Aunt Martha Does Dreadful Things
1988, (USA), color, 95 mins.
Minor thriller: Female psychopath terrifies

Sometimes They Come Back
1991, (USA), Paradise Films/Dino De Laurentiis, Made for TV, color, 95 mins.
W: Tim Matheson (*Jim Norman*), Brooke Adams (*Sally*), Robert Rusler (*Lawson*), Chris Demetral (*Wayne*), Robert Hy Gorman (*Norman*), William Sanderson, Tasia Valenza, Nicholas Sadler, Bentley Mitchum, Matt Nolan, Don Ruffin, Chadd Nyerges, T. Max Graham, William Kuhlke, Duncan McLeod, Nancy McLoughlin, Zachary Ball, Rodney McKay, Dick Solowicz, Kimball Cummings
D: Tom McLoughlin TELEPLAY: Lawrence Konner & Mark Rosenthal, from a short story by Stephen King PHOTOG: Bryan England MUSIC: Terry Plumeri
TVM, standard horror-fantasy: Schoolteacher encounters vicious childhood ghosts

Sometimes They Come Back...Again
1996, (USA), color, 100 mins.
W: Michael Gross, Hilary Swank (*Michelle*), Alexis Arquette
D & SCR: Adam Grossman, from a novel by Stephen King
Standard horror-fantasy: Man's childhood demons are unleashed

Somewhere in the Night
1946, (USA), 20th-Fox, b&w, 110 mins.

W: John Hodiak, Nancy Guild Lloyd Nolan, Richard Conte, John Russell, Josephine Hutchinson, Fritz Kortner, Margo Woode, Sheldon Leonard, Houseley Stevenson
D: Joseph L. Mankiewicz PHOTOG: Norbert Brodine
Standard thriller

Somewhere in Time
1980, (USA), Rastar-Stephen Deutsch/Univ, color, 103 mins.
W: Christopher Reeve (*Richard Collier*), Jane Seymour (*Elise McKenna*), Christopher Plummer (*William F. Robinson*), Teresa Wright (*Laura Roberts*), Bill Erwin (*Arthur*), George Voskovec (*Dr. Finney*), John Alvin, Susan French, Maud Strand, Eddra Gale
P: Stephen Deutsch D: Jeannot Szwarc SCR: Richard Matheson, from his novel *Bid Time Return* PHOTOG: Isidore Markofsky SPCL-FX: Jack Faggard MUSIC: John Barry
Unusual fantasy-romance: Young playwright time-travels to 1912, shares love with beautiful actress

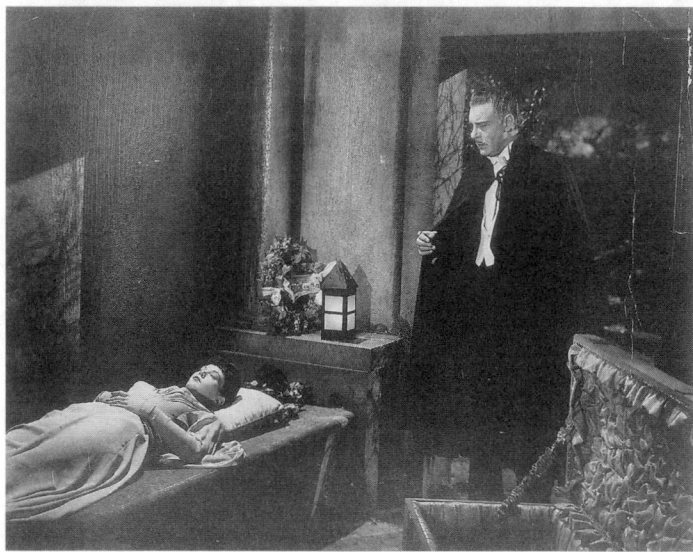
Son Of Dracula: LON CHANEY JR. AND LOUISE ALLBRITTON

Somewhere Tomorrow
1983, (USA), color, 95 mins.
W: Tom Shea, Sarah Jessica Parker Nancy Addison
D: Robert Wiemer
Standard fantasy: Teen romanced by boyfriend's ghost

Song of Abai
1945, (Russ), Alma-Ata Films, b&w
D: G. Roshal
Standard melodrama

Song of India
1949, (USA), Col, b&w, 77 mins.
W: Sabu, Gail Russell Turhan Bey, Anthony Caruso, Aminta Dyne
D: Albert S. Rogell
Standard adventure-thriller

Song of Scheherazade
1947, (USA), Univ, color, 106 mins.
W: Yvonne DeCarlo, Brian Donlevy, Jean-Pierre Aumont, Eve Arden, Philip Reed, John Qualen, Richard Lane, George Dolenz, Elena Verdugo
WRIT & D: Walter Reisch MUSIC: Miklos Rozsa
Standard adventure-romance: Exotic dancer inspires Russian naval cadet

Song of the South
1946, (USA), Walt Disney, color, 94 mins.
W: James Baskett (*Uncle Remus*), Ruth Warrick, Bobby Driscoll, Luana Patten, Hattie McDaniel, Eric Rolf
D: Wilfred Jackson & Harve Foster, from stories by Joel Chandler Harris
Classic musical-fantasy (blend of live action & animation): "Uncle Remus" tells amusing fables

Song of the Thin Man
1947, (USA), MGM, b&w, 86 mins.
W: William Powell (*Nick Charles*), Myrna Loy (*Nora Charles*), Keenan Wynn (*Clarence "Clinker" Krause*), Patricia Morison (*Phyllis Talbin*), Dean Stockwell (*Nick Charles Jr.*), Philip Reed (*Tommy Drake*), Gloria Grahame (*Fran Page*), Don Taylor (*Buddy Hollis*), Jayne Meadows (*Janet Thayar*), Ralph Morgan (*David L. Thayar*), Leon Ames (*Mitchell Talbin*), Warner Anderson (*Dr. Monolaw*), William Bishop (*Al Amboy*), Tom Dugan (*Davis*), Bruce Cowling (*Phil Brant*), Bess Flowers (*Jessica Thayar*), Connie Gilchrist (*Bertha*), James Burke (*Callahan*), Marie Windsor (*Helen Amboy*), James Flavin (*Reardon*), George Anderson (*Dunne*), Donald Kerr (*The News Photographer*), Alan Bridge (*Nagle*), Esther Howard (*The Woman at the Counter*), Matt McHugh

(The Taxi Driver), Clinton Sundberg *(The Desk Clerk)*, Earle Hodgins *(The Baggage Man)*, George Sorel *(The Headwaiter)*, Howard Negley *(Kramer)*, Morris Ankrum *(The Inspector)*, George Chan *(The Chinese Man)*
D: Edward Buzzell **SCR:** Steve Fisher, Nat Perrin, James O'Hanlon & Harry Crane, from characters created by Dashiell Hammett **PHOTOG:** Charles Rosher **MUSIC:** David Snell
Standard thriller (6th & last entry in **Thin Man** *series): Band leader on gambling ship murdered, urbane sleuth investigates*

The Song Spinner
1995, (USA), SHO-TV, color, 100 mins.
W: Patty LuPone, Meredith Henderson, David Hemblen
Made-for-Cable, standard fantasy: Mystery woman spreads gift of music in land where noise is forbidden

Son Of Frankenstein: BORIS KARLOFF

Sonka Zolotaya Ruchka (Sonka the Golden Hand)
1914-1916, (Russ), Drankov & Kinolenta, b&w
W: V. Hoffman, B. Svetlov, A. Varyagin, Chargonin
D: Y. Yurevsky, Vladimir Kasyanov & Alexander Chargonin **SCR:** V. Garlitsky, V. Rubinov & I. Rapgof [Count Amori] **PHOTOG:** Ivan Frolov
Standard melodrama (in 8 serial parts)

Sonny's Flight to the Moon
1963, (W. Ger), color
Standard juvenile fantasy

Son of Ali Baba
1952, (USA), Univ, color, 75 mins.
W: Tony Curtis *(Kasma Baba)*, Piper Laurie *(Kiki)*, William Reynolds *(Mustafa)*, Hugh O'Brian *(Hussein)*, Gregg Palmer *(Farouk)*, Victor Jory *(The Caliph)*, Philip Van Zandt *(Kareeb)*, Morris Ankrum *(Ali Baba)*, Barbara Knudson *(Theda)*, Leon Belasco *(Babu)*, Alice Kelley *(Calu)*, Milada Mladova *(Zaza)*, Gerald Mohr *(Capt. Youssef)*, Robert Barrat *(The Commandant)*, Katherine Warren *(Princess Karma)*, Sebastian Cabot Harry Guardino
P: Leonard Goldstein **D:** Kurt Neumann **SCR:** Gerald Drayson Adams **PHOTOG:** Maury Gertsman **MUSIC:** Joseph Gershenson
Standard adventure-thriller: Cadet outwits wicked caliph

Son of a Stranger
1957, (GB), Danziger/UA, b&w, 68 mins.
W: James Kenney *(Tom Adams)*, Ann Stephens *(Joannie)*, Basil Dignam *(Dr. Delaney)*, Victor Maddern *(Lenny)*, Catherine Finn *(Mrs. Adams)*, Diana Chesney *(Mrs. Peck)*
P: Edward J. & Harry Lee Danziger **D:** Ernest Morris **STORY:** Stanley Miller
Standard crime-thriller: Slum teenager searches for "rich" father

Son of Blob
see **Beware! The Blob**

The Son of Dr. Jekyll
1951, (USA), Col, b&w, 77 mins.
W: Louis Hayward, Jody Lawrance, Gavin Muir, Alexander Knox, Lester Matthews, Claire Carleton
D: Seymour Friedman **SCR:** Edward Huebsch, from a story by Mortimer Braus & Jack Pollexfen
Ger retitle, **The Second Face of Dr. Jekyll**
Standard horror-thriller: Son of maligned doctor tries to vindicate his father

Son of Dracula
1943, (USA), Univ, b&w, 80 mins.
W: Lon Chaney Jr. *("Count Alucard"/Dracula)*, Louise Allbritton *(Katherine Caldwell)*, Robert Paige *(Frank Stanley)*, J. Edward Bromberg *(Prof. Lazlo)*, Evelyn Ankers *(Claire Caldwell)*, Frank Craven *(Dr. Brewster)*, Samuel S. Hinds *(Judge Simmons)*, George Irving *(Col. Caldwell)*, Adeline DeWalt Reynolds *(Mme. Zimba)*, Patrick Moriarity *(Sheriff Dawes)*, Etta McDaniel *(Sarah)*
P: Ford Beebe **D:** Robert Siodmak **SCR:** Eric Taylor, from an orig. idea by Curt Siodmak **PHOTOG:** George Robinson **MUSIC:** H.J. Salter
Standard horror-fantasy: Vampire puts Southern belle under evil spell

Son of Dracula
1974, (GB), Apple/Cinemation, color, 90 mins.
W: Ringo Starr *(Merlin)*, Harry Nillson *(Count Dracula)*, Suzanna Leigh *(The Girl)*, Dennis Price *(Van)*, Freddie Jones *(Dr. Frankenstein)*, Peter Frampton, Keith Moon, John Bonham
P: Ringo Starr **D:** Freddie Francis **SCR:** Jay Fairbank **MUSIC:** Harry Nillson
Standard horror-spoof

Son of Flubber
1963, (USA), Walt Disney/Buena Vista, b&w, 100 mins.
W: Fred MacMurray *(Prof. Ned Brainard)*, Nancy Olson *(Betsy Brainard)*, Keenan Wynn *(Alonzo Hawk)*, Ken Murray *(Hurley)*, Tommy Kirk *(Biff Hawk)*, Elliott Reid *(Prof. Shelby Ashton)*, Joanna Moore *(Desiree de la Roche)*, Leon Ames *(Prof. Rufus Daggett)*, Charles Ruggles *(Judge Murdock)*, Ed Wynn *(A.J. Allen)*, Paul Lynde, William Demarest, Bob Sweeney, Edward Andrews, Jack Albertson, Stuart Erwin, Forrest Lewis, Alan Carney
D: Robert Stevenson **SCR:** Bill Walsh & Don Da Gradi, from characters created by Samuel W. Taylor **PHOTOG:** Edward Colman **MUSIC:** John Bruns
Standard SF-comedy (sequel to **The Absent-Minded Professor {1961}**)*: Professor's amusing adventures with anti-gravity substance*

Son of Frankenstein
1939, (USA), Univ, b&w, 80 mins.
W: Basil Rathbone *(Wolf von Frankenstein)*, Boris Karloff *(The Monster)*, Bela Lugosi *(Ygor)*, Josephine Hutchinson *(Elsa von Frankenstein)*, Lionel Atwill *(Insp. Krogh)*, Donnie Dunagan *(Peter von Frankenstein)*, Michael Mark, Edgar Norton, Emma Dunn, Perry Ivins, Lionel Belmore, Gustav von Seyffertitz, Lorimer Johnston, Lawrence Grant
P & D: Rowland V. Lee **SCR:** Willis Cooper **PHOTOG:** George Robinson **MUSIC:** Frank Skinner
"...it's a fascinating film...The performances are restrained, Lugosi being especially good and touching as Ygor (one of his best and most underrated performances)..." William K. Everson, Classics of the Horror Film
"...the climax, with all the principals converging on the laboratory—the Monster coming face to face with the police inspector (Lionel Atwill) and tearing his artificial arm off while holding the child under one of his boots had the same choreographic excitement of Lee's best work"—Carlos Clarens, An Illustrated History of the Horror Film
Classic horror-thriller: Scientist's son revives father's monstrous creation

Son of Godzilla
1968, (Jap), Toho/AIP-TV, color, 86 mins.
W: Tadao Takashima, Beverly Maeda, Akiro Kubo
P: Tomoyuki Tanaka **D:** Jun Fukuda **SCR:** Shinichi Sekizawa & Kazuo Shiba
Minor SF-fantasy: Giant reptiles endanger scientists

The Son of Hagar
see **Der Sohn der Hagar**

The Son of Hercules in the Land of Darkness
1964, (It), Embassy, color, 74 mins.
W: Dan Vadis, Spela Rozin, Carol Brown, Ken Clark, Janette Barton, John Simons, Hugo Arden, Red Ross, Sand Beanty
P & D: Al World **PHOTOG:** Claude Haroy
Minor "Sword & Sandal": Muscleman rescues captives from cruel queen of underground city

Son of Hercules in the Land of Fire
1962, (It), Cine Italia/Avco Embassy, color, 86 mins
W: Ed Fury, Claudia Mori
Minor "Sword & Sandal": Muscleman rescues king's daughter

Son of Ingagi
1940, (USA), Sack Amusement/Hollywood Prods., b&w, 70 mins.
W: Zack Williams, Laura Bowman, Alfred Grant, Spencer Williams Jr.

Son Of Godzilla

P & D: Richard C. Kahn **SCR:** Spencer Williams Jr.
Standard comedy-thriller (all-black cast): Love-starved apeman kidnaps bride

Son of Kong
1933, (USA), RKO, b&w, 69 mins.
W: Robert Armstrong (*Carl Denham*), Frank Reicher (*Capt. Englehorn*), Helen
   Mack, John Marston, Victor Wong, Noble Johnson, Ed Brady, Lee Kohlmar,
   Katherine Ward, Gertrude Sutton, Clarence Wilson, Gertrude Short
D: Ernest B. Schoedsack, from a story by Ruth Rose **PHOTOG:** Eddie Linden,
   Vernon Walker & J.O.Taylor **SPCL-FX:** Willis O'Brien **MUSIC:** Max
   Steiner **SONGS:** *Runaway Blues*
*Standard adventure-fantasy (sequel to **King Kong** {1933}): Showman seeks ancient treasure, finds giant ape*

The Son of Monte Cristo
1940, (USA), UA, b&w, 102 mins.
W: Louis Hayward, Joan Bennett, George Sanders, Montagu Love, Dwight Frye,
   Florence Bates (*Mathilde*), Ralph Byrd (*Gluck*), Lionel Royce (*Zimmerman*),
   Clayton Moore (*Dorner*), Jack Mulhall, George Renavent, Michael Visaroff,
   Theodore von Eltz, Rand Brooks, James Seay, Henry Brandon, Stanley
   Andrews, Edward Keane, Ernie Adams, Maurice Cass, Michael Mark,
   Charles Trowbridge, Ted Oliver, Charles Waldron Sr., Wyndham Standing,
   Lionel Belmore, Margaret Fealy
P & D: Rowland V. Lee **SCR:** George Bruce **PHOTOG:** George Robinson
   SPCL-FX: Howard A. Anderson **MUSIC:** Edward Ward
Standard adventure-thriller: Hero foils evil dictator

Son of Robin Hood
1958, (GB), Argo/20th-Fox, color, 77 mins.
W: Al (David) Hedison (*Jamie*), June Laverick (*Deering Hood*), David Farrar (*Des
   Roches*), Marius Goring (*Chester*), Philip Friend (*Dorchester*), Delphi Lawrence
   (*Sylvia*), George Coulouris (*Alan-a-Dale*), George Woodbridge (*Little John*),
   Humphrey Lestocq (*Blunt*), Shelagh Fraser (*Constance*), Jack Lambert (*Will
   Scarlet*), Maya Koumani (*The Lady in Waiting*)
P: Jack Lamont **D:** George Sherman **SCR:** George Sherman & George Slavin
   PHOTOG: Arthur Grant **MUSIC:** Leighton Lucas
Standard adventure-thriller: Outlaw's daughter saves boy prince from evil duke

Son of Samson
1960, (It-Fr-Yugo), Medallion, color, 89 mins.
W: Mark Forest (*Maciste*), Chelo Alonso (*Queen Smedes*), Vira Silenti (*Tekaet*),
   Angelo Zanolli (*Kenamun*), Federica Ranchi (*Nofret*), Carlo Tamberlani
   (*Armitee*), Peter Dorric (*The Vizier*)
P: Ermano Donati & Luigi Carpentieri **D:** Carlo Campogalliani **SCR:** Oreste
   Biancoli
Standard "Sword & Sandal": Hero saves Egypt from ruin

Son of Sinbad
1955, (USA), Howard Hughes/RKO, 3D, color, 88 mins.
W: Dale Robertson (*Sinbad*), Sally Forrest (*Ameer*), Vincent Price (*Omar*),Lily St.
   Cyr (*Nerissa*), Leon Askin (*Khalif*), Mari Blanchard (*Kristina*), Jay Novello
   (*Jiddah*), Ian MacDonald (*Murad*), Raymond Greenleaf (*Simon*), Donald
   Randolph (*The Councillor*), Larry Blake (*Samit*), Nejla Ates (*The Dancer in the
   Market*), Kalantan (*The Dancer in the Desert*), Kim Novak
P: Robert Sparks **D:** Ted Tetzlaff **SCR:** Aubrey Wisberg & Jack Pollexfen
   PHOTOG: William Snyder **MUSIC:** Victor Young
*A.k.a. **Nights in a Harem***
*Standard adventure-romance: Legendary sailor must perform difficult tasks to win freedom
   from wicked caliph*

Son of Spartacus
*see Il **Figlio di Spartacus***

The Sons of Satan
1915, (GB), London/Jury, b&w, 4,730 ft. (1441.8m)
W: Gerald Ames (*Henry Normand*), Blanche Bryan (*Winifred West*), Hayford Hobbs
   (*Dick Fenton*), Charles Rock (*Lord Desford*), Windham Guise (*Earl of
   Littleborough*), Lewis Gilbert (*William Freshley*), Arthur Cullin (*Felix Sawyer*),
   Douglas Munro (*Insp. Ransom*), George Bellamy (*The Editor*)
D: George Loane Tucker, from a novel by William le Qeux
*Standard crime-thriller: Detective secretly heads gang of jewel thieves, loves actress engaged
   to earl's son*

Sons of the Musketeers
*see **At Sword's Point***

Sooty Sketches
1909, (GB), Urban, b&w, 395 ft. (120.4m)
D: Walter R. Booth
Standard fantasy short: Artist's silhouette sketches come to life

Sorcellerie Culinaire (Culinary Sorcery)
1904, (Fr), Star, b&w, 84m (275.6 ft./4.7 mins.)
D: Georges Melies
*A.k.a. **The Cook in Trouble***
Standard comedy-fantasy: Chef stews in own juice

The Sorcerers
1967, (GB), Tigon/AA, color, 85 mins.
W: Boris Karloff (*Prof. Marcus Monserrat*), Catherine Lacey (*Estelle Monserrat*), Ian
   Ogilvy (*Mike*), Elizabeth Ercy (*Nicole*), Victor Henry (*Alan*), Dani Sheridan
   (*Laura*), Susan George (*Audrey*), Alf Joint (*Ron*), Ivor Dean (*Insp. Matalon*),
   Peter Fraser (*The Detective*), Bill Barnsley, Meier Tzelniker, Gerald Campion,

Martin Terry, Maureen Boothe
P: Tony Tenser **D:** Michael Reeves **SCR:** Michael Reeves & Tom Baker, from an idea by John Burke **PHOTOG:** Stanley A. Long **MUSIC:** Paul Ferris
SONGS: *Your Love & Sweet Nothing*, sung by Toni Daly
orig. to be titled **Before I Die**
Standard SF-thriller: Old couple dabbles in mind-control

Son Of King Kong: ROBERT ARMSTRONG

The Sorcerer's Egg
see L'Oeuf du Sorcier

The Sorcerer's Revenge
see Le Sorcier

The Sorcerer's Scissors
1907, (GB), Urban, b&w, 220 ft. (67.1m)
D: Walter R. Booth
Standard fantasy short: Scissors cut shapes that come to life

The Sorcerer, the Prince and the Good Fairy
see Le Sorcier, le Prince et le Bon Genie

Sorceress
1982, (USA-Mex), New World, color, 73 mins.
W: Leigh Harris *(Mira)*, Lynette Harris *(Mara)*, David Millbern *(Pando)*, Bob Helson *(Erlick)*, Bruno Rey *(Baldar)*, Ana de Sade *(Dellisia)*, Robert Ballesteros *(Traigon)*, Douglas Sanders *(Hunnu)*, Tony Stevens *(Khrakannon)*, Lucy Jensen *(The Dancer)*, Martin LaSalle *(Krona)*, Silvia Masters *(Kanti)*, William Arnold *(Dargon)*, Teresa Conway *(Amaya)*, Michael Fountain *(The Player)*, Peter Farmer *(The Armorer)*, Charles Rogers *(The Servant)*, Mark Arevan *(The Gambler)*, Phillip Garrigan *(The Soldier)*, Ginger Baum *(The Sister)*, Gloria Meister *(The Nursemaid)*, Marla Hill *(The Rich Lady)*, Randy Rothman *(The Peasant)*, Gerald Hood *(The Executioner)*
D: Brian Stuart **SCR:** Jim Wynorski **PHOTOG:** Alex Phillips Jr.
Minor adventure-fantasy: Female warrior twins share magic powers

Sorceress
1995, (USA), color
W: Larry Poindexter, Rochelle Swanson
Minor fantasy-thriller

Le Sorcier (The Sorcerer)
1903, (Fr), Star, b&w, 67m (219.8 ft./3.7 mins.)
WRIT & D: Georges Melies
GB retitle, **The Sorcerer's Revenge** *USA retitle,* **The Witch's Revenge**
Standard fantasy

La Sorciere (The Witch)
1955, (Fr-Swed), Iena/Ellis, b&w, 97 mins.
W: Marina Vlady *(Aino, the Sorceress)*, Maurice Ronet *(Laurent, the Engineer)*, Nicole Courcel *(Kristina)*, Michel Etcheverry *(Camoin)*, Ulf Palme *(Matti)*, Erik Hell *(Pullinen)*, Rune Lindstrom *(The Pastor)*, Ulla Lagnell *(The Pastor's Wife)*, Naima Wifstrand *(Maina)*
D: Andre Michel **SCR:** Jacques Companeez, from a novel by Alexander Kouprine
Standard fantasy

Les Sorcieres de Salem (The Witches of Salem)
1957, (Fr), b&w, 120 mins.
W: Simone Signoret *(Elizabeth Proctor)*, Yves Montand *(John Proctor)*, Mylene Demongeot *(Abigail Williams)*, Jean Debucourt *(Parris)*, Pierre Larquey *(Francis Nurse)*, Francoise Lugagne *(Jane Putnam)*, Raymond Rouleau *(Danforth)*, Jeanne Fusier-Gir *(Martha Corey)*, Alfred Adam *(Thomas Putnam)*, Yves Brainville *(Hale)*, Miss Darling *(Tituba)*, Alexandre Rignault *(Willard)*, Chantal Gozzi *(Francy Proctor)*, Jean Gaven *(Peter Corey)*, Pascale

Petit *(Mary Warren)*
P: Raymond Borderie **WRIT & D:** Raymond Rouleau, from Arthur Miller's play *The Crucible* **PHOTOG:** Claude Renoir **MUSIC:** Georges Auric
Superior thriller: Passion and hatred in Salem witch hunt of 1692

Le Sorcier, le Prince et le Bon Genie (The Sorcerer, the Prince and the Good Fairy)
1900, (Fr), Star, b&w, 40m (131.2 ft./2.2 mins.)
D: Georges Melies
A.k.a. **The Wizard, the Prince and the Good Fairy**
Standard fantasy

La Sorella di Satan (Satan's Sister)
1965, (It-Yugo), Europix, color, 71 mins.
W: Barbara Steele *(Veronica)*, Ian Ogilvy *(Philip)*, John Karlsen *(Van Helsing)*, Mel Welles *(Groper)*, Jay Riley, Ed Randolph, Richard Watson, Peter Grippe
D: Michael Reeves & Charles Griffith **SCR:** Michael Byron **PHOTOG:** G. Gengarelli **MUSIC:** Ralph Ferraro
GB retitle, **The Revenge of the Blood Beast** *USA retitle,* **The She Beast** *A.k.a.* **Queen of Evil**
Minor horror-thriller: Spirit of Transylvanian witch possesses honeymooning bride

Sorority Babes in the Slimeball Bowl-O-Rama
1987, (USA), Titan/Urban Classics, color, 80 mins.
W: Linnea Quigley, Andras Jones, Robin Rochelle, Michelle McClellan, Hal Havins, Brinke Stevens, Buck Flower Carla Baron, Kathi Obrecht, John Stuart Wildman
D: David DeCoteau **SCR:** Sergei Hasenecz **PHOTOG:** Stephen Ashley Blake **MUSIC COMPOSER:** Guy Moon **SONG:** *Here in Darkness*
Minor fantasy: Coeds meet evil imp

Sorority Girl
1957, (USA), AIP, b&w, 60 mins.
W: Susan Cabot, Dick Miller, Barboura O'Neill, Fay Baker, Barbara Crane, June Kenney, Jeane Wood
P & D: Roger Corman
A.k.a. **The Bad One**
Standard melodrama: Malicious coed causes grief

Sorority Girls and the Creature from Hell
1990, (USA), McBrearty/ACM, color
W: Len Lesser, Debbie Dutch, Eric Clark, Carl Johnson, Doug Koth, Gloria Hylton, Dori Courtney, Wynn Reichert, Glen Vincent, Stacy Lynn
P, D, & SCR: John McBrearty **STORY:** Lynette McBrearty & John McBrearty **PHOTOG:** Vincent C. Ellis **MUSIC:** Jim Fox
Minor comedy thriller: Collegians stalked at mountain cabin

Sorority House Massacre
1986, (USA), WB, color, 74 mins.
W: Angela O'Neill *(Beth)*, John C. Russell *(Bobby)*, Wendy Martel, Pamela Ross, Nicole Rio
P: Ron Diamond **WRIT & D:** Carol Frank **MUSIC:** Michael Wetherwax
blurb: "Who'll survive the final exam?"
Standard thriller: Crazed killer stalks coeds

Sorority House Massacre 2
1992, (USA), color, 80 mins.
W: Melissa Moore, Robyn Harris, Mike Elliott, Stacia Zhivago Dana Bentley
D: Jim Wynorski
A.k.a. **Sorority House Massacre 2: Nighty Nightmare**
Minor thriller: Coeds in mansion haunted by killer's ghost

The Sorrows of Satan
1917, (GB), G.B. Samuelson/Walker, b&w, 5,000 ft. (1524m)
W: Gladys Cooper *(Lady Sybil Elton)*, Owen Nares *(Geoffrey Tempest)*, Cecil Humphreys *(Prince Ramirez)*, Lionel d'Aragon *(Earl Elton)*, Winifred Delevanti *(Diana Chesney)*, Alice de Winton, Minna Grey
D: Alexander Butler **SCR:** Harry Engholm, from a novel by Marie Corelli
Standard fantasy: Girl loves prince who is really Satan

The Sorrows of Satan
1925, (USA), Famous Players-Lasky/Para, b&w, 9 reels (8,691 ft./2649m)
W: Adolphe Menjou *(Prince Lucio di Rimanez)*, Ricardo Cortez *(Geoffrey Tempest)*, Lya de Putti *(Princess Olga)*, Lawrence D'Orsay *(Lord Elton)*, Carol Dempster *(Mavis Claire)*, Ivan Lebedeff *(Amiel)*, Marcia Harris *(The Landlady)*, Nellie Savage *(The Dancing Girl)*, Dorothy Hughes *(Mavis' Chum)*, Josephine Dunn, Dorothy Nourse, Jeanne Morgan *(Jean Fenwick)*
D: D.W. Griffith **SCR:** Forrest Halsey, from Marie Corelli's novel **PHOTOG:** Harry Fischbeck & Arthur De Titta
Standard fantasy: Prince of Darkness infiltrates high society

The Sorrows of Selina
1914, (GB), Martin Films/DFSA, b&w, 595 ft. (181.4m)
D: Dave Aylott
Standard fantasy: Maid dreams she uses magic lamp to rescue suffragette from sultan

Sorry, Wrong Number
1948, (USA), Hal Wallis/Para, b&w, 90 mins.
W: Barbara Stanwyck *(Leona Stevenson)*, Burt Lancaster *(Henry Stevenson)*, Wendell Corey *(Dr. Alexander)*, Ed Begley *(James Cotterell)*, Ann Richards *(Sally Lord*

S

Dodge), William Conrad (*Morano*), Leif Erickson (*Fred Lord*), Paul Fierro (*Harpootlian*), John Bromfield (*Joe, the Detective*), Harold Vermilyea (*Waldo Evans*), Jimmy Hunt (*Jimmy Lord*), Dorothy Neumann (*Miss Jennings*), Cliff Clark (*Sgt. Duffy*), Kristine Miller (*Dolly, Dr. Alexander's Girlfriend*), Suzanne Dalbert (*The Cigarette Girl*), Tito Vuolo (*Albert, the Waiter*), Joyce Compton (*The Blonde*), Grace Poggi, Igor Dega
P: Hal Wallis & Anatole Litvak   **D:** Anatole Litvak   **SCR:** Lucille Fletcher, from her radio-play   **PHOTOG:** Sol Polito   **SPCL-FX:** Gordon Jennings   **MUSIC:** Franz Waxman
Classic thriller: Invalid woman hears murder plot over the telephone

Sorry, Wrong Number
1989, (USA), Wilshire Court, Made for TV, color, 90 mins.
W: Loni Anderson (*Madeleine Stevenson*), Carl Weintraub (*Charlie Stevenson*), Patrick Macnee (*Evans*), Hal Holbrook (*Jim Coltrane*), Diane D'Aquila (*Sally*), Miguel Fernandes (*Diaz*), Helen Hughes (*Ms. Jennings*), Barry Flatman (*Dr. Levine*), Harvey Atkin (*Det. Kiley*), Alan Jordan (*Jerry Luntschild*), Bernard Behrens (*Dr. Fisher*), Geoffrey Bowes (*Rob*), Ted Simonett (*Dave*), Keri Lyn (*Levine's Girl*), J. Winston Carroll (*Sgt. Crowley*), Marilyn Peppiatt (*Helen*), Bruce McFee (*Risner*), Michael J. Reynolds (*Henry*), Elliot McIver (*The Headwaiter*), Tom Melissis (*The Waiter*), Lorne Cossette (*The Preacher*), Jillian Cook (*The Housekeeper*), Victor Ertmanis (*The Dispatcher*), Ric Sarabia (*The Cabbie*)
D: Tony Wharmby   **TELEPLAY:** Ann Louise Burdach, based on scr & radio-play by Lucille Fletcher   **PHOTOG:** Frank Tidy   **MUSIC:** Bruce Broughton
TVM, standard thriller: Wealthy invalid overhears murder plot on telephone

So Sad About Gloria
1975, (USA), Centronics Int'l, color, 83 mins.
W: Lori Saunders (*Gloria Wellman*), Dean Jagger (*Frederic Wellman*), Bob Ginnaven (*Chris Kenner*), Seymour Treitman (*Mr. Ballinger*), Lou Hoffman (*The Psychiatrist*), Melanie Wadkins (*Mary*), Linda Wyse (*Janie Mylan*), Joe Barone (*The Ax-Man*), John Brown (*The Servant*), Etta Jagger (*The Nurse*), George Stewart (*Death*), Brenda Evans (*The Victim*), Jerald Reed (*The Chauffeur*)
D: Harry Thomason   **SCR:** Marshall Riggan   **PHOTOG:** Bob Dracup   **SPCL-FX:** Jack Bennett   **MUSIC:** Hank Levine   **SONGS:** *Today, Tonight and Tomorrow*
A.k.a. **Visions of Evil**
Minor thriller: Woman terrorized by apparition

S.O.S. Coast Guard
1942, (USA), Rep, b&w
W: Ralph Byrd, Bela Lugosi, Maxine Doyle
Minor thriller (feature version of 1937 serial)

A Soul for Sale
see **The Woman Who Dared**

Soul of a Monster
1944, (USA), Col, b&w, 61 mins.
W: George Macready, Rose Hobart, Jim Bannon, Jeanne Bates Will Jason
Minor fantasy-thriller: Dying man makes supernatural pact with satanic woman

Souls for Sale
see **Confessions of an Opium Eater**

Soultaker
1990, (USA), Action International, color, 95 mins.
W: Joe Estevez (*Soultaker*), Vivian Schilling (*Natalia*), Gregg Thomsen (*Zach*), David Shark (*Brad*), Jean Reiner, Robert Z'Dar, David Fawcett, Chuck Williams
D: Michael Rissi   **SCR:** Vivian Schilling
Standard fantasy-thriller: Mysterious agent stalks four car-crash "survivors"

The Sound Barrier
1951, (GB), Alexander Korda/British Lion, b&w, 118 mins.
W: Ralph Richardson (*John Ridgefield*), Ann Todd (*Susan Garthwaite*), Nigel Patrick (*Tony Garthwaite*), John Justin (*Philip Peel*), Dinah Sheridan (*Jess Peel*), Joseph Tomelty (*Will Sparks*), Denholm Elliott (*Chris Ridgefield*), Leslie Phillips (*The Controller*), Jack Allen (*Windy Williams*), Ralph Michael (*Fletcher*), Jolyon Jackley (*The Baby*) Vincet Holman (*The A.T.A. Officer*), Robert Brooks Turner (*The Test Bed Operator*), Anthony Snell (*Peter Makepeace*), Douglas Muir
P & D: David Lean   **SCR:** Terence Rattigan   **PHOTOG:** Jack Hildyard   **MUSIC:** Muir Mathieson
USA retitle, **Breaking the Sound Barrier** *UA, 1952*
Engrossing melodrama: British industrial family tries to perfect supersonic flight

The Sound of Fury
1950, (USA), UA, b&w, 92 mins.
W: Frank Lovejoy, Lloyd Bridges, Richard Carlson, Kathleen Ryan, Katherine Locke, Adele Jergens, Irene Vernon, Art Smith, Renzo Cesana
D: Cy Endfield
Standard thriller: War veteran drifts into crime, becomes involved in botched kidnapping

Sound of Horror
1965, (Sp), Gregorio Sacristan/Zurbano Films/Europix, b&w, 95 mins.
W: James Philbrook (*Pete*), Soledad Miranda (*Maria*), Ingrid Pitt (*Sofia*), Antonio Casas (*Andre*), Jose Bodalo, Arturo Fernandez, Lola Gaos, Francisco Piquer
D: Jose Antonio Nieves-Conde   **SCR:** Sam X. Abarbanel, Gregg Tallas, Jose Antonio Nieves-Conde & Gregorio Sacristan   **ORIG STORY:** Sam X. Abarbanel   **PHOTOG:** Manuel Berenguer   **SPCL-FX:** Manuel Baquero   **MUSIC:** Luis De Pablo
Minor horror-thriller: Invisible monster hatches from prehistoric egg

Sous le Soleil de Satan (Under Satan's Sun)
1987, (Fr), color, 103 mins.
W: Gerard Depardieu, Sandrine Bonnaire, Maurice Pialat, Alain Artur, Yann Dedet, Brigitte Legendre, Philippe Pallut, Jean-Claude Bourlat, Jean-Christophe Bouvet, Marcel Anselin, Yvette Lavogez, Pierre D'Hoffelize
D: Maurice Pialat   **SCR:** Sylvie Danton, from Georges Bernanos' novel   **PHOTOG:** Willy Kurant   **MUSIC:** Henri Dutilleux
Unusual psychodrama: Troubled priest wrestles with world's evils

The Southern Star
1969, (GB-Fr), Eurofrance/Capitole/Col, color, 104 mins.
W: George Segal (*Dan Rockland*), Ursula Andress (*Erica Kramer*), Ian Hendry (*Karl Ludwig*), Orson Welles (*Plankett*), Harry Andrews (*Kramer*), Johnny Sekka (*Matakit*), Michael Constantine (*Jose*), Guy Delorme (*Michael*), George Geret (*Andre*), Sylvain (*Louis*), Charles Lamb (*Todd*)
P: Robert Duchet   **D:** Sidney Hayers   **SCR:** David Pursall & Jack Seddon, from a story by Jules Verne   **PHOTOG:** Raoul Coutard   **MUSIC:** George Garvarentz
Standard adventure-romance: Gem hunting in French West Africa, circa 1912

South of Algiers
see **The Golden Mask**

South of Panama
see **Panama Menace**

South of Tahiti
1941, (USA), Univ, b&w, 75 mins.
W: Maria Montez, Broderick Crawford
D: George Waggner
Standard adventure-thriller

Soylent Green
1973, (USA), MGM, color, 97 mins.
W: Charlton Heston (*Thorn*), Edward G. Robinson (*Sol Roth*), Leigh Taylor-Young (*Shirl*), Brock Peters (*Hatcher*), Chuck Connors (*Tab*), Mike Henry (*Kulozik*), Paula Kelly (*Martha*), Joseph Cotten (*Simonson*), Stephen Young (*Gilbert*), Celia Lovsky (*The Exchange Leader*), Whit Bissell (*Santini*), Dick Van Patten (*The Usher*), Lincoln Kilpatrick (*The Priest*), Roy Jenson (*Donovan*), Leonard Stone (*Charles*), Jane Dulo (*Mrs. Santini*), Tim Herbert (*Brady*), John Dennis (*Wagner*), Jan Bradley (*The Bandana Woman*), Carlos Romero (*The New Tenant*), Pat Houtchens (*The Fat Guard*), Morgan Farley (*Book #1*), John Barclay (*Book #2*), Belle Mitchell (*Book #3*), Cyril Delevanti (*Book #4*), Forrest Wood, Faith Quabius, Cheri Howell, Joyce Williams, Beverly Gill, Jennifer King, Erica Hagen, Suesie Eejima, Kathy Silva, Marion Charles
D: Richard Fleischer   **SCR:** Stanley R. Greenberg, from Harry Harrison's novel *Make Room! Make Room!*   **PHOTOG:** Richard H. Kline   **MUSIC:** Fred Myrow
Superior SF-thriller (Edward G. Robinson's last film): Intrigue in overpopulated future

Space Amoeba
see **Yog—Monster from Space**

Space Avenger
see **Alien Space Avenger**

Spaceballs
1987, (USA), Brooksfilms/MGM, color, 96 mins.
W: Mel Brooks, John Candy, Bill Pullman, Daphne Zuniga, Rick Moranis, Dick Van Patten, George Wyner, Joan Rivers (*Voice of Dot Matrix*)
P & D: Mel Brooks   **SCR:** Mel Brooks, Thomas Meehan & Ronny Graham   **PHOTOG:** Nick McLean   **MUSIC:** John Morris   **SONGS:** *Good Enough, Hot Together & Raise Your Hands*
Standard SF-satire (spoof of Star Wars): Youth opposes evil galactic empire

Spacecamp
1986, (USA), ABC/20th Cnetury-Fox, color, 115 mins.
W: Kate Capshaw (*Ande*), Lea Thompson (*Kathryn*), Larry B. Scott (*Rudy*), Kelly Preston (*Tish*), Leaf Phoenix (*Max*), Tate Donovan (*Kevin*), Tom Skerritt (*Zach*), Barry Primus, Terry O'Gunn, Mitchell Anderson, T. Scott Coffey, Peter Scranton, Daryl Roach, Terry White, Kathy Hanson, Scott Holcomb, Ron Harris, Bill Phillips, Adrian Wells, Frank Welker, Jon Stegman
D: Harry Winer   **SCR:** W.W. Wicket & Casey T. Mitchell   **STORY:** Patrick Bailey & Larry B. Williams   **PHOTOG:** William A. Fraker   **MUSIC:** John Williams
Modest SF-adventure: Teens launched into space

The Space Children
1958, (USA), Para, b&w, 79 mins.
W: Johnny Washbrook, Peggy Webber, Jackie Coogan, Richard Shannon, Michel Ray, Adam Williams, Raymond Bailey, Sandy Descher, Russell Johnson,

Larry Pennell, John Crawford, Peter Baldwin, Jean Engstrom, David Bair, Ty Hungerford(Hardin), Eilene Janssen, Vera Marshe
P: William Alland **D:** Jack Arnold **SCR:** Bernard Schoenfeld, from a story by Tom Filer **PHOTOG:** Ernest Laszlo **SPCL-FX:** John P. Fulton **MUSIC:** Van Cleave
Standard SF-thriller: Amorphous space-alien makes telepathic contact with kids at military base

Space Demon
1962, (USA), Arcadia-Int'l, color
P: Mark McGee
not in general release
Stop-motion short, standard SF-horror

Spaced Out
see Outer Touch

Spaceflight IC-1
1965, (GB), Lippert/20th-Fox, b&w, 65 mins.
W: Bill Williams (*Mead Ralston*), Kathleen Breck (*Kate Saunders*), John Cairney (*Steven Thomas*), John Cairney (*Steven Thomas*), Donald Churchill (*Carl Walcott*), Jeremy Longhurst (*John Saunders*), Linda Marlowe (*Helen Thomas*), Margo Mayne (*Joyce Walcott*), Norma West (*Jan Ralston*), Tony Doonan John Lee, James Terry, Chuck Julian, Mark Lester, Tony Honour, Stewart Middleton
P: Robert L. Lippert & Jack Parsons **D:** Bernard Knowles **SCR:** Harry Spalding **PHOTOG:** Geoffrey Faithfull **MUSIC:** Elisabeth Lutyens
Standard SF-thriller: Mutiny on spaceship

Spacehunter: Adventures in the Forbidden Zone
1983, (Can), Ivan Reitman/Col, 3D, color, 88 mins.
W: Peter Strauss (*Wolff*), Molly Ringwald (*Niki*), Michael Ironside (*Overdog*), Ernie Hudson (*Washington*), Andrea Marcovicci (*Chalmers*), Beeson Carroll (*Patterson*), Deborah Pratt (*Meagan*) Grant Alianak (*Chemist*), Aleisha Shirley (*Reena*), Paul Boretski (*Jarrett*), Cali Timmins (*Nova*), Reggie Bennett (*Barracuda Leader*), Patrick Rowe (*Duster*)
D: Lamont Johnson **SCR:** Edith Rey, David Preston, Dan Goldberg & Len Blum **STORY:** Stewart Harding & Jean Lafleur **PHOTOG:** Frank Tidy **SPCL-FX:** Mike Minor **MUSIC:** Elmer Bernstein
Minor SF-adventure: Space jockey battles dictator of hostile planet

Space-Invasion of Lappland
see Rymdinvasion i Lappland

Spacejacked
1997, (USA), color
W: Amanda Pays
Standard SF-adventure

Spacejacked
1999, (USA-Ire), Roger Corman, color
Standard SF-thriller

Space Jam
1996, (USA), WB, color, 99 mins.
W: Michael Jordan, Bill Murray, Theresa Randle, Larry Bird, Charles Barkley, Wayne Knight, Patrick Ewing, Muggsey Bogues
VOICES: Danny DeVito (*Swackhammer*), Billy West (*Bugs Bunny & Elmer Fudd*), Bradley Baker (*Daffy Duck, Tasmanian Devil & Bull*), Bob Bergen (*Bertie, Hubie, Marvin the Martian, Porky Pig, Speedy Gonzales & Tweety*), Bill Farmer (*Sylvester, Yosemite Sam & Foghorn Leghorn*), Kath Soucie (*Lola Bunny*)
P: Ivan Reitman, Joe Medjuck & Daniel Goldberg **D:** Joe Pytka **SCR:** Leo Benvenuti, Steve Rudnick, Timothy Harris & Herschel Weingrod **PHOTOG:** Michael Chapman **MUSIC:** James Newton Howard **SONGS:** *Fly Like an Eagle* & *I Believe I Can Fly*
Standard comedy-fantasy (mix of live action & animation): Basketball star meets toons

The Spaceman and King Arthur
1979, (GB), Walt Disney, color, 93 mins.
W: Dennis Dugan (*Tom Trimble*), Jim Dale (*Sir Mordred*), Ron Moody (*Merlin*), Kenneth More (*King Arthur*), Sheila White (*Alisande*), John LeMesurier (*Sir Gawain*), Rodney Bewes (*Clarence*), Robert Beatty (*Sen. Millburn*), Cyril Shaps (*Dr. Zimmerman*), Kevin Brennan (*Winston*), Reg Lye (*The Prisoner*), Ewen Solon (*Watkins*), Pat Roach (*Oaf*)
P: Ron Miller **D:** Russ Mayberry **SCR:** Don Tait, from Mark Twain's novel *A Connecticut Yankee in King Arthur's Court* **PHOTOG:** Paul Beeson **MUSIC:** Ron Goodwin
USA retitle, Unidentified Flying Oddball
Standard fantasy: Naif time-travels to Arthurian period

Space Marines
1996, (USA), SHO-TV, color, 94 mins.
W: Billy Wirth, James Shigeta, Meg Foster, Edward Albert
Made-for-Cable, standard space-opera: Ambassador taken hostage in 21st century

Spacemaster X-7
1958, (USA), Regal/20th-Fox, b&w, 71 mins.
W: Bill Williams, Lyn Thomas, Paul Frees, Robert Ellis, Nesdon Booth, Moe Howard, Fred Sherman, Joan Nixon Barry, Thomas B. Henry, Jess Kirkpatrick, Rhoda Williams, Thomas Wilde, Carol Varga, Gregg Martell,

Court Shepard, Al Baffert, Bob Bice, Don Lamond, Judd Holdren, John Ward, Lane Chandler, Ellen Shaw, Helen Jay, Edward McNally, Joseph Becker
D: Edward Bernds **SCR:** Daniel Mainwaring & George Worthington Yates
orig. co-billed with The Fly (1958)
Minor SF-thriller: Alien fungus threatens Earth

Space Men
see Assignment—Outer Space

Spacemen Appear in Tokyo
see Uchujin Tokyo Ni Arawaru

Spacemen Saturday Night
see Invasion of the Saucer Men

Space Mission of the Lost Planet
see Horror of the Blood Monsters

Space Monster
1964, (USA), AIP, b&w, 80 mins.
W: James B. Brown, Francine York, Baynes Barron, Russ Bender
WRIT & D: Leonard Katzman **PHOTOG:** Robert Tobey **MUSIC:** Marlin Skiles
A.k.a. First Woman into Space
Minor SF-thriller

Space Mutiny
1988, (USA), color, 93 mins.
W: Reb Brown, James Ryan, John Phillip Law, Cameron Mitchell
D: David Winters **SCR:** Maria Dante
Minor SF-thriller: Spaceship passengers repel attack

Space People Attack Tokyo
see Uchujin Tokyo No Arawaru

Space Probe
see The Black Hole

Space Rage
1985, (USA), color, 77 mins.
W: Michael Pare, Richard Farnsworth (*The Colonel*), John Laughlin (*Walker*)
Minor SF-adventure: Bounty hunters of future vs. violent escapee

Space Raiders
1983, (USA), Millennium/New World, color, 84 mins.
W: Vince Edwards (*Hawk*), David Mendenhall (*Peter*), Patsy Pease (*Amanda*), Thom Christopher (*Flightplan*), Ray Stewart (*Zariatin*), Luca Bercovici (*Ace*), Drew Snyder (*Aldebaran*), George Dickerson (*Tracton*), Michael Miller (*Lou*), Virginia Kiser (*Janeris*), Don Washburn (*Jessup*), Dick Miller (*Crazy Mel*), William Boyett (*Taggart*), Howard Dayton (*Emler*), Suzan Hollis (*The Space Hooker*), Elizabeth Charlton (*Cookie*), Claude Johnson (*The Technician*), Laura Coles (*The Singer*), James Mendenhall (*The 1st Guard*), Patrick Close (*The 2nd Guard*)
P: Roger Corman **WRIT & D:** Howard R. Cohen **PHOTOG:** Alec Hirschfeld **SPCL VS-FX SPRVSR:** Tom Campbell **MUSIC:** James Horner **ORIG. SONGS:** Murphy Dunne
A.k.a. Star Child
Minor SF-adventure: Young earthling used as pawn by space aliens

Spaceship
see The Creature Wasn't Nice

Spaceship to the Unknown
1936, (USA), Univ, b&w, 97 mins.
W: Buster Crabbe (*Flash Gordon*), Jean Rogers (*Dale Arden*), Charles Middleton (*Ming the Merciless*), Frank Shannon (*Dr. Zarkoff*)
D: Frederick Stephani
A.k.a. Rocket Ship
Standard space-opera (feature version of 1936 serial Flash Gordon)

Spaceship Venus Does Not Reply
see Milczaca Gwiazda

Space Station, U.S.A.
see Gog

Space Station X
see Mutiny in Outer Space

Space-Thing
1968, (USA), B&B-F.P.S. Ventures/Entertainment Ventures, color, 69 mins.
Minor SF-nudie

Space 2074
see Star Quest (1989)

Space Vampires (1968)
see Astro Zombies

S

Space Vampires (1985)
see *Lifeforce*

Spaceways
1953, (GB), Hammer/Lippert, b&w, 76 mins.
W: Howard Duff (*Steve Mitchell*), Eva Bartok (*Lisa Frank*), Alan Wheatley (*Smith*), Philip Leaver (*Dr. Keppler*), Hugh Moxey (*Col. Daniels*), Michael Medwin (*Toby Daniels*), Cecile Chevreau (*Vanessa Mitchell*), Andrew Osborn (*Philip Crenshaw*), Anthony Ireland (*Gen. Hayes*), David Horne (*The Minister*), Leo Phillips, Joan Webster-Brough, Marianne Stone
P: Michael Carreras   D: Terence Fisher   SCR: Paul Tabori & Richard Landau, from a radio-play by Charles Eric Maine   PHOTOG: Reginald Wyer
Standard SF-melodrama: Scientist accused of stowing wife's corpse in space rocket

Spaceways

The Spaniard's Curse
1958, (GB), British Lion/Wentworth/IFD, b&w, 80 mins.
W: Tony Wright (*Charlie Manton*), Lee Patterson (*Mark Brett*), Michael Hordern (*Judge Manton*), Susan Beaumont (*Margaret Manton*), Ralph Truman (*Sir Robert Wyvern*), Henry Oscar (*Mr. Fredericks*), Brian Oulton (*Frank Porter*), Olga Dickie (*Hannah*), Roddy Hughes (*Jody*), Basil Dignam (*Guy Stevenson*)
P: Roger Proudlock   D: Ralph Kemplen   SCR: Kenneth Hyde, from Edith Pargiter's novel *The Assize of the Dying*
Standard thriller: Innocent man levies death curse on judge and jury

The Spanish Cape Mystery
1935, (USA), Rep, b&w, 65 mins.
W: Donald Cook (*Ellery Queen*), Helen Twelvetrees (*Stella Godfrey*), Berton Churchill (*Judge Macklin*), Frank Sheridan (*Godfrey*), Harry Stubbs (*Moley*), Guy Usher (*Insp. Queen*), Huntley Gordon (*Kummer*), Betty Blythe (*Mrs. Godfrey*), Olaf Hytten (*DuPre*), Ruth Gillette (*Mrs. Constable*), Jack LaRue (*Gardner*), Frank Leigh (*Tiller*), Donald Kerr (*Hendricks*), Barbara Bedford (*Mrs. Munn*), George Cleveland (*Jorum*)
D: Lewis D. Collins   SCR: Albert DeMond, from Ellery Queen's novel   PHOTOG: Gilbert Warrenton
*Standard thriller (**Ellery Queen** mystery): Vacationing detective becomes involved in four murders*

The Spanish Gardener
1956, (GB), Rank/RFD, color, 97 mins.
W: Dirk Bogarde (*Jose Santero*), Jon Whiteley (*Nicholas Brande*), Michael Hordern (*Harrington Brande*), Maureen Swanson (*Maria*), Cyril Cusack (*Garcia*), Lyndon Brook (*Robert Burton*), Josephine Griffin (*Carol Burton*), Bernard Lee (*Leighton Bailey*), Ina de la Haye (*Mrs. Santero*), Rosalie Crutchley (*Magdalena*), Geoffrey Keen
P: John Bryan   D: Philip Leacock   SCR: John Bryan & Lesley Storm, from a novel by A.J. Cronin   PHOTOG: Christopher Challis
Standard crime-thriller: Gardener jailed for theft committed by chauffeur

The Spanish Inquisition
see *La Cremation*

The Spanish Main
1945, (USA), RKO, color, 100 mins.
W: Paul Henreid, Maureen O'Hara, Walter Slezak, John Emery, Binnie Barnes, Barton MacLane, J.M. Kerrigan, Nancy Gates, Fritz Leiber
D: Frank Borzage   SCR: Herman J. mankiewicz & George Worthington Yates   PHOTOG: George Barnes   MUSIC: Hanns Eisler
Entertaining adventure-thriller: Pirate rescues beauty from villainous viceroy

Spara Forte, Piu Forte...Non Capisco (Shoot Loud, Louder...Don't Understand)
1966, (It), Embassy, color, 100 mins.
W: Marcello Mastroianni, Raquel Welch, Eduardo De Filippo, Leopoldo Trieste, Rosalba Grottesi, Franco Parenti, Regina Bianchi, Ignazio Spalla, Ugo

D'Alessio, Biagio Pelligra, Alessio Ruggeri, Tecla Scarano, Silvano, Tranquilli, Nino Vingelli, Pia Morra
D: Eduardo De Filippo   MUSIC: Nino Rota
Standard comedy-thriller

Sparkling Cyanide
1983, (USA), Stan Margulies/WB-TV/CBS-TV, color, 95 mins.
W: Anthony Andrews (*Tony Browne*), Deborah Raffin (*Iris Murdoch*), Harry Morgan (*Capt. Kemp*), Pamela Bellwood (*Ruth Lessing*), Christine Belford (*Rosemary Barton*), Josef Sommer (*George Barton*), Nancy Marchand (*Lucilla Drake*), Michael Woods, David Huffman, June Chadwick, Barrie Ingham, Anne Rogers, Shera Danese, Ismael Carlo, Linda Hoy, Abby Haman, Juan Fernandez, Eric Sinclair
D: Robert Lewis   TELEPLAY: Robert Malcolm Young, Sue Grafton & Steven Humphrey, from Agatha Christie's novel   PHOTOG: Ted Voigtlander   MUSIC: James Di Pasquale
TVM, standard thriller: Murder among beautiful people of Southern California

Spasmo
1976, (It), Libra, color, 88 mins.
W: Suzy Kendall (*Barbara*), Robert Hoffmann (*Christian*), Monica Monet (*Clorinda*), Ivan Rassimov, Guido Alberti
D: Umberto Lenzi   MUSIC: Ennio Morricone
Standard thriller

Spasms
1982, (Can), Producers Distribution Co., color, 87 mins.
W: Peter Fonda, Oliver Reed, Kerrie Keane, Al Waxman, Angus MacInnes, Miguel Fernandes, Marilyn Lightstone, Al Maini, Laurie Brown, Gerard Parkes, William Needles, David Bolt, Denis Simpson, Patrick Brymer, George Bloomfield, Denise Fergusson, John Bayliss, Barry Flatman, Les Rubie, Walker Boone, Don Buchsbaum, Harvey Chow, Peter McConnell, Julie Khaner, Sandra Awalt, Moira Shone, Douglas (*Scotty*)
D: William Fruet   SPCL-FX DIR: Brian Warner
*A.k.a. **Death Bite**, US release 1984*
Minor thriller: Monstrous snake imperils San Diego

Spawn of the Slithis
1978, (USA), Fabtrax/Cinema Shares Int'l, color, 86 mins.
W: Alan Blanchard, J.C. Claire, Dennis Lee Falt, Hy Pyke, Mello Alexandria, Win Condict, Judy Motulsky, Gary Dyer, Rocky Fumarelli, John Hatfield, Daphne Cohen, Dave Carlton, Stephen J. Hoag, Wendy Rastattar, Don Cummins, Dale Caldwell, David Ridenour, Ken Stimson, Gregory Clemmons, Prudie Butler, Ed Fournier, Jack Kelly, Alexandro Vass, Alisa Estes, Abraham Columbus, Drew Deeter, Michael Hudson, Marcus Harvey
P: Stephen Traxler & Paul Fabian   WRIT & D: Stephen Traxler   PHOTOG: Robert Caramico   MUSIC: Steve Zuckerman
*A.k.a. **Slithis***
Minor SF-satire: Scientists hunt primitive monstrosities

Speaking of Murder (Le Rouge Est Mis, The Red Light is On)
1957, (Fr), Cite Films/UMPD/Gaumont, b&w, 80 mins.
W: Jean Gabin, Annie Girardot
D: Gilles Grangier
Standard melodrama

Special Agent
1949, (USA), Pine Thomas/Para, b&w, 70 mins.
W: William Eythe, Laura Eliot
Standard thriller

Special Effects
1984, (USA), New Line Cinema, color, 103 mins.
W: Zoe Tamerlis, Brad Rijn Eric Bogosian, Kevin O'Connor, Bill Oland
D: Larry Cohen
Standard thriller: Embittered director films woman's murder

Special Investigator
1936, (USA), b&w, 60 mins.
W: Richard Dix, J. Carrol Naish, Margaret Callahan, Erik Rhodes, Owen Davis Jr., Ray Mayer, Joseph Sawyer
D: Louis King, from a novel by Erle Stanley Gardner
Standard thriller: Attorney exposes mob

Special Report: Journey to Mars
1996, (USA), CBS-TV, color, 95 mins.
W: Keith Carradine (*Slader*), Judge Reinhold (*West*), Alfre Woodard (*O'Neil*), Phillip Casnoff (*Van Pelt*), Rosalind Chao (*Yu*)
TVM, standard SF-adventure: Sabotage feared on first manned mission to red planet

Species
1995, (USA), MGM, color, 108 mins.
W: Ben Kingsley (*Fitch*), Natasha Henstridge (*Sil*), Michael Madsen (*Press*), Whip Hubley (*John F. Carey*), Marg Helgenberger (*Laura*), Forest Whitaker (*Dan*), Alfred Molina (*Arden*), Michelle Williams (*Young Sil*), Jordan Lund (*An Aide*), Scott Sproule (*The Team Driver*), Scott McKenna (*The Train Hobo*), Don Fischer (*An Aide*), Virginia Morris (*Mother*), David K. Schroeder (*The German Tourist*), Jayne Luke (*The Snack Shop Clerk*), David Jensen (*The Conductor*), Esther Scott (*The Female Conductor*), Herta Ware (*Mrs. Morris*),

Shirley Prestia (*Dr. Roth*), William Utay (*The Colleague*), David Selburg (*The Gov't Man*), Melissa Bickerton (*Fitch's Sec'y*), Lucy Rodriguez (*The Wedding Dress Saleswoman*), Ed Stone (*The Waiter*), Stogie Kenyatta (*The Cop*), Gary Bullock (*The Motel Clerk*), Susan Hauser (*The Lab Worker*), William Bumiller (*The Bouncer*), Sarah S. Leese (*The Screaming Woman*), Caroline Barclay (*The Drunken Girl*), Matthew Ashford (*The Guy in the Club*), Anthony Guidera (*Robbie*), Patricia Belcher (*The Admittance Clerk*), Richard Fancy (*The Doctor*), Leslie Ishii (*The Nurse*), Marliese K. Schneider (*The Abducted Woman*), Robert Mendelson (*The Homeless Man*), Dendrie Taylor (*Marie*), Lisa Liberati (*The Bathroom Bimbo*), Pam Cook (*The Commercial Model*), Kurtis Burow (*The Baby Boy*), Dana Hee (*The Creature Performer*), Frank Welker (*The Voice of Alien Sil*)
P: Frank Mancuso Jr. & Dennis Feldman **D:** Roger Donaldson **SCR:** Dennis Feldman **PHOTOG:** Andrzej Bartkowiak **VS-FX SPRVSR:** Richard Edlund **MUSIC:** Christopher Young "Sil" designed by H.R. Giger
Intense SF-horror: Scientist combines human and space-alien DNA, creates predatory female

Species II
1998, (USA), FGM/MGM, color, 88 mins.
W: Michael Madsen, Natasha Henstridge, Marg Helgenberger, Justin Lazard, Mykelti Williamson, George Dzundza, James Cromwell
D: Peter Medak **SCR:** Chris Brancato, from characters created by Dennis Feldman **PHOTOG:** Matthew F. Leonetti **MUSIC:** Edward Shearmur
Standard SF-horror: Hybrid alien compelled to mate

The Speckled Band
1912, (GB-Fr), Franco-British Film Co.-Eclair/Fenning, b&w, 1,700 ft. (518.2m)
W: Georges Treville (*Sherlock Holmes*), Mr. Moyse (*Dr. John Watson*)
D: Georges Treville, from Sir Arthur Conan Doyle's story
Standard thriller

The Speckled Band
1931, (GB), B&D/W&F, b&w, 90 mins.
W: Lyn Harding (*Dr. Grimesby Rylott*), Raymond Massey (*Sherlock Holmes*), Athole Stewart (*Dr. John Watson*), Nancy Price (*Mrs. Staunton*), Angela Baddeley (*Helen Stonor*), Marie Ault (*Mrs. Hudson*), Stanley Lathbury (*Rodgers*), Charles Paton (*The Builder*), Joyce Moore (*Violet*)
D: Jack Raymond **SCR:** W.P. Lipscomb, from Sir Arthur Conan Doyle's short story
Standard thriller: Sleuth solves snake-bite murder

Le Spectre (The Spectre)
1899, (Fr), Star, b&w, 20m (65.6 ft./1.1 mins.)
D: Georges Melies
*A.k.a. **Murder Will Out***
Standard thriller

Spectre
1977, (GB), Norway/20th-Fox/NBC-TV, color, 104 mins.
W: Robert Culp (*Sebastian*), Gig Young (*Hamilton*), Gordon Jackson (*The Inspector*), Ann Bell (*Anitra*), James Villiers (*Cyon*), John Hurt (*Mitri*), Majel Barrett (*Lilith*), Angela Grant (*The Butler*), Jenny Runacre (*Sydna*), Michael Latimer (*The Co-Pilot*), Penny Irving (*The 1st Maid*), Vicki Michelle (*The 2nd Maid*)
D: Clive Donner **TELEPLAY:** Gene Roddenberry & Samuel A. Peeples **STORY:** Gene Roddenberry **PHOTOG:** Arthur Ibbetson **MUSIC:** John Cameron
TVM, modest horror-fantasy: Criminologist and physician investigate psychic phenomena in financier's household

Le Spectre du Professeur Hichcock
*see **Raptus***

The Spectre of Edgar Allan Poe
1974, (USA), Cintel/CRC, color, 89 mins.
W: Robert Walker Jr. (*Edgar Allan Poe*), Mary Grover (*Lenore*), Cesar Romero

Spectre Of Edgar Allen Poe: Robert Walker Jr.

(*Grimaldi*), Tom Drake (*Forrest*), Carol Ohmart (*Lisa*), Mario Milano (*Joseph*), Karen Hartford (*The Nurse*), Dennis Fimple (*Farron*), Paul Bryar (*White*), Frank Packard (*Jonah*), Marsha Mae Jones (*Sarah*)
WRIT, P & D: Mohy Quandour **PHOTOG:** Robert Birchal **MUSIC:** Allen D. Allen
Standard horror-thriller: Literary master of macabre tries to restore lost love to land of living

Le Spectre Vert (The Green Ghost)
1930, (USA-Fr), MGM, b&w, 10 reels
W: Andre Luguet (*Lord Montague*), Jetta Goudal (*Lady Efra*), Pauline Garon (*Lady Vi*), Georges Renevant (*Dr. Ballou*), Jules Rancourt (*Sir James Ramsay*)
D: Jacques Feyder **SCR & DIALOG:** Yves Mirande, from a story by Ben Hecht **PHOTOG:** William Daniels
*Standard thriller (French-language version of **The Unholy Night**): Scotland Yard inspector probes deaths of regiment members*

Le Spectre Vert: Lionel Belmore and Andre Luguet

The Spell
1977, (USA), NBC-TV, color, 86 mins.
W: Lee Grant (*Marion Matchett*), Susan Myers (*Rita Matchett*), James Olson (*Glenn Matchett*), Helen Hunt (*Kristina*), Lelia Goldoni (*Jo Standish*), Jack Colvin (*Dale Boyce*), Barbara Bostock (*Jill*), Wright King (*Rian*), James Greene (*Stan*), Richard Carlyle (*Hugh*), Doney Oatman (*Jackie Siegel*)
D: Lee Phillips **TELEPLAY:** Brian Taggart
TVM, standard fantasy-thriller: Young witch raises havoc

Spellbinder
1988, (USA), Wizan/MGM-UA, color, 99 mins.
W: Timothy Daly (*Jeff Mills*), Kelly Preston (*Miranda Reed*), Rick Rossovich (*Derek Clayton*), Audra Lindley (*Mrs. White*), Anthony Crivello (*Aldys*), Diana Bellamy (*Grace Woods*), M.C. Gainey (*Brock*), Cary-Hiroyuki Tagawa (*Lt. Lee*), Sally Kemp (*Marilyn DeWitt*), James Louis Watkins (*Tim Weatherly*), Bob McCracken (*Simmons*), Kyle Heffner (*Herbie Green*), Cynthia Steele (*The Receptionist*), Stefan Gierasch (*Edgar DeWitt*), Karen Baldwin (*Mona*), Roderick Cook (*Ed Kennerie*), Richard Fancy (*Sgt. Barry*), Peter Schreiner (*Barry*), Diane Racine (*The Woman in the Coven*), John DeMita (*Brad*), Christopher Lawford (*Phil*), Alexandra Morgan (*Pamela*), Dale Cummings (*Frye*), Harold Diamond (*The Man*), Marisa Redanty (*Alice*), Don Woodard (*Steve*), Thomas F. Maguire (*The Priest*)
D: Janet Greek **SCR:** Tracy Torme **PHOTOG:** Adam Greenberg **MUSIC:** Basil Poledouris **SONGS:** Blind Alley, If My Love is Blind & Siren's Song
Standard fantasy-thriller: Young lawyer drawn into satanic nightmare

Spellbreaker: Secret of the Leprechauns
1995, (USA), color, 85 mins.
W: Gregory Edward Smith, John Bluthal
Made-for-Cable, standard fantasy: Boy visits Ireland, meets witch and "wee folk"

Spellbound
1941, (GB), Pyramid/UA, b&w, 82 mins.
W: Derek Farr (*Laurie Baxter*), Vera Lindsay (*Diana Hilton*), Frederick Leister (*Mr. Vincent*), Felix Aylmer (*Mr. Morton*), Hay Petrie (*Cathcart*), Diane King (*Amy Nugent*), W.G. Fay (*Johnnie*), Marian Spencer (*Mrs. Stapleton*), Gibb McLaughlin (*Gibb*), Hannen Swaffer
D: John Harlow **SCR:** Miles Malleson, from Robert Benson's novel *The Necromancers*
*USA retitle, **The Spell of Amy Nugent**, PRC, 1945 reissued (1946) as **Passing Shadows***
Standard fantasy: Spiritualist materializes man's dead fiancee

Spellbound
1945, (USA), Vanguard/UA, b&w, 111 mins.

S

<u>W:</u> Gregory Peck (*J.B.*), Ingrid Bergman (*Dr. Constance Peterson*) (*Miss Carmichael*), Leo G. Carroll (*Dr. Murchison*), Michael Chekhov (*Dr. Alex Brulov*), Jean Acker (*The Matron*), Donald Curtis (*Harry*), John Emery (*Dr. Fleurot*), Paul Harvey (*Dr. Hanish*), Steven Geray (*Dr. Graff*), Victor Kilian (*The Sheriff*), Erskine Sanford (*Dr. Galt*), Wallace Ford (*The Stranger*), Bill Goodwin (*The House Detective*), Dave Willock (*The Bellboy*), Janet Scott (*Norma*), Regis Toomey (*Sgt. Gillespie*), Addison Richards (*The Police Captain*), Art Baker (*Lt. Cooley*)
<u>P:</u> David O. Selznick   <u>D:</u> Alfred Hitchcock   <u>SCR:</u> Ben Hecht   <u>ADAPT:</u> Angus Macphail, from Francis Beeding's novel *The House of Doctor Edwards*
<u>PHOTOG:</u> George Barnes   <u>SPCL-FX:</u> Jack Cosgrove   <u>MUSIC:</u> Miklos Rozsa (Academy Award Winner)
Classic psychodrama: Lady psychiatrist shields amnesiac accused of murder. Dream sequence by Salvador Dali

Spellcaster
1991, (USA), color, 84 mins.
<u>W:</u> Richard Blade, Gail O'Grady, Adam Ant Harold Pruett, Bunty Bailey, Rafal Zeilinski
<u>D:</u> Rafal Zeilinski
Minor fantasy-thriller: Evil wizard engages rock 'n' roll fanatics in castle treasure hunt

The Spell of Amy Nugent
see *Spellbound* (1941)

Spell of Evil
1973, (GB), ITC/ABC-TV, color, 74 mins.
<u>W:</u> Diane Cilento (*Clara*), Edward De Souza (*Tony Mansell*), Jeremy Longhurst (*George*), Jennifer Daniel (*Liz*), William Dexter (*Pritchard*), Iris Russell (*Mrs. Roberts*), Martin Wyldeck (*Mr. Laker*), Philip Anthony (*Mr. Todd*), Linda Cunningham (*Suzy*), David Belcher, Reg Lye, Patricia Kneale
<u>P & D:</u> John Sichel   <u>TELEPLAY:</u> Terence Feely   <u>STORY:</u> Brian Clemens
<u>PHOTOG:</u> Roy Simper   <u>MUSIC:</u> Laurie Johnson
TVM, standard fantasy-thriller: Medieval witch exists in form of beautiful, contemporary woman

Spell of the Hypnotist
see *Fright* (1957)

Spermula
1975, (Fr), PPFC, color
<u>W:</u> Dayle Haddon, Udo Keir
<u>P:</u> Bernard Lenteric   <u>D & SCR:</u> Charles Matton
Minor eroto-SF: Vampiric female space-aliens feed on human sperm

Spettri (Ghosts)
1987, (It), color 95 mins
<u>W:</u> Donald Pleasence John Pepper, Erna Schurer
<u>D:</u> Marcello Avallone
Minor fantasy-thriller: Catacomb excavation opens gates of hell

Lo Spettro (The Ghost)
1963, (It), Panda-Magna, color, 93 mins.
<u>W:</u> Barbara Steele, Peter Baldwin, Elio Jotta, Umberto Raho, Harriet White, Carol Bennet, Charles Kechler, Reginald Price Anderson
<u>D:</u> Robert Hampton (Riccardo Freda)   <u>SCR:</u> Riccardo Freda & Robert Davidson (Oreste Biancoli)   <u>PHOTOG:</u> Donald Green (Raffaele Masciocchi)
<u>MUSIC:</u> Franck Wallace
Standard horror-thriller: Terror reaches from grave

Sphere
1998, (USA),Baltimore/Constant C-Punch/WB, color, 133 mins.
<u>W:</u> Dustin Hoffman (*Dr. Norman Goodman*), Sharon Stone (*Beth Halperin*), Samuel L. Jackson (*Harry Adams*), Peter Coyote (*Barnes*), Liev Schreiber (*Ted Fielding*), Queen Latifah (*Fletcher*), Marga Gomez, Haley Lewis, James Pickens Jr., Bernard Hocke, Michael Keys Hall, Ralph Tabakin
<u>D:</u> Barry Levinson   <u>SCR:</u> Stephen Hauser & Paul Attanasio   <u>ADAPT:</u> Kurt Wimmer, from Michael Crichton's 1987 novel   <u>PHOTOG:</u> Adam Greenberg   <u>MUSIC:</u> Elliot Goldenthal
Engrossing SF-thriller: Alien spacecraft found in ocean

The Sphinx
1933, (USA), Mono, b&w, 63 mins.
<u>W:</u> Lionel Atwill, Sheila Terry, Paul Fix, Luis Alberni, Theodore Newton, Paul Hurst, Robert Ellis, Lucien Prival, Lillian Leighton, George Hayes, Hooper Atchley, Wilfred Lucas
<u>D:</u> Philip Rosen   <u>SCR:</u> Albert DeMond   <u>PHOTOG:</u> Gilbert Warrenton
Minor thriller: Philanthropist goes on murder spree
cf. *Phantom Killer*

Sphinx
1981, (USA), Orion/WB, color, 116 mins.
<u>W:</u> Lesley-Anne Down (*Erica*), Frank Langella (*Ahmed Khazzan*), Sir John Gielgud (*Abdu Hamdi*), Maurice Ronet (*Yvon de Margeau*), Martin Benson (*Muhammed*), John Rhys-Davies (*Stephanos*), Tutte Lemkow (*Tewfik*), Nadim Sawalha (*Gamal*), Vic Tablian (*Khalifa*), Saeed Jaffrey (*Selim*), Eileen Way (*Aida*), William Hootkins (*Don*), Mark Kingston (*Carter*), James Cossins (*Lord Carnarvon*), Victoria Tennant (*Lady Carnarvon*), Ismat Rafat, Cengiz Saner, Kevork Malikyan, Yashar Adem, Ahmed Abdel Wareth, Ahmed

Hegazi, Abdullah Mahmoud, Mohamed Metwalli, Seif Allah Mokhtar, Abdel Reheim El Zorkani, Behrouz Vossoughi, Ahmed Salem Mohamed
<u>P:</u> Stanley O'Toole   <u>D:</u> Franklin J. Schaffner   <u>SCR:</u> John Byrum, from Robin Cook's novel   <u>PHOTOG:</u> Ernest Day   <u>SPCL-FX:</u> Roy Whybrow
<u>MUSIC:</u> Michael J. Lewis
Superior thriller: Woman archeologist seeks lost Egyptian tomb, finds romance and danger

The Spider
1931, (USA), Fox, b&w, 65 mins.
<u>W:</u> Edmund Lowe, Lois Moran
<u>D:</u> William Cameron Menzies
Standard thriller: Stage magician solves murder. Remade in 1945

The Spider
1939, (GB), Admiral-Wembley/GFD, b&w, 81 mins.
<u>W:</u> Diana Churchill (*Sally Silver*), Derrick de Marney (*Gilbert Silver*), Jean Gillie (*Clare Morley*), Frank Cellier (*Julian Ismay*), Cecil Parker (*Lawrence Bruce*), Edward Lexy (*Insp. Horridge*), Allan Jeayes (*George Hackett*), Jack Melford (*Duke*), Jack Lambert (*Smith*), Moira Lynd (*The Nurse*), Antony Holles (*The Manager*)
<u>D:</u> Maurice Elvey   <u>SCR:</u> Victor M. Greene, Kenneth Horne & Reginald Long, from Henry Holt's novel *Night Mail*
Minor thriller: Detective's wife foils murderous gem-thief

The Spider
1945, (USA), 20th-Fox, b&w, 62 mins.
<u>W:</u> Richard Conte, Faye Marlowe, Kurt Kreuger, Martin Kosleck John Harvey, Mantan Moreland, Walter Sande, Cara Williams, Ann Savage
<u>D:</u> Robert Webb
Minor thriller: Murder in New Orleans' French Quarter. Remake of 1931 film

The Spider
1958, (USA), AIP, b&w, 62 mins.
<u>W:</u> Edward Kemmer (*Kingman*), June Kenny (*Carol Flynn*), Gene Persson (*Mike Simpson*), Sally Fraser (*Helen Kingman*), Gene Roth (*Sheriff Cagle*), Troy Patterson, June Jocelyn, Mickey Finn, Skip Young, Hal Torey, Howard Wright, Jack Kosslyn, Bill Giorgio, Hank Patterson, Bob Garnet, Nancy Kilgas, Bob Tetrick, Shirley Falls, George Stanley, David Tomack, Merritt Stone
<u>P, D & SPCL-FX:</u> Bert I. Gordon   <u>SCR:</u> Laszlo Gorog & George Worthington Yates   <u>STORY:</u> Bert I. Gordon   <u>PHOTOG:</u> Jack Marta
A.k.a. **Earth vs. the Spider** *Ger retitle,* **Die Rache der Schwarzen Spinne (The Revenge of the Black Spider)** *orig. co-billed with* **The Brain Eaters**
blurb: "It must eat you to live!"
Standard SF-horror: Teens trapped in cave with giant, mutant spider. cf. **Journey to the Seventh Planet**

The Spider and the Fly
1949, (GB), Pinewood-Mayflower/GFD, b&w, 95 mins.
<u>W:</u> Eric Portman (*Insp. Fernand Maubert*), Guy Rolfe (*Philippe de Ledocq*), Nadia Gray (*Madeleine Saincaize*), Edward Chapman (*The War Minister*), George Cole (*Marc*), Maurice Denham (*Col. de la Roche*), John Carol (*Jean/Alfred Louis*), Harold Lang (*Belfort*), May Hallatt (*Monique*), James Hayter (*The Mayor*), Jeremy Spenser (*Jacques*), Sebastian Cabot (*The Inspector*), Natasha Sokolova (*Nicole Porte*)
<u>P:</u> Maxwell Setton & Aubrey Baring   <u>D:</u> Robert Hamer   <u>SCR:</u> Robert Westerby
<u>PHOTOG:</u> Geoffrey Unsworth
Standard thriller: Thief freed to crack German safe in World War I. US Releade: Rank, 1952

The Spider and the Fly
1994, (USA), color, 87 mins.
<u>W:</u> Mel Harris, Ted Shackleford, Kim Coates, Irwin Stroud, Colm Feore, Frankie R. Faison, Cynthia Beliveau, Kenneth Welsh, Peggy Lipton, Phillip Jarrett, Elias Zarou, Peter Langley, Ron Small, Angela Moore
<u>D:</u> Michael Katleman   <u>SCR:</u> Robert Pucci & Alanna Hamill   <u>MUSIC:</u> Richard Bellis
Made-for-Cable, standard thriller: Murders surround woman mystery writer

Spider Baby
1968, (USA), American General, color, 80 mins.
<u>W:</u> Lon Chaney Jr., Carol Ohmart, Mantan Moreland, Sid Haig Jill Banner, Beverly Washburn
<u>P:</u> Paul Monka & Gil Laskey   <u>D & SCR:</u> Jack Hill
Filmed in 1964 as **Cannibal Orgy, or The Maddest Story Ever Told** *A.k.a.* **The Liver Eaters**
Minor thriller: Inbred family becomes cannibalistic

Spider-Man
1977, (USA), CBS-TV/CPT, color, 74 mins.
<u>W:</u> Nicholas Hammond (*Peter Parker/"Spider-Man"*), Thayer David (*Byron*), David White (*Jameson*), Hilly Hicks (*Robbie*), Michael Pataki (*Capt. Barbera*), Robert Hastings (*Monahan*), Lisa Eilbacher
<u>TELEPLAY:</u> Alvin Boretz
A.k.a. **The Amazing Spider-Man**
TVM, standard SF-thriller: Scientist becomes super-hero

The Spiders
see *Die Spinne*

The Spider's Web
1960, (GB), Danziger/UA, color, 89 mins.
__W:__ Glynis Johns (*Clarissa Hailsham-Brown*), John Justin (*Henry Hailsham-Brown*), Jack Hulbert (*Sir Rowland Delahaye*), Cicely Courtneidge (*Miss Peake*), Ronald Howard (*Jeremy*), David Nixon (*Elgin*), Wendy Turner (*Pippa*), Basil Dignam (*Hugo*), Joan Sterndale-Bennett (*Mrs. Elgin*), Ferdy Mayne (*Oliver*), Peter Butterworth (*Insp. Lord*)
__P:__ Edward J. & Harry Lee Danziger   __D:__ Godfrey Grayson   __SCR:__ Albert G. Miller & Eldon Howard, from a play by Agatha Christie
Standard thriller: Guardian helps diplomat's wife hide corpse of stepdaughter's father

Spider Woman
1944, (USA), Univ, b&w, 63 mins.
__W:__ Basil Rathbone (*Sherlock Holmes*), Nigel Bruce (*Dr. John Watson*), Gale Sondergaard (*Adrea Spedding*), Dennis Hoey (*Insp. Lestrade*), Vernon Downing (*Locke*), Mary Gordon (*Mrs. Hudson*), Alec Craig (*Radlik*), Arthur Hohl (*Gilflower*), Gene Roth (*Taylor*)
__D:__ Roy William Neill   __SCR:__ Bertram Millhauser, from a story by Sir Arthur Conan Doyle   __PHOTOG:__ Charles Van Enger   __MUSIC:__ H.J. Salter
Good "Sherlock Holmes" thriller: "Suicides" plague London

The Spider Woman Strikes Back
1946, (USA), Univ, b&w, 59 mins.
__W:__ Gale Sondergaard, Brenda Joyce, Kirby Grant, Rondo Hatton
Standard thriller: Mistress of crime conspires

Der Spieler
see Doctor Mabuse

Spies
see Spione

Spies-A-Go-Go
see The Nasty Rabbit

Spin a Dark Web
see Soho Incident

Die Spinne (The Spiders)
1919, (Ger), Decla-Bioscop, b&w, 137 mins
__W:__ Carl de Vogt, Georg John, Lil Dagover, Ressel Orla, Edgar Pauly, Paul Morgan, Bruno Littinger, Paul Biensfeldt
__P:__ Erich Pommer   __WRIT & D:__ Fritz Lang   __SETS:__ Otto Hunte & Carl Kirms
Unusual crime-thriller, in 2 parts: (1) Der Goldene See (The Golden Lake)—PHO-TOG: *Emile Schonemann, & (2)* Das Brillanten Schiff (The Diamond Ship)—PHOTOG: *Karl Freund*
*2 other films of same series were planned but unfilmed (*Secrets of the Sphinx *and* For the Crown of Asia*)*

Spione (Spies)
1927, (Ger), Fritz Lang Film G.M.B.H.-Ufa, b&w, 14,317.6 ft. (4364m)
__W:__ Rudolf Klein-Rogge (*Haghi*), Gerda Maurus (*Sonia*), Lien Dyers, Willy Fritsch, Fritz Rasp, Paul Hoerbiger, Hertha von Walter, Craighall Sherry, Lupu Pick, Greta Berger
__P:__ Erich Pommer   __D:__ Fritz Lang   __SCR:__ Fritz Lang & Thea von Harbou   __PHOTOG:__ Fritz Arno Wagner   __SETS:__ Otto Hunte & Karl Vollbrecht
Classic thriller: Mastermind causes mayhem

The Spiral Staircase: ETHEL BARRYMORE AND DOROTHY MCGUIRE

The Spiral Staircase
1946, (USA), Dore Schary/Selznick/RKO, b&w, 83 mins.
__W:__ Dorothy McGuire (*Helen*), Ethel Barrymore (*Mrs. Warren*), George Brent (*Prof. Albert Warren*), Kent Smith (*Dr. Parry*), Rhonda Fleming (*Blanche*), Elsa Lanchester (*Mrs. Oates*), Rhys Williams (*Oates*), Gordon Oliver (*Stephen Warren*), Sara Allgood (*Nurse Barker*), James Bell (*The Constable*), Ellen Corby
__P:__ Dore Schary   __D:__ Robert Siodmak   __SCR:__ Mel Dinelli, from Ethel Lina White's

---

novel *Some Must Watch*   __PHOTOG:__ Nicholas Musuraca   __SPCL-FX:__ Vernon L. Walker   __MUSIC:__ Roy Webb
Classic thriller: Psychopath kills handicapped

The Spiral Staircase
1975, (GB), Raven/WB, color, 89 mins.
__W:__ Jacqueline Bisset (*Helen*), Mildred Dunnock (*Mrs. Sherman*), Christopher Plummer (*Dr. Sherman*), John Phillip Law (*Steven*), Gayle Hunnicutt (*Blanche*), Sam Wanamaker (*Lt. Fields*), Elaine Stritch (*The Nurse*), Sheila Brennan (*Mrs. Oates*), John Ronane (*Dr. Rawley*), Ronald Radd (*Oates*), Heather Lowe (*The Blind Girl*), Christopher Malcolm (*The Policeman*)
__P:__ Josef Shaftel & Peter Shaw   __D:__ Peter Collinson   __SCR:__ Allan Scott & Chris Bryant, from Ethel Lina White's novel *Some Must Watch*   __PHOTOG:__ Ken Hodges   __MUSIC:__ David Lindup
Minor thriller: Mute girl fears for her life when slayer of handicapped prowls

The Spirit
1987, (USA), ABC-TV, color, 69 mins.
__W:__ Sam Jones (*Denny Colt/"The Spirit"*), Nana Visitor (*Ellen Dolan*), Bumper Robinson (*Eubie*), Garry Walberg (*Commissioner Dolan*), McKinlay Robinson (*P'Gell*), Daniel Davis (*Simon Teasdale*), John Allen (*Bruno*), Les Lannom (*Officer Kling*)
__D:__ Michael Schultz   __TELEPLAY:__ Steven De Souza, from Will Eisner's 1940's comic-book character
TVM, standard comedy-thriller: Mystery man aids cause of Justice

Spiritism
1959, (Mex), Calderon/K. Gordon Murray, b&w, 85 mins.
__W:__ Joseph Louis Jiminez [Jose Luis Jiminez], Nora Veyran
loosely based on W.W. Jacob's short story "The Monkey's Paw"
Minor horror-thriller: Midnight seance leads to terror

Spiritisme Abracadabrant (Spiritual Abracadabra)
1900, (Fr), Star, b&w, 20m (65.6 ft./1.1 mins.)
__D:__ Georges Melies
USA retitle, Up-to-Date Spiritualism
Standard fantasy

The Spirit is Willing
1966, (USA), Para, color, 100 mins.
__W:__ Sid Caesar (*Helen*), Vera Miles, Barry Gordon, Cass Daley, John McGiver, Nestor Paiva, John Astin, Jay C. Flippen, Jesse White, Mary Wickes
__P & D:__ William Castle   __SCR:__ Ben Starr, from Nathaniel Benchley's novel *The Visitors*   __PHOTOG:__ Harold Stine   __MUSIC:__ Vic Mizzy
Minor comedy-fantasy: Female ghost seduces teenaged boy

Spirit Lost
1996, (USA), color, 95 mins.
__W:__ Leon, Regina Taylor (*Willy*), Cynda Williams (*Arabella*), Juanita Jennings (*Vera*)
Standard eroto-fantasy: Artist meets venal ghost

The Spirit of '76
1991, (USA), color, 85 mins.
__W:__ David Cassidy, Leif Garrett, Olivia d'Abo (*Chanel-6*) Geoff Hoyle, Jeff McDonald, Steve McDonald, Barbara Bain, Julie Brown, Tommy Chong, Iron Eyes Cody, Carl Reiner, Rob Reiner, Moon Zappa
__D:__ Lucas Reiner
Minor SF-adventure: Time travelers from future visit 1976 California

Spirit of the Dead
see The Asphyx

The Spirit of the Heath
1921, (GB), Zodiac, b&w, 1,000 ft. (304.8m)
__D:__ Fred Paul & Jack Raymond
Standard fantasy: Puck shows beauty of world to foolish young wife

Spirit of the Night
1991, (USA), color, 90 mins.
__W:__ Jenna Bodner, Michael Wiseman
Standard horror-thriller: Woman architect falls victim to family curse

The Spirit Portrait
see Le Portrait Spirite

Spirits
1914, (Den), b&w
__D:__ Forrest Holger Madsen
Standard fantasy

Spirits of the Dead
1969, (It-Fr), Les Films Marceau-P.E.A. Rome/Cocinor/AIP, color, 120 mins.
__W:__ Jane Fonda (*Countess Frederica*), Peter Fonda (*Baron Wilhelm*), Alain Delon (*Wilson*), Terence Stamp (*Toby Dammit*), Brigitte Bardot (*Giuseppina*), Carla Marlier (*Claude*), Francoise Prevost (*Frederica's Friend*), James Robertson Justice (*Frederica's Advisor*), Annie Duperey (*The First Guest*), Andreas Voutsinas (*The Second Guest*), Audoin de Bardot (*The Page*), Philippe Lemaire (*Philippe*), Serge Marquand (*Hugues*), Douking (*du Lissier*), Katia Cristina

(*The Young Girl*), Umberto D'Orsi (*Hans*), Daniele Vargas (*The Professor*), Renzo Palmer (*A Priest*), Salvo Randone (*A Priest*), Marina Yaru (*The Child*), Fabrizio Angeli (*The First Director*), Ernesto Colli (*The Second Director*), Anna Tonietti (*The TV Commentator*), Aleardo Ward (*The First Interviewer*), Paul Cooper (*The Second Interviewer*)
D: Roger Vadim; **PHOTOG:** Claude Renoir; **MUSIC:** Jean Prodromides), William Wilson (**D & SCR:** Louis Malle; **PHOTOG:** Tonino Delli Colli; **MUSIC:** Diego Masson), & *Never Bet the Devil Your Head* (**D:** Federico Fellini; **SCR:** Federico Fellini & Bernardino Zapponi; **PHOTOG:** Giuseppe Rotunno; **MUSIC:** Nino Rota
orig. to be titled **Extraordinary Stories**
Unusual fantasy-thriller, trio of Edgar Allan Poe tales: Metzengerstein

Spirit Summoning
see **Evocation Spirite**

Spiritual Abracadabra
see **Spiritisme Abracadabrant**

Spiritualism Exposed
1913, (GB), Motograph, b&w, 2,840 ft. (865.6m)
W: Louis Nikola (*The Chief*), Violet Stacey (*Norah*), Harry Gower (*Jules*), Douglas Payne (*Clipper Burke*), Luna Lindon (*The Palmist*), Nessie Blackford (*Mrs. Hearn*)
WRIT & D: Charles Raymond
USA retitle, **The Seer of Bond Street** *(Paul H. Cromelin/Motograph, 1914) A.k.a.* **Fraudulent Spiritualism Exposed**
Standard melodrama: Fake medium tries to con heiress

Spiritualism Exposed
1926, (GB), FHC Prods., b&w, 2,800 ft. (853.4m)
W: Arthur Prince (*The Doctor*), Yvonne Thomas (*Mrs. Cathcart*), Charles Ashton (*Mr. Cathcart*)
D & STORY: A.E. Coleby
A.k.a. **Fake Spiritualism Exposed**
Minor thriller: Obsessed woman cured by exposure of phony medium

The Spiritualist
see **The Amazing Mr. X**

A Spiritualistic Meeting
see **Le Fantome d'Alger**

A Spiritualistic Photographer
see **Le Portrait Spirite**

Splash
1984, (USA), Brian Grazer-Ron Howard/Touchstone/Buena Vista, color, 107 mins.
W: Tom Hanks (*Allen Bauer*), Daryl Hannah (*Madison*), John Candy (*Freddie Bauer*), Eugene Levy (*Walrer Kornbluth*), Dody Goodman (*Mrs. Stimler*), Shecky Greene (*Mr. Bayrite*), Howard Morris (*Dr. Zidell*), Richard B. Shull (*Dr. Rose*), Bobby Di Cicco (*Jerry*), Tony Di Benedetto (*Tim the Doorman*), Charles Macaulay, Patrick Cronin
D: Ron Howard   SCR: Lowell Ganz, Babaloo Mandel, & Bruce Jay Friedman
SCREEN STORY: Bruce Jay Friedman   PHOTOG: Don Peterman
MUSIC: Lee Holdridge   SONG: *Love Came for Me*, sung by Rita Coolidge
orig. to be titled **Wet**
Amusing fantasy: Mermaid and mortal fall in love

Splash, Too
1988, (USA), Made for TV, color, 95 mins.
W: Todd Waring, Amy Yasbeck, Donovan Scott (*Freddie*), Rita Taggart (*Fern*)
TVM, standard comedy-fantasy: Marital problems of man and his mermaid mate

Splatter
1983, (USA), Magic Shadows Distribution, color
W: Marilyn Burns (*Dorothy Grim*), Edwin Neal (*Splatter*)
D: Ronald Moore   SCR: Ronald Moore & John Best   SPCL-FX: Bob Burns
Standard SF-thriller: Future social conflict

Splatter University
1984, (USA), color, 79 mins.
W: Francine Forbes, Dick Biel, Cathy Lacommaro, Dan Eaton, Ric Randing
D: Richard W. haines   MUSIC: Chris Burke
Minor thriller: Asylum escapee slays coeds

The Splendid Coward
1918, (GB), Harma, b&w, 5,835 ft. (1776m)
W: James Knight (*Dick Swinton*), Joan Legge (*Dora Dundas*), Roy Travers (*Vivian Ormsby*), Wilifred Evans (*Lady Mary Swinton*), Sydney Lewis Ransome (*Trimmer*), Jeff Barlow (*Earl of Heresford*), Thomas Canning (*Col. Dundas*), Edward Arundell (*Jack Lorrimer*)
D: F. Martin Thornton, from a novel by Houghton Townley
Standard crime-thriller: Noblewoman's son takes blame for her forgery

The Split
see **The Manster**

Split Second
1953, (USA), Edmund Grainger/RKO, b&w, 85 mins.
W: Stephen McNally (*Sam Hurley*), Alexis Smith (*Kay Garven*), Richard Egan (*Dr. Garven*), Jan Sterling (*Dottie*), Arthur Hunnicutt (*Asa*), Keith Andes (*Larry Fleming*), Paul Kelly (*Bart Moore*), Robert Paige (*Arthur Ashton*), Frank de Kova (*Dummy*), Nestor Paiva
P: Edmund Grainger   D: Dick Powell   SCR: Edmund Grainger & William Bowers   PHOTOG: Nicholas Musuraca   MUSIC: Roy Webb
Standard thriller: Escaped convicts hold hostages in Nevada A-bomb test site

Split Second
1992, (USA), Muse/InterStar, color, 90 mins.
W: Rutger Hauer (*Harley Stone*), Kim Cattrall, Neil Duncan, Michael J. Pollard
P: Laura Gregory   D: Tony Maylam   SCR: Gary Scott Thompson   PHOTOG: Clive Tickner   SPCL-FX: Ace Effects Ltd.   MUSIC: Stephen Parsons & Francis Haines
Standard SF-thriller: Future cop hunts serial killer

Splitting Heirs
1993, (GB), color, 87 mins.
W: Eric Idle, Rick Moranis, Barbara Hershey, John Cleese, Catherine Zeta Jones, Sadie Frost, Stratford Johns, Eric Sykes, Brenda Bruce, William Franklyn
D: Robert Young   SCR: Eric Idle   PHOTOG: Tony Pierce-Roberts
Minor comedy-thriller: Heir plots rival's demise

Spontaneous Combustion
1990, (USA), color, 97 mins.
W: Brad Dourif, Cynthia Bain, Jon Cypher, William Prince, Dey Young, Melinda Dillon, Dale Dye, Dick Butkus, John Landis
D: Tobe Hooper   MUSIC: Graeme Revell
Minor SF-horror: Man's powers cause people to ignite

Spontaneous Creations
see **Creations Spontanees**

Spoof for Oof
1915, (GB), Martin/DFSA, b&w, 478 ft. (145.7m)
D: Edwin J. Collins
Standard fantasy: Hypnotized man dreams he is mesmerist

Spook Busters
1946, (USA) Mono/AA, b&w, 68 mins.
W: Leo Gorcey, Huntz Hall, Douglass Dumbrille, Vera Lewis, Gabriel Dell, Bobby Jordan, David Gorcey, Charles Middleton, Bernard Gorcey Billy Benedict, Tanis Chandler, Maurice Cass
P: Jan Grippo   D: William Beaudine   SCR: Edmond Seward & Tim Ryan
PHOTOG: Harry Neumann
Standard "Bowery Boys" comedy-thriller

Spook Chasers
1957, (USA), AA, b&w, 62 mins.
W: Huntz Hall, Stanley Clements, David Gorcey (*Condon*), William Henry, Darlene Fields, Jimmy Murphy, Robert Shayne, Ben Welden, Percy Helton, Eddie LeRoy, Robert Christopher, Peter Mamakos, Pierre Watkin
P: Ben Schwalb   D: George Blair   SCR: Elwood Ullman   PHOTOG: Harry Neumann
Standard "Bowery Boys" comedy-thriller

Spookies
1988, (USA), Twisted Souls Inc/Sefir/Sony., color, 85 mins.
W: Felix Ward (*Kreon*), Dan Scott (*Kreon's Servant*), Alec Nemser (*Billy*), Maria Pechukas (*Isabelle*), A.J. Lowenthal (*Korda*), Pat Wesley Bryan (*The Drifter*), Peter Dain (*Peter*), Nick Gionta (*Duke*), Lisa Friede (*Carol*), Charlotte Seely (*Adrienne*), Joan Ellen Delaney (*Linda*), Kim Merrill (*Meegan*), Peter Iasillo Jr. (*Rick*), Soo Paek (*The Spider Woman*), Anthony Valbiro, Gabriel Bartalos, John Beatty, Peter Delynn, Robert Epstein, Bill Adams, Paige M. Alexander, William Cam, Patrick Gilroy, William Kaplan, Zack Lazarus, Jon Meyers, David Ritch
D: Eugenie Joseph, Thomas Doran & Brendan Faulkner   SCR: Frank M. Farel, Thomas Doran & Brendan Faulkner   PHOTOG: Robert Chappel & Ken Kelsch   MUSIC: Kenneth Higgins & James Calabrese
Minor horror-fantasy: Sorcerer labors to raise dead

Spooks Run Wild
1941, (USA), Banner/Astor/Mon, b&w, 68 mins.
W: Bela Lugosi (*Nardo*), Leo Gorcey (*Muggs*), Huntz Hall (*Glimpy*), Bobby Jordan (*Danny*), Sunshine Sammy Morrison (*Scruno*), David O'Brien (*Jeff Dixon*), Dennis Moore (*Dr. Von Grosch*), Dorothy Short (*Linda Mason*), David Gorcey (*Peewee*), Donald Haines (*Skinny*), Angelo Rossitto (*Luigi*), P.J. Kelley (*Lem Harvey*), Guy Wilkerson (*The Constable*)
P: Sam Katzman   D: Phil Rosen   SCR: Charles R. Marion & Carl Foreman
PHOTOG: Marcel LePicard
Standard comedy-thriller: Dead End kids meet magician, escaped killer

The Spooky Movie Show
see **The Mask** *(1961)*

The Sporting Mice
1909, (GB), Armstrong/C&M, b&w, 300 ft. (91.5m)
D & STORY: Charles Armstrong
Standard fantasy: Acrobatic rodents cavort in silhouette

The Sport of Fate
1913, (GB), Cricks & Martin, b&w, 1,095 ft. (333.8m)
D: Edwin J. Collins
Standard crime-thriller: Farmer framed for killing miser, escapes jail

Sports in Moggyland
1912, (GB), Diamond Films/Cosmopolitan, b&w, 340 ft. (103.6m)
Standard fantasy: Wooden toys hold sports gala

Sports in Toyland
1914, (GB), Excel, b&w, 310 ft. (94.5m)
D: Stuart Kinder
Standard fantasy: Toys hold sports day

Spotlight on Murder
1961, (Fr), b&w, 95 mins.
W: Pierre Brasseur, Jean-Louis Trintignant
D: Georges Franju   **PHOTOG:** Marcel Fradetal   **MUSIC:** Maurice Jarre
Standard thriller

The Spring
1989, (USA), color, 110 mins.
W: Dack Rambo, Gedde Watanabe, Shari Shattuck, Steven Keats
D: John D. Patterson
Standard thriller: Archeologists seek Fountain of Youth

Sputnik
see A Dog, a Mouse and a Sputnik

The Spy
1909, (GB), Hepworth, b&w, 350 ft. (106.7m)
D: Lewin Fitzhamon
Standard crime-thriller: Spy drugs soldier, steals plans

The Spy
1914, (GB), Searchlight, b&w, 985 ft. (300.2m)
Standard thriller: Woman tends wounded spy, lets him go after learning he killed her son

Spy Chasers
1955, (USA), AA, b&w, 61 mins.
W: Leo Gorcey, Bernard Gorcey, Leon Askin, Sig Rumann, Lisa Davis, Veola Vonn, David Condon [Gorcey], Bennie Bartlett, Richard Benedict, Frank Richards, Linda Bennett
D: Edward Bernds   **SCR:** Bert Lawrence & Jerome S. Gottler   **MUSIC:** Marlin Skiles
Standard "Bowery Boys" comedy-thriller

Spy for Germany
1956, (W. Ger), WB-TV, b&w, 109 mins.
W: Martin Held, Nadja Tiller
Minor thriller: Nazi spy seeks American A-bomb secrets

Spy Hunt
1950, (USA), Univ, b&w, 74 mins.
W: Howard Duff (*Roger*), Marta Toren (*Catherine*), Walter Slezak (*Stahl*), Robert Douglas (*Paradou*), Philip Friend (*Chris*), Kurt Kreuger, Aram Katcher, Philip Dorn
D: George Sherman   **SCR:** George Zuckerman & Leonard Lee, from Victor Canning's novel *Panther's Moon*   **PHOTOG:** Irving Glassberg   **SPCL-FX:** David Horsley   **MUSIC:** Joseph Hershenson
*GB retitle, **Panther's Moon***
Standard thriller: Spies seek microfilm hidden in collar of vicious black panther

The Spy I Love
1964, (Fr), 4 Star-TV, color, 111 mins.
W: Virna Lisi, Jacques Balutin, Dominique Paturel
Standard thriller: Beauty aids secret agents in search for stolen atomic device

The Spy in Black
1939, (GB), Harefield/Alexander Korda/Col, b&w, 82 mins.
W: Conrad Veidt (*Capt. Ernst Hardt*), Valerie Hobson (*Jill Blacklock*), Sebastian Shaw (*Cdr. David Blacklock*), Marius Goring (*Lt. Schuster*), June Duprez (*Anne Burnett*), Athole Stewart (*Rev. Hector Matthews*), Agnes Lauchlan (*Mrs. Matthews*), Helen Haye (*Mrs. Sedley*), Cyril Raymond (*Rev. John Harris*), Hay Petrie (*James*), Grant Sutherland (*Bob Bratt*), Robert Rendel (*The Admiral*), Mary Morris (*Edwards*), Torin Thatcher (*The Officer*), Skelton Knaggs (*The Sailor*)
D: Michael Powell   **SCR:** Emeric Pressburger & Roland Pertwee, from a novel by J. Storer Clouston   **MUSIC:** Miklos Rozsa
*USA retitle, **U-Boat 29**, reissued 1944*
Standard thriller: Female spy poses as schoolmistress

The Spy in the Green Hat
1967, (USA), MGM, color, 92 mins.
W: Robert Vaughn (*Napoleon Solo*), David McCallum, Letitia Roman, Jack Palance, Elisha Cook Jr., Janet Leigh, Leo G. Carroll, Maxie Rosenbloom, Allen Jenkins, Joan Blondell, Jack LaRue, Eduardo Ciannelli
P: Boris Ingster   **D:** Joseph Sargent   **SCR:** Peter Allan Fields
Standard adventure-thriller (culled from episodes of teleseries "The Man from U.N.C.L.E."): Villain plans to divert Gulf Stream

Spy in the Sky
1958, (USA), AA, b&w, 74 mins.
W: Steve Brodie, Sandra Francis, Bob De Lange, George Coulouris, Andrea Domburg, Hans Tiemeyer, Herbert Curiel, Doty Oorthuis
WRIT, P & D: Myles Wilder, from A.S. Fleischman's novel *Counterspy Express*   **PHOTOG:** Jim Harvey   **MUSIC:** Hugo de Groot
*orig. co-billed with **Frankenstein—1970***
Minor thriller: Runaway Soviet scientist has code for deciphering Sputnik signals

The Spy in White
see The Secret of Stamboul

Spy in Your Eye
see Berlino Appuntamento per le Spie

The Spy is a Girl
1959, (Fr), Henri Decoin, b&w

Spy Today, Die Tomorrow: LEX BARKER AND BRAD HARRIS

W: Francoise Arnoul, Horst Frank, Francois Guerin, Jacques Fabri, Harold Kay
D: Eugene Tucherer   **SCR:** Jacques Remy
Minor thriller

Spymaker
*see **The Secret Life of Ian Fleming***

The Spy Ring
1938, (USA), Univ, b&w, 56 mins.
W: Jane Wyman
D: Joseph H. Lewis
A.k.a. ***International Spy***
Minor thriller

Spy Smasher Returns
1966, (USA), Rep, b&w, 100 mins.
W: Kane Richmond (*Jack Armstrong/Alan "Spy Smasher" Armstrong*), Sam Flint (*Adm. Corby*), Marguerite Chapman (*Eve Corby*), Hans Schumm ("*The Mask*"), Tristram Coffin (*Drake*), Frank (Franco) Corsaro (*Durand*), Hans von Morhart (*Capt. Gerhardt*), Richard Bond (*Hayes*), George Renavent (*The Governor*), Paul Bryar (*Lawlor*), Robert O. Davis [Rudolph Anders] (*Col. Von Kohr*), Tom London (*Crane*), Henry Zynda (*Lazar*), Crane Whitley (*Dr. Hauser*)
D: William Witney   **SCR:** Ronald Davidson, Norman S. Hall, Joseph Poland, William Lively & Joseph O'Donnell   **SPCL-FX:** Howard Lydecker
MUSIC: Mort Glickman
Standard thriller (feature version of 1942 serial 'The Spy Smasher'): Super-hero fights enemy agents

Spy Squad
*see **Capture That Capsule!***

Spy Story
1976, (GB), color, 102 mins.
W: Michael Petrovitch, Philip Latham, Don Fellows, Michael Gwynne, Nicholas Parsons, Tessa Wyatt, Derren Nesbitt
D: Lindsay Shonteff, from a novel by Len Deighton
Minor thriller: Power-mongering in world of espionage

The Spy Strikes Silently
1965, (It), color
W: Lang Jeffries, Emma Danieli
Minor thriller: Scotland Yard agent pobes deaths of scientist and his daughter

Spy Today, Die Tomorrow
1967, (W. Ger), ITC, color, 93 mins.
W: Lex Barker, Eddi Arent, Brad Harris
Minor thriller

The Spy Who Came in from the Cold
1965, (GB), Salem/Para, b&w, 112 mins.
W: Richard Burton (*Alec Leamas*), Claire Bloom (*Nan Perry*), Oskar Werner (*Fiedler*), Sam Wanamaker (*Peters*), Peter Van Eyck (*Hans-Dieter Mundt*), George Voskovec (*The Defense Attorney*), Rupert Davies (*Smiley*), Cyril Cusack (*Control*), Michael Hordern (*Ashe*), Robert Hardy (*Carlton*), Bernard Lee (*Patmore*), Beatrix Lehmann (*The President*), Esmond Knight (*The Judge*), Niall MacGinnis (*The Guard*), Warren Mitchell (*Zanfrello*), Kathy Keeton (*The Stripper*)
P & D: Martin Ritt   **SCR:** Paul Dehn & Guy Trosper, from John Le Carre's novel
PHOTOG: Oswald Morris   **MUSIC:** Sol Kaplan
Superior thriller: British spy seeks enemy agent in East Germany

The Spy Who Loved Me
1976, (GB), Eon/UA, color, 120 mins.
W: Roger Moore (*James Bond*), Barbara Bach (*Anya Amasova*), Curt Jurgens (*Stromberg*), Richard Kiel ("*Jaws*"), Caroline Munro (*Naomi*), Walter Gotell (*Maj. Gogol*), Lois Maxwell (*Miss Moneypenny*), Bernard Lee ("*M*"), Milton Reid (*Shandor*), Desmond Llewelyn ("*Q*"), Geoffrey Keen (*The Minister*), Sydney Tafler (*The Captain*), Edward De Souza (*Sheik Hosein*), George Baker (*Capt. Benson*), Vernon Dobtcheff (*Max Kalba*), Michael Billington (*Sergei*), Olga Bisera (*Felicca*), Valerie Leon (*The Receptionist*), Eve Rueber-Staier (*Rublevitch*), Cyril Shaps (*Bechmann*), Robert Brown (*Adm. Hargreaves*), Anika Pavel, Shane Rimmer, Bryan Marshall, Bob Sherman, Sue Vanner, Nadim Sawalha
P: Albert R. Broccoli   **D:** Lewis Gilbert   **SCR:** Christopher Wood & Richard Maibaum, from Ian Fleming's *James Bond* novel   **PHOTOG:** Claude Renoir
SPCL-FX: Derek Meddings   **MUSIC:** Marvin Hamlisch   **SONG:** (sung by Carly Simon), *Nobody Does It Better*
Superior thriller: Secret agent opposes wealthy terrorist

The Spy with a Cold Nose
1966, (GB), Assoc. London-Embassy/Para, color, 93 mins.
W: Laurence Harvey (*Francis Trevellyan*), Lionel Jeffries (*Stanley Farquhar*), Daliah Lavi (*Princess Natasha Romanova*), Eric Sykes (*Wrigley*), Eric Portman (*The Ambassador*), Denholm Elliott (*Pond-Jones*), Colin Blakely (*The Russian Prime Minister*), Robert Flemyng (*Director M15*), Paul Ford (*The General*), June Whitfield (*Elsie Farquhar*), Bernard Archard (*The Russian Chief*), Robin Bailey (*The Man*), Nai Bonet (*The Bellydancer*), RSM Ronald Brittain (*The Commissionaire*), Julian Orchard, Bernard Lee

P: Leonard Lightstone   **D:** Daniel Petrie   **SCR:** Ray Galton & Alan Simpson
PHOTOG: Kenneth Higgins   **MUSIC:** Riz Ortolani
Standard spy-farce: Electronically-bugged pooch is gift to Soviet Prime Minister

The Spy Within
1994, (USA), color, 90 mins.
W: Theresa Russell, Scott Glenn, Lane Smith (*Stephen*), Joe Pantoliano (*Brezner*), Terence Knox (*J.B.*), Katherine Helmond (*Dr. Schilling*), Alex Rocco (*The Bartender*)
Standard thriller: Fugitive woman agent becomes involved with jaded explosives expert

The Spy with My Face
1966, (USA), MGM, color, 86 mins.
W: Robert Vaughn (*Napoleon Solo*), David McCallum, Senta Berger, Jan Arvan, Nancy Hsueh
D: John Newland   **SCR:** Clyde Ware & Joseph Cavelli
*Standard thriller (expanded 1964 episode from teleseries **The Man from U.N.C.L.E.**): Spies abduct secret agent, replace him with double*

The Square Mile Murder
1961, (GB), Merton Park/Anglo-Amalgamated, b&w, 28 mins.
W: John Welsh (*Supt. Hicks*), Stanley Morgan (*Possner*), Delphi Lawrence (*Sylvia Possner*)
P: Jack Greenwood   **D:** Allan Davis   **STORY:** James Eastwood, from a novel by Edgar Lustgarten
Standard short crime-thriller: Woman safecracker pursued

The Squeaker
1930, (GB), British Lion, b&w, 90 mins.
W: Percy Marmont (*Capt. Leslie*), Anne Grey (*Beryl Stedman*), Gordon Harker (*Bill Annerley*), Trilby Clark (*Millie Trent*), Alfred Drayton (*Lew Friedman*), W. Cronin Wilson (*The Inspector*), Eric Maturin (*Frank Sutton*), Nigel Bruce (*Collie*)
D & SCR: Edgar Wallace, from his play
Standard thriller: Detective poses as ex-convict, exposes master criminal

The Spy Who Loved Me: BARBARA BACH

The Squeaker
1937, (GB), London/UA, b&w, 77 mins.
W: Edmund Lowe (*Insp. Barrabal*), Ann Todd (*Carol Stedman*), Sebastian Shaw (*Frank Sutton*), Tamara Desni (*Tamara*), Robert Newton (*Larry Graeme*), Allan Jeayes (*Insp. Elford*), Alastair Sim (*Joshua Collie*), Gordon McLeod

S

(*Field*), Mabel Terry-Lewis (*Mrs. Stedman*), Stewart Rome (*Supt. Marshall*)
D: William K. Howard **SCR:** Edward O. Berkman & Bryan Wallace, from a play by Edgar Wallace **PHOTOG:** Georges Perinal
USA retitle, **Murder on Diamond Row** *reissued 1943*
Standard thriller: Detective unmasks fence

The Squeaker
1965, (W. Ger), Gold Key, b&w, 95 mins.
W: Heinz Drache, Barbara Rueting
D: Alfred Vohrer, from a play by Edgar Wallace
Minor thriller: Scotland Yard hunts robber-murderer who dispatches victims with snake venom

The Squeeze
1977, (GB), Martinat/WB, color, 107 mins.
W: Stacy Keach (*Jim Naboth*), David Hemmings (*Keith*), Edward Fox (*Foreman*), Stephen Boyd (*Vic*), Carol White (*Jill*), Freddie Starr (*Teddy*), Hilary Gasson (*Barbara*), Stewart Harwood (*Des*), Rod Beacham (*Dr. Jenkins*), Alison Portes (*Christine*), Alan Ford (*Taff*), Lucinda Duckett (*Sharon*), Leon Greene (*The Commissionaire*), Maureen Sweeney (*The Receptionist*), Lionel Ngakane (*The West Indian*)
P: Stanley O'Toole **D:** Michael Apted **SCR:** Leon Griffiths, from a novel by David Craig **PHOTOG:** Dennis Lewiston **MUSIC:** David Hentschel
Standard crime-thriller: Fired police inspector seeks kidnapped ex-wife and daughter

Squirm
1976, (USA), Edgar Lansbury-Joseph Beruh/AIP, color, 92 mins.
W: Don Scardino (*Mick*), Fran Higgins (*Alma*), Jean Sullivan (*Naomi*), Patricia Pearcy (*Geri*), R.A. Dow (*Rogers*), Peter MacLean (*The Sheriff*), William Newman (*Quigley*), Barbara Quinn (*The Sheriff's Girl*), Carl Dagenhart (*Willie*), Kim Iocouvozzi (*Hank*), Angel Sande (*Millie*), Carol Jean Owens (*Bonnie*), Walter Dimmick (*Danny*), Julia Klopp (*Mrs. Klopp*)
P: George Manasse **WRIT & D:** Jeff Leiberman **PHOTOG:** Joseph Mangine **MUSIC:** Robert Prince
Minor SF-thriller: Worms terrorize Georgia community

Sredni Vashtar
1981, (GB), Laurentic/Fox, color, 27 mins.
W: Alexander Puttnam (*Conradin*), Judy Campbell (*Aunt Augusta*), Lila Kaye (*Mrs. Woolridge*), Patty Hancock (*Effie*), Gordon Kaye (*Ogden*),Vernon Dobtcheff (*Dr. Russell*), Alan Corduna (*Mortimer*), Shona Morris (*Vera*)
P: Harvey Bernard **D & SCR:** Andrew Birkin **STORY:** Saki **PHOTOG:** Peter Hannan **MUSIC:** Carl Orff
Standard short fantasy: Persecuted boy invokes supernatural to kill his guardian aunt

Sssssss
1973, (USA), Zanuck Brown/Univ, color, 99 mins.
W: Strother Martin (*Dr. Carl Stoner*), Dirk Benedict (*David Blake*), Heather Menzies (*Kristina Stoner*), Richard B. Shull (*Dr. Ken Daniels*), Tim O'Connor (*Kagen*), Reb Brown (*Steve Randall*), Jack Ging (*Sheriff Hardisson*), Ted Grossman (*The Deputy*), Kathleen King (*Kitty*), Charles Seel (*The Old Man*), Ray Ballard (*The Waggish Tourist*), Brendan Burns (*Jock #1*), Rick Beckner (*Jock #2*), James Drum (*Hawker #1*), Ed McReady (*Hawker #2*), Frank Kowalski (*Hawker #3*), Ralph Montgomery (*Hawker #4*), Michael Masters (*Hawker #5*), Charlie Fox (*Arvin*), Felix Silla (*The Seal Boy*), Nobel Craig (*Tim, the "Snake Man"*), Bobbi Kiger (*The Kootch Dancer*), J.R. Clark (*The Station Attendant*), Chip Potter (*The Postal Clerk*)
D: Bernard L. Kowalski **SCR:** Hal Dresner **PHOTOG:** Gerald Perry Finnerman **MUSIC:** Pat Williams
A.k.a. Sssssnake
Entertaining SF-fantasy: Experiments turns humans into reptiles

S.T.A.B.
1975, (Thai), color, 91 mins.
W: Greg Morris, Sombat Metanee, Krung Srivilai, Tham Thuy Hang
D: Chalong Pakdivijt
Minor thriller: Bounty hunter seeks skyjacked gold

Stage Fright
1950, (GB), WB, b&w, 110 mins.
W: Jane Wyman (*Eve Gill*), Richard Todd (*Jonathan Cooper*), Michael Wilding (*Smith*), Marlene Dietrich (*Charlotte Inwood*), Kay Walsh (*Nellie*), Alastair Sim (*Commodore Gill*), Sybil Thorndike (*Mrs. Gill*), Miles Malleson (*The Bibulous Gent*), Joyce Grenfell (*The Shooting Gallery Attendant*), Pat Hitchcock (*Chubby*), Hector MacGregor (*Freddie*), Andre Morell (*Insp. Byard*)
P & D: Alfred Hitchcock **SCR:** Whitfield Cook, from Selwyn Jepson's novel Man Running **PHOTOG:** Wilkie Cooper **MUSIC:** Leighton Lucas **SONG:** *The Laziest Gal in Town*
Unusual thriller: Young woman aids drama student accused of murder

Stage Fright
1983, (USA), color, 82 mins.
W: Jenny Neumann, Gary Sweet
Minor thriller: Actress becomes homicidal

Stagefright
1987, (USA), color, 95 mins.
W: David Brandon, Barbara Cupisti, Robert Gligorov

D: Michele Soavi
Minor thriller: Serial killer joins cast of play

Stairway to Heaven
see A Matter of Life and Death

Stalker
1979, (Russ), Mosfilm, color & b&w, 160 mins.
D: Andrei Tarkovsky
Superior SF: Adventure in future

Stalking Laura
1993, (USA), Leonard Hill/ACI, color, 93 mins.
W: Brooke Shields, Richard Thomas, Viveka Davis, Scott Bryce, William Allen Young, Richard Yniguez, Linda Edmond, T. Max Graham (*Capt. Olson*), Kevin Brief (*Lt. Mark Shagan*), Tim Snay (*SWAT Lt. Bannister*), Dick Mueller (*Tom Black*), Ben Stephenson (*Mike Pratt*), Donna Thomason (*Glenda Moritz*), Mark McCarthy (*Wayne Williams*), Dean Vivian (*Gary Fromm*), Caroline Vinciguerra (*Sarah Black*), Merle Moores (*Donna Black*), Carmen Rupe (*Helen Lamparter*), Hollis McCarthy (*Phyllis*), Barbara Houston (*Nancy Hammond*), John Durbin (*Lawrence Kane*), Connie Ventress (*Mary Bird*), C. Andrew Garrison (*The Process Server*), Ken Boehr (*Brad Jansen*), Annette John (*Dr. Peggy Knudsen*), Buck Baker (*Aviala*), David Snell (*Mark Blauvelt*), Jeff Hopkins (*Greg Scott*)
D: Michael Switzer **TELEPLAY:** Frank Abatemarco **PHOTOG:** Rob Draper **MUSIC:** Sylvester Levay
TVM, standard fact-based thriller: Co-worker stalks career woman

The Stand
1994, (USA), Laurel/ABC-TV, color, approx. 360 mins.
W: Gary Sinise (*Stu Redman*), Robe Lowe (*Nick Andros*), Molly Ringwald (*Fran Goldsmith*), Jamey Sheridan (*Randall Flagg*), Laura San Giacomo (*Nadine*), Adam Storke (*Larry*), Ruby Dee (*Mother Abigail*), Matt Frewer (*Trashcan Man*), Ray Walston (*Glen Bateman*), Bill Fagerbakke (*Tom Cullen*), Ossie Davis (*Judge Farris*), Rick Aviles (*Rat Man*), Peter Van Norden (*Ralph*), Miguel Ferrer (*Lloyd*), Mike Westenskow (*Paul Bulson*), Stephen King (*Teddy Weizak*), Corin Nemec, Max Wright, Ed Harris, Kathy Bates, John Bloom, Kevin Doyle, Bridgit Ryan, Shawnee Smith, Jeff Gelb, Kellie Overbey, Sam Anderson, Ken Jenkins, Warren Frost
D: Mick Garris **TELEPLAY:** Stephen King, from his novel **PHOTOG:** Edward Pei **MUSIC:** W.G. Snuffy Walden
4-part TVM, standard SF-fantasy: Virus decimates Earth's human population, satanic demagogue arises

Stanley
1972, (USA), Crown Int'l, color, 103 mins.
W: Chris Robinson (*Tim*), Alex Rocco (*Thomkins*), Susan Carroll (*Susie*), Steve Alaimo (*Crail*), Mark Harris (*Bob*), Rey Baumel (*Sidney*), Paul Avery (*Psycho*), Gary Crutcher (*Dr. Everett*), Marcie Knight (*Gloria*), Mel Pape (*The Guard*), Butterball Smith (*The Stage Manager*), Pamela Talus (*The Girl Friend*), Bill Marquez (*Wachula*), Charles Kaufman
P & D: William Grefe **SCR:** Gary Crutcher, from an orig. story by William Grefe **PHOTOG:** Cliff Poland **SONGS:** *Sparrow & Start a New World*
Minor thriller: Man commits murders with pet snakes

Stanley

S

Stanley's Dragon
1995, (USA), color, 92 mins.
<u>W:</u> Judd Trichter, Mia Fothergill
Standard juvenile fantasy: College student and journalist friend protect dragon hatchling

The Star and Crescent
1913, (GB), Searchlight Films/Phoenix, b&w, 1,700 ft. (518.2m)
Standard crime-thriller: Solicitor's typist tries to kill heir

Starchaser: The Legend of Orin
1985, (USA), color, 107 mins.
<u>D:</u> Steven Hahn   <u>MUSIC:</u> Andrew Belling
Standard animated SF-fantasy: Boy saves world from evil hordes

Star Child
see Space Raiders

Star Command
1996, (USA), UPN-TV, color, 95 mins.
<u>W:</u> Chad Everett (*Cdr. Shade Ridnaur*), Morgan Fairchild (*Cdr. Ivorstetter*), Jay Underwood (*Ken Oort*), Jennifer Bransford (*Ali McGinty*), Chris Conrad (*Tully Vallis*), Tembi Locke (*Meg Dundee*), Ivan Sergei, Kelly Hu
<u>D:</u> Jim Johnston   <u>TELEPLAY:</u> Melinda M. Snodgrass   <u>MUSIC:</u> Lee Holdridge
TVM, standard SF-adventure: Cadets face warring colonists on distant planet

Star Crash
1979, (It), New World, color, 92 mins.
<u>W:</u> Marjoe Gortner (*Akton*), Caroline Munro (*Stella*), David Hasselhoff (*Simon*), Robert Tessier (*Thor*), Joe Spinell (*Count Zarth Arn*), Christopher Plummer (*The Emperor*), Judd Hamilton (*Elle*), Nadia Cassini (*Queen of the Amazon*), Hamilton Camp (*Voice of Elle*)
<u>D:</u> Lewis Coates [Luigi Cozzi]   <u>SCR:</u> Lewis Coates & Nat Wachsberger   <u>PHOTOG:</u> Paul Beeson & Roberto D'Ettorre   <u>MUSIC:</u> John Barry, title sung by Cher Winz
A.k.a. Stella Star
Minor SF-adventure: Space pilot saves galaxy from evil fiend

Starcrossed
1985, (USA), Fries Entertainment/ABC-TV, color, 95 mins.
<u>W:</u> James Spader (*Joey Callan*), Belinda Bauer (*Mary*), Pete Kowanko (*Stewy*), Jacqueline Brookes (*Prof. Hobbs*), Clark Johnson (*Ralph*), Chuck Shamata (*The Chairman*), Fred Lee (*The Waiter*), Ed Groenenberg (*Alien #1*), Roland Groenenberg (*Alien #2*), James Kidnie (*The Federal Agent*), Andy Maton (*Frankie*), Barbara Barnes (*The Waitress*)
<u>WRIT & D:</u> Jeffrey Bloom   <u>PHOTOG:</u> Gil Hubbs   <u>SPCL-FX SPRVSR:</u> Louis Craig   <u>MUSIC:</u> Gil Melle   <u>SONGS:</u> I'm Restless & Out on the Run
TVM, standard SF-romance: Space-alien girl aided by Earth boy in her flight from sinister agents

Star Crystal
1985, (USA), Balcor Film Investors/New World, color, 93 mins.
<u>W:</u> C. Jutson Campbell (*Roger*), Faye Bolt (*Adrian*), John W. Smith, Taylor Kingsley, Macia Linn, Lance Bruckner, Eric Moseng, Thomas William, Don Kingsley, Robert Allen, Emily Longstreth, Lisa Goulian, Charles Linza, Frank Alexander
<u>P:</u> Eric Woster   <u>D & SCR:</u> Lance Lindsay   <u>STORY:</u> Lance Lindsay & Eric Woster   <u>SPCL VS-FX:</u> Lewis Abernathy   <u>MUSIC:</u> Doug Katsaros
Minor SF-thriller: Astronauts find dangerous alien

The Starfish
1952, (GB), Mount Pleasant/JPD, b&w, 38 mins.
<u>W:</u> Kenneth Griffith (*Jack Trevennick*), Nigel Finzi (*Tim Wilson*), Susan Schlesinger (*Jill*), Ursula Wood (*Mrs. Wilson*), Margaret Webber (*Witch Meg*), Christopher Finzi (*Michael*)
<u>WRIT, P & D:</u> Alan Cooke & John Schlesinger
Standard short fantasy: Cornish fisherman helps children rescue child from witch

Starflight One
see Starflight: The Plane That Couldn't Land

Starflight: The Plane That Couldn't Land
1983, (USA), Orion/Filmways/ABC-TV, color, 114 mins.
<u>W:</u> Lee Majors (*Cody Briggs*), Hal Linden (*Josh Gilliam*), Lauren Hutton (*Erika Hansen*), Robert Webber (*Felix Duncan*), Ray Milland (*Q.T. Thornwell*), Tess Harper (*Janet Briggs*), Gail Strickland (*Nancy Gilliam*), Pat Corley (*Joe Pedowski*), George DiCenzo (*Bowdish*), Terry Kiser, Heather McAdam, Michael Sacks, Gary Bayer Jocelyn Brando, Robert Englund, Kirk Cameron
<u>D:</u> Jerry Jameson   <u>TELEPLAY:</u> Robert Malcolm Young   <u>STORY:</u> Peter R. Brooke & Gene Warren   <u>PHOTOG:</u> Hector Figueroa   <u>SPCL-FX:</u> John Dykstra   <u>MUSIC:</u> Lalo Schifrin
A.k.a. Starflight One
TVM, standard thriller: Hypersonic passenger plane forced into orbit

Stargate
1994, (USA-Ger), Centropolis/MGM, color, 119 mins.
<u>W:</u> Kurt Russell (*Col. Jonathan "Jack" O'Neil*), James Spader (*Dr. Daniel Jackson*), Viveca Lindfors (*Catherine*), Jaye Davidson (*Ra*), Alexis Cruz, Leon Rippy, Mili Avital, Gianin Loffler, John Diehl, Carlos Lauchu, Djimon, French

Stewart, Erick Avari, Christopher John Fields, Derek Webster, Jack Moore, Steve Giannelli, David Pressman, Scott Smith, Cecil Hoffman, Rae Allen, Richard Kind, John Storey, Kelly Vint, Lee Taylor-Allan, Erik Holland, George Gray, Nick Wilder, Sayed Badreya, Michael Concepcion, Jerry Gilmore, Kenneth Danziger, Michel Jean-Phillipe, Dialy N'Daiye, Roger Til, Gladys Holland, Christopher West, Robert Ackerman, Kieron Lee, Frank Welker
<u>D:</u> Roland Emmerich   <u>WRIT:</u> Dean Devlin & Roland Emmerich   <u>PHOTOG:</u> Karl Walter Lindenlaub   <u>DIGITAL & VS-FX SPRVSR:</u> Jeffrey A. Okun   <u>MUSIC:</u> David Arnold
Standard SF-adventure: Portal to far side of universe discovered in Egypt

The Star Globe–Trotter
1908, (GB), Urban Trading Co., b&w, 320 ft. (97.8m)
<u>D:</u> W.R. Booth
Standard fantasy: Hypnotized gymnast circumvents Earth

Star Hunter
1998, (USA), color, 85 mins.
<u>W:</u> Roddy McDowall, Stella Stevens
Standard SF-thriller: Convicts flee space prison

Stark Fear
1963, (USA), B.H.S./Ellis Films, b&w, 86 mins.
<u>W:</u> Beverly Garland, Skip Homeier, Kenneth Tobey
<u>P:</u> Joe E. Burke, Ned Hockman, & Dwight V. Swain   <u>D:</u> Ned Hockman   <u>SCR:</u> Dwight V. Swain
Minor melodrama: Woman flees sadistic husband

Star Kid
1998, (USA), Trimark, color
<u>W:</u> Joseph Mazzello, Richard Gilliland
<u>D:</u> Manny Coto
Standard juvenile SF-adventure

Star Knight
see The Knight of the Dragon

Starlight Slaughter
see Eaten Alive! (1976)

Starman
1984, (USA), Michael Douglas-Larry J. Franco/Col, color, 115 mins.
<u>W:</u> Jeff Bridges (*The Starman*), Karen Allen (*Jenny Hayden*), Charles Martin Smith (*Mark Shermin*), Lu Leonard (*The Waitress*), Richard Jaeckel (*George Fox*), Tony Edwards
<u>D:</u> John Carpenter   <u>SCR:</u> Bruce A. Evans & Raynold Gideon   <u>PHOTOG:</u> Donald M. Morgan   <u>MUSIC:</u> Jack Nitzsche
Superior SF-romance: Extraterrestrial visitor takes form of woman's deceased husband

Star of India
1956, (GB), Raymond Stross/Eros/UA color, 84 mins.
<u>W:</u> Cornel Wilde (*Pierre St. Laurent*), Jean Wallace (*Katrina*), Herbert Lom (*Vicomte de Narbonne*), Yvonne Sanson (*Mme. de Montespan*), Basil Sydney (*Louis XIV*), Walter Rilla (*Van Horst*), John Slater (*Emile*), Leslie Linder (*Moulai*), Arnold Bell (*The Captain*)
<u>D:</u> Arthur Lubin   <u>SCR:</u> Seton I. Miller & C. Denis Freeman   <u>STORY:</u> Herbert Dalmas
Standard adventure-thriller: 17th-century nobleman helps Dutch widow recover stolen gem

Star Pilot
1966, (It), Monarch, color, 95 mins.
<u>W:</u> Kirk Morris, Leonora Ruffo, Gordon Mitchell
Minor space-opera: Earthlings captured by space-aliens

Star Portal
1998, (USA), color, 80 mins.
<u>W:</u> Athena Massey, Steven Bauer
Made-for-Video, standard SF-thriller (loose remake of Not of This Earth): Space-alien female takes human form

Star Quest
1989, (USA), color, 90 mins.
<u>W:</u> Tracy Davis, Jane Bachman, Michael Mack
<u>D:</u> Phillip Cook
A.k.a. Beyond the Rising Moon and Space 2074
Minor SF-thriller (Blade Runner imitation): Genetically-engineered woman seeks freedom

Star Quest
1994, (USA), color, 95 mins.
<u>W:</u> Steven Bauer, Emma Samms, Alan Rachins, Brenda Bakke, Ming-Na Wen, Gregory McKinney, Cliff DeYoung
<u>D:</u> Rick Jacobson
Standard SF-thriller: Astronauts find human race destroyed by nuclear holocaust

Starship
1987, (GB), color, 91 mins.
<u>W:</u> John Tarrant, Cassandra Webb, Donough Rees, Deep Roy, Ralph Cotterill
<u>D:</u> Roger Christian

*A.k.a. **Lorca and the Outlaws***
Minor SF-thriller: Human slaves on robot-controlled planet

Starship Invasions
1977, (Can), Hal Roach/WB, color, 89 mins.
<u>W</u>: Robert Vaughn (*Prof. Duncan*), Daniel Pilon (*Anaxi*), Tiiu Leek (*Phi*), Christopher Lee (*Capt. Rameses*), Helen Shaver (*Betty*), Henry Ramer (*Malcolm*), Ted Turner (*Zbender*), Kate Parr (*Diane*), Victoria Johnson (*Gezeth*), Sherri Ross (*Sagnac*), Doreen Lipson (*Dorothy*), Linda Rennhofer (*Joan*), Bob Warner (*The Air Force General*), Richard Fitzpatrick (*Job*), Sean McCann (*Carl*), Jonathan Welsh (*The Missile Officer*), Kurt Schiegl (*Rudi*), George Raymond, Harry Russell, Errol J. Ramsay, Kenneth Gordon, Catherine Marielle, Alan Rosenthal, Barb Richardson, Shirley Solomon, Arta Abele, Daubin Burke, Jack Anthony, Al Bernardo, Eric Braslis, Holly Dale, Alan Bridle, Paul Campbell, Jan Chamberlain, Chris Gillet, Terence Durant, Rob Garrison, Arno Gotthardt, Steven Klys, Laurie Haines, Dan Hennessey, Dave Musgrave, Robert O'Ree, Raymond O'Neill, Daniel Sampson, J. Roger Periard, Valeria Warburton, Gordon Thomason, Emily Wilkes, Donald Young, Ed Wiltshear, Janis Youngren
<u>WRIT & D</u>: Ed Hunt <u>PHOTOG</u>: Mark Irwin <u>SPCL-FX</u>: Dennis Pike <u>MUSIC</u>: Gil Melle
Minor SF-thriller: Aliens from dying world try to conquer Earth, induce mass suicide

Starship Troopers
1997, (USA), Sony/TriStar, color, 129 mins.
<u>W</u>: Casper Van Dien Neil Patrick Harris, Dina Meyer, Michael Ironside, Patrick Muldoon, Denise Richards
<u>D</u>: Paul Verhoeven <u>MUSIC</u>: Basil Poledouris
Big-budget ($100 million) space-opera: Giant alien insects attack Earth

Star Slammer
1987, (USA), color, 85 mins.
<u>W</u>: Ross Hagen, John Carradine, Sandy Brooke, Aldo Ray
<u>D</u>: Fred Olen Ray
Minor SF-comedy: Beauty unjustly sentenced to brutal prison spaceship

Star Trek
1979, (USA), Para, color, 131 mins. (video: 143 mins.)
<u>W</u>: William Shatner (*Adm. James T. Kirk*), Leonard Nimoy (*Mr. Spock*), DeForest Kelley (*Dr. Leonard "Bones" McCoy*), James Doohan ("*Scotty*"), Stephen Collins (*Cmdr. Decker*), Persis Khambatta (*Ilia*), George Takei (*Sulu*), Majel Barrett (*Lt. Christine Chappel*), Nichelle Nichols (*Uhura*), Walter Koenig (*Chekov*), Grace Lee Whitney (*Rand*), Mark Lenard (*The Klingon Captain*), Billy Van Zandt (*The Alien Boy*), Roger Aaron Brown (*The Epsilon Technician*), Gary Faga (*The Airlock Technician*), David Gauteaux (*Cmdr. Branch*), John D. Gowans (*The Ass't to Rand*), Howard Itzkowitz (*The Cargo Deck Ensign*), Jon Rashad Kamal (*Lt. Cmdr. Sonak*), Marcy Lafferty (*Chief DiFalco*), Jeri McBride (*The Technician*), Terrence O'Connor (*Chief Ross*), Michele Ameen Billy (*The Lieutenant*), Michael Rougas (*Lt. Cleary*), Susan J. Sullivan, Ralph Brannen, Ralph Byers, Tom Morga, Paula Crist, Iva Lane, Franklyn Seales, Momo Yashima, Jimmie Booth, Joel Kramer, Bill McTosh, Dave Moordigan, Tony Rocco, Joel Schultz, Craig Thomas, Edna Glover, Norman Stuart, Paul Weber, Joshua Gallegos, Junero Jennings, Leslie C. Howard, Sayra Hummel
<u>P</u>: Gene Roddenberry <u>D</u>: Robert Wise <u>SCR</u>: Harold Livingston <u>PHOTOG</u>: Richard H. Kline <u>SPCL-FX</u>: Douglas Trumbull & John Dykstra <u>MUSIC</u>: Jerry Goldsmith
Big-budget, Apollonian space-opera: Federation starship seeks to halt planet-destroying enigma

Star Trek II: The Wrath of Khan
1982, (USA), Para, color, 113 mins.
<u>W</u>: William Shatner (*Adm. James T. Kirk*), Leonard Nimoy (*Mr. Spock*), DeForest Kelley (*Dr. Leonard "Bones" McCoy*), George Takei (*Sulu*), Nichelle Nichols (*Uhura*), Walter Koenig (*Chekov*), Ricardo Montalban (*Khan*), James Doohan ("*Scotty*"), Bibi Besch, Kirstie Alley, Paul Winfield, Merritt Butrick
<u>D</u>: Nicholas Meyer <u>MUSIC</u>: James Horner
Exciting space-opera: Star Fleet admiral reunited with nemesis

Star Trek III: The Search for Spock
1984, (USA), Harve Bennett/Para, color, 105 mins.
<u>W</u>: William Shatner (*Adm. James T. Kirk*), DeForest Kelley (*Dr. Leonard "Bones" McCoy*), Mark Lenard (*Sarek*), George Takei (*Sulu*), James Doohan ("*Scotty*"), Walter Koenig (*Chekov*), Nichelle Nichols (*Uhura*), Merritt Butrick (*Dr. David Marcus*), Christopher Lloyd (*Lord Kruge*), John Larroquette (*Maltz*), Stephen Liska (*Torg*), Cathie Shirriff (*Valkris*), Robin Curtis (*Lt. Saavik*), Robert Hooks (*Adm. Morrow*), Dame Judith Anderson (*T'Lar*), James B. Sikking (*Capt. Styles*), Leonard Nimoy (*Spock*), Sharon Thomas, Majel Barrett, Grace Lee Whitney, Allan Miller, Carl Steven, Vadia Potenza, Joe W. Davis, Stephen Manley, Phil Morris, Bob Cummings, Scott McGinnis, Paul Sorensen, Dave Cadiente, Mario Marcelino, Branscombe Richmond, Phillip Richard Allen, Jeanne Mori, Conroy Gideon, Miguel Ferrer, Katherine Blum, Douglas Alan Shanklin, Dennis C. Ott
<u>WRIT & P</u>: Harve Bennett <u>D</u>: Leonard Nimoy <u>PHOTOG</u>: Charles Correll <u>SPCL-FX SPRVSR</u>: Bob Dawson <u>VS-FX</u>: Industrial Light & Magic <u>MUSIC</u>: James Horner
Above-average space-opera: Starship commander seeks reborn crewman

Star Trek III: The Search For Spock: DeForest Kelley, James Doohan, William Shatner and George Takei

Star Trek IV: The Voyage Home
1986, (USA), Harve Bennett/Para, color, 119 mins.
<u>W</u>: William Shatner (*Adm. James T. Kirk*), Leonard Nimoy (*Mr. Spock*), DeForest Kelley (*Dr. Leonard "Bones" McCoy*), Catherine Hicks (*Gillian Taylor*), Robert Ellenstein (*The Federation President*), Brock Peters (*Adm. Cartwright*), James Doohan ("*Scotty*"), John Schuck (*The Klingon Ambassador*), Jane Wyatt (*Amanda, Spock's Mother*), Mark Lenard (*Sarek, Spock's Father*), George Takei (*Sulu*), Walter Koenig (*Chekov*), Nichelle Nichols (*Uhura*), Robin Curtis (*Lt. Saavik*), Majel Barrett, Michael Snyder, Michael Berryman
<u>D</u>: Leonard Nimoy <u>SCR</u>: Steve Meerson, Peter Krikes, Harve Bennett & Nicholas Meyer <u>STORY</u>: Leonard Nimoy & Harve Bennett <u>PHOTOG</u>: Donald Peterman <u>VS-FX SPRVSR</u>: Ken Ralston <u>MUSIC</u>: Leonard Rosenman
Well-made space-opera: Starship time-travels to save Earth from alien probe

Star Trek V: The Final Frontier
1989, (USA), Harve Bennett/Para, color, 105 mins.
<u>W</u>: William Shatner (*Adm. James T. Kirk*), Leonard Nimoy (*Mr. Spock*), DeForest Kelley (*Dr. Leonard "Bones" McCoy*), James Doohan ("*Scotty*"), Walter Koenig (*Chekov*), Nichelle Nichols (*Uhura*), George Takei (*Sulu*), David Warner (*St. John Talbot*), Laurence Luckinbill (*Sybok*), Charles Cooper, Cynthia Gouw, Todd Bryant, Spice Williams, Rex Holman, Bill Quinn, George Murdock, Jonathan Simpson, Beverly Hart, Steve Susskind, Harve Bennett, Cynthia Blaise, Melanie Shatner
<u>D</u>: William Shatner <u>SCR</u>: David Loughery <u>STORY</u>: William Shatner, Harve Bennett & David Loughery, from *Star Trek* teleseries created by Gene Roddenberry <u>PHOTOG</u>: Andrew Laszlo <u>VS-FX</u>: Bran Ferren <u>MUSIC</u>: Jerry Goldsmith <u>SONGS</u>: *The Moon's a Window to Heaven*
Modest space-opera: Renegade usurps command of starship, seeks legendary "Eden"

Star Trek VI: The Undiscovered Country
1991, (USA), Para, color, 110 mins.
<u>W</u>: William Shatner (*Adm. James T. Kirk*), Leonard Nimoy (*Mr. Spock*), DeForest Kelley (*Dr. Leonard "Bones" McCoy*), Walter Koenig (*Chekov*), James Doohan ("*Scotty*"), Nichelle Nichols (*Uhura*), George Takei (*Sulu*), Kim Cattrall (*Lt. Valeris*), Christopher Plummer (*Gen. Chang*), David Warner (*The Klingon Chancellor*), Kurtwood Smith (*The Federation President*), Rosana DeSoto (*Azetbar*), Christian Slater, Michael Dorn, John Schuck, Iman, Dennis C. Ott
<u>D</u>: Nicholas Meyer <u>SCR</u>: Nicholas Meyer & Denny Martin Flynn <u>STORY</u>: Leonard Nimoy, Lawrence Konner & Mark Rosenthal, from characters created by Gene Roddenberry <u>PHOTOG</u>: Hiro Narita <u>MUSIC</u>: Cliff Eidelman
Modest space-opera

Star Trek: First Contact
1996, (USA), Para, color, 112 mins.
<u>W</u>: Patrick Stewart (*Picard*), Jonathan Frakes (*Riker*), Alice Krige (*The Borg Queen*), Alfre Woodard (*Lily*), Brent Spiner (*Data*), James Cromwell (*Zefram Cochran*), Michael Dorn, LeVar Burton, Gates McFadden, Marina Sirtis
<u>D</u>: Jonathan Frakes <u>SCR</u>: Brannon Braga & Ronald D. Moore <u>PHOTOG</u>: Matthew F. Leonetti <u>SPCL-FX</u>: Industrial Light & Magic <u>MUSIC</u>: Jerry Goldsmith
Standard space-opera: Aliens time travel to prevent creation of galactic federation

Star Trek: Generations
1994, (USA), Para, color, 117 mins.
<u>W</u>: Patrick Stewart (*Picard*), William Shatner (*Kirk*), Malcolm McDowell (*Soran*), Jonathan Frakes (*Riker*), Brent Spiner (*Data*), LeVar Burton (*Geordi*), James Doohan (*Scotty*), Michael Dorn (*Worf*), Marina Sirtis (*Troi*), Gates McFadden (*Beverly*), Walter Koenig (*Chekov*), Alan Ruck (*Capt. Harriman*), Jenette Goldstein (*The Science Officer*), Jacqueline Kim (*Demora*), Thomas Kopache (*The Com Officer*), Glenn Morshower (*The Navigator*), Tim Russ (*The Lieutenant*), Tommy Hinkley (*A Journalist*), John Putch (*A Journalist*), Christine Jansen (*A Journalist*), Michael Mack (*Ensign Hayes*), Patti Yasutake (*Nurse Ogawa*), Dendrie Taylor (*Lt. Farrell*), Granville Ames (*The Transporter Chief*), Henry Marshall (*The Security Officer*), Brittany Parkyn (*The Girl with the Teddy Bear*), Rif Hutton (*The Klingon Guard*), Majel Barrett (*The Computer*

S

Voice), Barbara March (*Lursa*), Gwynyth Walsh (*B'Etor*), Kim Braden (*Picard's Wife*), Brian Thompson (*The Klingon Helm*), Marcy Goldman (*An El Aurian Survivor*), Jim Krestalude (*An El Aurian Survivor*), Judy Levitt (*An El Aurian Survivor*), Gwen Van Dam (*An El Aurian Survivor*), Kristopher Logan (*An El Aurian Survivor*), Christopher James Miller (*Picard's Nephew*), Matthew Collins, Mimi Collins, Olivia Hack, Thomas Alexander Dekker, Whoopi Goldberg
<u>P</u>: Rick Berman   <u>D</u>: David Carson   <u>SCR</u>: Ronald D. Moore & Brannon Braga   <u>STORY</u>: Rick Berman & Ronald D. Moore, from characters created by Gene Roddenberry   <u>PHOTOG</u>: John A. Alonzo   <u>SPCL-FX SPRVSR</u>: Terry D. Frazee   <u>MUSIC</u>: Dennis McCarthy
Modest SF-adventure: Time warp unites space captains

Star Trek: Insurrection
1998, (USA), Para, color
<u>W</u>: Patrick Stewart (*Capt. Jean-Luc Picard*), Jonathan Frakes (*Cmdr. William Riker*), F. Murray Abraham (*Ru'afo*), Brent Spiner (*Data*), Marina Sirtis (*Deanna Troi*), Michael Dorn (*Worf*), Gates McFadden (*Dr. Beverly Crusher*), Anthony Zerbe (*Adm. Dougherty*), LeVar Burton (*Geordi*), Donna Murphy (*Anij*)
<u>D</u>: Jonathan Frakes   <u>SCR</u>: Michael Pillar
Standard SF-adventure

Starvengers
1982, (Jap), color, 105 mins.
Standard animated SF-adventure: Robot's intelligence is greatly increased

Star Wars
1977, (USA), 20th-Fox, color, 123 mins. (Special Edition {1997}: 125 mins.)
<u>W</u>: Mark Hamill (*Luke Skywalker*), Carrie Fisher (*Princess Leia Organa*), Harrison Ford (*Han Solo*), Alec Guinness (*Obi Wan "Ben" Kenobi*), Peter Cushing (*Grand Moff Tarkin*), Dave Prowse (*Darth Vader*), Anthony Daniels (*C3PO*), Kenny Baker (*R2D2*), Peter Mayhew (*Chewbacca*), Phil Brown (*Uncle Owen*), Shelagh Fraser (*Aunt Beru*), Jack Purvis (*Chief Jawa*), Alex McCrindle (*Gen. Dadonna*), James Earl Jones (*Voice of Darth Vader*), Eddie Byrne
<u>P</u>: Gary Kurtz   <u>WRIT & D</u>: George Lucas   <u>PHOTOG</u>: Gil Taylor   <u>SPCL-FX</u>: John Dykstra   <u>MUSIC</u>: John Williams
Classic SF-fantasy: Youth opposes evil galactic empire. cf. **The Empire Strikes Back** *and* **Return of the Jedi**

Star Wars Episode I—The Phantom Menace
1999, (USA), 20th-Fox, color
<u>W</u>: Ewan McGregor, Liam Neeson, Jake Lloyd, Samuel L. Jackson, Natalie Portman
<u>D</u>: George Lucas
Long-awaited "prequel" to Star Wars trilogy

State Department—File 649
1949, (USA), Film Classics, color, 87 mins.
<u>W</u>: William Lundigan, Virginia Bruce Raymond Bond, Nana Bryant
<u>D</u>: Peter Stewart (Sam Newfield)
Standard thriller: American agent vs. Oriental warlord

The Stateless Man
1955, (GB), Merton Park/Anglo-Amalgamated, b&w, 29 mins.
<u>W</u>: Frank Leighton (*Insp. Parry*), May Hallatt (*Mrs. Fenton*), Robin Wentworth (*The Sgt.*), Theodore Wilhelm (*Slavik*), Tom Clegg (*Bill Fenton*)
<u>P</u>: Alec Snowden   <u>D</u>: Paul Gherzo   <u>STORY</u>: James Eastwood
Standard short crime-thriller: Landlady's son stabs girl lodger

State Secret
1950, (GB), London/British Lion/Col, b&w, 104 mins.
<u>W</u>: Douglas Fairbanks Jr. (*Dr. John Marlowe*), Glynis Johns (*Lisa*), Jack Hawkins (*Col. Galcon*), Herbert Lom (*Theodor*), Walter Rilla (*Gen. Niva*), Karel Stepanek (*Dr. Revo*), Carl Jaffe (*Janovik Prada*), Gerard Heinz (*Bendel*), Hans Moser (*Sigrist*), Gerik Schjelderup (*Bartorek*), Peter Illing (*Macco*), Guido Lorraine (*Lt. Prachi*), Anton Diffring (*The Policeman*)
<u>P</u>: Frank Launder & Sidney Gilliat   <u>WRIT & D</u>: Sidney Gilliat, from Roy Huggins' novel *Appointment with Fear*   <u>PHOTOG</u>: Robert Krasker   <u>MUSIC</u>: William Alwyn
USA retitle, **The Great Manhunt** *reissued 1964*
Standard thriller: Dead general's supporters seek to silence surgeon

Station Six—Sahara
1962, (GB-W. Ger), British Lion/AA, b&w, 101 mins.
<u>W</u>: Carroll Baker, Peter Van Eyck, Ian Bannen, Jorg Felmy, Denholm Elliott, Mario Adorf, Biff McGuire
<u>D</u>: Seth Holt   <u>SCR</u>: Bryan Forbes & Brian Clemens
A.k.a. **Endstation 13 Sahara**
Unusual eroto-melodrama: Lone female excites passions at remote desert pumping station

Station 3 Ultra-Secret
see **The Satan Bug**

La Statue Animee (The Animated Statue)
1903, (Fr), Star, b&w, 48m (157.5 ft./2.7 mins.)
<u>D</u>: Georges Melies
USA retitle, **The Drawing Lesson: or, The Living Statue**
Standard fantasy

La Statue de Neige (The Snow Man)
1899, (Fr), Star, b&w, 20m (65.6 ft./1.1 mins.)
<u>D</u>: Georges Melies
Standard fantasy

Stay Awake
1987, (S. Afr), color, 90 mins.
<u>W</u>: Shirley Jane Harris, Tanya Gordon, Jayne Hutton, Heath Porter
<u>D</u>: John Bernard
Minor horror-fantasy: Demon stalks Catholic schoolgirls

Stay Tuned
1992, (USA), WB, color, 90 mins.
<u>W</u>: John Ritter (*Roy Knable*), Pam Dawber (*Helen Knable*), Jeffrey Jones (*Spike*), Eugene Levy (*Crowley*), David Tom (*Darryl Knable*), Heather McComb (*Diane Knable*), Salt-n-Pepa (*The Rap Artists*)
<u>D & PHOTOG</u>: Peter Hyams   <u>SCR</u>: Tom S. Parker & Jim Jennewein, from a story by Tom S. Parker, Jim Jennewein & Richard Siegel   <u>MUSIC</u>: Bruce Broughton
Modest fantasy: Couch potatoes sucked into TV set

Steel and Lace
1990, (USA), color, 92 mins.
<u>W</u>: Bruce Davison, Clare Wren, Stacy Haiduk, David Naughton, David Lander
<u>D</u>: Ernest Fario   <u>SCR</u>: Joseph Dougherty & Dave Edison
Minor SF-thriller: Scientist turns sister into cyborg

Steel Dawn
1987, (USA), Silver Lion/Vestron, color, 102 mins.
<u>W</u>: Patrick Swayze (*Nomad*), Lisa Niemi (*Kasha*), Christopher Neame (*Sho*), Brion James (*Tark*), Anthony Zerbe (*Damnil*), Brett Hool (*Jux*), John Fujioka (*Cord*), Marcel Van Heerden (*Lann*), Arnold Vosloo (*Makker*), James Whyle (*Tooey*), Alex Heyns (*The Priest*), Russell Savadier (*Off*), Joe Ribeiro (*Cali*), Brad Morris (*Bluto*), Tullio Moneta (*The Henchman*), David Sherwood (*The Merchant*)
<u>D</u>: Lance Hool   <u>SCR</u>: Doug Lefler   <u>PHOTOG</u>: George Tirl   <u>MUSIC</u>: Brian May
Standard SF-adventure: Post-nuke survivors vs. murderous tyrant

Steel Frontier
1995, (USA), color, 101 mins.
<u>W</u>: Joe Lara, Bo Svenson, Stacie Foster Brion James
<u>D</u>: Paul G. Volk & Jacobsen Hart   <u>SCR</u>: Jacobsen Hart
Minor SF-adventure: Gunslinger vs. post-nuke outlaws

The Steel Key
1952, (GB), Tempean/Eros, b&w, 69 mins.
<u>W</u>: Terence Morgan (*Johnny O'Flynn*), Joan Rice (*Doreen Wilson*), Raymond Lovell (*Insp. Forsythe*), Hector Ross (*Beroni*), Dianne Foster (*Sylvia Newman*), Colin Tapley (*Dr. Crabtree*), Esmond Knight (*Prof. Newman*), Arthur Lovegrove (*Gilchrist*)
<u>P</u>: Robert S. Baker & Monty Berman   <u>D</u>: Robert S. Baker   <u>SCR</u>: John Gilling, from a story by Roy Chanslor
Standard thriller: Ex-crook saves inventor from asylum run by spies

The Steel Trap
1952, (USA), Thor/20th-Fox, b&w, 85 mins.
<u>W</u>: Joseph Cotten, Teresa Wright, Tom Powers, Walter Sande, Jonathan Hale, Eddie Marr, Aline Towne, Sam Flint, Benny Burt, Bill Hudson, Joey Ray, Charlie Collins, Kurt Martell, Stephanie King, Carleton Young, Katherine Warren
<u>WRIT & D</u>: Andrew L. Stone   <u>PHOTOG</u>: Ernest Laszlo   <u>MUSIC</u>: Dimitri Tiomkin
Superior thriller: Bank executive absconds with stolen cash

Der Steinerne Reiter (The Stone Rider)
1923, (Ger), Decla-Bioscop, b&w
<u>W</u>: Rudolf Klein-Rogge, Lucie Mannheim, Georg John, Fritz Kampers, Otto Framer, Paul Biensfeldt, Gustav von Wangenheim
<u>D</u>: Fritz Wendhausen   <u>SCR</u>: Thea von Harbou   <u>PHOTOG</u>: Karl Hoffmann   <u>SETS</u>: Heinrich Heuser
Standard melodrama

Stellar Brothers—From the Kremlin to the Cosmos
1963, (Russ), Moscow Popular Science Film/Artkino, color
<u>W</u>: Andrian Nikolayev, Pavel Popovich
<u>D</u>: Dmitri Bogolepov   <u>SCR</u>: Yevgeni Ryabchikov
Standard docu: Promise of spaceflight

Stella Star
see **Star Crash**

Step by Step
1946, (USA), RKO, b&w, 62 mins.
<u>W</u>: Lawrence Tierney, Anne Jeffreys
Standard thriller

S

Step Down to Terror
1958, (USA), Univ, b&w, 75 mins.
<u>W:</u> Charles Drake, Colleen Miller, Rod Taylor, Josephine Hutchinson, Jocelyn Brando Alan Dexter, Rickey Kelman
<u>D:</u> Harry Keller   <u>SCR:</u> Chris Cooper   <u>PHOTOG:</u> Russell Metty   <u>SPCL-FX:</u> Clifford Stine   <u>MUSIC:</u> Joseph Gershenson
GB retitle, **The Silent Stranger**
Minor thriller (remake of **Shadow of a Doubt***): Son returns to family, is revealed to be psychotic killer*

The Stepfather
1986, (Can), ITC, color, 89 mins.
<u>W:</u> Terry O'Quinn (*Jerry Blake*), Jill Schoelen (*Stephanie*), Shelley Hack (*Susan*), Charles Lanyer (*Dr. Bondurant*), Jeff Schultz (*Paul Baker*), Stephen Shellen (*Jim Ogilvie*), Robyn Stevan (*Karen*), Stephen E. Miller (*Al Brennan*), Anna Hagan (*Mrs. Leitner*), Lindsay Bourne (*The Art Teacher*), Gillian Barber (*Annie Barnes*), Blu Mankuma (*Lt. Jack Wall*), Margot Pinvidic (*Mrs. Anderson*), Jackson Davies (*Mr. Chesterton*), Sandra Head (*The Receptionist*), Rochelle Greenwood (*Cindy Anderson*), Gabrielle Rose (*Dorothy Rinehard*), Dale Wilson (*Frank*), Richard Sargent (*Mr. Anderson*), Don S. Williams (*Mr. Stark*), Don MacKay (*Joe*), Gary Hetherington (*Herb*), Andrew Snider (*Mr. Grace*), Marie Stillin (*Mrs. Fairfax*), Paul Batten (*Mr. Fairfax*), Sheila Paterson (*Dr. Barbara Faraday*)
<u>D:</u> Joseph Ruben   <u>SCR:</u> Donald E. Westlake   <u>STORY:</u> Carolyn Lefcourt, Brian Garfield & Donald E. Westlake   <u>PHOTOG:</u> John W. Lindley   <u>MUSIC:</u> Patrick Moraz   <u>SONGS:</u> *Run Between the Raindrops, Sleeping Beauty & I Want You*
Unusual thriller: Psycho seeks perfect family

Stepfather II
1989, (Can), ITC/Millimeter, color, 88 mins.
<u>W:</u> Terry O'Quinn (*The Stepfather*), Meg Foster (*Carol Grayland*), Caroline Williams (*Matty Crimmins*), Jonathan Brandis (*Todd Grayland*), Henry Brown, Mitchell Laurance, Miriam Byrd-Nethery, Leon Martell, Renata Scott, Glen Adams, John O'Leary, Eric Brown
<u>D:</u> Jeff Burr   <u>SCR:</u> John Auerbach, from characters created by Carolyn Lefcourt, Brian Garfield & Donald E. Westlake   <u>PHOTOG:</u> Jacek Laskus   <u>MUSIC:</u> Jim Manzie (in assoc. with Pat Regan)
Standard thriller: Psychotic killer returns

Stepfather III: Father's Day
1991, (USA), ITC, color, 110 mins.
<u>W:</u> Robert Wightman, Priscilla Barnes, David Tom, Season Hubley, John Ingle
<u>D:</u> Guy Magar, from characters created by Carolyn Lefcourt, Brian Garfield & Donald E. Westlake   <u>PHOTOG:</u> Alan Caso   <u>MUSIC:</u> Patrick C. Regan
Minor thriller: Asylum escapee ensnares divorcee

The Stepford Children
1987, (USA), Taft Entertainment/NBC-TV, color, 96 mins.
<u>W:</u> Barbara Eden (*Laura Harding*), Don Murray (*Steven Harding*), Tammy Lauren (*Mary Harding*), Randall Batinkoff (*David Harding*), Pat Corley (*Sheriff Weston*), Ken Swofford (*Frank Gregson*), Richard Anderson (*Lawrence Danton*), Dick Butkus (*Tom Wilcox*), Sharon Spelman (*Sandy Gregson*), Debbie Barker (*Lois Gregson*), James Coco (*The Cooking Teacher*), Michael Murray, James Staley, Raye Birk, Judy Baldwin, Toni Sawyer, John Cameron Mitchell, Peter Elbling, Pirie Jones, Barbara Altz, Pamela Newman, John Hotstetter, Ronnie Carol, Philip Waller, Amy Lynne, Ryan Francis, Pat Darling, Holly Dorff, Erick Ratliff, Kim Scolari, Sheryl Staples
<u>D:</u> Alan J. Levi   <u>TELEPLAY:</u> Bill Bleich, based on characters created by Ira Levin   <u>PHOTOG:</u> Steve Shaw   <u>MUSIC:</u> Joseph Conlan
TVM, standard SF-thriller: Urban family finds strange perfection in suburbs

The Stepford Husbands
1996, (USA), Victor/CBS-TV, color, 96 mins.
<u>W:</u> Donna Mills (*Jodie*), Michael Ontkean (*Mick*), Cindy Williams (*Caroline*), Louise Fletcher (*Maryam Benton*), Sarah Douglas, Caitlin Clarke
<u>D:</u> Fred Walton   <u>TELEPLAY:</u> Ken & Jim Wheat, based on characters created by Ira Levin   <u>PHOTOG:</u> Don E. Fauntleroy   <u>MUSIC:</u> Dana Kaproff
TVM, standard SF-thriller: Mysterious clinic produces affable husbands

The Stepford Wives
1975, (USA), Palomar/Col, color, 114 mins.
<u>W:</u> Katharine Ross (*Joanna*), Paula Prentiss (*Bobby*), Peter Masterson (*Walter*), Nanette Newman (*Carol*), Patrick O'Neal (*Dale Coba*), Tina Louise (*Charmaine*), Carol Rossen (*Dr. Fancher*), William Prince (*Ike*), Carole Mallory, Barbara Rucker, Dee Wallace, George Coe
<u>P:</u> Edgar J. Scherick   <u>D:</u> Bryan Forbes   <u>SCR:</u> William Goldman, from Ira Levin's novel   <u>PHOTOG:</u> Owen Roizman   <u>MUSIC:</u> Michael Small
"...a chilling, cerebral thriller that works on more than one level"—Playboy
"Wonderfully ridiculous black humored satire"—Hollywood Reporter
Superior SF-horror: Suburban community has "perfect" women. cf. **Revenge of the Stepford Wives**

Stephen Crane's "The Monster"
1998, (USA), NBC-TV, color, 95 mins.
<u>W:</u> Danny Glover
from Stephen Crane's story
TVM, standard thriller: Man horribly disfigured in fire. cf. **Face of Fire**

Stepmonster
1993, (USA), color, 86 mins.
<u>W:</u> Alan Thicke Robin Riker, Corey Feldman, John Astin, Geoge Gaynes, Ami Dolenz
Minor horror-fantasy: Boy believes stepmother is murderous monster

The Stepmother
1971, (USA), color, 94 mins.
<u>W:</u> Alejandro Rey, John Anderson, Katherine Justice, John D. Garfield, Marlene Schmidt, Claudia Jennings, Duncan McLeod
<u>D:</u> Hikmet Avedis
Minor thriller

The Stepmother
1973, (USA), Crown Int'l, color, 94 mins.
<u>W:</u> Alejandro Rey (*Frank*), John Anderson (*The Inspector*), Katherine Justice (*Margo*), Larry Linville (*Dick*), John D. Garfield (*Goof*), Marlene Schmidt (*Sonja*), Claudia Jennings (*The Nude*), Rudy Herrera Jr. (*Steve*), DavidRenard (*Petro*), Priscilla Garcia (*Petro's Girl*)
<u>WRIT, P & D:</u> Hikmet Avedis   <u>MUSIC & LYRICS:</u> Sammy Fain & Paul Francis Webster   <u>SONG:</u> *Strange Are the Ways of Love*
Minor thriller

Steppenwolf
1974, (USA), color, 106 mins.
<u>W:</u> Max von Sydow, Dominique Sanda, Pierre Clementi, Carl Romanelli, Roy Bosier, Alfred Baillou
<u>D:</u> Fred Haines, from Hermann Hesse's novel
Unusual psychodrama: Intellectual and emotional crisis of middle-aged man

The Stepsister
1996, (USA), color
<u>W:</u> Linda Evans, Alan Rachins
Minor melodrama

Steps from Hell
1992, (USA), color, 90 mins.
<u>W:</u> Bernardo Rosa, Rocky Tucker, Ron Odell, Philip Cable, Liz Stoeckel, Steve Quimby, Lisa Lund
<u>D & SCR:</u> James Tucker
Minor horror-fantasy: Evil immortal controls cult of zombie women

Steps Towards the Moon
1965, (Ruman), color
<u>D:</u> Popescu Gopo
Outstanding comedy-docu: History of flight

Stewed Missionary
1904, (GB), Gaumont, b&w, 165 ft. (50.3m)
<u>D:</u> Alf Collins
Standard comedy-thriller: Cannibals cook cleric

The Stickpin
1933, (GB), British Lion/Fox, b&w, 44 mins.
<u>W:</u> Henry Kendall (*Paul Rayner*), Betty Astell (*Eve Marshall*), Francis L. Sullivan (*Jacob Volke*), Lawrence Anderson (*Tom Marshall*), Henry Caine (*Dixon*), Pope Stamper (*Simms*)
<u>D:</u> Leslie Hiscott   <u>STORY:</u> Michael Barringer
Standard thriller: Man framed for killing blackmailer of friend's wife

Stigma
1972, (USA), CRC, color, 93 mins.
<u>W:</u> Philip M. Thomas (*Dr. Crosse*), Harlan Cary Poe (*Bill*), Josie Johnson (*D.D.*), Peter H. Clune (*The Sheriff*), Kathy Joyce (*Kathleen*), Connie Van Ess (*Tassie*), William Magerman (*Jeremy*), Richard Geisman (*Joe*), Raina Barrett (*The "B" Girl*), Carter Courtney (*The Homosexual*), Edwin Mills (*The Choir Leader*), Rhonda Fuller (*Rhoda*), "Cousin" Bruce Morrow (*himself*), Jim Grace (*Ed*)
<u>P:</u> Charles B. Moss Jr.   <u>WRIT & D:</u> David E. Durston   <u>PHOTOG:</u> Robert M. Baldwin
Standard thriller: Social disease becomes epidemic

Still Life
1992, (USA), color, 83 mins.
<u>W:</u> Jason Gedrick, Jessica Steen, Stephen Shellan
<u>D:</u> Graeme Campbell   <u>MUSIC:</u> Mychael Danna
Minor thriller: Serial killer turns victims into sculptures

Still of the Night
1982, (USA), UA, color, 91 mins.
<u>W:</u> Roy Scheider (*Dr. Sam Rice*), Meryl Streep (*Brooke Reynolds*), Jessica Tandy (*Grace Rice*), Joe Grifasi (*Joseph Vitucci*), Sara Botsford (*Gail Phillips*), Josef Sommer (*George Bynum*)
<u>D & SCR:</u> Robert Benton   <u>PHOTOG:</u> Nestor Almendros   <u>MUSIC:</u> John Kander
Modest thriller, homage to Hitchcock: Psychiatrist investigates mystery woman in brutal murder case

Still Not Quite Human
1992, (USA), color, 84 mins.
<u>W</u>: Alan Thicke, Jay Underwood, Christopher Neame, Betsy Palmer, Adam Philipson, Rosa Nevin, Kenneth Pogue
<u>D & SCR</u>: Eric Luke
Standard SF-comedy: Robot tribulations

Still Waters Run Deep
1916, (GB), Ideal, b&w, 4,500 ft. (1371.6m)
<u>W</u>: Lady Tree (*Mrs. Sternbold*), Milton Rosmer (*John Mildmay*), Rutland Barrington (*Mr. Potter*), Sydney Lewis Ransome (*Capt. Hawksley*), Hilda Bruce-Potter (*Mrs. Mildmay*), E.H. Brooke
<u>D</u>: Fred Paul <u>SCR</u>: Dane Stanton, from a play by Tom Taylor
Standard crime-thriller: Captain installs himself in wealthy home, uses letters for blackmail

Sting of Death
1966, (USA), Essen/Thunderbird-Unt'l, color, 81 mins.
<u>W</u>: Joe Morrison, Valerie Hawkins, John Vella
<u>D</u>: William Grefe <u>SCR</u>: Richard S. Flink
Minor horror-hokum: Swamp monster terrorizes

Stole Assignment
1955, (GB), ACT Films-Unit/British Lion, b&w, 62 mins.
<u>W</u>: John Bentley (*Mike Billings*), Hy Hazell (*Jenny Drew*), Eddie Byrne (*Insp. Corcoran*), Joyce Carey (*Ida Garnett*), Patrick Holt (*Henry Crossley*), Charles Farrell (*Percy Simpson*), Kay Callard (*Stella Watson*), Jessica Cairns (*Marilyn Dawn*)
<u>P</u>: Francis Searle <u>D</u>: Terence Fisher <u>SCR</u>: Kenneth R. Hayles <u>STORY</u>: Sidney Nelson & Maurice Harrison
Standard crime-thriller: Reporter and girl aid woman accused of killing niece

The Stolen Airship Plans
1912, (GB), Urban Trading Co., b&w, 807 ft. (246m)
<u>W</u>: Irene Vernon (*The Spy*), Spot the Urbanora Dog
<u>WRIT & D</u>: Stuart Kinder
reissued (1914) as **The Regimental Pet**
Standard thriller: Inventor's partner and pet dog catch spy

A Stolen Face
1952, (GB), Hammer/Lippert, b&w, 72 mins.
<u>W</u>: Paul Henreid (*Dr. Philip Ritter*), Lizabeth Scott (*Alice Brent/Lily*), Andre Morell (*David*), Susan Stephen (*Betty*), Mary Mackenzie (*Lily*), John Wood (*Dr. Jack Wilson*), Cyril Smith (*Alf*), Arnold Ridley (*Dr. Russell*), Everley Gregg (*Lady Haringay*), Diana Beaumont (*May*)
<u>P</u>: Anthony Hinds <u>D</u>: Terence Fisher <u>SCR</u>: Martin Berkeley & Richard H. Landau
Unusual thriller from pre-horror Hammer studios: Plastic surgeon transforms prison inmate into image of his unattainable love

The Stolen Heirlooms
1915, (GB), I.B. Davidson/Walturdaw, b&w, 3,000 ft. (914.4m)
<u>W</u>: Harry Lorraine (*Sexton Blake*), Bert Rex (*Tinker*)
<u>D</u>: Charles Raymond, from characters created by Harry Blyth
Standard crime-thriller: Detective drugged with flowers and tied to sawmill while saving ex-gambler from jewel theft charge

The Stolen Masterpiece
1914, (GB), Big Ben Films-Union/Pathe, b&w, 3,245 ft. (989.1m)
<u>W</u>: H.O. Martinek (*Dick Steele*), Ivy Montford (*Kate Halifax*), Douglas Payne (*The Thief*)
<u>D</u>: H.O. Martinek <u>STORY</u>: L.C. MacBean
Standard crime-thriller: The "Sleuth Hounds" catch clubman after rescue from snakepit and fight in morass

The Stolen Papers
1912, (GB-Fr), Franco-British Film Co.-Eclair/Fenning, b&w, 1,400 ft. (426.7m)
<u>W</u>: Georges Treville (*Sherlock Holmes*), Mr. Moyse (*Dr. John Watson*)
<u>D</u>: Georges Treville, from a story by Sir Arthur Conan Doyle
Standard thriller

The Stolen Plans
1914, (GB), Edison, b&w, 1,040 ft. (317m)
<u>W</u>: Marc McDermott (*Capt. West*), Miriam Nesbitt (*Miss Ashmay*), Charles Vernon (*Capt. Ashmay*), Winifred Albion (*Mary*), William Luft (*Burgovitch*)
<u>D</u>: Charles Brabin <u>STORY</u>: Goring Chalmers
Standard thriller: Blackmailing spy seeks bi-plane plans

The Stolen Plans
1952, (GB), G.B. Instructional/ABFD-CFF, b&w, 57 mins.
<u>W</u>: Mavis Sage (*Nicolette Renaud*), Lance Secretan (*Michael Foster*), Peter Neil (*Tony Burton*), Pamela Edmunds (*Mrs. Foster*), Peter Burton (*Dr. Foster*), Patrick Boxill (*Mr. Palmer*), Len Sharp (*Tod*), Geoffrey Goodheart (*The Boss*), Ludmilla Tchakalova
<u>D & SCR</u>: James Hill <u>STORY</u>: Michael Poole
Standard juvenile thriller: French girl helps boy catch spies

The Stolen Sacrifice
1916, (GB), Renaissance/Gerrard, b&w, 4,000 ft. (1219.2m)
<u>W</u>: Peggy Richards (*Nancy Wilford*)
<u>D & STORY</u>: Sidney Morgan
Standard thriller: Detective saves girl from being sacrificed by Hindu sect

Stolen Time
1955, (GB), Charles Deane/British Lion, b&w, 69 mins.
<u>W</u>: Richard Arlen (*Tony Pelassier*), Constance Leigh (*Marie*), Susan Shaw (*Carole Carlton*), Vincent Ball (*Johnson*), Andrea Malandrinos (*Papa Pelassier*), Alathea Siddons (*Mama Pelassier*)
<u>D & STORY</u>: Charles Deane
USA retitle, **Blonde Blackmailer**
Standard crime-thriller: Ex-convict tracks man who framed him for murder

Stone Cold Dead
1980, (Can), Dimension, color, 97 mins.
<u>W</u>: Richard Crenna, Paul Williams, Linsa Sorenson, Belinda J. Montgomery Charles Shamata, Alberta Watson, Monique Mercure, Andree Cousineau, Frank Moore, George Chuvalo, George Touliatos, Dennis Strong, Jennifer Dale
<u>P</u>: George Mendeluk & John Ryan <u>D & SCR</u>: George Mendeluk Sorenson, from Hugh Garner's novel *Sniper* <u>PHOTOG</u>: Dennis Miller
Minor thriller: Psycho kills prostitutes

Stoner
1974, (Hong Kong), Golden Harvest/World Northal, color, 105 mins.
<u>W</u>: George Lazenby, Angela Mao, Betty Ting Pei, Wong In-Sik, Joji Takagi
<u>D</u>: Huang Feng
Minor thriller: Secret agent confronts "passion ray"

The Stone Rider
see **Der Steinerne Reiter**

Stones of Death
1988, (Austral), color, 90 mins.
<u>W</u>: Tom Jennings, Natalie McCurry, Zoe Carides, Eric Oldfield
<u>D</u>: James Bagle
Minor horror-thriller: Burial site disturbed, aboriginal curse awakened

Stop Me!
see **Silent Night, Evil Night**

Stop Me Before I Kill
see **The Full Treatment**

Stopover Forever
1964, (GB), A.B. Pathe/WPD, b&w, 59 mins.
<u>W</u>: Ann Bell (*Sue Chambers*), Anthony Bate (*Trevor Graham*), Conrad Phillips (*Eric Cunningham*), Bruce Boa (*Freddie*), Julian Sherrier (*Capt. Carlos Mordente*), Britta von Krogh (*Jane Watson*)
<u>P</u>: Terry Ashwood <u>D</u>: Frederic Goode <u>STORY</u>: David Osborne
Standard crime-thriller: Killer menaces airline hostess

Stop Press Girl
1949, (GB), Aquila Films/GFD, b&w, 78 mins.
<u>W</u>: Sally Ann Howes (*Jennifer Peters*), Gordon Jackson (*Jock Melville*), Basil Radford (*The Engine Driver/Bus Driver/Fred/Projectionist/Pilot*), Naunton Wayne (*The Fireman/Conductor/Fred's Boy Projectionist/Co-Pilot*), James Robertson Justice (*Mr. Peters*), Sonia Holm (*Angela Carew*), Campbell Cotts (*Mr. Fairfax*), Nigel Buchanan (*Roy Fairfax*), Joyce Barbour (*Miss Peters*), Julia Lang (*Carole Saunders*), Cyril Chamberlain (*Johnnie*), Michael Goodliffe (*McPherson*), Humphrey Lestocq (*The Commentator*), Kenneth More (*The Sgt.*), Vincent Ball (*The Hero*), Ann Valery (*The Heroine*)
<u>P</u>: Donald B. Wilson <u>D</u>: Michael Barry <u>STORY</u>: T.J. Morrison & Basil Thomas
Standard fantasy: Everything mechanical stops working when girl is near

Stories from a Flying Trunk
1979, (GB), Sands Films, color, 88 mins.
<u>W</u>: Murray Melvin (*Hans Christian Andersen*), Ann Firbank (*Mother*), Tasneem Maqsood (*The Little Match Girl*), John Tordoff (*The Tramp*), John Dalby (*Queen Victoria*), Gerd Larsen (*The Ballet Mistress*), Johanna Sonnex (*Little Ida*), Patricia Napier (*Lettuce*), Graham Fletcher (*Prince Potato*), Lesley Collier (*The Princess*), Christopher Carr
<u>P</u>: John Brabourne & Richard Goodwin <u>WRIT & D</u>: Christine Edzard, from Hans Christian Andersen's stories "The Kitchen", "The Little Match Girl" & "Little Ida" <u>PHOTOG</u>: Robin Browne <u>MUSIC</u>: Gioacchino Rossini
Standard fantasy: Danish author tells three fairy stories

Storm Bound
1951, (It), Rep, b&w, 60 mins.
<u>W</u>: Constance Dowling, Andrea Checchi
Minor melodrama

Storm Chasers: Revenge of the Twister
1998, (USA), Shavick-Regent/FAM-TV, color, 95 mins.
<u>W</u>: Kelly McGillis, Adrian Zmed, Wolf Larson, Liz Torres, David Millbern, James MacArthur

S

D: Mark Sobel   **TELEPLAY:** Jeff Wynne   **PHOTOG:** Miklos Lente   **MUSIC:** Ken Williams
TVM, standard thriller: Man vs. tornados

Storm Fear
1956, (USA), UA, b&w, 88 mins.
W: Cornel Wilde, Jean Wallace, Dan Duryea Lee Grant
P & D: Cornel Wilde   **PHOTOG:** Joseph La Shelle   **MUSIC:** Elmer Bernstein
Standard melodrama: Wounded bank robber hides at brother's home

Storm of the Century
1999, (USA), ABC-TV, color, approx. 280 mins.
W: Timothy Daly *(Mike Anderson)*, Debrah Farentino *(Molly Anderson)*, Colm Feore *(Andre Linoge)*, Dyllan Christopher *(Ralph Anderson)*, Casey Siemaszko *(Alton "Hatch" Hatcher)*, Jeffrey DeMunn *(Robbie Beals)*, Julianne Nicholson *(Cat)*, Becky Ann Baker *(Ursala)*, Torri Higginson *(Angie Carver)*, Spencer Breslin Myra Carter, Nada Despotovich, Kathleen Chalfant, Jeremy Jordan, Ron Perkins, Steve Rankin, Adam Zolotin, Adam LeFevre, Denis Forest, Peter macNeill, Soo Garay, Beth Dixon, Christopher Morren, Leif Aderson, Sam Morton, Marcia Loskowski, John Innes, Jack Jessop, Nancy Beatty, Rita Tuckett, Richard Blackburn, Gaylyn Britton, David Ferry, Tyler Bannerman, Harley English-Dixon, Skye McCole Bartusiak, Stephen Joffe, Kristin Baxley, Michael Copeman, Cayda Rubin, Shawn Doyle, Norma Edwards, Victor Ertmanis, Richard Fitzpatrick, Joan Gregson, Jennifer Griffin, Lynne Griffin, David Hughes, Helen Hughes, Joel Keller, Nicky Guadagni, Hardee T. Lineham, Gerard Parkes, Arlene Mozerolle, Michael Rhoades
D: Craig R. Baxley WRIT: Stephen King   **PHOTOG:** David Connell   **VS-FX SPRVSR:** Boyd Shermis   **MUSIC:** Gary Chang
3-part TVM, well-made fantasy-thriller: Killer terrorizes storm-locked Maine island

Storm Over Tibet
1951, (USA), Summit/Col, b&w, 87 mins.
W: Rex Reason, Diana Douglas, Myron Healey, Robert Karnes, Harold Fong, Strother Martin, Harald Dyrenforth, Jarmila Marton, William Schallert, John Dodsworth, M. Concepcion
D: Andrew Marton   **SCR:** Ivan Tors & Sam Mayer   **PHOTOG:** George E. Diskant & Richard Angst   **MUSIC:** Arthur Honegger
Minor fantasy-thriller: Explorer steals holy mask, bad luck follows

Storm Planet
see Planeta Bura

Stormquest
1987, (Sp), color, 90 mins.
W: Kai BakBrent Huff
D: Alex Sessa
Minor thriller: Jungle women wage war of sexes

Stormswept
1995, (USA), color, 94 mins.
W: Julie Hughes, Melissa Moore, Kathleen Kinmont
D: David Marsh
Standard thriller: Actress and friends stranded in haunted Louisiana mansion

The Storm Within
see Les Parents Terribles

Stormy Crossing
1958, (GB), Tempean/Eros, b&w, 69 mins.
W: John Ireland *(Griff Parker)*, Derek Bond *(Paul Seymour)*, Leslie Dwyer *(Bill Harris)*, Maureen Connell *(Shelley Baxter)*, Sheldon Lawrence *(Danny Parker)*, Sam Rockett *(himself)*, Jack Taylor *(The Navigator)*, Joy Webster *(Kitty Tyndall)*, Cameron Hall *(Insp. Parry)*
P: Robert Baker & Monty Berman   **D:** Penington Richards   **SCR:** Brock Williams   **STORY:** Sid Harris & Lou Dyer
Standard crime-thriller: Girl cross-channel swimmer murdered

Stormy Nights
1997, (USA), color, 87 mins.
W: Shannon Tweed
Made-for-Video, standard thriller: Widow deceives

Storybook
1995, (USA), color, 90 mins.
W: William McNamara, Swoosie Kurtz, Sean Fitzgerald, Milton Berle, Robert Costanzo, James Doohan, Brenda Epperson, Richard Moll, Gary Morgan, Jack Scalia
D: Lorenzo Doumani   **SCR:** Lorenzo Doumani & Susan Bowen
Standard juvenile fantasy: Magic book transports boy to evil queen's domain

Story of a Crime
see Les Incendiaires

The Story of a Cross
1914, (GB), B&C/DFSA, b&w, 1,165 ft. (355.1m)
Standard crime-thriller: 'Dead' miner returns to kill partner who has married his ex-fiancee and caused her death

Story of Fairies
see Cuento de Hadas

The Story of Gosta Berling
1924, (Swed), Svensk Filmindustri, b&w, 9,104.3 ft. (2775m)
W: Greta Garbo *(Gosta Berling)*, Lars Hanson, Ellen Cederstrom, Mona Martenson, Svend Tornbech, Jenny Hasselquist, Otto Elg Lundberg, Karin Swanstrom, Gerda Lundequist, Torsten Kammeren, Sixten Malmerfelt
D: Mauritz Stiller   **ADAPT:** Mauritz Stiller & Ragnar Hylten-Cavallius, from Selma Lagerlof's novel   **PHOTOG:** Julius Jaenzon
edited version released in USA (1928) as **Legend of Gosta Berling** *A.k.a.* **Gosta Berling's Saga** *&* **Atonement of Gosta Berling**
Standard melodrama

The Story of Mankind
1957, (USA), Cambridge/WB, color, 100 mins.
W: Ronald Colman *("The Spirit of Man")*, Vincent Price *("Mr. Scratch")*, Hedy Lamarr *(Joan of Arc)*, Jim Ameche *(Alexander Graham Bell)*, Agnes Moorehead *(Elizabeth I)*, Reginald Gardner *(William Shakespeare)*, Virginia Mayo *(Cleopatra)*, Marie Wilson *(Marie Antoinette)*, Peter Lorre *(Nero)*, Dennis Hopper *(Napoleon)*, Groucho Marx *(Peter Minuit)*, Chico Marx *(The Monk)*, Harpo Marx *(Sir Isaac Newton)*, Melville Cooper *(The Major Domo)*, Charles Coburn *(Hippocrates)*, Sir Cedric Hardwicke *(The Judge)*, John Carradine *(Khufu)*, Henry Daniell *(Bishop of Beauvais)* *(Moses)*, Cesar Romero *(The Spanish Envoy)*, Helmut Dantine *(Marc Antony)*, Austin Green *(Lincoln)*, Marie Windsor *(Josephine)*, Cathy O'Donnell *(The Early Christian Woman)*, Edward Everett Horton *(Sir Walter Raleigh)*, Anthony Dexter *(Columbus)*, Dani Crayne *(Helen of Troy)*, Franklin Pangborn *(Marquis de Varennes)*, Reginald Sheffield *(Julius Caesar)*, Robert Watson *(Hitler)*, George E. Stone, David Bond, Nick Cravat, Richard Cutting, Marvin Miller, Toni Gerry, Eden Hartford, Alexander Lockwood, Abraham Sofaer, Don Megowan, Melinda Marx, Bart Mattson, Nancy Miller, Leonard Mudie, Burt Nelson, Tudor Owen, Ziva Rodann, William Schallert, Harry Ruby, Angelo Rossitto
P & D: Irwin Allen   **SCR:** Irwin Allen & Charles Bennett, suggested by Hendrik van Loon's book   **PHOTOG:** Nicholas Musuraca   **MUSIC:** Paul Sawtell
Standard comedy-drama: Excursion through pages of history

The Story of Robin Hood
1952, (GB), Walt Disney/RKO, color, 84 mins.
W: Richard Todd *(Robert Fitzooth/Robin Hood)*, Peter Finch *(DeLacy)*, Joan Rice *(Maid Marian)*, Martita Hunt *(Queen Eleanor)*, James Hayter *(Friar Tuck)*, Hubert Gregg *(Prince John)*, James Robertson Justice *(Little John)*, Patrick Barr *(King Richard I)*, Bill Owen *(Stutely)*, Michael Hordern *(Scathelock)*, Elton Hayes *(Allan-a-Dale)*, Reginald Tate *(Hugh Fitzooth)*, Anthony Forwood *(Will Scarlett)*, Hal Osmonde *(Midge)*, Clement McCallin, Louise Hampton, Antony Eustrel, Archie Duncan
P: Perce Pearce   **D:** Ken Annakin   **SCR:** Laurence E. Watkin   **PHOTOG:** Geoffrey Unsworth & Guy Green   **MUSIC:** Clifton Parker
reissued 1972
Standard adventure-thriller: Youth aids oppressed of 13th-century England

The Story of Snow White
1987, (USA), color, 83 mins.
W: Diana Rigg, Billy Barty
Standard juvenile fantasy: Wicked queen casts spell upon princess

The Story of the Count of Monte Cristo
see Le Comte de Monte Cristo

The Story of the Rosary
1920, (GB), Master Films/BEF, b&w, 5,000 ft. (1524m)
W: Malvina Longfellow *(Venetia)*, Dick Webb *(Paul Romaine)*, Charles Vane *(Prince Sabran)*, Marjorie Day *(Princess Venetia)*, Cameron Carr *(Venetia's Lover)*, Frank Tennant *(Philip Romaine)*, Irene Rooke *(Mother Superior)*, Victor Luske *(Father Theodore)*, E.F. Wallace *(The Colonel)*
D: Percy Nash   **SCR:** W. Courtenay Rowden, from a play by Walter Howard
Standard melodrama: Man escapes revolution, saves princess from crooked brother

A Story of Tutankhamun
1975, (GB), Ginger Films, color, 52 mins.
W: Domini Blyth *(Christine)*, Ezzat Elalaily *(Ahmed)*, John Welsh *(Grandfather)*, Barbara Bolton *(Mother)*, Abdel Monem Fetoh *(Ay)*, Ahmed Hanan *(Horemheb)*, Seif El Din *(Tutankhamun)*, Magged Tawfik *(The Boy King)*, Saad Zaaglol *(The High Priest)*, Nagwa Fouad *(The Dancer)*
P: Brian Jackson   **D:** Kevin Scott   **STORY:** Yusuf Idris   **PHOTOG:** Lewis McLeod   **MUSIC:** Ron Grainer
Standard thriller: Girl believes she is heir to death curse

Stowaway to the Moon
1975, (USA), 20th-Fox/CBS-TV, color, 100 mins.
W: Michael Link *(E.J.)*, Lloyd Bridges *(Charlie Engelhardt)*, Jeremy Slate *(Lawrence)*, Morgan Paull *(Anderson)*, James McMullen *(Pelham)*, John Carradine *(Jacob Avril)*, Pete Conrad *(The TV Commentator)*, James Callahan *(Jack Smathers)*, Stephen Rogers *(Joey)*, Walter Brooke *(Whitehead)* Keene Curtis
D: Andrew V. McLaglen   **TELEPLAY:** William R. Shelton & Jon Boothe
TVM, standard SF-adventure: Boy finds himself aboard space capsule headed for moon

S

La Strage dei Vampiri (Slaughter of the Vampires)
1962, (It), Mercury, b&w, 81 mins.
W: Dieter Eppler, Walter Brandi, Graziella Granata
P: Dino sant'Ambrogio **WRIT & D:** Roberto Mauri
reissued (1969) by Pacemaker Films as Curse of the Blood-Ghouls
Minor horror-fantasy: Honeymooners meet Undead

Straight On Till Morning
1972, (GB), Hammer/MGM-EMI, color, 96 mins.
W: Rita Tushingham (*Brenda Thompson*), Shane Briant (*Peter*), Tom Bell (*Jimmy Lindsay*), Annie Ross (*Liza*), Katya Wyeth (*Caroline*), James Bolam (*Joey*), Claire Kelly (*Margo Thompson*), John Clive (*The Newsagent*), Harold Berens (*Harris*), Tommy Godfrey (*The Customer*), Mavis Villiers (*Princess*)
P: Roy Skeggs **D:** Peter Collinson **SCR:** Michael Peacock **PHOTOG:** Brian Probyn **MUSIC:** Roland Shaw
A.k.a. Till Dawn Do Us Part video title, Dressed for Death
Intriguing psychodrama (not distrib. theatrically in USA): Shy girl atracted to mysterious young man

Strait-Jacket
1964, (USA), Col, b&w, 92 mins.
W: Joan Crawford (*Lucy Harbin*), Diane Baker (*Carol*), Leif Erickson (*Bill Cutler*), George Kennedy (*Leo Krause*), John Anthony Hayes (*Michael Fields*), Howard St. John (*Raymond Fields*), Rochelle Hudson (*Emily Cutler*), Mitchell Cox (*Dr. Anderson*), Edith Atwater (*Mrs. Fields*), Lee Yeary (*Frank Harbin*), Patricia Krest (*Stella Fulton*), Lyn Lundgren (*The Beauty Operator*), Robert Ward (*The Shoe Clerk*), Laura Hess, Vickie Cos
P & D: William Castle **SCR:** Robert Bloch **PHOTOG:** Arthur E. Arling **SPCL-FX:** Richard Albain **MUSIC:** Van Alexander **SONGS:** *There Goes That Song Again*
blurb: "...vividly depicts axe murders!"
Entertaining thriller: Axe-murderess released from prison

Stranded
1988, (USA), New Line, color, 80 mins.
W: Ione Skye, Joe Morton, Maureen O'Sullivan, Brendan Hughes, Cameron Dye
D: Tex Fuller **SCR:** Alan Castle
Minor SF-fantasy: Rural family befriends space aliens

Stranded in Space
see *The Stranger (1973)*

A Strange Adventure
1932, (USA), Mono, b&w, 62 mins.
W: Regis Toomey, Jason Robards Sr., Dwight Frye, June Clyde
P: I.E. Chadwick, from a story by Arthur Hoerl
TV-retitle, The Wayne Murder Case
Minor thriller: Rich man murdered as he reads will

The Strange Adventure of David Gray
see *Vampyr*

The Strange Affair
1968, (GB), Para, color, 106 mins.
W: Michael York (*Peter Strange*), Jeremy Kemp (*Sgt. Pierce*), Susan George (*Frederika March*), Jack Watson (*Quince*), Bigel Davenport (*The Defense*), George A. Cooper (*Supt. Kingley*), George Benson (*Uncle Bertrand*), Barry Fantoni (*Charley Small*), Artro Morris (*Insp. Evans*), Richard Pearson (*The Constable*), Madge Ryan (*Aunt Mary*), Terence de Marney (*Mahon*)
P: Howard Harrison & Stanley Mann **D:** David Greene **SCR:** Stanley Mann, from a novel by Bernard Toms
Standard crime-thriller: Detective blackmails police recruit, pursues drug peddlers

The Strange Affair of Uncle Harry
1945, (USA), Univ, b&w, 82 mins.
W: George Sanders, Geraldine Fitzgerald, Ella Raines, Sara Allgood, Moyna MacGill, Samuel S. Hinds
D: Robert Siodmak
A.k.a. Uncle Harry & The Zero Murder Case
Standard thriller: Scheming sister disrupts man's life

The Strange and Deadly Occurrence
1974, (USA), NBC-TV, color, 72 mins.
W: Robert Stack, Vera Miles, Margaret Willock, L.Q. Jones, Herb Edelman, Dena Dietrich, Aldine King, James McCallion, Ted Gehring
P & TELEPLAY: Sandor Stern **STORY:** Sandor Stern & Lane Slate **D:** John Llewellyn Moxey **MUSIC:** Robert Prince
TVM, standard thriller: New homeowners find domicile plagued by seemingly supernatural phenomena

The Strange Awakening
1958, (GB), Merton Park/Anglo-Amalgamated, b&w, 69 mins.
W: Lex Barker (*Peter Chance*), Carole Matthews (*Selena Friend*), Lisa Gastoni (*Marny Friend*), Peter Dyneley (*Dr. Rene Normand*), Nora Swinburne (*Mrs. Friend*), John Serrat (*Commissaire Sagain*), Joe Robinson (*Sven*), Malou Pantera (*Isabella*)
P: Alec Snowden **D:** Montgomery Tully **SCR:** J. McLaren Ross, from Patrick Quentin's novel *Puzzle for Fiends*
Modest thriller: Amnesiac drawn into swindle scheme

Strange Behavior
1981, (N. Zeal), World Northal, color, 99 mins.
W: Michael Murphy (*John Brady*), Louise Fletcher (*Barbara*), Dan Shor (*Pete*), Fiona Lewis (*Gwen*), Arthur Dignam (*Dr. LaSange*), Dey Young (*Caroline*), Marc McClure (*Oliver*), Scott Brady (*Shea*), Beryl TeWiata (*Mrs. Haskell*), William Hayward (*Robinson*), Jim Boelson (*Waldo*), Charles Lane (*Donovan*), Elizabeth Cheshire (*Lucy*), B. Courtenay Leigh (*Paula*), Jack Haines (*Randy*), William Condon (*Bryan*), Billy Al Bengston (*Felix*), Nicole Anderson (*The Flying Nun*), Richard Moore, Cindy Arnold, Howard Crothall, John Clarke, Andrew Glover, Joe Harner, Mary Ruth Harner, Susanna Moore, Lulu Sylbert, Summer Ramer, Bob Houston, Susan Van Ravenswaav, Jessica Kenny, Neil Mclachlan, Alma Woods, Maurice Keene, Brenda Casey, Stephen Jackson, Bob Gentil, Greg Dower, Jane Dower, Simon Nesbitt, Rod Collison, Terry Donovan, Maryke Mann, Wally Parks, Campbell Hegan, Le Roy Sisnett, Kerry Brown, Peter Walker, Mark Hadlow, Melodie Batchelor, Kathryn Collins, Michael Hammond, Ngila Dickson, Louise Franklin, Marcus Le Grice, Adair Wheeler, Peta Rutter, Janet Wells
D: Michael Laughlin **SCR:** William Condon & Michael Laughlin **PHOTOG:** Louis Horvath **MUSIC:** Tangerine Dream
A.k.a. Dead Kids and Small Town Massacre
Unusual thriller: Brutal murders in college town

Strange Behaviour: MICHAEL MURPHY

Strange Behaviour
1988, (GB), Penrose Prods./ITC, color, 14 mins.
W: Anthony Vankaast (*The Man*), Rebecca Harbord (*The Woman*), Fred Baker (*The Gardener*), Robert Isaac (*A Policeman*), John Wyndham (*A Policeman*)
WRIT, P & D: Anthony Penrose **PHOTOG:** Adrian Jeakins **MUSIC:** Ron Geesin
Standard short fantasy: Commuter daydreams of nesting in tree with woman

The Strange Case of Blondie
1954, (GB), Merton Park/Anglo-Amalgamated, b&w, 32 mins.
W: Russell Napier (*Insp. Harmer*), Derek Aylward (*Langham*), Lee Sinclair (*Eddie Leroy*), Cyril Smith (*Wilson*), Barbara James (*Mrs. Dexter*)
P: Alec Snowden **D:** Ken Hughes **STORY:** Basil Francis, from a novel by Edgar Lustgarten
Standard short crime-thriller: Murderous cat-burglar disguised as blonde

The Strange Case of Dr. Manning
1958, (GB), Winwell/Rep/Astral, b&w, 75 mins.
W: Ron Randell, Greta Gynt
D: Arthur Crabtree
Minor thriller: Scotland Yard trails kidnappers. GB release: Morning Call

The Strange Case of Dr. Rx
1942, (USA), Univ, b&w, 66 mins.
W: Lionel Atwill, Patric Knowles, Anne Gwynne, Samuel S. Hinds, Mantan Moreland, Shemp Howard, Mona Barrie, Paul Cavanagh, Ray Corrigan
D: William Nigh **SCR:** Clarence Upson Young **PHOTOG:** Elwood Bredell
Minor thriller: Mysterious avenger commits murder

The Strange Case of Dr. Faustus
see *El Extrano Caso del Dr. Fausto*

The Strange Case of Mrs. Ward
see *Lo Strano Caso della Signora Ward*

The Strange Case of Mr. Todmorden
1935, (GB), Monarch/Zenifilms, b&w, 20 mins.
W: F. Bellenden Clark (*Mr. Todmorden*), Douglas Phillips (*Insp. Mason*), Vera Gerald (*Miss Hartley*), Peter Northcote (*George*), Clifford Cobbe (*PC Wilson*)
D: Fraser Foulsham & A.B. Imeson **SCR:** James Riddell, from a story by F. Britten Austin
Standard short thriller: Sleepwalking lawyer kills rich woman

S

The Strange Case of Philip Kent
1916, (GB), Barker-Neptune/KTC, b&w, 3,500 ft. (1066.8m)
W: Cyril Morton (*Dr. Cecil Mortimer*), J. Hastings Batson (*Sir George Terry*)
D: Fred W. Durrant   **STORY:** Rowland Talbot
Standard crime-thriller: Man persuades dying friend to insure, weds and murders widow

Strange Confession
1945, (USA), Univ, b&w, 62 mins.
W: Lon Chaney Jr., Brenda Joyce, Addison Richards, Milburn Stone, Lloyd
  Bridges, Mary Gordon, George Chandler, Wilton Graff, J. Carrol Naish,
  Jack Norton, Christian Rub, Francis McDonald
P: Ben Pivar   **D:** John Hoffman   **SCR:** M. Coates Webster   **PHOTOG:** Maury
  Gertsman
reissued as **The Missing Head**
Minor thriller (remake of **The Man Who Reclaimed His Head***): Scientist gains grisly
  revenge when wife and formula are stolen*

Strange Fascination: Cleo Moore and Genevieve Aumont

The Strange Countess
1961, (W. Ger), b&w, 96 mins.
W: Joachim Berger, Marianne Hoppe, Lil Dagover Brigitte Grothum
D: Josef Von Baky, from a story by Edgar Wallace
Minor thriller: Series of murders connected to countess and woman released from prison

The Strange Creature of the Black Lake
see **Creature from the Black Lagoon**

Strange Days
1995, (USA), Lightstorm/20th-Fox, color, 145 mins.
W: Ralph Fiennes (*Lenny Nero*), Angela Bassett (*Lornette "Mace" Mason*), Juliette
  Lewis (*Faith Justin*), Vincent D'Onofrio (*Burton Steckler*), Tom Sizemore
  (*Max*), Brigitte Bako (*Iris*), Michael Wincott (*Philo Gant*), Joe Uala (*Keith*),
  Glenn Plummer (*Jeriko One*), Richard Edson (*Tick*), Josef Sommer (*Deputy
  Commissioner Palmer Strickland*), William Fichtner (*Dwayne*), Malcolm
  Norrington (*Replay*), Nicky Katt (*Joey*), Michael Jace, David Carrera, Louise
  LeCavalier, Jim Ishida, Todd Graff, Brandon Hammond, Anais Munoz, Rio
  Hachford, Ted Kaler, James Muro, Donald "Donnie" Young, David Packer,
  Brook Susan Parker, B.J. Crockett, Erica Kelly, Dex Elliott Sanders, Raul
  Reformina, Ronnie Willis, Kylie Ireland, Ron Young, Marlana Young, Billy
  Worley, Ray Chang, Amon Bourne, Lisa Picotte, John Francis, Stefan
  Arngrim, Agustin Rodriguez, Kelly Hu, Nynno Anderson, Honey Labrador,
  Delane Vaughn, Russell W. Smith, Mark Arneson, James Acheson, Royce
  Minor, Milan Reynolds
D: Kathryn Bigelow   **SCR:** James Cameron & Jay Cocks   **STORY:** James
  Cameron   **PHOTOG:** Matthew F. Leonetti   **SPCL VS-FX:** Digital
  Domain   **MUSIC:** Graeme Revell   **MUSIC SPRVSR:** Randy Gerston
SONGS: *Selling Jesus, Lost in the Night, Get Your Gunn, No White Clouds,
  Overcome, Here We Come, Walk in Freedom, The Real Thing, Undone, Hardly
  Wait, Dance Me to the End of Love, Therapy, Rid of Me, Drink My Honey, Feed,
  Fall in the Light & New Eyes of Old*
Unusual futuristic thriller: Device transfers sensory stimuli

The Strange Death of Adolf Hitler
1943, (USA), Univ, b&w, 74 mins.
W: Ludwig Donath (*Franz Huber/Hitler*), Gale Sondergaard (*Anna Huber*), George
  Dolenz (*Herman Harbach*), Fritz Kortner (*Bauer*), Ludwig Stossel (*Graub*),
  William Trenk (*Von Zechwitz*), Rudolph Anders, Ivan Triesault, Erno
  Verebes, Kurt Katch, Fred Gierman, Hans Schumm, John Mylong, Kurt
  Kreuger, Lester Sharpe, Hans von Twardowski
D: James Hogan   **SCR:** Fritz Kortner   **ORIG STORY:** Fritz Kortner & Joe May
  PHOTOG: Jerome Ash   **MUSIC:** H.J. Salter
Minor thriller: Gestapo plot to create Hitler lookalike

Strange Deception
see **The Accused** (1948)

The Strange Door
1951, (USA), Univ, b&w, 81 mins.
W: Charles Laughton, Boris Karloff, Sally Forrest, Richard Stapley, Paul
  Cavanagh, Alan Napier, Michael Pate
P: Ted Richmond   **D:** Joseph Pevney   **SCR:** Jerry Sackheim, loosely based on
  Robert Louis Stevenson's short story *The Sire de Maletroit's Door*   **PHOTOG:**
  Irving Glassberg   **MUSIC:** Joseph Gershenson
Belg retitle, **Buried Alive** *Fr retitle,* **The Castle of Terror** *Ger retitle,* **Behind the
  Doors of Horror**
Standard thriller: Man seeks revenge in 17th-century London

A Strange Evening
see **The Old Dark House** (1932)

Strange Evidence
1933, (GB), London/Para, b&w, 71 mins.
W: Leslie Banks (*Francis Relf*), George Curzon (*Stephen Relf*), Carol Goodner
  (*Marie/Barbara Relf*), Frank Vosper (*Andrew Relf*), Norah Baring (*Clare Relf*),
  Haidee Wright (*Mrs. Relf*), Lyonel Watts (*Henry Relf*), Diana Napier (*Jean*),
  Lewis Shaw (*Larry*)
D: Robert Milton   **SCR:** Miles Malleson, from a story by Lajos Biro
Standard thriller: Faithless wife suspected of poisoning invalid husband

Strange Experiment
1937, (GB), Fox British, b&w, 74 mins.
W: Donald Gray (*James Martin*), Ann Wemyss (*Joan*), Mary Newcomb (*Helen
  Rollins*), Ronald Ward (*Waring*), Henri de Vries (*Prof. Bauer*), Alastair Sim
  (*Lawler*), James Carew (*Dr. Rollins*)
D: Albert Parker   **SCR:** Edward Dryhurst, from the play *Two Worlds* by Hubert
  Osborne & John Golden
Standard thriller: Chemist feigns amnesia, foils robbery gang

Strange Fascination
1952, (USA), Col, b&w, 80 mins.
W: Hugo Haas, Cleo Moore, Rick Vallin, Mona Barrie
WRIT, P & D: Hugo Haas
Minor melodrama: Middle-aged immigrant pianist weds venal young dancer

The Strange Girl
see **Das Fremde Madchen**

Strange Illusion
see **Out of the Night**

Strange Impersonation
1946, (USA), Rep, b&w, 68 mins.
W: William Gargan, Brenda Marshall
D: Anthony Mann
Minor melodrama

Strange Intruder
1956, (USA), AA, b&w, 82 mins.
W: Ida Lupino, Edmund Purdom
D: Irving Rapper   **PHOTOG:** Ernest Haller
Standard thriller

Strange Invaders
1983, (USA), Orion, color, 94 mins.
W: Paul LeMat (*Charles Bigelow*), Nancy Allen (*Betty Walker*), Louise Fletcher
  (*Mrs. Benjamin*), Diana Scarwid (*Margaret*), June Lockhart (*Mrs. Bigelow*),
  Kenneth Tobey (*Arthur Newman*), Lulu Sylbert (*Elizabeth*), Wallace Shawn
  (*Earl*), Michael Lerner (*Willie Collins*), Fiona Lewis (*The Waitress/Avon Lady*),
  Charles Lane (*Prof. Hollister*), Joel Cohen (*Tim*), Dan Shor (*Teen Boy in
  Prologue*), Dey Young (*Teen Girl in Prologue*), Jack Kehler (*The Gas Station
  Attendant*), Mark Goddard (*The Detective*), Al Roberts (*The Man in Dark
  Glasses*), Thomas Kopache (*The State Trooper*), Bobby Pickett (*The Editor*),
  Ron Gillham (*The First Alien*), Connie Kellers (*Connie*), Nancy Johnson
  (*Stewardess #1*), Betsy Pickerin (*Stewardess #2*), Jonathan Ulmer (*The Room
  Service Waiter*), Edwina Follows (*The Nurse*), Patti Medwid (*The Room Service
  Waitress*)
D: Michael Laughlin   **SCR:** Michael Laughlin & William Condon   **PHOTOG:**
  Louis Horvath   **SPCL VS-FX:** Private Stock Effects Inc.   **MUSIC:** John
  Addison
Standard SF-thriller: Space aliens detected on Earth

Strange Journey
see **Fantastic Voyage**

Strange Justice
1932, (USA), RKO, b&w, 72 mins.
W: Preston Foster, Irving Pichel
D: Victor Schertzinger
Standard melodrama

S

The Strange Love of Martha Ivers

1946, (USA), b&w, 117 mins.
W: Barbara Stanwyck, Van Heflin, Kirk Douglas (film debut), Lizabeth Scott, Judith Anderson, Roman Bohnen, Frank Orth
D: Lewis Milestone   SCR: Robert Rossen   PHOTOG: Victor Milner   MUSIC: Miklos Rozsa
Gripping "noir:" Calculating woman in love triangle

Strange Madame X

see L'Etrange Madame X

Strange Mr. Gregory

1946, (USA), Mono, b&w, 63 mins.
W: Edmund Lowe, Jean Rogers, Don Douglas, Frank Reicher, Jonathan Hale Marjorie Hoshelle, Robert Emmett Keane
P: Louis Berkoff   D: Phil Rosen
blurb: "Love thief by day...fiend by night"
Minor thriller: Villainous hypnotist fakes death

The Strangeness

1983, (USA), Stellarwind, color, 90 mins.
W: Dan Lunham (*Geoff Calvert*), Terri Berland (*Cindy Flanders*), Rolf Theison (*Myron Hemmings*), Keith Hurt (*Morgan*), Mark Sawicki (*Dan Flanders*), Chris Huntley (*Tony Ruggles*), Diane Borcyckowski (*Angela Platt*), Robin Sortman (*Brian*), Arlene Buchmann (*Amy*)
D: David Michael Hillman   SCR: David Michael Hillman & Chris Huntley   PHOTOG: Kevin O'Brien & Stephen Greenfield   SPCL VS-FX: Mark Sawicki & Chris Huntley
Minor horror-thriller: Abandoned mine harbors terror

Strange New World

1975, (USA), WB/ABC-TV, color, 100 mins.
W: John Saxon (*Capt. Anthony Vico*), Kathleen Miller (*Dr. Allison Crowley*), Keene Curtis (*Dr. Scott*), Ford Rainey, Reb Brown, James Olson, Martine Beswick, Catherine Bach, Gerrit Graham, Cynthia Wood, Bill McKinney
D: Robert Butler   TELEPLAY: Al Ramrus, Ronald F. Graham & Walon Green   PHOTOG: Michael Margulies
TVM, minor SF: Adventures in world of future

Strange Obsession

see La Strega in Amore

The Strange Ones

see Les Enfants Terribles

The Strange Possession of Mrs. Oliver

1977, (USA), NBC-TV, color, 76 mins.
W: Karen Black (*Mrs. Oliver*), George Hamilton (*Greg Oliver*), Robert F. Lyons (*Mark*), Jean Allison (*Mrs. Dempster*), Lucille Benson (*The Housekeeper*), Gloria LeRoy (*The Saleslady*), Burke Byrnes (*The Bartender*)
D: Gordon Hessler   TELEPLAY: Richard Matheson
TVM, standard thriller: Neurotic housewife affects alter ego, finds her life threatened

The Stranger

1946, (USA), RKO, b&w, 95 mins.
W: Orson Welles, Edward G. Robinson, Loretta Young, Richard Long, Billy House, Konstantin Shayne, Philip Merivale
D: Orson Welles   PHOTOG: Russell Metty   MUSIC: Bronislau Kaper
Unusual thriller: Nazi hides out in small Connecticut college town

The Stranger

1973, (USA), Bing Crosby Prods./NBC-TV, color, 98 mins.
W: Glenn Corbett, Sharon Acker, Lew Ayres, Dean Jagger, Cameron Mitchell, Tim O'Connor, George Coulouris, Steve Franken, Virginia Gregg
D: Lee H. Katzin   TELEPLAY: Gerald Sanford
A.k.a. Stranded in Space
TVM, standard SF-thriller (similar to Doppelganger): Astronaut stranded on sinister Earthlike planet

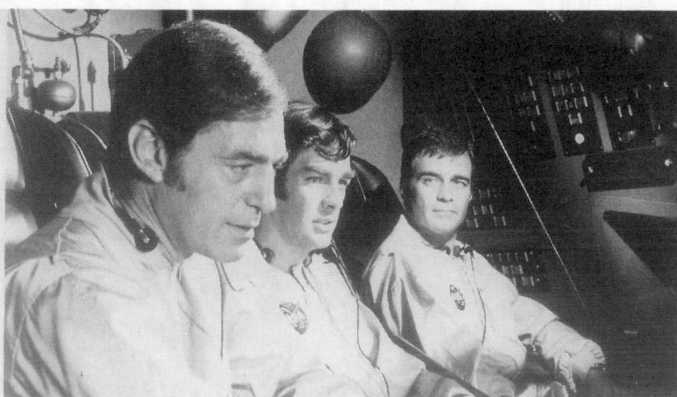

The Stranger: H.M. WYNANT, JERRY DOUGLAS AND GLENN CORBETT

Stranger at My Door

1956, (USA), Rep, b&w, 85 mins.
W: Macdonald Carey, Patricia Medina
Standard melodrama-western

The Stranger Came Home

1954, (GB), Hammer/Exclusive, b&w, 80 mins.
W: Paulette Goddard (*Angie Vickers*), William Sylvester (*Philip Vickers*), Patrick Holt (*Job Crandall*), Paul Carpenter (*Bill Saul*), Alvys Maben (*Joan Merrill*), Russell Napier (*Insp. Treherne*), Pat (Patricia) Owens (*The Blonde*), David King Wood (*Sessions*), Kay Callard (*Jenny*), Jeremy Hawk (*Sgt. Johnson*)
P & SCR: Michael Carreras   D: Terence Fisher, from George Sanders' novel *Stranger at Home*
USA retitle, The Unholy Four
Standard thriller: Amnesiac financier returns from "death," is framed for murder

Stranger from Venus

1954, (GB), Rich & Rich-Princess/Eros, b&w, 75 mins.
W: Patricia Neal (*Susan North*), Helmut Dantine (*The Stranger*), Derek Bond (*Arthur Walker*), Cyril Luckham (*Dr. Meinard*), Willoughby Gray (*Tom*), Marigold Russell (*Gretchen*), Arthur Young (*The Scientist*)
P: Burt Balaban & Gene Martel   D: Burt Balaban   SCR: Hans Jacoby, from a story by Desmond Leslie
USA retitle, Immediate Disaster A.k.a. The Venusian
Standard SF-thriller: Visiting Venusian wants Earth to abandon atomic experiments

The Stranger in Between

see Hunted (1952)

Stranger in Our House

1978, (USA), InterPlanetary/NBC-TV, color, 100 mins.
W: Linda Blair (*Rachel Bryant*), Carol Lawrence (*Leslie Bryant*), Lee Purcell (*Julia*), Jeremy Slate (*Tom Bryant*), Jeff East (*Peter Bryant*), Macdonald Carey (*Prof. Jarvis*), James T. Jarnigin (*Bobby Bryant*), Patricia Wilson (*Mrs. Gallagher*), Fran Drescher (*Carolyn*), Jeffrey McCracken (*Mike*)
P: Pat & Bill Finnegan   D: Wes Craven   TELEPLAY: Max A. Keller & Glenn M. Benest, based on the novel *Summer of Fear*
TVM, standard fantasy-thriller: Teenaged witch exercises her supernatural powers

Stranger in the House

1967, (GB), De Grunwald/RFD, color, 104 mins.
W: James Mason (*John Sawyer*), Geraldine Chaplin (*Angela Sawyer*), Bobby Darin (*Barney Teale*), Paul Bertoya (*Jo Christophorides*), Ian Ogilvy (*Desmond Flower*), Bryan Stanton (*Peter Hawkins*), Pippa Steele (*Sue Phillips*), Clive Morton (*Col. Flower*), James Hayter (*Harry Hawkins*), Megs Jenkins (*Mrs. Christophorides*), Moira Lister (*Mrs. Flower*), Marjie Lawrence (*Brenda*), Lisa Daniely (*Diana*)
P: Dimitri De Grunwald   D & SCR: Pierre Rouvel, from Georges Simenon's novel *Les Inconnus dans la Maison*
Standard thriller: Drunken ex-barrister defends daughter's lover on murder charges. Remake of 1942 film

Stranger in the House (1974)

see Silent Night, Evil Night

Stranger in Town

1957, (GB), Tempean/Eros, b&w, 73 mins.
W: Alex Nicol (*John Madison*), Anne Page (*Vicky Leigh*), Mary Laura Wood (*Lorna Ryland*), Mona Washbourne (*Agnes Smith*), Charles Lloyd Pack (*Capt. Nash*), Bruce Beeby (*William Ryland*), John Horsley (*Insp. Powell*), Colin Tapley (*Henry*), Betty Impey (*Geraldine Nash*)
P: Robert Baker & Monty Berman   D: George Pollock   SCR: Norman Hudis & Edward Dryhurst, from Frank Chittenden's novel *Uninvited*
Minor crime-thriller: Reporter solves blackmailer's shooting

A Stranger in Town

1998, (USA), SHO-TV, color, 95 mins.
W: Harry Hamlin, Graham Greene, Trevor Blumas, Rebecca Jenkins, Carly McKillip
Made-for-Cable, standard thriller: Handyman has troubled past

A Stranger is Watching

1982, (USA), MGM, color, 92 mins.
W: Rip Torn, Kate Mulgrew, James Naughton, Barbara Baxley, Shawn Von Schreiber, Stephen Joyce, James Russo, Maurice Copeland, Frank Hamilton, Maggie Task, Roy Poole, JoAnne Dorian, Eleanor Phelps, Read Morgan, Stephen Strimpell, David Brooks, William Hickey, Jenny Ventriss
D: Sean S. Cunningham   SCR: Earl Mac Rauch & Victor Miller, from Mary Higgins Clark's novel   PHOTOG: Barry Abrams   MUSIC: Lalo Schifrin
Standard thriller: Murderer menaces girl

The Stranger Left No Card

1953, (GB), Meteor/British Lion, b&w, 23 mins.
W: Alan Badel (*The Stranger*), Cameron Hall (*Latham*), Eileen Way (*The Secretary*)
P: George K. Arthur   D: Wendy Toye   STORY: Sidney Carroll
Standard short thriller: Weird eccentric murders man who framed him

S

Stranger on the Prowl
1953, (It), UA, b&w, 82 mins.
<u>W</u>: Paul Muni, Joan Lorring
Standard thriller

Stranger on the Third Floor
1940, (USA), RKO, b&w, 64 mins.
<u>W</u>: Peter Lorre, Margaret Tallichet, John McGuire, Charles Waldron, Elisha Cook Jr., Charles Halton, Ethel Griffies
<u>P</u>: Lee Marcus   <u>D</u>: Boris Ingster   <u>STORY & SCR</u>: Frank Partos   <u>PHOTOG</u>: Nicholas Musuraca   <u>MUSIC</u>: Roy Webb
Standard thriller (credited as the first true film noir): Reporter tracks mad killer

The Strangers
1980, (It), Angiolo Stella-Ciro Ippolito/Cinema Shares Int'l, color, 84 mins.
<u>W</u>: Belinda Mayne (*Thelma*), Marc Bodin, Robert Barrese, Judy Perrin, Benny Aldrich, Michael Shaw, Don Parkinson, Claudio Falanga
<u>WRIT, P & D</u>: Sam Cromwell   <u>PHOTOG</u>: Silvio Fraschetti   <u>SPCL-FX</u>: Donald Patterly   <u>MUSIC</u>: The Oliver Onions
Minor SF-horror: Colorado cave houses other-worldly force

The Stranger's Hand
1954, (GB), British Lion/DCA, b&w, 86 mins.
<u>W</u>: Trevor Howard (*Maj. Court*), Alida Valli (*Roberta*), Eduardo Ciannelli (*Dr. Vivaldi*), Richard Basehart (*Joe Hamstringer*), Richard O'Sullivan (*Roger Court*), Stephen Murray (*The Consul*), Giorgio Constantini (*Pescovitch*)
<u>P</u>: John Stafford & Graham Greene   <u>D</u>: Mario Soldati   <u>SCR</u>: Guy Elmes & Georgino Bassani, from a story by Graham Greene
Standard thriller: Schoolboy seeks father kidnapped by communist spies

Strangers in the House
see Les Inconnus dans la Maison

Strangers in the Night
1944, (USA), Rep, b&w, 56 mins.
<u>W</u>: William Terry, Virginia Grey
<u>D</u>: Anthony Mann
Standard thriller

Strangers in Town
see Bay Coven

Strangers' Meeting
1957, (GB), Parroch/RFD, b&w, 64 mins.
<u>W</u>: Peter Arne (*Harry Bellair*), Delphi Lawrence (*Margot Sanders*), Conrad Phillips (*David Sanders*), David Ritch (*Giovanni*), Barbara Archer (*Rosie Foster*), David Lodg (*Fred*), Selma Vaz Diaz (*Magda Mayer*), Victor Maddern (*Willie Fisher*)
<u>P</u>: Jack Parsons & E. Smedley Aston   <u>D</u>: Robert Day   <u>STORY</u>: David Gordon
Standard crime-thriller: Acrobat flees prison to locate partner's killer

Strangers on a Train
1951, (USA), WB, b&w, 101 mins.
<u>W</u>: Farley Granger (*Guy Haines*), Robert Walker (*Bruno Antony*), Ruth Roman (*Ann Morton*), Pat Hitchcock (*Barbara*), Marion Lorne (*Mrs. Antony*), Leo G. Carroll (*Sen. Morton*), Howard St. John (*Police Chief Turley*), Laura Elliot, John Brown, Robert Gist
<u>P & D</u>: Alfred Hitchcock   <u>SCR</u>: Raymond Chandler & Czenzi Ormonde, from Patricia Highsmith's novel   <u>PHOTOG</u>: Robert Burks   <u>MUSIC</u>: Dmitri Tiomkin
*Classic thriller: Demented playboy involves socialite in weird murder. pact cf. **Once You Meet a Stranger***

A Stranger Waits
1987, (USA), color, 95 mins.
<u>W</u>: Suzanne Pleshette, Tom Atkins, Justin Deas, Paul Benjamin, Ann Wedgeworth, Kenneth Welsh, Jesse Welles, Alexandra Johnson, Bill Ontiveros
<u>D</u>: Robert Lewis   <u>TELEPLAY</u>: Durrell Royce Crays   <u>PHOTOG</u>: John Lindley   <u>MUSIC</u>: James Di Pasquale
TVM, standard thriller: Caretaker has evil designs on widow

A Stranger Walked In
see Love from a Stranger (1947)

The Stranger Within
1974, (USA), Lorimar/ABC-TV, color, 72 mins.
<u>W</u>: Barbara Eden, George Grizzard, Joyce Van Patten, David Doyle, Nehemiah Persoff
<u>P</u>: Neil T. Maffeo   <u>D</u>: Lee Philips   <u>TELEPLAY</u>: Richard Matheson, from his short story   <u>PHOTOG</u>: Michael Margulies
orig. to be titled Trespass
*TVM, standard SF-thriller (similar to **The Village of the Damned**): Woman impregnated by alien force*

Strange Shadows in an Empty Room
1977, (It-Can), AIP, color, 97 mins.
<u>W</u>: Stuart Whitman, Martin Landau, John Saxon, Tisa Farrow
Minor thriller: Detective probes sister's murder, uncovers sordid past

Strangest Dreams: Invasion of the Space Preachers
1990, (USA), Big Pictures/Troma, color
<u>W</u>: Jim Wolfe (*Walter*), Guy Nelson (*Rick*), Eliska Hahn (*Nova*), Gary Brown (*Rev. Lash*), Jesse Johnson
<u>WRIT & D</u>: Daniel Boyd   <u>PHOTOG</u>: Bill Hogan   <u>MUSIC</u>: Michael Lipton
Minor SF-comedy: Intergalactic evangelists influence town

The Strange Story of Judge Cordier
see Diary of a Madman

Strange Triangle: ANABEL SHAW, JOHN SHEPPERD

Strange Triangle
1946, (USA), 20th-Fox, b&w, 65 mins.
<u>W</u>: Signe Hasso, John Sheppard (Shepperd Strudwick), Preston Foster
Minor melodrama

Strange World of Coffin Joe
1968, (Brz), color
<u>W</u>: Jose Mojica Marins
<u>D</u>: Jose Mojica Marins
Minor trilogy of terror tales: (1) Dollmaker tempted by human-like creations, (2) Balloon seller is necrophile, & (3) Doctor is sadist

The Strange World of Planet X
1958, (GB), Artistes Alliance/Eros/DCA, b&w, 75 mins.
<u>W</u>: Forrest Tucker (*Gil Graham*), Gaby Andre (*Michele Dupont*), Martin Benson (*Smith*), Alec Mango (*Dr. Laird*), Hugh Latimer (*Jimmy Murray*), Wyndham Goldie (*Cartwright*), Richard Warner (*Insp. Burns*), Patricia Sinclair (*Helen Forsythe*), Geoffrey Chater (*Gerald Wilson*)
<u>P</u>: George Maynard   <u>D</u>: Gilbert Gunn   <u>SCR</u>: Paul Ryder & Joe Ambor, from a TV serial by Rene Ray
*USA retitle, **The Cosmic Monster***
Minor SF-thriller: Extraterrestrial emissary destroys Earth doctor's device for enlarging insects

Stranglehold
see Grip of the Strangler

The Strangler
1932, (GB), BIP/Pathe, b&w, 45 mins.
<u>W</u>: Jack Morrison (*Johnnie Scott*), Moira Lynd (*Rosie Platt*), Lewis Dayton (*Lee MacArthur*), Molly Lamont (*Frances Marsden*), Cecil Ramage (*Dr. Bevan*), Hal Gordon (*Loveridge*), Patrick Susands (*Eckersley*), Carol Coombe (*Billie Southgate*)
<u>WRIT & D</u>: Norman Lee
Standard thriller: Actor killed during play rehearsal

The Strangler (1941)
see East of Piccadilly

The Strangler
1963, (USA), AA, b&w, 89 mins.
<u>W</u>: Victor Buono (*Leo*), David McLean (*Benson*), Diane Sayer (*Barbara*), Davey

S

Davison *(Tally)*, Ellen Corby *(Leo's Mother)*, Michael M. Ryan, Baynes Barron, Russ Bender, Jeanne Bates

P: Samuel Bischoff & David Diamond   **D:** Burt Topper   **SCR:** Bill S. Ballinger   **PHOTOG:** Jacques Marquette   **MUSIC:** Marlin Skiles
Minor thriller: Psychotic murders young women

The Strangler of Blackmoor Castle
1960, (W. Ger.), CCC/Telewide, b&w, 89 mins.
W: Ingmar Zeisberg, Karin Dor
Minor thriller

The Strangler of London
see Der Henker von London

Strangler of the Swamp
1945, (USA), PRC, b&w, 60 mins.
W: Robert Barrett, Rosemary La Planche, Charles Middleton, Frank Conlan, Blake Edwards
D & SCR: Frank Wisbar
Standard thriller: Vengeful "ghost" haunts backwater

Strangler of the Tower
1966, (W. Ger.), ITC, b&w, 92 mins.
W: Ady Berber
Minor thriller: Deranged killer holds city in grip of fear

Strangler of Vienna
see The Mad Butcher

The Stranglers of Bombay
1959, (GB), Hammer/Col, b&w, 81 mins.
W: Guy Rolfe *(Capt. Lewis)*, Andrew Cruickshank *(Col. Henderson)*, Allan Cuthbertson *(Capt. Connaught-Smith)*, Marne Maitland *(Patel Shan)*, George Pastell *(The High Priest)*, Jan Holden *(Mary)*, Paul Stassino *(Silver)*, David Spenser *(Gopali)*, Tutte Lemkow *(Ram Das)*, Marie Devereaux *(Karim)*
P: Anthony Hinds   **D:** Terence Fisher   **SCR:** David Z. Goodman   **PHOTOG:** Arthur Grant   **MUSIC:** James Bernard
Standard thriller: British captain unmasks Hindu cultists

Strangler's Web
1965, (GB), Merton Park/Anglo-Amalgamated, b&w, 55 mins.
W: John Stratton *(Lewis Preston)*, Pauline Munro *(Melanie)*, Griffith Jones *(Jackson Delacourt)*, Gerald Harper *(Insp. Murray)*, Maurice Hedley *(Amos Colfax)*, Pauline Boty *(Nell Pretty)*, Michael Balfour *(John Vichelski)*, Patricia Burke *(Norma Brent)*
P: Jack Greenwood   **D:** John Moxey   **STORY:** George Baxt
Standard thriller: Disfigured actor suspected of killing bigamous wife

Lo Strano Caso della Signora Ward (The Strange Case of Mrs. Ward)
1970, (It-Sp), MLR-Laurie Int'l/Gemini/Maron, color, 81 mins.
W: George Hilton *(George)*, Edwige Fenech *(Julie)*, Cristina Airoldi *(Carol)*, Alberto De Mendoza *(Neil)*, Ivan Rassimov *(Jean)*, Manuel Gill, Carlo Alighiero, Marella Corbi, Luis De Tejada, Bruno Corazzari, Miguel del Castillo, Pouchie, Brizio Montinaro, Mira Vidotto
D: Sergio Martino   **SCR:** Eduardo M. Brochero & Ernesto Gastaldi   **STORY:** Eduardo M. Brochero   **PHOTOG:** Emilio Foriscot   **MUSIC:** Nora Orlandi
A.k.a. Next! and Next Victim
Minor thriller: Sex maniac loose in Vienna

Strategy
1915, (GB), B&C/Pioneer, b&w, 2,330 ft. (710.2m)
W: Fay Temple *(The Woman)*, A.V. Bramble *(The Detective)*, Marjorie Unett *(A Crook)*, M. Gray Murray *(A Crook)*, James Dale *(A Crook)*
D & STORY: Harold Weston
A.k.a. Society Crooks
Standard crime-thriller: Disguised thieves use mechanical devices to steal pearls from hotel room

Strategy of Terror
1967, (USA), Univ/CBS-TV, color, 90 mins.
W: Barbara Rush, Hugh O'Brian *(Lacey)*, Neil Hamilton *(Harkin)*, Harry Townes *(Richard)*, Jan Merlin *(Jon)*, Frederick O'Neal *(Serrac)*, Will Corry *(Wally)*
D: Jack Smight   **TELEPLAY:** Robert L. Joseph   **PHOTOG:** Bud Thackery   **MUSIC:** Lyn Murray
TVM, standard thriller: Woman journalist uncovers UN assassination plot

Straw Dogs
1971, (GB), ABC Pictures/CRC, color, 118 mins.
W: Dustin Hoffman *(David)*, Susan George *(Amy)*, Peter Vaughan *(Tom Hedden)*, T.P. McKenna *(Maj. Scott)*, Ken Hutchinson *(Scutt)*, Del Henney *(Venner)*, Colin Welland *(Rev. Hood)*, Jim Norton *(Cawsey)*, Sally Thomsett *(Janice)*, Len Jones *(Bobby Hedden)*, Donald Webster *(Riddaway)*, Peter Arne *(John Niles)*, Michael Mundell *(Bertie Hedden)*, Robert Keegan *(Harry Ware)*, June Brown *(Mrs. Hedden)*, Cherina Mann *(Mrs. Hood)*, Chloe Franks *(Emma Hedden)*
D: Sam Peckinpah   **SCR:** Sam Peckinpah & David Zelag Goodman, from Gordon Williams' novel Trencher's   **PHOTOG:** John Coquillon   **MUSIC:** Jerry Fielding
Classic thriller: Villagers terrorize couple

The Straw Man
1953, (GB), Hedgerley/UA, b&w, 74 mins.
W: Dermot Walsh *(Mal Farris)*, Clifford Evans *(Jeff Howard)*, Lana Morris *(Ruth Hunter)*, Amy Dalby *(Lucy Graham)*, Ronald Ward *(Clay Rushlow)*, Josephine Stuart *(Miss Ward)*, Philip Saville *(Link Hunter)*, Peter Williams *(Insp. Conrad)*, John Forrest *(Johnny Gordon)*, Neal Arden *(Geoff)*, Lloyd Lamble *(The Doctor)*
WRIT, P & D: Donald Taylor, from a novel by Doris Miles Disney
Standard thriller: Detective captures strangler

The Street Fighter
1974, (Jap), color, 95 mins.
W: Sonny Chiba, Gerald Yamada *(Ratnose)*
Standard action-thriller: Adventures of mercenary assassin

Street Fighter II: The Animated Movie
1996, (USA), color, 100 mins.
VOICES: Hank Smith, Ted Richards, Mary Briscoe
Standard animated action-thriller: Sinister organization brainwashes street fighters, turns them into criminals

Street of Darkness
1958, (USA), Rep, b&w, 60 mins.
W: Robert Keys, John Close
Standard thriller

Street of Shadows
1953, (GB), Merton Park/Anglo-Amalgamated, b&w, 84 mins.
W: Cesar Romero *(Luigi)*, Kay Kendall *(Barbara Gale)*, Edward Underdown *(Insp. Johnstone)*, Victor Maddern *(Limpy)*, Simone Silva *(Angele)*, John Penrose *(Capt. Gerald Gale)*, Annaconda *(Darrell)*, Molly Hamley-Clifford *(Starry Darrell)*, Bill Travers *(Nigel Langley)*, Liam Gaffney, Robert Cawdron, Eileen Way, Paul Hardtmuth
P: W.H. Williams   **D & SCR:** Richard Vernon, from Lawrence Meynell's novel The Creaking Chair   **MUSIC:** Eric Spear
USA retitle, Shadow Man, Lippert, 1953
Modest thriller: London gambling saloon owner involved in murder

Streets of Fire
1984, (USA), Gordon-Silver/Univ-RKO, color, 94 mins.
W: Michael Pare, Diane Lane, Rick Moranis, Willem Dafoe, Amy Madigan, Deborah Van Valkenburgh, Richard Lawson, Stoney Jackson, Rick Rossovich, Bill Paxton, Lee Ving, Mykel T. Williamson, Robert Townsend, Grand Bush
D: Walter Hill   **SCR:** Walter Hill & Larry Gross   **PHOTOG:** Andrew Laszlo   **MUSIC:** Ry Cooder
Unusual futuristic rock-fantasy: Girl kidnapped by street thugs

Street Trash
1987, (USA), Lightning, color, 91 mins.
W: Mike Lackey *(Fred)*, Vic Noto *(Bronson)*, Mark Sferrazza *(Kevin)*, Bill Chepil *(Bill the Cop)*, Tony Darrow *(Nick Duran)*, Jane Arakawa *(Wendy)*, Nicole Potter *(Winette)*, Bernard Perlman *(Wizzy)*, R.L. Ryan *(Frank Schnizer)*, Miriam Zucker *(The Drunken Wench)*, Clarenze Jarmon *(Burt)*, James Lorinz *(The Doorman)*, M D'Jango Krunch *(Ed)*, Morty Storm *(Black Suit)*, Sam Blasco *(Jimmy the Doorman)*, Gary Auerbach *(The Hit Man)*, Bruce Torbet *(Paulie)*, Roman Zack *(The Forensics Expert)*, Roy Frumkes *(The Melted Businessman)*, Eddie Bay *(The Exploding Derelict)*, Jeanne Laporta *(The Bitchy Businesswoman)*, Colin Derouin *(The Concerned Businessman)*, Julian Davis *(The Husband in the Car)*, Victoria Lacas *(The Wife in the Car)*, Frank Farel *(The Dismembered Derelict)*, Robynne White *(The Old Lady Shopper)*, Kevin Simmons *(The Store Manager)*, Glenn Andreiev *(Mario)*, Stephen Patterson *(Alfalfa)*, Allan Lozito *(Delancey)*, Karl Schroeder *(The Desk Sergeant)*, Bill Bondanza *(Discount)*, Fred Schomaker *(Yellowman)*, Peter Iasillo *(Hefty)*, Stephen Santiago *(The Wheelchair Derelict)*, Julie McQuain *(The Receptive Whore in the Van)*, Carmel Pugh *(The Whore on the Telephone)*, Marilyn Kray, Kristin Kirkconnell, Nora Maher, Gina Menza, Nadine Garcia, Craig Edwards, Robert Jonathan, Raul Velez, Chris McNamee, Leslie Pascal, Nick Gianta, Dave Weinstein, Ramon Ybarra, Robert Depietro, Frank Dassaro, Joseph Vero, Raymond Ristau, Thomas Fuzia, Donald Ascher, John Hukushi, Gary Rozanski, Bobby Faust, Sylvia Wong, Judy Chin, Robert Audin, Kevin Chin, William Elijah Tyre, Paul Sansone, Alan Brustein, David Paul Rubenstein, Nathaniel Young, James D. Clements, Michael Maurer, Terrence Devlin, Robert Jockers, Eliezer Diaz, Lawrence Sufrin, Gail Feinsod, Buddy Mantia, Charlene Krista, Baron, Jet, Vince Anderson, Bernard Lunnon, Curtis Gaither, Sky Owens, Bill Gram, Christopher Perry
WRIT & P: Roy Frumkes   **D:** Jim Muro   **PHOTOG:** David Sperling   **MUSIC:** Rick Ulfik   **SONGS:** We Do Things My Way
Bizarre SF-satire: Toxic booze causes skidrow horrors

The Street with No Name
1948, (USA), 20th-Fox, b&w, 91 mins.
W: Mark Stevens, Richard Widmark, Lloyd Nolan, Barbara Lawrence, Ed Begley, Donald Buka, Joseph Pevney, John McIntire
D: William Keighley   **PHOTOG:** Joe Macdonald
Standard thriller: FBI agent infiltrates gang

La Strega in Amore (The Witch in Love)
1966, (It), Arco/Embassy, b&w, 103 mins.
W: Richard Johnson (*Sergio*), Rosanna Schiaffino (*Aura*), Gian Maria Volonte,
Sarah Ferrati, Ivan Rassimov, Margherita Guzzinati, Ivan Scratuglia, Vittorio
Venturoli, Elisabetta Wilding
D: Damiano Damiani   **SCR:** Ugo Liberatore & Damiano Damiani, from Carlos
Fuentes' novel *Aura*   **PHOTOG:** Leonida Barboni   **SPCL-FX:** Giuseppe
Metalli   **MUSIC:** Luis E. Bacalov
A.k.a. **The Strange Obsession & The Witch**
Standard eroto-fantasy: Sinister woman hires jaded roue as librarian, introduces him to her
bewitching daughter

The Strength That Failed
1914, (GB), Martin Films/DFSA, b&w, 714 ft. (217.6m)
W: Ernie Westo
D: Dave Aylott
Standard fantasy: Tired man becomes super-strong after taking doctor's pills

The Stress of Circumstance
1914, (GB), Hepworth, b&w, 1,100 ft. (335.3m)
W: Stewart Rome (*Ralph Densmore*), Violet Hopson (*Roma Barton*), Lionelle
Howard (*Lawrence Steynor*), Henry Vibart (*Mr. Barton*)
D: Warwick Buckland
Standard crime-thriller: Ex-tramp becomes magistrate's secretary, takes blame for theft

The Strife Eternal
see **Jane Shore** *(1915)*

The Striped Stocking Gang
1915, (GB), Barker-Neptune/Anima, b&w, 3,527 ft. (1075m)
W: Margaret Belona (*Viola Cassell*), Miriam Ferris (*Mrs. Cassell*)
D: Fred W. Durrant   **SCR:** Irene Miller, from her novel
A.k.a. **Mrs. Cassell's Profession**
Standard crime-thriller: Girl posing as maid takes blame when her milliner mother's gang
steals lady's pearls

Striptease Lady
see **Lady of Burlesque**

Strip Tease Murder
1961, (GB), Danziger/Para, b&w, 66 mins.
W: John Hewer (*Bert Black*), Ann Lynn (*Rita*), Jean Muir (*Diane*), Kenneth J.
Warren (*Branco*), Michael Peake (*Martin*), Carl Duering (*Rocco*), Leon Cortez
(*Lou*), Vanda Hudson (*Angelina*)
P: Ralph Ingram & John Elton   **D:** Ernest Morris   **STORY:** Paul Tabori
Standard crime-thriller: Woman electrocuted in mistake for crook's blackmailing girlfriend

The Strongest Man in the World
1974, (USA), Walt Disney/Buena Vista, color, 92 mins.
W: Kurt Russell (*Dexter Riley*), Joe Flynn (*Dean Higgins*), Eve Arden (*Harriet*),
Cesar Romero (*A.J. Arno*), Phil Silvers (*Krinkle*), Dick Van Patten (*Harry*),
Dick Bakalyan (*Cookie*), Michael McGreevey (*Richard Schuyler*), Harold
Gould (*Dietz*), William Schallert (*Quigley*), Benson Fong (*Ah Fong*),
Raymond Bailey, Roy Roberts, James Gregory, Burt Mustin, Fritz Feld,
Eddie Quillan
D: Vincent McEveety   **SCR:** Joseph L. McEveety & Herman Groves   **PHOTOG:**
Andrew Jackson   **MUSIC:** Robert F. Brunner
Standard SF-fantasy: College student develops vitamin formula, acquires superhuman
strength

A Strong Man's Love
1913, (GB), Clarendon, b&w, 2,095 ft. (638.6m)
W: Dorothy Bellew (*Elizabeth*)
D: Wilfred Noy   **STORY:** Marchioness of Townshend
Standard crime-thriller: Vicar's daughter elopes with actor who killed manager

Strong Room
1962, (GB), Theatrecraft/Bry, b&w, 80 mins.
W: Derren Nesbitt (*Griff*), Colin Gordon (*Spencer*), Ann Lynn (*Rose Taylor*), Keith
Faulkner (*Len*), Morgan Sheppard (*Alec*), Hilda Fenemore (*A Charlady*),
Diana Chesney (*A Charlady*), Jack Stewart (*Sgt. McIntyre*), Colin Tapley
(*Haynes*), Ian Colin (*Creighton*)
P: Guido Coen   **D:** Vernon Sewell   **SCR:** Richard Harris & Max Marquis
STORY: Richard Harris
Standard crime-thriller: Thieves lock bank manager and his secretary in airtight vault

Stryker
1983, (Phil), color, 86 mins.
W: Steve Sandor, Andria Fabio
D: Cirio H. Santiago   **SCR:** Howard R. Cohen
Minor SF-thriller: Post-nuke humans battle for scarce water

Student Bodies
1981, (USA), Para, color, 84 mins.
W: Kristen Riter (*Toby*), Matt Goldsby (*Hardy*), Mimi Weddell (*Miss Mumsley*),
Richard Brando (*The Breather*), Carl Jacobs (*Dr. Sigmund*), Joe Flood
(*Dumpkin*), Joe Talarowski (*Peters*), Peggy Cooper (*Ms. Van Dyke*), Kevin
Mannis (*Scott*), Janice E. O'Malley (*Nurse Krud*), Sara Eckhardt (*Patti*),
Cullen G. Chambers (*Charles*), Brian Batytis (*Wheels*), Joan Browning Jacobs
(*Mrs. Hummers*), Angela Bressler (*Julie*), Kay Ogden (*Ms. LeClair*), Douglas
Cotner (*Mr. Hummers*), Robyn Flanery (*Joan*), Charles L. Trotter (*The
Announcer*), Brenda Maduzia (*The Punker*), Jonathan Walling (*Al*), Thomas
D. Cannon II (*Ralph*), Keith Singleton (*Charlie*), Oscar James (*The Coach*),
Dario O. Jones (*Mawamba*), Tammie M. Tignor (*Dagmar*), Anita Taylor
(*Bertha*), John M. Armstrong (*Joe*), Dorothy Rich (*Mrs. Peters*), Anne Bell
(*The Teacher*), Kathryn Reve Doster (*Sue*), Janice Elaine Berridge (*The
Student*)
WRIT & D: Mickey Rose   **PHOTOG:** Robert Ebinger   **MUSIC:** Gene Hobson
Standard horror-satire: Killer plagues high school

Der Student von Prag (The Student of Prague)
1913, (Ger), Bioscop, b&w, 56 mins.
W: Paul Wegener (*Baldwin*), John Gottowt, Greta Berger, Lyda Salmonova,
Lothar Korner
D: Stellan Rye   **SCR:** Hanns Heinz Ewers & Paul Wegener, based on the writings
of E.T.A. Hoffmann, the Faust legend & Edgar Allan Poe's short story
William Wilson   **PHOTOG:** Guido Seeber   **SETS:** K. Richter & Robert A.
Dietrich
Classic fantasy-thriller: Student makes satanic pact

Der Student von Prague (The Student of Prague)
1926, (Ger), Sokal, b&w, 10,410.1 ft. (3173m)
W: Conrad Veidt, Agnes Esterhazy, Eliza La Porte, Ferdinand von Alten, Werner
Krauss
D & SCR: Henrik Galeen, based on a novel by Hanns Heinz Ewers   **PHOTOG:**
Gunther Krampf & Erich Nietzchmann   **SETS:** Hermann Warm
Standard fantasy-thriller: Student sells his reflection to Satan

Der Student von Prag (The Student of Prague)
1935, (Ger), b&w, 87 mins.
W: Adolph Wohlbruck [Anton Walbrook]
D: Arthur Robison
Standard fantasy-thriller: Student makes deal with Devil

The Studio Murder Mystery
1929, (USA), Para, b&w, 6,070 ft. (1850.1m), 62 mins.
W: Fredric March
D: Frank W. Tuttle   **PHOTOG:** Victor Milner
Minor thriller

A Study in Scarlet
1914, (GB), G.B. Samuelson/Moss, b&w, 5,749 ft. (1752.3m)
W: Fred Paul (*Jefferson Hope*), Agnes Glynne (*Lucy Ferrier*), James Braginton
(*Sherlock Holmes*), James Le Fre (*Father*), Harry Paulo (*John Ferrier*), Winifred
Pearson (*Young Lucy*)
D: George Pearson   **SCR:** Harry Engholm, from characters created by Sir Arthur
Conan Doyle
Standard thriller: Detective solves murder rooted in Mormon trek of 1850

A Study in Scarlet
1933, (USA), Tiffany/Fox, b&w, 73 mins.
W: Reginald Owen (*Sherlock Holmes*), Anna May Wong (*Mrs. Pyke*), June Clyde
(*Eileen Forrester*), Alan Dinehart (*Merrydew*), John Warburton (*John Stanford*),
Warburton Gamble (*Dr. John Watson*), J.M. Kerrigan (*Jabez Wilson*), Leila
Bennett (*Daffy Dolly*), Doris Lloyd (*Mrs. Hudson*), Billy Bevan (*Will
Swallow*), Wyndham Standing (*Capt. Pyke*), Halliwell Hobbes (*Dearing*)
D: Edwin L. Marin, from Sir Arthur Conan Doyle's "Sherlock Holmes" story
PHOTOG: Arthur Edeson
Standard thriller: Master sleuth encounters baffling murders

A Study in Skarlit
1915, (GB), Comedy Combine-Sunny South/Pioneer, b&w, 2,000 ft. (609.6m)
W: Fred Evans (*Sherlokz Homz*), Will Evans (*Prof. Moratorium*)
WRIT & D: Fred & Will Evans, inspired by characters created by Sir Arthur
Conan Doyle
Standard spoof: Private detective vs. master criminal

A Study in Terror
1965, (GB), Compton-Sir Nigel/Herman Cohen/Col, color, 94 mins.
W: John Neville (*Sherlock Holmes*), Donald Houston (*Dr. John Watson*), Judi Dench
(*Sally*), John Fraser (*Lord Carfax*), Anthony Quayle (*Dr. Murray*), Robert
Morley (*Mycroft Holmes*), Peter Carsten (*Max*), Adrienne Corri (*Angela
Osborne*), Frank Finlay (*Insp. Lestrade*), Barbara Windsor (*Annie Chapman*),
Kay Walsh (*Cathy Eddowes*), Dudley Foster (*The Home Sec'y*), Barry Jones
(*Duke of Shires*), Georgia Brown (*The Singer*), Cecil Parker (*The Prime
Minister*), Terry Downes (*Chunky*), Edina Ronay (*Mary Kelly*), Charles
Regnier (*Joseph Beck*), John Cairney
P: Henry E. Lester   **D:** James Hill   **ORIG. STORY & SCR:** Donald & Derek
Ford, from a novel by Ellery Queen   **PHOTOG:** Desmond Dickinson
MUSIC: John Scott   **SONG:** *In These Hard Times*
Modest thriller: Famed sleuth tracks Jack the Ripper

The Stuff
1985, (USA), Larco/New World, color, 87 mins.
W: Michael Moriarty (*David Rutherford*), Andrea Marcovicci (*Nicole*), Garrett
Morris ("*Chocolate Chip*" *Charlie*), Paul Sorvino (*Col. Spears*), Scott Bloom
(*Jason*), Danny Aiello (*Vickers*), James Dixon (*The Postman*), Alexander

S

Scourby (Evans), Russell Nype (Richards), Gene O'Neill (The Scientist), Cathy Schultz (The Waitress), Jim Dukas (The Gas Attendant), Peter Hock (The State Trooper), Frank Telfer (Jason's Father), Colette Blonigan (Jason's Mother), Beth Teagarden (The Investigator), Marilyn Staley (The Stuff Girl), Brian Bloom (Jason's Brother), Patrick O'Neal, Ann Dane, Rutanya Alda
P: Paul Kurta   WRIT & D: Larry Cohen   PHOTOG: Paul Glickman   MUSIC: Anthony Guefen
Modest SF-satire: Popular food controls humans' minds

Stuff Stephanie in the Incinerator
1989, (USA), Troma, color, 97 mins.
W: Catherine Dee, William Dame, Dennis Cunningham, M.R. Murphy
D: Don Nardo
Minor satire: Sexy snob's demise is plotted

Stunts Unlimited
1980, (USA), Par-TV/ABC-TV, color, 74 mins.
W: Chip Mayer (Matt), Susanna Dalton (C.C.), Sam J. Jones (Bo), Glenn Corbett (Macauley), Linda Grovernor (Jody), Alejandro Rey (Castilla), Stefan Gierasch (Kalb)
TVM, minor thriller: Hollywood stunt performers recruited for secret CIA operation

Submarine
1928, (USA), Col, b&w, 9 reels
D: Frank Capra   PHOTOG: Joseph Walker
Standard melodrama: Peril beneath the waves

The Submarine Plans
1912, (GB), GS Films/Hepworth, b&w, 675 ft. (205.7m)
D: Gilbert Southwell
Standard thriller: Lieutenant's sister stops adventuress from stealing plans

The Submersion of Japan
1974, (Jap), Toho, color, 90 mins.
W: Tetsuro Tamba, Hiroshi Fujioka, Keiju Kobayashi, Rhonda Leigh Hopkins, Marvin Miller, Ayumi Ishida
D: Shiro Moritani
released in USA (1975) by New World as Tidal Wave (with added scenes starring Lorne Greene, and added direction by Andrew Meyer)
Standard SF-thriller: Seismic activity threatens Nippon

Subspecies
1990, (USA), Full Moon, color, 88 mins.
W: Michael Watson, Laura Tate, Anders Hove, Angus Scrimm, Michelle McBride, Irina Movila Ivan J. Rado
D: Ted Nicolaou   SCR: Jackson Barr & David Pabian, from an orig. idea by Charles Band   PHOTOG: Vlad Baunescu
Minor fantasy-thriller: Student falls prey to lovestruck vampire

Subspecies II
see Bloodstone: Subspecies II

Subspecies III
see Bloodlust: Subspecies III

A Substantial Ghost
1903, (GB), Gaumont, b&w, 90 ft. (27.4m)
D: Alf Collins
Standard comedy short: Cop poses as ghost, scares cardplaying tramps in cemetery

Subterfuge
1968, (GB), Intertel/VTR/Commonwealth United, color, 92 mins.
W: Gene Barry (Donovan), Joan Collins (Anne), Richard Todd (Redmayne), Michael Rennie (Goldsmith), TomAdams (Langey), Suzanna Leigh (Donetta), Scott Forbes (Pannell), Marius Goring (Shevik), Colin Gordon (Kitteridge), Guy Deghy (Dr. Lundgren), Dermot Kelly, Stuart Cooper, John Welsh, Ron Pember, Gary Clifford, Jane Blackburn, Clifford Earl, Harry Locke, Fred Peisley, Sidney Vivien, Robert Raglan, Graham Lines, John Clifford, Bill Nagy, Freda Dowie, Charles Lamb, Gretchen Franklin, Marion Diamond, Carmen Dean, Lyn Marshall, Donna Reading, Valerie Hudson, Sheila Sands, Wendy Ascot
D: Peter Graham Scott   TELEPLAY: David Whitaker   PHOTOG: Roy Fuller   MUSIC: Cyril Ornadel
Minor thriller: CIA operative seeks double agent

Suburban Commando
1991, (USA), New Line, color, 85 mins.
W: Hulk Hogan (Shep Ramsey), Christopher Lloyd (Charlie Wilcox), Shelley Duvall (Jenny Wilcox), Jack Elam (Col. Dustin McHowell), Larry Miller (Adrian Beltz), William Ball (Gen. Suitor), Jo Ann Dearing (Margie Tanen), Roy Dotrice (Zanuck), Michael Faustino, Tony Longo, Laura Mooney
EXEC P: Hulk Hogan, kevin Moreton, Deborah Moore   D: Burt Kennedy   SCR: Frank Cappello   PHOTOG: Bernd Heinl   VS-FX: Jeffrey Okun   MUSIC: David Michael Frank   SONGS: Almost Like Paradise, Ramsey, It's a Nice Place to Live, Do You Want to Party? & Black Book
Standard SF-comedy: Alien warrior visits Earth

Subway in the Sky
1959, (GB), Orbit/Britannia, b&w, 86 mins.

W: Van Johnson (Maj. Baxter Grant), Hildegarde Neff (Lilli Hoffman), Albert Lieven (Carl von Schecht), Cec Linder (Capt. Carson), Katherine Kath (Anna Grant), Vivian Matalon (Stefan), Carl Jaffe (Adler), Chuck Keyser (Harwell), Edward Judd (Molloy)
P: Sydney Box, John Temple-Smith & Patrick Filmer-Sankey   D: Muriel Box   SCR: Jack Andress, from a play by Ian Main
Standard crime-thriller: Army deserter accused of drug-trafficking

Succubus
see Necronomicon

Such Men Are Dangerous
1930, (USA), Fox, b&w, 8 reels (7,400 ft./2255.5m), 83 mins.
W: Warner Baxter (Ludwig Kranz), Catherine Dale Owen (Elinor), Albert Conti (Paul Strohm), Hedda Hopper (Muriel Wyndham), Claude Allister (Frederick Wyndham), Bela Lugosi (Dr. Erdmann)
D: Kenneth Hawks   ADAPT & DIALOG: Ernest Vajda   STORY: Elinor Glyn   PHOTOG: L. William O'Connell & George Eastman   MUSIC: Dave Stamper
Standard thriller: Disfigured financier seeks vengeance on wife

Sudan
1945, (USA), Univ, color, 69 mins.
W: Maria Montez (Naila), Jon Hall (Merab), Turhan Bey (Herua), Andy Devine (Nebka), George Zucco (Horadef), Robert Warwick (Maatat), Harry Cording (Uba), Charles Arnt, Phil Van Zandt, George Lynn
P: Paul Malvern   D: John Rawlins   ORIG. SCR: Edmund L. Hartmann   PHOTOG: George Robinson   SPCL-PHOTOG: John P. Fulton   MUSIC: Milton Rosen
Standard adventure-romance: Egyptian princess seeks father's slayer

Sudden Danger
1955, (USA), AA, b&w, 65 mins.
W: Bill Elliott, Tom Drake Beverly Garland, Lucien Littlefield, Minerva Urecal, Lyle Talbot, Frank Jenks
D: Hubert Cornfield
Standard thriller: Murderer hunted

Sudden Fear
1952, (USA), RKO, b&w, 110 mins.
W: Joan Crawford (Myra Hudson), Bruce Bennett (Steve Kearney), Jack Palance (Lester Blaine), Gloria Grahame (Irene Neves), Virginia Huston (Ann Taylor), Michael "Touch" Connors (Junior Kearney)
P: Joseph Kaufman   D: David Miller   SCR: Lenore Coffee & Robert Smith, from a story by Edna Sherry   PHOTOG: Charles B. Lang Jr.   MUSIC: Elmer Bernstein
Effective suspense-thriller: Wealthy woman writer marries worthless actor with murderous designs

Suddenly
1954, (USA), b&w, 77 mins.
W: Frank Sinatra, Sterling Hayden, James Gleason, Nancy Gates, Willis Bouchey, Kim Charney, Paul Frees
D: Lewis Allen
Standard thriller: Assassins target U.S. president

Suddenly Last Summer
1959, (USA-GB), Horizon/Col, b&w, 114 mins.
W: Elizabeth Taylor (Catherine Holly), Montgomery Clift (Dr. Cukrowicz), Katharine Hepburn (Violet Venable), Albert Dekker (Dr. Hockstader), Mercedes McCambridge (Mrs. Holly), Gary Raymond (George Holly), Mavis Villiers (Miss Foxhill), Joan Young (Sister Felicity), Patricia Marmont (Nurse Benson)
P: Sam Spiegel   D: Joseph L. Mankiewicz   SCR: Gore Vidal & Tennessee Williams, from Tennessee Williams' play   PHOTOG: Jack Hildyard   MUSIC: Buxton Orr & Malcolm Arnold
Superior melodrama: Surgeon probes homosexual's bizarre death

Sudden Terror
1970, (GB), Anglo-EMI/National General, color, 95 mins.
W: Mark Lester (Ziggy), Susan George (Pippa), Tony Bonner (Tom), Lionel Jeffries (The Colonel), Peter Vaughan (Paul), Jeremy Kemp (Galleria), Peter Bowles (Victor), Betty Marsden (Mme. Robiac), Anthony Stamboulieh (Tacherie), John Allison (The Boutique Boy), Robert Russell (The H.Q. Sergeant), Joseph Furst (The Local Station Sergeant), Jonathan Burn (The Waiter), Christopher Robbie (The First Policeman), Jeremy Young (The Monk), Tom Eytle (The President), Maxine Kalli (Anne Marie), David Lodge (The Policeman in the Jeep)
D: John Hough   SCR: Ronald Harwood, from Mark Hebden's novel Eyewitness   PHOTOG: David Holmes   MUSIC: Fairfield Parlour & David Whitaker
Standard thriller: Assassin pursues boy who witnessed crime

Sugar Hill
1974, (USA), AIP, color, 91 mins.
W: Marki Bey (Diana "Sugar" Hill), Robert Quarry (Morgan), Don Pedro Colley (The Baron), Betty Ann Rees (Celeste), Ed Geldhart (O'Brien),Richard Lawson (Valentine), Zara Culley (Mama Maitresse), Larry D. Johnson (Langston), Charles Robinson (Fabulous), Rick Hagood (Tank), Raymond E. Simpson (The King), Thomas C. Carroll (Baker), Peter Harrell III (The Photographer), Albert J. Baker (George) Charles Krohn (The Captain), Jack Dull (Davidson),

Judy Hanson (*The Masseuse*), Walter Price (*The Preacher*), Tony Brubaker (*The Head Zombie*)
P: Elliott Schick **D:** Paul Maslansky **SCR:** Tim Kelly **PHOTOG:** Robert Jessup
A.k.a. **Voodoo Girl** *and* **Zombies of Sugar Hill**
Standard horror-fantasy: Woman seeks revenge, uses zombies

The Suicide Club
1914, (GB), B&C/Renters, b&w, 3,386 ft. (1032.1m)
W: Montagu Love (*Prince Florizel*), Elisabeth Risdon (*Zephyrine*), Fred Groves (*The President*), M. Gray Murray (*Col. Geraldine*)
D: Maurice Elvey, from a story by Robert Louis Stevenson
Standard thriller: Colonel saves princess from murderous society

The Suicide Club
1988, (USA), Angelika, color, 90 mins.
W: Mariel Hemingway (*Sasha*), Robert Joy (*Michael*), Madeleine Potter (*Nancy*), Lenny Henry (*Cam*), Michael O'Donoghue, Anne Carlisle
D: James Bruce **SCR:** Matthew Gaddis, Suzan Kouguell, & Carl Caportoto loosely based on a story by Robert Louis Stevenson
Minor thriller: Bored heiress mixes with bizarre types

Suicide Cult
1977, (USA), color, 82 mins.
Minor thriller: CIA employee predicts Christ's second coming

Suicide Mission
1971, (Mex), color
W: Santo
Minor thriller

The Sultan's Daughter
1943, (USA), Mono, b&w, 64 mins.
W: Ann Corio, Charles Butterworth
Minor adventure-romance

Summer Camp Nightmare
1986, (USA), color, 89 mins.
W: Chuck Connors, Charles Stratton, Harold Pruett, Adam Carl, Tom Fridley
D: Bert L. Dragin, from William Butler's novel *Butterfly Revolution*
A.k.a. **The Butterfly Revolution**
Minor thriller: Fascist uprising at summer camp

Summer Girl
1983, (USA), Lansbury/Haynes/Finnegan/CDS-TV, color, 100 mins.
W: Diane Franklin, Barry Bostwick (*Gavin Shelburne*), Kim Darby (*Mary Shelburne*), Martha Scott (*Martina Shelburne*), Murray Hamilton (*Jack Reardon*), Hunt Block (*Peter Mitchell*), Millie Slavin (*Esther Reardon*), David Faustino (*Jason Shelburne*)
TVM, minor thriller

Summer of Fear
1996, (USA), CBS-TV, color, 95 mins.
W: Gregory Harrison (*Lucas*), Corin Nemec (*Simon*), Glynnis O'Connor (*Cat*), Lee Garlington (*Winnie*), David Gallagher (*Zach*), Natalie Shaw (*Haley*), David Jaynes, Kathleen Walsh
D: Mike Robe **TELEPLAY:** John Gay, from Gloria Murphy's novel *Simon Says* **PHOTOG:** Alan Caso **MUSIC:** Mark Snow
TVM, standard thriller: Mysterious teen wages campaign of terror against business executive

Suna No Onna: KYOKO KISHIDA

Summoning the Spirits
see **Evocation Spirite**

Sumuru
see **The Million Eyes of Sumuru**

Sumurun
1920, (Ger), Ufa, b&w, 85 mins.
W: Pola Negri, Ernst Lubitsch, Paul Wegener
D: Ernst Lubitsch, from Max Reinhardt's stage pantomime **PHOTOG:** Theodor Sparkuhl
USA retitle, **One Arabian Night**, *First National, 1921*
Standard comedy-adventure: Exotic dancer charms sultan and his son

Suna No Onna (Woman in the Dunes)
1964, (Jap), Pathe-Contemporary, b&w, 127 mins.
W: Eiji Okada, Kyoko Kishida (*Woman*) Koji Mitsui, Sen Yano, Hiroko Ito, Ginzo Sekigushi, Kiyohiko Ichida, Tamutsu Tamura
D: Hiroshi Teshigahara **PHOTOG:** Hiroshi Segawa **MUSIC:** Toru Takemitsu
Celebrated fantasy-allegory: Antagonistic man and woman trapped in sand pit

The Sun Demon
see **The Hideous Sun Demon**

Sundown: The Vampire in Retreat
1990, (USA), Vestron, color, 105 mins.
W: David Carradine, Jim Metzler, Morgan Brittany (*Sarah*), Maxwell Caulfield (*Shane*), Deborah Foreman, John Ireland, Bruce Campbell, M. Emmet Walsh, Dana Ashbrook, Buck Flower John Hancock, Dabbs Greer, Bert Remsen
D: Anthony Hickox **SCR:** Anthony Hickox & John Burgess **PHOTOG:** Levie Isaacks
Minor horror-thriller: Rival bloodsuckers at plasma plant

A Sunken World
see **Die Versunkene Welt**

The Sun's Death
see **Le Mort du Soleil**

Sunset Boulevard
1950, (USA), Para, b&w, 111 mins.
W: Gloria Swanson (*Norma Desmond*), William Holden (*Joe Gillis*), Erich von Stroheim (*Max Von Mayerling*), Nancy Olson (*Betty Schaefer*), Jack Webb (*Artie Green*), Franklyn Farnum (*The Undertaker*), Fred Clark (*Sheldrake*), Ruth Clifford (*Sheldrake's Sec'y*), Lloyd Gough (*Morino*), Michael Brandon (*Archie Twitchell*) (*The Salesman*), Gertrude Messinger (*The Hairdresser*), Bert Moorhouse (*Gordon Cole*), Len Hendry (*The Sergeant*), Howard Negley (*The Police Captain*), Ken Christy (*The Homicide Captain*), Cecil B. DeMille (*himself*), H.B. Warner, Ray Evans, Buster Keaton, Anna Q. Nilsson, Jay Livingston, Hedda Hopper
P: Charles Brackett **D:** Billy Wilder **SCR:** Charles Brackett, Billy Wilder & D.M. Marshman Jr., based on story *A Can of Beans* by Billy Wilder & Charles Brackett **PHOTOG:** John F. Seitz **SPCL-FX:** Gordon Jennings **MUSIC:** Franz Waxman **SET DECORATION:** Sam Comer & Ray Moyer
Classic "Grand Guignol:" Silent-movie queen dreams of return to films

Sunset Grill
1993, (USA), Movie Group/New Line, color, 103 mins.
W: Peter Weller, Lori Singer, Stacy Keach, John Rhys-Davies, Alexandra Paul, Michael Anderson Jr.
D: Kevin Connor **PHOTOG:** Douglas Milsome **MUSIC:** Ken Thorne
Standard thriller: Private investigator probes murders

Sunstroke
1992, (USA), color, 95 mins.
W: Jane Seymour, Stephen Meadows (*Greg*), Don Ameche (*Jake*), Steve Railsback, Ray Wise
D: James Keach **TELEPLAY:** Duane Poole **PHOTOG:** Ross A. Maehl **MUSIC:** John Debney
TVM, standard thriller: Death trails mystery woman traversing desert

Superargo
see **Superargo e i Giganti Senzo Volto**

Superargo e i Giganti Senzo Volto (Superargo and the Faceless Giants)
1967, (It-Sp), GV/SEC/IzaroFanfare, color, 80 mins.
W: Guy Madison, Ken Wood (*Giovanni Cianfrigli*), Liz Barrett
D: Paolo Bianchini **SCR:** Julio Buchs
A.k.a.Superargo, **Superargo the Giant**, *and* **Il Rei de Criminali** *(The King of Criminals)*
Minor SF-thriller: Kidnapped athletes turned into electronic monsters

Superargo the Giant
see **Superargo e i Giganti Senzo Volto**

Superargo vs. Diabolicus
1966, (It-Sp), Liber/SEC/Balcazar/Col, color, 87 mins.

<u>W:</u> Ken Wood [Giovanni Cianfriglia], Gerard Tichy
<u>P:</u> Ottavio Poggi & J.J. Balcazar   <u>D:</u> Nick Nastro   <u>SCR:</u> Giarda Balcazar & J.J. Balcazar
Minor fantasy-thriller: Villain manufactures gold

Superbeast
1972, (Phil), A&S/UA, color, 90 mins.
<u>W:</u> Antoinette Bower
<u>P:</u> Aubrey Schenck   <u>D & SCR:</u> George Schenck
Minor horror-thriller: Doctor turns into ape-like monster

Superbug
1975, (W. Ger), Barbara Films/AA-TV, color
<u>W:</u> Robert Mark
Standard juvenile fantasy: Flying car pursues thief

Superbug, Super Agent
1976, (W. Ger), Barbara/Central Park/Telefilm Sales, color, 92 mins.
<u>W:</u> Robert Mark, Heidi Hansen, George Goodman
*Minor juvenile fantasy (sequel to **Superbug**): Flying car pursues villains*

Superchick
1973, (USA), Marimark/Crown Int'l, color, 94 mins.
<u>W:</u> Joyce Jillson (*Tara B. True*), John Carradine
<u>D:</u> Ed Forsythe
Minor comedy-thriller: Lovely stewardess doubles as crimefighter

Super Fuzz
1981, (USA-It), Transcinema/Avco Embassy, color, 97 mins.
<u>W:</u> Terence Hill (*Dave*), Ernest Borgnine (*Willy*), Joanne Dru (*Rosy*), Marc Lawrence (*Tropedo*), Julie Gordon (*Evelyn*), Lee Sandman (*The Chief*), Herb Goldstein (*Silvius*), Don Sebastian (*Dingo*), Sal Borghese (*Paradise Alley*), Sergio Smacchi (*Slot Machine*), Claudio Ruffini (*Tragedy Row*)
<u>D:</u> Sergio Corbucci   <u>SCR:</u> Sergio Corbucci & Sabatino Ciuffino   <u>PHOTOG:</u> Silvano Ippoliti
A.k.a. **Supersnooper**
Minor comedy-thriller: Law enforcer gains super powers

Supergirl
1971, (W. Ger), Thome, b&w, 100 mins.
<u>W:</u> Iris Berben, Fritzling Daunzungs-schnapps, Friedrich Schitzoff, Heinz-Gergesmuller von Griffensteinbrunner, Jess Hahn, Marquard Bohm
Minor SF-fantasy

Supergirl
1984, (USA-GB), TriStar, color, 104 mins.
<u>W:</u> Helen Slater (*Linda Lee/Supergirl*), Peter O'Toole (*Zaltar*), Faye Dunaway (*Selena*), Brenda Vaccaro (*Bianca*), Hart Bochner (*Ethan*), Pete Cook (*Nigel*), Marc McClure (*Jimmy Olsen*), Mia Farrow (*Alura*), Simon Ward (*Zor-El*), Maureen Teefy (*Lucy Lane*), David Healy (*Danvers*), Sandra Dickinson (*The Lady*), Robyn Mandell (*Myra*), Jenifer Landor (*Muffy*), Diana Ricardo (*Mrs. Murray*), Nancy Lippold (*Billy-Jo*), Zoot Money (*The Guest*), Sonya Leite (*Betsy*), Linsey Beauchamp (*Ali*), Virginia Greig (*Jody*), Sandra Martin (*The Astral Image*), Michelle Taylor (*Amy*), Julia Lewis
<u>D:</u> Jeannot Szwarc   <u>SCR:</u> David Odell   <u>PHOTOG:</u> Alan Hume   <u>SPCL-FX:</u> Derek Meddings   <u>MUSIC:</u> Jerry Goldsmith
Standard SF-fantasy-satire: Superman's cousin visits Earth to retrieve lost power source

Superman
1978, (USA), Alexander Salkind/WB, color, 143 mins. (TV-version, 192 mins.)
<u>W:</u> Marlon Brando (*Jor-El*), Christopher Reeve (*Clark Kent/"Superman"*), Margot Kidder (*Lois Lane*), Gene Hackman (*Lex Luthor*), Jackie Cooper (*Perry White*), Valerie Perrine (*Eve Teschmacher*), Ned Beatty (*Otis*), Glenn Ford (*Jonathan Kent*), Phyllis Thaxter (*Martha Kent*), Terence Stamp (*Gen. Zod*), Marc McClure (*Jimmy Olsen*), Jack O'Halloran (*Non*), Trevor Howard (*The First Elder*), Maria Schell (*Vond-Ah*), Jeff East (*Young Clark Kent*), Harry Andews (*The Second Elder*), Larry Hagman (*The Major*), Diane Sherry (*Lana Lang*), Rex Reed, Aaron Smolinski, Noel Neill, Vass Anderson, John Hollis, John Stuart, James Garbutt, Michael Glover, David Neal, William Russell, Penelope Lee, Alan Cullen, Billy J. Mitchell, Lee Quigley, Jeff Atcheson, David Petrou, Brad Flock, Robert Henderson, Larry Lamb, John F. Parker, James Brockington, John Cassady, Antony Scott, Ray Evans, Su Shifrin, Miquel Brown, Vincent Marzello, Leueen Willoughby, Benjamin Feitelson, Lise Hilboldt, Jill Ingham, Pieter Stuyck, Weston Gavin, Stephen Kahan, Matt Russo, Ray Hassett, Randy Jurgenson, Paul Avery, Colin Skeaping, Bo Rucker, George Harris II, David Maxt, Oz Clarke, Michael Harrigan, Jayne Tottman, John Cording, Raymond Thompson, Robert Whelan, Rex Everhardt, Frank Lazarus, Brian Protheroe, Lawrence Trimble, David Calder, Chief Tug Smith, Norwick Duff, Keith Alexander, Michael Ensign, Paul Tuerpe, Graham McPherson, Phil Brown, David Yorston, Robert O'Neill, Robert MacLeod, Mark Wynter, John Ratzenberger, Roy Stevens, Alan Tilvern, Bill Bailey, Chuck Julian, Burnell Tucker, Norman Warwick, Colin Etherington, Kirk Alyn
<u>P:</u> Pierre Spengler   <u>D:</u> Richard Donner   <u>SCR:</u> Mario Puzo, David Newman, Leslie Newman & Robert Benton   <u>PHOTOG:</u> Geoffrey Unsworth   <u>SPCL-FX:</u> Wally Veevers, Colin Chilvers, John Richardson & Les Bowie   <u>MUSIC:</u> John Williams (Academy Award)
Lavish SF-fantasy: Orphaned extraterrestrial becomes crime fighter

Superman: GEORGE REEVES

Superman II
1981, (USA), Alexander Salkind/WB, color 127 mins.
<u>W:</u> Christopher Reeve (*Clark Kent/"Superman"*), Gene Hackman (*Lex Luthor*), Margot Kidder (*Lois Lane*), E.G. Marshall (*The President*), Valerie Perrine (*Eve Teschmacher*), Marc McClure (*Jimmy Olsen*), Terence Stamp (*Gen. Zod*), Sarah Douglas (*Ursa*), Jackie Cooper (*Perry White*), Clifton James (*The Sheriff*), Jack O'Halloran (*Non*), Ned Beatty (*Otis*), Hal Galili (*The Man at the Bar*), Susannah York (*Lara*), Melissa Wiltsie (*The Nun*), Leueen Willoughby (*Leueen*), Robin Pappas (*Alice*), Roger Kemp (*The Spokesman*), Alain DeHay (*The Gendarme*), Jim Dowdell (*Boris*), Marc Boyle (*The C.R.S. Man*), Angus McInnes (*The Warden*), Alan Stuart (*The Cab Driver*), Todd Woodcroft (*The Father*), Elva May Hoover (*The Mother*), Peter Whitman (*The Deputy*), John Norton (*Nate*), Hadley Kay (*Jason*), Antony Sher (*The Bellboy*), John Hollis (*The Krypton Elder*), Bill Bailey (*J.J.*), Dinny Powell (*Boog*), Marcus D'Amico (*Willie*), Gordon Rollings (*The Fisherman*), Richard Parmentier (*The Reporter*), Don Fellows (*The General*), Michael J. Shannon (*The President's Aide*), Tony Sibald (*The Presidential Imposter*), Tommy Duggan (*The Diner Owner*), Pepper Martin (*Rocky*), Pamela Mandell (*The Waitress*), Eugene Lipinski (*The Newsvendor*), Anthony Milner, Roger Brierley, Richard Griffiths, Carl Parris, John Ratzenberger, Shane Rimmer, Cleon Spencer
<u>P:</u> Pierre Spengler   <u>D:</u> Richard Lester   <u>SCR:</u> Mario Puzo, David Newman & Leslie Newman   <u>PHOTOG:</u> Geoffrey Unsworth & Robert Paynter   <u>SPCL-FX:</u> Colin Chilvers   <u>MUSIC:</u> Ken Thorne (from John Williams' orig. music)
"It is that rarity of rarities, a sequel that readily surpasses the original"—Richard Schickel, Time
Standard SF-fantasy: Further exploits of Man of Steel

Superman III
1983, (USA), Alexander & Ilya Salkind/WB, color 122 mins.
<u>W:</u> Christopher Reeve (*Clark Kent/"Superman"*), Richard Pryor (*Gus Gorman*), Jackie Cooper (*Perry White*), Margot Kidder (*Lois Lane*), Marc McClure (*Jimmy Olsen*), Annette O'Toole (*Lana Lang*), Robert Vaughn (*Webster*), Annie Ross (*Vera*), Pamela Stephenson (*Lorelei Ambrosia*), Nancy Roberts (*The Clerk*), Gavan O'Herlihy (*Brad*), Graham Stark (*The Blind Man*), Henry Woolf (*The Penguin Man*), Gordon Rollings (*The Man*), Justin Case (*The Mime*), Bob Todd (*The Gent*), Helen Horton (*Miss Henderson*), Lou Hirsch (*Fred*), Shane Rimmer (*The Policeman*), Barry Dennen (*Dr. McClean*), John Bluthal (*The Vendor*), Enid Saunders (*Minnie Bannister*), Robert Beatty (*The Captain*), Paul Kaethler (*Ricky*), Ronnie Brody (*The Husband*), Sandra Dickinson (*The Wife*), George Chisholm (*The Sweeper*)
<u>P:</u> Pierre Spengler   <u>D:</u> Richard Lester   <u>SCR:</u> David & Leslie Newman   <u>PHOTOG:</u> Robert K. Paynter   <u>SPCL-FX:</u> Colin Chilvers   <u>MUSIC:</u> Ken Thorne   <u>SONGS:</u> Giorgio Moroder
Standard SF-fantasy: Man of Steel vs. evil industrialist

Superman IV: The Quest for Peace
1987, (USA), Golan-Globus/Cannon/WB, color, 85 mins.
W: Christopher Reeve (*Clark Kent/"Superman"*), Gene Hackman (*Lex Luthor*), Margot Kidder (*Lois Lane*), Jon Cryer (*Lenny*), Jackie Cooper (*Perry White*), Marc McClure (*Jimmy Olsen*), Sam Wanamaker (*David Warfield*), Mariel Hemingway (*Lacy Warfield*), Mark Pillow (*The Nuclear Man*)
D: Sidney J. Furie **SCR:** Lawrence Konner & Mark Rosenthal **PHOTOG:** Ernest Day **VS-FX SPRVSR:** Harrison Ellenshaw **MUSIC:** John Williams
Standard SF-fantasy: Man of Steel seeks global disarmament

Superman and the Mole Men
1951, (USA), Lippert, b&w, 67 mins.
W: George Reeves, Phyllis Coates, Jeff Corey, Walter Reed, J. Farrell MacDonald, Stanley Andrews, Billy Curtis
P: Barney A. Sarecky **D:** Lee Sholem **SCR:** Richard Fielding
televised as **The Unknown People** *GB retitle,* **Superman and the Strange People**
Minor SF-fantasy: Superhero aids subterranean dwarves

Superman and the Strange People
see **Superman and the Mole Men**

Super Mario Bros.
1993, (USA), Hollywood, color, 104 mins.
W: Bob Hoskins, John Leguizamo, Dennis Hopper (*King Koopa*), Samantha Davis (*Daisy*), Fiona Shaw, Fisher Stevens, Richard Edson, Lance Henriksen Dana Kaminski, Mojo Nixon
D: Rocky Morton & Annabel Jankel **SCR:** Parker Bennett, Terry Runte & Ed Solomon **SPCL-FX COORD:** Dean Semler **PHOTOG:** Paul Lombardi **MUSIC:** Alan Silvestri **SONGS:** *Almost Unreal, Walk the Dinosaur, Love is a Drug, I Would Stop the World & Speed of Light*
Unusual adventure-fantasy (inspired by video game): Two plumbers enter parallel universe

Supernatural
1933, (USA), Para, b&w, 67 mins.
W: Carole Lombard, Randolph Scott, Vivienne Osborne, H.B. Warner, Alan Dinehart, Beryl Mercer, William Farnum, Lyman Williams, Willard Robertson, George Burr McAnnan
P: Edward Halperin **D:** Victor Halperin **SCR:** Harvey Thew & Brian Marlowe, from a story by Garnett Weston **PHOTOG:** Arthur Martinelli
Unusual fantasy-thriller: Dead murderess' spirit takes possession of socialite's body

Supernatural (1964)
see **The Gorgon**

The Supernaturals
1986, (USA), Embassy, color, 86 mins.
W: Maxwell Caulfield (*Ellis*), Nichelle Nichols (*Leona*), Talia Balsam (*Lejune*) Bradford Bancroft, Margaret Shendal, Bobby DiCicco
D: Armand Mastroianni **SCR:** Joel Soisson & Michael S. Murphey **MUSIC:** Robert O. Ragland
Minor horror-fantasy: Confederate ghosts seek revenge

Supersnooper
see **Super Fuzz**

Supersonic Man
1979, (Sp), Topaz, color 85 imns.
W: Cameron Mitchell, Michael Coby Richard Yesteran, Diana Polakov, Jose Maria Caffarel, Frank Brana, Javier de Campos, Tito Garcia, Angel Ter, Quique Camoiras, Louis Barboo
D: Juan Piquer **SCR:** Juan Piquer & Sebastian Moi **PHOTOG:** Juan Marine **MUSIC:** Gino Peguri, Juan Luis Izaguirre & Carlos Attias
Minor SF-thriller: Mad doctor vs. superhero from outer space

Supersonic Saucer
1956, (GB), Gaumont/British Lion-CFF, b&w, 50 mins.
W: Fella Edmonds (*Rodney*), Donald Gray (*The Headmaster*), Marcia Monolescu (*Sumac*), Raymond Rollett (*No. 1*), Tony Lyons (*No. 13*), Gillian Harrison (*Greta*), Hilda Fenemore (*Mother*)
P & STORY: Frank Wells **D:** S.G. Ferguson **SCR:** Dallas Bowers
Minor juvenile fantasy: Children thwart crooks, save Venusian spacecraft

Superstition
1985, (USA), Mario Kassar-Andrew Vajna/Almi, color, 85 mins.
W: James Houghton (*Rev. David Thompson*), Lynn Carlin (*Melinda Leahy*), Larry Pennell (*George Leahy*), Albert Salmi (*Insp. Sturgess*), Maylo McCaslin, Heidi Bohay, Jacquelyn Hyde, Billy Jacoby, Kim Marie, Stacy Keach Sr., Bennett Liss, Joshua Cadman, Robert Symonds, Carole Goldman, John Alderman, Johnny Doran, Casey King, Nova Ball
D: James W. Roberson **SCR:** Donald G. Thompson, Michael O. Sajbel, Bret Plate & Brad White **STORY:** Michael O. Sajbel **PHOTOG:** Leon Blank **MUSIC:** David Gibney
A.k.a. **The Witch**
Minor horror-thriller: Witch enacts horrible vengeance

Superstitious
1996, (USA), Miramax, color

---

from R.L. Stine's novel
Standard horror-fantasy: Beautiful grad student drawn to Irish professor of folklore; ghastly events ensue

Superwheels
1978, (W. Ger), Konstantin W. Nowak/Barbara, color, 93 mins.
W: Robert Mark (*Jimmy Bondi*), Salvatore Borgese, Kathrin Oginski, Walter Giller, Walter Roderer, Ruth Recklin, Evelin Kraft, Ullrich Beiger, Peter W. Staub, Gerhard Frickhofer, Walter Feuchtenberg, Marion Winter
D: Rudolf Zehetgruber **SCR:** Gregor V. Nazzani **PHOTOG:** Rudiger Meichsner **MUSIC:** Gerhard Heinz
Minor juvenile fantasy (sequel to **Superbug***): Sentient auto enters car race*

Superzan and the Space Boy
1972, (Mex), Tikal International, color, 130 mins.
Minor fantasy

Sure Cure for Indigestion
see **Une Indigestion**

Surf Nazis Must Die
1987, (USA), Troma, color, 83 mins.
W: Gail Neely (*Mama*), Barry Brenner (*Adolf*), Dawn Wildsmith (*Eva*), Robert Harden (*Leroy*), Michael Sonye (*Mengele*), Joel Hile (*Hook*), Gene Mitchell (*Brutus*), Tom Shell (*Smeg*), John Willamette (*Mex*), Bobbie Bresee (*Smeg's Mom*), Brian Krutoff (*Curl*), Ty Thomas (*Aerial*), Rand Hogen (*Teeth*), Daniel Kong (*Wang*), Steve Reid (*Yin*), Terry Lee (*Yang*), Berta Dahl (*The Matron*), Ted Prior (*Blow*), Andrew Bick (*Dry*), Dawne Ellison (*Nurse Withers*), Willa Reynolds (*Anne*), Cristina Garcia (*The Waitress*), Esther Lloyd (*Esther*), Thomas Searle (*Wheels*), Karan Hanson (*Wheels' Lady*), Ross Allman (*Sex Puppy*), Dominique (*The Dominatrix*), Jason Collier (*Jet*), Ross Allman (*Sex Puppy*), Sherry Dreizen (*The Leather Lady*), Josh M (*The Purse Snatcher*), Antonyia Verna (*Lizard Lady*), John Bick (*Benny*), Jodi Shapiro (*Didi*), Kenneth Scherr (*Sly*), Dianne Copeland (*Smeg's Girl in Pink*), Laura Gregory (*Smeg's Girl in White*), Peter George (*The Boat Fisherman*), Mel Sparks (*The Elder Fisherman*), Gary Levinson (*The Dead Fisherman*), Carrie Joseph (*The Woman who has Purse Snatched*), Jan-Ove Hogman (*The Hippie Surfer*), Robert Tinnell (*Jake*), Anders Olausson (*Rabbit*), Maurice E. Brooks III, Daniel R. Flynn, Cosme T. Mata, Douglas D. Meyer, Don Lee Weiller, Scott Baker, Brian Curry, Jason Dreizen, Gary Frye, Miles Guarneri, Ian Meno, Justin Dalton, Jeremy Mullen, Jessica Mullen, Mike Yoder, Eric de Young, Andrew Sands, Dave Bergeson
D: Peter George **SCR:** Jon Ayre based on an orig. story by Peter George & Jon Ayre **PHOTOG:** Rolf Kestermann **MUSIC:** Jon McCallum
Minor SF-satire: Earthquake devastates California, vicious beach gangs prowl

The Surf Terror
see **Beach Girls and the Monster**

The Surgeon
1996, (USA), color
W: Peter Boyle, Isabel Glasser Charles Dance, Charles Bailey-Gates, Gregory West, Mother Love
D: Carl Schenkel **SCR:** Patrick Cirillo **PHOTOG:** Thomas Burstyn **MUSIC:** Christopher Frank
A.k.a. **Exquisite Tenderness**
Standard horror-thriller: Madman experiments on patients

The Surgeon
(Ger), 100 mins.
W: Isabel Glasser (*Dr. McCann*), Malcolm McDowell (*Dr. Stein*), James Remar (*Dr. Hendricks*), Sean Haberle (*Dr. Matar*)

The Surgen's Knife
1957, (GB), Gibraltar/Grand Nat'l, b&w, 83 mins.
W: Donald Houston (*Dr. Alex Waring*), Adrienne Corri (*Laura Shelton*), Lyndon Brook (*Dr. Ian Breck*), Sydney Tafler (*Dr. Hearne*), Jean Cadell (*Henrietta*), Mervyn Johns (*Mr Waring*), Marie Ney (*Matron Fiske*), Ronald Adam (*Maj. Tilling*), John Welsh (*Insp. Austen*), Beatrice Varley (*Mrs. Waring*)
P: Charles Leeds **D:** Gordon Parry **SCR:** Robert Westerby, from Anne Hocking's novel *Wicked*
Standard crime-thriller: Surgeon kills blackmailer

Survival 1990
1984, (Can), color
W: Jeff Holec, Nancy Scer
Minor SF-thriller: Post-nuke couple struggles for life

Survival Zone
1984, (USA), color, 90 mins.
W: Gary Lockwood, Morgan Stevens, Camilla Sparv
D: Percival Rubens
Standard SF-thriller: Post-nuke survivors vs. marauding motorcyclists

Les Survivants de l'Infini
see **This Island Earth**

Survive!
1976, (Mex), Robert Stigwood-Allan Carr/Para, color, 86 mins.

S

W: Pablo Ferrel (*Raul*), Norma Lazaren (*Sylvia*), Luz Maria Aguilar (*Mrs. Madero*), Hugo Stiglitz (*Francisco*), Fernando Larranga (*Madero*), Lorenzo de Rodas, Gloria Chavez, Carlos Camara, Jose Elias Moreno, Fernando Palaviccini, Sara Guash
WRIT, P & D: Rene Cardona Jr., from a book by Clay Blair Jr.   **MUSIC:** Gerald Fried
Minor thriller: Grisly tale of cannibalism after 1972 Andes plane crash

Surviving the Game
1994, (USA), color, 94 mins.
W: Rutger Hauer, Ice-T, F. Murray Abraham, Gary Busey, Jeff Corey, Charles S. Dutton, John C. McGinley, William McNamara
D: Ernest R. Dickerson   **SCR:** Eric Bernt   **MUSIC:** Stewart Copeland
Minor thriller: Sportsman hunts homeless man

Survivor
1980, (Austral), color, 91 mins.
W: Robert Powell, Jenny Agutter, Joseph Cotten, Angela Punch McGregor
D: David Hemmings   **SCR:** David Ambrose
Minor fantasy-thriller: Ghosts plague plane-crash survivor

Survivor
1987, (USA), Matrix-Martin Wragge, color, 92 mins.
W: Chip Mayer, Richard Moll (*Kragg*), Sue Kiel (*The Woman*)
D: Michael Shackleton   **SCR:** Bima Stagg   **ORIG. STORY:** Bima Stagg & Martin Wragge   **PHOTOG:** Fred Tammes   **MUSIC:** Adriaan Strydom
SONGS: *We Are Survivors*
Standard SF-adventure: Astronaut vs. post-nuke dictator

The Survivors of Infinity
*see **This Island Earth***

Susie Q
1995, (USA), Libra Pictures color, 90 mins.
W: Justin Whalin (*Zach*), Amy Jo Johnson (*Susie Q*), Shelley Long (*Penny Sands*), Andrea Libman (*Teri Sands*) Ernie Prentice, Bentley Mitchum, Tasha Simms, Lloyd Berry, Allan Morgan, Chris Martin, John Johnston
Minor fantasy: Teen aids ghost of girl who's haunting his house

The Suspect
1944, (USA), Univ, b&w, 85 mins.
W: Charles Laughton, Ella Raines, Henry Daniell, Rosalind Ivan, Molly Lamont, Dean Harens
D: Robert Siodmak   **SCR:** Bertram Millhauser, from a novel by James Ronald
PHOTOG: Paul Ivano
Taut thriller: Man plots wife's murder

Suspect Device
1995, (USA), color, 90 mins.
W: C. Thomas Howell, Stacy Travis, Jed Allan, John Beck, Marcus Aurelius, Jonathan Fuller
D: Rick Jacobson   **SCR:** Alex Simon   **PHOTOG:** John Aronson   **MUSIC:** Christopher Lennertz
Made-for-Cable, standard SF-thriller: Computer researcher becomes assassination target

Suspected: or, The Mysterious Lodger
1909, (GB), R.W. Paul, b&w, 300 ft. (91.4m)
D: Jack Smith
Standard comedy short: Landlady mistakes lodger's dummy for corpse

Suspended Alibi
1957, (GB), ACT Films/RFD, b&w, 64 mins.
W: Patrick Holt (*Paul Pearson*), Honor Blackman (*Lynn Pearson*), Valentine Dyall (*Insp. Kayes*), Naomi Chance (*Diana*), Lloyd Lamble (*Waller*), Andrew Keir (*Sandy*)
D: Alfred Shaughnessy   **STORY:** Kenneth R. Hayles
Standard thriller: Wrong man accused of murder

Suspense
1946, (USA), King Bros./Mono, b&w, 101 mins.
W: Belita, Barry Sullivan Albert Dekker, Bonita Granville, Eugene Pallette
D: Frank Tuttle   **SCR:** Philip Yordan
Standard thriller: Ambitious cad pursues ice-skating star

Suspicion
1941, (USA), RKO, b&w, 99 mins.
W: Joan Fontaine, Cary Grant, Sir Cedric Hardwicke, Dame May Whitty, Nigel Bruce, Isabel Jeans, Heather Angel, Leo G. Carroll, Auriol Lee
D: Alfred Hitchcock   **SCR:** Samson Raphaelson, Alma Reville & Joan Harrison, from Francis Iles' novel *Before the Fact*   **PHOTOG:** Harry Stradling   **SPCL-FX:** Vernon L. Walker   **MUSIC:** Franz Waxman
Academy Award, Joan Fontaine, Best Actress
Modest thriller: Woman weds playboy, comes to fear for her life

Suspicion
1987, (GB), color, 90 mins.
W: Anthony Andrews, Jane Curtin, Jonathan Lynn, Michael Hordern, Betsy Blair
D: Andrew Grieve, from Francis Iles' novel, *Before*
TVM, standard thriller (tepid remake of Hitchcock classic)

Suspiria
1977, (It), Salvatore Argento/Int'l Classics/20th Century-Fox, color, 92 mins. (uncut, 97 mins.)
W: Jessica Harper (*Susy Banyon*), Joan Bennett, Alida Valli, Stefania Casini, Udo Keir, Miguel Bose
D: Dario Argento   **PHOTOG:** Luciano Tovoli   **MUSIC:** Goblin
Tense thriller: Murders at dancing school

Suture
1994, (USA), Samuel Goldwyn, b&w, 96 mins.
W: Dennis Haysbert, Mel Harris, Michael Harris, Sab Shimono Dina Merrill, David Graf, Fran Ryan, John Ingle
WRIT & D: Scott McGhee & David Siegel   **PHOTOG:** Greg Gardiner
MUSIC: Cary Berger
Unusual thriller: Amnesiac involved in murder plot

Svengali
1927, (Ger), Terra-film, b&w
W: Paul Wegener
D & SCR: Paul Wegener, based on George du Maurier's novel *Trilby*
Standard thriller: Hypnotist enslaves girl

Svengali
1931, (USA), WB, b&w, 81 mins.
W: John Barrymore (*Svengali*), Marion Marsh (*Trilby*), Bramwell Fletcher, Luis Alberni, Donald Crisp, Carmel Myers, Paul Porcasi, Lumsden Hare
D: Archie Mayo   **SCR:** J. Grubb Alexander, from George du Maurier's novel *Trilby*   **PHOTOG:** Barney McGill
Classic thriller: Sinister hypnotist turns nonentity into opera star

Svengali
1954, (GB), Alderdale/Renown/MGM, color, 82 mins.
W: Donald Wolfit (*Svengali*), Hildegarde Neff (*Trilby*), Terence Morgan (*Billy*), Derek Bond (*The Laird*), Hubert Gregg (*Durien*), Noel Purcell (*Patrick O'Ferral*), Joan Haythorne (*Mrs. Bagot*), David Kossoff (*Gecko*), Alfie Bass (*Carrel*), Harry Secombe (*Barizel*), Peter Illing (*The Police Inspector*), Paul Rogers (*Taffy*), Hugh Cross (*Dubose*), David Oxley (*Dodor*), Richard Pearson (*Lambert*), Rica Fox, Toots Pound, Michael Craig, Neville Phillips, Arnold Bell, Cyril Smith, Joan Heal, Martin Boddey, Marne Maitland, The Voice of Mme. Elisabeth Schwarzkopf
P: George Minter   **WRIT & D:** Noel Langley, from George du Maurier's novel *Trilby*   **PHOTOG:** Wilkie Cooper   **MUSIC:** William Alwyn
Standard thriller: Mesmerist turns girl into singer

Svengali
1983, (USA), CBS-TV, color, 96 mins.
W: Peter O'Toole, Jodie Foster, Larry Joshua (*Johnny Rainbow*), Elizabeth Ashley (*Eve Swiss*), Pamela Blair (*Trish*), Barbara Bryne (*Mrs. Burns-Rizzo*), Ronald Weyland, Robin Thomas
D: Anthony Harvey   **TELEPLAY:** Frank Cucci   **STORY:** Sue Grafton, inspired by George du Maurier's novel *Trilby*   **PHOTOG:** Larry Pizer   **MUSIC:** John Barry   **SONGS:** *One Dream at a Time*
TVM, standard melodrama: Maestro turns girl into star

Swamp Diamonds
*see **Swamp Women***

Swamp Fire
1946, (USA), Para, b&w, 69 mins.
W: Johnny Weissmuller, Buster Crabbe, Virginia Grey, Carol Thurston, David Janssen, Edwin Maxwell, Pedro de Cordoba, Pierre Watkin
P: William Pine & William Thomas   **D:** William Pine   **SCR:** Geoffrey Holmes
blurb: "Twin water wizards clash in deadly bayou love feud!"
Standard thriller: Navy man vs. bayou king for "a tiger girl's love"

Swamp of the Lost Monster
*see **Swamp of the Lost Souls***

Swamp of the Lost Souls
1962, (Mex), Azteca/Young America, color, 76 mins.
W: Gaston Santos, Manuel Donde
D: Raphael Baledon   **SCR:** Ramon Obon   **PHOTOG:** Raoul Martinez Solares   **MUSIC:** Gustavo C. Carrion
*A.k.a. **Swamp of the Lost Monster***
Minor juvenile thriller: Hacienda murder mystery, "fish man" prowls

Swamp Thing
1982, (USA), Melniker-Uslan/Embassy, color, 91 mins.
W: Adrienne Barbeau, Louis Jourdan, Ray Wise, Don Knight, David Hess, Nicholas Worth, Dick Durock (*The Swamp Thing*), Al Ruban, Ben Bates, Nannette Brown, Reggie Batts, Tommy Madden, Mimi Meyer, Karen Price, Bill Erickson, Dov Gottesfeld
D & SCR: Wes Craven, from comic-book character created by Len Wein, Joe Orlando & Bernie Wrightson   **PHOTOG:** Robin Goodwin   **MUSIC:** Harry Manfredini
Standard SF-satire: Scientist becomes loathsome monster

Swamp Women
1956, (USA), Woolner/Screen Guild, color, 72 mins.
W: Marie Windsor, Michael Connors, Carole Mathews, Jill Jarmyn, Beverly
  Garland, Lou Place, Jonathan Haze
P: Bernard Woolner D: Roger Corman SCR: David Stern
A.k.a. **Swamp Diamonds** & **Cruel Swamp** *orig. co-billed with* **Blonde Bait**
Standard melodrama: Female convicts seek stolen diamonds in Louisiana bayou

Swanker and the Witch's Curse
1914, (GB), Cricks/DFSA, b&w, 510 ft. (155.4m)
D: Edwin J. Collins
Standard fantasy: Beggar woman's curse makes man's shopping come to life

Swanker Meets His Girl
1914, (GB), Cricks, b&w, 460 ft. (140.2m)
D: Edwin J. Collins
Standard fantasy: Girl's father chases her magical suitor

The Swan Princess
1994, (USA), WB, color, 90 mins.
VOICES: Jack Palance, Michelle Nicastro, Howard McGillin, Liz Callaway, John
  Cleese, Steven Wright, Mark Harelik, Steve Vinovich, Dakin Matthews,
  Sandy Duncan, James Arrington, Davis Gaines, Joel McKinnon Miller
D: Richard Rich SCR: Richard Rich & Brian Nissen MUSIC: Lex de Azevedo
SONG: *Far Longer Than Forever*
Standard animated fantasy: Girl escapes enchantment

The Swan Princess: Escape from Castle Mountain
1997, (USA), WB, color, 75 mins.
VOICES: Michelle Nicastro (*Odette*), Douglas Sills (*Derek*), Jake Williamson
  (*Clavius*)
D: Richard Rich
Standard animated fantasy

The Swan Princess: Mystery of the Enchanted Treasure
1998, (USA), color, 75 mins.
D: Richard Rich
Made-for-Video, standard animated fantasy

The Swarm
1978, (USA), WB, color, 116 mins.
W: Michael Caine (*Brad Crane*), Katharine Ross (*Helena*), Richard Widmark (*Gen.
  Slater*), Lee Grant (*Anne MacGregor*), Richard Chamberlain (*Dr. Hubbard*),
  Fred MacMurray (*Clarence*), Olivia de Havilland (*Maureen*), Ben Johnson
  (*Felix*), Henry Fonda (*Dr. Krim*), Jose Ferrer (*Dr. Andrews*), Patty Duke
  Astin (*Rita Bard*), Slim Pickens (*Jud Hawkins*), Bradford Dillman (*Maj.
  Baker*), Christian Juttner (*Paul Durant*), Cameron Mitchell (*Gen. Thompson*),
  Alejandro Rey (*Dr. Martinez*), Morgan Paull (*Dr. Newman*), Don "Red" Barry
  (*Pete Harris*), Doria Cook (*Mrs. Durant*), Robert Varney (*Mr. Durant*), Ernie
  Orsatti (*The Duty Officer*), Patrick Culliton (*Sheriff Morrison*), John Furlong
  (*The Cameraman*), Chris Petersen (*Hal*), Jerry Toomey (*Eddie*), Mara Cook
  (*The Secretary*), Joey Eis-nach (*The Bee Boy*), Stephen Powers (*The Radarman*),
  Chris Capen (*The Lieutenant*), George Simmons (*The Nurse*), Tony Haig
  (*Officer #2*), Bill Snider (*Radarman #2*), Arell Blanton (*The Sergeant*), Phil
  Montgomery (*The Mechanic*), John Williams (*The Launching Officer*), Trent
  Dolan (*The Radio Sergeant*), Steve Marlo (*Pilot #1*), James Austin Turley (*The
  Reverend*), Frank Blair (*himself*), Art Ballinger (*The Announcer*), Marcia
  Nicholson (*The Captain*), Arthur Space (*The Engineer*), Chuck Hayward (*The
  Standby Engineer*), Michael Sheehan (*Airman #1*), Howard Culver (*Airman
  #2*), Glenn Charles Lewis (*The Chemical Warfare Guard*)
P & D: Irwin Allen SCR: Stirling Silliphant, from a novel by Arthur Herzog
PHOTOG: Fred J. Koenekamp SPCL-FX: L.B. Abbott MUSIC: Jerry
  Goldsmith
Standard SF-thriller: Killer bees attack USA

Sweeney Todd
1928, (GB), QTS/Ideal, b&w, 6,500 ft. (1981.2m)
W: Moore Marriott (*Sweeney Todd*), Zoe Palmer (*Johanna*), Charles Ashton (*Mark
  Ingestre*), Iris Darbyshire (*Amelia Lovett*), Judd Green (*Simon Podge*), Philip
  Hewland (*Ben Wagstaffe*), Brian Glenny (*Tobias Wragge*), Harry Lorraine
  (*Mick Todd*)
D: Walter West, from the play by George Dibdin Pitt & C. Hazleton
Standard thriller: Man dreams he is murderous barber

Sweet Evil
1995, (USA), color, 100 mins.
W: Bridgette Wilson, Peter Boyle, Scott Cohen
Made-for-Video, standard thriller: Surrogate proves deadly

Sweet Kill
1972, (USA), New World, color, 84 mins.
W: Tab Hunter Cherie Latimer, Linda Leider, Isabel Jewell, Nadyne Turney,
  Roberta Collins, Brandy Jerred, Rory Guy, Angel Fox, Katie McKeown,
  John Aprea, Josh Green, Sandy Kenyon
P: Tamara Asseyev D & SCR: Curtis Hanson PHOTOG: Daniel Lacambre,
  Edmund Anderson & Floyd Crosby MUSIC: Charles Bernstein
A.k.a. **The Arousers, A Kiss From Eddie**
"...a milestone in Tab Hunter's career"—L.A. Times
Minor thriller with Psycho-type elements: Impotent gym teacher fixated on dead mother

Sweet Movie
1973, (Fr-Can-W. Ger), V.M./Mojack/Maran/Biograph, color, 99 mins.
W: Anna Prucnal, Carole Laure, John Vernon, Marpessa Dawn, Pierre Clementi,
  Sami Frey, Roland Topor, Jane Mallet
WRIT & D: Dusan Makavejev MUSIC: Manos Hadjidakis
*"A far-out political fantasy featuring sex in a bed of loose sugar and a chocolate-
covered nude bathing scene"—Bruce Williamson, Playboy*
Unusual satire: Bizarre blend of eroticism, vampirism & cannibalism

Sweet Murder
1993, (USA), color, 101 mins.
W: Helene Udy, Embeth Davidtz, Russell Todd
D: Percival Rubens
*Minor thriller (*Single White Female *imitation): Woman soon regrets sharing apartment*

The Sweet Scent of Death
1985, (GB), color
W: Dean Stockwell, Shirley Knight, Michael Gothard
Minor thriller: Couple at country retreat terrorized

Sweet Sixteen
1983, (USA), Productions Two/CIF, color, 88 mins.
W: Bo Hopkins (*Dan Burke*), Susan Strasberg (*Joanne Morgan*), Patrick Macnee
  (*Dr. Morgan*), Don Stroud (*Billy T.*), Aleisa Shirley (*Melissa Morgan*), Dana
  Kimmell (*Marci Burke*), Don Shanks (*Jason*), Steve Antin (*Hank Burke*),
  Michael J. Cutt (*Frank*), Sharon Farrell (*Kathy*), Tony Perfit (*Tommy Jackson*),
  Logan Clarke (*Jimmy*), Michael Pataki (*George Martin*), Henry Wilcoxon
  (*Greyfeather*), Larry Storch (*Johnny*), Sandy Charles (*The Lab Technician*)
P & D: Jim Sotos SCR: Erwin Goldman PHOTOG: James L. Carter
  MUSIC: Tommy Vig SONGS: *Melissa, How Long, 5 O'Clock World, Whole
  Lot to Learn* & *S.O.S.*
Minor thriller: Puzzling murders in Southwest town

Sweet, Sweet Rachel
1971, (USA), ABC-TV/Worldvision, color, 74 mins.
W: Stefanie Powers, Alex Dreier, Pat Hingle
P: Stan Shpetner D: Sutton Roley TELEPLAY: Anthony Lawrence
*TVM, standard thriller (feature-pilot for teleseries "The Sixth Sense"): ESP expert hunts
psychic killer*

A Swelled Head
see **The Man with the Rubber Head**

The Swimmer
1968, (USA), Col, color, 95 mins.
W: Burt Lancaster, Janet Landgard, Marge Champion, Janice Rule, Kim Hunter,
  Nancy Cushman, John Garfield Jr., Diana Muldaur, Cornelia Otis Skinner,
  Joan Rivers, Dolph Sweet, Charles Drake
P: Frank Perry & Roger Lewis D: Frank Perry & Sidney pollack SCR: Eleanor
  Perry, based on a story by John Cheever PHOTOG: David L. Quaid
  MUSIC: Marvin Hamlisch
Offbeat fable: Man's devastating vision of suburbia

Switch
1991, (USA), Beco/WB, color, 104 mins.
W: Ellen Barkin (*Amanda Brooks*), Jimmy Smits (*Walter Stone*), JoBeth Williams
  (*Margo Brofman*), Lorraine Bracco (*Sheila Faxton*), Tony Roberts (*Arnold
  Freidkin*), Lysette Anthony (*Liz*), Perry King (*Steve Brooks*), Basil Hoffman
  (*Higgins*), Victoria Mahoney (*Felicia*), Bruce Martyn Payne (*The Devil*),
  Catherine Keener (*Steve's Sec'y*), David Wohl (*Att'y Caldwell*), Kevin Kilner
  (*Dan Jones*), James Harper (*Lt. Laster*), John Lafayette (*Sgt. Phillips*), Emma
  Walton (*The Fur Protester*), Jim J. Bullock (*The Psychic*), Diana Chesney
  (*Mrs. Witherspoon*), Joe Flood (*Mac the Guard*), Ben Hartigan (*The Minister*),
  Louis Eppolito (*Al the Guard*), Yvette Freeman (*Mae the Maid*), Dennis
  Paladino (*Duke*), F. William Parker (*The Barber*), Tea Leoni (*The Dream
  Girl*), Rick Aiello (*The Wise Guy at Duke's*), David Gale (*The Doctor*), Jessie
  Jones (*Arnold's Sec'y*), Savant Tanney, Marti Muller, Virginia Morris, Robert
  Clotworthy, Robert Elias, Patricia Clipper, Michelle Wong, Mindy Lawson,
  Teri Gold, Kimberly Oja, Lily Marige, William Shockley, Dena Burton,
  Jennie Nauman, Annette Quinn, Michelle Reese, Karen Medak, Alana
  Silvani, Jacqulyn Moen, Tracy Lambert, Michael Badalucco, Taunie Vrenon,
  Gregory Barnett, Fred Lerner, Jay R. Goldenberg, Faith Minton, Rebecca
  Wood, Helena Apothaker, Linda Dona, Elena Statheros, Jim Lovelett,
  Robert Towers, Barbara Schillaci, Tony Genaro, Ross Brittain, Linda Gary,
  Richard Provost, Molly Okuneff
P: Tony Adams WRIT & D: Blake Edwards PHOTOG: Dick Bush MUSIC:
  Henry Mancini
Amusing comedy-fantasy: Playboy reincarnated in woman's body. cf. **Goodbye Charlie**

Switched Brains
see **The Man Who Changed His Mind**

The Sword and the Dragon
see **Ilya Mourometz**

The Sword and the Sorcerer
1982, (USA), Brandon Chase/Univ, color, 100 mins.
W: Lee Horsley (*Talon*), Kathleen Beller, Simon MacCorkindale, Richard Lynch,

S

George Maharis, Richard Moll, Robert Tessier, Anthony De Longis, Nina Van Pallandt, Jeff Corey, Anna Bjorn, Joe Regalbuto, Joseph Ruskin, Russ Marin, Reb Brown, Earl Maynard, George Murdock, John Davis Chandler, Emily Yancy, Christopher Cary, Peter Breck, Alan Caillou, Michael Evans, Jay Robinson, Simmy Bow, Eric Cord, George Fisher, Jo-Jo D'Amore, Steve Davis, Anthony Farrar, Tammi Furness, Greg Finley, Hubie Kerns, James Jarnigan, Lennie Geer, Michael Hoit, Edgy Lee, Shelley Taylor Morgan, Gina Smika, Charlie Messenge, Christina Nigra, Buckley Norris, Patrick O'Moore, Thomas Rosales, William Watson, Corinne Calvet, Alvah Stanley, Mark Steffan, Barry Chase

D: Albert Pyun   **SCR:** Tom Karnowski, John Stuckmeyer & Albert Pyun   **PHOTOG:** Joseph Mangine   **MUSIC:** David Whitaker
Modest adventure-fantasy: Evil sorcerer rules ancient kingdom

The Sword and the Dragon: ILYA MOUROMETZ

The Sword in the Stone
1963, (USA), Walt Disney, color, 80 mins.
VOICES: Ricky Sorenson, Sebastian Cabot, Karl Swenson, Alan Napier, Junius Matthews, Norman Alden, Barbara Jo Allen, Martha Wentworth
D: Wolfgang Reitherman, from a story by T.H. White   **MUSIC:** George Bruns
Standard animated fantasy: Wizard tutors fledgling king

The Sword of Ali Baba
1965, (USA), Univ, color, 81 mins.
W: Peter Mann (*Ali Baba*), Loycelyn Lane (*Amara*), Frank Puglia (*Prince Cassim*), Frank McGrath (*Pindar*), Peter Whitney (*Abou*), Gavin MacLeod (*Hulagu Khan*), Greg Morris (*Yusuf*), Frank DeKova (*Baba*), Morgan Woodward (*The Captain of the Guard*)
P: Howard Christie   **D:** Virgil W. Vogel   **SCR:** Oscar Brodney   **PHOTOG:** William Margulies
Minor adventure-fantasy (with much stock-footage from **Ali Baba and the Forty Thieves** *{1944}):* **Turmoil in Old Arabia**

Sword of Damascus
1962, (It), AIP Filmways, color, 93 mins.
W: Tony Russel, Gianni Solaro
Minor adventure-thriller

The Sword of Damocles
1920, (GB), B&C/Butcher, b&w, 4,920 ft. (1499.6m)
W: Jose Collins (*Leonie Paoli*), H.V. Esmond (*Hugh Maltravers*), Claude Fleming (*Geoffrey Moray*), Bobbie Andrews (*Jack Moray*), Thomas Nesbitt (*Bruce Leslie*), Chigquita de Lorenzo (*Una Paoli*), Edward Sorley (*Raikes*)
P: Edward Godal   **D & SCR:** George Ridgwell, from H.V. Esmond's play *Leonie*
Standard crime-thriller: Barrister's letter proves bride shot aged husband who was bigamist

Sword of Lancelot
see *Lancelot and Guinevere*

The Sword of Monte Cristo
1951, (USA), 20th Century-Fox, color, 80 mins.
W: George Montgomery, Paula Corday, William Conrad, Berry Kroeger
Modest adventure-thriller: Wicked gov't minister seeks key to fabulous treasure

Sword of Sherwood Forest
1960, (GB), Hammer-Yeoman/Col, color, 80 mins.
W: Richard Greene (*Robin Hood*), Peter Cushing (*The Sheriff of Nottingham*), Niall MacGinnis (*Friar Tuck*), Sarah Branch (*Lady Marian Fitzwater*), Richard Pasco (*Earl of Newark*), Jack Gwillim (*Archbishop Hubert*), Nigel Green (*Little John*), Dennis Lotis (*Alan A'Dale*), Vanda Godsell (*The Prioress*), Derren Nesbitt (*Martin*), Oliver Reed (*Melton*)
P: Richard Greene & Sidney Cole   **D:** Terence Fisher   **SCR:** Alan Hackney   **PHOTOG:** Ken Hodges   **MUSIC:** Alun Hoddinott
Standard adventure-thriller: Outlaw thwarts sheriff's plot to overthrow Archbishop of Canterbury

Sword of the Avenger
1948, (USA), UPA/Eagle Lion, sepia, 76 mins.
W: Ramon Del Gado, Sigrid Gurie
Standard adventure-thriller

Sword of the Conqueror
1961, (It), Titanus/UA, color, 85 mins.
W: Jack Palance, Guy Madison, Eleonrora Rossi-Drago, Carlo D'Angelo, Andrea Bosic, Edy Vessel, Ivan Palance, Vittorio Sanipoli
D: Carlo Campogalliani   **SCR:** Roberto Gianviti & Alessandro Ferrau   **STORY:** Paola Barbara & Primo Zeglio   **MUSIC:** Carlo Rustichelli
Standard action-thriller: Leader of violent empire covets opposition beauty

Sword of the Valiant
1985, (GB), Cannon, color, 102 mins.
W: Miles O'Keeffe (*Sir Gawain*), Sean Connery (*The Green Knight*), Trevor Howard (*King Arthur*), Peter Cushing (*The Seneschal*), Ronald Lacey (*Oswald*), Cyrielle Claire (*Linet*), Lila Kedrova (*Morgan le Fay*), Emma Sutton (*The Lady of Lyonesse*), Douglas Wilmer (*The Black Knight*), Leigh Lawson (*Humphrey*), John Rhys-Davies (*Baron Fortinbras*), Thomas Heathcote (*The Armourer*), Bruce Lidington (*Sir Bertilak*), John Serret (*The Priest*), Brian Coburn (*Friar Vosper*), David Rappaport, Wilfrid Brambell
D: Stephen Weeks   **SCR:** Stephen Weeks, Howard Pen, Philip Breen, Roger Towne, Rosemary Sutcliff & Therese Burdon   **PHOTOG:** Freddie Young   **MUSIC:** Ron Geesin
Standard adventure-fantasy: Knight uses magic ring to rescue maiden from baron's evil son

Sword of Venus
1953, (USA), RKO, b&w, 73 mins.
W: Robert Clarke, Catherine McLeod, Dan O'Herlihy, William Schallert
D: Harold Daniels
A.k.a. **Island of Monte Cristo**
Minor adventure-thriller: Son of Count of Monte Cristo fights family's enemies

The Swordsman
1976, (GB), Rank/20th-Fox, color, 91 mins.
W: Linda Marlowe (*Harriet Zapper*), Alan Lake (*Reynaud Deval*), Jason Kemp (*Karel Duval*), Tony Then (*Hock*), Noel Johnson (*Christian Duval*), Edina Ronay (*Guy Champion*), Michael O'Malley (*The Gendarme*), Peter Halliday (*Rabelais*), David Robb (*Alex Zendor*), William Ridoutt (*Insp. Cook*), Rex Grey
P: Lindsay Shonteff & Elizabeth Gray   **D:** Lindsay Shonteff   **STORY:** Ellis Hugh Brody   **PHOTOG:** Les Young   **MUSIC:** Colin Pearson
Standard crime-thriller: Fencing-school proprietor kills millionaire father

The Swordsman
1992, (USA), color, 98 mins.
W: Lorenzo Lamas
Standard fantasy-thriller: Fabled sword draws ancient enemies across time and space

Swords of Blood
see *Cartouche (1962)*

Swords of the Space Ark
1977, (Jap), color

WRIT & P: Bunker Jenkins   **MUSIC:** Doug Lackey & Joseph Zappala
TVM, minor space-opera: Alien kingdoms war

Sylvie and the Phantom
1946, (Fr), Discina, b&w, 97 mins.
W: Jacques Tati, Odette Joyeux
D: Claude Autant-Lara
US Release: Distinguished Films, 1950
Standard comedy-fantasy: Girl wooed by ghost of grandmother's lover

Symptoms
1976, (GB), Finiton/New Realm, color, 91 mins.
W: Angela Pleasence (*Helen Ramsey*), Peter Vaughan (*Brady*), Lorna Heilbron (*Anne*), Nancy Nevinson (*Hannah*), Marie-Paul Mailleux (*Cora*), Raymond Huntley (*Burke*), Ronald O'Neil (*John*), Michael Grady (*Nick*)
P: Jean Dupuis   **D:** Jose Larraz   **STORY:** Jose Larraz & Stanley Miller
   PHOTOG: Trevor Wrenn   **MUSIC:** John Scott
reissued (1977) as **Blood Virgin**
Standard horror-thriller: Mad girl commits murders

Synapse
1996, (USA), color, 90 mins.
W: Karen Duffy, Saul Rubinek, Matt McCoy (*Gabriel*), Lynne McCormack (*Dr. Merain*), Torri Higginson (*Kristen*) Chris Makepeace
D: Allan Goldstein
Standard SF-thriller: Corporate tyrants of 2015 put mind of rebel leader into body of his ex-lover

Syngenor
1990, (USA), color 98 imns
W: Starr Andreeff (*Susan*), Mitchell Laurance, David Gale Charles Lucia, Riva Spier, Jeff Doucette, Lewis Arquette, Bill Gratton, Jon Korkes, Melanie Shatner
D: George Elanjian Jr.   **MUSIC:** Tom Chase & Steve Rucker
Minor SF-thriller: Deadly desert-combat robot runs amok

Le Systeme du Docteur Goudron et du Professeur Plume (The System of Dr. Tarr and Professor Fether)
1909, (Fr), b&w
D: Maurice Tourneur, from Edgar Allan Poe's short story
Standard thriller

Le Systeme du Docteur Sonflamort (The System of Dr. Deathcheater)
1905, (Fr), Star, b&w, 93m (305.1 ft./5.2 mins.)
D: Georges Melies
A.k.a. 'Life-Saving Up-to-Date'
Standard fantasy

The System of Dr. Deathcheater
see Le Systeme du Docteur Sonflamort

The System of Dr. Tarr and Professor Fether
see Le Systeme du Docteur Goudron et du Professeur Plume

Sylvie et le Fantome: ODETTE JOYEAUX AND JACQUES TATI

Table Turning
1905, (GB), Hepworth, b&w, 100 ft. (30.5m)
D: Lewin Fitzhamon
Standard comedy short: Revolving table causes pandemonium at spiritualist's seance

Taboos of the World
1963, (It), Royal Films/AIP, color, 97 mins, also 86 mins.
W: Vincent Price *(narrator)*
P: Guido Giambartolomei **D & SCR:** Romolo Marcellini
US Release: AIP, 1965
Standard docu: Bizarre happenings (A-bomb victims, blood drinking, drug addicts selling their babies, etc.)

Tabu
1931, (USA), Golden Bough/Para, b&w, 90 mins.
W: Reri Matahi
P: Robert Flaherty & F.W. Murnau **D:** F.W. Murnau *(Flaherty quit as co-dir because of disagreement over directorial style)* **PHOTOG:** Floyd Crosby
MUSIC: Hugo Reisenfeld
Classic adventure-romance: South Seas boy has forbidden love for girl consecrated to island gods. cf. She-Gods of Shark Reef

Tag: The Assassination Game
1982, (USA), color, 92 mins.
W: Robert Carradine, Linda Hamilton, Michael Winslow, Perry Lang, Kristine DeBell
D & SCR: Nick Castle
Minor thriller: College "killing game" becomes real

Tails You Live, Heads You're Dead
1995, (USA), USA-TV, color
W: Corbin Bernsen, Ted McGinley, Maria Del Mar, Jeff Pustil, Tim Matheson (McKinley)
D: Tim Matheson **TELEPLAY:** Miguel Tejada-Flores, from Bill Pronzini's short story *Liar's Dice* **PHOTOG:** Francois Protat **MUSIC:** David Michael Frank
Made-for-Cable, standard thriller: Family man targeted as next victim of game-playing serial killer

Tainted Blood
1993, (USA), Wilshire Court/Para, color, 96 mins.
W: Raquel Welch, Alley Mills, Joan Van Ark
D: Matthew Patrick **PHOTOG:** Billy Dickson **MUSIC:** Dana Kaproff
TVM, minor thriller: Writer seeks lost twin, finds girl with killer gene

Tainted Image
1991, (USA), color, 95 mins.
W: Tom Saunders, Sandra Frances, Ken La Mothe, Annetta Arpin, Heidi Emerich, Steve Kornacki
Standard thriller: Woman artist goes mad

Tainted Love
1996, (USA), color, 100 mins.
W: Lee Anne Beaman, Doug Jeffrey
Made-for-Video, minor thriller: Undercover policewoman hunts serial killer

Tajemnica Doliny Los Hermanos
see Rekopios Znaleziony w Saragossie

Take My Life
1947, (GB), Cineguild/Independant Producers, b&w, 79 mins.
W: Hugh Williams *(Nicholas Talbot)*, Greta Gynt *(Philippa Bentley)*, Marius Goring *(Sidney Fleming)*, Henry Edwards *(Insp. Archer)*, Rosalie Crutchley *(Liz Rusman)*, Francis L. Sullivan *(The Prosecution)*, Marjorie Mars *(Mrs. Newcome)*, Ronald Adam *(The Deaf Man)*, Maurice Denham *(The Defense)*, Eleanor Summerfield *(Miss Carteret)*
P: Anthony Havelock-Allan **D:** Ronald Neame **SCR:** Winston Graham, Valerie Taylor & Margaret Kennedy **STORY:** Winston Graham & Valerie Taylor **PHOTOG:** Guy Green **MUSIC:** William Alwyn
US Release: Eagle-Lion, 1948
Standard thriller: Opera star's husband arrested for murder

Take One False Step
1949, (USA), Univ, b&w, 94 mins.
W: William Powell, Shelley Winters, James Gleason, Marsha Hunt, Dorothy Hart, Felix Bressart, Sheldon Leonard, Art Baker, Howard Freeman, Housely Stevenson, Paul Harvey, Minerva Urecal, Marjorie Bennett
D: Chester Erskine **SCR:** Chester Erskine & Irwin Shaw, from a novel by Irwin & David Shaw
Amusing thriller: Man's old girlfriend involves him in murder

Tale of a Vampire
1992, (GB-Jap), color, 93 mins.
W: Julian Sands, Kenneth Cranham, Suzanna Hamilton
D: Shimako Sato **SCR:** Jane Corbett & Shimako Sato **MUSIC:** Julian Joseph
Standard horror-fantasy: Vampire pursues lookalike of lost love

Tale of Fairies
see Cuento de Hadas

The Tale of Sweeney Todd
1998, (USA), SHO-TV, color, 95 mins.
W: Ben Kingsley *(Sweeney Todd)*, Campbell Scott *(Ben)*, Joanna Lumley *(Mrs. Lovett)*, Selina Boyack *(Alice)*, David Wilmot *(Tom)*
Made-for-Cable, standard thriller: Mad barber slays. cf. The Demon Barber of Fleet Street

A Tale of Tails
1933, (GB), Saturn-Inspiration, b&w, 19 mins.
W: Bert Coote *(The Drunk)*
D: Horace Shepherd
Standard comedy-fantasy short: Drunkard's dream of animated models

The Tale of the Ark
1909, (GB), Alpha Trading Co., b&w, 440 ft. (134.1m)
WRIT & D: Arthur Cooper
Standard fantasy: Child dreams of Bible tale enacted by toys

The Tale of the Fox
see Le Roman de Renard

Tales from the Crypt
1971, (GB), Amicus/CRC/Metromedia, color, 92 mins.
W: Joan Collins *(Joanne)*, Sir Ralph Richardson *(The Crypt Keeper)*, Peter Cushing *(Arthur Grimsdyke)*, Geoffrey Bayldon *(The Guide)*, Ian Hendry *(Carl Maitland)*, Chloe Franks *(Carol)*, Tony Wall *(The Attendant)*, Patrick Magee *(George)*, Martin Boddey *(Richard)*, Oliver MacGreevy *(The Maniac)*, Susan Denny *(Mrs. Maitland)*, Frank Forsyth *(The Tramp)*, Paul Clere *(Maitland's Son)*, Harry Locke *(The Cook)*, Nigel Patrick *(William)*, George Herbert *(The Old Blind Man)*, Hugo De Vernier *(A Blind Man)*, John Barrard *(A Blind Man)*, Chris Cannon *(A Blind Man)*, Louis Mansi *(A Blind Man)*, Edward Evans *(Ramsay)*, Robin Phillips *(James)*, David Markham *(Edward)*, Ann Sears *(Mrs. Carter)*, Irene Gawne *(Mrs. Phelps)*, Kay Adrian *(Mrs. Davies)*, Roy Dotrice *(Charles)*, Clifford Earl *(The Police)*, Peter Thomas *(The Pallbearer)*, Manning Wilson *(The Vicar)*, Dan Caulfield *(The Postman)*, Robert Hutton *(Baker)*, Melinda Clancy *(Miss Carter)*, Stafford Medhurst *(Phelps' Son)*, Carlos Baker *(Davies' Son)*, Richard Greene *(Ralph)*, Barbara Murray *(Enid)*, Hedger Wallace *(The Detective)*, Carl Bernard *(A Blind Man)*, Bartlett Mullins *(A Blind Man)*, Bert Palmer *(A Blind Man)*
P: Max J. Rosenberg & Milton Subotsky **D:** Freddie Francis **SCR:** Milton Subotsky **PHOTOG:** Norman Warwick **MUSIC:** Douglas Gamley
"A thriller that will grasp your attention throughout, as well as give you goose bumps along the way"—Ann Guarino, New York Daily News
Entertaining horror-fantasy anthology: Five strangers, lost in British catacombs, have eerie visions revealed to them

Tales From The Crypt: PETER CUSHING

Tales from the Crypt
1989, (USA), HBO-TV, color, 81 mins.
W: William Sadler, Mary Ellen Trainor, Larry Drake, Robert Wuhl, Joe Pantoliano, Gustav Vintas
D: Walter Hill, Robert Zemeckis & Richard Donner **MUSIC:** Ry Cooder & Alan Silvestri
Made-for-Cable, standard trilogy of fantasy-thrillers: "The Man Who Was Death," "'Twas the Night Before" & "Dig That Cat...He's Real Gone"

Tales from the Crypt II
see The Vault of Horror

Tales from the Crypt Presents Bordello of Blood
1996, (USA), Univ, color, 87 mins.
W: Dennis Miller *(Rafe Guttman)*, Angie Everhart *(Lilith)*, Erika Eleniak *(Katherine Verdoux)*, Chris Sarandon *(Rev. Current)*, Corey Feldman *(Caleb*

Verdoux), John Kassir (*The Voice of the Cryptkeeper*)
P & D: Gilbert Adler **SCR:** A.L. Katz & Gilbert Adler, from a story by Bob Gale & Robert Zemeckis **PHOTOG:** Tom Priestley **MUSIC SCORE:** Chris Boardman **THEME:** Danny Elfman
Standard horror-comedy-satire: Brothel conceals vampire nest

Tales from the Darkside
1990, (USA), Para, color, 93 mins.
W: Deborah Harry (*Betty*), Christian Slater (*Andy*), William Hickey (*Drogan*), David Johansen (*Halston*), Rae Dawn Chong (*Carola*), Robert Klein (*Wyatt*), James Remar (*Preston*), David Forrester, Matthew Laurance, Robert Sedgwick, Julianne Moore, Steve Buscemi, Donald Van Horn, Michael Deak, Ralph Marrero, George Guidall, Kathleen Chalfant, Mark Margolis, Paul Greeno, Alice Drummond, Delores Sutton, Joe Dabenigno, Ashton Wise, Philip Lenkowsky, Larry Silvestri, Donna Davidge, Nicole Leach, Daniel Harrison
D: John Harrison **SCR:** Michael McDowell & George A. Romero, from stories by Michael McDowell, Sir Arthur Conan Doyle & Stephen King **PHOTOG:** Robert Draper **SPCL-FX:** Dick Smith **MUSIC:** John Harrison, Chaz Jankel, Jim Manzie & Pat Regan
Standard fantasy-thriller: Trilogy of terror tales

Tales from the Hood
1995, (USA), 40 Acres and a Mule Filmworks/Savoy, color, 102 mins.
W: Corbin Bernsen (*Duke Metger*), Rosalind Cash (*Dr. Cushing*), Clarence Williams III (*Mr. Simms*), David Alan Grier (*Carl*), Paula Jai Parker (*Sissy*), Brandon Hammond (*Walter*), Tom Wright (*Martin Moorehouse*), Rusty Cundieff (*Richard*), Wings Hauser (*Strom*), Lamont Bentley (*Crazy K*), De'Aundre Bonds (*Ball*), Joe Torry (*Stack*), Samuel Monroe Jr. (*Bulldog*), Anthony Griffith (*Clarence*), Michael Massee (*Newton*), Art Evans (*Eli*), Duane Whitaker (*Billy*), Roger Smith (*Rhodie*), Don Dowe (*Cell Orderly #1*), Moon Jones (*Cell Orderly #2*), Chris Edwards (*Ty*), Christina Cundieff (*Miss Cobbs*), Troy Cartwright (*Craig*), Bobby McGee (*The Limo Driver*), Branden Jefferson (*Snoop*), Erika Hansen (*The Anchorwoman*), John A. Cundieff (*The Funeral Priest*), Tim Hutchinson (*Councilman Rogers*), Joseph Anthony Farris (*Reporter #1*), Dawn Gilliam (*Reporter #2*), April Barnett (*Reporter #3*), Ricky Harris (*Lil' Deke*), Darin Scott (*The Top Cop*), Rick Dean (*The Tattooed Man*), Lira Angel (*Nurse Roland*), Mark Christopher Lawrence (*The Prison Guard*), Scotty Brulee (*Young Tracy*), Ryan Williams (*Gangster #1*), Kamau Holloway (*Gangster #2*), Tasha Johnson (*The Little Shot Girl*)
P: Darin Scott **EXEC P:** Spike Lee **D:** Rusty Cundieff **SCR:** Rusty Cundieff & Darin Scott **PHOTOG:** Anthony Richmond **MUSIC:** Christopher Young **MUSIC SPRVSR:** Larry Robinson
blurb: "Your most terrifying nightmare and your most frightening reality are about to meet on the streets"
"A Powerhouse Of A Movie! 'Tales From the Hood' is greatlooking, fast-moving, action-filled, tough-minded and bursting with imagination!"—Los Angeles Times
"One of the best horror films of the decade! This is one 'Hood' that's definitely worth visiting"—Los Angeles Daily News
Unusual horror-fantasy anthology: Weird mortician tells homeboys three scary tales of urban angst

Tales of a Pale and Mysterious Moon after the Rain
see Ugetsu Monogatari

Tales of Robin Hood
1951, (USA), Hal Roach Jr./Lippert, b&w, 59 mins.
W: Robert Clarke, Mary Hatcher
D: James Tinling
Minor adventure-thriller

Tales of Terror
1962, (USA), AltaVista/AIP, color, 90 mins.
W: Vincent Price (*Locke/Fortunato/Valdemar*), Debra Paget (*Helene*), Basil Rathbone (*Carmichael*), Peter Lorre (*Montresor*), Joyce Jameson (*Annabel*), David Frankham (*Dr. James*), Maggie Pierce (*Lenora*), Wally Campo (*The Bartender*), Leona Gage (*Morella*), Ed Cobb (*The Driver*), Scotty Brown (*The Servant*), Lenny Weinrib (*A Policeman*), John Hackett (*A Policeman*), Alan Dewit (*The Chairman*)
P & D: Roger Corman **SCR:** Richard Matheson, trilogy of tales based on short stories by Edgar Allan Poe ***Morella*** (based on "Morella & Ligeia"—featuring Price, Pierce & Gage), ***The Black Cat*** (based on "The Black Cat" & "The Cask of Amontillado"—featuring Price, Lorre, Jameson & Campo), & ***The Facts in the Case of M. Valdemar*** (featuring Price, Paget, Rathbone & Frankham) **PHOTOG:** Floyd Crosby **MUSIC:** Les Baxter **DESIGN:** Daniel Haller
Standard horror-fantasy anthology: (1) Man's wife returns from dead, (2) Drunk gains grisly vengeance on faithless wife and her lover, & (3) Lecherous mesmerist prolongs life of invalid

Tales That Witness Madness
1973, (GB), World Film/Para, color, 90 mins.
W: Joan Collins (*Bella*), Kim Novak (*Auriol*), Jack Hawkins (*Nicholas*), Georgia Brown (*Mother*), Suzy Kendall (*Ann/Beatrice*), Donald Pleasence (*Tremayne*), Mary Tamm (*Ginny*), Michael Jayston (*Brian*), Donald Houston (*Father*), Michael Petrovitch (*Kimo*), Peter McEnery (*Timothy*), Russell Lewis (*Paul*), David Wood (*The Tutor*), Beth Morris (*Polly*), Leon Lissek (*Keoki*), Frank Forsyth (*Uncle Albert*), Zohra Segal (*Malia*), Leslie Nunnerley (*Vera*), Neil

---

Kennedy, Richard Connaught
P: Norman Priggen **D:** Freddie Francis **SCR:** Jay Fairbank **PHOTOG:** Norman Warwick **MUSIC:** Bernard Ebbinghouse
Standard anthology of terror tales: Bizarre case histories of patients at mental hospital

Talisman
1998, (USA), color, 83 mins.
W: Jason Adelman
Standard fantasy-thriller: Angel must perform seven human sacrifices

Talk about a Stranger
1952, (USA), MGM, b&w, 65 mins.
W: George Murphy (*Robert Fontaine Sr.*), Nancy Davis (Reagan) (*Marge Fontaine*), Billy Gray (*Robert Fontaine Jr.*), Kurt Kasznar (*Matlock*), Lewis Stone (*Mr. Wardlaw*), Anna Glomb (*Mrs. Wardlaw*), Tudor Owen, Katherine Warren, Stanley Andrews, Sarah Sachs, Harry Hines, Les O'Pace, Bill Tannen, Ed Cassidy, Mitchell Lewis
D: David Bradley **SCR:** Margaret Pitts, from a novel by Charlotte Armstrong **PHOTOG:** John Alton **MUSIC:** David Buttolph
Standard thriller

Talk of the Devil
1967, (GB), Chairene/Monarch, color, 27 mins.
W: Tim Barrett (*Stephen Wallace*), Suzan Farmer (*Wendy*), Hugh Latimer (*Nick Beelzebub*), Victor Maddern (*Cinders*), Robert Gallico (*Harvey*), Louise Leigh (*Lucy*), Jane Sharman (*Devilette*), Vicky Udal (*Jezebel*)
P: Robert Gallico & Lionel Grose **D:** Francis Searle **SCR:** Ian Finlay & Francis Searle **STORY:** Anthony Sheppard
Standard short fantasy: Henpeck changes places with Satan

Tall, Dark and Deadly
1995, (USA), USA-TV, color, 95 mins.
W: Kim Delaney, Jack Scalia, Todd Allen (*Sam*)
Made-for-Cable, standard thriller: Deranged man stalks woman architect

Tam Lin
1970, (GB), Jerry Gershwin-Elliott Kastner/Commonwealth United/AIP, color, 107 mins.
W: Ava Gardner (*Michaela*), Ian McShane (*Tom*), Cyril Cusack (*The Vicar*), Richard Wattis (*Elroy*), Madeline Smith (*Sue*), Stephanie Beacham (*Janet*), David Whitman (*Oliver*), Jennie Hanley (*Caroline*), Fabia Drake (*Miss Gibson*), Sinead Cusack (*Rose*), Rosemary Blake (*Kate*), Peter Henwood (*Guy*), Joanna Lumley (*Georgia*), Pamela Farbrother (*Vanna*), Heyward Morse (*Andy*), Bruce Robinson (*Alan*), Michael Bills (*Michael*), Julian Barnes (*Terry*), Oliver Norman (*Peter*), Virginia Tingwell (*Lottie*)
P: Alan Ladd Jr. & Stanley Mann **D:** Roddy McDowall **SCR:** William Spier, from Robert Burns poem *The Ballad of Tam Lin* **PHOTOG:** Billy Williams **MUSIC:** Stanley Myers **SONG:** *Sun in My Eyes*
USA retitle, **The Devil's Widow,** *USA release, 1971, GB release, 1977*
Unusual psychodrama, reworking of Celtic legend: Society matron enslaves youth

Tammy and the T-Rex
1994, (USA), Platinic Films, color, 82 mins.
W: Terry Kiser, Denise Richards, George Pilgrim, Ellen Dubin, Theo Forsett, J. Jay Saunders, Ken Carpenter, Sean Whalen, John Edmondson, Buck Flower, John Franklin, Ken Chandler, Efrem Ramirez
D: Stewart Raffill **SCR:** Stewart Raffill & Gary Brockette **PHOTOG:** Roger Olkowski
Minor SF-comedy: Teen's brain placed in mechanical dinosaur

Tangier
1946, (USA), Univ, b&w, 76 mins.
W: Maria Montez, Sabu
D: George Waggner
Standard adventure-thriller

Tangier Assignment
1955, (GB), Rock Pictures/New Realm, b&w, 64 mins.
W: Robert Simmons (*Valentine*), Fernando Rey (*The Inspector*), June Powell (*Vicky*)
P: Cyril Parker **D & STORY:** Ted Leversuch
Standard crime-thriller: Secret agent and nightclub singer nab gun runners

Tangier Incident
1953, (USA), AA, b&w, 77 mins.
W: George Brent, Mari Aldon
Standard thriller

Tangled Destinies
1932, (USA), b&w, 64 mins.
W: Lloyd Whitlock, Glenn Tryon, Vera Reynolds, Doris Hill, Sidney Bracy
D: Frank Strayer **SCR:** Edward T. Lowe
Standard thriller: Murder in old mansion

Tangled Evidence
1934, (GB), Real Art/Radio, b&w, 57 mins.
W: Sam Livesey (*Insp. Drayton*), Joan Marion (*Anne Wilmot*), Michael Hogan (*Ingram Underhill*), Michael Shepley (*Gilbert Morfield*), Reginald Tate (*Ellaby*), Dick Francis (*Frame*), Edgar Norfolk (*Dr. Ackland*), John Turnbull (*Moore*), Davina Craig (*Faith*)
D: George A. Cooper **SCR:** H. Fowler Mear, from a novel by Mrs. Champion de Crespigny

T

Standard thriller: Inspector proves girl did not kill occultist uncle

The Tangram
1914, (GB), Kineto, b&w, 370 ft. (112.8m)
D: Walter R. Booth
Standard fantasy: Pieces of Chinese puzzle form Henry VIII, Lloyd George and Chinese love drama

Tanin No Kao (The Face of Another)
1967, (Jap), Rising Sun/Toho International, color, 124 mins.
W: Tatsuya Nakadai (*Okuyama*), Kyoko Kishida (*The Nurse*), Mikijiro Hira (*The Doctor*), Machiko Kyo (*Mrs. Okuyama*), Eiji Okada (*The Director*), Miki Irie (*The Girl*)
P & D: Hiroshi Teshigahara   **STORY & SCR:** Kobo Abe   **PHOTOG:** Hiroshi Segawa   **MUSIC:** Toru Takemitsu
Classic psychodrama: Man has plastic surgery, loses his identity

Tank Cartoons
see Tanks

Tank Girl
1995, (USA), Trilogy/MGM/UA, color, 105 mins.
W: Lori Petty, Malcolm McDowell, Ice-T (*T-Saint*), Naomi Watts (*Jet Girl*), Don Harvey (*Small*), Jeff Kober (*Booga*), Reg E. Cathey, Scott Coffey, Iggy Pop, Brian Wimmer, Ann Cusack, Staci Linn Ramsower, Ann Magnuson
SCR: Tedi Sarafian   **MUSIC:** Graeme Revell   **SONGS:** Army of Me
Standard SF-satire: Post-nuke punk heroine vs. evil megalomaniac

Tanks
1916, (GB), Kineto, b&w, 470 ft. (143.3m)
D & STORY: Walter R. Booth
A.k.a. **Tank Cartoons**
Standard fantasy: Imaginative depiction of new secret weapon

Tanya's Island
1980, (Can), Fred Baker Films/International Film Exchange, color, 82 mins.
W: D.D. Winters (*Tanya*), Richard Sargent (*Lobo*), Don McCloud (*Blue*), Mariette Levesque (*The Commercial Producer*)
P & SCR: Pierre Brousseau   **D:** Alfred Sole   **PHOTOG:** Mark Irwin
Unusual fantasy (with footage from **Mighty Joe Young**): *Abused woman dreams of life on tropic isle*

Tarantula
1955, (USA), Univ, b&w, 80 mins.
W: John Agar (*Dr. Matt Hastings*), Mara Corday (*Stephanie Clayton*), Leo G. Carroll (*Dr. Gerald Deemer*), Edwin Rand (*Lt. John Nolan*), Ross Elliott (*Burch*), Nestor Paiva (*The Sheriff*), Raymond Bailey, Ed Parker, Steve Darrell, Bert Holland, Clint Eastwood
P: William Alland   **D:** Jack Arnold   **SCR:** Robert M. Fresco   **PHOTOG:** George Robinson   **SPCL-FX:** Clifford Stine   **MUSIC:** Joseph Gershenson
reissued 1965
"one of [Arnold's] most accomplished films...In a remarkable final sequence among the most impressive in the field, the spider burns like a creature of straw as the jets wheel around it, pouring down napalm. No monster ever had a more spectacular burial"—John Baxter, Science Fiction in the Cinema
Vintage SF-thriller: Scientist's secret formula causes giantism in animals, acromegaly in humans

Tarantulas: The Deadly Cargo
1977, (USA), Alan Landsburg/CBS-TV, color, 96 mins.
W: Claude Akins (*Bert Springer*), Charles Frank (*Joe Harmon*), Deborah Winters (*Cindy Beck*), Sandy McPeak (*Chief Beasley*), Bert Remsen (*Mayor Douglas*), Pat Hingle (*Doc Hodgins*), John Harkins (*Sylvan*), Tom Atkins (*Buddy*), Noelle North (*Honey Lamb*), Howard Hesseman (*Fred*), Edwin Owens (*Frank*), Charles Siebert (*Rich Finley*), Alex Colon (*Hector*), Jerome Guardino (*H.L. Williams*), Lanny Horn (*Harry Weed*), Jorge Cervera Jr. (*The Official*), Bill Striglos (*Ralph*), Steve Bonino (*Spud*), Mary-Nancy Burnett (*The Teacher*), Anita Keith (*Mary*), Bill Erwin (*Mr. Schneider*), Iris Korn (*Dorothy*), Matthew Laborteaux (*Matthew*), John Medici (*The Driver*), Laird Williamson (*Smitty*), Ruben Moreno (*Pedro*), Joseph Reale (*The Lineman*), Penelope Windust
D: Stuart Hapmann   **TELEPLAY:** John Groves & Guerdon Trueblood   **PHOTOG:** Robert Morrison   **SPCL-FX:** Roy Downey   **MUSIC:** Mudell Lowe
TVM, standard thriller: Plane crash brings venomous spiders to Southwest community

Target
1985, (USA), color, 118 mins.
W: Gene Hackman, Matt Dillon, Gayle Hunnicutt, Ilona Grubel, Victoria Fyodorova, Herbert Berghof, Josef Sommer
D: Arthur Penn
Standard thriller: Woman vanishes on trip to Paris

Target Earth
1954, (USA), Abtcon/AA, b&w, 75 mins.
W: Richard Denning, Kathleen Crowley, Richard Reeves, Mort Marshall, Virginia Grey, Robert Roark, Arthur Space, Steve Pendleton, Whit Bissell, House Peters Jr.
P: Herman Cohen   **D:** Herman A. Rose   **SCR:** Bill Raynor   **PHOTOG:** Guy Roe

Modest SF-thriller: Robots from space invade metropolis

Target Earth
1998, (USA), ABC-TV, color, 95 mins.
W: Christopher Meloni, Marcia Cross (*Karen*), John C. McGinley (*Agent Naples*), Dabney Coleman (*Sen. Ben Arnold*), Courtney Crumpler (*Tammy*), Chad

Target Earth

Lowe (*Comm. Faulk*)
TVM, standard SF-thriller

Target...Earth?
1980, (USA), Film Farm Inc./Gold Key, color, 95 mins.
W: Victor Buono (*Homer the Archivist*), Rick Overton (*Ino the Computer*), Alicia Heineman (*The Alien Captain*), Liza O'Keefe (*Alien Fish*), Patricia Manceri (*Alien Girl #1*), Maybelle Munoz (*Alien Girl #2*)
D: Joost Van Rees   **SCR:** Iris Van Rees   **SPCL-FX:** Patrick Firpo & Claudia Katayanagi   **MUSIC:** Joe Levine & Chris Palmaro
Minor docu in SF guise: Space-alien researcher probes mystery of Tunguska Event

Target: Embassy
see Embassy

A Target for Killing
1966, (Austrian-It), Gold Key/PEA/Intercontinental, color, 93 mins
W: Stewart Granger, Curt Jurgens, Molly Peters, Adolfo Celi, Klaus Kinski, Rupert Davies
D: Manfred Kohler
Minor thriller: Secret agent tries to prevent heiress' murder
Aka **How To Kill a Lady**

Target: Harry
1969, (USA), ABC Pictures Int'l, color, 85 mins.
W: Vic Morrow, Victor Buono, Suzanne Pleshette, Charlotte Rampling, Cesar Romero, Stanley Holloway, Michael Ansara, Milton Reid
P: Gene Corman   **D:** Henry Neill [Roger Corman]   **TELEPLAY:** Bob Barbash   **MUSIC:** Les Baxter
A.k.a. **What's in It for Harry?** *and* **How to Make It**
TVM, standard spy-thriller (shown in Europe with added nude scenes): Villain seeks plates stolen from British mint

Targets
1968, (USA), Saticoy/Para, color, 90 mins.
W: Boris Karloff, Tim O'Kelly, Nancy Hsueh, James Brown, Arthur Peterson, Mary Jackson, Tanya Morgan, Sandy Baron, Monty Landis, Paul Condylis, Mark Dennis, Frank Marshall, Stafford Morgan, Daniel Ades, Peter Bogdanovich, Raymond Roy, Tim Burns, Warren White, Geraldine Baron, Ellie Wood Walker, Gary Kent, Byron Betz, Mike Farrell, Jay Daniel, Carol Samuels, James Morris, Elaine Partnow, James Bowie, Pete Belcher, Anita Poree, Robert Cleaves, Susan Douglas, Kay Douglas, Diana Ashley, Kirk Scott, Randy Quaid
WRIT, P & D: Peter Bogdanovich   **PHOTOG:** Laszlo Kovacs
Modest thriller: Aged horror-film star attends drive-in theater; sniper menaces

The Tartar Invasion
1960, (It-Fr), color
W: Yoko Tani, Akim Tamiroff, Roland Lesaffre, Joe Robinson
Minor adventure thriller: Barbarians capture muscleman and son during 17th-century invasion of Poland

The Tartars
1960, (It-Yugo), Lux/MGM, color, 105 mins.
W: Orson Welles (*Burundai*), Victor Mature (*Oleg*), Folco Lulli (*Togrul*), Liana Orfei (*Helga*), Bella Cortez (*Samia*), Luciano Marin (*Eric*), Arnoldo Foa (*Chu-Lung*), Furio Meniconi (*Sigrun*)

Targets: BORIS KARLOFF

D: Richard Thorpe & Ferdinando Baldi   **SCR:** Sabatino Ciuffino, Ambrogio Molteni, Gaio Fratini, Oreste Palella & Emimmo Salvi
Standard adventure-thriller: Vikings battle Tartars on Asian steppes

Tarzan and His Mate
1934, (USA), MGM, b&w, 105 mins.
W: Johnny Weissmuller *(Tarzan)*, Maureen O'Sullivan *(Jane Parker)*, Neil Hamilton *(Harry Holt)*, Paul Cavanagh *(Martin Arlington)*, Forrester Harvey *(Beamish)*, Nathan Curry *(Saidi)*
D: Cedric Gibbons & Jack Conway   **SCR:** James Kevin McGuinness, from characters created by Edgar Rice Burroughs   **PHOTOG:** Charles G. Clarke & Clyde DeVinna
Classic adventure-thriller: Jungle man faces challenges

Tarzan and Jane Regained Sort Of
1964, (USA), Andy Warhol, Film-Makers Cooperativecolor & b&w, 120 mins.
W: Taylor Mead, Naomi Levine, Dennis Hopper
P & D: Andy Warhol
Standard "underground" fantasy, 16mm silent

Tarzan and the Amazons
1945, (USA), RKO, b&w, 76 mins.
W: Johnny Weissmuller *(Tarzan)*, Brenda Joyce *(Jane)*, Johnny Sheffield *(Boy)*, Maria Ouspenskaya, Henry Stephenson, J.M. Kerrigan, Don Douglas, Shirley O'Hara, Barton MacLane, Steven Geray
P: Sol Lesser   **D:** Kurt Neumann, from characters created by Edgar Rice Burroughs   **PHOTOG:** Archie Stout   **MUSIC:** Paul Sawtell
blurb: "Lovely pagans vs. white man's evil!"
Standard adventure-thriller: Jungle man opposes tribe of deadly females

Tarzan and the Golden Lion
1927, (USA), R-C Pictures/FBO, b&w, 6 reels (5,807 ft./1770m)
W: James Pierce *(Tarzan, Lord Greystoke)*, Frederic Peters *(Esteban Miranda)*, Edna Murphy *(Ruth Porter)*, Harold Goodwin *(Burton Bradney)*, Liu Yu-Ching *(Cadj, the High Priest)*, Dorothy Dunbar *(Lady Greystoke)*, D'Arcy Corrigan *(Weesimbo)*, Boris Karloff *(Owaza)*, Robert Bolder *(John Peebles)*, Jad Bal-Ja *(himself, the Golden Lion)*
D: J.P. McGowan   **ADAPT:** William E. Wing, from Edgar Rice Burroughs' novel   **PHOTOG:** Joe Walker
Standard adventure-thriller: Jungle man seeks city of diamonds

Tarzan and the Great River
1967, (USA-Switz), Para, color, 88 mins.
W: Mike Henry *(Tarzan)*, Jan Murray, Manuel Padilla Jr., Diana Millay, Rafer Johnson
P: Sy Weintraub   **D:** Robert Day   **SCR:** Bob Barbash   **STORY:** Bob Barbash & Lewis Reed, from characters created by Edgar Rice Burroughs   **PHOTOG:** Irving Lippman   **MUSIC:** William Loose
Standard adventure-thriller: Jungle man vs. evil chief of Amazon tribe

Tarzan and the Green Goddess
1938, (USA), Ashton-Dearholt/Expedition/New Realm, b&w, 72 mins.
W: Herman Brix (Bruce Bennet) *(Tarzan)*, Frank Baker *(Martling)*, Don Castello *(Raglan)*, Lew Sargent *(George)*, Ula Holt
D: Edward Kull   **SCR:** Charles F. Royal, from characters created by Edgar Rice Burroughs   **PHOTOG:** Ernest Smith   **SPCL-FX:** Ray Mercer & Howard Anderson
Standard adventure-thriller (feature version of serial The New Adventures of Tarzan): Expeditions seek legendary treasure

Tarzan and the Huntress
1947, (USA), RKO, b&w, 72 mins.
W: Johnny Weissmuller *(Tarzan)*, Brenda Joyce *(Jane)*, Johnny Sheffield Patricia Morison, Barton MacLane, Charles Trowbridge, Ted Hecht, Wallace Scott, Mickey Simpson, John Warburton
P: Sol Lesser   **D:** Kurt Neumann   **SCR:** Jerry Gruskin & Rowland Leigh, from characters created by Edgar Rice Burroughs   **PHOTOG:** Archie Stout   **MUSIC:** Paul Sawtell
Standard adventure-thriller: Jungle man opposes expedition to collect animals for zoos

Tarzan and the Jungle Boy
1968, (USA-Switz), Para, color, 90 mins.
W: Mike Henry *(Tarzan)*, Rafer Johnson, Aliza Gur, Ronald Gans
P: Robert Day   **D:** Robert Gordon   **SCR:** Stephen Lord, from characters created by Edgar Rice Burroughs   **PHOTOG:** Ozen Sermet   **MUSIC:** William Loose
Standard adventure-thriller: Jungle man aids woman photographer in search for scientist's missing son

Tarzan and the Jungle Queen
see Tarzan's Peril

Tarzan and the Leopard Woman
1946, (USA), RKO, b&w, 72 mins.
W: Johnny Weissmuller *(Tarzan)*, Brenda Joyce *(Jane)*, Johnny Sheffield *(Boy)*, Acquanetta, Tommy Cook
D: Kurt Neumann, from characters created by Edgar Rice Burroughs   **PHOTOG:** Karl Struss
Standard adventure-thriller: Jungle man meets deadly tribe

Tarzan and the Lost City
1998, (USA), WB, color
W: Casper Van Dien, Jane March, Steve Waddington
D: Carl Schenkel, from characters created by Edgar Rice Burroughs
Standard adventure-thriller

Tarzan and the Lost Safari
1957, (GB), MGM, color, 84 mins.
W: Gordon Scott *(Tarzan)*, Betta St. John *(Diana Penrod)*, Robert Beatty *("Tusker" Hawkins)*, Peter Arne *(Dick Penrod)*, Wilfrid Hyde-White *("Doodles" Fletcher)*, George Coulouris *(Carl Kraski)*, Yolande Donlan *(Gamage Dean)*, Orlando Martins *(Chief Ogonooro)*
D: H. Bruce Humberstone   **SCR:** Montgomery Pittman & Lillie Hayward, from characters created by Edgar Rice Burroughs   **PHOTOG:** C. Pennington-Richards   **MUSIC:** Clifton Parker
Standard adventure-thriller: Jungle man rescues survivors of airplane crash

Tarzan and the Mermaids
1948, (USA), RKO, b&w, 68 mins.
W: Johnny Weissmuller *(Tarzan)*, Brenda Joyce *(Jane)*, Linda Christian, Fernando Wagner, George Zucco, Edward Ashley, Andrea Palma
P: Sol Lesser   **D:** Robert Florey   **SCR:** Carroll Young, from characters created by Edgar Rice Burroughs   **PHOTOG:** Jack Draper   **MUSIC:** Dimitri Tiomkin
Standard adventure-thriller: Jungle man discovers community of reclusive females

Tarzan and the She-Devil
1953, (USA), RKO, b&w, 76 mins.
W: Lex Barker *(Tarzan)*, Joyce MacKenzie *(Jane)*, Raymond Burr *(Vargo)*, Monique Van Vooren *(Lyra)*, Tom Conway *(Fidel)*, Robert Bice *(Maka)*, Mike Ross *(Selim)*, Henry Brandon *(M'Tara)*, Michael Granger *(Lavar)*, Lillian Molieri
D: Kurt Neumann   **SCR:** Karl Kamb & Carroll Young, from characters created by Edgar Rice Burroughs   **PHOTOG:** Karl Struss   **MUSIC:** Paul Sawtell
Standard adventure-thriller: Ruthless ivory hunters menace jungle man and his spouse

Tarzan and the Slave Girl
1950, (USA), RKO, b&w, 74 mins.
W: Lex Barker *(Tarzan)*, Vanessa Brown, Hurd Hatfield, Robert Alda, Denise Darcel
Standard adventure-thriller: Jungle man aids captive girls

Tarzan and the Trappers
1958, (USA), WB-TV, Made for TV, b&w, 74 mins.
W: Gordon Scott *(Tarzan)*, Eve Brent, Ricki Sorenson, Sherman "Scatman" Crothers
D: Charles Haas & Sandy Howard   **SCR:** Frederick Schlick & Robert Leach   **PHOTOG:** William Snyder & Alan Stensvold   **MUSIC SPRVSR:** Audrey Granville
Standard adventure-thriller: Jungle man aids native chief

Tarzan and the Valley of Gold
1966, (USA-Switz), AIP, color, 99 mins.
W: Mike Henry *(Tarzan)*, Nancy Kovack, David Opatoshu, Don Megowan, Manuel Padilla Jr.
P: Sy Weintraub   **D:** Robert Day   **SCR:** Clair Huffaker, from characters created by Edgar Rice Burroughs   **PHOTOG:** Irving Lippman   **SPCL-FX:** Ira Anderson Sr. & Ira Anderson Jr.   **MUSIC:** Van Alexander
Standard adventure-thriller: Jungle man seeks kidnapped boy

T

Tarzana, The Wild Girl
1973, (USA), Ellman, color
W: Ken Clark, Beryl Cunningham, Franca Polesello, Andrew Ray, Frank Ressel, Alfred Thomas
D: James Reed   SCR: Philip Shaw
Minor adventure-thriller: female Tarzan conquers

Tarzan des Mers
see The Amphibian Man

Tarzan Escapes
1936, (USA), MGM, b&w, 95 mins.
W: Johnny Weissmuller (*Tarzan*), Maureen O'Sullivan (*Jane*), John Buckler (*Capt. Fry*), Benita Hume (*Rita*), E.E. Clive (*Masters*), William Henry (*Eric*), Herbert Mundin (*Rawlins*), Darby Jones (*Bomba*)
D: Richard Thorpe   SCR: Cyril Hume, from characters created by Edgar Rice Burroughs   PHOTOG: Leonard Smith
Standard adventure-thriller: Jungle man fears desertion by spouse

Tarzan Finds a Son!
1939, (USA), MGM, b&w, 90 mins.
W: Johnny Weissmuller (*Tarzan*), Maureen O'Sullivan (*Jane*), Johnny Sheffield (*Boy*), Frieda Inescort, Ian Hunter
D: Richard Thorpe, from characters created by Edgar Rice Burroughs
Standard adventure-thriller: Jungle couple adopts youth

Tarzan Goes to India
1962, (GB-US-Switz), MGM, color, 87 mins.
W: Jock Mahoney (*Tarzan*), Jai (*The Elephant Boy*), Mark Dana (*O'Hara*), Leo Gordon (*Bryce*), Feroz Khan (*Rama*), Murad (*The Maharajah*), Simi (*Princess Kamara*), Jagdish Raaj, Aaron Joseph, G. Raghaven, Abas Khan, Peter Cooke
D: John Guillermin   SCR: Robert Hardy Andrews & John Guillermin, from characters created by Edgar Rice Burroughs   PHOTOG: Paul Beeson   MUSIC: Ken Jones
Standard adventure-thriller: Jungle man champions animals imperiled by dam construction

Tarzan in Manhattan
1989, (USA), American First Run Studios, Made for TV, color, 100 mins.
W: Joe Lara (*Tarzan*), Kim Crosby (*Jane*), Tony Curtis (*Archimedes Porter*), Jan-Michael Vincent (*Brightmore*), Jimmy Medina Taggert, Joe Seneca, Peter Sherayko, Joel Carlson, Robert Benedetti, Jim Doughan, Oliver Muirhead, Darnelle Gregorio, Jerry Queeney, Sloan Fischer, Don McLeod, Terry Millines, Rodney Saulsberry, Christopher Carroll, Buck Young
D: Michael Schultz   TELEPLAY: Anna Sandor & William Gough, from characters created by Edgar Rice Burroughs   PHOTOG: Laszlo George   SPCL-FX: Image Engineering Inc.   MUSIC: Charles Fox   SONGS: *Pull Up to the Bumper & Leave My Monkey Alone*
TVM, standard adventure-thriller: Jungle man uncovers plot to monkey with simian intelligence

Tarzan of the Apes
1918, (USA), First Nat'l, b&w, 61 mins.
W: Elmo Lincoln (*Tarzan*), Enid Markey (*Jane*), Virginia True Boardman, Thomas Jefferson, George French, Kathleen Kirkham, Bessie Toner, Gordon Griffith, Rex Ingram
D: Scott Sidney, from Edgar Rice Burroughs' novel
Classic silent adventure: Man raised by apes

Tarzan of the Seas
see The Amphibian Man

Tarzan's Deadly Silence
1970, (USA), National General, color, 88 mins
W: Ron Ely (*Tarzan*), Manuel Padilla Jr. (*Jai*), Jock Mahoney (*The Colonel*), Woody Strode (*Marshak*), Nichelle Nichols (*Ruana*), Gregorio Acosta (*Chico*), Robert DoQui (*Metusa*), Virgil Richardson (*Tabor*), Rudolph Charles (*The Officer*), Kenneth W. Washington (*Akaba*), Lupe Garnica (*Boru*), Jose Chavez (*Okala*)
D: Robert L. Friend   SCR: Lee Erwin, Jack A. Robinson, John Considine & Tim Considine, from characters created by Edgar Rice Burroughs
Standard adventure-thriller

Tarzan's Desert Mystery
1943, (USA), RKO, b&w, 70 mins.
W: Johnny Weissmuller (*Tarzan*), Johnny Sheffield (*Boy*), Nancy Kelly, Otto Kruger, Joe Sawyer, Robert Lowery, Lloyd Corrigan, Frank Puglia, Philip Van Zandt
P: Sol Lesser   D: William Thiele   SCR: Edward T. Lowe   STORY: Carroll Young, from characters created by Edgar Rice Burroughs   PHOTOG: Harry J. Wild & Russell Harlan   MUSIC: Paul Sawtell   MUSIC DIR: C. Bakaleinikoff
Standard adventure-thriller (incorporating stock-footage from One Million B.C.): Jungle man vs. Nazis, jungle horrors

Tarzan's Fight for Life
1958, (USA), MGM, color, 86 mins.
W: Gordon Scott (*Tarzan*), Eve Brent, Rickie Sorenson, Carl Benton Reid, Woody

Strode, Harry Lauter, James Edwards
P: Sol Lesser   D: H. Bruce Humberstone   SCR: Thomas Hal Phillips, from characters created by Edgar Rice Burroughs   PHOTOG: William Snyder   MUSIC: Ernest Gold
Standard adventure-thriller: Jungle man helps combat plague

Tarzan's Greatest Adventure
1959, (GB), Solar/Para, color, 84 mins.
W: Gordon Scott (*Tarzan*), Anthony Quayle (*Slade*), Sara Shane (*Angie*), Sean Connery (*O'Bannion*), Niall MacGinnis (*Kruger*), Scilla Gabel (*Toni*), Al Mulock (*Dino*)
P: Sy Weintraub & Harvey Hayutin   D: John Guillermin   SCR: John Guillermin & Bernie Giler, from a story by Les Crutchfield, based on characters created by Edgar Rice Burroughs   PHOTOG: Ted Scaife   MUSIC: Douglas Gamley
Exciting adventure-thriller: Jungle man pursues crooks who seek diamond mine

Tarzan's Hidden Jungle
1955, (USA), RKO, b&w, 75 mins.
W: Gordon Scott (*Tarzan*), Vera Miles (*Jill Hardy*), Peter Van Eyck (*Dr. Celliers*), Jack Elam (*Burger*), Charles Fredericks (*De Groot*), Richard Reeves (*Reeves*), Maidie Norman (*Suma*), Don Beddoe (*Johnson*), Ike Jones (*Malenki*), Jester Hairston (*The Witch Doctor*), Rex Ingram (*Sukulu Makumwa*)
P: Sol Lesser   D: Harold Schuster   SCR: William Lively, from characters created by Edgar Rice Burroughs   PHOTOG: William Whitley   MUSIC: Paul Sawtell
Standard adventure-thriller: Jungle man vs. villainous hunters

Tarzan's Jungle Rebellion
1970, (USA), Nat'l General, color, 92 mins.
W: Ron Ely, Manuel Padilla Jr.
Standard action-thriller

Tarzan's Magic Fountain
1949, (USA), RKO, b&w, 73 mins.
W: Lex Barker (*Tarzan*), Brenda Joyce (*Jane*), Albert Dekker (*Trask*), Evelyn Ankers (*Gloria James*), Charles Drake (*Dodd*), Alan Napier (*Douglas Jessup*), Ted Hecht, Henry Brandon
P: Sol Lesser   D: Lee Sholem   SCR: Curt Siodmak & Harry Chandlee, from characters created by Edgar Rice Burroughs   PHOTOG: Karl Struss   MUSIC: Alexander Laszlo
Standard adventure-thriller: Jungle man discovers mythical paradise

Tarzan's New Adventure
1935, (USA), Ashton-Dearholt/Expedition/New Realm, b&w
W: Herman Brix (*Tarzan*), Ula Holt (*Ula*), Frank Baker (*Martling*), Dale Walsh (*Alice*), Harry Ernest, from characters created by Edgar Rice Burroughs
Minor adventure-thriller: Jungle man seeks missing friend in Central America. From serial 'The New Adventures of Tarzan', B-T, 1935

Tarzan's New York Adventure
1942, (USA), MGM, b&w, 71 mins.
W: Johnny Weissmuller (*Tarzan*), Maureen O'Sullivan (*Jane*), Johnny Sheffield (*Boy*), Charles Bickford (*Buck Rand*), Paul Kelly (*Jimmie Shields*), Virginia Grey (*Connie Beach*), Cy Kendall (*Col. Ralph Sargent*), Russell Hicks (*Judge Abbotson*), Chill Wills (*Manchester Mountford*), Howard Hickman (*Blake Norton*), Charles Lane (*Gould Beaton*), Miles Mander (*The Postmaster*)
D: Richard Thorpe   SCR: William P. Lipman & Myles Connolly, from a story by Myles Connolly, based on characters created by Edgar Rice Burroughs   PHOTOG: Sidney Wagner   SPCL-FX: Arnold Gillespie & Warren Newcombe   MUSIC SCORE: David Snell
Lively adventure-thriller: Circus men abduct jungle man's son

Tarzan's Peril
1951, (USA), RKO, b&w, 79 mins.
W: Lex Barker (*Tarzan*), Virginia Huston, George Macready, Glenn Anders, Alan Napier, Douglas Fowley, Dorothy Dandridge, Frederick O'Neal
P: Sol Lesser   D: Byron Haskin, from characters created by Edgar Rice Burroughs   PHOTOG: Karl Struss   MUSIC: Michel Michelet
*GB retitle, **Tarzan and the Jungle Queen***
Standard adventure-thriller: Jungle man vs. gunrunners

Tarzan's Revenge
1938, (USA), Principal/20th-Fox, b&w, 70 mins.
W: Glenn Morris (*Tarzan*), Eleanor Holm (*Eleanor*), Hedda Hopper (*Fanny*), C. Henry Gordon, George Barbier, Joseph Sawyer, George Meeker, Corbet Morris, Frederick Clarke, John Lester Johnson
D: D. Ross Lederman   SCR: Robert Lee Johnson & Jay Vann, from a novel by Edgar Rice Burroughs   PHOTOG: George Meehan   MUSIC SCORE: Hugo Reisenfeld
Minor adventure-thriller: Jungle man helps safari girl elude lecherous potentate

Tarzan's Savage Fury
1952, (USA), RKO, b&w, 80 mins.
W: Lex Barker (*Tarzan*), Dorothy Hart (*Jane*), Charles Korvin (*Rokov*), Tommy Carlton (*Joey*), Patric Knowles (*Edwards*)
P: Sol Lesser   D: Cy Endfield   SCR: Cyril Hume, Hans Jacoby & Shirley White, from characters created by Edgar Rice Burroughs   PHOTOG: Karl Struss   MUSIC: Paul Sawtell
Standard adventure-thriller: Jungle man tricked into leading crooks to treasure

Tarzan's Secret Treasure

1941, (USA), MGM, b&w, 69 mins.
W: Johnny Weissmuller (*Tarzan*), Maureen O'Sullivan (*Jane*), Johnny Sheffield (*Boy*), Reginald Owen (*Prof. Elliott*), Tom Conway (*Medford*), Barry Fitzgerald (*O'Doul*), Philip Dorn (*Vandermeer*), Cordell Hickman (*Tumbo*)
D: Richard Thorpe   ORIG. SCR: Myles Connolly & Paul Gangelin, from characters created by Edgar Rice Burroughs   PHOTOG: Clyde DeVinna   SPCL-FX: Warren Newcombe   MUSIC SCORE: David Snell
Modest adventure-thriller: Scientists seek gold, invade jungle lord's domain

Tarzan's Three Challenges

1963, (USA), MGM, color, 92 mins.
W: Jock Mahoney (*Tarzan*), Ricky Der, Woody Strode
D: Robert Day
Standard adventure-thriller: Jungle man protects heir to Asian kingdom

Tarzan the Ape Man

1932, (USA), MGM, b&w, 99 mins.
W: Johnny Weissmuller (*Tarzan*), Maureen O'Sullivan (*Jane*), Forrester Harvey, Doris Lloyd
D: W.S. Van Dyke, from Edgar Rice Burroughs' novel *Tarzan of the Apes*   PHOTOG: Hal Rosson
Classic adventure-thriller: Safari finds man raised by apes

Tarzan, the Ape Man

1959, (USA), MGM, color, 82 mins.
W: Denny Miller (*Tarzan*), Joanna Barnes (*Jane*), Cesare Danova
D: Joseph Newman, from Edgar Rice Burroughs' novel *Tarzan of the Apes*
Standard adventure-thriller: Explorers seek Elephants' Graveyard, find jungle man

Tarzan, the Ape Man

1981, (USA), Svengali/MGM-UA, color, 112 mins.
W: Bo Derek (*Jane Parker*), Miles O'Keeffe (*Tarzan*), Richard Harris (*James Parker*), John Phillip Law (*Harry Holt*), Steven Strong (*The Ivory King*), Akushula Selayah (*Africa*)
P: Bo Derek   D & PHOTOG: John Derek   SCR: Gary Goddard & Tom Rice, from Edgar Rice Burroughs' novel *Tarzan of the Apes*   MUSIC: Perry Botkin
Standard adventure-thriller: Girl seeks explorer father, also finds jungle man

Tarzan the Fearless

1933, (USA), Sol Lesser/Wardour/Principal, b&w, 78 mins.
W: Buster Crabbe (*Tarzan*), Jacqueline Wells (Julie Bishop) (*Mary*), Philo McCullough (*Jeff*), Mischa Auer (*The High Priest*), E. Alyn Warren, Eddie Woods, Mathew Betz
D: Robert F. Hill, from characters created by Edgar Rice Burroughs   PHOTOG: Harry Neumann & Joseph Brotherton
Minor adventure-thriller (feature version of serial): Jungle man opposes ruthless humans

Tarzan the Magnificent

1960, (GB), Solar/Para, color, 88 mins.
W: Gordon Scott (*Tarzan*), Jock Mahoney (*Coy Banton*), Betta St. John (*Fay Ames*), John Carradine (*Abel Banton*), Lionel Jeffries (*Ames*), Alexandra Stewart (*Laurie*), Gary Cockrell (*Johnny Banton*), Earl Cameron (*Tate*), Charles Tingwell (*Conway*), Al Mulock (*Martin Banton*)
P: Sy Weintraub & Harvey Hayutin   D: Robert Day   SCR: Bernie Giler, from characters created by Edgar Rice Burroughs   PHOTOG: Ted Scaife   MUSIC: Ken Jones
Standard adventure-thriller: Jungle man contends with family of criminals

Tarzan Triumphs

1943, (USA), RKO, b&w, 75 mins.
W: Johnny Weissmuller (*Tarzan*), Frances Gifford (*Zandra*), Johnny Sheffield (*Boy*), Stanley Ridges (*Von Reichart*), Sig Rumann, Philip Van Zandt, Pedro de Cordoba
P: Sol Lesser   D: William Thiele   SCR: Roy Chanslor & Carroll Young, from characters created by Edgar Rice Burroughs   PHOTOG: Harry J. Wild   MUSIC: Paul Sawtell
Standard adventure-thriller: Jungle man vs. Nazis

Tarzan vs. IBM

see *Alphaville, une Etrange Aventure de Lemmy Caution*

A Taste for Flesh and Blood

1990, (USA), color, 84 mins.
W: Rubin Santiago, Lori Karz, Tim Ferrante
Standard homage to 1950's "B" movies: Space monster eats humans

A Taste of Blood

1967, (USA), Creative Film Enterprises/Ajay, color, 120 mins.
W: Bill Rogers, Elizabeth Wilkinson, Thomas Wood, Herschell Gordon Lewis (A.k.a. Sheldon Seymour), Otto Schlesinger
P & D: Herschell Gordon Lewis   SCR: Donald Standford
A.k.a. **The Secret of Dr. Alucard**
Minor horror-fantasy: Descendant of Dracula becomes Undead

A Taste of Evil

1971, (USA), Aaron Spelling/ABC-TV, color, 74 mins.
W: Barbara Parkins (*Susan Wilcox*), Barbara Sranwyck (*Miriam Jennings*), Roddy McDowall (*Dr. Michael Lomas*), Bing Russell (*The Sheriff*), Arthur O'Connell (*John*), William Windom (*Harold Jennings*), Dawn Frame (*Young Susan*)
P: Aaron Spelling   D: John Llewellyn Moxey   TELEPLAY: Jimmy Sangster   PHOTOG: Arch Dalzell   MUSIC: Robert Drasnin
TVM, standard thriller: Former mental patient terrorized by weird memories

Taste of Excitement

1969, (GB), Trio-Group W/Crispin, color, 99 mins.
W: Eva Renzi (*Jane Kerrell*), David Buck (*Paul Hedley*), Peter Vaughan (*Insp. Malling*), Paul Hubschmid (*Hans Beiber*), Sophie Hardy (*Michela*), Kay Walsh (*Miss Barrow*), Francis Matthews (*Mr. Breese*), Peter Bowles (*Alfredo Guardi*), George Pravda (*Dr. Forla*)
P: William Gell & George Willoughby   D: Don Sharp   SCR: Brian Carton & Don Sharp, from Ben Healey's novel *Waiting*
Stadard crime-thriller: Painter saves girl ivolved in murder plot

A Taste of Fear

1961, (GB), Hammer/Col, b&w, 82 mins.
W: Susan Strasberg (*Penny Appleby*), Ronald Lewis (*Bob*), Ann Todd (*Jane Appleby*), Christopher Lee (*Dr. Gerrard*), Leonard Sachs (*Spratt*), Ann Blake (*Marie*), Fred Johnson (*Father*), John Serret (*Insp. Legrand*)
WRIT & P: Jimmy Sangster   D: Seth Holt   PHOTOG: Douglas Slocombe   MUSIC: Clifton Parker
*USA retitle, **Scream of Fear***
Standard thriller: Crippled heiress terrorized by father's reappearing corpse

Taste the Blood of Dracula

1969, (GB), Hammer/WB, color, 95 mins.
W: Christopher Lee (*Count Dracula*), Ralph Bates (*Lord Courtley*), Linda Hayden (*Alice Hargood*), Geoffrey Keen (*William Hargood*), Anthony Corlan (*Paul Paxton*), Peter Sallis (*Samuel Paxton*), John Carson (*Jonathan Secker*), Gwen Watford (*Martha Hargood*), Isla Blair (*Lucy Paxton*), Martin Jarvis (*Jeremy Secker*), Roy Kinnear (*Weller*), Michael Ripper (*Cobb*), John Garrie (*The Father*), Shirley Jaffe (*Hargood's Maid*), Russell Hunter (*Felix*), Reginald Barrett (*The Vicar*), Peter May (*The Son*), Maddy Smith (*Dolly*), Mai Ling (*The Chinese Girl*), Malaika Martin (*The Snake Girl*)
P: Aida Young   D: Peter Sasdy   SCR: John Elder [Anthony Hinds]   PHOTOG: Arthur Grant   MUSIC: James Bernard
Standard horror-fantasy: Thrill-seeking Victorians revive vampire

The Tattered Dress

1957, (USA), Univ, b&w, 93 mins.
W: Jeff Chandler, Jeanne Crain, Jack Carson, Gail Russell, Edward C. Platt, Paul Birch, William Schallert, Elaine Stewart, George Tobias, Edward Andrews, Philip Reed, Alexander Lockwood, Edwin Jerome, June McCall, Frank Scannell, Ingrid Goude
P: Albert Zugsmith   D: Jack Arnold   SCR: George Zuckerman   PHOTOG: Carl E. Guthrie   MUSIC: Frank Skinner   MUSIC DIR: Joseph Gershenson

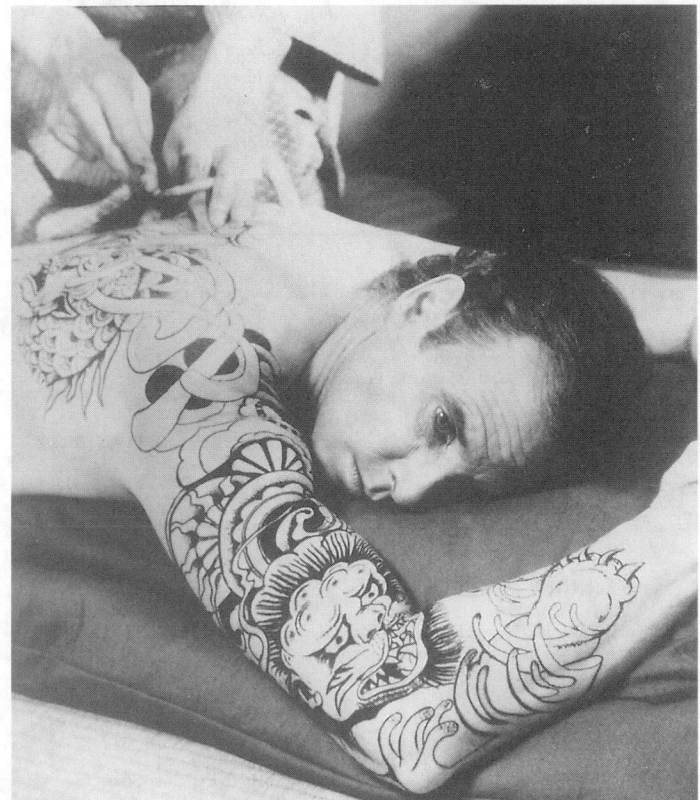

Tattoo: BRUCE DERN

Standard melodrama: Socialite accused of killing man who assaulted wife

Tattoo
1981, (USA), 20th-Fox, color, 103 mins.
<u>W</u>: Bruce Dern (*Karl*), Maud Adams (*Maddy*), Leonard Frey (*Halsey*), Rikke Borge (*Sandra*), John Getz (*Buddy*), Peter Iacangelo (*Dubin*), Alan Leach (*The Customer*), Lex Monson (*Dudley*), Cynthia Nixon (*Cindy*), Trish Doolan (*Cheryl*), Anthony Mannino (*George*), Patricia Roe (*Doris*), Robert Burr (*Ralph*), Jane Hoffman (*Teresa*), John Snyder (*Hawker*)
<u>D</u>: Bob Brooks   <u>SCR</u>: Joyce Bunuel   <u>PHOTOG</u>: Arthur Ornitz   <u>MUSIC</u>: Barry DeVorzon
Unusual thriller: Obsessed artist kidnaps model

The Tattooed Stranger
1950, (USA), RKO, b&w, 64 mins.
<u>W</u>: John Miles, Patricia White (*Barry*)
Standard thriller

Taur the Mighty
1961, (It), AIP-TV, color, 89 mins.
<u>W</u>: Joe Robinson, Bella Cortez
Minor "Sword & Sandal": Muscleman opposes slavers

Die Tausend Augen des Dr. Mabuse (The Thousand Eyes of Dr. Mabuse)
1960, (W. Ger-It-Fr), CCC/Omnia/Ajay, b&w, 103 mins.
<u>W</u>: Peter Van Eyck, Wolfgang Preiss, Dawn Addams, Gert Frobe, Lupe Prezzo, Howard Vernon
<u>P</u>: Artur Brauner   <u>D</u>: Fritz Lang   <u>SCR</u>: Fritz Lang & Heinz Oskar Wuttig
A.k.a. Eyes of Evil, The Diabolical Dr. Mabuse and The Secret of Dr. Mabuse
Standard thriller (Fritz Lang's last film): Murders at hotel run by criminal genius

The Taxi Mystery
1926, (USA), b&w, 50 mins.
<u>W</u>: Edith Roberts, Robert Agnew, Virginia Pearson, Phillips Smalley
<u>D</u>: Fred Windermere
Standard thriller: Starlet rescued from sinister understudy

Tchin-Chao, the Chinese Conjurer
1904, (Fr), Star, b&w, 60m (196.9 ft./3.3 mins.)
<u>D</u>: Georges Melies
Standard fantasy

TC 2000
1993, (USA), color, 95 mins.
<u>W</u>: Billy Blanks, Bobbie Phillips, Jalal Merhi, Bob Yeung, Matthias Hues
<u>D & SCR</u>: T.J. Scott
Minor SF-thriller: Cop's partner becomes killer cyborg

The Teckman Mystery
1954, (GB), London-Corona/British Lion, b&w, 89 mins.
<u>W</u>: Margaret Leighton (*Helen Teckman*), John Justin (*Philip Chance*), Roland Culver (*Insp. Harris*), George Coulouris (*Garvin*), Michael Medwin (*Martin Teckman*), Duncan Lamont (*Insp. Hilton*), Raymond Huntley (*Maurice Miller*), Frances Rowe (*Eileen Miller*), Jane Wenham (*Ruth Wade*), Meier Tzelniker (*John Rice*), Harry Locke (*Leonard*), Barbara Murray (*The Girl in the Plane*)
<u>P</u>: Josef Somlo   <u>D</u>: Wendy Toye   <u>SCR</u>: Francis Durbridge & James Matthews, from a TV-serial by Francis Durbridge
Minor thriller: Pilot's biographer catches spies

Teenage Catgirls in Heat
1993, (USA), color, 90 mins.
<u>W</u>: Gary Graves
Minor SF-thriller: Felines transformed into murderous young women

Teenage Cave Man
1958, (USA), AIP, b&w, 66 mins.
<u>W</u>: Robert Vaughn, Darah Marshall, Frank de Kova, Ed Nelson, June Jocelyn, Leslie Bradley, Charles Thompson, Jonathan Haze, Robert Shayne, Marshall Bradford, Beech Dickerson, Joseph Hamilton
<u>P & D</u>: Roger Corman   <u>SCR</u>: R. Wright Campbell   <u>PHOTOG</u>: Floyd Crosby   <u>MUSIC</u>: Albert Glasser
orig. co-billed with How to Make a Monster, GB retitle, Out of the Darkness, A.k.a. Prehistoric World, with stock-footage from Day the World Ended (1955)
Standard SF-thriller (using "monster" costume from Night of the Blood Beast): Primitive youth enters "forbidden zone"

Teenage Exorcist
1993, (USA), color, 90 mins.
<u>W</u>: Brinke Stevens, Eddie Deezen, Michael Berryman, Robert Quarry, Jay Richardson, Tom Shell, Elena Sahagun
<u>D</u>: Grant Austin Waldman   <u>SCR</u>: Brinke Stevens
Minor horror-spoof: Haunted house turns woman into killer

Teenage Monster
1957, (USA), Marquette/Howco-Int'l, b&w, 64 mins.
<u>W</u>: Anne Gwynne, Gloria Castillo, Stuart Wade, Gilbert Perkins, Charles Courtney, Stephen Parker
<u>P & D</u>: Jacques Marquette   <u>SCR</u>: Ray Buffum   <u>PHOTOG</u>: Taylor Byars &

Teenage Monster: STUART WADE

Jacques Marquette   <u>MUSIC</u>: Walter Greene
A.k.a. Monster on the Hill, TV retitle, Meteor Monster
Standard SF-horror: Meteor blast mutates son of Old West widow

Teenage Mutant Ninja Turtles
1990, (USA), Limelight/Golden Harvest/ New Line, color, 95 mins.
<u>W</u>: Judith Hoag (*April O'Neil*), Elias Koteas (*Casey Jones*), Josh Pais (*Raphael/The Passenger in the Cab*), Michelan Sisti (*Michelangelo/The Pizza Man*), Raymond Serra (*Chief Sterns*), James Saito (*The Shredder*), Toshishiro Obata (*Tatsu*), Leif Tilden (*Donatello/The Foot Messenger*), David Forman (*Leonardo/The Gang Member*), Sam Rockwell (*The Head Thug*), Kitty Fitzgibbon (*June*), Louis Cantarini (*The Cab Driver*), Joseph D'Onofrio (*Movie Hoodlum #1*), John D. Ward (*Movie Hoodlum #2*), Michael Turney, Jay Patterson, Ju Yu, John Rogers, Cassandra Ward-Freeman, Mark Jeffrey Miller, Tae Pak, Kenn Troum, Robert Haskell, Joshua Bo Lozoff, Winston Hemingway, Joe Inscoe
<u>D</u>: Steve Barron   <u>SCR</u>: Todd W. Langen & Bobby Herbeck   <u>STORY</u>: Bobby Herbeck, from characters created by Kevin Eastman & Peter Laird   <u>PHOTOG</u>: John Fenner   <u>MUSIC</u>: John DuPrez
Standard comedy-fantasy: Toxic waste turns reptiles into superheroes

Teenage Mutant Ninja Turtles II: The Secret of the Ooze
1991, (USA), Golden Harvest/New Line, color, 87 mins.
<u>W</u>: Paige Turco, David Warner
<u>D</u>: Michael Pressman   <u>SCR</u>: Todd W. Langen, from characters created by Kevin Eastman & Peter Laird   <u>PHOTOG</u>: Shelly Johnson   <u>MUSIC</u>: John DuPrez
Standard comedy-fantasy

Teenage Mutant Ninja Turtles III
1993, (USA), New Line, color, 95 mins.
Standard juvenile adventure-fantasy

The Teenage Psycho Meets Bloody Mary
see The Incredibly Strange Creatures Who Stopped Living and Became Mixed-Up Zombies

Teenagers from Outer Space
1959, (USA), Topaz/WB, b&w, 86 mins.
<u>W</u>: David Love, Dawn Anderson, Harvey B. Dunn, Tom Lockyear, Bryan Grant, King Moody, Bill DeLand, Billy Bridges, Helen Sage, Frederic Welch, Carl Dickensen, Sonia Torgeson
<u>WRIT, P & D</u>: Tom Graeff
blurb: "They blast the flesh off humans!"
Minor SF-thriller: Space-aliens seek to use Earth as pasture for monstrous creatures

Teen-Age Strangler
1967, (USA), Creative Film Enterprises/Ajay, color, 61 mins.
<u>W</u>: Bill A. Bloom, Jo Canterbury, John Ensign, Jim Asp, Bill Mills, Johnny Haymer
<u>P & SCR</u>: Clark Davis   <u>D</u>: Bill Posner
Minor thriller: Deeds of high-school "Bluebeard." Made in 1964 in West Virginia

Teenage Zombies
1960, (USA), Governor, b&w, 73 mins.
<u>W</u>: Don Sullivan (*Regg*), Katherine Victor, Nan Green, Steve Conte, Jay Hawk, Bri Murphy, Paul Pepper, Mitzi Albertson, Mike Concannon, J.L.D. Morrison, Chuck Niles
<u>P & D</u>: Jerry Warren   <u>SCR</u>: Jacques Lecoutier

Teenage Mutant Ninja Turtles

Minor SF-thriller: Mad woman doctor captures water-skiers. Made in 1957

Teen Agent
1991, (USA), color, 88 mins.
W: Richard Grieco (*Michael Corben*), Linda Hunt (*Ilsa Grunt*), Roger Rees (*Augustus Steranko*), Robin Bartlett, Gabrielle Anwar, Geraldine James, Michael Siberry, Carole Davis, Roger Daltrey
D: William Dear   **SCR:** Darren Star
Minor thriller: Highschooler in Paris mistaken for spy

Teen Alien
1988, (USA), color, 88 mins.
W: Vern Adix
D: Peter Senelka
A.k.a. **The Varrow Mission**
Minor SF-thriller: Teens meet hostile space alien on Halloween night

Teen Vamp
1988, (USA), color, 87 mins.
W: Clu Gulager, Karen Carlson, Angela Brown
D: Samuel Bradford
Minor horror-comedy: High-school boy bitten by prostitute, becomes vampire

Teen Witch
1989, (USA), Trans World, color, 95 mins.
W: Robyn Lively (*Louise*), Dan Gauthier (*Brad*), Caren Kaye (*Margaret*), Joshua Miller (*Richie*), Zelda Rubinstein (*Serena*), Dick Sargent, Marcia Wallace, Shelley Berman, Mandy Ingber, Noah Blake, Brett Clark, Ralph Baker
D: Dorian Walker   **SCR:** Robin Menken & Vernon Zimmerman   **PHOTOG:** Marc Reshovsky   **MUSIC:** Richard Elliot   **SONGS:** (by Larry Weir) *Finest Hour, I Like Boys & Popular Girl*
Minor fantasy: Fairy godmother changes girl's life

Teen Wolf
1985, (USA), Thomas Coleman-Michael Rosenblatt/Atlantic, color, 93 mins.
W: Michael J. Fox (*Scott Howard*), James Hampton (*Harold Howard*), Susan Ursitti (*Lisa "Boof" Marconi*), Jerry Levine (*Rupert "Stiles" Stilinsky*), Matt Adler (*Lewis*), Lorie Griffin (*Pamela*), Mark Arnold (*Mick*), Mark Holton (*Chubby*), James McKrell (*Mr. Thorne*), Jay Tarses (*Coach Finstock*), Scott Paulin (*Kirk Lolley*), Elizabeth Gorcey
D: Rod Daniel   **SCR:** Joseph Loeb III & Matthew Weisman   **PHOTOG:** Tim Suhrstedt   **MUSIC:** Miles Goodman
Modest horror-comedy: Youth becomes lycanthropic

Teen Wolf Too
1987, (USA), Kent Bateman/Atlantic, color, 95 mins.
W: Jason Bateman (*Todd Howard*), Kim Darby (*Prof. Brooks*), John Astin (*Dean Dunn*), Paul Sand (*Coach Finstock*), James Hampton (*Uncle Harold*), Mark

Holton (*Chubby*), Estee Chandler (*Nicki*), Stuart Fratkin, Robert Neary, Beth Ann Miller, Rachel Sharp, Kathleen Freeman, David Burton, William H. Burton, Eric Matthew
D: Christopher Leitch   **SCR:** R. Timothy Kring   **STORY:** Joseph Loeb III & Matthew Weisman   **PHOTOG:** Jules Brenner   **MUSIC:** Mark Goldenberg
Standard fantasy-comedy: Highschooler develops lycanthropy

Tekwar
1994, (USA), color, 92 mins.
W: Greg Evigan, Eugene C. Clark, Tom Higginson, William Shatner
D: William Shatner
Standard SF-thriller: Future cop hunts missing scientist

The Telephone Book
1971, (USA), Rosebud, color, 88 mins.
W: Sarah Kennedy (*Alice*), Norman Rose (*Smith*), James Harder (*Caller #1*), Jill Clayburgh (*Eyemask*), Ondine (*The Narrator*), Barry Morse (*Har Poon*), Ultra Violet (*The Whip Woman*), Roger C. Carmel (*The Analyst*), Geri Miller (*The Dancer*), William Hickey (*The Man in Bed*), Matthew Tobin (*The Mugger*), Jan Farrand (*The Woman in the Park*), David Dozer (*Caller #2*), Lucy Lee Flippen (*Caller #3*), Dolph Sweet (*Caller #4*), Joan Ziehl (*The Young Girl*), Margaret Brewster (*The Old Lady*), Arthur Haggerty (*The D.A.*)
WRIT & D: Nelson Lyon   **PHOTOG:** Leon Perer   **MUSIC:** Nate Sassover   **SONG:** *Something to Remember You By* (by Howard Dietz & Arthur Schwartz)
Minor thriller: Obscene phonecaller seduces victims

The Telephone Call
1910, (GB), Hepworth, b&w, 425 ft. (129.5m)
D: Lewin Fitzhamon
Standard crime-thriller: Wife holds burglar at gunpoint

Television Spy
1939, (USA), Para, b&w, 58 mins.
W: Anthony Quinn
D: Edward Dmytryk
Minor thriller

Tell Me Whom to Kill (Dis-moi Qui Tuer)
1965, (Fr), Gold Key/CIPRA/MGM, color, 93 mins.
W: Michele Morgan, Paul Hubschmid (*Christien*)
Minor thriller: Hunt for sunken Nazi loot

The Tell-Tale Globe
1915, (GB), Bamforth/YCC, b&w, 956 ft. (291.4m)
D: Cecil Birch
Standard comedy-fantasy: Magic orb reveals husband's flirtations

The Tell-Tale Heart
1934, (GB), Clifton-Hurst/Fox, b&w, 49 mins.
W: Norman Dryden (*The Boy*), John Kelt (*The Old Man*), Yolande Terrell (*The Girl*), Thomas Shenton (*The 1st Investigator*), James Fleck (*The 2nd Investigator*), Colonel Cameron (*The Colonel*)
D: Brian Desmond Hurst   **SCR:** David Plunkett Greene, from Edgar Allan Poe's short story
USA retitle, **Bucket of Blood**
Standard horror-thriller: Psychotic plots murder

The Tell-Tale Heart
1941, (USA), MGM, b&w, 2 reels
W: Joseph Schildkraut
D: Jules Dassin, based on Edgar Allan Poe's short story
Standard horror-thriller: Madness prompts murder

The Tell-Tale Heart
1953, (GB), Film Alliance/Adelphi, b&w, 20 mins.
W: Stanley Baker (*Edgar Allan Poe*)
P: I.G. Goldsmith   **D & SCR:** J.B. Williams, from Edgar Allan Poe's short story
Standard short horror-thriller: Mad killer hallucinates

The Tell-Tale Heart
1953, (USA), UPA/Stephen Bosustow/Col., color, 7 mins.
D: Ted Parmalee, based on Edgar Allan Poe's short story   **NARRATED BY:** James Mason (Academy Award Nominee)
Animated short: Old man's baleful eye prompts youth to kill

The Tell-Tale Heart
1960, (GB), Brigadier/Danziger, b&w, 78 mins.
W: Laurence Payne (*Edgar Allan Poe*), Adrienne Corri (*Betty Clare*), Dermot Walsh (*Carl Loomis*), Selma Vas Dias (*Mrs. Vine*), John Scott (*The Inspector*), John Martin (*The Sgt.*), Annette Carell (*The Landlady*), Yvonne Buckingham (*Mina*), David Lander, Rosemary Rotheray, Susanne Fuller, Richard Bennett, David Courtney, Joan Peart, Elizabeth Paget, Nada Beall, Frank Thornton, Pamela Plant, Graham Ashley, Brian Cobby, Madeline Leon, Patsy Smart
P: Edward J. & Harry Lee Danziger   **D:** Ernest Morris   **SCR:** Brian Clemens & Eldon Howard, inspired by Edgar Allan Poe's short story   **MUSIC:** Tony Crombie & Bill LeSage
reissued 1972
Standard horror-thriller: Author dreams of madness and murder

T

The Temp
1993, (USA), Par, color, 99 mins.
W: Timothy Hutton, Lara Flynn Boyle, Faye Dunaway (Charlene), Dwight Schultz (Roger), Dwight Schultz, Oliver Platt, Steven Weber, Scott Coffey, Colleen Flynn, Dakin Matthews, Maura Tierney
D: Tom Holland   SCR: Kevin Falls
Standard thriller: Temporary office worker kills her way up corporate ladder

The Tempest
1905, (GB), Urban, b&w, 150 ft. (45.7m)
based on Shakespeare's play
Standard fantasy short: Shipwreck scenes from "His Majesty's Theatre" production

The Tempest
1908, (GB), Clarendon, b&w, 765 ft. (233.2m)
D: Percy Stow   SCR: Langford Reed, from William Shakespeare's play
Standard fantasy: Magician regains dukedom by bewitching shipwrecked usurper

The Tempest
1980, (GB), Boyd's Co./Berwick Street/No. 8 Films/Mainline, color, 95 mins.
W: Heathcote Williams (Prospero), Karl Johnson (Ariel), Toyah Willcox (Miranda), Peter Bull (Alonso), Richard Warwick (Antonio), Elisabeth Welch (The Goddess), Jack Birkett (Caliban), Ken Campbell (Gonzalo), David Meyer (Ferdinand), Neil Cunningham (Sebastian), Christopher Biggins (Stephano), Peter Turner (Trinculo), Claire Davenport (Sycorax), Kate Temple (Miranda as a Child), Helen Wellington-Lloyd (The Spirit)
P: Guy Ford & Mordecai Schreiber   D & SCR: Derek Jarman, from William Shakespeare's play   PHOTOG: Peter Middleton   MUSIC: Brian Hodgson, Wavemaker & John Lewis
Standard fantasy: Deposed duke casts spell on enemies. cf. **Prospero's Books**

The Tempest
1998, (USA), NBC-TV, color, 95 mins.
W: Peter Fonda (Gideon Prosper), Katherine Heigl (Miranda), John Glover (Anthony Prosper), Harold Perrineau (Ariel), Eddie Mills (Frederick)
D: Jack Bender   TELEPLAY: James Henerson, from Shakespeare's play
TVM, unusual update of fantasy classic: Conjure magic on Civil War bayou

Tempest in a Bedroom
see **Une Tempete dans une Chambre a Coucher**

Une Tempete dans une Chambre a Coucher (Tempest in a Bedroom)
1901, (Fr), pathe, b&w, 50m (164 ft.)
W: Ferdinand Zecca
D: Ferdinand Zecca
Standard short comedy-fantasy

Tempi Duri per i Vampiri (Hard Times for Vampires)
1959, (It-Fr), Maxima/Embassy, color, 98 mins.
W: Renato Rascel, Christopher Lee, Sylva Koscina
P: Mario Cecchi Gori   D: Pio Angeletti   SCR: Mario Cecchi Gori, Eduardo Anton, Dino Verde & Alessandro Continenza
USA retitle, **Uncle was a Vampire**
Standard horror-farce: Hotel porter has problems when his uncle turns up in vampire form

Le Temple de la Magie (The Temple of Magic)
1901, (Fr), Star, b&w, 40m (131.2 ft./2.2 mins.)
D: Georges Melies
USA retitle, **The Temple of the Sun**
Standard fantasy

Temple of a Thousand Lights
1964, (It), Teleworld, color, 103 mins.
W: Richard Harrison, Luciana Gilli, Wilbert Bradley
Minor adventure-thriller

The Temple of Magic
see **Le Temple de la Magie**

The Temple of the Sun
see **Le Temple de la Magie**

Temple of the White Elephants
1963, (It), AIP-TV, color
W: Sean Flynn, Marie Versini
Minor adventure-thriller: Lancer rescues viceroy's daughter from jungle tribe

The Temple of Venus
1923, (USA), Fox, b&w, 7 reels (6,695 ft./2040.6m)
W: William Walling (Dennis Dean), Mary Philbin (Moira), Mickey McBan (Mickey), Alice Day (Peggy), David Butler (Nat Harper), William Boyd (Stanley Dale), Phyllis Haver (Constance Lane), Leon Barry (Phil Greyson), Senorita Consuella (Thetis), Celeste Lee (Venus), Robert Klein (Neptune), Marilyn Boyd (Juno), Frank Keller (Jupiter), Lorraine Eason (Echo), Helen Vigil (Diana)
D: Henry Otto   STORY & SCR: Henry Otto & Catherine Carr   PHOTOG: Joe August
Standard allegorical fantasy: Venus sends Cupid to Earth to find if romance still exists

Temple Tower
1930, (USA), Fox, b&w, 7 reels, 58 mins.
W: Kenneth MacKenna (Bulldog Drummond), Marceline Day (Patricia Verney), Henry B. Walthall (Blackton), Ivan Linow (Gaspard), Cyril Chadwick (Peter Darrell), Peter Gawthorne (Matthews), Frank Lanning (The Nightingale), Yorke Sherwood (The Constable)
D: Donald Gallagher   SCR & DIALOG: Llewellyn Hugges, from Sapper's novel   PHOTOG: Charles G. Clarke
Standard thriller: Sleuth seeks stolen emeralds, faces Masked Strangler. Bulldog Drummond feature

Temptation
1914, (GB), Cricks/KTC, b&w, 3,000 ft. (914.4m)
W: Jack Leigh (Jack Newton)
D: Charles Calvert
Standard thriller: Girl thwarts spies

Temptation
1946, (USA), Edward Small/Univ, b&w, 92 mins.
W: Merle Oberon, George Brent, Charles Korvin, Paul Lukas, Lenore Ulric, Arnold Moss, Ludwig Stossel, Ilka Gruning, Gavin Muir, Andre Charlot
D: Irving Pichel   SCR: Robert Thoeren, from Robert Hichens' novel Bella Donna   PHOTOG: Lucien Ballard   MUSIC: Daniele Amfitheatrof
Standard melodrama: Woman poisons archeologist-husband, blackmailing lover

The Temptation of Joseph
1914, (GB), Kineto, b&w, 1,265 ft. (385.6m)
WRIT & D: Langford Reed
Standard comedy-fantasy: Amorous mummy revives, embarrasses antiquarian

The Temptation of Saint Anthony
1898, (Fr), Star, b&w, 20m (65.6 ft./1.1 mins.)
W: Georges Melies, Jehanne d'Alcy
D: Georges Melies
Standard comedy-fantasy: Female demons lure holy man

The Tempter
1913, (GB), Natural Colour Kinematograph Co., color, 2,483 ft. (756.8m)
W: H. Agar Lyons (The Husband), Alfred de Manby (The Devil), F. Martin Thornton (The Drunkard), Leedham Bantock (The Gambler)
D: F. Martin Thornton & R.H. Callum   STORY: Leedham Bantock & Alfred de Manby
Standard fantasy: Satan tells stories illustrating drink, deceit and greed

The Tempter
1973, (GB-It), color, 106 mins.
W: Glenda Jackson, Claudio Cassinelli, Lisa Harrow, Adolfo Celi, Arnoldo Foa, Francisco Rabal
D: Damiano Damiani
A.k.a. **Il Sorriso Del Grande Tentatore (Smile of the Great Tempter)**
Standard melodrama: Corruption in convent

The Tempter (1974)
see **Anticristo**

Tempting Fate
1998, (USA), Pearson/ABC-TV, color, 95 mins.
W: Tate Donovan (Dr. Ben Creed), Ming-Na Wen (Ellen Moretti), Abraham Benrubi (John Bollandine), Grace Phillips (Melody), Matt Craven, Fran Bennett, Philip Baker Hall, Steve Murphy
D: Peter Werner   TELEPLAY: Gerald & Justin DiPego   PHOTOG: Neil Roach   MUSIC: Martin Davich
TVM, modest SF-thriller: Scientist finds "window" to alternate Earth

Temptress
1995, (USA), color, 90 mins.
W: Kim Delaney, Chris Sarandon, Corbin Bernsen, Dee Wallace Stone, Jessica Walter, Ben Cross
D: Lawrence Lanoff   SCR: Melissa Mitchell   MUSIC: Michael Stearns
Standard fantasy-thriller: Woman photographer possessed by spirit of ancient Indian goddess

The Temptress and the Monk
1963, (Jap), Toho, color, 88 mins
Minor fantasy

The Tenant
1976, (Fr), Marianne/Para, color, 124 mins.
W: Roman Polanski (Trelkovsky), Isabelle Adjani (Stella), Melvyn Douglas (Mr. Zy), Shelley Winters (The Concierge), Lila Kedrova (Mme. Gaderian), Claude Dauphin (The Husband), Jo Van Fleet (Mme. Dioz), Bernard Fresson (Scope), Claude Pieplu (The Neighbor), Rufus (Badar), Romain Bouteille (Simon), Jacques Monod, Patrice Alexsandre, Michel Blanc, Jean Pierre Bagot, Josiane Balasko, Florence Blot, Louba Chazel
D: Roman Polanski   SCR: Roman Polanski & Gerard Brach, from Roland Topor's novel   PHOTOG: Sven Nykvist   MUSIC: Philippe Sarde
Unusual thriller: Neurotic young man begins to assimilate personality of his apartment's former female tenant

Tender Dracula

1974, (Fr), Art Greenfield/AMLF, color, 98 mins.
W: Peter Cushing, Miou-Miou, Alida Vallie
orig. to be titled **The Big Funk**
Standard horror-satire: Vampire pursues nymph. Aka **La Grande Trouille** *(The Big Score)*

Tender Flesh

see **Welcome to Arrow Beach**

Tenebrae

1983, (It), color, 91 mins, also 100 mins.
W: Anthony Franciosa *(Peter Neal)*, Mirella D'Angelo *(Tilde)*, John Steiner *(Christiano Bruni)*, John Saxon *(Bulmer)*, Daria Nicolodi *(Anne)*, Christian Borromeo, Ania Pieroni, Carola Stagnard, Lara Wendel
D: Dario Argento **PHOTOG:** Luciano Tovoli
A.k.a. **Unsane & Sotto Gli Oochi Dell' Assassino (Under the Eye of the Assassin)**
Standard thriller: Novelist suspected in murders

Tenemos 18 Anos (We Have 18 Years)

1960, (Sp), Auster Films, b&w
W: Terele Penella, Isana Medel, Antonio Ozores, Luis Pena
D: Jesus Franco **PHOTOG:** Eloy Mella **MUSIC:** Enrique & Jesus Franco
Minor thriller

Ten Hats in 60 Seconds

see **Dix Chapeaux en 60 Secondes**

Tennis Court

1985, (GB), Hammer/Fox Mystery Theatre, Made for TV, color, 69 mins.
W: Peter Graves *(John Bray)*, Hannah Gordon *(Maggie Dowl)*, Jonathan Newth *(Harry)*, Cyril Shaps *(Magnusson)*, George Little *(Eldridge)*, Ralph Arliss *(Redmond Maryott)*, Isla Blair *(Eileen)*, Marcus Gilbert *(Young Bray)*, Peggy Sinclair *(The Matron)*, Annis Joslin *(Innes)*, David Cheesman *(Bobby)*
D: Cyril Frankel **TELEPLAY:** Andrew Sinclair, from a short story by Michael Hastings **PHOTOG:** Frank Watts **MUSIC:** Anthony Payne **MUSIC SPRVSR:** Philip Martell
TVM, minor thriller: Woman acquires country estate with haunted tennis court

Ten Little Indians

1965, (GB), Tenlit/7 Arts, b&w, 92 mins.
W: Hugh O'Brian *(Hugh Lombard)*, Shirley Eaton *(Ann Clyde)*, Leo Genn *(Gen. Mandrake)*, Wilfrid Hyde-White *(Judge Cannon)*, Daliah Lavi *(Ilona Bergen)*, Dennis Price *(Dr. Armstrong)*, Fabian *(Mike Raven)*, Stanley Holloway *(William Blore)*, Mario Adorf *(Groman)*, Marianne Hoppe
D: George Pollock **SCR:** Peter Yeldham & Peter Welbeck, from Agatha Christie's novel *And Then There Were None* **PHOTOG:** Ernest Steward **MUSIC:** Malcolm Lockyer
Modest thriller: Unknown assassin kills stranded guests

Ten Little Indians

1974, (GB-Sp), Filibuster/Avco Embassy, color, 98 mins.
W: Oliver Reed *(Hugh Lombard)*, Elke Sommer *(Vera Clyde)*, Stephane Audran *(Ilona Bergen)*, Herbert Lom *(Dr. Armstrong)*, Adolfo Celi *(Gen. Soule)*, Richard Attenborough *(Judge Cannon)*, Gert Frobe *(Wilhelm Blore)*, Charles Aznavour *(Michel Raven)*, Alberto De Mendoza *(Martino)*, Maria Rohm *(Elsa Martino)*, Nasser Malak Motli *(The Inspector)*, Orson Welles *(Voice of "U.N. Owen")*, Rick Battaglia
P: Harry Alan Towers **D:** Peter Collinson **SCR:** Peter Welbeck, from Agatha Christie's novel *And Then There Were None* **PHOTOG:** Fernando Arribas **MUSIC:** Bruno Nicolai
Minor thriller: Mysterious assassin kills travelers near ancient ruins of Persepolis

Ten Little Indians

1989, (GB), Breton/Cannon, color, 100 mins.
W: Donald Pleasence *(Judge Wargrave)*, Frank Stallone *(Capt. Lombard)*, Brenda Vaccaro *(Marion Marshall)*, Herbert Lom *(Gen. Romensky)*, Sarah Maur Thorp *(Vera Claythorne)*, Neil McCarthy *(Anthony Marston)*, Warren Berlinger *(Mr. Blore)*, Yehuda Efroni *(Dr. Werner)*, Moira Lister *(Mrs. Rodgers)*, Paul L. Smith *(Mr. Rodgers)*
P: Harry Alan Towers **D:** Alan Birkinshaw **SCR:** Jackson Hunsicker & Gerry O'Hara, from Agatha Christie's novel *And Then There Were None*
PHOTOG: Arthur Lavis **MUSIC:** George S. Clinton
Minor thriller: Safari members killed by unknown avenger

Ten Little Nigger Boys

1912, (GB), Empire Films/MP, b&w, 380 ft. (115.8m)
WRIT & D: Arthur Cooper
Standard fantasy: Nursery rhymes enacted by toys

Ten Little Niggers

see **And Then There Were None**

10 Rillington Place

1971, (GB), Filmways/Col, color, 109 mins.
W: Richard Attenborough *(John Reginald Christie)*, Judy Geeson *(Beryl Evans)*, John Hurt *(Timothy John Evans)*, Pat Heywood *(Mrs. Ethel Christie)*, Isobel

Black *(Alice)*, Sam Kydd *(The Furniture Dealer)*, Geoffrey Chater *(Christmas Humphreys)*, Robert Hardy *(Malcolm Morris)*, Andre Morell *(Judge Lewis)*, Ray Barron *(Workman Willis)*, Phyllis McMahon *(Muriel Eady)*, Miss Riley *(Baby Geraldine)*, Gabrielle Daye *(Mrs. Lynch)*, Douglas Blackwell *(Workman Jones)*, Edward Evans *(Insp. A)*, Jimmy Gardner *(Mr. Lynch)*, Tenniel Evans *(The Detective Sgt.)*, Edwin Brown *(The Hangman)*, Norma Shebbeare *(The Woman in the Cafe)*, Reg Lye *(The Tramp)*, Bernard Lee *(Insp. J)*, Robert Keegan *(Insp. K)*, David Jackson *(Constable C)*, George Lee, Richard Coleman, Jack Carr, Basil Dignam, Norman Henry, Rudolph Walker, Edward Burnham, Tommy Ansah
P: Martin Ransohoff & Leslie Linder **D:** Richard Fleischer **SCR:** Clive Exton, from Ludovic Kennedy's novel **PHOTOG:** Denys Coop **MUSIC:** John Dankworth
Semi-docu thriller: Britain's sensational Christie-Evans murder case

Tentacles

1977, (USA-It), AIP, color, 90 mins.
W: John Huston *(Ned Turner)*, Henry Fonda *(Whitehead)*, Shelley Winters *(Tillie Turner)*, Claude Akins *(Capt. Robards)*, Bo Hopkins *(Will Gleason)*, Delia Boccardo *(Vicky Gleason)*, Cesare Danova *(John Corey)*, Alan Boyd, John White, Alessandro Poggi
P: E.F. Doria **D:** Oliver Hellman [Olvidio Assonitis] **SCR:** Jerome Max, Tito Carpi & Steve Carabatsos
Minor SF-horror: Monster octopus terrorizes

The Tenth Victim

see **La Decima Vittima**

Tenture

1998, (USA), TNT-TV, color, 95 mins.
W: Shari Belafonte *(Trent)*, Bruce Boxleitner, Mira Furlan, Claudia Christian, Richard Biggs, Jeff Conaway, Stephen Furst, Patricia Tallman, Clyde Kusatsu
D: Jesus Salvador Trevino **TELEPLAY:** J. Michael Straczynski **PHOTOG:** John C. Flinn III **MUSIC:** Christopher Franke
TVM, standard SF-adventure

Teodora, Imperatrice di Bisanzio (Theodora, Empress of Byzantium)

1953, (It), I.F.E./Lux, color, 124 mins.
W: Gianna Maria Canale *(Theodora)*, Irene Papas *(Faidia)*, Georges Marchal *(Justinian)*, Renato Baldini *(Arcal)*, Henri Guisol *(Cappodocia)*, Carletto Sposito *(Scarpios)*, Umberto Silvestri *(The Executioner)*, Nerio Bernardi *(Belisario)*, Olga Solbelli *(Egina)*, Loris Gizzi *(Smirnos)*, Alessandro Fersen *(Metropolita)*, Mario Siletti *(The Magistrate)*, Oscar Andriani *(Scarpios' Attorney)*, Giovanni Fagioli *(The Court Chancellor)*
D: Riccardo Freda **SCR:** Rene Wheeler, Ranieri Cochetti, Claude Accursi & Riccardo Freda **MUSIC:** Renzo Rossellini
A.k.a. **Theodora, Slave Empress**
Standard adventure-thriller: Intrigue in Rome of the East

Teorema (Theorem)

1968, (It), color, 98 mins.
W: Terence Stamp, Silvana Mangano, Massimo Girotti, Andres Jose Cruz, Anne Wiazemsky, Laura Betti, Ninetto Davoli
WRIT & D: Pier Paolo Pasolini
Unusual allegorical thriller: Mystery man seduces family

Terminal

1996, (USA), NBC-TV, color, 95 mins.
W: Doug Savant, Nia Peeples, Michael Ironside, Roy Thinnes, Gregg Henry, Jenny O'Hara, Khandi Alexander, Richard Riehle, Jamie Rose, Joe E. Tata, James Eckhouse
D: Larry Elikann **TELEPLAY:** Nancy Isaak, from Robin Cook's novel **PHOTOG:** Eric Van Haren Noman **MUSIC:** Garry Schyman
TVM, standard thriller: Murder mystery surrounds cancer cure

Terminal Entry

1987, (USA), color, 98 mins.
W: Yaphet Kotto, Paul Smith, Edward Albert Jr.
Made-for-Video, standard thriller: Terrorists try to take over USA

Terminal Island

1973, (USA), Dimension, color, 88 mins.
W: Ena Hartman, Barbara Leigh, Don Marshall, Phyllis Davis, Tom Selleck
P: Charles Swartz **D:** Stephanie Rothman **SCR:** Stephanie Rothman, Charles Swartz & Jim Barnett
Minor melodrama: Four female prisoners banished to convict isle

Terminal Justice

1995, (USA), color, 95 mins.
W: Lorenzo Lamas, Chris Sarandon, Peter Coyote, Kari Salin, Barry Flatman, Tod Thawley
Standard SF-adventure: 21st-century policeman tries to free actress from clutches of video-game mogul

The Terminal Man

1974, (USA), WB, color, 104 mins.
W: George Segal *(Harry Benson)*, Jill Clayburgh *(Angela Black)*, Joan Hackett *(Dr. Janet Ross)*, Richard A. Dysart *(Dr. John Ellis)*, Donald Moffat *(Dr.*

T

McPherson), Michael C. Gwynne (*Dr. Robert Morris*), Matt Clark (*Gerhard*), Ian Wolfe (*The Priest*), Normann Burton (*Det. Capt. Anders*), James Sikking (*Ralph Friedman*), Jim Antonio (*Richards*), Jason Wingreen (*The Instructor*), William Hansen (*Dr. Ezra Manon*), Jordan Rhodes (*Questioner #1*), Dee Carroll (*The Night Nurse*), Steve Kanaly (*Edmonds*), Fred Sadoff (*The Police Doctor*), Robert Ito (*The Anesthetist*), Victor Argo (*The Orderly*), Lee DeBroux (*The Reporter*), Gene Borkan, Burke Byrnes
<u>WRIT, P & D</u>: Mike Hodges, from Michael Crichton's novel <u>PHOTOG</u>: Richard H. Kline.
Unusual SF-thriller: Experiments in computer-control of human emotions go horrendously awry

Terminal Virus
1995, (USA), color, 80 mins.
<u>W</u>: James Brolin
Made-for-Cable, minor SF-thriller: Destruction of ozonosphere makes sexes poisonous to each other

The Terminator
1984, (USA), Pacific Western/Hemdale/Orion, color, 104 mins.
<u>W</u>: Arnold Schwarzenegger, Linda Hamilton (*Sarah Connor*), Michael Biehn (*Reese*), Paul Winfield (*Traxler*), Dick Miller (*The Gun Salesman*), Lance Henriksen, Bess Motta, Rick Rossovich
<u>D</u>: James Cameron <u>SCR</u>: James Cameron & Gale Anne Hurd <u>PHOTOG</u>: Adam Greenberg <u>SPCL-FX</u>: Roger George & Frank DeMauro <u>MUSIC</u>: Brad Fiedel
Classic SF-thriller: Robot from future seeks woman's life

Terminator 2: Judgment Day
1991, (USA), Carolco/TriStar, color, 135 mins.
<u>W</u>: Arnold Schwarzenegger, Linda Hamilton, Robert Patrick, Edward Furlong, Joe Morton, Earl Boen, Danny Cooksey, S. Epatha Merkerson, Xander Berkeley, Jenette Goldstein
<u>P & D</u>: James Cameron <u>SCR</u>: James Cameron & William Wisher <u>PHOTOG</u>: Adam Greenberg <u>MUSIC</u>: Brad Fiedel
Superior SF-thriller: Robot from future seeks to kill boy

Terminus
1986, (Fr.-W. Ger), Hemdale, color, 110 mins. (also 137 mins.)
<u>W</u>: Johnny Hallyday, Karen Allen, Jurgen Prochnow, Gabriel Damon, Julie Glenn, Dieter Schidor, Dominique Valera, Janos Kulka, Jean-Luc Montama, Ray Montama, David Jalil, Bruno Ciarrochi, Andre Nocquet
<u>D</u>: Pierre-William Glenn <u>SCR</u>: Pierre-William Glenn & Patrice Duvic <u>FROM</u>: an orig. idea by Alain Gillot <u>PHOTOG</u>: Jean-Claude Vicquery <u>MUSIC</u>: David Cunningham
Minor SF-adventure: Rebels evade evil doctor and gov't forces

A Terra-Cotta Warrior
1990, (Hong Kong-Can), color, 120 mins.
<u>W</u>: Zhang Yimou, Gong Li, Yu Yung Kang
<u>D</u>: Ching Siu-Tung
Standard fantasy-adventure-comedy: Qin Dynasty guardsman seduces virgin, is turned into terra-cotta soldier

Terra em Transe (Land in Trance)
1966, (Brz), color, 105 mins.
<u>D</u>: Glauber Rocha
Standard allegory-thriller: Political turmoil in mythical third-world state

Terreur (Terror)
1924, (Fr), b&w
<u>W</u>: Pearl White
*USA retitle, **Perils of Paris** (Anderson Pictures, 1924)*
Standard melodrama

Terreur sans Nom
*see **The Blob** (1958)*

The Terrible Children
*see **Les Enfants Terribles***

A Terrible Night
*see **Une Nuit Terrible***

The Terrible Parents
*see **Les Parents Terribles***

The Terrible People
*see **The Hand of the Gallows***

The Terrible 'Tec
1916, (GB), Homeland/Globe, b&w, 3,000 ft. (914.4m)
<u>W</u>: Billy Merson (*Sherlock Blake*), Winifred Delevanti (*The Sec'y*), Blanche Bella (*The Mother*), Fred Dunning (*The Crook*)
<u>D</u>: W.P. Kellino <u>STORY</u>: Reuben Gillmer
Standard comedy-thriller: Detective wears disguises, catches diamond thieves

The Terrible Truth about Witchcraft
*see **Witchcraft** (1964)*

Terrified
1963, (USA), Bern-Field/Crown Int'l, b&w, 80 mins.
<u>W</u>: Rod Lauren (*Ken*), Steve Drexel (*David*), Tracy Olsen (*Marge*), Denver Pyle (*Sheriff Dixon*), Barbara Luddy, Lee Bradley, Robert Towers, Sherwood Keith, Ben Frank, Danny Welton, Nona Carver, Michael Fellen, Stephen Roberts, Angelo Rossitto
<u>WRIT & P</u>: Richard Bernstein <u>D</u>: Lew Landers <u>PHOTOG</u>: Curt Fetters <u>SPCL-FX</u>: Charles Duncan <u>MUSIC</u>: Michael Andersen
Minor thriller: Hooded killer terrorizes Western town

Terrified
1995, (USA), color, 90 mins.
<u>W</u>: Heather Graham, Lisa Zane
Standard eroto-thriller: Nymphomaniac stalked by mystery assailant

Terror (1924)
*see **Terreur***

The Terror
1928, (USA), WB, b&w, 9 reels (7,654 ft./2332.9m/approx. 82 mins.)
<u>W</u>: May McAvoy (*Olga Redmayne*), Louise Fazenda (*Mrs. Elvery*), Alec B. Francis (*Dr. Redmayne*), John Miljan (*Alfred Katman*), Edward Everett Horton (*Ferdinand Fane*), Mathew Betz (*Joe Connors*), Holmes Herbert (*Goodman*), Joseph W. Girard (*Supt. Hallick*), Otto Hoffman (*Soapy Marks*), Frank Austin (*Cotton*)
<u>D</u>: Roy Del Ruth <u>SCR</u>: Harvey Gates, from a play by Edgar Wallace <u>PHOTOG</u>: Barney McGill
*Standard thriller (first talking "horror" film): Guests at inn murdered. cf. **Return of the Terror***

The Terror
1938, (GB), ABPC/Alliance, b&w, 73 mins.
<u>W</u>: Wilfrid Lawson (*Mr. Goodman*), Bernard Lee (*Ferdy Fane*), Arthur Wontner (*Col. Redmayne*), Linden Travers (*Mary Redmayne*), Henry Oscar (*Connor*), Alastair Sim (*Soapy Marks*), Iris Hoey (*Mrs. Elvery*), Lesley Wareing (*Veronica Elvery*), John Turnbull (*Insp. Hallick*), Richard Murdoch (*PC Lewis*), Edward Lexy (*Insp. Dobie*), Kathleen Harrison (*Gladys*), Stanley Lathbury, Irene Handl
<u>D</u>: Richard Bird <u>SCR</u>: William Freshman, from a play by Edgar Wallace
reissued 1942
Standard thriller: Ex-convict seeks hidden bullion

The Terror
1963, (USA), Filmgroup/AIP, color, 81 mins.
<u>W</u>: Boris Karloff (*Baron Victor Frederick von Leppe*), Jack Nicholson (*Andre DuVallier*), Sandra Knight (*Helene/Ilsa*), Dorothy Neumann (*Catherina*), Richard Miller (*Stefan*), Jonathan Haze (*Gustav*)
<u>P & D</u>: Roger Corman <u>SCR</u>: Leo Gordon & Jack Hill <u>PHOTOG</u>: John

The Terror: JACK NICHOLSON AND SANDRA KNIGHT

Nickolaus <u>MUSIC</u>: Ronald Stein
*orig. to be titled **The Lady of the Shadows***
*Minor horror-fantasy ("quickie" made from sets and color film left over from **The Raven** {1963}): Mysterious beauty lures Napoleonic soldier*

Terror
1979, (GB), Crystal/Crown Int'l, color, 87 mins.
<u>W</u>: John Nolan (*James Garrick*), Carolyn Courage (*Ann*), James Aubrey (*Philip*), Sarah Keller (*Suzy*), Tricia Walsh (*Viv*), Glynis Barber (*Carol*), Rosie Collins (*Diane*), Chuck Julian (*Phil*), Michael Craze (*Gary*), Elaine Ives-Cameron (*Dolores Hamilton*), Patti Love (*Hannah*), Mary Maude (*Lady Garrick*), William Russell (*Lord Garrick*), Peter Craze (*Les*), Milton Reid (*The Bouncer*), Tanya Ferova (*The Stripper*), L.E. Mack (*Mad Dolly*), David McGillivray (*The TV Reporter*), Peter Attard, Peter Sproule, Colin Howells, Mike O'Malley, Peter Mayhew
<u>P</u>: Les Young & Richard Crafter <u>D</u>: Norman J. Warren <u>SCR</u>: David

McGillivray **STORY:** Les Young & Moira Young **PHOTOG:** Les Young
MUSIC: Ivor Slaney
orig. co-billed with **Dracula's Dog**
Standard horror-fantasy: Witch materializes to conclude 300-year-old curse on filmmaker's family

Terror at Halfday
see **Monster A-Go-Go**

Terror at London Bridge
see **Bridge Across Time**

Terror at Midnight
1956, (USA), Rep, b&w, 70 mins.
W: Scott Brady, Joan Vohs, Frank Faylen, John Dehner
D: Franklin Adreon
Standard thriller

Terror at Red Wolf Inn
see **The Folks at Red Wolf Inn**

Terror at the Opera
1988, (It), color, 90 mins.
W: Christina Marsillach, Urbano Barberini, Daria Nicolodi, Ian Charleson, Antonella Vitale, William McNamara, Barbara Cupisti, Coralina Cataldi Tassoni
D & SCR: Dario Argento
A.k.a. **Opera**
Standard thriller: Murderer stalks La Scala opera company

Terror Beneath the Sea
1966, (Jap), Toei/Teleworld, color, 85 mins.
W: Sonny Chiba, Mike Daneen, Peggy Neal, Franz Gruber, Gunther Braun, Andrew Hughes
D: Hajime Sato
A.k.a. **Water Cyborgs**
Standard SF-thriller: Mad scientist in underwater city

Terror by Night
1946, (USA), Univ, b&w, 60 mins.
W: Basil Rathbone (*Sherlock Holmes*), Nigel Bruce (*Dr. John Watson*), Dennis Hoey (*Insp. Lestrade*), Mary Forbes (*Lady Margaret*), Alan Mowbray (*Bleek*), Renee Godfrey (*Vivian*), Frederick Worlock, Skelton Knaggs, Geoffrey Steele, Billy Bevan
P & D: Roy William Neill **SCR:** Frank Gruber, from characters created by Sir Arthur Conan Doyle **PHOTOG:** Maury Gertsman **MUSIC:** Milton Rosen
Standard thriller: Famed detective protects valuable jewel

Terror Castle
see **La Vergine di Norimberga**

Terror Circus
see **Barn of the Naked Dead**

Terror-Creatures from the Grave
see **Cinque Tombe per un Medium**

Il Terror dei Barberi (Terror of the Barbarians)
1959, (It), AIP, color, 86 mins.
W: Steve Reeves, Chelo Alonso, Bruce Cabot
P: Emimmo Salvi **D:** Carlo Campogalliani **SCR:** Emimmo Salvi & Gino Mangini
USA retitle, **Goliath and the Barbarians**
Standard "Sword & Sandal": Goths invade 5th-century Europe

Terrore Nello Spazio (Terror in Space)
1965, (It-Sp), AIP, color, 86 mins.
W: Barry Sullivan (*Capt. Mark Markary*), Norma Bengell, Evi Marandi, Angel Aranda, Fernando Villena, Franco Andrei, Mario Morales
P: Fulvio Lucisano **D:** Mario Bava **SCR:** Ib Melchior & Louis M. Heyward, from Renato Pestriniero's short story "One Night of 21 Hours" **PHOTOG:** Antonio Rinaldi **MUSIC:** Gino Marinuzzi
orig. to be titled **Haunted World**, *USA retitle,* **Planet of the Vampires**, *USA TV-retitle,* **The Demon Planet**
Unusual SF-horror: Vampiric happenings on desolate planet

Terror Eyes
see **Night School**

Terror Eyes
1987, (USA), color, 90 mins.
W: Daniel Roebuck, Vivian Schilling, Dan Bell, Lance August
Standard fantasy-spoof: Satanic agent recruits writers for horror film

The Terror Factor
see **Scared to Death (1980)**

Terror from the Sun
see **The Hideous Sun Demon**

Terror from the Year 5,000
1958, (USA), AIP, b&w, 68 mins.
W: Ward Costello, Joyce Holden, Frederic Downs, Beatrice Furdeaux, John Stratton, Jack Diamond, Fred Herrick, Fred Taylor, Salome Jens (*The Terror*)
P D & SCR: Robert J. Gurney Jr, loosely based on Henry Slesar's short story *Bottle Baby* **PHOTOG:** Arthur Florman
orig. to be titled **Girl from 5,000 A.D.**, *reissued 1961*
Unusual SF-thriller: Mutant woman from future seeks males for breeding purposes

Terror from Under the House
see **Revenge (1971, GB)**

Terror from Within
1975, (GB), Made for TV, color
W: Pamela Franklin, Ian Bannen, Suzanne Neve, Oliver Tobias
TVM, minor thriller: Visitor to artists' colony has haunting experiences

Terrorgram
1990, (USA), color, 88 mins.
W: Michael Hartson, J.T. Wallace, James Earl Jones (*voice*)
Minor thriller: Two tales of the bizarre, each starting with the receipt of a sinister package

Terror Hospital
see **Beyond the Living**

Terror House (1942)
see **The Night Has Eyes**

Terror House (1972)
see **The Folks at Red Wolf Inn**

Terror in Space
see **Terrore Nello Spazio**

Terror in the Aisles
1984, (USA), Kaleidoscope/Univ, color, 80 mins.
W: Donald Pleasence, Nancy Allen
D: Andrew J. Kuehn **SCR:** Margery Doppelt **PHOTOG:** John A. Alonzo **MUSIC:** John Beal
Standard compendium of film clips: Pleasence and Allen introduce scenes from numerous cinema thrillers

Terror in the Crypt
see **La Maldicion de los Karnsteins**

Terror in the Haunted House
1958, (USA), Howco Int'l/AA, b&w, 90 mins.
W: Cathy O'Donnell, Gerald Mohr, William Ching, John Qualen, Barry Bernard
P: William S. Edwards **D:** Harold Daniels **SCR:** Robert C. Dennis **PHOTOG:** Frederick West

Terror In The Haunted House: CATHY O'DONNELL AND GERALD MOHR

A.k.a. **My World Dies Screaming**
Standard thriller: Girl gets bad vibrations in murder mansion

Terror in the Jungle
1969, (USA), Crown Int'l, b&w, 82 mins.
W: Robert Burns, Fawn Silver, Jimmy Angle
D: Tom DeSimone **MUSIC:** Les Baxter
Minor adventure-thriller

Terror in the Midnight Sun
see Rymdinvasion i Lappland

Terror in the Shadows
1995, (USA), Lifetime, color, 95 mins.
W: Genie Francis, Marcy Walker, Leigh J. McCloskey, Victoria Wyndham, Mark Damon Espinoza, Jacob Loyst
D: William Graham   **TELEPLAY:** Matt Dorff   **PHOTOG:** Robert Steadman   **MUSIC:** Chris Boardman
TVM, standard thriller: Escaped madwoman terrorizes family

Terror in the Swamp
1985, (USA), color, 89 mins.
W: Billy Holliday
D: Joe Catalanotto
Minor horror-thriller: Swamp creature besets small town

Terror in the Wax Museum
1973, (USA), Bing Crosby Prods./CRC, color, 94 mins.
W: Broderick Crawford (*Burns*), Ray Milland (*Flexner*), Elsa Lanchester (*Julia Hawthorn*), Louis Hayward (*Fowley*), John Carradine (*Claude Dupree*), Shani Wallis (*Laurie*), Patric Knowles (*Southcott*), Maurice Evans (*Insp. Daniels*), Lisa Lu (*Mme. Yang*), Steven Marlo (*Karkov*), Nicole Shelby (*Meg*), Mark W. Edwards (*Sgt. Hawks*), Ben Wright (*A Constable*), Matilda Calnan (*A Charwoman*), Peggy Stewart (*A Charwoman*), Leslie Thompson (*A Constable*), Don Herbert, Judy Wetmore, Jo Williamson, George Farina, Diane Wahrman, Rosa Huerta, Ben Brown, Rickie Weir, Paul Wilson, Ralph Cunningham, Don Williamson, Evelyn Reynolds
P: Andrew J. Fenady   **D:** George Fenady   **SCR:** Jameson Brewer   **STORY:** Andrew J. Fenady   **PHOTOG:** William Jurgensen   **MUSIC:** George Duning
Minor thriller: Murders center on waxworks

Terror in Toyland
see You Better Watch Out

Terror is a Man
1959, (USA), Lynn-Romero/Valiant, b&w, 89 mins.
W: Francis Lederer, Richard Derr, Greta Thyssen, Oscar Keesee, Lilia Duran, Flory Carlos, Payton Keesee
P: Kane W. Lynn & Edgar F. Romero   **D:** Gerardo de Leon   **SCR:** Harry Paul Harber   **PHOTOG:** Emmanuel I. Rojas
reissued (1965) as **The Blood Creature**
Standard SF-horror (similar to **Island of Lost Souls***): Scientist labors to transform jungle cat into human being*

Terror Is A Man: GRETA THYSSEN

Terror Island
1920, (USA), Para, b&w, 5 reels
W: Harry Houdini, Lila Lee
D: James Cruze
Standard thriller

The Terrornauts
1966, (GB), Amicus/Embassy, color, 75 mins.
W: Simon Oates (*Burke*), Zena Marshall (*Sandy*), Charles Hawtrey (*Yellowlees*), Patricia Hayes (*Mrs. Jones*), Max Adrian (*Shore*), Stanley Meadows (*Keller*), Frank Barry (*Burke as a Child*), Richard Carpenter (*Danny*), Leonard Cracknell (*Nick*), Robert Jewell (*The Robot Operator*), Frank Forsyth (*Uncle*), Andre Maranne (*The Gendarme*)
P: Milton Subotsky & Max J. Rosenberg   **D:** Montgomery Tully, based on Murray Leinster's novel *The Wailing Asteroid*   **PHOTOG:** Geoffrey Faithfull   **SPCL-FX:** Bowie Films Ltd.   **MUSIC:** Elisabeth Lutyens   **MUSIC CONDUCT:** Philip Martell
Standard SF-adventure: Scientist discovers space-alien plot

The Terror of Dr. Mabuse
see The Testament of Dr. Mabuse (1960)

Terror of Frankenstein
1975, (Swed-Ire), FAW, color, 96 mins.
W: Leon Vitali, Per Oscarsson, Nicholas Clay, Stacey Dorning
P & D: Calvin Floyd   **SCR:** Yvonne Floyd & Calvin Floyd, based on Mary Shelley's novel *Frankenstein*
A.k.a. **Victor Frankenstein**
Standard horror-fantasy: Scientist creates life

The Terror of Godzilla
1975, (Jap), Toho/Bob Conn Entertainment, color, 83 mins.
D: Inoshiro Honda   **SCR:** Yukiko Takayama
Standard SF-fantasy: Giant reptile vs. robot and avian horror

Terror of Mechagodzilla
1978, (Jap), Toho/UPA, color, 89 mins.
W: Katsuhiko Sasake, Tomoke Ai
D: Ishiro Honda   **SCR:** Yukiko Takayama   **PHOTOG:** Mototaka Tomioka   **SPCL-FX:** Teruyoshi Nakano   **MUSIC:** Akira Ifukube
A.k.a. **The Escape of Mechagodzilla** *and* **Monster from the Unknown Planet**
Standard SF-fantasy: Aliens covet Earth, enlist robot monster

Terror of Rome Against the Son of Hercules
1963, (It-Fr), Prometo & Sancro Films-Les Films Jacques Lettienne & Unicite/Embassy, color, 101 mins.
W: Mark Forest (*Poseidon*), Marilu Tolo, Elizabeth Fanty, Robert Hundar, Peter White, Giuseppe Addobbati, Ferruccio Amendola, Ugo Attanasio, Lea Monaco, Jacques Stany, Bruno Ukmar, Renato Navarrini, Enrico Salvatore
D: Mario Caiano   **SCR:** Mario Amendola & Albert Valentin   **STORY:** Mario Amendola & Alfonso Brescia   **PHOTOG:** Pier Ludovico Pavoni   **MUSIC:** Carlo Franci
A.k.a. **Maciste, Gladiatore di Sparta** *(Maciste, Gladiator of Sparta)*
Standard "Sword & Sandal": Gladiator aids Christians, battles gorilla

Terror of Sheba
see Persecution

The Terror of the Air
1914, (GB), Hepworth, b&w, 2,300 ft. (701m)
W: Tom Powers (*Roger Doubleday*), Stewart Rome (*Philip Townsend*), Violet Hopson (*Gabrielle Townsend*), Harry Royston (*The Spy*), Henry Vibart (*Prof.Doubleday*)
D: Frank Wilson
Standard thriller: Spy steals secret ray, destroys liner

Terror of the Barbarians
see Il Terror dei Barberi

Terror of the Black Mask
1960, (It-Fr), SNC/Romana/Embassy, color, 96 mins.
W: Pierre Brice, Helene Chanel
Minor adventure-thriller: Masked cavalier defends downtrodden

Terror of the Bloodhunters
1962, (USA), ADP, b&w, 60 mins.
W: Robert Clarke, Dorothy Haney, William White, Robert Christopher, Steve Conte, Niles Andrus
P & D: Jerry Warren   **ORIG. STORY & SCR:** Jacques Lecoutier
Minor thriller: Writer attempts escape from Devil's Island

Terror of the Mad Doctor
see Das Testament des Dr. Mabuse (1962)

Terror of the Red Mask
1960, (It), color, 90 mins.
W: Lex Barker, Chelo Alonso, Massimo Serato
D: Piero Pierotti
Standard thriller: Hero fights way through castle of horror

The Terror of the Tongs
1961, (GB), Hammer/Col., color, 79 mins.
W: Christopher Lee (*Chung King*), Geoffrey Toone (*Capt. Jackson*), Yvonne Monlaur (*Lee*), Barbara Brown (*Helena Jackson*), Marne Maitland (*The Beggar*), Brian Worth (*Harcourt*), Ewen Solon (*Tang How*), Roger Delgado (*Wang How*), Richard Leech (*Insp. Dean*), Charles Lloyd-Pack (*The Doctor*), Marie Burke (*Maya*), Burt Kwouk, Bandana Das Gupta, Milton Reid, Michael Hawkins
P: Kenneth Hyman **D:** Anthony Bushell **SCR:** Jimmy Sangster **PHOTOG:** Arthur Grant **MUSIC:** John Hollingsworth
Standard thriller: Opium-smuggler unmasked

Terror on a Train
see Time Bomb

Terror on Blood Island
see Brides of Blood

Terror on the Beach
1973, (USA), 20th Century-Fox-TV/CBS-TV, color, 74 mins.
W: Dennis Weaver, Estelle Parsons, Susan Dey
P: Allan Jay Factor **D:** Paul Wendkos **TELEPLAY:** Bill Suande
TVM, standard thriller: Vacationing family terrorized by Manson-type gang

Terror on the 40th Floor
1974, (USA), Metromedia/NBC-TV, color, 98 mins.
W: John Forsythe, Joseph Campanella, Anjanette Comer
P: Ed Montagne **D:** Jerry Jameson **TELEPLAY:** Jack Turley
TVM, standard thriller ('Towering Inferno' imitation): People trapped in penthouse of burning skyscraper

Terror Out of the Sky
1978, (USA), CBS-TV, color, 97 mins.
W: Efrem Zimbalist Jr. (*David Martin*), Tovah Feldshuh (*Jeannie Devereaux*), Dan Haggerty (*Nick Willis*), Lonny Chapman (*Earl Logan*), Ike Eisenmann (*Eric*), Richard Herd (*Col. Mangus*), Steve Franken (*Gladstone*), Joe E. Tata, Charles Hallahan, Bruce French
D: Lee H. Katzin **TELEPLAY:** Guerdon Trueblood & Dorothy Silverton **PHOTOG:** Michel Hugo
TVM, standard thriller: Killer bees accidentally released

Terrors
1930, (GB), Erle O. Smith, b&w, 47 mins.
W: Erle Smith Jr., Ronald Smith, Graham Smith
D & STORY: Erle O. Smith
Minor fantasy: Scots boys tell of adventures with prehistoric monsters

Terror Ship
1954, (GB), Merton Park/Anglo-Amalgamated/Lippert, b&w, 72 mins.
W: William Lundigan (*Peter Duncan*), Naomi Chance (*Joan Drew*), Vincent Ball (*John Drew*), Jean Lodge (*Vivian Bolton*), Kenneth Henry (*Insp. Neal*), Richard Stewart (*Sgt. French*), John Warwick (*Carter*), Beresford Egan (*Hartnell*)
P: W.H. Williams **D & STORY:** Vernon Sewell **SCR:** Julian Ward
reissued 1958
*Standard thriller: Gang steals uranium derivative. A.k.a. **Dangerous Voyage***

Terror Street
see Thirty-Six Hours (1954)

The Terror Strikes
see War of the Colossal Beast

Terror Train
1980, (USA), Astral Bellevue Pathe/Sandy Howard Prods./20th-Fox, color, 96 mins.
W: Ben Johnson (*Carne*), Jamie Lee Curtis (*Alana*), Hart Bochner (*Doc*), Timothy Webber (*Mo*), Sandee Currie (*Mitchy*), Derek MacKinnon (*Kenny*), Anthony Sherwood (*Jackson*), Howard Busgang (*Ed*), Steve Michaels (*The Brakeman*), Joy Boushel, Victor Knight, Greg Swanson, D.D. Winters
P: Howard Greenberg **D:** Roger Spottiswoode **SCR:** T.Y. Drake **PHOTOG:** John Alcott **MUSIC:** John Mills-Cockell **SONGS:** include *Funky Love* & *Broken Man*
Standard thriller: Collegians meet death on party train

Terrorvision
1986, (USA), Altar/Empire, color, 84 mins.
W: Diane Franklin (*Suzy*), Gerrit Graham (*Stan*), Mary Woronov (*Raquel*), Chad Allen (*Sherman*), Jonathan Gries (*O.D.*), Bert Remsen (*Grampa*), Alejandro Rey (*Spiro*), Randi Brooks (*Cherry*), Jennifer Richards (*Medusa*), Sonny Carl Davis (*Norton*), Ian Patrick Williams, William Paulson, John Leamer
WRIT & D: Ted Nicolaou **PHOTOG:** Romano Albani **MUSIC:** Richard Band
Modest SF-satire: Alien beast emerges from TV set

The Terror Within
1989, (USA), Roger Corman/Concorde, color, 99 mins.
W: George Kennedy, Andrew Stevens, Starr Andreeff, Terri Treas, John LaFayette, Tommy Hinchley

D: Thierry Notz **SCR:** Thomas M. Cleaver **MUSIC:** Rick Conrad
Minor SF-thriller: Post-apocalypse mutants crave flesh

The Terror Within II
1991, (USA), color, 89 mins.
W: Andrew Stevens, Stella Stevens, Chick Vennera, R. Lee Ermey, Burton "Bubba" Gilliam, Clare Hoak

Terrorvision: CHAD ALLEN

D: Andrew Stevens
Minor SF-thriller: Warrior of future battles mutants to save remnants of mankind from deadly virus

Terror without Name
see The Blob (1958)

Teseo Contro il Minotauro
see The Minotaur

Das Testament des Dr. Mabuse (The Testament of Dr. Mabuse)
1932, (Ger), Nero, b&w, 120 mins.
W: Rudolf Klein-Rogge (*Dr. Mabuse*), Otto Wernicke (*The Inspector*), Gustav Diesl (*Kent*), Oscar Beregi (*Dr. Baum*), Vera Liessem, Camilla Spira, Karl Meixner, Klaus Pohl
D: Fritz Lang **SCR:** Fritz Lang & Thea von Harbou, from a novel by Norbert Jacques **PHOTOG:** Fritz Arno Wagner **MUSIC:** Hans Erdmann **SETS:** Karl Vollbrecht & Emil Hasler
*Standard thriller: Criminal genius continues grab for power. cf. **Doctor Mabuse***

Le Testament d'Orphee (The Testament of Orpheus)
1958, (Fr), Films Around the World/Brandon, b&w, 83 mins.
W: Edouard Dermithe, Jean Cocteau, Jean-Pierre Leaud, Lucia Bose, Jean Marais, Pablo Picasso, Daniel Gelin, Luis Miguel Dominguin, Charles Aznavour, Yul Brynner, Brigitte Bardot, Maria Casaresi
P: Jean Thuillier **WRIT & D:** Jean Cocteau
Unusual docu: Overview of Jean Cocteau's life and cinematic oeuvre

Le Testament du Dr. Cordelier (The Testament of Dr. Cordelier)
1961, (Fr), Jean Renoir-Sofirad/RTE, b&w, 100 mins.
W: Jean-Louis Barrault, Micheline Gary, Andre Certes, Jean Topart, Michel Vitold, Teddy Bilis, Jean-Pierre Granval, Jacqueline Morane, Jacques Dannouville, Gaston Modot
WRIT & D: Jean Renoir, based on Robert Louis Stevenson's *Dr. Jekyll and Mr. Hyde* **PHOTOG:** Georges Leclerc **MUSIC:** Joseph Kosma
*A.k.a. **Experiment in Evil***
Standard fantasy-thriller: Man releases alter ego

The Testament of Dr. Mabuse (1932)
see Das Testament des Dr. Mabuse

The Testament of Dr. Mabuse
1960, (W. Ger), CCC/Omnia/Thunder Pictures, b&w, 87 mins.
W: Gert Frobe, Senta Berger, Alain Dijon, Wolfgang Preiss, Helmut Schmid, Walter Rilla
P: Artur Brauner **D:** Werner Klinger **SCR:** Ladislas Fodor & Robert A. Stemmle
*USA retitle, **The Terror of Dr. Mabuse**, A.k.a. **Terror of the Mad Doctor***
Standard thriller: Predations of criminal genius

The Testament of Orpheus
see Le Testament d'Orphee

Test Tube Teens from the Year 2000
1993, (USA), Torchlight/Full Moon, color, 74 mins.

W: Morgan Fairchild, Ian Abercrombie, Brian Bremer, Christopher Wolf, Laurel Wiley, Michelle Matheson, Sara Suzanne Brown, Don Dowe, Robin Joi Brown, Tamara Tohill
D: Ellen Cabot SCR: Kenneth J. Hall PHOTOG: James Lawrence Spencer MUSIC: Reg Powell
A.k.a. *Virgin Hunters*
Minor eroto-SF: Randy teens time-travel to escape sexually-oppressive future

Die Teufelsanbeter (The Devil-Worshippers)
1920, (Ger), Ustad-Film/Dr. Droop & Co., b&w, 1684 m.
W: Bela Lugosi
Standard thriller: Satanists conspire

The Texas Chainsaw Massacre
1974, (USA), Bryanston, color, 81 mins.
W: Marilyn Burns (*Sally*), Gunnar Hansen (*Leatherface*), Paul A. Partain (*Franklin*), Allen Danziger (*Jerry*), William Vail (*Kirk*), Edwin Neal (*The Hitchhiker*), Teri McMinn (*Pam*), Jim Siedow (*The Old Man*), John Dugan (*Grandfather*), Jerry Lorenz (*The Pickup Driver*), John Larroquette (*Narrator*)
D: Tobe Hooper STORY & SCR: Kim Hensel & Tobe Hooper PHOTOG: Daniel Pearl MUSIC: Tobe Hooper & Wayne Bell
reissued (1981) by New Line Pictures
Cult-classic horror-thriller: Demented family butchers unwary

The Texas Chainsaw Massacre 2
1986, (USA), Golan-Globus/Cannon, color, 98 mins.
W: Dennis Hopper (*Lefty Enright*), Jim Siedow (*Drayton Sawyer*), Caroline Williams (*Stretch*), Bill Mosely (*Chop-Top*), Bill Johnson (*Leatherface*), Ken Evert, Harlan Jordan
D: Tobe Hooper SCR: L.M. Kit Carson PHOTOG: Richard Kooris MUSIC: Tobe Hooper & Jerry Lambert
Standard horror-thriller: Murderous family wreaks havoc. cf. Leatherface: Texas Chainsaw Massacre III

T-Force
1994, (USA), color
W: Jack Scalia, Erin Gray
Standard SF-adventure: Policeman of year 2007 stalks renegade robots

Thank You, Mr. Moto
1937, (USA), 20th-Fox, b&w, 66 mins.
W: Peter Lorre (*Mr. Moto*), Pauline Frederick (*Mme. Chung*), Thomas Beck (*Tom Nelson*), Jayne Regan (*Eleanor Joyce*), Sidney Blackmer (*Eric Koerger*), John

Carradine (*Pereira*), William von Bricken (*Schneider*), John Bleifer (*Ivan*), Nedda Harrigan (*Mme. Tchernov*), Philip Ahn (*Prince Chung*), James Leong (*The Officer*), Sig Rumann, Charles Stevens, Chester Gan
D: Norman Foster SCR: Norman Foster & Willis Cooper, from John P. Marquand's novel PHOTOG: Virgil Miller MUSIC: Samuel Kaylin
Fr retitle, Le Serment de M. Moto (Mr. Moto's Promise)
Exciting thriller (most elaborate of 'Moto' series): Lost scroll holds key to treasure

Thark
1932, (GB), B&D/W&F, b&w, 79 mins.
W: Tom Walls (*Sir Hector Benbow*), Ralph Lynn (*Ronald Gamble*), Mary Brough (*Mrs. Todd*), Robertson Hare (*Hook*), Joan Brierley (*Cherry Buck*), Claude Hulbert (*Lionel Todd*), Gordon James (*Death*), Evelyn Bostock (*Kitty Stratton*), Beryl de Querton (*Lady Benbow*), Marjorie Corbett (*Warner*)
D: Tom Walls, from a play by Ben Travers
reissued 1937 & 1945
Standard comedy-thriller: Friends spend night in "haunted" house

That Darn Sorceress
1988, (USA), color, 89 mins.
W: Pauline Adams, Betty Page
D: Whitney Bain
Minor horror-fantasy: Witch performs horrible deeds

That Eternal Ping-Pong
1902, (GB), Hepworth, b&w, 100 ft. (30.5m)
W: May Clark (*The Girl*)
D: Percy Stow
Standard fantasy short: Boy and girl start table tennis game in 1900; their skeletons are still playing in 2000

That Eye, the Sky
1994, (Austral), color, 105 mins.
W: Lisa Harrow, Peter Coyote, James Croft, Amanda Dogue, Mark Fairall
D: John Ruane
Unusual thriller: Charismatic stranger heals boy's injured father

That Fatal Sneeze
1907, (GB), Hepworth, b&w, 350 ft. (106.7m)
W: Thurston Harris (*The Uncle*), Gertie Potter (*The Nephew*)
D: Lewin Fitzhamon
Standard comedy-fantasy: Boy shakes pepper on uncle, sneezes wreck house

Theatre Of Blood: Robert Morley, Vincent Price, Dennis Price, Robert Coote and Ian Hendry

Them: JAMES WHITMORE

That Mysterious Fez
1914, (GB), Hepworth, b&w, 450 ft. (137.2m)
<u>D:</u> Hay Plumb
Standard fantasy: Magic fez grants any wish, save wish for money

That They May Live
see J'Accuse (1937)

That Woman Opposite
see City After Midnight

Theatre of Blood
1973, (GB), Cineman/UA, color, 104 mins.
<u>W:</u> Vincent Price (*Edward Lionheart*), Diana Rigg (*Edwina*), Ian Hendry (*Devlin*), Robert Morley (*Meredith Merridew*), Jack Hawkins (*Solomon Psaltery*), Diana Dors (*Mrs. Psaltery*), Coral Browne (*Miss Chloe Moon*), Milo O'Shea (*Insp. Boot*), Harry Andrews (*Trevor Dickman*), Robert Coote (*Oliver Larding*), Michael Hordern (*George Maxwell*), Renee Asherson (*Mrs. Maxwell*), Arthur Lowe (*Horace Sprout*), Dennis Price (*Hector Snipe*), Eric Sykes (*Sgt. Dogge*), Joan Hickson (*Mrs. Sprout*), Madeline Smith (*Rosemary*), Brigid Eric Bates (*Agnes*), Tony Calvin (*The Police Photographer*), Bunny Reed, John Gilpin, Peter Thornton, Tutte Lemkow, Jack Maguire, Joyce Graham, Eric Francis, Sally Gilmore, Declan Mulholland, Stanley Bates
<u>P:</u> John Kohn & Stanley Mann <u>D:</u> Douglas Hickox <u>SCR:</u> Anthony Greville-Bell <u>PHOTOG:</u> Wolfgang Suschitzky <u>SPCL-FX:</u> John Stears <u>MUSIC:</u> Michael J. Lewis
Superior satire-thriller: Embittered Shakespearean actor doles out "poetic justice" to snooty theater critics

Theatre of Death
1965, (GB), Pennea/London Independent, color, 91 mins.
<u>W:</u> Christopher Lee (*Philippe Darvas*), Lelia Goldoni (*Dani Cirreaux*), Julian Glover (*Charles Marquis*), Evelyn Laye (*Mme. Angele*), Jenny Till (*Nicole Chapel*), Ivor Dean (*Insp. Micheaud*)
<u>P:</u> William Gell & Michael Smedley-Aston <u>D:</u> Sam Gallu <u>SCR:</u> Ellis Kadison & Roger Marshall <u>STORY:</u> Ellis Kadison
A.k.a. **Blood Fiend** *(Hemisphere, 1967)*
Minor horror-thriller: Surgeon helps police unmask necrophiliac vampire

The Theban Prophetess
see La Prophetesse de Thebes

Thelma: or, Saved from the Sea
1914, (GB), Cygnet/Bio, b&w, 2,500 ft. (762m)
<u>W:</u> Dorothy Keen (*Esme Villiers*), Arthur D. Mavity (*David Trelawney*), Arthur Charrington (*Derek Villiers*)
<u>WRIT & D:</u> Harold Brett
Standard thriller: Fisherman saves amnesiac heiress from being drowned by her cousin

Them!
1954, (USA), WB, b&w, 94 mins.
<u>W:</u> Edmund Gwenn (*Dr. Harold Medford*), James Whitmore (*Sgt. Ben Peterson*), Joan Weldon (*Patricia Medford*), James Arness (*Robert Graham*), Onslow Stevens (*Brig. Gen. O'Brien*), Sean McClory (*Maj. Kibbee*), Mary Ann Hokanson (*Mrs. Lodge*), Olin Howlin (*Jensen*), Chris Drake (*Ed Blackburn*), Fess Parker (*Crotty*), Dub Taylor, Richard Deacon, Don Shelton, Leonard Nimoy
<u>P:</u> David Weisbart <u>D:</u> Gordon Douglas <u>SCR:</u> Ted Sherdeman, from a story by George Worthington Yates <u>PHOTOG:</u> Sid Hickox <u>MUSIC:</u> Bronislau Kaper
Fr retitle, **The Monsters are Attacking the Town**
Classic SF-thriller: Nuclear testing creates gargantuan ants

Them
1996, (USA), UPN-TV, color, 95 mins.
<u>W:</u> Tony Todd (*Berlin*), Scott Patterson (*Simon Trent*), Dustin Voigt (*Jake*), Clare Carey, Caprice Benedetti, Lochlin Munro, Andrea Libman
<u>D:</u> Bill L. Norton <u>TELEPLAY:</u> Charles Grant Craig <u>PHOTOG:</u> Tobias Schliessler <u>MUSIC:</u> John R. Graham
TVM, standard SF-thriller: To save their race from extinction, alien invaders begin secret takeover of Earth

Theodora, Empress of Byzantium
see Teodora, Imperatrice di Bisanzio

Theodora, Slave Empress
see Teodora, Imperatrice di Bisanzio

Theodore Rex
1996, (USA), TNT-TV, color, 95 mins.
<u>W:</u> Whoopi Goldberg, Armin Mueller-Stahl (*Dr. Kane*), Juliet Landau (*Dr. Shade*), Richard Roundtree, Bud Cort, Stephen McHattie, Charles Chiodo, Jack Riley
<u>D & SCR:</u> Jonathan Betuel <u>PHOTOG:</u> David Tattersall <u>MUSIC:</u> Robert Folk
TVM, minor SF-fantasy: Woman cop teamed with dinosaur

Theorem
see Teorema

There Goes the Bride
1980, (GB), Lonsdale/Enterprise, color, 91 mins.
<u>W:</u> Tom Smothers (*Timothy Westerby*), Twiggy (*Polly Perkins*), Martin Balsam (*Elmer Babcock*), Michael Whitney (*Bill Shorter*), Sylvia Syms (*Ursula Westerby*), Geoffrey Sumner (*Gerald Drimond*), Graham Stark (*The Headwaiter*), Margot Moser (*Mrs. Babcock*), Hermione Baddeley (*Daphne Drimond*), Phil Silvers (*The Psychiatrist*), Broderick Crawford (*The Attendant*), Jim Backus (*Perkins*), John Terry (*Nicholas Babcock*), Toria Fuller (*Judy Westerby*), Carmen Zapata (*Mrs. Ramirez*), Gonzales Gonzales (*Ramirez*), April Cloud (*The Sec'y*)
<u>P:</u> Martin Chute & Ray Cooney <u>D:</u> Ray Cooney <u>SCR:</u> Ray Cooney & Terence Marcel, from a play by Ray Cooney <u>PHOTOG:</u> James Devis <u>MUSIC:</u> Harry Robinson
Standard fantasy: Flapper's ghost haunts ad executive

There's No Place Like Space
see Hold On!

There's Nothing Out There
1992, (USA), Rolfe Kanefsky, Valkhn Film, color, 90 mins.
<u>W:</u> Craig Peck (*Mike*), Wendy Bednarz (*Doreen*), Mark Collver (*Jim*), Bonnie Bowers (*Stacy*), John Carhart 3rd (*Nick*), Jeff Dachis (*David*), Claudia Flores (*Janet*)
<u>WRIT & D:</u> Rolfe Kanefsky <u>PHOTOG:</u> Ed Hershberger <u>MUSIC:</u> Christopher Thomas
Unusual horror-satire: Vacationing neurotic fears the worst

These are the Damned
see The Damned

Theseus vs. the Minotaur
see The Minotaur

They
1993, (USA), color, made for TV, 100 mins.
<u>W:</u> Patrick Bergin, Vanessa Redgrave
A.k.a. **They Watch**
TVM, Standard thriller: Grieving father turns to psychic when apparitions haunt family

They All Died Laughing
see A Jolly Bad Fellow

They Bite
1995, (USA), color, 96 mins.
<u>W:</u> Donna Frotscher, Nick Baldasare, Charlie Barnett
<u>D:</u> Bret Piper
Minor SF-spoof: Aquatic monsters plague porno-film shoot

They're Coming to Get You
see Dracula vs. Frankenstein

They Call Him Marcado
1972, (Mex), color, 82 mins.
<u>W:</u> Antonio Aguilar, Flor Silvestre, Eric Del Castillo, Juan Carlos Ruiz, Javier Ruan
<u>D:</u> Alberto Mariscal
A.k.a. **Los Marcados (The Scarred)**
Perverse religious allegory-western: Psychopath heads outlaw band

They Call It Murder
1969, (USA), Parsons/20th-Fox/NBC-TV, color, 97 mins.
<u>W:</u> Jim Hutton (*Doug Selby*), Jessica Walter (*Jane*), Lloyd Bochner (*Carr*), Carmen

T

Mathews, Leslie Nielsen, Robert J. Wilke, Nita Talbot, Ed Asner
D: Walter Grauman **TELEPLAY:** Sam Rolfe, based on Erle Stanley Gardner's novel *The D.A. Draws a Circle*
TVM, standard thriller: D.A. finds corpse in swimming pool

They Came from Another World (1956)
see Invasion of the Body Snatchers (1956)

They Came from Another World (1966)
see They Came from Beyond Space

They Came from Beyond Space
1966, (GB), Amicus/Embassy, color, 85 mins.
W: Robert Hutton (*Dr. Curtis Temple*), Jennifer Jayne (*Lee Mason*), Zia Moyheddin (*Farge*), Bernard Kay (*Richard Arden*), Michael Gough (*Monj*), Maurice Good (*Stilwell*), John Harvey (*Bill Trethowan*), Luanshya Greer (*The Attendant*), Geoffrey Wallace (*Allan Mullane*), Diana King (*Mrs. Trethowan*), Kenneth Kendall (*The Commentator*), Katy Wild, Dermot Cathie, Paul Bacon, Leonard Grahame, Jack Lambert, Frank Forsyth, Edward Rees, Christopher Banks, Norman Claridge, Michael Hawkins, Robin Parkinson
P: Milton Subotsky & Max J. Rosenberg **D:** Freddie Francis **SCR:** Milton Subotsky, based on Joseph Millard's novel *The Gods Hate Kansas* **PHOTOG:** Norman Warwick **MUSIC COMPOSED:** James Stevens **MUSIC CONDUCT:** Philip Martell
orig. to be titled **They Came from Another World**
Standard SF-thriller: Energy-beings control human hosts

They Came from Within
see Shivers

They Came to a City
1944, (GB), Ealing/Univ, b&w, 77 mins.
W: John Clements (*Joe Dinmore*), Googie Withers (*Alice Foster*), Raymond Huntley (*Malcolm Stritton*), Ada Reeve (*Mrs. Batley*), Renee Gadd (*Mrs. Stritton*), Frances Rowe (*Philippa Loxfield*), A.E. Matthews (*Sir George Gedney*), Ralph Michael (*Sgt. Jimmy*), Norman Shelley (*Cudworth*), Mabel Terry-Lewis (*Lady Loxfield*), Brenda Bruce, J.B. Priestley
P: Michael Balcon **D:** Basil Dearden **SCR:** Basil Dearden & Sidney Cole, from a play by J.B. Priestley
reissued 1948
Standard fantasy: Assorted people find themselves outside gates of mysterious city

They Can't Hang Me
1955, (GB), Vandyke/IFD/BL, b&w, 75 mins.
W: Terence Morgan (*Insp. Brown*), Yolande Donlan (*Jill*), Andre Morell (*Robert Pitt*), Ursula Howells (*Antonia Pitt*), Anthony Oliver (*Newcome*), Reginald Beckwith (*Harold*), Raymond Rollett (*Sir Robert Rosper*), Guido Lorraine (*Piotr Revsky*), Basil Dignam (*Riddle*)
P: Roger Proudlock **D:** Val Guest **SCR:** Val Guest & Val Valentine, from a novel by Leonard Moseley
Standard thriller: Inspector unmasks scientist behind spy ring

They Live
1988, (USA), Larry Franco/Alive/Univ, color, 97 mins.
W: Roddy Piper (*Nada*), Keith David (*Frank*), Meg Foster (*Holly*), George "Buck" Flower (*Drifter*), Peter Jason (*Gilbert*), Raymond St. Jacques (*The Street Preacher*), Susan Blanchard, Jason Robards III (*The Family Man*), John Lawrence (*The Bearded Man*), Susan Barnes (*The Brown-Haired Woman*), Sy Richardson (*The Black Revolutionary*), Wendy Brainard (*The Family Man's Daughter*), Norman Alden (*The Foreman*), Susan Blanchard (*The Ingenue*), Dana Bratton (*The Black Junkie*), Lucille Meredith (*The Female Interviewer*), John F. Goff (*The Well-Dressed Customer*), Norm Wilson (*The Vendor*), Thelma Lee (*The Rich Lady*), Stratton Leopold (*The Depressed Human*), Norman Howell (*The Blond-Haired Cop*), Rezza Shan (*The Arab Clerk*), Robert Grasmere (*The Scruffy Blond Man*), Tom Searle (*The Biker*), Larry Franco (*The Neighbor*), Vince Inneo (*The Passageway Guard*), Bob Hudson (*Passageway Guard #2*), Dennis Michael (*The Male News Anchor*), Nancy Gee (*The Female News Anchor*), Cibby Danyla (*The Naked Lady*), Jon Paul Jones (*The Manager*), Claudia Stanlee (*The Young Female Executive*), Christine Baur (*The Woman on the Phone*), Jeff Imada (*The Male Ghoul*), Eileen Wesson (*The Pregnant Sec'y*), Gregory Barnett (*Security Guard #1*), Jim Nickerson (*Security Guard #2*), Kerry Rossall (*The 2nd Unit Guard*), Michelle Costello (*The Female Ghoul*)
D: John Carpenter **SCR:** Frank Armitage [John Carpenter], from Ray Nelson's short story "Eight O'Clock in the Morning" **PHOTOG:** Gary B. Kibbe **SPCL-FX COORD:** Roy Arbogast **MUSIC:** John Carpenter & Alan Howarth
Standard SF-satire: Drifter discovers space-alien infiltration

They Live in Fear
1944, (USA), Col, b&w, 65 mins.
W: Cliff Severn, Otto Kruger
Standard thriller

They Made Me a Fugitive
1947, (GB), Gloria-Alliance/WB, b&w, 103 mins.
W: Sally Gray (*Sally*), Trevor Howard (*Clem Morgan*), Griffith Jones (*Narcey*), Rene Ray (*Cora*), Mary Merrall (*Aggie*), Vida Hope (*Mrs. Fenshawe*), Charles Farrell (*Curley*), Phyllis Robins (*Olga*), Eve Ashley (*Ellen*), Jack

McNaughton (*Soapy*), Ballard Berkeley (*Insp. Rockliffe*), Peter Bull (*Fidgetty Phil*), Sebastian Cabot (*The Proprietor*), Cyril Smith
P: Nat Bronsten & James Carter **D:** Cavalcanti **SCR:** Noel Langley, from Jackson Budd's Novel *A Convict Has Escaped*
USA retitle, **I Became a Criminal,** *reissued (1950) with 10 mins. cut*
Standard crime-thriller: Framed crook breaks jail, avenges himself on Soho dope-peddlers

They Made Me a Killer
1946, (USA), Pine-Thomas/Para, b&w, 64 mins.
W: Robert Lowery, Barbara Britton
Standard melodrama

They Might Be Giants
1971, (USA), Newman-Foreman/Univ, color, 88 mins.
W: George C. Scott (*Justin Playfair*), Joanne Woodward (*Dr. Watson*), Jack Gilford (*Wilbur Peabody*), Kitty Winn (*Grace*), Lester Rawlins (*Blevins Playfair*), Rue McClanahan (*Daisy*), Sudie Bond (*Maud*), Ron Weyand (*Dr. Strauss*), Worthington Miner (*Mr. Bagg*), Al Lewis (*The Messenger*), Staats Cotsworth (*Winthrop*), Jenny Egan (*Miss Finch*), Theresa Merritt (*Peggy*), Peter

Thief Of Bagdad: DOUGLAS FAIRBANKS

Fredericks (*Grace's Boyfriend*), Michael McGuire (*The Telephone Guard*), Oliver Clark (*Mr. Small*), F. Murray Abraham (*The Usher*), Eugene Roche (*The Policeman*), James Tolkan (*Mr. Brown*), Jacques Sandulescu (*Mr. Brown's Driver*), Frances Fuller (*Mrs. Bagg*), Matthew Coles (*The Teenage Boy*), Candy Azzara (*The Teenage Girl*), Ted Beniades (*The Cab Driver*), Tony Capodilupo (*The Chief*), John McCurry (*The Police Lieutenant*), Ralph Clanton (*The Store Manager*), Paul Benedict (*The Chestnut Vendor*), M. Emmet Walsh, Jane Hoffman, Dorothy Greener, Louis Zorich
P: John Foreman **D:** Anthony Harvey **STORY & SCR:** James Goldman **PHOTOG:** Victor Kemper **MUSIC:** John Barry
Standard comedy-thriller: Man thinks he is Sherlock Holmes. cf. **The Return of the World's Greatest Detective**

They Never Learn
1956, (GB), E.J. Fancey/New Realm, b&w, 47 mins.
W: John Blythe (*Frankie*), Jackie Collins (*Lil Smith*), Adrienne Scott (*PCW Watson*), Graham Stark (*Plum*)
D & SCR: Denis Kavanagh
Standard crime-thriller: Policewoman poses as ex-convict, catches forger

They Ran for Their Lives
1968, (USA), Masterpiece/Color Vision Int'l, color, 92 mins.
W: Luana Patten, Scott Brady, Jim Davis, John Payne, John Carradine, Anthony Eisley
P: Samuel Ray Calabrese **D:** John Payne **SCR:** Monroe Manning
Minor thriller: Dead geologist's daughter pursued by thugs

They Saved Hitler's Brain
see Madman of Mandoras

They Won't Believe Me
1947, (USA), RKO, b&w, 79 mins.
W: Susan Hayward (*Verna*), Robert Young (*Lawrence Ballantine*), Jane Greer (*Janice*), Rita Johnson (*Gretta*), Frank Ferguson (*Cahill*), Tom Powers, Don Beddoe, Edith Barrett, George Tyne, Harry Harvey
D: Irving Pichel **SCR:** Jonathan Latimer **PHOTOG:** Harry J. Wild **SPCL-FX:** Russell A. Cully **MUSIC:** Roy Webb **MUSIC DIR:** C. Bakaleinikoff
Well-made melodrama: Philanderer's involvement with three women leads to tragedy

The Thief
1912, (GB), Cricks & Martin, b&w, 720 ft. (219.5m)
W: Una Tristram (*Cissie Dalmaine*), Jack Jarman (*Jack Spicer*), Leah Marlborough (*Mrs. Spicer*)

T

D: Edwin J. Collins
Standard crime-thriller: Sailor blamed when sweetheart's brother steals

The Thief
1952, (USA), Fran/UA, b&w, 85 mins.
W: Ray Milland, Rita Gam, Martin Gabel, Harry Bronson, Rita Vale, Rex O'Malley
P: Clarence Greene **D** Russell Rouse **SCR:** Clarence Greene & Russell Rouse
Unusual experimental film (no dialog): Atomic scientist forced into espionage

The Thief at the Casino
1908, (GB), Hepworth, b&w, 600 ft. (182.9m)
D: Lewin Fitzhamon
Minor crime-thriller: Thief frames drunkard, is blackmailed by witness

The Thief of Bagdad
1924, (USA), UA, b&w, 12 reels (11,230 ft./3422.9m)
W: Douglas Fairbanks Sr. (*The Thief of Bagdad*), Julanne Johnston (*The Princess*), Anna May Wong (*The Mongol Slave*), Sojin (*The Mongol Prince*), K. Nambu (*The Mongol Prince's Counselor*), Sadakichi Hartmann (*The Mongol Prince's Court Magician*), Snitz Edwards (*The Evil Associate*), Charles Belcher (*The Holy Man*), Winter-Blossom (*The Slave of the Lute*), Etta Lee (*The Slave of the Sand Board*), Tote Du Crow (*The Soothsayer*), Brandon Hurst (*The Caliph*), Noble Johnson (*The Indian Prince*), Mathilde Comont (*The Persian Prince*), Charles Stevens, Sam Baker, Jess Weldon, Scotty Mattraw, Charles Sylvester
WRIT & P: Douglas Fairbanks Sr. **D:** Raoul Walsh **STORY:** Elton Thomas [Douglas Fairbanks Sr.] **PHOTOG:** Arthur Edeson
Classic silent fantasy: Arabian Nights adventures

The Thief of Bagdad
1940, (GB), London/UA, color, 106 mins.
W: Conrad Veidt (*Jaffar*), Sabu (*Abu*), John Justin (*Ahmad*), June Duprez (*The Princess*), Adelaide Hall (*The Singer*), Mary Morris (*Halima*), Rex Ingram (*The Djinni*), Hay Petrie (*The Astrologer*), Morton Selten (*The King*), Miles Malleson (*The Sultan*), Bruce Winston (*The Merchant*), Allan Jeayes (*The Storyteller*), Roy Emerton (*The Jailer*)
P: Alexander Korda **D:** Ludwig Berger, Tim Whelan & Michael Powell **SCR:** Lajos Biro & Miles Malleson **PHOTOG:** Georges Perinal & Osmond Borradaile **SPCL-FX:** Lawrence Butler **MUSIC:** Miklos Rozsa
Classic fantasy: Youth opposes evil magician. Academy Awards: Color Photography, Art Direction, Special Effects

The Thief of Baghdad
1961, (It-Fr), Titanus/Lux/Joseph E. Levine/MGM, color, 100 mins.
W: Steve Reeves, Georgia Moll, Arturo Dominici, Edy Vessel, George Charmarat
P: Bruno Vailati **D:** Arthur Lubin **SCR:** Bruno Vailati, Augusto Frassinetti & Filippo Sanjust **PHOTOG:** Tonino Delli Colli
Standard adventure-fantasy: Daring thief seeks blue rose that will cure ailing princess

The Thief of Baghdad
1978, (USA-GB), Palm/Victorine/NBC-TV, color, 102 mins.
W: Roddy McDowall (*Hasan*), Terence Stamp (*Wazir Jaudur*), Peter Ustinov (*The Caliph*), Kabir Bedi (*Prince Taj*), Pavla Ustinov (*Princess Yasmine*), Frank Finlay (*Abu Bakar*), Marina Vlady (*Perizadah*), Daniel Emilfork (*The Genie*), Ian Holm (*The Gatekeeper*), Ahmed El Shenawi (*Kanishka*), Neil McCarthy (*The Aide*), Leon Greene (*The Guard*), Arnold Diamond (*The Minister*)
P: Aida Young **D:** Clive Donner **STORY:** A.J. Carothers & Andrew Birkin **PHOTOG:** Denis Lewiston **MUSIC:** John Cameron
TVM, standard fantasy: Rogue thwarts evil wazir

Thief of Damascus
1952, (USA), Col, color, 78 mins.
W: Paul Henreid, John Sutton, Jeff Donnell, Elena Verdugo, Lon Chaney Jr., Helen Gilbert, Robert Clary, Nelson Leigh, Edward Colmans, Philip Van

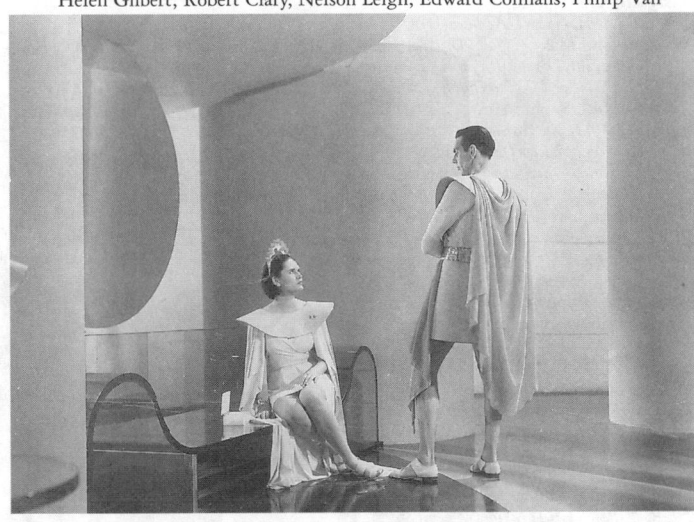

Things To Come: MARGARETTA SCOTT AND RAYMOND MASSEY

Zandt, Larry Stewart, Leonard Penn, Robert Conte
P: Sam Katzman **D:** Will Jason **SCR:** Robert E. Kent **PHOTOG:** Ellis W. Carter **MUSIC:** Mischa Bakaleinikoff
Standard adventure fantasy

The Thief of Venice
see Il Ladro di Venezia

The Thieves' Decoy
1910, (GB), Hepworth, b&w, 475 ft. (144.8m)
D: Bert Haldane
Standard crime-thriller: Father forces child to beg, attacks benefactor

Thieves of the Moon
see O Dwoch Takich Co Ukradli Ksiezyc

Thigh Line Lyre Triangular
1961, (USA), Stan Brakhage, color, 5 mins.
D: Stan Brakhage
Short "underground" film (16mm): Birth scenes with artistic embellishments

Thin Air
see The Body Stealers

The Thing
1982, (USA), Turman-Foster/Univ, color, 102 mins.
W: Kurt Russell, Richard Dysart, A. Wilford Brimley, T.K. Carter, David Clennon, Donald Moffat, Richard Masur
D: John Carpenter **SCR:** Bill Lancaster, from John W. Campbell's novella *Who Goes There?* **PHOTOG:** Dean Cundey **SPCL-FX:** Albert Whitlock **MUSIC:** Ennio Morricone
Modest SF-horror: Antarctic base menaced by space-alien monstrosity

The Thing from Another World
1951, (USA), Winchester/RKO, b&w, 87 mins.
W: Kenneth Tobey (*Capt. Patrick Hendry*), Margaret Sheridan (*Nikki Nicholson*), Robert Cornthwaite (*Dr. Carrington*), Eduard Franz (*Dr. Stern*), Royal Dano (*Dr. Chapman*), Douglas Spencer (*Ned Scott*), Sally Creighton (*Mrs. Chapman*), Dewey Martin (*The Crew Chief*), Robert Nichols (*Lt. Ken Erickson*), William Self (*Cpl. Barnes*), James Arness (*The Thing*), James Young, George Fenneman
P: Howard Hawks **D:** Christian Nyby **SCR:** Charles Lederer, based on John W. Campbell's novella *Who Goes There?* **PHOTOG:** Russell Harlan **SPCL-FX:** Donald Steward **MUSIC:** Dimitri Tiomkin
"...the blueprint for the science fiction films of its decade. The same paranoia, the same fear of the unknown, the same militaristic defensiveness that characterized the fifties were all clearly established in Howard Hawks' film"—Gary Gerani, "The Space Monster Book—Chapter Two: The Universe Next Door," Monster Fantasy, Vol. 1, No. 4 (August, 1975), p. 25
Classic SF-thriller: Blood-drinking vegetable being from space terrorizes arctic army base

T

Things Happen at Night
1948, (GB), Tudor-Alliance/Renown, b&w, 79 mins.
W: Gordon Harker (*Joe Harris*), Alfred Drayton (*Wilfred Prescott*) (*Vincent Ebury*), Olga Lindo (*Mrs. Ebury*), Gwyneth Vaughan (*Audrey Prescott*), Garry Marsh (*Spender*), Wylie Watson (*Watson*), Joan Young (*Mrs. Venning*), Beatrice Campbell (*Joyce Prescott*)
P: A.R. Shipman & James Carter **D:** Francis Searle **SCR:** St. John Legh Clowes, from Frank Harvey's play *The Poltergeist*
reissued 1953
Standard fantasy-thriller: Insurance agent finds psychic maid is activating poltergeist

Things to Come
1936, (GB), London/UA, b&w, 100 mins.
W: Raymond Massey (*John/Oswald Cabal*), Ralph Richardson (*Rudolph*), Edward Chapman (*Pippa/Raymond Passworthy*), Margaretta Scott (*Roxana*), Cedric Hardwicke (*Theotocopulos*), Maurice Braddell (*Dr. Harding*), Ann Todd (*Mary Gordon*), Sophie Stewart (*Mrs. Cabal*), Derrick de Marney (*Richard Gordon*), Pearl Argyle (*Katherine Cabal*), Kenneth Villiers (*Maurice Passworthy*), Ivan Brandt (*Morden*) Allan Jeayes (*Cabal*), Patricia Hilliard (*Janet*), Charles Carson (*Grandfather*), Abraham Sofaer (*Watsky*), Anthony Holles (*Simon Burton*), Patrick Barr (*An Airman*), John Clements (*An Airman*), Anne McLaren (*The Child*), George Sanders
P: Alexander Korda **D:** William Cameron Menzies **SCR:** H.G. Wells, from his writings **PHOTOG:** Georges Perinal **SPCL-FX:** Ned Mann, Edward Cohen & Lawrence Butler **MUSIC:** Arthur Bliss
*A.k.a. **The Shape of Things to Come***
SF classic: Scientists rebuild war-ravaged world

Things We Want to Know
1915, (GB), Hepworth, b&w, 650 ft. (198.1m)
W: Lionelle Howard (*The Husband*)
D: Hay Plumb **STORY:** Lionelle Howard
Standard fantasy: Man dreams he murders wife's lover

The Thing That Couldn't Die
1958, (USA), Univ, b&w, 69 mins.
W: William Reynolds, Carolyn Kearney, Andra Martin, Robin Hughes ("*The Thing*"), Jeffrey Stone, James Anderson, Peggy Converse, Charles Horvath
P & D: Will Cowan **SCR:** David Duncan **PH:** Russell Metty **MUSIC:** Joseph Gershenson
*Fr retitle, **Le Decapite Vivant (The Living Beheaded)***
Minor horror-fantasy: Ranch inhabitants fall under evil spell of severed head

The Thing That Leapt from Nowhere
see The Deadly Mantis

The Thing with Two Heads
1972, (USA), Sabre/AIP, color, 93 mins.
W: Ray Milland (*Maxwell Kirshner*), Roosevelt "Rosey" Grier (*Jack Moss*), Don Marshall (*Dr. Fred Williams*), Roger Perry (*Dr. Philip Desmond*), Chelsea Brown (*Lila*), Kathy Baumann (*Patricia*), Lee Frost (*Sgt. Hacker*), John Bliss (*Donald*), Bruce Kimball (*The Police Lieutenant*), Jane Kellem (*Miss Mullen*), John Dullaghan (*Thomas*), Wes Bishop (*Dr. Smith*), Britt Nilsson (*The Nurse*), Roger Gentry (*The Police Sergeant*), Rick Baker (*The Gorilla*), Rod Steel (*The Medical Salesman*), Phil Hoover (*The Policeman*), Michael Viner (*The Prison Guard*)
P: Wes Bishop **D:** Lee Frost **SCR:** Lee Frost, Wes Bishop & James Gordon

Thinner: ROBERT JOHN BURKE AND JOE MANTEGNA

White **PHOTOG:** Jack Steely **MUSIC:** Robert O. Raglan
Standard SF-thriller: White bigot's head grafted onto body of black man

Think Fast, Mr. Moto
1937, (USA), 20th-Fox, b&w, 66 mins.
W: Peter Lorre (*Mr. Moto*), Virginia Field (*Gloria Danton*), Thomas Beck (*Bob Hitchings*), Sig Rumann (*Nicholas Marloff*), Murray Kinnell (*Wilkie*), Lotus Long (*Lola*), George Cooper (*Muggs Blake*), John Rogers (*Carson*), J. Carroll Naish (*Adram*), Sammee Tong (*Chee*), George Hassell (*Hitchings*), Tom Ung (*The Scarfaced Coolie*), Charles Tannen (*The Man*), Virginia Sale (*The*

Stewardess*), Ray Hendricks (*The Soloist*), Howard Wilson (*Jack*), Charles Irwin (*The Steward*), Isabel La Mal, Tom Herbert, Frank Mayo, Bert Roach, Dick Alexander, Frederick Vogeding, William Law
D: Norman Foster **SCR:** Howard Ellis Smith & Norman Foster, from John P. Marquand's novel **PHOTOG:** Harry Jackson **MUSIC DIR:** Samuel Kaylin **SONGS:** by Sidney Clare & Harry Akst
Fr retitle, L'Enigmatique M. Moto (The Enigmatic Mr. Moto)
Above-average thriller: Japanese sleuth ferrets out jewel smuggler

The Thin Man
1934, (USA), MGM, b&w, 93 mins.
W: William Powell (*Nick Charles*), Myrna Loy (*Nora Charles*), Maureen O'Sullivan (*Dorothy Wynant*), Minna Gombell (*Mimi Wynant*), Nat Pendleton (*Lt. John Guild*), Porter Hall (*McCauley*), Harold Huber (*Nunheim*), Henry Wadsworth (*Andrew*), Cesar Romero (*Chris Jorgenson*), Natalie Moorhead (*Julia Wolf*), Edward Brophy (*Joe Morelli*), Clay Clement (*Quinn*), Ruth Channing (*Mrs. Jorgenson*), Gertrude Short (*Marion*), Edward Ellis (*Clyde Wynant*), Cyril Thornton (*Tanner*), Raymond Brown (*Dr. Walton*), Robert E. Homans (*Bill*), Kenneth Gibson (*The Apartment Clerk*), Walter Long (*Stutsy Burke*), Fred Malatesta (*The Headwaiter*), Tui Lorraine (*The Stenographer*), Bert Roach (*Foster*), Huey White (*Tefler*), Ben Taggart (*The Police Captain*), Charles Williams (*The Fight Manager*), Thomas Jackson, William Henry, Leo White, Rolfesedan, Douglas Fowley, Sherry Hall, Creighton Hale, Garry Owen
D: W.S. Van Dyke **SCR:** Albert Hackett & Frances Goodrich, from Dashiell Hammett's novel **PHOTOG:** James Wong Howe **MUSIC:** William Axt
Classic thriller: Urbane sleuth aids girl who seeks missing father

The Thin Man Goes Home
1944, (USA), MGM, b&w, 100 mins.
W: William Powell (*Nick Charles*), Myrna Loy (*Nora Charles*), Lucile Watson (*Mrs. Charles*), Gloria De Haven (*Laura Ronson*), Anne Revere (*Crazy Mary*), Minor Watson (*Sam Ronson*), Harry Davenport (*Dr. Charles*), Lloyd Corrigan (*Bruce Clayworth*), Helen Vinson (*Helena Draque*), Wally Cassell (*Bill Burns*), Donald MacBride (*Chief MacGregory*), Anita Bolster (*Hilda*), Charles Halton (*Tatum*), Nora Cecil (*Miss Peavy*), Morris Ankrum (*Willoughby*), Arthur Hohl (*Charles*), Harry Hayden (*The Conductor*), Anthony Warde (*The Captain*), Rex Evans (*The Fat Man*), Connie Gilchrist (*The Woman with the Baby*), Irving Bacon (*Tom*), Virginia Sale (*Tom's Wife*), Edward Gargan (*Mickey*), Garry Owen (*The Pool Player*), Chester Clute (*The Drunk*), Clarence Muse (*The Porter*), Catherine McLeod (*The Daughter*), Bill Smith, Lucille Brown, Mitchell Lewis, Mike Mazurki, Ray Teal
D: Richard Thorpe **SCR:** Robert Riskin, Dwight Taylor & Harry Kurnitz, from characters created by Dashiell Hammett **PHOTOG:** Karl Freund **MUSIC:** David Snell
Standard thriller (5th entry in "Thin Man" series): Artist murdered, urbane sleuth investigates

Thinner
1996, (USA), Spelling/Para, color, 92 mins.
W: Robert John Burke (*Billy Halleck*), Joe Mantegna (*Richie Ginelli*), Michael Constantine (*Tadzu Lempke*), Kari Wuhrer (*Gina Lempke*), Lucinda Jenney (*Heidi Halleck*), John Horton (*Judge Cary Rossington*), Sam Freed (*Dr. Mike Houston*), Joy Lenz (*Linda Halleck*), Stephen King (*The Pharmacist*), Daniel Von Bargen, Elizabeth Franz, Walter Bobbie, Time Winters, Ruth Miller, Howard Erskine, Sean Hewitt, Terrence Garmey, Randy Jurgensen, Jeff Ware, Adriana Delphine, Antonette Schwartzberg, Terrence Kava, Irma St. Paule, Mitchell Greenberg, Patrick Farrelly, Bridget Marks, Angela Pietropinto, Michael Walker, Ed Wheeler, Peter Maloney, Robert Fitch Sr., Josh Holland, Allelon Ruggiero
D: Tom Holland **SCR:** Michael McDowell & Tom Holland, from Stephen King's novel **PHOTOG:** Kees Van Oostrum **MUSIC:** Daniel Licht
Standard fantasy-thriller: Gypsy curse causes man to lose weight

The Third Alibi
1961, (GB), Eternal/Grand Nat'l, b&w, 68 mins.
W: Laurence Payne (*Norman Martell*), Patricia Dainton (*Helen Martell*), Jane Griffiths (*Peggy Hill*), Edward Underdown (*Dr. Murdoch*), John Arnatt (*Supt. Ross*), Lucy Griffiths (*Miss Potter*), Humphrey Lestocq (*The Producer*), Cleo Laine (*The Singer*)
P: Maurie J. Wilson **D:** Montgomery Tully **SCR:** Maurice J. Wilson & Montgomery Tully, from the play *Moment Blindness* by Pip & Jane Baker
Standard crime-thriller: Composer plots wife's murder

The Third Clue
1934, (GB), Fox British, b&w, 72 mins.
W: Basil Sydney (*Reinhardt/James Conway*), Molly Lamont (*Rosemary Clayton*), Robert Cochran (*Peter Kerrigan*), Alfred Sangster (*Rupert Clayton*), Frank Atkinson (*Lefty*), C.M. Hallard (*Gabriel Wells*), Raymond Lovell (*Robinson*), Ernest Sefton (*Newman*), Ian Fleming (*Mark Clayton*), Eric Fawcett (*Jack Tully*), Quinton McPherson (*Reuben*), Bruce Lister (*Derek Clayton*)
D: Albert Parker **SCR:** Michael Barringer, Lance Sieveking & Frank Atkinson, from Neil Gordon's novel *The Shakespeare Murders*
Standard thriller: Crooks seek jewels hidden in old house

The Third Key
see The Long Arm

The Third Man
1949, (GB), British Lion/Korda/Selzvick, b&w, 104 mins (also 93 mins.).

W: Orson Welles (*Harry Lime*), Joseph Cotten (*Holly Martins*), Wilfrid Hyde-White (*Crabbin*), Trevor Howard (*Calloway*), Siegfried Breuer (*Popesco*), Valli (*Anna*), Erich Ponto (*Winkel*), Paul Hoerbiger (*Harry's Porter*), Bernard Lee (*Paine*), Hedwig Bleibtreu (*Anna's Old Woman*), Ernst Deutsch (*Kurtz*), Herbert Halbik (*Hansel*), Frederick Schreicker (*Hansel's Father*), Jenny Werner (*Winkel's Maid*), Nelly Arno (*Kurtz' Mother*), Alexis Chesnakov (*Brodsky*), Leo Bieber (*Casanova, the Barman*)
D: Carol Reed   **SCR:** Graham Greene, from his novel   **PHOTOG:** Robert Krasker (Academy Award winner)   **MUSIC:** Anton Karas   **ZITHER MUSIC:** Anton Karas
Classic mystery-thriller: American writer in post-war Vienna probes life of strange friend

Third Party Risk
1955, (GB), Hammer/Exclusive, b&w, 70 mins.
W: Lloyd Bridges (*Philip Graham*), Finlay Currie (*Mr. Darius*), Maureen Swanson (*Lolita*), Simone Silva (*Mitzi*), Russell Waters (*Dr. Zeissman*), Ferdy Mayne (*Maxwell Carey*), Mary Parker (*Mrs. Zeissman*), Peter Dyneley (*Tony Roscoe*), Roger Delgado (*Gonzales*), George Woodbridge (*Insp. Goldfinch*)
P: Robert Dunbar   **D & SCR:** Daniel Birt, from a novel by Nicolas Bentley
Standard crime-thriller: American in Spain suspected of killing wartime friend to gain microfilm

The Third Secret
1964, (GB), Hubris/20th-Fox, b&w, 103 mins.
W: Stephen Boyd (*Alex Stedman*), Jack Hawkins (*Sir Frederick Belline*), Richard Attenborough (*Alfred Price-Gorham*), Diane Cilento (*Anne Tanner*), Pamela Franklin (*Catherine Whitset*), Paul Rogers (*Dr. Milton Gillen*), Alan Webb (*Alden Hoving*), Rachel Kempson (*Mildred Hoving*), Freda Jackson (*Mrs. Bales*), Peter Sallis (*Lawrence Jacks*), Patience Collier (*Mrs. Pelton*), Judi Dench (*Miss Humphries*), Peter Copley (*Dr. Leo Whitset*), Nigel Davenport (*Lew Harding*), Charles Lloyd-Pack (*Dermot McHenry*)
P: Robert L. Joseph & Hugh Perceval   **D:** Charles Crichton   **SCR:** Robert L. Joseph   **PHOTOG:** Douglas Slocombe   **MUSIC:** Richard Arnell
Minor thriller: TV star solves psychiatrist's murder

The Third Solution
see Russicum

Thirdspace: A Babylon 5 Adventure
1998, (USA), TNT-TV, color, 95 mins.
W: Shari Belafonte (*Trent*), Bruce Boxleitner, Mira Furlan, Claudia Christian, Richard Biggs, Jeff Conaway, Stephen Furst, Patricia Tallman, Clyde Kusatsu
D: Jesus Salvador Trevino   **TELEPLAY:** J. Michael Straczynski   **PHOTOG:** John C. Flinn III   **MUSIC:** Christopher Franke
TVM, standard SF-adventure

The Third Visitor
1951, (GB), Elvey-Gartside/Eros, b&w, 85 mins.
W: Sonia Dresdel (*Steffy Millington*), Guy Middleton (*Insp. Mallory*), Hubert Gregg (*Jack Kurton*), Colin Gordon (*Bill Millington*), Karel Stepanek (*Richard Carling*), Eleanor Summerfield (*Vera Kurton*), John Slater (*James Oliver*), Cyril Smith (*Horton*), Michael Martin-Harvey (*Hewson*)
D: Maurice Elvey   **SCR:** Gerald Anstruther & David Evans, from a play by Gerald Anstruther
Standard crime-thriller: Crooked German kills ex-partner, fakes own death

The Third Witness
1917, (GB), I.B. Davidson/LIFT, b&w, 2,830 ft. (862.6m)
W: Arthur Rooke (*John Drew*), Joan Legge (*Pickles*)
D: A.E. Coleby
Standard crime-thriller: Detective uses photograph to trace crook, who tries to kill him in fire

Thirst
1979, (Austral), New South Wales Film Corp.-Victorian Film Corp./Marvin/New Line, color, 98 mins.
W: Chantal Contouri (*Kate Davis*), Max Phipps (*Mr. Hodge*), Shirley Cameron (*Mrs. Barker*), Henry Silva (*Dr. Gauss*), Rod Mullinar (*Derek*), David Hemmings (*Dr. Fraser*), Walter Pym (*Dichter*), Rosie Sturgess (*Lori*), Robert Thompson (*Sean*), Amanda Muggleton (*Martha*), Lulu Pinkus (*A Nurse*), Stephan Clark (*The Barman*), Chris Milne (*David*), Ben Nightingale (*The Tourist Driver*), Jacqui Gordon (*Leah*), Val Christensen (*Toni*), Glenys O'Brien (*The Guide*), Stewart Faichney (*A Security Man*), David Vella (*A Security Man*), Yvette Rees (*A Nurse*), Paddy Burnet (*The Blue Rinse Lady*), Vicki Andonopoulos (*The Child Kate*)
D: Rod Hardy   **SCR:** John Pinkney   **PHOTOG:** Vincent Monton   **SPCL-FX:** Conrad C. Rothmann & Chris Murray   **MUSIC:** Brian May
Standard horror-thriller: Woman forced to join cult of blood-drinkers

The Thirsty Dead
1975, (USA), Walter E. De Pue/Int'l Amusement, color, 83 mins.
W: Jennifer Billingsley, John Considine, Frederick Myers, Judith McConnell, Tani Guthrie, Chiqui de Rosa, Mary Walters, Elena Sampson
D: Terry Becker   **SCR:** Charles Dennis   **PHOTOG:** Nonong Rasca   **MUSIC:** Richard LaSalle
A.k.a. **The Blood Cult of Shangri-la**, *video title,* **Blood Hunt**
Minor fantasy-thriller: Ancients stay youthful on young women's blood

13
see Eye of the Devil

Thirteen at Dinner
1985, (GB), color, 100 mins.
W: Peter Ustinov (*Hercule Poirot*), Faye Dunaway, Lee Horsley, David Suchet, Amanda Pays, Jonathan Cecil, Diane Keen, Benedict Taylor
D: Lou Antonio   **TELEPLAY:** Rod Browning, from Agatha Christie's novel
TVM, standard thriller: Belgian sleuth probes British lord's murder

13 East Street
1952, (GB), Tempean/Eros, b&w, 71 mins.
W: Patrick Holt (*Gerald Blake*), Sandra Dorne (*Judy*), Robert Ayres (*Larry Conn*), Sonia Holm (*Joan*), Michael Balfour (*Joey Long*), Dora Bryan (*Valerie*), Michael Brennan (*George Mack*)
P: Robert Baker & Monty Berman   **D & STORY:** Robert Baker   **SCR:** John Gilling
Standard crime-thriller: Detective poses as escaped convict, nabs warehouse robbers

13 Frightened Girls
1963, (USA), Col, color, 89 mins.
W: Kathy Dunn (*Candace*), Murray Hamilton (*Wally*), Joyce Taylor (*Soldier*), Hugh Marlowe (*Hull*), Lynne Sue Moon (*MaiLing*), Khigh Dhiegh (*Kang*), Charlie Briggs, Norma Varden, Janet Mary Prance, Garth Benton, Penny Anne Mills, Ariane Glaser, Maria Cristina Servera, Alexandra Bastedo, Ilona Schutze, Judy Pace
P & D: William Castle   **SCR:** Robert Dillon   **STORY:** Otis Guernsey Jr.
A.k.a. **The Candy Web**
Standard thriller: Diplomat's daughter involved in espionage

13 Ghosts
1960, (USA), Col, b&w and color, 88 mins.
W: Charles Herbert, Donald Woods, Jo Morrow, Martin Milner, Rosemary De Camp, Margaret Hamilton, John Van Dreelen
P & D: William Castle   **SCR:** Robb White   **PHOTOG:** Joseph Biroc   **MUSIC:** Von Dexter
Standard thriller: Museum curator inherits occultist uncle's creepy house

13 Lead Soldiers
1948, (USA), Bernard Small/Reliance/20th-Fox, b&w, 64 mins.
W: Tom Conway (*Bulldog Drummond*), Maria Palmer (*Estelle*), Helen Westcott (*Cynthia*), John Newland (*Algy Longworth*), Terence Kilburn (*Seymour*), Gordon Richards (*Insp. McIver*), William Stelling (*Coleman*), Harry Cording (*Vane*), William Edmunds (*Collier*), John Goldsworthy (*Steadman*)
D: Frank McDonald   **SCR:** Irving Elman, from a short story by Sapper   **PHOTOG:** George Robinson   **MUSIC:** Milton Rosen
Standard thriller: Famed sleuth solves three murders surrounding hidden treasure.("Bulldog Drummond" series)

The Thirteenth Candle
1933, (GB), First Nat'l/WB, b&w, 68 mins.
W: Isobel Elsom (*Lady Sylvia Meeton*), Arthur Maude (*Sir Charles Meeton*), Gibb McLaughlin (*Capt. Blyth*), Claude Fleming (*Sgt. Harris*), Joyce Kirby (*Marie*), Louis Hayward (*Paul Marriott*), Louis Goodrich (*Tarrant*), Winifred Oughton (*Pettit*), D.A. Clarke-Smith (*Blades*), Charles Childerstone (*Insp. Hart*)
D: John Daumery   **STORY:** Brock Williams
Standard thriller: Search for hated squire's killer

The Thirteenth Chair
1929, (USA), MGM, b&w, 8 reels (6,571 ft./2002.8m/73 mins.)
W: Conrad Nagel (*Richard Crosby*), Margaret Wycherly (*Mme. Rosalie La Grange*), Leila Hyams (*Helen O'Neill*), Helene Millard (*Mary Eastwood*), Mary Forbes (*Lady Crosby*), Bela Lugosi (*Insp. Delzante*), Lal Chand Mehra (*Chotee*), Holmes Herbert (*Sir Roscoe Crosby*), Moon Carroll (*Helen Trent*), Gretchen Holland (*Grace Standish*), Cyril Chadwick (*Brandon Trent*), John Davidson (*Edward Wales*), Charles Quartermaine (*Dr. Philip Mason*), Frank Leigh (*Prof. Feringeea*), Clarence Geldert (*Comm. Grimshaw*), Bertram Johns (*Howard Standish*),
D: Tod Browning   **SCR:** Elliot Clawson, from a play by Bayard Veiller   **PHOTOG:** Merritt B. Gerstad
Standard thriller: Seance used to unmask killer

T

The 30-Foot Bride of Candy Rock: DOROTHY PROVINE AND LOU COSTELLO

The 13th Chair

1937, (USA), MGM, b&w, 66 mins.
W: Dame May Whitty, Lewis Stone, Henry Daniell, Elissa Landi
P: J.J. Cohn   **D:** George B. Seitz   **SCR:** Marion Parsonnet
Standard thriller: Murder at a seance

The 13th Floor

1988, (USA), color, 86 mins.
W: Lisa Hensley, Tim McKenzie, Miranda Otto
D: Chris Roach
Minor fantasy-thriller: Young girl fuses with spirit of murdered boy

The Thirteenth Guest

1932, (USA), Mono, b&w, 70 mins.
W: Ginger Rogers, Lyle Talbot, James Eagles, J. Farrell MacDonald, Eddie Phillips, Erville Alderson
P: M.H. Hoffman   **D:** Albert Ray   **SCR:** Frances Hyland & Arthur Hoerl, from a novel by Armitage Traill   **PHOTOG:** Harry Neumann & Tom Galligan
Standard thriller: Black-hooded killer electrocutes people by telephone. cf. **The Mystery of the 13th Guest**

The Thirteenth Hour

1927, (USA), MGM, b&w, 6 reels (5,252 ft./1600.8m)
W: Lionel Barrymore (*Prof. Leroy*), Jacquelin Gadsdon (*Jane Daly*) (*Mary Lyle*),

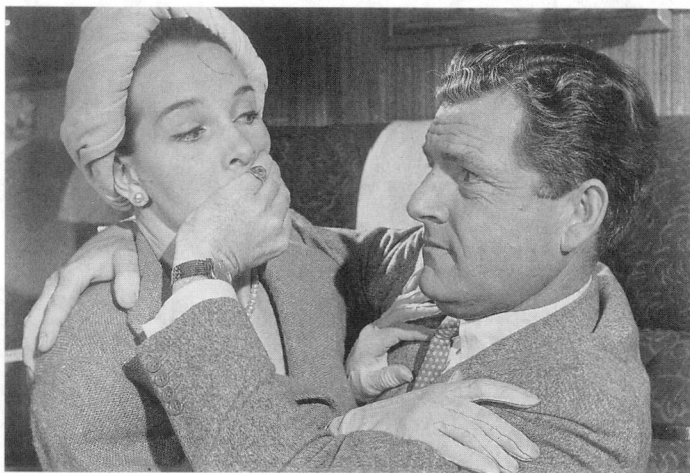

The Thirty-Nine Steps: Taina Elg and Kenneth More

Charles Delaney (*Matt Gray*), Fred Kelsey (*Det. Shaw*), Polly Moran (*Polly*), Napoleon (*The Dog*)
D: Chester Franklin   **STORY & SCR:** Douglas Furber & Chester Franklin
PHOTOG: Maximilian Fabian
Standard thriller: Noted criminologist exposed as murderer

The Thirteenth Hour

1947, (USA), Col, b&w, 85 mins.
W: Richard Dix, Karen Morley, Mark Dennis, John Kellogg, Bernadene Hayes, Jim Bannon, Regis Toomey
D: William Clemens
Standard thriller. (entry in "Whistler" series; Richard Dix's last film): Trucking-company owner suspected of murder

The Thirteenth Instant

1940, (GB), British Foundation/Kinograph, b&w, 17 mins.
W: Lionel Gamlin (*narrator*)
D: Ronald Haines
Standard comedy-fantasy short: Magic ring turns man into monkey

The Thirteenth Letter

1951, (USA), 20th-Fox, b&w, 85 mins.
W: Charles Boyer, Linda Darnell, Constance Smith, Michael Rennie, Francoise Rosay, Judith Evelyn
D: Otto Preminger   **SCR:** Howard Koch   **PHOTOG:** Joseph La Shelle
MUSIC: Alex North
Standard thriller (remake of **Le Corbeau***): Outbreak of poison-pen letters in small French-Canadian town*

The Thirteenth Man

1937, (USA), b&w, 70 mins.
W: Weldon Heyburn, Inez Courtney, Selmer Jackson, Milburn Stone, Matty Fain
D: William Nigh
Entertaining thriller: Gossip columnist probes murders

The Thirteenth Reunion

see *Charlie Boy/The Thirteenth Reunion*

The Thirteen Trunks of Mr. O.F.

see *Die Dreizehn Koffer des Herrn O.F.*

13 West Street

1962, (USA), Ladd Enterprises/Col, b&w, 80 mins.
W: Alan Ladd, Rod Steigerk, Jeanne Cooper, Michael Callan, Dolores Dorn
D: Philip Leacock, from Leigh Brackett's novel
Standard melodrama: Man stalks hoodlums

The 30 Foot Bride of Candy Rock

1959, (USA), D.R.B./Col, b&w, 75 mins.
W: Lou Costello, Dorothy Provine, Gale Gordon, Jimmy Conlin, Charles Lane, Robert Burton, Robert Nichols, Peter Leeds, Will Wright, Lenny Kent, Ruth Perrott, Veola Vonn, Jack Straw
P: Lewis J. Rachmil   **D:** Sidney Miller   **SCR:** Rowland Barber & Arthur Ross, from a story by Lawrence L. Goldman   **PHOTOG:** Frank G. Carson
MUSIC: Raoul Kraushaar
Standard SF-comedy: Amateur inventor turns girlfriend into giantess. (Lou Costellos' last film in Wonderama)

The 39 Steps

1935, (GB), Gaumont, b&w, 87 mins.
W: Robert Donat (*Richard Hannay*), Madeleine Carroll (*Pamela*), Godfrey Tearle (*Prof. Jordan*), John Laurie (*John*), Lucie Mannheim (*Anabella Smith*), Helen Haye (*Mrs. Jordan*), Peggy Ashcroft (*Margaret*), Frank Cellier (*Sheriff Watson*), Wylie Watson (*Memory*), Hilda Trevelyan (*The Innkeeper's Wife*), Peggy Simpson (*The Maid*), Gus McNaughton (*A Traveller*), Jerry Verno (*A Traveller*), Miles Malleson
D: Alfred Hitchcock   **SCR:** Charles Bennett, Ian Hay & Alma Reville, from John Buchan's novel   **PHOTOG:** Bernard Knowles   **MUSIC:** Louis Levy
reissued 1939 & 1942
Classic thriller: Innocent embroiled in espionage

The 39 Steps

1959, (GB), Rank/20th Century Fox, color, 93 mins.
W: Kenneth More (*Richard Hannay*), Taina Elg (*Miss Fisher*), Brenda de Banzie (*Nellie Lumsden*), Reginald Beckwith (*Lumsden*), Barry Jones (*Prof. Logan*), James Hayter (*Mr. Memory*), Sidney James (*Perce*), Faith Brook (*Nannie*), Jameson Clark (*McDougal*), Michael Goodliffe (*Brown*), Andrew Cruickshank (*The Sheriff*), Duncan Lamont (*Kennedy*), Leslie Dwyer (*The Milkman*), Joan Hickson (*Miss Dobson*)
P: Betty E. Box   **D:** Ralph Thomas   **SCR:** Frank Harvey, from a script by Charles Bennett, Ian Hay & Alma Reville, based on John Buchan's novel
PHOTOG: Ernest Steward   **MUSIC:** Clifton Parker
Standard thriller: Framed man exposes spy ring in Scotland

The 39 Steps

1978, (GB), Media Management/Norfolk Int'l/Rank/Int'l Picture Show, color, 102 mins.
W: Robert Powell (*Ruchard Hannay*), David Warner (*Edmund Appleton*), Eric Porter (*Insp. Lomas*), Karen Dotrice (*Alexandra Mackenzie*), John Mills (*Col. Scudder*), George Baker (*Sir Walter Bullivant*), Ronald Pickup (*Bayliss*), Donald Pickering (*Marshall*), Timothy West (*Porton*), Andrew Keir (*Lord Rohan*), Miles Anderson (*David Hamilton*), John Welsh (*Lord Belthane*), Robert Flemyng (*The Magistrate*), William Squire (*Harkness*), Paul McDowell (*McLean*), David Collings (*Tillotson*), Edward De Souza (*Woodville*), Donald Bissett (*Renfrew*), John Grieve (*PC Forbes*), John Normington (*Fletcher*), Tony Steedman (*The Admiral*), Andrew Downie (*Stewart*), Derek Anders (*Donald*), Oliver Maguire (*Martins*), Joan Henley (*Lady Nettleship*), Artro Morris (*Scott*), Prentis Hancock (*Perryman*), Leo Dolan (*The Milkman*), James Garbutt (*Miller*), Robert Gillespie (*Crombie*), Raymond Young (*The Guide*), Paul Jerricho (*PC Scott*), Michael Bilton (*The Vicar*)
P: Greg Smith   **D:** Don Sharp   **SCR:** Michael Robson, from John Buchan's novel
PHOTOG: John Coquillon   **MUSIC:** Ed Welch
Standard thriller: Spies pursue mining engineer for notebook containing secret of bomb in Big Ben

Thirty-Six Hours

1954, (GB), Hammer/Lippert, b&w, 80 mins.
W: Dan Duryea (*Bill*), Elsy Albiin (*Katie*), Eric Pohlmann (*Slauson*), Ann Gudrun (*Jenny*), John Chandos (*Orville Hart*), Kenneth Griffith (*Henry*), Jane Carr (*Sister Clair*), Harold Lang (*Harry*), Michael Golden (*Insp. Kevin*), Lee Patterson (*Joe*)
P: Anthony Hinds   **D:** Montgomery Tully   **STORY:** Steve Fisher
USA retitle, **Terror Street**
Standard thriller: Air Force pilot proves he did not kill wife

36 Hours

1965, (USA), MGM, b&w, 115 mins.
W: James Garner (*Maj. Jefferson Pike*), Eva Marie Saint (*Anna Hedler*), Rod Taylor (*Maj. Walter Gerber*), Werner Peters (*Otto Schack*), John Banner (*Ernst*), Russell Thorson (*Gen. Allison*), Alan Napier (*Col. Peter MacLean*), Oscar Beregi (*Lt. Col. Osterman*), Ed Gilbert (*Capt. Abbott*), Martin Kosleck (*Kraatz*), Sig Ruman (*The German Guard*), Celia Lovsky (*Elsa*), Karl Held (*Cpl. Kenter*), Walter Friedel (*Lemke*), Joseph Mell (*Lemke*), Marjorie Bennett (*The Charwoman*), Hilda Plowright (*The German Agent*), Henry Rowland (*A German Soldier*), Otto Reichow (*A German Soldier*)
D & SCR: George Seaton   **PHOTOG:** Philip Lathrop

Unusual thriller: Allied soldier made to believe war is over

30-Years-to-Life
1998, (USA), UPN-TV, color, 95 mins.
W: Robert Hays
TVM, standard SF-thriller: Innocent teen is aged 30 years for mysterious murder

This Gun for Hire
1942, (USA), Para, b&w, 80 mins.
W: Alan Ladd, Veronica Lake, Robert Preston, Laird Cregar, Tully Marshall, Marc Lawrence, Pamela Blake, Yvonne DeCarlo
D: Frank Tuttle   SCR: W.R. Burnett & Albert Maltz, from Graham Greene's novel
Classic melodrama: Hoodlum seeks revenge

This Gun for Hire
1991, (USA), color, 100 mins.
W: Robert Wagner, Nancy Everhard, Fredric Lehne, John Harkins
D: Lou Atonio, from Graham Greene's novel
TVM, tepid remake: Man hunts double-crosser

This House Possessed
1981, (USA), Mandy/ABC-TV, color, 100 mins.
W: Parker Stevenson (*Gary*), Lisa Eilbacher (*Sheila*), Joan Bennett (*The Rag Lady*), Shelley Smith (*Tanya*), K Callan (*Lucille*), Slim Pickens (*Keene*)
TVM, minor thriller: Rock performer buys home that is controlled by mysterious force

This Island Earth
1955, (USA), Univ, color, 86 mins.
W: Jeff Morrow (*Exeter*), Faith Domergue (*Ruth Adams*), Rex Reason (*Cal Meacham*), Douglas Spencer (*The Monitor*), Lance Fuller (*Brack*), Russell Johnson (*Steve Carlson*), Karl L. Lindt (*Adolph Engelborg*), Robert Nichols (*Joe Wilson*), Regis Parton (*The Metaluna Mutant*)
P: William Alland   D: Joseph Newman   SCR: Edward G. O'Callaghan & Franklin Coen, from Raymond F. Jones' novel   PHOTOG: Clifford Stine   SPCL-FX: Charlie Baker & Stanley Horsley   MUSIC: Joseph Gershenson
Fr retitle, Les Survivants de l'Infini (The Survivors of Infinity). Ger retitle, Metaluna Does Not Answer
"...over two and a half years in preparation. It was adapted from the novel by star science-fictioneer, Raymond F. Jones. Universal Pictures paid one of the most unbelievable figures in cinema history for the film rights"—Anon., "This Island Earth," Fantastic Monsters of the Film, Vol. I, No. 2 (1962), p. 18
Impressive space-opera: Aliens from warring planet seek aid of Earth scientists. cf. Mystery Science Theater 3000: The Movie

This is My Love
1954, (USA), RKO, color, 91 mins.
W: Linda Darnell (*Vida*), Dan Duryea (*Murray*), Rick Jason (*Glenn*), Faith Domergue (*Evelyn*), Hal Baylor (*Eddie*), Kam Tong (*Harry*), Jerry Mathers (*David Myer*), Susie Mathers (*Shirley Myer*), Mary Young (*Mrs. Timberly*), William Hopper (*The D.A.*), Stuart Randall (*The Investigator*), Judd Holdren (*Dr. Raines*)
P: Hugh Brooke   D: Stuart Heisler   SCR: Hagar Wilde & Hugh Brooke   PHOTOG: Ray June   MUSIC: Franz Waxman
Glossy melodrama: Wife of unpleasant cripple lusts after younger sister's "panther-eyed" beau

This is Not a Test
1962, (USA), GPA/Modern/AA-TV, b&w, 73 mins.
W: Seamon Glass, Thayer Roberts, Aubrey Martin, Mary Morlas, Mike Green, Alan Austin, Carol Kent, Norman Winston, James George Jr., Ron Starr, Don Spruance, William Flaherty, Jay Della, Norm Bishop, Ralph Manza, Phil Donati, Doyle Cooper
D: Fredric Gadette   SCR: Peter Abenheim, Betty Lasky & Fredric Gadette   PHOTOG: Brick Marquard   MUSIC: Greig McRitchie
Minor SF-thriller: Atom war promotes hysteria. (No US theatrical release)

This Man is Dangerous (1941)
see The Patient Vanishes

This Man is Dangerous (1953)
see Cet Homme est Dangereux
This Man Must Die
1970, (Fr), AA, color, 115 mins.
W: Michel Duchaussoy, Caroline Cellier
Standard thriller

This Side of the Law
1950, (USA), WB, b&w, 74 mins.
W: Viveca Lindfors, Kent Smith
Standard melodrama

Thomasina
see The Three Lives of Thomasina

Thomas l'Imposteur (Thomas the Imposter)
1965, (Fr), Filmel/CCFC, b&w, 93 mins.
W: Emmanuele Riva, Jean Servais, Fabrice Rouleau (*Thomas*)
D: Georges Franju   SCR: Georges Franju, Jean Cocteau, Michel Worms &

Raphael Clazel, from a novel by Jean Cocteau   PHOTOG: Marcel Fradetal   MUSIC: Georges Auric
Standard thriller

Thor and the Amazons (Thor and the Amazon Women)
1960, (It), C&M/Ambassador, color, 95 mins.
W: Joe Robinson, Susy Andersen
Minor "Sword & Sandal": Amazon queen keeps love slaves

The Thornton Jewel Mystery
1915, (GB), I.B. Davidson-St. George/Serra, b&w, 2,600 ft. (792.5m)
W: Harry Lorraine (*Sexton Blake*), Bert Rex (*Tinker*), Miss Vere (*Flash Kate*)
D: Charles Raymond, from characters created by Harry Blyth
Standard thriller: Girl frames drunkard for gem theft

Those Fantastic Flying Fools
1967, (USA-GB), AIP, color, 101 mins.
W: Burl Ives (*Phineas T. Barnum*), Troy Donahue (*Gaylord Sullivan*), Gert Frobe (*Prof. Von Bulow*), Terry-Thomas (*Sir Harry Washington-Smythe*), Daliah Lavi (*Madelaine*), Lionel Jeffries (*Sir Charles Dilworthy*), Hermione Gingold (*Angelica*), Dennis Price (*The Duke of Barset*), Stratford Johns (*The Warrant Officer*), Graham Stark (*Grundle*), Edward De Souza (*Henry*), Jimmy Clitheroe (*Gen. Tom Thumb*), Allan Cuthbertson (*Col. Scutling*), Judy Cornwell (*Electra*), Joan Sterndale Bennett (*Queen Victoria*)
P: Harry Alan Towers   D: Don Sharp   SCR: Dave Freeman   ORIG. STORY: Peter Welbeck, from a novel by Jules Verne   GB TITLE: Jules Verne's Rocket to the Moon
A.k.a. Blast-Off! orig. to be titled Rocket to the Moon, P.T. Barnum's Rocket to the Moon, Journey That Shook the World or What a Way to Fly
Standard SF-comedy: American showman and British lord finance rocket to send midget to moon

The Thousand and One Girls of Bagdad
see Babes in Bagdad

A Thousand and One Nights
1945, (USA), Col, color, 95 mins.
W: Cornel Wilde (*Aladdin*), Evelyn Keyes, Rex Ingram, Phil Silvers, Shelley Winters, Nestor Paiva, Adele Jergens, Dusty Anderson, Dennis Hoey
P: Samuel Bischoff   D: Alfred E. Green   SCR: Richard English, Jack Henley & Wilfred H. Petit
Standard fantasy: Youth finds lamp with female genie

A Thousand and One Nights
1968, (It-Sp), Group W/Filmways, color, 87 mins.
W: Luciana Paluzzi (*Mizziana*), Jeff Cooper (*Omar*), Perla Cristal (*The Favorite*), Raf Vallone (*Hixem*), Rueben Rojo (*Ali*), Ricardo Palacios (*Ahmed*), Tomas Blanco (*Cassim*)
D: Joe Lacy (*Jose Maria Elorrieta*)   SCR: Joe Lacy & J.L. Navarre   MUSIC: Nico Fidenco
Modest adventure-fantasy: Genie helps swordsman oppose usurper

The Thousand Eyes of Dr. Mabuse
see Die Tausend Augen des Dr. Mabuse

Thou Shalt Not Kill
see The Avenging Conscience

Threads
1984, (GB-Austral), Western-World & Nine Network/BBC-TV, color, 104 mins.
W: Karen Meagher (*Ruth Beckett*), Reece Dinsdale (*Jimmy Kemp*), David Brierley (*Mr. Kemp*), Rita May (*Mrs. Kemp*), Nicholas Lane (*Michael Kemp*), Henry Moxon (*Mr. Beckett*), Jane Hazlegrove (*Alison Kemp*), Harry Beety (*Mr. Sutton*), June Broughton (*Mrs. Beckett*), Ruth Holden (*Mrs. Sutton*), Sylvia Stoker (*Granny Beckett*), Ashley Barker (*Bob*), Phil Rose (*The Medical Officer*), Michael O'Hagan (*Chief Supt. Hirst*), Steve Halliwell (*The Information Officer*), Brian Grellis (*The Accommodation Officer*), Peter Faulkner (*The Transport Officer*), Anthony Collin (*The Food Officer*), Michael Ely (*The Scientific Advisor*), Sharon Baylis (*The Manpower Officer*), David Stutt (*The Works Officer*), Phil Askham (*Mr. Stothard*), Anna Seymour (*Mrs. Stothard*), Joe Belcher (*The Shopkeeper*), Fiona Rook (*Carol Stothard*), Christine Buckley (*The Woman in the Supermarket*), Maggie Ford (*The Peace Speaker*), David Major (*The Boy in the Supermarket*), Mike Kay (*The Trade Unionist*), Ted Beyer (*A Policeman*), Dean Williamson (*A Policeman*), John Livesey (*The Street Trader*), Richard Albrecht (*The Officer at the Food Depot*), Joe Holmes (*Mr. Langley*), Greta Dunn (*The Woman at the Hospital*), Andy Fenn-Rodgers (*The Patrol Officer*), Graham Hill (*The 1st Soldier*), Nigel Collins (*The 2nd Soldier*), Jerry Ready (*A Looter*), Dennis Conlon (*A Looter*), Nat Jackley (*The Old Man in the Graveyard*), Lee Daley (*Spike*), Dorothy Ford (*The Stunt Person*), Lesley Judd (*A Newscaster*), Colin Ward-Lewis (*A Newscaster*), Victoria O'Keefe (*Jane*), Marcus Lund (*Gaz*), Paul Vaughan (*The Narrator*)
D & TELEPLAY: Barry Hines   PHOTOG: Andrew Dunn & Paul Morris
TVM, unusual SF-thriller: Gripping vision of survival after nuclear holocaust

The Threat
1949, (USA), RKO, b&w, 66 mins.
W: Michael O'Shea, Virginia Grey, Charles McGraw, Julie Bishop, Robert Shayne, Anthony Caruso
D: Felix Feist

Standard thriller: Escaped thug seeks revenge

The Threat
1960, (USA), WB, b&w, 66 mins.
W: Robert Knapp, Linda Lawson, Lisabeth Hush, James Seay, Mary Castle, Barney Phillips
D: Charles R. Rondeau
Standard thriller: Killer hunted

The Three Avengers
1964, (It), color, 97 mins.
W: Alan Steel, Rosalba Neri, Mimmo Palmara, Lisa Gastoni
D: Gianfranco Parolini
Minor adventure-thriller: Freedom fighters oppose wicked ruler

The Three Bacchantes
see Les Trois Bacchantes

Three Bad Sisters
1956, (USA), UA, b&w, 75 mins.
W: Kathleen Hughes, Marla English, John Bromfield, Brett Halsey, Sara Shane, Jess Barker, Madge Kennedy
P: Howard Koch   **D:** Gilbert L. Kay   **SCR:** Gerald Drayson Adams
Minor melodrama: Inheritance causes division among siblings

The Three Caballeros
1945, (USA), Walt Disney, color, 71 mins.
W: Aurora Miranda, Carmen Melinda, Dora Luz
VOICES: Sterling Holloway, Clarence Nash, Jose Oliveira, Joaquin Garay   **D:** Norman Ferguson   **PHOTOG:** Ray Rennahan   **SONG:** *Baia*
Colorful blend of live action & animation: Salute to Latin America

Three Came to Kill
1960, (USA), Premium/UA, b&w, 70 mins.
W: Cameron Mitchell, John Lupton
Standard thriller

Three Cases of Murder
1955, (GB), Wessex/British Lion/Assoc. Artists, b&w, 99 mins.
W: Orson Welles (*Lord Mountdrago*), Alan Badel (*Mr. X/Harry/Owen*), Eammon Andrews (*The Host*), Hugh Pryse (*Jarvis*), John Salew (*Rooke*), Leueen McGrath (*Mrs. X*), Eddie Byrne (*Snyder*), Harry Welchman (*The Visitor*), Anne Hanslip (*A Girl*), John Gregson (*Edgar Curtain*), Elizabeth Sellars (*Elizabeth Grange*), Emrys Jones (*George Wheeler*), Jack Lambert (*Insp. Atcheson*), Maurice Kaufman (*Frank*), Andre Morell (*Dr. Audlin*), Helen Cherry (*Lady Elizabeth*), Arthur Wontner (*The Prime Minister*), Henry Oscar (*An MP*), David Horne (*The Doctor*), Zena Marshall (*A Girl*), Vera Pearce (*An MP*)
P: Ian Dalrymple, Alexander Paal & Hugh Perceval   **D:** Wendy Toye   **SCR:** Donald Wilson; from a story by Roderick Wilkinson

Three Crooked Men
1958, (GB), Danziger/Para, b&w, 71 mins.
W: Gordon Jackson (*Don Wescott*), Sarah Lawson (*May Wescott*), Warren Mitchell (*Prinn*), Philip Saville (*Seppy*), Michael Mellinger (*Vince*), Eric Pohlmann (*Masters*), Arnold Bell (*Mr. Brady*), Kenneth Edwards (*Insp. Wheeler*)
P: Edward J. & Harry Lee Danziger   **D:** Ernest Morris   **STORY:** Brian Clemens & Eldon Howard
Standard crime-thriller: Suspect tracks down bank robbers

3 Days of the Condor
1975, (USA), Dino De Laurentiis/Para, color, 118 mins.
W: Robert Redford (*Joe Turner*), Faye Dunaway (*Kathy*), Max von Sydow (*Joubert*), Cliff Robertson (*Higgins*), Addison Powell (*Atwood*), John Houseman (*Mr. Wabash*), Michael Kane (*Wicks*), Walter McGinn (*Sam Barber*), Tina Chen
P: Stanley Schneider   **D:** Sydney Pollack   **SCR:** Lorenzo Semple Jr. & David Rayfiel, based on James Grady's novel *Six Days of the Condor*   **PHOTOG:** Owen Roizman   **MUSIC:** David Grusin
Superior thriller: CIA office reader finds out too much, becomes hunted man

The Three Faces of Eve
1957, (USA), 20th-Fox, b&w, 95 mins.
W: Joanne Woodward (*Eve*), Lee J. Cobb (*Dr. Luther*), David Wayne (*Ralph White*), Edwin Jerome (*Dr. Day*), Alena Murray (*The Sec'y*), Nancy Kulp (*Mrs. Black*), Douglas Spencer (*Mr. Black*), Terry Ann Ross (*Bonnie*), Ken Scott (*Earl*), Vince Edwards (*The Soldier*), Mimi Gibson (*Eve, age 8*), Alistair Cooke (*Narrator*)
WRIT, P & D: Nunnally Johnson, from the book by Corbett H. Thigpen, M.D. & Hervey M. Cleckley, M.D.   **PHOTOG:** Stanley Cortez   **MUSIC:** Robert Emmett Dolan   **SONG:** *Hold Me*
Superior melodrama: Fact-based tale of woman with multiple personality. cf. Lizzie.
Joanne Woodward: Academy Award, Best Actress

The Three Faces of Fear
see I Tre Volti della Paura

Three Ghosts
see Ghosts—Italian Style

Three Hours to Kill
1954, (USA), Col, color, 77 mins.
W: Dana Andrews, Donna Reed
Standard melodrama. Western

The Three Lights
see Der Mude Tod

The Three Lives of Karen
1997, (USA), Spinnaker Films/USA-TV, color, 95 mins.
W: Gail O'Grady, Dennis Boutsikaris, Tim Guinee, Michelle White
D: David Burton Morris   **TELEPLAY:** David Chisholm   **PHOTOG:** John L. Demps Jr.   **SPCL-FX:** Stephen H. Lanier   **MUSIC:** Pray For Rain
TVM, standard thriller

The Three Lives of Thomasina
1963, (GB), Walt Disney/Buena Vista, color, 97 mins.
W: Patrick McGoohan (*Andrew McDhui*), Susan Hampshire (*Lori MacGregor*), Karen Dotrice (*Mary McDhui*), Vincent Winter (*Hughie Stirling*), Denis Gilmore (*Jamie McNab*), Francis De Wolff (*Targu*), Laurence Naismith (*Rev. Angus Peddie*), Jean Anderson (*Mrs. MacKenzie*), Wilfred Brambell (*Willie Bannock*), Finlay Currie (*Grandpa Stirling*), Oliver Johnston (*Mr. Dobbie*), Jack Stewart, Alex Mackenzie, Elspeth March (*Voice of Thomasina*)
P: Hugh Attwooll   **D:** Don Chaffey   **SCR:** Robert Westerby, from Paul Gallico's novel *Thomasina*   **PHOTOG:** Paul Beeson   **MUSIC:** Paul Smith
Standard fantasy: Ginger-colored cat alters lives of veterinarian and his daughter

Three Murderesses
1960, (Fr), 20th-Fox, b&w, 98 mins.
W: Alain Delon, Mylene Demongeot
Standard thriller

The Three Musketeers
1916, (USA), b&w, 74 mins.
W: Orin Johnson, Dorothy Dalton, Louise Glaum, Walt Whitman
D: Charles Swickard, from Alexandre Dumas' novel
A.k.a. D'Artagnan
Standard adventure-thriller: French queen saved from evil plot

The Three Musketeers
1921, (USA), UA, b&w, 11,700 ft. (3566.2m)
W: Douglas Fairbanks Sr., Adolphe Menjou, Mary MacLaren, Leon Barry, George Siegmann, Eugene Pallette, Boyd Irwin, Thomas Holding, Sidney Franklin, Charles Stevens, Willis Robards, Nigel de Brulier
P: Douglas Fairbanks Sr.   **D:** Fred Niblo, from Alexandre Dumas' novel   **PHOTOG:** Arthur Edeson
Standard adventure-thriller: Swordsmen oppose court intrigue

The Three Musketeers
1923, (Russ), b&w
D & PHOTOG: Mikhail Kaufman, from Alexandre Dumas' novel
Standard adventure thriller: Daring swordsmen defend France

The Three Musketeers
1935, (USA), b&w, 90 mins.
W: Walter Abel, Paul Lukas, Ian Keith, Onslow Stevens, Ralph Forbes, Margot Grahame, Heather Angel, Moroni Olsen, Miles Mander
D: Rowland V. Lee, from Alexandre Dumas' novel   **MUSIC:** Max Steiner
Dullest film-version of literary classic: Swordsmen aid France

The Three Musketeers
1939, (USA), 20th-Fox, b&w, 73 mins.
W: The Ritz Brothers, Don Ameche, Gloria Stuart, Binnie Barnes, John Carradine, Lionel Atwill, Joseph Schildkraut, Miles Mander, Pauline Moore, Moroni Olsen
P: Darryl F. Zanuck   **D:** Allan Dwan   **SCR:** M.M. Musselman, William A. Drake & Sam Hellman, from Alexandre Dumas' novel   **PHOTOG:** J. Peverell Marley
GB retitle, The Singing Musketeer
Standard adventure-comedy-musical: Zanies aid swordsmen

The Three Musketeers
1948, (USA), MGM, color, 127 mins.
W: Lana Turner, Gene Kelly, June Allyson, Van Heflin, Gig Young, Vincent Price, Angela Lansbury, John Sutton, Frank Morgan, Keenan Wynn, Robert Coote, Reginald Owen, Patricia Medina, Ian Keith, Marie Windsor
D: George Sidney   **SCR:** Robert Ardrey, from Alexandre Dumas' novel   **PHOTOG:** Robert Planck   **MUSIC:** Herbert P. Stothart
Superior adventure-thriller: Intrigue at court of Louis XIII

The Three Musketeers
1974, (GB-Panama), 20th-Fox, color, 107 mins.
W: Oliver Reed (*Athos*), Raquel Welch (*Constance*), Richard Chamberlain (*Aramis*), Michael York (*D'Artagnan*), Frank Finlay (*Porthos*), Christopher Lee (*Rochefort*), Faye Dunaway (*Milady*), Jean-Pierre Cassel (*Louis XIII*), Charlton Heston (*Cardinal Richelieu*), Geraldine Chaplin (*Anne of Austria*), Simon Ward (*Buckingham*), Spike Milligan (*M. Bonancieux*), Roy Kinnear, Nicole Calfan, Sybil Danning

D: Richard Lester **SCR:** George MacDonald Fraser, from Alexander Dumas' novel **PHOTOG:** David Watkins **MUSIC:** Michel Legrand
Humorous, fast-paced adventure-thriller: French swordsmen fight for queen and country. Sequel, **The Four Musketeers** *(1975)*

The Three Musketeers
1993, (USA), Walt Disney/Buena Vista, color, 105 mins.
W: Charlie Sheen *(Aramis)*, Kiefer Sutherland *(Athos)*, Tim Curry *(Cardinal Richelieu)*, Chris O'Donnell *(D'Artagnan)*, Rebecca De Mornay *(Milady)*, Gabrielle Anwar *(Queen Anne)*, Michael Wincott *(Rochefort)*, Hugh O'Conor *(King Louis)*, Julie Delpy *(Constance)*, Paul McGann
D: Stephen Herek **SCR:** David Loughery, from Alexandre Dumas' novel **MUSIC:** Michael Kamen **SONG:** All for Love
Well-made action-thriller: Swordsmen oppose scheming cardinal

The Three Musketeers and Their Sexual Adventures
see **The Erotic Adventures of the Three Musketeers**

Three Nuts for Cinderella
1973, (Czech), color
W: Libuse Safrankova, Ralf Hoppe, Carola Braunbock, Pavel Travnicek
Standard fantasy: Magic hazelnuts help girl realize dreams

Three Strangers: SYDNEY GREENSTREET, GERALDINE FITZGERALD AND PETER LORRE

Three on a Meathook
1973, (USA), Studio One, color
W: Charles Kissinger, James Pickett, Carolyn Thompson
P: John Asman & Lee Jones **D & SCR:** William Girdler
Standard horror-thriller: Cannibalistic madman kills girls, son is blamed

Three on a Ticket
1947, (USA), PRC, b&w, 64 mins.
W: Hugh Beaumont *(Michael Shayne)*, Cheryl Walker *(Phyllis Hamilton)*, Ralph Dunn *(Rafferty)*, Paul Bryar, Louise Currie, Gavin Gordon, Noel Cravat, Charles Quigley, Douglas Fowley, Charles King, Brooks Benedict
D: Sam Newfield **SCR:** Fred Myton, from characters created by Brett Halliday **PHOTOG:** Jack Greenhalgh **MUSIC:** Emil Cadkin
Exciting "Michael Shayne" thriller: Detective encounters gang seeking plans for secret weapons

Three Silent Men
1940, (GB), Butcher, b&w, 72 mins.
W: Sebastian Shaw *(Sir James Quentin)*, Patricia Roc *(Pat Quentin)*, Derrick de Marney *(Capt. John Mellish)*, Arthur Hambling *(Ginger Brown)*, Meinhart Maur *(Karl Zaroff)*, Andre Morell *(Klein)*, Peter Gawthorne *(Gen. Bullington)*, John Turnbull *(Insp. Gill)*
D: Thomas Bentley **SCR:** Dudley Leslie & John Byrdm, from a novel by E.P. Thorne
reissued 1942 & 1947
Standard thriller: Pacifist surgeon framed for killing secret weapon's inventor

Three Steps in the Dark
1953, (GB), Corsair/ABP, b&w, 60 mins.
W: Greta Gynt *(Sophy Burgoyne)*, Hugh Sinclair *(Philip Burgoyne)*, Sarah Lawson *(Dorothy)*, Elwyn Brook-Jones *(Wilbrahim)*, Helene Cordet *(Esme)*, John Van Eyssen *(Henry Burgoyne)*, Nicholas Hannen *(Arnold Burgoyne)*, Alistair Hunter *(Insp. Forbes)*, Katie Johnson *(Mrs. Riddle)*
P: Harold Richmond **D:** Daniel Birt **SCR:** Brock Williams **STORY:** Roger East
Standard crime-thriller: Crime authoress exposes rich uncle's killer

3 Steps to the Gallows
1953, (GB), Tempean/Eros, b&w, 81 mins.
W: Scott Brady *(Gregor Stevens)*, John Blythe *(Dave Leary)*, Mary Castle *(Yvonne Durante)*, Gabrielle Brune *(Lorna Dryhurst)*, Colin Tapley *(Winslow)*, Lloyd Lamble *(James Sith)*, Ferdy Mayne *(Sartago)*, Ballard Berkeley *(Insp. Haley)*, Paul Erickson *(Larry)*
P: Robert Baker & Monty Berman **D & SCR:** John Gilling **STORY:** Paul Erickson
Standard crime-thriller: American seaman exposes jewel smugglers

The Three Stooges in Orbit
1962, (USA), Normandy/Col, b&w, 87 mins.
W: Moe Howard, Larry Fine, Joe De Rita, Emil Sitka *(Prof. Danforth)*, Carol Christensen *(Carol Danforth)*, Edson Stroll *(Capt. Andrews)*, Nestor Paiva *(The Warlord of Mars)*, Peter Dawson *(Gen. Bixby)*, Peter Brocco *(Dr. Appleby)*, Rayford Barnes *(Zogg)*, George Neise *(Og)*, Norman Leavitt *(Williams)*, Don Lamond
P: Norman Maurer **D:** Edward Bernds **SCR:** Elwood Ullman **STORY:** Norman Maurer **MUSIC:** Paul Dunlap
orig. to be titled **The Three Stooges Meet the Martians**
Standard SF-comedy: Zanies meet space-alien meanies

The Three Stooges Meet Hercules
1962, (USA), Normandy/Col, b&w, 89 mins.
W: Moe Howard, Larry Fine, Joe De Rita, Vicki Trickett *(Diane Quigley)*, Quinn Redeker *(Schuyler Davis)*, George Neise *(Ralph Dimsal/Odius)*, Samson Burke *(Hercules)*, Hal Smith *(Thesus)*, Lewis Charles *(Achilles)*, Mike McKeever *(Ajax)*, Barbara Hines *(Anita)*, Gene Roth *(The Captain)*, Emil Sitka *(Shepherd)*, John Cliff *(Ulysses)*, Marlon McKeever *(Argo)*, Terry Huntington *(Hecuba)*, Gregg Martell *(Simon)*, Diana Piper *(Helen)*, Edward Foster *(Freddie)*, Cecil Elliott *(Matron)*, Rusty Wescoatt *(Philo)*
P: Norman Maurer **D:** Edward Bernds **SCR:** Elwood Ullman **STORY:** Norman Maurer **PHOTOG:** Charles S. Welbourne **MUSIC:** Paul Dunlap
Standard comedy-fantasy: Zanies time-travel

The Three Stooges Meet the Martians
see **The Three Stooges in Orbit**

Three Strangers
1946, (USA), WB-FN, b&w, 92 mins.
W: Sydney Greenstreet *(Jerome K. Arbutney)*, Peter Lorre *(Johnny West)*, Joan Lorring *(Icy)*, Geraldine Fitzgerald *(Crystal Shackelford)*, Rosalind Ivan *(Lady Rhea Belladon)*, Alan Napier *(David Shackelford)*, Peter Whitney *(Timothy "Gabby" Delaney)*, John Alvin *(The Clerk)*, Robert Shayne *(Bertram Fallon)*, Marjorie Riordan *(Janet)*, Doris Lloyd *(Mrs. Proctor)*, Arthur Shields, Reginald Sheffield
D: Jean Negulesco **SCR:** Howard Koch & John Huston **PHOTOG:** Arthur Edeson **MUSIC:** Adolph Deutsch
Unusual thriller: Three people form odd partnership on Chinese New Year

Three Sundays to Live
1957, (GB), Danziger/UA, b&w, 71 mins.
W: Kieron Moore *(Frank Martin)*, Jane Griffiths *(Judy Allen)*, Sandra Dorne *(Ruth Chapman)*, Basil Dignam *(Davitt)*, John Stone *(The Detective)*, Hay Ayer *(Al Murray)*, John Longden *(The Warder)*
P: Edward J. & Harry Lee Danziger **D:** Ernest Morris **STORY:** Brian Clemens
Standard crime-thriller: Band leader breaks jail, seeks girl witness to prove his innocence

The Three Swords of Zorro
1963, (It-Sp), color
W: Guy Stockwell, Mikaela Wood, Gloria Milland, Antonio Prieto
Standard adventure-thriller: Masked hero reunites with long-lost son

3000 A.D.
see **Captive Women**

Three Wax Men
see **Das Wachsfigurenkabinett**

The Three Weird Sisters
1948, (GB), British Nat'l/Pathe, b&w, 83 mins.
W: Nancy Price *(Gertrude Morgan-Vaughan)*, Mary Clare *(Maud Morgan-Vaughan)*, Mary Merrall *(Isobel Morgan-Vaughan)*, Nova Pilbeam *(Claire Prentiss)*, Anthony Hulme *(David Davies)*, Raymond Lovell *(Owen Morgan-Vaughan)*, Edward Rigby *(Waldo)*, Elwyn Brook-Jones *(Thomas)*, Hugh Griffith *(Mabli Hughes)*, Marie Ault *(Beattie)*
P: Louis H. Jackson **D:** Dan Birt **SCR:** Louise Birt, David Evans & Dylan Thomas, from Charlotte Armstrong's novel *The Case of the Three Weird Sisters*
Standard thriller: Crippled sisters plot to kill rich half brother

Three Wise Fools
1946, (USA), MGM, b&w, 90 mins.
W: Margaret O'Brien, Lionel Barrymore, Lewis Stone, Edward Arnold, Thomas Mitchell, Ray Collins, Jane Darwell, Henry O'Neill, Cyd Charisse [*Rina Fairchild*], Cameron Mitchell, Charles Dingle, Harry Davenport, Raymond Hatton, Prince Denis
P: William H. Wright **D:** Edward Buzzell, from Austin Strong's play **PHOTOG:** Harold Rosson **MUSIC:** Bronislau Kaper
Standard fantasy: Irish girl tries to lift curse placed on three old men

The Three Wishes
1954, (GB), b&w, 1 reel
D: Lotte Reiniger, from story by Brothers Grimm
Animated fantasy short

Three Wishes
1995, (USA), Rysher/Savoy, color, 108 mins.
W: Patrick Swayze, Mary Elizabeth Mastrantonio, Joseph Mazzello, Seth Mumy, Michael O'Keefe, David Marshall Grant, John Diehl, Jay O. Sanders, Diane

T

Venora

D: Martha Coolidge   **SCR:** Elizabeth Anderson   **STORY:** Clifford & Ellen Green   **PHOTOG:** Johnny E. Jensen   **VS-FX SPRVSR:** Phil Tippett   **MUSIC:** Cynthia Millar

blurb: "When you really believe, magic can find you"
Unusual romance-fantasy: Widowed mother meets mystery man

The Three Worlds of Gulliver
1960, (GB), Morningside/Col, color, 98 mins.
W: Kerwin Mathews (*Lemuel Gulliver*), Jo Morrow (*Gwendolyn*), June Thorburn (*Elizabeth*), Lee Patterson (*Reldresal*), Basil Sydney (*The Emperor of Lilliput*), Sherry Alberoni (*Glumdalclitch*), Gregoire Aslan (*King Brobdingnag*), Martin Benson (*Flimnap*), Charles Lloyd-Pack (*Makovan*), Mary Ellis (*Queen Brobdingnag*), Peter Bull (*Lord Bermogg*), Marian Spencer, Alec Mango
P: Charles H. Schneer   **D:** Jack Sher   **SCR:** Arthur Ross & Jack Sher, from Jonathan Swift's satire *Gulliver's Travels*   **PHOTOG:** Wilkie Cooper   **SPCL-FX:** Ray Harryhausen   **MUSIC:** Bernard Herrmann
Standard fantasy: Shipwrecked doctor's adventures in fantastic lands

Thrill
1996, (USA), FAM-TV, color, 95 mins.
W: Antonio Sabato Jr. (*Jack*), Stepfanie Kramer (*Theresa*), Ted Marcoux, Christine Harnos, Larry Joshua, Bill Cobbs
D: Sam Pillsbury   **TELEPLAY:** Betty Goldberg, from Robert Byrne's novel   **PHOTOG:** Alan Caso   **MUSIC:** Michael Hoenig
TVM, minor thriller

A Thrilling Story
1910, (GB), Cricks & Martin, b&w, 330 ft. (100.6m)
D: Dave Aylott
Standard fantasy: Maid dreams she is Puritan saved by Cavalier

The Thrill Killers
1964, (USA), Fairway-Int'l, color, 72 mins.
W: Cash Flagg [Ray Dennis Steckler], Liz Renay, George Morgan, Erina Enyo, Atlas King, Lonnie Lord, Brick Bardo, Gary Kent, Carolyn Brandt, Titus Moede, Ron Haydock
P: George J. Morgan   **D:** Ray Dennis Steckler   **SCR:** Ray Dennis Steckler & Gene Pollock
reissued (1972) as **Maniacs on the Loose**, *A.k.a.* **The Monsters are Loose**
Standard horror-satire: Asylum inmates escape, create havoc

Throne of Blood
1957, (Jap), Toho/Brandon Films, b&w, 105 mins.
W: Toshiro Mifune (*Washizu*), Isuzu Yamada (*Asaji*), Takashi Shimura (*Odagura*), Minoru Chiaki, Akira Kubo
D: Akira Kurosawa   **SCR:** Hideo Oguni, Shinobu Hashimoto, Riyuzo Kikushima & Akira Kurosawa, based on Shakespeare's play *Macbeth*   **MUSIC:** Masaru Sato
A.k.a. **Cobweb Castle** *and* **The Castle of the Spider's Web**
Classic thriller: Samurai saga of ambitious warlord

Through a Glass Darkly (Sasom I En Spegel)
1961, (Swed), Svensk Filmindustri/Janus, b&w, 91 mins.
W: Gunnar Bjornstrand (*David, the Father*), Harriet Andersson (*Karin, the Daughter*), Max von Sydow (*Martin, the Husband*), Lars Passgard (*Minus, the Brother*)
D: Ingmar Bergman   **PHOTOG:** Sven Nykvist   **MUSIC:** Johann Sebastian Bach
Classic melodrama: Wife goes mad

Through Fire to Fortune
1911, (GB), Kineto, b&w, 630 ft. (192m)
D: Theo Bouwmeester
Standard adventure-thriller: Shipwrecked elopers find treasure cave, are rescued in time to save father from poverty

Through Naked Eyes
1983, (USA), Fries Entertainment, color, 95 mins.
W: David Soul, Pam Dawber, Fionnuala Flanagan, Rod McCary, William Schallert, Dick Anthony Williams, Gerald Castillo
D: John Llewellyn Moxey   **TELEPLAY:** Jeffrey Bloom   **PHOTOG:** Jack L. Richards   **MUSIC:** Gil Melle
TVM, standard thriller (with echoes of **Rear Window***): Murders in highrise*

Through Stormy Water
1920, (GB), Goddard Films/Cinematography, b&w, 6,000 ft. (1828.8m)
W: Eileen Bellamy (*Eileen Donovan*), George Keene (*Frank Evans*), Harry J. Worth (*The Employer*), Fred Morgan (*The Manager*)
D & STORY: Frederick Goddard
Standard crime-thriller: Amnesia victim cleared when hypnotist reveals real thief

Through the Ages
1914, (GB), Martin/DFSA, b&w, 965 ft. (294.1m)
W: Ernie Westo, Bob Reed, Sid Butler
D: Dave Aylott
Standard comedy-fantasy: Knocked-out boxer dreams of fighting in Stone Age

Through the Clouds
1913, (GB), B&C/Ruffells, b&w, 3,158 ft. (962.6m)

W: Ernest G. Batley (*Halifax Hilliard*), Marie Pickering (*Kitty Hilliard*), George Foley (*Lord Denison*), Harry Lorraine (*Silk Hat Harry*), Jack Jarman (*Rudolf Berkman*)
WRIT & D: Charles Weston
Standard adventure-thriller: Girl flies airplane, saves detective father from jewel thief's balloon

Through the Dark
1924, (USA), Goldwyn, b&w, 8 reels
W: Colleen Moore (*Mary McGinn*), Forrest Stanley (*Boston Blackie*), Margaret Seddon (*Mother McGinn*), George Cooper (*Travel*), Hobart Bosworth (*The Warden*), Edward Phillips (*The "Glad Rags" Kid*), Wade Boteler (*Det. O'Leary*), Tom Bates (*Sandy*), Carmelita Geraghty (*Ethel Grayson*)
D: George Hill   **SCR:** Frances Marion, from characters created by Jack Boyle   **PHOTOG:** L. William O'Connell & Allen Siegler
Standard "Boston Blackie" thriller: Girl helps rogue elude law

Through the Flames
1912, (GB), John Bull Films/Cosmo, b&w, 1,250 ft. (380m)
W: Dorothy Batley (*Peggy*), Ernest G. Batley
D: Ethyle Batley   **STORY:** Ernest G. Batley
Standard crime-thriller: Child traverses telephone wire when cousin sets house afire

Through the Magic Pyramid
1981, (USA), Major H/NBC-TV, color
W: Chris Barnes (*Bobby Tuttle*), Hans Conried (*Ay*), Olivia Barash (*Baket*), Vic Tayback (*Horemheb*), Jo Anne Worley (*Mutnedjmet*), Betty Beaird (*Eleanor Tuttle*), Gino Conforti (*Hotep*), Elaine Giftos (*Nefertiti*), James Hampton (*Sam Tuttle*), Eric Greene (*Tut*), Robbie Rist (*Bonkers*), Kario Salem (*Akhenaten*), Mel Berger, Mary Carver, Hoke Howell, Kurt Christian, Woodrow Chambliss, David Darlow, Richard Moll, Ralph Dougherty, Mike Johnson, Angelo Lamonea, Len Lesser, Daniel Leon, Sydney Penny, Linda Zernecke
D: Ron Howard   **TELEPLAY:** Rance Howard & Herbert J. Wright   **PHOTOG:** Gary Graver   **MUSIC:** Joe Renzetti
edited-down version titled **Tut and Tuttle**
2-part TVM, minor adventure-fantasy: Boy time-travels to ancient Egypt

Thumbelina
1955, (GB), b&w, 1 reel
D: Lotte Reiniger, from Hans Christian Andersen's fairy tale
Animated fantasy short

Thumbelina
1994, (USA), color, 89 mins.
VOICES: Jodi Benson, Gary Imhoff, Gino Conforti, Barbara Cook, Will Ryan,

Thunderball: SEAN CONNERY AND BOB SIMMONS

Kenneth Mars, Charo, June Foray, Gilbert Gottfried, John Hurt, Carol Channing

D: Don Bluth & Gary Goldman **SCR:** Don Bluth, from Hans Christian Andersen's fairy tale **MUSIC:** William Ross, Barry Manilow, Jack Feldman & Bruce Sussman **SONG:** *Marry the Mole*, by Barry Manilow
Standard animated fantasy: Prince loves diminutive fairy

Thunderball
1965, (GB), Eon/UA, color, 132 mins.
W: Sean Connery (*James Bond*), Claudine Auger (*Domino*), Adolfo Celi (*Largo*), Luciana Paluzzi (*Fiona*), Bernard Lee ("*M*"), Rik Van Nutter (*Felix Leiter*), Lois Maxwell (*Miss Moneypenny*), Martine Beswick (*Paula*), Molly Peters (*The Masseuse*), Desmond Llewelyn ("*Q*"), Guy Doleman (*Count Lippe*), Michael Brennan (*Janni*), Patrick Holt (*Dawson*), Roland Culver (*The Foreign Sec'y*), Paul Stassino (*Palazzi*), Earl Cameron (*Pinder*), Edward Underdown (*Air Vice Marshal*), Reginald Beckwith (*Kenniston*), Philip Locke, Rose Alba
P: Kevin McClory **D:** Terence Young **SCR:** Richard Maibaum & John Hopkins, from orig. story by Kevin McClory, Jack Whittingham & Ian Fleming **PHOTOG:** Ted Moore **SPCL-FX:** John Stears **MUSIC:** John Barry **TITLE SUNG BY:** Tom Jones
Exciting thriller: Master criminal uses atomic devices to blackmail Great Britain and USA. cf. Never Say Never Again

Thunderbirds are Go
1966, (GB), Animated Pictures/UA, color, 94 mins.
VOICES: Sylvia Anderson (*Lady Penelope*), Ray Barrett (*John Tracy/The Controller*), Peter Dyneley (*Jeff Tracy*), David Graham (*Gordon Tracy/ Parker/Brains*), Shane Rimmer (*Scott Tracy*), Jeremy Wilkin (*Virgil Tracy/The President*), Matt Zimmerman (*Alan Tracy/The Messenger*), Bob Monkhouse (*Brad Newman*), Neil McCallum (*Dr. Pierce*), Charles Tingwell (*Dr. Grant/PRO/The Man*)
WRIT & P: Gerry & Sylvia Anderson **D:** David Lane
Juvenile SF-fantasy (enacted by puppets): Mars exploration ship saved from crashing

Thunderbirds in Outer Space
1981, (GB), color
SPCL-FX: Derek Meddings & Brian Johnson
Juvenile SF-fantasy (enacted by puppets): Daring rescuers try to halt runaway rocketship

Thunderbird 6
1968, (GB), A.P. Films-Century 21/UA, color, 90 mins.
VOICES: Peter Dyneley (*Jeff Tracy*), Christine Finn (*TinTin*), Keith Alexander (*Black Phantom/John Tracy*), Jeremy Wilkin (*Virgil Tracy/Hogarth*), Gary Files (*Foster/Lane*), John Carson (*Foster 2*), Sylvia Anderson (*Lady Penelope*), David Graham (*Brains/Gordon/Parker*), Matt Zimmerman (*Alan Tracy*), Geoffrey Keen (*The Controller*), Shane Rimmer (*Scott Tracy*)
WRIT & P: Gerry & Sylvia Anderson **D:** David Lane
Standard juvenile SF-fantasy (enacted by puppets): Rescue organization saves new skyship from pirate

Thunderbirds to the Rescue
1980, (GB), color, 90 mins.
Juvenile SF-fantasy (enacted by puppets): Rescue at sea

Thunder over Sangoland
1955, (USA), Arrow/Lippert, b&w, 73 mins.
W: Jon Hall, Marjorie Lord
Minor adventure-thriller. From the "Ramar of the Jungle" TV series

Thunder Over Tangier
see Man from Tangier

Thunder Rock
1942, (GB), Charter/MGM, b&w, 112 mins.
W: Michael Redgrave (*David Charleston*), Barbara Mullen (*Ellen Kirby*), James Mason (*Streeter*), Lilli Palmer (*Melanie Kurtz*), Finlay Currie (*Capt. Joshua*), Frederick Valk (*Dr. Kurtz*), Sybilla Binder (*Anne-Marie*), Miles Malleson (*The Chairman*), Frederick Cooper (*Ted Briggs*), Jean Sheperd (*Mrs. Briggs*), Barry Morse (*Robert*), George Carney (*Harry*), A.E. Matthews (*Kirby*), Olive Sloane (*The Director*)
P: John Boulting **D:** Roy Boulting **SCR:** Wolfgang Wilhelm, Jeffrey Dell, Bernard Miles & Anna Reiner, from a play by Robert Ardrey **PHOTOG:** Mutz Greenbaum [Max Greene] **MUSIC:** Hans May
reissued 1947
Standard fantasy: World-weary journalist retires to Canadian lighthouse, is haunted by ghosts of drowned immigrants

Thursday the 12th
see Pandemonium

THX 1138
1971, (USA), American Zoetrope/WB, color, 95 mins.
W: Robert Duvall (*THX 1138*), Maggie McOmie (*LUH 3417*), Don Pedro Colley (*SRT*), Donald Pleasence (*SEN 5241*), Sid Haig, Ian Wolfe, Marshall Efron, Claudette Bessing, Irene Forrest, David Ogden Stiers, John Pearce
D: George Lucas Jr. **SCR:** George Lucas Jr. & Walter Murch **PHOTOG:** Dave Meyers & Albert Kihn **MUSIC:** Lalo Schifrin
Classic SF-thriller (expanded remake of celebrated short 'THX 1138 4EB'): Intriguing vision of subterranean life in 25th century

THX 1138 4EB
1968, (USA), George Lucas Jr., color, 15 mins.
WRIT & D: George Lucas Jr.
Imaginative amateur film: Man flees computer-dominated future society

Thy Neighbor's Wife
1953, (USA), 20th-Fox, b&w, 77 mins.
W: Hugo Haas, Cleo Moore, Ken Carlton, Katherine Hughes
WRIT, P & D: Hugo Haas, based on novellete *The Peasant Judge* by Oskar Jellinek
Minor melodrama: Ruthless 19th-century judge hangs for murder of young wife's lover

Tickled Pink
see Magic Spectacles

Ticks
1993, (USA), color, 83 mins.
W: Rosalind Allen, Ami Dolenz, Peter Scolari
Minor SF-thriller: Campers encounter mutated insects

Tidal Wave
see The Submersion of Japan

Tidal Wave: No Escape
1997, (USA), ABC-TV, color, 95 mins.
W: Corbin Bernsen, Julianne Phillips, Harve Presnell (*Dr. Stanley Schiff*), Gregg Henry (*Edgar Purcell*), Larry Brandenburg (*Frank Brisick*), Lawrence-Hilton Jacobs (*Marlan Clark*), Aki Aleong (*Dr Agamo*), Gene Wolande (*Jules Benard*), Lance Wilson-White (*Chick*)
D: George Miller
TVM, standard disaster-thriller: Man-made tidal waves threaten

Tiempo de Morir (Time to Die)
1985, (Colomb-Cuba), color, 98 mins.
W: Gustavo Angarita, Sebastian Ospina, Jorge Emilio Salazar, Maria Eugenia Davis, Lina Botero
D: Jorge Ali Triana **SCR:** Gabriel Garcia Marquez
Standard thriller: Ex-convict target of assassination

Tiffany Jones
1973, (GB), Pete Walker/Heritage/Hemdale, color, 90 mins.
W: Anouska Hempel (*Tiffany Jones*), Ray Brooks (*Guy*), Susan Sheers (*Jo*), Damien Thomas (*Salvador*), Eric Pohlmann (*Pres. Jabal*), Richard Marner (*Vorjak*), Ivor Salter (*Karatik*), Lynda Baron (*Anna Karekin*), Martin Benson (*Petcek*), Alan Curtis (*Marocek*), John Clive (*Stefan*), Geoffrey Hughes (*Georg*), Bill Kerr (*Morton*), Nick Zaran (*Anton*), Martin Wyldeck (*Brodsky*), Walter Randall (*Jan*), Kim Alexander (*Harry Wheeler*), Tony Sympson (*The Man*), Pearl Hackney (*The Demonstrator*), Tom Mennard (*The Board of Trade Man*), David Hamilton
P & D: Pete Walker **SCR:** Alfred Shaughnessy, from a comic strip by Pat Tourret & Jenny Butterworth **PHOTOG:** Peter Jessop **MUSIC:** Cyril Ornadel
Standard thriller: Model helps overthrow foreign president

Tiger by the Tail
1955, (GB), Tempean/Eros, b&w, 85 mins.
W: Larry Parks (*John Desmond*), Constance Smith (*Jane Claymore*), Lisa Daniely (*Anna Ray*), Cyril Chamberlain (*Foster*), Donald Stewart (*Macaulay*), Thora Hird (*Mary*), Joan Heal (*Annabelle*), Alexander Gauge (*Fitzgerald*), Ronan O'Casey (*Mick*), Marie Bryant (*Melodie*)
P: Robert Baker & Monty Berman **D:** John Gilling **SCR:** Willis Goldbeck & John Gilling, from John Mair's novel
USA retitle: Crossup
Standard crime-thriller: Counterfeiters seek dead girl's diary, kidnap American reporter

Tiger Claws
1992, (USA), HBO-TV, color, 93 mins.
W: Cynthia Rothrock, Jalal Mehri
Made-for-Cable, standard thriller: Killer claws victims to death

Tiger in the Smoke
1956, (GB), Rank/RFD, b&w, 94 mins.
W: Donald Sinden (*Geoffrey Levett*), Muriel Pavlow (*Meg Elkin*), Tony Wright (*Jack Havoc*), Bernard Miles (*Tiddy Doll*), Alec Clunes (*Oates*), Laurence Naismith (*Canon Avril*), Christopher Rhodes (*Insp. Luke*), Charles Victor (*Will Talisman*), Thomas Heathcote (*Rolly Gripper*), Sam Kydd (*Tom Gripper*), Beatrice Varley (*Mrs. Cash*), Kenneth Griffith (*Crutches*)
P: Leslie Parkyn **D:** Roy Baker **SCR:** Athony Pelissier, from a novel by Margery Allingham **PHOTOG:** Geoffrey Unsworth
Standard crime-thriller: Escaped convict hunts treasure

Tiger Man
see The Lady and the Monster

Tiger of Bengal
see Journey to the Lost City

T

The Tiger of Eschnapur
see *Journey to the Lost City*

The Tiger of San Pedro
1921, (GB), Stoll, b&w, 2,080 ft. (634m)
<u>W</u>: Eille Norwood *(Sherlock Holmes)*, Hubert Willis *(Dr. John Watson)*, Lewis Gilbert *(Murillo)*, Arthur Walcott *(Garcia)*, George Harrington *(Scott Eccles)*, Mme. d'Esterre *(Mrs. Hudson)*, Arthur Bell *(Insp. Lestrade)*
<u>D</u>: Maurice Elvey   <u>SCR</u>: William J. Elliott, from the writings of Sir Arthur Conan Doyle
Standard crime-thriller (episode in "Adventures of Sherlock Holmes" series)

Tiger of the Seven Seas
1962, (It-Fr), color, 90 mins.
<u>W</u>: Gianna Maria Canale, Anthony Steel, Grazia Maria Spina, Ernesto Calindri
<u>D</u>: Luigi Capuano
*Standard action-thriler (sequel to **Queen of the Pirates**): Pirate queen inspires romance and swordfighting*

The Tiger Woman
1945, (USA), Rep, b&w, 57 mins.
<u>W</u>: Adele Mara, Kane Richmond
Standard adventure-thriller

Tigris
1913, (It), Silvio Villa/Itala Pictures, b&w
Standard thriller: Master criminal plots

Till Dawn Do Us Part
see *Straight On Till Morning*

Till Death
1978, (USA), color, 89 mins.
<u>W</u>: Keith Atkinson, Belinda Balaski, Marshall Reed, Jonathan Hale, Bert Freed
<u>D</u>: Walter Stocker
Modest thriller: "Murdered" woman found alive in crypt

Till Death Do Us Part
see *The Blood Spattered Bride*

Till the End of the Night
1994, (USA), color
<u>W</u>: Scott Valentine
Minor melodrama

Time After Time
1979, (USA), Orion/WB, color, 112 mins.
<u>W</u>: Malcolm McDowell *(H.G. Wells)*, David Warner *(Dr. John Leslie Stevenson/"Jack the Ripper")*, Mary Steenburgen *(Amy Robbins)*, Charles Cioffi *(Lt. Mitchell)*, Andonia Katsaros *(Mrs. Turner)*, Kent Williams *(The Assistant)*, Geraldine Baron *(Carol)*, Joseph Maher *(Adams)*, Patti D'Arbanville *(Shirley)*, James Garrett *(Edwards)*, Keith McConnell *(Harding)*, Leo Lewis *(Richardson)*, Byron Webster *(McKay)*, Karin Mary Shea *(Jenny)*, Laurie Main *(Insp. Gregson)*, Bob Shaw, Michael Evans, Ray Reinhardt, Stu Klitsner, Hilda Haynes, Nicholas Shields, Gene Hartline, Clement St. George, Read Morgan, Shirley Marchant, Larry J. Blake, Antonie Becker, Mike Gainey,

Timecop: JEAN-CLAUDE VAN DAMME

Jim Haynic, Wayne Storm, John Colton, James Cranna, Corey Feldman, Earl Nicols, Bill Bradley, Shelley Hack, Clete Roberts, Rita Conde, Gail Hyatt
<u>P</u>: Herb Jaffe   <u>D & SCR</u>: Nicholas Meyer   <u>STORY</u>: Steve Hayes & Karl Alexander, from Karl Alexander's novel *The Time Traveler*   <u>PHOTOG</u>: Paul Lohmann   <u>MUSIC</u>: Miklos Rozsa
"A time-of-your-life movie... A film that is refreshingly different"—Rex Reed, Vogue
"A wonderful adventure, richly veined with humor and give added depth by its love story"—Omni
"MAGICAL! An adult's movie with the shimmer of a new toy"— New York Times
"...witty, scary, and also romantic. Meyer's direction is lucid and uncluttered, Paul Lohmann's foggy London photography and crystal-clear San Francisco photography heighten the film's mood, and Donn Cambern has edited with a sure hand. The casting is particularly felicitous, with Malcolm McDowell's H.G. Wells being frighteningly accurate"—After Dark
Superior SF-thriller: H.G. Wells time-travels to capture Jack the Ripper

Time at the Top
1999, (USA), SHO-TV, color, 100 mins.
<u>W</u>: Elisha Cuthbert, Gabrielle Boni, Timothy Busfield
Made-for-Cable, standard fantasy: Girl time-travels to 1881

Time Bandits
1981, (GB), Handmade/Avco Embassy, color, 114 mins.
<u>W</u>: John Cleese *(Robin Hood)*, Sean Connery *(Agamemnon)*, Sir Ralph Richardson *(The Supreme Being)*, Shelley Duvall *(Pansy)*, Michael Palin *(Vincent)*, Peter Vaughan *(The Ogre)*, Katherine Helmond *(Mrs. Ogre)*, Ian Holm *(Napoleon)*, David Warner *(The Evil Genius)*, Craig Warnock *(Kevin)*, Malcolm Dixon *(Strutter)*, Kenny Baker *(Fidget)*, David Rappaport *(Randall)*, Jack Purvis *(Wally)*, Mike Edmonds *(Og)*, Tiny Ross *(Vermin)*, Jim Broadbent *(Compere)*, David Daker *(Father)*, Sheila Fearn *(Mother)*, Myrtle Devenish *(Beryl)*, Preston Lockwood *(Neguy)*, John Hughman *(Great Rumbozo)*, Jerold Wells *(Benson)*, Martin Carroll *(Baxi Brazilia)*
<u>P & D</u>: Terry Gilliam   <u>SCR</u>: Terry Gilliam & Michael Palin   <u>PHOTOG</u>: Peter Biziou   <u>MUSIC</u>: Mike Moran   <u>SONGS</u>: George Harrison
Unusual fantasy: Boy time-travels with larcenous dwarves

Time Bomb
1953, (GB), MGM British, b&w, 72 mins.
<u>W</u>: Glenn Ford *(Peter Lyncourt)*, Anne Vernon *(Janine Lyncourt)*, Maurice Denham *(Jim Warrilow)*, Harcourt Williams *(The Vicar)*, Victor Maddern *(The Saboteur)*, Campbell Singer *(Insp. Branson)*, Harold Warrender *(Sir Evelyn Jordan)*, John Horsley *(PC Charles Baron)*, Bill Fraser *(PC Reed)*, Herbert C. Walton *(Old Charlie)*, Ada Reeve *(The Old Lady)*, Frank Atkinson *(The Guard)*, Ernest Butcher *(Martindale)*
<u>P</u>: Richard Goldstone   <u>D</u>: Ted Tetzlaff   <u>SCR</u>: Kem Bennett, from his novel *Attention*   <u>PHOTOG</u>: Frederick A. Young
USA retitle, ***Terror on a Train***
Tense thriller: Engineer must dismantle time bomb planted in trainload of naval mines

Time Chasers
1995, (USA), color, 90 mins.
<u>W</u>: Matthew Burch, Bonnie Pritchard, Peter Harrington
<u>D</u>: David Giancola
Standard SF-thriller: Time-travel device lays waste the future

Timecop
1994, (USA), Largo-JVC/Univ, color, 99 mins.
<u>W</u>: Jean-Claude Van Damme *(Walker)*, Mia Sara *(Melissa)*, Ron Silver *(McComb)*, Bruce McGill *(Matuzak)*, Brad Loree *(Reyes)*, Gloria Reuben *(Fielding)*, Scott Bellis *(Ricky)*, Shane Kelly *(Rollerblades)*, Jason Schombing *(Atwood)*, Scott Lawrence *(Spota)*, Kenneth Welsh *(Utley)*, Brent Woolsey *(Shotgun)*, Richard Faraci *(Cole)*, Steve Lambert *(Lansing)*, Jacob Rupp *(Palmer)*, Kevin McNulty *(Parker)*, J.J. Makaro *(McComb Guard #1)*, Yves Cameron *(McComb Guard #2)*, David Jacox *(McComb Man #1)*, Mike Mitchell *(McComb Man #2)*, Sean O'Byrne *(Aide Lawrence)*, Gabrielle Rose *(Judge Marshall)*, Malcolm Stewart *(Nelson)*, Alfonso Quijada *(The Photographer)*, Duncan Fraser *(The Irish Cop)*, Yvette Ferguson *(The Atwood Sec'y)*, Glen Roald *(The Doorman)*, Theodore Thomas *(Pete)*, Lon Katzmann *(Handlebar)*, Tony Morelli *(Tweed)*, Nick Hyams *(The Newsboy)*, Kelli Fox *(The Aide)*, Pamela Martin *(The TV Commentator)*, Tom McBeath *(The T.E.C. Technician)*, Veena Sood *(The Nurse)*, Frank Cassini *(The T.E.C. Agent)*, Kim Kondrashoff *(Security Agent #1)*, Cole Bradsen *(The Boy)*, James Lew *(Knife #1)*, Charles Andre *(Knife #2)*, Scott Nicholson *(Guard #1)*, Ernie Jackson *(Guard #2)*, Tom Eirikson *(Guard #3)*, Laura Murdoch *(The Virtual Reality Woman)*, Ian Tracey *(The Soldier)*, Dalton Fisher *(The Washington Cop)*, Callum Keith Rennie *(The Stranger)*, Tom Glass *(The Wagon Driver)*, Doris Blomgren *(The Old Woman)*
<u>D & PHOTOG</u>: Peter Hyams   <u>SCR</u>: Mark Verheiden   <u>STORY</u>: Mike Richardson & Mark Verheiden, based on their comic-book series   <u>SPCL-FX</u>: Woody Lawhon, Don B. Leask, Clay Scheirer, Joel Shist, Michael Steffe & Tim Storvik   <u>SPCL-FX CO-ORD</u>: John Thomas   <u>MUSIC</u>: Mark Isham   <u>MUSIC SPRVSR</u>: Karyn Rachtman
Standard SF-thriller: Gov't agent prevents tampering with space-time continuum

Time Flies
1913, (GB), Cricks & Martin, b&w, 276 ft. (84.1m)

<u>W:</u> Edwin J. Collins (*Prof. Collins*)
<u>D:</u> Edwin J. Collins
Standard fantasy: Policeman pursues vanishing tramp

Time Flies
1944, (GB), Gainsborough/GFD, b&w, 88 mins.
<u>W:</u> Tommy Handley (*Tommy*), Evelyn Dall (*Susie Barton*), John Salew (*William Shakespeare*), George Moon (*Bill Barton*), Felix Aylmer (*Prof. MacAndrew*), Moore Marriott (*The Soothsayer*), Graham Moffatt (*The Soothsayer's Nephew*), Leslie Bradley (*Walter Raleigh*), Olga Lindo (*Queen Elizabeth I*), Roy Emerton (*Capt. John Smith*), Iris Lang (*Princess Pocahontas*), Stephane Grappelly (*The Troubadour*), Lloyd Pearson (*The Tavern Keeper*), Robert Atkins (*The Town Crier*)

<u>P:</u> Edward Black   <u>D:</u> Walter Forde   <u>STORY:</u> Howard Irving Young, J.O.C. Orton & Ted Kavanagh
Standard comedy-fantasy: Time machine lets tricksters visit medieval days

Time Flyer
1985, (USA), Three Blind Mice/Walt Disney, color, 95 mins.
<u>W:</u> Peter Coyote (*Max Knickerbocker*), Huckleberry Fox (*Jonathan Knicks*), Art Carney (*Henry Coogan*), Dennis Lipscomb (*Finch*), Joe Flood (*Sgt. Leary*), Frank Simons (*Young Henry Coogan*), Mittie Smith (*Helen Knickerbocker*), Stu Klitsner (*Mr. Knicks*), Morgan Upton (*The Police Captain*), Bennett Gale (*Dooley*), Cyril Clayton (*The Drunk*), Gretchen Grant (*Mrs. Knicks*), Charles Adams (*The Newsstand Man*), Howard Goodwin, Doug Morrison, Lew Horn,

The Time Of Their Lives: Lou Costello and Marjorie Richards

Hugh Gillin, Tommy Rosenkranz, Edith Fields, Crane Jackson, Ted Sawyer, Jimmy Powell, Jerry Landis, Jo Mohrbach, Eric Barnes, Stephen Prior, Art Scholl, Scott Devenney, Buck McDancer, Sandra Gimpel, Alan Gibb
<u>WRIT & D:</u> Mark Rosman   <u>PHOTOG:</u> Hiro Narita   <u>MUSIC:</u> David Shire
A.k.a. **The Blue Yonder**
Made-for-Cable, standard SF-fantasy: Boy time-travels to prevent grandfather's death

The Time Guardian
1989, (Austral), Hemdale, color, 91 mins.
<u>W:</u> Tom Burlinson (*Ballard*), Nikki Coghill (*Annie*), Dean Stockwell (*The Boss*), Carrie Fisher (*Petra*), Peter Merrill (*Zuryk*), Tim Robertson (*McCarthy*), Jim Holt (*Rafferty*), Peter Merrill, Wan Thye Liew, Damon Sanders
<u>D:</u> Brian Hannant   <u>SCR:</u> John Baxter & Brian Hannant   <u>PHOTOG:</u> Geoff Burton   <u>MUSIC:</u> Allan Zavod
Minor SF-adventure: Androids threaten survivors of neutron wars

Time is My Enemy
1954, (GB), Vandyke/IFD, b&w, 64 mins.
<u>W:</u> Dennis Price (*Martin Radley*), Renee Asherson (*Barbara Everton*), Susan Shaw (*Evelyn Gower*), Patrick Barr (*John Everton*), Bonar Colleano (*The Roommate*), Alfie Bass (*Ernie Gordon*), Duncan Lamont (*Charles Wayne*), William Franklyn (*Peter Thompson*), Brenda Hogan (*Diana*), Agnes Lauchlan (*Aunt Laura*)
<u>P:</u> Roger Proudlock   <u>D:</u> Don Chaffey   <u>SCR:</u> Allan Mackinnon, from Ella Adkins' play *Second Chance*
Standard thriller: Murder results when criminal tries to blackmail former wife

Time is Terror
see Flesh Feast

The Time Killer
see The Night Strangler

Timelock
1998, (USA), SCI-TV, color, 95 mins.
<u>W:</u> Maryam D'Abo, Arye Gross, Jeffrey Meek, Jeff Speakman
Made-for-Cable, standard SF-thriller: Woman spaceship captain trapped on penal asteroid

The Time Machine
1960, (USA), Galaxy/MGM, color, 103 mins.
<u>W:</u> Rod Taylor (*George, the Time Traveler*), Yvette Mimieux (*Weena*), Alan Young

(*David Filby/James Filby*), Sebastian Cabot (*Dr. Hillyer*), Doris Lloyd (*Mrs. Watchett*), Tom Helmore (*Bridewell*), Whit Bissell (*Walter*)
<u>P & D:</u> George Pal   <u>SCR:</u> David Duncan, from H.G. Wells' novel   <u>PHOTOG:</u> Paul C. Vogel   <u>OSCAR-WINNING SPCL-FX:</u> Gene Warren, Wah Chang, Tim Barr & Bill Brace   <u>MUSIC:</u> Russell Garcia
Classic SF-adventure: Victorian time-travels to future

The Time Machine
1978, Classics Illustrated/NBC-TV, color, 100 mins.
<u>W:</u> John Beck (*Neil Perry*), Priscilla Barnes (*Weena*), John Hansen (*Ariel*), Rosemary De Camp (*Agnes*), Andrew Duggan (*Bean*), Parley Baer (*Henry Haverson*), Whit Bissell (*Ralph Branly*), R.G. Armstrong (*The General*), John Doucette (*The Sheriff*), Bill Zuckert (*Charlie*), Jack Kruschen, Michael Ruud, John Zaremba, Peg Stewart, Hyde Clayton
<u>D:</u> Henning Schellerup   <u>TELEPLAY:</u> Wallace Bennett, loosely based on H.G. Wells' novel   <u>SPCL-FX:</u> Harry Woolman   <u>MUSIC:</u> John Cacavas
TVM, minor SF-adventure: Man time-travels

Timemaster
1995, (USA), color, 100 mins.
<u>W:</u> Pat Morita, Jesse Cameron-Glickenhaus, Joanna Pacula, Michael Dorn, Duncan Regehr, Michelle Williams
<u>D & SCR:</u> James Glickenhaus
Made-for-Video, standard SF-adventure: Era-hopping expedition

Time of the Apes
1987, (Jap), color, 98 mins.
<u>W:</u> Reiko Tokunaga
Minor SF-thriller: Three humans find simian society of future

Time of the Beast
see Mutator

The Time of Their Lives
1946, (USA), Univ, b&w, 82 mins.
<u>W:</u> Bud Abbott, Lou Costello, Marjorie Reynolds, John Shelton, Gale Sondergaard, Binnie Barnes, Robert Barrat, Lynn Baggett, Jess Barker, Ann Gillis, Donald MacBride, William Hall, Rex Lease
<u>D:</u> Charles Barton   <u>SCR:</u> Val Burton, Walter DeLeon & Bradford Ropes   <u>PHOTOG:</u> Charles Van Enger   <u>SPCL-PHOTOG:</u> D.S. Horsley & Jerome Ash   <u>MUSIC:</u> Milton Rosen
A.k.a. **The Ghost Steps Out**
Standard comedy-fantasy: Ghost from Revolutionary Period tries to clear maligned name

Time Raiders
see Warriors of the Apocalypse

Timerider
1982, (USA), Michael Nesmith/Jensen Farley Pictures, color, 93 mins.
<u>W:</u> Fred Ward (*Lyle Swann*), Belinda Bauer (*Claire Cygne*), Ed Lauter (*The Padre*), Peter Coyote (*Reese*), Richard Masur (*Claude*), Tracey Walter (*Carl Dorsett*), L.Q. Jones (*Ben Potter*), Chris Mulkey (*Daniels*), Macon McCalman (*Dr. Sam*), Laurie O'Brien (*Terry*), Jonathan Bahnks (*Jesse*), William Dear (*The 3rd Technician*)
<u>WRIT & D:</u> William Dear & Michael Nesmith   <u>PHOTOG:</u> Larry Pizer   <u>MUSIC:</u> Michael Nesmith
Minor SF-adventure: Motorcycle racer time-travels to 1875

Time Runner
1992, (USA), Cinemax, color, 90 mins.
<u>W:</u> Mark Hamill, Brion James, Rae Dawn Chong, Marc Baur, Gordon Tipple, Allen Forget, Barry W. Levy
<u>D:</u> Michael Mazo   <u>PHOTOG:</u> Danny Nowak   <u>MUSIC:</u> Braun Farnon & Robert Smart
Made-for-Cable, standard SF-adventure: 21st-century space-station captain travels back in time to 1990's

Timeslip
1955, (GB), Todon/AA, b&w, 93 mins.
<u>W:</u> Gene Nelson (*Mike Delaney*), Faith Domergue (*Jill Friday*), Joseph Tomelty (*Insp. Cleary*), Vic Perry (*Vasquo*), Donald Gray (*Maitland*), Peter Arne (*Stephen Maitland*), Launce Maraschal (*The Editor*), Charles Hawtrey (*Scruffy*), Martin Wyldeck (*Dr. Preston*), Carl Jaffe (*Dr. Marks*), Barry MacKay (*Insp. Hammond*), Paul Hardtmuth
<u>P:</u> Alec C. Snowden   <u>D & SCR:</u> Ken Hughes, from Charles Eric Maine's play *The Isotope Man*
USA retitle, **The Atomic Man**
Standard SF-thriller: Reporter investigates nefarious scientist

Timestalkers
1987, (USA), Fries Entertainment/CBS-TV, color, 95 mins.
<u>W:</u> William Devane, Lauren Hutton, Klaus Kinski (*Cole*), John Ratzenberger (*Gen. Brodsky*), Forrest Tucker (*Cody*), James Avery (*The Blacksmith*), John Considine (*Dr. Crawford*), Gail Youngs (*Mrs. McKenzie*), Tracey Walter, R.D. Call, Patrick Baldauff, Danny Pintauro, Ritch Brinkley, A.J. Freeman, J. Michael Flynn, Deborah Levin, Tim Russ, Begona Plaza, John Wesley, Michael Strasser, Monty Cox, Buck Taylor, Robert Braiver, Burke Denis, Joshua Devane, Lane Leavitt, Terry Funk, Christopher Doyle, Tim Gilbert, Tommy Lamey, George Parrish, Eric Mansker, Beth Mitchell, Jed Naboneal,

Dean Smith, Ben Rawnsley, Arnold Roberts, Merritt Yohnka, John Timothy Williams

D: Michael Schultz   **TELEPLAY:** Brian Clemens   **STORY:** Ray Brown & Brian Clemens   **PHOTOG:** Harry Mathias   **SPCL-FX:** Dick Albain & Jon Alexander   **MUSIC:** Craig Safan

TVM, standard SF-adventure: History prof and woman from future hunt villain in 19th-century West

Times to Come

1981, (Argent), color, 98 mins.

W: Hugo Soto, Juan Leyrado, Charly Garcia

D: Gustavo Mosquera

Unusual SF-thriller: Three people struggle to survive in desolate future

Time to Kill

1942, (USA), 20th-Fox, b&w, 61 mins.

W: Lloyd Nolan (*Michael Shayne*), Heather Angel (*Merle*), Ralph Byrd (*Louis Venter*), Richard Lane (*Lt. Breeze*), Ted Hecht (*Phillips*), Sheila Bromley (*Lois Morney*), William Pawley (*Hench*), Morris Ankrum (*Alex Morney*), James Seay (*Leslie Murdock*), Ethel Griffies (*Mrs. Murdock*), Lester Sharpe (*Washburn*), Syd Saylor (*The Postman*), Bruce Wong (*The Houseboy*), Charles Williams (*The Dental Ass't*), LeRoy Mason (*The Headwaiter*), Phyllis Kennedy (*Ena*), Paul Guilfoyle (*The Manager*), Helen Flint (*Marge*)

D: Herbert I. Leeds   **SCR:** Clarence Upson Young, from Raymond Chandler's novel *The High Window* and characters created by Brett Halliday   **PHOTOG:** Charles Clarke   **MUSIC:** Emil Newman

Superior "Michael Shayne" thriller: Murders surround theft of valuable coin

A Time to Kill

1996, (USA), WB, color

W: Sandra Bullock, Matthew McConaughey, Samuel L. Jackson, Brenda Fricker, Kevin Spacey, Oliver Platt, Charles S. Dutton, Patrick McGoohan, Ashley Judd, Donald Sutherland

D: Joel Schumacher   **SCR:** Akiva Goldsman, from John Grisham's novel   **PHOTOG:** Peter Menzies Jr.   **MUSIC:** Elliot Rosenthal

Tense thriller: Race-charged trial of vicious abusers

Time to Remember

1962, (GB), Merton Park/Anglo-Amalgamated, b&w, 58 mins.

W: Yvonne Monlaur (*Suzanne*), Robert Rietty (*Victor*), Harry H. Corbett (*Jack Burgess*), Ernest Clark (*Cracknell*), David Lodge (*Jumbo Johnson*), Ray Barrett (*Sammy*), Jack Watson (*Insp. Bolam*), Genine Graham (*Mrs. Johnson*), Patricia Mort (*Vera*)

P: Jack Greenwood   **D:** Charles Jarrett   **SCR:** Arthur la Bern, from Edgar Wallace's novel *Bought London*

Standard crime-thriller: Estate agent finds gem-thief's cache

A Time to Run

see **The Female Bunch**

Time Trackers

1989, (USA), Roger Corman/Concorde, color, 90 mins.

W: Ned Beatty (*Harry*), Wil Shriner (*Charles*), Kathleen Beller, Bridget Hoffman, Alex Hyde-White, Lee Bergere, Robert Cornthwaite

WRIT & D: Howard R. Cohen

Standard SF-adventure: Scientists time-travel to 1146, try to prevent murder

Time Trap

see **The Time Travelers (1964)**

The Time Travelers

1964, (USA), Dobie/AIP, color, 82 mins.

W: Preston Foster (*Von Steiner*), Philip Carey (*Steve*), John Hoyt, Merry Anders, Dennis Patrick, Joan Woodbury, Dolores Wells, Steve Franken, Forrest J. Ackerman

P: William Redlin   **WRIT & D:** Ib Melchior   **PHOTOG:** William Zsigmond   **SPCL-FX:** David Hewitt   **MUSIC:** Richard LaSalle

orig. to be titled **Depths of the Unknown** *and* **Time Trap**

Standard SF-adventure: Time travelers find future Earth ravaged by war and hideous mutants

Time Travelers

1976, (USA), 20th-Fox/ABC-TV, color

W: Sam Groom (*Dr. Clinton Earnshaw*), Richard Basehart (*Dr. Henderson*), Francine York (*Dr. Helen Sanders*), Tom Hallick (*Jeff Adams*), Trish Stewart (*Jane Henderson*), Booth Colman (*Dr. Cummings*), Baynes Barron (*Chief Williams*), Dort Clark (*Sharkey*), Walter Brooke (*Dr. Stafford*), Patrick Gulliton (*Jim Younger*), Jon Cedar (*Pegleg*), Gil Lamb, Richard Webb, Ed Ness, Kathleen Bracken, Victoria Meyerink, Fred Borden, Albert Cole, Rita Lupino

P: Irwin Allen   **D:** Alexander Singer   **TELEPLAY:** Jackson Gillis   **STORY:** Rod Serling   **PHOTOG:** Fred Jackman   **MUSIC:** Morton Stevens   **MUSIC DIR:** Lionel Newman

TVM, standard SF-adventure (feature-pilot for unsold teleseries): Scientists seek cure to virulent disease, time-travel to Chicago on eve of 1871 fire

Time Troopers

see **Morgen Grauen**

Time Walker

1982, (USA), Dimitri Villard/Wescom, color, 86 mins.

W: Ben Murphy (*Doug*), Nina Axelrod (*Susy*), Kevin Brophy (*Peter*), James Karen (*Wendell*), Robert Random (*Parker*), Shari Belafonte-Harper, Sam Chew Jr., Melissa Prophet, Austin Stoker, Gerard Prendergast, Antoinette Bower, Ken Gibbel, Darwin Jostin, Greta Blackburn, John Lavachielle, Clint Young, Gary Dubin, Greta Stapf, Vanna Bonta, Royce Alexander, Michelle Avonne, Marie Briguglio, Joy Grdnic, Sandra Carey, Susan Curtis, Warrington Gillette, Richard Hoyes, J. Michael Hunter, Kelly Junkerman, Alan Rachins, Don LaFontaine, Jack Olson, Allene Simmons, Diane Terry, Hugo L. Stanger, Alan Stock, Ann Trussell, Victoria Von Voorhees, Dimitri Villard, Behrouz Vossoughi, Jeff Yesko, Jason Williams, Annie Barbieri

D: Tom Kennedy   **SCR:** Tom Friedman & Karen Levitt   **STORY:** Jason Williams & Tom Friedman   **PHOTOG:** Robbie Greenberg   **MUSIC:** Richard H. Band

Minor SF-horror: Predations of space-alien mummy

Time Warp Terror

1987, (GB), color

D: Norman J. Warren

Minor SF-horror

Time Without Pity

1957, (GB), b&w, 88 mins.

W: Michael Redgrave, Ann Todd, Leo McKern, Peter Cushing, Alec McCowen, Renee Houston, Paul Daneman, Lois Maxwell, George Devine, Richard Wordsworth, Joan Plowright

D: Joseph Losey   **SCR:** Ben Barzman, from Emlyn Williams' play *Someone Waiting*   **PHOTOG:** Freddie Francis

Unusual thriller: Man wrongly convicted of murder

Tim the Messenger

1913, (GB), Phoenix Film Agency, b&w, 690 ft. (210.3m)

Standard crime-thriller: Messenger boy prevents girl's kidnapping

The Tingler

1959, (USA), Col, b&w, 82 mins.

W: Vincent Price, Judith Evelyn, Patricia Cutts (*Isabel*), Pamela Lincoln (*Lucy*), Darryl Hickman, Philip Coolidge

P & D: William Castle   **SCR:** Robb White   **PHOTOG:** Wilfrid M. Cline   **MUSIC:** Von Dexter

Classic horror-thriller (featuring film clips from 'Tol'able David' {1921}): Scientist finds organism on human spine that causes death from fright

The Tinted Venus

1921, (GB), Hepworth, b&w, 5,200 ft. (1585m)

W: Alma Taylor (*Matilda Collum*), George Dewhurst (*Leander Tweddle*), Maud Cressall (*Venus*), Eileen Dennes (*Bella Parkinson*), Hugh Clifton (*Jauncey*), Mary Brough (*The Landlady*), Gwynne Herbert (*Mrs. Collum*)

D: Cecil M. Hepworth   **SCR:** Blanche McIntosh, from a novel by F. Anstey

Standard fantasy: Statue of Venus comes to life. cf. **One Touch of Venus**

Tintorera...Bloody Waters

1977, (GB-Mex), United Film Distribution, color

W: Susan George (*Gabriella*), Jennifer Ashley (*Kelly*), Fiona Lewis (*Patricia*), Hugo Stiglitz (*Stephen*), Andres Garcia (*Miguel*), Laura Lyons (*Cynthia*), Robert Guzman (*Colorado*), Priscilla Barnes (*A Girl*), Pamela Garner (*A Girl*), Erika

To Commit A Murder: SENTA BERGER AND LOUIS JOURDAN

Carlson (*A Girl*)

P: Gerald Green   **D:** Rene Cardona Jr.   **SCR:** Ramon Bravo & Rene Cardona Jr., from a novel by Ramon Bravo   **PHOTOG:** Leon Sanchez   **MUSIC:** Basil Poledouris

*Minor thriller (***Jaws*** imitation): Love triangle complicates hunt for great white shark*

The Tired Death
see Der Mude Tod

Titan Find
see Creature

Les Titans (The Titans)
1962, (It-Fr), UA, color, 110 mins.
W: Pedro Armendariz, Jacqueline Sassard
P: Franco Cristaldi D: Duccio Tessari SCR: Ennio De Concini & Duccio Tessari *(USA dialog, T. Rowe)*
USA retitle, My Son, the Hero
Standard fantasy-comedy: Mythological hero battles assorted foes

To All a Goodnight
1980, (USA), Intercontinental Releasing Corp., color, 90 mins.
W: Jennifer Runyon, Forrest Swanson *(Alex)*, Linda Gentile *(Melody)*, William Lauer *(T.J.)*, Judith Bridges *(Leia)*, Katherine Herrington *(Mrs. Jensen)*, Sam Shamshak *(Polansky)*, Buck West *(Ralph)*, Angela Bath *(Trisha)*, Jeff Butts *(Blake)*, Denise Stearns *(Sam)*, Bill Martins *(Jim)*, Solomon Trager *(Tom)*, Jay Rasumny *(Dan)*, Judy Hess *(Mrs. Ronsoni)*, Dan Stryker *(The Pilot)*, Carrie Cobb *(Mrs. Jensen's Daughter)*, Lisa Labowskie *(Cynthia)*, Vivienne Kove *(The Sincere Mother)*, Harry Sethe *(The Irate Father)*, Ann Tucker, Alain Clenet, Dori Tressler, Michael George, Lori Eiseman, Jamie Nielsen, Jennifer Howard, Robin Theriault, Cathy Hicky, Mary Hicky, Cathy Fisher, Mary Wagner, Robin Olsen, Toby Sternlieb, Virginia Quiria, Donald Kinn, Jane Osborn, Justin Zach-ary, Linda Mersman
D: David Hess SCR: Alex Rebar PHOTOG: Bil Godsey
Minor thriller: Psycho "Santa" slays school sluts

Tobe Hooper's Night Terrors
1995, (USA), color
W: Robert Englund, Zoe Trilling
Standard horror-fantasy

Tobor the Great
1954, (USA), Dudley/Para., b&w, 77 mins.
W: Charles Drake *(Harrison)*, Karin Booth *(Janice)*, Billy Chapin *(Gadge)*, Taylor Holmes *(Nordstrom)*, Lyle Talbot *(The Admiral)*, Steven Geray *(The Man with the Glasses)*, Henry Kulky, Hal Baylor, Alan Reynolds, Helen Winston, Peter Brocco, Norman Field, Robert Shayne, Emmett Vogan, William Schallert
P: Richard Goldstone D: Lee Sholem SCR: Philip MacDonald, from a story by Card Dudley PHOTOG: John L. Russell MUSIC: Howard Jackson
Juvenile SF-thriller: Boy befriends robot

Toby and the Koala Bear
1979, (Austral), color
Juvenile fantasy-adventure (animated characters on live backgrounds): Boy has amazing friend

To Catch a Thief
1955, (USA), Para, color, 107 mins.
W: Cary Grant *(John Robie)*, Grace Kelly *(Frances Stevens)*, Charles Vanel *(Bertani)*, John Williams *(H.H. Hughson)*, Jessie Royce Landis *(Mrs. Stevens)*, Brigitte Auber *(Danielle)*, Jean Martinelli *(Foussard)*, Georgette Anys *(Geramine)*, Jean Hebey *(Mercier)*, Roland Lesaffre *(Claude)*, Marie Stoddard *(Mrs. Sanford)*, Rene Blancard *(Lepic)*, Russell Gaige *(Mr. Sanford)*, John Alderson, Don Megowan, Bela Kovacs, Edward Manouk, Guy DeVestel, Wee Willie Davis, Dominique Davray, Paul Newlan, Lewis Charles, Aimee Torriani, Otto Schulze, Frank Chelland, Martha Bamattre
P & D: Alfred Hitchcock SCR: John Michael Hayes from David Dodge's novel PHOTOG: Robert Burks MUSIC: Lyn Murray
Classic thriller: Suspected thief romances rich girl on Riviera

To Catch a Yeti
1993, (USA), Walt Disney, color, 89 mins.
W: Meat Loaf
Standard juvenile fantasy: Miniature sasquatch complicates mountain climber's life

To Commit a Murder
1966, (Fr), Gaumont-Int'l/Cinerama, color, 90 mins.
W: Louis Jourdan *(Charles)*, Senta Berger *(Gertrud)*, Edmond O'Brien *(Sphax)*, Bernard Blier *(Rhome)*, Fabrizzio Capucci *(Cecil)*, Giuseppe Addobbati *(Moranez)*, Patricia Scott *(La Nordique)*, Maurice Garrel *(Banck)*, Gamil Ratib *(Belloum)*
D: Edouard Molinaro SCR: Edouard Molinaro & Jacques Robert, from a novel by Jacques Robert PHOTOG: Ray LeMoigne MUSIC: Jose Berghmans
Standard thriller: Agents try to prevent French scientist from defecting to Red China

To Die For
1989, (USA), Skouras, color, 94 mins.
W: Brendan Hughes *(Vlad Tepish)*, Sydney Walsh *(Kate Wooten)*, Scott Jacoby *(Martin Planting)*, Amanda Wyss *(Celia Kett)*, Micah Grant *(Mike Dunn)*, Duane Jones *(Simon Little)*, Steve Bond *(Tom)*, Remy O'Neill *(June)*, Al Fann *(Lt. Williams)*, Philip Granger *(Det. Bocco)*, Lloyd Alan *(Rich)*, Ava Fabian *(Franny)*, Julie Maddalena *(Paula Higgins)*, Eloise Broady *(The Girl at the Party)*, Cate Caplin *(Michelle)*, Richard Sarafian *(The Bartender)*, Dean Anthony *(Ben)*, Fred Waugh *(The Bum)*, Bill Handy *(The Dumptruck Driver)*,

Sharon Mullings *(The Woman on the Yacht)*
D: Deran Sarafian SCR: Leslie King PHOTOG: Jacques Haitkin SPCL-FX SPRVSR: Eddie Surkin MUSIC: Cliff Eidelman SONGS: *Where Are You, Can't Let Go, Torn and Tattered, Always, Dancing Doll, For You I'd Die, It's You Who Said It & Tyranny*
Standard horror-fantasy: Vampire stalks Los Angeles

To Die For II: Son of Darkness
1991, (USA), Arrowhead-Lee Caplin/Trimark, color, 95 mins.
W: Rosalind Allen *(Nina)*, Steve Bond *(Tom)*, Scott Jacoby *(Martin)*, Michael Praed *(Max)*, Jay Underwood *(Danny)*, Remy O'Neill *(Jane)*, Amanda Wyss *(Celia)*, Michael Eric Kramer *(The Bartender)*, Devin Corrie Sims *(Tyler)*, Jann Carl *(The Field Reporter)*, Elizabeth Woods *(The Wife)*, Jim Price *(The Husband)*, George Fisher *(Joe)*, Scott Heath *(The Teenage Boy)*, Gayle Phelps *(The Woman Attacked)*, Doug Collins *(The Man Outside the House)*, Donald Redding *(The Man in the Tavern)*, Vince Edwards, Melody Doff, Kathryn Atwood, Bonnie Moore, Valencia Bilyeu, Therese Price, Jeff Phillips, Karen Soroca
D: David F. Price SCR: Leslie King PHOTOG: Gerry Lively MUSIC: Mark McKenzie SONGS: *Rumanian Folk Dance, Enemy Lines, Caught in a Web of Love, Love Attack, Midnight & Reach Out and Rock Somebody*
Standard horror-fantasy: Master vampire seeks parental rights

The Todd Killings
1971, (USA), color, 93 mins.
W: Robert F. Lyons, Richard Thomas, Barbara Bel Geddes, Ed Asner, Sherry Miles, Gloria Grahame, Belinda J. Montgomery
D: Barry Shear SCR: Jel Oliansky
A.k.a. A Dangerous Friend and Skipper
Minor thriller: Psycho kills young women

To Gillian on Her 37th Birthday
1996, (USA), Triumph, color, 93 mins.
W: Peter Gallagher *(David Lewis)*, Michelle Pfeifer *(Gillian Lewis)*, Claire Danes *(Rachel Lewis)*, Kathy Baker *(Esther Wheeler)*, Wendy Crewson *(Kevin Dollof)*, Bruce Altman *(Paul Wheeler)*, Laurie Fortier *(Cindy Bayles)*, Freddie Prinze Jr. *(Joey Bost)*
D: Michael Pressman SCR: David E. Kelley, from Michael Brady's play PHOTOG: Tim Suhrstedt MUSIC: James Horner
Standard fantasy-romance: Man communes with wife's ghost

To Have and to Hold
1963, (GB), Merto Park/Anglo-Amalgamated, b&w, 71 mins.
W: Ray Barrett *(Henry Fraser)*, Katharine Blake *(Claudia Lyon)*, Nigel Stock *(George Lyon)*, William Hartnell *(Insp. Roberts)*, Patricia Bredin *(Lucy)*, Richard Clarke *(Charles Wagner)*, Noel Trevarthen *(Blake)*
P: Jack Greenwood D: Herbert Wise SCR: John Sansom, from Edgar Wallace's story "The Breaking Point"
Standard crime-thriller: Woman involves policeman in scheme to murder her husband

To Kill a Clown
1972, (GB), Palomar/20th-Fox, color, 104 mins.
W: Alan Alda *(Maj. Ritchie)*, Blythe Danner *(Lily Frischer)*, Heath Lamberts *(Timothy Frischer)*, Eric Clavering *(Stanley)*
P: Theodore Sills D: George Bloomfield SCR: George Bloomfield & I.C. Rapoport, from Algis Budrys' novel *Master of the Hounds* PHOTOG: Walter Lassally MUSIC: Richard Hill
Standard thriller: Crippled Vietnam veteran holds painter and wife prisoner on island

To Let
1919, (GB), Harma Photoplays, b&w, 1,788 ft. (545m)
W: James Reardon *(Mr. Briggs)*, Peggy Patterson *(Mrs. Briggs)*, James Prior *(The Husband)*, Ida Fane *(The Wife)*
D: James Reardon, from a story by Reuben Gillmer
Standard comedy: Retired conjurer tries to scare couple from his house

To Love a Vampire
see Lust for a Vampire

Tom and Jerry: The Movie
1992, (USA), color, 84 mins.
VOICES: Richard Kind, Dana Hill, Andi McAfee, Henry Gibson D: Phil Roman
Dull animated fantasy: Cat and mouse become friends

The Tomb
1985, (USA), Trans World, color, 84 mins.
W: Cameron Mitchell *(Dr. Howard Phillips)*, John Carradine *(Mr. Andoheb)*, Sybil Danning *(Jade)*, Susan Stokey *(Helen)*, Richard Alan Hench *(David Manners)*, Michelle Bauer *(Nefratis)*, David Pearson *(John Banning)*, Craig Hamann *(Tyler)*, George Hoth *(Dr. Stewart)*, Stu Weltman *(Det. Sullivan)*, Emanuel Shipow *(Youssef)*, Jack Frankel *(Dr. Manners)*, Dawn Wildsmith *(Anna Conda)*, Peter Conway *(Customs Agent #1)*, Brad Arrington *(Customs Agent #2)*, Frank McDonald *(Officer Ullman)*, Kitten Natividad *(The Stripper)*, Victor von Wright *(The Detective)*, Morrie Eisenman *(The Airport Cabbie)*, Martin Nicholas *(The Janitor)*, Dutch Polder *(The Bar Swinger)*, Michael D. Sonye *(The Waiter)*, Katina Garner *(Old Nefratis)*, Gertie the Rat *(herself)*
D: Fred Olen Ray SCR: Kenneth J. Hall PHOTOG: Paul Elliott MUSIC: Drew Neumann SONGS: *Try Me, Twisted, Kick Around Me, Danger Boy &*

Saturday Nite Rockers
Minor horror-thriller: Stolen artifacts, Egyptian curse

The Tomb of Ligeia
1964, (USA-GB), Ata Vista/AIP, color, 82 mins.
W: Vincent Price *(Verden Fell)*, Elizabeth Shepherd *(Rowena/Ligeia)*, Derek Francis *(Lord Trevanion)*, Frank Thornton *(Peperel)*, John Westbrook *(Christopher Gough)*, Oliver Johnston *(Kenrick)*, Richard Vernon *(Dr. Vivian)*, Ronald Adam *(The Parson)*, Penelope Lee *(The Maid)*, Denis Gilmore
P & D: Roger Corman **SCR:** Robert Towne, from Edgar Allan Poe's short story *Ligeia* **PHOTOG:** Arthur Grant **SPCL-FX:** Ted Samuels **MUSIC:** Kenneth V. Jones **DESIGN:** Colin Southcott
orig. to be titled *The Last Tomb of Ligeia*
Superior horror-fantasy (ultimate Corman-Price-Poe film): Dark spirit of recluse's first wife seeks vehicle to return from dead

Tomb of the Living Dead
see Mad Doctor of Blood Island

Tomb of the Undead
see Garden of the Dead

Tomb of Torture
1963, (It), Trans-Lux, b&w, 88 mins.
W: Anne Albert, Elizabeth Queen, Marc Marian, Bernard Blay, Thony Maky
P: Frank Campitelli **D:** Antonio Boccaci **SCR:** Antonio Boccaci & Giorgio Simonelli
Minor thriller: Girl believes she is reincarnation of sanguine countess

The Tombs of Horror
see Cinque Tombe per un Medium

Tombs of the Blind Dead
1972, (Sp-Port), Plata-Interfilme/Atlas, color, 86 mins.
W: Lone Fleming, Cesar Burner, Helen Harp, Joseph Thelman, Rufino Ingles, Veronica Llimera, Simon Arriaga, Francisco Sanz, Juan Cortes, Andres Speizer, Antonio Orengo, Maria Sylva, Jose Camoiras
WRIT & D: Armando De Ossorio **PHOTOG:** Pablo Ripoll **MUSIC:** Anton Garcia Abril
A.k.a. The Blind Dead
Minor horror-fantasy: Ruined monastery harbors satanic zombies

Tomcat: Dangerous Desires
1993, (USA), color, 95 mins.
W: Richard Grieco, Natalie Radford
Minor SF-thriller: Genetic experiment has unforseen effects on terminally-ill dancer

Tommy
1974, (GB), Hemdale/Col, color, 108 mins.
W: Ann-Margret *(Nora Walker)*, Oliver Reed *(Frank Hobbs)*, Roger Daltrey *(Tommy Walker)*, Elton John *(The Pinball Wizard)*, Eric Clapton *(The Preacher)*, Jack Nicholson *(The Doctor)*, Keith Moon *(Uncle Ernie)*, Paul Nicholas *(Cousin Kevin)*, Robert Powell *(GC Walker)*, Tina Turner *(The Acid Queen)*, Barry Winch *(Tommy as a Boy)*, Victoria Russell *(Sally Simpson)*, Ben Aris *(Rev. Simpson)*, Mary Holland *(Mrs. Simpson)*, Jennifer Baker *(A Nurse)*, Susan Baker *(A Nurse)*, Arthur Brown *(The Priest)*, John Entwistle *(himself)*, Pete Townshend *(himself)*
P: Robert Stigwood & Ken Russell **D:** Ken Russell **SCR:** Ken Russell, John Entwistle & Keith Moon, from the rock-opera by Pete Townshend & The Who **PHOTOG:** Dick Bush **MUSIC:** The Who
Unusual psychedelic musical: Handicapped youth becomes pinball wizard

The Tommyknockers
1993, (USA), color, approx. 190 mins.
W: Jimmy Smits, Marg Helgenberger, E.G. Marshall, Robert Carradine, Traci Lords, John Ashton, Joanna Cassidy, Alyce Beasley, Annie Corley, Cliff DeYoung, Leon Woods, Chuck Henry, Jim McLarty, Paul McIver
D: John Power **TELEPLAY:** Lawrence D. Cohen, from Stephen King's novel **PHOTOG:** Danny Burstall & David Eggby **MUSIC:** Christopher Franke
2-part TVM, standard SF-thriller: Woman uncovers alien spacecraft

Tommy Tricker and the Stamp Traveller
1988, (Can), color, 105 mins.
W: Lucas Evans *(Ralph)*, Anthony Rogers *(Tommy)*
Standard juvenile fantasy (blend of animation and live action): Stampcollectors have magical adventure

Tom Old Boot
1896, (Fr), Star, b&w, 20m (65.6 ft./1.1 mins.)
D: Georges Melies
Standard comedy-fantasy: Tale of grotesque dwarf

Tomorrow at Ten
1962, (GB), Blakeley's Films/Planet, b&w, 80 mins.
W: John Gregson *(Insp. Parnell)*, Robert Shaw *(Marlow)*, Alec Clunes *(Anthony Chester)*, Alan Wheatley *(Bewley)*, Helen Cherry *(Robbie)*, Kenneth Cope *(Sgt. Grey)*, Ernest Clark *(Dr. Towers)*, William Hartnell *(Freddy)*, Betty McDowall *(Mrs. Parnell)*, Renee Houston *(Mrs. Maddox)*
P: Tom Blakeley **D:** Lance Comfort **STORY:** Peter Millar & James Kelly

Too Hot To Handle: CLARK GABLE

Standard crime-thriller: Rich man kills kidnapper, seeks son menaced by time bomb

The Tomorrow Man
see 984: Prisoner of the Future

Tomorrow Never Comes
1978, (GB-Can), Classic Film Industries/Montreal Trust/Neffbourne/Rank, color, 109 mins.
W: Oliver Reed *(Jim Wilson)*, Susan George *(Janie)*, Raymond Burr *(Burke)*, John Ireland *(The Captain)*, John Osborne *(Lyne)*, Stephen McHattie *(Frank)*, Donald Pleasence *(Dr. Todd)*, Paul Koslo *(Willy)*, Cec Linder *(Milton)*, Richard Donat *(Ray)*, Dolores Etienne *(Hilde)*, James Eastwood *(Lois)*, Sammy Snyder *(Joey)*
P: Julian Melzack & Michael Klinger **D:** Peter Collinson **STORY:** David Pursall, Jack Seddon & Sydney Banks **PHOTOG:** Francois Protat **MUSIC:** Roy Budd
Standard crime-thriller: Jealous man holds girlfriend captive

Tomorrow Never Dies
1997, (USA-GB), UA, color
W: Pierce Brosnan *(James Bond)*, Teri Hatcher, Jonathan Pryce, Michelle Yeoh, Gotz Otto, Joe Don Baker, Judy Dench, Desmond Llewelyn
from characters created by Ian Fleming
Lavish adventure-thriller

Tomorrow's Child
1982, (USA), 20th-Fox/ABC-TV, color, 95 mins.
W: William Atherton *(Dr. Spence)*, Stephanie Zimbalist *(Kay Spence)*, Ed Flanders *(Anders Stenslund)*, Arthur Hill *(Dr. Glenn Gorham)*, Bruce Davison *(Cliff Bender)*, Salome Jens *(Dr. Laura Pressburg)*, Susan Oliver *(Marilyn Hurst)*, J. Victor Lopez *(Roy)*, James Shigeta *(Dr. Shibura)*, Stephen Douglas Helm *(The Man at the Accident)*, Dave Turner *(Lt. Wolders)*, Teddi Siddall *(Janice Bender)*, Jerry McNeely *(Dr. Sargent)*, Virginia Bingham *(Cheryl)*, Freddye Chapman *(The Nurse)*, Lance Rosen *(Chuck)*, Jody Myler *(Arlene)*, Shelly O'Neil *(The Sec'y)*
D: Joseph Sargent **TELEPLAY:** Jerry McNeely **PHOTOG:** Hector R. Figueroa **MUSIC:** Patrick Williams **MUSIC CONDUCT:** Lionel Newman
TVM, standard thriller: Eugenics and "test-tube babies"

Tom Thumb
1958, (SA-GB), Galaxy/MGM, color, 92 mins.
W: Russ Tamblyn *(Tom Thumb)*, Alan Young *(Woody)*, June Thorburn *(Fairy Queen of the Forest)*, Peter Sellers *(Antony)*, Terry Thomas *(Ivan)*, Jessie Matthews *(Anna)*, Bernard Miles *(Jonathan)*, Ian Wallace *(The Shoemaker)*, Peter Butterworth
P & D: George Pal **SCR:** Ladislas Fodor, based on stories from the pen of the Brothers Grimm **PHOTOG:** Georges Perinal **OSCAR-WINNING SPCL-FX:** Tom Howard **MUSIC:** Muir Mathieson **SONGS:** After All These Years, Dancing Shoes, Are you a Dream?, The Yawning Song & The Talented Shoes
Well-made fantasy: Two-inch boy thwarts thieves

Tom Tight et Dum Dum
1903, (Fr), Star, b&w, 50m (164 ft./2.8 mins.)
D: Georges Melies
A.k.a. Jack Jaggs and Dum Dum and The Rival Music Hall Artistes
Standard comedy-fantasy: Magician treats man like nail, hammers him into stage

Le Tonnerre de Jupiter (Jupiter's Thunder)
1903, (Fr), Star, b&w, 70m (229.7 ft./3.9 mins.)
D: Georges Melies
A.k.a. Jupiter's Thunderbolt or, The Home of the Muses
Standard fantasy

T

Too Good to be True
1988, (USA), NBC-TV, color, 95 mins.
W: Loni Anderson, Patrick Duffy, Julie Harris, Glynnis O'Connor, Larry Drake, Neil Patrick Harris, Carmen Argenziano, Elizabeth Norment, James B. Sikking, Ted Gehring, Lorinne Vozoff, Carl Franklin, Daniel Baldwin, Leeza Vinnichenko, Arnold Turner, Areta Farrell, Randy Josselyn, Michael Blue
D: Christian I. Nyby II **TELEPLAY:** Timothy Bradshaw, from Ben Ames Williams' novel *Leave Her to Heaven* **PHOTOG:** Michael D. Margulies **MUSIC:** Michel Rubini
TVM, minor melodrama: Neurotic woman destroys lives about her

Too Hot to Handle
1960, (GB), Wigmore/WPD, color, 100 mins.
W: Jayne Mansfield (*Midnight Franklin*), Leo Genn (*Johnny Solo*), Carl Boehm (*Robert Jouvel*), Patrick Holt (*Insp. West*), Danik Patisson (*Lilliana Decker*), Christopher Lee (*Novak*), Kai Fischer (*Cynthia*), Martin Boddey (*Mr. Arpels*), Sheldon Lawrence (*Diamonds Dinelli*), Barbara Windsor (*Ponytail*), Tom Bowman (*Flash Gordon*)
P: Selim Cattan & Ronald Rietti **D:** Terence Young **SCR:** Herbert Kretzmer **STORY:** Harry Lee **PHOTOG:** Otto Heller

Topkapi: MAXIMILIAN SCHELL AND MELINA MERCOURI

Standard crime-thriller: Strip-club owner involved in death

The Toolbox Murders
1978, (USA), EFI/Cal-AM/Selected, color, 93 mins.
W: Cameron Mitchell (*Kingsley*), Pamelyn Ferdin (*Laurie*), Wesley Eure (*Kent*), Nicholas Beauvy (*Joey*), Tim Donnelly (*The Detective*), Aneta Corsaut (*Joanne*), Evelyn Guerrero, Faith McSwain, Marciee Drake, Mariane Walter, Kelly Nichols
P: Tony Didio **D:** Dennis Donnelly **STORY & SCR:** Robert Easter & Ann Kindberg **PHOTOG:** Gary Graver
Minor thriller: Crazed aparent superintendant kills "sinful" women

Too Many Chefs
see Who Is Killing the Great Chefs of Europe?

Too Many Detectives
1953, (GB), Collingwood/New Realm, b&w, 33 mins.
W: John Laurie (*Edward Potter*), Hector Ross (*Insp. Greenaway*), Mavis Villiers, Jack Stewart, Howard Connell
P & D: Oscar Burn & John Wall
Standard short crime-thriller: Scotland Yard clerk proves embezzler was murdered

Topper: ROLAND YOUNG AND MINERVA URECAL

Too Many Winners
1947, (USA), PRC, b&w, 60 mins.
W: Hugh Beaumont (*Michael Shayne*), Trudy Marshall (*Phyllis Hamilton*), Ralph Dunn (*Rafferty*), John Hamilton (*Payson*), Claire Carleton (*Mayme Marin*), Grandon Rhodes (*Hardessan*), Charles Mitchell (*Tim Rourke*), Ben Welden (*Madden*), Byron Foulger (*Edwards*), Jean Andrews (*Mrs. Edwards*), Maurice B. Mozelle (*Poak*), George Meader (*Clarence*), Frank Hagney (*Joe*)
D: William Beaudine **SCR:** Fred Myton & Scott Darling, from characters created by Brett Halliday **PHOTOG:** Jack Greenhalgh **MUSIC:** Alvin Levin
Standard "Michael Shayne" thriller: Detective investigates counterfeit racetrack tickets

Toomorrow
1970, (GB), Lowndes-Sweet Music/RFD, color, 95 mins.
W: Olivia Newton-John (*Olivia*), Benny Thomas (*Benny*), Vic Cooper (*Vic*), Karl Chambers (*Karl*), Roy Dotrice (*John Williams*), Imogen Hassall (*Amy*), Tracey Crisp (*Suzanne Gilmore*), Margaret Nolan (*Johnson*), Roy Marsden (*Alpha*), Carl Rigg (*Matthew*), Maria O'Brien (*Francoise*), Stuart Henry
P: Harry Saltzman & Don Kirschner **WRIT & D:** Val Guest
Standard SF-musical: Teen pop group kidnapped by extraterrestrials

Too Much Lobster
1909, (GB), Hepworth, b&w, 275 ft. (83.8m)
D: Lewin Fitzhamon
Standard comedy-fantasy: Husband overeats, dreams of girls

Too Much Sausage
1916, (GB), Kineto, b&w, 475 ft. (144.8m)
D: Walter R. Booth
Standard fantasy: Man dreams sausage turns into zeppelin

Too Scared to Scream
1982, (USA), Doorman Co. Ltd., color, 99 mins.
W: Mike Connors (*Lt. Dinardo*), Ian McShane (*Vincent Hardwick*), Anne Archer (*Kate*), Leon Issac Kennedy (*Frank*), Maureen O'Sullivan (*Mother*), Ruth Ford (*Irma*), Ken Norris (*Mike*), John Heard (*The Lab Technician*), Murray Hamilton (*Jack*), Carrie Nye (*Graziella*), Chet Doherty (*Edward*), Sully Boyar (*Sydney Blume*), Karen Rushmore (*Nadine*), Val Avery (*The Medical Examiner*), Rony Clanton (*The Barker*), Beeson Carroll (*Barry Moyer*), Victoria Bass (*Cynthia Oberman*), Dick Boccelli (*Benny*), Yvonne Talton Kersey (*Mamie*), Fred Ford (*The Man at the Bar*), Ernesto Gasco (*The Waiter*), Adrienne Howard (*Louise*), Gaetano Lisi (*The Guard*), Harry Madsen (*Lyman*), John Ring (*The Irishman*)
P: Mike Connors **D:** Tony Lo Bianco **SCR:** Neal Barbera & Glenn Leopold **PHOTOG:** Larry Pizer **MUSIC:** George Garvarentz **SONG:** sung by Charles Aznavour & Phyllis Hyman, *I'll Be There*
Standard thriller: Killer plagues apartment building

Toothless
1997, (USA), Walt Disney, color, 95 mins.
W: Kirstie Alley, Dale Midkiff, Ross Malinger, Daryl "Chill" Mitchell, Marcus Toji, Melanie Mayron, Lynn Redgrave
D: Melanie Mayron **TELEPLAY:** Mark S. Kaufman **PHOTOG:** Dansi Sissel **MUSIC:** David Michael Frank
TVM, standard comedy-fantasy: Deceased lady dentist must become Tooth Fairy

Topkapi
1964, (Fr), Filmways/UA, color, 122 mins.
W: Melina Mercouri, Maximilian Schell, Peter Ustinov, Akim Tamiroff, Robert Morley, Gilles Segal, Joseph Dassin, Jess Hahn
P & D: Jules Dassin **SCR:** Monja Danischewsky, based on Eric Ambler's novel *The Light of Day* **PHOTOG:** Henri Alekan **MUSIC:** Manos Hadjidakis
Superior comedy-thriller (Best Supporting Actor, Peter Ustinov): Thieves covet emerald-encrusted dagger in Istanbul museum

Top Kids
1988, (W. Ger), color, 80 mins.
W: Ross Harris, Niki Lauda
Minor SF-adventure: Young computer hacker time-travels

Topper
1937, (USA), MGM, b&w, 97 mins.
W: Roland Young (*Cosmo Topper*), Cary Grant, Constance Bennett, Billie Burke, Virginia Sale, Alan Mowbray, Eugene Pallette, Hoagy Carmichael, Ward Bond, Arthur Lake, Hedda Hopper, J. Farrell MacDonald, Doodles Weaver
P: Hal Roach **D:** Norman Z. McLeod, from Thorne Smith's novel The Jovial Ghosts **PHOTOG:** Norbert Brodine **MUSIC DIR:** Arthur Morton **SONG:** *Old Man Moon*
Classic comedy-fantasy: Socialite haunted by deceased madcap couple

Topper
1979, (USA), ABC-TV, color, 95 mins.
W: Jack Warden (*Cosmo Topper*), Andrew Stevens (*George Kirby*), Kate Jackson (*Marion Kirby*), Rue McClanahan (*Clara Topper*), James Karen (*Korbell*), Macon McCalman (*Wilkins*), Charles Siebert (*Ogilvy*), Larry Gelman (*The Mechanic*), Estelle Owens (*Miss Johnson*), Gloria LeRoy (*The Salesady*)
D: Charles S. Dubin **TELEPLAY:** George Kirgo, Maryanne Kasica & Michael Scheff, from Thorne Smith's novel *The Jovial Ghosts* **PHOTOG:** Robert Caramico **MUSIC:** Fred Karlin
TVM, standard comedy-fantasy: Ghosts plague socialite

T

Topper Returns

1941, (USA), MGM, b&w, 87 mins.
W: Roland Young (*Cosmo Topper*), Carole Landis (*Ann Carrington*), Joan Blondell (*Gail Richards*), Dennis O'Keefe (*Bob*), H.B. Warner (*Mr. Carrington*), Billie Burke (*Mrs. Topper*), Rafaela Ottiano (*Lillian*), Patsy Kelly (*The Maid*), George Zucco (*Dr. Jeris*), Eddie "Rochester" Anderson (*The Chauffeur*), Donald MacBride (*Sgt. Roberts*), Trevor Bardette (*Rama*)
P: Hal Roach   **D:** Roy Del Ruth   **SCR:** Jonathan Latimer & Gordon Douglas, from characters created by Thorne Smith
Standard comedy-fantasy: Ghosts encounter foul play

Topper Takes a Trip

1939, (USA), UA, b&w, 85 mins.
W: Roland Young (*Cosmo Topper*), Billie Burke (*Mrs. Topper*), Constance Bennett (*Marion Kirby*), Veree Teasdale, Franklin Pangborn, Alan Mowbray, Alex D'Arcy
P: Hal Roach   **D:** Norman Z. McLeod   **SCR:** Eddie Moran, Jack Jevne & Corey Ford, from characters created by Thorne Smith   **PHOTOG:** Norbert Brodine
Standard comedy-fantasy: Socialite haunted on Riviera

Top Secret

1952, (GB), Transocean/ABP, b&w, 94 mins.
W: Oscar Homolka (*Zekov*), Nadia Gray (*Tania Ivanova*), George Cole (*George Potts*), Wilfrid Hyde-White (*Sir Hubert*), Charles Goldner (*Gaston*), Irene Handl (*Mrs. Tidmarsh*), Gerard Heinz (*A Director*), Frederick Leister (*The Prime Minister*), Michael Medwin (*Smedley*), Edwin Styles (*The Superintendent*), Olaf Pooley (*Roblettski*), Geoffrey Sumner (*Pike*), Frederick Valk (*Rakov*), Eleanor Summerfield (*Cecilia*), Kynaston Reeves (*A Director*), Richard Wattis (*Barnes*)
P & D: Mario Zampi   **STORY:** Michael Pertwee & Jack Davies
USA retitle: **Mr. Potts Goes to Moscow**
Standard comedy-thriller: Soviet spies kidnap sanitary engineer, mistaking him for atom scientist

Top Secret

1978, (USA), Jemmin-Sheldon Leonard/ABC-TV, color, 96 mins.
W: Bill Cosby, Tracy Reed, Sheldon Leonard, Gloria Foster, George Brenlin (*Murphy*), Paolo Turco (*Gino*), Luciano Bartoli (*Pietro*), Maris Merlini (*Rosa*), Leonardo Traviglio, Bryan Rostran, Francesca De Sapio, Walter Williams, Craig Hill, Paul Leaf, Nat Bush
PHOTOG: Gabor Pogany   **MUSIC:** Stu Gardner & Teo Macero
TVM, standard comedy-thriller: U.S. agents in Italy seek stolen plutonium

Top Secret!

1984, (GB), Kingsmere/Para, color, 87 mins.
W: Val Kilmer (*Nick Rivers*), Lucy Gutteridge (*Hillary Flammond*), Peter Cushing (*Jorgensen*), Michael Gough (*Dr. Flammond*), Jeremy Kemp (*The General*), Omar Sharif (*Cedric*), Warren Clarke (*Col. Von Horst*), Harry Ditson (*Dr. Quois*), Gertan Klauber (*The Mayor*), John Sharp (*The Maitre d'*), Christopher Villiers (*Nigel*), Jim Carter (*Deja Vu*), Eddie Tagoe (*Chocolate Mousse*), Tristram Jellinek (*Maj. Crumpler*), Richard Mayes (*Biletnikov*), Vyvyan Lorrayne (*Mme. Bergerone*), John Craney (*Klaus*), Sydney Arnold (*Albert Potato*), Billy J. Mitchell (*Martin*), Dimitri Andreas (*Latrine*)
P: Jon Davison & Hunt Lowry   **D:** Jim Abrahams, David Zucker & Jerry Zucker   **SCR:** Jim Abrahams, David Zucker, Jerry Zucker & Martyn Burke   **PHOTOG:** Christopher Challis   **MUSIC:** Maurice Jarre
Standard farce: Rock star helps girl rescue scientist-father from East Germany

Topsy's Dream of Toyland

1911, (GB), Cricks & Martin, b&w, 1,050 ft. (320m)
W: Dorothy St. John (*Topsy*), Edwin J. Collins (*The Rich Man*)
WRIT & D: A.E. Coleby
Standard fantasy: Waif faints, dreams she weds prince

Topsy-Turvy Villa

1900, (GB), Hepworth, b&w, 75 ft. (22.9m)
W: Cecil Hepworth (*The Policeman*), May Clark (*The Cook*)
D: Cecil Hepworth
Standard fantasy: Cop, cook and boy walk on ceiling

Tora No O O Fumu Otokotachi (Walkers on the Tiger's Tail)

1945, (Jap), Toho, b&w, 58 mins.
W: Denjiro Okochi, Susumu Fujita, Masayuki Mori, Takashi Shimura, Aritake Kono
D & SCR: Akira Kurosawa
Standard adventure-thriller: Feudal nobleman flees vengeful brother

Les Torches Humaines (The Human Torches)

1908, (Fr), Star, b&w, 57m (187 ft./3.2 mins.)
D: Georges Melies
A.k.a. **Justinian's Human Torches**
Standard melodrama: Roman tyrant executes hapless

Torchy Blane in Chinatown

1939, (USA), First Nat'l, b&w, 58 mins.
W: Glenda Farrell (*Torchy Blane*), Barton MacLane (*Steve McBride*), Henry O'Neill (*Sen. Baldwin*), Patric Knowles (*Capt. Condon*), Tom Kennedy (*Gahagan*),

James Stephenson (*Mansfield*), Janet Shaw (*Janet*), Frank Shannon (*Capt. McTavish*), George Guhl (*The Desk Sergeant*), Anderson Lawlor (*Fitzhugh*), Eddy Chandler (*Capt. McDonald*), Richard Bond (*Staunton*)
D: William Beaudine   **SCR:** George Bricker, from characters created by Frederick Nebel   **PHOTOG:** Warren Lynch
Standard thriller (7th "Torchy Blane" mystery): Adventurers involved with priceless jade tablets are murdered, girl reporter investigates

Torchy Blane in Panama

1938, (USA), First Nat'l, b&w, 58 mins.
W: Lola Lane (*Torchy Blane*), Paul Kelly (*Steve McBride*), Tom Kennedy (*Gahagan*), Anthony Averill (*Crofton*), Larry Williams (*Bill Canby*), Betty Compson (*Kitty*), James Conlin (*Botkin*), Hugh O'Connell (*Skinner*), Joe Cunningham (*Maxie*), Frank Shannon (*Capt.McTavish*), George Guhl (*The Desk Sergeant*), John Ridgely, George Lloyd, James Nolan, George Regas, John Harron
D: William Clemens   **SCR:** George Bricker, from characters created by Frederick Nebel   **PHOTOG:** Tony Gaudio
Standard thriller (5th "Torchy Blane" mystery): Girl reporter trails killer to convention

Torchy Blane, the Adventurous Blonde

see The Adventurous Blonde

Torchy Gets Her Man

1938, (USA), WB, b&w, 62 mins.
W: Glenda Farrell (*Torchy Blane*), Barton MacLane (*Steve McBride*), Tom Kennedy (*Gahagan*), Willard Robertson (*$100 Bailey*), George Guhl (*The Desk Sergeant*), Frank Reicher (*The Professor*), John Ridgely (*Bugs*), Nat Carr

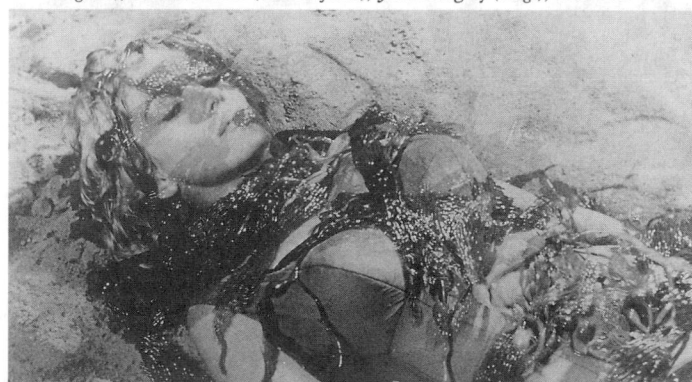

Tormented: JULI REDING

(*Schmidt*), Tommy Jackson (*Gloomy*), Edward Raquello (*Gonzales*), Frank Shannon (*Capt. McTavish*), Ed Keane (*Stoneham*), Cliff Saum (*O'Brien*), Joe Cunningham (*Maxie*), John Harron (*Wilkins*), Herbert Rawlinson (*Breenan*), Lois Cheaney (*Moll*), Greta Meyer (*Mrs. Schmidt*)
D: William Beaudine   **SCR:** Albert DeMond, from characters created by Frederick Nebel   **PHOTOG:** Arthur Todd & Warren Lynch
Standard thriller (6th "Torchy Blane" mystery): Girl reporter tracks counterfeiter

Torchy Plays with Dynamite

1939, (USA), WB, b&w, 59 mins.
W: Jane Wyman (*Torchy Blane*), Allen Jenkins (*Steve McBride*), Tom Kennedy (*Gahagan*), Joe Cunningham (*Maxie*), Sheila Bromley (*Jackie McGuire*), Frank Shannon (*Insp. McTavish*), Eddie Marr (*Denver Eddie*), Edgar Dearing (*Jim Simmons*), Bruce MacFarlane (*Bugsie*), George Lloyd (*Harp*), Aldrich Bowker (*The Police Court Judge*), Creighton Hale (*The Hotel Clerk*), Cliff Clark (*Kelly*), Ruth Robinson (*The Head Matron*), Tiny Roebuck (*Bone Crusher*), Pat Flaherty (*Crusher's Handler*), John Sheehan (*Desk Sergeant O'Toole*), Nat Carr (*The Book Store Clerk*), William Gould (*The Fire Chief*), Frank Mayo (*The Detective*), Cliff Saum (*The Bailiff*), Sol Gross (*The Court Attendant*), Charles Sullivan (*Charlie*), Bess Meyers (*The Night Matron*), Vera Lewis (*The Landlady*), Glen Cavender (*The Landlord*), Harry Hollingsworth (*The Officer*), Frank Moran (*The Handler*), Eddy Chandler (*The Announcer*), Bob Perry (*The Referee*), John Ridgely, Larry Williams, John Harron, Kate Lawson, Dudley Dickerson, Mme. Sultewan, Ralph Sanford, Jack Mower, Lois Cheaney, Jessie Perry, John "Skins" Miller, Jack Richardson
D: Noel Smith   **SCR:** Earle Snell & Charles Belden, from characters created by Frederick Nebel   **PHOTOG:** Arthur L. Todd
Standard thriller (9th & last "Torchy Blane" mystery): Reporter seeks gangster's moll

Torchy Runs for Mayor

1939, (USA), WB, b&w, 60 mins.
W: Glenda Farrell (*Torchy Blane*), Barton MacLane (*Steve McBride*), Tom Kennedy (*Gahagan*), Frank Shannon (*Capt. McTavish*), Joe Cunningham (*Maxie*), John Miljan (*Dr. Dolan*), George Guhl (*The Desk Sergeant*), Joe Downing (*O'Brien*), Irving Bacon (*Hogarth Ward*), Charles Richman (*The Mayor*), John Butler (*Chuck Ball*), Joe Devlin (*Stone*), John Harron (*Dibble*), Walter Fenner (*Skinner*), Kenneth Harlan (*The Advertising Manager*), Millard Vincent (*Reynolds*), Larry Williams (*The Reporter*), Jack Mower (*Duncan*), Chester Gan (*Ling*), Tommy Bupp (*The Urchin*), Claude Wisberg (*The Newsboy*), James Conlin (*The Coroner*), Sidney Bracy (*The Butler*), Stuart Holmes (*Mr. James*), Hal Craig (*Hill*), Eddie Graham (*Stone's Companion*), Jeffrey Sayre (*The Radio Manager*), John Ridgely (*The Photographer*), Dave Roberts (*The Radio

T

Announcer), Kit Guard (*Hoppy*), Jack Daly, Wedgewood Nowell, Fern Barry, Alice Con-nors, Jack Goodrich, Glen Cavender
D: Raymond McCarey   **SCR:** Earle Snell, from characters created by Frederick Nebel   **PHOTOG:** Warren Lynch
Standard thriller (8th & best "Torchy Blane" mystery): Reporter bugs mayor's home, gets goods on political boss

Torment (1944)
see Hets

Torment
1949, (GB), Advance/Adelphi, b&w, 78 mins.
W: Dermot Walsh (*Cliff Brandon*), Rona Anderson (*Joan*), John Bentley (*Jim Brandon*), Michael Martin-Harvey (*Curley Wilson*), Valentine Dunn (*Mrs. Crier*), Dilys Laye (*Violet Crier*)
P: Robert Jordan Hill & John Guillermin   **WRIT & D:** John Guillermin
USA retitle, Paper Gallows
Standard thriller: Jealous novelist essays perfect crime

Torment
1986, (USA), Aslanian-Hopkins/New World, color, 85 mins.
W: Taylor Gilbert, William Witt, Eve Brenner, Stan Weston, Warren Lincoln, Najean Cherry, Al Droyan, Gar Grover
WRIT, P & D: Samson Aslanian & John Hopkins   **PHOTOG:** Stephen Carpenter   **MUSIC:** Christopher Young
Minor thriller: Madman terrorizes woman and her future daughter-in-law

Torment
1993, (Fr), color, 103 mins.
W: Emmanuelle Beart, Francois Cluzet, Nathalie Cardone, Andre Wilms, Marc Lavoine, Dora Doll, Jean-Pierre Cassel
D: Claude Chabrol, from a screenplay by Henri-Georges Clouzot
Engrossing melodrama: Husband's jealousy approaches dementia

Tormented
1960, (USA), AA, b&w, 75 mins.
W: Richard Carlson, Juli Reding, Lugene Sanders, Lillian Adams, Susan Gordon (*Sandy*), Joe Turkel, Gene Roth, Vera Marshe, Dick Walsh, Harry Fleer, Merritt Stone, George Stanley, Leslie Thomas
P: Bert I. Gordon & Joe Steinberg   **D:** Bert I. Gordon   **SCR:** George Worthington Yates   **STORY:** Bert I. Gordon   **PHOTOG:** Ernest Laszlo
SPCL-FX: Bert I. Gordon & Flora M. Gordon   **MUSIC:** Albert Glasser
Minor fantasy-thriller: Dead songstress haunts former lover

The Tormented
1977, (It), Tiberia Film Int'l/21st Century, color
W: Stella Carnachia, Chris Auram, Lucretia Love
P: Justin Reid   **D:** Mario Gariazzo
A.k.a. The Sexorcists and Eerie Midnight Horror Show
Minor eroto-horror: Art student ravished by living statue

Tornado!
1996, (USA), Fox-TV, color, 95 mins.
W: Bruce Campbell, Ernie Hudson, Shannon Sturges, Bo Eason (*Tex*), L.Q. Jones (*Ephram*), Carrie Boren (*Mattie*)
D: Noel Nosseck   **TELEPLAY:** John Logan   **MUSIC:** Garry Schyman
TVM, standard thriller (inspired by Twister): Weather menaces meteorologist and Gov't accountant in Texas panhandle

Torn Curtain
1966, (USA), Univ, color, 119 mins.
W: Paul Newman, Julie Andrews, Lila Kedrova, Ludwig Donath, David Opatoshu, Tamara Toumanova, Hans-Joerg Felmy, Wolfgang Kieling
P & D: Alfred Hitchcock   **SCR:** Brian Moore   **PHOTOG:** John F. Warren
   MUSIC: John Addison
Standard thriller: American scientist pretends to defect

The Torpedo of Doom
1966, (USA), Rep, b&w, 100 mins.
W: Lee Powell, Herman Brix, Eleanor Stewart, Montagu Love
P: Robert Beche   **D:** William Witney & John English   **SCR:** Barry Shipman, Franklin Adreon, Ronald Davidson & Sol Shor
Minor thriller (feature version of 1938 serial The Fighting Devil Dogs): Hooded villain seeks world conquest

La Torre de los Siete Jorobados (The Tower of the Seven Hunchbacks)
1944, (Sp), b&w
W: Isabel de Pomes, Julia Lajos, Manolita Moran, Felix de Pomes, Antonio Riquelme, Julia Pachelo, Guillermo Marin, Antonio Casal
D: Edgar Neville   **SCR:** Emilio Carrere
Standard thriller

Torso
1974, (It), Carlo Ponti/Joseph Brenner, color, 89 mins.
W: Suzy Kendall (*Jane*), Tina Aumont (*Dani*), Luc Merenda (*Roberto*), John Richardson (*Franz*), Roberto Bisacco (*Stefano*), Angela Covello (*Katia*), Carla Brait (*Ursula*), Patricia Adiutori (*Flo*), Cristina Airoldi (*Carol*)
P: Antonio Cervi   **D:** Sergio Martino   **SCR:** E. Gastaldi & Sergio Martino
PHOTOG: Giancarlo Ferrando

Standard eroto-thriller: Murderous psycho stalks coed

Torticola Contre Frankensberg (Torticola vs. Frankensberg)
1952, (Fr), Les Films Marceau, b&w, 36 mins.
W: Vera Norman, Roger Blin, Marc Boussac, Francois Patrice, Michel Piccoli, Daniel Gelin, Helena Manson, Pierre Brasseur
D & ADAPT: Paul Paviot   **SCR & DIALOG:** Louis Sapin & Albert Vidalie
   PHOTOG: Andre Thomas   **MUSIC:** Joseph Kosma
Standard horror-satire

The Torture Chamber of Baron Blood
see Gli Orrori del Castello di Nuremberga

The Torture Chamber of Dr. Sadism
see Die Schlangengrube und das Pendel

Torture Dungeon
1969, (USA), Mishkin, color
W: Jeremy Brooks, Patricia Dillon, Susan Cassidy
P: William Mishkin   **D:** Andy Milligan   **SCR:** Andy Milligan & John Borske
orig. co-billed with Bloodthirsty Butchers
Minor horror-thriller: Duke of Norwich tortures and kills successors to English throne

Torture Garden
1967, (GB), Amicus/Col, color, 93 mins.
W: Burgess Meredith (*Dr. Diablo*), Jack Palance (*Ronald Wyatt*), Beverly Adams (*Carla Hayes*), Peter Cushing (*Canning*), Maurice Denham (*Uncle Roger*), John Standing (*Leo Winston*), Michael Bryant (*Colin Williams*), Robert Hutton (*Bruce Benton*), John Phillips (*Eddie Storm*), Michael Ripper (*Gordon Roberts*), Bernard Kay (*Dr. Heim*), Barbara Ewing (*Dorothy Endicott*), Catherine Finn (*Nurse Parker*), Ursula Howells (*Maxine Chambers*), David Bauer (*Mike Charles*), Niall MacGinnis (*The Doctor*), Clytie Jessop
P: Max J. Rosenberg & Milton Subotsky   **D:** Freddie Francis   **SCR:** Robert Bloch, based on several of his short stories (e.g., "Terror Over Hollywood" & "The Man Who Collected Poe")   **PHOTOG:** Norman Warwick
Standard horror-fantasy anthology: Satanic fairground barker predicts horrendous futures

Torture Zone
see The Fear Chamber

To Save a Child
1991, (USA), ABC-TV, color, 95 mins.
W: Marita Geraghty (*Isabella*), Pete Kowanko (*Garth*), Janel Moloney (*Janelle*), Shirley Knight (*Rinda*), Anthony Zerbe (*Lewis*), Joseph Runningfox (*Toby Coldcreek*), Sarah Jane Jackson (*Taryn*), Spalding Gray (*Hobart*), Phil Mead (*Dr. Bob*), Steven Gregory Tyler (*Det. Wetzel*)
TVM, standard thriller: Pregnant woman meets coven

To Save the King
1914, (GB), Martin Films/Thanhouser, b&w, 955 ft. (291.1m)
W: Harry Granville
D: Dave Aylott
reissued (1915) as The Enemy Within
Standard thriller: Detective saves Ruritanian king from anarchists

To Sleep with a Vampire
1992, (USA), color, 90 mins.
W: Scott Valentine, Charlie Spradling, Richard Zobel, Ingrid Vold, Stephanie Hardy
D: Adam Friedman
Minor horror-fantasy (remake of Dance of the Damned): Vampire seeks normal existence, stalks stripper

Total Recall
1990, (USA), Carolco/Tri-Star, color, 116 mins.
W: Arnold Schwarzenegger (*Quaid*), Rachel Ticotin (*Melina*), Sharon Stone (*Lori*), Ronny Cox (*Cohaagen*), Michael Ironside (*Richter*), Marshall Bell (*George/Kuato*), Mel Johnson Jr. (*Benny*), Roy Brocksmith (*A Doctor*), George P. Wilbur, Michael Champion, Ray Baker, Rosemary Dunsmore, Debbie Lee Carrington, David Knell, Alexia Robinson, Dean Norris, Ken Strausbaugh, Mark Carlton, Lycia Naff, Bobby Costanzo, Bob Tzudiker, Michael LaGuardia, Priscilla Allen, Marc Alaimo, Michael Gregory, Ken Gildin, Mickey Jones, Parker Whitman, Ellen Gollas, Gloria Dorson, Erika Carlson, Benny Corral, Erik Cord, Frank Kopvc, Chuck Sloan, Dave Nicolson, Paula McClure, Rebecca Ruth, Milt Tarver, Roger Cudney, Monica Steuer, Sasha Rionda, Linda Howell, Robert Picardo (*Voice of Johnnycab*)
D: Paul Verhoeven   **SCR:** Ronald Shusett, Dan O'Bannon & Gary Goldman
   SCREEN STORY: Ronald Shusett, Dan O'Bannon & Jon Povill, inspired by Philip K. Dick's short story "We Can Remember It for You Wholesale"   **PHOTOG:** Jost Vacano   **VS-FX:** Dream Quest   **MUSIC:** Jerry Goldsmith
   Fr retitle: Voyage to the Center of Memory
Superior SF-adventure: Man visits Mars, seeks his true identity

Die Toten Augen von London (Dead Eyes of London)
1960, (W. Ger), Magna, b&w
W: Joachim Fuchsberger, Karin Baal, Klaus Kinski, Dieter Borsche, Ady Berber
P: Herbert Sennewald   **D:** Alfred Vohrer   **SCR:** Trygve Larsen, from Edgar Wallace's novel *Dark Eyes of London*
Standard thriller: Nasty insurance murders. cf. Dark Eyes of London

T

To the Devil a Daughter

1975, (GB-W. Ger), Hammer-Terra Filmkunst/EMI, color, 93 mins.
W: Richard Widmark (*John Verney*), Christopher Lee (*Father Michael Rayner*), Honor Blackman (*Anna Fountain*), Denholm Elliott (*Henry Beddows*), Nastassia Kinski (*Catherine Beddows*), Michal Goodliffe (*George De Grass*), Derek Francis (*The Bishop*), Eva-Marie Meineke (*Eveline DeGrass*), Irene Prador (*The Matron*), Anthony Valentine (*David*), Isabella Telezynska (*Margaret*), Brian Wilde (*The Attendant*), Anna Bentinck (*Isabel*), Frances de la Tour (*The SA Major*), Constantin De Goguel (*Kolide*)
P: Roy Skeggs **D:** Peter Sykes **SCR:** Christopher Wicking & John Peacock, from a novel by Dennis Wheatley **PHOTOG:** David Watkin **MUSIC:**

The Tourist Trap: TANYA ROBERTS

Paul Glass
video title: **Child of Satan**
Minor horror-fantasy: Novelist saves girl from possession by evil spirit

To the Ends of the Earth

1948, (USA), Col, b&w, 109 mins.
W: Dick Powell, Signe Hasso
Standard melodrama

To the Ends of Time

1996, (GB), color
W: Joss Ackland, Michael Silverback
Made-for-Cable, standard juvenile fantasy: King of Floating city seeks to end all war

To the Starry Island

see **Gesom E Kako Shipta**

To Trap a Spy

1966, (USA), MGM, color, 92 mins.
W: Robert Vaughn, Patricia Crowley, David McCallum, Fritz Weaver, William Marshall, Luciana Paluzzi, Victoria Shaw, Will Kuluva, Ivan Dixon
D: Don Medford **PHOTOG:** Joseph Biroc
Minor thriller (created by lengthening pilot for teleseries "The Man from U.N.C.L.E.")

Touch

1997, (USA), Lumiere Int'l/UA, color, 100 mins.
W: Bridget Fonda (*Lynn Faulkner*), Christopher Walken (*Bill Hill*), Skeet Ulrich (*Juvenal*), Tom Arnold (*August Murray*), Gina Gershon (*Debra Lusanne*), Paul Mazursky (*Artie*), Janeane Garofalo (*Kathy Worthington*), Lolita Davidovich
P: Lila Cazes & Fida Attieh **WRIT & D:** Paul Schrader, from Elmore Leonard's 1977 novel **PHOTOG:** Ed Lachman **MUSIC:** David Grohl
Unusual comedy-melodrama: Mysterious youth has healing powers

Touch of Death

1962, (GB), Helion/Planet, b&w, 58 mins.
W: William Lucas (*Pete Mellor*), David Sumner (*Len Williams*), Ray Barrett (*Maxwell*), Jan Waters (*Jackie*), Frank Coda (*Sgt. Byrne*), Roberta Tovey (*Pam*), Geoffrey Denton (*Baxter*)
P: Lewis Linzee **D:** Lance Comfort **SCR:** Lyn Fairhurst **STORY:** Aubrey Cash & Wilfred Josephs
Standard crime-thriller: Crook steals poisoned money

A Touch of Hydrophobia

1911, (GB), Hepworth, b&w, 400 ft. (121.9m)
W: Johnny Butt (*The Man*)
D: Frank Wilson
Standard fantasy: Mad dog bites man, causes him to act like canine

The Touch of Melissa

see **The Touch of Satan**

The Touch of Satan

1971, (USA), Futurama Int'l, color
W: Emby Mellay
P: George E. Carey **D:** Don Henderson **SCR:** James E. McLarty
A.k.a. **The Touch of Melissa** *and* **Night of the Demon**

A Touch of the Other

1970, (GB), Global/Queensway, color, 92 mins.
W: Kenneth Cope (*Delger*), Shirley Anne Field (*Elaine*), Noel Davis (*Max Ronleau*), Helene Francois (*Wendy*), Timothy Craven (*Webber*), Vasco Koulolia (*Hughes*), Renny Lister (*Sheila*), Gypsy Kemp (*Shirley*), Paul Stassino (*Connely*)
P: Leslie Berens, Arnold Louis Miller & Sheila Miller **D:** Arnold Louis Miller **STORY:** Frank Wyman
Standard crime-thriller: Prostitute helps detective framed for murder

A Touch of Zen

1969, (Thai), color, 175 mins.
W: Shih Chun, Hsu Feng, Pai Ying, Tien Peng, Roy Chiao
D: King Hu
Visually-stunning melodrama: Tale of Ming Dynasty moves from ghost story to political thriller

La Tour de Londres et les Derniers Moments d'Anne de Boleyn (The Tower of London and the Last Moments of Anne Boleyn)

1905, (Fr), Star, b&w, 103m (337.9 ft./5.7 mins.)
D: Georges Melies
A.k.a. **The Tower of London**
Standard melodrama (in 5 scenes): English queen beheaded

Tourist Trap

1979, (USA), Charles Band/Compass Int'l, color, 85 mins.
W: Chuck Connors (*Slausen*), Jocelyn Jones (*Molly*), Tanya Roberts (*Becky*), Jon Van Ness (*Jerry*), Dawn Jeffory (*Tina*), Robin Sherwood (*Eileen*), Keith McDermott (*Woody*)
D: David Schmoeller **SCR:** David Schmoeller & J. Larry Carroll **PHOTOG:** Nicholas Von Sternberg **MUSIC:** Pino Donaggio
Standard thriller: Mannequins terrorize teens

La Tour Maudite (The Cursed Tower)

1901, (Fr), Star, b&w, 60m (196.9 ft./3.3 mins.)
D: Georges Melies
USA retitle, **The Bewitched Dungeon**
Standard fantasy

Toward the Terra

1980, (Jap), color, 112 mins.
Standard SF-thriller: Space colonists revolt

The Tower

1983, (Can), Lionel Shenken/Emmeritus, color, 90 mins.
W: Ray Paisley, Jackie Wray, George West
WRIT & D: James Makichuk
TVM, minor SF: Computer traps exec in office high-rise

The Towering Inferno

1974, (USA), 20th-Fox & WB, color, 165 mins.
W: Steve McQueen (*Michael O'Hallorhan*), Paul Newman (*Doug Roberts*), Faye Dunaway (*Susan Franklin*), Jennifer Jones (*Lisolette*), Fred Astaire (*Harlee Claiborne*), O.J. Simpson (*Jernigan*), William Holden (*James Duncan*), Richard Chamberlain (*Roger Simmons*), Susan Blakely (*Patty Simmons*), Robert Vaughn (*Sen. Gary Parker*), Gregory Sierra (*Carlos*), Robert Wagner (*Bigelow*), Susan Flannery (*Laurie*), Normann Burton (*Will Giddings*), Jack Collins (*Mayor Ramsey*), Ross Elliott, Paul Comi, Dabney Coleman, Sheila Mathews, Ernie Orsatti, Don Gordon, Norman Grabowski, Felton Perry
P: Irwin Allen **D:** John Guillermin **SCR:** Stirling Silliphant **PHOTOG:** Fred J. Koenekamp & Joseph Biroc **SPCL-FX:** L.B. Abbott **MUSIC:** John Williams **SONG:** sung by Maureen McGovern, *We May Never Love Like This Again*
Superior thriller: San Francisco skyscraper burns

Tower of Evil

1972, (GB), Grenadier/Fanfare/Anglo-EMI, color, 89 mins.
W: Bryant Halliday (*Evan Brent*), Jill Haworth (*Rose Mason*), Anna Palk (*Nora Winthrop*), William Lucas (*Supt. Hawk*), Anthony Valentine (*Dr. Simpson*), Jack Watson (*Hamp Gurney*), Mark Edwards (*Adam*), Derek Fowlds (*Dan Winthrop*), Candace Glendenning (*Penny Read*), John Hamill (*Gary*), Dennis Price (*Laurence Bakewell*), Gary Hamilton (*Brom*), Serretta Wilson (*Mae*), George Coulouris (*John Gurney*), Robin Askwith (*Des*), Frederic Abbott (*Saul Gurney*), Mark McBride (*Michael Gurney*), Marianne Stone (*The Nurse*)

T

P: Richard Gordon **D & SCR:** Jim O'Connolly **STORY:** George Baxt **PHO-TOG:** Desmond Dickinson **MUSIC:** Kenneth V. Jones
USA retitle: Horror on Snape Island, A.k.a. Beyond the Fog
Standard thriller: Archeologists murdered by mad lighthouse keeper

The Tower of Lies
1925, (USA), MGM, b&w, 6,500 ft. (1981.2m)
W: Lon Chaney Sr., Norma Shearer, William Haines
D: Victor Seastrom
Standard melodrama

The Tower of London (1905)
see La Tour de Londres et les Derniers Moments d'Anne de Boleyn

The Tower of London
1909, (GB), Williamson, b&w, 1,125 ft. (342.9m)
D: James Williamson, from a novel by Harrison Ainsworth
Standard melodrama: Nobleman escapes from jealous jailer to wed Lady's maid

The Tower of London
1939, (USA), Univ, b&w, 92 mins.
W: Boris Karloff (*Mord*), Basil Rathbone (*Richard III*), Nan Grey (*Lady Alice*), Barbara O'Neil (*Queen Elizabeth*), Vincent Price (*Duke of Clarence*), John Sutton, Ian Hunter, Rose Hobart, John Rodion, Ralph Forbes, Ernest Cossart, Leo G. Carroll, Miles Mander, Frances Robinson, Lionel Belmore, Ronald Sinclair, G.P. Huntley Jr., Walter Tetley, Donnie Dunagan, John Herbert-Bond, Georgia Caine
P & D: Rowland V. Lee **SCR:** Robert N. Lee **PHOTOG:** George Robinson **MUSIC:** Charles Previn
"Tower of London brought the mechanics of horror to historical spectacle and was, in essence, Shakespeare's Richard III minus the text but with every behead-ing, drowning, stabbing and smothering lovingly intact"—Carlos Clarens, An Illustrated History of the Horror Film
Modest thriller: English tyrant kills to acquire crown

Tower of London
1962, (USA), Admiral/UA, b&w, 79 mins.
W: Vincent Price (*Richard III*), Sandra Knight, Joan Freeman, Michael Pate, Robert Brown, Bruce Gordon, Sara Taft, Joan Camden, Richard Hale, Charles Macaulay, Sarah Selby, Justice Watson, Donald Losby, Eugene Martin
P: Gene Corman **D:** Roger Corman **SCR:** Leo V. Gordon, Amos Powell & James B. Gordon **STORY:** Leo V. Gordon & Amos Powell **PHOTOG:** Arch Dalzell **SPCL-FX:** Modern Film Effects **MUSIC DIR:** Michael Andersen
Standard thriller: English king's infamies

The Tower of London and the Last Moments of Anne Boleyn
see La Tour de Londres et les Derniers Moments d'Anne de Boleyn

Tower of Terror
1941, (GB), Assoc. British/Pathe, b&w, 68 mins.
W: Wilfrid Lawson (*Wolfe Kristan*), Movita (*Marie Durand*), Michael Rennie (*Anthony Hale*), George Woodbridge (*Rudolf Jurgens*), Morland Graham (*Herr Kleber*), Edward Sinclair (*Fletcher*), John Longden (*The Commandant*), Charles Rolfe (*Albers*), Richard George (*Capt. Borkmann*), Victor Weske (*Peters*), Olive Sloane (*The Florist*)
D: Lawrence Huntington **SCR:** John Reinhart **ADAPT:** John Argyle **PHOTOG:** Walter Harvey & Ronald Anscombe **MUSIC:** Eddie Benson
Unusual thriller: Fugitive beauty causes conflict between British agent and mad German lighthouse keeper

Tower of the Screaming Virgins
1968, (W. Ger), color, 89 mins.
W: Terry Torday, Jean Piat
loosely based on an Alexandre Dumas novel
Minor thriller: French queen murders her lovers

The Tower of the Seven Hunchbacks
see La Torre de los Siete Jorobados

Towers Open Fire
1963, (GB), Anthony Balch/Connoisseur, b&w, 11 mins.
W: William Burroughs, Alexander Trocchi, David Jacobs, Ian Sommerville, Brion Gysin, Bachoo Sen, John Gillett, Liam O'Leary
P & D: Antony Balch **STORY:** William Burroughs
Standard short fantasy: Melange of images concerning drugs, homosexuality, masturbation & violence

A Town has Turned to Dust
1998, (USA), SCI-TV, color
W: Ron Perlman, Stephen Lang, Judy Collins, from a story by Rod Serling
TVM, standard SF-fantasy

Town on Trial
1957, (GB), Marksman/Col, b&w, 96 mins.
W: John Mills (*Supt. Mike Halloran*), Charles Coburn (*Dr. John Fenner*), Barbara Bates (*Elizabeth Fenner*), Derek Farr (*Mark Roper*), Elizabeth Seal (*Fiona Dixon*), Alec McCowen (*Peter Crowley*), Fay Compton (*Mrs. Crowley*),

Geoffrey Keen (*Mr. Dixon*), Harry Locke (*Sgt. Beale*), Margaretta Scott (*Helen Dixon*), Meredith Edwards (*Sgt. Rogers*), Raymond Huntley (*Dr. Reese*), Maureen Connell (*Mary Roper*), John Warwick (*Insp. Hughes*), Magda Miller (*Molly Stevens*)
P: Maxwell Setton **D:** John Guilermin **STORY:** Robert Westerby & Ken Hughes
Modest crime-thriller: Nurse's uncle suspected of strangling pregnant girl

The Town That Dreaded Sundown
1977, (USA), AIP, color
W: Ben Johnson, Andrew Prine, Charles B. Pierce, Dawn Wells
P & D: Charles B. Pierce **SCR:** Earl E. Smith
Unusual, fact-based thriller: Hooded killer terrorizes Texas town

The Toxic Avenger
1984, (USA), H.C.H./Troma, color, 82 mins.
W: Andree Maranda (*Sara*), Mitchell Cohen (*The Toxic Avenger*), Pat Ryan Jr. (*Mayor Belgoody*), Cindy Manion (*Julie*), Jennifer Baptist (*Wanda*), Robert Prichard (*Slug*), Charles Lee Jr. (*Nipples*), Gary Schneider (*Bozo*), Dick Martinson (*Officer O'Clancy*), Mark Torgl (*Melvin*), Dan Snow (*Cigar Face*), Chris Liano (*Walter Harris*), Larry Sutton (*Frank*), David Weiss (*The Chief of Police*), Pat Kilpatrick (*Leroy*), Doug Isbecque (*Knuckles*), Mike Russo (*Rico*), Norma Pratt (*Mrs. Haskell*), Andrew Craig (*Fred*), Ryan Sexton (*Johnny*), Sarabel Levinson (*Melvin's Mom*), Al Pia (*Tom Wrightson*), Reuben Guss (*Dr. Snodburger*), Barbara J. Gurskey (*Barbie*), Donna Winter (*The Mayor's Sec'y*), Mary Ellen David, Dennis Souder, Joe Zarro, William Christopher Weiss, Sherry Park, Dan Hogan, Myrna Williams, Richard Duggan, Xavier Barquet, Bruce Morton, John Stobaeus, Joe Supor Jr., D.J. Calvitto, Cosmo Wilder, Brigitte Douglaston, Nancy Compansanto, Matt Klan, Andrea Suter, Joey Calderone, Vickie Usher, Roxanne Maranda, Barry Shapiro, Andy Stamatin, Betty Pia, Jessica Perkins, Teddy Copley, Dolly Hall, Alisha Riggs, Mary Cox, Vicki Juditz, Maxine Hayt, Teresa Simpson, Margaret Riley, Don Costello, June DeYoung, Jon Curtis, Peter Racini, Skip Hamra, Martin Scott McMann, Ed Carrion, Bruce Zimmerman, Charles DiCagno, Eileen Nad Castaldi, Nathan Jon Castaldi, Britt Martinsen, Kristen Martinsen, Lisa Martinsen, DonnaMarie Stipo, Dianna-Jean Flaherty, Giorgio Calderone, Wil-liam Klan, Kenneth Kessler (*Voice of the Toxic Avenger*)
D: Michael Herz & Samuel Weil **SCR:** Joe Ritter **ORIG. STORY:** Lloyd Kaufman **PHOTOG:** James London & Lloyd Kaufman **SONGS:** *Body Talk, It's This Love, Lay It on the Line & Nothing at All*
Modest cult classic, standard SF-satire: Nerd becomes super hero

The Toxic Avenger, Part II
1989, (USA), Troma, color
W: Ron Fazio, Phoebe Legere, John Altamura, Rick Collins, Rikiya Yasuoka, Tsutomu Sekine, Lisa Gaye, Jessica Dublin, Shinoburyu, Mayako Katsuragi, Jack Cooper, Erika Schickel, Bonnie Garvin, Karen King, Didi Mancuso, Melissa Osborne, Helen Wheels, Raven Skye, Traci Mann, Paul Davis, Fernando Antonio, Paul Borgese, Sylvester Covin, William Decker, Joe Fleishaker, Marc Fusile, Marc Allan Ginsberg, Benny Nieves, Sal Lioni, Doug McDonald, Karum Ratcliff, Eric Alan, Felix Cortes, Michael White, Susan Whitty, Jeremiah Yates, Andrew Wolk, Dan Snow, Florence Gummersbach, Bill Ferris, Michael Drummer, Irene Scase Summerville, Alex Cserhart, John Mollica, Theresa Faw, Thomas Harding, Bryan Per-kins, Michael Leoce, Keith Allen, Elliot Weiss, Emmy Meyer, Matt Miller, Phil Rivo, Arthur Jolly, Frank Kramer, Doug Wright, Carol Mazzei, Char-lotte Kaufman, Lisbeth Kaufman, Patricia Kaufman, Lily Hayes Kaufman, Sloane Herz, Anthony Caputo, Ron Goldberg, Darel Chase, Kevin Colby, Lorna Courtney, Alexis Grey, Kayko Kawamoto, Chris McNamee, Louie Ortiz, Valentine Smith,Tony Peters, John Reidy, Raymond Seiden, Lily Smith, Richard Sparks, Roy Sundance, Tom Vigarito, Paul Weatherbee, Jim Woyt, Orentha Alva, Anne Charbonneau, Lori Corby, Julie Fried, Kathleen Footer, Jennifer Furillo, David Greenspan, David Glover, Robert Hoffer Sr., Robert Hoffer Jr., Beverly Irish, Don Kaplan, Glenn Keet, Lis Kuzman, William Leone, Robert Libby Sr., Ted Lyon, Larry Mardany, Cariann Mazzei, Dominick Mastrianna, Carol Morrissey, J.W. Sass, Takayuki Arafuka, Karen Silvernail, Susan Slutsky, Jon Stern, Myron Smith, Debi Staron, Harry Williams Jr., Steven Young, Maya Shiraki, Yoko Ohshima, Kenji Nara, Kenji Nakajima, Yutaka Kondo, Hidenori Takahashi, Masahiro Ishii, Kei Nakada, Tadayuki Sugiyama, Hiroaki Matsuya, Eiji Kobayashi, Yasuhiro Tanogashira, Yuji Kobayashi, Yoshikazu Fukunaga, Yasutaka Tezuka, Wataru Tsukada, Satoshi Morioka, Toshimi Yamaguchi, Wataru Fukuda, Yoshiko Nagashima, Kazumi Kanebako, Shunsako Nakayama, Nao Kotetsu, Masao Machitani, Masahiro Fujiyoshi, Yoshiaki Okuten, Saburo Isobe, Masanori Sato, Akito Oshima, Ichiro Yamanak, Go Nagai, Sayuri Niida, Isamu Gosha, Jiiko Uchiyama, Katsuyaki Sato, Satoe Nanaki, Yoko Kuriki, Keiko Kano, Masamori Kanbe, Morikazu Kanbe, Daisuke Kato, Wataru Ohashi, Hiroshi Mitsui, Toyoko Kunisawa, Makoto Fukutomi, Hitomi Tawara, Shizuka Mukai, Masayoshi Hosokawa, Kazumasa Suzuki, Takeshi Takimoto, Wasaburo Nakamura, Sora Yamada, Fukawa Masaaki, Sonoda Hideki
D: Michael Herz & Lloyd Kaufman **SCR:** Gay Partington Terry & Lloyd Kaufman **ORIG. STORY:** Lloyd Kaufman **PHOTOG:** James London **MUSIC:** Barrie Guard **SONGS:** *Turn to Me & Toxic Lover*
Minor SF-satire: Grotesque superhero returns

The Toxic Avenger, Part III: The Last Temptation of Toxie
1989, (USA), Troma, color, 89 mins.

W: Ron Fazio, Phoebe Legere, John Altamura, Rick Collins, Lisa Gaye, Jessica Dublin, Michael Kaplan
D: Michael Herz & Lloyd Kaufman   **SCR:** Gay Partington Terry & Lloyd Kaufman   **ORIG. STORY:** Lloyd Kaufman   **PHOTOG:** James London   **MUSIC:** Christopher DeMarco (based on music by Antonin Dvorak)
Minor SF-satire: Grotesque superhero faces mid-life crisis

Toxic Zombies
1980, (USA), CM Prods., color, 83 mins.
W: Charles Austin (*Cole*), Beverly Shapiro (*Polly*), Dennis Helfend, Kevin Hanlon, Judy Brown, Bob Larson
WRIT, P & D: Charles McCrann   **PHOTOG:** David Sperling   **SPCL-FX:** Craig Harris   **MUSIC:** Ted Shapiro
Minor horror-thriller: Marijuana growers mutated by defoliant

Toy Factory
see Necromancy

The Toymaker's Dream
1910, (GB), Alpha Trading Co., b&w, 420 ft. (128m)
WRIT & D: Arthur Cooper
Standard fantasy: Toymaker dreams of toy airplanes crashing

Toy Story
1995, (USA), Walt Disney, color, 81 mins.
VOICES: Tom Hanks (*Woody*), Tim Allen (*Buzz Lightyear*), Don Rickles (*Mr. Potato Head*), Jim Varney (*Slinky Dog*), John Ratzenberger (*Hamm the Pig*), Annie Potts (*Bo Peep*), Wallace Shawn, John Morris, R. Lee Ermey, Laurie Metcalf, Erik von Detten
D: John Lasseter   **SCR:** Joss Whedon, Joel Cohen & Alec Sokolow   **MUSIC:** Randy Newman   **SONG:** *You've Got a Friend in Me*
Engrossing juvenile fantasy (first feature made entirely by computer): Boy's playthings come to life when unobserved

Toy Story II
1997, (USA), Walt Disney, color
VOICES: Tom Hanks, Tim Allen
Made-for-Video, standard fantasy: Further adventures of living toys

Traces of Red
1992, (USA), Samuel Goldwyn, color, 105 mins.
W: James Belushi, Lorraine Bracco, Tony Goldwyn, William Russ, Faye Grant, Michelle Joyner, Joe Lisi, Julian Byrd
D: Andy Wolk
Minor thriller: Serial killer pursued

Track of the Cat
1954, (USA), WB, color, 102 mins.
W: Robert Mitchum, Teresa Wright, Tab Hunter, Diana Lynn, Beulah Bondi, Philip Tonge, William Hopper, Carl Switzer
D: William A. Wellman, from a novel by Walter Van Tilburg Clark   **PHOTOG:** William H. Clothier
Gripping psychodrama-Western: Mountain lion menaces family

Track of the Moon Beast
1977, (USA), Cinema Shares, color, 90 mins.
W: Chase Cordell, Gregorio Sala (*Salinas*), Donna Leigh Drake (*Cathy*), Patrick Wright (*McCabe*)
D: Richard Ashe
Minor horror-thriller: Mineralogist becomes killer lizard by moonlight

Track of the Vampire
see Blood Bath (1966)

Tracks of a Killer
1996, (USA), color
W: James Brolin, Kelly LeBrock, Wolf Larsen, Courtney Taylor, George Touliatos
Standard thriller: Vengeful executive stalks corporate bigwig and his wife at mountain retreat

Track the Man Down
1955, (GB), Rep, b&w, 75 mins.
W: Kent Taylor (*Don Ford*), Petula Clark (*June Dennis*), Mary Mackenzie (*Mrs. Norman*), Renee Houston (*Pat Sherwood*), Kenneth Griffith (*Ken Orwell*), Walter Rilla (*Austin Melford*), George Rose (*Rick Lambert*), Ursula Howells (*Mary Dennis*), Lloyd Lamble (*Insp. Barnet*)
P: William N. Boyle   **D:** R.G. Springsteen   **SCR:** Paul Erickson & Kenneth R. Hayles
Standard crime-thriller: Reporter collars dogtrack-takings thief on long-distance bus

Track 29
1987, (GB), color, 90 mins.
W: Theresa Russell, Gary Oldman, Christopher Lloyd, Colleen Camp, Sandra Bernhard, Seymour Cassel, Leon Rippy
D: Nicolas Roeg   **SCR:** Dennis Potter
Standard psychodrama: Neglected wife discovers long-lost illegitimate son

Trader Horn
1931, (USA), MGM, b&w, 105 mins.
W: Harry Carey (*Trader Horn*), Edwina Booth, Duncan Renaldo, Olive Golden,

Mutia Omoolu, C. Aubrey Smith
D: W.S. van Dyke II   **SCR:** Cyril Hume, Richard Schayer, Dale Van Every & John Thomas Neville   **PHOTOG:** Clyde De Vinna
Classic thriller (first African melodrama filmed on location): Safari finds "white goddess"

Trader Horn
1973, ven (USA), MGM, color, 105 mins.
W: Rod Taylor (*Trader Horn*), Anne Heywood (*Nicole*), Jean Sorel (*Emil*), Don Knight (*Sinclair*), Ed Bernard (*Apaque*), Stack Pierce (*Malugi*), Erik Holland (*Medford*), Robert Miller Driscoll (*Alfredo*), King Solomon III (*Red Sun*), Willie Harris (*Blue Star*), Caro Kenyatta (*Umbopa*), Curt Lowens (*Schmidt*), John Siegfried (*The German Officer*), Oliver Givens
D: Reza S. Badiyi   **SCR:** William Norton & Edward Harper   **STORY:** Edward Harper   **PHOTOG:** Ronald W. Browne   **MUSIC:** Shelly Manne
Minor adventure-thriller (listless remake of cinema classic)

Traffic in Crime
1946, (USA), Rep, b&w, 56 mins.
W: Kane Richmond, Adele Mara
Standard melodrama

Tragedy at Holly Cottage
1916, (GB), British Oak/New Agency, b&w, 1,070 ft. (326.1m)
D: Ernest G. Batley
Standard crime-thriller: Rich man strangled by disowned son

The Tragedy of Basil Grieve
1914, (GB), Hepworth/Feature, b&w, 3,250 ft. (990.6m)
W: Violet Hopson (*Vera Duncan*), Stewart Rome (*Basil Grieve*), Cyril Morton (*Roland Nashley*), Harry Gilbey (*Fothergill*), Marie de solla (*Brenda Welham*), John MacAndrews (*The Detective*)
D: Frank Wilson
A.k.a. The Great Poison Mystery
Standard crime-thriller: Woman poisons husband, is killed fleeing to lover

The Tragedy of Carmen
1983, (Fr), color, 85 mins.
W: Helene Delavault, Howard Hensel, Agnes Host, Jake Gardner, Jean-Paul Denizon, Alain Maratrat
D: Peter Brook, from Bizet's opera, based on Prosper Merimee's story   **PHOTOG:** Sven Nykvist
Fast-paced musical thriller: Gypsy stirs passions

A Tragedy of the Cornish Coast
1912, (GB), B&C/MP, b&w, 1,050 ft. (320m)
W: Wallett Waller (*Tom Leigh*), Dorothy Foster (*Mary Trelawney*), O'Neil Farrell (*A Villain*), Sidney Northcote (*A Villain*)
D: Sidney Northcote   **STORY:** Harold Brett
Standard crime-thriller: Fishergirl escapes abduction

A Tragedy of the Olden Times
1911, (GB), Natural Colour Kinematograph Co., color, 590 ft. (179.8m)
D: Theo Bouwmeester
Standard melodrama: 1830s innkeeper tries to poison farmer, kills highwayman son by mistake

A Tragedy of the Truth
1909, (GB), Precision Films, b&w, 730 ft. (222.5m)
D: T.J. Gobbett
Standard crime-thriller: Snubbed man robs nobleman, frames rival

The Trail of Sand
1911, (GB), Hepworth, b&w, 450 ft. (137.2m)
W: Flora Morris (*The Girl*)
D: Bert Haldane
Standard crime-thriller: Workman robs foreman, is trailed by girl and scouts

Train Ride to Hollywood
1975, (USA), color, 95 mins.
W: Charles Love, Willis Draffen, Harry Williams
Standard fantasy: Rock singer dreams he's aboard train filled with old-time movie stars

Trial by Combat
see A Choice of Weapons

The Trail of the Fatal Ruby
1912, (GB), Barker, b&w, 980 ft. (298.7m)
D: Bert Haldane   **STORY:** Rowland Talbot
Standard thriller: Bad luck follows theft of mummy's gem

Traitement de Choc (Shock Treatment)
1972, (It-Fr), Lira/AJ, color, 91 mins.
W: Alain Delon, Annie Girardot, Michel Duchaussoy, Bernard Hirsch
WRIT & D: Alain Jessua   **PHOTOG:** Jacques Robin   **SPCL-FX:** Andre Pierdel   **MUSIC:** Rene Koering & Alain Jessua
GB retitle, The Doctor in the Nude, USA retitle, Shock
Standard satire-thriller: Woman discovers gruesome source of rejuvenation treatments

The Traitors

1962, (GB), Ello/RFD, b&w, 69 mins.
W: Patrick Allen (*John Lane*), James Maxwell (*Ray Ellis*), Ewan Roberts (*Col. Burlington*), Jacqueline Ellis (*Mary*), Zena Walker (*Annette Lane*), Jeffrey Segal (*Dr. Lindt*), Harold Goodwin (*Edwards*)
P & SCR: James O'Connolly **D:** Robert Tronson **STORY:** J.P. O'Connolly & J. Levy
Standard crime-thriller: Communist spies behind scientist's death

Traitor's Gate
1964, (GB), Summit/Col, b&w, 80 mins.
W: Albert Lieven (*Trayne*), Gary Raymond (*Graham/Lt. Dick Lee-Carnby*), Margot Trooper (*Dinah*), Catherina Von Schell (*Hope*), Eddie Arent (*Hector*), Klaus Kinski (*Kinski*), Anthony James (*John*), Tim Barrett (*Lloyd*), Dave Birks (*Spider*), Heinz Bernard (*Martin*), Alec Ross (*Sgt. Carter*), Edward Underdown (*Insp. Gray*), Julie Mendez (*The Stripper*)
P: Ted Lloyd **D:** Freddie Francis **SCR:** John Sansom, from an Edgar Wallace novel
Standard crime-thriller: Executive robs Tower of London

The Tramp's Cycling Mania
1908, (GB), Urban Trading Co., b&w, 315 ft. (96m)
D: W.R. Booth
Standard comedy-fantasy: Bicycle-stealing tramp squashed flat

The Tramp's Dream
1906, (GB), Hepworth, b&w, 450 ft. (137.2m)
W: Sebastian Smith (*The Tramp*), Hetty Potter (*The Fairy*)
D: Lewin Fitzhamon
Standard comedy-fantasy: Hobo dreams fairy takes him to be Marquis' guest

A Tramp's Dream of Wealth
1907, (GB), Hepworth, b&w, 425 ft. (129.5m)
W: Thurston Harris (*The Tramp*), Hetty Potter (*The Mermaid*)
D: Lewin Fitzhamon
Standard comedy-fantasy: Tramp dreams mermaid leads him to ship full of money

Trancers
1984, (USA), Charles Band/Empire, color, 76 mins.
W: Tim Thomerson (*Jack Deth*), Helen Hunt (*Lena*), Michael Stefani (*Martin Whistler*), Art La Fleur (*McNulty*), Telma Hopkins (*Engineer Ruth Raines*), Richard Herd (*Chairman Spencer*), Anne Seymour (*Chairman Margaret Ashe*), Miguel Fernandez (*Officer Lopez*), Biff Manard (*Hap Ashby*), Pete Schrum (*Santa Claus*), Barbara Perry (*Mrs. Santa Claus*), Brad Logan (*Bull*), Richard Erdman (*The Drunken Wise Man*), Wiley Harker (*The Dapper Old Man*), Minnie Lindsay ("*Mom*"), Allyson Croft (*Baby McNulty*), Michael McGrady (*Chris Lavery*), Edward McClarty (*Jerry the Punk*), Don Ross (*The Security Guard*), Michael Heldebrant (*The Boy with Santa*), Kim Sheppard, Steve "O" Jensen, Nicky Beat, Tony Malone, Lantza Krantz
D: Charles Band **SCR:** Danny Bilson & Paul DeMeo **PHOTOG:** Mac Ahlberg **MUSIC:** Mark Ryder & Phil Davies
*Intriguing SF-adventure (***Terminator***-type thriller): 23rd-century detective pursues evil zombie-maker in 1985 Los Angeles*

Trancers II: The Return of Jack Deth
1991, (USA), Full Moon/Para, color, 86 mins.
W: Tim Thomerson (*Jack Deth*), Helen Hunt (*Lena Deth*), Megan Ward (*Alice Stillwell*), Biff Manard (*Hap Ashby*), Art La Fleur (*Old McNulty*), Martine Beswicke (*Nurse Trotter*), Jeffrey Combs (*Dr. Pyle*), Allyson Croft (*Baby McNulty*), Richard Lynch (*Dr. Wardo*), Barbara Crampton (*Sadie Brady*), Telma Hopkins (*Commander Raines*), Sonny Carl Davis (*Rabbit*), Rhino Michaels, Michael Secora, Willy Parsons, Don Dowe, Dani Klein, Gary Rooney, B.J. Davis, Juan Barrie, Neal Parrow, Chris Doyle, Gordon Hunt, Albert Band, John Chandler, Irwin Moseley Jr., Albert Henderson, Gregory Niebel, Paul Roache, Curtis Shaw, Karl Bakke, Kristopher Antekleier, Christopher Lynch, Kevin O'Hara
P & D: Charles Band **SCR:** Jackson Barr **ORIG. STORY:** Jackson Barr & Charles Band **PHOTOG:** Adolfo Bartoli **MUSIC:** Mark Ryder & Phil Davies
Confused SF-thriller: Time-traveling detective has further adventures

Trancers III: Deth Lives
1992, (USA), color, 83 mins.
W: Tim Thomerson, Melanie Smith, Andrew Robinson, Tony Pierce, Dawn Ann Billings, Helen Hunt, Megan Ward, Stephen Macht, Telma Hopkins
D & SCR: C. Courtney Joyner **MUSIC:** Richard Band
Minor SF-thriller: Man time-trips to 2005, battles government-made zombies

Trancers 4: Jack of Swords
1993, (USA), color, 74 mins.
W: Tim Thomerson, Stacie Randall, Ty Miller, Terri Ivens, Mark Arnold, Clare Hartley, Alan Oppenheimer, Stephen Macht, David Nutter
SCR: Peter David **MUSIC:** Gary Fry
Standard SF-thriller: Time traveler vs. killer zombies

Trancers 5: Sudden Deth
1994, (USA), color, 73 mins.
W: Tim Thomerson, Stacie Randall, Ty Miller, Terry Ivens, Mark Arnold, Clare Hartley, Alan Oppenheimer, Jeff Moldovan, Stephen Macht, Lochlyn Munro
D: David Nutter **SCR:** Peter David **MUSIC:** Gary Fry

Standard SF-thriller

Un Tranquillo Posto di Campagna (A Quiet Place in the Country)
1968, (It), PEA Cinematografica/Lopert, color, 106 mins.
W: Vanessa Redgrave, Franco Nero, Georges Geret
D: Elio Petri
Standard melodrama

Transatlantic
1961, (GB), Danziger/UA, b&w, 63 mins.
W: Peter Murray (*Robert Stanton*), June Thorburn (*Judy*), Malou Pantera (*Gina*), Bill Nagy (*Fabroni*), Neil Hallatt (*Evans*), Jack Melford (*Capt. Brady*), Sheldon Lawrence (*Capt. Ives*), Robert Ayres (*Hotchkiss*), Anthony Oliver (*Wentworth*)
P: Brian Taylor **D:** Ernest Morris **STORY:** Brian Clemens & James Eastwood
Standard crime-thriller: FBI agent and dead pilot's sister pursue diamond thieves

Transatlantic Tunnel
see **The Tunnel**

Trans-Europe Express
1966, (Fr), Trans-American, b&w, 92 mins.
W: Jean-Louis Trintignant, Alain Robbe-Grillet, Catherine Robbe-Grillet, Marie-France Pisier
WRIT & D: Alain Robbe-Grillet
Minor thriller

Transformations
1914, (GB), Kineto, b&w, 470 ft. (143.3m)
D: F. Percy Smith
Standard fantasy: Pictures of famous people transform into related objects

Transformations
1989, (USA), color, 85 mins.
W: Rex Smith, Lisa Langlois
Minor SF-thriller: Plague turns intergalactic pilot into killer

Transmutations
1985, (GB), Limehouse-Greenman, color, 103 mins.
W: Denholm Elliott (*Savary*), Steven Berkoff (*Motherskille*), Larry Lamb (*Roy Bain*), Nicola Cowper (*Nicole*), Ingrid Pitt (*Pepperdine*), Miranda Richardson (*Oriel*), Irina Brook (*Bianca*), Art Malik (*Fluka*), Brian Croucher (*Darling*), Trevor Thomas (*Ricardo*), Clive Panto (*Abbott*), Candy Davis (*The Barmaid*), Sean Chapman (*Buchanan*), Karen Gould (*A Dancer*), Jeanette Landry (*A Dancer*), Mark West (*A Dancer*), Philip Davis (*Lazarus*), Gary Olsen (*Red Dog*), Paul Mari (*Dudu*), Paul Bown (*Nygaard*), Philip Tan (*Tung*), Tina Maskell (*Chevron*), Jim Dowdell (*Underworlder #1*), Mathew Zajac (*Underworlder #2*), Guy Dartnell (*Underworlder #3*)
D: George Pavlou **SCR:** Clive Barker & James Caplin **STORY:** Clive Barker **PHOTOG:** Sydney Macartney **MUSIC:** Freur **SONG:** *Nicole*
A.k.a. **Underworld**
Minor SF-thriller: Drugs create human monstrosities

Les Transmutations Imperceptibles (Imperceptible Transmutations)
1904, (Fr), Star, b&w, 38m (124.7 ft./2.1 mins.)
D: Georges Melies
Standard fantasy

The Transvestite
see **Glen or Glenda?**

Transylvania 6-5000
1985, (USA), Mace Neufeld/New World, color, 93 mins.
W: Jeff Goldblum, Joseph Bologna, Ed Begley Jr., Carol Kane, Jeffrey Jones, John Byner, Geena Davis, Michael Richards, Donald Gibb, Norman Fell, Teresa Ganzel, Rudy De Luca (*The Wolfman*), Inge Apelt
WRIT & D: Rudy De Luca **MUSIC:** Lee Holdridge
Minor horror-farce: Tabloid reporters meet Old World monsters

Transylvania Twist
1989, (USA), color, 85 mins.
W: Robert Vaughn, Teri Copley (*Marisa*)
Standard horror-spoof: Career of venomous vampire

The Trap
1947, (USA), Mono, b&w, 62 mins.
W: Sidney Toler (*Charlie Chan*), Mantan Moreland (*Birmingham Brown*), Victor Sen Yung (*Tommie Chan*), Larry Blake (*Rick Daniels*), Tanis Chandler (*Adelaide*), Rita Quigley (*Clementine*), Kirk Alyn (*Sgt. Reynolds*), Anne Nagel (*Marcia*), Lois Austin (*Mrs. Thorn*), Helen Gerald (*Ruby*), Barbara Jean Wong (*San Toy*), Howard Negley (*Cole King*), Minerva Urecal (*Mrs. Webbles*), Margaret Brayton (*Madge Mudge*), Walden Boyle (*Dr. George Brandt*), Bettie Best (*Winifred*), Jan Bryant (*Lois*)
D: Howard Bretherton **SCR:** Miriam Kissinger, from characters created by Earl Derr Biggers **PHOTOG:** James Brown **MUSIC:** Edward J. Kay
Standard "Charlie Chan" thriller: Showgirl murdered

Trapped
1949, (USA), Eagle Lion, b&w, 78 mins.

W: Lloyd Bridges, Barbara Payton, John Hoyt, James Todd, Russ Conway, Robert Karnes
D: Richard Fleischer
Standard thriller: FBI hunts counterfeiters

Trapped by Boston Blackie
1948, (USA), Col, b&w, 67 mins.
W: Chester Morris (*Boston Blackie*), June Vincent (*Doris Bradley*), Richard Lane (*Insp. Farraday*), Patricia White (*Joan Howell*), Edward Norris (*Igor Borio*), Frank Sully (*Sgt. Matthews*), George E. Stone (*Runt*), William Forrest (*Carter*), Fay Baker (*Sandra Doray*), Mary Currier (*Mrs. Kenyon*), Sarah Selby (*Mrs. Carter*), Pierre Watkin (*Dunn*), Ben Welden (*Louis*), Abigail Adams (*The Receptionist*), Ray Harper (*The Clerk*)
D: Seymour Friedman   SCR: Maurice Tombragel, Charles Marion & Edward Beck, from characters created by Jack Boyle   PHOTOG: Philip Tanura   MUSIC: Mischa Bakaleinikoff
Standard thriller: Sleuth guards society party, expensive necklace stolen

Trapped by the London Sharks
1916, (GB), Barker/Magnet, b&w, 4,464 ft. (1360.6m)
W: Blanche Forsythe (*Hilda Manton*), Bertram Burleigh (*Insp. James Graham*), Maud Yates (*Countess Zena*), High Nicholson (*Baron Slomann*), Humbertson Wright (*John Manton*)
D: L.C. MacBean
Standard crime-thriller: Conniving cardsharps gas drunkard, make him think he has killed his wife

Trapped in Space
1994, (USA), color, 87 mins.
W: Jack Wagner, Jack Coleman, Sigrid Thornton, Craig Wasson, Kay Lenz
D: Arthur Seidelman   SCR: John Vincent Curtis & Melinda M. Snodgrass, from a short story by Arthur C. Clarke   MUSIC: Jay Gruska
Standard SF-thriller: Asteroid hits space shuttle

Trauma
1963, (USA), Parade, b&w, 92 mins.
W: John Conte, Lynn Bari, David Garner, Warren Kemmerling, Lorrie Richards, Bond Blackman, William Bissell, Renee Mason, Ruby Borner, Robert Totten, LeRoy Lennaert, Alfred Chafe
P: Joseph Cranston   WRIT & D: Robert Malcolm Young
Standard thriller: Woman keeps dangerous, retarded son secreted on creepy estate

Trauma
1993, (It), ADC/Overseas Filmgroup, color, 106 mins.
W: Christopher Rydell (*David Parsons*), Asia Argento (*Aura Petrescu*), Piper Laurie (*Adriana Petrescu*), Frederic Forrest (*Dr. Judd*), Laura Johnson (*Grace Harrington*), James Russo (*Capt. Travis*), Dominique Serrano (*Stefan Petrescu*), Ira Belgrade (*Arnie*), Hope Alexander-Willis (*Linda Quirk*), Brad Dourif (*Dr. Lloyd*), Sharon Barr, Isabell Monk, Lester Purry, Cory Garvin, Terry Perkins, Tony Saffold, Stephen D'Ambrose, Peter Moore, David Chase, Jacqui Kim, Gregory Beech, Rita Vassallo, Bonita Parsons, Kevin Dutcher, E.A. Violet Boor, Kathy Quirk
P & D: Dario Argento   SCR: Dario Argento & T.E.D. Klein, based on a story by Franco Ferrini, Gianni Romoli & Dario Argento   PHOTOG: Raffaele Mertes   MUSIC: Pino Donaggio
Standard thriller: Daughter of murdered psychic hunts serial decapitator

Treachery and Greed on the Planet of the Apes
1974, (USA), 20th-Fox, color
W: Roddy McDowall (*Galen*), Ron Harper (*Alan*), James Naughton (*Ted*), John Hoyt (*Barlow*), Mark Leonard (*Urko*), Morgan Woodward, Richard Devon, Percy Rodrigues
from characters created by Pierre Boulle, PHOTOG: Gerald Perry Finnerman
*TVM, minor SF-adventure (feature culled from episodes of **Planet of the Apes** teleseries): Stranded astronauts contend with villainous simians of future Earth. cf. **Back to the Planet of the Apes**, **Farewell to the Planet of the Apes**, **Forgotten City of the Planet of the Apes** and **Life, Liberty and Pursuiton the Planet of the Apes***

Tread Softly
1952, (GB), Albany/Apex, b&w, 70 mins.
W: Frances Day (*Madeleine Peters*), Patricia Dainton (*Tangye Ward*), John Bentley (*Keith Gilbert*), John Laurie (*Angus MacDonald*), Olaf Olsen (*Philip Defoe*), Nora Nicholson (*Isobel Mayne*), Harry Locke (*Nutty Potts*), Betty Baskcomb (*Olivia Winter*), Robert Urquhart (*Clifford Brett*), Michael Ward (*Alexander Mayne*)
P: Donald Ginsberg & Vivian A. Cox   D: David Macdonald   SCR: Gerald Verner, Donald Ginsberg & Vivian A. Cox, from Gerald Verner's radio-serial *The Show Must Go On*
Standard thriller: Murders in mad woman's old theater

Tread Softly Stranger
1958, (GB), Alderdale/Renown, b&w, 90 mins.
W: Diana Dors (*Calico*), George Baker (*Johnny Mansell*), Jane Griffiths (*Sylvia*), Terence Morgan (*Dave Mansell*), Betty Warren (*Flo*), Patrick Allen (*Paddy Ryan*), Maureen Delany (*Mrs. Finnegan*), Thomas Heathcote (*Sgt. Lamb*), Russell Napier (*Potter*), Norman MacOwen (*Danny*), Wilfrid Lawson (*Holroyd*), Joseph Tomelty (*Joe Ryan*), Andrew Keir (*Insp. Harris*)
P: Denis O'Dell & George Minter   D: Gordon Parry   SCR: George Minter & Denis O'Dell, from Jack Popplewell's play

Standard crime-thriller: Gambler's brother robs steel mill

Treason
1933, (USA), Col, b&w, 61 mins.
D: George B. Seitz
Minor melodrama

Treasure at the Mill
1957, (GB), Wallace/British Lion-CFF, b&w, 60 mins.
W: Richard Palmer (*John Adams*), John Ruddock (*Mr. Wilson*), Hilda Fenemore (*Mrs. Adams*), The Pettit Family (*themselves*)
P: A.V. Curtice   D: Max Anderson   SCR: Mary Cathcart Borer   STORY: Malcolm Saville
reissued 1974 (9 mins. cut)
Standard juvenile thriller: Children help widow's son find cavalier's treasure

Treasure Island
1920, (USA), MGM, b&w, 6 reels
W: Charles Ogle (*Long John Silver*), Shirley Mason (*Jim Hawkins*), Lon Chaney Sr.
P & D: Maurice Tourneur, from Robert Louis Stevenson's novel
Standard thriller: Boy meets treasure-hunting pirates

Treasure Island
1934, (USA), MGM, b&w, 103 mins.
W: Jackie Cooper (*Jim Hawkins*), Wallace Beery (*Long John Silver*), Lionel Barrymore (*Billy Bones*), Lewis Stone (*Capt. Smollett*), Otto Kruger (*Livesey*), Nigel Bruce (*Squire Trelawney*), Chic Sale (*Ben Gunn*)
D: Victor Fleming   SCR: John Lee Mahin, from Robert Louis Stevenson's novel   PHOTOG: Ray June & Harold Rosson   MUSIC: Herbert P. Stothart
Classic adventure-thriller: Dead pirate's cache sought

Treasure Island
1950, (USA), Walt Disney/RKO, color, 96 mins.
W: Robert Newton (*Long John Silver*), Bobby Driscoll (*Jim Hawkins*), Basil Sydney (*Capt. Smollett*), Denis O'Dea (*Dr. Livesey*), Walter Fitzgerald (*Squire Trelawney*), Finlay Currie (*Capt. Billy Bones*), Ralph Truman (*George Merry*), John Laurie (*Pew*), Francis De Wolff (*Black Dog*), Geoffrey Wilkinson (*Ben Gunn*), David Davies, Sam Kydd, Jack Arrow, Geoffrey Keen, William Devlin, Eddie Moran, Leo Phillips, Harry Locke, Harold Jamieson, Stephen Jack, Chris Adcock, Reginald Drummond, Gordon Mulholland, Patrick Troughton, Fred Clark, Tom Lucas, Bob Head, Andrew Blackett, Howard Douglas, Paddy Brannigan, Ken Buckle, John Gregson
D: Byron Haskin   SCR: Laurence Edward Watkin, from Robert Louis Stevenson's novel   PHOTOG: Frederick A. Young   MUSIC: Clifton Parker
*Well-made adventure-thriller: Pirate befriends boy, seeks long-lost fortune. cf. **Long John Silver***

Treasure Island
1971, (GB-W. Ger-Sp-Fr), Massfilms/Productions FDL/CCC Filmkunst/Eguiluz/Nat'l General, color, 95 mins.
W: Orson Welles (*Long John Silver*), Kim Burfield (*Jim Hawkins*), Maria Rohm (*Mrs. Hawkins*), Walter Slezak (*Squire Trelawney*), Lionel Stander (*Capt. Billy Bones*), Angel Del Pozo (*Dr. Livesey*), Paul Muller (*Blind Pew*), Rik Battaglia (*Capt. Smollett*), Michel Garland (*George Merry*), Jean Lefevbre (*Ben Gunn*), Aldo Sambrell (*Israel Hands*), Alibe (*Mrs. Silver*), Chinchilla (*Anderson*)
P: Harry Alan Towers   SCR: John Hough & Orson Welles, from Robert Louis Stevenson's novel   PHOTOG: Cecilio Paniagua   MUSIC: Natale Massara
Minor adventure-thriller: Boy sails on voyage to find buried treasure

Treasure Island
1976, (USA-GB), color
W: Ashley Knight (*Jim Hawkins*), Alfred Burke (*Long John Silver*), Jack Watson (*Billy Bones*), Anthony Bate
from Robert Louis Stevenson's novel
Minor adventure-thriller

Treasure Island
1990, (USA-GB), Agamemnon-British Lion/TNT-TV, color
W: Charlton Heston (*Long John Silver*), Christian Bale (*Jim Hawkins*), Oliver Reed (*Capt. Billy Bones*), Julian Glover (*Dr. Livesey*), Richard Johnson (*Squire Trelawney*), Clive Wood (*Smollett*), Christopher Lee (*Blind Pew*), Isla Blair (*Mrs. Hawkins*), Michael Thoma (*Hunter*), Nicholas Amer (*Ben Gunn*), Robert Putt (*Job Anderson*), James Cosmo (*Redruth*), John Benfield (*Black Dog*), John Abbott (*Joyce*), Bill Sloan (*Scarface*), James Coyle (*Morgan*), Michael Halsey (*Israel Hands*), Peter Postlethwaite (*George Merry*), Richard Beale (*Mr. Arrow*), Brett Fancy (*Young Tom*), Steven Mackintosh (*Dick*)
WRIT, P & D: Fraser C. Heston, from Robert Louis Stevenson's novel   PHOTOG: Robert Steadman   MUSIC: Paddy Moloney
TVM, standard adventure-thriller: Boy meets pirates, seeks fabulous booty

Treasure of Bengal
1953, (It), b&w, 72 mins.
W: Sabu, Luisa Boni, Luigi Tosi, Georges Poujouly
Minor adventure-thriller: Native youth saves sweetheart from slave traders

Treasure of Fear
see Scared Stiff (1945)

T

The Treasure of Lost Canyon
1951, (USA), Univ, color, 82 mins.
W: William Powell, Julie Adams, Tommy Ivo, Rosemary De Camp, Chubby Johnson, John Doucette, Charles Drake, Henry Hull, Marvin Press, Frank Wilcox
D: Ted Tetzlaff   SCR: Brainerd Duffield & Emerson Crocker, from Robert Louis Stevenson's novel *The Treasure of Franchard*   PHOTOG: Russell Metty
MUSIC: Joseph Gershenson
Standard adventure-thriller: Buried fortune changes lives

Treasure of Monte Cristo
1949, (USA), Lippert, b&w, 78 mins.
W: Glenn Langan, Adele Jergens
Standard adventure-thriller

The Treasure of Monte Cristo
1961, (GB), Mid-Century/MGM, color, 95 mins.
W: Rory Calhoun (*Capt. Adam Corbett*), Patricia Bredin (*Pauline Jackson*), John Gregson (*Renato*), Gianna Maria Canale (*Lucetta*), Peter Arne (*Count Boldoni*), Francis Matthews (*Auclair*), Sam Kydd (*Albert*), Ian Hunter (*Col. Jackson*), David Davies (*Van Ryman*), Tutte Lemkow (*Gino*), C. Denier Warren (*The Proprietor*)
P & PHOTOG: Robert S. Baker & Monty Berman   D: Monty Berman
STORY: Leon Griffiths   MUSIC: Clifton Parker
USA retitle, Secret of Monte Cristo
Standard adventure-thriller: Captain seeks treasure, rescues colonel's daughter

The Treasure of San Teresa
see Long Distance

Treasure of Silver Lake
1965, (W. Ger), Col, color
W: Lex Barker, Herbert Lom, Gotz George, Pierre Brice
D: Harald Reinl, from a novel by Karl May
Minor adventure-thriller

Treasure of the Four Crowns
1982, (USA-Sp), Cannon, 3D, color, 100 mins.
W: Tony Anthony (*J.T. Striker*), Ana Obregon (*Liz*), Francisco Rabal (*Socrates*), Gene Quintana (*Edmund*), Jerry Lazarus (*Rick*), Emiliano Redondo (*Brother Jonas*), Francisco Villena (*The Professor*)
D: Ferdinando Baldi   SCR: Lloyd Battista, Jim Bryce & Jerry Lazarus   ORIG. STORY: Tony Anthony & Gene Quintana   PHOTOG: Marcello Masciocchi & Giuseppe Ruzzolini   MUSIC: Ennio Morricone
Minor thriller: Adventurers vs. messianic sect

Treasure of the Petrified Forest
1964, (It), Asteria-Olga Chart, color, 81 mins.
W: Gordon Mitchell, Eleonora Bianchi, Ivo Payer, Pamela Tudor, Luisa Rivelli, Nat Koster
ORIG. STORY: Emimmo Salvi   PHOTOG: Mario Parapetti   ORIG. MUSIC: Ralf Ferraro
Minor myth-adventure: Legendary hero Sigmund vs. villainous Vikings

Treasure of the Piranha
see Killer Fish

The Treasures of Satan
see Les Tresors de Satan

The Treasurous Policeman
1909, (GB), Hepworth, b&w, 675 ft. (205.7m)
D: Theo Bouwmeester
Standard crime-thriller: Crooked cop runs over girl's father, blames rival

Tree of Hands
1988, (GB), color, 89 mins.
W: Helen Shaver, Lauren Bacall, Malcolm Stoddard, Peter Firth, Paul McGann, Kate Hardie, Tony Haygarth, Phyllida Law
D: Giles Foster, from Ruth Rendell's novel
Standard thriller: Abused child kidnapped

Tremors
1990, (USA), Univ, color, 98 mins.
W: Kevin Bacon (*Valentine McKee*), Fred Ward (*Earl Basset*), Finn Carter (*Rhonda LeBeck*), Michael Gross (*Burt Gummer*), Reba McEntire (*Heather Gummer*), Bobby Jacoby (*Melvin Plug*), Charlotte Stewart (*Nancy*), Tony Genaro, Ariana Richards, Richard Marcus, Victor Wong, Sunshine Parker, Michael Dan Wagner, Conrad Bachmann, Bibi Besch, John Goodwin, John Pappas
D: Ron Underwood   SCR: S.S. Wilson & Brent Maddock   STORY: S.S. Wilson, Brent Maddock & Ron Underwood   PHOTOG: Alexander Gruszynski
MUSIC: Ernest Troost   SONGS: *You Are the One, It's a Cowboy Lovin' Night, Drop Kick Me Jesus, Heart of a Working Man & Why Not Tonight*
Amusing SF-thriller: Monstrous slugs attack inhabitants of desert community

Tremors 2: Aftershocks
1996, (USA), color, 100 mins.
W: Michael Gross (*Burt Gummer*), Fred Ward (*Earl*), Christopher Gartin (*Grady*),

Helen Shaver (*Kate*), Marcelo Tubert (*Ortega*),
D: S.S. Wilson   SCR: Brent Maddock & S.S. Wilson   PHOTOG: Virgil Harper
MUSIC: Jay Ferguson
Made-for-Video, standard SF-comedy: "Graboids" menace mining site

I Tre Moschettieri (The Three Musketeers)
1909, (It), b&w
D: Mario Caserini, from Alexander Dumas' novel
Standard adventure-romance: Swordsmen defend France

Trent's Last Case
1920, (GB), Broadwest/Walturdaw, b&w, 5,500 ft. (1676.4m)
W: Gregory Scott (*Philip Trent*), Pauline Peters (*Mabel Manderson*), Clive Brook (*John Marlow*), George Foley (*Sigsbee Manderson*), Cameron Carr (*Insp. Murch*), P.E. Hubbard (*Nathaniel Cupples*), Richard Norton (*Martin*)
D: Richard Garrick   SCR: P.L. Mannock, from a novel by E.C. Bentley
Standard thriller: Millionaire commits suicide, frames secretary for murder

Trent's Last Case
1929, (USA), Fox, b&w, 96 mins.
W: Donald Crisp, Raymond Hatton
D: Howard Hawks, from a novel by E.C. Bentley   PHOTOG: Harold Rosson
Standard thriller: Mystery surrounds millionaire's death

Trent's Last Case
1952, (GB), British Lion/Rep, b&w, 90 mins.
W: Margaret Lockwood (*Margaret Manderson*), Michael Wilding (*Philip Trent*), Orson Welles (*Sigsbee Manderson*), John McCallum (*John Marlowe*), Miles Malleson (*Burton Cupples*), Hugh McDermott (*Calvin C. Bunner*), Sam Kydd (*Insp. Murch*), Jack McNaughton (*Martin*), Henry Edwards (*The Coroner*), Kenneth Williams (*Horace Evans*), Eileen Joyce (*The Pianist*)
P & D: Herbert Wilcox   SCR: Pamela Bower, from a novel by E.C. Bentley
PHOTOG: Max Greene   MUSIC: Anthony Collins
Standard thriller: Secretary framed for murder

Les Tresors de Satan (The Treasures of Satan)
1902, (Fr), Star, b&w, 50m (164 ft./2.8 mins.)
W: Georges Melies
D: Georges Melies
GB retitle, The Devil's Money Bags
Standard comedy-fantasy

Trespass
see The Stranger Within

I Tre Volti della Paura (The Three Faces of Fear)
1963, (It), Emmepi/Galatea/Lyre/AIP, color, 95 mins.
W: Boris Karloff, Michele Mercier, Mark Damon, Jacqueline Pierreux, Milly Monti, Suzy Andersen, Lidia Alfonsi, Rika Dialina
D: Mario Bava   SCR: Mario Bava, Marcello Fondato & Alberto Bevilacqua
PHOTOG: Ubaldo Terzano
USA retitle, Black Sabbath
Unusual trilogy of terror tales: (1) The Drop of Water {from a short story by Chekhov}, (2) The Telephone, & (3) The Wurdalak {from a story by Tolstoy}

The Trial
1963, (Fr), Astor, b&w, 118 mins.
W: Anthony Perkins, Jeanne Moreau, Orson Welles, Madeleine Robinson, Elsa Martinelli, Romy Schneider, Suzanne Flon, Akim Tamiroff, Arnoldo Foa, Fernand Ledoux, William Chappell, Bill Kearns
P: Alexander Salkind   D & ADAPT: Orson Welles, from Franz Kafka's novel
Classic thriller: Man persecuted for unknown crime

The Trial of Abraham's Faith
1909, (GB), Empire Films/Butcher, b&w, 460 ft. (140.2m)
Standard biblical melodrama: Patriarch ordered to sacrifice son

Trial of Joan of Arc
see Proces de Jeanne d'Arc

The Trial of the Incredible Hulk
1989, (USA), NBC-TV, color
W: Bill Bixby, Lou Ferrigno, John Rhys-Davies, Rex Smith (*Matt Murdock*), Marta Du Bois (*Ellie Mendez*), Joseph Mascolo (*Tendelli*), Nancy Everhard (*Christa Klein*), Richard Cummings Jr. (*Al Pettiman*), Nicholas Hormann (*Edgar*)
TVM, minor SF-fantasy: Scientist involved with mobster and crime fighter

Trial Run
1984, (New Zeal), color, 89 mins.
W: Annie Whittle, Judith Gibson, Christopher Broun, Philippa Mayne, Stephen Tozer, Martyn Sanderson
D: Melanie Read
Standard thriller: Woman menaced in isolated beach house

The Tribe
1974, (USA), Univ/ABC-TV, color, 72 mins.
W: Victor French, Warren Vanders, Mark Gruner, Jeannine Brown, Stewart Moss, Henry Wilcoxon, Sam Gilman, Adriana Shaw, Meg Wyllie, Nancy Elliott, Tani Phelps Guthrie, Niles Brown

P: George Eckstein **D:** Richard A. Colla **TELEPLAY:** Lane Slate **PHOTOG:** Rexford Metz **MUSIC:** David Shire **NARRATION:** Paul Richards
TVM, standard melodrama: Cromagnons vs. primitive Nature and marauding Neanderthals

Trick or Treat
1986, (USA), DEG, color, 97 mins.
W: Mark Price, Tony Fields, Lisa Orgolini, Elaine Joyce, Doug Savant, Glen Morgan, Gene Simmons, Ozzy Osbourne, Richard Doyle
D: Charles Martin Smith **SCR:** Michael S. Murphey, Joel Soisson & Rhet Topham **STORY:** Rhet Topham **PHOTOG:** Robert Elswit **MUSIC SCORE:** Christopher Young, orig. music composed & performed by Fastway
Standard horror-fantasy: Teen conjures up evil spirit of rock star

Trick or Treats
1982, (USA), Gary Graver/Lone Star Pictures Int'l, color, 90 mins.
W: Jackelyn Giroux (*Linda*), Peter Jason (*Malcolm O'Keefe*), Chris Graver (*Christopher O'Keefe*), Carrie Snodgress, David Carradine (*Richard Adams*), Jillian Kesner (*Andrea*), Steve Railsback, (*Bret*), Dan Pastorini (*The 1st Attendant*), Tim Rossovich (*The 2nd Attendant*), Paul Bartel (*The Bum*), J.L. Clark (*Bert*), John Blyth Barrymore, (*The Mad Doctor*), Catherine Coulson (*The Nurse*), Maria Dillon (*The TV Reporter*), Jason Bernard, Owen Orr, Allen Wisch, Patricia Callahan, Debbi Drissi, Tara Hupp, Glenn Jacobson, Butch Sanders, Jono Kouzouyan, Sylvester Stewart, Nike Zachmanoglou, Murray Bolen, Herb Franklin, Thomas Ellison, Wayne Stringer, James E. Johnson, Angela Uva, Michael Stringer, David Lane, Barron, Bill Bridges, Annette Dugdale, Glenn Alexakis, Jason Richards, Rashell Travis, David Uva, Lisa Travis, Alfredo Botello, Har-El Dar-Noy, Orin Dar-Noy
WRIT, D & PHOTOG: Gary Graver
Minor thriller (amateurish 'Halloween' clone): Escaped madman stalks babysitter

The Tricky Convict: or, The Magic Cap
1908, (GB), Walter Tyler, b&w, 440 ft. (134.1m)
D: Dave Aylott
Standard fantasy: Convict finds cap that makes wearer disappear

The Tricky Stick
1914, (GB),Martin Films/DFSA, b&w, 465 ft. (141.7m)
D: Dave Aylott
Standard fantasy: Boy finds magic wand that reverses people and objects

Tried in the Fire
1913, (GB), Hepworth, b&w, 1,215 ft. (370.3m)
W: Alec Worcester (*Rev. Paul Brayton*), Alma Taylor (*Thelma*), Harry Royston (*Denzil*)
D: Warwick Buckland
Standard crime-thriller: Cleric foils kidnapping of spoiled rich girl

The Trigger Effect
1996, (USA), color, 95 mins.
W: Kyle MacLachlan, Elisabeth Shue, Dermot Mulroney
Standard thriller: Power failure causes breakdown of society

Trifling Women
1922, (USA), Metro, b&w, 8,000 ft. (2438.4m)
W: Barbara LaMarr, Ramon Novarro, Edward Connelly, Lewis Stone
WRIT, P & D: Rex Ingram **PHOTOG:** John F. Seitz
Standard melodrama

Trilby
1914, (GB), London/Jury, b&w, 3,400 ft. (1036.3m)
W: Sir Herbert Tree (*Svengali*), Viva Birkett (*Trilby O'Ferrall*), Ion Swinley (*Little*

The Trip: PETER FONDA AND BRUCE DERN

Billee), Charles Rock (*Sandy McAllister*), Phillip Merivale (*Taffy Wynne*), Wyndham Guise (*Mr. O'Ferrall*), Cicely Richards (*Mme. Vinard*), Douglas ⬛⬛⬛⬛
D: Harold Shaw **SCR:** Bannister Merwin, from George du Maurier's novel

Standard thriller: Hypnotist turns artist's model into singer

Trilby
1915, (USA), Equitable-World, b&w
W: Clara Kimball Young (*Trilby*), Wilton Lackaye, Chester Barnett, Paul McAllister, James Young
D: Maurice Tourneur, from George du Maurier's novel
Standard thriller: Charlatan mesmerizes girl

Trilby
1922, (GB), Master Films/BEF, b&w, 1,300 ft. (396.2m)
W: Phyllis Neilson-Terry (*Trilby*), Charles Garry (*Svengali*)
SCR: W.C. Rowden, from George du Maurier's novel
Standard thriller: Hypnotist controls waif

Trilby
1923, (USA), First Nat'l, b&w
W: Andree Lafayette (*Trilby*), Arthur Edmund Carewe, Philo McCullough, Wilfred Lucas, Creighton Hale, Maurice Cannon, Francis McDonald
D: James Young **SCR:** Richard Walton Tully, from George du Maurier's novel **PHOTOG:** George Benoit
Standard thriller: Mesmerist turns girl into singer

Trilogy of Terror
1975, (USA), ABC-TV, color, 72 mins.
W: Karen Black, Skip Burton (*Chad*), John Karlen (*Anman*), George Gaynes (*Dr. Ramsay*), Kathryn Reynolds, Orin Cannon, James Storm, Tracy Curtis, Gregory Harrison
P & D: Dan Curtis **PHOTOG:** Paul Lohmann **MUSIC:** Robert Cobert
TVM, standard trio of terror tales (based on short stories by Richard Matheson): (1) **Julie** *{teleplay, William F. Nolan}, (2)* **Millicent and Therese** *{teleplay, William F. Nolan}, & (3)* **Amelia** *{teleplay, Richard Matheson, from his short story "Prey"}*

Trilogy of Terror II
1996, (USA), USA-TV, color, 95 mins.
W: Lysette Anthony, Geraint Wyn Davies, Matt Clark, Geoffrey Lewis, Blake Heron, Gerry Quigley, Norm Spence, Dennis O'Connor, Philip Williams
D & CO-TELEPLAY: Dan Curtis **PHOTOG:** Elemer Ragalyi **MUSIC:** Bob Cobert
TVM, standard fantasy-thriller

Le Trio Infernal (The Infernal Trio)
1974, (Fr), Levitt-Pickman, color, 106 mins.
W: Michel Piccoli (*George*), Romy Schneider (*Philomene*), Mascha Gomska (*Catherine*), Andrea Ferreol (*Noemie*), Monica Fiorentini (*Magali*), Hubert Deschamps (*Chambon*)
D: Francois Girod **SCR:** Francois Girod & Jacques Rouffio, from a novel by Solange Fasquelle **PHOTOG:** Andrea Winding **MUSIC:** Ennio Morricone
Standard thriller

Il Trionfo di Ercole (The Triumph of Hercules)
1964, (It-Fr), P.C. Produzione Cinematografica-Les Films Jacques Letienne-Unicite/Walter Manley, color, 92 mins.
W: Dan Vadis, Marilu Tolo, Pierre Cressoy, Moira Orfei, Piero Lulli, Enzo Fiermonte, Renato Rossini, Aldo Cecconi, Pietro Capanna, Franco Daddi, Nino Marchetti, Anna Maria Mustari, Gaetano Quartararo, Jacques Stany, Nazzarano Zamperla
P: Alberto Chimino **D:** Alberto De Martino **STORY & SCR:** Roberto Gianviti & Alessandro Ferraro **PHOTOG:** Pier Ludovico Pavoni **MUSIC:** Francesco De Masi
A.k.a. **Hercules vs. the Giant Warriors**
Standard myth-adventure: Hero battles sorceress in Hades

The Trip
1967, (USA), AIP, color, 85 mins.
W: Peter Fonda, Susan Strasberg, Dennis Hopper, Bruce Dern, Dick Miller, Salli Sachse
P & D: Roger Corman **SCR:** Jack Nicholson **PHOTOG:** Arch Dalzell **MUSIC:** The American Musical Band
Standard thriller: Man has LSD experience

The Triple Conjurer and the Living Head
see **L'Illusioniste Double et la Tete Vivante**

Triple Deception
see **House of Secrets** *(1956)*

The Triple Lady
1898, (Fr), Star, b&w, 20m (65.6 ft./1.1 mins.)
D: Georges Melies
Standard comedy-fantasy: Woman becomes multiple

A Trip to Mars
1910, (USA), Edison, b&w
D: Edwin S. Porter
Standard SF-fantasy: Anti-gravity concoction enables man to visit red planet

A Trip to the Moon
see **Le Voyage dans la Lune**

Tristana
1970, (Sp-Fr), Maron, color, 105 mins.
W: Catherine Deneuve *(Tristana)*, Fernando Rey *(Don Lope)*, Franco Nero *(Horacio)*, Lola Gaos *(Saturna)*, Antonio Casas *(Don Cosme)*, Jesus Fernandez *(Saturno)*, Vicente Soler *(Don Ambrosio)*, Sergio Mendizabal *(The Professor)*, Jose Calvo *(The Bellringer)*, Mary Paz Pondal *(The Girl)*, Candida Losada *(The Bourgeois)*, Fernando Cebrian *(Dr. Miquis)*, Juanjo Menendez *(Don Candido)*
D: Luis Bunuel SCR: Luis Bunuel & Julio Alejandro, from a novel by Benito Perez Galdos PHOTOG: Jose F. Aguayo
Surrealist horror-psychodrama: Virginal schoolgirl takes up residence with impoverished aristocrat

Tristan and Isolt
see Lovespell

The Triumph of Hercules
see Il Trionfo di Ercole

Triumph of Robin Hood
1962, (It), color
W: Don Burnett, Gia Scala
Standard adventure-thriller: Outlaw aids King Richard in his battle against Normans

The Triumph of Sherlock Holmes
1935, (GB), Gaumont, b&w, 84 mins.
W: Arthur Wontner *(Sherlock Holmes)*, Lyn Harding *(Prof. Moriarty)*, Leslie Perrins *(John Douglas)*, Ian Fleming *(Dr. John Watson)*, Jane Carr *(Ettie Douglas)*, Charles Mortimer *(Insp. Lestrade)*, Minnie Rayner *(Mrs. Hudson)*, Ben Welden *(Ted Balding)*, Michael Shepley *(Cecil Barker)*, Roy Emerton *(Boss McGinty)*, Conway Dixon *(Ames)*, Wilfred Caithness
D: Leslie H. Hiscott SCR: H. Fowler Mear & Cyril Twyford, from Sir Arthur Conan Doyle's short story *Valley of Fear* PHOTOG: William Luff MUSIC: W.L. Trytel
Standard thriller: Secret society behind revenge killing

The Triumph of the Scarlet Pimpernel
1928, (GB), B&D/W&F, b&w, 7,946 ft. (2421.9m)
W: Matheson Lang *(Sir Percy Blakeney)*, Juliette Compton *(Theresa Cabbarrus)*, Nelson Keys *(Robespierre)*, Marjorie Hume *(Lady Blakeney)*, Haddon Mason *(Tallien)*, H. Fisher White *(St. Just)*, Douglas Payne *(Rateau)*, Harold Huth *(Fouquier-Tinville)*
D: T. Hayes Hunter SCR: Angus Macphail, from a novel by Baroness Orczy
*USA retitle, **The Scarlet Daredevil***
Standard adventure: Dandy saves wife from guillotine

Triumph of the Son of Hercules
1963, (It), color
W: Kirk Morris, Cathia Caro
Minor "Sword & Sandal": Muscleman opposes wicked queen

Triumph of the Ten Gladiators
1964, (It), color, 94 mins.
W: Dan Vadis, Helga Line, Stanley Kent, Gianni Rizzo, John Heston, Halina Zalewska
D: Nick Nostro
Standard "Sword & Sandal": Unrest in ancient Rome

Trog
1970, (GB), Herman Cohen/WB, color, 93 mins.
W: Joan Crawford *(Dr. Brockton)*, Bernard Kay *(Insp. Greenham)*, Michael Gough *(Sam Murdock)*, David Griffin *(Malcolm Travers)*, Kim Braden *(Anne Brockton)*, Thorley Walters *(The Magistrate)*, John Hamill *(Cliff)*, Jack May *(Dr. Selbourne)*, Paul Hansard *(Dr. Kurtlimer)*, Robert Crewdson *(Dr. Pierre Duval)*, Robert Hutton *(Dr. Richard Warren)*, David Warbeck *(Alan Davis)*, Brian Grellis *(John Dennis)*, Joe Cornelius *(Trog)*, Simon Lack *(Col. Vickers)*, John Baker *(The Anesthetist)*, Bartlett Mullins *(The Butcher)*, Chloe Franks *(The Little Girl)*, Geoffrey Case *(Bill)*, Maurice Good, Shirley Conklin, Rona Newton-John
P: Herman Cohen D: Freddie Francis SCR: Aben Kandel PHOTOG: Desmond Dickinson MUSIC: John Scott
*Standard SF-thriller (with stock-footage from **The Animal World**): Woman scientist studies ape man found in cave*

Les Trois Bacchantes (The Three Bacchantes)
1900, (Fr), Star, b&w, 20m (65.6 ft./1.1 mins.)
D: Georges Melies
Standard fantasy: Greek demi-gods revel

Les Trois Lumieres
see Der Mude Tod

Les Trois Mousquetaires (The Three Musketeers)
1921, (Fr), b&w
W: Albert Prejean
from Alexandre Dumas' novel
Standard melodrama: Swordsmen defend France

The Trojan Horse
1961, (It-Fr), Europa/Les Films Modernes/Colorama, color, 92 mins.
W: Steve Reeves *(Aeneas)*, John Drew Barrymore *(Ulysses)*, Juliette Mayniel *(Creusa)*, Hedy Vessel *(Helen)*, Lydia Alfonsi *(Cassandra)*, Warner Bentivegna, Arturo Dominici, Mimmo Palmara, Luciana Angiolillo, Nerio Bernardi, Carlo Tamberlani, Nando Tamberlani, Giancarlo Bastianoni, Giovanni Cianfriglia, Luigi Ciavarro, Giovanni Pazzafini, Giulio Maculani
P: Gianpaolo Bigazzi D: Giorgio Ferroni SCR: Ugo Liberatore, Giorgio Stegani, Federico Zardi & Giorgio Ferroni STORY: Ugo Liberatore & Giorgio Stegani
*A.k.a. **The Trojan War***
Standard "Sword & Sandal": Passions rise as fall of Troy nears

The Trojan War
see The Trojan Horse

The Trojan Women
1971, (GB-Sp), CRC, color, 102 mins.
W: Katharine Hepburn *(Queen Hecuba)*, Vanessa Redgrave *(Andromache)*, Genevieve Bujold *(Cassandra)*, Patrick Magee *(Menelaus)*, Irene Papas *(Helen)*, Brian Blesed *(Talthybius)*, Alberto Sanz
P: Josef Shaftel D & SCR: Michael Cacoyannis, from Euripedes' play PHOTOG: Alfio Contini MUSIC: Mikis Theodorakis
Superior psychodrama: Women of Troy await fates at hands of conquering Greeks

Troll
1986, (USA-It), Charles Band/Empire, color, 82 mins.
W: Noah Hathaway, Michael Moriarty, Shelley Hack, Jenny Beck, Sonny Bono, Brad Hall, Anne Lockhart, Dale Wyatt, Julia Louis-Dreyfus, Gary Sandy, June Lockhart *(Eunice St. Clair)*, Phil Fondacaro, Robert Hathaway, James Beck, Debra Dion
D: John Carl Buechler SCR: Ed Naha PHOTOG: Romano Albani MUSIC: Richard Band
Minor fantasy-thriller: Family rents apartment, evil critter terrorizes

Troll II
1992, (USA), color, 95 mins.
W: Michael Stephenson, Connie McFarland, George Hardy, Margo Prey
Minor fantasy-thriller: Evil creatures plague vacationing family

The Trollenberg Terror
1957, (GB), Tempean/Eros/DCA, b&w, 87 mins.
W: Forrest Tucker *(Alan Brooks)*, Laurence Payne *(Philip Truscott)*, Janet Munro *(Anne Pilgrim)*, Jennifer Jayne *(Sarah Pilgrim)*, Warren Mitchell *(Prof. Crevatt)*, Frederick Schiller *(Klein)*, Andrew Faulds *(Brett)*, Stuart Saunders *(Dewhurst)*, Colin Douglas *(Hans)*, Derek Sydney *(Wilde)*, Anne Sharp, Richard Golding, George Herbert, Jack Taylor, Leslie Heritage, Jeremy Longhurst, Anthony Parker, Garard Green, Theodore Wilhelm, Caroline Glaser
P: Robert S. Baker & Monty Berman D: Quentin Lawrence SCR: Jimmy Sangster, from a story by Peter Kay PHOTOG: Monty Berman MUSIC: Stanley Black
*orig. to be titled **The Flying Eye**, USA retitle, **The Crawling Eye***
Minor classic, engrossing SF-horror: Psychic girl detects lurking monstrosity

A Troll in Central Park
1994, (USA), Walt Disney, color, 90 mins.
VOICES: Dom DeLuise, Cloris Leachman, Charles Nelson Reilly, Phillip Glasser, Jonathan Pryce, Hayley Mills, Robert Morley, Tawney Sunshine Glover, Sy Goraleb, Jordan Metzner
D: Don Bluth & Gary Goldman SCR: Stu Krieger MUSIC: Robert Folk
Standard animated fantasy: Magical creature befriends unhappy children

Troma's War
1988, (USA), Troma, color, 90 mins. (also 105 mins.)
W: Carolyn Beauchamp, Ara Romanoff, Michael Ryder, Sean Bowen
D: Michael Herz & Lloyd Kaufman
Minor thriller: Tourists vs. terrorists

Tromba, the Tiger Man
1952, (USA), Lippert, b&w, 63 mins.
Minor adventure-thriller

Tromeo and Juliet
1997, (USA), Troma, color, 107 mins.
W: Jane Jensen *(Juliet)*, Will Keenan *(Tromeo Que)*, Valentine Miele *(Murray Martini)*, Lemmy *(The Narrator)*
D: Lloyd Kaufman SCR: James Gunn & Lloyd Kaufman, based on Shakespeare's play *Romeo and Juliet* PHOTOG: Brendan Flynt MUSIC: Willie Wisely
Bizarre spoof: Grotesque tale of star-crossed lovers

Tron
1982, (USA), Walt Disney/Buena Vista, color, 96 mins.
W: Jeff Bridges *(Flynn)*, Bruce Boxleitner *(Tron)*, David Warner *(Sark)*, Cindy Morgan *(Lora)*, Barnard Hughes
D & SCR: Steven Lisberger STORY: Steven Lisberger & Bonnie MacBird MUSIC: Wendy Carlos
Standard SF-fantasy: Youth drawn into electronic world of computer

T

Le Trou (The Hole)

1959, (It-Fr), b&w, 140 mins.

W: Philippe Leroy, Marc Michel, Jean Keraudy, Andre Bervil, Raymond Meunier, Michel Constantin, Catherine Spaak

D: Jacques Becker & Jose Giovanni   **SCR:** Jacques Becker, Jose Giovanni & Jean Aurel, from a novel by Jose Giovanni   **PHOTOG:** Ghislain Cloquet

A.k.a. **The Night Watch**

Classic fact-based melodrama: Four prisoners attempt to tunnel to freedom

Trouble at 16

see **Platinum High School**

Troubled Waters

1964, (GB), Parroch-McCallum-Lippert/British Lion, b&w, 70 mins.

W: Tab Hunter (*Alex Carswell*), Zena Walker (*Janet Carswell*), Michael Goodliffe (*Jeff Driscoll*), Yvette Rees (*Sally Driscoll*), Stanley Maxted (*Rev. Wilcox*), Marianne Stone (*Miss James*), Andy Myers (*Ronnie Carswell*), Arnold Bell (*The Attendant*)

P: C. Jack Parsons   **D:** Stanley Goulder   **SCR:** Al Rosen & Tudor Gates   **STORY:** Al Rosen

USA retitle, **The Man with Two Lives**

Standard crime-thriller (shown only on TV): Jealous ex-con tries to kill his son

Trouble for Two

1936, (USA), MGM, b&w, 75 mins.

W: Robert Montgomery (*Prince Florizel*), Rosalind Russell (*Miss Vandeleur/Princess Brenda*), Frank Morgan (*Col. Geraldine*), Reginald Owen (*Dr. Franz Noel, President of the Club*), E.E. Clive (*The King*), Louis Hayward (*The Young Man with Cream Tarts*), Pedro de Cordoba (*Sergei*), Ivan Simpson (*Collins*), Walter Kingsford (*Malthus*), Robert Greig (*The Fat Man*), Tom Moore (*Mayor O'Rork*), Leland Hodgson (*Capt. Rich*), Guy Bates Post (*The Ambassador*), Pat Flaherty (*The Ship Captain*), Frank Darien (*The King's Aide*), Sidney Bracy (*The Henchman*), Tom Ricketts (*The Excited Club Member*), Pat O'Malley (*The Purser*), Leonard Carey (*The Valet*), Bill O'Brien (*The Club Waiter*), Paul Porcasi (*The Cafe Proprietor*), Frank McGlynn Jr. (*A Club Member*), Larry Steers (*The Officer*), Olaf Hytten (*The Butler*), Edgar Norton (*The Herald*), Fred Graham (*The Club Guard*)

P: Louis D. Lighton   **D:** J. Walter Ruben   **SCR:** Manuel Seff & Edward E. Paramore Jr., from Robert Louis Stevenson's short story "The Suicide Club"   **PHOTOG:** Charles Clarke   **MUSIC:** Franz Waxman

Standard thriller: Couple involved with murderous society

The Troubles of a Hypochondriac

1915, (GB), Bamforth/YCC, b&w, 431 ft. (131.4m)

W: Reggie Switz (*Winky*)

D: Cecil Birch

Standard comedy-fantasy: Liquid electricity cures old man

The Trouble with Harry

1955, (USA), Para, color, 99 mins.

W: John Forsythe (*Sam Marlowe*), Shirley MacLaine (*Jennifer Rogers*), Royal Dano (*Calvin Wiggs*), Edmund Gwenn (Capt. Albert Wiles), Mildred Natwick (*Miss Graveley*), Jerry Mathers (*Arnie Rogers*), Parker Fennelly (*The Millionaire*), Barry Macollum (*The Tramp*), Dwight Marfield (*Dr. Greenbow*), Leslie Wolf (*The Art Critic*), Philip Truex (*Harry Worp*), Ernest Curt Bach (*The Chauffeur*)

P & D: Alfred Hitchcock   **SCR:** John Michael Hayes, from Jack Trevor's novel   **PHOTOG:** Robert Burks   **MUSIC:** Bernard Herrmann

Unusual comedy-thriller: Attempts to conceal corpse

Trucks

1997, (USA), Leider-Reisberg/Trimark/USA-TV, color, 95 mins.

W: Timothy Busfield, Brenda Bakke, Aidan Devine, Brendan Fletcher, Amy Stewart, Victor Cowie, Sharon Bajer

D: Chris Thomson   **TELEPLAY:** Brian Taggert, from: a short story by Stephen King   **PHOTOG:** Rob Draper   **SPCL-FX SPRVSR:** Rory P.M. Cutler   **MUSIC:** Michael Richard Plowman

TVM, standard SF-fantasy: Driverless vehicles threaten humans. cf. **Maximum Overdrive**

True Crime

1996, (USA), Jonathan Furie/Trimark, color

W: Alicia Silverstone, Kevin Dillon, Bill Nunn, Jennifer Savidge, Michael Bowen, Joshua Schaefer, Marla Sokoloff, Ann Devaney, Sean Moran

WRIT & D: Pat Verducci   **PHOTOG:** Chris Squires   **MUSIC:** Blake Leyh   **SONGS:** *Blue Death Cold, Bad Seed & Journey Through the Heart*

Standard thriller: Girl hunts killer

A True Scout

1913, (GB), Cricks/C&M, b&w, 915 ft. (278.9m)

D: Charles Calvert

Standard crime-thriller: Office boy tortured, but refuses to reveal hidden money

True Till Death

1907, (GB), Warwick Trading Co., b&w, 480 ft. (146.3m)

D: Charles Raymond

Standard short thriller: Man frees fiancee from cavalier's dungeon; they are tracked by bloodhounds, caught and executed

The Truman Show

1998, (USA), Para, color, 104 mins.

W: Jim Carrey, Ed Harris, Laura Linney, Natascha McElhone, Noah Emmerich, Holland Taylor

D: Peter Weir   **SCR:** Andrew Niccol   **PHOTOG:** Peter Biziou   **MUSIC:** Burkhard Dallwitz

Classic satire: Man finds his life is calculated teleshow

The Trunk

1961, (GB), Donwin/Col, b&w, 72 mins.

W: Phil Carey (*Stephen Dorning*), Julia Arnall (*Lisa Maitland*), Dermot Walsh (*Henry Maitland*), Vera Day (*Diane*), Peter Swanwick (*Nicholas Steiner*), John Atkinson (*Matt*), Betty le Beau (*Maria*), Tony Quinn

P: Lawrence Huntington   **D & SCR:** Donovan Winter   **STORY:** Edward & Valerie Abraham

Standard thriller: Blackmailer frames girl for murder of her husband's mistress

Trunk Crime

1939, (GB), Charter/Anglo, b&w, 51 mins.

W: Manning Whiley (*Bentley*), Barbara Everest (*Ursula*), Michael Drake (*Gierson*), Hay Petrie (*Old Dan*), Thorley Walters (*Frazier*), Eileen Bennett (*Eve*), Lewis Stringer (*Hearty*)

D: Roy Boulting   **SCR:** Francis Miller, from a play by Edward Percy & Reginald Denham

USA retitle, **Design for Murder**

Standard thriller: Taunted student goes mad, tries to bury tormentor alive

The Truth about Murder

1946, (USA), RKO, b&w

W: Bonita Granville, Morgan Conway

Standard thriller

The Truth Will Out

1910, (GB), Clarendon, b&w, 680 ft. (275.2m)

D: Percy Stow

Standard crime-thriller: Office boy witnesses robbery, saves clerk from being framed

The Trygon Factor

1966, (GB), Rank/Rialto/20th-Fox, color, 87 mins.

W: Stewart Granger (*Supt. Cooper-Smith*), Susan Hampshire (*Trudy Emberday*), Cathleen Nesbitt (Livia Emberday), Robert Morley (*Hubert Hamlyn*), James Robertson Justice (*Sir John*), Brigitte Horney (*Sister General*), James Culliford (*Luke Emberday*), Sophie Hardy (*Sophie*), Eddi Arent (*Emil Clossen*), Diane Clare (*Sister Clare*), Allan Cuthbertson (*Thompson*), Colin Gordon (*Dice*), Russell Waters (*Sgt. Chivers*), Jeremy Hawk (*The Manager*)

P: Ian Warren & Brian Taylor   **D:** Cyril Frankel   **SCR:** Derry Quinn, Stanley Munro & Kingsley Amis   **PHOTOG:** Harry Waxman   **MUSIC:** Peter Thomas

Standard thriller: Convent fronts for gold smugglers

Tuareg, the Desert Warrior

1984, (It), color

W: Mark Harmon (*Tuareg*), Luis Prendes (*Abdul*)

Minor adventure-thriller

The Tube of Death

1913, (GB), Barker/Royal, b&w, 2,790 ft. (850.4m)

W: Fred Paul (*M. Sardies*), Blanche Forsythe (*Mary Dacre*), Rolf Leslie (*John Dacre*)

D: Alexander Butler   **STORY:** Rowland Talbot

A.k.a. **The Anarchist's Doom**

Standard thriller: Inventor's wife avenges death

Tuck Everlasting

1981, (USA), Natalie Babbitt Prods., color, 98 mins.

W: Fred A. Keller, James McGuire, Paul Flessa, Margaret Chamberlain, Sonia Raimi, Bruce D'Auria, Barbara Harmon, Frank O'Hara, Marvin Macnow, Mark Callen, Bill Klaiber, Mary Gulino, Tom Kelly, Eric Harris, Halle Sims, Edward Granger, Joe Marshall, Pam Reed, Joey Glambra, Gretchen Lopez, Ron Swick, Howard Wyrauch

D: Frederick King Keller   **SCR:** Stratton Rawson, Fred A. Keller, Frederick King Keller & Jim Bisco, from Natalie Babbitt's best-selling story   **PHOTOG:** Michael G. Matthews   **MUSIC:** Malcolm Daiglish & Grey Larsen

Minor fantasy: Small community has immortality secret

La Tulipe Noire (The Black Tulip)

1963, (Fr), color, 115 mins.

W: Alain Delon, Virna Lisi, Akim Tamiroff

D: Christian-Jaque, from Alexander Dumas' novel   **PHOTOG:** Henri Decae

Standard adventure-thriller

Tumak, Fils de la Jungle

see **One Million B.C.**

The Tunnel

1935, (GB), Gaumont, b&w, 94 mins.

W: Richard Dix (*McAllan*), Madge Evans (*Ruth McAllan*), Leslie Banks (*Robbie*), Helen Vinson (*Varlia*), C. Aubrey Smith (*Lloyd*), George Arliss (*The Prime Minister*), Walter Huston (*The President*), Basil Sydney (*Mostyn*), Henry

Oscar (*Grellier*), Jimmy Hanley (*Geoffrey*), Cyril Raymond (*Harriman*), Hilda Trevelyan (*Mary*), James Carew (*Jim Bardon*), Percy Parsons (*The Financier*), Cyril Smith (*The Man*)
D: Maurice Elvey   **SCR:** Curt Siodmak, L. DuGarde Peach & Clemence Dane, from Bernhard Kellerman's novel   **PHOTOG:** Gunther Krampf   **MUSIC DIR:** Louis Levy
USA retitle, **Transatlantic Tunnel**
Classic SF-thriller: Engineers build undersea tunnel from Britain to USA

Tunneling the English Channel
see **Le Tunnel sous la Manche ou le Cauchemar Franco-Anglais**

Le Tunnel sous la Manche ou le Cauchemar Franco-Anglais (The Tunnel Under the English Channel: or, The Franco-English Nightmare
1907, (Fr), Star, b&w, 307m (1,007.2 ft./17 mins.)
D: Georges Melies
A.k.a. **Tunneling the English Channel**
Standard SF-fantasy

Tunnel Vision
1995, (Austral), color, 90 mins.
W: Patsy Kensit
Minor thriller: Woman detective and partner hunt serial killer

Tup, Tup
1972, (Yugo), Zagreb Studios, color
Standard animated fantasy: Lack of privacy causes frustrations

Turbo: A Power Rangers Movie
1997, (USA-Jap), Saban-Toei/20th-Fox, color, 100 mins.
W: Johnny Yong Bosch, Nakia Burrise, Steve Cardenas, Jason David Frank, Austin St. John, Catherine Sutherland, Jason Narvy, Paul Schrier, Blake Foster, Hilary Shepard, Amy Jo Johnson
P: Jonathan Tzachor   **D:** David Winning & Shuki Levy   **SCR:** Shuki Levy & Shell Danielson   **PHOTOG:** Ilan Rosenberg   **MUSIC:** Shuki Levy
MUSIC SPRVSRS: Ron Kenan & David Ari Leon
Minor SF-fantasy (inspired by juvenile teleseries): Superheroes oppose demonic conqueror

Turkey Shoot
see **Escape 2000**

Die Tur mit den Sieben Schlossern (The Door with Seven Locks)
1962, (W. Ger), UCC-TV, b&w, 96 mins.
W: Heinz Drache, Klaus Kinski, Sabrina Sesselmann, Hans Nielsen, Ady Berber, Jan Hendricks
D: Alfred Vohrer, from an Edgar Wallace novel
Standard thriller: Cad imperils heiress

Turnabout
1940, (USA), UA, b&w, 83 mins.
W: John Hubbard, Carole Landis, Adolphe Menjou, Mary Astor, William Gargan, Joyce Compton, Verree Teasdale, Donald Meek
D: Hal Roach, from a story by Thorne Smith   **PHOTOG:** Norbert Brodine
Standard comedy-fantasy: Magic Buddha causes husband and wife to switch personalities

Turn Back the Clock
1989, (USA), NBC-TV, color, 95 mins.
W: Connie Sellecca (*Sheila Powers*), David Dukes (*Barney Powers*), Wendy Kilbourne (*Tracy Alexander*), Gene Barry (*John Forrest*), Dina Merrill (*Maureen Dowd*), Joan Leslie (*New York Woman '88*), Franc Luz (*Michael Dean*), Pat Cupo (*The Cab Driver*), Christopher Judges, Frank Coppola, Thomas H. Middleton, Dennis Paladino, Carmela Rioseco, Pat Sturges, Jeannine Wiest
D: Larry Elikann   **TELEPLAY:** Lee Hutson & Lindsay Harrison, based on a scr by Walter Bullock & a novel by William O'Farrell   **PHOTOG:** Laszlo George   **MUSIC:** Nan Schwartz
TVM, modest fantasy-thriller (remake of **Repeat Performance***): Murderess relives previous year*

Turning the Tables
1909, (GB), Walturdaw, b&w, 528 ft. (160.9m)
Standard fantasy: Magic wand helps henpeck gain revenge on wife

The Turn of the Screw
1992, (GB-Fr), color, 95 mins.
W: Patsy Kensit, Stephane Audran, Julian Sands, Marianne Faithful, Clare Szekeres, Joseph England
D: Rusty Lemorande, from Henry James' classic novel   **MUSIC:** Simon Boswell
Standard thriller: Governess fears supernatural. cf. **The Innocents**

Turn the Key Softly
1953, (GB), Chiltern/Astor, b&w, 81 mins.
W: Yvonne Mitchell (*Monica Marsden*), Terence Morgan (*David*), Joan Collins (*Stella Jarvis*), Kathleen Harrison (*Mrs. Quilliam*), Thora Hird (*The Landlady*), Glyn Houston (*Bob*), Dorothy Alison (*Joan*), Geoffrey Keen (*Gregory*), Richard Massingham (*The Bystander*), Russell Waters (*Jenkins*), Clive Morton (*Walters*)
P: Maurice Cowan   **D:** Jack Lee   **SCR:** John Brophy & Maurice Cowan, from a novel by John Brophy
Standard melodrama: Burglar, shoplifter, and prostitute released from Holloway prison on

same day

Tut and Tuttle
see **Through the Magic Pyramid**

Tut-Tut and His Terrible Tomb
1923, (GB), Bertram Phillips/Butcher, b&w, 2,000 ft. (609.6m)
W: Queenie Thomas, Peter Upcher, Frank Stanmore, Adeline Hayden Coffin, Jeff Barlow, Fatty Phillips
D: Bertram Phillips   **STORY:** Frank Miller
Standard comedy-fantasy (episode from **Syncopated Picture Plays** *series): Mummy's crypt provides chills and laughs*

A TV Dante: Cantos I-VIII
1989, (GB), color & b&w, 88 mins.
W: Sir John Gielgud (*Vergil*), Bob Peck (*Dante*), Joanne Whalley-Kilmer (*Beatrice*), David Attenborough, David Rudkin
D: Peter Greenaway & Tom Phillips, from Dante's *Divina Commedia*
TVM, exceptional fantasy: Writer's allegorical descent into hell

'Twas Only a Dream
see **The Hunger Strike**

The 12th Hour
1947, (USA), Col, b&w
W: Richard Dix
Minor thriller

Twelve Hours to Live
see **His Last 12 Hours**

12 Monkeys
1995, (USA), Atlas-Classico/Univ, color, 130 mins.
W: Bruce Willis (*James Cole*), Brad Pitt (*Jeffrey Goines*), Madeleine Stowe (*Kathryn Railly*), Cjristopher Plummer (*Dr. Leland Goines*), Frank Gorshin (*Dr. Fletcher*), Simon Jones, Jon Seda, Bill Raymond, Carol Florence, Bob Adrian, Terry Jackson, Joseph Melito, Michael Chance, Vernon Campbell, H. Michael Walls, Joey Perillo, Irma St. Paule, Thomas Roy, Rick Warner, John Copeman, Kevin Thigpen, Bruce Kirkpatrick, Stan Kang, Pat Das, Wilfred Williams, Nell Johnson, Franklin Huffman, Fred Strother, David Morse, Christopher Melon, Jack Dougherty, Stephen Bridgewater, Aaron Michael Lacey, Jann Ellis, Harry O'Toole, Lisa Gay Hamilton, Larry Daly, Chuck Jeffreys, Matthew Ross, Barry Price, Arthur Fennell, Karl Warren, Lee Golden, Sean Kelly, John Panzarella, Jeff Tanner, Joseph McKenna, Anne Golden, Faith Potts, Michael Ryan Segal, JoAnn S. Dawson, Lenny Daniels, Carolyn Walker
P: Charles Roven   **D:** Terry Gilliam   **SCR:** David & Janet Peoples, inspired by Chris Marker's film **La Jetee**   **PHOTOG:** Roger Pratt   **MUSIC:** Paul Buckmaster
Unusual, thought-proviking SF-thriller: Future convict time-travels to locate source of deadly virus plague

12:01
1993, (USA), color
W: Jonathan Silverman
from a 1973 short story by Richard A. Lupoff
Standard SF-comedy: Experiment allows bemused clerk to relive and correct worst day of his life

12-10
1919, (GB), B&C/World, b&w, 4,894 ft. (1491.7m)
W: Marie Doro (*Marie Fernando*), Ben Webster (*Lord Chatterton*), Geoffrey Kerr (*Geoffrey Brooke*), James Carew (*Arthur Newton*), Fred Kerr (*Dr. Wrightman*)
P: Edward Godal   **D:** Herbert Brenon   **SCR:** George Edwardes Hall   **STORY:** Earle Carroll
Standard thriller: Lord fakes death with life-suspending drug, stops secretary from killing adopted orphan

12 to the Moon
1960, (USA), Col, b&w, 74 mins.
W: Ken Clark (*Anderson*), Tom Conway (*Orloff*), Tony Dexter (*Vargas*), Anna-Lisa, Michi Kobi, Francis X. Bushman, John Wengraf, Philip Baird, Tema Bey, Roger Til, Richard Weber, Robert Montgomery Jr., Cory Devlin
P: Fred Gebhardt   **D:** David Bradley   **SCR:** DeWitt Bodeen   **STORY:** Fred Gebhardt   **PHOTOG:** John Alton   **SPCL-FX:** Howard Anderson Co.   **MUSIC:** Michael Andersen
Minor SF-thriller: Lunarites repulse first expedition to moon

24 Hours to Kill
1965, (GB), Grixflag/WPD, color, 83 mins.
W: Lex Barker (*Jamie*), Mickey Rooney (*Norman Jones*), Michael Medwin (*Tommy*), Wolfgang Lukschy (*Kurt*), Helga Somerfield (*Louise*), France Anglade (*Francoise*), Walter Slezak (*Malouj*), Helga Lehner (*Helga*)
P: Bernard Coote & Harry Alan Towers   **D:** Peter Bezencenet   **SCR:** Peter Yeldham   **STORY:** Harry Alan Towers
Standard thriller: Airline pilots save hostess from kidnap by gold smugglers

Twentieth Century Conjuring
see **La Clownesse Fantome**

T

The 20th Century Illustrationist
see *Extraordinary Illusions*

20th Century Oz
1977, (GB), Interplanetary Pictures, color
W: Graham Matters, Joy Dunstan, Bruce Spence, Gary Waddell, Michael Carman, Paula Maxwell, Ned Kelly, Robin Ramsay
P: Chris Lofven & Lyne Helms   WRIT & D: Chris Lofven   MUSIC: Ross Wilson
Standard fantasy-satire

20 Million Miles to Earth
1957, (USA), Morningside/Col, b&w, 82 mins.
W: William Hopper, Joan Taylor, Kenneth Tobey, Thomas B. Henry, Frank Puglia, John Zaremba, Tito Vuolo, Jan Arvan, Arthur Space, Bart Bradley, George Pelling, Don Orlando, George Khoury, Rollin Moriyama
P: Charles H. Schneer   D: Nathan Juran   SCR: Bob Williams & Christopher Knopf, from a story by Charlotte Knight   PHOTOG: Irving Lippman & Carlos Ventigmilia   SPCL-FX: Ray Harryhausen   MUSIC: Mischa Bakaleinikoff
Ger retitle, The Beast from Space
"Harryhausen's stop motion work was flawless, and the dramatic and imaginative image of the Ymir makes one wonder why more outerspace entities weren't animated for the screen"—Gary Gerani, "The Space Monster Book—Chapter Four: Other Invasions," Monster Fantasy, Vol. 1, No. 4 (August, 1975), p. 32
orig. co-billed with The 27th Day
Classic SF-thriller (Harryhausen's best b&w animation): Hideous lifeform that increases in size is brought to Earth by first spaceship to probe Venus

The Twenty Questions Murder
1950, (GB), Pax-Pendennis/Grand Nat'l, b&w, 95 mins.
W: Robert Beatty (*Bob Beacham*), Rona Anderson (*Mary Game*), Clifford Evans (*Tom Harmon*), Edward Lexy (*Insp. Charlton*), Olga Lindo (*Olive Tavy*), Frederick Leister (*The Commissioner*), Harold Scott (*Maurice Emery KC*), Meadows White (*Frederick Tavy*), Kynaston Reeves (*Gen Maitland Webb*), Wally Patch (*Tiny White*), Stewart MacPherson, Jack Train, Daphne Padel, Richard Dimbleby, Jeanne de Casalis, Norman Hackforth
P: Steven Pallos & Victor Katona   D: Paul Stein   SCR: Patrick Kirwin & Victor Katona   STORY: Charles Leeds
reissued (1952) as Murder on the Air
Standard thriller: Reporter unmasks killer who sends clues to radio quiz show

The 27 days of the Planet Sigma
see *The 27th Day*

The 27th Day
1957, (USA), Romson/Col, b&w, 75 mins.
W: Gene Barry, Valerie French, George Voskovec, Paul Birch, Arnold Moss, Stefan Schnabel, Friedrich Ledebur, Philip Van Zandt, Ralph Clanton, Azemat Janti, Marie Tsien, Ed Hinton, Grandon Rhodes
P: Helen Ainsworth   D: William Asher   SCR: John Mantley, from his novel   PHOTOG: Henry Freulich   MUSIC: Mischa Bakaleinikoff
Sp retitle, The 27 Days of the Planet Sigma, USA TV-retitle, Kidnappers from Space, orig. co-billed with 20 Million Miles to Earth
Unusual SF-thriller: Space aliens test Earthlings by offering devices of mass destruction

20,000 Leagues Under the Sea (1907)
see *Deux Cent Mille Lieues sous les Mers*

20,000 Leagues Under the Sea
1916, (USA), b&w, 105 mins.
W: Matt Moore, Allen Holubar, June Gail, William Welsh, Dan Hamlon, Chris Benton
D & SCR: Stuart Paton, from Jules Verne's novel
Standard adventure-thriller: Renegade captain in mystery submarine

20,000 Leagues Under the Sea
1954, (USA), Walt Disney/Buena Vista, color, 126 mins.
W: James Mason (*Capt. Nemo*), Kirk Douglas (*Ned Land*), Paul Lukas (*Prof. Aronnax*), Peter Lorre (*Conseil*), Robert J. Wilke (*Captain's First Mate*), Ted de Corsia (*Capt. Farragut*), Carleton Young (*John Howard*)
D: Richard Fleischer   SCR: Earl Felton, from Jules Verne's novel   PHOTOG: Franz Planer   OSCAR-WINNING SPCL-FX: Ub Iwerks   MUSIC: Paul Smith   SONG: A Whale of a Tale
Classic SF-adventure: Vengeful captain terrorizes sea lanes with his fantastic submarine

20,000 Leagues Under the Sea
1997, (USA), CBS-TV, color
W: Ben Cross (*Capt. Nemo*), Richard Crenna (*Prof. Aronnax*), Paul Gross, (*Ned Land*), Julie Cox (*Sophie*), Michael Jayston
D: Michael Anderson   TELEPLAY: Joe Wiesenfeld, from Jules Verne's novel   PHOTOG: Alan Hume   MUSIC: John Scott
TVM, listless adventure-thriller (no giant squid {or octopi, as in novel}): Enigmatic submarine captain opposes world's navies

20,000 Leagues Under the Sea
1997, (USA), ABC-TV, color, 192 mins.
W: Michael Caine (*Capt. Nemo*), Patrick Dempsey (*Pierre Arronax*), Bryan Brown (*Ned Land*), Adewale (*Cabel*), Mia Sara
D: Rod Hardy   TELEPLAY: Brian Nelson, from Jules Verne's novel   PHOTOG: James Bartle   MUSIC: Mark Snow
2-part TVM, standard SF-adventure

23 1/2 Hours Leave
1919, (USA), Famous Players-Lasky, b&w, 5 reels
P: Thomas H. Ince   D: Henry King, from a story by Mary Roberts Rinehart
Standard thriller

23 Paces to Baker Street
1956, (USA), 20th-Fox, color, 103 mins.
W: Van Johnson (*Phillip Hannon*), Vera Miles (*Jean Lennox*), Maurice Denham (*Insp. Grovening*), Cecil Parker (*Matthews*), Estelle Winwood (*The Barmaid*), Patricia Laffan (*Miss MacDonald*), Liam Redmond (*Mr. Murch*), Martin Benson (*Pilling*), Isobel Elsom (*Lady Syrett*), Natalie Norwick (*Janet Murch*), Terence de Marney (*Sgt. Luce*), Charles Keane (*The Policeman*), Queenie Leonard (*Miss Schuyler*), Lucie Lancaster (*Miss Marston*), A. Cameron Grant, Ashley Cowan, Ben Wright, Les Sketchly, Reginald Sheffield, Phyllis Montifiere, Arthur Gomez, Janice Kane, Robert Raglan, Howard Lang, Fred Griffith, Margaret McGrath, Walter Horsborough, Charles Stanley, Robin Alalouf, Yorke Sherwood
D: Henry Hathaway   SCR: Nigel Balchin, from Philip MacDonald's novel   PHOTOG: Milton Krasner   MUSIC: Leigh Harline
Standard thriller: Blind playwright probes kidnap-murder case

2020 Texas Gladiators
1984, (USA-It), Continental/American Nat'l, color
W: Harrison Muller, Al Cliver, Sabrina Siani, Daniel Stephen, Peter Hooten, Donal O'Brien
D: Kevin Mancuso   PHOTOG: John Larson   MUSIC: Francis Taylor
Minor SF-adventure (Euro-imitation of The Road Warrior): Wheeled mayhem in future

2267 A.D.—When the Sleeper Wakes
1267, (USA), AIP, color
W: Vincent Price, Martha Hyer
from a novel by H.G. Wells
orig. to be titled 2165 A.D.—When the Sleeper Wakes
SF-thriller (unfinished): Man revives from suspended animation

Twice Dead
1988, (USA), Concorde, color, 90 mins.
W: Tom Breznahan (*Scott*), Jill Whitlow (*Robin-Myrna*), Sam Melville (*Harry*), Jonathan Chapin (*Crip-Tyler*), Christopher Burgard (*Silk*), Brooke Bundy (*Sylvia*), Todd Bridges (*Petie*)
D: Bert Dragin   SCR: Bert Dragin & Robert McDonnell   PHOTOG: Zoran Hochstatter   MUSIC: David Bergeaud
Minor horror-thriller: Family inherits haunted house in bad neighborhood

Twice-Told Tales
1963, (USA), Admiral/UA, color, 119 mins.
W: Vincent Price, Joyce Taylor, Sebastian Cabot, Mari Blanchard, Richard Denning (*Maulle*), Beverly Garland (*Alice*), Abraham Sofaer (*Baglioni*), Brett Halsey (*Giovanni*), Edith Evanson, Jacqueline Floyd, Gene Roth
WRIT & P: Robert E. Kent   D: Sidney Salkow, from stories by Nathaniel Hawthorne
orig. to be titled The Corpse Makers
Standard trilogy of terror tales: (1) Dr. Heidegger's Experiment—Fountain of Youth discovered, (2) Rapaccini's Daughter—Girl given fatal touch, & (3) House of the Seven Gables—Family curse endures

Twice Upon a Time
1983, (USA), color, 75 mins.
VOICES: Lorenzo Music, Judith kahan Kampmann, Marshall Efron, James Cranna, Julie Payne, Hamilton Camp, Paul Frees
D: John Korty & Charles Swenson
Unusual animated fantasy (never given full theatrical release): Evil technocrats plot to blanket world with perpetual nightmares

Twice Upon a Time
1998, (USA), Lifetime, color, 95 mins.
W: Molly Ringwald, George Newbern, Melora Walters, Shawnee Smith, Michael Whaley, Ellen Crawford, Rob Youngblood, Timothy Blake, Brian Pope
D: Thom Eberhardt   TELEPLAY: Scott Fifer   PHOTOG: Barry M. Wilson   MUSIC: Brian Adler
TVM, minor comedy-fantasy: Woman finds romance in alternate universe

Twilight of the Cockroaches
1989, (Jap), Tyo/Streamline Pictures, color, 105 mins.
W: Kaoru Kobayashi (*Saito*), Setsuko Karasumaru (*The Neighbor*)
WRIT & D: Hiroaki Yoshida
Unusual fantasy-allegory (mixture of animation & live action): Roaches relate to humans with whom they live

Twilight of the Dead
see *The Gates of Hell*

Twilight People

1972, (Phil), Four Assocs. Ltd./Dimension, color, 84 mins.
W: John Ashley, Pat Woodell, Jan Merlin, Charles Macaulay, Eddie Garcia *(Pereira)*, Pam Grier *(The Panther Woman)*, Ken Metcalfe *(The Antelope Man)*, Kim Ramos *(The Ape Man)*, Tony Gosalvez *(The Bat Man)*, Mona Morena *(The Wolf Woman)*, Angelo Ventura, Johnny Long, Andres Centenera, Letty Mirasol, Max Rojo, Cenon Gonzalez, Roger Ocampo, Romeo Mabuto, Vic Unson, Brooke Mills
P: Eddie Romero & John Ashley   **D:** Eddie Romero   **ORIG. SCR:** Jerome Small & Eddie Romero   **PHOTOG:** Fredy Conde   **MUSIC:** Ariston Avelino & Tito Arevalo
video title: *Beasts*
Minor SF-thriller: Mad doctor essays creation of supermen

Twilight's Last Gleaming

1977, (USA-W. Ger), color, 146 mins.
W: Burt Lancaster, Richard Widmark, Charles Durning, Melvyn Douglas, Paul Winfield, Burt Young, Joseph Cotten, Roscoe Lee Browne, Gerald S. O'Loughlin, Richard Jaeckel
D: Robert Aldrich, based on Walter Wager's novel *Vipers*
Standard thriller: Nuclear paranoia grows

Twilight Zone

1983, (USA), WB, color, 102 mins.
W: Dan Aykroyd *(The Passenger)*, Albert Brooks *(The Driver)*, Vic Morrow *(Bill)*, Doug McGrath *(Larry)*, Charles Hallahan *(Ray)*, John Larroquette *(A K.K.K. Man)*, Steven Williams *(The Bar Patron)*, Annette Claudier *(The French Mother)*, Stephen Bishop *(The Charming G.I.)*, Bill Quinn *(Conroy)*, Scatman Crothers *(Bloom)*, Norbert Weisser *(Soldier #1)*, Martin Garner *(Weinstein)*, Selma Diamond *(Mrs. Weinstein)*, Helen Shaw *(Mrs. Dempsey)*, Murray Matheson *(Agee)*, Peter Brocco *(Mute)*, Priscilla Pointer *(Miss Cox)*, Scott Nemes *(Young Mr. Weinstein)*, Tanya Fenmore *(Young Mrs. Weinstein)*, Evan Richards *(Young Mr. Agee)*, Laura Mooney *(Young Mrs. Dempsey)*, Christopher Eisenmann *(Young Mr. Mute)*, Richard Swingler *(The Grey Panther)*, Elsa Raven *(The Nurse)*, Alan Haufrect *(Conroy's Son)*, Cheryl Socher *(Conroy's Daughter-in-Law)*, Kathleen Quinlan *(Helen)*, Jeremy Licht *(Anthony)*, Kevin McCarthy *(Uncle Walt)*, Patricia Barry *(Anthony's Mother)*, William Schallert *(Anthony's Father)*, Nancy Cartwright *(Ethel)*, Abbe Lane *(The Senior Stewardess)*, Dick Miller *(Paisley)*, Cherie Currie *(Sara)*, Bill Mumy *(Tim)*, John Lithgow *(Valentine)*, Jeffrey Bannister *(Charlie)*, Donna Dixon *(The Junior Stewardess)*, John Dennis Johnston *(The Co-Pilot)*, Larry Cedar *(The Creature)*, Charles Knapp *(The Sky Marshal)*, Christina Nigra *(The Little Girl)*, Lonna Schwab *(The Little Girl's Mother)*, Margaret Wheeler *(The Old Woman)*, Eduard Franz *(The Old Man)*, Margaret Fitzgerald, Jeffrey Weissman, Jeffrey Lambert, Frank Toth, Remus Peets, Kai Wulff, Sue Dugan, Debby Porter, Joseph Hieu, Vincent J. Isaac, Albert Leong, Thomas Byrd, William B. Taylor, Domingo Ambriz, Eddie Donno, Michael Milgram
D: John Landis, Steven Spielberg, Joe Dante & George Miller   **SCR:** John Landis, George Clayton Johnson, Josh Rogan & Richard Matheson, from stories by George Clayton Johnson, Richard Matheson & Jerome Bixby   **MUSIC:** Jerry Goldsmith
Standard anthology of 4 SF-fantasy tales

Twinkle, Twinkle, Killer Kane

1980, (USA), New World, color, 118 mins.
W: Stacy Keach *(Col. Kane)*, Scott Wilson *(Capt. Cutshaw)*, Ed Flanders *(Col. Fell)*, Jason Miller *(Lt. Reno)*, Neville Brand *(himself)*, George DiCenzo *(Capt. Fairbanks)*, Moses Gunn *(Maj. Nammack)*, Robert Loggia *(Lt. Bennish)*, Joe Spinell *(Spinell)*, Alejandro Rey *(Lt. Gomez)*, Tom Atkins *(Sgt. Krebs)*, Steve Sandor, Richard Lynch, Mark Gordon, Bill Lucking, Stephen Powers, David Healy, William Paul, Tom Shaw, Gordon K. Kee, Bruce Boa, Linda Blatty, Marilyn Raymon, Hobby Gilman, Bobby Bass, Billy Blatty
WRIT & D: William Peter Blatty   **PHOTOG:** Gerry Fisher   **MUSIC:** Barry DeVorzon
A.k.a. The Ninth Configuration
Unusual surrealist thriller: Servicemen treated for nervous disorders

The Twin Pawns

1920, (USA), Pathe, b&w
WRIT & D: Leonce Perret, from Wilkie Collins' novel *The Woman in White*
Standard thriller: Imprisoned beauty, inheritance scheme

Twin Peaks: Fire Walk with Me

1992, (USA), New Line, color, 135 mins.
W: Sheryl Lee *(Laura Palmer)*, Ray Wise *(Leland Palmer)*, Kyle MacLachlan *(Special Agent Dale Cooper)*, Madchen Amick *(Shelly Johnson)*, Dana Ashbrook *(Bobby Briggs)*, Phoebe Augustine *(Ronette Pulaski)*, David Lynch *(Gordon Cole)*, Pamela Gidley *(Teresa Banks)*, Chris Isaak *(Special Agent Chester Desmond)*, Miguel Ferrer *(Albert Rosenfeld)*, Eric DaRe *(Leo Johnson)*, Heather Graham *(Annie Blackburn)*, David Bowie *(Phillips Jeffries)*, James Marshall *(James Hurley)*, Moira Kelly *(Donna Hayward)*, Jurgen Prochnow *(Woodsman)*, Kiefer Sutherland *(Sam Stanley)*, Lenny Von Dohlen *(Harold Smith)*, Harry Dean Stanton *(Carl Rodd)*, Grace Zabriskie *(Sarah Palmer)*, Catherine E. Coulson *(The Log Lady)*, Peggy Lipton *(Norma Jennings)*, Frances Bay, Michael J. Anderson, Frank Silva, Walter Olkewicz, Al Strobel, Gary Hershberger, Sandra Kinder, Jon Huck, Chris Pedersen, Victor Rivers, Rick Aiello, Audra L. Cooper, Gary Bullock, Mike Malone, Joe Berman, Yvonne Roberts, John Hoobler, Kimberly Ann Cole, Elizabeth Ann McCarthy, C.H.

Evans, Paige Bennett, G. Kenneth Davidson, Ingrid Brucato, Chuck McQuarry, Andrea Hays, Margaret Adams, Carlton L. Russell, Calvin Lockhart, Jonathan J. Leppell, David Brisbin, Julee Cruise, Jane Jones, Steven Hodges, William Ungerman, Joseph "Simon" Szeibert, Gregory "Smokey" Hormel, Joseph L. Altruda, James Parks, Karin Robison, Lorna MacMillan
D: David Lynch   **SCR:** David Lynch & Robert Engels   **PHOTOG:** Ron Garcia   **MUSIC:** Angelo Badalamenti
Bizarre thriller ("prequel" to the teleseries "Twin Peaks"): Events leading to girl's rape and murder

Twins

1988, (USA), color, 107 ins.
W: Arnold Schwarzenegger, Danny DeVito, Kelly Preston, Trey Wilson, Chloe Webb, Bonnie Bartlett, Marshall Bell
D: Ivan Reitman   **SCR:** William Davies, William Osborne, Timothy Harris & Herschel Weingrod   **MUSIC:** Georges Delerue & Randy Edelman
Standard SF-comedy: Genetically-engineered twins reunited

Twinsanity

1970, (GB), color, 91 mins.
W: Judy Geeson, Martin Potter, Michael Redgrave
Standard thriller: Twins implicated in murder

Twins of Evil

1971, (GB), Hammer/Univ, color, 87 mins.
W: Inigo Jackson *(Woodman)*, Judy Matheson *(Woodman's Daughter)*, Peter Cushing *(Gustav)*, Alex Scott *(Hermann)*, Harvey Hall *(Franz)*, Sheelah Wilcox *(The Lady in the Coach)*, Mary Collinson *(Maria)*, Madelaine Collinson *(Frieda)*, Kathleen Byron *(Katy)*, Damien Thomas *(The Count)*, David Warbeck *(Anton)*, Roy Stewart *(Joachim)*, Dennis Price *(Dietrich)*, Luan Peters *(Gerta)*, Maggie Wright *(Aleta)*, Kirsten Lindholm *(The Young Girl at the Stake)*, Katya Wyeth *(The Countess)*, Isobel Black *(Ingrid)*, Peter Thompson *(The Gaoler)*
P: Harry Fine & Michael Style   **D:** John Hough   **SCR:** Tudor Gates, loosely based on Sheridan LeFanu's novel *Carmilla*   **PHOTOG:** Dick Bush   **MUSIC:** Harry Robinson
"The film is done with Hammer's obvious care for details and a sobriety which creates the proper mood of unexpected evil in attractive, tranquil surroundings. It is also well-played, mostly at a gallop, by Madelaine and Mary Collinson, as the lovely double-dish of feminine splendor; Damien Thomas, as the pleasure-mad Count Karnstein...and Peter Cushing, the grand old man of British fright films, who gives the twisted witch-hunting uncle and almost sympathetic bent as he travels the lonely road of evil-doing in the Lord's name"—Robert L. Jerome, Cinefantastique
Unusual horror-fantasy: Count turns Puritan's niece into vampiress

Twisted

1985, (USA), Greenroom, color
W: Lois Smith *(Helen Giles)*, Christian Slater *(Mark Collins)*, Tandy Cronyn *(Evelyn Collins)*, Dina Merrill *(Nell Kempler)*, Dan Ziskie *(Phillip Collins)*, John Cunningham *(Jim Kempler)*, Brooke Tracy *(Susan Collins)*, J.C. Quinn *(The Sheriff)*, Edward Marshall *(Karl Yaeger)*, Laurie Kennedy *(Peg Yaeger)*, Ralph Buckley *(The Deputy)*, Charlotte Jones *(Mrs. Murtagh)*, Karl Taylor *(Williams)*, Chip Olcott *(Sam, the Grocer)*, Noelle Parker *(Jeanette)*, Andre Morgan *(The Drug Emergency Man)*, Michael Benhar *(Metz)*, William Meyers *(The Pharmacist)*, Richard Thomsen *(Elsworth Peale)*, Deanna Wemble *(Mrs. Peale)*, Dan Lounsbery *(The Chemistry Teacher)*, Mercedes Rule *(Cybelle)*, Anthony Herrera *(The Orator)*, Charly Slagle *(A Paramedic)*, Bill Vasaturo *(A Paramedic)*, K. Mayr *(Kaye)*, Howard Henick *(A Party Man)*, Harry Kiernan *(A Party Man)*
D: Adam Holender   **SCR:** Glenn Kershaw & Bruce Graham, based on Jack Horrigan's play *Children! Children!*   **PHOTOG:** Alexander Gruszynski   **MUSIC:** Michael Bacon
Minor thriller: Teen torments babysitter

Twisted Brain

see Horror High

Twisted Justice

1989, (USA), color, 90 mins.
W: David Heavener, Erik Estrada, Jim Brown, Shannon Tweed, James Van Patten, Don Stroud, Karen Black, Lori Warren
D & SCR: David Heavener
Minor SF-thriller: 21st-century cop pursues killer

Twisted Nightmare

1987, (USA), color
Minor horror-thriller: Spirit of murdered child menaces campers

The Twisted Nerve

1968, (GB), Boulting Bros./Nat'l General, color, 118 mins.
W: Hayley Mills *(Susan Harper)*, Hywel Bennett *(Martin Durnley/Georgie Clifford)*, Billie Whitelaw *(Joan Harper)*, Barry Foster *(Gerry Henderson)*, Phyllis Calvert *(Enid Durnley)*, Thorley Walters *(Sir John Forrester)*, Salmaan Peer *(Shashi Kumar)*, Christian Roberts *(Philip)*, Gretchen Franklin *(Mrs. Clarke)*, Timothy West *(Supt. Dakin)*, Clifford Cox *(Insp. Goddard)*, Frank Finlay *(Henry Durnley)*, Brian Peck *(Det. Sgt. Thompson)*, Richard Davies *(Taffy Evans)*, Michael Cadman *(Mac)*, Russell Napier *(Prof. Fuller)*, Russell Waters

(*The Hospital Attendant*), Mary Land (*Judy*), Hazel Bainbridge (*The Nursing Sister*)
D: Roy Boulting **SCR:** Leo Marks & Roy Boulting **PHOTOG:** Harry Waxman **MUSIC:** Bernard Herrmann
"...suspense that gives your nerves a helluva workout!" —Cue
Unusual thriller: Youth feigns retardation, commits brutal murders

Twister
1996, (USA), Amblin/WB-Univ, color, 113 mins.
W: Helen Hunt (*Jo*), Bill Paxton (*Bill*), Jami Gertz (*Melissa*), Cary Elwes (*Jonas*), Lois Smith (*Aunt Meg*), Jeremy Davies (*Laurence*), Joey Slotnick (*Joey*), Philip Seymour Hoffman (*Rabbit*), Alan Ruck (*Dusty*), Todd Field, Zach Grenier, Jake Busey, Nicholas Sadler, Scott Thomson, Abraham Benrubi, Ben Weber, Wendle Josepher, Gregory Sporleder, Melanie Hoopes, Patrick Fischler, Anthony Rapp, Eric LaRay, J. Dean Lindsay, Dan Kelpine, Sharonlyn Morrow, Alexa Vega, Bruce Wright, Richard Lineback, Rusty Schwimmer, Taylor Gilbert, Rick Mitchell, Gary England, Jeff Lazauer, Samantha McDonald, Jennifer Hamilton, John Thomas Rhyne, Paul Douglas, Anneke De Bont
D: Jan De Bont **SCR:** Michael Crichton & Anne-Marie Martin **PHOTOG:** Jack N. Green **MUSIC:** Mark Mancina
Impressive thriller: Tornado hunters imperiled

Twist of Fate
see **Beautiful Stranger**

Twists of Terror
1997, (Can), color, 95 mins.
W: Jennifer Rubin, Nick Mancuso
Made-for-Cable, standard thriller trilogy: (1) Man bitten by rabid dog, (2) Backwoodsmen terrorize couple, and (3) Woman has date with stranger

Twitch of the Death Nerve
1972, (It), Hallmark, color, 87 mins.
W: Claudine Auger, Claudio Volonto, Ana Maria Rosati, Laura Betti, Luigi Pistilli, Brigitte Skay
WRIT & D: Mario Bava **MUSIC:** Stelvio Cipriani

Two Lost Worlds: GLORIA PETROFF, LAURA ELLIOT, JIM ARNESS AND BILL KENNEDY

A.k.a. (USA) **Carnage** and **Last House on the Left Part II**, released (USA) on video-cassette as **Bay of Blood**
blurb: "13 periods of intense shock"
Minor thriller: Series of murders perplexes

Two Beautiful Cracksmen
1910, (GB), Warwick Trading Co., b&w, 417 ft. (127.2m)
Standard crime-thriller: Crooks pursued

Two Before Zero
1962, (USA), Ellis Films, color, 78 mins.
W: Basil Rathbone, Mary Murphy
P: Fred A. Niles **D:** William Faralla
A.k.a. **Red Hell** and **Russian Roulette**
Unusual anti-communist allegory/fantasy/docu: "Everywoman" probes history of Marxism

Two Brothers and a Spy
1912, (GB), Hepworth, b&w, 850 ft. (259.1m)
W: Alec Worcester (*Lt. Dick Fenton*), Madge Campbell (*The Colonel's Daughter*)
D: Hay Plumb
Standard crime-thriller: Lieutenant takes blame when brother steals plans

Two Evil Eyes
1990, (It), Taurus, color
W: Harvey Keitel, Adrienne Barbeau, Aamy Zada, John Amos, Sally Kirkland, Martin Balsam, E.G. Marshall, Kim Hunter, Madeleine Potter

D: George Romero & Dario Argento **SCR:** George Romero, Dario Argento & Franco Ferrini, based on stories by Edgar Allan Poe **MUSIC:** Pino Donaggio
Minor horror-thriller

The Two Faces of Dr. Jekyll
1960, (GB), Hammer/AIP, color, 88 mins.
W: Paul Massie (*Dr. Henry Jekyll*), Dawn Addams (*Kitty Jekyll*), Christopher Lee (*Paul Allen*), David Kossoff (*Ernest Litauer*), Francis De Wolff (*The Inspector*), Norma Marla (*Maria*), Joy Webster (*A Sphinx Girl*), Magda Miller (*A Sphinx Girl*), William Kendall (*The Clubman*), Joe Robinson (*Corinthian*), Oliver Reed
P: Michael Carreras **D:** Terence Fisher **SCR:** Wolf Mankowitz, from Robert Louis Stevenson's novel *Dr. Jekyll and Mr. Hyde* **PHOTOG:** Jack Asher **MUSIC:** John Hollingsworth
USA retitle, **House of Fright**, *orig. to be titled* **Jekyll's Inferno**
Standard horror-thriller: Drug turns old doctor into murderous young sadist

The Two-Headed Spy
1958, (GB), Sabre/Col, b&w, 93 mins.
W: Jack Hawkins (*Gen. Alex Scottland*), Gia Scala (*Lili Geyr*), Erik Schumann (*Capt. Kurt Reinisch*), Felix Aylmer (*Cornaz*), Alexander Knox (*Mueller*), Laurence Naismith (*Gen. Hauser*), Edward Underdown (*Kaltenbrunner*), Martin Benson (*Gen. Wagner*), Donald Pleasence (*Gen. Hardt*), Walter Hudd (*Adm. Canaris*), Kenneth Griffith (*Adolph Hitler*), Harriet Johns (*Karen Corscher*), Geoffrey Bayldon (*Dietz*), Richard Grey (*Marshal Keitel*)
P: Hal E. Chester & Bill Kirby **D:** Andre de Toth **SCR:** James O'Donnell, from a story by J. Alvin Kugelmass **PHOTOG:** Ted Scaife **SPCL-FX:** George Blackwell **MUSIC:** Gerard Schurmann
Unusual, fact-based thriller: British spy serves on German general staff

Two Letter Alibi
1962, (GB), Playpnt/ritish Lion, b&w, 60 mins.
W: Peter Williams (*Charles*), Petra Davies (*Kathy*), Ursula Howells (*Louise*), Ronald Adam (*Sir John Fawcett*), Peter Howell (*Carlton*), Bernard Archard (*Duke*), Stratford Johns (*Bates*)
P: E.M. Smedley Aston **D:** Robert Lynn **SCR:** Roger Marshall, from Andrew Garve's novel
Standard crime-thriller: TV star's lover accused of killing his alcoholic wife

Two Lost Worlds
1950, (USA), Eagle Lion, b&w, 63 mins.
W: James Arness, Laura Elliot, William Kennedy, Hank Mann, Gloria Petroff, Tom Hubbard, Jane Harlan, Fred Kohler Jr., Tim Monroe
P: Boris Petroff **D:** Norman Dawn **SCR:** Tom Hubbard, from a story by B. Petroff **SPCL-FX:** Jack Glass **MUSIC:** Alex Alexander
Standard SF-thriller (with stock-footage from **One Million B.C.**): *Adventurers face pre-historic terrors*

Two Mafia Guys from the FBI
see **Dr. Goldfoot and the Girl Bombs**

Two Mafia Guys vs. Goldginger
1965, (It), color
W: Franco Franchi, Ciccio Ingrassia, Fernando Rey, Gloria Paul
USA retitle, **The Amazing Dr. G**
Minor SF-comedy: Idiots tangle with mastermind bent on robotizing gov't personnel. cf. **Dr. Goldfoot and the Girl Bombs**

The Two Mrs. Carrolls
1947, (USA), WB, b&w, 99 mins.
W: Humphrey Bogart (*Geoffrey Carroll*), Barbara Stanwyck (*Sally Morton Carroll*), Alexis Smith (*Cecily Latham*), Pat O'Moore (*Charles Pennington*), Nigel Bruce (*Dr. Tuttle*), Isobel Elsom (*Mrs. Latham*), Ann Carter (*Beatrice Carroll*), Barry Bernard (*Mr. Bingdon*), Anita Bolster (*Christine*), Colin Campbell (*MacGregor*), Leland Hodgson (*The Inspector*), Peter Godfrey (*A Tout*), Creighton Hale (*A Tout*)
P: Mark Hellinger **D:** Peter Godfrey **SCR:** Thomas Job, from Martin Vale's stage play **PHOTOG:** J. Peverell Marley **MUSIC:** Franz Waxman **MUSIC DIR:** Leo F. Forbstein
Standard melodrama: Artist murders wives

The Twonky
1953, (USA), UA, b&w, 72 mins.
W: Hans Conried, Billy Lynn, Gloria Blondell, Janet Warren, Ed Max, Al Jarvis, Norman Field, Trilby Conried, William Phipps, Steve Roberts, Florence Ravenel
WRIT, P & D: Arch Oboler, from Henry Kuttner's story **PHOTOG:** Joseph Biroc **MUSIC:** Jack Meakin
Classic SF-comedy: Android from totalitarian future assumes form of TV set

Two on a Guillotine
1964, (USA), WB, b&w, 107 mins.
W: Connie Stevens (*Melinda & Cassie Duquesne*), Dean Jones (*Val Henderson*), Cesar Romero ("*Duke*" *Duquesne*), Parley Baer ("*Buzz*" *Sheridan*), Virginia Gregg (*Dolly Bast*), John Hoyt (*Carl Vickers*), Connie Gilchrist (*Ramona Ryerdon*), Russell Thorson (*Carmichael*), Robert Adler, Denise Monroe
P & D: William Conrad **SCR:** John Kneubuhl & Henry Slesar, from an orig. story by Henry Slesar **PHOTOG:** Sam Laevitt **MUSIC:** Max Steiner

Modest thriller: To collect inheritance, girl must spend several nights in eerie mansion of her stage-magician father

The Two Roads

1915, (GB), London/Jury, b&w, 4,070 ft. (1240.5m)

<u>W</u>: Edna Flugrath (*Linda Murdoch*), Ben Webster (*Sir Cuthbert Maclaine*), Fred Groves (*Rev. Basil Egerton*), Douglas Munro (*Toby Murdoch*), Wallace Bosco (*Taplow*), Florence Nelson (*Lady Maclaine*)

<u>D</u>: Harold Shaw, from a play by Ben Landeck

Standard crime-thriller: Counterfeiter's daughter blackmailed by father's partner, forced to steal secret formula

2000 Maniacs

1964, (USA), Boxoffice Spectaculars, color, 75 mins.

<u>W</u>: Connie Mason, Thomas Wood, Ben Moore, Jeffrey Allen, Shelby Livingston, Mark Douglas, Jerome Eden, Yvonne Gilbert, Linda Cochran, Gary Bakeman, Michael Korb, Vincent Santo, Andy Wilson

<u>P</u>: David F. Friedman   <u>D</u>: Herschell G. Lewis

Standard satire-thriller: Inhabitants of Southern town execute Yankee strangers

2001: A Space Odyssey

1968, (USA-GB), MGM, color, 139 mins.

<u>W</u>: Keir Dullea (*David Bowman*), Gary Lockwood (*Frank Poole*), William Sylvester (*Dr. Heywood Floyd*), Robert Beatty (*Halvorsen*), Leonard Rossiter (*Smyslov*), Daniel Richter (*Moonwatcher, the Primate*), Douglas Rain (*Voice of "Hal 9000"*), Margaret Tyzack (*Elena*), Sean Sullivan (*Michaels*), Frank Miller (*The Controller*), Alan Gifford

<u>P & D</u>: Stanley Kubrick   <u>SCR</u>: Stanley Kubrick & Arthur C. Clarke, inspired by Arthur C. Clarke's short story "The Sentinel"   <u>PHOTOG</u>: Geoffrey Unsworth   <u>SPCL-FX</u>: Wally Veevers, Douglas Trumbull, Con Pederson & Tom Howard   <u>MUSIC</u>: Richard Strauss, Johann Strauss, Aram Khachaturian & Gyorgy Ligeti   <u>ART DIRECTION</u>: John Hoesli

"Stanley Kubrick has created a film destined to become a major breakthrough in motion picture technique. It is an epic of mankind, its pre-history and its future. It is an astonishingly beautiful visual experience seen in the breathtaking sweep of Cinerama. You will be projected into an adventure of exploration from Earth to Moon; through the Solar System; out to Jupiter and then on to the Stars" —Anon., "What's New in Monsterdom," Monster Mania, No. 3 (April, 1967), p. 35

"...a magnificent achievement. No humans and little humanity but over-powering visuals, impeccable cinematics, and awing concept. Evolution-causing monolithic life force is discovered on moon and space flight heads toward Jupiter in search of its origins. Easily the best made science fantasy film ever"—Anon., "Frankenstein TV Movieguide," Castle of Frankenstein, Vol. IV, No. 1 (Spring, 1969), p. 62

Classic SF-adventure: Malfunctioning computer threatens astronauts on secret mission

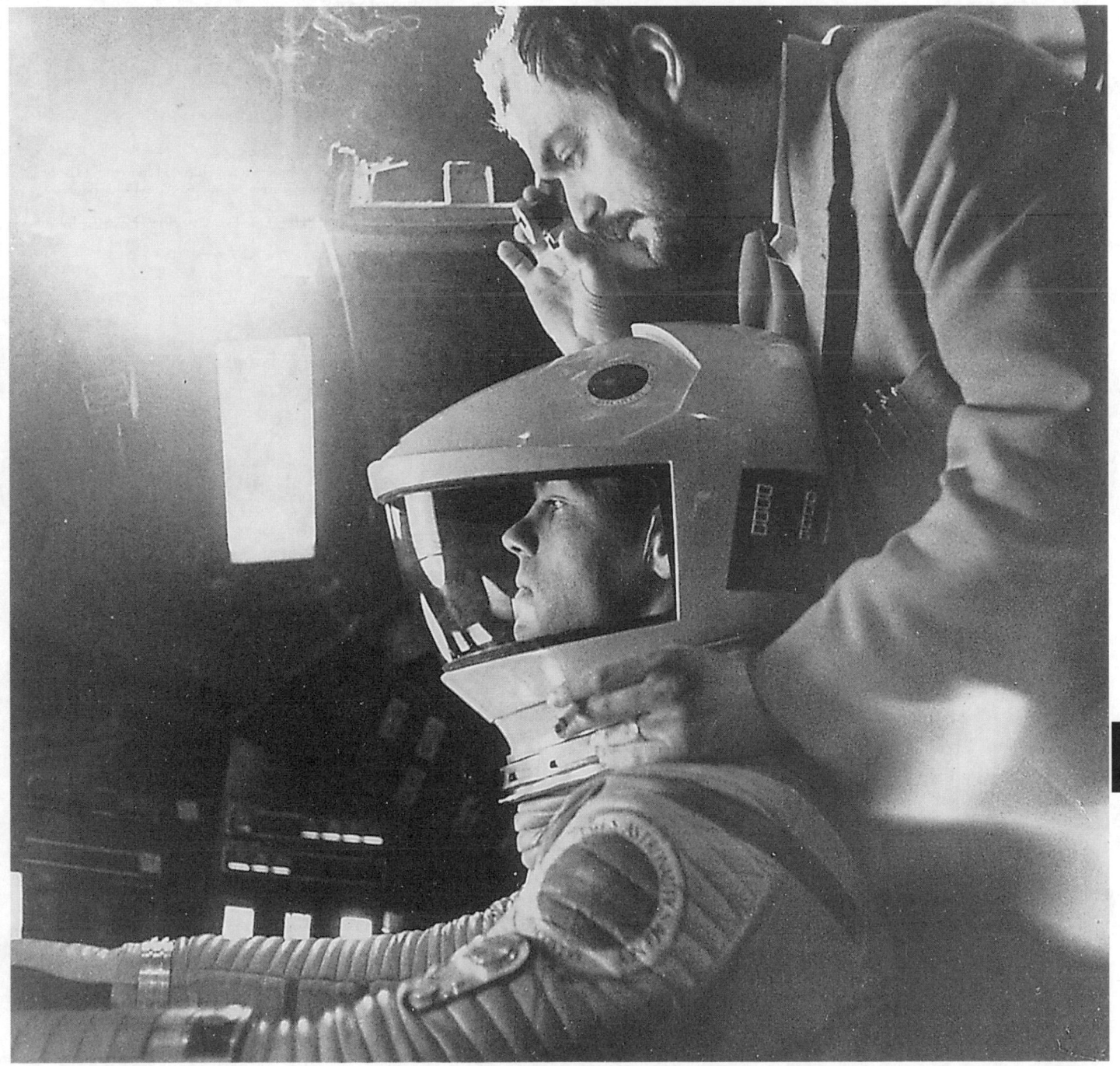

2001: A Space Odyssey: GARY LOCKWOOD AND STANLEY KUBRICK

2010
1984, (USA), MGM-UA, color, 115 mins.
<u>W</u>: Roy Scheider (*Dr. Heywood Floyd*), John Lithgow (*Walter Curnow*), Helen Mirren (*Capt. Tanya Kirbuk*), Bob Balaban (*Dr. Chandra*), Keir Dullea (*Dave Bowman*), Madolyn Smith, Dana Elcar, Elya Baskin, Douglas Rain (*Voice of "Hal 9000"*), James McEachin
<u>P, D, SCR & PHOTOG:</u> Peter Hyams, from Arthur C. Clarke's novel   <u>SPCL-FX:</u> Richard Edlund   <u>MUSIC:</u> David Shire
Standard SF-adventure: US-Soviet mission to locate lost spacecraft near moon of Jupiter

2069: A Sex Odyssey
1974, (W. Ger), color, 73 mins.
<u>W</u>: Nina Frederic, Alena Penz, Gerti Sneider, Raul Retzer, Catherine Conti, Heidi Hammer, Michael Mein, Herb Heesel
<u>D</u>: George Keil
Minor sex-farce: Five beauties on erotic space mission

2002: Rape of Eden
1994, (USA), color, 90 mins.
<u>W</u>: Jeff Conaway, Vernon Wells, Phil Nordell
Minor SF-thriller: Madman loose in future desert

2000 Years Later
1968, (USA), WB-7Arts, color
<u>W</u>: John Abbott (*Gregorius*), Terry-Thomas (*Charles*), Lisa Seagram (*Cindy*), Edward Everett Horton (*Evermore*), Monte Rock III (*Tomorrow's Leader*), John Myhers (*The General*), Pat Harrington Jr. (*Franchot*), Tom Melody (*The Senator*), Myrna Ross (*Miss Forever*), Murray Roman (*Superdude*), Michael Christian (*The Piston Kid*), Casey Kasem (*The Disc Jockey*), Rudi Gernreich
<u>WRIT & D:</u> Bert Tenzer   <u>PHOTOG:</u> Mario DiLeo   <u>MUSIC:</u> Stu Phillips
Standard SF-satire

Two Wives at One Wedding
1961, (GB), Danziger/Para, b&w, 66 mins.
<u>W</u>: Gordon Jackson (*Tom*), Christina Gregg (*Janet*), Lisa Daniely (*Annette*), Andre Maranne (*Paul*), Viola Keats (*Mrs. Ervine*), Humphrey Lestocq (*Mark*), Douglas Ives (*Jessop*), John Serrett (*Larouche*)
<u>P</u>: Brian Taylor   <u>D</u>: Montgomery Tully   <u>STORY:</u> Brian Clemens & Eldon Howard
Standard crime-thriller: Doctor marries socialite, then is blackmailed by French girl who claims to be his wife

The Two Worlds of Jennie Logan
1979, (USA), Fries Enterprises/CBS-TV, color, 94 mins.
<u>W</u>: Lindsay Wagner (*Jennie*), Marc Singer (*David*), Henry Wilcoxon (*Harrington*), Alan Feinstein (*Michael*), Linda Gray (*Elizabeth*), Joan Darling (*Dr. Lauren*), Irene Tedrow (*Mrs. Bates*), Peter Hobbs, Constance McCashin, Pat Corley, Charles Thomas Murphy, Allen Willims, John Hawkins, Robert Nadder, Layla Galloway
<u>P</u>: Paul B. Radin   <u>D & TELEPLAY:</u> Frank De Felitta, from David Williams' novel *Second Sight*   <u>PHOTOG:</u> Al Francis   <u>MUSIC:</u> Glenn Paxton
"A silly mix of **Berkeley Square** and **Portrait of Jennie**" —Judith Crist, TV Guide
TVM, standard fantasy-romance: Mysterious dress transports woman to turn of century

The Tyborn Case
1957, (GB), Merton Park/Anglo-Amalgamated, b&w, 32 mins.
<u>W</u>: John Warwick (*Supt. Reynolds*), Patricia Marmont (*Nora Sims*), Howard Marion Crawford (*Peter Shilling*), Genine Graham (*Mrs. Sandford*)
<u>P</u>: Alec Snowden   <u>D:</u> David Paltenghi   <u>STORY:</u> James Eastwood, from a novel by Edgar Lustgarten
Standard short crime-thriller: Lawyer drowns widow to gain insurance

Tyrant of Lydia Against the Son of Hercules
1963, (It), color
<u>W</u>: Gordon Scott, Massimo Serato
Minor "Sword & Sandal"

Tyrant of the Sea
1950, (USA), Col, b&w, 70 mins.
<u>W</u>: Ron Randell, Rhys Williams
Minor adventure-thriller

Tystnaden (The Silence)
1963, (Swed), Svensk Filmindustri/Janus, b&w, 95 mins.
<u>W</u>: Gunnel Lindblom (*Anna*), Ingrid Thulin (*Ester*), Jorgen Lindstrom (*The Boy*), Hakan Jahnberg (*The Old Waiter*), Birger Malmsten (*The Man*), Eduardo Gutierez
<u>WRIT, P & D:</u> Ingmar Bergman   <u>PHOTOG:</u> Sven Nykvist   <u>MUSIC:</u> Johann Sebastian Bach
Complex melodrama: Tragic relationship between two sisters

2010: The Year We Make Contact: KEIR DULLEA

U-Boat Prisoner
1944, (Col), b&w, 65 mins.
W: Bruce Bennett, John Abbott, John Wood, Kenneth MacDonald, Erik Rolf, John Wengraf
D: Lew Landers
Minor thriller

U-Boat 29
see The Spy in Black

L'Uccello delle Piume di Cristallo (The Bird with the Crystal Plumage)
1969, (It), UMC, color, 98 mins.
W: Tony Musante (*Sam*), Suzy Kendall (*Julia*), Eva Renzi (*Monica*), Enrico Maria Salerno (*Morosini*), Mario Adorf (*Berto*), Renato Romano (*Dover*), Umberto Raho (*Ranieri*), Reggie Nalder
WRIT & D: Dario Argento **PHOTOG:** Vittorio Storaro **MUSIC:** Ennio Morricone
A.k.a. **The Gallery Murders** and **Phantom of Terror**
Elaborate thriller: Baffling murders of beautiful women

Uchujin Tokyo Ni Arawaru (Space people Attack Tokyo)
1957, (Jap), Toho, color, 87 mins.
W: Keizo Kawasaki, Toyomi Karita, Bontaro Miake, Kiyoko Hirai, Shozo Nanbu, Isao Yamagata, Mieko Nagai
P: Masaichi Nagata **D:** Koji Shima **SCR:** Hideo Oguni
USA release, 1963 A.k.a. **Mysterious Satellite**, **Warning from Space**, **The Cosmic Man Appears In Tokyo**, **Space Men Appear in Tokyo**, *and* **Unknown Satellite over Tokyo**
Standard SF-thriller: Space creatures warn Earth of disaster

U.F.O.
1956, (USA), Greene-Rouse/UA, b&w (minimal color footage), 91 mins.
W: Tom Powers (*Chop*), Robert Phillips (*Ruppelt*)
P: Clarence Greene **D:** Winston Jones **SCR:** Francis Martin **MUSIC:** Ernest Gold
Minor SF-thriller: Detailed reconstruction of Air Force investigation into "flying saucer" reports

The UFO Incident
1975, (USA), NBC-TV, color, 100 mins.
W: James Earl Jones (*Barney Hill*), Estelle Parsons (*Betty Hill*), Barnard Hughes (*Dr. Benjamin Simon*), Dick O'Neill (*Gen. Davidson*), Beeson Carroll (*McRainey*), Jeanne Joe (*The Examiner*), Terrence O'Connor (*Lisa McRainey*), Lou Wagner (*The Leader*), Joe Stefano (*Henderson*), Tony Swartz (*Gill*)
P: Joe L. Cramer **D:** Richard A. Colla, from John G. Fuller's book *The Interrupted Journey* **PHOTOG:** Rexford Metz **MUSIC:** Billy Goldenberg
TVM, fact-based thriller: Space-alien abduction of couple

UFOria
1986, (USA), color, 105 mins.
W: Cindy Williams, Harry Dean Stanton, Fred Ward
D & SCR: John Binder **MUSIC:** Richard Baskin
Standard thriller: Con man in desert town encounters phony faith healer and UFO visionary

UFOs are Coming Wednesday
1990, (Russ), color
W: Eric Sykes
Standard SF-thriller

U.F.O.: Target Earth
1974, (USA), Centrum Int'l, color, 80 mins.
W: Nick Plakias, Cynthia Cline, Phil Erickson
P & D: Michael A. de Gaetano
Minor SF-thriller: Scientists salvage space-alien "saucer"

Ugetsu Monogatari (Tales of a Pale and Mysterious Moon after the Rain)
1953, (Jap), Daiei, b&w, 96 mins.
W: Machiko Kyo (*Lady Wakasa*), Masayuki Mori (*Genjuro*), Sakae Ozawa (*Tobei*), Kinuyo Tanaka (*Miyagi*), Mitsuko Mito (*Ohama*)
P: Masaichi Nagata **D:** Kenji Mizoguchi from classic stories by Akinari Ueda **PHOTOG:** Kazuo Miyagawa
Standard fantasy-thriller: Greedy brothers-in-law have lives drastically changed by lustful soldiers and castle of ghosts

The Ugly
1997, (New Zeal), color
Minor horror-thriller

The Ugly Duckling
1959, (GB), Hammer/Col, b&w, 84 mins.
W: Bernard Bresslaw (*Henry Jekyll/Teddy Hyde*), Jon Pertwee (*Victor Jekyll*), Reginald Beckwith (*Reginald*), Maudie Edwards (*Henrietta Jekyll*), Jean Muir (*Snout*), David Lodge (*Peewee*), Richard Wattis (*Barclay*), Michael Ripper (*Benny*), Elwyn Brook-Jones
P: Tommy Lyndon-Hayes **D:** Lance Comfort **SCR:** Sid Colin & Jack Davies, inspired by Robert Louis Stevenson's *Dr. Jekyll and Mr. Hyde*
Standard comedy-fantasy: Great-grandfather's formula turns chemist's assistant into jewel thief

L'Ultima Preda del Vampiro (The Last Prey of the Vampire)
1960, (It), Tiziano Longo/Nord Film Italiana/Richard Gordon, b&w, 80 mins.
W: Lyla Rocco (*Vera*), Walter Brandi (*Count Gabor/The Vampire*), Maria Giovannini (*Katia*), Alfredo Rizzo, Ivy Holzer, Erika Di Centa, Tilde Damiani, Corinne Fontaine, Leonardo Botta, Antoine Nicos, Marisa Quattrini, Enrico Salvatore
D & SCR: Piero Regnoli **PHOTOG:** Ugo Brunelli **MUSIC:** Aldo Piga **MUSIC CONDUCT:** Pier Luigi Urbini
Fr retitle, Des Filles pour un Vampire (Some Girls for a Vampire) USA retitle (1963), The Playgirls and the Vampire A.k.a. Curse of the Vampire
Standard horror-thriller with "jiggle": Stranded showgirls meet Undead nobleman

The Ultimate Impostor
1979, (USA), Univ/CBS-TV, color, 86 mins.
W: Joseph Hacker (*Frank Monihan*), Keith Andes (*Eugene Danziger*), Macon McCalman (*Dr. Jake McKeever*), Thomas Bellin (*Joe Maslan*), Erin Gray (*Beatrice "Bucky" Tate*), W.T. Zacha (*Weeks*), Chip Johnson (*Martin*), Joseph Hardin (*Eddie*), Mark Garcia (*Felipe*), Loren Berman (*Dominic*), John Van Dreelen, Tracy Brooks Swope, Rosalind Chao, Robert Phillips, Normann Burton, Bobby Riggs, Mike Kulcsar, Tommy Reamon, Graydon Gould
D: Paul Stanley **TELEPLAY:** Lionel E. Siegel **STORY:** William T. Zacha & Lionel E. Siegel **PHOTOG:** Vincent A. Martinelli **MUSIC:** Dana Kaproff
TVM, minor SF-thriller: Secret agent implanted with computer brain

The Ultimate Warrior
1975, (USA), Weintraub-Heller/WB, color, 94 mins.
W: Yul Brynner (*Carson*), Max von Sydow (*The Baron*), Joanna Miles (*Melinda*), William Smith (*Carrot*), Stephen McHattie (*Robert*), Richard Kelton (*Cal*), Darrell Zwerling (*Silas*), Lane Bradbury (*Barrie*), Nate Esformes (*Garon*), Mel Novak (*Lippert*), Mickey Caruso (*B. Harkness*), Gray Johnson (*L. Harkness*), Susan Keener (*The Angry Woman*), Fred Slyter (*The Store Room Clerk*), Stevie Myers (*The Ice House Woman*), Pat Johnson, Alex Colon, Reggie Parton, Larry Bischof, Henry Kingi
WRIT & D: Robert Clouse **PHOTOG:** Gerald Hirschfeld **SPCL-FX:** Gene Griggs **MUSIC:** Gil Melle
A.k.a. **The Barony**
Minor SF-thriller: Post-plague survivors in New York City, A.D. 2012

Ultimatum
1938, (Fr), b&w
W: Erich Von Stroheim, Dita Parlo
D: Robert Wiene & Robert Siodmak (uncredited)
Standard melodrama

Ultimatum to Earth
see The Day the Earth Stood Still

Gli Ultimi Giorni di Pompei (The Last Days of Pompeii)
1908, (It), b&w
D: Luigi Maggi
from Bulwer-Lytton's novel
Standard thriller: Volcano destroys Roman town

Gli Ultimi Giorni di Pompei (The Last Days of Pompeii)
1913, (It), b&w
D: Mario Caserini
from Bulwer-Lytton's novel
Standard thriller: Volcano razes Roman resort

Ultraviolet
1992, (USA), color, 79 mins.
W: Esai Morales
Standard thriller: Deranged stranger turns couple's romantic desert weekend into terrifying nightmare

Ultra Warrior
1992, (USA), color, 80 mins.
W: Dack Rambo, Meshach Taylor, Clare Beresford
A.k.a. **Welcome to Oblivion**
Minor SF-thriller: Warfare on post-nuke Earth

Ultus 1: The Townsend Mystery
see Ultus, the Man from the Dead

Ultus 2: The Ambassador's Diamond
see Ultus, the Man from the Dead

Ultus 3: The Grey Lady
see Ultus and the Grey Lady

Ultus 4: The Traitor's Fate
see Ultus and the Grey Lady

Ultus 5: The Secret of the Night
see Ultus and the Secret of the Night

Ultus 6: The Three-Button Mystery
see Ultus and the Three-Button Mystery

Ultus 7

see Ultus and the Three-Button Mystery

Ultus and the Grey Lady

1916, (GB), Gaumont-Victory, b&w, 4,488 ft. (1367.8m)
<u>W</u>: Aurele Sydney *(Ultus)*, Mary Dibley *(Mary Ferris)*, Jack Leigh *(Conway Bass)*, Frank Dane *(Dick)*, M. Gouget *(Eugene Lester)*
<u>D & STORY</u>: George Pearson
USA retitles (shown in 2 parts), **Ultus and the Grey Lady** *and* **Ultus 4: The Traitor's Fate**
Standard crime-thriller: Girl helps "Avenger" trace her father's killer

Ultus and the Secret of the Night

1916, (GB), Gaumont-Victory, b&w, 4,000 ft. (1219.2m)
<u>W</u>: Aurele Sydney *(Ultus)*, Mary Dibley *(Mary Ferris)*, J.L.V. Leigh *(Coway Bass)*, Lionel d'Aragon *(Banks)*, Mary Forbes *(Lady Fleet)*, Leonard Shepherd *(Sir Miles Fleet)*, Frank Dane
<u>D & STORY</u>: George Pearson
USA retitle: **Ultus 5: The Secret of the Night**
Standard crime-thriller: Girl helps "Avenger" save child heiress from killers

Ultus and the Three-Button Mystery

1917, (GB), Gaumont-Victory, b&w, 4,650 ft. (1417.6m)
<u>W</u>: Aurele Sydney *(Ultus)*, Manora Thew *(Elsie Meredith)*, Charles Rock *(Derwent)*, Alice de Winton, Fred Morgan, Frank Dane
<u>D & STORY</u>: George Pearson
USA retitles (shown in 2 parts), **Ultus 6: the Three-Button Mystery** *and* **Ultus 7**
Standard crime-thriller: "Avenger" rescues kidnapped statesman

Ultus, the Man From the Dead

1915, (GB), Gaumont-Victory, b&w, 6,147 ft. (1873.6m)
<u>W</u>: Aurele Sydney *(Dick Morgan)*, J.L.V. Leigh *(Conway Bass)*, Marjorie Dunbar *(Lady Townsend)*, A. Caton Woodville *(Sir Gilbert Townsend)*, M. Gouget *(Eugene Lester)*
<u>D</u>: George Pearson   <u>STORY</u>: George Pearson & Thomas Welsh
USA retitles (shown in 2 parts), **Ultus 1: The Townsend Mystery** *and* **Ultus 2: the Ambassador's Diamond**
Standard crime-thriller: Diamond miner survives attack, dons disguises to kill partner

Ulysses

1954, (It), Lux/Para, color, 104 mins.
<u>W</u>: Kirk Douglas *(Ulysses)*, Silvana Mangano *(Circe/Penelope)*, Rossana Podesta *(Nausicaa)*, Anthony Quinn *(Antinous)*, Sylvie *(Euriclea)*, Daniel Ivernel *(Euriloco)*, Jacques Dumesnil *(Al Cinous)*, Franco Interlenghi, Umberto Silvestri, Piero Lulli, Elena Zareschi, Evi Maltagliati, Ludmilla Dudarova, Teresa Pellati, Tania Weber, Ferruccio Stagni, Alessandro Fersen, Oscar Andriani, Gualtiero Tumiati, Mario Felicianni, Michele Riccardini
<u>P</u>: Dino De Laurentiis   <u>D</u>: Mario Camerini   <u>SCR</u>: Franco Brusati, Ennio De Concini, Hugh Gray, Ben Hecht, Ivo Perilli & Irwin Shaw, based on Homer's epic *The Odyssey*   <u>PHOTOG</u>: Harold Rosson   <u>SPCL-FX</u>: Eugen Shuftan   <u>MUSIC</u>: Alessandro Cicognini
Well-made myth-adventure: Exploits of Greek hero on return from Trojan War cf. **The Odyssey**

Ulysses Against the Son of Hercules

1962, (It), Embassy, color
<u>W</u>: Georges Marchal, Michael Lane, Eleonora Bianchi, Yvette Lebon
<u>WRIT & D</u>: Mario Caiano   <u>PHOTOG</u>: Alvaro Mancori
A.k.a. **Hercules vs. Ulysses**
Minor "Sword & Sandal"

The Unbelievable Varan

see Varan the Unbelievable

The Umbrellas of Cherbourg

see Les Parapluies de Cherbourg

The Unborn

1991, (USA), color, 85 mins.
<u>W</u>: Brooke Adams, Jeff Hayenga, James Karen, K Callan, Jane Cameron, Kathy Cameron, Kathy Griffin
<u>D</u>: Rodman Flender
Minor SF-thriller: Artificial insemination experiment goes awry

The Unborn II

1994, (USA), color, 84 mins.
<u>W</u>: Michele Greene, Scott Valentine, Robin Curtis
<u>D</u>: Rick Jacobson
Standard SF-thriller: Woman hunts mutant infants

The Uncanny

1977, (Can-GB), Cinevideo-Tor/Rank, color, 85 mins.
<u>W</u>: Peter Cushing *(Wilbur Gray)*, Ray Milland *(Frank Richards)*, Joan Greenwood *(Miss Malkin)*, Roland Culver *(Wallace)*, John Vernon *(Pomeroy)*, Susan Penhaligon *(Janet)*, Simon Williams *(Michael)*, Alexandra Stewart *(Joan Blake)*, Katrina Holden *(Lucy)*, Donald Pilon *(Mr. Blake)*, Chloe Franks *(Angela)*, Renee Girard *(Mrs. Maitland)*, Donald Pleasence *(Valentine De'Ath)*, Samantha Eggar *(Edina Hamilton)*, Sean McCann *(The Inspector)*, Catherine Begin *(Madeleine)*, Jean Leclerc *(Bruce Barrington)*

<u>P</u>: Claude Heroux & Rene Dupont   <u>D</u>: Denis Heroux   <u>SCR</u>: Michel Parry   <u>PHOTOG</u>: Harry Waxman   <u>SPCL-FX</u>: Michael Albrechtsen   <u>MUSIC COMP</u>: Wilfred Josephs   <u>MUSIC CONDUCT</u>: Philip Martell
Minor thriller: Writer recounts three tales of feline terror

Uncharted Seas

see The Lost Continent

The Unclean World: The Suburban-Bunkum Microbe-Guyoscope

1903, (GB), Hepworth, b&w, 100 ft. (30.5m)
<u>W</u>: Cecil Hepworth *(The Professor)*
<u>D</u>: Percy Stow
Standard SF-comedy (burlesque of **The Unseen World: The Urban-Duncam Micro-Bioscope***): Professor peers into microscope, sees clockwork fly, etc.*

Uncle Sam

1996, (USA), color, 88 mins.
<u>W</u>: Bo Hopkins, Timothy Bottoms
Standard horror-fantasy: Soldier returns from death when pranksters burn U.S. flag over grave

Uncle Silas

1947, (GB), Two Cities/GFD, b&w, 103 mins.
<u>W</u>: Jean Simmons *(Caroline Ruthyn)*, Katina Paxinou *(Mme. de la Rougierre)*, Derrick de Marney *(Uncle Silas)*, Derek Bond *(Lord Richard Ibury)*, Esmond Knight *(Dr. Bryerley)*, Sophie Stewart *(Lady Monica Waring)*, Reginald Tate *(Austin Ruthyn)*, Manning Whiley *(Dudley Ruthyn)*, Marjorie Rhodes *(Mrs. Rusk)*, John Laurie *(Giles)*, Frederick Burtwell *(Branston)*, George Curzon *(Sleigh)*, O.B. Clarence *(The Vicar)*, Guy Rolfe *(Sepulchre Hawkes)*
<u>P</u>: Josef Somio & Laurence Irving   <u>D</u>: Charles Frank   <u>SCR</u>: Ben Travers, from a novel by Sheridan LeFanu
USA retitle, **The Inheritance**
Standard thriller: Evil guardian plots girl's death

Uncle Silas: KATINA PAXINOV AND JEAN SIMMONS

Uncle Was a Vampire

see Tempi Duri per i Vampiri

The Undead

1956, (USA), AIP, b&w, 71 mins.
<u>W</u>: Pamela Duncan *(Diana Love/Helene)*, Allison Hayes *(Livia)*, Richard Garland *(Quintus Ratcliff)*, Dorothy Neumann *(Meg Maud)*, Richard Devon, Billy Barty, Bruno Ve Sota, Richard Miller, Val Dufour, Aaron Saxon
<u>P & D</u>: Roger Corman   <u>SCR</u>: Charles Griffith & Mark Hanna   <u>MUSIC</u>: Ronald Stein
blurb: "A thousand years of naked TERROR!"
orig. co-billed with **Voodoo Woman**
Modest horror-fantasy: Hypnotist regresses street-walker to former life in medieval England, where she was accused of witchcraft

Under Capricorn

1949, (GB), Transatlantic/WB, color, 116 mins.
<u>W</u>: Ingrid Bergman *(Lady Henrietta Flusky)*, Joseph Cotten *(Sam Flusky)*, Margaret Leighton *(Milly)*, Michael Wilding *(Hon. Charles Adare)*, Cecil Parker *(The Governor)*, Denis O'Dea *(Corrigan)*, Jack Watling *(Winter)*, Harcourt Williams *(The Coachman)*, John Ruddock *(Mr. Potter)*, Ronald Adam *(Mr. Riggs)*, Francis De Wolff *(Maj. Wilkins)*, Olive Sloane *(Sal)*, G.H. Mulcaster *(Dr. McAllister)*, Maureen Delany *(Flo)*
<u>P</u>: Sydney M. Bernstein & Alfred Hitchcock   <u>D</u>: Alfred Hitchcock   <u>SCR</u>: James Bridie, from a novel by Helen Simpson   PHOTOG: Jack Cardiff   MUSIC: Richard Addinsell
Gripping psychodrama: Australian wife battles alcoholism and plot to drive her insane

Undercover Agent
see *Counterspy*

Undercover Girl
1950, (USA), Univ, b&w, 83 mins.
W: Alexis Smith, Scott Brady (*Trent*), Richard Egan (*Jess*), Gerald Mohr (*Menig*), Gladys George (*Liz*)
D: Joseph Pevney
Standard thriller: Policewoman works incognito, nails narcotics ring to avenge father's death

Undercover Girl
1958, (GB), Luckwell/Butcher, b&w, 68 mins.
W: Paul Carpenter (*Johnny Carter*), Kay Callard (*Joan Foster*), Monica Grey (*Evelyn King*), Bruce Seton (*Ted Austin*), Jackie Collins (*Peggy Foster*), Maya Koumani (*Miss Brazil*), Kim Parker (*The Maid*), Tony Quinn (*Mike O'Sullivan*)
P: Kay Luckwell & Derek Winn **D:** Francis Searle **SCR:** Bernard Lewis & Bill Luckwell **STORY:** Bernard Lewis
Standard thriller: Dead reporter's brother unmasks nightclub owner as blackmailing drug peddler

The Undercover Kid
1995, (USA), color, 85 mins.
W: Bradley Pierce (*Max*)
Made-for-Video, standard juvenile thriller: 10-year-old communicates with pets, tries to thwart plot to kill U.S. president

Undercover Woman
1946, (USA), Rep, b&w, 56 mins.
W: Stephanie Bachelor, Robert Livingston
Standard thriller

Underground
1970, (USA), UA, color, 100 mins.
W: Robert Goulet, Daniele Gaubert
Minor melodrama

Under Lock and Key
1995, (USA), color, 90 mins.
W: Wendi Westbrook, Barbara Niven, Taylor Leigh (*Slash*), Stephanie Ann Smith (*Sarah*)
Minor thriller: Female FBI agent infiltrates women's prison

Under Satan's Sun
see *Sous le Soleil de Satan*

Undersea Girl
1957, (USA), AA, b&w, 66 mins.
W: Mara Corday, Pat Conway, Myron Healey, Brick Sullivan, Dan Seymour, Florence Marly
P: Norman T. Herman **D:** John Peyser **SCR:** Arthur V. Jones
A.k.a. Crime Beneath the Sea, orig. co-billed with Teenage Doll
Standard thriller: Female skindiver involved in murder mystery, missing millions

Under Secret Orders
1937, (GB), b&w
W: Dita Parlo, John Loder, Erich von Stroheim
Minor thriller: Mata Hari-type German spy pursues secret British plans

The Understudy: Graveyard Shift II
1989, (Can), Cannon, color, 90 mins.
W: Silvio Oliveiro, Wendy Gazelle
Minor horror-thriller: Vampire becomes actor in fright film

Under Suspicion
see *The Game of Liberty*

The Undertaker and His Pals
1967, (USA), Howco, color, 70 mins.
W: Ray Dennis, Robert Lowery, Brad Fulton, Sally Frei
P & D: David C. Graham **SCR:** T.L.P. Swicegood
Standard horror-comedy: Two maniacs drum up business for mortician friend

Under The Eyes of the Assassin
see *Tenebrae*

Under the Gun
1950, (USA), Univ, b&w, 84 mins.
W: Richard Conte, Sam Jaffe, John McIntire, Royal Dano
D: Ted Tetzlaff
Effective melodrama: Gangsters behind bars

Under the Phrygian Star
see *Pod Gwiazda Frygijska*

Under the Red Robe
1915, (GB), Clarendon/Gaumont, b&w, 3,747 ft. (1142.1m)
W: Owen Roughwood (*Gil de Berault*), Dorothy Drake (*Renée de Cochefort*), Jakson

Wilcox (*Richelieu*), Sydney Bland (*M. de Cochefort*)
D: Wilfred Noy, from a play by Edward Rose, based on a novel by Stanley Weyman
Standard adventure-thriller: Cardial's emissary forced to betray brother

Under the Seas
see *Deux Cent Mille Lieues sous les Mers*

Undertow
1996, (USA), SHO-TV, color, 93 mins.
W: Lou Diamond Phillips, Mia Sara, Charles Dance
Made-for-Cable, standard thriller: Mad moonshiner menaces drifter

The Underwater City
1961, (USA), Neptune/Col, b&w, 78 mins.
W: William Lundigan, Julie Adams, Carl Benton Reid, Kathie Brown, Roy Roberts, Chet Douglas, Karen Norris, Paul Dubov, Edward Mallory, George DeNormand, Roy Damron, Edmund Cobb, Paul Power
P: Alex Gordon **D:** Frank McDonald **SCR:** Owen Harris **PHOTOG:** Gordon Avil **MUSIC:** Ronald Stein
Minor SF-adventure: Architects plan city beneath the waves

An Underwater Odyssey
see *The Neptune Factor*

Underworld (1985)
see *Transmutations*

Underworld
1997, (USA), Touchstone, color
from a story by Barry Clifford
Exciting SF-adventure: Treasure hunt in underground rivers

Underworld After Dark
see *Big Town After Dark*

Underworld Informers
1965, (GB), Continental, b&w, 105 mins.
W: Nigel Patrick, Catherine Woodville
Standard melodrama

The Underworld of London
1915, (GB), Weston FeatureFilms/Powers, b&w, 3,511 ft. (1070.2m)
W: Arthur Finn (*Dan*), Lily Saxby, Winnie Fitch, Harry Webb, Gordon Begg, Thomas Brooklyn, Guy Rupert Lane, Frank R. Growcott, Rowland Moore
D: Charles Weston
Standard crime-thriller: Lord gives unwanted girl to Jewish crook whotrains her to beg

Under Wraps
1997, (USA), color, 90 mins.
W: Adam Wylie, Bill Fagerbakke, Mario Yedidia, Clara Bryant, Ken Campbell, Penny Peyser, Ed Lauter
D: Greg Beeman **TELEPLAY:** Don Rhymer **PHOTOG:** Mark Gray **MUSIC:** David Michael Frank
Made-for-Cable, juvenile fantasy: Kids unleash ancient mummy

The Undesirable Neighbour
1963, (GB), Merton Park/Anglo-Amalgamated, b&w, 29 mins.
W: Vanda Godsell (*Agnes Chester*), Bridget Armstrong (*Anna Bosworth*), Anthony Newlands (*Strang*), Dorinda Stevens (*Mary Bennett*), Ronald Hatton (*Peter Bosworth*), Howard Pays (*Harry Finch*)
P: Jack Greenwood **D:** Gordon Hales **STORY:** James Eastwood, from a novel by Edgar Lustgarten
Standard short crime-thriller: Newlyweds slandered by gossiping neighbor

Undressing Extraordinary: or, The Troubles of a Tired Traveller
1901, (GB), R.W. Paul, b&w, 200 ft. (61m)
D: Walter R. Booth
Standard fantasy: Seaside lodger finds lively skeleton in bed

The Undying Monster
1942, (USA), 20th-Fox, b&w, 63 mins.
W: James Ellison, Heather Angel, Bramwell Fletcher, Aubrey Mather, John Howard, Heather Thatcher, Alec Craig, Matthew Boulton, Holmes Herbert, Eily Malyon, Heather Wilde, Donald Stuart, Halliwell Hobbes, Dave Thursby, John Rogers
P: Bryan Foy **D:** John Brahm **SCR:** Lillie Hayward & Michel Jacoby, from a novel by Jessie D. Kerruish **PHOTOG:** Lucien Ballard **MUSIC:** Emil Newman
GB retitle, The Hammond Mystery
Standard thriller: Old family curse engenders modern horror

The Unearthing
1993, (USA), color, 83 mins.
W: Norman Moses, Tina Ona Paukstelis
D & SCR: Wyre Martin & Barry Poltermann
Minor horror-thriller: Woman's in-laws prove cannibalistic

U

The Unearthly

1957, AB-PT/Rep, b&w, 76 mins.

W: John Carradine, Allison Hayes, Myron Healey, Sally Todd, Tor Johnson, Marilyn Buferd, Arthur Batanides, Roy Gordon, Harry Fleer, Guy Prescott, Paul MacWilliams

P & D: Brooke L. Peters **PHOTOG:** W. Merle Connell

blurb: "Guaranteed to frighten!"

Standard thriller: Experiments to control mental illness have unpleasant results

Unearthly Stranger

1963, (GB), Julian Wintle-Leslie Parkyn/Independent Artists/AIP, b&w, 75 mins.

W: John Neville (*Dr. Mark Davidson*), Gabriella Licudi (*Julie Davidson*), Philip Stone (*Prof. John Lancaster*), Jean Marsh (*Miss Ballard*), Patrick Newell (*Maj. Clarke*), Warren Mitchell (*Dr. Munro*)

P: Albert Fennell **D:** John Krish **SCR:** Rex Carlton, from an idea by Jeffrey Stone **PHOTOG:** Reg Wyer **MUSIC:** Edward Williams **MUSIC DIR:** Marcus Dods

Modest SF-thriller: Scientist researches space travel via telekinesis, finds wife controlled by other-world powers

Unforgettable

1996, (USA), MGM, color, 116 mins.

W: Ray Liotta (*David Krane*), Linda Fiorentino (*Dr. Martha Briggs*), Peter Coyote (*Det. Don Bresler*), Christopher McDonald (*Stewart Gleick*), Kim Cattrall (*Kelly*), David Paymer (*Curtis*), Duncan Fraser (*Michael Stratton*), Kim Coates (*Eddie Dutton*), Caroline Elliott, Suzy Joachim, Garwin Sanford, Colleen Rennison, Stellina Rusich, Jenafor Ryane, Nathaniel Deveaux, Dean Choe, Jimmy Broyden, Mike Cresijo, Joanna Piros, Cheryl Wilson, Kevin Hayes, Dwight McFee, Arien Jones, Claudio De Victor, Siddnie Boll, Eric Pospisil, Cory Dagg, Bob Wilde, Brock Chapman, Rondel Reynoldson, Henry Watson, Robert Metcalfe, William B. Davis, Tong Lung, Tom Davies, Robin Douglas, Callum Keith Rennie, Roland Corkum, Leslie Graham, David Sobolov, Isabel Price, Kate Lancaster, Dave St. Pierre, Dale Villeneuve, Azalea Davila

D: John Dahl **SCR:** Bill Geddie **PHOTOG:** Jeffrey Jur **MUSIC:** Christopher Young

Unusual SF-thriller: Husband of murdered woman engages in unorthodox thought-transference experiment

The Unguarded Moment

1956, (USA), Univ, color, 95 mins.

W: Esther Williams, John Saxon, George Nader, Les Tremayne, Edward Andrews, Jack Albertson, Edward C. Platt, Dani Crayne, John Wilder, Eleanor Audley, Robert B. Williams

P: Gordon Kay **D:** Harry Keller **SCR:** Herb Meadows & Larry Marcus **PHOTOG:** William Daniels **MUSIC:** Herman Stein **MUSIC SPRVSR:** Joseph Gershenson

Standard thriller: Disturbed student menaces female teacher

The Unholy

1988, (USA), Team Effort/Vestron, color, 100 mins.

W: Ben Cross (*Father Michael*), Ned Beatty (*Lt. Stern*), Hal Holbrook (*Archbishop Mosely*), Trevor Howard (*Father Silva*), William Russ (*Luke*), Jill Carroll (*Millie*), Ruben Rabasa, Peter Frechette, Claudia Robinson, Nicole Fortier, Ellen Cody

D: Camilo Vila **WRIT:** Philip Yirdan & Fernando Fonseca **PHOTOG:** Henry Vargas **SPCL VS-FX:** Bob Keen **MUSIC:** Roger Bellon

Standard horror-fantasy: Demon tempts priest

The Unholy Four

see *The Stranger Came Home*

Unholy Love

see *Alraune* (1928)

The Unholy Night

1929, (USA), MGM, b&w, 9,442.2 ft. (2878m)

W: Ernest Torrence (*Ballou*), Dorothy Sebastian (*Efra*), Roland Young (*Montague*), Nathalie Moorehead (*Vi*), K. Sojin, Polly Moran, Sidney Jarvis, John Miljan, Philip Strange, George Cooper, Boris Karloff, Richard Tucker, John Roche, John Loder, Lionel Belmore, Claude Fleming, Gerard Barry, Clarence Geldert

D: Lionel Barrymore **SCR:** Dorothy Farnum & Edwin Justus Mayer, from a story by Ben Hecht **PHOTOG:** Ira Morgan

orig. to be titled The Green Ghost

Standard thriller: Scotland Yard probes murders cf. Le Spectre Vert

The Unholy Quest

1934, (GB), Equity British Film Prods., b&w, 56 mins.

W: Claude Bailey (*Prof. Sorotoff*), Terence de Marney (*Frank Davis*), Cristine Adrien (*Vera*), John Milton (*Hawkins*), Ian Wilson (*Wilky*), Harry Terry (*Soapy*)

D: R.W. Lotinga **STORY:** Widgey Newman

Standard horror-thriller: Doctor revives embalmed Crusader

The Unholy Three

1925, (USA), MGM, b&w, 6,848 ft. (2087.3m)

W: Lon Chaney Sr., Mae Busch, Victor McLaglen, Marjorie Morton, Harry Earles,

Mathew Betz, Walter Perry, Violet Crane, Percy Williams, Lou Morrison, John Merkyl, Edward Connelly, A.E. Warren, William Humphreys

D: Tod Browning **SCR:** Waldemar Young, based on novel by Clarence Aaron "Tod" Robbins **PHOTOG:** David Kesson

Classic thriller: Carnival types plot series of crimes

The Unholy Three

1930, (USA), MGM, b&w, 75 mins.

W: Lon Chaney Sr., Lila Lee, John Miljan, Harry Earles, Clarence Burton, Elliott Nugent, Ivan Linow, Crauford Kent

D: Jack Conway **SCR:** J.C. Nugent & Elliott Nugent, from novel by Clarence Aaron "Tod" Robbins **PHOTOG:** Percy Hilburn

Standard thriller (remake of 1925 hit, Chaney Sr.'s only "talkie" & last film): Criminals operate out of carnival

Unico in the Island of Magic

1984, (Jap), color, 92 mins.

Minor animated fantasy: Unicorn has adventures

Unidentified Flying Objects

see *U.F.O.*

Unidentified Flying Oddball

see *The Spaceman and King Arthur*

The Uninvited

1944, (USA), Para, b&w, 98 mins.

W: Ray Milland, Ruth Hussey, Gail Russell, Cornelia Otis Skinner, Alan Napier, Donald Crisp, Dorothy Stickney, Barbara Everest, Holmes Herbert

P: Charles Brackett **D:** Lewis Allen **SCR:** Dodie Smith & Frank Partos, from Dorothy Macardle's novel **PHOTOG:** Charles Lang **MUSIC:** Victor Young **SONG:** *Stella by Starlight* **DESIGN:** Hans Drier & Ernst Fegte

"...quite probably the movies' best ghost story"—William K. Everson, Classics of the Horror Film

Classic fantasy-thriller: Brother and sister find spectral presence has grim designs on life of young girl

Uninvited

1987, (USA), Heritage/Amazing, color, 92 mins.

W: George Kennedy (*Mike*), Alex Cord (*Walter*), Clu Gulager (*Albert*), Toni Hudson (*Rachel*), Eric Larson (*Martin*), Rob Estes (*Corey*), Clare Carey (*Bobbie*), Beau Dremann (*Lance*), Shari Shattuck (*Suzanne*), Michael Holden (*Daryl Perkins*), Cecile Callan (*The Girl in the Pizza Parlor*), Jack Heller (*The Concierge*), Austin Stoker (*The Caribbean Officer*), Gina Schinasi (*The Bartender*), Mike Tillman, Ron Presson, Noon Orsatti, Richard Warlock, Spice Williams, Greydon Clark, Paul Martin, Trevor Clark

WRIT, P & D: Greydon Clark **PHOTOG:** Nicholas Von Sternberg **MUSIC:** Dan Slider **SONGS:** *Uninvited, Seasons of Love, Hard to Find, One More Try & String Quartet in G*

Minor thriller: Mutant feline spreads death on luxury yacht

Uninvited

1993, (USA), color

W: Jack Elam, Christopher Boyer, Erin Noble, Bari Buckner, Jerry Rector, Zane Paolo, Dennis Gibbs, Ted Haler, Eno Brutto

D & SCR: Michael Derek Bohusz

Standard thriller: Fortune hunters defile Amerind burial ground

The Uninvited

1996, (USA), CBS-TV, color, 95 mins.

W: Sharon Lawrence (*Patricia*), Beau Bridges (*Charlie*), Shirley Knight (*Delia*), Alex D. Linz (*Jonathan*), Emily Bridges (*Molly*), Lesley Woods, Lawrence Pressman, Kathleen Lloyd, Slim Pickens Jr.

D: Larry Shaw **TELEPLAY:** Karen Clark **PHOTOG:** Bryan England **MUSIC:** Wendy Blackstone

*TVM, standard "fact-based" fantasy-thriller (similar to **Poltergeist**): Family bedeviled by haunted house*

Universal Soldier

1992, (USA-Ger), TriStar, color, 98 mins.

W: Jean Claude Van Damme (*Luc*), Dolph Lundgren (*Scott*), Ally Walker (*Veronica*), Ed O'Ross (*Col. Perry*), Jerry Orbach (*Dr. Gregor*), Leon Rippy (*Woodward*), Tico Wells (*Garth*), Ralph Moeller

D: Roland Emmerich **SCR:** Richrd Rothstein, Christopher Leitch & Dean Devlin **PHOTOG:** Karl Walter Lindenlaub **MUSIC:** Christopher Franke

Standard SF-thriller: Warriors battle in bleak future

Universal Soldier II: Brothers in Arms

1998, (USA), color, 95 mins.

W: Gary Busey

Made-for-Cable, standard SF-thriller: Vietnam casualty resurrected as robotic killing machine

Universal Soldier III: Unfinished Business

1998, (USA), color, 95 mins.

W: Burt Reynolds, Matt Battaglia, Chandra West

Made-for-Cable, standard SF-thriller: Evil Genius unleashes new generation of fighting machines

The Universe
1959, (Can), Nat'l Film Board of Canada, color, 29 mins.
P & D: Colin Low & Roman Kroitor   **STORY:** Roman Kroitor   **SPCL-FX:** Wally Gentleman   **MUSIC:** Eldon Rathburn
Seminal documentary (influenced many subsequent films): A night in an astronomer's life provides realistic galactic vistas

The Unknown
1927, (USA), MGM, b&w, 5,517 ft. (1681.6m)
W: Lon Chaney Sr. (*Alonzo*), Joan Crawford (*Estrellita*), Norman Kerry (*Malabar*), Frank Lanning (*Costra*), Nick de Ruiz (*Zanzi*), John George (*Cojo*)
D: Tod Browning   **SCR:** Waldemar Young, from a story by Tod Browning   **PHOTOG:** Merritt B. Gerstad
Standard thriller

The Unknown
1946, (USA), Col, b&w, 70 mins.
W: Karen Morley, Jim Bannon, Jeff Donnell, Robert Scott, Robert Wilcox
P: Wallace MacDonald   **D:** Henry Levin   **SCR:** Malcolm Stuart Boylan & Julian Harmon, based on episode of radio-series *I Love a Mystery*
Minor thriller: Detectives nab graverobber at haunted Southern mansion

The Unknown Guest
1943, (USA), b&w, 64 mins.
W: Victor Jory, Pamela Blake, Veda Ann Borg, Harry Hayden, Emory Parnell
D: Kurt Neumann
Standard whodunit

Unknown Island
1948, (USA), Film Classics, color, 75 mins.
W: Richard Denning, Virginia Grey, Barton MacLane, Philip Reed
P: Albert Jay Cohen   **D:** Jack Bernhard   **SCR:** Robert T. Shannon & Jack Harvey, from a story by Robert T. Shannon   **SPCL-FX:** Howard Anderson   **MUSIC:** Ralph Stanley
Minor SF-adventure: Prehistoric monsters found on uncharted Pacific isle

UNKNOWN ISLAND: BARTON MACLANE

The Unknown People
see *Superman and the Mole Men*

Unknown Powers
1980, (USA), color, 97 mins.
W: Samantha Eggar, Jack Palance, Will Geer, Roscoe Lee Browne
D: Don Como
Minor speculation-docu: ESP and magic examined

The Unknown Terror
1957, (USA), Regal-Emirau/20th-Fox, b&w, 77 mins.
W: John Howard (*Dan*), Mala Powers (*Gina*), Paul Richards (*Pete*), May Wynn (*Concha*), Gerald Milton, Charles Postal, Duane Gray, Patrick O'Moore, William Hamel, Sir Lancelot, Richard Gilden, Martin Garralaga
P: Robert Stabler   **D:** Charles Marquis Warren   **SCR:** Kenneth Higgins   **PHOTOG:** Joseph Biroc   **SPCL-FX:** Jack Rabin & Louis DeWitt   **MUSIC:** Raoul Kraushaar
Standard horror-thriller: Doctor nurtures carnivorous fungi in West Indian cave

Unknown World
1951, (USA), Lippert, b&w, 74 mins.
W: Victor Kilian (*Prof. Morley*), Bruce Kellogg, Jim Bannon, Marilyn Nash, Otto Waldis, Tom Handley, Dick Cogan, George Baxter
D: Terrell O. Morse   **ORIG. SCR:** Millard Kaufman   **PHOTOG:** Allen G. Siegler & Henry Freulich   **PRODUCTION DESIGN & SPCL-FX:** Irving Block & Jack Rabin   **MUSIC:** Ernest Gold
Minor SF-thriller: Scientists seek sub-Earth refuge from A-bomb fears

Unlikely Angel
1996, (USA), CBS-TV, color, 95 mins.
W: Dolly Parton, Roddy McDowall (*Saint Peter*), Brian Kerwin (*Ben Bartilson*), Allison Mack (*Sarah Bartilson*), Ely Marienthal (*Matthew Bartilson*), Maria Del Mar, Gary Sandy
D: Michael Switzer   **TELEPLAY:** Liz Coe & Robert L. Freedman   **PHOTOG:** Robert Draper   **MUSIC:** Velton Ray Bunch   **ORIG. SONGS:** Dolly Parton
TVM, standard fantasy: Deceased country singer earns her wings by helping distressed family

The Unnamable
1988, (USA), Yankee Classics/K.P., color, 87 mins.
W: Charles King (*Howard Damon*), Mark Kinsey Stephenson (*Randolph Carter*), Alexandra Durrell (*Tanya Heller*), Eben Ham (*Bruce Weeks*), Laura Albert (*Wendy Barnes*), Delbert Spain (*Joshua Winthrop*), Blane Wheatley (*John Babcock*), Mark Parra (*Joel Manton*), Colin Cox (*Mr. Craft*), Paul Farmer (*The Mortician*), Paul Pajor (*Gravedigger #1*), Marcel Lussier (*Gravedigger #2*), Lisa Wilson (*Student #1*), Nancy Kreisel (*Student #2*), Katrin Alexandre (*Alyda Winthrop, the Creature*)
D & SCR: Jean-Paul Ouellette, from H.P. Lovecraft's short story   **PHOTOG:** Tom Fraser   **MUSIC:** David Bergeaud   **SONG:** *Up There*
Standard horror-fantasy: Collegians meet arcane monster

The Unnamable II
1993, (USA), color, 104 mins.
W: John Rhys-Davies, David Warner, Mark Kinsey Stephenson, Maria Ford
*A.k.a. **The Unnamable II: The Statement of Randolph Carter***
Standard fantasy-thriller: Ancient warlock engineers bizarre murders

The Unnamable II: The Statement of Randolph Carter
see *The Unnamable II*

Unnatural
see *Alraune (1952)*

Unsane
see *Tenebrae*

The Unseeing Eye
1959, (GB), Merton Park/Anglo-Amalgamated, b&w, 28 mins.
W: Russell Napier (*Supt. Duggan*), John Stone (*Sgt. Nixon*), Denny Dayviss (*Wendy Green*), John Stuart (*The Doctor*)
P: Jack Greenwood   **D:** Geoffrey Muller   **SCR:** James Eastwood
Standard short thriller: Glass eye leads to capture of murderous arsonist

The Unseen
1945, (USA), Para, b&w, 81 mins.
W: Joel McCrea, Gail Russell, Herbert Marshall, Tom Tully, Phyllis Brooks, Isobel Elsom, Mikhail Rasumny, Nona Griffith, Richard Lyon
P: John Houseman   **D:** Lewis Allen, from Ethel Lina White's novel *Her Heart in Her Throat*   **PHOTOG:** John F. Seitz   **MUSIC:** Ernst Toch
Well-made thriller: Girl replaces murdered governess

The Unseen
1981, (USA), World Northal, color, 89 mins.
W: Barbara Bach (*Jennifer*), Sydney Lassick (*Ernest Keller*), Stephen Furst (*Junior Keller*), Lelia Goldoni (*Virginia*), Karen Lamm (*Karen*), Doug Barr (*Tony*), Lois Young (*Vicki*), Maida Severn (*The Solvang Lady*)
D: Peter Foleg   **SCR:** Michael L. Grace   **PHOTOG:** Roberto Quezada   **SPCL-FX:** Harry Woolman   **MUSIC:** Michael J. Lewis
Minor horror-thriller: Human monster stalks newswoman

The Unseen Witness
1914, (GB), Hepworth, b&w, 1,750 ft. (533.4m)
W: Tom Powers (*Brian Foster*), Chrissie White (*Anne*), Ruby Belasco (*Mrs. Foster*), Violet Hopson (*Ethel*), William Felton (*The Footman*)
D: Frank Wilson
Standard crime-thriller: Companion blamed when employer's necklace stolen by son's fiancee

The Unstoppable Man
1960, (GB), Argo/Anglo-Amalgamated, b&w, 68 mins.
W: Cameron Mitchell (*James Kennedy*), Marius Goring (*Insp. Hazelrigg*), Harry H. Corbett (*Feist*), Lois Maxwell (*Helen Kennedy*), Denis Gilmore (*Jimmy Kennedy*), Ann Sears (*Pat Delaney*), Humphrey Lestocq (*Sgt. Plummer*), Timothy Bateson (*Rocky*), Kenneth Cope (*Benny*), Tony Hawes (*The TV Interviewer*)
P: Jack Lamont & John Pellatt   **D:** Terry Bishop   **SCR:** Alun Falconer, P. Manning O'Brine & Terry Bishop, from Michael Gilbert's novel *Amateur Violence*
Standard crime-thriller: Industrialist's son kidnapped

An Unsuitable Job for a Woman
1982, (GB), Boyd's Co./Goldcrest, color, 94 mins.
W: Billie Whitelaw (*Elizabeth Laeming*), Pippa Guard (*Cordelia Gray*), Paul Freeman (*James Callender*), Elizabeth Spriggs (*Miss Markland*), Dominic Guard (*Andrew Lunn*), Alex Guard (*Mark Callender*), David Horovitch (*Sgt. Maskell*), Dawn Archibald (*Isobel*), Bernadette Short (*The Temp*), James

Gilbey (*The Boy*), Kelda Holmes (*The Girl*)
P: Michael Relph & Peter McKay **D:** Christopher Petit **SCR:** Elizabeth McKay, Brian Scobie & Christopher Petit, from a novel by P.D. James **PHOTOG:** Martin Schafer **MUSIC:** Chas Jankel
Standard crime-thriller: Woman detective poses as gardener, probes suicide of rich man's son

The Unsuspected
1947, (USA), WB, b&w, 103 mins.
W: Joan Caulfield (*Matilda Frazier*), Claude Rains (*Victor Grandison*), Constance Bennett (*Jane Moynihan*), Hurd Hatfield (*Oliver Keane*), Audrey Totter (*Althea Keane*), Fred Clark (*Richard Donovan*), Michael North (*Steven Francis Howard*), Harry Lewis (*Max*), Nana Bryant (*Mrs. White*), Ray Walker (*Donovan's Ass't*), Jack Lambert (*Mr. Press*), Walter Baldwin (*Justice of the Peace*)
D: Michael Curtiz **SCR:** Ranald MacDougall, based on Charlotte Armstrong's novel **PHOTOG:** Woody Bredell **SPCL-FX:** David C. Kertes & Harry Barndollar **MUSIC:** Franz Waxman
Standard thriller: Clever killer baffles

Untamed Mistress
1960, (USA), Brenner, color
W: Jacqueline Fontaine, Allan Nixon
P, D & SCR: Ron Ormond
Minor adventure-thriller: Explorer meets jungle woman

Untamed Women
1952, (USA), Jewell/UA, b&w, 70 mins.
W: Mikel Conrad, Lyle Talbot, Doris Merrick, Morgan Jones, Richard Monahan, Mark Lowell, Midge Ware
D: W. Merle Connell **SCR:** George W. Sayre **MUSIC:** Raoul Kraushaar
blurb: "Savage beauties who feared no animal...yet fell before the touch of men!"
Minor adventure-thriller: Servicemen find primitive isle ruled by women

Until the End of the World
1991, (Austral), WB, color, 158 mins.
W: William Hurt, Solveig Dommartin, Sam Neill, Rudiger Vogler, Max von Sydow, Jeanne Moreau, Ernie Dingo
D: Wim Wenders **SCR:** Peter Carey & Wim Wenders, from an orig. idea by Wim Wenders & Solveig Dommartin **ORIG. SCORE:** Graeme Revell
Bizarre SF-thriller: Scientists pursue unusual experiment as Earth faces annihilation

Unusual Tales
see Histoires Extraordinaires

The Unwritten Code
1944, (USA), Col, b&w, 61 mins.
W: Tom Neal, Ann Savage
Standard melodrama

Up from the Depths
1979, (Phil), New World, color, 75 mins.
W: Sam Bottoms, Suzanne Reed, Virgil Frye (*Earl*), Kedric Wolfe (*Oscar*), Charles Howerton
D: Charles Griffith **SCR:** Anne Dyer
Minor SF-thriller: Monster terrorizes natives and tourists on tropic isle

Up in Smoke
1957, (USA), AA, b&w, 64 mins.
W: Huntz Hall (*Sach*), Byron Foulger (*Satan*), Judy Bamber (*Mabel*), Eddie LeRoy, David Gorcey, Jack Mulhall, Stanley Clements (*Duke*), Ric Roman (*Tony*), Fritz Feld (*Bluzak*), Joe Devlin (*Al*), Benny Rubin, Dick Elliott, Ralph Sanford
P: Richard Heermance **D:** William Beaudine **SCR:** Jack Townley **PHOTOG:** Harry Neumann
Minor comedy-fantasy: Bowery Boy sells soul to Devil in exchange for racing tips

Upior (Vampire)
1968, (Pol), color
Standard horror-fantasy

Uproar in Heaven
1966, (Red China), color
W: Peking Opera
Standard fantasy: Monkey king causes chaos in afterlife

Upside Down: or, The Human Flies
1899, (GB), R.W. Paul, b&w, 80 ft. (24.4m)
D: Walter Booth
Standard fantasy: Spiritualist causes group to walk on ceiling

An Up to Date Conjuror (1899)
see L'Impressioniste Fin de Siecle

The Up-to-Date Conjurer
1900, (GB), Warwick Trading Co.-Biokam, b&w, 50 ft. (15.2m)
Standard fantasy short

Up-to-Date Spiritualism
see Spiritisme Abracadabrant

Up-to-Date Surgery
see Une Indigestion

Up to His Tricks
1904, (GB), Mutoscope & Biograph/Gaumont, b&w, 185 ft. (56.4m)
W: John Warren
Standard fantasy: Conjurer plays tricks on friends

Upworld
1994, (USA), color, 95 mins.
W: Anthony Michael Hall, Jerry Orbach, Claudia Christian, Eli Danker, Mark Harelik
Minor fantasy-thriller: Detective and subterranean creature pursue thieves

The Uranium Conspiracy
1978, (It), color, 100 mins.
W: Fabio Testi
Minor adventure-thriller: Secret agent and mercenary soldier protect precious ore

Urban Legends
1998, (USA), Phoenix/TriStar, color
W: Jared Leto, Alicia Witt, Joshua Jackson, John Neville, Rebecca Gayheart, Robert Englund, Loretta Devine, Tara Reid, Michael Rosenbaum
D: Jamie Blanks
Standard thriller: Bizarre deaths among students

Urban Warriors
1975, (USA), color, 90 mins.
W: Karl Landgren, Alex Vitale, Deborah Keith
D: Joseph Warren
Minor SF-thriller: Post-nuke barbarians pillage Earth

Urge to Kill
1960, (GB), Merton Park/Anglo-Amalgamated, b&w, 58 mins.
W: Patrick Barr (*Supt. Allen*), Howard Pays (*Charles Ramskill*), Ruth Dunning (*Auntie B*), Terence Knapp (*Hughie*), Anna Turner (*Lily Willis*), Christopher Trace (*Sgt. Grey*), Margaret St. Barbe West (*Mrs. Willis*), Yvonne Buckingham (*Gwen*)
P: Jack Greenwood **D:** Vernon Sewell **SCR:** James Eastwood, from story *Hand in Glove* by Gerald Savory & Charles Freeman
Minor thriller: Retarded youth framed for girl's mutilation murder

Urotsukidoj 1: Legend of the Overfiend
1993, (Jap), color, 108 mins.
A.k.a. The Wandering Kid
Standard animated SF-fantasy: Youth battles monster tyrant

Urotsukidoj 2: Legend of the Demon Womb
1993, (Jap), color, 88 mins.
Standard animated SF-fantasy: Doctor's cousin accidentally receives monstrous powers

Ursus in the Land of Fire
1963, (It), color, 87 mins.
W: Ed Fury, Claudia Mori, Adriano Micantoni, Luciana Gilli
D: Giorgio Simonelli

Ursus nella Valle dei Leoni (Ursus in the Valley of the Lions)
1961, (It), color, 92 mins.
W: Ed Fury (*Ursus*), Moira Orfei
D: Carlo Ludovico Bragaglia
USA retitle, Valley of the Lions
Minor "Sword & Sandal": Abandoned infant prince raised by lions

U.S. Marshals
1998, (USA), WB, color
W: Wesley Snipes, Tommy Lee Jones, Robert Downey Jr., Joe Pantoliano, Kate Nelligan, Tom Wood, Irene Jacob
D: Stuart Baird **SCR:** John Pogue, from characters created by Roy Huggins **PHOTOG:** Andrzej Bartkowiak **MUSIC:** Jerry Goldsmith
Standard thriller (spin-off from 1993's The Fugitive)

The Usual Suspects
1995, (USA), Polygram, color, 108 mins.
W: Gabriel Byrne, Kevin Spacey, Stephen Baldwin, Giancarlo Esposito, Chazz Palminteri, Pete Postlethwaite, Kevin Pollak, Suzy Amis, Dan Hedaya, Benicio del Toro
D: Bryan Singer **SCR:** Christopher McQuarrie
Superior crime-thriller

Utopia
see Atoll K

U-238 and the Witch Doctor
1966, (USA), Rep, b&w, 99 min, 205 mins.
W: Clayton Moore, Phyllis Coates, Johnny Spencer, Roy Glenn, John Cason
D: Fred C. Brannon
Standard thriller (feature version of 1953 serial Jungle Drums of Africa)

V

1983, (USA), NBC-TV, color

W: Marc Singer (*Mike Donovan*), Faye Grant (*Juliet Parrish*), Jane Badler (*Diana*), Jenny Sullivan (*Kristine*), Evan C. Kim (*Tony*), Richard Herd (*John*), Richard Lawson (*Ben*), Leonardo Cimino (*Abraham*), Andrew Prine (*Steven*), Jason Bernard (*Caleb*), Peter Nelson (*Brian*), Blair Tefkin (*Robin Maxwell*), David Packer (*Daniel Bernstein*), Frank Ashmore (*Martin*), Michael Durrell (*Robert Maxwell*), Rafael Campos (*Sancho*), Michael Wright (*Elias Taylor*), Neva Patterson, David Hooks, Bonnie Bartlett, Hansford Rowe, Penelope Windust, George Morfogen, Myron Healey, Curt Lowens, Harry Reasoner

WRIT & D: Kenneth Johnson **PHOTOG:** John McPherson **SPCL-FX:** Tom Ryea **MUSIC:** Joe Harnell

TVM, standard SF-thriller: Carnivorous aliens invade Earth

A Vacation in Hell

1979, (USA), ABC-TV, color, 97 mins.

W: Michael Brandon (*Alan*), Priscilla Barnes (*Denise*), Andrea Marcovicci (*Barbara*), Maureen McCormick (*Margaret*), Barbara Feldon (*Evelyn*), Ed Ka'Ahea (*The Hunter*)

D: David Greene **TELEPLAY:** Shelley Katz & D.B. Ledrov **PHOTOG:** Harry May **SPCL-FX:** John Frazier **MUSIC:** Gil Melle

TVM, standard thriller: Feminist saga of jungle survival

The Vacuum Cleaner Nightmare

1906, (GB), Urban Trading Co., b&w, 275 ft. (83.8m)

D: Walter R. Booth

Standard fantasy short: Salesman sucked into cleaner, is turned into rubbish

A Vagabond's Revenge

1915, (GB), Cunard/King, b&w, 4,770 ft. (1453.9m)

W: Agnes Glynne (*Enid*), Jack Morrison (*Clive Emmett*), Alice de Winton (*Sarah*), Lyston Lyle (*Lord Hayhurst*), Sydney Paxton (*The Doctor*)

D: Wallett Waller **STORY:** Florence Britton

Standard melodrama: Lord's blind daughter kidnapped by gypsy

Valerie

1957, (USA), UA, b&w, 84 mins.

W: Sterling Hayden, Anita Ekberg, Anthony Steel, Malcolm Atterbury

D: Gerd Oswald

Unusual melodrama-Western: Beauty accused of murder

Valerie and her Week of Wonders

1970, (Czech), color, 77 mins.

W: Jaroslava Schallerova, Helena Anyzkova, Petr Kopriva, Jiri Prymek, Jan Kluzak

D: Jaromil Jires

Unusual fantasy: Bizarre figments of girl's subconscious (e.g., devils, vampires, black magic)

Valley of Blood

1973, (USA), Mica, color, 64 mins.

W: Penny DeHaven, Ernie Ashworth, Zeke Clements, Wayne Forsythe, Rita Cristinziano, Joseph Turner, Herman Floyd

D: Dean Turner **SCR:** Wayne Forsythe **PHOTOG:** Craig Faulkner, Ron Evans & John Evans **MUSIC:** Don Green

Minor thriller

The Valley of Fear

1916, (GB), G.B. Samuelson/Moss, b&w, 6,500 ft. (1981.2m)

W: H.A. Saintsbury (*Sherlock Holmes*), Booth Conway (*Prof. Moriarty*), Daisy Burrell (*Ettie Shafter*), Arthur M. Cullin (*Dr. Watson*), Jack Macaulay (*McGinty*), Cecil Mannering (*John McMurdo*), Lionel d'Aragon (*Capt. Marvin*), Bernard Vaughan (*Shafter*), Jack Clair (*Ted Baldwin*)

D: Alexander Butler **SCR:** Harry Engholm, from stories by Sir Arthur Conan Doyle

Standard thriller: Ex-convict tries to kill detective

Valley of Fear

1964, (W. Ger), CCC, b&w

W: Christopher Lee (*Sherlock Holmes*), Thorley Walters (*Dr. John Watson*), Hans Nielsen, Hans Sohnker

D: Terence Fisher, from a Sherlock Holmes short story by Sir Arthur Conan Doyle

Standard thriller: Famed detective faces nemesis

The Valley of Gwangi

1969, (USA), WB-7Arts, color, 95 mins.

W: James Franciscus (*Tuck Kirby*), Gila Golan (*T.C. Breckinridge*), Richard Carlson (*Champ*), Laurence Naismith (*Prof. Horace Bromley*), Curtis Arden (*Lope*), Gustavo Rojo (*Carlos*), Freda Jackson (*Tia Zorina*), Dennis Kilbane (*Rowdy*), Mario de Barros

P: Charles H. Schneer **D:** James O'Connolly **SCR:** William E. Bast & Julian More **PHOTOG:** Erwin Hillier **SPCL ANIMATION:** Ray Harryhausen **MUSIC:** Jerome Moross

orig. to be titled **Lost Valley, Valley Time Forgot** *or* **The Valley Where Time Stood Still**
Standard SF-adventure (inspired by unfinished 'Gwangi'): Circus performers find valley with prehistoric life. cf. **Gwangi, Mighty Joe Young** *and* **The Black Scorpion**

Valley of the Dragons

1961, (USA), ZRB/Col, b&w, 79 mins.

W: Cesare Danova, Sean McClory, Joan Staley, Danielle De Metz, Gregg Martell,

---

I. Stanford Jolley, Roger Til, Mike Lane, Gil Perkins, Mark Dempsey, Dolly Gray, Jerry Sunshine

P: Byron Roberts **D & SCR:** Edward Bernds **STORY:** Donald Zimbalist loosely based on Jules Verne's novel *Off on a Comet* (A.k.a. *Career of a Comet*)

PHOTOG: Brydon Baker **SPCL-FX:** Dick Albain **MUSIC:** Ruby Raksin

GB retitle, **Prehistoric Valley**

Standard SF-adventure (with stock-footage from **One Million B.C.**): *Comet sweeps two men into primitive world. cf.* **Na Komete**

Valley of the Eagles

1951, (GB), Independent Sovereign/GFD, b&w, 86 mins.

W: Jack Warner (*Insp. Petersen*), Nadia Gray (*Kara Niemann*), John McCallum (*Dr. Nils Ahlen*), Anthony Dawson (*Sven Nystrom*), Mary Laura Wood (*Helga Ahlen*), Norman MacOwan (*McTavish*), Alfred Maurstad (*Trerik*), Martin Boddey (*The Headman*), Christopher Lee (*A Detective*), Ewen Solon (*A Detective*), Naima Wifstrand (*Baroness Erland*), George Willoughby (*Bertil*)

P: Nat A. Bronsten & George Willoughby **D & SCR:** Terence Young **STORY:** Paul Tabori & Nat A. Bronsten

Standard thriller: Scientist seeks stolen invention that produces power from sound

Valley of the Headhunters

1953, (USA), Col, b&w, 67 mins.

W: Johnny Weissmuller, Christine Larson, Robert Foulk, Don Blackman, Steven Ritch, Nelson Leigh, Joseph Allen Jr., George Eldredge, Neyle Morrow, Vince M. Townsend Jr., Paul Thompson

P: Sam Katzman **D:** William Berke **SCR:** Samuel Newman

Standard "Jungle Jim" adventure: Jungle hero helps Gov't agent make deal with natives for mineral deposits

Valley of the Lions

see Ursus nella Valle dei Leoni

Valley of Mystery

1967, (USA), Univ, color, 94 mins.

W: Richard Egan, Peter Graves

Minor adventure-thriller

Valley of the Zombies

1946, (USA), Rep, b&w, 58 mins.

W: Robert Livingston, Adrian Booth, Ian Keith, Charles Trowbridge, Thomas Jackson, LeRoy Mason

P: Darrell McGowan **D:** Philip Ford **SCR:** Darrell McGowan & Stuart McGowan, from a story by Royal K. Cole & Sherman T. Lowe

Minor horror-thriller

Valley Time Forgot

see The Valley of Gwangi

The Valley Where Time Stood Still

see The Valley of Gwangi

Vamp

1986, (USA), Donald P. Borchers/New World, color, 92 mins.

W: Grace Jones (*Katrina*), Chris Makepeace (*Keith*), Sandy Baron (*Vic*), Robert Rusler (*A.J.*), Gedde Watanabe (*Duncan*), Dedee Pfeiffer (*Allison*), Billy Drago (*Snow*), Brad Logan (*Vlad*), Lisa Lyon (*Cimmaron*), Jim Boyle (*The Fraternity Leader*), Larry Spinak, Eric Welch, Gary Swailes, Stuart Rogers, Ray Ballard, Paunita Nichols, Bob Schott, Trudel Williams, Marlon McGann, Thomas Bellin, Francine Swift, Bryan McGuire, Leila Hee Olsen, Hilary Carlip, Tricia Brown, Naomi Shohan, Janeen Davis, Roger Hampton, Ytossie Patterson, Tanya Papanicolas, Robin Kaufman, Hy Pike, Pops, Adam Barth, Bill Morphew, Simmy Bow, Julius LeFlore, Andy Rivas, Greg Lewis, Dar Robinson

D & SCR: Richard Wenk **STORY:** Donald P. Borchers & Richard Wenk **PHOTOG:** Elliot Davis **MUSIC:** Jonathan Elias

Modest horror-comedy: Frat pledges seek stripper, find Undead

Vampira

1974, (GB), World Film/AIP, color, 89 mins.

W: Teresa Graves (*Countess Vampira*), David Niven (*Count Dracula*), Jennie Linden (*Angela*), Nicky Henson (*Marc Williams*), Bernard Bresslaw (*Pottinger*), Peter Bayliss, Linda Hayden (*Helga*), Freddie Jones (*Gilmore*), Andrea Allan (*Eve*), Veronica Carlson (*Ritva*), Frank Thornton (*King*), Kenneth Cranham (*Paddy*), Cathie Shirriff (*Nancy*), Minah Bird (*Rose*), Christopher Sandford (*Milton*), Aimi MacDonald (*The Woman*), Carol Cleveland (*Jane*), Luan Peters, Patrick Newell

P: Jack Wiener **D:** Clive Donner **SCR:** Jeremy Lloyd **PHOTOG:** Tony Richmond **MUSIC:** David Whitaker

Standard horror-farce: Vampire revives dead bride. USA retitle, **Old Dracula**

Las Vampiras (1960)

see El Santo Contra las Vampiras

Las Vampiras (The Vampire Women)

1969, (Mex), Col, color

W: John Carradine, Maria Duval, Mils Mascaras

P: Luis Enrique Vergara **D:** Federico Curiel **SCR:** Adolfo Torres Portillo & Federico Curiel

Minor horror-fantasy

The Vampire
1913, (GB), Searchlight Films/Phoenix, b&w, 1,020 ft. (310.9m)
Standard horror-fantasy: Explorer shoots vampiress, she becomes snake

The Vampire
1913, (USA), Kalem, b&w, 40 mins.
<u>W</u>: Alice Eis, Bert French, Marguerite Courtot, Harry Millarde, Alice Hollister
<u>D</u>: Robert Vignola
Standard thriller

The Vampire
1920, (USA), Metro, b&w
Standard thriller

The Vampire (1943)
see *Dead Men Walk*

The Vampire
1957, (USA), Gramercy/UA, b&w, 74 mins.
<u>W</u>: John Beal, Coleen Gray, Kenneth Tobey, James Griffith, Dabbs Greer, Hallene Hill, Paul Brinegar, Lydia Reed, Ann Staunton, Herb Vigran, Natalie Masters, Louise Lewis, Brad Morrow, Wood Romoff, Raymond Greenleaf, George Selk, Anne O'Neal, Mauritz Hugo, Walter A. Merrill, Arthur Gardner, Christine Rees
<u>P</u>: Arthur Gardner & Jules V. Levy   <u>WRIT & D</u>: Pat Fielder   <u>MUSIC</u>: Gerald Fried
*TV retitle, **Mark of the Vampire***
Standard horror-thriller: Doctor turns self into monster

The Vampire (1959)
see *El Vampiro*

Vampire (1968)
see *Upior*

Vampire
1979, (USA), MTM/ABC-TV, color
<u>W</u>: Richard Lynch (*Anton Voytek, the Vampire*), E.G. Marshall (*Harry Kilcoyne*), Jason Miller (*John Rawlins*), Kathryn Harrold (*Leslie Rawlins*), Barrie Youngfellow (*Andrea*), Jessica Walter (*Nicole*), Adam Starr (*Tommy*), Michael Tucker (*Christopher Bell*), Jonelle Allen (*Brandy*), Wendy Cutler (*Iris*), David Hooks, Brendan Dillon
<u>P</u>: Gregory Hoblit   <u>D</u>: E.W. Swackhammer   <u>TELEPLAY</u>: Steven Bocho & Michael Kozoll   <u>PHOTOG</u>: Dennis Dalzell   <u>MUSIC</u>: Fred Karlin
TVM, standard horror-thriller: Demonic killer menaces San Francisco

The Vampire and Sex
1968, (Mex), color
<u>W</u>: Santo
*A.k.a. **Santo and the Treasures of Dracula***
Minor horror-fantasy: Muscleman meets erotic Undead

The Vampire and the Ballerina
see *L'Amante del Vampiri*

Vampire at Midnight
1987, (USA), Vampire Ltd. Partners, color, 94 mins.
<u>W</u>: Jason Williams (*Roger Sutter*), Gustav Vintas (*Victor Radkoff*), Lesley Milne (*Jenny Carlon*), Esther Alise (*Lucia Giannini*), Jeanie Moore (*Amalia*), Shendt (*Raoul*), Robert Random (*Al Childress*), Jonny Solomon (*Lee Keller*), Celia Kaye (*Sandra*), Ted Hamaguchi (*Capt. Takato*), Mike Wiles (*Gunman #1*), Mike Tino (*Gunman #2*), Richard Kory (*Gunman #3*), Mike Kehoe (*Jon*), Eddie Jr. (*Bobby Rio*), Jeff Bardo (*Ptn. Buccola*), Mark Nordike (*Ptn. Gray*), Angela Worthy (*Anna*), Camille Lund (*The Female Paramedic*), Tom Friedman (*The M.C.*), Richmond Shepard (*Chapman*), Barbara Hammond (*Kelly*), Tom De Antonio (*John*), Kathrine Bates (*Ellen*), Kathryn Lee (*Patsy Subaru*), David Gilbert (*The Newscaster*), Eric Leviton (*Lasky*), Christina Whitaker (*Ingrid*), Frank the Fish (*himself*)
<u>D</u>: Gregory McClatchy   <u>SCR</u>: Dulany Ross Clements   <u>PHOTOG</u>: Daniel Yarussi   <u>MUSIC</u>: Robert Etoll   <u>SONGS</u>: *Midnight Kiss, American Dream, Get It Right, Another Goodbye & Steppin' Right*
Standard thriller: Cop hunts bestial slayer

The Vampire Bat
1933, (USA), Majestic, b&w, 71 mins.
<u>W</u>: Lionel Atwill, Fay Wray (*Ruth*), Melvyn Douglas (*Karl*), Dwight Frye (*Herman*), Maud Eburne (*Aunt Gussie*), George E. Stone, Robert Fraser, Lionel Belmore, Paul Weigel, Stella Adams, Rita Carlisle, William V. Mong, Fern Emmett, Carl Stockdale, Harrison Greene
<u>D</u>: Frank Strayer   <u>SCR</u>: Edward T. Lowe   <u>PHOTOG</u>: Ira Morgan
" ...despite a good cast...the film is basically a primitive, creaky old relic with astonishingly little to recommend it...A forerunner of equally poor melodramas made in the fabulous Forties by Monogram and PRC"—Gary Gerani, "The Vampire Book—Chapter Four: Vampire Films of the Thirties," *Monster Fantasy, Vol. 1, No. 1 (April, 1975) pp. 26-27*
Standard horror-thriller: Mad scientist creates monstrosity, feeds it human blood

Vampire Circus
1971, (GB), Hammer/20th-Fox, color, 87 mins.
<u>W</u>: Adrienne Corri (*The Gypsy*), Laurence Payne (*Mueller*), Thorley Walters (*The Burgomeister*), John Moulder-Brown (*Anton Kersh*), Lynne Frederick (*Dora Mueller*), Anthony Corlan (*Emil*), Elizabeth Seal (*Gerta Hauser*), Richard Owens (*Dr. Kersh*), Domini Blythe (*Anna Mueller*), Robin Hunter (*Hauser*), Robert Tayman (*Count Mitterhouse*), Mary Wimbush (*Elvira*), Lalla Ward (*Helga*), Robin Sachs (*Heinrich*), Dave Prowse (*The Strongman*), Roderick Shaw (*John Hauser*), Barnaby Shaw (*Gustav Hauser*), Christina Paul (*Rosa*), Jane Darby (*Jenny*), Skip Martin (*Michael*), John Bown (*Schilt*), Milovan & Serena (*The Webbers*)
<u>P</u>: Wilbur Stark   <u>D</u>: Robert Young   <u>SCR</u>: Judson Kinberg   <u>STORY</u>: George Baxt & Wilbur Stark   <u>PHOTOG</u>: Murray Grant   <u>MUSIC</u>: David Whitaker
Unusual horror-fantasy: Doctor finds circus run by vampiric shapeshifters

Vampire Cop
1990, (USA), color, 89 mins.
<u>W</u>: Melissa Moore, Ed Cannon, Terence Jenkins
Minor action-horror: Undead cop stalks drug kingpin

Le Vampire de Dusseldorf (The Vampire of Dusseldorf)
1964, (Fr), b&w
<u>W</u>: Robert Hossein
<u>P</u>: Carlo Ponti   <u>WRIT & D</u>: Robert Hossein
Standard thriller

The Vampire Doll
1972, (Jap), Toho, color, 85 mins.
<u>W</u>: Yokiko Kobayashi, Yoko Manakaze
<u>D</u>: Michio Yamamoto
Standard horror-fantasy

The Vampire Girls
1978, (Phil), Capricorn Three, color, 82 mins
<u>W</u>: John Carradine, Bruce Fairbairn, Trey Wilson, Karen Stride, Lenka Novak, Katie Dolan, Lex Winter
<u>P</u>: Robert E. Waters   <u>D</u>: Cirio H. Santiago   <u>SCR</u>: Howard Cohen   <u>MUSIC</u>: Jaime Mendoza-Nava
*A.k.a. **Sensuous Vampires**, **Night of the Bloodsuckers** and **Vampire Hookers***
Minor eroto-horror: Vampire's harem provides victims

The Vampire Happening
1971, (W. Ger), Acquila Films, color, 90 mins.
<u>W</u>: Ferdy Mayne
<u>P</u>: Pier A. Caminneci   <u>D</u>: Freddie Francis   <u>SCR</u>: August Rieger
Minor horror-thriller: Actress meets Undead

Vampire Hookers
see *The Vampire Girls*

Vampire Hunter D
1985, (USA), color, 90 mins.
<u>VOICES</u>: Michael McConnohie
Standard animated horror-fantasy: Bloodsucking hybrid tails Dracula's descendants

Vampire in Brooklyn
1995, (USA), Para, color, 103 mins.
<u>W</u>: Eddie Murphy (*Maximillian*), Angela Bassett (*Rita*), Allen Payne (*Justice*),

Vampire In Brooklyn: Eddie Murphy and Kadeem Hardison

Kadeem Hardison (*Julius*), Zakes Mokae, Jerry Hall, Joanna Cassidy, John Witherspoon
P: Eddie Murphy & Mark Lipsky   **D:** Wes Craven   **SCR:** Charles Murphy, Michael Lucker & Chris Parker   **STORY:** Eddie Murphy, Vernon Lynch Jr. & Charles Murphy   **MUSIC:** J. Peter Robinson
Standard horror-comedy: World's last vampire seeks bride

Vampirella
1978, (GB), Hammer, color
W: Barbara Leigh (*Vampirella*)
film never completed

Vampirella
1996, (USA), SHO-TV, color, 90 mins.
W: Talisa Soto (*Vampirella*), Roger Daltrey (*Vlad*), Brian Bloom (*Demos*), Tom Deters (*Traxx*), Carina Harney (*Sallah*)
from the comic-book characters
Made-for-Cable, standard horror-fantasy: Alien vampiress champions humankind. cf. **Vampirella** *(1978)*

The Vampire Journals
1997, (USA), color, 85 mins.
W: David Gunn, Jonathon Morris
Made-for-Video, minor horror-thriller: Pianist menaced by Undead

The Vampire Lovers
1970, (GB), Hammer/AIP, color, 91 mins.
W: Peter Cushing (*The General*), Ingrid Pitt (*Carmilla*), Kate O'Mara (*The Governess*), George Cole (*Morton*), Dawn Addams (*The Countess*), Ferdy Mayne (*The Doctor*), Douglas Wilmer (*The Baron*), Madeline Smith (*Emma*), Kirsten Betts (*The Vampire*), John Forbes-Robertson (*The Man in Black*), Pippa Steele (*Laura*), John Finch (*Carl*), Charles Farrell (*The Landlord*), Harvey Hall (*Renton*), Janet Key (*Gretchen*)
P: Harry Fine & Michael Style   **D:** Roy Ward Baker   **SCR:** Tudor Gates   **ADAPT:** Harry Fine, Tudor Gates & Michael Style, loosely based on J. Sheridan LeFanu's novel *Carmilla*
Adult horror-fantasy: Lesbian vampire returns to enslave girls. cf. **Et Mourir de Plaisir**

Vampire Men of the Lost Planet
see Horror of the Blood Monsters

The Vampire of Dusseldorf
see Le Vampire de Dusseldorf

The Vampire of Notre Dame
see I Vampiri

The Vampire of the Opera
see Il Vampiro dell'Opera

The Vampire of Utopia
see El Vampiro de la Utopista

Vampire on Bikini Beach
1988, (USA), Beacon, color, 80 mins.
W: Jennifer Badham (*Judy*), Todd Kaufmann (*Harold*), Stephen Mathews (*Bob*), Nancy Rogers (*Kim*), Amanda Hughes (*Clarke*), Jennifer Jostyn (*Wynette*), William Hao (*Demos*), Mariusz Olbrychowski (*Falto*), Robert Ankers (*Gnordron*), Neal Jano (*The Servant*), Jacques Dury (*Dr. Gower*), Chet Maxwell (*The Bookstore Clerk*), Richard Reiner (*Dick*), Ken Abraham (*The Beach Storyteller*), Gary Don Cox (*The Biker*), Carol Dinova (*The Biker Girl*), Bon Dinwiddie (*The Pizza Boy*), Peter Fox (*The Surfboard Boy*), Sharon Scimeca (*The Surfer Girl*), Louie Franco (*Louie*), Scot Harger (*The Dark Figure*), Charles Glazer, Sherry Dill, Nelly Pereira, Joel Rabb, Sonia Beck, Guillermo Barreta, Guy Jones, Sandra Benedict, Jane Bryant, Jeanie Daniels, Karen Ellis, Lauri Polo, Laura Bryant, Ted Yonenaka, Flora Dolnikov, Jennifer Logan, Banca Palacios, Georgia Low, Lisa Melbe, Heidi Brennan, Barbara Buck, Debra Montana, Bobby Sands, Chris Larsen, Richard Bustos, Jessica Doran, Robert Daniels, Roseann Harris, Richard Allen, Ivan Hernandez, Kastle Waserman, Ricker Machado
P: Richard A. Jones   **D:** Jerry Brady   **ORIG. SCR:** Mark Headley   **PHOTOG:** John Bilecky   **SPCL-FX:** Edward Wilde   **ORIG. DRAMATIC MUSIC SCORE:** Miguel Alonso   **ORIG. ROCK-MUSIC SCORE:** Brian Cadd & Max Merritt   **SONGS:** *Loaded with Love, Sucker, Living on the Edge, Ain't Got You & Runaway*
Amateurish horror-fantasy: Teens find vampire nest

A Vampire Out of Work
1916, (USA), Vitagraph, b&w
Minor melodrama

Vampire over London
see Mother Riley Meets the Vampire

Vampire People
see The Blood Drinkers

Vampire Playgirls (1971)
see The Devil's Nightmare

Vampire Playgirls (1972)
see Gran Amore del Conde Dracula

The Vampires (1956)
see I Vampiri

The Vampires (1961)
see Maciste Contro il Vampiro

Vampires
1998, (USA), Largo/Dimension, color
W: James Woods (*Jack Crow*), Daniel Baldwin (*Montoya*), Sheryl Lee (*Katrina*), Thomas Ian Griffith (*Valek*), Tim Guinee (*Father Adam*)
D: John Carpenter, from a novel by John Steakley
Modest horror-fantasy: Exploits of determined vampire-slayers

Vampires Against Hercules
see Ercole al Centro della Terra

The Vampire's Clutch
1915, (USA), Knight, b&w
Minor melodrama

The Vampire's Coffin
see El Ataud del Vampiro

The Vampire's Ghost
1945, (USA), Rep, b&w, 59 mins.
W: John Abbott, Charles Gordon, Peggie Stewart, Adele Mara, Roy Barcroft, Grant Withers
D: Lesley Selander   **SCR:** Leigh Brackett & John K. Butler   **STORY:** Leigh Brackett   **PHOTOG:** Bud Thackeray & Robert Pittack   **MUSIC DIR:** Richard Cherwin
Unusual horror-thriller: Undead haunts African village

Vampires in Havana
1986, (Cuba), color, 80 mins.
WRIT, P & DESIGNED: Juan Padrone
Animated horror-comedy: Predicaments of Undead in 1930's Cuba

Vampire's Kiss
1989, (USA), Magellan/Hemdale, color, 105 mins.
W: Nicholas Cage (*Peter Loew*), Maria Conchita Alonso (*Alva Restrepo*), Jennifer Beals (*Rachel*), Elizabeth Ashley (*Dr. Glaser*), Kasi Lemmons (*Jackie*), Bob Lujan (*Emilio*), Boris Leskin (*The Fantasy Cabbie*), Jessica Lundy (*Sharon*), John Walker (*Donald*), Michael Knowles (*Andrew*), John Michael Higgins (*Ed*), Jodie Markell, Marc Coppola, David Pierce, Amy Stiller, Sol Echeverria, Helen Lloyd Breed, Robert Dorfman, Jill Gatsby, Rex Robbins, William DeAcutis, David Holbrook, Yanni Sfinnias, Rogerio Triandade, Robyn Knoll, Jennifer Butt, Jacques Sandlescu, Jorgen Schiott, Christopher Sluka, Stephen Chen, Jennifer Spinner, Paul Sansone, Cheryl Henry, Herschel Rosen, Phil Ballou, Reggie Rock Bythewood, Jerry Rector, Mark Oates, John Epperson, Pamela Dean Kelly, John McLaughlin, Jonathan Gold, Renee Scroggins, Valerie Jean Scroggins, Helen Scroggins, David Miles, Peter Hock, Derek Gibson, Mike Estler, Allen McCullogh, Gwendolyn Bucci, John Daly
D: Robert Bierman   **SCR:** Joseph Minion   **PHOTOG:** Stefan Czapsky   **MUSIC:** Colin Towns
Unusual horror-satire: Businessman fears becoming Undead

The Vampire's Lover
see L'Amante del Vampiri

The Vampires' Night Orgy
see La Orgia Nocturna de los Vampiros

Vampires of Prague
see The Mark of the Vampire (1935)

The Vampire's Tower
1914, (USA), Ambrosia, b&w
Minor horror-thriller

The Vampire Women (1960)
see El Santo Contra las Vampiras

The Vampire Women (1969)
see Las Vampiras (1969)

Vampire Vixens from Venus
1994, (USA), color, 90 mins.
W: Michelle Bauer, Charlie Callas
Minor SF-satire: Drug-smuggling female space aliens prey on Earth men

I Vampiri (The Vampires)
1956, (It), Titanus/Athena, b&w, 90 mins.
W: Gianna Maria Canale, Antoine Balpetre, Paul Muller, Carlo D'Angelo, Wandisa Guida, Renato Tontini, Charles Fawcett, Dario Michaelis

P: Ermano Donati & Luigi Carpentieri   D: Riccardo Fred   SCR: Piero Regnoli & Rik Sjostrom   PHOTOG: Mario Bava   MUSIC: Roman Vlad & Franco Mannino   SETS: Beni Montresor
cut & dubbed for export as **The Devil's Commandment** *A.k.a.* **The Vampire of Notre Dame** *and* **Lust of the Vampire**
Standard horror-fantasy: Doctor uses blood to restore countess' youth

El Vampiro (The Vampire)
1957, (Mex), Abel Salazar-Cinematografica ABSA, b&w, 95 mins.
W: German Robles, Ariadne Welter, Abel Salazar, Mercedes Soler, July Danery, Joseph Chavez, Jose Luis Simenez, Carmen Montejo, Lydia Mellon
P: Abel Salazar   D: Fernando Mendez   SCR: Heinrich Rodriguez & Ramon Obon   MUSIC: Gustavo Carrea
Fr retitle, **Les Proies du Vampire** *(The Prey of the Vampire)*
Standard horror-fantasy: Girl visits ailing aunt, discovers vampire nest. cf. **El Ataud del Vampiro**

El Vampiro Acecha (The Lurking Vampire)
1956, (Argent), b&w
W: Blanca del Prado, Nestor Zarvade
Minor horror-fantasy

El Vampiro de la Utopista (The Vampire of Utopia)
1970, (Sp), Paragon/Amati, color
W: Waldemar Wohlfahrt
P: Edmondo Amanti   D: Jose Luis Madrid
USA retitle, **The Horrible Sexy Vampire**
Minor horror-fantasy: Vampiric baron reincarnated

Il Vampiro dell'Opera (The Vampire of the Opera)
1961, (It), N.I.F. Rome, color
W: Vittoria Prada
D: Renato Polselli
Minor horror-fantasy

El Vampiro Sangriento (The Bloody Vampire)
1961, (Mex), AIP, b&w, 107 mins.
W: Carlos Agosti (*Count Frankenhausen*), Begona Palacios (*Ines*), Antonio Raxel (*Cagliostro*), Erna Bauman, Francisco A. Cordoba, Raul Farrell, Bertha Moss, Lupe Carrillo, Enrique Lucero
P: Rafael Perez Grovas   WRIT & D: Miguel Morayta   PHOTOG: Manuel Fontanels   MUSIC: Luis Hernandez Breton
Standard horror-fantasy

Vampyr
1932, (Ger-Fr), Tobis Klangfilm-Dreyer, b&w, 66 mins. (also 83 mins.)
W: Sybille Schmitz, Julian West (*Baron Nicholas de Gunzburg*), Henriette Gerard, Albert Bras, Jan Hieronimko, N. Babanini, Maurice Schutz, Rena Mandel
P & D: Carl Dreyer   SCR: Carl Dreyer & Christen Jul, based on J. Sheridan LeFanu's novel *Carmilla*   PHOTOG: Rudolph Maté   MUSIC: Wolfgang Zeller
A.k.a. **The Strange Adventure of David Gray.** *USA retitle,* **Castle of Doom** *&* **Not Against the Flesh** *(General Pictures, 1934)*
Classic horror-fantasy: Youth meets Undead. cf. **Dr. Terror's House of Horrors** *(1943)*

Vampyre
1990, (USA), color
D: Bruce Hallenbeck
Unusual horror-fantasy: Mysterious stranger helps timeless town battle evil forces

Vampyres...Daughters of Dracula
1975, (GB), Essay/Cambist/Fox/Rank, color, 84 mins.
W: Marianne Morris (*Fran*), Anulka Dziubinska (*Miriam*), Murray Brown (*Ted*), Brian Deacon (*John*), Sally Faulkner (*Harriet*), Michael Byrne (*Playboy*), Karl Lanchbury (*Rupert*), Margaret Heald (*The Receptionist*), Douglas Jones (*The Manager*), Gerald Case (*The Agent*), Bessie Love (*The American*)
P: Brian Smedley-Aston   D: Jose Larraz   STORY: D. Daubeney   PHOTOG: Harry Waxman   MUSIC: James Clarke
Standard horror-thriller: Female hitchhikers become Undead

Vampyrn
1912, (Swed), b&w
Standard horror-fantasy

The Vanishing
1988, (Neth-Fr), color, 106 mins.
W: Bernard Pierre Donnadieu (*Raymond Lemorne*), Gene Bervoets (*Rex*), Johanna Ter Stegge (*Saskia*), Bernadette Le Sache, Gwen Eckhaus
D: George Sluizer, from Tim Krabbe's novel *Golden*
Celebrated thriller: Man's girlfriend disappears

The Vanishing
1993, (USA), color, 110 mins.
W: Jeff Bridges, Kiefer Sutherland, Nancy Travis, Sandra Bullock, Lisa Eichhorn, Park Overall, George Hearn, Lynn Hamilton, Maggie Linderman
D: George Sluizer   SCR: Todd Graff, from Tim Krabbe's novel *Golden*   MUSIC: Jerry Goldsmith
Standard thriller (remake): Psycho killer hunted

The Vanishing Body
see **The Black Cat** *(1934)*

The Vanishing Lady
1896, (Fr), Star, b&w, 20m (65.6 ft./1.1 mins.)
W: Jehanne d'Alcy
WRIT, P & D: Georges Melies
Standard fantasy

The Vanishing Lady
1897, (GB), R.W. Paul, b&w, 40 ft. (12.2m)
W: Charles Bertram
Standard fantasy: Conjurer makes girl disappear

Vanishing Point
1971, (USA), Cupid/20th-Fox, color, 107 mins.
W: Barry Newman (*Kowalski*), Cleavon Little (*Super Soul*), Dean Jagger (*The Prospector*), Victoria Medlin (*Vera*), Paul Koslo (*The Young Cop*), Bob Donner (*The Older Cop*), Timothy Scott (*Angel*), Gilda Texter (*The Nude Rider*), Karl Swenson (*The Clerk*), Anthony James (*The 1st Male Hitchhiker*), Arthur Malet (*The 2nd Male Hitchhiker*), Severn Darden (*J. Hovah*), Lee Weaver (*Jake*), Tom Reese (*Sheriff*), Owen Bush (*The Communications Officer*), Cherie Foster, Valerie Kairys, Tom Reese (*The Sheriff*), Owen Bush (*The Communications Officer*), Cherie Foster (*The First Girl*), Valerie Kairys (*The Second Girl*)
D: Richard Sarafian   SCR: Guillermo Cain   STORY: Malcolm Hart   PHOTOG: John A. Alonzo   MUSIC: Jimmy Bowen
Unusual psychodrama: Ex-marine obsessed with speed

Varan the Unbelievable
1962, (USA-Jap), Toho/Dallas/Crown Int'l, b&w, 70 mins.
W: Myron Healey Tsuruko Kobayashi, Clifford Kawada, Derick Shimatsu, Hideo Imamura, George Sasaki, Hiroshi Hisamune, Yoneo Iguchi, Roy K. Ogata, Michael Sung
P & D: Jerry A. Baerwitz, Inoshiro Honda   SCR: Sid Harris   PHOTOG: Jack Marquette   PHOTOG-FX: Howard Anderson Co.
orig. to be titled **Baran**, *Japanese release:* **Daikaiju Baran**, *1958, 87 mins. TV retitle,* **The Unbelievable Varan**, *A.k.a.* **The Monster Baran**
Minor SF-fantasy (re-edited from 1958 Japanese thriller): Prehistoric horror rampages

Vargtimmen (Hour of the Wolf)
1967, (Swed), Svensk Filmindustri/Lopert, b&w, 89 mins.
W: Max von Sydow, Liv Ullmann, Ingrid Thulin, Gudrun Brost, Georg Rydeberg, Erland Josephson, Gertrud Fridh
WRIT & D: Ingmar Bergman   PHOTOG: Sven Nykvist
"Bergman's adline tells us that 'the hour of the wolf is the time when nightmares are most real.' This strange and powerful film certainly belongs to that time"—Anon., "Frankenstein TV Movieguide," Castle of Frankenstein, Vol. IV, No. 1 (Spring, 1969), p. 63
Unusual thriller: Artist descends into madness, draws wife into world of eerie hallucinations

The Vatican Affair
1969, (It), 20th Century-Fox-TV, color, 120 mins. (also 94 mins)
W: Walter Pidgeon, Ira Furstenberg, Marino Mase, Klaus Kinski, Tino Carraro
D: Emilio Miraglia
Standard thriller: Elderly professor plans heist of St. Peter's art treasures

Vault of Horror
1973, (GB), Amicus/Metromedia/Fox-Rank/CRC, color, 93 mins.
W: Curt Jurgens (*Sebastian*), Dawn Addams (*Inez*), Michael Craig (*Maitland*), Daniel Massey (*Rogers*), Denholm Elliott (*Diltant*), Anna Massey (*Donna*), Tom Baker (*Moore*), Edward Judd (*Alex*), Glynis Johns (*Eleanor*), Terry Thomas (*Critchit*), John Witty (*Gaskill*), Geoffrey Davies (*Jerry*), Erik Chitty (*The Old Waiter*), Jasmina Hilton (*The Indian Girl*), Mike Pratt (*Clive*), Jerold Wells (*The Waiter*), Ishaq Bux (*The Fakir*), Robin Nedwell (*Tom*), Marianne Stone (*Jane*), Arthur Mullard (*The Gravedigger*), John Forbes-Robertson (*Wilson*), Terence Alexander (*Breedley*), Frank Forsyth (*Waiter*), Roy Evans
P: Max J. Rosenberg & Milton Subotsky   D: Roy Ward Baker   SCR: Milton Subotsky   PHOTOG: Denys Coop   MUSIC: Douglas Gamley
"Of blood, there is plenty"—Independent Film Journal
A.k.a. **Tales from the Crypt II**
Modest anthology of terror tales (based on popular comic book of early 1950s): Five dead men recount their dreams

Vegas in Space
1993, (USA),Troma, color, 88 mins.
W: Doris Fish, Ginger Quest
D & SCR: Phillip R. Ford
Minor SF-comedy: All-male spaceship crew changes sex to pass as lounge act on pleasure planet of women

The Veil
see **Haunts**

The Veils of Bagdad
1953, (USA), Univ, color, 82 mins.
W: Victor Mature, Mari Blanchard, Virginia Field, Palmer Lee [Gregg Palmer], Guy Rolfe, James Arness, Nick Cravat, Ludwig Donath, Dave Sharpe, Jackie

Loughery, Leon Askin, Howard Petrie, Charles Arnt, Glenn Strange, Sam Stein
D: George Sherman   STORY & SCR: William R. Cox
Modest action-romance: Adventurer seeks to preserve Ottoman Empire

Velvet House
see The Corpse

The Velvet Touch
1948, (USA), Independent Artists/RKO, b&w, 97 mins.
W: Rosalind Russell (*Valerie Stanton*), Leo Genn (*Michael Morrell*), Claire Trevor (*Marian Webster*), Lex Barker (*Paul Banton*), Sydney Greenstreet (*Capt. Danbury*), Frank McHugh (*Ernie Boyle*), Leon Ames (*Gordon Dunning*), Theresa Harris (*Nancy*), Walter Kingsford (*Peter Gunther*), Dan Tobin (*Jeff Trent*), Nydia Westman (*Susan Crane*), Irving Bacon (*Albert*), Esther Howard (*Pansy Dupont*), Harry Hayden (*Mr. Crouch*), Martha Hyer (*Helen Adams*), James Flavin (*Sgt. Oliphant*), Louis Mason (*Terry*), Jeni LeGon, John Archer, Allen Ray, Helen Perry, Bessie Wade, Jim Drum, Bess Flowers, Gill Wallace
P: Frederick Brisson   **D:** John Gate   SCR: Leo Rosten   ORIG. SCREEN STORY: William Mercer & Annabel Ross   PHOTOG: Joseph Walker   MUSIC: Leigh Harline   MUSIC DIR: C. Bakaleinikoff   SPCL-FX: Russell A. Cully
Standard thriller: Stage actress murders producer, allows another actress to take blame

The Velvet Vampire
1971, (USA), New Wold, color, 82 mins.
W: Michael Blodgett (*Lee*), Sherry Miles (*Susan*), Celeste Yarnall (*Diane*), Jerry Daniels (*Juan*), Gene Shane (*Carl*), Paul Prokop (*Cliff*), Sandy Ward (*Amos*), Chris Woodley (*Cliff's Girlfriend*)
P: Charles S. Swartz   **D:** Stephanie Rothman   SCR: Maurice Jules, Charles S. Swartz & Stephanie Rothman   PHOTOG: Daniel Lacambre   MUSIC: Clancy B. Grass & Roger Dollarhide
blurb: "Climax after climax of terror and desire"
Standard horror-fantasy: Couple visits vampiress in Mojave Desert

Vendetta
1950, (USA), RKO, b&w, 84 mins.
W: Faith Domergue, George Dolenz, Hillary Brooke, Nigel Bruce, Joseph Calleia, Hugo Haas
D: Mel Ferrer
Standard thriller: Beauty must avenge family's honor

La Vendetta di Ercole (The Vengeance of Hercules)
1960, (It), AIP, color, 88 mins.
W: Mark Forest, Broderick Crawford, Eleonora Ruffo, Sandro Maretti, Philippe Hersent, Gaby Andre, Federica Ranchi
P: Achille Piazzi & Gianni Fuchs   **D:** Vittorio Cottafavi, from a story by Marco Piccolo & Archibald Zounds Jr.
USA retitle, **Goliath and the Dragon**
Standard "Sword & Sandal": Muscleman undergoes ordeals to save land from evil ruler

Vault of Horror: GLYNIS JOHNS

Vendetta for the Saint
1968, (GB), ITC/CBS-TV, color, 98 mins.
W: Roger Moore (*Simon Templar*), Ian Hendry (*Alexander Destamio*), Rosemary Dexter (*Gina*), Aimi MacDonald (*Lily*), Finlay Currie, George Pastell, Marie Burke, Anthony Newlands, Alex Scott, Marco Ponti
D: Jim O'Connolly   TELEPLAY: Harry W. Junkin & John Kruse, from characters created by Leslie Charteris   PHOTOG: Brendan J. Stafford   MUSIC: Edwin Astley
TVM, standard thriller (culled from teleseries "The Saint"): Sleuth battles Sicilian Mafia

The Venetian Affair
1967, (USA), MGM, color, 92 mins.
W: Robert Vaughn, Elke Sommer, Felicia Farr, Boris Karloff, Luciana Paluzzi, Fabrizio Mioni, Edward Asner, Karl Boehm, Joe DeSantis, Roger C. Carmel, Wesley Lau
P: Jerry Thorpe & E. Jack Neuman   **D:** Jerry Thorpe   SCR: E. Jack Neuman, from Helen MacInnes' novel   PHOTOG: Milton Krasner   MUSIC: Lalo Schifrin
Standard thriller: Reporter works for CIA, imperils life

Venetian Bird
1952, (GB), Rank/UA, b&w, 95 mins.
W: Richard Todd (*Edward Mercer*), Eva Bartok (*Adrianna Medova*), John Gregson (*Cassana*), George Coulouris (*Spedoni*), Margot Grahame (*Rosa Melitus*), Walter Rilla (*Count Boria*), John Bailey (*Lt. Longo*), Sidney James (*Bernardo*), Michael Balfour (*Moretto*), Martin Boddey (*Gufo*), Eric Pohlmann (*Gostini*), Sydney Tafler (*Boldesca*), David Hurst (*Minelli*), Miles Malleson (*Crespi*), Raymond Young, Eileen Way, Janice Kane, Toni Lucarda
P: Betty E. Box   **D:** Ralph Thomas   SCR: Victor Canning, from his novel   PHOTOG: Ernest Steward   MUSIC: Nino Rota
USA retitle, **The Assassin**
Standard thriller (slight **Third Man** *imitation): Private eye scours Venice for missing ex-partisan*

La Venganza de Don Mendo (The Vengeance of Don Mendo)
1962, (Sp), b&w
W: Fernando Fernan Gomez, Paloma Valdes, Joaquin Roa, Juan Jose Menendez, Paula Martel, Maria Luisa Ponte, Antonio Garisa
WRIT & D: Fernando Fernan Gomez, from a story by Pedro Munos Seca   PHOTOG: Jose F. Aguayo
Standard melodrama

Vengeance
1962, (GB-W. Ger), Raymond Stross/CCC, b&w, 83 mins.
W: Peter Van Eyck (*Dr. Peter Corrie*), Anne Heyward (*Anna Holt*), Cecil Parker (*Stevenson*), Ellen Schwiers (*Ella*), Bernard Lee (*Frank Shears*), Miles Malleson (*Dr. Miller*), Jack MacGowran (*Furber*), Maxine Audley (*Marion Fane*), Siegfried Lowitz (*Walters*), Jeremy Spenser (*Martin Holt*), George A. Cooper (*Gabler*), Allan Cuthbertson (*Dr. Silva*), Kenneth Kendall (*The Newscaster*), Irene Richmond, Bandana Das Gupta, Hans Nielsen, Ann Sears, Victor Brooks, Alistair Williams, John Junkin, Richard McNeff, Frank Forsythe, John Watson, Patsy Rowlands, Brian Pringle
P: Raymond Stross   **D:** Freddie Francis   SCR: Robert Stewart & Philip Mackie loosely based on Curt Siodmak's novel *Donovan's Brain*   PHOTOG: Bob Huke   MUSIC: Ken Jones
USA retitle, **The Brain** *(Governor Films, 1964), A.k.a.* **Over My Dead Body**
Grim SF-thriller: Brain of murdered industrialist seeks revenge

Vengeance is Mine
1908, (GB), Walter Tyler, b&w, 530 ft. (161.5m)
Standard melodrama: Blacksmith killed by lightning when he tries to blind wife's lover

The Vengeance of Daniel Whidden
1912, (GB), Cricks & Martin, b&w, 1,000 ft. (304.8m)
W: Una Tristam (*Mary Whidden*), Jack Leigh (*Jan Stewer*)
D: Edwin J. Collins
Standard melodrama: Fisherman takes blame when girl's father stabs rival

The Vengeance of Don Mendo
see La Venganza de Don Mendo

The Vengeance of Egypt
1912, (Fr), b&w
Standard thriller

The Vengeance of Fu Manchu
1967, (GB), Hallam-7Arts/WB, color, 89 mins.
W: Christopher Lee (*Dr. Fu Manchu*), Douglas Wilmer (*Nayland Smith*), Howard Marion-Crawford (*Dr. Petrie*), Eddie Byrne (*The Captain*), Tsai Chin (*Lin Tang*), Tony Ferrer (*Insp. Ramos*), Susanne Roquette (*Maria Lieberson*), Horst Frank (*Rudy Moss*), Noel Trevarthen (*Mark Weston*), Peter Carsten (*Kurt Heller*), Wolfgang Kieling (*Dr. Lieberson*), Maria Rohm (*Ingrid*)
P: Harry Alan Towers   **D:** Jeremy Summers   SCR: Peter Welbeck [Harry Alan Towers], from characters created by Sax Rohmer   PHOTOG: John Von Kotze   MUSIC: Malcolm Lockyer   SONG: *The Real Me*
Standard thriller: Oriental villain tries to form int'l crime ring

The Vengeance of She
1967, (GB), Hammer-7Arts/20th-Fox, color, 101 mins.
W: John Richardson (*Killikrates*), Olinka Berova (*Carol*), Edward Judd (*Philip Smith*), Colin Blakely (*George Carter*), Jill Melford (*Sheila Carter*), George Sewell (*Harry Walker*), Andre Morell (*Kassim*), Noel Willman (*Za-Tor*), Derek Godfrey (*Men-Hari*), Daniele Noel (*Sharna*), Gerald Lawson (*The Seer*), Derrick Sherwin (*No. 1*), William Lyon Brown (*The Magus*), Charles O'Rourke (*The Servant*), Zohra Segal (*Putri*), Christine Pockett (*The Dancer*), Dervis Ward (*The Lory Driver*)
P: Aida Young   **D:** Cliff Owen   SCR: Peter O'Donnell, suggested by H. Rider Haggard's novel *Ayesha: The Return of She*   PHOTOG: Wolfgang Suschitzky

SPCL-FX: Bowie Films Ltd.   **MUSIC:** Mario Nascimbene   **MUSIC SPRVSR:** Philip Martell   **SONG:** *Who is She?*
working title, ***Ayesha, Daughter of She***
Modest adventure-fantasy (sequel to She *{1965}): Mental call draws young beauty to lost city in North Africa*

The Vengeance of the Air
1914, (GB), Martin/Pathe, b&w, 2,450 ft. (746.8m)
W: Ivan Cleveland (*Lt. Douglas Blake*), Constance Little (*Dora Frazer*), Lionel d'Aragon (*Capt. Kesdale*), Margaret Scudamore (*Enid Mortimer*), Donald Bruce (*Col. Frazer*)
D: Dave Aylott
Standard crime-thriller: Framed lieutenant flies to save colonel's daughter from being kidnapped by rival

The Vengeance of the 47 Ronin
see ***Chushingura*** *(1932)*

Vengeance of the Three Musketeers
1963, (Fr), color
W: Gerard Barray, Mylene Demongeot
Minor adventure-thriller

Vengeance of the Zombies
1972, (Sp), Intervid, color, 90 mins.
W: Paul Naschy, Mirta Miller, Romy, Luis Ciges, Vic Winner
D: Leon Klimovsky   **JAZZ SCORE:** Juan Carlos Calderon
USA retitle, ***Walk of the Dead***
Standard horror-fantasy: Voodoo reanimates dead

Venom (1971/1974)
see ***The Legend of Spider Forest***

Venom
1982, (GB), Morison Film Group/Para, color, 93 mins.
W: Sterling Hayden (*Howard Anderson*), Sarah Miles (*Dr. Marion Stowe*), Klaus Kinski (*Jacmel*), Cornelia Sharpe (*Ruth Hopkins*), Nicol Williamson (*Cmdr. William Bulloch*), Susan George (*Louise*), Lance Holcomb (*Philip Hopkins*), Oliver Reed (*Dave*), Michael Gough (*David Ball*), Mike Gwilym (*Det. Constable Dan Spencer*), Rita Webb (*Mrs. Loewenthal*), Peter Porteous (*Hodges*), Maurice Colbourne (*Sampson*), Moti Makan (*Murkerjee*), Nicholas Donnelly (*The Superintendent*), Katherine Wilkinson (*Susan Stowe*), Arnold Diamond (*The Waiter*), Alan Ford, Howard Bell, David Sterne, Cyril Conway, Sally Lahee, Michael Watkins, Gerard Ryder, Norman Mann, Tony Meyer, Eric Richard, Hugh Lloyd, John Forbes-Robertson, Edward Hardwicke, Paul Williamson, Ian Brimble, Charles Cork
P: Martin Bregman   **D:** Piers Haggard   **SCR:** Robert Carrington, from Alan Scholefield's novel   **PHOTOG:** Gilbert Taylor & Denys Coop   **SPCL-FX:** Alan Whibley & Richard Dean   **MUSIC:** Michael Kamen
Unusual thriller: Kidnapping thwarted by deadly snake

Venus Against the Son of Hercules
1962, (It), color
W: Roger Brown, Jackie Lane
Minor "Sword & Sandal"

Venus Rising
1996, (USA), color, 91 mins,
W: Billy Wirth, Morgan Fairchild, Costas Mandylor, Audie England
D & SCR: Leora Barish
Standard SF-thriller: Couple flees future prison isle

The Venusian
see ***Stranger from Venus***

Venus in Furs
see ***Paroxysmus***

The Verdict
1946, (USA), WB, b&w, 86 mins.
W: Peter Lorre, Sydney Greenstreet, Joan Lorring (*Lottie*), Paul Cavanagh (*Russell*), Rosalind Ivan (*Mrs. Benson*), Morton Lowry (*Kendall*), George Coulouris (*Buckley*), Arthur Shields (*Holbrook*), Art Foster (*Warren*)
D: Don Siegel   **SCR:** Peter Milne, from Israel Zangwill's novel *The Big Ben Mystery*   **PHOTOG:** Ernest Haller   **MUSIC:** Frederick Hollander
Well-made thriller: Scotland Yard inspector comes out of retirement to solve case

The Verdict
1964, (GB), Merton Park/Anglo-Amalgamated, b&w, 55 mins.
W: Cec Linder (*Joe Armstrong*), Zena Marshall (*Carola*), Paul Stassino (*Danny Thorne*), Nigel Davenport (*Larry Mason*), Derek Francis (*Supt. Brett*), John Bryan (*Prendergast*), Derek Partridge (*Peter*), Glyn Jones (*Harry*), Dorinda Stevens (*Molly*)
P: Jack Greenwood   **D:** David Eady   **SCR:** Arthur la Bern, from Edgar Wallace's *story The Big Four*
Standard crime-thriller: Jailed killer has partner rig jury

El Verdugo
see ***Not on Your Life!***

La Vergine di Norimberga (The Virgin of Nuremberg)
1963, (It-W Ger), Gladiator/Zodiac, color, 82 mins.
W: Christopher Lee, Rossana Podesta, George Riviere, Jim Dolen, Mirko Valentin, Anny Delli Uberti
P: Marco Vicario   **D:** Anthony Dawson [Antonio Margheriti]   **SCR:** Antonio Margheriti, G. Green & Edmond T. Greville
GB retitle, ***The Castle of Terror***, *USA retitle,* ***Horror Castle*** *(Walter Manley/Zodiac, 1965), A.k.a.* ***Terror Castle*** *(1966 reissue)*
Standard thriller: Young bride finds horror in husband's ancestral home

La Vergine di Roma (The Virgin of Rome)
1961, (It-Fr), Cine Italia/UA, color, 98 mins.
W: Louis Jourdan, Sylvia Syms
D: Carlo Ludovico Bragaglia & Vittorio Cottafavi (uncredited)
A.k.a. ***Amazons of Rome*** *and* ***Warrior Women***
Minor "Sword & Sandal"

Der Verlorene (The Lost One)
1951, (W. Ger), Arnold Pressburger, b&w, 98 mins.
W: Peter Lorre, Karl John, Helmut Rudolph
D: Peter Lorre   **SCR:** Peter Lorre, Axel Eggebrecht & Benno Vigny
reissued (1964) by Atlas Films
Unusual thriller, strongly anti-Nazi film: Scientist in bombed-out Hamburg becomes killer

Der Verlorene Schuh (The Lost Shoe)
1922, (Ger), Decla-Bioscop, b&w, 7,706.7 ft. (2349m)
W: Renate Mannhardt, Johanna Hofer
D: Ludwig Berger   **PHOTOG:** Gunther Krampf
USA retitle, ***Cinderella***
Standard fantasy: Scullery maid wooed by prince

Eine Versunkene Welt (A Sunken World)
1922, (Austria), Sascha Film-AG, b&w
Standard SF-thriller

Vertigo
1958, (USA), Para, color, 128 mins.
W: James Stewart (*John "Scotty" Ferguson*), Kim Novak (*Madeleine Elster/Judy Barton*), Barbara Bel Geddes (*Midge*), Raymond Bailey (*The Psychiatrist*), Tom Helmore (*Gavin Elster*), Henry Jones (*The Coroner*), Ellen Corby (*The Desk Clerk*), Lee Patrick, Konstantin Shayne
P & D: Alfred Hitchcock   **SCR:** Alec Coppel & Samuel Taylor, from novel *D'entre les Morts (Among the Dead)* by Pierre Boileau & Thomas Narcejac   **PHOTOG:** Robert Burks   **SPCL-FX:** John P. Fulton   **MUSIC:** Bernard Herrmann
Classic thriller: Retired police officer suffers from fear of heights, suicidal woman leads him to high places. cf. ***Body Double***

Vertigo: KIM NOVAK

The Very Edge
1962, (GB), Garrick/British Lion, b&w, 89 mins.
W: Richard Todd (*Geoffrey Lawrence*), Anne Heywood (*Tracey Lawrence*), Nicole Maurey (*Helen*), Jack Hedley (*McInnes*), Barbara Mullen (*Dr. Shaw*), Jeremy Brett (*Mullen*), Maurice Denham (*Crawford*), William Lucas (*Insp. Davies*), Patrick Magee (*Simmonds*), Gwen Watford (*Sister Holden*)
P: Raymond Stross   **D:** Cyril Frankel   **SCR:** Elizabeth Jane Howard   **STORY:** Vivian Cox, Leslie Bricusse & Raymond Stross   **PHOTOG:** Bob Huke   **MUSIC:** David Lee
Standard psychodrama: Architect's wife becomes frigid after being attacked

A Very Missing Person

1972, (USA), Univ-MCA/ABC-TV, color, 73 mins.

<u>W</u>: Eve Arden (*Hildegarde Withers*), James Gregory (*Oscar Piper*), Julie Newmar (*Aletha*), Skye Aubrey (*Isobel/Lenore Gregory*), Ray Danton (*Capt. Westering*), Dennis Rucker (*Al Fisher*), Robert Easton (*Onofre*), Woodrow Parfrey (*Eberhardt*), Bob Hastings (*Malloy*), Pat Morita, Ezra Stone, Sherry Bain

<u>D</u>: Russell Mayberry <u>TELEPLAY</u>: Philip H. Reisman Jr., from characters created by Stuart Palmer

TVM, minor thriller: Woman sleuth probes heiress' disappearance

A Very Old Man with Enormous Wings

1988, (Sp), color, 90 mins.

<u>D</u>: Fernando Birri <u>STORY</u>: Gabriel Garcia Marquez

Standard fantasy: Allegorical tale of mysterious human freak

A Very Powerful Voice

1911, (GB), Hepworth, b&w, 400 ft. (121.9m)

<u>D</u>: Lewin Fitzhamon

Standard comedy-fantasy: Singer's voice makes bus go backwards, wrecks recording studio

The Veteran

see Deathdream

Viaje al Centro de la Tierra (Journey to the Center of the Earth)

1977, (Sp), Almena, color

<u>P & D</u>: Juan Piquer <u>SCR</u>: Carlos Puerto, John Melson & Juan Piquer, from Jules Verne's novel

Minor adventure-thriller

Viaggio Immaginario (Imaginary Voyage)

1963, (Ruman), color

<u>D</u>: Mircea Popescu

Standard fantasy

Vibes

1988, (USA), Imagine Entertainment/Col, color, 99 mins.

<u>W</u>: Cyndi Lauper (*Sylvia Pickel*), Jeff Goldblum (*Nick Deezy*), Julian Sands (*Dr. Steele*), Googy Gress (*Ingo Swedlin*), Peter Falk (*Harry Buscafusco*), Karen Akers, Elizabeth Pena, Michael Lerner, Ramon Bieri

<u>D</u>: Ken Kwapis <u>SCR</u>: Lowell Ganz & Babaloo Mandel <u>STORY</u>: Deborah Blum, Lowell Ganz & Babaloo Mandel <u>PHOTOG</u>: John Bailey <u>VS-FX</u>: Richard Edlund <u>MUSIC</u>: James Horner

Minor SF-comedy-fantasy: Psychics seek fabulous treasure Vice and Virtue. cf. Le Vice et la Vertu

Vice and Virtue: or, The Tempters of London

1915, (GB), Weston Feature Films/Standard, b&w, 3,200 ft. (975.4m)

<u>W</u>: Rowland Moore (*Jack*), Alice Inward (*Alice Brown*), Lily Saxby (*Bella Brown*), Charles Weston (*Bob the Dip*), Gordon Begg (*Father*), Harry Webb (*The Detective*)

<u>D & STORY</u>: Charles Weston

Standard crime-thriller: Disowned man framed for shooting his wealthy father

Le Vice et la Vertu (Vice and Virtue)

1963, (Fr-It), Gaumont/MGM, color, 100 mins.

<u>W</u>: Catherine Deneuve (*Justine*), Annie Girardot (*Juliette*), Serge Marquand (*Ivan*), Philippe Lemaire (*Hans*), Robert Hossein (*Schondorff*), Luciana Paluzzi (*Helena*)

<u>P, D & SP</u>: Roger Vadim, based on Marquis de Sade's novels *Juliette* and *Justine*

Standard melodrama: Two sisters find different fates in Nazi Europe

Vice Girls

1995, (USA), color, 85 mins.

<u>W</u>: Lana Clarkson, Lita Goodson

Minor thriller: Female cops track psychopathic filmmaker

Vice Versa

1910, (GB), Cricks & Martin, b&w, 465 ft. (141.7m)

<u>W</u>: A.E. Coleby

<u>D</u>: Dave Aylott

Standard fantasy: Boy uses magic wand to reverse policemen with sandwichmen, sailors with suffragettes

Vice Versa

1916, (GB), London/Jury, b&w, 3,900 ft. (1188.7m)

<u>W</u>: Charles Rock (*Paul Bultitude*), Douglas Munro (*Marmaduke Paradine*), Edward O'Neill (*Dr. Grimstone*), Guy Newall (*Dick Bultitude*)

<u>D</u>: Maurice Elvey, from a novel by F. Anstey

Standard fantasy: Pompous father magically changes places with schoolboy son

Vice Versa

1947, (GB), Two Cities/Rank, b&w, 111 mins.

<u>W</u>: Roger Livesey (*Paul Bultitude*), Kay Walsh (*Florence Verlaye*), Petula Clark (*Dulcie Grimstone*), Anthony Newley (*Dick Bultitude*), David Hutcheson (*Marmaduke Paradine*), Patricia Raine (*Alice*), James Robertson Justice (*Dr. Grimstone*), Vida Hope (*Nanny*), Joan Young (*Mrs. Grimstone*), Kynaston Reeves (*Dr. Chawner*), Ernest Jay (*Boaler*), Harcourt Williams (*The Judge*), Bill Shine (*Lord Gosport*), Alfie Bass (*The Urchin*), Robert Eddison (*Mr.*

Blinkhorn), James Hayter (*The Bandmaster*), Hugh Dempster (*Col. Ambrose*), James Kenney (*Coggs*), Peter Jones (*Chawner Jr.*), Cyril Smith (*The Inspector*), Vi Kaley

<u>P</u>: Peter Ustinov & George H. Brown <u>D & SCR</u>: Peter Ustinov, from a novel by F. Anstey

Standard comedy-fantasy: Magic stone enables Victorian boy to change places with father

Vice Versa

1988, (USA), Col, color, 97 mins.

<u>W</u>: Judge Reinhold (*Marshall*), Fred Savage (*Charlie*), Jane Kaczmarek (*Robyn*), Corinne Bohrer (*Sam*), William Prince (*Avery*), Swoosie Kurtz (*Tina*), David Proval (*Turk*), Harry Murphy (*Larry*), Gloria Gifford (*Marcie*), Kevin O'Rourke (*Brad*), Beverly Archer (*Mrs. Luttrell*), Chip Lucia (*Cliff*), Richard Kind (*Floyd*), Ajay Naidu (*Dale*), Raymond Rosario (*Dooley*), Elya Baskin (*Kerschner*), James Hong (*Kwo*), Jane Lynch (*Ms. Lindstrom*), Anuwat Tiernate (*A Tomb Robber*), Surasri Klangsuwan (*A Tomb Robber*), Penjit Prembudd (*The Interpreter*), Ram Waratum (*The Gov't Spokesman*), Tuantone Kammesri (*The Man in the Warehouse*), Sulaleewan Suwanatat (*The Old Lady*), Danielle Kohl (*Lori*), Jason Late (*Eric*), Tom Crawford (*Judd*), Christian Fitzpatrick (*Clipper*), Joe Guastaferro (*Mr. Ferriera*), Martyn St. David (*The Rich Customer*), Peggy Roeder (*The Principal's Sec'y*), Paul Greatbatch (*The Teacher*), Robert Bundy (*The Music Salesman*), Jeff Kahn (*The Music Kid*), P.J. Brown (*The Hockey Coach*), Robert Petkoff (*The Sporting Goods Salesman*), Harry Yorku (*The Guru*), Alan Shearman (*The Security Salesman*), Bernie Landis (*Santa Claus*), Michelle Philpot (*The Cosmetic Salesgirl*), Mike Bacarella (*The Limo Driver*), Bettina Wendt (*The Babysitter*), Ralph Foody (*The Doorman*), Steve Assad (*The Waiter*), Danny Goldring (*The Motorcycle Cop*), Rick Hall (*The Shotgun Cop*), Garrett Hohimer, Steve Cohen, Albert Fields, Dayna O'Brien, John T. Stibich, Darlene Anderson, Stella Vaicik, Garrick Paul Axelrod, Kathleen B. Scott, Linda Jaffe, Cindy Legler

<u>D</u>: Brian Gilbert <u>SCR</u>: Dick Clement & Ian La Frenais <u>PHOTOG</u>: King Baggott <u>MUSIC</u>: David Shire <u>SONGS</u>: Set the Night to Music & Crazy in the Night

Modest comedy-fantasy: Father and son switch bodies

Vicious Circle

1947, (USA), UA, b&w, 77 mins.

<u>W</u>: Conrad Nagel, Lyle Talbot

A.k.a. Women in Brown

Standard melodrama

The Vicious Circle

1957, (GB), Beaconsfield/Romulus, b&w, 84 mins.

<u>W</u>: John Mills (*Dr. Howard Latimer*), Noelle Middleton (*Laura James*), Derek Farr (*Ken Palmer*), Wilfrid Hyde-White (*Maj. Harrington*), Roland Culver (*Insp. Dane*), Mervyn Johns (*Dr. George Kimber*), Rene Ray (*Mrs. Amhler*), Lionel Jeffries (*Jeffrey Windsor*), Lisa Daniely (*Frieda Veldon*), Fritz Kortner

<u>P</u>: Peter Rogers <u>D</u>: Gerald Thomas <u>SCR</u>: Francis Durbridge <u>PHOTOG</u>: Otto Heller <u>MUSIC</u>: Stanley Black

USA retitle, The Circle (Kassler Films, 1959)

Standard thriller: Police use framed doctor to trap actress' murderer

Victim Five

1964, (GB-W. Ger), Towers of London/British Lion/Col, color, 88 mins.

<u>W</u>: Lex Barker (*Steve Martin*), Ronald Fraser (*Insp. Lean*), Ann Smyrner (*Helga*), Veronique Vendell (*Gina*), Dietmar Schonherr (*Paul*), Walter Rilla (*Wexler*), Howard Davies (*Rawling*), Gert Van den Bergh (*Vanberger*), Percy Sieff (*Anderson*)

<u>P</u>: Harry Alan Towers & Skip Steloff <u>D</u>: Robert Lynn <u>SCR</u>: Peter Yeldham <u>STORY</u>: Peter Welbeck

USA retitle, Code 7...Victim 5

Standard thriller: Millionaire hires American detective to solve murder of his valet

Victim of Desire

1995, (USA), color, 90 mins.

<u>W</u>: Marc Singer, Shannon Tweed, Julie Strain, Wings Hauser, Johnny Williams

<u>D</u>: Jim Wynorski

Standard thriller: Gov't investigator tracks embezzled millions, becomes involved with murder victim's wife

Victims

1980, (GB), Jennie & Co./Para/CIC, color, 29 mins.

<u>W</u>: Angela Morant (*The Wife*), Warren Clarke (*The Husband*), Adam Bareham (*The Milkman*), Wayne Brooks (*The Boy*), Winnie Holman (*The Cashier*), Julie Jupp (*The Ass't*), Barbara Johnson (*The Passenger*)

<u>P</u>: Gower Frost <u>D & STORY</u>: Alan Blake <u>PHOTOG</u>: John Crawford <u>MUSIC</u>: David Lawson

Standard short thriller: Housewife dreams of stabbing milkman

Victims of Blackmail

see The Sins of Harvey Clare

Victor Frankenstein

see Terror of Frankenstein

The Video Dead

1987, (USA), Highlight Prods.-Interstate 5, color, 90 mins.

<u>W</u>: Roxanna Augesen, Rocky Duvall, Vickie Bastel, Michael St. Michaels, Sam David McClelland, Jennifer Miro, Cliff Watts, Thaddeus Golas, Al Millan,

Patrick Treadway
WRIT, P & D: Robert Scott   **PHOTOG:** Greg Becker   **ORIG. MUSIC:** Stuart Rabinowitsh, Leonard Marcel & Kevin McMahon   **SONG:** *Dizzy Tonite*
Minor horror-fantasy: Ghouls emerge from boob tube

Videodrome
1983, (Can), Pierre David-Victor Solnicki/Filmplan Int'l II/Univ, color, 88 mins.
W: James Woods (*Max Renn*), Deborah Harry (*Nicki Brand*), Sonja Smits (*Bianca O'Blivion*), Jack Creley (*Prof. Brian O'Blivion*), Peter Dvorsky (*Harlan*), Les Carlson (*Barry Convex*), Lynne Gorman (*Masha*), Julie Kahner, Julie Khaner (*Bridey*), Reiner Schwarz (*Moses*), David Bolt (*Raphael*), Lally Cadeau (*Rena*), Henry Gomez (*Brolley*), Kay Hawtry (*The Matron*), Sam Malkin (*The Derelict*), Bob Church (*The Newscaster*), Jayne Eastwood (*The Caller*), Franciszka Hedland (*The Bellydancer*), David Tsubouchi (*A Salesman*), Harvey Chao (*A Salesman*)
P: Claude Heroux   **WRIT & D:** David Cronenberg   **PHOTOG:** Mark Irwin   **MUSIC:** Howard Shore   **SPCL MAKEUP:** Rick Baker
Unusual SF-horror: Insidious TV broadcasts control minds, destroy life

Vierges et Vampires (Virgins and Vampires)
1973, (Fr), Les Films ABC/National Cinema Corp./Box Office Int'l, color, 75 mins.
P: Sam Selsky   **D:** Jean Rollin
A.k.a. **Caged Virgins, Crazed Vampire** *and* **Dungeons of Terror**
Standard eroto-horror: Vampire king traps two girls

A View to a Kill
1985, (GB), MGM-UA, color, 131 mins.
W: Roger Moore (*James Bond*), Tanya Roberts (*Stacey Sutton*), Grace Jones (*May Day*), Christopher Walken (*Max Zorin*), Patrick Macnee (*Tibbett*), Lois Maxwell (*Miss Moneypenny*), Desmond Llewelyn ("*Q*"), Walter Gotell (*Gen. Gogol*), David Yip (*Chuck Lee*), Geoffrey Keen (*The Minister*), Patrick Bauchau (*Scarpine*), Robert Brown ("*M*"), Fiona Fullerton (*Pola Ivanova*), Manning Redwood (*Bob Conley*), Alison Doody (*Jenny Flex*), Willoughby Gray (*Dr. Carl Mortner*), Jean Rougerie (*Aubergine*), Bogdan Kominowski (*Klotkoff*), Papillon Soo Soo (*Pan Ho*), Mary Stavin (*Kimberley Jones*), Dominique Risbourg (*Compere*), Daniel Benzali
P: Albert Broccoli & Michael Wilson   **D:** John Glen   **SCR:** Richard Maibaum & Michael G. Wilson, from characters created by Ian Fleming   **PHOTOG:** Alan Hume   **SPCL-FX:** John Richardson   **MUSIC:** John Barry title song performed by Duran Duran
Exciting thriller: Magnate plots destruction of Silicon Valley

The Viking
1928, (USA), MGM, color
W: Donald Crisp, Pauline Starke, Le Roy Mason, Roy Stewart, Anders Randolph, Richard Alexander, Harry Lewis Woods, Albert MacQuarrie, Toben Meyer, Claire MacDowell, Julia Swayne Gordon
D: R. William Neill, from Ottillie A. Liljencrantz's novel *Thrall*
Unusual (early Technicolor) adventure-thriller: Norsemen seek new world

Viking Massacre
see **Knives of the Avenger**

The Viking Queen
1966, (GB), Hammer-7Arts/20th-Fox, color, 91 mins.
W: Don Murray (*Justinian*), Carita (*Salina*), Andrew Keir (*Octavian*), Donald Houston (*Maelgan*), Adrienne Corri (*Beatrice*), Niall MacGinnis (*Tiberian*), Wilfrid Lawson (*The King*), Nicola Pagett (*Talia*), Percy Herbert (*Catus*), Denis Shaw (*Osiris*), Patrick Troughton (*Tristram*), Sean Caffrey (*Fergus*), Philip O'Flynn (*The Merchant*), Brendan Matthews (*Nigel*), Gerry Alexander (*Fabian*), Patrick Gardiner (*Benedict*), Paul Murphy (*Dalan, Maelgan's Son*), Cecil Sheridan (*The Shopkeeper at the Protest Gathering*), Arthur O'Sullivan (*The Old Man at the Tax-Enquiry*), Anna Mannahan (*The Shopkeeper's Wife*), Nita Lorraine (*The Nubian Slave-Girl*)
P: John Temple-Smith   **D:** Don Chaffey   **SCR:** Clarke Reynolds, from an orig. story by John Temple-Smith   **PHOTOG:** Stephen Dade   **SPCL-FX:** Allan Bryce   **MUSIC:** Gary Hughes   **MUSIC SPRVSR:** Philip Martell
Standard adventure-romance: Celts of ancient Britain revolt against Roman conquerors

The Viking's Bride
1907, (GB), Hepworth, b&w, 400 ft. (121.9m)
D: Lewin Fitzhamon
Standard adventure-thriller: Vikings help chief save bride from rival tribe

The Viking Women and the Sea Serpent
1957, (USA), Malibu/AIP, b&w, 66 mins.
W: Abby Dalton (*Desir*), Susan Cabot (*Enger*), Brad Jackson (*Vedric*), Richard Devon (*Stark*), Jonathan Haze (*Ottar*), Jay Sayer (*Senja*), June Kenney, Lynne Bernay, Gary Conway, Sally Todd, Betsy Jones-Moreland, Michael Forrest
P & D: Roger Corman   **SCR:** Lawrence Louis Goldman   **STORY:** Irving Block   **SPCL-FX:** Jack Rabin, Louis DeWitt & Irving Block   **MUSIC:** Albert Glasser
Full-length title, **The Saga of the Viking Women and Their Voyage to the Waters of the Great Sea Serpent**
Standard adventure-thriller: Viking women go in search of their long absent men

La Villa dei Mostri (House of Monsters)
1950, (It), b&w, 10 mins.
WRIT & D: Michelangelo Antonioni   **MUSIC:** Giovanni Fusco
Standard short thriller

Village in the Mist
1983, (S. Korea), color, 90 mins.
W: Ahn Song-Ki, Chong Yun-Hee, Lee Yea-Min, Kim Ji-Yung, Choi Dong-Jun, Jin Bong-Jin
D: Lim Kwon-Taek
Unusual thriller (variation on 'Straw Dogs'): Woman schoolteacher finds sinister mystery in remote village

The Village of the Damned
1960, (GB), MGM, b&w, 78 mins.
W: George Sanders (*Gordon Zellaby*), Barbara Shelley (*Anthea Zellaby*), Martin Stephens (*David Zellaby*), Michael Gwynn (*Alan Bernard*), Laurence Naismith (*Dr. Willers*), Richard Vernon (*Sir Edgar Hargreaves*), John Phillips (*Gen. Leighton*), Jenny Laird (*Mrs. Harrington*), Richard Warner (*Harrington*), Thomas Heathcote (*James Pawle*), Bernard Archard (*The Vicar*), Charlotte Mitchell (*Janet Pawle*), John Stuart (*Prof. Smith*), Sarah Long, Susan Richards, Peter Vaughan, Rosamund Greenwood, Pamela Buck, June Coswell, Keith Pyott, Alexander Archdale, Sheila Robins, Tom Bowman, Carlo Cura, Anthony Harrison, Diane Aubrey, John Kelly, Linda Bateson, Gerald Paris, Roger Malik, Mark Mileham, Elizabeth Munden, Theresa Scoble, Peter Taylor, Peter Preidel, Howard Knight, Brian Smith, Paul Norman, Janice Howley, Robert Marks, John Bush, Billy Lawrence
P: Ronald Kinnoch   **D:** Wolf Rilla   **SCR:** Stirling Silliphant, Wolf Rilla & George Barclay, from John Wyndham's novel *The Midwich Cuckoos*   **PHOTOG:** Geoffrey Faithfull   **SPCL-FX:** Tom Howard   **MUSIC:** Ron Goodwin
Classic SF-thriller: Earth children sired by alien force. cf. **Children of the Damned**

Village of the Damned
1995, (USA), Alphaville/Univ, color, 95 mins.
W: Christopher Reeve (*Alan Chaffee*), Kirstie Alley (*Dr. Susan Verner*), Linda Kozlowski (*Jill McGowan*), Michael Pare (*Frank McGowan*), Mark Hamill (*Rev. George*), Meredith Salenger (*Melanie Roberts*), Peter Jason, Pippa Pearthree, Thomas Dekker, Constance Forslund, Lindsey Haun, Karen Kahn
P: Michael Preger & Sandy King   **D:** John Carpenter   **SCR:** David Himmelstein, from John Wyndham's novel *The Midwich Cuckoos* and the 1960 screenplay by Stirling Silliphant, Wolf Rilla & George Barclay   **PHOTOG:** Gary B. Kibbe   **EDIT:** Edward A. Warschilka   **PRODUCTION DESIGN:** Rodger Maus   **MUSIC:** John Carpenter & Dave Davies
Unusual SF-thriller: Children spawned by alien force

Village of the Giants
1965, (USA), Bert I. Gordon/Embassy, color, 82 mins.
W: Tommy Kirk (*Mike*), Johnny Crawford (*Horsey*), Joy Harmon (*Merrie*), Beau Bridges (*Fred*), Ronny Howard, Mike Clifford, Freddy Cannon, Charla Doherty, Bob Random, Tisha Sterling, Tim Rooney, Kevin O'Neal, Joseph Turkel, Gail Gilmore, Toni Basil, Hank Jones, Jim Begg, Vicki London
P & D: Bert I. Gordon   **SCR:** Alan Caillou loosely based on H.G. Wells' novel *The Food of the Gods*   **PHOTOG:** Paul C. Vogel   **SPCL-FX:** Bert I. Gordon & Flora M. Gordon
blurb: "See them burst out of their clothes and bust up a town!"
Standard SF-comedy: Teens turned into gargantuans.   cf. **Empire of the Ants** *and* **The Food of the Gods**

A Village Tragedy
1911, (GB), Tress Film Co., b&w, 780 ft. (237.7m)
P: Henry Tress
Standard thriller: 17th-century innkeeper kills own son in mistake for rich guest

The Villain's Downfall
1909, (GB), Hepworth, b&w, 725 ft. (221m)
D: Lewin Fitzhamon
Standard thriller: Rich man kidnaps girl

The Villain Still Pursued Her
1940, (USA), RKO, b&w, 66 mins.
W: Hugh Herbert, Anita Louise, Buster Keaton, Alan Mowbray, Joyce Compton, Richard Cromwell, Margaret Hamilton, Billy Gilbert
D: Edward Cline   **PHOTOG:** Lucien Ballard   **MUSIC:** Frank Tours
Standard satire: Broad, labored spoof of silent melodramas

The Vindicator
1986, (Can), Michael T. Levy/20th-Fox, color, 92 mins.
W: David McIlwraith, Teri Austin, Richard Cox (*Whyte*), Maury Chaykin (*Burt*), Pam Grier (*Hunter*)
D: Jean-Claude Lord   **SCR:** Edith Rey & David Preston
Minor SF-thriller: Hunt for missing humanoid. A.k.a. **Frankenstein '88**

The Vineyard
1989, (USA), color, 95 mins.
W: James Hong, Karen Witter, Michael Wong
D: James Hong & Bill Rice
Mior horror-thriller: Japanese madman seeks immortality, drinks human blood

Les Vingt Mille Lieues sous les Mers (20,000 Leagues under the Sea)
1916, (Fr), b&w, 105 mins.
D: Stuart Paton, from Jules Verne's novel
Standard adventure-thriller: Saga of vengeful submarine captain

Violated
1954, (USA), Palace, b&w, 78 mins.
<u>W</u>: Mitchell Kowal, Wim Holland, Lili Dawn, Vicki Carlson, William Martel, Jason Niles
<u>P</u>: Wim Holland   <u>D</u>: Walter Strate   <u>SCR</u>: William Paul Mishkin
   HARMONICA SCORE: Tony Mottola
Standard thriller: Hair-fetish killer interrogated

Violence
1947, (USA), Mono, b&w, 72 mins.
<u>W</u>: Nancy Coleman, Michael O'Shea
Standard thriller

The Violence of Desire
1965, (It), color
<u>D</u>: Enzo di Gianni
Minor fantasy

A Violent Journey
see The Fool Killerv

Violent Midnight
see Psychomania (1964)

Violent Moment
1959, (GB), Independent Artists/Anglo-Amalgamated, b&w, 61 mins.
<u>W</u>: Lyndon Brook (*Douglas Baines*), Jane Hylton (*Daisy Harker*), Jill Browne (*Janet Greenway*), John Paul (*Sgt. Ranson*), Rupert Davies (*Bert Glennon*), Moira Redmond (*Kate Glennon*), Bruce Seton (*Insp. Davis*), Martin Miller (*Hendricks*)
<u>P</u>: Bernard Coote   <u>D</u>: Sidney hayers   **STORY**: Peter Barnes
Standard crime-thriller: Army deserter strangles mistress

Violent Playground
1958, (GB), Rank/RFD, b&w, 108 mins.
<u>W</u>: Stanley Baker (*Sgt. Truman*), Peter Cushing (*The Priest*), Anne Heywood (*Cathie Murphy*), David McCallum (*Johnny Murphy*), John Slater (*Sgt. Walker*), Moultrie Kelsall (*The Supt.*), Clifford Evans (*Heaven Evans*), George A. Cooper (*The Chief Insp.*), Brona Boland (*Mary Murphy*), Fergal Boland (*Patrick Murphy*), Tsai Chin (*Primrose*), Michael Chow (*Alexander*)
<u>P</u>: Michael Relph   <u>D</u>: Basil Dearden   <u>SCR</u>: James Kennaway, from his novel
Standard crime-thriller: Detective loves sister of psycho teen arsonist

Violent Rage
see Fearmaker

Violent Women
1960, (USA), Exploit Films/Brenner, b&w, 63 mins.
<u>W</u>: Jennifer Statler, Jo Ann Kelly, Pamela Perry, Elinor Blair, Sandy Lyn, Patty Magee
<u>D</u>: Barry Mahon
Minor melodrama: Bad broads behind bars

Violette Noziere
1977, (Fr-Can), color, 122 mins.
<u>W</u>: Isabelle Huppert, Jean Carmet, Stephane Audran, Lisa Langlois, Mario David, Bernadette Lafont, Jean-Francois Garreaud
<u>D</u>: Claude Chabrol
Standard fact-based thriller: Girl poisons parents

Virgin Among the Living Dead
1971, (Sp), color, 90 mins.
<u>W</u>: Christina von Blanc, Britt Nichols, Howard Vernon, Anne Libert, Rose Kiekens, Paul Muller
<u>D</u>: Jesus Franco
Minor horror-thriller: Young woman finds terror in remote castle

Virgin Hunters
see Test Tube Teens from the Year 2000

The Virgin of Nuremberg
see La Vergine di Norimberga

The Virgin of Rome
see La Vergine di Roma

Virgins and Vampires
see Vierges et Vampires

Virgin Witch
1970, (GB), Univista/Tigon/Joseph Brenner, color, 89 mins.
<u>W</u>: Ann Michelle (*Christine*), Vicky Michelle (*Betty*), Keith Buckley (*Johnny*), Patricia Haines (*Sybil Waite*), Neil Hallett (*Gerald Amberley*), James Chase (*Peter*), Paula Wright (*Mrs. Wendell*), Helen Dennis Durack, Edward Brady, & Ralph Solomons
<u>D</u>: Ray Austin   <u>SCR</u>: Klaus Vogel (from his novel)   **PHOTOG**: Gerald Moss
   MUSIC: Ted Dicks
A.k.a. Lesbian Twin
Standard thriller: Psychic lesbian tries to turn her girlfriend into witch

Viridiana
1961, (Sp), Uninei S.A. Films, b&w, 90 mins.
<u>W</u>: Silvia Pinal, Francisco Rabal, Fernando Rey, Margarita Lozano, Victoria Zinny, Teresa Rabal, Jose Calvo, Luis Heredia, Joaquin Roa, Jose Manuel Martin
<u>D</u>: Luis Bunuel   <u>SCR</u>: Luis Bunuel & Julio Alejandro   **PHOTOG**: Jose Aguayo
Arresting psychodrama: Novice nun corrupted by nasty uncle

Virtual Assasin
1995, (Can-Jap), color, 99 mins.
<u>W</u>: Michael Dudikoff, Brion James, Jon Cuthbert, Suki Kaiser
<u>D</u>: Robert Lee   <u>SCR</u>: Eric Poppen
A.k.a. Cyberjack
Minor SF-thriller: 21st-century thugs try to steal computer virus

Virtual Combat
1995, (USA), color, 90 mins.
<u>W</u>: Don "The Dragon" Wilson, Michael Bernardo, Athena Massey, Loren Avedon, Kenneth McLeod, Turhan Bey, Stella Stevens
<u>D</u>: Andrew Stevens
Minor SF-thriller: Futuristic border policeman pursues villainous escapee from world of virtual reality

Virtual Girl
1998, (USA), color, 86 mins.
<u>W</u>: Charlie Curtis, Max Dixon
Minor SF-thriller: Computer genius creates virtual-reality simulation of perfect woman

Virtual Obsession
1998, (USA), Von Zerneck/USA-TV, color, 143 mins.
<u>W</u>: Peter Gallagher, Bridgette Wilson (*Juliet*), Mimi Rogers (*Karen*), Andy Comeau (*Tom Inman*), Robert Vaughn (*Adam Spring*), Jake Lloyd, Lee Garlington, Michael O'Neill, Dan Martin, Tom Nibley, Charles Gruber, David Jensen, Cynthia Garris, Frank Gerrish, Nicole Guertin, Mary Bishop
<u>D</u>: Mick Garris   **TELEPLAY**: Preston Sturges & Mick Garris, from Peter James' novel   **PHOTOG**: Shelly Johnson   **VS-FX SPRVSR**: Craig Weiss
   MUSIC: Nicholas Pike
2-part TVM, standard SF-thriller: Dead woman's mind transmitted to computer

Virtual Seduction
1995, (USA), color, 90 mins.
<u>W</u>: Jeff Fahey (*Liam Bass*), Carrie Genzel (*Paris*)
Made-for-Cable, standard SF-thriller: Man's deceased love returns in virtual-reality experiment

Virtuosity
1995, (USA), Para, color, 105 mins.
<u>W</u>: Denzel Washington (*Parker Barnes*), Kelly Lynch (*Madison Carter*), Russell Crowe (*Sid 6.7*), Louise Fletcher (*Elizabeth Deane*), Stephen Spinella (*Lindenmeyer*), William Forsythe (*William Cochran*), William Fichtner (*Wallace*), Costas Mandylor (*John Donovan*), Kevin J. O'Connor (*Clyde Reilly*), Kaley Cuoco (*Karin*), Christopher Murray (*Matthew Grimes*), Heidi Schanz (*Sheila 3.2*), J. Gordon Noice (*Big Red*), Traci Lords (*The Media Zone Singer*), Mari Morrow (*Linda Barnes*), Michael Buffer (*The Emcee*), Mara Duronslet (*The Beautiful Woman at Olympic Stadium*), Karen Annarino (*The 1st TV Reporter*), Miguel Najera (*Rafael Debaca*), Randall Fontana (*Ed*), Danny Goldring (*John Symes*), Allen Scotti (*The Surgeon*), Dwayne Chattman (*The Stripped Man in the Media Zone*), Ed Marques, Cheryl Lawson, Kevin Loreque, Eiko Nijo, Amy Smallman, Gauravani Buchwald, Rolando Molina, Marva Hicks, Laura Leigh Hughes, Steven R. Barnett, Gary Anthony Sturgis, Monica Allison, Susan Mohun, David Asman, Anthony C. Hall, Brogan Young, Ahmed Ahmed, Juan A. Riojas, John Walcutt, Michael Buchman Silver, Jordan Marder, Tony Winters, Dustin Nguyen, Virginia Watson, Margot Hope, Beverly Cohen, Una Damon, Mary-Rachel Foot,

Virtuosity: DENZEL WASHINGTON

Jennifer Greenhut, Alanna Ubach, Lesa Noelle, Michelle Smith, Brit Thompson, Eric Bernt, Kevin La Presle, Daniel Anderson, Michael Tamburro, Robert John Gomes
<u>P:</u> Gary Lucchesi   <u>D:</u> Brett Leonard   <u>SCR:</u> Eric Bernt   <u>PHOTOG:</u> Gale Tattersall   <u>VS-FX SPRVSR:</u> Jon Townley   <u>MUSIC:</u> Christopher Young   <u>SONGS:</u> *A Big Day in the North, I Can't Get No Sleep, Build It with Love, Samurai, Into the Paradise, Young Boys, Ka-Pow, No Talking Just Head, Fallen Angel, The Loyaliser, Two into One & Party Man*
Standard SF-thriller: Cyber-space criminal gains android body, then spreads reign of terror

Virus
1980, (Jap-Can), Toho/Media/Broadwood, color, 106 mins.
<u>W:</u> Chuck Connors (*Capt. McCloud*), Glenn Ford (*Pres. Richardson*), Olivia Hussey (*Marit*), Robert Vaughn (*Barkley*), George Kennedy (*Adm. Conway*), Masao Kusakari (*Yoshizumi*), Bo Svenson (*Maj. Carter*), Henry Silva (*Garland*), Stephanie Faulkner (*Sarah*), Edward J. Olmos (*Capt. Lopez*), Stuart Gillard (*Dr. Mayer*), Cec Linder (*Dr. Latour*), Isao Natsuki (*Dr. Nakanishi*), Nicholas Campbell, Tsunehiko Natase, John Evans, Shinichi (Sonny) Chiba, Kensaku Morita, Chris Wiggins, John Granik, Toshiyuki Nagashima, Eve Crawford, John Bayliss, Ted Follows, Ara Hovanessian, Daniele Schneider, J. Roger Periard, Diane Lasko, Laura Pennington, George Touliatos, Julie Khaner, Larry Reynolds, David Gardner, Ron Hartman, Dan Kippy, William Binney, Gordon Thompson, Jim Bearden, Ken Pogue, Wally Bondarenko, Lt. Comm. David Griffiths, John Rutter, Ken Camroux, Alfred Humphreys, Michael Tough, Peter Heppleston, Matt Hawthorne, Jan Muszynski, Charles Northcote, Yumi Takigawa, Ken Ogata, Keiko Ito, Ichiro Kijima, Takashi Noguchi, Nenji Kobayashi, Tayori Hinatsu, Tomoko Igarashi, Sachiko Sato, Sanae Nakahara, Colin Fox, Yukiko Watanabe, Dick Grant, Richard Ayres, Tyler Miller, Jefferson Mappin, Charles L. Campbell, Terry Martin, George Wilbur
<u>D:</u> Kinji Fukasaku   <u>SCR:</u> Koji Takada, Gregory Knapp & Kinji Fukasaku, from a novel by Sakyo Komatsu   <u>PHOTOG:</u> Daisaku Kimura   <u>MUSIC:</u> Teo Macero
Minor SF-thriller (Chushingura meets The Satan Bug while on the beach): Man-made virus depopulates world

Visa to Canton
1960, (GB), Swallow-Hamme/Col, color, 75 mins.
<u>W</u>: Richard Basehart (*Don Benton*), Athene Seyler (*Mao Tai Tai*), Lisa Gastoni (*Lola Sanchez*), Eric Pohlmann (*Ivano Kang*), Marne Maitland (*Han Po*), Bernard Cribbins (*Periera*), Alan Gifford (*Orme*), Bert Kwouk (*Jimmy*)
<u>P & D:</u> Michael Carreras   <u>STORY:</u> Gordon Wellesley
USA retitle, **Passport to China**
Standard crime-thriller: Communists frame travel agent's half-brother

The Vision
1987, (GB), color, 103 mins.
<u>W:</u> Lee Remick, Dirk Bogarde, Helena Bonham Carter, Eileen Atkins
<u>D:</u> Norman Stone
Unusual thriller: Televangelists attempt to control viewers' minds

The Visions of an Opium Smoker
1905, (GB), R.W. Paul, b&w, 262 ft. (79.9m)
<u>D:</u> J.H. Martin
Standard fantasy: Man smokes opium in Chinese den, has weird dream

Visions of Evil
see So Sad about Gloria

Visions of Murder
1994, (USA), Bar-Gene/Hearst/NBC-TV, color, 95 mins.
<u>W:</u> Barbara Eden (*Jessie Newman*), James Brolin (*Hal*), Joan Pringle (*Gwen*), Terry O'Quinn (*Adm. Hagar*), Scott Bryce, Erika Flores, Anita Finlay, Jack Shearer, Ray Reinhardt
<u>D:</u> Michael Rhodes   <u>PHOTOG:</u> Steven Shaw   <u>MUSIC:</u> Michael Hoenig
TVM, standard thriller: Psychic phenomena reveal killer to woman psychiatrist

Visitants
1987, (USA), color, 93 mins.
<u>W:</u> Marcus Vaughter, Johanna Grika, Joel Hile, Nicole Rio
<u>D:</u> Rick Sloane
Minor SF-comedy: Space aliens descend on small 1950's town

Les Visiteurs du Soir (The Evening Visitors)
1942, (Fr), Andre Paulve, b&w, 110 mins.
<u>W:</u> Jules Berry, Alain Cuny, Maria Dea, Arletty, Marcel Herrand, Fernand Ledoux, Gabriel Gabrio, Roger Blin
<u>D:</u> Marcel Carne
A.k.a. **The Devil's Envoys** *(US release:* **Superfilm,** *1947)*
Unusual allegorical fable: Satan's minions interfere with 13th-century lovers

Visiting Hours
1982, (Can), Pierre David-Victor Solnicki/Filmplan Int'l/20th-Fox, color, 104 mins.
<u>W:</u> Lee Grant, William Shatner, Michael Ironside, Linda Purl
<u>P:</u> Claude Heroux   <u>D:</u> Jean-Claude Lord   <u>SCR:</u> Brian Taggart
Standard thriller: Psycho stalks newswoman

The Visit of Santa Claus
see Santa Claus (1898)

The Visitor
1979, (USA-It), International Picture Show, color, 96 mins.
<u>W:</u> Paige Conner, John Huston, Mel Ferrer, Shelley Winters, Glenn Ford
<u>D:</u> Michael J. Paradise   <u>SCR:</u> Lou Comici & Robert Mundy   <u>SPCL-FX:</u> Robert Shelley & Vernon Hyde
Minor horror-thriller: Child has supernatural powers

The Visitors
1989, (Swed), MVM/Vidmark, color, 102 mins.
<u>W:</u> Keith Berkeley, Lena Enore, John Force, Brent Landiss, Joanna Berg, John Olson, Patrik Ersgard
<u>D:</u> Joakim Ersgard   <u>SCR:</u> Patrik Ersgard & Joakim Ersgard   <u>PHOTOG:</u> Hans Lerin   <u>SPCL-FX:</u> Olov Nylander   <u>MUSIC:</u> Peter Wallin
*Standard horror-thriller (**Amityville Horror/Poltergeist** imitation): Family buys haunted house in Sweden*

The Visitors
1993, (Fr), Alpilles-Amigo/Miramax Zoe, color, 106 mins.
<u>W:</u> Christian Clavier (*Jacquouille/Jacquart*), Jean Reno (*Godefroy*), Valerie Lemercier (*Frenegonde/Beatrice*), Marie-Anne Chazel (*Ginette*), Christian Bujeau (*Jean-Pierre*), Didier Pain (*Louis VI*), Isabelle Nanty
<u>P:</u> Alain Terzian   <u>D:</u> Jean-Marie Poire   <u>SCR:</u> Christian Clavier & Jean-Marie Poire   <u>PHOTOG:</u> Jean-Yves Le Mener   <u>MUSIC:</u> Eric Levi
USA release, 1996
Unusual fantasy-satire: Potion hurls two 12th-century warriors into 20th-century France

Visitors of the Night
1995, (USA), NBC-TV, color, 95 mins.
<u>W:</u> Markie Post, Candace Cameron
<u>D:</u> Jorge Montesi
TVM, standard SF-thriller: Woman fears teenage daughter was conceived during alien abduction

Visit to a Small Planet
1960, (USA), Para, b&w, 101 mins.
<u>W:</u> Jerry Lewis (*Kreton*), Fred Clark (*Roger Putnam Spelding*), Joan Blackman (*Ellen Spelding*), Lee Patrick (*Reba Spelding*), Earl Holliman (*Conrad*), John Williams (*Mr. Delton*), Gale Gordon (*Bob Mayberry*), Ellen Corby (*Mabel Mayberry*), Jerome Cowan (*George Abercrombie*), Barbara Lawson (*The Beatnik Girl*), Milton Frome
<u>P:</u> Hal B. Wallis & Joseph H. Hazen   <u>D:</u> Norman Taurog   <u>SCR:</u> Edmund Beloin & Henry Garson, from an orig. teleplay by Gore Vidal   <u>PHOTOG:</u> Loyal Griggs   <u>SPCL-FX:</u> John P. Fulton   <u>MUSIC:</u> Leigh Harline

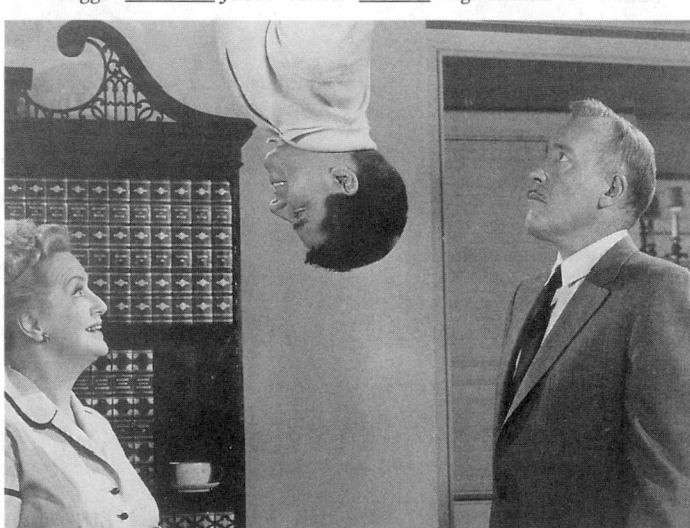

Visit To A Small Planet: LEE PATRICK, JERRY LEWIS AND FRED CLARK

Standard SF-comedy: Alien causes amusing situations when he visits Earth

A Visit to a Spiritualist
1906, (GB), Alpha Trading Co., b&w, 120 ft. (36.6m)
<u>D:</u> Arthur Cooper
Standard fantasy: Man visits medium, sees ghost

A Voice in the Night
see Wanted for Murder

The Voice of Merrill
1952, (GB), Tempean/Eros, b&w, 84 mins.
<u>W:</u> Valerie Hobson (*Alycia Roach*), Edward Underdown (*Hugh Allen*), James Robertson Justice (*Jonathan Roach*), Henry Kendall (*Ronald Parker*), Garry Marsh (*Insp. Thornton*), Daniel Wherry (*Pierce*), Sam Kydd (*Sgt. Baker*), Daphne Newton (*Miss Quinn*), Ian Fleming (*Dr. Forrest*), Alvar Liddell (*The Announcer*)
<u>P:</u> Robert Baker & Monty Berman   <u>D & SCR:</u> John Gilling   <u>STORY:</u> Gerald Landeau & Terence Austin

*USA retitle, **Murder Will Out** (Kramer Hyams, 1953)*
Standard thriller: Dying author frames radio narrator for killing his secretary

Voice of the Whistler
1945, (USA), Col, b&w, 61 mins.
<u>W</u>: Richard Dix
<u>D</u>: William Castle
Standard thriller: Greedy nurse weds patient

Voice Over
1981, (GB), Welsh Arts, color, 105 mins.
<u>W</u>: Ian McNeice (*Ed "Fats" Bannerman*), John Cassady (*F.X. Jones*), Bish Nethercote (*Bitch/Elizabeth*), Sarah Martin (*Celia*), David Pearce (*Frank*), Stuart Hutton (*The Doctor*), Eira Moore (*PAP Boss*), Paul Chandler (*RDOV Boss*), Carol Owen (*Bitch's Friend*), Jon Groome (*Capt. Thompson*)
<u>WRIT & D</u>: Chris Monger
Bizarre thriller: Radio personality becomes demented

Voices
1973, (GB), Warden/Hemdale, color, 91 mins
<u>W</u>: David Hemmings (*Robert*), Gayle Hunnicutt (*Claire*), Lynn Farleigh (*Mother*), Russell Lewis (*John*), Peggy Ann Clifford (*The Medium*), Eva Griffith (*Jessica*), Adam Bridge (*David*)
<u>D</u>: Kevin Billington   <u>SCR</u>: George Kirgo & Robert Enders, from a play by Richard Lortz   <u>PHOTOG</u>: Geoffrey Unsworth   <u>MUSIC</u>: Richard Rodney Bennett
*USA retitle, **Nightmare***
Minor fantasy: Mother of drowned boy sees ghosts of dead family

A Voice Said Goodnight
1932, (GB), First Nat'l/WB, b&w, 35 mins.
<u>W</u>: Nora Swinburne (*Joan Creighton*), Jack Trevor (*Gerald Creighton*), D.A. Clarke-Smith (*Philip Gaylor*), Wilfred Caithness (*Beldon*), John Turnbull (*Insp. Lavory*), Daphne Scorer (*Annie*), Roland Culver (*The Reporter*)
<u>D</u>: William McGann   <u>SCR</u>: Roland Pertwee & John Hastings Turner, from a story by Roland Pertwee
Standard thriller: Usurer murdered

Volcano
1997, (USA), 20th-Fox, color, 104 mins.
<u>W</u>: Tommy Lee Jones (*Mike Roark*), Anne Heche (*Dr. Amy Barnes*), Gaby Hoffman (*Kelly Roark*), Don Cheadle (*Emmit Reese*), Keith David
<u>D</u>: Mick Jackson   <u>SCR</u>: Jerome Armstrong & Billy Ray   <u>PHOTOG</u>: Theo van de Sande   <u>MUSIC</u>: Alan Silvestri
Exciting thriller: Earthquake precipitates volcanic eruption in Los Angeles

Volcano: Fire on the Mountain
1997, (USA), ABC-TV, color, 95 mins.
<u>W</u>: Dan Cortese, Cynthia Gibb, Don Davis, Lynda Boyd, John Novak, Brian Kerwin
<u>D</u>: Graeme Campbell   <u>TELEPLAY</u>: Craig Spector & Steve Womack   <u>PHOTOG</u>: Tobias Schliessler   <u>MUSIC</u>: David Michael Frank
TVM, standard thriller: Seismic terror in rural community

The Volcano Monsters
*see **Godzilla Raids Again***

Les Voleurs de la Lune
*see **O Dwoch Takich Co Ukradli Ksiezyc***

Voodoo
1995, (USA), A-Pix, color, 91 mins
<u>W</u>: Corey Feldman, Jack Nance, Sarah Douglas
<u>D</u>: Rene Eram   <u>SCR</u>: Brian DiMuccio & Dino Vindeni   <u>MUSIC</u>: Keith Bilderbeck
Standard horror-fantasy: Transfer student finds priestess has lured him into fraternity of Undead

Voodoo Black Exorcist
1974, (Sp), color
<u>W</u>: Aldo Sambrell, Luis Marin, Ferdinand Sancho
<u>D</u>: M. Cano   <u>PHOTOG</u>: Robert Ochoa
Minor horror-fantasy: Mummified native returns to life

Voodoo Blood Bath
1964, (USA), Jerry Gross/Cinemation, b&w, 85 mins.
<u>W</u>: William Joyce (*Tom Harris*), Heather Hewitt (*Jeannine*), Betty Hyatt Linton (*Coral*), Dan Stapleton (*Duncan*), Robert Stanton
<u>WRIT, P & D</u>: Del Tenney   <u>PHOTOG</u>: Francois Farkas   <u>MUSIC</u>: Lon E. Norman
*reissued (with **I Drink Your Blood**) in 1970 as **I Eat Your Skin**, A.k.a. **Zombies***
Minor horror-thriller: Vacationers encounter voodoo, grotesque experiments

Voodoo Blood Death
*see **Curse of Simba***

Voodoo Dawn
1990, (USA), color, 85 mins.
<u>W</u>: Raymond St. Jacques, Theresa Merritt, Gina Gershon, Kirk Baily, Billy "Sly"

Williams, J. Grant Albrecht, Tony Todd
<u>D</u>: Steven Fierberg   <u>SCR</u>: John Russo & Jeffrey Delman
Minor horror-thriller: Demonic doings at labor camp

Voodoo Girl
*see **Sugar Hill***

Voodoo Heartbeat
1972, (USA), TWI, color, 88 mins.
<u>W</u>: Ray Molina, Philip Ahn, Ern Dugo, Forrest Duke, Ebby Rhodes, Mike Zapata, Ray Molina Jr., Stan Mason, Mary Martinez, Mike Meyers
<u>P</u>: Ray Molina   <u>D & SCR</u>: Charles Nizet
Standard horror-satire: Serum turns man into blood-drinking monster

Voodoo Island
1957, (USA), Bel-Air/UA, b&w, 76 mins.
<u>W</u>: Boris Karloff, Beverly Tyler, Rhodes Reason, Murvyn Vye, Elisha Cook Jr., Jean Engstrom, Frederick Ledebur, Glen Dixon, Owen Cunningham, Herbert Patterson, Jerome Frank
<u>P</u>: Howard K. Koch   <u>D</u>: Reginald LeBorg   <u>SCR</u>: Raymond T. Marcus   <u>MUSIC</u>: Les Baxter
*reissued (1963) as **Silent Death***
Minor horror-thriller: Witchcraft and monsters on tropic isle

Voodoo Man
1944, (USA), Banner/Mono, b&w, 62 mins.
<u>W</u>: Bela Lugosi (*Dr. Richard Marlowe*), George Zucco (*Nicholas*), John Carradine (*Toby*), Wanda McKay (*Betty*), Michael Ames (Tod Andrews) (*Ralph*), Louise Currie (*Sally*), Terry Walker (*Alice*), Ellen Hall (*Mrs. Marlowe*), Mary Currier (*Mrs. Benton*), Dan White (*The Deputy*), Henry Hall (*The Sheriff*), Cilare James (*The Zombie*), Pat McKee (*Grego*), Mici Goty (*The Housekeeper*)
<u>P</u>: Sam Katzman & Jack Dietz   <u>D</u>: William Beaudine   <u>ORIG. STORY & SCR</u>: Robert Charles   <u>PHOTOG</u>: Marcel LePicard   <u>MUSIC DIR</u>: Edward Kay
*Standard horror-thriller: Sinister trio turns lovelies into zombies. cf. **Lock Up Your Daughters***

Voodoo Tiger
1952, (USA), Col, b&w, 67 mins.
<u>W</u>: Johnny Weissmuller, Jean Byron, James Seay, Charles Horvath, Jeanne Dean, Robert Bray, Michael Fox, Richard Kipling, Rick Vallin, John Cason, Paul Hoffman, William R. Klein, Fredcric Berest, Alex Montoya, Tamba
<u>P</u>: Sam Katzman   <u>D</u>: Spencer G. Bennet   <u>STORY & SCR</u>: Samuel Newman
Standard "Jungle Jim" adventure-thriller: Jungle hero battles Nazis, headhunters, and gangsters

Voodoo Woman
1957, (USA), Carmel/AIP, b&w, 77 mins.
<u>W</u>: Marla English (*Marilyn Blanchard*), Tom Conway (*Dr. Roland Gerard*), Mary Ellen Kaye (*Susan Gerard*), Lance Fuller, Touch (Mike) Connors, Martin Wilkins, Paul Dubov, Norman Willis, Paul Blaisdell, Emmett E. Smith, Giselle D'Arc, Jean Davis
<u>P</u>: Alex Gordon   <u>D</u>: Edward L. Cahn   <u>SCR</u>: Russell Bender & V.I. Voss   <u>MUSIC</u>: Darrell Calker
*script orig. titled **Black Voodoo**, orig. co-billed with **The Undead***
Standard horror-fantasy ($60,000 budget): Scientist uses jungle medecine and voodoo to turn beautiful criminal into loathsome monster

Voodoo Woman

Vormittaggspuk (Ghosts Before Breakfast)
1928, (Ger), b&w, 450 ft. (137.2m)
<u>D</u>: Hans Richter
Standard fantasy

Vortex
see The Day Time Ended

Vous Pigez? (You Dig?) (You Get It!)
1956, (Fr-It), Dismage/Transalpin, b&w, 98 mins.
W: Eddie Constantine (*Lemmy Caution*), Maria Frau, Yves Royan
D: Pierre Chevalier   SCR: Jacques Doniol-Valcroze, Victor Trivas, from Peter Cheyney's novel *Don't Get Me Wrong*
Standard thriller (7th "Lemmy Caution" adventure): Secret agent counters criminals

A Vow to a Kill
1995, (USA), (cable), color
W: Richard Grieco, Julianne Phillips, Gordon Pinsent, Peter MacNeill, Tom Cavanagh
D: Harry S. Longstreet   TELEPLAY: Sean Silas, Renee Longstreet & Harry S. Longstreet   PHOTOG: Francois Protat   MUSIC: John M. Keane
Made-for-Cable, standard thriller: Magazine photographer weds wealthy woman, holds her hostage on remote island

Le Voyage a Travers l'Impossible (The Impossible Voyage)
1904, (Fr), Star, b&w, 434m (1,423.9 ft./24.1 mins.); abbrev. version: 378m (1,240.2 ft./21 mins.)
W: Georges Melies
WRIT & D: Georges Melies
A.k.a. Whirling the Worlds
Standard SF-fantasy: Journey to surface of sun and bottom of ocean

Le Voyage dans la Lune (A Trip to the Moon)
1902, (Fr), Star, b&w, 260m (845 ft./14.3 mins.)
W: Georges Melies, Victor Andre, Farjaux-Kelm-Brunnet, Delpierre, Bluette Bernon (*The Girl in the Crescent*), Ballerinas of the Theatre du Chatelet (*The Girls in the Stars*), Acrobats of the Folies-Bergere (*The Selenites*)
WRIT, P & D: Georges Melies   PHOTOG: Lucien Tainguy
Classic SF-fantasy (in 30 scenes): Improbable expedition to Earth's satellite

Le Voyage Imaginaire (The Imaginary Voyage)
1924, (Fr), De Mare, b&w, 80 mins. (also 62 mins.)
W: Albert Prejean
WRIT & D: Rene Clair
Standard fantasy

Voyage into Space
1968, (Jap), Toei/AIP, color, 98 mins.
W: Mitsundbu Kaneko, Akjo Ito
Standard juvenile SF-fantasy (animation & live action)

Voyage of the Rock Aliens
1987, (USA), color, 97 mins.
W: Pia Zadora, Tom Nolan, Craig Sheffer, Ruth Gordon, Rhema, Michael Berryman, Jermaine Jackson
D: James Fargo
Minor SF-farce: Competing space-alien rock stars

Voyage of Terror
1998, (USA), Shavick/FAM-TV, color, 95 mins.
W: Lindsay Wagner, Martin Sheen, Brian Dennehy, Michael Ironside, Horst Buchholz, William B. Davis, Katharine Isabelle, Nathaniel Deveaux, David Lewis, Steve Bacic
D: Brian Trenchard-Smith   TELEPLAY: Mel Frohman   MUSIC: Brahm Wenger
TVM, standard thriller: Plague on cruise ship

Voyage to a Prehistoric Planet
1968, (USA), AIP-TV, color, 78 mins.
W: Mamie Van Doren, Mary Frank, Paige Lee
P: Roger Corman   D: Peter Bogdanovich   SCR: Henry Ney

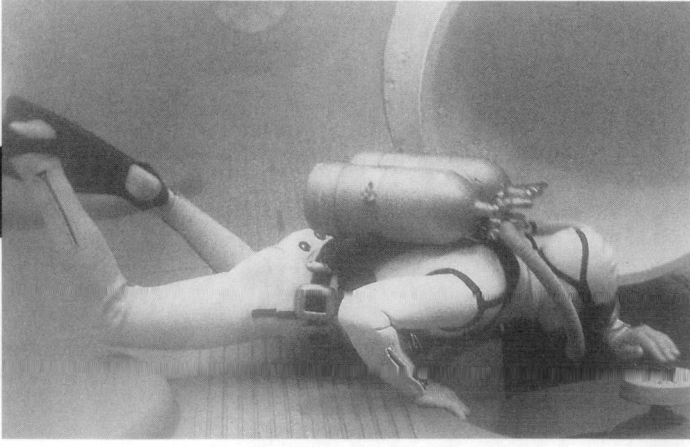

Voyage To The Bottom Of The Sea

A.k.a.: Voyage to the Planet of Prehistoric Women
Standard SF-adventure

Voyage to the Bottom of the Sea
1961, (USA), Windsor/20th-Fox, color, 105 mins.
W: Joan Fontaine (*Dr. Susan Hiller*), Walter Pidgeon (*Adm. Nelson*), Peter Lorre (*Lucius*), Barbara Eden (*Lt. Kathy Connors*), Robert Sterling (*Lee*), Regis Toomey (*Dr. Jameson*), Michael Ansara (*Alvarez*), Frankie Avalon (*Romano*), Robert Easton ("*Sparks*"), John Litel, Henry Daniell, Howard McNear, Mark Slade, Delbert Monroe, Charles Tannen, Skip Ward
P & D: Irwin Allen   SCR: Irwin Allen & Charles Bennett, from a story by Irwin Allen   PHOTOG: Winton C. Hoch   SPCL-FX: L.B. Abbott   MUSIC: Paul Sawtell & Bert Shefter
Modest SF-thriller: Futuristic submarine saves Earth from destruction

Voyage to the Center of Memory
see Total Recall

Voyage to the End of the Universe
see Ikaria XB1

Voyage to the Outer Planets
1973, (USA), Showsphere/Graphic Films Corp., color, 28 mins.
WRIT & D: Colin Cantwell   SPCL-FX: John Dykstra   MUSIC: Paul Novros
Standard SF-docu short

Voyage to the Prehistoric Planet
see Planeta Bura

Les Voyages de Gulliver (The Voyages of Gulliver)
1902, (Fr), Star, b&w, 80m (262.5 ft./4.4 mins)
D: Georges Melies, based on Jonathan Swift's novel *Gulliver's Travels*
Standard fantasy: Shipwrecked man finds bizarre lands

Le Voyeur
see Peeping Tom

Vrazda Po Cesku (Murder Czech Style)
1967, (Czech), Royal Films, b&w & color, 87 mins.
D: Jiri Weiss
Standard thriller

Vredens Dag (Day of Wrath)
1943, (Den), Palladium-Copenhagen/Brandon Films, b&w, 105 mins. (also 97 mins.)
W: Thorkild Roose (*Absalon*), Lisbeth Movin (*Anne*), Sigrid Neeiendam (*Meret*), Preben Lerdorff (*Martin*), Anna Svierkier (*Herlofs Marte*), Albert Hoeberg (*The Bishop*)
P & D: Carl Dreyer   SCR: Carl Dreyer, Poul Knudsen & Mogens Skot-Hansen, from Wiers Jenssen's play *Anne Pedersdotter*   PHOTOG: Carl Andersson   MUSIC: Poul Schierbeck
Standard melodrama

Vulcan, Son of Jupiter
1963, (It), Joseph E. Levine/Embassy, color, 75 mins.
W: Rod Flash Ilush, Gordon Mitchell, Bella Cortez, Omero Gargano, Furio Meniconi, Roger Browne, Annie Gorassini
D: Emimmo Salvi   PHOTOG: Mario Parapetti
Standard myth-adventure: Mars leads Thracian mortals in overthrow of gods

The Vulture
1937, (GB), First Nat'l/WB, b&w, 67 mins.
W: Claude Hulbert (*Cedric Gull*), Lesley Brook (*Sylvia*), Hal Walters (*Stiffy Mason*), Frederick Burtwell (*Jenkinson*), George Merritt (*Spicer*), Arthur Hardy (*Li Fu*), Archibald Batty (*McBride*), George Carr (*Charlie Yen*)
D: Ralph Ince, from a story by Stafford Dickens
Standard comedy-thriller: Detective poses as Chinese, catches jewel thieves

The Vulture
1966, (GB), Homeric-Iliad-Financial/Para, color, 91 mins.
W: Robert Hutton (*Eric Lutyens*), Akim Tamiroff (*Prof. Koniglich*), Broderick Crawford (*Brian Stroud*), Diane Clare (*Trudy Lutyens*), Philip Friend (*The Vicar*), Monty Landis (*The Driver*), Patrick Holt (*Jarvis*), Edward Caddick (*The Sexton*), Annette Carell (*Ellen West*), Gordon Sterne (*Edward Stroud*), Margaret Robertson, Keith McConnell
WRIT, P & D: Lawrence Huntington   PHOTOG: Stephen Dade
Standard thriller: Futuristic experiments produce horrifying mutant

The Vultures of London
1915, (GB), Martin/KTC, b&w, 3,000 ft. (916.9m)
W: H. St. Barbe Wst (*The Artist*), Dora de Winton (*Cora l'Estrange*), Mollie vaughan (*The Girl*), Alfred Brandon (*The Crook*), Edwin Beach (*The Accomplice*)
D: R. Harley West
Standard crime-thriller: Girl crook poses as model, helps gang rob artist

W
1973, (USA), Bing Crosby Prods./CRC, color, 95 mins.
W: Twiggy (*Katie*), Michael Witney (*Ben*), Dirk Benedict (*William*), Alfred Ryder
    (*The Investigator*), Eugene Roche (*Charles*), Michael Conrad (*Whitfield*), Peter
    Walker (*The Prison Official*), John Vernon (*Arnie*), Ken Lynch (*The Guard*),
    Carmen Zapata (*Betty*), Dave Morick (*Paul*)
P: Mel Ferrer   D: Richard Quine   SCR: Gerald Di Pego & James Kelly
    STORY: Ronald Shusett & James Kelly   PHOTOG: Gerald Hirschfeld
    MUSIC: Johnny Mandel
A.k.a. *I Want Her Dead*
"a suspense thriller...Twiggy in her first dramatic role"—Film Newsletter
"A thriller in the great Hitchcock tradition"—James Bacon, United Feature
    Syndicate
Unusual thriller: Girl stalked by maniacal first husband

Das Wachsfigurenkabinett (The Cabinet of Wax Figures)
1924, (Ger), Neptun-Film, b&w, 7,044 ft. (2147m/62 mins.)
W: Emil Jannings, Conrad Veidt, Werner Krauss, Olga von Balieff, Wilhelm
    Dieterle, John Gottowt
D: Paul Leni   SCR: Henrik Galeen   PHOTOG: Helmar Lerski   SETS: Paul
    Leni & Ernst Stern
GB retitle, **Waxworks**, USA retitle, **Three Wax Men** (Viking Productions, 1929)
Unusual, impressionistic thriller: Terror in wax museum

The Wacky World of Dr. Morgus
1962, (USA), b&w
W: Sid Noel (*Dr. Morgus*), Dana Barton, Jeanne Teslof, David Kleinberger
D: Roul Haig   SCR: Sid Noel & Roul Haig
Minor SF-fantasy: Machine turns humans into sand

The Wages of Fear
see *Le Salaire de la Peur*

The Wager
1913, (GB), B&C/MP, b&w, 1,061 ft. (323.4m)
W: George Foley (*Bill McCann*), Harold Brett (*Cavendish*)
D & SCR: Harold Brett
Standard crime-thriller: Rich man bets he can reform thief

The Waif and the Statue
1907, (GB), Urban, b&w, 240 ft. (73.2m)
D: Walter R. Booth
Standard fantasy: Statue of Hope revives, finds home for waif

The Waif and the Wizard: or, The Home Made Happy
1901, (GB), R.W. Paul, b&w, 90 ft. (27.4m)
D: Walter R. Booth
Standard fantasy: Conjurer changes bailiff into waiter with food

The Waif's Christmas
1908, (GB), Walturdaw, b&w, 320 ft. (97.5m)
Standard fantasy: Santa gives orphans cracker that produces boongiving fairy

Wake Up!: or, A Dream of Tomorrow
1914, (GB), Union Jack Photoplays/Eclair, b&w, 3,500 ft. (1066.8m)
W: Bertram Burleigh
D & STORY: Lawrence Cowen
*Standard fantasy: Pacifist secretary of war converted after dreaming England is invaded by
    "Valvictians"*

Wakamba
1955, (USA), RKO, color, 65 mins.
Standard adventure: Intrigue in Africa

Waldo Warren: Private Dick Without a Brain
see *Maximum Thrust*

Walk a Tightrope
1963, (GB), Oarroch-McCallum/British Lion, b&w, 78 mins.
W: Dan Duryea (*Lutcher*), Patricia Owens (*Ellen*), Terence Cooper (*Jason*), Richard
    Leech (*Doug*), Neil McCallum (*The Counsel*), Trevor Reid (*Insp. McMitchell*),
    A.J. Brown (*The Magistrate*)
P: Jack Parsons   D: Frank Nesbitt   SCR: Neil McCallum   STORY: Manny
    Rubin
Standard crime-thriller: Mad killer claims woman hired him to shoot her husband

The Walking Dead
1936, (USA), WB, b&w, 66 mins.
W: Boris Karloff, Marguerite Churchill, Edmund Gwenn, Warren Hull, Ricardo
    Cortez, Barton MacLane, Henry O'Neill, Ruth Robinson, Eddie Acuff,
    Addison Richards, Joe Sawyer, Kenneth Harlan, Adrian Rosley, Robert
    Strange, Miki Morita, Paul Joseph King
D: Michael Curtiz   SCR: Ewart Adamson, Robert Adams, Lillie Hayward &
    Peter Milne   PHOTOG: Hal Mohr
*Excellent horror-thriller (classic Karloff performance): Electrocuted man revived, seeks
    vengeance*

A Walking Nightmare
see *The Living Ghost* (1942)

The Walk in the Night
see *Der Januskopf*

Walk in the Shadow
see *Life for Ruth*

Walk of the Dead
see *Vengeance of the Zombies*

Walk the Dark Street
1956, (USA), Dominant, color, 74 mins.
W: Chuck Connors, Don Ross, Regina Gleason, Eddie Kafafian
WRIT, P & D: Wyott Ordung
*Modest thriller: Big-game hunter and army officer stalk each other through downtown Los
    Angeles*

Wall of Death
1952, (GB), Realart, b&w, 90 mins.
W: Maxwell Reed, Susan Shaw, Laurence Harvey
GB title: *There is Another Sun* (Butcher's, 1951, 95 mins.)
Standard melodrama

Wall of Death
1956, (GB), Merton Park/Anglo-Amalgamated, b&w, 30 mins.
W: Cyril Chamberlain (*Insp. Harris*), Vanda Godsell (*Mrs.Hartier*), Vernon Greeves
    (*Schmidt*)
P: Alec Snowden   D & SCR: Montgomery Tully   STORY: Judith Warden, from
    a novel by Edgar Lustgarten
Standard short crime-thriller: Inspector probes death of fairground worker

Walpurgis Night
see *La Noche de Walpurgis*

Wand-erful Will
1916, (GB), Cricks/DFSA, b&w, 663 ft. (202.1m)
W: Jack Jarman (*The Man*)
D: Toby Cooper
*Standard fantasy: Penniless man shares lodgings with professor whose magic wand makes
    furniture move*

The Wandering Jew (1904)
see *Le Juif Errant*

The Wandering Jew
1920, (Austria), b&w, 65 mins.
W: Rudolf Schildkraut, Joseph Schildkraut
Standard fantasy: Jew cursed with immortality

The Wandering Jew
1933, (GB), Twickenham/Gaumont, b&w, 111 mins.
W: Conrad Veidt (*Matathias*), Marie Ney (*Judith*), Cicely Oates (*Rachel*), Basil
    Gill (*Pontius Pilate*), Anne Grey (*Joanne de Beaudricourt*), Dennis Hoey (*de
    Beaudricourt*), Jack Livesey (*Duke Godfrey*), Bertram Wallis (*Prince Boemund*),
    Joan Maude (*Gianella*), John Stuart (*Pietro Morelli*), Arnold Lucy (*Andrea
    Michelotti*), Peggy Ashcroft (*Olalla Quintana*), Francis L. Sullivan (*Juan de
    Texada*), Felix Aylmer (*Ferera*), Ivor Barnard (*Castro*), Abraham Sofaer
    (*Zapportas*)
D: Maurice Elvey   SCR: H. Fowler Mear, from a play by E. Temple Thurston
US release: Olympic, 1935, 85 mins.
Elaborate fantasy: Jew cursed to live through ages

Wanted For Murder: ERIC PORTMAN

Wanted, a Mummy

1910, (GB), Cricks & Martin, b&w, 525 ft. (160m)
D: A.E. Coleby
Standard comedy: Tramp poses as mummy, partner sells him to professor

Wanted for Murder

1946, (GB), Excelsio/20th Century-Fox, b&w, 103 mins. (also 91 mins.)
W: Eric Portman (*Victor Colebrooke*), Dulcie Gray (*Anne Fielding*), Derek Farr (*Jack Williams*), Stanley Holloway (*Sgt. Sullivan*), Rolnad Culver (*Insp. Conway*), Barbara Everest (*Mrs. Colebrooke*), Bonar Colleano (*Cpl. Mappolo*), Jenny Laird (*Jeannie McLaren*), Kathleen Harrison (*Florrie*), Bill Shine (*Ellis*), Viola Lyel (*Mabel Cooper*), John Salew (*Walters*), John Ruddock (*Glover*), Wally Patch (*The Showman*), George Carney (*The Boatman*), Wilfrid Hyde-White (*The Guide*), Moira Lister (*Miss Willis*), Beatrice Campbell
D: Lawrence Huntington   **SCR:** Emeric Pressburger, Rodney Ackland, & Maurice Cowan, from a play by Percy Robinson & Terence de Marney   **PHOTOG:** Max Greene   **MUSIC:** Mischa Spoliansky
A.k.a. A Voice in the Night, reissued 1952
Standard thriller: Scotland Yard hunts demented strangler

War Between the Planets

1971, (It), Mercury-Int'l/Fanfare, color, 80 mins.
W: Giacomo Rossi-Stuart (*Rod*), Amber Collins (*Terry Sanchez*)
D: Anthony Dawson [Antonio Margheriti]
Original title Missione Planete Errante (Operation Wandering Planet)
Minor SF-adventure.

Ward 13

see Hospital Massacre

The War Eagle

1939, (USA), RKO, b&w
production abandoned after filming of several spcl-fx scenes (by Willis O'Brien)
War Eagle scenario: Prehistoric natives make aerial attack on New York City

The Ware Case

1917, (GB), Broadwest, b&w, 6,191 ft. (1887m)
W: Matheson Lang (*Sir Hubert Ware*), Violet Hopson (*Ware*), Ivy Close (*Marian Scales*), Gregory Scott (*Michael Ayde*), George Foley (*Sir Henry Egerton*)
P & D: Walter West   **SCR:** J. Bertram Brown, from a play by George Pleydell Bancroft
reissued 1919
Standard crime-thriller: Acquitted knight admits to drowning wife's rich brother

Wargames

1983, (USA), MGM-UA, color, 113 mins.
W: Matthew Broderick (*David*), Dabney Coleman (*McKittrick*), Ally Sheedy (*Jennifer*), John Wood (*Falken*), Barry Corbin (*Gen. Beringer*), Juanin Clay (*Pat*), Joe Dorsey (*Conley*), Dennis Lipscomb (*Watson*), Irving Metzman (*Richter*), Michael Ensign (*Beringer's Aide*), William Bogert (*Mr. Lightman*), Susan Davis (*Mrs. Lightman*), James Tolkan (*Wigan*), David Clover (*Stockman*), Drew Snyder (*Ayers*), John Garber, Duncan Wilmore, John Spencer, Billy Ray Sharkey, Michael Madsen, Erik Stern, Gary Sexton, Jason Bernard, Frankie Hill, Jesse Goins, Alan Blumenfeld, Len Lanson, Maury Chaykin, Stephen Lee, Eddie Deezen, Lucinda Crosby, Stack Pierce, Art Lafleur, Brad David Berwick, Martha Shaw, James Ackerman, Howie Allen, Mike Adams, Jim Marriott, Tom Lawrence, Frances Nealy, Charles Akins, Glenn Standifer, Edward Jahnke
D: John Badham   **SCR:** Lawrence Lasker & Walter F. Parkes   **PHOTOG:** William A. Fraker   **MUSIC:** Arthur B. Rubinstein   **SONG:** Video Fever
Modest SF-thriller: High-schooler dabbles on computer, gains access to U.S. missile-warning system

War Gods of Babylon

1962, (It), AIP-TV, color, 88 mins.
W: Howard Duff, Jackie Lane, Luciano Marin, Giancarlo Sbragia
Minor "Sword & Sandal": Brothers vie for girl, defying decree of gods

War-Gods of the Deep

see The City Under the Sea

Warhead

1996, (USA), color
W: Joe Lara, Frank Zagarino
Minor thriller

The War in Space

1978, (Jap), Toho, color, 91 mins.
W: Kensaku Morita, Yoko Asano, Masaya Oki, Akihiko Hirata, William Ross, David Perin, Shuji Otaka, Ryo Ikebe
D: Jun Fukuda   **PHOTOG:** Jo Aizawo   **MUSIC:** Toshiaki Tsushima
Minor SF-adventure: Earth vs. alien attackers

Warlock

1991, (USA), Trimark, color, 102 mins.
W: Julian Sands (*The Warlock*), Lori Singer (*Kassandra*), Richard E. Grant (*Giles Redferne*), Kevin O'Brien (*Chas*), Mary Woronov (*The Channeler*), Richard Kuss (*The Mennonite*), Allan Miller, Anna Levine, David Carpenter, Frank Renzulli, Kay E. Kuter, Ian Abercrombie, Robert Breeze, Kenneth

Danziger, Art Smith, Brandon Call, Rob Paulsen, Nancy Fox, Harry Johnson, Juli Burkhart, Peter Sherayko, Gyl Roland, Meta King, Bill Dunnam, Wendy Feiner
P & D: Steve Miner   **SCR:** D.T. Twohy   **PHOTOG:** David Eggby   **MUSIC:** Jerry Goldsmith
Standard horror-fantasy: Male witch seeks to undo universe

Warlock: The Armageddon

1993, (USA), Tapestry/Trimark, color, 98 mins.
W: Julian Sands, Chris Young, Paula Marshall, Joanna Pacula, Bruce Glover, R.G. Armstrong, Steve Kahan, Charles Hallahan, Joanna Pacula, Craig Hurley, Bruce Glover
D: Anthony Hickox, from characters created by David N. Twohy
SCR: Kevin Rock & Sam Bernard   **STORY:** Kevin Rock   **PHOTOG:** Gerry Lively   **MUSIC:** Mark McKenzie
Standard horror-fantasy: Satanic agent returns to threaten world

Warlock Moon

1975, (USA), color, 75 mins
W: Laurie Walters, Joe Spany, Harry Bauer, Robert Walker Jr., Cesar Romero, Tom Drake
D: Bill Herbert
Minor fantasy-thriller: Couple meets witch's coven at abandoned spa

The War Lord

1965, (USA), Univ, color, 122 mins.
W: Charlton Heston (*Chrysagon*), RoseMary Forsyth (*Bronwyn*), Richard Boone (*Bors*), Maurice Evans (*The Priest*), Henry Wilcoxon (*The Frisian Prince*), Guy Stockwell (*Draco*), Niall MacGinnis (*Odin*), James Farentino (*Marc*), Sammy Ross (*Volc*), Woodrow Palfrey (*Piet*), John Alderson (*Holbracht*), Allen Jaffe (*Tybald*), Dal Jenkins (*Dirck*), Michael Conrad (*Rainault*), Johnny Jensen (*The Boy Prince*), Forrest Wood (*The Chrysagon Man*), Belle Mitchell (*The Old Woman*),
D: Franklin Schaffner   **SCR:** John Collier & Millard Kaufman, from Leslie Stevens' play Lovers   **PHOTOG:** Russell Metty   **MUSIC:** Jerome Moross
Engrossing melodrama: Passion and upheaval during Norman occupation of Britain

The Warlord: Battle for the Galaxy

1998, (USA), Renfield-Para/UPN-TV, color, 95 mins.
W: John Corbett, Rod Taylor (*Gen. Sorenson*), John Pyper-Ferguson (*Heenoc Xian*), Carolyn McCormick, Elisabeth Harnois, J. Madison Wright, Darryl Theirse, Marjorie Monaghan, Joel Swetow, Philip Moon, Lilyan Chauvin, Rhino Michaels, Dick Miller, John Marlo, Rob Elk, Dyrk Ashton, Dorothy A. Gallagher, Michael Quill, Dawn Ann Billings, Shannon Welch, Leslie Redden, Belinda Balaski, Tom Billett, Steven E. Daniels, Gregory Kargianis
D: Joe Dante   **TELEPLAY:** Caleb Carr   **PHOTOG:** Jamie Anderson   **SPCL-FX:** Ron Zarro   **SPCL-FX SPRVSR:** Ric Zarro
TVM (made in 1996), minor SF-adventure (feature-pilot for unsold teleseries): Space rogue seeks to rescue kidnapped sister

Warlords

1988, (USA), color, 87 mins.
W: David Carradine, Sid Haig, Ross Hagen, Fox Harris, Dawn Wildsmith, Robert Quarry, Victoria Sellers, Brinke Stevens
D: Fred Olen Ray
Minor SF-thriller: Lone soldier vs. mutant hordes in post-nuke desert

Warlords of Atlantis

see Warlords of the Deep

Warlords of the Deep

1978, (GB), John Dark-Kevin Connor/Col-EMI, color, 96 mins.
W: Doug McClure (*Greg*), Cyd Charisse (*Atsil*), Shane Rimmer (*Daniels*), Lea Brodie (*Delphine*), Peter Gilmore (*Charles*), Michael Gothard (*Atmir*), Hal Galili (*Grogan*), Derry Power (*Jacko*), John Ratzenberger (*Fenn*), Donald Bissett (*Aitken*), Ashley Knight (*Sandy*), Robert Brown (*Briggs*), Daniel Massey (*Atraxon*)
P: John Dark   **D:** Kevin Connor   **SCR:** Brian Hayles   **PHOTOG:** Alan Hume   **SPCL-FX:** John Richardson & Roger Dicken   **MUSIC:** Mike Vickers
A.k.a. Warlords of Atlantis
Minor SF-adventure: 1890's archeologists find undersea civilization

Warlords of the 21st Century

1982, (USA), color, 91 mins.
W: Michael Beck, Anne McEnroe, James Wainwright
D: Harley Cokliss   **SCR:** Harley Cokliss, Irving Austin & John Beech   **PHOTOG:** Chris Menges
A.k.a. Battletruck
Minor SF-thriller

Warlords 3000

1993, (USA), color, 92 mins.
W: Jay Roberts Jr., Denise Marie Duff, Steve Blanchard, Wayne Duvall
D: Faruque Ahmed   **SCR:** Ron Herbst & Faruque Ahmed
Minor SF-thriller: Drug lords control devastated future Earth

Warning from Space

see Uchujin Tokyo No Arawaru

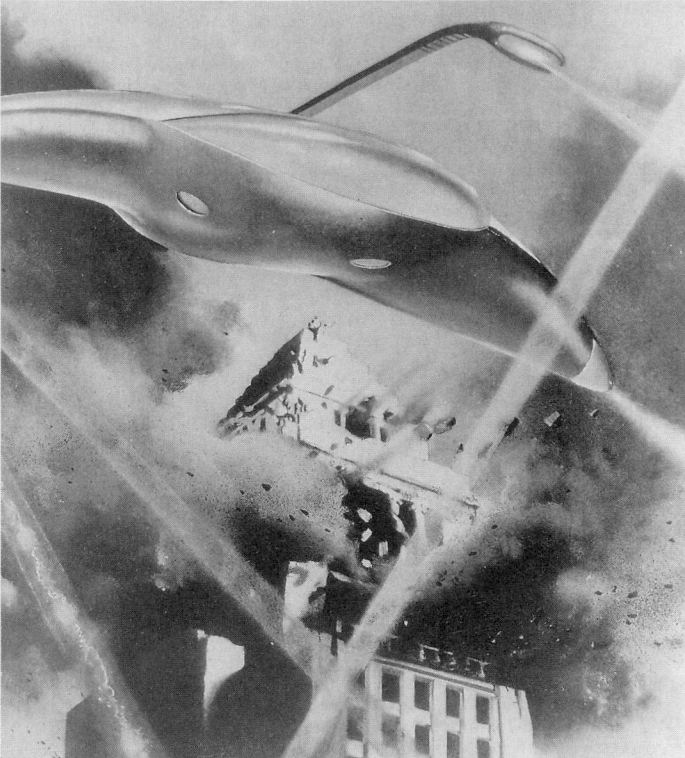

War Of The Worlds

Warning Shadows
see Schatten, eine Nachtliche Halluzination

Warning Sign
1985, (USA), Barwood-Robbins/20th-Fox, color, 100 mins.
<u>W</u>: Sam Waterston, Kathleen Quinlan, Yaphet Kotto, Jeffrey DeMunn, Richard Dysart, G.W. Bailey, Jerry Hardin, Keith Szarabajka, Rick Rossovich, Cynthia Carle, Scott Paulin, Kavi Raz, Jack Thibeau, J. Patrick McNamara, Tom McFadden, Kyle Heffner, Meshach Taylor, Lori Hallier, Jeanne Epper, Gilbert Smith
<u>D</u>: Hal Barwood   <u>SCR</u>: Hal Barwood & Matthew Robbins   <u>PHOTOG</u>: Dean Cundey   <u>SPCL-FX SPRVSR</u>: J. Kelvin Pike   <u>MUSIC</u>: Craig Safan
Standard SF-thriller: Lab mishap creates genetic zombies

War of the Colossal Beast
1958, (USA), Carmel/AIP, b&w (last seconds in color), 67 mins.
<u>W</u>: Dean Parkin *(Col. Glenn Manning)*, Sally Fraser *(Joyce)*, Roger Pace, Russ Bender, George Becwar, Rico Alaniz, June Jocelyn, Charles Stewart, Robert Hernandez, John McNamara, Loretta Nicholson, Jack Kosslyn, Raymond Winston, George Navarro, Bob Garnet, Stan Chambers, June Burt, Rod Dana, Howard Wright, Mary Hennessy, George Alexander, Bill Giorgio, George Milan, Warren Frost, Bob Tetrick
<u>P, D & STORY</u>: Bert I. Gordon   <u>SCR</u>: George Worthington Yates   <u>PHOTOG</u>: Jack Marta   <u>MUSIC</u>: Albert Glasser
orig. to be titled Revenge of the Colossal Man, orig. co-billed with Attack of the Puppet People, GB retitle, The Terror Strikes
Standard SF-thriller (sequel to The Amazing Colossal Man): Mutated giant returns to plague civilization

War of the Fools
1964, (Czech), b&w
<u>D</u>: Karel Zeman   <u>SCR</u>: Karel Zeman & Pavel Juracek
Standard fantasy: Three 17th-century people seek land without warfare

The War of the Gargantuas
1966, (Jap), Toho/UPA/Henry G. Saperstein/Maron, color, 93 mins.
<u>W</u>: Russ Tamblyn, Kipp Hamilton, Kenji Sahara, Kumi Mizuno, Jun Tazaki
<u>D</u>: Inoshiro Honda   <u>SCR</u>: Inoshiro Honda & Kaoru Mabuchi   <u>SONG</u>: *The Words Get Stuck in My Throat*
Minor SF-thriller: American scientist copes with prehistoric monsters, volcanic explosion

War of the Monsters
see Godzilla vs. Gigan

War of the Planets
1978, (It), Picturmedia Ltd., color, 89 mins.
<u>W</u>: John Richardson *(Hamilton)*, Yanti Somer, Max Karis, West Buchanan, Kathy Christine, Elly King, Percy Hogan, John Fortis, Dan Dublin, Romeo Constantin, Malisa Longo, Charles Borromel, Max Bonus, Aldy Canti
<u>D</u>: Al Bradley   <u>SCR</u>: Al Bradley & Al Crydo   <u>PHOTOG</u>: S. Fraschetti   <u>SPCL-FX</u>: Aldi Frollini   <u>MUSIC</u>: Marcel Giombrini & National Music

A.k.a. Cosmos-War of the Planets and *Cosmo 2000: Planet Without a Name*
Standard SF-thriller: Astronauts find world ruled by evil computer

War of the Robots
1978, (USA), color, 99 mins.
<u>W</u>: Antonio Sabato, Melissa long, James R. Stuart
Minor SF-thriller (similar to This Island Earth): Scientists from Earth kidnapped to save dying civilization

War of the Satellites
1958, (USA), AA, b&w, 72 mins.
<u>W</u>: Dick Miller, Susan Cabot, Richard Devon, Michael Fox, Eric Sinclair, Robert Shayne, Jerry Barclay, Jay Sayer, Mitzi McCall, Bruno Ve Sota, John Brinkley, Beech Dickerson
<u>P & D</u>: Roger Corman   <u>SCR</u>: Lawrence Louis Goldman   <u>PHOTOG</u>: Floyd Crosby   <u>MUSIC</u>: Walter Greene
Minor SF-melodrama

War of the Wizards
1983, (Taiwan), 21st Century, color, 72 mins.
<u>W</u>: Richard Kiel, Charles Lang, Betty Noonan
<u>D</u>: Richard Caan & Sam Arikawa   <u>SCR</u>: F. Kenneth Lin   <u>PHOTOG</u>: Mike Tomioka   <u>SPCL-FX</u>: Sam Arikawa   <u>MUSIC</u>: Lawrence Borden
A.k.a. The Phoenix
Minor action-fantasy: Space Alien Woman tries to conbquer Earth

The War of the Worlds
1953, (USA), Para, color, 85 mins.
<u>W</u>: Gene Barry *(Dr. Clayton Forrester)*, Ann Robinson *(Sylvia Van Buren)*, Les Tremayne *(Gen. Mann)*, Sandro Giglio *(Dr. Bilderbeck)*, Robert Cornthwaite *(Dr. Pryor)*, Lewis Martin *(Rev. Collins)*, Bill Phipps *(Wash Perry)*, Vernon Rich, Paul Frees, Henry Brandon, Jack Kruschen, Carolyn Jones, Ned Glass, Houseley Stevenson Jr., Walter Sande, Ivan Lebedeff, Pierre Cressoy, Nancy Hale, Alex Frazer, Virginia Hall, Charles Gemora, Ann Codee, John Maxwell, Robert Rockwell, Alvy Moore, Paul Birch, Frank Kreig
<u>P</u>: George Pal   <u>D</u>: Byron Haskin   <u>SCR</u>: Barre Lyndon, from H.G. Wells' novel   <u>PHOTOG</u>: George Barnes   <u>OSCAR-WINNING SPCL-FX</u>: Gordon Jennings, W. Wallace Kelley, Paul Lerpae, Ivyl Burks, Jay Domella & Irwin Roberts   <u>MUSIC</u>: Leith Stevens   <u>NARRATION</u>: Sir Cedric Hardwicke
"...the property sat on the Paramount shelves for almost twenty years before Pal decided to take a whack at filming it. A reported $2,000,000 was spent for this purpose, most of it for elaborate special effects. What ultimately emerged was a neatly directed thriller...highlighted by the stupendous visuals and a brilliant use of Technicolor"—Gary Gerani, "The Space Monster Book — Chapter Three: 'The War of the Worlds,'" Monster Fantasy, Vol. 1, No. 4 (August, 1975), p. 27
Classic SF-thriller: Martian war-machines ravage Earth

War of the Zombies
see Roma Contra Roma

The Warren Case
1934, (GB), BIP/Pathe, b&w, 75 mins.
<u>W</u>: Richard Bird *(Louis Bevan)*, Nancy Burne *(Mary Clavering)*, Diana Napier *(Pauline Warren)*, Edward Underdown *(Hugh Waddon)*, Iris Ashley *(Elaine de Lisle)*, A. Bromley Davenport *(Sir Richard Clavering)*
<u>D & SCR</u>: Walter Summers, from Arnold Ridley's play *The Last Chance*
Standard thriller: Mad reporter strangles mistress, frames fiance of employer's daughter

The Warrior and the Slave Girl
1958, (It), color, 84 mins.
<u>W</u>: Ettore Manni, Georges Marchal, Gianna Maria Canale, Rafael Calvo
<u>D</u>: Vittorio Cottafavi
Standard "Sword & Sandal": Roman subdues wicked princess

The Warrior and the Sorceress
1984, (USA), color, 76 mins.
<u>W</u>: David Carradine, Luke Askew, Maria Socas, Harry Townes, Anthony DeLongis, William Marin
<u>D</u>: John Broderick
Minor eroto-SF: Lone fighter in mythical kingdom on far planet. Conflict over water rights

Warrior Queen
1986, (GB), Harry Alan Towers/Lightning Pictures, color, 70 mins.
<u>W</u>: Sybil Danning, Donald Pleasence, Richard Hill, Tally Chanel, Josephine Jacqueline Jones, Stasia Micula, Suzanna Smith
<u>D</u>: Chuck Vincent   <u>SCR</u>: Rick Marx   <u>ORIG. STORY</u>: Peter Welbeck [Harry Alan Towers]   <u>MUSIC</u>: Ian Shaw & Kai Joffe
US release: Seymour Borde & Associates, 1987, 69 mins.
Minor "Sword & Sandal": Eve of destruction in Pompeii

Warriors of the Apocalypse
1985, (USA), color, 96 mins.
<u>W</u>: Michael James, Debrah Moore, Ken Metcalfe, Franco Guerrero
<u>D</u>: Bobby Suarez
A.k.a. Searchers of the Voodoo Mountain and Time Raiders
Minor SF-adventure: Post-nuke humans seek eternal life

Warriors of the Lost World
see *Warriors of the Wasteland*

Warriors of the Wasteland
1983, (It), Eduard Sarlui/A.D.I./New Line, color, 90 mins.
<u>W:</u> Robert Ginty, Persis Khambatta (*Nastasia*), Donald Pleasence (*Prossor*) Fred Williamson, Harrison Muller, Vinicio Recchi, Philip Dallas, Laura Nucci, Janna Ryan, Consuelo Marcaccini, Dan Stephen, Stefano Mior, Scott Coffey, Urs Althaus, Goffredo Marcaccini, Lucien Bruchon, Nguyen Huu Phu, Harrison Muller Jr., Giuliano Rosati, Russell Case, Ennio Antonelli, Hernani Moreira, Massimo Liti, Samuele Goldzader
<u>WRIT & D:</u> David Worth   <u>PHOTOG:</u> Giancarlo Ferrando   <u>MUSIC:</u> Daniele Patucchi
video-cassette retitle, **Warriors of the Lost World**
*Minor SF-thriller (**Road Warrior** imitation): Antagonistic sects in postnuke future*

Warriors of the Wind
1987, (Jap), New World, color, 95 mins.
<u>WRIT & D:</u> Hayao Miyazaki   <u>ANIMATION:</u> Kazuo Komatsubara
Standard SF-fantasy (animated): Space princess rules giant insects

Warriors of Virtue
1997, (USA–Hong Kong), MGM, color, 103 mins.
<u>W:</u> Mario Yedidia (*Ryan Jeffers*), Angus Macfayden (*Komodo*), Dennis Mung (*Ming*), Chao-Li Chi (*Master Chang*), Marley Shelton (*Elysia*), Stuart Kingston (*Dullard*), Qu Ying (*Barbarotious*), Lee Arenberg (*Mantose*)
<u>D:</u> Ronny Yu   <u>SCR:</u> Michael Vickerman & Hugh Kelley   <u>PHOTOG:</u> Peter Pau   <u>MUSIC:</u> Don Davis
Standard juvenile fantasy: Youth aids residents of mystical land

Warrior Women
see *La Vergine di Roma*

War Shock
see *A Woman's Devotion*

The Wasp Woman
1959, (USA), Filmgroup/AA, b&w, 73 mins.
<u>W:</u> Susan Cabot (*Janice Starlin*), Fred (Anthony) Eisley (*Bill Lane*), Barboura Morris (*Mary Dennison*), Michael Mark (*Eric Zinthrop*), William Roerick (*Arthur Cooper*), Roy Gordon (*Paul Thompson*), Bruno Ve Sota (*The Watchman*), Carolyn Hughes (*Jean Carson*), Lynn Cartwright (*Maureen Reardon*), Frank Gerstle (*Les Hellman*), Frank Wolff, Lani Mars, Aron Kincaid, Phillip Barry
<u>P & D:</u> Roger Corman   <u>SCR:</u> Leo Gordon , from a story by Kinta Zertuche   <u>PHOTOG:</u> Harry C. Newman   <u>MUSIC:</u> Fred Katz   <u>DESIGN:</u> Daniel Haller
orig. co-billed with **Beast from Haunted Cave**
blurb: "A beautiful woman by day—a lusting queen wasp by night!"
Standard SF-horror: Insect enzymes rejuvenate aging cosmetics tycoon

The Wasp Woman
1995, (USA), color, 90 mins.
<u>W:</u> Jennifer Rubin, Doug Wert, Daniel J. Travanti
Made-for-Cable, standard SF-horror (remake of cult classic): Businesswoman rejuvenated

The Watcher in the Woods
1980, (GB), Walt Disney/Buena Vista, color, 100 mins.
<u>W:</u> Bette Davis (*Mrs. Aylwood*), Carroll Baker (*Helen Curtis*), David McCallum (*Paul Curtis*), Lynn-Holly Johnson (*Jan Curtis*), Kyle Richards (*Ellie Curtis*), Ian Bannen (*John Keller*), Richard Pasco (*Tom Colley*), Frances Cuka (*Mary Fleming*), Benedict Taylor (*Mike Fleming*), Eleanor Summerfield (*Mrs. Thayer*), Georgina Hale (*Young Mrs. Aylwood*), Katherine Levy (*Karen Aylwood*)
<u>P:</u> Ron Miller   <u>D:</u> John Hough   <u>PHOTOG:</u> Alan Hume   <u>MUSIC:</u> Stanley Myers
Standard fantasy-thriller: Girl trapped in other dimension

Watchers
1988, (Can-USA), Rose & Ruby/Centaur/Concorde, color, 95 mins.
<u>W:</u> Corey Haim (*Tavis*), Barbara Williams (*Nora*), Michael Ironside (*Lem*), Lala (*Tracey*), Christopher Carey (*The TV Newscaster*), Graeme Campbell, Dan O'Dowd, Colleen Winton, Dale Wilson, Blu Mankuma, Duncan Fraser, Jason Priestley, Lou Bollo, Matt Hill, Andrew Markey, Norman Browning, Don S. Davis, Ghislaine Crawford, Justine Crawford, Frank C. Turner, Tong Lung, Keith Wardlow, Freda Perry, William Samples, Suzanne Ristic, Boyd MacConnachie, Phillip Wong, Sandy the Dog
<u>D:</u> Jon Hess   <u>SCR:</u> Bill Freed & Damian Lee, from Dean R. Koontz' novel   <u>PHOTOG:</u> Richard Leiterman   <u>MUSIC:</u> Joel Goldsmith
Standard SF-thriller: Mutants escape laboratory

Watchers Reborn
1998, (USA), color
<u>W:</u> Mark Hamill
Made-for-Video, standard SF-horror: Mutants rampage

Watchers II
1990, (USA-Can), Concorde/New Horizons, color, 97 mins.
<u>W:</u> Marc Singer (*Paul Ferguson*), Tracy Scoggins (*Barbara White*), Jonathan Farwell

(*Steve Maleno*), Irene Miracle (*Sarah Ferguson*), Mary Woronov (*Dr. Glatman*), Thomas W. Poster (*The Outsider*), Donald Pugsley (*Smith*), Joseph Hardin (*Wesson*), Kurt Braunreiter (*MP #1*), Merritt Yohnka (*MP #2*), Diana James (*Bell*), John LaFayette (*Watson*), Tom Hinkley (*The Lab Ass't*), Jeffrey Arbaugh (*Lead Protestor #1*), Stirling Bradley (*Lead Protestor #2*), Diedre Conrad (*The Female Protestor*), Eric Louis Levy (*Protestor #2*), Garon Grigsby (*The Security Guard*), Phil Nordell (*The Detective*), Jeremy Stanford (*The Policeman*), Kip Addota (*The Motel Clerk*), Christopher Thornton (*The Boy at the Motel*), Raquel Rios (*The Woman at the Motel*), Mary Ingersoll (*The Anchorwoman*), Dhiru Shah (*The Convenience Store Clerk*), Frank Roman (*The Puerto Rican*), Stan Yale (*Wino #1*), Sam Goffredo (*Wino #2*), Daryl Haney (*The Panhandler*), Harriet Price (*The Bag Lady*), James Smith (*The Gang Kid*), Dakai (*Einstein the Dog*)
<u>P:</u> Roger Corman   <u>D:</u> Thierry Notz   <u>SCR:</u> Henry Dominic, based on Dean R. Koontz' novel *Watchers*   <u>PHOTOG:</u> Edward Pei   <u>MUSIC:</u> Rick Conrad
Standard SF-thriller: Mutants flee gov't lab

Watchers III
1994, (USA), New Horizons, color, 84 mins.
<u>W:</u> Wings Hauser, Gregory Scott Cummins, Daryl Roach, John K. Linton, Lolita Ronalds, Frank Novak
<u>D:</u> Jeremy Stanford, inspired by Dean R. Koontz' novel *Watchers*
Standard SF-thriller: Scientist and intelligent dog vs. killer canine

Watch Me When I Kill
1981, (It), color, 95 mins.
<u>W:</u> Richard Stewart, Sylvia Kramer, Anthony Bido
Minor thriller: Murder ensnares nightclub dancer

The Water Babies
1979, (GB-Pol), Pethurst/Prods. Assocs./Ariadne/Studio Miniatur/WB, color, 92 mins.
<u>W:</u> James Mason (*Grimes*), Billie Whitelaw (*Mrs. Doasyouwouldbedoneby*), Bernard Cribbins (*Masterman*), Samantha Gates (*Ellie*), Joan Greenwood (*Lady Harriet*), David Tomlinson (*Sir John*), Tommy Pender (*Tom*), Paul Luty (*Sladd*)
<u>P:</u> Peter Shaw   <u>D:</u> Lionel Jeffries   <u>SCR:</u> Michael Robson, Lionel Jeffries & Denis Norden, from Charles Kingsley's novel   <u>PHOTOG:</u> Ted Scaife   <u>MUSIC:</u> Phil Coulter   <u>VOICES:</u> Jon Pertwee, Olive Gregg, Lance Percival, David Jason & Una Stubbs
Standard fantasy (live action & animation): Oppressed orphan becomes aquatic creature

The Water Babies: or, The Little Chimney Sweep
1907, (GB), Clarendon, b&w, 955 ft. (291.1m)
<u>D:</u> Percy Stow   <u>SCR:</u> Langford Reed, from Charles Kingsley's novel
Standard fantasy: Boy-sweep drowns while fleeing cruel master, is transformed into water sprite

Water Cyborgs
see *Terror Beneath the Sea*

The Water Rats of London
1914, (GB), B&C/DFSA, b&w, 1,846 ft. (562.7m)
<u>W:</u> Lillian Wiggins (*May*), Fred Morgan (*Dr. Chatiet*), Gladys Johnson (*Chariet's Daughter*)
<u>D & STORY:</u> James Youngdeer
Standard crime-thriller: Black Cross Gang woman returns doctor's kidnapped daughter

Watership Down
1978, (GB), Nepenthe Prods. Lmtd./Arco Embassy, color, 92 mins.
<u>VOICES:</u> John Hurt (*Hazel*), Richard Briers (*Fiver*), Denholm Elliott (*Cowslip*), Harry Andrews (*Gen. Woundwort*), Michael Hordern (*The Narrator*), Ralph Richardson (*The Chief Rabbit*), Zero Mostel (*Kehaar*), Michael Graham-Cox (*Bigwig*), John Bennett (*Capt. Holly*), Simon Cadell (*Blackberry*), Roy Kinnear (*Pipkin*), Richard O'Callaghan (*Dandelion*), Terence Rigby (*Silver*), Lyn Farleigh (*Cat*), Mary Maddox (*Clover*), Hannah Gordon (*Hyzenthlay*), Nigel Hawthorne (*Campion*), Clifton Jones (*Blackavar*), Joss Ackland (*Black Rabbit*)
<u>WRIT, P, & D:</u> Martin Rosen, from Richard Adams' best-selling novel   <u>MUSIC COMPOSED & ARRANGED:</u> Angela Morley   <u>MUSIC DIR:</u> Marcus Dods   <u>INCIDENTAL MUSIC:</u> Malcolm Williamson   <u>SONG:</u> (composed, Mike Batt; sung by Art Garfunkel), *Bright Eyes*
Animated classic: Allegorical tale of life among rabbits

Waterworld
1995, (USA), Univ, color, 120 mins.
<u>W:</u> Kevin Costner (*Mariner*), Jeanne Tripplehorn (*Helen*), Dennis Hopper (*Deacon*), Tina Majorino (*Enola*), Michael Jeter (*Gregor*), Gerard Murphy (*Nord*), R.D. Call (*Enforcer*), John Fleck (*Doctor*), Robert Joy (*Ledger Guy*)
<u>D:</u> Kevin Reynolds   <u>SCR:</u> Peter Rader & David Twohy   <u>PHOTOG:</u> Dean Semler   <u>MUSIC:</u> James Newton Howard
Lavish SF-adventure: Global warming causes polar caps to melt, sea level rises, survivors seek "Dryland"

The Watts Monster
see *Dr. Black Mr. Hyde*

Watusi
1959, (USA), Al Zimbalist/MGM, color, 85 mins.
<u>W:</u> George Montgomery, Taina Elg, David Farrar, Rex Ingram, Dan Seymour
<u>D:</u> Kurt Neumann   <u>SCR:</u> James Clavell, from characters created by H. Rider

Haggard **PHOTOG:** Harold E. Wellman
Standard adventure-thriller (sequel to 'King Solomon's Mines' {1950}): Adventurers seek fabulous treasure

Wavelength
1982, (USA), Wavelength Film Co./New World, color, 87 mins.
W: Robert Carradine (*Bobby Sinclair*), Cherie Currie (*Iris Longacre*), Keenan Wynn (*Dan*), Cal Bowman (*Gen. Milton Ward*), James Hess (*Col. James MacGruder*), Terry Burns (*Capt. Hinsdale*), Eric Morris (*Dr. Vernon Cottrell*), Bob McLean (*Dr. Benjamin Stern*), Eric Heath (*Dr. Stacy*), Dov Young (*Gamma*), Joshua Oreck (*Beta*), Christian Morris (*Delta*), Robert Glaudini (*Dr. Wolf*), George O. Petrie (*Saviland*), George Skaff (*Gen. Hunt*), Milt Kogan (*The Chief Pathologist*), Jim Elk (*Flemming*), Ivan Naranjo (*Warren*), Alan Koss (*The Military Attache*), Kent Butler (*The Young Lieutenant*), Brooke Hudson (*The Undercover Cop*), Cecil Jordan (*The Navajo Sheriff*), Marianne Bunch (*Laurie McCall*), Bobby DiCicco (*Marvin Horn*), Jamie Horton (*The Radioman*), Judd Laurance (*The Studio Engineer*), Jim Gosa (*Vince*), Dale E. House (*The Helicopter Pilot*), Ricardo T. Lopez, Brad M. Bucklin, David Carlton, Greg Hunter, Kelly Zapp, Al Kyper, Steve Rapp, Rif Hutton, Nugget (*Frank the Dog*)
WRIT & D: Mike Gray **PHOTOG:** Paul Goldsmith **SPCL-FX:** Mike Menzel **MUSIC:** Tangerine Dream **SONG:** *No More Lonely Days & All I Know for Sure*
Modest SF-thriller: Army studies aliens from downed UFO

Waxwork
1988, (USA), Vestron, color, 97 mins.
W: David Warner, Patrick Macnee, Zach Galligan, Deborah Foreman, Miles O'Keeffe, Michelle Johnson
D: Anthony Hickox
Minor horror-thriller: Teens terrorized by sinister proprietor of wax museum

Waxwork II: Lost in Time
1991, (USA), Electric Pictures, color, 104 mins.
W: Zach Galligan (*Mark Loftmore*), Alexander Godunov (*Lord Scarabus*), Monika Schnarre (*Sarah Brightman*), Martin Kemp (*Baron Von Frankenstein*), Bruce Campbell (*John Loftmore*), Michael Des Barres (*George*), Jon Metzler (*Roger*), Patrick Macnee (*Sir Wilfred*), Sophie Ward (*Elenore*), Marina Sirtis (*Gloria*), Billy Kane (*Nigel*), John Ireland (*King Arthur*), Juliet Mills (*The Defense Lawyer*), Joe Baker (*The Peasant*), David Carradine (*The Beggar*), Jack Eiseman (*The Cabbie*), George Buck Flower (*Stepfather*), Paul Hampton (*The Prosecution*), Buckley Norris (*The Judge*), Stanley Sheff (*The Speaker for the Jury*), John O'Leary (*Herr Vogel*), Elisha Shapiro (*Felix*), Stefanos Miltsakakis (*Frankenstein's Monster*), Maxwell Caulfield (*Mickey*), Erin Gourlay (*The Ghost Girl*), Bryan "Travis" Smith (*The Peasant Boy*), Guy Luthan (*The Master's Officer*), Steve Matteucci (*The Master's Guard*), Kate Murtagh (*The Matron*), Eyal Rimmon (*The Chief Worshipper*), Shanna L. Teare (*The Panther Girl*), Anthony Hickox (*The King's Officer*), Piers R.C. Plowden (*The King's Guard*), Harrison Young (*James Westbourne*), Ivan S. Markota (*The Press Man*), Marie Foti (*The Press Woman*), Frank Anthony Zagarino (*Zombie Killer #1*), Martin C. Jones (*Zombie Killer #2*), Darryl Pierce (*Zombie Killer #3*), John Breznikar (*Mark's Father*), Lisa Oestreich (*Mark's Mother*), Caron K. Berstein (*The Master's Girl*), Brent Bolthouse (*Cabbie #2*), Bob Keen (*The Mad Monk*), Chris Breed (*The King's Announcer*), Emile Gladstone (*The Jester*), Michael Viela (*Dr. Jekyll*), Gerry Lively, Yanko Damboulev, Jim Silverman, Paul Madigan, Kim Henderson, Treasure Little, Lisa Jay, Elizabeth Notteli, Achena Massey, Marcia Santos, Felicia Hernandez, Cristal Calderoni, Greg Woertz, Ilona Margolis, Martin Mercer, Dorian Langdon, John Mushroom Mappin, James Hickox, Erin Breznikar, Jonathan Breznikar, Mark Courier, Robert Kass, Steve Painter, Drew Barrymore, Hadria Lawner, Paul Jones, Alex Butler, Yolanda Jilot
WRIT & D: Anthony Hickox **PHOTOG:** Gerry Lively **ORIG. SCORE:** Steve Schiff
Standard SF-fantasy: Young couple flees through time

Waxworks
see Das Wachsfigurenkabinett

The Way
1923, (GB), b&w
D: Francis Bruguiere
Minor thriller

The Wayne Murder Case
see Strange Adventure

The Way Out
see Dial 999

Way...Way Out
1966, (USA), Way Out Co./20th-Fox, color, 101 mins.
W: Jerry Lewis, Connie Stevens (*Eileen Forbes*), Dick Shawn (*Igor*), Anita Ekberg (*Anna*), Robert Morley (*Harold Quonset*), Dennis Weaver (*Hoffman*), Howard Morris (*Schmidlap*), Brian Keith (*Gen. Hallenby*), Bobo Lewis (*Esther Davenport*), Sig Rumann, William O'Connell, Linda Harrison, Alex D'Arcy, James Brolin, Milton Frome
P: Malcolm Stuart **D:** Gordon Douglas **SCR:** William Bowers & Laszlo Vadnay **PHOTOG:** William H. Clothier **SPCL-FX:** L.B. Abbott, Emil Kosa Jr. & Howard Lydecker **MUSIC:** Lalo Schifrin, title sung by Gary Lewis & the Playboys
Standard SF-comedy: Misfit chosen for lunar tour of duty

The Weapon
1956, (GB), Periclean/Eros, b&w, 81 mins.
W: Steve Cochran (*Mark Andrews*), Herbert Marshall (*Insp. Mackenzie*), Lizabeth Scott (*Elsa Jenner*), George Cole (*Joshua Henry*), Nicole Maurey (*Vivienne*), Denis Shaw (*Groggins*), Jon Whiteley (*Eric Jenner*), John Horsley (*Johnson*), Laurence Naismith (*Jamison*), Stanley Maxted (*The Colonel*), Richard Goolden (*The Man*)
P: Hal E. Chester & Frank Bevis **D:** Val Guest **SCR:** Fred Freiberger **STORY:** Hal E.Chester
Standard crime-thriller: Runaway boy finds gun, is pursued by police and killer

Weapons for Vengeance
see Arms of the Avenger

We're Back! A Dinosaur's Story
1993, (USA), Steven Spielberg/Univ, 3D, color, 79 mins.
VOICES: Joey Shea (*Louie*), John Goodman (*Rex*), Felicity Kendal (*Elsa*), Walter Cronkite (*Capt. NewEyes*), Jay Leno (*Vorb*), Julia Child (*Dr. Bleeb*), Martin Short (*Stubbs the Clown*), Kenneth Mars (*Prof. Screw Eyes*), Rhea Perlman (*Mama Bird*)
P: Stephen Hickner **D:** Dick Zondag, Ralph Zondag, Phil Nibbelink & Simon Wells **SCR:** John Patrick Shanley, from Hudson Talbott's book **MUSIC:** James Horner
Standard animated fantasy: Dinosaurs visit New York City

The Weary Death
see Der Mude Tod

Weary Willie Steals a Fish
1908, (GB), Hepworth, b&w, 575 ft. (175.3m)
D: Lewin Fitzhamon
Standard fantasy: Tramp dreams of adventures under sea with submarine, mermaid, policeman, etc.

The Web
1947, (USA), Univ, b&w, 87 mins.
W: Ella Raines, Edmond O'Brien, William Bendix, Vincent Price, John Abbott, Maria Palmer, Fritz Leiber, Howland Chamberlin
D: Michael Gordon **SCR:** William Bowers **STORY:** Harry Kurnitz **PHOTOG:** Irving Glassberg **MUSIC:** H.J. Salter
Standard thriller: Bodyguard kills boss' arch enemy, finds himself double-crossed

Web of Danger
1947, (USA), Rep, b&w, 58 mins.
W: Adele Mara, Bill Kennedy
Minor thriller

Web of Deceit
1990, (USA), Sankan/Wilshire Court/Para, color, 95 mins.
W: Linda Purl, James Read, Paul de Souza, Larry Black, Len Birman, Barbara Rush (*Judith*), Ray McKinnon (*Stuart Troxel*), Danny Fendley (*The Mercedes Man*), Randi Layne (*The Mercedes Woman*), Tom Nowicki (*Det. Burdock*), Linda Pierce (*Ann Sorva*), Amy Bryson (*Mary Ellen Reese*), Tony Franciscus (*Officer #1*), Summer Still (*The Woman*), Jill Jane Clements (*Waitress #2*), Karen Beyer (*The Sec'y*), Len Harper (*Dr. Dubrow*), Patty Mack (*Reynolds*), Edith Ivey (*Binnie*), Alex Van (*Pryor*), Judson Vaughn (*Earl Culver*), Christina Reguli (*The Newswoman*), Robby Preddy (*Amanda*), Diana Brittain (*Helen*), Robert Harter (*Scott Ranfield*), Deborah Duke (*The Maid*), Benji Wilhoite (*The Valet*), Joan Riordan (*Gloria Grant*), Elizabeth Omilami (*The Hospital Receptionist*), Ric Reitz (*The Emergency Room Doctor*), Afemo Omilami (*The Bailiff*), Kathryn Roth (*Det. Broder*), Cavanaugh Yelling (*Willie*), Kenny Leon (*Dr. Poole*), Eric Ware (*Ken Houseman*)
WRIT & D: Sandor Stern **PHOTOG:** Chuck Arnold **MUSIC:** J.A.C. Redford
TVM, standard thriller: Woman attorney involved with murder suspect

Web of Evidence
see Beyond This Place

Web of Passion
see Leda

Web of Suspicion
1959, (GB), Danziger/Para, b&w, 70 mins.
W: Philip Friend (*Bradley Wells*), Susan Beaumont (*Janet Shenley*), John Martin (*Eric Turner*), Peter Sinclair (*Tom Wright*), Robert Raglan (*Insp. Clark*), Peter Elliott (*Watson*), Ian Fleming (*Forbes*), Rolf Harris (*Ben*), Hal Osmond (*Charlie*)
P: Edward J. & Harry Lee Danziger **D:** Max Varnel **STORY:** Brian Clemens & Eldon Howard
Standard thriller: Art mistress helps accused games master prove music teacher killed girl

Web of the Spider
1972, (It-Fr-Ger),Cinema Shares, color, 93 mins.
W: Tony Franciosa, Michele Mercier (*Elizabeth*), Klaus Kinski (*Edgar Allan Poe*), Peter Carsten
D: Anthony M. Dawson [Antonio Margheriti] **SCR:** Bruno Corbucci **MUSIC:** Riz Ortolani
A.k.a. In the Grip of the Spider, Dracula in the Castle of Blood, and And Comes the Dawn . . . But Colored Red

*Standard horror-fantasy (arty remake of **La Danza Macabra**): Journalist accepts wager, spends night in "haunted house"*

Wedding in Blood
1973, (Fr-It), New Line Cinemas, color, 98 mins.

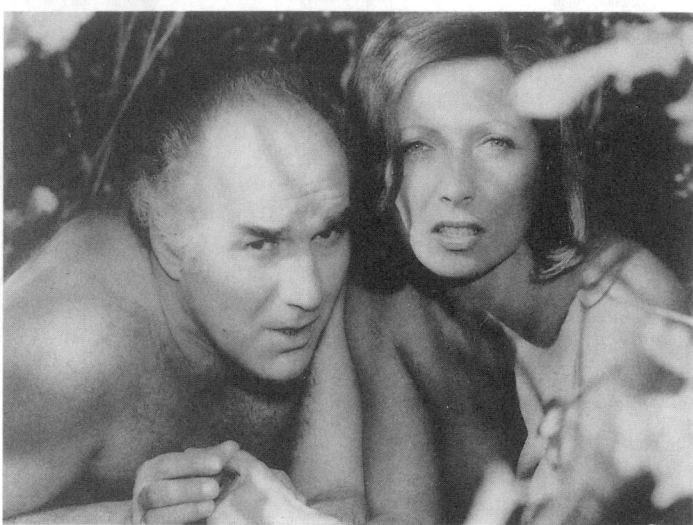

Wedding In Blood: MICHEL PICCOLI AND STEPHAN AUDRAN

<u>W:</u> Stephane Audran, Michel Piccoli
<u>D:</u> Claude Chabrol
Unusual thriller: Lovers conspire to kill spouses

We Do Believe in Ghosts
1947, (GB), WW British, b&w, 36 mins.
<u>W:</u> John Latham (*Gray*), Arthur Dibbs (*Henry VIII*), Valerie Carlish (*Anne Boleyn*)
<u>P & D:</u> Walter West
Standard fantasy short: Spirits of historical figures appear

Weekend of Fear
1966, (USA), J.D. Prods., b&w, 63 mins.
<u>W:</u> Ruth Trent, Kenneth Washman, Tory Alburn, Micki Malone, Dianne Danford
<u>P, D & SCR:</u> Joe Danford
Minor thriller: Widow hires deaf mute to eliminate girlfriend of handsome local boy

We Have 18 Years
*see **Tenemos 18 Anos***

Das Weib des Pharao (The Loves of Pharao)
1921, (Ger), Ufa/Par, b&w, 6 reels
<u>W:</u> Emil Jannings, Paul Wegener
<u>D:</u> Ernst Lubitsch
Standard melodrama

The Weird Ones
1962, (USA), Crescent/Colonial Int'l, b&w, 76 mins.
<u>W:</u> Mike Braden, Rudy Duran, Phyllis Warren, Lee Morgan
<u>P, D & SCR:</u> Pat Boyette
Minor SF-thriller: Press agents try to capture alien "astronik"

Weird Science
1985, (USA), Univ, color, 92 mins.
<u>W:</u> Anthony Michael Hall (*Gary*), Kelly LeBrock (*Lisa*), Ilan Mitchell-Smith (*Wyatt*), Bill Paxton (*Chet*), Suzanne Snyder (*Deb*), Judie Aronson (*Hilly*), Robert Downey (*Ian*), Robert Rusler (*Max*), Vernon Wells (*Lord General*), Britt Leach (*Al*), Barbara Lang (*Lucy*), Michael Berryman (*The Mutant Biker*), Ivor Barry (*Henry*), Anne Bernadette Coyle (*Carmen*), Suzy J. Kellems (*The Gymnast*), John Kapelos (*The Kandy Bar Owner*), Fred D. Scott, Vince Monroe Townsend, Chino Williams, Jill Whitlow, Theodocia Goodrich, Wally Ward, Johnny Timko, Kym Malin, Mikul Robins, Darren Harris, Babette Props, Michael Cramer, Todd Hoffman, D'Mitch Davis, Mary Steelsmith, Jeff Jensen, Robin Frohman, Alison Carole Lowe, Kevin Thompson, Jennifer Balgobin, Prince A. Hughes, Rick LeFevor, Pamela Gordon, Rock Walker, Joe Gieb, Doug MacHugh
<u>WRIT & D:</u> John Hughes <u>PHOTOG:</u> Matthew F. Leonetti <u>SPCL-FX:</u> Henry Millar, David M. Blitstein, Doug Hubbard, Roger Lifsey, Mike Millar & Richard Thompson <u>MUSIC:</u> Ira Newborn <u>SONG:</u> *Turn It On, Deep in the Jungle, Tesla Girls, Private Joy, Wanted Man, Method to My Madness, The Circle, Eighties & Nervous and Shakey*
Modest comedy-fantasy: High-school boys use computer wizardry to create ideal woman

Weird Woman
1944, (USA), Univ, b&w, 64 mins.
<u>W:</u> Lon Chaney Jr., Anne Gwynne, Evelyn Ankers, Samuel S. Hinds, Ralph Morgan, Lois Collier, Elizabeth Russell, Phil Brown, Elisabeth Risdon, Jackie Lou Harding, Harry Hayden
<u>D:</u> Reginald LeBorg <u>SCR:</u> Brenda Weisberg, loosely based on Fritz Leiber's clas-

sic novel *Conjure Wife* <u>PHOTOG:</u> Virgil Miller <u>MUSIC:</u> Paul Sawtell
*Standard thriller: College professor weds superstitious girl from Pacific island. cf. **Night of the Eagle** and **Witches' Brew***

Welcome to Arrow Beach
1974, (USA), Brut/WB, color, 89 mins.
<u>W:</u> Laurence Harvey (*Jason Henry*), Joanna Pettet (*Grace Henry*), Stuart Whitman (*Deputy Rakes*), Meg Foster (*Robbin Stanley*), John Ireland (*Sheriff H. "Duke" Bingham*), David Macklin (*Alex Heath*), Gloria LeRoy (*Ginger*), Altovise Gore (*Deputy Molly*), Elizabeth St. Clair (*The Head Nurse*), Tony Ballen (*Clifford*), Robert Lussier (*Deputy Lippencott*), Andy Romano (*Bryant*), Jesse Vint (*The Hot Rod Driver*), John Hart (*The Doctor*), Florence Lake (*The Landlady*), June Hedin (*The Hostess*), Janear Hines (*The Underground Reporter*), Winston Pruett (*Ape*), Peter Ireland (*Dale*)
<u>D:</u> Laurence Harvey <u>STORY & SCR:</u> Wallace C. Bennett <u>ADAPT:</u> Jack Gross Jr. <u>PHOTOG:</u> Gerald Perry Finnerman <u>MUSIC:</u> Tony Camillo
*A.k.a. **Tender Flesh***
blurb: "He killed more than he could eat"
Minor thriller: Psycho menaces girl drifter

Welcome to Blood City
1977, (GB-Can), Blood City/EMI/Famous Players, color, 96 mins.
<u>W:</u> Jack Palance (*Frendlander*), Keir Dullea (*Michael Lewis*), Samantha Eggar (*Katherine*), Barry Morse (*The Supervisor*), Hollis McLaren (*Martine*), Chris Wiggins (*Gellor*), Allan Royale (*Peter*), Henry Ramer (*Chumley*), John Evans (*Lyle*), Ken James (*Flint*), Larry Reynolds (*Bates*), Alan Crofoot (*Sarge*), Jack Creley (*Webb*), Chuck Shamata (*Ricardo*)
<u>P:</u> Marilyn Stonehouse <u>D:</u> Peter Sasdy <u>STORY:</u> Stephen Schneck & Michael Winder <u>PHOTOG:</u> Reginald Morris <u>MUSIC:</u> Roy Budd
Standard SF-thriller: Abductees trained to become assassins

Welcome to Oblivion
*see **Ultra Warrior***

Welcome II the Terrordome
1994, (GB), color, 94 mins.
<u>W:</u> Suzette Llewellyn, Saffron Burrows, Brian Bovell, Felix Joseph, Valentine Nonyela, Ben Wynter
<u>D:</u> Ngozi Onwurah
Unusual low-budget SF-thriller: Dystopic society of future black ghetto

The Well
1951, (USA), UA, b&w, 85 mins.
<u>W:</u> Richard Rober, Henry Morgan, Barry Kelley, Christine Larson, Maidie Norman, Ernest Anderson
<u>D:</u> Leo Popkin & Russell Rouse <u>SCR:</u> Russell Rouse & Clarence Greene <u>PHOTOG:</u> Ernest Laszlo
Well-made thriller: Child trapped in well

Well I'm—
1915, (GB), Martin/DFSA, b&w, 456 ft. (139m)
<u>D:</u> Edwin J. Collins
Standard fantasy: Man under hypnosis dreams he is the hypnotist

Went the Day Well?
1942, (GB), UA, b&w, 92 mins.
<u>W:</u> Leslie Banks, Elizabeth Allan, Frank Lawton, Basil Sydney, Valerie Taylor, Mervyn Jones, Marie Lohr, Edward Rigby, David Farrar, Thora Hird, Harry Fowler, John Slater
<u>P:</u> Michael Balcon <u>D:</u> Alberto Cavalcanti <u>STORY:</u> Graham Greene
Well-made wartime thriller: Undercover Nazis take over English town

We're Back ! A Dinosaur's Story
<u>VOICES:</u> Rene LeVant, Blaze Berdahl, Charles Fleischer, Yeardley Smith

The Werewolf
1913, (USA), Univ/Bison, b&w, 2 reels
<u>W:</u> Clarence Burton, Marie Walcamp
<u>D:</u> Henry McRae
Standard fantasy-thriller: Indian girl returns from death, takes form of wolf to avenge lover's murder

The Werewolf (1923)
*see **Le Loup-Garou***

The Werewolf
1956, (USA), Clover/Col, b&w, 83 mins.
<u>W:</u> Steven Ritch, Don Megowan, Joyce Holden, Kim Charney, Eleanore Tanin, Harry Lauter, James Gavin, George Cisar, Larry J. Blake, Ken Christy, S. John Launer, George E. Lynn
<u>P:</u> Sam Katzman <u>D:</u> Fred F. Sears <u>STORY & SCR:</u> Robert E. Kent & James B. Gordon <u>PHOTOG:</u> Lionel Linden <u>MUSIC:</u> Mischa Bakaleinikoff
Fr retitle: L'Empreinte du Loup-Garou (Mark of the Werewolf) orig. co-billed with Earth vs. the Flying Saucers
Standard horror-thriller: Scientists experiment on accident victim, turn him into lycanthrope

The Werewolf and the Yeti
*see **La Maldicion de la Bestia***

Werewolf in a Girl's Dormitory
see Lycanthropus

Werewolf of London
1935, (USA), Carl Laemmle/Univ, b&w, 74 mins.
<u>W</u>: Henry Hull (*Dr. Glendon*), Valerie Hobson (*Lisa Glendon*), Warner Oland (*Dr. Yogami*), Lawrence Grant (*Col. Forsythe*), Lester Matthews (*Paul Ames*), Spring Byington (*Miss Ettie Coombs*), Clark Williams (*Hugh Benwick*), Charlotte Granville (*Lady Forsythe*), J.M. Kerrigan (*Hawkins*), Reginald Barlow (*Dr. Phillips*), Louis Vincenot (*The Cooley*), Ethel Griffies, Jeanne Bartlett, Zeffie Tilbury
<u>P</u>: Stanley Bergerman <u>D</u>: Stuart Walker <u>SCR</u>: John Colton, from an orig. story by Robert Harris <u>PHOTOG</u>: Charles Stumar
Fr retitle, Le Monstre de Londres (The Monster of London)
Classic horror-fantasy: Scientist seeks rare Himalayan plant, is infected by lycanthrope

Werewolf of Washington
1973, (USA), Millco/Diplomat, color, 90 mins.
<u>W</u>: Dean Stockwell (*Jack*), Biff McGuire (*The President*), Clifton James (*The Attorney General*), Jane House (*Marion*), Beeson Carroll (*Cmdr. Salmon*), Michael Dunn (*Dr. Kiss*), Stephen Cheng (*The Foreign Minister*), Nancy Andrews (*Mrs. Captree*), Ben Yaffe (*The Judge*), Jacqueline Brookes (*The Publisher*), Barbara Siegel (*A Hippy*), Thurman Scott (*A Hippy*), Tom Scott (*The Reporter*), Dennis McMullen (*The Astronaut*), Jack Waltzer (*The Appointments Sec'y*), Randy Phillips (*The Federal Agent*), Glenn Kezer (*The Admiral*), Lenka Peterson, James Tolkan, John Garson, Danna Hansen, Richard Wexler, Mark Mezendez, Michael Sarossy, Richard Sorrentino, Li Ling Ai, Jim Campagna, Robert Patterson, Al Schneiderman, Robert Sheridan, Kenneth Moore, Edmond Dante, Rusty Blitz, Derek Steeley, Anita Daniels, Jerry Roth, Phil Denman, Jane Marla Robbins, Harry Stockwell, Norman Beim, Spencer Davis, Richard Marr, Charles Regan, Terry Alexander, John Henry Redwood, Joel Levitch, Kyle Rote, Jim Simpson, Jan Welt
<u>WRIT & D</u>: Milton Moses Ginsberg <u>PHOTOG</u>: Bob Baldwin <u>MUSIC</u>: Arnold Freed
Minor horror-spoof: Presidential aide becomes monster

Werewolf Woman
see The Legend of the Wolf Woman

The Werewolf vs. the Vampire Woman
see La Noche de Walpurgis

Werewolves on Wheels
1971, (USA), Fanfare, color, 85 mins.
<u>W</u>: Barry McGuire (*Scarf*), Billy Gray (*Bill*), Stephen Oliver (*Adam*), Severn Darden (*The High Priest*), D.J. Anderson (*Helen*), Duece Berry (*Tarot*), Gray Johnson (*Movie*), Owen Orr (*Mouse*), Anna Lynn Brown (*Shirley*), Leonard Rogel (*The Gas Station Operator*)
<u>P</u>: Paul Lewis <u>D</u>: Michel Levesque <u>SCR</u>: Michel Levesque & David M. Kaufman <u>PHOTOG</u>: Isidore Mankofsky <u>MUSIC</u>: Don Gere
Minor horror-thriller: Satanists turn two bikers into lycanthropes

Wes Craven Presents Mind Ripper
1995, (USA), color, 94 mins.
<u>W</u>: Lance Henriksen, John Diehl, Natasha Gregson Wagner, Dan Blom, Claire Stansfield
<u>D</u>: Joe Gayton <u>WRIT</u>: Jonathan Craven & Phil Mittleman <u>PHOTOG</u>: Fernando Arguelles <u>MUSIC</u>: J. Peter Robinson
A.k.a. Mind Ripper
Standard SF-horror: Monstrous beast stalks scientists in secret underground lab

Wes Craven's New Nightmare
1994, (USA), New Line, color, 111 mins.
<u>W</u>: Heather Langenkamp (*herself*), Robert Englund (*himself*), John Saxon (*himself*), Miko Hughes (*Dylan*), Tracy Middendorf (*Julie*), David Newsom (*Chase Porter*), Matt Winston (*Chuck*), Fran Bennett (*Dr. Heffner*), Rob LaBelle (*Terry*), Wes Craven (*himself*), Marianne Maddalena (*herself*), Robert Shaye (*himself*), Cully Fredricksen (*The Limo Driver*), Gretchen Oehler, Jeffrey John Davis, Bodhi Elfman, Sam Rubin, Claudia Haro, Sara Risher, Cindy Guidry, Ray Glanzmann, Michael Hagiwara, Yonda Davis, W. Earl Brown, Kenneth Zanchi, Tuesday Knight, Nick Corri, Beans Morocco, Tamara Mark, Lin Shaye, Deborah Zara Kobylt, Diana Nadeau, Star-Shemah, Lou Thornton, Tina Vail, Sandra Ellis Lafferty, Cynthia Savage, Jessica Craven, Thomas G. Burt
<u>WRIT & D</u>: Wes Craven <u>PHOTOG</u>: Mark Irwin <u>MUSIC</u>: J. Peter Robinson
Unusual horror-fantasy: Demonic forces terrorize horror-film actress

We Shall See
1964, (GB), Merton Park/Anglo-Amalgamated, b&w, 61 mins.
<u>W</u>: Maurice Kaufmann (*Evan Collins*), Faith Brook (*Alva Collins*), Alec Mango (*Ludo*), Alex McIntosh (*Greg Thomas*), Hugh Paddick (*Connell*), Talitha Pol (*Jirina*), Bridget Armstrong (*Rosemary Layton*), William Abney (*Shaw*)
<u>P</u>: Jack Greenwood <u>D</u>: Quentin Lawrence <u>SCR</u>: Donal Giltinian, from a novel by Edgar Wallace
Standard crime-thriller: Pilot's psychopathic wife murdered

West 11
1963, (GB), Dial Films/WPD, b&w, 93 mins.

<u>W</u>: Alfred Lynch (*Joe Beckett*), Kathleen Breck (*Ilsa Barnes*), Eric Portman (*Richard Dyce*), Diana Dors (*Georgia*), Sean Kelly (*Larry*), Kathleen Harrison (*Mrs. Beckett*), Finlay Currie (*Cash*), Freda Jackson (*Mrs. Hartley*), Harold Lang (*Silent*), Peter Reynolds (*Jacko*), Patrick Wymark (*Father Hogan*), Marie Ney (*Mildred Dyce*)
<u>P</u>: Daniel M. Angel <u>D</u>: Michael Winner <u>SCR</u>: Keith Waterhouse & Willis Hall, from Laura Del Rivo's novel *Furnished*
Standard crime-thriller: Ex-officer hires drifter to kill rich aunt

The Westland Case
1937, (USA), Univ, b&w, 64 mins.
<u>W</u>: Preston Foster (*Bill Crane*), Carol Hughes, Frank Jenks, Barbara Pepper, Astrid Allwyn, George Meeker, Arthur Hoyt, Theodore von Eltz, Clarence Wilson, Russell Hicks, Bryant Washburn, Rollo Lloyd, Selmer Jackson
<u>D</u>: Christy Cabanne <u>SCR</u>: Robertson White, from Jonathan Latimer's novel *Headed for a Hearse*
Standard thriller (1st "Bill Crane" mystery): Detective investigates girl's murder

West of Shanghai
1937, (USA), WB, b&w, 7 reels (64 mins.)
<u>W</u>: Boris Karloff, Gordon Oliver, Beverly Roberts, Ricardo Cortez, Sheila Bromley, Vladimir Sokoloff, Richard Loo
<u>D</u>: John Farrow <u>PHOTOG</u>: L. William O'Connell
Standard melodrama: Chinese warlord holds Westerners hostage

West of Suez
1957, (GB), Winwell/Astral, b&w, 75 mins.
<u>W</u>: Keefe Brasselle (*Brett Manders*), Kay Callard (*Pat*), Maya Koumani (*Men Hassa*), Karel Stepanek (*Langford*), Ursula Howells (*Eileen*), Bruce Seton (*Maj. Osborne*), Richard Shaw (*Cross*), Harry Fowler (*Tommy*), Sheldon Lawrence (*Jeff*)
<u>D</u>: Arthur Crabtree <u>SCR</u>: Norman Hudis <u>STORY</u>: Lance Z. Hargreaves
USA retitle, Fighting Wildcats
Standard crime-thriller: Gun traffickers plot to assassinate Arab leader

West of Zanzibar
1928, (USA), MGM, b&w, 6,150 ft. (1874.5m)
<u>W</u>: Lon Chaney Sr., Mary Nolan, Lionel Barrymore, Warner Baxter
<u>D</u>: Tod Browning, from a play by Chester de Vonde & Kilbourn Gordon
Standard thriller: Evil-doing in jungle. cf. Kongo

Westworld
1973, (USA), MGM, color, 91 mins.
<u>W</u>: Yul Brynner (*The Gunslinger*), James Brolin (*John Blane*), Richard Benjamin (*Peter Martin*), Dick Van Patten (*The Banker*), Alan Oppenheimer (*The Chief Supervisor*), Linda Scott (*Arlette*), Norman Bartold (*The Medieval Knight*), Victoria Shaw (*The Medieval Queen*), Steve Franken (*The Technician*), Michael Miller (*The Black Knight*), Julie Marcus (*The Girl in the Dungeon*), Robert Hogan (*The TV Announcer*), Majel Barrett (*Miss Carrie*), Nora Marlowe (*The Hostess*), Terry Wilson (*The Sheriff*), Anne Randall (*The Servant Girl*), Sharyn Wynters (*The Apache Girl*), Anne Bellamy (*The Middle-Aged Woman*), Chris Holter (*The Stewardess*), Charles Seel (*The Bellhop*), Wade Crosby (*The Bartender*), Will J. White, Ben Young, Tom Falk, Orville Sherman, Lindsay Workman, Howard Platt, Lauren Gilbert, Davis Roberts, Jared Martin, David Frank, Richard Roat, Kenneth Washington, Kip King, Robert Patten, David Man, Larry Delaney
<u>P</u>: Paul N. Lazarus III <u>WRIT & D</u>: Michael Crichton <u>PHOTOG</u>: Gene Polito <u>MUSIC</u>: Fred Karlin
Modest SF-thriller: Malfunctioning robots at adult resort. cf. Futureworld

Wet
see Splash

What!
see La Frusta e il Corpo

What a Carve Up!
1961, (GB), New World/Joseph E. Levine/Embassy, b&w, 88 mins.
<u>W</u>: Sidney James (*Syd*), Kenneth Connor (*Ernie*), Shirley Eaton (*Linda*), Dennis Price (*Guy*), Michael Gough (*Fisk*), Donald Pleasence (*Mr. Sloane*), Esma Cannon (*Aunt Emily*), Michael Gwynn (*Malcolm*), Valerie Taylor (*Janet*), George Woodbridge (*Dr. Edward*), Timothy Bateson (*The Porter*), Philip O'Flynn (*Gabriel/Arkwright*), Frederick Piper (*The Hearse Driver*), Adam Faith
<u>P</u>: Robert S. Baker & Monty Berman <u>D</u>: Pat Jackson <u>SCR</u>: Ray Cooney & Tony Hilton, based on Frank King's novel *The Ghoul* <u>PHOTOG</u>: Monty Berman
USA retitle, No Place Like Homicide
Standard comedy-thriller: Rich madman fakes own death, stalks relatives

What a Night!
1931, (GB), BIP/First Nat'l-Pathe, b&w, 58 mins.
<u>W</u>: Leslie Fuller (*Bill Grimshaw*), Molly Lamont (*Nora Livingstone*), Frank Stanmore (*Mr. Livingstone*), Charles Paton (*Grindle*), Syd Courtenay (*Mr. Merry*), Ernest Fuller (*The Landlord*), Molly Hamley-Clifford (*The Landlady*), Olivette (*Rose*)
<u>D</u>: Monty Banks <u>STORY</u>: Syd Courtenay & Lola Harvey
Standard comedy-thriller: Traveler catches burglar at "haunted" inn

What a Way to Fly
see Those Fantastic Flying Fools

What a Woman Will Do
1914, (GB), Regent/MP, b&w, 3,000 ft. (916.9m)
D: Charles Weston
Standard crime-thriller: Girl seeks to avenge her innocent father's conviction, tries to kill judge's son

What Became of Jack and Jill
1972, (GB), Amicus/Palomar/20th-Fox, color, 93 mins.
W: Paul Nicholas (*Jack*), Vanessa Howard (*Jill*), Mona Washbourne (*Gran*), Peter Jeffrey (*Dr. Graham*), Peter Copley (*Dickson*), Patricia Fuller (*Frankie*), Renee Roberts (*The Neighbor*), George A. Cooper (*Trouncer*), Angela Down (*The Jehovah's Witness*), Lillias Walker (*The Secretary*), George Benson (*The Minister*)
P: Max J. Rosenberg & Milton Subotsky   **D:** Bill Bain   **SCR:** Roger Marshall based on Laurence Moody's novel *The Ruthless Ones*   **PHOTOG:** Gerry Turpin   **MUSIC:** Carl Davis
Off-beat thriller: Youth plots to kill aged grandmother

What Dreams May Come
1998, (USA), Polygram, color
W: Robin Williams, Cuba Gooding Jr., Annabella Sciorra, Max von Sydow
D: Vincent Ward   **SCR:** Ron Bass   MUSIC: Michael Kamen
Lavish fantasy-melodrama: Suicide seeks lost love in the afterlife

What Ever Happened to Aunt Alice?
1969, (USA), Assocs. & Aldrich-Palomar/CRC, color, 101 mins.
W: Geraldine Page (*Mrs. Mirabel*), Ruth Gordon (*Mrs. Dimmock*), Rosemary Forsyth (*Harriet Vaughn*), Robert Fuller (*Mike*), Mildred Dunnock (*Miss Edna Tinsley*), Peter Bonerz (*Mr. Bentley*), Joan Huntington, Peter Brandon, Lou Kane, Michael Barbera, Valerie Allen, Claire Kelly, Seth Riggs, Jack Bannon
P: Robert Aldrich   **D:** Lee H. Katzin   **SCR:** Theodore Apstein, from Ursula Curtiss' novel *The Forbidden Garden*   **PHOTOG:** Joseph Biroc   **MUSIC:** Gerald Fried

Whatever Happened To Aunt Alice? : JOAN HUNTINGTON, CLAIRE KELLY AND VALERIE ALLEN

Modest thriller: Sinister widow murders paid companions

What Ever Happened to Baby Jane?
1962, (USA), 7Arts/WB, b&w, 132 mins.
W: Bette Davis ("*Baby Jane*" *Hudson*), Joan Crawford (*Blanche Hudson*), Victor Buono (*Edwin Flagg*), Anna Lee (*Mrs. Bates*), Maidie Norman (*Elvira Stitt*), Marjorie Bennett (*Mrs. Flagg*), Julie Allred (*Young Jane*), Gina Gillespie (*Young Blanche*), Barbara Merrill (*Liza Bates*), Dave Willock (*Ray Hudson*), Bert Freed (*The Producer*), Wesley Addy (*The Director*), Ann Barton (*Cora Hudson*), Robert Cornthwaite (*The Doctor*), Bobs Watson, Ernest Anderson, Michael Fox
P & D: Robert Aldrich   **SCR:** Lukas Heller, from Henry Farrell's novel   **PHOTOG:** Ernest Haller   **SPCL-FX:** Don Steward   **MUSIC:** Frank De Vol   **SONG:** *I've Written a Letter to Daddy*
"Achieves its goals with something breathlessly close to perfection...A shocker in the best Hitchcock tradition" —Arthur Knight, Saturday Review
"The year's scariest, funniest and most sophisticated chiller"—Time
Classic thriller: Faded child actress torments crippled sister

What Ever Happened to Baby Jane?
1991, (USA), ABC-TV, color, 95 mins.
W: Vanessa Redgrave (*Blanche Hudson*), Lynn Redgrave (*Jane Hudson*), John Glover (*Billy Cork*), Amy Steel (*Connie Trotter*), John Scott Clough (*Frank Trotter*), Bruce A. Young (*Dominick*)
D: David Greene   **TELEPLAY:** Brian Taggert, from Henry Farrell's novel
PHOTOG: Stevan Larner   **MUSIC:** Peter Manning Robinson
TVM, standard thriller: Former child star becomes demented

What Ever Happened to Cousin Charlotte?
see Hush...Hush, Sweet Charlotte

What's Bred...Comes Out in the Flesh
1916, (GB), Master/Kino Exclusives, b&w, 3,374 ft. (1028.4m)
W: Janet Alexander (*Elma*), Lauderdale Maitland (*Judge Gildersleve*), Frank Tennant (*Kelvin Scott*), Richard Norton (*Nevitt*), H.J. Lord (*Guy*), Rupert Stutfield (*Cyril*)
D & SCR: Sidney Morgan, from Grant Allen's novel *What's Bred in the Bone*
Standard crime-thriller: Judge tries man for his own crime, but confesses in court when gypsy makes him "see" event

What Lies Beneath
1999, (USA), Dreamworks SKG, color
W: Harrison Ford, Michelle Pfeiffer
D: Robert Zemeckis
Standard SF-thriller

What Lola Wants
see Damn Yankees

What Men Will Do
1914, (GB), B&C/DFSA, b&w, 1,972 ft. (601.1m)
W: Arthur Finn, Marie Pickering
D: Charles Weston
Standard crime-thriller: Man robs remarried wife's house, gets trapped in safe

What on Earth?
1967, (Can), color
Minor fantasy-thriller

What Price Murder
1957, (Fr), Speva Films/UMPO, b&w, 105 mins.
W: Henri Vidal, Mylene Demongeot, Isa Miranda, Jean Lou Philippe, Alfred Adam, Simone Bach, Antonin Berval, Ky Duyen, Jean Galland, Andre Roanne, Marc Vabbel
D: Henri Verneuil   **SCR:** Henri Verneuil, Annette Wademant & Francois Boyer, from a novel by James Hadley Chase
orig to be titled Une Manche et la Belle (Beauty is Only Skin Deep)
Modest thriller

What's in It for Harry?
see Target: Harry

What's the Matter with Helen?
1971, (USA), Filmways-Raymax/UA, color, 101 mins.
W: Shelley Winters (*Helen Hill*), Debbie Reynolds (*Adelle Bruckner*), Dennis Weaver (*Lincoln Palmer*), Agnes Moorehead (*Sister Alma*), Sammee Lee Jones (*Winona Palmer*), Helene Winston (*Mrs. Greenbaum*), Molly Dodd (*Mrs. Rigg*), Michael MacLiammoir (*Hamilton Starr*), Robbi Morgan (*Rosalie Greenbaum*), Pamelyn Ferdin (*The Kiddy M.C.*), Timothy Carey (*The Tramp*), Peggy Rea (*Mrs. Schultz*), Debbie Van Den Houten (*Sue Anne Schultz*), Yvette Vickers (*Mrs. Barker*), Paulle Clark (*Mrs. Plumb*), Tammy Lee (*Charlene Barker*), Teresa De Rose (*Donna Plumb*), Swen Swenson (*The Gigolo*), Harry Stanton (*Malcolm Hays*), James Dobson (*The Cab Driver*), Logan Ramsey (*Det. West*), Peggy Lloyd Patten (*Ellie Banner*), Gary Combs (*Matt Hill*), Sadie Delfino (*The Midget Lady*), Annette Davis (*The Spinster*), Helene Heigh (*The Widow*), Peter Brocco (*The Old Man*), Minta Durfee Arbuckle (*The Old Lady*), Peggy Walton (*The Young Girl*), Douglas Deane (*The Fanatical Man*), Reggie Nalder
P: George Edwards   **D:** Curtis Harrington   **SCR:** Henry Farrell   **PHOTOG:** Lucien Ballard   **MUSIC:** David Raksin
Standard thriller: Madness and murder among Hollywood set

What The?
1915, (GB), Bamforth/YCC, b&w, 411 ft. (125.3m)
W: Alf Scotty (*Alf*)
D: Cecil Birch
Standard fantasy: Butcher has nightmare

What the Peeper Saw
see Night Hair Child

What Waits Below
see Secrets of the Phantom Caverns

What We Did That Night
1999, (USA), Rysher/ABC-TV, color, 95 mins.
W: Rick Schroder, Jack Noseworthy, Michael Easton, Jayce Bartok, Tara Reid, Jillian Berard, Maryann McKellor, Koi Soremekun, Andi Motheny
D: Paul Shapiro   **TELEPLAY:** Eric Harlacher   **PHOTOG:** Brian J. Reynolds   **MUSIC:** Dana Kaproff
TVM, standard thriller: Old crime threatens to be revealed

The Wheel of Death
1910, (GB), E.B. Davidson/Tilly, b&w, 3,000 ft. (914.4m)
W: Arthur Rooke (*John Drew*), Joan Legge (*Pickles*), Frank Rosbert Cheroka (*Hastings*), Charles Vane (*The Professor*), Peggy Richards (*Mrs. Merton*)

D: A.E. Coleby
Standard crime-thriller: Blackmailer kidnaps woman, traps detective in mad professor's torture chamber

Wheel of Fire
see **Pyro**

Wheels of Terror
1990, (USA), Wilshire Court/USA-TV, color, 95 mins.
W: Joanna Cassidy (*Laura*), Marcie Leeds (*Stephanie*), Arlen Dean Snyder (*Det. Drummond*), Carlos Cervantes (*Luis*), Henry Max Kendrick (*Kellogg*), Sharon Thomas (*Amy Donaldson*), Jacob Kenner (*Brad*), Julie Hasel (*The Girl on the Bus*), Kimberly Duncan (*Kimberly Donaldson*), Jon Conrad Pochron (*The Motorcycle Officer*), Mindy Spence (*Stacy Harrison*), Kirk Nelson (*The Sheriff*), Kristina Betts (*The Girl Victim*), Bill Yarbrough (*The Girl's Father*), Roger Roon (*The Pastor*), "Bear" Cheney (*The Gym Trainer*), Liz Romero (*The Police Clerk*), John McCabe (*The Boy*), Robert Elliott (*Mr. Donaldson*), Fred Sugarman, Richard Hardy, Maria Amarocho, Carolyn Pain
D: Christopher Cain **TELEPLAY:** Alan B. McElroy **PHOTOG:** Richard Bowen **SPCL-FX:** Mike Woods **MUSIC:** Jay Gruska
TVM, minor thriller: Sinister car menaces young girls

When a Stranger Calls
1979, (USA), Col, color, 97 mins.
W: Carlo Kane (*Jill Johnson*), Charles Durning (*John Clifford*), Colleen Dewhurst (*Tracy Fuller*), Rachel Roberts (*Dr. Monk*), Tony Beckley (*Curt Duncan*), Ron O'Neal (*Lt. Charlie Garber*), Steve Anderson (*Stephen Lockhart*), Joe Reale (*The Bartender*), Rutanya Alda (*Mrs. Mandrakis*), Carmen Argenziano (*Dr. Mandrakis*), Kirsten Larkin (*Nancy*), Bill Boyett (*Sgt. Sacker*), Heetu (*The Houseboy*), Michael Champion (*Bill*), Ed Wright (*The Retired Man*), Louise Wright (*The Retired Woman*), Carol O'Neal (*Mrs. Garber*), Dennis McMullen (*The Maintenance Man*), Wally Taylor (*The Cheater*), John Tobyansen (*The Bar Customer*), Sarah Dammann (*Bianca Lockart*), Richard Bail (*Stevie Lockart*), Lenora May (*Sharon*), Randy Holland (*The Maitre d'*), Trent Dolan, Frank Dielsi, Arell Blanton, DeForest Covan, Charles Boswell
P: Doug Chapin & Steve Feke **D:** Fred Walton **SCR:** Fred Walton & Steve Feke **PHOTOG:** Don Peterman **MUSIC:** Dana Kaproff
"*Unequivocally the most terrifying movie I've ever seen*" —After Dark
Gripping thriller: Psycho terrorizes babysitter

When a Stranger Calls Back
1993, (USA), Krost-Chapin/Prods. Entertainment Group/Pacific/Univ, (cable), color, 96 mins.
W: Carol Kane, Charles Durning, Jill Schoelen, Gene Lythgow, Kevin McNulty
P: Tom Rowe **WRIT & D:** Fred Walton, from characters created by Steve Feke & Fred Walton **PHOTOG:** David Geddes **MUSIC:** Dana Kaproff
Made-for-Cable, standard thriller (sequel to **When a Stranger Calls***): Phantom maniac stalks coed*

When Boys Leave Home
see **Downhill**

When Clubs Were Clubs
1915, (GB), Martin/DFSA, b&w, 700 ft. (213.4m)
W: Ernie Westo, Bob Reed, Johnny Butt
D: Dave Aylott
Standard comedy-fantasy: Prehistoric caveman rescues girl from ruffians

When Dinosaurs Ruled the Earth
1969, (GB), Hammer/WB, color, 100 mins.
W: Victoria Vetri (*Sanna*), Robin Hawdon (*Tara*), Drewe Henley (*Khaku*), Patrick Allen (*Klingsor*), Sean Caffrey (*Kane*), Connie Tilton (*The Sand Mother*), Patrick Holt (*Ammon*), Jan Rossini (*The Rock Girl*), Imogen Hassall (*Ayak*), Magda Konopka (*Ulido*), Maria O'Brien (*Omah*), Carol-Anne Hawkins (*Yani*), Maggie Lynton (*The Rock Mother*), Jimmy Lodge, Ray Ford, Billy Cornelius
P: Aida Young **WRIT & D:** Val Guest **PHOTOG:** Dick Bush **SPCL-FX:** Jim Danforth **MUSIC:** Mario Nascimbene
Well-made SF-fantasy: Prehistoric beauty flees tribe to avoid becoming human sacrifice

When East Meets West
1915, (GB), Clarendon, b&w, 3,000 ft. (914.4m)
W: Dorothy Bellew (*The Girl*)
D: Wilfred Noy **STORY:** Marchioness of Townshend
Standard thriller: Indian fakir hypnotizes officer's daughter

When Knights Were Bold
1916, (GB), London/Jury, b&w, 4,800 ft. (1463m)
W: James Welch (*Sir Guy de Vere*), Gerald Ames (*Sir Brian Ballymote*), Hayford Hobbs (*Widdicombe*), Gwynne Herbert (*Isaacson*), Philip Hewland (*Barker*), Bert Wynne (*Whittle*), Edna Maude (*Aunt Thornridge*), Marjorie Day (*The Maid*)
D: Maurice Elvey **SCR:** Frank Miller, from a play by Charles Marlow
Standard comedy-fantasy: Commoner dreams of medieval days

When Knights Were Bold
1929, (GB), B&D/W&F, b&w, 7,213 ft. (2198.5m)
W: Nelson Keys (*Sir Guy de Vere*), Miriam Seegar (*Lady Rowena*), Eric Bransby Williams (*Sir Brian Ballymote*), Lena Halliday (*Lady Walgrave*), Wellington

Briggs (*Widdicombe*), Martin Adeson (*Barker*), Hal Gordon (*Whittle*), E.L. Frewen (*Dean*), Edith Kingdon (*Aunt Thornridge*)
D: Tim Whelan **SCR:** Tim Whelan & Herbert Wilcox, from a play by Charles Marlow
Standard fantasy: Unpopular heir dreams of medieval days

When Knights Were Bold
1936, (GB), Capitol/GFD, b&w, 75 mins.
W: Jack Buchanan (*Sir Guy de Vere*), Fay Wray (*Lady Rowena*), Garry Marsh (*Brian Ballymote*), Kate Cutler (*Aunt Agatha*), Martita Hunt (*Aunt Esther*), Robert Horton (*Cousin Bertie*), Aubrey Mather (*Canon*), Aubrey Fitzgerald (*Barker*), Robert Nainby (*Whittle*), Moore Marriott (*The Tramp*)
D: Jack Raymond **SCR:** Austin Parker & Douglas Furber, from a play by Charles Marlow
US release: Fine Arts, 1942, 57 mins., reissued 1942 & 1947
Standard musical-fantasy: Lieutenant dreams of medieval days

When London Burned
see **Old St. Paul's**

When London Sleeps
1914, (GB), B&C/Ideal, b&w, 3,357 ft. (1023.2m)
W: Lillian Wiggins (*Queenie Carruthers*), Douglas Mars (*David Engelhardt*), George Foley (*The Captain*)
D: Ernest G. Batley, from a play by Charles Darrell
Standard crime-thriller: Captain tries to kill heiress by fire

When Michael Calls
1972, (USA), 20th-Fox/NBC-TV, color, 73 mins.
W: Ben Gazzara, Elizabeth Ashley, Michael Douglas, Albert S. Waxman, Karen Pearson, Larry Reynolds, Marian Waldman, Christopher Pellett, Alan McRae, Steve Weston, John Bethune, Robert Warner, Michael Chicoine
D: Philip Leacock **TELEPLAY:** Jim Bridges **MUSIC:** Lionel Newman
A.k.a. **Shattered Silence** *or* **House on Highway 5**
TVM, standard thriller: Telephone calls from boy believed dead

When Other Lips . . .
1908, (GB), Warwick Trading Co., b&w
D: Charles Raymond
Standard melodrama: 18th-century general duels cavalier who eloped with his wife

When Paths Diverge
1913, (GB), Barker, b&w, 1,295 ft. (395m)
W: Thomas H. MacDonald (*Jack Cotterell*), Irene Vernon (*Mary Milton*), Fred Paul (*Squire Miton*), Edward Viner (*The Hunchback*), Roy Travers (*Jim*), Rachel de Solla (*Mrs. Cotterell*)
D: Bert Haldane **SCR:** Rowland Talbot
Standard crime-thriller: Crooks steal squire's keys, frame ex-convict secretary

When Passions Rise
1915, (GB), Clarendon/Walturdaw, b&w, 2,855 ft. (870.2m)
D: Wilfred Noy
Standard crime-thriller: Villain abducts rival's fiancee

When Pigs Fly
1996, (USA), Panorama Entertainment, color, 94 mins.
W: Alfred Molina (*Marty*), Marianne Faithfull (*Lilly*), Seymour Cassel (*Frank*), Rachael Bella (*Ruthie*), Maggie O'Neill (*Sheila*), Tarzan (*Dolphy the dog*)
D: Sara Driver **SCR:** Ray Dobbins **PHOTOG:** Roby Muller **MUSIC:** Joe Strummer
Unusual fantasy: Lonely musician meets ghosts of woman and little girl

When Quackel Did Hyde
1920, (USA), Gold Seal/Aywon, b&w, 5 reels
W: Charlie Joy
D: Charles Gramlich, based on Robert Louis Stevenson's *Dr. Jekyll and Mr. Hyde*
Standard spoof: Man transmogrified by potion

When the Bough Breaks
1993, (USA), Osmosis/Prism, color, 106 mins.
W: Ally Walker (*Audrey Macleah*), Martin Sheen (*Capt. J.S. Swaggert*), Ron Perlman (*Dr. Eben*), Ron Knepper (*Creedmore*), Tara Subkoff (*Jordan/Jenny*), Scott Lawrence (*Foots*), John P. Conolly (*Belvin*), Dick Welsbacher (*Hess*), Jimmy Medina (*Delarand*), Ron Recasner (*Singer*), Juan Antonio Devoto (*Danny*), Christopher Doyle (*Speckett*), Michael Raysses (*The Sonar Technician*), Mark Daneri (*Det. Sam*), William A. Porter (*The Old Man*), Taylor Brock (*The Anchor*), Karen Radcliffe (*Mrs. Klugman*), Tim Halligan (*Mr. Klugman*), Steve Kehela (*Policeman #1*), Julianna McCarthy (*Mrs. Voss*), Rod Britt (*The Father*), Gina Phillips (*The Teenage Girl*), Richard Morrison (*The Custodian*), Jack Anker (*The Taxi Driver*), Don Pugsley (*The Crew Foreman*), Melissa Clayton (*Jenny Double*)
WRIT & D: Michael Cohn **PHOTOG:** Michael Bonvillain **MUSIC:** Ed Tomney **SONG:** *My Heroine, Enough Is Never Enough, I Can't Stop & Two Marys*
Standard thriller: Woman detective hunts killer of children

When the Dark Man Calls
1995, (USA), USA-TV, color, 96 mins.
W: Joan Van Ark, Chris Sarandon, Geoffrey Lewis, James Read. Frances Hyland,

Janet-Laine Green
D: Nathaniel Gutman **TELEPLAY:** Pablo F. Fenjves, from a novel by Stuart M. Kaminsky
TVM, standard thriller: Killer stalks woman radio psychologist

When the Devil Drives
1907, (GB), Urban, b&w, 390 ft. (118.9m)
D: Walter R. Booth
reissued 1913
Standard fantasy: Satan drives train over telegraph wires, under sea, etc.

When the Earth is Opening
see Crack in the World

When the Man in the Moon Seeks a Wife
1908, (GB), Clarendon, b&w, 970 ft. (295.7m)
D: Percy Stow **STORY:** Langford Reed
Standard fantasy: Man in the Moon comes to Earth in gas balloon

When the Screaming Stops
1973, (Sp), Independent Artists/Intervid, color, 86 mins.
W: Tony Kendall, Helga Line, Silvia Tortosa
P: Ricardo Sanz & Ricardo Munoz Suay **D & SCR:** Armando De Ossorio
Standard horror-fantasy: Beauty turns into reptile monster

When the Wind Blows
1986, (GB), John Coates/Kings Road/Int'l Video, color, 81 mins.
W: Dame Peggy Ashcroft *(Hilda's Voice)*, Sir John Mills *(James' Voice)*
D: Jimmy T. Murakami **SCR:** Raymond Briggs, from his novel
USA release, 1988
Standard animated satire: Elderly couple faces nuclear holocaust

When Time Expires
1996, (USA), color
W: Richard Grieco, Mark Hamill *(Bill)*, Cynthia Geary *(June)*
Standard SF-thriller: Time-traveler must save Earth

When Time Ran Out
1980, (USA), WB, color, 110 mins (video version: 141 mins.).
W: Paul Newman *(Hank Anderson)*, Jacqueline Bisset *(Kay Kirby)*, William Holden *(Shelby Gilmore)*, Edward Albert *(Brian)*, Red Buttons *(Francis Fendly)*, Valentina Cortese *(Rose Valdez)*, Barbara Carrera *(Iolani)*, Ernest Borgnine *(Tom Conti)*, James Franciscus *(Bob Spangler)*, Veronica Hamel *(Nikki)*, Alex Karras *(Tiny Baker)*, John Considine *(Webster)*, Burgess Meredith *(Rene Valdez)*, Sheila Allen *(Mona)*, Pat Morita *(Sam)*, Darrell Larson Lonny Chapman *(Kelly)*, Sandy Kenyon *(Henderson)*, Marcus Mukai *(Wrangler)*, Ted Gehring *(Durant)*, Joe Papalimu Ijaylin Maureen Acol, Reed Derwin Acol, Barbara Costello, Ava Readdy, Glynn Rubin, Takayo Doran, James Gavin, M. James Arnett, Marcia Nicholson, Bill Smillie, Steven Marlo, Esmond Chung, Jeffrey McDevitt, John Springer Jr.
P: Irwin Allen **D:** James Goldstone
orig. to be titled **Day the World Ended**, *TV retitle,* **Earth's Final Fury**
Standard thriller: Volcano and tidal wave threaten tropic isle

When Woman Hates
1916, (GB), British Empire Films, b&w, 5,500 ft. (1676.4m)
W: Henry Lonsdale, Mercy Hatton, Jose Brooks
D & SCR: Albert Ward, from a play by Fred Bulmer
Standard crime-thriller: Gambler forces girl to rob father and frame her brother for murder

When Women Had Tails
1973, (It), Clesi/Film Ventures-Int'l, color, 99 mins.
W: Senta Berger, Frank Wolff, Paolo Corboni, Lino Toffolo, Giuliano Gemma, Lando Buzzanca, Aldo Giuffre, Marcello Coscia, Ottavio Jemma
D: Pasquale Festa Campanile **PHOTOG:** Franco DiGiacomo **MUSIC:** Ennio Morricone
Standard SF-comedy: Caveman brothers discover opposite sex

When Women Lost Their Tails
1975, (It), color, 94 mins.
W: Senta Berger
Minor SF-comedy: Adventures of Cromagnon beauty

When Worlds Collide
1951, (USA), Para, color, 81 mins.
W: Barbara Rush *(Joyce Hendren)*, Richard Derr *(Dave Randall)*, Peter Hansen *(Dr. Tony Drake)*, John Hoyt *(Stanton)*, Larry Keating, Ralph Brooks, Mary Murphy, Stephen Chase, Judith Ames, Sandro Giglio, Frank Cady, Hayden Rorke, James Congdon, Stuart Whitman
P: George Pal **D:** Rudolph Maté **SCR:** Sydney Boehm, based on the Baumer-Wylie SF classic **PHOTOG:** John F. Seitz & W. Howard Greene
OSCAR-WINNING SPCL-FX: Harry Barndollar & Gordon Jennings
MUSIC: Leith Stevens
Classic SF-thriller: Rogue star threatens Earth, "Noah's Ark" spaceship hastily assembled cf. Deep Impact

Where Danger Lives
1950, (USA), RKO, b&w, 84 mins.
W: Robert Mitchum, Faith Domergue, Maureen O'Sullivan, Claude Rains,

Maureen O'Sullivan, Charles Kemper, Ralph Dumke, Billy House, Jack Kelly, Philip Van Zandt, Harry Shannon, Jack Kruschen, Lillian West
D: John Farrow **PHOTOG:** Nicholas Musuraca **MUSIC:** Roy Webb
Standard thriller: Scheming beauty involves man in murder

Where East is East
1929, (USA), MGM, b&w, 70 mins.
W: Lon Chaney Sr., Lope Velez, Estelle Taylor, Lloyd Hughes
WRIT, P & D: Tod Browning
Standard melodrama

Where Has Poor Mickey Gone?
1964, (GB), Ledeck-Indigo/Compton/Cameo, b&w, 59 mins.
W: Warren Mitchell *(Emilio Dinelli)*, John Malcolm *(Mick)*, Raymond Armstrong *(Ginger)*, John Challis *(Tim)*, Christopher Robbie *(Kip)*, Karol Hagar *(The Girl)*, Joseph Cook *(The Boy)*
P & D: Gerry Levy **STORY:** Peter Marcus
Standard fantasy: Persecuted carnival magician makes hooligans vanish

Where Have All the People Gone?
1974, (USA), Jozak-Alpine/Metromedia/NBC-TV, color, 72 mins.
W: Peter Graves, Verna Bloom, George O'Hanlon Jr., Noble Willingham, Kathleen Quinlan, Jay W. MacIntosh, Michael James Wixted
P: Gerald I. Isenberg **D:** John Llewellyn Moxey **TELEPLAY:** Lewis John Carlino & Sandor Stern **PHOTOG:** Michael Margulies
TVM, standard SF-thriller: Solar flares produce mutated virus, most of human race killed

Where's Johnny?
1974, (GB), Eady-Barnes/CFF, color, 59 mins.
W: Raymond Boal *(Johnny)*, Kim Clifford *(Becky)*, Perry Benson *(Maurice)*, Graham Stark *(Prof. Graham)*, Patrick Newell *(Basil)*, George Innes *(Fingers)*, Dennis Ramsden *(Bagshawe)*, Donald Morley *(Jones)*, Audrey Nicholson *(Mrs. Jones)*
P: David Eady & Mike Gorell Barnes **D:** David Eady **STORY:** Mike Gorell Barnes **PHOTOG:** Jo Jago **MUSIC:** Harry Robinson
Standard juvenile thriller: Crooks covet secret of boy's invisible dog

Where the Bullets Fly
1966, (GB), Puck/GEF/Avco Embassy, color, 88 mins.
W: Tom Adams *(Charles Vine)*, Dawn Addams *(Fiz)*, Sidney James *(The Mortician)*, Wilfrid Brambell *(The Guard)*, Joe Baker *(The Minister)*, Tim Barrett *(Seraph)*, Michael Ripper *(Angel)*, Suzan Farmer *(Caron)*, Maggie Kimberley *(Jacqueline)*, Heidi Erich *(Carruthers)*, Garry Marsh *(The Major)*, Julie Martin *(The Girl)*, John Arnott *(Rockwell)*, Ronald Leigh-Hunt *(Thursby)*, Michael Ward *(Michael)*
P: Joseph E. Levine & James Ward **D:** John Gilling **STORY:** Michael Pittock
Minor comedy-thriller: Spies seek nuclear device, secret agent opposes

Where the Rainbow Ends
1921, (GB), British Photoplay Prods./Pioneer, b&w, 5,000 ft. (1524m)
W: Babs Farren *(Rosamund Carey)*, B. Cave Chinn *(Crispian Carey)*, Muriel Pointer *(Betty Blunders)*, Eric Gray *(Jin Blunders)*, Roger Livesey *(Cubby the Lion)*, Vesta Sylva *(Will o' the Wisp)*, Harold Deacon *(Saint George)*, Ruth Maitland *(Mrs. Carey)*, George Bishop *(The Dragon King)*, Walter Gay *(Capt. Carey)*, Fred Glover *(Joseph Flint)*, Ernest A. Trimingham *(The Genie)*
P: Edward Godal **D:** H. Lisle Lucoque, from a play by Clifford Mills & John Ramsey
Standard juvenile fantasy: Children find magic carpet, rescue shipwrecked parents from dragon

Where the Spies Are
1965, (GB), MGM, color, 113 mins.
W: David Niven *(Dr. Jason Love)*, Francoise Dorleac *(Vikki)*, Cyril Cusack *(Rosser)*, John LeMesurier *(Macgillivray)*, Eric Pohlmann *(Farouk)*, Nigel Davenport *(Parkington)*, Ronald Radd *(Stanislaus)*, Paul Stassino *(Simmias)*, Noel Harrison *(Jackson)*, George Pravda *(The Agent)*, Basil Dignam *(Maj. Harding)*, Robert Raglan *(Sir Robert)*, George Mikell *(The Assassin)*, Dennis Quilley *(The Dentist)*, Russell Napier *(The Man)*
P: Val Guest & Steven Pallos **D:** Val Guest **SCR:** Val Guest, Wolf Mankowitz & James Leasor, from James Leasor's novel *Passport to Oblivion*
Standard thriller: Russian agents plot assassination of prince

Where Time Began
1978, (Sp), Int'l Picture Show, color, 87 mins.
W: Kenneth More *(Prof. Lindenbrock)*, Pep Munne *(Axel)*, Ivonne Sentis *(Glauben)*, Jack Taylor *(Olsen)*, Jose Maria Cafarell *(Prof. Fridleson)*, Lone Fleming *(Molly)*, Emiliano Redondo *(Prof. Kristoff)*, Frank Branna
D: Juan Piquer **SCR:** Juan Piquer & Carlos Puerto, loosely based on Jules Verne's novel *A Journey to the Center of the Earth* **PHOTOG:** Andres Berenguer **MUSIC:** Juan Jose Farcia Caffi
Standard SF-adventure: Prehistoric terrors found at Earth's core

Which is Witch?
1915, (GB), Martin/DFSA, b&w, 533 ft. (162.5m)
D: Edwin J. Collins
Standard fantasy: Old hag curses rich landowner

While I Live
1947, (GB), Edward Dryhurst/20th Century-Fox, b&w, 85 mins.

W: Tom Walls (*Nehemiah*), Clifford Evans (*Peter Sloane*), Carol Raye (*Sally Grant*), Patricia Burke (*Christine Sloane*), Sonia Dresdel (*Julia Trevelyan*), John Warwick (*George Grant*), Edward Lexy (*Selby*), Audrey Fildes (*Olwen Trevelyan*), Charles Victor (*Sgt. Pearne*), Johnnie Schofield (*Alfie*), Ernest Butcher (*Ambrose*), Sally Rogers (*Hannah*)
D: John Harlow   **SCR:** John Harlow & Doreen Montgomery, from Robert Bell's play *This Same Garden*
*reissued (1950) as **Dream of Olwen***
Standard thriller: Woman believes reporter's amnesiac wife is her reincarnated sister

While Paris Sleeps
1923, (USA), W.W. Hodkinson/, b&w, 6 reels
W: Lon Chaney Sr., Jack (John) Gilbert, J. Farrell MacDonald, Mildred Manning, Harden Kirtland
D: Maurice Tourneur, based on *The Glory of Love* by "Pan" (Leslie Beresford)   **PHOTOG:** Rene Guissart
*orig. to be titled **The Glory of Love** (produced in 1920)*
Standard melodrama

While the City Sleeps
1956, (USA), RKO, b&w, 100 mins.
W: Dana Andrews, Ida Lupino, Vincent Price, Rhonda Fleming, Thomas Mitchell, James Craig, Sally Forrest, George Sanders, John Drew Barrymore, Howard Duff
P: Bert Friedlob   **D:** Fritz Lang   **SCR:** Casey Robinson
Unusual thriller: Cops and newspaper reporters hunt "lipstick killer"

While the Cook Slept
1912, (GB), Cricks & Martin, b&w, 425 ft. (129.5m)
D: A.E. Coleby
Standard fantasy: Food prepares itself while cook dozes

While Under a Hypnotist's Influence
see Le Magnetiseur

The Whip and the Body
see La Frusta e il Corpo

The Whip Hand
1951, (USA), RKO, b&w, 82 mins.
W: Elliott Reid, Carla Balenda, Raymond Burr, Edgar Barrier, Lurene Tuttle
WRIT & D: William Cameron Menzies   **PHOTOG:** Nicholas Musuraca
Standard thriller: Communists menace

Whirling the Worlds
see Le Voyage a Travers l'Impossible

Whirlpool
1959, (GB), Rank/RFD, color, 95 mins.
W: Juliette Greco (*Lora*), O.W. Fischer (*Rolph*), Muriel Pavlow (*Dina*), William Sylvester (*Herman*), Marius Goring (*George*), Richard Palmer (*Derek*), Lily Kann (*Mrs. Steen*), Geoffrey Bayldon (*Wendel*), Peter Illing (*Braun*), Harold Kasket (*Steibel*)
P: George Pitcher   **D:** Lewis Allen   **SCR:** Lawrence P. Bachmann, from his novel *Lorelei*
Standard crime-thriller: Barge captain shelters killer's accomplice

Whirlpool
1970, (Den), Cinemation, color, 92 mins. (also 75 mins.)
W: Vivian Neves (*Tulia*), Karl Lanchbury (*Theo*), Pia Anderson (*Sara*), Johanna Hegger, Andrea Grant, Ernest Jenning, Edwin Brown, Larry Dann, Alan Charles, Barrie Craine, John Davenport
D & SCR: J.R. Larrath
Standard melodrama

A Whisper to a Scream
1988, (Can), color, 96 mins.
W: Nadia Capone, Yaphet Kotto, Lawrence Bayne, Silvio Oliviero
D: Robert Bergman   **SCR:** Robert Bergman & Gerard Ciccoritti
Standard thriller: Murders surround phone-sex operator

Whiskers
1996, (USA), color, 105 mins.
W: Brent Carver, Michael Caloz
Standard comedy-fantasy: Boy prays to Egyptian goddess to make his cat human

The Whispering
1994, (USA), color, 88 mins.
W: Leif Garrett, Leslie Danon, Tom Patton, Mette Holt, Maxwell Rutherford
D: Gregory Gieras   **SCR:** Leslie Danon
Modest horror-fantasy: Insurance investigator looks into murders, meets female Grim Reaper

Whispering Death
1971, (USA), CBS-TV, color
W: Roy Thinnes, John Rubinstein, Jim Hutton, Kate Woodville, Jonathan Brooks, B.J. Mason
TVM, minor thriller (feature culled from 1971 teleseries "The Psychiatrist")

Whispering Ghosts
1942, (USA), 20th-Fox, b&w, 75 mins.

W: Milton Berle, Willie Best, John Carradine, Brenda Joyce, Grady Sutton, Milton Parsons, John Shelton
D: Alfred Werker   **SCR:** Lou Breslow
Standard comedy-thriller: Radio detective probes sea captain's murder

Whispering Smith
1949, (USA), Para, color, 89 mins.
W: Alan Ladd, Brenda Marshall, Robert Preston, Donald Crisp, Fay Holden, William Demarest
D: Leslie Fenton, from a novel by Frank H. Spearman   **PHOTOG:** Ray Rennahan   **MUSIC:** Adolph Deutsch
Standard western melodrama: Railroad detective foils train robbers

Whispering Smith Hits London
1952, (GB), Hammer-Lesser/RKO, b&w, 82 mins.
W: Richard Carlson (*Whispering Smith*), Greta Gynt (*Louise*), Herbert Lom (*Ford*), Rona Anderson (*Anne*), Reginald Beckwith (*Manson*), Alan Wheatley (*Hector Reith*), Danny Green (*Cecil*), Dora Bryan (*La Fosse*), James Raglan (*Supt. Meaker*)
P: Anthony Hinds & Julian Lesser   **D:** Francis Searle   **SCR:** John Gilling, from a story by Steve Fisher
*USA retitle, **Whispering Smith vs. Scotland Yard***
Standard thriller: American detective unmasks blackmail gang behind girl's "suicide"

Whispering Smith vs. Scotland Yard
see Whispering Smith Hits London

Whispering Tongues
1934, (GB), Real Art/Radio, b&w, 55 mins.
W: Reginald Tate (*Alan Norton*), Jane Welsh (*Claudia Mayland*), Russell Thorndike (*Fenwick*), Malcolm Keen (*Insp. Dawley*), Felix Aylmer (*Supt. Fulton*), Tonie Edgar Bruce (*Lady Weaver*), Charles Carson (*Roger Mayland*), Victor Stanley (*The Steward*)
D: George Pearson   **SCR:** H. Fowler Mear   **STORY:** Bernerd Mainwaring
Standard thriller: Man and butler steal gems from those responsible for father's suicide

Whisper Kill
1988, (USA), color
W: Loni Anderson, Joe Penny
Minor thriller: Reporter and newspaper editor stalk slasher

Whispers
see Dean R. Koontz' Whispers

The Whistler
1944, (USA), Col, b&w, 60 mins.
W: Richard Dix, Gloria Stuart, J. Carrol Naish, Robert Emmett Keane, Alan Dinehart, Don Costello, Joan Woodbury
D: William Castle   **SCR:** Eric Taylor, from a story by J. Donald Wilson   **PHOTOG:** James S. Brown   **MUSIC:** Wilbur Hatch
Standard thriller: Man believes himself responsible for wife's death, arranges his own execution. First of 'Whistler' series

White Angel
1993, (GB), color, 96 mins.
W: Harriet Robinson, Peter Firth, Don Henderson, Harry Miller, Joe Collins, Anne-Catherine Arton
D: Chris Jones
Standard thriller: Transvestite-dentist serial killer and authoress form strange alliance

White Captive
see White Savage

The White Cliffs Mystery
1957, (GB), Merton Park/Anglo-Amalgamated, b&w, 32 mins.
W: Russell Napier
P: Alec Snowden   **D:** Montgomery Tully   **STORY:** James Eastwood, from a novel by Edgar Lustgarten
Standard short crime-thriller: Secretary blackmails rocket engineer

The White Cockatoo
1935, (USA), WB, b&w, 73 mins.
W: Jean Muir, Ricardo Cortez, Ruth Donnelly
D: Alan Crosland   **PHOTOG:** Tony Gaudio
Standard mystery-thriller: Heiress menaced

White Dog
1981, (USA), color, 90 mins.
W: Kristy McNichol, Paul Winfield, Jameson Parker, Burl Ives, Lynne Moody, Marshall Thompson, Christa Lang, Paul Bartel, Samuel Fuller, Dick Miller
D: Samuel Fuller   **PHOTOG:** Bruce Surtees   **MUSIC:** Ennio Morricone
Well-made controversial thriller: Canine trained to attack blacks

White Dwarf
1995, (USA), American Zoetrope/Fox-TV, color, 95 mins.
W: Paul Winfield (*Dr. Akada*), Neal McDonough (*Driscoll Rampart*), CCH Pounder (*Shabana*), Joey Andrews (*Never*), Chip Heller (*Osh*), Katy Boyer (*Lady X*), Ele Keats, Ray Brocksmith, Beverly Mitchell, Robert Cornthwaite, Kevin Brophy

D: Peter Markle **TELEPLAY:** Bruce Wagner **PHOTOG:** Phaedon Papa Michael **MUSIC:** Stewart Copeland
TVM (feature-pilot for unsold teleseries), standard SF-fantasy: Young doctor meets bizarre types on distant planet

The White Goddess
1953, (USA), Lippert, b&w, 73 mins.
W: Jon Hall, Ray Montgomery, M'liss McClure, Ludwig Stossel, James Fairfax, Darby Jones, Lucien Prival, Millicent Patrick, Robert Williams, Joel Fluellen
D: Wallace Fox **SCR:** Sherman L. Lowe & Eric Taylor **MUSIC:** Irving Gertz
*Minor adventure-thriller (culled from 1950's teleseries **Ramar of the Jungle**): American doctor seeks medicinal herbs, finds African tribe ruled by white girl*

The White Gorilla
1945, (USA), Special Attractions, b&w, 62 mins.
W: Ray "Crash" Corrigan, Lorraine Miller
P: Adrian Weiss **D:** Harry L. Fraser
*Minor adventure-thriller (incorporating portions of **Perils of the Jungle** serial{1927}): Ape exiled from his tribe*

White Huntress
*see **Golden Ivory***

White Light
1991, (Can), color, 95 mins.
W: Martin Kove, Allison Hossack
Minor thriller: Cop seeks woman he met during out-of-body experience

White Lilac
1935, (GB), Fox British, b&w, 67 mins.
W: Basil Sydney (*Ian Mackie*), Judy Gunn (*Mollie*), Claude Dampier (*Percy*), Percy Marmont (*Tollitt*), Gwenllian Gill (*Muriel*), Leslie Perrins (*Iredale*), Constance Travers (*Jessie*), Billy Holland (*Harvey*), Marjorie Hume (*Mrs. Lyall*)
D: Albert Parker, from Ladislas Fodor's play
Standard thriller: Too many suspects in murder of unpopular villager

White of the Eye
1987, (USA), Cannon/Palisades Entertainment, color, 111 mins.
W: David Keith (*Paul White*), Cathy Moriarty (*Joan White*), Alan Rosenberg (*Mike Desantos*), Art Evans (*Mendoza*), Marc Hayashi (*Stu*), Michael Greene (*Phil Ross*), Danielle Smith (*Danielle White*), Alberta Watson (*Anna Mason*), William G. Schilling (*Harold Gideon*), David Chow (*Fred Hoy*), Pamela Seamon (*Caryanne*), Mimi Lieber (*Liza Manchester*), Danko Gurovich (*Arnold White*), Bob Zache (*Lucas Herman*), China Cammell (*Ruby Hoy*), Jim Wirries (*Grunveldt*), Kate Waring (*Joyce Patell*), Fred Allison (*The TV Newsman*), Clyde Pitfarkin (*The Hairdresser*)
D: Donald Cammell **SCR:** China & Donald Cammell, from Margaret Tracy's novel *Mrs. White* **PHOTOG:** Larry McConkey **MUSIC:** Nick Mason & Rick Fenn
Standard thriller: Psycho-killer in Arizona town

The White Orchid
1954, (USA), UA, color, 80 mins.
W: William Lundigan, Peggie Castle, Carlos Rivas, Rosenda Monteros, Armando Silvestre, Jorge Trevino, Alejandro de Montenegro, Miguel A. Gallardo
P & D: Reginald LeBorg **SCR:** David Duncan & Reginald LeBorg
Standard thriller: Adventurers probe pre-Colombian ruins

White Pongo
1945, (USA), PRC, b&w, 73 mins.
W: Richard Fraser, Maris Wrixon, Lionel Royce, Al Eben, Gordon Richards, Egon Brecher, Joel Fluellen, Michael Dyne, George Lloyd, Milton Kibbee, Larry Steers
P: Sigmund Neufeld **D:** Sam Newfield **SCR:** Raymond L. Schrock **PHOTOG:** Jack Greenhalgh
*edited-down version sold under title **Blond Gorilla***
Inept thriller, "camp" classic: Explorers meet albino gorilla

The White Raven
1998, (USA), color, 90 mins.
W: Roy Scheider, Joan Severance, Ron Silver
Standard thriller: Journalist seeks missing diamond

White Room
1990, (GB-Can), color, 90 mins.
W: Kate Nelligan, Maurice Godin, Margot Kidder, Barbara Gordon, Sheila McCarthy
D: Patricia Rozema
Unusual thriller: Voyeur witnesses pop star's murder, meets mystery woman with dead singer's voice

White Savage
1943, (USA), Univ, color, 75 mins.
W: Maria Montez, Jon Hall, Sabu, Thomas Gomez, Paul Guilfoyle, Sidney Toler, Don Terry
D: Arthur Lubin **SCR:** Richard Brooks **PHOTOG:** Lester White & William Snyder **MUSIC:** Frank Skinner

*GB retitle, **White Captive***
Standard adventure-thriller: Island princess opposes jewel hunters

The White Sheik
*see **Lo Sceicco Bianco***

The White Slave
1900, (USA), Vitagraph, b&w
D: J. Stuart Blackton
Standard melodrama

The White Spider
1963, (W. Ger), Gold Key, b&w, 105 mins.
W: Joachim Fuchsberger, Karin Dor, Mady Rahl, Horst Frank
Minor thriller

The White Witch
1913, (GB), Herkomer/Tyler, b&w, 1,690 ft. (515.1m)
W: Hubert von Herkomer (*The Witch*)
WRIT & D: Hubert von Herkomer
Standard fantasy: Witch's magic saves woodman's daughter from evil baron

White Woman
1933, (USA), Para, b&w, 68 mins.
W: Charles Laughton, Carole Lombard, Kent Taylor, Charles Middleton, Noble Johnson, Charles Bickford
P: E. Lloyd Sheldon **D:** Stuart Walker **SCR:** Samuel Hoffenstein & Gladys Lehman
blurb: "Woman Hunger. Crazed Men Who Lived Without Love—Sly Whispers!"
*Standard thriller (using sets from **Island of Lost Souls**): Evil jungle ruler tyrannizes. cf. **Island of Lost Men***

White Zombie
1932, (USA), Halperin/UA, b&w, 73 mins.
W: Bela Lugosi, Madge Bellamy (*Madeline*), John Harron (*Neil*), Joseph Cawthorn (*Bruner*), Robert Frazer, George Burr McAnnan, Clarence Muse, Brandon Hurst, Dan Crimmins, Frederick Peters, Annette Stone, John Printz, Claude Morgan, John Fergusson, Velma Gresham
P: Edward Halperin **D:** Victor Halperin **ORIG. STORY & SCR:** Garnett Weston, inspired by William Seabrook's book *The Magic Island* **PHOTOG:** Arthur Martinelli **MUSIC ARRANGED:** Abe Meyer
Semi-classic horror-thriller ("A beautiful girl torn from her lover on her bridal night—Rendered lifeless...Soulless...Then brought to life again by a fiend and made to perform his every desire!"):
*Sexual Thriller. Lovers run afoul of zombie master. cf. **Dr. Terror's House of Horrors** (1943)*

Who?
1973, (GB), Lorimar/Lion Int'l/Hemisphere/Maclean & Co./Col/EMI Warner, color, 93 mins.
W: Elliott Gould (*Sean Rogers*), Trevor Howard (*Col. Azarin*), Joseph Bova (*Dr. Lucas Martino*), James Noble (*Gen. Deptford*), John Lehne (*Haller*), Lyndon Brook (*Dr. Barrister*), Kay Tornborg (*Edith*), Joy Garrett (*Barbara*), Michael Lombard (*Dr. Besser*), Ivan Desny (*Gen. Sturmer*), John Stewart (*Frank Heywood*), Alexander Allerson (*Dr. Kothu*), Bruce Boa (*Miller*), Dan Sazarino (*Uncle Lucas*)
P: Barry Levinson & Kurt Berthold **D:** Jack Gold **SCR:** John Gould (Jack Gold), from a novel by Algis Budrys **PHOTOG:** Petrus Schloemp **MUSIC:** John Cameron
*USA retitle, **Man without a Face**, A.k.a. **Roboman***
Standard SF-thriller: Superpowers vie for possession of android

Who Done It?
1942, (USA), Univ, b&w, 75 mins.
W: Bud Abbott, Lou Costello, William Bendix, Louise Allbriton, William Gargan, Patric Knowles, Thomas Gomez, Don Porter, Jerome Cowan, Mary Wickes, Ludwig Stossel
D: Erle C. Kenton **SCR:** Stanley Roberts, Edmund Joseph & John Grant **ORIG. STORY:** Stanley Roberts **PHOTOG:** Stanley Van Enger **MUSIC:** Frank Skinner **MUSIC DIR:** Charles Previn
Modest comedy-thriller: Two bumbling soda jerks involved in murder at a radio station

Who Done It?
1956, (GB), Ealing/Rank, b&w, 82 mins.
W: Benny Hill (*Hugo*), Belinda Lee (*Frankie*), David Kossoff (*Zacco*), Garry Marsh (*Hancock*), Ernest Thesiger (*Sir Walter*), George Margo (*Barakov*), Denis Shaw (*Stumpf*), Philip Stainton (*Frankie's Agent*), Frederick Schiller (*Gruber*), Thorley Walters (*Raymond Courtney*), Warwick Ashton, Peter Bull, Ernest Jay, Stratford Johns, Nicholas Phipps, Norah Blane, Gibb McLaughlin, Harold Scott, Charles Hawtrey, Jeremy Hawk
P: Michael Relph **D:** Basil Dearden **STORY & SCR:** T.E.B. Clarke **PHOTOG:** Otto Heller **MUSIC:** Philip Green
Broad farce with SF element: Would-be sleuth trails spies

Whodunit
1982, (USA), color, 82 mins.
W: Rick Bean, Gary Phillips
D: Bill Naud **SCR:** Anthony Shaffer
Minor thriller: Murders on remote isle

Who Fears the Devil?

1973, (USA), Jack H. Harris, color, 89 mins.
<u>W</u>: Susan Strasberg, Denver Pyle, Hedge Capers, Severn Darden
<u>P</u>: Barney Rosenzweig <u>D</u>: John Newland <u>SCR</u>: Melvin Levy <u>SPCL-FX</u>: Gene Warren
A.k.a. **The Legend of Hillbilly John**
Standard fantasy-thriller: Wandering ballad singer finds black magic in Appalachians

Who Framed Roger Rabbit

1988, (USA), Amblin/Touchstone, color, 96 mins. (also 103 mins.)
<u>W</u>: Bob Hoskins, Christopher Lloyd, Joanna Cassidy
<u>D</u>: Robert Zemeckis <u>ANIMATION D</u>: Richard Williams (Academy Award) <u>SCR</u>: Jeffrey Price & Peter Seaman, from Gary K. Wolf's book *Who Censored Roger Rabbit?* <u>SPCL VS-FX</u>: Industrial Light & Magic (Academy Award) <u>MUSIC</u>: Alan Silvestri
Superior comedy-fantasy (mix of animation & live action): Detective probes world of cartoons

Who Is Killing the Great Chefs of Europe ?

1978, (USA-W. Ger), WB, color, 112 mins.
<u>W</u>: George Segal *(Robby)*, Jacqueline Bisset *(Natasha)*, Robert Morley *(Max)*, Jean-Pierre Cassel *(Kohner)*, Philippe Noiret *(Moulineau)*, Madge Ryan *(Beecham)*, Jean Rochefort *(Grand-villiers)*, Luigi Proietti *(Ravello)*, Stefano Satta Flores *(Fausto Zoppi)*, Frank Windsor *(Blodgett)*, Peter Sallis *(St. Claire)*, Tim Barlow *(Doyle)*, John LeMesurier *(Dr. Deere)*, Joss Ackland *(Cantrell)*, Jean Gaven *(Salpetre)*, Daniel Emilfork *(Saint-Juste)*, Jacques Marin *(Massenet)*, Jacques Balutin *(Chappemain)*, Jean Paredes *(Brissac)*, Michael Chow *(Soong)*, Anita Graham *(The Blonde)*, Nicholas Ball *(Skeffington)*, David Cook *(Bussingbill)*, Nigel Havers *(The Counterman)*, John Carlisle *(The Actor)*, Sheila Ruskin *(The Actress)*, Kenneth Fortescue *(The Director)*, Strewan Rodger *(The Ass't Director)*, Marjorie Smith *(The Receptionist)*, Sylvia Kay *(The Reporter)*, Aimee Delamain *(The Old Woman)*, Lyall Jones *(The Driver)*, Eddie Tagoe *(Mumbala)*, Caroline Langrishe *(Loretta)*
<u>D</u>: Ted Kotcheff <u>SCR</u>: Peter Stone, from the novel *Someone Killing Europe* by Nan & Ivan Lyons <u>MUSIC</u>: Henry Mancini
A.k.a. **Too Many Chefs**
Standard comedy-thriller: Gourmets eliminated in various nasty ways

Who Killed Gail Preston?

1938, (USA), b&w, 60 mins.
<u>W</u>: Don Terry, Rita Hayworth, Robert Paige, Wyn Cahoon, Gene Morgan, Marc Lawrence, Arthur Loft
<u>D</u>: Leon Barsha
Minor whodunit: Murder in a nightclub

Who Killed Teddy Bear?

1965, (USA), Magna, color, 90 mins.
<u>W</u>: Sal Mineo, Juliet Prowse, Jan Murray, Elaine Stritch, Bruce Glover, Margot Bennett, Dan Travanty, Diana Moore, Tom Aldredge, Frank Campanella, Rex Everhart, Alex Fisher, Stanley Beck, Casey Townsend
<u>D</u>: Joseph Cates
Minor thriller: Sex-crazed busboy terrorizes nightclub dancer

Who Killed the Cat?

1966, (GB), Eternal/Grand Nat'l, b&w, 76 mins.
<u>W</u>: Mary Merrall *(Janet Bowering)*, Ellen Pollock *(Ruth Prendergast)*, Amy Dalby *(Lavinia Goldsworthy)*, Mervyn Johns *(Henry Fawcett)*, Vanda Godsell *(Eleanor Trellington)*, Conrad Phillips *(Insp. Bruton)*, Gregory Phillips *(Peter Parsons)*, Natasha Pyne *(Mary Trellington)*, Ronald Adam *(Gregory)*
<u>P</u>: Maurice J. Wilson <u>D</u>: Montgomery Tully <u>SCR</u>: Maurice J. Wilson & Montgomery Tully, from the play *Tabitha* by Arnold Ridley & Mary Cathcart Borer
Standard thriller: Old spinsters suspected of poisoning vicious landlady

The Whole Truth

1958, (GB), Romulus-Valiant/Col, b&w, 85 mins.
<u>W</u>: Stewart Granger *(Max Poulton)*, Donna Reed *(Carol Poulton)*, George Sanders

Who Killed The Cat: VANDA GODSELL AND MERVYN JOHNS

(Carliss), Michael Shillo *(Insp. Simon)*, Gianna Maria Canale *(Gina Bertini)*, Peter Dyneley *(Willy Reichel)*, Hy Hazell *(The American)*, Jimmy Thompson *(The Ass't)*, Richard Molinas *(Gilbert)*, Philip Vickers *(Jack Leslie)*, John Van Eyssen *(Archer)*, Carlo Justini *(The Leading Man)*
<u>P</u>: Jack Clayton <u>D</u>: John Guillermin <u>SCR</u>: Jonathan Latimer, from a teleplay by Philip Mackie
Standard crime-thriller: Actress' husband frames producer for murder

Who Slew Auntie Roo?

1971, (GB), Hemdale/AIP, color, 91 mins.
<u>W</u>: Shelley Winters *(Mrs. Forrest, "Auntie Roo")*, Mark Lester *(Christopher)*, Judy Cornwell *(Clarine)*, Lionel Jeffries *(Insp. Willoughby)*, Ralph Richardson *(Mr. Benton)*, Rosalie Crutchley *(Miss Henley)*, Chloe Franks *(Katy)*, Pat Heywood *(Dr. Mason)*, Hugh Griffith *(Mr. Harrison, the Pigman)*, Marianne Stone *(Miss Wilcox)*, Michael Gothard *(Albie)*, Richard Beaumont *(Peter)*, Jacqueline Cowper *(Angela)*, Charlotte Sayce *(Katherine)*
<u>P</u>: Samuel Z. Arkoff & James H. Nicholson <u>D</u>: Curtis Harrington <u>SCR</u>: Robert Blees & Jimmy Sangster <u>STORY</u>: David Osborn <u>PHOTOG</u>: Desmond Dickinson <u>MUSIC</u>: Ken Jones
orig. to be titled **The Gingerbread House** *or* **Gingerbread Lady**
Standard satire-thriller (reworking of "Hansel & Gretel"): Children suspect aunt is witch

Whoso Diggeth a Pit

1915, (GB), London/Jury, b&w, 3,660 ft. (1115.6m)
<u>W</u>: Gerald Ames *(Dr. Hartley)*, Charles Rock *(Frank Edwards)*, Gwynne Herbert *(Mrs. Warde)*, Mary Dibley *(Grace Warde)*
<u>D</u>: Ralph Dewsbury <u>STORY</u>: Frank Fowell
Standard crime-thriller: Financier kills tramp in mistake for his partner, is exposed by doctor's injection of death simulant

Whosoever Shall Offend

1919, (GB), Windsor/Walturdaw, b&w, 5,900 ft. (1798.3m)
<u>W</u>: Kenelm Foss *(Guido Folco)*, Odette Goimbault *(Aurora)*, Mary Marsh Allen *(Regina)*, Hayford Hobbs *(Marcello Consalvi)*, Evelyn Harding *(Signora Consalvi)*, Charles Vane *(Ercole)*, Maud Cressall *(Countess Del Armi)*, Barbara Everest *(Maddalena)*, Philip Hewland *(Prof. Kalmon)*, Joyce Templeton *(Regina as a Child)*
<u>D</u>: Arrigo Bocchi <u>SCR</u>: Kenelm Foss, from a novel by Marion Crawford
Standard crime-thriller: Wife-murderer weds rich widow, tries to eliminate her

Who Stole the Body?

1962, (Fr), Official Films, b&w, 92 mins.
<u>W</u>: Francis Blanche *(Edouard)*, Daryl Cowl *(Felix)*, Elke Sommer, Clement Harari, Daniel Ceccaldi, Mario David
<u>D</u>: Jean Girault
orig: **Les Bricoleurs**
Minor comedy-thriller: Real-estate agents find corpse in house

Who Was Maddox?

1964, (GB), Merton Park/Anglo-Amalgamated, b&w, 62 mins.
<u>W</u>: Bernard Lee *(Supt. Meredith)*, Jack Watling *(Jack Heath)*, Suzanne Lloyd *(Diane Heath)*, Richard Gale *(Maddox)*, Finlay Currie *(Alec Campbell)*, James Bree *(Reynolds)*, Dora Reisser *(Anne Wildig)*, Christa Bergmann *(Greta)*, Billy Milton *(Chandler)*
<u>P</u>: Jack Greenwood <u>D</u>: Geoffrey Nethercott <u>SCR</u>: Roger Marshall, from Edgar Wallace's story "The Undisclosed Client"
Standard crime-thriller: Blackmailer murders publisher's chairman

Why Must I Die?

1960, (USA), AIP, b&w, 86 mins.
<u>W</u>: Terry Moore, Debra Paget, Bert Freed, Julie Reding
<u>P</u>: Richard Bernstein <u>D</u>: Roy Del Ruth <u>SCR</u>: George Waters & Richard Bernstein
Standard melodrama (I Want to Live imitation): Innocent woman executed

Why Would Anyone Want to Kill a Nice Girl Like You?

1969, (GB),Trio/Group W/Crispen, color, 99 mins.
<u>W</u>: David Buck, Eva Renzi, Paul Hubschmid, Peter Vaughan
<u>D</u>: Don Sharp
original title: Taste of Excitement
Minor thriller: Tourist imperiled on Riviera

The Wicked

1989, (Austral), color, 87 mins.
<u>W</u>: Brett Cumo, Richard Morgan, Angela Kennedy, John Doyle, Maggie Blinco
<u>D</u>: Colin Eggleston
Minor horror-spoof: Folks meet vampiric family

Wicked City

1992, (Hong Kong), color, 88 mins.
<u>W</u>: Jacky Cheung, Leon Lai, Michelle Li
<u>D</u>: Peter Mak
Standard SF-thriller: Reptilian race plots demise of humans

The Wicked Lady

1983, (GB), London Cannon/Col-EMI-WB, color, 99 mins.
<u>W</u>: Faye Dunaway *(Lady Barbara Skelton)*, Alan Bates *(Capt. Jerry Jackson)*, Sir John Gielgud *(Hogarth)*, Denholm Elliott *(Sir Ralph Skelton)*, Prunella Scales *(Lady Henrietta Kingsclere)*, Oliver Tobias *(Kit Locksby)*, Glynis Barber *(Lady*

Caroline), Joan Hickson (*Aunt Agatha*), Nicholas Gecks (*Ned Cotterell*), Helena McCarthy (*Moll Skelton*), Mollie Maureen (*Doll Skelton*), John Savident (*Squire Thornton*), Derek Francis (*Lord Kingsclere*), Mark Burns (*King Charles II*), Hugh Millais (*Uncle Martin*), Dermot Walsh (*Lord Marwood*), Marc Sinden (*Lord Dolman*), Ewen Solon (*The Cleric*), Tersa Codling (*Nell Gwynne*), Ellen Pollock (*Mrs. Munce*)
P: Menehem Golan & Yoram Globus **D:** Michael Winner **SCR:** Leslie Arliss, Michael Winner, Gordon Glennon & Aimee Stuart, from Magdalen King-Hall's novel *Wicked Skelton* **PHOTOG:** Jack Cardiff **MUSIC:** Tony Banks
Modest adventure-thriller: Nobleman's wife becomes partner of highwayman

Wicked Stepmother
1988, (USA), Larco/MGM, color, 90 mins.
W: Bette Davis (*Miranda*), Barbara Carrera (*Priscilla*), Colleen Camp (*Jenny*), Lionel Stander (*Sam*), David Rasche (*Steve*), Shawn Donahue (*Mike*), Tom Bosley (*Lt. MacIntosh*), Richard Moll (*Nat*), Evelyn Keyes (*The Witch Instructor*), James Dixon (*Det. Flynn*), Seymour Cassel (*Feldshine*), Bob Goen (*The Game Show Host*), Susie Garrett (*Mandy*), Laurene Landon (*Vanilla*), Robert Frank Telfer (*The Game Show Producer*), Richard Duggan (*The Page*), Ed Vandell (*The Police Chief*), Ernest Harada (*Nukumoto*), Helen Shaw (*Sadie*), Eve Smith (*Mamie*), Maxine Elliott (*Mathilda*), Mary M. Egan (*Henrietta*), Rose Parenti (*Bernice*), Jennifer Roach (*The Child Witch*), Michael Kaufman (*The Prosecutor*), Laurie Main (*The Client*), Robert Dowdell (*The Judge*), Dawn Mazzella (*The Beach Bunny*), James Garrick (*The Ass't Prosecutor*), Christopher James Tylor (*A Bully*), Robert Keller (*A Bully*), Anthony Torn (*The Street Hustler*)
WRIT & D: Larry Cohen **PHOTOG:** Bryan England **MUSIC:** Robert Folk
Standard comedy-fantasy: Scheming witch disrupts family. Bette Davis' last film

Wicked, Wicked
1973, (USA), MGM, color, 95 mins.
W: Tiffany Bolling, Randy Roberts, Scott Brady, Arthur O'Connell, Diane McBain, Edd Byrnes
P, D & SCR: Richard L. Bare
Standard comedy-thriller: Psychotic handyman dismembers blondes. Split screens used throughout

Wicked Wife
see Grand National Night

The Wicker Man
1973, (GB), British Lion/WB, color, 99 mins. (also 102 mins.)
W: Christopher Lee (*Lord Summerisle*), Britt Ekland (*Willow*), Edward Woodward (*Sgt. Neil Howie*), Ingrid Pitt (*The Librarian*), Diane Cilento (*Miss Rose*), Lindsay Kemp (*Alder MacGregor*), Russell Waters (*The Harbour Master*), Irene Sunter (*May Morrison*), Aubrey Morris (*The Gardener*), Walter Carr (*The Schoolmaster*), Ian Campbell (*Oak*), Kevin Collins (*The Fisherman*), Geraldine Cowper (*Rowan Morrison*), Donald Eccles (*T.H. Lenox*), Lesley Mackie (*Daisy*), Leslie Blackwater, Roy Boyd, Peter Brewis, Ross Campbell, Penny Cluer, Barbara Ann Brown, Juliette Cadzow, Michael Cole, Ian Cutler, John Hallam, Myra Forsyth, Alison Hughes, Helen Norman, Charles Kearney, Fiona Kennedy, John MacGregor, Lorraine Peters, Jimmy MacKenzie, Jennifer Martin, Tony Roper, Bernard Murray, Tony Roper, John Sharp, Andrew Tompkins, Elizabeth Sinclair, Ian Wilson, John Young, Richard Wren
P: Peter Snell **D:** Robin Hardy **SCR:** Anthony Shaffer **PHOTOG:** Harry Waxman **MUSIC COMPOSED:** Paul Giovanni **SONGS:** *Corn Rigs* & *Gently Johnny*, music performed by Lodestone
"PURE, BRILLIANT, SPINE-TINGLING FUN! IT'S THE MOST INSPIRED MYSTERY I'VE SEEN IN AGES, A KNOCKOUT!
It's intriguing, suspenseful and thought-provoking. It's literate, witty, ironic, and sophisticated. It's an absolute gem of a film!"—Bruce McCabe, Boston Globe
"A wickedly ingenious and mesmerizing movie that will come back to haunt you time and time again!"—Frank Dolan, WEEI-AM
Superior eroto-thriller: Policeman probes child disappearance, finds modern-day paganism on Channel isle

The Wickham Mystery
1931, (GB), Samuelson/UA, b&w, 84 mins.
W: Eve Gray (*Joan Hamilton*), John Longden (*Harry Crawford*), Lester Matthews (*Charles Wickham*), Sam Livesey (*Insp. Cobb*), Walter Piers (*George Beverley*), John Turnbull (*Howard Clayton*), Wally Bosco (*Edward Hamilton*), Doris Clemence (*Mrs. Wickham*)
D: G.B. Samuelson, based on John McNally's play *The Paper Chase*
Standard thriller: Crooks steal pearls and helicopter plans

Wide Boy
1952, (GB), Merton Park/Anglo-Amalgamated, b&w, 67 mins.
W: Sydney Tafler (*Benny*), Susan Shaw (*Molly*), Ronald Howard (*Insp. Carson*), Melissa Stribling (*Caroline*), Laidman Brown (*Pop*), Colin Tapley (*Mannering*), Helen Christie (*Sally*), Martin Benson (*Rocco*)
P: W.H. Williams **D:** Ken Hughes **STORY:** Rex Rienits
Standard crime-thriller: Girl tracks murderous blackmailer

Wide Sargasso Sea
1993, (USA-Australia), HBO-TV/Fine Line Features, color, 96 mins.
W: Karina Lombard, Nathaniel Parker, Rachel Ward, Michael York, Martine Beswicke, Claudia Robinson

D: John Duigan, from a novel by Jean Rhys, based on characters in Charlotte Bronte's novel *Jane Eyre* **PHOTOG:** Geoffrey Burton **MUSIC:** Stewart Copeland
Standard thriller: Superstition and Jamaican voodoo complicate marriage of madwoman's daughter

Widow in Scarlet
1932, (USA), Action/Mayfair, b&w, 64 mins.
W: Dorothy Revier
D: George Seitz **PHOTOG:** Edward Cronjager
Minor melodrama

Widow's Kiss
1995, (USA), HBO-TV, color, 105 mins.
W: Beverly D'Angelo, Mackenzie Astin, Dennis Haysbert
D: Peter Foldy
Made-for-Cable, standard thriller: Young man connects oft-widowed stepmother with father's death

Widow Twan-Kee
1923, (GB), Stoll, b&w, 6,050 ft. (1844m)
W: George Robey (*Widow Twan-Kee*), Lionelle Howard (*Aladdin*), Julia Kean (*The Princess*), Edward O'Neill (*Abanazar*), Aubrey Fitzgerald (*The Servant*), W.G. Saunders (*The Emperor*), Basil Saunders (*The Slave of the Lamp*), H. Agar Lyons (*Li-Pong*), Julie Suedo (*The Fairy of the Ring*)
D & SCR: Sinclair Hill, based on the pantomime *Aladdin*
A.k.a. One Arabian Night
Standard comedy-fantasy: Magic lamp helps washerwoman's son attain princess

Wielka, Wielka i Najwieksza (Big, Big and Highest)
1962, (Pol), Film Polski, b&w, 103 mins.
W: Kinga Sienko, Wojciech Puzynski, Zbigniew Jozefowicz, J. Klosinski, M. Stoor, B. Bilewski, Z. Kucowna, B. Pawlik, Z. Malawski, E. Radzikowska, E.B. Mickus, U. Modrzynska, A. Szczepkowski
D: Anna Sokolowska **SCR:** Jerzy Broszkiewicz & Anna Sokolowska **STORY:** Jerzy Broszkiewicz **PHOTOG:** Kazimierz Wawrzyniak & Jacek Korcelli **MUSIC:** Andrzej Markowski
Fr retitle, Le Grand Monde des Petits Enfants (The Big World of Little Children)
Standard fantasy

Wife of a Thief
1914, (GB), Regent/MP, b&w, 2,000 ft. (609.6m)
W: Gordon Begg
D: Charles Weston
Standard crime-thriller: Thief fakes own drowning, saves remarried wife from gambler

The Wife of Monte Cristo
1946, (USA), PRC, b&w, 80 mins.
W: Lenore Aubert, John Loder, Eva Gabor, Charles Dingle, Eduardo Ciannelli, Eva Gabor, Martin Kosleck
D: Edgar G. Ulmer
Standard adventure-thriller

The Wife Of Monte Cristo

A Wife's Revenge; or A Gambler's End
1904, (GB), Cricks & Sharp, b&w, 240 ft. (73.1m)
Standard crime-thriller (in 2 scenes): Cardsharp kills victim in duel

The Wild Beast of Crete
see The Minotaur

The Wild Child
see L'Enfant Sauvage

Wilder Napalm
1993, (USA), Baltimore Pictures/Tri Star, color, 109 mins.

<u>W</u>: Debra Winger, Dennis Quaid, Arliss Howard, M. Emmet Walsh, Jim Varney, Mimi Lieber, Marvin J. McIntyre
<u>D</u>: Glenn Gordon Caron   <u>SCR</u>: Vince Gilligan   MUSIC: Michael Kamen
Standard thriller: Man starts fires by power of thought via brother

Wildest Dreams
1990, (USA), color, 84 mins.
<u>W</u>: James Davies, Heidi Paine, Ruth Collins, Jane Hamilton, Deborah Blaisdell, Jill Johnson
<u>D</u>: Chuck Vincent
A.k.a. Bikini Genie
Minor comedy-fantasy: Genie helps youth meet girls

Wildfire
see It's a Dog's Life

Wildflower
1914, (GB), Hepworth, b&w, 1,050 ft. (320m)
<u>W</u>: Chrissie White (*Priscilla Angelina*)
<u>D</u>: Warwick Buckland
Standard crime-thriller: Orphan girl, adopted by gypsies, warns rich man of impending robbery

Wild in the Streets
1968, (USA), Jack Cash/AIP, color, 97 mins.
<u>W</u>: Shelley Winters, Christopher Jones, Diane Varsi, Hal Holbrook, Millie Perkins, Richard Pryor, Kevin Coughlin, Walter Winchell, Ed Begley, Bert Freed, Larry Bishop
<u>D</u>: Barry Shear   <u>SCR</u>: Robert Thom, based on story "The Day It All Happened, Baby"   <u>PHOTOG</u>: Richard Moore   <u>MUSIC</u>: Les Baxter
Unusual SF-thriller: Singing idol becomes U.S. dictator

Wild is My Love
1963, (USA), Mishkin, b&w, 74 mins.
<u>W</u>: Paul Hampton, Ray Fulmer, Bob Alexander
<u>P & D</u>: Richard Hilliard   <u>SCR</u>: Otto Lemming
Minor psychodrama: Tensions arise when stripper spends weekend with three college boys

Wild Jungle Captive
see Jungle Captive

The Wild Man of Borneo
1902, (GB), Haggar & Sons, b&w, 150 ft. (45.7m)
<u>D</u>: William Haggar
Standard fantasy: Knight battles forest hermit

Wild Strawberries
see Smultronstallet

Wild Thing
1987, (Can), Filmline Int'l/Atlantic, color, 92 mins.
<u>W</u>: Ron Knepper (*Wild Thing*), Kathleen Quinlan (*Jane*), Robert Davi (*Chopper*), Maury Chaykin (*Trask*), Betty Buckley (*Leah*), Guillaume Lemay-Thivierge (*Wild Thing, 10 years*), Robert Bednarski (*Wild Thing, 3 years*), Clark Johnson (*Winston*), Sean Hewitt (*Father Quinn*), Teddy Abner (*Rasheed*), Cree Summer Francks (*Lisa*), Shawn Levy (*Paul*), Rod Torchia, Christine Jones, Robert Austern, Tom Rack, Alexander Chapman, Robert Ozores, Lorena Gale, Sonny Forbes, Johnny O'Neil, Alastair Chartey, Richard Raybourne, Freddie James, George Popovich, Ken Roberts, Ron Lea, Jose Miguel Luis, Claire Rodger, Lynne Adams, Elizabeth Turbide, Diana Sookedeo, Doug Price, Patricia Hanganu, Mitsumi Takahashi, Michael Hunter, Audie Grant, Susan Seymour, Wally Martin, Jodie Resther, Carol Ann Francis, Douglas Leopold, Neil Kroetsch, Arthur Corber, Harry Standjofski, Tyrone Benskin, Neil Affleck, Arthur Holden, Griffith Brewer, Anthony Sherwood, Joe Cazalet, Donald Lamoreux, Sandra Blackie, Ray Roth, Bonnie Beck, Real Andrews, Jeffrey Chong, Richard Campbell, Leon Darnell Ramsoondar
<u>D</u>: Max Reid   <u>SCR</u>: John Sayles   <u>STORY</u>: John Sayles & Larry Stamper
<u>PHOTOG</u>: Rene Verzier   <u>MUSIC</u>: George S. Clinton
Modest adventure-thriller: Exploits of urban Tarzan

Wild, Wild Planet
see I Criminali della Galassia

Wild Women
1953, (USA), color
<u>W</u>: Lewis Wilson, Frances Dubay, Dana Wilson
Minor thriller: Jungle women capture safari white men

Wild Women of Wongo
1958, (USA), Wolcott/Tropical, color, 73 mins.
<u>W</u>: Ed Fury, Adrienne Bourbeau, Jean Hawkshaw, Johnny Walsh
<u>P</u>: George R. Black   <u>D</u>: James Wolcott   <u>SCR</u>: Cedric Rutherford
Amusing SF-adventure: Prehistoric tribes war

The Wild World of Batwoman
1966, (USA), ADP, b&w, 70 mins.
<u>W</u>: Katherine Victor, Steve Brodie, Lloyd Nelson, George Andre
<u>P, D & SCR</u>: Jerry Warren
A.k.a. She Was a Hippy Vampire
Minor SF-satire: Superheroine vs. evil scientist

Willard
1971, (USA), Bing Crosby Prods./CRC, color, 95 mins.
<u>W</u>: Bruce Davison (*Willard Stiles*), Ernest Borgnine (*Al Martin*), Elsa Lanchester (*Henrietta Stiles*), Sondra Locke (*Joan*), Joan Shawlee (*Alice*), Michael Dante (*Brandt*), Jody Gilbert (*Charlotte Stassen*), William Hansen (*Barskin*), J. Pat O'Malley (*Jonathan Farley*), John Myhers (*Carlson*), Almira Sessions (*Carrie Smith*), Helen Spring (*Mrs. Becker*), Pauline Drake (*Ida Stassen*), Alan Baxter, Sherry Presnell, Lola Kendrick, Robert Golden, Minta Durfee Arbuckle, Louise De Carlo, Arthur Tovey, Shirley Lawrence
<u>D</u>: Daniel Mann   <u>SCR</u>: Gilbert A. Ralston, from Stephen Gilbert's novel *Ratman's Notebooks*   <u>PHOTOG</u>: Robert B. Hauser   <u>MUSIC</u>: Alex North
"Davison's performance is a moving psychological portrait of frustrated loneliness and desperation verging on madness. Miss Lanchester, as a pathetic woman...is alternately moving and bizarre and the sequences between them are charged with tension"—Motion Picture Daily
Unusual thriller: Loner's trained rats help him gain revenge, cf. Ben

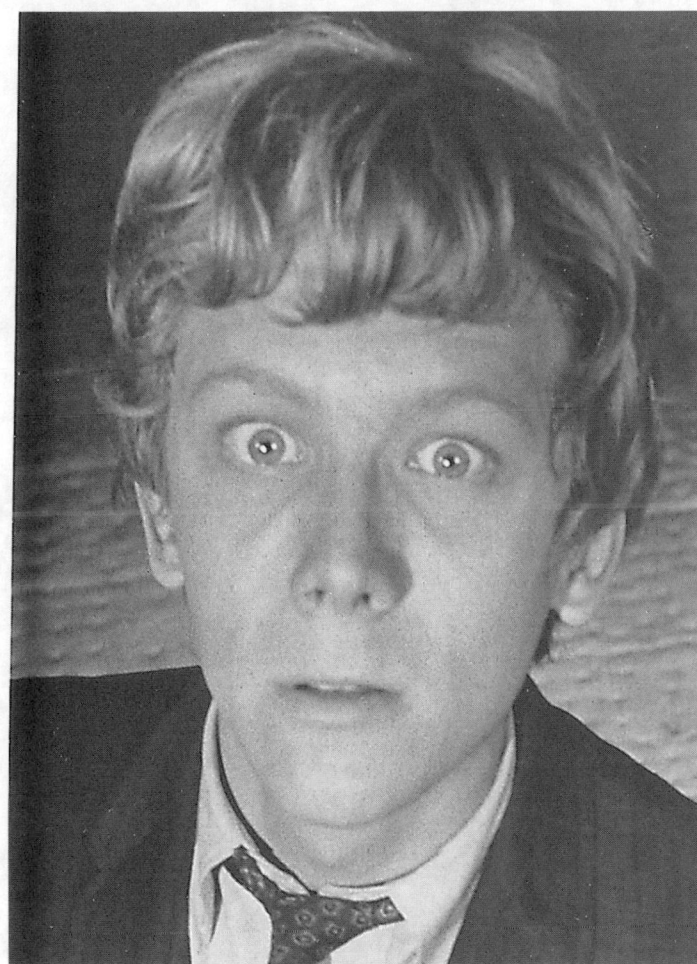

Willard: BRUCE DAVISON

William Drake, Thief
1912, (GB), Cricks & Martin, b&w, 1,020 ft. (310.9m)
<u>D</u>: Charles Calvert
Standard thriller: Suspected man proves maid stole jewels

William Tell (1896)
see Guillaume Tell

William Tell
1901, (GB), R.W. Paul, b&w, 100 ft. (30.5m)
Standard adventure: Archer shoots apple off son's head

William Tell
1901, (GB), Warwick Trading Co., b&w, 150 ft. (45.7m)
Standard adventure: "The row about an apple"

The Willies
1990, (USA), color, 120 mins.
<u>W</u>: James Karen, Sean Astin, Kathleen Freeman, Jeremy Miller
<u>D</u>: Brian Peck
Standard thriller: Three youngsters camp out in backyard, tell each other terror tales

Willie's Dream
1907, (GB), Sheffield Photo Co., b&w, 400 ft. (121.9m)
W: Mabel Strickland, Lenore Fisher
D: Frank Mottershaw
Standard comedy-fantasy: Boy dreams of playing pranks

Willie's Dream of Mick Squinter
1913, (GB), Martin/Thanhouser, b&w, 674 ft. (205.4m)
D: Dave Aylott
Standard comedy-fantasy: Boy reads "penny dreadful," dreams of being captured by gang

Willie's Magic Wand
1907, (GB), Urban, b&w, 320 ft. (97.5m)
D: Walter R. Booth
Standard fantasy: Magician's son plays tricks with father's magic wand

Willow
1988, (USA), Imagine Entertainment/Lucasfilm Ltd./MGM, color, 124 mins.
W: Val Kilmer (*Madmartigan*), Joanne Whalley (*Sorsha*), Warwick Davis (*Willow*), Jean Marsh (*Queen Bavmorda*), Patricia Hayes (*Raziel*), Billy Barty (*High Aldwin*), Pat Roach (*Kael*), Gavan O'Herlihy (*Airk*), Mark Northover (*Burglekutt*), Maria Holvoe (*Cherlindrea*), Julie Peters (*Kiaya*), Ruth & Kate Greenfield (*Elora Danan*), David Steinberg, Phil Fondacaro, Kevin Pollak, Rick Overgon
D: Ron Howard   SCR: Bob Dolman   STORY: George Lucas   PHOTOG: Adrian Biddle   MUSIC: James Horner
Ambitious fantasy: Adventurers protect infant from evil queen

Willy McBean and His Magic Machine
1965, (Jap), Magna, color, 94 mins.
VOICES: Larry Mann, Bille Richards & Alfie Scopp, Paul Ligman, Bunny Cowan, Paul Soles, Pegi Loder
MUSIC & LYRICS: Edward Thomas, Gene Forrell & James Polack
Juvenile fantasy (enacted by puppets)

Willy the Sparrow
1993, (USA), color
VOICE: Aaron Bybee
Standard animated fantasy: Boy becomes bird

Willy Wonka and the Chocolate Factory
1971, (USA), David L. Wolper/Para, color, 110 mins. (also 98 mins.)
W: Gene Wilder (*Willy Wonka*), Jack Albertson (*Grandpa Joe*), Michael Bollner (*Augustus Gloop*), Peter Ostrum (*Charlie Bucket*), Leonard Stone (*Beauregarde*), Ursula Reit (*Mrs. Gloop*), Denise Nickerson (*Violet*), Peter Capell (*Tinker*), Julie Dawn Cole (*Veruca*), Roy Kinnear (*Mr. Salt*), Aubrey Woods (*Mr. Bill*), Paris Themmen (*Mike Teevee*), Werner J. Heyking (*Jopeck*), Dodo Denney (*Mrs. Teevee*), Diana Sowle (*Mrs. Bucket*), David Battley (*Mr. Turkentine*), Dora Altmann (*Grandma Georgina*), Gunter Meisner (*Mr. Slugwork*), Ernest Ziegler (*Grandpa George*), Franziska Liebing (*Grandma Josephine*)
D: Mel Stuart   STORY & SCR: Roald Dahl, from his book *Charlie and the Chocolate Factory*   PHOTOG: Arthur Ibbetson   MUSIC & LYRICS: Leslie Bricusse & Anthony Newley   SONGS: *Candyman*
Standard fantasy: Dictatorial magnate runs bizarre candy factory

Willy Wonka and the Choclate Factory: JACK ALBERTSON AND PETER OSTRUM

Wimpy
see *Psycho*

The Wind in the Willows
1985, (USA), Disney, color, 100 mins.
VOICES: Paul Frees, from Kenneth Grahame's novel
Standard animated fantasy: Adventures of English animals

A Wind Named Amnesia
1993, (Jap), color, 80 mins.
D: Kazuo Yakmazaki
SCR: Hideyuki Kikuchi
Unusual SF-thriller: Strange wind erases mankind's memory

The Wind of Change
1961, (GB), Cresswell/Bry, b&w, 64 mins.
W: Donald Pleasence (*Pop*), Johnny Briggs (*Frank*), Ann Lynn (*Josie*), Hilda Fenemore (*Gladys*), Glyn Houston (*Sgt.Parker*), Norman Gunn (*Ron*), Bunny May, David Hemmings (*Ginger*)
P: John Dark   D: Vernon Sewell   STORY: Alexander Dore & John McLaren
Standard crime-thriller: Teen involved with vicious gang

The Window
1949, (USA), RKO, b&w, 73 mins.
W: Arthur Kennedy, Barbara Hale, Ruth Roman, Bobby Driscoll, Paul Stewart
D: Ted Tetzlaff   SCR: Mel Dinelli, from a story by Cornell Woolrich   PHOTOG: William Steiner   MUSIC: Roy Webb   MUSIC DIR: C. Bakaleinikoff   SPECIAL ACADEMY AWARD: Bobby Driscoll
Classic thriller: Boy witnesses murder, no one believes him. cf. **Cloak and Dagger** *(1984),* **The Boy Cried Murder** *(1965)*

Window to Paris
1994, (Russ-Fr), color, 95 mins.
W: Sergei Dontsov, Agnes Soral, Viktor Mikhailov, Nina Ousatova
Standard fantasy: Magical window frees beleaguered Soviet

Windows
1980, (USA), Michael Lobell/UA, color, 96 mins.
W: Talia Shire (*Emily Hollander*), Elizabeth Ashley (*Andrea Glassen*), Joseph Cortese (*Bob Luffrono*), Kay Medford (*Ida Marx*), Michael Gorrin (*Sam Marx*), Russell Horton (*Steven Hollander*), Michael Lipton (*Dr. Marin*), Linda Gillin (*The Policewoman*), Ron Ryan (*Det. Swid*), Rick Petrucelli (*Obecny*), Tony Di Benedetto (*Nick*), Bryce Bond (*The Voice Over*), Ken Chapin (*The Renting Agent*), Marty Greene (*Ira*), Robert Hodge (*The Desk Sgt.*), Bill Handy (*The Desk Officer*), Pat McNamara (*The Doorman*), Kyle Scott Jackson (*The Detective*), Gerry Vichi (*Ben*)
D: Gordon Willis   SCR: Barry Siegel   MUSIC: Ennio Morricone
Standard thriller: Lesbian terrorizes Manhattan woman

The Winged Serpent
see *Q*

Wings of Death
1961, (GB), Merton Park/Anglo-Amalgamated, b&w, 29 mins.
W: Harry H. Corbett (*Supt. Hammond*), Shelagh Fraser (*Diane Wilson*), Simon Lack (*Swain*)
P: Jack Greenwood   D: Allan Davis   STORY: James Eastwood, from a novel by Edgar Lustgarten
Standard short crime-thriller: Pilot's wife and her lover plant bomb in airplane

Wings of Desire
1987, (Fr-W. Ger), Orion Classics, color, 128 mins.
W: Bruno Ganz, Solveig Dommartin, Otto Sander, Curt Bois, Peter Falk
D: Wim Wenders   SCR: Wim Wenders & Peter Handke   PHOTOG: Henri Alekan   MUSIC: Jurgen Knieper
A.k.a. **Der Himmel Uber Berlin** *(Heaven Over Berlin)*
Unusual philosophical fantasy: Angel falls in love with mortal woman. cf. **City of Angels**

Wings of Fame
1990, (Neth), color, 109 mins.
W: Peter O'Toole, Colin Firth, Marie Trintignant, Gottfried John, Ellen Umlauf, Andrea Ferreol, Robert Stephens, Maria Becker
D: Otakar Votocek   PHOTOG: Alex Thomson
Unusual fantasy: Assassinated actor meets killer in the afterlife

Wink of an Eye
1958, (USA), UA, b&w, 72 mins.
W: Jonathan Kidd, Doris Dowling, Barbara Turner
P: Fernando Carrere   D: Winston Jones   SCR: Robert Radnitz, Robert Presnell Jr. & James Edmiston
Standard horror-comedy: Chemist suspected of killing wife

Winning His Stripes
1913, (GB), Hepworth, b&w, 875 ft. (266.7m)
W: Cyril Morton (*Jack Harris*), Alma Taylor (*Mrs. Harris*), Harry Royston (*PC Warner*)
D: Frank Wilson
Standard crime-thriller: Policeman and escaped convict capture bank robbers

Winterbeast
1992, (USA), color, 77 mins.
W: Tim R. Morgan, Mike Magri
Minor fantasy: Workmen figure enemy protagonist

Winter Kills
1979, (USA), Winter Gold/ICA/Embassy, color, 96 mins.

W: Jeff Bridges, John Huston, Anthony Perkins, Eli Wallach, Sterling Hayden, Dorothy Malone, Ralph Meeker, Belinda Bauer, Richard Boone, Elizabeth Taylor, Brad Dexter, Tomas Milian, Toshiro Mifune, Donald Moffat, David Spielberg, Michael Toma, Ed Madsen, Irving Selbst, Chris Soldo, Tisa Farrow, Joe Spinell
D & SCR: William Richert, from a novel by Richard Condon   **PHOTOG:** Vilmos Zsigmond   **MUSIC:** Maurice Jarre
Superior thriller: Brother of murdered U.S. president seeks real assassin

Wired to Kill
1986, (USA), color, 96 mins.
W: Merritt Butrick, Emily Longstreth, Devin Hoelscher, Frank Collison
D: Francis Schaeffer
Minor SF-thriller: Teens engineer device for revenge

Wishes
1934, (GB), BIP/Pathe, b&w, 35 mins.
W: Wallace Lupino (*Wally*), Barry Lupino (*Barry*), Gus McNaughton, Hal Gordon
D: W.P. Kellino   **STORY:** Wallace Lupino
Standard fantasy: Tramp finds magic talisman

Wishful Thinking
1992, (USA), color, 94 mins.
W: Murray Langston, Michelle Johnson, Ruth Buzzi, Johnny Dark, Billy Barty, Ray "Boom Boom" Mancini, Vic Dunlop, Kip Addotta
D: Murray Langston
Standard fantasy: Screenwriter acquires magical power

The Wishmaker
1985, (USA), color, 54 mins.
Minor fantasy: Youth squanders three wishes

Wishman
1993, (USA), Curb Esquire/Monarch, color, 89 mins.
W: Paul Le Mat, Geoffrey Lewis, Paul Gleason, Quinn Kessler, Nancy Parsons, Gailard Sartain, Brion James
D & SCR: Mike Marvin
Standard fantasy: Garbageman aids homeless genie

Wishmaster
1997, (USA), color, 90 mins.
W: Robert Englund (*Beaumont*), Tony Todd (*Johnny*), Wendy Benson (*Shannon*), Tony Crane (*Josh*), Tammy Lauren, Andrew Divoff, Kane Hodder
D: Robert Kurtzman   **SCR:** Peter Atkins
Standard horror-fantasy: Evil genie freed from precious stone

Wish Me Luck
1995, (USA), color
W: Avalon Anders, Zen Gesner
D: Philp J. Jones
Minor comedy-fantasy: Genie and trio of cheerleaders help nerd lose his virginity

Wish Upon a Star
1996, (USA), Leucadia, color
W: Danielle Harris, Katherine Heigl, Don Jeffcoat, Scott Wilkinson, Mary Parker Williams, Lois Chiles
D: Blair Treu   **SCR:** Jessica Barondes   **PHOTOG:** Brian Sullivan   **MUSIC:** Ray Colcord
Standard comedy: Sisters trade places

The Witch
1906, (Fr), Star, b&w, 252m (826.8 ft./14 mins.)
WRIT, P & D: Georges Melies
Standard fantasy

The Witch (1955)
see La Sorciere

The Witch (1966)
see La Strega in Amore

The Witch (1985)
see Superstition

Witch Academy
1993, (USA), color
W: Priscilla Barnes
Standard fantasy-thriller: Devil turns college misfit into deadly seductress

Witch and Warlock
see Witchcraft (1964)

Witchblade
1999, (USA), WB-TV, color
TVM, standard SF-fantasy

Witchboard
1987, (USA), Paragon Arts Int'l/Cinema Group, color, 97 mins.
W: Todd Allen (*Jim*), Tawny Kitaen (*Linda*), Stephen Nichols (*Brandon*), Kathleen

Wilhoite (*Zarabeth*), Burke Byrnes (*Lt. Dewhurst*), Rose Marie (*The Landlady*), Judy Tatum, James W. Quinn, Susan Nickerson, J.P. Luebsen, Clare Bristol
WRIT & D: Kevin S. Tenney   **PHOTOG:** Roy H. Wagner   **SPCL-FX:** Tassilo Baur   **MUSIC:** Dennis Michael Tenney
Standard horror-thriller: Ouija board conjures demonic forces. cf. **Witchtrap**

Witchboard 2: The Devil's Doorway
1993, (USA), color, 100 mins.
W: Ami Dolenz, Laraine Newman, Timothy Gibbs, John Gatins
D & SCR: Kevin S. Tenney   **MUSIC:** Dennis Michael Tenney
Standard SF-horror: Artist experiments with ouija board, opens gateway to pure evil

Witchboard: The Possession
1995, (USA), color, 95 mins.
W: David Nerman, Locky Lambert, Cedric Smith, Donna Sarrasin
D: Peter Svatek   **SCR:** Kevin S. Tenney & Jon Ezrine   **PHOTOG:** Barry Gravelle
Standard horror-fantasy: Bedevilled ouija board provides stock tips

Witchcraft (1920)
see Haxan

Witchcraft
1964, (GB), Parroch-McCallum/20th-Fox, b&w, 80 mins.
W: Lon Chaney Jr. (*Morgan Whitlock*), Jack Hedley (*Bill Lanier*), Jill Dixon (*Tracy Lanier*), Marie Ney (*Malvina Lanier*), Viola Keats (*Helen Lanier*), David Weston (*Todd Lanier*), Yvette Rees (*Vanessa Whitlock*), Victor Brooks (*Insp. Baldwin*), Diane Clare (*Amy Whitlock*)
P: Robert L. Lippert & Jack Parsons   **D:** Don Sharp   **SCR:** Harry Spalding   **PHOTOG:** Arthur Lavis   **MUSIC:** Carlos Martelli   **DESIGN:** George Provis
orig. to be titled **The Terrible Truth About Witchcraft** *or* **Witch and Warlock**
Standard horror-fantasy: 300-year-old witch thwarts plans for development of cemetery

Witchcraft
1988, (USA), color
W: Anat "Topol" Barzilai, Gary Sloan, Lee Kisman, Deborah Scott
D: Robert Spera
Minor horror-fantasy: Young couple burned at stake, compelled to wander hell until agreing to bear Satan's son

Witchcraft 2: The Temptress
1990, (USA), color, 88 mins.
W: Charles Solomon, Mia Ruiz, Delia Sheppard
D: Mark Woods
Minor fantasy-thriller: Seductress lures youth into occult

Witchcraft 3: The Kiss of Death
1991, (USA), Vista Street, color
W: Charles Solomon, Lisa Toothman, William L. Baker, Lena Hall
D: R.L. Tillmanns
Minor horror-fantasy: Satanic beauty lures former master of occult

Witchcraft 4: Virgin Heart
1992, (USA), color, 92 mins.
W: Charles Solomon, Julie Strain, Clive Pearson, Barbara Dow, Jason O'Gulihar, Lisa Jay Harrington
D: James Merendino
Minor fantasy-thriller: Attorney falls into satanic trap

Witchcraft 5: Dance with the Devil
1992, (USA), color, 94 mins.
W: Marlen Kennedy, Carolyn Taye-Loren, Nicole Sassaman, Aysha Hauer
D: Talun Hsu
Minor fantasy-thriller: Unpleasant loopholes in satanic contracts

Witchcraft 6: The Devil's Mistress
1994, (USA), color, 86 mins.
W: Kurt Alan, John E. Holiday, Bryan Nutter, Jerry Spicer, Shannon Lead
D & SCR: Julie Davis
Minor fantasy-thriller: Satanic disciple attempts virgin sacrifice

Witchcraft 7: Judgement hour
1995, (USA), color, 91 mins.
W: David Byrnes, April Breneman, Alisa Christensen, John Cragen, Loren Schmalle
D: Michael Paul Girard   **SCR:** Peter Fleming   **PHOTOG:** Denis Maloney   **MUSIC:** Miriam Cutler
Minor fantasy-thriller: Modern warlock vs. evil vampire

Witchcraft Through the Ages
see Haxan

Witchery
1989, (USA), Filmirage/Vidmark, (video), color, 96 mins.
W: Linda Blair (*Jane Brooks*), David Hasselhoff (*Gary*), Catherine Hickland (*Linda Sullivan*), Annie Rosss (*Rose Brooks*), Hildegard Knef (*The Lady in Black*), Kara Lynch (*Cindy*), Leslie Cumming (*Leslie*), Victoria Biggers (*The Secretary*), Bob Champagne (*Freddie Brooks*), James Hanes (*Jon*), Rick Farnsworth (*Jerry Giordano*), Frank Cammarata (*Tony Giordano*), Michael

Manchester *(Tommy Brooks)*, Ely Coughlin *(Satan)*, Richard Ladenburg *(The Sheriff)*, George Stevens *(The Fisherman)*
D: Martin Newlin **PHOTOG:** John Wynn **SPCL-FX:** Maurizio Trani
Made-for-Video, minor horror-fantasy: Stranded group encounters satanism

The Witches
1966, (GB), Hammer-7Arts/20th-Fox, color, 91 mins.
W: Joan Fontaine *(Gwen Mayfield)*, Kay Walsh *(Stephanie Bax)*, Alec McCowen *(Alan Bax)*, Duncan Lamont *(Bob Curd)*, Martin Stephens *(Ronnie Dowsett)*, Gwen Ffrangcon-Davies *(Granny Rigg)*, John Collin *(Dowsett)*, Ingrid Brett *(Linda Rigg)*, Leonard Rossiter *(Dr. Wallis)*, Michele Dotrice *(Valerie)*, Ann Bell *(Sally)*
P: Anthony Nelson Keys **D:** Cyril Frankel **SCR:** Nigel Kneale, from a novel by Peter Curtis **PHOTOG:** Arthur Grant **MUSIC:** Richard Rodney Bennett
*USA retitle, **The Devil's Own***
Unusual thriller: Headmistress finds black arts flourishing in English countryside

The Witches
1990, (GB), Lorimar/WB, color, 92 mins.
W: Anjelica Huston *(Miss Ernst/Grand High Witch)*, Jasen Fisher *(Luke)*, Mai Zetterling *(Helga)*, Rowan Atkinson *(Mr. Stringer)*, Bill Paterson *(Mr. Jenkins)*, Charlie Potter *(Bruno Jenkins)*, Brenda Blethyn *(Mrs. Jenkins)*, Annabel Brooks *(Nicola)*, Anne Lambton *(The Woman in Black)*, Jane Horrocks *(Miss Irvine)*, Sukie Smith *(Marlene)*, Rosamund Greenwood *(Janice)*, Rose English *(Dora)*, Jenny Runacre *(Elsie)*, Emma Relph *(Millie)*, Nora Connolly *(Beatrice)*, Anjelique Rockas *(Henrietta)*, Ann Tirard *(Lady #1)*, Leila Hoffman *(Lady #2)*, Jim Carter *(The Head Chef)*, Roberta Taylor *(The Witch Chef)*, Debra Gillett *(The Waitress)*, Brian Hawksley *(The Elderly Waiter)*, Darcy Flynn *(Luke's Mother)*, Vincent Marzello *(Luke's Father)*, Greta Nordra *(The Norwegian Witch)*, Serena Harragin *(The Doctor)*, Elsie Eide *(Erica)*, Kristin Steinsland *(Child Helga)*, Ola Otnes *(Erica's Father)*, Merete Armand *(Erica's Mother)*, Sverre Rossummoen *(A Policeman)*
EXEC P: Jim Henson **D:** Nicolas Roeg **SCR:** Allan Scott, from Roald Dahl's book **PHOTOG:** Harvey Harrison **MUSIC:** Stanley Myers
Superior fantasy-thriller: Sorceress plots to turn children into mice

The Witches and the Grinnygog
1983, (GB), TVS, (Made for TV Movie), color, 102 mins.
W: Zoe Loftin, Adam Woodyatt, Giles Harper, Heidi Mayo, Patricia Hayes, Robert Swann, Paul Curtis, John Barrard, Olu Jacobs, Jane Wood, Eva Griffith, Anne Dyson, Sheila Grant, Anna Wing
D: Diarmuid Lawrence **TELEPLAY:** Roy Russell, from Dorothy Edwards' book
TVM, minor fantasy: Pagan statue introduces children to world of wicca

The Witches Attack
1965, (Mex), b&w
Minor fantasy-thriller

The Witches' Black Sabbath
1988, (It), color
W: Raffaella Rossellini, Daniel Ezralov
Minor fantasy-thriller

Witches' Brew
1980, (USA), Herbert L. Struck/Joshua Lightman/Donna Ashbrook/NBC-TV, color, 98 mins.
W: Richard Benjamin *(Joshua Lightman)*, Teri Gart *(Margaret Lightman)*, Lana Turner *(Vivian Cross)*, Kathryn Leigh Scott *(Susan Carey)*, James R. Winker *(Linus Cross)*, Elen Farran *(Joanna Arnholt)*, Bill Sorrels *(Nick Carey)*, Nathan Roth *(Ben Cohn)*, Kelly Jean Peters *(Linda Reynolds)*, Lawrence Guy *(Carl Groton)*, Jordan Charney *(Charlie Reynolds)*, Barbara Minkus-Barron *(The Saleswoman)*, Bonnie Gondell *(Marcia Groton)*, Carlos Royval *(Patrol Officer #1)*, Tony Kulik *(Patrol Officer #2)*, Gerald Ray *(Motor Officer #1)*, Charles "Corky" Behrle *(Motor Officer #2)*, Leonard Chichester *(Motor Officer #3)*, Richard Stobie *(The Security Officer)*, Joyce McNeal *(The Nurse)*, Edmund Stoiber *(The Doctor)*, Jon Reigrod *(Schwartz)*, Kerry Stein *(The Funeral Director)*, Shepard Saunders *(The Minister)*, Deborah Kim Moore *(The Female Student)*, Steve Bond *(Mike)*, Gaye Nelson *(Tina)*, Al Ginsburg *(The History Professor)*, Lennie Bleecher *(The Literature Professor)*, Robert Zaigue *(The French Professor)*
D: Richard Shorr (additional dir by Herbert L. Strock) **SCR:** Syd Dutton & Richard Shorr, loosely based (uncredited) on Fritz Leiber's novel *Conjure Wife* **PHOTOG:** Norman Gerard (additional photog by Joao Fernandes) **SPCL-FX:** Conrad Rothman **MUSIC:** John Parker
A.k.a. "Which Witch is Which?"
*Minor fantasy-thriller: Faculty wives practice witchcraft. Lana Turner's last film. Made in 1978; unreleased, debuted on Showtime Cable. cf. **Night of the Eagle** and **Weird Woman***

Witches' Mountain
1970, (Sp), Avco Embassy, color, 98 mins.
W: Patty Shepard, John Caffari, Monica Randall
D: Raul Artigot
Minor horror-thriller: News photographer visits site of witch burning

The Witches of Eastwick
1987, (USA), Guber-Peters/WB, color, 118 mins.
W: Jack Nicholson *(Daryl Van Horne)*, Cher *(Alexandra)*, Susan Sarandon *(Jane)*, Michelle Pfeiffer *(Sukie)*, Veronica Cartwright, Carel Struycken, Helen Lloyd Breed, Keith Jochim, Lansdale Chatfield, Sean O'Sullivan

D: George Miller **SCR:** Michael Cristofer, from John Updike's novel **PHOTOG:** Vilmos Zsigmond **MUSIC:** John Williams
Superior fantasy-thriller: Three women conjure devil

The Witches of Salem
*see **Les Sorcieres de Salem***

Witch Finder General
1968, (GB), Tigon/AIP, color, 87 mins.
W: Vincent Price *(Matthew Hopkins)*, Ian Ogilvy *(Richard Marshall)*, Rupert Davies *(John Lowes)*, Wilfrid Brambell *(Master Coach)*, Patrick Wymark *(Oliver Cromwell)*, Nicky Henson *(Trooper Swallow)*, Robert Russell *(John Stearne)*, Hilary Dwyer *(Sara)*, Tony Selby *(Salter)*, Michael Beint *(Capt. Gordon)*, Peter Haigh *(The Magistrate)*, Alf Joint, Bernard Kay, Godfrey James
P: Tony Tenser, Arnold Miller & Louis M. Heyward **D:** Michael Reeves **SCR:** Tom Baker & Michael Reeves, from a novel by Ronald Bassett **PHOTOG:** John Coquillon **MUSIC:** Paul Ferris & Jim Morahan
*USA retitle, **Conqueror Worm***
Standard horror-thriller: Lawyer tortures to obtain confessions of witchcraft

The Witch House
*see **La Maldicion de La Llorona***

Witch House (1968)
*see **Curse of the Crimson Altar***

Witch Hunt
1994, (USA), HBO-TV, color, 100 mins.
W: Dennis Hopper, Penelope Ann Miler, Eric Bogosian, Sheryl Lee Ralph, Julian Sands, Alan Rosenberg, Valerie Mahaffey, Debi Mazar
D: Paul Schrader **WRIT:** Joseph Dougherty **MUSIC:** Angelo Badalamenti
Standard fantasy-thriller: Private eye seeks killer of movie mogul in bewitched Hollywood

The Witching
*see **Necromancy***

The Witching of Ben Wagner
1990, (USA), color, 97 mins.
W: Justin Gocke, Sam Bottoms *(Sam Wagner)*, Harriet Hall *(Kathy Wagner)*
D: Paul Annett
Standard fantasy: Boy suspects magical stranger is responsible for family problems

Witching Time/The Silent Scream
1980, (GB), (Made fot TV Movie), color
W: Peter Cushing, Brian Cox, Patricia Quinn, Jon Finch
*TVM, minor thriller (2 episodes of teleseries **House of Horror**)*

The Witch in Love
*see **La Strega in Amore***

A Witch in Paradise
*see **Bell, Book and Candle***

Witchkill
*see **The Witchmaker***

The Witch Kiss
1907, (Fr), b&w
Standard fantasy

The Witchmaker
1969, (USA), LQ-Jaf/Excelsior, color, 97 mins.
W: John Lodge *(Luther)*, Alvy Moore *(Dr. Hayes)*, Anthony Eisley *(Victor)*, Thordis Brandt *(Tasha)*, Helene Winston *(Jessie #1)*, Warene Ott *(Jessie #2)*, Kathy Lynn *(Patty)*, Shelby Grant *(Maggie)*, Sue Bernard *(Felicity)*, Carolyn Rhodimer *(Marta)*, Howard Viet *(San Blas)*, Diane Webber *(Nautch)*, Nancy Crawford *(Goody)*, Patty Wymer *(The Hag of Devon)*, Larry Vincent *(Amos)*, Gwen Lipscomb *(Fong)*, Del Kaye *(Le Singe)*, Valya Garanda *(El A Haish Ma)*, Tony Benson, Robyn Millan, Burt Mustin
WRIT & D: William O. Brown **PHOTOG:** John Arthur Morrill **MUSIC:** Jaime Mendoza-Nava
*A.k.a. **Legend of Witch Hollow** and **Witchkill***
Minor thriller: Murder and satanism in Louisiana swamps

The Witch of the Welsh Mountains
1912, (GB), B&C/MP, b&w, 990 ft. (301.8m)
W: Dorothy Foster *(Catrin Morgan)*, Sidney Cairns *(Ewan ap Ewan)*, Beatrice de Burgh *(Yeda)*, Lady Georgina St. George *(Widow Evans)*
D: Sidney Northcote **STORY:** Harold Brett
Standard thriller: Wounded widow recovers in time to save wrong girl from being burned at stake

The Witch's Curse
*see **Maciste al Inferno***

The Witch's Mirror
*see **El Espejo de la Bruja***

The Witch's Revenge
see Le Sorcier

Witchtrap
1989, (USA), color, 87 mins.
W: James W. Quinn, Kathleen Bailey, Linnea Quigley
D: Kevin S. Tenney
Minor fantasy-thriller (a sequel to **Witchboard***): Mansion's new owner hires psychics to exorcise disturbed ghost*

A Witch without a Broom
1966, (Sp), Sidney W. Pink/Ufa Int'l/Lacy Int'l, color, 71 mins (also 86 mins.).
W: Jeff Hunter (*Prof. Logan*), Maria Perschy (*Marianna*), Gustavo Rojo (*Caius*), Perla Cristal (*Octavia*), Reginald Gilliam, Katherine Ellison, Al Mulock, Carl Rapp, Gillian Simpson, John Clark, May Johnson, Lewis Gordon, Susan Talbot
D: Joe Lacy [Jose E. Lorietta]   SCR: Howard Berk (J. L. Navarro Basso)   ORIG. STORY: Jose Luis Navarro Basso & Jose Maria Elorrietta   PHOTOG: Al Nieva   MUSIC: F. Garcia Morcillo
Standard SF-fantasy: Medieval sorceress transports history professor through time and space

With a Vengeance
1992, (USA), color, 95 mins.
W: Melissa Gilbert Brinkman, John Scalia, Matthew Lawrence, Roger Aaron Brown, Michael Gross
D: Michael Switzer   PHOTOG: Robert Draper   MUSIC: J. Peter Robinson
TVM, standard thriller: Killer stalks woman witness, from Charlotte Armstrong's novel Mischief

With Human Instinct
1913, (GB), B&C/MP, b&w, 845 ft. (283m)
W: George Foley (*Mr. West*), Alice Moseley (*Janet*), Henry Harrison (*Crooky*), Minnie Levine (*Mrs. West*), Francis Everard (*Ginger*), Ida Strathan (*Baby West*)
D: H.O. Martinek
Standard crime-thriller: Pet bulldog rescues kidnapped baby

With Mask and Pistol
1911, (GB), Urban Trading Co., b&w, 860 ft. (262.1m)
Standard adventure-thriller: Earl's disowned son turns highwayman, forces brother to return father's jewels

Without a Clue
1988, (GB), ITC/Orion, color, 107 mins.
W: Michael Caine (*Sherlock Holmes*), Ben Kingsley (*Dr. John Watson*), Jeffrey Jones (*Insp. Lestrade*), Lysette Anthony (*The Fake Leslie*), Paul Freeman (*Prof. Moriarty*), Matthew Savage (*Wiggins*), Nigel Davenport (*Lord Smithwick*), Peter Cook (*Greenhough*), Pat Keen (*Mrs. Hudson*), Tim Killick (*Sebastian*), John Warner (*Peter Giles*), Matthew Sim (*The Real Leslie*), Harold Innocent (*Mayor Johnson*), George Sweeney (*John Clay*), Murray Ewan (*Archie*), Stephen Tiller (*Reporter #1*), Michael O'Hagan (*Reporter #2*), Ivor Roberts (*Reporter #3*), Martin Pallot (*The Photographer*), James Bree (*The Barrister*), Caroline Milmoe (*Constance*), Clive Mantle (*Thug #1*), Dave Cooper (*Thug #2*), Gregor Fisher (*The Bobby at the Warehouse*), Steven O'Donnell (*The Bartender*), Sarah Parr-Byrne (*The Singer*), Richard Henry, Lesley Daine, John Tordoff, Jennifer Guy, Alexandra Spencer, Sam Davies, Adam Kotz, Elizabeth Spencer, John Surman, Andy Bradford, Chris Webb, Les White, Evan Russell, Alan Bodenham, Prince the Wonder Dog (*The Duke*)
D: Thom Eberhardt   SCR: Gary Murphy & Larry Strawther   PHOTOG: Alan Hume   MUSIC: Henry Mancini
orig. to be titled **Sherlock and Me**
Modest comedy-thriller: Fake sleuth stalks master criminal

Without Apparent Motive
1972, (Fr), 20th-Fox, color, 102 mins.
W: Jean-Louis Trintignant, Dominique Sanda
Standard thriller

Without Warning (1938)
see **The Invisible Menace**

Without Warning
1980, (Can), Filmways, color, 89 mins.
W: Jack Palance (*Taylor*), Martin Landau (*Fred*), Tarah Nutter (*Sandy*), Christopher S. Nelson (*Greg*), Cameron Mitchell (*Hunter*), Neville Brand (*Leo*), Sue Ane Langdon (*Aggie*), Ralph Meeker (*Dave*), Larry Storch (*The Scoutmaster*), Lynn Theel (*Beth*), David Caruso (*Tom*), Darby Hinton (*Randy*)
P & D: Greydon Clark   SCR: Lyn Freeman, Daniel Grodnik, Ben Nett & Steve Mathis   PHOTOG: Dean Cundey   MUSIC: Dan Wyman
Minor SF-thriller: Alien beings prey on small town

The Witness
1959, (GB), Merton Park/Anglo-Amalgamated, b&w, 58 mins.
W: Dermot Walsh (*Richard Brinton*), Greta Gynt (*May*), John Chandos (*Lodden*), Russell Napier (*Insp. Rosewarne*), Martin Stephens (*Peter Brinton*), Derek Hedger Wallace (*Manbre*)
P: Jack Greenwood   D: Geoffrey Muller   SCR: Julian Bond   STORY: John Salt
Standard crime-thriller: Boy betrays ex-convict father to police

Witness for the Prosecution
1957, (USA), UA, b&w, 116 mins.
W: Charles Laughton (*Sir Wilfrid Robarts*), Marlene Dietrich (*Christine Vole*), Tyrone Power (*Leonard Vole*), Elsa Lanchester (*Miss Plimsoll*), Torin Thatcher (*Mr. Meyers*), Una O'Connor (*Janet MacKenzie*), Henry Daniell (*Mayhew*), Ruta Lee (*Diana*), John Williams (*Brogan-Moore*), Ian Wolfe (*Carter*), Philip Tonge (*Insp. Hearne*), Norma Varden (*Mrs. French*), Francis Compton (*The Judge*), Molly Roden (*Miss McHugh*), Ottola Nesmith (*Miss Johnson*), Marjorie Eaton (*Miss O'Brien*)
D: Billy Wilder   SCR: Billy Wilder & Harry Kurnitz, from play based on the novel by Agatha Christie   PHOTOG: Russell Harlan   MUSIC: Ernest Gold
Superior thriller: Man accused of murder, scheming wife undermines defense

Witness in the Dark
1959, (GB), Ethiro/RFD, b&w, 62 mins.
W: Patricia Dainton (*Jane Pringle*), Conrad Phillips (*Insp. Coates*), Madge Ryan (*Mrs. Finch*), Nigel Green (*The Intruder*), Enid Lorimer (*Mrs. Temple*), Richard O'Sullivan (*Don Theobold*), Stuart Saunders (*Mr. Finch*), Ian Colin (*Supt. Tompson*)
P: Norman Williams   D: Wolf Rilla   STORY: Leigh Vance & John Lemont
Standard thriller: Blind girl helps police trap old lady's killer

Witness to Murder
1954, (USA), UA, b&w, 83 mins.
W: Barbara Stanwyck (*Cheryl Draper*), Gary Merrill (*Lawrence Mathews*), George Sanders (*Albert Richter*), Harry Shannon (*Capt. Donnelly*), Jesse White (*Eddie Vincent*), Claire Carleton (*The Blonde*), Lewis Martin (*The Psychiatrist*), Dick Elliott (*The Apartment Manager*), Harry Tyler (*Charlie*), Juanita Moore (*The Woman*), Joy Hallward (*The Woman's Co-worker*), Gertrude Graner (*The Policewoman*), Adeline DeWalt Reynolds (*The Old Lady*)
WRIT & P: Chester Erskine   D: Roy Rowland   PHOTOG: John Alton   MUSIC: Herschel Burke Gilbert
Standard thriller: Woman sees neighbor kill, no one believes her

Witness to the Execution
1994, (USA), NBC-TV, color, 95 mins.
W: Sean Young, Tim Daly, Dee Wallace Stone, Alan Fudge, Len Cariou, George Newbern
D: Tommy Lee Wallace   TELEPLAY: Thomas Baum
TVM, standard thriller: Man's execution televised

The Wiz
1978, (USA), Motown/Univ, color, 133 mins.
W: Diana Ross (*Dorothy*), Michael Jackson (*The Scarecrow*), Nipsey Russell (*The Tin Man*), Mabel King (*Evillene*), Ted Ross (*The Lion*), Lena Horne (*Glinda the Good*), Richard Pryor (*The Wiz*), Theresa Merritt (*Aunt Em*), Thelma Carpenter (*Miss One*), Stanley Greene (*Uncle Henry*), Clyde J. Barrett (*The Subway Peddler*), Carlos Cleveland, Glory Van Scott, Carlton Johnson, Harry Madsen, Vicki Baltimore, Roderick Spencer Sibert, Derrick Bell, Kashka Banjoko, Damon Pearce, Ronald Smokey Stevens, Tony Brealond, Clinton Jackson, Joe Lynn, Charles Rodriguez, Ted Williams, Mabel Robinson, Gay Faulkner, Ted Butler, Donna Patrice Ingram, Mariann Aalda, Aaron Boddie, T.B. Skinner, Jamie Perry, Daphne McWilliams, Douglas Berring, James Shaw, Johnny Brown, Kevin Stockton, Gyle Waddy, Dorothy Fox, Frances Salisbury, Claude Brooks, Beatrice Dunmore, Traci Core, Donald King, Billie Allen, Willie Carpenter, Denise DeJon, Alvin Alexis
D: Sidney Lumet   SCR: Joel Schumacher, from stage musical based on L. Frank Baum's classic *The Wonderful Wizard of Oz*   PHOTOG: Oswald Morris   SPCL-FX: Albert Whitlock   MUSIC ADAPT & SUPERVISED: Quincy Jones   SONGS: Ease on Down the Road, He's the Wizard, Believe in Yourself, You Can't Win, What Would I Do If I Could Feel?, Be a Lion, A Brand New Day, Is This What Feeling Gets? & Home
Lavish musical-fantasy: Young schoolteacher is transported to magical land. All black cast

The Wizard
1927, (USA), Fox, b&w, 60 mins.
W: Edmund Lowe, Leila Hyams, George Kotsonaros, Gustav von Seyffertitz, Barry Norton, Norman Trevor
D: Richard Rosson   SCR: Harry O. Hoyt & Andrew Bennison, based on Gaston Leroux's play *Balaoo*   PHOTOG: Frank B. Good
Standard thriller: Mad surgeon creates murderous ape man

The Wizard and the Brigands
1911, (GB), Natural Colour Kinematograph Co., color, 410 ft. (125m)
D: Walter R. Booth & Theo Bouwmeester
Standard fantasy: Wizard causes Spanish brigands to vanish

The Wizard of Baghdad
1960, (USA), 20th-Fox, color, 92 mins.
W: Dick Shawn, Diane Baker, Barry Coe, John Van Dreelen, Robert F. Simon, Vaughn Taylor, Kim Hamilton, Don Beddoe, Michael David, Stanley Adams, Leslie Warner, William Edmonson, Michael Burns
P: Sam Katzman   D: George Sherman   SCR: Jesse Lasky Jr. & Pat Silver, from a story by Samuel Newman   PHOTOG: Ellis W. Carter   MUSIC: Irving Gertz
Standard comedy-fantasy: Genie assigned tasks

The Wizard of Gore

1970, (USA), Mayflower/Boxoffice Spectaculars, color, 96 mins.
W: Ray Sager, Judy Cler, Wayne Rattay, Jim Rau, Monika Blackwell, Phil Laurensen, Don Alexander, John Elliott, Corinne Kirkin
P & D: Herschell Gordon Lewis **SCR:** Allen Kahn **PHOTOG:** Eskandar Ameripoor **MUSIC:** Larry Wellington
Standard horror-satire: Stage magician inspires suicides

The Wizard of Mars

1964, (USA), Karston-Hewitt/American General, color, 81 mins.
W: John Carradine, Roger Gentry, Vic McGee, Eve Bernhardt, Jerry Rannow
P, D, & SCR: David L. Hewitt **STORY:** David L. Hewiyy & Armando Busick
PHOTOG: Austin McKinney **SPCL-FX:** Cinema Research
video-cassette retitle, **Horrors of the Red Planet**
Minor SF-adventure: Astronauts find lost Martian city

The Wizard of Oz

1910, (USA), Selig, b&w
W: Romola Remus *(Dorothy)*
based on L. Frank Baum's The Wonderful Wizard of Oz
Standard fantasy: Girl visits land of fantasy

The Wizard of Oz

1925, (USA), Chadwick, b&w, 7 reels (93 mins.)

The Wizard of Oz: JACK HALEY, BERT LAHR, JUDY GARLAND, FRANK MORGAN AND RAY BOLGER

W: Dorothy Dwan *(Dorothy)*, Larry Semon, Oliver Hardy, Josef Swickard, Virginia Pearson, Bryant Washburn
D: Larry Semon, from L. Frank Baum's *The Wonderful Wizard of Oz*
Standard fantasy: Girl's adventures in fantastic land

The Wizard of Oz

1939, (USA), MGM, color & b&w, 101 mins.
W: Judy Garland *(Dorothy)*, Bert Lahr *(The Cowardly Lion)*, Ray Bolger *(The Scarecrow)*, Jack Haley *(The Tin Man)*, Margaret Hamilton *(The Wicked Witch of the West)*, Frank Morgan *(The Wizard of Oz)*, Billie Burke *(Glinda, the Good Witch of the North)*, Clara Blandick *(Aunty Em)*, Charley Grapewin, Pat Walshe, Prince Denis
P: Mervyn LeRoy **D:** Victor Fleming **SCR:** Noel Langley, Florence Ryerson & Edgar Allan Woolf, from L. Frank Baum's *The Wonderful Wizard of Oz*
PHOTOG: Harold Rosson **SPCL-FX:** A. Arnold Gillespie **MUSIC:** Harold Arlen. Academy Award Score by Herbert Stothart **LYRICS:** E.Y. "Yip" Harburg **SONGS:** *If I Only Had a Brain, Over the Rainbow* (Oscar), *Follow the Yellow Brick Road, Ding Dong, the Witch is Dead & We're Off to see the Wizard*
Classic fantasy: Tornado transports girl to land of bizarre wonders. Special Academy Award, Judy Garland

The Wizard of Oz

1983, (Jap), color
from L. Frank Baum's The Wonderful Wizard of Oz
Minor fantasy (animated)

Wizards

1977, (USA), 20th-Fox, color, 81 mins.

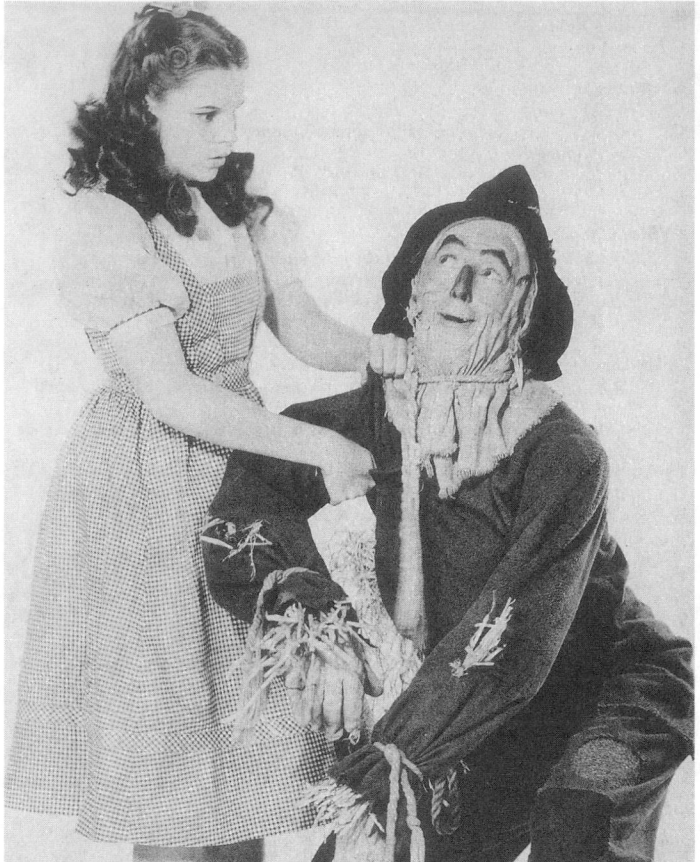

The Wizard of Oz:

VOICES: Bob Holt, Jesse Wells, Richard Romanus, David Proval, Steve Gravers
D & SCR: Ralph Bakshi **MUSIC:** Andrew Belling
Standard animated fantasy: Two brothers grow up to become opposing Wizards

Wizards of the Demon Sword

1991, (USA), color
W: Lyle Waggoner
Minor fantasy-thriller: Swashbuckler helps woman rescue her father from evil sorcerer

Wizards of the Lost Kingdom

1985, (USA-Argent), Frank Isaac-Alex Sessa/Concorde, color, 75 mins.
W: Bo Svenson *(Kor)*, Vidal Peterson *(Simon)*, Maria Socas *(Acrasia)*, Thom Christopher *(Shurka)*, Barbara Stock *(Udea)*, Dolores Michaels *(Aura)*, Edward Morrow *(Wulfrick/Old Simon/Gilfax)*, August Laretta *(King Tylor)*, Mark Welles *(Rongar)*, Michael Fontaine *(Hurla)*, Mary Gale *(Linnea)*, Mark Peters *(Timmon)*, Norton Freeman *(Sipra)*, Arch Gallo *(Bobino)*, Rick Gallo *(Malkon)*, Patrick Duggan *(The Advisor)*, Ernie Smith *(The Friar)*, Nick Cord *(The Bat Creature)*, Carl Garcia *(The Lizardtaur)*, Art Tass *(A Warrior)*, Carl Fountain *(A Warrior)*, Helen Grant, J.C. Topper, Richard Paley, Guy Reed
D: Hector Olivera **SCR:** Tom Edwards **PHOTOG:** Leonard Solis **SPCL-FX:** Richard Lennox **MUSIC:** James Horner & Chris Young
Minor fantasy-adventure: Boy prince avenges father's death

The Wizard's Walking Stick

1909, (GB), Urban, b&w, 410 ft. (125m)
D: Walter R. Booth
Standard fantasy (in 15 scenes): Magic wand enables wizard to elude police

The Wizard, the Prince and the Good Fairy

see **Le Sorcier, le prince et le Bon Genie**

Wolf

1994, (USA), Col, color, 125 mins.
W: Jack Nicholson *(Will Randall)*, Michelle Pfeiffer *(Laura Alden)*, James Spader *(Stewart Swinton)*, Christopher Plummer *(Raymond Alden)*, Kate Nelligan *(Charlotte Randall)*, Richard Jenkins *(Det. Bridges)*, Eileen Atkins *(Mary)*, Om Puri *(Dr. Vijay Alezals)*, David Hyde Pierce *(Roy)*, Ron Rifkin *(The Doctor)*, Prunella Scales *(Maude)*, Bradford English *(Keyes)*, Peter Gerety *(George)*, Brian Markinson *(Det. Wade)*, Stewart J. Zully *(Gary)*, Thomas F. Duffy *(Tom)*, Tom Oppenheim, Madhur Jaffrey, Shirkin Devrim, Allison Janney, William Hill, Kirby Mitchell, Cynthia O'Neal, Timothy Thomas, Lisa Emery, Leigh Carlson, Alice Liu, Max Weitzenhoffer, Irene Forrest, Jennifer Nicholson, Jack Nisbet, Dale Kasman, Jeffrey Allen O'Den, Jose Soto, Van Dallay, Dwayne McClary, Liz Chang, Elizabeth Morrie, Joanna Sanchez, Eva Rodriguez, Starletta Du-Pois, Osgood Perkins, David Schwimmer, Christopher Birt, Kaity Tong

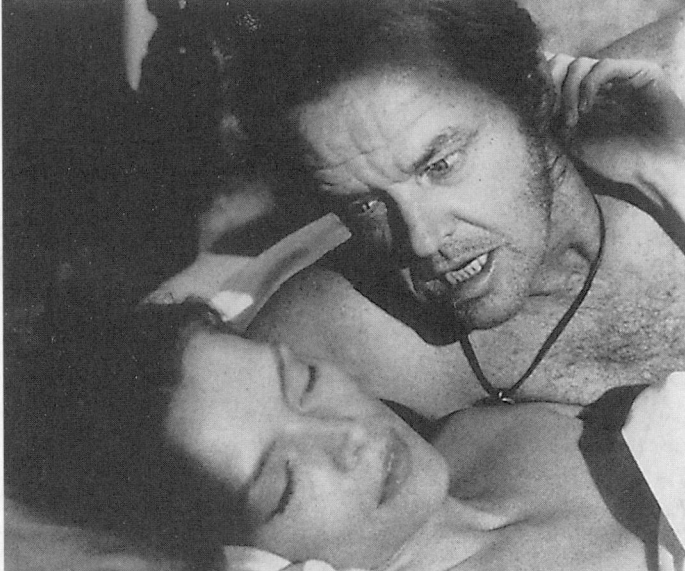

Wolf: MICHELLE PFEIFFER AND JACK NICHOLSON

D: Mike Nichols   **SCR:** Jim Harrison & Wesley Strick   **PHOTOG:** Giuseppe Rotunno   **SPCL VS-FX:** Sony Pictures Imageworks   **MUSIC:** Ennio Morricone
Unusual horror-thriller: Publishing executive becomes werewolf

Wolf Blood
1925, (USA), b&w, 68 mins.
W: George Chesebro, Marguerite Clayton, Ray Hanford, Roy Watson, Milburn Morante
D: George Chesebro & George Mitchell
Unusual thriller: Unexplained deaths ensue when accident victim transfused with wolf's blood

Wolfen
1981, (USA), King-Hitzig/Orion/WB, color, 111 mins.
W: Albert Finney *(Dewey Wilson)*, Diane Venora *(Rebecca Neff)*, Gregory Hines *(Whittington)*, Edward James Olmos *(Eddie Holt)*, Tom Noonan *(Ferguson)*, Dick O'Neill *(Warren)*, Sam Gray *(The Mayor)*, Peter Michael Goetz *(Ross)*, Dehl Berti *(The Old Indian)*, Max M. Brown *(Christopher Vanderveer)*, Ralph Bell *(The Commissioner)*, Anne Marie Pohtamo *(Pauline Vanderveer)*, Sarah Felder *(Cicely Rensselaer)*, Reginald Vel Johnson *(The Morgue Attendant)*, John McCurry *(Sayad Alve)*, James Tolkan *(Baldy)*, Donald Symington *(The Lawyer)*, Chris Minor *(The Janitor)*, Frank Adonis *(Scola)*, Jeffery Ware *(The Interrogation Operator)*, E. Brian Dean *(Foucher)*, Jeffrey Thompson *(Harrison)*, Victor Arnold *(Roundenbush)*, Richard Minchenberg *(The Policeman)*, Ray Serra, Thomas Ryan, Tony Latham, David Connell, Jery Hewitt, Ray Brocksmith, Michael Wadleigh, Joaquin Rainbow, John Ferraro, Rino Thunder, Glenn Benoit, Eddy Navas, Ricky Hawkeye, Peter Dyer, Paul Skyhorse, Gordon Eagle, Javier First-Day-of-Light, George Stonefish, Jane Lind, Julie Evening Lilly
P: Rupert Hitzig   **D:** Michael Wadleigh   **SCR:** David Eyre & Michael Wadleigh, from Whitley Strieber's novel   **PHOTOG:** Gerry Fisher   **SPCL-FX:** Ronnie Ottesen & Conrad Brink   **MUSIC:** James Horner
Standard thriller: Intelligent wolves prowl Manhattan

The Wolf Man
1941, (USA), Univ, b&w, 75 mins.
W: Lon Chaney Jr. *(Larry Talbot)*, Claude Rains *(Sir John Talbot)*, Evelyn Ankers *(Gwen Conliffe)*, Bela Lugosi *(Bela)*, Ralph Bellamy *(Capt. Paul Montford)*, Patric Knowles *(Frank Andrews)*, Maria Ouspenskaya *(Maleva)*, Warren William *(Dr. Richard Lloyd)*, Fay Helm *(Jenny Williams)*, J.M. Kerrigan *(Charles Conliffe)*, Doris Lloyd *(Mrs. Williams)*, La Riana *(The Gypsy Dancer)*, Forrester Harvey *(Twiddle)*, Chisco de Verdi *(The Lead Gypsy Violinist)*
P & D: George Waggner   **SCR:** Curt Siodmak   **PHOTOG:** Joseph Valentine   **MUSIC:** Charles Previn   **DESIGN:** Jack Otterson
orig. to be titled **Destiny**
"...misty atmospheric photography, believable script and unforced dialogue, and restrained sincere playing by Lon Chaney (Jr.) and others"—Ivan Butler, The Horror Film
Classic horror-fantasy: Heir to estate is bitten by lycanthropic gypsy. cf. **Frankenstein Meets the Wolf Man**

Wolfman
1979, (USA), E.O. Corp./Omni, color, 91 mins.
W: Earl Owensby, Kristina Reynolds, Sid Rancer, Brownlee Davis, Edward Grady, Richard Dedmon, Maggie Lauterer, Al Meyers, Helene Tryon, Mike Allen, Victor Smith, Charles Reynolds, Julian Morton, Dick Rice
WRIT & D: Worth Keeter   **PHOTOG:** Darrell Cathcart   **MUSIC:** Arthur Smith & David Floyd
Minor horror-fantasy: Heir finds he carries werewolf curse

Wolf's Clothing
1927, (USA), WB, b&w, 6,400 ft. (1950.7m)
W: Monte Blue, Patsy Ruth Miller
D: Roy Del Ruth   **SCR:** Darryl F. Zanuck
Standard thriller

Wolf's Clothing
1936, (GB), Wainwright/Univ, b&w, 80 mins.
W: Claude Hulbert *(Ambrose Girling)*, Gordon Harker *(Prosser)*, George Graves *(Sir Roger Balmayne)*, Lilli Palmer *(Lydia)*, Helen Haye *(Mildred Girling)*, Peter Gawthorne *(Sir Hector)*, Shayle Gardner *(Babo)*, Frank Birch *(Rev. Laming)*, George Hayes *(Yassiov)*, Joan Swinstead *(Mary Laming)*, Ernest Sefton *(Finden Charvet)*
D: Andrew Marton   **SCR:** Evadne Price & Brock Williams, from play *The Emancipation of Ambrose*
Standard comedy-thriller: Spy mistakes innocent for assassin

Wolves of the Underworld
see **Puppets of Fate**

A Woman Alone
see **Sabotage**

The Woman Eater
1958, (GB), Fortress/Eros/Col, b&w, 71 mins.
W: George Coulouris *(Dr. James Moran)*, Vera Day *(Sally)*, Peter Wayn *(Jack Venner)*, Joyce Gregg *(Margaret Santer)*, Joy Webster *(Judy Ryan)*, Jimmy Vaughan *(Tanga)*, Maxwell Foster *(Insp. Brownlow)*, Sara Leighton *(Susan Curtis)*, Robert MacKenzie, Edward Higgins, Marpessa Dawn, Harry Ross, Alexander Field, Norman Claridge
P: Guido Coen   **D:** Charles Saunders   **STORY & SCR:** Brandon Fleming
USA TV-retitle, **The People Eater**
Standard horror-thriller: To obtain fluid that can revive dead, scientist feeds young girls to carnivorous plant

Woman Hunt
1972, (Phil), color, 81 mins.
W: John Ashley, Lisa Todd, Eddie Garcia, Laurie Rose
D: Eddie Romero
A.k.a. **The Highest Bidder**
Minor thriller: Men kidnap women, hunt them in jungle

The Woman Hunter
1972, (USA), Jerome L. Epstein/ABC-TV, color, 74 mins.
W: Barbara Eden, Stuart Whitman, Robert Vaughn, Sydney Chaplin, Larry Storch, Enrique Lucero, Victor Hugo Jauregui
D: Bernard L. Kowalski   **TELEPLAY:** Brian Clemens
TVM, standard thriller: Socialite involved with international thief

The Woman in Green
1945, (USA), Univ, b&w, 68 mins.
W: Basil Rathbone *(Sherlock Holmes)*, Nigel Bruce *(Dr. John Watson)*, Henry Daniell *(Prof. Moriarty)*, Paul Cavanagh *(Sir George)*, Hillary Brooke *(Lydia Marlowe)*, Mary Gordon *(Mrs. Hudson)*, Tom Bryson, Matthew Boulton, Sally Shepherd, Eve Amber, Frederick Worlock

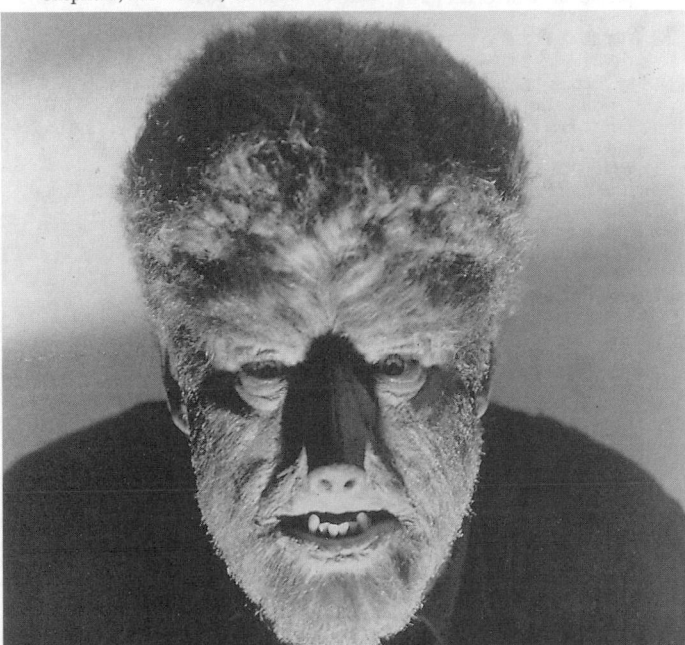

The Wolfman: LON CHANEY, JR.

P & D: Roy William Neill **SCR:** Bertram Millhauser, from Sir Arthur Conan Doyle's short story "The Adventure of the Empty House" **PHOTOG:** Virgil Miller **SPCL-FX:** John P. Fulton **MUSIC DIR:** Mark Levant
Standard thriller: Famed detective probes puzzling murders, contends with lady hypnotist

Woman in Hiding
1950, (USA), Univ, b&w, 92 mins.
W: Ida Lupino, Howard Duff, Stephen McNally, Stephen McNally, Peggy Dow, John Litel, Taylor Holmes, Joe Besser, Irving Bacon, Don Beddoe
D: Michael Gordon **SCR:** Oscar Saul **PHOTOG:** William Daniels
Standard thriller: Woman flees homicidal spouse

The Woman in Question
1950, (GB), Javelin-Vic/GFD/Col, b&w, 88 mins.
W: Jean Kent (*Astra Houston*), Dirk Bogarde (*Bib Baker*), Susan Shaw (*Catherine Taylor*), John McCallum (*Michael Murray*), Hermione Baddeley (*Mrs. Finch*), Charles Victor (*Albert Pollard*), Duncan Macrae (*Supt. Lodge*), Duncan Lamont (*Barney*), Lana Morris (*Lana Clark*), Bobbie Scroggins (*Alfie Finch*), Joe Linnane (*Insp. Butler*), Vida Hope (*Shirley Jones*), Anthony Dawson (*Insp. Wilson*), Albert Chevalier (*Gunter*), Ian Fleming (*The Doctor*)
P: Joseph Janni & Teddy Baird **D:** Anthony Asquith **STORY:** John Cresswell
USA retitle (1953), **Five Angles on Murder**
Standard crime-thriller: Fortune-teller's demise probed

Woman in the Dark
1952, (USA), Rep, b&w, 60 mins.
W: Penny Edwards, Ross Elliott
Standard thriller

Woman in the Dunes
see **Suna No Onna**

Woman in the Moon
see **Die Frau im Mond**

The Woman in the Window
1944, (USA), Int'l Independent/RKO, b&w, 99 mins.
W: Edward G. Robinson, Joan Bennett, Dan Duryea, Raymond Massey, Edmund Breon, Bobbie Blake
WRIT & P: Nunnally Johnson, from J.H. Wallis' novel *Once Off Guard* **D:** Fritz Lang **PHOTOG:** Milton Krasner **MUSIC:** Arthur Lang
Unusual thriller: Beautiful stranger lures middle-aged man into web of murder

The Woman in White
1929, (GB), B&D/W&F, b&w, 6,702 ft. (2042.8m)
W: Blanche Sweet (*Laura Fairlie/Anne*), Haddon Mason (*Walter Hartwright*), Cecil Humphreys (*Sir Percival Glyde*), Louise Prussing (*Marian Fairlie*), Frank Perfitt (*Count Fosco*), Minna Grey (*Countess Fosco*)
P & D: Herbert Wilcox **SCR:** Herbert Wilcox & Robert J. Cullen, from Wilkie Collins' novel
Standard thriller: Impostor confines wife, kills her insane double

The Woman in White
1948, (USA), WB, b&w, 109 mins.
W: Alexis Smith, Gig Young, Eleanor Parker, John Abbott, Sydney Greenstreet, Agnes Moorehead, Curt Bois, Matthew Boulton, John

The Woman in White
1998, (GB), PBS-TV, color, 95 mins.
W: Tara Fitzgerald, Justine Waddell, James Wilby, Simon Callow, Andrew Lincoln, Corin Redgrave, John Standing, Susan Vidler, Anne Bell, David Barry, Eric Carte
D: Tim Fywell **TELEPLAY:** David Pirie, from Wilkie Collins' novel **PHOTOG:** Richard Greatrex
TVM, standard thriller: Mystery surrounds lookalikes

The Woman on Pier 13
see **I Married a Communist**

A Woman Possessed
1958, (GB), Danziger/UA, b&w, 68 mins.
W: Margaretta Scott (*Katherine Winthrop*), Francis Matthews (*John Winthrop*), Kay Callard (*Ann Winthrop*), Ian Fleming (*Walter*), Alison Leggatt (*Emma*), Denis Shaw (*The Bishop*), Jan Holden (*Mary*), Totti Truman Taylor (*Miss Frobisher*)
P: Edward J. & Harry Lee Danziger **D:** Max Varnel **STORY:** Brian Clemens & Eldon Howard
Standard crime-thriller: Doctor suspects widowed mother is poisoner

A Woman's Temptation
1959, (GB), Danziger/British Lion, b&w, 60 mins.
W: Patricia Driscoll (*Betty*), Robert Ayres (*Mike*), John Pike (*Jimmy*), Neil Hallett (*Glyn*), John Longden (*Insp. Syms*), Kenneth Warren (*Warner*), Robert Raglan (*The Constable*)
P: Edward J. & Harry Lee Danziger **D:** Godfrey Grayson **STORY:** Brian Clemens & Eldon Howard
Standard crime-thriller: Seaman saves widow from crooks

A Woman's Vanity
1909, (GB), Hepworth, b&w, 450 ft. (137.2m)

D: Theo Bouwmeester
Standard crime-thriller: Woman's wine drugged by rich lover

A Woman's Vengeance
1948, (USA), Univ, b&w, 96 mins.
W: Charles Boyer, Jessica Tandy, Ann Blyth, Mildred Natwick, Sir Cedric Hardwicke, Cecil Humphreys, Hugh French, John Williams, Rachel Kempson
P & D: Zoltan Korda, from a story by Aldous Huxley **PHOTOG:** Russell Metty **MUSIC:** Miklos Rozsa
Standard thriller: Philanderer's wife murdered

The Woman Who Wouldn't Die
see **Catacombs** *(1964)*

A Woman's Wit
1912, (GB), Hepworth, b&w, 625 ft. (190.5m)
W: Alec Worcester (*Jack Dale*), Gladys Sylvani (*Lucy Price*), John MacAndrews (*Sir William Drainger*)
D: Warwick Buckland
Standard crime-thriller: Engineer's fiancee steals airplane plans, saves him from conniving rivals

Wombling Free
1978, (GB), Shand/Q/Rank, color, 96 mins.
W: David Tomlinson (*Roland Frogmorton*), Frances de la Tour (*Julia Frogmorton*), Bonnie Langford (*Kim Frogmorton*), Bernard Spear (*Arnold Takahashi*), Yasuko Nagazumi (*Doris Takahashi*), John Junkin (*The Surveyor*), Reg Lye (*The Assistant*), Jack Purvis (*Great Uncle Bulgaria*), Kenny Baker (*Bungo*), Marcus Powell (*Orinoco*), Sadie Corrie (*Mme. Cholet*), Eileen Baker (*Tobermory*), John Lummiss (*MacWomble*), Brian Jones (*Wellingtom*), Albert Wilkonson (*Tomski*), Tony Friel (*Womble*)
P: Ian Shand **D & SCR:** Lionel Jeffries **PHOTOG:** Alan Hume **MUSIC:** MikeBatt **VOICES:** Lionel Jeffries, David Jason, Janet Brown & Jon Pettwee
Standard fantasy: Underground creatures oppose littering humans

Women and Bloody Terror
1970, (USA), Howco, color, 97 mins.
W: Gerald McRaney, Georgine Darcy, Christa Hart, Michael Anthony, Marcus J. Grapes
P: Albert J. SalzerWeaver & Albert J. Salzer **D:** Joy N. Houck, Jr. **PHOTOG:** Robert A. Weaver **MUSIC:** Jim Helms, Gary LeMel & Norma Green

Women in Cages
1973, (USA), New World, color, 78 mins.
W: Jennifer Gan, Judy Brown
Minor thriller: Angst in women's prisons

Women in Cell Block 7
1977, (It), color, 100 mins.
W: Anita Strindberg, Eve Czemeys, Olga Bisera, Jane Avril, Valeria Fabrizi, Jenny Tamburi
D: Rino Di Silvestro
Minor thriller: Abuse in women's prison

Women in Fury
1984, (Brz), color, 94 mins.
W: Suzanne Carvalho, Gloria Cristal, Leonardo Jose, Zeni Pereira
Minor thriller: Hellish conditions in Brazilian women's prison

Women of All Nations
1931, (USA), Fox, b&w, 72 mins.
W: Victor McLaglen, Greta Nissen, Edmund Lowe, El Brendel, Fifi D'Orsay, Bela Lugosi, Humphrey Bogart
D: Raoul Walsh **SCR:** Barry Connors **PHOTOG:** Lucien Andriot **MUSIC:** Reginald H. Bassett
Standard adventure-comedy: Soldiers invade harem of sinister Turkish prince

Women of Devil's Island
1960, (Fr), AIP-TV, color, 86 nins.
W: Guy Madison, Michele Mercier, Paul Muller, Federica Ranchi
Minor thriller: Pirates seek prison-camp gold

The Women of Fire
see **Les Filles du Diable**

Women of Pitcairn Island
1956, (USA), 20th-Fox, b&w, 72 mins.
W: James Craig, Lynn Bari, John Smith, Arleen Whelan, Sue England, Carol Thurston, Charlita
D: Jean Yarbrough
Standard adventure-thriller

Women of the Prehistoric Planet
1966, (USA), J. Broder-G. Edwards/United Screen, color, 92 mins. (also 87 mins.)
W: Wendell Corey, Keith Larsen (*Sota*), Irene Tsu (*Linda*), John Agar (*Dr. Farrell*), Merry Anders, Paul Gilbert, Suzie Kaye, Stuart Margolin
D & SCR: Arthur C. Pierce **SPCL-FX:** Howard Anderson
orig. to be titled **Prehistoric Planet Women**

Minor SF-adventure
Women's Penitentiary
see *Caged Women (1984)*

Women's Prison Massacre
1985, (It), color, 89 mins.
<u>W</u>: Laura Gemser, Lorraine De Selle, Francoise Perrot, Ursula Flores, Gabriele Truti
<u>D</u>: Gilbert Roussel
Minor thriller: Male convicts take female inmates hostage

The Wonderful Invention
see *The Diabolical Invention*

The Wonderful Land of Oz
1972, (USA), Classic/Cinetron, color, 72 mins.
<u>P & D</u>: Barry Mahon, from L. Frank Baum's *The Wonderful Wizard of Oz*
Minor fantasy

The Wonderful Living Fan
see *Le Merveilleux Eventail Vivant*

The Wonderful Rose-Tree
see *Le Rosier Miraculeux*

The Wonderful World of the Brothers Grimm
1962, (USA), MGM, Cinerama, color, 134 mins. (also 129 mins.)
<u>W</u>: Laurence Harvey, Carl Boehm, Claire Bloom, Barbara Eden, Walter Slezak, Jim Backus, Oscar Homolka, Buddy Hackett, Russ Tamblyn, Yvette Mimieux, Terry Thomas, Martita Hunt, Robert Crawford, Beulah Bondi, Otto Kruger, Arnold Stang, Peter Whitney, Clinton Sundberg, Ian Wolfe, Walter Rilla
<u>P</u>: George Pal   <u>D</u>: Henry Levin (fairy-tale sequences dir by George Pal)   <u>SCR</u>: David P. Harmon, Charles Beaumont & William Roberts   <u>STORY</u>: David P. Harmon, based on Dr. Hermann Gerstner's biography *Die Bruder Grimm (The Brothers Grimm)*   <u>PHOTOG</u>: Paul C. Vogel   <u>MUSIC</u>: Leigh Harline
Academy Award winning costumes by Mary Wills
Lavish bio of Brothers Grimm, incorporating 3 of their fanciful tales (**The Dancing Princess, The Cobbler and the Elves & The Singing Bone**)

Wonder Man
1945, (USA), RKO, color, 98 mins.
<u>W</u>: Danny Kaye, Virginia Mayo, Vera-Ellen, Donald Woods, S.Z. Sakall, Allen Jenkins, Ed Brophy, Otto Kruger
<u>D</u>: H. Bruce Humberstone
<u>SPCL-FX</u> (Oscar-winning): John P. Fulton

The Wonders of Aladdin: DONALD O'CONNOR

Standard comedy-fantasy: Spirit of man's murdered twin shares his body

The Wonders of Aladdin
1961, (USA-It), Lux/MGM, color, 92 mins.
<u>W</u>: Donald O'Connor (*Aladdin*), Noelle Adam, Michele Mercier, Vittorio De Sica, Aldo Fabrizi, Milton Reid, Mario Girotti [Terence Hill], Fausto Tozzi, Marco Tulli, Raymond Bussieres
<u>P</u>: Joseph E. Levine   <u>D</u>: Henry Levin & Mario Bava   <u>SCR</u>: Luther Davis   <u>PHO-TOG</u>: Tonino Delli Colli   <u>MUSIC</u>: Angelo Lavagnino
Juvenile comedy-fantasy: Youth meets genie

Wonders of the Deep
see *Le Royaume de Fees*

Wonders of Aladdin: DONALD O'CONNOR

Wonder Woman
1974, (USA), WB/ABC-TV, color, 75 mins.
<u>W</u>: Cathy Lee Crosby (*Diana Prince/Wonder Woman*), Andrew Prine (*George*), Kaz Garas (*Steve Trevor*), Ricardo Montalban (*Abner Smith*), Anitra Ford, Robert Porter, Charlene Holt, Donna Garrett, Beverly Gill, Jordan Rhodes
<u>D</u>: Vincent McEveety   <u>TELEPLAY</u>: John D.F. Black, from comic-book characters created by Charles Moulton   <u>PHOTOG</u>: Joseph Biroc   <u>MUSIC</u>: Artie Butler
TVM, minor fantasy-thriller: Superheroine aids humankind
cf. **The New, Original Wonder Woman**

Wonder Women
1973, (Phil), General Film Corp., color, 82 mins.
<u>W</u>: <u>W</u>: Nancy Kwan (*Dr. Tsu*), Ross Hagen (*Mike*), Sid Haig (*Gregorius*), Maria De Aragon (*Linda*), Robert Collins (*Laura*), Tony Lorea (*Paulson/Lorenzo*), Vic Dias (*Lapu*), Claire Hagen (*Vera*), Shirley Washington (*Maggie*), Gail Hansen (*Gail*), Eleanor Siron (*Mei-Ling*), Rudy De Jesus (*The Boy*), Rick Reveke (*The Attendant*), Bruno Punzalan (*Nono*), Joonee Gamboa (*Won Ton Charlie*), Wendy Greene (*The Swimmer*), Leila Benitez (*Lillian*), Ross Rival (*Ramon*)
<u>P</u>: Ross Hagen   <u>D</u>: Robert O'Neill   <u>SCR</u>: Lou Whitehill   <u>PHOTOG</u>: Ricardo M. David   <u>MUSIC</u>: Carson Whitsett
Minor SF-thriller: Female army traffics in spare body parts

Wooden Soldiers
see *Babes in Toyland (1934)*

Woodchipper Massacre
1989, (USA), color, 90 mins.
<u>W</u>: Jon McBride, Patricia McBride
<u>D</u>: Jon McBride
Minor thriller: Nasty relatives vie for inheritance

Woof!
1990, (GB), (Made for TV Movie), color, 95 mins.
<u>W</u>: Edward Fidoe, Liza Goddard, John Ringham, Sheila Steafel
TVM, standard fantasy: Boy turns into dog

Woof Too! A Girl and Her Dog
1991, (GB), (Made for TV Movie), color, 75 mins.
<u>W</u>: Edward Fidoe, Sarah Smart, Liza Goddard (*Mrs. Jessop*), John Ringham (*Blocker*)
TVM, standard fantasy: Boy who can turn into dog befriends aspiring bicycling champ

Woof Again! Why Me?
1992, (GB), (Made for TV Movie), color, 75 mins.
<u>W</u>: Edward Fidoe, Sarah Smart
TVM, standard fantasy: Boy with canine alter ego meets man who can turn into a Labrador

Woof Returns! A Kid's Best Friend
1994, (GB), (Made for TV Movie), color, 75 mins.
<u>W</u>: Edward Fidoe
TVM, standard fantasy: Boy who can turn into dog replaces injured friend in race

Work is a Four Letter Word
1968, (GB), Cavalcade/Univ, color, 93 mins.
<u>W</u>: David Warner (*Val Brose*), Cilla Black (*Betty Dorrick*), Zia Moyheddin (*Dr. Narayana*), David Waller (*Mr. Price*), Elizabeth Spriggs (*Mrs. Murray*), Alan

Howard (*Rev. Mort*), Jan Holden (*Mrs. Price*), Tony Church (*Arkwright*), Julie May (*Mrs. Dorrick*), Joe Gladwin (*Pa Brose*)
D: Peter Hall   **SCR:** Jeremy Brooks, from Henry Livings' play *Eh?*   **PHOTOG:** Gilbert Taylor   **MUSIC:** Guy Woolfenden
Bizarre comedy: Man devotes life to growing hallucinogenic mushrooms

A Workman's Honour
1912, (GB), Cricks & Martin, b&w, 990 ft. (201.8m)
D: Charles Calvert

Wonder Woman: CATHY LEE CROSBY

Standard crime-thriller: Crooked manager frames laborer

The Work of Death
1969, (Mex), color
W: Santo
Minor fantasy-thriller

World by Night No. 2
1965, (It), Cresa Roma/AIP, color, 100 mins.
NARRATOR: George Sanders   **P:** Francesco Mazzei   **D:** Gianni Proia   **SCR:** R.W. Cresse
USA retitle, Ecco
Standard docu-thriller: Anthology of bizarre practices (e.g., black mass)

World for Ransom
1954, (USA), Mono/AA, b&w, 82 mins.
W: Dan Duryea, Gene Lockhart, Patric Knowles, Reginald Denny, Nigel Bruce, Marian Carr, Arthur Shields, Douglass Dumbrille
D: Robert Aldrich   **PHOTOG:** Joseph Biroc
Standard thriller: Private eye seeks kidnapped nuclear scientist

World Gone Wild
1988, (USA), Apollo, color, 94 mins.
W: Bruce Dern (*Ethan*), Michael Paré (*George*), Catherine Mary Stewart (*Angie*),

Adam Ant (*Derek*), Larry Ketchum
D: Lee H. Katzin   **SCR:** Jorge Zamacona   **PHOTOG:** Don Burgess
Minor SF-satire: Post-nuke settlers struggle for survival

World of Dracula
1979, (USA), Univ, (Made for TV Movie), color, 96 mins.
W: Michael Nouri (*Dracula*), Carol Baxter, Stephen Johnson, Bever-Leigh Banfield, Louise Sorel, Antoinette Stella, Mark Montgomery
D: Jeffrey Hayden, Sutton Roley & Kenneth Johnson   **SCR:** Craig Buck, Myla Lichtman, Renee Longstreet, Harry Longstreet & Kenneth Johnson   **CREATED BY:** Kenneth Johnson   **PHOTOG:** Robert F. Liu & Mario DiLeo   **MUSIC SCORE:** Les Baxter & Joe Harnell
TVM, standard horror-thriller (culled from teleseries "Cliffhanger"): Vampire pursues girl

World of the Depraved
1967, (USA), color, 73 mins.
W: Tempest Storm, Johnnie Decker, Larry Reed
D & SCR: Herbert Jeffries
Minor eroto-thriller: Detectives hunt sex killer

The World of the Vampires
see *El Mundo de los Vampiros*

The World's Greatest Sinner
1962, (USA), Frenzy Prods., b&w, 82 mins.
W: Timothy Carey, Gil Baretto, Betty Rowland, Doris Carey, George F. Carey, James Farley, Titus Moede
WRIT, P & D: Timothy Carey   **MUSIC:** Frank Zappa
Unusual satire: Insurance salesman decides he's God, becomes rock 'n' roll evangelist

The World's Wizard
1906, (GB), R.W. Paul, b&w, 350 ft. (106.7m)
D: J.H. Martin
Standard fantasy: Wizard emerges from exploding Earth, turns countries into girls

The World's Worst Wizard
1915, (GB), Kineto, b&w, 440 ft. (134.1m)
D: Walter R. Booth
Standard fantasy: Mechanical goose spoils conjurer's tricks

The World, the Flesh and the Devil
1959, (USA), Sol C. Siegel/MGM, b&w, 95 mins.
W: Harry Belafonte, Inger Stevens, Mel Ferrer
P: George Englund   **D & SCR:** Ranald MacDougall   **SCREEN STORY:** Ferdinand Reyher, suggested by Matthew Phipps Shiel's 1902 novel *The Purple Cloud*   **PHOTOG:** Harold J. Marzorati   **MUSIC:** Miklos Rozsa
Classic SF-thriller: Three people survive nuclear war

World War III
1982, (USA), David Greene Productions/NBC-TV, color, 186 mins.
W: Rock Hudson (*Pres. McKenna*), David Soul (*Caffrey*), Cathy Lee Crosby (*Kate*), Brian Keith (*Sec'y Gorny*), Jeroen Krabbe (*Col. Vorashin*), Robert Prosky (*Gen. Rudenski*), Lee Wallace (*Farber*), Katherine Helmond (*Dorothy*), James Hampton (*Rickman*), Richard Yniguez, Herbert Jefferson Jr.
P: Bruce Lansbury   **D:** David Greene   **TELEPLAY:** Robert L. Joseph   **PHOTOG:** Stevan Larner   **MUSIC:** Gil Melle
TVM, unusual thriller: Russian seizure of Alaskan pipeline threatens nuclear holocaust

World War Three Breaks Out
see *The Final War*

World without End
1956, (USA), AA, color, 80 mins.
W: Hugh Marlowe, Nancy Gates, Rod Taylor, Christopher Dark, Shawn Smith (*Shirley Patterson*), Lisa Montell, Nelson Leigh, Booth Colman, Paul Brinegar, Stanley Fraser, Everett Glass, Rankin Mansfield, William Vedder, Mickey Simpson
P: Richard Heermance   **WRIT & D:** Edward Bernds   **PHOTOG:** Ellsworth Fredericks   **SPCL-FX:** Milt Rice, Jack Rabin & Irving Block
orig. co-billed with **Indestructible Man**
Standard SF-thriller: Astronauts break time barrier

The Worm Eaters
1973, (USA), Geneni, color, 75 mins.
W: Herb Robins, Lindsay Armstrong Black, Joseph Sacket, Robert Garrison, Muriel Cooper, Mike Garrison, Barry Hostetler
P: Ted V. Mikels   **D & SCR:** Herb Robins   **STORY:** Nancy Kapner   **PHOTOG:** Willis Hawkins   **MUSIC:** Theodore Stern
blurb: "An immortal film of our time"
Minor horror-thriller: Vengeful nerd turns townspeople into half-human creatures

The Worst Agents
1966, (It), AA, b&w, 83 mins.
W: Franco Franchi
Minor spy spoof

The Worst Witch
1986, (USA), color, 70 mins.
W: Fairuza Balk, Charlotte Rae, Diana Rigg, Tim Curry

D: Robert M. Young
Made-for-Cable, standard fantasy: Girl studies witchcraft

The Would-Be Conjurer
1899, (GB), Riley Bros./Bamforth, b&w, 65 ft. (19.8m)
Standard fantasy: Yokel helps conjurer, tries tricks on wife

The Wraith
1986, (USA), Alliance Entertainment-John Kemeny/New Century, color, 91 mins.
W: Charlie Sheen *(Jake/The Wraith)*, Sherilyn Fenn *(Keri)*, Nick Cassavetes *(Packard)*, Randy Quaid *(Sheriff Loomis)*, Matthew Barry *(Billy)*, David Sherrill *(Skank)*, Jamie Bozian *(Gutterboy)*, Clint Howard *(Rughead)*, Griffin O'Neal *(Oggie)*, Chris Nash *(Minty)*, Vickie Benson *(The Waitress)*, Jeffrey Sudzin *(Redd)*, Peder Melhuse *(Murphy)*, Elizabeth Cox *(The Girl in the Daytona)*, Steven Eckholdt *(The Boy in the Daytona)*, Michael Hungerford *(Stokes)*, Dick Alexander *(Sandeval)*, Christopher Bradley *(Jamie)*, Joan H. Reynolds *(The Policewoman)*
WRIT & D: Mike Marvin   **PHOTOG:** Reed Smoot   **MUSIC:** Michael Hoenig & J. Peter Robinson   **SONGS:** *Where's the Fire, Secret Loser, Wake Up Call, Hearts vs. Heads, Smokin' in the Boys Room, Scream of Angels, Addicted to Love, Power Love, Those Were the Days, Never Surrender, Matter of the Heart, Hold on Blue Eyes, Rebel Yell, Young Love, Hot Love & Bad Mistake*
Minor SF-fantasy: Spectral drag-racer erases hoodlums in Arizona

The Wraith of the Tomb
1915, (GB), Cricks/Ogden, b&w, 3,000 ft. (914.4m)
W: Dorothy Bellew *(Natalie Vaughan)*, Sydney Vauthier *(Harry Newby)*, Douglas Payne
D: Charles Calvert   **STORY:** William J. Elliott
A.k.a. **The Avenging Hand**
Standard fantasy: Ghost of Egyptian princess curses archeologist who stole her mummified hand

The Wrecker of Lives
1914, (GB), Cricks/Ruffells, b&w, 3,000 ft. (914.4m)
W: Jack Leigh *(Vivian Raymond)*, Una Tristram *(Alice Graham)*, Lionel d'Aragon *(Bill Blake)*, Edward Sydney *(Jack Courtney)*, Fred Morgan *(Gen. Graham)*
D: Charles Calvert
Standard crime-thriller: Spy poses as secretary to kill general and frame his daughter's fiance

The Wrecking Crew
1969, (USA), Col, color, 104 mins.
W: Dean Martin *(Matt Helm)*, Elke Sommer *(Linka Karensky)*, Sharon Tate *(Freya Carlson)*, Tina Louise *(Lola Medina)*, Nancy Kwan *(Ya-Rang)*, Nigel Green *(Count Contini)*, Weaver Levy *(Kim)*, John Larch *(MacDonald)*, John Brascia *(Karl)*, Wilhelm von Homburg *(Gregor)*, Bill Saito *(Ching)*, Pepper Martin *(Frankie)*, Fuji *(Toki)*
D: Phil Karlson   **SCR:** William McGivern, from Donald Hamilton's *Matt Helm* novels   **PHOTOG:** Sam Leavitt   **MUSIC:** Hugo Montenegro
Standard comedy-thriller: Super-agent vs. gold hijackers. ('Matt Helm' series). cf. **The Ambushers, Murderers' Row** & **The Silencers** *(1966)*

Wrestling Women vs. the Aztec Mummy
1963, (Mex), Calderon/AIP-TV, b&w, 88 mins.
W: Lorena Velazquez, Armando Silvestre, Elizabeth Campbell
D: Rene Cardona   **SCR:** Abel Salazar
Minor fantasy-thriller: Lady wrestlers troubled by vengeful mummy

Writer's Block
1991, (USA), Skylark/Wilshire Court/USA-TV, color, 95 mins.
W: Morgan Fairchild *(Magenta Hart)*, Joe Regalbuto *(Det. Browning)*, Michael Praed *(Andrew)*, Mary Ann Pascal, Ned Bellamy, Cheryl Anderson, Douglas Rowe, Anthony Herrera, David Grant Wright, Danae Torn, Tokeli Le Claire, Marnie Andrews, Janet Haley, John Flaiz, David J. Partington, Debi Fares, Johnnie Johnson III, Barry Grayson, Clement Blake, Eileen Bowman
D: Charles Correll   **TELEPLAY:** Elisa Bell, based on a story by Elisa Bell & Tracy Barone   **PHOTOG:** Tobias Schliessler   **SPCL-FX:** Robin D'Arcy & Larry Fioritto   **MUSIC:** Nan Schwartz
TVM, standard thriller: Authoress' homicidal creation becomes reality

The Wrong Box
1966, (GB), Col, color, 110 mins. (also 95 mins.)
W: Michael Caine *(Michael Finsbury)*, John Mills *(Uncle Masterman)*, Ralph Richardson *(Joseph Finsbury)*, Nanette Newman *(Julia)*, Peter Sellers *(Dr. Pratt)*, Dudley Moore *(John)*, Peter Cook *(Morris)*, Thorley Walters *(The Solicitor)*, Tony Hancock *(The Detective)*, John LeMesurier *(Dr. Slattery)*, Tutte Lemkow *(The Balmouth Strangler)*, Graham Stark *(Ian)*, Wilfrid Lawson *(Peacock)*, Leonard Rossiter *(Vyvyan)*, Cicely Courtneidge *(Maj. Martha)*, Irene Handl *(Mrs. Hackett)*, Peter Graves *(The Officer)*, Norman Bird *(The Clergyman)*, Norman Rossington *(Rough)*, Diane Clare *(Mercy)*, Nicholas Parsons *(Alan Scrope)*, Avis Bunnage *(Queen Victoria)*, Valentine Dyall *(Oliver Pike Harmsworth)*, Andre Morell *(The Servant)*, Lionel Gamlin *(The Driver)*, Temperance Seven *(The Band)*, Jeremy Lloyd, Michael Bird, Gerald Sim, Timothy Bateson, Vanda Godsell, James Villiers, Dick Gregory
P & D: Bryan Forbes   **SCR:** Larry Gelbart & Burt Shevelove, based on a novel by Robert Louis Stevenson & Lloyd Osbourne   **PHOTOG:** Gerry Turpin   **MUSIC:** John Barry   **SETS:** Ray Sim
Classic comedy-thriller: Inheritance inspires mayhem

The Wrong Cab
1909, (GB), Hepworth, b&w, 425 ft. (129.5m)
D: Lewin Fitzhamon
Standard comedy: Father chases elopers' cab, finds it contains lunatic

The Wrong Man
1957, (USA), WB, b&w, 105 mins.
W: Henry Fonda, Vera Miles, Anthony Quayle, Charles Cooper, Harold J. Stone, Natalie Priest, Peggy Webber, Nehemiah Persoff
P & D: Alfred Hitchcock   **SCR:** Maxwell Anderson & Angus Macphail   **PHOTOG:** Robert Burks   **MUSIC:** Bernard Herrmann
Tense, fact-based thriller: Musician wrongly convicted of murder

Wrong Number
1959, (GB), Merton Park/Anglo-Amalgamated, b&w, 59 mins.
W: Peter Reynolds *(Angelo)*, Lisa Gastoni *(Maria)*, Peter Elliot *(Dr. Pole)*, Olive Sloane *(Miss Crystal)*, Paul Whitsun-Jones *(Cyril)*, Barry Keegan *(Max)*, John Horsley *(Supt. Blake)*, Harold Goodwin *(Bates)*
P: Jack Greenwood   **D:** Vernon Sewell   **SCR:** James Eastwood, from a play by Norman Edwards
Standard crime-thriller: Old lady's telephone mistake helps police nab mail thieves

Wunder der Schopfung (Miracles of Creation) (Our Heavenly Bodies)
1925, (Ger), Ufa, b&w
Standard science-docu

Wuthering Heights
1920, (GB), Ideal, b&w, 6,230 ft. (1898.9m)
W: Milton Rosmer *(Heathcliff)*, Colette Brettel *(Catherine Hareton)*, Warwick Ward *(Hindley Earnshaw)*, Cyril Raymond *(Hareton)*, Anne Trevor *(Cathy)*, John L. Anderson *(Edgar Linton)*, Cecil Morton *(Earnshaw)*, Aileen Bagot *(Frances Earnshaw)*, Dora de Winton *(Mrs. Linton)*, Mrs. Templeton *(Nelly Dean)*, George Traill *(Joseph)*, Alfred Bennett *(Rev. Shields)*, Albert Brantford *(Young Heathcliff)*, Lewis Barber *(Young Hareton)*
D: A.V. Bramble   **SCR:** Eliot Stannard, from Emily Bronte's novel
reissued (with 4 rls cut), 1922
Standard melodrama: Tragedy parts lovers

Wuthering Heights
1939, (USA), Samuel Goldwyn/UA, b&w, 103 mins.
W: Laurence Olivier *(Heathcliff)*, Merle Oberon *(Cathy)*, David Niven *(Edgar)*, Flora Robson *(Ellen Dean)*, Geraldine Fitzgerald *(Isabella)*, Donald Crisp *(Dr. Kenneth)*, Hugh Williams *(Hindley)*, Cecil Humphreys *(Judge Linton)*, Leo G. Carroll *(Joseph)*, Miles Mander *(Lockwood)*, Romaine Callender *(Robert)*, Rex Downing *(Heathcliff as a Child)*, Sarita Wooton *(Cathy as a Child)*, Douglass Scott *(Hindley as a Child)*, Cecil Kellaway *(Earnshaw)*
D: William Wyler   **SCR:** Ben Hecht & Charles MacArthur , from Emily Bronte's novel   **PHOTOG:** Gregg Toland (Academy Award winner)   **MUSIC:** Alfred Newman
Classic melodrama: Girl and gypsy find haunting love

Wuthering Heights (1953)
see **Cumbres Borrascosas**

Wuthering Heights
1970, (GB), Anglo-EMI/AIP, color, 105 mins.
W: Anna Calder-Marshall *(Catherine)*, Timothy Dalton *(Heathcliff)*, Harry Andrews *(Mr. Earnshaw)*, Ian Ogilvy *(Edgar)*, Judy Cornwell *(Nellie)*, Hugh Griffith *(Dr. Kenneth)*, James Cossins *(Mr. Linton)*, Pamela Brown *(Mrs. Linton)*, Rosalie Crutchley *(Mrs. Earnshaw)*, Julian Glover *(Hindley)*, Aubrey Woods *(Joseph)*, Hilary Dwyer *(Isabella)*, Peter Sallis *(Mr. Shielders)*, Morag Hood *(Frances)*
P: Louis M. Heyward   **D:** Robert Fuest   **SCR:** Patrick Tilley, from Emily Bronte's novel   **PHOTOG:** John Coquillon   **MUSIC:** Michel Legrand
Standard melodrama: Doomed love on English moors

Wuthering Heights
1998, (GB), PBS-TV, color
W: Orla Brady *(Catherine)*, Robert Cavanah *(Heathcliff)*, from Emily Bronte's novel
TVM, modest melodrama: Doomed love on moors

Wuthering Heights
1998, (USA), NBC-TV, color
W: Gabriel Byrne
from Emily Bronte's novel
TVM, standard melodrama: Gypsy loves English girl

Wycieczka w Kosmos (Excursion in the Cosmos)
1961, (Pol), Film Polski, b&w
D: Krzysztof Debowski   **SCR:** Stanislaw Lem
Speculative SF: Space-race adventure

Xanadu

1980, (USA), Lawrence Goldman/Univ, color, 93 mins. (also 88 mins.)
W: Olivia Newton-John, Michael Beck (*Sonny Malone*), Gene Kelly (*Danny McGuire*), James Sloyan (*Simpson*), Dimitra Arliss (*Helen*), Katie Hanley (*Sandra*), Fred McCarren (*Richie*), Ren Woods (*Jo*), Sandahl Bergman, Lynn Latham, Melinda Phelps, Cherise Bate, Juliette Marshall, Marilyn Tokunda, Yvette Van Voorhees, Teri Beckerman, Robert Pereno (*Ben*)
D: Robert Greenwald   **PHOTOG:** Victor J. Kemper   **MUSIC SCORING:** Barry DeVorzon   **SONGS:** *Magic & I'm Alive*
*Standard musical-fantasy (lavish but uneven rehash of **Down to Earth** and **One Touch of Venus**): Beautiful muse inspires dispirited artist*

X-15

1961, (USA), Essex/UA, color, 105 mins.
W: Charles Bronson, Brad Dexter, Mary Tyler Moore, Kenneth Tobey, James Gregory, Patricia Owens, Stanley Livingston, David McLean, Lisabeth Hush, Ralph Taeger, James Stewart (*narrator*)
P: Henry Sanicola & Tony Lazzarino   **D:** Richard D. Donner   **SCR:** Tony Lazzarino   **PHOTOG:** Carl E. Guthrie   **MUSIC:** Nathan Scott
Standard thriller: Pilots on missile project

The X-Files

1998, (USA), 20th-Fox, color, 115 mins.
W: David Duchovny, Gillian Anderson, Martin Landau, William B. Davis, Blythe Danner, John Neville, Mitch Pileggi, Armin Mueller-Stahl
D: Rob Bowman   **SCR:** Chris Carter   **STORY:** Chris Carter & Frank Spotnitz, From characters created by Chris Carter   **PHOTOG:** Ward Russell   **MUSIC:** Mark Snow
Lavish SF-thriller: Agents probe earth-shaking conspiracy

The X from Outer Space

1966, (Jap), Shochiku/AIP, color, 85 mins.
W: Toshiya Wazaki, Peggy Neal, Eibi Motomochi, Itoko Harada, Shinichi Yanagisawa, Franz Gruber, Mike Daning, Keisuke Sonoi, Torahiko Hamada
D: Kazui Nihomatsu   **SCR:** Eibi Motomochi, Moriyoshi Ishida & Kazui Nihomatsu   **SPCL-FX:** Hiroshi Ikeda
Minor SF-thriller: Giant space-chicken attacks Earth

Xmas Greeting Film

1911, (GB), Brighton & County Films, b&w, 65 ft. (19.8m)
D: W. Harold Speer
Standard fantasy: Father Christmas magically produces Cinderella

X-Ray Fiend

see X-Rays

X-Rays

1897, (GB), G.A. Smith, b&w, 54 ft. (16.5m)
W: Tom Green (*The Professor*)
D: George Albert Smith
*A.k.a. **X-Ray Fiend***
Standard SF-comedy: Prof turns X-ray machine on courters, reveals embracing skeletons

X—The Man with the X-Ray Eyes

1963, (USA), Alta-Vista/AIP, color, 80 mins.
W: Ray Milland (*Dr. James Xavier*), Diana van der Vlis (*Dr. Diane Fairfax*), Harold J. Stone (*Dr. Sam Brant*), John Hoyt (*Dr. Benson*), Don Rickles (*Crane*), Barboura Morris (*The Nurse*), Dick Miller (*John Trask*), John Dierkes (*The Preacher*), Vicki Lee, Kathryn Hart, Morris Ankrum, Lorie Summers, Carol Irey
P & D: Roger Corman   **SCR:** Robert Dillon & Ray Russell   **PHOTOG:** Floyd Crosby   **SPCL-FX:** Butler-Glouner, Inc.   **MUSIC:** Les Baxter   **DESIGN:** Daniel Haller
Modest SF-thriller: Experimental drug expands doctor's sight and consciousness

X...The Unknown

1956, (GB), Hammer/WB, b&w, 81 mins.
W: Dean Jagger (*Dr. Adam Royston*), Edward Chapman (*Elliott*), William Lucas (*Peter Elliott*), Leo McKern (*McGill*), Peter Hammond (*Lt. Bannerman*), Anthony Newley ("*Spider*" *Webb*), Marianne Brauns (*Zena*), Michael Ripper (*Sgt. Grimsdyke*), Kenneth Cope (*Pvt. Lancing*), Jameson Clark (*Jack Harding*), Edward Judd (*A Soldier*), Ian McNaughton (*Haggis*), John Harvey (*Maj. Cartwright*), Jane Aird (*Mrs. Harding*), Michael Brooke (*Ian Osborne*), Fraser Hines (*Willie Harding*), Edwin Richfield
P: Anthony Hinds   **D:** Leslie Norman   **STORY & SCR:** Jimmy Sangster   **PHOTOG:** Gerald Gibbs   **MUSIC:** John Hollingsworth
*orig. co-billed with **The Curse of Frankenstein***
Modest SF-horror: Radioactive mass oozes forth from Earth

Xtro

1982, (GB), Ashley/Amalgamated Film Enterprises, color, 82 mins.
W: Bernice Stegers (*Rachel Phillips*), Philip Sayer (*Sam Phillips*), Danny Brainin (*Joe Daniels*), Maryam d'Abo (*Analise*), Simon Nash (*Tony Phillips*), Peter Mandell (*The Clown*), Robert Fyfe (*The Doctor*), Katherine Best (*Jane*), David Cardy (*Michael*), Anna Wing (*Miss Goodman*), Arthur Whybrow (*The Knight*), Anna Mottram (*The Teacher*), David Henry (*The Gynecologist*), Vanya Seager (*Paula*), Tik (*The Monster*), Tok (*The Commando*), Robert Austin
P: Mark Forstater

D & MUSIC: Harry Bromley Davenport   **SCR:** Iain Cassie & Robert Smith, from an orig. story by Michel Parry & Harry Bromley Davenport   **PHOTOG:** John Metcalfe   **SPCL-FX SPRVSR:** Tom Harris
distrib. in USA (1983) by New Line Films
Standard SF-horror: British father gruesomely altered by nasty extraterrestrials

Xtro II: The Second Encounter

1991, (USA), color, 92 mins.
W: Jan-Michael Vincent, Paul Koslo, Tara Buckman (*Julie*), Jano Frandsen (*McShane*), Nicholas Lea, W.F. Wadden, Rolf Reynolds, Nic Amoroso, Tracy Westerholm
D: Harry Bromley Davenport
Minor SF-horror: Blood-drinking aliens invade Earth

Xtro 3: Watch the Skies

1995, (Can), color, 90 mins.
W: Sal Landi, Jim Hanks, Robert Culp, Andrew Divoff, Karen Moncrieff
D: Harry Bromley Davenport
Standard SF-horror: Space alien inhabits remote island

Yabu No Naka No Kuroneko

see Kuroneko

A Yankee in King Arthur's Court

see A Connecticut Yankee in King Arthur's Court (1949)

Year 2889

see In the Year 2889

A Yell of a Night

1932, (GB), b&w, 42 mins.
W: Mickey Brantford (*The Boy*), Mignon Swaffer (*The Girl*), M. Huntington (*The Father*), Sam Lee (*The Crook*)
D: Gustave Minzenty   **STORY:** Gustave Minzenty & C. Becket Williams
Minor comedy-thriller: Crooks search waxworks for stolen jewels

The Yellow Balloon

1952, (GB), Marble Arch/ABP/AA, b&w, 80 mins.
W: William Sylvester (*Len*), Kenneth More (*Ted*), Kathleen Ryan (*Em*), Andrew Ray (*Frankie*), Bernard Lee (*PC Chapman*), Hy Hazell (*Mary*), Veronica Hurst (*The Teacher*), Campbell Singer (*Potter*), Sandra Dorne (*Iris*), Eliot Makeham (*The Pawnbroker*), Sidney James (*Barrowboy*), Marjorie Rhodes (*Mrs. Stokes*), Peter Jones, Stephen Fenemore
WRIT & D: J. Lee Thompson, from a story by Anne Burnaby   **PHOTOG:** Gilbert Taylor   **MUSIC:** Philip Green
Standard thriller: Crook manipulates small boy

Yellowbeard

1983, (USA), Orion, color, 101 mins.
W: Graham Chapman (*Yellowbeard*), Peter Boyle (*Moon*), Richard "Cheech" Marin (*El Segundo*), Tommy Chong (*El Nebuloso*), Peter Cook (*Lord Lambourn*), Marty Feldman (*Gilbert*), Eric Idle (*Cmdr. Clement*), Martin Hewitt (*Dan*), Michael Hordern (*Dr. Gilpin*), Madeline Kahn (*Betty*), James Mason (*Capt. Hughes*), John Cleese (*Blind Pew*), Stacey Nelkin (*Triola*), Kenneth Mars (*Crisp/Verdugo*), Spike Milligan (*Flunkie*), Nigel Planer (*Mansell*), Susannah York (*Lady Churchill*), Beryl Reid (*Lady Lambourn*), Ferdinand Mayne (*Beamish*), John Francis (*The Chaplain*), Peter Bull (*Queen Anne*), Bernard Fox (*Tarbuck*), Ronald Lacey, Nigel Stock, Greta Blackburn, Kenneth Danziger, Monte Landis, John Diar, Gillian Eaton, Bernard McKenna, Carlos Romano, Alvaro Carcano, Leopoldo Frances, Ava Harela, Garry O'Neill, David Bowie
D: Mel Damski   **SCR:** Graham Chapman, Peter Cook & Bernard McKenna   **PHOTOG:** Gerry Fisher   **MUSIC:** John Morris
Standard satire: Pirates seek buried treasure

The Yellow Claw

1920, (GB), Stoll, b&w, 6,029 ft. (1837.6m)
W: Kitty Fielder (*The Lady of the Poppies*), Norman Page (*Soames*), Harvey Braban (*Gaston Max*), Sydney Seaward (*Insp. Dunbar*), Kiyoshi Takase (*Ho-Pin*), Fothringham Lysons (*Henry Leroux*), Mary Massart (*Helen Cumberley*), Arthur Cullin (*Dr. Cumberley*), Cyril Percival (*John Howard Exel*), Eric Albury (*Gianopolis*), Ivy King (*Mrs. Leroux*), Annie Esmond (*Denise Ryland*), Geoffrey Benstead (*Sowerby*)
D: Rene Plaisetty   **SCR:** Gerald Fort Buckle, from a novel by Sax Rohmer
Standard crime-thriller: French and English detectives nab opium smugglers who killed novelist's wife

Yellow Dog

1973, (GB), Akari/Scotia-Barber, color, 101 mins.
W: Jiro Yamiya (*Kimura*), Robert Hardy (*Alexander*), Carolyn Seymour (*Della*), Joseph O'Conor (*Dover*), Hilary Tindall (*Helen*), Jonathan Newth (*Tim*), Keith Drinkel (*Eric*), Gay Singleton (*Della 2*), Madge Ryan (*Mother*), Angela Thorne (*Jenny Alexander*), Rupert Lord (*Daniel Alexander*), Annabel Lord (*Paulie Alexander*), Geoffrey Lumsden (*Sir William Renfrew*), Belina Carroll (*Miss Henderson*), John M. Bray (*Galloway*), Harvey Hall (*Alin*), Harold Innocent (*Marceau*), Richard Pendrey (*Ed Fisher*), Noel Davis (*Norman*), James Willis (*Hugh Curtis*), John Welsh (*Dr. Beasley*), Michael Godfrey (*Insp. Morgan*), Esmond Knight (*Mundt*), Richard Hampton (*Capt. Exelby*), Fiona Curzon (*The Hostess*)
P, D & STORY: Terence Donovan   **SCR:** Shinobu Hashimoto, John Bird & Prof.

Alan Turney   **PHOTOG:** David Watkin   **MUSIC:** Ron Grainer
Unusual thriller: Japanese private eye has mission in London

Yellow Face
1921, (GB), Stoll, b&w, 2,020 ft. (615.7m)
W: Eille Norwood (*Sherlock Holmes*), Hubert Willis (*Dr. John Watson*), Clifford Heatherley (*Grant Munro*), Norma Whalley (*Effie Munro*)
D: Maurice Elvey   **SCR:** William J. Elliott, from the writings of Sir Arthur Conan Doyle
Standard crime-thriller (episode in "Adventures of Sherlock Holmes" series)

The Yellow Mask
1930, (GB), BIP/Wardour, b&w, 95 mins.
W: Lupino Lane (*Sam Slipper*), Warwick Ward (*Li San*), Dorothy Seacombe (*Mary Trayne*), Wilfred Temple (*John Carn*), Haddon Mason (*Ralph Carn*), Frank Cochrane (*Ah Sing*), Wallace Lupino (*The Steward*), Winnie Collins (*Molly*), William Shine (*Sunshine*)
D: Harry Lachman   **SCR:** Val Valentine, Miles Malleson, George Arthurs, Walter C. Mycroft & W. David, from Edgar Wallace's play *Traitor's Gate*
Standard musical-thriller: Chinese potentate steals British crown jewels

Yellow Peril
see Chinese Magic

Yesterday's Target
1996, (USA), SHO-TV, color, 85 mins.
W: Daniel Baldwin, Malcolm McDowell
Made-for-Cable, standard SF-thriller: Threatened time travelers are stranded in past

Yeti
1977, (It), Stefano, color, 105 mins.
W: Phoenix Grant (*Jane*), John Stacy (*Wasserman*), Mimmo Crau (*The Yeti*), Jim Sullivan, Tony Kendall, Eddy Fay, Steve Elliot, Loris Bazoky
P: Mario Di Nardo, Gianfranco Paolini, Nicolo Pomilia & Wolfranco Coccia   **D:** Frank Kramer (Gianfranco Paolini)   **SCR:** Mario Di Nardo & Frank Kramer   **PHOTOG:** Sandro Mancori   **OPTIC-FX:** Ermanno Biamonte   **MUSIC:** Sante Maria Romitelli
Minor horror-thriller: Giant bigfoot befriends mute boy

The Yesterday Machine
1963, (USA), b&w, 85 ins.
W: Tim Holt, James Britton, Jack Herman
D: Russ Marker
Minor SF-thriller: Mad doctor tries to bring back Hitler

Les Yeux sans Visage (Eyes without a Face)
1959, (It Fr), Lopert/UA, b&w, 90 mins.
W: Pierre Brasseur, Alida Valli, Edith Scob, Juliette Mayniel, Beatrice Alta Lriba, Rene Genin, Francois Guerin, Alexandre Rignault
D: Georges Franju   **SCR:** Pierre Boileau, Thomas Narcejac, Jean Redon & Claude Sautet   **DIALOG:** Pierre Gascar   **PHOTOG:** Eugen Shuftan   **MUSIC:** Maurice Jarre   **DESIGN:** Auguste Capelier
USA retitle, **Horror Chamber of Dr. Faustus** *(Lopert, 1962), remake:* **Mansion of the Doomed**
Poetic horror-thriller: Doctor performs unorthodox operations to repair daughter's disfigured face

Yield to the Night
1956, (GB), Kenwood/ABP, b&w, 99 mins.
W: Diana Dors (*Mary Hilton*), Yvonne Mitchell (*Macfarlane*), Michael Craig (*Jim Lancaster*), Marie Ney (*The Governor*), Geoffrey Keen (*The Chaplain*), Olga Lindo (*Hill*), Athene Seyler (*Miss Bligh*), Mary Mackenzie (*Maxwell*), Marjorie Rhodes (*Brandon*), Joan Miller (*Barker*), Liam Redmond (*The Doctor*), Molly Urquhart (*Mason*), Michael Ripper (*Roy*), Harry Locke (*Fred Hilton*)
P: Kenneth Harper   **D:** J. Lee Thompson   **SCR:** Joan Henry & John Cresswell, from a novel by Joan Henry   **PHOTOG:** Gilbert Taylor
USA retitle, **Blonde Sinner**
Modest crime-thriller: Woman shoots mistress of her pianist lover

Yogi
1916, (Ger), b&w
Standard thriller

Yog—Monster from Space
1970, (Jap), Toho/AIP, color, 84 mins.
W: Akira Kubo (*Taro*), Atsuko Takahashi (*Ayako*), Noritake Saito (*Rico*), Yoshio Tsuchiya (*Kyoichi*), Yukiko Kobayashi (*Saki*), Kenji Sahara (*Makoto*)
P: Tomoyuki Tanaka & Fumio Tanaka   **D:** Inoshiro Honda   **SCR:** Ei Ogawa   **PHOTOG:** Taiichi Kankura   **MUSIC:** Akira Ifukube
A.k.a. Space Amoeba
Standard SF-horror: Alien creature takes form of octopus

Yolanta
1964, (Russ), Artkino, color, 82 mins.
W: Natalya Rudnaya, Yuri Petrov
Standard melodrama

Yongary, Monster from the Deep
1967, (Jap-Korea), Toei/Filmways, color, 72 mins. (100 mins.)
W: Yungil Oh, Chung-Im Nam, Soonjai Lee, Moon Kang, Lee Kyang Ho, Lee Chai
D: Kim Ki-Duk   **SP:** Yunsung Suh   **PHOTOG:** Byon Inchib & Kenichi Nakagawa   **MUSIC:** Chun Jung-Kun
Minor SF-horror: Earthquake frees gargantuan beast

Yor, the Hunter from the Future
1983, (Turk-It), Diamant/Kodiak/Col, color, 93 mins.
W: Marina Rocchi (*Tarita*), Ayshe Gul (*Roa*), Aytekin Akkaya (*Ukan*), Sergio Nicolai (*Kay*), Reb Brown (*Yor*), Corinne Clery (*Ka-Laa*), John Steiner (*The Overlord*), Carole Andre (*Ena*), Alan Collins (*Pag*), Marina Rocchi
D: Anthony M. Dawson [Antonio Margheriti]   **SCR:** Robert Bailey & Anthony M. Dawson, based on novel *Yor* by Juan Zanotto & Ray Collins   **PHOTOG:** Marcello Masciocchi   **SPCL-FX:** Edward & Tony Margheriti   **MUSIC:** John Scott
Minor SF-fantasy: Man transported to prehistory, faces space invaders

Yoru No Tsuzumi (Night Drum)
1958, (Jap), Shochiku, b&w, 95 mins.
W: Rentaro Mikuni, Ineko Arima, Masayuki Mori, Sumiko Hidaka
P: Tengo Yamada   **D:** Tadashi Imai   **SCR:** Kaneto Shindo, from a play by Chikamatsu
A.k.a. **The Adulteress**
Neo-realistic thriller: Adultery and revenge in 17th-century Japan

You Better Watch Out
1980, (USA), color, 100 mins.
W: Brandon Maggart, Dianne Hull, Scott McKay, Joe Jamrog, Peter Friedman, Ray Barry, Bobby Lesser, Sam Gray
D: Lewis Jackson
A.k.a. **Christmas Evil** *and* **Terror in Toyland**
Unusual thriller: Killer disguised as Santa Claus. cf. **Tales from the Crypt**

You Can't Escape
1956, (GB), Forth Films/ABP, b&w, 77 mins.
W: Noelle Middleton (*Kay March*), Robert Urquhart (*Peter Darwin*), Guy Rolfe (*David Anstruther*), Peter Reynolds (*Rodney Nixon*), Elizabeth Kentish (*Claire Segar*), Barbara Cavan (*Aunt Sue*), Martin Boddey (*Insp. Crane*), Thorley Walters (*Chadwick*), Jacqueline Mackenzie (*Mrs. Baggerley*)
P: Robert Hall   **D:** Wilfred Eades   **SCR:** Robert Hall & Doreen Montgomery, from Alan Kennington's novel
Standard crime-thriller: Heiress' fiance kills his former fiancee and blackmailer

You're Driving Me Crazy
1991, (USA), Magnum, (video), color
W: Norman Fell
Made-for-Video, standard thriller: Three demented doctors swap asylum tales

You Never Can Tell
1951, (USA), Univ, b&w, 78 mins.
W: Dick Powell, Peggy Dow, Joyce Holden, Charles Drake, Albert Sharpe, Lou Polan, Frank Nelson, Will Vedder
P: Leonard Goldstein   **D:** Lou Breslow   **SCR:** Lou Breslow & David Chandler   **PHOTOG:** Maury Gertsman   **MUSIC:** Hans Salter
GB retitle, **You Never Know**
Standard comedy-fantasy: German shepherd dog returns from death as human being, seeks his killer. cf. **Oh Heavenly Dog**

You Never Know
see You Never Can Tell

Young Again
1986, (USA), Sharmhill/Disney/ABC-TV, color, 90 mins.
W: Robert Urich, Lindsay Wagner (*Laura*), Keanu Reeves (*Young Michael*)
TVM, standard fantasy: 40-year-old executive granted wish to be 17 again

Young and Evil
see Cry of the Bewitched

The Young, The Evil and The Savage
1968, (USA), AIP, color, 82 mins.
W: Michael Rennie, Eleanor Brown
Minor melodrama

Young and Innocent
1937, (GB), Gaumont/GFD, b&w, 82 mins.
W: Nova Pilbeam (*Erica Burgoyne*), Derrick de Marney (*Robert Tisdall*), Percy Marmont (*Col. Burgoyne*), Mary Clare (*Aunt Margaret*), Edward Rigby (*Old Will*), John Longden (*Insp. Kent*), George Curzon (*Guy*), Basil Radford (*Uncle Basil*), Pamela Carme (*Christine Clay*), George Merritt (*Sgt. Miller*), J.H. Roberts (*Henry Briggs*), Jerry Verno (*The Driver*), H.F. Maltby (*The Sgt.*), Gerry Fitzgerald (*The Singer*), John Miller (*The Constable*), Beatrice Varley (*Mrs. Vessons*), Frank Atkinson (*Venner*), Bill Shine (*Bill*), Torin Thatcher (*Guvnor*), Syd Crossley
D: Alfred Hitchcock   **SCR:** Charles Bennett, Alma Reville, Anthony Armstrong, Edwin Green-wood & Gerald Savory, from Josephine Tey's novel *A Shilling*

for Candles
USA retitle, **The Girl was Young** (GB, 1938)
Standard thriller: Innocent man accused of murder

The Young and the Immoral
see The Sinister Urge

The Young Captives
1959, (USA), Para, b&w, 66 mins.
W: Tom Selden, Luana Patten, Steven Marlo, Herb Armstrong, Ed Nelson
WRIT & P: Andrew J. Fenady D: Irvin Kershner
blurb: "Teenage elopers' love turns to terror as they battle crazed killer!"
Minor thriller: Hitchhiker terrorizes couple

Young Diana
1922, (USA), Cosmopolitan-Para, b&w, 7 reels
W: Marion Davies, Pedro de Cordoba, Maclyn Arbuckle, Gypsy O'Brien, Forrest Stanley
D: Albert Capellani & Robert Vignola SCR: Luther Reed, based on a novel by Marie Corelli PHOTOG: Harold Wenstrom SETS: Joseph Urban
Unusual SF-fantasy (inspired by contemporary experiments with monkey glands): Scientist covets secret of immortality

Young Dracula
see Dracula (1974)

The Youngest Spy
see My Name is Ivan

Young Frankenstein
1974, (USA), 20th-Fox, b&w, 104 mins.
W: Gene Wilder (*Baron Frederick von Frankenstein*), Peter Boyle (*The Monster*), Madeline Kahn (*Elizabeth*), Teri Garr (*Inga*), Cloris Leachman (*Frau Bluecher*), Marty Feldman (*Igor*), Gene Hackman (*The Blind Hermit*), Kenneth Mars (*Insp. Kemp*), Richard Haydn (*Falkstein*), Danny Goldman (*The Medical Student*), Oscar Beregi (*The Sadistic Jailer*), Arthur Malet (*The Village Elder*), Anne Beesley (*The Little Girl*), Liam Dunn (*Mr. Hilltop*), Leon Askin (*Herr Waldman*), Lou Cutell (*The Frightened Villager*), Terrence Pushman (*The 1st Villager*), Ian Abercrombie (*The 2nd Villager*), Randolph Dobbs (*The 3rd Villager*), Richard Roth (*Insp. Kemp's Aide*), Monty Landis, Rusty Blitz, Michael Fox, John Madison, Norbert Schiller, Lidia Kristen
P: Michael Gruskoff D: Mel Brooks SCR: Gene Wilder & Mel Brooks PHOTOG: Gerald Hirschfeld SPCL-FX: Henry Millar Jr. & Hal Millar MUSIC: John Morris
Madcap horror-comedy: Grandson of Good Doctor creates life

Young Hercules
1998, (USA), Renaissance/FAM-TV, color, 95 mins.
W: Ian Bohnen (*Hercules*), Chris Conrad (*Jason*), Kevin Smith (*Ares*), Johna Stewart (*Yvenna*), Dean O'Gorman
D: T.J. Scott PHOTOG: John Mahaffie VS-FX: Flat Earth MUSIC: Joseph LoDuca
TVM, standard adventure-fantasy: Demigod's early years

Young Indiana Jones and the Attack of the Hawkmen
1995, (USA), (Made for TV Movie), color, 90 mins.
W: Sean Patrick Flanery (*Indiana Jones*)
TVM, standard adventure-thriller: Youth gets perilous assignment as reconnaisance photographer in World war I

Young Indiana Jones: Travels with Father
1996, (USA), (Cable), color
W: Corey Carrier (*Indiana Jones*), Michael Gough (*Leo Tolstoy*), George Jackos (*Nikos Kazantzakis*), Lloyd Owen (*Prof. Jones*), George Yiasoumi (*Aristotle*)
D: Michael Schultz
Made-for-Cable, standard adventure-thriller: 10-year-old meets famous authors

The Young Magician
1987, (Can-Pol), color, 100 mins.
W: Rusty Jedwab, Natasza Maraszek (*Margaret*), Edward Garson (*Alexander*)
Standard fantasy: Telekinetic boy seeks acceptance

The Young Poisoner's Handbook
1995, (GB-Ger), color, 100 mins.
W: Hugh O'Conor, Antony Sher, Ruth Sheen (*Molly*), Charlotte Coleman (*Winnie*), Roger Lloyd Pack (*Fred*), Paul Stacey, Samantha Edmonds, Charlie Creed-Miles
D: Benjamin Ross SCR: Benjamin Ross & Jeff Rawle PHOTOG: Hubert Taczanowski MUSIC: Robert Lane & Frank Strobel
Unusual satire: Disgruntled teen essays career of poisoning

Young Sherlock Holmes
1985, (GB), Amblin/Para, color, 110 mins.
W: Nicholas Rowe (*Sherlock Holmes*), Alan Cox (*John Watson*), Sophie Ward (*Elizabeth*), Anthony Higgins (*Rathe*), Freddie Jones (*Cragwitch*), Susan Fleetwood (*Mrs. Dribb*), Nigel Stock (*Dr. Waxflatter*), Roger Ashton-Griffiths (*Lestrade*), Earl Rhodes (*Dudley Babcock*), Donald Eccles (*Rev. Nesbitt*), Patrick Newell (*Bentley Bobster*), Brian Oulton
P: Steven Spielberg D: Barry Levinson SCR: Chris Columbus, from characters

created by Sir Arthur Conan Doyle PHOTOG: Stephen Goldblatt SPCL-FX: Kit West VS-FX: Industrial Light & Magic MUSIC: Bruce Broughton
Unusual adventure-thriller: Teenage sleuth uncovers cult of assassins

Young Torless
see Der Junge Torless

Young Warlord
see King Arthur, the Young Warlord

You Only Die Twice
see Solo Se Muere Dos Veces

You Only Live Twice
1967, (GB), Eon/UA, color, 116 mins.
W: Sean Connery (*James Bond*), Mie Hama (*Kissy Suzuki*), Akiko Wakabayashi (*Aki*), Karin Dor (*Miss Brandt*), Tetsuro Tamba (*Tiger Tanaka*), Bernard Lee ("*M*"), Desmond Llewelyn ("*Q*"), Lois Maxwell (*Miss Moneypenny*), Donald Pleasence (*Blofeld*), Teru Shimada (*Osato*), Charles Gray (*Henderson*), Tsai Chin (*The Girl*), Alexander Knox (*The President*), Robert Hutton (*The Aide*)
P: Albert R. Broccoli & Harry Saltzman D: Lewis Gilbert SCR: Roald Dahl, from characters created by Ian Fleming PHOTOG: Frederick A. Young MUSIC: John Barry DESIGN: Ken Adam, TITLE: Nancy Sinatra
Lavish thriller: Secret agent finds danger on Japanese isle

You Pay Your Money
1957, (GB), Butcher's Films, b&w, 67 mins.
W: Hugh McDermott (*Bob Westlake*), Jane Hylton (*Rosemary Delgardo*), Honor Blackman (*Susie Westlake*), Hugh Moxey (*Tom Cookson*), Ivan Samson (*Steve Mordaunt*), Shirley Deane (*Doris Squire*), Ferdy Mayne (*Delal*), Gerard Heinz (*Dr. Burger*), Ben Williams (*Seymour*), Basil Dignam (*Currie*)
P: W.G. Chalmers D & SCR: Maclean Rogers, from a novel by Michael Cronin
Standard crime-thriller: Arab league seeks rare books, kidnaps girl

Your Turn, Darling
see A Toi de Faire, Migonne

Your Teeth in My Neck
see The Fearless Vampire Killers or: Pardon Me, But Your Teeth are in My Neck

Your Witness
1950, (GB), Coronado/WB, b&w, 100 mins.
W: Robert Montgomery (*Adam Heywood*), Leslie Banks (*Col. Summerfield*), Felix Aylmer (*The Judge*), Andrew Cruickshank (*Sir Adrian North KC*), Patricia Wayne (*Cutts*) (*Alex Summerfield*), Harcourt Williams (*Beamish*), Jenny Laird (*Mary Baxter*), Michael Ripper (*Sam Baxter*), Ann Stephens (*Sandy Summerfield*), Wylie Watson (*Widgery*), James Hayter (*Prouty*), Noel Howlett (*Martin Foxglove KC*)
P: David E. Rose & Joan Harrison D: Robert Montgomery SCR: Hugo Butler, Ian Hunter & William Douglas Home STORY: Hugo Butler
USA retitle, **Eye Witness** (Eagle Lion, 1950)
Standard crime-thriller: American lawyer seeks witness to prove innocence of wartime friend

You'll Find Out
1940, (USA), RKO, b&w, 96 mins.
W: Boris Karloff, Bela Lugosi, Peter Lorre, Dennis O'Keefe, Ginny Simms, Kay Kyser, Helen Parrish, Alma Kruger, Ish Kabibble
P & D: David Butler SCR: James V. Kern & David Butler PHOTOG: Frank Redman MUSIC: Jimmy McHugh LYRICS: Johnny Mercer
blurb: "A seance in swing with the ha-ha-horror boys"
Standard comedy musical-thriller: Seances and skullduggery

You'll Like My Mother
1972, (USA), Bing Crosby Prods./Univ, color, 92 mins.
W: Patty Duke (*Francesca*), Richard Thomas (*Kenny*), Rosemary Murphy (*Mrs. Kinsolving*), Sian Barbara Allen (*Kathleen*), Dennis Rucker (*Red Cooper*), Harold Congdon (*The Man*), James Glazman (*The Breadman*), James Neumann (*Joey*)
P: Mort Briskin D: Lamont Johnson SCR: Jo Heims, from a novel by Naomi A. Hintze PHOTOG: Jack A. Marta MUSIC: Gil Melle
"...a scare show which knows how to say 'Boo!' with finesse"—Robert L. Jerome, Cinefantastique
Gripping thriller: Pregnant widow trapped in snowbound house

Ysani the Priestess
1934, (GB), Int'l Prods., b&w, 32 mins.
W: Raven Wood (*himself*), Vivienne Bell (*Ysani*), Charles Hay (*The Man*)
D: Gordon Sherry STORY: Raven Wood
Standard fantasy: Mummified priestess tells fortunes

Zaat
see Blood Waters of Dr. Z

Zakoldovannoye Mesto
see Zvenigora

Zamba

1949, (USA), Eagle Lion, b&w, 75 mins.
W: Jon Hall, June Vincent, Jane Nigh, Beau Bridges
Minor adventure-thriller

The Zany Adventures of Robin Hood

1984, (USA-GB), Bobka/CBS-TV, color, 97 mins.
W: George Segal (*Robin Hood*), Morgan Fairchild (*Lady Marian*), Janet Suzman (*Eleanor of Acquitaine*), Roddy McDowall (*Prince John*), Tom Baker (*Sir Guy*), Robin Nedwell (*Will Scarlett*), Robert Hardy (*King Richard*), Neil Hallett (*The Sheriff*), Kenneth Griffith (*Isaac*), Roy Kinnear, Michelle Newell, Pat Roach, Melvyn Hayes, Michael Hordern, Fenella Fielding, Aubrey Morris, Bruce Purchase, Tony Steedman, Roger Ashton-Griffiths, Paul Brooke, Angus Lennie
D: Ray Austin **TELEPLAY:** Robert Kaufman **PHOTOG:** Jack Hildyard
MUSIC: Stanley Myers
TVM, standard spoof: Noble outlaw opposes tyrant

Zanzibar

1940, (USA), Univ, b&w, 69 mins.
W: Lola Lane, James Craig
Standard thriller (remake of Nagana): Adventurers seek skull of African sultan

Zapped!: Scott Baio

Zapped!

1982, (USA), Apple-Rose/Embassy, color, 96 mins.
W: Scott Baio (*Barney Springboro*), Willie Aames (*Peyton*), Robert Mandan (*Walter Johnson*), Felice Schachter (*Bernadette*), Scatman Crothers (*Dexter Jones*), Roger Bowen (*Mr. Springboro*), Marya Small (*Mrs. Springboro*), Greg Bradford (*Robert Wolcott*), Heather Thomas (*Jane Mitchell*), Sue Ane Langdon (*Rose Burnhart*), Hilary Beane (*Corrine Updike*), Hardy Keith (*Roscoe Brown*), Curt Ayers (*Art*), Henry Ford Robinson (*The Umpire*), Merritt Butrick (*Gary Cooter*), Irwin Keyes ("*Too Mean*" *Levine*), Jennifer Chaplin (*Melissa Granger*), Dick Balduzzi (*The Waiter*), Bennett Liss (*The Croupier*), Ron Deutsch (*Larry*), Ed Deezen (*Sheldon*), Jan Leighton (*Albert Einstein*), Bryan O'Byrne (*Father Murray*), Ed Bakey (*Father Gallagher*), LaWanda Page (*Mrs. Jones*), Rosanne Katon (*Donna*), Sandy Serrano (*Amy*), Susan Ursitti (*Debby*), Corine Borher (*Cindy*), Michael Wainwright, Holly Rutherford, Jason Hickman, Phil Gilbreth, Richard Paine, Lisa Le Cover, P.J. Martin, Hyde Anderson, Kym Fisher, Mieke Lanter, James Loren, Dale Lott, Joshua Daniel, Lynn Seibel, Randy Patrick, Demetre Phillips, Daniel Dayan, Carlos Lacamara
D: Robert J. Rosenthal **SCR:** Bruce Rubin & Robert J. Rosenthal **PHOTOG:**

Daniel Pearl **SPCL VS-FX:** Robert Blalack **MUSIC:** Charles Fox
SONGS: *Shoot the Moon, Just for Fun, Ready or Not, Got to Believe in Magic, King and Queen of Hearts, Star Spangled Baby, Tryin to Kill a Saturday Night, Bomp Me, This Power of Ours & Updike's Theme*
Minor SF-comedy: Schoolboy develops telekinesis

Zapped Again

1989, (USA), color, 98 mins.
W: Todd Eric Andrews, Kelli Williams, Reed Rudy, Linda Blair, Karen Black, Lyle Alzado, Sue Ane Langdon
D: Douglas Campbell
Standard SF-fantasy: Outcast student employs telepathic powers

Zardoz

1973, (GB), 20th-Fox, color, 105 mins.
W: Sean Connery (*Zed*), Charlotte Rampling (*Consuela*), Sara Kestelman (*May*), John Alderton (*Friend*), Sally Anne Newton (*Avalow*), Niall Buggy (*Zardoz/Arthur*), Jessica Swift (*The Apathetic*), Bosco Hogan (*George*), Bairbre Dowling (*Star*), Christopher Casson (*The Scientist*), Reginald Jarman (*Death*)
WRIT, P & D: John Boorman **PHOTOG:** Geoffrey Unsworth **SPCL-FX:** Jerry Johnston **MUSIC:** David Munrow
"Both the story and style show enormous sophistication. Though at a pre-opening press conference Boorman denied having read much sf, there are overtones here of much of the best. I caught echoes (not imitations) of Wells, Weinbaum, Stapledon, van Vogt, Clarke, Asimov and Sturgeon"Baird Searles, "Films," The Magazine of Fantasy and Science Fiction, Vol. 46, No. 5 (May, 1974), p. 82
Superior SF-thriller: Barbarian of 2293 invades sterile, closed-circuit community of immortals

Zarkorr! The Invader

1996, (USA), color, 80 mins.
W: Rhys Pugh, Deprise Grossman, Mark Hamilton, Charles Schneider, Eileen Wesson
D: Aaron Osborne **SCR:** Benjamin Carr **PHOTOG:** Joe C. Maxwell **MUSIC:** Richard Band
Standard SF-thriller: Space Aliens study Earthlings

Zenabel

1969, (It), color
W: Lucretia Love, Mauro Parenti, Lionel Stander
Minor sex-fantasy: Adventures of medieval amazons

Zenom: Girl of the 21st Century

1999, (USA), Disney, color, 95 ins.
W: Kirsten Storms, Raven-Symone, Stuart Pankin, Frederick Coffin, Holly Fulger, Bob Bancroft, Greg Thriloway, Neil Denis, Phillip Rhys, Gwynyth Walsh, Lauren Maltby, Blair Slater, Danielle Fraser, Brenden Richard Jefferson, Zach Lipovsky,Gregory Smith
D: Kenneth Johnson **TELEPLAY:** Stu Krieger **PHOTOG:** Ron Orieux
MUSIC: Phil Marshall
TVM, standard juvenile SF-adventure: Space-station girl visits Earth

Zeppelin

1971, (GB), J. Ronald Getty-Leon Fromkess/WB, color, 101 mins.
W: Michael York (*Geoffrey*), Elke Sommer (*Erika*), Peter Carsten (*Maj. Tauntler*), Marius Goring (*Prof. Altschul*), Alan Rothwell (*Bradner*), Anton Diffring (*Col. Hirsch*), Alexandra Stewart (*Stephanie Ross*), Rupert Davies (*Capt. Whitney*), Andrew Keir (*Lt. Cmdr. von Gorian*), Ronald Adam (*The Prime Minister*), John Gill (*Meier*), William Marlow (*Lt. Cmdr. Anderson*), Clive Morton (*Lord Delford*), Richard Hurndall (*The Rear Admiral*), George Mikell (*The German Officer*), Michael Robbins (*The Scot's Sergeant*), Ben Howard (*Jamie*), Arnold Diamond (*Maj. Proudfoot*), Bryan Coleman (*Col. Whippen*), Gary Waldhorn (*Harlich*), Frazer Hines (*The Operator*)
P: Owen Crump **D:** Etienne Perier **SCR:** Arthur Rowe & Donald Churchill
PHOTOG: Alan Hume **SPCL-FX:** Cliff Richardson **MUSIC:** Roy Budd
Standard action-thriller: World War I German mission to destroy the Magna Carta

The Zero Boys

1986, (USA), Omega/Samuel Goldwyn, color, 70 mins.
W: Daniel Hirsch (*Steve*), Kelli Maroney (*Jamie*), Nicole Rio (*Sue*), Tom Shell (*Larry*), Jared Moses (*Rip*), Crystal Carson (*Trish*), Joe Phelan (*The Killer*), Gary Jochimsen (*Killer #2*), John Michaels (*Casey*), Elise Turner (*The Victim*), T.K. Webb (*Killer #3*), Steve Shaw (*The Coach*), Jason Pickets, Stephen Kay, Neil Weiss, Harry Donnenfeld, Dennis Ott, Patrick Hirsch, Trudy Adams, Jessica Tress, Angela High, Christina Cardan
P, D & STORY: Nico Mastorakis **SCR:** Nico Mastorakis & Fred C. Perry
PHOTOG: Steve Shaw **MUSIC:** Stanley Myers & Hans Zimmer
Minor thriller (Friday the 13th imitation): Campers are slaughtered

Zero Population Growth

see Z.P.G.

Zeta One

1969, (GB), Tigon, color, 82 mins.
W: Robin Hawdon (*James Word*), Yutte Stensgaard (*Ann Olsen*), James Robertson Justice (*Maj. Bourdon*), Charles Hawtrey (*Swyne*), Lionel Murton ("*W*"), Dawn Addams (*Zeta*), Anna Gael (*Clotho*), Brigitte Skay (*Lachesis*), Valerie Leon (*Atropos*), Carol-Anne Hawkins (*Zara*), Yolande Del Mar (*The Stripper*),

Wendy Lingham (*Edwina Strain*)

P: Tony Tenser & George Maynard   **D:** Michael Cort   <u>STORY</u>: Michael Cort & Alastair McKenzie

A.k.a. **The Love Factor**

Standard SF-thriller: Agent and stripper versus extraterrestrial super-women

Zex

1958, (GB), Nat Cohen-Stuart Levy/Anglo Amalgamated/Col, b&w, 72 mins.

<u>W:</u> Rod Cameron (*Jeff Keenan*), Mary Murphy (*Ruth Vance*), Meredith Edwards (*Dr. Maxwell*), Peter Illing (*Paul Zakon*), Carl Jaffe (*Dr. Hoff*), Kay Callard (*Laura Maxwell*), Carl Duering (*Blore*), Roberta Huby (*Verna Berteaux*), Felix Felton (*The Commissaire*), Larry Cross (*Brad Somers*), Jacques Cey (*The French Doctor*), Carlo Borelli (*Signore Kallini*), John McCarthy (*Calude Denver*), Armande Guinle (*The French Farmer*), Malou Pantera (*The Clinic Receptionist*), Alan Gifford (*Wayne*), Pat Clavin (*The Studio Receptionist*)

P: Alec C. Snowden   <u>D:</u> Montgomery Tully   <u>SCR:</u> Charles Eric Maine, from his novel *The Man Who Couldn't Sleep*   **PHOTOG:** Bert Mason   **MUSIC:** Richard Taylor

A.k.a. Escapement

USA retitle (1960), **The Electronic Monster**

Modest SF-thriller: Device produces dreams and nightmares

Zillah, a Story of Gipsy Life

1909, (GB), Anglo-American Films, b&w, 275 ft. (83.8m)

Standard melodrama: Gypsy girl tries to warn squire of impending burglary, is killed by tribe

Zipperface

1993, (USA), color, 90 mins.

<u>W:</u> Donna Adams

Minor thriller: Woman detective tracks killer of prostitutes

Zolotoye Ozero (The Golden Lake)

1935, (Russ), Mezhrabpom, b&w

<u>D:</u> Vladimir Shneiderov

<u>SCR:</u> A. Peregudov

Standard adventure-fantasy

Zoltan: Hound of Dracula

see **Dracula's Dog**

Zombi

see **Dawn of the Dead**

Zombie

1980, (It), Variety/Jerry Gross, color, 93 mins.

<u>W:</u> Richard Johnson, Tisa Farrow, Ian McCulloch, Auretta Gay, Al Cliver, Olga Kartalos

<u>D:</u> Lucio Fulci   <u>SCR:</u> Elisa Briganti   **PHOTOG:** Sergio Salvati

GB retitle, **Zombie Flesh Eaters**

Standard horror-fantasy: Corpses roam island paradise

Zombie Flesh Eaters

see **Zombie**

Zombie High

1987, (Can), Elliott Kastner/Cinema Group, color, 91 mins.

<u>W:</u> Virginia Madsen (*Andrea*), James Wilder (*Barry*), Paul Feig (*Emerson*), Richard Cox (*Philo*), Sherilyn Fenn, Kay E. Kuter

<u>D:</u> Ron Link   <u>SCR:</u> Elizabeth Passarelli, Tim Doyle & Aziz Ghazal   **MUSIC:** Daniel May   <u>LYRICS:</u> Kent Richards & Tymm Rocco   <u>SONG:</u> *Kiss My Butt*

A.k.a. **The School That Ate My Brain**

Modest horror-satire: Student finds suspicious doings

Zombie Holocaust

see **Queen of the Cannibals**

Zombie Island Massacre

1984, (USA), Troma, color, 86 mins.

<u>W:</u> David Broadnax (*Paul*), Rita Jenrette (*Sandy*), George Peters (*Whitney*), Tom Cantrell (*Steve*), Diane Clayre Holub (*Connie*), Ian McMillan (*Joe*), Dennis Stephenson (*The Tour Guide*), Debbie Ewing (*Helen*), Kristina Wetzel (*Barbie*), Harriet Rawlings (*Ethel*), Christopher Ferris (*Matt*), Ralph Monaco (*Jerry*), Deborah Jason (*Donna*), Luba Pinus (*Simmons*), Tom Fitzsimmons (*Ed*), Bruce Sterman (*Hogan*), Emmett Murphy (*George*), Trevor Reid (*The Voodoo Priest*), Mignon Lowe (*The Voodoo Priestess*), Oscar Lawson (*The Creature*)

P: David Broadnax   <u>D & ED:</u> John N. Carter   <u>SCR:</u> William Stoddard & Logan O'Neil   <u>ORIG. STORY:</u> David Broadnax & Logan O'Neil   **PHOTOG:** Robert M. Baldwin   <u>SPCL-FX:</u> Steve Kirshoff & Dennis Eger   <u>MUSIC:</u> Harry Manfredini

Minor horror-thriller: Tourists meet reanimated dead

Zombie Nightmare

1987, (USA), Gold-Gems Ltd., (video), color, 81 mins.

<u>W:</u> Adam West (*Churchman*), Jon-Mikl Thor (*Tony*), Manuska, Tia Carrere, Frank Dietz, Linda Singer, Mark Kulik, Allan Fisher, James Rae, Hamibh McEwen

<u>D:</u> Jack Bravman   <u>WRIT:</u> David Wellington   **PHOTOG:** Roger Racine

<u>MUSIC:</u> Motorhead, Girlschool, Thor, Deathmask & Fist   <u>SONGS:</u> *Out for the Kill, Rebirth & I'm Dangerous*

Made-for-Video, minor horror-fantasy: Hit-run victim revived, gets revenge

Zombies

see **Voodoo Blood Bath**

Zombies Lake

1980, (Sp-Fr), Eurocine/Cinema Shares Int'l, color, 96 mins.

<u>W:</u> Howard Vernon, Pierre Escourrou, Anouchka, Anthony Mayans, Nadine Pascale, Youri Rad, Burt Altman, Gilda Arancio, Marcia Sharif, Yvonne Dani, Jean-Rene Bleu, Jean Rollin

<u>D:</u> J.A. Laser   <u>SCR:</u> A.L. Mariaux   <u>STORY:</u> Julian Esteban   **PHOTOG:** Max Monteillet   <u>SPCL-FX:</u> Michael Nizza   **MUSIC:** Daniel White

Minor horror-thriller: Nazi dead rise from tarn

Zombies of Mora Tau

1957, (USA), Clover/Col, b&w, 70 mins.

<u>W:</u> Gregg Palmer, Allison Hayes, Gene Roth, Autumn Russell, Morris Ankrum, Philip Shankel, Edward Henderson, Marjorie Eaton, Joel Ashley, Karl Davis, William Baskin, Ray Corrigan, Lewis Webb, Mel Curtis, Frank Hagney

P: Sam Katzman   <u>D:</u> Edward L. Cahn   <u>SCR:</u> Raymond T. Marcus, from a story by George H. Plympton

Standard horror-thriller: Zombies guard fortune in pearls

Zombies of Sugar Hill

see **Sugar Hill**

Zombies on Broadway

1945, (USA), RKO, b&w, 68 mins.

<u>W:</u> Wally Brown, Alan Carney, Bela Lugosi, Anne Jeffreys, Sheldon Leonard, Frank Jenks, Russell Hopton, Ian Wolfe, Joseph Vitale, Darby Jones, Louis Jean Heydt, Sir Lancelot

P: Sid Rogell & Ben Stoloff   <u>D:</u> Gordon Douglas   <u>SCR:</u> Lawrence Kimble   <u>ADAPT:</u> Robert E. Kent   <u>ORIG. STORY:</u> Robert Faber & Charles Newman   **PHOTOG:** Jack MacKenzie   **MUSIC:** Roy Webb   <u>MUSIC DIR:</u> C. Bakaleinikoff

Minor horror-comedy: Bumblers encounter voodoo

Zone Troopers

1986, (USA-It), Empire/Vestron, color, 88 mins.

<u>W:</u> Tim Thomerson (*The Sarge*), Timothy Van Patten (*Joey*), Art La Fleur (*Mittens*), Biff Manard (*Dolan*), Peter Boom (*Col. Manheim*), William Paulson (*The Alien*), Max Turilli (*S.S. Sgt. Zeller*), Eugene Brell (*The Radioman*), Alviero Martin (*The Fuhrer*), John Leamer (*The Lieutenant*), Bruce McGuire (*The Medic*), Mike Manderville (*The S.S. Motorcyclist*), Archille Brunini (*The S.S. Radioman*), Joshua McDonald (*The Zone Trooper Captain*), Ole Jorgensen (*The S.S. Sentry*), Peter Hintz (*The S.S. Corporal*), Anita Zagaria (*The Dream Girl*)

<u>D:</u> Danny Bilson   <u>SCR:</u> Danny Bilson & Paul DeMeo   **PHOTOG:** Mac Ahlberg   <u>MUSIC:</u> Richard Band

Minor SF-thriller: World War II soldiers find alien spaceship

Zontar: The Thing from Venus

1966, (USA), Azalea/AIP, color, 73 mins.

<u>W:</u> John Agar, Susan Bjurman, Anthony Houston, Patricia Delany, Neil Fletcher, Warren Hammack, Colleen Carr, Jeff Alexander, Bill Thurman, Andrew Traister, George Edgley, Jonathan Ledford, Carol Gilley, Bertha Holmes

<u>D:</u> Larry Buchanan   <u>SCR:</u> Hillman Taylor & Larry Buchanan   **PHOTOG:** Robert B. Alcott

Minor SF-thriller (remake of **It Conquered the World***): Alien creature enslaves humans*

Zorro

1975, (It-Fr), Mondial-Artistes Associes, color, 93 mins.

<u>W:</u> Alain Delon (*Zorro*), Stanley Baker (*Col. Huerta*), Ottavia Piccolo (*Hortensia*), Moustache (*Sgt. Garcia*), Enzo Cerusico (*The Mute Servant*), Adriana Asti (*The Countess*), Giacomo Rossi-Stuart, Giampiero Albertini, Marino Mase, Rajka Jurcec

<u>D:</u> Duccio Tessari   <u>STORY & SCR:</u> Giorgio Arlorio, from Johnston McCulley's novel *The Curse of Capistrano*   **PHOTOG:** Giulio Arlorio   <u>SPCL-FX:</u> Cataldo Galiano   **MUSIC:** Guido De Angelis & Maurizio De Angelis

Standard adventure-thriller: Masked hero fights injustice

Zorro (1997)

see **The Mask of Zorro**

Zorro Contro Maciste (Zorro vs. Maciste)

1964, (It), AIP, color, 92 mins.

<u>W:</u> Alan Steel, Pierre Brice, Moira Orfei, Maria Grazia Spina

P: Fortunato Misiano   <u>D:</u> Umberto Lenzi   <u>SCR:</u> Guido Malatesta & Umberto Lenzi

USA retitle, **Samson and the Slave Queen**

Minor adventure-fantasy: Legendary heroes join forces to defeat evil queen

Zorro Rides Again

1959, (USA), Rep, b&w, 68 mins.

<u>W:</u> John Carroll, Helen Christian

Minor adventure-thriller (feature-version of serial, 1937)

X

Y

Z

Zorro, the Gay Blade
1981, (USA), Melvin Simon/20th-Fox, color, 93 mins.
<u>W</u>: George Hamilton (*Don Diego Vega/Bunny Wigglesworth*), Lauren Hutton (*Charlotte Wilson*), Brenda Vaccaro (*Florinda*), Ron Leibman (*Esteban*), Donovan Scott (*Paco*), James Booth (*Velasquez*), Helen Burns (*Consuela*), Clive Revill (*Garcia*), Carolyn Seymour (*Dolores*), Eduardo Noriega (*Don Francisco*), Jorge Russek (*Don Fernando*), Eduardo Alcaraz (*Don Jose*), Carlos Bravo (*Luis*), Roberto Dumont (*Ferraro*), Jorge Bolio (*Pablito*), Dick Balduzzi (*The Old Man*), Ana Elisa Perez Bolanos (*The Granddaughter*), Julian Colman (*Martinez*), Francisco Morayta (*Ramirez*), Owen Lee (*The Segeant*), Gustavo Ganem (*The Barman*), Armando Duarte (*The Soldier*), Norm Blankenship (*The Whipping Master*), Frank Welker (*The Narrator*)
<u>P</u>: George Hamilton & C.O. Erickson <u>D</u>: Peter Medak <u>SCR</u>: Hal Dresner. from a story by Hal Dresner, Greg Alt, Don Moriarty & Bob Randall, based on characters created by Johnston McCulley <u>PHOTOG</u>: John A. Alonzo <u>MUSIC</u>: Ian Frazer
Standard adventure-spoof: Masked hero has effeminate double

Zorro: The Legend Begins
1990, (USA), Ellipse/New World TV/FAM-TV, color, 95 mins.
<u>W</u>: Duncan Regehr (*Don Diego/Zorro*), Efrem Zimbalist Jr., Patrice Camhi, James Victor, Michael Tylo, Peter Diamond, Juan Diego Botto, Luis Lorenzo, Dennis Vaughan, Nur Al Levi, Jorge Bosso, Cesar A. Peralta
<u>D</u>: Ray Austin <u>TELEPLAY</u>: Robert L. McCullough, from characters created by Johnston McCulley <u>PHOTOG</u>: Manuel Teran <u>SPCL-FX</u>: Reyes Abades <u>MUSIC</u>: Jay Asher <u>LYRICS</u>: Dennis Spiegel
TVM, standard adventure-thriller (feature pilot for teleseries): Mystery man avenges down-trodden in Spanish California

Zorro vs. Maciste
see Zorro Contro Maciste

Zotz!
1962, (USA), Col, b&w, 85 mins.
<u>W</u>: Tom Poston (*Prof. Jonathan Jones*), Jim Backus (*Horatio Kellgore*), Julia Meade (*Prof. Virginia Fenster*), Margaret Dumont (*Persephone Updike*), Fred Clark (*Gen. Bulliver*), Carl Don (*Josh Bates*), Bart Patton (*Mr. Crane*), Zeme North (*Cynthia Jones*), Mike Mazurki (*Igor*), Jimmy Hawkins (*Jimmy Kellgore*), James Milhollin (*Dr. Kroner*), Michael Westfield (*Capt. Byron*), Judee Morton (*Miss Blakiston*), Susan Dorn (*The Nurse*), Russ Whiteman (*Maj. Folger*), George Moorman (*Lt. Stefanski*), Elaine Martone (*The Secretary*), Louis Nye, Cecil Kellaway
<u>P & D</u>: William Castle <u>SCR</u>: Ray Russell, from Walter Karig's novel <u>PHOTOG</u>: Gordon Avil <u>MUSIC</u>: Bernard Green
Standard comedy-fantasy: Man finds coin engraved with ancient word of power

Z.P.G.
1971, (USA-GB), Jagittarius/Para, color, 97 mins.
<u>W</u>: Oliver Reed, Geraldine Chaplin, Diane Cilento, Bill Nagy, Don Gordon, Aubrey Woods
<u>P</u>: Thomas F. Madigan <u>D</u>: Michael Campus <u>SCR</u>: Max Ehrlich & Frank De Felitta <u>SPCL-FX</u>: Derek Meddings <u>MUSIC</u>: Jonathon Hodge
Adult SF: Totalitarian future aims for zero population growth

Zu: Warriors of the Magic Mountain
1983, (Hong Kong), color, 95 mins.
<u>D</u>: Tsui Hark
Standard fantasy-thriller: Soldier battles evil spirits

Zvenigora
1927, (Russ), Vufku, b&w, 5,902.2 ft. (1799m)
<u>W</u>: Semyon Svashenko, Mikola Nademsky, Alexander Podorozhny
<u>D</u>: Alexander Dovzhenko <u>SCR</u>: Mikhail Johansen & Yuri Yurtik <u>PHOTOG</u>: Boris Zabelyov
A.k.a. Zakoldovannoye Mesto (Bewitched Place)
Modest myth-fantasy: Tableaux of 1,000 years of Ukrainian history

Z.P.G.: DIANE CILENTO

FIN

X
Y
Z

The Mask of Fu Manchu: BORIS KARLOFF

Adamson, Ray(mond) (act): *The Curse Of The Golem; The Orchard End Murder*
Adcock, Chris (act): *Treasure Island (1950)*
Adcock, Danny (act): *The Cars That Ate Paris; Chilling*
Adcox, Thom (act): *I Saw What You Did (1988); Popcorn*
Addams, Charles (wri): *The Addams Family; Addams Family Values*
Addams, Dawn (act, 1930–1985): *The Hour Of 13; Long Distance; Return To Treasure Island; Riders To The Stars; Die Tausend Augen Des Dr. Mabuse; The Two Faces Of Dr. Jekyll; The Vampire Lovers; The Vault Of Horror; Where The Bullets Fly; Zeta One*
Addario, Danny (act): *The Pink Chiquitas*
Addie, Robert (act): *Excalibur*
Addinsell, Richard (mus, b. 1904): *The Black Rose; Blithe Spirit; Scrooge (1951); Under Capricorn*
Addison, Bernard (act): *King Kong Lives*
Addison, Carlotta (act): *The Blue Bird (1910)*
Addison, John (mus, b. 1920): *The Black Knight; High Treason (1951); The Hour Of 13; The Loved One; Mistress Of Paradise; The Phantom Of The Opera (1990); Seven Days To Noon; The Seven-Per-Cent Solution; Sleuth; Strange Invaders; Torn Curtain*
Addison, Patrick (act): *The Greed Of William Hart*
Addison, Walter (act): *Ghost In The Machine*
Addiss, Justus (dir): *The Cry Baby Killer*
Addobbati, Giuseppe (act): *The Night Porter; Terror Of Rome Against The Son Of Hercules; To Commit A Murder*
Addota, Kip (act): *Watchers II*
Addy, Wesley (act, 1912-1996): *Hush...Hush, Sweet Charlotte; Seconds; What Ever Happened To Baby Jane? (1962)*
Adee, Richie (cin): *Oh Heavenly Dog*
Adejugbe, Ayo (act): *Congo*
Adele, Blanche (act): *I'm An Explosive*
Adeline, Sherri (act): *Phantom Of The Paradise*
Adell, Pearl (act): *Retribution (1988)*
Adelman, Julius (act): *Killer's Kiss*
Adelphi Girls, The (act): *Elstree Calling*
Adem, Yashar (act): *Sphinx (1981)*
Ademia, Mack (act): *The Dungeonmaster*
Adeney, Eric (act): *Castle Sinister (1932); The Merry Men Of Sherwood*
Ades, Daniel (act): *Targets*
Ades, Vivienne (wri): *Dual Alibi*
Adeson, Martin (act): *When Knights Were Bold (1929)*
Adet, Georges (act): *Aimez Vous Les Femmes?*
Adewale (act): *Congo; 20,000 Leagues Under The Sea (1997, ABC-TV)*
Adiutori, Patricia (act): *Torso*
Adkins, Ella (wri): *Time Is My Enemy*
Adjani, Isabelle (act, b. 1955): *Diabolique (1996); Nosferatu, The Vampyre; Possession (1981); The Tenant*
Adler, Alan (J.) (wri): *The Alchemist; Parasite*
Adler, Allen (wri): *Behemoth, The Sea Monster; Forbidden Planet*
Adler, Clyde (act): *Beach Girls And The Monster*
Adler, Felix (wri): *A Chump At Oxford*
Adler, Gilbert (dir & wri): *Tales From The Crypt Presents Bordello Of Blood*
Adler, Jay (act, 1896–1978): *The Curse Of The Undead; The Killing*
Adler, Jay (act): *Grave Of The Vampire*
Adler, Joseph (dir): *Scream, Baby, Scream*
Adler, Larry (mus): *A High Wind In Jamaica*
Adler, Luther (act, 1903–1984): *Cornered; D.O.A. (1949); Lancer Spy; M (1950)*
Adler, Matt (act): *Dream A Little Dream; Flight Of The Navigator; Teen Wolf*
Adler, Richard (mus): *Damn Yankees*
Adler, Robert (act): *Journey To The Center Of The Earth (1959); Prince Valiant; Two On A Guillotine*
Adler, Stella (act): *Shadow Of The Thin Man*
Adler, Susan (act): *She (1983)*
Adler, William (act): *I Was A Zombie For The F.B.I.*
Adley, Hawk (act): *Boarding House*
Adlum, Ed (dir): *Invasion Of The Blood Farmers*
Adlum, Ed (wri): *Invasion Of The Blood Farmers; Shriek Of The Mutilated*
Admoni, I. (mus): *Planeta Bura*
Adoch, Andy (act): *Shock Chamber*
Adolphe, Hylette (act): *Satyricon*
Adolphson, Kristina (act): *The Devil's Eye*
Adomaitis, Regimantis (act): *Korol Lir*
Adonis, Frank (act): *Wolfen*
Adoree, Renee (act, 1898–1933, nee Jeanne De La Fonte): *The Black Bird (1926); Mr. Wu (1927); Monte Cristo*
Adorf, Mario (act): *The Devil Strikes At Night; Ghosts-Italian Style; The Red Tent; Ten Little Indians (1965); L'uccello Delle Piume Di Cristallo*
Adorni, Dina (act): *Amarcord*
Adreon, Franklin (dir): *The Claw Monsters; Cyborg 2087; Dimension 5*
Adreon, Franklin (wri): *Dick Tracy Returns; Dick Tracy's G-Men; Dr. Satan's Robot; The Torpedo Of Doom*
Adrian, Bob (act): *12 Monkeys*
Adrian, Iris (act, b. 1913, nee Iris Hostetter): *The Barefoot Executive; Bluebeard (1944); Boston Blackie's Rendezvous; Horror Island; Lady Of Burlesque; Philo Vance Returns; The Shaggy D.A.; Shake Hands With Murder; The Sky Dragon*
Adrian, Kay (act): *—And Now The Screaming Starts!; Tales From The Crypt*
Adrian, Max (act, 1903–1973): *The Deadly Affair; Dr. Terror's House Of Horrors (1964); Pool Of London; The Terrornauts Adriance,*
Jane Sterling (act): see Sterling, Jan
Adrien, Cristine (act): *The Unholy Quest*
Adventures, The (mus): *Demons*
Aeriens, Elizabeth (act): *Jane Eyre (1921)*
Aeschylus (wri, 525–456 b.c.): *The Iliac Passion*
Affleck, Neil (act): *Armageddon, My Bloody Valentine; Oh Heavenly Dog; Scanners; Wild Thing*
Afonso, Yves (act): *The Black Windmill*
Afrakhan, Behrooz (act): *Party Line*
Afterman, Peter (mus): *Earth Girls Are Easy; The 6th Man*
Afzal, Safira (act): *Octopussy*
Agar, Ivan (act): *Shriek Of The Mutilated*
Agar, John (act,b. 1927): *Attack Of The Puppet People; Bait; The Brain From Planet Arous; Curse Of The Swamp Creature; Daughter Of Dr. Jekyll; Fear (1990); The Golden Mistress; Hand Of Death; Hold Back Tomorrow; Invisible Invaders; Journey To The Seventh Planet; King Kong (1976); The Magic Carpet (1951); Miracle Mile; The Mole People; Night Breed; Night Fright; The Perfect Bride; Revenge Of The Creature; Rocket Man; The St. Valentine's Day Massacre; Tarantula; Women Of The Prehistoric Planet; Zontar: The Thing From Venus*
Agar, Mona (act): *The Funhouse (1981)*
Agate, May (act): *I Was A Spy*
Age (wri): *Ok, Nero!*
Agee, James (wri, 1909–1955): *The Night Of The Hunter (1955)*
Ager, Diane (act): *Alien High*
Ager, Suzanne (act): *The Alien Within; Evil Toons*
Agnew, Daisy (act): *The Bells (1923)*
Agnew, Walter L. (act): see Fields, Stanley
Agosti, Carlos (act): *La Invasion De Los Vampiros; The Saint vs. The Zombies; El Vampiro Sangriento*
Agostini, Claude (cin): *Quest For Fire*
Agrama, Frank (dir & wri): *Dawn Of The Mummy*
Agren, Janet (act): *Aladdin (1987); Eaten Alive (1980); The Gates Of Hell; Panic (1983); Red Sonja*
Aguayo, Jose F. (cin): *La Cara Del Terror; Tristana; La Venganza De Don Mendo*
Aguiar, Marcia (act): *The Pink Chiquitas*
Aguilar, Cesar (act): *The Blood Drinkers*
Aguilar, George (act): *The Lightning Incident*
Aguilar, Luz Maria (act): *Survive!*
Aguilar, Scott (act): *The Brotherhood Of Satan*
Aguire, Sergio (act): *The Offspring*
Aguirre, Alma Rose (act): *The Phantom Of The Red House*
Aguirre, Javier (dir & wri): *Gran Amore Del Conde Dracula; El Jorobado De La Morgue*
Aguirre, Jose Luis (act): *A Midsummer Night's Dream (1985)*
Aguirre, Nina M. (act): *Distortions*
Agullo, Alfonso (mus): *Mystery On Monster Island*
Agutter, Jenny (act, b. 1952): *An American Werewolf In London; Child's Play 2; Dominique; I Start Counting; Logan's Run; The Savage Curse*
Ah-Ben-Aza (act): *The Mystery Film*
Ahern, Allegra (act): *The Sand Castle*
Ahern Jr., Lloyd (act): *Prince Valiant*
Ahern, Patrick (act): *Rocketship X-M*
Aherne, Brian (act, 1902–1986): *I Confess; Lancelot And Guinevere; The Locket; Prince Valiant; Sotto Contro La Morte*
Aherne, Lloyd (cin): *The Brasher Doubloon; For Heaven's Sake; Gorilla At Large; Miracle On 34th Street (1947)*
Aherne, Pat(Rick) (act, 1901–1970): *The Challenge; The Man Who Knew Too Much (1956); The Paradine Case; The Return Of Bulldog Drummond*
A'hiller, Lejaren (act & dir): *Devil's Angel*
Ahlberg, Mac (cin): *Crash And Burn; Deepstar Six; Dolls; The Dungeonmaster; The Eliminators; From Beyond; Ghost Town; Ghost Warrior; Ghoulies; Hell Night; House; House II: The Second Story; Innocent Blood; Meridian; Parasite; Prison (1988); Re-Animator; The Seduction; Trancers; Zone Troopers*
Ahlstedt, Borje (act): *I Am Curious (Yellow)*
Ahlstrand, Linne (act): *Beast From Haunted Cave*
Ahmed, Ahmed (act): *Virtuosity*
Ahmed, Benyahim (act): *The Jewel Of The Nile*
Ahmed, Makoula (act): *The Jewel Of The Nile*
Ahn, Philip (act, 1905–1978): *Boston Blackie's Chinese Venture; Charlie Chan In Honolulu; The Chinese Ring; Confessions Of An Opium Eater; The Creeper (1948); Daughter Of Shanghai; Destination Saturn; Fair Wind To Java; Shock Corridor; Thank You, Mr. Moto; Voodoo Heartbeat*
Ahn, Ralph (act): *Confessions Of An Opium Eater*
Ahui (act): *Robinson Crusoe And The Tiger*
Ai, Kyoko (act): *Destroy All Monsters*
Ai, Li Ling (act): *Werewolf Of Washington*
Ai, Tomoke (act): *Terror Of Mechagodzilla*
Aidman, Charles (act): *Countdown; The House Of The Dead*
Aiello, Danny (act, b. 1935): *Jacob's Ladder; The Stuff*
Aiello, Rick (act): *Switch*
Aime, Monique (act): *House Of 1,000 Dolls*
Aimee, Anouk (act, b. 1932, nee Francoise Sorya): *8 1/2; Paris Express; Sodom And Gomorrah*
Aimos (act): *Le Golem (1936)*
Ainley, Anthony (act): *The Blood On Satan's Claw; In The Devil's Garden; The Land That Time Forgot; Naked Evil*
Ainley, Henry (act): *Called Back; The Prisoner Of Zenda (1915); Rupert Of Hentzau (1915)*
Ainley, June (act): *Oh Heavenly Dog*
Ainley, Richard (act, 1910–1967): *Above Suspicion; The Frog; The Smiling Ghost*
Ainsley, Norman (act): *Charlie Chan On Broadway*
Ainsworth, Carole (act): *Peter Rabbit And The Tales Of Beatrix Potter*
Ainsworth, Harrison (wri): *Old St. Paul's; The Tower Of London (1909)*
Aird, Jane (act): *Death Goes To School; Hunted (1952); Quatermass II; X...The Unknown*
Airoldi, Conchita (act): *The Human Factor*
Airoldi, Cristina (act): *Lo Strano Caso Della Signora Ward; Torso*
Aitchison, Peggy (act): *Paint Me A Murder*
Aitchison, Suzy (act): *Bloody New Year*
Aitken, Spottiswoode (act): *The Avenging Conscience; The Flying Torpedo; Monte Cristo*
Aitkin, Michael (act): *The Mcguffin*
Aizawo, Jo (cin): *The War In Space*
Ajaye, Franklyn (act): *The 'Burbs*
Ajzenberg, Harold (act): see Woodlawn, Holly
Akagi, Ranko (act): *Kwaidan*
Akasaka, Koreyoshi (dir): *Atomic Rulers Of The World; Evil Brain From Outer Space*
Aked, Muriel (act): *Just William's Luck*
Akers, Andra (act): *Killer In The Mirror*
Akers, Karen (act): *Vibes*
Akers, Tom (act): *Premonition (1972)*
Akhan, Damien (act): *Echoes*
Aki, Haru (act): *The Fan*
Akin, Philip (act): *Iceman; Millennium*
Akins, Claude (act, 1918–1994): *Battle For The Planet Of The Apes; The Curse; Monster In The Closet; The Night Stalker (1971); The Norliss Tapes; Tarantulas: The Deadly Cargo; Tentacles*
Akitsu, Hiroshi (act): *Mothra*
Akiyama, Denis (act): *Johnny Mnemonic*
Akiyama, Miyuki (act): *Attack Of The Monsters*
Akman, Eris (act): *Slipstream*
Akst, Harry (mus): *Lady Of Burlesque; Think Fast, Mr. Moto*
Akune, Shuko (act): *Alien Nation*
Alaimo, Marc (act): *Dr. Black Mr. Hyde; Fugitive From The Empire; Matt Helm; Total Recall*
Alaimo, Michael (act): *The China Syndrome*
Alaimo, Steve (act): *Stanley*
Alain, Michael (act): *Paris Express*
Alalouf, Robin (act): *Paris Express; 23 Paces To Baker Street*
Alan, Eric (act): *The Toxic Avenger, Part II*
Alan, Lloyd (act): *To Die For*
Alaniz, Rico (act): *War Of The Colossal Beast*
Alazraki, Benito (dir, b. 1923): *The Saint vs. The Zombies*
Alba (act): *Bedazzled*
Alba, Alney (act): *Fright (1957)*
Alba, Jaime (act): *My Science Project*
Alba, Julia C. (act): *La Corona Negra*
Alba, Maria (act): *Chandu; El Cuerpo Del Lito*
Alba, Rafael Morena (dir & wri): *Exorcism's Daughter*
Alba, Rose (act): *Shadow Of A Man; Thunderball*
Albach—Retty, Rosemarie (act): *See Schneider, Romy*
Albain, Richard/Dick (Ccn): *Bog; Cruise Into Terror; Shadow Of The Hawk; Strait-Jacket; Timestalkers; Valley Of The Dragons*
Albanesi, Meggie (act): *Mr. Wu (1919)*
Albani, Romano (cin): *Inferno (1979); Terrorvision; Troll*
Albano, Bea (act): *Edward Scissorhands*
Albee, George Sumner (wri): *The Next Voice You Hear*
Albee, Mary (act): *The Monster Squad*
Albee, Roxanne (act): *Sisters Of Death*
Alben, Adrianna (act): *Kong Island*
Alberge, Betty (act): *Crucible Of Terror; Disciple Of Death*
Alberghetti, Anna Maria (act, b. 1936): *Cinderfella; The Medium (1951)*
Alberni, Luis (act, 1887–1962): *The Lone Wolf Meets A Lady; The Mad Genius; The Man From Beyond; The Sphinx (1933); Svengali (1931)*
Alberoni, Sherri/Sherry (act): *Barn Of The Naked Dead; Sisters Of Death; The Three Worlds Of Gulliver*
Albers, Hans (act, 1892–1960): *Die Avonturen Von Baron Munchhausen; F.P. 1 Antwortet Nicht; Gold (German- Speaking Version)*
Albershart, Albert (act): see Lane, Allan
Albert, Anne (act): *Le Manoir Maudit; Tomb Of Torture*
Albert, Arthur (cin): *Heart Condition; Night Of The Comet*
Albert, Eddie (act, b. 1908, nee Eddie Heimberger): *The Borrowers; Brenda Starr (1992); The Demon Murder Case; The Devil's Rain; Dreamscape; Escape To Witch Mountain; Goliath Awaits; Out Of The Fog (1941)*
Albert (Jr.), Edward (act, b. 1951): *Death Cruise; Demon Keeper; Distortions; The Fool Killer; Galaxy Of Terror; The House Where Evil Dwells; Killer Bees; Space Marines; When Time Ran Out*
Albert, Jerry (act): *Primal Scream*
Albert, Laura (act): *Dr. Caligari; The Unnamable*
Albert, Mary (act): *Remo Williams: The Adventure Begins*
Albertazzi, Giorgio (act): *L'annee Derniere A Marienbad*
Alberti, Barbara (wri): *The Night Porter*
Alberti, Flora (act): *The Jewel Of The Nile*
Alberti, Guido (act): *Aimez Vous Les Femmes?; 8 1/2; Spasmo*
Albertini, Giampiero (act): *Zorro (1975)*
Albertson, Coit (act): *The Return Of Boston Blackie*
Albertson, Frank (act, 1909–1964): *A Connecticut Yankee; Ellery Queen's Penthouse Mystery; House Of Menace; Just Imagine; Man-Made Monster; Nightfall (1956); Psycho*
Albertson, Jack (act, 1907–1981): *Dead And Buried; Man Of A Thousand Faces; Miracle On 34th Street (1947); The Poseidon Adventure; The Shaggy Dog; Son Of Flubber; Willy Wonka And The Chocolate Factory*
Albertson, Mabel (act): *Black Widow (1954); The Gazebo; The House That Wouldn't Die; On A Clear Day You Can See Forever*
Albertson, Mitzi (act): *Teenage Zombies*
Alberty, Karl Otto (act): *Slaughterhouse-Five*
Albiin, Elsy (act): *Intimate Relations; Rapture; Thirty-Six Hours*
Albin, Andy (act): *Bates Motel; Forgotten City Of The Planet Of The Apes*
Albin, Dolores (act): *Bates Motel*
Albin, Hans (dir): *No Survivors, Please*
Albion, Winifred (act): *The Daughter Of Romany; The Stolen Plans*
Albrecht, Richard (act): *Threads*
Albrechtsen, Michael (cin): *Corruption; The Uncanny*
Albright, Carlton J. (wri): *The Children*
Albright, Carol (act): *Dr. Caligari*
Albright, Hardie (act, b. 1903): *Angel On My Shoulder (1946); The Jade Mask; The Mad Doctor Of Market Street; The Scarlet Letter (1934)*
Albright, Lola (act, b. 1924): *Les Felins; The Helicopter Spies; The Monolith Monsters*
Albright, Sarah (act): *The Children*
Albright, Nathanael (act): *The Children*

Alburn, Tory (act): *Weekend Of Fear*
Albury, Eric (act): *The Yellow Claw*
Alcalde, Mario (act): *Dead Ringer*
Alcaraz, Eduardo (act): *El Ladron De Cadaveres; Zorro, The Gay Blade*
Alcaraz, Jose Antonio (act): *Dr. Tarr's Torture Dungeon*
Alcazar, Victor (act): *Nightmare Hotel*
Alcocer, S. (dir, a.k.a. Edward Mann): *Cauldron Of Blood*
Alcoriza, Luis (wri, b. 1920): *El Angel Exterminador; La Mort En Ce Jardin*
Alcorn, Olive Ann (act): *The Phantom Of The Opera (1925)*
Alcott, John (cin): *Baby: Secret Of The Lost Legend; The Beastmaster; A Clockwork Orange; Greystoke: The Legend Of Tarzan, Lord Of The Apes; No Way Out; The Shining; Terror Train*
Alcott, Robert (b.) (cin): *Don't Look In The Basement; It's Alive! (1968); Zontar: The Thing From Venus*
Alda, Alan (act, b. 1936): *The Extraordinary Seaman; Isn't It Shocking?; The Mephisto Waltz; To Kill A Clown*
Alda, Elizabeth (act): *Night Of The Creeps*
Alda, Robert (act, 1914—1986, nee Alphonso D'abruzzo): *The Beast With Five Fingers; Cloak And Dagger (1946); Deadly Dust; The Devil's Hand (1961); House Of Exorcism; The Serpent; Tarzan And The Slave Girl*
Alda, Rutanya (act): *Amityville II: The Possession; The Dark Half; The Fury; The Stuff; When A Stranger Calls*
Aldam, Gillian (act): *Fahrenheit 451*
Aldana, Vida (act): *Queen Of The Amazons (1947)*
Alden, Bob (act): *The Falcon's Alibi*
Alden, Cary Wilmot (act): *The Savage Bees*
Alden, John (act): *Deep Red (1994)*
Alden, Norman (act): *Ben; Ed Wood; The Nutty Professor (1963); Roller Blade Warriors: Taken By Force*
Alden, Richard (Can act): *The Pit (1983)*
Alden, Richard (USA act): *The Sadist*
Alden, Ronald (act): *The Projected Man*
Alden, Stacey (act): *A Nightmare On Elm Street 3: Dream Warriors*
Alden, Tom (act): *Mirrors*
Alden, Tom Smith (act): *The Savage Bees*
Alder, Don (act): *The Haunting Of Sarah Hardy*
Alder, Nick (cin): *Legend*
Alder, Thomas (act): *The Red Circle (1960)*
Alderdice, Alfred (act): see Drake, Tom
Alderman, John (act): *The Alpha Incident; Crypt Of The Living Dead; New Year's Evil; The Screaming Woman; Superstition*
Alderson, Erville (act): *The Bishop's Wife; The Feathered Serpent (1948); Nancy Drew, Troubleshooter; The Shanghai Chest; The Thirteenth Guest*
Alderson, George (act): *Dial M For Murder (1954)*
Alderson, John (act): *The Cat From Outer Space; Evil Under The Sun; To Catch A Thief*
Alderson, Judith (act): *Outland*
Alderton, John (act): *Zardoz*
Aldiss, Brian W. (wri, b. 1925): *Roger Corman's Frankenstein Unbound*
Aldo, G.R. (cin, 1905–1953): *Miracle In Milan*
Aldon, Mari (act): *A Race For Life; Tangier Incident*
Aldredge, John (act): *Murder On A Bridle Path*
Aldredge, Tom (act): **Batteries Not Included; The Mind Snatchers; The Mouse On The Moon*
Aldrich, Alida (act): *Hush...Hush, Sweet Charlotte*
Aldrich, Benny (act): *The Strangers*
Aldrich, Kelly (act): *Hush...Hush, Sweet Charlotte*
Aldrich, Robert (dir, 1918–1983): *Hush...Hush, Sweet Charlotte; Kiss Me Deadly; What Ever Happened To Baby Jane? (1962)*
Aldridge, Katharine (act): *Dead Men Tell*
Aldridge, Kay (act): *The Falcon's Brother; Nyoka And The Lost Secrets Of Hippocrates*
Aldridge, Kitty (act): *Slipstream*
Aldridge, Michael (act): *Life For Ruth*
Aldridge, Sidney (dir & wri): *Adventures Of Willie Woodbine And Lightning Larry-A Joyride To The Cannibal Islands*
Aldridge, Wallace (act): *The Cloister And The Woman*
Alejandro, Julio (wri): *H.G. Wells' New Invisible Man; Tristana*
Alekan, Henri (cin, b. 1909): *La Belle Et La Bete; Topkapi*
Aleksander, Grant (act): *Dark Mansions*
Aleman, Julio (act): *Los Automatas De La Muerte; Blood Of Nostradamus; La Maldicion De Nostradamus; Nostradamus Y El Destructor De Monstruos; Nostradamus Y El Genio De La Tinieblas*
Aleong, Aki (act): *Tidal Wave: No Escape*
Ales, John (act): *The Nutty Professor (1996)*
Alessandrini, Alessandro (mus): *The Devil's Nightmare; La Figlia Di Frankenstein*
Alessandrini, Goffredo (act & dir): *Rapture*
Alessandro, Anthony (act): *Jacob's Ladder*
Alessandro, Perrella (act): *El Castello Dell' Orrore*
Aletter, Frank (act): *Now You See Him, Now You Don't*
Aletter, Kyle (act): *The Day After*
Alexakis, Glenn (act): *Trick Or Treats*
Alexander, Alex (mus): *Two Lost Worlds*
Alexander, Arthur (act): *Bloodspell*
Alexander, Ben (act): *Buried Alive (1940)*
Alexander, Bob (act): *Wild Is My Love*
Alexander, Brett (act): *Cat People (1982)*
Alexander, Carmen J. (act): *Edward Scissorhands*
Alexander, Charles (act): *Just Imagine*
Alexander, David James (act): *Nightmare On The 13th Floor*
Alexander, Denyse (act): *The Medusa Touch*
Alexander, Dick (act): See Alexander, Richard/Dick
Alexander, Don (act): *The Wizard Of Gore*
Alexander, Dr. Donna (act): *Blink*
Alexander, E. Nick (wri): *Of Mice And Men (1981)*
Alexander, Eddie (act): *The Bees*
Alexander, Frank (act): *Star Crystal*
Alexander, George (act): *War Of The Colossal Beast*
Alexander, Gerry (act): *The Viking Queen*
Alexander, Howard (act): *Flesh Gordon*
Alexander, J. Grubb (wri): *The Chinese Parrot; The Lone Wolf Returns (1926); The Mad Genius; The Man Who Laughs (1928); Moby Dick (1930); Murder Will Out (1930); Outward Bound; Svengali (1931)*
Alexander, Jack (act): *The Chance Of A Lifetime*
Alexander, James/Jim (act): *Jack And The Beanstalk (1952); Skullduggery*
Alexander, Jane (act, b. 1939, nee Jane Quigley): *Miracle On 34th Street (1973)*
Alexander, Janet (act): *For All Eternity; God's Clay; I Hear You Calling Me; Queen Of The Wicked; What's Bred...Comes Out In The Flesh*
Alexander, Jason (act, b. 1959): *The Hunchback Of Notre Dame (1996); Jacob's Ladder*
Alexander, Jeff (act): *Curse Of The Swamp Creature; Horror High; Zontar: The Thing From Venus*
Alexander, Jeff (mus, 1910–1989): *The Gazebo*
Alexander, John (GB act): *Greystoke: The Legend Of Tarzan, Lord Of The Apes; Return To Oz*
Alexander, John (USA act, b. 1897): *Arsenic And Old Lace; The Horn Blows At Midnight*
Alexander, Jon (cin): *Timestalkers*
Alexander, Karl (wri): *Time After Time*
Alexander, Katherine (act, b. 1901): *Death Takes A Holiday (1934); The Hunchback Of Notre Dame (1939)*
Alexander, Keith (act): *Superman (1978); Thunderbird 6*
Alexander, Khandi (act): *Maid To Order; Terminal*
Alexander, Les (wri): *Not Of This World*
Alexander, Paige M. (act): *Spookies*
Alexander, Paul (act): *Schizo (1977)*
Alexander, Richard/Dick (act): *Boston Blackie's Rendezvous; Charlie Chan In Honolulu; The Clutching Hand; The Leopard Lady; Think Fast, Mr. Moto; The Wraith*
Alexander, Ross (act, 1907–1937): *A Midsummer Night's Dream (1935)*
Alexander, Royce (act): *Time Walker*
Alexander, Scott (wri): *Ed Wood*
Alexander, Silvan (act): *The Mutagen; Shock Chamber*
Alexander, Simon (act): *Blood Diner*
Alexander, Terence (act, b. 1923): *The Boy Who Never Was; Death Is A Number; Frankenstein (1984); The Magic Christian; Man At The Carlton Tower; The Mind Benders (1963); The Vault Of Horror*
Alexander, Terry (act): *Angel On My Shoulder (1980); Day Of The Dead; Fantasies; Werewolf Of Washington*
Alexander, Tom (act): *Dream A Little Evil*
Alexander, Van (mus): *The Atomic Kid; Platinum High School; The Private Lives Of Adam And Eve; Strait-Jacket; Tarzan And The Valley Of Gold*
Alexander, Victoria (act): *The Phantom Empire*
Alexander, Zoe (act): *The Night Digger*
Alexander-Willis, Hope (act): *The Long, Dark Night; Trauma (1993)*
Alexandra, Sarah (act): *Robin Hood: Prince Of Thieves*
Alexandre, Katrin (act): *The Unnamable*
Alexandria, Mello (act): *Spawn Of The Slithis*
Alexeyev, V. (cin): *Mezhplanetnaya Revolutsiya*
Alexious, Nicos (act): *The Day The Fish Came Out*
Alexis, Alvin (act): *The Brother From Another Planet; The Wiz*
Alexis, Nora (act): *The Gore-Gore Girls*
Alexsandre, Patrice (act): *The Tenant*
Alfa, Michele (act): *The Count Of Monte Cristo (1955)*
Alfieri, Richard (act): *Echoes*
Alfonsi, Lidia/Lydia (act): *Morgan The Pirate; I Tre Volti Della Paura; The Trojan Horse*
Alfonso, Maria Jose (act): *Behind The Mask Of Zorro*
Algren, Nelson (act): *Fearless Frank*
Ali, George (act): *Peter Pan*
Ali, Khalilah (act): *The China Syndrome*
Ali, Salwa (act): *Ed Wood*
Ali, Usaf (act): *The Falcon In Hollywood*
Aliba, Marc (act): *Anguish*
Alibe (act): *Treasure Island (1971)*
Alica, Maria (act): *Black Orpheus*
Alicia, Ana (act, b. 1955): *Halloween II*
Alicia, Marta (act): *Mindwarp*
Aliff, Lisa (act): *Remote Control (1988)*
Alighiero, Carlo (act): *The Cat O' Nine Tails; Lo Strano Caso Della Signora Ward*
Alis, Rene (act): *Dr. Tarr's Torture Dungeon*
Alise, Esther (act): *Vampire At Midnight*
Alison, Barbie (act): *Alice In Wonderland (1985)*
Alison, Dorothy (act, b. 1925): *The Amazing Mr. Blunden; Blind Terror; Child's Play (1954); Dr. Jekyll And Sister Hyde; The Man Upstairs; Turn The Key Softly*
Alkon, Simon (act): *Dr. Tarr's Torture Dungeon*
Allain, Marcel (wri): *Fantomas (1913); Fantomas Contro Scotland Yard*
Allais, Jean-Pierre (act): *The Black Windmill*
Allan, Andrea (act): *Scream And Die!; Vampira*
Allan, Charles (act): *Princess Clementina*
Allan, Douglas (Scotty) (act): *Spasms*
Allan, Elizabeth (act, b. 1908): *Alibi (1931); The Brain Machine; Grip Of The Strangler; The Lodger (1932); The Mark Of The Vampire (1935); The Mystery Of Mr. X; The Shadow (1933)*
Allan, Isaac (act): *Dead Of Night (1987)*
Allan, Jack (act): *Inn Of The Damned*
Allan, James Stuart (cin): *The Music Of The Spheres*
Allan, Jed (act): *Brenda Starr (1976)*
Allan, Lee (act): *The Silence Of The Hams*
Allan, Michael (act): *Dead Of Night (1945)*
Allan, Nancy (act): *Happy Birthday To Me*
Allan, Pamela (act): *Death Goes To School; Noose For A Lady*
Allan, Roger (act): *Lord Of The Flies (1963)*
Allan, Ross (act): *No Blade Of Grass*
Allan, Ted (cin): *Bride Of The Monster*
Alland, William (act): *Macbeth (1947)*
Alland, William (wri): *The Deadly Mantis*
Allanen, Merja (act): *Castle Keep*
Allardice, James B. (wri): *Francis Joins The Wacs*
Allas, Peter (act): *Cast A Deadly Spell*
Allaylis, Toni (act): *Mad Max Beyond Thunderdome*
Allbritton, Louise (act, 1920–1979): *Son Of Dracula (1943); Who Done It? (1942)*
Allder, Nick (cin): *The Jewel Of The Nile; Moon Zero Two*
Alldredge, Michael (act): *The Entity; Ghost Town; The Incredible Melting Man; Robot Jox*
Allef, Tony (act): *Slipstream*
Allegret, Marc (act, 1900–1973): *Et Mourir De Plaisir*
Allegret, Marc (dir, 1900–1973): *Blackmailed*
Allen, Adrianne (act): *The October Man*
Allen, Allen D. (mus): *The Clones; The Spectre Of Edgar Allan Poe*
Allen, Antony (act): *Hellraiser*
Allen, Bambi (act): *Hell's Bloody Devils; Satan's Sadists*
Allen, Barbara (Jo) (act, d. 1974, a.k.a. Vera Vague): *The Mad Doctor*
Allen, Barry (act): *Funeral Home*
Allen, Beverly (act): *Screams Of A Winter Night*
Allen, Billie (act): *The Wiz*
Allen, Bob (act): *Naked Evil; Raiders Of The Living Dead*
Allen, Buck (act): *The Alien's Return*
Allen, Carol (act): *The Flesh And Blood Show*
Allen, Chad (act): *The Bad Seed (1985); Terrorvision*
Allen, Chesney (act): *Alf's Button Afloat; Life Is A Circus*
Allen, Christi Michelle (act): *The Initiation*
Allen, Corey (act, b. 1934): *The Mad Magician; The Night Of The Hunter (1955); Private Property*
Allen, Corey (dir): *Avalanche; The Man In The Santa Claus Suit*
Allen, Corey (wri): *Avalanche*
Allen, David/Dave (cin): *The Dungeonmaster; Equinox; Flesh Gordon; Laserblast*
Allen, David (dir): *The Dungeonmaster; Puppet Master II*
Allen, David (wri): *The Dungeonmaster*
Allen, Diana (act): *Salome (1923)*
Allen, Edgar (act): *The Mandarin Mystery*
Allen, Edward Paul (act): *Monolith*
Allen, Florence (act): *The Lone Wolf's Daughter (1929)*
Allen, Gary (act): *Alice, Sweet Alice; Don't Answer The Phone!; Fright Night II; Pandemonium; The Sentinel*
Allen, George (act): *The Clutching Hand*
Allen, Gracie (act, 1906–1964): *The Gracie Allen Murder Case; International House*
Allen, Grant (wri): *What's Bred...Comes Out In The Flesh*
Allen, Greg (act): *The Resurrected*
Allen, Harry (act): *The Enchanted Cottage (1924); The Kennel Murder Case*
Allen, Irving (act): *On Her Majesty's Secret Service; The Road To Hong Kong*
Allen, Irving (dir): *16 Fathoms Deep*
Allen, Irwin (dir, 1916–1991): *The Animal World; Beyond The Poseidon Adventure; City Beneath The Sea (1970); Five Weeks In A Balloon; The Lost World (1960); The Story Of Mankind; The Swarm; Voyage To The Bottom Of The Sea*
Allen, Irwin (wri, 1916–1991): *The Animal World; Five Weeks In A Balloon; The Lost World (1960); The Story Of Mankind; Voyage To The Bottom Of The Sea*
Allen, Jack (act): *House Of Mortal Sin; She Shall Have Murder; The Sound Barrier*
Allen, Jay Presson (wri): *Marnie*
Allen, Jeffrey (act): *2000 Maniacs*
Allen, Joan (act): *The Crucible (1996)*
Allen, Joanie (act): *The Incredible Hulk Returns*
Allen, John (act): *The Spirit*
Allen, John H. (act): *Charlie Chan At The Race Track*
Allen, Jonelle (act): *The Midnight Hour; Vampire (1979)*
Allen, Joseph (act): *Seven Keys To Baldpate (1929)*
Allen Jr., Joseph/Joe (A.) (act, 1918–1962): *Cannibal Attack; Dangerous Money; Valley Of The Headhunters*
Allen, Karen (act, b. 1951): *Ghost In The Machine; Raiders Of The Lost Ark; Scrooged; Starman*
Allen, Keith (GB act): *Loch Ness*
Allen, Keith (USA act): *The Toxic Avenger, Part II*
Allen, Kenneth (act): *Just Imagine*
Allen, Lester (act): *The Dark Mirror (1946)*
Allen, Lewis (dir, b. 1905): *At Sword's Point; The Uninvited (1944); The Unseen (1945)*
Allen, Mark (act): *Child Of Darkness, Child Of Light; Neon Maniacs*
Allen, Marty (act, b. 1922): *The Last Of The Secret Agents?*
Allen, Mary (act): see Jerrold, Mary
Allen, Mary Marsh (act): *Whosoever Shall Offend*
Allen, Mel (act): *The Return Of Dracula*
Allen, Mike (act): *Wolfman (1979)*
Allen, Nancy (act, b. 1950): *Blow Out; Carrie; Dressed To Kill (1980); Memories Of Murder; The Philadelphia Experiment; Poltergeist III; Robocop; Robocop 2; Robocop 3; Strange Invaders; Terror In The Aisles*
Allen, Patrick (act, b. 1927): *The Body Stealers; Captain Clegg; Dial M For Murder (1954); Journey Into Darkness; Murder Is Easy; The Night Of The Big Heat; The Night Of The Generals; 1984 (1955); Persecution; Sign It Death; The Sinister Man; When Dinosaurs Ruled The Earth*
Allen, Peter (mus): *Cyborg 2: Glass Shadow*
Allen, Phillip Richard/R. (act): *Mortal Sins; Star Trek III: The Search For Spock*
Allen, Priscilla (act): *Total Recall*
Allen, Rae (act): *Damn Yankees; Stargate*
Allen, Randi (act): *Cauchemares*
Allen, Richard (act): *Vampire On Bikini Beach*
Allen, Robert (1930's act): *The Black Room; Crime And Punishment (1935)*
Allen, Robert (1980s act): *Star Crystal*
Allen, Ronald (act): *The Fiend (1972)*

Allen, Rosalind (act): Children Of The Corn II: The Final Sacrifice; Ticks; Pinocchio's Revenge; To Die For II: Son Of Darkness
Allen, Russell D. (mus): Offerings
Allen, Sage (act): Puppet Master II
Allen, Sam (act): The Sea Beast
Allen, Sarita (act): Angel Heart
Allen, Sheila (act): Alice In Wonderland (1985); The Alphabet Murders; The Legend Of Spider Forest
Allen, Sian Barbara (act): Scream, Pretty Peggy; You'll Like My Mother
Allen, Steve (act, b. 1921): Alice In Wonderland (1985); Amazon Women On The Moon
Allen, Steve (mus, b. 1921): Alice In Wonderland (1985)
Allen, Stewart (act): Richard III (1955)
Allen, Ted (wri): The Great Rupert
Allen, Thomas B. (wri): The Plutonium Incident
Allen, Tim (act, b. 1953): The Santa Clause; Toy Story; Toy Story II
Allen, Todd (act): Night Visitors; Tall, Dark And Deadly; Witchboard
Allen, Tyress (act): Robocop
Allen, Valerie (act): The Devil's Bedroom; I Married A Monster From Outer Space; What Ever Happened To Aunt Alice?
Allen, Woody (act, b. 1935, nee Allen Stewart Konigsberg): Casino Royale; Sleeper
Allen, Woody (dir, mus & wri, b. 1935): Sleeper
Allende, Fernando (act): The Phoenix (1981)
Alleney, Tamba (act): Moby Dick (1956)
Allerson, Alexander (act): Who?
Alley, Kirstie (act, b. 1951): Blind Date; Runaway; Star Trek II: The Wrath Of Khan; Village Of The Damned (1995)
Alleyne, Muriel (wri): The Dead Heart
Allgood, Sara (act, 1883-1950): Between Two Worlds; Blackmail (1929); Dr. Jekyll And Mr. Hyde (1941); Jane Eyre (1944); The Lodger (1944); The Passing Of The Third Floor Back (1935); The Spiral Staircase (1946)
Allin, Jeff (act): Remo Williams: The Adventure Begins
Allingham, Margery (wri): Room To Let
Allinson, Vera (wri): Crime On The Hill
Allison, Bart (act): It Happened Here
Allison, Cynthia (act): Roger Corman's Frankenstein Unbound
Allison, Dwayne (act): Secrets Of The Phantom Caverns
Allison, Eric (act): Blood Mania; The Cremators
Allison, Fred (act): White Of The Eye
Allison, Jean (act): The Devil's Partner; Edge Of Fury; The Strange Possession Of Mrs. Oliver
Allison, John (act, 1939–1985): Sudden Terror
Allison, Keith (act): Phantom Of The Paradise
Allison, Monica (act): Virtuosity
Allison, Patricia (act): The Seventh Sign
Allison, Patti (act): Orpheus Descending
Allister, Bunny (act): The Curious Female
Allister, Claud (act, 1893-1970, nee Claud Palmer): Arrest Bulldog Drummond; Bulldog Drummond (1929); Bulldog Drummond At Bay (1937); Dracula's Daughter; In The Next Room; Murder Will Out (1930); The Private Life Of Don Juan; The Return Of Bulldog Drummond; Such Men Are Dangerous
Allister, David (act): The Face Of Darkness
Allman, Elvia (act): Halloween With The Addams Family; The Nutty Profesor (1963)
Allman, Ross (act): Surf Nazis Must Die
Allman, Sheldon (act): The Man With The Power
Allphin, Pat (act): The Alien's Return
Allport, Christopher (act): Dead And Buried; Invaders From Mars (1986); Man On A Swing
Allred, Byron (mus): Don't Answer The Phone!
Allred, Julie (act): What Ever Happened To Baby Jane? (1962)
Allum, Victoria (act): Schizo (1977)
Allwood, Frederick (wri): No Haunt For A Gentleman
Allworthy, Margaret (act): Hour Of Decision
Allwyn, Astrid (act, 1910-1978): Charlie Chan's Secret; The Lone Wolf Strikes; Miracles For Sale; The Westland Case
Allyn, Alyce (act, d. 1976): The Manchurian Candidate
Allyn, Robin (act): My Science Project
Allyson, June (act, b. 1923, nee Ella Gaisman): Blackout (1978); Curse Of The Black Widow; The Kid With The Broken Halo; The Three Musketeers (1948)

Almanzar, James (act): The Island At The Top Of The World
Almendros, Nestor (cin, 1930–1992): L'enfant Sauvage; Perceval; Still Of The Night
Almereyda, Michael (dir): Nadja
Almodovar, Robert (act): Congo
Almond, Brittany (act): Deadly Game
Almond, Paul (dir & wri): Isabel
Almoney, Keith (act): The Blob (1958)
Almquist, Dean L. (act): Fright (1957)
Alonso, Chelo (act): Atlas In The Land Of Cyclops; Morgan The Pirate; The Pirate And The Slave Girl; Son Of Samson; Il Terror Dei Barberi
Alonso, Johnny (act): Serial Mom
Alonso, Maria Conchita (act, b. 1957): Predator 2; The Running Man; Vampire's Kiss
Alonso, Miguel (act): El Castillo De Las Bofetadas
Alonso, Miguel (mus): Vampire On Bikini Beach
Alonzo, Alicia (act): Mad Doctor Of Blood Island
Alonzo, John (act): Hand Of Death
Alonzo, John A. (cin): Black Sunday (1977); Cool World; Farewell, My Lovely; The Guardian; Look What's Happened To Rosemary's Baby; The Meteor Man; Runaway; Star Trek: Generations; Terror In The Aisles; Vanishing Point; Zorro, The Gay Blade
Alper, Murray (act): After The Thin Man; Another Thin Man; Black Friday; Hold That Hypnotist; Jalopy; The Lone Wolf Strikes; Lost Continent (1951); The Maltese Falcon (1941); The Phantom Thief
Alpert, David (act): Gog
Alpert, Herbert S. (cin): The Mask (1961)
Alpert, Lee (act): Premonition (1972)
Alphen, Corinne (act): Shadow Of Death (1983)
Alquist, James (act): The Fish Men
Alric, Catherine (act): Mas Alla De La Aventura
Alsberg, Arthur (wri): The Munsters' Revenge
Alskog, Kristine (act): Evilspeak
Alston, Andy (act): Dr. Blood's Coffin
Alston, Emmett (dir): Demonwarp; New Year's Evil
Alston, Karen (act): Halloween 4: The Return Of Michael Myers
Alston, Peggy (act): The Exorcist III
Alsup, Andy (act): Slugs
Alt, Greg (wri): Zorro, The Gay Blade
Alt, Sally (act): Flesh Gordon
Altamura, John (act, b. 1966): The Toxic Avenger, Part II; The Toxic Avenger, Part III: The Last Temptation Of Toxie
Altan, Laura (act): Ercole Alla Conquista Della Atlantide
Alta Riba, Beatrice (act): Les Miserables (1957); Les Yeux Sans Visage
Altaskaya, V. (act): Jack Frost
Alten, Frank (act): Dick Tracy vs. Crime, Inc.
Altenbay, Enver (act): The Green Slime
Altenburger, Alida Maria (act): see Valli, Alida
Alter, Robert Edmond (wri): Ravagers
Alterio, Hector (act): Flesh & Blood
Althaus, Urs (act): Warriors Of The Wasteland
Altman, Bruce (act) To Gillian On Her 37th Birthday
Altman, Burt (act): Zombies Lake
Altman, John (act): Memoirs Of A Survivor
Altman, Richard (act): The Hand (1981)
Altman, Robert (dir, b. 1925): Countdown; Images; Quintet
Altman, Robert (wri, b. 1925): Images; Quintet
Altmann, Dora (act): Willy Wonka And The Chocolate Factory
Alton, John (cin, b. 1901): The Black Book; The Lady And The Monster; Mystery Street; Pearl Of The South Pacific; Talk About A Stranger; 12 To The Moon; Witness To Murder
Alton, Kenneth (act): Kronos (1957)
Alton, Walter George (act): The Puma Man
Altz, Barbara (act): The Stepford Children
Alva, Orentha (act): The Toxic Avenger, Part II
Alvarado, Angela (act): Night Visions
Alvarado, Aurora (act): Blood Of Nostradamus; La Maldicion De Nostradamus; Nostradamus Y El Destructor De Monstruos; Nostradamus Y El Genio De La Tinieblas
Alvarado, Don (act): The Bridge Of San Luis Rey (1929); Loves Of Carmen; The Monkey Talks; On Secret Service
Alvarado, Fernando (act): The Falcon In Mexico
Alvarado, Trini (act): The Frighteners
Alvaredo, Crox (act): El Ladron De Cadaveres; La Momia Contra El Robot Humano
Alvarez, Abraham (act): Alien Nation
Alvarez, Alisa (act): Blood Diner

Alvarez, Angel (act): The Cauldron Of Death
Alvarez, Edmundo Rivera (act): Creature From The Haunted Sea; The Possession Of Joel Delaney
Alvarez, Juanita (act): Curse Of The Cat People; The Falcon And The Co-Eds; The Falcon In Mexico
Alvarez, Miguel Angel (act): Pacto Diabolico
Alvarez, Roma (act): Dr. Black Mr. Hyde
Alvarez, Ruth (act): The Falcon And The Co-Eds; The Falcon In Mexico
Alvarez, Santiago (act): Slugs
Alvarez, Tere (act): Caveman (1981)
Alvarez, Tito (act): Anguish
Alvedrez, David (act): Cavegirl (1985)
Alverson, Charles (wri): Jabberwocky
Alverson, Tammy (act): Pandemonium
Alves, Joe (dir): Jaws 3-D
Alvey Jr., Glenn H. (dir & wri): The Door In The Wall
Alvin, Harry (act): Secrets In The Attic
Alvin, John (act): The Beast With Five Fingers; The Couch; Crackle Of Death; The Shanghai Chest; Somewhere In Time; Three Strangers
Alwin, John (wri): The Black Spot
Alwyn, William (mus, b. 1905): The Fallen Idol; I Accuse (1958); In Search Of The Castaways; The Naked Edge; Night Of The Eagle; The October Man; The Rocking Horse Winner; Saturday Island; State Secret; Svengali (1954); Take My Life
Alyn, Glen (act): The Dark Stairway; Law And Disorder; The Perfect Crime
Alyn, Kirk (act): Atom Man vs. Superman; The Trap
Alyse, Esther (act): Hollywood Chainsaw Hookers
Alzado, Lyle (act, 1949–1992): Destroyer
Alzola, Mickey (act): Gargoyles
Amabile, Vincent (act): Lord Of The Flies (1990)
Amachi, Shigeru (act): Onna Kyuketsuki
Amadio, Silvio (dir): The Minotaur
Amadio, Silvio (wri): The Prisoner Of The Iron Mask
Amador, Andrew (act): The First Power
Amadoro, Ugo (cin): Atom Age Vampire
Amagas, Nydia (act): Phantom Of The Paradise
Amagula, Nanjiwarra (act): The Last Wave
Amagula, Walter (act): The Last Wave
Amakye, Willie (act): Congo
Amandes, Tom (act): The Long Kiss Goodnight
Amanitis, Antigone (act): Blind Date
Amann, Betty (act): Nancy Drew, Reporter; Rich And Strange
Amante, James (dir): The Alchemist
Amar, Leonora (act): Captain Scarlett
Amaral, Bob (act): Heart And Souls
Amarilis (act): Generation X
Amarocho, Maria (act): Wheels Of Terror
Amateau, Chloe (act): Miracle Mile
Amateau, Rod (dir, b. 1923): The Garbage Pail Kids; Hitler's Son
Amateau, Rod (wri, b. 1923): The Garbage Pail Kids
Amato, Mary Margaret (act): Phantom Of The Paradise
Amatrudo, Ed (act): Popcorn
Amazan Jr., Eriberto (act): The Blood Drinkers
Amber, Eve (act): The Woman In Green
Ambesi, Adriana (act): The Bible; Fangs Of The Living Dead; La Maldicion De Los Karnsteins
Ambler, Eric (wri, b. 1909): Background To Danger; Highly Dangerous; Journey Into Fear (1942 & 1975); The Mask Of Dimitrios; The October Man; Topkapi
Ambler, Joss (act): Candles At Nine; The Claydon Treasure Mystery; Ghost Ship (1952); Halfway House; Soho Incident
Ambor, Joe (wri): The Strange World Of Planet X
Ambrose, David (wri): D.A.R.Y.L.; The Fifth Musketeer; The Final Countdown
Ambrosio, Fred (act): Making Contact
Ambroso, Roberto (wri): Secret Agent Superdragon
Ambuehl, Cindy (act): Phantasm III: Lord Of The Dead
Ameche, Don (act, 1908-1993, nee Dominic Amichi): Cocoon; Cocoon: The Return; The Happy Land; Harry And The Hendersons; Heaven Can Wait (1942); Picture Mommy Dead; Sleep, My Love; The Three Musketeers (1939)
Ameche, Jim (act, d. 1983): The Story Of Mankind
Amedee (act): Un Amour De Poche; Jeux Interdits
Ameen, Michael (act): Silent Night, Deadly Night III

Amendola, Ferruccio (act): Terror Of Rome Against The Son Of Hercules
Amendola, Mario (wri): Battle Of The Amazons; Behind The Mask Of Zorro; Terror Of Rome Against The Son Of Hercules
Amendolia, Don (act): Ed Wood
Amer, Nicholas/Nick (act): Disciple Of Death; Treasure Island (1990)
American Musical Band, The (mus): The Trip
Ameripoor, Eskandar (cin): The Gore-Gore Girls; The Wizard Of Gore
Ames, Adrienne (act): The Death Kiss
Ames, Allyson (act): Simon, King Of The Witches
Ames, Brian (act): Roger Corman's Frankenstein Unbound
Ames, Delano (wri): She Shall Have Murder
Ames, Elsie (act): Houdini
Ames, Florenz (act): The Deadly Mantis
Ames, Gerald (act): Alf's Button (1920); Arsene Lupin; The Black Spot; Boundary House; The Cage; The Game Of Liberty; The King's Daughter; The King's Minister; Paste; The Princess Of Happy Chance; The Prisoner Of Zenda (1915); Robin Hood's Men; Rupert Of Hentzau (1915); The Sons Of Satan; When Knights Were Bold (1916); Whoso Diggeth A Pit
Ames, Granville (act): Star Trek: Generations
Ames, Heather (act): Blood Of Dracula; How To Make A Monster
Ames, Judith (act): When Worlds Collide
Ames, Kelly (act): Bates Motel
Ames, Leon (act, b. 1903, nee Leon Wycoff): The Absent-Minded Professor (1961); Charlie Chan On Broadway; The Cockeyed Miracle; Crime Doctor; Ellery Queen And The Murder Ring; Hammersmith Is Out; Lady In The Lake; The Misadventures Of Merlin Jones; Mr. Moto In Danger Island; The Monkey's Uncle; The Murders In The Rue Morgue (1932); The Mysterious Mr. Moto; On A Clear Day You Can See Forever; Sherlock Holmes In New York; Song Of The Thin Man; Son Of Flubber; The Velvet Touch
Ames, Michael (act): Heaven Can Wait (1942); Return Of The Ape Man; Voodoo Man
Ames, Rachel (act): Daddy's Gone A-Hunting
Ames, Ramsay (act, b. 1924): Ali Baba And The Forty Thieves (1943); Below The Deadline; Calling Dr. Death; The Mummy's Ghost; Philo Vance Returns
Ames, Robert (act): Black Waters
Ames, Totty (act): Skullduggery
Amey, Marlena (act): Midnight Lace (1981)
Amfitheatrof, (Daniele) (mus, 1901-1983): An Act Of Murder (1948); Angels In The Outfield (1951); The Beginning Or The End?; The Last Hunt; The Lost Moment; The Naked Jungle; Salome (1953); Temptation (1946)
Amichi, Dominic (act): see Ameche, Don
Amick, Madchen (act): The Courtyard; I'm Dangerous Tonight; Sleepwalkers
Amick, Ryan Paul (act): The Exorcist III
Amidor, Erick (act): Blood Diner
Amiel, Jon (dir): Copycat
Amigo, Cesar (wri): The Blood Drinkers
Amigo, Hank (act): The Outing
Amis, Kingsley (wri, 1922–1995): The Trygon Factor
Amis, Martin (act): A High Wind In Jamaica
Amis, Martin (wri): Saturn 3
Amis, Suzy (act): The Ex
Amman, Alicia (act): Journey Into Fear (1975)
Amman, Sara (act): Rocket Attack U.S.A.
Ammerman, Dan (act): Red Alert
Ammons, Mike (act): Ghostriders
Amodio, Amedeo (act): The Night Porter
Amor, Christine (act): The Day After Halloween
Amori, Count (wri): see Rapgof, I.
Amoroso, Nick (act): Empire Of Ash III
Amoruzo, Alice (act): Blind Date
Amos, Beth (act): Prom Night
Amos, Diane (act): Copycat
Amos, Emma (act): A Ghost In Monte Carlo
Amos, John (act, b. 1939): The Beastmaster; Dance Of The Dwarfs; Future Cop; Two Evil Eyes
Amouroux, Clementine (act): Perceval
Amplas, John (act): Bloodeaters; Martin; Midnight (1980)
Amram, David (mus): The Manchurian Candidate
Amyl, Max (act): Fantastic Planet
An, Feng Ko (act): Legend Of The Seven Golden Vampires
Anamoto, Eisei (act): King Kong Escapes
Anaya, Reynaldo (act): Blood Diner

Anchia, Juan Ruiz (cin): The Seventh Sign
Anchoriz, Leo (act): Horror; Perseus The Invincible
Ancira, Carlos (act): El Ataud Del Vampiro
Andar, David (act): House Of Usher
Andelman, Juli (act): Silent Scream (1979)
Anderberg, Bertil (act): Det Sjunde Inseglet
Anders, Avalon (act): Wish Me Luck
Anders, Donna (act): Count Yorga, Vampire
Anders, Ed (act): Pumpkinhead II: Blood Wings
Anders, Glenn (act, b. 1889): The Lady From Shanghai; M (1950); Tarzan's Peril
Anders, Gunther (cin): The Last Ten Days Of Adolf Hitler
Anders, Ina (act): 48 Hours To Live
Anders, Karen (act): Fright Night II
Anders, Luana (act, b. 1940): B.J. Lang Presents; Dementia 13; Heart And Souls; The Killing Kind; Night Tide; The Pit And The Pendulum (1961)
Anders, Merry (act, b. 1932): Beauty And The Beast (1962); Desk Set; House Of The Damned (1962); The Hypnotic Eye; Legacy Of Blood; Les Miserables (1952); Raiders From Beneath The Sea; The Time Travelers (1964); Women Of The Prehistoric Planet
Anders, Ralph (wri): The Big Game
Anders, Rudolph (act): Frankenstein (1970); Jungle Gents; Phantom From Space; She Demons; Sherlock Holmes And The Voice Of Terror; The Snow Creature; The Strange Death Of Adolf Hitler
Andersen, Bridgette (act): Nightmares (1983)
Andersen, Dana (act): Outbreak
Andersen, Elga (act): A Toi De Faire, Migonne; Frantic; Run, Psycho, Run
Andersen, Gerald (act): Horrors Of The Black Museum; The Sinister Man
Andersen, Hans Christian (wri, 1805-1875): Cisaruv Slavik; The Little Match Girl (1914); The Little Match Seller; Mr. H.C. Andersen; Stories From A Flying Trunk; Thumbelina (1955 & 1994)
Andersen, John (act): Haxan
Andersen, Michael (mus): Tower Of London (1962); Terrified; 12 To The Moon
Andersen, Scott (act): Empire Of Ash III
Andersen, Suzy/Susi (act): Roma Contra Roma; Thor And The Amazons; I Tre Volti Della Paura
Anderson, Agnes (act): The Plot Thickens
Anderson, Andy (cin): The Man From Planet X
Anderson, Angry (act): Mad Max Beyond Thunderdome
Anderson, Annette (act): Flesh Gordon
Anderson, Arline (act): The Hound Of The Baskervilles (1972); The Magician (1973)
Anderson, Asbjorn (act): Reptilicus
Anderson, Barbara (act): Don't Be Afraid Of The Dark; The Six Million Dollar Man
Anderson, Blair (act): Iceman
Anderson, Brent (act): D.O.A. (1988)
Anderson, Brooke (act): The Punisher
Anderson, Bryan (act): Quarantine
Anderson, Carl (act): Mind Over Murder
Anderson, Chantel (act): Phoenix The Warrior
Anderson, Cheryl (act): Writer's Block
Anderson, Choanne (act): Making Contact
Anderson, Christina (act): Charley And The Angel; The Shaggy D.A.
Anderson, Dana (act): Alien Nation: The Enemy Within
Anderson, Daniel (act): Virtuosity
Anderson, Daphne (act, b. 1922, nee Daphne Scrutton): Captain Clegg; Cloudburst; A Kid For Two Farthings
Anderson, Darlene (act): Vice Versa (1988)
Anderson, Daryl (act): The Monster Squad; The Phoenix (1981)
Anderson, Dawn (act): Teenagers From Outer Space
Anderson, Deke (act): Curse II: The Bite; The Hidden; School Spirit
Anderson, Donna (act): On The Beach
Anderson, Dusty (act): Crime Doctor's Warning; The Phantom Thief
Anderson, E. Erich (act): Friday The 13th-The Final Chapter
Anderson, Eddie "Rochester" (act, 1905-1977): Cabin In The Sky; Green Pastures; Topper Returns
Anderson, Elizabeth (wri): Three Wishes (1995)
Anderson, Erika (act): A Nightmare On Elm Street 5: The Dream Child
Anderson, Ernest (act): The Alien's Return; Coma; What Ever Happened To Baby Jane? (1962)
Anderson, Gene (act): The Day The Earth Caught Fire; The Shakedown
Anderson, George (act): A Night Of Mystery (1937); Song Of The Thin Man
Anderson, Georgine (act): A Place To Die
Anderson, Gerry (wri): Doppelganger; Thunderbirds Are Go; Thunderbird 6
Anderson, Gordon (act): A Reflection Of Fear
Anderson, Harry (1940s act): Meet Boston Blackie
Anderson, Harry (act, b. 1952): It (1990)
Anderson, Hedli (act): Colonel Bogey
Anderson, Helen (act): The Annihilator
Anderson, Herb (act): I Bury The Living
Anderson, Hillyard (act): The Computer Wore Tennis Shoes
Anderson (Co.), Howard (A.) (cin): Escape From The Planet Of The Apes; Invasion Of The Saucer Men; Jack The Giant Killer; King Dinosaur; The Son Of Monte Cristo; Tarzan And The Green Goddess; 12 To The Moon; Unknown Island; Varan The Unbelievable; Women Of The Prehistoric Planet
Anderson, Hyde (act): Zapped!
Anderson, Ingrid (act): Hercules (1983)
Anderson (Sr.), Ira (cin): Curse Of The Faceless Man; Frankenstein's Daughter (1958); Missile To The Moon; The Night Strangler; Tarzan And The Great River; Tarzan And The Valley Of Gold
Anderson Jr., Ira (cin): Tarzan And The Valley Of Gold
Anderson, Isa (act): Night Angel
Anderson, James (act): Five; I Married A Monster From Outer Space; The Thing That Couldn't Die
Anderson, Jamie (cin): Piranha (1978)
Anderson, Jan (act): The Pink Chiquitas
Anderson, Jean (act, b. 1908): The Lady Vanishes (1979); The Night Digger; Screamtime; The Three Lives Of Thomasina
Anderson, Jerry (act): Attack Of The Killer Tomatoes
Anderson, Jo (act): Daylight; Dead Again; I Saw What You Did (1988); Jamaica Inn (1985)
Anderson, John (act, 1923–1992): Brock's Last Case; Psycho; The Satan Bug; Smile, Jenny, You're Dead
Anderson, John L. (act): Wuthering Heights (1920)
Anderson, (Dame) Judith (act, 1898–1992): And Then There Were None; The Borrowers; Cinderfella; Inn Of The Damned; Laura; Rebecca; The Red House; Salome (1953); Star Trek III: The Search For Spock
Anderson, Jurgen (act): The Boys From Brazil
Anderson, Keith (act): Murder Motel
Anderson, Ken (act): Phobia
Anderson, Kevin (act): Orpheus Descending
Anderson, Larry (act): Dr. Strange; Eve Of Destruction
Anderson, Larz (cin): Gremlins 2: The New Batch
Anderson, Lawrence (act): Bluff; The Stickpin
Anderson, Leif (act): Of Unknown Origin
Anderson, Leona (act): House On Haunted Hill
Anderson, Loni (act, b. 1944): Sorry, Wrong Number (1989); Too Good To Be True; Whisper Kill
Anderson, Louie (act): Ratboy
Anderson, M.A. (cin): Condemned To Live
Anderson, Mary (act): The False Faces; Lifeboat
Anderson, Matthew (act): Leprechaun 2
Anderson, Max (act): In The Year 2889
Anderson, Max (dir): Treasure At The Mill
Anderson, Max W. (cin): Children Of The Corn; The Ice Pirates; The Philadelphia Experiment
Anderson, Maxwell (mus): Midnight Lace (1960)
Anderson, Maxwell (wri, 1888–1959): The Bad Seed (1956 & 1985); Death Takes A Holiday (1934); The Wrong Man
Anderson, Mckee (act): Night Of The Living Dead (1990)
Anderson, Mel (act): The Dark (1979)
Anderson, Melissa Sue (act, b. 1962): Dark Mansions; Happy Birthday To Me; Midnight Offerings
Anderson, Melody (act): Dead And Buried; Firewalker; Flash Gordon; Hitler's Daughter
Anderson, Michael (dir, b. 1920): Around The World In 80 Days; Chase A Crooked Shadow; Doc Savage, The Man Of Bronze; Dominique; The House Of The Arrow (1953); Logan's Run; Millennium; The Naked Edge; 1984 (1955); Operation Crossbow; Orca; The Quiller Memorandum; 20,000 Leagues Under The Sea (1997, CBS-TV)
Anderson Jr., Michael (act, b. 1943): The House That Wouldn't Die; In Search Of The Castaways; Logan's Run
Anderson, Miles (act): The 39 Steps (1978)
Anderson, Mitchell (act): Jaws: The Revenge; Spacecamp
Anderson, Nancy (act): The Ghost Of Dragstrip Hollow
Anderson, Natalie (act): Silent Night, Deadly Night III
Anderson, Nelson D. (act): Alien Warrior
Anderson, Nicole (act): Strange Behavior
Anderson, Nina (act): Sampa
Anderson, Nynno (act): Strange Days
Anderson, Paul (dir): Mortal Kombat
Anderson, Pia (act): Whirlpool
Anderson, Raymond L. (act): Mr. Destiny
Anderson, Reginald Price (act): Lo Spettro
Anderson, Reid (act): Secrets Of Sex
Anderson, Richard (act, b. 1926): The Astronaut; Bionic Showdown: The Six Million Dollar Man And The Bionic Woman; A Cry In The Night (1956); Curse Of The Faceless Man; Dead Men Tell No Tales; Forbidden Planet; It's A Dog's Life; Johnny Cool; The Night Strangler; The Return Of The Six Million Dollar Man And The Bionic Woman; The Search For Bridey Murphy; Seconds; Seven Days In May; The Stepford Children
Anderson, Richard Dean (act): Pandora's Clock
Anderson, Robert (act): The Falcon Out West
Anderson, Rona (act, b. 1926): The Black Rider; Black 13; Devils Of Darkness; Little Red Monkey; Noose For A Lady; Scrooge (1951); Shadow Of A Man; Sleeping Car To Trieste; Soho Incident; The Solitary Child; Torment (1949); The Twenty Questions Murder; Whispering Smith Hits London
Anderson, Sam (act): Critters 2: The Main Course; I Come In Peace
Anderson, Sharon (act): Fargo
Anderson, Stanley (act): Primal Fear
Anderson, Steve (act): When A Stranger Calls
Anderson, Sylvia (act): Thunderbirds Are Go; Thunderbird 6
Anderson, Sylvia (wri): Doppelganger; Thunderbirds Are Go; Thunderbird 6
Anderson, Vass (act): Superman (1978)
Anderson, Vince (act): Street Trash
Anderson, Warner (act, 1911–1976): The Beginning Or The End?; Destination Moon; Song Of The Thin Man
Anderson, Wesley (cin): The Beast With Five Fingers
Anderson, William Wycliff (act): see Erickson, Leif
Andersson, Bibi (act, b. 1935): Ansiktet; The Devil's Eye; Herr Arnes Pengar (1954); The Kremlin Letter; Persona; Quintet; Det Sjunde Inseglet; Smultronstallet
Andersson, Carl (cin & mus): Vredens Dag
Andersson, Harriet (act, b. 1932): The Deadly Affair; Through A Glass Darkly
Andes, Keith (act, b. 1920): Blackbeard The Pirate; Hell's Bloody Devils; A Life At Stake; Model For Murder; Project X (1949); Split Second (1953); The Ultimate Impostor
Andonopolous, Vicki (act): Thirst
Andor-Palfi, Lotta (act): Marathon Man
Andra, Fern (act, 1893–1974): Genuine
Andre The Giant (act, 1946–1993): The Princess Bride
Andre, Carole (act): Yor, The Hunter From The Future
Andre, Charles (act): I Confess; The Little Match Girl (1987); Timecop
Andre, E.J. (act, 1908-1984): Dead Of Night (1977); Haunts; Magic; The Mysterious Two
Andre, Gaby (act): Duel At The Rio Grande; The Green Glove; The Strange World Of Planet X; La Vendetta Di Ercole
Andre, Gwili (act): The Falcon's Brother
Andre, Lona (act): International House
Andre, Marcel (act): La Belle Et La Bete; Les Parents Terribles
Andre, Nicki (act): Phantom Of The Opera (1943)
Andre, Victor (act): Le Voyage Dans La Lune
Andre, Yvonne (act): Return From The Ashes
Andreas, Dimitri (act): Evil Under The Sun; Top Secret! (1984)
Andreas, Luke (act): Modern Problems
Andreas, Michael (act): Day Of The Animals
Andree, Victor (act): Caltiki, Il Mostro Immortale
Andreeff, Starr (act): Dance Of The Damned; Ghoulies II; Nightfall (1988); Syngenor; The Terror Within
Andrei, Damir (act): Happy Birthday To Me
Andrei, Franco (act): Doctor Jekyll (1964); Terrore Nello Spazio
Andrei, Marcello (dir & wri): Deborah
Andreiev, Glenn (act): Street Trash
Andreiev, Leonid (wri): He Who Gets Slapped
Andren, Jean (act): Invasion Of The Body Snatchers (1956)
Andreozzi, Jack (act): Deep Red (1994); Lady In White
Andreschlin, Hans (cin): Orlacs Haende
Andress, Herb (act): Enemy Mine
Andress, Ursula (act, b. 1936): Casino Royale; Clash Of The Titans; La Decima Vittima; Dr. No; The Fifth Musketeer; Il Montagna Di Dio Cannibale; Nightmare In The Sun; She (1965); The Southern Star
Andreu, Simon (act): The Blood Spattered Bride; Flesh & Blood; Night Of The Sorcerers
Andrew, Sylvia (act): The Snake Pit (1948)
Andrews Sisters, The (act): Hold That Ghost
Andrews, Andy (act): The Crawling Hand; Gog
Andrews, Anthony (act, b. 1948): Hands Of A Murderer; Mistress Of Paradise; The Scarlet Pimpernel (1982); Sparkling Cyanide
Andrews, Augustus George (act): see Arliss, George
Andrews, Barry (act): The Blood On Satan's Claw; Dracula Has Risen From The Grave; Revenge (1971, GB)
Andrews, Bobbie (act): The Sword Of Damocles
Andrews, Brian (act): Halloween
Andrews, Brian J. (act): Cocoon: The Return
Andrews, Carol (act): Murder Is My Business
Andrews, Christian (act): Radioactive Dreams
Andrews, Dana (act, 1909–1992): Assignment-Paris; Berlino Appuntamento Per Le Spie; Beyond A Reasonable Doubt; Brain Storm (1965); The Cobra; Crack In The World; Duel In The Jungle; Enchanted Island; The Fearmakers; The Forbidden Street; The Frozen Dead; Laura; The Loved One; Night Of The Demon (1957); The Satan Bug; Three Hours To Kill; While The City Sleeps
Andrews, David (GB act): Dracula A.D. 1972
Andrews, David (USA act): Cherry 2000; Graveyard Shift (1990)
Andrews, Deirdre (act): Return Of The Killer Tomatoes
Andrews, Eammon (act): Three Cases Of Murder
Andrews, Edward (act, 1914–1985): The Absent-Minded Professor (1961); Birds Do It; The Brass Bottle (1964); Charley And The Angel; Gremlins; Kisses For My President; Now You See Him, Now You Don't; The Return (1973, Can); Son Of Flubber; The Unguarded Moment
Andrews, Geno (act): Hard Rock Zombies
Andrews, Harry (act, b. 1911): The Big Sleep (1978); The Blue Bird (1976); Burke And Hare; The Curse Of King Tut's Tomb; A Dandy In Aspic; The Deadly Affair; Death On The Nile; Hawk The Slayer; I Accuse (1958); The Last Days Of Man On Earth; The Medusa Touch; Moby Dick (1956); Modesty Blaise; The Nightcomers; Night Hair Child; The Night Of The Generals; The Ruling Class; The Southern Star; Superman (1978); Theater Of Blood; Watership Down; Wuthering Heights (1970)
Andrews, Janine (act): Octopussy
Andrews, Jean (act): Too Many Winners
Andrews, Joey (act): Sleepstalker; White Dwarf
Andrews, John (act): Orgy Of The Dead (1965)
Andrews, Julie (act, b. 1935, nee Julia Elizabeth Wells): Mary Poppins; The Singing Princess; Torn Curtain
Andrews, Kenny (act): The Mcguffin
Andrews, Mark (act): The Attic
Andrews, Marnie (act): Writer's Block
Andrews, Matthew (wri): The Fat Spy
Andrews, Nancy (Lee) (act): Saturday The 14th; Werewolf Of Washington
Andrews, Real (act): Wild Thing
Andrews, Robert D. (wri): Before I Hang; The Devil Commands
Andrews, Robert Hardy (wri): Bagdad; Tarzan Goes To India
Andrews, Stanley (act, 1892–1969): Dead Men Tell; The Docks Of New Orleans; The Son Of Monte Cristo; Superman And The Mole Men; Talk About A Stranger
Andrews, Tod (act): The Baby; Beneath The Planet Of The Apes; From Hell It Came
Andrews, Todd Eric (act): Zapped Again
Andrews, V.C. (wri, D. 1986): Flowers In The Attic
Andrews, William Forrest (act): see Forrest, Steve
Andreyev, Boris (act): Ilya Mourometz
Andriani, Oscar (act): Teodora, Imperatrice Di Bisanzio; Ulysses
Andrieux, Nicole (act): see Courcel, Nicole
Andriot, Lucien (cin, b. 1897): And Then There Were None; Balaoo; Charlie Chan At The Opera; The Hairy Ape; In The Palace Of The King; Just Off Broadway; Loves Of

Carmen; Mr. Moto In Danger Island; Mr. Moto's Gamble; Monte Cristo; The Return Of Peter Grimm (1934); Secret Agent Of Japan; Women Of All Nations

Androsky, Carol (act): Saturday The 14th
Andrus, Mark (wri): Late For Dinner
Andrus, Niles (act): Terror Of The Bloodhunters
Andruschak, Kevin (act): Quarantine
Andrusco, Gene (act): The Screaming Woman
Anemone (act): El Mono Loco
Anfinsen, Tom (act): The Barefoot Executive
Angarola, Richard (act): The Amazing Captain Nemo
Angel (act): The Attic
Angel, Heather (act, 1909–1986): Arrest Bulldog Drummond; Berkeley Square; The Bold Caballero; Bulldog Drummond Escapes; Bulldog Drummond In Africa; Bulldog Drummond's Bride; Bulldog Drummond's Secret Police; Charlie Chan's Greatest Case; The Hound Of The Baskervilles (1931); Lifeboat; The Mystery Of Edwin Drood (1935); The Premature Burial; Suspicion; Time To Kill (1942); The Undying Monster
Angel, Lira (act): Tales From The Hood
Angel, Mike (wri): Grotesque; Psychic Killer
Angel, Mikel (dir): Love Butcher
Angelelli, Guillermo (act): Moebius
Angeles, Jack (act): Death Dreams
Angeles, Luz (act): Curse Of The Vampires
Angeletti, Pio (dir): Tempi Duri Per I Vampiri
Angeli, Fabrizio (act): Spirits Of The Dead
Angeli, Pier (act, 1932–1971): Berlino Appuntamento Per Le Spie; M.M.M. 83; Octaman; Shadow Of Evil (1964); Sodom And Gomorrah
Angeline, Judith (act): Dr. Black Mr. Hyde
Angelini, Nando (act): Operation Kid Brother
Angelis, Paul (act): For Your Eyes Only; If It's A Man, Hang Up; Otley
Angelle, Bobby (act): Dr. Black Mr. Hyde
Angelo, Jean (act): L'atlantide (1920)
Angelo, Olga (act): Roger Corman's 'Frankenstein Unbound'
Angelo, Tony (act): Oh Heavenly Dog; Rabid
Angelucci, Mario (act): The Mcguffin
Angelus, Muriel (act): Red Aces; The Ringer (1928)
Angelyne (act): Earth Girls Are Easy
Anger, Kenneth (act, cin, edit, & wri, b. 1932): Prisoner Of Mars
Angers, Avril (act, b. 1922): Devils Of Darkness; The Green Man
Angiolillo, Luciana (act): The Trojan Horse
Anglade, France (act): 24 Hours To Kill
Anglim, Philip (act, b. 1954): Haunted Summer
Anglin, Anne (act): Scanners
Angold, Edit (act): Above Suspicion; The Ambushers
Angotti, Nick (act): Assassin (1986)
Angst, Richard (cin): Storm Over Tibet
Angwin, Neil (cin): The Last Wave
Anhalt, Edna (wri): Bulldog Drummond Strikes Back (1947); The Sniper
Anhalt, Edward (wri, b. 1914): The Boston Strangler; Bulldog Drummond Strikes Back (1947); Crime Doctor's Diary; The Satan Bug; The Sniper
Anholt, Christien (act): Hamlet (1990)
Anholt, Tony (act): Appointment With A Killer; Fear Is The Key
Aniston, Jennifer (act, b. 1969): Leprechaun
Anka, Paul (act, b. 1941): The Private Lives Of Adam And Eve
Anker, Jack (act): When The Bough Breaks
Ankers, Evelyn (act, 1918–1985): Captive Wild Woman; The Claydon Treasure Mystery; The Fatal Witness; Flight To Nowhere; The French Key; The Frozen Ghost; The Ghost Of Frankenstein; The Great Impersonation (1942); Hold That Ghost; The Invisible Man's Revenge; The Jungle Woman; The Lone Wolf In London; The Mad Ghoul; The Pearl Of Death; Sherlock Holmes And The Voice Of Terror; Son Of Dracula (1943); Tarzan's Magic Fountain; Weird Woman; The Wolf Man (1941)
Ankers, Robert (act): Vampire On Bikini Beach
Ankerstjerne, Johan (cin): Haxan
Ankrum, Morris (act, 1896–1964): The Beginning Of The End; The Cockeyed Miracle; Earth Vs. The Flying Saucers; Flight To Mars; From The Earth To The Moon; The Giant Claw; Giant From The Unknown; The Hidden Eye; How To Make A Monster; Invaders From Mars (1953); I Wake Up Screaming; Kronos (1957); Lady In The Lake; The Lion Hunters; Most Dangerous Man Alive; The Naked Gun; Omar Khayyam; Red Blood...

Thin Man; Son Of Ali Baba; The Thin Man Goes Home; Time To Kill (1942); X-The Man With The X-Ray Eyes; Zombies Of Mora Tau
Anna, Julie (act): Rabid
Annabel (act): Mr. Arkadin
Annaconda (act): Street Of Shadows
Annakin, Ken (dir, b. 1914): Double Confession; The Fifth Musketeer; Miranda; The Story Of Robin Hood
Anna–Lisa (act): Have Rocket, Will Travel; 12 To The Moon
Annamaria, Tornello (act): El Castello Dell'orrore
Annand, James (act): The Bargain; The Mystery Of Edwin Drood (1909)
Annarino, Karen (act): Virtuosity
Annaud, Jean–Jacques (dir, b. 1943): The Name Of The Rose; Quest For Fire
Anne, Cheryl (act): Octopussy
Anne, Tiffani (act): Demon Knight
Anneman, Bill (cin): The Corpse Grinders
Annen, Glory (act): Outer Touch; Prey (1978)
Anesley, Imogen (act): Howling III
Annett, Paul (dir): The Beast Must Die; Never-Never Land
Annette (act): See Funicello, Annette
Annin, Joanna (act): No Blade Of Grass
Annis, Francesca (act, b. 1944): Dune; The Eyes Of Annie Jones; Krull; Macbeth (1971); Murder Most Foul; Sign It Death
Ann–Margret (act, b. 1941): Magic; Murderers' Row; Tommy
Anon, Marisol (act): House Of 1,000 Dolls
Anouchka (act): Zombies Lake
Ansah, Tommy (act): 10 Rillington Place
Ansara, Edward (act): Beyond Evil
Ansara, Michael (act, b. 1922): Abbott And Costello Meet The Mummy; The Bandits Of Corsica; Day Of The Animals; Dear, Dead Delilah; The Destructors; The Diamond Queen; The Doll Squad; It's Alive (1974); The Lone Ranger; The Manitou; The Saracen Blade; Slaves Of Babylon; Target: Harry; Voyage To The Bottom Of The Sea
Anscombe, Ronald (cin): Tower Of Terror
Ansell, Eric (mus): I Met A Murderer
Anselmo, Ginger (act): Flesh-Eating Mothers
Anselmo, Paul (act): Nomads
Anson, G.W. (act): Desire
Anson, Jay (wri, 1921–1980): The Amityville Horror
Anson, Joe (wri): Babes In Bagdad
Anspach, Susan (act, b. 1944): Blue Monkey; The Devil And Max Devlin
Anstey, F. (wri): The Brass Bottle (1914, 1923, & 1964); One Touch Of Venus; The Tinted Venus; Vice Versa (1916 & 1947)
Anstey, Jill (act): Murder At The Windmill
Anstey, Norman (act): Howling IV
Anstruther, Gerald (wri): Master Spy
Ant, Adam (act): Nomads; Spellcaster; World Gone Wild
Antekleier, Kristopher (act): Trancers II: The Return Of Jack Deth
Antheil, George (mus, 1900–1959): Repeat Performance; The Sniper
Anthelme, Paul (wri): I Confess
Anthes, Eva (act): Fellowship Of The Frog
Anthony, Brian (act): Doomwatch
Anthony, Carl (act): Plan 9 From Outer Space; The Sinister Urge
Anthony, Dean (act): To Die For
Anthony, Ellen (act): The Day After
Anthony, Jack (act): Starship Invasions
Anthony, Joseph (act, b. 1912): Shadow Of The Thin Man
Anthony, Joseph (wri): Crime And Punishment (1935); Meet Nero Wolfe
Anthony, Lee (act): Howard The Duck
Anthony, Lysette (act, b. 1962): Dr. Jekyll And Ms. Hyde; Dracula: Dead And Loving It; A Ghost In Monte Carlo; Krull; Switch; Trilogy Of Terror II; Without A Clue
Anthony, Mark (act): The Alien Within
Anthony, Michael (act): I Accuse (1958); Mata Hari (1985); Women And Bloody Terror
Anthony, Olga (act): Captain Kronos: Vampire Hunter; The Mutations; Macbeth (1971)
Anthony, Philip (act): Melody Of Death; The Private Life Of Sherlock Holmes; Spell Of Evil
Anthony, Richard J. (wri): Echoes
Anthony, Stuart (wri): Charlie Chan In Paris; The Monster And The Girl
Antille, Lisa (act): Beyond Evil
Antin, Steve (act): The Goonies; Sweet Sixteen
Antivo, Philip (act): The Blood Drinkers
Antoine, Andre–Paul (wri): Le Golem (1936)
Anton, Amerigo (dir): Maciste Alla Corte Della Zar
Anton, Eduardo (wri): Robin Hood And The Pirates; Tempi Duri Per I Vampiri
Anton, Guillermo (act): ...

Anton, Karl (dir): Der Raecher
Antonelli, Ennio (act): Warriors Of The Wasteland
Antonelli, Laura (act): Dr. Goldfoot And The Girl Bombs
Antonini, Gabriele (act): Ercole E La Regina Di Lidia
Antonio, Fernando (act): The Toxic Avenger, Part II
Antonio, Jim/James D. (act): Blood Pen; Eve Of Destruction; Futureworld; Outbreak; Planet Earth; The Terminal Man
Antonioni, Michelangelo dir, b. 1912): Red Desert; La Villa Dei Mostri
Antonioni, Michelangelo (wri, b. 1912): Lo Sceicco Bianco; La Villa Dei Mostri
Antoniou, Michael (act): Moon 44
Antony, Scott (act): The Mutations
Antrim, Paul (act): Evil Under The Sun; The Man Who Would Be King
Antrobus, John (wri, b. 1933): The Bed-Sitting Room
Antrobus, Yvonne (act): Dr. Who And The Daleks
Anty, Nadia (act): Sei Donne Per L'assassino
Antzes, Louis (cin): Silent Night, Bloody Night
Anwar, Gabrielle (act, b. 1970): The Body Snatchers; The Grave; The Three Musketeers (1993)
Anys, Georgette (act): To Catch A Thief
Anzai, Kyoko (act): Battle In Outer Space
Aoyama, Kazuya (act): Godzilla vs. The Bionic Monster
Aoyama, Yoshihiko (act): Majin, Monster Of Terror
Apelt, Inge (act): Transylvania 6-5000
Aperlo, Allan (act): Neon Maniacs
Apfel, Oscar (act): The Maltese Falcon (1931); The Plot Thickens
Apfel, Oscar (act): Bulldog Drummond (1923)
Apicella, John (act): Full Eclipse
Apostoloff, Stephen C. (dir): Orgy Of The Dead (1965)
Apostolou, Scott (act, dir & wri): Mutants In Paradise
Apothaker, Helena (act): Switch
Appice, Carmine (act): Black Roses
Apple, Chris (mus): The Fearmakers
Applebaum, Louis (mus): The Mask (1961)
Appleby, Basil (act): The Black Knight; 49th Parallel; Pimpernel Smith
Appleby, Dorothy (act): Charlie Chan In Paris
Appleby, Noel (act): The Navigator: An Odyssey Across Time
Appleby, Shiri (act): Curse II: The Bite
Appleby, Suki (act): Bunny Lake Is Missing; Eye Of The Devil
Applegate, Christina (act, b. 1971): Jaws Of Satan; Mars Attacks!
Applegate, Phyllis (act): The Arrival
Appleseth, Mary (act): Planet Of Dinosaurs
Appleton, Dudi (act): Mary Shelley's Frankenstein
Aprelat, Werner (act): The Castle Of Fu Manchu
Apstein, Norman (dir): Ice Cream Man
Apstein, Theodore (wri): Baffled!; What Ever Happened To Aunt Alice?
Apted, Michael (dir, b. 1941): Agatha; Blink; Extreme Measures
Aquino, John (act): Blow Out
Arafuka, Takayuki (act): The Toxic Avenger, Part II
Arago, Chico (act): Killer Fish
Aragon, Louis (act): El Baron Del Terror
Arajol, Juan (wri):El Castillo De Las Bofetadas
Arakawa, Jane (act): Street Trash
Arancio, Gilda (act): Zombies Lake
Aranda, Angel (act): The Colossus Of Rhodes; The Last Days Of Pompeii (1959); Terrore Nello Spazio
Aranda, Michael (act): Creepozoids
Aranda, Ricardo Lopez (wri): Marta
Aranda, Vicente (dir & wri): The Blood Spattered Bride
Aranoff, Maria (act): Flesh Gordon
Aranson, Jack (act): Murder In Eden
Araojo, Johnny (cin): Equalizer 2000
Araskog, Julie (act): Freeway; Outbreak; Seven
Arata, Ubaldo (cin): Black Magic (1949)
Aratama, Michiyo (act): Kwaidan
Ararow, Paul (dir): Dr. Dracula
Arau, Alfonso (act): Romancing The Stone
Araujo Jr., Ismael (act): Earth Girls Are Easy
Aravindan, G. (dir): The Bogey Man
Araya, Hochui (act): Onibaba
Arbaugh, Jeffrey (act): Watchers II
Arbenina, Stella (act): The Secret Kingdom
Arbez, Nicholas (act): Moonraker
Arbiter, Petronius (wri): Satyricon
Arbo, Manuel (act): Goliath Against The Giants...

Arbogast, Bob (act): The Adventures Of The American Rabbit
Arbogast, Michael (cin): Edward Scissorhands
Arbogast, Roy (cin): Christine; Return Of The Jedi
Arbogast, Thierry (cin): The Fifth Element
Arbuckle, Linda (act): The Pink Chiquitas
Arbuckle, Maclyn (act): Young Diana
Arbuckle, Minta Durfee (act): What's The Matter With Helen?; Willard
Arbus, Allan (act): Damien-Omen II; Scream, Pretty Peggy
Arce, Eddie (act): The Blood Drinkers
Arceo, Gil (act): Beyond Atlantis; Dance Of The Dwarfs
Archainbaud, George (dir, 1890–1959): The Millerson Case; Murder On The Blackboard; The Penguin Pool Murder
Archainbaud, George (wri, 1890–1959): The Lost Squadron
Archambault, Arch (act): Ravagers
Archambault, Arch (cin): Count Yorga, Vampire
Archard, Bernard (act, b. 1922): The Clue Of The New Pin (1961); Fragment Of Fear; Horror Of Frankenstein; Krull; The List Of Adrian Messenger; Macbeth (1971); Man Detained; The Spy With A Cold Nose; The Village Of The Damned (1960)
Archard, Marcel (wri): Alibi (1942)
Archdale, Alexander (act): The Headless Ghost; House Of Darkness; The Village Of The Damned (1960)
Archer, Anne (act, b. 1947): The Man In The Attic (1995); The Mark Of Zorro (1974); Narrow Margin; Too Scared To Scream
Archer, Barbara (act): Horror Of Dracula; Model For Murder
Archer, Beverly (act): Vice Versa (1988)
Archer, Jim (act): Agatha
Archer, John (act, b. 1915, nee Ralph Bowman): Bowery At Midnight; Destination Moon; Dragon's Gold; I Saw What You Did (1965); King Of The Zombies; The Lost Moment; The Scarlet Spear; She-Devil; Sherlock Homes In Washington; The Velvet Touch
Archer, Steve (act): Bridge Across Time
Archer, William (wri): The Green Goddess (1923 & 1929)
Archerd, Army (act, b. 1922): Escape From The Planet Of The Apes; Repossessed
Archerd, Selma (act): Alice In Wonderland (1985); Fantasies
Archibald, Dawn (act):The Company Of Wolves
Archibald, William (wri): I Confess; The Innocents
Archie, John (act): Flight Of The Navigator
Ardant, Fanny (act): Afraid Of The Dark
Ardao, David (act): A Return To Salem's Lot
Arden, Arianne (act): Beyond The Time Barrier
Arden, Curtis (act): The Valley Of Gwangi
Arden, Eve (act, 1908-1990, nee Eunice Quedens): One Touch Of Venus; Pandemonium; Sergeant Deadhead The Astronaut!; Song Of Scheherazade; The Strongest Man In The World; A Very Missing Person
Arden, Hugo (act): The Son Of Hercules In The Land Of Darkness
Arden, Mary (act): Master Stroke; Sei Donne Per L'assassino
Arden, Neal (act): Behemoth, The Sea Monster; The Straw Man
Arden, Robert (act, b. 1921): Condorman; The Final Conflict; Little Shop Of Horrors (1986); Mr. Arkadin; Soho Incident
Ardisson, Giorgio/George (act): Agent 383/Passport To Hell; Ercole Al Centro Della Terra; The Eyes Behind The Stars; Last Of The Vikings; I Lunghi Capelli Della Morte; The Masked Conqueror; Morgan The Pirate; Operation Counterspy
Ardolino, Emile (dir, d. 1993): Chances Are
Ardrey, Robert (wri, b. 1908): The Three Musketeers (1948); Thunder Rock
Arena, Maurizio (act): The Man Who Wagged His Tail
Arenas, Pilar (act): The Emerald Of Artatama
Arenas, Rosita (act): La Casa Viviente; El Espejo De La Bruja; La Maldicion De La Llorona; La Momia; La Momia Contra El Robot Humano
Arenberg, Lee (act): Warriors Of Virtue
Areno, Lois (act): Are You In The House Alone?
Arent, Eddi (act): Circus Of Fear; Spy Today, Die Tomorrow; The Trygon Factor
Aresco, Joey (act): The Hidden
Arevalo, Tito (mus): Beast Of Blood; The Blood Drinkers; Curse Of The Vampires; Twilight People
Argent, Maurice (act): Invasion Of The Body Snatchers (1978)
Argentiogorgis, Nicos (act): The Offspring
Argento, Asia (act): Demons 2; Trauma (1993)

Argento, Dario (dir, b. 1943): *The Cat O' Nine Tails; Inferno (1979); Phenomena; Profundo Rosso; Quatro Mosche Di Velluto Gris; Suspiria; Tenebrae; Terror At The Opera; Trauma (1993); Two Evil Eyes; L'uccello Delle Piume Di Cristallo*
Argento, Dario (wri, b. 1943): *The Cat O' Nine Tails; Demons 2; Inferno (1979); Phenomena; Profundo Rosso; Quatro Mosche Di Velluto Gris; Trauma (1993); Two Evil Eyes; L'uccello Delle Piume Di Cristallo*
Argento, Fiore (act): *Demons; Phenomena*
Argenziano, Carmen (act): *The First Power; Graduation Day; Grave Of The Vampire; The Man Who Fell To Earth (1987); Rave Review; Search For The Gods; Too Good To Be True; When A Stranger Calls*
Argiro, Vinny (act): *Date With An Angel; Ed Wood; Mars Attacks!*
Argo, Victor (act): *The Terminal Man*
Argue, David (act): *Razorback*
Argyle, John (dir): *The Hills Of Donegal*
Argyle, John/J.F. (wri): *Dark Eyes Of London; The Door With Seven Locks (1940); The Patient Vanishes; Tower Of Terror*
Argyle, Pearl (act): *Chu Chin Chow (1934); Things To Come*
Arias, John (act): *Elvira, Mistress Of The Dark*
Arias, Joseph (act): *Deadly Game*
Aries, Anna (act): *Invasion Of The Bee Girls*
Arikawa, Sadamasa (dir): *The Phoenix (1980)*
Arima, Ineko (act): *Yoru No Tsuzumi*
Ariola, Julie (act): *Fire In The Sky (1993); Running Against Time*
Aris, Ben (act): *Digby-The Biggest Dog In The World; Hamlet (1969); The Plague Of The Zombies; Tommy*
Arishima, Ichiro (act): *King Kong Vs. Godzilla*
Aristides, Colleen (act): *Princess Warrior*
Arit, Lewis (act): *He Knows You're Alone*
Ariznavarreta, Roman (act): *The Fifth Musketeer*
Arizono, Yoshiki (act): *The Crazy Family*
Arjuna, Tony (act): *Octopussy*
Arkin, Adam (act, b. 1956): *Full Moon High; The Monitors*
Arkin, Alan (act, b. 1934): *Doomsday Gun; Edward Scissorhands; Full Moon High; The Monitors; The Rocketeer; The Seven-Per-Cent Solution; Simon*
Arkush, Alan (dir): *Deathsport; Heartbeeps*
Arlen, Elizabeth (act): *D.O.A. (1988); The First Power*
Arlen, Harold (mus, 1905–1986): *Cabin In The Sky; The Wizard Of Oz (1939)*
Arlen, Michael (wri, 1895-1956): *Appointment With Murder; A Date With The Falcon; The Devil's Cargo; The Falcon And The Co-Eds; The Falcon In Danger; The Falcon In Hollywood; The Falcon In Mexico; The Falcon In San Francisco; The Falcon Out West; The Falcon's Adventure; The Falcon's Alibi; The Falcon Strikes Back; The Falcon Takes Over; The Fatal Night; The Gay Falcon; Search For Danger*
Arlen, Richard (act, 1900-1976): *Accomplice; Alice In Wonderland (1933); The Crawling Hand; The Human Duplicators; Identity Unknown; Island Of Lost Souls; The Lady And The Monster; The Phantom Speaks*
Arlen, Roxanne (act): *The Loved One*
Arletty (act): *Les Visiteurs Du Soir*
Arley, Catherine (wri): *Woman Of Straw*
Arling, Arthur E. (cin, b. 1906): *The Glass Slipper; Strait—Jacket*
Arliss, Dimitra (act): *The Fall Of The House Of Usher (1982); Xanadu*
Arliss, George (act, 1868-1946, nee Augustus George Andrews): *The Devil (1921); Dr. Syn; The Green Goddess (1923 & 1929); Tunnel, The*
Arliss, Mrs. George (act): *The Devil (1921)*
Arliss, Leslie (dir, 1901-1987): *A Man About The House; The Man In Grey; The Night Has Eyes*
Arliss, Leslie (wri, 1901-1987): *A Man About The House; The Man In Grey; The Saint Meets The Tiger*
Arliss, Ralph (act): *The Asphyx; Dead Man's Folly; The Quatermass Conclusion; Tennis Court*
Arlorio, Giorgio (wri): *Zorro (1975)*
Arlorio, Giulio (cin): *Zorro (1975)*
Arlt, Lewis (act): *Orpheus Descending*
Arlton, Frank (act): *The Last Hour; The Romany Rye*
Armand, Margot (act): *Maria Marten (1928)*
Armand, Merete (act): *The Witches (1990)*
Armenaki, Arledge (cin): *Howling V: The Rebirth*
Armendariz, Pedro (act, 1912–1963): *Captain Sinbad; From Russia With Love; The Little Savage; Lucrezia Borgia (1952); Les Titans*
Armendariz Jr., Pedro (act): *Chosen Survivors; Don't Be Afraid Of The Dark; Earthquake; Licence To Kill (1989)*
Armetta, Henry (act, 1888–1945): *The Black Cat (1934); The Man Who Reclaimed His Head; Night Life Of The Gods*
Armida (act): *Jungle Goddess*
Armitage, Frank (wri): *They Live*
Armitage, George (wri): *Gas-S-S-S!*
Armitage, Graham (act): *The Devils; The Private Life Of Sherlock Holmes*
Armitage, Walter (act): *Great Expectations (1934)*
Armitrij, Vijay (act): *Octopussy*
Armond, John (act): *Blood Of Ghastly Horror*
Armont, Paul (wri): *Love Me Tonight*
Armstrong, Alun (act): *The Eyes Have It; Krull*
Armstrong, Anthony/Antony (wri): *The Man In The Road; The Man Who Haunted Himself; Young And Innocent*
Armstrong, Bess (act, b. 1953): *Jaws 3-D; Jekyll And Hyde...Together Again; Second Sight*
Armstrong, Charlotte (wri): *Talk About A Stranger; The Three Weird Sisters; The Unsuspected*
Armstrong, Curtis (act): *The Clan Of The Cave Bear*
Armstrong, David (act): *On The Threshold Of Space*
Armstrong, Gerard (act): *Mad Max Beyond Thunderdome*
Armstrong, H.C. (wri): *Dead Men Are Dangerous*
Armstrong, Herb (act): *Cape Fear (1961); Something Evil; The Young Captives*
Armstrong, Hugh (act): *Deathline*
Armstrong, Jack (act): *The Guyver*
Armstrong, Jerome (wri): *Volcano*
Armstrong, John M. (act): *Student Bodies*
Armstrong, Katherine (act): *Crash And Burn*
Armstrong, Kathy (act): *Phoenix The Warrior*
Armstrong, Lee (act): *Leprechaun 3; Magic Island*
Armstrong, Leslie (act): *The Fatal Night*
Armstrong, Louis (act, 1900–1971): *Cabin In The Sky*
Armstrong, Louis (mus, 1900–1971): *On Her Majesty's Secret Service*
Armstrong, Mary (act): *Hello Again*
Armstrong, Michael (dir): *The Haunted House Of Horror; Mark Of The Devil (1972)*
Armstrong, Michael (wri): *The Haunted House Of Horror; House Of The Long Shadows*
Armstrong, Peter (act): *Blood And Lace; The Cars That Ate Paris; Howling III*
Armstrong, R.G. (act): *The Beast Within; The Car; Children Of The Corn; Devil Dog: The Hound Of Hell; Dick Tracy (1990); Evilspeak; The Fugitive Kind; Heaven Can Wait (1978); Predator; Race With The Devil; Reflections Of Murder; The Time Machine (1978)*
Armstrong, Ray (act): *Jekyll And Hyde*
Armstrong, Raymond (act): *Where Has Poor Mickey Gone?*
Armstrong, Richard (act): *La Decima Vittima*
Armstrong, Robert (act, 1890–1973): *Crime Doctor's Diary; The Falcon In San Francisco; King Kong (1933); The Leopard Lady; The Lost Squadron; The Mad Ghoul; Mighty Joe Young; The Most Dangerous Game; The Penguin Pool Murder; Son Of Kong*
Armstrong, Ron (act): *Night Of The Zombies (1981)*
Armstrong, Tex (act): *The Destructors; Dimension 5*
Armstrong, Todd (act): *Jason And The Argonauts*
Armstrong, Valorie (act): *A Nightmare On Elm Street 5: The Dream Child*
Armstrong, William (act): *Riders Of The Storm*
Armus, Sidney (act): *Making Mr. Right*
Arnall, Julia (act, b. 1931): *The Double Man; The Man Without A Body; Mark Of The Phoenix; Model For Murder; The Trunk*
Arnatt, John (act): *A Challenge For Robin Hood; Clash By Night; Crucible Of Terror; Dick Barton At Bay; Dr. Crippen; House Of Blackmail; Licensed To Kill; Licensed To Love And Kill; Out Of The Fog (1962)*
Arnau, B.J. (act): *Live And Let Die*
Arnaud, Daniele (act): *School Spirit*
Arnaud, Georges (wri, 1917–1987): *Le Salaire De La Peur*
Arnaud, Marie-Helene (act): *Fantomas Contro Scotland Yard*
Arnaud, Yvonne (act, 1892–1958): *Desire; The Ghosts Of Berkeley Square*
Arnaz Jr., Desi (act, b. 1953): *Automan; House Of The Long Shadows*
Arndt, Denis (act): *Asteroid; The Beast (1996); Nightscream*
Arndt, Jacques (act): *Amazons (1986)*
Arne, Peter (act, 1921–1983): *Agatha; Battle Beneath The Earth; Black Torment; Chitty Chitty Bang Bang; The Hell-Fire Club; Men Of Sherwood Forest; Murders In The Rue Morgue (1971); The Oblong Box; The Pirates Of Blood River; Tarzan And The Lost Safari; Timeslip; The Treasure Of Monte Cristo (1961)*
Arnell, Richard (mus): *The Third Secret*
Arneric, Neda (act): *The Legend Of Spider Forest*
Arneson, Mark (act): *Strange Days*
Arness, James (act, b. 1923): *Them! (1954); The Thing From Another World; Two Lost Worlds; The Veils Of Bagdad*
Arnett, David (act): *The Punisher*
Arnett, James (act): *Nightwing*
Arngrim, Stefan/Steven (act): *Class Of '84; Fear No Evil (1981); Strange Days*
Arno, Nelly (act): *The Third Man*
Arno, Nick (act): *Houdini*
Arno, Siegfried/Sig (act, b. 1895): *The Mummy's Hand; Passport To Suez*
Arnold, Bert (act): *Phantom From Space*
Arnold, Charles/Chuck (G.) (cin): *Assassin (1986); Don't Go To Sleep; The Possessed (1977)*
Arnold, Cindy (act): *Strange Behavior*
Arnold, Danny (act, 1920–1995): *Scared Stiff (1953)*
Arnold, David (mus): *Independence Day; Stargate*
Arnold, Denny (act): *Logan's Run*
Arnold, Dick (act): *Pandora's Clock*
Arnold, Dickie (act): *Santa Claus (1985)*
Arnold, Dorothy (act, 1919–1985): *Lizzie; The Phantom Creeps*
Arnold, Edward (act, 1890–1956, nee Guenther Schneider): *All That Money Can Buy; Crime And Punishment (1935); Eyes In The Night; The Hidden Eye; Kismet (1944); Main Street After Dark; Meet Nero Wolfe; Rasputin And The Empress; Roman Scandals; The Secret Of The Blue Room; Three Wise Fools*
Arnold, Frank (act): *Flesh And Fantasy*
Arnold, Gertrud (act): *Chronik Von Grieshuus; Die Nibelungen*
Arnold, Grace (act): *Konga*
Arnold, Hewton Dennis (act): *The Goonies*
Arnold, Irene (act): *Night Train For Inverness*
Arnold, Jack (dir, b. 1916): *Creature From The Black Lagoon; The Glass Web; Hello Down There; The Incredible Shrinking Man; It Came From Outer Space; Monster On The Campus; The Mouse That Roared; Revenge Of The Creature; The Space Children; Tarantula; The Tattered Dress*
Arnold, Jack (wri, b. 1916): *The Monolith Monsters; Tarantula*
Arnold, Jeanne (act): *Munster, Go Home!*
Arnold, Jessie (act): *Boston Blackie Goes to Hollywood; The Chance Of A Lifetime*
Arnold, Joann (act): *The Adventures Of Hajji Baba*
Arnold, John (act): *Mad Max*
Arnold, John (cin): *Mr. Wu (1927)*
Arnold, Lamont (act): *The Dark Half; The Silence Of The Lambs*
Arnold, Mal (act): *Blood Feast*
Arnold, Malcolm (mus, b. 1921): *Four Sided Triangle; The Key; The Ringer (1952); Suddenly Last Summer*
Arnold, Marcel (act): *Mr. Peek-A-Boo*
Arnold, Mark (act): *Teen Wolf*
Arnold, Mason (act): *The Gifted One*
Arnold, Melbourne (cin): *Psycho II*
Arnold, Newton/Newt (dir): *Hands Of A Stranger; The Horror From Beyond*
Arnold, Newton (wri): *Hands Of A Stranger*
Arnold, Newton D. (act): *Skullduggery*
Arnold, Peter (wri): *Sisters Of Death*
Arnold, Sean (act): *Haunters Of The Deep*
Arnold, Steven (cin, dir & wri): *Luminous Procuress*
Arnold, Susan (act): *Empire Of Ash III*
Arnold, Sydney (act): *Top Secret! (1984)*
Arnold, Tichina (act): *Little Shop Of Horrors (1986)*
Arnold, Tom (act): *Touch*
Arnold, Victor (act): *Wolfen*
Arnott, David (act): *Blood Song; House II; The Second Story*
Arnott, John (act): *Where The Bullets Fly*
Arnoul, Francoise (act, b. 1931, nee Francoise Annette Gautsch): *Le Diable Et Les Dix Commandements; The Spy Is A Girl*
Arnoux, Robert (act): *Liliom (1933)*
Arnova, Alba (act): *Miracle In Milan; Ok, Nero!*
Arnsen, David (act): *The China Syndrome*
Arnt, Charles (act, 1907–1990): *Boston Blackie's Chinese Venture; Crime Doctor's Courage; Dangerous Intruders; Dressed To Kill (1941); The Falcon's Brother; Just Before Dawn (1946); Paris Calling; Sudan; The Veils Of Bagdad*
Arnt, Jake (act): *Deathstalker II: Duel Of The Titans*
Arntzen, David (act): *Phantasm*
Aron, Jean (act): *La Poupee*
Aronberg, Chuck (act): *Pumpkinhead II: Blood Wings*
Aronesty, Scott (act): *Santa Claus Conquers The Martians*
Aronin, Michael (act): *The Fifth Missile*
Aronson, Judie (act): *The Sleeping Car; Weird Science*
Arosenius, Per—Axel (act): *Topaz*
Arpino, Tony (act): *Evil Of Frankenstein*
Arpon, Maria Elena (act): *El Jorobado De La Morgue*
Arpuco, Ike (act): *Dance Of The Dwarfs*
Arquette, Alexis (act): *Of Mice And Men (1992)*
Arquette, David (act): *Scream; Scream II*
Arquette, Lewis (act): *The China Syndrome*
Arquette, Patricia (act, b. 1968): *Ed Wood; A Nightmare On Elm Street 3: Dream Warriors; Lost Highway; The Secret Agent (1996)*
Arquette, Richard (act): *Seven*
Arquette, Rosanna (act): *Amazon Women On The Moon; Black Rainbow; Crash (1996); The Dark Secret Of Harvest Home*
Arrants, Rod (act): *A*P*E*
Arriaga, Simon (act): *Tombs Of The Blind Dead*
Arribas, Fernando (cin): *The Blood Spattered Bride; Night Fiend; Ten Little Indians (1974)*
Arrighi, Nike (act): *Countess Dracula; The Devil Rides Out*
Arrington, Brad (act): *The Tomb*
Arroita—Jauregui, Marcelo (act): *El Secreto Del Doctor Orlof*
Arrow, Jack (act): *Treasure Island (1950)*
Arroyo, Alexis (act): *Dr. Tarr's Torture Dungeon*
Arroyo, Tita (act): *Dr. Tarr's Torture Dungeon*
Artaud, Antonin (act, 1896–1948): *Liliom (1933)*
Artaud, Antonin (wri, 1896–1948): *La Coquille Et Le Clergyman*
Artemiev/Artemeyev, Eduard/Edward (mus): *The Odyssey; Solaris*
Arthur, Art (wri): *Around The World Under The Sea; Birds Do It; Heaven Only Knows*
Arthur, Edward (act): *Morons From Outer Space*
Arthur, Hartney (act): *Devotion*
Arthur, Jean (act, 1901–1991, nee Gladys Green): *The Canary Murder Case; The Greene Murder Case; The Mysterious Dr. Fu Manchu; The Return Of Dr. Fu Manchu*
Arthur, Johnny (act): *The Monster (1925); Sakima And The Masked Marvel*
Arthur, Karen (dir): *Lady Beware; The Mafu Cage; Shadow Of A Doubt (1991)*
Arthur, Maureen (act): *A Man Called Dagger*
Arthur, Michelle (act): *Goldeneye*
Arthur, Roy (act): *Great Expectations (1946)*
Arthurs, George (wri): *The Yellow Mask*
Arthuys, Philippe (act): *La Prima Donna*
Arthy, Judith (act): *The Shuttered Room*
Artigot, Raul (dir): *Witches' Mountain*
Art Of Noise (mus): *Demons 2*
Arton, Anne-Catherine (act): *White Angel*
Artus, Ashley (act): *Judge Dredd*
Arue, Andrew (act): *Fear (1996)*
Arums, Mudite (act): *Something Weird*
Arundale, Sybil (act): *The Chinese Puzzle*
Arundell, Dennis (act, b. 1898): *The Echo Murders; Meet Sexton Blake; Pimpernel Smith; The Saint Meets The Tiger*
Arundell, Edward (act): *The Lyons Mail*
Arundell, Teddy (act): *The Amazing Partnership; At The Villa Rose (1920); The Elusive Pimpernel (1919); Mr. Wu (1919); The Mystery Of Mr. Bernard Brown*
Arvan, Jan (act, 1912–1979): *The Brass Bottle (1964); Curse Of The Faceless Man; The Poseidon Adventure; The Screaming Woman; The Spy With My Face; 20 Million Miles To Earth*
Arvide, Manuel (act): *The Beast Of Hollow Mountain*
Arvidson, Frank (act): *The Monster Of Piedras Blancas*
Arvidson, Linda (act): *Edgar Allan Poe; The Scarlet Letter (1913)*
Arywitz, Mark (wri): *Just Before Dawn (1980)*
Asali, Donna (act): *Raiders Of The Living Dead*
Asano, Yoko (act): *The War In Space*
Asato, Reid (act): *The Odyssey*
Asbury, Anthony (act): *Labyrinth (1986)*

Asche, Oscar (act): Kismet (1914); Scrooge (1935)
Asche, Oscar (wri): Chu Chin Chow (1923 & 1934)
Ascher, Donald (act): Street Trash
Ascher, Shoshana (act): Night Of The Zombies (1981)
Ascot, Wendy (act): Subterfuge
Asghar, Maiser (act): Slipstream
Ash, Arty (act): Dr. Sin Fang
Ash, Bill (act): Plan 9 From Outer Space
Ash, Gordon (act): A Message From Mars (1921)
Ash, Jerome/Jerry (cin): Abbott And Costello Meet Frankenstein; The Cat Creeps (1930); Destination Saturn; The Mad Doctor Of Market Street; Peril From The Planet Mongo; The Phantom Creeps; Pillow Of Death; Purple Death From Outer Space; The Strange Death Of Adolf Hitler; The Time Of Their Lives
Ash, Monty (act): Bell, Book And Candle
Ash, Sam (act): Charlie Chan On Broadway; Dick Tracy (1945)
Ashana, Rochelle (act): Fright Night II
Ashbrook, Dana (act): Girlfriend From Hell; Return Of The Living Dead, Part II; Sundown: The Vampire In Retreat
Ashbrook, Daphne (act): Automatic; Doctor Who
Ashbrooke, Florence (act): The Lone Wolf (1917)
Ashby, Carole (act): Arthur The King; Octopussy
Ashby, Harvey (act): Jekyll And Hyde
Ashby, John (act): The Entity
Ashby, Linden (act): Dark Angel; Mortal Kombat; Night Angel
Ashby, Sally (act): Peter Rabbit And The Tales Of Beatrix Potter
Ashcroft, (Dame) Peggy (act, 1907–1991): Secret Ceremony; The 39 Steps (1935); The Wandering Jew (1933); When The Wind Blows
Ashcroft, Ronnie (dir):The Astounding She-Monster
Ashe, Eve Brent (act): Fade To Black; Shadow Of Death (1983)
Ashe, Richard (dir): Track Of The Moon Beast
Ashe, Warren (act): Boston Blackie And The Law; One Dangerous Night
Asher, Jack (cin, b. 1916): Brides Of Dracula; The Camp On Blood Island; The Curse Of Frankenstein; Horror Of Dracula; The Hound Of The Baskervilles (1959); The Man Who Could Cheat Death; The Mummy (1959); The Revenge Of Frankenstein; The Scarlet Blade; The Secret Of Blood Island; The Snorkel; The Two Faces Of Dr. Jekyll
Asher, Jane (act, b. 1946): Dreamchild; The Masque Of The Red Death (1964)
Asher, Jay (mus): Zorro: The Legend Begins
Asher, John Mallory (act): The Haunted (1991)
Asher, Max (act): Rip Van Winkle (1921)
Asher, Ron (act): Echoes
Asher, William (dir, b. 1919): Butcher, Baker (Nightmare Maker); How To Stuff A Wild Bikini; I Dream Of Jeannie: Fifteen Years Later; Johnny Cool; The 27th Day
Asher, William (wri, b. 1919): How To Stuff A Wild Bikini
Asherson, Renee (act, b. 1920): Black Limelight; The Day The Earth Caught Fire; Pool Of London; Rasputin, The Mad Monk; Theater Of Blood; Time Is My Enemy
Asheton, Ron (act): Frostbiter: Wrath Of The Wendigo
Ashford, David (act): The Quatermass Conclusion
Ashford, Matthew (act): Species
Ashida, Isamu (cin):Rodan, The Flying Monster
Ashida, Toyoo (dir): Fist Of The North Star
Ashley, Angel (act): Sleepstalker
Ashley, Charles (act): The Silver Greyhound (1919)
Ashley, Diana (act): Corruption; Targets
Ashley, Edward (act, b. 1904, nee E.A. Cooper): The Black Swan; Dick Tracy Meets Gruesome; Sky Murder; Tarzan And The Mermaids
Ashley, Elizabeth (act, b. 1939): Coma; A Fire In The Sky (1978); The Magician (1973); Svengali (1983); Vampire's Kiss; When Michael Calls; Windows
Ashley, Eve (act): They Made Me A Fugitive
Ashley, George (act): The Cloister And The Woman
Ashley, Graham (act): The Tell-Tale Heart (1960)
Ashley, [illegible]
Ashley, Herbert (act):League Of Frightened Men
Ashley, Iris (act): Blind Man's Bluff (1936); The Warren Case

Ashley, Jennifer (act): Guyana, Cult Of The Damned; Inseminoid; Phantom Of The Paradise; Tintorera...Bloody Waters
Ashley, Joel (act): Zombies Of Mora Tau
Ashley, John (act): Beast Of Blood; Beast Of The Yellow Night; Beyond Atlantis; Brides Of Blood; The Eye Creatures; Frankenstein's Daughter (1958); How To Make A Monster; How To Stuff A Wild Bikini; Mad Doctor Of Blood Island; Sergeant Deadhead The Astronaut!; Twilight People
Ashley, Karan (act): Mighty Morphin Power Rangers
Ashley, Lyn (act): Quest For Love
Ashman, Howard (wri, 1950–1991): Little Shop Of Horrors (1986)
Ashmore, Frank (act): The Clonus Horror; Monster In The Closet; V
Ashmore, Jonathan (act): A Kid For Two Farthings
Ashmore, Peter (act): The Ipcress File
Ashokan, Master (act): The Bogey Man
Ashton, Charles (act): Maria Marten (1928); The Monkey's Paw (1923); Spiritualism Exposed (1926); Sweeney Todd
Ashton, Frederick (act): Peter Rabbit And The Tales Of Beatrix Potter
Ashton, Harry (act): In The Days Of Robin Hood
Ashton, Iris (act): The Dancer Of The Nile
Ashton, James (wri): The Devil's Rain
Ashton, John (act): King Kong Lives
Ashton, Judy (act): Dead And Buried
Ashton, Nigel (act): Macbeth (1971)
Ashton, Pat (act): Blood Bath At The House Of Death
Ashton, Rachel (act): Return To Oz
Ashton, Sylvia (act): The Leopard Lady
Ashton, Warwick (act): Who Done It? (1956)
Ashton-Griffiths, Roger (act): Brazil; Dreamchild; Haunted Honeymoon (1986); The Odyssey; Young Sherlock Holmes; The Zany Adventures Of Robin Hood
Ashwell, Charles (act): The Price He Paid
Ashworth, Dicken (act): Krull
Asimov, Dr. Isaac (wri, 1920–1992):Fantastic Voyage; Light Years; Nightfall (1988)
Askew, Alice (wri): God's Clay; The Pleydell Mystery
Askew, Claude (wri): God's Clay; The Pleydell Mystery
Askew, Luke (act): Dune Warriors
Askey, Arthur (act, b. 1900): The Ghost Train (1941); King Arthur Was A Gentleman
Askham, Phil (act): Threads
Askin, Leon (act, b. 1920): Desert Legion; Doctor Death: Seeker Of Souls; Frightmare (1983); Hammersmith Is Out; The Perils Of Pauline; The Road To Bali; Secret Of The Incas; Son Of Sinbad; Spy Chasers; The Veils Of Bagdad; Young Frankenstein
Askins, Monroe (cin): Blood Of Dracula; The House On Skull Mountain; The Human Duplicators
Askwith, Robin (act): The Flesh And Blood Show; Horror Hospital; Otley; Tower Of Evil
Aslan, Coco (act): Sleeping Car To Trieste
Aslan, G. (act): L'auberge Rouge
Aslan, Gregoire (act, b. 1908, nee Kridor Aslanian): Aimez Vous Les Femmes?; Cage Of Gold; Cet Homme Est Dangereux; The Golden Voyage Of Sinbad; Last Holiday; Mr. Arkadin; Moment To Moment; Our Man In Marrakesh; Paris When It Sizzles; The Snorkel; The Three Worlds Of Gulliver
Aslanian, Kridor (act): see Aslan, Gregoire
Aslanian, Samson (dir & wri): Torment (1986)
Asman, David (act): Virtuosity
Asman, William (cin): Abby
Asner, Edward (act, b. 1929): Daughter Of The Mind; Haunts Of The Very Rich; The Last Child; Pinocchio And The Emperor Of The Night; The Satan Bug; They Call It Murder; The Venetian Affair
Asner, Kate (act): Dr. Jekyll And Ms. Hyde
Asner, Matthew (act): Neon Maniacs
Asoka (act): Desert Legion; The Diamond Queen
Asp,Jim (act): Teen-Age Strangler
Asparagus, Fred (act): Galaxis
Aspel, Michael (act): The Magic Christian
Aspin, Max (act): Howling III
Asprey, George (act): Mary Shelley's 'Frankenstein'
Asquerino, Maria (act): Amador
Asquith, Anthony (dir, 1902–1968): Fanny By Gaslight; The Net; The Woman In Question
Asquith, Anthony (wri, 1902–1968):Boadicea
Assan, Dana (act): The Man With The Power; 976-Evil II: The Astral Factor
Assad, Richard (act): Mars Attacks!
Assad, Steve (act): Vice Versa (1988)
Assael, David (act): Schizoid (1980)

Assael, David (wri): The London Connection
Assante, Armand (act, b. 1949): Human Feelings; I, The Jury (1982); Judge Dredd; The Odyssey; Prophecy (1979)
Assonitis, Olvidio (dir, a.k.a. Oliver Hellman): Beyond The Door; Tentacles
Ast, Pat (act): Pandemonium
Astaire, Fred (act, 1899-1987, nee Frederick Austerlitz): Ghost Story (1981); The Man In The Santa Claus Suit; On The Beach; The Towering Inferno
Astan, Thomas (act): Jonathan
Astar, Ben (act): Five Weeks In A Balloon
Astell, Betty (act): Flat No. 3; The Mind Of Mr. Reeder; A Piece Of Cake; The Stickpin
Astell, Betty (wri): A Piece Of Cake
Asterova, Jitka (act): Howling III
Asther, Nils (act, 1897–1981): Bluebeard (1944); The Feathered Serpent (1948); Himmelskibet; Laugh, Clown, Laugh; The Man In Half Moon Street; Night Monster
Asti, Adriana (act): Zorro (1975)
Astin, John (act, b. 1930): The Frighteners; Gremlins 2: The New Batch; Halloween With The Addams Family; Night Life (1989, Usa); Return Of The Killer Tomatoes; The Silence Of The Hams; The Spirit Is Willing; Teen Wolf Too
Astin, Mackenzie (act): The Garbage Pail Kids; I Dream Of Jeannie: Fifteen Years Later; Widow's Kiss
Astin, Patty Duke (act): see Duke (Astin), Patty
Astin, Sean (act): Encino Man; The Goonies; Kurt Vonnegut's Harrison Bergeron
Astley, Edwin (T.) (mus): Digby- The Biggest Dog In The World; The Fiction-Makers; Kadoyng; Kill Her Gently; Koroshi; The Mouse That Roared; Vendetta For The Saint
Astley, Susan (act): It (1990)
Astor, Avice (act): Shadow Of Death (1939)
Astor, Gertrude (act, 1887-1977): The Cat And The Canary (1927); The Devil's Hand (1961); Dick Tracy (1945); Rupert Of Hentzau (1923)
Astor, Mary (act, 1906–1987, nee Lucile Langhanke): The Case Of The Howling Dog; Don Juan (1927); Don Q, Son Of Zorro; Hush...Hush, Sweet Charlotte; The Kennel Murder Case; The Lash; The Lost Squadron; The Maltese Falcon (1941); The Prisoner Of Zenda (1937); Puritan Passions; Return Of The Terror
Astral Warriors, The (mus): A Nymphoid Barbarian In Dinosaur Hell
Astyr, Bobby (act): The Amazing Dr. Jekyll
Atasanoff, Pete (act): From Dusk Till Dawn
Atchelor, Jack (cin): The Haunted House Of Horror
Atcheson, James (act): Neon Maniacs
Atcheson, Jeff (act): Superman (1978)
Atchley, Hooper (act): Dick Tracy vs. Crime, Inc.; Mr. Wong, Detective; The Mystery Of Mr. Wong; The Sphinx (1933)
Ateah, Scott (act): The Resurrected
Ates, Nejla (act): Son Of Sinbad
Ates,Roscoe (act, 1892–1962): Alice In Wonderland (1933); Freaks
Athens, Vi (act): Crime Doctor
Atherley, Frank (act): Sexton Blake, Gambler; Silken Threads
Atherton, Edward (act):The Hunchback (1997)
Atherton, Vernie (act): Jane Eyre (1921)
Atherton, William (act, b. 1947): Bio-Dome; Ghostbusters; Grim Prairie Tales; Tomorrow's Child
Athey, Ron (act): Single White Female
Atkey, Bertram (wri): The Secret Kingdom
Atkin, Harvey (act): Funeral Home; Incubus (1982); Sorry, Wrong Number (1989)
Atkins, Bruce (act): Scalpel
Atkins, Chris(topher) (act, b. 1961): Dead Man's Island; Die Watching; Dracula Rising; Project Shadowchaser III; Secret Weapons; Shakma
Atkins, Eileen (act): The Avengers; I Don't Want To Be Born; Wolf
Atkins, Pat (act): Death Dreams
Atkins, Peter (wri): Hellbound: Hellraiser II; Hellraiser III: Hell On Earth; Hellraiser: Bloodline
Atkins, Robert (act): Hamlet (1913); The House In The Square; A Matter Of Life And Death; Time Flies (1944)
Atkins, Tom (act): Escape From New York; The Fog; Halloween III: Season Of The Witch; Maniac Cop; Night Of The Creeps; Tarantulas: The Deadly Cargo
Atkinson, Frank (act): At The Stroke Of Nine; Before I Wake; The Body Vanishes; Cat Girl; Great Expectations (1946); The Limping Man (1936); The Man In The White Suit; The Third Clue; Young And Innocent
Atkinson, Frank (wri): The Third Clue
Atkinson, George (act): The Conquering Power
Atkinson, John (act): The Savage Curse; The Trunk
Atkinson, Rowan (act): Bernard And The Genie; Never Say Never Again; The Witches (1990)
Atkinson, Steve (act): The Haunting Of Hamilton High
Atkinstall, Lorna (act): Phoenix The Warrior
Atkyns, Norman (act): Frankenstein And The Monster From Hell; No Blade Of Grass
Atlanta, Joe (act): Satanik
Atlantis, Paul (act): The Boy Who Never Was
Attanasio, Ugo (act): Terror Of Rome Against The Son Of Hercules
Attard, Peter (act): Terror (1979)
Attard, Tony (wri): Haunters Of The Deep
Attaway, Ruth (act, 1910–1987): The Bermuda Depths
Attell, Toni (act): The Annihilator
Attenborough, (Sir) Richard (act, b. 1923): Dr. Dolittle; Jurassic Park; The Lost World: Jurassic Park; The Magic Christian; The Man Upstairs; A Matter Of Life And Death; Miracle On 34th Street (1994); Seance On A Wet Afternoon; Ten Little Indians (1974); 10 Rillington Place; The Third Secret
Attenborough, (Sir) Richard (dir, b. 1923): Magic
Atterbury, Malcolm (act): The Birds; Blood Of Dracula; How To Make A Monster; I Was A Teenage Werewolf; North By Northwest
Attias, Daniel (dir): Silver Bullet
Atwater, Barry (act): Night Gallery; The Night Stalker (1971)
Atwater, Edith (act): The Body Snatcher (1945); Family Plot; Strait-Jacket
Atwill, Lionel (act, 1885–1946): Charlie Chan In Panama; Charlie Chan's Murder Cruise; Doctor X; Fog Island; Frankenstein Meets The Wolf Man; Genius At Work; The Ghost Of Frankenstein; The Gorilla (1939); The Hound Of The Baskervilles (1939); House Of Dracula; House Of Frankenstein; Lady In The Death House; Lancer Spy; The Mad Doctor Of Market Street; Man-Made Monster; The Man Who Reclaimed His Head; The Mark Of The Vampire (1935); Mr. Moto Takes A Vacation; Murders In The Zoo; Mystery Of The Wax Museum; Night Monster; The Secret Of Madame Blanche; The Secret Of The Blue Room; Secrets Of Scotland Yard; Sherlock Holmes And The Secret Weapon; Son Of Frankenstein; The Sphinx (1933); The Strange Case Of Dr. Rx; The Three Musketeers (1939); The Vampire Bat
Atwood, Kathryn (act):Jason Goes To Hell: The Final Friday; To Die For II: Son Of Darkness
Atwood, Margaret (wri): The Handmaid's Tale
Atwood, Rhonda (act): Mountaintop Motel Massacre
Auber, Brigitte (act): To Catch A Thief
Auberjonois, Rene (act, 1940): Batman Forever; A Connecticut Yankee In King Arthur's Court (1989); The Dark Secret Of Harvest Home; Eyes Of Laura Mars; Images; King Kong (1976); Little Nemo: Adventures In Slumberland; My Best Friend Is A Vampire
Aubert, Lenore (act, b. 1918): Abbott And Costello Meet Frankenstein; Abbott And Costello Meet The Killer; The Catman Of Paris; The Return Of The Whistler; The Wife Of Monte Cristo
Aubin, Tony (mus): Le Corbeau
Aubrey, Angharad (act): The Nanny
Aubrey, Anne (act): The Man Inside; The Secret Man
Aubrey, Diane (act): Grip Of The Strangler; Invasion (1965); The Pirates Of Blood River; The Village Of The Damned (1960)
Aubrey, James (act): Endless Descent; The Hunger; Lord Of The Flies (1963); Riders Of The Storm; Terror (1979)
Aubrey, Jean (act): The Angel Who Pawned Her Harp; Date At Midnight; Man Detained; Model For Murder
Aubrey, Jimmie (act): Arrest Bulldog Drummond; Charlie Chan In Panama; Mr. Moto's Last Warning; Mr. Moto Takes A Vacation; The Mysterious Mr. Moto
Aubrey, Larry (act): Clarence
Aubrey, Skye (act): Ellery Queen: Don't Look Behind You; The Phantom Of Hollywood; A Very Missing Person
Aubry, Cecile (act, b. 1929, nee Anne-José Benard): The Black Rose
Aubuchon, Jacques (act): The Shaggy Dog

Auclair, Michel (act, b. 1922, nee Vladimir Vujovic): La Belle Et La Bete
Audet, Daniel Vincent (act): Galaxina
Audiard, Michel (wri): Les Miserables (1957); Mr. Peek-A-Boo
Audin, Robert (act): Street Trash
Audley, Maxine (act, b. 1923): Bluebeard's Ten Honeymoons; A Ghost In Monte Carlo; Frankenstein Must Be Destroyed; Koroshi; Man At The Carlton Tower; Never Mention Murder; Peeping Tom; Vengeance
Audouard, Yvan (wri): Le Saint Mene La Dance
Audran, Edmond (act): The Elusive Pimpernel (1950)
Audran, Stephane (act, b. 1933): The Black Bird (1975); Le Boucher; The Discreet Charm Of The Bourgeoisie; Landru; Ten Little Indians (1974); Violette Noziere; Wedding In Blood
Audray, Elvire (act): Ironmaster
Auel, Jean M. (wri): The Clan Of The Cave Bear
Auen, Signe (act): see Owen, Seena
Auer, Greg (cin): Attack Of The Killer Tomatoes; The Hills Have Eyes; Kingdom Of The Spiders
Auer, John (dir): The Crime Of Dr. Crespi
Auer, Mischa (act, 1905–1967, nee Misha Ounskowsky): And Then There Were None; The Benson Murder Case; Bulldog Drummond Strikes Back (1934); The Christmas That Almost Wasn't; Condemned To Live; Cracked Nuts (1941); A Dog, A Mouse And A Sputnik; Drums Of Jeopardy (1931); Faust And The Devil; For You I Die; Hellzapoppin; Hold That Ghost; Just Imagine; Lady In The Dark; Mr. Arkadin; The Monster Walks; One Night Of Fame; Tarzan The Fearless
Auer, Tony (act): Nightmare On The 13th Floor
Auerbach, Gary (act): Street Trash
Auerbach, John (wri): Stepfather II
Auerbach, Marshall (act): Mother's Day
Auger, Claudine (act, b. 1942): The Black Belly Of The Tarantula; Il Diavolo Innamorato; The Killing Game; The Man In The Iron Mask (1962); Snuff; Thunderball; Twitch Of The Death Nerve
Augesen, Roxanna (act): The Video Dead
Aughenbaugh, Charles (act): Raiders Of The Living Dead
August, Helen (wri): The Monkey's Uncle
August, Joseph/Joe (cin, 1890–1947): All That Money Can Buy; Dante's Inferno (1924); The Hunchback Of Notre Dame (1939); Portrait Of Jennie; The Saint In New York; The Temple Of Venus
August, Ken (wri): The Sins Of Dorian Gray
August, Kim (act): No Way To Treat A Lady
August, Lance (act): Project X (1987)
August, Tom (wri): The Monkey's Uncle
Augustin, Christina (act): Alien Predators
Augustine, Jill (act): Fright Night II
Augustyn, Joe (wri): Night Of The Demons
Aukin, Liane (act): The Phantom Of The Opera (1962)
Aulin, Ewa (act, b. 1950): Ceremonia Sangrienta; Death Smiles On A Murderer; Plucked
Ault, Ann (act): The Green Slime
Ault, Marie (act, 1870–1951, nee Marie Cragg): The Lodger (1926); The Monkey's Paw (1923); The Speckled Band (1931); The Three Weird Sisters
Aumont, Alexandre (act): Alien High
Aumont, Jean-Pierre (act, b. 1913, nee Jean-Pierre Salomons): Atlantis (1948); Blackout (1978); Castle Keep; Cauldron Of Blood; The Memory Of Eva Ryker; Song Of Scheherazade
Aumont, Tina (act): Torso
Auram, Chris (act): The Tormented (1977)
Aured, Carlos (dir): Horror Rises From The Tomb; House Of Doom (1973); The Mummy's Revenge
Aured, Carlos (wri): House Of Doom (1973)
Aurel, Jean (dir, b. 1925): Les Aventures Extraordinaires De Jules Verne
Aureli, Andrea (act): Gli Amori Di Ercole; Last Of The Vikings
Aurenche, Jean (wri, b. 1904): L'auberge Rouge; The Hunchback Of Notre Dame (1957); Jeux Interdits
Auric, Georges (mus, 1899–1983): L'aigle A Deux Tetes; La Belle Et La Bete; The Burning Court; Cage Of Gold; Corridor Of Mirrors; Dead Of Night (1945); L'eternel Retour; The Hunchback Of Notre Dame (1957); The Innocents; The Lavender Hill Mob; Lola Montes; The Mind Benders (1963); Orphee; Parents Terribles; The Queen Of Spades (1948); Le Salaire De La Peur; Le Sang D'un Poete; Les Sorcieres De Salem; Thomas L'imposteur
Aurichio, Jimmy (act): Maniac (1980)
Aurio, Gina Malia (act): The Presence
Aurthur, Robert Alan (wri, 1922–1978): All That Jazz; Lilith
Aussey, Germaine (act): Le Golem (1936)
Austerlitz, Frederick (act): see Astaire, Fred
Austern, Robert (act): Wild Thing
Austin, Alan (act): This Is Not A Test
Austin, Amber (act): Neon Maniacs
Austin, Cathy (act): Slaughter
Austin, Charles (act): Toxic Zombies
Austin, Charlotte (act): The Bride And The Beast; Frankenstein- 1970; Gorilla At Large; The Man Who Turned To Stone
Austin, F. Britten (wri): The Strange Case Of Mr. Todmorden
Austin, Frank (act): The Terror (1928)
Austin, George (act): The Monster (1925)
Austin, Jeanne (act): The Funhouse (1981)
Austin, Jerry (act): The Adventures Of Don Juan
Austin, Karen (act): Assassin (1986); The Clan Of The Cave Bear; Fantasies
Austin, Lauraine (act): Class Of Nuke'em High
Austin, Lois (act): The Golden Eye; The Shanghai Chest; The Trap
Austin, May (wri): The King's Romance
Austin, Michael (wri): Greystoke: The Legend Of Tarzan, Lord Of The Apes; The Shout
Austin, Pamela (GB act): Agatha
Austin, Pamela (USA act, b. 1941): The Perils Of Pauline
Austin, Ray (dir): House Of The Living Dead; The Return Of The Man From U.N.C.L.E.; The Return Of The Six Million Dollar Man And The Bionic Woman; Virgin Witch; The Zany Adventures Of Robin Hood; Zorro: The Legend Begins
Austin, Robert (act): Morons From Outer Space; Xtro
Austin, Ron (wri): The Horror At 37,000 Feet
Austin, Terence (wri): The Voice Of Merrill
Austin, Teri (act): Raising Cain; The Vindicator
Austin, Terry (act): Philo Vance Returns; Philo Vance's Gamble
Austin, William (act): Alice In Wonderland (1933); The Garden Murder Case; The Mysterious Dr. Fu Manchu; The Return Of Dr. Fu Manchu
Autant-Lara, Claude (dir, b. 1903): L'auberge Rouge; Le Comte De Monte Cristo; Le Plus Vieux Metier Du Monde; Sylvia And The Phantom
Auten, Cindy (act): The Pit (1983)
Auten, John (act): The Pit (1983)
Auther, Ana Maria (act): Curse II: The Bite
Autry, Alan (act, b. 1942): House; Nomads
Autry, Gene (act, b. 1907): Radio Ranch
Avacado, Bob (act): Blood Diner
Avallone, Francis Thomas (act): see Avalon, Frankie
Avalon, Frankie (act, b. 1940, nee Francis Thomas Avallone): Alakazam The Great; Blood Song; Dr. Goldfoot And The Bikini Machine; Drums Of Africa; The Haunted House Of Horror; How To Stuff A Wild Bikini; The Million Eyes Of Sumuru; Panic In Year Zero; Sergeant Deadhead The Astronaut!; Voyage To The Bottom Of The Sea
Avalon, Phil (act): Inn Of The Damned
Avalos, Luis (act): Ghost Fever; The Ghost Of Flight 401
Avari, Erick (act): Stargate
Avdan, Nilufer (act): The Devil's Castle (1963)
Avedis, Howard (dir & wri): The Fifth Floor; Mortuary
Avedon, Caren (act): Distortions
Avelino, Ariston (mus): Twilight People
Avellana, Joe Mari (wri): Equalizer 2000
Avenetti, Phillip (act): Night Of The Lepus
Averback, Hy (dir, b. 1925): Chamber Of Horrors (1966)
Avergon, Ruth (wri): Night School
Averill, Anthony (act): The Phantom Creeps; Torchy Blane In Panama
Avery, Belle (act): Repossessed
Avery, Bob (act): Haunts
Avery, Brian (act): Sleeper
Avery, Carol (act): Deathmoon
Avery, David (act): Secrets Of The Phantom Caverns
Avery, James (act): Beastmaster 2: Through The Portal Of Time; Condor; Nightflyers; Timestalkers
Avery, Margaret (act): The Folks At Red Wolf Inn; The Lathe Of Heaven; Something Evil
Avery, Paul (act): Stanley; Superman (1978)
Avery, Phyllis (act): The Last Child
Avery, Scott (act): Barracuda
Avery, Stephen Morehouse (wri): The Woman In White (1948)
Avery, Tol (act): It Came From Beneath The Sea; The Magician (1973)
Avery, Val (act): The Amityville Horror; Too Scared To Scream
Avianca, Frank (act): The Human Factor
Avianca, Frank (wri): Blood Song
Aviks, Valda (act): Nightbreed
Avil, Gordon (cin): The Black Sleep; King Dinosaur; The Sign Of Zorro; The Underwater City; Zotz!
Avildsen, John G. (dir, b. 1936): Neighbors
Aviles, Rick (act, 1953–1995): Ghost (1990)
Avison, John (act): No Blade Of Grass
Avital, Mili (act): Stargate
Avon, Roger (act): Daleks' Invasion Earth 2150 A.D.; Electric Eskimo; Kill Her Gently; Quatermass And The Pit
Avonne, Michelle (act): Time Walker
Avramovic, Milance (act): Arthur The King
Avranitis, Betty (act): The Next One
Avrech, Robert J. (wri): Body Double; The Secret Life Of Ian Fleming
Awalt, Sandra (act): Spasms
Awosika, Gregory (act): Dr. Black Mr. Hyde
Axberg, Ric (act): The Doll (1963, Swed)
Axel, Gabriel (dir): The Red Mantle
Axelrod, David (wri): Charlie Chan And The Curse Of The Dragon Queen
Axelrod, Garrick Paul (act): Vice Versa (1988)
Axelrod, George (wri, b. 1922): Goodbye Charlie; The Lady Vanishes (1979); The Manchurian Candidate; Paris When It Sizzles
Axelrod, Nina (act): Motel Hell; Time Walker
Axelrod, Robert (act): Alice In Wonderland (1985); Bates Motel
Axman, Hanne (act): The Red Menace
Axt, William (mus): Gabriel Over The White House; The Thin Man
Axton, Hoyt (act, b. 1938): Endangered Species; Gremlins; Retribution (1988)
Ayars, Ann (act): Nazi Agent
Ayer, Harold (act): Saturday Island; Tarzan, The Ape Man (1981)
Ayer, Lewis (act): see Ayres, Lew
Ayers, Curt (act): Midnight Offerings; Mortuary; Zapped!
Aykroyd, Dan (act, b. 1952): Casper; Coneheads; Exit To Eden; Ghostbusters; Ghostbusters II; My Stepmother Is An Alien; Neighbors; Nothing But Trouble; Twilight Zone
Aykroyd, Dan (dir, b. 1952): Nothing But Trouble
Aykroyd, Dan (wri, b. 1952): Ghostbusters; Ghostbusters II; Nothing But Trouble
Aykroyd, Danielle (act): Nothing But Trouble
Aykroyd, P.H. (act): Nothing But Trouble
Aykroyd, Peter (act & wri): Nothing But Trouble
Aylen, Richard (act): Possession (1973)
Aylett, Carole-Ann (act): Patrick
Aylett, Martin (act): Honey, I Shrunk The Kids
Aylesworth, Arthur (act): The Plot Thickens; The Return Of Dr. X; Shadow Of The Thin Man
Aylmer, Felix (act, 1889–1979): Alice In Wonderland (1950); The Angel Who Pawned Her Harp; The Case Of The Frightened Lady; The Clairvoyant (1934); Escape To Danger; The Frog; Gestapo; The Ghost At St. Michael's; The Ghost Camera; The Ghosts Of Berkeley Square; The Girl In The News; Hamlet (1948); The Hands Of Orlac (1959); The House In The Square; I Accuse (1958); Knights Of The Round Table; The Laughing Lady; A Man About The House; The Man In The Mirror; Masquerade; The Mummy (1959); The October Man; Paris Express; The Road To Hong Kong; The Saint's Vacation; She Shall Have Murder; So Long At The Fair; Spellbound (1941); Time Flies (1944); The Two-Headed Spy; The Wandering Jew (1933); Whispering Tongues; Your Witness
Aylott, Dave (act): Scouts To The Rescue
Aylott, Dave (dir): The Cakes Of Khandipore; The Charm That Charmed; The Club Of Pharos; The Crimson Triangle; Erratic Power; The Fairy Bottle; For East Is East; The Gloves Of Ptames; Her Fatal Hand; The Hindoo's Treachery; His Phantom Burglar; Hypnotic Suggestion; The Invisible Button; Jollyboy's Dream; The Kweer Kuss; A Merry Night; Mike And The Miser; Mike Murphy's Dream Of Love And Riches; Mike Murphy's Dream Of The Wild West; The Misadventures Of Mike Murphy; Mr. Tubby's Triumph; The Murder Of Squire Jeffrey; The Mystic Mat; The Mystic Moonstone; The Mystic Ring; Paul Sleuth, Crime Investigator: The Burglary Syndicate; The Pirates Of 1920; The Price He Paid; Professor Hoskin's Patent Hustler; The Rajah's Revenge; The Ring That Wasn't; Scouts To The Rescue; Selina-Ella; A Shattered Idyll; A Shocking Complaint; Some Fish!; The Sorrows Of Selina; The Strength That Failed; A Thrilling Story; Through The Ages; To Save The King; The Tricky Convict: or, The Magic Cap; The Tricky Stick; The Vengeance Of The Air; Vice Versa (1910); When Clubs Were Clubs; Willie's Dream Of Mick Squinter
Aylott, Dave (wri): The Price He Paid; Scouts To The Rescue
Aylward, Derek (act): The House On Marsh Road
Ayme, Marcel (wri): Mr. Peek-A-Boo
Ayre, Jon (wri): Surf Nazis Must Die
Ayre, Robert (wri): Mr. Sycamore
Ayres, Leah (act): The Burning
Ayres, Lew (act, 1908-1996, nee Lewis Ayer): Battle For The Planet Of The Apes; Battlestar Galactica; Damien-Omen II; The Dark Mirror (1946); Donovan's Brain; Earth Ii; End Of The World (1977); Fingers At The Window; The Last Generation; Of Mice And Men (1981); The Questor Tapes; Salem's Lot; She Waits; The Stranger
Ayres, Nancy (act): Flesh Gordon
Ayres, Richard (act): The House By The Lake; Virus
Ayres, Robert (act, 1914–1968): Battle Beneath The Earth; Cat Girl; Cosh Boy; Date At Midnight; First Man Into Space; Night Without Stars; The Road To Hong Kong
Ayres, Rosalind (act): Cry Wolf (1980); From Beyond The Grave; The Slipper And The Rose
Ayrton, Randle (act): Chu Chin Chow (1923)
Ayrton, Randle (dir): The Sands Of Time
Azab, Ali (act): Dawn Of The Mummy
Azman, Jank (act): Millennium
Aznavour, Charles (act, b. 1924): Le Diable Et Les Dix Commandements; Ten Little Indians (1974); Le Testament D'orphee
Aznavour, Charles (mus, b. 1924): Too Scared To Scream
Azulay, Ricardo (act): Anguish
Azuma, Tatsuya (act): Fugitive Alien
Azzara, Candy (act): Pandemonium; They Might Be Giants
Azzarelli, Itala (act): Forever Evil
Azzato, Joe (act): Making Contact
B. Lisa (act): Serpent's Lair
Baal, Karin (act): Die Toten Augen Von London
Babanini, N. (act): Vampyr
Babasa, Telly (act): Dance Of The Dwarfs
Babatunde, Obba (act): The Silence Of The Lambs
Babbage, Wilfred (act): Peter Rabbit And The Tales Of Beatrix Potter
Babbatunde, Obba (act): Dead Again
Babbins, Barbara (act): Blood Diner
Babbitt, Natalie (wri): Tuck Everlasting
Babcock, Barbara (act, b. 1937): Chosen Survivors
Babcock, David (act): The Brother From Another Planet
Babcock, Dwight V. (wri): Dead Man's Eyes; Devil Goddess; The Devil's Mask; House Of Horrors (1946); Jungle Captive; Jungle Moon Men; Pillow Of Death
Babcock, Larry (act): The Being Babel (Mus): Howling II
Baberske, Robert (wri): On Secret Service
Babo, Jennine (act): The Coming
Babson, Thomas W. (act): Snowbeast
Babus, Hulya (act): Countess Dracula
Baby Peggy (act, b. 1920): Jack And The Beanstalk (1924)
Baby Rose Marie (act): see Rose Marie, "Baby"
Bacall, Lauren (act, b. 1924, nee Betty Jean Perske): The Big Sleep (1946); Confidential Agent; The Fan; Misery; Murder On The Orient Express; Shock Treatment (1964)
Bacalov, Luis Enriquez (mus): Ghosts-Italian Style; La Strega In Amore
Bacarella, Mike (act): Primal Fear; The Relic; Vice Versa (1988)
Baccala, Donna (act): Brainscan; The Dunwich Horror
Bacci, Magasoli Erasmo (cin): The Last Days Of Pompeii (1959)
Bach, Barbara (act, b. 1949): The Black Belly Of The Tarantula; Caveman (1981); The Fish Men; The Great Alligator; The Humanoid; The Spy Who Loved Me; The Unseen (1981)
Bach, Catherine (act, b. 1954): Strange New World
Bach, Danilo (wri): April Fool's Day
Bach, Ernest Curt (act): The Trouble With Harry
Bach, Johann Sebastian (mus, 1685–1750): Les Enfants Terribles; Through A Glass Darkly; Tystnaden
Bach, Reginald (act): The Chinese Puzzle; The Hound Of The Baskervilles (1931)

Bach, Simone (act): *The Queen Of Spades (1966); What Price Murder*
Bach, Vivi (act): *Assignment K*
Bacharach, Burt (mus, b. 1928): *Casino Royale; Lizzie; Lost Horizon (1973)*
Bachardy, Don (wri): *Frankenstein: The True Story*
Bachelder, John (act): *Deadtime Stories*
Bachelor, Stephanie (act): *Lady Of Burlesque; Passkey To Danger; Port Of 40 Thieves; Secrets Of Scotland Yard; Undercover Woman*
Bachman, Harold (act): *The Pink Chiquitas*
Bachman, Richard (wri): see King, Stephen
Bachmann, Conrad (act): *Outbreak; Tremors*
Bachmann, Lawrence P. (wri): *Fingers At The Window*
Bachus, Michael (act): *The Couch*
Back, Ingrit (act): *The Ape Creature; On Her Majesty's Secret Service*
Backer, Brian (act): *The Burning*
Backes, Alice (act): *The Cat From Outer Space*
Backlinie, Susan (act): *Jaws*
Backner, Constance (act): *Hamlet (1912); The Mystery Of A London Flat*
Backus, Jim (act, 1913–1989): *Androcles And The Lion; Chomps; Francis In The Navy; Half Angel; Hello Down There; Johnny Cool; Macabre (1958); Man Of A Thousand Faces; The Man With A Cloak; Miracle On 34th Street (1973); Myra Breckinridge; Now You See Him, Now You Don't; Pete's Dragon; The Wonderful World Of The Brothers Grimm; Zotz!*
Backus, Richard (act): *Deathdream*
Baclanova, Olga (act, 1899–1974): *Freaks; The Man Who Laughs (1928)*
Bacmeister, Nelia (act): *Maniac (1980)*
Bacon, Buni (act): *The Private Lives Of Adam And Eve*
Bacon, Irving (act, 1893–1965): *The Gracie Allen Murder Case; The Lone Wolf Spy Hunt; The Lone Wolf Takes A Chance; Mr. Moto's Gamble; Shadow Of A Doubt (1943); The Thin Man Goes Home; Torchy Runs For Mayor; The Velvet Touch*
Bacon, James (act): *Charlie Chan And The Curse Of The Dragon Queen; Escape From The Planet Of The Apes; Planet Earth; Skullduggery*
Bacon, Kevin (act, b. 1958): *Apollo 13; The Demon Murder Case; Flatliners; Tremors*
Bacon, Lloyd (act, 1889–1955): *It Happens Every Spring; Miss Pinkerton; Moby Dick (1930)*
Bacon, Max (act): *Chitty Chitty Bang Bang; The Eyes Of Annie Jones; King Arthur Was A Gentleman; Privilege*
Bacon, Michael (mus): *Twisted*
Bacon, Norman (act): *Dracula Has Risen From The Grave*
Bacon, Paul (act): *The Asphyx; They Came From Beyond Space*
Badal, Jean (cin, b. 1927): *The Accident; La Poursuite*
Badalamenti, Angelo (mus): *Blue Velvet; The City Of Lost Children; Lost Highway; A Nightmare On Elm Street 3: Dream Warriors; Twin Peaks: Fire Walk With Me*
Badalucco, Michael (act): *Switch*
Badcoe, Brian (act): *Mata Hari (1985)*
Baddeley, Angela (act, 1904–1976): *The Ghost Train (1931); The Speckled Band (1931)*
Baddeley, Hermione (act, 1906–1986): *The Black Windmill; Cosh Boy; Counterspy; Information Received; Mary Poppins; Midnight Lace (1960); Scrooge (1951); The Secret Of Nimh; The Woman In Question*
Baddeley, John (act): *The Dark Crystal*
Badel, Alan (act, 1923–1982): *Agatha; Children Of The Damned; The Medusa Touch; Otley; Salome (1953); The Stranger Left No Card; Three Cases Of Murder*
Badger, Clarence (dir, 1880–1964): *Murder Will Out (1930)*
Badger, Russ (act): *The Gore-Gore Girls*
Badham, Jennifer (act): *Vampire On Bikini Beach*
Badham, John (dir): *Dracula (1979); Isn't It Shocking?; Reflections Of Murder; Short Circuit*
Badham, Mary (act, b. 1952): *Let's Kill Uncle*
Badie, Laurence (act): *Jeux Interdits*
Badila, John (act): *Serial Mom*
Badiyi, Reza (S.) (dir): *The Eyes Of Charles Sand; Of Mice And Men (1981)*
Badland, Annette (act): *Jabberwocky*
[illegible]
[illegible]
Baecker, Otto (cin): *Gold (German-Speaking Version)*
Baena, Carlos (act): *Adam And Eve*
Baer, Bill (wri): *The Quiet Earth*
Baer, Buddy (act, b. 1915, nee Jacob Henry Baer): *Africa Screams; Fair Wind To Java; Giant From The Unknown; Jack And The Beanstalk (1952); Snow White And The Three Stooges*
Baer, Byron (cin): *The Brain That Wouldn't Die*
Baer, Hanania (cin): *The Being; Echoes; Elvira, Mistress Of The Dark; Masters Of The Universe*
Baer, Jacob Henry (act): see Baer, Buddy
Baer, Johanna (act): *The People*
Baer, John (act): *City Of Shadows; Night Of The Blood-Beast*
Baer, Max (act): *Africa Screams*
Baer, Parley (act): *The Brass Bottle (1964); Cry For The Strangers; Halloween With The Addams Family; Killer In The Mirror; The Time Machine (1978); Two On A Guillotine*
Baer, Richard (wri): *Poor Devil*
Baere, Geoffrey (wri): *School Spirit*
Baerwitz, Jerry A. (dir): *Varan The Unbelievable*
Baez, Joan (mus, b. 1941): *Silent Running*
Baez, Sonya (act): *Blood Diner*
Baffert, Al (act): *Space Master X-7*
Bagdadi, Cecile (act): *Final Exam*
Bagdasarian, Carol (act): *Aurora Encounter; The Octagon*
Bagdasarian, Ross (act): *Rear Window*
Bagetta, Vincent (act): *Embryo; The Man Who Wasn't There*
Baggett, Jeffrey P. (act): *Nothing But Trouble*
Baggett, Lynn (act): *D.O.A. (1949); The Time Of Their Lives*
Baggett, Wendell (act): *Skullduggery*
Baggoo, Tosca (act): *The Little Match Girl (1987)*
Baggott, King (act, 1874–1948): *Dr. Jekyll And Mr. Hyde (1913, Imp); The Secret Of The Air*
Baggott, King (cin): *Dream A Little Dream; The Hand (1981); The Last Starfighter; Oh, God! You Devil; Vice Versa (1988)*
Bagot, Aileen (act): *Wuthering Heights (1920)*
Bahn, Roma (act): *Confess, Dr. Corda*
Baide, Doon (act): *Creatures The World Forgot*
Baietti, Al (act): *The China Syndrome*
Bail, Richard (act): *When A Stranger Calls*
Bailey, Anthony (act): *Captain Nemo And The Underwater City; The Deadly Bees; Robin Hood Junior (1975)*
Bailey, Bill (act): *Notorious (1992); Outland; Superman (1978); Superman II*
Bailey, Blake (act): *Lurking Fear*
Bailey, Bunty (act): *Dolls*
Bailey, Charles (act): *Robocop 2*
Bailey, Charles J. (act): *Red Alert*
Bailey II, Charles W. (wri): *Seven Days In May*
Bailey, Claude (act): *The Saint Meets The Tiger; The Unholy Quest*
Bailey, Cliff (act): *Between Midnight And Dawn*
Bailey, David (act): *Change Of Mind*
Bailey, Dulcie (act): See Gray, Dulcie
Bailey, Ewan (act): *Judge Dredd*
Bailey, Frederick (act & wri): *Equalizer 2000*
Bailey, G.W. (act): *The Gifted One; Mannequin; Runaway; Short Circuit; Warning Sign*
Bailey, Horace (act): *Change Of Mind*
Bailey, Jeff (act): *I Was A Zombie For The F.B.I.*
Bailey, John (act): *Celia; Circle Of Danger; High Treason (1951); It Happened Here; Journey To The Unknown; Man On The Run; Rasputin, The Mad Monk; Venetian Bird*
Bailey, John (cin): *Cat People (1982); Extreme Measures; Groundhog Day; Premonition (1972); Vibes*
Bailey, Leonard (act): *Tarzan, The Ape Man (1981)*
Bailey, Loretta (act): *The Haunting Of Hamilton High*
Bailey, Mark (act): *Doomsday Machine*
Bailey, Patrick (wri): *Spacecamp*
Bailey, Pearl (act): *The Last Generation*
Bailey, Raymond (act, b. 1907): *Five Weeks In A Balloon; The Incredible Shrinking Man; I've Lived Before; The Space Children; The Strongest Man In The World; Tarantula; Vertigo*
Bailey, Richard (act): *Captain Mephisto And The Transformation Machine*
Bailey, Robert (wri): *Yor, The Hunter From The Future*
Bailey, Robin (act, b. 1919): *Blind Terror; Danger Route; The Diplomatic Corpse;* [illegible]
Bailey, Thomas (act): [illegible] *Warriors: Taken By Force*
Bailey, Thomas (act): *I Was A Zombie For The F.B.I.*
Bailey, Van (act): *Wolf*
Bailey, Wanda (act): *Arnold*
Bailey, William N. (act): *Charlie Chan's Secret; The House Without A Key*
Bailie, David (act): *The Creeping Flesh; Legend Of The Werewolf*
Baily, Don (act): *Blackie's Redemption*
Baily, Hugh (act): *The Mutations*
Bain, Bill (dir): *What Became Of Jack And Jill*
Bain, Cynthia (act): *Pumpkinhead*
Bain, Gerard (act): *M.M.M. 83*
Bain, Imogen (act): *Robin Hood: Prince Of Thieves*
Bain, Sherry (act): *A Very Missing Person*
Bainborough, Bob (act): *Millennium*
Bainbridge, Hazel (act): *The Twisted Nerve*
Baines, John (wri): *Colonel Bogey; Dead Of Night (1945); The Hands Of Orlac (1959); Seven Thunders*
Bainridge, Jane (act): *The Ivory Ape*
Bainter, Fay (act, 1892–1968): *Dark Waters*
Baio, Scott (act, b. 1961): *Alice In Wonderland (1985); Zapped!*
Bair, David (act): *The Space Children*
Bair, Dina (act): *The Relic*
Baird, Alecs (act): *Children Shouldn't Play With Dead Things*
Baird, Anthony (act): *Dead Of Night (1945); The Hangman Waits; The Laughing Girl Murder; Night Comes Too Soon*
Baird, Dorothea (act): *Princess Clementina*
Baird, Harry (act): *Castle Keep; The Oblong Box; The Road To Hong Kong; Sapphire*
Baird, Jimmy (act): *The Return Of Dracula*
Baird, Leah (act): *The Secret Of The Air*
Baird, Leah (wri): *The Return Of Boston Blackie*
Baird, Peter (act): *Howard The Duck; Howling II*
Baird, Philip (act): *Quatermass II; 12 To The Moon*
Baird, Sharon (act): *Ratboy*
Baird, Yogi (act): *Robocop 2*
Bairn, William A. (wri): *Gli Orrori Del Castello Di Norimberga*
Bairnsfather, Bruce (act & wri): *Old Bill Through The Ages*
Baisho, Mitsuko (act): *The Crazy Family*
Bajema, Don (act): *976-Evil*
Bakaleinikoff, C. (mus, 1898–1966): *Dick Tracy (1945); Dick Tracy Meets Gruesome; The Falcon And The Co-Eds; The Falcon In Danger; The Falcon In Hollywood; The Falcon In Mexico; The Falcon In San Francisco; The Falcon Out West; The Falcon's Adventure; The Falcon's Alibi; The Falcon Strikes Back; The Falcon Takes Over; Genius At Work; Gildersleeve's Ghost; Journey Into Fear (1942); The Locket; Mystery In Mexico; The Velvet Touch; Window, The; Zombies On Broadway*
Bakaleinikoff, Mischa (mus): *Boston Blackie And The Law; Boston Blackie's Chinese Venture; Boston Blackie's Rendezvous; Bulldog Drummon At Bay (1947); A Close Call For Boston Blackie; Crime Doctor's Gamble; Crime Doctor's Manhunt; Have Rocket, Will Travel; It Came From Beneath The Sea; The Lone Wolf And His Lady; The Lone Wolf In London; The Lone Wolf In Mexico; The Millerson Case; One Mysterious Night; The Phantom Thief; The Saracen Blade; Screaming Mimi; Shadowed; Slaves Of Babylon; Thief Of Damascus; Trapped By Boston Blackie; 20 Million Miles To Earth; The 27th Day; The Werewolf (1955)*
Bakalyan, Richard/Dick (act): *The Bonnie Parker Story; Charley And The Angel; The Computer Wore Tennis Shoes; Now You See Him, Now You Don't; Panic In Year Zero; Return From Witch Mountain; The St. Valentine's Day Massacre; The Shaggy D.A.; The Strongest Man In The World*
Baker Twins, The (act): *No. 1 Of The Secret Service*
Baker, Aaron (act): *Repossessed*
Baker, Albert J. (act): *Sugar Hill*
Baker, Art (act): *The Beginning Or The End?; The Decision Of Christopher Blake; Once Upon A Time (1944)*
Baker, Becky Ann (act): *Jacob's Ladder*
Baker, Benny (act): *It Came Upon The Midnight Clear*
Baker, Blanche (act, b. 1956): *The Awakening Of Candra; The Handmaid's Tale*
Baker, Bradley (act): *Space Jam*
Baker, Brian (act): *Final Eye*
Baker, Brydon (cin): *Return Of The Fly; Valley Of The Dragons*
Baker, Buddy (mus): *Charley And The Angel; The Devil And Max Devlin; The Gnome-Mobile; The Monkey's Uncle; The Shaggy D.A.*
Baker, Carlos (act): *Tales From The Crypt*
Baker, Carroll (act, b. 1931): *A Kiss To Die For; The Miracle (1959); The Next Victim (1975); Orgasmo; A Quiet Place To Kill; Something Wild; The Watcher In The Woods*
Baker, Charles L. (act): *Witchcraft II: The Kiss Of Death*
Baker, Charlie (cin): *Abbott And Costello Go To Mars; This Island Earth*
Baker, Cynthia (act): *Blood Diner*
Baker, Daisy (act): see Dumont, Margaret
Baker, Del (act): *Batman (1989); The Black Windmill*
Baker, Diane (act, b. 1940): *The Cable Guy; The Haunted (1991); Journey To The Center Of The Earth (1959); Marnie; The Silence Of The Lambs; Strait-Jacket; The Wizard Of Baghdad*
Baker, Dylan (act): *Love Potion No. 9*
Baker, Eileen (act): *Wombling Free*
Baker, Everett (cin): *The Beast With A Million Eyes*
Baker, Fay (act): *The Gentleman From Nowhere; She-Devil; Trapped By Boston Blackie*
Baker, Frank (act): *Arrest Bulldog Drummond; Counterespionage; The Lone Wolf Spy Hunt; Tarzan And The Green Goddess; Tarzan's New Adventure*
Baker, Fred (act): *Strange Behaviour*
Baker, George (act, b. 1931): *Curse Of The Fly; Lancelot And Guinevere; The Laughing Girl Murder; On Her Majesty's Secret Service; The Spy Who Loved Me; The 39 Steps (1978)*
Baker, George (wri): *One Million B.C.; One Million Years B.C.*
Baker, George D. (dir & wri): *Buried Treasure*
Baker, Graham (dir): *Alien Nation; The Final Conflict; Impulse (1984)*
Baker, Graham (wri): *Crime Doctor*
Baker, Henry (act): *Seizure*
Baker, Henry Judd (act): *Neighbors*
Baker, Herbert (wri): *The Ambushers; Murderers' Row; Scared Stiff (1953)*
Baker, Ian (cin): *Iceman; The Punisher*
Baker, Iris (act): *The Crime At Blossoms; The Feathered Serpent (1934)*
Baker, James (act): *The Adventures Of Robin Hood*
Baker, Jane (wri): *Captain Nemo And The Underwater City; The Night Of The Big Heat*
Baker, Jay (act): *April Fool's Day; The Incredible Hulk Returns*
Baker, Jennifer (act): *Tommy*
Baker, Joe (GB act): *Where The Bullets Fly*
Baker, Joe (USA act): *Waxwork II: Lost In Time*
Baker, Joe Don (act, b. 1936): *Cape Fear (1991); Congo; Goldeneye; The Living Daylights; The Long, Dark Night; Mars Attacks!*
Baker, John (act): *Cat Girl; The Curse Of The Golem; Satellite In The Sky; Trog*
Baker, Jolyon (act): *A Ghost In Monte Carlo*
Baker, Kathy (act, b. 1950): *Diabolique (1996); Edward Scissorhands; Misery; Mr. Frost; To Gillian On Her 37th Birthday*
Baker, Kelly (act): *Slaughter High*
Baker, Ken (act): *Dressed To Kill (1980)*
Baker, Kenny (act): *Circus Of Horrors; The Empire Strikes Back; Labyrinth (1986); Return Of The Jedi; Star Wars; Time Bandits; Wombling Free*
Baker, Kent (act): *The Flesh And Blood Show*
Baker, Kirsten (act): *Friday The 13th-Part 2*
Baker, Lee Anne (act): *Breeders*
Baker, Lorris (act): *Kismet (1930)*
Baker, Mark (act): *The Man Inside*
Baker, Mark H. (wri): *Flight Of The Navigator*
Baker, Melville (wri): *Above Suspicion; Darkened Rooms; The Last Days Of Pompeii (1935)*
Baker, Michelle (act): *The Pink Chiquitas*
Baker, Nat (act): *Anguish*
Baker, Nellie Bly (act): *The Bishop Murder Case*
Baker, Nina (act): *The Dungeonmaster*
Baker, Norma Jean (act): see Monroe, Marilyn
Baker, Pip (wri): *Captain Nemo And The Underwater City; The Night Of The Big Heat*
Baker, Ralph (act): *Teen Witch*
Baker, Ray (act): *Dark Angel; Ed Wood; Heart Condition; Total Recall*
Baker, Rebekah (act): *Secrets In The Attic*
Baker, Richard A. (act): *The Incredible Shrinking Woman*
Baker, Rick (act): *The Thing With Two Heads*
Baker, Robert (S.) (cin): *The Hell-Fire Club; Jack The Ripper (1958); The Treasure Of Monte Cristo (1961)*
Baker, Robert S. (dir): *The Hell-Fire Club; Jack The Ripper (1958); Passport To Treason; The Steel Key*
Baker, Roy (Ward) (dir, b. 1916): *And Now The Screaming Starts!; The Anniversary; Asylum; Dr. Jekyll And Sister Hyde; The*

Fiction-Makers; Highly Dangerous; The House In The Square; Journey To Midnight; Legend Of The Seven Golden Vampires; The Monster Club; Moon Zero Two; The October Man; Quatermass And The Pit; Scars Of Dracula; The Vampire Lovers; The Vault Of Horror
Baker, Rupert (act): Lifeforce
Baker, Ruth (act): Dear, Dead Delilah
Baker, Sam (act): The Lost City; The Sea Beast; The Thief Of Bagdad (1924)
Baker, Scott (Thompson) (act): Rest In Pieces; Surf Nazis Must Die
Baker, Sean (act):An American Werewolf In London
Baker, (Sir) Stanley (act, 1928–1976): Cloudburst; Knights Of The Round Table; A Lizard In A Woman's Skin; The Man Who Finally Died; Richard II (1955); Sodom And Gomorrah; The Tell-Tale Heart (1953, Gb); Zorro (1975)
Baker, Susan (act): Tommy
Baker, Tom (act): The Curse Of King Tut's Tomb; Frankenstein: The True Story; The Golden Voyage Of Sinbad; The Mutations; Rollercoaster; The Vault Of Horror; The Zany Adventures Of Robin Hood
Baker, Tom (wri): The Sorcerers; Witch-Finder General
Baker, W. Howard (wri): Murder At Site Three
Bakewell, William (act): The Bat Whispers; Beyond Tomorrow; Cheaters At Play; The Iron Mask; Retik, The Moon Menace
Bakey, Ed (act): Dead And Buried; The Evil; The Other (1972); Zapped!
Bakke, Brenda (act):Demon Knight; Solar Crisis
Bakke, Karl (act): Trancers II: The Return Of Jack Deth
Bakken, George (cin): Kiss Daddy Goodbye
Bako, Brigitte (act): Strange Days
Bakshi, Ralph (dir, b. 1939): Cool World; The Lord Of The Rings
Bakula, Scott (act): Color Of Night; Lord Of Illusions
Balaban, Bob (act, b. 1945): Altered States; Close Encounters Of The Third Kind; 2010
Balaban, Bob (dir, b. 1945): Parents
Balaban, Burt (dir, 1922–1965): Lady Of Vengeance; Stranger From Venus
Balamos, John (mus): Hercules In New York
Balandin, John (cin): Alien Predators
Balaski, Belinda (act): Explorers; The Food Of The Gods; Gremlins; Gremlins 2: The New Batch; The Howling; Matinee; Piranha (1978)
Balasko, Josiane (act): The Tenant
Balbo, Ennio (act): Cinque Tombe Per Un Medium
Balcazar, Alfonso (wri): Lightning Bolt
Balcazar, J.J. (wri): Superargo vs. Diabolicus
Balcerzak, Chris (act): The Gifted One
Balch, Anthony/Antony (dir & wri): Horror Hospital; Secrets Of Sex
Balchin, Nigel (wri, 1908–1970): 23 Paces To Baker Street
Baldassarre, Raf (act): The Adventures Of Hercules
Baldauff, Patrick (act): Timestalkers
Balderama, Tony (act): School Spirit
Balderston, John L. (wri, 1889–1954): Berkeley Square; Bride Of Frankenstein; Dracula (1931 {English-Speaking Version} & 1979); The House In The Square; Mad Love; The Man Who Changed His Mind; The Mummy (1932); The Mystery Of Edwin Drood (1935); The Prisoner Of Zenda (1937 & 1952); Red Planet Mars; Scotland Yard (1941)
Baldi, Ferdinando (dir): David And Goliath
Baldi, Marcello (dir & wri): Marte, Dio Della Guerra
Balding, Rebecca (act): The Boogens; Silent Scream (1979)
Baldini, Renato (act): Teodora, Imperatrice Di Bisanzio
Baldoni, Sam (act): Evilspeak
Balduzzi, Dick (act): Zapped!; Zorro, The Gay Blade
Baldwin, Adam (act): Predator 2
Baldwin, Alan (act): The Devil Bat
Baldwin, Alec (act, b. 1958): Beetlejuice; Prelude To A Kiss; The Shadow (1994)
Baldwin, Caitlin (act): Eyes Of Fire
Baldwin, Daniel (act, b. 1959): Attack Of The 50-Foot Woman (1993); Bodily Harm; Nothing But Trouble; Too Good To Be True; Yesterday's Target
Baldwin, Dick (act): Mr. Moto's Gamble
Baldwin, Earl (wri): Africa Screams; Doctor X
Baldwin, Greta (act): Project X (1967)
Baldwin, Janit (act): Humongous; Phantom Of The Paradise; Ruby
Baldwin, Joan (act): Maniac (1980)
Baldwin, Judy (act): The Stepford Children
Baldwin, Karen (act): Spellbinder
Baldwin, Ken (act): Demon Knight
Baldwin, (A.) Michael (act): Phantasm; Phantasm II: Lord Of The Dead
Baldwin, Peter (It act): Lo Spettro
Baldwin, Peter (USA act): Houdini; I Married A Monster From Outer Space; The Space Children
Baldwin, Raaf (act): Echoes
Baldwin, Rebecca (act): The Fear (1994)
Baldwin, Robert (act): The Girl From Scotland Yard
Baldwin, Robert/Bob (M.) (cin): Basket Case 2; Frankenhooker; Let's Scare Jessica To Death; Stigma; Werewolf Of Washington; Zombie Island Massacre
Baldwin, Stephen (act): Bio-Dome; Dead Weekend
Baldwin, Walter (act): After Midnight With Boston Blackie; The Devil Commands; The Unsuspected
Baldwin, William (act, b. 1963): Curdled; Flatliners; Sliver
Baldwin, Zac (act): Neon Maniacs
Bale, Andy (act): Darkman (1990)
Bale, Christian (act, b. 1974): The Secret Agent (1996); Treasure Island (1990)
Bale, Ernest (act): The Man Without A Body
Baledon, Rafael/Raphael (dir): El Hombre Y El Monstruo; La Maldicion De La Llorona; Orlak, El Infierno De Frankenstein; Swamp Of The Lost Souls
Baledon, Rafael (wri): La Maldicion De La Llorona
Baleno, Frank (act): Neon Maniacs
Balentine, Dan (wri): Rattlers
Baley, Heather L. (act): Deadtime Stories
Balfour, Betty (act, b. 1903): Champagne
Balfour, Eve (act): The Mystery Of The Diamond Belt; Royal Love; The Woman Of The Iron Bracelets
Balfour, Michael (act, b. 1918): Barbados Quest; Batman (1989); Black 13; Cage Of Gold; The Diamond; Fahrenheit 451; Fiend Without A Face; The Flesh And The Fiends; Macbeth (1971); The Monster Of Highgate Ponds; The Oblong Box; Obsession (1949); The Prisoner Of Zenda (1979); The Private Life Of Sherlock Holmes; Quatermass II; The Secret Of The Forest; Secret Venture; Strangler's Web; Venetian Bird
Balfour, Noelle (act): Amazons (1986)
Balgobin, Jennifer (act): Dr. Caligari; Weird Science
Balik, Shelby (act): The Incredible Shrinking Woman
Balin, Ina (act, 1937–1990, Nee Ina Rosenberg): The Projectionist
Balin, Richard (act): Graduation Day; Schizoid (1980)
Balk, Fairuza (act): The Craft; The Island Of Dr. Moreau (1996); Return To Oz; The Worst Witch
Ball, Bob (act): Invasion Of The Star Creatures
Ball, David (wri): Hard Rock Zombies
Ball, Lucille (act, 1911–1989): Bulldog Drummond Strikes Back (1934); Lured; The Magic Carpet (1951); Roman Scandals
Ball, Nicholas (act): Lifeforce
Ball, Nova (act): Superstition
Ball, Robert F. (act): Doctor Death: Seeker Of Souls; Sherlock Holmes In New York
Ball, Robert Kent (act): Grim Prairie Tales
Ball, Suzan (act, 1933–1955): City Beneath The Sea (1952)
Ball, Vincent (act): The Black Rider; Blood Of The Vampire; Face In The Night; The Secret Of The Forest; Stop Press Girl
Ball, Warren (act): The Corpse Grinders
Ball, William (act): Suburban Commando
Ball, Zachary (act): Sometimes They Come Back
Ballantine, Sara (act): The Nutty Professor (1996); Phantom Of The Paradise
Ballantyne, William (act): An American Christmas Carol
Ballard, Gary (act): Bates Motel
Ballard, J.G. (wri): Crash (1996)
Ballard, John (dir & wri): Friday The 13th...The Orphan
Ballard, Kaye (act, b. 1926): Pandemonium
Ballard, Lucien (cin, 1904–1988): Berlin Express; Blind Alley; Crime And Punishment (1935); The Killing; The Lodger (1944); The Lone Wolf In Paris; Prince Valiant; Temptation (1946); The Undying Monster; The Villain Still Pursued Her; What's The Matter With Helen?
Ballard, Ray (act): Ssssss; Vamp
Ballatore, Thomas (act): Once Bitten
Ballen, Tony (act): Rattlers; Welcome To Arrow Beach
Ballesteros, Antonio (cin): The Colossus Of Rhodes; La Corona Negra; The Last Days Of Pompeii (1959)
Ballesteros, Maria Paz (act): Amador
Ballhaus, Michael (cin): Bram Stoker's Dracula; Outbreak
Ballin, Hugo (dir & wri): Jane Eyre (1921)
Ballin, Mabel (act): Jane Eyre (1921)
Ballinger, Art (act): The Swarm
Ballinger, Bill S. (wri): Crackle Of Death; The Strangler (1963)
Balliol & Merton (act): Champagne
Ballistrada, Lucio (wri): The Dead Are Alive
Ballos, D. (act): Blind Date
Ballou, Phil (act): Vampire's Kiss
Balme, Timothy (act): Dead Alive
Balogh, Emese (act): Mata Hari (1985)
Balpetre, Antoine/Antonio (act): The Burning Court; I Vampiri
Balrice, Brian (act): Dr. Caligari
Balsam, Martin (act, 1919-1996): The Bedford Incident; Cape Fear (1961 & 1991); Death Rage; The Eyes Behind The Stars; Murder On The Orient Express; Night Of Terror (1972); Psycho; The Sentinel; Seven Days In May; The Silence Of The Hams; The Six Million Dollar Man; Two Evil Eyes
Balsam, Talia (act): The Companion (1994); Crawlspace; The Initiation Of Sarah; The Kindred; The Supernaturals
Balson, Allison (act): The Hearse; Looker
Balter, Allan (wri): Earth II; The Man With The Power
Balter, Sam (act): Abbott And Costello Meet The Invisible Man
Balthoff, Alfred (act): Confess, Dr. Corda
Baltimore, Vicki (act): The Wiz
Baltzell, Deborah (act): The Devil And Max Devlin
Balutin, Jacques (act): The Great Spy Chase; The Spy I Love
Baly, Michele (act): Marte, Dio Della Guerra
Balzagette, Michael (act): The Hangman Waits
Bamattre, Martha (act): To Catch A Thief
Bamber, Judy (act): A Bucket Of Blood (1959); Up In Smoke
Bamberger, Hilary (act): Inn Of The Damned
Bamford, Freda (act): The Ipcress File; Sapphire
Bamford, Simon (act): Hellbound: Hellraiser II; Nightbreed
Banahan, Susan (act): The Face Of Darkness
Bancroft, Anne (act, b. 1931, Nee Anna Maria Luisa Italiano): Don't Bother To Knock; The Girl In Black Stockings; Gorilla At Large; Love Potion No. 9; Nightfall (1956)
Bancroft, George Pleydell (wri): Princess Clementina; The Ware Case
Bancroft, John (act): Holocaust 2000
Band, Albert (act): End Of The World (1977); Trancers II: The Return Of Jack Deth
Band, Albert (dir, b. 1924): Dracula's Dog; Face Of Fire; Ghoulies II; I Bury The Living
Band, Alex (act): Puppet Master II
Band, Bertha (act): End Of The World (1977)
Band, Charles (dir): Crash And Burn; Death Ride; The Dungeonmaster; Meridian; Metalstorm: The Destruction Of Jared-Syn; Parasite; Trancers; Trancers II: The Return Of Jack Deth
Band, Charles (wri): The Dungeonmaster; Meridian; Puppet Master; Puppet Master II; Subspecies; Trancers II: The Return Of Jack Deth
Band, Jackie (act): End Of The World (1977)
Band, Meda (act): End Of The World (1977)
Band, Richard (H.) (mus): The Alchemist; Bride Of Re-Animator; Crash And Burn; Dr. Heckyl & Mr. Hype; Dolls; The Dungeonmaster; From Beyond; Ghost Warrior; Ghoulies; The House On Sorority Row; Laserblast; Mutant; Parasite; Prison (1988); Puppet Master; Puppet Master II; Re-Animator; The Resurrected; Shadowzone; Silent Night, Deadly Night 4: Initiation; Terrorvision; Time Walker; Troll; Zone Troopers
Band, Taryn (act): Puppet Master II
Bandel, Murray (act): Angel Heart
Bandemer, John (act): Fargo
Bandera, Sergio (mus): A Polish Vampire In Burank
Banderas, Antonio (act, b. 1960): Eaters Of The Dead; Interview With The Vampire; The Mask Of Zorro; Never Talk To Strangers
Bane, Holly (act): Radar Secret Service
Banes, Lisa (act): Mother, May I Sleep With Danger?; The Presence
Banfield, Bever-Leigh (act): The Loves Of Dracula; World Of Dracula
Banfield, George J. (dir): Sexton Blake, Gambler
Bang, Joy (act): Dead People; Night Of The Cobra Woman
Bang, Poul (dir): Reptilicus
Banionis, Donatis (act): Korol Lir; The Red Tent; Solaris
Banjoko, Kashka (act): The Wiz
Bank, Ashley (act): The Haunted (1991); The Monster Squad
Bankerd, Chad (act): Serial Mom
Bankhead, Tallulah (act, 1903–1968): Fanatic; Lifeboat
Banks, Anthony (mus): The Shout
Banks, Brian (mus): Graveyard Shift (1990)
Banks, Christopher (act): They Came From Beyond Space
Banks, Don (mus): The Brigand Of Kandahar; Captain Clegg; Evil Of Frankenstein; The Frozen Dead; Hysteria!; Monster Of Terror; The Mummy's Shroud; Nightmare (1963); Rasputin, The Mad Monk; The Reptile
Banks, Doug (act): The Brain Eaters
Banks, Ernie (act): It Came Upon The Midnight Clear
Banks, Harold (cin): Giant From The Unknown; Missile To The Moon
Banks, Howard (act): The Living Ghost (1942)
Banks, Jonathan (act): Assassin (1986); The Fifth Missile; Freejack; Gremlins; She's Dressed To Kill
Banks, Leslie (act, 1890–1952): Busman's Honeymoon; The Door With Seven Locks (1940); Jamaica Inn (1939); The Man Who Knew Too Much (1934); The Most Dangerous Game; Strange Evidence; The Tunnel; Your Witness
Banks, Lynne Reid (wri): The Indian In The Cupboard
Banks, Marcia (act): Howard The Duck
Banks, Marilyn (act): Angel Heart
Banks, Monty (dir): What A Night!
Banks, Peter (act): Dreamchild; Highlander; Sebastian Star Bear: First Mission
Banks, Richard (act): Frankenstein Island
Banks, Spencer (act): A Christmas Carol (1984)
Bankston, Scott (act): The Outing
Bannen, Ian (act, b. 1928): Doomwatch; Fright (1971); From Beyond The Grave; Ghost Dad; Jane Eyre (1970); Psyche 59; Terror From Within; The Watcher In The Woods
Banner, Jill (act): The President's Analyst
Banner, John (act, 1910–1973): Black Angel (1946)
Bannerjee, Karuna (act): Devil
Bannerman, Margaret (act): Flames; Lady Audley's Secret (1920)
Bannister, Monica (act): Mystery Of The Wax Museum
Bannister, Reggie (act): Phantasm; Phantasm II; Phantasm II: Lord Of The Dead; Silent Night, Deadly Night 4: Initiation
Banno, Yoshimitu (dir & wri): Godzilla Vs. The Smog Monster
Bannon, Jack (act): What Ever Happened To Aunt Alice?
Bannon, Jim (act, b. 1911): Daughter Of The Jungle; The Devil's Mask; I Love A Mystery (1945); The Missing Juror; Phantom From Space; Soul Of A Monster; The Unknown (1946); Unknown World
Bannor, Marcy (act): Forever Evil
Bantock, Leedham (act): Santa Claus (1912); Scrooge (1913); The Tempter (1913)
Bantock, Leedham (dir): The Beggar Girl's Wedding; The Girl Who Took The Wrong Turning; Kismet (1914); A Prehistoric Love Story; Scrooge (1913)
Bantock, Leedham (wri): Mephisto; Santa Claus (1912); The Tempter (1913)
Baptist, Jennifer (act): The Toxic Avenger
Baptiste, Thomas (act): Dr. Terror's House Of Horrors (1964); The Ipcress File
Baquero, Manuel (cin): Sound Of Horror
Bara, Nina (act, 1920–1990): Missile To The Moon
Bara, Roy (act): The Last Wave
Bara, Theda (act, 1890–1955, nee Theodosia Goodman): Salome (1917)
Baragrey, John (act): The Colossus Of New York; Gammera, The Invincible
Barajas, Fausto (act): Cat People (1982)
Baran, Edward (act): The Brother From Another Planet
Baranski, Christine (act, b. 1952): Addams Family Values
Barash, Olivia (act): Grave Secrets; I Was A Teenage Sex Mutant; Through The Magic Pyramid
Baratelli, Joseph (act): Dr. Caligari
Baratier, Jacques (dir, b. 1918): L'or Du Duc; La Poupee
Baratier, Jacques (wri, b. 1918): La Poupee
Barba, Norberto (dir): Solo
Barbara, Paola (wri): Sword Of The Conqueror

Barbarian Brothers, The (act): Ghost Writer
Barbaossa, Joscik (act): 1984 (1984)
Barbash, Bob (wri): The Black Hole; Target: Harry; Tarzan And The Great River
Barbe, John (act): Scalpel
Barbeau, Adrienne (act, b. 1946): Bridge Across Time; Creepshow; The Darker Side Of Terror; Escape From New York; The Fog; The Great Houdinis; The Next One; Red Alert; Return To Fantasy Island; Silk Degrees; Someone's Watching Me!; Swamp Thing; Two Evil Eyes; Wild Women Of Wongo
Barbee, Buzz (act): Outbreak
Barber, Ellen (act): The Premonition (1975)
Barber, Gillian (act): The Stepfather
Barber, Glynis (act): Edge Of Sanity; Terror (1979)
Barber, J. Edwards (act): Forty Winks; Love In The Welsh Hills; My Lord Conceit; The Sands Of Time
Barber, John (mus): The Incredible 2-Headed Transplant
Barber, Lewis (act): Wuthering Heights (1920)
Barber, Nigel (act): Attack Of The Killer Tomatoes
Barber, Rowland (wri): The 30 Foot Bride Of Candy Rock
Barbera, Joseph (act): The Flintstones
Barbera, Joseph (dir): Jetsons: The Movie
Barbera, Michael (act): What Ever Happened To Aunt Alice?
Barbera, Neal (F.) (wri): The Prowler (1981); Too Scared To Scream
Barberi, Katie (act): The Garbage Pail Kids
Barberi, Paul (act): The Offspring
Barberini, Urbano (act): Demons; Terror At The Opera
Barbi, Vince(nt) (act): Astro Zombies; The Blob (1958); The Corpse Grinders; Sherlock Holmes In New York
Barbier, George (act, 1865–1945): Tarzan's Revenge
Barbieri, Annie (act): Time Walker
Barbieri, Franco (wri): Shock (1978)
Barbieri, Urbano (act): Gor; Outlaw Of Gor
Barboni, Enzo (cin): Kemek
Barboni, Leonida (cin): La Strega In Amore
Barbour, Bruce (Paul) (act): Endangered Species; Piranha (1978)
Barbour, Joyce (act): Sabotage; Stop Press Girl
Barbour, Terry (wri): Haunters Of The Deep
Barbour, Thomas (act): Dr. Cook's Garden
Barbour, Vincent (act): My Science Project
Barbro, Steve (act): Monolith
Barckhausen, J. (wri): Milczaca Gwiazda
Barclay, Caroline (act): American Gothic; Candyman: Farewell To The Flesh; Species
Barclay, David (GB act): —And Now The Screaming Starts!; Return Of The Jedi
Barclay, David (USA act): see O'brien, Dave
Barclay, Don (act):After Midnight With Boston Blackie; The Falcon's Brother; Frankenstein Meets The Wolf Man
Barclay, Elizabeth (act): The Resurrected
Barclay, Eric (act): Faust (1926)
Barclay, George (wri): Devil Doll (1963); The Village Of The Damned (1960 & 1995)
Barclay, Jerry (act): War of the Satellites
Barclay, Joan (act): Black Dragons; Blake Of Scotland Yard; The Corpse Vanishes; The Falcon In Danger; The Falcon Out West; The Falcon Strikes Back; The Shanghai Cobra
Barclay, John (Act): The Brotherhood Of Satan; Soylent Green
Barclay, Mary M. (act): The Headless Ghost
Barcroft, John (act): Morons From Outer Space
Barcroft, Roy (act): Another Thin Man; Billy The Kid vs. Dracula; Captain Mephisto And The Transformation Machine; Destination Inner Space; Retik, The Moon Menace; The Vampire's Ghost
Bard, Ben (act): The Bat Whispers; Black Angel (1946); The Leopard Man; The Seventh Victim
Bardawil, George ("Gallimard") (wri): Aimez-Vous Les Femmes?
Bardem, Juan Antonio (dir & wri): The Mysterious Island Of Captain Nemo
Bardem, Pilar (act): The Mummy's Revenge
Bardem, Rafael (act): The Mysterious Island Of Captain Nemo
Barden, James H. (dir, mus & wri): The Judas Project
Bardette, Trevor (act): The Beginning Or The End?; The Chance Of A Lifetime; Charlie Chan At Treasure Island; Dick Tracy (1945); The Monolith Monsters; Murder Over New York; Topper Returns
Bardo, Brick (act): The Thrill Killers
Bardo, Jeff (act): Vampire At Midnight
Bardot, Brigitte (act, b. 1934, nee Camille Javal):Spirits Of The Dead; Le Testament D'orphee
Bardot, Mijanou (act): Pirate Of The Black Hawk; Sex Kittens Go To College
Bare, Ashli (act): The Offspring
Bare, Jane (act): The Lost Boys
Bare, Richard (L.) (dir): Prisoners Of The Casbah; Wicked, Wicked
Bare, Richard L. (wri): Wicked, Wicked
Bareham, Adam (act): Return Of The Jedi
Baretto, Gil (act): Mermaids Of Tiburon; The World's Greatest Sinner
Barford (Films), Bent (cin): Journey To The Seventh Planet
Barge, Gene (act): Chain Reaction (1996)
Barham, Debi (act): I Was A Zombie For The F.B.I.
Barhydt, Frank (wri): Quintet
Bari, Lynn (act, 1913–1989, nee Marjorie Schuyler Fisher): The Amazing Mr. X; The Bridge Of San Luis Rey (1944); Charlie Chan In City In Darkness; The Falcon Takes Over; Francis Joins The Wacs; Home, Sweet Homicide; Mr. Moto's Gamble; Secret Agent Of Japan; Shock (1946); Sleepers West; Trauma (1963); Women Of Pitcairn Island
Barich, Robert (cin & wri): Mausoleum
Barilla, Giuseppe (wri): Sei Donne Per L'assassino
Barilla, John (act): Night Of The Zombies (1981)
Barille, Anthony (act): Friday The 13th-Part V: A New Beginning
Baring, Aubrey (act): The Golden Mask
Baring, Norah (act): Murder; Strange Evidence
Baring, Victor (act): Corruption; The Secret Life Of Ian Fleming
Barish, Mildred (wri): The Phantom Creeps
Barjavel, Rene (wri): Les Miserables (1957)
Bark, Peter (act): Burial Ground
Bark, William J. (act): The Search For Bridey Murphy
Barka, Badel (act): La Captive Du Desert
Barkas, Geoffrey (dir): King Solomon's Mines (1937)
Barker, Alexander Crichlow (act): see Barker, Lex
Barker, Ambrose (act): Peter Ibbetson; The Return Of Dr. Fu Manchu
Barker, Antonio (wri): The Amazing Mr. Blunden
Barker, Art (act): Mission Mars
Barker, Ashley (act): Threads
Barker, Chris (act): Short Circuit 2
Barker, Clive (dir, b. 1953): Hellraiser; Lord Of Illusions; Nightbreed
Barker, Clive (wri, b. 1953): Candyman; Candyman: Farewell To The Flesh; Hellbound: Hellraiser II; Hellraiser; Hellraiser II: Hell On Earth; Hellraiser: Bloodline; Lord Of Illusions; Nightbreed; Rawhead Rex; Transmutations
Barker, Danny (act): The Savage Bees
Barker, Debbie (act): The Stepford Children
Barker, Dennis (act): The China Syndrome
Barker, Eric (act): Carry On Spying; Maroc 7; The Mouse On The Moon
Barker, Florence (act): Jane Shore (1911)
Barker, Jess (act, b. 1914): The Night Walker; The Time Of Their Lives
Barker, Kenneth (act): The Kidnapped Child
Barker, Lex (act, 1919–1973, nee Alexander Crichlow Barker): The Battles Of Chief Pontiac; Black Devils Of Kali; Dick Tracy Meets Gruesome; The Girl In Black Stockings; The Girl In The Kremlin; In The Steel Net Of Dr. Mabuse; The Invisible Dr. Mabuse; Jungle Heat; The Pirate And The Slave Girl; The Price Of Fear; Robin Hood And The Pirates; Die Schlangengrube Und Das Pendel; Spy Today, Die Tomorrow; The Strange Awakening; Tarzan And The She-Devil; Tarzan And The Slave Girl; Tarzan's Magic Fountain; Tarzan's Peril; Tarzan's Savage Fury; 24 Hours To Kill; The Velvet Touch; Victim Five
Barker, Reginald (dir): Seven Keys To Baldpate (1929)
Barker, Ronnie (act): A Ghost Of A Chance (1968); Kill Or Cure; The Man Outside (1967); Robin And Marian
Barker, Tim (act): Morons From Outer Space
Barker, Will (dir): Princess Clementina; She (1916)
Barkev, Aram (act): Happy Birthday To Me
Barkham, Don (act): Inn Of The Damned
Barkhurst, Vernon (act): Fire In The Sky (1993)
Barkin, Ellen (act, b. 1954): The Adventures Of Buckaroo Banzai; Switch
Barkley, Charles (act): Space Jam
Barkley, Lucille (act): Bedtime For Bonzo; The Big Clock; Flight To Mars; Prisoners Of The Casbah
Barkoff, Victoria (act): Alien High
Barkworth, Peter (act): Downfall
Barlatier, Andre (cin): The Flying Dutchman
Barle, Gail (act): Alfred Hitchcock Presents
Barlow, Jeff (act): Chu Chin Chow (1923); Faust (1923); Further Exploits Of Sexton Blake-The Mystery Of The S.S. Olympic; A Garret In Bohemia; The House Of Peril; The Man In Motley; Rupert Of Hentzau (1915); The Sands Of Time; The Silver Greyhound (1919); Tut-Tut And His Terrible Tomb
Barlow, Jennifer (act): Grim Prairie Tales
Barlow, John Perry (act): Endangered Species
Barlow, Pat (act): April Fool's Day
Barlow, Reginald (act): Bride Of Frankenstein; The Mad Monster; Werewolf Of London
Barlow, Tim (act): Mary Reilly
Barnabe, Bruno (act): The Mummy's Shroud; Sinbad And The Eye Of The Tiger
Barnabo, Guglielmo (act): Miracle In Milan
Barnard, Ivor (act, 1887–1953): Beat The Devil; The Crime At Blossoms; Death At Broadcasting House; Escape To Danger; The Man Behind The Mask (1936); The Queen Of Spades (1948); Secret Lives; The Wandering Jew (1933)
Barnard, Michael (cin): The Invisible Kid
Barndollar, Harry (cin): The Unsuspected; When Worlds Collide
Barnell, Jane (act): see Roderick, Olga
Barner, Robert (act): Martin
Barnes, Barbara (act): Starcrossed
Barnes, Barry K. (act, 1906–1965): Bedelia; The Girl In The News; Law And Disorder; The Midas Touch; The Return Of The Scarlet Pimpernel
Barnes, Binnie (act, b. 1906): I Married An Angel; Murder At Covent Garden; No Escape (1934); I Pirati Di Capri; The Private Life Of Don Juan; Shadow Of The Eagle; The Three Musketeers (1939); The Time Of Their Lives
Barnes, Bob (act): Psycho IV: The Beginning
Barnes, Chris (act): Mary Shelley's 'Frankenstein'; Through The Magic Pyramid
Barnes, Christopher Daniel (act):Frankenstein: The College Years
Barnes, David (act): The Handmaid's Tale
Barnes, Deryck (act): The Cars That Ate Paris
Barnes, Donna (act): Dr. Jekyll And Ms. Hyde
Barnes, Eric (act): Time Flyer
Barnes, George (cin, 1893–1953): The Boy With Green Hair; Bulldog Drummond (1929); Condemned; Jane Eyre (1944); Ladies In Retirement; Rebecca; The Road To Bali; Samson And Delilah; Sherlock Holmes (1932); Sinbad The Sailor; Spellbound (1945); The War Of The Worlds
Barnes, Glenn (act): The Galaxy Invader; Nightbeast
Barnes, Gordon (act): The Angry Red Planet
Barnes, J.H. (act): Hamlet (1913)
Barnes, Joanna (act, b. 1934): Goodbye Charlie; Tarzan, The Ape Man (1959)
Barnes, Julian (act): Frankenstein: The True Story; The Haunted House Of Horror; Tam Lin
Barnes, Mike Gorell (wri): Where's Johnny
Barnes, Nicholas (act): Outland
Barnes, Patrick (act): Metamorphosis: The Alien Factor
Barnes, Peter (wri): Ring Of Spies; The Ruling Class
Barnes, Priscilla (act, b. 1956): Licence To Kill (1989); Lords Of The Deep; Stepfather II: Father's Day; The Time Machine (1978); A Vacation In Hell; Witch Academy
Barnes, Rayford (act): The Beginning Of The End; Bowery To Bagdad; The Three Stooges In Orbit
Barnes, Raymond (act): Jesse James Meets Frankenstein's Daughter
Barnes, Roger (act): Friday The 13th, Part VIII-Jason Takes Manhattan; I Still Dream Of Jeannie
Barnes, Ronald C. (act): Secrets Of The Phantom Caverns
Barnes, Sarah (act): Revenge Of The Teenage Vixens From Outer Space
Barnes, Susan (act): Bad Dreams; Freeway; Meet The Applegates
Barnes, Suzanne (act): The Children; Hello Again
Barnes, Theo (act): Brain Damage
Barnes, Tom (act): Freejack
Barnes, Walter (act): Blood Pen; Captain Sinbad; Day Of The Animals; Escape To Witch Mountain
Barnete, Robert (act): The Secret Of My Success
Barnett, Alan (act): Happy Birthday To Me
Barnett, April (act): Tales From The Hood
Barnett, Charles (act & wri): The Amazing Partnership
Barnett, Chester (act): Trilby (1915)
Barnett, Craig (act): Eraser
Barnett, David (dir): Faust (1910)
Barnett, Eileen (act): Killer In The Mirror
Barnett, Gregory (act): Switch
Barnett, Griff (act): Dick Tracy Vs. Crime, Inc.; The Millerson Case; Possessed (1947)
Barnett, Ivan (cin & dir): The Fall Of The House Of Usher (1950)
Barnett, Jim (wri): Death At Love House; Terminal Island
Barnett, Ken (wri): Secrets Of The Phantom Caverns
Barnett, Laurel (act): The Child
Barnett, Madge (act): The Mutations
Barnett, Patrice (mus): Carnival Of Blood
Barnett, Robbie (act): Return To Oz
Barnett, Steve (dir): Mindwarp
Barnett, Steven R. (act): Virtuosity
Barnett, Trevor (act): The Headless Ghost
Barnett, Vince (act, b. 1902): After The Thin Man; Bowery At Midnight; Captive Wild Woman; The Corpse Vanishes; The Death Kiss; The Falcon's Alibi; Jungle Man; Red Planet Mars
Barney, Maria (act): Lady Beware
Barnhouse, James (cin): Invasion Of The Girl Snatchers
Barnsley, Bill (act): The Sorcerers
Barolsky, Martin (act): Carnival Of Blood
Baron (Dog act): Street Trash
Baron, Carla (act): Sorority Babes In The Slimeball Bowl-O-Rama
Baron, Cherie (act): The Exorcist II
Baron, David (act): The Reptile
Baron, Geraldine (act):Targets; Time After Time
Baron, Helen (act): The Return Of Count Yorga
Baron, Joan-Carrol (act): The Monster Squad
Baron, Leo (act): Aimez-Vous Les Femmes
Baron, Lita (act): Savage Drums
Baron, Lunda (act): Hands Of The Ripper
Baron, Sandy (act): Leprechaun 2; The Munsters' Scary Little Christmas; Targets; Vamp
Baron, Sidney (act): The Adventures Of Robin Hood
Barondes, Elizabeth (act): Not Of This Earth (1995)
Barondess, Barbara (act): The Plot Thickens
Barone, Joe (act): So Sad About Gloria
Barone, Tracy (wri): Writer's Block
Barquet, Xavier (act): I'm Dangerous Tonight; The Toxic Avenger
Barr, Byron (act): see Young, Gig
Barr, Christopher (act): Lifeforce
Barr, Doug (Act): Deadly Blessing; The Unseen (1981)
Barr, Jackson (wri): Subspecies; Trancers II: The Return Of Jack Deth
Barr, Leonard (act): Diamonds Are Forever
Barr, Matthew (wri): Deadly Blessing
Barr, Patrick (act, 1908–1985): At The Stroke Of Nine; Black Orchid; Black 13; The Black Windmill; The Brain Machine; The Case Of The Frightened Lady; Death Of An Angel; The Flesh And Blood Show; The Gaunt Stranger; A Ghost For Sale; The Godsend; House Of Whipcord; Lady Of Vengeance; The Lavender Hill Mob; The Merry Men Of Sherwood Forest; Midnight At Madame Tussaud's; Murder At Scotland Yard; Murder At The Grange; Octopussy; The Return Of The Scarlet Pimpernel; Ring Of Spies; The Satanic Rites Of Dracula; The Story Of Robin Hood; Time Is My Enemy; Urge To Kill
Barr, Robert (wri): The Oracle (1952)
Barr, Sharon (act): Fugitive From The Empire; Trauma (1993)
Barr, Tim (cin): Atlantis, The Lost Continent; Dinosaurus!; The Time Machine (1960)
Barr, Tony (act): Between Midnight And Dawn; Scared Stiff (1953)
Barraclough, Roy (act): The Slipper And The Rose
Barrad, John (act): Santa Claus (1985)
Barragan, Ramon (act): Dr. Tarr's Torture Dungeon
Barrager, Nate (act): Just Imagine
Barrard, John (act): Tales From The Crypt; The Witches And The Grinnygog
Barrat, Robert (act, 1891–1970): The Baron Of Arizona; Charlie Chan In Honolulu; The Dragon Murder Case; Flight To Mars; The Florentine Dagger; Just Before Dawn (1946); The Kennel Murder Case; The Lone Wolf And His Lady; Marie Antoinette (1938); Son Of Ali Baba; The Time Of Their Lives
Barratt, Andy (act): The Bride (1985)
Barratt, Michael (act): The Magic Christian
Barraud, George (act): After Dark; Charlie Chan In London; Great Expectations (1934)

Barrault, Jean-Louis (Act, 1910–1994): Chappaqua; Le Testament Du Dr. Cordelier
Barrault, Marie-Christine (Act, B. 1946): The Medusa Touch; Perceval
Barray, Gerard (act): Baraka X-77; Scheherazade; Vengeance Of The Three Musketeers
Barre, Gabriel (act): Eat And Run
Barreiro, Ramon (dir & wri): El Otro Fu Manchu
Barrera, Rene (act): Dr. Tarr's Torture Dungeon
Barrese, Robert (act): The Strangers
Barret, Earl (wri): Poor Devil
Barreta, Guillermo (act): Vampire On Bikini Beach
Barrett, Adrienne (act): Dementia
Barrett, Amy (act): The House Where Evil Dwells
Barrett, Beatrice (act): Flesh And Fantasy
Barrett, Bob (act): Howling II
Barrett, Brandy (act): Screams Of A Winter Night
Barrett, Claudia (act): Robot Monster
Barrett, Clyde J. (act): The Wiz
Barrett, David (cin): The Fear (1994)
Barrett, Edith (act): Ghost Ship (1943); I Walked With A Zombie; Jane Eyre (1944); Ladies In Retirement
Barrett, Frank (wri): The Woman Of The Iron Bracelets
Barrett, Harold (act): The Fish And The Ring
Barrett, Jack (act): Just Imagine
Barrett, James Lee (wri): On The Beach
Barrett, Jane (act): Colonel Bogey
Barrett, Joe (act): Eat And Run
Barrett, John (GB act): Robin And Marian
Barrett, John (USA act): The Octagon
Barrett, Judith (act): The Gracie Allen Murder Case
Barrett, June (act): Dr. Strange
Barrett, Lawrence (dir): Discipline
Barrett, Liz (act): Superargo E I Giganti Senza Volto
Barrett, Majel (act): The Man In The Santa Claus Suit; Planet Earth; The Questor Tapes; Spectre (1977); Star Trek; Star Trek II: The Search For Spock; Star Trek IV: The Voyage Home; Star Trek: Generations; Westworld
Barrett, Nancy (GB act): The Fish And The Ring
Barrett, Nancy (USA act): House Of Dark Shadows; Night Of Dark Shadows
Barrett, Paula (act): Millennium
Barrett, Raina (act): Stigma
Barrett, Ray (act): The Reptile; Revenge (1971, Gb); Thunderbirds Are Go
Barrett, Reginald (act): Taste The Blood Of Dracula
Barrett, Robert (act): Strangler Of The Swamp
Barrett, Sean (act): The Dark Crystal; Four Sided Triangle; Return To Oz; Robin Hood Junior (1975)
Barrett, Tim (act): Blood Bath At The House Of Death; The Boy Cried Murder; The Deadly Bees; The Flying Sorceror; The Mummy's Shroud; The Slipper And The Rose; Talk About A Stranger; Where The Bullets Fly
Barrett, Tony (act): Dick Tracy Meets Gruesome; Dick Tracy's Dilemma; The Falcon's Adventure; Mystery In Mexico
Barretto, Amber (act): Little Monsters
Barrie, Amanda (act, b. 1939, nee Amanda Broadbent): Koroshi; One Of Our Dinosaurs Is Missing
Barrie, Barbara (act, b. 1931): The Caretakers; Child Of Glass; Guess Who's Coming For Christmas?
Barrie, Clive (act): Scars Of Dracula
Barrie, Frank (act): Jekyll And Hyde
Barrie, H.E. (wri): Frankenstein's Daughter (1958); Missile To The Moon; She Demons
Barrie, James M. (wri, 1860–1937): Male And Female; Peter Pan
Barrie, John (act): Lancelot And Guinevere; The Laughing Girl Murder; Life For Ruth
Barrie, Juan (act): Trancers II: The Return Of Jack Deth
Barrie, Maxine (act): The Fiend (1972)
Barrie, Michael (wri): Amazon Women On The Moon
Barrie, Mona (act, b. 1909, nee Mona Smith): Charlie Chan In London; The Devil's Mask; Ellery Queen And The Murder Ring; Just Before Dawn (1946); One Dangerous Night; Strange Fascination
Barrie, Nigel (act): Passenger To London; The Ringer (1928)
Barrie, Wendy (act, 1912–1978, nee Wendy Jenkins): The Barton Mystery (1932); The Callbox Mystery; A Date With The Falcon; The Gay Falcon; The Hound Of The Baskervilles (1939); Murder At The Inn; The Saint In Palm Springs; The Saint Strikes Back; The Saint Takes Over
Barrier, Edgar (act, 1906–1964): Arabian Nights; Cobra Woman; Eyes Of The Jungle; Flesh And Fantasy; A Game Of Death; The Giant Claw; The Golden Blade; Hurricane Island; Journey Into Fear (1942); Macbeth (1947); Phantom Of The Opera (1943); The Saracen Blade; Secrets Of Scotland Yard; Snow White And The Three Stooges
Barrier, Ernestine (act): Project Moonbase
Barringer, Barry (wri): The Death Kiss
Barringer, Dan(iel) (act): Deep Red (1994); Eve Of Destruction
Barringer, Michael (dir): Murder At Covent Garden
Barringer, Michael (wri): The Dummy Talks; Flat No. 3; The Man Who Made Diamonds; Murder At Covent Garden; Murder At Monte Carlo; Passing Shadows; Sexton Blake And The Mademoiselle; The Stickpin; The Third Clue
Barringer, Pat (act): Orgy Of The Dead (1965)
Barringer, Paul (act): The Monster Squad
Barrington, Clare (act): The Case Of A Doped Actress
Barrington, Rutland (act): Still Waters Run Deep
Barrio, Cusi (cin): Crime Zone
Barris, Don (act): Blood Diner
Barron (act): Trick Or Treats
Barron, Allison (act): Beverly Hills Bodysnatchers; The Haunted (1991)
Barron, Baynes (act): From Hell It Came; Space Monster; The Strangler (1963); Time Travelers (1976)
Barron, Bebe (mus): Forbidden Planet
Barron, Dana (act): He Knows You're Alone
Barron, Donald (act): La Casa Del Terror
Barron, Doug (act):Jacob's Ladder; Mr. Destiny
Barron, John (act): Hitler: The Last Ten Days
Barron, Keith (act, b. 1936): At The Earth's Core; The Land That Time Forgot; Mirror Of Deception; Nothing But The Night
Barron, Louis (mus): Forbidden Planet
Barron, Ray (act): The Legend Of Spider Forest; 10 Rillington Place
Barron, Steve (dir): The Adventures Of Pinocchio; Coneheads; Electric Dreams
Barron, Steve (wri):The Adventures Of Pinocchio
Barros, Esmeralda (act): The Devil's Wedding Night; Kong Island
Barrow, Arthur (mus): Beverly Hills Bodysnatchers
Barrow, Janet (act): Night Of The Demon (1957)
Barrow, John (wri): After Dark
Barrows, Dan (act): It Came Upon The Midnight Clear; Jekyll And Hyde...Together Again; Once Bitten
Barrows, George (act): Frankenstein's Daughter (1958); The Ghost In The Invisible Bikini; Hillbillys In A Haunted House; She Demons
Barrows, Henry (act): The Shock (1923)
Barrows, James (act): The Sea Beast
Barr-Smith, A. (dir): Death In The Hand; The Hangman Waits
Barr-Smith, A. (wri): The Hangman Waits
Barry, Alan (act): Captain Nemo And The Underwater City
Barry, Bruce (act): Patrick
Barry, Don "Red" (act): The Swarm
Barry, Donald (act, nee Donald Barry De Acosta): Dr. Dracula; Frankenstein (1970)
Barry, Fern (act): The Attic; Torchy Runs For Mayor
Barry, Frank (act): The Terrornauts
Barry, Gene (act, b. 1921, nee Eugene Klass): The Atomic City; The Devil And Miss Sarah; Guyana, Cult Of The Damned; L.A. 2017; Maroc 7; Subterfuge; Turn Back The Clock; The 27th Day; The War Of The Worlds
Barry, Georgetta (act): See King, Andrea
Barry, Gerald (act): The Crimes Of Stephen Hawke; Once In A New Moon
Barry, Gerard (act): The Unholy Night
Barry, Hilda (act): Fragment Of Fear; Horrors Of The Black Museum; House Of Mortal Sin
Barry, Ian (dir): The Chain Reaction (1980)
Barry, Ivor (act): Daughter Of The Mind; Fear No Evil (1969); The Island At The Top Of The World; The Six Million Dollar Man; Weird Science
Barry, Joan (act): Hutch Stirs 'em Up; Rich And Strange
Barry, Joan Nixon (act): Space Master X-7
Barry, Joe (act): Bell, Book And Candle
Barry, John (act): Dark Interval
Barry, John (mus, b. 1933): Alice's Adventures In Wonderland (1972); The Black Hole; The Deep; Diamonds Are Forever; From Russia With Love; Goldfinger; Howard The Duck; The Ipcress File; King Kong (1976); The Legend Of The Lone Ranger; The Living Daylights; The Man With The Golden Gun; Moonraker; Octopussy; On Her Majesty's Secret Service; The Quiller Memorandum; Robin And Marian; The Scarlet Letter (1995); Seance On A Wet Afternoon; Somewhere In Time; Star Crash; Svengali (1983); They Might Be Giants; Thunderball; A View To A Kill; The Wrong Box; You Only Live Twice
Barry, John (wri): Saturn 3
Barry, Julian (wri): Rhinoceros (1974)
Barry, Leon (act): The Iron Mask; The Temple Of Venus
Barry, Matthew (act): Ed Wood; The Wraith
Barry, Michael (dir): Stop Press Girl
Barry, Neill (act, b. 1965): Amityville 3-D
Barry, Patricia (act, a.k.a. Patricia White): The Beast With Five Fingers; Cry Wolf (1947); Dead Men Tell No Tales; The Tattooed Stranger; Trapped By Boston Blackie; Twilight Zone
Barry, Patrick (act): See Sullivan, Barry
Barry, Phillip (act): The Wasp Woman
Barry, Phyllis (act): The Invisible Menace
Barry, Raymond J. (act): Nothing But Trouble
Barry, Thom (act): Congo
Barry, Toni (act): Proteus
Barry, Tracy (act): The Being
Barry, Wendy (act): The Slipper And The Rose
Barry, Wesley (act): Bits Of Life
Barry, Wesley E. (dir): Creation Of The Humanoids
Barrymore, Drew (act, b. 1975): Babes In Toyland (1986); Batman Forever; Cat's Eye; E.T.-The Extra-Terrestrial; Firestarter; Scream; Waxwork II: Lost In Time
Barrymore, Ethel (act, 1879–1959, nee Ethel Blythe): Kind Lady (1951); Moss Rose; The Paradine Case; Portrait Of Jennie; Rasputin And The Empress; The Spiral Staircase (1946)
Barrymore (Sr.), John (act, 1882–1942, nee John Blythe): Bulldog Drummond Comes Back; Bulldog Drummond's Peril; Bulldog Drummond's Revenge; Dr. Jekyll And Mr. Hyde (1920, Famous Players/Para); Don Juan (1927); The Invisible Woman (1941); The Mad Genius; Marie Antoinette (1938); Moby Dick (1930); Rasputin And The Empress; The Sea Beast; Sherlock Holmes (1922); Svengali (1931)
Barrymore, John Blyth (act): Trick Or Treats
Barrymore (Jr.), John (Drew) (act, b. 1932): Arms Of The Avenger; The Clones; Nights Of Rasputin; Roma Contro Roma; The Trojan Horse; While The City Sleeps
Barrymore, Lionel (act, 1878-1954, nee Lionel Blythe): The Bells (1926); Devil Doll (1936); The Face In The Fog (1922); A Guy Named Joe; It's A Wonderful Life; The Mark Of The Vampire (1935); Mata Hari (1932); The Mysterious Island (1929); On Borrowed Time; Rasputin And The Empress; The Return Of Peter Grimm (1934); The Thirteenth Hour (1927); Three Wise Fools; Treasure Island (1934); West Of Zanzibar
Barrymore, Lionel (dir, 1878–1954): The Unholy Night
Barselow, Paul (act): The Comedy Of Terrors
Barsi, Judith (act, 1977–1988): Jaws: The Revenge
Bart, Jean (wri): The Man Who Reclaimed His Head
Bartalos, Gabriel (act): Spookies
Bartel, Paul (act): Amazon Women On The Moon; Chopping Mall; Gremlins 2: The New Batch; Heartbeeps; Killer Party; Out Of The Dark; Piranha (1978); Trick Or Treats
Bartel, Paul (dir): Death Race 2000; Private Parts
Bartel, Wendy (act): Death Race 2000
Bartell, Dick (act): Possessed (1947)
Bartelme, Jane (act): Evilspeak
Bartels, Louis John (act): The Canary Murder Case
Barth, Adam (act): Vamp
Barth, Ed(Die) (act): The Amityville Horror; The Man In The Santa Claus Suit
Barth, Helmut (cin): The Hellstrom Chronicle
Barth, Julie (act): Octopussy
Barthelmess, Richard (act, 1895–1963): Alias The Doctor; The Enchanted Cottage (1924); The Lash
Bartholomae, Hubert (cin): Making Contact
Bartholomae, Tricia (act): Explorers
Bartilson, Lynsey (act): Mrs. Santa Claus
Bartkowiak, Andrzej (cin): Species
Bartlam, Dorothy (act): The Ringer (1931)
Bartle, Claire (act): Killer Klowns From Outer Space
Bartle, James (cin): Death Warmed Up; My Best Friend Is A Vampire; The Quiet Earth; 20,000 Leagues Under The Sea (1997, Abc-TV)
Bartlett, Bennie (act): The Bowery Boys Meet The Monsters; Bowery To Bagdad; Dig That Uranium!; Jalopy; Jungle Gents; Master Minds (1950); Rear Window; Spy Chasers
Bartlett, Bonnie (act): The Legend Of Lizzie Borden; Salem's Lot; V
Bartlett, Cal (act): Invitation To Hell
Bartlett, Charles (act): Just Before Dawn (1980)
Bartlett, Hal (dir): The Caretakers
Bartlett, Hetta (act): Honour In Pawn; Melody Of Death
Bartlett, Jeanne (act): Werewolf Of London
Bartlett, Jeanne (wri): Man-Eater Of Kumaon
Bartlett, Juanita (wri): Midnight Offerings; Planet Earth
Bartlett, Martine (act): No Way To Treat A Lady
Bartlett, Rhett (act): Blood Diner
Bartlett, Richard (dir): I've Lived Before
Bartlett, Ronnie (act): Bulldog Drummond's Revenge
Bartlett, Vernon (act): Death At Broadcasting House
Bartley, Opelene (act): Once Bitten
Barto, Dominic (act): The Hearse
Bartok, Bela (mus, 1881–1945): The Shining
Bartok, Eva (act, b. 1926, nee Eva Sjoke): The Crimson Pirate; The Gamma People; Orient Express; Sei Donne Per L'assassino; Spaceways; Venetian Bird
Bartold, Norman (act): Capricorn One; Something Evil; Westworld
Bartold, Sheila (act): Project X (1967); Something Evil
Bartoli, Adolfo (Cin): Trancers II: The Return Of Jack Deth
Bartoli, Luciano (act): Top Secret (1978)
Bartolucci, Anita (act): Demons 2
Barton, Ann (act): What Ever Happened To Baby Jane? (1962)
Barton, Benita (act): Attack Of The Killer Tomatoes
Barton, Charles (T.) (dir, 1902-1981): Abbott And Costello Meet Frankenstein; Abbott And Costello Meet The Killer; Africa Screams; Island Of Doomed Men; The Shaggy Dog; The Time Of Their Lives
Barton, Dana (act): The Wacky World Of Dr. Morgus
Barton, Dee (mus): Play Misty For Me
Barton, Derek (act): Eve Of Destruction
Barton, Don (dir): Blood Waters Of Dr. Z
Barton, Dora (act): The Answer; The House Opposite (1917); Maria Marten (1928)
Barton, Gary (act): Coma
Barton, James (act, 1890–1962): The Scarf
Barton, Jannette (act): The Son Of Hercules In The Land Of Darkness
Barton, Joe (act): Blood Diner
Barton, Larry (act): The Human Duplicators
Barton, Michael (act): Blood Diner
Barton, Olivia (act): Ravagers
Barton, Peter (act, b. 1958): Friday The 13th-The Final Chapter; Hell Night
Barton, Rodger (act): Never Talk To Strangers
Barton, Winnie (act): The Brigand's Daughter
Bartram, Laurie (act): Friday The 13th (1980)
Bartsch, Ted (act): Flight Of The Navigator
Barty, Billy (act, b. 1924): Legend; Masters Of The Universe; A Midsummer Night's Dream (1935); Pygmy Island; Rumpelstiltskin (1987); The Story Of Snow White; The Undead; Willow
Barty, Jack (act): Gaslight (1940)
Barwell, Peggy (wri): Mrs. Pym Of Scotland Yard
Barwood, Hal (dir): Warning Sign
Barwood, Hal (wri): Dragonslayer; Warning Sign
Bary, Leon (dir): In The Hands Of The Spoilers
Barzell, Wolfe (act, 1896–1969): Atlantis, The Lost Continent; Bell, Book And Candle; Frankenstein's Daughter (1958); Homicidal
Barzman, Ben (wri, 1910–1989): The Boy With Green Hair
Barzyk, Fred (dir): The Lathe Of Heaven
Basaraba, Gary (act): One Magic Christmas
Basch, Felix (act): Enemy Agents Meet Ellery Queen; The Falcon In Danger
Basch, Hannes (act): I Love You, I Kill You
Basch, Harry (act): Coma; The Love War
Bascoe, Wally (act): Richard II (1955)
Basehart, Richard (act, 1914–1984): The Black Book; Cartouche (1957); City Beneath The Sea (1970); Cry Wolf (1947); Flood; The

Intimate Stranger; The Island Of Dr. Moreau (1977); Mansion Of The Doomed; Moby Dick (1956); Rage; Repeat Performance; The Satan Bug; Sole Survivor; The Stranger's Hand; Time Travelers (1976)

Basham, Jerry (act): Deadly Game; Fire In The Sky (1993)

Basham, Tom (act): Colossus: The Forbin Project; Night Gallery; The Psychopath (1973)

Basie, (William) "Count" (act & mus, 1904–1984): Cinderfella; Crazy House (1943)

Basil, Harry W. (act): The Seventh Sign

Basil, Toni (act): Rockula; Slaughterhouse Rock

Basile, Costy (act): The Power (1980)

Basili, Cristina (act):The Adventures Of Hercules

Basinger, Kim (act, b. 1953):Batman (1989); Cool World; The Ghost Of Flight 401; My Stepmother Is An Alien; Never Say Never Again

Baskcomb, A.W. (act): The Lodger (1932)

Baskcomb, Betty (act): The Man Who Knew Too Much (1956); Tread Softly

Baskcomb, John (act): The Final Conflict

Baskcomb, Lawrence (act): The Man in Black

Baskin, Alan (act): Chilling

Baskin, Ilya (act): Deepstar Six; The Name Of The Rose; 2010; Vice Versa (1988)

Baskin, William (act): Dr. Goldfoot And The Bikini Machine; The Raven (1963); Zombies Of Mora Tau

Bass, Alfie (act, b. 1920): The Angel Who Pawned Her Harp; The Bespoke Overcoat; A Challenge For Robin Hood; The Fearless Vampire Killers Or: Pardon Me, But Your Teeth Are In My Neck; A Kid For Two Farthings; The Lavender Hill Mob; Moonraker; Murder By Proxy; Pool Of London; Svengali (1954); Time Is My Enemy; Vice Versa (1947)

Bass, Bobby (act): Blood Beach

Bass, George (act): The Ghost Walks (1935)

Bass, Harriet (act): Madman

Bass, Jules (dir): The Hobbit; Mad Monster Party

Bass, Jules (mus): The Hobbit; The Return Of The King

Bass, Mony (act): Grim Prairie Tales

Bass, Ronald (wri): Black Widow (1987)

Bass, Saul (dir, b. 1920): Phase IV

Bass, Timothy (act): Matinee

Bass, Victoria (act): Too Scared To Scream

Bassani, Georgino (wri): The Stranger's Hand

Bassermann, Albert (act, 1867–1952): Der Andere; Foreign Correspondent; Invisible Agent

Bassett, Angela (act, b. 1958): Contact; Critters 4; Strange Days; Vampire In Brooklyn

Bassett, John C. (act): The Pit (1983)

Bassett, Linda (act): Mary Reilly

Bassett, Reginald H. (mus): Women Of All Nations

Bassett, Ronald (wri): Witch-Finder General

Bassett, Steve (act): Endangered Species

Bassett, William H. (act): Creator

Bassetti, Catherine (act): Hundra

Bassey, Jennifer (act): The Goddess Of Love

Bassey, Shirley (act, b. 1937): The Satanist

Bassham, Cynthia (act): Flatliners

Bassinson, Kevin (mus): Cyborg (1989)

Bassman, George (mus): The Canterville Ghost (1944)

Basso, Bob (act): Fantasies; Love At First Bite

Basson, Limpie (act): House Of The Living Dead

Bassuk, Craig (cin): Deathrow Gameshow; A Polish Vampire In Burbank

Bast, William (E.) (wri): The Legend Of Lizzie Borden; Mistress Of Paradise; The Valley Of Gwangi

Bastard (mus): She (1983)

Bastedo, Alexandra (act): The Blood Spattered Bride; The Ghoul (1974)

Bastel, Vickie (act): The Video Dead

Bastel, Victoria (act): Romeo Is Bleeding

Bastian, Stephan (act): The Fifth Musketeer

Bastiani, William (act): Blood And Concrete

Bastianoni, Giancarlo (act): Battle Of The Amazons; The Trojan Horse

Baston, Jack (act): Loves Of Carmen

Bastos, Othon (act): Os Deuses E Os Mortos

Bataille, Henri (wri): The Private Life Of Don Juan

Batalla, Rick (act): Eraser

Baralov, Alexei (act, b. 1928): Deryat'dney Odnogo Goda

Batalov, Nikolai (act): Aelita

Batanides, Arthur (act): The Leech Woman; The Unearthly

Barcheller, Richard (cin): Night Gallery

Batchelor, Graham (act): Scanners

Batchelor, Joy (dir, b. 1914): Animal Farm

Batchelor, Joy (wri, b. 1914): Animal Farm; The Monster Of Highgate Ponds

Batchelor, Melodie (act): Strange Behavior

Batchler, Lee (wri): Batman Forever

Bate, Anthony (act): Act Of Murder (1964); Ghost Story (1975); Treasure Island (1976)

Bate, Tom (act): Beverly Hills Bodysnatchers

Bateke, Fidel (act): Congo

Bateman, Charles (act): The Brotherhood Of Satan

Bateman, Frederick (act): Jekyll And Hyde

Bateman, Jason (act, b. 1969): Bates Motel; Teen Wolf Too

Bateman, Susanne (act): Friday The 13th-Part V: A New Beginning

Bates, Alan (act, b. 1934): Dr. M; Frankenstein (1993); Hamlet (1990); Mr. Frost; Royal Flash; The Shout

Bates, Barbara (act, 1925–1969): Fabulous Joe

Bates, Ben (act): Swamp Thing

Bates, Brigid Eric (act): Theater Of Blood

Bates, Charles (act):Shadow Of A Doubt (1943)

Bates, Florence (act, 1888–1954, nee Florence Rabe): The Brasher Doubloon; Heaven Can Wait (1942); Kismet (1944); The Mask Of Dimitrios; Les Miserables (1952); Portrait Of Jennie; Rebecca; The Secret Life Of Walter Mitty; The Son Of Monte Cristo

Bates, Harry (wri, b. 1900): The Day The Earth Stood Still

Bates, Jeanne (act): Back From The Dead; The Chance Of A Lifetime; Eraserhead; The Mask Of Dijon; Mom; Sabaka; Shadows In The Night; Silent Night, Deadly Night 4: Initiation; Soul Of A Monster; The Strangler (1963)

Bates, Jo (act): Fear (1996)

Bates, Kathrine (act): Vampire At Midnight

Bates, Kathryn (act): Arrest Bulldog Drummond

Bates, Kathy (act, b. 1948): Diabolique (1996); Dick Tracy (1990); Dolores Claiborne; Misery; Prelude To A Kiss

Bates, Kathy D. (act): My Best Friend Is A Vampire

Bates, Ken (act): Invaders From Mars (1986)

Bates, Michael (act, b. 1929): Bedazzled; A Clockwork Orange; Frenzy; Gulliver's Travels (1977)

Bates, Ralph (act): Dr. Jekyll And Sister Hyde; Fear In The Night (1972); Horror Of Frankenstein; I Don't Want To Be Born; Lust For A Vampire; Murder Motel; Persecution; Taste The Blood Of Dracula

Bates, Stanley (act): Theater Of Blood

Bates, Tom (act): In The Next Room; Through The Dark

Bates, William (act): Orgy Of The Dead (1965)

Bateson, Linda (act): The Village Of The Damned (1960)

Bateson, Timothy (act): The Anniversary; A Christmas Carol (1984); Evil Of Frankenstein; The Golden Rabbit; The Mouse That Roared; Nightmare (1963); Richard II (1955); What A Carve Up!; The Wrong Box

Bath, Angela (act): To All A Goodnight

Bathurst, Peter (act): Babes In Bagdad

Batinkoff, Randall (act): The Stepford Children

Batistelli, Luigi (cin): Dawn Of The Mummy

Batiz-Macaria, Javier (act): Dr. Tarr's Torture Dungeon

Batley, Dorothy (act): Kleptomania Tablets; The Master Crook Outwitted By A Child

Batley, Ernest G. (act): Guy Fawkes And The Gunpowder Plot; Kleptomania Tablets; The Master Crook Outwitted By A Child; The Master Crook Turns Detective; Through The Clouds

Batley, Ernest G. (dir): The Black Circle Gang; A Cry In The Night (1915); The Eleventh Hour (1916); The Enemy Amongst Us; The Foundling; Guy Fawkes And The Gunpowder Plot; Judgement; The King's Romance; Kleptomania Tablets; Lieutenant Daring, Aerial Scout; Lieutenant Daring And The Stolen Invention; The Man Who Forgot; The Master Crook Outwitted By A Child; The Master Crook Turns Detective; Retribution (1916); Tragedy At Holly Cottage; When London Sleeps; A Woman's Hate

Batley, Ernest G. (wri): Kleptomania Tablets

Batley, Ethyle (act): The King's Romance

Batley, Ethyle (dir):England's Future Safeguard; Into The Light; Saved By A Dream (1914)

Batley, Ethyle (wri): The Foundling; A Woman's Hate

Bators, Stiv (act): Polyester

Batory, Jan (dir & wri): O Dwoch Takich Co Ukradli Ksiezyc

Batson, John/J. Hastings (act): The Devil's Bondman; The German Spy Peril; God's Clay; The House Opposite (1917); The Lights O' London; London By Night (1913); Royal Love; She (1916); The Silver Bridge; The Strange Case Of Philip Kent

Batt, Bret (wri): Frankenstein Must Be Destroyed

Batt, Mike (mus): Wombling Free; Watership Down

Battaglia, Gianlorenzo/Lorenzo (cin): Demons; Demons 2; Miami Golem

Battaglia, John (act): Slugs

Battaglia, Rick/Rik (act): The Minotaur; The Mysterious Island Of Captain Nemo, The; Roland The Mighty; Ten Little Indians (1974); Treasure Island (1971)

Batten, Paul (act): Runaway; The Stepfather

Battiste, Arienne (act): I Come In Peace

Battistelli, Nino (cin): Gli Amori Di Ercole

Battistone, Catherine (act): Condor

Battle, Ed (act): Mother's Day

Battle, Lois (act): Something Evil

Battley, David (act): Krull; The London Connection; Rentadick; Willy Wonka And The Chocolate Factory

Batts, Reggie (act): Swamp Thing

Batty, Archibald (act): The Drum; The Vulture (1937)

Battyn, Skip (act): Doomsday Machine

Batytis, Brian (act): Student Bodies

Bauchau, Patrick (act): Phenomena; A View To A Kill

Baud, Antoine (act): Perceval

Baudish, Dominic (act): The Punisher

Bauer, Belinda (act): Fugitive From The Empire; RoboCop 2; The Servants Of Twilight; The Sins Of Dorian Gray; Starcrossed; Timerider

Bauer, Bill (wri): Slipstream

Bauer, Charita (act, 1922–1985): The Cradle Will Fall

Bauer, David (act): Danger Route; Diamonds Are Forever; Embassy; Endless Night; Torture Garden

Bauer, Frieda (act): The Cradle Will Fall

Bauer, Hans (wri): Anaconda

Bauer, Harry (act): Warlock Moon

Bauer, Kristin (act): Galaxis

Bauer, Michelle (act): Blonde Heaven; Cavegirl (1985); Death Row Diner; Hollywood Chainsaw Hookers; The Phantom Empire; The Tomb

Bauer, Steven (act, b. 1956): Alfred Hitchcock Presents; Primal Fear; Raising Cain; Snapdragon

Baum, L. Frank (wri, 1856–1919): The Patchwork Girl Of Oz; Return To Oz; The Wiz; The Wizard Of Oz (1910, 1925, 1939, & 1983); The Wonderful Land Of Oz

Baum, Ralph (dir): Diabolically Yours

Baum, Thomas (wri): The Haunting Of Sarah Hardy; The Manhattan Project; Night Visions; Secret Weapons; The Sender; Simon; Witness To The Execution

Bauman, Erna (act): El Vampiro Sangriento

Baumann, Anne Marie (act): The Last Days Of Pompeii (1959)

Baumann, Kathy (act): The Thing With Two Heads

Baumel, Rey (act): Stanley

Baumer (wri): When Worlds Collide

Baumert, Hank (act): Party Line

Baumgarner, James (act): see Garner, James

Baumgarten, Adam (act): Impulse (1984)

Baumgartner, James (act): Making Contact

Baums, Wilford Lloyd (wri): The Cat Creature

Baunescu, Vlad (cin): Subspecies

Baur, Harry (act, 1880–1943): Le Golem (1936); Rasputin (1938)

Baur, Tassilo (cin): Return (1985); Witchboard

Bautista, Aurora (act): Nightmare Hotel

Bava, Lamberto (dir): Blastfighter; Demons; Demons 2; The House With The Dark Staircase; Macabre (1980); Red Ocean

Bava, Lamberto (wri): Demons 2; Shock (1978)

Bava, Mario (cin, 1914–1980, a.k.a. John Foam): La Battaglia Di Maratona; Caltiki, Il Mostro Immortale; Hatchet For A Honeymoon; Hercules (1957); Shock (1978); I Vampiri

Bava, Mario (dir, 1914–1980, a.k.a. John M. Old): The Adventures Of Ulysses; La Battaglia Di Maratona; Diabolik; Dr. Goldfoot And The Girl Bombs; Ercole Al Centro Della Terra; Five Dolls For An August Moon; La Frusta E Il Corpo; Hatchet For A Honeymoon; House Of Exorcism; Gli Invasori; Knives Of The Avenger; La Maschera Del Demonio; Operazione Paura; Gli Orrori Del Castello Di Noremberga; La Ragazza Che Sapeva Troppo; Sei Donne Per L'assassino; Shock (1978); Terrore Nello Spazio; I Tre Volti Della Paura; Twitch Of The Death Nerve; The Wonders Of Aladdin

Bava, Mario (wri, 1914–1980): Diabolik; Ercole Al Centro Della Terra; La Ragazza Che Sapeva Troppo; Sei Donne Per L'assassino; I Tre Volti Della Paura; Twitch Of The Death Nerve

Bavier, Frances (act, 1903–1989): The Day The Earth Stood Still; Man In The Attic (1953)

Bawden, Nina (wri): The Solitary Child

Bax (mus): Alien Warrior

Baxley, Barbara (act, 1927–1990): Countdown; The Exorcist II; No Way To Treat A Lady; A Stranger Is Watching

Baxley, Craig (act): Mind Over Murder; Nightwing

Baxley, Craig R. (dir): I Come In Peace

Baxley, Gary (act): I Come In Peace

Baxley, Jack (act):The Gracie Allen Murder Case

Baxley, Kristin (act): I Come In Peace

Baxley, Paul (act): The Boy Who Cried Werewolf

Baxt, David (act): Batman (1989); Inseminoid; The Shining

Baxt, George (wri): Circus Of Horrors; City Of The Dead; The Shadow Of The Cat; Strangler's Web; Tower Of Evil; Vampire Circus

Baxter, Alan (act, 1909–1976): The End Of The Line; The Lone Wolf Strikes; The Night Key; Phantom Lady; Saboteur; The Set-Up; Shadow Of The Thin Man; Willard

Baxter, Anne (act, 1923–1985): Angel On My Shoulder (1946); The Busy Body; Chase A Crooked Shadow; Guest In The House; I Confess; The Luck Of The Irish; Masks Of Death; Nero Wolfe; Ritual Of Evil

Baxter, Beryl (act): Counterspy; The Man With The Twisted Lip

Baxter, Carol (act): The Loves Of Dracula; World Of Dracula

Baxter, Deborah (act):A High Wind In Jamaica

Baxter, George (act): She-Devil; Unknown World

Baxter, Jane (act, b. 1909, nee Feodora Forde): All Hallowe'en; The Clairvoyant (1934); Death Of An Angel; The Man Behind The Mask (1936)

Baxter, Jerry M. (act): Jaws 2

Baxter, John (dir): The Dragon Of Pendragon Castle; Old Mother Riley's Ghosts

Baxter, John (wri): The Time Guardian

Baxter, Keith (act, b. 1933): Melody Of Hate

Baxter, Les (mus): The Beast Within; The Black Sleep; The Bride And The Beast; The Comedy Of Terrors; Cry Of The Banshee; Dr. Goldfoot And The Bikini Machine; The Dunwich Horror; Frogs; The Ghost In The Invisible Bikini; House Of Usher; How To Stuff A Wild Bikini; The Invisible Boy; The Lone Ranger And The Lost City Of Gold; The Loves Of Dracula; Macabre (1958); Master Of The World; Gli Orrori Del Castello Di Noremberga; Panic In Year Zero; Pharaoh's Curse; The Pit And The Pendulum (1961); The Raven (1963); Tales Of Terror; Target: Harry; Voodoo Island; Wild In The Streets; A Woman's Devotion; World Of Dracula; X—The Man With The X-Ray Eyes

Baxter, Lynsey (act): The Girl In A Swing

Baxter, Meredith (act, b. 1947): Ben; The Cat Creature; The Night That Panicked America

Baxter, Mort (act): The Devil's Wedding Night

Baxter, Warner (act, 1893–1951): Behind That Curtain; Crime Doctor; Crime Doctor's Courage; Crime Doctor's Diary; Crime Doctor's Gamble; Crime Doctor's Manhunt; Crime Doctor's Strangest Case; Crime Doctor's Warning; The Devil's Henchman; Earthbound (1940); The Gentleman From Nowhere; Just Before Dawn (1946); Lady In The Dark; The Millerson Case; Shadows In The Night; Such Men Are Dangerous; West Of Zanzibar

Bay, Eddie (act): Street Trash

Bay, Frances (act): The Attic; Blue Velvet; Nomads; The Pit And The Pendulum (1990); Single White Female

Bay, Michael (dir): Armageddon

Bay, Sara (act, nee Rosalba Neri): Devil's Wedding Night; The; La Figlia Di Frankenstein

Bayer, Al (act): Gog

Bayer, Daniel (act): Making Contact

Bayer, Gary (act): Creator; It Came Upon The Midnight Clear; Psycho II; Sanctuary Of Fear; Starflight: The Plane That Couldn't Land

Bayfield, Peggy (act): Sherlock Holmes (1922)

Bayldon, Geoffrey (act, b. 1929): Assignment K; Asylum; Casino Royale; Dead Man's Chest; Frankenstein Must Be Destroyed; Gawain And The Green Knight; Horror Of Dracula; The House That Dripped Blood; Journey To The Unknown; The Monster Club; Otley; Scrooge (1970); The Slipper And The Rose; Tales From The Crypt; The 2-Headed Spy

Bayler, Terence (act): Brazil; Macbeth (1971)

Bayley, E.T. (wri): The Mistletoe Bough

Bayley, Hilda (act): The Barton Mystery (1920)

Bayley, Laura (act): Cinderella And The Fairy Godmother
Bayliff, H. Lane (act): The Shadow Between
Baylis, Sharon (act): Threads
Bayliss, Claire (act): Deja Vu
Bayliss, Jean (act): Lady In The Fog
Bayliss, John (act): The Intruder (1981); Spasms; Virus
Bayliss, Peter (act): From Russia With Love; Mr. Selkie; Vampira
Baylor, Hal (act): The Barefoot Executive; A Boy And His Dog; Prince Valiant; This Is My Love; Tobor The Great
Bayly, Frank G. (dir): The Lifeguardsman
Bayly, Johnson (act): How To Murder A Rich Uncle
Baynes, Gay (act): Slipstream
Bayonas, Andreas (act): Howling II
Bazaldua, Charles (act): Nightmare On The 13th Floor
Bazelli, Bojan (cin): The Body Snatchers; The Haunting Of Sarah Hardy; Pumpkinhead
Baziga (act): King Solomon's Mines (1949)
Bazoky, Loris (act): Yeti
Bazzoni, Camillo (dir): Invasione
Beach, Jill (act): Flight Of The Navigator
Beach, Larry (act): James Tont: Operation Goldsinger
Beach, Laurie (act): The Aliens Are Coming
Beach, Michael (act): Late For Dinner
Beach, Richard (act): Dick Tracy (1937); The Mandarin Mystery
Beacham, Stephanie (act, b. 1949): And Now The Screaming Starts!; A Distant Scream; Dracula A.D. 1972; House Of Mortal Sin; Inseminoid; The Nightcomers; Schizo (1977); Tam Lin
Beach Boys, The (act): The Monkey's Uncle
Beagle, E. Hampton (act): The China Syndrome; Demon Seed
Beagle, Peter S. (wri): The Lord Of The Rings
Beahan, Charles (wri): Murder By The Clock
Beaird, Betty (act): Through The Magic Pyramid
Beaird, John (wri): My Bloody Valentine
Beal, Cindy (act): Slavegirls From Beyond Infinity
Beal, John (act, 1909-1997, nee J. Alexander Bliedung): Amityville 3-D; The Bride (1973); The Cat And The Canary (1939); Ellery Queen And The Perfect Crime; Key Witness; The Legend Of Lizzie Borden; Les Miserables (1935); The Vampire (1957)
Beal, John (mus): The Funhouse (1981); Terror In The Aisles
Beal, Kay (act): The New House On The Left
Bealby, George (act): The Last Hour
Beale, Chris (act): Copycat
Beale, Richard (act): Treasure Island (1990)
Beall, Betty (act): The Day Mars Invaded Earth
Beall, Nada (act): The Tell-Tale Heart (1960)
Beals, Jennifer (act, b. 1963): Blood And Concrete; The Bride (1985); Dr. M; Night Owl; Vampire's Kiss
Beames, David (act): Dark Water
Bean, Alan L. (act): For All Mankind
Bean, Orson (act, b. 1928): The Hobbit; Innerspace; The Return Of The King
Bean, Robert (act): Creature From The Haunted Sea
Bean, Sean (act, b. 1959): Goldeneye
Beane, Hilary (act): Zapped!
Beano (act): Deathrow Gameshow
Beanty, Sand (act): The Son Of Hercules In The Land Of Darkness
Beard, Jocelyn (wri): Igor And The Lunatics
Bearden, Jim (act): Haunted By Her Past; Rona Jaffe's Mazes And Monsters; Virus
Beardley, Richard (act): La Figlia Di Frankenstein
Beardsley, Alice (act): *Batteries Not Included
Bearse, Amanda (act): Fright Night; The Goddess Of Love
Beart, Emmanuelle (act, b. 1965): Date With An Angel; Mission: Impossible
Beascoeche, Frank (cin): Buck Rogers In The 25th Century; Deadly Game
Beasley, Allyce (act): Rumpelstiltskin (1996); Silent Night, Deadly Night 4: Initiation
Beasley, Darrel (act): Angel Heart
Beasley, Nicolette (cin): The Quilt Of Hathor
Beasley, Stephen (act): Angel Heart
Beat, Nicky (act): Trancers
Beatie, May (act): Mad Love
Beaton, Betsy (wri): The Boy With Green Hair
Beaton, Bruce (act): Never Talk To Strangers
Beaton, Mary Louise (act): Message From Mars (1921)
Beaton, Timothy (act): Return Of A Stranger
Beattie, Alan (dir): Delusion
Beattie, John McIntosh (act): see Warwick, John
Beatts, Anne (wri): Nightlife (1989)
Beatty, Chuck (act): Horror High
Beatty, Clyde (act, 1904–1965): Africa Screams; Darkest Africa; The Lost Jungle; Perils Of The Jungle (1953); Ring Of Fear
Beatty, Diane (act): Dawn Of The Mummy
Beatty, John (act): Spookies
Beatty, May (act): The Benson Murder Case; Dressed To Kill (1941); I Wake Up Screaming
Beatty, Ned (act, b. 1937): Alfred Hitchcock Presents; Captain America (1992); Dying Room Only; Ed And His Dead Mother; Exorcist II: The Heretic; The Incredible Shrinking Woman; Prelude To A Kiss; Purple People Eater; Repossessed; Rolling Vengeance; Superman (1978); Superman II; Time Trackers; The Unholy
Beatty, Robert (act, 1909–1992): Calling Bulldog Drummond; Counterblast; The Net; The Oracle (1952); Portrait From Life; Postmark For Danger; The Shakedown; Sleepwalker (1975); The Spaceman And King Arthur; Superman II; Tarzan And The Lost Safari; The Twenty Questions Murder; 2001: A Space Odyssey
Beatty, Scott (act): Killer Klowns From Outer Space
Beatty, Warren (act, b. 1937): Dick Tracy (1990); Heaven Can Wait (1978); Lilith
Beatty, Warren (dir & wri, b. 1937): Heaven Can Wait (1978)
Beau, Bill (act): The Octagon
Beau, Kitty (act): The Octagon
Beauchamp, D.D. (wri): Abbott And Costello Go To Mars
Beauchamp, Linsey (act): Supergirl (1984)
Beauchamp, Richard (act): Secrets Of The Phantom Caverns
Beauchard, Jean-Guy (act): Oh Heavenly Dog
Beaudine, William (dir, 1892–1970): The Ape Man; Billy The Kid Vs. Dracula; The Boys From Brooklyn; The Chinese Ring; The Face Of Marble; The Feathered Serpent (1948); Ghost Chasers; Ghost Crazy; Ghosts On The Loose; The Golden Eye; Hold That Line; Jalopy; The Living Ghost (1942); Mr. Hex; The Mystery Of The 13th Guest; No Holds Barred; Paris Playboys; Phantom Killer; Philo Vance Returns; The Shanghai Chest; Spook Busters; Too Many Winners; Torchy Blane In Chinatown; Torchy Gets Her Man; Up In Smoke; Voodoo Man
Beaulieu, Candice (act): Darkman II: The Return Of Durant
Beaulieu, Robert (act): The Annihilator
Beaulieu, Trace (act & wri): Mystery Science Theater 3000: The Movie
Beaumont, Charles (Can wri): Brain Dead
Beaumont, Charles (USA wri, 1929–1967): The Haunted Palace (1963); Journey Into Darkness; The Masque Of The Red Death (1964); Night Of The Eagle; The Premature Burial; Queen Of Outer Space; 7 Faces Of Dr. Lao; The Wonderful World Of The Brothers Grimm
Beaumont, Diana (act): Black Limelight; Murder On Monday; The Old Man; A Stolen Face
Beaumont, Ena (act): The Girl From Downing Street; The Golden Web
Beaumont, Evelyn (act): A Message From Mars (1913)
Beaumont, Gabrielle (dir): Beastmaster II: The Eye Of Braxus; The Godsend
Beaumont, Hugh (act, 1909–1982): Apology For Murder; Blonde For A Day; The Human Duplicators; The Lady Confesses; Larceny In Her Heart; Lost Continent (1951); The Mole People; Money Madness; Murder Is My Business; Pier 23; The Seventh Victim; Three On A Ticket; Too Many Winners
Beaumont, Lucy (act): Devil Doll (1936)
Beaumont, Richard (act): Digby-The Biggest Dog In The World; Only A Scream Away; Scrooge (1970); Who Slew Auntie Roo?
Beaumont, Roger (act): The Bible
Beaumont, Susan (act): The Spaniard's Curse; Web Of Suspicion
Beaumont, Victor (act): The Kremlin Letter; Shoot To Kill (1961)
Beaune, Caroline (act): The Phantom Of The Opera (1990)
Beautiful Bobby (act): Blood Diner
Beauvais, David (act): The Iliac Passion
Beauvais, Marie-Claude (act): Alien High
Beauvais, Richard (act): The Iliac Passion
Beauvy, Nicholas (act): Rage; The Toolbox Murders
Beaver, Jack (mus): Alibi (1942); It Happened Here
Beaver, Paul (mus): The Last Days Of Man On Earth
Beavers, Louise (act, 1904–1962): Shadow Of The Thin Man
Beavis, Arthur (cin): The Quiller Memorandum
Bebout, Amy (act): Night Of The Hunter (1991)
Beccaria, Mario (act): Le Boucher
Bechard, Gorman (dir & wri, b. 1959): Psychos In Love
Becher, John C. (act, 1923–1986): Gremlins
Bechner, Renata (act): Making Contact
Bechthold, Keri (act): Offerings
Beck, Billy (act): The Blob (1988); Invitation To Hell; Leprechaun 2
Beck, Bonnie (act): Wild Thing
Beck, Christophe (mus): Crossworlds
Beck, Christopher (act): Greystoke: The Legend Of Tarzan, Lord Of The Apes
Beck, Cornish (act): The Lone Wolf (1917)
Beck, Danny (act): The Living Ghost (1942); Man Of A Thousand Faces
Beck, Edward (wri): Trapped By Boston Blackie
Beck, Glen(n) (act): The Bedford Incident; Dr. Strangelove, Or: How I Learned To Stop Worrying And Love The Bomb
Beck, James (act): Troll
Beck, Jenny (act): Troll
Beck, John (1920s act): The Cave Girl (1921); The Shock (1923)
Beck, John (act): Audrey Rose; Cyborg 2087; Nightmare Honeymoon; Rollerball; Sleeper; The Time Machine (1978)
Beck, Julian (act): Poltergeist II: The Other Side
Beck, Karen (act): Party Line
Beck, Kimberly (act): Friday The 13th-The Final Chapter; Maid To Order
Beck, Martin (act): Hellhole
Beck, Maureen (act): The Golden Rabbit
Beck, Michael (act, b. 1948): Chiller; Deadly Game; Megaforce; Xanadu
Beck, Peggy (act): Just Imagine
Beck, Sonia (act): Vampire On Bikini Beach
Beck, Thomas (act): Charlie Chan At The Opera; Charlie Chan At The Race Track; Charlie Chan In Egypt; Charlie Chan In Paris; Thank You, Mr. Moto; Think Fast, Mr. Moto
Beck, Vincent (act): The Immortal; Santa Claus Conquers The Martians
Becke, Eve (act): Death At Broadcasting House
Becker, Antonie (act): Time After Time
Becker, David (act): Pandemonium
Becker, Frank (mus): Monolith
Becker, Fred (act): The Black Pirate
Becker, Gerry (act): Asteroid; Eraser
Becker, Greg (cin): The Video Dead
Becker, Gretchen (act): Ed Wood
Becker, Jacques (dir, 1906–1960): Ali-Baba Et Les Quarante Voleurs; L'or Du Cristobal
Becker, Joseph (act): Space Master X-7
Becker, Ken (act): The Atomic Submarine
Becker, Lauren (act): Silent Night, Deadly Night II
Becker, Martin (cin): Friday The 13th, Part VI: Jason Lives
Becker, Rolf (act): I Love You, I Kill You
Becker, Terry (dir): The Thirsty Dead
Beckett, David (act): Lifeforce
Beckett, Jack (wri): Please Don't Eat My Mother
Beckett, Scott(y) (act, 1929–1968): Ali Baba And The Forty Thieves (1943); The Blue Bird (1940); The Climax; Dante's Inferno (1935)
Beckinsale, Kate (act): Haunted (1996)
Beckinsale, Richard (act): Rentadick
Beckles, Gordon (wri): East Of Piccadilly
Beckley, Barbara (act): Condor
Beckley, Tony (act): Beware, My Brethren; Diagnosis: Murder; The Fiend (1972); In The Devil's Garden; The Penthouse (1967); Uncharted Seas; When A Stranger Calls
Beckley, William (act): Daughter Of The Mind; The President's Analyst
Beckman, Henry (act): The Brood; The Satan Bug
Beckman, John (act): A Nightmare On Elm Street 4: The Dream Master
Beckman, Peter (act): C.H.U.D. II
Beckner, Michael Frost (wri): Cutthroat Island
Beckner, Rick (act): Ssssss
Beckwith, Alan (act): The China Syndrome
Beckwith, Reginald (act, 1908–1965): Another Man's Poison; Circle Of Danger; The Day The Earth Caught Fire; Lancelot And Guinevere; The March Hare; Men Of Sherwood Forest; Mr. Drake's Duck; Night Of The Demon (1957); Night Of The Eagle; They Can't Hang Me; The 39 Steps (1959); Thunderball; The Ugly Duckling; Whispering Smith Hits London
Becwar, George (act): Bride Of The Monster; War Of The Colossal Beast
Bedden, Perry (act): Shock Treatment! (1981)
Beddoe, Don(ald T.) (act, b. 1891): Before I Hang; Beware, Spooks!; The Boogie Man Will Get You; Charlie Chan's Murder Cruise; Crime Doctor's Diary; The Face Behind The Mask; The Great Rupert; Island Of Doomed Men; Jack The Giant Killer; The Lone Wolf Keeps A Date; The Lone Wolf Spy Hunt; The Lone Wolf Strikes; The Lone Wolf Takes A Chance; The Man They Could Not Hang; The Night Of The Hunter (1955); The Notorious Lone Wolf; Tarzan's Hidden Jungle; The Wizard Of Baghdad
Beddor, Frank (act): Remote Control (1988)
Bedelia, Bonnie (act, b. 1948): The Boy Who Could Fly; Needful Things; Salem's Lot; Sandcastles
Bedell, Rodney (act): The Gruesome Twosome
Bedells, Mrs. (act): The Man Behind "The Times"
Bedells, Phyllis (act): Fairyland
Bedford, Barbara (act): The Death Kiss; The Haunted House (1929); Mockery; The Spanish Cape Mystery
Bedford, Brian (act): Number Six
Bedford, David (mus): Mark Of The Devil (1985)
Bedford, Terry (cin): Jabberwocky; Monty Python And The Holy Grail
Bedi, Kabir (act, b. 1945): Fugitive From The Empire; Octopussy; Satan's Mistress; The Thief Of Baghdad (1978)
Bedker, Edith (act): The Pit (1983)
Bednarek, Tomczek (act): Silent Night, Deadly Night II
Bednarski, Andrew (act): Eternal Evil
Bednarski, Robert (act): Wild Thing
Bednarz, Wendy (act): There's Nothing Out There
Bedos, Guy (act): Aimez-Vous Les Femmes?
Bedoya, Alfonso (act): The Black Rose
Bedoya, Ingrid (act): The Devil's Messenger
Bedrosian, Hunter (act): The Fear (1994)
Bee, Molly (act): Hillbillys In A Haunted House
Bee, Richard (wri): The Haunted House (1929); The House Of Horror (1929); Seven Footprints To Satan
Beebe, Dick (act & wri): Into The Badlands
Beebe, Ford (dir, b. 1888): African Treasure; Bomba And The Hidden City; Bomba, The Jungle Boy; The Deadly Ray From Mars; Destination Saturn; The Golden Idol; The Invisible Man's Revenge; Killer Leopard; Lord Of The Jungle; The Lost Volcano; Night Monster; Panther Island; Peril From The Planet Mongo; The Phantom Creeps; Purple Death From Outer Space; Safari Drums
Beebe, Ford (wri, b. 1888): African Treasure; The Golden Idol; Killer Leopard; Lord Of The Jungle; The Lost Volcano; Panther Island; Safari Drums
Beebe, Matthew (act): Addams Family Values
Beebe, Reda (act): Demon Knight
Beeby, Bruce (act): The Devil-Ship Pirates; The Golden Link; The Limping Man (1953); The Man In The Road
Beech, Gregory (act): Trauma (1993)
Beecham, Charles (act): D.O.A. (1988)
Beechcroft, David (act): The Rain Killer
Beecher, Alan (act): Razorback
Beecher, Janet (act, 1886–1955): The Mark Of Zorro (1940)
Beecher, Robert (act): Dick Tracy (1990); Phantasm II: Lord Of The Dead
Beechner, Ed (act): Outbreak
Beecroft, David (act): Shadowzone
Beecroft, Eleanor (act): Funeral Home; The Mask (1961)
Beeding, Francis (wri): Spellbound (1945)
Beedle Jr., William Franklin (act): see Holden, William
Beekman, Tim (act): Nosferatu, The Vampyre
Beeman, Greg (dir): Mom And Dad Save The World
Beeman, Terry (act): Eraser
Been, Patti (act): Dark Mirror (1984)
Beeny, Christopher (act): Child's Play (1954)
Beer, Daniel (act): Night Visions
Beer, Robert (act): My Science Project
Beerbohm, Max (wri): Death In The Hand
Beery (Sr.), Noah (act, 1884–1946): Bits Of Life; The Crimson Circle (1936); The Frog; The Mark Of Zorro (1920); Murder Will Out (1930); Someone At The Door
Beery Jr., Noah (act, 1913–1994): The Cat Creeps (1946); The Crimson Canary; The

Benedict, William/Bill/Billy (act, b. 1917): The Adventures Of Nick Carter; Bride Of The Monster; Confessions Of Boston Blackie; Final Eye; Ghost Chasers; Ghosts On The Loose; The Lady And The Monster; The Magnetic Monster; Master Minds (1950); Meet Nero Wolfe; Mr. Hex; Sherlock Holmes In New York

Benedicto, Luis (act): The Blood Drinkers

Benesh, Amy (act): Amazons (1984)

Benesh, Natalie (act): Babes In Bagdad

Benest, Glenn M. (wri): Deadly Blessing; Stranger In Our House

Benet, Stephen Vincent (wri, 1898–1943): All That Money Can Buy

Beneveds, Bob (act): The Monster That Challenged The World

Benfield, Derek (act): The Boy Who Never Was; I Don't Want To Be Born; Lifeforce

Benfield, John (act): Treasure Island (1990)

Benford, Timothy B. (wri): Hitler's Daughter

Benge, Wilson (act): The Bat Whispers; Bulldog Drummond (1929); Bulldog Drummond Strikes Back (1934); Queen Of The Amazons (1947); Robin Hood (1922)

Bengell, Norma (act): Os Deuses E Os Mortos; Terrore Nello Spazio

Bengs, Carl (act): The Green Slime

Bengston, Billy Al (act): Strange Behavior

Bengston, Ray (act): It Came Upon The Midnight Clear

Benham, Harry (act): Dr. Jekyll And Mr. Hyde (1912)

Benham, Joan (act): Limbo Line; Peter Rabbit And The Tales Of Beatrix Potter; Saturday Island

Benhar, Michael (act): Twisted

Beniades, Ted (act): They Might Be Giants

Bening, Annette (act, b. 1958): In Dreams, Mars Attacks!; Richard II (1995)

Benitez, Andres (act): The Blood Drinkers; Curse Of The Vampires

Benjamin, Al (cin): Empire Of Ash II

Benjamin, Alan (act): Silent Night, Deadly Night II

Benjamin, Arthur (mus, b. 1893): The Clairvoyant (1934); The Man Who Knew Too Much (1934); The Scarlet Pimpernel (1934)

Benjamin, Christopher (act): Baffled!; Hawk The Slayer; Koroshi; The Secret Life Of Ian Fleming

Benjamin, Darwin Lee (act): Galaxina

Benjamin, Floella (act): I Don't Want To Be Born

Benjamin, Richard (act, b. 1938): Love At First Bite; Portnoy's Complaint; Saturday The 14th; Westworld; Witches' Brew

Benjamin, Richard (dir, b. 1938): My Stepmother Is An Alien

Benjamin, Sonyia (act): The Return Of Mr. Moto

Benji (act): Oh Heavenly Dog

Benktsson, Benkt-Ake (act): Det Sjunde Inseglet

Bennell, Cyril (act): The Girl Who Wrecked His Home

Bennent, David (act): Legend

Bennent, Heinz (act): Possession (1981)

Benner, Brenda (act): The 'Burbs

Benner, Yale (act): The Man From Beyond

Bennet, Carol (act): Lo Spettro

Bennet, Spencer G. (dir, 1893–1987): The Atomic Submarine; Atom Man vs. Superman; Captain Mephisto And The Transformation Machine; Devil Goddess; The House Without A Key; Jungle Gold; Killer Ape; Phantom Of The Jungle; Sakima And The Masked Marvel; Savage Mutiny; Sombra, The Spider Woman; Voodoo Tiger

Bennett, Mrs. (act): The Pleydell Mystery

Bennett, Alayna (act): The Outing

Bennett, Alfred (act): Wuthering Heights (1920)

Bennett, Alma (act): The Lost World (1925)

Bennett, Arnold (wri): The Grand Babylon Hotel

Bennett, Audra (act): The Outing

Bennett, Belle (act): The Iron Mask

Bennett, Billie (act): Robin Hood (1922)

Bennett, Brian (mus): Riders Of The Storm

Bennett, Bruce (act, b. 1909, a.k.a. Herman Brix): The Alligator People; Angels In The Outfield (1951); Before I Hang; The Clones; The Cosmic Man; The Lone Wolf Keeps A Date; The Lone Wolf Meets A Lady; Lost Island Of Kioga; Mystery Street; Sudden Fear; Tarzan And The Green Goddess; Tarzan's New Adventure; The Torpedo Of Doom; U-Boat Prisoner

Bennett, Charles (wri, 1899–1995): Black Magic (1949); Blackmail (1929); The City Under The Sea; The Clairvoyant (1934); Dangerous Mission; Five Weeks In A Balloon; The Green Glove; Kind Lady (1951); King Solomon's Mines (1937); The Last Hour; The Lost World (1960); The Man Who Knew Too Much (1934 & 1956); Midnight (1931); Night Of The Demon (1957); Sabotage (1936); The Secret Agent (1936); The Secret Of The Loch (1934); The Story Of Mankind; The 39 Steps (1935 & 1959); Voyage To The Bottom Of The Sea; Young And Innocent

Bennett, Chuck (act): Project X (1987)

Bennett, Compton (dir, 1900–1974): King Solomon's Mines (1949)

Bennett, Constance (act, 1905–1965): Topper (1937); Topper Takes A Trip; The Unsuspected

Bennett, Dean (act): Blow Out

Bennett, Dorothy (wri): The Brasher Doubloon

Bennett, Edna (act): The Casino Murder Case

Bennett, Eileen (act): Trunk Crime

Bennett, Enid (act): Robin Hood (1922)

Bennett, Faith (act): Eyes Of Fate

Bennett, Fran (act): Wes Craven's New Nightmare

Bennett, Frances (act): The Snake Woman

Bennett, Frank (act): It Happened Here

Bennett, Harold (act): A Place To Die

Bennett, Harve (act): Star Trek V: The Final Frontier

Bennett, Harve (wri): The Invisible Man (1975); Star Trek II: The Search For Spock; Star Trek Iv: The Voyage Home; Star Trek V: The Final Frontier

Bennett, Helen (act): On The Threshold Of Space

Bennett, Hywel (act, b. 1944): Alice's Adventures In Wonderland (1972); Endless Night; Percy; The Twisted Nerve

Bennett, Jack (cin): Don't Look In The Basement; The Initiation; In The Year 2889; It's Alive! (1968); So Sad About Gloria

Bennett, Jajary (act): The Offspring

Bennett, Jay (wri): Catacombs

Bennett, Jesse (act): Earthbound (1981)

Bennett, Jill (act, b. 1931): For Your Eyes Only; Full Circle; The Nanny; The Skull

Bennett, Joan (act, 1910–1990): Bulldog Drummond (1929); The Eyes Of Charles Sand; For Heaven's Sake; Green Hell; House Of Dark Shadows; The Man In The Iron Mask (1939); The Man Who Reclaimed His Head; Moby Dick (1930); Scotland Yard (1930); Secret Beyond The Door; The Son Of Monte Cristo; Suspiria; This House Possessed; The Woman In The Window

Bennett, Joan Sterndale (act): Those Fantastic Flying Fools

Bennett, Joel (act): Hellhole

Bennett, John (act): The Face Of Darkness; Hitler: The Last Ten Days; The House In Nightmare Park; The House That Dripped Blood; The Pirates Of Blood River

Bennett, Julie (act): Goliath Awaits

Bennett, Kevin (act): Otley

Bennett, Lee (act): Larceny In Her Heart

Bennett, Leila (act): Doctor X; The Mark Of The Vampire (1935); A Study In Scarlet (1933)

Bennett, Linda (act): Creature With The Atom Brain; Spychasers

Bennett, Marcia (act): The Pink Chiquitas

Bennett, Marjorie (act): Billy The Kid vs. Dracula; Games; The Night Walker; Sherlock Holmes In New York; What Ever Happened To Baby Jane? (1962)

Bennett, Maureen (act): The Mirror Crack'd

Bennett, Mickey (act): The Ghost Talks

Bennett, Nicolas (act): Konga

Bennett, Nigel (act): Bay Coven; Hitler's Daughter; Narrow Margin

Bennett, Randy (act): Pandemonium

Bennett, Raphael (act): Dick Tracy Returns

Bennett, Richard (GB act): The Pirates Of Blood River; Richard II (1955); The Tell-Tale Heart (1960)

Bennett, Richard (USA act, 1873–1944): Journey Into Fear (1942)

Bennett, Richard (Rodney) (mus, b. 1936): Billion Dollar Brain; Face In The Night; Murder On The Orient Express; Murder With Mirrors; The Nanny; Secret Ceremony; Sherlock Holmes In New York; Voices; The Witches (1966)

Bennett, Richard (wri): The Food Of The Gods II

Bennett, Ruth (act): Killers From Space

Bennett, Steve (wri): Madman Of Mandoras

Bennett, Wallace (C.) (wri): The Philadelphia Experiment; Philadelphia Experiment II; Silent Scream (1979); The Time Machine (1978); Welcome To Arrow Beach

Benninghofen, Jeff (act): King Kong Lives

Bennison, Ishia (act): The Awakening

Benny, Jack (act, 1894–1974, nee Benjamin Kubelsky): The Horn Blows At Midnight

Benoist, Michel (act): Les Parapluies De Cherbourg

Benoit, George (cin): Trilby (1923)

Benoit, Glenn (act): Wolfen

Benoit, Pierre (wri, 1886-1962): Antinea, L'amante Della Citta Sepolta; L'atlantide (1920); Die Herrin Von Atlantis

Benrubi, Abraham (act): Twister

Benscoter, Robert (act): Copycat

Bensen, Carle (act): Death Race 2000

Benskin, Tyrone (act): The Kiss (1988); Wild Thing

Benson, Annette (act): Downhill; The Ringer (1928)

Benson, Anthony (act): 1984 (1984)

Benson, Constance (act): Macbeth (1911); Richard II (1911)

Benson, Deborah (act): Ghost Fever; Just Before Dawn (1980)

Benson, Douglas (act): Return Of The Living Dead, Part II

Benson, E.F. (wri, 1867–1940): Dead Of Night (1945)

Benson, Eddie (mus): Tower Of Terror

Benson, Esther (act): The Fan

Benson, Frank (act): Macbeth (1911); Richard II (1911)

Benson, George (act, b. 1911): Cage Of Gold; The Creeping Flesh; Highly Dangerous; Horror Of Dracula; The Man In The White Suit; Model For Murder; The October Man; Pool Of London; The Private Life Of Sherlock Holmes; What Became Of Jack And Jill

Benson, Hugh (wri): Goliath Awaits

Benson, Ivy (act): The Dummy Talks

Benson, Jay (wri): Deathmoon

Benson, Jodi (act): Thumbelina (1994)

Benson, Joey (act): Blood Of Ghastly Horror; Gallery Of Horror; Horror Of The Blood Monsters

Benson, John (act): The Blob (1958)

Benson, Kevin (mus): My Demon Lover

Benson, Lucille (act, 1914–1984): Betrayal; The Devil's Daughter (1972); The Fugitive Kind; Halloween II; Private Parts; Reflections Of Murder; Slaughterhouse-Five; The Strange Possession Of Mrs. Oliver

Benson, Martin (act, b. 1918): Battle Beneath The Earth; Captain Clegg; Goldfinger; Gorgo; Mystery Junction; Night Without Stars; The Omen; Soho Incident; Sphinx (1981); The Strange World Of Planet X; The Three Worlds Of Gulliver; 23 Paces To Baker Street; The Two-Headed Spy

Benson, Perry (act): Where's Johnny

Benson, Peter (act): Hawk The Slayer; The Shout

Benson, Richard (dir): Lycanthropus

Benson, Robby (act): Beauty And The Beast (1991); Homewrecker

Benson, Robert (wri): Spellbound (1941)

Benson, Ron (act): Mutants In Paradise

Benson, Sally (wri): Shadow Of A Doubt (1943 & 1991)

Benson, Steven (dir & wri) Endgame

Benson, Tony (act): The Witchmaker

Benson, Vickie (act): The Wraith

Benson, Wendy (act): Pretty Poison (1996)

Benson, Wilfred (act): The Disappearance Of The Judge

Bensoussan, Michelle (act): Grotesque

Benstead, Geoffrey (act): The Yellow Claw

Bentall, Paul (act): First Knight

Bentinck, Anna (act): To The Devil A Daughter

Bentine, Michael (act): Rentadick

Bentivegna, Warner (act): The Trojan Horse

Bentley, Dick (act): The Golden Rabbit

Bentley, E.C. (wri): Trent's Last Case (1920, 1929 & 1952)

Bentley, Grendon (act): Hamlet (1913)

Bentley, John (act, b. 1916): Black Orchid; Golden Ivory; The Hills Of Donegal; The Lost Hours; Paul Temple Returns; Paul Temple's Triumph; She Shall Have Murder; The Sinister Man; Torment (1949); Tread Softly

Bentley, Lamont (act): Tales From The Hood

Bentley, Thomas (dir, 1890?-1950?): The Chimes; Old Bill Through The Ages; The Scotland Yard Mystery; Silver Blaze (1937); Three Silent Men; The Woman Who Dared

Bentley, Thomas (wri, 1890?-1950?): The Chimes

Benton, Barbi (act, b. 1950): And The Wall Came Tumbling Down; Deathstalker; Hospital Massacre

Benton, Charles (act): Bridge Across Time; The Gifted One

Benton, Craig (act): The Lawnmower Man

Benton, Deane (act): Chandu

Benton, Eddie (act): Dr. Strange; Prom Night; The Shape Of Things To Come (1979)

Benton, Garth (act): 13 Frightened Girls

Benton, Robert (dir, b. 1932): Still Of The Night

Benton, Robert (wri, b. 1932): Still Of The Night; Superman (1978)

Benton, Susanne (act): A Boy And His Dog

Bentzen, Paul (act): The Alpha Incident; Invasion From Inner Space

Benussi, Femi (act): Hatchet For A Honeymoon

Benveniste, Michael (dir & wri): Flesh Gordon

Benvenuti, Leo (wri): The Santa Clause; Space Jam

Benvictor, Paul (act): Body Parts

Benyaer, Michael (act): Friday The 13th, Part VIII—Jason Takes Manhattan

Benyon, Nancy (act): The Beetle

Benz, Donna (act): Looker

Benzali, Daniel (act): The Return Of Sherlock Holmes (1986)

Beradino, John (act, b. 1917): Do Not Fold, Spindle Or Mutilate; Moon Of The Wolf

Beranger, Clara S. (wri, 1886–1956): Dr. Jekyll And Mr. Hyde (1920, Famous Players/Para)

Beranger, George (act): Nightmare Alley

Berben, Iris (act): Supergirl (1971)

Berber, Ady (act): Strangler Of The Tower; Die Toten Augen Von London; Die Tur Mit Den Sieben Schlossern

Berber, Anita (act): Doctor Mabuse

Bercovici, Eric (wri): The Other Man

Bercovici, Leonardo (wri): The Bishop's Wife; The Lost Moment; Portrait Of Jennie; The Preacher's Wife

Bercovici, Luca (act): Frightmare (1983); Pacific Heights; Parasite; Space Raiders

Bercovici, Luca (dir & wri): Ghoulies

Bercu, Michaela (act): Bram Stoker's Dracula

Berdahl, Blaze (act): Pet Sematary

Berdahl, Sky (act): Mr. Destiny

Beregi, Oscar (act, 1917–1976): Desert Legion; The Incredible Mr. Limpet; Das Testament Des Dr. Mabuse; Young Frankenstein

Berenger, Tom (act, b. 1949): The Sentinel; Sliver

Berenguer, Andres (cin): Mystery On Monster Island; Where Time Began

Berenguer, Manuel (cin): Crack In The World; The House That Screamed; Murders In The Rue Morgue (1971); Pyro; Sound Of Horror

Berenoff (act): The Face At The Window (1932)

Berens, Harold (act): Bluebeard's Ten Honeymoons; Dual Alibi; A Kid For Two Farthings; The Magic Christian; Straight On Till Morning

Berensford, Marcus (act): Ladyhawke

Berenson, Berry (act): Cat People (1982)

Berenson, Marisa (act, b. 1948): Killer Fish; Notorious (1992)

Beresford, Elisabeth (wri): Wombling Free

Beresford, Harry (act): Charlie Chan Carries On; Doctor X

Beresford, Leslie ("Pan") (wri): While Paris Sleeps

Beresford, Susan (act): Flesh & Blood

Berest, Frederic (act): Jungle Jim In The Forbidden Land; Voodoo Tiger

Berfield, Barry (act): Powder

Berg, Alex (wri): Creature With The Blue Hand

Berg, Axel (act): Making Contact

Berg, Gene (act): see Nelson, Gene

Berg, Joanna (act): The Visitors (1989)

Berg, Jon (cin): Piranha (1978)

Berg, Katherine (act): The Secret Of Seagull Island

Berg, Nancy (act): Fail-Safe

Berg, Peter (act): Fire In The Sky (1993); Late For Dinner; Miracle Mile; Shocker

Berg, Tracy (act): Piranha II: The Spawning

Bergdall, Tamara (act): The Premonition (1975)

Berge, Colette (act): Les Abysses

Berge, Francine (act): Les Abysses; Judex

Bergeaud, David (mus): Twice Dead; The Unnamable

Bergen, Avril (act): Peter Rabbit And The Tales Of Beatrix Potter

Bergen, Bob (act): Space Jam

Bergen, Candice (act, b. 1946): Arthur The King; The Day The Fish Came Out; The Magus

Bergen, Connie (act): Man-Made Monster

Bergen, Edgar (act, 1903–1978): The Hanged Man

Bergen, Elizabeth (act): Sisters Of Death

Bergen, Polly (act, b. 1930): Anatomy Of Terror; Cape Fear (1961); The Caretakers; Death Cruise; Dr. Jekyll And Ms. Hyde; The Haunting Of Sarah Hardy; Kisses For My President; The Lightning Incident; Making Mr. Right; Murder On Flight 502

Berger, Alan (act): Beverly Hills Bodysnatchers; Miracle Mile

Berger, Carl (cin): Jungle Goddess

Berger, Fred (act): The Perfect Woman

Berger, Greg (act):Attack Of The Killer Tomatoes
Berger, Greta (act): Doctor Mabuse; Spione; Der Student Von Prag (1913)
Berger, Helmut (act, b. 1944): Dorian Gray
Berger, Howard (act): Night Of The Creeps
Berger, Joachim (act): see Fuchsberger, Joachim
Berger, Ludwig (dir, 1892–1969): The Thief Of Bagdad (1940); Der Verlorene Schuh
Berger, Mal (act): Hammersmith Is Out
Berger, Mel (act): Through The Magic Pyramid
Berger, Senta (act, b. 1941): The Ambushers; De Sade; Diabolically Yours; I Spy, You Spy; Operation Solo; Our Man In Marrakesh; The Quiller Memorandum; The Scarlet Letter (1972); The Secret Of The Black Trunk; Sherlock Holmes And The Deadly Necklace; The Spy With My Face; The Testament Of Dr. Mabuse (1960); To Commit A Murder; When Women Had Tails; When Women Lost Their Tails
Berger, Sidney (act): Carnival Of Souls
Berger, Thomas (wri): Neighbors
Berger, William (act, b. 1928): The Adventures Of Hercules; The Fifth Missile; Hercules (1983); I'm Dangerous Tonight; Ironmaster; The Murder Clinic
Bergerac, Jacques (act, b. 1927): Fury Of Achilles; The Hypnotic Eye; Mother Goose A Go-Go
Bergere, Ouida (wri): Bella Donna (1923)
Bergeron, Loys T. (act): Angel Heart
Bergeron, Michael (act): Candyman: Farewell To The Flesh
Bergese, Micha (act): The Company Of Wolves
Bergeson, Dave (act): Surf Nazis Must Die
Berghmans, Jose (mus): To Commit A Murder
Berghof, Herbert (act, 1909–1990): Red Planet Mars
Bergin, Emmet (act): Excalibur
Bergin, Patrick (act): Frankenstein (1993); Highway To Hell; The Lawnmower Man 2: Beyond Cyberspace; Robin Hood (1991); They
Berglas, Ron (act): Dreamchild; Highlander
Berglevist, Megan (act): Dr. Caligari
Bergman, Alan (mus): Never Say Never Again
Bergman, Andrew (act): Oh, God! You Devil
Bergman, Harold (act): Cocoon: The Return
Bergman, Henry (act): Modern Times
Bergman, Ingmar (dir, b. 1918): Ansiktet; The Devil's Eye; The Devil's Wanton; Persona; Det Sjunde Inseglet; Smultronstallet; Through A Glass Darkly; Tystnaden; Vargtimmen
Bergman, Ingmar (wri, b. 1918): Ansiktet; The Devil's Eye; The Devil's Wanton; Hets; Persona; Det Sjunde Inseglet; Smultronstallet; Tystnaden; Vargtimmen
Bergman, Ingrid (act, 1915–1982): Dr. Jekyll And Mr. Hyde (1941); Gaslight (1944); Murder On The Orient Express; Notorious (1946); Spellbound (1945); Under Capricorn
Bergman, Marilyn (mus): Never Say Never Again
Bergman, Peter (act): Fantasies
Bergman, Robert (cin): Graveyard Shift (1987); Psycho Girls
Bergman, Sandahl (act): All That Jazz; Conan The Barbarian; Hell Comes To Frogtown; Ice Cream Man; Inner Sanctum 2; Programmed To Kill; Raw Nerve; Red Sonja; She (1983)
Bergner, Elisabeth (act, b. 1900): Cry Of The Banshee; Paris Calling
Bergquist, Peter L. (wri): Monster In The Closet
Bergryd, Ulla (act): The Bible
Bergstrom, Catherine (act): Halloween II
Berini, Paul (act): Mr. Sycamore
Beristain, Gabriel (cin): Dolores Claiborne
Berk, Ailsa (act): Greystoke: The Legend Of Tarzan, Lord Of The Apes; Return To Oz
Berk, Howard (wri): The Bang-Bang Kid; A Witch Without A Broom
Berk, Michael (wri): The Haunting Passion
Berk, Robert (act): The Bat People
Berke, Ed (act): Retribution (1988)
Berke, Irwin (act): Frankenstein (1970)
Berke, (Lester) William (dir, 1904–1958): Captive Girl; Dick Tracy (1945); The Falcon In Mexico; The Falcon's Adventure; Fury Of The Congo; The Jungle; The Lost Missile; The Lost Tribe; Mark Of The Gorilla; Pygmy Island; Savage Drums; Valley Of The Headhunters
Berke, Lester William (wri, 1904–1958): The Lost Missile
Berkeley, Ballard (act): China's Play (1934); Men Of Sherwood Forest; Night Caller From Outer Space; Passport To Treason; The Playbirds; The Saint In London; They Made Me A Fugitive

Berkeley, Billie (act): The Shadow Between
Berkeley, Keith (act): The Visitors (1989)
Berkeley, Martin (wri): The Deadly Mantis; The Notorious Lone Wolf; Revenge Of The Creature; A Stolen Face; Tarantula
Berkeley, Xander (act): Barb Wire; Candyman; Not Of This World; Terminator 2: Judgment Day
Berkely, George (act): Devil Goddess
Berkman, Edward O. (wri): The Squeaker (1937)
Berkoff Dancers, The (act): Elstree Calling
Berkoff, Steven (act): A Clockwork Orange; Octopussy; Outland; Prehistoric Women (1966); Transmutations
Berland, Jacques (wri): Cet Homme Est Dangereux; La Mome Vertde-Gris
Berland, Terri (act): The Strangeness
Berlanga, Luis Garcia (dir, b. 1921): Not On Your Life!; A Rocket From Calabuch
Berle, Milton (act, b. 1908, nee Milton Berlinger): The Loved One; Storybook; Whispering Ghosts
Berlin, Brigid (act): Serial Mom
Berlin, Jeannie (act & wri): In The Spirit
Berlin, Michael (act): Anguish
Berliner, Rudolph (mus): The Road To Yesterday
Berlinger, Michael (act): Deadtime Stories
Berlinger, Milton (act): see Berle, Milton
Berlinger, Warren (act, b. 1937): Ellery Queen; Platinum High School; The Shaggy D.A.; Ten Little Indians (1989)
Berlitz, Charles (wri): The Philadelphia Experiment
Berlyn, Ivan (act): Honour In Pawn; The Phantom Picture
Berman, Barry (wri): The Adventures Of Pinocchio
Berman, Jane (act): Jaws Of Satan
Berman, Loren (act): The Ultimate Impostor
Berman, Monty (cin, b. 1913): Blood Of The Vampire; The Flesh And The Fiends; The Hell-Fire Club; Jack The Ripper (1958); The Treasure Of Monte Cristo (1961); The Trollenberg Terror; What A Carve Up!
Berman, Monty (dir, b. 1913): Hell-Fire Club, The; Jack The Ripper (1958); The Treasure Of Monte Cristo (1961)
Berman, Rick (wri): Star Trek: Generations
Berman, Sam (wri): The Scarlet Pimpernel (1934)
Berman, Shelley (act, b. 1924): Beware! The Blob; The St. Valentine's Day Massacre; Teen Witch
Berman, Susan (act): Making Mr. Right
Bermejo, Chiro (act): Amador
Bermingham, Rev. T. (act): The Exorcist
Bern, Tonia (act): The Glass Tomb
Bernal, Francisco (act): Goliath Against The Giants; A Rocket From Calabuch
Bernaola, Carmelo (mus): Gran Amore Del Conde Dracula
Bernard, Andrew Paul (act):The Pink Chiquitas
Bernard, Anna (act): Doctor Death : Seeker Of Souls
Bernard, Barry (act): Bulldog Drummond Strikes Back (1947); Charlie Chan In The Secret Service; Cry Wolf (1947); Houdini; Killer Leopard; Return Of The Fly; The Rocks Of Valpre; Terror In The Haunted House; The Two Mrs. Carrolls; The Woman In White (1948)
Bernard, Carl (act): Doctor Of Seven Dials; The Headless Ghost; Hour Of Decision; Tales From The Crypt
Bernard, Charles (act): The Haunting Of Sarah Hardy
Bernard, Crystal (act, b. 1964): Slumber Party Massacre II
Bernard, Ed (act): Reflections Of Murder
Bernard, Ian (wri):Oh Dad Poor Dad, Mamma's Hung You In The Closet And I'm Feelin' So Sad
Bernard, Iris Quinn (act): Hideaway
Bernard, Ivor (act): Great Expectations (1946); The Saint's Vacation
Bernard, Jacques (act): Les Enfants Terribles
Bernard, James (mus, b. 1925): The Curse Of Frankenstein; The Damned; The Devil Rides Out; Dracula Has Risen From The Grave; Dracula, Prince Of Darkness; Frankenstein And The Monster From Hell; Frankenstein Created Woman; Frankenstein Must Be Destroyed; The Gorgon; Horror Of Dracula; Horror Of Frankenstein; The Hound Of The Baskervilles (1959); Kiss Of The Vampire; Legend Of The Seven Golden Vampires; The Plague Of The Zombies; The Quatermass Experiment; Quatermass II; Scars Of Dracula; The Secret Of Blood Island; She (1965); The

Stranglers Of Bombay; Taste The Blood Of Dracula
Bernard, James (wri): Seven Days To Noon
Bernard, Jason (act): All Of Me; Liar Liar; Trick Or Treats; V
Bernard, Jay (act): The Philadelphia Experiment
Bernard, Joseph/Joe (E.) (act): The Baby; Death At Love House; House Of Dracula; The Immortal
Bernard, Maurice (act): The Incredible Petrified World
Bernard, Napoleon (act): The Golden Mistress
Bernard, Nicolette (act): It Happened Here
Bernard, Sue (act): Faster, Pussycat! Kill! Kill!; Necromancy; The Witchmaker
Bernardi, Herschel (act, 1923–1986): Sandcastles
Bernardi, Nerio (act): The Conquest Of Mycenae; The Lion Of Thebes; The Minotaur; Satanik; Teodora, Imperatrice Di Bisanzio; The Trojan Horse
Bernardo, Al (act): Starship Invasions
Bernardo, Michael (act): Virtual Combat
Bernay, Lynne (act): I Bury The Living; The Pit And The Pendulum (1961); The Viking Women And The Sea Serpent
Bernds, Edward (dir, b. 1905): The Bowery Boys Meet The Monsters; Bowery To Bagdad; Dig That Uranium!; Jungle Gents; Private Eyes; Queen Of Outer Space; Return Of The Fly; Space Master X-7; Spy Chasers; The Three Stooges In Orbit; The Three Stooges Meet Hercules; Valley Of The Dragons; World Without End
Bernds, Edward (wri, b. 1905): The Bowery Boys Meet The Monsters; Bowery To Bagdad; Jungle Gents; Private Eyes; Return Of The Fly; Valley Of The Dragons; World Without End
Bernede, Arthur (wri): Judex
Berneis, Peter (dir): No Survivors, Please
Berneis, Peter (wri): No Survivors, Please; Portrait Of Jennie
Berner, Robby (act): Empire Of Ash II
Berner, Sara (act): Rear Window
Berners, Lord (mus): Halfway House
Bernhard, Harvey (wri): Damien-Omen II
Bernhard, Jack (dir): Appointment With Murder; Unknown Island
Bernhard, Manfred (act): Dr. Black Mr. Hyde
Bernhard, Sandra (act): The Apocalypse
Bernhardt, Curtis (dir, 1899–1981):Devotion; Kisses For My President; Possessed (1947)
Bernhardt, Eve (act): The Wizard Of Mars
Bernhardt, Kevin (act): Hellraiser II: Hell On Earth
Bernhardt, Sarah (act, 1844–1923): Le Duel D'hamlet
Bernheim, Shirl (act): Frankenhooker
Berni, Mara (act): Samson
Bernon, Bluette (act): Barbe-Bleue; Jack Le Ramoneur; Le Voyage Dans La Lune
Berns, Gerald (act): Eraser; Running Against Time
Bernsen, Collin (act): Mr. Destiny; Puppet Master II
Bernsen, Corbin (act, b. 1954): Bloodhounds; The Dentist; Grey Knight; Hello Again; Inhumanoid; Love Can Be Murder; Tails You Live, Heads You're Dead; Tales From The Hood; Tidal Wave: No Escape
Bernstein, Ben (act): see Blue, Ben
Bernstein, Charles (mus): April Fool's Day; Are You In The House Alone?; Blood Pen; Covenant; Cujo; Deadly Friend; The Entity; Ghost Of A Chance (1987); Invasion Of The Bee Girls; Look What's Happened To Rosemary's Baby; Love At First Bite; A Nightmare On Elm Street; Secret Weapons
Bernstein, Elmer (mus, b. 1922): The Amazing Mr. Blunden; An American Werewolf In London; Blind Terror; Cape Fear (1991); Cat-Women Of The Moon; Ellery Queen; Ghostbusters; The Good Son; Heavy Metal; It's A Dog's Life; The Miracle (1959); Nightmare Honeymoon; Rampage; Robot Monster; Saturn 3; The Silencers (1966); Slipstream; Spacehunter: Adventures In The Forbidden Zone; Sudden Fear
Bernstein, Morey (wri): The Search For Bridey Murphy
Bernstein, Nat (act): Bates Motel
Bernstein, Noga (act): The Punisher
Bernstein, Peter (mus): The Ewok Adventure; Ewoks: The Battle For Endor; My Science Project; Remote Control (1988)
Bernstein, Richard (wri): From Hell It Came;

Bernstein, Sheryl (act): Repossessed
Bernstein, Steven (cin): Curdled
Bernstein, Walter (wri): Fail-Safe

Bernt, Eric (act & wri): Virtuosity
Bernuth, Charles P. (act): Slaughterhouse Rock
Berova, Olinka (act): The Vengeance Of She
Berrell, Lloyd (act): Long John Silver
Berri, Robert (act): Lemmy Pour Les Dames
Berridge, Elizabeth (act, b. 1962): The Funhouse (1981)
Berridge, Janice Elaine (act): Student Bodies
Berridge, Rob (act): Empire Of Ash II
Berrier, Stephen (act): Robocop
Berring, Douglas (act): The Wiz
Berroatua, Mario (act): The Last Days Of Pompeii (1959)
Berry, Al (act): Ghost Warrior; The Last Starfighter; Reanimator
Berry, Barah (act): C.H.U.D. II
Berry, Bert (act): Detective Daring And The Thames Coiners
Berry, Bill (act): Firebird 2015 A.D.
Berry, Christine Louise (act): The Craft
Berry, Eric (act): The Diamond
Berry, Frank (act): Dr. Strangelove, or: How I Learned To Stop Worrying And Love The Bomb
Berry, Halle (act, b. 1968): The Flintstones; The Rich Man's wife
Berry, Hugh (act): I Was A Zombie For The F.B.I.
Berry, Jack (act): Abide With Me
Berry, John (dir): Angel On My Shoulder (1980)
Berry, Jules (act, 1889-1951): Les Visiteurs Du Soir
Berry, Julian (wri): see Gastaldi, (Ernesto)
Berry, June (act): The Children; The Nesting
Berry, Ken (act): The Cat From Outer Space; Hello Down There
Berry, Lloyd (act): April Fool's Day; The Plutonium Incident; Runaway
Berry, Mike (act): I Was A Zombie For The F.B.I.
Berry, Owen (act): Fire Maidens Of Outer Space
Berry, Patrick H. (act): Offerings
Berry, Sarah (act): Evil Dead 2: Dead By Dawn
Berry, Stephanie (act): Jacob's Ladder
Berry, Tim (act): Cavegirl (1985)
Berry, Vincent (act): Sleepstalker
Berryhill, Betsy (act): Phenomenon
Berryhill, Sharon (act): Simon, King Of The Witches
Berryman, Michael (act, b. 1948): Beastmaster 2: Through The Portal Of Time; Deadly Blessing; Doc Savage, The Man Of Bronze; Haunting Fear; The Hills Have Eyes; The Hills Have Eyes II; Invitation To Hell; My Science Project; Star Trek Iv: The Voyage Home; Weird Science
Berset, Fernand (act): Aimez-Vous Les Femmes?
Bershad, Sheldon (act): see Leonard, Sheldon
Berstein, Caron K. (act): Waxwork II: Lost In Time
Bertazzolo, Riccardo (act): Miracle In Milan
Bertea, Roberto (act): Atom Age Vampire
Bertelsen, Tommy (act): Ed Wood
Bertelson, Emily Marie (act): see Windsor, Marie
Bertheau, Julien (act): The Discreet Charm Of The Bourgeoisie
Berthier, Jacques (act): Lemmy Pour Les Dames
Berthron, Dierdre (act): Carrie
Berti, Dehl (act): Ritual Of Evil; Wolfen
Berti, Pierre (act): Orphee
Bertin, Yori (act): Frantic
Bertinelli, Valerie (act, b. 1960): Chomps; The Haunting Of Helen Walker
Bertish, Jane (act): Paperhouse; The Quatermass Conclusion
Bertl, Pavel (act): Order And Disorder
Bertolini, Angelo (act): Lady In White
Berton, Kenneth J. (dir & wri): The Devil's Gift
Bertoya, Paul (act): Stranger In The House (1967)
Bertram, Charles (act): Hail Britannia!; The Vanishing Lady (1897)
Bertrand, Claude (act): And Soon The Darkness
Bertrand, Rachel (act):Dr. Jekyll And Ms. Hyde
Bertrand, Ralph (act): Isle Of The Snake People; Misterios Del Ultratumba
Beruh, Joe (act): Remote Control (1988)
Berval, Annie (act): Death Comes From Space
Berval, Antonin (act): What Price Murder
Berwick, Irvin (dir): The Monster Of Piedras Blancas
Berwick, James (act): Outland
Berwick, John (act): Goliath Awaits; I, Desire
Berwick, Mike (cin): Eclipse (1977)
Besbas, Peter (act): Master Of The World
Besch, Bibi (act): Mr. Don't Walk; The Day After; Kill Me Again; The Lonely Lady; Rattled; Star Trek II: The Wrath Of Khan; Tremors
Besnak, Greg (act): Midnight (1980)

Bess, Ardon (act): Prom Night; The Shape Of Things To Come (1979)
Bessell, Ted (act, 1935–1996): Scream, Pretty Peggy
Besselo, George (act): see Reeves, George
Besser, Joe (act, 1907–1988): Africa Screams; Hand Of Death
Besserer, Eugenie (act): The Bridge Of San Luis Rey (1929)
Bessho, Tetsuya (act): Solar Crisis
Bessiere, Christine (act): Princess Warrior
Bessing, Claudette (act): Thx 1138
Bessler, Albert (act): Confess, Dr. Corda
Besson, Luc (dir): Le Dernier Combat; The Fifth Element
Besson, Luc (wri): The Fifth Element
Best, Bettie (act): The Trap
Best, Deannie (act): The Shanghai Chest
Best, Edna (act, 1900–1974): The Ghost And Mrs. Muir; The Man Who Knew Too Much (1934)
Best, James (act, b. 1926): The Beast From 20,000 Fathoms; Francis Goes To West Point; The Killer Shrews; Man On The Prowl; Riders To The Stars; The Savage Bees; Shock Corridor
Best, John (wri): Splatter
Best, Jonathan (act): Silent Night, Deadly Night
Best, Katherine (act): Xtro
Best, Oscar (act): Angel Heart
Best, Peggy (act): The Black Bird (1926)
Best, Peri (act): Quarantine
Best, Wayne (act): Short Circuit 2
Best, Willie (act, 1916–1962, a.k.a. Sleep'n'Eat): A-Haunting We Will Go; The Body Disappears; Dangerous Money; The Face Of Marble; The Ghost Breakers; The Hidden Hand; Mr. Moto In Danger Island; Mr. Moto Takes A Vacation; The Monster Walks; Murder On A Bridle Path; Murder On A Honeymoon; Nancy Drew, Troubleshooter; The Red Dragon (1945); The Shanghai Chest; Whispering Ghosts
Bestaeva, T. (act): The Shadows Of Forgotten Ancestors
Bestar, Barbara (act): Killers From Space; Safari Drums
Bester, Diane (act): Maroc 7; Model For Murder
Bestolarides, Bill (act): The Dungeonmaster
Beswick, Doug (cin): The Cremators
Beswick(e), Martine (act, b. 1941): Devil Dog: The Hound Of Hell; Dr. Jekyll And Sister Hyde; From Russia With Love; The Offspring; One Million Years B.C.; The Penthouse (1967); Prehistoric Women (1966); Seizure; Strange New World; Thunderball; Trancers II: The Return Of Jack Deth; Wide Sargasso Sea
Betancourt, Anne (act): Jack's Back
Beth, Kay (act): Pranks
Bethel, Dawn (act): see North, Sheree
Bethman, Sabina (act): Journey To The Lost City
Bethune, Ivy (act): Dark Night Of The Scarecrow; Eyes Of Fire
Bethune, John (act): When Michael Calls
Bethune, Zina (act, b. 1945): Forgotten City Of The Planet Of The Apes
Betsworth, Sommer (act): Curse II: The Bite
Bettger, Lyle (act, b. 1915): The Lone Ranger
Betti, Laura (act): Hatchet For A Honeymoon; Twitch Of The Death Nerve
Bettin, Val (act): The Man Who Wasn't There
Bettinson, Ralph (Gilbert) (wri): Doomed To Die; 1984 (1955); Rogues Of Sherwood Forest
Bettoia, Franca (act): The Last Man On Earth
Betts, Bert (act): The Pit (1962)
Betts, Kirsten (act): Crescendo; The Vampire Lovers
Betts, Kristina (act): Wheels Of Terror
Betts, Nigel (act): Jekyll And Hyde
Bettus, Ken (wri): The Adventures Of Nick Carter
Betuel, Jonathan R. (dir): My Science Project
Betuel, Jonathan (R.) (wri): The Last Starfighter; My Science Project
Betz, Byron (act): Targets
Betz, Carl (act, 1920–1978): The Deadly Dream; Killdozer
Betz, Donna Lee (act): Orpheus Descending
Betz, Jimmy (act): Pranks
Betz, Mathew (act): Mystery Of The Wax Museum; Tarzan The Fearless; The Terror (1928); The Unholy Three (1925)
Betzler, Geri (act): Amityville: The Evil Escapes
Betzner, Christine (act): A Bell From Hell
Beuth, Robert Alan (act): Ghostbusters II; Graveyard Shift (1990); Outbreak
Bevan, Billy (act): see Bevan, William/Billy
Bevan, Isla (act): The Face At The Window (1932); Puppets Of Fate; The Sign Of Four (1932)
Bevan, Stewart/Stuart (act): The Flesh And Blood Show; The Ghoul (1974); House Of Mortal Sin
Bevan, William/Billy (act, 1887–1957, nee William Bevan Harris): Arrest Bulldog Drummond; Counterespionage; Devotion; Dr. Jekyll And Mr. Hyde (1941); Dracula's Daughter; The Invisible Man's Revenge; The Lodger (1944); The Lost Patrol (1934); The Man Who Wouldn't Die; The Mysterious Mr. Moto; The Picture Of Dorian Gray (1945); Rogues Of Sherwood Forest; A Study In Scarlet (1933); Terror By Night
Bevani, Alexander (act): The Phantom Of The Opera (1925)
Bevans, Clem (act): The Millerson Case; Portrait Of Jennie; Saboteur
Beveridge, Mal (act): Quarantine
Beverley, Joan (act): At The Villa Rose (1920)
Beverly, Helen (act): Black Magic (1944)
Bevilacqua, Alberto (wri): Atom Age Vampire; I Tre Volti Della Paura
Bevington, Nancy (act): The Mystery Of Edwin Drood (1909)
Bevis, Leslie (act): Alien Nation; Amazons (1984)
Bewes, Rodney (act): Alice's Adventures In Wonderland (1972); Jabberwocky; The Spaceman And King Arthur
Bey, John Toles (act): Endless Descent
Bey, Marki (act): Sugar Hill
Bey, Tema (act): 12 To The Moon
Bey, Turhan (act, b. 1920): Ali Baba And The Forty Thieves (1943); The Amazing Mr. X; Arabian Nights; Background To Danger; The Climax; The Falcon Takes Over; The Gay Falcon; The Mad Ghoul; The Mummy's Tomb; A Night In Paradise; Prisoners Of The Casbah; Sudan; White Savage
Beyer, Hanne Karin (act): see Karina, Anna
Beyer, Ted (act): Threads
Beyer, Uwe (act): The Nibelungs (1966)
Beyerle, Clinton (act): Halloween With The Addams Family
Beymer, Richard (act): A Face To Die For; The Presence; Silent Night, Deadly Night II
Bezencenet, Peter (dir): 24 Hours To Kill
Bezzerides, I.A. (wri): Kiss Me Deadly
Bhaskar (act): I Drink Your Blood
Bhat, Rishi (act): The Indian In The Cupboard
Bhutto, Chuck (act): Phantasm II: Lord Of The Dead
Bialik, Mayim (act): Pumpkinhead
Biamonte, Ermanno (cin): Cameron's Closet; Yeti
Bianchi, Andrea (dir): Burial Ground
Bianchi, Daniela (act, b. 1942): Code Name: Tiger; From Russia With Love; Operation Kid Brother; Requiem For A Secret Agent
Bianchi, Edward (dir): The Fan
Bianchi, Eleonora (act): Treasure Of The Petrified Forest; Ulysses Against The Son Of Hercules
Bianchi, Paolo (dir): Superargo E I Giganti Senza Volto
Bianchi, Regina (act): Spara Forte, Piu Forte...Non Capisco
Bianchi, Tino (act): La Maschera Del Demonio
Bianchine, Jill (act): My Best Friend Is A Vampire
Biancoli, Oreste (wri, a.k.a. Robert Davidson): Gli Invasori; Maciste Al Inferno; Maciste Alla Corte Del Gran Khan; Son Of Samson; Lo Spettro
Biao, Yuen (act): The Dead And The Deadly; Mr. Vampire II
Biberman, Abner (act, b. 1909): Another Thin Man; The Bridge Of San Luis Rey (1944); Captain Kidd; The Golden Mistress; The Leopard Man
Biberman, Herbert J. (dir, 1900–1971): Meet Nero Wolfe
Bibic, Vladimir (act): Gremlins 2: The New Batch
Bicat, Nick (mus): A Christmas Carol (1984); The Reflecting Skin
Bice, Robert/Bob (act, b. 1914): The Adventures Of Hajji Baba; Bowery To Bagdad; Captive Women; Invasion U.S.A.; It!—The Terror From Beyond Space; Port Sinister; The Snow Creature; Space Master X-7; Tarzan And The She-Devil
Bick, Andrew (act): Surf Nazis Must Die
Bick, John (act): Surf Nazis Must Die
Bick, Joni (act): Last Bride Of Salem
Bickel, Frederick McIntyre (act): see March, Fredric
Bickel, Ray (act): Creature; Shocker
Bickerton, Melissa (act): Species
Bickford, Charles (act, 1891–1967): Of Mice And Men (1939); Tarzan's New York Adventure; White Woman
Bicknell, Gene (act): Condor; Neon Maniacs
Biddle, Adrian (cin): Aliens; The Princess Bride; Willow
Bide, Yan (act): Buddha's Lock
Bider, Robyn (act): The Black Cat (1965)
Biderman, Ann (wri): Copycat; Primal Fear
Bidlake, Richard (act): Island Of Terror
Bie, Sherry (act): Memories Of Murder; The Reflecting Skin
Bieber, Leo (act): The Third Man
Biehn, Michael (act, b. 1956): The Abyss; Aliens; Asteroid; Conundrum; Deep Red (1994); The Fan; A Fire In The Sky (1978); Jade; The Seventh Sign; The Terminator
Bien, Robert Taylor (act): see Warwick, Robert
Bienert, Gerhard (act): M (1931)
Biensfeldt, Paul (act): Doctor Mabuse; Die Spinnen; Der Steinerne Reiter
Bierce, Ambrose (wri, 1842–1914?): Au Coeur De La Vie; The Return (1973, GB)
Bieri, Ramon (act): The Andromeda Strain; Demon And The Mummy; Vibes
Bierko, Craig (act): The Long Kiss Goodnight
Bierle, Natalie (act): see Birell, Tala
Bierman, Robert (dir): Vampire's Kiss
Biesk, Adam (act): Leprechaun 2; Meet The Applegates
Bigagli, Claudio (act): Fiorile
Bigelow, Kathryn (dir): Near Dark; Strange Days
Bigelow, Kathryn (wri): Near Dark
Biggart, Brad (act): Blood Diner
Bigger, Hal (cin): Return From Witch Mountain
Biggers, Earl Derr (wri, 1884–1953): Castle In The Desert; Charlie Chan And The Curse Of The Dragon Queen; Charlie Chan At Monte Carlo; Charlie Chan At The Circus; Charlie Chan At The Olympics; Charlie Chan At The Opera; Charlie Chan At The Race Track; Charlie Chan At The Wax Museum; Charlie Chan At Treasure Island; Charlie Chan Carries On; Charlie Chan: Happiness Is A Warm Clue; Charlie Chan In City In Darkness; Charlie Chan In Egypt; Charlie Chan In Honolulu; Charlie Chan In London; Charlie Chan In Panama; Charlie Chan In Paris; Charlie Chan In Reno; Charlie Chan In Rio; Charlie Chan In Shanghai; Charlie Chan In The Secret Service; Charlie Chan On Broadway; Charlie Chan's Chance; Charlie Chan's Courage; Charlie Chan's Greatest Case; Charlie Chan's Murder Cruise; Charlie Chan's Secret; The Chinese Cat; The Chinese Parrot; The Chinese Ring; Dangerous Money; Dark Alibi; Dead Men Tell; The Docks Of New Orleans; The Feathered Serpent (1948); The Golden Eye; House Of The Long Shadows; The Jade Mask; Murder Over New York; The Red Dragon (1945); The Scarlet Clue; Seven Keys To Baldpate (1917, 1925 & 1929); Shadows Over Chinatown; The Shanghai Chest; The Sky Dragon; The Trap
Biggers, Victoria (act): Witchery
Biggins, Christopher (act): The Rocky Horror Picture Show; The Tempest (1980)
Biggins, Jonathan (act): Those Dear Departed
Biggs, Rickie (act): Miracle Mile
Biggs, Roxann (act): Mortal Sins
Bignamini, Nino (act): The Night Porter
Biheller, Robert (act): Fire In The Sky (1993)
Bikel, Theodore (act, b. 1924): I Bury The Living; Murder On Flight 502; The Return Of The King
Bilas, Jay (act): I Come In Peace
Bilbao, Fernando (act, a.k.a. Fred Harris): Les Experiences Erotiques De Frankenstein; Exterminators Of The Year 3000; Hundra
Bilbrey, Effie (act): Blood Diner
Bilbrook, Lydia (act): The Picture Of Dorian Gray (1945)
Bildt, Paul (act): Das Kalte Herz; Schloss Vogelod
Bilecky, John (cin): Vampire On Bikini Beach
Bilewski, B. (act): Wielka, Wielka I Najwieksza
Bilis, Teddy (act): Le Testament Du Dr. Cordelier
Bill, John (act): The Resurrection Of Zachary Wheeler
Bill, Tony (act, b. 1940): Are You In The House Alone?; Castle Keep; Haunts Of The Very Rich; How To Steal The World; The Initiation Of Sarah
Billecard, Denise (act): see Darcel, Denise
Biller, Brigitte (act): The Pink Chiquitas
Billerey, Raoul (act): Perceval
Billings, Earl (act): Something Is Out There
Billings, Ted (act): Bride Of Frankenstein
Billingslea, Beau (act): The Blob (1988)
Billingsley, Barbara (act): Bay Coven; Shadow On The Wall
Billingsley, Jennifer (act): Lady In A Cage; The Thirsty Dead
Billingsley, Peter (act): Death Valley
Billington, Kevin (dir, b. 1933): The Light At The Edge Of The World; Voices
Billington, Michael (act): The Spy Who Loved Me
Billock, Rik (act): The Dark Half
Bills, Michael (act): Tam Lin
Billy Merrin and His Commanders (act): The Dance Of Death
Billy Smart Circus, The (act): Berserk
Billy, Michele Ameen (act): Star Trek
Bilotta, Bruno (act): Demons 2
Bilotta, Furio (act): Demons 2
Bilson, Danny (dir): Zone Troopers
Bilson, Danny (wri): Eliminators; The Flash; The Rocketeer; Trancers; Zone Troopers
Bilson, David (act): Eraser
Bilyeu, Valencia (act): To Die For II: Son Of Darkness
Bilzerian, Laurence (act): Nothing But Trouble
Bimchy, Kate (act): The Mind Of Mr. Soames
Binder, John (act & wri): Endangered Species
Binder, Maurice (cin): The Final Countdown
Binder, Sybilla (act): Counterblast; Portrait From Life; Thunder Rock
Bindi, Clara (act): La Maschera Del Demonio
Binet, Catherine (dir): The Games Of Countess Dolingen Of Gratz
Binford, Robert (act): Ed Wood
Bing, Herman (act): The Florentine Dagger
Bingham, Barbara (act): Bridge Across Time; Friday The 13th, Part VIII-Jason Takes Manhattan
Bingham, Cindy (act): I Was A Zombie For The F.B.I.
Bingham, Daryl (act): Earthbound (1981)
Bingham, Gena (act): Copycat
Bingham, John (wri): Fragment Of Fear
Bingham, Lucy (act): Seizure
Bingham, Stanley (act): Robin Hood Jr. (1923)
Bingham, Traci (act, b. 1973): Demon Knight; The Nutty Professor (1996)
Bingham, Virginia (act): Tomorrow's Child
Binion, Crawford (act): Creator
Binkowski, Bruce (act): Return Of The Killer Tomatoes
Binner, Hans (act): Confess, Dr. Corda
Binney, Geoffrey (act): Battlestar Galactica
Binney, William (act): Virus
Binns, Edward (act, 1916–1990): Beyond A Reasonable Doubt; The Curse Of The Undead; Fail-Safe; North By Northwest
Binns, Colonel Percy (act): It Happened Here
Binyon, Claude (wri, 1905–1978): Kisses For My President
Biolos, Leigh (act): Howling II
Biondolillo, Gaspare (act): see LaRue, Jack
Birbichi, Enrico (cin): The Grim Reaper
Birch, Cecil (dir): Monty's Monocle; The Scarecrow; The Tell-Tale Globe; The Troubles Of A Hypochondriac; What The?
Birch, Derek (act): Grip Of The Strangler
Birch, Don (act): Attack Of The Killer Tomatoes
Birch, Frank (act): Dracula (1979); Lady In The Fog; Wolf's Clothing (1936)
Birch, Frank (dir): Ashes
Birch, Paul (act): The Beast With A Million Eyes; Bonzo Goes To College; Day The World Ended (1955); Not Of This Earth (1957); Queen Of Outer Space; The Tattered Dress; The 27th Day; The War Of The Worlds
Birch, Rebecca (act): Attack Of The Killer Tomatoes
Birch, Thora (act, b. 1982): Hocus Pocus
Birch, Wyrley (act): The Last Days Of Pompeii (1935); The Lone Wolf Returns (1935)
Birch, Yan (act): The People Under The Stairs
Birchal, Robert (cin): The Spectre Of Edgar Allan Poe
Birchard, Paul (act): Batman (1989)
Bird, Billie (act): Ernest Saves Christmas
Bird, Bobby (act): Dead Of Night (1987)
Bird, Brad (wri): *Batteries Not Included
Bird, Charlie (act): Nightwing
Bird, John (act): A Dandy In Aspic; Jabberwocky; The Seven-Per-Cent Solution
Bird, Kristi (act): Phantom Of The Paradise
Bird, Larry (act): Space Jam
Bird, Michael (act): The Wrong Box
Bird, Michael (cin): Oh Heavenly Dog
Bird, Minah (act): Vampira
Bird, Norman (act, b. 1920): Black Torment; Cash On Demand; A Dandy In Aspic; Doomwatch; The Final Conflict; First Men In The Moon (1964); Hands Of The Ripper; Hot Enough For June; In Search Of The Castaways; An Inspector Calls; Limbo Line; Maniac (1963); Man In The Moon (1960); The Medusa Touch; The Mind Benders (1963); Night Of The Eagle; The Slipper And The Rose
Bird, Richard (act, b. 1894): Bulldog Drummond At Bay (1937); Death Trap

(1962); The Door With Seven Locks (1940); Forbidden; Halfway House; The Warren Case
Bird, Richard (dir, b. 1894): The Terror (1939)
Bird, T.H. (wri): The March Hare
Birdwell, Russell (dir): The Girl In The Kremlin
Birell, Tala (act, 1908-1959, nee Natalie Bierle): Crime And Punishment (1935); The Frozen Ghost; The Lone Wolf Returns (1935); The Monster Maker (1943); Nagana; One Dangerous Night; Philo Vance's Gamble; Philo Vance's Secret Mission
Birinski, Leo (wri): Mata Hari (1932)
Birk, Raye (act): Deadly Messages; The Stepford Children
Birkenfeld, Bobby (act): Phantom Of The Paradise
Birkett, Bernadette (act): Jekyll And Hyde...Together Again
Birkett, Jack (act): The Bride (1985); The Tempest (1980)
Birkett, Viva (act): Trilby (1914)
Birkin, Andrew (dir): Sredni Vashtar
Birkin, Andrew (wri): The Final Conflict; The Name Of The Rose; The Pied Piper (1971); Sredni Vashtar; The Thief Of Baghdad (1978)
Birkin, Jane (act, b. 1947): Dark Places; Death On The Nile; Evil Under The Sun; Seven Deaths In The Cat's Eye
Birkinshaw, Alan (dir): Killer's Moon; Ten Little Indians (1989)
Birkinshaw, Alan (wri): Killer's Moon
Birks, David (act): The Hound Of The Baskervilles (1959)
Birman, Len (act): Assassin (1986); Captain America (1978); Captain America II
Birmingham, Gil (act): House II: The Second Story
Birnbaum, Nathan (act): see Burns, George
Birney, David (act, b. 1939): Caravan To Vaccares; Nightfall (1988); Oh, God! Book II; Someone's Watching Me!
Birney, Frank (act): The Babysitter; C.H.U.D. II; The Clonus Horror; Critters 2: The Main Course; Fear No Evil (1981); Modern Problems
Biro, Lajos (wri, 1880–1948): Dark Journey; The Drum; The Ghost Train (1931); The Haunted House (1929); Knight Without Armour; The Man Who Could Work Miracles; The Private Life Of Don Juan; The Return Of The Scarlet Pimpernel; The Scarlet Pimpernel (1934); Strange Evidence; The Thief Of Bagdad (1940)
Biroc, Joseph (cin, 1903-1996): The Amazing Colossal Man; The Bat (1959); Beyond The Poseidon Adventure; The Clone Master; Confessions Of An Opium Eater; Donovan's Brain; Escape From The Planet Of The Apes; Hush...Hush, Sweet Charlotte; I Saw What You Did (1965); It's A Wonderful Life; Nightmare (1956); Red Planet Mars; Shanks; 13 Ghosts; To Trap A Spy; The Towering Inferno; The Twonky; The Unknown Terror; What Ever Happened To Aunt Alice?; Wonder Woman
Birri, Fernando (dir): A Very Old Man With Enormous Wings
Birriel, Felippe (act): Flight Of The Lost Balloon
Birt, Christopher (act): Wolf
Birt, Dan(iel) (dir): The Interrupted Journey; She Shall Have Murder; The Three Weird Sisters
Birt, Louise (wri): The Three Weird Sisters
Biryukov, P. (act): Pikovaya Dama (1910)
Bisacco, Roberto (act): Torso
Bisbee, Aileen (act): see Pringle, Aileen
Bischof, Larry (act): The Ultimate Warrior
Bisco, Jim (wri): Tuck Everlasting
Bisera, Olga (act): The Spy Who Loved Me
Bishop, Alfred (act): The Brass Bottle (1914); The Lifeguardsman
Bishop, Anthony (act): Eat And Run
Bishop, Arland (act): Ghostriders
Bishop, Barbara (act): Blood Of Dracula's Castle
Bishop, Donald (act): The China Syndrome
Bishop, Doug (act): Secrets Of The Phantom Caverns
Bishop, Ed(ward) (act): Battle Beneath The Earth; Diamonds Are Forever; Doppelganger; The Fifth Missile; Quiller: Price Of Violence; Saturn 3
Bishop, George (act): The Flesh And The Fiends; The Mysterious Mr. Nicholson; Where The Rainbow Ends
Bishop, Jennifer (act): The Female Bunch; Horror Of The Blood Monsters; Impulse! (1974); The Mad Room
Bishop, Jim (act): Santa Claus Conquers The Martians
Bishop, Joey (act, b. 1918, nee Joseph Abraham Gottlieb): Johnny Cool
Bishop, Julie (act, b. 1917, a.k.a. Jacqueline Wells): The Black Cat (1934); The Hidden Hand; Tarzan The Fearless
Bishop, Larry (act): Shanks; Wild In The Streets
Bishop, Mark (wri): Demon Knight
Bishop, Melanie (act): The Lost Boys
Bishop, Norm (act): This Is Not A Test
Bishop, Phillan (mus): Kiss Of The Tarantula
Bishop, Robert (act): Richard II (1955)
Bishop, Rummy (act): Short Circuit 2
Bishop, Stephen (mus): The China Syndrome
Bishop, Terry (dir & wri): Cover Girl Killer; Model For Murder
Bishop, Tony (act): Road Games
Bishop, Wes (act): The Thing With Two Heads
Bishop, Wes (wri): Race With The Devil; The Thing With Two Heads
Bishop, William (act): Port Said; Song Of The Thin Man
Bislani, Fernando (act): The Devil's Men
Bisley, Steve (act): The Chain Reaction (1980); Mad Max
Bisoglio, Val (act, b. 1926): Matt Helm
Bissell, Whit (act, 1909-1996): The Atomic Kid; City Beneath The Sea (1970); Creature From The Black Lagoon; Crime Doctor's Diary; A Double Life; Flood; For Heaven's Sake; Invasion Of The Body Snatchers (1956); I Was A Teenage Frankenstein; I Was A Teenage Werewolf; Lost Continent (1951); The Manchurian Candidate; Monster On The Campus; Psychic Killer; Seven Days In May; Soylent Green; Target Earth; The Time Machine (1960 & 1978)
Bissell, William (act): Trauma (1963)
Bisset, Jacqueline (act, b. 1944): Casino Royale; Cul-De-Sac; The Deep; The Mephisto Waltz; Murder On The Orient Express; Once You Meet A Stranger; Secret Agent (1974); The Spiral Staircase (1975); When Time Ran Out
Bissett, Donald (act): Blind Terror; Eye Of The Devil; The Headless Ghost; Little Red Monkey; The 39 Steps (1978); Warlords Of The Deep
Bissett, Josie (act): All-American Murder
Biswanger, Erwin (act): Metropolis (1926)
Biswas, Chhabi (act): Devi
Bitterman, Shem (wri): Halloween 5: The Revenge Of Michael Myers
Bitzer, G.W./Billy (cin, 1870–1944): The Avenging Conscience; The Midnight Girl
Bitzer, John (cin): King Tut-Ankh-Amen's Eighth Wife
Bivens, J.B. (act): The Resurrected
Bivens, Loren (act & cin): Blood Simple
Bixby, Bill (act, 1934–1993): The Death Of The Incredible Hulk; Fantasy Island; The Great Houdinis; The Incredible Hulk; The Incredible Hulk, Part 2; The Incredible Hulk Returns; The Magician (1973); Murder Is Easy; The Trial Of The Incredible Hulk
Bixby, Bill (dir, 1934–1993): The Death Of The Incredible Hulk
Bixby, Jay Lewis (wri): Fantastic Voyage
Bixby, Jerome (wri, b. 1923): Curse Of The Faceless Man; It!—The Terror From Beyond Space; The Lost Missile; Twilight Zone
Bixler, Denise (act): Evil Dead 2: Dead By Dawn
Bizet, Georges (wri): Gipsy Blood
Biziou, Peter (cin): Richard II (1995); Time Bandits
Bizley, Roger (act): The Face Of Darkness
Bjorck, Hauck (act): Roger Corman's Frankenstein Unbound
Bjorn, Anna (act): The Sword And The Sorcerer
Bjornstrand, Gunnar (act, b. 1909): Ansiktet; The Devil's Eye; Hets; Persona; The Red Mantle; Det Sjunde Inseglet; Smultronstallet; Through A Glass Darkly
Bjurman, Susan (act): Zontar: The Thing From Venus
Blaazer, Louis (act): Dr. No
Blache, Herbert (dir): Secrets Of The Night
Black Sabbath (mus): Heavy Metal
Black, Bill (act): Kill, Kill, Overkill
Black, Cilla (act, b. 1943): Work Is A Four Letter Word
Black, Don (mus): Alice's Adventures In Wonderland (1972); Gulliver's Travels (1977)
Black, Don (wri): Gulliver's Travels (1977)
Black, Dorothy (act): The Night Has Eyes
Black, Gabriel (mus): The Initiation
Black, George (wri): The Perfect Woman
Black, Gerry (act): Re-Animator
Black, Ian (act): Memories Of Murder
Black, Ian Stuart (wri): The Limping Man (1953); Shadow Of The Past; Soho Incident
Black, Isobel (act): Kiss Of The Vampire; 10 Rillington Place; Twins Of Evil
Black, J.R. (wri): Shadow Zone: The Undead Express
Black, Jack (act): Mars Attacks!
Black, Jeremy (act): The Boys From Brazil
Black, John (dir): Robin Hood Junior (1975)
Black, John D.F. (wri): The Clone Master; Do Not Fold, Spindle Or Mutilate; Wonder Woman
Black, Karen (act, b. 1943, nee Karen Ziegler): Burnt Offerings; Capricorn One; Children Of The Night (1992); Eternal Evil; Evil Spirits; Family Plot; Haunting Fear; Invaders From Mars (1986); The Invisible Kid; It's Alive II: Island Of The Alive; Killer Fish; Mirror, Mirror; Night Angel; Out Of The Dark; Portnoy's Complaint; Rhinoceros (1974); The Strange Possession Of Mrs. Oliver; Trilogy Of Terror
Black, Kelly (act): Looker
Black, Lewis (act): Jacob's Ladder
Black, Lindsay Armstrong (act): The Worm Eaters
Black, Lorne (act): Maid To Order
Black, Lucas (act): Sling Blade
Black, Noel (dir, b. 1937): Mirrors; Pretty Poison (1968)
Black, Noel (wri, b. 1937): Mirrors
Black, Shane (act): Predator
Black, Shane (wri, b. 1961): The Long Kiss Goodnight; The Monster Squad
Black, Stanley (mus, b. 1913): Blood Of The Vampire; The City Under The Sea; The Day The Earth Caught Fire; The Fatal Night; The Flesh And The Fiends; The Full Treatment; Hour Of Decision; Jack The Ripper (1958); The Trollenberg Terror; The Vicious Circle (1957)
Black, Stewart (act): Dorian Gray
Black, Terry (wri): Dead Heat
Blackburn, Arline (act): Annabel Lee
Blackburn, Clarice (act): Man On A Swing; Night Of Dark Shadows; Pretty Poison (1968)
Blackburn, Greta (act): Party Line; Time Walker
Blackburn, Jane (act): Subterfuge
Blackburn, John (wri): Nothing But The Night
Blackburn, Joy (act): Anguish
Blackburn, Ken (act): The Frighteners
Blackburn, Richard (act, dir & wri): Lemora, The Lady Dracula
Blackburn, Tom (wri): Mara Of The Wilderness
Blacker, Tina (act): see Louise, Tina
Blacker, Vera (act): The Demon (1981)
Blackett, Andrew (act): Treasure Island (1950)
Blackett, Anthony (act): The Medusa Touch
Blackford, Nessie (act): Maria Marten: Or, The Murder In The Red Barn (1913); Spiritualism Exposed (1913)
Blackie, Sandra (act): Wild Thing
Blackman, Bond (act): Trauma (1963)
Blackman, Don (act): Desert Legion; Scream, Blacula, Scream; Valley Of The Headhunters
Blackman, Honor (act, b. 1926): The Cat And The Canary (1978); Daughter Of Darkness (1948); Fright (1971); The Glass Tomb; Goldfinger; Jason And The Argonauts; Moment To Moment; The Secret Of My Success; So Long At The Fair; Suspended Alibi; To The Devil A Daughter
Blackman, Joan (act): The Destructors; Visit To A Small Planet
Blackman, Ronald (act): The Pirates Of Blood River
Blackman, Wanda (act): Obsession (1976)
Blackmer, Sidney (act, 1895–1973): Beyond A Reasonable Doubt; Charlie Chan At Monte Carlo; The Count Of Monte Cristo (1934); Deluge; Ellery Queen And The Perfect Crime; Kismet (1930); The Lady And The Monster; Rosemary's Baby; Thank You, Mr. Moto
Blackmon, Esther (act): The Mutations; The Sentinel
Blackmore, Peter (wri): Child's Play (1954); Mad About Men; Miranda
Blackmore, R.D. (wri, 1825–1900): Lorna Doone (1912, 1920 & 1922)
Blackmore, Stephanie (act): Revenge Of The Stepford Wives
Blackoff, Edward (act): Chiller
Black Shadow (act): El Santo Contra Las Vampiras
Blackshaw, Anthony (act): Evil Of Frankenstein
Blackstone, Wendy (mus): The Uninvited (1996)
Blackton, J. Stewart (dir, 1875–1941): The Adventures Of Sherlock Holmes (1905); The Life Of Moses; Shakespeare's Tragedy, King Lear; The White Slave
Blackwater, Leslie (act): The Wicker Man
Blackwell, Carlyle (act, 1888–1955): Bulldog Drummond (1923); The Hound Of The Baskervilles (1929); She (1925)
Blackwell, Charles (act): The Fan
Blackwell, Charles (mus): Some Girls Do
Blackwell, Douglas (act): Robin Hood: Prince Of Thieves; 10 Rillington Place
Blackwell, George (cin): The Abominable Dr. Phibes; The Masque Of The Red Death (1964); Saturday Island; The Two-Headed Spy
Blackwolf, Mike (act): Princess Warrior
Blackwood, Kael (act): Charlie Chan And The Curse Of The Dragon Queen
Blackwood, Steve (act): Monolith
Blacque, Taurean (act): Deepstar Six
Blade, Richard (act): Spellcaster
Blades, Ruben (act): Color Of Night; Predator 2
Bladh, Hilding (cin): Rymdinvasion I Lappland
Blagdon, Michael (act): The Seven-Per-Cent Solution
Blaho, John (act): Midnight (1980)
Blahova, Dasha (act): Howling II
Blain, Estella (act): The Diabolical Dr. Z
Blain, Luci (act): Dinosaurus!
Blain, Pierre (act): The Golden Mistress
Blaine, Frank (act): Karate, The Hand Of Death
Blaine, James (act): The Lone Wolf Spy Hunt
Blaine, Jerry (act): Blood Of Dracula
Blaine, Martin (act): The Satan Bug
Blaine, Ruby (act): The Midnight Girl
Blaine, Vivian (act, 1921–1995): The Dark (1979); Parasite
Blair, Barbara (act): Bedelia; The Frightened Bride; I Killed The Count
Blair, Bernard (act): The Great Spy Chase
Blair, Betsy (act, b. 1923, nee Betsy Boger): Kind Lady (1951); Mystery Street; The Snake Pit (1948)
Blair, Bonnie (act): The Falcon's Alibi
Blair Jr., Clay (wri): Survive!
Blair, Don (act): Santa Claus Conquers The Martians
Blair, Elinor (act): Violent Women
Blair, Frank (act): The Swarm
Blair, George (dir): Daughter Of The Jungle; The Hypnotic Eye; Sabu And The Magic Ring; Secrets Of Scotland Yard; Spook Chasers
Blair, Isla (act): Dr. Terror's House Of Horrors (1964); Taste The Blood Of Dracula; Tennis Court; Treasure Island (1990)
Blair, Janet (act, b. 1921, nee Martha Jane Lafferty): Night Of The Eagle; Once Upon A Time (1944)
Blair, Joyce (act): Number Six
Blair, June (act): Island Of Lost Women
Blair, Kevin (act): Bloodstone: Subspecies II; Friday The 13th, Part VII-The New Blood; The Hills Have Eyes II
Blair, Linda (act, b. 1959): The Exorcist; Exorcist II: The Heretic; Grotesque; Hell Night; Repossessed; Stranger In Our House; Witchery
Blair, Lionel (act): The Limping Man (1953); Maroc 7
Blair, Nicky (act): Crashing Las Vegas; Diamonds Are Forever
Blair, Pamela (act): Svengali (1983)
Blair, Pat (act): Cage Of Evil
Blair, Ron (act): Seven
Blaisdell, Anne (wri): Fanatic
Blaisdell, Paul (act): Day The World Ended (1955); The Ghost Of Dragstrip Hollow; It Conquered The World; The She-Creature; Voodoo Woman
Blaise, Cynthia (act): Star Trek V: The Final Frontier
Blake, Alfonso Corona (dir): El Mundo De Los Vampiros; The Saint In The Wax Museum; El Santo Contra Las Vampiras
Blake, Alfonso Corona (wri): El Santo Contra Las Vampiras
Blake, Amanda (act, 1929–1989, nee Beverly Neill): The Adventures Of Hajji Baba; Betrayal; Counterspy Meets Scotland Yard; The Glass Slipper; Smuggler's Gold
Blake, Andre (act): The Silence Of The Lambs
Blake, Angela (act): I Was A Teenage Frankenstein
Blake, Ann (act): The Curse Of Frankenstein; The Curse Of The Werewolf; The Door In The Wall; Murder Reported; The Private Life Of Sherlock Holmes; A Taste Of Fear
Blake, Arthur (act): Quatermass II
Blake, Beverly (act): Creatures The World Forgot
Blake, Bobbie (act): see Blake, Robert
Blake, Clement (act): Writer's Block
Blake, Denis (act): Carry On Screaming
Blake, Ellen (act): The Being
Blake, Geoffrey (act): Philadelphia Experiment II
Blake, Gerald (dir): The Dance Of Death
Blake, Gladys (act): Phantom Of The Opera (1943)

Blake, Grey (act): Paul Temple Returns
Blake, Howard (act): Agatha
Blake, Howard (mus): Amityville 3-D; Flash Gordon
Blake, John A. (act): Offerings
Blake, Jon (act): Chilling
Blake, Josephine (act): The Headless Ghost
Blake, Julia (act): The Day After Halloween; Patrick
Blake, Katharine (act): Saturday Island
Blake, Larry (J.) (act): The Beginning Of The End; Creature With The Atom Brain; Demon Seed; Diamonds Are Forever; Earth vs. The Flying Saucers; Son Of Sinbad; Time After Time; The Trap; The Werewolf (1955)
Blake, Madge (act): Batman (1966); Between Midnight And Dawn; Please Murder Me; The Prowler (1951)
Blake, Marie (act): Blue, White And Perfect; Gildersleeve's Ghost; The Snake Pit (1948)
Blake, Noah (act): Teen Witch
Blake, Oliver (act): The Challenge; Giant From The Unknown; Houdini; Nightmare Alley; Shadow Of The Thin Man
Blake, Pamela (act): The Hat Box Mystery; Highway 13
Blake, Patricia (act): The Black Sleep
Blake, Paul (act): The Crimson Circle (1936)
Blake, Peter (act): Panic (1979)
Blake, Richard (wri): Invaders From Mars (1953 & 1986)
Blake, Robert/Bobbie/Bobby (act, b. 1934): The Black Rose; The Horn Blows At Midnight; Lost Highway; Of Mice And Men (1981); The Woman In The Window
Blake, Rosemary (act): Tam Lin
Blake, Stephen Ashley (cin): Sorority Babes In The Slimeball Bowl-O-Rama
Blake, T.C. (dir): Nightflyers
Blake, Tom (act): The Face In The Fog (1922)
Blake, Whitney (act): My Gun Is Quick
Blake, Willie (cin): The God King
Blake, Yvonne (act): Fahrenheit 451
Blakeley, James Barry (act): Nightfall (1988)
Blakely, Colin (act, 1930–1987): The Big Sleep (1978); The Day The Fish Came Out; Evil Under The Sun; Murder On The Orient Express; The Private Life Of Sherlock Holmes; The Spy With A Cold Nose; The Vengeance Of She
Blakely, Don (act): In The Shadow Of Kilimanjaro
Blakely, Gene (act): Everything's Ducky
Blakely, Ronee (act, b. 1946): A Nightmare On Elm Street; A Return To Salem's Lot
Blakely, Susan (act, b. 1950): The Annihilator; Color Me Perfect; Dream A Little Dream; Ladykillers (1988); The Towering Inferno
Blakely, Susie (act): Savages
Blakeney, Eric (wri): Generation X
Blakeney, Olive (act): Roogie's Bump
Blakey, John (act): First Knight; Judge Dredd
Blakey, Ken (cin): The Power Within
Blakiston, Caroline (act): The Magic Christian; Return Of The Jedi
Blalack, Robert (cin): Zapped!
Blamauer, Karoline (act): see Lenya, Lotte
Blanc, Erika (act): The Devil's Nightmare; Mark Of The Devil II; The Night Evelyn Came Out Of The Grave; Operazione Paura
Blanc, Mel (act, 1908–1989): Buck Rogers In The 25th Century; Champagne For Caesar; The Flintstones; Jetsons: The Movie
Blanc, Michel (act):Prospero's Books; The Tenant
Blancard, Jarred (act): It (1990)
Blancard, Rene (act): La Poursuite; To Catch A Thief
Blanch, Jewel (act): Baffled!
Blanchar, Pierre (act, 1892–1963): Gold (French-Speaking Version); The Queen Of Spades (1937)
Blanchard, Alan (act): Spawn Of The Slithis
Blanchard, Brianna (act): Candyman: Farewell To The Flesh
Blanchard, Francoise (act): Revenge In The House Of Usher
Blanchard, Mari (act, 1927–1970): Abbott And Costello Go To Mars; The Crooked Web; Jungle Heat; She-Devil; Son Of Sinbad; Twice-Told Tales; The Veils Of Bagdad
Blanchard, Rachel (act): Clarence
Blanchard, Susan (act): Prince Of Darkness; They Live
Blanchard-Power, Christie (act): The Nutty Professor (1996)
Blanche, Francis (act, b. 1921): Belle De Jour; The Great Spy Chase; L'ours; Who Stole The Body?
Blanche, Margaret (act): The Cobweb; The Grand Babylon Hotel; The Woman Of The Iron Bracelets
Blanche, Marie (act): The Elusive Pimpernel (1919); The Prehistoric Man (1924)
Blanco, Hugo (act): El Secreto Del Doctor Orlof
Blanco, Tomas (act):Faustina; The House That Screamed; A Thousand And One Nights (1968)
Blanco, Victorio (act): Dr. Tarr's Torture Dungeon
Bland, Joyce (act): The Barton Mystery (1932); The Crime At Blossoms
Bland, Rita (act): Dick Tracy (1990)
Bland, Sydney (act): The Picture Of Dorian Gray (1916); She (1916)
Blandick, Clara (act, 1881–1962): Charlie Chan's Greatest Case; Drums Of Jeopardy (1931); Philo Vance Returns; Pillow Of Death; The Wizard Of Oz (1939)
Blanding, Bernard (act): Matinee
Blane, Barbara (act): Satan Met A Lady
Blane, Norah (act): Who Done It? (1956)
Blane, Sally (act, b. 1910):Charlie Chan At Treasure Island; Crime On The Hill; Night Of Terror (1933)
Blaney, Tim (act): Short Circuit; Short Circuit 2
Blanguernon, Karen (act): Castle Keep; The Deadly Trap
Blank, Dorothee (act): L'or Du Duc; Les Parapluies De Cherbourg
Blank, Harrod (act): Killer Klowns From Outer Space
Blank, Leon (cin): Superstition
Blankenship, Linda (act): Mountaintop Motel Massacre
Blankenship, Norm (act): Zorro, The Gay Blade
Blankfield, Mark (act): The Incredible Shrinking Woman; Jekyll And Hyde...Together Again; The Midnight Hour; Robin Hood: Men In Tights
Blankfort, Albert (wri): Blind Alley
Blankfort, Michael (wri, b. 1907): An Act Of Murder (1948); The Other Man
Blanks, Billy (act): Tc 2000
Blanks, Brenda (act): Nightbeast
Blanshard, Joby (act): Doomwatch; Moon Zero Two
Blanton, Arell (act): Blood Mania; The Gifted One; The Swarm; When A Stranger Calls
Blanton, Nina Lynn (act): The Handmaid's Tale
Blas, Anibal (act): Slugs
Blasco, Ricardo (dir):Behind The Mask Of Zorro
Blasco, Sam (act): Street Trash
Blasi, Silvana (act): Quelqu'un Derriere La Porte
Blasko, Bela (act): see Lugosi, Bela
Blasko, Dan (act): Jaws 3-D
Blatchford, Frederick (wri): The Elusive Pimpernel (1919); Mr. Wu (1919)
Blatchley, Joseph (act): Arthur The King
Blatt, Edward A. (dir, b. 1905): Between Two Worlds
Blatty, William Peter (dir): The Exorcist II; Twinkle, Twinkle, Killer Kane
Blatty, William Peter (wri): The Exorcist; Exorcist II: The Heretic; The Exorcist II; Twinkle, Twinkle, Killer Kane
Blau, Beatrice Manley (act): The Baby
Blaustein, Barry W. (wri): The Nutty Professor (1996)
Blay, Bernard (act): Tomb Of Torture
Blaze, Tommy (act): Rumpelstiltskin (1996)
Blazickova, Nadezda (act):Baron Prasil
Bleasdale, Gary (act): Paperhouse
Blech, Hans Christian (act): The Scarlet Letter (1972)
Blechman, Corey (wri): Dark Mirror (1984)
Bleckner, Jeff (dir): The Beast (1996)
Bledsoe, Will(iam) (act): The Dark Side Of The Moon; The Return Of The Six Million Dollar Man And The Bionic Woman
Bleecher, Lennie (act): Witches' Brew
Blees, Robert (wri): The Black Scorpion; Curse Of The Black Widow; Dr. Phibes Rises Again; From The Earth To The Moon; The Glass Web; Screaming Mimi; Who Slew Auntie Roo?
Bleesz, Regina (act): From Beyond
Bleeth, Yasmine (act): A Face To Die For
Bleibtreu, Hedwig (act): The Third Man
Bleich, William/Bill (wri):Deadly Massages; The Hearse; The Midnight Hour; The Presence; The Stepford Children
Bleifer, John (act): The Black Room; Charlie Chan At Monte Carlo; Mr. Moto Takes A Vacation; Thank You, Mr. Moto
Bleiler, Weldon (act): The Bad Seed (1985)
Blessed, Brian (act): Apointment With A Killer; Flash Gordon; The Hound Of The Baskervilles (1982); The Trojan Women
Blessing, Ann (act): I, Desire
Blessing, Jack (act): Galaxy Of Terror
Bletcher, William/Billy (act): The Lost City; Satan Met A Lady
Blethyn, Brenda (act): The Witches (1990)
Bleu, Jean-Rene (act): Zombies Lake
Blick, Hugo E. (act): Batman (1989); A Connecticut Yankee In King Arthur's Court (1989)
Blick, John (cin): The Frighteners
Blick, Jonathan (act): The Frighteners
Blick, Newton (act): Man In The Moon (1960); Ring Of Spies
Bliedung, J. Alexander (act): see Beal, John
Blier, Bernard (act, 1916–1989): Catch Me A Spy; Les Miserables (1957); The Seventh Juror; To Commit A Murder
Bliesener, Jack (act): Hard Rock Zombies
Bligh, Jack (act): The Horror Of It All; The Night Of The Big Heat
Blin, Roger (act): Aimez-Vous Les Femmes?; The Hunchback Of Notre Dame (1957); Orphee; Torticola Contre Frankensberg; Les Visiteurs Du Soir
Blish, James (wri, 1921–1975): The Beast Must Die
Bliss, (Sir) Arthur (mus, 1891–1975): Things To Come
Bliss, John (act):The Thing With Two Heads
Bliss, Lela (act): The Dark Mirror (1946); Ghost Chasers; The Snake Pit (1948)
Bliss, Lucille (act): Miracle Mile
Bliss, Roy (act): Meet Nero Wolfe
Blitstein, David M. (cin): Weird Science
Blitz, Rusty (act): Werewolf Of Washington; Young Frankenstein
Blizzard, Helen (wri): The Beetle
Bloch, Andrew (act): Fugitive From The Empire; Hangar 18; Jason Goes To Hell: The Final Friday
Bloch, Charles B. (wri): The Hypnotic Eye
Bloch, Robert (wri, 1917–1994): Asylum; Bates Motel; The Cabinet Of Caligari; The Cat Creature; The Couch; The Dead Don't Die; The Deadly Bees; The House That Dripped Blood; Journey To Midnight; The Night Walker; Psycho; Psycho II; Psycho II; Psycho IV: The Beginning; The Psychopath (1965); The Skull; Strait-Jacket; Torture Garden
Block, Diane (act): Getting Lucky
Block, Hunt (act): Secret Weapons; Summer Girl
Block, Irving (cin): Behemoth, The Sea Monster; Flight To Mars; Queen Of Outer Space; Unknown World; The Viking Women And The Sea Serpent; World Without End
Block, Irving (wri): Forbidden Planet; The Viking Women And The Sea Serpent
Block, Larry (act): Heaven Can Wait (1978)
Block, Lawrence J./Larry (wri): Captain America (1992); The Funhouse (1981)
Block, Libbie (wri): Caught
Block, Oliver (act): Big
Blocker, Dirk (act): Prince Of Darkness
Blodgett, Carol (act): Race With The Devil
Blodgett, Michael (act): The Velvet Vampire
Blom, August (dir, 1869–1942): Atlantis (1913)
Blomberg, Jan (act): The Devil's Messenger
Blomfield, Derek (act, 1920–1964): Alibi (1942); The Ghost At St. Michael's
Blomgren, Bengt (act): Rymdinvasion I Lappland
Blomgren, Doris (act): Timecop
Blommaert, Susan J. (act): Edward Scissorhands; Pet Sematary
Blomquist, Marianne (act): I Love You, I Kill You
Blondell, Gloria (act): The Twonky
Blondell, Joan (act, 1909–1979): The Dead Don't Die; Death At Love House; Desk Set; For Heaven's Sake; Lizzie; Miss Pinkerton; Nightmare Alley; The Spy In The Green Hat; Topper Returns
Blondell, Simone (act): El Castello Dell'orrore
Blondheim, George (mus): Gate II
Blonigan, Colette (act): The Stuff
Blood, William (act): The Curse Of The Living Corpse
Bloom, Anne (act): I, Desire
Bloom, Bill A. (act): Teen-Age Strangler
Bloom, Brian (act): The Stuff; Vampirella (1996)
Bloom, Claire (act, b. 1931): Brainwashed; Charly; Clash Of The Titans; Daylight; Deja Vu; The Haunting; The Illustrated Man; Richard II (1955); The Spy Who Came In From The Cold; The Wonderful World Of The Brothers Grimm
Bloom, David (act): The Reflecting Skin
Bloom, Eric L. (wri): Eyes Of A Stranger
Bloom, Harold Jack (wri): Land Of The Pharaohs
Bloom, Jason (dir): Bio-Dome
Bloom, Jeffrey (dir): Blood Beach; Flowers In The Attic; Starcrossed
Bloom, Jeffrey (wri): Blood Beach; Flowers In The Attic; Nightmares (1983); Starcrossed
Bloom, John (F.) (act): Brain Of Blood; The Dark (1979); Dracula vs. Frankenstein; Harry And The Hendersons; The Hills Have Eyes II; The Incredible 2-Headed Transplant
Bloom, Judi (act): Scream And Scream Again
Bloom, Lindsay (act): Bridge Across Time
Bloom, Scott (act): The Stuff
Bloom, Verna (act): Where Have All The People Gone?
Bloomfield, Angela (act): The Frighteners
Bloomfield, George (act): Spasms
Bloomfield, George (dir & wri): To Kill A Clown
Bloomfield, John (act): The Adding Machine
Bloomstein, Henry (wri): Human Feelings
Blore, Eric (act, 1887–1959): Bowery To Bagdad; The Casino Murder Case; Counter-Espionage; The Lone Wolf In London; The Lone Wolf In Mexico; The Lone Wolf Keeps A Date; The Lone Wolf Meets A Lady; The Lone Wolf Strikes; The Lone Wolf Takes A Chance; The Notorious Lone Wolf; One Dangerous Night; Passport To Suez; Secrets Of The Lone Wolf
Blossom, Roberts (act): Always; Christine; Close Encounters Of The Third Kind; Deranged (1974); Slaughterhouse-Five
Blot, Florence (act): The Tenant
Blount, Lisa (act): The Annihilator; Dead And Buried; Nightflyers; Prince Of Darkness; Radioactive Dreams; Secrets Of The Phantom Caverns
Blount, Sheraton (act): The Deadly Affair
Blowers, Sean (act): First Knight
Blue Oyster Cult (mus): Heavy Metal
Blue, Ben (act, 1901–1975, nee Ben Bernstein): The Busy Body
Blue, Michael (act): Too Good To Be True
Blue, Monte (act, 1890–1963): The Hidden Hand; The Mask Of Dimitrios; Possessed (1947); Sharad Of Atlantis; Wolf's Clothing (1927)
Blue, Simone (act): Explorers
Blue, Sugar (act): Angel Heart
Bluel, Richard (wri): Goliath Awaits
Bluemke, Ralph (dir): I Was A Teen-Age Mummy
Bluestone, Harry (mus): The Killer Shrews; Mara Of The Wilderness
Blum, Deborah (wri): Vibes
Blum, Edwin (wri): The Adventures Of Sherlock Holmes (1939); The Boogie Man Will Get You; Down To Earth
Blum, Jack (act): Happy Birthday To Me
Blum, Katherine (act): Star Trek II: The Search For Spock
Blum, Len (wri): Heavy Metal
Blum, Sammy (act): The Falcon In Hollywood
Blume, Jochen (act): Confess, Dr. Corda
Blumenfeld, Alan (act): The Dark Side Of The Moon; Friday The 13th, Part VI: Jason Lives
Blumenfeld, Arthur (cin): The Monster In The Basement
Blumenthal, Jason (wri): Bio-Dome
Blumenthal, Jim (act): Outbreak
Blumner, Rudolf (act): M (1931)
Blumsack, Gary (act): The Return Of The Six Million Dollar Man And The Bionic Woman
Blundell, Graeme (act): Those Dear Departed
Blunt, Augie (act): Ghost (1990); Princess Warrior
Bluth, Don (dir): The Secret Of Nimh
Bluthal, John (act): Carry On Spying; Digby-The Biggest Dog In The World; The Flying Sorceror; A Ghost Of A Chance (1968); Leapin' Leprechauns!; The Mouse On The Moon; Superman II
Bluto, Tony (act): Nightbreed
Blyden, Larry (act): On A Clear Day You Can See Forever
Blye, Margaret (act, b. 1942): The Entity
Blystone, John (dir): Charlie Chan's Chance
Blystone, Stanley (act): Charlie Chan At The Opera; Mr. Moto Takes A Vacation
Blyth, Ann (act, b. 1928): The House In The Square; Mr. Peabody And The Mermaid
Blyth, David (dir): Death Warmed Up; Red Blooded American Girl
Blyth, David (wri): Death Warmed Up
Blyth, Domini (act): A Story Of Tutankhamun; Vampire Circus
Blyth, Harry (wri): The Council Of Three; The Counterfeiters; Further Exploits Of Sexton Blake-The Mystery Of The S.S. Olympic; The Great Cheque Fraud; The Jewel Thieves Run To Earth By Sexton Blake; The Kaiser's Spies; The Mystery Of The Diamond

Belt; The Stolen Heirlooms; The Thornton Jewel Mystery
Blythe, Betty (act, 1899–1972): *The Chinese Cat; Chu Chin Chow (1923); The Scarlet Letter (1934); She (1925); The Spanish Cape Mystery*
Blythe, Erik (act): *Invasion U.S.A.*
Blythe, Ethel (act): see Barrymore, Ethel
Blythe, Janus (act): *The Hills Have Eyes; The Hills Have Eyes II; The Incredible Melting Man*
Blythe, John (GB act): *Dear Murderer; Portrait From Life*
Blythe, John (USA act): see Barrymore (Sr.), John
Blythe, Lionel (act): see Barrymore, Lionel
Blythe, Peter (act): *Arthur The King; A Challenge For Robin Hood; Frankenstein Created Woman*
Blythe, Robin (act): *Deathrow Gameshow*
Blythe, Sidney (cin): *Juggernaut; Scrooge (1935)*
Blyton, Enid (wri): *Noddy In Toyland*
Bo, Angela (act): *Death Smiles On A Murderer*
Boa, Bruce (act): *The Adding Machine; The London Connection; Man In The Moon (1960); Octopussy; The Omen; Return To Oz; Screamers (1996); Slipstream; Who?*
Boal, Raymond (act): *Where's Johnny*
Boam, Jeff(rey) (wri): *The Dead Zone; Indiana Jones And The Last Crusade; Innerspace; The Lost Boys; The Phantom (1996)*
Board, Paul (act): *Happy Birthday To Me*
Boardman, Chris (mus): *Tales From The Crypt Presents Bordello Of Blood*
Boardman, Virginia True (act): *A Blind Bargain; Tarzan Of The Apes*
Boasberg, Al (wri): *Freaks*
Boatman, Bob (cin): *The Resurrection Of Zachary Wheeler*
Boatman, Michael (act, b. 1964): *Donor*
Boaz, Charles (act): *The Search For Bridey Murphy*
Bobbie, Walter (act): *Thinner*
Bobby Breen Quintet, The (act): *Curse Of Simba*
Bobby, Anne (act): *Nightbreed*
Bobenko, Mike (act): *Laserblast*
Bobin, John W. (wri): *The Counterfeiters*
Boccaci, Antonio (dir & wri): *Tomb Of Torture*
Boccardo, Delia (act): *Deborah; Hercules (1983); Tentacles*
Boccelli, Dick (act): *Too Scared To Scream*
Bocchi, Arrigo (dir): *The Polar Star; Whosoever Shall Offend*
Boccia, Tanio (wri): *Maciste Alla Corte Della Zar*
Boccoli, Brigitta (act): *Manhattan Baby*
Boch, Edward (wri): *Crime Doctor's Gamble*
Boche, Herbert (act): *Ed Wood*
Bochenko, Irka (act): *Moonraker*
Bochner, Hart (act, b. 1957): *Making Mr. Right; Mr. Destiny; Supergirl (1984); Terror Train*
Bochner, Lloyd (act, b. 1924): *Crowhaven Farm; The Dunwich Horror; A Fire In The Sky (1978); Millennium; The Night Walker; The Return (1973, Can); Rona Jaffe's Mazes And Monsters; Satan's School For Girls; They Call It Murder*
Bocho, Steve(n) (wri): *The Invisible Man (1975); Silent Running; Vampire (1979)*
Bockman, Michael (wri): *Beyond The Living*
Bod, Terez (act): *Phantom Of The Opera (1983)*
Boda, Benjamin (act): *Judex*
Bodalo, Jose (act): *Sound Of Horror*
Boddey, Martin (act): *Cage Of Gold; Cloudburst; Dark Places; How To Murder A Rich Uncle; Psychomania (1972); Secret Venture; Svengali (1954); Tales From The Crypt; Valley Of The Eagles; Venetian Bird*
Boddicker, Michael (mus): *The Adventures Of Buckaroo Banzai; Solar Crisis*
Boddie, Aaron (act): *The Wiz*
Bode, Ralf (cin): *Dressed To Kill (1980)*
Bodeen, DeWitt (wri, b. 1908): *Cat People (1942 & 1982); Curse Of The Cat People; The Enchanted Cottage (1945); The Girl In The Kremlin; The Seventh Victim; 12 To The Moon*
Bodelstein, Christel (act): *Das Singende Ringende Baumchen*
Boden, Anthony (act): *Murder In Mind*
Boden, Petra (act): *Fargo*
Bodenham, Alan (act): *Without A Clue*
Boder, Lada (act): *Dick Tracy (1990)*
Bodie, Jamie (act): *Secrets Of The Phantom Caverns*
Bodin, IVor (act): *Santa Claus Conquers The Martians*
Bodin, Marc/Mark (act): *The Grim Reaper; The Strangers*
Bodinus, Carsten (act): *Nosferatu, The Vampyre*
Bodison, Wolfgang (act): *Freeway*
Bodkin, Tain (act): *Frankenstein Island*
Bodnar, Erika (act): *Daughter Of Darkness (1990)*
Bodnar, Jenna (act): *Cellblock Sisters: Banished Behind Bars*
Boehlke, Bain (act): *Fargo*
Boehm, Carl/Karl (act, b. 1928): *Alraune (1952); Peeping Tom; The Venetian Affair; The Wonderful World Of The Brothers Grimm*
Boehm, David (wri): *The Raven (1935)*
Boehm, Herbert (act): *Il Mulino Delle Donne Di Pietra*
Boehm, Karl (act): see Boehm, Carl/Karl
Boehm, Marc (wri): *In The Steel Net Of Dr. Mabuse*
Boehm, Susan (act): *Ghostbusters II*
Boehm, Sydney (wri, b. 1908): *The Atomic City; Mystery Street; Second Chance; Secret Of The Incas; Shock Treatment (1964); When Worlds Collide*
Boeke, Jim (act): *Heaven Can Wait (1978); In The Shadow Of Kilimanjaro; Pandemonium*
Boekelheide, Todd (mus): *The Blood Of Heroes*
Boelson, Jim (act): *Strange Behavior*
Boen, Earl (act): *Alien Nation; The Annihilator; The Companion (1994); Miracle Mile; Terminator 2: Judgment Day*
Boepple, Beatrice (act): *Quarantine*
Boergadine, Steve (act): *Sasquatch, The Legend Of Bigfoot*
Boers Jr., Frank (act): *Equinox*
Boese, Carl (dir): *The Golem: How He Came Into The World*
Boesen, Kurt (act): *Outbreak*
Boessow, Mary (act): *Pumpkinhead*
Boeta, Jose R. (wri): *El Principe Encadenado*
Boetticher Jr., Oscar "Budd" (dir, b. 1916): *Behind Locked Doors; City Beneath The Sea (1952); Escape In The Fog; One Mysterious Night*
Boffety, Jean (cin): *Au Coeur De La Vie*
Bogard, A.R. (act): *Mr. Moto's Last Warning*
Bogarde, Dirk (act, b. 1921, nee Derek Van Den Bogaerd): *Blackmailed; Hot Enough For June; Hunted (1952); The Mind Benders (1963); Modesty Blaise; The Night Porter; Our Mother's House; The Serpent; The Servant; So Long At The Fair; The Woman In Question*
Bogart, Hal (act): *Attack Of The Puppet People*
Bogart, Humphrey (act, 1899–1957): *Beat The Devil; The Big Sleep (1946); The Maltese Falcon (1941); The Return Of Dr. X; The Two Mrs. Carrolls; Women Of All Nations*
Bogart, Paul (dir, b. 1919): *Oh, God! You Devil*
Bogarth, Harry (act): *Bulldog Drummond (1923)*
Bogdanovich, Peter (act & wri, b. 1937): *Targets*
Bogdanovich, Peter (dir, b. 1937): *Targets; Voyage To A Prehistoric Planet*
Boger, Betsy (act): see Blair, Betsy
Bogert, William (act): *A Fire In The Sky (1978); Heaven Can Wait (1978)*
Boggetti, Vera (act): *Candles At Nine; The Girl In The Flat; Inside The Room*
Boggs, Doris (act): *The Handmaid's Tale*
Boggs, Gail (act): *Ghost (1990)*
Boggs, Haskell (cin): *Cinderfella; I Married A Monster From Outer Space*
Bogle, Andrew (dir & wri): *Dark Water; Haunters Of The Deep*
Bogner, Jonathan Scott (mus): *Ghoulies II*
Bogner, Ludek (cin): *Red Blooded American Girl*
Bogner, Norman (wri): *Privilege*
Bogolepov, Dmitri (wri): *Stellar Brothers-From The Kremlin To The Cosmos*
Bogomolov, Vladimir (wri): *My Name Is Ivan*
Bogosian, Eric (act): *Dolores Claiborne*
Bogot, Jean Pierre (act): *The Tenant*
Bogues, Muggsey (act): *Space Jam*
Bogusslavski, Axel (act): *Docteur Petiot*
Bohan, James (act): *Phantom Of The Paradise*
Bohay, Heidi (act): *Superstition*
Bo-Hee, Lee (act): *The Man With Three Coffins*
Bohem, Leslie (act): *School Spirit*
Bohem, Leslie (wri): *Dante's Peak; Daylight; The Horror Show; A Nightmare On Elm Street 5: The Dream Child*
Bohn, Chris (act): *Fright (1957)*
Bohne, Bruce (act): *Fargo*
Bohne, Werner (cin): *Gold (German-Version)*
Bohnen, Michael (act): *Gold (German Version)*
Bohnen, Roman (act, 1894–1949): *The Hairy Ape; Of Mice And Men (1939)*
Bohnet, Mirjam (act): *The Handmaid's Tale*
Bohnsch, Ina (act): *Making Contact*
Bohny, Lilian (act): see Dove, Billie
Bohr, Robert (wri): *I Lunghi Capelli Della Morte*
Bohrer, Corinne (act): *Vice Versa (1988)*
Bohrman, Stan (act): *The China Syndrome*
Boht, Jean (act): *The Girl In A Swing*
Boht, Margot (act): *Scars Of Dracula*
Bohun, Carol (act): *The Beast Must Die*
Boileau, Peter (act): *Kemek*
Boileau, Pierre (wri, b. 1906): *Body Parts; Diabolique (1955 & 1996); Faces In The Dark; Reflections Of Murder; Vertigo; Les Yeux Sans Visage*
Bois, Curt (act, 1900–1992): *Blue, White And Perfect; Caught; Gypsy Wildcat; The Hunchback Of Notre Dame (1939); The Woman In White (1948)*
Bois, Ilse (act): *The Ghost Train (1927)*
Boisseau, Jocelyne (act): *Perceval*
Boissery, Jean (act): *Perceval*
Boize, Sandra (act): *Hysteria!*
Bokar, Hal (act): *Graduation Day; Lady In White*
Bokhari, Yousaf (act): *Alien Predators*
Bolam, James (act): *Crucible Of Terror; Murder Most Foul; Otley; Straight On Till Morning*
Boland, Bridget (wri): *Gaslight (1940)*
Boland, Mary (act, 1880–1965): *Four Frightened People*
Bolanos, Ana Elisa Perez (act): *Zorro, The Gay Blade*
Bolden, Bernhard (act): *Moon 44*
Bolder, Cal (act): *Jesse James Meets Frankenstein's Daughter; One Spy Too Many*
Bolder, Robert (act): *Tarzan And The Golden Lion*
Boldoay y Castilla, Marguerita Guadalupe (act): see Margo
Bolen, Murray (act): *Trick Or Treats*
Bolender, Bill (act): *D.O.A. (1988); RoboCop 2*
Bolender, Charles (act): *Dark Intruder*
Boler, Robert (act): *Dead And Buried*
Boles, Barbara (act): *Doctor Death: Seeker Of Souls*
Boles, Eric (act): *Doctor Death: Seeker Of Souls*
Boles, Jim (act): *Doctor Death: Seeker Of Souls*
Boles, John (act, 1895–1969): *Babes In Bagdad; Frankenstein (1931); The Last Warning (1929)*
Boleslawsky, Richard (dir, 1889–1937): *The Last Of The Lone Wolf; Les Miserables (1935)*
Boley, Mary (act): *Moby Dick (1930)*
Bolger, Ray (act, 1906–1987): *Babes In Toyland (1961); The Wizard Of Oz (1939)*
Bolin, Nick (act): *Blackenstein*
Bolin, Shannon (act): *The Children; Damn Yankees*
Bolinger, Terrie (act): *Scalpel*
Bolio, Jorge (act): *Zorro, The Gay Blade*
Bolkan, Florinda (act, b. 1941): *A Lizard In A Woman's Skin; Royal Flash*
Boll, Helen (act): *Poltergeist II: The Other Side*
Boll, Siddnie (act): *Unforgettable*
Bolling, Angie (act): *Robocop; Robocop 2*
Bolling, Bettie (act): *Kingdom Of The Spiders*
Bolling, Claude (mus): *The Awakening; Catch Me A Spy; The Hands Of Orlac (1959)*
Bolling, Tiffany (act): *Kingdom Of The Spiders; Wicked, Wicked*
Bollinger, Alun (cin): *The Frighteners*
Bollman, Ryan (act): *Children Of The Corn II: The Final Sacrifice*
Bollner, Michael (act): *Willy Wonka And The Chocolate Factory*
Bollo, Lou (act): *Watchers*
Bologna, Joe (act): *Transylvania 6-5000*
Bologna, Ugo (act): *City Of The Walking Dead*
Bolognini, Mauro (dir, b. 1923): *Le Plus Vieux Metier Du Monde*
Bolshoi Ballet, The (act): *Cinderella (1961)*
Bolsover, Edith (act): *Funeral Home*
Bolster, Anita (Sharp) (act): *Craze; Dead Men Are Dangerous; The Hands Of Orlac (1959); The House On Marsh Road; Jabberwocky; The Lodger (1944); The Lost Weekend; The Perfect Woman; The Thin Man Goes Home; The Two Mrs. Carrolls*
Bolt, Anne (act): *All Clear: No Need To Take Cover*
Bolt, Crispan (wri): *Solar Crisis*
Bolt, David (act): *Millennium; Phobia; Prom Night; Spasms*
Bolt, Faye (act): *Star Crystal*
Bolthouse, Brent (act): *Full Eclipse; Waxwork II: Lost In Time*
Bolton, Barbara (act): *A Story Of Tutankhamun*
Bolton, Charles (act): *The Quatermass Conclusion*
Bolton, Christopher (act): *I Still Dream Of Jeannie*
Bolton, Emily (act): *Moonraker*
Bolton, Guy (wri): *The Cave Girl (1921); Secrets Of The Night*
Bolton, Heather (act): *Dark Of The Night*
Bolton, Lyn (act): *Blood Feast*
Bolton, Muriel Roy (wri): *The Amazing Mr. X*
Bolvary, Geza M. (dir): *The Ghost Train (1927)*
Bolzoni, Adriano (wri): *Il Figlio Di Spartacus; The Humanoid*
Bomba, Leo (wri): *Robin Hood And The Pirates*
Bon, Sheila (act): *Curse Of The Stone Hand*
Bonada, Eduardo (act): *El Santo Contra Las Vampiras*
Bonaduce, Danny (act): *Murder On Flight 502*
Bonales, Boby (act): *El Santo Contra Las Vampiras*
Bonanova, Fortunio (act, 1895–1969): *The Red Dragon (1945); Second Chance*
Bonar, Ivan (act): *The Haunting Passion; Project X (1967)*
Bond, Cynthia (act): *Def By Temptation*
Bond, David (act): *The Return Of The Living Dead (1985); The Story Of Mankind*
Bond, Derek (act, b. 1920): *Gideon's Day; The Hand (1960); The Hour Of 13; Not Guilty; Stranger From Venus; Svengali (1954); Uncle Silas*
Bond, Diane (act): *House Of 1,000 Dolls; In Like Flint*
Bond, Gary (act): *The House That Bled To Death/Growing Pains*
Bond III, James (act, dir & wri): *Def By Temptation*
Bond, Julian (wri): *The Man Outside (1967)*
Bond, Lillian (act, 1907–1991): *Desperate Chance For Ellery Queen; Man In The Attic (1953); The Maze; The Old Dark House (1932); The Picture Of Dorian Gray (1945)*
Bond, Lorraine (act): *Just Imagine*
Bond, Margery (act): *Endangered Species*
Bond, Michael (act): *Are You In The House Alone?*
Bond, Raleigh (act): *Elvira, Mistress Of The Dark; Nightmares (1983); Salvage*
Bond, Raymond (act): *The Man From Planet X*
Bond, Renee (act): *Invasion Of The Bee Girls; Please Don't Eat My Mother*
Bond, Rhonda (act): *The Handmaid's Tale*
Bond, Richard (act): *Spy Smasher Returns; Torchy Blane In Chinatown*
Bond, Rudy (act): *Hercules In New York; Nightfall (1956)*
Bond, Serena (act): *Goldeneye*
Bond, Sidonie (act): *Demons Of The Mind*
Bond, Steve (act): *The Prey (1980); To Die For; To Die For II: Son Of Darkness; Witches' Brew*
Bond, Sudie (act): *Sanctuary Of Fear; They Might Be Giants*
Bond, Sue (act): *Secrets Of Sex*
Bond, Timothy (dir): *The Quilt Of Hathor*
Bond, Timothy (wri): *Happy Birthday To Me*
Bond, Walter (act): see Fitzgerald, Walter
Bond, Ward (act, 1904–1960): *The Falcon Takes Over; A Guy Named Joe; The Maltese Falcon (1941); The Man Who Lived Twice; Mr. Moto In Danger Island; Mr. Moto's Gamble; The Night Key; On Dangerous Ground; Topper (1937)*
Bondanza, Bill (act): *Street Trash*
Bondarchuk, Natalie (act): *Solaris*
Bondarenko, Wally (act): *Virus*
Bondi, Beulah (act, 1892–1981): *The Baron Of Arizona; The Black Book; The Invisible Ray; It's A Wonderful Life; On Borrowed Time; She Waits; The Snake Pit (1948); The Wonderful World Of The Brothers Grimm*
Bonds, Bill (act): *Escape From The Planet Of The Apes*
Bonds, De'Aundre (act): *Tales From The Hood*
Bone, Kristen (act): *The Long Kiss Goodnight*
Bone, Stephen (act): *Kadoyng*
Bonerz, Peter (act, b. 1938): *What Ever Happened To Aunt Alice?*
Bonestell, Chesley (wri): *Conquest Of Space*
Bonet, Lisa (act, b. 1967): *Angel Heart*
Bonet, Nai (act): *Nocturna, Granddaughter Of Dracula; The Spy With A Cold Nose*
Bongfeld, Mary (act): *Phantom Of The Paradise*
Bong-Jin, Jin (act): *Village In The Mist*
Bonham, Bill (act): *Copycat*
Bonham, John (act): *Son Of Dracula (1974)*
Bonham-Carter, Helena (act, b. 1966): *Hamlet (1990); Mary Shelley's 'Frankenstein'*
Boni, Luisa (act): *Land Of The Pharaohs; Treasure Of Bengal*
Bonicelli, Vittorio (wri): *Barbarella*
Bonifas, Paul (act): *Les Abyses; The Green Glove*
Bonifassy, Luce (act): *La Decima Vittima*
Bonilla, Arturo (act): *Return Of The Living Dead, Part II*
Bonino, Steve (act): *Tarantulas: The Deadly Cargo*
Bonios, Irving (act): *Cyborg 2: Glass Shadow*
Bonn, Curt (act): *Empire Of Ash II: Quarantine*
Bonnaire, Sandrine (act): *La Captive Du Desert*

Bonnard, Mario (dir): The Last Days Of Pompeii (1959)
Bonne, Shirley (act): It's Alive! (1968)
Bonnefous, Jean Pierre (act): Diabolique (1955)
Bonnell, Lee (act): The Saint In Palm Springs
Bonnell, Vivian (act): Ghost (1990)
Bonner, Beverly (act): Basket Case; Frankenhooker
Bonner, Frank (act): Fer-De-Lance
Bonner, Tony (act): Creatures The World Forgot; Inn Of The Damned; Sudden Terror
Bonner, William (act): Angels' Wild Women
Bonnet, James (act): The Blob (1958)
Bonnet, Vicki (act): Those Dear Departed
Bonneville, Richard (act): Mary Shelley's 'Frankenstein'
Bonney, Gail (act): Bell, Book And Candle
Bonney, John (act): Paranoiac
Bonney, Lawrence A. (act): The Silence Of The Lambs
Bonns, Miguel Iglesias (dir): La Maldicion De La Bestia
Bono and the Edge (mus): Goldeneye
Bono, Sonny (act, b. 1935): Murder On Flight 502; Troll
Bonomo, Joe (act): Island Of Lost Souls
Bonos, Gigi (act): The Flower In His Mouth
Bonos, Luigi (act): La Ragazza Che Sapeva Troppo
Bons, Ida (act): Flesh & Blood
Bonta, Vanna (act): Time Walker
Bonthuys, Gerard (act): Creatures The World Forgot
Bonucci, Alberto (act): Et Mourir De Plaisir
Bonus, Max (act): War Of The Planets
Bonvillain, Michael (cin): When The Bough Breaks
Bonvoisin, Berangere (act): Docteur Petiot
Booke, Sorrell (act, 1930–1994): The Adventures Of Nick Carter; Adventures Of The Queen; Brenda Starr (1976); Demon And The Mummy; Fail-Safe; Les Felins; The Horrible House On The Hill; Slaughterhouse-Five
Booker, Thom (act): Lifeforce
Boolsen, Bjorn Watt (act): The Night Visitor
Boom, Peter (act): The Great Alligator; The Secret Of Seagull Island; Zone Troopers
Boon, Robert (act): Queen Of Blood
Boone, Brendon (act): The Big Game
Boone, Daniel (act): Mr. Moto's Last Warning
Boone, Norman (act): The Creeping Terror
Boone, Pat (act, b. 1934): Goodbye Charlie; The Horror Of It All; Journey To The Center Of The Earth (1959); The Perils Of Pauline
Boone, Richard (act, 1917–1981): The Big Sleep (1978); The Hobbit; I Bury The Living; The Kremlin Letter; The Last Dinosaur; Lizzie
Boone, Walker (act): Spasms
Boor, E.A. Violet (act): Trauma (1993)
Booraem, Abigail (act): Impulse (1984)
Boorman, Charles/Charley (act): Excalibur; Mr. Frost
Boorman, Imogen (act): Dreamchild; Hellbound: Hellraiser II
Boorman, Joanne (act): The Godsend
Boorman, John (dir, b. 1933): Excalibur; Exorcist II: The Heretic; Zardoz
Boorman, John (wri, b. 1933): Excalibur; Zardoz
Boorman, Katrine (act): Excalibur
Boorstin, Jon (wri): Dream Lover
Boot, Gladys (act): Murder Reported
Booth, Adrian (act): Valley Of The Zombies
Booth, Anthony (act): Corruption; Neither The Sea Nor The Sand; The Return Of Mr. Moto
Booth, Calvin (act): Invasion Of The Saucer Men
Booth, Connie (act): High Spirits; Monty Python And The Holy Grail; The Return Of Sherlock Holmes (1986)
Booth, Harry (dir): The Flying Sorceror
Booth, Harry (wri): At The Stroke Of Nine; The Flying Sorceror
Booth, James (act, b. 1930): Deep Space; Programmed To Kill; Rentadick; Revenge (1971, Gb); The Secret Of My Success; Zorro, The Gay Blade
Booth, Jimmie (act): Star Trek
Booth, Karin (act): African Manhunt; Jungle Man-Eaters; Tobor The Great
Booth, Nesdon (act): Damn Yankees; Space Master X-7
Booth, Susan (act): The Pink Chiquitas
Booth, Walter (R.)/W.R. (dir): An Absorbing Tale; Adventurous Voyage Of 'The Arctic'; The Aerial Anarchists; The Aerial Submarine; The Airship Destroyer; Animated Cotton; Animated Toys; The Apple Of Discord; Artistic Creation; The Automatic Motorist; The Bewitched Boxing Gloves; Bobby Wideawake; The Cap Of Invisibility; Card Manipulations; The Cheese Mites: Or, Lilliputians In A London Restaurant; Chinese Magic; Clever Egg Conjuring; Comedy Cartoons; The Conjurer's Pupil; The Conjuror As A Good Samaritan; The Devil In The Studio; A Devil Of A Honeymoon; Diablo Nightmare; Dreamland Adventures; The Drunkard's Conversion; An Eccentric Sportsman; The Electric Servant; The Electric Vitalizer; The Enchanted Cup; An Extraordinary Cab Accident; The Extraordinary Waiter; The Fakir's Fan; The Famous Illusion Of Kolta; Father Thames' Temperance Cure; The Freezing Mixture; Giles Has His Fortune Told; The Hand Of The Artist; The Hands Of A Wizard; Hanky Panky Cards; The Haunted Bedroom; The Haunted Curiosity Shop; The Haunted Scene Painter; How I Cooked Peary's Record; In Fairyland; The Invisible Dog; The Jester's Joke; The Joker's Mistake; A Juvenile Hypnotist; Kitty In Dreamland; The Last Days Of Pompeii (1900); The Lightning Postcard Artist; Little Lady Lafayette; Little Mickey The Mesmerist; Love And Magic; Magical Mysteries; The Magic Bottle; The Magic Carpet (1909); The Magic Sword: Or, A Mediaeval Mystery; Mischievous Puck; The Miser's Doom; Modelling Extraordinary; A Modern Galatea; A Modern Mystery; The Modern Pygmalion And Galatea; Monty Learns To Swim; The Music Hall Manager's Dilemma; Mystic Manipulations; Ora Pro Nobis: Or, The Poor Orphan's Last Prayer; The Over-Incubated Baby; Paper Tearing; Pocket Boxers; The Portrait Of Dolly Grey; The Prehistoric Man (1908, Urban); Prof. Puddenhead's Patents- The Aerocab And Vacuum Provider; Professor Puddenhead's Patents- The Electric Enlarger; The Professor's Dream; The Automatic Motorist; The Quick-Change Mesmerist; Santa Claus (1912); Scrooge: or, Marley's Ghost; The Shirker's Nightmare; Sooty Sketches; The Sorcerer's Scissors; The Tangram; Tanks; Too Much Sausage; Undressing Extraordinary: or, The Troubles Of A Tired Traveller; Upside Down: Or, The Human Flies; The Vacuum Cleaner Nightmare; The Waif And The Statue; The Waif And The Wizard: or, The Home Made Happy; When The Devil Drives; Willie's Magic Wand; The Wizard And The Brigands; The Wizard's Walking Stick; The World's Worst Wizard
Booth, Walter R. (wri): An Eccentric Sportsman; The Joker's Mistake; The Magic Sword: Or, A Mediaeval Mystery; A Modern Mystery; The Portrait Of Dolly Grey; The Shirker's Nightmare; Tanks
Booth, Webster (act): Faust (1936); The Laughing Lady
Boothby, Larry (act): Deadly Game
Boothby, Mark (act): Secrets In The Attic
Boothe, Jon (wri): Stowaway To The Moon
Boothe, Maureen (act): The Sorcerers
Boothe, Powers (act): Bio-Force I; The Plutonium Incident
Boothroyd, Kaaren (act): Single White Female
Bor, Hanus (act): Rocket To Nowhere
Boras, Ferike (act): Sleepers West
Boratto, Caterina (act): Castle Keep; Giulietta Degli Spiriti
Borchaca, Josephine (act): Anguish
Borchers, Donald P. (dir): Grave Secrets
Borchers, Donald P. (wri): Vamp
Borchert, Rudolph (wri): Crackle Of Death
Borcia, Jose (act): Jekyll And Hyde...Together Again
Borcyckowski, Diane (act): The Strangeness
Bordellier, Clotiel (act): Candyman: Farewell To The Flesh
Borden, Eddie (act): The Falcon's Alibi
Borden, Eugene (act): Charlie Chan In City In Darkness; Charlie Chan In Rio; Charlie Chan On Broadway; Dr. Renault's Secret; The Fly (1958)
Borden, Fred (act): Time Travelers (1976)
Borden, Jeff (act): Princess Warrior
Borden, Lynn (act): Frogs; Hellhole
Borden, Olive (act, 1907–1947): The Monkey Talks
Borden, Roger (act): Logan's Run
Borderie, Bernard (dir & wri): A Toi De Faire, Migonne; Comment Qu'ella Est!; Les Femmes S'en Balancent; Lemmy Pour Les Dames; La Mome Vert-De-Gris
Bordiggi, Al (act): Invasion Of The Bee Girls
Bordiu, J. Martinez (act): Endless Descent
Bordona, Dan (cin): The Alien Within
Bordy, Bill (act): The Bees
Borel, Matt (act): Screams Of A Winter Night
Borel, Raymond (wri): Shadow Of Evil (1964)
Borelli, Carla (act): Ritual Of Evil
Borelli, Carlo (act): Zex
Borelli, Claude (act): Cet Homme Est Dangereux
Boren, Carrie (act): Tornado!
Boren, Lamar (cin): Around The World Under The Sea; Flood
Boreo, Emile (act): The Lady Vanishes (1938)
Borer, Mary Cathcart (wri): The Dragon Of Pendragon Castle; The Monster Of Highgate Ponds; One Wish Too Many; Treasure At The Mill; Who Killed The Cat?
Boretz, Alvin (wri): Spider-Man
Borg, George (act): I Was A Zombie For The F.B.I.
Borg, Sven-Hugo (act): Above Suspicion
Borg, Veda Ann (act, 1915–1973): Accomplice; Blonde Savage; The Corsican Brothers (1941); Dangerous Intruders; The Face Of Marble; The Falcon In Hollywood; The Fearmakers; Fog Island; Hold That Line; The Naked Gun; Revenge Of The Zombies (1943)
Borgato, Augostino (act): The Maltese Falcon (1931)
Borgato, Emilio (act): The Private Life Of Helen Of Troy
Borge, Rikke (act): Tattoo
Borgenicht, Nancy (act): Halloween 4: The Return Of Michael Myers
Borgese, Paul (act): The Toxic Avenger, Part II
Borg(h)ese, Sal(vatore) (act): Super Fuzz; Superwheels
Borgmann, Hans-Otto (mus): Gold (German-Speaking Version)
Borgnine, Effron (act): see Borgnine, Ernest
Borgnine, Ernest (act, b. 1918, nee Effron Borgnine): Alice In Wonderland (1985); The Black Hole; Deadly Blessing; The Devil's Rain; Escape From New York; Future Cop; The Ghost Of Flight 401; The Neptune Factor; The Poseidon Adventure; Ravagers; Super Fuzz; When Time Ran Out; Willard
Borher, Corine (act): Zapped!
Borienko, Yuri (act): On Her Majesty's Secret Service
Borisenko, Don (act): The Psychopath (1965)
Bork, Hanne (act): The Night Visitor; Relax, Freddie
Bork, Tomeck (act): Murder By Moonlight
Borkan, Gene (act): The Silence Of The Lambs; The Terminal Man
Borkowski, Andrzei (act): Mission: Impossible
Borland, Barlowe (act): The Hound Of The Baskervilles (1939); A Night Of Mystery (1937)
Borland, Carol (act, b. 1914): The Mark Of The Vampire (1935); Scalps
Born, Max (act): Satyricon
Born, Roscoe (act): End Of The World (1977); The Haunting Of Sarah Hardy
Borneman, Mick (cin): Color Me Dead
Borner, Ruby (act): Trauma (1963)
Bornheimer, Larry (act): Slugs
Bornstein, Norm (act): Shock Chamber
Borowczyk, Walerian (dir & wri, b. 1923): The Beast (1974); Contes Immoraux; Le Dernier Voyage De Gulliver
Borradaile, Osmond (cin, b. 1892): The Thief Of Bagdad (1940)
Borrel, Mimi (act): Prisoners Of The Casbah
Borrini, Angelo (act): see Ventura, Lino
Borromel, Charles (act): Ladyhawke; War Of The Planets
Borromeo, Christian (act): Tenebrae
Borsche, Dieter (act): The Black Abbot (1963); Dr. Mabuse vs. Scotland Yard; Der Henker Von London; The Phantom Of Soho; Die Toten Augen Von London
Borske, John (wri): Torture Dungeon
Borsody, Eduard (dir): Liane, Das Madchen Aus Dem Urwald
Borsody, Hans (act): Candidate For Murder
Bortman, Michael (wri): Chain Reaction (1996)
Borzage, Bill (act): House Of Usher
Borzage, Frank (dir, 1893–1962): Liliom (1930)
Borzage, Raymond (act): Meet Nero Wolfe
Bosacki, Dean (act): Prom Night
Bosch, Johnny Yong (act): Mighty Morphin Power Rangers; Turbo: A Power Rangers Movie
Boschen, Steve (act): The Henderson Monster
Boschero, Dominique (act): Demons Of The Dead; Secret Agent Fireball
Bosco, Wallace/Wally (act): The House Of Peril; Lady Audley's Secret (1920); The Lion's Cubs; Old Bill Through The Ages; Repulsion; The Shadow Between; The Two Roads; The Wickham Mystery
Bosco, Wally (wri): Death Is A Woman
Boscoe Holder Dancers, The (act): The Hand Of Night
Bose, Lucia (act, b. 1931): Ceremonia Sangrienta; Satyricon; Le Testament D'orphee
Bose, Miguel (act): Suspiria
Bosetti, Giulio (act): Morgan The Pirate; The Reluctant Saint
Boshears, Michael (act): Blood Diner
Bosic, Andrea (act): Manhattan Baby; The Prisoner Of The Iron Mask; Sword Of The Conqueror
Bosley, Tom (act, b. 1927): The Bang-Bang Kid; Death Cruise; Miracle On 34th Street (1973); Night Gallery; The Night That Panicked America; Pinocchio And The Emperor Of The Night; Wicked Stepmother
Boss Film Corp. (cin): Solar Crisis
Bossick, Barney (act): The Cremators
Bosso, George (act): see Bosso, Jorge
Bosso, J.O. (act): Alien Predators
Bosso, Jorge (act, a.k.a. George Bosso): Flesh & Blood; Hundra; Mystery On Monster Island; Zorro: The Legend Begins
Bosson, Barbara (act, b. 1939): The Last Starfighter
Bost, Pierre (wri, 1901–1975): L'auberge Rouge; Jeux Interdits
Bostock, Barbara (act): The Spell
Bostock, Evelyn (act): Thark
Boston, David (wri): The London Connection
Boston, J.L. (act): At The Villa Rose (1920)
Bostwick, Barry (act, b. 1945): Megaforce; Project: Metalbeast, DNA Overload; The Rocky Horror Picture Show; Summer Girl
Bostwick, Jackson (act): My Science Project; The Prey (1980); Secrets Of The Phantom Caverns
Boswall, John (act): 1984 (1984)
Boswell, Charles (act): When A Stranger Calls
Boswell, Peter (act): Razorback
Boswell, Simon (mus): Demons 2; Hardware; Lord Of Illusions
Bosworth, Brian (act, b. 1964): Blackout (1995)
Bosworth, Hobart (act, 1867–1943): The Chinese Parrot; Dirigible; In The Palace Of The King; Just Imagine; Rupert Of Hentzau (1923); Through The Dark
Bota, Rick (cin): Barb Wire; The Companion (1994); Demon Knight
Boteler, Wade (act, 1891-1943): Blue, White And Perfect; Charlie Chan At The Circus; The Death Kiss; The Kennel Murder Case; The Mandarin Mystery; Seven Keys To Baldpate (1925); Through The Dark
Botello, Alfredo (act): Trick Or Treats
Botello, Catalina (act): The Arrival
Botero, Rodrigo (act): Cave Girl Island
Bothelo, Niki (act): Ewoks: The Battle For Endor
Botkin, Perry (mus): Dance Of The Dwarfs; Silent Night, Deadly Night; Tarzan, The Ape Man (1981)
Botsford, Sara (act): Deadly Eyes; Still Of The Night
Botta, Leonardo (act): L'ultima Preda Del Vampiro
Bottaro, Pamela (act): Planet Of Dinosaurs
Bottcher, Gabrielle (act): The Alien's Return
Bottcher, Gritt (act): The Black Abbot (1963)
Bottcher, Neil (act): The Alien's Return
Botterill, Joyce (act): see Carne, Judy
Botto, Juan Diego (act): Zorro: The Legend Begins
Bottomley, Roland (act): The Devil (1921)
Bottoms, Joseph (act, b. 1954): The Black Hole; Blind Date; The Intruder Within; The Sins Of Dorian Gray
Bottoms, Sam (act): Dolly Dearest; Hunter's Blood; Project Shadowchaser II; Up From The Depths; The Witching Of Ben Wagner
Bottoms, Timothy (act, b. 1951): Death Game; The Drifter; In The Shadow Of Kilimanjaro; Invaders From Mars (1986); Rollercoaster; Secrets Of The Phantom Caverns
Botts, Jacquie (act): Snowbeast
Boty, Pauline (act): Strangler's Web
Botz, Gustav (act): Der Januskopf; Nosferatu, Eine Symphonie Des Grauens
Boucher, Bob (act): Prehistoric Peeps; The Faithful Clock
Boucher, Evelyn (act): My Lord Conceit
Boucher, Savannah Smith (act): Meet The Applegates
Boucher, Sherry (act): Sisters Of Death
Boucher, Suzette (act): Silent Night, Deadly Night II
Bouchet, Barbara (act, b. 1943): Agent For H.A.R.M.; Amuck; The Black Belly Of The Tarantula; Casino Royale; The Cauldron Of Death; Danger Route; Death Rage; Man With Icy Eyes
Bouchey, Willis (act, b. 1895): Red Planet Mars
Bouchier, Chili (act, b. 1909, nee Dorothy Bouchier): The Dark Stairway; The Ghost Goes West; The Laughing Lady; The Mind Of Mr. Reeder; Murder In Reverse

Bouchier, Dorothy (act): see Bouchier, Chili
Boucicault, Nina (act): *Juggernaut*
Boudot, Sabrina (act): *The Kiss (1988)*
Bouillon, Jean-Claude (act): *The Phantom Of The Opera (1990)*
Boulanger, Daniel (act): *La Mariee Etait En Noir*
Boulanger, Jamieson (act): *Frankenstein And Me*
Bould, Becket (act): *The Flesh And The Fiends*
Boulle, Pierre (wri, 1912–1994): *Back To The Planet Of The Apes; Battle For The Planet Of The Apes; Beneath The Planet Of The Apes; Conquest Of The Planet Of The Apes; Escape From The Planet Of The Apes; Farewell To The Planet Of The Apes; Forgotten City Of The Planet Of The Apes; Life, Liberty And Pursuit On The Planet Of The Apes; Planet Of The Apes; Treachery And Greed On The Planet Of The Apes*
Boulos, Afif (act): *Embassy*
Boulter, Rosalyn (act): *For Them That Trespass*
Boulting, John (dir, 1913–1985): *Seven Days To Noon*
Boulting, Roy (dir, b. 1913): *High Treason (1951); Run For The Sun; Thunder Rock; Trunk Crime; The Twisted Nerve*
Boulting, Roy (wri, b. 1913): *High Treason (1951); Run For The Sun; Seven Days To Noon; The Twisted Nerve*
Boulton, David (cin): *Children Of The Damned; The Curse Of The Golem; The Frozen Dead; The Haunting; Modesty Blaise; The Secret Of My Success*
Boulton, Matthew (act, b. 1893): *Bulldog Drummond In Africa; Bulldog Drummond's Peril; Bulldog Drummond Strikes Back (1947); Counter-Espionage; Creeping Shadows; Night Must Fall (1937); Phantom Raiders; Sabotage; Secrets Of Scotland Yard; The Undying Monster; The Woman In Green; The Woman In White (1948)*
Bouquet, Carole (act, b. 1957): *For Your Eyes Only*
Bouquet, Michel (act): *La Mariee Etait En Noir; The Serpent*
Bourgeois, Gerard (dir): *The Mummy And King Ramses*
Bourgeois, John (act): *Never Talk To Strangers*
Bourgoin, Jean (cin, b. 1913): *Black Orpheus; Mr. Arkadin*
Bourke Jr., Terry (act): *Inn Of The Damned*
Bourke (Jr.), Terry (dir & wri): *Inn Of The Damned*
Bourlessi, K. (act): *Blind Date*
Bourne, Adeleine (act): *Hamlet (1913)*
Bourne, Amon (act): *Strange Days*
Bourne, Lindsay (act): *The Death Of The Incredible Hulk; The Stepfather*
Bourne, Molly Ann (act): *The Blob (1958)*
Bourne, Tammy (act): *An American Christmas Carol; Prom Night*
Bourneuf, Philip (act, 1907–1979): *Beyond A Reasonable Doubt; Chamber Of Horrors (1966)*
Bourton, Rayner (act): *Outland*
Bourvil (act, 1913–1970, nee Andre Raimbourg): *Don't Look Now; Don't Tempt The Devil; Les Miserables (1957); Mr. Peek-A-Boo*
Boushel, Joy (act): *The Fly (1986)*
Bou-Sliman, Noelle (act): *Something Is Out There*
Boussac, Marc (act): *Torticola Contre Frankensberg*
Bouteille, Romain (act): *The Tenant*
Boutros, Maher (act): *Jekyll And Hyde... Together Again*
Boutsikaris, Dennis (act): **Batteries Not Included*
Boutte, Lillian (act): *Angel Heart*
Bouvencourt, Laurence (act): *Notorious (1992)*
Bouwmeester, Theo (dir): *Buffalo Bill On The Brain; The Cap Of Invisibility; Dandy Dick Of Bishopsgate; His Conscience; Little Lady Lafayette; The Magic Ring (1911); Mischievous Puck; Mistaken Identity; The Modern Pygmalion And Galatea; Mystic Manipulations; The Sleepwalker (1909); Through Fire To Fortune; A Tragedy Of The Olden Times; The Wizard And The Brigands; A Woman's Treachery*
Boux, Claude (mus): *The Music Of The Spheres*
Bova, Joseph (act): *Pretty Poison (1968); Who!*
Boverio (act): *Forces Occultes*
Bovo, Brunella (act): *Miracle In Milan; Lo Sceicco Bianco*
Bow, Simmy (act): *Beetlejuice; Dracula's [illegible] Warrior; Laserblast; The Sword And The Sorcerer; Vamp*
Bowden, George (act): *The Corpse Grinders*

Bowditch, Frederick W. (act): see Richmond, Kane
Bowe, Cornelius (act): *The Medusa Touch*
Bowe, Merlin (act): *Empire Of Ash II*
Bowe, Rosemarie (act): *The Adventures Of Hajji Baba; The Golden Mistress*
Bowen, B.B. (act): *Phoenix The Warrior*
Bowen, Jimmy (mus): *Vanishing Point*
Bowen, John (wri): *The Mcguffin*
Bowen, Marjorie (wri): *The Black Tulip (1921)*
Bowen, Michael (act): *Forbidden World; Night Of The Comet*
Bowen, Richard (cin): *Wheels Of Terror*
Bowen, Roger (act, 1932-1996): *Heaven Can Wait (1978); Zapped!*
Bowen, Terry (cin): *Laserblast*
Bowen, Trevor (act): *I Hired A Contract Killer*
Bowens, Malick/Malik (act): *The Believers; Outbreak*
Bowens, Shereil L. (act): *Always*
Bower, Antoinette (act): *Blood Song; Prom Night; Superbeast; Time Walker*
Bower, Hugo (act): *Octopussy; The Secret Life Of Ian Fleming*
Bower, Ingrid (act): *The Pink Chiquitas*
Bower, Marion (wri): *The Chinese Puzzle*
Bower, Pamela (wri): *Trent's Last Case (1952)*
Bower, Tom (act): *Lady In White; Love Can Be Murder; Raising Cain*
Bowers, Bonnie (act): *There's Nothing Out There*
Bowers, Dallas (dir, b. 1907): *Alice In Wonderland (1950)*
Bowers, Dallas (wri): *Supersonic Saucer*
Bowers, George (dir): *The Hearse*
Bowers, James (act): *The Savage Bees*
Bowers, John (act): *Bits Of Life; Lorna Doone (1922)*
Bowers, Lally (act): *Dracula A.D. 1972; The Slipper And The Rose*
Bowers, Raymond (act): *Schizo (1977)*
Bowers, Tanya (act): *The Hearse*
Bowers, Wendy (act): *Misery*
Bowers, William (J.) (wri, b. 1916): *The Notorious Lone Wolf; Split Second (1953); Way...Way Out; The Web*
Bowes, Geoffrey (act): *Sorry, Wrong Number (1989)*
Bowie, David (act, b. 1947): *The Hunger; Labyrinth (1986); The Man Who Fell To Earth (1976); Twin Peaks: Fire Walk With Me*
Bowie, James (act): *Rat Pfink & Boo Boo; Targets*
Bowie, Les(lie)/Bowie Films Ltd. (cin): *The City Under The Sea; The Curse Of The Werewolf; The Day The Earth Caught Fire; The Devil-Ship Pirates; Dracula, Prince Of Darkness; Evil Of Frankenstein; Frankenstein And The Monster From Hell; Frankenstein Created Woman; Kiss Of The Vampire; Legend Of The Seven Golden Vampires; Moon Zero Two; The Mummy's Shroud; Nothing But The Night; Paranoiac; Quatermass And The Pit; The Quatermass Experiment; The Quiller Memorandum; The Shadow Of The Cat; She (1965); Superman (1978); The Terrornauts; The Vengeance Of She*
Bowie, Trixxie (act): *Fraternity Demon*
Bowker, Aldrich (act): *Nancy Drew, Troubleshooter; Torchy Plays With Dynamite*
Bowker, Judi (act, b. 1954): *Clash Of The Titans*
Bowker, Norman (act): *Jamaica Inn (1985)*
Bowler, Richard (act): *I Drink Your Blood*
Bowles, Billy (act): *The Hound Of The Baskervilles (1972); How Awful About Allan*
Bowles, Peter (act): *Dead Man's Chest; Endless Night; The Legend Of Hell House; Sudden Terror*
Bowman, Cal (act): *Wavelength*
Bowman, Don (act): *Hillbillys In A Haunted House*
Bowman, Eileen (act): *Writer's Block*
Bowman, Laura (act): *Son Of Ingagi*
Bowman, Lee (act, 1914–1979): *Another Thin Man; Miracles For Sale*
Bowman, Loretta Leigh (act): *Offerings*
Bowman, Nellie (act): *Eyes Of Fate*
Bowman, Pamela (act): *Scared To Death (1980)*
Bowman, Ralph (act): see Archer, John
Bowman, Richard (act): *Nightbreed*
Bowman, Tom (act): *Men Of Sherwood Forest; The Village Of The Damned (1960)*
Bowman, William (act): *The False Faces*
Bown, John (act): *Dr. Who And The Daleks; Fear In The Night (1972); Vampire Circus*
Bown, Paul (act): *Morons From Outer Space; Transmutations*
[illegible] *Werewolf In London*
Bowz, Eddie (act): *The Fear (1994)*

Box, Muriel (wri): *Dear Murderer; Portrait From Life*
Boxer, Stephen (act): *Mary Reilly*
Box, Sydney (wri): *Dear Murderer; Portrait From Life*
Boxer, John (act): *Frenzy; The October Man; Secret Venture*
Boxleitner, Bruce (act, b. 1950): *From The Dead Of Night; Tron*
Boyar, Sully (act): *The Entity; The Manhattan Project; Too Scared To Scream*
Boyce, Christiane (act): *The Clan Of The Cave Bear*
Boyce, James Reid (act): *Ed Wood*
Boyce, Jim (act): *The Slumber Party Massacre*
Boyce, Todd (act): *The Punisher*
Boyce, William (act): *The Slime People*
Boyd, Alan (act): *Tentacles*
Boyd, Betty (act): *The Green Goddess (1929)*
Boyd, Campbell (act): *Secrets Of The Phantom Caverns*
Boyd, Chris (act): *Akiss To Die For*
Boyd, Daniel (dir & wri): *Strangest Dreams: Invasion Of The Space Preachers*
Boyd, David (act): *Puppet Master*
Boyd, Dorothy (act): *Birds Of Prey; Inside The Room; The Shot In The Dark*
Boyd, Guy (act): *Body Double; The Ewok Adventure; Eyes Of Fire*
Boyd, Jerry (act): *The Annihilator*
Boyd, Jimmy (act): *Platinum High School*
Boyd, Lynda (act): *Volcano: Fire On The Mountain*
Boyd, Margaret (act): *Murder At The Grange*
Boyd, Marilyn (act): *The Temple Of Venus*
Boyd, Mildred (act): *The Red Dragon (1945)*
Boyd, Ralph (act): *Blake Of Scotland Yard*
Boyd, Robert (act): *Scanners*
Boyd, Roy (act): *The Wicker Man*
Boyd, Russell (cin): *Forever Young; The Last Wave; Liar Liar; Picnic At Hanging Rock*
Boyd, Stephen (act, 1928–1977, nee William Miller): *Assignment K; The Bible; The Big Game; Evil In The Deep; Fantastic Voyage; Marta; Seven Thunders; The Third Secret*
Boyd, William (cowboy-film act, 1898–1972): *The Benson Murder Case; The Road To Yesterday*
Boyd, William (stage act, 1890–1935): *The Lost City; Murder By The Clock; The Temple Of Venus*
Boyden, Peter (act): *Blow Out*
Boyden, Raymond (act): *The Boogeyman*
Boyer, Alfred (act): *Neon Maniacs*
Boyer, Andrew (act): *Night Of The Comet*
Boyer, Chance (act): *Night Of The Comet*
Boyer, Charles (act, 1899–1978): *Around The World In 80 Days; Casino Royale; Confidential Agent; Flesh And Fantasy; Gaslight (1944); Liliom (1933); Lost Horizon (1973); The Thirteenth Letter*
Boyer, Christopher (act): *Sleepstalker*
Boyer, Francois (wri): *Jeux Interdits; What Price Murder*
Boyer, Jean (dir & wri): *Mr. Peek-A-Boo*
Boyer, Katy (act): *White Dwarf*
Boyer, Philip (act): *Look What's Happened To Rosemary's Baby*
Boyett, William/Bill (act): *The Hidden; Space Raiders; When A Stranger Calls*
Boyette, Pat (act): *Dungeons Of Horror*
Boyette, Pat (dir): *Dungeons Of Horror; The Weird Ones*
Boyette, Pat (wri): *The Weird Ones*
Boykin, Nancy (act): *The Kirlian Witness*
Boylan, John (act): *Rabid*
Boylan, Lee (act): *Invasion Of The Girl Snatchers*
Boylan, Malcolm Stuart (wri): *Boston Blackie Booked On Suspicion; Cheaters At Play; The Lone Wolf And His Lady; The Unknown (1946)*
Boyle, Bill (act): *Shock Chamber*
Boyle, Charles P. (cin): *City Beneath The Sea (1952)*
Boyle, David (act): *Revenge Of The Stepford Wives*
Boyle, Jack (wri): *After Midnight With Boston Blackie; Alias Boston Blackie; Blackie's Redemption; Boston Blackie; Boston Blackie And The Law; Boston Blackie Booked On Suspicion; Boston Blackie Goes Hollywood; Boston Blackie's Chinese Venture; Boston Blackie's Little Pal; Boston Blackie's Rendezvous; The Chance Of A Lifetime; A Close Call For Boston Blackie; Confessions Of Boston Blackie; Crooked Alley; The Face In The Fog (1922); Meet Boston Blackie; Missing Millions; One Mysterious Night; The Phantom Thief; The Return Of Boston Blackie; Through [illegible]*
Boyle, Jim (act): *Vamp*
Boyle, John W. (cin): *The Bridge Of San Luis Rey (1944)*

Boyle, Lara Flynn (act, b. 1970): *Past Tense; Poltergeist II; The Temp*
Boyle, Lisa (act): *The Nutty Professor (1996)*
Boyle, Marc (act): *The Final Conflict; Outland; Superman II*
Boyle, Michael (act): *Bridge Across Time*
Boyle, Peter (act, b. 1933): *Beyond The Poseidon Adventure; A Deadly Vision; Outland; The Santa Clause; The Shadow (1994); Solar Crisis; The Surgeon; Young Frankenstein*
Boyle, Ray (act): *Satan's Satellites*
Boyle, Richard (act): *The Savage Bees*
Boyle, Robert F. (act): *Explorers*
Boyle, Walden (act): *The Trap*
Boyne, Clifton (act): *The Crimson Circle (1922)*
Boynton, Peter (act): *Hellraiser II: Hell On Earth*
Boys, Arthur (wri): *The Queen Of Spades (1948)*
Bozian, Jamie (act): *The Wraith*
Bozizio, Liu (act): *Frankenstein (1974)*
Bozzetta, Angela (act): *Road Games*
Bozzi, Marie Anita (act): *The Prisoner Of Zenda (1915)*
Bozzuffi, Marcel (act, 1929–1988): *Caravan To Vaccares; Images; Sky Above Heaven*
Braban, Harvey (act): *Alibi (1931); Blackmail (1929); Bulldog Jack; The Callbox Mystery; The Yellow Claw*
Brabin, Charles (J.) (dir, 1883–1957): *The Antique Brooch; The Bridge Of San Luis Rey (1929); The Daughter Of Romany; The Mask Of Fu Manchu; The Stolen Plans*
Bracco, Lorraine (act): *Switch; Traces Of Red*
Brace, Bill (cin): *The Time Machine (1960)*
Brace, Peter (act): *A Ghost In Monte Carlo; The Saint And The Brave Goose*
Bracewell, Ethel (act): *The Beggar Girl's Wedding; The King's Romance; The Master Crook Outwitted By A Child; The Master Crook Turns Detective*
Brach, Gerard (wri): *Cul-De-Sac; The Fearless Vampire Killers Or: Pardon Me, But Your Teeth Are In My Neck; The Name Of The Rose; Quest For Fire; Repulsion; The Tenant*
Bracho, Mario Castillon (act): *Dr. Tarr's Torture Dungeon*
Brack, Claudia (act): *Black Zoo*
Bracken, Eversley (wri): *A Night Of Magic*
Bracken, Kathleen (act): *Time Travelers (1976)*
Brackett, Charles (wri, 1892–1969): *Journey To The Center Of The Earth (1959); Niagara; Sunset Boulevard*
Brackett, Leigh (wri, 1915-1978): *The Big Sleep (1946); Crime Doctor's Manhunt; The Empire Strikes Back; The Vampire's Ghost*
Brackett, Sarah (act): *Battle Beneath The Earth; The Masque Of The Red Death (1964)*
Bracy, Charles (act): *Human Feelings*
Bracy, Sidney (act): *The Bishop Murder Case; The Black Bird (1926); Crooked Alley; The Haunted House (1929); The Monster Walks; Torchy Runs For Mayor; Trouble For Two*
Bradbury Sr., James (act): *The Leopard Lady*
Bradbury Jr., James (act): *Bits Of Life*
Bradbury, Lane (act): *The Ultimate Warrior*
Bradbury, Ray (wri, b. 1920): *The Beast From 20,000 Fathoms; Fahrenheit 451; The Illustrated Man; It Came From Outer Space; Little Nemo: Adventures In Slumberland; Moby Dick (1956); The Screaming Woman; Something Wicked This Way Comes*
Bradbury, Robert (act): see Steele, Bob
Braddell, Maurice (act, 1900–1990): *Things To Come*
Braddock, Martin (act): *The Ghost Of Dragstrip Hollow*
Braddock, R.E. (cin): *Offerings*
Braddock, Reb (dir & wri): *Curdled*
Braddon, Dorothy (wri): *Lady Audley's Secret (1906 & 1920)*
Braddon, Russell (wri): *Night Of The Lepus*
Braden, Bernard (act, b. 1916): *The Day The Earth Caught Fire; The Full Treatment*
Braden, Kim (act): *Star Trek: Generations; Trog*
Braden, Mike (act): *The Weird Ones*
Bradford, Andy (act): *Krull; Octopussy; Without A Clue*
Bradford, Ernie (wri): *Burke And Hare*
Bradford, Greg (act): *Zapped!*
Bradford, Hank (wri): *Ghost Of A Chance (1987)*
Bradford, James/Jim (act): *Mountaintop Motel Massacre; Sasquatch; The Legend Of Bigfoot*
Bradford, Lane (act, 1920–1973): *African Treasure; The Golden Idol; The Lone Ranger And The Lost City Of Gold; Satan's Satellites*
Bradford, Marshall (act): *Ghost Chasers; It [illegible] Frankenstein; The Neanderthal Man; Teenage Cave Man*

Bradford, Richard (act): *Dr. Giggles; The Servants Of Twilight*
Bradford, Roark (wri): *Green Pastures*
Bradford, Robert (act): *The Alien's Return*
Bradford (Dwiggins), Sue (wri): *Indestructible Man; Monstrosity*
Bradford, William (cin): *Port Sinister; Return To Treasure Island; Secrets Of Scotland Yard*
Bradigan, Bonnie (act): *Blood Diner*
Bradin, Jean (act): *Champagne*
Bradley, Al (dir): *Battle Of The Amazons; Iron Warrior...The Legend!; War Of The Planets*
Bradley, Al (wri): *Iron Warrior...The Legend!; War Of The Planets*
Bradley, Bart (act): *20 Million Miles To Earth*
Bradley, Bill (act): *The Goonies; The Lost Missile; Time After Time*
Bradley, Christopher (act): *The Initiation; The Wraith*
Bradley, Dan (act): *Hellhole*
Bradley, David (act): *Blood Run; Cyborg Cop; Cyborg Cop II*
Bradley, David (dir): *Madman Of Mandoras; Talk About A Stranger; 12 To The Moon*
Bradley, Doug (act, b. 1954): *Hellbound: Hellraiser II; Hellraiser II: Hell On Earth; Hellraiser: Bloodline; Nightbreed*
Bradley, Elizabeth (act): *An American Werewolf In London; The Flesh And Blood Show*
Bradley, Elizabeth (wri): *Cocoon: The Return*
Bradley, Ellen (act): *The Arrival*
Bradley, Grace (act): *Invisible Killer*
Bradley, Harold (act): *Daylight*
Bradley, Harry C. (act): *Peril From The Planet Mongo; Purple Death From Outer Space*
Bradley, J.V. (act): *Cry For The Strangers*
Bradley, Jan (act): *Soylent Green*
Bradley, Jordan (act): *Halloween 4: The Return Of Michael Myers*
Bradley, Josie (act): *The Mysterious Mr. Nicholson*
Bradley, Lee (act): *Terrified*
Bradley, Leslie (GB act): *Black Limelight; The Crimson Pirate; The Dragon Of Pendragon Castle; Just William's Luck; Time Flies (1944)*
Bradley, Leslie (USA act): *Attack Of The Crab Monsters; Teenage Cave Man*
Bradley, Pat (act): *Capture That Capsule!*
Bradley, Robin (act): *Screams Of A Winter Night*
Bradley, Stephen (act): *Disciple Of Death*
Bradley, Stewart (act): *The Burglar*
Bradley, Stirling (act): *Watchers II*
Bradley, Truman (act, 1905–1974): *Charlie Chan In Rio; Dead Men Tell; The Horn Blows At Midnight; On Borrowed Time*
Bradley, Wilbert (act): *I Diavoli Della Spazio, I; Temple Of A Thousand Lights*
Bradsen, Cole (act): *Timecop*
Bradshaw, Booker (act): *Skullduggery*
Bradshaw, Irene (act): *Dr. Jekyll And Sister Hyde*
Bradshaw, Joan (act): *Back From The Dead; She-Devil*
Bradshaw, Timothy (wri): *Too Good To Be True*
Bradstreet, Charles (act): *Abbott And Costello Meet Frankenstein*
Brady, Alice (act, 1893–1939): *Missing Millions*
Brady, Bob (act): *Liquid Sky*
Brady, Brandon (act): *Billion Dollar Brain; Danger By My Side; The Double Man*
Brady, Buff (act): *Dr. Black Mr. Hyde*
Brady, Dan Patrick (act): *My Demon Lover*
Brady, Ed (act): *Son Of Kong*
Brady, Fred (act): *The Cat Creeps (1946)*
Brady, Fred (wri): *Champagne For Caesar*
Brady, Jack (act): *The Incredibly Strange Creatures Who Stopped Living And Became Mixed-Up Zombies*
Brady, James (act): *Howard The Duck*
Brady, Janelle (act): *Class Of Nuke'em High*
Brady, Janet (act): *Beyond The Poseidon Adventure*
Brady, Jerry (dir): *Vampire On Bikini Beach*
Brady, Joseph (act): *Cry Wolf (1980)*
Brady, Michael (wri): *To Gillian On Her 37th Birthday*
Brady, Moya (act): *Mary Reilly*
Brady, Robert H. (act): *Secrets Of The Phantom Caverns*
Brady, Ruth (act): *Caught*
Brady, Scott (act, 1924–1985, nee Jerry Tierney): *Castle Of Evil; The China Syndrome; Destination Inner Space; Gremlins; Hell's Bloody Devils; The Ice House; Journey To The Center Of Time; Marooned; The Mighty Gorga; Nightmare In Wax; The Night Strangler; Satan's Sadists; Strange Behavior; Terror At Midnight; They Ran For Their Lives; Undercover Girl (1950); Wicked, Wicked*

Braeden, Eric (act): *The Aliens Are Coming; The Ambulance; Colossus: The Forbin Project; Escape From The Planet Of The Apes; The Mask Of Sheba; The New, Original Wonder Woman*
Braga, Brannon (wri): *Star Trek: First Contact; Star Trek: Generations*
Bragado, Julio (cin): *Slugs*
Bragaglia, Arturo (act): *Gli Amori Di Ercole; Miracle In Milan*
Bragaglia, Carlo Ludovico (dir, b. 1894): *Gli Amori Di Ercole; Orient Express; The Queen Of Babylon; Il Segreto Delle Tre Punte; Ursus Nella Valle Dei Leoni; La Vergine Di Roma*
Bragaglia, Carlo Ludovico (wri, b. 1894): *The Queen Of Babylon*
Bragdon, Cliff (act): *The Saint In New York*
Braginton, James (act): *A Study In Scarlet (1914)*
Braha, Herb (act): *The Howling*
Braham, Lionel (act): *A Christmas Carol (1938); Don Juan (1927); Macbeth (1947)*
Brahm Hans (dir): see Brahm, John
Brahm, John (dir, 1893–1982, nee Hans Brahm): *Atlantis (1948); The Brasher Doubloon; The Diamond Queen; Guest In The House; Hangover Square; Il Ladro Di Venezia; The Locket; The Lodger (1944); The Mad Magician; The Undying Monster*
Brahm, Roberta (act): *Wonder Woman*
Brahms, Caryl (wri): *The Ghosts Of Berkeley Square*
Brahms, Penny (act): *The Private Life Of Sherlock Holmes*
Brainin, Danny (act): *Dreamchild; Xtro*
Brainville, Yves (act): *The Man Who Knew Too Much (1956); The Night Of The Generals; Les Sorcieres De Salem*
Brait, Carla (act): *Escape From The Bronx; Torso*
Braithwaite, Lilian (act): *The Chinese Puzzle; Downhill; A Man About The House; The Woman Who Was Nothing*
Braiver, Robert (act): *Timestalkers*
Brakhage, Stan (dir, b. 1933): *Thigh Line Lyre Triangular*
Bralver, Bob (act): *Beyond The Poseidon Adventure*
Brambell, Wilfrid (act, 1912–1985): *In Search Of The Castaways; Sword Of The Valiant; The Three Lives Of Thomasina; Where The Bullets Fly; Witch-Finder General*
Brambilla, Marco (dir): *Demolition Man*
Bramble, A.V. (act): *Beautiful Jim; Fatal Fingers; London's Yellow Peril; The Mystery Of A Hansom Cab; Strategy*
Bramble, A.V. (dir): *Fatal Fingers; A Smart Set; Wuthering Heights (1920)*
Bramble, Adam (act): *Darkman II: The Return Of Durant*
Bramhall, Dorothy (act): *The Clouded Crystal; Murder At Scotland Yard*
Brams, Julian (act): *The Companion (1994)*
Bramson, Danny (mus): *The Nutty Professor (1996)*
Brana, Francisco/Frank (act): *Crypt Of The Living Dead; Endless Descent; Hundra; Mystery On Monster Island; Pieces; Slugs*
Branagan, John (act): *The Entity*
Branagh, Kenneth (act & dir, b. 1960): *Dead Again; Hamlet (1996); Mary Shelley's 'Frankenstein'*
Branagh, Kenneth (wri, b. 1960): *Hamlet (1996)*
Branch, Houston (wri): *Mr. Wong, Detective*
Branch, Sarah (act): *Sword Of Sherwood Forest*
Branchu, Jacques (act): *La Jetee*
Brancia, Armando (act): *Amarcord*
Brand, Christianna (wri): *Green For Danger; The Mark Of Cain*
Brand, David (act): *Friday The 13th-Part 2*
Brand, George (act): *Island Of Lost Women*
Brand, Gibby (act): *Haunted, The (1991)*
Brand, Joline (act): *Giant From The Unknown*
Brand, Joshua (wri): *The London Connection*
Brand, Larry (dir): *The Drifter; Masque Of The Red Death (1989, Roger Corman/New World)*
Brand, Larry (wri): *The Drifter*
Brand, Millen (wri): *The Snake Pit (1948)*
Brand, Neville (act, 1921–1992): *The Adventures Of Nick Carter; The Alien's Return; Cry Terror!; D.O.A. (1949); Eaten Alive! (1976); Evils Of The Night; Killdozer; The Mad Bomber; Prince Valiant; Psychic Killer*
Brand, Roland (act): *Fear Is The Key*
Brand Sheila (act): *The Return Of Sherlock Holmes (1986)*
Brandauer, Klaus Maria (act): *Never Say Never Again*
Brandel, Marc (wri): *The Hand (1981); Return To Fantasy Island*

Brandenburg, Larry (act): *Fargo; Tidal Wave: No Escape*
Brander, Arthur (act): *Night Comes Too Soon; Panic At Madam Tussaud's*
Brandes, Richard (act & wri): *Party Line*
Brandi, Walter (act): *L'amante Del Vampiri; Cinque Tombe Per Un Medium; La Strage Dei Vampiri; L'ultima Preda Del Vampiro*
Brandis, Jock (act): *Scanners*
Brandis, Jonathan (act): *It (1990); The Neverending Story II: The Next Chapter; Stepfather II*
Brandner, Gary (wri): *Cameron's Closet; The Howling; Howling II; Howling II; Howling IV; Howling V: The Rebirth; The Howling: New Moon Rising*
Brandner, Uwe (dir, mus & wri): *I Love You, I Kill You*
Brando, Jocelyn (act, b. 1919): *Dark Night Of The Scarecrow; Nightfall (1956); Step Down To Terror*
Brando, Kevin (act): *The Octagon; Saturday The 14th*
Brando, Marlon (act, b. 1924): *The Fugitive Kind; The Island Of Dr. Moreau (1996); The Nightcomers; Reflections In A Golden Eye; Superman (1978)*
Brando, Richard (act): *Student Bodies*
Brandon, Bill (act): *The Black Knight*
Brandon, Catherine (act): *Persecution*
Brandon, David (act): *The Boys From Brazil; The Navy vs. The Night Monsters; She (1983)*
Brandon, Ella (act): *Rip Van Winkle (1914)*
Brandon, Henry (act, 1912–1990, a.k.a. Henry Kleinbach): *Babes In Toyland (1934); Captain Sinbad; Destination Saturn; Doomed To Die; The Land Unknown; Omar Khayyam; Raiders Of The Seven Seas; Scared Stiff (1953); The Son Of Monte Cristo; Tarzan And The Shedevil; Tarzan's Magic Fountain; The War Of The Worlds*
Brandon, John (act): *The Adding Machine; Billion Dollar Brain*
Brandon, John G. (wri): *The Silent House*
Brandon, Michael (act): *Deadly Messages; Quatro Mosche Di Velluto Gris; Red Alert; A Vacation In Hell*
Brandon, Peter (act): *Altered States; Battle Beneath The Earth; Final Eye; Good Against Evil; What Ever Happened To Aunt Alice?*
Brandon, William (act): *Further Exploits Of Sexton Blake-The Mystery Of The S.S. Olympic*
Brandorff, Stan (act): *Serial Mom*
Brandt, Astrid (act): *The Pink Chiquitas*
Brandt, Carolyn (act): *The Incredibly Strange Creatures Who Stopped Living And Became Mixed-Up Zombies; The Lemon Grove Kids Meet The Monsters; Rat Pfink & Boo Boo; The Thrill Killers*
Brandt, Hank (act): *The Aliens Are Coming; Dark Mirror (1984); Mandrake*
Brandt, Ivan (act): *The Man Who Could Work Miracles; Things To Come*
Brandt, Luci (act): *Shriek Of The Mutilated*
Brandt, Marilyn (act): *Outbreak*
Brandt, Max (act): *Frankenhooker*
Brandt, Rainer (act): *Funeral In Berlin*
Brandt, Thordis (act): *The Witchmaker*
Brandt, Victor Elliot (act): *Neon Maniacs*
Brandt, Walker (act): *Lunar Cop*
Brandt, William (act): *Just Imagine*
Brandy, Mycle (act): *Flesh Gordon*
Branham, Craig (act): *Philadelphia Experiment II*
Branna, Frank (act): *Where Time Began*
Brannan, Patrick (act): *The Dark Half*
Brannen, Richard H. (act): *Scalpel*
Brannen, Ralph (act): *Star Trek*
Brannigan, Paddy (act): *Treasure Island (1950)*
Brannon, Fred C. (dir): *Cyclotrode X; Flying Disc Man From Mars; Lost Planet Airmen; Missile Monsters; Retik, The Moon Menace; Satan's Satellites; Slaves Of The Invisible Monster; Sombra, The Spider Woman; U-238 And The Witch Doctor*
Bransfield, Marjorie (act): *Abraxas, Guardian Of The Universe*
Bransford, Jennifer (act): *Star Command*
Brant, Neil (wri): *International House*
Brantford, Albert (act): *Wuthering Heights (1920)*
Brantford, Mickey (act): *Blake The Law-breaker; The Clue Of The Second Goblet; The Great Office Mystery; The Mystery Of The Silent Death; The Phantom Light; Sexton Blake, Gambler; Silken Threads; The Stolen Necklace; A Yell Of A Night*
Brantley, Betsy (act): *I Come In Peace; Schizopolis; Shock Treatment! (1981)*
Brantlinger, Dee (act): *Alice In Wonderland (1985)*

Braque, Willy (act): *Aimez-Vous Les Femmes?*
Bras, Albert (act): *Vampyr*
Brascia, Dominic(k) (act): *Friday The 13th-Part V: A New Beginning; Once Bitten*
Brasica, John (act): *The Wrecking Crew*
Braslis, Eric (act): *Starship Invasions*
Brasno, George (act): *Charlie Chan At The Circus*
Brasno, Olive (act): *Charlie Chan At The Circus*
Brason, John (wri): *House Of The Living Dead*
Brass, David (act): *Quarantine*
Brass, Tinto (dir, b. 1933): *Il Disco Volante*
Brassett, Stephen (act): *Professor Potter's Magic Potions*
Brasseur, Claude (act): *Act Of Aggression*
Brasseur, Pierre (act, 1903–1972, nee Pierre Espinasse): *Agent Of Doom; Carthage In Flames; The Gentle Art Of Murder; Torticola Contre Frankensberg; Les Yeux Sans Visage*
Bratcher, Joe (act): *The Howling*
Bratt, Benjamin (act, b. 1963): *Demolition Man*
Bratton, Nathaniel (act): *Cavegirl (1985)*
Brauer, Jonathon (wri): *Not Of This World*
Braugher, Andre (act): *Primal Fear*
Braun, Harold (dir): *The Glass Tower*
Braun, Kurt (act): *The Dungeonmaster*
Braun, Marianne (act): *The End Of The Line*
Braun, Pinkas (act): *Curse Of The Yellow Snake; The Hunchback Of Soho; The Man Outside (1967); Mission Stardust*
Braunbock, Carola (act): *Three Nuts For Cinderella*
Brauner, Eva (act): *Necronomicon*
Brauner, Fritz (act): *Flight Of The Navigator*
Braunreiter, Kurt (act): *Watchers II*
Brauns, Marianne (act): *Kill Her Gently; X...The Unknown*
Braunstein, Joseph (dir): *Rest In Pieces*
Braus, Mortimer (wri): *The Son Of Dr. Jekyll*
Brauss, Art (act): *Hauser's Memory*
Braver, Billy (act): *Alice In Wonderland (1985)*
Braverman, Bart (act): *Alligator (1981)*
Braverman, Michael (wri): *Cruise Into Terror; Donor*
Braverman, Randy (act): *Distortions*
Bravman, Jack (dir): *Zombie Nightmare*
Bravman, Nancy (act): *Alien High*
Bravo, Carlos (act): *Zorro, The Gay Blade*
Bravo, Ramon (wri): *Tintorera...Bloody Waters*
Brawer, Alan (mus): *Outer Touch*
Bray, Isobel (wri): *The Shuttle Of Life*
Bray, Robert (act): *The Accursed; My Gun Is Quick; Voodoo Tiger*
Bray, Thom (act): *Deepstar Six; Prince Of Darkness*
Braya, Keith (act): *The Good Son*
Brayne, William (cin): *Disciple Of Death*
Brayshaw, Edward (act): *The Saint And The Brave Goose*
Brayton, Lily (act): *Kismet (1914)*
Brayton, Margaret (act): *The Trap*
Brazeale, Hal (act): *The Adventures Of Robin Hood*
Brazeau, Jay (act): *Prisoner Of Zenda, Inc.*
Brazelton, Conni Marie (act): *The People Under The Stairs*
Brazzel, Greg (act): *Mountaintop Motel Massacre*
Brazzi, Rossano (act, 1916–1994): *El Castello Dell'orrore; The Christmas That Almost Wasn't; La Corona Negra; The Final Conflict; Legend Of The Lost; Revenge Of The Black Eagle; Siege Of Syracuse*
Brdecka, Jiri (wri, b. 1917): *Cisaruv Pekar, Pekaruv Cisar; Cisaruv Slavik*
Breaks, Sebastian (act): *The Night Digger*
Breakston, George (P) (act, 1920–1973): *Great Expectations (1934); Jungle Stampede; The Return Of Peter Grimm (1934)*
Breakston, George (P) (dir, 1920–1973): *The Boy Cried Murder; Golden Ivory; The Manster*
Breakston, George P. (wri, 1920–1973): *The Manster*
Brealond, Tony (act): *The Wiz*
Breamer, Sylvia (act): *The Devil (1921)*
Brecher, Egon (act): *Above Suspicion; The Black Cat (1934); The Black Room; Charlie Chan's Secret; The Florentine Dagger; White Pongo*
Brecher, Irving (wri): *Shadow Of The Thin Man*
Brecht, Susan (act): *Fantasies*
Breck, Kathleen (act): *The Frozen Dead; Spaceflight IC-1*
Breck, Peter (act): *The Crawling Hand; I Still Dream Of Jeannie; Shock Corridor; The Sword And The Sorcerer*
Brecke, Norman (act): *Blood Song*
Breckenridge, Mano (act): *The God King*
Breckinridge, John (act): *Plan 9 From Outer Space*
Bredell, Elwood/Woody (cin): *The Adventures Of Don Juan; Black Friday; The Ghost Of*

Frankenstein; Hellzapoppin; Hold That Ghost; Horror Island; The Invisible Woman (1941); Man-Made Monster; The Mummy's Hand; The Mystery Of Marie Roget; Phantom Lady; Sherlock Holmes And The Voice Of Terror; The Unsuspected
Bredin, Patricia (act): *The Treasure Of Monte Cristo (1961)*
Bredin, Robert (act): *The Pink Chiquitas*
Bree, James (act): *Cry Wolf (1980); On Her Majesty's Secret Service; Satan's Slave; Without A Clue*
Breed, Chris (act): *Waxwork II: Lost In Time*
Breed, Helen Lloyd (act): *Vampire's Kiss; The Witches Of Eastwick*
Breeding, Richard (act): *The Man Who Fell To Earth (1976)*
Breedlove, John (act): *Fire In The Sky (1993)*
Breen, Paulette (act): *The Clonus Horror*
Breen, Philip (wri): *Gawain And The Green Knight; Sword Of The Valiant*
Breen, Richard L. (wri, 1919–1967): *Niagara*
Breese, Edmund (act, 1871–1936): *The Haunted House (1929); International House; Kismet (1930); Mata Hari (1932)*
Breeze, Robert (act): *Warlock*
Bregman, Tracy (act): *Happy Birthday To Me*
Breil, Joseph Carl (mus): *The Green Goddess (1923)*
Breillat, Catherine (act): *Dracula, Pere Et Fils*
Breillat, Marie-Helene (act): *Dracula, Pere Et Fils*
Breimer, Stephen (wri): *Butcher, Baker (Nightmare Maker)*
Breitbard, Earl (act): *Between Midnight And Dawn*
Brejchova, Jana (act): *Baron Prasil; Gentlemen, I Have Killed Einstein*
Brell, Eugene (act): *Zone Troopers*
Brembilla, Ferruccio (act): *Amarcord*
Bremer, Brian (act): *Pumpkinhead; Silent Night, Deadly Night 5: The Toymaker*
Bremer, Leslee (act): *School Spirit*
Bremer, Lucille (act, 1917-1996): *Adventures Of Casanova; Behind Locked Doors; Dark Delusion*
Bremner, Ewen (act): *Judge Dredd*
Brendel, El (act, 1891–1964): *House Of Fear (1939); Just Imagine; The She-Creature; Women Of All Nations*
Brenlin, George (act): *Top Secret (1978)*
Brennan, Brid (act): *Excalibur*
Brennan, Dolly (act): *Billion Dollar Brain*
Brennan, Don (act): *Funeral Home*
Brennan, Ed (wri): *Dark Places*
Brennan, Eileen (act, b. 1935): *Babes In Toyland (1986); Murder By Death; The Night That Panicked America*
Brennan, Frederick H. (wri): *The Ghost Talks*
Brennan, Heidi (act): *Vampire On Bikini Beach*
Brennan, John H. (act): *Galaxis*
Brennan, Kelly (act): *Full Eclipse*
Brennan, Kevin (act): *The Spaceman And King Arthur*
Brennan, Linda (act): *Repossessed*
Brennan, Marguerite (act): *Lady In The Fog*
Brennan, Martin (act): *The Children*
Brennan, Michael (act, b. 1912): *Circle Of Danger; The Devil's Agent; Doomwatch; Fright (1971); Lust For A Vampire; Nothing But The Night; No Trace; Thunderball*
Brennan, Patrick (act): *The Attic*
Brennan, Peggy Lee (act): *Message From Space*
Brennan, Peter (wri): *Razorback*
Brennan, Sheila (act): *The Curse Of The Werewolf; The Spiral Staircase (1975)*
Brennan, Walter (act, 1894–1974): *The Gnome-Mobile; Home For The Holidays*
Brennan, William M. (act): *Grim Prairie Tales*
Brenneman, Amy (act): *Casper; Daylight; Fear (1996)*
Brennen, Claire (act): *Planet Earth; She Freak*
Brenner, Barry (act): *Surf Nazis Must Die*
Brenner, Bettina (act): *Flesh & Blood; Hundra*
Brenner, Dori (act): *Altered States; I Dream Of Jeannie: Fifteen Years Later*
Brenner, Eve (act): *Torment (1986)*
Brenner, Faye (act): *Ghost (1990)*
Brenner, Jules (cin): *The Return Of The Living Dead (1985); Salem's Lot; S*H*E (1980); Teen Wolf Too*
Brennock, Rachel (act): *Robin Hood Junior (1975)*
Brenon, Herbert (act, 1880–1958): *The Secret Of The Air*
Brenon, Herbert (dir, 1880–1958): *Daughter Of The Gods; A Kiss For Cinderella; Laugh, Clown, Laugh; The Lone Wolf (1917); [illegible] The Secret Of The Air; Someone At The Door; 12-10*
Brenon, Herbert (wri, 1880–1958): *Daughter Of The Gods*
Brenon, Juliet (act): *A Kiss For Cinderella*
Brent, Doris (act): *The Brain That Wouldn't Die*
Brent, Earl (mus): *Snow White And The Three Stooges*
Brent, Eve (act): *The Barefoot Executive; Mara Of The Wilderness; Tarzan And The Trappers; Tarzan's Fight For Life*
Brent, Evelyn (act, 1899–1975, nee Mary Elizabeth Riggs): *Darkened Rooms; The Golden Eye; Mr. Wong, Detective; A Night Of Mystery (1928); The Seventh Victim; The Shuttle Of Life*
Brent, George (act, 1904–1979): *Charlie Chan Carries On; F.B.I. Girl; Miss Pinkerton; Slave Girl; The Spiral Staircase (1946); Tangier Incident; Temptation (1946)*
Brent, Lynton (act): *Mr. Wong, Detective*
Brent, Maya (act): *Il Planeta Degli Uomini Spenti*
Brent, Romney (act, 1902–1976): *The Adventures Of Don Juan; Screaming Mimi*
Brent, Simon (act): *The Legend Of Spider Forest*
Brent, Timothy (act): *Escape From The Bronx*
Brentano, Amy (act): *Breeders*
Brenton, Gilbert (act): *Class Of Nuke'em High*
Breon, Edmund (act, 1882–1951, nee E. MacLaverty): *Devotion; Dressed To Kill (1946); Gaslight (1944); The Lodger (1944); The Man In Half Moon Street; The Private Life Of Don Juan; The Return Of The Scarlet Pimpernel; The Scarlet Pimpernel (1934); The Woman In The Window*
Brereton, Arola (act): *The Houseboat Mystery*
Brereton, Tyrone (act): *Secrets Of The Night*
Brescia, Alfonso (wri): *Terror Of Rome Against The Son Of Hercule*
Bresee, Bobbie (act): *The Alien Within; Ghoulies; Mausoleum; Surf Nazis Must Die*
Bresin, Marty (cin): *The Hidden*
Bresk, Carl (act): *Darkman (1990)*
Breslau, Susan (act): *First Knight; Ghost (1990)*
Breslauer, Jeff (act): *Matinee*
Bresler, Jacob (act): *The Alien's Return*
Breslin, Howard (wri): *Platinum High School*
Breslin, Patricia (act): *Homicidal; I Saw What You Did (1965)*
Breslow, Lou (dir): *You Never Can Tell*
Breslow, Lou (wri, b. 1900): *A-Haunting We Will Go; Bedtime For Bonzo; Charlie Chan At The Race Track; The Gift Of Gab; Mr. Moto Takes Chance; Sleepers West; Whispering Ghosts; You Never Can Tell*
Bresnard, Nicole (act): *La Beaute Du Diable*
Bressart, Felix (act, 1890–1949): *Above Suspicion; Portrait Of Jennie*
Bresslaw, Bernard (act, 1934–1993): *Blood Of The Vampire; Carry On Screaming; The Fifth Musketeer; Hawk The Slayer; Jabberwocky; Krull; Men Of Sherwood Forest; Moon Zero Two; One Of Our Dinosaurs Is Missing; The Ugly Duckling; Vampira*
Bressler, Angela (act): *Student Bodies*
Bresson, Robert (act, b. 1907): *A Man Escaped*
Bresson, Robert (dir, b. 1907): *Lancelot Du Lac*
Brestoff, Richard (act): *The Entity; Return To Horror High*
Bretherton, Howard (dir, 1896–1969): *Return Of The Terror; The Trap*
Breton, Luis Hernandez (mus): *La Invasion De Los Vampiros; El Vampiro Sangriento*
Bretonniers, Jean (act): *The Green Glove*
Brett, Anna (act): *Dr. Jekyll And Sister Hyde*
Brett, (B.) Harold (act): *The Adventures Of Dick Turpin-The Gunpowder Plot*
Brett, (B.) Harold (dir): *The Houseboat Mystery; Thelma: Or, Saved From The Sea*
Brett, (B.) Harold (wri): *The Adventures Of Dick Turpin-The Gunpowder Plot; The Adventures Of Dick Turpin-The King Of Highwaymen; Detective Daring And The Thames Coiners; The Houseboat Mystery; The King's Peril; Robin Hood Outlawed; Thelma: Or, Saved From The Sea; The Witch Of The Welsh Mountains*
Brett, Ingrid (act): *The Witches (1966)*
Brett, Jeremy (act, 1935–1995, nee Jeremy Huggins): *The Medusa Touch; One Deadly Owner; The Secret Of Seagull Island; The Very Edge*
Brett, John (act): *Deranged (1987)*
Brettel, Colette (act): *Blood Money; Wuthering Heights (1920)*
Breuer, Siegfried (act): *The Third Man*
Breuil, Marcel (cin): *Johnny The Giant Killer*
Brewer, Art (cin): *Donor*
Brewer, Bill (act): *The Big Game*
Brewer, Griffith (act): *Happy Birthday To Me; Wild Thing*
Brewer, Jameson (wri): *Arnold; The Incredible Mr. Limpet; Terror In The Wax Museum*
Brewer, Jerry (act): *Offerings*
Brewer, Kyf (act): *Serial Mom*
Brewer, Leslie (act): *Phantom Of The Paradise*
Brewer, Ray (act): *Rocket Attack U.S.A.*
Brewis, Peter (act): *The Wicker Man*
Brewis, Peter (mus): *Morons From Outer Space*
Brewster, Carol (act): *Cat-Women Of The Moon*
Brewster, Diane (act): *The Invisible Boy; The Man In The Net; Pharaoh's Curse*
Brewster, E. Kim (wri): *The Food Of The Gods II*
Brewster, James (act): *Maniac (1980)*
Brewster, Margaret (act): *My Cousin Rachel; Savages; Second Chance*
Brez, Ethel (wri): *Castle Rock*
Brez, Mel (wri): *Castle Rock*
Breznahan, Tom (act): *Twice Dead*
Brezniak, David M.- (act): *Echoes*
Breznikar, Erin (act): *Waxwork II: Lost In Time*
Breznikar, John (act): *Waxwork II: Lost In Time*
Breznikar, Jonathan (act): *Waxwork II: Lost In Time*
Brialy, Jean-Claude (act, b. 1933): *The Burning Court; Le Diable Et Les Dix Commandements; A Killing Success; La Mariee Etait En Noir; Le Plus Vieux Metier Du Monde*
Brian, David (act, b. 1914): *Accused Of Murder; Castle Of Evil; The Destructors; No Place To Hide; A Perilous Journey*
Brian, Mary (act, b. 1908, nee Louise Dantzler): *Black Waters; Charlie Chan In Paris; Peter Pan*
Briansky, Oleg (act): *All Hallowe'en*
Briant, Shane (act): *Captain Kronos: Vampire Hunter; Cassandra; Demons Of The Mind; Frankenstein And The Monster From Hell; Hawk The Slayer; Murder Is Easy; Straight On Till Morning*
Bricard, Patrick (act): *Les Parapluies De Cherbourg*
Brice, Bridget (act): *No Blade Of Grass*
Brice, Derrick (act): *The Return Of The Living Dead (1985)*
Brice, Monte (wri): *Genius At Work*
Brice, Pierre (act): *The Bacchantes; Lipstick; Il Mulino Delle Donne Di Pietra; Operation Solo; Terror Of The Black Mask; Zorro Contro Maciste*
Brickell, Beth (act): *Brock's Last Case*
Bricker, Clarence (dir): *Robin Hood Jr. (1923)*
Bricker, George (wri, b. 1899): *The Brute Man; Buried Alive (1940); The Devil Bat; House Of Horrors (1946); Man In The Dark (1953); Mr. Moto In Danger Island; Pillow Of Death; She-Wolf Of London; Torchy Blane In Chinatown; Torchy Blane In Panama*
Bricker, Jack (act): *Something Is Out There*
Bricker, Sammy (act): *Darkened Rooms*
Brickman, Greg (act): *The Clonus Horror*
Brickman, Marshall (dir): *The Manhattan Project; Simon*
Brickman, Marshall (wri): *The Manhattan Project; Simon; Sleeper*
Bricusse, Leslie (mus, b. 1931): *Babes In Toyland (1986); Scrooge (1970); Willy Wonka And The Chocolate Factory*
Bricusse, Leslie (wri, b. 1931): *Scrooge (1970); The Very Edge*
Bridenbecker, Milton (cin): *The Phantom Of The Opera (1925)*
Bridge, Adam (act): *The Medusa Touch; Voices*
Bridge, Al(lan) (act): *The Falcon's Alibi; The Jade Mask; Shadows Over Chinatown; Song Of The Thin Man*
Bridges, Alan (dir): *Act Of Murder (1964); Invasion (1965)*
Bridges, Beau (act, b. 1941): *Alice In Wonderland (1985); The Fifth Musketeer; Guess Who's Coming For Christmas?; Hammersmith Is Out; The Uninvited (1996); Village Of The Giants*
Bridges, Bill (act): *Trick Or Treats*
Bridges, Billy (act): *Teenagers From Outer Space*
Bridges, Emily (act): *The Uninvited (1996)*
Bridges, Jack (act): *Midnight Offerings*
Bridges, James (dir, 1935–1993): *The China Syndrome*
Bridges, James/Jim (wri, 1935–1993): *Alfred Hitchcock Presents; The China Syndrome; Colossus: The Forbin Project; When Michael Calls*
Bridges, Jeff (act, b. 1949): *King Kong (1976); Starman; Tron*
Bridges, Jim (act): *Invasion Of The Saucer Men*
Bridges, Jimmy (act): *It Came Upon The Midnight Clear*
Bridges, Judith (act): *To All A Goodnight*
Bridges, Kenneth (act): *The Gifted One*
Bridges, Lloyd (act, b. 1913): *Alias Boston Blackie; Alice In Wonderland (1985); Around The World Under The Sea; Bear Island; Crime Doctor's Strangest Case; The Deadly Dream; The Fifth Musketeer; Haunts Of The Very Rich; Honey, I Blew Up The Kid; The Limping Man (1953); The Lone Wolf Takes A Chance; The Love War; Passport To Suez; Rocketship X-M; Secret Service Investigator; 16 Fathoms Deep; Stowaway To The Moon; Strange Confession; Trapped*
Bridges, Rand (act): *Phantom Of The Paradise*
Bridges, Ronald (act): *Naked Evil*
Bridges, Todd (act, b. 1965): *Twice Dead*
Bridgewater, Dee Dee (act): *The Brother From Another Planet*
Bridgewater, Stephen (act): *12 Monkeys*
Bridie, James (wri, 1888–1951): *The Paradine Case; Under Capricorn*
Bridle, Alan (act): *Starship Invasions*
Brienza, Anthony "Chip" (act): *Serial Mom*
Brienza, Linda Rae (act): *Ed Wood*
Brierley, David (act): *Threads*
Brierley, Joan (act): *Thark*
Brierley, Roger (act): *Superman II*
Briers, Richard (act, b. 1934): *Fathom; Hamlet (1996); Mary Shelley's 'Frankenstein'; Murder She Said; Rentadick; Watership Down*
Briganti, Elisa (Livia) (wri): *Exterminators Of The Year 3000; The House By The Cemetery; Manhattan Baby; Zombie*
Brigaud, Philippe (act): *Act Of Aggression*
Briggs, Charlie (act): *13 Frightened Girls*
Briggs, Donald (act, d. 1986): *Blondes At Work*
Briggs, Harlan (act): *After The Thin Man; Charlie Chan's Murder Cruise; The Missing Guest*
Briggs, Helen Virginia (act): see Bruce, Virginia
Briggs, Johnny (act): *The Devil-Ship Pirates*
Briggs, Raymond (wri): *When The Wind Blows*
Briggs, Wellington (act): *When Knights Were Bold (1929)*
Bright, Jeff (act): *The Silence Of The Hams*
Bright, John (wri, 1908–1989): *Sherlock Holmes And The Voice Of Terror*
Bright, Matthew (dir & wri): *Freeway*
Bright, Richard (act): *The Ambulance; Marathon Man*
Brighton, Bruce (act): *The Brain That Wouldn't Die*
Brighton, Peter (act): *Endgame*
Briguglio, Marie (act): *Time Walker*
Brikmanis, Peter (act): *The Music Of The Spheres*
Briley, John/Jack (wri): *Children Of The Damned; The Medusa Touch*
Briley-Strand, Gwendolyn (act): *Serial Mom*
Brill, Charlie (act): *The Man Who Wasn't There*
Brill, Michael (act): *The Abominable Snowman Of The Himalayas; The Camp On Blood Island*
Brill, Patti (act): *The Falcon And The Co-Eds; The Falcon In Hollywood; The Falcon Out West*
Brill, Steven (act): *Edward Scissorhands*
Brilli, Nancy (act): *Demons 2*
Brilliant, Arthur (wri): *Annabel Lee*
Brilliante, Sammy (act): *Dance Of The Dwarfs*
Brimble, Ian (act): *Jamaica Inn (1985); Venom (1982)*
Brimble, Nick (act): *Jamaica Inn (1985); Loch Ness; Robin Hood: Prince Of Thieves; Roger Corman's Frankenstein Unbound*
Brimley, (A.) Wilford (act, b. 1934): *Bio-Force I; The China Syndrome; Cocoon; Cocoon: The Return; Death Valley; Ewoks: The Battle For Endo; Remo Williams: The Adventure Begins; The Thing (1982)*
Brimmell, Max (act): *Grip Of The Strangler; Solution By Phone*
Brimmer, Ernest (act): see Dix, Richard
Brimo, Maurice (act): *The Punisher*
Brinckerhoff, Burt (dir): *Brave New World; Slaughter*
Brind, Smylla (act): see Brown, Vanessa
Brindley, Madge (act): *The Lady Killers (1956)*
Brinegar, Paul (act): *The Annihilator; How To Make A Monster; The Vampire (1957); World Without End*
Bringelson, Mark (act): *The First Power; The Lawnmower Man*
Brink, Conrad (cin): *Jacob's Ladder; Wolfen*
Brinkley, John (act): *A Bucket Of Blood (1959); War Of The Satellites*
Brinkley, Ritch (act): *Timestalkers*
Brinkman, Dolores (act): *The Mysterious Island (1929)*
Brinkman, Paul (act): *The Falcon's Alibi*
Brinkmann, Robert (cin): *The Cable Guy; Encino Man*
Brinton, Amy (act): *Midnight (1980)*
Brinton, Tim (act): *Information Received*
Brion, Francoise (act): *Caravan To Vaccares; Cartes Sur Table; Comment Qu'ella Est!; Lemmy Pour Les Dames; Le Saint Mene La Dance*
Briscoe, Donald (act): *House Of Dark Shadows*
Briscoe, Laurie (act): *The Resurrected*

Briscoe, Robert (act): *School Spirit*
Brisebois, Danielle (act, b. 1969): *The Premonition (1975)*
Brisigotti, Michele (act): *An American Werewolf In London*
Brismee, Jean (dir): *The Devil's Nightmare*
Brissac, Virginia (act): *The Adventurous Blonde; The Bandits Of Corsica; Black Friday; Crime Doctor's Strangest Case; Dressed To Kill (1941); The Ghost Breakers; The Mummy's Tomb; The Scarlet Clue; The Snake Pit (1948)*
Brisson, Carl (act, 1894–1958, nee Carl Pedersen): *Murder At The Vanities; The Ring*
Bristol, Clare (act): *Witchboard*
Bristow, Billie (wri): *Midnight (1931); The Secret Of The Loch (1934)*
Bristow, Douglas (act): *Cyborg Cop II*
Britt, Leo (act, b. 1908): *Dial M For Murder (1954); The Magnetic Monster*
Britt, Lisa (act): *The Haunting Passion*
Britt, May (act): *Haunts*
Britt, Rod (act): *The Craft; When The Bough Breaks*
Brittain, RSM Ronald (act): *The Spy With A Cold Nose*
Brittain, Ross (act): *Switch*
Brittany, Morgan (act, b. 1951): *The Initiation Of Sarah; Sundown: The Vampire In Retreat*
Britton, Barbara (act, b. 1920, nee Barbara Brantingham Czukor): *Bwana Devil; Captain Kidd; Champagne For Caesar; The Return Of Monte Cristo; They Made Me A Killer*
Britton, Christopher (act): *Millennium*
Britton, Florence (wri): *A Vagabond's Revenge*
Britton, Jacqueline (act): *A Return To Salem's Lot*
Britton, Jocelyn (act): *Sapphire*
Britton, Katherine (act): *Night Of The Creeps*
Britton, Malcolm (act): *The Keeper*
Britton, Mike (act): *Secrets Of Sex*
Britton, Pamela (act, 1923–1974): *D.O.A. (1949)*
Britton, Tony (act, b. 1924): *Agatha; Dr. Syn-Alias The Scarecrow; Night Watch; The People That Time Forgot*
Brix, Herman (act): see Bennett, Bruce
Brizzi, Anchise (cin): *Black Magic (1949)*
Broadbent, Amanda (act): see Barrie, Amanda
Broadbent, Dora (act): see Bryan, Dora
Broadbent, Jim (act): *The Avengers; Brazil; Richard II (1995); The Secret Agent (1996); The Shout; Time Bandits*
Broadbridge, Tom (act): *Mad Max*
Broadhurst, Kent (act): *The Dark Half*
Broadnax, David (act & wri): *Zombie Island Massacre*
Broady, Eloise (act): *To Die For*
Brocco, Fred (act): *Appointment With Murder*
Brocco, Peter (act): *The Balcony; The Bandits Of Corsica; Boston Blackie's Chinese Venture; Champagne For Caesar; Dark Intruder; Games; Jekyll And Hyde...Together Again; The Lone Wolf In Mexico; Our Man Flint; The Prisoner Of Zenda (1952); Search For Danger; The Three Stooges In Orbit; Tobor The Great; Twilight Zone; What's The Matter With Helen?*
Brocco, Peter (dir): *Homebodies*
Brochard, Jean (act): *Diabolique (1955)*
Brochero, Eduardo M. (wri): *Satanik; Lo Strano Caso Della Signora Ward*
Brock, Alan (act): *Shriek Of The Mutilated*
Brock, Hall (act): *Mr. Sycamore*
Brock, Lou (wri): *The Enchanted Forest*
Brock, Major (act): *Mountaintop Motel Massacre*
Brock, Phil (act): *Date With An Angel; Dollman vs. Demonic Toys*
Brock, Stanley (act): *The Devil And Max Devlin; Love At First Bite; Night Of The Comet*
Brock, Taylor (act): *When The Bough Breaks*
Brockett, Don (act, 1930–1995): *Day Of The Dead; Lady Beware; The Silence Of The Lambs*
Brockette, Garry (act): *The Philadelphia Experiment*
Brockington, James (act): *Superman (1978)*
Brockman, Jochen (act): *Fellowship Of The Frog*
Brockman, Michael (act): *Flight Of The Navigator*
Brocksmith, Ray (act): *Killer Fish; Total Recall; White Dwarf; Wolfen*
Brockwell, Gladys (act): *The Hunchback Of Notre Dame (1923)*
Brodell, Joan (act): see Leslie, Joan
Broder, Josh (act): *Silence Of The Lambs, The*
Broderick, Helen (act, 1891–1959): *Murder On A Bridle Path*
Broderick, Matthew (act, b. 1962): *The Cable Guy; Godzilla; Ladyhawke; Project X (1987)*
Broderick, Shirley (act): *Hideaway*
Brodie, Don (act): *Charlie Chan At The Olympics; Charlie Chan On Broadway; The Kennel Murder Case; Lady In The Morgue*
Brodie, Lea (act): *Warlords Of The Deep*
Brodie, Robert Stephen (wri): *Dick Tracy's Dilemma*
Brodie, Steve (act, b. 1919, nee Johnny Stevens): *Arson For Hire; The Beast From 20,000 Fathoms; Desperate; Donovan's Brain; The Falcon's Adventure; Frankenstein Island; The Giant Spider Invasion; I Cheated The Law; The Lady In The Iron Mask; M (1950); Spy In The Sky*
Brodine, Norbert (cin, 1897-1970): *A Blind Bargain; The Death Kiss; Deluge; Of Mice And Men (1939); One Million B.C.; The Silent Watcher; Topper (1937); Topper Returns; Topper Takes A Trip*
Brodney, Oscar (wri, b. 1905): *The Black Shield Of Falworth; Bobbikins; The Brass Bottle (1964); Francis Covers The Big Town; Francis Goes To The Races; Francis Goes To West Point; Harvey; The Sword Of Ali Baba*
Brodrick, Susan (act): *Dr. Jekyll And Sister Hyde; Journey To Midnight*
Brody, Adrien (act): *Solo*
Brody, Ann (act): *Alias The Lone Wolf; Drums Of Jeopardy (1931)*
Brody, Donald (act): *The Incredible 2-Headed Transplant*
Brody, Ronnie (act): *A Hitch In Time; Superman II*
Brody, Steve (act): *The Wild World Of Batwoman*
Brogan, Harry (act): *The Face Of Fu Manchu*
Brogan, Ron (act): *Gallery Of Horror*
Brogger, IVan (act): *C.H.U.D.*
Brok, Isabelle (act): *The Lift*
Broker, Lee (act): *Firebird 2015 A.D.; Scanners*
Brolin, James (act, b. 1940): *The Amityville Horror; Capricorn One; The Car; Fantastic Voyage; Nightmare On The 13th Floor; Relative Fear; Short Walk To Daylight; Tracks Of A Killer; Visions Of Murder; Way...Way Out; Westworld*
Brolin, Josh (act): *The Goonies*
Bromberg, Erich (mus): *Frankenstein Island*
Bromberg, J. Edward (act, 1903–1951): *Charlie Chan On Broadway; Cloak And Dagger (1946); Invisible Agent; Lady Of Burlesque; The Mark Of Zorro (1940); The Missing Corpse; Mr. Moto Takes A Chance; Phantom Of The Opera (1943); Pillow Of Death; Queen Of The Amazons (1947); Son Of Dracula (1943)*
Bromfield, Farron (act): see Bromfield, John
Bromfield, John (act, b. 1922, nee Farron Bromfield): *Curucu, Beast Of The Amazon; Hold That Line; Manfish; Revenge Of The Creature; Ring Of Fear; Sorry, Wrong Number (1948); Three Bad Sisters*
Bromfield, Valri (act): *Nothing But Trouble*
Bromiley, Dorothy (act): *The Servant*
Bromilow, Peter (act): *Camelot; Live Again, Die Again*
Bromley, Harold (act): *The Count Of Monte Cristo (1975)*
Bromley, Sheila (act): *Nancy Drew, Reporter; Time To Kill (1942); Torchy Plays With Dynamite*
Bromley, Sydney (act): *An American Werewolf In London; Captain Clegg; Dragonslayer; The Fearless Vampire Killers Or: Pardon Me, But Your Teeth Are In My Neck; Frankenstein And The Monster From Hell; Macbeth (1971); Monster Of Terror; The Neverending Story; The Night Of The Big Heat; Paranoiac; A Place To Die; Prehistoric Women (1966); Robin Hood Junior (1975)*
Bromly, Alan (dir): *The Angel Who Pawned Her Harp*
Bron, Eleanor (act, b. 1939): *Bedazzled*
Bronchalo, Domingo (act): *El Castillo De Las Bofetadas*
Bronfman, Robin (act): *The Kiss (1988)*
Bronner, Robert (cin): *It's Always Fair Weather; 7 Faces Of Dr. Lao*
Bronowski, Steven (act): *Howling II*
Bronsky, Brick (act): *Class Of Nuke'em High, Part 2: Subhumanoid Meltdown*
Bronson, Betty (act, 1906–1971, nee Elizabeth Ada Bronson): *A Kiss For Cinderella; Peter Pan*
Bronson, Charles (act, b. 1922, nee Charles Buchinsky): *Deep Freeze; House Of Wax; Master Of The World; Quelqu'un Derriere La Porte; X-15*
Bronson, Elizabeth Ada (act): *see Bronson, Betty*
Bronson, Harry (act): *The Thief*
Bronson, Lillian (act): *The Devil's Daughter; The Next Voice You Hear; Sleep, My Love*
Bronsten, Nat A. (wri): *Valley Of The Eagles*
Bronte, Charlotte (wri, 1816–1855): *Jane Eyre (1921, 1934, 1944, 1957, 1970 & 1996); Wide Sargasso Sea*
Bronte, Emily (wri, 1818–1848): *Cumbres Borrascosas; Wuthering Heights (1920, 1939 & 1970)*
Brook, Allen (act): *League Of Frightened Men*
Brook, Claudio (act): *The Bees; Cronos; Dr. Tarr's Torture Dungeon; The Saint In The Wax Museum*
Brook, Clifford (act): see Brook, Clive
Brook, Clive (act, 1887–1974, nee Clifford Brook): *The List Of Adrian Messenger; The Loudwater Mystery; The Return Of Sherlock Holmes (1929); Shanghai Express; Sherlock Holmes (1932); Trent's Last Case (1920)*
Brook, Faith (act, b. 1922): *Chase A Crooked Shadow; The Curse Of King Tut's Tomb; The Intimate Stranger; The Jungle Book (1942); Man In The Shadow; The 39 Steps (1959)*
Brook, Irina (act): *Transmutations*
Brook, Laura (act): *Mission: Impossible*
Brook, Lesley (act): *The Dark Stairway; House Of Darkness; The Man Who Made Diamonds; The Vulture (1937)*
Brook, Lindsey (act): *Hawk The Slayer*
Brook, Lyndon (act): *The Clue Of The Silver Key; Invasion (1965); Who?*
Brook, Peter (dir, b. 1925): *King Lear (1970); Lord Of The Flies (1963); The Persecution And Assassination Of Jean Paul Marat As Performed By The Inmates Of The Asylum Of Charenton Under The Direction Of The Marquis De Sade*
Brook, Peter (wri, b. 1925): *King Lear (1970); Lord Of The Flies (1963)*
Brooke, Clifford (act): *The Woman In White (1948)*
Brooke, Dinah (wri): *It Happened Here*
Brooke, E.H. (act): *Still Waters Run Deep*
Brooke, Hillary (act, b. 1914): *Abbott And Costello Meet Captain Kidd; The Adventures Of Sherlock Holmes (1939); Africa Screams; Big Town After Dark; Confidence Girl; Counter-Espionage; Crime Doctor's Courage; Dragon's Gold; The House Across The Lake; Invaders From Mars (1953); Jane Eyre (1944); Let's Live Again; Lost Continent (1951); The Man Who Knew Too Much (1956); The Maze; Ministry Of Fear; The Road To Utopia; Sherlock Holmes And The Voice Of Terror; Sherlock Holmes Faces Death; The Woman In Green*
Brooke, Hugh (act): *Dark World*
Brooke, Hugh (wri): *Dark World; Donovan's Brain; Saturday Island; This Is My Love*
Brooke, Lois (act): *Monster A-Go-Go*
Brooke, Michael (act): *X...The Unknown*
Brooke, Paul (act): *Agatha; For Your Eyes Only; Greystoke: The Legend Of Tarzan, Lord Of The Apes; The Lair Of The White Worm; Phantom Of The Opera (1983); The Zany Adventures Of Robin Hood*
Brooke, Peter R. (wri): *Starflight: The Plane That Couldn't Land*
Brooke, Ralph (dir): *Bloodlust!*
Brooke, Ralph (wri): *Bloodlust!; Giant From The Unknown*
Brooke, Sandy (act): *Nightmare Sisters*
Brooke, Walter (act): *The Astronaut; Black Sunday (1977); Bloodlust!; Conquest Of Space; Marooned; The Return Of Count Yorga; Stowaway To The Moon; Time Travelers (1976)*
Brooker, Richard (act): *Deathstalker; Friday The 13th-Part 3*
Brooker, William (act): *Something Weird*
Brookes, Jacqueline (act): *The Entity; Ghost Story (1981); The Good Son; Last Embrace; Starcrossed; Werewolf Of Washington*
Brookes, Olwen (act): *The Black Knight; An Inspector Calls*
Brookholt, Henry (act): see Buchholz, Horst
Brook-Jones, Elwyn (act): *The Three Weird Sisters; The Ugly Duckling*
Brooklyn, Thomas (act): *The Underworld Of London*
Brooklyn Dodgers, The (act): *Roogie's Bump*
Brooks Group, The (mus): *Carnival Of Blood*
Brooks, Aimee (act): *Critters 3*
Brooks, Albert (act, b. 1947): *Twilight Zone*
Brooks, Annabel (act): *Nightflyers; The Witches (1990)*
Brooks, Beverley (act): *Find The Lady*
Brooks, Bob (dir): *Tattoo*
Brooks, Claude (act): *The Wiz*
Brooks, Conrad (act, b. 1931): *The Beast Of Yucca Flats; Ed Wood; Glen Or Glenda?; Plan 9 From Outer Space; A Polish Vampire In Burbank*
Brooks, David (act): *A Stranger Is Watching*
Brooks, David Allen (act): *The Kindred*
Brooks, Edward (act): *The Man In The Iron Mask (1939)*
Brooks, Elisabeth (act): *The Howling*
Brooks, Eric (act): *The Mind Of Mr. Soames*
Brooks, Geraldine (act, b. 1925, nee Geraldine Stroock): *An Act Of Murder (1948); Cry Wolf (1947); The Green Glove; Possessed (1947)*
Brooks, Hazel (act): *Sleep, My Love*
Brooks, Hildy (act): *The Babysitter*
Brooks, Hillary (act): *Secrets In The Attic*
Brooks, Hugh (act): *I Was A Zombie For The F.B.I.*
Brooks, Iris (act): *I Drink Your Blood*
Brooks, J. Cynthia (act): *Human Timebomb*
Brooks, Jason (act): *I'm Dangerous Tonight*
Brooks, Jean (act, b. 1921): *The Falcon And The Co-Eds; The Falcon In Danger; The Falcon In Hollywood; The Falcon's Alibi; The Leopard Man; A Night Of Adventure; The Seventh Victim*
Brooks, Jeremy (act): *Torture Dungeon*
Brooks, Jeremy (wri): Our Mother's House; Work Is A Four Letter Word
Brooks, Jerry (act): *Simon, King Of The Witches*
Brooks, Joe (act): *Gremlins*
Brooks, John Jo (act): *Lovespell*
Brooks, Jonathan (act): *Whispering Death*
Brooks, Jose (act): *When Woman Hates*
Brooks, Leslie (act): *The Cobra Strikes; The Secret Of The Whistler*
Brooks, Lola (act): *On The Beach*
Brooks, Louise (act, 1900–1985): *The Canary Murder Case*
Brooks, Margaret (act): *Our Mother's House*
Brooks, Martin (E.) (act): *Bionic Showdown: The Six Million Dollar Man And The Bionic Woman; Colossus: The Forbin Project; The Return Of The Six Million Dollar Man And The Bionic Woman*
Brooks III, Maurice E. (act): *Surf Nazis Must Die*
Brooks, Mel (act, b. 1927): *Dracula: Dead And Loving It; Robin Hood: Men In Tights; The Silence Of The Hams; Spaceballs*
Brooks, Mel (dir, b. 1927): *Dracula: Dead And Loving It; Robin Hood: Men In Tights; Spaceballs; Young Frankenstein*
Brooks, Mel (wri, b. 1927): *Dracula: Dead And Loving It; The Nude Bomb; Robin Hood: Men In Tights; Spaceballs; Young Frankenstein*
Brooks, Michael (act): *Bulldog Drummond In Africa; Bulldog Drummond's Peril*
Brooks, Nola (act): *Dot And The Kangaroo*
Brooks, Pattie (mus): *Agatha*
Brooks, Phyllis (act, b. 1915, nee Phyllis Seiller): *Charlie Chan In Honolulu; Charlie Chan In Reno; The Unseen (1945)*
Brooks, Ralph (act): *When Worlds Collide*
Brooks, Rand (act): *The Son Of Monte Cristo*
Brooks, Randi (act): *Looker; Terrorvision*
Brooks, Ray (act, b. 1942): *Alice's Adventures In Wonderland (1972); Assassin (1973); Baffled!; Daleks' Invasion Earth 2150 A.D.; The Flesh And Blood Show; House Of Whip Cord*
Brooks, Richard (act): *The Crow: City Of Angels; The Hidden; Shocker*
Brooks, Richard (dir, 1912–1992): *The Last Hunt*
Brooks, Richard (wri, 1912–1992): *Cobra Woman; The Last Hunt; Mystery Street; White Savage*
Brooks, Rob (act): *Beverly Hills Bodysnatchers*
Brooks, Ron (act): *Leatherface: Texas Chainsaw Massacre II; The Offspring*
Brooks, Sabrina (act): *Blood Diner*
Brooks, Teri (act): *Homicidal*
Brooks, Van (act): *Blood Simple*
Brooks, Victor (act): *Brides Of Dracula; Cover Girl Killer; The Day Of The Triffids; Devils Of Darkness; Downfall; Electric Eskimo; The Eyes Of Annie Jones; The Road To Hong Kong; Witchcraft (1964)*
Broome, Marianne (act): *The Legacy; The Slipper And The Rose*
Broones, Martin (mus): *The Mysterious Island (1929)*
Broos, Huib (act): *The Lift*
Brophy, Ed(ward S.) (act, 1895–1960): *Calling Philo Vance; Exile Express; The Falcon In San Francisco; The Falcon's Adventure; Freaks; The Gay Falcon; The Invisible Woman (1941); It Happened Tomorrow; Mad Love; Sleepers West; The Thin Man; The Thin Man Goes Home*
Brophy, John (wri): *Turn The Key Softly*
Brophy, Kevin (act): *Hell Night; The Seduction; Time Walker; White Dwarf*

Brosnan, Pierce (act, b. 1953): *Dante's Peak; Goldeneye; The Lawnmower Man; Mars Attacks!; Nomads; Tomorrow Never Dies*
Bross, Jennifer (act): *Phantasm II: Lord Of The Dead*
Brossman, Robert L. (act): *Galaxina*
Brost, Gudrun (act): *Det Sjunde Inseglet; Vargtimmen*
Brostrom, Gunnel (act): *The Devil's Messenger; I Am Curious (Yellow)*
Broszkiewicz, Jerzy (wri): *Wielka, Wielka I Najwieksza*
Brotherhood, J.C. (cin): *Angel Heart*
Brothers, Dr. Joyce (act): *Embryo; Oh, God! Book II*
Brotherson, Eric (act): *Blacula*
Brotherton, Joseph (cin): *Tarzan The Fearless*
Brouett, Albert (act): *The Silent House*
Brough, Antonia (act): *Maria Marten: Or, The Murder In The Red Barn (1935)*
Brough, Arthur (act): *Dead Man's Chest; The Green Man*
Brough, Candi (act): *Pandemonium*
Brough, Mary (act): *The Brass Bottle (1914); A Christmas Carol (1914); The Golden Dawn; Thark; The Tinted Venus*
Brough, Randi (act): *Pandemonium*
Brough, Spangler Arlington (act): see Taylor, Robert
Broughton, Bruce (mus): *The Boy Who Could Fly; Harry And The Hendersons; Honey, I Blew Up The Kid; The Ice Pirates; Miracle On 34th Street (1994); The Monster Squad; Narrow Margin; A Simple Wish; Sorry, Wrong Number (1989); Stay Tuned; Young Sherlock Holmes*
Broughton, June (act): *Threads*
Broussard, Rebecca (act): *Mars Attacks!*
Brousse, Liliane (act): *Maniac (1963); Paranoiac*
Brousseau, Pierre (wri): *Tanya's Island*
Brower, Otto (dir): *Radio Ranch*
Brown, A.J. (act): *Clegg; Hands Of The Ripper*
Brown, Alex (A.) (act): *Earthquake; Night Of The Comet*
Brown, Alfred (act): *The 7th Voyage Of Sinbad*
Brown Jr., Alonzo (act): *The Hidden*
Brown, Andra (act): *Empire Of Ash II*
Brown, Anita (act): *Charlie Chan In Egypt*
Brown, Antony (act): *Brazil; Jekyll And Hyde*
Brown, Arthur (act): *Tommy*
Brown, Barbara (Ann) (GB act): *The Terror Of The Tongs; The Wicker Man*
Brown, Barbara (USA act): *The Beast With Five Fingers; The Falcon And The Co-Eds; Jack And The Beanstalk (1952)*
Brown, Barry (act, 1951–1978): *Piranha (1978); Premonition (1972)*
Brown, Barry (1980s act): *Offerings*
Brown, Ben (act): *Terror In The Wax Museum*
Brown, Bill (cin): *The Savage Curse*
Brown, Blair (act): *Altered States; The Bad Seed (1985)*
Brown, Bobbie (act): *Flash Gordon*
Brown, Bobby Baresford (act): *Ghostbusters II*
Brown, Bryan (act): *20,000 Leagues Under The Sea (1997, Abctv)*
Brown, Candida (act): *Only A Scream Away*
Brown, Caplan (act): *Making Contact*
Brown, Carlos (act): *No Exit*
Brown, Carol (act): *The Son Of Hercules In The Land Of Darkness*
Brown, Casey (act): *Ghost Warrior*
Brown, Charles (cin): *Cinque Tombe Per Un Medium*
Brown, Charles D. (act): *The Big Sleep (1946); Charlie Chan In Reno; Just Before Dawn (1946); Mr. Moto In Danger Island; Mr. Moto's Gamble*
Brown, Chelsea (act): *The Thing With Two Heads*
Brown, Cheryl (act): *Return To Oz*
Brown, Christopher (act): *Alien Avengers*
Brown, Claire (act): *It (1990)*
Brown, Clancy (act): *The Adventures Of Buckaroo Banzai; The Bride (1985); Cast A Deadly Spell; Highlander; Pet Sematary Two*
Brown, Clarence (dir, 1890–1987): *Angels In The Outfield (1951)*
Brown, Colin Eliot (act): *Lucifer Complex*
Brown, Courtney (act): *The Flight Of The Navigator*
Brown, Darcy (act): *Shriek Of The Mutilated*
Brown, David (It act): *Endgame*
Brown, David (USA act): *I Was A Zombie For The F.B.I.; The Quilt Of Hathor*
Brown, Dwier (act, b. 1958): *The Guardian; House II: The Second Story; Mom And Dad [illegible] The World*
Brown, Earl Jolly (act): *Live And Let Die*
Brown, Edward R. (cin): *The Henderson Monster*
Brown, Edwin (act): *10 Rillington Place; Whirlpool*
Brown, Edwin (Scott) (dir & wri): *The Prey (1980)*
Brown, Elaine (act): *Mutants In Paradise*
Brown, Ernie (act): *The Monster Squad*
Brown, Ewing (act): *The Astounding She-Monster*
Brown, Frederic (wri, 1907–1972): *Martians Go Home*
Brown, Frederick (wri): *Screaming Mimi*
Brown, Gary (act): *Strangest Dreams: Invasion Of The Space Preachers*
Brown, Gaye (act): *A Clockwork Orange; The Masque Of The Red Death (1964); Mata Hari (1985)*
Brown, Georg Stanford (act, b. 1943): *Colossus: The Forbin Project; The Kid With The Broken Halo; Ritual Of Evil*
Brown, Georgia (act): *Murder Reported; Nothing But The Night; The Seven-Per-Cent Solution; A Study In Terror; Tales That Witness Madness*
Brown, Harry (wri): *The Sniper*
Brown, Helen (act): see Hayes, Helen
Brown, Henry C. (act): *I'm Dangerous Tonight*
Brown, Capt. Horace (act): *The Destructors*
Brown, J. Bertram (wri): *The Ware Case*
Brown, J.P.S. (act): *Death Valley*
Brown, Jack (cin): *The Lone Wolf (1924)*
Brown, Jackie (mus): *The Accursed*
Brown, James (B.) (act, 1920–1992): *Space Monster; Targets*
Brown (Jr.), James (S.) (cin): *Close Call For Ellery Queen; Crime Doctor; Crime Doctor's Strangest Case; Desperate Chance For Ellery Queen; Ellery Queen And The Murder Ring; Ellery Queen And The Perfect Crime; Ellery Queen, Master Detective; Ellery Queen's Penthouse Mystery; Enemy Agents Meet Ellery Queen; Mr. Hex; Murder By Television; The Trap; The Whistler*
Brown, Janet (act): *The Adding Machine; For Your Eyes Only; Wombling Free*
Brown, Jeannine (act): *The Tribe*
Brown, Jim (act, b. 1936): *Mars Attacks!; The Running Man*
Brown, Jimmy (act): *The Company Of Wolves*
Brown, Joe (act): *Making Contact*
Brown, Joe (E.) (act, 1892–1973): *Around The World In 80 Days; Beware, Spooks!; The Comedy Of Terrors; The Ghost Talks; The Gladiator; A Midsummer Night's Dream (1935)*
Brown, John (Euro act): *Howling II; Master Spy*
Brown, John (USA act): *So Sad About Gloria; Strangers On A Train*
Brown, John P. (act): *The Dream Of A Rarebit Fiend*
Brown, Johnny (act): *The Wiz*
Brown, Jophery (C.) (act): *Jurassic Park; The Relic*
Brown, Jordan (act): *Dead Of Night (1987); Serial Mom*
Brown, Josephine (act): *The Man Inside*
Brown, Juanita (act): *Caged Heat!*
Brown, Judith (act): *Psychic Killer*
Brown, Judy (act): *Toxic Zombies*
Brown, Julie (act & wri): *Earth Girls Are Easy*
Brown, June (act): *Murder By Decree; Psychomania (1972)*
Brown, Karl (wri, 1896–1990): *The Ape Man; The Man They Could Not Hang; The Man With Nine Lives; Mr. District Attorney*
Brown, Kate (act): *Elvira, Mistress Of The Dark*
Brown, Kathie (act): *Brainstorm (1965); The Underwater City*
Brown, Kathryn (act): *Just Imagine*
Brown, Kathy (act): *Secrets Of The Phantom Caverns*
Brown, Kerry (act): *Strange Behavior*
Brown, Larry (dir & wri): *The Psychopath (1973)*
Brown, Laura (act): *Colossus And The Headhunters*
Brown, Laurie (act): *Spasms*
Brown, Les (act): *The Nutty Professor (1963)*
Brown, Lew (act): *The Clone Master; Colossus: The Forbin Project; Planet Earth; The Resurrection Of Zachary Wheeler*
Brown, Linda (act): *Inn Of The Damned*
Brown, Lita (act): *Panther Island*
Brown, Lowell (act): *The Day Mars Invaded Earth; Ghost Diver*
Brown, Lucille (act): *The Thin Man Goes Home*
Brown, Martha (act): *Nightbeast*
Brown, Martin (wri): *The Mad Genius*
Brown, Mary (act): *A Nightmare On Elm Street 3: Dream Warriors*
Brown, Matthew (act): *Plymouth*
Brown, Maureen (act): *Il Mostro Di Venezia*
Brown, Max M. (act): *Wolfen*
Brown, Michael (act): *Raiders Of The Living Dead*
Brown, Mike (act): *Echoes*
Brown, Miquel (act): *Superman (1978)*
Brown, Murray (act): *The Black Windmill; Dracula (1973); Vampyres...Daughters Of Dracula*
Brown, Nannette (act): *Swamp Thing*
Brown, Niles (act): *The Tribe*
Brown, Olivia (act): *Memories Of Murder*
Brown, P.J. (act): *Vice Versa (1988)*
Brown, P.L. (act): *Neighbors*
Brown, Pamela (GB act, b. 1917): *Alice In Wonderland (1950); Dracula (1973); The Night Digger; On A Clear Day You Can See Forever; Richard II (1955); Secret Ceremony; Wuthering Heights (1970)*
Brown, Pamela (USA act): *Fright Night*
Brown, Pat Crawford (act): *Elvira, Mistress Of The Dark*
Brown, Paulette K. (act): *Jekyll And Hyde...Together Again*
Brown, Penny (act): *A Lizard In A Woman's Skin*
Brown, Peter (act): *Aurora Encounter*
Brown, Phil (GB act): *The Adding Machine; Thebedford Incident; The Boy Cried Murder; The Camp On Blood Island; The Green Scarf; Obsession (1949); Star Wars; Superman (1978)*
Brown, Phil (USA act): *Jungle Captive; The Luck Of The Irish; Weird Woman*
Brown, Ralph (act): *Alien 3; The Devil's Messenger; Final Exam*
Brown, Ray (wri): *Timestalkers*
Brown, Raymond (act): *The Thin Man*
Brown, Raymonda (act): *Just Imagine*
Brown, Reb (act): *Captain America (1978); Captain America II; Howling II; Ssssss; Strange New World; The Sword And The Sorcerer; Yor, The Hunter From The Future*
Brown, Ricky (act): *I Was A Zombie For The F.B.I.*
Brown, Rita Mae (wri): *The Slumber Party Massacre*
Brown, Ritza (act): *Ator: The Fighting Eagle; The Mcguffin*
Brown, Robert (GB act, b. 1918): *The Abominable Snowman Of The Himalayas; Cloudburst; Demons Of The Mind; The Double; Kill Me Tomorrow; Licence To Kill (1989); The Living Daylights; The Masque Of The Red Death (1964); Octopussy; One Million Years B.C.; The Spy Who Loved Me; A View To A Kill; Warlords Of The Deep*
Brown, Robert (USA act): *The Flame Barrier; The Hidden; Tower Of London (1962)*
Brown, Robert Allen (act): *The Mummy And The Curse Of The Jackals*
Brown, Robert Howell (act): see Lansing, Robert
Brown, Roger Aaron (act): *Alien Nation; Bad Ronald; Galaxis; Robocop 2; Star Trek*
Brown, Rona (act): *Greystoke: The Legend Of Tarzan, Lord Of The Apes*
Brown, Rosey (act): *The Silence Of The Hams*
Brown, Russ (act): *Damn Yankees*
Brown, Scotty (act): *Tales Of Terror*
Brown, Stanley (act): *The Lone Wolf Spy Hunt; The Man With Nine Lives*
Brown, Stephen (act): *A Ghost Of A Chance (1968)*
Brown, Steven (act): *Anguish; Silent Running*
Brown, Summer (wri): *The Prey (1980)*
Brown, Susan (act): *Fear No Evil (1969)*
Brown, Sydney (act): *Change Of Mind*
Brown, T.K. (wri): *Haunts Of The Very Rich*
Brown, Tally (act, 1924–1989): *The Iliac Passion; Silent Night, Bloody Night*
Brown, Tane' Sally (act): *Crawlspace*
Brown, Teddy (act): *Elstree Calling*
Brown, Teresa (act): *I Was A Zombie For The F.B.I.*
Brown, Terry (act): *Copycat*
Brown, Thomas (act): *Honey, I Shrunk The Kids*
Brown, Timothy P. (act): *The Body Snatchers*
Brown, Tom (act): *The Naked Gun*
Brown, Tricia (act): *Hollywood Chainsaw Hookers; The Phantom Empire; Vamp*
Brown, Vanessa (act, b. 1928, nee Smylla Brind): *The Ghost And Mrs. Muir; Secret Of St. Ives; Tarzan And The Slave Girl*
Brown, Victoria (act): *Psycho II*
Brown, Vivian (act): *The Philadelphia Experiment*
Brown, W. Earl (act): *Wes Craven's New Nightmare*
Brown, Wally (act): *The Absent-Minded Professor (1961); Genius At Work; The Seventh Victim; Zombies On Broadway*
Brown, Walter (act): *The Brigand Of Kandahar; Dracula, Prince Of Darkness; Information Received; Locker 69*
Brown, Walter C. (wri): *The House In The Woods*
Brown, William Lyon (act): *One Million Years B.C.; The Vengeance Of She*
Brown, William O. (dir & wri): *The Witchmaker*
Brown, Woody (act): *Dominion*
Brown, Wren (T.) (act): *Heart And Souls; The Hidden*
Browne, Clarke (act): *The Giant Gila Monster*
Browne, Coral (act, 1913–1991): *Black Limelight; Dr. Crippen; Dreamchild; The Night Of The Generals; The Ruling Class; Theater Of Blood*
Browne, Derek (V.) (cin): *Prey (1978); Prisoners Of The Lost Universe*
Browne, Earle (wri): *Sherlock Holmes (1922)*
Browne, Howard (wri): *The St. Valentine's Day Massacre*
Browne, Irene (act): *The Bad Lord Byron; Berkeley Square; The House In The Square*
Browne, K.R.G. (wri): *Forging Ahead*
Browne, Kale (act): *Alfred Hitchcock Presents*
Browne, Kuri (act): *Dead Of Night (1987)*
Browne, Laidman (act): *Ghost Ship (1952)*
Browne, Robert Alan (act): *Psycho II; Psycho III*
Browne, Robin (cin): *House Of The Living Dead; The Keep; Stories From A Flying Trunk*
Browne, Roger (act): *Marte, Dio Della Guerra; Revenge Of The Gladiators; Vulcan, Son Of Jupiter*
Browne, Ronald W. (cin): *Captain America (1978); Crackle Of Death; Demon And The Mummy*
Browne, Roscoe Lee (act, b. 1925): *Dr. Scorpion; Logan's Run; Moon 44; Topaz*
Brownfield, Richard (cin): *The Hills Have Eyes II*
Browning, Alan (act): *Fury At Smugglers' Bay*
Browning, Irving (cin): *The House Of Secrets (1929)*
Browning, Norman (act): *Watchers*
Browning, Ricou (act, b. 1930): *The Creature Walks Among Us; Revenge Of The Creature*
Browning, Ricou (wri, b. 1930): *The Night Of The Claw*
Browning, Robert (wri, 1812–1889): *The Pied Piper (1907 & 1971); The Pied Piper Of Hamelin*
Browning, Rod (wri): *Oh Heavenly Dog*
Browning, Tod (dir, 1882–1962): *The Black Bird (1926); Devil Doll (1936); Dracula (1931, English-Speaking Version); The Eyes Of Mystery; Freaks; The Jury Of Fate; London After Midnight; The Mark Of The Vampire (1935); Miracles For Sale; The Mystic; Outside The Law; Revenge (1918); The Thirteenth Chair (1929); The Unholy Three (1925); The Unknown (1927); West Of Zanzibar; Where East Is East*
Browning, Tod (wri, 1882–1962): *The Black Bird (1926); Devil Doll (1936); London After Midnight; The Mark Of The Vampire (1935); The Mystic; Outside The Law; The Road To Mandalay; The Unknown (1927); Where East Is East*
Browning, William (act): *Bulldog Drummond (1923)*
Brownjohn, Robert (act): *Otley*
Brownlee, Frank (act): *Boston Blackie*
Brownlow, Jason (act): *The Reflecting Skin*
Brownlow, Kevin (dir & wri, b. 1938): *It Happened Here*
Brownrigg, S.F. (dir): *Don't Look In The Basement*
Brox, Michael (Denis) (act): *Galaxina; Ghost Warrior*
Broyden, Jimmy (act): *Unforgettable*
Broyles Jr., William (wri): *Apollo 13*
Brubaker, Robert (act): *Seconds*
Brubaker, Tony (act): *I Come In Peace; Sugar Hill*
Bruce, Brenda (act, b. 1918): *Nightmare (1963); Peeping Tom; The Secret World Of Polly Flynt; They Came To A City*
Bruce, Charles (act): *Secrets In The Attic*
Bruce, Colin (act): *Gotham*
Bruce, David (act, 1914–1976, nee Marden McBroom): *Calling Dr. Death; Cannibal Attack; Jungle Hell; The Mad Ghoul; Pygmy Island; Seeds Of Destruction*
Bruce, Donald (act): *The Vengeance Of The Air*
Bruce, Eddie (act): *The Chance Of A Lifetime*
Bruce, George (wri, b. 1898): *Beauty And The Beast (1962); The Corsican Brothers (1941); The Fifth Musketeer; The Man In The Iron Mask (1939); Mask Of The Avenger; The*

Return Of Monte Cristo; Rogues Of Sherwood Forest; The Son Of Monte Cristo
Bruce, Jim (act): A Polish Vampire In Burbank
Bruce, James (dir): The Suicide Club (1988)
Bruce, Jane (act): The Curse Of The Living Corpse
Bruce, Janet (act): Nothing But The Night
Bruce, Lenny (wri, 1925–1966): Rocket Man
Bruce, Nigel (act, 1895–1953): The Adventures Of Sherlock Holmes (1939); Birds Of Prey; The Blue Bird (1940); Bwana Devil; Crazy House (1943); Dressed To Kill (1946); Gypsy Wildcat; The Hound Of The Baskervilles (1939); The House Of Fear (1945); I Was A Spy; The Pearl Of Death; Pursuit To Algiers; Rebecca; Red Aces; The Scarlet Claw; The Scarlet Pimpernel (1934); She (1935); Sherlock Holmes And The Secret Weapon; Sherlock Holmes And The Voice Of Terror; Sherlock Holmes Faces Death; Sherlock Holmes In Washington; Spider Woman; The Squeaker (1930); Suspicion; Terror By Night; Treasure Island (1934); The Two Mrs. Carrolls; The Woman In Green
Bruce, Robert (act): I Was A Zombie For The F.B.I.
Bruce, Sally Jane (act): The Night Of The Hunter (1955)
Bruce, Tonie Edgar (act): Whispering Tongues
Bruce, Virginia (act, 1910–1982, nee Helen Virginia Briggs): The Garden Murder Case; The Invisible Woman (1941); Jane Eyre (1934); Kongo; Night Has A Thousand Eyes; State Department-File 649
Bruce-Potter, Hilda (act): Still Waters Run Deep
Bruchon, Lucien (act): Warriors Of The Wasteland
Bruck, Bella (act): Something Evil
Bruck, Karl (act, 1906–1987): Doomsday Machine; Escape From The Planet Of The Apes
Bruckman, Clyde (wri): Sherlock Jr.
Bruckner, Lance (act): Star Crystal
Bruckner, William (wri): Dr. Renault's Secret
Bruderlin, Brian (act): Boarding House
Bruehl, Heidi (act, 1942–1991): Captain Sinbad; The Eiger Sanction
Bruguiere, Francis (dir): The Way
Brule, Claude (wri): Et Mourir De Plaisir
Brulee, Scotty (act): Tales From The Hood
Brull, Pamela (act): The Guardian
Bruller, Jean (wri): see Vercors
Brummer, Andre (mus): Monster From The Ocean Floor
Brun, Joseph (dir): The Fat Spy
Brundin, Bo (act): I Saw What You Did (1988); Meteor
Brunel, Adrian (act, 1892–1958): The Man Without Desire
Brunel, Adrian (dir, 1892–1958): Elstree Calling; I'm An Explosive; The Man Without Desire; Menace (1934); The Shimmy Sheik
Brunel, Adrian (wri, 1892–1958): Elstree Calling; The Face At The Window (1920); I'm An Explosive; The Return Of The Scarlet Pimpernel; The Shimmy Sheik
Brunel, Bernard (act): Condemned To Death
Brunel-Cohen, Jane (act): Dr. Dracula
Brunelle, Tom (act): Misery
Brunelli, Ugo (cin): L'ultima Preda Del Vampiro
Bruner, Tom (mus): School Spirit
Brunet, Genevieve (act): The City Of Lost Children
Brunetti, Argentina (act): Ghost Chasers; Man-Eater Of Kumaon; My Cousin Rachel
Bruni, Robert (act): Alien High
Bruning, Robert (act): The Day After Halloween
Brunini, Archille (act): Zone Troopers
Brunius, Jacques (act): L'age D'or; The Golden Mask; Return From The Ashes
Brunjes, David (act): Lord Of The Flies (1963)
Brunner, Robert F. (mus): The Barefoot Executive; Blackbeard's Ghost; The Computer Wore Tennis Shoes; Now You See Him, Now You Don't; The Strongest Man In The World
Bruno, Frank (act): Mr. Wong, Detective
Brunot, Christophe (act): La Mariee Etait En Noir
Bruns, George (mus, 1914–1983): The Absent-Minded Professor (1961); Babes In Toyland (1961); The Love Bug; Son Of Flubber
Bruns, Philip (act): Return Of The Living Dead, Part II; Silent Night, Bloody Night
Brunskill, John (act): Long John Silver
Brunson, Glenda (act): The Legend Of Blood Mountain
Brusati, Franco (wri): Ulysses
Brustein, Alan (act): Street Trash
Bruton, Naomi (act): Curse Of The Swamp Creature
Brutsman, Joseph (act): Once Bitten
Bruyure, Christian (act): The Keeper; The Plutonium Incident
Bruyure, Margee (act): The Keeper
Bry, Ellen (act): The Chinese Web
Bryan, Arthur Q. (act): The Devil Bat; Samson And Delilah
Bryan, Blanche (act): The Man In The Attic (1915); The Sons Of Satan
Bryan, Brandy (act): The Angry Red Planet
Bryan, Dora (act, b. 1923, nee Dora Broadbent): Circle Of Danger; The Fallen Idol; The Green Man; Hands Of The Ripper; High Treason (1951); The Interrupted Journey; Mad About Men; Mother Riley Meets The Vampire; No Trace; The Perfect Woman; The Ringer (1952); Scarlet Thread; Whispering Smith Hits London
Bryan, Mitch (act): Killer Klowns From Outer Space
Bryan, Pat Wesley (act): Spookies
Bryan, Peggy (act): Dead Of Night (1945)
Bryan, Peter (wri): Brides Of Dracula; A Challenge For Robin Hood; The Deathshead Vampire; The Hound Of The Baskervilles (1959); The Plague Of The Zombies; The Projected Man; Seven Deaths In The Cat's Eye
Bryan, Zachery Ty (act, b. 1982): Magic Island
Bryans, John (act): The House That Dripped Blood
Bryant, Bill (act): King Dinosaur
Bryant, Bob (act): Curse Of The Faceless Man
Bryant, Charles (dir): Salome (1922)
Bryant, Chris (wri): The Awakening; Don't Look Now; The Spiral Staircase (1975)
Bryant, Curtis (act): Children Shouldn't Play With Dead Things
Bryant, Fred (act): For Your Eyes Only
Bryant, Gerard (wri): No Haunt For A Gentleman; The Secret Of The Forest
Bryant, Jan (act): The Trap
Bryant, Jane (act): Vampire On Bikini Beach
Bryant, John (act): The Bat (1959)
Bryant, Joshua (act): Black Noon; Salem's Lot
Bryant, Laura (act): Vampire On Bikini Beach
Bryant, Lee (act): Capricorn One; The Mysterious Two
Bryant, Michael (act): Caravan To Vaccares; The Deadly Affair; Girly; The Mind Benders (1963); The Ruling Class; Torture Garden
Bryant, Nana (act, 1888–1955): The Corsican Brothers (1941); Harvey; The Jungle Woman; League Of Frightened Men; The Lone Wolf Returns (1935); Meet Nero Wolfe; The Return Of October; The Unsuspected
Bryant, Pamela (act): Don't Answer The Phone!; The Return Of The Six Million Dollar Man And The Bionic Woman
Bryant, Peter (wri): Dr. Strangelove, Or: How I Learned To Stop Worrying And Love The Bomb
Bryant, Theona (act): The Private Lives Of Adam And Eve
Bryant, Todd (act): Friday The 13th-Part V: A New Beginning; Night Of The Creeps; Star Trek V: The Final Frontier
Bryant, Virginia (act): Demons 2
Bryant, William (act): Billion Dollar Threat; Black Noon; Experiment In Terror; The Resurrection Of Zachary Wheeler
Bryant III, Wilson (act): Dr. Black Mr. Hyde
Bryar, Claudia (act): The Immortal; I Was A Teenage Frankenstein; Psycho II
Bryar, Michael (act): Laserblast
Bryar, Paul (act): Blonde For A Day; The Chinese Ring; Larceny In Her Heart; Shadows Over Chinatown; The Spectre Of Edgar Allan Poe; Spy Smasher Returns; Three On A Ticket
Bryce, Alex (dir): The Black Tulip (1937); Sexton Blake And The Mademoiselle
Bryce, Allan (cin): The Viking Queen
Bryce, Scott (act): Pandora's Clock; Visions Of Murder
Brychta, Edita (act): The Secret Life Of Ian Fleming
Brychta, Jan (act): Do You Keep A Lion At Home?
Bryden, William (act): The Mask (1961)
Brydon, Jon (act): Runaway
Brydone, Alfred (act): The Lyons Mail; Richard II (1911)
Bryl, Barbara (act): Faraon
Brymer, Patrick (act): Bay Coven; Spasms
Bryniarski, Andre(w) (act): Batman Returns; Cyborg 3
Bryne, Barbara (act): Svengali (1983)
Brynner, Yul (act, 1915–1985): Death Rage; The Double Man; Futureworld; The Light At The Edge Of The World; The Magic Christian; The Serpent; Le Testament D'orphee; The Ultimate Warrior; Westworld
Brynych, Zbynek (dir & wri): The Fifth Horseman Is Fear
Bryson, Edith (act): Copycat
Bryson, James (act): The Fan
Bryson, Tom (act): The Woman In Green
Bryson, Winifred (act): Behind The Curtain (1924); The Hunchback Of Notre Dame (1923)
Brzechwa, Jan (wri): O Dwoch Takich Co Ukradli Ksiezyc
Bschliessmayer, O. Josef (act): see Werner, Oskar
B'Tiste, Illana (act): Flatliners
Bua, Anthony (act): Black Roses
Buba, Pasquale (act): Martin
Buba, Tony (act): Martin
Buber, Martin (wri, 1878–1965): Goldstein
Bublett, John W. (act): Cabin In The Sky
Bucci, Flavio (act): Murder On The Last Night Train
Bucci, Gwendolyn (act): Vampire's Kiss
Bucci, Marc (mus): Human Experiments
Bucciarelli, Lana (act): Matinee
Buccille, Ashley (act): Phenomenon
Buch, Fred (act): Cocoon: The Return; Shock Waves
Buchan, John (wri, 1875–1940): The 39 Steps (1935, 1959 & 1978)
Buchan, Josephine (act): Deja Vu
Buchanan, Barry (act): The Loch Ness Horror; Neon Maniacs
Buchanan, David (act): Buck Rogers In The 25th Century
Buchanan, Dee (act): The Loch Ness Horror
Buchanan, Donald I. (wri): Pawns Of Mars
Buchanan, Edgar (act, 1902–1979): The Bandit Of Sherwood Forest; The Devil's Partner
Buchanan, Elsa (act): Charlie Chan In London; Peter Ibbetson
Buchanan, Erin (act): Eyes Of Fire
Buchanan, Ian (act): The Seventh Sign
Buchanan, Jack (act, 1891–1957): Bulldog Drummond's Third Round; Bulldog Sees It Through; Her Heritage; When Knights Were Bold (1936)
Buchanan, James David (wri): Brenda Starr (1992)
Buchanan, Jennifer (act): Remote Control (1988)
Buchanan, Jim (wri): The Horror At 37,000 Feet
Buchanan, Larry (dir): Creature Of Destruction; Curse Of The Swamp Creature; The Eye Creatures; In The Year 2889; It's Alive! (1968); The Loch Ness Horror; Mars Needs Women; Mistress Of The Apes; Night Fright; Zontar: The Thing From Venus
Buchanan, Larry (wri): The Loch Ness Horror; Mars Needs Women; Mistress Of The Apes; Zontar: The Thing From Venus
Buchanan, Meriol (act): Dark Of The Night
Buchanan, Morris (act): Night Slaves
Buchanan, Nigel (act): Stop Press Girl
Buchanan, Robert (act): La Ragazza Che Sapeva Troppo
Buchanan, Robert (wri): Alone In London; The Charlatan; The English Rose; A Man's Shadow
Buchanan, Ruby (act): The Company Of Wolves; High Spirits
Buchanan, Russell (act): Candyman: Farewell To The Flesh
Buchanan, Sherry (act): The Eyes Behind The Stars; The Secret Of Seagull Island
Buchanan, Susan (act): Bloodspell
Buchanan, West (act): Party Line; War Of The Planets
Buchanan, William (wri): Dr. Syn-Alias The Scarecrow
Buchel, Brian (act): Bulldog Drummond At Bay (1937); Inside The Room; Murder At Monte Carlo
Buchet, Willis (act): Panic In Year Zero
Buchholz, Horst (act, b. 1933, a.k.a. Henry Brookholt): The Amazing Captain Nemo; Dead Of Night (1977); Return To Fantasy Island; The Savage Bees
Buchi, Ella (act): Faust (1963)
Buchinsky, Charles (act): see Bronson, Charles
Buchman, Sidney (wri, 1902–1975): Here Comes Mr. Jordan
Buchmann, Arlene (act): The Strangeness
Buchs, Julio (wri): Superargo E I Giganti Senza Volto
Buchsbaum, Don (act): Scanners; Spasms
Buchwald, Gauravani (act): Virtuosity
Buck, Barbara (act): Phoenix The Warrior; Vampire On Bikini Beach
Buck, Craig (wri): The Loves Of Dracula; World Of Dracula
Buck, David (act): The Dark Crystal; Dr. Syn-Alias The Scarecrow; The Mummy's Shroud; Why Would Anyone Want To Kill A Nice Girl Like You?
Buck, Frank (act, 1888–1950): Africa Screams
Buck, George (act): Angel Heart
Buck, Pamela (act): The Village Of The Damned (1960)
Buckingham, Jan (act): After Midnight With Boston Blackie
Buckingham, Robert (act): Bram Stoker's Dracula
Buckingham, Yvonne (act): Murder In Eden; Sapphire; The Sinister Man; The Tell-Tale Heart (1960); Urge To Kill
Buckland, Ray (act): Mutants In Paradise
Buckland, Vera (act): The Mystery Of Edwin Drood (1935)
Buckland, Warwick (act): The Chimes; The Grip Of Iron
Buckland, Warwick (dir): At The Eleventh Hour; At The Foot Of The Scaffold; The Avaricious Monk; The Curtain; Diamond Cut Diamond; The Heart Of A Woman; The Man Behind The Mask (1914); The Mystery Of Mr. Marks; On The Brink Of The Precipice; Partners In Crime; A Price On His Head; The Stress Of Circumstance
Buckland, Mrs. Wilfred (act): The Greene Murder Case
Buckle, Gerard Fort (wri): The Yellow Claw
Buckle, Ken (act): Fury At Smugglers' Bay; Treasure Island (1950)
Buckler, John (act): The Black Room; Tarzan Escapes
Buckley, Betty (act, b. 1947): Carrie; Wild Thing
Buckley, Christine (act): Threads
Buckley, Harold (wri): Nick Carter, Master Detective
Buckley, John (act): No Blade Of Grass
Buckley, Joss (act): Morons From Outer Space
Buckley, Keith (act): Dr. Phibes Rises Again; Excalibur; The Pied Piper (1971); Virgin Witch
Buckley, Pamela (act): The Haunting
Buckley, Ralph (act): Twisted
Bucklin, Brad M.(act): Wavelength
Buckman, Tara (act): The Man In The Santa Claus Suit; Xtro II: The Second Encounter
Buckmaster, Paul (mus): 12 Monkeys
Buckner, Parris (act): Flight Of The Navigator
Buckner, Robert (wri, b. 1906): Confidential Agent; Moon Pilot
Buckner, Susan (act): Deadly Blessing
Bucksey, Colin (dir): The Mcguffin; Notorious (1992)
Buckstone, Dorothy (act): Scrooge (1913)
Buckstone, J.C. (act): Scrooge (1913)
Buckton, Ben (act): The Glitterball
Buckton, Clifford (act): The Candlelight Murder
Bucossi, Peter (act): Serial Mom
Bucquet, Harold S. (dir, 1891–1946): On Borrowed Time
Buczachi, Jerzy (act): Faraon
Budahazi, Gabor (cin): A Connecticut Yankee In King Arthur's Court (1989)
Budashkin, N. (mus): Jack Frost
Buday, Don (wri): Kiss Meets The Phantom Of The Park
Budd, Jackson (wri): They Made Me A Fugitive
Budd, Julie (act): The Devil And Max Devlin
Budd, Norman (act): Alien Warrior; The Atomic City; Buried Alive (1940); One Million B.C.; Port Sinister
Budd, Roy (mus): The Black Windmill; Fear Is The Key; Sinbad And The Eye Of The Tiger; Zeppelin
Buddeke, Kate (act): Blink
Budrys, Algis (wri): To Kill A Clown; Who?
Buechler, John (Carl) (cin): From Beyond; Hard Rock Zombies
Buechler, John (Carl) (dir): Friday The 13th, Part VII-The New Blood; Troll
Buechler, John (wri): Demonwarp; The Dungeonmaster
Buel, Kenean (dir): She (1917)
Buenaflor, Jess (act): The Blood Drinkers
Buenaventura, Angel (act): Beast Of Blood; Dance Of The Dwarfs
Buferd, Marilyn (act): One Night Of Fame; Queeen Of Outer Space; The Unearthly
Buffa, Salvatore Amedeo (act): see Nazzari, Amedeo
Buffalo, Norton (act): Blood Beach
Buffer, Michael (act): Virtuosity
Buffett, Jimmy (act): Congo
Buffington, Sam (act): Invasion Of The Saucer Men
Buffington, Ted (act): The Jewel Of The Nile
Buffinton, Bryan (act): Mr. Destiny
Buffum, Ray (wri): The Brain From Planet Arous; Island Of Lost Women; Teenage Monster
Bufkin, William (act): The Clonus Horror
Bufler, Hugo (wri): A Christmas Carol (1938)

Bugarin, Rudy (act): *The Blood Drinkers*
Buggy, Niall (act): *Zardoz*
Bugner, Joe (act): *The Sheriff And The Satellite Kid*
Buheiry, Leila (act): *Embassy*
Buhr, Gerard (act): *The Night Of The Generals*
Bujeau, Christian (act): *The Visitors (1993)*
Bujold, Genevieve (act, b. 1944): *The Adventures Of Pinocchio; Coma; Dead Ringers; Earthquake; Isabel; Mistress Of Paradise; Murder By Decree; Obsession (1976); The Trojan Women*
Buka, Donald (act): *Between Midnight And Dawn*
Bukovy, William (mus): *Do You Keep A Lion At Home?*
Bulgarelli, Diane (mus): *Alien High*
Bull, Peter (act, b. 1912): *Alice's Adventures In Wonderland (1972); Dr. Dolittle; Dr. Strangelove: or, How I Learned To Stop Worrying And Love The Bomb; Footsteps In The Fog; Great Expectations (1974); Licensed To Kill; The Magic Shop; Marie Antoinette (1938); The Old Dark House (1963); Saadia; Scrooge (1951); The Tempest (1980); They Made Me A Fugitive; The Three Worlds Of Gulliver; Who Done It? (1956)*
Bull, Richard (act): *The Andromeda Strain; Mr. Sycamore; The Satan Bug*
Bullard, Nigel (act): *I, Desire*
Bullard, R.N. (act): *The Cremators*
Buller, Guy (act): *The Reflecting Skin*
Bullett, Gerald (wri): *The Last Man To Hang?*
Bullivant, Cecil (wri): *Blood Money*
Bulloch, Christian (act): *The Boy Who Never Was*
Bulloch, Jeremy (act): *The Lady Vanishes (1979); Octopussy; Only A Scream Away; Return Of The Jedi*
Bullock, Anna Mae (act & mus): see Turner, Tina
Bullock, Gary (act): *The Handmaid's Tale; Robocop 2; Species*
Bullock, Jim J. (act): *Switch*
Bullock, John (act): *Dark Of The Night*
Bullock, Sandra (act, b. 1967): *Bionic Showdown: The Six Million Dollar Man And The Bionic Woman; Demolition Man; Love Potion No. 9; A Time To Kill (1996)*
Bullock, Walter (wri, b. 1907): *Repeat Performance; Turn Back The Clock*
Bulmer, Fred (wri): *When Woman Hates*
Bulnes, Quintin (act): *Isle Of The Snake People*
Bulow, Gordon (act): *Mars Needs Women*
Bulwer-Lytton, Lord Edward George (wri, 1803–1873): *Les Derniers Jours De Pompeii; Eugene Aram; The Last Days Of Pompeii (1900 & 1959); Gli Ultimi Giorni Di Pompei (1908 & 1913)*
Bumatai, Ray (act): *The Presence*
Bumiller, William (act): *Species*
Bumpass, Roger (act): *Heavy Metal*
Bumstead, Henry (act): *Slaughterhouse-Five*
Bumstead, J.P. (act): *Fantasies*
Bunce, Alan (act): *Homicidal*
Bunce, Stuart (act): *First Knight*
Bunch, Betty (act): *Mars Attacks!*
Bunch, Farah (act): *The Alien's Return*
Bunch, Marianne (act): *Wavelength*
Bunch, Velton Ray (mus): *Unlikely Angel*
Bundy, Brooke (act): *The Adventures Of Nick Carter; Beverly Hills Bodysnatchers; Explorers; The Man In The Santa Claus Suit; A Nightmare On Elm Street 3: Dream Warriors; A Nightmare On Elm Street 4: The Dream Master; Twice Dead*
Bundy, Robert (act): *Vice Versa (1988)*
Bunin Puppets, The (act): *Alice In Wonderland (1950)*
Bunker, Edward (act): *Miracle Mile*
Bunker, Ralph (act): *The Ghost Goes West*
Bunnage, Avis (act): *Panic (1979)*
Bunny, George (act): *The Adventures Of Robin Hood; The Lost World (1925)*
Bunston, Herbert (act): *Charlie Chan's Chance; Dracula (1931, English-Speaking Version)*
Bunuel, Joyce (wri): *Black Moon (1975); Tattoo*
Bunuel, Luis (act, 1900–1983): *Un Chien Andalou*
Bunuel, Luis (dir, 1900–1983): *L'age D'or; El Angel Exterminador; Belle De Jour; Un Chien Andalou; Cumbres Borrascosas; The Discreet Charm Of The Bourgeoisie; La Mort En Ce Jardin; Tristana*
Bunuel, Luis (wri, 1900–1983): *L'age D'or; El Angel Exterminador; Un Chien Andalou; Cumbres Borrascosas; The Discreet Charm Of The Bourgeoisie; La Mort En Ce Jardin; Tristana*
Buono, Victor (act, 1938–1982): *Arnold; Beneath The Planet Of The Apes; Brenda Starr (1976); The Evil; Hush...Hush, Sweet Charlotte; The Mad Butcher; The Man From Atlantis; Man With Icy Eyes; Moonchild; The Silencers (1966); The Strangler (1963); Target...Earth?; Target: Harry; What Ever Happened To Baby Jane? (1962)*
Bupp, Tommy (act): *Mystery Plane; Nancy Drew, Detective; Torchy Runs For Mayor*
Buquet, August (act): *Empire Of Ash II*
Buquet, Ed (act): *Empire Of Ash II*
Bura, Dee (act): *The Mutations*
Bura, Fay (act): *The Mutations*
Burch, Curtis (wri): *The Alien's Return*
Burch, John (act): *Great Expectations (1946)*
Burcher, Tommy (act): *The Offspring*
Burchill, William (act): *Lady Audley's Secret (1920)*
Burchinal, William (act): *Night Of The Living Dead (1968)*
Burdach, Ann Louise (wri): *Sorry, Wrong Number (1989)*
Burden, Gary (act): *The Annihilator*
Burden, H.E. (wri): *Murder In Eden*
Burden, Hugh (act, 1913–1985): *Blood From The Mummy's Tomb; Funeral In Berlin; Ghost Ship (1952); The House In Nightmare Park; One Of Our Dinosaurs Is Missing; The Ruling Class; Sleeping Car To Trieste*
Burdette, Nicole (act): *Angel Heart*
Burdick, Eugene (wri): *Fail-Safe*
Burdis, Mark (act): *The Mcguffin; Never-Never Land*
Burdon, Therese (wri): *Sword Of The Valiant*
Burel, Leonce-Henri (cin, b. 1892): *J'accuse (1918)*
Buresh, Richard (act): *Attack Of The Killer Tomatoes*
Burfield, Kim (act): *The Flying Sorceror; Treasure Island (1971)*
Burford, Roger (wri): *Dr. Syn*
Burg, Emmy (act): *Confess, Dr. Corda*
Burgard, Christopher (act): *Twice Dead*
Burgdorph, Barbara (act): *The Clones*
Burge, James C. (act): *Castle Rock*
Burger, Gottfried (wri): *Baron Prasil*
Burger, Julie (act): *Echoes*
Burger, Neal (wri): *The Disappearance Of Flight 412*
Burger, Paul (wri): *Charlie Chan At The Olympics*
Burger, Robbyn (wri): *Asteroid*
Burger, Shereen (act): *Phoenix The Warrior*
Burgess, Anthony (wri, 1917–1993): *A Clockwork Orange; Quest For Fire*
Burgess, Christopher (act): *The Medusa Touch*
Burgess, Deborah (act): *Curtains*
Burgess, Don (cin): *The Night Stalker (1987); World Gone Wild*
Burgess, Helen (act): *A Night Of Mystery (1937)*
Burgess, James (act): *The Exorcist II*
Burgess, John (wri): *Sundown: The Vampire In Retreat*
Burgess, Lucinda (act): *Killer Klowns From Outer Space*
Burgess, Vivienne (act): *Maroc 7*
Burgess, Michael (act): *The Lottery*
Burghoff, Gary (act, b. 1943): *The Man In The Santa Claus Suit*
Burgin, Angus (act): *Lord Of The Flies (1990)*
Burgon, Geoffrey (mus): *Robin Hood (1991)*
Burgos, G. Moreno (wri): *Hipnosis*
Burgos, Gabriel (wri): *La Orgia Nocturna De Los Vampiros*
Burgos, Jose (act): *Masquerade*
Burgoyne, Victoria (act): *Death Ship*
Burgraff, Roger (act): *Shadow Of Death (1983)*
Burk, James H. (act): *Prophecy (1979)*
Burke, Alfred (act, b. 1918): *Children Of The Damned; Man At The Carlton Tower; The Man Inside; The Man Upstairs; Model For Murder; The Nanny; Night Caller From Outer Space; Treasure Island (1976)*
Burke, Barbara (act): *Jack The Ripper (1958)*
Burke, Beverly (act): *Seven*
Burke, Billie (act, 1885–1970, nee Mary William Ethelbert Appleton Burke): *Topper (1937); Topper Returns; Topper Takes A Trip; The Wizard Of Oz (1939)*
Burke, Brian (act): *Lady In The Morgue*
Burke, Calvin (act): *Moon 44*
Burke, Carlease (act): *Ghost In The Machine*
Burke, Charlotte (act): *Paperhouse*
Burke, Chris (act): *Nightbeast*
Burke, Chris (mus): *The Refrigerator*
Burke, Daubin (act): *Starship Invasions*
[illegible]
Burke, James (act, d. 1968): *The Big Clock; Charlie Chan's Murder Cruise; Close Call For Ellery Queen; Desperate Chance For Ellery Queen; Ellery Queen And The Murder Ring; Ellery Queen And The Perfect Crime; Ellery Queen, Master Detective; Ellery Queen's Penthouse Mystery; Enemy Agents Meet Ellery Queen; The Kennel Murder Case; The Maltese Falcon (1941); Nightmare Alley; Philo Vance's Gamble; The Saint Strikes Back; The Saint Takes Over; Song Of The Thin Man*
Burke, James H. (act): *Prophecy (1979)*
Burke, John (wri): *The Sorcerers*
Burke, Jonnie (cin): *Endangered Species; The Magician (1973)*
Burke, Kathleen (act): *Bulldog Drummond Strikes Back (1934); Island Of Lost Souls; Murders In The Zoo*
Burke, Marie (act, b. 1894, nee Marie Holt): *The Face In The Fog (1922); Face In The Night; The Flanagan Boy; Seance On A Wet Afternoon; The Snorkel; The Terror Of The Tongs; Vendetta For The Saint*
Burke, Martyn (dir): *The Last Chase*
Burke, Martyn (wri): *The Last Chase; Top Secret! (1984)*
Burke, Mary Ellen (act): *The Corpse Grinders*
Burke, Mary William Ethelbert Appleton (act): see Burke, Billie
Burke, Michael (act): *Boarding House*
Burke, Michael Reilly (act): *Bermuda Triangle; Mars Attacks!*
Burke, Patricia (act, b. 1917): *The Day The Fish Came Out; Forbidden; Strangler's Web; While I Live*
Burke, Patrick (Sullivan) (act): *The Brotherhood Of Satan; Equinox*
Burke, Paul (act, b. 1926): *Anatomy Of Terror; Crowhaven Farm; Daddy's Gone A-Hunting; The Disembodied; Francis Goes To West Point; Francis In The Navy; Psychic Killer*
Burke, Peter (act): *Children Shouldn't Play With Dead Things*
Burke, Richard (wri): *Dressed To Kill (1941)*
Burke, Robert (John) (act): *Dust Devil; Robocop 3; Thinner*
Burke, Ron (act): *Destination Inner Space; The Entity*
Burke, Samson (act): *Revenge Of Ursus; The Three Stooges Meet Hercules*
Burke, Sonny (mus): *Hand Of Death*
Burke, Sue (act): *Eve Of Destruction*
Burke, Thomas (act): *Gipsy Blood*
Burke, Thomas Robert (act): *Running Against Time*
Burke, Walter (act): *Beauty And The Beast (1962); Jack The Giant Killer; Mystery Street; The President's Analyst*
Burkett, Laura (act): *Blood Beach*
Burkhanov, Shukur (act): *Ilya Mourometz*
Burkhart, Juli (act): *Warlock*
Burkholder, Scott (act): *House IV*
Burkley, Dennis (act): *Laserblast*
Burks, Ivyl (cin): *Conquest Of Space; The War Of The Worlds*
Burks, Rick (act): *Blood Diner*
Burks, Robert (cin, 1910–1968): *Arsenic And Old Lace; The Birds; Dial M For Murder (1954); I Confess; The Man Who Knew Too Much (1956); Marnie; North By Northwest; Possessed (1947); Rear Window; Strangers On A Train; To Catch A Thief; The Trouble With Harry; Vertigo; The Wrong Man*
Burlaiev, Kolya (act): *My Name Is Ivan*
Burleigh, Bertram (act): *The Black Spider; The Crimson Circle (1922); The Sands Of Time; Trapped By The London Sharks; Wake Up!: Or, A Dream Of Tomorrow*
Burley, Matthew (act): *Pumpkinhead*
Burlinson, Tom (act): *Flesh & Blood; The Time Guardian*
Burls, Helene (act): *Dear Murderer; The Lady Killers (1956)*
Burman, Barney (act): *The Offspring*
Burman, Ellis (cin): *One Dark Night*
Burman, Hans (cin): *City Of The Walking Dead*
Burman, Tom (cin): *The Manitou; One Dark Night*
Burmeister, Augusta (act): *The Greene Murder Case*
Burmeister, Diane (act): *The Demon (1981)*
Burmester, Leo (act): *The Abyss*
Burn, Jonathan (act): *The Persecution And Assassination Of Jean-Paul Marat As Performed By The Inmates Of The Asylum Of Charenton Under The Direction Of The Marquis De Sade; Sudden Terror*
Burn, Oscar (dir): *Castle Sinister (1948)*
Burnaby, Anne (wri, b. 1922): *The Yellow Balloon*
Burnaby, Dave (act): *Murder At The Inn; The Shot In The Dark*
Burnam, Earl (act): *The Corpse Grinders*
Burne, Jonathan (act): *Blood From The Mummy's Tomb*
Burne, Nancy (act): *The Warren Case*
Burnell, Helen (act): *Elstree Calling*
Burner, Cesar (act): *Tombs Of The Blind Dead*
Burnet, Paddy (act): *Thirst*
Burnett, Al (act): *King Arthur Was A Gentleman*
Burnett, Don (act): *Triumph Of Robin Hood*
Burnett, J. Max (act): *Offerings*
Burnett, Mary-Nancy (act): *It's Alive (1974); Tarantulas: The Deadly Cargo*
Burnett, Nancy (act): *Alfred Hitchcock Presents*
Burnett, Ruth (act): *Edge Of Sanity*
Burnett, Ted (act): *A Hitch In Time*
Burnett, W.R. (wri): *Background To Danger; Dangerous Mission*
Burnette, Dorsey (mus): *Kingdom Of The Spiders*
Burnette, Justin (act): *The Flash*
Burnette, Smiley (act, 1911–1967): *Dick Tracy (1937); Radio Ranch; Sharad Of Atlantis*
Burney, Bruce (act): *Making Contact*
Burnham, Burnham (act): *Howling II*
Burnham, Edward (act): *The Abominable Dr. Phibes; In The Toils Of The Blackmailer; Murder On The Midnight Express; 10 Rillington Place*
Burnham, Jeremy (act): *The Brigand Of Kandahar*
Burnham, Jeremy (wri): *Horror Of Frankenstein; The Secret Of Seagull Island*
Burnier, Robert (act): *Landru*
Burnley, Fred (dir): *Neither The Sea Nor The Sand*
Burns, Bob (cin): *Splatter*
Burns, Brendan (act): *Ssssss*
Burns, David (act, 1902–1971): *I Killed The Count; It's Always Fair Weather; The Saint In London*
Burns, Diann (act): *Primal Fear*
Burns, Edmund (act): *The Chinese Parrot; The Death Kiss*
Burns, George (act, 1896-1996, nee Nathan Birnbaum): *18 Again!; International House; Oh, God!; Oh, God! Book II; Oh, God! You Devil*
Burns, Glen (act): *Into The Badlands*
Burns, Helen (act): *The Changeling; Zorro, The Gay Blade*
Burns, Jere (act): *Turn Back The Clock*
Burns, Leonard (act): *Impulse (1984)*
Burns, Lisa (act): *The Shining*
Burns, Marilyn (act): *Eaten Alive! (1976); Kiss Daddy Goodbye; Splatter; The Texas Chainsaw Massacre*
Burns, Mark (act): *The Curse Of The Golem; Death Is A Woman; House Of The Living Dead; The Maids*
Burns, Martha (act): *Never Talk To Strangers*
Burns, Michael (act): *Brock's Last Case; The Mad Room; The Wizard Of Baghdad*
Burns, Nancy (act): *Mermaids Of Tiburon*
Burns, Nora (act): *Jacob's Ladder*
Burns, Patricia (act): *Flesh Gordon*
Burns, Paul (E.) (act): *Crime Doctor's Manhunt; The Mummy's Tomb*
Burns, Ralph (mus): *All That Jazz; Phantom Of The Opera (1983)*
Burns, Richard (act): *Something Is Out There*
Burns, Robert (wri, 1759-1796): *Journey To The Center Of The Earth (1959); Tam Lin*
Burns, Robert A. (act): *Confessions Of A Serial Killer*
Burns, Ronald R. (act): *Nightfall (1988)*
Burns, Ronnie (act): *Anatomy Of A Psycho*
Burns, Stan (act): *Charlie Chan And The Curse Of The Dragon Queen*
Burns, Stephan W. (act): *Herbie Goes Bananas*
Burns, Terry (act): *Wavelength*
Burns, Tim (act): *Gargoyles; Mad Max; Targets*
Burns, William (1940s act): see Tyler, Tom
Burns, William (1970s act): *Mirrors*
Burns III, Yancy E. (act): *Blood Beach*
Burow, Kurtis (act): *Species*
Burr, David (cin): *Those Dear Departed*
Burr, Eugene (act): *The Clutching Hand; Jungle Trail Of The Son Of Tarzan*
Burr, Jeff (dir): *Leatherface: Texas Chainsaw Massacre II; The Offspring; Pumpkinhead II: Blood Wings; Stepfather II*
Burr, Jeff (wri): *The Offspring*
Burr, Lonnie (act): *The Silence Of The Hams*
Burr, Manuel Gomez (act): *Cuento De Hadas*
Burr, Randy (act): *Night Of The Living Dead (1968)*
Burr, Raymond (act, 1917–1993): *The Adventures Of Don Juan; The Alien's Return, The; The Amazing World Of Psychic Phenomena; The Bandits Of Corsica; Black Magic (1949); Bride Of The Gorilla; Bride Of Vengeance; A Cry In The Night (1956); The Curse Of King Tut's Tomb; Godzilla 1985; Gojira; Gorilla At Large; M (1950); The*

Magic Carpet (1951); Pitfall; Please Murder Me; Rear Window; Secret Of Treasure Mountain; Sleep, My Love; Tarzan And The She-Devil

Burr, Robert (act): Fer-De-Lance; The Possession Of Joel Delaney; A Return To Salem's Lot; Tattoo

Burr, Wally (act): Fist Of The North Star

Burrage, A.M. (wri): The Return (1973, GB)

Burrage, Avis (act): The Wrong Box

Burrell, Alan (act): Freejack

Burrell, Daisy (act): The Valley Of Fear (1916)

Burrell, Daniel (act): Neon Maniacs

Burrell, Fred (act): Dr. Cook's Garden

Burrell, George (act): The Sea Beast

Burrell, Jan (act): Mind Over Murder

Burrell, Maryedith (act): Eve Of Destruction; The Little Match Girl (1987)

Burrell, Maryedith (wri): The Little Match Girl (1987)

Burrell, Richard (act): Act Of Murder (1964); Murder At Site Three

Burrell, Sheila (act): Black Orchid; Cloudburst; The Man In Black; Paranoiac

Burress, William (act): After The Thin Man

Burridge, Geoffrey (act): An American Werewolf In London

Burris, Michael Harington (act): Killer Klowns From Outer Space

Burrise, Nakia (act): Turbo: A Power Rangers Movie

Burroughs, Edgar Rice (wri, 1875–1950): At The Earth's Core; Greystoke: The Legend Of Tarzan, Lord Of The Apes; Jungle Trail Of The Son Of Tarzan; The Land That Time Forgot; The People That Time Forgot; The Return Of Tarzan; Romance Of Tarzan; Tarzan And His Mate; Tarzan And The Amazons; Tarzan And The Golden Lion; Tarzan And The Great River; Tarzan And The Green Goddess; Tarzan And The Huntress; Tarzan And The Jungle Boy; Tarzan And The Leopard Woman; Tarzan And The Lost Safari; Tarzan And The Mermaids; Tarzan And The She-Devil; Tarzan And The Trappers; Tarzan And The Valley Of Gold; Tarzan Escapes; Tarzan Finds A Son!; Tarzan Goes To India; Tarzan In Manhattan; Tarzan Of The Apes; Tarzan's Deadly Silence; Tarzan's Desert Mystery; Tarzan's Fight For Life; Tarzan's Greatest Adventure; Tarzan's Hidden Jungle; Tarzan's Magic Fountain; Tarzan's New Adventure, Tarzan's New York Adventure; Tarzan's Peril; Tarzan's Revenge; Tarzan's Savage Fury; Tarzan's Secret Treasure; Tarzan, The Ape Man (1932, 1959 & 1981); Tarzan The Fearless; Tarzan Triumphs

Burroughs, Jackie (act): The Dead Zone; The Food Of The Gods II; Heavy Metal; The Housekeeper

Burroughs, William (act, b. 1914): Chappaqua

Burrow, Joe (act): The Cars That Ate Paris

Burrows, Blair (act): The Return Of The Living Dead (1985)

Burrows, Darren (E.) (act): Class Of '99; 976-Evil

Burrows, John (act): Kiss Of The Tarantula

Bursi, Danny (act): I Was A Zombie For The F.B.I.

Bursi, Raymond (act): I Was A Zombie For The F.B.I.

Burson, Greg (act): Jurassic Park

Burstyn, Ellen (act, b. 1932): A Deadly Vision; The Exorcist

Burstyn, Thom (cin): Dark Of The Night

Burt, Benny (act): The Steel Trap

Burt, Clarissa (act): The Neverending Story II: The Next Chapter

Burt, Corri (act): Raiders Of The Living Dead

Burt, Flo (act): The She-Creature

Burt, Frank (wri): The Bandits Of Corsica

Burt, June (act): War Of The Colossal Beast

Burt, Keith Erik (dir & wri): Night Of The Witches

Burt, Margaret (act): A Night Of Mystery (1928)

Burt, Thomas G. (act): Wes Craven's New Nightmare

Burt, William (P.) (act): The Leopard Lady; Midnight Mystery

Burtis, James (act): Satan Met A Lady

Burton, Bennah (act): End Of The World (1977)

Burton, Bill (act): The Entity

Burton, Chris(topher) (act): Ghoulies II; The Neverending Story II: The Next Chapter

Burton, Clarence (act): The Road To Yesterday; The Unholy Three (1930)

Burton, Colonel (act): Dr. No

Burton, David (dir): The Bishop Murder Case

Burton, Dena (act): Switch

Burton, Frederick (act): Bits Of Life; The Saint In New York

Burton, Geoff(rey) (cin): The Beast (1996); Something Is Out There; The Time Guardian; Wide Sargasso Sea

Burton, Geoffrey (act): Inn Of The Damned

Burton, J. Stephen (act): Deadly Messages

Burton, Jeff (act): Planet Of The Apes

Burton, Jhean (act): A Bucket Of Blood (1959)

Burton, Jim (act): Lost Prophet

Burton, John (act): Attack Of The Mayan Mummy; Boston Blackie's Little Pal; The Hound Of The Baskervilles (1939)

Burton, John Nelson (dir): Never Mention Murder

Burton, Julian (act): A Bucket Of Blood (1959); The Masque Of The Red Death (1964)

Burton, Kate (act): Big Trouble In Little China

Burton, Kim (act): I Was A Zombie For The F.B.I.

Burton, Langhorne (act): At The Villa Rose (1920); Blake The Lawbreaker; The Clue Of The Second Goblet; The Great Office Mystery; The King's Minister; A Man's Shadow; The Mystery Of The Silent Death; Sexton Blake, Gambler; Silken Threads

Burton, LeVar (act, b. 1957): The Midnight Hour; Star Trek: First Contact; Star Trek: Generations

Burton, Michael (wri): Flight Of The Navigator

Burton, Norman(n) (act): Deep Space; Diamonds Are Forever; Escape From The Planet Of The Apes; Fade To Black; Fright (1957); Hand Of Death; Life, Libery And Pursuit On The Planet Of The Apes; Mausoleum; The Reincarnation Of Peter Proud; Simon, King Of The Witches; The Terminal Man; The Towering Inferno; The Ultimate Impostor

Burton, Peter (act): Berserk; A Clockwork Orange; Dr. No; Soho Incident

Burton, Richard (act, 1925–1984, nee Richard Jenkins): Bluebeard (1972); Dr. Faustus; Exorcist II: The Heretic; Hammersmith Is Out; Lovespell; The Medusa Touch; A Midsummer Night's Dream (1959); My Cousin Rachel; 1984 (1984); The Spy Who Came In From The Cold; The Woman With No Name

Burton, Richard (dir, 1925–1984): Dr. Faustus

Burton, Robert (act): Curse Of The Black Widow; I Was A Teenage Frankenstein; Rymdinvasion I Lappland; The Slime People; The 30 Foot Bride Of Candy Rock

Burton, Skip (act): Trilogy Of Terror

Burton, Steve (act): Cyber-Tracker

Burton, Tim (dir, b. 1958): Batman (1989); Batman Returns; Beetlejuice; Edward Scissorhands; Ed Wood; Mars Attacks!

Burton, Tim (wri, b. 1958): Edward Scissorhands

Burton, Tom (act): The Falcon Out West

Burton, Tony (act): Cybertracker 2; The Shining

Burton, Val (wri): Bedtime For Bonzo; The Time Of Their Lives

Burtt, Jeff (act): End Of The World (1977)

Burtwell, Frederick (act): The Dark Tower; Dr. Syn; Inside The Room; The Laughing Lady; Uncle Silas; The Vulture (1937)

Burum, Stephen (H.) (cin): Body Double; The Bride (1985); Death Valley; The Entity; Mission: Impossible; Raising Cain; Something Wicked This Way Comes

Burwell, Carter (mus): Blood Simple; Buffy, The Vampire Slayer; Fargo; Fear (1996); Joe's Apartment; Psycho II

Bury, Sean (act): The Abominable Dr. Phibes

Burzynski, Lezlek (dir): Cry Wolf (1980)

Busby, Jane (act): Return Of The Jedi

Buscemi, Steve (act): Ed And His Dead Mother; Escape From L.A.; Fargo; Tales From The Darkside

Busch, Charles (act): Addams Family Values

Busch, Mae (act, 1897–1946): The Clutching Hand; Doctor X; The Mad Monster; Marie Antoinette (1938); Nancy Drew, Detective; The Unholy Three (1925)

Busch, Robert (act): The Lost Missile

Buschoff, Walter (act): Babes In Toyland (1986)

Busey, Gary (act, b. 1944): Hex; Lost Highway; Predator 2; Silver Bullet

Busey, Jake (act, b. 1971): The Frighteners; Twister

Bus-Fekete, Lazlo (wri): Heaven Can Wait (1942)

Bush, Beatrice (act): The Henderson Monster

Bush, Billy Green (act): Critters; The Hitcher; Jason Goes To Hell: The Final Friday

Bush, Dick (cin): The Blood On Satan's Claw; Dracula A.D. 1972; The Fan; The Hound Of The Baskervilles (1978); The Lair Of The White Worm; The Legacy; Little Monsters; Phase IV; The Philadelphia Experiment; Switch; Tommy; Twins Of Evil; When Dinosaurs Ruled The Earth

Bush, Grand L. (act): Demolition Man; The Exorcist II; The First Power; Freejack

Bush, James (H.) (act): The Beginning Or The End?; Beyond Tomorrow; Call Of The Jungle; A Night Of Mystery (1937)

Bush, John (act): The Village Of The Damned (1960)

Bush, Maurice (act): The Creeping Flesh

Bush, Morris (act): Scars Of Dracula

Bush, Nancy (act): The Edge Of Hell

Bush, Nat (act): Top Secret (1978)

Bush, Norman (act): Blood Bath (1975)

Bush, Owen (act): Alfred Hitchcock Presents; The Eyes Of Charles Sand; Poor Devil; Vanishing Point

Bush, Ron (act): Deadtime Stories

Bush, Tommy (act): Ed Wood; Mars Attacks!

Bushell, Anthony (act, b. 1904): The Black Knight; Crime On The Hill; Dark Journey; The Ghoul (1933); High Treason (1951); I Was A Spy; The Return Of The Scarlet Pimpernel; The Scarlet Pimpernel (1934); The Silver Greyhound (1932)

Bushell, Anthony (dir, b. 1904): The Terror Of The Tongs

Bushelman, John (dir): Day Of The Nightmare

Bushelman, John (wri): Daughters Of Satan

Bushman, Francis X. (act, 1883–1966): Dick Tracy (1937); The Ghost In The Invisible Bikini; The Phantom Planet; The Story Of Mankind; 12 To The Moon

Busia, Akosua (act): The Final Terror; The Seventh Sign

Busick, Armando (wri): The Wizard Of Mars

Busquets, Narciso (act): Demonoid

Buss, Harry (act): Ghosts (1912); Highwayman Hal; Mr. Poorluck's Dream; The Of-Course-I-Can Brothers

Buss, Harry (dir): Cinderella (1913)

Bussani, John (act): Empire Of Ash II

Busse, Jochen (act): Hauser's Memory

Bussey, Nicholas D. (act): Not Of This World

Bussieres, Raymond (act, b. 1907): Paris When It Sizzles; The Wonders Of Aladdin

Bustos, Richard (act): Vampire On Bikini Beach

Buswell, Richard A. (act): Offerings

Butcher, Ernest (act): Candles At Nine; Dear Murderer; Pimpernel Smith; While I Live

Butcher, Kim (act): Frightmare (1974); House Of Mortal Sin

Butcher, Oliver (wri): Dr. Jekyll And Ms. Hyde

Buthelezi, June (act): King Solomon's Mines (1985)

Butkus, Dick (act): The Eliminator; Gremlins 2: The New Batch; The Legend Of Sleepy Hollow; The Stepford Children

Butler, Aaron (act): Graduation Day

Butler, Alex (act): Waxwork II: Lost In Time

Butler, Alexander (act): She (1925)

Butler, Alexander (dir): The Beetle; The Disappearance Of The Judge; In The Toils Of The Blackmailer; London By Night (1913); The Passions Of Men; The Sorrows Of Satan (1917); The Tube Of Death; The Valley Of Fear (1916)

Butler, Artie (mus): Angel On My Shoulder (1980); Wonder Woman

Butler, Bill (cin): Anaconda; Bates Motel; Capricorn One; Child's Play (1988); Damien-Omen II; Demon Seed; Fearless Frank; Jaws; Something Evil

Butler, Blake (act): —And Now The Screaming Starts!; Journey To The Unknown

Butler, Calvin (act): Curtains

Butler, Cindy (act): Boggy Creek II-The Legend Continues

Butler, Dan (act): The Silence Of The Lambs

Butler, Dave (act): House Of Whipcord

Butler, David (1920s act): The Temple Of Venus

Butler, David (act): The Corpse; The Dark Half

Butler, David (cin): Simon, King Of The Witches

Butler, David (dir, 1894–1979): Ali Baba Goes To Town; A Connecticut Yankee; Just Imagine; You'll Find Out

Butler, David (wri, 1894–1979): Just Imagine; You'll Find Out

Butler, David (1980s wri): Bear Island

Butler, Duke (act): Buck Rogers In The 25th Century

Butler, Eugene (act): A Force Of One

Butler, Fonti (act): Demon Knight

Butler, Frank (wri, 1890–1967): Babes In Toyland (1934); Beyond The Blue Horizon; Golden Earrings; The Miracle (1959); The Road To Bali

Butler, Gerald (wri): The Fatal Night

Butler, Hugo (wri, 1914-1968): Your Witness

Butler, James (act): The Man From Downing Street

Butler, John (act): Torchy Runs For Mayor

Butler, John K. (wri): The Vampire's Ghost

Butler, Kathleen (wri): The Feathered Serpent (1934); Miracles Do Happen

Butler, Keith (act): Outbreak

Butler, Kent (act): Wavelength

Butler,Lawrence (cin): The Horn Blows At Midnight; The Jungle Book (1942); The Thief Of Bagdad (1940); Things To Come

Butler, Lori Lee (act): The Final Terror

Butler, Lucy (act): Matinee

Butler, Michael (cin): Dance Of The Dwarfs; Jaws 2; Megaforce

Butler, Michael (wri): The Car

Butler, Paul (act): Romeo Is Bleeding

Butler, Prudie (act): Spawn Of The Slithis

Butler, Richard (act): The Hidden Face

Butler, Robert (dir): The Barefoot Executive; The Computer Wore Tennis Shoes; Death Takes A Holiday (1971); Now You See Him, Now You Don't; Strange New World

Butler, Sid (act): Through The Ages

Butler, Ted (act): The Wiz

Butler, Tom (act): Ghost Of A Chance (1987); Hitler's Daughter

Butler, Vera (act): Dr. Caligari

Butler, Warde Q. (act): Scalpel

Butler, Werner (act): Confess, Dr. Corda

Butler, William (act): Ghoulies II; Leatherface: Texas Chainsaw Massacre II; Night Of The Living Dead (1990)

Butler, Wilmer C. (cin): The Deathmaster

Butler, Yancy (act): The Ex

Butler-Glouner, Inc. (cin): X-The Man With The X-Ray Eyes

Butlin, Jan (act): In The Devil's Garden

Butner, Cheryl (act): Phoenix The Warrior

Butrick, Merritt (act): Fright Night II; From The Dead Of Night; Star Trek II: The Wrath Of Khan; Star Trek II: The Search For Spock; Zapped!

Butt, Dale (mus): The Catman Of Paris

Butt, Jennifer (act): Vampire's Kiss

Butt, Johnny (act): The American Heiress; Blackmail (1929); The Bridge Destroyer; The Chimes; The Clue Of The New Pin (1929); The Fatal Appetizer; The Grand Babylon Hotel; Hot Pickles; The Man Behind "The Times;" The Monkey's Paw (1923); On The Brink Of The Precipice; The Prehistoric Man (1924); A Touch Of Hydrophobia; When Clubs Were Clubs

Butt, (W.) Lawson (act): Dante's Inferno (1924); The Flying Dutchman; The Miracle Man (1919); The Ringer (1928)

Butterfield, Catherine (act): Ed Wood

Butterfield, Keith (act): The Lost Boys

Butterfield, Marlene (act): The Ivory Ape

Butterfield, Max (act): The Camp On Blood Island

Butterworth, Charles (act, 1897–1946): The Boys From Syracuse; Bulldog Drummond Strikes Back (1934); Love Me Tonight; The Mad Genius; The Sultan's Daughter

Butterworth, Peter (act, b. 1923): Carry On Screaming; Kill Or Cure; Mr. Drake's Duck; Murder At The Windmill; Murder She Said; Never Mention Murder; Robin And Marian; Saturday Island; The Spider's Web; Tom Thumb

Buttery, Richard (act): For All Eternity; I Hear You Calling

Buttner, Cathy (act): Phantom Of The Paradise

Buttolph, David (mus): The Beast From 20,000 Fathoms; The Brasher Doubloon; House Of Wax; The Lone Ranger; Long John Silver; Phantom Of The Rue Morgue; Secret Of The Incas; Talk About A Stranger

Buttons, Red (act, b. 1919, nee Aaron Chwatt): Alice In Wonderland (1985); The Ambulance; Chomps; 18 Again!; Five Weeks In A Balloon; The New, Original Wonder Woman; Pete's Dragon; The Poseidon Adventure; When Time Ran Out

Buttram, Pat (act, 1915–1994): The Hanged Man

Butts, Jeff (act): To All A Goodnight

Bux, Ishaq (act): The Quatermass Conclusion; Raiders Of The Lost Ark; The Vault Of Horror

Buxer, Jon (act): Boarding House

Buxton, Judy (act): I Don't Want To Be Born

Buxton, Sheila (act): The Shakedown

Buzzanca, Lando (act): When Women Had Tails

Buzzell, Edward (dir, 1897–1985): Song Of The Thin Man; Three Wise Fools

Buzzi, Ruth (act, b. 1936): The Being

Byars, Floyd (wri): Making Mr. Right

Byars, Taylor (cin): Teenage Monster

Byass, Nigel (wri): Dr. Sin Fang

Byer, Denise (act): Gulliver's Travels (1977); Return To Oz

Byers, Bill (mus, 1926-1996): Hauser's Memory

Byers, Bo (act): The House Of The Dead
Byers, Frank (cin): Flowers In The Attic
Byers, Patrick (act): Screams Of A Winter Night
Byers, Ralph (act): The Cradle Will Fall; Star Trek
Byfield, Trevor (act): Goldeneye
Byford, Joan Roy (wri): The Phantom Light
Byford, Roy (act): Museum Mystery
Bygraves, Anthony (act): Maroc 7
Bygraves, Max (act, b. 1922): Bobbikins
Byington, Spring (act, 1893–1971): Angels In The Outfield (1951); The Blue Bird (1940); Dragonwyck; Ellery Queen And The Perfect Crime; The Enchanted Cottage (1945); The Great Impersonation (1935); Heaven Can Wait (1942); Rocket Man; Werewolf Of London
Bykov, Roland (act): The Overcoat
Byner, John (act): The Man In The Santa Claus Suit; Transylvania 6-5000
Bynum, Nate (act): Candyman: Farewell To The Flesh
Byrd, Bretton (mus): The Saint's Vacation
Byrd, David (act): School Spirit
Byrd, Jack (wri): The Man Behind The Mask (1936)
Byrd, John (wri): Three Silent Men
Byrd, Julian (act): Barracuda; Traces Of Red
Byrd, Ralph (act, 1909–1952): Dark Streets Of Cairo; Dick Tracy (1937); Dick Tracy Meets Gruesome; Dick Tracy Returns; Dick Tracy's Dilemma; Dick Tracy's G-Men; Dick Tracy Vs. Crime, Inc.; The Jungle Book (1942); Jungle Goddess; Radar Secret Service; The Son Of Monte Cristo; S.O.S. Coast Guard; Time To Kill (1942)
Byrd, Sandy (act): Candyman: Farewell To The Flesh
Byrde, Edye (act): Addams Family Values
Byrd-Nethery, Miriam (act): Leatherface: Texas Chainsaw Massacre III; The Offspring
Byrge, Bill (act): Ernest Saves Christmas
Byrne, Adrienne (act): Memoirs Of A Survivor
Byrne, Barbara (act): Excalibur
Byrne, Duane (act): The Lawnmower Man
Byrne, Eddie (act, b. 1911): Devils Of Darkness; Face In The Night; Floods Of Fear; Island Of Terror; Jack The Ripper (1958); A Kid For Two Farthings; Locker 69; The Mummy (1959); The Shakedown; Star Wars; Three Cases Of Murder; The Vengeance Of Fu Manchu
Byrne, Gabriel (act): Cool World; Excalibur; Gothic; Hello Again; The Keep
Byrne, Jenna (act): Outbreak
Byrne, John (wri): Nefertite, Regina Del Nilo; Rage Of The Buccaneers
Byrne, Michael (act): Indiana Jones And The Last Crusade; The Medusa Touch; Vampyres...Daughters Of Dracula
Byrne, Michael P. (act): Blink
Byrne, Muriel St. Claire (wri): Busman's Honeymoon
Byrne, Patsy (act): The Ruling Class
Byrne, Paula (act): The Key Man
Byrne, Robert (act): Rawhead Rex
Byrne, Stuart James (wri): Doomsday Machine
Byrnes, Burke (act): Meteor; Prophecy (1979); The Strange Possession Of Mrs. Oliver; The Terminal Man; Witchboard
Byrnes, Edd (act, b. 1933): Party Line; Wicked, Wicked
Byrnes, Jim (act): Omen IV: The Awakening
Byrnes, Pam (act): Party Line
Byrnes, Tom (act): Party Line
Byron, Arthur (act): The Casino Murder Case; Gabriel Over The White House; The Mummy (1932)
Byron, Carol (act): Dimension 5
Byron, Jean (act): Invisible Invaders; Jungle Moon Men; Themagnetic Monster; Voodoo Tiger
Byron, Jeffrey (act): The Dungeonmaster; The London Connection; Metalstorm: The Destruction Of Jared-Syn
Byron, Jeffrey (wri): The Dungeonmaster
Byron, Kathleen (act, b. 1922): Black Narcissus; Craze; The House In The Square; A Matter Of Life And Death; Night Of The Eagle; The Night Of The Full Moon; Nothing But The Night; One Of Our Dinosaurs Is Missing; Scarlet Thread; Secret Venture; Twins Of Evil
Byron, Kathryn (act): The Mummy (1932)
Byron, Michael (wri): La Sorella Di Satan
Byron, Walter (act): British Agent; Charlie Chan's Greatest Case; The Menace (1932)
Byron-Webber, R. (wri): The Barton Mystery (1920); First Men In The Moon (1919); The Rocks Of Valpre
Byrum, John (wri): Sphinx (1981)
Bythewood, Reggie Rock (act): The Brother From Another Planet; Vampire's Kiss
Bywaters, Yvonne (act): Angel Heart
C. Andy (act): Blackenstein
Caan, James (act, b. 1938): Alien Nation; Countdown; Dick Tracy (1990); Eraser; Games; Lady In A Cage; Misery; Rollerball
Caan, Richard (dir): The Phoenix (1980)
Cabal, Alan (act): Doctor Franken
Caballero, Joseph Luis (act): Primal Fear
Caballero, Magdalena (act): Doctor Of Doom
Caban, Angel (act): The Refrigerator
Cabanne, Christy (dir, 1888–1950): The Mummy's Hand; One Frightened Night; The Westland Case
Cable, Bill (act): Elvira, Mistress Of The Dark
Cabot, Bruce (act, 1904–1972, nee Jacques de Bujac): Diamonds Are Forever; King Kong (1933); Murder On The Blackboard; Mystery Of The White Room; Red Cloak, The; Il Terror Dei Barberi
Cabot, Ceil (act): It Happened One Christmas
Cabot, Sebastian (act, 1918–1977): Babes In Bagdad; Dick Barton At Bay; Dick Barton Strikes Back; Dual Alibi; Journey To Midnight; Miracle On 34th Street (1973); Old Mother Riley's Jungle Treasure; Omar Khayyam; Pimpernel Smith; The Secret Agent (1936); Son Of Ali Baba; The Spider And The Fly; They Made Me A Fugitive; The Time Machine (1960); Twice-Told Tales
Cabot, Susan (act, 1927–1986): On The Isle Of Samoa; The Viking Women And The Sea Serpent; War Of The Satellites; The Wasp Woman
Cabre, Mario (act): Pandora And The Flying Dutchman
Cabrera, John (cin): Hundra; Night Of The Zombies (1983)
Cacavas, John (mus): Cry For The Strangers; Hangar 18; Horror Express; Human Feelings; Mortuary; No Place To Hide (1981); The Satanic Rites Of Dracula; The Time Machine (1978)
Cacoyannis, Michael (dir & wri, b. 1922): The Day The Fish Came Out; Electra (1961); Iphigenia; The Trojan Women
Cadd, Brian (mus): Vampire On Bikini Beach
Caddick, Edward (act): The Vulture (1966)
Cadell, Ava (act): The Hound Of The Baskervilles (1978); Outer Touch
Cadell, Jean (act, b. 1884): Alf's Button (1920); The Late Edwina Black; Love From A Stranger (1937); The Man Who Stayed At Home; Meet Mr. Lucifer
Cadell, Patrick (act): Eclipse (1977)
Caden, Pierre (act): Les Parapluies De Cherbourg
Cadia, Octavian (act): Bram Stoker's 'Dracula'
Cadiente, David/Dave (act): Buck Rogers In The 25th Century; Star Trek III: The Search For Spock
Cadkin, Emil (mus): The Killer Shrews; Three On A Ticket
Cadman, Joshua (act): Superstition
Cadman, Michael (act): The Twisted Nerve
Cadman, Milton (act): Lifeforce
Cadogan, Alice (act): Night Of The Creeps
Cadora, Eric (act): Candyman: Farewell To The Flesh
Cady, Daniel B. (wri): Kiss Of The Tarantula
Cady, Frank (act): The Atomic City; The Bad Seed (1956); The Great Rupert; Rear Window; The Sky Dragon; When Worlds Collide
Cady, Jerry (wri): Charlie Chan At Monte Carlo; Charlie Chan On Broadway; Mr. Moto's Gamble; The Saint In Palm Springs
Cadzow, Juliette (act): The Wicker Man
Caer-Myrddin, Morgan (act): I Was A Zombie For The F.B.I.
Caesar, Harry (act): The Offspring; Retribution (1988)
Caesar, Sid (act, b. 1922): Alice In Wonderland (1985); The Busy Body; Curse Of The Black Widow; The Fiendish Plot Of Dr. Fu Manchu; The Munsters' Revenge; The Spirit Is Willing
Cafarell, Jose/Joe (Maria) (act): The Bang-Bang Kid; Hipnosis; Mi Adorable Esclava; Where Time Began
Caffarell, Jean (act): The Face Of Eve
Caffari, John (act): Witches' Mountain
Caffey, Michael (dir): The Devil And Miss Sarah
Caffi, Juan Jose Garcia (mus): Where Time Began
Caffrey, James (act): Island Of Terror
Caffrey, Sean (act): The Viking Queen; When Dinosaurs Ruled The Earth
Caffrey, Stephen (act): Buried Alive II
Cagan, Steve (mus): The Cat And The Canary (1978)
Cage, John (mus, 1912–1992): Dreams That Money Can Buy
Cage, Nicholas (act, b. 1963): Vampire's Kiss
Caggiano, Tim (act): Serial Mom
Cagne, Gil (act): Dracula (1974)
Cagney, James (act, 1899–1986): Man Of A Thousand Faces; A Midsummer Night's Dream (1935)
Cagney, Jeanne (act, 1919–1984): Don't Bother To Knock; Man Of A Thousand Faces
Cagney, William (act, 1905–1988): Lost In The Stratosphere
Cahall, Robin (act): King Kong Lives
Cahill, Barry (act): Daddy's Gone A-Hunting; The Groundstar Conspiracy
Cahill, David (act): Howling III
Cahill, James (act): Santa Claus Conquers The Martians
Cahill, Lynette (wri): Shadow Of The Hawk
Cahill, Samantha (act): Paperhouse
Cahill, Stan (act): Color Me Perfect
Cahn, Edward L. (dir, 1899–1963): Beauty And The Beast (1962); Creature With The Atom Brain; Curse Of The Faceless Man; The Four Skulls Of Jonathan Drake; Girls In Prison; Invasion Of The Saucer Men; Invisible Invaders; It!—The Terror From Beyond Space; The She-Creature; Voodoo Woman; Zombies Of Mora Tau
Cahn, Leo (cin): The Lift
Cahn, Sammy (mus, 1913–1993): Lady Of Burlesque
Caiano, Mario (dir): Amanti D'oltretomba; Terror Of Rome Against The Son Of Hercules; Ulysses Against The Son Of Hercules
Caiano, Mario (wri): The Nights Of Lucretia Borgia; Ulysses Against The Son Of Hercules
Caidin, Martin (wri, 1927-1997): Bionic Showdown: The Six Million Dollar Man And The Bionic Woman; Exo-Man; Marooned; The Return Of The Six Million Dollar Man And The Bionic Woman; The Six Million Dollar Man
Caillou, Alan (act): Beyond Evil; Five Weeks In A Balloon; The Hound Of The Baskervilles (1972); The Ice Pirates; The Questor Tapes; The Sword And The Sorcerer
Caillou, Alan (wri): Kingdom Of The Spiders; Rampage; Village Of The Giants
Caillou, Nadia (act): Kingdom Of The Spiders
Cain, Christopher (act): The Force On Thunder Mountain
Cain, Christopher (dir): Wheels Of Terror
Cain, Guillermo (wri): Vanishing Point
Cain, James M. (wri): Gypsy Wildcat
Cain, Lisa (act): Deadtime Stories
Cain, Tony (act): The Lost Boys
Caine, Georgia (act): The Lone Wolf Meets A Lady; Tower Of London (1939)
Caine, Harry (act): Richard III (1911)
Caine, Henry (act): The Ghost Train (1931); Number 17; The Stickpin
Caine, Jeffrey (wri): The Cold Room; Goldeneye
Caine, Michael (act, b. 1933, nee Maurice Mickelwhite): Beyond The Poseidon Adventure; Billion Dollar Brain; The Black Windmill; Bullet To Beijing; Dressed To Kill (1980); Funeral In Berlin; The Hand (1981); How To Murder A Rich Uncle; The Ipcress File; The Island; Jaws: The Revenge; Jekyll And Hyde; The Magus; The Man Who Would Be King; Mr. Destiny; Sleuth; The Swarm; 20,000 Leagues Under The Sea (1997, ABC-TV); Without A Clue; The Wrong Box
Caine, Sari (act): Mr. Destiny
Caine, Shakira (act, b. 1947): The Man Who Would Be King
Caine, Stanley (act): Billion Dollar Brain
Caine, Sylvia (act): Faust (1922)
Caird, Laurence (dir): The Fairy Doll
Caire, Audrey (act): Madman Of Mandoras
Cairney, John (act): The Devil-Ship Pirates; The Flesh And The Fiends; Jason And The Argonauts; Spaceflight IC-1; A Study In Terror
Cairns, Adrian (act): Diagnosis: Murder; Jamaica Inn (1985)
Cairns, Dallas (act): The Princess Of Happy Chance; The Silver Bridge; The Silver Greyhound (1919)
Cairns, Dallas (dir): The Silver Bridge
Cairns, Jessica (act): Grip Of The Strangler
Cairns, Sally (act): The Chance Of A Lifetime
Cairns, Sidney (act): The Witch Of The Welsh Mountains
Caithness, Wilfred (act): Death In The Hand; The Perfect Crime; The Triumph Of Sherlock Holmes; A Voice Said Goodnight
Caits, Joe (act): After The Thin Man
Cake, Jonathan (act): First Knight
Calabrese, Gina (act): The Dungeonmaster
Calabrese, James (mus): Spookies
Calamai, Clara (act): Profundo Rosso
Calandra, Giuliana (act): Profundo Rosso
Caldecott, Todd (act): Mother, May I Sleep With Danger?
Calder, David (act): Superman (1978)
Calder, King (act): On The Threshold Of Space
Calderisi, David (act): Millennium
Calder-Marshall, Anna (act): Wuthering Heights (1970)
Calderon, Juan Carlos (mus): House Of Doom (1973); Vengeance Of The Zombies
Calderon, Licia (act): Mi Adorable Esclava
Calderon, Norma (act): The Naked Jungle
Calderon, Paul (act): Dark Angel
Calderone, Giorgio (act): The Toxic Avenger
Calderone, Joey (act): The Toxic Avenger
Calderoni, Cristal (act): Waxwork II: Lost In Time
Caldicott, Richard (act): Clue Of The Twisted Candle
Caldinez, Sonny (act): Raiders Of The Lost Ark
Caldwell, Courtney (act): Phoenix The Warrior
Caldwell, Dale (act): Spawn Of The Slithis
Caldwell, Forbes (act): Carnival Of Souls
Caldwell, George (act): Rat Pfink & Boo Boo; Retribution (1988)
Caldwell, Jane (act): Mandroid
Caldwell, Janette (act): Heart And Souls
Caldwell, Orville (act): The Last Warning (1938)
Caldwell, Stephan (act): Primal Scream
Cale, John (mus): Caged Heat!
Calegory, Jade (act): Mac And Me
Calei, Noel (wri): Frantic
Calfa, Don (act): Chopper Chicks In Zombietown; The Return Of The Living Dead (1985); Rhinoceros (1974); Shanks
Calfan, Nicole (act): The Three Musketeers (1974)
Calhern, Louis (act, 1896–1956, nee Carl Vogt): The Bridge Of San Luis Rey (1944); The Count Of Monte Cristo (1934); Heaven Can Wait (1942); The Last Days Of Pompeii (1935); The Man With A Cloak; Notorious (1946); The Prisoner Of Zenda (1952)
Calhoun, Rory (act, b. 1923, nee Timothy Durgin): Adventure Island; The Colossus Of Rhodes; The Emerald Of Artatama; Hell Comes To Frogtown; Motel Hell; Night Of The Lepus; The Red House; River Of No Return; Roller Blade Warriors: Taken By Force; The Treasure Of Monte Cristo (1961)
Cali, Joseph (act): Something Is Out There
Calia, Hank (act): My Science Project
Caliban (act): The Mcguffin
Caliendo, Jeff (act): The Psychotronic Man
Calinieff, Martin (act): see Callan, Michael
Calker, Darrell (mus): Adventure Island; From Hell It Came; Voodoo Woman
Calkin, Elizabeth (act): Ora Pro Nobis
Calkins, John (act): The Boy With Green Hair
Call, Brandon (act): The Gifted One; Warlock
Call, Ed (act): Dark Night Of The Scarecrow
Call, John (act): Santa Claus Conquers The Martians
Call, Kenny (act): Near Dark
Call, R.D. (act): Timestalkers
Callaghan, Duke (cin): Conan The Barbarian
Callahan, David (act): Blink
Callahan, E.J. (act): Congo
Callahan, Edna (act): Just Imagine
Callahan, George (wri, b. 1902): Black Magic (1944); Charlie Chan In The Secret Service; The Chinese Cat; Dark Alibi; The Jade Mask; The Red Dragon (1945); The Scarlet Clue; The Shanghai Cobra
Callahan, James (act): She Waits; Stowaway To The Moon
Callahan, Marlene (act): The Magic Sword (1962)
Callahan, Patricia (act): Trick Or Treats
Callan, Cecile (act): Uninvited (1987)
Callan, K (act): This House Possessed
Callan, Kathleen (act): Raising Cain
Callan, Michael (act, b. 1935, nee Martin Calinieff): The Cat And The Canary (1978); Leprechaun 3; Mysterious Island (1961)
Callard, Kay (act): Cat Girl; Find The Lady; The Hypnotist (1957); Links Of Justice; Man In The Shadow; The Stranger Came Home; Undercover Girl (1958); Zex
Callas, Charlie (act): Amazon Women On The Moon; Pete's Dragon
Callaway, Cheryl (act): The Night Of The Hunter (1955)
Callaway, Paul (act): Rana: The Legend Of Shadow Lake
Callaway, Sage (act): Phenomenon
Callaway, Thomas/Tom (act): Creepozoids; The Gifted One; Slavegirls From Beyond Infinity
Callaway, Thomas L. (cin): Ghostriders

Callegari, Jean Paul (wri): *Black Devils Of Kali; The Minotaur*
Calleia, Joseph (act, 1887–1975, nee Joseph Spurin-Calleja): *After The Thin Man; The Beginning Or The End?; Gilda; The Gorilla (1939); The Jungle Book (1942); Lured; Marie Antoinette (1938); The Monster And The Girl; The Silk Noose*
Callejo, Cecilia (act): *The Falcon In Mexico*
Callen, Mark (act): *Tuck Everlasting*
Calles, Guillermo (act): *Run For The Sun*
Calliet, Lucien (mus): *Jamaica Run*
Callinan, Dick (act): *The Night Of The Claw*
Callow, Simon (act): *James And The Giant Peach*
Calloway, (Cabell) "Cab" (act, 1907–1994): *Cabin In The Sky; International House; The Littlest Angel (1969)*
Callum, R.H. (dir): *The Fish And The Ring; Santa Claus (1912); The Tempter (1913)*
Calnan, Matilda/Matilde (act): *Daddy's Gone A-Hunting; Roma Contra Roma; Terror In The Wax Museum*
Calo, Carla (act): *The Flower In His Mouth; Last Of The Vikings*
Caloz, Michael (act): *Screamers (1996); Whiskers*
Calpakis, Greg (act): *Alien High*
Caltaviano, Alfio (act): *The Colossus Of Rhodes*
Calthrop, Donald (act, 1888–1940): *Altar Chains; The Bells (1931); Blackmail (1929); The Clairvoyant (1934); The Clue Of The New Pin (1929); Elstree Calling; F.P. 1 Antwortet Nicht; The Ghost Train (1931); I Was A Spy; Love From A Stranger (1937); The Man Behind The Mask (1936); The Man Who Changed His Mind; Murder; Number 17; The Phantom Light; Scrooge (1935); Shadow Of Death (1939)*
Calvert, Bill (act): *C.H.U.D. II; Heart And Souls*
Calvert, C.C. (dir): *Silent Evidence*
Calvert, Charles (dir): *The Cellar Of Death; The Foreign Spy (1913); The Great Tiger Ruby; Guarding Britain's Secrets; In The Dead Man's Room; A London Mystery; The Missing Tiara; Mother Gets The Wrong Tonic; Paul Sleuth And The Mystic Seven; Secret Service; A Smoky Story, Snatched From Death; Temptation (1914); William Drake, Thief; The Wraith Of The Tomb; The Wrecker Of Lives*
Calvert, E.H. (act): *The Benson Murder Case; The Canary Murder Case; Darkened Rooms; The Greene Murder Case*
Calvert, Henry (act): *Phantom Of The Paradise*
Calvert, Jim (act): *House*
Calvert, John (act, a.k.a. John Trevlac): *Appointment With Murder; Dark Venture; The Devil's Cargo; Search For Danger*
Calvert, John (dir & wri): *Dark Venture*
Calvert, Leonard (act): *Scrooge (1913)*
Calvert, Phyllis (act, b. 1917): *Appointment With Danger; Fanny By Gaslight; A Lady Mislaid; The Man In Grey; Mr. Denning Drives North; The Net; The Twisted Nerve; The Woman With No Name*
Calvert, Steve (act): *The Bride And The Beast*
Calvet, Corinne (act, b. 1925, nee Corinne Dibos): *Bluebeard's Ten Honeymoons; Dr. Heckyl & Mr. Hype; Peking Express; The Phantom Of Hollywood; She's Dressed To Kill; The Sword And The Sorcerer*
Calvin, Henry (act): *Babes In Toyland (1961); The Sign Of Zorro*
Calvin, John (act): *The Dark Secret Of Harvest Home; Ghost Warrior; The Magic Bubble*
Calvin, Tony (act): *Dr. Jekyll And Sister Hyde; Theater Of Blood*
Calvitto, D.J. (act): *The Toxic Avenger*
Calvo, Armando (act): *Duel At The Rio Grande; El Espejo De La Bruja; Satanik*
Calvo, Eduardo (act): *House Of Doom (1973); The Mummy's Revenge*
Calvo, Jose (act): *Babes In Bagdad; Murders In The Rue Morgue (1971); Tristana*
Calvo, Maria (act): *El Cuerpo Del Lito*
Calvo, Pablito (act): *The Man Who Wagged His Tail*
Cam, William (act): *Spookies*
Camach, Art (dir): *The Power Within*
Camacho, Corinne (act): *The Mask Of Sheba; Planet Earth*
Camacho, Mark (act): *Dr. Jekyll And Ms. Hyde*
Camale, Alessandra (act): *Miami Golem*
Camara, Carlos (act): *Survive!*
Camardiel, Roberto (act): *The Colossus Of Rhodes; Perseus The Invincible*
Cambell, Samuel (act): *Blood Diner*
Cambert, Louise (act): *Fragment Of Fear*
Cambi, Flora (act): *Miracle In Milan*
Cambridge, Godfrey (act, 1933–1976): *Beware! The Blob; The Busy Body; The President's Analyst*
Camden, Joan (act): *Tower Of London (1962)*
Camel, Toni (act): *The Incredibly Strange Creatures Who Stopped Living And Became Mixed-Up Zombies*
Camelinat, Jacques (act): *Les Parapluies De Cherbourg*
Camen, Paul (act): *On A Clear Day You Can See Forever*
Camerini, Mario (dir, 1895-1981): *Kali-Yug, La Dea Della Vendetta; Ulysses*
Cameron (act): *Night Tide*
Cameron, Audrey (act): *The Crimson Candle*
Cameron, Candace (act): *I Saw What You Did (1988); Visitors Of The Night*
Cameron, Colin (act): *Phantom Of The Paradise*
Cameron, Colonel (act): *The Tell-Tale Heart (1934)*
Cameron, Dean (act): *Bad Dreams; Miracle Beach; Rockula*
Cameron, Douglas (act): *Alien Nation*
Cameron, Earl (act, b. 1925): *Battle Beneath The Earth; Pool Of London; Sapphire; Tarzan The Magnificent; Thunderball*
Cameron, Elaine Ives (act): *The Night Digger*
Cameron, Ian (wri, b. 1937): *The Island At The Top Of The World*
Cameron, Isla (act): *The Innocents; Nightmare (1963)*
Cameron, James (dir, writ): *The Abyss; Aliens; Piranha II: The Spawning; The Terminator; Terminator 2: Judgment Day Strange Days;*
Cameron, JoAnna (act): *Deadly Dust*
Cameron, John (act): *Darkman (1990)*
Cameron, John (mus): *Jekyll And Hyde; The London Connection; The Man From Nowhere; The Mirror Crack'd; Moments; Night Watch; The Ruling Class; Spectre (1977); The Thief Of Baghdad (1978); Who?*
Cameron, Kirk (act, b. 1970): *Goliath Awaits*
Cameron, Lloyd (act): *Man Beast*
Cameron, Lorne (wri): *Clarence; First Knight*
Cameron, Marlene (act): *Orpheus Descending*
Cameron, Michael (act): *Eraser*
Cameron, Nadia (act): *Merlin*
Cameron, Patricia (act): *Dressed To Kill (1946)*
Cameron, Patrick (act): *The Goonies*
Cameron, Pearl (act): *Mystery Junction*
Cameron, Ray (act, dir & wri): *Blood Bath At The House Of Death*
Cameron, Rod (act,1910–1983, nee Rod Cox): *Double Jeopardy; The Jungle; The Man Who Died Twice; The Monster And The Girl; Passport To Treason; Pirates Of Monterey; Psychic Killer; The Remarkable Andrew; Zex*
Cameron, Shirley (act): *Thirst*
Cameron, William (act): *The Dark Half; Day Of The Dead*
Cameron, Yves (act): *Timecop*
Cameron-Bure, Candace (act): *Nightscream*
Camhi, Patrice (act): *Zorro: The Legend Begins*
Camille, Sharen (act): *Psycho IV: The Beginning*
Camiller, George (act): *Slipstream*
Camilleri, Charles (mus): *The Castle Of Fu Manchu; House Of 1,000 Dolls*
Camilleri, Terry (act): *The Cars That Ate Paris; Encounter At Raven's Gate*
Camillo, Tony (mus): *Welcome To Arrow Beach*
Caminito, Augusto (wri): *The Secret Of Seagull Island*
Caminneci, Pier A. (act & wri): *Necronomicon*
Camino, Connie (act): *Endangered Species*
Cammarata, Frank (act): *Witchery*
Cammell, China (act & wri): *White Of The Eye*
Cammell, Donald (dir, 1933-1996): *Demon Seed; White Of The Eye*
Cammell, Donald (wri, 1933-1996): *White Of The Eye*
Camoin, Cora (act): *L'ours*
Camoiras, Jose (act): *Tombs Of The Blind Dead*
Camp, Austin (act): *Abide With Me; The Barton Mystery (1920); The Mystery Of The Diamond Belt; The Woman Who Dared*
Camp, Colleen (act, b. 1953): *D.A.R.Y.L.; The Eliminator; The Seduction; Sliver; Wicked Stepmother*
Camp, Hamilton (act): *Dick Tracy (1990); Evilspeak; Heaven Can Wait (1978); It Came Upon The Midnight Clear; The Perils Of Pauline; Star Crash*
Camp, Joe (act, dir & wri): *Oh Heavenly Dog*
Camp, Oscar (mus): *Amazons (1986)*
Camp, Robin (act): *My Cousin Rachel*
Camp, Shep (act): *The Greene Murder Case*
Camp, Wilson (act): *Night Of The Comet*
Campagna, Jim (act): *Werewolf Of Washington*
Campanaro, Paddy (act): *Phobia*
Campanella, Frank (act): *Angel On My Shoulder (1980); Dick Tracy (1990); Heaven Can Wait (1978); Matt Helm*
Campanella, Joseph (act, b. 1927): *Ben; Earthbound (1981); Hangar 18; Meteor; The Plutonium Incident; Return To Fantasy Island; The St. Valentine's Day Massacre; Seconds; Terror On The 40th Floor*
Campanella, Roy (act, 1921–1993): *Roogie's Bump*
Campanile, Pasquale Festa (dir): *When Women Had Tails*
Campanini, Carlo (act): *Ok, Nero!*
Campannini, Pietro (act): *The Lion Of Thebes*
Campbell (mus): *Blackmail (1929)*
Campbell, Alice (wri): *Juggernaut*
Campbell, Amelia (act): *The Exorcist III; Single White Female*
Campbell, Anthony B. (act): *Secrets Of The Phantom Caverns*
Campbell, Audrey Jo (act): *The Cradle Will Fall*
Campbell, Beatrice (act, b. 1923): *Grand National Night; The Hangman Waits; The House In The Square; Last Holiday; Things Happen At Night; Wanted For Murder*
Campbell, Beverly (act): see Garland, Beverly
Campbell, Bill (act, b. 1959): *Bram Stoker's Dracula; The Cold Equations; Out There; The Rocketeer*
Campbell, Billy (act): *Secrets Of The Phantom Caverns*
Campbell, Bruce (act): *Army Of Darkness; Congo; Darkman (1990); The Evil Dead; Evil Dead 2: Dead By Dawn; Maniac Cop; Maniac Cop 2; Mindwarp; Moontrap; Sundown: The Vampire In Retreat; Tornado!; Waxwork II: Lost In Time*
Campbell, Bruce (mus): *The Man In The Road; Mr. Drake's Duck*
Campbell, C. Jutson (act): *Star Crystal*
Campbell, Catina (act): *The Hound Of The Baskervilles (1921)*
Campbell, Charles L. (act): *Virus*
Campbell, Chellio (act): *The Lucifer Complex*
Campbell, Cheryl (act): *Greystoke: The Legend Of Tarzan, Lord Of The Apes; Hawk The Slayer*
Campbell, Chris (act): *Clarence*
Campbell, Colin (act): *The Lost World (1960); The Two Mrs. Carrolls*
Campbell, Courtney (act): *Secrets In The Attic*
Campbell, David (act): *Forever Evil*
Campbell, Don (act): *Mars Needs Women*
Campbell, Elizabeth (act): *Doctor Of Doom; Wrestling Women Vs. The Aztec Mummy*
Campbell, Gar (act): *Fright Night II*
Campbell, Gavin (act): *The Playbirds*
Campbell, George (act): *Monte Cristo*
Campbell, Glen P. (act): *I Was A Zombie For The F.B.I.*
Campbell, Graeme (act): *Watchers*
Campbell, Graeme (dir): *Volcano: Fire On The Mountain*
Campbell, Ian (act): *The Wicker Man*
Campbell, Ivar (dir): *Eyes Of Fate*
Campbell, J.A. (wri): *The Queen Mother*
Campbell, J. Kenneth (act): *Mars Attacks!*
Campbell, James (mus): *Elvira, Mistress Of The Dark*
Campbell Jr., John W. (wri, 1910–1971): *The Thing (1982); The Thing From Another World*
Campbell, Judy (act): *East Of Piccadilly; Green For Danger; Sredni Vashtar*
Campbell, Ken (act): *Dreamchild; The Tempest (1980)*
Campbell, Laura (act): *The Legend Of Sleepy Hollow*
Campbell, Lindsay (act): *A Clockwork Orange; The Curse Of The Golem; Schizo (1977)*
Campbell, Louise (act): *Bulldog Drummond Comes Back; Bulldog Drummond's Peril; Bulldog Drummond's Revenge*
Campbell, Mae (act): *Hellhole*
Campbell, Martin (dir): *Cast A Deadly Spell; Goldeneye; No Escape (1994)*
Campbell, Nell (act, a.k.a. Little Nell): *Liszt O' Mania; The Rocky Horror Picture Show; Shock Treatment! (1981)*
Campbell, Neve (act): *The Craft; Scream; Scream II*
Campbell, Nicholas (act): *The Brood; The Dead Zone; The Pink Chiquitas; The Shape Of Things To Come (1979); Virus*
Campbell, Mrs. Patrick (act, 1865–1940): *Crime And Punishment (1935)*
Campbell, Patrick (act): *Critters 2: The Main Course; Halloween With The Addams Family; Saturday The 14th*
Campbell, Patrick (wri): *The Oracle (1952)*
Campbell, Paul (act): *The Deadly Mantis; Starship Invasions*
Campbell, R. Wright (wri): *Captain Nemo And The Underwater City; Man Of A Thousand Faces; The Masque Of The Red Death (1964); Teenage Cave Man*
Campbell, Richard (act): *Wild Thing*
Campbell, Rob (act): *The Crucible (1996)*
Campbell, Robert (act): *Cell 2455, Death Row*
Campbell, Ross (act): *The Wicker Man*
Campbell, Sarah (act): *Body Parts*
Campbell, Scott (act): *The Dungeonmaster*
Campbell, Scott Michael (act): *Project: Alf*
Campbell, Shawn (act): *Man On A Swing*
Campbell, Tim (act): *Boarding House*
Campbell, Tisha (act, b. 1968): *Little Shop Of Horrors (1986)*
Campbell, Tom (cin): *Space Raiders*
Campbell, Vernon (act): *12 Monkeys*
Campbell, Violet (act): *The Lyons Mail; The Phantom Picture*
Campbell, Webster (act): *In The Next Room*
Campbell, William (act, b. 1926): *Blood Bath (1966); Cell 2455, Death Row; Dementia 13; Hush...Hush, Sweet Charlotte; Portrait In Terror; The Return Of The Six Million Dollar Man And The Bionic Woman*
Campion, Cyril (wri): *Juggernaut*
Campion, Gerald (act): *The Drum; The Sorcerers*
Campitelli, Tom (act): *I Come In Peace*
Campo, Tony (act): *The Psychotronic Man*
Campo, Wally (act): *Beast From Haunted Cave; The Little Shop Of Horrors (1960); Master Of The World; Tales Of Terror*
Campogalliani, Carlo (dir): *Mighty Ursus; Son Of Samson; Sword Of The Conqueror; Il Terror Dei Barberi*
Campos, Jose (act): *La Maldicion De Los Karnsteins*
Campos, Rafael (act, 1936–1985): *Agent For H.A.R.M.; Astro Zombies; Lady In A Cage; V*
Campos, Susan (act): *Nothing But Trouble*
Campos, Victor (act): *Black Sunday (1977); Demon And The Mummy; Fugitive From The Empire*
Campoy, Anna Maria (act): *Il Dottor Jekyll*
Campus, Michael (dir): *Z.P.G.*
Camroux, Ken (act): *The Resurrected; Virus*
Camus, Marcel (dir, b. 1912): *Black Orpheus*
Canaan, Christopher (wri): *Bridge Of Time; Hitler's Daughter*
Canale, Alessandra (act): *The Adventures Of Hercules*
Canale, Gianna Maria (act, b. 1927): *Il Figlio Di Spartacus; Hercules (1957); The Lebanese Mission; Maciste Contre Il Vampiro; Nights Of Rasputin; Queen Of The Pirates; La Regina Della Amazzoni; Revenge Of The Black Eagle; Teodora, Imperatrice Di Bisanzio; The Treasure Of Monte Cristo (1961); I Vampiri*
Canary, David (act): *The St. Valentine's Day Massacre*
Canaway, Bill (wri): *The Ipcress File*
Candelora, Joe (act): *Matinee*
Candido, Candy (act): *The Great Rupert*
Candido, Nino (act): *I Come In Peace*
Candoli, the Brothers (act & mus): *Bell, Book And Candle*
Candy, John (act, 1950–1994): *Heavy Metal; Little Shop Of Horrors (1986); Nothing But Trouble; Spaceballs; Splash*
Cane, Charles R. (act): *Revenge Of The Creature*
Cane, Elliot (act): *Greystoke: The Legend Of Tarzan, Lord Of The Apes*
Canedo, Roberto (act): *Doctor Of Doom*
Canegata, Leonard (act): see Lee, Canada
Canerday, Natalie (act): *Sling Blade*
Canfield, Gene (act): *Romeo Is Bleeding*
Canfield, Mary Grace (act): *Something Wicked This Way Comes*
Cann, David (act): *1984 (1984)*
Cannan, Debnis (wri): *A High Wind In Jamaica*
Cannata, Anthony (act): *Blink*
Cannata, Karen (act): *Shock Chamber*
Cannell, Stephen J. (wri): *Dr. Scorpion*
Canning, James (act): *The Fog*
Canning, Victor (wri, b. 1911): *Family Plot; Limbo Line; Masquerade; Spy Hunt; Venetian Bird*
Cannon, Bill (act): *The Capture Of Bigfoot*
Cannon, Chris (act): *Tales From The Crypt*
Cannon, Danny (dir): *Judge Dredd*
Cannon, Doran William (wri): *Hex*
Cannon, Dyan (act, b. 1937): *Arthur The King; Heaven Can Wait (1978)*
Cannon, Esma (act): *Crow Hollow; Double Confession; The Flesh And The Fiends; Guilt Is My Shadow; Hide And Seek; I Met A Murderer; Last Holiday; Poison Pen; What A Carve Up!*
Cannon, Freddy (act): *Village Of The Giants*

Cannon, Katherine (act): Trilby (1923)
Cannon, Maurice (act): The Hidden
Cannon, Orin (act): Burnt Offerings; Trilogy Of Terror
Cannon II, Thomas D. (act): Student Bodies
Cannon, Wanda (act): The Housekeeper
Canny, Mark (cin): Razorback
Cano, M. (dir): Voodoo Black Exorcist
Canovas, Ann (act): Revenge Of The Dead (1984)
Canovas, Antonio (cin): Parsifal
Canoy, Reuben (wri): Mad Doctor Of Blood Island
Cansino, Margarita Carmen (act): see Hayworth, Rita
Cansino, Rita (act): see Hayworth, Rita
Cantafora, Antonio (act): Demons 2; Gli Orrori Del Castello Di Noremberga
Cantarini, Louis (act): Teenage Mutant Ninja Turtles
Canterbury, Jo (act): Teen-Age Strangler
Canti, Aldy (act): War Of The Planets
Cantillion, Jane (act): Blood Diner
Cantinflas (act, 1911–1993, nee Mario Moreno): Around The World In 80 Days; Le Salaire De La Peur
Cantley, Charles (act): The Smugglers' Cave
Canton, Daniel B. (cin): Deadtime Stories
Cantor, Eddie (act, 1893–1964, nee Edward Itzkowitz): Ali Baba Goes To Town; Roman Scandals
Cantor, Eli (wri): The Nest
Cantor, Herman (act): The Golden Eye
Cantrell, Cynthia (act): Blood Diner
Cantrell, Early (act): One Mysterious Night
Cantrell, Mark (act): Secrets Of The Phantom Caverns
Cantrell, Tom (act): Zombie Island Massacre
Cantu, Reynaldo (act): Into The Badlands
Cantwell, Brian (act): Attack Of The Killer Tomatoes
Cantwell, Colin (dir & wri): Voyage To The Outer Planets
Canty, Marietta (act, 1906–1986): Lady In The Dark
Canutt, Yakima (act): The Clutching Hand
Canutt, Yakima (dir): Captain Mephisto And The Transformation Machine
Canzano, Pam (act): The Slumber Party Massacre
Capaldi, Peter (act): The Lair Of The White Worm
Capanna, Pietro (act): Il Trionfo Di Ercole
Capdevielle, Maria (act): see Maris, Mona
Capell, Barbara (act): Hauser's Memory; La Noche De Walpurgis
Capell, Peter (act): Hauser's Memory; I Aim At The Stars; Willy Wonka And The Chocolate Factory
Capellani, Albert (dir, 1870–1931): Young Diana
Capen, Chris (act): The Swarm
Caper, John (mus): Equinox
Capers, Hedge (act): Who Fears The Devil?
Capers, Virginia (act): Donor; Howard The Duck
Capes, Renault (wri): Dual Alibi
Capetillo, Christiana (act): Single White Female
Capizzi, Bill (act): Heart And Souls
Caplan, Neil (act): A Midsummer Night's Dream (1985)
Caplin, Cate (act): The Hidden; To Die For
Caplin, James (wri): Transmutations
Capo, Armand (act): Amazons (1986)
Capobianco, Carmine (act & wri): Psychos In Love
Capodice, John (act): Gremlins 2: The New Batch; Jacob's Ladder; Q
Capodilupo, Tony (act): They Might Be Giants
Capon, Paul (wri): Hidden Homicide
Capone, Gino (wri): Conquest
Capone, Vinny (act): Friday The 13th, Part VIII-Jason Takes Manhattan
Caporale, Aristide (act): Amarcord; El Castello Dell'orrore
Caportoto, Carl (wri): The Suicide Club (1988)
Capote, Truman (act, 1924–1984): Murder By Death
Capote, Truman (wri, 1924–1984): Beat The Devil; The Innocents
Capp, Al (wri, 1909–1979): Li'l Abner (1940 & 1959)
Cappell, Barbara (act): The Werewolf vs The Vampire Woman
Cappello, Frank (wri): Suburban Commando
Cappello, Timmy (act): The Lost Boys
Capponi, Claudio (mus): Jane Eyre (1996)
Capponi, Pier Paolo (act): The Cat O' Nine Tails
Capra, Francis (act): Kazaam

Capra, Frank (dir, 1897–1991): Arsenic And Old Lace; Dirigible; It's A Wonderful Life; Lost Horizon (1937)
Capra, Jordana (act): The Goddess Of Love; Miracle Mile
Capri, Ahna (act): The Brotherhood Of Satan
Capriolo, Vittorio (act): Secret Agent (1974)
Capshaw, Kate (act, b. 1954): Dreamscape; Indiana Jones And The Temple Of Doom; Spacecamp
Capua, Enzo (wri): Rorret
Capuano, Luigi (dir): Sandokan Against The Leopard Of Sarawak; Sandokan Fights Back
Capucci, Fabrizzio (act): To Commit A Murder
Capucine (act, 1933–1990, nee Germaine Lefebvre): Arabian Adventure; Satyricon
Caputo, Anthony (act): The Toxic Avenger, Part II
Caputo, Chris (act): Ghost Warrior; Midnight Lace (1981); Retribution (1988)
Caquelin, Cynthia (act): Flight Of The Navigator
Carabatsos, Steve (wri): Tentacles
Caradine, Philip (act): The Invincible Barbarian
Carafa, Sacha (act): The Kremlin Letter
Carafotes, Paul (act): The Clan Of The Cave Bear
Caramico, Robert (cin): The Cremators; Journey To The Center Of Time; Kiss Meets The Phantom Of The Park; Octaman; Spawn Of The Slithis; Topper (1979)
Carat, Jane (act): Les Parapluies De Cherbourg
Carayiannis, Costas (dir): The Devil's Men
Carbajal, Jose Antonio/Tony (act): Run For The Sun; A Woman's Devotion
Carbajal, Lonny (act): Charlie Chan And The Curse Of The Dragon Queen
Carballido, Emilio (wri): Macario
Carballo, Dick (act): Night Of The Zombies (1981)
Carbis, Christopher (act): The Psychotronic Man
Carbone, Anthony/Antony (act): Avalanche; A Bucket Of Blood (1959); Creature From The Haunted Sea; Last Woman On Earth; The Pit And The Pendulum (1961)
Carbonera, Gerard (mus): Dr. Cyclops
Carby, Fanny (act): A Distant Scream
Carcano, Gianfilippo (act): Amarcord
Card, Lamar (dir): The Clones
Cardan, Christina (act): The Zero Boys
Cardea, Frank (wri): It Came Upon The Midnight Clear
Cardea, Ugo (act): The Night Porter
Cardella, Richard (act & wri): The Crater Lake Monster
Cardenas, Colby (wri): The Night Of The Claw
Cardenas, Elsa (act): The Incredible Face Of Dr. B; Return From The Beyond; La Senora Muerte
Cardenas, Hernan (dir & wri): The Night Of The Claw
Cardenas, Steve (act): Mighty Morphin Power Rangers; Turbo: A Power Rangers Movie
Carder, Elizabeth (act): The Octagon
Cardew, Jane (act): The Flesh And Blood Show
Cardi, Pat (act): Battle For The Planet Of The Apes; Brainstorm (1965); Horror High; Let's Kill Uncle
Cardiff, Jack (cin, b. 1914): The Awakening; Black Narcissus; The Black Rose; Cat's Eye; Conan The Destroyer; Death On The Nile; The Fifth Musketeer; Ghost Story (1981); A Matter Of Life And Death; Pandora And The Flying Dutchman; Under Capricorn
Cardiff, Jack (dir, b. 1914): Beyond This Place; The Liquidator; The Mutations
Cardille, Bill "Chilly Billy" (act): Night Of The Living Dead (1968)
Cardille, Lori (act): Day Of The Dead
Cardinal, Tantoo (act): The Lightning Incident
Cardinale, Claudia (act, b. 1939): Cartouche (1962); 8 1/2; The Red Tent
Cardona, Rene (act): El Baron Del Terror
Cardona (Sr.), Rene (dir & wri): Night Of The Bloody Apes; Santa Claus (1959)
Cardona (Jr.), Rene (dir & wri): Doctor Of Doom; Guyana, Cult Of The Damned; The Night Of A Thousand Cats; Robinson Crusoe And The Tiger; Survive!; Tintorera...Bloody Waters; Night Of The Bloody Apes; Survive!
Cardona, Robert D. (dir): Not Guilty
Cardona, Roy (act): The Clutching Hand
Cardone, J.S. (dir): Shadowzone; The Slayer
Cardone, J.S. (wri): Crash And Burn; Shadowzone
Cardos, John (act): Blood Of Dracula's Castle; Nightmare In Wax [illegible]
Cardos, John (dir): The Dark (1979); Kingdom Of The Spiders; Mutant
Cardoso, Beny (act): Future Women
Cardoza, David (act): Deadly Eyes
Cardoza, Tony (act): The Beast Of Yucca Flats

Carducci, Mark Patrick (wri): Neon Maniacs; Pumpkinhead
Cardwell, Barry (act): The Sand Castle
Cardwell, Jack (act): Piranha (1978)
Cardwell, James (act): Daughter Of The Jungle; The Shanghai Cobra
Cardwell, Laurie (act): The Sand Castle
Cardy, David (act): Xtro
Careddu, Stefania (act): Johnny Hamlet
Carell, Annette (act): The Tell-Tale Heart (1960); The Vulture (1966)
Carena, Anna (act): Miracle In Milan
Carere, Christine (act, b. 1930): I Deal In Danger
Caresio, John (act): The Creeping Terror
Carette, Julien (act, 1897–1966): L'auberge Rouge; The Rules Of The Game
Carew, James (act): Alf's Button (1920); The Corner House Burglary; High Treason (1929); Midnight At Madame Tussaud's; The Mystery Of The Mary Celeste; The Rajah's Tiara; Strange Experiment; The Tunnel; 12-10
Carewe, Arthur Edmund (act): The Cat And The Canary (1927); Charlie Chan's Secret; Doctor X; Mystery Of The Wax Museum; The Phantom Of The Opera (1925); Trilby (1923)
Carewe, Edwin (dir): The Invisible Fear
Carey, Christopher (act): Watchers
Carey, Clare (act): Them (1996); Uninvited (1987)
Carey, Dave (act): Rawhead Rex
Carey, Denis (act): Psychomania (1972)
Carey, Doris (act): The World's Greatest Sinner
Carey, George F. (act): The World's Greatest Sinner
Carey (Sr.), Harry (act, 1878–1947): Among The Living; Beyond Tomorrow; The Happy Land
Carey Jr., Harry (act, b. 1921): Back To The Future, Part III; Billy The Kid vs. Dracula; Cyborg 2087; Endangered Species; The Exorcist III; Gremlins
Carey, John (act): I Lunghi Capelli Della Morte
Carey, Joyce (act, b. 1898, nee Joyce Lawrence): The Black Windmill; Blithe Spirit; The Eyes Of Annie Jones; The October Man; Only A Scream Away
Carey, Leonard (act): The Lone Wolf Spy Hunt; A Night Of Mystery (1937); Rebecca; Trouble For Two
Carey, Macdonald (act, 1913–1994): Bride Of Vengeance; The Damned; The Devil's Agent; Dream Girl; End Of The World (1977); It's Alive III: Island Of The Alive; Shadow Of A Doubt (1943); Stranger At My Door; Stranger In Our House
Carey, Michele (act): In The Shadow Of Kilimanjaro
Carey, Olive (act, 1896–1988): Billy The Kid Vs. Dracula
Carey, Peter (wri): Until The End Of The World
Carey, Phil(ip) (act, b. 1925): Crackle Of Death; Dead Ringer; Monstroid; Screaming Mimi; Scream Of The Wolf; The Shadow On The Window; The Time Travelers (1964); The Trunk
Carey, Reginald (act): see Harrison, Rex
Carey, Roland (act): Giants Of Thessaly
Carey, Sandra (act): Time Walker
Carey, Timothy (act, 1929–1994): The Boy And The Pirates; Francis In The Haunted House; The Killing; Mermaids Of Tiburon; What's The Matter With Helen?; The World's Greatest Sinner
Carey, Timothy (dir & wri): The World's Greatest Sinner
Cargher, Emilio (act): The Secret Of Stamboul
Carhart 3rd, John (act): There's Nothing Out There
Cargill, Patrick (act): The Clue Of The Silver Key; The Magic Christian
Cargol, Jean-Pierre (act): Caravan To Vaccares; L'enfant Sauvage
Carhart, Timothy (act): Candyman: Farewell To The Flesh
Cariaga, Marvelee (act): Dick Tracy (1990)
Caridi, Carmine (act): Kiss Meets The Phantom Of The Park
Caridia, Michael (act): The Gamma People
Carillo, Mario (act): The Private Life Of Helen Of Troy
Cariou, Len (act, b. 1939): Killer In The Mirror; Lady In White; The Man In The Attic (1995); Never Talk To Strangers
Carita (act): The Viking Queen
Carl, Adam (act): The Monster Squad
Carl, John (act): To Die For II: Son Of Darkness
[illegible] (act): Batman (1989)
Carle, Cynthia (act): Warning Sign
Carle, Cynthia (wri): The 6th Man
Carle, Richard (act): The Ghost Walks (1934)

Carlen, Catherine (act): Chopper Chicks In Zombietown
Carleo III, James A. (act): The Handmaid's Tale
Carleton, Claire (act, 1913–1979): The Black Sleep; A Close Call For Boston Blackie; Crime Doctor's Diary; Crime Doctor's Manhunt; A Double Life; The Son Of Dr. Jekyll; Too Many Winners; Witness To Murder
Carleton, George (act): Boston Blackie Booked On Suspicion; Daughter Of The Jungle; Just Off Broadway
Carleton, James (act): Atlas
Carleton, Lloyd B. (dir & wri): The Flying Dutchman
Carleton, Marjorie (wri): Cry Wolf (1947)
Carlile, Bob (act): Rawhead Rex
Carlile, C.A. (act): The Kidnapped King
Carlile, C. Douglas (act): The Kidnapped King
Carlile, C. Douglas (dir): Sexton Blake
Carlile, C. Douglas (wri): The Kidnapped King
Carlile, David (act): I'm Dangerous Tonight
Carlin, George (act, b. 1937): Bill & Ted's Bogus Journey; Bill & Ted's Excellent Adventure; Justin Case
Carlin, John (act): A Ghost In Monte Carlo; Holocaust 2000
Carlin, Leila (act): The Night Stalker (1987)
Carlin, Lynn (act): Deathdream; Superstition
Carlin, Thomas A. (act): Jacob's Ladder
Carlin, Tony (act): The Nutty Professor (1996)
Carling, William (mus): Berkeley Square
Carlini, Carlo (cin): Autopsy; Seven Deaths In The Cat's Eye
Carlino, Lewis John (wri): Haunted Summer; A Reflection Of Fear; Seconds; Where Have All The People Gone?
Carlip, Hilary (act): Vamp
Carlish, Valerie (act): We Do Believe In Ghosts
Carlisle, Anne (act): Liquid Sky
Carlisle, Kitty (act, b. 1914, nee Catherine Holzman): Murder At The Vanities
Carlisle, Mary (act, b. 1912): Beware, Spooks!; Dead Men Walk; House Of Menace; One Frightened Night
Carlisle, Peggy (act): The Rocks Of Valpre
Carlisle, Peter (act): Secrets Of Sex
Carlisle, Rita (act): The Vampire Bat
Carlisle, Spencer (act): The Devil's Partner
Carlisle, Steve (act): The Curse
Carlo, Ismael ("East") (act): Eraser; Sparkling Cyanide
Carlo, Joseph (act): Satan's Cheerleaders
Carlos, Christopher (act): Dr. Terror's House Of Horrors (1964); Fury At Smugglers' Bay
Carlos, Eugenio (act): Love Slaves Of The Amazons
Carlos, Flory (act): Terror Is A Man
Carlos, Franzi (act): Old Bill Through The Ages
Carlos, Walter (mus): A Clockwork Orange
Carlos, Wendy (mus): Tron
Carlson, Chad (act): Babes In Toyland (1986)
Carlson, Chrissie (act): Secrets In The Attic
Carlson, Erica (act): Caveman (1981)
Carlson, Erika (act): Total Recall
Carlson, Joel (act): Communion; Tarzan In Manhattan
Carlson, Karen (act): It Happened One Christmas; The Octagon
Carlson, Leigh (act): Wolf
Carlson, Les(lie) (act): The Dead Zone; Deranged (1974); The Fly (1986); The Neptune Factor; Videodrome
Carlson, Richard (act, 1912–1977): The Amazing Mr. X; Behind Locked Doors; Beyond Tomorrow; Creature From The Black Lagoon; The Ghost Breakers; Hold That Ghost; It Came From Outer Space; King Solomon's Mines (1949); The Magnetic Monster; The Maze; The Power (1967); Riders To The Stars; Tormented (1960); The Valley Of Gwangi; Whispering Smith Hits London
Carlson, Richard (dir, 1912–1977): Riders To The Stars
Carlson, Steve (act, b. 1943): Deadlier Than The Male
Carlson, Velletta (act): Mars Attacks!
Carlson, Veronica (act, b. 1944): Dracula Has Risen From The Grave; Frankenstein Must Be Destroyed; The Ghoul (1974); Horror Of Frankenstein; Vampira
Carlson, Vicki (act): Violated
Carlsson, Erika (act): Demonoid
Carlton, Dave (act): Spawn Of The Slithis
Carlton, David (act): Wavelength
Carlton, Hope Marie (act): Slaughterhouse Rock
Carlton, Ken (act): [illegible]
Carlton, Lewis (act): [illegible] The Mystery Of The Diamond Belt
Carlton, Mark (act): Endangered Species; RoboCop; Total Recall
Carlton, Mary (act): Just Imagine

Carlton, Rex (wri, b. 1918): Blood Of Dracula's Castle; The Brain That Wouldn't Die; Nightmare In Wax; Unearthly Stranger
Carlton, Tommy (act): Tarzan's Savage Fury
Carlton, Wilfred (dir): The Case Of A Doped Actress
Carlucci, Milly (act): The Adventures Of Hercules
Carlyle, David (act): Smart Blonde
Carlyle, Richard (1930s act): Kismet (1930)
Carlyle, Richard (1970s act): The Spell
Carman, Jeannie (act): The Devil's Hand (1961)
Carman, Michael (act): 20th Century Oz
Carme, Pamela (act): Young And Innocent
Carmel, Eddie (act): The Brain That Wouldn't Die
Carmel, Roger C. (act, 1932–1986): Goodbye Charlie; Myra Breckinridge; The Silencers (1966); Skullduggery; The Venetian Affair
Carmen, Jeanne (act): The Monster Of Piedras Blancas
Carmen, Jewel (act): The Bat (1926)
Carmen, Julie (act): Fright Night II; In The Mouth Of Madness
Carmet, Jean (act): And Soon The Darkness; Violette Noziere
Carmi, Maria (act): Homunculus
Carmi, Oded (act): Deadtime Stories
Carmichael, Hoagy (act, 1899–1981): Topper (1937)
Carmichael, Ian (act, b. 1920): From Beyond The Grave; Hide And Seek; The Lady Vanishes (1979); Meet Mr. Lucifer
Carmichael, Patricia (act): Dear, Dead Delilah
Carmichael, Ralph (mus): The Blob (1958); 4D Man
Carminatti, Tullio (act, 1894–1971): The Bat (1926)
Carmine, Michael (act): *Batteries Not Included; Leviathan
Carminoso, Mara (act): Sei Donne Per L'assassino
Carmody, Gareth (act): see Conway, Gary
Carnachia, Stella (act): The Tormented (1977)
Carnaghi, Roberto (act): Moebius
Carne, Judy (act, b. 1939, nee Joyce Botterill): Dead Men Tell No Tales; Someone At The Top Of The Stairs
Carne, Marcel (dir, 1906–1996): Les Visiteurs Du Soir
Carnegie, Robert (act): Mother's Day
Carnell, Cliff (act): Night Slaves
Carnera, Primo (act, 1907–1967): Ercole E La Regina Di Lidia; A Kid For Two Farthings; Mighty Joe Young; Prince Valiant
Carney, Alan (act, 1910–1973): The Absent-Minded Professor (1961); Genius At Work; Son Of Flubber; Zombies On Broadway
Carney, Art (act, b. 1910): Firestarter; The Night They Saved Christmas; Ravagers; Time Flyer
Carney, Brian (act): Ravagers
Carney, Chris (mus): The Howling
Carney, George (act): Miracles Do Happen; Thunder Rock; Wanted For Murder
Carney, James (act): Alf's Button Afloat; Busman's Honeymoon
Carney, John (J.) (act): A Clockwork Orange; Hamlet (1969); Hawk The Slayer
Carney, Thom (act): Dead Men Tell No Tales; It!—The Terror From Beyond Space; Wonder Woman
Carnivani, Maria Luisa (act): Deathstalker II: Duel Of The Titans
Carnovsky, Morris (act, 1897–1992): Man-Eater Of Kumaon
Caro, Cathia (act): Giants Of Thessaly; Triumph Of The Son Of Hercules
Caro, Marc (dir): The City Of Lost Children
Carol, Connie (act): Gregorio And His Angel
Carol, Jack (act): Devil Dog: The Hound Of Hell
Carol, Joan (act): Burke And Hare; Ghost Ship (1952); Mr. Moto's Last Warning
Carol, John (act): The Dark Stairway; The Dummy Talks; The Perfect Crime; The Spider And The Fly
Carol, Judith (act): Dear Murderer
Carol, Linda (act): Beverly Hills Bodysnatchers; School Spirit
Carol, Martine (act, 1922–1967, nee Maryse Mourer): Around The World In 80 Days; Atomic Agent; La Beaute Du Diable; Lola Montes; Lucrezia Borgia (1952); Madame Dubarry (1954); Nathalie, Agent Secret
Carol, Ronnie (act): Billion Dollar Threat; The Stepford Children
Carol, Sheila (act): Beast From Haunted Cave
Caroll, Staness (act): My Best Friend Is A Vampire
Caron, Leslie (act, b. 1931): The Glass Slipper; The Man With A Cloak
Caron, Marvin (act): Millennium
Caron, Richard (wri): Shadow Of Evil (1964)
Caron, Sandra (act): Digby-The Biggest Dog In The World; Dracula (1973)
Carothers, A.J. (wri): The Thief Of Baghdad (1978)
Carothers, Mariann V. (act): Phenomenon
Carothers, Veronica (act): Phoenix The Warrior
Carouso, Mickey (act): Beyond Evil
Carozzo, Pat (act): Moontrap
Carpenter, Charles E. (act): Nightfall (1988)
Carpenter, David (act): Warlock
Carpenter, Edward Childs (wri): The Leopard Lady
Carpenter, Francis (act): Jack And The Beanstalk (1917); Rip Van Winkle (1921)
Carpenter, Harry (act): The Magic Christian
Carpenter, John (act, b. 1948): The Silence Of The Hams
Carpenter, John (dir, b. 1948): Big Trouble In Little China; Christine; Dark Star; Escape From L.A.; Escape From New York; The Fog; Halloween; In The Mouth Of Madness; Memoirs Of An Invisible Man; Prince Of Darkness; Someone's Watching Me!; Starman; They Live; The Thing (1982); Village Of The Damned (1995)
Carpenter, John (mus, b. 1948): Big Trouble In Little China; Christine; Dark Star; Escape From New York; The Fog; Halloween; Halloween II; Halloween III: Season Of The Witch; Halloween 4: The Return Of Michael Myers; Halloween 5: The Revenge Of Michael Myers; Halloween: The Curse Of Michael Myers; In The Mouth Of Madness; Prince Of Darkness; They Live; Village Of The Damned (1995)
Carpenter, John (wri, b. 1948): Dark Star; Escape From L.A.; Escape From New York; Eyes Of Laura Mars; The Fog; Halloween; Halloween II; Someone's Watching Me!
Carpenter, Ken (act): Hellraiser III: Hell On Earth; Phantom Of The Paradise
Carpenter, Paul (act, 1921–1964): Call Me Bwana; Date At Midnight; Dr. Crippen; Fire Maidens Of Outer Space; First Men In The Moon (1964); The Hypnotist (1957); Murder Reported; Shadow Of A Man; The Stranger Came Home; Undercover Girl (1958)
Carpenter, Paul (1970s act): Blood Mania
Carpenter, Pete (mus): Captain America II; Dr. Scorpion
Carpenter, Peter (act): Point Of Terror
Carpenter, Randall (act): Cannibal Girls
Carpenter, Richard (act): The Terrornauts
Carpenter, Russ(ell) (cin): Cameron's Closet; Critters 2: The Main Course; Lady In White; The Lawnmower Man; Pet Sematary Two; Solar Crisis
Carpenter, Stephen (cin): The Kindred; The Power (1980); Pranks
Carpenter, Stephen (dir): The Kindred; The Power (1980); Pranks; Torment (1986)
Carpenter, Stephen (wri): The Kindred; The Power (1980); Pranks; The Servants Of Twilight; Torment (1986)
Carpenter, Sue Ann (act): The Resurrection Of Zachary Wheeler
Carpenter, Thelma (act): The Devil's Daughter (1972); The Wiz
Carpenter, Virginia (act): Phantom Of Chinatown
Carpenter, Willie (C.) (act): Full Eclipse; The Wiz
Carpi, Tito (wri): Escape From The Bronx; Hunters Of The Golden Cobra; Johnny Hamlet; Marta; Tentacles
Carr, Alexander (act): The Death Kiss
Carr, Betty Ann (act): Hangar 18
Carr, Cameron (act): The Loudwater Mystery; Trent's Last Case (1920)
Carr, Camilla (act): Logan's Run
Carr, Catherine (wri): The Temple Of Venus
Carr, Christopher (act): Stories From A Flying Trunk
Carr, Colleen (act): Zontar: The Thing From Venus
Carr, Comyns (wri): Called Back
Carr, Cynthia (act): The Last House On The Left
Carr, Darleen (act): The Beguiled; Sleepwalker (1975)
Carr, George (act): The Vulture (1937)
Carr, Geraldine (act): The Sniper
Carr, Jack (GB act): 10 Rillington Place
Carr, Jack (USA act): The Chance Of A Lifetime
Carr, Jane (act): Alibi (1942); Murder At The Inn; The Saint's Return; Thirty-Six Hours; The Triumph Of Sherlock Holmes
Carr, Joan (act): Moonbeam Magic
Carr, John Dickson (wri, 1905–1977): The Burning Court; The Man In Black; The Man With A Cloak
Carr, Larry (act): I Was A Teenage Frankenstein
Carr, Lena (act): Nightwing
Carr, Marion (act): Indestructible Man; Ring Of Fear
Carr, Marion (wri): Face To Face
Carr, Mary (act): Just Imagine
Carr, Michael (act): Missile Monsters
Carr, Nat (act): Torchy Gets Her Man; Torchy Plays With Dynamite
Carr, Patricia (act): The Murder Clinic
Carr, Paul (act): The Bat People; Ben; Sisters Of Death
Carr, Percy (act): One Exciting Night
Carr, Phillipe (act): Shadow Of Death (1983)
Carr, Robert (act): Dr. Dracula
Carr, Stephen (act): Jane Eyre (1921)
Carr, Thomas (dir, b. 1907): Superman's Perils
Carr, Walter (act): The Wicker Man
Carra, Michael J. (act): Pumpkinhead II: Blood Wings
Carradine, David (act, b. 1936): The Bad Seed (1985); The Best Of Sex And Violence; Circle Of Iron; Crime Zone; Death Race 2000; Deathsport; A Distant Scream; Dune Warriors; Future Zone; I Saw What You Did (1988); Q; Sundown: The Vampire In Retreat; Trick Or Treats; Waxwork II: Lost In Time
Carradine, John (act, 1906–1988, nee Richmond Reed Carradine): Ali Baba Goes To Town; The Alien Within; Around The World In 80 Days; Astro Zombies; Autopsia De Un Fantasma; The Bees; The Best Of Sex And Violence; Big Foot; Billy The Kid Vs. Dracula; The Black Sleep; The Black Swan; Blood Of Dracula's Castle; Blood Of Ghastly Horror; Bluebeard (1944); The Boogeyman; Bride Of Frankenstein; Captain Kidd; Captive Wild Woman; The Cat Creature; Charlie Chan At The Olympics; The Cosmic Man; Crowhaven Farm; Curse Of The Stone Hand; Dark Venture; Daughter Of The Mind; Death At Love House; Death Ride; Dr. Dracula; Evils Of The Night; The Face Of Marble; The Female Jungle; Frankenstein Island; Gallery Of Horror; Goliath Awaits; Half-Human; The Helicopter Spies; Hell's Bloody Devils; Hell Ship Mutiny; Hex; Hillbillys In A Haunted House; Horror Of The Blood Monsters; The Hostage; The Hound Of The Baskervilles (1939); House Of Dracula; House Of Frankenstein; The House Of Seven Corpses; House Of The Black Death; House Of The Long Shadows; The Howling; The Ice Pirates; The Incredible Petrified World; Invisible Invaders; The Invisible Man's Revenge; Is This Trip Really Necessary?; Journey Into Beyond; The Killer Inside Me; Legacy Of Blood; Mary, Mary, Bloody Mary; Les Miserables (1935); Mr. Moto's Last Warning; The Monster Club; Monster In The Closet; Monstroid; Moonchild; The Mummy And The Curse Of The Jackals; The Mummy's Ghost; Munster, Go Home!; Myra Breckinridge; The Nesting; The Night Strangler; Nocturna, Granddaughter Of Dracula; Pacto Diabolico; Portnoy's Complaint; Return Of The Ape Man; Revenge Of The Zombies (1943); Rymdinvasion I Lappland; Satan's Cheerleaders; Satan's Mistress; The Secret Of Nimh; La Senora Muerte; The Sentinel; Sex Kittens Go To College; Shock Waves; Silent Night, Bloody Night; The Story Of Mankind; Stowaway To The Moon; Superchick; Tarzan The Magnificent; Terror In The Wax Museum; Thank You, Mr. Moto; They Ran For Their Lives; The Three Musketeers (1939); The Tomb; The Unearthly; Las Vampiras (1969); The Vampire Girls; Voodoo Man; Whispering Ghosts; The Wizard Of Mars
Carradine, Keith (act, b. 1951): The Best Of Sex And Violence; Hex; Special Report: Journey To Mars
Carradine, Richmond Reed (act): see Carradine, John
Carradine, Robert (act, b. 1954): Blackout (1978); Clarence; I Saw What You Did (1988); Orca; Wavelength
Carraro, Tino (act): The Cat O' Nine Tails; Orgasmo; The Vatican Affair
Carras, Nicholas (mus): Missile To The Moon; She Demons
Carrau, Bob (wri): The Ewok Adventure
Carre, Lilliane (act): see Damita, Lili
Carrean, Gustavo C. (mus): The Fool Killer; El Vampiro
Carrel, Dany (act, b. 1936): The Hands Of Orlac (1959); Il Mulino Delle Donne Di Pietra
Carrera, Barbara (act, b. 1948): Condorman; Embryo; The Island Of Dr. Moreau (1977); I, The Jury (1982); Love At Stake; Never Say Never Again; When Time Ran Out; Wicked Stepmother
Carrera, David (act): Strange Days
Carreras, Enrique (dir): Master Of Horror
Carreras, Michael (dir, b. 1927): Call Him Mr. Shatter; The Curse Of The Mummy's Tomb; Maniac (1963); Prehistoric Women (1966); Uncharted Seas
Carreras, Michael (wri, b. 1927): Creatures The World Forgot; Moon Zero Two; One Million Years B.C.; The Stranger Came Home
Carrere, Emilio (wri): La Torre De Los Siete Jorobados
Carrere, Frank C. (cin): Bay Coven
Carrere, Tia (act, b. 1967): Covenant; Nothing But The Truth; Zombie Nightmare
Carrey, Jim (act, b. 1962): Batman Forever; The Cable Guy; Earth Girls Are Easy; Liar Liar; The Mask (1994); Once Bitten
Carriaga, Jean (wri): The Blood Rose
Carrick, Gene (act): Appointment With Murder
Carrier, Corey (act): The Adventures Of Pinocchio; Young Indiana Jones: Travels With Father
Carrier, Gabriel (act): Sleepstalker
Carrier, Julie (act): The Children
Carrier, Michael (act): The Children
Carriere, Jean-Claude (wri, b. 1931): The Diabolical Dr. Z; The Discreet Charm Of The Bourgeoisie
Carriere, Mathieu (act): Bluebeard (1972)
Carrigan, Caroline (act): Deadtime Stories
Carrigan, Thomas/Tom (J.) (act): Cinderella (1911, Selig); Crooked Alley; Nick Carter (1921)
Carriles, Lupe (act): The Beast Of Hollow Mountain
Carrillo, Elpidia (act): The Lightning Incident; Predator
Carrillo, Leo (act, 1880–1961): Four Frightened People; Ghost Catchers; Gypsy Wildcat; Horror Island; Phantom Of The Opera (1943)
Carrillo, Lupe (act): El Vampiro Sangriento
Carrington, Debbie (Lee) (act): The Ewok Adventure; Howard The Duck; Total Recall
Carrington, Jack (act): Crime Doctor's Courage
Carrington, Murray (act): Richard III (1911)
Carrington, Robert (wri): Fear Is The Key; Mind Over Murder; Venom (1982)
Carrington, William (act): Rip Van Winkle (1903)
Carrion, Ed (act): The Toxic Avenger
Carrion, Gustavo Cesar/C. (mus): El Ataud Del Vampiro; El Baron Del Terror; El Hombre Y El Monstruo; Swamp Of The Lost Souls
Carrol, Regina (act, 1943–1992): Angels' Wild Women; Blood Of Ghastly Horror; Brain Of Blood; Dr. Dracula; Dracula Vs. Frankenstein; The Female Bunch; Satan's Sadists
Carroll, Anne (act): Not Of This Earth (1957)
Carroll, Barbara (act): Goliath Against The Giants; The Last Days Of Pompeii (1959)
Carroll, Beeson (act): Spacehunter: Adventures In The Forbidden Zone; Too Scared To Scream; The Ufo Incident; Werewolf Of Washington
Carroll, Brian (act): Lifeforce
Carroll, Charles (act): Robocop
Carroll, Christopher (act): Primal Fear; Something Is Out There; Tarzan In Manhattan
Carroll, Dee (act): The Terminal Man
Carroll, Deryl (act): Elvira, Mistress Of The Dark
Carroll, Diahann (act, b. 1935): From The Dead Of Night
Carroll, Earle (wri): 12-10
Carroll, Eddy (act): The Clonus Horror
Carroll, J. Larry (wri): Tourist Trap
Carroll, J. Winston (act): Sorry, Wrong Number (1989)
Carroll, Janice (act): Killer In The Mirror
Carroll, Jax Jason (act): The Cremators; Octaman
Carroll, Jean (act): Mermaids Of Tiburon
Carroll, Jill (act): Psycho II; The Unholy
Carroll, Joann (act): Secrets Of The Phantom Caverns
Carroll, John (act, 1905-1970): Murder On A Bridle Path; Phantom Raiders; Zorro Rides Again
Carroll, Lane (act): Code Name Trixie; Hercules In New York
Carroll, Larry (dir): Ghost Warrior
Carroll, Leo G. (act, 1892–1972): Bulldog Drummond's Secret Police; The Casino Murder Case; Charlie Chan In City In Darkness; Charlie Chan's Murder Cruise; A Christmas Carol (1938); The Helicopter Spies; How To Steal The World; The Karate Killers; London By Night (1937); Murder On A Honeymoon; North By Northwest; One Of Our Spies Is Missing; One Spy Too Many; The Paradine

Case; Rebecca; Spellbound (1945); The Spy In The Green Hat; Strangers On A Train; Suspicion; Tarantula; Tower Of London (1939); Wuthering Heights (1939)
Carroll, Lewis (wri, 1832–1898): Alice In Wonderland (1903, 1933, 1950 & 1985); Alice's Adventures In Wonderland (1910 & 1972); Alice Through The Looking Glass; Jabberwocky
Carroll, Lisa Hart (act): Not Of This World
Carroll, Madeleine (act, 1906–1987, nee Marie-Madeleine Bernadette O'Carroll): I Was A Spy; The Prisoner Of Zenda (1937); The Secret Agent (1936); The 39 Steps (1935)
Carroll, Martin (act): Revenge (1971, Gb); Time Bandits
Carroll, Moon (act): Dracula (1931, English-Speaking Version); The Thirteenth Chair (1929)
Carroll, Paul Vincent (wri): The March Hare
Carroll, Peter (act): The Last Wave
Carroll, Richard (wri): The Ape (1940)
Carroll, Ron (act): Deepstar Six; House II: The Second Story
Carroll, Sharon (act): Night Of The Living Dead (1968)
Carroll, Sidney (wri): The Count Of Monte Cristo (1975); The Stranger Left No Card; Three Cases Of Murder
Carroll, Susan (act): Stanley
Carroll, Ted (act): Dracula (1979); Flash Gordon
Carroll, Thomas C. (act): Sugar Hill
Carroll, Thomas Joseph (act): The Relic
Carroll, Tony (act): Masters Of The Universe
Carroll, Victoria (act): The Lucifer Complex; Pandemonium
Carroll, Zelma (wri): The Lost City
Carrotes, Beal (act): Night Of The Creeps
Carruthers, Ben (act): Fearless Frank
Carruthers, Benito (act): A High Wind In Jamaica; Uncharted Seas
Carscallen, Helen (act): The Quilt Of Hathor
Carson, Bob (act): Radar Secret Service
Carson, Brian R. (act): The Dungeonmaster
Carson, Charles (act, b. 1885): Bobbikins; Curse Of The Fly; Dark Journey; The Dummy Talks; No Escape (1934); The Return Of The Frog; The Saint In London; Scrooge (1935); The Secret Agent (1936); Secret Lives; Things To Come; Whispering Tongues
Carson, Crystal (act): The Zero Boys
Carson, Darwyn (act): Deathrow Gameshow; The Seventh Sign
Carson, David (act): The Funhouse (1981)
Carson, David (dir): Star Trek: Generations
Carson, Frank G. (cin): The 30 Foot Bride Of Candy Rock
Carson, Fred (act): Crosscurrent
Carson, Hunter (act): Invaders From Mars (1986)
Carson, Jack (act, 1910–1963): Arsenic And Old Lace; The Saint In New York; The Tattered Dress
Carson, James B. (act): The Gracie Allen Murder Case
Carson, Jean (act): I Married A Monster From Outer Space
Carson, Jill (act): The Incredibly Strange Creatures Who Stopped Living And Became Mixed-Up Zombies
Carson, John (act): Act Of Murder (1964); Captain Kronos: Vampire Hunter; Come Out, Come Out, Wherever You Are; Locker 69; The Man Who Haunted Himself; Master Spy; Night Caller From Outer Space; The Plague Of The Zombies; Possession (1973); Taste The Blood Of Dracula; Thunderbird 6
Carson, John David (act, b. 1951): Creature From Black Lake; The Day Of The Dolphin; Empire Of The Ants; The Fifth Floor
Carson, L.M. Kit (wri): The Texas Chainsaw Massacre 2
Carson, Paul (act): The Bedford Incident
Carson, Renee/Renie (act): The Picture Of Dorian Gray (1945); Shock (1946)
Carson, Robert (act): Dick Tracy's G-Men; The Saint In Palm Springs
Carson, Shawn (act): Cry For The Strangers; The Funhouse (1981); Something Wicked This Way Comes
Carson, Sherry (act): The Wizard Of Gore
Carson, Willie May (act): The Leopard Lady
Carstairs, John Paddy (dir, 1910–1970): The Devil's Agent; The Saint In London; Sleeping Car To Trieste
Carsten, Peter (act, b. 1929, nee Peter Ransenthaler): The Quiller Memorandum; A Study In Terror; The Vengeance Of Fu Manchu; Web Of The Spider; Zeppelin
Carte, Eric (act): The Beast Must Die
Cartellieri, Carmen (act): Orlacs Haende
Carter (wri): Alibi (1942)
Carter, Angela (wri): The Company Of Wolves
Carter, Ann (act): A Connecticut Yankee In King Arthur's Court (1949); Curse Of The Cat People; The Two Mrs. Carrolls
Carter, Ben (act): Dark Alibi; Dressed To Kill (1941); The Scarlet Clue; Sleepers West
Carter, Bill (act): Il Planeta Degli Uomini Spenti
Carter, Claire (act): Blow Out
Carter, Dave (act): The Sexplorer
Carter, Deborah (act): Secrets Of The Phantom Caverns
Carter, Diane (act): The Alien's Return; The Dungeonmaster
Carter, Ellis (W.) (cin): The Curse Of The Undead; The Deadly Mantis; Diary Of A Madman; The Incredible Shrinking Man; The Land Unknown; The Leech Woman; The Mole People; The Monolith Monsters; Thief Of Damascus; The Wizard Of Baghdad
Carter, Finn (act): Tremors
Carter, Georgianna (act): Night Of The Blood-Beast
Carter, Harrison (wri): The Frozen Ghost
Carter, Harry (act): Black Widow (1954)
Carter, Helena (act, b. 1923, nee Helen Rickerts): Double Crossbones; Invaders From Mars (1953)
Carter, Hubert (act): The House Of Peril
Carter, Jack (act): Charlie Chan's Courage; The Octagon; Pocomania
Carter, Jack (act-comic, b. 1923): Alligator (1981); The Extraordinary Seaman; Human Feelings; The Resurrection Of Zachary Wheeler
Carter, James (L.) (cin): Don't Answer The Phone!; Leatherface: Texas Chainsaw Massacre III; Sweet Sixteen
Carter, Janis (act, 1914–1994, nee Janis Dremann): Framed; The Ghost That Walks Alone; The Girl In The Case; Just Off Broadway; Mark Of The Whistler; The Missing Juror; The Notorious Lone Wolf; One Mysterious Night; Power Of The Whistler; Secret Agent Of Japan
Carter, Jason (act): The Dark Dancer
Carter, Jim (act): Haunted Honeymoon (1986); Top Secret! (1984); The Witches (1990)
Carter, Joey (act): Around The World Under The Sea
Carter, John (act): The Andromeda Strain; Marooned; My Science Project
Carter, John N. (dir): Zombie Island Massacre
Carter, Julie (act): Mr. Moto Takes A Chance
Carter, Ken (act): I Was A Zombie For The F.B.I.
Carter, Laurence (act): The Boy Who Turned Yellow
Carter, Leslie (act): The Lifeguardsman
Carter, Lincoln J. (wri): The Eleventh Hour (1923)
Carter, Louise (act): The Mystery Of Edwin Drood (1935); Nancy Drew And The Hidden Staircase
Carter, Lynda (act, b. 1951): The New, Original Wonder Woman
Carter, Mel (act): The Cat From Outer Space
Carter, Michael (act): An American Werewolf In London; A Christmas Carol (1984); The Keep; Return Of The Jedi
Carter, Michael Patrick (act): Guess Who's Coming For Christmas?
Carter, Mitch (act): The First Power
Carter, Nancy (act): see Gombell, Minna
Carter, Nell (act, b. 1948): Modern Problems
Carter, Nina (act): An American Werewolf In London
Carter, Patrick (act): Blue Blood
Carter, Peter (dir): The Intruder Within; Rituals
Carter, Reginald (act): Dr. No
Carter, Ric (act): Howling III; The Punisher
Carter, Ron (act): End Of The World (1977)
Carter, Rosanna (act): The Brother From Another Planet
Carter, Terry (act): Abby; Battlestar Galactica
Carter, T.K. (act): The Thing (1982)
Carter, Trina (act): I Was A Zombie For The F.B.I.
Carter, Wylie (act): Capture That Capsule!
Carteris, Gabrielle (act): Raising Cain
Cartier, Francois (act): Modern Problems
Cartier, Rudolph (wri): Corridor Of Mirrors
Cartland, Barbara (wri, b. 1901): A Ghost In Monte Carlo
Carton, R.C. (wri): The Ashes Of Revenge
Cartwright, Angela (act, b. 1952): Beyond The Poseidon Adventure
Cartwright, Hank (act): Child Of Darkness, Child Of Light
Cartwright, Jean (act): Magic Spectacles
Cartwright, Lynn (act): The Lucifer Complex; Queen Of Outer Space; Something Evil; The Wasp Woman
Cartwright, Nancy (act): Flesh & Blood
Cartwright, Peggy (act): Robin Hood Jr. (1923)
Cartwright, Troy (act): Tales From The Hood
Cartwright, Veronica (act): Alien; The Birds; Candyman: Farewell To The Flesh; Flight Of The Navigator; Hitler's Daughter; Invasion Of The Body Snatchers (1978); The Lottery; Nightmares (1983); The Witches Of Eastwick
Carty, Todd (act): Krull
Caruana, Michael (act): Bay Coven
Caruso, Anthony (act, b. 1913): Blackbeard The Pirate; Bride Of Vengeance; Crime Doctor's Courage; Desert Legion; Most Dangerous Man Alive; Phantom Of The Rue Morgue; Raiders Of The Seven Seas
Caruso, David (act): Jade
Caruso, John (act): Making Contact
Caruso, Mickey (act): Invasion Of The Bee Girls; The Ultimate Warrior
Carvahal, Carl (cin): Most Dangerous Man Alive
Carvajal, Alfonso (act): Beast Of Blood; Mad Doctor Of Blood Island
Carver, Alex (wri): Endgame
Carver, Brent (act): Millennium; Whiskers
Carver, Lynne (act, 1917–1955): A Christmas Carol (1938)
Carver, Mary (act): Arachnophobia; Through The Magic Pyramid
Carver, Nona (act): Terrified
Carver, Steve (dir): The Arena (1973)
Carver, Tina (act): From Hell It Came; The Man Who Turned To Stone
Carwardine, Richard (act): Dr. Faustus
Cary, Christopher (act): Beyond The Universe; Captain America II; The Mask Of Sheba; Mind Over Murder; Planet Earth; The Sword And The Sorcerer
Cary, Claiborne (act): Doctor Franken
Cary, Falkland (wri): The Hypnotist (1957)
Cary, Jill (act): In The Devil's Garden
Cary, Tristam (mus): Blood From The Mummy's Tomb; The Lady Killers (1956); Quatermass And The Pit
Casal, Antonio (act): Faustina; Mi Adorable Esclava; La Torre De Los Siete Jorobados
Casal, Maria (act): Hundra
Casale, Gerald V. (mus): Slaughterhouse Rock
Casalini, Dario (act): Demons 2
Casanova, Tony (mus): Diary Of A High School Bride
Casaravilla, Carlos (act): La Cara Del Terror; Fangs Of The Living Dead; Pyro
Casares, Maria (act, b. 1922, nee Maria Casares Quiroga): Orphee; Le Testament D'orphee
Casas, Antonio (act): Los Muertos No Perdonan; Sound Of Horror; Tristana
Casas, Fernando Izcaino (wri): Battle Of The Amazons
Casci, David (wri): The Pagemaster
Casconi, Michael (act): Night Of The Zombies (1981)
Case, Allen (act): The Magician (1973); The Man From Atlantis
Case, Catherine (act): Dr. Caligari
Case, David (wri): —And Now The Screaming Starts!
Case, Geoffrey (act): Trog
Case, Gerald (act): The Candlelight Murder; Cloudburst; Murder On Monday; Museum Mystery; Vampyres...Daughters Of Dracula
Case, Justin (act): Hamlet (1990); Return To Oz; Superman III
Case, Kathleen (act): Calling Homicide
Case, Marianna (act): Dimension 5
Case, Russell (act): The Fifth Missile; Warriors Of The Wasteland
Case, Tom (act): Moontrap
Casella, Alberto (wri): Death Takes A Holiday (1934 & 1971)
Casella, Martin (act): Robocop 2
Casella, Max (act): Ed Wood
Casellato, Gigi (act): Deborah
Casenave, Jeannette (act): Oh Heavenly Dog; Rabid
Caserini, Mario (dir, 1874–1920): Lucrezia Borgia (1910); Macbeth (1909); I Tre Moschettieri; Gli Ultima Giorni Di Pompei (1913)
Casetti, Tiziana (act): The Minotaur
Casey, Bernie (act): Dr. Black Mr. Hyde; Gargoyles; In The Mouth Of Madness; It Happened At Lake Wood Manor; The Man Who Fell To Earth (1976); Never Say Never Again
Casey, Brenda (act): Strange Behavior
Casey, Dolores (act): Arrest Bulldog Drummond
Casey, Kimberley (act): Phoenix The Warrior
Casey, Richard (dir): Hellbent
Casey, Sally (act): Mars Needs Women
Casey, Sue (act): Beach Girls And The Monster; Evilspeak; The Scarf
Casey, Taggart (act): It Conquered The World
Casey, Thomas (wri): Flesh Feast
Cash, Aubrey (wri): Danger By My Side
Cash, "Bubbles" (act): Mars Needs Women
Cash, Cindy (act): The Cradle Will Fall
Cash, Jim (wr): Anaconda
Cash, Renata (act): La Figlia Di Frankenstein
Cash, Rosalind (act, 1938–1995): The Adventures Of Buckaroo Banzai; Dr. Black Mr. Hyde; The Offspring; The Omega Man; Tales From The Hood
Cashdollar, Gary (act): Critters 2: The Main Course
Casher, Del (mus): Nightmare Sisters
Casimir, Golda (act): Berserk; The Black Windmill
Casini, Stefania (act): Suspiria
Casnoff, Philip (act): Message From Space; Special Report: Journey To Mars
Caso, Alan (cin): A Deadly Vision; The Presence; Stepfather III: Father's Day; Summer Of Fear
Cason, Barbara (act, 1929–1990): She's Dressed To Kill
Cason, John (act): Voodoo Tiger
Caspary, Katrina (act): Mac And Me
Caspary, Vera (wri, 1900–1987): Bedelia; Laura
Casper, Billy (act): Now You See Him, Now You Don't
Casper, Robert (act): Demon And The Mummy
Casperson, Debbie (act): Flight Of The Navigator
Cass, Dave (act): The Boy Who Cried Werewolf; Endangered Species
Cass, Henry (dir, b. 1902): Blood Of The Vampire; The Hand (1960); Last Holiday
Cass, Henry (wri, b. 1902): The Earth Dies Screaming
Cass, Maurice (act): Charlie Chan At The Opera; The Lone Wolf In Paris; The Notorious Lone Wolf; The Son Of Monte Cristo
Cassady, Bill (act): The Amazing Colossal Man
Cassady, John (act): Highlander; Superman (1978)
Cassarino, Richard (act): The Hideous Sun Demon
Cassarino, Stephen J. (act): Princess Warrior
Cassavetes, John (act, 1929–1989): The Fury; Incubus (1982); Rosemary's Baby
Cassavetes, Nick (act): The Wraith
Cassel, Jean-Pierre (act, b. 1932, nee Jean-Pierre Crochon): The Discreet Charm Of The Bourgeoisie; The Killing Game; Mr. Frost; Murder On The Orient Express; Notorious (1992); The Phantom Of The Opera (1990); The Three Musketeers (1974)
Cassel, Judy (act): The Mummy And The Curse Of The Jackals
Cassel, Sandra (act): The Last House On The Left
Cassel, Seymour (act): Angel On My Shoulder (1980); Dick Tracy (1990); Ravagers; When Pigs Fly; Wicked Stepmother
Cassel, Wally (act): The Thin Man Goes Home
Cassell, Robert (act): Quarantine
Cassidy, B. Arthur (wri): Man Beast
Cassidy, David (act, b. 1950): The Spirit Of '76
Cassidy, Ed(ward) (act): Devil Bat's Daughter; The Mad Monster; Talk About A Stranger
Cassidy, Jack (act, 1927–1976): The Eiger Sanction; The Phantom Of Hollywood
Cassidy, Joanna (act, b. 1944): Blade Runner; Chain Reaction (1996); The Cursed Medallion; Invitation To Hell; She's Dressed To Kill; Vampire In Brooklyn; Wheels Of Terror; Who Framed Roger Rabbit
Cassidy, Matt (act): Roger Corman's 'Frankenstein Unbound'
Cassidy, Michael (act): Deadly Messages
Cassidy, Patrick (act): Hitler's Daughter; Love At Stake; Midnight Offerings
Cassidy, Rice (act): The Scarlet Letter (1922)
Cassidy, Susan (act): Torture Dungeon
Cassidy, Ted (act, 1933–1979): Genesis II; Halloween With The Addams Family; Planet Earth
Cassie, Iain (wri): Xtro
Cassinelli, Claudio (act, 1939–1985): The Adventures Of Hercules; The Fish Men; The Great Alligator; Hercules (1983); Il Montagna Di Dio Cannibale
Cassinelli, Dolores (act): The Midnight Girl
Cassini, Frank (act): Timecop
Cassini, John (act): Man's Best Friend; Seven
Cassini, Nadia (act): Star Crash

Cassini, Stefania (act): *Dracula (1974)*
Cassner, Sergio (wri): *Mark Of The Devil (1972)*
Casson, Anne (act): *Number 17*
Casson, Christopher (act): *Zardoz*
Casson, Lewis (act): *Crime On The Hill*
Cast, Edward (act): *Deadly Record; Person Unknown; Quest For Love*
Castagnoli, Fabrizia (act): *The Great Alligator*
Castaldi, Eileen Nad (act): *The Toxic Avenger*
Castaldi, Jean-Pierre (act): *Caravan To Vaccares; Moonraker*
Castaldi, Nathan Jon (act): *The Toxic Avenger*
Castaneda, Luis Aceves (act): *La Momia Contra El Robot Humano*
Castel, Colette (act): *Aimez-Vous Les Femmes?*
Castel, Lou (act): *Orgasmo; Rorret; The Scarlet Letter (1972)*
Castell, Andrew (act): *Jekyll And Hyde*
Castellani, Renato (dir, b. 1913): *Ghosts-Italian Style*
Castellano, Giuseppe (act): *The Fish Men*
Castellano, John (act): *Mother's Day*
Castellanos, Julio (act): *Hundra*
Castellanos, Vincent (act): *Anaconda*
Castellari, Enzo G./Girolami (dir): *Escape From The Bronx; Great White; Johnny Hamlet; Sinbad And The Seven Seas*
Castellari, Enzo G./Girolami (wri): *Escape From The Bronx; Johnny Hamlet*
Castelli, Giuseppe (act): *Deborah*
Castelli, Philippe (act): *Aimez-Vous Les Femmes?*
Castello, William (act): *Phantom Of Chinatown*
Castelnuovo, Nino (act): *Les Parapluies De Cherbourg*
Castiglioni, Iphigenie (act): *Conquest Of Space; Rear Window*
Castillo, Candy (act): *The Alien's Return*
Castillo, Enrique (act): *Mars Attacks!*
Castillo, Gloria (act): *Invasion Of The Saucer Men; The Night Of The Hunter (1955); Teenage Monster*
Castillo, Susan (act): *Fire In The Sky (1993)*
Castle, Aimee (act): *Of Unknown Origin*
Castle, Alan (wri): *Stranded*
Castle, David (act): *Midnight Lace (1981)*
Castle, Dolores (act): *Jungle Goddess*
Castle, Don (act): *The Guilty; In Self Defense; The Invisible Wall; Perilous Waters*
Castle, Georgiana (act): *Bug*
Castle, Jane (cin): *Leprechaun 2*
Castle, John (act): *Never-Never Land*
Castle, Mary (act, b. 1931): *Crashing Las Vegas*
Castle, Mike (act): *Galaxina*
Castle, Nick (act): *Halloween*
Castle, Nick (dir & wri): *The Boy Who Could Fly; The Last Starfighter; Escape From New York*
Castle, Peggie (act, 1927–1973): *Back From The Dead; The Beginning Of The End; The Finger Man; Invasion U.S.A.; I, The Jury (1953); The Long Wait; The White Orchid*
Castle, Roy (act): *Dr. Terror's House Of Horrors (1964); Dr. Who And The Daleks; Legend Of The Werewolf*
Castle, William (act, 1914–1979): *Shanks*
Castle, William (dir, 1914–1979): *The Busy Body; The Chance Of A Lifetime; Crime Doctor's Gamble; Crime Doctor's Manhunt; Crime Doctor's Warning; The Gentleman From Nowhere; Homicidal; House On Haunted Hill; I Saw What You Did (1965); Just Before Dawn (1946); Let's Kill Uncle; Macabre (1958); Mark Of The Whistler; Mr. Sardonicus; The Mysterious Intruder; The Night Walker; The Old Dark House (1963); Project X (1967); The Saracen Blade; Shanks; Slaves Of Babylon; The Spirit Is Willing; Strait-Jacket; 13 Frightened Girls; 13 Ghosts; The Tingler; The Voice Of The Whistler; Zotz!*
Castle, Wiliam (wri, 1914–1979): *Bug*
Castleton, Paul (wri): *The Bandit Of Sherwood Forest*
Castro, David (act): *Cavegirl (1985)*
Castro, German (act): *Dr. Tarr's Torture Dungeon*
Castro, Jack (act): *Dead Of Night (1987)*
Castro, Jay (act): *Secrets Of The Phantom Caverns*
Castronova, Tom (act): *Distortions*
Caswell, Ozzie (mus): *Bomba And The Hidden City; The Lost Volcano*
Catala, Muriel (act): *Faustine Et Le Bel Ete*
Catalano, Frank (act): *Dr. Strange*
Catching, Bill (act): *Fer-De-Lance*
Catching, Dottie (act): *Dead And Buried*
Catelot, Jacques (act): *Les Femmes S'en Balancent*
Cater, John (act): *The Abominable Dr. Phibes; Captain Kronos: Vampire Hunter; Dr. Phibes Rises Again; If It's A Man, Hang Up*
Cates, Joseph (dir): *Who Killed Teddy Bear?*
Cates, Madelyn (act): *The Devil And Max Devlin; Jekyll And Hyde... Together Again*
Cates, Phoebe (act, b. 1963): *Date With An Angel; Gremlins; Gremlins 2: The New Batch*
Cates, Steve (act): *Attack Of The Killer Tomatoes*
Cathay, James Earl (act): *Re-Animator*
Cathcart, Darrell (cin): *Final Exam; Wolfman (1979)*
Catherine, Susan (act): *Dr. Dracula*
Cathey, Reg E. (act): *Seven*
Cathie, Dermot (act): *They Came From Beyond Space*
Cathleen, Charlene (act): *Ghoulies*
Catlett, Mary Jo (act): *Blood Beach; Serial Mom*
Catlett, Walter (act, 1889-1960): *The Boy With Green Hair*
Catlin, Victoria (act): *Ghoulies; Howling V: The Rebirth; Maid To Order*
Catseli, Aleka (act): *Electra (1961)*
Catt, Dorothy (wri): *The Fall Of The House Of Usher (1950)*
Cattaneo, Bruno (act): *Don't Look Now*
Catto, Max (wri): *Daughter Of Darkness (1948); The Flanagan Boy*
Catton, Haji (act): *Demonoid*
Catton, Sandy (act): *Phantom Of The Paradise*
Cattrall, Kim (act): *Big Trouble In Little China; Deadly Harvest; Good Against Evil; Mannequin; Robin Cook's Invasion; Running Delilah; Split Second (1992); Star Trek Vi: The Undiscovered Country; Unforgettable*
Cauchoin, Lily (act): see Colbert, Claudette
Caudell, Lane (act): *Fugitive From The Empire; Satan's Cheerleaders*
Caulfield, Dan (act): *Tales From The Crypt*
Caulfield, Joan (act, 1922–1991): *Larceny; The Magician (1973); The Unsuspected*
Caulfield, Mason (act): *The Cremators*
Caulfield, Maxwell (act, b. 1960): *Electric Dreams; Fatal Sky; Sundown: The Vampire In Retreat; The Supernaturals; Waxwork II: Lost In Time*
Caunter, Julian (wri): *No Haunt For A Gentleman*
Caunter, Tony (act): *The Adding Machine; The Asphyx; Dark Water; The Mind Of Mr. Soames*
Caussimon, (Jean-Roger) (act): *L'auberge Rouge, Le Saint Mene La Dance*
Cauty, Leo (act): *A Newsboy's Christmas Dream*
Cavada, Alicia Fernandez (act): *Hundra*
Cavalcanti, (Alberto) (dir, 1897–1982): *Dead Of Night (1945); For Them That Trespass; The Monster Of Highgate Ponds; They Made Me A Fugitive*
Cavalier, Jason (act): *Screamers (1996)*
Cavallaro, A.A. (act): *Cavegirl (1985)*
Cavallaro, Gaylord (act): *Murder Reported*
Cavallone, Alberto (wri): *Ironmaster*
Cavan, James (act): *Parasite*
Cavanagh, James P. (wri): *Murder At The Gallop*
Cavanagh, Megan (act): *Robin Hood: Men In Tights*
Cavanagh, Paul (act, b. 1895): *The Bandits Of Corsica; Blonde Bait; Bride Of The Gorilla; The Four Skulls Of Jonathan Drake; Francis In The Haunted House; The House Of Fear (1945); House Of Wax; The Kennel Murder Case; The Man In Half Moon Street; The Man Who Turned To Stone; Port Sinister; Rogues Of Sherwood Forest; The Scarlet Claw; Secret Beyond The Door; She-Devil; The Strange Door; Tazan And His Mate; The Verdict; The Woman In Green*
Cavanaugh, Hobart (act, 1886–1950): *Black Angel (1946); Horror Island; Kismet (1944); A Midsummer Night's Dream (1935)*
Cavanaugh, Michael (act): *Dr. Scorpion*
Cavanaugh, Page (act): see Page Cavanaugh & his Trio
Cavani, Liliana (dir & wri, b. 1937): *The Night Porter*
Cavara, Paolo (dir): *The Black Belly Of The Tarantula*
Cavarozzi, Joyce (act): *The Attic*
Cavelli, Joseph (wri): *The Spy With My Face*
Cavellini, Ayn (act): *Beyond The Poseidon Adventure*
Cavender, Glen (act): *Torchy Plays With Dynamite; Torchy Runs For Mayor*
Cavendish, Brenda (act): *An American Werewolf In London*
Cavendish, Constance (act): *Mr. Sardonicus*
Cavendish, Kitty (act): *The Man Without A Soul*
Cavens, Al (act): *The Boy And The Pirates*
Cavestani, Frank (act): *The China Syndrome*
Cavett, Dick (act, b. 1936): *A Nightmare On Elm Street 3: Dream Warriors*
Ca Vinci, Elen (act): *Ghost Diver*
Cawdron, Robert (act): *The Candlelight Murder; October Moth; The Private Life Of Sherlock Holmes; Street Of Shadows; The Shuttered Room*
Cawthorn, James (wri): *The Land That Time Forgot*
Cawthorn, Joseph (act): *White Zombie*
Cawthorne, Alec (act): *Sleuth*
Cayetano, Calna (act): *The Ape Creature*
Caylor, Rose (wri): *Fingers At The Window*
Cayse, Harlo (act): *Invasion Of The Girl Snatchers*
Cayton, Elizabeth (act): *Slavegirls From Beyond Infinity*
Cazabon, John (act): *The Snake Woman*
Cazalet, Joe (act): *Wild Thing*
Cazelet, Isolde (act): *High Spirits*
Cazenove, Christopher (act, b. 1945): *Color Him Dead; Dead Man's Island; Mata Hari (1985); Royal Flash*
Ceballos, Rene (act): *The Fan*
Cebrian, Fernando (act): *Tristana*
Ceccaldi, Daniel (act): *El Mono Loco*
Cecchi, Nana (act): *Ladyhawke*
Cecchini, Mimi (act): *Eat And Run*
Cecconi, Aldo (act): *Behind The Mask Of Zorro; Il Trionfo Di Ercole*
Cecere, Tony (act): *Dead And Buried*
Cecil, Dorothy (act): *The Black Spider*
Cecil, Edward (act): *The Phantom Of The Opera (1925); Secrets Of The Night*
Cecil, Evelyn (act): *The Angel Of The Ward*
Cecil, Jonathan (act): *Catch Me A Spy; Dead Man's Folly; Otley*
Cecil, Nora (act): *A Night Of Mystery (1937); Seven Footprints To Satan; The Thin Man Goes Home*
Cedar, Jon (act): *Day Of The Animals; Kiss Daddy Goodbye; The Manitou; Time Travelers (1976)*
Cedar, Jon (wri): *The Manitou*
Cedar, Larry (act): *C.H.U.D. II; Donor; Dreamscape; Ghost Warrior; The Hidden; The London Connection; Philadelphia Experiment II*
Cederstrom, Ellen (act): *The Story Of Gosta Berling*
Ceelen, Aat (act): *The Lift*
Cegani, Elisa (act): *Perseus The Invincible; The Reluctant Saint*
Ceglia, Tom (cin): *The Lawnmower Man*
Ceily, Leonard (act): *The Grit Of A Dandy*
Cela, Violeta (act): *Conquest*
Celano, Guido (act): *Hipnosis; Il Ladro Di Venezia*
Celario, Mario (act): *Elvira, Mistress Of The Dark*
Cele, Henry (act): *The Ghost And The Darkness*
Celedonio, Maria (act): *The Presence*
Celeste, Suzanne (act): *Curse II: The Bite*
Celestin, Jack (wri): *Crime On The Hill; The Crimes Of Stephen Hawke; The Gables Mystery; The Man At Six*
Celi, Adolfo (act, 1922–1986): *Diabolik; Fragment Of Fear; Hitler: The Last Ten Days; Holocaust 2000; Master Stroke; Murders In The Rue Morgue (1971); Operation Kid Brother; A Target For Killing; Ten Little Indians (1974); Thunderball*
Celio, Mary (act): *Impulse (1984)*
Cellier, Antoinette (act): *At The Villa Rose (1939); The Gables Mystery; I Killed The Count*
Cellier, Frank (act, 1884–1948): *The Clairvoyant (1934); The Man Who Changed His Mind; The Midas Touch; The Passing Of The Third Floor Back (1935); The Spider (1939); The 39 Steps (1935)*
Cellier, Peter (act): *Holocaust 2000*
Celluci, Claire (act): *Clarence*
Celozzi, Nicholas (act): *Slaughterhouse Rock*
Cembrzynska, Iga (act): *Rekopis Znaleziony W Saragossie*
Cendrars, Blaise (act): *J'accuse (1918)*
Centa (act): *Le Salaire De La Peur*
Centenera, Andres/Andy (act): *Beyond Atlantis; Twilight People*
Centeno, Laura (act): *Shock Chamber*
Centeno, Raul (wri): *El Ataud Del Vampiro; El Hombre Y El Monstruo*
Cepek, Petr (act): *Gentlemen, I Have Killed Einstein*
Cerbonnet, Frederique (act): *Perceval*
Cerchio, Carlo (cin): *Rorret*
Cerchio, Fernando (dir): *The Last Musketeer; Nefertite, Regina Del Nilo*
Cerf, Norman A. (dir & wri): *Jungle Hell*
Cernan, Eugene A. (act): *For All Mankind*
Cernocka, Petra (act): *Girl On A Broom*
Cerny, Daniel (act): *Children Of The Corn III: Urban Sacrifice*
Cerny, Frantisek (act): *Cisaruv Pekar, Pekaruv Cisar*
Cerrella, Ginny (wri): *Sister, Sister*
Certes, Andre (act): *Le Testament Du Dr. Cordelier*
Cerullo, Al (act): *Eraser*
Cerusico, Enzo (act): *The Dead Are Alive; Hercules, Samson And Ulysses; Zorro (1975)*
Cervantes, Arthur "Turko" (act): *Dance Of The Dwarfs*
Cervantes, Carlos (act): *Secrets Of The Phantom Caverns; Wheels Of Terror*
Cervera Jr., Jorge (act): *Tarantulas: The Deadly Cargo*
Cervi, Bruce (act): *Joe & The Colonel*
Cervi, Gino (act, 1901–1974): *Les Miserables (1943); Mistress Of The World (1959); Ok, Nero!; Queen Of Sheba; Siege Of Syracuse*
Cesar, Julio (act): *The Bees*
Cestare, John (act): *Doomsday Machine*
Cey, Jacques (act): *Lady In The Fog; Links Of Justice; Return From The Ashes; Zex*
Chaback, J.J. (act): *Outbreak*
Chaber, M.E. (wri): *The Man Inside*
Chabing (act): *The Chinese Ring; The Shanghai Chest*
Chabrol, Claude (dir, b. 1930): *The Blue Panther; Le Boucher; Code Name: Tiger; Dr. M; Landru; Leda; Le Scandale; Violette Noziere; Wedding In Blood*
Chace, H. Haile (wri): *The Monster Of Piedras Blancas*
Chachornia, Constantine (wri): *Pumpkinhead II: Blood Wings*
Chachornia, Ivan (wri): *Pumpkinhead II: Blood Wings*
Chacko, Lori (act): *Dr. Caligari*
Chadbon, Tom (act): *The Beast Must Die; Electric Eskimo*
Chadbourne, Eugene (act): *Shocker*
Chadwick, Cyril (act): *Peter Pan; Temple Tower; The Thirteenth Chair (1929)*
Chadwick, June (act): *Distortions; Evil Below; Forbidden World; Headhunter; Sparkling Cyanide*
Chadwick, Marc (act): *Daylight*
Chadwick, Robin (act): *Hamlet (1969)*
Chaet, Mark (act): *The Haunted (1991)*
Chafe, Alfred (act): *Trauma (1963)*
Chaffee, Bob (act): *Secrets In The Attic*
Chaffey, Don (dir, b. 1917): *Chomps; Creatures The World Forgot; Jason And The Argonauts; The Man Upstairs; One Million Years B.C.; Persecution; The Three Lives Of Thomasina; Time Is My Enemy; The Viking Queen*
Chaffey, Don (wri, b. 1917): *The Man Upstairs*
Chagrin, Francis (mus, b. 1905): *An Inspector Calls; Last Holiday; The Snorkel*
Chagrin, Julian (act): *Alice's Adventures In Wonderland (1972)*
Chai, Lee (act): *Yongary, Monster From The Deep*
Chaia, Jorge (act): *Os Deuses E Os Mortos*
Chaikelson, Janice (act): *City On Fire*
Chaikelson, Steven (act): *City On Fire*
Chaiken, Ilene (wri): *Barb Wire*
Chailles, Joseph (act): *The Lone Wolf (1917)*
Chakiris, George (act, b. 1933): *The Big Cube; Jekyll And Hyde...Together Again; Pale Blood; Return To Fantasy Island; The Savage Curse*
Chakravarty, Khagesh (act): *Devi*
Chalee, William (act): *Billy The Kid Vs. Dracula; Moonchild*
Chalem, Brent (act): *The Monster Squad*
Chalfant, Kathleen (act): *Tales From The Darkside*
Chaliapin, Feodor (act, 1873–1938): *The Seventh Victim*
Chaliapin (Jr.), Feodor (act, 1905–1992): *Inferno (1979); The Name Of The Rose*
Chalk, Garry (act): *The Fly II; I Still Dream Of Jeannie; It (1990)*
Chalk, Harvey (act): *Curucu, Beast Of The Amazon; Love Slaves Of The Amazons*
Challenger, Rudy (act): *Change Of Mind*
Challenor, Pauline (act): *The House That Screamed*
Challis, Christopher (cin, b. 1919): *The Boy Who Turned Yellow; Catch Me A Spy; Chitty Chitty Bang Bang; A Dandy In Aspic; The Deep; The Elusive Pimpernel (1950); Evil Under The Sun; Footsteps In The Fog; The Little Prince; The Mirror Crack'd; The Private Life Of Sherlock Holmes; Return From The Ashes; Saadia; Top Secret! (1984)*
Challis, John (act): *Where Has Poor Mickey Gone?*
Challis, Tom (act): *The Fear (1994)*
Chalmers, Doreen (act): *Psycho IV: The Beginning*
Chalmers, Goring (wri): *The Stolen Plans*
Chalmers, Kitty (wri): *Cyborg (1989)*
Chalmers, Thomas (act): *Puritan Passions*

Chalupetz, Apollonia (act): see Negri, Pola
Chamarat, Georges (act): Diabolique (1955)
Chamberlain, Charles Agnew (wri): The Red House
Chamberlain, Cyril (act): The Bad Lord Byron; Blackmailed; Dead Men Are Dangerous; The Diamond; The Gamma People; The Net; Old Mother Riley's Jungle Treasure; Poison Pen; Scarlet Thread; Stop Press Girl
Chamberlain, Jan (act): Starship Invasions
Chamberlain, Lachelle (act): Captain America II
Chamberlain, Margaret (act): Tuck Everlasting
Chamberlain, Matthew (act): The Frighteners
Chamberlain, Richard (act, b. 1935): Allan Quatermain And The Lost City Of Gold; Bells (1983); The Count Of Monte Cristo (1975); King Solomon's Mines (1985); The Last Wave; Night Of The Hunter (1991); The Secret Of The Purple Reef; The Slipper And The Rose; The Swarm; The Three Musketeers (1974); The Towering Inferno
Chamberlain, Wilt (act, b. 1936): Conan The Destroyer
Chamberlin, Howland (act): Electric Dreams; Francis; The Web
Chamberlin, Jan (act): It Came Upon The Midnight Clear
Chamberlin, Mark (act): Ghost Story (1981)
Chambers, Bonita (act): The Premonition (1975)
Chambers, Cullen G. (act): Student Bodies
Chambers, David (act): Earthbound (1981)
Chambers, Elisabeth (act): Making Contact
Chambers, Everett (wri, b. 1926): Night Slaves
Chambers, John (act): Schlock
Chambers, Karl (act): Tomorrow
Chambers, Marilyn (act): Rabid
Chambers, Phil (act): The Mole People
Chambers, Stan (act): War Of The Colossal Beast
Chambers, Wheaton (act): The Baron Of Arizona; Between Midnight And Dawn; Crime Doctor's Gamble; Cyclotrode X; The Falcon In Hollywood; The Falcon Out West; Possessed (1947)
Chamblee, Robert (wri): The Killer Inside Me
Chambliss, Woodrow (act): The Devil's Rain; Gargoyles; Glen And Randa; Through The Magic Pyramid
Chaminade, Pierre (act): The Golden Mask
Champagne, Bob (act): Witchery
Champagne, Clarence (cin): Psycho
Champeaux, Albert (cin): Johnny The Giant Killer
Champion, Jean (act): Les Parapluies De Cherbourg
Champion, Marge (act, b. 1926): The Swimmer
Champion, Michael (act): Total Recall; When A Stranger Calls
Champion, Sandy-Alexander (act): The Munsters' Revenge
Champlin, Alice (act): The Power (1980)
Champreux, Jacques (act): Les Nuits Rouges
Champreux, Jacques (wri) Judex; The Mysterious Island Of Captain Nemo; Les Nuits Rouges
Chan, George (act): Song Of The Thin Man
Chan, Luke (act): The Chinese Cat; The Mysterious Mr. Wong
Chan, Michael Paul (act): Galaxis; The Goonies; Runaway
Chan, Spencer (act): The Chinese Ring
Chan, Wong Han (act): Legend Of The Seven Golden Vampires
Chance, The (mus): Outer Touch
Chance, Michael (act): 12 Monkeys
Chance, Naomi (act): The Man Inside; The Saint's Return; Suspended Alibi
Chancer, Norman (act): Outland
Chandlee, Harry (wri): Tarzan's Magic Fountain
Chandler, Barry (act): The Devil's Gift
Chandler, Chick (act, b. 1905): The Great Rupert; I Wake Up Screaming; Lost Continent (1951); Mr. Moto Takes A Chance; Murder On A Honeymoon; Nightmare In The Sun; Seven Doors To Death
Chandler, Dan (act): The Night Of The Claw
Chandler, David (wri): You Never Can Tell
Chandler, Don (cin): The Night Of The Claw
Chandler, Eddie/Eddy (act): The Chance Of A Lifetime; Charlie Chan In The Secret Service; The Lone Wolf Returns (1935); Torchy Blane In Chinatown; Torchy Plays With Dynamite
Chandler, Estee (act): Teen Wolf Too
Chandler, Evan (wri): Robin Hood: Men In Tights
Chandler, George (act, 1899–1985): Castle In The Desert; Charlie Chan At The Olympics; The Chinese Cat; Dead Ringer; The Ghost And Mr. Chicken; The Kennel Murder Case; Mr. Moto Takes A Vacation; Nightmare Alley; Strange Confession
Chandler, Helen (act, 1909–1968): Dracula (1931, English-Speaking Version); Outward Bound
Chandler, Jared (act): Blood Diner
Chandler, Jeff (act): Deported; Flame Of Araby; Smuggler's Island; The Tattered Dress
Chandler, Jeffrey (act): A High Wind In Jamaica
Chandler, Joan (act, 1923–1979): How To Make A Monster; Rope
Chandler, John (act): Crash And Burn; Moon Of The Wolf; Phantasm III: Lord Of The Dead; Trancers II: The Return Of Jack Deth
Chandler, John Davis (act): The Sword And The Sorcerer
Chandler, Karen Mayo (act): Party Line
Chandler, Lane (act, b. 1899): Charlie Chan In Panama; Creature With The Atom Brain; The Dark Mirror (1946); Flesh And Fantasy; The Lone Ranger; The Lone Wolf And His Lady; Return To Treasure Island; Samson And Delilah; Space Master X-7
Chandler, Michael (act): Anguish
Chandler, Patti (act): Dr. Goldfoot And The Bikini Machine; The Million Eyes Of Sumuru
Chandler, Raymond (wri, 1888–1959): The Big Sleep (1946 & 1978); The Brasher Doubloon; The Falcon Takes Over; Farewell, My Lovely; Lady In The Lake; Murder, My Sweet; Strangers On A Train; Time To Kill (1942)
Chandler, Tanis (act): Dick Tracy (1945); Lured; Shadows Over Chinatown; 16 Fathoms Deep; The Trap
Chandler, Vivienne (act): A Clockwork Orange
Chandos, John (act): 49th Parallel; The Green Man; I Accuse (1958); Thirty-Six Hours
Chandre (act): Pranks
Chanel, Helene (act): Hercules Of The Desert; Maciste Al Inferno; Operation Counterspy; Terror Of The Black Mask
Chanel, Tally (act): Warrior Queen
Chaney, Jason (act): The Outing
Chaney, Lesley (act): The Outing
Chaney (Sr.), Lon (act, 1883–1930): Bits Of Life; The Black Bird (1926); A Blind Bargain; The Chimney's Secret; The False Faces; He Who Gets Slapped; The Hunchback Of Notre Dame (1923); Laugh, Clown, Laugh; London After Midnight; The Miracle Man (1919); Mr. Wu (1927); Mockery; The Monster (1925); Outside The Law; The Penalty; The Phantom Of The Opera (1925); The Road To Mandalay; The Shock (1923); The Tower Of Lies; Treasure Island (1920); The Unholy Three (1925 & 1930); The Unknown (1927); West Of Zanzibar; Where East Is East; While Paris Sleeps
Chaney (Sr.), Lon (dir & wri): The Chimney's Secret
Chaney Jr., Lon (act, 1907–1973): Abbott And Costello Meet Frankenstein; The Alligator People; The Battles Of Chief Pontiac; The Black Castle; The Black Pirates; The Black Sleep; Bride Of The Gorilla; Calling Dr. Death; La Casa Del Terror; Charlie Chan In City In Darkness; Charlie Chan On Broadway; Cobra Woman; Crazy House (1943); The Cyclops; Dead Man's Eyes; The Devil's Messenger; Dracula vs. Frankenstein; Eyes Of The Underworld; The Female Bunch; Fireball Jungle; Frankenstein Meets The Wolf Man; The Frozen Ghost; Gallery Of Horror; Ghost Catchers; The Ghost Of Frankenstein; The Haunted Palace (1963); Hillbillys In A Haunted House; House Of Dracula; House Of Frankenstein; House Of The Black Death; Indestructible Man; Jivaro; Manfish; Man-Made Monster; Mr. Moto's Gamble; The Most Dangerous Game; The Mummy's Curse; The Mummy's Ghost; The Mummy's Tomb; Night Of The Beast; Night Of The Ghouls; Of Mice And Men (1939); One Million B.C.; Pillow Of Death; Raiders Of The Seven Seas; Scream In The Night; Sharad Of Atlantis; 16 Fathoms Deep; Son Of Dracula (1943); Spider Baby; Strange Confession; Thief Of Damascus; Weird Woman; Witchcraft (1964); The Wolf Man (1941)
Chaney, Warren (act & wri): The Outing
Chang, Gary (mus): Donor; Firewalker; Full Eclipse; The Island Of Dr. Moreau (1996)
Chang, Lia (act): Frankenhooker; Wolf
Chang, Paul (act): The Million Eyes Of Sumuru
Chang, Ray (act): Strange Days
Chang, Vincent (act): Manfish
Chang, Wah (cin): Atlantis, The Lost Continent; Dinosaurus!; The Time Machine (1960)
Chang-Ho, Lee (dir): The Man With Three Coffins
Channing, Carissa (act): Frankenhooker
Channing, Carol (act): Alice In Wonderland (1985)
Channing, Margo (act): Sleuth
Channing, Ruth (act): The Thin Man
Channing, Stockard (act, b. 1944): Meet The Applegates
Chanslor, Roy (wri): Black Angel (1946); Destiny (1944); The House Of Fear (1945); The Steel Key; Tarzan Triumphs
Chantler, David (T.) (wri): Cash On Demand; She (1965)
Chao, Harvey (act): Conundrum
Chao, Rosalind (act): The Chinese Web; Special Report: Journey To Mars; The Ultimate Impostor
Chao-Lichi (act): Fugitive From The Empire
Chapek, Peter (act): I Still Dream Of Jeannie
Chapin, Billy (act): The Night Of The Hunter (1955); Tobor The Great
Chapin, Doug (act): Ladybug, Ladybug
Chapin, Jonathan (act): Twice Dead
Chapin, Miles (act): The Funhouse (1981); Howard The Duck; Pandemonium
Chapin, Summer-Healy (act): Matinee
Chapin, Tom (act): Lord Of The Flies (1963)
Chaplin, Charles (act, dir & wri, 1889–1977): His Prehistoric Past; Modern Times
Chaplin Jr., Charles (act): Follow The Hunter; Sex Kittens Go To College
Chaplin, Geraldine (act, b. 1944): Gulliver's Travels (1996); Honeycomb; I Killed Rasputin; Jane Eyre (1996); The Mirror Crack'd; The Odyssey; Stranger In The House (1967); The Three Musketeers (1974); Z.P.G.
Chaplin, Jennifer (act): Zapped!
Chaplin, Josephine (act): Jack The Ripper (1979); Les Nuits Rouges
Chaplin, Paul (wri): Mystery Science Theater 3000: The Movie
Chaplin, Prescott (wri): Island Of Lost Women
Chaplin, Sydney (act, b. 1926): The Adding Machine; The Deadliest Sin; Land Of The Pharaohs; Satan's Cheerleaders; The Woman Hunter
Chapman, Alexander (act): Wild Thing
Chapman, Alexander Bacon (act): The Lost Boys
Chapman, Andi (act): Once You Meet A Stranger; Something Is Out There
Chapman (Jr.), Ben(jamin F.) (act): Creature From The Black Lagoon; Jungle Moon Men
Chapman, Brock (act): Unforgettable
Chapman, Constance (act): Doomwatch
Chapman, Edward (act, b. 1901): Hide And Seek; Law And Disorder; Man On The Run; The Man Who Could Work Miracles; The Man Who Haunted Himself; Murder; The October Man; Poison Pen; The Ringer (1952); Someone At The Door; The Spider And The Fly; Things To Come; X... The Unknown
Chapman, Edythe (act): Bits Of Life
Chapman, Eric (act): Pyro
Chapman, Freddye (act): Tomorrow's Child
Chapman, Graham (act, 1941–1989): The Magic Christian; Monty Python And The Holy Grail
Chapman, Graham (wri, 1941–1989): Monty Python And The Holy Grail; Rentadick
Chapman, Joseph (act): Final Eye; Killer In The Mirror
Chapman, Judith (act): Scalpel
Chapman, Leigh (wri): The Octagon
Chapman, Lonny (act): The Birds; The Screaming Woman; Terror Out Of The Sky
Chapman, Margaret (act): No Blade Of Grass
Chapman, Mark Lindsay (act): American Gothic; The Annihilator; Night Visions
Chapman, Marguerite (act, b. 1916): The Amazing Transparent Man; The Body Disappears; Charlie Chan At The Wax Museum; Flight To Mars; Mr. District Attorney; One Dangerous Night; Spy Smasher Returns
Chapman, Michael (act): Gotham
Chapman, Michael (cin): Ghostbusters II; Gotham; Invasion Of The Body Snatchers (1978); The Lost Boys; The Man With Two Brains; Primal Fear; Scrooged; Space Jam
Chapman, Michael (dir): The Annihilator; The Clan Of The Cave Bear
Chapman, Priscilla (wri): The Fan
Chapman, Robert (wri): Murder Reported
Chapman, Ron (cin): Class Of Nuke'em High, Part II: Subhumanoid Meltdown
Chapman, [illegible] (cin): Pumpkinhead; Hellraiser II; Hellraiser; Transmutations
Chapman, Tim (act): Empire Of Ash III
Chapman, Tom (wri): The Boogens; Hangar 18; The Legend Of Sleepy Hollow
Chapman, Vic (act): —And Now The Screaming Starts!
Chappel, Melissa (act): Inn Of The Damned
Chappel, Robert (cin): Spookies
Chappell, Anna (act): Mountaintop Motel Massacre
Chappell, Bertram (mus): Licensed To Kill
Chappell, Diana (act): The Fiend (1972)
Chappell, John (act): Kiss Meets The Phantom Of The Park; My Best Friend Is A Vampire
Chappell, William (act): The Trial
Chappelle, Dave (act): The Nutty Professor (1996); Robin Hood: Men In Tights
Chappelle, Joe (dir): Halloween: The Curse Of Michael Myers
Chappelle, Tom (act): Flesh-Eating Mothers
Chapple, Geoff (wri): The Navigator: An Odyssey Across Time
Chapple, Susan (act): Quarantine
Chappuis, Alan (act): The Octagon
Charbonneau, Anne (act): The Toxic Avenger, Part II
Charbonneau, Doc D. (act): Cameron's Closet
Charbonneau, Patricia (act): Brain Dead
Chard, Dave (act): Inn Of The Damned
Chard, Marjorie (act): Inside The Room
Chardynin, Pyotr (dir & wri): Pikovaya Dama (1910)
Charet, Francois (act): Les Parapluies De Cherbourg
Chargonin, Alexander (act & dir): Sonka Zolotaya Ruchka
Charise, Andre (act): Return From The Ashes
Charisse, Cyd (act, b. 1922, nee Tula Ellice Finkles): It's Always Fair Weather; Maroc 7; The Silencers (1966); Three Wise Fools; Warlords Of The Deep
Charles, Alan (act): Whirlpool
Charles, Charlie (act): Heaven Can Wait (1978)
Charles, Cindy (act): Attack Of The Killer Tomatoes
Charles, Colin (act): Greystoke: The Legend Of Tarzan, Lord Of The Apes
Charles, Ernest A. (wri): Point Of Terror
Charles, Frank (wri): Danger Tomorrow
Charles, John (act): Buried Treasure
Charles, John (mus): The Quiet Earth
Charles, Josh (act): Crossworlds; The Grave
Charles, Lewis (act, 1916–1979): 48 Hours To Live; I Love A Mystery (1966); Our Man Flint; The Three Stooges Meet Hercules; To Catch A Thief; Topaz
Charles, Marion (act): Soylent Green
Charles, Moie (wri): Bedelia; Dark Secret; Scarlet Thread
Charles, Nancy Linehan (act): Bram Stoker's 'Dracula'
Charles, Olivia (act): Shadow Of A Doubt (1991)
Charles, Paul (act): Never-Never Land
Charles, Robert (wri): Return Of The Ape Man; Voodoo Man
Charles, Rudolph (act): Tarzan's Deadly Silence
Charles, Sandy (act): Sweet Sixteen
Charles, Theresa (wri): The Woman With No Name
Charles, Vernon (act): The Fall Of The House Of Usher (1950)
Charles, Zachary B. (act): Asteroid
Charleson, Ian (act, 1949–1990): Greystoke: The Legend Of Tarzan, Lord Of The Apes; Terror At The Opera
Charleson, Leslie (act): The Day Of The Dolphin
Charleson, Ray (act): Fatal Sky; Hawk The Slayer; Prisoners Of The Lost Universe; Shock Treatment! (1981)
Charles-Williams, Liz (wri): Deadlier Than The Male; Some Girls Do
Charlesworth, John (act): The Adventures Of Hal 5; Date At Midnight; The Oracle (1952); Scrooge (1951)
Charlie (act): Meridian
Charlita (act): Billy The Kid vs. Dracula; The Boys From Brooklyn
Charlot (act): The Face At The Window (1932)
Charlot Girls, The (act): Elstree Calling
Charlot, Andre (act, b. 1882): The Falcon's Brother; The Falcon Strikes Back; Temptation (1946)
Charlot, Andre (dir): Elstree Calling
Charlot, Kawena (act): The Return Of The Six Million Dollar Man And The Bionic Woman
Charlots, Les (act): Bon Baisers De Hong Kong
Charlton, Althea (act): Someone At The Top Of The Stairs
Charlton, Elizabeth (act): Space Raiders
Charmarat, George (act): The Thief Of Baghdad (1960)
Charney, Eva (act): My Demon Lover

Charney, Jordan (act): *Amazons (1984); Creator; The Plutonium Incident; Witches' Brew*
Charney, Kim (act): *The Werewolf (1955)*
Charney, Susan (act): *Garden Of The Dead*
Charno, Stu(art) (act): *Friday The 13th-Part 2; Once Bitten*
Charnota, Anthony (act): *Human Feelings; Looker*
Charrier, Jacques (act): *Le Plus Vieux Metier Du Monde*
Charrington, Arthur (act): *Thelma: Or, Saved From The Sea*
Charteris, Leslie (wri, 1907–1993): *The Fiction-Makers; The Saint; The Saint And The Brave Goose; The Saint In London; The Saint In New York; The Saint In Palm Springs; The Saint Meets The Tiger; Le Saint Mene La Dance; Le Saint Prend L'affut; The Saint's Double Trouble; The Saint's Return; The Saint Strikes Back; The Saint's Vacation; The Saint Takes Over; Vendetta For The Saint*
Charters, Rodney (cin): *Psycho IV: The Beginning; The Quilt Of Hathor; Sleepwalkers*
Charters, Spencer (act, 1878–1943): *The Bat Whispers; The Hunchback Of Notre Dame (1939); The Kennel Murder Case; Murder On A Bridle Path; Murder On A Honeymoon; The Raven (1935)*
Chartey, Alastair (act): *Wild Thing*
Chartier, Urbain (act): *Empire Of Ash III*
Chase, Alden (act): *Buried Alive (1940); Forty Naughty Girls*
Chase, Arthur (act): *The Children*
Chase, Barrie (act): *Cape Fear (1961)*
Chase, Barry (act): *The Sword And The Sorcerer*
Chase, Borden (wri, 1900–1971): *Blue, White And Perfect*
Chase, Carl (act): *Alien 3; Batman (1989)*
Chase, Channing (act): *The Annihilator*
Chase, Chevy (act, b. 1943): *Memoirs Of An Invisible Man; Modern Problems; Nothing But Trouble; Oh Heavenly Dog*
Chase, Chris (act): *All That Jazz*
Chase, Darel (act): *The Toxic Avenger, Part II*
Chase, David (act): *Trauma (1993)*
Chase, David (wri): *Demon And The Mummy; Grave Of The Vampire*
Chase, Frank (act): *Attack Of The 50-Foot Woman (1958); The Beginning Of The End; The Creature Walks Among Us*
Chase, Harry (act): *Making Mr. Right*
Chase, James (act): *Virgin Witch*
Chase, James Hadley (wri): *What Price Murder*
Chase, Jeffrey (act): *Scream Of The Demon Lover*
Chase, Jo Flores (act): *Demon (1976)*
Chase, John (act): *Boarding House*
Chase, Libbie (act): *Dracula's Dog; Mansion Of The Doomed*
Chase, Mary C. (wri, 1907–1981): *Harvey*
Chase, Stephan (act): *A Ghost In Monte Carlo*
Chase, Stephen (GB act): *Cry Of The Banshee; A Distant Scream; Macbeth (1971)*
Chase, Stephen (USA act): *When Worlds Collide*
Chase, Steven (act): *The Blob (1958)*
Chase, Thomas/Tom (mus): *Creature; Little Nemo: Adventures In Slumberland; 976-Evil; Scared To Death (1980)*
Chase, Tiffany Gautier (act): *The Savage Bees*
Chasen, Debbie (act): *Child's Play (1985)*
Chasen, Heather (act): *The Deadly Females*
Chase/Rucker Productions (mus): *Alien Predators*
Chaskin, David (wri): *The Curse; I, Madman; A Nightmare On Elm Street, Part 2: Freddy's Revenge*
Chason, Gary (act): *My Best Friend Is A Vampire*
Chason, Myra (act): *Condor*
Chassagne, Micheline (act): see Presle, Micheline
Chatelain, Helene (act): *La Jetee*
Chater, Geoffrey (act): *Endless Night; Look Back In Darkness; The Secret Life Of Ian Fleming; The Strange World Of Planet X; 10 Rillington Place*
Chatfield, Karen (act): *Forever Evil*
Chatfield, Lansdale (act): *The Witches Of Eastwick*
Chatham, Jack (act): *The Mutilator*
Chatman, Glenndon (act): *Eraser*
Chatrian (wri): *The Bells (1926 & 1931)*
Chattaway, Jay (mus): *Maniac (1980); Silver Bullet*
Chatterjee, Anil (act): *Devi*
Chatterjee, Soumitra (act, b. 1935): *Devi*
Chatterton, Ann-Leizabeth (act): *Hellhole*
Chattin, Sara (act): *Planet Earth*
Chattman, Dwayne (act): *Virtuosity*
Chatto, Tom (act): *The Curse Of The Golem; The Frozen Dead; In The Devil's Garden*
Chaudet, Louis (dir): *The Devil Bear*
Chauffard, Jacques-Rene (act): *Et Mourir De Plaisir*
Chaumeau, Andre (act): *Docteur Petiot; The Phantom Of The Opera (1990)*
Chautard, Emile (act): *The House Of Horror (1929)*
Chauvet, Elisabeth (act): *Rattlers*
Chauvin, Lilyan/Lylyan (act): *Bloodlust!; The Mephisto Waltz; Predator 2; Pumpkinhead II: Blood Wings; Silent Night, Deadly Night*
Chavance, Louis (wri): *Le Corbeau*
Chaves, Richard (act): *Predator*
Chavez, Frank (act): *Fire In The Sky (1993)*
Chavez, Gloria (act): *Survive!*
Chavez, Jose(ph) (act): *The Beast Of Hollow Mountain; Tarzan's Deadly Silence; El Vampiro*
Chavez, Julio C. (cin): *Death Curse Of Tartu*
Chavez, Marga (act): *Eve Of Destruction*
Chayefsky, Paddy (wri, 1923–1981, a.k.a. Sidney Aaron): *Altered States*
Chayette, Jeff (act): *Cavegirl (1985)*
Chaykin, Maury (act): *Cutthroat Island; Def Con 4; Millennium; Mr. Destiny; Of Unknown Origin; The Vindicator; Wild Thing*
Chaza, Kubi (act): *Live And Let Die*
Chazel, Louba (act): *The Tenant*
Chazel, Marie-Anne (act): *The Visitors (1993)*
Cheadle, Don (act): *The Meteor Man; Volcano*
Cheaney, Lois (act): *Torchy Gets Her Man; Torchy Plays With Dynamite*
Cheap Trick (mus): *Heavy Metal*
Cheatham, Jack (act): *The Dark Mirror (1946)*
Chebotaryov, Vladimir (dir): *The Amphibian Man*
Checchi, Andrea (act, 1916–1974): *La Maschera Del Demonio; Storm Bound*
Chechik, Jeremiah (dir): *Diabolique (1996)*
Chee, Sebastian (act): *Hardware*
Cheek, Douglas (dir): *C.H.U.D.*
Cheeseman, Patrick (act): see Wymark, Patrick
Cheesman, David (act): *Tennis Court*
Cheever, John (wri, 1912–1982): *The Swimmer*
Chefe, Jack (act): *Appointment With Murder; Dick Tracy (1945); Murder Is My Business*
Cheff, Andre (act): *L'auberge Rouge*
Chegwin, Jeffrey (act): *Egghead's Robot*
Chegwin, Keith (act): *Egghead's Robot; Macbeth (1971); Robin Hood Junior (1975)*
Cheirel, Micheline/Michel (act): *Close Call For Ellery Queen; Cornered; Crime Doctor's Gamble; Flight To Nowhere; So Dark The Night*
Chekhov, Anton Pavlovich (wri, 1860–1904): *I Tre Volti Della Paura*
Chekhov, Michael (act, 1891–1955): *Spellbound (1945)*
Cheling, George (act): *RoboCop 2*
Chelland, Frank (act): *To Catch A Thief*
Chelton, Tsilla (act): *Shanks*
Chen, China (act): *Friday The 13th-Part 2*
Chen, Joan (act): *The Blood Of Heroes; Judge Dredd; Precious Find*
Chen, Li (wri): *Goliathon*
Chen, Lily (act): *RoboCop 2*
Chen, Moira (act): *Endgame*
Chen, Stefanie J. (act): *The Handmaid's Tale*
Chen, Stephen (act): *Vampire's Kiss*
Chen, Tina (act): *The Ghost Of Flight 401; 3 Days Of The Condor*
Chenal, Pierre (dir & wri): *Nights Of Rasputin*
Chendrikova, Valentina (act): *The Savage Hunt Of King Stakh*
Cheney, "Bear" (act): *Wheels Of Terror*
Cheney, Max (act): *I Was A Zombie For The F.B.I.*
Cheng, Mary (act): *The Million Eyes Of Sumuru*
Cheng, Stephen (act): *Werewolf Of Washington*
Chepil, Bill (act): *Street Trash*
Cher (act, b. 1946): *The Witches Of Eastwick*
Chermak, Cy (wri): *4D Man*
Cherney, Linda (act): *Screaming Mimi*
Cherniavsky, Joseph (mus): *The Last Warning (1929)*
Chernuchin, Michael S. (wri): *Eraser*
Cheroka, Frank Robert (act): *The Wheel Of Death*
Cheron, Andre (act): *The Black Cat (1934)*
Cherques, George (act): *Killer Fish*
Cherrill, Virginia (act): *Charlie Chan's Greatest Case*
Cherrington, Ruth (act): *The Lone Wolf's Daughter (1929)*
Cherry, Helen (act): *The Devil's Agent; For Them That Trespass; A Ghost In Monte Carlo; Last Holiday; The Mark Of Cain; Three Cases Of Murder; The Woman With No Name*
Cherry, John (dir): *Ernest Saves Christmas*
Cherry, Najean (act): *Torment (1986)*
Cherry III, William T. (cin): *Screams Of A Winter Night*
Cherwin, Richard (mus): *The Vampire's Ghost*
Chesewright, Grahame (act): *The Scarab Murder Case*
Chesire, Denise (act): *Graduation Day*
Chesire, Elizabeth (act): *Strange Behavior*
Chesire, Geoffrey (act): *Daleks' Invasion Earth 2150 A.D.; On Her Majesty's Secret Service*
Chesire, Harry (act): *Nightmare Alley*
Chesler, Wayne (dir & wri): *The Hotel Manor Inn*
Chesnakov, Alexis (act): *The Third Man*
Chesney, Arthur (act): *Forging Ahead; The Lights O' London; The Lodger (1926)*
Chesney, Diana (act): *Switch; A Woman Of Mystery*
Chesney, Peter (cin): *The Night They Saved Christmas*
Chesnut, James (act): *The Dungeonmaster*
Chesser, Chris (act): *Night Of The Comet*
Chester the Chimp (act): *Five Weeks In A Balloon*
Chester, Colby (act): *Death Takes A Holiday (1971); The Munsters' Revenge*
Chester, George Randolph (wri): *The Altar Stairs*
Chester, Hal E. (wri): *Night Of The Demon (1957)*
Chester, Vanessa Lee (act, b. 1984): *The Lost World: Jurassic Park*
Chesterman, Ben (act): *Mad Max Beyond Thunderdome*
Chesterman, Dan (act): *Mad Max Beyond Thunderdome*
Chesterton, G.K. (wri, 1874–1936): *Sanctuary Of Fear*
Chetwynd-Hayes, R. (wri): *From Beyond The Grave*
Cheung, George Kee (act): *Galaxis*
Cheung, Jacky (act): *A Chinese Ghost Story II*
Cheung, Leslie (act): *A Chinese Ghost Story; A Chinese Ghost Story II*
Cheung, Margaret (act): *The Million Eyes Of Sumuru*
Cheung, Shelly (act): *Quarantine*
Chevalier, Albert (act): *The Woman In Question*
Chevalier, Catherine (act): *Hellbound: Hellraiser II; Nightbreed*
Chevalier, Maurice (act, 1888–1972): *In Search Of The Castaways; Love Me Tonight*
Chevalier, Pierre (dir): *Vous Pegez?*
Chevreau, Cecile (act): *Death In The Hand; Spaceways*
Chevret, Lita (act): *The Fatal Hour (1940)*
Chew (Jr.), Sam (act): *Rattlers; Time Walker*
Chew, Virgilia (act): *The Fugitive Kind*
Cheyaroon, Permphol (cin): *Night Creature*
Cheyne, Hank (act): *Deep Red (1994)*
Cheyney, Peter (wri): *A Toi De Faire, Migonne; Cet Homme Est Dangereux; Comment Qu'ella Est!; Les Femmes S'en Balancent; Lemmy Pour Les Dames; La Mome Vert-De-Gris; Vous Pegez?*
Chi, Chao-Li (act): *The Nutty Professor (1996); Warriors Of Virtue*
Chi, Greta (act): *Fathom*
Chia, Essie Lin (act): *Doomsday Machine*
Chia, Jeni (act): *Copycat*
Chiaki, Mindru (act): *Godzilla Raids Again*
Chianetta, Maria (wri): *The Great Alligator*
Chiang, David (act): *Legend Of The Seven Golden Vampires*
Chiang, George (act): *Charlie Chan And The Curse Of The Dragon Queen*
Chiantoni, Renato (act): *Demons Of The Dead; Robin Hood And The Pirates*
Chiao, Roy (act): *Indiana Jones And The Temple Of Doom*
Chiari, Walter (act, b. 1930): *Ok, Nero!*
Chiba, Shinichi (act): *Invasion Of The Neptune Men; Virus*
Chiba, Sonny ("J.J.") (act): *Immortal Combat; Message From Space; Terror Beneath The Sea*
Chicago, Sonny (act): *Princess Warrior*
Chichester, Leonard (act): *Witches' Brew*
Chicoine, Michael (act): *When Michael Calls*
Chidnoff, Hal (act): *Attack Of The Killer Tomatoes*
Chieffet, Alexis (act): *The Exorcist III*
Chieffo, Michael (act): *Alice In Wonderland (1985)*
Chiesa, Guila (act): *The Clan Of The Cave Bear*
Chiffre, Yvan (dir & wri): *Bon Baisers De Hong Kong*
Chihara, Michael (mus): *A Fire In The Sky (1978)*
Chihara, Paul (mus): *The Bad Seed (1985); The Darker Side Of Terror; Deathmoon; Death Race 2000; Dr. Strange; Haunted By Her Past; The Haunting Passion; Impulse (1984); Mind Over Murder*
Chikamatsu (wri): *Yoru No Tsuzumi*
Chilcott, Barbara (act): *The Full Treatment*
Chilcott, Robert (act): *Demons 2*
Child, Beth (act): *Razorback*
Child, Jeremy (act): *Privilege; Quest For Love*
Child, Julia (act, b. 1912): *We're Back! A Dinosaur's Story*
Child, Kirsty (act): *Picnic At Hanging Rock*
Child, Lincoln (wri): *The Relic*
Childers, Hary Ann (act): *Primal Fear*
Childerstone, Charles (act): *The Cry For Justice; The Thirteenth Candle*
Childs, Doug (act): *Moontrap*
Childs, Lucy (act): *Blink*
Chiles, Linden (act): *Forbidden World*
Chiles, Lois (act): *Coma; Creepshow 2; Curdled; Dark Mansions; Death On The Nile; Moonraker*
Chilton, John (act): *Project X (1987)*
Chilvers, Colin (cin): *Condorman; Incubus (1982); Saturn 3; Superman (1978); Superman II; Superman III*
Chimene, Andre (act): *The Outing*
Chin, Carol (act): *The Pink Chiquitas*
Chin, Cathleen (act): *Distortions*
Chin, Glen (act): *Jekyll And Hyde...Together Again*
Chin, Judy (act): *Street Trash*
Chin, Kevin (act): *Street Trash*
Chin, Susan (act): *The Hand That Rocks The Cradle*
Chin, Tsai (act, b. 1938): *The Blood Of Fu Manchu; The Brides Of Fu Manchu; The Castle Of Fu Manchu; The Face Of Fu Manchu; Invasion (1965); Long Distance; Rentadick; The Vengeance Of Fu Manchu; You Only Live Twice*
Chinchilla (act): *Treasure Island (1971)*
Chinchilla, Jose' (act): *Exterminators Of The Year 3000*
Ching, William (act, b. 1913): *D.O.A. (1949); Scared Stiff (1953); Terror In The Haunted House*
Chinh, Kieu (act): *The Lucifer Complex*
Chinlund, Nick (act): *Eraser*
Chinn, Allan (act): *The China Syndrome*
Chinn, Anthony (act): *The Abominable Snowman Of The Himalayas; The Kremlin Letter; Mark Of The Devil (1985); Raiders Of The Lost Ark*
Chinn, B. Cave (act): *Where The Rainbow Ends*
Chinn, Mimi (act): *Hardware*
Chinnery, Dennis (act): *The Plague Of The Zombies*
Chinney, Sandy (act): *Prey (1978)*
Chinyamurindi, Michael (act): *Congo*
Chiodo, Charles (act & wri): *Killer Klowns From Outer Space*
Chiodo, Stephen (dir & wri): *Killer Klowns From Outer Space*
Chionetti, Carlo (act): *Red Desert*
Chiquita (act): *Jaguar*
Chiquita the Wonder Chicken (act): *Dance Of The Dwarfs*
Chiquete, Charles (act): *Eraser*
Chirello, George (act): *Macbeth (1947)*
Chisays, Bobby (act): *Popcorn*
Chisholm, Arthur (act): *The Angel Of The Ward*
Chisholm, George (act): *Superman III*
Chism, Glenda (act): *Matinee*
Chisnell, Frank (dir): *It Happened In Soho*
Chiswick, Jeffrey (act): *Dreamchild*
Chittell, Christopher (act): *Are You Dying Young Man?*
Chitty, Erik (act): *First Men In The Moon (1964); The Flying Sorceror; Great Expectations (1974); The Horror Of It All; Jabberwocky; Lust For A Vampire; One Of Our Dinosaurs Is Missing; The Seven-Per-Cent Solution; The Vault Of Horror*
Chitwood, Joie (act): *Live And Let Die*
Chivers, Steve (cin): *Hardware*
Chiverton, Lisa (act): *The Pink Chiquitas*
Chizat, Jean-Paul (act): *Les Parapluies De Cherbourg*
Chizmadia, Steve (act): *I Come In Peace*
Chmara, Grigor (act): *Raskolnikov*
Choate, Tim (act): *Def Con 4; Ghost Story (1981); Not Of This World*
Chodorov, Edward (wri, 1904–1988): *House Of Menace; Kind Lady (1951)*
Chodos, Daniel (act): *Outbreak*
Choe, Dean (act): *Unforgettable*
Choga, Innocent (act): *King Solomon's Mines (1985)*
Choice, Elisabeth (act): *Are You Dying Young Man?*
Chomsky, Marvin (J.) (dir): *Doctor Franken; The Magician (1973)*

Chomyn, Chris (cin): Phantasm III: Lord Of The Dead
Chong, Jeffrey (act): Wild Thing
Chong, Mona (act): Koroshi; On Her Majesty's Secret Service
Chong, Rae Dawn (act, b. 1961): The Borrower; Hideaway; Mask Of Death; Quest For Fire; Tales From The Darkside
Chong, Sheila (act): Saturday Island
Chopin, Frederic (mus, 1810–1849): The Little Girl Who Lives Down The Lane
Chopra, Ram (act): Dr. Faustus
Chorik, M. (mus): The Shadows Of Forgotten Ancestors
Chouchanian, Jack (act): Phenomenon
Choudhury, Arpen (act): Devi
Chow, David (act): Charlie Chan And The Curse Of The Dragon Queen; Conquest Of The Planet Of The Apes; Dimension 5; White Of The Eye
Chow, Harvey (act): Spasms
Chow, Leonard (act): Millennium
Choy, Brock (wri): Bionic Showdown: The Six Million Dollar Man And The Bionic Woman
Choy, Diana (act): Electric Dreams
Chraibi, Abdelhaq (act): The Man Who Knew Too Much (1956)
Chramostova, Vlasta (act): The Cremator
Chressanthis, James (cin): Death Dreams
Chris, Marilyn (act): Rhinoceros (1974)
Christenfeld, Karen (act): From Beyond
Christensen, Benjamin (act &wri, 1879–1959): Haxan; Det Hemmelighedsfulde X
Christensen, Benjamin (dir): The Haunted House (1929); Haxan; Det Hemmelighedsfulde X; The House Of Horror (1929); Mockery; The Mysterious Island (1929); Seven Footprints To Satan
Christensen, Carol (act): The Three Stooges In Orbit
Christensen, Greta (act): The Falcon In Hollywood
Christensen, Hugo (dir): Curse Of The Stone Hand
Christensen, Richard (act): Nightbeast
Christensen, Val (act): Thirst
Christenson, Irma (act): The Devil's Wanton
Christiaansen, Dana (cin): Second Sight
Christian, Brian (act): Retribution (1988)
Christian, Chad (act): The Power (1980)
Christian, Claudia (act): Arena (1989); Hexed; Maniac Cop 2
Christian, Daryk (act): Eve Of Destruction
Christian, Don (wri): The Mafu Cage
Christian, Gina (act): Death Valley
Christian, Helen (act): Zorro Rides Again
Christian, Kurt (act): Fragment Of Fear; The Golden Voyage Of Sinbad; Horror Hospital; Sinbad And The Eye Of The Tiger; Through The Magic Pyramid
Christian, Leigh (act): Beyond Atlantis
Christian, Linda (act, b. 1923, nee Blanca Rosa Welter): The Devil's Hand (1961); Slaves Of Babylon; Tarzan And The Mermaids
Christian, Mary (act): A Kiss For Cinderella
Christian, Michael (act): Doomsday Machine; 2000 Years Later
Christian, Natt (act): King Kong Lives
Christian, Patricia (act): Black Angel (1980)
Christian, Paul (act): see Hubschmid, Paul
Christian, Roger (dir): Black Angel (1980); Nostradamus; The Sender
Christian, Roger (wri): Black Angel (1980)
Christian, Thomas (act): Pranks
Christian, Wolf (act): First Knight
Christian-Jaque (dir, b. 1904, nee Christian Maudet): Carmen (1942); Lucrezia Borgia (1952); Madame Dubarry (1954); Le Saint Prend L'affut; La Tulipe Noire
Christian-Jaque (wri, b. 1904): Madame Dubarry (1954); Le Saint Prend L'affut
Christians, Mady (act): Address Unknown
Christiansen, Arthur (act): The Day The Earth Caught Fire
Christiansen, Harvey (act): My Best Friend Is A Vampire
Christianson, John (act): Remo Williams: The Adventure Begins
Christianson, Lila (act): Looker
Christianson, Lorna (act): Looker
Christie, Agatha (wri, 1891–1976): Alibi (1931); The Alphabet Murders; And Then There Were None; Dead Man's Folly; Death On The Nile; Endless Night; Evil Under The Sun; Five Dolls For An August Moon; Love From A Stranger (1937); The Mirror Crack'd; Murder At The Gallop; Murder Is Easy; Murder Most Foul; Murder On The Orient Express; Murder She Said; Murder With Mirrors; Sparkling Cyanide; The Spider's Web; Ten Little Indians (1965, 1974 & 1989); Witness For The Prosecution
Christie, Audrey (act, 1910–1989): Carousel
Christie, Campbell (wri): Grand National Night; Someone At The Door
Christie, Dick (act): Looker
Christie, Dorothy (act): Grand National Night; Radio Ranch
Christie, Dorothy (wri): Someone At The Door
Christie, Helen (act): Lust For A Vampire; Rasputin, The Mad Monk
Christie, Howard (wri): Abbott And Costello Go To Mars
Christie, Julianne (act): The Nutty Professor (1996)
Christie, Julie (act, b. 1941): Demon Seed; Don't Look Now; Dragonheart; Fahrenheit 451; Hamlet (1996); Heaven Can Wait (1978); Memoirs Of A Survivor
Christine, Angela (act): Mountaintop Motel Massacre
Christine, Kathy (act): War Of The Planets
Christine, Virginia (act, 1917-1996): Billy The Kid vs. Dracula; Daughter Of The Mind; House Of Horrors (1946); Invasion Of The Body Snatchers (1956); The Invisible Wall; The Mummy's Curse; Murder Is My Business; Nightmare (1956)
Christmas, Eric (act): All Of Me; The Andromeda Strain; Attack Of The Killer Tomatoes; The Changeling; Child Of Darkness, Child Of Light; The Philadelphia Experiment
Christodoulou, Raymond (wri): From Beyond The Grave
Christoff, Russ (act): Copycat
Christofferson, Debra (act): The Silence Of The Hams
Christophe, Francoise (act): Gli Invasori; Seven Deaths In The Cat's Eye
Christopher, Dennis (act, b. 1955): Alien Predators; Blood And Lace; Deadly Invasion: The Killer Bee Nightmare; Fade To Black; It (1990); Jake Speed; The Silencers (1995)
Christopher, Guy (act): Popcorn
Christopher, Jean (act): Decoy For Terror
Christopher, John (wri): No Blade Of Grass
Christopher, Jordan (act, b. 1940): Angel, Angel, Down We Go; Brainstorm (1983); The Fat Spy
Christopher, June (act): Misery
Christopher, Kathy (act): Snowbeast
Christopher, Kay (act): Dick Tracy's Dilemma
Christopher, Robert (act): Agent For H.A.R.M.; The Disembodied; Frankenstein Island; Terror Of The Bloodhunters
Christopher, Robin (act): Equinox
Christopher, Thom (act): Deathstalker III: Warriors From Hell; Space Raiders; Wizards Of The Lost Kingdom
Christopher, Tom (act): S*H*E (1980)
Christou, Angelo (act): The Pink Chiquitas
Christy, George (act): Outbreak; Seven
Christy, Ivan (act): Seven Footprints To Satan
Christy, James V. (act): The Right Hand Of The Devil
Christy, Ken (act): Shadow Of The Thin Man; Sunset Boulevard; The Werewolf (1955)
Chrystal, Belle (act): The Frightened Lady (1932); The Girl In The Flat; The House Of The Arrow (1940); Poison Pen; The Scotland Yard Mystery
Chubb, Gloria (act): Forever Evil
Chuck, Kenneth (act): The Chinese Ring
Chudney, Roger (act): Remo Williams: The Adventure Begins
Chudnow, David (mus): Buried Alive (1940); Captain Kidd; The Devil Bat; The Mad Monster; Nabonga
Chudzinski, Sandra (act): Forever Evil
Chukron, Dru-Ann (act): Neighbors
Chulla, Babs (act): Runaway
Church, Suzanne (act): Child's Play (1985)
Church, Thomas Haden (act): Demon Knight; George Of The Jungle
Church, Tony (act): Krull; Work Is A Four Letter Word
Churchill, Berton (act): The Spanish Cape Mystery
Churchill, Diana (act): The House Of The Arrow (1940); Law And Disorder; The Spider (1939)
Churchill, Donald (act, b. 1930): The Hound Of The Baskervilles (1982); Spaceflight IC-1
Churchill, Donald (wri): Zeppelin
Churchill, Marguerite (act, b. 1910): Charlie Chan Carries On; Dracula's Daughter; The Walking Dead
[illegible] Jack Frost
Chuvalo, George (act): The Fly (1986)
Chwalibog, Maria (act): Matka Joanna Od Aniolow
Chwatt, Aaron (act): see Buttons, Red
Cianci, Antonio (act): La Donna Scimmia
Cianfriglia, Giovanni (act): Hercules, The Avenger; Ironmaster; The Trojan Horse
Ciani, Sergio (act): see Steel, Alan
Ciani, Suzanne (mus): The Incredible Shrinking Woman
Ciannelli (wri): Ok, Nero!
Ciannelli, Eduardo (act, 1887–1969): Bulldog Drummond's Bride; The Creeper (1948); Crime Doctor's Gamble; Crime Doctor's Warning; Doctor Satan's Robot; Ellery Queen's Penthouse Mystery; Foreign Correspondent; The Girl From Scotland Yard; League Of Frightened Men; The Lost Moment; Love Slaves Of The Amazons; The Mask Of Dimitrios; The Monster From Green Hell; The Mummy's Hand; Paris Calling; Rapture; The Spy In The Green Hat; The Stranger's Hand
Ciarfalio, Carl (N.) (act): Candyman: Farewell To The Flesh; Eve Of Destruction; Freejack
Ciavarro, Luigi (act): Battle Of The Amazons; The Trojan Horse
Cicchetti, Tony (act): Princess Warrior
Ciccoritti, Gerard (dir): Graveyard Shift (1987); Psycho Girls
Ciccoritti, Gerard (wri): Graveyard Shift (1987)
Cicognini, Alessandro (mus, b. 1906): Il Ladro Di Venezia; Miracle In Milan; Ulysses
Cidre, Cynthia (wri): I Saw What You Did (1988)
Ciepielewska, Anna (act): Matka Joanna Od Aniolow
Ciesar, Jennifer (act): Inner Sanctum 2
Cieutat, Shirl (act): The Savage Bees
Cifariello, Antonio (act): In Search Of The Castaways
Ciges, Luis (act): Horror Rises From The Tomb
Cigoj, Laci (act): Cave Of The Living Dead
Cilento, Diane (act, b. 1933): All Hallowe'en; The Angel Who Pawned Her Harp; The Full Treatment; Hitler: The Last Ten Days; The Naked Edge; Negatives; Spell Of Evil; The Third Secret; The Wicker Man; Z.P.G.
Cilla, Felix (act): The Dungeonmaster
Cimber, Matt (dir & wri): Hundra
Cimino, Leonardo (act): The Monster Squad; V
Cimino, Mike (wri): Silent Running
Cimorelli, Frank J. (act): Death Valley
Cindrich, Reynold (act): Return Of The Living Dead, Part II
Cinema Research (cin): The Immortal; The Wizard Of Mars
Cinesite (cin): Lawnmower Man 2: Beyond Cyberspace
Cinnamon (act): The Boy Who Never Was
Cinque, Michele (act): Kemek
Cintra, Luis Miguel (act): The Convent
Cioffi, Charles (act): Remo Williams: The Adventure Begins; Time After Time
Ciorciolini, Marcello (wri): Robin Hood And The Pirates
Cipriani, Stelvio (mus): City Of The Walking Dead; The Great Alligator; Night Hair Child; Twitch Of The Death Nerve
Cirile, Jim (act): The Edge Of Hell
Cirillo, Joe (act): Beyond The Poseidon Adventure
Cirino, Chuck (mus): Chopping Mall; Deathstalker II: Duel Of The Titans; The Haunting Of Morella; Not Of This Earth (1988); The Return Of Swamp Thing
Ciron, Jacques (act): The Black Windmill
Cisar, George (act): Attack Of The Giant Leeches; Billy The Kid vs. Dracula; Nightfall (1956); The Werewolf (1955)
Cistheri, Raymond (wri): The Body Snatchers
Citicica, Sonia (act): Killer Fish
Cittini, Alberto (wri): House Of Exorcism
Ciuffi, Sonia (act): Battle Of The Amazons
Ciuffino, Sabatino (wri): Il Gigante Di Metropolis; Super Fuzz; The Tartars
Ciupka, Richard (cin): An Americam Christmas Carol; Secret Weapons
Civirani, Cristiano (cin): David And Goliath
Civirani, Oswaldo (dir & wri): Ercole Contro I Figli Del Sole
Civit, Josep M./J.M. (cin): Anguish; Silent Night, Deadly Night III
Clabaugh, Richard (cin): The Prophecy (1995)
Claflin, Ned (act): Dick Tracy (1990)
Clair, Jack (act): The Live Wire; The Valley Of Fear (1916)
Clair, Jany (act): The Conquest Of Mycenae; Fx 18, Secret Agent; Maciste E La Regina Di Samar; Planets Against Us; The Prisoner Of The Iron Mask
Clair, Rene (dir, 1898–1981): And Then There Were None; Le Beaute Du Diable; Le Fantome Du Moulin Rouge; The Ghost Goes West; I Married A Witch; It Happened Tomorrow; Paris Qui Dort; Le Voyage Imaginaire
Clair, Rene (wri, 1898–1981): It Happened Tomorrow; Paris Qui Dort; Le Voyage Imaginaire
Clair, Richard (wri): Beware! The Blob
Clair, Sidney (mus): Think Fast, Mr. Moto
Claire, Adele (act): The Destructors; Human Feelings
Claire, Cyrielle (act): Sword Of The Valiant
Claire, Imogen (act): The Lair Of The White Worm; Liszt O' Mania; Shock Treatment! (1981)
Claire, J.C. (act): Spawn Of The Slithis
Claire, Jan (act): Madman
Clama, Renee (act): The Man They Could Not Arrest
Clancey, Vernon (wri): Dangerous Fingers; Dead Men Are Dangerous
Clancy, Carl Stearns (wri): The Headless Horseman
Clancy, Melinda (act): Tales From The Crypt
Clancy, Tom (act): Final Eye; The Ghost Of Flight 401
Clanton, Ralph (act): Pharaoh's Curse; They Might Be Giants; The 27th Day
Clanton, Rony (act): Def By Temptation; Too Scared To Scream
Clapham, Peter (act): The Phantom Of The Opera (1989)
Clapton, Eric (act, b. 1944): Tommy
Clapton, Eric (mus, b. 1944): Communion; Phenomenon
Clare, Diane (act): The Double; The Hand Of Night; The Haunting; The Naked Edge; Night Caller From Outer Space; The Plague Of The Zombies; The Trygon Factor; The Vulture (1966); Witchcraft (1964); The Wrong Box
Clare, Frances (act): Panic At Madam Tussaud's
Clare, Gladys (act): see George, Gladys
Clare, Mary (act, 1894–1970): The Black Rose; The Black Spider; The Clairvoyant (1934); Fiddlers Three; Gipsy Blood; The Lady Vanishes (1938); Mrs. Pym Of Scotland Yard; The Night Has Eyes; The Passing Of The Third Floor Back (1935); The Patient Vanishes; The Three Weird Sisters; Young And Innocent
Clare, Phyllis (act): The Flaw
Clarence, O.B. (act, 1870–1955): The Barton Mystery (1932); The Bells (1931); Eyes Of Fate; The Feathered Serpent (1934); Great Expectations (1946); A Place Of One's Own; The Return Of The Scarlet Pimpernel; The Scarlet Pimpernel (1934); The Shot In The Dark; Uncle Silas
Clarendon, Wendye (act): D.O.A. (1988)
Claridge, Norman (act): Clegg; They Came From Beyond Space; The Woman Eater
Claridge, Wes (wri): Deadly Game
Claridge, Westbrook (act): The Incredible Melting Man
Clark, Andrew (act): Edward Scissorhands
Clark, Benjamin (dir & wri): Children Shouldn't Play With Dead Things
Clark, Blake (act): Love Potion No. 9
Clark, Bob (dir): Deathdream; Deranged (1974); Murder By Decree; Silent Night, Evil Night
Clark, Bobby (act): Invasion Of The Body Snatchers (1956)
Clark, Brett (act): Alien Warrior
Clark, Bridgetta (act): The Conquering Power
Clark, Bruce (dir & wri): Galaxy Of Terror
Clark, Candy (act, b. 1948): Amityville 3-D; The Big Sleep (1978); The Blob (1988); Buffy, The Vampire Slayer; Cat's Eye; The Man Who Fell To Earth (1976); Q
Clark, Carolyn Ann (act): The Cradle Will Fall
Clark, Charles Dow (act): The Bat Whispers
Clark, Chester (act): Mutant
Clark, Christie (act): Children Of The Corn II: The Final Sacrifice
Clark, Cliff (act): Blue, White And Perfect; Charlie Chan's Murder Cruise; Crime Doctor's Diary; The Falcon And The Co-Eds; The Falcon In Danger; The Falcon Out West; The Falcon's Brother; The Falcon Strikes Back; Miracles For Sale; Mr. Moto's Gamble; The Mummy's Tomb; Philo Vance's Gamble; The Sniper; Sorry, Wrong Number (1948); Torchy Plays With Dynamite
Clark, Colbert (wri): The Lost Jungle
Clark, Cordy (act): The Hills Have Eyes
Clark, Dane (act, b. 1915, nee Bernard Zanville): [illegible] Paid To Kill
Clark, Dan(iel B.) (cin): The Black Camel; Charlie Chan At Monte Carlo; Charlie Chan At The Circus; Charlie Chan At The Olympics; Charlie Chan In Egypt

Clark, Dave (1940s act): Charlie Chan In The Secret Service
Clark, Dave (1980s act): The Being
Clark, Davison (act): Samson And Delilah
Clark, Don (act): Distortions
Clark, Dorian Joe (act): The Kiss (1988)
Clark, Dort (Donald) (act): Cameron's Closet; Time Travelers (1976)
Clark, Duane B. (act): Remo Williams: The Adventure Begins
Clark, E. Holman (act): Her Heritage; A Message From Mars (1913)
Clark, Ed (act): Bog
Clark, Edward/Eddie (act): Amazon Quest; The Falcon Out West; The Falcon's Alibi; Nightmare Alley
Clark, Eric (act): Sorority Girls And The Creature From Hell
Clark, Ernest (act, b. 1912): Castle Keep; The Curse Of The Golem; The Devil-Ship Pirates; I Accuse (1958); Masquerade; Master Spy; 1984 (1955); A Woman Of Mystery
Clark, Eugene (act): Millennium
Clark, Francis (mus): Horror
Clark, Fred (act, 1914–1968): Alias Nick Beal; The Curse Of The Mummy's Tomb; Dr. Goldfoot And The Bikini Machine; The Face Of Eve; Mr. Peabody And The Mermaid; Ride The Pink Horse; Sergeant Deadhead The Astronaut!; Sunset Boulevard; Treasure Island (1950); The Unsuspected; Visit To A Small Planet; Zotz!
Clark, Gloria (act): Diary Of A Madman
Clark, Greydon (act): Psychic Killer; Uninvited (1987)
Clark, Greydon (dir & wri): The Alien's Return; Satan's Cheerleaders; Uninvited (1987), Satan's Sadists;
Clark, Harry J. (act): Outbreak
Clark, Harvey (act): Charlie Chan's Courage; Seven Keys To Baldpate (1929)
Clark, Holman (act): The Brass Bottle (1914)
Clark, J.J. (act): Frankenhooker
Clark, J.L. (act): Trick Or Treats
Clark, J. Nesbit (act): The Fan
Clark, J.R. (act): Ssssss
Clark, Jacqueline (act): Blithe Spirit
Clark, James (act): Eraser; Nothing But Trouble
Clark, James/Jim (dir): Madhouse; Rentadick
Clark, Jameson (act): Beyond This Place; The Key; The 39 Steps (1959); X...The Unknown
Clark, Jane (act): Galaxis
Clark, Jerry L. (act): The Initiation
Clark, Jessica (act): Phoenix The Warrior
Clark, John (act): A Witch Without A Broom
Clark, Johnny (act): The Locket
Clark, Jon (act): Slaughter High
Clark, Joseph (act): The Medusa Touch
Clark, Josh (act): Big
Clark, Karen (wri): The Uninvited (1996)
Clark, Ken (act): Attack Of The Giant Leeches; Fx 18, Secret Agent; None But The Lonely Spy; On The Threshold Of Space; The Son Of Hercules In The Land Of Darkness; 12 To The Moon
Clark, Lawrence Gordon (dir): Jamaica Inn (1985)
Clark, Louise Caire (act): Programmed To Kill
Clark, Lynda (A.) (act): The Alien's Return; It's Alive III: Island Of The Alive; A Return To Salem's Lot
Clark, Marguerite (act, 1883–1940): Snow White (1917)
Clark, Marlene (GB act): The Beast Must Die
Clark, Marlene (USA act): Beware! The Blob; Ganja And Hess; Lord Shango; Night Of The Cobra Woman
Clark, Martin (act): The Annihilator
Clark, Mary Higgins (act, b. 1929): Remember Me
Clark, Mary Higgins (wri): The Cradle Will Fall; Remember Me; A Stranger Is Watching
Clark, Matt (act): The Adventures Of Buckaroo Banzai; Back To The Future, Part III; Candyman: Farewell To The Flesh; The Legend Of The Lone Ranger; Return To Oz; The Terminal Man; Trilogy Of Terror II
Clark, May (act): Alice In Wonderland (1903); The Slavey's Dream; That Eternal Ping-Pong; Topsy-Turvy Villa
Clark, Michael (act): Dr. Strange; The Magician (1973); Prospero's Books
Clark, Mildred (act): Forever Evil
Clark, Oliver (act): Ernest Saves Christmas; Nightlife (1989, USA-Mex); They Might Be Giants
Clark, P.G. (act): The Lure
Clark, Paulle (act): The Night Walker; What's The Matter With Helen?
Clark, Petula (act, b. 1932): Murder In Reverse; Nevernever Land; Track The Man Down; Vice Versa (1947)
Clark, Phillip (act): Shark Kill
Clark, Roger (act): One Dangerous Night; Secrets Of The Lone Wolf
Clark, Roydon (act): Blood Song
Clark, Russ (act): A Date With The Falcon; The Lone Wolf Spy Hunt; Mr. Moto's Gamble
Clark, Russell (act): Fright Night II
Clark, Sanders (act): Les Miserables (1952)
Clark, Stephan (act): Mad Max; Thirst
Clark, Steve (act): Phantom From Space
Clark, Susan (act, b. 1940): The Astronaut; City On Fire; Colossus: The Forbin Project; Murder By Decree; Skullduggery
Clark, Thomas (cin): Full Circle
Clark, Tom (act): I Was A Zombie For The F.B.I.
Clark, Tracy (act): Secrets Of The Phantom Caverns
Clark, Trilby (act): Maria Marten (1928); The Squeaker (1930)
Clark, William (wri): Man On A Swing
Clark, William Baird (act): House Of The Living Dead
Clarke, Alexander (act): The Computer Wore Tennis Shoes
Clarke, Angela (act): The Ghost Of Flight 401; Houdini; House Of Wax; Killer In The Mirror
Clarke, Arthur C. (wri, b. 1917): 2001: A Space Odyssey; 2010
Clarke, Betsy Ross (act): The Man From Downing Street; The Murders In The Rue Morgue (1932)
Clarke, Caitlin (act): Dragonslayer; The Stepford Husbands
Clarke, Charles (G.) (cin, b. 1899): Black Widow (1954); Carousel; The Casino Murder Case; Charlie Chan In Honolulu; Dead Men Tell; The Garden Murder Case; Miracle On 34th Street (1947); Mr. Moto Takes A Vacation; Tarzan And His Mate; Temple Tower; Time To Kill (1942); Trouble For Two
Clarke, David (act): The Boy With Green Hair
Clarke, Donald Henderson (wri): Ghost Ship (1943)
Clarke, Frederick (act): Tarzan's Revenge
Clarke, Gage (act): The Absent-Minded Professor (1961); The Bad Seed (1956); The Invisible Boy; The Monkey's Uncle; The Return Of Dracula
Clarke, Gary (act): The Eyes Of Charles Sand; How To Make A Monster; The Lightning Incident; Missile To The Moon
Clarke, Gordon (act): The Octagon; One Spy Too Many
Clarke, Harvey (act): He Who Gets Slapped; In The Palace Of The King
Clarke, Hope (act): Angel Heart; Change Of Mind
Clarke, J.D. (act): The Children
Clarke, James (mus): Vampyres...Daughters Of Dracula
Clarke, Joe (act): Basket Case
Clarke, John (act): The Satan Bug; Strange Behavior; Those Dear Departed
Clarke, Justine (act): Mad Max Beyond Thunderdome
Clarke, Lisa (act): Empire Of Ash III
Clarke, Logan (act): Sweet Sixteen
Clarke, Lydia (act): The Atomic City
Clarke, Madison (act): The Incredibly Strange Creatures Who Stopped Living And Became Mixed-Up Zombies
Clarke, Mae (act, 1910–1992): Frankenstein (1931); Lost Planet Airmen; The Penguin Pool Murder
Clarke, Mamo (act, 1914–1986): One Million B.C.
Clarke, Margi (act): I Hired A Contract Killer
Clarke, Marilyn (act): The Horror Of Party Beach
Clarke, Mike (act): Mutants In Paradise
Clarke, Mindy (act): Return Of The Living Dead III
Clarke, Oz (act): Superman (1978)
Clarke, Philip (act): The Lure
Clarke, Richard (GB act): Siege Of The Saxons
Clarke, Richard (USA act): Charlie Chan In City In Darkness
Clarke, Robert (act, b. 1920): The Astounding She-Monster; Bedlam; Beyond The Time Barrier; The Body Snatcher (1945); Captive Women; A Date With Death; Dick Tracy Meets Gruesome; The Falcon In Hollywood; Frankenstein Island; A Game Of Death; The Hideous Sun Demon; The Incredible Petrified World; The Man From Planet X; Midnight Movie Massacre; Sword Of Venus; Tales Of Robin Hood; Terror Of The Bloodhunters
Clarke, Robert (dir & wri, b. 1920): The Hideous Sun Demon
Clarke, Robin (act): Cyberzone; Inseminoid; Midnight Lace (1981)
Clarke, Robin (wri): From Beyond The Grave
Clarke, Scott (act): Queenie Of The Circus
Clarke, Shelbi (act): Serial Mom
Clarke, Shirley (act): Galaxie
Clarke, Spencer (act): Jack's Back
Clarke, T.E.B. (wri, 1907–1989): Dead Of Night (1945); Gideon's Day; Halfway House; A Hitch In Time; The Lavender Hill Mob; Who Done It? (1956)
Clarke, Warren (act): A Clockwork Orange; The Cold Room; Hands Of A Murderer; Hawk The Slayer; The Hunchback Of Notre Dame (1977); Top Secret! (1984)
Clarke-Smith, D.A. (act, 1888–1959): Dangerous Fingers; The Feathered Serpent (1934); Flat No. 3; The Frightened Lady (1932); The Ghoul (1933); I'm An Explosive; The Man Who Knew Too Much (1934); Menace (1934); Murder By Rope; The Old Man; Passing Shadows; Sabotage; The Thirteenth Candle; A Voice Said Goodnight
Clarkson, Grady (act): Roger Corman's Frankenstein Unbound
Clarkson, Lana (act): Barbarian Queen II (The Empress Strikes Back); Blind Date; Deathstalker; The Haunting Of Morella
Clarkson, Stephen (dir): Death Goes To School
Clarkson, Stephen (wri): Death Goes To School; Dual Alibi
Clary, Charles (act): Behind The Curtain (1924); In The Palace Of The King; Kismet (1930); The Penalty; The Road To Yesterday
Clary, Robert (act, b. 1926): Thief Of Damascus
Clash, Kevin (act): Labyrinth (1986)
Claudier, Annette (act): Hellhole
Clausen, Liv (act): Rawhead Rex
Clauson, Dal (cin): The Lone Wolf (1924)
Clavell, James (wri, 1924–1994): The Fly (1958); The Satan Bug; Watusi
Clavell, Michaela (act): Octopussy
Claver, Bob (dir): Jaws Of Satan
Clavering, Eric (act): 49th Parallel; The Patient Vanishes; The Saint Meets The Tiger; To Kill A Clown
Clavier, Christian (act & wri): The Visitors (1993)
Clavillazo (act): El Castillo De Los Monstruos
Clavin, Pat (act): Zex
Clawsen, Mary Ellen (act): The Incredible 2-Headed Transplant
Clawson, Elliot (wri): The Phantom Of The Opera (1925); The Road To Mandalay; The Thirteenth Chair (1929)
Clawson, Steven (act): Heart And Souls
Claxton, Richard (act): First Knight
Claxton, William (F.) (dir): Follow The Hunter; Night Of The Lepus
Claxton, William (F.) (wri): Follow The Hunter
Clay, Andrew Dice (act): Brain Smasher...A Love Story
Clay, Carl (act): Gammera Vs. Viras
Clay, Harry (act): The Falcon Out West
Clay, Jerome (act): Secrets Of The Phantom Caverns
Clay, Juanin (act): The Legend Of The Lone Ranger
Clay, Nicholas (act): Child's Play (1985); Evil Under The Sun; Excalibur; The Hound Of The Baskervilles (1982); Lovespell; The Night Digger; The Odyssey; Terror Of Frankenstein
Clay, Philippe (act): Bell, Book And Candle; The Hunchback Of Notre Dame (1957); Shanks
Clay, Rachel (act): The Monster Of Highgate Ponds
Clay, Ray (act): Blink
Clay, Stanley (Bennett) (act): The Annihilator; The Disappearance Of Flight 412
Clayburgh, Jill (act, b. 1944): Fear Stalk; Portnoy's Complaint; The Terminal Man
Claycomb, Susy (act): The Crater Lake Monster
Claydon, George (act): Berserk; I Don't Want To Be Born
Clayton, Arthur (act): Charlie Chan In London
Clayton, Cyril (act): Time Flyer
Clayton, Elizabeth (act): Silent Night, Deadly Night, Part II
Clayton, Hyde (act): The Time Machine (1978)
Clayton, Jack (dir, 1921–1995): The Bespoke Overcoat; The Innocents; Our Mother's House; Something Wicked This Way Comes
Clayton, Kevin (act): Maid To Order
Clayton, Kristin (act): The Hidden; A Nightmare On Elm Street 3: Dream Warriors
Clayton, Lynn (act): Paint Me A Murder
Clayton, Melissa (act): When The Bough Breaks
Clayton, Merry (act): Maid To Order
Clayton, Richard (act): The Hunchback Of Notre Dame (1939)
Clayworth, June (act, 1913–1993): Dick Tracy Meets Gruesome; Rocket Man
Cleare, John (cin): The Eiger Sanction
Cleary, Brigid (act): Flight Of The Navigator
Cleave, Arthur (act): Old Bill Through The Ages
Cleave, Van (mus): Conquest Of Space; Project X (1967); Robinson Crusoe On Mars; The Space Children
Cleaver, Thomas M. (wri): The Terror Within
Cleaves, Robert (act): Don't Be Afraid Of The Dark; Project X (1967); Targets
Cleckley, M.D., Hervey M. (wri): The Three Faces Of Eve
Cleese, John (act, b. 1939): Erik The Viking; George Of The Jungle; The Jungle Book (1994); The Magic Christian; Mary Shelley's 'Frankenstein'; Monty Python And The Holy Grail; Time Bandits
Cleese, John (wri, b. 1939): Monty Python And The Holy Grail; Rentadick
Clegg, Brendan (act): The Hills Of Donegal
Clegg, Tom (act): Carry On Screaming; Moby Dick (1956)
Cleland, Sean C. (act): Blink
Clemant, Dora (act): The Phantom Creeps
Clemence, Doris (act): The Wickham Mystery
Clemens, Brian (dir): Captain Kronos: Vampire Hunter
Clemens, Brian (wri): And Soon The Darkness; Blind Terror; Captain Kronos: Vampire Hunter; Dr. Jekyll And Sister Hyde; The Golden Voyage Of Sinbad; Highlander 2: The Quickening; Links Of Justice; Mark Of The Devil (1985); Murder In Mind; Murder Motel; Murder On The Midnight Express; Not Guilty; Once The Screaming Starts; One Deadly Owner; Only A Scream Away; Possession (1973); Return Of A Stranger; The Savage Curse; Spell Of Evil; The Tell-Tale Heart (1960); Timestalkers; Web Of Suspicion; The Woman Hunter; A Woman Of Mystery
Clemens, Gunter (act): Mark Of The Devil (1972)
Clemens, Paul (act): The Beast Within; Communion
Clemens, William (dir): Calling Philo Vance; Devil's Island; The Falcon And The Co-Eds; The Falcon In Danger; The Falcon Out West; Nancy Drew, Detective; Nancy Drew, Reporter; Nancy Drew, Troubleshooter; Torchy Blane In Panama
Clemenson, Christian (act): Making Mr. Right
Clement, Clay (act): The Thin Man
Clement, David (act): Darkman II: The Return Of Durant
Clement, Dick (dir &wri, b. 1937): Catch Me A Spy; Otley; The Prisoner Of Zenda (1979); Vice Versa (1988)
Clement, Gene (dir): The Deadly Trap
Clement, Marc (act): King Kong Lives; Mutant
Clement, Myra (wri): Cauchemares
Clement, Pilar (act): Battle Of The Amazons
Clement, Rene (dir, 1913-1996): Les Felins; Jeux Interdits
Clement, Rene (wri, 1913-1996): Jeux Interdits
Clementi, Pierre (act, b. 1944): Belle De Jour; Sweet Movie
Clemento, Steve (act): Arrest Bulldog Drummond; King Kong (1933); The Most Dangerous Game
Clements, Calvin (wri): The Devil And Miss Sarah
Clements, Candace (act): Maniac (1980)
Clements, Dulany Ross (wri): Vampire At Midnight
Clements, James D. (act): Street Trash
Clements, (Sir) John (act, 1910–1988): Knight Without Armour; The Mind Benders (1963); Once In A New Moon; They Came To A City; Things To Come
Clements, Ron (dir & wri): Hercules (1997)
Clements, Stanley (act, 1926–1981): Destination Murder; Hold That Hypnotist; Panic In The City; Rocket Man; Spook Chasers; Up In Smoke
Clements, Stanley (wri): The Devil's Partner
Clemm, Susanna (act): Dressed To Kill (1980)
Clemmons, Gregory (act): Spawn Of The Slithis
Clemmons, Julie (act): The Hand That Rocks The Cradle
Clemons, Mary Ellen (act): The Night Of The Hunter (1955)
Clenard, Val (act): The China Syndrome
Clenet, Alain (act): To All A Goodnight
Clennon, David (act): Matinee; The Thing (1982)
Clensy, Rohan (act): The Devil's Profession
Cler, Judy (act): The Wizard Of Gore
Clere, Paul (act): Tales From The Crypt
Clere, Sharon (act): Tales From The Crypt
Clery, Corinne (act, b. 1950): The Humanoid; Moonraker; Yor, The Hunter From The Future
Cleveland, Carlos (act): The Wiz

Cleveland, Carol (act): The Adding Machine; Monty Python And The Holy Grail; Vampira

Cleveland, George (act, 1886–1965): All That Money Can Buy; Angel On My Shoulder (1946); It Happened Tomorrow; Pillow Of Death; Revolt Of The Zombies; The Spanish Cape Mystery

Cleveland, Ivan (act): Old St. Paul's; The Vengeance Of The Air

Cleveland, Madge (act): Indestructible Man

Clevenger, Billy (act): Dick Tracy (1990)

Cleverdon, Dean (act): House II: The Second Story

Cleverdon, Douglas (wri): Death In The Hand

Clewes, Lorraine (act): The Pirates Of Blood River

Cliff, John (act): I Was A Teenage Frankenstein; The Three Stooges Meet Hercules

Cliff, Nicola (act): The Frighteners

Cliffe, H. Cooper (act): Missing Millions

Clifford, Barry (wri): Underworld (1997)

Clifford, G.W. (wri): The Green Terror

Clifford, Gary (act): Subterfuge

Clifford, Jack (act): Confessions Of Boston Blackie; The Lone Wolf Returns (1935); Mr. Moto Takes A Vacation

Clifford, Jack (wri): The Dummy Talks

Clifford, Jill (act): Knights Of The Round Table

Clifford, Jim (act): Inn Of The Damned

Clifford, John (act): Curse Of The Crimson Altar; Subterfuge

Clifford, John (wri): Carnival Of Souls

Clifford, Kim (act): Where's Johnny

Clifford, Matt (mus): The Return Of The Living Dead (1985)

Clifford, Mike (act): Village Of The Giants

Clifford, Peggy Ann (act): Jabberwocky; Kind Hearts And Coronets; Voices

Clifford, Richard (act): Mary Shelley's 'Frankenstein'; The Secret Life Of Ian Fleming

Clifford, Ruth (act): Sunset Boulevard

Clifford, Veronica (act): Rentadick

Clift, Denison (dir, b. 1893): The Mystery Of The Mary Celeste

Clift, Denison (wri, b. 1893): The Mystery Of The Mary Celeste; Scotland Yard (1930 & 1941); Secrets Of Scotland Yard

Clift, Montgomery (act, 1920–1966): I Confess; Suddenly Last Summer

Clift, Ralph M. (act): Killer In The Mirror

Clifton, Herbert (act): Counter-Espionage

Clifton, Hugh (act): The Tinted Venus

Cline, Cynthia (act): U.F.O.: Target Earth

Cline, Eddie (act): The Haunted House (1921)

Cline, Edward (dir, 1892–1948): Cracked Nuts (1931); Crazy House (1943); Forty Naughty Girls; Ghost Catchers; In The Next Room; The Villain Still Pursued Her

Cline, Kathy (act): Ring Of Fear

Cline, Robert (cin): Nabonga

Cline, Wilfrid M. (cin): The Giant Gila Monster; The Killer Shrews; The Tingler

Clinton, George (S.) (mus): Brainscan; Gotham; A Kiss To Die For; Ten Little Indians (1989); Wild Thing

Clinton, Mildred (act): Alice, Sweet Alice

Clinton, Roger S. (act): Pumpkinhead II: Blood Wings

Clipper, Patricia (act): Switch

Clitheroe, Jimmy (act): Those Fantastic Flying Fools

Clive, Colin (act, 1898–1937, nee Clive Greig): Bride Of Frankenstein; Frankenstein (1931); Jane Eyre (1934); Mad Love

Clive, Donald (act): Murder At The Windmill

Clive, E.E. (act, 1879–1940): The Adventures Of Sherlock Holmes (1939); Arrest Bulldog Drummond; Bride Of Frankenstein; Bulldog Drummond Comes Back; Bulldog Drummond Escapes; Bulldog Drummond In Africa; Bulldog Drummond's Bride; Bulldog Drummond's Peril; Bulldog Drummond's Revenge; Bulldog Drummond's Secret Police; Bulldog Drummond Strikes Back (1934); Charlie Chan In London; Dracula's Daughter; The Hound Of The Baskervilles (1939); The Invisible Man (1933); The Last Warning (1938); Mr. Moto's Last Warning; The Mystery Of Edwin Drood (1935); Night Must Fall (1937); Tarzan Escapes; Trouble For Two

Clive, Iris (act): The Cat Creeps (1946)

Clive, John (act): A Clockwork Orange; Great Expectations (1974); Straight On Till Morning

Clive, Teagan (act): Sinbad And The Seven Seas

Clive, Vincent (act): Called Back; The Ring And The Rajah

Cliver, Al (act): The Black Cat (1980); Endgame; 2020 Texas Gladiators; Zombie

Clodfelter, Rick (act): I Was A Zombie For The F.B.I.

Cloerec, Rene (mus): Le Comte De Monte Cristo; Johnny The Giant Killer

Cloninger, Ralph (act): Monte Cristo

Clooney, George (act, b. 1961): Batman And Robin; From Dusk Till Dawn; The Magic Bubble; Return Of The Killer Tomatoes; Return To Horror High

Cloquet, Ghislain (cin, b. 1924): Un Amour De Poche; Peau D'ane

Close, Del (act): Beware! The Blob; The Blob (1988)

Close, Glenn (act, b. 1947): Hamlet (1990); Light Years; Mars Attacks!; Mary Reilly; 101 Dalmatians (1996)

Close, Ivy (act): Darkest London: or, The Dancer's Romance; Dream Paintings; Ghosts (1914); The Haunting Of Silas P. Gould; The House Opposite (1917); The Lady Of Shallot; The Legend Of King Cophetua; Mifanwy-A Tragedy; Pygmalion And Galatea (1912); The Sleeping Beauty (1912); The Ware Case

Close, John(ny) (act): The Beginning Of The End; The Girl On The Bridge; The Slime People; Street Of Darkness

Close, Patrick (act): Space Raiders

Clothier, William (H.) (cin): Killers From Space; Phantom From Space; Way...Way Out

Clotworthy, Robert (act): Switch

Cloud, Darrah (wri): The Haunted (1991)

Cloud, David (act): Leatherface: Texas Chainsaw Massacre III

Cloud, Paul (act): The Return Of The Living Dead (1985)

Clough, John Scott (act): Bad Dreams; What Ever Happened To Baby Jane? (1991)

Clouse, Robert (dir): Deadly Eyes; The London Connection; The Ultimate Warrior

Clouse, Robert (wri): Happy Mother's Day, Love George; Something Evil; The Ultimate Warrior

Clouston, J. Storer (wri): The Spy In Black

Clouzot, Henri-Georges (dir, b. 1907): Le Corbeau; Diabolique (1955); Le Salaire De La Peur

Clouzot, Henri-Georges (wri, b. 1907): Le Corbeau; Diabolique (1955); Les Inconnus Dans La Maison; Le Salaire De La Peur

Clouzot, Vera (act, 1921–1960): Diabolique (1955); Le Salaire De La Peur

Clover, David (act): The Loch Ness Horror

Clowater, Denise (act): Quarantine

Clowes, St. John L. (wri): Dear Murderer; Things Happen At Night

Cluer, Penny (act): The Wicker Man

Clugston, H.N. (act): Bulldog Drummond Strikes Back (1934); In The Palace Of The King

Clune, Anne (act): Hands Of The Ripper

Clune, Peter H. (act): Stigma

Clunes, Alec (act, b. 1912): Richard III (1955)

Clunie, Michelle (act): Jason Goes To Hell: The Final Friday

Cluny, Genevieve (act): Formula C-12/Beirut

Clute, Chester (act, 1891–1956): Arsenic And Old Lace; The Falcon In Hollywood; Just Off Broadway; Mr. Moto's Gamble; The Thin Man Goes Home

Clutesi, George (act): Nightwing; Prophecy (1979)

Clyde, Craig (act): Earthbound (1981)

Clyde, David (act): Arrest Bulldog Drummond; Bulldog Drummond Escapes; Bulldog Drummond's Secret Police; Devotion; The House Of Fear (1945); The Lodger (1944); The Scarlet Claw

Clyde, Jean (act): Poison Pen

Clyde, June (act): Midnight Mystery; Night Without Stars; Seven Doors To Death; A Study In Scarlet (1933)

Clyde, Louis (cin): Five

Clymer, Gail (act): Embassy

Clymire, Robert (act): The Curse Of Bigfoot

Coad, Joyce (act): The Scarlet Letter (1926)

Coady, Francis (act): Addams Family Values

Coady, Terry (act): Scanners

Coakley, Marion (act): The Enchanted Cottage (1924)

Coakley, Patty (act): A Kiss For Cinderella

Coates, Alan (act): The Arrival

Coates, Conrad (act): Clarence

Coates, Denton (act): The Keeper

Coates, Kevin (act): Buck Rogers In The 25th Century

Coates, Kim (act): Blind Fear; The Club (1994); Red Blooded American Girl; Unforgettable

Coates, Lewis (dir & wri): see Cozzi, Luigi

Coates, Phyllis (act): The Claw Monsters; The Incredible Petrified World; Invasion U.S.A.; I Was A Teenage Frankenstein; Superman And The Mole Men; Teenage Monster; The Woman Eater; The Witch Doctor

Coatman, Cindy (act): Princess Warrior

Coats, Athol (act): Possession (1973)

Cobb, Carrie (act): To All A Goodnight

Cobb, Christopher (act): The Offspring

Cobb, David (wri): Dr. Frankenstein On Campus

Cobb, Ed(mund) (act, 1891–1974): Alias Boston Blackie; The Amazing Colossal Man; Dick Tracy Vs. Crime, Inc.; The Falcon In San Francisco; The Falcon's Alibi; Girls In Prison; The Golden Eye; The Lone Wolf Spy Hunt; The Lone Wolf Strikes; The Phantom Thief; River Of No Return; The She-Creature; Tales Of Terror; The Underwater City

Cobb, Jerry (act): Agent 255/Desperate Mission

Cobb, Julie (act): Brave New World; Dr. Jekyll And Ms. Hyde; Salem's Lot

Cobb, Kacey (act): The Crater Lake Monster

Cobb, Lee J. (act, 1911–1978): Ali Baba Goes To Town; The Exorcist; Gorilla At Large; Green Mansions; In Like Flint; The Luck Of The Irish; Our Man Flint; Paris Calling; The Three Faces Of Eve

Cobb, Randall (act): The Golden Child

Cobb, Ron (cin): Dark Star

Cobb, Vincent (act): Creator

Cobbe, Clifford (act): Discipline; Flames; The Strange Case Of Mr. Todmorden

Cobbs, Bill (act): The Brother From Another Planet; Demolition Man; The People Under The Stairs

Cobby, Brian (act): The Tell-Tale Heart (1960)

Cobert, Robert (mus): Burnt Offerings; Curse Of The Black Widow; Dracula (1973); House Of Dark Shadows; Night Of Dark Shadows; The Night Stalker (1971); The Night Strangler; Scalpel; Trilogy Of Terror

Coburn, Brian (act): Octopussy; The Return Of Mr. Moto; Sword Of The Valiant

Coburn, Candy (act): The Relic

Coburn, Charles (act, 1877–1961): Around The World In 80 Days; Heaven Can Wait (1942); How To Murder A Rich Uncle; The Long Wait; Lured; Monkey Business; The Paradine Case; Rocket Man; The Story Of Mankind

Coburn, James (act, b. 1928): Eraser; A High Wind In Jamaica; In Like Flint; Looker; The Loved One; The Nutty Professor (1996); Our Man Flint; The President's Analyst

Coburn, Sandra (act): Reflections Of Murder

Coby, Fred (act): Jungle Goddess; The Night The World Exploded

Coby, Michael (act): Supersonic Man

Coca, Imogene (act, b. 1908): Alice In Wonderland (1985)

Coca Cola, Tony (act & mus): see Tony Coca Cola & the Roosters

Coch, Edward (act): Creature With The Atom Brain; The Saracen Blade

Cochetti, Ranieri (wri): Teodora, Imperatrice Di Bisanzio

Cochran, Linda (act): 2000 Maniacs

Cochran, Mimi (act): I Come In Peace

Cochran, Robert (act): The Limping Man (1936); The Man Who Could Work Miracles; Mr. Reeder In Room 13; Scrooge (1935); The Third Clue

Cochran, Robert Alexander (act): see Cochran, Steve

Cochran, Steve (act, 1917–1965, nee Robert Alexander Cochran): Boston Blackie Booked On Suspicion; Boston Blackie's Rendezvous; The Chase; Operation Secret

Cochrane, Frank (act): Bulldog Drummond At Bay (1937); Chu Chin Chow (1934); The Yellow Mask

Cochrane, Michael (act): Frankenstein (1984)

Cochrane, Tallie (act): Frightmare (1983)

Cociarelli, Maria Luisa (act): see Vitti, Monica

Cockburn, Adam (act): Mad Max Beyond Thunderdome

Cockram, Joan (act): Lorna Doone (1920)

Cockrell, Francis (wri, 1906–1987): On The Threshold Of Space

Cockrell, Frank (wri): Dark Waters

Cockrell, Gary (act): The Bedford Incident; The Man Outside (1967)

Cockrell, John Mills (mus): Humongous

Cockrell, Marian (wri): Dark Waters

Cockroft, Angee (act): I Was A Zombie For The F.B.I.

Cocks, Jay (wri): Strange Days

Coco, James (act, 1930–1987): The Littlest Angel (1969); Murder By Death; The Stepford Children

Cocteau, Jean (act, 1889–1963): Le Baron Fantome; Cisaruv Slavik; Le Testament D'orphee

Cocteau, Jean (dir, 1889–1963): L'aigle A Deux Tetes; La Belle Et La Bete; Orphee; Les Parents Terribles; Le Sang D'un Poete; Le Testament D'orphee

Cocteau, Jean (wri, 1889–1963): L'aigle A Deux Tetes; La Belle Et La Bete; La Corona Negra; Les Enfants Terribles; L'eternel Retour;

Intimate Relations; Orphee; Les Parents Terribles; Le Sang D'un Poete; Le Testament D'orphee; Thomas L'imposteur

Cocza, Frank (act): Amazons (1986)

Coda, Frank (act): The Final Conflict

Code, Grant (act): Silent Night, Bloody Night

Codee, Ann (act): The War Of The Worlds

Codiglia, John (act): The Children

Codling, Teresa (act): Kadoyng

Cody (act): The Lost Boys

Cody, Ellen (act): The Unholy

Cody, Iron Eyes (act, b. 1915): Green Hell; The Road To Yesterday; The Scarlet Letter (1934)

Cody, Joe (act): The Falcon Out West

Cody, Kathleen (act, b. 1953): Charley And The Angel

Cody, Lew (act, 1888-1934): Rupert Of Hentzau (1923)

Coe, Barry (act): Doctor Death: Seeker Of Souls; Fantastic Voyage; Jaws 2; On The Threshold Of Space; The Wizard Of Baghdad

Coe, George (act): The Entity; Remo Williams: The Adventure Begins; The Stepford Wives

Coe, Jennifer (act): Hard Rock Zombies

Coe, John A. (act): The Exorcist III

Coe, Liz (wri): Unlikely Angel

Coe, Miranda (act): The Lair Of The White Worm

Coe, Peter (act): Desert Legion; Gypsy Wildcat; Hell Ship Mutiny; House Of Frankenstein; The Mummy's Curse; The Road To Bali; Sabaka; Snow White And The Three Stooges

Coe, Richard (act): The House That Dripped Blood

Coe, Wayne (dir & wri): Grim Prairie Tales

Coen, Ethan (wri): Blood Simple; Fargo

Coen, Franklin (wri): This Island Earth

Coen, Joel (dir & wri): Blood Simple; Fargo

Coffee, Lenore (J.) (wri, 1898–1984): The Bishop Murder Case; Footsteps In The Fog; Four Frightened People; Lightning Strikes Twice; Sudden Fear

Coffey, Bob (act): Electric Dreams

Coffey, Charlie (wri): Earth Girls Are Easy

Coffey, Colleen (act): The Lawnmower Man

Coffey, Jean Marie (act): First Knight

Coffey, (T.) Scott (act): Spacecamp; Warriors Of The Wasteland

Coffin, Adeline Hayden (act): The Black Spider; Faust (1923); God's Clay; The Sands Of Time; Sexton Blake, Gambler; Tut-Tut And His Terrible Tomb

Coffin, Hayden (act): The Black Spider; Queen Of My Heart

Coffin, Tris(tram) (act): The Barefoot Executive; The Baron Of Arizona; The Corpse Vanishes; The Crawling Hand; Creature With The Atom Brain; Dangerous Money; Flight To Mars; Lost Planet Airmen; The Night The World Exploded; Nyoka And The Lost Secrets Of Hippocrates; Pygmy Island; Radar Secret Service; The Resurrection Of Zachary Wheeler; The Shanghai Chest; Spy Smasher Returns

Coffing, Barry (act): The Outing

Coffman, Josh (act): Offerings

Cogan, Dick (act): Missile Monsters; Unknown World

Cogan, Henri (act): A Toi De Faire, Mignonne; The Liquidator

Cogan, Shaye (act): Jack And The Beanstalk (1952)

Coger, D.M. (act): I Was A Zombie For The F.B.I.

Coggin, Linda (act): Gothic

Coggiola, Rossana (act): Rorret

Coghill, Ambrose (act): Dr. Faustus

Coghill, Bridget (act): Dr. Faustus

Coghill, Joy (act): The Little Match Girl (1987)

Coghill, Nevill (act, dir & wri, 1899–1980): Dr. Faustus

Coghill, Nikki (act): Dark Age; The Time Guardian

Coghlan (Jr.), Frank (act): The Adventures Of Captain Marvel; Charlie Chan At The Race Track; Murder Over New York

Coghlan, Junior (act): The Road To Yesterday

Coghlan, Phyllis (act): The Adventures Of Robin Hood; Charlie Chan In London

Cogie, Louie (act): Mother's Day

Cohan, George M. (wri): House Of The Long Shadows

Cohan, Theo (act): Class Of Nuke'em High

Cohen, Barney (wri): Friday The 13th-The Final Chapter

Cohen, Barry (act): Windom

Cohen, Charles (act): Andy Warhol's Dracula

Cohen, Chuck (act): Neon Maniacs

Cohen, Daphne (act): Spawn Of The Slithis

Cohen, David (wri): Friday The 13th-Part V: A New Beginning

Cohen, Edward (cin): Things To Come

Cohen, Emma (act): Horror Rises From The Tomb
Cohen, Gabe (act): The Power (1980)
Cohen, Harvey (act): Silent Night, Bloody Night
Cohen, Herman (act): How To Make A Monster
Cohen, Herman (wri): Berserk; Black Zoo; Craze; The Headless Ghost; Horrors Of The Black Museum; How To Make A Monster; Konga
Cohen, Howard R. (dir): Saturday The 14th; Space Raiders; Time Trackers
Cohen, Howard R. (wri): Deathstalker; Saturday The 14th; Space Raiders; Time Trackers; The Vampire Girls
Cohen, J.J. (act): 976-Evil
Cohen, Jack (act): The Jerusalem File
Cohen, Jacob (act): see Dangerfield, Rodney
Cohen, Jay (act): School Spirit
Cohen, Jeff (act): The Goonies
Cohen, Jerry (cin): The Monster In The Basement
Cohen, Joel (act): Strange Invaders
Cohen, Joel (wri): Sister, Sister
Cohen, Larry (dir): The Ambulance; Demon (1976); Full Moon High; It Lives Again; It's Alive (1974); It's Alive III: Island Of The Alive; Q; A Return To Salem's Lot; The Stuff; Wicked Stepmother
Cohen, Larry/Lawrence (D.) (wri): The Body Snatchers; Carrie; Daddy's Gone A-Hunting; Demon (1976); Full Moon High; Ghost Story (1981); I Deal In Danger; I, The Jury (1982); It Lives Again; It's Alive (1974); It's Alive III: Island Of The Alive; Maniac Cop; Maniac Cop 2; Q; A Return To Salem's Lot; The Stuff; Wicked Stepmother
Cohen, Laurence (act): Charlie Chan And The Curse Of The Dragon Queen
Cohen, Lawrence Robert (wri): Scream, Baby, Scream
Cohen, Marc (act): The Long Kiss Goodnight
Cohen, Max (wri): King Tut-Ankh-Amen's Eighth Wife
Cohen, Michael (act): The Body Snatchers
Cohen, Mitchell (act): The Toxic Avenger
Cohen, Richard (act): Octaman
Cohen, Rob (dir): Daylight; Dragonheart
Cohen, Sammy (act): The Return Of Peter Grimm (1926)
Cohen, Scott (act): Jacob's Ladder
Cohen, Steve (act): Vice Versa (1988)
Cohill, William W. (act): Life Without Soul
Cohn, Alfred A. (wri): The Cat And The Canary (1927); The Gorilla (1927); The Last Warning (1929)
Cohn, Jack (act): see Coogan, Jackie
Cohn, Michael (dir & wri): When The Bough Breaks
Cohn, Mindy (act, b. 1966): The Boy Who Could Fly
Coit, Stephen (act): Poor Devil
Coke, Edward (act): The Shanghai Chest
Coke, Peter (act): I Met A Murderer
Coker, Samali (act): Sinbad And The Eye Of The Tiger
Cokliss, Harley (dir & wri): The Glitterball
Colaizzi, Robert (act): The First Power
Colasanto, Nicholas (act, 1924–1985): Family Plot; The Return Of The World's Greatest Detective
Colbert, Angel (act): Dr. Black Mr. Hyde
Colbert, Claudette (act, 1905-1996, nee Lily Cauchoin): Four Frightened People; Sleep, My Love
Colbert, Curt (act): The Psychotronic Man
Colbert, Keith (act): Firestarter
Colbert, Robert (act): Amazon Women On The Moon; City Beneath The Sea (1970); Have Rocket, Will Travel
Colbourne, Maurice (act): Hawk The Slayer; Venom (1982)
Colby, Anita (act): The Living Dead At Manchester Morgue
Colby, Kevin (act): The Toxic Avenger, Part II
Colceri, Tim (act): Eraser
Coldewey, Anthony (wri): The Hidden Hand
Cole, Albert (act): Human Feelings; The Incredible 2-Headed Transplant; Time Travelers (1976)
Cole, Barry (mus): Sling Blade
Cole, Ben (act): Edge Of Sanity; Howling V: The Rebirth
Cole, Carol (act): The Mad Room
Cole, Chester (wri): The Invisible Man Returns
Cole, Corinne (act): The Lucifer Complex
Cole, Dona (act): The Beast With A Million Eyes
Cole, Emerson (act): Secrets Of The Phantom Caverns
Cole, Evan (act): Scared To Death (1980)
Cole, Frederick (act): Secrets Of The Night
Cole, George (act, b. 1925): The Anatomist; The Blue Bird (1976); Dr. Syn-Alias The Scarecrow; Fright (1971); The Green Man; An Inspector Calls; The Intruder (1955); Mary Reilly; Scrooge (1951); The Spider And The Fly; Top Secret (1952); The Vampire Lovers
Cole, Jack (act, b. 1914): Kismet (1944)
Cole, Jacqulin (act): Satan's Cheerleaders
Cole, Janet (act): see Hunter, Kim
Cole, Janine (act): Phobia
Cole, Julie Dawn (act): Willy Wonka And The Chocolate Factory
Cole, Kay (act): Coma
Cole, Kimberly L. (act): The Body Snatchers
Cole, Leslie (act): The Incredible 2-Headed Transplant
Cole, Lester (wri, 1904–1985): Among The Living; Charlie Chan's Greatest Case; The House Of The Seven Gables
Cole, Michael (GB act): The Wicker Man
Cole, Michael (USA act): The Bubble; The Last Child
Cole, Olivia (act): Mistress Of Paradise
Cole, Paul (act): Horror Of Dracula
Cole, Phyllis (act): The Hypnotic Eye
Cole, Rosalie (act): The Child
Cole, Royal (K.) (wri): Lost Planet Airmen; Valley Of The Zombies
Cole, Sidney (wri, b. 1908): The Angel Who Pawned Her Harp; They Came To A City
Cole, Ted (act): The Little Match Girl (1987)
Cole, Terence (cin): A Ghost In Monte Carlo
Cole, Tina (act): Omega Doom
Coleby, A.E. (act): For All Eternity; Vice Versa (1910)
Coleby, A.E. (dir): The Advantages Of Hypnotism; The Airtight Safe; And Then He Woke Up; A Bag Of Monkey Nuts; The Blackmailers; Brown Bewitched; A Case For Sherlock Holmes; Constable Smith In Trouble Again; The Convict's Dream; The Devil's Bargain; The Fate Of A King; For All Eternity; Have It Out, My Boy, Have It Out!; How The Artful Dodger Secured A Meal; The Hunchback (1911); I Hear You Calling Me; Little Red Riding Hood (1911); Little Jim; The Lonely Inn; The Mummy (1912); The Mysteries Of London; The Phantom Ship (1908); The Pirates Of 1920; The Prehistoric Man (1924); Professor Piecan's Discovery; Salome Mad; Satan's Amazon; Scroggins Goes In For Chemistry And Discovers A Marvellous Powder; Scroggins Has His Fortune Told; The Sculptor's Dream; Sleepy Sam's Awakening; Spiritualism Exposed (1926); The Third Witness; Topsy's Dream Of Toyland; Wanted, A Mummy; The Wheel Of Death; While The Cook Slept
Coleby, A.E. (wri): For All Eternity; The Mysteries Of London; Spiritualism Exposed (1926); Topsy's Dream Of Toyland
Coleby, Robert (act): The Plumber
Coleman, Alex (act): The Silence Of The Lambs
Coleman, Barbara (act): Mirrors
Coleman, Bill (wri): Secret Agent Superdragon
Coleman, Brady (act): Powder
Coleman, Brian/Bryan (act): Blood Of The Vampire; The Hand (1960); The Lost Hours; Zeppelin
Coleman, Charles (act): The Great Impersonation (1942); Michael Shayne, Private Detective
Coleman, Clarke (act): Jekyll And Hyde... Together Again; Neon Maniacs
Coleman, Dabney (act, b. 1932): Bad Ronald; Cloak And Dagger (1984); Devil's Food; Dying Room Only; Meet The Applegates; Modern Problems; The Towering Inferno
Coleman, David (wri): Endless Descent
Coleman, Frank (act): The Cave Girl (1921)
Coleman, Gary (act, b. 1968): The Kid With The Broken Halo
Coleman, George (act): Freejack
Coleman, Graeme (mus): Quarantine
Coleman, Jack (act): Daughter Of Darkness (1990)
Coleman, Lane (act): Humongous
Coleman, Layne (act): The Housekeeper
Coleman, Leo (act): The Medium (1951)
Coleman, Marilyn (act): The Meteor Man
Coleman, Michael (act): Peter Rabbit And The Tales Of Beatrix Potter
Coleman, Nancy (act, b. 1917): Devotion; Her Sister's Secret; Violence
Coleman, Noel (act): Edge Of Sanity
Coleman, Ornette (act): Chappaqua
Coleman, Patricia (wri): Above Suspicion
Coleman, Patrick (mus): Blue Monkey
Coleman, Richard (act): Naked Evil; 10 Rillington Place
Coleman, Robin Jo (act): The Cradle Will Fall
Coleman, Ruth (act): A Night Of Mystery (1937)
Coleman, Tom (act): Attack Of The Killer Tomatoes
Coleman, Vincent (act): Salome (1923)
Coleman, Wilson (act): Alf's Button Afloat; The Black Tulip (1937); Blind Man's Bluff (1936); Dr. Syn; Sexton Blake And The Mademoiselle
Colen, Beatrice (act): Brave New World
Colerider, Glenn (act): The Dark Half
Colerider-Krugh, Kyle (act): Primal Fear
Coleridge, Alison (act): The Shining
Coleridge, Ethel (act): The Clouded Crystal; Colonel Bogey
Coleridge, Sylvia (act): I Met A Murderer
Coles, Barbara (act): Aliens
Coles, John (cin): Midnight Offerings
Coles, Laura (act): Space Raiders
Coles, Michael (act): Dr. Who And The Daleks; Dracula A.D. 1972; Man Detained; Never Mention Murder; The Satanic Rites Of Dracula
Coletti, Duilio (wri): Operation Crossbow
Coletti, Russell (act): Getting Lucky
Coley, John Ford (act): Dream A Little Dream
Coley, Tom (act): Dr. Cyclops
Colgan, Joseph (act): Distortions
Colgan, Michael (act): Donovan's Brain
Colicos, John (act): Battlestar Galactica; The Changeling; King Solomon's Treasure; Passport To Treason; Phobia
Colin, Ferdinand (cin): La Maldicion De Nostradamus; Nostradamus Y El Destructor De Monstruos
Colin, Ian (act): Blind Man's Bluff (1936); Witness In The Dark
Colin, Jean (act): Last Holiday
Colin, John (act): The Pirates Of Blood River
Colin, Margaret (act): Independence Day; Martians Go Home; The Return Of Sherlock Holmes (1986)
Colin, Sid (wri): Carry On Spying; It's Not The Size That Counts; The Ugly Duckling
Coll, Julio (dir): Los Muertos No Perdonan; Pyro
Colla, Richard (A.) (dir): Battlestar Galactica; Live Again, Die Again; The Other Man; The Questor Tapes; Something Is Out There; The Tribe; The Ufo Incident
Collatina, Silvia (act): The Great Alligator
Colleano, Bonar (act, 1924–1958): The Man Inside; A Matter Of Life And Death; Pool Of London; Sleeping Car To Trieste; Time Is My Enemy; Wanted For Murder
Colleano, Mark (act): The Laughing Girl Murder
Collector, Robert (wri): Memoirs Of An Invisible Man
Collentine, Barbara (act): Deadly Messages
Coller, Robin (act): The Groundstar Conspiracy
Collet, Christopher (act): The Manhattan Project
Collet, Joris (act): Daughters Of Darkness
Colley, Don Pedro (act): Beneath The Planet Of The Apes; Crosscurrent; Sugar Hill; Thx 1138
Colley, Ken(neth) (act): The Devils; Hitler: The Last Ten Days; I Hired A Contract Killer; Liszt O' Mania; Return Of The Jedi
Colley, Michael (act): The House Of The Dead
Colli, Ernesto (act): Spirits Of The Dead
Colli, Mario (act): S*H*E (1980)
Colli, Ombretta (act, a.k.a. Amber Collins): I Diavoli Della Spazio; Planet On The Prowl
Collier, Constance (act, 1877–1955): Rope
Collier, Constance (wri): Downhill; Peter Ibbetson
Collier, Cosette (act): I Was A Zombie For The F.B.I.
Collier, Ed (act): The Groundstar Conspiracy
Collier, Ian (act): Hamlet (1969)
Collier, Jason (act): Surf Nazis Must Die
Collier, John (wri): Elephant Boy
Collier, Lesley (act): Peter Rabbit And The Tales Of Beatrix Potter; Stories From A Flying Trunk
Collier, Lois (act): The Cat Creeps (1946); Cobra Woman; The Crimson Canary; Flying Disc Man From Mars; The Jungle Woman; Missile Monsters; Out Of The Storm; Weird Woman
Collier, Patience (act): Countess Dracula; Endless Night; The Third Secret
Collier, Richard (act): Eve Of Destruction
Collier, Terence (act): The Lost Patrol (1929)
Collier Jr., William (act): A Night Of Mystery (1928)
Collin, Anthony (act): Threads
Collin, John (act): Dead Man's Chest; The Witches (1966)
Collinge, Patricia (act, 1894–1974): Shadow Of A Doubt (1943)
Collings, Andy (act): The Corpse Grinders
Collings, Anne (act): The Mask (1961)
Collings, C.F. (act): The Girl Who Took The Wrong Turning
Collings, David (act): Scrooge (1970); The 39 Steps (1978)
Collings, Lisa (act): Captain Kronos: Vampire Hunter; The Mutations
Collins, Alan (act): El Castello Dell'orrore; Cinque Tombe Per Un Medium; Demons Of The Dead; Exterminators Of The Year 3000; Hatchet For A Honeymoon; Hunters Of The Golden Cobra; Lycanthropus; Master Stroke; Gli Orrori Del Castello Di Noremberga; Yor, The Hunter From The Future
Collins, Alf (act): The Mysterious Mechanical Toy
Collins, Alf (dir): Dr. Cut'emup; The Drunkard's Dream; The Effects Of Too Much Scotch; The Electric Goose; From Servant Girl To Duchess; King Of Coins; The Marvellous Syringe; Mechanical Legs; Mr. Mosenstein; The Mysterious Mechanical Toy; A Photographic Episode; The Puzzle Maniac; Revenge! (1904); Rip Van Winkle (1903); A Substantial Ghost
Collins, Amber (act): see Colli, Ombretta
Collins, Anthony (mus): Trent's Last Case (1952)
Collins, Bette (act): Mutants In Paradise
Collins, Bill (Austral act): Howling III
Collins, Bill (USA act): The Incredible 2-Headed Transplant
Collins, Bob (act): Seven
Collins, Boon (wri): Butcher, Baker (Nightmare Maker)
Collins, Brian (act): Midnight Lace (1981)
Collins, Burton (act): Creator
Collins, Charlie (act): The Steel Trap
Collins, Chick (act): Mr. Moto Takes A Vacation
Collins, Chuck (act): The Saint In Palm Springs
Collins, Cora Sue (act): Mad Love; The Scarlet Letter (1934)
Collins, Doug (act): The Hidden; To Die For II: Son Of Darkness
Collins, Eddie (act): The Blue Bird (1940); Charlie Chan In Honolulu; Charlie Chan In Reno
Collins, Edwin J. (act): The Hunchback (1911); Little Red Riding Hood (1911); Nan In Fairyland; Time Flies (1913); Topsy's Dream Of Toyland
Collins, Edwin J. (dir): Boots From Bootle; Constable Smith And The Magic Baton; Constable Smith On The Warpath; A Daughter Of Satan (1914); Daydreams; A Deuce Of A Girl; The Devil To Pay; The Electric Doll; Esmeralda; Eugene Aram; A Fluke In The 'flu-ence; A Hairraising Episode In One Splash; The Harvest Of Sin; Here We Are Again; His Wonderful Lamp; The Masked Smuggler; Nan In Fairyland; A Newsboy's Christmas Dream; On The Carpet; The Pursuit Of Venus; Rays That Erase; Spoof For Oof; Swanker And The Witch's Curse; Swanker Meets His Girl; Time Flies (1913); The Vengeance Of Daniel Whidden; Well I'm—; Which Is Witch?
Collins, Edwin J. (wri): Eugene Aram
Collins, Frank (act): His Just Desserts
Collins, Gary (act, b. 1938): Dial A Deadly Number; Hangar 18; Houston, We've Got A Problem; Killer Fish; Only A Scream Away
Collins, Greg (act): The Annihilator; Eve Of Destruction; 976-Evil
Collins, Jack (act): Jekyll And Hyde...Together Again; Murder Is My Business; The Nest; The Other (1972); The Towering Inferno
Collins, Jackie (act): The Shakedown; Undercover Girl (1958)
Collins, Jesse (act): Darkman II: The Return Of Durant
Collins, Joan (act, b. 1933): The Big Sleep (1978); Cosh Boy; Dark Places; Empire Of The Ants; Fear In The Night (1972); I Don't Want To Be Born; Land Of The Pharaohs; Quest For Love; Revenge (1971, GB); The Road To Hong Kong; Subterfuge; Tales From The Crypt; Tales That Witness Madness; Turn The Key Softly
Collins, Joe (act): White Angel
Collins, Joely (act): Hideaway
Collins, John D. (act): Dracula Has Risen From The Grave; The Ghoul (1974)
Collins III, Johnnie (act): Scream, Pretty Peggy
Collins, Jose (act): The Sword Of Damocles
Collins, Kathryn (act): Strange Behavior
Collins, Kevin (act): The Wicker Man
Collins, Lewis (act): A Ghost In Monte Carlo
Collins, Lewis D. (dir): Jungle Goddess; The Spanish Cape Mystery
Collins, Lisa (act): Deep Red (1994)
Collins, Matthew (act): Star Trek: Generations
Collins, Michael (act): For All Mankind
Collins, Michael James (act): Single White Female
Collins, Michelle (act): The Haunted (1991)
Collins, Mimi (act): Star Trek: Generations

Collins, Monty (act): *The Gracie Allen Murder Case*
Collins, Monty (wri): *Atoll K*
Collins, Nigel (act): *Threads*
Collins, Noel (act): *Never-Never Land*
Collins, Pat (act): *Change Of Mind; Eraser*
Collins, Patricia (act): *Phobia*
Collins, Paul (act): *Rogues Of Sherwood Forest*
Collins, Paul (wri): *Johnny The Giant Killer*
Collins, Ray (act, 1890–1965): *Crime Doctor; A Double Life; Francis; The Hidden Eye; It Happens Every Spring; Leave Her To Heaven; A Night In Paradise; The Return Of Monte Cristo; Three Wise Fools*
Collins, Ray (wri): *Yor, The Hunter From The Future*
Collins, Reuben (act): *The China Syndrome*
Collins, Richard (wri, b. 1914): *The Adventures Of Hajji Baba; Cult Of The Cobra; My Gun Is Quick*
Collins, Rick (act): *The Toxic Avenger, Part II; The Toxic Avenger, Part III: The Last Temptation Of Toxie*
Collins, Robert (act): *Mother's Day*
Collins, Roberta (act): *Caged Heat!; Death Race 2000; Saturday The 14th; School Spirit*
Collins, Rosie (act): *Terror (1979)*
Collins, Rufus (act): *The Hunger; Shock Treatment! (1981)*
Collins, Russell (act, 1897–1965): *Fail-Safe; Niagara*
Collins, Ruth (act): *Doom Asylum*
Collins, Sean (act): *The Housekeeper*
Collins, Shannon (act): *Piranha (1978)*
Collins, Sheldon (act): *The President's Analyst*
Collins, Stephen (act, b. 1947): *Dark Mirror (1984); The Disappearance Of Nora; The Henderson Monster; Star Trek*
Collins, Stephen (wri): *The Legend Of Spider Forest*
Collins, Wilkie (wri, 1824–1889): *Crimes At The Dark House; The Moonstone (1915); The Twin Pawns; The Woman In White (1929 & 1948)*
Collins, Winnie (act): *The Yellow Mask*
Collinson, Madelaine (act): *Twins Of Evil*
Collinson, Mary (act): *Twins Of Evil*
Collinson, Peter (dir, 1936–1980): *Fright (1971); The Penthouse (1967); The Spiral Staircase (1975); Straight On Till Morning; Ten Little Indians (1974)*
Collinson, Peter (wri, 1936–1980): *The Penthouse (1967)*
Collinson, Tara (act): *Fright (1971)*
Collis, George (act): *Deadly Strangers*
Collis, Jack T. (act): *Impulse (1984)*
Collison, Frank (act): *Alien Nation; Elvira, Mistress Of The Dark; The Lawnmower Man*
Collison, Rod (act): *Strange Behavior*
Collister, Peter Lyons (cin): *Halloween 4: The Return Of Michael Myers*
Collo, Luigi (wri): *The Cat O' Nine Tails*
Collodi, Carlo (wri): *The Adventures Of Pinocchio; Pinocchio*
Collodi, Joseph G. (wri): *Puppet Master*
Collver, Mark (act): *There's Nothing Out There*
Collyer, June (act, 1907–1968, nee Dorothy Heermance): *Drums Of Jeopardy (1931); Face In The Fog (1935); The Ghost Walks (1934); Murder By Television*
Collyer, Pamela (act): *The Kiss (1988)*
Colman, Ben (cin): *Battlestar Galactica; The Eyes Of Charles Sand; Haunts Of The Very Rich*
Colman, Booth (act): *Forgotten City Of The Planet Of The Apes; Secret Of The Incas; Time Travelers (1976); World Without End*
Colman, Edward (act): *The Absent-Minded Professor (1961); The Ambushers; Babes In Toyland (1961); Blackbeard's Ghost; The Gnome-Mobile; The Love Bug; Mary Poppins; The Monkey's Uncle; The Shaggy Dog; Son Of Flubber*
Colman, Julian (act): *Zorro, The Gay Blade*
Colman, Ronald (act, 1891–1958): *Around The World In 80 Days; The Black Spider; Bulldog Drummond (1929); Bulldog Drummond Strikes Back (1934); Champagne For Caesar; Condemned; A Double Life; Kismet (1944); Lost Horizon (1937); The Prisoner Of Zenda (1937); The Story Of Mankind*
Colmans, Edward (act): *Diary Of A Madman; Secret Of The Incas; Thief Of Damascus*
Colmar, Eric (act): *Captive Women; The Neanderthal Man; Port Sinister*
Colmes, Walter (dir): *Woman Who Came Back*
Colobanane, Sadeke (act): *The Jewel Of The Nile*
Colobuci, Joel (act): *The Kirlian Witness*
Colombier, Michael (mus): *Barb Wire; The Golden Child*
Colombo, E. (wri): *Scream Of The Demon Lover*

Colomby, Scott (act, b. 1953): *Angel On My Shoulder (1980); Are You In The House Alone?*
Colon, Alex (act): *Tarantulas: The Deadly Cargo; The Ultimate Warrior*
Colon, Miriam (act): *The Lightning Incident; The Possession Of Joel Delaney*
Colon, William (act): *Cyborg 2: Glass Shadow*
Colonna, G.C. (act): *The Murdock Trial*
Colosimo, Clara (act): *The Great Alligator*
Colosimo, Sandy (act): *Frankenhooker*
Colourz, Captain (act): *The Lost Boys*
Colpi, Henri (dir): *The Mysterious Island Of Captain Nemo*
Colson, Kevin (act): *Night Watch*
Colt, Marshall (act): *Flowers In The Attic*
Colt, Zebedy (act): *The Amazing Dr. Jekyll*
Colti, Tony (act): *On A Clear Day You Can See Forever*
Colton, Jacque Lynn (act): *Gremlins 2: The New Batch*
Colton, John (act): *Time After Time*
Colton, John (wri): *The Invisible Ray; Werewolf Of London*
Colton, Rita (act): *Project X (1949)*
Coltrane, Tom (act): *The Punisher*
Coltrane, Rexx (act): *The Being*
Coltrane, Robbie (act, b. 1950): *Flash Gordon; Goldeneye; Krull; Slipstream*
Columbier, Michel (mus): *Colossus: The Forbin Project*
Columbo, Albert (mus): *Dick Tracy Returns; Murder On A Honeymoon*
Columbus, Abraham (act): *Spawn Of The Slithis*
Columbus, Chris (wri, b. 1959): *The Goonies; Gremlins; Little Nemo: Adventures In Slumberland; Young Sherlock Holmes*
Coluzzi, Francesca Romana (act): *Red Sonja*
Colvey, Peter (act): *Brainscan*
Colvig, Vance (act): *Maid To Order*
Colvin, Jack (act): *Child's Play (1988); Embryo; Exo-Man; The Incredible Hulk; The Incredible Hulk, Part 2; The Incredible Hulk Returns; The Spell*
Colwell, Chuck (cin): *The Death Of The Incredible Hulk; Galaxina; The Incredible Hulk Returns*
Colyer, Chris (act): *Jamaica Inn (1985)*
Comandini, Adele (wri): *Beyond Tomorrow*
Comanor, Jeffrey (act): *Phantom Of The Paradise*
Comar, Richard (act): *Short Circuit 2*
Comber, Bobbie (act): *Elstree Calling*
Combs, Gary (act): *Looker; What's The Matter With Helen?*
Combs, Holly Marie (act): *Dr. Giggles*
Combs, Jeffrey (act): *Bride Of Re-Animator; Castle Freak; Cellar Dweller; Cyclone; Dead Man Walking; Doctor Mordrid; Fortress; The Frighteners; Frightmare (1983); From Beyond; The Phantom Empire; The Pit And The Pendulum (1990); Re-Animator; Trancers II: The Return Of Jack Deth*
Combs, Mike (act): *Hex*
Combs, Thurman L. (act): *The Body Snatchers*
Comden, Betty (mus & wri, b. 1916): *It's Always Fair Weather*
Comencini, Luigi (dir, b. 1916): *Italian Secret Service*
Comer, Anjanette (act, b. 1942): *The Baby; Dead Of Night (1977); The Loved One; The Night Of A Thousand Cats; Terror On The 40th Floor*
Comer, John (act): *Memoirs Of A Survivor*
Comfort, Brian (wri): *The Asphyx; Beware, My Brethren; The Fiend (1972); Girly*
Comfort, Lance (dir, 1908–1966): *At The Stroke Of Nine; Bedelia; Daughter Of Darkness (1948); Devils Of Darkness; Escape To Danger; Face In The Night; The Girl On The Pier; The Man In The Road; The Ugly Duckling*
Comi, Paul (act): *Cape Fear (1961); Conquest Of The Planet Of The Apes; Howard The Duck; The Towering Inferno*
Comici, Lou (act): *The Visitor*
Comingore, Dorothy (act, 1918–1971): *The Hairy Ape*
Commander, Johnny (act): *The Being*
Commons, David (cin): *The Neanderthal Man*
Como, Rossella (act): *Gli Amori Di Ercole*
Comolli, Jean-Louis (act): *Alphaville, Une Étrange Aventure De Lemmy Caution*
Comont, Mathilde (act): *Loves Of Carmen; The Sea Beast; The Thief Of Bagdad (1924)*
Compan, Gilberto (act): *Nightlife (1989, Usa-Mex)*
Companeez, Jacques (wri): *Alibi (1942); Shadow Of The Eagle; La Sorciere*
Companeez, Nina (dir & wri): *Faustine Et Le Bel Ete*
Compansanto, Nancy (act): *The Toxic Avenger*

Compinsky, Manuel (mus): *Killers From Space; The Snow Creature*
Compson, Betty (act, 1897–1974): *Blondes At Work; The Great Gabbo; The Invisible Ghost; Midnight Mystery; The Miracle Man (1919); Torchy Blane In Panama*
Compton, Athol (act): *The Last Wave*
Compton, Fay (act, 1894–1978): *Blackmailed; The Haunting; The House Of Peril; I Start Counting; Journey To Midnight; Robinson Crusoe (1927)*
Compton, Francis (act): *Witness For The Prosecution*
Compton, Joyce (act, b. 1907, nee Eleanor Hunt): *Dark Alibi; The Last Warning (1938); Scared To Death (1947); Sky Murder; Sorry, Wrong Number (1948); The Villain Still Pursued Her*
Compton, Juliette (act): *Bulldog Drummond's Third Round; The Triumph Of The Scarlet Pimpernel*
Compton, Marjorie (act): *Honour In Pawn*
Compton, Richard (dir): *Ravagers*
Compton, Sharon (act): *Dr. Heckyl & Mr. Hype*
Compton, Viola (act): *Dark World; The Man In The Mirror; The Shadow (1933)*
Comstock, Howard W. (wri): *Doctor X*
Comyn, Charles (act): *Prisoners Of The Lost Universe'*
Conaway, Cristi (act): *Batman Returns*
Conaway, Curtis (act): *Friday the 13th- Part V: A New Beginning*
Conaway, Jeff (act): *Bay Coven; Elvira, Mistress Of The Dark; Ghost Writer; Mirror Images; Pete's Dragon; 2002: Rape Of Eden*
Concannon, Mike (act): *Teenage Zombies*
Concepcion, M. (act): *Storm Over Tibet*
Concepcion, Michael (act): *Stargate*
Conde, Antonio Diaz (mus): *Doctor Of Doom*
Conde, Fredy (cin): *Twilight People*
Conde, Rita (act): *Reflections Of Murder; Time After Time*
Conde, Zedra (act): *The Falcon Out West*
Conder, Robert (act): *Halloween 4: The Return Of Michael Myers*
Condict, Win (act): *Spawn Of The Slithis*
Condle, Molly (act): *Matinee*
Condon, Bill (dir): *Candyman: Farewell To The Flesh; Sister, Sister*
Condon, David (act): *The Bowery Boys Meet The Monsters; Bowery To Bagdad; Crashing Las Vegas; Dig That Uranium!; Hold That Hypnotist!; Jalopy; Jungle Gents; Spy Chasers*
Condon, Richard (wri, 1914-1996): *The Manchurian Candidate*
Condon, William (act): *Strange Behavior*
Condon, William/Bill (wri): *Sister, Sister; Strange Behavior; Strange Invaders*
Condron, Tim (act): *The Plague Of The Zombies*
Condylis, Paul (act): *Targets*
Cone, Bill (act): *Phantasm*
Conely, Sharon (act): *The Haunted (1991)*
Conforti, Donna (act): *Santa Claus Conquers The Martians*
Conforti, Gino (act): *Poor Devil; Through The Magic Pyramid*
Confrey, Wayne (act): *Empire Of Ash III*
Congdon, Harold (act): *You'll Like My Mother*
Congdon, James (act): *4D Man; When Worlds Collide*
Congia, Vittorio (act): *The Cat O' Nine Tails*
Conjiu, Nela (act): *La Maldicion De Los Karnsteins*
Conkel, Jeff (act): *The Hand That Rocks The Cradle*
Conklin, Chester (act, 1888–1971): *The Beast With A Million Eyes; The Haunted House (1929); The House Of Horror (1929); Modern Times; The Phantom Of The Opera (1925)*
Conklin, Heinie (act): *The Chance Of A Lifetime; Li'l Abner (1940)*
Conklin, Shirley (act): *The Adding Machine; Trog*
Conklin, Tracy (act): *The Haunting Of Sarah Hardy*
Conkling, Chris (wri): *The Lord Of The Rings*
Conkling, Donna King (act): *The Hideous Sun Demon*
Conkling, Xandra (act): *The Hideous Sun Demon*
Conlan, Christopher (act): *Boarding House*
Conlan, Frank (act, b. 1890): *All That Money Can Buy; Strangler Of The Swamp*
Conlan, Joseph (mus): *Joe & The Colonel; Memories Of Murder; Mortal Sins; The Stepford Children*
Conlan, Thomas J. (act): *The Resurrection Of Zachary Wheeler*
Conley, Amelia (act): *Fright (1957)*

Conley, Corinne (act): *The Return Of Count Yorga*
Conley, Sharon (act): *Nightmare On The 13th Floor*
Conley, Ted (act): *Quarantine*
Conlin Jr., David (act): *Beyond The Door; Shock (1978)*
Conlin, James/Jimmy (act, 1885–1962): *The Adventurous Blonde; Calling Philo Vance; Dick Tracy's Dilemma; The Great Rupert; The 30 Foot Bride Of Candy Rock; Torchy Blane In Panama; Torchy Runs For Mayor*
Conlon, Dennis (act): *Threads*
Conlon, Mark (act): *The Craft*
Conlon, Noel (act): *My Science Project*
Conlon, Tim (act): *Prom Night III: The Last Kiss*
Connah, Lit (act): *Mutant*
Connaught, Richard (act): *A Clockwork Orange; Tales That Witness Madness*
Connell, David (act): *Wolfen*
Connell, David (act): *The Neverending Story II: The Next Chapter*
Connell, Edward (act): *Equinox*
Connell, Jane (act): *Dr. Jekyll And Ms. Hyde; Ladybug, Ladybug*
Connell, Jim (act): *Gargoyles*
Connell, Kim (act): *The Dungeonmaster*
Connell, Linda (act): *The Cape Canaveral Monsters*
Connell, Maureen (act): *The Abominable Snowman Of The Himalayas; Danger By My Side; Golden Ivory; Kill Her Gently; The Man Upstairs*
Connell, Richard (wri, b. 1893): *Bloodlust!; A Game Of Death; The Most Dangerous Game; Run For The Sun*
Connell, Tracy (act): *The Return Of Mr. Moto*
Connell, W. Merle (cin): *The Unearthly*
Connell, W. Merle (dir): *Untamed Women*
Connelly (mus): *Blackmail (1929)*
Connelly, Christopher (act, 1941–1988): *Earthbound (1981); Manhattan Baby; The Norsemen*
Connelly, Edward (act): *The Conquering Power; The Prisoner Of Zenda (1922); Trifling Women; The Unholy Three (1925)*
Connelly, Erwin (act): *The Man From Beyond; Sherlock Jr.*
Connelly, Jane (act): *Sherlock Jr.*
Connelly, Jennifer (act, b. 1970): *Labyrinth (1986); Phenomena; The Rocketeer*
Connelly, Joe (wri): *Munster, Go Home!*
Connelly, Marc (act, 1890–1980): *Devil's Angel*
Connelly, Marc (dir, 1890–1980): *Green Pastures*
Connelly, Marc (wri, 1890–1980): *Green Pastures; I Married A Witch*
Conner, Marla (act): *Frankenstein Island*
Conner, Paige (act): *The Visitor*
Conners, Julie (act): *Count Yorga, Vampire*
Connery, Jason (act, b. 1963): *Bullet To Beijing; The Secret Life Of Ian Fleming*
Connery, Neil (act): *The Body Stealers; Operation Kid Brother*
Connery, Sean (act, b. 1930): *The Avengers; Darby O'gill And The Little People; Diamonds Are Forever; Dr. No; Dragonheart; First Knight; The Frightened City; From Russia With Love; Goldfinger; Highlander; Highlander 2: The Quickening; Indiana Jones And The Last Crusade; The Man Who Would Be King; Marnie; Meteor; Murder On The Orient Express; The Name Of The Rose; Never Say Never Again; Outland; The Red Tent; Robin And Marian; Robin Hood: Prince Of Thieves; Sword Of The Valiant; Tarzan's Greatest Adventure; Thunderball; Time Bandits; Woman Of Straw; You Only Live Twice; Zardoz*
Connick Jr., Harry (act, b. 1967): *Copycat; Independence Day*
Connolly, Myles (wri): *Tarzan's New York Adventure; Tarzan's Secret Treasure*
Connolly, Nora (act): *The Witches (1990)*
Connolly, Norma (act): *The Other (1972)*
Connolly, Patricia (act): *Color Me Dead*
Connolly, Walter (act, 1883–1940): *League Of Frightened Men*
Connor, Edric (act, 1915–1968): *Moby Dick (1956); Seven Thunders*
Connor, Frank (act): *The Beginning Of The End*
Connor, Keith (act): *Alien High*
Connor, Kenneth (act, b. 1924): *The Black Rider; Captain Nemo And The Underwater City; The Lady Killers (1956); Psion Pan; What A Carve Up!*
Connor, Kevin (dir): *Arabian Adventure; At The Earth's Core; From Beyond The Grave; Goliath Awaits; The House Where Evil Dwells; The Land That Time Forgot; Motel*

Hell; The People That Time Forgot; The Return Of Sherlock Holmes (1986); Warlords Of The Deep
Connor, Patrick (act): Brazil; The Headless Ghost; Kill Her Gently; Lifeforce
Connor, Randy (act): Android
Connor, Whitfield (act): The Saracen Blade
Connors, Alice (act): Torchy Runs For Mayor
Connors, Barry (wri): The Black Camel; Chandu The Magician; Charlie Chan Carries On; Charlie Chan's Chance; Women Of All Nations
Connors, Chuck (act, 1921–1992, nee Kevin Joseph Connors): Captain Nemo And The Underwater City; Embassy; The Horror At 37,000 Feet; The Mad Bomber; Night Of Terror (1972); 99 And 44/100% Dead; Soylent Green; Tourist Trap; Virus; Walk The Dark Street
Connors, Kathleen (act): Congo
Connors, Kathleen (wri): The Fatal Night
Connors, Kevin (act): Phantasm III: Lord Of The Dead
Connors, Kevin Joseph (act): see Connors, Chuck
Connors, Michael/Mike (act, b. 1925, nee Kreker Ohanian, a.k.a. Touch Connors): Day The World Ended (1955); Kiss The Girls And Make Them Die; Sudden Fear; Swamp Women; Too Scared To Scream; Voodoo Woman
Connors, Phillip Dennis (wri): Evils Of The Night
Conolly, John P. (act): When The Bough Breaks
Conover, Jean (wri): The Midnight Girl
Conover, Theresa Maxwell (act): Peter Ibbetson
Conquest, Arthur (act): The Showman's Dream
Conrad, Alan (act): Final Eye
Conrad, Barbara (act): A Princess Of The Blood
Conrad Jr., Charles (act): For All Mankind
Conrad, Chris (act): Star Command
Conrad, Chris (wri): Junior
Conrad, Diedre (act): Watchers II
Conrad, Eugene (wri): Philo Vance's Gamble
Conrad, Jess (act, b. 1940): The Assassination Bureau; The Flesh And Blood Show; Konga
Conrad, Joseph (wri, 1857–1924): Sabotage; The Secret Agent (1996)
Conrad, Kendall (act): Alien Nation
Conrad, Michael (act, 1925–1983): Castle Keep; Satan's Triangle; Scream, Blacula, Scream; W
Conrad, Mikel (act): The Flying Saucer (1950); Francis; Untamed Women
Conrad, Mikel (dir & wri): The Flying Saucer (1950)
Conrad, Paul (act): The Docks Of New Orleans
Conrad, Pete(r) (act): The Funhouse (1981); Stowaway To The Moon
Conrad, Rick (mus) The Nest; Watchers II
Conrad, Robert (act, b. 1935): The Adventures Of Nick Carter; Assassin (1986); The Fifth Missile
Conrad, Sid (act): King Kong (1976)
Conrad, Tom (act): The Green Slime
Conrad, William (act, 1920–1994): The Brotherhood Of The Bell; The Naked Jungle; The Return Of The King; Sorry, Wrong Number (1948); The Sword Of Monte Cristo
Conrad, William (dir, 1920–1994): Brainstorm (1965); My Blood Runs Cold; Two On A Guillotine
Conried, Hans (act, 1917–1982): The Cat From Outer Space (1943); Crazy House; A Date With The Falcon; The Falcon Takes Over; The 5000 Fingers Of Dr. T; The Gay Falcon; The Hobbit; Journey Into Fear (1942); The Monster That Challenged The World; Oh, God! Book II; The Shaggy D.A.; Siren Of Bagdad; Through The Magic Pyramid; The Twonky
Conried, Trilby (act): The Twonky
Conroy, Burt (act): Futureworld
Conroy, Frank (act, 1890–1964): Charlie Chan At The Opera; Charlie Chan In Egypt; The Day The Earth Stood Still; The Kennel Murder Case; Lady Of Burlesque; The Last Days Of Pompeii (1935); Lightning Strikes Twice; The Loves Of Edgar Allan Poe; Meet Nero Wolfe; The Snake Pit (1948)
Conroy, J.R. (act): My Best Friend Is A Vampire
Conroy, Jarlath (act): Day Of The Dead
Conroy, Kevin (act): Batman: Mask Of The Phantasm; Covenant; Island City
Conroy, Thom (act): Seconds
Conselman, William (wri): A Connecticut Yankee
Considine, John (act): Doctor Death: Seeker Of Souls; Endangered Species; Pandora's Clock; The Thirsty Dead; Timestalkers
Considine, John (wri): Tarzan's Deadly Silence
Considine, Robert (wri): The Beginning Or The End?
Considine, Tim (act): The Shaggy Dog
Considine, Tim (wri): Tarzan's Deadly Silence
Constance-Churcher, Pia (act): Arthur The King
Constantin, George (act): Getting Lucky
Constantin, Romeo (act): War Of The Planets
Constantine, Dorothy (act): The Alien's Return
Constantine, Eddie (act, b. 1917): Alphaville, Une Etrange Aventure De Lemmy Caution; A Toi De Faire, Mignonne; Cartes Sur Table; Cet Homme Est Dangereux; Comment Qu'ella Est!; Les Femmes S'en Balancent; Hi, Here's Eddie; Lemmy Pour Les Dames; Long Distance; La Mome Vert-De-Gris; Nick Carter Et Le Trefle Rouge; Nick Carter Va Tout Casser; Vous Pegez?
Constantine, Mathew (act): Mad Max
Constantine, Michael (act, b. 1927): Death Cruise; The Night That Panicked America; The Southern Star; Thinner
Constantini, Giorgio (act): The Stranger's Hand
Consuella, Senorita (act): The Temple Of Venus
Contandin, Fernand Joseph Desire (act): See Fernandel
Conte, John (act): Lost In A Harem; Trauma (1963)
Conte, Nicholas (act): see Conte, Richard
Conte, Richard (Act, 1914–1975, nee Nicholas Conte): Desert Legion; The Eyes Of Annie Jones; Little Red Monkey; A Race For Life; Slaves Of Babylon; The Spider (1945)
Conte, Robert (act): Appointment With Murder; Thief Of Damascus
Conte, Steve (act): La Casa Del Terror; The Kindred; The Resurrection Of Zachary Wheeler; Teenage Zombies; Terror Of The Bloodhunters
Conti, Albert (act): As You Desire Me; The Black Cat (1934); Charlie Chan In City In Darkness; The Chinese Parrot; Such Men Are Dangerous
Conti, Audrey (act): Invasion Of The Saucer Men
Conti, Bill (mus): Bionic Showdown: The Six Million Dollar Man And The Bionic Woman; For Your Eyes Only; Masters Of The Universe; Neighbors; Nomads
Conti, Eduardo Giorgio (wri): Perseus The Invincible
Conti, Richard (act): Copycat
Conti, Sam (act): Invasion Of The Body Snatchers (1978)
Conti, Tom (act, b. 1941): Eclipse (1977); Full Circle; If It's A Man, Hang Up
Continenza, (Alessandro/Sandro) (wri): Gli Amori Di Ercole; Ceremonia Sangriento; Ercole Al Centro Della Terra; Ercole Alla Conquista Della Atlantide; Marte, Dio Della Guerra; Ok, Nero!; Tempi Duri Per I Vampiri
Continenz, S. (wri): The Minotaur
Contini, Alfio (cin): The Night Porter; The Trojan Women
Contner, J. Burgi (cin): Fright (1957); Roogie's Bump
Contner, James A. (cin): Jaws 3-D
Contner, James A. (dir): Hitler's Daughter
Contouri, Chantal (act): The Day After Halloween; Thirst
Contreras, Ernie (wri): The Pagemaster
Contreras, Miguel (act): Secret Of The Incas
Contreras, Robert(O) (act): The Beast Of Hollow Mountain; The Dark (1979); The Flame Barrier; Mara Of The Wilderness
Converse, Anita (act): Fade To Black
Converse, Frank (act, b. 1938): Cruise Into Terror; Dr. Cook's Garden
Converse, Peggy (act): Just Before Dawn (1946); The Thing That Couldn't Die
Convertino, Michael (mus): The Hidden
Conville, David (act): Evil Of Frankenstein
Convy, Bert (act, 1933–1991): A Bucket Of Blood (1959); Death Takes A Holiday (1971); Jennifer (1978); The Man In The Santa Claus Suit
Conway, Blake (act): Jason Goes To Hell: The Final Friday
Conway, Booth (act): Esmeralda; The Valley Of Fear (1916)
Conway, Cyril (act): Evil Under The Sun; Venom (1982)
Conway, Gary (act, b. 1938, nee Gareth Carmody): How To Make A Monster; I Was A Teenage Frankenstein; The Viking Women And The Sea Serpent
Conway, Gerry (wri): Conan The Destroyer
Conway, Harold (act): Mothra
Conway, Hugh (wri): Called Back
Conway, Jack (dir, 1887–1952): The Unholy Three (1930)
Conway, James (L.) (dir & wri): The Boogens; Earthbound (1981); The Fall Of The House Of Usher (1982); Hangar 18
Conway, Jane R. (act): I Was A Zombie For The F.B.I.
Conway, Kevin (act, b. 1942): The Funhouse (1981); The Lathe Of Heaven; Lawnmower Man 2: Beyond Cyberspace; Portnoy's Complaint; Slaughterhouse-Five
Conway, Lyle (act): Return To Oz
Conway, Michael (act): I Was A Zombie For The F.B.I.
Conway, Morgan (act, 1900–1981): Charlie Chan In Reno; Desperate Chance For Ellery Queen; Dick Tracy (1945); Dick Tracy vs. Cueball; The Saint Takes Over; The Truth About Murder
Conway, Pat (act): The Deadly Mantis; Undersea Girl
Conway, Peter (act): The Tomb
Conway, Richard (cin): The Adventures Of Baron Munchausen (1989)
Conway, Russ (act): Jennifer (1953); Killer Leopard; One Girl's Confession; Our Man Flint; Safari Drums; The Screaming Skull
Conway, Tim (act, B. 1933): The Shaggy D.A.
Conway, Tom (act, 1904–1967, nee Thomas Sanders): The Atomic Submarine; Barbados Quest; Bride Of The Gorilla; Cat People (1942); The Challenge; Confidence Girl; The Falcon And The Co-Eds; The Falcon In Danger; The Falcon In Hollywood; The Falcon In Mexico; The Falcon In San Francisco; The Falcon Out West; The Falcon's Alibi; The Falcon's Brother; The Falcon Strikes Back; I Cheated The Law; I Walked With A Zombie; The Last Man To Hang?; A Night Of Adventure; One Touch Of Venus; Prince Valiant; Repeat Performance; The Seventh Victim; The She-Creature; Sky Murder; Tarzan And The She-Devil; Tarzan's Secret Treasure; 13 Lead Soldiers; 12 To The Moon; Voodoo Woman
Conyers, Darcy (dir & wri): The Secret Of The Forest
Coogan, Jackie (act, 1914–1984, nee Jack Cohn): Dr. Heckyl & Mr. Hype; Escape From Terror; Halloween With The Addams Family; Human Experiments; Mesa Of Lost Women; The Phantom Of Hollywood; Prehistoric Women (1950); The Prey (1980); Sex Kittens Go To College; Sherlock Holmes In New York; The Space Children
Coogan, Keith (act): The Power Within
Coogan, Robert (act): Ghost Chasers
Cook, Ancel (act): Frightmare (1983); Rattlers
Cook, Bonnie (act): King Kong Lives
Cook, Carole (act): The Incredible Mr. Limpet
Cook, Clyde (act, b. 1891): Arrest Bulldog Drummond; Bulldog Drummond Escapes; Bulldog Drummond's Secret Police; Counter-Espionage; He Who Gets Slapped
Cook, Diana (act): Mermaids Of Tiburon
Cook, Donald (act, 1900–1961): The Casino Murder Case; The Mad Genius; Murder In The Blue Room; The Penguin Pool Murder; The Spanish Cape Mystery
Cook, Doria (act): The Swarm
Cook, Earle Browne (act): The Dungeon
Cook Jr., Elisha (act, 1904–1995): A-Haunting We Will Go; The Big Sleep (1946); The Black Bird (1975); Black Zoo; Blacula; Born To Kill; Dark Waters; Dead Of Night (1977); Dead People; The Falcon's Alibi; The Glass Cage; The Haunted Palace (1963); Hellzapoppin ; House On Haunted Hill; It Came Upon The Midnight Clear; I, The Jury (1953); I Wake Up Screaming; Johnny Cool; The Killing; The Maltese Falcon (1941); The Night Stalker (1971); Phantom Lady; The Phantom Of Hollywood; Platinum High School; Rosemary's Baby; Salem's Lot; The Spy In The Green Hat; Stranger On The Third Floor; Voodoo Island
Cook, Fielder (dir, b. 1923): Miracle On 34th Street (1973)
Cook, Fredric (act): Schizoid (1980)
Cook, Gordon (act): Empire Of Ash III
Cook, Jacqui (act): Captain Kronos: Vampire Hunter
Cook, Jillian (act): Sorry, Wrong Number (1989)
Cook, John (act): The Adding Machine
Cook, Joseph (act): Where Has Poor Mickey Gone?
Cook, Larry (act): Primal Fear
Cook, Lawrence (act): Lord Shango
Cook, Mara (act): The Swarm
Cook, Marianne (act): Black Panther Of Ratana
Cook, Marlene (act): Ed Wood
Cook, Mary Lou (act): The Destructors
Cook, Myron (act): The Amazing Colossal Man; The Lost Missile
Cook, Nathan (act): Abby
Cook, Pam (act): Species
Cook, Patrick (act): Those Dear Departed
Cook, Peter (Act, 1937–1995): Bedazzled; The Bed-Sitting Room; A Dandy In Aspic; The Hound Of The Baskervilles (1978); The Princess Bride; Supergirl (1984); Without A Clue; The Wrong Box
Cook, Peter (wri): Bedazzled; The Hound Of The Baskervilles (1978)
Cook, Randall William (cin): The Gate; Gate II
Cook, Randy (act): Dr. Caligari
Cook, Robin (wri, b. 1940): Coma; Robin Cook's Harmful Intent; Robin Cook's Invasion; Sphinx (1981); Terminal
Cook, Ron (act): The Odyssey
Cook, Roderick (act): Spellbinder
Cook, Steve (act): Equalizer 2000
Cook, T.S. (wri): The China Syndrome
Cook, Tommy (act): Missile To The Moon; Tarzan And The Leopard Woman
Cook, Vera (act): Brides Of Dracula; Kiss Of The Vampire
Cook, Whitfield (wri): Stage Fright
Cook, Willis (cin): The Beast From 20,000 Fathoms
Cooke, Alan (dir): The Hunchback Of Notre Dame (1977); The Mind Of Mr. Soames; Paint Me A Murder; The Starfish
Cooke, Alan (wri): The Starfish
Cooke, Beryl (act): The Boy Who Never Was; The Monster Of Highgate Ponds
Cooke, C.J. (act): Nightmare (1981)
Cooke, Jennifer (Act): Friday The 13th, Part VI: Jason Lives
Cooke, Jill (act): Peter Rabbit And The Tales Of Beatrix Potter
Cooke, John B. (act): Missing Millions
Cooke, Keith H. (act): Heatseeker
Cooke, Peter (act): Tarzan Goes To India
Cooke, Steven (act): Getting Lucky
Cooke, Terry (act): One Wish Too Many
Cooke, Wendy (act): Cocoon: The Return; Donor; Grim Prairie Tales; 976-Evil
Cookerly, Jack (mus): Grotesque
Coo-Koo The Bird Woman (act): Freaks
Cooksey, Danny (act): Terminator 2: Judgment Day
Cookson, Barrie (act): A Clockwork Orange
Cookson, Georgina (act): Catacombs; The Shakedown; Solution By Phone
Cookson, Peter (act, 1913–1990): Adventures Of Kitty O'day; Fear (1946); Shadow Of Suspicion
Cookson, S.A. (act): Hamlet (1913)
Cookson, Tony (dir & wri): And You Thought Your Parents Were Weird
Cooley, B.J. (act): Secrets Of The Phantom Caverns
Cooley, Hallam (act): Black Waters; The Monster (1925)
Cooley, Isabel (act): Silent Night, Deadly Night III
Coolidge, Martha (dir): Three Wishes (1995)
Coolidge, Martha (wri): The London Connection
Coolidge, Philip (act): The Tingler
Coolidge, Rita (mus, b. 1945): Octopussy; Splash
Coombe, Carol (act): The Ghost Train (1931); The Strangler (1932)
Coombes, James (act): Murder With Mirrors
Coon, Caroline (act): House Of 1,000 Dolls
Coon, Gene (wri): The Questor Tapes
Coon, Jacque J. (act): Bloodspell
Coonan, Sheila (act): Echoes
Cooney, Helene (act): Haunted Palace (1949)
Cooney, Kevin (act): Deadly Blessing
Cooney, Ray (act & wri): The Hand (1960) What A Carve Up!
Coontz, Bill (act): Frankenstein's Daughter (1958); She Demons
Coop, Denys (cin, b. 1920): —And Now The Screaming Starts!; Asylum; Bunny Lake Is Missing; The Double Man; The Mind Benders (1963); Satellite In The Sky; 10 Rillington Place; The Vault Of Horror; Venom (1982)
Cooper, Alice (act, b. 1948): Freddy's Dead: The Final Nightmare; Prince Of Darkness
Cooper, Alice (mus, b. 1948): Class Of '84
Cooper, Arthur (dir): Animated Matches; The Cat's Cup Final; Cinderella (1912); Dolly's Toys; Dreams Of Toyland; The Enchanted Toymaker; The Fairy Godmother (1906); Father's Forty Winks; In The Land Of Nod; Larks In Toyland; The Motor Valet; Oh That Molar!; Old Mother Hubbard; An Old Toymaker's Dream; The Tale Of The Ark; Ten Little Nigger Boys; The Toymaker's Dream; A Visit To A Spritualist
Cooper, Arthur (wri): Animated Matches; The Cat's Cup Final; Cinderella (1912); Dreams Of Toyland; In The Land Of Nod;

Larks In Toyland; Old Mother Hubbard; An Old Toymaker's Dream; The Tale Of The Ark; Ten Little Nigger Boys; The Toymaker's Dream
Cooper, Ashley (act): Robin Hood Jr. (1923)
Cooper, Barry (act): Fear No Evil (1981)
Cooper, Betty (act): The Camp On Blood Island; Lady In The Fog; Obsession (1949)
Cooper, Bobby (act): Secrets Of Scotland Yard
Cooper, Buddy (dir & wri): The Mutilator
Cooper, Cami (act): Meet The Applegates; Shocker
Cooper, Camille (act): Lawnmower Man 2: Beyond Cyberspace
Cooper, Cathy (act): Blood Diner
Cooper, Charles (act): Angel On My Shoulder (1980); Star Trek V: The Final Frontier; The Wrong Man
Cooper, Chevis (act): Project X (1987)
Cooper, Chris (wri): Step Down To Terror
Cooper, Chuck (act): I Was A Zombie For The F.B.I.
Cooper, Clancy (act): The Great Rupert
Cooper, Dave (act): Without A Clue
Cooper, Dee (act): The Alien's Return
Cooper, Dennis (wri): Woman Who Came Back
Cooper, Douglas (act): Dragonslayer
Cooper, Doyle (act): This Is Not A Test
Cooper, E.A. (act): see Ashley, Edward
Cooper, Edmund (wri): The Invisible Boy
Cooper, Edna Mae (act): Male And Female
Cooper, Frank J. (act): see Cooper, Gary
Cooper, Frederick (act): Escape To Danger; Thunder Rock
Cooper, Gary (act, 1901–1961, nee Frank J. Cooper): Alice In Wonderland (1933); Cloak And Dagger (1946); The Naked Edge; Peter Ibbetson
Cooper, George (A.) (GB act, b. 1913): The Black Windmill; Dracula Has Risen From The Grave; A Ghost In Monte Carlo; Nightmare (1963); On Her Majesty's Secret Service; Vengeance; What Became Of Jack And Jill
Cooper, George (USA act): Behind The Curtain (1924); The Missing Guest; Think Fast, Mr. Moto; Through The Dark; The Unholy Night
Cooper, George A. (dir): The Black Abbot (1934); Blake The Lawbreaker; The Clue Of The Second Goblet; The Man Outside (1933); Puppets Of Fate; Sexton Blake And The Bearded Doctor; The Shadow (1933); Tangled Evidence
Cooper, George Lane (act): Batman (1989)
Cooper, Gladys (act, 1888–1971): At Sword's Point; The Bishop's Wife; The Black Cat (1941); The Cockeyed Miracle; The Gay Falcon; The List Of Adrian Messenger; Love Letters; Rebecca; The Sorrows Of Satan (1917)
Cooper, Helmar (act): Frankenhooker
Cooper, Henry (act): Royal Flash
Cooper, Inez (act): Flight To Nowhere; Shadow Of The Thin Man
Cooper, J. (act): Old St. Paul's
Cooper, Jack (act): The Toxic Avenger, Part II
Cooper, Jackie (act, b. 1921): The Astronaut; Chosen Survivors; Everything's Ducky; The Invisible Man (1975); Shadow On The Land; Superman (1978); Superman II; Superman III; Superman IV: The Quest For Peace; Treasure Island (1934)
Cooper, Jackie (dir, b. 1921): The Night They Saved Christmas
Cooper, Jeanne (act): Black Zoo
Cooper, Jeff (act): Circle Of Iron; A Thousand And One Nights (1968)
Cooper, Jeremy (act): The Reflecting Skin
Cooper, Joan (act): The Ruling Class
Cooper, John (dir): Murder On The Midnight Express; Possession (1973)
Cooper, John C. (wri): First Man Into Space; Grip Of The Strangler; The Projected Man
Cooper, Justin (act, b. 1988): Liar Liar
Cooper, Mark (act): Hawk The Slayer
Cooper, Maury (act): Coma
Cooper, Maxine (act): Kiss Me Deadly
Cooper, Melville (act, 1897–1973): The Adventures Of Robin Hood; Around The World In 80 Days; Blind Alley; Forging Ahead; From The Earth To The Moon; Murder Over New York; The Private Life Of Don Juan; Rebecca; The Scarlet Pimpernel (1934); Scotland Yard (1941); The Story Of Mankind
Cooper, Merian C. (dir, 1895–1973): King Kong (1933)
Cooper, Merian C. (wri, 1895–1973): King Kong (1933); King Kong Lives
Cooper, Muriel (act): The Worm Eaters
Cooper, Romolo Waddle (act): The Mutilator
Cooper, Paul (act): Lifeforce; Spirits Of The Dead
Cooper, Peggy (act): Student Bodies
Cooper, Ray (act): Brazil
Cooper, Richard (act): Alf's Button Afloat; The Black Abbot (1934); The House Of The Arrow (1930); The Last Hour
Cooper, Ronnie (act): Rocket Attack U.S.A.
Cooper, Rosemary (act): The Return Of Boston Blackie
Cooper, Rowena (act): Memoirs Of A Survivor
Cooper, Stanley (act): see Rosi, Stelvio
Cooper, Stuart (act): Subterfuge
Cooper, Stuart (dir): The Disappearance
Cooper, Tamar (act): Not Of This Earth (1957)
Cooper, Ted (act): Phantom From Space
Cooper, Terence (act): Casino Royale
Cooper, Toby (dir): Only A Room-er; Wand-erful Will
Cooper, Trace (act): The Mutilator
Cooper, Vic (act): Toomorrow
Cooper, Violet Kemble (act, 1886–1961): The Invisible Ray
Cooper, Wilkie (cin, b. 1911): Beyond This Place; Fiddlers Three; First Men In The Moon (1964); Green For Danger; Halfway House; I Aim At The Stars; Jason And The Argonauts; Maniac (1963); The Mouse On The Moon; Mysterious Island (1961); One Million Years B.C.; The 7th Voyage Of Sinbad; Siege Of The Saxons; Stage Fright; Svengali (1954); The Three Worlds Of Gulliver
Cooper, Willis (wri): Mr. Moto Takes A Chance; The Phantom Creeps; Son Of Frankenstein; Thank You, Mr. Moto
Cooper, Wilmuth (act): The Premonition (1975)
Coopersmith, Jerome (wri): An American Christmas Carol; The Cradle Will Fall
Coote, Bert (act): A Tale Of Tails
Coote, David (act): Murder Reported
Coote, Robert (act, 1909–1982): Berlin Express; The Elusive Pimpernel (1950); The Ghost And Mrs. Muir; House Of Fear (1939); Lured; A Matter Of Life And Death; Mr. Moto's Last Warning; The Prisoner Of Zenda (1952); Theater Of Blood; The Three Musketeers (1948)
Coover, Robert (wri): The Babysitter (1995)
Copage, John (act): Repossessed
Cope, Kenneth (act, b. 1931): The Damned; Death Trap (1962); The Night Of The Big Heat; Rentadick; X...The Unknown
Copeland, Derek (act): Oh Heavenly Dog
Copeland, Dianne (act): Surf Nazis Must Die
Copeland, James (act): The Private Life Of Sherlock Holmes
Copeland, Maurice (act): Blow Out; A Stranger Is Watching
Copeland, Stewart (mus): The First Power; Highlander 2: The Quickening; White Dwarf
Copeman, John (act): 12 Monkeys
Copeman, Michael (act): Dead Of Winter; The Fly (1986)
Copland, Aaron (mus, 1900–1990): Of Mice And Men (1939); Something Wild
Coplen, Yorke (act): Jungle Stampede
Copleston, Geoffrey (act): The Black Cat (1980); The Night Porter; Roger Corman's 'Frankenstein Unbound'
Copley, Peter (act, b. 1915): Frankenstein Must Be Destroyed; Gawain And The Green Knight; The Hour Of 13; Jane Eyre (1970); The Man Without A Body; Quatermass And The Pit; Saadia; The Third Secret; What Became Of Jack And Jill
Copley, Teddy (act): The Toxic Avenger
Copley, Teri (act, b. 1961): New Year's Evil; Transylvania Twist
Coppel, Alec (wri): The Black Night; The Gazebo; I Killed The Count; Mr. Denning Drives North; Moment To Moment; Obsession (1949); Vertigo
Copperfield, David (act, b. 1956): Terror Train
Coppersmith, Terry (act): Howling II
Coppin, Tyler (act): Something Is Out There
Copping, Sam (act): Fortress
Coppola, Andrea (act): Escape From The Bronx
Coppola, Francis (Ford) (cin, b. 1939): The Heaven's Call
Coppola, Francis (Ford) (dir, b. 1939): Bram Stoker's Dracula; Dementia 13; Jack
Coppola, Francis (Ford) (wri, b. 1939): Dementia 13; The Heavens Call
Coppola, Frank (act): Turn Back The Clock
Coppola, Marc (act): Dracula's Widow; Vampire's Kiss
Coppola, Sam (act): Jacob's Ladder
Coppola, Talia (act): see Shire, Talia
Coquillon, John (cin): The Changeling; Cry Of The Banshee; Curse Of The Crimson Altar; The Oblong Box; [illegible] Scream Again (1978); Witch-Finder General; Wuthering Heights (1970)
Corarito, Gary (act): Android
Coraut, Aneta (act): The Toolbox Murders
Corazzari, Bruno (act): The Black Cat (1980); Lo Strano Caso Della Signora Ward
Corbeil, Normand (mus): Screamers (1996)
Corben, Richard (wri): Heavy Metal
Corber, Arthur (act): Wild Thing
Corbett, Ed (act): Fright Night II; 976-Evil; Party Line
Corbett, Glenn (act): Homicidal; The Pirates Of Blood River; The Stranger; Stunts Unlimited
Corbett, Gretchen (act, b. 1947): Jaws Of Satan; Let's Scare Jessica To Death; Mandrake; The Savage Bees; She's Dressed To Kill
Corbett, Harry H. (act, b. 1925): Carry On Screaming; Cover Girl Killer; Floods Of Fear; Jabberwocky; The Shakedown
Corbett, Jim (wri): Man-Eater Of Kumaon
Corbett, Kristen (act): Night Visions
Corbett, Marjorie (act): Thark
Corbett, Ronnie (act): Casino Royale
Corbett, Skyler (act): Phoenix The Warrior
Corbett, Susannah (act): First Knight; Robin Hood: Prince Of Thieves
Corbi, Marella (act): Lo Strano Caso Della Signora Ward
Corbin, Barry (act): Critters 2: The Main Course; Curdled; Dead And Buried; Fantasies; My Science Project; Solo
Corbin, Martin (act): Dr. Caligari
Corbin, Virginia (Lee) (act): Aladdin And His Wonderful Lamp; Jack And The Beanstalk (1917)
Corbitt Jr., Chance (act): Pumpkinhead
Corbitt, Chance Michael (act): The Lost Boys
Corboni, Paolo (act): When Women Had Tails
Corbucci, Bruno (wri): Battle Of The Amazons; Il Figlio Di Spartacus; Web Of The Spider
Corbucci, Enzo (wri): La Ragazza Che Sapeva Troppo
Corbucci, Sergio (dir): Il Figlio Di Spartacus; Maciste Contre Il Vampiro; Romolo E Remo; Super Fuzz
Corbucci, Sergio (wri): Johnny Hamlet; The Last Days Of Pompeii (1959); Maciste Contre Il Vampiro; Romolo E Remo; Super Fuzz
Corby, Ellen (act, b. 1913, nee Ellen Hansen): Bedlam; The Bowery Boys Meet The Monsters; The Caretakers; Hush...Hush, Sweet Charlotte; Macabre (1958); The Locket; Mighty Joe Young; The Spiral Staircase (1946); The Strangler (1963); Vertigo; Visit To A Small Planet
Corby, Francis (cin): Babes In Toyland (1934)
Corby, Jennifer (act): The Hotel Manor Inn
Corby, Lori (act): The Toxic Avenger, Part II
Corbyn, Horace (act): The Shadow Between
Corchoran, Roy (wri): 7 Doors Of Death
Corcoran, Brian (act): Babes In Toyland (1961)
Corcoran, Donna (act): Angels In The Outfield (1951); Don't Bother To Knock
Corcoran, Hugh (act): The Manitou
Corcoran, Kevin (act): Babes In Toyland (1961); The Shaggy Dog
Corcoran, Michael (act): The Lady Killers (1956)
Cord, Alex (act, b. 1931, nee Alexander Viespi): Chosen Survivors; The Dead Are Alive; Genesis II; Goliath Awaits; Inn Of The Damned; The Scorpio Letters; Uninvited (1987)
Cord, Bill (act): She-Gods Of Shark Reef
Cord, Eric/Erik (act): The Prisoner Of Zenda (1979); Robocop 2; The Sword And The Sorcerer; Total Recall
Cord, Nick (act): Wizards Of The Lost Kingdom
Corda, Maria (act): The Private Life Of Helen Of Troy
Corday, Claudia (act): Doctor?? Coppelius!!
Corday, Mara (act, b. 1932, nee Marilyn Watts): The Black Scorpion; Francis Joins The Wacs; The Giant Claw; The Naked Gun; Tarantula; Undersea Girl
Corday, Marcelle (act): Above Suspicion; Midnight Mystery; Peter Ibbetson; The Scarlet Letter (1926)
Corday, Paula (act, b. 1924, a.k.a. Paule Croset & Rita Corday): The Black Castle; The Body Snatcher (1945); Dick Tracy vs. Cueball; The Falcon And The Co-Eds; The Falcon In Hollywood; The Falcon In San Francisco; The Falcon's Alibi; The Falcon Strikes Back; The Sword Of Monte Cristo
Corday, Rita (act): see Corday, Paula
Cordeau, Sonya (act): Danger By My Side; The Phantom Of The Opera (1962)
Cordell, Cathleen (act): Dark Mirror (1984); Gaslight (1940)
Cordell, Chase (act): Track Of The Moon Beast
Cordell, Daisy (act): The Devil's Bondman; The Disappearance Of The Judge; The Harbour Lights; His Just Desserts; The Romany Rye; [illegible]
Cordell, Frank (mus): Demon (1976)
Cordell, Shane (act): Fiend Without A Face
Corden, Henry (act): The Black Castle; Modern Problems
Cordero, Joaquim (act): 100 Cries Of Terror
Cordero, Laurencio (cin): Nightlife (1989, Usa-Mex)
Cordet, Helene(act): The Limping Man (1953)
Cordic, Regis J./Rege (act): The Man With The Power; Ritual Of Evil
Cording, Harry (act): The Adventures Of Robin Hood; The Black Cat (1934); Charlie Chan In Paris; Dressed To Kill (1946); Great Expectations (1934); Gypsy Wildcat; The House Of Fear (1945); Jungle Gents; Killer Leopard; Sudan; 13 Lead Soldiers
Cording, John (act): Superman (1978)
Cordio, Carlo Maria (mus): Ator: The Fighting Eagle; Curse II: The Bite; Endgame
Cordoba, Francisco (A.) (act): Dr. Tarr's Torture Dungeon; El Vampiro Sangriento
Cordova, Fred (act): The Feathered Serpent (1948)
Cordova, Samuel (act): The Resurrection Of Zachary Wheeler
Corduna, Alan (act): Sredni Vashtar
Cordy, Raymond (act, 1898–1956): La Beaute Du Diable; Les Inconnus Dans La Maison
Core, Natalie (act): The Ice Pirates
Core, Traci (act): The Wiz
Corea, Nicholas (dir): Fugitive From The Empire; The Incredible Hulk Returns
Corea, Nicholas (wri): Fugitive From The Empire; The Incredible Hulk Returns; Joe & The Colonel
Corell, Beth A. (act): Nightfall (1988)
Corelli, Marie (wri): Blade Af Satans Bog; The Sorrows Of Satan (1917 & 1925); Young Diana
Cores, Charles (act): Curse Of The Stone Hand
Corey, Brigitte (act): Samson
Corey, Isabelle (act): Last Of The Vikings
Corey, Jeff (act, b. 1914): All That Money Can Buy; Bagdad; The Balcony; Battle Beyond The Stars (1980); Beneath The Planet Of The Apes; The Boston Strangler; Color Of Night; Conan The Destroyer; Creator; Cry For The Strangers; Curse Of The Black Widow; Frankenstein Meets The Wolf Man; Jennifer (1978); The Judas Project; Lady In A Cage; The Man Who Wouldn't Die; The Next Voice You Hear; Oh, God!; The Premonition (1975); Seconds; Something Evil; Superman And The Mole Men; The Sword And The Sorcerer
Corey, Lois (act): The Resurrection Of Zachary Wheeler
Corey, Maggie (act): Blood And Lace
Corey, Wendell (act, 1914–1968): The Accused; Agent For H.A.R.M.; Astro Zombies; Cyborg 2087; Jamaica Run; The Killer Is Loose; Man-Eater Of Kumaon; Picture Mommy Dead; Rear Window; Sorry, Wrong Number (1948); Women Of The Prehistoric Planet
Corff, Robert (act): Fright Night; Gas-S-S-S!; Houston, We've Got A Problem
Corfman, Caris (act): Dreamchild
Corigliano, John (mus): Altered States
Corio, Ann (act): Call Of The Jungle; Jungle Siren; The Sultan's Daughter
Cork, Charles (act): I Hired A Contract Killer; Venom (1982)
Corkidi, Rafael (cin): Dr. Tarr's Torture Dungeon
Corkill, Danny (act): D.A.R.Y.L.
Corkum, Roland (act): Unforgettable
Corlan, Anthony (act, b. 1947): Taste The Blood Of Dracula; Vampire Circus
Corley, Bob (wri): The Legend Of Blood Mountain
Corley, David (wri): Solo
Corley, Pat (act): The Hand (1981); Mr. Destiny; Nightwing; Of Mice And Men (1981); Starflight: The Plane That Couldn't Land; The Stepford Children; The Two Worlds Of Jennie Logan
Cormack, Bartlett (wri): The Benson Murder Case; Four Frightened People; The Greene Murder Case; The Phantom Of Crestwood
Cormack, Lynn (act): Dead Ringers
Cormack, Paul (act): Eclipse (1977)
Corman, Avery (wri): Oh, God!
Corman, Catherine (act): Roger Corman's 'Frankenstein Unbound'
Corman, Gene (wri): Night Of The Blood-Beast
Corman, Leonard (act): Raiders Of The Living Dead
Corman, Roger (act, b. 1926): Apollo 13; The Cry Baby Killer; The Howling; The Silence Of The Lambs
Corman, Roger (dir, b. 1926): Atlas; Attack Of The Crab Monsters; A Bucket Of

Blood (1959); Creature From The Haunted Sea; Day The World Ended (1955); Gas-S-S-S!; The Haunted Palace (1963); House Of Usher; It Conquered The World; Last Woman On Earth; The Little Shop Of Horrors (1960); The Masque Of The Red Death (1964); Not Of This Earth (1957); The Pit And The Pendulum (1961); The Premature Burial; The Raven (1963); Roger Corman's Frankenstein Unbound; The St. Valentine's Day Massacre; She-Gods Of Shark Reef; Swamp Women; Tales Of Terror; Target: Harry; Teenage Cave Man; The Terror (1963); The Tomb Of Ligeia; Tower Of London (1962); The Trip; The Undead; The Viking Women And The Sea Serpent; War Of The Satellites; The Wasp Woman; X—The Man With The X-Ray Eyes

Corman, Roger (wri, b. 1926): *Roger Corman's Frankenstein Unbound*

Cormier, Al (act): *Barn Of The Naked Dead*

Cormier, Gerald (wri): *Barn Of The Naked Dead*

Cornaly, Anne (act): *Au Coeur De La Vie*

Corne, Leonce (act): *Forces Occultes*

Cornelius, Billy (act): *Carry On Screaming; The Mind Of Mr. Soames; When Dinosaurs Ruled The Earth*

Cornelius, Joe (act): *Trog*

Cornell, Ann(E) (act): *Dark Venture; Search For Danger*

Cornell, Ellie (act): *Halloween 4: The Return Of Michael Myers; Halloween 5: The Revenge Of Michael Myers*

Cornell, Phyllis (act): *Before I Wake*

Cornell, Sharon Breslau (act): *Ghost (1990)*

Cornfeld, Stuart (act): *Darkman (1990)*

Cornish, Richard (act): *Holocaust 2000*

Cornish, Vera (act): *Abide With Me; The Mystery Of A London Flat*

Cornthwaite, Robert (act, b. 1917): *Colossus: The Forbin Project; Crackle Of Death; The Devil's Daughter (1972); Futureworld; Matinee; Monkey Business; On The Threshold Of Space; The Thing From Another World; The War Of The Worlds; What Ever Happened To Baby Jane? (1962); White Dwarf*

Cornu, Richard (mus): *The Secret Of Magic Island*

Cornwell, Judy (act): *Santa Claus (1985); Those Fantastic Flying Fools; Who Slew Auntie Roo?; Wuthering Heights (1970)*

Cornwell, Stephen (dir): *Philadelphia Experiment II*

Corona, Alan (act): *Blood Diner*

Corona, Isabella (act): *El Espejo De La Bruja*

Coronado, Celestino (dir & wri): *A Midsummer Night's Dream (1985)*

Coronel, Maria Luisa (act): *The Arrival*

Corosky, Emma (act): *Never Talk To Strangers*

Corradi, Nelly (act): *Faust And The Devil*

Corrado, Gino (act): *Charlie Chan In City In Darkness; The Iron Mask*

Corraface, George (act): *Escape From L.A.*

Corral, Benny (act): *Total Recall*

Correale, Luigi (act): *Spara Forte, Piu Forte...Non Capisco*

Correia, David (act): *Seven*

Correll, Charles (cin): *Dr. Scorpion; Star Trek III: The Search For Spock*

Correll, Charles (dir): *Writer's Block*

Corri, Adrienne (act, b. 1933): *Bunny Lake Is Missing; A Clockwork Orange; Devil Girl From Mars; Doctor Of Seven Dials; The Hell-Fire Club; Journey Into Darkness; Lancelot And Guinevere; Madhouse; Moon Zero Two; A Study In Terror; The Tell-Tale Heart (1960); Vampire Circus; The Viking Queen*

Corri, Nick (act): *A Nightmare On Elm Street; Wes Craven's New Nightmare*

Corridori, (Giovanni/John) (cin): *The Adventures Of Hercules; Alien Contamination; Escape From The Bronx*

Corrie, Devin (act): *To Die For II: Son Of Darkness*

Corrie, Sadie (act): *Wombling Free*

Corrigan, "Crash" (act): see Corrigan, Ray "Crash"

Corrigan, D'arcy (act): *The Adventures Of Robin Hood; A Christmas Carol (1938); The Last Warning (1929); The Murders In The Rue Morgue (1932); Tarzan And The Golden Lion*

Corrigan, Kevin (act): *Cocoon: The Return; The Exorcist III*

Corrigan, Lee (act): *Dark Mansions*

Corrigan, Lloyd (act, 1900–1969): *After Midnight With Boston Blackie; Alias Boston Blackie; The Bandit Of Sherwood Forest; The Big Clock; Boston Blackie Booked On Suspicion; Boston Blackie Goes Hollywood; The Bowery Boys Meet The Monsters; Captive Wild Woman; The Chance Of A Lifetime; The Chase; Confessions Of Boston Blackie; Crime Doctor's Courage; The Ghost Breakers; Ghost Chasers; The Manchurian Candidate; The Mystery Of Marie Roget; The Return Of October; Shadowed; She-Wolf Of London; Tarzan's Desert Mystery; The Thin Man Goes Home*

Corrigan, Lloyd (dir, 1900–1969): *Murder On A Honeymoon; The Night Key*

Corrigan, Lloyd (wri, 1900–1969): *The Mysterious Dr. Fu Manchu; The Return Of Dr. Fu Manchu*

Corrigan, Ray "Crash" (act, 1903–1976): *Dante's Inferno (1935); It!—The Terror From Beyond Space; Killer Ape; Night Life Of The Gods; Sharad Of Atlantis; The White Gorilla; Zombies Of Mora Tau*

Corrington, John (William) (wri): *The Arena (1973); Battle For The Planet Of The Apes; Killer Bees*

Corrington, Joyce (H.) (wri): *The Arena (1973); Battle For The Planet Of The Apes; Killer Bees; The Omega Man*

Corriveau, Marguerite (act): *Oh Heavenly Dog*

Corry, Graham (act): *Inn Of The Damned*

Corry, Will (act): *Strategy Of Terror*

Corsaro, Franco/Frank (act): *Crime Doctor's Warning; Spy Smasher Returns*

Corseaut/Corsaut, Anita/Aneta (act, d. 1995): *Bad Ronald; The Blob (1958)*

Corsentino, Frank (act): *Moonchild*

Corso, Chris (act): *Roller Blade Warriors: Taken By Force*

Corso, John A. (cin): *Metamorphosis: The Alien Factor*

Cort, Bud (act, b. 1951): *Bates Motel; Brain Dead; Brave New World; Electric Dreams; Gas-S-S-S!; Hitler's Son; Invaders From Mars (1986); Love At Stake; Out Of The Dark*

Cort, Michael (dir & wri): *Zeta One*

Cort, William (act): *Elvira, Mistress Of The Dark; Ghost (1990)*

Corte, Frederic (dir & wri): Sse Cortes, Fernando

Cortes, Felix (act): *The Toxic Avenger, Part II*

Cortes, Fernando (dir & wri, a.k.a. Frederic Corte): *Creature Of The Walking Dead*

Cortes, Juan (act): *Tombs Of The Blind Dead*

Cortes, Mapita (act): *Misterios Del Ultratumba*

Cortese, Dan (act, b. 1967): *Demolition Man; The Lottery; Volcano: Fire On The Mountain*

Cortese, Joseph/Joe (act, b. 1950): *Computercide; Evilspeak; Final Eye; Something Is Out There; Windows*

Cortese, Luigi (act): *Judex*

Cortese, Valentina (act, b. 1925): *The Adventures Of Baron Munchausen (1989); Black Magic (1949); Giulietta Degli Spiriti; Les Miserables (1943); La Ragazza Che Sapeva Troppo; A Rocket From Calabuch; Shadow Of The Eagle; When Time Ran Out*

Cortez, Bella (act): *Ali Baba And The Sacred Crown; Ali Baba And The Seven Saracens; Il Gigante Di Metropolis; None But The Lonely Spy; The Tartars; Taur The Mighty; Vulcan, Son Of Jupiter*

Cortez, Carolyn (act): *Edge Of Sanity*

Cortez, Ricardo (act, b. 1899, nee Jack Kranz): *Charlie Chan In Reno; The Locket; The Lost Zeppelin; The Maltese Falcon (1931); Mr. Moto's Last Warning; Mockery; Murder Over New York; Mystery In Mexico; The Phantom Of Crestwood; The Private Life Of Helen Of Troy; The Sorrows Of Satan (1925); The Walking Dead*

Cortez, Stacey (act): *I Come In Peace*

Cortez, Stanley (cin, b. 1908, nee Stanley Kranz): *Abbott And Costello Meet Captain Kidd; The Angry Red Planet; The Black Cat (1941); The Diamond Queen; Dinosaurus!; Doomsday Machine; Flesh And Fantasy; The Ghost In The Invisible Bikini; Lady In The Morgue; Madman Of Mandoras; The Navy Vs. The Night Monsters; The Neanderthal Man; Nightmare In The Sun; The Night Of The Hunter (1955); Riders To The Stars; Secret Beyond The Door; Shock Corridor; The Three Faces Of Eve*

Corti, Jesse (act): *Nightlife (1989, Usa-Mex)*

Corti, Tony (wri): *City Of The Walking Dead*

Cortijo, Basilio (cin): *Endless Descent; Mystery On Monster Island*

Cortland, Nicholas (act, 1941–1988): *Frogs*

Cortwright, Jerry (act): *The Giant Gila Monster*

Corwin, Linda (act): *A Nymphoid Barbarian In Dinosaur Hell*

Corwin, Norman (wri, b. 1910): *Once Upon A Time (1944)*

Cory, Desmond (wri): *Mark Of The Phoenix*

Cory, Phil(Ip) (cin): *Bug; Flatliners*

Cory, Ray (cin): *Have Rocket, Will Travel*

Cory, Steve (act): *The Resurrection Of Zachary Wheeler*

Coryell, John R. (wri): *The Adventures Of Nick Carter; Nick Carter (1908 & 1921); Nick Carter And The Black-Coated Thieves; Nick Carter As An Acrobat; Nick Carter-Bandits In Evening Dress; Nick Carter Et Le Trefle Rouge; Nick Carter In Danger; Nick Carter, Master Detective; Nick Carter-Sleeping Pills; Nick Carter-The Mystery Of The White Bed; Nick Carter Va Tout Casser; Phantom Raiders; Sky Murder*

Cos, Vickie (act): *Strait-Jacket*

Cosby, Bill (act, b. 1937): *The Devil And Max Devlin; Ghost Dad; Jack; The Meteor Man; Top Secret (1978)*

Cosby, Vivian (wri): *The Mind Reader*

Coscarelli, Don (cin, b. 1954): *Phantasm*

Coscarelli, Don (dir, b. 1954): *The Beastmaster; Phantasm; Phantasm II; Phantasm III: Lord Of The Dead*

Coscarelli, Don (wri, b. 1954): *The Beastmaster; Beastmaster 2: Through The Portal Of Time; Beastmaster III: The Eye Of Braxus; Phantasm II; Phantasm III: Lord Of The Dead*

Coscia, Marcello (act): *When Women Had Tails*

Coscia, Marcello (wri): *Dorian Gray*

Cosell, Howard (act, 1918–1995): *Sleeper*

Cosgrave, Frankie (act): *Hawk The Slayer*

Cosgrove, Jack (act): *Monte Cristo*

Cosgrove, Jack (cin): *Beyond Tomorrow; The Prisoner Of Zenda (1937); Spellbound (1945)*

Cosima, Renee (act): *Les Enfants Terribles*

Cosma, Vladimir (mus): *Dracula, Pere Et Fils*

Cosmatos, George (dir): *Leviathan; Of Unknown Origin*

Cosmo, James (act): *Doomwatch; Highlander; In The Devil's Garden; Treasure Island (1990)*

Cossar, John (act): *The Hunchback Of Notre Dame (1923)*

Cossart, Ernest (act, 1876–1951): *Love Letters; Tower Of London (1939)*

Cossette, Lorne (act): *Sorry, Wrong Number (1989)*

Cossins, James (act): *The Anniversary; Blood From The Mummy's Tomb; The Deadly Bees; Deathline; Fear In The Night (1972); Hitler: The Last Ten Days; The Man With The Golden Gun; Otley; Possession (1973); Privilege; Sphinx (1981); Uncharted Seas; Wuthering Heights (1970)*

Costa, Cosie (act): *Remo Williams: The Adventure Begins*

Costa, Mario (dir): *Rage Of The Buccaneers*

Costa, Nick (act): *The Incredible Hulk Returns*

Costa, Sam (act): *One Wish Too Many; A Piece Of Cake*

Costa-Gavras, Costi (dir & wri, b. 1933): *The Sleeping Car Murders*

Costain, Thomas B. (wri, 1885–1965): *The Black Rose*

Costanzo, Robert/Bobby (act): *Dick Tracy (1990); Man's Best Friend; Total Recall*

Costello, Carmen (act): *Loves Of Carmen; The Man Who Laughs (1928)*

Costello, Daniel (act): *Midnight (1980)*

Costello, Deirdre (act): *Demons Of The Mind*

Costello, Delmar (act): *Secret Of The Incas*

Costello, Dolores (act, 1905–1979): *The Sea Beast*

Costello, Don (act): *Another Thin Man; Class Of Nuke'em High; Crime Doctor; Here Comes Mr. Jordan; Just Off Broadway; The Red Dragon (1945); Sleepers West; Tarzan And The Green Goddess; The Toxic Avenger; The Whistler*

Costello, Elvis (act): *Americathon*

Costello, Helene (act): *Don Juan (1927)*

Costello, John (act): *Les Miserables (1952)*

Costello, Lou (act, 1906–1959, Nee Louis Francis Cristillo): *Abbott And Costello Go To Mars; Abbott And Costello Meet Captain Kidd; Abbott And Costello Meet Dr. Jekyll And Mr. Hyde; Abbott And Costello Meet Frankenstein; Abbott And Costello Meet The Invisible Man; Abbott And Costello Meet The Killer; Abbott And Costello Meet The Mummy; Africa Screams; Hold That Ghost; Jack And The Beanstalk (1952); Lost In A Harem; The 30 Foot Bride Of Candy Rock; The Time Of Their Lives; Who Done It? (1942)*

Costello, Mariclare (act): *Let's Scare Jessica To Death; Nightmares (1983)*

Costello, Michael (act): *D.O.A. (1988)*

Costello, Shann (act): *Grim Prairie Tales*

Costello, Toni (act): *The Sinister Urge*

Costello, Ward (act): *Project X (1987); Return To Witch Mountain; Terror From The Year 5,000*

Costelloe, John (act): *Kazaam*

Coster, Claudine (act): *Le Comte De Monte Cristo; Lemmy Pour Les Dames*

Coster, Nicolas (act, b. 1934): *A Fire In The Sky (1978); My Blood Runs Cold*

Costikyan, Andrew (cin): *Beast From Haunted Cave*

Costner, Kevin (act, b. 1955): *No Way Out; Robin Hood: Prince Of Thieves; Waterworld*

Coswell, June (act): *The Village Of The Damned (1960)*

Cote, Tina (act): *Nemesis 2*

Cotler, George (wri): *The Black Bird (1975); Sanctuary Of Fear*

Cotner, Douglas/Doug (act): *The Gifted One; Student Bodies*

Coto, Manny (dir & wri): *Dr. Giggles*

Cotsworth, Staats (act, b. 1908): *Dr. Cook's Garden; Silent Night, Bloody Night; They Might Be Giants*

Cottafavi, Vittorio (dir, b. 1914): *Ercole Alla Conquista Della Atlantide; La Vendetta Di Ercole; La Vergine Di Roma*

Cottafavi, Vittorio (wri, b. 1914): *Ercole Alla Conquista Della Atlantide*

Cotten, Joseph (act, 1905–1994): *The Abominable Dr. Phibes; A Blueprint For Murder; City Beneath The Sea (1970); Delusion; The Devil's Daughter (1972); Doomsday Voyage; La Figlia Di Frankenstein; The Fish Men; From The Earth To The Moon; Gaslight (1944); Guyana, Cult Of The Damned; Half Angel; The Hearse; Hush...Hush, Sweet Charlotte; Journey Into Fear (1942); The Killer Is Loose; Latitude Zero; Love Letters; The Man With A Cloak; Niagara; Gli Orrori Del Castello Di Noremnerga; Peking Express; Portrait Of Jennie; Return To Fantasy Island; The Screaming Woman; Shadow Of A Doubt (1943); Soylent Green; The Steel Trap; The Third Man; Under Capricorn*

Cotten, Joseph (wri): *Journey Into Fear (1942)*

Cotter, Al (cin): *Prom Night*

Cotterill, Ralph (act): *The Chain Reaction (1980); Howling III*

Cottle, Josephine (act): see Storm, Gale

Cotton, George (act): *The Curse Of The Living Corpse*

Cotton, James (act): *Phenomenon*

Cotton, Joan (act): *Return Of The Fly*

Cotton, King (act): *Ed Wood*

Cotton, Lucy (act): *The Devil (1921); Life Without Soul*

Cottrell, Bill (act): see Cottrell, William/Bill

Cottrell, Mickey (act): *Ed Wood*

Cottrell, Mike (act): *Return Of The Jedi*

Cottrell, William/Bill (act): *Captain Kidd And The Slave Girl; Donovan's Brain; Les Miserables (1952); Return To Treasure Island*

Cotts, Campbell (act): *Barbados Quest; The Hour Of 13; Stop Press Girl*

Coubert, Chana (act): *La Ragazza Che Sapeva Troppo*

Couch (Sr.), Bill (act): *Dead And Buried; Earthbound (1981)*

Couch Jr., Bill (act): *Dead And Buried*

Couch, Charles (act): *Dead And Buried*

Couderc, Pierre (act): *The Patchwork Girl Of Oz*

Coufos, Paul (act): *Battlestar Galactica; Chopping Mall; The Food Of The Gods, Part II; The Lost Empire*

Cougar, James (act): *Blackenstein*

Coughlan, Mary (act): *High Spirits*

Coughlan, Phillis (act): *The Brotherhood Of Satan*

Coughlin, Ely (act): *Witchery*

Coughlin, Kevin (act, 1945–1976): *Wild In The Streets*

Coulouris, George (act, 1903–1989): *Anticristo; The Assassination Bureau; Between Two Worlds; Blood From The Mummy's Tomb; Bluebeard's Ten Honeymoons; Confidential Agent; Fury At Smugglers' Bay; I Accuse (1958); It's Not The Size That Counts; Kill Me Tomorrow; Kill Or Be Killed; Koroshi; The Last Days Of Man On Earth; The Manchurian Candidate; The Man Without A Body; Murder On The Orient Express; No Blade Of Grass; Seven Thunders; The Skull; Sleep, My Love; Son Of Robin Hood; Spy In The Sky; The Stranger; Tarzan And The Lost Safari; The Teckman Mystery; Tower Of Evil; Venetian Bird; The Verdict; The Woman Eater*

Coulouris, Keith (act): *Beastmaster III: The Eye Of Braxus*

Coulson, Catherine (act): *Trick Or Treats*

Coulson, Roy (act): *Don Q, Son Of Zorro; Robin Hood (1922)*

Coulson, Thomas (act): *Eraserhead*

Coulter, Craig (act): *Saturday The 14th*

Coulter, Jean (act): *Jaws 2*

Coulter, Phil (mus): The Water Babies
Coulter, Scott (cin): Class Of Nuke'em High
Coulter, Stephen (wri): Embassy
Cound, Tom (act): Beauty And The Beast (1962)
Counsell, Elisabeth (act): Killer's Moon
Couper, Barbara (act): Dark Secret; Face In The Night; Paul Temple's Triumph
Courage, Carolyn (act): Terror (1979)
Courant, Curtis (cin, b. 1895): The Man In The Mirror; The Man Who Knew Too Much (1934)
Courbois, Kitty (act): Flesh & Blood
Courcel, Nicole (act, b. 1930, Nee Nicole Andrieux): Nick Carter Et Le Trefle Rouge; La Sorciere
Courier, Mark (act): Waxwork II: Lost In Time
Court Wizard Productions (cin): Hell Night; Once Bitten
Court, Don (act): see Murray, Don
Court, Hazel (act, b. 1926): Counterspy; The Curse Of Frankenstein; Dear Murderer; Devil Girl From Mars; Dr. Blood's Coffin; Forbidden; Ghost Ship (1952); Hour Of Decision; The Man Who Could Cheat Death; The Man Who Was Nobody; The Masque Of The Red Death (1964); Model For Murder; The Premature Burial; The Raven (1963); The Shakedown; A Woman Of Mystery
Courtal, Suzanne (act): Jeux Interdits
Courtenay, Margaret (act): The Mirror Crack'd; Oh Heavenly Dog; Royal Flash
Courtenay, Syd (act & wri): What A Night! The Man Behind The Mask (1936)
Courtenay, Tom (act, b. 1937): Catch Me A Spy; A Dandy In Aspic; The Day The Fish Came Out; The Night Of The Generals; Operation Crossbow; Otley
Courtland, Jerome (act, b. 1926): Colossus And The Huns; Queen Of The Seas
Courtland, R. (act): The Charlatan
Courtley, Steve (cin): Mad Max Beyond Thunderdome
Courtneidge, Cicely (act, 1893–1980): Elstree Calling; The Ghost Train (1931); The Spider's Web
Courtney, Carter (act): Stigma
Courtney, Charles/Chuck (act): Assassin (1986); Billy The Kid Vs. Dracula; The Food Of The Gods; Teenage Monster
Courtney, Daphne (act): Murder By Rope
Courtney, David (act): Information Received; The Tell-Tale Heart (1960)
Courtney, Del (act): The Hideous Sun Demon; It Came From Beneath The Sea
Courtney, Don (cin): Kiss Meets The Phantom Of The Park
Courtney, Dori (act): Sorority Girls And The Creature From Hell
Courtney, Inez (act): The Raven (1935)
Courtney, James (act): Moontrap
Courtney, James Jude (act): Philadelphia Experiment II
Courtney, Jeni (act): The Secret Of Roan Inish
Courtney, Lorna (act): The Toxic Avenger, Part II
Courtney, Lynn (act): She Freak
Courtney, Mark (act): Dead And Buried
Courtney, Michael (act): Dead And Buried
Courtney, Therese (act): The Dark Half
Courtot, Marguerite (act): The Vampire (1913)
Cousins, Brian (act): Invisible: The Chronicles Of Benjamin Knight; Mandroid
Cousins, Julie (act): The Blob (1958)
Cousins, Kay (wri): Jennifer (1978)
Coussa, Sylvia (act): Ed Wood
Cousteau, Desiree (act): Caged Heat!
Coutard, Raoul (cin, b. 1924): Alphaville, Une Etrange Aventure De Lemmy Caution; Embassy; The Jerusalem File; La Mariee Etait En Noir; The Southern Star
Coutts, Julian (act): The Housekeeper
Couture, Jacques (act): The Music Of The Spheres
Couyoumdjian, Gianfranco (wri): Hunters Of The Golden Cobra
Couzin, Victor (act): The Fifth Musketeer
Covan, Deforest (act): Evilspeak; The Incredible Melting Man; Midnight Lace (1981); When A Stranger Calls
Covarrubias, Robert (act): Fire In The Sky (1993); Project X (1987)
Covay, Cab (act): Phenomenon
Cove, Kenneth (act): Evil Of Frankenstein
Covello, Angela (act): Torso
Covello, Dino (dir): Il Mostro Di Venezia
Coventry, Tom (act): The Girl Who Didn't Care; The House Of Peril; Jane Shore (1915); The Monkey's Paw (1923)
Coverly, Eric (act): Manfish
Covin, Sylvester (act): The Toxic Avenger, Part II
Covington, Bruce (act): The Phantom Of The Opera (1925)
Covington, Toni (act): The Private Lives Of Adam And Eve
Cowan, Ashley (act): The Snake Pit (1948); Sorry, Wrong Number (1948); 23 Paces To Baker Street
Cowan, Bob (act): The Eye Creatures
Cowan, Jerome (act, 1897–1972): Black Zoo; Crime By Night; Crime Doctor's Courage; Crime Doctor's Strangest Case; Cry Wolf (1947); Exile Express; Flight To Nowhere; Fog Island; The Gracie Allen Murder Case; Guest In The House; Have Rocket, Will Travel; Jungle Captive; The Maltese Falcon (1941); Miracle On 34th Street (1947); Night Has A Thousand Eyes; A Night In Paradise; Out Of The Fog (1941); The Saint Strikes Back; Visit To A Small Planet; Who Done It? (1942)
Cowan, Maurice (wri): Turn The Key Softly; Wanted For Murder
Cowan, Will (dir): The Thing That Couldn't Die
Coward, Noel (act, 1899–1973): Around The World In 80 Days; Bunny Lake Is Missing; Paris When It Sizzles
Coward, Noel (wri, 1899–1973): Blithe Spirit
Cowden, Jack (wri): The Night Of The Claw
Cowell, John (act): The Clutching Hand
Cowen, Lawrence (Dir & Wri): Wake Up!: or, A Dream Of Tomorrow
Cowen, William (dir): Kongo
Cowgill, Jackie (act): The Power (1980)
Cowgill, Richard (act): The Power (1980); Pranks
Cowie, Laura (act): The Game Of Liberty; The Secret Of Stamboul
Cowin, John (act): Empire Of Ash III
Cowl, Daryl (act): A Dog, A Mouse And A Sputnik; Who Stole The Body?
Cowles, Jules (act): The Lost World (1925); The Scarlet Letter (1926)
Cowles, Matthew (act): They Might Be Giants
Cowling, Brenda (act): The Black Windmill; Jabberwocky; Octopussy
Cowling, Bruce (act): Cannibal Attack; Song Of The Thin Man
Cowper, Geraldine (act): The Wicker Man
Cowper, Jacqueline (act): Who Slew Auntie Roo?
Cowper, Nicola (act): Dreamchild; Journey To The Center Of The Earth (1989); Transmutations
Cowper, Peter (act): My Bloody Valentine; Oh Heavenly Dog
Cox, Alan (act): The Odyssey; Young Sherlock Holmes
Cox, Ashley (act): Looker
Cox, Brian (act): Chain Reaction (1996); The Long Kiss Goodnight; Murder By Moonlight; Witching Time/The Silent Scream
Cox, Brian (cin): Mad Max Beyond Thunderdome
Cox, C.J. (act): Nightmare Sisters; The Offspring
Cox, Chad (act): Powder
Cox, Clifford (act): The Twisted Nerve
Cox, Colin (act): The Unnamable
Cox, Courteney (act, b. 1964): Cocoon: The Return; Masters Of The Universe; Mr. Destiny; Scream; Scream II
Cox, Darryl (act): Robocop
Cox, David A. (act): Galaxina
Cox, Dorothy Isobel (act): See Wynyard, Diana
Cox, Doug (act): Carrie; Creator
Cox, Douglas (act): The Picture Of Dorian Gray (1916); The Romany Rye
Cox, Elizabeth (act): Night Of The Creeps; The Wraith
Cox, Ernest A. (act): The Barton Mystery (1920)
Cox, Frank (act): Alice's Adventures In Wonderland (1972); Fahrenheit 451
Cox, Fred(die) (act): Alice's Adventures In Wonderland (1972); Fahrenheit 451
Cox, Gary Don (act): The Lost Empire; Vampire On Bikini Beach
Cox, Jack (cin): See Cox, John/Jack
Cox, Jacqueline (act): The Secret Of The Forest
Cox, John (act): See Howard, John
Cox, John/Jack (cin): Alias John Preston; Blackmail (1929); Devil Girl From Mars; The Lady Vanishes (1938); The Man Who Changed His Mind; Mr. Drake's Duck; Rich And Strange
Cox, Jon (act): Forever Evil
Cox, Joshua (act): The People Under The Stairs
Cox, Julie (act): 20,000 Leagues Under The Sea (1997, CBS-TV)
Cox, Linda (act): Phantom Of The Paradise
Cox, Mary (act): The Toxic Avenger
Cox, Mary Agen (act): Screams Of A Winter Night
Cox, Mitchell (act): Strait-Jacket
Cox, Monty (act): Timestalkers
Cox, Morgan (wri): Dick Tracy (1937)
Cox, Nikki (act): The Presence
Cox, Olive (act): Cinderella (1911, Selig)
Cox, Raymond (act): The Adventures Of Dick Turpin-The King Of Highwaymen
Cox, Richard (Can act): Hellhole; Seizure; The Vindicator; Zombie High
Cox, Richard (USA act): see Sargent, Richard
Cox, Rick (act): The Offspring
Cox, Rod (act): see Cameron, Rod
Cox, Ronny (act): The Beast Within; Captain America (1992); The Car; The Mind Snatchers; Robocop; Total Recall
Cox, Ruth (act): The Attic; Fantasies
Cox, Simon (act): Mary Shelley's 'Frankenstein'
Cox, Tony (act): The Ewok Adventure; Ewoks: The Battle For Endor; Jekyll And Hyde...Together Again; Leprechaun 2; Retribution (1988); The Silence Of The Hams
Cox, Vincent (cin): Creatures The World Forgot; The Demon (1981)
Cox, Vivian (A.) (wri, b. 1915): Deadly Record; Tread Softly; The Very Edge
Cox, Wally (act, 1924–1973): The Barefoot Executive; The Bedford Incident; The Night Strangler
Cox, William R. (wri): The Golden Blade; The Veils Of Bagdad
Coxe, George Harmon (wri): The Hidden Eye
Coxen, Ed(ward) (act): The Flying Dutchman; One Million B.C.
Coxon, Cole (act): The Gifted One
Coy, Durango (act): The Pink Chiquitas
Coy, Walter (act): Cult Of The Cobra
Coyle, Anne Bernadette (act): Weird Science
Coyle, Bob (act): Rawhead Rex
Coyle, James (act): Frankenstein (1984); Treasure Island (1990)
Coyne, Harold (act): The Bride (1985)
Coyne, Maureen (act): Howard The Duck
Coyne, Susan (act): Never Talk To Strangers
Coyote, Peter (act): Endangered Species; E.T.-The Extra-Terrestrial; Terminal Justice; That Eye, The Sky; Time Flyer; Timerider; Unforgettable
Cozart, Cylk (act): Eraser
Cozzi, Luigi (dir, a.k.a. Lewis Coates): Quatro Mosche Di Velluto Gris
Cozzi, Luigi (wri, a.k.a. Lewis Coates): The Adventures Of Hercules; Alien Contamination; Hercules (1983); Quatro Mosche Di Velluto Gris; Star Crash
Cozzo, Paola (act): Demons
Crabb, Chris (act): An American Christmas Carol; Funeral Home
Crabbe, Clarence Linden (act): see Crabbe, Larry "Buster"
Crabbe, James (act): Just William's Luck
Crabbe, Kerry (wri): Memoirs Of A Survivor
Crabbe, Larry "Buster" (act, 1908–1983, nee Clarence Linden Crabbe): Captive Girl; The Deadly Ray From Mars; Destination Saturn; His Brother's Ghost; It Fell From The Sky; Jungle Man; Jungle Siren; King Of The Jungle; Mars Attacks The World; Nabonga; Peril From The Planet Mongo; Purple Death From Outer Space; Spaceship To The Unknown; Swamp Fire; Tarzan The Fearless
Crabe, James (cin): Agent For H.A.R.M.; The China Syndrome; Covenant; The Dead Don't Die; Rhinoceros (1974)
Crabtree, Arthur (dir, b. 1900): Dear Murderer; Fiend Without A Face; Horrors Of The Black Museum; The Strange Case Of Dr. Manning
Crabtree, Brian (act): No Blade Of Grass
Crabtree, Loren (act): Biohazard
Cracknell, Derek (act): Oh Heavenly Dog
Cracknell, Leonard (act): The Terronauts
Craft, Gere (act): The Devil's Hand (1961)
Cragg, Marie (act): See Ault, Marie
Craig, Alec (act): Calling Dr. Death; A Date With The Falcon; The Jungle Woman; The Lone Wolf Spy Hunt; Phantom Raiders; Spider Woman; The Undying Monster
Craig, Andrew (act): Leprechaun 2; The Toxic Avenger
Craig, Blanche (act): Darkened Rooms; Peter Ibbetson
Craig, Carolyn (act): House On Haunted Hill
Craig, Catherine (act): Appointment With Murder; Doomed To Die
Craig, Charles (act): Night Of The Living Dead (1968)
Craig, Charles Grant (wri): Them (1996)
Craig, Colin (wri): Jack The Ripper (1958)
Craig, Dana (act): Nightmare On The 13th Floor
Craig, Davina (act): Tangled Evidence
Craig, Donald (act): Amazons (1984)
Craig, Edith (act): Her Greatest Performance
Craig, Edwin (act): Batman (1989); Hellbound: Hellraiser II
Craig, Hal (act): Torchy Runs For Mayor
Craig, Helen (act): The Legend Of Lizzie Borden; The Snake Pit (1948)
Craig, Howard (wri): No. 1 Of The Secret Service
Craig, Ivan (act): Panic At Madam Tussaud's
Craig, James (act, 1912–1985, nee James H. Meador): All That Money Can Buy; The Cyclops; Dark Delusion; Doomsday Machine; Ghost Diver; Kismet (1944); The Lone Wolf Spy Hunt; The Man They Could Not Hang; While The City Sleeps; Women Of Pitcairn Island
Craig, John (act): Shock Corridor
Craig, Louis (cin): Of Unknown Origin; Starcrossed
Craig, Michael (act, b. 1928, nee Michael Gregson): Escape 2000; Inn Of The Damned; Life For Ruth; Modesty Blaise; Mysterious Island (1961); Sapphire; Svengali (1954); The Vault Of Horror
Craig, Nell (act): Another Thin Man; Arrest Bulldog Drummond
Craig, Nobel (act): Poltergeist II: The Other Side; Ssssss
Craig, Phyllis (act): Deadtime Stories
Craig, Robert (act): Funeral Home
Craig, Simon (act): The Dead Zone
Craig, Wendy (act, b. 1934): The Mind Benders (1963); The Nanny; The Servant
Craig, Yvonne (act): In Like Flint; Mars Needs Women; One Of Our Spies Is Missing; One Spy Too Many
Crain, Jeanne (act, b. 1925): Duel In The Jungle; Leave Her To Heaven; Nefertite, Regina Del Nilo; The Night God Screamed; The Tattered Dress
Crain, William (dir): Blacula; Dr. Black Mr. Hyde
Craine, Barrie (act): Whirlpool
Craine, Barry (act): Haunters Of The Deep
Cram, Mildred (wri): Beyond Tomorrow
Cramer, Douglas S. (wri): The Cat Creature
Cramer, Fred (cin): Ravagers
Cramer, Grant (act): Killer Klowns From Outer Space; Leapin' Leprechauns!; New Year's Evil
Cramer, Joey (act): The Clan Of The Cave Bear; Flight Of The Navigator; Runaway
Cramer, Kay (act): Magic Spectacles
Cramer, Marc (act): Genius At Work; Isle Of The Dead (1945)
Cramer, Massey (dir & wri): The Legend Of Blood Mountain
Cramer, Michael (Euro act): Hipnosis
Cramer, Michael (USA act): Weird Science
Cramer, Nick (act): The People Under The Stairs
Crammond, James (act): Funeral Home
Crampton, Barbara (act, b. 1959): Castle Freak; Chopping Mall; From Beyond; Puppet Master; Re-Animator; Robot Wars; Trancers II: The Return Of Jack Deth
Crampton, Gerry (act): Deathline
Crampton, Howard (act): Black Orchids
Crampton, Jerry (act): Prey (1978)
Cramton, Ray (act): see Everett, Chad
Crane, Anita (act): New Year's Evil
Crane, Barry (dir): The Hound Of The Baskervilles (1972)
Crane, Brandon (act): It (1990)
Crane, Chilton (act): The Death Of The Incredible Hulk
Crane, Christian (act): Impulse (1984)
Crane, Frank H. (dir): Hutch Stirs 'Em Up
Crane, Harry (wri): Lost In A Harem; Song Of The Thin Man
Crane, Hilary (act): Mark Of The Devil (1985)
Crane, James (act): The Mummy (1932)
Crane, Jimmy (act): Dick Tracy vs. Cueball
Crane, Kenneth G. (dir): Half-Human; The Manster; The Monster From Green Hell
Crane, Les (act): I Love A Mystery (1966)
Crane, Michael (act): At The Earth's Core; Gawain And The Green Knight
Crane, Norma (act, 1931–1973): Night Gallery
Crane, Ogden (act): The Invisible Fear
Crane, Peter (dir): Assassin (1973); Moments
Crane, Randolph (act): see Scott, Randolph
Crane, Richard (act, 1918–1969): The Alligator People; Beyond The Moon; The Cold Sun; The Crash Of Moons; The Devil's Partner; Duel In Space; The Forbidden Moon; The Gypsy Moon; The Happy Land; House Of The Damned (1962); Manhunt In Space; The Neanderthal Man; The Saint In Palm Springs
Crane, Stephen (act): Crime Doctor's Courage; Cry Of The Werewolf

Crane, Stephen (wri, 1871–1900): Face Of Fire
Crane, Violet (act): The Unholy Three (1925)
Crane, Ward (act): The Phantom Of The Opera (1925); Sherlock Jr.
Craney, John (act): Top Secret! (1984)
Cranford, George (act): Matinee
Cranham, Kenneth (act): Dead Man's Folly; Fragment Of Fear; Hellbound: Hellraiser II; Otley; Prospero's Books; Robin And Marian; Vampira
Cranna, James (act): Time After Time
Cranner, Adam (act): Jason Goes To Hell: The Final Friday
Cranshaw, Pat(Rick) (act): The Amazing Transparent Man; Curse Of The Swamp Creature; Mars Needs Women
Cranston, Bryan (act): The Companion (1994); The Return Of The Six Million Dollar Man And The Bionic Woman
Cranston, Joseph L. (wri): The Corpse Grinders; The Crawling Hand
Crao, Mimmo (act): Yeti
Cravat, Nick (act, b. 1911): The Crimson Pirate; The Island Of Dr. Moreau (1977); The Story Of Mankind; The Veils Of Bagdad
Cravat, Noel (act): Captain Kidd And The Slave Girl; The 5000 Fingers Of Dr. T; Shadow Of The Thin Man; Three On A Ticket
Cravel, Rex (act): Mr. Reeder In Room 13
Craven, Eddie (act, 1907–1991): The Invisible Menace
Craven, Frank (act, 1875–1945): Destiny (1944); Miracles For Sale; Son Of Dracula (1943)
Craven, Frank (1980s act): Anguish
Craven, Gemma (act): The Slipper And The Rose
Craven, James (act): Flying Disc Man From Mars; Missile Monsters; Project Moonbase
Craven, Jessica (act): Night Visions; Shocker; Wes Craven's New Nightmare
Craven, John (act): Flight To Nowhere
Craven, Jonathan Christian (act): Shocker
Craven, Matt (act, b. 1956): Happy Birthday To Me; The Intruder Within; Jacob's Ladder
Craven, Mimi (act): Last Gasp
Craven, Wes (act, b. 1938): The Fear (1994); Shadow Zone: The Undead Express; Shocker; Wes Craven's New Nightmare
Craven, Wes (dir, b. 1938): Chiller; Deadly Blessing; Deadly Friend; The Hills Have Eyes; The Hills Have Eyes II; Invitation To Hell; The Last House On The Left; A Nightmare On Elm Street; Night Visions; The People Under The Stairs; Scream; The Serpent And The Rainbow; Shocker; Stranger In Our House; Swamp Thing; Vampire In Brooklyn; Wes Craven's New Nightmare
Craven, Wes (wri, b. 1938): Deadly Blessing; Freddy's Dead: The Final Nightmare; The Hills Have Eyes; The Hills Have Eyes II; The Last House On The Left; A Nightmare On Elm Street; A Nightmare On Elm Street, Part 2: Freddy's Revenge; A Nightmare On Elm Street 3: Dream Warriors; A Nightmare On Elm Street 4: The Dream Master; A Nightmare On Elm Street 5: The Dream Child; Night Visions; The People Under The Stairs; Shocker; Swamp Thing; Wes Craven's New Nightmare
Cravens, Rutherford (act): RoboCop 2
Craviotta, Darlene (act): Dracula's Dog; Human Experiments
Crawford, Alvin (act): Clarence
Crawford, Andrew (act, b. 1917): Dear Murderer; The Shadow Of The Cat
Crawford, Anne (act, 1920–1956, nee Imelda Crawford): Bedelia; The Dark Tower; Daughter Of Darkness (1948); Knights Of The Round Table; Mad About Men
Crawford, Broderick (act, 1911–1986): The Adventures Of Nick Carter; Black Angel (1946); The Black Cat (1941); Down Three Dark Streets; Embassy; Gregorio And His Angel; Harlequin; Hell's Bloody Devils; The Island Of Lost Men; Look What's Happened To Rosemary's Baby; Night Unto Night; The Phantom Of Hollywood; Terror In The Wax Museum; La Vendetta Di Ercole; The Vulture (1966)
Crawford, Dallas J. (act): Blink
Crawford, Dana (act): Phoenix The Warrior
Crawford, David (act): Lady Beware
Crawford, Don (act): Change Of Mind
Crawford, Eve (act): Short Circuit 2; Virus
Crawford, Francis Marion (wri): In The Palace Of The King
Crawford, Ghislaine (act): Watchers
Crawford, Gwen (act): The Falcon In Hollywood
Crawford, Harold A. (act): From Scotland Yard
Crawford, Imelda (act): see Crawford, Anne
Crawford, James M. (act): Howling II
Crawford, Joan (Act, 1908–1977): Above Suspicion; Berserk; The Caretakers; I Saw What You Did (1965); Journey To The Unknown; The Karate Killers; Night Gallery; Possessed (1947); Strait-Jacket; Sudden Fear; Trog; The Unknown (1927); What Ever Happened To Baby Jane? (1962)
Crawford, John (act): The Boogens; Captain Kidd And The Slave Girl; Captain Sinbad; The Devil's Messenger; Floods Of Fear; Grave Secrets; I Saw What You Did (1965); Jason And The Argonauts; The Key; The Man Who Was Nobody; The Poseidon Adventure; Satan's Satellites
Crawford, Johnny (act): The Naked Ape; The Space Children; Village Of The Giants
Crawford, Justine (act): Watchers
Crawford, Katherine (act): Code Name: Minus One
Crawford, Les (act): On Her Majesty's Secret Service
Crawford, Lilybelle (act): The Man Who Fell To Earth (1976)
Crawford, Marion (wri): Whosoever Shall Offend
Crawford, Michael (act, b. 1942): Alice's Adventures In Wonderland (1972); Condorman
Crawford, Nancy (act): The Witchmaker
Crawford, Pauline (act): Empire Of Ash III
Crawford, Robert (act): The Wonderful World Of The Brothers Grimm
Crawford, Thomas/Tom (act): Outbreak; Vice Versa (1988)
Crawford, Wayne (David) (act): Barracuda; Evil Below; Headhunter; Jake Speed; Rising Storm
Crawford, Wayne (David) (wri): Barracuda; Jake Speed
Crayden, Johanna (act): An American Werewolf In London
Crayford, Jonathan (act & mus): Dark Of The Night
Crayne, Dani (act): The Story Of Mankind
Craze, Michael (act): Journey To The Unknown; Neither The Sea Nor The Sand; Satan's Slave; Terror (1979)
Craze, Peter (act): Are You Dying Young Man?; Terror (1979)
Creach, Everett L. (act): Prophecy (1979)
Creach, Lauri (act): Hellhole
Creagan, Linda (act): Jack's Wife
Creamer, John (act): Obsession (1976)
Creamer, William (act): Blood Simple
Creasey, John (wri): Gideon's Day
Creber, Lewis (cin): The Mysterious Mr. Moto
Crechales, Tony (wri): The Attic; Blood Mania; Point Of Terror
Crechalon, Lenny (wri): The Killing Kind
Credel, Curtis (act): The Aliens Are Coming; Firestarter
Creed, Roger (act): Endangered Species; Piranha (1978)
Creel, Monica (act): Rattled
Creelman, James A./Ashmore (wri): King Kong (1933); The Last Days Of Pompeii (1935); The Most Dangerous Game; Puritan Passions
Creer, Erica (act): Circle Of Iron
Creevay, Lori (act): Popcorn
Cregar, Laird (act, 1916–1944): The Black Swan; Hangover Square; Heaven Can Wait (1942); I Wake Up Screaming; The Lodger (1944)
Crehan, Dorothy (act): I Was A Teenage Werewolf
Crehan, Joseph (act, 1884–1966): Amazon Quest; Behind The Mask (1932); Black Magic (1944); Dangerous Money; Dick Tracy (1945); Dick Tracy Meets Gruesome; Dick Tracy vs. Cueball; The Falcon's Adventure; One Mysterious Night; The Phantom Thief; Philo Vance's Gamble; The Return Of Dr. X; Smart Blonde
Crehuet, Elisa (act): Anguish
Creighton, Sally (act): The Thing From Another World
Creley, Jack (act): Change Of Mind; Dr. Strangelove: or, How I Learned To Stop Worrying And Love The Bomb; Gotham; Rituals; Videodrome; Welcome To Blood City
Cremer, Lance (act): Mr. Sycamore
Cremieux, Henri (act): Orphee
Crenna, Richard (act, b. 1926): Death Ship; Devil Dog: The Hound Of Hell; The Evil; A Fire In The Sky (1978); It Grows On Trees; Jade; Leviathan; Marooned; Stone Cold Dead; 20,000 Leagues Under The Sea (1997, CBS-Tv)
Cresijo, Mike (act): Unforgettable
Crespi, Todd (act): The Magician (1973)
Crespin, Claudia (act): Phenomenon
Crespinel, Bill (act): Radar Secret Service
Crespo, Maria Luisa (act): Hundra
Cressall, Maud (act): The Barton Mystery (1920); The Tinted Venus; Whosoever Shall Offend
Cresse, Bob (act): House On Bare Mountain
Cresse, R.W. (wri): World By Night No. 2
Cressoy, Pierre (act): David And Goliath; The Lion Of Thebes; Il Trionfo Di Ercole; The War Of The Worlds
Cresswell, Jane (act): The Boy From Andromeda
Cresswell, John (wri): The Woman In Question
Cresswell, Paul (act): Jamaica Inn (1985)
Crevenna, Alfredo (dir): H.G. Wells' 'The New Invisible Man'
Crew, Carl (act): Blood Diner
Crewdson, Robert (act): Night Caller From Outer Space; The Psychopath (1965); Trog
Crewe, Bob (mus): Barbarella
Crews, Laura Hope (act, 1880–1942): The Blue Bird (1940)
Crewson, Wendy (act): The Good Son; Rona Jaffe's Mazes And Monsters; The Santa Clause; To Gillian On Her 37th Birthday
Cribben, Mik (act): Nightmare (1981)
Cribbins, Bernard (act, b. 1928): Carry On Spying; Casino Royale; Daleks' Invasion Earth 2150 A.D.; Frenzy; A Ghost Of A Chance (1968); The Mouse On The Moon; She (1965); The Water Babies
Crichton, Charles (dir, b. 1910): Dead Of Night (1945); Floods Of Fear; Hunted (1952); The Lavender Hill Mob; The Third Secret
Crichton, Charles (wri, b. 1910): Floods Of Fear
Crichton, David (act): Black Roses
Crichton, Michael (dir, b. 1942): Coma; Looker; Pursuit (1972); Runaway; Westworld
Crichton, Michael (wri, b. 1942): The Andromeda Strain; Coma; Congo; Eaters Of The Dead; Jurassic Park; Looker; The Lost World: Jurassic Park; Pursuit (1972); Runaway; Sphere; The Terminal Man; Twister; Westworld
Cricks, R. Howard (act): A Newsboy's Christmas Dream
Crider, Missy (act): The Beast (1996); Eyes Of Terror; Powder
Crimmins, Dan (act): White Zombie
Crimson, King (mus): Devil's Triangle
Cripps, Kernan (act): The Falcon Out West; The Lone Wolf Returns (1935); The Scarlet Clue
Crisa, Erno (act): Mata Hari's Daughter
Criscuolo, Lou (act): Eat And Run; King Kong Lives
Crisman, Jerry (act): Revenge Of The Teenage Vixens From Outer Space
Crisp, Donald (act, 1880–1974): The Avenging Conscience; The Black Pirate; Dr. Jekyll And Mr. Hyde (1941); Don Q, Son Of Zorro; Prince Valiant; Scotland Yard (1930); Svengali (1931); Trent's Last Case (1929); The Uninvited (1944); Whispering Smith; Wuthering Heights (1939)
Crisp, Donald (dir, 1880–1974): Don Q, Son Of Zorro
Crisp, Frank (wri): Night Caller From Outer Space
Crisp, Quentin (act, b. 1908): The Bride (1985)
Crisp, Tracey (act): Casino Royale; The Projected Man; Too-Morrow
Crispino, Armando (dir): Autopsy; The Dead Are Alive
Crispino, Armando (wri): The Dead Are Alive
Criss, Peter (act): Kiss Meets The Phantom Of The Park
Crist, Paula (act): The Dark (1979); Star Trek
Cristal, Linda (act, b. 1935, nee Victoria Moya): The Dead Don't Die; Panic In The City; Slave Girls Of Sheba
Cristal, Perla (act): The Awful Dr. Orlof; Las Cuatro Noches De La Luna Llena; The Fury Of The Wolfman; El Secreto Del Doctor Orlof; A Thousand And One Nights (1968); A Witch Without A Broom
Cristiani, Pedro (wri): Moebius
Cristillo, Louis Francis (act): see Costello, Lou
Cristin, Chris (act): Boarding House
Cristina, Katia (act): Spirits Of The Dead
Cristino, Tony (act): Human Feelings
Cristofer, Michael (wri): The Witches Of Eastwick
Cristos (act): From Dusk Till Dawn
Criswell (act, d. 1982): Orgy Of The Dead (1965); Plan 9 From Outer Space
Criswell, Billy (act): Pranks
Critchlow, Keith (wri): Night Life (1989, USA)
Crivello, Anthony (act): Spellbinder
Crivello, Guerrino (act): The Black Belly Of The Tarantula
Croall, John (act): see Stuart, John
Croccolo, Carlo (act): The Reluctant Saint
Crocetti, Dino (act): see Martin, Dean
Crochon, Jean-Pierre (act): see Cassel, Jean-Pierre
Crocker, Emerson (wri): The Treasure Of Lost Canyon
Crocker-King, C.H. (act): One Exciting Night
Crockett, B.J. (act): Strange Days
Crockett, Dick (act): Experiment In Terror; Moon Of The Wolf
Crockett, Ellie (act): Mary Reilly
Crockett, Karlene (act): Charlie Chan And The Curse Of The Dragon Queen; Eyes Of Fire; Return (1985)
Crockett, Samuel (wri): The Secret Of The Loch (1957)
Crofoot, Alan (act): Welcome To Blood City
Crofoot, Leonard (John) (act): Echoes; A Reflection Of Fear
Croft, Al (act): Night Of The Living Dead (1968)
Croft, Alyson/Allyson (act): Maid To Order; Trancers; Trancers II: The Return Of Jack Deth
Croft, Colin (act): The Accursed
Croft, James (act): That Eye, The Sky
Croft, Jon (act): The Black Windmill; The Mind Of Mr. Soames
Croft, Peter (act): The Gaunt Stranger
Croft-Cooke, Rupert (wri): Clash By Night; Seven Thunders
Crofton, Kelli (act): Edward Scissorhands
Crofts, Charles (act): Glen Or Glenda?
Crognale, Thomas (act): Frankenhooker
Croise, Hugh (act): The Game Of Liberty; The Mystery Of A London Flat
Croise, Hugh (dir): Scrooge (1928)
Croll, Don Alan (act): Donor
Croman, Richard (act): Aladdin And His Lamp
Cromarty, Andree (act): At The Earth's Core
Crombie, Jonathan (act): The Housekeeper
Crombie, Peter (act): Seven
Crombie, Tony (mus): The Tell-Tale Heart (1960)
Cromer, Dean (act): The Monolith Monsters
Crompton, R. (act): A Message From Mars (1913)
Crompton, Richmal (wri): Just William's Luck
Cromwell Brothers Trapeze Act (act): Dual Alibi
Cromwell, James (act, b. 1939): Eraser; Explorers; The Man With Two Brains; Murder By Death; Oh, God! You Devil; Romeo Is Bleeding; Star Trek: First Contact
Cromwell, John (dir, 1888–1979): The Enchanted Cottage (1945); The Prisoner Of Zenda (1937); The Scavengers
Cromwell, Richard (act): The Villain Still Pursued Her
Cromwell, Sam (dir & wri): The Strangers
Crone, Glenn (act): The Henderson Monster
Crone, Penny (act): Daylight
Cronenberg, David (act, b. 1943): Extreme Measures; The Fly (1986); Nightbreed
Cronenberg, David (dir, b. 1943): The Brood; Crash (1996); Dead Ringers; The Dead Zone; The Fly (1986); Rabid; Scanners; Shivers; Videodrome
Cronenberg, David (wri, b. 1943): The Brood; Crash (1996); Dead Ringers; The Fly (1986); Rabid; Scanners; Shivers; Videodrome
Cronenweth, Jordan (cin): Altered States; Blade Runner
Cronin, A.J. (wri, 1896–1981): Beyond This Place
Cronin, Joe (act): The Haunting Of Sarah Hardy
Cronin, Michael (act): Mark Of The Devil (1985); The Sexplorer
Cronin, Patrick (act): Brave New World; Splash
Cronin, Paul (act): Children Shouldn't Play With Dead Things
Cronjager, Edward (cin, 1904–1960): The Gorilla (1939); Heaven Can Wait (1942); I Wake Up Screaming; The Lost Squadron; Seven Keys To Baldpate (1929); Widow In Scarlet
Cronjager, Henry (cin): Hands Of A Stranger
Cronjager, Jules (cin): The Dancer Of The Nile; The Monster Walks
Cronjager, William (cin): Joe & The Colonel
Cronkite, Walter (act): We're Back! A Dinosaur's Story
Cronyn, Hume (act, b. 1911): *Batteries Not Included; The Beginning Or The End?; Cocoon; Cocoon: The Return; Impulse (1984); Lifeboat; Phantom Of The Opera (1943); Shadow Of A Doubt (1943)
Cronyn, Tandy (act): Twisted
Crooke, Leland (act): Maid To Order
Cropper, Steve (act): Empire Of Ash III
Crosbie, Annette (act): Hawk The Slayer; The Slipper And The Rose

Crosbie, Craig (act): Jekyll And Hyde

Crosby, Bing (act, 1904–1977, nee Harry Lillis Crosby): A Connecticut Yankee In King Arthur's Court (1949); Dr. Cook's Garden; The Road To Bali; The Road To Hong Kong; The Road To Utopia; Scared Stiff (1953)

Crosby, Bob (act, b. 1913): The Road To Bali

Crosby, Cathy Lee (act, b. 1948): The Dark (1979); Wonder Woman; World War III

Crosby, Denise (act): Bio-Force I; Dolly Dearest; The Eliminators; Miracle Mile; Pet Sematary

Crosby, Floyd (D.) (cin, b. 1899): Attack Of The Crab Monsters; Black Zoo; The Comedy Of Terrors; Crime And Punishment, U.S.A.; Hand Of Death; The Haunted Palace (1963); House Of Usher; How To Stuff A Wild Bikini; Monster From The Ocean Floor; Pajama Party; The Pit And The Pendulum (1961); The Premature Burial; The Raven (1963); The Screaming Skull; She-Gods Of Shark Reef; The Snow Creature; Tabu; Tales Of Terror; Teenage Caveman; War Of The Satellites; X—The Man With The X-Ray Eyes

Crosby, Gary (act, 1933–1995): The Night Stalker (1987); Sandcastles

Crosby, Harry (act): Friday The 13th (1980)

Crosby, Harry Lillis (act): see Crosby, Bing

Crosby, Joan (act): Planet Earth; The Shaggy D.A.

Crosby, Kathryn (act): see Grant (Crosby), Kathryn

Crosby, Katja (act): It's Alive III: Island Of The Alive; A Return To Salem's Lot

Crosby, Kim (act): Tarzan In Manhattan

Crosby, Lindsay (act): Big Foot

Crosby, Mary (act, b. 1959): The Berlin Conspiracy; Child's Play (1985); The Ice Pirates; Midnight Lace (1981)

Crosby, Randy (act): The Night They Saved Christmas

Crosby, Wade (act): Invasion U.S.A.; Prisoners Of The Casbah; Westworld

Croset, Paule (act): see Corday, Paula

Crosland, Alan (dir, 1894–1936): The Case Of The Howling Dog; Don Juan (1927); The Face In The Fog (1922); The Great Impersonation (1935)

Crosman, Henrietta (act, 1861–1944): Charlie Chan's Secret

Cross, Ben (act): First Knight; Nightlife (1989, Usa-Mex); Paperhouse; 20,000 Leagues Under The Sea (1997, CBS-TV); The Unholy

Cross, Beverly (wri): Clash Of The Titans; Jason And The Argonauts; Sinbad And The Eye Of The Tiger

Cross, Cyril (act): Doomwatch; The Orchard End Murder

Cross, David (act): Creation Of The Humanoids; The Magic Sword (1962)

Cross, Dennis (act): How To Make A Monster

Cross, Gerrards (act): see More, Kenneth

Cross, H.B. (wri): Chosen Survivors

Cross, Harley (act): The Believers; The Fly II

Cross, Hugh (act): Just William's Luck; Seven Days To Noon; Svengali (1954)

Cross, Jimmy (act): The Amazing Colossal Man

Cross, Larry (act): Embassy; The Girl Hunters; The Man Outside (1967); The Mouse That Roared; Zex

Cross, Marcia (act): Mantis

Cross, Paul (act): Amazons (1984)

Cross, Roger R. (act): Hideaway

Cross, Sally (act): Slaughter High

Cross, Thomas (act): The Invisible Kid

Crossley, Syd (act): The Gorilla (1927); The Man In The Mirror; Young And Innocent

Crosthwaite, Julie (act): Madhouse

Crothall, Howard (act): Strange Behavior

Crothers, (Sherman) Scatman (act, 1910–1986, Nee Benjamin Sherman Crothers): Deadly Eyes; Lady In A Cage; The Shining; Tarzan And The Trappers; Twilight Zone; Zapped!

Croucher, Brian (act): The Quatermass Conclusion; Transmutations

Crouse, Avery (dir & wri): Eyes Of Fire; The Invisible Kid

Crouse, Lindsay (act, b. 1948): The Arrival; Communion; Iceman; The Indian In The Cupboard

Crow, Alvin (act): Endangered Species

Crow, Angela (act): Morons From Outer Space

Crow, Ashley (act): Dark Angel; The Good Son

Crow, Carl (act): Premonition (1972); Shell Shock

Crow, Clarence (act): The Other (1972)

Crow, Emilia (act): Disaster In Time

Crow, Julie (act): The Phantom Empire

Crow, Kim (act): Raptors

Crowcroft, Peter (act): On A Clear Day You Can See Forever

Crowden, Graham (act): The Company Of Wolves; Dead Man's Chest; For Your Eyes Only; Jabberwocky; The Last Days Of Man On Earth; The Little Prince; The Night Digger; The Ruling Class

Crowder, John (act): The Crater Lake Monster

Crowdy, Francis (wri): The Mark Of Cain

Crowe, Christopher (wri): Alfred Hitchcock Presents; Fear (1996); Nightmares (1983)

Crowe, Rick (act): I Was A Zombie For The F.B.I.

Crowe, Russell (act): Virtuosity

Crowe, Tonya (act): Dark Night Of The Scarecrow

Crowell Jr., Henry (act): I Still Dream Of Jeannie

Crowell, Josephine (act): The Man Who Laughs (1928); Rupert Of Hentzau (1923)

Crowell, W.B.F. (act): The Dungeon

Crowell, William (act): Revolt Of The Zombies

Crowley, David (L.) (act): Donor; The Flash

Crowley, Dermot (act): Octopussy; Return Of The Jedi

Crowley, Ed (act): The Fan

Crowley, Joy (wri): The Night Digger

Crowley, Kathleen (act): The Curse Of The Undead; The Female Jungle; The Flame Barrier; Target Earth

Crowley, Pat(ricia) (act, b. 1933): Return To Fantasy Island; To Trap A Spy

Crowley, Rory L. (act): The Clan Of The Cave Bear

Croxton, Dee (act): Fugitive From The Empire

Croydon, Joan (act): The Bad Seed (1956)

Croydon, John (wri): A Piece Of Cake

Croyle, Kenneth (act): Midnight (1980)

Cruchley, Murray (act): Clarence

Crudden, Coleen (act): Phantom Of The Paradise

Crugnali, Louis (act): Robin Cook's 'Invasion'

Cruickshank, Andrew (act): Forbidden; The Mark Of Cain; Murder Most Foul; Richard III (1955); The Stranglers Of Bombay; The 39 Steps (1959); Your Witness

Cruickshank, Art (cin): City Beneath The Sea (1970); Condorman; Daughter Of The Mind; Escape To Witch Mountain; Fantastic Voyage; The Island At The Top Of The World

Cruickshank, James (wri): Mr. Destiny

Cruickshank, Rufus (act): No Haunt For A Gentleman

Cruickshank, Su (act): Those Dear Departed

Cruickshanks, Reid (act): Dark Mirror (1984); Ed Wood

Cruise, Al (act): Alien High

Cruise, Tom (act, b. 1962): Interview With The Vampire; Legend; Mission: Impossible

Cruise, Yvette (act): Ghostbusters II

Crumb, Anthony (act): The Mutagen

Crume, Louis (act): Psycho IV: The Beginning

Crump, Owen (dir & wri): The Couch

Crumpacker, Amy (act): Revenge Of The Teenage Vixens From Outer Space

Cruse, Charles (act): Secrets Of The Phantom Caverns

Cruse, Gerald (act): Blood Waters Of Dr. Z

Crutcher, Gary (act): Giant From The Unknown; Stanley

Crutcher, Gary (wri): Stanley

Crutcher, Jack (wri): Jalopy; No Holds Barred

Crutchfield, Jim (wri): The Nasty Rabbit

Crutchfield, Les (wri): Tarzan's Greatest Adventure

Crutchley, Jeremy (act): The Mangler

Crutchley, Rosalie (act, b. 1921): And Now The Screaming Starts!; Beyond This Place; Blood From The Mummy's Tomb; Creatures The World Forgot; The Gamma People; The Haunting; The House In Nightmare Park; The Hunchback Of Notre Dame (1982); The Return (1973, GB); Seven Thunders; Take My Life; Who Slew Auntie Roo?; Wuthering Heights (1970)

Cruz, Alejandro (act): El Ladron De Cadaveres

Cruz, Alexis (act): Stargate

Cruz, Bob (act): Making Mr. Right

Cruz, Celia (act): The Mummy's Revenge

Cruz, Conchita (act): The Blood Drinkers

Cruz, Francisco (act): Curse Of The Vampires

Cruz, Ismael (act): Howling II

Cruz, Mara (act): Hipnosis

Cruz, Raymond (act): Dead Again; Gremlins 2: The New Batch

Cruze, James (act, 1884–1942): Dr. Jekyll And Mr. Hyde (1912); She (1911)

Cruze, James (dir, 1884–1942): The Great Gabbo

Cruze, Josh (act): The Fluid

Cryde, Al (wri): War Of The Planets

Cryer, Barry (act & wri): Blood Bath At The House Of Death

Cryer, David (act): Gotham

Cryer, Jon (act, b. 1965): Heads; Superman IV: The Quest For Peace

Crystal, Billy (act, b. 1947): Hamlet (1996); Human Feelings; The Princess Bride

Cserhart, Alex (act): The Toxic Avenger, Part II

Cuadrado, Luis (cin): Night Hair Child

Cucci, Frank (wri): Svengali (1983)

Cucinelli, Enrico (act): Just Imagine

Cudco, Kaley (act): Virtuosity

Cudney, Cliff (act): Friday The 13th-Part 2; The Nesting

Cudney, Roger (act): The Bees; Final Eye; Total Recall

Cuetos, Concha (act): Slugs

Cuetos, Conchita (act): La Cara Del Terror

Cuevas, Guy (act): The Jewel Of The Nile

Cuff, John Haslett (act): Psycho Girls

Cuff, Max (wri): Prey (1978)

Cuffling, Bernard (act): The Little Match Girl (1987); The Resurrected

Cugat, Xavier (act, 1900–1990): The Monitors

Cuka, Frances (act): The Watcher In The Woods

Cukor, George (Dir, 1899–1983): The Blue Bird (1976); A Double Life; Gaslight (1944)

Culea, Melinda (act): Buried Secrets

Culkin, Macaulay (act, 1980): The Good Son; The Pagemaster

Culkin, Michael (act): Candyman: Farewell To The Flesh

Culkin, Quinn (act): The Good Son

Culkin, Rory (act): The Good Son

Cullen, Alan (act): Superman (1978)

Cullen, Carmel (act): Inn Of The Damned

Cullen, Hedley (act): The Last Wave

Cullen, Katharine (act): The Girl From Tomorrow; Mad Max Beyond Thunderdome

Cullen, Kerrie (act): Endangered Species

Cullen, Max (act): Encounter At Raven's Gate

Cullen, Robert J. (wri): The Woman In White (1929)

Cullen, William Kirby (act): Blood Song

Culley, Frederick (act): The Drum; Knight Without Armour

Culley, John K. (cin): Attack Of The Killer Tomatoes

Culley, Zara (act): Sugar Hill

Culliford, James (act): Deathline; The Trygon Factor

Cullimore, Alan (dir): The Clouded Crystal

Cullin, Arthur (M.) (act): The Answer; Blood Money; A Christmas Carol (1914); The Devil's Bondman; The Sign Of Four (1923); A Smart Set; The Sons Of Satan; The Valley Of Fear (1916); The Yellow Claw

Cullinan, Thomas (wri): The Beguiled

Culliton, Patrick (act): Beyond The Poseidon Adventure; Future Zone; The Swarm

Cullum, John (act, b. 1930): The Day After

Cully, Russell A. (act): Dick Tracy Meets Gruesome; The Locket; The Velvet Touch

Culotta, Ann (act): My Science Project

Culotta, Phil (act): The Monster Squad; Remo Williams: The Adventure Begins

Culp, Joseph (act): Full Eclipse

Culp, Robert (act, b. 1930): A Cold Night's Death; Flood; The Hanged Man; Houston, We've Got A Problem; Silent Night, Deadly Night III; Spectre (1977)

Culp, Steven (act): Dead Again; Jason Goes To Hell: The Final Friday

Culpan, Peter (act): Mad Max; Patrick

Culpepper, Stuart (act): Mutant

Cult, The (mus): Demons 2

Culture Club (mus): Electric Dreams

Culver, Carmen (wri): Murder Is Easy

Culver, Howard (act): The Swarm

Culver, Jim (act): Nightmare Sisters

Culver, Lillian (act): Nightfall (1956)

Culver, Michael (act): The Body Stealers; Devil's Web

Culver, Roland (act, 1900–1984): Dead Of Night (1945); Down To Earth; Fragment Of Fear; Gestapo; The Hour Of 13; The Hunchback Of Notre Dame (1982); The Hypnotist (1957); The Late Edwina Black; The Legend Of Hell House; The Magic Christian; Never-Never Land; Puppets Of Fate; The Teckman Mystery; Thunderball; The Uncanny; A Voice Said Goodnight; The Vicious Circle (1957); Wanted For Murder

Culver, Veronica (act): Demon Knight

Cumba, Richy (act): Halloween 4: The Return Of Michael Myers

Cumberland, Marten (wri): Inside The Room

Cumbuka, Ji-Tu (act): Blacula; Covenant; Dr. Black Mr. Hyde; Mandrake

Cumer, Jill (act): Deranged (1987)

Cummiford, Daniel (act): Chiller

Cummings, Alan (act): Bernard And The Genie; Goldeneye

Cumming, Dorothy (act): A Kiss For Cinderella

Cumming, Kristin (act): Don't Go To Sleep

Cumming, Leslie (act): Witchery

Cummings, Bob (act): The Hidden; Star Trek III: The Search For Spock

Cummings, Constance (act, b. 1910, nee Constance Halverstadt): Behind The Mask (1932); Blithe Spirit; Busman's Honeymoon; Dead Man's Folly; The Intimate Stranger; Jane Eyre (1970); The Mind Reader

Cummings, Dale (act): Spellbinder

Cummings, Irving (act, 1888–1959): Rupert Of Hentzau (1923)

Cummings, Irving (dir, 1888–1959): Behind That Curtain

Cummings, Kimball (act): Sometimes They Came Back

Cummings, Quinn (act, b. 1967): The Babysitter

Cummings Jr., Richard (act): Eve Of Destruction; Project X (1987); The Trial Of The Incredible Hulk

Cummings, Robert (act, 1910–1990): The Accused; The Black Book; The Chase; Dial M For Murder (1954); Five Golden Dragons; Flesh And Fantasy; For Heaven's Sake; Heaven Only Knows; The Lost Moment; Saboteur; Sleep, My Love

Cummins, Don (act): Spawn Of The Slithis

Cummins, Gregory Scott (act): Phantom Of The Mall: Eric's Revenge

Cummins, Juliette (act): Friday The 13th, Part V: A New Beginning

Cummins, Martin (act): Friday The 13th, Part VIII-Jason Takes Manhattan

Cummins, Peggy (act, b. 1926): The March Hare; Meet Mr. Lucifer; Moss Rose; My Daughter Joy; Night Of The Demon (1957)

Cummins, Ron (act): Ghostbusters II; The Relic

Cunard, Grace (act): Bride Of Frankenstein

Cunati, Edwige (act): see Feuillere, Edwige

Cundell, Pamela (act): Memoirs Of A Survivor

Cundey, Dean (act): Jurassic Park

Cundey, Dean (cin): Amazons (1984); Apollo 13; Back To The Future; Back To The Future, Part II; Big Trouble In Little China; Creature From Black Lake; Death Becomes Her; Escape From New York; The Flintstones; The Fog; Galaxina; Halloween; Halloween II; Halloween III: Season Of The Witch; The Invisible Woman (1983); Invitation To Hell; It Came Upon The Midnight Clear; Jaws Of Satan; Jurassic Park; Nothing But Trouble; Project X (1987); Psycho II; Romancing The Stone; Satan's Cheerleaders; The Thing (1982); Warning Sign

Cundieff, Christina (act): Tales From The Hood

Cundieff, John A. (act): Tales From The Hood

Cundieff, Rusty (act, dir & wri): Tales From The Hood

Cunha, Kathy (act): End Of The World (1977)

Cunha, Richard (cin): Giant From The Unknown

Cunha, Richard (E.) (dir): Frankenstein's Daughter (1958); Giant From The Unknown; Missile To The Moon; She Demons

Cunha, Richard (E.) (wri): She Demons

Cunniffe, R. (act): Blind Date

Cunning, Joyce (act): The Screaming Woman

Cunning, Pat (act): Charlie Chan At The Opera

Cunningham, Beryl (act): Curse Of Simba; Dorian Gray; Exterminators Of The Year 3000; The Fish Men

Cunningham, Bob (act): Earthquake

Cunningham, Cecil (act): Above Suspicion

Cunningham, Chris (act): Dracula Has Risen From The Grave; Frankenstein And The Monster From Hell

Cunningham, Copper (act): The Brother From Another Planet

Cunningham, Dan (act): Richard III (1955)

Cunningham, Danny (act): Little Shop Of Horrors (1986)

Cunningham, George T. (act): Shock Chamber

Cunningham, Jack (act): The Snake Woman

Cunningham, Jack (wri): The Black Pirate; Don Q, Son Of Zorro

Cunningham, James (act): Copycat

Cunningham, Joe (act): Blondes At Work; Torchy Blane In Panama; Torchy Gets Her Man; Torchy Plays With Dynamite; Torchy Runs For Mayor

Cunningham, John (act): Hello Again; Twisted

Cunningham, June (act): Horrors Of The Black Museum

Cunningham, Liam (act): First Knight

Cunningham, Linda (act): Spell Of Evil

Cunningham, Neil (act): The Tempest (1980)

Cunningham, Owen (act): Yankee Island

Cunningham, Peggy (act): Just Imagine

Cunningham, Ralph (act): Terror In The Wax Museum

Cunningham, Robert (act): No Survivors, Please
Cunningham, Sarah (act): Nero Wolfe
Cunningham, Sean S. (dir): Case Of The Full Moon Murders; Deepstar Six; Friday The 13th (1980); A Stranger Is Watching
Cuny, Alain (act, b. 1908): The Hunchback Of Notre Dame (1957); Satyricon; Les Visiteurs Du Soir
Cupo, Pat (act): Turn Back The Clock
Cupp, David (act): Mutants In Paradise
Cura, Carlo (act): The Village Of The Damned (1960)
Curacao, Harcourt (act): The Boy Who Never Was
Curcio, E.J. (act): Hard Rock Zombies
Curiel, Federico/Frederick (dir): Los Automatas De La Muerte; La Maldicion De Nostradamus; Nostradamus Y El Destructor De Monstruos; Nostradamus Y El Genio De La Tinieblas; Las Vampiras (1969)
Curiel, Federico/Frederick (wri): El Baron Del Terror; La Cabeza Viviente; Nostradamus Y El Destructor De Monstruos; Las Vampiras (1969)
Curiel, Herbert (act): Spy In The Sky
Curley, Pauline (act): Life Without Soul
Curley, Thom (act): Ghost (1990)
Curnen, Tim (wri): Forbidden World; Ghost Warrior
Curnick, David (wri): The Keeper
Curnow, Graham (act): Horrors Of The Black Museum
Curran, Larry (act): Beyond The Universe
Curran, Pamela (act): The Blob (1958); Mutiny In Outer Space
Curran, Paul (act): Jabberwocky
Curran, Robert (wri): The Haunted (1991)
Curran, Thomas (act): The Black Pearl
Currens, Cal (act): The Destructors
Currie, Anthony (dir & wri): The Pink Chiquitas
Currie, Bill (act): The Hideous Sun Demon
Currie, Cherie (act): Parasite; Wavelength
Currie, Clive (act): Old Bill Through The Ages
Currie, Donald (act): Mr. Selkie
Currie, Finlay (act, 1878–1968): Around The World In 80 Days; The Black Rose; Bunny Lake Is Missing; The Claydon Treasure Mystery; The Clue Of The Silver Key; Doctor Of Seven Dials; Footsteps In The Fog; 49th Parallel; The Frightened Lady (1932); Great Expectations (1946); Murder At The Gallop; My Daughter Joy; The Old Man; Sleeping Car To Trieste; The Three Lives Of Thomasina; Thunder Rock; Treasure Island (1950); Vendetta For The Saint
Currie, Gordon (act): Blood & Donuts; Friday The 13th, Part VII- Jason Takes Manhattan; Puppet Master 4; Puppet Master 5
Currie, Jean (act): The Pink Chiquitas
Currie, Louise (act): The Ape Man; The Chinese Ring; Sakima And The Masked Marvel; Three On A Ticket; Voodoo Man
Currie, Michael (act): Dead And Buried; Halloween III: Season Of The Witch; The Philadelphia Experiment
Currie, Sandee (act): Terror Train
Currie, Sondra (act): Demon And The Mummy
Currie, Tad (act): Scalpel
Currier, Frank (act): A Message From Mars (1921)
Currier, Lauren (wri): Cujo
Currier, Mary (act): Dick Tracy (1945); The Falcon In Mexico; Return Of The Ape Man; Trapped By Boston Blackie; Voodoo Man
Currier, Terrence (act): Blow Out
Currin, Brenda (act): C.H.U.D.
Curry, Bill (act): Alien High
Curry, Brian (act): Surf Nazis Must Die
Curry, Christopher (act): C.H.U.D.
Curry, Nathan (act): Tarzan And His Mate
Curry, Shaun (act): Death Is A Woman
Curry, Steven (act): Glen And Randa
Curry, Tim (act, b. 1946): Beauty And The Beast: The Enchanted Christmas; Congo; It (1990); Legend; The Rocky Horror Picture Show; The Shadow (1994); The Shout; The Three Musketeers (1993); The Worst Witch
Curtain, Hoyt (mus): Kiss Meets The Phantom Of The Park
Curteis, Ian (dir): The Projected Man
Curthan, John (act): Making Contact
Curtin, Jane (act, b. 1947): Coneheads
Curtin, Jerry (act): Alfred Hitchcock Presents
Curtin, Lionel (act): Howling III
Curtin, Valerie (act): Brave New World
Curtis, Alan (GB act): The Flesh And Blood Show
Curtis, Alan (USA act, 1909–1953, Nee Harold Neberroth): Destiny (1944); Flight To Nowhere; The Invisible Man's Revenge; Philo Vance's Gamble; Philo Vance's Secret Mission
Curtis, Beatrice (act): The Lone Wolf Spy Hunt
Curtis, Billy (act, 1909–1988): The Incredible Shrinking Man; It Came Upon The Midnight Clear; Jungle Moon Men; The Night They Saved Christmas; Pygmy Island; Superman And The Mole Men
Curtis, Bob (act): The Sky Dragon
Curtis, Dan (dir): Burnt Offerings; Curse Of The Black Widow; The Norliss Tapes; Scream Of The Wolf; Trilogy Of Terror
Curtis, Dan (wri): Burnt Offerings; Night Of Dark Shadows
Curtis, Dick (act): The Lone Wolf In Paris; The Lone Wolf Spy Hunt; The Man They Could Not Hang
Curtis, Dick (act): Secrets Of The Phantom Caverns
Curtis, Donald (act): The Amazing Mr. X; Earth Vs. The Flying Saucers; It Came From Beneath The Sea; Spellbound (1945)
Curtis, Greg (cin): Impulse (1984); The Lightning Incident; Nightmare On The 13th Floor
Curtis, Jack (dir): The Flesh Eaters
Curtis, Jacqueline (act): Fire Maidens Of Outer Space
Curtis, Jamie Lee (act, b. 1958): The Fog; Forever Young; Halloween; Halloween II; Prom Night; Road Games; Terror Train
Curtis, Jon (act): The Toxic Avenger
Curtis, Keene (act, b. 1925): Blade; Heaven Can Wait (1978); Macbeth (1947); The Magician (1973); Sliver; Strange New World
Curtis, Kelly (act): The Devil's Daughter (1995)
Curtis, Kelly Leigh (act): La Setta
Curtis, Ken (act, 1916–1991): The Killer Shrews
Curtis, Liane (act): The Brother From Another Planet; Critters 2: The Main Course; Girlfriend From Hell
Curtis, Medelon (act): Jason Goes To Hell: The Final Friday
Curtis, Mel (act): Zombies Of Mora Tau
Curtis, Nat (wri): Jack And The Beanstalk (1952)
Curtis, Oren (act): Black Zoo
Curtis, Paul (act): The Witches And The Grinnygog
Curtis, Peter (wri): Guilt Is My Shadow; The Witches (1966)
Curtis, Richard (act): Attack Of The Killer Tomatoes
Curtis, Robin (act): Northstar; Star Trek III: The Search For Spock; Star Trek IV: The Voyage Home
Curtis, Ronald (act): The Great Office Mystery
Curtis, Scott (act): Cameron's Closet
Curtis, Sonia (act): The Monster Squad
Curtis, Susan (act): Time Walker
Curtis, Tony (act, b. 1925, nee Bernard Schwartz): The Black Shield Of Falworth; The Boston Strangler; Chamber Of Horrors (1966); The Count Of Monte Cristo (1975); Francis; Goodbye Charlie; Houdini; The List Of Adrian Messenger; Lobster Man From Mars; The Manitou; Midnight (1989); The Mirror Crack'd; The Mummy Lives; Paris When It Sizzles; The Purple Mask; Shadow Of Death (1983); Son Of Ali Baba; Tarzan In Manhattan
Curtis, Tracy (act): Trilogy Of Terror
Curtis, Wanda (act): King Dinosaur
Curtis, Willy (cin): The Incredible Melting Man
Curtiss, Jacqueline (act): The Camp On Blood Island
Curtiss, Ursula (wri): I Saw What You Did (1965 & 1988); What Ever Happened To Aunt Alice?
Curtiz, Gabor (act): Doomsday Machine
Curtiz, Michael (dir, 1888–1962): The Adventures Of Robin Hood; Alias The Doctor; British Agent; The Case Of The Curious Bride; Doctor X; The Kennel Murder Case; Labyrinth Des Grauens; The Mad Genius; The Man In The Net; Mystery Of The Wax Museum; Samson And Dalila; The Unsuspected; The Walking Dead
Curwen, Patric(k) (act): The Echo Murders; The Ringer (1931)
Curzon, Fiona (act): Frightmare (1974); Licensed To Love And Kill; No. 1 Of The Secret Service
Curzon, George (act, 1898–1976): For Them That Trespass; Jamaica Inn (1939); The Man Who Knew Too Much (1934); The Mind Of Mr. Reeder; Murder At Covent Garden; The Scotland Yard Mystery; Sexton Blake And The Bearded Doctor; Sexton Blake And The Hooded Terror; Sexton Blake And The Mademoiselle; Strange Evidence; Uncle Silas; Woman Of Straw; Young And Innocent
Curzon, Jill (act): Daleks' Invasion Earth 2150 A.D.
Cusack, Bill (act): Ed Wood
Cusack, Cyril (act, 1910–1993): The Elusive Pimpernel (1950); Fahrenheit 451; Floods Of Fear; Gideon's Day; King Lear (1970); Lovespell; The Man In The Road; The March Hare; 1984 (1984); Saadia; The Spy Who Came In From The Cold; Tam Lin; Where The Spies Are
Cusack, Joan (act, b. 1962): Addams Family Values
Cusack, Sinead (act): The Eyes Have It; Quiller: Price Of Violence; Revenge (1971, Gb); Tam Lin
Cusack, Sorcha (act): A Hitch In Time
Cushing, Peter (act, 1913–1994): The Abominable Snowman Of The Himalayas; — And Now The Screaming Starts!; Arabian Adventure; Asylum; At The Earth's Core; The Beast Must Die; Biggles: Adventures In Time; The Black Knight; Brides Of Dracula; Call Him Mr. Shatter; Captain Clegg; Cash On Demand; A Chump At Oxford; Corruption; The Creeping Flesh; The Curse Of Frankenstein; Daleks' Invasion Earth 2150 A.D.; The Deathshead Vampire; The Devil's Agent; The Devil's Men; Dr. Phibes Rises Again; Doctors Wear Scarlet; Dr. Terror's House Of Horrors (1964); Dr. Who And The Daleks; Dracula A.D. 1972; Evil Of Frankenstein; Fear In The Night (1972); The Flesh And The Fiends; Frankenstein And The Monster From Hell; Frankenstein Created Woman; Frankenstein Must Be Destroyed; From Beyond The Grave; Fury At Smugglers' Bay; The Ghoul (1974); The Gorgon; The Great Houdinis; Hamlet (1948); The Hell-Fire Club; Hitler's Son; Horror Express; Horror Of Dracula; The Hound Of The Baskervilles (1959); House Of The Long Shadows; The House That Dripped Blood; I, Monster; Island Of Terror; Legend Of The Seven Golden Vampires; Legend Of The Werewolf; Madhouse (1974); The Man In The Iron Mask (1939); The Man Who Finally Died; Masks Of Death; The Mummy (1959); Mystery On Monster Island; The Naked Edge; The Night Of The Big Heat; Nothing But The Night; The Revenge Of Frankenstein; The Satanic Rites Of Dracula; The Satanist; Scream And Scream Again; She (1965); Shock Waves; The Skull; Star Wars; Sword Of Sherwood Forest; Sword Of The Valiant; Tales From The Crypt; Tender Dracula; Top Secret! (1984); Torture Garden; Twins Of Evil; The Uncanny; The Vampire Lovers; Witching Time/The Silent Scream
Cushing, Tom (wri): Laugh, Clown, Laugh
Cushman, Nancy (act): The Swimmer
Cushner, George (act): Mutants In Paradise
Cutcliffe-Hyne, C.J. (wri): The Desert Island; The Kaiser's Dream; The Man With A Scar; The People Of The Rocks
Cutell, Lou (act): Frankenstein Meets The Space Monster; Honey, I Shrunk The Kids; Rhinoceros (1974); Young Frankenstein
Cuthbertson, Allan (act, b. 1921): The Body Stealers; Captain Nemo And The Underwater City; Cloak Without Dagger; In The Devil's Garden; The Malpas Mystery; Man At The Carlton Tower; The Mirror Crack'd; The Mouse On The Moon; Operation Crossbow; The Stranglers Of Bombay; Those Fantastic Flying Fools; The Trygon Factor; Vengeance
Cutler, Adele (act): Just Imagine
Cutler, Barry (act): Laserblast
Cutler, Ian (act): The Wicker Man
Cutler, Kate (act): When Knights Were Bold (1936)
Cutler, Miriam (mus): Getting Lucky
Cutler, Wendy (act): Primal Fear; Vampire (1979)
Cutolo, Louis (act): Flight Of The Navigator
Cutrara, Joel (act): Batman (1989)
Cutt, Michael (J.) (act): Something Is Out There; Sweet Sixteen
Cuttall, Christina (act): Mary Shelley's 'Frankenstein'
Cutter, Rex (act): Equalizer 2000
Cutting, Richard (act): Attack Of The Crab Monsters; Black Widow (1954); The Monolith Monsters; The Story Of Mankind
Cutts, Dale (act): Howling IV
Cutts, Graham (dir, 1885–1958): The Sign Of Four (1932)
Cutts, Meredith (act): Sherlock Holmes In New York
Cutts, Patricia (act, 1927–1974): The Tingler
Cuva, Frank (act): The Psycho Lover
Cuyler, Audrey (act): Ed Wood
Cybelle, Roxanne (act): Blood Diner
Cybulski, Zbigniew (Act, 1928–1967): La Poupee; Rekopis Znaleziony W Saragossie; Salto
Cyliakus, Marie (act): Les Enfants Terribles
Cypher, Jon (act): The Food Of The Gods; Masters Of The Universe
Cyphers, Charles (act): Escape From New York; The Fog; A Force Of One; Halloween; Halloween II; Someone's Watching Me!
Cyphert, D. Wayne (act): Attack Of The Killer Tomatoes
Cyr, Amy (act): The Clan Of The Cave Bear
Cyr, Myriam (act): Gothic; Roger Corman's Frankenstein Unbound
Czapsky, Stefan (cin): Batman Returns; Child's Play 2; Edward Scissorhands; Ed Wood; Prelude To A Kiss; Vampire's Kiss
Czemerys, Eva (act): Escape From The Bronx
Czerkas, Steve (cin): Monstroid
Czerniuk, Edward (act): Rocket Attack U.S.A.
Czerny, Henry (act): Mission: Impossible
Czerny, Jan (wri): Niebespieczenstwo
Czukor, Barbara Brantingham (act): see Britton, Barbara
Czyzewska, Elzbieta (Act): Rekopis Znaleziony W Saragossie

Daans, Layra (act): The Edge Of Hell
D'abbes, Ingram (wri): The Laughing Lady
Dabenigno, Joe (act): Tales From The Darkside
Dabernon-Stoke, Hugh (act): The Rocks Of Valpre
Dabner, Abbie (act): Little Shop Of Horrors (1986)
D'abo, Maryam (act, b. 1961): Arthur The King; The Living Daylights; Nightlife (1989, USA-Mex); Something Is Out There; Xtro
D'abo, Olivia (act): Conan The Destroyer; The Spirit Of '76
D'abruzzo, Alphonso (act): see Alda, Robert
Dacascos, Mark (act): D.N.A.; The Island Of Dr. Moreau (1996)
Dachis, Jeff (act): There's Nothing Out There
Dachman, Alan J. (wri): The Gore-Gore Girls
Dacia (act): Chu Chin Chow (1923)
Dacoda, Chayse (act): Deep Red (1994)
Da Conquista, Victoria (dir): see Rocha, Glauber
Dacqmine, Jacques (act): Leda
Dacre, Susan (act): Return To Oz
Da Cunha, Maria Do Carmo Miranda (act): see Miranda, Carmen
D'adderio, Areno (act): Ironmaster
Daddi, Franco/Frank (act): Iron Warrior...The Legend!; Il Trionfo Di Ercole
Dade, Frances (act): Dracula (1931, English-Speaking Version)
Dade, Stephen (cin, b. 1909): The Bad Lord Byron; The City Under The Sea; Dear Murderer; Dr. Blood's Coffin; The Late Edwina Black; The Man Who Finally Died; A Place Of One's Own; The Snake Woman; The Viking Queen; The Vulture (1966)
Dagelet, Hans (act): The Lift
Dagenhart, Carl (act): Squirm
Dagg, Cory (act): Unforgettable
Daggett, Jensen (act): Asteroid; Friday The 13th, Part VIII-Jason Takes Manhattan; Project: Alf
Dagnall, Ernest A. (act): The Charlatan
Dagover, Lil (act, 1897–1980, nee Martha Maria Lilitts): Chronik Von Grieshuus; Das Kabinett Des Dr. Caligari; Der Mude Tod; Phantom (1922); Die Spinnen; The Strange Countess
Dagradi, Don (wri): Bedknobs And Broomsticks; Blackbeard's Ghost; The Love Bug; Mary Poppins; Son Of Flubber
D'aguilar, Thelma (act): Chase A Crooked Shadow
Dahl, Arlene (act, b. 1927): The Black Book; Desert Legion; The Diamond Queen; Jamaica Run; Journey To The Center Of The Earth (1959); Kisses For My President
Dahl, Berta (act): Surf Nazis Must Die
Dahl, John (dir): Unforgettable
Dahl, Pat (act): It's Only Money
Dahl, Roald (wri, 1916–1990): Alfred Hitchcock Presents; Chitty Chitty Bang Bang; James And The Giant Peach; The Night Digger; Willy Wonka And The Chocolate Factory; The Witches (1990); You Only Live Twice
Dahl, Tessa (act): The Slipper And The Rose
Dahlbeck, Eva (act, b. 1920): Morianna; The Red Mantle
Dahle, Keith (act): Madman Of Mandoras
Dahlgren, Tom (act): Invasion Of The Body Snatchers (1978)
Dahlin, Bob (dir & wri): Monster In The Closet

Dahlke, Paul (act): The Naked Woman And Satan
Dai, Lin (act): Madam White Snake
Daichi, Kiwako (act):Live Today, Die Tomorrow
Daiglish, Malcolm (mus): Tuck Everlasting
Daikun, Alex (act): Firebird 2015 A.D.
Dailes, Dee Dee (act): Flesh Gordon
Dailey, Catherine (act): see Daley, Cass
Dailey, Dan (act, 1914–1978): Las Cuatro Noches De La Luna Llena; It's Always Fair Weather
Dailey, Irene (act): The Amityville Horror; No Way To Treat A Lady
Dailey, Susanne (act): Revenge Of The Teenage Vixens From Outer Space
Daily, Bill (act): The Barefoot Executive; I Dream Of Jeannie: Fifteen Years Later; I Still Dream Of Jeannie
Daily, Dan (act): Daylight
Daily, E.G. (act): Bad Dreams
Daily, Elizabeth (act): One Dark Night
Daimon, Masaaki (act): Godzilla Vs. The Bionic Monster
Dain, Peter (act): Spookies
Daine, Lesley (act): Without A Clue
Daine, Lois (act): Captain Kronos: Vampire Hunter
Dainton, Joanne (act): Holocaust 2000
Dainton, Noel (act): The Saint Meets The Tiger
Dainton, Patricia (act, b. 1930): At The Stroke Of Nine; The House On Marsh Road; Paul Temple Returns; Tread Softly; Witness In The Dark
Dair, John (act): Batman (1989)
Daire, George (act): Bulldog Drummond's Bride
Daisika (act): Disciple Of Death
Daix, Didier (wri): How To Murder A Rich Uncle
Dakai (act): Watchers II
Daker, David (act): The Black Windmill; Time Bandits
Dakin, Philip (act): Great Expectations (1934)
Dakkar (act): Ator: The Fighting Eagle
Dakota, Tony (act): It (1990)
Dakshinamoorthy (mus): The Jungle
Dal, Oleg (act): Korol Lir
Dalbert, Suzanne (act): Mark Of The Gorilla; Sorry, Wrong Number (1948)
D'alberti, Della (act): Maciste E La Regina Di Samar
Dalbes, Alberto (act): El Jorobado De La Morgue; Los Muertos No Perdonan; Murder Mansion
D'albrook, Sidney (act): The Bat Whispers; Midnight Mystery
Dalby, Amy (act, 1888–1969): The Haunting; The Night Has Eyes; The Secret Of My Success; The Straw Man; Who Killed The Cat?
Dalby, John (act): Stories From A Flying Trunk
Dalby, Linda (act): Funeral Home
Dalby, Lynn (act): Legend Of The Werewolf
Dalby, W. Barrington (act): The Magic Christian
D'alcy, Jehanne (act): Barbe-Bleue; The Temptation Of Saint Anthony; The Vanishing Lady
Dale, Badgett (act): Lord Of The Flies (1990)
Dale, Cynthia (act): My Bloody Valentine
Dale, Ellis (act): Blood Bath At The House Of Death
Dale, Esther (act, 1886–1961): Monkey Business
Dale, Holly (act): Starship Invasions
Dale, James (act): The Mystery Of A Hansom Cab; Strategy
Dale, Jennifer (act): Of Unknown Origin
Dale, Jim (act, b. 1935): Carry On Screaming; Carry On Spying; Digby-The Biggest Dog In The World; The Hunchback (1997); Pete's Dragon; The Spaceman And King Arthur
Dale, Margaret (act): One Exciting Night
Dale, Philip (act): Mystery Junction
Dale, Stan (act): Something Weird
Dale, Virginia (act): The Docks Of New Orleans; The Gay Falcon
D'alessio, Ugo (act): Spara Forte, Piu Forte...Non Capisco
Daley, Cass (act, b. 1915, nee Catherine Dailey): Crazy House (1943); The Spirit Is Willing
Daley, Lee (act): Threads
Daley, Tom (dir): The Outing
D'algy, Helena (act): Don Juan (1927)
Dali', Fabienne (act): Operazione Paura
Dali, Salvador (act, dir & wri, 1904–1989): Un Chien Andalou
Dalio, Marcel (act, 1900–1983): The Beast (1974); Cartouche (1962); The Monocle; The Rules Of The Game
Dall, Evelyn (act, b. 1914): King Arthur Was A Gentleman; Time Flies (1944)
Dall, John (act, 1918–1971, nee John Jenner Thompson): Atlantis, The Lost Continent; Rope
Dallamano, Massimo (cin): The Nights Of Lucretia Borgia
Dallamano, Massimo/Max (dir & wri): The Cursed Medallion; Dorian Gray
Dallamano, Max (dir & wri): see Dallamano, Massimo/Max
Dallas, Jean (act): Kadoyng
Dallas, Peter (dir): Broken Goddess
Dallas, Philip (act): Warriors Of The Wasteland
Dallesandro, Joe (act, b. 1948): Black Moon (1975); Dracula (1974); Frankenstein (1974); Seeds Of Evil
Dallimore, John (act): Robin Hood: Prince Of Thieves
Dallimore, Maurice (act, d. 1973): The Collector
Dalmatoff, M. (act): Atoll K
D'almeida, Elaine (act): Lemmy Pour Les Dames
Dalrymple, Ian (wri): Pimpernel Smith; Three Cases Of Murder
Dalton, Abby (act, b. 1935): Cyber-Tracker; Roller Blade Warriors: Taken By Force; The Viking Women And The Sea Serpent
Dalton, Audrey (act, b. 1934): The Deadliest Sin; Mr. Sardonicus; The Monster That Challenged The World; My Cousin Rachel
Dalton, Bebby (act): Making Contact
Dalton, Deborah (wri): A Kiss To Die For
Dalton, Dorothy (act): The Lone Wolf (1924)
Dalton, Justin (act): Surf Nazis Must Die
Dalton, Oakley (act): Angel Heart
Dalton, Sam (act): The Elixir Of Life; The Magic Extinguisher; The Marvellous Hair Restorer
Dalton, Susanna (act): Stunts Unlimited
Dalton, Timothy (act, b. 1946): Agatha; Brenda Starr (1992); The Doctor And The Devils; Flash Gordon; Licence To Kill (1989); The Living Daylights; The Rocketeer; Wuthering Heights (1970)
Dalton, Valda (act): Rabid
Dalton, Wally (act): Deadly Messages
Daltrey, Roger (act, b. 1944): The Legacy; Liszt O' Mania; Tommy; Vampirella (1996)
D'alvarez, Margarita (act): Pandora And The Flying Dutchman
Daly, Brian (act): Flying From Justice; The Harbour Lights; The Romany Rye
Daly, Brian (wri): The Harbour Lights; The Romany Rye
Daly, Candice (act): Liquid Dreams
Daly, Cindy (act): Carrie
Daly, Gerry (wri): Bloodspell; Dead Of Night (1987)
Daly, Jack (act): Champagne For Caesar; For Heaven's Sake; Killers From Space; Return Of The Fly; Search For Danger; The Snow Creature; Torchy Runs For Mayor
Daly, James (act, 1918–1978): I Aim At The Stars; Planet Of The Apes; The Resurrection Of Zachary Wheeler
Daly, Jane (1920's act): The Mysterious Island (1929)
Daly, Jane (1970's act): Children Shouldn't Play With Dead Things
Daly, John (act): Vampire's Kiss
Daly, Jonathan (act): The Shaggy D.A.
Daly, Larry (act): 12 Monkeys
Daly, Mark (act, 1887–1957): The Ghost Goes West; The Man Who Could Work Miracles
Daly, Tim(othy) (act, b. 1956): Caroline At Midnight; Dr. Jekyll And Ms. Hyde; Made In Heaven; Spellbinder; Witness To The Execution
Daly, Tom (act): The Angry Red Planet; Gog; Phantom From Space
Daly, Toni (mus): The Sorcerers
Daly, Tyne (act, b. 1947): A Howling In The Woods
Dalya, Jacqueline (act): Charlie Chan In Rio; Mystery In Mexico; One Million B.C.
Dalzell, Arch(ie) (cin): Cruise Into Terror; Fantasy Island; The Hypnotic Eye; The Little Shop Of Horrors (1960); Planet Earth; Return To Fantasy Island; A Taste Of Evil; Tower Of London (1962); The Trip
Dalzell III, Bill (act): The Silence Of The Lambs
Dalzell, Dennis (cin): Death At Love House; Mind Over Murder; Vampire (1979)
Damas, Bertila (act): Nothing But Trouble
D'amato, Joe (dir): The Grim Reaper
D'amato, Pina (act): Spara Forte, Piu Forte...Non Capisco
D'amboise, Jacques (act): Carousel
Damboulev, Yanko (act): Waxwork II: Lost In Time
D'ambricourt, Adrienne (act): Bulldog Drummond's Bride; Charlie Chan In City In Darkness; Peter Ibbetson
D'ambrose, Stephen (act): Trauma (1993)
D'ambrosio, Vito (act): The Flash
Dame, Beverly (act): The Medium (1951)
Damia, Ema (act): The Invisible Terror
Damian, Leo (act): Ghosts Can't Do It
Damiani, Damiano (dir, b. 1922): Amityville II: The Possession; La Strega In Amore
Damiani, Damiano (wri, b. 1922): La Strega In Amore
Damiani, Tilde (act): L'ultima Preda Del Vampiro
Damiano, Gerard (Dir & Wri): Legacy Of Satan
D'amico, Gary (cin): The Haunting Of Sarah Hardy
D'amico, Marcus (act): Superman II
D'amico, Suso Cecchi (wri): Spara Forte, Piu Forte...Non Capisco
Damita, Lili (act, 1901–1994, nee Lilliane Carre): The Bridge Of San Luis Rey (1929)
Damler, John (act): The Atomic City
Dammann, Sarah (act): When A Stranger Calls
Dammett, Blackie (act): The Lost Empire; Midnight Lace (1981)
Damon, Bruno (act): I Drink Your Blood
Damon, Cathryn (act): Midnight Offerings
Damon, Craig Winston (act): Blink
Damon, Gabriel (act): Little Nemo: Adventures In Slumberland; RoboCop 2
Damon, Jack (act): Roller Blade Warriors: Taken By Force
Damon, John (act): I Drink Your Blood
Damon, Kenny (act): The Adding Machine
Damon, Mark (act): Beauty And The Beast (1962); Crypt Of The Living Dead; The Devil's Wedding Night; House Of Usher; The Scalawag Bunch; I Tre Volti Della Paura
Damon, Peter (act): Crack In The World
Damon, Stuart (act, b. 1937): Fantasies; Melody Of Hate
Damon, Una (act): Virtuosity
D'amore, Jojo/Jo-Jo (act): Dracula's Dog; The Sword And The Sorcerer
Dampier, Claude (act): White Lilac
Damron, Roy (act): The Underwater City
Damski, Mel (dir): A Connecticut Yankee In King Arthur's Court (1989)
Dana, Barbara (act): Daughter Of The Mind; The Monitors
Dana, Bill (act, b. 1924): The Busy Body; The Nude Bomb
Dana, Bill (wri, b. 1924): The Nude Bomb
Dana, Justin (act): The Incredible Shrinking Woman
Dana, Leora (act, 1923-1983): Amityville 3-D
Dana, Mark (act): Pharaoh's Curse; Tarzan Goes To India
Dana, Mike (act): Killer's Kiss
Dana, Rod (act): How To Make A Monster; War Of The Colossal Beast
Danare, Malcolm (act): The Curse; Popcorn
Danby, Ian (wri): The Devil's Wedding Night
Dance, Charles (act, b. 1946): Alien 3; For Your Eyes Only; The Golden Child; The Mcguffin; The Phantom Of The Opera (1990); Undertow
Dance, Eric (act): Discipline
Dance, William (act): Elvira, Mistress Of The Dark
Danch, William (wri): Monster From The Ocean Floor
Dancz, Steve (mus): Grim Prairie Tales
Dand, C.H. (wri): The Bells (1931)
Dand, Rod (act): Ladyhawke
D'andre, Dante (act): Phantom Of The Mall: Eric's Revenge
D'andrea, John (mus): Child's Play 3
D'andrea, Tom (act): The Next Voice You Hear
Dandridge, Dorothy (act, 1923–1965): Tarzan's Peril
Dane, Alexandra (act): Corruption; The Creeping Flesh; Jabberwocky
Dane, Ann (act): It's Alive III: Island Of The Alive; The Stuff
Dane, Clemence (wri): Murder; The Tunnel
Dane, Cyril (act): Old Bill Through The Ages
Dane, Frank (act): The Black Tulip (1921); Blood Money; Further Exploits Of Sexton Blake-The Mystery Of The S.S. Olympic; Lorna Doone (1920); Silent Evidence
Dane, Ila (act): Silent Night, Deadly Night III
Dane, Karl (act, 1886–1934): The Scarlet Letter (1926)
Dane, Lawrence (act): Bionic Showdown: The Six Million Dollar Man And The Bionic Woman; Darkman II: The Return Of Durant; Happy Birthday To Me; Millennium; Of Unknown Origin; Rituals; Rolling Vengeance; Scanners
Dane, Robert (act): The Girl On The Bridge
Daneen, Mike (act): Terror Beneath The Sea
Danell, Carol (act): Il Planeta Degli Uomini Spenti
Daneman, Paul (act): The Clue Of The New Pin (1961); Locker 69
Daneri, Mark (act): When The Bough Breaks
Danery, July (act): El Vampiro
Danes, Claire (act, b. 1979): To Gillian On Her 37th Birthday
Danese, Shera (act): Sparkling Cyanide
Danet, Jean (act): The Hunchback Of Notre Dame (1957)
Danford, Dianne (act): Weekend Of Fear
Danford, Joe (dir & wri): Weekend Of Fear
Danforth, Dan (act): Impulse (1984)
Danforth, Jim (cin): Equinox; Flesh Gordon; When Dinosaurs Ruled The Earth
D'angelo, Beverly (act, b. 1953): High Spirits; Maid To Order; The Man Who Fell To Earth (1987); Pacific Heights; The Sentinel; Widow's Kiss
D'angelo, Carlo (act): Ercole E La Regina Di Lidia; Il Planeta Degli Uomini Spenti; Sword Of The Conqueror; I Vampiri
D'angelo, Gerry (act): Mad Max Beyond Thunderdome
D'angelo, Giulia (act): The Great Alligator
D'angelo, Jesse (act): Black Roses; The Edge Of Hell
D'angelo, Mirella (act): Hercules (1983); Tenebrae
Dangerfield, Diana (act): Inn Of The Damned
Dangerfield, Ernest (wri): Only A Room-er
Dangerfield, Mrs. (Ernest) (act): Only A Room-Er
Dangerfield, Rodney (act, b. 1921, nee Jacob Cohen): The Projectionist
Dangler, Anita (act): Cry For The Strangers; The Munsters' Revenge
Dani, Yvonne (act): Zombies Lake
Daniel, Alexis (act): Judge Dredd
Daniel, Cormel (act): The Amazing Transparent Man
Daniel, Gregg (act): Mars Attacks!
Daniel, Jay (act): Targets
Daniel, Jennifer (act): The Clue Of The Silver Key; Kiss Of The Vampire; The Reptile; Spell Of Evil
Daniel, Joshua (act): Zapped!
Daniel, Leslie (act): The Brain That Wouldn't Die
Daniel, Paul (act): Mad Max Beyond Thunderdome
Daniel, Rod (dir): Teen Wolf
Daniel, Sean (act): Darkman (1990)
Danielewski, Ted (dir): No Exit
Danieli, Emma (act): The Last Man On Earth; The Spy Strikes Silently
Daniell, Henry (act, 1894–1963): Atlantis (1948); The Bandit Of Sherwood Forest; The Body Snatcher (1945); Captain Kidd; Castle In The Desert; Dressed To Kill (1941); Five Weeks In A Balloon; The Four Skulls Of Jonathan Drake; From The Earth To The Moon; The Great Impersonation (1942); Jane Eyre (1944); The Last Of The Lone Wolf; Marie Antoinette (1938); Sherlock Holmes And The Secret Weapon; Sherlock Holmes And The Voice Of Terror; Sherlock Holmes In Washington; The Story Of Mankind; The Suspect; The Thirteenth Chair (1929 & 1937); Voyage To The Bottom Of The Sea; Witness For The Prosecution; The Woman In Green
Danielle, Suzanne (act): Arabian Adventure; Flash Gordon
Daniels, Alex (act): Cyborg (1989); Meridian
Daniels, Anita (act): Werewolf Of Washington
Daniels, Anthony (act): The Empire Strikes Back; Return Of The Jedi; Star Wars
Daniels, Bebe (act, 1901–1971, nee Virginia Daniels): Male And Female; The Maltese Falcon (1931)
Daniels, Billy (act): The Gracie Allen Murder Case
Daniels, Danice (act): Magic Spectacles
Daniels, Danny (act): Prehistoric Women (1966); Woman Of Straw
Daniels, Danny D. (act): The Outing; Retribution (1988)
Daniels, David Mason (act): One Dark Night
Daniels, Diane (act): Damien-Omen II
Daniels, Don (act): Bog
Daniels, Gray (act): Gallery Of Horror; Gremlins 2: The New Batch
Daniels, Harold (dir): A Date With Death; House Of The Black Death; Port Sinister; Terror In The Haunted House
Daniels, J.D. (act): Man's Best Friend
Daniels, Jeanne (act): Vampire On Bikini Beach

Daniels, Jeff (act): *Arachnophobia; The Butcher's Wife; Disaster In Time; 101 Dalmatians (1996)*
Daniels, John (act): *Flesh-Eating Mothers*
Daniels, Joseph (act): *Scared To Death (1980)*
Daniels, Karil (cin): *The Devil's Gift*
Daniels, Lenny (act): *12 Monkeys*
Daniels, Leonard (act): *The Ivory Ape*
Daniels, Lisa (act): *The Glass Slipper*
Daniels, Marc (act): *Slaughterhouse Rock*
Daniels, Marc (dir): *Planet Earth*
Daniels, Mark (act): *Bury Me Dead; The Invisible Avenger*
Daniels, Phil (act): *The Bride (1985)*
Daniels, Robert (act): *Vampire On Bikini Beach*
Daniels, Virginia (act): see Daniels, Bebe
Daniels, Wayne (act): *The People Under The Stairs*
Daniels, William (act, b. 1927): *Black Sunday (1977); The Incredible Hulk, Part 2; Ladybug, Ladybug; The Little Match Girl (1987); The Lottery; Oh, God!; The President's Analyst*
Daniels, William (H.) (Cin, 1895–1970): *Another Thin Man; As You Desire Me; Harvey; In Like Flint; Lured; Marie Antoinette (1938); Mata Hari (1932); Rasputin And The Empress; Shadow Of The Thin Man; Le Spectre Vert*
Danielson, Cliff (act): *Shadow Of The Thin Man*
Danielson, Lynn (act): *Out Of The Dark*
Danielson, Shell (wri): *Turbo: A Power Rangers Movie*
Daniely, Lisa (act): *Curse Of Simba; Danger Tomorrow; The Last Train; The Man In The Road; The Man Who Was Nobody; Stranger In The House (1967); The Vicious Circle (1957)*
Danilova, Raissa (act): *Graveyard Shift (1990)*
Danischewsky, Monja (wri, b. 1911): *Meet Mr. Lucifer; Topkapi*
Danko, Jim (act): *Red Alert*
Danks, Jeff (act): *My Bloody Valentine*
Dankworth, John (mus, b. 1927): *Fathom; The Magus; Modesty Blaise; Return From The Ashes; The Servant; 10 Rillington Place*
Danmar (act): *Enemy Mine*
Dann, Larry (act): *Ghost Story (1975); Whirlpool*
Dann, Roger (act): *Crime Doctor's Gamble; I Confess*
Danner, Blythe (act, b. 1943): *Are You In The House Alone?; Dr. Cook's Garden; Futureworld; To Kill A Clown*
Danner, Frederick (act): *Privilege*
Danning, Sybil (act): *Amazon Women On The Moon; Battle Beyond The Stars (1980); Bluebeard (1972); Hercules (1983); Howling II; The Phantom Empire; The Three Musketeers (1974); The Tomb; Warrior Queen*
Dannis, Ray (act): *The Corpse Grinders; The Undertaker And His Pals*
Dannouville, Jacques (act): *Le Testament Du Dr. Cordelier*
Danny The Wonder Pony (act): *From Dusk Till Dawn*
Dano, Calvin (act): *The Trouble With Harry*
Dano, Royal (act, b. 1922): *The Dark Half; Dead People; Face Of Fire; Ghoulies II; House II: The Second Story; The Killer Inside Me; Killer Klowns From Outer Space; Moby Dick (1956); Moon Of The Wolf; 7 Faces Of Dr. Lao; Something Wicked This Way Comes; The Thing From Another World*
Danon, Marcello (wri): *The Black Belly Of The Tarantula*
Danova, Cesare (act, b. 1926): *Chamber Of Horrors (1966); Death Cruise; Don Juan (1956); The Love Of Three Queens; Tarzan, The Ape Man (1959); Tentacles; Valley Of The Dragons*
Danquah, Paul (act): *Maroc 7*
Dansereau, Anne (act): *The Music Of The Spheres*
Danson, Linda (act): *The Adventures Of Hajji Baba*
Danson, Ted (act, b. 1947): *Creepshow; Gulliver's Travels (1995); Loch Ness; Once Upon A Spy*
Dante The Magician (act): *A-Haunting We Will Go*
Dante Alighieri (wri, 1265-1321): *Il Conte Ugolino; Dante's Inferno (1912 & 1924)*
Dante, Carl (mus): *Cellar Dweller; Slavegirls From Beyond Infinity*
Dante, Edmond (act): *Werewolf Of Washington*
Dante, Jean (act): *L'enfant Sauvage*
Dante, Joe (act): *The Silence Of The Hams*
Dante, Joe (dir): *Amazon Women On The Moon; The 'Burbs; Explorers; Gremlins; Gremlins 2: The New Batch; The Howling; Innerspace; Matinee; Piranha (1978); Twilight Zone*
Dante, Michael (act, b. 1931, nee Ralph Vitti): *Beyond Evil; Willard*
Dantes, Claude (act): *The Masked Man Against The Pirates; Sei Donne Per L'assassino*
D'antin, Mary (act): *She (1983)*
Dantine, Helmut (act, 1918–1982): *The Fifth Musketeer; Hell On Devil's Island; Operation Crossbow; Shadow Of A Woman; The Story Of Mankind; Stranger From Venus*
Danton, Geoffrey (act): *The Snake Woman*
Danton, Ray (act, 1931–1992): *Code Name: Jaguar; Sandokan Against The Leopard Of Sarawak; Sandokan Fights Back; Secret Agent Superdragon; A Very Missing Person*
Danton, Ray(Mond) (dir, 1931–1992): *Crypt Of The Living Dead; The Deathmaster; Psychic Killer*
Danton, Raymond (wri, 1931–1992): *Psychic Killer*
D'antonio, Carmen (act): *Salome (1953)*
Dantzler, Louise (act): see Brian, Mary
Danube, Maria (act): *Castle Keep*
Danvers, Ivor (act): *Dick Barton, Special Agent; Electric Eskimo*
Danvers-Walker, Michael (act): *Night Watch*
Danyon, Pipa (act): *Phoenix The Warrior*
Danza, Tony (act, b. 1950): *Angels In The Outfield (1994)*
Danziger, Allen (act): *The Texas Chainsaw Massacre*
Danziger, Cory (act): *The 'Burbs*
Danziger, Kenneth (act): *Stargate; Warlock*
Danziger, Maia (act): *Dr. Heckyl & Mr. Hype*
Dapkunaite, Ingeborga (act): *Mission: Impossible*
D'aquila, Diane (act): *Sorry, Wrong Number (1989)*
Darabont, Frank (wri): *The Blob (1988); The Fly II; A Nightmare On Elm Street 3: Dream Warriors*
D'aragon, Lionel (act): *A Daughter Of Satan (1914); Eugene Aram; First Men In The Moon (1919); London's Enemies; Paul Sleuth And The Mystic Seven; The Price He Paid; The Sorrows Of Satan (1917); The Valley Of Fear (1916); The Vengeance Of The Air; The Wrecker Of Lives*
D'arbanville, Patti (act): *The Fifth Floor; Modern Problems; Time After Time*
Darbo, Patrika (act): *The 'Burbs; Gremlins 2: The New Batch*
Darbowitz, Seymour (Dir & Wri): *Psychophobia*
Darby, Jane (act): *Vampire Circus*
Darby, Kim (act, b. 1948, nee Deborah Zerby): *Don't Be Afraid Of The Dark; The Karate Killers; Mirror Of Deception; The People; Summer Girl; Teen Wolf Too*
Darbyshire, Iris (act): *Sweeney Todd*
D'arc, Giselle (act): *Voodoo Woman*
Darc, Mirielle (act, b. 1939): *The Great Spy Chase*
Darcel, Denise (act, b. 1925, nee Denise Billecard): *Tarzan And The Slave Girl*
Darcey, Jeffrey (act): *I Lunghi Capelli Della Morte*
Darchi, Bob (act): *Silent Night, Bloody Night*
D'arcy, Alex (act, b. 1908, nee Alexander Sarruf): *Another Thin Man; Blood Of Dracula's Castle; Champagne; Horrors Of Spider Island; The Prisoner Of Zenda (1937); The St. Valentine's Day Massacre; Topper Takes A Trip; Way...Way Out*
D'arcy, Gene (act): *The Saracen Blade*
Darcy, Georgine (act): *Rear Window; Women And Bloody Terror*
Darcy, Robert (act): *Hellhole*
D'arcy, Robin (cin): *Writer's Block*
D'arcy, Roy (act, 1894–1969): *The Last Warning (1929); Revolt Of The Zombies*
D'arcy, Sheila (act): *Arrest Bulldog Drummond; Jungle Man*
D'arcy, Tim (act): *Repossessed*
Darden, Severn (act, 1930–1995): *Battle For The Planet Of The Apes; Conquest Of The Planet Of The Apes; The Day Of The Dolphin; Fearless Frank; Goldstein; The Mad Room; The New, Original Wonder Woman; The President's Analyst; Saturday The 14th; Vanishing Point; Who Fears The Devil?*
Dardick, Ruth (act): *Don't Go In The House*
Dare, Aldo (act): see Ray, Aldo
Dare, Dorothy (act): *A Shattered Idyll*
Da Re, Eric (act): *The Flash; Silent Night, Deadly Night III*
Dare, Eva (act): *The Girl Who Took The Wrong Turning*
Dare, Phyllis (act): *Crime On The Hill*
Dargin, Alan (act): *Howling III*
Darien, Frank (act): *The Flying Saucer (1950); Trouble For Two*
Darin, Bobby (act, 1936–1973): *Happy Mother's Day, Love George; Stranger In The House (1967)*
Daring, Mason (mus): *The Brother From Another Planet*
Dario, Sascha (act): *Atlas*
Darius, Elizabeth (act): *Castle Keep*
Dark, Bobby (act): *Deadly Blessing*
Dark, Christopher (act, D. 1971): *World Without End*
Dark, Johnny (act): *The Being; Communion; Repossessed*
Darla (Animal Act): *The Silence Of The Lambs*
Darley, Bert (act): *The Shuttle Of Life*
Darling, Ann (act): *Bride Of Frankenstein*
Darling, Candy (act, 1947–1974, nee James Slat- Tery): *Silent Night, Bloody Night*
Darling, Jamie (act): *Justice; The Night Bell*
Darling, Joan (act): *Fearless Frank; The President's Analyst; The Two Worlds Of Jennie Logan*
Darling, Miss (act): *Les Sorcieres De Salem*
Darling, Pat (act): *The Stepford Children*
Darling, (W.) Scott (wri): *Charlie Chan At The Opera; The Chinese Ring; Cobra Woman; The Docks Of New Orleans; The Fatal Hour (1940); The Ghost Of Frankenstein; The Golden Eye; The Great Impersonation (1942); Mr. Wong In Chinatown; The Mystery Of Mr. Wong; No Escape (1934); The River House Ghost; The Shanghai Chest; Sherlock Holmes And The Secret Weapon; The Stolen Necklace; Too Many Winners*
Darlington, W.A. (wri): *Alf's Button (1920 & 1930); Alf's Button Afloat; Alf's Carpet*
Darlow, David (act): *Through The Magic Pyramid*
Darlow, Linda (act): *Memories Of Murder*
Darmon, Gerard (act): *Obsession: A Taste For Fear*
Darmora Ballet, The (act): *Gaslight (1940)*
Darmour, Roy (act): *Invasion Of The Saucer Men*
Darmstatter, Percy (wri): *Cinder-Elfred*
Darnborough, Anthony (dir): *So Long At The Fair*
Darnell, Deborah (act): *Count Yorga, Vampire*
Darnell, Linda (act, 1923–1965, nee Manetta Eliosa Darnell): *Angels Of Darkness; Blackbeard The Pirate; Hangover Square; It Happened Tomorrow; The Mark Of Zorro (1940); Saturday Island; Second Chance; The Thirteenth Letter; This Is My Love*
Darnell, Manetta Eloisa (act): see Darnell, Linda
Darnell, Vicki (act): *Frankenhooker*
Darnley, Louis (act): *Dr. Sin Fang*
Darnley-Smith, Jan (dir): *A Ghost Of A Chance (1968); A Hitch In Time*
Dar-Noy, Har-El (act): *Trick Or Treats*
Dar-Noy, Orin (act): *Trick Or Treats*
Darrell, Charles (wri): *When London Sleeps*
Darrell, Dominique (act): *Dracula (1974)*
Darrell, Steve (act): *Cannibal Attack; The Monolith Monsters; Tarantula*
Darren, Eva (act): *Brides Of Blood*
Darren, James (act, b. 1936, nee James Ercolani): *City Beneath The Sea (1970); Paroxysmus*
Darrieux, Danielle (act, b. 1917): *Le Diable Et Les Dix Commandements; The Gentle Art Of Murder; Landru*
Darrin, Diana (act): *The Amazing Colossal Man; Girls In Prison; The Incredible Shrinking Man*
Darro, Frankie (act, 1917–1976, nee Frank Johnson): *Charlie Chan At The Race Track; The Mad Genius; Radio Ranch*
Darrow, Barbara (act): *The Monster That Challenged The World; Queen Of Outer Space*
Darrow, Henry (act): *Beyond The Universe; Brock's Last Case; Halloween With The Addams Family; The Hitcher; The Invisible Man (1975)*
Darrow, Tony (act): *Street Trash*
Darski, Bronislaw (act): *O Dwoch Takich Co Ukradli Ksiezyc*
Darst, Danny (act): *The Silence Of The Lambs*
Darteuil (act): *Forces Occultes*
Dartnell, Guy (act): *Transmutations*
Darvi, Bella (act, 1928–1971, nee Bella Wegier): *Lipstick; The Mask Of The Gorilla*
Darvos, Kim (act): *Danger By My Side*
Darwell, Jane (act, 1880–1967, nee Patti Woodward): *All That Money Can Buy; Before Dawn; Girls In Prison; The Loves Of Edgar Allan Poe; Mary Poppins; Roman Scandals; Three Wise Fools*
Dary, Rene (act): *Gli Amori Di Ercole*
Das, Eddie (act): *Man-Eater Of Kumaon*
Das, Pat (act): *12 Monkeys*
Das Bolas, Xan (act): *Faustina*
Das Gupta, Bandana (act): *The Terror Of The Tongs; Vengeance*
Dash, Simone (act): *Those Dear Departed*
Da Silva, Howard (act, 1909–1986, nee Howard Silverblatt): *The Lost Weekend; M (1950); Smile, Jenny, You're Dead*
Daskawisz, Steve (act): *Friday The 13th-Part 2*
Dassaro, Frank (act): *Street Trash*
Dassin, Jo(Seph) (act): *Nick Carter Et Le Trefle Rouge; Topkapi*
Dassin, Jules (dir, b. 1911): *The Canterville Ghost (1944); Nazi Agent; The Tell-Tale Heart (1941); Topkapi*
D'assunto, Rocco (act): *Ok, Nero!*
Dastagir, Sabu (act): see Sabu
Daston, John (act): *The Human Duplicators*
Datcher, Alex (act): *Body Bags*
Dattilo, Kristin (act): *Child Of Darkness, Child Of Light; Mirror, Mirror*
Dau, Brigitta/Bridgitta (act): *Alien Nation: The Enemy Within; I Still Dream Of Jeannie*
Daubeney, D. (wri): *Vampyres...Daughters Of Dracula*
D'auburn, Denis (act): *The Adventures Of Robin Hood; Mr. Moto's Last Warning*
Dauer, Roger (act): *Blood Diner*
Daugherty, Mary (act): *End Of The World (1977)*
Daughton, James (act): *Blind Date; Future Cop; Girlfriend From Hell*
Daumery, Carrie (act): *The Conquering Power; The Last Warning (1929)*
Daumery, John (dir): *The Thirteenth Candle*
Daumier, Sophie (act): *Aimez-Vous Les Femmes?; A Killing Success*
Daunzungs-Schnapps, Fritzling (act): *Supergirl (1971)*
Dauphin, Claude (act, 1903–1978, nee Claude Franc-Nohain): *Barbarella; Le Diable Et Les Dix Commandements; The Full Treatment; Phantom Of The Rue Morgue; The Tenant*
Dauphin, Jean-Claude (act): *Dracula, Pere Et Fils*
D'auria, Bruce (act): *Tuck Everlasting*
Davalos, Dick (act): *The Cabinet Of Caligari*
Davalos, Dominique (act): *Howard The Duck*
Davalos, Elyssa (act): *Good Against Evil; Herbie Goes Bananas*
Daveikis, John (act): *Nothing But Trouble*
Daven, Gregory (act): *Donor*
Davenport, A. Bromley (act): *The Face At The Window (1932); Old Mother Riley's Ghosts; The Pointing Finger; The Scarlet Pimpernel (1934); The Shot In The Dark; The Stolen Necklace; The Warren Case*
Davenport, Claire (act): *Return Of The Jedi; The Tempest (1980)*
Davenport, Harry (act, 1866–1949): *The Decision Of Christopher Blake; The Enchanted Forest; Fly-Away Baby; Foreign Correspondent; The Hunchback Of Notre Dame (1939); Kismet (1944); Marie Antoinette (1938); The Thin Man Goes Home; Three Wise Fools*
Davenport, Harry Bromley (dir & mus): *Xtro*
Davenport, Harry Bromley (wri): *Full Circle; Xtro*
Davenport, Havis (act): *Rear Window*
Davenport, John (act): *Whirlpool*
Davenport, Johnny Lee (act): *Chain Reaction (1996)*
Davenport, Mary (act): *Dressed To Kill (1980); Sisters*
Davenport, Milla (act): *Rip Van Winkle (1921)*
Davenport, Ned (act): *Giant From The Unknown*
Davenport, Nigel (act, b. 1928): *A Christmas Carol (1984); Dracula (1973); Greystoke: The Legend Of Tarzan, Lord Of The Apes; A High Wind In Jamaica; The Island Of Dr. Moreau (1977); The London Connection; The Mind Of Mr. Soames; No Blade Of Grass; Peeping Tom; Phase IV; The Third Secret; Where The Spies Are; Without A Clue*
Daves, Delmer (act, b. 1904): *The Bishop Murder Case*
Daves, Delmer (dir & wri, b. 1904): *The Red House*
Daves, Diana (act): *Premonition (1972)*
Davi, Carina (act): *Deathstalker II: Duel Of The Titans*
Davi, Robert (act): *The Goonies; License To Kill (1989); Maniac Cop 2; Mardi Gras For The Devil; Peacemaker; Predator 2; Wild Thing*
Daviau, Allen (cin): *Congo; E.T.-The Extra-Terrestrial; Harry And The Hendersons*
David Stipes Prods. Inc. (cin): *The Pink Chiquitas*

David, Agnes (act): Phantom Of The Opera (1983)
David, Clifford (act): The Exorcist III
David, Davilia (act): Blood Bath At The House Of Death
David, Eleanor (act): The Scarlet Pimpernel (1982); Slipstream
David, Elizabeth (act): The Gruesome Twosome
David, Ernesto (act): The Blood Drinkers
David, Hal (mus): Journey Into Fear (1975); Lizzie; Lost Horizon (1973); Moonraker
David, Keith (act): Always; Armageddon; The Puppet Masters; They Live; Volcano
David, Lolita (act): The Pink Chiquitas
David, Lou (act): The Burning; The Ivory Ape
David, Mack (mus, 1912–1993): The Quiller Memorandum
David, Mario (act): Violette Noziere
David, Marjorie (wri): Into The Badlands
David, Mary Ellen (act): The Toxic Avenger
David, Michael (act): Capture That Capsule!; Pandora's Clock; Snow White And The Three Stooges; The Wizard Of Baghdad
David, Nick (act): Exo-Man
David, Saul (act): Skullduggery
David, Shannon Scott (act): The Octagon
David, Thayer (act, 1926–1978): The Eiger Sanction; Happy Mother's Day, Love George; House Of Dark Shadows; Journey To The Center Of The Earth (1959); Nero Wolfe; Night Of Dark Shadows; Savages; Spider-Man
David, W. (wri): The Yellow Mask
David, Zorro (act): Reflections In A Golden Eye
Davidescu, Andreas (cin): The Final Terror
Davidge, Donna (act):Tales From The Darkside
David-Djerf, Karl (act): Addams Family Values
Davidovich, Lolita (act): Raising Cain; Touch
Davidson, Ben (act): Conan The Barbarian
Davidson, Boaz (dir): American Cyborg: Steel Warrior; Hospital Massacre
Davidson, Boaz (wri): American Cyborg: Steel Warrior
Davidson, Brett (act): Funeral Home
Davidson, Claire (act): Our Mother's House
Davidson, Diana (act): Scared To Death (1980)
Davidson, Eileen (act): The House On Sorority Row
Davidson, Jack (act): Shock Waves
Davidson, James (act): Parasite
Davidson, Jaye (act): Stargate
Davidson, John (act): Arrest Bulldog Drummond; Charlie Chan In Egypt; The Chinese Cat; The Devil Bat; Dick Tracy vs. Crime, Inc. The Last Days Of Pompeii (1935); Mr. Moto's Last Warning; Mr. Moto Takes A Vacation; Prince Valiant; The Thirteenth Chair (1929)
Davidson, John (1990s Act): Edward Scissorhands
Davidson, L.W. (wri): Hands Of The Ripper
Davidson, Lawford (act): The Crimson Circle (1922); Faust (1922); The Mysterious Dr. Fu Manchu
Davidson, Lewis (wri): Act Of Murder (1964)
Davidson, Lionel (wri): Hot Enough For June
Davidson, Marsella (act): Mother's Day
Davidson, Martin (wri): Moon Zero Two
Davidson, Peter (act): Captain Kronos: Vampire Hunter
Davidson, Robert (wri): See Biancoli, Oreste
Davidson, Roger (act): The Secret Life Of Ian Fleming
Davidson, Ronald (wri): The Adventures Of Captain Marvel; Dick Tracy Returns; Dick Tracy's G-Men; Dick Tracy vs. Crime Inc.; Dr. Satan's Robot; Flying Disc Man From Mars; Missile Monsters; Nyoka And The Lost Secrets Of Hippocrates; Retik, The Moon Menace; Satan's Satellites; Spy Smasher Returns
Davidson, Roscoe (act): Seven
Davidson, Suzanne (act): Miracle On 34th Street (1973)
Davidson, Sven (wri): Ice Cream Man
Davidson, Tania (act): Kemek
Davidson, William b. (act): Dick Tracy's Dilemma; The Dragon Murder Case; Hold That Ghost; Man-Made Monster; The Menace (1932); The Notorious Lone Wolf; The Most Dangerous Game
Davie, Cedric Thorpe (mus): The Bad Lord Byron; The Green Man
Davies, Amanda (act): The Clonus Horror
Davies, Anne-Marie (act): An American Werewolf In London
Davies, Batty (wri): House Of Darkness
Davies, Betty Ann (act, 1910–1955): Alias John Preston; Cosh Boy; Death At Broadcasting House; Grand National Night; The Man In Black; Murder By Proxy; The Woman With No Name
Davies, Brian (act): The Bedford Incident
Davies, Daniel (act): Pandemonium
Davies, Danny (act):A Christmas Carol (1984)
Davies, Dave (mus): Village Of The Damned (1995)
Davies, David (act): The Frightened City; The Masque Of The Reddeath (1964); Treasure Island (1950); The Treasure Of Monte Cristo (1961)
Davies, Frances (act): The Girl Who Wrecked His Home
Davies, Gary Michael (act): Shocker
Davies, Geoffrey (act): The Vault Of Horror
Davies, George (act): The Offspring
Davies, Geraint Wyn (act): Bionic Showdown: The Six Million Dollar Man And The Bionic Woman; Trilogy Of Terror II
Davies, Gron (act): The Quatermass Experiment
Davies, Henry Wayne (act): see Wayne, Naunton
Davies, Howard (GB act): Victim Five
Davies, Howard (USA act): Boston Blackie's Little Pal; Devotion
Davies, Iva (mus): Razorback
Davies, Ivor Novello (act): see Novello, Ivor
Davies, Jack (wri): Someone At The Door; Top Secret (1952); The Ugly Duckling
Davies, Jackson (act): I Still Dream Of Jeannie; The Plutonium Incident; Runaway; The Stepfather
Davies, James (cin): Endgame
Davies, Jeremy (act): Twister
Davies, Joan C. (act): The Night Evelyn Came Out Of The Grave
Davies, John (act): RoboCop
Davies, John Howard (act, b. 1939): The Rocking Horse Winner
Davies, Kathy (act): Octopussy
Davies, L.P. (wri): The Groundstar Conspiracy; Journey Into Darkness
Davies, Lew (mus): Fright (1957)
Davies, Marion (act, 1897–1961, nee Marion Cecilia Douras): Buried Treasure; Young Diana
Davies, Megan (act): Howling IV
Davies, Naunton (wri): The Cobweb
Davies, Peter Maxwell (mus): The Devils
Davies, Phil (mus): Trancers; Trancers II: The Return Of Jack Deth
Davies, Piers (wri): The Cars That Ate Paris
Davies, Ray (act): Percy
Davies, Richard (GB act): Blue Blood; The Mutations; The Twisted Nerve
Davies, Richard (USA act): The Falcon In Danger; The Mad Doctor Of Market Street
Davies, Rita (act): Monty Python And The Holy Grail
Davies, Robin (act):The Blood On Satan's Claw
Davies, Rosemary (wri): Neither The Sea Nor The Sand
Davies, Rupert (act, b. 1916): The Accursed; Bobbikins; The Brides Of Fu Manchu; Curse Of The Crimson Altar; Danger Tomorrow; Dracula Has Risen From The Grave; Five Golden Dragons; Frightmare (1974); The Key; The Night Visitor; The Oblong Box; Sapphire; The Spy Who Came In From The Cold; Witchfinder General; Zeppelin
Davies, Sam (act): Without A Clue
Davies, Stephen (act): The Nest
Davies, Tom (act): Unforgettable
Davies, Valentine (wri): It Happens Every Spring; Miracle On 34th Street (1947, 1973 & 1994)
Davies, Victor (mus): The Pit (1983)
Davies, Walter Langdon (act): Empire Of Ash III
Davies, Whit (act): The Offspring
Davies, William (mus): Model For Murder
Davies, William (wri): Dr. Jekyll And Ms. Hyde; Ghost In The Machine
Davies, William C. (cin): Doomsday Machine
Davies, Windsor (act): The Playbirds
Davila, Azalea (act): Primal Fear; Unforgettable
Davila, Francesca Romana (act): The Devil's Wedding Night
Davila, Luis (act): Mission Stardust; The Mummy's Revenge; Scalawag Bunch
Davila, Raul (act): The Believers
Davin, Robert Gwyn (act): First Knight
Davion, Alex(Ander) (act, b. 1929): Doctors Wear Scarlet; The Hunchback Of Notre Dame (1965); Paranoiac; The Plague Of The Zombies; Richard III (1955)
Davis, Allan (dir): The Clue Of The New Pin (1961); The Clue Of The Twisted Candle
Davis, Altovise (act): Kingdom Of The Spiders
Davis, Andrew (cin): Mansion Of The Doomed
Davis, Andrew (dir): Chain Reaction (1996); The Final Terror
Davis, Andy (act): Journey To The Center Of Time; The Resurrection Of Zachary Wheeler
Davis, Annette (act): What's The Matter With Helen?
Davis, b.J. (act): Trancers II: The Return Of Jack Deth
Davis, Barry (act): Pumpkinhead II: Blood Wings
Davis, Bart (wri): Impulse (1984)
Davis, Becki (act): Mirrors
Davis, Bette (act, 1908–1989): The Anniversary; Another Man's Poison; Burnt Offerings; The Dark Secret Of Harvest Home; Dead Ringer; Death On The Nile; Hush...Hush, Sweet Charlotte; Madame Sin; The Menace (1932); Murder With Mirrors; The Nanny; Return From Witch Mountain; Satan Met A Lady; Scream, Pretty Peggy; The Watcher In The Woods; What Ever Happened To Baby Jane? (1962); Wicked Stepmother
Davis, Bill (act): The Little Match Girl (1987)
Davis, Boyd (act): Samson And Delilah
Davis, Brad (act, 1950–1991): Child Of Darkness, Child Of Light
Davis, Brownlee (act): Wolfman (1979)
Davis, Bud (act): Jekyll And Hyde...Together Again
Davis, Candy (act): Transmutations
Davis, Carl (mus): I, Monster; Rentadick; Roger Corman's Frankenstein Unbound; The Secret Life Of Ian Fleming; What Became Of Jack And Jill
Davis, Carole (act): Mannequin
Davis, Charles (act): The Man From Planet X
Davis, Chet (act): The Eye Creatures; Mars Needs Women
Davis, Clark (wri): Teen-Age Strangler
Davis, Colonius (act): I Was A Zombie For The F.B.I.
Davis, Craig (act): Raiders Of The Living Dead
Davis, Dale (act): Beach Girls And The Monster
Davis, Damita (act): Offerings
Davis, Daniel (act): Glen Or Glenda?; The Spirit
Davis, Darryl Rocky (act): Blink
Davis Jr., Darvel (act): The Preacher's Wife
Davis, Deddie (act): The Amazing Mr. Blunden
Davis, Desmond (dir): Clash Of The Titans
Davis, Desmond (wri): An Inspector Calls
Davis, D'mitch (act): Weird Science
Davis, Don(ald S.) (act): Hideaway; Hitler's Daughter; Memories Of Murder; Omen IV: The Awakening; Volcano: Fire On The Mountain; Watchers
Davis, Don (mus): The Beast (1996); Notorious (1992); Pandora's Clock; Running Against Time; Warriors Of Virtue
Davis, Donald (wri): One Dangerous Night
Davis, Dorothy (act): The Little Girl Who Lives Down The Lane
Davis, Duane (act): The Adventures Of Captain Zoom In Outer Space; The Hidden; A Nightmare On Elm Street 4: The Dream Master
Davis, Ed (wri): All Of Me
Davis, Eddie (dir): Color Me Dead; Panic In The City
Davis, Eddie (wri): Panic In The City
Davis, Elaine (act): The Atomic Kid
Davis, Elizabeth (wri): Revenge (1971, USA)
Davis, Elliot (cin): Vamp
Davis, Eugene (act): The Hitcher
Davis, Frank (act): Return Of The Killer Tomatoes
Davis, Frank G. (act): Monolith
Davis, Geena (act, b. 1957): Beetlejuice; Cutthroat Island; Earth Girls Are Easy; The Fly (1986); The Long Kiss Goodnight; Secret Weapons; Transylvania 6-5000
Davis, Gene (act): The Relic
Davis, George (act): The Black Cat (1934); Charlie Chan At Monte Carlo; Charlie Chan In City In Darkness; Crime Doctor's Gamble; He Who Gets Slapped; Nightmare Alley; Sherlock Jr.
Davis, Gerry (wri): Doomwatch; The Final Countdown
Davis, Gilbert (act): Quatermass II; The Sign Of Four (1932)
Davis, Gunnis (act): Bulldog Drummond Escapes; Bulldog Drummond Strikes Back (1934)
Davis, Guy (act): Def By Temptation
Davis, Harry (act): Fear No Evil (1969)
Davis, Honey (act): Dr. Caligari
Davis, Hope (act): Flatliners
Davis, Humphrey (act): Fright (1957)
Davis, Ivan (wri): The Hunger
Davis, J.C. (act): Charlie Chan Carries On
Davis, Jack (act): Endgame
Davis, Janeen (act): Vamp
Davis, Jared (act): Kiss Of The Tarantula
Davis, Jean (act): Voodoo Woman
Davis, Jeffrey John (act): Wes Craven's New Nightmare
Davis,Jerry (wri, 1917–1991): Cult Of The Cobra; Kind Lady (1951)
Davis, Jim (act, 1915–1981): The Beginning Or The End?; Blonde Bait; Dracula Vs. Frankenstein; Jesse James Meets Frankenstein's Daughter; The Monster From Green Hell; Satan's Triangle; They Ran For Their Lives
Davis, Joan (act, 1908–1961): Hold That Ghost
Davis, Jodie (act): Dr. Caligari
Davis, Joe W. (act): Star Trek III: The Search For Spock
Davis, Joel (act): Curse Of The Cat People
Davis, John Walter (act): Alice In Wonderland (1985); Phantom Of The Mall: Eric's Revenge
Davis, Julian (act): Street Trash
Davis, Karen (act): Angel Heart
Davis, Karl (act): Creature With The Atom Brain; Salome (1953); Zombies Of Mora Tau
Davis, Ken (act): Night Life (1989, USA)
Davis, Kenn (wri): Nightmare In Blood
Davis, Kenny (act): Flight Of The Navigator
Davis, Kimberlee M. (act): Big
Davis, Kristin (act): Alien Nation: Body And Soul; A Deadly Vision
Davis, Led (wri): Colonel March Investigates
Davis, Leon (act): Hellraiser
Davis, Lilian Hall (act): Boadicea; The Ring
Davis, Lisa (GB Act): Edge Of Sanity
Davis, Lisa (USA Act): Queen Of Outer Space; Spy Chasers
Davis, Lou (act): The Lone Wolf Spy Hunt
Davis, Luther (wri, b. 1921): Daughter Of The Mind; Lady In A Cage; The Wonders Of Aladdin
Davis, Marty (act): The Goddess Of Love
Davis, Michael (act): The Moon-Spinners
Davis, Miles (Mus, 1926–1991): Frantic
Davis, Mimi (act): Sandcastles
Davis, Monica (act): The Dead One; Rocket Attack U.S.A.
Davis, Nancy (act, b. 1921): Crash Landing; Donovan's Brain; The Next Voice You Hear; Night Into Morning; The Shadow In The Sky; Shadow On The Wall; Talk About A Stranger
Davis, Nathan (act): Chain Reaction (1996); Flowers In The Attic; Poltergeist III
Davis, Nick (wri): Galaxis
Davis, Noel (act): Clegg; Macbeth (1971)
Davis, Ossie (act, b. 1917): The Android Affair; Night Gallery; Shock Treatment (1964)
Davis, Owen (wri): The Haunted House (1929)
Davis Jr., Owen (act): Murder On A Bridle Path; The Plot Thickens
Davis, Paul (act): The Toxic Avenger, Part II
Davis, Philip (act): Dark Water; Howling V: The Rebirth; Trans-Mutations
Davis, Phyllis (act): The Day Of The Dolphin; Terminal Island
Davis, Preston (act): I Was A Zombie For The F.B.I.
Davis, Rachel (act): The House That Bled To Death/Growing Pains
Davis, Redd (dir): The Girl In The Flat
Davis, Rex (act): The Crimson Circle (1922)
Davis, Richard (act): Horror
Davis, Richard Harding (wri):It's A Dog's Life
Davis, Rick (act): Secrets Of The Phantom Caverns
Davis, Robert O. (act): The Great Impersonation (1942); Spy Smasher Returns
Davis, Rochelle (act): The Crow (1994)
Davis, Rod (act): King Kong Lives
Davis, Roger (act): House Of Dark Shadows; Killer Bees; Ruby
Davis, Samantha (act): Super Mario Bros.
Davis, Sammi (act): The Lair Of The White Worm
Davis Jr., Sammy (act, 1925–1990): Alice In Wonderland (1985); Johnny Cool; Nightmare In The Sun; Poor Devil
Davis, Sarah (act): Phantasm III: Lord Of The Dead
Davis, Silas (act): Mother's Day
Davis, Sonny (act): Project X (1987)
Davis, Sonny Carl (act): Terrorvision; Trancers II: The Return Of Jack Deth
Davis, Spencer (act): Werewolf Of Washington
Davis, Steve (act): The Curse; The Sword And The Sorcerer
Davis, Stratford (wri): Man In The Shadow
Davis, Stringer (act): Murder At The Gallop; Murder Most Foul; Murder She Said
Davis, Suzanne (act): Generation X
Davis, Ted (act): Beverly Hills Bodysnatchers
Davis, Terry (act): Mars Needs Women

Davis, Tudor (act): *Koroshi*
Davis, Ursula (act): *La Maldicion De Los Karnsteins*
Davis, Wade (wri): *The Serpent And The Rainbow*
Davis, Walt (act): *The Shaggy D.A.*
Davis, Warwick (act): *The Ewok Adventure; Ewoks: The Battle For Endor; Leprechaun; Leprechaun 2; Leprechaun 3; Return Of The Jedi; Willow*
Davis, William/"Wee Willie" (act): *Above Suspicion; Arabian Nights; Samson And Delilah; Shadow Of The Thin Man; To Catch A Thief*
Davis, William b. (act): *It (1990); Unforgettable*
Davis, Yonda (act): *Wes Craven's New Nightmare*
Davison, Bruce (act, b. 1948): *Alfred Hitchcock Presents; The Crucible (1996); The Jerusalem File; The Lathe Of Heaven; Mind Over Murder; Tomorrow's Child; Willard*
Davison, Davey (act): *The Strangler (1963)*
Davison, Michelle (act): *Endangered Species*
Davison, Parnell (act): *Blood Diner*
Davison, Tito (dir): *The Big Cube*
Davitian, Kenneth (act): *The Silence Of The Hams*
Davray, Dominique (act): *To Catch A Thief*
Davreux, Denise (act): *The Million Eyes Of Sumuru*
Davy, Peter (act): *Lord Of The Flies (1963)*
Daw, Marjorie (act, b. 1902): *Rupert Of Hentzau (1923)*
Dawber, Pam (act, b. 1951): *Stay Tuned*
Dawe, Carlton (wri): *The Black Spider; Shadow Of Evil (1921)*
Dawe, Kathryn (act): *Egghead's Robot*
Dawe, Robert Shaen (act): see Shayne, Robert
Dawes, Anthony (act): *One Deadly Owner*
Dawes, Deborah (act): *Evilspeak*
Dawley, J. Searle (dir, D. 1950): *Frankenstein (1910); Rescued From An Eagle's Nest*
Dawn, Hazel (act, 1890–1988): *The Lone Wolf (1917)*
Dawn, Lili (act): *Violated*
Dawn, Marpessa (act): *Black Orpheus; Sweet Movie; The Woman Eater*
Dawn, Norman (dir): *Two Lost Worlds*
Dawn, Vincent (dir): see Mattei, Bruno
Dawne, Doreen (act): *The Masque Of The Red Death (1964)*
Dawson, Anna (act): *Blood Bath At The House Of Death*
Dawson, Anthony (act, b. 1916): *The Count Of Monte Cristo (1975); The Curse Of The Werewolf; Dial M For Murder (1954); Dr. No; Grip Of The Strangler; Hour Of Decision; Midnight Lace (1960); Operation Kid Brother; The Queen Of Spades (1948); Valley Of The Eagles; The Woman In Question*
Dawson, Anthony (M.) (dir): see Margheriti, Antonio
Dawson, Basil (wri): *The Devil's Daffodil*
Dawson, Bob (cin): *Star Trek III: The Search For Spock*
Dawson, Cristy (act): *Earth Girls Are Easy*
Dawson, Curt (act): *Blood Bath (1975)*
Dawson, Forbes (act): *Scrooge (1923)*
Dawson, Freddie (act): *Scared To Death (1980)*
Dawson, Gordon (wri): *Into The Badlands*
Dawson, Ivo (act): *The Other Person*
Dawson, Joann S. (act): *12 Monkeys*
Dawson, Maurine (act): *The Mummy And The Curse Of The Jackals*
Dawson, Patrick (act): *Rawhead Rex*
Dawson, Peter (act): *The Three Stooges In Orbit*
Dawson, Ralph (wri): *The Dance Of Death*
Dawson, Richard (act, b. 1932): *Munster, Go Home!; The Running Man*
Dawson, Robert (cin): *Prophecy (1979); Rhinoceros (1974)*
Dawson, Vicky (act): *The Prowler (1981)*
Dawson, Wendy (act): *Oh Heavenly Dog*
Dax, Danielle (act): *The Company Of Wolves*
Dax, Earl (act): *The People Under The Stairs*
Day, Alexandra (act): *Boarding House*
Day, Alice (act): *The Gorilla (1927); In The Next Room; The Temple Of Venus*
Day, Baybi (act): *Driller Killer*
Day, Clayton (act): *The Day After*
Day, Cora Lee (act): *Dr. Black Mr. Hyde*
Day, Daniel (mus): *Chopper Chicks In Zombietown*
Day, Diana (act): *The Secret Of The Forest*
Day, Doris (act, b. 1924, nee Doris Kappelhoff): *Julie; The Man Who Knew Too Much (1956); Midnight Lace (1960)*
Day, Ernest (cin): *Parents; Sphinx (1981); Superman IV: The Quest For Peace*
Day, Frances (act, b. 1908): *Fiddlers Three; Tread Softly*
Day, Gabrielle (act): *Cry Wolf (1980)*
Day, Gary (act): *Death Warmed Up*
Day, Gerry (wri): *The Black Hole*
Day, Jerry (Austral act): *Mad Max*
Day, Jerry (USA act): *Cavegirl (1985)*
Day, Joe (cin): *Coma*
Day, John (act): *Abbott And Costello Meet The Invisible Man; The Claw Monsters*
Day, Josette (act, 1914–1978): *La Belle Et La Bete; Les Parents Terribles*
Day, Laraine (act, b. 1920, nee Laraine Johnson): *Fingers At The Window; Foreign Correspondent; The Locket; Murder On Flight 502; Return To Fantasy Island*
Day, Lynda (act): see George, Lynda Day
Day, Marceline (act): *London After Midnight; Temple Tower*
Day, Margaret (act): see Lockwood, Margaret
Day, Marjorie (act): *When Knights Were Bold (1916); The Woman Who Was Nothing*
Day, Percy (cin): *A Matter Of Life And Death*
Day, Robert (dir, b. 1922): *The Big Game; Bobbikins; Doctor Of Seven Dials; First Man Into Space; The Green Man; Grip Of The Strangler; The Initiation Of Sarah; Ritual Of Evil; She (1965); Tarzan And The Great River; Tarzan And The Valley Of Gold; Tarzan's Three Challenges; Tarzan The Magnificent*
Day, Shannon (act): *The Gypsy Romance*
Day, Stewart G. (act): *A Return To Salem's Lot*
Day, Venecia (act): *Craze*
Day, Vera (act): *Grip Of The Strangler; A Kid For Two Farthings; Quatermass II; The Trunk; The Woman Eater*
Day, Yvonne (act): *Don Juan (1927)*
Dayan, Daniel (act): *Zapped!*
Dayan, David (act): *Ghoulies*
Daybell, Eileen (act): *Detective Daring And The Thames Coiners; A Newsboy's Christmas Dream*
Daye, Gabrielle (act): *10 Rillington Place*
Dayle, Daphne (act): *Nick Carter Va Tout Casser*
Dayle, Ellis (act): *Madhouse*
Day-Lewis, Daniel (act, b. 1957): *The Crucible (1996)*
Daymore, Reginald Leigh (act): see Denny, Reginald
Dayton, Charles (act): *Bride Of Vengeance; School Spirit*
Dayton, Danny (act): *Ed Wood; Love At First Bite*
Dayton, Howard (act): *Space Raiders*
Dayton, Kurt (cin): *El Ataud Del Vampiro*
Dayton, Lewis (act): *The Mystery Of Mr. Bernard Brown; The Shadow Between; The Strangler (1932)*
Dayviss, Denny (act): *The Unseeing Eye*
Dea, Gloria (act): *Plan 9 From Outer Space*
Dea, Maria (act): *Orphee; Les Visiteurs Du Soir*
Deacon, Brian (act): *And The Wall Came Tumbling Down; Vampyres...Daughters Of Dracula*
Deacon, Harold (act): *Where The Rainbow Ends*
Deacon, Richard (act, 1922–1984): *Abbott And Costello Meet The Mummy; The Birds; Blackbeard's Ghost; Carousel; Everything's Ducky; Francis In The Haunted House; The Gnome-Mobile; Invasion Of The Body Snatchers (1956); Piranha (1978); Them! (1954)*
De Acosta, Donald Barry (act): see Barry, Donald
Deacutis, William (act): *Vampire's Kiss*
Dead Can Dance (mus): *Demons 2*
Deadman, Derek (act): *Brazil; Robin Hood: Prince Of Thieves*
Deadrick, Vince (act): *Beyond The Poseidon Adventure*
Deak, Michael (S.) (act): *The Alien Within; Cellar Dweller; Ghoulies II; Tales From The Darkside*
Deakin, Rufus (act): *An American Werewolf In London*
Deakins, Lucy (act): *The Boy Who Could Fly*
Deakins, Roger (cin): *Fargo; 1984 (1984)*
Dealessandro, Mark (act): *Daylight*
De Alonso, Luis Antonio Damaso (act): see Roland, Gilbert
Deamer, Angela (act): *The Godsend*
Dean, Alfie (act): *The Bespoke Overcoat*
Dean, Basil (Dir & wri, 1888–1978): *Birds Of Prey*
Dean, Bill (act): *Night Watch*
Dean, Carmen (act): *Subterfuge*
Dean, E. Brian (act): *Wolfen*
Dean, Fabian (act): *The Barefoot Executive; The Computer Wore Tennis Shoes*
Dean, Gerald (act): *Bulldog Drummond (1923)*
Dean, Isabel (act, b. 1918, nee Isabel Hodgkinson): *Catch Me A Spy; A High Wind In Jamaica*
Dean, Ivor (act, 1916–1974): *Dr. Jekyll And Sister Hyde; The Oblong Box; The Sorcerers; Theatre Of Death*
Dean, James F. (Ac): *C.H.U.D. II*
Dean, Jeanne (act): *Blood Of Dracula; Gog; Voodoo Tiger*
Dean, Jimmy (act, b. 1928): *Diamonds Are Forever*
Dean, John (act): *Mutants In Paradise*
Dean, Julia (act, 1878–1952): *Curse Of The Cat People; Nightmare Alley*
Dean, Karyn J. (act): *The Craft*
Dean, Lalla (act): *For Your Eyes Only*
Dean, Lerae (act): *Class Of Nuke'em High*
Dean, Man Mountain (act): *The Gladiator*
Dean, Margia (act): *The Baron Of Arizona; Follow The Hunter; Moro Witch Doctor; The Quatermass Experiment; Secret Of The Purple Reef*
Dean, Max (act): *The Murder Clinic*
Dean, Patricia (act): *The Beginning Of The End*
Dean, Priscilla (act, b. 1896): *Outside The Law*
Dean, Raye (act): *A Message From Mars (1921)*
Dean, Richard (cin): *Venom (1982)*
Dean, Rick (act): *Carnosaur 2; Tales From The Hood*
De Anda, Olivia (act): *Cavegirl (1985)*
De Andrade, Joaquim Pedro (dir): *Macunaima*
Deane, Douglas (act): *What's The Matter With Helen?*
Deane, Hamilton (wri): *Dracula (1931 {English-Speaking Version} & 1979)*
Deane, Lezlie (act): *Freddy's Dead: The Final Nightmare; 976-Evil*
Deane, Shirley (act): *Charlie Chan At The Circus; The Deadly Ray From Mars; Peril From The Planet Mongo; Purple Death From Outer Space*
Deane, Sydney (act): *Missing Millions*
Deane, Teddy (act): *The Haunting Of Sarah Hardy*
De Angelis, Guido (mus): *Ironmaster; Killer Fish; Il Montagna Di Dio Cannibale; Zorro (1975)*
De Angelis, Maurizio (mus): *Ironmaster; Killer Fish; Il Montagna Di Dio Cannibale; Zorro (1975)*
Deans, Marjorie (wri, b. 1901): *Someone At The Door*
De Antonio, Tom (act): *Vampire At Midnight*
Dear, Elizabeth (act): *Captain Kronos: Vampire Hunter*
Dear, Leslie (cin): *The Flying Sorceror*
Dear, William (act): *Darkman (1990)*
Dear, William (dir): *Angels In The Outfield (1994); Harry And The Hendersons; Timerider*
Dear, William (wri): *Harry And The Hendersons; The Rocketeer; Timerider*
De Aragon, Maria (act): *Blood Mania*
Dearden, Basil (dir, 1911–1971): *The Assassination Bureau; Cage Of Gold; Dead Of Night (1945); Halfway House; Life For Ruth; Man In The Moon (1960); The Man Who Haunted Himself; Masquerade; The Mind Bender (1963); Pool Of London; Sapphire; They Came To A City; Who Done It? (1956); Woman Of Straw*
Dearden, Basil (wri, 1911–1971): *The Man Who Haunted Himself; They Came To A City*
Dearden, James (dir & wri): *The Cold Room; Panic (1979)*
Deare, Morgan (act): *Mission: Impossible*
Dearing, Edgar (act): *Boston Blackie's Chinese Venture; The Gracie Allen Murder Case; Nick Carter, Master Detective; Shadow Of The Thin Man; Torchy Plays With Dynamite*
Dearing, Jo Ann (act): *Cat People (1982); C.H.U.D. II; Suburban Commando*
Dearlove, Jack (act): *Raiders Of The Lost Ark*
Dearman, Glyn (act): *Four Sided Triangle; Scrooge (1951)*
Dearman, Jennifer (act): *Four Sided Triangle*
Dearth, Bill (act): *Chiller*
Dearth, John (act): *The Road To Hong Kong*
Dearth, William E. (act): *Alien Nation*
Deary, Tony (act): *Howling III*
Deas, Justin (act): *Dream Lover*
De Ately, Murray (cin): *Frankenstein Island*
Deathmask (mus): *Zombie Nightmare*
De Avila, Michael (dir, cin & wri): *Lost Prophet*
Debaer, Jean (act): *The Fan*
De Balzac, Honore (wri, 1799-1850): *The Conquering Power; Desire*
De Banzie, Brenda (act, 1915–1981): *A Kid For Two Farthings; The Man Who Knew Too Much (1956); The 39 Steps (1959)*
Debanzie, Lois (act): *Addams Family Values*
De Bardot, Audoin (act): *Spirits Of The Dead*
De Barros, Mario (act): *Flesh & Blood; Hundra; The Valley Of Gwangi*
Debeausset, Michael (act): *Mission Mars*
De Becker, Marie (act): *The Chance Of A Lifetime; Devotion*
De Bello, James (act): *Attack Of The Killer Tomatoes*
Debello, John (act, dir & wri): *Attack Of The Killer Tomatoes; Return Of The Killer Tomatoes*
De Benedictus, Dick (mus): *The Return Of The World's Greatest Detective*
De Benedittis, Laura (act): *El Castello Dell'orrore*
Debenning, Burr (act): *The Amazing Captain Nemo; City Beneath The Sea (1970); The House Of The Dead; The Incredible Melting Man; A Nightmare On Elm Street 5: The Dream Child*
De Beranger, Andre (act): *The Bat (1926)*
Debert, Dragicia (act): *Fortress*
De Blain, Luis G. (wri): *Murder Mansion*
De Blas, Manuel (act): *Slugs*
Debney, John (mus): *The Curse; Cutthroat Island; Doctor Who; Into The Badlands; Liar Liar; The Relic*
De Boer, Nikki (act): *Prom Night IV: Deliver Us From Evil*
Debois, Velvet (act): *Re-Animator*
Debont, Anneke (act): *Twister*
Debont, Jan (cin): *Cujo; Flatliners; Flesh & Blood; The Jewel Of The Nile*
Debont, Jan (dir): *Twister*
De Bor, Curt (act): *The Dark Half*
Debowski, Krzysztof (dir): *Bezludna Planeta; Wycieczka W Kosmos*
De Boysson, Pascale (act): *Les Abysses; Perceval*
De Bray, Yvonne (act, 1889–1954): *Les Parents Terribles*
Debrett, Hal (wri): *Before I Wake*
Debreuil, Andre (cin): *I Love You, I Kill You*
De Broca, Philippe (dir, b. 1933): *Cartouche (1962); Dear Detective; Le Plus Vieux Metier Du Monde*
De Broca, Philippe (wri, b. 1933): *Cartouche (1962)*
Debroux, Lee (act): *Bates Motel; Pumpkinhead; Robocop; The Terminal Man*
De Brugada, Philippe (act): *The Phantom Of The Opera (1990)*
Debruine, Delight (act): *The Day It Came To Earth*
De Brulier, Nigel (act, 1878–1948): *Charlie Chan In Egypt; Don Juan (1927); The Eleventh Hour (1923); The Hound Of The Baskervilles (1939); The Hunchback Of Notre Dame (1923); The Iron Mask; Moby Dick (1930); One Million B.C.; Rasputin And The Empress; Ruper Of Hentzau (1923); Salome (1922)*
Debucourt, Jean (act, 1894–1958): *Les Sorcieres De Salem*
De Bujac, Jacques (act): see Cabot, Bruce
De Burgh, Beatrice (act): *The Witch Of The Welsh Mountains*
Decae, Henri (cin, b. 1915): *The Boys From Brazil; Castle Keep; Les Enfants Terribles; Les Felins; Leda; The Light At The Edge Of The World; The Night Of The Generals; La Tulipe Noire*
De Camp, Marianne (act): *The Monster Squad*
De Camp, Rosemary (act, b. 1914): *Eyes In The Night; The Jungle Book (1942); Night Unto Night; Saturday The 14th; 13 Ghosts; The Time Machine (1978); The Treasure Of Lost Canyon*
De Carlo, Louise (act): *Willard*
Decarlo, Mark (act): *Buffy, The Vampire Slayer*
Decarlo, Yvonne (act, b. 1924, nee Peggy Middleton): *American Gothic; Buccaneer's Girl; Cellar Dweller; Guyana, Cult Of The Damned; Kismet (1944); The Mark Of Zorro (1974); Munster, Go Home!; The Munsters' Revenge; Nocturna, Granddaughter Of Dracula; The Power (1967); Satan's Cheerleaders; Silent Scream (1979); Slave Girl; Song Of Scheherazade*
Decarlton, George (act): *Life Without Soul*
De Carolis, Cinzia (act): *The Cat O' Nine Tails*
De Casalis, Jeanne (act): *Jamaica Inn (1939); The Twenty Questions Murder*
De Castilla, Elena (act): *El Castillo De Las Bofetadas*
Decastro, Travis (act): *Earthbound (1981)*
De Chalonge, Christian (dir): *Docteur Petiot*
Deckard, Diane (act): *The Children*
Decker, Alan (act): *Rattlers*
Decker, Diana (act, b. 1926): *Devils Of Darkness; Fiddlers Three; Murder At The Windmill; Saturday Island*
Decker, Lionel (act): *Ed Wood*
Decker, Marc (mus): *Princess Warrior*

Decker, William (act): *The Toxic Avenger, Part II*
Deckers, Eugene (act, b. 1917): *The Assassination Bureau; Dual Albi; The Elusive Pimpernel (1950); Highly Dangerous; Limbo Line; Night Without Stars; Seven Thunders; Sleeping Car To Trieste*
Deckert, Blue (act): *The Outing*
Decleux, John (act): *I Was A Zombie For The F.B.I.*
De Closs, James (act): *Alien Nation*
Decoin, Henri (dir, 1896–1969): *Les Inconnus Dans La Maison; Nathalie, Agent Secret; Nick Carter Va Tout Casser*
De Coligny, Andrey (wri): *The Lion Of Thebes*
Decomble, Guy (act): *Cet Homme Est Dangereux*
De Concini, Ennio (dir): *Hitler: The Last Ten Days*
De Concini, Ennio (wri): *La Battaglia Di Maratona; Bluebeard (1972); Carthage In Flames; The Colossus Of Rhodes; Ercole E La Regina Di Lidia; Hitler: The Last Ten Days; The Last Days Of Pompeii (1959); La Maschera Del Demonio; The Queen Of Babylon; La Ragazza Che Sapeva Troppo; The Red Tent; Romolo E Remo; Les Titans; Ulysses*
De Cordoba, Pedro (act, 1881–1950): *The Beast With Five Fingers; Before I Hang; Charlie Chan In City In Darkness; Condemned To Live; The Corsican Brothers (1941); Devil Doll (1936); The Falcon In Mexico; The Ghost Breakers; Samson And Delilah; Tarzan Triumphs; Trouble For Two; Young Diana*
De Cordova, Arturo (act, 1907–1973, nee Arturo Garcia): *Adventures Of Casanova; H.G. Wells' The New Invisible Man*
De Cordova, Frederick (dir, b. 1910): *Bedtime For Bonzo; Bonzo Goes To College*
De Cordova, Joseph (act): *The Omegans*
De Cordova, Leander (dir): *She (1925)*
De Cordova, Rafael (act): *El Amor Brujo (1972)*
De Cordova, Rudolph (act): *The Secret Kingdom*
De Corsia, Ted (act, b. 1906): *Enchanted Island; It Happens Every Spring; The Killing; The Lady From Shanghai; Man In The Dark (1953); 20,000 Leagues Under The Sea (1954)*
Decosta, Michelle (act): *The Refrigerator*
Decoteau, David/Dave (dir): *Creepozoids; I Was A Teenage Sex Mutant; Nightmare Sisters; Puppet Master III: Toulon's Revenge; Sorority Babes In The Slimeball Bowl-O-Rama*
Decoteau, David (wri): *Creepozoids*
De Crespigny, Mrs. Champion (wri): *Tangled Evidence*
De Crosset, Francois (wri): *Arsene Lupin*
Dedmon, Richard (act): *Wolfman (1979)*
Dee, Frances (act, b. 1907, nee Jean Dee): *The Happy Land; I Walked With A Zombie; King Of The Jungle*
Dee, Frankie (act): *The Mummy And The Curse Of The Jackals*
Dee, Jean (act): see Dee, Frances
Dee, John (act): *Bay Coven*
Dee, Protacio (act): *Hunters Of The Golden Cobra*
Dee, Ruby (act, b. 1924, nee Ruby Ann Wallace): *The Balcony; Cat People (1982)*
Dee, Sandra (act, b. 1942, nee Alexandra Zuck): *The Dunwich Horror; Fantasy Island; Houston, We've Got A Problem; Portrait In Black*
Deed, Andre (act): *Dislocation Mysterieuse*
Deeley, Michael (wri): *At The Stroke Of Nine*
Deemer, Susan (act): *Kill, Kill, Overkill*
Deems, Mickey (act): *The Munsters' Revenge*
Deering, Dee Dee (act): *The Night Of The Claw*
Deering, Olive (act): *Samson And Delilah; Shock Treatment (1964)*
Deery, Jack (act): *The Adventures Of Robin Hood*
Dees, Stephanie (act): *Halloween 4: The Return Of Michael Myers*
Deeter, Drew (act): *Spawn Of The Slithis*
Deeter, Jasper (act): *The Blob (1958); 4D Man*
Deeth, James/Jim (act): *Cat People (1982); Seven*
Deezen, Ed(Die) (act): *Beverly Hills Vamp; Laserblast; A Polish Vampire In Burbank; The Silence Of The Hams; Zapped!*
De Falla, (Don) Manuel (mus & wri): *El Amor Brujo (1972 & 1986)*
De Faut, Richard (act): *Night Of The Zombies (1981)*
Defazio, Sam (act): *Devil's Express*
De Felice, J. Greg (wri): *Out Of The Dark*
De Felice, Lionello (wri): *Maciste, L'eroe Piu Grande Del Mondo*
De Felitta, Frank (dir): *Killer In The Mirror; The Two Worlds Of Jennie Logan*
De Felitta, Frank (wri): *Audrey Rose; The Entity; Killer In The Mirror; The Two Worlds Of Jennie Logan; Z.P.G.*
De Feo, Francesco (dir & wri): *The Prisoner Of The Iron Mask*
Defillipis, Tony (act): *Blood Diner*
De Filippo, Eduardo (act & dir, 1900–1984): *Spara Forte, Piu Forte...Non Capisco*
De Filippo, Eduardo (wri, 1900–1984): *Ghosts—Italian Style; Spara Forte, Piu Forte... Non Capisco*
Defoe, Daniel (wri, 1660-1731): *Robinson Crusoe (1902 & 1927); Robinson Crusoe And The Tiger; Robinson Crusoe On Mars*
Deford, Jane (act): *Phantom Of The Paradise*
Deforest, Calvert (act): *My Demon Lover*
De France, Stephen (act): *Night Of The Lepus*
De Francesco, Louis (mus): *Berkeley Square*
Defrancisco, Michael (act): *Shadow Of Death (1983)*
Defranco, Tom (act): *Alien Nation; I Was A Teenage Sex Mutant*
Defrank, Bob (act): *Driller Killer*
De Frates, Jami (mus): *Blood Waters Of Dr. Z*
Defries, Diana (act): *Slipstream*
Defru, Paul (cin): *The Devil's Nightmare*
De Funes, Louis (act, 1914–1983): *Le Diable Et Les Dix Commandements; Fantomas Contro Scotland Yard; A Killing Success; Poison (1951)*
Dega, George (act): *Wonder Woman*
Dega, Igor (act): *Sorry, Wrong Number (1948)*
De Gaetano, Michael A. (dir): *U.F.O.: Target Earth*
Degagne, Marc (act): *Happy Birthday To Me*
Degan, Justin (act): *Jekyll And Hyde*
Degas, Brian (wri): *Barbarella; Diabolik*
Degeneres, Ellen (act): *Infernal Affairs*
Deghy, Guy (act): *The Kremlin Letter; Subterfuge*
Deghy, Guy (wri): *Danger Tomorrow*
Degnan, Martina (act): *Ghost (1990)*
Degni, Lou (act): see Forest, Mark
De Gogual, Constantin (act): *Diamonds Are Forever; To The Devil A Daughter*
De Gooyer, Ryk (act): *Nosferatu, The Vampyre*
De Gortner, Fred (wri): *The Phantom Planet*
De Gostrie, Roland (dir): see Neill, Roy William
De Goya, Liza (act): *Kemek*
De Graaf, Manfred (act): *The Lift*
De Grado, Conchita (act): *Hundra*
De Grandy, Miguel (act): *Slugs*
De Grasse, Robert (cin, 1900-1971): *The Body Snatcher (1945); A Date With The Falcon; Genius At Work; Lady Of Burlesque; The Leopard Man*
De Grasse, Sam (act, 1875–1953): *The Black Pirate; The Dancer Of The Nile; In The Palace Of The King; The Man Who Laughs (1928); Robin Hood (1922)*
Degrave, Jean (act): *Judex*
De Greenlaw, Jennifer (act): *The Last Wave*
De Grey, Sydney (act): *Just Imagine; The Mark Of Zorro (1920)*
De Groot, Hugo (mus): *Spy In The Sky*
De Grunwald, Anatole (wri, 1910–1967): *Murder On Monday; Pimpernel Smith*
Deguere, Philip (Dir & Wri): *Dr. Strange*
De Guiche, Dorothy (act): see Gish, Dorothy
De Guiche, Lillian (act): see Gish, Lillian
De Gunzburg, Baron Nicolas (dir): see West, Julian
De Guzman, Michael (wri): *Jaws: The Revenge*
Dehart, Judith (act): *Dead Men Tell No Tales*
Dehart, Wayne (act): *I Come In Peace; RoboCop 2*
De Hartog, Jan (wri): *The Key*
De Haven, Gloria (act, b. 1925): *Bog; Scene Of The Crime; The Thin Man Goes Home*
Dehaven, Richard (act): *Night Of The Creeps*
De Havilland, Joan (act): see Fontaine, Joan
De Havilland, Olivia (act, b. 1916): *The Adventures Of Robin Hood; The Dark Mirror (1946); Devotion; The Fifth Musketeer; Hush...Hush, Sweet Charlotte; Lady In A Cage; A Midsummer Night's Dream (1935); Murder Is Easy; My Cousin Rachel; The Screaming Woman; The Snake Pit (1948); The Swarm*
De Havos, Jorge Martinez (act): *The Littlest Angel (1960)*
Dehay, Alain (act): *Superman II*
Dehecq, Madeleine (act): *Amador*
De Heer, Rolf (dir & wri): *Encounter At Raven's Gate*
De Heredia, Jose Luis Saenz (dir & wri): *Faustina*
De Herrera, Nana (act): *The 7th Voyage Of Sinbad*
Dehetre, Katherine (act): *Looker; Meteor*
Dehn, Paul (wri, 1912–1976): *Battle For The Planet Of The Apes; Beneath The Planet Of The Apes; Conquest Of The Planet Of The Apes; The Deadly Affair; Escape From The Planet Of The Apes; Fragment Of Fear; Goldfinger; Murder On The Orient Express; The Night Of The Generals; Seven Days To Noon; The Spy Who Came In From The Cold*
Dehner, John (act, b. 1915): *The Bowery Boys Meet The Monsters; The Boys From Brazil; Captive Girl; Carousel; Creator; The Day Of The Dolphin; Please Murder Me; Rogues Of Sherwood Forest; Slaughterhouse-Five*
Deighton, Len (wri, b. 1929): *Billion Dollar Brain; Funeral In Berlin; The Ipcress File*
Deignan, Martina (act): *The Night Of The Claw*
Dein, Edward (dir): *The Curse Of The Undead; The Leech Woman*
Dein, Edward (wri): *Boston Blackie's Rendezvous; Calling Dr. Death; The Cat Creeps (1946); The Curse Of The Undead; The Falcon Strikes Back; The Jungle Woman; The Leopard Man; The Lone Wolf And His Lady; The Notorious Lone Wolf*
Dein, Mildred (wri): *The Curse Of The Undead*
Dejarnatt, Steve (dir): *Alfred Hitchcock Presents; Cherry 2000; Miracle Mile*
Dejarnatt, Steve (wri): *Alfred Hitchcock Presents; Miracle Mile*
De Jerez, Gomez (act): *El Amor Brujo (1986)*
De Jesus, Luchi (mus): *Crackle Of Death*
De Jesus, Wanda (act): *RoboCop 2*
Dejon, Denise (act): *The Wiz*
De Jong, Holly (act): *Electric Dreams*
De Keyser, David (act): *Diamonds Are Forever*
De Keyzer, Bruno (cin): *Afraid Of The Dark; The Murders In The Rue Morgue (1986)*
Dekker, Albert (act, 1905–1968): *Among The Living; Bride Of Vengeance; Dr. Cyclops; The French Key; Gammera, The Invincible; Kiss Me Deadly; The Last Warning (1938); The Lone Wolf In Paris; The Man In The Iron Mask (1939); Marie Antoinette (1938); Search For Danger; She-Devil; Suddenly Last Summer; Tarzan's Magic Fountain*
Dekker, Ben (act): *House Of The Living Dead*
Dekker, Chris (act): *Night Of The Creeps*
Dekker, Fred (dir): *The Monster Squad; Night Of The Creeps; RoboCop 3*
Dekker, Fred (wri): *House; The Monster Squad; Night Of The Creeps; RoboCop 3*
Dekker, Thomas (Alexander) (act): *Star Trek: Generations; Village Of The Damned (1995)*
De Koron, Chris Maria (act): *The Oracle (1985)*
De Kova, Frank (act, 1910–1981): *Atlantis, The Lost Continent; Hold Back Tomorrow; The Lone Ranger; Raiders Of The Seven Seas; Split Second (1953); Teenage Cave Man*
De Kovan, Roger (act): *Seizure*
De La Barca, Pedro Calderon (wri): *El Principe Encadenado*
De Laberdesque, Caridad (act): *L'age D'or*
De La Croix, Raven (act): *The Lost Empire*
De Lacey, Phillipe (act): *Don Juan (1927); Peter Pan*
De La Iglesia, Eloy (dir): *Apartment On The Thirteenth Floor*
Delafield, E.M. (wri): *Crime On The Hill*
De La Fonte, Jeanne (act): see Adoree, Renee
De La Haye, Ina (act): *The Private Life Of Sherlock Holmes*
De-La-Haye, Lysandre (act): *Dark Places*
Delahaye, Michel (act): *Alphaville, Une Etrange Aventure De Lemmy Caution*
Delair, Suzy (act, b. 1916): *Atoll K*
Del-Aires, The (act & mus): *The Horror Of Party Beach*
De La Loma (Sr.), Jose (wri): *Conquest; Lightning Bolt*
Delamain, Aimee (act): *High Spirits; The House In Nightmare Park; I, Monster; Santa Claus (1985)*
Delamare, Gil (act): *Les Femmes S'en Balancent*
Delamare, Lise (act): *Lola Montes*
Delamere, Louise (act): *Judge Dredd*
De La Motte, Marguerite (act, 1903–1950): *The Iron Mask; The Mark Of Zorro (1920)*
De La Motte, Mischa (act): *Endless Night; Frankenstein And The Monster From Hell; Return From The Ashes*
Delan, Anthony (act): *The Haunted (1991)*
De Lancie, John (act): *Deep Red (1994); The Hand That Rocks The Cradle; The Man With The Power*
Deland, Bill (act): *Deadly Messages; The Midnight Hour; Teen-Agers From Outer Space*
De Landa, Juan (act): *Beat The Devil; Faustina*
Delaney, Charles (act): *The Thirteenth Hour (1927)*
Delaney, Joan (act, b. 1943): *The President's Analyst*
Delaney, Joan Ellen (act): *Spookies*
Delaney, Kim (act, b. 1964): *Body Parts; Closer And Closer; Darkman II: The Return Of Durant; The Drifter; Project: Metalbeast; Project: Metalbeast, DNA Overload; Serial Killer; Something Is Out There; Tall, Dark And Deadly; Temptress*
Delaney, Larry (act): *Westworld*
Delaney, Leon (act): *Kiss Meets The Phantom Of The Park*
Delaney, Tom J. (act): *The Fish Men*
De Lange, Bob (act): *Spy In The Sky*
Delannoy, Jean (dir, b. 1908): *L'eternel Retour; Marie Antoinette (1953); Obsession (1954)*
Delano, Diane (act): *Miracle Mile*
Delano, Lee (act): *Project X (1967)*
Delano, Michael (act): *Curse Of The Black Widow; Not Of This Earth (1988)*
De Lanti, Stella (act): *Don Q, Son Of Zorro*
Delany, Dana (act, b. 1957): *Batman: Mask Of The Phantasm; Exit To Eden; The Fan*
Delany, Maureen (act): *The March Hare; The Mark Of Cain; Under Capricorn*
Delany, Pat(ricia) (act): *The Bat People; Charley And The Angel; Creature Of Destruction; Ellery Queen: Don't Look Behind You; Mars Needs Women; Now You See Him, Now You Don't; Zontar: The Thing From Venus*
De La Paz, Danny (act): *Alfred Hitchcock Presents; Freejack; Miracle Mile*
De La Pena, Angel (act): *The Arrival*
Delapparent, Hubert (act): *L'ours*
De Lara, Frederick (act): *The Charlatan*
De La Rosa, Nelson (act): *The Island Of Dr. Moreau (1996)*
De La Tour, Andrew (act): *The Bride (1985)*
De La Tour, Charles (dir): *The Limping Man (1953)*
De La Tour, Frances (act): *Murder With Mirrors; To The Devil A Daughter; Wombling Free*
Delaurentis, Robert (wri): *Bionic Showdown: The Six Million Dollar Man And The Bionic Woman*
De Laurentis, Simona (act): *The Mcguffin*
Delay, Carol (act): *Hush, Hush, Sweet Charlotte*
Del Balzo, Liana (act): *Il Ladro Di Venezia*
Delbo, Jean Jacques (act): *Death Comes From Space*
Del Castillo, Erick (act): *The Incredible Face Of Dr. B*
Del Castillo, Miguel (act): *Lo Strano Caso Della Signora Ward*
Del Cielo, Mona (act): *The Blood Drinkers*
Delcour, Mike (act): *Secrets Of The Phantom Caverns*
Delecluze, Guy (cin): *The Mysterious Island Of Captain Nemo*
Delegall, Bob (act): *Dr. Strange*
De Leon, Enedina Diaz (act): *Run For The Sun*
De Leon, Gerardo/Gerry (dir): *The Blood Drinkers; Curse Of The Vampires; Mad Doctor Of Blood Island; Terror Is A Man De Leon, Jack (Act): The Hobbit*
De Leon, Jack (wri): *Crime On The Hill; The Gables Mystery; The Man At Six*
Deleon, Walter (wri): *The Cat And The Canary (1939); The Ghost Breakers; International House; Scared Stiff (1953); The Time Of Their Lives*
Delerue, Georges (mus, 1925–1992): *Cartouche (1962); The Day Of The Dolphin; Maid To Order; Mata Hari, Agent H21; Our Mother's House*
Delevanti, Cyril (act, b. 1887): *Crowhaven Farm; Dead Ringer; The Jade Mask; Mary Poppins; Oh Dad Poor Dad, Mamma's Hung You In The Closet And I'm Feelin' So Sad; Soylent Green*
Delevanti, Winifred (act): *The Sorrows Of Satan (1917); The Terrible 'Tec*
De Leyse, Marietta (act): *London's Enemies*
Delfino, Sallie (act): *What's The Matter With Helen?*
Delfosse, Raoul (act): *Aimez-Vous Les Femmes?*
Delgado, Adelaida (act): see Mara, Adele
Delgado, Jose Luis (wri): *City Of The Walking Dead*
Delgado, Miguel (act): *Flatliners*
Del Gado, Ramon (act): *Sword Of The Avenger*
Delgado, Roger (act, 1920–1973): *First Man Into Space; Hot Enough For June; In Search Of The Castaways; Masquerade; The Mind Benders (1963); The Mummy's Shroud; The Road To Hong Kong; The Terror Of The Tongs*
Del Genio, Tom (cin): *Cat People (1982)*
Del Grande, Louis (act): *Clarence; Happy Birthday To Me; Of Unknown Origin; Scanners*

Del Grosso, Remigio (wri): The Conquest Of Mycenae; Il Mulino Delle Donne Di Pietra; Secret Agent Superdragon
Delhoyo, George (act): The Crying Child
Delia, Joseph/Joe (mus): The Body Snatchers; Driller Killer
Delibes, Leo (mus): Doctor?? Coppelius!!
Delinsky, Anna (act): Death Takes A Holiday (1934)
De Lirio, Carmen (act): Goliath Against The Giants
Deliso, Debra (act): Dr. Caligari; The Slumber Party Massacre
Delk, Denny (act): Howard The Duck
Dell, Claudia (act, b. 1910): Black Magic (1944); The Lost City
Dell, Edith (wri): Satellite In The Sky
Dell, Ethel M. (wri): The Rocks Of Valpre
Dell, Gabriel (act, 1920–1988): Earthquake; Master Minds (1950); Mr. Hex; Spook Busters
Dell, Jeffrey (dir): The Dark Man (1951)
Dell, Jeffrey (wri): The Dark Man (1951); The Saint's Vacation; Thunder Rock
Dell, Myrna (act): The Falcon In San Francisco; The Falcon's Adventure; The Falcon's Alibi; The Locket; The Lost Tribe; Radar Secret Service; Search For Danger
Della, Jay (act): This Is Not A Test
Dell'acqua, Matilde (act): Deborah
Della Sorte, Joseph (act): Psychic Killer
Delli Colli, Franco (cin): Morgan The Pirate
Delli Colli, Tonino (cin): Ghosts-Italian Style; Morgan The Pirate; The Name Of The Rose; Spirits Of The Dead; The Thief Of Baghdad (1960); The Wonders Of Aladdin
Dellos, Dove (act): Repossessed
Delman, Jeffrey (act, dir & wri): Deadtime Stories
Del Mar, Dolores (act): The Last Days Of Man On Earth
Del Mar, Maria (act): Unlikely Angel
Del Mar, Pola (act): Jack's Back
Del Mar, Yolande (act): Zeta One
Delmolino, Ray (act): The Children
Delo, Ken (act): Destination Inner Space
Deloach, Quitman (act): I Was A Zombie For The F.B.I.
Deloe, Jan Hathaway (act): Secrets In The Attic
Delon, Alain (act, b. 1935): Le Diable Et Les Dix Commandements; Diabolically Yours; Les Felins; Spirits Of The Dead; Three Murderesses; Traitement De Choc; La Tulipe Noire; Zorro (1975)
Delon, Nathalie (act): Bluebeard (1972); The Eyes Behind The Stars
De Long, Daniel (act): Equalizer 2000
De Longis, Anthony (act): The Sword And The Sorcerer
Delora, Jennifer (act): Deranged (1987); Frankenhooker
De Lorenzo, Chigquita (act): The Sword Of Damocles
Delorme, Danielle (act, b. 1926, nee Gabrielle Girard): Les Miserables (1957); The Seventh Juror
Delorme, Guy (act):Perceval; The Southern Star
De Lory, Al (mus): The Devil's Rain
De Los Arcos, Louis (wri): Pyro
De Los Rios, Waldo (mus): The House That Screamed; Murders In The Rue Morgue (1971)
Delphine, Adriana (act): Thinner
Delpierre (act): Le Voyage Dans La Lune
Del Pilar, Rosario (act): Curse Of The Vampires
Delpozo,Angel (act): Treasure Island (1971)
Del Prado, Blanca (act): El Vampiro Acecha
Delpy, Julie (act): The Three Musketeers (1993)
Del Rey, Pilar (act): The Flame Barrier; The Naked Jungle
Del Rio, Dolores (act, 1905–1983, nee Lolita Dolores Asunsolo De Martinez): C'era Una Volta; The Fugitive; Journey Into Fear (1942); Lancer Spy; Loves Of Carmen; Madame Dubarry (1934); La Otra
Del Rio, Isabelle (act): Quelqu'un Derriere La Porte
Del Rio, Jack (act): Between Midnight And Dawn
Del Rio, Teresa (act): Honeycomb
Del Ruth, Hampton (wri): The Invisible Fear
Del Ruth, Roy (dir, 1895–1961): The Alligator People; Bulldog Drummond Strikes Back (1934); The Maltese Falcon (1931); The Mind Reader; Phantom Of The Rue Morgue; The Terror (1928); Topper Returns; Why Must I Die?; Wolf's Clothing (1927)
Del Ruth, Thomas/Tom (cin):Asteroid; Impulse (1984); The Running Man; She's Dressed To Kill
Del Santo, Lory (act): The Great Alligator
Delschaft, Maly (act): Der Letzte Mann
Delsol, Gerald (act): Children Of The Damned
Del Sol, Laura (act): El Amor Brujo (1986)
Deltgen, Rene (act): Journey To The Lost City
Del Toro, Guillermo (dir & wri): Cronos
Deluando, Poppy (act): The Saracen Blade
De Luca, Giovanna (act): The Eyes Behind The Stars
Deluca, Michael (wri): Freddy's Dead: The Final Nightmare; In The Mouth Of Madness; Judge Dredd
Deluca, Peppino (mus): Dorian Gray
De Luca, Rudy (act): Dracula: Dead And Loving It; The Return Of Count Yorga; The Silence Of The Hams; Transylvania 6-5000
De Luca, Rudy (dir): Transylvania 6-5000
De Luca, Rudy (wri): Caveman (1981); Transylvania 6-5000
Delugg, Anne (mus): Sleeping Beauty (1965, W. Ger)
Delugg, Milton (mus): Gulliver's Travels Beyond The Moon; Santa Claus Conquers The Martians; Sleeping Beauty (1965, W. Ger)
Delugo, Winston (act): Doomsday Machine
De Luise, Alfonso (act): Kemek
Deluise, David (act): The Silence Of The Hams
Deluise, Dom (act, b. 1933): The Adventures Of Sherlock Holmes' Smarter Brother; The Busy Body; Failsafe; Haunted Honeymoon (1986); Robin Hood: Men In Tights; The Secret Of Nimh; The Silence Of The Hams; A Troll In Central Park
Deluise, Peter (act): Children Of The Night (1992); The Midnight Hour
De Luna, Alvaro (act): Gran Amore Del Conde Dracula
De Lungo, Toni (act): The House Of The Arrow (1930)
Del Val, Jean (act): Charlie Chan In City In Darkness; Crime Doctor's Gamble; Fantastic Voyage; The Return Of Monte Cristo
Del Valle, Juan (act): The Power (1980)
Delynn, Peter (act): Spookies
Delysia, Alice (act): She (1916)
Del Zoppo, Alex (Act & Mus): Premonition (1972)
Demain, Gordon (act): The Mad Monster
De Malero, Betty (act): The House Of The Arrow (1930)
De Manby, Alfred (act): Mephisto; The Tempter (1913)
De Manby, Alfred (dir): Mephisto
De Manby, Alfred (wri): Mephisto; Santa Claus (1912); The Tempter (1913)
Demara, Fred "The Great Impostor" (act, 1922–1982): The Hypnotic Eye
Demarco, Christopher (mus): The Toxic Avenger, Part III: The Last Temptation Of Toxie
De Marco, Dino (act): El Espejo De La Bruja
Demarest, William (act, 1892–1983): The Casino Murder Case; Charlie Chan At The Opera; Don't Be Afraid Of The Dark; Dressed To Kill (1941); The Gracie Allen Murder Case; Miracles For Sale; Night Has A Thousand Eyes; Once Upon A Time (1944); Son Of Flubber; Whispering Smith
De Marinis, Nick (act): It Came Upon The Midnight Clear
De Mario, Tony (act): Black Widow (1954)
Demarne, Denis (act): The Man With Two Heads
De Marney, Derrick (act, 1906–1978): The March Hare; Once In A New Moon; The Projected Man; She Shall Have Murder; Sleeping Car To Trieste; The Spider (1939); Things To Come; Three Silent Men; Uncle Silas; Young And Innocent
De Marney, Terence (act, b. 1909): Confessions Of An Opium Eater; Death Is A Woman; Dual Alibi; Eyes Of Fate; The Hand Of Night; I Killed The Count; The Merry Men Of Sherwood Forest; Monster Of Terror; The Mystery Of The Mary Celeste; Pharaoh's Curse; 23 Paces To Baker Street; The Unholy Quest
De Marney, Terence (wri, b. 1909): Wanted For Murder
De Martinez, Lolita Dolores Asunsolo (act): see Del Rio, Dolores
Demartino, Alberto (dir, a.k.a. Martin Herbert): Anticristo; Holocaust 2000; Horror; Miami Golem; Operation Kid Brother; Perseus The Invincible; Il Trionfo Di Ercole
Demartino, Alberto (wri): Anticristo; Holocaust 2000; Miami Golem; Perseus The Invincible
De Martino, Kelly (act): Copycat
De Masi, Francesco (mus): Escape From The Bronx; The Lion Of Thebes; Il Trionfo Di Ercole
De Maupassant, Guy (wri, 1850-1893):Diary Of A Madman; Le Horla (1967); Night Fiend
Demaurey, Edna (act): The Conquering Power
Demauro, Frank (cin): The Terminator
Demauro, Gino (act): Invitation To Hell
Demauro, Nick (act): Amazons (1984)
De Mejo, Carlo (act): The Dead Are Alive; Manhattan Baby
De Melo, Anais (act): Caveman (1981)
De Mendoza, Alberto (act): Horror Express; A Lizard In A Woman's Skin; Lo Strano Caso Della Signora Ward; Ten Little Indians (1974)
Demenno, Lou (act): The Resurrection Of Zachary Wheeler
Demeo, Angelo (act): Dead And Buried
Demeo, Paul (wri): Eliminators; The Flash; The Rocketeer; Trancers; Zone Troopers
Demerest, Rube (act): The Gracie Allen Murder Case
De Mering, David (act): Plan 9 From Outer Space
Demeritt, Matthew (act): Cyborg 2: Glass Shadow
Demetral, Chris (act): Sometimes They Come Back
Demetriou, Theodore (act): Electra (1961)
De Metz, Danielle (act): Duel At The Rio Grande; The Magic Sword (1962); Return Of The Fly; Valley Of The Dragons
Demicheli, Tulio (dir): The Cauldron Of Death
Demille, Cecil b. (act, 1881–1959): Sunset Boulevard
Demille, Cecil b. (dir, 1881–1959): Adam's Rib; Four Frightened People; Male And Female; The Road To Yesterday; Samson And Delilah
Demille, Don (act): Empire Of Ash III
Demille, Katherine (act, 1911–1995, nee Katherine Lester): The Black Room; Charlie Chan At The Olympics; Dark Street Of Cairo; Ellery Queen, Master Detective
Demin, Peter (act): The Adventures Of Robin Hood
Deming, Peter (cin): Joe's Apartment; Lost Highway; Martians Go Home
Deming, W.R. (act): Mr. Moto In Danger Island
Demita, John (act): Child Of Darkness, Child Of Light; Leprechaun 3; Spellbinder
Demitri, Ann (act): Appointment With Murder
Demme, Jonathan (act, b. 1944): The Incredible Melting Man
Demme, Jonathan (dir, b. 1944): Caged Heat!; Last Embrace; The Silence Of The Lambs
Demme, Jonathan (wri, b. 1944):Caged Heat!
Demmon, Chad (act): Attack Of The Killer Tomatoes
Demonaco, James (wri): Jack
Demond, Albert (wri, b. 1901): Blondes At Work; Captain Mephisto And The Transformation Machine; Cyclotrode X; The House Of (1931); Shock (1946); The Spanish Cape Mystery; The Sphinx (1933); Torchy Gets Her Man
Demongeot, Mylene (act, b. 1936): Fantomas Contro Scotland Yard; Gold For The Caesars; Oss 117-Mission For A Killer; Romulus And The Sabines; Les Sorcieres De Salem; Three Murderesses; Vengeance Of The Three Musketeers; What Price Murder
De Montenegro, Alejandro (act): The White Orchid
Demontmollin, Gabrielle (wri): The Music Of The Spheres
De Mora Y Aragon, Jaime (act): Las Cuatro Noches De La Luna Llena
De Mornay, Rebecca (act, b. 1961): The Hand That Rocks The Cradle; The Murders In The Rue Morgue (1986); Never Talk To Strangers; The Three Musketeers (1993)
De Moro, Pierre (dir): Hellhole
Demorton, Reggie (act): Alien Warrior
Demoss, Darcy (act): Friday The 13th, Part VI: Jason Lives; Return To Horror High
De Moye, Diane (act): The Alien's Return
De Moye, James (act): The Alien's Return
Dempsey, Clifford (act): The Ghost Talks
Dempsey, Lee (act): Alien High
Dempsey, Marion (act): Carousel
Dempsey, Mark (act): Valley Of The Dragons
Dempsey, Patrick (act): Bloodknot; Outbreak; 20,000 Leagues Under The Sea (1997, ABC-TV)
Dempster, Austin (cin): Bedazzled; Otley
Dempster, Camilla (act): A Connecticut Yankee In King Arthur's Court (1989)
Dempster, Carol (act, b. 1902): One Exciting Night; Sherlock Holmes (1922); The Sorrows Of Satan (1925)
Dempster, Hugh (act): Babes In Bagdad; Candles At Nine; The Curse Of Frankenstein; The Frightened Bride; The House Across The Lake; Paul Temple's Triumph; Scrooge (1951); Vice Versa (1947)
Demsky, Issur Danielovitch (act): see Douglas, Kirk
Demunn, Jeffrey (act): The Blob (1988); The Haunted (1991); The Hitcher; Phenomenon; Sanctuary Of Fear; Warning Sign
Demy, Jacques (dir & wri, 1931–1990): Les Parapluies De Cherbourg; Peau D'ane; The Pied Piper (1971)
De Naleche, Francoise Bandy (act): See Rosay, Francoise
De Nardo, Luca (act): Demons 2
De Nava, Giovanni (act): The House By The Cemetery
Demberg, Susan (act): Frankenstein Created Woman
Denbeigh-Russell, Grace (act): The Camp On Blood Island; Great Expectations (1946); The Intimate Stranger
Dench, Jeffery (act): First Knight
Dench, Judi (act, b. 1934): Goldeneye; A Study In Terror; The Third Secret
Deneuve, Catherine (act, b. 1943): Act Of Aggression; Belle De Jour; The Convent; The Hunger; Les Parapluies De Cherbourg; Peau D'ane; Repulsion; Tristana; Le Vice Et La Vertu
Denevi, Marco (wri): Secret Ceremony
Dengate, Dennis (act): Prehistoric Women (1950)
Denger, Fred (wri): Mark Of The Devil II
Denham, Maurice (act, b. 1909): The Alphabet Murders; Animal Farm; Countess Dracula; Danger Route; Downfall; Hysteria!; Miranda; The Nanny; Negatives; The Net; Night Caller From Outer Space; Night Of The Demon; Operation Crossbow; Paranoiac; Some Girls Do; The Spider And The Fly; Take My Life; Torture Garden; 23 Paces To Baker Street; The Very Edge
Denham, Reginald (dir): The Crimson Circle (1936); Death At Broadcasting House; The Silent Passenger
Denham, Reginald (wri) Ladies In Retirement; The Mad Room; Trunk Crime
Denier, Lydie (act): Red Blooded American Girl
De Niro, Robert (act, b. 1943): Angel Heart; Brazil; Cape Fear (1991); Mary Shelley's 'Frankenstein'
Denis, Burke (act): The Incredible Hulk Returns; Timestalkers
Denis, Prince (act, 1900–1984): Three Wise Fools; The Wizard Of Oz (1939)
Denise, Denise (act): Doctor Death: Seeker Of Souls
Denise, Gita (act): Dracula (1973)
Denisof, Alexis (act): First Knight
Denison, Anthony John (act): Child Of Darkness, Child Of Light; Full Eclipse
Denison, Jane (Act & Dir): All Clear: No Need To Take Cover
Denison, Leslie (act): Bulldog Drummond Strikes Back (1947); Charlie Chan In Rio; Counter-Espionage; Dangerous Money; The Feathered Serpent (1948); The Return Of The Vampire; The Snow Creature
Denison, Michael (act, b. 1915): Faces In The Dark; The Frightened Bride
Deniz, Umit (wri): Drakula Istanbulda
Denker, Henry (wri): The Only Way Out Is Dead
Denman, Phil (act): Werewolf Of Washington
Denman, Tony (act): Fargo
Dennae, Jerome L. (act): Neon Maniacs
Dennehy, Brian (act, b. 1939): Cocoon; Cocoon: The Return; It Happened At Lake Wood Manor
Dennen, Barry (act): The Dark Crystal; Madhouse; The Shining; Shock Treatment! (1981); Superman III
Denner, Charles (act, b. 1933): Landru; La Mariee Etait En Noir; The Night Caller
Dennes, Eileen (act): Alf's Button (1920); The Tinted Venus
Dennett, Peter (act): Night Of The Red Hunter
Denney, Dodo (act): Willy Wonka And The Chocolate Factory
Denney, Julie (act): Cat People (1982)
Denning, Richard (act, b. 1916, nee Louis A. Denninger): Beyond The Blue Horizon; The Black Scorpion; Creature From The Black Lagoon; Creature With The Atom Brain; Day The World Ended (1955); Girls In Prison; The Glass Web; The Gracie Allen Murder Case; Insurance Investigator; Lady At Midnight; Target Earth; Twice-Told Tales; Unknown Island
Denninger, Louis A. (act): see Denning, Richard
Dennis, Alfred (act): Demon Seed
Dennis, Charles (wri): The Thirsty Dead
Dennis, Fred (act): Amazons (1984)
Dennis, Gill (act): Eraserhead
Dennis, Gill (wri): Return To Oz
Dennis, John (act): Conquest Of Space; Conquest Of The Planet Of The Apes; Dead

Men Tell No Tales; Earthquake; End Of The World (1977); Garden Of The Dead; Psychic Killer; Soylent Green
Dennis, Judy (act): The Horror From Beyond
Dennis, Mark (act): The Millerson Case; Secret Beyond The Door; Targets
Dennis, Matt (act & mus): Jennifer (1953)
Dennis, Robert C. (wri): Terror In The Haunted House
Dennis, Sandy (act, 1937–1992): Demon (1976); Mr. Sycamore; 976-Evil; The Only Way Out Is Dead; Parents; Something Evil
Dennis, Winifred (act): Her Heritage
Dennis, Winston (act): The Adventures Of Baron Munchausen (1989); Brazil
Dennis-Leigh, Patrick (act): Doctor Death: Seeker Of Souls
Dennison, Jo Carroll (act): Prehistoric Women (1950)
Denny, Reginald (act, 1891–1967, nee Reginald Leigh Daymore): Abbott And Costello Meet Dr. Jekyll And Mr. Hyde; Around The World In 80 Days; Arrest Bulldog Drummond; Batman (1966); Bulldog Drummond Comes Back; Bulldog Drummond Escapes; Bulldog Drummond In Africa; Bulldog Drummond's Bride; Bulldog Drummond's Peril; Bulldog Drummond's Revenge; Bulldog Drummond's Secret Police; Crime Doctor's Strangest Case; Eyes In The Night; The Great Gambini; The Locket; The Lost Patrol (1934); Love Letters; Rebecca; Sabaka; Sherlock Holmes (1922); Sherlock Holmes And The Voice Of Terror
Denny, Susan (act): Tales From The Crypt
Denoble, Alphonso (act): Alice, Sweet Alice; Night Of The Zombies (1981)
Denormand, George (act): Dick Tracy (1937); The Falcon In Hollywood; The Underwater City
Denove, Thomas F. (cin): Puppet Master II
Densham, Nevin (act): The Kiss (1988)
Densham, Pat (dir): The Kiss (1988)
Densham, Pen (wri): Lifepod; Robin Hood: Prince Of Thieves
Dent, Lester (wri, a.k.a. Kenneth Robeson): Doc Savage, The Man Of Bronze
Dent, Vernon (act): The Lone Wolf Spy Hunt
Denton, Christa (act): The Bad Seed (1985); Explorers; The Gate
Denton, Donna (act): Slaughterhouse Rock
Denton, Geoffrey (act): Nothing But The Night
Denton, Jack (act): Flying From Justice; Old Bill Through The Ages; Scrooge (1923); She (1916)
Denton, Jack (dir): The Airman's Children; ; Lady Audley's Secret (1920)
Denton, Scot (act): The Gate
Denton-Thompson, J. (act): A Man's Shadow
De Nuccio, Lorie (act): Phoenix The Warrior
Denver, Bob (act, b. 1935): The Invisible Woman (1983)
Denver, John (act, b. 1943): Oh, God!
Denver, Tom (act): Sherlock Holmes In New York
Deodato, Ruggero (dir): Cannibal
De Oliveira, Lourdes (act): Black Orpheus
De Oliveira, Manoel (dir): The Convent
De Oliveira, Sergio (act): Curucu, Beast Of The Amazon
De Olivera, Isaura (act): The Blood Of Fu Manchu
De Orazal, J. (dir):El Castillo De Las Bofetadas
De Ossorio, Armando (dir): El Ataque De Los Muertos Sin Ojos; Demon Witch Child; Fangs Of The Living Dead; Horror Of The Zombies; Night Of The Seagulls; Night Of The Sorcerers; People Who Own The Dark; Tombs Of The Blind Dead; When The Screaming Stops
De Ossorio, Armando (wri): Horror Of The Zombies; Night Of The Seagulls; Night Of The Sorcerers; People Who Own The Dark; Tombs Of The Blind Dead; When The Screaming Stops
De Pablo, Luis (mus): Sound Of Horror
De Palma, Brian (dir, b. 1941): Blow Out; Body Double; Carrie; Dressed To Kill (1980); The Fury; Mission: Impossible; Obsession (1976); Phantom Of The Paradise; Raising Cain; Sisters
De Palma, Brian (wri, b. 1941): Blow Out; Body Double; Dressed To Kill (1980); Raising Cain; Sisters
De Palma, Cameron (act): Carrie
De Palma, Peter (act): The Jewel Of The Nile
Depardieu, Gerard (act, b. 1948): Bogus; Hamlet (1996); The Machine; The Man In The Iron Mask (1998); Secret Agent (1996)
Depardon, Raymond (dir & cin): La Captive Du Desert
Depatie, Beth (act): Leatherface: Texas Chainsaw Massacre III
De Paul, Gene (mus): Li'l Abner (1959)
De Pencier, Miranda (act): Alien High; Kurt Vonnegut's Harrison Bergeron
Depersia, Brian (act): Deadtime Stories
Depew, Hap (cin): The Black Pearl
Depietro, Robert (act): Street Trash
De Pinto, Joey (act): Full Eclipse
De Plata, Manitas (act): Caravan To Vaccares
De Poliakoff-Baidaroff, Marina (act): see Vlady, Marina
De Poliakoff-Baidarov, Militza (act): see Versois, Odile
De Poligny, Serge (dir): Le Baron Fantome; Gold (1934, French-Speaking Version)
De Poligny, Serge (wri): Le Baron Fantome
De Pomes, Felix (act): Parsifal; La Torre De Los Siete Jorobados
De Pomes, Isabel (act): The Man Who Wagged His Tail; La Torre De Los Siete Jorobados
De Ponti, Cinzia (act): Manhattan Baby
Depp, Harry (act): Black Magic (1944); Charlie Chan On Broadway; The Living Ghost (1942); The Lone Wolf Returns (1935)
Depp, Johnny (act, b. 1963): Edward Scissorhands; Ed Wood; A Nightmare On Elm Street
Deprume, Cathryn (act): Deadtime Stories
De Putti, Lya (act, 1901–1931): The Sorrows Of Satan (1925)
Depyer, Julia (act): Outland
De Querton, Beryl (act): Thark
Dequincey, Thomas (wri, 1785-1859): Confessions Of An Opium Eater; Histoires Extraordinaires
Der, Ricky (act): Tarzan's Three Challenges
Deragon, Lynne (act): Rabid
Deraita, Clif (act): The Fan
Derbyshire, Delia (mus): The Legend Of Hell House
Dercal, Colette (act):Cet Homme Est Dangereux
Dere, Charly (act): Making Contact
De Re, Michel (act): La Poupee
Dereham, Cecil (act): In The Days Of Robin Hood
Derek, Bo (act, b. 1957): Ghosts Can't Do It; Orca; Tarzan, The Ape Man (1981)
Derek, John (act, b. 1926, nee Derek Harris): The Adventures Of Hajji Baba; Mask Of The Avenger; Nightmare In The Sun; Omar Khayyam; Prince Of Pirates; Rogues Of Sherwood Forest
Derek, John (Dir & Cin, b. 1926): Ghosts Can't Do It; Tarzan, The Ape Man (1981)
Derek, John (wri, b. 1926):Ghosts Can't Do It
Deren, Bobby (act): The Exorcist III
Derevitsy, Alexander (mus): The Nights Of Lucretia Borgia
Deriane, Muna (act): Slaughterhouse Rock
De Ricci, Rona (act): The Pit And The Pendulum (1990)
De Riso, Arpad (act): Ercole Contro Roma; Goliath Against The Giants; Maciste E La Regina Di Samar; Marquis De Sade: Justine
Deriso, Tony (act): Flesh-Eating Mothers
De Rita, Joe (act): Have Rocket, Will Travel; Snow White And The Three Stooges; The Three Stooges In Orbit; The Three Stooges Meet Hercules
Derleth, August (wri, 1909–1971): The Shuttered Room
Derloshon, Jerry (wri): The Legend Of The Lone Ranger
Dermithe, Edouard (act): Les Enfants Terribles; Orphee; Le Testament D'orphee
Dern, Bruce (act, b. 1936): Black Sunday (1977); The 'Burbs; Castle Keep; Family Plot; Hush...Hush, Sweet Charlotte; The Incredible 2-Headed Transplant; Into The Badlands; Marnie; Mrs. Munck; Psych-Out; The St. Valentine's Day Massacre; Silent Running; Tattoo; The Trip; World Gone Wild
Dern, Laura (act, b. 1967): Blue Velvet; Haunted Summer; Jurassic Park
Dernier, Lydie (act): Blood Relations
De Rochbrune, Jean (act): see Sorel, Jean
Deroche, Chris (wri): The Day After Halloween
Deroche, Everett (wri): The Day After Halloween; Harlequin; Link; Patrick; Razorback; Road Games
De Rodas, Lorenzo (act): Survive!
Derogatis, Al (act): Heaven Can Wait (1978)
De Rosa, Chiqui (act): The Thirsty Dead
Derosa, Franco (act): Doppelganger; Return From The Ashes
Derosa, Justin (act): Beyond The Poseidon Adventure
Derose, Chris (act): The Man Who Fell To Earth (1987)
De Rosa, [illegible] (act): What's The Matter With Helen?
De Rossi, Alberto (wri): Maciste Alla Corte Della Zar
Derossi, Gianetto (cin): The Living Dead At Manchester Morgue
De Rossi, Gino (cin): Burial Ground; Exterminators Of The Year 3000
De Roubiax, Francois (mus): Daughters Of Darkness
De Rouen, Reed (act): Billion Dollar Brain; The Hand (1960); Lady In The Fog; Murder At Site Three
Derouin, Colin (act): Street Trash
Deroy, Richard (wri): A Howling In The Woods
Derr, Celia (act): Phantom Of The Paradise
Derr, Richard (act, 1917–1992): Castle In The Desert; Charlie Chan In Rio; The Invisible Avenger; Just Off Broadway; The Man Who Wouldn't Die; Terror Is A Man; When Worlds Collide
Derrick, William (act): Mark Of The Devil (1985)
Derringer, William (act): The Dark (1979)
Derry, Kim (cin): Nothing But Trouble
De Ruiz, Nick (act): The Altar Stairs; The Hunchback Of Notre Dame (1923); The Man Who Laughs (1928); The Unknown (1927)
Derval, Jacqueline (act): Il Planeta Degli Uomini Spenti
Derval, Lamya (act): Hellhole; Howling IV
Derwent, Clarence (act): Fetters Of Fear
De S. Wentworth James, Gertie (wri): The Devil's Profession
De Sabata, Eliana (wri): La Ragazza Che Sapeva Troppo
De Sade, Ana (act): Caveman (1981); Sorceress
De Sade, Marquis (wri, 1740-1814): Le Vice Et La Vertu
Desai, Shelly (act): Project X (1987); The Silence Of The Hams
Desailly, Jean (act, b. 1920): Le Saint Mene La Dance
De Saint-Colombe, Paul (wri): Secret Lives
De Saint-Exupery, Antoine (wri): The Little Prince
De Santis, Dina (act): Giant Of Evil Island
Desantis, Gino (wri): Atom Age Vampire
Desantis, Joe (act, 1909–1989): The Last Hunt; The Man With A Cloak; The Venetian Affair
De Santis, Pasqualino (cin, b. 1927): Sheena
Desantis, Stanley (act): Ed Wood
Desantis, Tony (act): Short Circuit 2
De Sapio, Francesca (act): Top Secret (1978)
De Satti, Alan (act): Philadelphia Experiment II
De Savitch, Igor (act): Notorious (1992)
De Sax, Guillaume (act): La Main Du Diable
Desbarates, Gabrielle (act): The Mutagen
Des Barres, Michael (act): Deep Red (1994); Ghoulies; Nightflyers; Silk Degrees; Waxwork II: Lost In Time
Desbordes, Jean (act): Le Sang D'un Poete
Desborough, Clifford (act): The English Rose
Desborough, Philip (act): Blake The Lawbreaker
Desbrow, Audie (act): Maid To Order
Des Cars, Guy (wri): The Green Scarf
Deschamps, Hubert (act): Le Trio Infernal
Deschenes, Manon (act): Dr. Jekyll And Ms. Hyde
De Schepper, Luc (act): Ed Wood
Descher, Sandy (act): It Grows On Trees; The Space Children; Them! (1954)
Descombes, Collette (act): Orgasmo
De Segurola, Andres (act): Il Cuerpo Del Lito
Desert, Alex (act): The Flash
Desfassiaux, Maurice (cin): Paris Qui Dort
Deshales, Marc (act): A Nymphoid Barbarian In Dinosaur Hell
Deshields, Andre (act): I Dream Of Jeannie: Fifteen Years Later; Prison (1988)
De Sica, Vittorio (act, 1901–1974): Dracula (1974); The Wonders Of Aladdin
De Sica, Vittorio (dir, 1901–1974): Miracle In Milan
Desiderio, Robert (act): Oh, God! You Devil; Once You Meet A Stranger
Desimone, John (act): Missile Monsters
De Simone, Tom (dir): Hell Night
Deslauriers, Nicole (act): Marathon Man
Des Ligneris, Francois (wri): Psyche 59
Deslys, Kay (act): The Leopard Lady
Desmarestz, Erick (act): The Murders In The Rue Morgue (1986)
Desmond, Eric (act): The Bridge Destroyer; The Magic Glass; A Price On His Head
Desmond, Florence (act): The River House Ghost; Some Girls Do
Desmond, John (dir): Castle Rock
Desmond, Johnny (act, 1920–1985): The Bubble
Desmond, Patrick (act): Fury At Smugglers' Bay
Desmond, Roy (act): Macbeth (1971)
Desmond, Shaun (act):The Scarab Murder Case
Desmond, Shaw (act): Haunted Palace (1949)
Desmond, Will (act): The Dumb Man Of Manchester
Desmond, William (act): The Clutching Hand
Desmonde, Jerry (act, 1908–1967): The Angel Who Pawned Her Harp; The Perfect Woman
Desni, Tamara (act, b. 1913): Dark World; Dick Barton At Bay; The Hills Of Donegal; The Squeaker (1937)
Desny, Ivan (act, b. 1922): The Becket Affair; I Killed Rasputin; The Invisible Terror; Lola Montes; The Mystery Of Thug Island; Number Six; Who?
De Solla, Marie (act): Gipsy Nan; Justice; The Tragedy Of Basil Grieve
De Solla, Rachel (act): Creatures Of Clay; In The Toils Of The Blackmailer; Jane Shore (1915); The Shuttle Of Life
Desoto, Alfredo (act): The Killer Shrews
Desoto, Rosana (act): Star Trek VI: The Undiscovered Country
De Souza, Edward (act, b. 1933):Kiss Of The Vampire; The Phantom Of The Opera (1962); Spell Of Evil; The Spy Who Loved Me; The 39 Steps (1978); Those Fantastic Flying Fools
De Souza, Noel (act):The Man With The Power
De Souza, Ruth (act): Macumba Love
De Souza, Steven (E.) (wri): The Flintstones; Judge Dredd; The Running Man; The Spirit
Despotovich, Nada (act): The First Power
Dessinees, Bandes (cin): The Killing Game
Dest, Jo (act): Le Salaire De La Peur
Desteffani, Joseph (act): The Man They Could Not Hang
D'esterre, Mme. (act): Abide With Me; Bluff; The Hound Of The Baskervilles (1921); The Sign Of Four (1923)
D'esterre, Lisa (act): Knight Without Armour
Destri, Robert (act): Psycho II
Destry, John (act): Memories Of Murder
De Sue, Joe (act): Blackenstein
Desy, Victor (act): Oh Heavenly Dog; Rabid; Scanners
Desylva, Brown & Henderson (wri): Just Imagine
De Sylva, Marcia (wri): Elephant Boy
De Tejada, Luis (act): Satanik; Lo Strano Caso Della Signora Ward
Deters, Tom (act): Vampirella (1996)
De Terville, Gillian (act): Octopussy
De Titta, Arthur (cin): The Sorrows Of Satan (1925)
De Toth, Andre (dir, b. 1910): Dark Waters; Gold For The Caesars; House Of Wax; Morgan The Pirate; Passport To Suez; Pitfall; The 2-Headed Spy
De Toth, Andre (wri, b. 1910): Morgan The Pirate
Detoth, Nicolas (act): The Invisible Kid
De Treaux, Tamara (act): Ghoulies
Detrick, Bruce (act): Invasion Of The Blood Farmers
De Troyes, Chretien (wri): Perceval
D'ettorre, Roberto (cin): Star Crash
Detweiler, Amanda (act): Nightmare Sisters
Deus, Beni(act): Operation Atlantis
Deutsch, A.J. (wri): Moebius
Deutsch, Adolph (mus, 1897–1980): The Maltese Falcon (1941); The Mask Of Dimitrios; Three Strangers; Whispering Smith
Deutsch, Ernst (act, 1890–1969): The Golem: How He Came Into The World; The Third Man
Deutsch, Helen (wri, 1906–1992): The Glass Slipper; Golden Earrings; King Solomon's Mines (1949)
Deutsch, Kurt (act): Nothing But The Truth
Deutsch, Ron (act): Zapped!
Deutschendorf, Hank (act): Ghostbusters II
Deutschendorf, Will (act): Ghostbusters II
De Valvert, Isabelle (act): The Count Of Monte Cristo (1975)
Devane, Joshua (act): Timestalkers
Devane, William (act, b. 1939): The Dark (1979); Family Plot; Marathon Man; Red Alert; Timestalkers
Devaney, Richie (act): Mr. Destiny
Devant, David (act): D. Devant, Conjurer; The Egg-Laying Man; The Mysterious Rabbit
Devarona, Joanna (act): A*P*E
Devasquez, Devin (act): House II: The Second Story
Devaul, Ken (act): Edward Scissorhands
Deveau, Robert (act): Raiders Of The Living Dead
[illegible]
Deveaux, Nathaniel (act): Color Me Perfect; Unforgettable

De Velasco, Mercedes (act): Behind That Curtain
Devenie, Stuart (act): The Frighteners
Devenish, Myrtle (act): Brazil; Time Bandits
Devenney, Scott (act): Copycat; Time Flyer
Deveraux, William (wri): The Lifeguardsman
De Verdi, Chisco (act): The Wolf Man (1941)
De Vere, Harry (act): The Altar Stairs; The Shock (1923)
De Vere, Horace (act): Bulldog Drummond (1923)
Devereau, Audrey (act): The Brain That Wouldn't Die
Devereaux, Helen (act): The Scarlet Clue
Devereaux, Jan (act): Death Dreams
Devereaux, Marie (act): Brides Of Dracula; The Pirates Of Blood River; The Stranglers Of Bombay
Devereaux, Rex (mus): New Year's Evil
Deverell, John (act): Alibi (1931)
De Vernier, Hugo (act): Tales From The Crypt
Devestel, Guy (act): To Catch A Thief
Devi Dja And Her Balinese Dancers (act): The Picture Of Dorian Gray (1945)
Devi, Chitra (act): The Jungle
Devi, Kamala (act): The Brass Bottle (1964)
De Victor, Claudio (act): Unforgettable
De Villalonga, Jose (act): Giulietta Degli Spiriti
Deville, Paul R. (act): Moon Of The Wolf
De Vilmorin, Louise (wri): The Secret Of Magic Island
Devine, Andy (act, 1905–1977, nee Jeremiah Schwartz): Ali Baba And The Forty Thieves (1943); Around The World In 80 Days; Ghost Catchers; The Gift Of Gab; Myra Breckinridge; Sudan
Devine, J. Llewellyn (wri): The Gorgon
De Vine, Janet (act): Just Imagine
Devine, Jerry (act): Sherlock Holmes (1922)
Devine, Loretta (act): The Preacher's Wife
Devink, Darline (act): Empire Of Ash III
Devinna, Clyde (Cin, 1892-1953): The Jungle; Tarzan And His Mate; Tarzan's Secret Treasure
Devis, Pamela (act): The Perfect Woman
Devito, Danny (act, b. 1944): Batman Returns; Hercules (1997); The Jewel Of The Nile; Junior; Mars Attacks!; Romancing The Stone; Space Jam
Devlin (act): Return Of The Killer Tomatoes
Devlin, Cory (act): 12 To The Moon
Devlin, Dean (act): Moon 44
Devlin, Dean (wri): Independence Day; Stargate; Universal Soldier
Devlin, Don (act): Anatomy Of A Psycho; Blood Of Dracula
Devlin, Frank (act): Flesh-Eating Mothers
Devlin, J.G. (act): Attempt To Kill; Darby O'gill And The Little People
Devlin, Joe (act): Another Thin Man; Boston Blackie's Rendezvous; The Devil Checks Up; The Shanghai Cobra; Torchy Runs For Mayor; Up In Smoke
Devlin, Terrence (act): Street Trash
Devlin, Tony (act): Prehistoric Women (1950)
Devlin, William (act, 1911–1987): Blood Of The Vampire; I Met A Murderer; The Shuttered Room; Treasure Island (1950)
De V Marais, Marc (wri): House Of The Living Dead
Devnarian, Jack (act): The Ghost And The Darkness
Devo (mus): Heavy Metal; Slaughterhouse Rock
De Voe, Theo (act): Just Imagine
De Vogt, Carl (act): Die Spinnen
De Vol, (Frank) (mus): Hush...Hush, Sweet Charlotte; What Ever Happened To Baby Jane? (1962)
Devol, Gordon (act): A Reflection Of Fear
Devon, Laura (act, b. 1939): Chamber Of Horrors (1966); Goodbye Charlie
Devon, Richard (act): Blood Of Dracula; The Silencers (1966); Treachery And Greed On The Planet Of The Apes; The Undead; The Viking Women And The Sea Serpent; War Of The Satellites
De Vonde, Chester (wri): Kongo; West Of Zanzibar
Devonshire, Felicity (act): Liszt O' Mania
De Vore, Christopher (wri): Hamlet (1990)
Devorzon, Barry (mus): The Exorcist III; Jekyll And Hyde...Together Again; Looker; Night Of The Creeps; Tattoo; Xanadu
Devoto, Juan Antonio (act): When The Bough Breaks
Devries, David (act): King Kong Lives
Devries, Diana (act): Class Of Nuke'em High
Devries, George (act): Around The World Under The Sea; Mission Mars
De Vries, Hans (act): Billion Dollar Brain
De Vries, Henri (act): Murder At Covent Garden; Paste; The Scarab Murder Case; Strange Experiment
Devrim, Shirin (act): Wolf
Devry, Elaine (act): The Boy Who Cried Werewolf; Diary Of A Madman
De Vylars, Celia (wri): The Medium (1934)
Dew, Edward (act): The Adventures Of Robin Hood
Dew, Edward (dir): The Naked Gun
Dew, Rod (acr): Mutants In Paradise
Dewar, Ian (act): The Satanic Rites Of Dracula
Dewey-Carter, John (act): Beyond The Universe; Buck Rogers In The 25th Century
Dewhurst, Colleen (act, 1926-1991): The Boy Who Could Fly; The Dead Zone; When A Stranger Calls
Dewhurst, George (act): The Crimson Circle (1922); The Tinted Venus
Dewhurst, George (dir & wri): The Shadow Between
Dewhurst William (act): Bulldog Drummond At Bay (1937); Dark Journey; Sabotage
de Winter, Arion (act): Cat People (1982)
deWinter, Jo(hanna) (act): Planet Earth; Poor Devil
de Winton, Alice (act): Creatures Of Clay; The Dead Heart; The Fairy Doll; the Guest Of The Evening; The Sorrows Of Satan (1917); A Vagabond's Revenge; The Woman Of The Iron Bracelets
de Winton, Dora (act): The Chinese Puzzle; The House Opposite (1917); Jane Shore (1915); Wuthering Heights (1920)
Dewit, Alan (act): Tales Of Terror
de Wit, Jacqueline (act): Black Magic (1944); Fog Island; The Lone Wolf in Mexico; The Snake Pit (1948)
de Witt, Jack (wri, b. 1900): Bomba, The Jungle Boy; Cell 2455, Death Row; the Lost Volcano; The Neptune Factor
DeWitt, James (act): Invasion Of The Girl Snatchers
DeWitt, Louis (cin): Back From The Dead; The Beast Of Hollow Mountain; Behemoth, The Sea Monster; Daughter Of Dr. Jekyll; The Night Of The Hunter (1955); The Phantom Planet; Pharaoh's Curse; The Unknown Terror; The Viking Women And The Sea Serpent
DeWolfe (mus): Horror Hospital; Jabberwocky; Robin Hood Junior (1975)
de Wolfe, Karen (wri): Condemned To Live
De Wolff, Francis (act): Black Torment; Clue Of The Twisted Candle; Devil Doll (1963); The Diamond; Doctor Of Seven Dials; From Russia With Love; The Hound Of The Baskervilles (1959); Licensed To Kill; The Man who Could Cheat Death; Moby Dick (1956); Scrooge (1951); Siege Of The Saxons; The Three Lives Of Thomasina; Treasure Island (1950); The Two Faces Of Dr. Jekyll; Under Capricorn
DeWoody, Crystal (act): Amazons (1984)
Dewsbury, Ralph (dir): The Golden Dawn; The Lion's CubS; The Man In Motley; The Man In ThE Attic (1915); Paste; Whoso Diggeth A Pit
Dexter, Alan (act): I Married A Monster From Outer Space; It Came from Outer Space
Dexter, Anthony (act, b. 1919, nee Walter Reinhold Alfred FleischmaNn): The Black Pirates; Capt. John Smith And Pocahontas; Captain Kidd And The Slave Girl; Fire Maidens Of Outer Space; The Phantom Planet; The Story Of Mankind
Dexter, Aubrey (act): Rich And Strange
Dexter, Brad (act, b. 1922): Johnny Cool; X-15
Dexter, Elliott (act, 1870-1941): Adam's Rib
Dexter, John William (mus): Dream A Little Dream
Dexter, Maury (dir, b. 1927): The Day Mars Invaded Earth; House Of The Damned (1962)
Dexter, Pete (wri): Michael
Dexter, Rosemary (act): Vendetta For The Saint
Dexter, Tony (act): 12 To The Moon
Dexter, Von (mus): House On Haunted Hill; Mr. Sardonicus; 13 Ghosts; The Tingler
Dexter, William (GB act): Death Is A Woman; The Hand Of Night; Spell Of Evil
Dexter, William (USA act): The Capture Of Bigfoot
Dey, Janet (act): Dr. Black Mr. Hyde; Laserblast
Dey, Susan (act, b. 1952): Bridge Of Time; Deadly Love; Looker; Terror On the Beach
de Yonson, Carlotta (act): The Kidnapped King
De Young, Cliff (act, b. 1945): The Awakening Of Candra; Carnosaur 2; The Craft; dr. Giggles; Flight Of The Navigator; The Hunger; Immortal Sins; Love Can Be Murder; The Night that Panicked America; Pulse; Shock Treatment! (1981)
de Young, Eric (act): Surf Nazis Must Die
DeYoung, June (act): The Toxic Avenger
de Zarn, Tim (act): Demon Knight; Running Against Time
Dheran, Bernard (act): Le Comte De Monte Cristo
Dhiegh, Khigh (act, 1910-1991): The Destructors; The Manchurian Candidate; The Mephisto Waltz; Seconds; 13 Frightened Girls
Diablo, John (act): Empire Of Ash III
Diak, Rodney (act): Fire Maidens Of Outer Space; The Flesh And Blood Show
Diakun, Alex (act): Friday The 13th, Part VIII-Jason Takes Manhattan
Dialina, Rika (act): I Tre Volti Della Paura
Diamant, Otto (act): Liszt O' Mania
Diamond, Arnold (act): The Anniversary; The Final Conflict; Frankenstein: The True Story; The Golden Mask; The Hands Of Orlac (1959); Madame Sin; Maniac (1963); Paranoiac; Return From The Ashes; The Revenge Of Frankenstein; The Thief Of Baghdad (1978); Venom (1982); Zeppelin
Diamond, Barry (act): Heartbeeps
Diamond, David (wri): The Adventurous Blonde
Diamond, Don (act): The Kid With The Broken Halo
Diamond, Harold (act): Spellbinder
Diamond, I.A.L. (wri, 1920-1988): Monkey Business; The Private Life Of Sherlock Holmes
Diamond, Jack (act): Terror From The Year 5,000
Diamond, James (cin): The Drums Of Jeopardy (1923); Jane Eyre (1921)
Diamond, Judi (act): Bram Stoker's 'Dracula'
Diamond, Keith (act): Dr. Giggles
Diamond, Marcia (act): Deranged (1974)
Diamond, Marion (act): Not Guilty; Subterfuge
Diamond, Peter (act): Highlander; Zorro: The Legend Begins
Diamond, Rick (act): The Hidden
Diamond, Ron (act): Cat People (1982)
Diamond, Selma (act, 1920-1985): All Of Me; Twilight Zone
Diamond, T.C. (act): Earth Girls Are Easy
Diamont, Sherry (act): Making Mr. Right
Diana Nellis Dancers, The (act): She Demons
DiAngelo, Rick (act): The Clonus Horror
DiAquino, John (act): Pumpkinhead
Di Aragon, Maria (act): The Cremators
Diaz, Cameron (act, b. 1972): Head Above Water; The Mask (1994)
Diaz, Eliezer (act): Street Trash
Diaz, Guillermo (act): Freeway
Diaz, Vic (act): Beast Of The Yellow Night; Beyond Atlantis; Daughters Of Satan; Equalizer 2000
Dibble, Daphne (act): Jaws 2
Dibbs, Arthur (act): We Do Believe In Ghosts
Dibbs, Kem (act): Omar Khayyam; Riders To The Stars
Dibdin-Pitt, George (wri): The Demon Barber Of Fleet Street
di Benedetti, Aldo (wri): Shadow Of The Past
Di Benedetto, Gianni (act): La Ragazza Che Sapeva Troppo
Di Benedetto, Tony (act): Splash
Dibley, Mary (act): The Bargain; Shadow Of Evil (1921); The Silver Greyhound (1919); Who So Diggeth A Pit
Dibos, Corinne (act): see Calvet, Corinne
DiCagno, Charles (act): The Toxic Avenger
DiCandia, Denise (act): The Edge Of Hell
DiCaprio, Leonardo (act): The Man In The Iron Mask (1998)
Di Centa, Erika (act): L'ultima Preda Del Vampiro
DiCenzo, George (act): Close Encounters Of The Third Kind; The Exorcist III; Starflight: The Plane That Couldn't Land
DiCicco, Bobby (act): The Baby Doll Murders; The Philadelphia Experiment; Splash; Wavelength
Dick, Danny (act): The Dungeonmaster
Dick, Douglas (act): The Accused; Rope
Dick, Gina (act): Happy Birthday To Me; My Bloody Valentine
Dick, Keith Joe (act): Ghoulies; Maid To Order
Dick, Michael (wri): Bad Dreams
Dick, Peter (mus): Shock Chamber
Dick, Philip K. (wri, 1928-1982): Blade Runner; Screamers (1996); Total Recall
Dick, R.A. (wri): The Ghost And Mrs. Muir
Dicken, Roger (cin): The Land That Time Forgot; Scars of Dracula; Warlords Of The Deep
Dickens, Charles (wri, 1812-1870): An American Christmas Carol; The Chimes; A Christmas Carol (1914, 1938, 1982 & 1984); Ebbie; Gabriel Grubb The Surly Sexton; Great Expectations (1934, 1946 & 1974); The Mystery Of Edwin Drood (1909 & 1935); Scrooge (1913, 1922, 1923, 1928, 1935, 1951 & 1970); Scrooge: or, Marley's Ghost; Scrooged
Dickens, Joanna (act): Morons From Outer Space
Dickens, Stafford (wri): The Vulture (1937)
Dickensen, Carl (act): Teenagers From Outer Space
Dickenson, Bikk (cin): The Crater Lake Monster
Dickenson, Ron E. (act): Slaughterhouse Rock
Dickerson, Beech (act): Attack Of The Crab Monsters; Bury Me An Angel; Creature From The Haunted Sea; The Dunwich Horror; School Spirit; Shell Shock; Teenage Cave Man; War Of The Satellites
Dickerson, Dan (act): The Initiation
Dickerson, Dudley (act): Dangerous Money; Torchy Plays With Dynamite
Dickerson, Ernest (R.) (cin): The Brother From Another Planet; Def By Temptation
Dickerson, Ernest (R.) (dir): Demon Knight
Dickerson, George (act): Blue Velvet; Death Dreams; Psycho II; Space Raiders
Dickey, Basil (wri): Captain Mephisto And The Transformation Machine; Cyclotrode X; The Deadly Ray From Mars; Peril From The Planet Mongo; The Phantom Creeps; Purple DeatH From Outer Space
Dickey, Candace (act): Blood Song
Dickey, Paul (act): Robin Hood (1922)
Dickey, Paul (wri): Scared Stiff (1953)
Dickie, Olga (act): Horror Of Dracula; Kiss Of The Vampire; The Spaniard's Curse
Dickinson, Angie (act, b. 1932): Charlie Chan And The Curse Of The Dragon Queen; Cry Terror!; Dial M For Murder (1981); Dressed To KilL (1980); The Love War; The Maddening; The Norliss Tapes; The Resurrection Of Zachary Wheeler
Dickenson, Desmond (cin, b. 1902): The Alphabet Murders; Are You Dying Young Man?; Berserk; Burke And Hare; City Of The Dead; The Fiend (1972); Hamlet (1948); The Hands Of Orlac (1959); Horrors Of The Black Museum; Konga; the Man From Nowhere; Meet Mr. Lucifer; The Net; the Rocking Horse Winner; A Study In Terror; Tower of Evil; Trog; Who Slew Auntie Roo?
Dickinson, Dick (act): House Of Frankenstein
Dickinson, Sandra (act): The Last Days Of Man On Earth; Supergirl (1984); Superman III
Dickinson, Thorold (dir, b. 1903): Gaslight (1940); The Queen Of Spades (1948)
Dickman, Robert (act): Popcorn
Dickson, Bill(y) (cin): Grotesque; Halloween: The Curse Of Michael Myers; Tainted Blood
Dickson, Brenda (act): The Deathmaster
Dickson, Gloria (act): Crime Doctor's Strangest Case; Lady Of Burlesque
Dickson, Hugh (act): Deathline
Dickson, Neil (act, b. 1956): Biggles: Adventures In Time; A Ghost In Monte Carlo; The Murders In The Rue Morgue (1986)
Dickson, Ngila (act): Strange Behavior
Dickson, Paul (act): A Woman Of Mystery
Dickson, Paul (dir, b. 1920): Satellite In The Sky
Di Clemente, Giovanni (wri): Conquest
Di Cola, Emanuele (cin): Scream Of The Demon Lover
DiDio Jr., Tony (cin): Dawn Of The Mummy
Di Donato, Mario (act): Seven
Diedrich, Robert (act): Blood Song
Diehl, Carl Ludwig (act): On Secret Service
Diehl, John (act): The Dark Side Of The Moon; The Grave; Stargate; Wes Craven Presents Mind Ripper
Diehl, William (wri): Primal Fear
DiElsi, Frank (act): I'm Dangerous Tonight; When A Stranger Calls
Diener, Arpad (act): I Aim At The Stars
Dierkes, John (act, b. 1906): Abbott And Costello Meet Dr. Jekyll And Mr. Hyde; Daughter Of Dr. Jekyll; The Haunted Palace (1963); Macbeth (1947); Les Miserables (1952); The Naked Jungle; The Premature Burial; Prince Valiant; X— The Man With The X-Ray Eyes
Dierkop, Charles (act): Grotesque; Silent Night, Deadly Night
Diesl, Gustav (act): Das Testament Des Dr. Mabuse
Diestel, George (act): Attack Of The Killer Tomatoes
Dieterle, Wilhelm/William (act, 1893-1972): Faust (1926); Lucrezia Borgia (1922); Das Wachsfigurenkabinett
Dieterle, William (dir, 1893-1972): The Accused; All That Money Can Buy; The Hunchback Of Notre Dame (1939); Kismet (1944); Love Letters; Madame Dubarry

(1934); A Midsummer Night's Dream (1935); Mistress Of the World (1959); Omar Khayyam; Peking Express; Portrait Of Jennie; Salome (1953); Satan Met A lady
Dietlein, Marsha (act): Return Of The Living Dead, Part II
Dietrich, Dena (act): The Strange And Deadly Occurrence
Dietrich, Marc (act): Silent Night, Deadly Night III
Dietrich, Marlene (act, 1902-1992, nee Maria Magdalena Dietrich von Losch): Around The World In 80 Days; Golden Earrings; Kismet (1944); Knight Without Armour; Paris When It Sizzles; Shanghai Express; Stage Fright; Witness For The Prosecution
Dietz, Eileen (act): The Clonus Horror
Dietz, Frank (act): Black Roses; The Edge Of Hell; Zombie Nightmare
Dietze, Max (act): Metropolis (1926)
Dieudonne, Albert (act): La Folie Du Docteur Tube
DiFalco, Marcello (act): Amarcord; Satyricon
Diffenderfer, Craig (act): Monolith
Diffring, Anton (act, b. 1918): The Accursed; The Beast Must Die; Call Him Mr. Shatter; Circus Of Horrors; The Double Man; Fahrenheit 451; Incident At Midnight; Lady Of Vengeance; The Man Who Could Cheat Death; Mark Of The Devil II; Mark Of The Phoenix; Operation Crossbow; The Savage Curse; Seven Deaths In The Cat's Eye; Seven Thunders; State Secret; Zeppelin
Digges, Dudley (act, 1879-1947): Before Dawn; Condemned; House of Menace; The Invisible Man (1933); The Maltese Falcon (1931); Outward Bound
Diggle, Tim (act): Jekyll And Hyde
Diggs, Andrew (act): I Was A Zombie For The F.B.I.
Dightam, Mark (act): Macbeth (1971)
Dighton, John (wri, b. 1909): The Ghost At St. Michael's; Kind Hearts And Coronets; The Man In The White Suit
DiGiacomo, Franco (cin): Amityville II: The Possession; When Women Had Tails
di Gianni, Enzo (dir): The Violence Of Desire
DiGioila, Doug (act): Premonition (1972)
DiGiovanni, Gastone (cin): The Night Evelyn Came Out Of The Grave
Digital Domain (cin): Apollo 13; Strange Days
Dignam, Arthur (act): Strange Behavior; Those Dear Departed
Dignam, Basil (act, b. 1909): Doctor Of Seven Dials; Gorgo; The Intimate Stranger; Life For Ruth; Naked Evil; The Spaniard's Curse; The Spider's Web; 10 Rillington Place; They Can't Hang Me; Where The Spies Are
Dignam, Mark (act, b. 1907): The Boy Who Turned Yellow; Clash By Night; The Eyes Of Annie Jones; Hamlet (1969); Lancelot And Guinevere; Memoirs Of A Survivor; Siege Of The Saxons
Dignam, Rebecca (act): The Damned
Dignard, Paul (act): Empire Of Ash III
Dignon, Edward (act): Sexton Blake And The Bearded Doctor; Someone at the Door
Dijon, Alain (act): Assignment-Outer Space; The Invisible Dr. Mabuse; The Testament Of Dr. Mabuse (1960)
Dikker, Loek (mus): Body Parts
Di Lazzaro, Dalila (act): Frankenstein (1974); Phenomena
DiLeo, Antone (act): Day Of The Dead
Di Leo, Fernando (dir & wri): Slaughter Hotel (1972)
DiLeo, Mario (cin): Alfred Hitchcock Presents; The Evil; The Loves of Dracula; Nightmares (1983); 2000 Years Later; World Of Dracula
Dilian, Irasema (act): Cumbres Borrascosas
Dill, Kevin (act): The Ivory Ape
Dill, Sherry (act): Vampire On Bikini Beach
Dill, William (cin): Jason Goes To Hell: The Final Friday; Mantis; Pumpkinhead II: Blood Wings
Dillane, Stephen (act): Hamlet (1990)
Dillard, Alan (act): Miracle Mile
Dillard, Mimi (act): The Immortal
Diller, Phyllis (act, b. 1917): The Adding Machine; Dr. Hackenstein; The Fat Spy; Mad Monster Party; The Silence Of The Hams
Dillinger, Chris (act): Moonraker
Dillman, Bradford (act, b. 1930): Adventures Of The Queen; Bug; Chosen Survivors; Covenant; Deborah; The Disappearance Of Flight 412; Escape From The Planet Of The Apes; The Eyes of Charles Sand; Fear No Evil (1969); Guyana, Cult oF The Damned; The Helicopter Spies; Last Bride Of Salem; Look Back In Darkness; Lords Of The Deep; the Memory Of Eva Ryker; The Mephisto Waltz; Monstrosity; Moon Of The Wolf; 99 And 44/100% Dead; Piranha (1978); The Resurrection Of Zachary Wheeler; Revenge (1971, Usa); The Swarm
Dillman Jr., Dean (wri): Monstrosity
Dillon, Basil (wri): The Dark Stairway
Dillon, Brendan (act): Bug; The Hound Of The Baskervilles (1972); The Island At The Top Of The World; The Premature Burial; The Vampire (1979
Dillon, C.J. "Clark" (act): Attack Of The Killer Tomatoes; Return Of The Killer Tomatoes
Dillon, Constantine (wri): Return Of The Killer Tomatoes
Dillon, Costa (wri): Attack Of The Killer Tomatoes
Dillon, Edward (dir): The Drums Of Jeopardy (1923)
Dillon, Efemia (act): Attack Of The Killer Tomatoes
Dillon, George (act): I'm An Explosive
Dillon, John Francis (dir): Behind The Mask (1932); Kismet (1930)
Dillon, John Webb (act): The House Without A Key; Jane EyRE (1921)
Dillon, Kevin (act, b. 1965): The Blob (1988); No Escape (1994); Remote Control (1988)
Dillon, Maria (act): Trick Or Treats
Dillon, Melinda (act, b. 1939): Captain America (1992); Close Encounters Of The Third Kind; Harry And The Hendersons
Dillon, Oscar (act): Magic Island
Dillon, Patricia (act): Torture Dungeon
Dillon, Paul (act): Blink
Dillon, Robert (wri): The Lost City; 99 And 44/100% Dead; The Old Dark House (1963); 13 Frightened Girls; X—The Man With The X-Ray Eyes
Dillon, Tom (act): Night Tide
Dills-Vozoff, Lorinne (act): Heart And Souls
Di Lorenzo, Edward (wri): La Figlia Di Frankenstein
Dilson, John (act): Dick Tracy (1937); Dick Tracy vs. Crime, Inc.; Man-Made Monster; ThE Man With Nine Lives; Phantom Of Chinatown; Shadow Of The Thin Man
Di Luia, Bruno (act): The Eyes Behind The Stars
Dilullio, Ron (mus): Mountaintop Motel Massacre
Dilworth, Carol (act): The Haunted House Of Horror
Dilworth, Gabriel (act): Mad Max Beyond Thunderdome
Di Maggio, Ross (mus): The Man Who Turned To Stone; The Night The World Exploded
DiMarco, Steve (dir & wri): Shock Chamber
Di Mario, Raffaele (act): Deborah
Di Mascio, Angelo (act): Ghostbusters II
Dimbleby, Richard (act): The Twenty Questions Murder
Di Milo, Cardella (act): Blackenstein
Di Mino, James (act): The Dungeonmaster
Dimitri, Nick (act): Forgotten City Of The Planet Of The Apes; The Norliss Tapes
Dimitri, Richard (act): Human Feelings
Dimitriou, Theodore (act): Atlas
Dimitrova, Yelena (act): The Savage Hunt Of King Stakh
Dimmick, Walter (act): Squirm
Dimon, Elizabeth (act): Matinee
Dimond, A.S. (mus): The Goddess Of Love
Dimopoulos, Stephen (act): The Little Match Girl (1987)
Dimsdale, Howard (wri): Abbott And Costello Meet Captain Kidd; The Living Ghost (1942)
Dinardi, Gerard (act): Slaughterhouse Rock
Di Nardo, Mario (wri): Yeti
Dinehart, Alan (act, 1886-1944): Charlie Chan At The Race Track; Dante's Inferno (1935); A Study In Scarlet (1933); Supernatural (1933); The Whistler
Dinehart, Mason Alan (act): Platinum High School
Dinelli, Mel (wri, 1912-1991): Beware, My Lovely; Lizzie; The Spiral Staircase (1946); The Window
Dinga, Pat (cin): Bride Of The Monster; House Of Usher; The Raven (1963); Return To Treasure Island
Dingle, Charles (act, 1887-1956): The Beast With Five Fingers; Lady Of Burlesque; Three Wise Fools
Dingo, Ernie (act): Until The End Of The World
Dinner, William (wri): The Late Edwina Black
Dinning, Isabel (act): The Secret Life Of Ian Fleming
Dinova, Carol (act): Vampire On Bikini Beach
Dinovi, Gene (act): Body Parts
Dinsdale, Reece (act): Threads
Dinsmore, Bruce (act): Relative Fear
Dinwiddie, Bob (act): Vampire On Bikini Beach
Diol, Susan (act): Alien Nation: Millennium
Dion, Daniel (act): The Dungeonmaster
Dion, Debra (act): Troll
Dione, Rose (act): Freaks; Salome (1922)
Dionisio, Felipe (act): The Blood Drinkers
Dionisio, Felix (act): The Blood Drinkers
Dionne, Monica (act): The Arrival
Di Palma, Carlo (cin, b. 1925): L'assassino; Omicron; Red Desert
Di Palma, Dario (cin): Perseus The Invincible
Di Paolo, Daniel (mus): Jack's Back
Di Paolo, Dante (act): Marte, Dio Della Guerra; La Ragazza Che Sapeva Troppo
Di Pasquale, James (mus): Sparkling Cyanide
di Pego, Gerald (wri): The Astronaut; The Death Of The Incredible Hulk; Phenomenon; Short Walk To Daylight; W
di Pego, Justin (act): The Death Of The Incredible Hulk; Phenomenon
D'Ippolito, Ron (act): Mr. Sycamore
Direda, Joe (act): The Andromeda Strain
Di Rigo, Guy (act): Moonraker
Dirksen, Sen. Everett (act, 1896-1969): The Monitors
Dirlam, John (cin): Distortions
DiSanti, John (act): Batteries Not Included; Beyond the Bermuda Triangle; Eyes Of A Stranger; The Relic
Discombe, Will (act): Detective Daring And The Thames Coiners
Disher, Catherine (act): Haunted By Her Past
Disico, Dean (act): Boarding House
Di Silvestro, Rino (dir & wri): The Legend Of The Wolf Woman
DiSimone, Bob (act): Friday The 13th-Part V: A New Beginning
Diskant, George (E.) (cin, 1907-1965): Beware, My Lovely; Dick Tracy vs. Cueball; On Dangerous Ground; Storm Over Tibet
Disney, Doris Miles (wri): Do Not Fold, Spindle Or Mutilate; The Straw Man
Disney, Tom (act): I Was A Zombie For The F.B.I.
DiStefano, Dan (wri): Covenant; Nightmare On The 13th Floor
DiStefano, James (act): Running Against Time
Ditano, Anna (act): King Solomon's Mines (1985)
Ditchburn, Anne (act): Curtains
Ditillo, Larry (wri): The Secret Of The Sword
Ditky, Judy (wri): The Cremators
Ditson, Harry (act): Incubus (1982); The Sender; Top Secret! (1984)
Di Venanzo, Gianni (cin, 1920-1966): La Decima Vittima; 8 1/2; Giulietta Degli Spiriti
Divine (act, d. 1989): Out Of The Dark; Polyester
Divoff, Andrew (act): Graveyard Shift (1990); Neon Maniacs
Dix, Beulah Marie (wri): The Leopard Lady; Midnight Mystery; The Road To Yesterday
Dix, Billy (act): Giant From The Unknown; She Demons
Dix, Bob (act): see Dix, Robert
Dix, Richard (act, 1894-1949, nee Ernest Brimmer): Eyes Of The Underworld; Ghost SHIP (1943); The Lost Squadron; Mark Of The Whistler; Power Of the Whistler; The Return Of The Whistler; The Secret of The Whistler; Seven Keys To Baldpate (1929); The Thirteenth Hour (1947); The Tunnel; The 12th hour; The Whistler
Dix, Richard (1980s act): Fugitive From The Empire
Dix, Robert/Bob (act): Blood Of Dracula's Castle; Forbidden Planet; Frankenstein's Daughter (1958); Hell's Bloody Devils; Horror Of The Blood Monsters; Satan's Sadists
Dix, William (act, b. 1956): Dr. Dolittle; The Nanny
Dixey, Phyllis (act): Dual Alibi
Dixion, Raymond (act): Endangered Species
Dixon, Beverly (act): Beyond Evil; Graduation Day
Dixon, Campbell (wri): The Secret Agent (1936)
Dixon, Conway (act): The Triumph Of Sherlock Holmes
Dixon Jr., D. (wri): Angels' Wild Women
Dixon, Dianne (act): The Cradle Will Fall
Dixon, Donna (act): Lucky Stiff
Dixon, Earl (act): Nothing But Trouble
Dixon, Floyd (act): Invasion Of The Saucer Men
Dixon, Glen (act): The Barefoot Executive; Voodoo Island
Dixon, Gordon C. (act): Night Of The Zombies (1981)
Dixon, Ivan (act, b. 1931): Fer-De-Lance; To Trap A Spy
Dixon, James (act): Demon (1976); It Lives Again; It's Alive (1974); It's Alive III: Island Of The Alive; A Return To Salem's Lot; The Stuff; Wicked Stepmother
Dixon, James (wri): A Return To Salem's Lot
Dixon, Jamie (cin): Heart And Souls
Dixon, Jill (act): The Hidden Face; Witchcraft (1964)
Dixon, John Robert (act): Friday The 13th-Part V: A New Beginning
Dixon, Ken (dir): The Best Of Sex And Violence
Dixon, MacIntyre (act): *Batteries Not Included
Dixon, Malcolm (act): Return Of The Jedi; Time Bandits
Dixon, Pat (wri): Night Comes Too Soon
Dixon, Richard (act): Jekyll And Hyde
Dja, Devi (act): see Devi Dja and Her Balinese Dancers
Djimon (act): Stargate
Djola, Badja (act): The Serpent And The Rainbow
Dloughy, Edward (act): Bloodspell
Dmitravitch, Maroussia (act): The Queen Of Spades (1948)
Dmytryk, Edward (dir, b. 1908): Bluebeard (1972); Captive Wild Woman; Confessions Of Boston Blackie; Counter-Espionage; The Devil Commands; The Falcon Strikes Back; The Human Factor; Murder, My Sweet; Mystery Sea Raider; Obsession (1949); The Reluctant Saint; Secrets of The Lone Wolf; The Sniper; Television Spy
Dmytryk, Edward (wri, b. 1908): Bluebeard (1972)
Doak, Frank (act): Night Of The Living Dead (1968)
Doba, Wayne (act): The Funhouse (1981)
Dobbins, Ray (wri): When Pigs Fly
Dobbs, Randolph (act): Young Frankenstein
D'Obici, Valeria (act): Escape From The Bronx
Dobie, Alan (act, b. 1932): Dr. Syn-Alias The Scarecrow; Madame Sin
Dobkin, David (wri): Ice Cream Man
Dobkin, Lawrence/Larry (act): Beastmaster 2: Through The Portal Of Time; The Cabinet Of Caligari; D.O.A. (1949); Riders To The Stars; Sabaka
Dobrin, Ronald (wri): Dawn Of The Mummy
Dobry, Karel (act): Mission: Impossible
Dobson, James (act, 1920-1987): Captain Sinbad; Cult Of The Cobra; Impulse! (1974); Mutiny In Outer Space; What's The Matter With Helen?
Dobson, Peggy (act): The Cradle Will Fall
Dobson, Peter (act): Bates Motel; The Frighteners
Dobson, Tamara (act, b. 1947): Amazons (1984)
Dobtcheff, Vernon (act): Are You Dying Young Man?; The Assassination Bureau; Condorman; Hamlet (1990); The Hidden face; MaTA Hari (1984); Murder On The Orient Express; The Spy Who Loved Me; Sredni Vashtar
Doby, Kathryn (act): All That Jazz; The Handmaid's Tale
Dochtermann, Rudy (wri): The Fiendish Plot Of Dr. Fu Manchu; The Night they Saved Christmas
Dockrey, Sam (cin): The Night Of The Claw
Dockstader, Ted (mus): Satyricon
Doctors, Melanie (act): A Nightmare On Elm Street 3: Dream Warriors
Dodd, Claire (act, 1908-1973): The Black Cat (1941); Charlie Chan in Honolulu; the Mad Doctor Of Market Street; Secret Of The Chateau
Dodd, Judy (act): The Coming
Dodd, Molly (act): How Awful About Allan; What's The Matter With Helen?
Dodds, K.K. (act): Flatliners
Dodge, David (wri): To Catch A Thief
Dodge, Estelle (act): Man-Eater Of Kumaon
Dodgers, The (act): see Brooklyn Dodgers, The

Dodimead, David (act): *Are You Dying Young Man?*
Dods, Marcus (mus): *The Awakening; Unearthly Stranger; Watership Down*
Dodson, Eric (act): *Jekyll And Hyde*
Dodsworth, John (act): *The Maze; Storm Over Tibet*
Doe, Barry (act): *Raiders Of The Living Dead*
Doederlein, Fred (act): *Scanners*
Doel, Frances (wri): *Avalanche; Deathsport*
Doff, Melody (act): *To Die For II: Son Of Darkness*
Doggart, Evelyn (act): *Mary Reilly*
Dogue, Amanda (act): *That Eye, The Sky*
Doheny, Lawrence (dir, 1924-1982): *Houston, We've Got A Problem*
Doherty, Charla (act, 1947-1988): *In The Year 2889; Village Of The Giants*
Doherty, Chet (act): *Too Scared To Scream*
Dohler, Don (dir & wri): *Fiend (1980); The Galaxy Invader; Nightbeast*
Dohler, Greg (act): *Fiend (1980); The Galaxy Invader; Nightbeast*
Dohler, Kim (act): *Fiend (1980); The Galaxy Invader; Nightbeast*
Dohler, Pam (act): *Nightbeast*
Do Kahu, Rongo (act): *Night Of The Red Hunter*
Dokic, Maya (act): *Mission: Impossible*
Dokshnimurti (mus): *Sabaka*
Dolan, Charles E. (cin): *The Man Who Fell To Earth (1987)*
Dolan, Charlie (wri): *Ghoulies*
Dolan Don (act, b. 1938): *Haunts*
Dolan, Frank (act): *The Coming*
Dolan, Julie (act): *Blood Beach*
Dolan, Katie (act): *The Vampire Girls*
Dolan, Michael (act): *Scrooge (1951)*
Dolan, Robert Emmett (mus, 1908-1972): *Mr. Peabody And The Mermaid; The Three Faces of Eve*
Dolan, Trent (act): *The Clone Master; Damnation Alley; How Awful About Allan; The Swarm; When A Stranger Calls*
Dolby, Thomas (act): *Howard The Duck*
Dolby, Thomas (mus): *Gothic*
Dolce, Donnah (act): *Death May Be Your Santa Claus*
Dolce, Ignazio (act): *Goliath Against The Giants*
Doldinger, Klaus (mus): *The Neverending Story*
Dole, Julie (act): *Getting Lucky*
Doleman, Guy (act, b. 1923): *Billion Dollar Brain; Captain Sinbad; Chilling; the Deadly Bees; Funeral In Berlin; The Ipcress File; on The Beach; Thunderball*
Dolen, Jim (act): *Il Planeta Degli Uomini Spenti; La Ragazza Che Sapeva Troppo*
Dolenz, Ami (act): *Children Of The Night; Miracle Beach; Pumpkinhead II: Blood Wings; Ticks; Witchboard 2: The Devil's Doorway*
Dolenz, George (act, 1908-1963): *The Climax; My Cousin Rachel; A Night In Paradise; Scared Stiff (1953); Song Of Scheherazade; The Strange Death Of Adolf Hitler; Vendetta*
Dolfin, Giorgio/George (act): *The Black Belly Of The Tarantula; The Devil's Wedding Night*
Dolinsky, Meyer (wri): *The Fifth Floor*
D'Olive, Wendy (act): *The Dead Are Alive*
D'Oliveira, Damon (act): *Short Circuit 2*
Dollarhide, Jessica (act): *Castle Freak*
Dolman, Bob (wri): *Willow*
Dolman, Richard (act): *The Man Who Changed His Name*
Dolnikov, Flora (act): *Vampire On Bikini Beach*
Dolphe, Hal (mus): *Rich And Strange*
Dombasle, Arielle (act): *El Mono Loco; Perceval*
Dombo, Kathy (act): *Edward Scissorhands*
Domburg, Andrea (act): *Spy In The Sky*
Domella, Jan (cin): *Conquest Of Space; The War Of The Worlds*
Domenici, Beppe (cin): *Goliath Against The Giants*
Domenico, Pat (cin): *Cat People (1982)*
Domerel, Myrtle (act): *A Bucket Of Blood (1959)*
Domergue, Faith (act, b. 1925): *Cult Of The Cobra; The House Of Seven Corpses; It Came From Beneath The Sea; Legacy Of Blood; man In the Shadow; Man With Icy Eyes; Planeta Bura; Soho Incident; This Island Earth; This Is My Love; Timeslip; Vendetta; Where Danger Lives*
Domingo, Anni (act): *Outland*
Domingo, Placido (mus): *Hamlet (1996)*
Domingue, Norris (act): *The Kiss (1988)*
Dominguez, Columba (act): *El Ladron De Cadaveres*
Dominguin, Luis (Miguel) (act): *Around The World In 80 Days; Le Testament D'orphee*
Dominic, Henry (wri): *Watchers II*
Dominici, Arturo (act): *Caltiki, Il Mostro Immortale; The Conquest Of Mycenae; La Maschera Del Demonio; Perseus The Invincible; The Thief Of Baghdad (1960); The Trojan Horse*
Dominici, Franca (act): *Operazione Paura*
Dominici, Germana (act): *La Maschera Del Demonio*
Dominique (act): *Surf Nazis Must Die*
Dominique, Fritz (act): *Cocoon: The Return*
Dommartin, Solveig (act & wri): *Until The End Of The World*
Don, Carl (act): *Hammersmith Is Out; Santa Claus Conquers The Martians; Zotz!*
Dona, Linda (act): *Switch*
Donaggio, Pino (mus): *The Adventures Of Hercules; Beyond Evil; The black Cat (1980); Blow Out; Body Double; Carrie; Crawlspace; Hercules (1983); The Howling; Meridian; Never Talk To Strangers; Piranha (1978); Raising Cain; Tourist Trap; Trauma (1993); Two evil Eyes*
Donahue, Jill (act): *Face Of Fire*
Donahue, Pat (act): *My Gun Is Quick*
Donahue, Patricia (act): *Once The Killing Starts*
Donahue, Shawn (act): *Wicked Stepmother*
Donahue, Troy (act, b. 1937, nee Merle Johnson): *I Was A Teenage Sex Mutant; Monster On The Campus; My Blood Runs Cold; Seizure; Those Fantastic Flying Fools*
Donald, Henry (wri): *The Adventures Of Hal 5*
Donald, James (act, 1917-1993): *The Big Sleep (1978); Cage Of Gold; The Net; Quatermass And The Pit*
Donald, Juli (act): *Nightmare On The 13th Floor*
Donald, Terry (act): *Rabid*
Donaldson, b.J. (act): *Jacob's Ladder*
Donaldson, Lesleh (act): *Curtains; Deadly Eyes; Funeral Home; Happy Birthday To Me*
Donaldson, Martin (wri): *Brock's Last Case*
Donaldson, Roger (dir): *Dante's Peak; No Way Out; Species*
Donaldson, Sandy (act): *Blood Bath At The House Of Death*
Donaldson, Ted (act, b. 1933): *The Decision Of Christopher Blake; Once Upon A time (1944)*
Donaldson, Tex (act): *Night Of The Creeps*
Donan, Martin (dir): *Killers Are Challenged*
Donat, Lucas (act): *Damien-Omen II*
Donat, Peter (act, b. 1928): *Charlie Chan: Happiness Is A Warm Clue; The China Syndrome; Mirrors; Rona Jaffe's Mazes And Monsters*
Donat, Richard (act): *City On Fire*
Donat, Robert (act, 1905-1958) *The Count Of Monte Cristo (1934); The Ghost goes West; Knight Without Armour; The 39 Steps (1935)*
Donath, Louis (act): *Enemy Agents Meet Ellery Queen*
Donath, Ludwig (act, 1900-1967): *Gilda; The Return Of Monte Cristo; The Strange death Of Adolf Hitler; Torn Curtain; The Veils Of Bagdad*
Donati, Phil (act): *This Is Not A Test*
Donati, Sergio (wri): *The Fish Men; Holocaust 2000; Orca*
Donde, Manuel (act): *Swamp Of The Lost Souls*
Donella, Chad (act): *The Long Kiss Goodnight*
Donelson, Sue (act): *I Was A Zombie For The F.B.I.*
Donelson, Virginia (act): *I Was A Zombie For The F.B.I.*
Donemeyer, Steve (act): *Blood Diner*
Donen, Peter (cin): *Flatliners*
Donen, Stanley (dir, b. 1924): *Bedazzled; Damn Yankees; It's Always Fair Weather; The Little Prince; Saturn 3*
Donen, Sue (wri): *Gold Of The Amazon Women*
Doner, Jack (act): *Hand Of Death*
Dong-Jun, Choi (act): *Village In The Mist*
Donham, David (act): *The Goddess Of Love*
Donini, Giulio (act): *Robin Hood And The Pirates*
Doniol-Valcroze, Jacques (wri): *Vous Pegez?*
Donlan, Cindy (act): *Schizoid (1980)*
Donlan, James/Jimmy (act): *The Bishop Murder Case; The Death Kiss; Murder on A Bridle Path; The Penguin Pool Murder; The Plot Thickens*
Donlan, Yolande (act, b. 1920): *Mr. Drake's Duck; Tarzan And The Lost Safari; They Can't Hang Me*
Donlevy, Brian (act, 1900-1972): *The Beginning Or The End?; Crack-Up; A Cry In The Night (1956); Curse Of the Fly; The Fat Spy; Five Golden Dragons; Gammera, The Invincible; Heaven Only Knows; How To Stuff a Wild Bikini; The Quatermass Experiment; Quatermass II; The Remarkable Andrew; Song Of Scheherazade*
Donlin, Mike (act): *The Sea Beast*
Donne, Carol (act): *Amazon Quest; Appointment With Murder*
Donnell, Jean (act): see Donnell, Jeff
Donnell, Jeff (act, 1921-1988): *The Boogie Man Will Get You; The Phantom Thief; Power Of The Whistler; Thief Of Damascus; The Unknown (1946)*
Donnelly, Bud (wri): *Cinderella 2000*
Donnelly, Dennis (dir): *The Toolbox Murders*
Donnelly, Donal (act): *The Mind Of Mr. Soames*
Donnelly, Elaine (act): *Sleepwalker (1975)*
Donnelly, Jesse J. (act): *Mr. Destiny*
Donnelly, Nicholas (act): *Lifeforce; Venom (1982)*
Donnelly, Ruth (act, 1896-1982): *The Snake Pit (1948)*
Donnelly, Tim(othy) (act): *The Clonus Horror; The Toolbox Murders*
Donnenfeld, Harry (act): *The Zero Boys*
Donner, Clive (dir, b. 1926): *Arthur The King; Babes In Toyland (1986); Charlie Chan And The Curse of The Dragon Queen; A Christmas Carol (1984); Dead Man's Folly; The nude Bomb; The Sinister Man; Spectre (1977); The Thief Of Baghdad (1978); Vampira*
Donner, Judith (act): *Seance On A Wet Afternoon*
Donner, Richard (D.) (dir): *The Goonies; Ladyhawke; The Omen; Scrooged; Superman (1978); X-15*
Donner, Robert/Bob (act): *Allan Quatermain And The Lost City Of Gold; Damnation Alley; Vanishing Point*
Donnilias, Myrte (act): *Charlie Chan At The Opera*
Donnini, Giulio (act): *Gli Amori Di Ercole; Beat The Devil; Ok, Nero!*
Donno, Eddy (act): *The Entity*
D'Onofrio, Joseph (act): *Teenage Mutant Ninja Turtles*
D'Onofrio, Vincent (act, b. 1959): *The Blood Of Heroes; Ed Wood; Men In Black; Strange Days*
Donoghue, Quinn (wri): *Prey (1978)*
Donoho, David (act): *Nightbeast*
Donoho, David (cin): *The Galaxy Invader*
Donohoe, Amanda (act, b. 1962): *The Lair Of The White Worm; Liar Liar*
Donohr, Albert (act): *Nosferatu, Eine Symphonie Des Grauens*
Donohue, Jack (dir): *Babes In Toyland (1961)*
Donovan (act, b. 1943): *The Pied Piper (1971)*
Donovan (mus, b. 1943): *Jack's Wife; The Pied Piper (1971)*
Donovan, Elizabeth (act): *Dr. Faustus*
Donovan, Gwen (act): *Behind Locked Doors*
Donovan, John (act): *The Clonus Horror*
Donovan, King (act, 1918-1987): *Alias Nick Beal; The Beast From 20,000 Fathoms; Invasion Of The Body Snatchers (1956); The Magnetic Monster; Mystery Street; Riders To The Stars; The Scarf*
Donovan, Martin (dir): *Death Dreams*
Donovan, Martin (wri): *Death Becomes Her*
Donovan, Mike Pat (act): *Confessions Of Boston Blackie*
Donovan, Paul (dir & wri): *Def Con 4*
Donovan, Peter (act): *Rawhead Rex*
Donovan, Tate (act): *Hercules (1997); Love Potion No. 9; Spacecamp*
Donovan, Terry (act): *Strange Behavior*
Donovan, Tom (dir): *Last Bride Of Salem; Lovespell*
Donovan, William (act): *Phantom Of The Paradise*
Donovon, Linda (act): *The Curse Of The Living Corpse*
Donte, Joel (act): *Most Dangerous Man Alive*
Doody, Alison (act): *Indiana Jones And The Last CrusaDE; A View To a kill*
Doogh, Desmond (act): *The Giant Gila Monster*
Doohan, Anita (wri): *Embryo*
Doohan, James (act, b. 1920): *One Of Our Spies Is Missing; Star Trek; Star Trek II: The Wrath Of Khan; Star Trek III: The Search For Spock; Star Trek IV: The Voyage Home; Star Trek V: The Final Frontier; Star Trek VI: The Undiscovered Country; Star Trek: Generations*
Doolan, Trish (act): *Neon Maniacs; Tattoo*
Dooley, Anita Donna (act): see Naldi, Nita
Dooley, John (dir & wri): *The Assistant*
Dooley, Paul (act): *Endangered Species; Guess Who's Coming For Christmas?; Monster in The Closet*
Dooline, Lucinda (act): *The Alchemist*
Doolittle, Don (act): *Creation Of The Humanoids*
Doolittle, John (act): *The Clan Of The Cave Bear; RoboCop 2*
Doonan, Anthony/Tony (act): *Cover Girl Killer; Escape From Broadmoor; Spaceflight IC-1*
Doonan, Patric (act, 1927-1958): *Calling Bulldog Drummond; High Treason (1951); Highly Dangerous; The Man In The White Suit; The Net*
Doppelt, Margery (wri): *Terror In The Aisles*
DoQui, Robert (act): *Dark Mirror (1984); Miracle Mile; My Science Project; RoboCop; RoboCop 2; Tarzan's Deadly Silence*
Dor, Karin (act): *The Face Of Fu Manchu; The Green Archer; The Hand of The Gallows; The Invisible Dr. Mabuse; The Nibelungs (1966); Die Schlangengr Ube Und Das Pendel; The Strangler Of Blackmoor Castle; Topaz; The White Spider; You Only Live Twice*
Doran, Ann (act, b. 1914): *Blue, White And Perfect; The Brass Bottle (1964); Charlie Chan In London; Dead Of Night (1977); Ellery Queen's Penthouse Mystery; Fear In The Night (1947); It!—The Terror From Beyond Space; The Man They Could Not Hang; The Man Who Turned To Stone; Pitfall; The Snake Pit (1948)*
Doran, James (wri): *The Ipcress File*
Doran, Jesse (act): *Cat's Eye*
Doran, Jessica (act): *Vampire On Bikini Beach*
Doran, Johnny (act): *Superstition*
Doran, Mary (act): *Electric Dreams*
Doran, Thomas (dir & wri): *Spookies*
Doran, Tokayo (act): *Doctor Franken*
Doran, Veronica (act): *The Haunted House Of Horror*
Dorat, Charles (act): *Le Golem (1936)*
Dorat, Jean-Pierre (act): *Les Parapluies De Cherbourg*
D'Orazio, Pier Luigi (act): *The Dead Are Alive*
Dorbett, Anna (act): *Fiend (1980)*
Dore, Alexander (act): *Chitty Chitty Bang Bang*
Dore, Ella (act): *The Case Of A Doped Actress*
Dorery, Paula (act): *Captive Women*
Dorff, Holly (act): *The Stepford Children*
Dorff, Matt (wri): *Nothing But The Truth*
Dorff, Stephen (act): *The Gate*
Dorff, Steve (mus): *Alien Nation: The Enemy Within; My Best Friend is a Vampire*
Dorfman, Robert (act): *Vampire's Kiss*
Doria, Daniela (act): *The Gates Of Hell; The House By the Cemetery*
Doria, Luciano (wri): *Gli Amori Di Ercole*
Dorian, Angela (act): see Vetri, Victoria
Dorian Elsa (act): *No Exit*
Dorian, Ernst (act): *Enemy Agents Meet Ellery Queen; Isle Of The Dead (1945)*
Dorian, Joanne (act): *A Stranger Is Watching*
Dorini, Ed (act): *The Dungeonmaster*
Dorio, Daniela (act): *The Black Cat (1980)*
Dorken, Rosemary (act): *The Haunting*
Dorleac, Francoise (act, 1941-1967): *Billion Dollar Brain; Cul-De-Sac; Where The Spies are*
Dorn, Dolores (act, b. 1935): *Phantom Of The Rue Morgue*
Dorn, Michael (act): *Star Trek VI: The Undiscovered Country; Star Trek: First Contact; Star Trek: Generations*
Dorn, Philip (act, 1901-1975, nee Fritz van Dungen): *Spy Hunt; Tarzan's Secret Treasure*
Dorn, Susan (act): *Zotz!*
Dorne, Sandra (act, b. 1925): *Alias John Preston; Devil Doll (1963); The House on Marsh Road; The Malpas Mystery; The Playbirds; The Secret Door; The Yellow Balloon*
Dorning, Robert (act): *The Black Windmill; Cul-De-Sac; Evil Under The Sun; Fanatic; The Man Who Was Nobody; Murder In Mind*
Dorning, Stacey (act): *Terror Of Frankenstein*
Dorny, Therese (act): *Diabolique (1955)*
Dornys, Judith (act): *The Curse Of The Hidden Vault*
Doro, Marie (act, 1882-1956): *12-10*
Doro, Mino (act): *The Last Days Of Pompeii (1959); Roma Contra roma*
d'Oro, Virginia (act): *La Ragazza Che Sapeva Troppo*
Doronin (act): *Portret Doriana Greya*

Dorr, Leslie (act): Killers From Space
Dorr, Lester (act): Charlie Chan On Broadway; The Jade Mask; Missile Monsters; Mr. Moto in Danger Island
Dorric, Peter (act): Son Of Samson
Dors, Diana (act, 1931-1984, nee Diana Fluck): The Amazing Mr. Blunden; Berserk; Code Of Scotland Yard; Craze; Danger Route; Devil's Web; From Beyond The Grave; A Kid For Two Farthings; Nothing But The Night; The Pied Piper (1971); The Saint's Return; The Shop At Sly Corner; Theater Of Blood
D'Orsay, Fifi (act, 1904-1983): Assignment To Kill; Just Imagine; Nabonga; Women Of All Nations
Dorsay, J.P. (mus): The Blood Rose
D'Orsay, Lawrence (act): The Sorrows Of Satan (1925)
Dorsch, Bobbi (act): A Polish Vampire In Burbank
Dorsch, Steve (act): A Polish Vampire In Burbank
Dorsett, Chuck (act): Impulse (1984)
Dorsey, Jimmy (act & mus, 1904-1957): Lost In A Harem
Dorsey, Joe (act): Brainstorm (1983); The PhiladelphIA Experiment
Dorsey, Nay (act): 976-Evil
D'Orsi, Umberto (act): Spirits Of The Dead
Dorson, Gloria (act): Total Recall
Dortort, David (wri): A Cry In The Night (1956)
Dorziat, Gabrielle (act, 1886-1979, nee Gabrielle Moppert): Les Parents Terribles
Dossett, Chappell (act): The Mysterious Dr. Fu Manchu
Doster, Kathryn Reve (act): Student Bodies
Dostoevski, Fedor Mikhailovich (wri, 1821-1881): Crime And Punishment (1935, 1958 & 1975); Crime And Punishment, U.S.A.; Fear (1946); Raskolnikov
Dotrice, Karen (act, b. 1955): The Gnome-Mobile; Mary Poppins; The 39 Steps (1978); The Three Lives Of Thomasina
Dotrice, Michele (act): And Soon The Darkness; The Blood On Satan's Claw; Jane Eyre (1970); The Witches (1966)
Dotrice, Roy (act, b. 1923): The Eliminators; The Scarlet Letter (1995); Suburban Commando; Tales From The Crypt; Toomorrow
Dotson, Rhonda (act): Solar Crisis
Dotto, Steve (act): Quarantine
Doubet, Steve (act): Silent Scream (1979)
Doublin, Anthony (cin): From Beyond; Re-Animator
Doucette, Diane (act): Shadow Of Death (1983)
Doucette, John (act): Sabu And The Magic Ring; 7 Faces of Dr. Lao; The Time Machine (1978); The Treasure Of Lost Canyon
Doucette, Rudy (act): Gremlins
Doucette, Suzanne (act): Mission: Impossible
Doudy, Reginald (act): see Garrick, John
Doughan, Jim (act): Tarzan In Manhattan
Dougherty, Charles (act): Alice In Wonderland (1985)
Dougherty, Jack (act): 12 Monkeys
Dougherty, Joseph (wri): Attack Of The 50-Foot Woman (1993); Cast A Deadly Spell
Dougherty, Ralph (act): Through The Magic Pyramid
Dougherty, Walter Hampden (act): see Hampden, Walter
Doughton Jr., Russell S. (dir): The Hostage
Douglas, Angela (act): Carry On Screaming; Digby-The Biggest Dog In the World; Maroc 7; The Shakedown
Douglas, Buddy (act): It Came Upon The Midnight Clear; The Night They Saved Christmas
Douglas, Chet (act): The Underwater City
Douglas, Christopher (act): Jamaica Inn (1985)
Douglas, Colin (act): Captain Clegg; Ghost Ship (1952); The Trollenberg Terror
Douglas, Diana (act): A Fire In The Sky (1978); Jaws Of Satan; Let's Live Again; Storm Over Tibet
Douglas, Don(ald) (act): Calling Philo Vance; Charlie Chan in Panama; Dead Men Tell; The Falcon Out West; Fright (1957); Mr. Moto in Danger Island; Murder, My Sweet; Sleepers West; Strange Mr. Gregory; Tarzan And The Amazons
Douglas, Freddie (act): The Odyssey
Douglas, George (act): Attack Of The 50-Foot Woman (1958); Dick Tracy's g-Men; The Snow Creature
Douglas, Gordon (M.) (dir, b. 1909): Aladdin's Lantern; Between Midnight And Dawn; call Me Bwana; Dick Tracy vs. Cueball; The Falcon in Hollywood; Gildersleeve's Ghost; In Like Flint; Rogues Of Sherwood Forest; Roland The Mighty; Skullduggery; Them! (1954); Way... Way Out; Zombies On Broadway
Douglas, Gordon (wri): Topper Returns
Douglas, Howard (act): Dear Murderer; Night Comes Too Soon; Treasure Island (1950)
Douglas, Illeana (act): Hello Again
Douglas, J.b. (act): The Barefoot Executive
Douglas, James (b.) (act): An American Christmas Carol; Deadly Eyes; Last Bride Of Salem; Mr. Destiny
Douglas, Jerry (act): Black Zoo; The Dead Don't Die; Looker
Douglas, Jimmy (act): The Intruder (1981)
Douglas, John (mus): Crack In The World
Douglas, Katya (act): The Full Treatment; Kill Or Cure; Murder At The Gallop; The Road To Hong Kong
Douglas, Kay (act): Targets
Douglas, Keith (act): see Kennedy, Douglas (R.)
Douglas, Kirk (act, b. 1916, nee Issur Danielovitch Demsky): Catch Me A Spy; The Final Countdown; The Fury; Holocaust 2000; The Light At The Edge Of The World; The List Of Adrian Messenger; Saturn 3; Seven Days In May; 20,000 Leagues Under The Sea (1954); Ulysses
Douglas, Larry (act): Fugitive From The Empire
Douglas, Leal (act): The Beetle
Douglas, Mark (act): 2000 Maniacs
Douglas, Melvyn (act, 1901-1981, nee Melvyn Hesselberg): As You Desire Me; The Changeling; Death Takes A Holiday (1971); Ghost Story (1981); The Lone Wolf Returns (1935); Nagana; The Old Dark House (1932); The Tenant; The Vampire Bat
Douglas, Michael (act, b. 1944): The China Syndrome; Coma; The Ghost And The Darkness; The Jewel Of The Nile; Romancing The Stone; When Michael Calls
Douglas, Morgan (act): Chopping Mall
Douglas, Paul (act, 1907-1959): Angels In The Outfield (1951); The Gamma People; It Happens Every Spring
Douglas, Paul (1990s act): Twister
Douglas, Pavel (act): Goldeneye; Jamaica Inn (1985)
Douglas, R.H. (wri): Puppets Of Fate
Douglas, Rita (wri): Jungle Man
Douglas, Robert (act, b. 1909): The Adventures Of Don Juan; At Sword's Point; The Decision Of Christopher Blake; Dick Tracy (1945); Fair Wind To Java; Homicide; The Prisoner Of Zenda (1952); The Questor Tapes; Spy Hunt
Douglas, Robin (act): Unforgettable
Douglas, Sally (act): Carry On Screaming
Douglas, Sam (act): Batman (1989); Dreamchild; Mission: Impossible
Douglas, Sarah (act): Beastmaster 2: Through The Portal Of Time; Conan The Destroyer; Dracula (1973); The Last Days Of Man On Earth; Nightfall (1988); The People That Time Forgot; Puppet Master III: Toulon's Revenge; The Return Of Swamp Thing; The Stepford Husbands; Superman (1978); Superman II
Douglas, Sharon (act): Fog Island
Douglas, Shirley (act): Dead Ringers
Douglas, Susan (act): Five; Targets
Douglas, Tom (act): The Phantom Of Crestwood
Douglas, Warren (act): Below The Deadline; The Chinese Ring; Homicide For Three; Incident; The Inner Circle; Post Office Investigator; Secrets Of Monte Carlo
Douglass, Robyn (act): The Clone Master
Douglaston, Brigitte (act): The Toxic Avenger
Doukas, Nike (act): Running Against Time
Doukas, Susan (act): Liquid Sky
Douking (act): Spirits Of The Dead
Doung, Mang (act): Blood Diner
Douras, Marion Cecilia (act): see Davies, Marion
Dourif, Brad (act, b. 1950): Blackout (1995); Blue Velvet; Body Parts; Child's Play (1988); Child's Play 2; Child's Play 3; Color Of Night; Death Machine; Dune; The Exorcist III; Eyes Of Laura Mars; Graveyard Shift (1990); Grim Prairie Tales; I, Desire; Trauma (1993)
Douthette, Dani (act): Repossessed
Dova, Ben (act): Marathon Man
Dove, Andrew (act): One Of Our Dinosaurs Is Missing
Dove, Billie (act, b. 1904, nee Lilian Bohny): The Black Pirate; The Lone Wolf Returns (1926)
Dovzhenko, Alexander (dir, 1894-1956): Zvenigora
Dow, Mindy (act): Earthbound (1981)
Dow, Peggy (act, b. 1928, nee Peggy Varnadow): Harvey; You Never Can Tell
Dow, R.A. (act): Squirm
Dow, Tony (cin): Doctor Who
Dowd, Ned (act): Endangered Species
Dowdell, Jim (act): Superman II; Transmutations
Dowdell, Robert (act): The Initiation; Wicked Stepmother
Dowe, Don (act): Tales From The Hood; Trancers II: The Return Of Jack Deth
Dower, Greg (act): Strange Behavior
Dower, Jane (act): Strange Behavior
Dowie, Freda (act): Subterfuge
Dowling, Alison (act): Memoirs Of A Survivor
Dowling, Bairbre (act): Zardoz
Dowling, Barbara (act): Dementia 13
Dowling, Constance (act, 1923-1969): Black Angel (1946); Blind Spot; Boston Blackie And The Law; Gog
Dowling, Doris (act, b. 1921): Birds Do It; The Crimson Key; The Lost Weekend; Storm Bound; Wink Of An Eye
Dowling, Joan (act): For Them That Trespass; Murder Without Crime; Pool Of London
Dowling, Joseph (act): Another Thin Man; The Miracle Man (1919)
Dowling, Kathryn (act): Lovespell
Down, Angela (act): What Became Of Jack And Jill
Down, Lesley-Anne (act, b. 1954): Beastmaster III: The Eye Of Braxus; Countess Dracula; From Beyond The Grave; The Hunchback Of Notre Dame (1982); In The Devil's Garden; Ladykillers (1988); Munchie Strikes Back; Murder Is Easy; Nomads; Sphinx (1981)
Downe, A./Allison Louis (wri): Blood Feast; The Gruesome Twosome; She-Devils On Wheels
Downer, Herb (act): The Brother From Another Planet
Downes, Anson (act): Carrie
Downes, Terry (act): The Fearless Vampire Killers Or: Pardon Me, But Your Teeth Are In My Neck; A Study In Terror
Downey, Deborah (act): Remote Control (1988)
Downey, Jed (act): Endless Descent
Downey Jr., Morton (act): Predator 2
Downey Jr., Robert (act, b. 1965): Chances Are; Heart And Souls; Richard III (1995); Weird Science
Downey, Roy (cin): Child Of Darkness, Child Of Light; It Happened At Lake Wood Manor; Tarantulas: The Deadly Cargo
Downing, Frank (act): Coma
Downing, Helen (act): Virgin Witch
Downing, J. (act): Ghoulies II
Downing, Joseph/Joe (act): Lady In The Morgue; Torchy Runs For Mayor
Downing, Lauren (act): The Coming
Downing, Rupert (wri): The Ghoul (1933)
Downing, Vernon (act): Spider Woman
Downs, Cathy (act, b. 1924): The Amazing Colossal Man; For You I Die; Missile To The Moon; The Phantom From 10,000 Leagues; The She-Creature
Downs, Fred(eric) (act): Bug; Terror From The Year 5,000
Downs, Hugh (act, b. 1921): The Littlest Angel (1960); Oh, God! Book II
Downs, Johnny (act, b. 1913): Babes In Toyland (1934); The Mad Monster
Downs, Richard (act): Rocket Attack U.S.A.
Downs, Watson (act): The Magnetic Monster
Doxat-Pratt, b.E. (dir): The Other Person
Doxat-Pratt, C.b. (wri): Bulldog Drummond (1923)
Doyka, Mimi (act): Outbreak
Doyle, Sir Arthur Conan (wri, 1859-1930): The Adventures of Sherlock Holmes (1905 & 1939); The Beryl Coronet; A Case For Sherlock Holmes; The Copper Beeches; Dressed To Kill (1946); The Firm Of Girdlestone; Hands Of A Murderer; The Hound Of The Baskervilles (1917, 1921, 1929, 1931, 1939, 1959, 1972, 1978 & 1982); The House Of Fear (1945); The Lost World (1925 & 1960); The Man With The Twisted Lip; Masks Of Death; The Missing Rembrandt; The Musgrave Ritual; The Mystery Of Boscombe Vale; The Pearl Of Death; Pursuit To Algiers; The Reigate Squires; The Return Of Sherlock Holmes (1929 & 1986); The Scarlet Claw; Sherlock And Me; Sherlock Holmes (1909, 1922 & 1932); Sherlock Holmes And The Deadly Necklace; Sherlock Holmes And The Secret Weapon; Sherlock Holmes And The Voice Of Terror; Sherlock Holmes Faces Death; Sherlock Holmes In New York; Sherlock Holmes In Washington; The Sign Of Four (1923, 1932 & 1983); Silver Blaze (1912 & 1937); The Sleeping Cardinal; The Speckled Band (1912 & 1931); Spider Woman; The Stolen Papers; A Study In Scarlet (1914 & 1933); A Study In Skarlit; Tales From The Darkside; Terror By Night; The Triumph Of Sherlock Holmes; Valley Of Fear (1916 & 1964); The Woman In Green; Young Sherlock Holmes
Doyle, Carolyn (act): Howling II
Doyle, Chris (act): Galaxis; Trancers II: The Return Of Jack Deth
Doyle, Christopher (act): Timestalkers; When The Bough Breaks
Doyle, Colin (act): The Clan Of The Cave Bear
Doyle, David (act, 1929-1997): The Adventures Of Pinocchio; Capricorn One; Crackle Of Death; The Day The Screaming Stopped; Ghost Writer; The Invisible Woman (1983); Miracle On 34th Street (1973); The Stranger Within
Doyle, Jim (cin): The Haunting Of Hamilton High
Doyle, John Calvin (act): Serial Mom
Doyle, Kathleen (act): The Body Snatchers
Doyle, Laird (wri): British Agent
Doyle, Martin (act): The Clan Of The Cave Bear
Doyle, Maxine (act): Condemned To Live; S.O.S. Coast Guard
Doyle, Patrick (act): Dead Again
Doyle, Patrick (mus): Dead Again; Hamlet (1996); Mary Shelley's 'Frankenstein'
Doyle, Richard (act): Coma; Trick Or Treat
Doyle, Ron (act): Gallery Of Horror
Doyle, Sharon (act): The Long Kiss Goodnight
Doyle, Tim (wri): Zombie High
Doyle-Murray, Brian (act): Groundhog Day; Modern Problems; Nothing But Trouble
D'Oyly-Rhind, Warren (act): Shriek Of The Mutilated
Dozier, Robert (wri): Dead Men Tell No Tales; Pursuit (1972)
Drache, Heinz (act): Black Panther Of Ratana; The Brides Of Fu Manchu; Circus Of Fear; Hipnosis; The Indian Scarf; The Inn On Dartmoor; The Mysterious Magician; Der Raecher; The Squeaker (1965); Die Tur Mit Den Sieben Schlossern
Draco, Ely (act): Ercole Al Centro Della Terra
Dracup, Bob (cin): So Sad About Gloria
Drage, Prudence (act): A Clockwork Orange; The Sexplorer
Dragin, Bert (dir & wri): Twice Dead
Drago, Billy (act): Cyborg 2: Glass Shadow; Lunar Cop; Vamp
Drago, Joseph (act): The Fifth Missile
Dragon, Carmen (mus, 1914-1984): Invasion Of The Body Snatchers (1956)
Dragoti, Stan (dir): Love At First Bite
Draheim, Jack (act): Re-Animator
Draizin, Doug (act): Repossessed
Drake, Arnold (wri): The Flesh Eaters
Drake, Betsy (act): Intent To Kill
Drake, Charles (act, 1918-1994, nee Charles Ruppert): Bonzo Goes To College; Harvey; It Came From Outer Space; The Maltese Falcon (1941); The Screaming Woman; Scream, Pretty Peggy; Step Down To Terror; The Swimmer; Tarzan's Magic Fountain; Tobor The Great; The Treasure Of Lost Canyon; You Never Can Tell
Drake, Charlie (act): The Golden Link; Professor Popper's Problem
Drake, Chris (act): The Falcon In Hollywood; Them! (1954)
Drake, Claudia (act): The Face Of Marble
Drake, Colin (act): Goliath Awaits; Inn Of The Damned
Drake, Colleen (act): Queen Of Outer Space
Drake, Delores (act): I Still Dream Of Jeannie
Drake, Dick (act): Evilspeak
Drake, Dodie (act): The Little Shop Of Horrors (1960)
Drake, Dona (act, b. 1920, nee Rita Novella): The Bandits Of Corsica; Dangerous Millions
Drake, Donna Leigh (act): Track Of The Moon Beast
Drake, Fabia (act, 1904-1990): The Hour Of 13; Man In The Shadow; Tam Lin

Drake, Frances (act.): The Invisible Ray; The Lone Wolf In Paris; Mad Love; Les Miserables (1935)
Drake, Jackie (act.): Dracula's Dog
Drake, Jennifer (act.): Fantastic Planet
Drake, Jim (dir.): The Goddess Of Love
Drake, Jonathan (act.): The Invisible Woman (1983)
Drake, Judith (act.): Angel Heart
Drake, Larry (act.): The Beast (1996); Darkman (1990); Darkman II: The Return Of Durant; Dark Night Of The Scarecrow; Dr. Giggles; Too Good To Be True
Drake, Laura (act.): Ghost (1990)
Drake, Marciee (act.): The Toolbox Murders
Drake, Mervyn (act.): Razorback
Drake, Michael (act.): Trunk Crime
Drake, Oliver (dir.): The Mummy And The Curse Of The Jackals
Drake, Oliver (wri.): The Feathered Serpent (1948); Sharad Of Atlantis; The Sky Dragon
Drake, Pauline (act.): The Fatal Hour (1940); Willard
Drake, T.Y. (dir.): The Keeper
Drake, T.Y. (wri.): The Keeper; Terror Train
Drake, Tom (act, 1919-1982, nee Alfred Alderdice): The Beginning Or The End?; Betrayed Women; City Beneath The Sea (1970); Crackle Of Death; The Cyclops; The Great Rupert; House Of The Black Death; The Spectre Of Edgar Allan Poe; Sudden Danger; Warlock Moon
Drake, Walter (act.): The Case Of A Doped Actress
Drake, William (A.) (wri.): The Adventures Of Sherlock Holmes (1939); The Three Musketeers (1939)
Drake-Massey, Bebe (act.): Alien Nation
Draper, Jack (cin): Mystery In Mexico; Tarzan And The Mermaids
Draper, Polly (act.): Making Mr. Right
Draper, Ralph (act.): Howling IV
Draper, Rob(ert) (cin): Dr. Giggles; Halloween 5: The Revenge Of Michael Myers; Nothing But The Truth; Remember Me; Tales From The Darkside; Unlikely Angel
Drasin, Richard (act.): Ben
Drasnin, Robert (mus): Daughter Of The Mind; Dr. Cook's Garden; The Kremlin Letter; A Taste Of Evil
Dratfield, Jim (act.): The Silence Of The Lambs
Dratler, Jay (wri, b. 1911): Confessions Of Boston Blackie; I Aim At The Stars; Laura; Meet Boston Blackie
D'Ray, Anita (act.): Murder At The Windmill; Old Mother Riley's Jungle Treasure
Drayton, Alfred (act, 1881-1949, nee Alfred Varick): The Crimson Circle (1936); Halfway House; Iron Justice; The Squeaker (1930); Things Happen At Night
Drayton, Noel (act.): Blackbeard The Pirate
Drazen, Julie (act.): The Incredible Melting Man
Dream Quest (Images) (cin): Alien Nation: Body And Soul; Dr. Jekyll And Ms. Hyde; A Nightmare On Elm Street 3: Dream Warriors; Total Recall
Dreger, Reg (act.): Millennium; Never Talk To Strangers
Dreghorn, Lea (act.): The Slipper And The Rose
Dreier, Alex (act.): Sweet, Sweet Rachel
Dreifuss, Arthur (dir.): Boston Blackie Booked On Suspicion; Boston Blackie's Rendezvous
Dreith, Dennis (mus): The Goddess Of Love; The Punisher
Dreizen, Jason (act.): Surf Nazis Must Die
Dreizen, Sherry (act.): Surf Nazis Must Die
Dremann, Beau (act.): My Science Project; Uninvited (1987)
Dremann, Janis (act.): see Carter, Janis
Drenth, Jan Anne (act.): The Lift
Drescher, Adam (act.): Ed Wood
Drescher, Fran (act, b. 1957): Jack; Stranger In Our House
Dresdel, Sonia (act, 1909-1976, nee Lois Obee): The Fallen Idol; While I Live
Dresden, John (act.): The Dark (1979)
Dresner, Hal (wri.): The Eiger Sanction; The Extraordinary Seaman; Sssssss; Zorro, The Gay Blade
Dress, Michael (mus): The House That Dripped Blood; The Mind Of Mr. Soames
Dressel, David (act.): Blood Diner
Dresser, Louise (act, 1878-1965): Mr. Wu (1927)
Dressler, David (wri.): Crime Doctor's Diary
Dressler, Lieux (act.): Grave Of The Vampire; Kingdom Of The Spiders
Dressler, Roger (act.): The Groundstar Conspiracy
Dreville, Jean (dir.): A Dog, A Mouse And A Sputnik
Drew, Bob (act.): Repossessed
Drew, Ellen (act, b. 1915, a.k.a. Terry Ray): The Baron Of Arizona; Crime Doctor's Manhunt; The Gracie Allen Murder Case; Isle Of The Dead (1945); The Mad Doctor; The Monster And The Girl; A Night Of Mystery (1937); The Remarkable Andrew
Drew, Griffen (act.): Sinful Intrigue
Drew, Lee (act.): Secrets Of The Phantom Caverns
Drew, Linzi (act.): The Lair Of The White Worm
Drew, Lowell (act.): The Greene Murder Case
Drew, Roland (act, 1900-1988): Invisible Killer; Lady In The Morgue; The Last Warning (1938); Peril From The Planet Mongo; Purple Death From Outer Space; The Saint Takes Over
Drewett, Pauline (act.): The Gamma People
Drewniak, Jozef (act.): Those Dear Departed
Drews, Karl (cin): Chronik Von Grieshuus
Drexel, Steve (act.): Terrified
Drexler, Ellen (act.): Attack Of The Killer Tomatoes
Dreyer, Carl (Theodor) (dir, 1889-1968): Blade Af Satans Bog; Vampyr; Vredens Dag
Dreyer, Carl Theodor (wri, 1889-1968): Vampyr; Vredens Dag
Dreyfus, Jean-Claude (act.): The City Of Lost Children
Dreyfus, Jean-Paul (dir & wri): see Le Chanois, Jean-Paul
Dreyfuss, Richard (act, b. 1947): Always; Close Encounters Of The Third Kind; Hello Down There; James And The Giant Peach; Jaws
Driant, Jean (act.): Return From The Ashes
Drier, Moosie (act.): It Happened At Lake Wood Manor
Drier, Peggy (act.): The Beguiled
Driest, Burkhard (wri.): Hitler's Son
Driggs, Deborah (act.): Night Rhythms
Driggs, Pearl (act.): The Hideous Sun Demon
Drimmer, John (wri.): Iceman
Drinkwater, Carol (act.): A Clockwork Orange; The Haunted School; The Shout
Driscoll, Bobby (act, b. 1937): Treasure Island (1950); The Window
Driscoll, Chris (act.): The Quatermass Conclusion
Driscoll, R.C. (act.): No Blade Of Grass
Driscoll, Toni (act.): Night Of The Red Hunter
Drissi, Debbie (act.): Trick Or Treats
Dristas, William (act.): Nightmare Sisters
Drivas, Robert (act, b. 1938): Demon (1976); The Illustrated Man
Driver, Donald (dir & wri): The Naked Ape
Driver, Edgar (act.): The Hypnotist (1957)
Driver, Frances (act.): Black Widow (1954)
Driver, Keno (act.): Offerings
Driver, Minnie (act.): Goldeneye
Driver, Sara (dir.): Sleepwalk; When Pigs Fly
Drogue, Evelyn (act.): For Your Eyes Only
Dromgoole, Patrick (dir.): Dead Man's Chest; The Hidden Face
Droney, Kevin (wri.): Mortal Kombat
Dropko, Whitey (act.): Quarantine
Drouet, Soo (act.): Robin Hood: Prince Of Thieves
Drouineau, Francois (act.): see Villard, Frank
Drouot, Jean-Claude (act.): The Light At The Edge Of The World
Drouot, Pierre (wri.): Daughters Of Darkness
Drown, Mark (act.): Outbreak
Droyan, Al (act.): Torment (1986)
Dru, Joanne (act, 1922-1996, nee Joanne Letitia La Cock, a.k.a. Joanne Marshall): September Storm; Super Fuzz
Drudi, Vera (act.): Demons Of The Dead
Drum, James (act.): Ssssss
Drum, Jim (act.): The Velvet Touch
Drummer, Michael (act.): The Toxic Avenger, Part II
Drummond, Alice (act.): Ghostbusters; Man On A Swing; Sanctuary Of Fear; Tales From The Darkside
Drummond, Reginald (act.): Treasure Island (1950)
Drummond-Hay, Cecil (act.): Empire Of Ash III
Drummond-Hay, Charlie (act.): Empire Of Ash III
Drury, James (act, b. 1934): The Devil And Miss Sarah; Forbidden Planet
Drury, Patrick (act.): The Awakening
Drury, Susan (act.): The Assistant
Druyan, Ann (wri.): Contact
Dryden, Jane (act.): The Man Without Desire
Dryden, John (wri.): The Hills Of Donegal
Dryden, Norman (act.): The Tell-Tale Heart (1934)
Dryden, Richard (act.): Man On A Swing
Dryden, Victoria (act.): The Oracle (1985)
Dryer, Robert (act.): Cyborg 2: Glass Shadow; Kiss Daddy Goodbye
Dryhurst, Edward (wri.): The Case Of The Frightened Lady; The Claydon Treasure Mystery; Crimes At The Dark House; Double Alibi; The House Of The Arrow (1953); The Patient Vanishes; Strange Experiment
Drynan, Judith (act.): Fahrenheit 451
Drysdale, Bill (act.): Macbeth (1971)
Drysdale, Denise (act.): The Day After Halloween
D'Salva, Ramon (act.): Equalizer 2000
Duane, Michael (act.): The Devil's Mask; The Return Of The Whistler
Duarte, Armando (act.): Zorro, The Gay Blade
Duarte, Felix (act.): The Mutations
Dubac, Robert (act.): Alien High
DuBarry, Denise (act.): The Darker Side Of Terror; The Devil And Max Devlin; Monster In The Closet
Dubbins, Don (act.): Enchanted Island; From The Earth To The Moon; The Illustrated Man
Dubencourt, Jean (act.): La Chute De La Maison Usher
Duberg, Axel (act.): Ansiktet; The Devil's Eye
Dubin, Alexis (act.): Madman
Dubin, Charles S. (dir.): Topper (1979)
Dubin, Gary (act.): Jaws 2; Midnight Offerings; Time Walker
Dubin, Mitchell (cin): Meet The Applegates
Dubin, Steven (cin): Godzilla 1985
Dublin, Dan (act.): War Of The Planets
Dublin, Jessica (act.): Fragment Of Fear; The Toxic Avenger, Part II; The Toxic Avenger, Part III: The Last Temptation Of Toxie
Dublino, Daniele (act.): The Black Belly Of The Tarantula
DuBois, Kit (wri.): Cellar Dweller
Dubois, Marie (act, b. 1937): The Serpent
Du Bois, Marta (act.): The Trial Of The Incredible Hulk
Dubose, Tyrone (act.): A Polish Vampire In Burbank
Dubost, Paulette (act.): Lola Montes; The Rules Of The Game
Dubov, Paul (act.): The Atomic Submarine; Day The World Ended (1955); The She-Creature; The Underwater City; Voodoo Woman
DuBrey, Claire (act.): Charlie Chan's Murder Cruise; Close Call For Ellery Queen; Devil Doll (1936); Gabriel Over The White House; Raiders Of The Seven Seas
Ducados, Coco (act.): Perceval
Duce, Sharon (act.): Outland
Duchaussoy, Michel (act.): The Killing Game; Traitement De Choc
Duchesne, Roger (act.): Le Golem (1936)
Duckworth, Todd (act.): Runaway
DuClos, Danielle (act.): The Cradle Will Fall
Ducommun, Rick (act.): The 'Burbs; Ghost In The Machine; Gremlins 2: The New Batch; Groundhog Day; Little Monsters
Du Crow, Tote (act.): Don Q, Son Of Zorro; The Thief Of Bagdad (1924)
Duda, John Joseph (act.): Flatliners
Dudarova, Ludmilla (act.): The Kremlin Letter; Ulysses
Dydek, Marty (act.): Party Line
Dudgeon, Elspeth (act.): Bulldog Drummond's Secret Police; Bulldog Drummond Strikes Back (1947); Devotion
Dudgeon, John (act.): The Old Dark House (1932)
Dudikoff, Michael (act.): Radioactive Dreams
Dudko, Appolonari (dir & wri): The Sleeping Beauty (1965, Russ)
Dudley, Bernard (dir.): Love In The Welsh Hills
Dudley, Carl (wri.): Tobor The Great
Dudley, Lucas (act.): Outbreak
Dudley, Ninon (act.): The Lifeguardsman
Dudley, Robert (act.): Portrait Of Jennie
Duell, William (act.): Elvira, Mistress Of The Dark
Duering, Carl (act.): The Boys From Brazil; A Clockwork Orange; Seven Thunders; Zex
Dufaux, Georges (cin): Isabel
Duff, Amanda (act.): The Devil Commands; Mr. Moto In Danger Island
Duff, Denice (act.): Bloodstone: Subspecies II
Duff, Howard (act, 1913-1990): Illegal Entry; Jennifer (1953); Monster In The Closet; No Way Out; Oh, God! Book II; Panic In The City; Spaceways; Spy Hunt; War Gods Of Babylon; Woman In Hiding
Duff, Norwich (act.): Short Circuit 2
Duff, Norwick (act.): Superman (1978)
Duff, Warren b. (wri, b. 1904): Deluge
Duffell, Bee (act.): Battle Beneath The Earth; Fahrenheit 451; Monty Python And The Holy Grail; Quatermass And The Pit
Duffell, Peter (dir.): The House That Dripped Blood
Duff-Griffin, William (act.): Romeo Is Bleeding
Duffield, Brainerd (act.): Macbeth (1947)
Duffield, Brainerd (wri.): The Treasure Of Lost Canyon
Duffield, Michael (act.): The Last Wave
Duffin, Robert (cin): Princess Warrior
Duffy (act.): The Phantom Empire
Duffy, Albert (wri, b. 1903): The Lone Wolf Strikes
Duffy, Dave (act.): Hamlet (1990)
Duffy, Jack (act.): Blackie's Redemption
Duffy, Jesse (wri.): Captain Mephisto And The Transformation Machine; Cyclotrode X
Duffy, Karen (act.): Synapse
Duffy, Michael (wri.): Blind Alley
Duffy, Patrick (act, b. 1949): Alice In Wonderland (1985); Cry For The Strangers; 14 Going On 30; The Man From Atlantis; Too Good To Be True
Duffy, Quinn (act.): The Nutty Professor (1996)
Duffy, Thomas F. (act.): Wolf
Duffy, William (act.): No Blade Of Grass
Dufilho, Jacques (act.): Nosferatu, The Vampyre; La Poupee; Saadia
Dufour, Val (act, b. 1927): The Undead
Dufour, Yvon (act.): King Solomon's Treasure
Dugan, Dennis (act.): The Howling; The Spaceman And King Arthur
Dugan, Earle (act.): Creature
Dugan, John (act.): The Texas Chainsaw Massacre
Dugan, Michael (act.): The Destructors; Ghost Diver; The Monster That Challenged The World
Dugan, Michael (dir.): Mausoleum
Dugan, Michael J. (cin): Beyond Atlantis
Dugan, Tom (act, 1889-1958): Doctor X; Ellery Queen And The Murder Ring; Ellery Queen's Penthouse Mystery; The Ghost Breakers; The Lone Wolf Spy Hunt; The Shadow Returns; Song Of The Thin Man
Dugan, Tom (1980s act): Ghostbusters II
Dugay, Yvette (act.): Ali Baba And The Forty Thieves (1943); Francis Covers The Big Town; Hiawatha
Dugdale, Annette (act.): Trick Or Treats
Dugdale, George (dir & wri): Slaughter High
Duggan, Andrew (act, 1923-1988): A Fire In The Sky (1978); Frankenstein Island; The Incredible Mr. Limpet; In Like Flint; It Lives Again; It's Alive (1974); A Return To Salem's Lot; Seven Days In May; The Time Machine (1978)
Duggan, Cal (act.): Curse Of The Swamp Creature; Mars Needs Women
Duggan, Gerry (act.): Goldfinger
Duggan, Nancy (act.): A Return To Salem's Lot
Duggan, Patrick (act.): Wizards Of The Lost Kingdom
Duggan, Richard (act.): It's Alive III: Island Of The Alive; A Return To Salem's Lot; The Toxic Avenger; Wicked Stepmother
Duggan, Terry (act.): Murder By Decree; Schizo (1977)
Duggan, Tom (act.): Frankenstein (1970)
Duggan, Tommy/Thomas (act.): The Adding Machine; The Final Conflict; Fury At Smugglers' Bay; The Omen; Superman II
Dugo, Ern (act.): Voodoo Heartbeat
Duguay, Christian (dir.): Screamers (1996)
du Gue, Cecil (act.): The Beggar Girl's Wedding; The Green Terror; Silent Evidence
Duhaime, Terri (act.): The Fan
Duhamel, Andre (wri.): Cet Homme Est Dangereux
Duigan, John (dir.): Wide Sargasso Sea
Dukakis, John (act.): Delusion; Jaws 2
Dukakis, Olympia (act.): In The Spirit
Dukas, Jim (act.): The Stuff
Duke (act.): The Girl In A Swing
Duke, Bill (act.): Predator
Duke Jr., Charles M. (act.): For All Mankind
Duke, Daryl (dir.): Charlie Chan: Happiness Is A Warm Clue
Duke, Forrest (act.): Voodoo Heartbeat
Duke, Freddie (act.): Nomads
Duke (Astin), Patty (act, b. 1946): Amityville: The Evil Escapes; The Babysitter; Curse Of The Black Widow; 4D Man; Journey To The Unknown; Look What's Happened To Rosemary's Baby; Prelude To A Kiss; She Waits; The Swarm; You'll Like My Mother
Duke, Robin (act.): Blue Monkey
Dukes, David (act.): Date With An Angel; A Fire In The Sky (1978); The Handmaid's Tale; Rawhead Rex; Turn Back The Clock
Dukinfield, William Claude (act.): see Fields, W.C.

Dulac, Germaine (dir, 1882-1942): *La Coquille Et Le Clergyman*
Dullaghan, John (act): *The Thing With Two Heads*
Dullea, Keir (act, b. 1936): *The Alien Oro; The Beginning; Blind Date; Brave New World; Bunny Lake Is Missing; De Sade; Full Circle; The Next One; No Place To Hide; The Return (1973, Can); Shadow Of Death (1983); Silent Night, Evil Night; 2001: A Space Odyssey; 2010; Welcome To Blood City*
Dulo, Jane (act): *Soylent Green*
Dumar, Louis (act): *Salome (1922)*
Dumas, Alexander (wri, 1802-1870): *The Bandits Of Corsica; Black Magic (1949); The Black Tulip (1921 & 1937); Le Comte De Monte Cristo; The Corsican Brothers (1897, 1902, 1941 & 1960); The Count Of Monte Cristo (1912, 1934, 1955 & 1975); Fencing Contest From 'The Three Musketeers'; The Fifth Musketeer; The Iron Mask; The King's Daughter; The Lady In The Iron Mask; The Man In The Iron Mask (1939, 1962 & 1998); Monte Cristo; The Three Musketeers (1921, 1923, 1939, 1948, 1974 & 1993); I Tre Moschettieri, Les Trois Mousquetaires; La Tulipe Noire*
Dumas, C. (act): *Raiders Of The Living Dead*
Dumat, Philippe (act): *Les Parapluies De Cherbourg*
du Maurier, Daphne (wri, 1907-1989): *The Birds; Don't Look Now; Jamaica Inn (1939 & 1985); My Cousin Rachel; Rebecca*
du Maurier, George (wri, 1834-1896): *Peter Ibbetson; Svengali (1927, 1931, 1954 & 1983); Trilby (1914, 1915, 1922 & 1923)*
du Maurier, Gerald (act): *I Was A Spy; The Scotland Yard Mystery*
du Maurier, Gerald (wri): *Bulldog Drummond (1929)*
Dumbrille, Douglass (act, 1890-1974): *Castle In The Desert; The Cat Creeps (1946); The Catman Of Paris; Charlie Chan At Treasure Island; Charlie Chan In City In Darkness; Crime And Punishment (1935); Ellery Queen And The Perfect Crime; The Frozen Ghost; Gypsy Wildcat; I Married An Angel; The Jungle Woman; King Of The Jungle; The Lone Wolf And His Lady; The Lone Wolf Returns (1935); Lost In A Harem; Michael Shayne, Private Detective; Mr. Moto In Danger Island; A Night In Paradise; Peter Ibbetson; Rapture; The Road To Utopia; Spook Busters*
Dumbrowski, Jim (act): *Mutants In Paradise*
Dumesnil, Jacques (act): *Gold (French-Speaking Version); Ulysses*
Dumke, Ralph (act): *Francis In The Haunted House; Invasion Of The Body Snatchers (1956); Mystery Street*
Dumont, Danielle (act): *The Hunchback Of Notre Dame (1957)*
Dumont, Guy (act): *The Boys From Brazil*
Dumont, J.K. (act): *Dead Of Night (1987)*
Dumont, J.M. (act): *The Miracle Man (1919)*
Dumont, Margaret (act, 1889-1965, nee Daisy Baker): *The Horn Blows At Midnight; Zotz!*
Dumont, Richard (act): *The Kiss (1988)*
Dumont, Roberto (act): *Dr. Tarr's Torture Dungeon; Zorro, The Gay Blade*
Dumouchel, Steve (act): *Matinee*
Dumur, Michel (act): *Diabolique (1955)*
Dun, Dennis (act): *Big Trouble In Little China; Prince Of Darkness*
Duna, Steffi (act): *Phantom Raiders*
Dunagan, Donnie (act): *Son Of Frankenstein; Tower Of London (1939)*
Dunard, David (act): *Retribution (1988)*
Dunaway, Don Carlos (wri): *Cujo; Impulse (1984)*
Dunaway, Faye (act, b. 1941): *The Deadly Trap; The Extraordinary Seaman; Eyes Of Laura Mars; The Handmaid's Tale; Supergirl (1984); 3 Days Of The Condor; The Three Musketeers (1974); The Towering Inferno*
Dunbar, David (act): *The Return Of Dr. Fu Manchu*
Dunbar, Dorothy (act): *Tarzan And The Golden Lion*
Dunbar, John (act): *The Quatermass Conclusion*
Dunbar, Olive (act): *The Hearse*
Dunbar, Robert (act): *Nightwing*
Dunbar, Robert (wri): *The Man Upstairs; Model For Murder; The Solitary Child*
Dunbar, Viola (act): *Angel Heart*
[illegible] *(1963); The Phoenix (1981); Simon, King Of The Witches*
Duncan, Ann (act): *The Black Cat (1934)*
Duncan, Archie (act, b. 1914): *The Bad Lord Byron; The Boy And The Pirates; Counterspy; The Horror Of It All; Lancelot And Guinevere; The Story Of Robin Hood*
Duncan, Arlene (act): *An American Christmas Carol; Body Parts*
Duncan, Barbara (act): *The Clan Of The Cave Bear*
Duncan, Betty (act): *Neither The Sea Nor The Sand*
Duncan, Carmen (act): *Harlequin*
Duncan, Charles (cin): *Plan 9 From Outer Space; Terrified*
Duncan, Craig (act): *Blood Of Dracula*
Duncan, David (wri, b. 1913): *The Black Scorpion; Fantastic Voyage; The Leech Woman; Monster On The Campus; The Monster That Challenged The World; The Thing That Couldn't Die; The Time Machine (1960); The White Orchid*
Duncan, F. Martin (dir): *Cheese Mites*
Duncan, Frank (act): *Assassin (1973)*
Duncan, J. (act): *The Kidnapped King*
Duncan, Jayson (act): *Mystery Island*
Duncan, Kenne(th) (act): *The Astounding She-Monster; Cyclotrode X; Destination Saturn; Night Of The Ghouls; Radar Secret Service; The Sinister Urge*
Duncan, Kimberly (act): *Wheels Of Terror*
Duncan, Kirk (act): *Blood Of Ghastly Horror; Seconds*
Duncan, Lanny (act): *Mind Over Murder*
Duncan, Lindsay (act): *Body Parts; The Reflecting Skin*
Duncan, Mary (act, b. 1903): *Kismet (1930); The Phantom Of Crestwood*
Duncan, Mary Davis (act): *The Initiation*
Duncan, Michael Clarke (act): *Armageddon*
Duncan, Neil (act): *Split Second (1992)*
Duncan, Pamela (act): *Attack Of The Crab Monsters; It Conquered The World; My Gun Is Quick; The Saracen Blade; The Undead*
Duncan, Peter (act): *Flash Gordon*
Duncan, Robert (act): *Rasputin, The Mad Monk*
Duncan, Sandy (act, b. 1946): *The Cat From Outer Space; Pinocchio*
Duncan, Ted (act): *The Octagon*
Duncan, Trevor (mus): *La Jetee; Little Red Monkey*
Duncanson, Jon (act): *Primal Fear*
Dundee, Jimmie (act): *Mr. Moto In Danger Island*
Dundom, Tim (act): *The Plutonium Incident*
Dunham, George (act): *The Sand Castle*
Dunham, Joanna (act): *The House That Dripped Blood; Possession (1973)*
Dunham, Maudie (act): *The Beetle*
Dunham, Phil (act): *The Man With A Cloak*
Dunham, Phillip (act): *Robin Hood Jr. (1923)*
Dunham, Robert (act): *The Green Slime; Mothra*
Dunhill, Mark (act): *The Lost Missile*
Duning, George (mus, b. 1908): *Arnold; Bell, Book And Candle; Brainstorm (1965); Goliath Awaits; How Awful About Allan; Mask Of The Avenger; My Blood Runs Cold; Nightfall (1956); The Return Of October; Terror In The Wax Museum*
D'Union, Sheila (act): *Frankenstein And The Monster From Hell*
Dunk, Albert J. (cin): *Incubus (1982)*
Dunk, Bert (cin): *Haunted By Her Past; I Still Dream Of Jeannie*
Dunker, Brad (act): *Class Of Nuke'em High*
Dunkin, Claude (act): *Red Planet Mars*
Dunkley, Doretta (act): *Flash Gordon*
Dunlap, Al (act): *Rattlers*
Dunlap, Dawn (act): *Forbidden World*
Dunlap, Jane (act): *Just Imagine*
Dunlap, Pamela (act): *Retribution (1988)*
Dunlap, Paul (mus): *The Angry Red Planet; The Baron Of Arizona; Black Zoo; Blood Of Dracula; Cyborg 2087; Destination Inner Space; The Destructors; Dimension 5; Follow The Hunter; The Four Skulls Of Jonathan Drake; Frankenstein (1970); How To Make A Monster; Invisible Invaders; I Was A Teenage Frankenstein; I Was A Teenage Werewolf; Lost Continent (1951); The Three Stooges In Orbit; The Three Stooges Meet Hercules*
Dunlap, Scott (dir): *Boston Blackie*
Dunlop, G. Thomas (act): *Jaws 2*
Dunlop, Joe (act): *Disciple Of Death*
Dunlop, Lesley (act): *A Distant Scream; The Monster Club*
[illegible]
[illegible] *Devlin; Martians Go Home*
Dunmore, Beatrice (act): *The Wiz*
Dunmyre, Louis (cin): *The Man From Beyond*
Dunn, Andrew (cin): *The Crucible (1996); Threads*
Dunn, Bridgett (act): *Phantom Of The Paradise*
Dunn, Carlyn (act): *Hitler's Daughter; The Quilt Of Hathor*
Dunn, Clara (act): *Scalpel*
Dunn, Clive (act): *The Magic Christian; The Mouse On The Moon*
Dunn, Edward/Eddie (F.) (act): *Boston Blackie And The Law; Dead Man's Eyes; The Falcon In Danger; The Falcon's Brother; The Gay Falcon; The Phantom Thief; The Saint In Palm Springs*
Dunn, Emma (act, 1875-1966): *The Bridge Of San Luis Rey (1944); I Married A Witch; Ladies In Retirement; Son Of Frankenstein; The Woman In White (1948)*
Dunn, Ethne (act): *Dementia 13; The Mutations*
Dunn, Greta (act): *Threads*
Dunn, Harvey b. (act): *Bride Of The Monster; Teenagers From Outer Space*
Dunn, James (act, 1905-1967): *The Ghost And The Guest; The Ghost Goes Wild; The Living Ghost (1942)*
Dunn, Josephine (act, 1906-1983): *The Sorrows Of Satan (1925)*
Dunn, Kathy (act): *13 Frightened Girls*
Dunn, Kevin (act): *Chain Reaction (1996); The 6th Man*
Dunn, Liam (act, 1916-1973): *Charley And The Angel; Miracle On 34th Street (1973); A Reflection Of Fear; Young Frankenstein*
Dunn, Linwood (cin): *The Bible; Damnation Alley*
Dunn, Louise (act): *The Liquidator*
Dunn, Marie (act): *Moonchild*
Dunn, Michael (act, 1934-1973, nee Gary Neil Miller): *El Castello Dell'orrore; The House Of The Damned (1974); Murders In The Rue Morgue (1971); The Mutations; No Way To Teeat A Lady; Werewolf Of Washington*
Dunn, Nicholas (act): *Robin Hood Junior (1975)*
Dunn, Ralph (act): *Boston Blackie Goes Hollywood; Dick Tracy (1945); Gaslight (1944); Genius At Work; The Golden Eye; Larceny In Her Heart; Laura; The Lost Tribe; Mr. Moto In Danger Island; Mr. Moto's Gamble; Mr. Moto Takes A Vacation; Murder Is My Business; Possessed (1947); Three On A Ticket; Too Many Winners*
Dunn, Stephen (act): *Candyman: Farewell To The Flesh*
Dunn, Valentine (act): *Torment (1949)*
Dunn, Violet (act): *The Black Camel*
Dunnam, Bill (act): *Warlock*
Dunnam, Virginia (act): *Piranha (1978)*
Dunne, Dominique (act, 1960-1982): *Poltergeist*
Dunne, Donelda (act): *Silent Night, Bloody Night*
Dunne, Elizabeth (act): *Cat People (1942); A Double Life*
Dunne, Griffin (act, b. 1955): *Amazon Women On The Moon; An American Werewolf In London; The Android Affair; The Fan; Me And Him*
Dunne, Irene (act, 1902-1990): *A Guy Named Joe; It Grows On Trees*
Dunne, James (act): *Echoes*
Dunne, Joe (act): *The Prisoner Of Zenda (1979)*
Dunne, Michael (act): see Dunne, Steve
Dunne, Murphy (mus): *Space Raiders*
Dunne, Philip (wri, 1908-1992): *The Count Of Monte Cristo (1934); The Ghost And Mrs. Muir; Lancer Spy; The Luck Of The Irish*
Dunne, Steve/Stephen (act, a.k.a. Michael Dunne): *Crime Doctor's Diary; Hand Of Death; Shock (1946); The Return Of October*
Dunning, Ellen (act): *Elvira, Mistress Of The Dark*
Dunning, Fred (act): *A Daughter Of Satan (1913); The Terrible 'Tec*
Dunning, Jessica (act): *Night Of The Eagle*
Dunning, Ruth (act): *The House In Nightmare Park; Intimate Relations; Urge To Kill*
Dunnington, Steve (act): *Alien High*
Dunnock, Mildred (act, 1901-1991): *Something Wild; The Spiral Staircase (1975); What Ever Happened To Aunt Alice?*
Dunnock, Patricia (act): *Serial Mom*
[illegible]
[illegible] *Happened Tomorrow*
Dunsmore, Rosemary (act): *Total Recall*
Dunst, Kirsten (act, b. 1982): *Interview With The Vampire; Jumanji*
Dunstan, Eric (act): *Death At Broadcasting House*
Dunstan, Joy (act): *20th Century Oz*
Dunstan, Tom (act): *Goliath Awaits*
Dunstedter, Eddie (mus): *Donovan's Brain*
DuPar, Edwin b. (cin): *From The Earth To The Moon; Ring Of Fear*
Duperey, Annie (act, b. 1947): *The Blood Rose; Spirits Of The Dead*
Duphilo (act): *The Hunchback Of Notre Dame (1957)*
DuPois, Starletta (act): *Chiller; Wolf*
Dupont, Daniel (act): *Candyman: Farewell To The Flesh*
Dupont, Danielle (act): *Invasion Of The Bee Girls*
Dupont, E.A. (Ewald-Andre) (dir, 1891-1956): *The Neanderthal Man; A Night Of Mystery (1937); Return To Treasure Island; The Scarf*
Dupont, Elaine (act): *Beach Girls And The Monster; The Ghost Of Dragstrip Hollow*
duPont, Michael (act): *Hands Of A Stranger*
du Pont, Michael (dir): *The Bloodless Vampire*
Dupouy, Jean (act): *The Phantom Of The Opera (1990)*
Duppin, Andy (act): *Angel Heart*
Du Pratt, Paul (act): *Jack's Back*
Dupree, J.H. (act): *The Killer Shrews*
Dupree, Rick (cin): *I Was A Zombie For The F.B.I.*
DuPree, V.C. (act): *Friday The 13th, Part VIII-Jason Takes Manhattan*
Duprez, Fred (act): *Dark World*
Duprez, John (mus): *Once Bitten; Teenage Mutant Ninja Turtles; Teenage Mutant Ninja Turtles II: The Secret Of The Ooze*
Duprez, June (act, 1918-1984): *And Then There Were None; The Brighton Strangler; The Crimson Circle (1936); The Thief Of Bagdad (1940); The Spy In Black*
Dupuis, Joan (act): *Invasion Of The Saucer Men*
Dupuis, Matthew (act): *Relative Fear*
Dupuis, Paul (act): *The Laughing Lady; Sleeping Car To Trieste*
Dupuis, Roy (act): *Screamers (1996)*
Duralia, Darlene (act): *The Incredible 2-Headed Transplant*
Duran, Javier (act): *Anguish*
Duran, Jim (act): *Equinox*
Duran, Larry (act): *Buck Rogers In The 25th Century; Charlie Chan And The Curse Of The Dragon Queen; The Flame Barrier*
Duran, Lilia (act): *Terror Is A Man*
Duran, Lorene (act): *Phoenix The Warrior*
Duran, Raphael (act): *Babes In Bagdad*
Duran, Richard (act): *Deadly Game*
Duran, Rudy (act): *The Weird Ones*
Durand, Edouard (act): *The Lone Wolf (1924)*
Durand, Jean (act): *The House On Skull Mountain*
Durand, Larry (act): *Lost Horizon (1973)*
Durand, Paul (mus): *Le Saint Mene La Dance*
Duran Duran (mus): *A View To A Kill*
Durang, Christopher (act): *The Butcher's Wife; In The Spirit*
Durant, Don (act): *She-Gods Of Shark Reef*
Durant, Jack (act): *Journey Into Fear (1942)*
Durant, Marjorie (act): *Queen Of Outer Space*
Durant, Maurice (act): *Murder Reported; Peeping Tom*
Durant, Teddy (act): *The Night Walker*
Durante, Jimmy (act, 1893-1980): *The Great Rupert*
Duray, Bill (act): *Desk Set*
Durbin, John (act): *The Annihilator; Cyborg 2: Glass Shadow; Dr. Caligari; Heart And Souls*
Durbridge, Francis (wri): *Paul Temple Returns; Paul Temple's Triumph; The Teckman Mystery; The Vicious Circle (1957)*
Durden, Richard (act): *Batman (1989); Scars Of Dracula*
Durfee, Minta (act, 1897-1975): *The Chance Of A Lifetime*
Durfee, Ross (act): *The Lucifer Complex*
Durgin, Francis Timothy (act): see Calhoun, Rory
Durham, Brad (act): *Dr. Caligari*
Durham, Cathy (act): *Dr. Caligari*
Durham, Donna (act): *A Nightmare On Elm Street 3: Dream Warriors*
[illegible]
Durie, Frederic (act): *The Phantom Of The Opera (1990)*
Durin, John (wri): *B.J. Lang Presents*

Durkin, Father John (act): The Exorcist III
Durkin, Keith C. (act): Galaxina
Durkin, Patrick (act): Raiders Of The Lost Ark
Durkin, Shevonne (act): Ghost In The Machine; Leprechaun 2
Durkus, Jaye (act): Prophecy (1979)
Durning, Bernard (act): Blackie's Redemption
Durning, Bernard J. (dir): The Eleventh Hour (1923)
Durning, Charles (act, b. 1933): Brenda Starr (1992); Dark Night Of The Scarecrow; Dick Tracy (1990); Fatal Sky; The Final Countdown; The Fury; Mrs. Santa Claus; Sisters; Solarbabies; When A Stranger Calls; When A Stranger Calls Back
Durock, Dick (act): Remote Control (1988); The Return Of Swamp Thing; Swamp Thing
Duronslet, Mara (act): Hideaway; The Lawnmower Man; Virtuosity
Durrant, Edward (act): The Fairy Doll; Robin Hood Outlawed
Durrant, Fred W. (dir): The Girl Who Didn't Care; The Picture Of Dorian Gray (1916); The Strange Case Of Philip Kent; The Striped Stocking Gang
Durrant, Terence (act): Starship Invasions
Durrell, Alexandra (act): The Unnamable
Durrell, Michael (act): V
Durren, John (act & wri): The Horrible House On The Hill
d'Urrutia, Frederico (wri): Mission Stardust
Durst, John (dir): One Wish Too Many
Durston, David (E.) (dir & wri): I Drink Your Blood; Stigma
Dury, Ian (act): Judge Dredd
Dury, Jacques (act): Vampire On Bikini Beach
Dury, Susan (act): Jamaica Inn (1985)
Duryea, Dan (act, 1907-1968): The Bamboo Saucer; Black Angel (1946); The Burglar; Five Golden Dragons; Ministry Of Fear; Platinum High School; Storm Fear; Thirty-Six Hours; This Is My Love; The Woman In The Window
Duryea, Peter (act): Is This Trip Really Necessary?
Dusay, Debra (act): Blink
Dusay, Marj (act): A Fire In The Sky (1978)
Duse, Carlo (act): Il Mostro Dell'isola
Dusenberry, Ann (act): Jaws 2; The Possessed (1977)
Dussart, Ghislain (act): The Sand Castle
d'Usseau, Armand (wri): Horror Express; Psychomania (1972)
d'Usseau, Arnaud (wri, 1916-1990): Just Off Broadway; The Man Who Wouldn't Die
d'Usseau, Leon (wri): The Lost City
d'Usseau, Louis (wri): The Clutching Hand
Dussolier, Andre (act): Perceval
Dutch, Debbie (act): The Haunting Of Morella; Sorority Babes And The Creature From Hell
Dutcher, Kevin (act): Trauma (1993)
Dutra, John (act): Rocketship X-M
Dutsch, Nikolaus (act): I Love You, I Kill You
Dutson, Todd (act): The Force On Thunder Mountain
Dutton, Charles S. (act): Alien 3; Night Visitors; A Time To Kill (1996)
Dutton, Syd (cin): Roger Corman's 'Frankenstein Unbound'
Dutton, Syd (wri): Witches' Brew
Duval, Juan (act): Mr. Moto In Danger Island
Duval, Maria (act): The Living Coffin; El Santo Contra Las Vampiras; Las Vampiras (1969)
Duval, Paulette (act): Alias The Lone Wolf; He Who Gets Slapped
Duvall, Robert (act, b. 1930): Countdown; Deep Impact; The Handmaid's Tale; Invasion Of The Body Snatchers (1978); Nightmare In The Sun; Phenomenon; The Scarlet Letter (1995); The Seven-Per-Cent Solution; Sling Blade; Thx 1138
Duvall, Rocky (act): The Video Dead
Duvall, Shelley (act, b. 1949): Mother Goose Rock 'N' Rhyme; The Shining; Suburban Commando; Time Bandits
Duvall, Susan (act): Serial Mom
Duvalles (act): The Burning Court
Duverger, Albert (cin): L'age D'or
Duvernoy, Claude (act): Schizoid (1980)
Duvitski, Janine (act): Dracula (1979)
Duvivier, Julien (dir, 1896-1967): The Burning Court; Le Diable Et Les Dix Commandements; Flesh And Fantasy; Le Golem (1936)
Divibier, Julien (wri, 1896-1967): The Burning Court; Paris When It Sizzles
Dux, Eckard (act): Das Singende Ringende Baumchen
Dux, Frank (act): Highlander; Little Shop Of Horrors (1986)
Duyen, Ky (act): What Price Murder
Dvorak, Ann (act, 1912-1979, nee Anna McKim): Blind Alley; Escape To Danger
Dvorak, Antonin (mus, 1841-1904): The Toxic Avenger, Part III: The Last Temptation Of Toxie
Dvorjetski, Vladislav (act): Solaris
Dvorsky, Peter (act): The Dead Zone; The Kiss (1988); Millennium; Videodrome
Dwan, Allan (dir, 1885-1981): Enchanted Island; The Gorilla (1939); The Iron Mask; Most Dangerous Man Alive; Pearl Of The South Pacific; Robin Hood (1922); The Three Musketeers (1939)
Dwan, Dorothy (act): The Wizard Of Oz (1925)
Dwiggins, Sue Bradford (wri): see Bradford (Dwiggins), Sue
Dwight, Reginald Kenneth (act & mus): see John, Elton
Dwire, Earl (act): Peril From The Planet Mongo; Purple Death From Outer Space
Dworakowski, Marian (act): Those Dear Departed
Dworet, Laurence (wri): Outbreak
Dwyer, David (act): The Exorcist III; Freejack; Robocop 2
Dwyer, Frederick (act): The Resurrection Of Zachary Wheeler
Dwyer, Hilary (act): The Body Stealers; Cry Of The Banshee; The Oblong Box; Witch-Finder General; Wuthering Heights (1970)
Dwyer, Leslie (act, b. 1906): The Bad Lord Byron; The Black Rider; Cloak Without Dagger; Dominique; Double Confession; Face In The Night; The Hour Of 13; Monster Of Terror; One Of Our Dinosaurs Is Missing; The 39 Steps (1959)
Dwyer, Marlo (act): Secrets Of The Lone Wolf; The Sniper
Dyall, Franklin (act): Alibi (1931); Creeping Shadows; The Ringer (1931)
Dyall, Valentine (act, 1908-1985): Casino Royale; City Of The Dead; Corridor Of Mirrors; First Men In The Moon (1964); For Them That Trespass; The Haunting; The Horror Of It All; The Man In Black; Night Comes Too Soon; Night Train For Inverness; Paul Temple Returns; The Queen Of Spades (1948); Room To Let; The Slipper And The Rose; Suspended Alibi; The Wrong Box
Dyce, Hamilton (act): The Double; The Pied Piper (1971)
Dyck, Gerald (act): Empire Of Ash III
Dyck, Jim (act): Empire Of Ash III
Dycus, Thomas (act): The Resurrection Of Zachary Wheeler
D'Yd, D. (act): L'auberge Rouge
Dye, Cameron (act): The Apocalypse; Out Of The Dark; Stranded
Dye, Dale (act): Always; Outbreak
Dyer, Ann(e) (wri): Battle Beyond The Stars (1980); Up From The Depths
Dyer, Dwight Brad (act): Primal Fear
Dyer, Elmer (cin): Dirigible
Dyer, Fred (act): The Lost Patrol (1929)
Dyer, Gary (act): Spawn Of The Slithis
Dyer, Lee (cin): Something Wicked This Way Comes
Dyer, Percy (act): The Fairy Doll; The Fish And The Ring
Dyer, Pete (act): Wolfen
Dyer, Sharon (act): The Pink Chiquitas
Dyer, Stewart (act): A Letter To The Princess
Dyers, Lien (act): Gold (German-Speaking Version); Spione
Dyke, John Hart (act): Assassin (1973)
Dyke, Robert (dir): Moontrap
Dykstra, John (cin): Alice In Wonderland (1985); Batman And Robin; Batman Forever; Invaders From Mars (1986); Lifeforce; Starflight: The Plane That Couldn't Land; Star Trek; Star Wars; Voyage To The Outer Planets
Dylinsky, Bina (act): Shock Chamber
Dymon Jr., Frankie (dir & wri): Death May Be Your Santa Claus
Dynarski, Gene (act): Earthquake
Dyne, Aminta (act): Bulldog Drummond At Bay (1947)
Dyne, Michael (act, 1918-1989): White Pongo
Dyne, Michael (wri, 1818-1989): The Moon-Spinners
Dyneley, Peter (act): Call Me Bwana; Deadly Record; House Of Mystery (1961); The Manster; October Moth; The Strange Awakening; Thunderbirds Are Go; Thunderbird 6
Dyrenforth, Harald (act): Storm Over Tibet
Dyrenforth, James (act): Fiend Without A Face; Floods Of Fear; The Girl Hunters
Dysart, Richard (A.) (act, b. 1929): Back To The Future, Part III; Code Name: Minus One; It Happened One Christmas; Meteor; Prophecy (1979); The Terminal Man; The Thing (1982); Warning Sign
Dyson, Anne (act): The Witches And The Grinnygog
Dyson, Reginald (act): Room To Let
Dyszel, Richard (act): The Galaxy Invader; Nightbeast
Dziubinska, Anulka (act): Liszt O' Mania; Vampyres...Daughters Of Dracula
Dzundza, George (act): The Butcher's Wife; The Limbic Region; Salem's Lot; Something Is Out There

Eadie, Dennis (act): The Man Who Stayed At Home
Eady, David (dir): Faces In The Dark; The Laughing Girl Mystery; Three Cases Of Murder; Where's Johnny
Eady, Piers (act): The Godsend
Eagle, Gordon (act): Wolfen
Eagle, Jim (act): Beastmaster 2: Through The Portal Of Time
Eagle, Roger (act): Howling III; Something Is Out There
Eagle, James (act): Charlie Chan In Egypt; The Thirteenth Guest
Eames, Ian (dir): The Magic Shop; The Munsters' Scary Little Christmas
Earl, Clifford (act): Attempt To Kill; The Haunted House Of Horror; Scream And Scream Again; Subterfuge; Tales From The Crypt
Earl, John St. John (cin): Island Of Terror
Earl, Randy (act): Distortions
Earle, Blanche Taylor (wri): The Dancer Of The Nile
Earle, Edward (act): The Beginning Or The End?; Black Magic (1944); Blue, White And Perfect; Buried Alive (1940); Dark Alibi; Flight To Mars; In The Next Room; Mr. Moto's Gamble; The She-Creature
Earle, Frank (act): Jungle Trail Of The Son Of Tarzan
Earle, Freddie (act): Alice's Adventures In Wonderland (1972)
Earle, Jack (act, 1906-1952): Jack And The Beanstalk (1924)
Earle, Marilee (act): The Lost Missile
Earle, William P.S. (dir & wri): The Dancer Of The Nile
Earles, Daisy (act): Freaks
Earles, Harry (act, b. 1902, nee Kurt Schneider): Freaks; The Unholy Three (1925 & 1930)
Earley, Andrew (act): The Henderson Monster
Earls, Claude (act): Mars Needs Women
Early, David (act): The Dark Half; The Silence Of The Lambs
Easdale, Brian (mus, b. 1909): Black Narcissus; The Elusive Pimpernel (1950); Peeping Tom
Easom, Paul (act): The Lair Of The White Worm
Eason, Bo (act): Tornado!
Eason, B. Reeves ("Breezy") (dir, 1886-1956): Darkest Africa; Radio Ranch; Sharad Of Atlantis
Eason, David (act): Getting Lucky
Eason, Lorraine (act): The Temple Of Venus
East, Carlos (act): The Fear Chamber
East, Charles (act): Isle Of The Snake People
East, Jeff (act): The Day After; Deadly Blessing; Pumpkinhead; Stranger In Our House; Superman (1978)
East, John (act): The Playbirds; Shoot To Kill (1961)
East, John (M.) (act): The Bargain; The Harbour Lights; In The Days Of Robin Hood; The Little Match Girl (1914); The Man In Motley; The Romany Rye
East, John (M.) (wri): The Harbour Lights; The Romany Rye
East, Susanna (act): Captain Kronos: Vampire Hunter; The Fiend (1972)
Easter, Robert (wri): The Toolbox Murders
Eastham, Richard (act): Battle For The Planet Of The Apes; Murderers' Row
Eastin, Steve (act): The Clone Master; The Hidden; Nightmare On The 13th Floor
Eastlake, William (wri, 1918-1997): Castle Keep
Eastman, George (act): Endgame; The Grim Reaper; Ironmaster
Eastman, George (cin): Such Men Are Dangerous
Eastman, Kevin (wri): Teenage Ninja Turtles; Teenage Ninja Turtles II: The Secret Of The Ooze
Eastman, Lynn (act): Phantasm; Project X (1987)
Eastman, Marilyn (act): Night Of The Living Dead (1968)
Eastman, Rodney (act): Beverly Hills Bodysnatchers; A Nightmare On Elm Street 3: Dream Warriors; A Nightmare On Elm Street 4: The Dream Master
Easton, Barbara (act): Those Dear Departed
Easton, Charles (act): The Ghost Talks
Easton, David (act): Cocoon: The Return
Easton, Jacki (act): School Spirit
Easton, Jane (act): Jalopy
Easton, Joyce (act): The Brotherhood Of Satan; The Fury
Easton, Richard (act): Dead Again
Easton, Robert (act, b. 1930): The Giant Spider Invasion; The Loved One; Mr. Sycamore; The Neanderthal Man; A Very Missing Person; Voyage To The Bottom Of The Sea
Easton, Robert (wri, b. 1930): The Giant Spider Invasion
Easton, Sheena (mus, b. 1959): For Your Eyes Only; Santa Claus (1985)
Eastwood, Clint (act, b. 1931): The Beguiled; The Eiger Sanction; Francis In The Navy; Play Misty For Me; Revenge Of The Creature; Tarantula
Eastwood, James (wri): Crossroad Gallows; Devil Girl From Mars; Fatal Journey; The Ghost Train Murder; The Hidden Face; The Last Train; Little Red Monkey; The Man Who Was Nobody; Person Unknown; The Unseeing Eye; Urge To Kill
Easy Squeezin' Alice (act): Attack Of The Killer Tomatoes
Eaton, Charles (act): Double Alibi; The Gaunt Stranger
Eaton, Ken (act): Flesh-Eating Mothers
Eaton, Marjorie (act): The Attic; Hammersmith Is Out; Monstrosity; Night Tide; Witness For The Prosecution; Zombies Of Mora Tau
Eaton, Shirley (act, b. 1937): Around The World Under The Sea; The Blood Of Fu Manchu; Future Women; The Girl Hunters; Goldfinger; Life Is A Circus; The Million Eyes Of Sumuru; Rio 70; The Scorpio Letters; Ten Little Indians (1965); What A Carve Up!
Eaton, Wallas (act): Dark Interval; The Last Wave
Eaves, Carl (act): I Was A Zombie For The F.B.I.
Eaves, Hilary (act): Crimes At The Dark House
Ebara, Shinjiro (act): Invasion Of The Neptune Men
Ebbe, Annevig Schelde (act): The Kingdom
Ebbin, Michael (act): Live And Let Die
Ebbinghouse, Bernard (mus): Invasion (1965); Naked Evil; Tales That Witness Madness
Ebbutt, P.G. (act): Old St. Paul's
Ebdon, James (act): Forever Evil
Ebeier, Jacqueline (act): How To Make A Monster
Eben, Al (act): White Pongo
Eberhardt, Norma (act): The Return Of Dracula
Eberhardt, Thom (dir): Night Of The Comet; Without A Clue
Eberhardt, Thom (wri): Honey, I Blew Up The Kid; Night Of The Comet
Eberhart, Mignon G. (wri): The Dark Stairway
Eberle, Ingo (act): Moon 44
Eberle, Oliver (wri): Moon 44
Ebersole, Christine (act): Dead Again; Mac And Me
Ebert, Carl (act): Der Golem (1914)
Ebinger (Jr.), Robert (cin): The Being; The Loch Ness Monster; School Spirit; Student Bodies
Ebsen, Buddy (act, b. 1908): The Horror At 37,000 Feet
Eburne, Maude (act, 1875-1960): Among The Living; The Bat Whispers; The Boogie Man Will Get You; The Chance Of A Lifetime; L'il Abner (1940); The Vampire Bat
Eby, David (act): Return Of The Living Dead, Part II
Eby-Rock, Helyn (act): The Man With A Cloak
Eccles, Aimee (act): Joe & The Colonel
Eccles, Donald (act): The Quatermass Conclusion; The Wicker Man; Young Sherlock Holmes
Eccles, Jeremy (act): Dr. Faustus
Eccles, Ted (act): Bad Ronald
Echard, Margaret (wri): Lightning Strikes Twice
Echeverria, Sol (act): Vampire's Kiss
Echols, Frank (act): Ed Wood
Echols, J. Kermit (act): Scalpel
Echols, Jill (act): House Of 1,000 Dolls
Eck, Johnny (act, b. 1911): Freaks
Eckart, Norma Jean (act): Houdini
Eckelmann, Thomas (act): I Love You, I Kill You

Eckemyr, Agneta (act): The Island At The Top Of The World
Eckert, David (act): Primal Fear
Eckford, Janet (wri): Mr. Selkie
Eckhardt, Sara (act): Student Bodies
Eckholdt, Steve(n) (act): 14 Going On 30; The Wraith
Eckhouse, James (act): Terminal
Eckstein, George (wri): The Bad Seed (1985); Murder With Mirrors
Eckstein, Hannah (act): Ed Wood
Eckstein, Paul S. (act): Seven
Eco, Umberto (wri): The Name Of The Rose
Eddie Jr. (act): Vampire At Midnight
Eddington, Paul (act, 1927-1995): The Devil Rides Out; The Man Who Was Nobody
Eddins, Beverly (act): Kiss Of The Tarantula
Eddins, Rebecca (act): Kiss Of The Tarantula
Eddins, Susan (act): Kiss Of The Tarantula
Eddins, W. James (act): Kiss Of The Tarantula
Eddison, Robert (act, b. 1908): The Angel Who Pawned Her Harp; The Boy Who Turned Yellow; Indiana Jones And The Last Crusade; Vice Versa (1947)
Eddy, Bonny Kay (act): The Atomic City
Eddy, Helen Jerome (act, 1897-1990): Mata Hari (1932)
Eddy, Nelson (act, 1901-1967): I Married An Angel; Phantom Of The Opera (1943)
Edel, Udi (dir): Rasputin (1996)
Edelman, Herb (act, 1934-1996): The Strange And Deadly Occurrence
Edelman, Randy (mus): Anaconda; Daylight; Diabolique (1996); Dragonheart; Ghostbusters II; The Indian In The Cupboard
Edelman, Steve (act): Fargo
Eden, Barbara (act, b. 1934, nee Barbara Moorhead): The Brass Bottle (1964); Dead Man's Island; Eyes Of Terror; Five Weeks In A Balloon; A Howling In The Woods; I Dream Of Jeannie: Fifteen Years Later; I Still Dream Of Jeannie; 7 Faces Of Dr. Lao; The Stepford Children; The Stranger Within; Visions Of Murder; Voyage To The Bottom Of The Sea; The Woman Hunter; The Wonderful World Of The Brothers Grimm
Eden, Daniel (act): Fear No Evil (1981)
Eden, Jerome (act): 2000 Maniacs
Eden, Mark (act): Curse Of The Crimson Altar; Seance On A Wet Afternoon
Eden, Richard (act): Solar Crisis
Edeson, Arthur (cin, 1891-1970): The Bat (1926); Frankenstein (1931); The Gorilla (1927); The The Invisible Man (1933); The Lost World (1925); The Maltese Falcon (1941); The Mask Of Dimitrios; The Old Dark House (1932); Robin Hood (1922); Satan Met A Lady; A Study In Scarlet (1933); The Thief Of Bagdad (1924); The Three Musketeers (1921); Three Strangers
Edeson, Robert (act, 1868-1931): The Prisoner Of Zenda (1922)
Edgar, Graham (cin): Deadly Strangers
Edgar, Hindle (act): The Scarlet Pimpernel (1934)
Edgar, Marriott (wri): Alf's Button Afloat; The Ghost Train (1941); King Arthur Was A Gentleman
Edgar Kelly Band, The (mus): The Lucifer Complex
Edgcomb, James (act): The Goddess Of Love; The Philadelphia Experiment
Edge, Francis (wri): Black Orchid
Edgerton, Earle (act): Carnival Of Blood
Edgerton, Justin (wri): Last Bride Of Salem
Edgley, George (act): Mars Needs Women; Zontar: The Thing From Venus
Edlin, Tubby (act): Alf's Button (1930)
Edlund, Richard (cin): Alien 3; Big Trouble In Little China; The Boy Who Could Fly; Date With An Angel; Fright Night; Ghostbusters; Masters Of The Universe; The Monster Squad; Multiplicity; Poltergeist II: The Other Side; Return Of The Jedi; Solarbabies; Species; 2010; Vibes
Edmiston, James (wri): Wink Of An Eye
Edmiston, Walker (act): Beach Girls And The Monster; Dick Tracy (1990); Everything's Ducky; Scared To Death (1980)
Edmond, J. Trevor (act): Pumpkinhead II: Blood Wings; Return Of The Living Dead III
Edmond, James (act): Devil Girl From Mars
Edmonds, Don (wri): The Night Stalker (1987)
Edmonds, E.V. (wri): The King's Romance
Edmonds, Fella (act): Supersonic Saucer
Edmonds, James (act): Silent Night, Evil Night
Edmonds, Louis (act): House Of Dark Shadows
Edmonds, Mike (act): Return Of The Jedi; [illegible]
Edmonds, Mitchell (act): It's Alive III: Island Of The Alive

Edmonson, William (act): The Wizard Of Baghdad
Edmund, Justin Pierre (act): The Preacher's Wife
Edmund, Peter (act): Octopussy
Edmunds, John (act): Lifeforce
Edmunds, Jon (act): The Phantom Empire
Edmunds, Robert (wri): The Clairvoyant (1934)
Edmunds, William (act): The Beast With Five Fingers; The Climax; House Of Frankenstein; The Lost Moment; 13 Lead Soldiers
Edney, Beatie (act): Highlander
Edouart, Farciot (cin): Dr. Cyclops
Edsman, Elza (act): Abbott And Costello Go To Mars
Edson, Richard (act): Howard The Duck; Strange Days; Super Mario Bros.
Edwall, Allan (act): The Devil's Eye
Edward, Marion (act): Road Games
Edwardes, Olga (act): Black Orchid
Edwards, Alan (act): Forty Naughty Girls; The Lone Wolf In Mexico
Edwards, Anne (wri): Haunted Summer
Edwards, Anthony (act, b. 1962): Charlie's Ghost Story; Landslide; Miracle Mile; Pet Sematary Two
Edwards, Bill (act): The Bedford Incident; First Man Into Space
Edwards, Blake (act, b. 1922): Strangler Of The Swamp
Edwards, Blake (dir, b. 1922): Experiment In Terror; Justin Case; Switch
Edwards, Blake (wri, b. 1922): The Atomic Kid; The Couch; Switch
Edwards, Bob (cin): The Curse Of King Tut's Tomb; Diagnosis: Murder
Edwards, Bruce (act): Dangerous Money; Dick Tracy (1945); The Falcon In Danger; Queen Of The Amazons (1947); Sombra, The Spider Woman
Edwards, Chris (act): Tales From The Hood
Edwards, Cliff (act, 1895-1971): The Falcon Strikes Back; The Monster And The Girl; Platinum High School
Edwards, Craig (act): Street Trash
Edwards, Darryl (act): The Brother From Another Planet
Edwards, Dorothy (wri): The Witches And The Grinnygog
Edwards, Edgar (act): The Deadly Ray From Mars; Nancy Drew, Troubleshooter; One Million B.C.; Peril From The Planet Mongo; Purple Death From Outer Space
Edwards, Edward (act): RoboCop
Edwards, Elaine (act): The Bat (1959); Curse Of The Faceless Man
Edwards, Elizabeth (act): The Pink Chiquitas
Edwards, Ella (act): Crackle Of Death; Dead Men Tell No Tales
Edwards, Frank (act): The Frighteners
Edwards, Gail (act): Joe & The Colonel
Edwards, George (dir): The Attic
Edwards, George (wri): The Attic; Ruby
Edwards, Glyn(n) (act): Burke And Hare; The Deathshead Vampire; Fragment Of Fear; A Place To Die; The Playbirds
Edwards, Henry (act, 1882-1952): Alone In London; The Bargain; The Cobweb; Double Confession; East Of Piccadilly; The Failure; The Man Who Stayed At Home; A Place Of One's Own; Take My Life
Edwards, Henry (dir, 1882-1952): The Bargain; The Barton Mystery (1932); The Failure; Juggernaut; The Man Who Changed His Name; Scrooge (1935); Trent's Last Case (1952)
Edwards, Henry (wri, 1882-1952): The Bargain; The Failure
Edwards, Henryetta (act): She Shall Have Murder
Edwards, Hugh (act): Lord Of The Flies (1963)
Edwards, J. Gordon (dir): Salome (1917)
Edwards, Ian (act): Gold Of The Amazon Women
Edwards, James (act, 1922-1970): The Manchurian Candidate; The Set-Up; Tarzan's Fight For Life
Edwards, James (wri): Midnight At Madame Tussaud's
Edwards, Jason (act): The Hidden
Edwards, Jeillo (act): Memoirs Of A Survivor; Paint Me A Murder
Edwards, Jimmy (act): The Bed-Sitting Room; A Ghost Of A Chance (1968); Murder At The Windmill
Edwards, Judy (act): Mermaids Of Tiburon
Edwards, Kate (act): Howling IV
Edwards, Keith (act): Batman (1989)
[illegible]
Edwards, Lance (act): Peacemaker
Edwards, Leon (act): The Offspring

Edwards, Leslie (act): Peter Rabbit And The Tales Of Beatrix Potter
Edwards, Luke (act): Not Of This World
Edwards, Mark (act): Blood From The Mummy's Tomb; Tower Of Evil
Edwards, Mark W. (act): Terror In The Wax Museum
Edwards, Maudie (act): The Key Man; Murder In Reverse; The Ugly Duckling
Edwards, Meredith (act): Gulliver's Travels (1977); The Lavender Hill Mob; Mad About Men; Zex
Edwards, Neely (act): Mr. Moto In Danger Island
Edwards, Paddi (act): It Came Upon The Midnight Clear
Edwards, Patty (act): The New House On The Left
Edwards, Penny (act): Missing Women; Woman In The Dark
Edwards, Percy (act): The Dark Crystal
Edwards, Ronnie Claire (act): Future Cop
Edwards, Sarah (act): Charlie Chan In The Secret Service
Edwards, Snitz (act): The Mysterious Island (1929); The Phantom Of The Opera (1925); The Thief Of Bagdad (1924)
Edwards, Stacy (act): The Fear (1994)
Edwards, Stephen (mus): Orpheus Descending
Edwards, Thornton (act): The Chinese Ring; The False Faces
Edwards, Tim (act): Making Contact
Edwards, Tom (wri): Wizards Of The Lost Kingdom
Edwards, Tony (act): C.H.U.D. II; Starman
Edwards, Vince (act, 1928-1996): Cellar Dweller; Cell 2455, Death Row; Do Not Fold, Spindle Or Mutilate; The Fear (1994); Hiawatha; Island Women; The Killing; The Mad Bomber; Murder By Contract; Return To Horror High; The Scavengers; The Seduction; Sole Survivor; Space Raiders; The Three Faces Of Eve; To Die For II: Son Of Darkness
Edwards, Whit (act): Mr. Destiny
Edwards, William C. (wri): The Mummy And The Curse Of The Jackals
Edwards, William (dir & wri): Dracula (The Dirty Old Man)
Edzard, Christine (dir): Stories From A Flying Trunk
Edzard, Christine (wri): Peter Rabbit And The Tales Of Beatrix Potter; Stories From A Flying Trunk
Eejima, Suesie (act): Soylent Green
Eero, Joseph (act): Igor And The Lunatics
Effa, Karel (act): Baron Prasil
Effects Associates (cin): Hawk The Slayer; The Quatermass Conclusion
Effel, Jean (dir): La Creation Du Monde
Efremov, Ivan (wri): The Andromeda Nebula
Efron, David (act): Fright Night II
Efron, Marshall (act): Blade
Efroni, Yehuda (act): Ten Little Indians (1989)
Egan, Aeryk (act): Flatliners; Shrunken Heads
Egan, Bernard (act): The Plague Of The Zombies
Egan, Eddie (act): Night Of Terror (1972)
Egan, Jenny (act): They Might Be Giants
Egan, Maggie (act): Communion
Egan, Mary (M.) (act): Return Of The Killer Tomatoes; Wicked Stepmother
Egan, Richard (act, 1921-1987): The Big Cube; Blackbeard The Pirate; The Destructors; Gog; The House That Wouldn't Die; Split Second (1953); Undercover Girl (1950)
Egan, Sam (wri): Elvira, Mistress Of The Dark
Egan, Terence (wri): The Shadow (1933)
Egbert, Albert (act & wri): The Dustman's Nightmare
Egbert, Seth (act & wri): The Dustman's Nightmare
Ege, Julie (act): Craze; Creatures The World Forgot; It's Not The Size That Counts; The Last Days Of Man On Earth; Legend Of The Seven Golden Vampires; The Mutations; On Her Majesty's Secret Service; Rentadick
Egelhof, Kurt (act): The Ghost And The Darkness
Eger, Harvey (act): Martin
Eggar, Samantha (act, b. 1940): The Brood; The Collector; Curtains; The Dead Are Alive; Demonoid; Dr. Crippen; Dr. Dolittle; A Ghost In Monte Carlo; The Light At The Edge Of The World; Psyche 59; Return From The Ashes; The Seven-Per-Cent Solution; The Uncanny; Welcome To Blood City
Eggby, David (cin): The Blood Of Heroes; Chilling; Daylight; Dragonheart; Fortress; Mad Max; Warlock
[illegible]
Eggen, Albert (act): Runaway
Eggenton, Joseph (act): Black Dragons
Eggericks, Marianne (act): Caravan To Vaccares

Eggers, Fred (wri): The Return Of Mr. Moto
Eggert, Konstantin (act): Aelita
Eggert, Nicole (act): Amanda And The Alien; The Annihilator; The Clan Of The Cave Bear; The Demolitionist; The Haunting Of Morella
Eggett, John (cin): Fear No Evil (1981)
Eggleston, Estelle (act): see Stevens, Stella
Egilsson, Eagle (cin): A Face To Die For
Eginton, Madison (act): Star Trek: Generations
Eglee, Charles (wri): Deadly Eyes
Egleton, Clive (wri): The Black Windmill
Ego, Sandra (act): Fer-De-Lance
Egon, Robert (act): Captain America (1992)
Ehlers, Beth (act): The Hunger
Ehlers, Paul (act): Madman
Ehrlich, Jesse (act): Frightmare (1983)
Ehrlich, Max (Simon) (wri, 1909-1983): The Glass Web; The Naked Edge; The Reincarnation Of Peter Proud; Z.P.G.
Ehrlich, Peter (act): Hauser's Memory
Ehrlich, Suzanne (act): Flesh-Eating Mothers
Ehser, Else (act): Das Schloss
Eichberger, Willy (act): see Esmond, Carl
Eichelberger, Ezra (act): The Cradle Will Fall
Eichhorn, Lisa (act, b. 1952): Grim Prairie Tales; Moon 44
Eichhorst, Adam (act): Mr. Destiny
Eide, Elsie (act): The Witches (1990)
Eidelman, Cliff (mus): The Meteor Man; Star Trek VI: The Undiscovered Country; To Die For
Eikenberry, Jill (act, b. 1947): The Manhattan Project
Eilbacher, Cynthia/Cindy (act): Bad Ronald; A Fire In The Sky (1978); Shanks
Eilbacher, Lisa (act): Bad Ronald; Deadly Intent; Leviathan; Spider-Man; This House Possessed
Eilber, Janet (act): The Craft
Eilers, Kurt (act): The Last Ten Days Of Adolf Hitler
Eilers, Sally (act): The Black Camel
Eimerman, John (act): The Capture Of Bigfoot
Einer, Bob (act): Invasion Of The Saucer Men
Einfeld, Richard (dir & wri): Ghost Diver
Einhorn, RichArd (mus): Dead Of Winter; The Prowler (1981); Shock Waves; Sister, Sister
Eirik, Sten (act): Darkman II: The Return Of Durant; Electra (1995)
Eirikson, Tom (act): Timecop
Eis, Alice (act): The Vampire (1913, USA)
Eis, Elizabeth (act): Dear, Dead Delilah
Eisele, Robert (wri): Darkman II: The Return Of Durant
Eiseman, Jack (act): Waxwork II: Lost In Time
Eiseman, Lori (act): To All A Goodnight
Eisen, Hal (act): Body Parts
Eisenberg, Aaron (act): Amityville: The Evil Escapes
Eisenberg, Avner (act): The Jewel Of The Nile
Eisenberg, D.F. (wri): Dream A Little Dream
Eisenberg, Ned (act): The Burning
Eisenbise, David (act): The China Syndrome
Eisenhart, Tim (act): Earthbound (1981)
Eisenman, Morrie (act): The Tomb
Eisenmann II, Al (act): Remote Control (1988)
Eisenmann, Ike (act): Devil Dog: The Hound Of Hell; Escape To Witch Mountain; Return From Witch Mountain; Terror Out Of The Sky
Eisenstein, Harry (cin): Flesh-Eating Mothers
Eisinger, Jo (wri): Mistress Of The World (1959); The Scorpio Letters
Eisley, Anthony/Tony (act): The Doll Squad; Dracula Vs. Frankenstein; Journey To The Center Of Time; Lightning Bolt; The Mighty Gorga; Monstroid; The Mummy And The Curse Of The Jackals; The Navy vs. The Night Monsters; They Ran For Their Lives; The Witchmaker
Eisley, Fred (act): The Wasp Woman
Eisley, Jonathan (act): The Brotherhood Of Satan
Eisnach, Joey (act): The Swarm
Eisner, David (act): Happy Birthday To Me; Phobia
Eisner, Will (wri): The Spirit
Eitner, Don(ald) (act): The Beginning Of The End; Kronos (1957); Queen Of Blood
Ek, Anders (act): Det Sjunde Inseglet
Ekberg, Anita (act, b. 1931): Abbott And Costello Go To Mars; The Alphabet Murders; Call Me Bwana; The Cobra; Fangs Of The Living Dead; The Glass Sphinx; The Golden Blade; Gold Of The Amazon Women; The Man Inside; Screaming Mimi; S*H*E (1980); Valerie; Way...Way Out
Ekborg, Lars (act): Ansiktet
Ekerot, Bengt (act): Ansiktet; Det Sjunde Inseglet
[illegible]
Ekland, Britt (act, b. 1942): Asylum; The Double Man; Endless Night; King Solomon's Treasure; The Man With The Golden Gun;

The Monster Club; Moon In Scorpio; Night Hair Child; Percy; Royal Flash; Satan's Mistress; The Wicker Man
Ekman, Gosta (act, 1888-1937): *Faust (1926)*
Ekman, Hasse (act, b. 1915): *The Devil's Wanton*
Ekstrom, Jan (wri): *Morianna*
Elalaily, Ezzat (act): *A Story Of Tutankhamun*
Elam, Greg (act): *Endangered Species*
Elam, Jack (act, b. 1916): *Aurira Encounter; Creature From Black Lake; Kiss Me Deadly; The Norsemen; Suburban Commando; Tarzan's Hidden Jungle*
Elan, Joan (act): *Jane Eyre (1957)*
Elbein, Jan (wri): *Capture That Capsule!*
Elbling, Peter (act): *Once Bitten; The Stepford Children*
Elbling, Peter (wri): *Honey, I Blew Up The Kid*
Elcar, Dana (act): *All Of Me; Code Name: Minus One; Condorman; Dying Room Only; The Fool Killer; The Nude Bomb; 2010*
Elder, Charles (act): *Change Of Mind*
Elder, Gordon (act): *Lord Of The Flies (1990)*
Elder, John (dir & wri): see Hinds, Anthony
El Din, Seif (act): *A Story Of Tutankhamun*
Eldred, Stig (act): *Dick Tracy (1990)*
Eldredge, John (act, 1904-1960): *The Black Cat (1941); Champagne For Caesar; Charlie Chan At The Olympics; Dark Alibi; Horror Island; I Married A Monster From Outer Space; Sh! The Octopus; The Sky Dragon; Valley Of The Headhunters*
Eldridge, Craig (act): *The Long Kiss Goodnight*
Eldridge, Florence (act, 1901-1988): *An Act Of Murder (1948); The Greene Murder Case; Les Miserables (1935)*
Eldridge, George (act): *Calling Dr. Death; The Corpse Vanishes; Dark Alibi; Jungle Jim In The Forbidden Land; The Living Ghost (1942); Riders To The Stars; Shadows Over Chinatown; The Shanghai Chest; The Sky Dragon*
Eldridge, James Henry (act): *Skullduggery*
Eldridge, John (wri): *One Wish Too Many; Pool Of London*
Eldridge, June (act): *The Dancer Of The Nile*
Elen, Cissie (act): *The Bishop's Silence*
Eleniak, Erika (act): *Tales From The Crypt Present Bordello Of Blood*
Elerick, John (act): *Demon And The Mummy; Earthquake; Embryo*
Eles, Sandor (act): *And Soon The Darkness; Countess Dracula; Evil Of Frankenstein; The Kremlin Letter; The Naked Edge*
Elfers, Konrad (mus): *Funeral In Berlin*
Elfman, Bodhi (act): *Wes Craven's New Nightmare*
Elfman, Danny (act, b. 1955): *The Nightmare Before Christmas*
Elfman, Danny (mus, b. 1955): *Batman (1989); Beetlejuice; Darkman (1990); Darkman II: The Return Of Durant; Dick Tracy (1990); Dolores Claiborne; Edward Scissorhands; Extreme Measures; The Flash; Freeway; The Frighteners; Mars Attacks!; Mission: Impossible; Nightbreed; The Nightmare Before Christmas; Scrooged; Tales From The Crypt Presents Bordello Of Blood*
Elg, Taina (act, b. 1931): *The Bacchantes; Hercules In New York; The 39 Steps (1959); Watusi*
Elgar, Avril (act): *The Medusa Touch*
Elhardt, Ingrid (act): *Sampa*
Elian, Yona (act): *The Jerusalem File*
Elias, Alix (act): *Pandemonium*
Elias, Arie (act): *The Jerusalem File*
Elias, Cyrus (act): *Roger Corman's 'Frankenstein Unbound'; She (1983)*
Elias, Hector (act): *It Came Upon The Midnight Clear*
Elias, Jeannie (act): *The Pit (1983)*
Elias, Jonathan (mus): *Children Of The Corn; Grave Secrets; Leprechaun 2; Parents; Vamp*
Elias, Robert (act): *Switch*
Elic, Joe (act): *Santa Claus Conquers The Martians*
Elikann, Larry (dir): *Terminal; Turn Back The Clock*
Eliot, John (wri): *Secrets Of Sex*
Eliot, Laura (act): *Jamaica Run; Samson And Delilah; Special Agents; Strangers On A Train; Two Lost Worlds*
Eliot, Mary (act): *The Crater Lake Monster*
Elise, Christine (act): *The Body Snatchers; Child's Play 2*
Elise, Marie (act): *Arthur The King*
Elizabeth of Toro (act): *Sheena*
Elizabeth, Kathleen (act): *Roller Blade Warriors: Taken By Force*
Elizondo, Chuy (cin): *Destroyer*
Elizondo, Evangelina (act): *El Castillo De Los Monstruos; Flying Saucers*
Elizondo, Everado (act): *Lord Of The Flies (1990)*
Elizondo, Hector (act, b. 1936): *Exit To Eden; The Fan; Leviathan*
Elizondo, Jesus (cin): *In The Shadow Of Kilimanjaro*
Elk, Jim (act): *Wavelength*
El-Kadi, Nameer (act): *Quest For Fire*
Elkin, Clifford (act): *The Scarlet Blade*
Elkins, Marvin (act): *Shocker*
Elkins, Michael (wri): *Dog Eat Dog*
Elkins, Saul (wri): *Charlie Chan At The Race Track*
Elkus, Geri (act): *Bloodspell*
Ellen, Jack (act): *The Headless Ghost*
Ellenshaw, Harrison (cin): *Superman IV: The Quest For Peace*
Ellenshaw, P.S./Peter (cin): *The Man Who Fell To Earth (1976); Mary Poppins*
Ellenstein, Robert (act): *Love At First Bite; Star Trek IV: The Voyage Home*
Eller, Kermit (act): *Scared To Death (1980)*
Eller, M. (wri): *El Invencible Hombre Invisible*
Ellerbe, Harry (act, 1901-1992): *Desk Set; The Haunted Palace (1963); House Of Usher; The Magnetic Monster; Murder On A Honeymoon*
Elles, Fred (dir & wri): *Mrs. Pym Of Scotland Yard*
Ellingson, Brad (act): *Rana: The Legend Of Shadow Lake*
Ellington, "Duke" (Edward Kennedy) (act, 1899-1974): *Cabin In The Sky*
Ellington, "Duke" (Edward Kennedy) (mus, 1899-1974): *Change Of Mind*
Ellington, E.A. (wri): *Gilda*
Elliot, Biff (act): *The Dark (1979); Destination Inner SPACE*
Elliot, Erika (act): *Creation Of The Humanoids*
Elliot, Gertrude (act): *Hamlet (1913)*
Elliot, Gizelle (act): *Flight Of The Navigator*
Elliot, John (act): *The Clutching Hand*
Elliot, Lillian (act): *Liliom (1930)*
Elliot, Mark (GB act): *Edge Of Sanity*
Elliot, Mark (USA act): *Raiders Of The Living Dead*
Elliot, Patricia (act): *The Green Slime*
Elliot, Paul (cin): *976-Evil*
Elliot, Peter (act): *King Kong Lives; Missing Link*
Elliot, Peter (mus): *House Of The Living Dead*
Elliot, Richard (mus): *Teen Witch*
Elliot, Rosalind (act): *Murders In The Rue Morgue (1971)*
Elliot, Steve (act): *Yeti*
Elliot, Tim (act): *Avengers Of The Reef*
Elliot, Yves (act): *Quelqu-Un Derriere La Porte*
Elliott, Alison (act): *Killer's Moon*
Elliott, Biff (act): *I, The Jury (1953)*
Elliott, Bill (act): *Calling Homicide; Chain Of Evidence; Footsteps In The Night; Sudden Danger*
Elliott, Caroline (act): *Unforgettable*
Elliott, Cecil (act): *The Lost Missile; The Three Stooges Meet Hercules*
Elliott, Chris (act): *Groundhog Day*
Elliott, David (act): *Jaws 2; The Possession Of Joel Delaney*
Elliott, Dean (mus): *The Phantom Tollbooth*
Elliott, Denholm (act, 1922-1992): *The Boys From Brazil; The Hound Of The Baskervilles (1978 & 1982); The House That Dripped Blood; Indiana Jones And The Last Crusade; It's Not The Size That Counts; Madame Sin; Maroc 7; Percy; Quest For Love; Raiders Of The Lost Ark; The Ringer (1952); Robin And Marian; The Sound Barrier; The Spy With A Cold Nose; To The Devil A Daughter; Transmutations; The Vault Of Horror; Watership Down*
Elliott, Dick (act): *After Midnight With Boston Blackie; Another Thin Man; Dangerous Money; Hold That Hypnotist; The Lone Wolf Spy Hunt; Mr. Moto's Gamble; Nancy Drew And The Hidden Staircase; Up In Smoke; Witness To Murder*
Elliott, Edythe (act): *Dick Tracy (1945)*
Elliott, Frank (act, b. 1880): *Bulldog Drummond Escapes*
Elliott, Gerald (wri): *The Fatal Hour (1937); The Frog; Museum Mystery; The Return Of The Frog*
Elliott, Gordon (act): *Lady In The Morgue; The Private Life Of Helen Of Troy*
Elliott, Helen (act): *The Adding Machine*
Elliott, Jack (mus): *Final Eye; Oh, God!; Sanctuary Of Fear*
Elliott, John (act): *Calling Dr. Death; Charlie Chan At Treasure Island; Cry Wolf (1947); The Mad Monster; Satan Met A Lady; The Wizard Of Gore*
Elliott, John (1980s act): *The Being*
Elliott, Maxine (act): *Wicked Stepmother*
Elliott, Mike (act): *Sorority House Massacre 2*
Elliott, Nancy (act): *The Tribe*
Elliott, Paul (cin): *And You Thought Your Parents Were Weird; The Tomb*
Elliott, Peter (act): *Battle Beneath The Earth; The Island Of Dr. Moreau (1996); Night Of The Demon (1957); Noddy In Toyland; Return To Oz; Web Of Suspicion*
Elliott, Peter J. (act): *The Demon (1981)*
Elliott, Robert (act): *The Lone Wolf's Daughter (1929); The Maltese Falcon (1931); The Saint Strikes Back*
Elliott, Robert (1990s act): *Wheels Of Terror*
Elliott, Ross (act): *Alfred Hitchcock Presents; The Beast From 20,000 Fathoms; The Crawling Hand; Indestructible Man; Monster On The Campus; Tarantula; The Towering Inferno; Woman In The Dark*
Elliott, Sam (act, b. 1944): *The Blue Lightning; Frogs; The Legacy*
Elliott, Stephen (act): *Prototype*
Elliott, Ted (wri): *Little Monsters; The Puppet Masters*
Elliott, Tim (act): *The Fan*
Elliott, Tom (act): *The Darker Side Of Terror*
Elliott, William (act): *Night Of The Lepus*
Elliott, William J. (wri): *The Hound Of The Baskervilles (1921); The Wraith Of The Tomb*
Ellis, Chris (act): *Addams Family Values; Ghost In The Machine*
Ellis, Christopher (act): *The Nightcomers*
Ellis, Dave (act): *Nightbeast*
Ellis, Desmond Walter (act): *The Hell-Fire Club*
Ellis, Don (act): *The Corpse Grinders*
Ellis, Don (mus): *Moon Zero Two; Ruby*
Ellis, Earl (act): *Night Of The Creeps*
Ellis, Edward (act, 1872-1952): *The Return Of Peter Grimm (1934); The Thin Man*
Ellis, Edwin (act): *Eyes Of Fate; The Hangman Waits; The Man Without A Body*
Ellis, George (act): *The Legend Of Blood Mountain*
Ellis, Ian (act): *The Sky Bike*
Ellis, Jacqueline (act): *The Sinister Man*
Ellis, James (GB act): *Mark Of The Devil (1985)*
Ellis, James (USA act): *Re-Animator*
Ellis, Jann (act): *12 Monkeys*
Ellis, Jeffrey (wri): *D.A.R.Y.L.*
Ellis, John (act): *The Devil Bat*
Ellis, Joshua (act): *Making Contact*
Ellis, June (act): *The Angel Who Pawned Her Harp; The Devil-Ship Pirates; Frenzy*
Ellis, June C. (act): *Earth Girls Are Easy*
Ellis, Karen (act): *Vampire On Bikini Beach*
Ellis, Magdalen (act): see Lorring, Joan
Ellis, Marvin (act): *Indestructible Man*
Ellis, Mary (act, b. 1900, nee Mary Elsas): *Bella Donna (1934); The Three Worlds Of Gulliver*
Ellis, Mitzi (act): *The Haunting Of Sarah Hardy*
Ellis, Patricia (act, 1916-1970): *Lady In The Morgue*
Ellis, Paul (act): *The Bridge Of San Luis Rey (1929)*
Ellis, Ray (mus): *Cauldron Of Blood*
Ellis, Robert (act): *Spacemaster X-7; The Sphinx (1933)*
Ellis, Robert (wri): *Charlie Chan At Monte Carlo; Charlie Chan At The Circus; Charlie Chan At The Olympics; Charlie Chan At The Race Track; Charlie Chan In City In Darkness; Charlie Chan In Egypt; Charlie Chan In Shanghai; Charlie Chan's Secret; The Monster Walks*
Ellis, Robin (act): *The Curse Of King Tut's Tomb*
Ellis Tawm (act): *Shriek Of The Mutilated*
Ellis, Vincent C. (cin): *Sorority Girls And The Creature From Hell*
Ellis, William (act): *Dracula A.D. 1972*
Ellison, Art (act): *Carnival Of Souls*
Ellison, Brian (act): *Mad Max Beyond Thunderdome*
Ellison, David (act): *Macbeth (1971)*
Ellison, Dawne (act): *Surf Nazis Must Die*
Ellison, Harlan (wri, b. 1934): *A Boy And His Dog*
Ellison, James (act, b. 1910, nee James Ellison Smith): *The Ghost Goes Wild; I Walked With A Zombie; The Undying Monster*
Ellison, Joseph (dir): *Don't Go In The House*
Ellison, Katherine (act): *A Witch Without A Broom*
Ellison, Thomas (act): *Trick Or Treats*
Elloy, Max (act): *Atoll K*
Ellsworth, Christine (act): *The Savage Bees*
Ellsworth, Scott (act): *Dead Men Tell No Tales*
Ellsworth, Stephen (act): *Screaming Mimi*
Ellwanger, W.T. (act): *The Green Terror*
Elmaloglou, Rebekah (act): *Mad Max Beyond Thunderdome*
Elman, Irving (wri): *The Challenge; 13 Lead Soldiers*
Elmendorf, Raymond (act): *Project X (1987)*
Elmer, William (act): *Condemned*
Elmes, Frederick (cin): *Blue Velvet*
Elmes, Guy (wri, b. 1920): *Counterspy; The Flanagan Boy; The Night Visitor; The Stranger's Hand*
Elmi, Nicole(tta) (act): *The Cursed Medallion; Gli Orrori Del Castello Di Norembergа*
Elms, Albert (mus): *Manfish; The Man Without A Body; The Omegans; Satellite In The Sky*
El-Naswari, Issam (act): *The Mcguffin*
Elorrietta, Jose Maria (dir): *Mi Adorable Esclava*
Elorrietta, Jose Maria (wri): *Mi Adorable Esclava; A Witch Without A Broom*
Elphick, Jeanette (act): see Shaw, Victoria
Elphick, Michael (act): *Blind Terror; Cry Of The Banshee; Hamlet (1969)*
Elrady, Joe (act): *The Gifted One*
El Razzac, Abdul Salaam (act): *Deadly Game*
Elsas, Mary (act): see Ellis, Mary
Elsendoorn, Arnica (act): *The Lift*
El Shenawi, Ahmed (act): *The Thief Of Baghdad (1978)*
Elsom, Isobel (act, 1893-1981, nee Isobel Reed): *Between Two Worlds; Ladies In Retirement; Love From A Stranger (1947); The Miracle (1959); A Prehistoric Love Story; The Sign Of Four (1923); The Thirteenth Candle; 23 Paces To Baker Street; The Two Mrs. Carrolls; The Unseen (1945)*
Elsom, Jonathan (act): *The Face Of Darkness; Only A Scream Away*
Elson, Don(ald) (act): *Escape From The Planet Of The Apes; Gremlins*
Elswit, Robert (cin): *The Hand That Rocks The Cradle; Return Of The Living Dead, Part II; Trick Or Treat*
Elton, Edmund (act): *The Saint In Palm Springs*
Elton, Eileen (act): *Lady Of Vengeance*
Elton, Ray (cin): *Last Holiday; Miranda*
Eluard, Paul (act): *L'age D'or*
Elung-Jensen, Soeren (act): *King Lear (1970)*
Elvey, Maurice (act, 1887-1967): *Maria Marten Or, The Murder In The Red Barn (1913)*
Elvey, Maurice (dir, 1887-1967): *At The Villa Rose (1920); Beautiful Jim; The Clairvoyant (1934); Flames; The Elusive Pimpernel (1919); High Treason (1929); The Hound Of The Baskervilles (1921); House Of Blackmail; The King's Daughter; The Late Edwina Black; The Lodger (1932); London's Yellow Peril; Maria Marten: Or, The Murder In The Red Barn (1913); Mr. Wu (1919); Popsy Wopsy; The Princess Of Happy Chance; The Return Of The Frog; The Rocks Of Valpre; The Sign Of Four (1923); The Spider (1939); The Suicide Club (1914); The Tunnel; Vice Versa (1916); The Wandering Jew (1933); When Knights Were Bold (1916); The Woman Who Was Nothing*
Elvey, Maurice (wri, 1897-1967): *The Last Man To Hang?; Maria Marten: Or, The Murder In The Red Barn (1913); The Sign Of Four (1923)*
Elvidge, June (act): *The Eleventh Hour (1923)*
Elvin, June (act): *Mr. H.C. Andersen; She Shall Have Murder*
Elvin, Violetta (act): *The Queen Of Spades (1948)*
Elwell, Tom (act): *The Mutagen*
Elwenspoek, Hans (act): *Hauser's Memory*
Elwes, Cary (act, b. 1962): *Bram Stoker's Dracula; The Jungle Book (1994); Liar Liar; The Princess Bride; Robin Hood: Men In Tights; Twister*
Elwes, Cassian (act): *Jack's Back*
Elwes, Mark (act): *Billion Dollar Brain; Maroc 7*
Elwin, Roger (act): *Lord Of The Flies (1963)*
Elwyn, Michael (act): *The Private Life Of Sherlock Holmes*
Ely, David (wri): *Seconds*
Ely, Dennis (act): *Pranks*
Ely, John (act): *Slaughter Hotel (1972)*
Ely, Michael (act): *Threads*
Ely, Ron (act, b. 1938, nee Ronald Pierce): *Doc Savage, The Man Of Bronze; Tarzan's Deadly Silence*
El Zorkani, Abdel Reheim (act): *Sphinx (1981)*
Elzy, Lula (act): *Angel Heart*
Emanuel, Michael (act): *Outbreak*
Embree, Coleen (act): *Phobia*

Emelin, Georgia (act): Fire In The Sky (1993)

Emenegger, Robert (dir, mus & wri): Beyond The Universe

Emerald, Charles (act): The Lost Patrol (1929); The Ringer (1928)

Emerald, Nell (act): A Bold Adventuress; Dr. Sin Fang

Emerson, Douglas (act): Alfred Hitchcock Presents

Emerson, Faye (act, 1917-1983): Between Two Worlds; Danger Signal; Guilty Bystander; The Mask Of Dimitrios

Emerson, John (act): The Flying Torpedo

Emerson, Jonathan (act): Graveyard Shift (1990); Mars Attacks!; Nightfall (1988)

Emerson, Karrie (act): Chopping Mall; Evils Of The Night

Emerson, Keith (mus): Inferno (1979)

Emerson, Michael (act): Orpheus Descending

Emerson, Steve (act): Billion Dollar Brain

Emerton, Roy (act, 1892-1944): Busman's Honeymoon; The Case Of The Frightened Lady; Dr. Syn; The Drum; The Man In Grey; The Sign Of Four (1932); The Thief Of Bagdad (1940); Time Flies (1944); The Triumph Of Sherlock Holmes

Emery, Gilbert (act, 1889-1945): Behind That Curtain; The Brighton Strangler; Dracula's Daughter; Peter Ibbetson; The Return Of The Vampire; The Saint Strikes Back; Scotland Yard (1941)

Emery, James (H.) (act): Phoenix The Warrior; Something Is Out There

Emery, John (act, 1905-1964): Between Two Worlds; The Corsican Brothers (1941); Eyes In The Night; Here Comes Mr. Jordan; Kronos (1957); Let's Love Again; The Mad Magician; Rocketship X-M; Spellbound (1945); The Woman In White (1948)

Emery, Julie (act): Child Of Darkness, Child Of Light

Emery, Katherine (act): Eyes In The Night; Isle Of The Dead (1945); The Locket; The Maze

Emery, Lisa (act): Wolf

Emery, Pollie (act): After Dark; The Case Of Lady Camber

Emery, Robert (J.) (dir): My Brother Has Bad Dreams; Scream Bloody Murder

Emery, Robert (J.) (wri): Scream Bloody Murder

Emge, David (act): Dawn Of The Dead

Emhardt, Robert (act, b. 1901): It's Alive (1974)

Emhe, Stephen (act): Primal Scream

Emi, Sanae (act): Lake Of Dracula

Emil, Michael (act): In The Spirit

Emilfork, Daniel (act): The City Of Lost Children; The Devil's Nightmare; The Liquidator; La Poupee; The Thief Of Baghdad (1978)

Emilia, Reggio (act): see Reggiani, Serge

Emling Jr., Edward L. (act): The Premonition (1975)

Emm, Andrew (act): The Girl Who Took The Wrong Turning; The Girl Who Wrecked His Home

Emmanouil/Emmanuel, Takis (act): Electra (1961); The Golden Voyage Of Sinbad; The Magus

Emmanuel, Alphonsia (act): Murder By Moonlight

Emmerich, Roland (dir): Independence Day; Making Contact; Moon 44; Stargate; Universal Soldier

Emmerich, Roland (wri): Independence Day; Making Contact; Moon 44; Stargate

Emmerson, Kris (act): Electric Eskimo

Emmet, Michael (act): Attack Of The Giant Leeches; Night Of The Blood-Beast

Emmett, Basil (cin): Curse Of The Fly; The Return Of Mr. Moto

Emmett, E.V.H. (wri): Sabotage

Emmett, Fern (act): Pillow Of Death; The Vampire Bat

Emmett, Steve (act): I Was A Teen-Age Mummy

Emmich, Cliff (act): Barracuda; Halloween II; Hellhole; Invasion Of The Bee Girls; Return To Horror High

Emmons, William (act): Sasquatch, The Legend Of Bigfoot

Emney, Fred (act): Bunny Lake Is Missing; The Magic Christian

Emney, Mrs. Fred (act): The Mystery Of The Silent Death; Silken Threads

Emory, Richard (act): The Beginning Of The End

Emrys, James (act): Dragonslayer

Emukoro, Teyoko (act): Daimajin Vs. Dragon

Enberg, Alexander (act): Last Gasp

Enberg, Dick (act): Heaven Can Wait (1978)

Encinas, Alicia (act): The Bees

Enden, David (act): Greystoke: The Legend Of Tarzan, Lord Of The Apes

Enders, Robert (wri): The Maids; Voices

Endfield, Cy (dir, b. 1914): De Sade; Hide And Seek; The Limping Man (1953); Mysterious Island (1961); Tarzan's Savage Fury

Endfield, Cyril (wri): Mr. Hex

Endore, Guy (wri, 1901-1970): The Curse Of The Werewolf; Devil Doll (1936); Fear No Evil (1969); League Of Frightened Men; Mad Love; The Mark Of The Vampire (1935)

Endoso, Kenny (act): Buck Rogers In The 25th Century; The Entity

Engel, Alexander (act): Das Kalte Herz

Engel, Billie (act): The Cat And The Canary (1927)

Engel, Iya (act): Dr. Tarr's Torture Dungeon

Engel, Paula (act): Powder

Engel, Roy (act): Charley And The Angel; The Flying Saucer (1950); Indestructible Man; Kingdom Of The Spiders; The Magnetic Monster; The Man From Planet X; Not Of This Earth (1957); Satan's Satellites

Engel, Samuel G. (wri): Blue, White And Perfect; Charlie Chan In Rio; Scotland Yard (1941)

Engel, Susan (act): King Lear (1970)

Engel, Volker (cin): Independence Day; Moon 44

Engelbach, David (dir & wri): America 3000

Engels, Robert (wri): Twin Peaks: Fire Walk With Me

Engels, Vera (act): The Great Impersonation (1935)

Engholm, Harry (wri): Buttons; The Lights O' London; London By Night (1913); The Sorrows Of Satan (1917); A Study In Scarlet (1914); The Valley Of Fear (1916)

England, Bryan (act): Friday The 13th, Part VIII-Jason Takes Manhattan; Gate II; I, Madman; The Judas Project; Robin Cook's Invasion; Sometimes They Come Back; The Uninvited (1996); Wicked Stepmother

England, David (act): Mars Needs Women

England, Gary (act): Twister

England, Jo (act): Hawk The Slayer; The Last Wave

England, Sue (act): Bomba And The Hidden City

England, Thomas (act): Mary Shelley's 'Frankenstein'

England, Virginia (act): The Psychotronic Man

Engle, Peter King (act): see Whitney, Peter

Engleberg, Fred (act): Dinosaurus!; The Lost Missile

Engleman, David (act): The Keeper

Engleman, Roy (act): Children Shouldn't Play With Dead Things

English, Bradford (act): Wolf

English, David (act): Lifeforce; The Saint And The Brave Goose

English, Diane (wri): The Lathe Of Heaven

English, Elizabeth (act): Flat No. 3

English, Jack (act): The Incredible 2-Headed Transplant

English, James (act): Bloodspell

English, John (dir): The Adventures Of Captain Marvel; Dick Tracy Returns; Dick Tracy's G-Men; Dick Tracy Vs. Crime, Inc.; Dr. Satan's Robot; Lost Island Of Kioga; The Torpedo Of Doom

English, Louise (act): House Of The Long Shadows

English, Marla (act): Rear Window; The She-Creature; Shield For Murder; Three Bad Sisters; Voodoo Woman

English, Richard (wri): A Thousand And One Nights (1945)

English, Robert (act): The Crimson Circle (1922); The Hound Of The Baskervilles (1921); Mrs. Pym Of Scotland Yard; The Secret Of Stamboul

English, Rose (act): The Witches (1990)

Englund, Jan (act): Invasion Of The Saucer Men; Lizzie

Englund, Ken (wri, 1914-1993): The Secret Life Of Walter Mitty

Englund, Pat (act): The Day Of The Dolphin

Englund, Paul (act): Charlie Chan In London

Englund, Robert (act, b. 1948): Dead And Buried; The Fifth Floor; Freddy's Dead: The Final Nightmare; Galaxy Of Terror; The Mangler; Mind Over Murder; A Nightmare On Elm Street; A Nightmare On Elm Street, Part 2: Freddy's Revenge; A Nightmare On Elm Street 3: Dream Warriors; A Nightmare On Elm Street 4: The Dream Master; A Nightmare On Elm Street 5: The Dream Child; The Phantom Of The Opera (1989); Tobe Hooper's Night Terrors; Wes Craven's New Nightmare

Englund, Robert (dir, b. 1948): 976-Evil

Engstrom, Jean (act): The Space Children; Voodoo Island

Enke, Elizabeth Edith (act): see Adams, Edie

Ennals, Roger (act): Return To Oz

Enns, Paul (act): Cavegirl (1985)

Eno, Brian (mus): The Devil's Men; For All Mankind

Eno, Roger (mus): For All Mankind

Enoch, Russell (act): Intimate Relations; The Saint's Return

Enoki, Kazuo (cin): Onibaba

Enore, Lena (act): The Visitors (1989)

Enos, John (act): Demolition Man

Enrico, Robert (dir & wri, b. 1931): Au Coeur De La Vie

Enright, Don (wri): Not Of This World

Enright, Kevin (act): Hand Of Death

Enriton, G. (act): Portret Doriana Greya

Ensign, John (act): Teen-Age Strangler

Ensign, Michael (act): All Of Me; Ghostbusters; House; Jekyll And Hyde...Together Again; Superman (1978)

Enskat, Jennifer (act): Blood Song

Ensor, David (act): Information Received

Entwistle, John (act & mus): Tommy

Enyart, Tom (act): Deadly Game; The Haunting Of Sarah Hardy

Enyo, Erina (act): The Incredibly Strange Creatures Who Stopped Living And Became Mixed-Up Zombies; The Thrill Killers

Eory, Iran (act): Horror; Los Muertos No Perdonan

Epcar, Richard (act): Not Of This World

Ephron, Delia (wri): Michael

Ephron, Henry (wri, 1911-1992): Carousel; Desk Set

Ephron, Marshall (act): Thx 1138

Ephron, Nora (dir & wri): Michael

Ephron, Phoebe (wri, 1914-1971): Carousel; Desk Set

Epper, Andrew (act): Phantom Of The Paradise

Epper, Daniel (act): The Exorcist III

Epper, Gary (act): Nightwing

Epper, Jeanne (act): Warning Sign

Epper, Tony (act): Beyond The Poseidon Adventure; Condor; Dick Tracy (1990); Freejack

Epperson, John (act): Vampire's Kiss

Epple, Cindy (act): Earthbound (1981)

Eppler, Dieter (act): The Naked Woman And Satan; La Strage Dei Vampiri

Eppolito, Louis (act): Switch

Epps Jr., Jack (wri): Anaconda

Epps, Mickey (cin): The Alien's Return

Epps, Omar (act): Daybreak

Epstein, David (wri): The Murders In The Rue Morgue (1986)

Epstein, Jean (dir, 1897-1953): La Chute De La Maison Usher; La Glace A Trois Faces

Epstein, Jep (mus): Mutants In Paradise

Epstein, Jerome (dir): The Adding Machine

Epstein, Jerome (wri): The Adding Machine; Search For Danger

Epstein, Julius J. (cin, b. 1909): Arsenic And Old Lace

Epstein, Julius J. (wri, b. 1909): Return From The Ashes

Epstein, Philip G. (cin): Arsenic And Old Lace

Epstein, Robert (act): Spookies

Equiluz, Enrique L. (dir): La Marca Del Hombre Lobo

Equini, Arrigo (wri): The Conquest Of Mycenae

Eram, Rene (dir): Voodoo

Erangey, Paul (act): The Magic Shop

ERckmann (wri): The Bells (1926 & 1931)

Ercolani, James (act): see Darren, James

Ercolono, Carol (act): Dr. Caligari

Ercy, Elizabeth (act): Fathom; The Sorcerers

Erdman, N. (wri): Jack Frost

Erdman, Richard (act, b. 1925): Face Of Fire; Francis In The Navy; Trancers

Erdmann, Hans (mus): Das Testament Des Dr. Mabuse

Erdody, (Leo) (mus): Blonde For A Day; Bluebeard (1944); Dead Men Walk; Larceny In Her Heart; Murder Is My Business; Shinel

Eremeeva, A. (act): Shinel

Erham, Kevin (cin): The Curse

Erhard, Bernard (act): Little Nemo: Adventures In Slumberland

Erhardt, Catharine (act): Cinderella 2000; Naked Evil

Erhardy, Catherine (act): The Phantom Of The Opera (1990)

Erhart, Thomas (act): Goldstein

Eric, Barry (act): Echoes

Eric, James (act): The Gifted One

Erich, Field (act): Deat...

Erichsen, Mark (act): American Gothic

Erickson, Bill (act): Swamp Thing

Erickson, Carl (wri): Mystery Of The Wax Museum

Erickson, Clem (act): Jungle Jim In The Forbidden Land

Erickson, Kathleen (act): The Lightning Incident

Erickson, Knute (act): The Clutching Hand; The Monster (1925)

Erickson, Leif (act, 1911-1986, nee William Wycliff Anderson): Abbott And Costello Meet Captain Kidd; Arabian Nights; Blonde Savage; The Deadly Dream; Invaders From Mars (1953); I Saw What You Did (1965); Meet Nero Wolfe; Night Monster; The Snake Piy (1948); Sorry, Wrong Number (1948); Straitjacket

Erickson, Lisa (act): The Power (1980)

Erickson, Paul (wri): The End Of The Line; Find The Lady; The Green Buddha; Kill Her Gently; Secret Venture; Shadow Of A Man; Track The Man Down

Erickson, Phil (act): U.F.O.: Target Earth

Ericson, Devon (act): Night Of The Comet

Ericson, Helen (act): The Blue Bird (1940); Charlie Chan In Panama

Ericson, John (act, b. 1926, nee Joseph Meibes): The Bamboo Saucer; Bedknobs And Broomsticks; Death Ride; The Destructors; The House Of The Dead; Operation Atlantis; 7 Faces Of Dr. Lao; Slave Queen Of Babylon

Eriksen, Kaj-Erik (act): Quarantine

Erikson, Diane (act): Jack's Back

Ermey, R. Lee (act): The Body Snatchers; Endless Descent; The Frighteners; I'm Dangerous Tonight; Seven

Ernest, George (act): The Mystery Of Edwin Drood (1935)

Ernest, Harry (act): Tarzan's New Adventure

Ernest, Philippe (act): La Mome Vert-De-Gris

Ernest, Rick (act): Nightbeast

Ernryd, Bengt (mus): I Am Curious (Yellow)

Ernsberger, Duke (act): King Kong Lives

Ernst, Kaye (act): Raiders Of The Living Dead

Ernst, Max (act, 1891-1976): L'age D'or

Errickson, Krista (act): Jekyll And Hyde... Together Again

Erroll, Leon (act, 1881-1951): Alice In Wonderland (1933); The Invisible Man's Revenge

Erschbamer, George (cin): The Plutonium Incident

Ersgard, Joakim (dir & wri): The Visitors (1989)

Ersgard, Patrik (act & wri): The Visitors (1989)

Erskine, Chester (dir & wri 1905-1986): Androcles And The Lion, Witness To Murder

Erskine, Eileen (act): Great Expectations (1946); The Midas Touch

Erskine, Howard (act): Thinner

Erskine, John (wri): The Private Life Of Helen Of Troy

Erskine, Madelyn (act): Rawhead Rex

Ertmanis, Victor (act): Brainscan; Haunted By Her Past; Sorry, Wrong Number (1989)

Ervolina, Tony (act): Jason Goes To Hell: The Final Friday

Erwin, Bill (act): see Erwin, William/Bill

Erwin, Edward (act): The Amazing Transparent Man

Erwin, Lee (wri): Tarzan's Deadly Silence

Erwin, Stu(art) (act, 1903-1967): Before Dawn; Cracked Nuts (1941); Drums Of The Congo; Heaven Only Knows; International House; Son Of Flubber

Erwin, William/Bill (act): How Awful About Allan; Invitation To Hell; Somewhere In Time; Tarantulas: The Deadly Cargo

Esbern, Stig (wri): Mockery

Escalante, Dana (wri): Return To Horror High

Escalante, Henry (act): Creature From The Black Lagoon

Escamilla, Teo (cin): El Amor Brujo (1986)

Escane, Stanley (act): Cosh Boy

Escober, Adrian (act): Jurassic Park

Escoffier, Jean Yves (cin): The Crow: City Of Angels

Escourrou, Pierre (act): Zombies Lake

Escribano, Antonio Gimenez (act): Scream Of The Demon Lover

Escriva, Javier (act): Los Muertos No Perdonan; El Principe Encadenado

Escriva, V. (wri): El Principe Encadenado

Esdra, Michela (act): Deborah

Esformes, Nate (act): The Ultimate Warrior

Eshley, Norman (act): Blind Terror; The Carnation Killer; House Of Mortal Sin;

Esmelton, Fred(erick) (act): Boston Blackie; The Chinese Parrot

Esmond, Annie (act): Alf's Button (1930); Bulldog Drummond At Bay (1937); The Claydon Treasure Mystery; The Mystery Of Mr. Bernard Brown; The Yellow Claw
Esmond, Carl (act, b. 1906, nee Willy Eichberger): Address Unknown; Agent For H.A.R.M.; The Catman Of Paris; From The Earth To The Moon; Lola Montes; Ministry Of Fear
Esmond, H.V. (act): Scrooge (1922); The Sword Of Damocles
Esmond, H.V. (wri): The Sword Of Damocles
Esmond, Jill (act, 1908-1990): The Bandit Of Sherwood Forest; Bedelia; F.P. 1 Antwortet Nicht
Esnaught, Anne-Laure (act): Those Dear Departed
Espe, Mike (Act): The Incredible 2-Headed Transplant
Esperon, Manuel (mus): The Living Idol
Espinasse, Pierre (act): see Brasseur, Pierre
Espinoza, Jose (act): Hammersmith Is Out
Espinoza, Salvador R. (act): Dr. Caligari
Esposito, Gianni (act): Les Miserables (1957)
Esposito, John (wri): Graveyard Shift (1990)
Espy, William Gray (act): Haunts
Esser, Paul (act): Daughters Of Darkness; Das Kalte Herz
Essex, David (act): In The Devil's Garden; Octaman
Essex, Harry (dir, b. 1910): The Cremators; I, The Jury (1953); Octaman
Essex, Harry (J.) (wri, b. 1910): Boston Blackie And The Law; Creature From The Black Lagoon; The Cremators; It Came From Outer Space; I, The Jury (1953); Octaman
Essex, Robert (act): Castle Sinister (1948)
Essler, Fred (act, 1896-1973): Houdini
Essoe, Gabe (wri): The Devil's Rain
Esson, Robert (wri): The Fall Of The House Of Usher (1958)
Estabrook, Howard (wri, 1894-1978): The Bridge Of San Luis Rey (1944); Kismet (1930)
Esteban, Adela (act): El Otro Fu-Manchu
Esteban, Julian (wri): Zombies Lake
Estela, Alfonso (act): Parsifal
Estelita (act): Jesse James Meets Frankenstein's Daughter
Estelle, Don (act): Santa Claus (1985)
Esterhazy, Agnes (act): Der Student Von Prag (1926)
Esterhazy, Andrea (act): Obsession (1976)
Esterman, Laura (act): Addams Family Values
Estes, Alisa (act): Spawn Of The Slithis
Estes, Rob (act): Phantom Of The Mall: Eric's Revenge; Uninvited (1987)
Estevez, Emilio (act, b. 1962): Freejack; Maximum Overdrive; Mission: Impossible; Nightmares (1983)
Estevez, Joe (act): Beach Babes From Beyond; Blonde Heaven; Soultaker
Estevez, Ramon (act): see Sheen, Martin
Estevez, Rene (act): Single White Female
Estey, William Bruce (act): Earthbound (1981)
Estivill, Jordi (act): Anguish
Estler, Mike (act): Vampire's Kiss
Estrada, Angelina (act): Ghost (1990)
Estrada, Bianca (act): Mystery On Monster Island
Estrada, Carlos (act): Master Of Horror
Estrada, Erik (act, b. 1949): Alien Seed; Demon And The Mummy; Earth Angel
Estridge, Robin (wri, b. 1920): Eye Of The Devil; House Of Darkness
Estrin, Patricia (act): Crackle Of Death
Estrom, Pamela (act): Beyond The Poseidon Adventure
Estruado, David (act): Cameron's Closet
Eszterhas, Joe (wri): Jade
Etaix, Pierre (dir, b. 1928): Insomnia
Etcheverry, Fred (cin): The Alligator People
Etcheverry, Michel (act): Perceval; La Sorciere
Etherington, Colin (act): Superman (1978)
Etherington, James (act): The Hills Of Donegal
Ethier, Alphonse/Alphonz (act): Alias The Lone Wolf; The Lone Wolf (1924); The Lone Wolf Returns (1926); A Message From Mars (1921); Secret Of The Chateau
Etievant, Yvette (act): L'ours
Etoll, Robert (mus): Vampire At Midnight
Etra, Will (act): Return To Horror High
Etting, Ruth (act, 1897-1978): Roman Scandals
Ettinger, Cynthia (act): The Silence Of The Lambs
Eubank, Victoria (act): The Hearse
Eunson, Dale (wri): Guest In The House
Eunson, Joan (act): see Evans, Joan
Eure, Tom (act): The China Syndrome
Eure, Wesley (act): The Toolbox Murders
Euripedes (wri, 480?-406 B.C.): The Trojan Women
Eurythmics (mus): 1984 (1984)
Eustace, David F. (dir): The Intruder (1981)
Eustis, Helen (wri, b. 1916): The Fool Killer
Eustrel, Antony (act): Counterblast; The Story Of Robin Hood
Evanou, Daniele (act): Le Saint Prend L'affut
Evans, Andy (cin): Remo Williams: The Adventure Begins
Evans, Art (J.) (act): Fright Night; Tales From The Hood; White Of The Eye
Evans, Barry (act): Die Screaming, Marianne
Evans, BrendA (act): So Sad About Gloria
Evans, Bruce A. (wri): Cutthroat Island; Made In Heaven; Starman
Evans, Charles (E.) (act): Beyond A Reasonable Doubt; Cannibal Attack; Creature With The Atom Brain; The Dark Mirror (1946); Earth Vs. The Flying Saucers; The Greene Murder Case; The Night The World Exploded
Evans, Clara (act): The Children
Evans, Clifford (act, b. 1912): At The Stroke Of Nine; At The Villa Rose (1939); The Curse Of The Werewolf; Face In The Night; The House Of The Arrow (1940); Kiss Of The Vampire; Passport To Treason; The Saint Meets The Tiger; Solution By Phone; The Straw Man; The Twenty Questions Murder; While I Live
Evans, David (wri): The Late Edwina Black; Passenger To London; Portrait From Life; The Three Weird Sisters
Evans, Douglas (act): The Beginning Of The End; Champagne For Caesar; I Saw What You Did (1965)
Evans, (Dame) Edith (act, 1888-1976): Craze; The Queen Of Spades (1948); Scrooge (1970); The Slipper And The Rose
Evans, Edward (act): The Angel Who Pawned Her Harp; Cosh Boy; Lifeforce; Tales From The Crypt; 10 Rillington Place
Evans, Elizabeth (act): see Risdon, Elizabeth
Evans, Estelle (act): The Invisible Fear
Evans, Evans (act): Prophecy (1979)
Evans, Frank Howel (wri): In The Shadow Of Big Ben
Evans, Fred (GB act, dir & wri; 1889-1915): Aladdin (1915); Diche Turpin's Ride To Yorke (1913, Folly Films/ Phoenix); Lieutenant Pimple And The Stolen Submarine; Once Upon A Time (1913); Pimple And Galatea; Pimple's Inferno; Pimple's Midsummer Night's Dream; Sexton Pimple; A Study In Skarlit
Evans, Fred (USA act): Prophecy (1979)
Evans, Gene (act, b. 1922): Behemoth, The Sea Monster; Donovan's Brain; The Golden Blade; The Horrible House On The Hill; The Long Wait; Matt Helm; Shock Corridor
Evans, George Ewart (wri): The Secret Of The Forest
Evans, Harry (act): Desk Set
Evans, Harvey (act): Experiment In Terror; Ravagers
Evans, Helena P. (act): Nancy Drew, Detective
Evans, Herbert (act): The Adventures Of Robin Hood; The Black Room; The Mysterious Mr. Moto
Evans, Jack (act): The Hand (1981)
Evans, Jeanne (act): The She-Creature
Evans, Jeptha (act): The Children
Evans, Jerry (wri): Hell's Bloody Devils
Evans, Jessie (act): Countess Dracula; The Orchard End Murder
Evans, Joan (act, b. 1934, nee Joan Eunson): It Grows On Trees
Evans, Joe (act): Joey's Dream; Once Upon A Time (1913); Pearls Of Death
Evans, Joe (dir & wri): Aladdin (1915); Dicke Turpin's Ride To Yorke (1913, Folly Films/Phoenix); Joey's Dream; Lieutenant Pimple And The Stolen Submarine; Once Upon A Time (1913); Pearls Of Death; Pimple And Galatea; Pimple's Inferno; Pimple's Midsummer Night's Dream; Sexton Pimple
Evans, John (act): Virus; Welcome To Blood City
Evans, John (cin): Hands Of A Murderer
Evans, John H. (act): Assassin (1986)
Evans, Josh (act): Dream A Little Dream
Evans, Laramie G. (act): Slugs
Evans, Larry (act): Journey To The Center Of Time
Evans, Lucas (act): Tommy Tricker And The Stamp Traveller
Evans, Lyn (act): Cloudburst; Kind Hearts And Coronets
Evans, Madge (act, 1909-1981): The Tunnel
Evans, Maurice (act, b. 1901): Androcles And The Lion; Beneath The Planet Of The Ape; The Body Stealers; The Brotherhood Of The Bell; Kind Lady (1951); One Of Our Spies Is Missing; Planet Of The Apes; Rosemary's Baby; Scrooge (1935); Terror In The Wax Museum
Evans, Michael/Mike (act): Cliath Awaits; The Haunting Of Hamilton High; The House On Skull Mountain; Now You See Him, Now You Don't; The Sword And The Sorcerer; Time After Time
Evans, Mitch (act): Gallery Of Horror
Evans, Murray (act): The Shuttered Room
Evans, Patrick (act): The Hand (1981)
Evans, Peggy (act): Calling Bulldog Drummond
Evans, Peter (act, 1950-1989): The Henderson Monster
Evans, Randy (act): The Hand (1981)
Evans, Ray (act): Sunset Boulevard; Superman (1978)
Evans, Reg (act): Mad Max
Evans, Rex (act, 1903-1969): The Brighton Strangler; Frankenstein Meets The Wolf Man; The Great Impersonation (1942); Jamaica Run; Midnight Lace (1960); Pursuit To Algiers; The Thin Man Goes Home
Evans, Richard (act): The Return Of Mr. Moto
Evans, Robert J. (act, b. 1930): Man Of A Thousand Faces
Evans, Robin (act): One Dark Night
Evans, Roy (act): The Company Of Wolves; Dark Places; Dr. Jekyll And Sister Hyde; Hamlet (1990); Psychomania (1972); The Vault Of Horror
Evans, Scott (act): The Hand (1981)
Evans, Tenniel (act): 10 Rillington Place
Evans, Terrence (act): Curse II: The Bite; Phantom Of The Mall: Eric's Revenge
Evans, Tom (act): Mutants In Paradise
Evans, Tom (cin): Secrets In The Attic
Evans, Tracie (act): Maniac (1980)
Evans, Troy (act): Bodily Harm; Deadly Messages; Demolition Man; The Frighteners; The Lawnmower Man; Near Dark; Phenomenon
Evans, Will (act & wri): The Showman's Dream; A Study In Skarlit
Evans, Will (dir): A Study In Skarlit
Evans, Winifred (act): Shadow Of Death (1939)
Evanson, Edith (act): The Day The Earth Stood Still; The Jade Mask; The Notorious Lone Wolf; Rope; Twice-Told Tales
Evans-Wilson, Augusta J. (wri): St. Elmo
Eve (act): Bella Donna (1934)
Eve, Leslie (act): The Alien Within
Eve, Trevor (act): Dracula (1979); Jamaica Inn (1985)
Eveleigh, Leslie (dir): The Mystery Of The Silent Death; Silken Threads
Evelyn, Judith (act, 1913-1967): Rear Window; The Thirteenth Letter; The Tingler
Evening Lilly, Julie (act): Wolfen
Evennett, Wallace (act): The Face At The Window (1939)
Evenson, Wayne (act): Fargo
Everage, Gregory L. (act): Lady In White
Everest, Barbara (act, 1891-1967): The Damned; Gaslight (1944); An Inspector Calls; Jane Eyre (1944); The Lodger (1932); The Man Who Finally Died; The Man Without A Soul; The Passing Of The Third Floor Back (1935); Passing Shadows; The Patient Vanishes; Phantom Of The Opera (1943); Scrooge (1935); Trunk Crime; The Uninvited (1944); Wanted For Murder; Whosoever Shall Offend
Everett, Chad (act, b. 1936, nee Ray Cramton): The Intruder Within; Journey To Midnight; Mistress Of Paradise; Star Command
Everett, Gimel (wri): The Lawnmower Man
Everett, Kenny (act): Blood Bath At The House Of Death
Everett, Peter (wri): Negatives
Everett, Richard (act): Cry Of The Banshee; Hamlet (1969)
Everett, Rupert (act): Arthur The King; Cemetery Man
Everett, Tom (act): Leatherface: Texas Chainsaw Massacre III
Evergreen, James (wri): Love Butcher
Everhard, Nancy (act): Deepstar Six; The Punisher; The Trial Of The Incredible Hulk
Everhardt, Rex (act): Superman (1978)
Everhart, Angie (act): Tales From The Crypt Presents Bordello Of Blood
Everly, Viviane (act): Quelqu'un Derriere La Porte
Evers, Brian (act): Eat And Run; Seven
Evers, Bruce (act): Mr. Destiny
Evers, Jason (act): Barracuda; Basket Case 2; The Brain That Wouldn't Die; Escape From The Planet Of The Apes; Fer-De-Lance; The Illustrated Man
Evert, Ken (act): The Texas Chainsaw Massacre 2
Everts, Juke (act): Play Misty For Me
Evigan, Greg (act, b. 1953): Deepstar Six; House Of The Damned (1996); Northstar
Evirust (mus): I Lunghi Capelli Della Morte
Evors, Bobbi (act): Psycho IV: The Beginning
Ewalt, Jack (act): Around The World Under The Sea
Ewan, Murray (act): Without A Clue
Ewart, John (act): Razorback
Ewer, Donald (act): The Housekeeper
Ewers, H.H./Hanns Heinz (wri): Alraune (1928, 1930 & 1952); Der Student Von Prag (1913 & 1926)
Ewert, Renate (act): The Red Circle (1960)
Ewing, Barbara (act): Dracula Has Risen From The Grave; Haunters Of The Deep; Torture Garden
Ewing, Bill (act): The Deathmaster
Ewing, Debbie (act): Zombie Island Massacre
Ewing, Jon (act): Howling III
Ewing, Loren (act): El Castello Dell'orrore
Ewing, Patrick (act): The Exorcist III; Space Jam
Exarchos, Christos (act): Atlas
Experimental Opera Company (act): Magic Lotus Lantern
Experimental Studio of Polish Radio (cin): Przyjaciel
Exton, Clive (wri): The Awakening; Doomwatch; The House In Nightmare Park; Night Must Fall (1964); Red Sonja; 10 Rillington Place
Eyer, Richard (act): The Invisible Boy; The 7th Voyage Of Sinbad
Eynon, Howard (act): Mad Max
Eyraud, Marc (act): Aimez-Vous Les Femmes?; Perceval
Eyre, David (wri): Wolfen
Eyre, Peter (act): Dragonslayer; The Pied Piper (1971)
Eyre, Richard (wri): Richard III (1995)
Eyres, John (dir): Monolith
Eyres, John (wri): Empire Of Ash III
Eythe, William (act): Special Agent
Eytle, Tom (act): Sudden Terror
Eyton, Bessie (act): The Long Ago
Ezra, Mark (dir & wri): Slaughter High
Ezralov, Daniel (act): The Witches' Black Sabbath

Faa'DiBruno, Antonino (act): Amarcord
Fabares, Shelley (act, b. 1944): Hold On!
Faber, Leslie (act): The Ringer (1928)
Faber, Robert (wri): Zombies On Broadway
Faber, Ron (act): The Exorcist
Fabian (act, b. 1943, nee Fabian Forte): Dr. Goldfoot And The Girl Bombs; Five Weeks In A Balloon; Kiss Daddy Goodbye; Ten Little Indians (1965)
Fabian, Ava (act): To Die For
Fabian, Diane (act): The Housekeeper
Fabian, John (act): First Man Into Space; Grip Of The Strangler; Quatermass II
Fabian, John (cin): Sasquatch, The Legend Of Bigfoot
Fabian, Maximilian (cin): The Thirteenth Hour (1927)
Fabiani, Joel (act): Brenda Starr (1976)
Fabiolo (act): see de Mora y Aragon, Jaime
Fabislak, Kazimierz (act): Matka Joanna Od Aniolow
Fabray, Nanette (act, b. 1920): The Man In The Santa Claus Suit
Fabri, Jacques (act): The Spy Is A Girl
Fabrizi, Aldo (act, 1905-1990): The Wonders Of Aladdin
Fabrizi, Franco (act, b. 1926): The Flower In His Mouth; A Rocket From Calabuch
Fabrizi, Mario (act): The Mouse On The Moon
Fabrizio, Alvaro (wri): Deborah
Factory, The (mus): Howling V: The Rebirth
Fadden, Tom (act): Invasion Of The Body Snatchers (1956)
Fadule, John (act): The Silence Of The Hams
Faella, Michael (act): Sleepstalker
Fafard, Steve (act): Mutants In Paradise
Faga, Gary (act): Star Trek
Fagan, James B. (wri): Bella Donna (1934)
Fagan, Sean (act): The Gate
Fagen, Donald (mus): Heavy Metal
Faggard, Jack (cin): Somewhere In Time
Fagioli, Giovanni (act): Teodora, Imperatrice Di Bisanzio
Fahey, Jeff (act): Body Parts; Darkman III: Die Darkman Die; The Lawnmower Man; Psycho III; Serpent's Lair
Fahey, Myrna (act): House Of Usher
Faiad, Zulma (act): The Night Of A Thousand Cats
Faichney, Stewart (act): Thirst
Fain, Matty (act): Another Thin Man
Fair, Florence (act): The Florentine Dagger
Fair, Herbert (act): Miracle Mile

Fair, Jody (act): *The Brain Eaters; The Ghost Of Dragstrip Hollow*
Fair, William (act): *The First Power*
Fairall, Mark (act): *That Eye, The Sky*
Fairbairn, Bruce (act): *The Vampire Girls*
Fairbank, Chris(topher) (act): *Agatha; Alien 3; The Awakening; Batman (1989); Cry Wolf (1980); Hamlet (1990); Murder With Mirrors*
Fairbank, Jay (wri): *Son Of Dracula (1974); Tales That Witness Madness*
Fairbanks (Sr.), Douglas (act, 1883-1939, nee Douglas Elton Ulman, a.k.a. Elton Thomas): *The Black Pirate; Don Q, Son Of Zorro; The Mark Of Zorro (1920); The Private Life of Don Juan; Robin Hood (1922); The Thief of Bagdad (1924); The Three Musketeers (1921)*
Fairbanks Jr., Douglas (act, b. 1909, nee *Elton Ulman Jr.*): *The Corsican Brothers (1941); Ghost Story (1981); Green Hell; Mr. Drake's Duck; Outward Bound; The Prisoner of Zenda (1937); Sinbad the Sailor; State Secret*
Fairbrass, Craig (act): *Galaxis*
Fairbrother, Sydney (act, 1873-1941, nee Sydney Tapping): *Chu Chin Chow (1934); The Game Of Liberty; The Golden Dawn; Iron Justice; King Solomon's Mines* (1937)
Fairbrother, Violet (act): *Downhill; Murder*
Fairchild, Charlotte (act): *Silent Night, Bloody Night*
Fairchild, Edgar (mus): *House Of Dracula; Pursuit To Algiers*
Fairchild, Margaret (act): *Grave Of The Vampire*
Fairchild, Max (act): *Howling III; Mad Max*
Fairchild, Morgan (act, b. 1950): *Dead Man's Island; The Haunting Of Sarah Hardy; The Initiation Of Sarah; The Memory Of Eva Ryker; Phantom of the Mall: Eric's Revenge; The Seduction; Sleeping Beauty (1986); Star Command; Test Tube Teens From The Year 2000; Writer's Block; The Zany Adventures of Robin Hood*
Fairchild, William (wri): *Colonel Bogey; Embassy; The Net*
Faire, Betty (act): *Bulldog Drummond's Third Round*
Faire, Bill (act): *Biohazard*
Faire, Virginia Brown (act): *The Lost World (1925); Monte Cristo; Peter Pan*
Fairfax, Deborah (act): *Frightmare (1974)*
Fairfax, Ferdinand (dir): *The Secret Life Of Ian Fleming*
Fairfax, James (act): *The Challenge; My Cousin Rachel; The White Goddess*
Fairfax, Lance (act): *Gipsy Blood*
Fairfax, Marion (wri): *The Lost World (1925); Sherlock Holmes (1922)*
Fairfax, Sarah (act): *The Bad Seed (1985)*
Fairfax, Thur (act): *The Gypsy Romance*
Fairhurst, Lyn (wri, b. 1920): *Devils Of Darkness*
Fairley, Victor (act): *The Stolen Necklace*
Fairlie, Gerard (wri): *Bulldog Jack; Bulldog Sees It Through; Calling Bulldog Drummond; The Shot in the Dark*
Fairman, Austin (act): *The Adventures Of Robin Hood*
Fairman, Blain (act): *Aliens*
Fairman, Churten (wri): *Disciple Of Death*
Fairman, Michael (act): *Charlie Chan And The Curse Of The Dragon Queen*
Fairman, Paul (wri): *Invasion Of The Saucer Men*
Fairweather, Helen (act): *The Private Life Of Helen Of Troy*
Faison, Ellene (act): *Dawn Of The Mummy*
Faison, Frankie (act): *Cat People (1982); Freejack; The Silence Of The Lambs*
Faison, Matthew (act): *Something Is Out There*
Faith, Adam (act): *What A Carve Up!*
Faith, Dolores (act): *The Human Duplicators; Mutiny In Outer Space; The Phantom Planet*
Faithfull, Geoffrey (act): *Alice In Wonderland (1903)*
Faithfull, Geoffrey (cin, b. 1894): *Doctor Of Seven Dials; First Man Into Space; Naked Evil; Spaceflight Ic-1; The Terrornauts; The Village of the Damned (1960)*
Faithfull, Marianne (act): *Ghost Story (1975); Hamlet (1969); When Pigs Fly*
Faithfull, Stanley (act): *Alice In Wonderland (1903)*
Fajardo, Eduardo/Edward (act): *The Cauldron Of Death; Exterminators Of The Year 3000; House Of Exorcism*
Fajardo, Joaquin (act): *The Omegans*
Fakackt, X. Ben (act): *The Children*
Falanga, Claudio (act): *The Strangers*
Falanga, Nino (act): *The 7th Voyage Of Sinbad*
Falardo, Eduardo (act): *Hundra*
Falchi, Anna (act): *Cemetery Man*
Falconer, Alun (wri): *The Man Upstairs*
Falconer, John (act): *The Pied Piper (1971)*
Falconer, Peter (act): *Def Con 4*
Falconer, Robert (wri): *Kill Me Tomorrow*
Falconetti, Gerard (act): *Perceval*
Falk, Harry (dir): *Mandrake*
Falk, Lee (wri): *The Phantom (1996)*
Falk, Peter (act, b. 1927): *The Balcony; Castle Keep; In The Spirit; Murder By Death; The Princess Bride; Vibes*
Falk, Rossella (act): *The Black Belly Of The Tarantula; 8 1/2; Modesty Blaise*
Falk, Tom (act): *Westworld*
Falkenberg, Kort (act): *The Loch Ness Horror*
Falkenstein, Julius (act): *Doctor Mabuse*
Falko, Alexei (wri): *Aelita*
Fall, Richard (mus): *Liliom (1930)*
Fall, Timothy (act): *Bates Motel*
Fallender, Deborah (act): *Jabberwocky*
Fallenstein, Karina (act): *The German Chainsaw Massacre*
Fallman, Gilbert (act): *The Man From Planet X*
Fallon, Edward (act): *Primal Scream*
Fallon, John (act): *Final Exam*
Fallon, Phillipa (act): *The Private Lives Of Adam And Eve*
Fallon, Thomas F. (wri): *The Last Warning (1929)*
Falls, Mat (act): *Popcorn*
Falls, Shirley (act): *The Spider (1958)*
Falode, Charmain (act): *Never-Never Land*
Falt, Dennis Lee (act): *Spawn Of The Slithis*
Faltermeyer, Harold (mus): *The Running Man*
Fame, Maki (act): *Popcorn*
Fanara, Shauna (act): *The Clan Of The Cave Bear*
Fancher, Hampton (wri): *Blade Runner*
Fancy, Brett (act): *Treasure Island (1990)*
Fancy, Richard (act): *From The Dead Of Night; Species; Spellbinder*
Fane, Dorothy (act): *Blood Money; Bulldog Drummond (1923); The Picture Of Dorian Gray (1916)*
Fane, Ida (act): *To Let*
Fanelli, John (act): *Mother's Day*
Fanfulla (act): *Satyricon*
Fankboner, Sarah (act): *The Shaggy D.A.*
Fann, Al (act): *Creator; Curse II: The Bite; Parasite; Return To Horror High; To Die For*
Fannon, Kathy (act): *Serial Mom*
Fant, Carl-Henrik (act): *The Devil's Wanton*
Fantasia, Andrea (act): *Ercole E La Regina Di Lidia*
Fantasia, Franco (act): *Il Montagna Di Dio Cannibale; Murder Mansion*
Fantasy II Film Effects (cin): *Captain America (1992); Killer Klowns From Outer Space*
Fante, John (wri): *The Reluctant Saint*
Fantini, Dino (act): *The Sinister Urge*
Fantini, Giancarlo (act): *Scream Of The Demon Lover*
Fantoni, Barry (act): *Otley*
Fantoni, Cesare (act): *Gli Amori Di Ercole; Ercole E La Regina Di Lidia*
Fantoni, Sergio (act, b. 1930): *Atom Age Vampire; Ercole E La Regina Di Lidia; Kali-Yug, La Dea Della Vendetta*
Fanty, Elizabeth (act): *Terror Of Rome Against The Son Of Hercules*
Fapp, Daniel (L.) (cin): *Bride Of Vengeance; Dream Girl; Golden Earrings; Li'l Abner (1959); Marooned; Our Man Flint*
Faraci, Richard (act): *Timecop*
Faracy, Peggy (act): *Repossessed*
Faracy, Stephanie (act): *Heaven Can Wait (1978)*
Faragoh, Francis Edward (wri): *Frankenstein (1931)*
Faraizl, Adam (act): *It (1990); RoboCop 2*
Faraj, Said (act): *Darkman (1990); Ghost (1990)*
Faralla, William (dir): *Two Before Zero*
Farbman, Paul (act): *A Polish Vampire In Burbank*
Farbrother, Pamela (act): *Cry Of The Banshee; Frightmare (1974); Tam Lin*
Fardo, Maurizio (act): *Escape From The Bronx*
Farebrother, Violet (act): *Richard III (1911); The Solitary Child*
Farel, Frank (act): *Street Trash*
Farel, Frank M. (wri): *Spookies*
Farelley, Patrick (act): *The Nesting*
Farentino, James (act, b. 1938): *The Cradle Will Fall; Dead And Buried; The Final Countdown; The Possessed 1977); Psychomania (1964)*
Fares, Debi (act): *Writer's Block*
Fares, Debra (act): *Return Of The Killer Tomatoes*
Fargas, Antonio (act): *The Borrower; Firestarter*
Fargo, George (act): *Play Misty For Me*
Fargo, James (wri): *Blood Song*
Faria, Celso (act): *Killer Fish*
Farina, Dennis (act, b. 1944): *The Disappearance Of Nora; Out Of Annie's Past*
Farina, George (act): *Terror In The Wax Museum*
Farino, Ernest (D.) (cin): *Lady In White; Screamers (1996)*
Farinon, Gabriella/Gaby (act): *Assignment-Outer Space; Et Mourir De Plaisir*
Farish, Christine (act): *Raiders Of The Living Dead*
Farjaux-Kelm-Brunnet (act): *Le Voyage Dans La Lune*
Farjeon, J. Jefferson (wri): *After Dark; The Ghost Camera; The House Opposite (1931); Number 17*
Farkas, Francois (cin): *Voodoo Blood Bath*
Farkas, Pedro (cin): *The Dolphin*
Farkas, Victor P. (act): *Shock Chamber*
Farleigh, Lynn (act): *Voices*
Farley, James (act): *The Phantom Creeps; The World's Greatest Sinner*
Farley, Morgan (act, 1901-1988): *The Barefoot Executive; The Greene Murder Case; Heaven Can Wait (1978); Macbeth (1947); Soylent Green*
Farley, Teresa (act): *Breeders*
Farmer, Bill (act): *RoboCop; Space Jam*
Farmer, Bill (cin): *Sasquatch, The Legend Of Bigfoot*
Farmer, Ellen (act): *Les Parapluies De Cherbourg*
Farmer, Frances (act, 1917-1970): *Among The Living*
Farmer, Gary (act): *Demon Knight*
Farmer, Ken (act): *Empire Of Ash III*
Farmer, Mark (act): *Memoirs Of A Survivor*
Farmer, Mimsy (act): *Autopsy; The Black Cat (1980); Quatro Mosche Di Velluto Gris*
Farmer, Paul (act): *The Unnamable*
Farmer, Suzan (act): *The Devil-Ship Pirates; Dracula, Prince Of Darkness; Monster Of Terror; Persecution; Rasputin, The Mad Monk; The Scarlet Blade; Talk of the Devil; Where The Bullets Fly*
Farnay, Stephanie (act): *A Date With Death*
Farndale, John (act): *Mad Max*
Farnese, Alberto (act): *Giants Of Thessaly; Siege Of Syracuse*
Farnon, Robert (mus): *Circle Of Danger; The Road To Hong Kong*
Farnon, Shannon (act): *Night Gallery*
Farnsworth, Hill (act): *Piranha (1978)*
Fransworth, Richard (act): *Misery; Space Rage*
Farnsworth, Rick (act): *Witchery*
Farnum, Dorothy (wri): *The Unholy Night*
Farnum, Franklyn (act, 1876-1961): *Charlie Chan At The Circus; The Clutching Hand; Dick Tracy (1945); The She-Creature; Sunset Boulevard* Farnum, William (act, 1876-1963): *Captain Kidd; The Clutching Hand; A Connecticut Yankee; The Corsican Brothers (1941); The Count Of Monte Cristo (1934); Jack and the Beanstalk (1952); Les Miserables (1918_; The Mummy's Curse; Samson And Delilah; The Scarlet Letter (1934); Sharad Of Atlantis;* supernatural (1933)
Farquhar, Betty (act): *Lady Audley's Secret (1920); The Silver Bridge*
Farquharson, Robert (act): *The Man They Could Not Arrest*
Farr, Derek (act, 1912-1986): *Attempt To Kill; Double Confession; The Man In The Road; The Man On The Run; Murder Without Crime; The Shop at Sly Corner; Spellbound (1941); The Vicious Circle (1957); Wanted For Murder*
Farr, Felicia (act, b. 1932): *Asylum For A Spy; The Venetian Affair*
Farr, Jamie (act, b. 1936): *Arnold; Curse II: The Bite*
Farr, Kevin (act): *Deadly Blessing*
Farr, Michele (act): *Single White Female*
Farran, Elen (act): *Witches' Brew*
Farran, Mark (act): *Kong Island*
Farrands, Daniel (wri): *Halloween: The Curse Of Michael Myers*
Farrar, Anthony (act): *The Sword and the Sorcerer*
Farrar, David (act, b. 1908): *Black Narcissus; The Black Shield Of Falworth; Cage Of Gold; The Dark Tower; The Echo Murders; I Accuse (1958); The Late Edwina Black; Meet Sexton Blake; Night Without Stars; Pearl Of The South Pacific; Sexton Blake And The Hooded Terror; Son Of Robin Hood; Watusi*
Farrar, Jane (act): *The Climax; Phantom Of The Opera (1943)*
Farrar, Robert (mus): *Don't Look In The Basement*
Farrar, Scott (cin): *Congo*
Farrar, Vincent (cin): *Behind That Curtain; Boston Blackie's Chinese Venture; Crime Doctor's Diary; The Red Dragon (1945); The Shanghai Cobra*
Farrel, Bernard (act): *Saadia*
Farrell, Amy (act): *The Gore-Gore Girls*
Farrell, Areta (act): *Too Good To Be True*
Farrell, Charles (GB act): *The Abominable Dr. Phibes; Countess Dracula; Creeping Shadows; The Diplomatic Corpse; The Girl Hunters; Hidden Homicide; The House Opposite (1931); The Man at Six; The Ring; The Stolen Necklace; They Made Me A Fugitive; The Vampire Lovers*
Farrell, Charles (USA act, 1901-1990): *Liliom (1930)*
Farrell, Colin (act): *The Land That Time Forgot*
Farrell, Major Fred (act): *Charlie Chan In City In Darkness*
Farrell, Glenda (act, 1904-1971): *The Adventurous Blonde; Blondes At Work; Fly-Away Baby; Mystery Of The Wax Museum; Secret Of The Incas; Smart Blonde; Totchy Blane in Chinatown; Torchy Gets Her Man; Torchy Runs For Mayor*
Farrell, Henry (wri): *The Eyes Of Charles Sand; The House That Wouldn't Die; How Awful About Allan; Hush...Hush, Sweet Charlotte; What Ever Happened to Baby Jane?* (1962 & 1991)
Farrell, John (act): *Portrait Of Jennie*
Farrell, Keith (act): *The Return Of The Six Million Dollar Man And The Bionic Woman*
Farrell, Mike (act, b. 1939): *Doomsday Machine; Live Again, Die Again; The Questor Tapes; Targets*
Farrell, Molly (act): *The Brass Bottle (1914)*
Farrell, Nicholas (act): *Greystoke: The Legend Of Tarzan, Lord Of The Apes*
Farrell, Paul (act): *A Clockwork Orange; Monster Of Terror; The Monsters Christmas*
Farrell, Raul (act): *El Vampiro Sangriento*
Farrell, Richard (act): *Rabid*
Farrell, Ronald (act): *Luminous Procuress*
Farrell, Sharon (act, b. 1948): *The Eyes Of Charles Sand; The Fifth Floor; It's Alive (1974); L.A. 2017; Night Of The Comet; The Premo-nition (1975); Sweet Sixteen*
Farrell, Susan (act): *Primal Scream*
Farrell, Terry (act): *Hellraiser III: Hell On Earth*
Farrell, Timothy (act): *Glen Or Glenda?*
Farrell, Tommy (act): *Pygmy Island*
Farrelly, Patrick (act): *Thinner*
Farren, Babs (act): *Fairyland; Where The Rainbow Ends*
Farren, Fred (act): *Adventurous Voyage Of 'The Arctic'*
Farren, Terry W. (act): *Final Exam*
Farrington, Betty (act): *The Saint In Palm Springs*
Farris, Howard E. (act): *Secrets Of The Phantom Caverns*
Farris, John (dir): *Dear, Dead Delilah*
Farris, John (wri): *Dear, Dead Delilah; The Fury*
Farris, Joseph Anthony (act): *Tales From The Hood*
Farrish, Mike (act): *I Was A Zombie For The F.B.I.*
Farrow, John (dir, 1904-1963): *Alias Nick Beal; The Big Clock; The Invisible Menace; Night Has A Thousand Eyes; The Saint Strikes Back*
Farrow, John (wri, 1904-1963): *Around The World In 80 Days*
Farrow, Mia (act, b. 1945): *Avalanche; Blind Terror; A Dandy In Aspic; Death On The Nile; Full Circle; Rosemary's Baby; Secret Ceremony; Supergirl (1984)*
Farrow, Tisa (act): *The Grim Reaper; The Initiation Of Sarah; Some Call It Loving; Strange Shadows In An Empty Room; Zombie*
Farrow, Yvonne (act): *Mantis*
Farwell, Jonathan (act): *C.H.U.D. II; The Haunting Of Morella; Watchers II*
Fasano, John (dir): *Black Roses; The Edge Of Hell*
Fasano, John (wri): *The Hunchback (1997)*
Fash, Michael (cin): *Orpheus Descending*
Fasmer, Per Didrik (act): *Outbreak*
Fasquelle, Solange (wri): *Le Trio Infernal*
Fassler, Ron (act): *Alien Nation: Body And Soul; Alien Nation: Millennium; Alien Nation: The Enemy Within; Gremlins 2: The New Batch*
Fast, Alvin (wri): *Eaten Alive! (1976); Satan's Cheerleaders*
Fast, Russ (act): *Child Of Darkness, Child Of Light; Deadly Game; The Haunting Of Sarah Hardy*
Fastway (mus): *Trick Or Treat*

Fatooh, John (act): *Headhunter*
Faucett, William (act): *Jesse James Meets Frankenstein's Daughter*
Fauchois, Rene (wri): *The Monkey Talks*
Faulcon, Kent (act): *Dream A Little Dream*
Faulds, Andrew (act): *Blood Of The Vampire; The Devils; The Flesh And The Fiends; The Hellfire Club; Jason And The Argonauts; Liszt o' Mania; Passport to Treason; The Trollenberg Terror*
Faulkner, Brendan (dir & wri): *Spookies*
Faulkner, Carl (act): *Dick Tracy (1945)*
Faulkner, Edward (act): *The Barefoot Executive; The Navy Vs. The Night Monsters*
Faulkner, Gay (act): *The Wiz*
Faulkner, James (act): *Great Expectations (1974)*
Faulkner, Max (act): *Blind Terror*
Faulkner, Peter (act): *Threads*
Faulkner, Sally (act): *The Body Stealers; Prey (1978); Vampyres...Daughters Of Dracula*
Faulkner, Stephanie (act): *Beyond The Universe; Heartbeeps; Howling V: The Rebirth; Virus*
Faulkner, Stephenie (act): *The Philadelphia Experiment*
Faulkner, Trader (act): *Mr. Denning Drives North*
Faulkner, William (wri, 1897-1962): *The Big Sleep (1946); Land Of The Pharaohs*
Fauntelle, Diane (act): *The Docks Of New Orleans*
Fauntleroy, Don E. (cin): *The Stepford Husbands*
Fausak, Robert (act): *Raiders Of The Living Dead*
Faust, Bobby (act): *Street Trash*
Faust, Joe (act): *Nightmare On The 13th Floor*
Faust, Martin (act): *The Face In The Fog (1922)*
Faust, Victoria (act): *Lady Of Burlesque; The Scarlet Clue*
Faustino, David (act): *Alien Nation: Millennium; Dead Man's Island; Summer Girl*
Faustino, Michael (act): *The Monster Squad; Suburban Commando*
Faustino, Randy (act): *Exo-Man*
Favero, Ray (act): *Bridge Across Time*
Faversham, Alec (act): *Night Comes Too Soon*
Favorite, Jack (act): *Death Race 2000*
Favronova, Margaret (act): *Santa Claus (1912)*
Faw, Theresa (act): *The Toxic Avenger, Part II*
Fawcett, Alan (act): *Secret Weapons*
Fawcett, Charles (act): *Captain Sinbad; The Emerald Of Artatama; I Vampiri*
Fawcett, David (act): *Soultaker*
Fawcett, Eric (act): *The Third Clue*
Fawcett, Farrah (act): see Fawcett (Majors), Farrah
Fawcett, George (act, 1860-1939): *Drums Of Jeopardy (1931); The Private Life Of Helen Of Troy*
Fawcett, L'Estrange (wri): *Alf's Button (1930); High Treason (1929)*
Fawcett, William (act): *Jungle Jim In The Forbidden Land*
Fawcett(-Majors), Farrah (act, b. 1947): *Logan's Run; Murder On Flight 502; Myra Breckinridge; Saturn 3*
Fax, Jesslyn (act): *Desk Set; Rear Window*
Fay, Brendan (act): *Man On A Swing*
Fay, Eddy (act): *The Count Of Monte Cristo (1975); Yeti*
Fay, W.G. (act): *Spellbound (1941)*
Fay, William (wri): *Alfred Hitchcock Presents*
Faye, Janina (act): *The Adventures Of Hal 5; The Day Of The Triffids; The Hands Of Orlac (1959); Horror Of Dracula*
Faye, Julia (act, 1896-1966): *A Connecticut Yankee In King Arthur's Court (1949); Male And Female; The Road To Yesterday; Samson and Delilah*
Faye, Randall (wri): *The Face At The Window (1939); Maria Marten: Or, The Murder In The Red Barn (1935); Murder At The Inn*
Faylen, Frank (act, 1906-1985): *The Falcon Strikes Back; Francis; The Invisible Menace; It's A Wonderful Life; The Lost Weekend; The Monkey's Uncle; Nick Carter, Master Detective; The Sniper*
Fayth, Gloria (act): *Just Imagine*
Fazenda, Louise (act, 1895-1962): *Alice In Wonderland (1933); The Bat (1926); The Casino Murder Case; The House Of Horror (1929); The Terror (1928)*
Fazio, Ron (act): *The Toxic Avenger, Part II; The Toxic Avenger, Part III: The Last Temptation Of Toxie*
Feagin, Hugh (act): *In The Year 2889*
Fealy, Margaret (act): *The Return Of Dr. Fu Manchu; The Son Of Monte Cristo*
Fearing, Kenneth (wri): *The Big Clock; No Way Out*
Fearn, Sheila (act): *Time Bandits*
Feast, Michael (act): *I Start Counting*
Featherstone, Angela (act): *Dark Angel: The Ascent*
Featherstone, Vane (act): *The Brass Bottle (1914)*
Fechner, Christian (wri): *Bon Baisers De Hong Kong*
Fedack, Mike (act): *Scalpel*
Feder, Michel (act): *The Phantom Of The Opera (1990)*
Feder, Todd (act): *The Lost Boys*
Federkievicz, Stefania (act): see Powers, Stephanie
Federov, Oleg (act): *Mission: Impossible*
Fee, Melinda (O.) (act): *The Aliens Are Coming; Fade To Black; The Invisible Man (1975); A Nightmare On Elm Street 2: Freddy's Revenge*
Feely, Eleanor (act): *Rawhead Rex*
Feely, Terence (wri): *A Ghost In Monte Carlo; Only A Scream Away; A Place To Die; Quest For Love; The Savage Curse; Spell Of Evil*
Feeney, F.X. (wri): *Roger Corman's 'Frankenstein Unbound'*
Feeney, Francis (act): see Ford, Francis
Feeney, Katharine Scully (act): see Forrest, Sally
Feero, Robert (act): *Fugitive From The Empire*
Fega, Russ (act): *Galaxis*
Fegan, Jack (act): *Picnic At Hanging Rock*
Fegan, Roy (act): *The Meteor Man*
Fehmiu, Bekim (act): *Black Sunday (1977)*
Fehrson, Honor (act): *It Happened Here*
Feig, Paul (act): *Zombie High*
Feigelson, J.D. (wri): *Chiller; Covenant; Cry For The Strangers; Dark Night Of The Scarecrow; Nightmare On The 13th Floor*
Feihu, Sun (act): *Buddha's Lock*
Feil, Gerald (cin): *He Knows You're Alone; Lord Of The Flies (1963); Friday The 13th-Part 3*
Fein, David Lee (wri): *Demonoid*
Feinberg, Ron(ald) (act): *A Boy And His Dog; Dying Room Only; The Man In The Santa Claus Suit*
Feinberg, Steven (wri): *Fortress*
Feindel, J. Arthur (cin): *Revolt Of The Zombies*
Feindel, Jock(ey A.) (cin): *Bluebeard (1944); Day The World Ended (1955)*
Feiner, Wendy (act): *Warlock*
Feinsod, Gail (act): *Street Trash*
Feinstein, Alan (act): *The Two Worlds Of Jennie Logan*
Feirstein, Bruce (wri): *Goldeneye*
Feist, Felix (wri): *Babes In Bagdad*
Feist Jr., Felix (dir, 1910-1965): *Deluge; Donovan's Brain*
Feist, Frances (act): *Carnival Of Souls*
Feitelson, Benjamin (act): *Superman (1978)*
Feke, Steve (wri): *Mac And Me; When A Stranger Calls; When A Stranger Calls Back*
Felcan, Tom (act): *Empire Of Ash III*
Feld, Fritz (act, 1900-1993): *The Computer Wore Tennis Shoes; Lancer Spy; The Secret Life Of Walter Mitty; The Strongest Man In the World; Up in Smoke*
Feld, Gay (act): *The Man With Two Heads*
Felder, Clarence (act): *The Hidden; Man On A Swing*
Felder, Don (mus): *Heavy Metal*
Felder, Sarah (act): *Wolfen*
Feldman, Corey (act): *The 'Burbs; Dream A Little Dream; Dream A Little Dream 2; Friday The 13th-The Final Chapter; Friday the 13th-Part V: A New Beginning; The Goonies; Gremlins; The Lost Boys; Tales From The Crypt Presents Bordello Of Blood; Time After Time; Voodoo*
Feldman, Dennis (wri): *The Golden Child; Species*
Feldman, Marty (act, 1933-1982): *The Adventures Of Sherlock Holmes' Smarter Brother; The Bed-Sitting Room; Young Frankenstein*
Feldman, Randolph (wri): *Hell Night*
Feldman, William (act): *Deathstalker II: Duel Of The Titans*
Feldner, Sheldon (act): *Howard The Duck; Revenge Of The Stepford Wives*
Feldon, Barbara (act, b. 1941): *A Vacation In Hell*
Feldshuh, Tovah (act, b. 1952): *Scream, Pretty Peggy; Terror Out Of The Sky*
Feleo, Ben (wri): *Curse Of The Vampires*
Felice, Lindade (act): *La Donna Scimmia*
Felice, Lyle (act): *Blood Of Ghastly Horror*
Felicianni, Mario (act): *Devil Of The Desert Against The Son Of Hercules; Ulysses*
Feliciano, Jose (act): *Fargo*
Felio, Gordon (act): *Aimez-Vous Les Femmes?; Nick Carter Et Le Trefle Rouge*
Felio, Santesso (act): *Nick Carter Et Le Trefle Rouge*
Felisatti, Masimo (wri): *The Night Evelyn Came Out Of The Grave*
Felix, Art (act): *The Clutching Hand*
Felix, Geoff (act): *Return To Oz*
Felix, J.P. (wri): *Edge Of Sanity*
Felix, Maria (act, b. 1915): *Affairs Of Messalina; La Corona Negra; Faustina*
Fell, Norman (act, b. 1924): *C.H.U.D. II; The Hanged Man; Transylvania 6-5000; You're Driving Me Crazy*
Felleghy, Tom (act): *The Cat O' Nine Tails; City Of The Walking Dead; Demons Of The Mind; Escape From The Bronx; The Eyes Behind the Stars; Mission Stardust*
Fellen, Michael (act): *Terrified*
Feller, Catherine (act): *The Curse Of The Werewolf; The Malpas Mystery; Murder In Eden*
Fellini, Federico (act, 1920-1993): *Il Miracolo*
Fellini, Federico (dir, 1920-1993): *Amarcord; City Of Women; 8 1/2; Giulietta Degli Spiriti; Satyricon; Lo Sceicco Bianco; Spirits Of The Dead*
Fellini, Federico (wri, 1920-1993): *Amarcord; City Of Women; 8 1/2; Giulietta Degli Spiriti; Il Miracolo; Satyricon; Lo Sceicco Bianco; Spirits Of the Dead*
Fellous, Roger (cin): *The Blood Rose*
Fellowes, Edith (act, b. 1923): *Jane Eyre (1934)*
Fellowes, Julian (act): *Baby: Secret Of The Lost Legend*
Fellowes, Rockliffe (act): *Bits Of Life*
Fellows, Don (act): *Electric Dreams; Haunted Honeymoon (1986); Licensed To Love And Kill; The London Connection; Raiders of the Lost Ark; Superman II*
Fellows, Robert (wri): *The Girl Hunters*
Felmingham, Peter (act): *Mad Max*
Felmy, (Hans)jorg/Hans-Joerg (act): *Brainwashed; Der Henker Von London; Legacy Of Horror (1964); The Monster Of London (1964); Torn Curtain*
Felony (act & mus): *Graduation Day*
Felperlaan, Marc (cin): *The Lift*
Felton, Earl (wri, b. 1913): *20,000 Leagues Under The Sea (1954)*
Felton, Felix (act): *Chitty Chitty Bang Bang; Licensed To Kill; Zex*
Felton, William (act): *The Basilisk; Boundary House; The Bridge Destroyer; The Dead Heart; Face To Face; A Grain Of Sand; Morphia, The Death Drug; The Murdock Trial; The Unseen Witness*
Feltron, Ross (act): *Empire Of Ash III*
Felty, Beth (act): *Deadtime Stories*
Fenady, Andrew J. (wri, b. 1928): *Black Noon; Terror In The Wax Museum; The Young Captives*
Fenady, George (dir): *Arnold; Terror In The Wax Museum*
Fenby, Eric (mus): *Jamaica Inn (1939)*
Fenech, Edwige (act): *Demons Of The Dead; Lo Strano Caso Della Signora Ward*
Fenemore, Hilda (act): *Clash By Night; Full Circle; Saturday Island; Supersonic Saucer; Treasure At The Mill*
Fenemore, Stephen (act): *The Yellow Balloon*
Feng, Huang (dir): *Stoner*
Fenlon, Bernie (mus): *Devils Of Darkness*
Fenn, Leo (act): *The Secret Life Of Ian Fleming*
Fenn, Rick (mus): *White Of The Eye*
Fenn, Sherilyn (act, b. 1965): *Crime Zone; Desire And Hell At Sunset Motel; Meridian; Of Mice And Men (1992); The Wraith; Zombie High*
Fennel, Tod (act): *Brainscan*
Fennell, Arthur (act): *12 Monkeys*
Fennelly, Parker (W.) (act, 1891-1988): *The Trouble With Harry*
Fenner, John (cin): *Teenage Mutant Ninja Turtles*
Fenner, Walter (act): *The Shanghai Cobra; Torchy Runs For Mayor*
Fenniman, George (act, 1920-1997): *The Thing From Another World*
Fenning, Stephen (act): *Scared To Death (1980)*
Fenn-Rodgers, Andy (act): *Threads*
Fenollar, Pedro (act): *Satanik*
Fenske, Annemarie (act): *The Handmaid's Tale*
Fenton, Earl (wri): *The Lone Wolf Keeps A Date; The Lone Wolf Takes A Chance*
Fenton, Frank (act, 1906-1957): *Eyes Of The Jungle; Lady Of Burlesque; Philo Vance's Secret Mission*
Fenton, Frank (wri): *A Date With The Falcon; The Falcon Takes Over; The Gay Falcon; The Man With A Cloak; River Of No Return; The Saint in London; The Saint Takes Over*
Fenton, George (mus): *The Company Of Wolves; The Crucible (1996); Groundhog Day; High Spirits; Mary Reilly; Multiplicity*
Fenton, Leonard (act): *The Devil-Ship Pirates; Morons From Outer Space; Panic (1979)*
Fenton, Leslie (act, 1901-1978): *The Casino Murder Case; F.P. 1 Antwortet Nicht; Murder On A Bridle Path*
Fenton, Leslie (dir, 1901-1978): *The Saint's Vacation; Whispering Smith*
Fenton, Mark (act): *The Conquering Power*
Fenton, Simon (act): *Matinee*
Fenwick, Jean (act): *Arrest Bulldog Drummond; Ellery Queen And The Murder Ring*
Fenwick, Moya (act): *Last Bride Of Salem*
Fenwick, T. Gilly (act): *Escape From Broadmoor*
Ferber, Dorin (act): *The Pink Chiquitas*
Ferdin, Pamelyn (act): *The Beguiled; Daughter Of The Mind; The Mephisto Waltz; The Toolbox Murders; What's The Matter With Helen?*
Fere, Tawny (act): *Rockula*
Ferens, Buddy (act): *Change Of Mind*
Fergelic, Stephen (act): *Martin*
Fergus, Adele (act): *Just Imagine*
Ferguson, Al (act): *Mr. Moto In Danger Island*
Ferguson, Allyn (mus): *The Count Of Monte Cristo (1975); Final Eye; Sanctuary Of Fear; Shadow Of A Doubt (1991)*
Ferguson, Anne (act): *The Human Factor*
Ferguson, Carson (act): *Empire Of Ash III*
Ferguson, Casson (act): *The Road To Yesterday*
Ferguson, David (act): *Copycat*
Ferguson, Frank (act, 1899-1978): *Abbott And Costello Meet Frankenstein; The Beast From 20,000 Fathoms; The Beginning Or The End?; Blonde for a Day; Caught; Hush... Hush, Sweet Charlotte; It Grows On Trees*
Ferguson, J. Don (act): *Freejack*
Ferguson, Jane (act): *Fire In The Sky (1993)*
Ferguson, Jay (act): *Offerings*
Ferguson, Jay (mus): *Bad Dreams; A Nightmare On Elm Street 5: The Dream Child*
Ferguson, Jessie Lawrence (act): *Amazons (1984); Neon Maniacs; Prince Of Darkness*
Ferguson, John (act): *The Haunting Of Hamilton High*
Ferguson, Kate (act): *Outer Touch*
Ferguson, Kathleen (act): *Nightmare (1981)*
Ferguson, Larry (wri): *Alien 3; Highlander*
Ferguson, Lester (act): *The Fatal Night*
Ferguson, Michael (act): *The Pink Chiquitas*
Ferguson, S.G. (dir): *Supersonic Saucer*
Ferguson, Sherry (act): *Edward Scissorhands*
Ferguson, Virginia (act): *Alien High*
Ferguson, Yvette (act): *Timecop*
Fergusson, Denise (act): *Spasms*
Fergusson, John (act): *White Zombie*
Ferlan, Dominic (act): *Dracula's Dog*
Ferland, Guy (dir & wri): *The Babysitter (1995)*
Fern, Robert (wri): *Lemora, The Lady Dracula*
Fernald, John (act): *The Night Has Eyes*
Fernandel (act, 1903-1971, nee Fernand Joseph Desire Contandin): *Ali-Baba Et Les Quarante Voleurs; Around The World In 80 Days; L'auberge Rouge; Le Diable et les Dix Commandements*
Fernandes, Colin (act): *An American Werewolf In London*
Fernandes, Joao (cin): *The Nesting; Witches' Brew*
Fernandes, Miguel (act): *Ghost Story (1981); Rabid; Sorry, Wrong Number (1989); Spasms*
Fernandez, Abel (act): *Devil Goddess*
Fernandez, Arturo (act): *Sound Of Horror*
Fernandez, Eddie (act): *The Blood Drinkers*
Fernandez, Evelina (act): *Flatliners*
Fernandez, Felix (act): *The Colossus Of Rhodes*
Fernandez, Jaime (act): *Return From The Beyond; El Santo Contra Las Vampiras*
Fernandez, Jesus (act): *Tristana*
Fernandez, Jose (act): *The Possession Of Joel Delaney*
Fernandez, Juan (act): *Sparkling Cyanide*
Fernandez, M. Cruz (act): *The Mummy's Revenge*
Fernandez, Margarita (act): *The Ewok Adventure; Howard The Duck*
Fernandez, Mario (act): *Anguish*
Fernandez, Miguel (act): *Trancers*
Fernando, Felix (act): *A Rocket From Calabuch*
Fernau, Rudolf (act): *Confess, Dr. Corda; The Invisible Dr. Mabuse*
Fernberger, Peter (cin): *Nightlife (1989, USA-Mex)*
Fernetz, Charlene (act): *Sabrina The Teenage Witch*
Ferone, Pasquale (act): *Le Boucher*
Ferova, Tanya (act): *The Sexplorer; Terror (1979)*
Ferraday, Lisa (act): *Last Train From Bombay*

Ferral, Alain (act): Le Comte De Monte Cristo
Ferrandini, Dean (act): Beyond The Poseidon Adventure
Ferrando, Giancarlo (cin): The Fish Men; The Great Alligator; Ironmaster; Il Montagna Di Dio Cannibale; Torso; Warriors Of The Wasteland
Ferrara, Al (act): Dracula's Dog
Ferrara, Ed (wri): The Munsters' Scary Little Christmas
Ferrara, Frank (act): Remo Williams: The Adventure Begins
Ferrara, Romano (dir & wri): Planets Against Us
Ferrare, Ashley (act): Cyclone
Ferrare, Cristina (act): Mary, Mary, Bloody Mary
Ferrari, Georgio (cin): Popcorn
Ferrari, Marco (dir, b. 1928): La Donna Scimmia
Ferraro, Alessandro (wri): Il Trionfo Di Ercole
Ferraro, John (act): Wolfen
Ferraro, Ralf/Ralph (mus): Flesh Gordon; La Sorella Di Satan; Treasure Of The Petrified Forest
Ferrati, Sarah (act): La Strega In Amore
Ferratti, Rebecca (act): Outlaw Of Gor
Ferrau, Alessandro (wri): Sword Of The Conqueror
Ferrel, Pablo (act): Survive!
Ferrell, Conchata (act): Edward Scissorhands; Freeway
Ferrell, Denise (act): Slaughterhouse Rock
Ferrell, Jeff (cin, dir & wri): Revenge Of The Teenage Vixens From Outer Space
Ferrell, Tyra (act): The Exorcist III; Lady Beware
Ferren, Bran (cin): Altered States; Making Mr. Right; The Manhattan Project; Star Trek V: The Final Frontier
Ferreol, Andrea (act): The Phantom Of The Opera (1990); Le Trio Infernal
Ferrer, Jorge (act): Anguish
Ferrer, Jose (act, 1909-1992): The Amazing Captain Nemo; The Aquarians; The Being; Covenant; Crosscurrent; Death Ride; Demon Isalnd, Dracula's Dog, Dune. Exoman; The Fifth Musketeer; I Accuse (1958); The Sentinel; The Swarm
Ferrer, Jose (dir, 1909-1992): I Accuse (1958)
Ferrer, Mel (act, b. 1917, nee Melchor Gaston Ferrer): The Amazing Captain Nemo; Anticristo; City Of The Walking Dead; Le Diable et les Dix Commandements; Eaten Alive! (1976); Et Mourir de Plaisir; The Fifth Floor; The Fish Men; The Great Alligator; The Hands of Orlac (1959); Knights of the Round Table; The Memory of Eva Ryker; The Norsemen; Paris When It Sizzles; Saadia; The Visitor; The World, the Flesh and the Devil
Ferrer, Mel (dir, b. 1917): Green Mansions
Ferrer, Melchor Gaston (act & dir): see Ferrer, Mel
Ferrer, Miguel (act): Deepstar Six; The Guardian; Project: Alf; Robocop; Star Trek III: The Search For Spock
Ferrer, Tony (act): The Vengeance Of Fu Manchu
Ferrera, Abel (dir): The Addiction; The Body Snatchers; Driller Killer; Ms. 45
Ferrero, Martin (act): High Spirits; Jurassic Park
Ferrero, Rossella (act): El Castello Dell'orrore
Ferrers, Helen (act):The River
Ferret, Eve (act): Haunted Honeymoon (1986)
Ferri, Laura (act): The Hand That Rocks The Cradle
Ferrier, Noel (act): Avengers Of The Reef
Ferrier, Russell (act): Shock Chamber
Ferrier, Willard G. (cin): Fantasies
Ferrigno, Carla (act): Black Roses; The Death Of The Incredible Hulk
Ferrigno, Lou (act, b. 1951): The Adventures Of Hercules; The Death Of The Incredible Hulk; Hercules (1983); The Incredible Hulk; The Incredible Hulk, Part 2; The Incredible Hulk Returns; Sinbad; Sinbad And The Seven Seas; The Trial Of The Incredible Hulk
Ferrin, Frank (dir & wri): Sabaka
Ferrini, Franco (wri): Demons 2; Phenomena; Trauma (1993); Two Evil Eyes
Ferrio, Gianni (mus): The Mysterious Island Of Captain Nemo
Ferris, Barbara (act, b. 1943): Children Of The Damned
Ferris, Bill (act): The Toxic Avenger, Part II
Ferris, Christopher (act): Zombie Island Massacre
Ferris, Mark (act): Invasion Of The Star Creatures
Ferris, Miriam (act): The Picture Of Dorian Gray (1916); The Striped Stocking Gang
Ferris, Paul (mus): The Creeping Flesh; Persecution; The Sorcerers; Witch-Finder General
Ferris, Walter (wri, b. 1886): At Sword's Point; Death Takes A Holiday (1934)
Ferro, Frank (act): Galaxina
Ferro, Scott (act): A Nymphoid Barbarian In Dinosaur Hell
Ferroni, Giorgio (dir): The Conquest Of Mycenae; The Lion Of Thebes; Il Mulino Delle Donne Di Pietra; The Trojan Horse
Ferrucci, Frank (act): Quarantine
Ferrugiaro, Kenny (act): Evilspeak
Ferry, David (act): Darkman II: The Return Of Durant
Ferry, Isidoro Martinez (dir): La Cara Del Terror
Ferry, Jean (wri): Le Saint Prend L'affut
Fersen, Alessandro (act): Teodora, Imperatrice Di Bisanzio; Ulysses
Ferth, Karl (act): The Fifth Musketeer
Fertis, Yannis (act): Electra (1961)
Ferzetti, Gabriele (act, b. 1927, nee Pasquale Ferzetti): The Bible; Il Diavolo Innamorata; The Gentle Art Of Murder; Hitler, The Last Ten Days; Night Porter; On Her Majesty's Secret Service; The psychic; The St. Valentine's Day Massacre
Ferzetti, Pasquale (act): see Ferzetti, Gabriele
Fescourt, Henri (dir, 1880-1966): Les Miserables (1925)
Fescud, Richard (act): Hitler: The Last Ten Days
Fesette, Doris (act): Edge Of Fury
Festa Campanile, Pasquale (wri, b. 1927): L'Assassino
Fetchit, Stepin (act, 1902-1985, nee Lincoln Perry): Charlie Chan In Egypt; The Ghost Talks
Fetherston, Eddie (act): Boston Blackie And The Law; The Lone Wolf In Paris; The Lone Wolf Spy Hunt; The Phantom Thief
Fethke, J. (wri): Milczaca Gwiazda
Fetoh, Abdel Monem (act): A Story Of Tutankhamun
Fetters, Curt (cin): Terrified
Fetty, Darrell (act): Blood Beach; Endangered Species
Feuchtenberg, Walter (act): Superwheels
Feuer, Cy (mus): Dick Tracy Vs. Crime, Inc.
Feuer, Debra (act): Night Angel
Feuer, Michael (act): Flesh-Eating Mothers
Feuillade, Louis (dir, 1873-1925): Fantomas (1913)
Feuillade, Louis (wri, 1873-1925): Judex
Feuillere, Edwige (act, b. 1907, nee Edwige Cunati): L'aigle A Deux Tetes; Aimez-Vous Les Femmes?; The Gentle Art Of Murder
Feury, Peggy (act): Friday The 13th...The Orphan
Fey, Stephane (act): Au Coeur De La Vie
Feyder, Jacques (dir, 1887-1948): L'atlantide (1920); Knight Without Armour; Le Spectre Vert
Feyder, Jacques (wri, 1887-1948): L'atlantide (1920)
Feyer, Friedrich (act): Das Kabinett Des Dr. Caligari
Ffolliott, Gladys (act): Old Bill Through The Ages
Ffrangcon-Davies, Gwen (act, 1891-1992): The Devil Rides Out; The Witches (1966)
Fiander, Lewis (act): Dr. Jekyll And Sister Hyde; Dr. Phibes Rises Again
Fichter, Rick (cin): Bride Of Re-Animator
Fichtner, William (act): Strange Days; Virtuosity
Fidello, Manuel (wri): Friday The 13th, Part VII-The New Blood
Fidenco, Nico (mus): The Bang-Bang Kid; A Thousand And One Nights (1968)
Fidler, Cindy (act): Red Blooded American Girl
Fidoe, Edward (act): Woof!; Woof Too! A Girl And Her Dog; Woof Again! Why Me?; Woof Returns! A Kid's Best Friend
Fiedel, Brad (mus): Blink; Deadly Messages; Eyes Of Fire; Fright Night; Fright Night II; Johnny Mnemonic; Just Before Dawn (1980); The Midnight Hour; Night School; Night Visions; Northstar; Plymouth; Rasputin (1996); The Serpent and the Rainbow; The Terminator; The Terminator 2: Judgement Day
Fiedler, Eric (act): Full Eclipse
Fiedler, John (act, b. 1925): Bad Ronald; The Deathmaster; Human Feelings; The Shaggy D.A.
Field, Alexander (act): Dark Eyes Of London; F.P. 1 Antwortet Nicht; The Last Hour; The Woman Eater
Field, Ben (act): The Clairvoyant (1934); The Face At The Window (1920); Secret Lives; The Secret of the Loch (1934)
Field, Betty (act, 1918-1973): Flesh And Fantasy; Of Mice And Men (1939)
Field, Chelsea (act): The Birds II: Land's End; The Dark Half; Masters Of The Universe; Prison (1988)
Field, Gladys (act): Dr. Jekyll And Mr. Hyde (1919)
Field, Karin (act): Cave Of The Living Dead; The Mad Butcher
Field, Logan (act): Blacula; The Brotherhood Of The Bell
Field, Marc (act): The Dark Half
Field, Margaret (act): The Big Clock; Captive Women; Chain Of Circumstance; The Man From Planet X
Field, Margaret Cynthia (act): see Field, Virginia
Field, Mark (act): The Creeping Terror
Field, Mary (act): A Connecticut Yankee In King Arthur's Court (1949)
Field, Nicholas (act): Mark Of The Devil
Field, Norman (act): Tobor The Great; The Twonky
Field, Pamela (act): Ironmaster
Field, Patrick (act): Howling II
Field, Robert Nathan (act): Cavegirl (1985)
Field, Sally (act, b. 1946): Beyond The Poseidon Adventure; Home For The Holidays
Field, Shirley Anne (act, b. 1938): The Damned; Horrors Of The Black Museum; House Of The Living Dead; Man In the Moon (1960); Peeping Tom; Seven Thunders
Field, Steven (act): Beverly Hills Bodysnatchers
Field, Susan (act): Mary Shelley's 'Frankenstein'
Field, Todd (act): Twister
Field, Virginia (act, 1917-1992, nee Margaret Cynthia Field): Charlie Chan At Monte Carlo; A Connecticut Yankee in King Arthur's Court; Dream Girl; The Earth; Dies Screaming; Lancer Spy; Mr. Moto's Last Warning; Mr. Moto Takes a Vacation; Repaet Performance; Think Fast, Mr. Moto; The Veils of Bagdad
Field, Walter Logan (act): Halloween 4: The Return Of Michael Myers
Fielder, Kitty (act): The Yellow Claw
Fielder, Pat (dir): The Vampire (1957)
Fielder, Pat (wri): The Flame Barrier; Goliath Awaits; The Monster That Challenged The World; The Return of Dracula; The Vampire (1957)
Fielding, Dorothy (act): Fright Night
Fielding, Edward (act): Dead Man's Eyes; Flesh And Fantasy; The Invisible Man Returns; Rebecca
Fielding, Fenella (act, b. 1930): Carry On Screaming; The Old Dark House (1963); The Zany Adventures Of Robin Hood
Fielding, Gerald (act): Last Rites
Fielding, Guy (act): Candles At Nine
Fielding, Jerry (mus): Beyond The Poseidon Adventure; The Big Sleep (1978); The Black Bird (1975); Crackle of Death; Demon and the Mummy; Demon Seed; Funeral Home; The Nightcomers
Fielding, Marjorie (act, 1892-1956): Circle Of Danger; The Lavender Hill Mob; The Net
Fielding, Richard (wri): Superman And The Mole Men
Fields, Albert (act): Vice Versa (1988)
Fields, Charlie (act): The Demon Murder Case
Fields, Chip (act): The Chinese Web
Fields, Christopher (act): Jacob's Ladder
Fields, Christopher John (act): Alien 3; Jurassic Park; Stargate
Fields, Darlene (act): The Snow Creature; Spook Chasers
Fields, Don (dir): The Curse Of Bigfoot
Fields, Eddy (act): Prisoners Of The Casbah
Fields, Edith (act): Fantasies; Time Flyer
Fields, Holly (act): Communion
Fields, Hugh O. (act): A Polish Vampire In Burbank
Fields, J.T. (wri): The Curse Of Bigfoot
Fields, Jere (act): Friday The 13th-Part V: A New Beginning
Fields, John H. (act): Cat People (1982)
Fields, Kim (act, b. 1969): The Kid With The Broken Halo
Fields, Lindsey (act): The Goddess Of Love
Fields, Lloyd (act): Moon 44
Fields, Lois (act): Crime Doctor's Diary
Fields, Marneen (act): Beyond The Poseidon Adventure; Hellhole
Fields, Norman (act): Octaman
Fields, Peter Allan (wri): The Spy In The Green Hat
Fields, Robert (act): The Blob (1958); Rhinoceros (1974)
Fields, Sid(ney) (act): Charlie Chan On Broadway; For Heaven's Sake
Fields, Sidney (wri): Abbott And Costello Meet Dr. Jekyll And Mr. Hyde
Fields, Stanley (act, 1880-1941, nee Walter L. Agnew): Cracked Nuts (1931); Island Of Lost Souls
Fields, Suzanne (act): Flesh Gordon
Fields, Thor (act): Hello Again
Fields, Tony (act): Trick Or Treat
Fields, W.C. (act, 1879-1946, nee William Claude Dukinfield): Alice In Wonderland (1933); International House
Fieldsteel, Robert (act): Beastmaster 2: Through The Portal Of Time
Fienhage, Joyce (mus): The Howling
Fienhage, Rick (mus): The Howling
Fiennes, Ralph (act, b. 1963): The Avengers; Strange Days
Fierberg, Steven (cin): A Nightmare On Elm Street 4: The Dream Master
Fiermonte, Enzo (act): The Lion Of Thebes; Il Trionfo Di Ercole
Fierro, Lee (act): Jaws; Jaws: The Revenge
Fierro, Paul (act): The Creature Walks Among Us; Dig That Uranium!; Sisters Of Death; Sorry, Wrong Number (1948)
Fierstein, Harvey (act): Dr. Jekyll And Ms. Hyde; Independence Day
Fieschi, Jean-Andre (act): Alphaville, Un Etrange Aventure De Lemmy Caution
Fieweger, Thomas J. (act): Copycat
Fife, Jason (act): Addams Family Values
Fife, Maxine (act): One Body Too Many
Figaro, Dominique (act): Notorious (1992)
Figueroa, Gabriel (cin, b. 1907): El Angel Exterminador; Macario
Figueroa, Hector (R.) (cin): Midnight Offerings; Starflight: The Plane That Couldn't Land; Tomorrow's Child
Figueroa, Juan Ancona (act): Caveman (1981)
Filardi, Jason (act): The Craft
Filardi, Peter (wri): The Craft; Flatliners
Fildes, Audrey (act): Kind Hearts And Coronets; While I Live
Fildew, William (cin): Outside The Law
Filer, Tom (wri): The Beast With A Million Eyes; The Space Children
Files, Gary (act): Thunderbird 6
Filip, Josef (act): Do You Keep A Lion At Home?
Filipovsky, Frantisek (act): Na Komete
Filippidis, Andreas (act): Atlas
Fillali, Hamid (act): The Jewel Of The Nile
Fillali, Mohammed (act): The Jewel Of The Nile
Fillmore, Clyde (act, b. 1876): The Hidden Eye; Laura
Fillmore, Trish (act): Retribution (1988)
Filloon, Mike (act): Re-Animator
Filozov, Albert (act): The Savage Hunt Of King Stakh
Filpi, Carmen (act): Bates Motel; Ed Wood; Halloween 4: The Return Of Michael Myers
Filson, Al (act): Monte Cristo
Fimberg, Hal (wri, 1916-1974): In Like Flint; Our Man Flint
Fimiani, Maria (act): A Man About The House
Fimple, Dennis (act): Creature From Black Lake; King Kong (1976); Of Mice And Men (1981); The Spectre of Edgar Allen Poe
Finazzo, Anthony (act): Cocoon: The Return
Finch, Charles (act): Amazons (1986)
Finch, Flora (act, 1869-1940): The Cat And The Canary (1927); The Haunted House (1929); A Kiss For Cinderella
Finch, Gloria Stuart (act): see Stuart, Gloria
Finch, Howard (act): Red Alert
Finch, Jennifer (act): Serial Mom
Finch, John (act): The Vampire Lovers
Finch, Jon (act, b. 1941): Death On The Nile; Diagnosis: Murder; Frenzy; The Last Days Of Man On Earth; Lurking Fear; Macbeth (1971)
Finch, Peter (act, 1916-1977, nee William Mitchell): First Men In The Moon (1964); Lost Horizon (1973); The Red Tent; The Story of Robin Hood
Finch, Scott (act): The Liquidator
Fincham, Lindsay (act): The Romany Rye
Fincher, David (dir): Alien 3; Seven
Finch-Smiles, Frank (act, a.k.a. Finch Smiles): Behind That Curtain; The Lost World (1925)
Findlater, John (act): Meteor
Findlay, Alistair (act): Highlander
Findlay, Michael (dir): Shriek Of The Mutilated
Findlay, Roberta (cin): The Oracle (1985); Shriek Of The Mutilated
Findlay, Roberta (dir): The Oracle (1985); Prime Evil
Findlay, Thomas (act): Buried Treasure
Findley, Diane (act): Gammera, The Invincible
Findley, Freddie (act): Rasputin (1996)
Fine, Harry (act): Panic At Madam Tussaud's
Fine, Harry (wri): The Vampire Lovers

Flanders, Ed (act, 1934-1995): The Exorcist III; The Legend Of Lizzie Borden; Salem's Lot; Tomorrow's Child; Twinkle, Twinkle, Killer Kane
Flanders, Susan (act): Secrets Of The Phantom Caverns
Flanders, Traci (act): Secrets Of The Phantom Caverns
Flanery, Sean Patrick (act, b. 1965): Guinevere; Powder; Young Indiana Jones And The Attack Of The Hawkmen
Flanery, Robyn (act): Student Bodies
Flannery, Erin (act): Incubus (1982)
Flannery, Susan (act, b. 1943): Melody Of Hate; The Towering Inferno
Flather, Catherine (act): The Clan Of The Cave Bear
Flatman, Barry (act): Short Circuit 2; Sorry, Wrong Number (1989); Spasms; Terminal Justice
Flato, Herbert (act): Rocket Attack U.S.A.
Flato, Richard (act): Return Of The Fly
Flaven, Arthur (wri): Jungle Trail Of The Son Of Tarzan
Flavin, James (act, 1906-1976): Abbott and Costello Go To Mars; Abbott and Costello Meet The Killer; Angel On My Shoulder (1946); The Barefoot Executive; Francis in the Haunted House; the Gracie Allen Murder Case; Hold That Hypnotist; King Kong (1933); Laura; League of Frightened Men; Mighty Joe Young; Mr. Wong in Chinatown; Nightmare Alley; One Touch of Venus; Shadow of the Thin Man; The Shanghai Cobra; Song of the Thin Man; Spellbound (1945); The Velvet Touch
Flax, Phyllis (act): Nightmare On The 13th Floor
Flaxman, Harvey (wri): Grizzly
Fleck, James (act): The Tell-Tale Heart (1934)
Fleck, Jerry (act): Earthbound (1981)
Fleck, John (act): Howard The Duck
Fleck, Lois (act): Red Alert
Fleder, Gary (dir): The Companion (1994)
Fleeks, Eric (act): Deep Red (1994)
Fleer, Harry (act): Tormented (1960); The Unearthly
Fleetwood, James (act): Inferno (1979)
Fleetwood, Susan (act): Clash Of The Titans; Young Sherlock Holmes
Fleig, Kathy (act): Deadtime Stories
Fleischer, Charles (act): Back To The Future, Part Ii; Demon Knight; Dick Tracy (1990); The Hand (1981)
Fleischer, Richard (dir, b. 1916): Amityville 3-D; Blind Terror; The Boston Strangler; Conan The Destroyer; Dr. Dolittle; Fantastic Voyage; Red Sonja; Soylent Green; 10 Rillington Place; 20,000 Leagues Under the Sea (1954)
Fleischman, A.S. (wri): Spy In The Sky
Fleischmann, Harry (act): Charlie Chan In City In Darkness
Fleischmann, Herbert (act): Future Women; Hauser's Memory
Fleischmann, Walter Reinhold Alfred (act): See Dexter, Anthony
Fleishaker, Joe (act): The Toxic Avenger, Part II
Fleming, Al (act): Slaughterhouse Rock
Fleming, Andrew (dir & wri, b. 1962): Bad Dreams; The Craft
Fleming, Athole (act): Bulldog Jack
Fleming, Brandon (wri): The Flaw; Forging Ahead; Solution By Phone; The Woman Eater
Fleming, Brendan (act): Judge Dredd
Fleming, Claude (act): The Sword Of Damocles; The Thirteenth Candle; The Unholy Night
Fleming, Cliff (act): Darkman (1990)
Fleming, Cynthia (act): Invasion Of The Blood Farmers
Fleming, Edyie (act): The Fan
Fleming, Eric (act, 1924-1966): Conquest Of Space; The Curse of the Undead; Fright (1957); Queen of Outer Space
Fleming, Erin (act): The Legend Of Blood Mountain
Fleming, Frances (act): Jack's Back
Fleming, Ian (act, 1888-1969): After Dark; The Missing Rembrandt; Return of a Stranger; The Return of Mr. Moto; Sexton Blake and the Mademoiselle; Silver Blaze (1937); The Sleeping Cardinal; The Third Clue; The Triumph of Sherlock Holmes; The Voice of Merrill; The Web of Suspicion; The Woman In Question
Fleming, Ian (wri, 1908-1964): Casino Royale; Chitty Chitty Bang Bang; Diamonds Are Forever; Dr. No; For Your Eyes Only; From Russia With Love; Goldeneye, Goldfinger; Licence to Kill (1989); Live and Let Die; The Living Daylights; The Man With the Golden Gun; Moonraker; Never Say Never Again; Octopussy; On Her Majesty's Secret Service; The Spy Who Loved Me; Thunderball; Tomorrow Never Dies; A View to a Kill; You Only Live Twice
Fleming, Joan (wri): Family Doctor
Fleming, John J. (act): Eat And Run
Fleming, Lone (act): Tombs Of The Living Dead; Where Time Began
Fleming, Marvin (act): Heaven Can Wait (1978)
Fleming, Michael (act): The Man With The Golden Gun
Fleming, Paul (act): Revenge Of The Teenage Vixens From Outer Space
Fleming, Rhonda (act, b. 1923, nee Marilyn Louis): Adventure Island; A Connecticut Yankee In King Arthur's Court (1949); Cry Danger; Jivaro; The Killer is Loose; The Nude Bomb; The Queen Of Babylon; Spellbound (1945); The Spiral Staircase (1946); While the City Sleeps
Fleming, Tom (act): King Lear (1970)
Fleming, Victor (dir, 1883-1949): Dr. Jekyll And Mr. Hyde (1941); Treasure Island (1934); The Wizard Of Oz (1939)
Flemyng, Gordon (dir, b. 1934): Daleks' Invasion Earth 2150 A.D.; Dr. Who And The Daleks
Flemyng, Robert (act, b. 1912): Blackmailed; The Body Stealers; The Deadly Affair; The Deathshead Vampire; The Medusa Touch; The Quiller Memorandum; Raptus; The Spy With a Cold Nose; The 39 Steps (1978)
Flender, Rodman (dir): Leprechaun 2
Flessa, Paul (act): Tuck Everlasting
Fletcher, Barrie (act): Only A Scream Away
Fletcher, Bill (act): The Man With The Power
Fletcher, Bramwell (act, b. 1904): The Mummy (1932); The Scarlet Pimpernel (1934); Svengali (1931); The Undying Monster
Fletcher, Buffy (act): Phoenix The Warrior
Fletcher, Cecil (act): Iron Justice
Fletcher, Cyril (act): A Piece Of Cake
Fletcher, Dexter (act): Gothic; El Mono Loco
Fletcher, Diane (act): Macbeth (1971)
Fletcher, Graham (act): Peter Rabbit And The Tales Of Beatrix Potter; Stories From A Flying Trunk
Fletcher, Jack (act): Elvira, Mistress Of The Dark
Fletcher, Kent (act): Lord Of The Flies (1963)
Fletcher, Lawrence (act): The Search For Bridey Murphy
Fletcher, Louise (act, b. 1934): The Boy Who Could Fly; Brainstorm (1983); Exorcist II: The Heretic; Firestarter; Flowers in the Attic; Frankenstein and Me; Invaders From Mars (1986); Mama Dracula; Nightmare On the 13th Floor; Shadowzone; The Stepford Husbands; Strange Behavior; Strange Invaders; Virtuosity
Fletcher, Louise (wri): Night Watch
Fletcher, Lucille (wri): Sorry, Wrong Number (1948 & 1989)
Fletcher, Neil (act): Deadly Blessing; In The Year 2889; Mars Needs Women; Zontar: The Thing From Venus
Fletcher, Page (act): Haunted By Her Past; Humongous
Fletcher, Suzanne (act): Sleepwalk
Fletcher, Tommy (cin): A Hitch In Time
Fletcher, Tony (act): The Intruder (1981)
Fletcher, Wilfred (act): The House Of Thof The Arrow (1930)
Fletcher, William (act): The Lost City
Flick, Pat C. (act): The Missing Guest
Flickenschildt, Elisabeth (act): The Hand Of The Gallows; The Phantom Of Soho
Flicker, Theodore J. (dir & wri, b. 1930): Jacob Two-Two Meets The Hooded Fang; The President's Analyst
Flink, Richard S. (wri): Sting Of Death
Flint, Helen (act): Time To Kill (1942)
Flint, John (act): A Place To Die
Flint, Sam (act): The Chinese Cat; Crime Doctor's Strangest Case; Cyclotrode X; The Monster Maker (1943); Spy Smasher Returns; The Steel Trap
Flintoft, Jason (act): The Outing
Flippen, Jay C. (act, 1899-1971): It's Always Fair Weather; The Killing; The Spirit Is Willing
Flippin, Lucy Lee (act): Earth Girls Are Easy; Lady In White
Flitner, Ellen (act): Endangered Species
Flitton, Sheila (act): Rawhead Rex
Floche, Sebastien (act): The Phantom Of The Opera (1990)
Flock, Brad (act): Superman (1978)
Floersheim, Patrick (act): The Murders In The Rue Morgue (1986)
Flon, Suzanne (act): Mr. Arkadin; The Trial
Flood, Ellen (act): Change Of Mind
Flood, Joe (act): Student Bodies; Switch; Time Flyer
Flood, Kevin (act): Frankenstein Created Woman
Flood, Patricia (act): Eye Of The Alien
Flood, Shari (act): Mad Max Beyond Thunderdome
Floores, Brian (act): The Outing
Florek, Dann (act): Angel Heart; The Flintstones
Florek, Dave (act): Ghostbusters II
Florelle (act): Liliom (1933)
Florence, Carol (act): 12 Monkeys
Florence, Sheila (act): Mad Max
Flores, Claudia (act): There's Nothing Out There
Flores, Erika (act): Buried Secrets; Visions Of Murder
Flores, Von (act): Conundrum
Florey, Robert (dir, 1900-1979): The Beast With Five Fingers; The Face Behind The Mask; The Florentine Dagger; Meet Boston Blackie; The Murders In The Rue Morgue (1932); The Preview Murder Mystery; Tarzan And The Mermaids
Florey, Robert (wri, 1900-1979): Frankenstein (1931)
Floria, Emma (act): The Clan Of The Cave Bear
Florian, Barbara (act): Gli Amori Di Ercole
Florman, Arthur (cin): Terror From The Year 5,000
Flory, Med (act): The Amazing Captain Nemo; The Boogens; The Hearse; Home For The Holidays; The Nutty Professor(1963)
Flourney, Don (act): Beyond The Time Barrier; The Giant Gila Monster
Flower, (George) "Buck" (act): The Alpha Incident; Bates Motel; The Capture Of Bigfoot; Drive-In Massacre; Pumpkinhead; Puppet Master II; Sundown, The Vampire In Retreat; They Live; Waxwork II: Lost In Time
Flower, Newman (wri): The Answer
Flower, Verkina (act): Beyond Evil; The Capture Of Bigfoot
Flowers, A.D. (cin): Red Alert; Sleeper
Flowers, Bess (act): The Ghost Talks; The Lone Wolf In Paris; Song Of The Thin Man; The Velvet Touch
Floyd, Alton (wri): Finger Prints
Floyd, Calvin (dir): In Search Of Dracula; Terror Of Frankenstein
Floyd, Calvin (wri): Terror Of Frankenstein
Floyd, Courtney (act): The Ivory Ape
Floyd, David (mus): Wolfman (1979)
Floyd, Jacqueline (act): Twice-Told Tales
Floyd, P.R. (act): Making Mr. Right
Floyd, Yvonne (wri): In Search Of Dracula; Terror Of Frankenstein
Fluck, Diana (act): see Dors, Diana
Fluegel, Darlanne (act): Battle Beyond The Stars (1980); Darkman III: Die Darkman Die; Fatal Sky; Pet Sematary Two; Relative Fear; Scanner Cop
Fluellen, Joel (act): Jungle Gents; The Monster From Green Hell; The White Goddess; White Pongo
Flugrath, Edna (act): The Ashes Of Revenge; A Christmas Carol (1914); The Firm Of Girdlestone; A Garret In Bohemia; The King's Minister; The Man Without A Soul; The Ring And The Rajah; The Two Roads
Flugrath, Leona (act): see Mason, Shirley
Flying Zacchinis, The (act): Phantom Of The Rue Morgue
Flynn, Bill (act): House Of The Living Dead; Prisoners Of The Lost Universe
Flynn, Colleen (act): Late For Dinner
Flynn, Daniel R. (act): Surf Nazis Must Die
Flynn, Darcy (act): The Witches (1990)
Flynn, Denny Martin (wri): Star Trek VI: The Undiscovered Country
Flynn, Emmett (J.) (dir): A Connecticut Yankee In King Arthur's Court (1921); In The Palace Of The King; Monte Cristo
Flynn, Eric (act): A Challenge For Robin Hood; Dr. Syn-Alias The Scarecrow
Flynn, Errol (act, 1909-1959): Adventures Of Captain Fabian; The Adventures Of Don Juan; The Adventures Of Robin Hood; The Case of the Curious Bride; Cry Wolf (1947); Murder At Monte Carlo
Flynn, Errol (wri, 1909-1959): Adventures Of Captain Fabian
Flynn, Frederick (act): Shadowzone
Flynn, Gertrude (act): Devil Dog: The Hound Of Hell
Flynn, J. Michael (act): Timestalkers
Flynn, Janet (act): see Malo, Gina
Flynn, Joe (act, 1924-1974): The Barefoot Executive; The Computer Wore Tennis Shoes; Indestructible Man; The Love Bug; Now You See Him, Now You Don't; The Strongest Man In The World
Flynn, John (dir): Brainscan; The Jerusalem File
Flynn, Joni (act): Octopussy
Flynn, Kelly (act): Hush...Hush, Sweet Charlotte
Flynn, Mannix (act): Excalibur
Flynn, Michael (act): Halloween 4: The Return Of Michael Myers
Flynn, Miriam (act): 18 Again!
Flynn, Pat (act): Not Of This Earth (1957)
Flynn, Sean (act, b. 1941): Duel At The Rio Grande; Mission To Venice; Temple Of The White Elephants
Flynn, Steven (act): Alien Nation: Millennium
Flynn, William J. (wri): Behind The Curtain (1924)
Flynt, Brendan (cin): Tromeo And Juliet
Flyswatter, Dukey (act): Nightmare Sisters
FM (mus): The Intruder (1981)
Foa, Arnoldo (act): The Nights Of Lucretia Borgia; The Reluctant Saint; The Tartars; The Trial
Foad, Gene (act): The Lake
Foam, John (cin, dir & wri): see Bava, Mario
Focarille, James (act): Raiders Of The Living Dead
Focas, Spiros (act): Holocaust 2000; The Jewel Of The Nile; Psycosissimo
Foch, Nina (act, b. 1924): Boston Blackie's Rendezvous; Cry Of The Werewolf; Escape In The Fog; I Love A Mystery (1945); Jennifer (1978); Nomads; The Return Of The vampire; Shadows In The Night; Sliver
Fodor, ladislas (wri): Charlie Chan In City In Darkness; In The Steel Net Of Dr. Mabuse; The Invisible Dr. Mabuse; The Nibelungs (1966); The Phantom Of Soho; The Secret Of Dr. Mabuse; Das Testament Des Dr. Mabuse (1962); Tom Thumb; White Lilac
Fogarty, Mary (act): Hello Again
Fogel, Vladimir (act): Luch Smerti
Fogg, David (act): The Force On Thunder Mountain
Fogle, Adeen (act): Little Shop Of Horrors (1986)
Foglietti, Mario (wri): Quatro Mosche Di Velluto Gris
Folbigge, Dennis (act): Howling IV
Foldes, Yolanda (wri, b. 1903): Golden Earrings
Foldi, Erzebet (act, b. 1967): All That Jazz
Foleg, Peter (dir): The Unseen (1981)
Foley, George (act): Abide With Me; The Adventures Of Dick Turpin-The Gunpowder Plot; The Answer; The Grip of Iron; The King's Romance; Lieutenant Daring And The Stolen Invention; The Mystery Of A London Flat; The Price He Paid; Robin Hood Outlawed; Through The Clouds; Trent's Last Case (1920); The Ware Case; When London Sleeps
Foley, James (dir): Fear (1996)
Foley, Joan (act): Ghost Warrior
Foley, Macka (act): Ghost (1990)
Foley, Patty (act): In The Shadow Of Kilimanjaro
Folies-Bergere, Acrobats of the (act): Le Voyage Dans La Lune
Folies-Bergere, Girls from the (act): Long-Distance Wireless Photography
Folk, Alexander (act): Maid To Order
Folk, Robert (mus): Beastmaster 2: Through The Portal Of Time; Lawnmower Man 2: Beyond Cyberspace; The Never Ending Story II: The Next Chapter; Wicked Stepmother
Folker, Sydney (act): The English Rose
Follansbee, Julie (act): The Day Of The Dolphin
Follows, Edwina (act): Strange Invaders
Follows, Megan (act): Silver Bullet
Follows, Ted (act): Virus
Folse, Gabriel (act): D.O.A. (1988)
Folse, Marisa (act): Cat People (1982)
Folsey, George (J.) (cin, 1898-1988): The Balcony; The Enchanted Cottage (1924); Forbidden Planet; A Guy Named Joe; House of Menace; The Man With A Cloak; The Savage
Folsom (act): The Lost Boys
Fonda, Bridget (act, b. 1964): Roger Corman's 'Frankenstein Unbound'; Single White Female; Touch
Fonda, Henry (act, 1905-1982): The Boston Strangler; City On Fire; Fail-Safe; The Fugitive; Meteor; Rollercoaster; The Serpent; Tenticles; The Swarm; The Wrong Man
Fonda, Jane (act, b. 1937): Barbarella; The Blue Bird (1976); The China Syndrome; Les Felins; Spirits Of The Dead
Fonda, Peter (act, b. 1939): Dance Of The Dwarfs; Escape From L.A.; Futureworld; Lilith; Nadja; Race With The Devil; Spasms; Spirits of the Dead; The Trip
Fondacaro, Phil (act): Condor; The Dungeonmaster; Ghoulies II Meridian; Troll
Fondacaro, Sal (act): The Dungeonmaster
Fondato, Marcello (wri): Sei Donne Per L'assassino; I Tre Volti Della Paura

Fong, Benson (act): *Boston Blackie's Chinese Venture; Charlie Chan In The Secret Service; The Chinese Cat; The Chinese Web; Conquest of Space; Dark Alibi; The Love Bug; Our Man Flint; The Red Dragon (1945); The Scarlet Clue; The Shanghai Cobra; The Strongest Man In The World*
Fong, Harold (act): *Not Of This Earth (1957); Storm Over Tibet*
Fong, Jason (act): *Shadow Of Death (1983)*
Fong, Jon (act): *The Million Eyes Of Sumuru*
Fons, Angelino (wri): *Amador*
Fonseca, Fernando (wri): *The Unholy*
Fonseca, Roger (act): *I Was A Zombie For The F.B.I.*
Fonss, Olaf (act): *Homunculus*
Fontages, Francoise (act): *House Of 1,000 Dolls*
Fontaine, Char (act): *The Punisher*
Fontaine, Corinne (act): *L'ultima Preda Del Vampiro*
Fontaine, Eddie (act): *Forgotten City Of The Planet Of The Apes*
Fontaine, Frank (act, 1920-1978): *Scared Stiff (1953)*
Fontaine, Jacqueline (act): *Untamed Mistress*
Fontaine, Jean (act): *The Sinister Urge*
Fontaine, Joan (act, b. 1917, nee Joan de Havilland): *Beyond A Reasonable Doubt; Dark Mansions; Jane Eyre (1944); Kiss The Blood Off My Hands, Rebecca; Suspicion; Voyage To The Bottom Of The Sea; The Witches (1966)*
Fontaine, Lilian (act): *The Locket; The Lost Weekend*
Fontaine, Michael (act): *The Man Who Fell To Earth (1987); Wizards Of The Lost Kingdom*
Fontana, Linda (act): *Arthur The King*
Fontana, Randall (act): *The Lawnmower Man; Virtuosity*
Fontanals, Manuel (cin): *El Vampiro Sangriento*
Fontanarosa, Frederique (act): *La Mariee Etait En Noir*
Fontanarosa, Renaud (act): *La Mariee Etait En Noir*
Fontelieu, Stocker (act): *Angel Heart; Obsession (1976)*
Fonvielle, Lloyd (dir): *Gotham*
Fonvielle, Lloyd (wri): *The Bride (1985); Gotham*
Foo, Lee Tong (act): *The Chinese Ring; The Golden Eye; Mr. Wong, Detective; Mr. Wong In Chinatown; The Mystery Of Mr. Wong; The Phantom Of Chinatown*
Foody, Ralph (act): *Vice Versa (1988)*
Foote, Hallie (act): *The Little Match Girl (1987)*
Foote, Horton (wri): *Of Mice And Men (1992)*
Foote, Jennifer (act): *Oh Heavenly Dog*
Foote, John Tainton (wri): *The Mark Of Zorro (1940)*
Footer, Kathleen (act): *The Toxic Avenger, Part II*
Foraker, Lois (act): *The Exorcist III; Gremlins*
Foran, Dick (act, 1910-1979): *The Atomic Submarine; The Fear Makers; Horror Island; The House Of The Seven Gables; The Mummy's Hand; The Mummy's Tomb; Please Murder Me*
Foran, Mary (act): *The Hypnotic Eye*
Foray, June (act, b. 1919): *Sabaka*
Forbes, Archibald (act): *The Grit Of A Dandy*
Forbes, Bryan (act, b. 1926): *An Inspector Calls; The Key; Quatermass II; Satellite In The Sky; The Slipper And The Rose*
Forbes, Bryan (dir, b. 1926): *Seance On A Wet Afternoon; The Slipper And The Rose; The Stepford Wives; The Wrong Box*
Forbes, Bryan (wri, b. 1926): *The Black Knight; Man In The Moon (1960); Seance On A Wet Afternoon; The Slipper And The Rose*
Forbes, C. Scott (wri): *The Penthouse (1967)*
Forbes, Chris (act): *Sleeper*
Forbes, Elwood (act): *The Relic*
Forbes, Karen (act): *Prom Night*
Forbes, Lou(is) (mus): *The Bat (1959); From The Earth To The Moon; Most Dangerous Man Alive; Pearl Of The South Pacific*
Forbes, Mary (act, 1883-1974): *The Adventures Of Sherlock Holmes (1939); Flesh And Fantasy; The Great Impersonation (1942); Les Miserables (1935); The Picture Of Dorian Gray (1945); Terror By Night; The Thirteenth Chair (1929)*
Forbes, Meriel (act, b. 1913): *Murder On Monday*
Forbes, Ralph (act, 1902-1951): *Calling Philo Vance; The Green Goddess (1929); The Hound Of The Baskervilles (1939); Mr. Wu (1927); The Mystery of Mr. X; The Tower Of London (1939)*
Forbes, Scott (act): *The Mind Of Mr. Soames; Subterfuge*
Forbes, Sonny (act): *City On Fire; Scanners; Wild Thing*
Forbes, Stanton (wri): *A Reflection Of Fear*
Forbes, Violet (act): *Hutch Stirs 'Em Up*
Forbes-Robertson, Eric (act): *The Murdock Trial*
Forbes-Robertson, James (act): *Lifeforce*
Forbes-Robertson, John (act): *Legend Of The Seven Golden Vampires; The Man From Nowhere; The Vampire Lovers; The Vault Of Horror; Venom (1982)*
Forbes-Robertson, Johnston (act, 1853-1937): *Hamlet (1913); The Passing Of The Third Floor Back (1918)*
Forbes-Robertson, Peter (act): *Gawain And The Green Knight; Island Of Terror; Scream And Die!*
Forbstein, Leo F. (mus): *Cry Wolf (1947); The Florentine Dagger; Rope; Satan Met A Lady; The Two Mrs. Carrolls*
Force, John (act): *The Visitors (1989)*
Forchion, Ray(mond) (act): *Flight Of The Navigator; The Night Of The Claw*
Ford, Alan (act): *Venom (1982)*
Ford, Aleksander (dir, b. 1908): *Knights Of The Teutonic Order*
Ford, Anitra (act): *Invasion Of The Bee Girls; Wonder Woman*
Ford, Ann (act): *Logan's Run*
Ford, Brylo (act): *Naked Evil*
Ford, Buck (act): *King Kong Lives*
Ford, Carole Ann (act): *The Day Of The Triffids; The Man Outside (1967)*
Ford, Chris (act): *The Outing*
Ford, Cia (act): *Arthur The King*
Ford, Constance (act): *The Cabinet Of Dr. Caligari; The Last Hunt*
Ford, Corey (wri): *Topper Takes A Trip*
Ford, David (act): *The Offspring*
Ford, Derek (dir): *Secret Rites; The Sexplorer*
Ford, Derek (wri): *Black Torment; Corruption; The Legend Of Spider Forest; Scream And Die!; Secret Rites; The Sexplorer; A Study In Terror*
Ford, Donald (wri): *Black Torment; Corruption; The Legend Of Spider Forest; A Study In Terror*
Ford, Dorothy (GB act): *Threads*
Ford, Dorothy (USA act): *Jack And The Beanstalk (1952)*
Ford, Edwina (act): *Jamaica Inn (1985)*
Ford, Faith (act): *Night Visitors*
Ford, Francis (act, 1883-1953, nee Francis Feeney): *Charlie Chan At The Circus; Charlie Chan's Courage; Charlie Chan's Greatest Case; Charlie Chan's Secret; Hangover Square; The Man Who Wouldn't Die*
Ford, Fred (act): *Too Scared To Scream*
Ford, Fritz (act): *Damien-Omen II*
Ford, George (act): *Dick Barton At Bay; Dick Barton, Special Agent*
Ford, Glenn (act, b. 1917, nee Gwyllin Ford): *The Brotherhood Of The Bell; The Disappearance Of Flight 412; Experiment In Terror; Framed; Gilda; The Green Glove; Happy Birthday To Me; Raw Nerve; The Return Of October; Superman (1978); Virus; The Visitor*
Ford, Grace (act): *Devil Doll (1936)*
Ford, Gwyllin (act): see Ford, Glenn
Ford, Harriet (wri): *In The Next Room*
Ford, Harrison (act, b. 1943): *Blade Runner; The Empire Strikes Back; Indiana Jones And The Last Crusade; Indiana Jones And The Temple Of Doom; The Possessed (1977); Raiders Of The Lost Ark; Return Of The Jedi; Star Wars*
Ford, Jack (act): *Murder Is My Business*
Ford, James (act): *The House Of Horror (1929)*
Ford, John (dir, 1895-1973): *Gideon's Day; The Lost Patrol (1934)*
Ford, Lee (act): *Dick Tracy Returns*
Ford, Maggie (act): *Threads*
Ford, Maria (act): *Alien Terminator; The Haunting Of Morella; The Unnamable II*
Ford, Mary (act): *Missile To The Moon; Queen Of Outer Space*
Ford, Matt (act): *Cocoon: The Return*
Ford, Michael (act): *Rawhead Rex*
Ford, Michael C. (act): *Simon, King Of The Witches*
Ford, Paul (act, 1901-1976): *The Spy With A Cold Nose*
Ford, Peter (act): *Mad Max*
Ford, Philip (dir): *Valley Of The Zombies*
Ford, Rana (act): *Jack's Back*
Ford, Ray (act): *When Dinosaurs Ruled The Earth*
Ford, Ron (act & wri): *The Fear (1994)*
Ford, Ross (act): *Project Moonbase*
Ford, Roy (cin): *Legend Of The Seven Golden Vampires; On Her Majesty's Secret Service*
Ford, Ruth (act): *Secrets Of The Lone Wolf; Too Scared To Scream; Woman Who Came Back*
Ford, Steve (act): *Eraser*
Ford, Steve (dir): *The Dungeonmaster*
Ford, Wallace (act, 1897-1966, nee Sam Grundy): *The Ape Man; Black Angel (1946); Freaks; Harvey; The Lost Patrol (1934); The Man Who Reclaimed His Head; The Mummy's Hand; The Mummy's Tomb; The Mysterious Mr. Wong; Night Of Terror (1933); One Frightened Night; The Set-Up; Shadow Of A Doubt (1943)*
Ford, William (act): *Forever Evil*
Forde, Eugene (dir, b. 1898): *Charlie Chan At Monte Carlo; Charlie Chan In London; Charlie Chan On Broadway; Charlie Chan's Courage; Charlie Chan's Murder Cruise; Crime Doctor's Strangest Case; Dressed To Kill (1941); Michael Shayne, Private Detective; Shadows In The Night; Sleepers West*
Forde, Feodora (act): see Baxter, Jane
Forde, Leila (act): *The Phantom Of The Opera (1962)*
Forde, Walter (dir, b. 1896): *Bulldog Jack; Chu Chin Chow (1934); Condemned To Death; The Gaunt Stranger; The Ghost Train (1931 & 1941); The Last Hour; The Ringer (1931); The Silent House; Time Flies (1944)*
Fordyce, Ian (dir): *One Deadly Owner*
Fore, Mark (act): *Flesh Gordon*
Foree, Ken (act): *Dawn Of The Dead; The Dentist; From Beyond; Knightriders; Leatherface: Texas Chainsaw Massacre III; Northstar; Phantom Of The Mall: Eric's Revenge; Sleepstalker*
Foreman, Amanda (act): *Forever Young*
Foreman, Carl (wri, 1914-1984): *The Key; Spooks Run Wild*
Foreman, Deborah (act): *April Fool's Day; Destroyer; Lobster Man From Mars; Sundown: The Vampire In Retreat; Waxwork*
Forest, Denis (act): *Eraser*
Forest, Emil (wri): *Behind The Curtain (1924)*
Forest, Jean-Claude (wri): *Barbarella*
Forest, Mark (act, b. 1933, nee Lou Degni): *Colossus Of The Arena; Ercole Contro I Figli Del Sole; Hercules Against The Barbarian; Kindar The Invulnerable; The Lion Of Thebes; Maciste, L'eroe Piu Grande Del Mondo; Molemen Against The Son Of Hercules; Sins Of Babylon; Son Of Samson; Terror Of Rome Against The Son Of Hercules; La Vendetta Di Ercole*
Forest, Michael (act): *King Kong Lives*
Forest, Peter (act): *Billion Dollar Brain; Cry Of The Banshee*
Forestal, Sean (wri): *No Blade Of Grass*
Forestier, Louis (cin): *Pikovaya Dama (1910)*
Forgeham, John (act): *Sheena*
Forges, Robert D. (cin): *The Curse*
Forin, Laura (act): *The Kremlin Letter*
Foriscot, Emilio (cin): *Lo Strano Caso Della Signora Ward*
Forman, Carol (act): *The Docks Of New Orleans; The Falcon's Adventure; The Feathered Serpent (1948); Sombra, The Spider Woman*
Forman, David (act): *Teenage Mutant Ninja Turtles*
Forman, Joey (act): *The Atomic Kid; Earthbound (1981)*
Forner, Michael (act): *Phenomenon*
Forney, Jay Speed (act): *Congo*
Forney, Sam (act): *Phantom Of The Paradise*
Foronjy, Richard (act): *Ghostbusters II*
Forrest, Allan (act): *The Invisible Fear*
Forrest, Anthony (act): *Killer's Moon*
Forrest, Christine (act): *The Dark Half; Martin; Monkey Shines*
Forrest, Daniel (wri): *One Of Our Dinosaurs Is Missing*
Forrest, Donald (act): *Outbreak*
Forrest, Frederic (act, b. 1936): *Gotham; Hidden Fears; It Lives Again; Return (1985); Trauma (1993)*
Forrest, Ingeborg (act): *Martin*
Forrest, Irene (act): *Bride Of Re-Animator; Communion; Heartbeeps; Thx 1138; Wolf*
Forrest Jr., J. Clifford (act): *Martin*
Forrest, James (act): *Mr. Sardonicus; Nightmare In Wax*
Forrest, John (act): *Black 13; Great Expectations (1946); The Straw Man*
Forrest, Lottie Pickford (act): *Don Q, Son Of Zorro*
Forrest, Michael (act): *Atlas; Beast From Haunted Cave; Deathwatch; The Viking Women And The Sea Serpent*
Forrest, Ray (act): *Marzipan Of The Shapes*
Forrest, Sally (act, b. 1928, nee Katharine Scully Feeney): *Mystery Street; Son Of Sinbad; The Strange Door; While The City Sleeps*
Forrest, Sombra (act): *Deadly Game*
Forrest, Steve (act, b. 1924, nee William Forrest Andrews): *Amazon Women On The Moon; Captain America (1978); The Living Idol; Phantom Of The Rue Morgue*
Forrest, William (act): *The Bandits Of Corsica; Billy The Kid vs. Dracula; The Lone Wolf Meets A Lady; The Lone Wolf Takes A Chance; Sakima And The Masked Marvel; Trapped By Boston Blackie*
Forrestal, Terry (act): *Brazil*
Forrester, Cay (act): *D.O.A. (1949); Queen Of The Amazons (1947)*
Forrester, David (act): *Tales From The Darkside*
Forrester, Holgie (act): *Impulse (1984)*
Forrester, Larry (wri, b. 1924): *Fathom*
Forry, Angela (act): *A Ghost In Monte Carlo*
Forsche, Bull (act): *Howling IV*
Forslund, Constance (act): *Village Of The Damned (1995)*
Forster, Jaime (act): *Attack Of The Puppet People*
Forster, Peter (act): *Escape From The Planet Of The Apes*
Forster, Robert (act, b. 1941): *Alligator (1981); Avalanche; The Banker; The Black Hole; Committed; The Darker Side Of Terror; Goliath Awaits; In-Between; Peacemaker; Reflections In A Golden Eye*
Forster, Rudolph (act, 1884-1969): *Chronik Von Grieshuus*
Forston, Don (act): *Blink*
Forsyth, Brigit (act): *The Night Digger*
Forsyth, Bruce (act): *Bedknobs And Broomsticks*
Forsyth, Edward (act): *Fatal Journey*
Forsyth, Frank (act): *—And Now The Screaming Starts!; Asylum; Before I Wake; Carry On Screaming; Dr. Terror's House Of Horrors (1964); Evil Of Frankenstein; The Man Without A Body; The Psychopath (1965); The Skull; Tales From The Crypt; Tales That Witness Madness; The Terrornauts; They Came From Beyond Space; The Vault Of Horror*
Forsyth, Myra (act): *The Wicker Man*
Forsyth, Rory (mus): *Dark Water*
Forsyth, Rosemary (act, b. 1944): *The Brotherhood Of The Bell; City Beneath The Sea (1970); Daylight; What Ever Happened To Aunt Alice?*
Forsyth, Stephen (act): *Hatchet For A Honeymoon*
Forsythe, Bill (act): *The Man Who Wasn't There*
Forsythe, Blanche (act): *His Sister's Honour; In The Toils Of The Blackmailer; Jane Shore (1915); The Rogues Of London; She (1916); Trapped By The London Sharks*
Forsythe, Ed (dir): *Superchick*
Forsythe, John (act, b. 1918, nee John Freund): *Cruise Into Terror; The Glass Web; The Mysterious Two; Scrooged; Shadow On The Land; Terror On The 40th Floor; Topaz; The Trouble With Harry*
Forsythe, William (act): *Dick Tracy (1990); A Kiss To Die For; Virtuosity*
Fort, Garrett (wri): *Among The Living; Devil Doll (1936); Dracula (1931, English-Speaking Version); Dracula's Daughter; Frankenstein (1931); Ladies In Retirement; The Lost Patrol (1934); The Man In Half Moon Street; The Mark Of Zorro (1940); The Midnight Girl; Scotland Yard (1930)*
Fort, Mary-Rachel (act): *Virtuosity*
Forte, Fabian (act): see Fabian
Forte, Joe (act): *Cyclotrode X; Homicidal*
Fortescue, Kenneth (act): *The Brides Of Fu Manchu; The Golden Rabbit; How To Murder A Rich Uncle; The Mirror Crack'd*
Fortier, Laurie (act, b. 1975): *To Gillian On Her 37th Birthday*
Fortier, Nicole (act): *The Unholy*
Fortin, Robert (act): *Pharaoh's Curse*
Fortis, Giuseppe/John (act): *The Black Belly Of The Tarantula; War Of The Planets*
Fortunato, Sondra (act): *Mother's Day*
Fortune, John (act): *Blood Bath At The House Of Death*
Fortune, John (wri): *Rentadick*
Fortune, Kim (act): *Moonraker*
Forum Quorum, The (mus): *Mission Mars*
Forward, Bob (wri): *Bravestarr-The Movie; The Secret Of The Sword*
Forward, Robert (act): *Code Name: Minus One*
Forward, William (act): *Chiller; D.O.A. (1988)*
Forwood, Anthony (act): *Knights Of The Round Table; The Man In Black; The Story Of Robin Hood*
Fos, Antonio (F.) (wri): *Ella Y El Miedo; La Orgia Nocturna De Los Vampiros*
Foschi, Massimo (act): *Holocaust 2000*
Foshko, Robert (wri): *Hide And Seek*
Foss, F.A. (wri): *Blood Pen*
Foss, Kenelm (act): *Trapped By The London Sharks; Whosoever Shall Offend*
Foss, Kenelm (dir): *The House Of Peril*

Foss, Kenelm (wri): *Asthore; The House Of Peril; The Man Without A Soul; Trapped By The London Sharks; Whosoever Shall Offend*
Fosse, Bob (act, 1927-1987): *The Little Prince*
Fosse, Bob (dir & wri, 1927-1987): *All That Jazz*
Fosse, Jill (act): *Dead And Buried*
Fossey, Brigitte (act, b. 1947): *Jeux Interdits; Quintet*
Foster, Al (act): *Def Con 4*
Foster, Alan (act): *Man-Eater Of Kumaon*
Foster, Alan Dean (wri): *Star Trek*
Foster, Art (act): *The Verdict*
Foster, Barry (act, b. 1931): *Frenzy; Playback; The Twisted Nerve*
Foster, Bennett (wri): *Mistress Of Paradise*
Foster, Bill (act): *Kingdom Of The Spiders*
Foster, Blake (act): *Turbo: A Power Rangers Movie*
Foster, Bob (wri): *I, Desire*
Foster, Cherie (act): *Vanishing Point*
Foster, Cheryl (act): *The Initiation*
Foster, Clayton (act): *Beyond The Living*
Foster, Dianne (act, b. 1928): *Gideon's Day; The Lost Hours; The Steel Key*
Foster, Dorothy (act): *The Great Anarchist Mystery; Hamlet (1912); The Witch Of The Welsh Mountains*
Foster, Dudley (act): *Moon Zero Two; Never Mention Murder; Quest For Love; A Study In Terror*
Foster, Edward/Eddie (act): *Dick Tracy Returns; Killer Ape; The Mummy's Hand; The Three Stooges Meet Hercules*
Foster, Eve (act): *The Body Vanishes*
Foster, Gloria (act): *The Angel Levine; Top Secret (1978)*
Foster, Harold (wri, 1893-1982): *Prince Valiant*
Foster, Hebden (act): *The Beetle*
Foster, Henry (act): *Eugene Aram*
Foster, J. Byron (act): *The Corpse Grinders*
Foster, Jodie (act, b. 1963): *Contact; The Little Girl Who Lives Down The Lane; The Silence Of The Lambs; Smile, Jenny, You're Dead; Svengali (1983)*
Foster, Kathy (act): *Flesh Gordon*
Foster, Kenneth (act): *The Mutagen*
Foster, Kitty (act): *Moonbeam Magic*
Foster, Lewis R. (dir, 1900-1974): *Jamaica Run; The Sign Of Zorro*
Foster, Lewis R. (wri, 1900-1974): *Jamaica Run*
Foster, Maurice (wri): *Assignment K*
Foster, Meg (act): *Hidden Fears; Immortal Combat; The Legend Of Sleepy Hollow; Leviathan; Masters Of The Universe; Project: Shadowchaser; Space Marines; Stepfather II; They Live; Welcome To Arrow Beach*
Foster, Norman (act, 1903-1976, nee Norman Hoeffer): *Alias The Doctor*
Foster, Norman (dir, 1903-1976): *Charlie Chan At Treasure Island; Charlie Chan In Panama; Charlie Chan In Reno; The Green Hornet; Journey Into Fear (1942); Mr. Moto's Last Warning; Mr. Moto Takes A Vacation; The Mysterious Mr. Moto; Scotland Yard (1941); The Sign Of Zorro; Thank You, Mr. Moto; Think Fast, Mr. Moto*
Foster, Norman (wri, 1903-1976): *Mr. Moto's Last Warning; Mr. Moto Takes A Chance; Mr. Moto Takes A Vacation; The Mysterious Mr. Moto; The Sign Of Zorro; Thank You, Mr. Moto; Think Fast, Mr. Moto*
Foster, Pam (act): *Macbeth (1971)*
Foster, Phil (act, 1914-1985): *Conquest Of Space*
Foster, Preston (act, 1901-1970): *Bermuda Mystery; Doctor X; The Hunted (1948); I, The Jury (1953); Lady In The Morgue; The Last Days Of Pompeii (1935); The Last Warning (1938); Secret Agent Of Japan; The Time Travelers (1964); The Westland Case*
Foster, Robert (wri): *Final Eye*
Foster, Ronald (act): *Cage Of Evil; Diary Of A High School Bride; House Of The Damned (1962)*
Foster, Ruth (act): *Dimension 5*
Foster, Sadie (act): *Bram Stoker's Dracula*
Foster, Stacie (act): *Cyber-Tracker; Cybertracker 2; Steel Frontier*
Foster, Stan (act): *Project X (1987)*
Foster, Steffen Gregory (act): *The Lawnmower Man*
Foster, Susan (act): *The Boy Who Cried Werewolf; Haunts Of The Very Rich*
Foster, Susanna (act, b. 1924, nee Suzan Larsen): *The Climax; Phantom Of The Opera (1943)*
Foster, Tiffany (act): *Hideaway*
Foster, Walter (act): *Phantom Of The Paradise*
Foster, Wayne (act): *Forgotten City Of The Planet Of The Apes*
Foster, William (wri): *Blind Man's Bluff (1936)*
Foster, Zenna (act): *The Corpse Grinders*
Foster-Davis, William (act): *Dr. No*
Fothergill, Mia (act): *Stanley's Dragon*
Foti, Marie (act): *Waxwork II: Lost In Time*
Fotre, Vincent (wri): *Missile To The Moon; Gli Orrori Del Castello Di Norembega*
Fouad, Nagwa (act): *A Story Of Tutankhamun*
Fouchaud, Pierre (wri): *Fantomas Contro Scotland Yard; Oss 117-Mission For A Killer; Shadow Of Evil (1964)*
Foulger, Byron (act, b. 1902): *Champagne For Caesar; The Chinese Ring; The Devil's Partner; Dick Tracy (1937); Dick Tracy vs. Cueball; Ellery Queen, Master Detective; The Falcon Strikes Back; The Gnome-Mobile; The Hidden Eye; Lightning Strikes Twice; The Love War; The Magnetic Monster; Man-Made Monster; The Man They Could Not Hang; The Man With Nine Lives; Meet Boston Blackie; Peril From The Planet Mongo; The Prisoner Of Zenda (1937); Purple Death From Outer Space; The Return Of October; Run For The Hills; Sky Murder; Too Many Winners; Up In Smoke*
Foulk, Robert (act): *Hold That Hypnotist; Indestructible Man; Valley Of The Headhunters*
Foulkrod, Anne Horne (act): *Primal Scream*
Foulsham, Fraser (dir): *The Strange Case Of Mr. Todmorden*
Fountain, Carl (act): *Wizards Of The Lost Kingdom*
Fountaine, William E. (act): *The Dungeon*
Fournery, Mary (act): *Amazons (1986)*
Fournier, Ed (act): *Spawn Of The Slithis*
Fournier, Marcel (act): *Rabid*
Fournier, Pedro (act): *Hundra*
Fournier, Silvia (act): *El Mundo De Los Vampiros*
Fouser, Scott (act): *The Man Who Fell To Earth (1987)*
Fowell, Frank (wri): *The Man Without Desire; Whoso Diggeth A Pit*
Fowlds, Derek (act): *Frankenstein Created Woman; Tower Of Evil*
Fowler, Frank (act): *Monstrosity*
Fowler Jr., Gene (dir): *I Married A Monster From Outer Space; I Was A Teenage Werewolf*
Fowler, Harry (act, b. 1926): *Clash By Night; The Diplomatic Corpse; Fire Maidens Of Outer Space; For Them That Trespass; The Nanny; A Piece Of Cake; Scarlet Thread; She Shall Have Murder*
Fowler, Harry (cin): *Crooked Alley*
Fowler, Jake (wri): *Horror High*
Fowler, Joan (act): *Phobia*
Fowles, John (wri, b. 1926): *The Collector; The Magus*
Fowley, Douglas (act): *Behind Locked Doors; The Chance Of A Lifetime; Charlie Chan At Treasure Island; Charlie Chan On Broadway; The Docks Of New Orleans; Ellery Queen, Master Detective; Larceny In Her Heart; Mighty Joe Young; Mr. Moto's Gamble; The Naked Jungle; One Body Too Many; Scared To Death (1947); Search For Danger; Tarzan's Peril; The Thin Man; Three On A Ticket*
Fowley, Douglas (dir, b. 1911): *Macumba Love*
Fox, Alan (act): *The Pink Chiquitas*
Fox, Allen (act): *Charlie Chan On Broadway; Dr. Cyclops*
Fox, Bernard (act): *Arnold; The Hound Of The Baskervilles (1972); The House Of The Dead; Munster, Go Home!; Soho Incident*
Fox, Carla M. (act): *Slugs*
Fox, Cary (act): *Hell Night*
Fox, Charles/Charlie (act): *The Corpse Grinders; The New, Original Wonder Woman; Oh, God! Book II; Repossessed; Short Circuit 2; Ssssss; Tarzan In Manhattan; Zapped!*
Fox, Colin (R.) (act): *Daylight; The Food Of The Gods, Part II; Hello Again; Virus*
Fox, Dorothy (act): *The Wiz*
Fox, Earle (act): *The Ghost Talks; The Mind Reader*
Fox, Edward (act, b. 1937): *The Big Sleep (1978); The Cat And The Canary (1978); Journey To Midnight; The Mind Benders (1963); The Mirror Crack'd; Never Say Never Again; Robin Hood (1991); Skullduggery*
Fox, Ferris (wri): *Blackie's Redemption*
Fox, Fred S. (wri): *Oh, God! Book II*
Fox, George (wri): *Earthquake*
Fox, Huckleberry (act): *Time Flyer*
Fox, James (act, b. 1939): *Afraid Of The Dark; Greystoke: The Legend Of Tarzan, Lord Of The Apes; The Servant*
Fox, Jerry (act): *The Alien Within; Hollywood Chainsaw Hookers*
Fox, Jim (mus): *Sorority Girls And The Creature From Hell*
Fox, John (J.) (act): *Someone's Watching Me!; Something Evil*
Fox, Kelli (act): *Timecop*
Fox, Kerry (act): *Night Of The Red Hunter*
Fox, Lee (act): *A Clockwork Orange*
Fox, Lucy (act): *The Lone Wolf (1924)*
Fox, Marcia (act): *Creatures The World Forgot*
Fox, Michael (act, 1921-1996): *The Beast From 20,000 Fathoms; Class Of '84; Conquest Of Space; Crackle Of Death; The Dunwich Horror; Gog; The Magnetic Monster; Riders To The Stars; Voodoo Tiger; War Of The Satellites; What Ever Happened To Baby Jane? (1962); Young Frankenstein*
Fox, Michael J. (act, b. 1961): *Back To The Future; Back To The Future, Part II; Back To The Future, Part III; The Frighteners; Mars Attacks!; Teen Wolf*
Fox, Mickey (act): *Blood Beach*
Fox, Nancy (act): *Warlock*
Fox, Neal (mus): *Return Of The Killer Tomatoes*
Fox, Norman (wri): *The Intruder (1981)*
Fox, Peter (act): *The Munsters' Revenge; Night Of The Comet; Vampire On Bikini Beach*
Fox, Reginald (act): *Robinson Crusoe (1927); Shadow Of Evil (1921)*
Fox, Rex (act): *Edward Scissorhands*
Fox, Rica (act): *Return From The Ashes; Svengali (1954)*
Fox, Robbie (act): *The Mutagen*
Fox, Roberta (act): *Slipstream*
Fox, Sidney (act): *The Murders In The Rue Morgue (1932)*
Fox, Sonny (act): *The Christmas That Almost Wasn't*
Fox, Sydney (mus): *The Diabolical Invention*
Fox, Teresa (act): *Fire In The Sky (1993)*
Fox, Terry Curtis (wri): *Fortress*
Fox, Vivica A. (act): *Batman And Robin; Independence Day*
Fox, Wallace (dir): *Bowery At Midnight; The Corpse Vanishes; Pillow Of Death; The White Goddess*
Fox, William (act): *The Final Conflict; Mata Hari (1985)*
Fox-Brenton, David (act): *Bridge Across Time*
Foxwell, Ivan (wri): *Guilt Is My Shadow*
Foxworth, Robert (act, b. 1941): *Damien—Omen II; Deathmoon; The Devil's Daughter (1972); It Happened At Lake Wood Manor; The Memory Of Eva Ryker; Prophecy (1979); The Questor Tapes*
Foxx, Elizabeth (act): *School Spirit*
Foxx, Redd (act, 1922-1991): *Ghost Of A Chance (1987)*
Foy, Bryan (dir): *The Gorilla (1931)*
Foy, Charles (act): *The Adventurous Blonde*
Foy Jr., Eddie (act): *Murder In The Air (1940)*
Foy, Mary (act): *The Headless Horseman*
Fradet, Bernard (act): *Les Parapluies De Cherbourg*
Fradet, Roger (act): *Judex*
Fradetal, Marcel (cin, b. 1908): *Judex; Thomas L'imposteur*
Fraenkel, Heinrich/H. (wri): *Juggernaut; Menace (1934)*
Fragosa, Oscar (act): *Grim Prairie Tales*
Frahse, Mary Jane (act): see Frazee, Jane
Fraile, Alfredo (cin): *Faustina*
Fraim, Tracy (act): *Fear (1996); Running Against Time*
Frain, James (act): *Loch Ness*
Fraker, William (A.) (dir): *The Legend Of The Lone Ranger; A Reflection Of Fear*
Fraker, William A. (cin): *Chances Are; The Day Of The Dolphin; Exorcist II: The Heretic; Games; Heaven Can Wait (1978); The Island Of Dr. Moreau (1996); Memoirs Of An Invisible Man; The President's Analyst; Rosemary's Baby; Spacecamp*
Frakes, Jonathan (act): *Star Trek: First Contact; Star Trek: Generations*
Frakes, Jonathan (dir): *Star Trek: First Contact*
Frakes, Randall (wri): *Hell Comes To Frogtown*
Frame, Dawn (act): *A Taste Of Evil*
Frame, Grazina (act): *The Alphabet Murders*
Frame, Philip (act): *The Return Of Count Yorga*
Framer, Otto (act): *Der Steinerne Reiter*
Frampton, Peter (act): *Son Of Dracula (1974)*
France, C.V. (act, 1868-1949): *The Blue Bird (1910); Gestapo; Halfway House; Scrooge (1935)*
France, Ketty (act): *Judex*
France, Michael (wri): *Goldeneye*
France, Richard (act): *Code Name Trixie; Graveyard Shift (1990)*
France, Ronald (act): *House Of The Living Dead; Nukie*
Francen, Victor (act, b. 1888): *Adventures Of Captain Fabian; The Beast With Five Fingers; The Beginning Or The End?; Confidential Agent; The Conspirators; Devotion; J'accuse (1937); The Mask Of Dimitrios*
Frances, Vera (act): *King Arthur Was A Gentleman*
Francey, Micheline (act): *Le Corbeau*
Franchetti, Rina (act): *Atom Age Vampire*
Franchi, Franco (act): *Dr. Goldfoot And The Girl Bombs; Two Mafia Guys vs. Goldginger*
Franci, Carlo (mus): *Maciste E La Regina Di Samar; Perseus The Invincible; Terror Of Rome Against The Son Of Hercules*
Francine, Anne (act): *Savages*
Franciosa, Anthony/Tony (act, b. 1928, nee Anthony Papaleo): *Curse Of The Black Widow; Earth Ii; Fathom; Ghost Writer; Julie Darling; Matt Helm; Tenebrae; Web Of The Spider*
Francis, Al (cin): *Goliath Awaits; The Two Worlds Of Jennie Logan*
Francis, Alec B. (act): *The Bishop Murder Case; Mata Hari (1932); Murder Will Out (1930); The Mystery Of Mr. X; Outward Bound; The Return Of Peter Grimm (1926); The Terror (1928)*
Francis, Ann (act): *Agatha*
Francis, Anne (act, b. 1932): *Brainstorm (1965); Forbidden Planet; Haunts Of The Very Rich; Love Can Be Murder; Portrait Of Jennie; Rocket Man; Rona Jaffe's Mazes And Monsters; The Satan Bug*
Francis, Anne Lloyd (act): *Return (1985)*
Francis, Arlene (act, b. 1908, nee Arlene Kazanjian): *The Murders In The Rue Morgue (1932)*
Francis, Barbara (act): *The Beast Of Yucca Flats*
Francis, Carol (act): *Crawlspace*
Francis, Carol Ann (act): *Wild Thing*
Francis, Charles (act): *The Pearl Of Death*
Francis, Clive (act): *A Clockwork Orange*
Francis, Coleman (dir & wri): *The Beast Of Yucca Flats*
Francis, Derek (act): *Captain Clegg; A Christmas Carol (1984); Electric Eskimo; Jabberwocky; Murder Motel; Rasputin, The Mad Monk; Scrooge (1970); The Tomb Of Ligeia; To The Devil A Daughter*
Francis, Dick (act): *Tangled Evidence*
Francis, Eric (act): *The Private Life Of Sherlock Holmes; Theater Of Blood*
Francis, Freddie (cin, b. 1918): *Beat The Devil; Brenda Starr (1992); Cape Fear (1991); Dune; The Innocents; Night Must Fall (1964)*
Francis, Freddie (dir, b. 1918): *Craze; The Creeping Flesh; The Deadly Bees; The Doctor And The Devils; Dr. Terror's House Of Horrors (1964); Dracula Has Risen From The Grave; Evil Of Frankenstein; The Ghoul (1974); Girly; Hysteria!; Legend Of The Werewolf; Nightmare (1963); Paranoiac; The Psychopath (1965); The Skull; Son Of Dracula (1974); Tales From The Crypt; Tales That Witness Madness; They Came From Beyond Space; Torture Garden; Trog; The Vampire Happening; Vengeance*
Francis, Ivor (act, 1918-1986): *The Eyes Of Charles Sand; The House Of The Dead; The Night Strangler; The Return Of The World's Greatest Detective*
Francis, Jan (act): *Dracula (1979); File It Under Fear*
Francis, Jeremy Lee (wri): *Licensed To Love And Kill*
Francis, John (act): *Robin Hood: Prince Of Thieves; Strange Days*
Francis, Kay (act, 1899-1968, nee Katherine Gibbs): *British Agent*
Francis, Larry (act): *Murder By Television*
Francis, Missy (act): *Bad Dreams; Midnight Lace (1981)*
Francis, Nina (act): *Deadly Strangers*
Francis, Olin (act): *The Clutching Hand; Kismet (1930)*
Francis, Rodney (act): *Howling III*
Francis, Ryan (act): *The Stepford Children*
Francis, Sandra (act): *Spy In The Sky*
Francis, Sylvia (act): *Night Train For Inverness*
Francis, Tom (act): *The Hand That Rocks The Cradle*
Francis, Vera (act): *Devil Goddess*
Francisci, Pietro (dir): *Ercole E La Regina Di Lidia; Hercules (1957); Hercules, Samson And Ulysses; Siege Of Syracuse*
Francisci, Pietro (wri): *Ercole E La Regina Di Lidia; Hercules, Samson And Ulysses*
Francisco, Betty (act): *Charlie Chan Carries On; Seven Keys To Baldpate (1925)*
Francisco, Manuel (mus): *The Devil's Hand (1961)*
Franciscus, James (act, 1934-1991): *Beneath The Planet Of The Apes; The Cat O' Nine Tails; City On Fire; Great White; Killer Fish;*

Marooned; Night Slaves; Secret Weapons; The Valley Of Gwangi; When Time Ran Out

Franck, A.M. (dir): Revenge In The House Of Usher

Franckhauser, Tom (act): The Alien's Return

Francks, Cree Summer (act): Bay Coven; Wild Thing

Francks, Don (act): Heavy Metal; My Bloody Valentine

Francks, Lili (act): Short Circuit 2

Franc-Nohain, Claude (act): see Dauphin, Claude

Franco, Doro (act): Luminous Procuress

Franco, Enrique (mus): Tenemos 18 Anos

Franco, Jesus/Jess (dir): The Awful Dr. Orlof; Barbed Wire Dolls; The Blood Of Fu Manchu; Cartes Sur Table; The Castle Of Fu Manchu; Count Dracula; The Diabolical Dr. Z; Eugenie...The Story Of Her Journey Into Perversion; Jack The Ripper (1979); Marquis De Sade; Justine; Necronomicon; Night Of The Blood Monster; Paroxysmus; Rio 70; El Secreto Del Doctor Orlof; Tenemos 18 Anos

Franco, Jesus (mus): Tenemos 18 Anos

Franco, Jesus/Jess (wri): The Awful Dr. Orlof; The Diabolical Dr. Z; Jack The Ripper (1979); Night Of The Blood Monster; Paroxysmus; El Secreto Del Doctor Orlof

Franco, Louie (act): Vampire On Bikini Beach

Francois, Jacques (act): The Golden Mask

Francois, Nicole (act): La Prima Donna

Francoise, Nina (act): Outland

Frandsen, Jano (act): I Still Dream Of Jeannie; Xtro Ii: The Second Encounter

Franju, Georges (dir, 1912-1987): Judex; Les Nuits Rouges; Thomas L'imposteur; Les Yeux Sans Visage

Franju, Georges (wri, 1912-1987): Thomas L'imposteur

Frank the Fish (act): Vampire At Midnight

Frank, Ben (act): Assassin (1986); Don't Answer The Phone!; Terrified

Frank, Brian (act): Hell Comes To Frogtown

Frank, Bruno (wri): The Hunchback Of Notre Dame (1939)

Frank, Carol (dir & wri): Sorority House Massacre

Frank, Charles (act): Covenant; Tarantulas: The Deadly Cargo

Frank, Charles (dir): Intimate Relations; Johnny The Giant Killer; Uncle Silas

Frank, Charles (wri): Intimate Relations; Johnny The Giant Killer; The Late Edwina Black

Frank, David (act): Dead Men Tell No Tales; Westworld

Frank, David (Michael) (mus): Dead Of Night (1987); The Lottery; Suburban Commando; Volcano: Fire On The Mountain

Frank, Frederick M. (wri): Samson And Delilah

Frank, Gary (act): Midnight Lace (1981)

Frank, Gerold (wri): The Boston Strangler

Frank, Horst (act): The Cat O' Nine Tails; The Dead Are Alive; I Deal In Danger; Johnny Hamlet; The Naked Woman And Satan; Red Dragon (1965); Secret Agent 077-Operation Hong Kong; The Spy Is A Girl; The Vengeance Of Fu Manchu; The White Spider

Frank, Janice (act): Making Mr. Right

Frank, Jason David (act): Mighty Morphin Power Rangers; Turbo: A Power Rangers Movie

Frank, Jerome (act): Voodoo Island

Frank, Jerry (act): The Lost City

Frank, Joanne (act): Philo Vance's Gamble

Frank, Joshua (act): Angel Heart

Frank, Kevin (act): Clarence

Frank, Laurie (wri): Making Mr. Right

Frank, Marilyn Dodds (act): Blink; Flatliners

Frank, Mary (act): Voyage To A Prehistoric Planet

Frank, Melvin (dir, 1913-1988): L'il Abner (1959)

Frank, Melvin (wri, 1913-1988): L'il Abner (1959); The Return Of October; The Road To Hong Kong; The Road To Utopia

Frank, Modi (act): Dark Night Of The Scarecrow

Frank, Nick (wri): El Secreto Del Doctor Orlof

Frank, Robert (cin, b. 1924): Chappaqua

Frank, Scott (wri): Dead Again

Frank, Tony (act): Alfred Hitchcock Presents

Frankau, Nicholas (act): The Secret Life Of Ian Fleming

Frankau, Ronald (act, 1894-1951): Dual Alibi; The Ghosts Of Berkeley Square

Franke, Anthony (act): The Blob (1958)

Franke, Christopher (mus): A Face To Die For; Solo; Universal Soldier

Frankel, Art (act): Critters

Frankel, Benjamin (mus, b. 1906): The Curse Of The Werewolf; Footsteps In The Fog; A Kid For Two Farthings; The Man In The White Suit; Mr. Denning Drives North; The Net; Paris Express

Frankel, Cyril (dir, b. 1921): The Sain And The Brave Goose; Tennis Court; The Trygon Factor; The Very Edge; The Witches (1966)

Frankel, Jack (act): The Tomb

Franken, Steve (act): The Fiendish Plot Of Dr. Fu Manchu; Houston, We've Got A Problem; It Happened At Lake Wood Manor; The Stranger; Terror Out Of The Sky; The Time Travelers (1964); Westworld

Frankenberg, Jane (act): see Seymour, Jane

Frankenfield, Cindy (act): Offerings

Frankenheimer, John (dir, b. 1930): Black Sunday (1977); The Extraordinary Seaman; The Island Of Dr. Moreau (1996); The Manchurian Candidate; 99 And 44/100% Dead; Prophecy (1979); Seconds; Seven Days In May

Frankeur, Paul (act): The Discreet Charm Of The Bourgeoisie; Nick Carter Va Tout Casser

Frankham, David (act): Master Of The World; Return Of The Fly; Tales Of Terror

Frankiel, Eric (act): Au Coeur De La Vie

Frankiel, Francois (act): Au Coeur De La Vie

Frankish, Brian (act): Haunts

Frankland, Peter (act): Puppet Master

Frankle, Chuck (act): The Nest Of The Cuckoo Birds

Franklin, Albert (act): Devil's Island

Franklin, Carl (act): Too Good To Be True

Franklin, Chester (M.) (dir): Behind The Curtain (1924); The Thirteenth Hour (1927)

Franklin, Christopher (act): Blood Beach

Franklin, Daniel (act): The Fear (1994)

Franklin, Daniel Jay (wri): Dream A Little Dream

Franklin, David (act): Chilling

Franklin, Diane (act): Amityville II: The Possession; Deadly Lessons; Summer Girl; Terrorvision

Franklin, Gretchen (act): Before I Wake; The Hidden Face; Monster Of Terror; The Quatermass Conclusion; Subterfuge; The Twisted Nerve

Franklin, Herb (act): Trick Or Treats

Franklin, Howard (wri): The Name Of The Rose

Franklin, Hugh (act): The Curse Of The Living Corpse

Franklin, John (act): The Addams Family; Addams Family Values; Children Of The Corn

Franklin, Joseph (act): The Hand That Rocks The Cradle

Franklin, Louise (Austral Act): Strange Behavior

Franklin, Louise (USA act): Jungle Man-Eaters; The Sky Dragon

Franklin, Martha (act): Don Q, Son Of Zorro

Franklin, Pamela (act, b. 1949): And Soon The Darkness; The Food Of The Gods; The Innocents; The Legend Of Hell House; The Nanny; Necromancy; Our Mother's House; Satan's School For Girls; Screamer; Terror From Within; The Third Secret

Franklin, Richard (dir, b. 1947): Cloak And Dagger (1984); Link; Patrick; Psycho Ii; Road Games

Franklin, Shane (act): The Man From Nowhere

Franklin, Steve (act): Empire Of Ash III

Franklyn, Fredric (act): The Hearse

Franklyn, John (act): And Soon The Darkness

Franklyn, William (act): Cul-De-Sac; Fury At Smugglers' Bay; Quatermass II; The Satanic Rites Of Dracula; The Snorkel; Time Is My Enemy

Franklyn-Robbins, John (act): Asylum; Dr. Jekyll And Ms. Hyde; Memoirs Of A Survivor

Frankoff, Kevin (act): The Pink Chiquitas

Franks, Chloe (act): The House That Dripped Blood; Tales From The Crypt; Trog; The Uncanny; Who Slew Auntie Roo?

Franks, Judy (act): Haunts

Franks, Laurie (act): Bram Stoker's Dracula

Frann, Mary (act, b. 1943): I'm Dangerous Tonight

Franquelli, Fely (act): The Leopard Man

Franz, Arthur (act, b. 1920): Abbott And Costello Meet The Invisible Man; The Atomic Submarine; Back From The Dead; Beyond A Reasonable Doubt; The Flame Barrier; Flight To Mars; The Human Factor; Invaders From Mars (1953); Monster On The Campus; Sisters Of Death; The Sniper

Franz, Dennis (act): Blow Out; Body Double; Deadly Messages; Dressed To Kill (1980); Psycho II

Franz, Eduard (act, b. 1902): Beauty And The Beast (1962); The Brotherhood Of The Bell; Cyborg 2087; The Four Skulls Of Jonathan Drake; Francis; The Miracle (1959); The President's Analyst; Shadow In The Sky; The Thing From Another World; Twilight Zone

Franz, Elizabeth (act): Thinner

Franz, Joseph J. (dir): The Cave Girl (1921)

Franzen, Charles (act): Mutant

Fraschetti, Silvio/S. (cin): The Strangers; War Of The Planets

Fraschetti, Yvonne (act): Demons 2

Frase, Harry (dir): Jungle Man

Fraser, Alec (act): The Lure

Fraser, Angus (wri): Kissed

Fraser, Bill (act, b. 1908): Alias John Preston; Captain Nemo And The Underwater City; Lady In The Fog; Masquerade; Moments

Fraser, Brendan (act, b. 1968): Child Of Darkness, Child Of Light; Encino Man; George Of The Jungle

Fraser, Brent (act): Plymouth

Fraser, Constance (act): A Lady Mislaid

Fraser, Dennis (act): An American Werewolf In London

Fraser, Duncan (act): The Death Of The Incredible Hulk; The Reflecting Skin; Timecop; Unforgettable; Watchers

Fraser, Elisabeth (act): Seconds

Fraser, Elizabeth (act): The Hidden Hand

Fraser, Fiona (act): King Solomon's Treasure

Fraser, George MacDonald (wri): Octopussy; Red Sonja; Royal Flash; The Three Musketeers (1974)

Fraser, Harry L. (dir): Chained For Life; The White Gorilla

Fraser, Helen (act): Repulsion

Fraser, Ian (mus): Babes In Toyland (1986); Scrooge (1970); Zorro, The Gay Blade

Fraser, John (act, b. 1931): Fury At Smugglers' Bay; Operation Crossbow; Repulsion; Schizo (1977); A Study In Terror

Fraser, Liz (act): Fury At Smugglers' Bay

Fraser, Peter (act): The Sorcerers

Fraser, Peter (wri): Model For Murder

Fraser, Richard (act, b. 1913): Bedlam; Blonde For A Day; The Fatal Witness; The Lone Wolf In London; The Picture Of Dorian Gray (1945); Shadow Of Terror; White Pongo

Fraser, Robert (Austral act): The Punisher

Fraser, Robert (USA act): Robin Hood (1912); The Vampire Bat

Fraser, Ronald (act, b. 1930): The Bed-Sitting Room; Fathom; In Search Of The Castaways; The Model Murder Case; Rentadick; Victim Five

Fraser, Rupert (act): The Girl In A Swing

Fraser, Sally (act): Giant From The Unknown; It Conquered The World; It's A Dog's Life; North By Northwest; The Spider (1958); War Of The Colossal Beast

Fraser, Shelagh (act): The Body Stealers; Death In The Hand; Doomwatch; Nothing But The Night; Persecution; Son Of Robin Hood; Star Wars

Fraser, Stanley (act): The Maze; World Without End

Fraser, Tom (cin): Chopper Chicks In Zombietown; The Unnamable

Fraser, Tony (act): The Scarlet Letter (1922)

Frassinetti, Augusto (wri): La Battaglia Di Maratona; The Thief Of Bagdad (1960)

Frates, Mervin W. (act): Play Misty For Me

Frates, Robin (act): Plymouth; Puppet Master

Fratini, Gaio (wri): The Tartars

Fratis, William (act): Glen And Randa

Fratkin, Stewart/Stuart (act): I'm Dangerous Tonight; I Was A Teenage Sex Mutant; Teen Wolf Too

Frattali, Dick (act): Neon Maniacs

Frau, Maria (act): Vous Pegez?

Frawley, John (act): The Last Wave

Frawley, Tim (act): The Cremators; Play Misty For Me

Frawley, William (act, 1887-1966): Abbott And Costello Meet The Invisible Man; Crime Doctor's Manhunt; The Lone Wolf And His Lady; Miracle On 34th Street (1947)

Frazee, Jane (act, 1918-1985, nee Mary Jane Frahse): Hellzapoppin; Homicide For Three; Incident

Frazee, Terry D. (cin): Star Trek: Generations

Frazee, Tim (act): Outbreak

Frazer, Alex (act): The War Of The Worlds

Frazer, Evelyn (wri): Frozen Alive

Frazer, Harold (act): see Pollard, Snub

Frazer, Robert (act): Black Dragons; The Clutching Hand; Dick Tracy Vs. Crime, Inc.; White Zombie

Frazer, Wally (act): Slugs

Frazer-Simpson, Cicely (wri): The Fatal Hour (1937)

Frazier, Alan (act): I Was A Zombie For The F.B.I.

Frazier, John (cin): Cry For The Strangers; The Hills Have Eyes; It Came Upon The Midnight Clear; Outbreak; A Vacation In Hell

Frazier, Randy (act): The Brother From Another Planet

Frazier, Richard (act): Glen And Randa

Frazier, Ron (act): D.A.R.Y.L.

Frears, Stephen (dir): Mary Reilly

Frechette, Peter (act): The Hills Have Eyes II; The Kindred; The Unholy

Freda, Riccardo (dir, b. 1909, a.k.a. Robert Hampton): Caltiki, Il Mostro Immortale; Il Conte Ugolino; Giants Of Thessaly; Gold For The Caesars; Maciste Al Inferno; Maciste Alla Corte Del Gran Khan; Raptus; The Seventh Sword; Lo Spettro; Teodora, Imperatrice Di Bisanzio; I Vampiri

Freda, Riccardo (wri, b. 1909): Il Conte Ugolino; Lo Spettro; Teodora, Imperatrice Di Bisanzio

Freddie, Lottie (act): The Night Visitor

Frederic, Nina (act): 2069: A Sex Odyssey

Frederici, Blanche (act): The Cat Creeps (1930); Kismet (1930); Love Me Tonight; Mata Hari (1932); Murder By The Clock

Frederick, Christopher (act): Raiders Of The Lost Ark

Frederick, Geoffrey (act): Lifeforce; Man At The Carlton Tower; Nothing But The Night

Frederick, Hal (act): Daughter Of The Mind

Frederick, Lynne (act, 1954-1994): The Amazing Mr. Blunden; No Blade Of Grass; Phase Iv; The Prisoner Of Zenda (1979); Schizo (1977); Vampire Circus

Frederick, Pauline (act, 1883-1938): The Phantom Of Crestwood; Thank You, Mr. Moto

Frederick, Robert (act): Pranks

Frederick, Vicki (act): Chopper Chicks In Zombietown

Fredericks, Carl (act): Madman

Fredericks, Charles (act, 1919-1970): The Cabinet Of Caligari; Tarzan's Hidden Jungle

Fredericks, David (act): Fear (1996)

Fredericks, Dean (act): The Phantom Planet

Fredericks, James (act): Beverly Hills Bodysnatchers

Fredericks, Peter (act): They Might Be Giants

Fredericks, Scott (act): Blind Terror; The Deadly Females

Frederickson, Lynne (act): The Green Slime

Fredric, Norman (act): The Disembodied; The Lone Ranger And The Lost City Of Gold

Fredrick, Miranda (act): Phoenix The Warrior

Fredricksen, Cully (act): Bram Stoker's 'Dracula'; Wes Craven's New Nightmare

Fredrickson, Robert (act): Pumpkinhead

Fredsti, Dana (act): Princess Warrior

Free, Bill (act): Nightmare Alley

Freeborn, Denise (act): The Search For Bridey Murphy

Freed, Arnold (mus): Werewolf Of Washington

Freed, Arthur (cin): Murder By Television

Freed, Bert (act, 1919-1994): The Atomic City; Barracuda; The Gazebo; Shock Treatment (1964); What Ever Happened To Baby Jane? (1962); Why Must I Die?; Wild In The Streets

Freed, Bill (act): Madman Of Mandoras

Freed, Bill (wri): Watchers

Freed, Don (act): On The Threshold Of Space

Freed, Herb (dir & wri): Beyond Evil; Graduation Day; Haunts

Freed, Sam (act): Thinner

Freeding, Sandra (act): Making Contact

Freedman, Ben (act): The Octagon

Freedman, Benedict (wri): The Atomic Kid; Everything's Ducky; Sabu And The Magic Ring

Freedman, Harry (mus): Isabel

Freedman, Jerrold (dir): A Cold Night's Death

Freedman, Robert L. (wri): Unlikely Angel

Freedman, Winifred (act): C.H.U.D. II

Freeman, A.J. (act): Timestalkers

Freeman Jr., Al (act, b. 1934): Castle Keep

Freeman, Alan (act): Dr. Terror's House Of Horrors (1964)

Freeman, Alfonso (act): Seven

Freeman, Anthony (act): The Eyes Behind The Stars

Freeman, Bill (act): Basket Case

Freeman, Charles (wri): Urge To Kill

Freeman, Christine (act): Jaws 2

Freeman, Damita Jo (act): Bad Dreams; Elvira, Mistress Of The Dark

Freeman, Dave (wri): Those Fantastic Flying Fools

Freeman, Devery (wri, b. 1913): Francis In The Navy; Francis Joins The Wacs

Freeman, Eric (act): Silent Night, Deadly Night, Part II

Freeman, Ernie (mus): The Double Man

Freeman, Everett (wri): The Maltese Bippy

Freeman, Helen (act): Bulldog Drummond Comes Back

Freeman, Howard (act, 1899-1967): House Of Horrors (1946); Once Upon A Time (1944); The Snake Pit (1948)

Freeman, J.E. (act): Copycat

Freeman, Jane (act): *Dark Water*
Freeman, Joan (act): *Deathmoon; Panic In Year Zero; The Reluctant Astronaut; Tower Of London (1962)*
Freeman, K. Todd (act): *Eraser*
Freeman, Kathleen (act, b. 1919): *Behind Locked Doors; Bonzo Goes To College; The Fly (1958); The Glass Web; Gremlins 2: The New Batch; Heartbeeps; The Helicopter Spies; Innerspace; The Magnetic Monster; Myra Breckinridge; The Norsemen; The Nutty Professor (1963); The Prisoner Of Zenda (1952)*
Freeman, Margaret (act): *King Kong Lives*
Freeman, Mike (act): *Condor*
Freeman, Mona (act, b. 1926): *Before I Wake*
Freeman, Morgan (act): *Chain Reaction (1996); Deep Impact; Outbreak; Robin Hood: Prince Of Thieves; Seven*
Freeman, Norton (act): *Wizards Of The Lost Kingdom*
Freeman, Paul (act): *Mighty Morphin Power Rangers; Raiders Of The Lost Ark; The Sender; Without A Clue*
Freeman, Sandy (act): *Dark Mirror (1984)*
Freeman, Stella (act): *The House Of The Arrow (1930)*
Freeman, Yvette (act): *Dead Again; Switch*
Frees, Paul (act): *The Hobbit; Space Master X-7; The War Of The Worlds; The Wind In The Willows*
Fregoli, Leopoldo (act): *The Lightning Change Artist*
Fregonese, Hugo (cin, b. 1908): *Man In The Attic (1953)*
Fregonese, Hugo (dir, b. 1908): *Man In The Attic (1953); Seven Thunders*
Frehley, Ace (act): *Kiss Meets The Phantom Of The Park*
Freiberger, Fred (wri): *Crash Landing*
Freiberger, Manfred (act): *The Night Porter*
Freindikh, Alice (act): *Rasputin (1985)*
Freiwald, Eric (wri): *The Lone Ranger And The Lost City Of Gold*
Freley, Pat (act): *The Adventures Of The American Rabbit*
Fremault, Anita (act): see Louise, Anita
Fremont, Al (act): *The Fatal 30*
French, Allen (act): *I Was A Zombie For The F.B.I.*
French, Bert (act): *The Vampire (1913, USA)*
French, Bruce (act): *Curse Of The Black Widow; It Happened At Lake Wood Manor; Man On A Swing; The Mysterious Two; The Savage Bees; Terror Out Of The Sky*
French, Charles K. (act): *The Last Warning (1929); Murder By Television; Radio Ranch*
French, Ed (act): *Breeders*
French, Gay (act): *Kiss Daddy Goodbye*
French, George (act): *The Black Pearl; Tarzan Of The Apes*
French, Harold (act): *The Callbox Mystery; Murder At The Inn*
French, Harold (dir, b. 1900): *Dead Men Are Dangerous; The Hour Of 13; The House Of The Arrow (1940); Paris Express*
French, Howard (act): *I Come In Peace*
French, Hugh (act): *Mr. Peabody And The Mermaid; Shadow Of The Eagle*
French, Leslie (act): *C'era Una Volta; The Malpas Mystery*
French, Mary Meade (act): *Doomsday Machine*
French, Mitchell (act): *Beverly Hills Bodysnatchers*
French, Rita (act): *Kiss Of The Tarantula*
French, Sadie (act): *The Black Cat (1965)*
French, Susan (act): *Captain America II; Flatliners; House; Jaws 2; Somewhere In Time*
French, Tami (act): *The Gifted One*
French, Valerie (act, 1931-1990): *The Four Skulls Of Jonathan Drake; The 27th Day*
French, Victor (act, 1935-1989): *The House On Skull Mountain; The Other (1972); The Tribe*
Frend, Charles (dir, 1909-1977): *Return Of The Vikings; The Sky Bike*
Frend, Charles (wri, 1909-1977): *The Sky Bike*
Frenguelli, A.G. (dir): *The Cry For Justice*
Frenguelli, Tony (dir): *Dr. Sin Fang*
Frere, Dorothy (act): *The Curse Of The Golem; The Snake Woman*
Frerichs, Reed (act): *Powder*
Fresco, Jacques (cin): *Project Moonbase*
Fresco, Robert (cin): *Firebird 2015 A.D.*
Fresco, Robert M. (wri, b. 1928): *The Monolith Monsters; Tarantula*
Freshman, William (act): *F.P. 1 Antwortet Nicht; The Scarlet Pimpernel (1934)*
Freshman, William (wri): *[illegible] Terror (1938)*
Fresnay, Pierre (act, 1897-1975, nee Pierre Laudenbach): *Le Corbeau; La Main Du Diable; The Man Who Knew Too Much (1934)*
Fresson, Bernard (act): *The Tenant*
Fresson, Theresa (act): *Mary Shelley's 'Frankenstein'*
Freulich, Henry (cin): *The Boogie Man Will Get You; Boston Blackie Goes Hollywood; Bulldog Drummond Strikes Back (1947); It Came From Beneath The Sea; The Lone Wolf In London; The Lone Wolf Meets A Lady; The Lone Wolf Returns (1935); The Lone Wolf Strikes; Meet Nero Wolfe; The Saracen Blade; Shadowed; Slaves Of Babylon; The 27th Day; Unknown World*
Freund, Herta (act): *The Invisible Terror*
Freund, John (act): see Forsythe, John
Freund, Karl (cin, 1890-1969): *The Decision Of Christopher Blake; Dracula (1931, English-Speaking Version); The Golem: How He Came Into The World; Green Hell; A Guy Named Joe; Der Januskopf; Der Letzte Mann; Metropolis (1926); The Murders In The Rue Morgue (1932); Satanas; Die Spinnen; The Thin Man Goes Home*
Freund, Karl (dir, 1890-1969): *Madame Spy; Mad Love; The Mummy (1932)*
Freur (mus): *Transmutations*
Frewen, E.L. (act): *My Lord Conceit; When Knights Were Bold (1929)*
Frewer, Matt (act, b. 1957): *Generation X; Honey, I Shrunk The Kids; Lawnmower Man 2: Beyond Cyberspace*
Frey, Katherine (act): *A Midsummer Night's Dream (1935)*
Frey, Leonard (act, 1938-1988): *The Magic Christian; Tattoo*
Frey, Mary (act): *Night Of Terror (1933)*
Frey, Nathaniel (act): *Damn Yankees*
Frey, Sami (act): *Black Widow (1987); Sweet Movie*
Frezza, Giovanni (act): *Manhattan Baby*
Friberg, John (cin): *Alice, Sweet Alice*
Fric, Martin/Mac (dir & wri, 1902-1968): *Cisaruv Pekar, Pekaruv Cisar*
Frick, Elise (act): *The Bermuda Depths*
Fricker, Brenda (act): *The Quatermass Conclusion; A Time To Kill (1996)*
Frickert, Joseph (wri): *One Million B.C.; One Million Years B.C.*
Frickhofer, Gerhard (act): *Superwheels*
Frid, Jonathan (act): *The Devil's Daughter (1972); House Of Dark Shadows; Seizure*
Friday (act): *Eyes In The Night; The Hidden Eye*
Fridell, Ake (act): *Ansiktet; Det Sjunde Inseglet*
Fridell, Squire (act): *Human Feelings*
Fridh, Gertrud (act): *Ansiktet; The Devil's Eye; Vargtimmen*
Fridley, Tom (act): *Friday The 13th, Part Vi: Jason Lives; Phantom Of The Mall: Eric's Revenge; Phenomenon*
Friebel, Sandra (act): *Blood Beach*
Fried, Adam (act): *The Edge Of Hell*
Fried, Gerald (mus): *The Baby; The Cabinet Of Caligari; Cruise Into Terror; Curse Of The Faceless Man; I Bury The Living; Killer's Kiss; The Killing; The Lost Missile; Murder Is Easy; One Spy Too Many; The Return Of Dracula; Survive!; The Vampire (1957); What Ever Happened To Aunt Alice?*
Fried, Julie (act): *The Toxic Avenger, Part II*
Fried, Justin (act): *The Magic Snowman*
Fried, Suzy (act): *Mother's Day*
Friedberger, Fred (wri): *The Beast From 20,000 Fathoms; The Beginning Of The End*
Friede, Lisa (act): *Spookies*
Friedhofer, Hugo (mus, 1902-1981): *The Bishop's Wife; Bride Of Vengeance; Homicidal; The Lodger (1944)*
Friedkin, David (wri): *The Fool Killer*
Friedkin, William (dir, b. 1939): *The Exorcist; The Guardian; Jade*
Friedkin, William (wri, b. 1939): *The Guardian*
Friedl, Fritz V. (act): *The Fifth Musketeer*
Friedlander, Louis (act): see Landers, Lew
Friedlob, Ellen (act): see Parker, Eleanor
Friedman, Bernie (act): *Neighbors*
Friedman, Brent V. (wri): *The Resurrected*
Friedman, Bruce Jay (wri): *Splash*
Friedman, Daniel (H.) (act): *Chain Reaction (1996); School Spirit*
Friedman, David F. (wri): *She Freak*
Friedman, Irving (mus): *Love From A Stranger (1947); Philo Vance's Gamble*
Friedman, Jill (act): *The Hidden*
Friedman, Josh (wri): *Chain Reaction (1996)*
Friedman, Ken (dir & wri): *Death By Invitation*
Friedman, Kinley (act): *The Being*
Friedman, Peter (act): *Blink; The Seventh Sign; Single White Female*
Friedman, Philip (wri): *Rage*
Friedman, Richard (dir): *Phantom Of The Mall: Eric's Revenge*
Friedman, Seymour (dir, b. 1915): *Boston Blackie's Chinese Venture; Crime Doctor's Diary; The Saint's Return; The Son Of Dr. Jekyll; Trapped By Boston Blackie*
Friedman, Tom (act): *Vampire At Midnight*
Friedman, Tom (wri): *Time Walker*
Friedrich, John (act): *The Final Terror*
Friedrichsen, Uwe (act): *The Ape Creature*
Friedson, Adam (act): *Silent Night, Deadly Night III*
Friedstand, Bob (act & cin): *I Was A Zombie For The F.B.I.*
Friel, Cassy (act): *Late For Dinner*
Friel, Tony (act): *Wombling Free*
Friels, Colin (act): *Darkman (1990)*
Friend, Andrew W. (cin): *The Alchemist*
Friend, Bob (act): *Mission: Impossible*
Friend, J.B. (act): *Neighbors*
Friend, Jessie-Ann (act): *Magic Island*
Friend, Philip (act, b. 1915): *Buccaneer's Girl; Cloak Without Dagger; The Diamond; The Midas Touch; Pimpernel Smith; The Solitary Child; Son Of Robin Hood; Spy Hunt; The Vulture (1966); Web Of Suspicion*
Friend, Robert L. (dir): *Tarzan's Deadly Silence*
Fries, Brooke (act): *Flowers In The Attic*
Friese-Greene, Claude (cin): *The Saint In London*
Friganza, Trixie (act, 1871-1955): *The Road To Yesterday*
Frings, Ketti (wri, 1915-1981): *The Accused; Guest In The House; Mr. Sycamore*
Frink, Jeff (cin): *Eve Of Destruction*
Frisco, Joe (act, 1889-1958): *The Gorilla (1931)*
Frishman, Dan(iel) (act): *The Ewok Adventure; Ewoks: The Battle For Endor; Night Of The Creeps*
Fritchie, Barbara (act): *Murder On The Blackboard*
Frith, Anne (act): *Fiend (1980); The Galaxy Invader; Nightbeast*
Frith, Steve (act): *Fiend (1980)*
Fritsch, Willy (act, 1901-1973): *Die Frau Im Mond; Spione*
Fritzell, Jim (wri): *The Ghost And Mr. Chicken; The Reluctant Astronaut*
Frizzell, John (mus): *Dante's Peak*
Frizzell, Lou (act): *Capricorn One; Devil Dog: The Hound Of Hell; The Other (1972)*
Frizzi, Fabio (mus): *The Gates Of Hell; Manhattan Baby*
Frobe, Gert (act, 1912-1988): *Chitty Chitty Bang Bang; Enough Rope; Goldfinger; The Green Archer; A High Wind In Jamaica; I Killed Rasputin; In The Steel Net Of Dr. Mabuse; It Happened In Broad Daylight; Les Nuits Rouges; Die Tausend Augen Des Dr. Mabuse; Ten Little Indians (1974); The Testament Of Dr. Mabuse (1960); Those Fantastic Flying Fools*
Froehlich, Bill (dir & wri): *Return To Horror High*
Froelich, Gustav (act, b. 1902): *Metropolis (1926)*
Froeschel, George (wri, b. 1891): *I Aim At The Stars*
Frohman, Robin (act): *Weird Science*
Frollini, Aldi (cin): *War Of The Planets*
Frolov, Diane (wri): *Alien Nation: The Enemy Within*
Frolov, Ivan (cin): *Sonka Zolotaya Ruchka*
Fromdahl, Jonathan (act): *Communion*
Frome, Milton (act, 1910-1989): *The Nutty Professor (1963); The St. Valentine's Day Massacre; The Shaggy D.A.; Visit To A Small Planet; Way...Way Out*
Frommer, Ben (act): *Bride Of The Monster; Plan 9 From Outer Space; Psycho II*
Frondaroli, Angela (act): *Demons 2*
Frontiere, Dominic (mus): *Dark Mirror (1984); Fer-De-Lance; Hammersmith Is Out; Haunts Of The Very Rich; The Immortal; Modern Problems; Probe*
Froom, Mitchell (mus): *Dr. Caligari*
Frost, Alan (act): *The Brain Eaters; Something Evil*
Frost, Jack (act): *Just Imagine*
Frost, Jackie (act): *Ok, Nero!*
Frost, Lee (act & dir): *The Thing With Two Heads*
Frost, Lee (wri): *Race With The Devil; The Thing With Two Heads*
Frost, Lindsay (act): *Dead Heat; Monolith*
Frost, Maria (act): *Secrets Of Sex*
Frost, Mark (wri): *The Believers*
Frost, Philip (act): *Scrooge (1935)*
Frost, R.L. (dir): *The Defilers; House On Bare Mountain*
Frost, Robert (act): *The Black Cat (1965)*
Frost, Sadie (act): *A Ghost In Monte Carlo; Magic Hunter*
Frost, Terry (act): *The Baron Of Arizona; Crashing Las Vegas; The Monster Maker (1943); The Night The World Exploded*
Frost, Warren (act): *Psycho IV: The Beginning; War Of The Colossal Beast*
Froud, Toby (act): *Labyrinth (1986)*
Fruet, Allison (act): *Funeral Home*
Fruet, William (dir): *Blue Monkey; Funeral Home; The House By The Lake*
Fruet, William (wri): *The House By The Lake*
Frugoni, Cesare (wri): *The Fish Men; The Great Alligator; Il Montagna Di Dio Cannibale*
Frumkes, Roy (act & wri): *Street Trash*
Frumkin, Marla (act): *Bates Motel*
Fry, Herald (avt): *The Invincible Barbarian*
Fry, Iris (act): *Murder By Decree*
Fry, James (act): *It Came Upon The Midnight Clear*
Fry, Kevin (act): *Eraser*
Fry, Ricky (wri): *Bride Of Re-Animator*
Fry, Robert (act): *Bog*
Fry, Taylor (act): *Death Dreams*
Frydman, Stuart (act): *Chilling*
Frye, Christopher (wri, b. 1907): *The Bible*
Frye, Dwight (act, 1899-1943): *The Black Camel; Bride Of Frankenstein; The Crime Of Dr. Crespi; Dead Men Walk; Dracula (1931, English-Speaking Version); Frankenstein (1931); Frankenstein Meets The Wolf Man; The Ghost Of Frankenstein; The Great Impersonation (1935); The Invisible Man (1933); The Maltese Falcon (1931); Phantom Raiders; The Son Of Monte Cristo; Strange Adventure; The Vampire Bat*
Frye, Gary (act): *Surf Nazis Must Die*
Frye, Gil (act): *The Bride And The Beast; The Monster That Challenged The World*
Frye, Marie (act): see MacDonald, Marie
Frye, Peter (act): *1984 (1984)*
Frye, Soleil Moon (act, b. 1976): *Invitation To Hell; Pumpkinhead II: Blood Wings*
Frye, Virgil (act): *The Cat Creature; Dr. Heckyl & Mr. Hype; Graduation Day; Queen Of Blood; Up From The Depths*
Fryers, Austin (wri): *The Charlatan*
Fucco, Richard (act): *Alien High*
Fuchs, Daniel (wri): *Between Two Worlds*
Fuchs, Eddie (act): *Skullduggery*
Fuchs, Gaby (act): *Mark Of The Devil (1972); La Noche De Walpurgis*
Fuchs, Hannes (act): *I Love You, I Kill You*
Fuchs, Hilda (act): *Hundra; Pieces*
Fudge, Alan (act): *Are You In The House Alone? Brainstorm (1983); Bug; Capricorn One; Chiller; Edward Scissorhands; Galaxis; Goliath Awaits; I Saw What You Did (1988); Mantis; My Demon Lover; Nightmare On The 13th Floor; Witness To The Execution*
Fuentes, Acencion (act): *Always*
Fuentes, Amalia (act): *The Blood Drinkers; Curse Of The Vampires*
Fuentes, Carlos (wri, b. 1928): *La Strega In Amore*
Fuentes, Daisy (act): *Curdled*
Fuentes, Miguel Angel (act): *Caveman (1981)*
Fuentes, Tony (act): *Flesh-Eating Mothers*
Fuest, Robert (dir): *The Abominable Dr. Phibes; And Soon The Darkness; The Devil's Rain; Dr. Phibes Rises Again; The Last Days Of Man On Earth; Revenge Of The Stepford Wives; Wuthering Heights (1970)*
Fuest, Robert (wri): *Dr. Phibes Rises Again; The Last Days Of Man On Earth*
Fuglsang, Frederik (cin): *Himmelskibet*
Fugs, The (act & mus): *Chappaqua*
Fuhrer, Martin (cin): *Lord Of The Flies (1990)*
Fuhrmann, E.O. (act): *Das Schloss*
Fuji (act): *The Wrecking Crew*
Fuji, Tatsuya (act): *Gappa, The Triphibian Monster*
Fujii, Kazuo (cin): *Gammera Vs. Zigra*
Fujikawa, Jerry (act): *The Cat From Outer Space*
Fujiki, Yu (act): *Atragon; Godzilla vs. Mothra; King Kong vs. Godzilla*
Fujimaki, Jun (act): *Majin, Monster Of Terror*
Fujimoto, Tak (cin): *Cocoon: The Return; Death Race 2000; Dr. Black Mr. Hyde; Last Embrace; The Silence Of The Lambs*
Fujioka, Hiroshi (act): *Catastrophe 1999: The Prophecies Of Nostradamus; Ghost Warrior; The Submersion Of Japan*
Fujioka, John (act): *Futureworld; The Octagon; Steel Dawn*
Fujioka, Yutaka (wri): *Little Nemo: Adventures In Slumberland*
[illegible]
[illegible]
Fujita, Toyo (act): *The Return Of Dr. Fu Manchu*
Fujiwara, Kay (act): *The Neptune Factor*

Fujiwara, Kei (act): *Iron Man*

Fujiyama, Koji (act): *Gammera Vs. Zigra*

Fujiyama, Yoko (act): *Atragon; Dogora*

Fujiyoshi, Masaharu (act): *The Toxic Avenger, Part II*

Fukasaku, Kinji (dir): *The Green Slime; Message From Space; Samurai Reincarnation; Virus*

Fukasaku, Kinji (wri): *Virus*

Fukotomi, Makoto (act): *The Toxic Avenger, Part II*

Fukuda, Jun (wri): *Godzilla Vs. Megalon*

Fukuda, Wataru (act): *The Toxic Avenger, Part II*

Fukunaga, Takehiko (wri): *Mothra*

Fukunaga, Yoshikazu (act): *The Toxic Avenger, Part II*

Fulcher, Stedwell (act): *Horror Of Dracula*

Fulci, Lucio (act): *Manhattan Baby*

Fulci, Lucio (dir, a.k.a. Louis Fuller): *The Black Cat (1980); Conquest; The Conspiracy Of Torture; Eyes Of The Evil Dead; The Gates Of Hell; The House By The Cemetery; A Lizard In A Woman's Skin; Manhattan Baby; New York Ripper; The Psychic; 7 Doors Of Death; Zombie*

Fulci, Lucio (wri): *The Black Cat (1980); The Gates Of Hell; A Lizard In A Woman's Skin*

Fulks, Sarah Jane (act): see Wyman, Jane

Fullam, Kevin (act): *Millennium*

Fullenwider, Fran (act): *The Monster Club; The Mutations*

Fuller, Dale (act): *The House Of Horror (1929)*

Fuller, Dolores (act, b. 1923): *Bride Of The Monster; Glen Or Glenda?*

Fuller, Ernest (act): *What A Night!*

Fuller, Erwin (act): *Beyond The Living; Deadly Messages; It Came Upon The Midnight Clear*

Fuller, Frances (act): *Homebodies; They Might Be Giants*

Fuller, John G. (wri): *The Ghost Of Flight 401; The Ufo Incident*

Fuller, Jonathan (act): *Castle Freak; The Pit And The Pendulum (1990)*

Fuller, Kurt (act): *Elvira, Mistress Of The Dark; Eve Of Destruction; Ghostbusters II; Miracle Mile; Pandora's Clock; Reflections In The Dark*

Fuller, Lance (act): *The Bride And The Beast; Girls In Prison; Pearl Of The South Pacific; The She-Creature; This Island Earth; Voodoo Woman*

Fuller, Leslie (act): *What A Night!*

Fuller, Lisa (act): *Earth Girls Are Easy; The Monster Squad; Night Life (1989, USA)*

Fuller, Louis (dir & wri): see Fulci, Lucio

Fuller, Mary (act): *A Letter To The Princess*

Fuller, Parmer (mus): *Saturday The 14th*

Fuller, Patricia (act): *What Became Of Jack And Jill*

Fuller, Rhonda (act): *Stigma*

Fuller, Robert (act, b. 1934): *The Brain From Planet Arous; Repossessed; What Ever Happened To Aunt Alice?*

Fuller, Roy (cin): *Subterfuge*

Fuller, Samuel (act, b. 1911): *A Return To Salem's Lot*

Fuller, Samuel (dir & wri, b. 1911): *The Baron Of Arizona; Shock Corridor*

Fuller, Susanne (act): *The Tell-Tale Heart (1960)*

Fuller, Tex (act): *No Blade Of Grass*

Fuller, Tex (dir): *Stranded*

Fullerton, Fiona (act, b. 1958): *Alice's Adventures In Wonderland (1972); A Ghost In Monte Carlo; The Secret Life Of Ian Fleming; A View To A Kill*

Fullerton, Karen (act): *Scanners*

Fullerton, Melanie (act): *Night Of The Lepus*

Fulmer, Ray (act): *Wild Is My Love*

Fulton, Jeff (act): *My Bloody Valentine*

Fulton, Joan (act): *House Of Horrors (1946)*

Fulton, John P. (cin, b. 1902): *The Bishop's Wife; The Black Cat (1941); Cobra Woman; The Colossus Of New York; Conquest Of Space; Great Expectations (1934); Gypsy Wildcat; House Of Frankenstein; I Married A Monster From Outer Space; Invisible Agent; The Invisible Man (1933); The Invisible Man Returns; The Invisible Man's Revenge; The Invisible Ray; The Invisible Woman (1941); Man-Made Monster; The Man Who Knew Too Much (1956); The Murders In The Rue Morgue (1932); Omar Khayyam; Rear Window; The Search For Bridey Murphy; The Space Children; Sudan; Vertigo; Visit To A Small Planet; The Woman In Green*

Fulton, Maude (wri): *The Maltese Falcon (1931)*

Fulton, Rad (act): *Antinea, L'amante Delle Citta Sepolta*

Fultz, Ronda (act): *I Drink Your Blood*

Fumarelli, Rocky (act): *Spawn Of The Slithis*

Funakoshi, Eiji (act): *Gammera, The Invincible*

Funfrok, Huguette (act): *Bon Baisers De Hong Kong*

Fung, Paul (act): *The Lone Wolf In London*

Fung, Willie (act): *The Gay Falcon; The Gracie Allen Murder Case*

Funicello, Annette (act, b. 1942): *Babes In Toyland (1961); Dr. Goldfoot And The Bikini Machine; How To Stuff A Wild Bikini; The Misadventures Of Merlin Jones; The Monkey's Uncle; Pajama Party; The Shaggy Dog*

Funk, Terry (act): *Timestalkers*

Funkquist, Georg (act): *The Devil's Eye*

Funston, Lance (act): *The Initiation*

Furber, Douglas (wri): *The Thirteenth Hour (1927); When Knights Were Bold (1936)*

Furdeaux, Beatrice (act): *Terror From The Year 5,000*

Furey, John (act): *Friday The 13th-Part 2; Guess Who's Coming For Christmas?; The Night Of The Claw*

Furey, Louis (mus): *Jacob Two-Two Meets The Hooded Fang*

Furey, Martha (act): *Glen And Randa*

Furie, Daniel (act): *The Entity*

Furie, Sid(ney) J. (dir, b. 1933): *Dr. Blood's Coffin; The Entity; The Ipcress File; The Snake Woman; Superman Iv: The Quest For Peace*

Furillo, Jennifer (act): *The Toxic Avenger, Part II*

Furlin, Matthew Daniel Moses (act): *The Relic*

Furlong, Edward (act, b. 1977): *Brainscan; Pet Sematary Two; Terminator 2: Judgment Day*

Furlong, John (act): *The Swarm*

Furnari, Salvatore (act): *Escape From The Bronx*

Furneaux, Yvonne (act, b. 1928): *Le Comte De Monte Cristo; The House Of The Arrow (1953); The Lion Of Thebes; The Mummy (1959); Repulsion; Le Scandale; The Secret Of Dr. Mabuse; Slave Queen Of Babylon*

Furness, Tammi (act): *The Sword And The Sorcerer*

Furnival, Don (act): *The House Of The Living Dead*

Furrer, Urs (cin): *Dr. Cook's Garden*

Furrh, Chris (act): *Lord Of The Flies (1990)*

Furry, Elda (act): see Hopper, Hedda

Furse, Judith (act, b. 1912): *Black Narcissus; Carry On Spying; Mad About Men; The Man In The White Suit; Mother Riley Meets The Vampire*

Furst, Esther (act): *Ring Of Terror*

Furst, Joseph (act): *The Brides Of Fu Manchu; Diamonds Are Forever; Inn Of The Damned; Sudden Terror*

Furst, Stephen (act): *The Unseen (1981)*

Furst, Timothy Daniel (act): *The Jewel Of The Nile*

Furstenberg, Ira (act): *Matchless; The Vatican Affair*

Furth, George (act, b. 1932): *Megaforce; Myra Breckinridge; Oh, God!*

Furth, Jaro (act): *Der Januskopf*

Furthman, Jules (wri, 1888-1966): *The Big Sleep (1946); Moss Rose; Nightmare Alley; Peking Express; Shanghai Express*

Furuta, Toshihiko (act): *Mothra*

Fury, Ed (act): *Mighty Ursus; La Regina Delle Amazzoni; Samson Against The Sheik; Son Of Hercules In The Land Of Fire; Ursus Nella Valle Dei Leoni; Wild Women Of Wongo*

Fury, Loretta (act): *Man On A Swing*

Fusco, Anthony (act): *Eraser; Highlander*

Fusco, Giovanni (mus, b. 1906): *Black Devils Of Kali; Red Desert; La Villa Dei Mostri*

Fusco, John (wri): *Loch Ness*

Fusco, Maria Pia (wri): *Bluebeard (1972); Hitler: The Last Ten Days*

Fusco, Paul (wri): *Project: Alf*

Fusier-Gir, Jeanne (act): *Les Sorcieres De Salem*

Fusile, Marc (act): *The Toxic Avenger, Part II*

Fuss, Harry (act): *The Invisible Terror*

Futcher, Hugh (act): *Repulsion*

Futrelle, Jacques (wri): *The Man Behind The Mask (1936)*

Futterer, Werner (act): *Faust (1926)*

Fux, Herbert (act): *The Ape Creature; La Figlia Di Frankenstein; Funeral In Berlin; House Of 1,000 Dolls; The Invisible Terror; Jack The Ripper (1979); Mark Of The Devil (1972)*

Fuxa, Chris (act): *Cocoon: The Return*

Fuzia, Thomas (act): *Street Trash*

Fyfe, Jim (act): *The Frighteners*

Fyfe, Robert (act): *Xtro*

Fyffe, Will (act, 1885-1947): *Elstree Calling; The Mind Of Mr. Reeder; The Missing People*

Fyodorova, Victoria (act): *Crime And Punishment (1975)*

Gaba, Marianne (act): *Missile To The Moon*

Gabai, Richard (act): *Dinosaur Island (1994); Nightmare Sisters*

Gabay, Trissa (act): *Silent Night, Deadly Night III*

Gabbard, Glendon (act): *Blink*

Gabel, Martin (act, 1912-1986): *Goodbye Charlie; M (1950); Marnie; The Thief*

Gabel, Martin (dir, 1912-1986): *The Lost Moment*

Gabel, Scilla (act): *Arms Of The Avenger; Colossus Of The Arena; Knights Of Terror; Modesty Blaise; Il Mulino Delle Donne Di Pietra; Queen Of The Pirates; Revenge Of The Gladiators; Tarzan's Greatest Adventure*

Gabin, Jean (act, 1904-1976, nee Alexis Moncorge): *Crime And Punishment (1958); His Last 12 Hours; Les Miserables (1957); Speaking Of Murder*

Gable, Christopher (act, b. 1960): *The Hunchback Of Notre Dame (1977); The Lair Of The White Worm; The Slipper And The Rose*

Gable, June (act): *Brenda Starr (1992)*

Gabold, Anne-Lise (act): *King Lear (1970)*

Gabor, Eva (act, 1921-1995): *Captain Kidd And The Slave Girl; The Mad Magician*

Gabor, Sara (act): see Gabor, Zsa Zsa

Gabor, Zsa Zsa (act, b. 1917, nee Sara Gabor): *The Girl In The Kremlin; A Nightmare On Elm Street 3: Dream Warriors; Picture Mommy Dead; Queen Of Outer Space*

Gabriel, Ana (act): *The Nature Of The Beast*

Gabriel, John (GB act): *The Curse Of The Werewolf; Doomsday Voyage; A Place To Die*

Gabriel, John (USA act): *Fantasies; The Incredible Hulk Returns; Hell's Bloody Devils*

Gabriel, Larry (act): *Cavegirl (1985)*

Gabrielle, Monique (act): *Amazon Women On The Moon; Deathstalker II: Duel Of The Titans; Not Of This Earth (1988)*

Gabrielle, Nancy (act): *The Black Windmill*

Gabrio, Gabriel (act): *Les Visiteurs Du Soir*

Gachman, Dan (act): *The Monster That Challenged The World; The Return Of Dracula*

Gadbois, Margaret (act): *Scanners*

Gadd, Renee (act): *The Crimson Circle (1936); Dead Of Night (1945); The Man In The Mirror; The Man Who Made Diamonds; They Came To A City*

Gaddis, Matthew (wri): *The Suicide Club (1988)*

Gade, Analia (act): *Las Cuatro Noches De La Luna Llena; Exorcism's Daughter; Murder Mansion*

Gades, Antonio (act): *El Amor Brujo (1972 & 1986)*

Gades, Antonio (wri): *El Amor Brujo (1986)*

Gadette, Fredric (dir & wri): *This Is Not A Test*

Gadney, Alan (dir & wri): *Moonchild*

Gadsden, Terence (wri): *The Mutagen*

Gadsdon, Jacquelin (act): *The Thirteenth Hour (1927)*

Gael, Anna (act): *Blue Blood; Dracula, Pere Et Fils; Zeta One*

Gael, Josseline (act): *La Main Du Diable*

Gaffe, Donna (act): *The Alien's Return*

Gaffe, James (act): *The Alien's Return*

Gaffin, Melanie (act): *The Entity*

Gaffney, Liam (act): *The Bad Lord Byron; Island Of Terror; Street Of Shadows*

Gaffney, Marjorie (wri): *The Mind Of Mr. Reeder*

Gaffney, Robert (dir, b. 1931): *Frankenstein Meets The Space Monster*

Gage, Erford (act): *Curse Of The Cat People; The Falcon In Danger; The Falcon Strikes Back; The Seventh Victim*

Gage, Kevin (act): *The 'Burbs*

Gage, Leona (act): *Four Sided Triangle; Tales Of Terror*

Gage, Neva (act): *Cat People (1982)*

Gage, Pat(ricia) (act): *Charlie Chan: Happiness Is A Warm Clue; Hello Again; Rabid*

Gage, Rooney (act): *Runaway*

Gagliardi, Vincenzo (act): *Modern Problems*

Gagnon, Andre (mus): *Phobia*

Gagnon, Lee (mus): *Seizure*

Gagnon, Steven H. (act): *Blood Run*

Gagnon, Terry (act): *Maniac (1980)*

Gago, Jenny (act): *Alien Nation: Body And Soul; Alien Nation: Millennium*

Gahagan, Heln (act, 1900-1980): *She (1935)*

Gaige, Russell (act): *To Catch A Thief*

Gail, Albert (wri): *Five Weeks In A Balloon*

Gail, David (act): *Full Eclipse*

Gail, Jane (act): *The Black Spot; Called Back; Dr. Jekyll And Mr. Hyde (1913, Imp); The Prisoner Of Zenda (1915); Rupert Of Hentzau (1915)*

Gail, Jeanne (act): *Woman Who Came Back*

Gail, Max (act. b. 1943): *The Aliens Are Coming; Curse Of The Black Widow; Killer In The Mirror*

Gail, Scanlon (act): *Fright Night II*

Gaillard, Roger (act): *Les Enfants Terribles*

Gaines, Ardis Anderson (act): see Marshall, Brenda

Gaines, Richard (act, b. 1904): *Flight To Mars; Francis In The Haunted House; Ride The Pink Horse*

Gainey, M.C. (act): *Spellbinder*

Gainey, Mike (act): *Time After Time*

Gains, Courtney (act): *The 'Burbs; Children Of The Corn*

Gainsborough, Louise (act): *Shadow Of The Past*

Gainsborough, Michael (act): *Looker*

Gainsbourg, Charlotte (act): *Jane Eyre (1996)*

Gainsbourg, Serge (act, 1928-1991): *Mister Freedom; Samson; Seven Deaths In The Cat's Eye*

Gaintner, G. Leroy (act): *Night Of The Lepus*

Gaisford, Bonnie (act): *Silent Night, Deadly Night III*

Gaisman, Ella (act): see Allyson, June

Gaither, Curtis (act): *Street Trash*

Gaj, Grigori (act): *The Red Tent*

Gajadhar, Ken (act): *Death May Be Your Santa Claus*

Gajdecki, John (cin): *The Quilt Of Hathor*

Gajoni, Cristina (act): *Mighty Ursus*

Gal, Emil (act): *Shinel*

Galadzhev, Pyotr (act): *Luch Smerti*

Galante, James Joseph/Jim (act): *Alice In Wonderland (1985); Death Sport*

Galasso, Dave (act): *The Arrival*

Galbo, Cristina (act): *The House That Screamed; The Living Dead At Manchester Morgue*

Galbraith, Robert (act): *The Intruder (1981)*

Galdos, Benito Perez (wri): *Tristana*

Gale, Bennett (act): *Time Flyer*

Gale, Bob (wri): *Back To The Future; Back To The Future, Part II; Back To The Future, Part III; Tales From The Crypt Presents Bordello Of Blood*

Gale, David (act): *The Brain (1988); Bride Of Re-Animator; The First Power; Re-Animator; Switch*

Gale, Ed (act): *Howard The Duck; Lifepod; The Munsters' Scary Little Christmas*

Gale, Eddra (act): *Somewhere In Time*

Gale, John (mus): *Dr. Phibes Rises Again; Mr. Selkie*

Gale, Johnnie (act): *Murder At The Windmill*

Gale, June (act): *Charlie Chan At Treasure Island*

Gale, Lorena (act): *Wild Thing*

Gale, Mary (act): *Wizards Of The Lost Kingdom*

Gale Peter (1910s act): *In The Toils Of The Blackmailer*

Gale, Peter (act): *Hamlet (1969); Jekyll And Hyde*

Gale, Ricardo Jacques (cin): *The Nest*

Gale, Richard (cin): *Alien Warrior*

Galeen, Henrik (act, 1882-1949): *Der Golem (1914)*

Galeen, Henrik (dir, 1882-1949): *Alraune (1928); Der Golem (1914); Der Student Von Prag (1926)*

Galeen, Henrik (wri, 1882-1949): *Alraune (1928); The Golem: How He Came Into The World; Nosferatu, Eine Symphonie Des Grauens; Der Student Von Prag (1926); Das Wachsfigurenkabinett*

Galetti, April (act): *The Demon (1981)*

Galfas, Timothy (cin): *The Lord Of The Rings*

Galiana, Fernando (wri): *The Saint In The Wax Museum*

Galiano, Cataldo (cin): *Zorro (1975)*

Galich, Steve (cin): *Endangered Species*

Galicia, Maria Luz (act): *The Shadow Of Zorro*

Galiena, Anna (act): *Rorret*

Galik, Denise (act): *Don't Answer The Phone!; The Eliminator; Humanoids From The Deep*

Galili, Hal (act): *The Adding Machine; Arabian Adventure; Outland; Superman II; Warlords Of The Deep*

Galindo, Cavernario (act): *El Santo Contra Las Vampiras*

Gallager, Bronagh (act): *Mary Reilly*

Gallagher, Carole (act): *The Falcon Out West*

Gallagher, David (act): *Bermuda Triangle; Phenomenon; Summer Of Fear; Syngenor*

Gallagher, Donald (dir): *Temple Tower*

Gallagher, Gina (act): *Edward Scissorhands*

Gallagher, Maurie (act): *Chopping Mall*

Gallagher, Megan (act): *The Ambulance*

Gallagher, Peter (act): *Dreamchild; High Spirits; Late For Dinner; To Gillian On Her 37th Birthday*

Gallagher, Richard "Skeets" (act): *The Phantom Of Crestwood*

Gallagher, Thomas (act): The Angel Who Pawned Her Harp; Babes In Baghdad; The Saint's Return
Galland, Jean (act): What Price Murder
Gallardo, Lucas (wri): Behind The Mask Of Zorro
Gallardo, Miguel A. (act): The White Orchid
Gallaudet, John (act): The Beginning Or The End?; The Docks Of New Orleans; Julie; The Lone Wolf In Mexico; Shadows Over Chinatown
Gallea, A. (cin): Faust And The Devil
Gallegher, Pattie (act): King Dinosaur
Gallego, Gina (act): My Demon Lover
Gallegos, Joshua (act): Star Trek
Galleon, George (act): The Man Who Made Diamonds
Gallery, James (act): Salem's Lot
Galletti, Giovanna (act): Gli Amori Di Ercole
Galli, Ida (act, a.k.a. Evelyn Stewart): Murder Mansion; Roma Contra Roma
Galli, Rosina (act): Phantom Of The Opera (1943)
Galliano, Vittorio (cin): Goliath Against The Giants
Gallico, Paul (wri, 1897-1976): Beyond The Poseidon Adventure; Daughter Of The Mind; The Poseidon Adventure; The Three Lives Of Thomasina
Gallico, Robert (act): Behemoth, The Sea Monster; Talk Of The Devil
Gallier, Alex (act): The Curse Of Frankenstein; The Man Inside
Galligan, Tom (cin): The Thirteenth Guest
Galligan, Zach (act, b. 1964): Cyborg 3; Gremlins; Gremlins 2: The New Batch; Rising Storm; Waxwork; Waxwork II: Lost In Time
"Gallimard" (wri): see Bardawil, George
Gallo, Arch (act): Wizards Of The Lost Kingdom
Gallo, Jacques (act): The Magic Sword (1962)
Gallo, Mario (act): The Incredible Hulk; King Kong (1976)
Gallo, Phil (mus): Mother's Day
Gallo, Rick (act): Wizards Of The Lost Kingdom
Gallo, William (act): Night Of The Demons
Gallon, Tom (wri): The Man In Motley; The Princess Of Happy Chance; The Woman Who Was Nothing
Gallone, Carmine (dir, 1886-1973): Carthage In Flames; Faust And The Devil
Gallone, Carmine (wri, 1886-1973): Carthage In Flames
Galloni, Cristiana (act): Scream Of The Demon Lover
Gallow, Janet Ann (act): The Ghost Of Frankenstein
Galloway, Fred (act): The Plutonium Incident
Galloway, Jack (act): Possession (1973)
Galloway, Jenny (act): Mary Shelley's 'Frankenstein'
Galloway, L. (act): The Glittering Sword
Galloway, Layla (act): The Two Worlds Of Jennie Logan
Galloway, Lindsay (wri): The Double
Galloway, Paul (act): Blood Waters Of Dr. Z
Gallu, Sam(uel) (dir, b. 1918): Limbo Line; The Man Outside (1967); Theatre Of Death
Gallu, Samuel (wri, b. 1918): The Man Outside (1967)
Gallup, Bonnie (act): Powder
Gallup, Michael (act): Dick Tracy (1990)
Gallus, Agi (act): Psycho Girls
Galter, Sam (act): Death Comes From Space
Galton, Ray (wri): The Spy With A Cold Nose
Galtress, Trevor (act): Honey, I Shrunk The Kids
Galvan, Pedro (act): The Black Scorpion
Galvani, Dino (act): The Clouded Crystal; The Missing Rembrandt; The Secret Agent (1936); The Silver Greyhound (1932)
Galvani, Graziella (act): Nick Carter Et Le Trefle Rouge
Galvez, Jose (act): Macario
Galvez, Venchito (act): Dance Of The Dwarfs
Galvin, James (act): Man On A Swing
Galvin, Ray (act): Simon, King Of The Witches
Galvino, Tony (act): Flight Of The Navigator
Gam, Rita (act, b. 1928): Distortions; Midnight (1989); No Exit; Saadia; Seeds Of Evil; The Thief
Gamal, Samia (act): Ali-Baba Et Les Quarante Voleurs
Gaman, Tom (act): Lord Of The Flies (1963)
Gambina, Frank (act): Doomsday Machine
Gambino, James (act): Phantom Of The Paradise
Gamble, Duncan (act): Running Against Time
Gamble, John (act): Mutants In Paradise
Gamble, Mason (act): Bad Moon
Gamble, Warburton (act): As You Desire Me; Blind Man's Bluff (1936); A Study In Scarlet (1933)
Gambon, Michael (act): The Beast Must Die; Mary Reilly; Nothing But The Night
Gamet, Kenneth (wri): Devil's Island
Gamin, Poupee (act): Journey To The Center Of Time
Gamley, Douglas (mus): —And Now The Screaming Starts!; Asylum; The Beast Must Die; Beyond This Place; City Of The Dead; From Beyond The Grave; Gideon's Day; The Land That Time Forgot; Madhouse; The Monster Club; The Return Of Mr. Moto; Tales From The Crypt; Tarzan's Greatest Adventure; The Vault Of Horror
Gamlin, Lionel (act): Man In The Moon (1960); Seance On A Wet Afternoon; The Thirteenth Instant; The Wrong Box
Gammell, Robin (act): Full Circle; Nightmares (1983); Project X (1987); Rituals
Gammon, James (act): Made In Heaven; Silver Bullet
Gampel, C.M. (act): Beyond The Universe
Gampu, Ken (act): King Solomon's Mines (1985); King Solomon's Treasure
Gamut, Kenneth (wri): Fly-Away Baby; Nancy Drew And The Hidden Staircase; Nancy Drew, Detective; Nancy Drew, Reporter; Nancy Drew, Troubleshooter; Smart Blonde
Gan, Chester (act): Man-Made Monster; The Mystery Of Mr. Wong; Thank You, Mr. Moto; Torchy Runs For Mayor
Ganapoler, Martin (act): Howard The Duck
Gance, Abel (act, 1889-1981): La Fin Du Monde
Gance, Abel (cin, 1889-1981): J'accuse (1918)
Gance, Abel (dir & wri, 1889-1981): La Fin Du Monde; La Folie Du Docteur Tube; J'accuse (1918 & 1937)
Gance, Margaret (act): La Chute De La Maison Usher
Ganem, Gustavo (act): Zorro, The Gay Blade
Gangel, Ed (act): Capture That Capsule!
Gangelin, Paul (wri, b. 1897): The Giant Claw; The Mad Ghoul; Nazi Agent; Tarzan's Secret Treasure
Ganger, Ben (Ryan) (act): Ed Wood; Flowers In The Attic
Ganley, Gail (act): Blood Of Dracula; Not Of This Earth (1957)
Gann, Merrilyn (act): It (1990)
Gannascoli, Joseph R. (act): Ed Wood; Never Talk To Strangers
Gannes, Gayle (act): The Prey (1980)
Gannon, Joe (wri): Solar Crisis
Gano, Glen (cin): The Incredible 2-Headed Transplant
Gans, Ronald (act): Hell Night; Tarzan And The Jungle Boy
Gans, Sharon (act): Slaughterhouse-Five
Gans, Victor (act): Hundra
Gant, John (cin): Lifeforce; Link
Gant, Marya (act): A Polish Vampire In Burbank
Gant, Richard (act): Jason Goes To Helll: The Final Friday
Ganthony, Richard (wri): A Message From Mars (1913)
Gantman, Ron (wri): Slugs
Ganus, Paul (act): Crash And Burn; Monolith
Ganz, Bruno (act): The Boys From Brazil; Nosferatu, The Vampyre
Ganz, Lowell (wri): Multiplicity; Splash; Vibes
Ganzel, Teresa (act): Transylvania 6-5000
Gaona, Alex (act): Monolith
Gaos, Lola (act): Sound Of Horror; Tristana
Garabedian, Robert (act): Satan's Satellites
Garady, Ken (act): Dr. Who And The Daleks
Garanda, Valya (act): The Witchmaker
Garandza, Nestor (act): Empire Of Ash III
Garas, Dezso (act): Daughter Of Darkness (1990)
Garas, Kaz (act): Ben; Wonder Woman
Garay III, Joaquin (act): Herbie Goes Bananas
Garber, Esther (act): Houdini
Garber, Hope (act): The Haunted (1991)
Garber, John (act): Short Circuit
Garber, Matthew (act, b. 1956): The Gnome-Mobile; Mary Poppins
Garbett, Dean (act): Funeral Home
Garbo, Greta (act, 1905-1990, nee Greta Louisa Gustafsson): As You Desire Me; Mata Hari (1932); The Story Of Gosta Berling
Garbo, Ingrid (act): Gran Amoro Dol Condo Dracula
Garbutt, James (act): Superman (1978)
Garces, Mauricio (act): El Baron Del Terror; La Cabeza Viviente; El Mundo De Los Vampiros
Garcia, Allan (act): Modern Times
Garcia, Andy (act, b. 1956): Dead Again
Garcia, Arturo (act): see de Cordova, Arturo
Garcia, Carl (act): Wizards Of The Lost Kingdom
Garcia, Cristina (act): Surf Nazis Must Die
Garcia, David (act): Monster From The Ocean Floor
Garcia, Eddie (act): Beast Of Blood; Beast Of The Yellow Night; Beyond Atlantis; Curse Of The Vampires; Twilight People
Garcia, Ernest (act): From Dusk Till Dawn
Garcia, Henry (wri): Dungeons Of Horror
Garcia, Ignacio (act): Anguish
Garcia, John (act): Anguish
Garcia, Jose (act): The Arrival; Curse II: The Bite
Garcia, Joseph (act): The China Syndrome
Garcia, Juan (act): I'm Dangerous Tonight; Run For The Sun
Garcia, Lea (act): Black Orpheus
Garcia, Mark (act): The Ultimate Impostor
Garcia, Nadine (act): Street Trash
Garcia, Pablo (act): Alien Predators
Garcia, Raymond (act): Maid To Order
Garcia, Ron (cin): Alien Nation: The Enemy Within; Twin Peaks: Fire Walk With Me
Garcia, Russell (mus): Atlantis, The Lost Continent; The Time Machine (1960)
Garcia, Sandra E. (act): The Lost Boys
Garcia, Sara (act): The Living Idol
Garcia, Stella (act): The Private Lives Of Adam And Eve
Garcia, Tito (act): The Light At The Edge Of The World
Garcin, Henri (act): Quelqu'un Derriere La Porte
Garde, Annie Birgit (act): Journey To The Seventh Planet
Garden, John (wri): Double Confession
Gardenia, Vincent (act, 1921-1992): Dark Mirror (1984); Heaven Can Wait (1978); Little Shop Of Horrors (1986)
Gardett, Robert (act): Fright (1957)
Gardiner, Patrick (act): The Viking Queen
Gardiner, Reginald (act, 1903-1980): Androcles And The Lion; Black Widow (1954); The Horn Blows At Midnight; Marie Antoinette (1938); The Story Of Mankind
Gardner, Arthur (act): The Vampire (1957)
Gardner, Ava (act, 1922-1990, nee Lucy Johnson): Around The World In 80 Days; The Bible; The Blue Bird (1976); The Bribe; City On Fire; Earthquake; Ghosts On The Loose; The Kidnapping Of The President; Knights Of The Round Table; One Touch Of Venus; On The Beach; Pandora And The Flying Dutchman; The Sentinel; Seven Days In May; Tam Lin
Gardner, Brooks (act): Phantasm III: Lord Of The Dead
Gardner, Caron (act): Death Is A Woman; Evil Of Frankenstein
Gardner, Craig (act): The Demon (1981); Short Circuit 2
Gardner, Cyril (dir): El Cuerpo Del Lito
Gardner, David (act): Prom Night; Virus
Gardner, Dick (act): Desk Set
Gardner, Earle Stanley (wri, 1889-1970): The Case Of The Curious Bride; The Case Of The Howling Dog; They Call It Murder
Gardner, Helen (act): Devil's Angel
Gardner, Hy (act): The Girl Hunters
Gardner, Jack (act): Flesh And Fantasy
Gardner, Jerry (act): Into The Badlands
Gardner, Jimmy (act): The Company Of Wolves; Dead Man's Folly; Robin Hood: Prince Of Thieves; 10 Rillington Place
Gardner, Joan (act, b. 1914): Dark Journey; The Man Outside (1933); The Man Who Could Work Miracles; The Private Life Of Don Juan; The Scarlet Pimpernel (1934)
Gardner, Joan (wri): Beach Girls And The Monster
Gardner, John (wri): The Liquidator
Gardner, Louanna (act): The Black Sleep
Gardner, Marcella (mus): Liliom (1930)
Gardner, Sandra (act): Those Dear Departed
Gardner, Shayle (act): The Lodger (1932); The Medium (1934); Menace (1934); The Return Of Dr. Fu Manchu; The River House Ghost; St. Elmo; Wolf's Clothing (1936)
Gardner, Stu (mus): Top Secret (1978)
Gardner, Suzi (act): Serial Mom
Gardner, Terri M. (act): The Cradle Will Fall
Garen, Leo (dir & wri): Hex
Garfein, Jack (dir & wri, b. 1930): Something Wild
Garfias, Ruben (act): Full Eclipse
Garfield, Allen (act): Cyborg 2: Glass Shadow; Diabolique (1996); Dick Tracy (1990); Killer In The Mirror
Garfield, Brian (wri): The Stepfather; Stepfather II; Stepfather III: Father's Day
Garfield, Frank (act): Night Of The Zombies (1983)
Garfield, John (act, 1913-1952, nee Julius Garfinkle): Between Two Worlds; Out Of The Fog (1941)
Garfield Jr., John (act): The Swimmer
Garfield, John D. (act): The Golden Voyage Of Sinbad
Garfield, Michael (act): Slugs
Garfinkle, Gayle (act): Of Unknown Origin; Oh Heavenly Dog
Garfinkle, Julius (act): see Garfield, John
Garfinkle, Louis (wri, b. 1925): Face Of Fire; I Bury The Living
Garfunkle, Art (mus): Watership Down
Gargan, Edward/Ed (act, 1902-1964): A-Haunting We Will Go; Another Thin Man; Charlie Chan In Pamama; A Date With The Falcon; The Falcon And The Co-Eds; The Falcon In Danger; The Falcon Out West; The Falcon's Brother; The Falcon Strikes Back; The Falcon Takes Over; The Lone Wolf Keeps A Date; The Saint Strikes Back; The Thin Man Goes Home
Gargan, Jack (act): The Dark Mirror (1946); Dick Tracy (1945)
Gargan, William (act, 1905-1979): The Argyle Secrets; British Agent; The Canterville Ghost (1944); Close Call For Ellery Queen; Desperate Chance For Ellery Queen; Enemy Agents Meet Ellery Queen; Follow That Woman; Four Frightened People; House Of Fear (1939); Isle Of Destiny; I Wake Up Screaming; Who Done It? (1942)
Gargano, Omero (act): Vulcan, Son Of Jupiter
Gargiulo, Arnold (cin): Alien High
Garia, Rick (act): It's Alive III: Island Of The Alive; A Return To Salem's Lot
Gariazzo, Mario (dir): The Tormented (1977)
Garibba, Mario (act): Deborah
Garinei, Andrea (act): Demons 2
Garino, Gerard (act): The Phantom Of The Opera (1990)
Garisa, Antonio (act): La Venganza De Don Mendo
Garko, John (act): Hercules (1983)
Garland, Prof. (act): Professor Garland The Conjurer
Garland, Beverly (act, b. 1930, nee Beverly Campbell): The Alligator People; Curucu, Beast Of The Amazon; D.O.A. (1949); The Glass Web; It Conquered The World; Killer Leopard; Life, Liberty And Pursuit On The Planet Of The Apes; The Mad Room; The Neanderthal Man; Not Of This Earth (1957); Pretty Poison (1968); Rocket Man; Stark Fear; Swamp Women; Twice-Told Tales
Garland, David (act): Phantom Of The Paradise
Garland, Frank (act): Hercules (1983)
Garland, Judy (act, 1922-1969, nee Frances Gumm): The Wizard Of Oz (1939)
Garland, Kenneth (act): Funeral Home
Garland, Michel (act): Treasure Island (1971)
Garland, Richard (act): Attack Of The Crab Monsters; Mutiny In Outer Space; My Gun Is Quick; Panic In Year Zero; The Undead
Garland, Robert (wri): No Way Out
Garland, Tom (act): Ghost Diver
Garlick, Stephen (act): The Dark Crystal
Garlington, Lee (act): The Babysitter (1995); Psycho II; Psycho III, The Seventh Sign; Summer Of Fear
Garlitsky, V. (wri): Sonka Zolotaya Ruchka
Garmes, Lee (cin, 1898-1978): Caught; Guest In The House; The Jungle Book (1942); Lady In A Cage; Land Of The Pharaohs; Love Letters; Nightmare Alley; The Paradine Case; The Private Life Of Helen Of Troy; The Secret Life Of Walter Mitty; Shanghai Express
Garmey, Terrence (act): Thinner
Garner, David (act): Trauma (1963)
Garner, Ed (act): The Ghost In The Invisible Bikini
Garner, Jack (act): Fantasies; Midnight Offerings
Garner, James (act, b. 1928, nee James Baumgarner): The Fan; Fire In The Sky (1993)
Garner, Jay (act): Silent Night, Bloody Night
Garner, Jimmy (act): Frenzy
Garner, Katina (act): A Polish Vampire In Burbank; The Tomb
Garner, Martin (act): Twilight Zone
Garner, Paul "Mousie" (act): Saturday The 14th
Garner, Peggy Ann (act, 1931-1984): Black Widow (1954); Bomba, The Jungle Boy; Jane Eyre (1944)
Garner, Shay (act): Humongous
Garner, Stan (act): Nothing But Trouble
Garner, Bob (act): The Spider (1958); War Of The Colossal Beast
Garnett, Gale (act): The Children
Garnett, Richard (act): Link

Garnett, Tay (dir, 1898-1977): The Black Knight; A Connecticut Yankee In King Arthur's Court (1949)
Garnett, Tony (act): Incident At Midnight
Garnica, Lupe (act): Tarzan's Deadly Silence
Garnier, Bernard (act): Les Parapluies De Cherbourg
Garofalo, Franco (act): The Eyes Behind The Stars
Garofalo, Janeane (act): The Cable Guy; Touch
Garofalo, Joseph (wri): Evilspeak
Garon, Pauline (act): Adam's Rib; Le Spectre Vert
Garr, Frances (act): The Fool Killer
Garr, Teri (act, b. 1950): Close Encounters Of The Third Kind; Doctor Franken; Mom And Dad Save The World; Nightscream; Oh, God!; Witches' Brew; Young Frankenstein
Garralaga, Martin (act): African Treasure; Another Thin Man; The Feathered Serpent (1948); Secret Of The Incas; The Unknown Terror
Garrani, Ivo (act): Atom Age Vampire; Death Comes From Space; Hercules (1957); Holocaust 2000; La Maschera Del Demonio; Morgan The Pirate
Garras, Robert (cin): Dr. Heckyl & Mr. Hype
Garratt, Donna (act): Diamonds Are Forever
Garreaud, Jean-Francois (act): Violette Noziere
Garrel, Maurice (act): To Commit A Murder
Garret, George (wri): Frankenstein Meets The Space Monster
Garrett, Andi (act): I Saw What You Did (1965)
Garrett, Betty (act): The Shadow On The Window
Garrett, Donna (act): The Entity; Wonder Woman
Garrett, Drum (act): It (1990)
Garrett, George (wri): The Playground
Garrett, Grant (wri): Abbott And Costello Meet Dr. Jekyll And Mr. Hyde
Garrett, Hank (act): The Sentinel
Garrett, James (act): Time After Time
Garrett, Jane (act): Slaughter Hotel (1972)
Garrett, Joy (act): Who?
Garrett, Leif (act): The Horrible House On The Hill; Party Line' The Spirit Of '76
Garrett, Oliver H.P. (wri): Moby Dick (1930)
Garrett, Otis (dir): Lady In The Morgue
Garrett, Richard (act): Cinque Tombe Per Un Medium
Garrett, Robert (mus): The Phantom Empire; Roller Blade Warriors: Taken By Force
Garrett, Roger (act): Night Of The Cobra Woman
Garrett, Roy (dir & wri): The Eyes Behind The Stars
Garrett, Scott (act): Ben; Magic
Garrett, Steve (act): Galaxis
Garrett, Susie (act): Wicked Stepmother
Garrett, William (wri): The Man In The Mirror
Garrick, Curtis Lee (act): The Dungeonmaster
Garrick, James (act): Wicked Stepmother
Garrick, John (act, b. 1902, nee Reginald Doudy): Charlie Chan Carries On; Chu Chin Chow (1934); Just Imagine
Garrick, Kathy (act): Schizoid (1980)
Garrick, Richard (dir): Trent's Last Case (1920)
Garrie, John (act): Koroshi; Madhouse; The Private Life Of Sherlock Holmes; Taste The Blood Of Dracula
Garris, Cynthia (act): Critters 2: The Main Course; Psycho Iv: The Beginning; Sleepwalkers
Garris, Mick (dir): Critters 2: The Main Course; Psycho Iv: The Beginning; Sleepwalkers
Garris, Mick (wri): *Batteries Not Included; Critters 2: The Main Course; The Fly II
Garris, Phil (act): Francis In The Navy
Garrison, Harold (act): Arrest Bulldog Drummond
Garrison, Mike (act): The Corpse Grinders; The Worm Eaters
Garrison, Pat (act): The Flying Saucer (1950)
Garrison, Richard (act): The Crater Lake Monster; Northstar
Garrison, Rob (act): Prom Night; Starship Invasions
Garrison, Robert (act): The Worm Eaters
Garrison, Sean (act, b. 1937): The Adventures Of Nick Carter; Moment To Moment
Garrity, Peter (wri): Destroyer
Garron, Victor (act): Earth Girls Are Easy
Garrone, Riccardo (act): The Bang-Bang Kid
Garry, Charles (act): Trilby (1922)
Garry, Robert (act): The Hideous Sun Demon
Garsen, Bernard J. (act): Nightfall (1988)
Garson, Edward (act): The Young Magician
Garson, Henry (wri): Visit To A Small Planet
Garson, John (act): Werewolf Of Washington
Garson, Mort (mus): Beware! The Blob
Garson, Willie (act): Mars Attacks!; Repossessed
Garth, David (act): Neither The Sea Nor The Sand
Garth, Michael (act): The Phantom From 10,000 Leagues
Garth, Raymond (act): The Woman Who Wouldn't Die (1965)
Gartin, Christopher (act): Tremors 2: Aftershocks
Garvarentz, George(s) (mus): Quelqu'un Derriere La Porte; The Southern Star; Too Scared To Scream
Garver, John (act): Mr. Destiny
Garvey, Steve (act): Ice Cream Man
Garvie, Parker (act): Murder Is My Business
Garvin, Bonnie (act): The Toxic Avenger, Part II
Garvin, Cory (act): Trauma (1993)
Gary, Ann Pearl (act): The Fan; Jacob's Ladder
Gary, Linda (act): Switch
Gary, Lorraine (act): Jaws; Jaws 2; Jaws: The Revenge
Gary, Micheline (act): Le Testament Du Dr. Cordelier
Gary, Dr. Norman (act): The Savage Bees
Garza, Juan (act): Dr. Tarr's Torture Dungeon
Gascar, Pierre (wri): Les Yeux Sans Visage
Gasco, Ernesto (act): Too Scared To Scream
Gascon, Merche (act): Anguish
Gascoyne, Brian (mus): Blue Blood; Phase Iv
Gaslini, Giorgio (mus): Profundo Rosso
Gasnier, Louis (dir): Darkened Rooms
Gaspar, Luis (act): The Mummy's Revenge
Gaspard, Ray (act): Screams Of A Winter Night
Gasparri, Gianfranco (act):Goliath Against The Giants
Gass, Kyle (act): Jacob's Ladder
Gassman, Vittorio (act, b. 1922): La Corona Negra; Il Diavolo Innamorato; Ghosts-Italian Style; The Miracle (1959); The Nude Bomb; Quintet; Slalom
Gastaldi, (Ernesto) (wri, a.k.a. Julian Berry): L'amante Del Vampiri; La Frusta E Il Corpo; The Great Alligator; Lycanthropus; The Murder Clinic; Perseus The Invincible; Lo Strano Caso Della Signora Ward; Torso
Gastoni, Lisa (act, b. 1935): Colossus And The Huns; I Criminali Della Galassia; The Deadly Diaphanoids; Face In The Night; Family Doctor; The Man Who Laughs (1965); Messalina Against The Son Of Hercules; Queen Of The Seas; The Strange Awakening
Gate, John (dir): The Velvet Touch
Gatehouse, Robin (act): The Mouse That Roared
Gatell, Clyde (act): Batman (1989)
Gately, Frederick (cin): I Bury The Living
Gatenby, Ray (act): Agatha
Gates, Deborah (act): Return Of The Killer Tomatoes
Gates, Gilbert (dir): Oh, God! Book II
Gates, Harvey (M.) (wri): Behind The Curtain (1924); Black Dragons; The Corpse Vanishes; In The Next Room; The Terror (1928)
Gates, Larry (act, 1915-1996): Francis Covers The Big Town; The Henderson Monster; Invasion Of The Body Snatchers (1956)
Gates, Nancy (act, b. 1926): The Atomic City; At Sword's Point; The Search For Bridey Murphy; World Without End
Gates, Richard (act): The House Of The Dead
Gates, Rick (act): Fantasies
Gates, Samantha (act): Full Circle; The Water Babies
Gates, Tudor (wri): Barbarella; Diabolik; Fright (1971); Lust For A Vampire; Twins Of Evil; The Vampire Lovers
Gatherum, Jimmy (act): The Hearse
Gathrid, Brett (act): Sleepstalker
Gati, Kathi (act): Frankenhooker
Gatins, John (act): Leprechaun 3; Pumpkinhead II: Blood Wings
Gatley, Dorothy Walton (act): see Harding, Ann
Gatliff, Frank (act): Deja Vu; The Ipcress File
Gator, Linus (act): Flesh Gordon
Gatrell, John (act): The Private Life Of Sherlock Holmes
Gatrell, Robert (act): Funeral Home
Gatsby, Jill (act): It's Alive III: Island Of The Alive; A Return To Salem's Lot; Vampire's Kiss
Gatti, Marcello (cin): The Black Belly Of The Tarantula
Gatto, Gregory (act): Cat People (1982)
Gaubert, Christian (mus): The Little Girl Who Lives Down The Lane
Gauch, Steve (cin): Amazons (1984)
Gaudio, Bob (mus): Little Shop Of Horrors (1986)
Gaudio, Tony (cin, 1885-1951): The Adventures Of Robin Hood; Background To Danger; The Bandit Of Sherwood Forest; The Dragon Murder Case; Love From A Stranger (1947); The Mark Of Zorro (1920); The Mask Of Fu Manchu; Torchy Blane In Panama
Gauge, Alexander (act, 1914-1960): Before I Wake; Counterspy; The Golden Link; The Green Man; House Of Blackmail; The Interrupted Journey
Gaugh, Homer (dir): Goliathon
Gaughan, Michael (act): Edward Scissorhands
Gauguin, Lorraine (act): One Million B.C.
Gaul, Patricia (act): Deadly Messages
Gaulke, James (act): Fargo
Gaulke, Peter (act): Repossessed
Gault, Greg (act): The Capture Of Bigfoot
Gaunt, Valerie (act): The Curse Of Frankenstein; Horror Of Dracula
Gauntley, John (act): Castle Sinister (1948)
Gauthier, Dan (act): Teen Witch
Gauthier, Dave (cin): The Little Match Girl (1987)
Gauthier, Merrily (act): Alien High
Gauthier, Nathalie (act): Alien High
Gautreaux, David (act): The Hearse; Star Trek
Gautsch, Francoise Annette (act): see Arnoul, Francoise
Gava, Cassandra (act): Condor
Gavaldon, Roberto (dir & wri): Macario
Gaven, Jean (act): Les Sorcieres De Salem
Gaver, Duffy (act): Seven
Gavia, Raquel (act): Blood Simple
Gavigan, John (act): Shadow Of A Doubt (1991)
Gavin, Erica (act): Caged Heat!
Gavin, James (act): The Werewolf (1955)
Gavin, John (act, b. 1934): Jennifer (1978); Midnight Lace (1960); Oss 117-Double Agent; Psycho
Gavin, Mary (act): Flesh Gordon
Gavin, Weston (act): Superman (1978)
Gaviola, Cassandra (act): Conan The Barbarian
Gaviola, Sandy (act): Wonder Woman
Gavon, Igors (act): Neighbors
Gawne, Irene (act): Tales From The Crypt
Gawthorne, Coomarie (act): My Lord Conceit
Gawthorne, Peter (act): Alf's Button Afloat; Behind That Curtain; Charlie Chan Carries On; Dead Men Are Dangerous; Death Is A Number; The Lodger (1932); The Man Behind The Mask (1936); Murder At Monte Carlo; Old Mother Riley's Ghosts; Paul Temple Returns; Pimpernel Smith; Temple Tower; Three Silent Men; Wolf's Clothing (1936)
Gawthrop, Grace (act): Flesh-Eating Mothers
Gay, Auretta (act): Zombie
Gay, Gregory (act): Charlie Chan At The Opera; Creature With The Atom Brain; Flying Disc Man From Mars; I Love A Mystery (1945); I Wake Up Screaming; Jungle Man-Eaters; Meteor; Missile Monsters; One Dangerous Night; Savage Mutiny
Gay, John (act): On Her Majesty's Secret Service
Gay, John (wri): Adventures Of The Queen; Dial M For Murder (1981); The Hunchback Of Notre Dame (1982); No Way To Treat A Lady; The Power (1967); Shadow Of A Doubt (1991); Summer Of Fear
Gay, Maisie (act): The Old Man
Gay, Ramon (act): Cry Of The Bewitched; The Curse Of The Doll People; La Momia; La Momia Contra El Robot Humano
Gay, Walter (act): Where The Rainbow Ends
Gaybis, Anne/Annie (act): Beyond Evil; The Lost Empire
Gaye, Howard (act): Dante's Inferno (1924)
Gaye, Lisa (act): La Cara Del Terror; Castle Of Evil; Class Of Nuke'em High, Part 2: Subhuman-oid Meltdown; The Toxic Avenger, Part Ii; The Toxic Avenger, Part III: The Last Temptation Of Toxie
Gaye, Vivian (act): The Frog
Gayford, John (act): Kill Her Gently
Gayheart, Rebecca (act): Robin Cook's 'Invasion'
Gaylin, Michael (wri): No Escape (1994)
Gaylor, Anna (act): Seven Thunders
Gaylor, Gerry (act): Queen Of Outer Space
Gaylord, Raymond (act): La Casa Del Terror
Gaynes, George (act): The Boy Who Cried Werewolf; It Came Upon The Midnight Clear; Trilogy Of Terror
Gaynor, Janet (act, b. 1906): The Return Of Peter Grimm (1926)
Gaynor, Joey (act): Galaxis
Gayson, Eunice (act, b. 1931): Dr. No; From Russia With Love; It Happened On Soho; The Last Man To Hang?; The Revenge Of Frankenstein
Gazelle, Frederick C. (act): Galaxina
Gazelle, Wendy (act): Remo Williams: The Adventure Begins; The Understudy: Graveyard Shift II
Gazzana, Nic (act): Mad Max
Gazzara, Ben (act, b. 1930): The Neptune Factor; Pursuit (1972); When Michael Calls
Gazzo, Michael V. (act, 1923-1995): Black Sunday (1977)
Gearon, Valerie (act): Invasion (1965)
Gearson, Monica (act): The Boys From Brazil
Geary, Anthony (act, b. 1947): The Amazing Captain Nemo
Geary, Bud (act): Alias Boston Blackie; Charlie Chan At The Opera
Geary, Dick (act): The Prisoner Of Zenda (1979)
Geary, Maine (act): Robin Hood (1922)
Geary, Richard (act): Ghost Diver
Geasland, Jack (wri): Dead Ringers
Gebhardt, Fred (wri, b. 1925): The Phantom Planet; 12 To The Moon
Gebuhr, Otto (act): The Golem: How He Came Into The World
Geddes, David (cin): Bridge Of Time; When A Stranger Calls Back
Geddie, Bill (wri): Unforgettable
Gedrick, Jason (act): The Heavenly Kid
Gee, Buck (act): Satan's Triangle
Gee, Donald (act): Murder In Mind
Gee, Prunella (act): Never Say Never Again
Geeling (act): Mad Max Beyond Thunderdome
Geer, Andy (act): Enemy Mine
Geer, Ellen (act): Creator; Phenomenon
Geer, Kevin (act): A Force Of One
Geer, Lennie (act): The Destructors; The Sword And The Sorcerer
Geer, Lenny (act): Mind Over Murder
Geer, Noel (act): It (1990)
Geer, Thad (act): The Octagon
Geer, Will (act, 1902-1978): The Blue Bird (1976); Brock's Last Case; The Brotherhood Of The Bell; Dear, Dead Delilah; Isn't It Shocking?; The Mafu Cage; The Night That Panicked America; Seconds
Geeseman, Jane (act): The Haunting Of Sarah Hardy
Geesin, Ron (cin): Ghost Story (1975); Strange Behaviour; Sword Of The Valiant
Geeson, Judy (act, b. 1948): Berserk; Diagnosis: Murder; Dominique; Doomwatch; Fear In The Night (1972); Inseminoid; It's Not The Size That Counts; Murder On The Midnight Express; Nightmare Hotel; 10 Rillington Place; Twinsanity
Geeson, Sally (act): Cry Of The Banshee; The Oblong Box
Geeves, Peter (act): Jekyll And Hyde
Geffner, Deborah (act): All That Jazz
Gehring, Ted (act): Are You In The House Alone?; The Invisible Man (1975); The Strange And Deadly Occurrence; Too Good To Be True
Geiduschek, Joss (cin): Nothing But Trouble
Geier, Ruthe (act): Making Mr. Right
Geiger, William (act): Roger Corman's 'Frankenstein Unbound'
Geisel, Theodor Seuss (wri): see Seuss, Dr.
Geisman, Richard (act): Stigma
Geissendorfer, Hans W. (dir & wri): Jonathan
Gwiwitz, Richard (act): Nightbeast
Geiwitz, Richard (cin): Fiend (1980); Nightbeast
Gelbart, Larry (wri): Neighbors; Oh, God!; The Wrong Box
Geldenhuys, Peter (act): House Of The Living Dead
Geldert, Clarence (act): Behind The Curtain (1924); The Thirteenth Chair (1929); The Unholy Night
Geldhart, Ed (act): RoboCop 2; Sugar Hill
Geldman, Mark (D.) (wri): Cyborg 2: Glass Shadow; The Jungle Book (1994)
Gelfan, Barney (act): Blood Of Ghastly Horror
Gelfman, Sam (act): The Incredible Melting Man
Gelgur, Donna (act): Night Of The Lepus
Gelin, Daniel (act, b. 1921): Carthage In Flames; The Man Who Knew Too Much (1956); Mr. Frost; The Sleeping Car Murders; The Snow Was Black; Le Testament D'orphee; Torticola Contre Frankensberg
Gellar, Sarah Michelle (act): Scream II
Geller, Bruce (dir): The Savage Bees
Geller, Bruce (wri): Mission: Impossible
Geller, Harold (mus): Fury At Smugglers' Bay
Geller, Judith (act): Hellhole
Geller, Stephen (wri): Pretty Poison (1968 & 1996); Slaughterhouse-Five
Gelman, Janice (act): The Incredible 2-Headed Transplant
Gelman, Larry (act): Dreamscape; She Demons; Topper (1979)
Gelpi, Juan (cin): Crypt Of The Living Dead
Gemier, Firmin (act): The Magician (1926)
Gemma, Giuliano (act): When Women Had Tails

Gemora, Charles (act): *The War Of The Worlds*
Gems, Jonathan (wri): *Mars Attacks!*
Gems, Pam (act): *1984 (1984)*
Gemser, Laura (act): *Ator: The Fighting Eagle*
Genaro, Tony (act): *The Craft; Heart And Souls; Phenomenon; Switch; Tremors*
Gendre, Louis (act): see Jourdan, Louis
Gendron, Pierre (wri): *Bluebeard (1944); Fog Island; The Monster Maker (1943)*
Geneen, Jan (act): *Blind Date*
Genesse, Bryan (act): *Cyborg Cop III; Human Timebomb*
Genest, Emile (act): *Rampage*
Genet, Jean (wri, 1910-1986): *The Balcony; The Maids*
Genevie, Michael (act): *Mr. Destiny*
Gengarelli, G. (cin): *La Sorella Di Satan*
Genik, Ihsan (act): *Crypt Of The Living Dead*
Genin, Rene (act): *The Burning Court; Judex; Les Yeux Sans Visage*
Genina, Augusto (dir, 1892-1957): *Lucrezia Borgia (1919)*
Genkins, Harvey (cin): *The Garbage Pail Kids*
Genn, Leo (act, 1905-1978): *Circus Of Fear; Die Screaming, Marianne; The Dream Doctor; Endless Night; Frightmare (1974); Green For Danger; The Green Scarf; I Accuse (1958); Law And Disorder; A Lizard In A Woman's Skin; Moby Dick (1956); Night Of The Blood Monster; The Snake Pit (1948); Ten Little Indians (1965); The Velvet Touch*
Gennaro, Karen (act): *Demons 2*
Genova III, Anthony T. (act): *The Dungeonmaster*
Genovese, Michael/Mike (act): *Dark Angel: The Ascent; Eyes Of Fire; The Invisible Kid*
Genschow, Fritz (dir & wri): *Sleeping Beauty (1965, W. Ger)*
Gentil, Bob (act): *Strange Behavior*
Gentil, Luc (act): *The Phantom Of The Opera (1990)*
Gentile, Denise (act): *Netherworld*
Gentile, Linda (act): *To All A Goodnight*
Gentilomo, Giacomo (dir): *Last Of The Vikings; Maciste Contro Il Vampiro; Maciste E La Regina Di Samar*
Gentle, Roslyn (act): *The Punisher*
Gentleman, Wally (cin): *Iron Warrior...The Legend!*
Gentry, Mike (act): *I Drink Your Blood; The Projectionist*
Gentry, Minnie (act): *The Brother From Another Planet; Def By Temptation*
Gentry, Mojo (act): *Serial Mom*
Gentry, Paul (cin): *The Crater Lake Monster*
Gentry, Robert (act): *Dear, Dead Delilah*
Gentry, Roger (act): *Gallery Of Horror; The Thing With Two Heads; The Wizard Of Mars*
Geoffrey, Paul (act): *Excalibur; Greystoke: The Legend Of Tarzan, Lord Of The Apes*
Geoffrey, Wallace (act): *The House Opposite (1931); On Secret Service; The Return Of Bulldog Drummond; The Scarab Murder Case*
Geoffrey, Wallace (wri): *The Perfect Woman; The Scotland Yard Mystery*
Geoffreys, Stephen (act, b. 1964): *Fright Night; Moon 44; 976-Evil*
George, Chris (act): *Dracula's Dog*
George Christopher (act, 1929-1983): *Cruise Into Terror; Day Of The Animals; Dead Men Tell No Tales; Escape; The Gates Of Hell; Graduation Day; Grizzly; The Immortal; Mortuary; Not Guilty; Pieces; Project X (1967)*
George, Chief Dan (act, 1899-1981): *Americathon; Shadow Of The Hawk*
George, David (mus): *Howling IV*
George, Don E. (mus): *The House Of Fear (1945); The Pearl Of Death; Phantom Lady*
George, Eric (act): *My Lord Conceit*
George, Frank (cin): *The City Under The Sea; Dr. No; Dracula Has Risen From The Grave; Quatermass II*
George, George (W.) (wri): *Rocket Man; Son Of Robin Hood*
George, Gladys (act, 1902-1954, nee Gladys Clare): *The Maltese Falcon (1941); Marie Antoinette (1938); Undercover Girl (1950)*
George, Gotz (act): *The Blood Of Fu Manchu; Hipnosis; Out Of Order*
George, Heinrich (act): *Metropolis (1926); She (1925)*
George Howard (act): *Jekyll And Hyde...Together Again; Killer In The Mirror*
George, Isabel (act): *Death Is A Number*
George, Jack (act): *Amazon Quest; Queen Of The Amazons (1947)*
George Jr., James (act): *This Is Not A Test*
George, John (act): *Don Juan (1927); Island Of Lost Souls; The Road To Mandalay; The Unknown (1927)*
George, Jon (wri): *The Final Terror*
George, Kent (act): *The Relic*
George, Laszlo (cin): *Rolling Vengeance; Rona Jaffe's Mazes And Monsters; Something Is Out There; Tarzan In Manhattan; Turn Back The Clock*
George, Lynda Day (act, b. 1946): *The Amazing Captain Nemo; Beyond Evil; Come Out, Come Out, Wherever You Are; Cruise Into Terror; Day Of The Animals; Fear No Evil (1969); It Happened At Lake Wood Manor; Mortuary; Pieces*
George, Maude (act): *The Drums Of Jeopardy (1923); Monte Cristo*
George, Michael (act): *To All A Goodnight*
George, Muriel (act): *Alibi (1942); Dr. Syn; Last Holiday; The Man From Scotland Yard; A Place Of One's Own*
George, Peter (act & dir): *Surf Nazis Must Die*
George, Peter (wri, 1924-1966): *Dr. Strangelove: or, How I Learned To Stop Worrying And Love The Bomb*
George, Raymond (act): *The Flesh And Blood Show*
George, Richard (act): *Dick Barton At Bay; 49th Patallel; Great Expectations (1946); Tower Of Terror*
George, Roger (W./Inc.) (cin): *Cyborg 2087; Destination Inner Space; The Destructors; Dimension 5; The Howling; The Human Duplicators; Humanoids From The Deep; Invisible Invaders; The Kid With The Broken Halo; Maid To Order; Mutiny In Outer Space; The Terminator*
George, Ron Howard (act): *Night Visions*
George, Susan (act, b. 1950): *Billion Dollar Brain; Computercide; Die Screaming, Marianne; Final Eye; Fright (1971); The House Where Evil Dwells; The Sorcerers; Sudden Terror; Tintorera...Bloody Waters; Venom (1982)*
George, Wally (act): *Repossessed*
Georger, Diana (act): *Jason Goes To Hell: The Final Friday*
Georgeson, Tom (act): *The Assistant*
Georges-Picot, Olga (act): *The Man Who Haunted Himself; Persecution*
Georgiade, Nick (act): *Poor Devil*
Georgitsis, Phaedon (act): *The Next One*
Gerace, Michael (act): *The Pink Chiquitas*
Geraghty, Carmelita (act): *Through The Dark*
Geraghty, Erin (act): *Peter Rabbit And The Tales Of Beatrix Potter*
Geraghty, Gerald (wri): *The Falcon And The Co-Eds; The Falcon In Hollywood; The Falcon In Mexico; The Falcon Strikes Back*
Geraghty, Leslie March (act): see Marsh, Garry
Geraghty, Maria (act): *Groundhog Day*
Geraghty, Marita (act): *To Save A Child*
Geraghty, Maurice (wri, b. 1908): *Sharad Of Atlantis*
Gerald, Helen (act): *The Trap*
Gerald, Jim (act): *Bulldog Drummond At Bay (1937)*
Gerald, Vera (act): *The Flaw; The Strange Case Of Mr. Todmorden*
Gerani, Gary (wri): *Pumpkinhead*
Gerard, Bryson (cin): *Nothing But Trouble*
Gerard, Edyie (act): *The Questor Tapes*
Gerard, George (act): *Metamorphosis: The Alien Factor*
Gerard, Gil (act, b. 1943): *Buck Rogers In The 25th Century; Man On A Swing*
Gerard, Hal (act): *Ghost Chasers; The Lady In The Iron Mask*
Gerard, Henriette (act): *Vampyr*
Gerard, Maurice (wri): *The Secret Of The Moor*
Gerard, Merwin (wri): *The Screaming Woman*
Gerard, Norman (cin): *Witches' Brew*
Gerard, Teddie (act): *The Cave Girl (1921)*
Gerard, Will (act): *Covenant*
Gerassimov, Sergei (act, b. 1906): *Shinel*
Geray, Noel Steven (act): *The Nest*
Geray, Steve(n) (act, 1899-1973, nee Stefan Gyergyay): *Above Suspicion; Blue, White And Perfect; Castle In The Desert; Crime Doctor's Gamble; Eyes In The Night; Gilda; The Golden Blade; Jesse James Meets Frankenstein's Daughter; The Lone Wolf And His Lady; The Mask Of Dimitrios; Phantom Of The Opera (1943); Pygmy Island; The Return Of Monte Cristo; Secret Agent Of Japan; So Dark The Night; Spellbound (1945); Tarzan And The Amazons; Tobor The Great*
Gerber, Joanie (act): *Explorers*
Gerber, Kathy (act): *The Exorcist III*
Gerber, Steve (wri): *Howard The Duck*
Gerbereck, George (act): *The Blob (1958)*
Gerdes, George (act): *Single White Female*
Gere, Richard (act, b. 1947): *First Knight; Primal Fear*
Geret, George(s) (act): *The Southern Star; Un Tranquillo Posto Di Campagna*
Gerety, Peter (act): *Wolf*
Germain, Andre (act): *The Golden Mistress*
Germain, Lud (act): *L'auberge Rouge*
Germain, Stuart (act): *Oh Heavenly Dog*
Germaine, Maeve (act): *Rawhead Rex*
Germaine, Mary (act, b. 1933): *Cloudburst; The Green Buddha; House Of Blackmail*
Germani, Gaia (act): *A Toi De Faire, Migonne; Castle Of The Living Dead*
Germann, Cory (act): *The Being*
Germi, Pietro (wri): *Black 13*
Germon, N. (act): *L'auberge Rouge*
Germon, Nane (act): *La Belle Et La Bete*
Gernreich, Rudi (act): *2000 Years Later*
Gerome, Raymond (act): *The Deadly Trap; Secret Agent (1974)*
Geronimi (wri): *Diabolique (1955)*
Geronimi, Clyde (dir): *101 Dalmatians (1960)*
Gerovitz, Lee N. (act): *Princess Warrior*
Gerrard, Charles (act): *Dracula (1931, English-Speaking Version); The Lone Wolf's Daughter (1929); The Menace (1932)*
Gerrard, Douglas (act): *Bulldog Drummond Strikes Back (1934)*
Gerrard, Frank (act): *The Silver Greyhound (1919)*
Gerrard, Henry (cin): *The Greene Murder Case; The Most Dangerous Game; The Penguin Pool Murder; The Phantom Of Crestwood*
Gerrard, Sean (act): *The Legend Of Spider Forest*
Gerrard, Tom (act): *Dracula's Dog*
Gerrault, William (act): *Le Boucher*
Gerringer, Robert (act, 1926-1989): *The Exorcist; Fail-Safe*
Gerrish, Flo (act): *Don't Answer The Phone!; Schizoid (1980)*
Gerritsen, Lisa (act): *A Howling In The Woods*
Gerry, Toni (act): *The Story Of Mankind*
Gersak, Savina (act): *Curse II: The Bite; Iron Warrior ...The Legend!*
Gershenson, Joseph (mus, b. 1904): *Abbott And Costello Go To Mars; Abbott And Costello Meet Dr. Jekyll And Mr. Hyde; Abbott And Costello Meet The Invisible Man; Abbott And Costello Meet The Mummy; The Black Castle; The Black Shield Of Falworth; Creature From The Black Lagoon; The Creature Walks Among Us; Cult Of The Cobra; The Deadly Mantis; Francis Covers The Big Town; Francis Goes To West Point; Francis In The Navy; Francis Joins The Wacs; The Glass Web; The Golden Blade; The Incredible Shrinking Man; I Saw What You Did (1965); It Came From Outer Space; I've Lived Before; The Land Unknown; Man Of A Thousand Faces; The Mole People; The Monolith Monsters; The Night Walker; Revenge Of The Creature; Son Of Ali Baba; Spy Hunt; Step Down To Terror; The Strange Door; Tarantula; The Thing That Couldn't Die; This Island Earth; The Treasure Of Lost Canyon*
Gershman, Gerry (mus): *Freeway*
Gershom Parkington Quintet, The (act): *Death At Broadcasting House*
Gershon, Gina (act): *Touch, Voodoo Dawn*
Gershuny, Theodore (dir & wri): *Kemek; Silent Night, Bloody Night*
Gershwin, Ira (mus, 1896-1983): *Lady In The Dark*
Gerson, Betty Lou (act): *The Fly (1958)*
Gerson, Jeanne (act): *The Bride And The Beast; She-Gods Of Shark Reef*
Gerstad, Merritt (B.) (cin): *The Bridge Of San Luis Rey (1929); Bulldog Drummond's Secret Police; Freaks; London After Midnight; The Man Who Reclaimed His Head; Mockery; The Road To Mandalay; The Thirteenth Chair (1929); The Unknown (1927)*
Gerstein, Ellen (act): *I'm Dangerous Tonight; It Came Upon The Midnight Clear*
Gerstle, Frank (act): *Killers From Space; The Magnetic Monster; Monstrosity*
Gerstner, Dr. Hermann (wri): *The Wonderful World Of The Brothers Grimm*
Gerston, Randy (mus): *Strange Days*
Gertie the Rat (animal act): *The Tomb*
Gertsman, Maury (cin, b. 1910): *The Brute Man; The Creature Walks Among Us; Dressed To Kill (1946); The Four Skulls Of Jonathan Drake; The Glass Web; The Golden Blade; House Of Horrors (1946); How To Make A Monster; I've Lived Before; Invisible Invaders; It Grows On Trees; Jungle Captive; She-Wolf Of London; Son Of Ali Baba; Strange Confession; Terror By Night; You Never Can Tell*
Gertz, Irving (mus, b. 1915): *The Alligator People; The Bandits Of Corsica; The Curse Of The Undead; Jungle Goddess; The Leech Woman; The White Goddess; The Wizard Of Baghdad*
Gertz, Jami (act, b. 1966): *The Lost Boys; Solarbabies; Twister*
Gervasone, Ana (act): *Hundra*
Gesner, Zen (act): *Wish Me Luck*
Gessner, Nicolas (dir): *The Little Girl Who Lives Down The Lane; Quelqu'un Derriere La Porte*
Gessner, Nicolas (wri): *Quelqu'un Derriere La Porte*
Gester, Stan (act): *Rymdinvasion I Lappland*
Getcher, J.R. (act): *Mutants In Paradise*
Geter, Leo (act): *Silent Night, Deadly Night*
Getty, Alexander (act): *The Devil's Wedding Night*
Getty, Balthazar (act): *Judge Dredd; Lord Of The Flies (1993); Lost Highway*
Getty, Estelle (act, b. 1923): *Mannequin*
Getz, John (act): *Blood Simple; The Fly (1986); The Fly II; Killer Bees; Tattoo*
Getz, Lorry (act): *Rana: The Legend Of Shadow Lake*
Getz, Robert (act): *Bram Stoker's Dracula*
Ghadban, Alle (act): *Prom Night IV: Deliver Us From Evil*
Ghaffari, Earl (wri): *The Kindred*
Ghaffari, John (act): *Hundra*
Ghazal, Aziz (wri): *Zombie High*
Gherzo, Paul (dir): *Fatal Journey*
Ghia, Dana (act): *Seven Deaths In The Cat's Eye*
Ghiglia, Benedetto (mus): *Secret Agent Superdragon*
Ghostley, Alice (act): *Blue Sunshine*
Giachino, Stacey (wri): *Pranks*
Giacobini, Franco (act): *Operation Kid Brother*
Giafalio, Carl Nick (act): *The Incredible Hulk Returns*
Giagnoni, Piero (act): *Land Of The Pharaohs*
Gialanella, Victor (wri): *Frankenstein (1984)*
Giambalvo, Louis (act): *Bad Dreams*
Giammarco, Terese (act): *The Coming*
Gian, Joey (act): *The Night Stalker (1987)*
Gianasi, Rick (act): *Mutant Hunt*
Giannelli, Steve (act): *Stargate*
Gianni, Branduani (act): *Miracle In Milan*
Giannini, Christian (act): *Impulse (1984)*
Giannini, Giancarlo (act, b. 1942): *The Black Belly Of The Tarantula*
Giannone, Joe (dir & wri): *Madman*
Giannoni, Marco (act): *The Great Alligator*
Gianopoulos, David (act): *Candyman: Farewell To The Flesh*
Gianta, Nick (act): *Street Trash*
Gianviti, Roberto (wri): *A Lizard In A Woman's Skin; Maciste, L'eroe Piu Grande Del Mondo; Psycosissimo; Sword Of The Conqueror; Il Trionfo Di Ercole*
Gibb, Alan (act): *Time Flyer*
Gibb, Cynthia (act): *Jack's Back; Short Circuit 2; Volcano: Fire On The Mountain*
Gibb, Donald (act): *Transylvania 6-5000*
Gibb, Hunter (act): *Mad Max*
Gibb, James (act): *Black Angel (1980)*
Gibb, Ken (cin): *The House Of The Dead*
Gibbel, Ken (act): *The Octagon; Time Walker*
Gibbins, Duncan (dir & wri, 1952-1993): *Eve Of Destruction*
Gibboney, Kathie (act): *The House Of The Dead*
Gibbons, Cedric (dir, 1893-1960): *Tarzan And His Mate*
Gibbons, Edward Peter (act): *Invasion Of The Saucer Men*
Gibbons, Leeza (act, b. 1957): *RoboCop; RoboCop 2*
Gibbons, Robert (act): *Death At Love House*
Gibbons, Rodney (cin): *My Bloody Valentine; Screamers (1996)*
Gibbons, Sandy (act): *The Gifted One*
Gibbs, Angela (act): *Party Line*
Gibbs, Anne (act): *Dear, Dead Delilah*
Gibbs, Frank (act): *An American Christmas Carol*
Gibbs, George (cin): *Alien 3; Brazil; Labyrinth (1986)*
Gibbs, Gerald (cin, b. 1910): *Curse Of Simba; The Green Man; The Intimate Stranger; The Man Upstairs; Quatermass II; X... The Unknown*
Gibbs, Janet (act): *The Entity*
Gibbs, Katherine (act): see Francis, Kay
Gibbs, Louis (act): *James Tont: Operation Goldsinger*
Gibbs, Marla (act): *The Meteor Man*
Gibbs, Michael (mus): *Madame Sin*
Gibbs, Nigel (act): *Ghost In The Machine*
Gibbs, Philip Hamilton (wri): *Darkened Rooms*
Gibbs, Roberta (act): *No. 1 Of The Secret Service*
Gibbs, Sheila Shand (act): *A Lady Mislaid; Mr. Denning Drives North; The Seven-Per-Cent Solution*
Gibbs, Timothy (act): *The Kindred*

Giblyn, Charles (act): The Mysterious Dr. Fu Manchu
Gibmeyer, Fred (act): Nightbeast
Gibney, Barbara (act): Mutants In Paradise
Gibney, David (mus): Superstition
Gibney, Rebecca (act): Dark Of The Night
Gibney, Sheridan (wri, b. 1903): The Locket
Gibney, Susan (act): And You Thought Your Parents Were Weird
Gibson, Alan (dir): Crescendo; Dracula A.D. 1972; Journey To Midnight; Murder In Mind; The Satanic Rites Of Dracula
Gibson, Beau (act): The Hidden
Gibson, Billie (act): The Shining
Gibson, Brian (dir): Poltergeist II: The Other Side
Gibson, Cal (act): Something Is Out There
Gibson, Derek (act): Vampire's Kiss
Gibson, Donal (act): The Punisher
Gibson, Doug (act): Dead Dudes In The House
Gibson, H. Edmund (cin): Barracuda
Gibson, Henry (act, b. 1935): Brenda Starr (1992); The 'Burbs; Gremlins 2: The New Batch; The Incredible Shrinking Woman; Innerspace; Monster In The Closet; The New, Original Wonder Woman; The Nutty Professor (1963)
Gibson, Hoot (act): Flight To Nowhere
Gibson, Judith (act): Return Of The Ape Man
Gibson, Julia (act): Android
Gibson, Kenneth (act): The Thin Man
Gibson, Lois (wri): Crypt Of The Living Dead
Gibson, Mary Ann (act): The Shaggy D.A.
Gibson, Mel (act, b. 1956): Forever Young; Hamlet (1990); Mad Max; Mad Max Beyond Thunderdome; The Road Warrior
Gibson, Mimi (act): The Monster That Challenged The World; The Three Faces Of Eve
Gibson, Paul (cin): The Refrigerator
Gibson, Sarah (act): Jane Eyre (1970)
Gibson, Thomas (act): Night Visitors
Gibson, William (wri): Johnny Mnemonic
Gibson, Wynne (act, b. 1889): The Falcon Strikes Back
Gicca, Fulvio (wri): Sandokan The Great
Gidding, Nelson (wri, b. 1915): The Andromeda Strain; Beyond The Poseidon Adventure; The Haunting; Skullduggery
Gideon, Bond (act): Gold Of The Amazon Women
Gideon, Conroy (act): Star Trek III: The Search For Spock
Gideon, Lee (act): D.O.A. (1988)
Gideon, Raynold (wri): Cutthroat Island; Starman
Gidley, Pamela (act): Cherry 2000; The Crew; Disturbed
Gieb, Joe (act): Weird Science
Giehse, Therese (act): The Mark Of Cain
Gielgud, Irwin (wri): Amazon Quest
Gielgud, (Sir) John (act, b. 1904): Around The World In 80 Days; Assignment To Kill; The Canterville Ghost (1986); The Clue Of The New Pin (1929); First Knight; Frankenstein (1984); Frankenstein: The True Story; Gulliver's Travels (1996); Hamlet (1996); The Hunchback Of Notre Dame (1982); Lost Horizon (1973); The Loved One; Murder By Decree; Murder On The Orient Express; Probe; Prospero's Books; Richard III (1955); The Secret Agent (1936); Sphinx (1981)
Gielgud, Val (act & wri): Death At Broadcasting House
Gierasch, Stefan (act): Blood Beach; Carrie; Spellbinder; Stunts Unlimited
Gierman, Fred (act): Calling Dr. Death; The Strange Death Of Adolf Hitler
Giese, Therese (act): Black Moon (1975)
Gieske, Paul (act): The Lift
Gifford, Alan (act, b. 1905): Devil Doll (1963); Hour Of Decision; Phase IV; The Road To Hong Kong; Satellite In The Sky; Screaming Mimi; 2001: A Space Odyssey; Zex
Gifford, Frances (act): The Remarkable Andrew; Tarzan Triumphs
Gifford, Gloria (act): Halloween II; Vice Versa (1988)
Gifford, Wendy (act): The Medusa Touch
Giftos, Elaine (act): Crackle Of Death; Gas-S-S-S!; On A Clear Day You Can See Forever; Through The Magic Pyramid
Gigante, Elio (act): Satyricon
Gigante, Marcello (mus): El Castello Dell'orrore
Gigante, Tony (act): Metamorphosis: The Alien Factor
Giglio, Sandro (act): Second Chance; The War Of The Worlds; When Worlds Collide
Gignoux, Hubert (act): Perceval
Gil, Arturo (act): Leprechaun 2; The Munsters' Scary Little Christmas
Gil, Joane A. (wri): Deja Vu
Gil, Vicente (act): Anguish
Gil, Vince (act): Encounter At Raven's Gate; Mad Max
Gilan, Yvonne (act): Agatha
Gilb, Leslie (act): Lemora, The Lady Dracula
Gilbert, Anthony (wri): Candles At Nine
Gilbert, Arthur (dir): The Mystery Of Edwin Drood (1909)
Gilbert, Ben (act): The Power (1980)
Gilbert, Billy (act, 1894-1971): Arabian Nights; Bride Of Vengeance; Crazy House (1943); Five Weeks In A Balloon; Ghost Crazy; The Villain Still Pursued Her
Gilbert, Brian (dir): Vice Versa (1988)
Gilbert, Carolyn (act): The Incredible 2-Headed Transplant
Gilbert, Cicely (act): The Rajah's Revenge
Gilbert, David (act): Vampire At Midnight
Gilbert, Eugenia (act): The Man From Downing Street
Gilbert, Florence (act): The Return Of Peter Grimm (1926)
Gilbert, Gordon (act): Children Shouldn't Play With Dead Things
Gilbert, Gregory (act): Frankenhooker
Gilbert, Helen (act): Beyond The Blue Horizon; The Falcon Takes Over; Girls In Prison; Thief Of Damascus
Gilbert, Henry (act): Long John Silver; The Return Of Mr. Moto
Gilbert, Herschel Burke (mus): Beyond A Reasonable Doubt; Crime And Punishment, U.S.A.; I Dismember Mama; Nightmare (1956); Project Moon Base; The Scarf; Witness To Murder
Gilbert, J. Renee (act): The Devil's Gift
Gilbert, Jack (act): While Paris Sleeps
Gilbert Jo(anne) (act): Houdini; Hurricane Island; On The Threshold Of Space
Gilbert, Jody (act, 1915-1979): Shadow Of The Thin Man; Willard
Gilbert, John (Can act): Rabid
Gilbert, John (USA act, 1897-1936): He Who Gets Slapped; Monte Cristo
Gilbert, Lauren (act): Westworld
Gilbert, Lee (act): The Kidnapped King
Gilbert, Lewis (act): The Hound Of The Baskervilles (1921); The House Of Peril; The Sons Of Satan
Gilbert, Lewis (dir, b. 1920): Cosh Boy; Moonraker; Scarlet Thread; The Spy Who Loved Me; You Only Live Twice
Gilbert, Lewis (wri, b. 1920): Cosh Boy
Gilbert, Lou (act, 1909-1978): Fearless Frank; Giulietta Degli Spiriti; Goldstein; Marathon Man
Gilbert, Marcus (act): A Ghost In Monte Carlo; Tennis Court
Gilbert, Melissa (act): see Gilbert-Brinkman
Gilbert, Mickey (act): Ghost In The Machine; The Intruder Within; The Prisoner Of Zenda (1979)
Gilbert, Nina (act): Nightmare Alley
Gilbert, Pamela (act): The Alien Within; Demonwarp
Gilbert, Paul (act, b. 1924, nee Paul MacMahon): Women Of The Prehistoric Planet
Gilbert, Philip (act): Fanatic
Gilbert, Philip (dir): Blood And Lace
Gilbert, Stephen (wri, b. 1912): Ben; Willard
Gilbert, Taylor (act): Torment (1986); Twister
Gilbert, Ted (act): Blink
Gilbert, Tim (act): Timestalkers
Gilbert, Virginia (act): Beverly Hills Bodysnatchers
Gilbert, Yvonne (act): 2000 Maniacs
Gilbert-Brinkman, Melissa (act, b. 1964): Donor; House Of Secrets (1993)
Gilbert-Hill, Richard (act): Running Against Time
Gilbey, Harry (act): At The Foot Of The Scaffold; The Chimes; The Confession; Creatures Of Clay; The Dead Heart; The Incorruptible Crown; The Man Behind "The Times"; The Man With The Scar; On The Brink Of The Precipice; Partners In Crime; The Tragedy Of Basil Grieve
Gilbreth, Phil (act): Zapped!
Gilbride, Joe (act): The Hidden
Gilchrist, Connie (act, 1902-1985): Houdini; Long John Silver; The Monkey's Uncle; Song Of The Thin Man; The Thin Man Goes Home; Two On A Guillotine
Gilchrist, James (act): The Power (1980)
Gilden, Richard (act): The Unknown Terror
Gilder, Colin (act): Enemy Mine
Gildin, Ken (act): Total Recall
Giler, Bernie (wri): Tarzan's Greatest Adventure; Tarzan The Magnificent
Giler, David (dir): The Black Bird (1975)
Giler, David (wri): Alien; Alien 3; The Black Bird (1975)
Giles, Marleta (act): Blood Beach
Giles, Nancy (act): Secrets In The Attic
Giles, Sandra (act): Are You In The House Alone?
Gilford, Gwynne (act): Beware! The Blob; Fade To Black; Satan's School For Girls
Gilford, Jack (act, 1907-1990): Caveman (1981); Cocoon; Cocoon: The Return; They Might Be Giants
Gilgreen, John (act): The Aliens Are Coming
Gili, Gustavo (act): Anguish
Gilinsky, William (act): The Outing
Gill, Basil (act): The Crimson Circle (1936); High Treason (1929); Knight Without Armour; The Rocks Of Valpre; The Wandering Jew (1933)
Gill, Beverly (act): Haunts Of The Very Rich; Scream, Blacula, Scream; Soylent Green; Wonder Woman
Gill, Elizabeth (act): Not Of This World
Gill, Gwenllian (act): White Lilac
Gill, Helen (act): At The Earth's Core
Gill, Inga (act): Det Sjunde Inseglet
Gill, John (act): Night Must Fall (1964); Zeppelin
Gill, Manuel (act): Lo Strano Caso Della Signora Ward
Gill, Maud (act): The Crime At Blossoms
Gill, Philippa (act): The Perfect Woman
Gill, Robert (mus): The Golden Mask
Gill, Tom (act): Mr. Drake's Duck
Gill Jr., Will (act): Chopping Mall
Gillam, Reg (act): Color Me Dead
Gillam, Reginald (act): A Witch Without A Broom
Gillard, Nick (act): Roger Corman's 'Frankenstein Unbound'
Gillard, Stuart (act): The Neptune Factor; Virus
Gillen, Arlene (act): Deranged (1974)
Gillen, Jeff (dir): Deranged (1974)
Gillen, Jeffrey (act): Children Shouldn't Play With Dead Things
Gillen, Jim (act): Crack In The World
Giller, Walter (act): The Burning Court; Superwheels
Gilles, Mike (act): The Outing
Gillespie, (A.) Arnold (cin, b. 1899): Atlantis, The Lost Continent; The Beginning Or The End?; Forbidden Planet; Tarzan's New York Adventure; The Wizard Of Oz (1939)
Gillespie, Dana (act): The Hound Of The Baskervilles (1978); The People That Time Forgot; Uncharted Sea
Gillespie, Gina (act): What Ever Happened To Baby Jane? (1962)
Gillespie, Robert (act): At The Earth's Core; Otley
Gillet, Chris (act): Starship Invasions
Gillet, Rachel (act): L'ange De Noel; Le Petit Chaperon Rouge
Gillett, Chris (act): Darkman II: The Return Of Durant
Gillett, Debra (act): The Witches (1990)
Gillett, Jane Goodnow (act): The Invisible Man (1975)
Gillette, Anita (act): It Happened At Lake Wood Manor
Gillette, Betty (act): The Falcon's Alibi
Gillette, Robert (act): Flight Of The Lost Balloon
Gillette, Ruth (act): The Shaggy D.A.; The Spanish Cape Mystery
Gillette, Warrington (act): Friday The 13th-Part 2; Time Walker
Gilley, Carol (act): Zontar: The Thing From Venus
Gillham, Ron (act): Strange Invaders
Gilli, Luciana (act): Conqueror Of Atlantis; Temple Of A Thousand Lights
Gilliam, David (act): Frogs
Gilliam, Dawn (act): Tales From The Hood
Gilliam, Holly (act): Brazil
Gilliam, Stu (act): The Devil And Max Devlin; Dr. Black Mr. Hyde
Gilliam, Terry (act): Monty Python And The Holy Grail
Gilliam, Terry (dir): The Adventures Of Baron Munchausen (1989); Brazil; Jabberwocky; Monty Python And The Holy Grail; Time Bandits; 12 Monkeys
Gilliam, Terry (wri): The Adventures Of Baron Munchausen (1989); Brazil; Jabberwocky; Monty Python And The Holy Grail; Time Bandits
Gilliat, Sidney (dir, b. 1908): Endless Night; Green For Danger; State Secret
Gilliat, Sidney (wri, b. 1908): Bulldog Jack; Chu Chin Chow (1934); Endless Night; The Gaunt Stranger; Gestapo; The Girl In The News; Green For Danger; The Green Man; Jamaica Inn (1939); The Lady Vanishes (1938 & 1979); The Man Who Changed His Mind; State Secret
Gillick, John (act & wri): I Was A Zombie For The F.B.I.
Gillie, Jean (act): Decoy; The Saint Meets The Tiger; The Spider (1939)
Gillies, Fiona (act): Frankenstein (1993)
Gillies, Jacques (wri): Cash On Demand
Gillies, Max (act): The Cars That Ate Paris
Gilliland, John (act): Mutants In Paradise
Gilliland, Richard (act): Bug
Gillin, Hugh (act): Doin' Time On Planet Earth; Elvira, Mistress Of The Dark; Psycho II; Psycho III; Time Flyer
Gillin, Linda (act): Final Eye; The Folks At Red Wolf Inn
Gilling, John (dir, 1910-1984): The Brigand Of Kandahar; Escape From Broadmoor; The Flesh And The Fiends; Fury At Smugglers' Bay; The Gamma People; The Man Inside; Mother Riley Meets The Vampire; The Mummy's Shroud; Night Caller From Outer Space; No Trace; The Pirates Of Blood River; The Plague Of The Zombies; The Scarlet Blade; The Shadow Of The Cat; The Voice Of Merrill; Where The Bullets Fly
Gilling, John (wri, 1910-1984): The Brigand Of Kandahar; Dark Interval; Escape From Broadmoor; The Flesh And The Fiends; Fury At Smugglers' Bay; The Gamma People; A Ghost For Sale; The Gorgon; The Greed Of William Hart; Guilt Is My Shadow; House Of Darkness; The Lost Hours; The Man In Black; The Man Inside; The Mummy's Shroud; Murder At Scotland Yard; Murder At The Grange; No Trace; The Pirates Of Blood River; Room To Let; The Scarlet Blade; The Secret Of Blood Island; The Steel Key; The Voice Of Merrill; Whispering Smith Hits London
Gillingham, Kim (act): Captain America (1992)
Gillingwater, Claude (act, 1870-1939): The Gorilla (1927); Green Eyes
Gillis, Alec (act): Alien Nation
Gillis, Ann (act, b. 1927, nee Alma O'Connor): The Time Of Their Lives
Gillis, Jackson (wri): Time Travelers (1976)
Gillis, Jamie (act): Night Of The Zombies (1981)
Gillis, Jim (act): A Return To Salem's Lot
Gullis, Philip A. (act): Darkman (1990)
Gillis, Richard (mus): The Bees; Demonoid
Gillmer, Reuben (wri): A Fight For Life; Hamlet (1915); The House Opposite (1917); Queen Of My Heart; The Sands Of Time; The Terrible 'Tec; To Let
Gilmain, Janice (act): Rocket Attack U.S.A.
Gilman, Sam (act): The Tribe
Gilmer, Pauline (act): The Blue Bird (1910)
Gilmore, Andrew (act): Mad Max
Gilmore, Denis (act): Fahrenheit 451; Psychomania (1972); The Three Lives Of Thomasina; The Tomb Of Ligeia
Gilmore, Jerry (act): Stargate
Gilmore, Lowell (act, b. 1907): Androcles And The Lion; Dream Girl; Francis Covers The Big Town; King Solomon's Mines (1949); The Picture Of Dorian Gray (1945); Rogues Of Sherwood Forest
Gilmore, Peter (act): The Abominable Dr. Phibes; Warlords Of The Deep
Gilmore, Sally (act): Theater Of Blood
Gilmore, Scott (act): Nightbreed
Gilmore, Stuart (dir): Captive Women
Gilmore, Virginia (act, 1919-1986): The Loves Of Edgar Allan Poe
Gilmore, Wendy (act): Schizo (1977)
Gilmour, Sally (act): All Hallowe'en
Gilpin, April (act): Earthbound (1981); Jaws 2
Gilpin, John (act): Theater Of Blood
Gilpin, Marc (act): Earthbound (1981); Jaws 2
Gilpin, Toni (act): The Gorgon; The Mummy's Shroud
Gilreath, Paul (mus): Making Contact
Gilroy, Dan (act): Mother Goose Rock 'N' Rhyme
Gilroy, Dan (wri): Freejack
Gilroy, Gabrielle (act): St. Elmo
Gilroy, Patrick (act): Spookies
Gilroy, Tony (wri): Dolores Claiborne; Extreme Measures
Giltinian, Donal (wri): Dead Man's Chest
Gimbel, Norman (mus): The Man In The Santa Claus Suit
Gimello, Jean (act): Castle Keep
Gimeno, Nuria (act): A Bell From Hell
Gimpel, Sandra (Lee) (act): Night Of The Comet; Time Flyer
Gimpera, Teresa (act): Crypt Of The Living Dead
Ginever, Aveling (dir): A Dickensian Fantasy

Ging, Jack (act, b. 1932): *The Ghost Of Dragstrip Hollow; Play Misty For Me; Sssssss*
Gingell, George (act): *Kiss Of The Tarantula*
Gingold, Hermione (act, 1897-1987): *Bell, Book And Candle; Cosh Boy; Munster, Go Home!; The Naked Edge; Someone At The Door; Those Fantastic Flying Fools*
Ginnaven, Bob (act): *The Day It Came To Earth; So Sad About Gloria*
Ginsberg, Allen (act, 1926-1997): *Chappaqua*
Ginsberg, Donald (wri): *The Clouded Crystal; Tread Softly*
Ginsberg, Marc Allan (act): *The Toxic Avenger, Part II*
Ginsberg, Milton Moses (dir & wri): *Werewolf Of Washington*
Ginsburg, Al (act): *Witches' Brew*
Ginter, Brad F. (dir & wri): *Flesh Feast*
Ginther, Brad (act): *The Being*
Ginty, Robert (act, b. 1948): *The Alchemist; Programmed To Kill; Warriors Of The Wasteland*
Ginzburg, Alexander (wri): *Cinderella (1961)*
Gioielli, Lorenzo (act): *Demons 2*
Giombrini, Marcel(lo) (mus): *The Eyes Behind The Stars; Murder Mansion; War Of The Planets*
Giono, Jean (wri): *La Poursuite*
Gionta, Nick (act): *Spookies*
Giordana, Carlo (act): *Satyricon*
Giordano, Aldo (cin): *Atom Age Vampire; The Minotaur*
Giordano, Daniela (act): *The Girl In Room 2a*
Giordano, Domiziana (act): *Interview With The Vampire*
Giordano, Mariangela (act): *La Setta*
Giorgi, Eleonora (act): *Inferno (1979)*
Giorgio, Bill (act): *Attack Of The Puppet People; The Spider (1958); War Of The Colossal Beast*
Giosa, Sue (act): *The First Power*
Giovana (act): *El Amor Brujo (1986)*
Giovanni, Paul (mus): *The Wicker Man*
Giovannini, Giorgio (act): *Gli Invasori*
Giovannini, Maria (act): *L'ultima Preda Del Vampiro*
Gipps-Kent, Simon (act): *Great Expectations (1974)*
Giraci, May (act): *Jungle Trail Of The Son Of Tarzan; Lorna Doone (1922)*
Giraldi, Jill (act): *The Omega Man*
Girard, Bernard (dir, b. 1929): *The Mad Room; The Mind Snatchers*
Girard, Bernard (wri, b. 1929): *The Mad Room*
Girard, Gabrielle (act): see Delorme, Daniele
Girard, J.W. (act): *Just Imagine*
Girard, Joseph (W.) (act): *The Clutching Hand; The Terror (1928)*
Girard, Michael (act): *Princess Warrior*
Girard, Michael Paul (dir, mus & wri): *Getting Lucky*
Girard, Renee (act): *The Uncanny*
Girardin, Ray (act): *Midnight Offerings*
Girardon, Michele (act): *Devil Of The Desert Against The Son Of Hercules*
Girardot, Annie (act, b. 1931): *Dear Detective; La Donna Scimmia; The Gentle Art Of Murder; Speaking Of Murder; Traitement De Choc; Le Vice Et La Vertu*
Girardot, Etienne (act, 1856-1939): *The Dragon Murder Case; The Garden Murder Case; The Hunchback Of Notre Dame (1939); The Kennel Murder Case*
Giraud, Claude (act): *La Poursuite*
Giraud, Jean Mobius (wri): *Little Nemo: Adventures In Slumberland*
Giraud, Roland (act): *Mr. Frost*
Giraut, Leila (act): *From Russia With Love*
Girdler, William (dir): *Abby; Asylum Of Satan; Day Of The Animals; Grizzly; The Manitou; Three On A Meathook*
Girdler, William (wri): *Abby, Asylum Of Satan; The Manitou; Three On A Meathook*
Girling, Cindy (act): *Castle Rock; The Kidnapping Of The President*
Girlschool (mus): *Zombie Nightmare*
Girod, Francois (dir & wri): *Le Trio Infernal*
Girolami, Enio (act): *Johnny Hamlet*
Girolami, Mario (dir): *My Friend, Dr. Jekyll*
Girolani, Bob (act): *Rabid*
Girotti, Mario (act, b. 1941, a.k.a. Terence Hill): *The Nibelungs (1966); Super Fuzz; The Wonders Of Aladdin*
Girotti, Massimo (act, b. 1918): *Giants Of Thessaly; Gold For The Caesars; Gli Orrori Del Castello Di Noremberga; The Red Tent; Romolo E Remo; Il Segreto Delle Tre Punte; Sins Of Rome*
Giroux, Jackelyn/Jackie (act): *Distortions; Trick [illegible]*
Giroux, Lee (act): *The Resurrection Of Zachary Wheeler*
Girvin, Richard A. (mus): *The Alpha Incident*
Gish, Dorothy (act, 1898-1968, nee Dorothy De Guiche): *The Avenging Conscience*
Gish, Lillian (act, 1894-1993, nee Lillian De Guiche): *Daphne And The Pirate; The Night Of The Hunter (1955); Portrait Of Jennie; The Scarlet Letter (1926)*
Gish, Sheila (act): *Highlander; Hitler: The Last Ten Days*
Gist, Robert (act): *Jack The Giant Killer; Strangers On A Train*
Gist, Rod (act): *Deadly Messages*
Gitonga, Jackson (act): *Congo*
Gittelson, June (act): *The Mark Of The Vampire (1935)*
Gittens, Wyndham (wri): *Lorna Doone (1922)*
Giuffre, Aldo (act): *The Flower In His Mouth; Ghosts-Italian Style; When Women Had Tails*
Giuffria, April (act): *Earth Girls Are Easy*
Giurato, Blasco (cin): *Escape From The Bronx*
Giustini, Carlo (act): *I Criminali Della Galassia*
Given, Eddy H. (wri): *Maciste Al Inferno*
Givens, Jack (act): *Night Of The Living Dead (1968)*
Givens, Robin (act): *A Face To Die For; The Penthouse (1989)*
Givney, Kathryn (act, 1896-1978): *Lightning Strikes Twice*
Givot, George (act, b. 1903): *The Falcon And The Co-Eds*
Gizzi, Claudio (mus): *Frankenstein (1974)*
Gizzi, Loris (act): *Teodora, Imperatrice Di Bisanzio*
Gl, Vincent (act): *The Day After Halloween*
Glabov, Yevgeny (mus): *The Savage Hunt Of King Stakh*
Glaccum, Joy (act): *The Children*
Gladstein, Richard N. (act): *Silent Night, Deadly Night III; Silent Night, Deadly Night 4: Initiation*
Gladstone, Dana (act): *I Saw What You Did (1988)*
Gladstone, Emile (act): *Waxwork II: Lost In Time*
Gladstone, John (dir): *Discipline*
Gladstone, Steve (act): *Flesh-Eating Mothers*
Gladwell, David (dir & wri): *Memoirs Of A Survivor*
Gladwin, Joe (act): *The Mind Of Mr. Soames; Night Must Fall (1964); Work Is A Four Letter Word*
Glaister, Gerard (dir): *The Clue Of The Silver Key*
Glambra, Joey (act): *Tuck Everlasting*
Glanzmann, Ray (act): *Ghostbusters II; Wes Craven's New Nightmare*
Glas, Uschi (act): *The Ape Creature*
Glascow, Gil (act): *Screams Of A Winter Night*
Glaser, Ariane (act): *13 Frightened Girls*
Glaser, Bunny (act): *Orgy Of The Dead (1965)*
Glaser, Caroline (act): *The Trollenberg Terror*
Glaser, Jake (act): *Kazaam*
Glaser, Paul Michael (act, b. 1943): *The Great Houdinis; Phobia*
Glaser, Paul Michael (dir, b. 1943): *Amazons (1984); Kazaam; The Running Man*
Glaser, Vaughan (act): *Arsenic And Old Lace*
Glasner, Christine (act): *The Fifth Musketeer*
Glass, Everett (act): *Flight To Mars; Invasion Of The Body Snatchers (1956); World Without End*
Glass, Gaston (act): *The Clutching Hand; The Gorilla (1927); Monte Cristo*
Glass, Jack (R.) (cin): *The Lost Missile; The Magnetic Monster; Two Lost Worlds*
Glass, Michael (act): *Demon Seed*
Glass, Ned (act, 1906-1984): *The Adventures Of Nick Carter; Back From The Dead; Dick Tracy Returns; Experiment In Terror; Fright (1957); Jennifer (1953); North By Northwest; The War Of The Worlds*
Glass, Paul (act): *Bunny Lake Is Missing; Nightmare In The Sun; To The Devil A Daughter*
Glass, Philip (mus): *Candyman; Candyman: Farewell To The Flesh; The Secret Agent (1996)*
Glass, Robert (wri): *Death Dreams; Not Of This World; Running Against Time*
Glass, Ron (act, b. 1945): *Deep Space*
Glass, Seamon (act): *This Is Not A Test*
Glass, Tom (act): *Timecop*
Glassberg, Irving (cin): *The Black Castle, The Black Shield Of Falworth; Francis; Francis Goes To The Races; Francis Joins The Wacs; Spy Hunt; The Strange Door; The Web*
Glasse, Kayce (act): *Forever Evil*
Glasser, Albert (mus, b. 1916): *The Amazing Colossal Man; Attack Of The Puppet People; The Beginning Of The End; The Boy And The Pirates; Confessions Of An Opium Eater; The Cremators; The Cyclops; Giant From The Unknown; Indestructible Man; Invasion U.S.A.; The Monster Maker (1943); The Neanderthal Man; Port Sinister; Rocketship X-M; Teenage Cave Man; Tormented (1960); The Viking Women And The Sea Serpent; War Of The Colossal Beast*
Glasser, Isabel (act): *Forever Young; The Surgeon*
Glasser, Phillip (act): *A Troll In Central Park*
Glassman, A.J. (act): *Sleepstalker*
Glassmire, Gus (act): *The Living Ghost (1942)*
Glaudini, Robert (act): *The Alchemist; Parasite; Wavelength*
Glaum, Louise (act): *The Lone Wolf's Daughter (1919)*
Glave, Matthew (act): *Ghost In The Machine*
Glazer, Benjamin (wri): *Mata Hari (1932); Paris Calling*
Glazer, Charles (act): *Vampire On Bikini Beach*
Glazer, Eugene Robert (act): *Eve Of Destruction*
Glazer, Mitch (wri): *Scrooged*
Glazier, Gene (act): *The Clonus Horror*
Glazman, James (act): *You'll Like My Mother*
Gleaming Spires, The (mus): *School Spirit*
Gleason, Colin (act): *The Pink Chiquitas*
Gleason, James (act, 1886-1959): *Arsenic And Old Lace; The Bishop's Wife; A Date With The Falcon; Down To Earth; The Falcon Takes Over; Forty Naughty Girls; A Guy Named Joe; Here Comes Mr. Jordan; Murder On A Bridle Path; Murder On A Honeymoon; Murder On The Blackboard; The Night Of The Hunter (1955); Once Upon A Time (1944); The Penguin Pool Murder; The Plot Thickens; The Return Of October*
Gleason, James (1990s act): *Jason Goes To Hell: The Final Friday*
Gleason, Lucile (act): *The Gay Falcon*
Gleason, Paul (act): *Doc Savage, The Man Of Bronze; Ewoks: The Battle For Endor; He Knows You're Alone; Wishman*
Gleason, Russell (act): *Condemned To Live*
Gleason-Kennedy, Carrie (act): *The Pink Chiquitas*
Gleckler, Robert (act): *Bulldog Drummond's Revenge; Dante's Inferno (1935)*
Gledhill, Karen (act): *Paperhouse*
Gleen, Montgomery (act): *La Danza Macabra; Raptus*
Gleeson, Patrick (act): *Flatliners*
Gleeson, Redmond (act): *Dreamscape; The Octagon*
Gleise, Rochus (dir): *Der Golem Und Die Tanzerin*
Glen, Edward (act): *Odin: Photon Space Sailor Starlight*
Glen, John (dir): *For Your Eyes Only; Licence To Kill (1989); The Living Daylights; Octopussy; A View To A Kill*
Glendenning, Candace (act): *The Flesh And Blood Show; Satan's Slave; Tower Of Evil*
Glenn, Carrick (act): *The Burning*
Glenn, Jacqueline (act): *The Projectionist*
Glenn, James M. (act): *Spookies*
Glenn, Raymond (act): *The Return Of Boston Blackie*
Glenn (Sr.), Roy (E.) (act, 1914-1971): *Escape From The Planet Of The Apes; The Golden Idol; Jungle Gents; Killer Leopard*
Glenn, Scott (act): *Gargoyles; Hex; The Keep; Past Tense; Shadowhunter; The Silence Of The Lambs; The Spy Within*
Glennon, Bert (cin, 1893-1967): *Alice In Wonderland (1933); Gabriel Over The White House; House Of Wax; The Mad Magician; The Red House*
Glennon, James (cin): *Flight Of The Navigator*
Glenny, Brian (act): *Sweeney Todd*
Glenwright, Gordon (act): *Inn Of The Damned*
Gless, Sharon (act, b. 1943): *Revenge Of The Stepford Wives*
Glick, James (act): *Grim Prairie Tales*
Glickman, Mort (mus): *Cyclotrode X; Spy Smasher Returns*
Glickman, Paul (cin): *The Stuff*
Gliddon, John (act): *The Sands Of Time*
Glindemann, Ib (mus): *Journey To The Seventh Planet*
Gloag, Helena (act): *Scrooge (1970)*
Gloag, Julian (wri): *Our Mother's House*
Glomb, Anna (act): *Talk About A Stranger*
Gloriani, Tina (act): *L'amante Del Vampiri; Gli Amori Di Ercole*
Glouner, Richard (C.) (cin): *The Awakening Of Candra; Charlie Chan: Happiness Is A Warm Clue; The Dunwich Horror; The Savage Bees*
Glover, Andrew (act): *Strange Behavior*
Glover, Barbara (act): *Curse II: The Bite; The Lightning Incident*
Glover, Brian (act): *Alien 3; An American Werewolf In London; The Company Of Wolves; Jabberwocky; The Mcguffin*
Glover, Bruce (act): *Diamonds Are Forver; Ghost Town; Popcorn; Who Killed Teddy Bear?*
Glover, Christopher (act): *Judge Dredd*
Glover, Crispin (act): *Back To The Future; Friday The 13th-The Final Chapter*
Glover, Danny (act, b. 1947): *Angels In The Outfield (1994); Iceman; Predator 2*
Glover, David (GB act): *Fahrenheit 451*
Glover, David (USA act): *The Toxic Avenger, Part II*
Glover, Don (act): *Halloween 4: The Return Of Michael Myers*
Glover, Edmund (act): *Dick Tracy (1945); The Falcon Out West*
Glover, Edna (act): *Star Trek*
Glover, Fred (act): *Where The Rainbow Ends*
Glover, Gail (act): *Endangered Species*
Glover, John (act): *Gremlins 2: The New Batch; The Incredible Shrinking Woman; In The Mouth Of Madness; Last Embrace; RoboCop 2; Scrooged; What Ever Happened To Baby Jane? (1991)*
Glover, Julian (act, b. 1935): *The Adding Machine; The Alphabet Murders; For Your Eyes Only; Gulliver's Travels (1977); Hitler: The Last Ten Days; Indiana Jones And The Last Crusade; The Magus; Mirror Of Deception; Quatermass And The Pit; Theatre Of Death; Treasure Island (1990); Wuthering Heights (1970)*
Glover, Kevin (act): *Jack's Back*
Glover, Michael (act): *A Clockwork Orange; Superman (1978)*
Glover, Susan (act): *Dr. Jekyll And Ms. Hyde*
Gluckstadt (dir): *The Isle Of The Dead (1913)*
Glueckman, Alan Jay (wri): *Butcher, Baker (Nightmare Maker)*
Gluskin, Lud (mus): *The Return Of Monte Cristo*
Glyn, Celia (act): *The House Opposite (1931)*
Glyn, Elinor (wri): *Such Men Are Dangerous*
Glyn-Jones, John (act): *The Adventures Of Hal 5; Dark Places; Locker 69; Man In The Moon (1960); The Sinister Man*
Glynn, Henry (act): *Above Suspicion*
Glynn, Tamara (act): *Halloween 5: The Revenge Of Michael Myers*
Glynne, Agnes (act): *A Study In Scarlet (1914); A Vagabond's Revenge*
Glynne, Ashley (act): *Mr. H.C. Andersen*
Glynne, Mary (act, 1898-1954): *The Cry For Justice; Flat No. 3; Scrooge (1935)*
Gmur, Leslie (act): *Empire Of Ash III*
Gnass, Fritz (act): *M (1931)*
Gobel, George (act, 1920-1991): *Alice In Wonderland (1985); The Day It Came To Earth; The Invisible Woman (1983)*
Goblin(s), (The) (mus): *Alien Contamination; Dawn Of The Dead; Night Of The Zombies (1983); Profundo Rosso*
Goblirsch, Fritz (act): *The Fifth Musketeer*
Gocha (act): *L'ours*
Gochis, Constantine S. (dir): *The Redeemer*
Gocke, Justin (act): *The Witching Of Ben Wagner*
Gockiman, Al (act): *The Punisher*
Godar, Godfrey (cin): *Howling IV; The London Connection*
Godard, Alain (wri): *Dracula, Pere Et Fils; The Name Of The Rose*
Godard, Jean-Luc (dir & wri, b. 1930): *Alphaville, Une Etrange Aventure De Lemmy Caution; Le Plus Vieux Metier Du Monde*
Godbout, Jacques (cin): *Of Unknown Origin*
Goddard, Alf (act): *Alf's Button (1930); Downhill; The Drum; High Treason (1929); King Solomon's Mines (1937); The Saint Meets The Tiger*
Goddard, Charles W. (wri): *Scared Stiff (1953)*
Goddard, Frederick (dir & wri): *Through The Stormy Waters*
Goddard, Gary (dir): *Masters Of The Universe*
Goddard, Liza (act): *Woof!; Woof Too! A Girl And Her Dog*
Goddard, Mark (act, b. 1936): *Blue Sunshine; Strange Invaders*
Goddard, Paulette (act, 1905-1990, nee Paulette Levy): *Babes In Bagdad; Bride Of Vengeance; The Cat And The Canary (1939); The Ghost Breakers; Modern Times; Sins Of Jezebel; The Stranger Came Home*
Goddard, Willoughby (act): *Gawain And The Green Knight; The Golden Rabbit; Jabberwocky*
Golden, Jimmy (act): *Crime On The Hill, The Dance Of Death; Someone At The Door*
Godden, (Margaret) Rumer (wri, b. 1907): *Black Narcissus*
Godderis, Drew (act): *The Alien Within; [illegible]*
Goddet, Anne-Julia (act): *The Phantom Of The Opera (1990)*
Godee, Ann (act): *Charlie Chan In Rio*

Godet, Danielle (act): *The Elusive Pimpernel (1950)*
Godfrey, Derek (act): *The Abominable Dr. Phibes; Hands Of The Ripper; The Vengeance Of She*
Godfrey, Mary (act): *The House On The Marsh*
Godfrey, Michael (act): *Men Of Sherwood Forest*
Godfrey, Peter (act, 1899-1970): *Dr. Jekyll And Mr. Hyde (1941); Please Murder Me; The Two Mrs. Carrolls*
Godfrey, Peter (dir, 1899-1970): *Cry Wolf (1947); The Decision Of Christopher Blake; The Lone Wolf Spy Hunt; Please Murder Me; The Two Mrs. Carrolls; The Woman In White (1948)*
Godfrey, Philip (wri): *The Black Abbot (1934)*
Godfrey, Renee (act): *Terror By Night*
Godfrey, Terry (act): *The Majorettes*
Godfrey, Tommy (act): *From Beyond The Grave; Straight On Till Morning*
Godin, Maurice (act): *White Room*
Goding, Gittan (act): *Frankenhooker*
Godowsky, Dagmar (act): *The Altar Stairs*
Godoy, Fred (act): *The Lone Wolf In Mexico*
Godreau, Miguel (act): *Altered States*
Godridge, Constance (act): *Murder By Rope*
Godsell, Peter (act): *The Adventures Of Hal 5*
Godsell, Vanda (act, b. 1919): *The Brain Machine; Candidate For Murder; Clash By Night; The Earth Dies Screaming; Hour Of Decision; Konga; The Man Who Was Nobody; The Shadow Of The Cat; Sword Of Sherwood Forest; Who Killed The Cat?; The Wrong Box*
Godsey, Bil (cin): *To All A Goodnight*
Godshall, Liberty (act): *Human Feelings*
Godunov, Alexander (act, 1950-1995): *Waxwork II: Lost In Time*
Godwin, Frank (dir): *The Boy Who Never Was; Electric Eskimo*
Godwin, Frank (wri): *Demons Of The Mind; Electric Eskimo*
Goebbels, Christine (act): *Making Contact*
Goebbels, Michael (act): *Making Contact*
Goelz, David (act): *Labyrinth (1986)*
Goen, Bob (act): *Wicked Stepmother*
Goeppinger, Jim (act): *The Crater Lake Monster*
Goethals, Stanley (act): *Outside The Law*
Goethe, Johann Wolfgang von (wri, 1749-1832): *Faust And The Devil*
Goetz, Peter (Michael) (act): *King Kong Lives; Roger Corman's 'Frankenstein Unbound'; Wolfen*
Goetzke, Bernhard (act): *Doctor Mabuse; Der Mude Tod; Die Nibelungen*
Goff, Greer (act): *Angel Heart*
Goff, Ivan (wri, b. 1910): *The Legend Of The Lone Ranger; Man Of A Thousand Faces; Midnight Lace (1960); Portrait In Black*
Goff, Joanna (act): *The Haunting Of Sarah Hardy*
Goff, John (act): *The Alpha Incident; The Capture Of Bigfoot; Distortions; Grotesque*
Goff, John (wri): *Distortions; Drive-In Massacre; Hundra; The Night Stalker (1987)*
Goffage, John (act): see Rafferty, Chips
Goffe, Rusty (act): *Disciple Of Death*
Goffredo, Sam (act): *Watchers II*
Goggins, Walt (act): *Forever Young*
Gogol, Nikolai Vasilievich (wri, 1809-1852): *The Bespoke Overcoat; La Maschera Del Demonio; The Overcoat; Shinel*
Gohar, Ali (act): *Dawn Of The Mummy*
Goimbault, Odette (act): *Whosoever Shall Offend*
Goins, Jesse (act): *Jekyll And Hyde...Together Again; Robocop*
Gokul (act): *The First Power*
Golan, Gila (act, b. 1940): *Our Man Flint; The Valley Of Gwangi*
Golas, Thaddeus (act): *The Video Dead*
Golburt, Akiba (wri): *The Amphibian Man*
Gold, Brandy (act): *Amityville: The Evil Escapes*
Gold, David (act): *End Of The World (1977)*
Gold, Ernest (mus, b. 1921): *Jennifer (1953); On The Beach; The Screaming Skull; Tarzan's Fight For Life; U.F.O.; Unknown World; Witness For The Prosecution*
Gold, Harry (act): *Carrie*
Gold, Jack (dir, b. 1930): *The Medusa Touch; Who?*
Gold, Jimmy (act): *Alf's Button Afloat; Life Is A Circus*
Gold, Jonathan (act): *Vampire's Kiss*
Gold, Kimberlye (act): *Once Bitten*
Gold, L. Harvey (act): *Fear (1996)*
Gold, Max (act): *Mary Shelley's 'Frankenstein'*
Gold, Myron J. (wri): *The Monitors*
Gold, Robert (cin): *Endgame*
Gold, Ron (act): *Rattlers*
Gold, Teri (act): *Switch*
Gold, Tony (act): *Slugs*
Gold, Travis (act): *Rattlers*
Gold, William (act): *The Murder Clinic*
Goldbeck, Willis (wri, b. 1900): *The Colossus Of New York; Freaks; A Kiss For Cinderella; Murder On The Blackboard; The Penguin Pool Murder; Peter Pan*
Goldberg, Adam (act): *The Prophecy (1995)*
Goldberg, Barry (mus): *Captain America (1992)*
Goldberg, Dan (wri): *Heavy Metal*
Goldberg, Gary (act): *The Alien's Return*
Goldberg, Marcy (act): *I Still Dream Of Jeannie*
Goldberg, Ron (act): *The Toxic Avenger, Part II*
Goldberg, Whoopi (act, b. 1955): *Bogus; Ghost (1990); The Pagemaster; Star Trek: Generations; Theodore Rex*
Goldblatt, Harold (act): *Children Of The Damned; The Mind Benders (1963); The Reluctant Saint; The Scarlet Blade*
Goldblatt, Mark (dir): *Dead Heat; The Punisher*
Goldblatt, Stephen (cin): *Batman And Robin; Batman Forever; Outland; Young Sherlock Holmes*
Goldblum, Jeff (act, b. 1952): *The Adventures Of Buckaroo Banzai; Earth Girls Are Easy; The Fly (1986); Hideaway; Independence Day; Invasion Of The Body Snatchers (1978); Jurassic Park; The Legend Of Sleepy Hollow; The Lost World: Jurassic Park; Mr. Frost; El Mono Loco; Powder; Transylvania 6-5000; Vibes*
Golden, Anne (act): *12 Monkeys*
Golden, John (wri): *Strange Experiment*
Golden, Lee (act): *12 Monkeys*
Golden, Michael (act): *The Black Rider; The Man Without A Body; Murder By Proxy; Pool Of London; Thirty-Six Hours*
Golden, Mildred (act): *The Greene Murder Case*
Golden, Rachel (act): *I Married A Vampire*
Golden, Robert/Bob (act): *Planet Earth; Willard*
Goldenberg, Billy (mus): see Goldenberg, William
Goldenberg, Emmanuel (act): see Robinson, Edward G.
Goldenberg, Jay R. (act): *Switch*
Goldenberg, Karl (act): *The Creeping Terror*
Goldenberg, Mark (mus): *Teen Wolf Too*
Goldenberg, Michael (wri): *Contact*
Goldenberg, William/Billy (mus): *Code Name: Minus One; 18 Again!; Fear No Evil (1969); Future Cop; Night Gallery; Reflections Of Murder; Ritual Of Evil; Search For The Gods; The UFO Incident*
Goldenthal, Elliot (mus): *Alien 3; Batman And Robin; Batman Forever; Demolition Man; Interview With The Vampire; Pet Sematary*
Goldert, Clarence (act): *The Bishop Murder Case*
Goldfinger, Michael (act): *The Goddess Of Love*
Goldie, Michael (act): *Jamaica Inn (1985); Robin Hood: Prince Of Thieves*
Goldie, Wyndham (act): *The Girl In The News; The Strange World Of Planet X*
Goldin, Daniel (wri): *Darkman (1990)*
Goldin, Joshua (wri): *Darkman (1990)*
Goldin, Ricky Paull (act): *The Blob (1988); A Face To Die For; Hyper Sapien: People From Another Star*
Golding, Richard (act): *The Man Inside; The Trollenberg Terror*
Golding, (Sir) William (wri, 1911-1993): *Lord Of The Flies (1963 & 1990)*
Goldman, Carole (act): *Superstition*
Goldman, Danny (act): *Young Frankenstein*
Goldman, Erwin (wri): *Sweet Sixteen*
Goldman, Gary (wri): *Big Trouble In Little China; Total Recall*
Goldman, Hal (wri): *Oh, God! Book II*
Goldman, Harold (wri): *Busman's Honeymoon*
Goldman, James (wri): *Robin And Marian; They Might Be Giants*
Goldman, Lawrence Louis (wri): *Kronos (1957); The 30 Foot Bride Of Candy Rock; The Viking Women And The Sea Serpent; War Of The Satellites*
Goldman, Marcy (act): *Star Trek: Generations*
Goldman, Roy (act): *Sherlock Holmes In New York*
Goldman, Shannon (act & wri): *Lost Prophet*
Goldman, Wendy (act): *Chiller*
Golden, William (wri, b. 1931): *The Ghost And The Darkness; Magic; Marathon Man; Masquerade; Memoirs Of An Invisible Man; Misery; No Way To Treat A Lady; The Princess Bride; The Stepford Wives*
Goldner, Charles (act, 1900-1955): *Black Magic (1949); The Golden Mask; The Laughing Lady; The Rocking Horse Winner; Shadow Of The Eagle; Top Secret (1952)*
Goldoni, Leila/Lelia (act, b. 1938): *Good Against Evil; Hysteria!; Invasion Of The Body Snatchers (1978); Mistress Of Paradise; The Spell; Theatre Of Death; The Unseen (1981)*
Goldring, Danny (act): *Vice Versa (1988); Virtuosity*
Goldsberry, Steven (act): *The Presence*
Goldsby, Matt (act): *Student Bodies*
Goldsman, Akiva (wri): *Batman And Robin; Batman Forever; A Time To Kill (1996)*
Goldsmith, Frank (act): *Bulldog Drummond's Third Round; The Secret Kingdom*
Goldsmith, Frederic (wri): *Hour Of Decision*
Goldsmith, George (wri): *Blue Monkey; Children Of The Corn*
Goldsmith, I.G. (wri): *The Scarf*
Goldsmith, Isadore (wri): *Bedelia*
Goldsmith, Jerry (act, b. 1929): *Gremlins 2: The New Batch*
Goldsmith, Jerry (mus, b. 1929): *Alien; Baby: Secret Of The Lost Legend; The Boys From Brazil; The Brotherhood Of The Bell; The 'Burbs; Capricorn One; Chain Reaction (1996); Coma; Congo; Damien-Omen II; Damnation Alley; Escape From The Planet Of The Apes; Explorers; The Final Conflict; First Knight; Forever Young; The Ghost And The Darkness; Gremlins; Gremlins 2: The New Batch; The Illustrated Man; In Like Flint; Innerspace; King Solomon's Mines (1985); Link; The List Of Adrian Messenger; Logan's Run; Magic; Matinee; The Mephisto Waltz; Mom And Dad Save The World; The Omen; The Other (1972); Our Man Flint; Outland; Planet Of The Apes; Poltergeist; Poltergeist II: The Other Side; Powder; Psycho Ii; The Reincarnation Of Peter Proud; Runaway; The Satan Bug; Seconds; Seven Days In May; The Shadow (1994); Shock Treatment (1964); Star Trek; Star Trek V: The Final Frontier; Star Trek: First Contact; Supergirl (1984); The Swarm; Total Recall; Twilight Zone; Warlock*
Goldsmith, Joel (mus): *Endless Descent; Laserblast; Man's Best Friend; The Man With Two Brains; Moon 44; Watchers*
Goldsmith, Jonathan (act): *Alfred Hitchcock Presents; Phantom Of The Mall: Eric's Revenge*
Goldsmith, Martin (wri): *The Lone Wolf In Mexico*
Goldsmith, Merwin (act): *Making Mr. Right*
Goldsmith, Paul (cin): *The Annihilator; Wavelength*
Goldsmith, Saul (act): *The Mummy And The Curse Of The Jackals*
Goldstein, Elliott (act): see Gould, Elliott
Goldstein, Herb (act): *Dr. Jekyll And Ms. Hyde; Super Fuzz*
Goldstein, Jenette (act, b. 1960): *Aliens; Miracle Mile; Near Dark; Star Trek: Generations; Terminator 2: Judgment Day*
Goldstein, Josh (wri): *18 Again!*
Goldstein, Leonard (wri): *Day Of The Nightmare*
Goldstein, Ron (cin): *Nothing But Trouble*
Goldstein, William (mus): *The Aliens Are Coming; A Connecticut Yankee In King Arthur's Court (1989); Hello Again; Shocker*
Goldstein, William (wri): *The Abominable Dr. Phibes; Dr. Phibes Rises Again*
Goldstone, James (dir): *Rollercoaster; When Time Ran Out*
Goldthwait, Bobcat (act): *Scrooged*
Goldthwaite, Anne (act): *Devotion*
Goldwyn, Tony (act): *Ghost (1990); Traces Of Red*
Goldzader, Samuele (act): *Warriors Of The Wasteland*
Golia, David (act): *The Coming*
Golia, David (cin): *Midnight (1989)*
Golightly, Herman (act): *Princess Warrior*
Golightly, John (act): *Lifeforce*
Golightly, Joseph (act): *Ed Wood*
Golino, Valeria (act, b. 1966): *Blind Date*
Golisano, Francesco (act): *Miracle In Milan*
Gollas, Ellen (act): *Total Recall*
Gollomb, Joseph (wri): *Murder At The Vanities*
Gollova, Natasa (act): *Cisaruv Pekar, Pekaruv Cisar*
Golm, Lisa (act): *Above Suspicion; Calling Dr. Death; Cry Wolf (1947); Possessed (1947)*
Golonka, Arlene (act): *The Busy Body; I Was A Teenage Sex Mutant*
Golovnya, Anatoli (cin): *Mekhanikha Golovnovo Mozga*
Golsby, Kevin (act): *The Cars That Ate Paris*
Goltsworthy, John (act): *13 Lead Soldiers*
Gombell, Minna (act, 1891-1973, a.k.a. Winifred Lee & Nancy Carter): *The Hunchback Of Notre Dame (1939); The Snake Pit (1948); The Thin Man*
Gomes, Robert John (act): *Virtuosity*
Gomez, Arthur (act): *The End Of The Line; 23 Paces To Baker Street*
Gomez, Carlos (act): *A Kiss To Die For*
Gomez, Fernando Fernan (act): *Faustina; La Venganza De Don Mendo*
Gomez, Fernando Fernan (dir & wri): *La Venganza De Don Mendo*
Gomez, Glen (act): *Candyman: Farewell To The Flesh*
Gomez, Mayra (act): *Death Curse Of Tartu*
Gomez, Panchito (act): *Return To Horror High*
Gomez, Pilarin (act): *Pyro*
Gomez, Rita (act): *Maid To Order*
Gomez, Sylvia (act): *Primal Fear*
Gomez, Thomas (act, 1905-1971): *The Adventures Of Hajji Baba; Arabian Nights; Beneath The Planet Of The Apes; The Climax; Crazy House (1943); Dead Man's Eyes; A Night In Paradise; Phantom Lady; Ride The Pink Horse; Sherlock Holmes And The Voice Of Terror; White Savage; Who Done It? (1942)*
Gomi, Kosuke (wri): *Secret Scrolls—Parts I & II*
Gomi, Ryutaro (act): *Majin, Monster Of Terror*
Gomperts, Natasha (act): *The Mcguffin*
Gomska, Mascha (act): *Le Trio Infernal*
Goncharova, A. (act): *Pikovaya Dama (1910)*
Gondek, Beth (act): *The Haunting Of Hamilton High*
Gondell, Bonnie (act): *Witches' Brew*
Gong, Michael Gregory (act): *Eraser*
Gonneau, Pierre (act): *Doctor Death: Seeker Of Souls*
Gonshaw, Francesca (act): *A Ghost In Monte Carlo*
Gonzales, Augustin (act): *Behind The Mask Of Zorro*
Gonzales, Ernesto (act): *The Possession Of Joel Delaney*
Gonzales, John (act): *The Phantom Empire*
Gonzales, Servando (dir): *The Fool Killer*
Gonzales(-Gonzales), Jose (act): *Kronos (1957); Mermaids Of Tiburon*
Gonzales-Gonzales, Pedro (act, b. 1926): *Bates Motel*
Gonzalez, Carlos (act): *Cocoon: The Return; Nightlife (1989, USA-Mex)*
Gonzalez, Cenon (act): *Twilight People*
Gonzalez, Clifton Gonzalez (act): *Fortress*
Gonzalez, Gonzo (act): *Flatliners*
Gonzalez, Jaime (act): *A Woman's Devotion*
Gonzalez, Joseph/Joe (act): *Frankenhooker; Matinee*
Gonzalez, Joseph Julian (mus): *Curdled*
Gonzalez, Manuel (cin): *El Santo Contra Las Vampiras*
Gonzalez, Mary (act): *El Otro Fu Manchu*
Gonzalez, Pedro Gonzalez (act): *Ring Of Fear*
Gonzalez, Sonia Noemi (act): *Creature From The Haunted Sea*
Gonzalez-Gonzalez, Pedro (act): *Donor*
Good, Frank B. (cin): *The Wizard*
Good, Jo-Anne (act): *Killer's Moon*
Good, Maurice (act): *Quatermass And The Pit; The Skull; They Came From Beyond Space; Trog*
Good, Peter B. (dir): *The Force On Thunder Mountain*
Good, Ray (act): *Raiders Of The Living Dead*
Goodchild, George (wri): *Condemned To Death*
Goode, Frederic (dir): *Death Is A Woman; The Hand Of Night*
Goode Jr., Jack (act): *Dick Tracy (1990)*
Goodell, Gregory (dir): *Human Experiments*
Gooden, Robert (act): *Night Of The Lepus*
Goodeve, Grant (act): *Pandora's Clock*
Goodger, Michele (act): *Quarantine*
Goodhart, Geoffrey (act): *Solution By Phone*
Goodhart, William (wri): *Exorcist II: The Heretic*
Goodich, Fred (cin): *Fear No Evil (1981)*
Goodier, Robert (act): *The Only Way Out Is Dead*
Gooding, Bruce (act): *Happy Birthday To Me*
Gooding Jr., Cuba (act, b. 1967): *Daybreak; Outbreak*
Goodis, David (wri): *The Burglar; Nightfall (1956)*
Goodkind, Saul (A.) (dir): *Destination Saturn; The Phantom Creeps*
Goodliffe, Michael (act, 1914-1976): *The Camp On Blood Island; The Day The Earth Caught Fire; The Gorgon; Hitler: The Last Ten Days; The Hour Of 13; Number Six; Peeping Tom; Stop Press Girl; The 39 Steps (1959); To The Devil A Daughter*
Goodlin, Chalmers (act): *The Devil's Messenger*
Goodman, Coley (act): *The Harper Mystery*
Goodman, David Zelag (wri): *Eyes Of Laura Mars; Farewell, My Lovely; Man On A Swing; The Stranglers Of Bombay*
Goodman, Dody (act, b. 1929): *I Dream Of Jeannie: Fifteen Years Later; Splash*
Goodman, George (act): *Superbug, Super Agent*
Goodman, Henry (act): *Mary Reilly*

Goodman, J. Kenneth (act): *The Dungeon*
Goodman, John (act): *Always; Arachnophobia; The Flintstones; Matinee; We're Back! A Dinosaur's Story*
Goodman, Karen (act): *Mermaids Of Tiburon*
Goodman, Kelly L. (act): *Graveyard Shift (1990)*
Goodman, Leonard (act): *Flesh Gordon*
Goodman, Miles (mus): *Little Shop Of Horrors (1986); The Man Who Wasn't There; Rattlers; Teen Wolf*
Goodman, Nora (wri): *Slaughterhouse Rock*
Goodman, Richard (act): *The Nylon Noose*
Goodman, Robert (act): *Flight Of The Navigator*
Goodman, Ron J. (act): *The First Power*
Goodman, Theodosia (act): see Bara, Theda
Goodner, Carol (act): *The Frog; The Ringer (1931); Strange Experiment*
Goodnoff, Irv (cin): *Evilspeak; The Resurrected*
Goodrich, Deborah (act): *April Fool's Day; Remote Control (1988)*
Goodrich, Eva (act): *Surf Nazis Must Die*
Goodrich, Frances (wri, 1891-1984): *After The Thin Man; Another Thin Man; It's A Wonderful Life; Lady In The Dark; The Thin Man*
Goodrich, Jack (act): *The Man Who Laughs (1927); Torchy Runs For Mayor*
Goodrich, John (wri): *Deluge*
Goodrich, Louis (act): *The Sleeping Cardinal; The Thirteenth Candle*
Goodrich, Theodocia (act): *Weird Science*
Goodricke, Bridget (act): *Peter Rabbit And The Tales Of Beatrix Potter*
Goodrow, Garry (act): *Glen And Randa; Invasion Of The Body Snatchers (1978); It Came Upon The Midnight Clear; The Lost Empire; Night Gallery; Once Bitten; The Prey (1980)*
Goodrow, Garry (wri): *Honey, I Blew Up The Kid*
Goods, Olivia (act): *Ator: The Fighting Eagle*
Goodspeed, Marjorie (act): see Reynolds, Marjorie
Goodwin, Alan (act): *I Was A Zombie For The F.B.I.*
Goodwin, Angela (act): *Autopsy*
Goodwin, Bill (act, 1910-1959): *The Atomic Kid; Heaven Only Knows; House Of Horrors (1946)*
Goodwin, Estelle (act): see Winwood, Estelle
Goodwin, Fred (dir): *Curse II: The Bite*
Goodwin, George (act): *The Secret Of The Moor*
Goodwin, Gordon (mus): *Attack Of The Killer Tomatoes*
Goodwin, Harold (GB act, b. 1924): *The Curse Of The Mummy's Tomb; Frankenstein Must Be Destroyed; Jabberwocky; The Lady Killers (1956); The Man In The White Suit; Monster Of Terror; The Mummy (1959); Number Six; The Phantom Of The Opera (1962)*
Goodwin, Harold (USA act): *The Boy Who Cried Werewolf; Charlie Chan At The Wax Museum; The Great Rupert; Tarzan And The Golden Lion*
Goodwin, Howard (act): *Time Flyer*
Goodwin, Jerem (act): *The Good Son*
Goodwin, Jimbo (act): *School Spirit*
Goodwin, John (act): *Heart And Souls; Tremors*
Goodwin, Moya (act): *Distortions*
Goodwin, Richard (wri): *Peter Rabbit And The Tales Of Beatrix Potter*
Goodwin, Robin (cin): *Swamp Thing*
Goodwin, Ron (mus): *The Alphabet Murders; Children Of The Damned; The Day Of The Triffids; Deadly Strangers; Frenzy; Gawain And The Green Knight; Lancelot And Guinevere; One Of Our Dinosaurs Is Missing; Operation Crossbow; The Spaceman And King Arthur; The Village Of The Damned (1960)*
Goodwin, Ruby (act): *The Alligator People*
Goodwin, Suki (act): *Hell Night*
Goodwins, Fred (act): *Blood Money*
Goodwins, Fred (dir): *Blood Money; The Chinese Puzzle*
Goodwins, Fred (wri): *The Chinese Puzzle*
Goodwins, Leslie (dir, 1899-1969): *Genius At Work; The Lone Wolf In London; The Mummy's Curse; Murder In The Blue Room*
Goodwyn, Anne (act): *The Henderson Monster*
Gool, Amina (act): *House Of The Living Dead*
Goulden, Richard (act): *The Curse Of The Golem; Once In A New Moon*
Goomas, Deborah (act): *Flatliners*
Goorjian, Michael (act): *Forever Young*
Goorney, Howard (act): [illegible] *The Blood On Satan's Claw; The Corpse; Evil Of Frankenstein; Jamaica Inn (1985)*
Gopo, Popescu (dir): *Steps Towards The Moon*

Gora, Claudio (act): *The Flower In His Mouth; La Poupee*
Goraguer, Alain (mus): *Fantastic Planet*
Goranson, Linda (act): *An American Christmas Carol; Millennium*
Goranzon, Marie (act): *I Am Curious (Yellow)*
Gorassini, Annie (act): *Vulcan, Son Of Jupiter*
Gorcey, Bernard (act, 1888-1955): *The Bowery Boys Meet The Monsters; Bowery To Bagdad; Dig That Uranium!; Ghost Chasers; Jalopy; Jungle Gents; Spook Busters; Spy Chasers*
Gorcey, David (act): *Ghost Chasers; Jalopy; Master Minds (1950); Mr. Hex; Spook Busters; Spooks Run Wild*
Gorcey, Elizabeth (act): *Teen Wolf*
Gorcey, Leo (act, 1915-1969): *The Bowery Boys Meet The Monsters; Bowery To Bagdad; Crashing Las Vegas; Dig That Uranium!; Ghost Chasers; The Ghost Creeps; Ghosts On The Loose; Hold That Line; Jalopy; Jungle Gents; Master Minds (1950); Mr. Hex; No Holds Barred; Out Of The Fog (1941); Paris Playboys; Private Eyes; Smuggler's Cove; Spook Busters; Spooks Run Wild; Spy Chasers*
Gordan, Jack (act): *Jaws Of Satan*
Gordey, Keith (act): *Runaway*
Gordian, Fortune (act): *Prince Valiant*
Gordon, Alan (act): *Cannibal Girls*
Gordon, Alex (wri): *Bride Of The Monster; Brock's Last Case*
Gordon, Angela (act): *Monolith*
Gordon, Barbara (act): *Dead Ringers; White Room*
Gordon, Barry (act): *Hands Of A Stranger; Love At First Bite; The Spirit Is Willing*
Gordon, Bert I. (cin, b. 1922): *The Amazing Colossal Man; The Beginning Of The End; Empire Of The Ants; The Food Of The Gods; The Spider (1958); Tormented (1960); Village Of The Giants*
Gordon, Bert I. (dir, b. 1922): *The Amazing Colossal Man; Attack Of The Puppet People; The Beginning Of The End; The Boy And The Pirates; The Coming; The Cyclops; Empire Of The Ants; The Food Of The Gods; King Dinosaur; The Mad Bomber; The Magic Sword (1962); Necromancy; Picture Mommy Dead; Serpent Island; The Spider (1958); Tormented (1960); Village Of The Giants; War Of The Colossal Beast*
Gordon, Bert I. (wri, b. 1922): *The Amazing Colossal Man; Attack Of The Puppet People; The Boy And The Pirates; The Coming; The Cyclops; Empire Of The Ants; The Food Of The Gods; King Dinosaur; The Mad Bomber; The Magic Sword (1962); Necromancy; Serpent Island; The Spider (1958); Tormented (1960); War Of The Colossal Beast*
Gordon, Bertie (act): *Lorna Doone (1920)*
Gordon, Betty (act): *Just Imagine*
Gordon, Bruce (GB act): *Elephant Boy; First Men In The Moon (1919)*
Gordon, Bruce (USA act, b. 1919): *The Curse Of The Undead; Hello Down There; Piranha (1978); Tower Of London (1962)*
Gordon, C. Henry (act, 1878-1940): *The Black Camel; Charlie Chan At The Olympics; Charlie Chan At The Wax Museum; Charlie Chan Carries On; Charlie Chan In City In Darkness; Gabriel Over The White House; Kongo; Mata Hari (1932); Miss Pinkerton; Rasputin And The Empress; Tarzan's Revenge*
Gordon, Carl (act): *The Brother From Another Planet*
Gordon, Charles (act): *The Vampire's Ghost*
Gordon, Christine (act): *I Walked With A Zombie*
Gordon, Claire (act): *Konga; Licensed To Kill*
Gordon, Colin (act, b. 1911): *Bobbikins; Casino Royale; Circle Of Danger; The Devil's Agent; Grand National Night; The Green Man; The Hour Of 13; House Of Mystery (1961); The Key Man; The Liquidator; Little Red Monkey; The Man In The White Suit; The Mouse That Roared; Night Of The Eagle; The Psychopath (1965); Subterfuge; The Trygon Factor*
Gordon, Debbie (act): *Oh Heavenly Dog*
Gordon, Denis (act): *Daughter Of Darkness (1948)*
Gordon, Denni (act): *Fortress*
Gordon, Don (act): *The Beast Within; The Borrower; Charlie Chan: Happiness Is A Warm Clue; Equalizer 2000; The Exorcist III; The Final Conflict; The Towering Inferno; Z.P.G.*
Gordon, Dorothy (act): *Grip Of The Strangler; House Of Whipcord*
Gordon, Eddie (act): *Lady Of Burlesque*
Gordon, Eric (act): *The Boy Who Cried Werewolf*

Gordon, Esther (act): *Hello Again*
Gordon, Eve (act): *Honey, We Shrunk Ourselves*
Gordon, Flora M. (cin): *Tormented (1960); Village Of The Giants*
Gordon, Frank (act): *Hercules In The Vale Of Woe*
Gordon, Gale (act, 1906-1995): *The 'Burbs; Francis Covers The Big Town; Sergeant Deadhead The Astronaut!; The 30 Foot Bride Of Candy Rock; Visit To A Small Planet*
Gordon, Gavin (act, b. 1901): *The Bat (1959); Bride Of Frankenstein; Mystery Of The Wax Museum; The Phantom Of Crestwood; Philo Vance's Gamble; Three On A Ticket*
Gordon, Gerald (M.) (act): *It Happened At Lake Wood Manor; The Judas Project*
Gordon, Gerti (act): *The Boys From Brazil*
Gordon, Hal (act): *Crime On The Hill; The Man Behind The Mask (1936); The Strangler (1932); When Knights Were Bold (1929); Wishes*
Gordon, Hannah (act): *Miss Morison's Ghosts; Tennis Court*
Gordon, Huntley (act, 1887-1956): *Mr. Wong In Chinatown; Murder By Television; Phantom Of Chinatown; The Spanish Cape Mystery*
Gordon, Jack (act): *A Close Call For Boston Blackie*
Gordon, Jacqui (act): *The Day After Halloween; Thirst*
Gordon, James B. (cin): *Journey To The Center Of The Earth (1959); The Lost World (1960); The Mask (1961)*
Gordon, James B. (wri): *Tower Of London (1962); The Werewolf (1955)*
Gordon, Jamie (act): *Addams Family Values*
Gordon, Jeffrey Pratt (act): *Serial Mom*
Gordon, Jessie (act): *Shadow Of Death (1983)*
Gordon, John (act): *Macbeth (1971);*
Gordon, Joyce (act): *The Housekeeper*
Gordon, Julie (act): *Super Fuzz*
Gordon, Kay (act): *Just Imagine*
Gordon, Keith (act): *All That Jazz; Christine; Dressed To Kill (1980); Jaws 2*
Gordon, Kenneth (act): *The Music Of The Spheres; Starship Invasions*
Gordon, Kilbourn (wri): *Kongo; West Of Zanzibar*
Gordon, Lance (act): *The Hills Have Eyes; The Hills Have Eyes Ii*
Gordon, Leo (act, b. 1922): *Bog; The Cry Baby Killer; The Haunted Palace (1963); The Man Who Knew Too Much (1956); The St. Valentine's Day Massacre; Tarzan Goes To India*
Gordon, Leo (V.) (wri, b. 1922): *Attack Of The Giant Leeches; The Cry Baby Killer; The Terror (1963); Tower Of London (1962); The Wasp Woman*
Gordon, Leon (wri): *Freaks; The Hour Of 13; Kongo*
Gordon, Leslie Howard (wri): *Melody Of Death*
Gordon, Lewis (act): *A Witch Without A Broom*
Gordon, Mack (mus): *Charlie Chan In Rio*
Gordon, Marianne (act): *The Being*
Gordon, Mark (act): *Freejack*
Gordon, Mary (act, 1882-1963): *After The Thin Man; The Black Camel; Bride Of Frankenstein; The Hound Of The Baskervilles (1939); The Mummy's Tomb; The Pearl Of Death; Shadows Over Chinatown; Sherlock Holmes And The Secret Weapon; Sherlock Holmes And The Voice Of Terror; Sherlock Holmes Faces Death; Spider Woman; Strange Confession; The Woman In Green*
Gordon, Maude Turner (act): *After The Thin Man*
Gordon, Michael (dir, b. 1909): *An Act Of Murder (1948); All Hallowe'en; Boston Blackie Goes Hollywood; Crime Doctor; One Dangerous Night; Portrait In Black; The Web*
Gordon, Neil (wri): *The Claydon Treasure Mystery; The Third Clue*
Gordon, Nora (act): *The Glass Tomb; Horrors Of The Black Museum; The Nanny*
Gordon Pam(ela) (act): *Alien Nation: Body And Soul; The Borrower; Weird Science*
Gordon, Pat (act): *Lizzie*
Gordon, Pattie (act): *Getting Lucky*
Gordon, Peter (act): *The Black Sleep*
Gordon, Phillip (act): *Dark Of The Night*
Gordon, Phyllis (act): *Another Thin Man*
Gordon, Richard (act): *Black Magic (1944)*
Gordon Jr., Richard F. (act): *For All Mankind*
Gordon, Robert (dir): *Black Zoo; It Came From Beneath The Sea; Tarzan And The Jungle Boy*
Gordon, Roy (act): *Attack Of The 50-Foot Woman (1958); Hand Of Death; The Lone Wolf Strikes; The Shanghai Cobra; The Unearthly; War Of The Colossal Beast; The Wasp Woman*

Gordon, Rueben (wri): *Alien Warrior*
Gordon, Ruth (act, 1896-1985, nee Ruth Jones): *Don't Go To Sleep; The Great Houdinis; Isn't It Shocking?; Look What's Happened To Rosemary's Baby; What Ever Happened To Aunt Alice?*
Gordon, Ruth (wri, 1896-1985): *A Double Life*
Gordon, Serena (act): *Goldeneye*
Gordon, Stafford (act): *Captain Kronos: Vampire Hunter*
Gordon, Stuart (dir): *Daughter Of Darkness (1990); Dolls; Fortress; From Beyond; The Pit And The Pendulum (1990); Re-Animator; Robot Jox*
Gordon, Stuart (wri): *The Body Snatchers; From Beyond; Honey, I Blew Up The Kid; Honey, I Shrunk The Kids; Re-Animator*
Gordon, Susan (act): *Attack Of The Puppet People; The Boy And The Pirates; Picture Mommy Dead; Tormented (1960)*
Gordon, Vera (act, 1886-1948): *The Living Ghost (1942)*
Gordone, Charles (act): *Angel Heart*
Gordy, Alison (act): *Jacob's Ladder*
Gore Avenue Sound Project, The (mus): *Empire Of Ash III*
Gore, Altovise (act): *Welcome To Arrow Beach*
Gore, Michael (mus): *The Butcher's Wife*
Gore, Steven (act): *Forever Evil*
Gorenchstein, F. (wri): *Solaris*
Gorg, Galyn (act): *RoboCop 2*
Gorham, Charles (act): *In The Palace Of The King*
Gorham, Mel (act): *Curdled*
Gori, Connie (act): *Midnight (1980)*
Gori, Mario Cecchi (wri, 1920-1993): *Tempi Duri Per I Vampiri*
Gorine, Owen (act): *Crooked Alley*
Goring, Marius (act, b. 1912): *The Case Of The Frightened Lady; Charlie Boy/The Thirteenth Reunion; Circle Of Danger; The Devil's Agent; The Devil's Daffodil; Family Doctor; Highly Dangerous; A Matter Of Life And Death; Pandora And The Flying Dutchman; Paris Express; Son Of Robin Hood; The Spy In Black; Subterfuge; Take My Life; Zeppelin*
Gorini, Arianna (act): *Sei Donne Per L'assassino*
Gorman, Buddy (act): *Ghost Chasers*
Gorman, Chip (act): *Johnny Hamlet*
Gorman, Cliff (act, b. 1936): *All That Jazz*
Gorman, James (wri): *Cutthroat Island*
Gorman, Lynne (act): *Videodrome*
Gorman, Patrick (act): *Assassin (1986); In The Shadow Of Kilimanjaro*
Gorman, Reg (act): *Inn Of The Damned*
Gorman, Robert (Hy) (act): *Forever Young; Leprechaun; Sometimes They Come Back*
Gorman, Shay (act): *The Eyes Of Annie Jones; Island Of Terror; Kill Her Gently*
Gorme, Eydie (act, b. 1932): *Alice In Wonderland (1985)*
Gorn, Lester (wri): *The Beginning Of The End*
Gorn, Steve (mus): *Jack's Wife*
Gorney, Walter (act): *Friday The 13th (1980); Friday The 13th-Part 2*
Gornick, Michael (cin): *Dawn Of The Dead; Day Of The Dead; Martin*
Gornick, Michael (dir): *Creepshow 2*
Gorog, Laszlo (wri, b. 1903): *The Land Unknown; The Mole People; The Spider (1958)*
Gorre, Leilani (act): *Mother's Day*
Gorshin, Frank (act, b. 1934): *Batman (1966); Beverly Hills Bodysnatchers; Goliath Awaits; Invasion Of The Saucer Men; The Meteor Man; Midnight (1989); 12 Monkeys*
Gorson, Arthur H. (wri): *Silent Night, Deadly Night Iii; Silent Night, Deadly Night 4: Initiation*
Gorson, Corrie (act): *Silent Night, Deadly Night III*
Gorst, Derek (act): *The Fatal Hour (1937); The Gables Mystery; The Mind Of Mr. Reeder*
Gort the Robot (act): *The Day The Earth Stood Still*
Gortner, Marjoe (act, b. 1944): *Earthquake; The Food Of The Gods; Hellhole; Mausoleum; Star Crash*
Gosa, Jim (act): *Wavelength*
Gosalvez, Tony (act): *Twilight People*
Gosha, Isamu (act): *The Toxic Avenger, Part II*
Goslar, Jurgen (dir): *Amuck*
Goslins, Maarten (act): *RoboCop*
Gosnell, Robert (wri): *Firewalker*
Goss, David (act): *She (1983)*
Goss, Helen (act): *The Hound Of The Baskervilles (1959); Jane Eyre (1970); A Place Of One's Own*
Goss, Victor (cin): *The Lightning Incident*

Gossage, John (wri): The Gamma People
Gossen, Suzanne (act): Judex
Gossett (Jr.), Lou(is) (act, b. 1936): The Deep; Firewalker; In His Father's Shoes; Jaws 3-D; J.D.'s Revenge; Monolith; The Punisher
Gossett, Tracy (act): I Was A Zombie For The F.B.I.
Gotell, Walter (act): Black Sunday (1977); The Boys From Brazil; The Damned; The Devil's Daffodil; Endless Night; For Your Eyes Only; From Russia With Love; Lancelot And Guinevere; The Living Daylights; The London Connection; The Man Inside; The Man With The Twisted Lip; Moonraker; Octopussy; The Road To Hong Kong; The Spy Who Loved Me; A View To A Kill
Gotfurt, Frederick (wri): A Lady Mislaid
Gotham Quartette, The (act): Alf's Button (1930)
Gothard, Michael (act): The Devils; For Your Eyes Only; Frankenstein (1993); Lifeforce; Scream And Scream Again; The Sweet Scent Of Death; Warlords Of The Deep; Who Slew Auntie Roo?
Gotho, Heinrich (act): Metropolis (1926)
Gott, Barbara (act): The Crime At Blossoms; Downhill; The Ghost Walks (1935); The House Of The Arrow (1930); The Medium (1934)
Gottesfeld, Dov (act): Swamp Thing
Gotthardt, Arno (act): Starship Invasions
Gottler, Jerome S. (wri): Spy Chasers
Gottlieb, Carl (act): Jaws; Something Evil
Gottlieb, Carl (dir): Amazon Women On The Moon; Caveman (1981)
Gottlieb, Carl (wri): Caveman (1981); Jaws; Jaws 2; Jaws 3-D
Gottlieb, Frank (dir): Curse Of The Yellow Snake
Gottlieb, Franz Josef (dir): The Phantom Of Soho
Gottlieb, Joseph Abraham (act): see Bishop, Joey
Gottlieb, Michael (dir): A Kid In King Arthur's Court; Mannequin
Gottlieb, Michael (wri): Mannequin
Gottlieb, Stan (act): Slaughterhouse-Five
Gottlieb, Theodore (act): The Lone Wolf In Mexico
Gottowt, John (act): Genuine; Nosferatu, Eine Symphonie Des Grauens; Der Student Von Prag (1913); Das Wachsfigurenkabinett
Gottschalk, Ferdinand (act): Secret Of The Chateau
Gottshall, D. Christian (act): Matinee
Goty, Mici (act): Voodoo Man
Goudal, Jetta (act, 1898-1985): The Green Goddess (1923); The Road To Yesterday; Le Spectre Vert
Goude, Ingrid (act): The Killer Shrews
Gougey, Rosalind (act): One Wish Too Many
Gough, John(ny) (act): The Haunted House (1929); The Gorilla (1927)
Gough, Lloyd (act): Earthquake; Sandcastles; The Scarf; Sunset Boulevard
Gough, Michael (act, b. 1917): Arthur The King; Batman (1989); Batman And Robin; Batman Forever; Batman Returns; Berserk; Blackmailed; Black Zoo; The Boys From Brazil; Candidate For Murder; A Christmas Carol (1984); The Corpse; Curse Of The Crimson Altar; Dr. Terror's House Of Horrors (1964); Horror Hospital; Horror Of Dracula; Horrors Of The Black Museum; The House In The Woods; Konga; The Legend Of Hell House; The Man In The White Suit; Model For Murder; Nostradamus; The Phantom Of The Opera (1962); Richard III (1955); Satan's Slave; The Serpent And The Rainbow; The Skull; They Came From Beyond Space; Top Secret! (1984); Trog; Venom (1982); What A Carve Up!; Young Indiana Jones: Travels With Father
Gough, Simon (act): The Corpse
Gough, William (wri): Tarzan In Manhattan
Gould, Brewster (act): The Haunting Of Morella
Gould, Charles S. (dir): Jungle Moon Men
Gould, Chester (wri, 1900-1985): Dick Tracy (1937, 1945 & 1990); Dick Tracy Meets Gruesome; Dick Tracy Returns; Dick Tracy's Dilemma; Dick Tracy's G-Men; Dick Tracy Vs. Crime, Inc.; Dick Tracy vs. Cueball
Gould, Duncan (act): Jekyll And Hyde
Gould, Elliott (act, b. 1938, nee Elliott Goldstein): Capricorn One; The Devil And Max Devlin; The Lady Vanishes (1979); Who?
Gould, Glenn (mus, 1932-1982): Slaughterhouse-Five
Gould, Graydon (act): Mission: Impossible; The Ultimate Impostor
Gould, Harold (act, b. 1923): The Man In The Santa Claus Suit; Project X (1967); The Strongest Man In The World
Gould, Harvey (cin): The Invisible Ghost
Gould, Heywood (wri): The Boys From Brazil
Gould, Howard (act): The Lone Wolf Returns (1935)
Gould, John (wri): Journey Into Darkness; Who?
Gould, Karen (act): Transmutations
Gould, Karsen Lee (act): Heartbeeps
Gould, Michael (act): Mary Shelley's 'Frankenstein'
Gould, Robert (act): Philadelphia Experiment II
Gould, Sandra (act): The Barefoot Executive
Gould, William (act): Destination Saturn; Mr. Wong, Detective; Nancy Drew And The Hidden Staircase; Torchy Plays With Dynamite
Goulder, Stanley (dir & wri): Naked Evil
Goulding, Alfred (dir): A Chump At Oxford; Dick Barton, Special Agent
Goulding, Alfred (wri): Dick Barton, Special Agent
Goulding, Edmund (dir, 1891-1959): Nightmare Alley
Goulding, Edmund (wri, 1891-1959): Dante's Inferno (1924); The Devil (1921)
Gould-Porter, Arthur E. (act): Bedknobs And Broomsticks
Goulet, Robert (act, b. 1933): I Deal In Danger
Goulian, Lisa (act): Star Crystal
Goullet, Arthur (act): The Crimson Candle; Silver Blaze (1937)
Gounod, Charles (wri, 1818-1893): Faust (1910, 1911, 1922 & 1936); Faust And The Devil
Gouriet, Gerald (mus): Death Dreams; Philadelphia Experiment II
Gourlay, Erin (act): Waxwork II: Lost In Time
Gout, Albert (dir): Adam And Eve
Goutman, Christopher (act): The Prowler (1981)
Gouw, Cynthia (act): Star Trek V: The Final Frontier
Goux, John (mus): Alfred Hitchcock Presents
Govar, Rene (dir & wri): Las Noches Del Hombre Lobo
Gover, Victor M. (dir): A Ghost For Sale; Murder At Scotland Yard; Murder At The Grange
Governor, Mark (mus): Pet Sematary Two
Governor, Richard (dir): Ghost Town
Gow, James (wri): Murder On A Bridle Path
Gow, Keith (wri): The Cars That Ate Paris
Gow, Ronald (dir & wri): The Glittering Sword
Gowans, John (D.) (act): Fantasies; Star Trek
Gowdy, Barbara (wri): Kissed
Gowdy, Curt (act): Heaven Can Wait (1978)
Gower, Andre (act): The Man In The Santa Claus Suit; The Monster Squad
Gower, Harry (act): Spiritualism Exposed (1913)
Gowers, Patrick (mus): The Boy Who Turned Yellow; Hamlet (1969)
Go West (mus): Demons
Gowland, Gibson (act, 1882-1951): Don Juan (1927); Hutch Stirs 'Em Up; The Mysterious Island (1929); The Mystery Of The Mary Celeste; The Phantom Of The Opera (1925); The Private Life Of Don Juan; The Secret Of The Loch (1934)
Goya, Mona (act): Juggernaut
Goya, Tito (act, b. 1951): Marathon Man
Goyer, David S. (wri): The Crow: City Of Angels; The Puppet Masters
Gozier, Bernie (act): City Beneath The Sea (1952); Creature From The Black Lagoon; The Flame Barrier; The Naked Jungle
Gozzi, Chantal (act): Les Sorcieres De Salem
Graas, John Christian (act): Philadelphia Experiment II
Grabert, Fred (act): Zapped!
Grable, Betty (act, 1916-1974, nee Elizabeth Grasle): I Wake Up Screaming
Grabowski, Norman (act): The Gnome-Mobile; The Monkey's Uncle; The Towering Inferno
Grace, Billy (act): I Was A Zombie For The F.B.I.
Grace, Howard (act): Judge Dredd
Grace, Jim (act): Stigma
Grace, Meyer (act): Dark Alibi
Grace, Michael L. (wri): The Unseen (1981)
Grace, Sally (act): Ghost Story (1975)
Grace, Tre (act): I Was A Zombie For The F.B.I.
Grace, Wayne (act): Fire In The Sky (1993)
Gracen, Elizabeth (act): The Death Of The Incredible Hulk
Gracia, Angel (act): Hundra
Gracia, (Felix) Sancho (act): Behind The Mask Of Zorro; House Of 1,000 Dolls
Gracia, Juana (act): Hundra
Gracia, Maria (act): The Littlest Angel (1960)
Grad, Genevieve (act): Beast Of Babylon Against The Son Of Hercules
Gradoli, Antonio (act): Gli Amori Di Ercole
Gradussov, Alex (act): Skullduggery
Gradwell, Michael (act): The Playbirds
Grady, Ed L. (act): D.A.R.Y.L.; The Handmaid's Tale
Grady, Edward (act): Wolfman (1979)
Grady, James (wri): 3 Days Of The Condor
Grady, Michael (act): Symptoms
Graeff, Tom (dir & wri): Teenagers From Outer Space
Graeme, Bruce (wri): Face In The Night
Graetz, Paul (act): Bulldog Jack; Murder At Monte Carlo; The Scotland Yard Mystery
Graf, David (act): Love At Stake
Graf, Peter (act): The Erotic Adventures Of The Three Musketeers
Grafe, Judy (act): The Dark Half; Frankenhooker
Graff, Fred (act): Boston Blackie And The Law
Graff, Todd (act): The Abyss; Strange Days
Graff, Wilton (act, 1904-1969): Bloodlust!; Bulldog Drummond Strikes Back (1947); Just Before Dawn (1946); Operation Secret; The Phantom Thief; Pillow Of Death; Rogues Of Sherwood Forest; Shadowed; Strange Confession
Graffis, William H. (wri): Dick Tracy Meets Gruesome
Graffitti, Andy (act): Empire Of Ash III
Grafton, Sue (wri): Sparkling Cyanide; Svengali (1983)
Graham, Aimee (act): From Dusk Till Dawn
Graham, Alec (wri): Meet Mr. Lucifer
Graham, Barbara (act): Crackle Of Death
Graham, Ben (act): The Lone Wolf (1917)
Graham, Bruce (wri): Twisted
Graham, Charles (act): The Headless Horseman
Graham, Clive (act): Hamlet (1969)
Graham, David (act): Thunderbirds Are Go; Thunderbird 6
Graham, David C. (dir): The Undertaker And His Pals
Graham, Eddie (act): Torchy Runs For Mayor
Graham, Fred (act): Cyclotrode X; The Giant Gila Monster; The Last Hunt; Rear Window; Trouble For Two
Graham, Gary (act): Alien Nation: Body And Soul; Alien Nation: Millennium; Alien Nation: The Enemy Within; No Place To Hide (1981); The Presence; Robot Jox
Graham, Genine (act): Black 13; The Crossroad Gallows; Murder At The Windmill
Graham, Gerrit (act): Child's Play 2; Chopping Mall; C.H.U.D. II; The Creature Wasn't Nice; Demon Seed; It's Alive III: Island Of The Alive; Phantom Of The Paradise; Philadelphia Experiment II; Ratboy; Strange New World; Terrorvision
Graham, Guy (act): Bluff
Graham, Harry (act): The Mystery Of The Diamond Belt
Graham, Herschel (act): Charlie Chan At The Opera
Graham, Holter (act): Maximum Overdrive
Graham, Hugh (act): The Blob (1958)
Graham, Imogen (act): Repulsion
Graham, John (act): The Lost World (1960)
Graham, John Michael (act): Halloween
Graham, John R. (mus): Them (1996)
Graham, Joyce (act): Theater Of Blood
Graham, Kirsten (act): Alien Nation
Graham, Kirsty (act): Loch Ness
Graham, Leslie (act): Unforgettable
Graham, Lewis (wri): The Crime Of Dr. Crespi
Graham, Lillian (act): The Pit (1983)
Graham, Margaret (act): The Premonition (1975)
Graham, Michael (act): Curse Of The Fly
Graham, Morland (act, 1891-1949): The Ghost Train (1941); Gestapo; Jamaica Inn (1939); The Scarlet Pimpernel (1934); Tower Of Terror
Graham, Norman (wri): Macumba Love
Graham, Rachel (act): Mad Max Beyond Thunderdome
Graham, Ranald (wri): Shanks
Graham, Reavis (act): Moontrap
Graham, Ronald F. (wri): Strange New World
Graham, Ronny (wri): Spaceballs
Graham, Rose (act): Psycho Girls
Graham, Sammy (act): Shock Waves
Graham, Scott (act): The Brotherhood Of The Bell
Graham, T. Max (act): Sometimes They Come Back
Graham, Tara (act): White Dwarf
Graham, Tim (act): The Brain From Planet Arous
Graham, Tracie (act): Pumpkinhead II: Blood Wings
Graham, Violet (act): The Charlatan; A Man's Shadow
Graham, William (act): Just William's Luck
Graham, William (A.) (dir, b. 1930): Beyond The Bermuda Triangle; The Last Generation; Shark Kill
Graham, Winston (wri): Marnie; Night Without Stars; Take My Life
Grahame, David (act): Octopussy
Grahame, Gloria (act, 1929-1981, nee Gloria Grahame Hallward): Black Noon; Blood And Lace; Escape; Mansion Of The Doomed; Naked Alibi; The Nesting; Prisoners Of The Casbah; Song Of The Thin Man; Sudden Fear
Grahame, Kenneth (wri, 1859-1932): The Wind In The Willows
Grahame, Leonard (act): They Came From Beyond Space
Grahame, Margot (act, b. 1911): Black Magic (1949); Creeping Shadows; The Crimson Pirate; Forging Ahead; Venetian Bird
Grahame, Ronald (wri): Queen Of The Wicked
Grahame-White, Claude (act): The Secret Of The Air
Graig, Davina (act): The Demon Barber Of Fleet Street
Grail, Tom (act): Shriek Of The Mutilated
Grainer, Ron (mus, b. 1925): The Assassination Bureau; I Don't Want To Be Born; The Moon-Spinners; The Mouse On The Moon; Never-Never Land; Night Must Fall (1964); The Omega Man; A Story Of Tutankhamun
Grainger, Edmund (wri): Split Second (1953)
Grais, Michael (wri): Cool World; Poltergeist; Poltergeist Ii: The Other Side
Gram, Bill (act): Street Trash
Gramatica, Emma (act): Miracle In Milan
Gramlich, George (act): Just Imagine
Granach, Alexander (act, 1890-1945): Nosferatu, Eine Symphonie Des Grauens
Granada, Maria (act): Operation Atlantis
Granata, Graziella (act): Aimez-Vous Les Femmes?; La Strage Dei Vampiri
Granberry, Don (act): The Groundstar Conspiracy; The House By The Lake
Granby, Joe (act): Amazon Quest
Grand Funk Railroad (mus): Heavy Metal
Grandel, Janine (act): Return Of The Fly
Grandey, Teddy B. (act): Secrets Of The Phantom Caverns
Grandi, Serena (act): The Adventures Of Hercules
Grandin, Elmer (act): The House Of Secrets (1929)
Grando, Kelley (act): Never Talk To Strangers
Grandpre, Gisele (act): Les Parapluies De Cherbourg
Grandstaff, Olive/Kathryn (act): see Grant (Crosby), Kathryn
Grandy, Fred (act): Death Race 2000
Graneman, Eddie (wri): The Lost City
Graner, Gertrude (act): Witness To Murder
Granger Dorothy (act, b. 1914): The Jade Mask; One Body Too Many; Shadows Over Chinatown
Granger, Edward (act): Tuck Everlasting
Granger, Farley (act, b. 1925): Amuck; Arnold; Penetration; The Prowler (1981); Rope; The Serpent; Strangers On A Train
Granger, Marc (act): The Amazing Mr. Blunden
Granger, Michael (act, 1923-1981): Creature With The Atom Brain; Jungle Moon Men; The Magnetic Monster; Murder By Contract; Salome (1953); Tarzan And The She-Devil
Granger, Philip (act): To Die For
Granger, Stewart (act, 1913-1993, nee James LaBlache Stewart): Fanny By Gaslight; Footsteps In The Fog; The Hound Of The Baskervilles (1972); King Solomon's Mines (1949); The Last Hunt; The Man In Grey; The Prisoner Of Zenda (1952); Red Dragon (1965); Requiem For A Secret Agent; Salome (1953); Sodom And Gomorrah; A Target For Killing; The Trygon Factor
Grangier, Gilles (dir): Speaking Of Murder
Granik, John (act): Virus
Granowski, Alexis (dir): Die Dreizehn Koffer Des Herrn O.F.
Granpree, Colin (act): Mutants In Paradise
Granstedt, Greta (act): The Return Of Dracula
Grant, Alexander (act): Peter Rabbit And The Tales Of Beatrix Potter
Grant, Alfred (act): Son Of Ingagi
Grant, Andrea (act): Whirlpool
Grant, Andrew (act): The Sexplorer
Grant, Angela (act): Spectre (1977); Tales From The Crypt
Grant, Arthur (cin): The Abominable Snowman Of The Himalayas; The Angel Who Pawned Her Harp; Blood From The Mummy's Tomb; Captain Clegg; A Challenge For Robin Hood; The Curse Of The Werewolf; The Damned; Demons Of The Mind; The Devil Rides Out; Dracula Has Risen From The

Grave; Fear In The Night (1972); Frankenstein Created Woman; Frankenstein Must Be Destroyed; The Mummy's Shroud; The Old Dark House (1963); Paranoiac; The Phantom Of The Opera (1962); The Pirates Of Blood River; The Plague Of The Zombies; Quatermass And The Pit; The Reptile; Rx Murder; The Shadow Of The Cat; Son Of Robin Hood; The Stranglers Of Bombay; Taste The Blood Of Dracula; The Terror Of The Tongs; The Tomb Of Ligeia; The Witches (1966)

Grant, Audie (act): *Wild Thing*

Grant, Barra (act): *Daughters Of Satan*

Grant, Belinda (act): *Not Of This Earth (1988)*

Grant, Beth (act): *Child's Play 2; The Dark Half; Flatliners*

Grant, Bryan (act): *Teenagers From Outer Space*

Grant, (A.) Cameron (act): *The Man With A Cloak; 23 Paces To Baker Street*

Grant, Cary (act, 1904-1986, nee Alexander Archibald Leach): *Alice In Wonderland (1933); Arsenic And Old Lace; The Bishop's Wife; Monkey Business; North By Northwest; Notorious (1946); Once Upon A Time (1944); Suspicion; To Catch A Thief; Topper (1937)*

Grant, Clare (act): *The Island Of Dr. Moreau (1996)*

Grant, Cy (act): *At The Earth's Core*

Grant, David Marshall (act): *Forever Young*

Grant, Dick (act): *Virus*

Grant, Donald (act): *Monster In The Closet*

Grant, Faye (act): *Omen IV: The Awakening; Traces Of Red; V*

Grant, Garry (act): *Peter Rabbit And The Tales Of Beatrix Potter*

Grant, Gilly (act): *Clegg*

Grant, Gretchen (act): *Time Flyer*

Grant, Helen (act): *Wizards Of The Lost Kingdom*

Grant, Helena (act): *Charlie Chan In London; Jungle Goddess*

Grant, Hugh (act, b. 1961): *Extreme Measures; The Lair Of The White Worm*

Grant, James (act): *The Resurrected*

Grant, James Edward/E. (dir, 1904-1966): *Ring Of Fear*

Grant, James E. (wri, 1904-1966): *Miracles For Sale; Ring Of Fear*

Grant, John (wri): *Abbott And Costello Go To Mars; Abbott And Costello Meet Captain Kidd; Abbott And Costello Meet Dr. Jekyll And Mr. Hyde; Abbott And Costello Meet Frankenstein; Abbott And Costello Meet The Killer; Abbott And Costello Meet The Mummy; Hold That Ghost; Lost In A Harem; Who Done It? (1942)*

Grant, Julian (act): *The Pink Chiquitas*

Grant, Julian (dir): *Electra (1995)*

Grant (Crosby), Kathryn (act, b. 1933, nee Olive Grandstaff): *Cell 2455, Death Row; The Initiation Of Sarah; The Night The World Exploded; Rear Window; The 7th Voyage Of Sinbad*

Grant, Kirby (act, 1911-1985, nee Kirby Grant Horn): *Fangs Of The Arctic; Ghost Catchers; Snow Dog; The Spider Woman Strikes Back*

Grant, Lawrence (act): *Bulldog Drummond (1929); The Canary Murder Case; The Cat Creeps (1930); The Living Ghost (1942); The Man Who Reclaimed His Head; The Mask Of Fu Manchu; Shanghai Express; Son Of Frankenstein; Werewolf Of London*

Grant, Lee (act, b. 1927, nee Lyova Rosenthal): *The Balcony; Charlie Chan And The Curse Of The Dragon Queen; Damien-Omen II; The Last Generation; The Mafu Cage; Marooned; Night Slaves; Portnoy's Complaint; The Spell; The Swarm; Visiting Hours*

Grant, Leon W. (act): *The Brother From Another Planet*

Grant, Micah (act): *To Die For*

Grant, Moira (act): *Labyrinth (1986)*

Grant, Morton (wri): *The Falcon Out West*

Grant, Murray (cin): *Horror Of Frankenstein; I, Monster; Scars Of Dracula; Vampire Circus*

Grant, Paul (act): *The Beginning Of The End*

Grant, Phoenix (act): *Yeti*

Grant, Richard (act): *Forbidden Planet; On The Threshold Of Space*

Grant, Richard E. (act): *Bram Stoker's 'Dracula'; Warlock*

Grant, Rita (act): *Crimes At The Dark House*

Grant, Sandra (act): *I Still Dream Of Jeannie*

Grant, Sarina (act): *The Howling*

Grant, Seafield (act): see Hayward, Louis

Grant, Sheila (act): *The Witches And The [illegible]*

Grant, Shelby (act): *Fantastic Voyage; The Witchmaker*

Grant, Steve (act): *La Momia*

Grant, Winston E. (act): *The Body Snatchers*

Grantham, Ken (act): *Shadow Of A Doubt (1991)*

Grantham, Lesley (act): *Morons From Outer Space*

Grantham, Lucy (act): *The Last House On The Left*

Grantham, Mark (wri): *Date At Midnight; Night Train For Inverness*

Grant-Minchen, Bill (act): *Powder*

Granval, Jean-Pierre (act): *Le Testament Du Dr. Cordelier*

Granville, Audrey (mus): *Tarzan And The Trappers*

Granville, Bonita (act, 1923-1988): *The Guilty; The Lone Ranger; Nancy Drew And The Hidden Staircase; Nancy Drew, Detective; Nancy Drew, Reporter; Nancy Drew, Troubleshooter; The Truth About Murder*

Granville, Charlotte (act): *Werewolf Of London*

Granville, Harry (act): *To Save The King*

Grapes, Marcus J. (act): *Women And Bloody Terror*

Grapewin, Charley (act, 1875-1956): *Close Call For Ellery Queen; Desperate Chance For Ellery Queen; Ellery Queen And The Murder Ring; Ellery Queen And The Perfect Crime; Ellery Queen, Master Detective; Ellery Queen's Penthouse Mystery; Enemy Agents Meet Ellery Queen; One Frightened Night; The Wizard Of Oz (1939)*

Grappelly, Stephane (act): *Time Flies (1944)*

Grasis, Jesse (act): *Of Unknown Origin*

Grasle, Elizabeth (act): see Grable, Betty

Grasmere, Robert (act): *Prince Of Darkness*

Grass, Sandra (act): *School Spirit*

Grassby, Bertram (act): *The Dancer Of The Nile; The Lone Wolf's Daughter (1919)*

Grasshoff, Alex (dir): *Crackle Of Death; The Last Dinosaur*

Gratsch, Carolyn (act): *Flesh-Eating Mothers*

Grattan, Stephen (act): *The Lone Wolf (1917)*

Gratton, Bill (act): *Eve Of Destruction*

Grau, Albin (wri): *Schatten, Eine Nachtliche Halluzination*

Grau, Jorge (dir): *Ceremonia Sangrienta; Night Fiend*

Graubart, David (act): *The Relic*

Graubart, Judy (act): *Simon*

Grauer, Ben (act): *Annabel Lee*

Grauer, Marshall (act): *Blood Waters Of Dr. Z*

Grauman, Walter (E.) (dir, b. 1922): *Are You In The House Alone?; Covenant; Crowhaven Farm; Daughter Of The Mind; Dead Men Tell No Tales; The Disembodied; I Deal In Danger; Lady In A Cage; The Memory Of Eva Ryker; Nightmare On The 13th Floor; They Call It Murder*

Gravage, Bob (act): *Earthquake*

Gravance, Louie (act): *Evilspeak*

Graver, Chris (act): *Trick Or Treats*

Graver, Gary (cin): *The Attic; The Clones; Deathsport; Dr. Dracula; Invasion Of The Bee Girls; The Kid With The Broken Halo; Mortuary; The Phantom Empire; Through The Magic Pyramid; The Toolbox Murders; Trick Or Treats*

Graver, Gary (dir & wri): *Trick Or Treats*

Graves, Ann (act): *The Magic Sword (1962)*

Graves, Eric (act): *The Lost Boys*

Graves, Florence (act): *Mr. Reeder In Room 13*

Graves, Gary (act): *Teenage Catgirls In Heat*

Graves, George (act): *Wolf's Clothing (1936)*

Graves, Leslie (act): *Piranha II: The Spawning*

Graves, Peter (GB act): *I Hired A Contract Killer; King Arthur Was A Gentleman; The Laughing Lady; The Magic Christian; The Slipper And The Rose; Tennis Court; The Wrong Box*

Graves, Peter (USA act, b. 1926): *Addams Family Values; The Beginning Of The End; The Clonus Horror; Death In Small Doses (1957); It Conquered The World; Killers From Space; The Memory Of Eva Ryker; The Mysterious Monsters; The Night Of The Hunter (1955); Red Planet Mars; Scream Of The Wolf; Where Have All The People Gone?*

Graves, Ralph (act): *Amazon Quest; Dirigible*

Graves, Robert (wri): *The Shout*

Graves, Teresa (act): *Vampira*

Gravina, Carla (act): *Anticristo*

Gravina, Cesare (act): *The Man Who Laughs (1928); The Phantom Of The Opera (1925)*

Gray, Allan (mus): *The Late Edwina Black; A Matter Of Life And Death*

Gray, Barry (mus): *Daleks' Invasion Earth 2150 A.D.; Doppelganger*

Gray, Beatrice (act): *House Of Dracula*

Gray, Bill(y) (act, b. 1938): *The Day The Earth Stood Still; The Navy vs. The Night Monsters; Talk About A Stranger; Werewolves On Wheels*

Gray, Bruce (act): *Invitation To Hell*

Gray, Carole (act): *The Brides Of Fu Manchu; Curse Of The Fly; Devils Of Darkness; Island Of Terror*

Gray, Charles (act, b. 1928, nee Donald M. Gray): *The Beast Must Die; The Devil Rides Out; Diamonds Are Forever; I Accuse (1958); The Legacy; Man In The Moon (1960); The Man Outside (1967); Masquerade; The Mirror Crack'd; Murder On The Midnight Express; The Night Of The Generals; The Rocky Horror Picture Show; The Seven-Per-Cent Solution; Shock Treatment! (1981); You Only Live Twice*

Gray, Charles H. (act): *Prophecy (1979)*

Gray, Christopher (act): *Fear (1996); Night Visitors*

Gray, Coleen (act, b. 1922, nee Doris Jensen): *Ellery Queen: Don't Look Behind You; The Killing; The Leech Woman; Nightmare Alley; The Phantom Planet; The Vampire (1957)*

Gray, David (act): *The Savage Bees*

Gray, Denis (act): *A Dog, A Mouse And A Sputnik*

Gray, Dolly (act): *Valley Of The Dragons*

Gray, Dolores (act, b. 1924): *It's Always Fair Weather*

Gray, Donald (act): *The Diamond; Murder On The Campus; The Quatermass Experiment; Satellite In The Sky; Saturday Island; Strange Experiment; Supersonic Saucer; Timeslip*

Gray, Donald M. (act): see Gray, Charles

Gray, Dorian (act): *La Regina Delle Amazzoni*

Gray, Duane (act): *The Unknown Terror*

Gray, Dulcie (act, b. 1919, nee Dulcie Bailey): *A Man About The House; A Place Of One's Own; Wanted For Murder*

Gray, Eddie (act): *Life Is A Circus*

Gray, Elspet (act): *The Girl In A Swing*

Gray, Eric (act): *Where The Rainbow Ends*

Gray, Erin (act, b. 1950): *Buck Rogers In The 25th Century; Jason Goes To Hell: The Final Friday; T-Force; The Ultimate Impostor*

Gray, Eve (act): *The Crimson Candle; The Flaw; Midnight (1931); Murder At Monte Carlo; Scrooge (1935); Silver Blaze (1937); The Wickham Mystery*

Gray, Gary (act, b. 1936): *The Next Voice You Hear*

Gray, George (act): *Stargate*

Gray, Harry (mus): *The Mandarin Mystery*

Gray, Helen (dir): *Grimm's Fairy Tales For Adults*

Gray, Hugh (wri): *The Drum; Ulysses*

Gray, Jack (act): *The Lone Wolf Returns (1935)*

Gray, John (act): *Mars Attacks!*

Gray, John (cin): *Dark Mansions*

Gray, John (mus): *Metamorphosis: The Alien Factor*

Gray, John (wri): *Forty Naughty Girls*

Gray, Julie (act): *I Was A Teenage Sex Mutant; School Spirit*

Gray, Kenneth (act): *Retribution (1988)*

Gray, Leo (act): *Nightmare Alley*

Gray, Linda (GB act): *Dark Places*

Gray, Linda (USA act, b. 1940): *Slaughter; The Two Worlds Of Jennie Logan*

Gray, Lisa (act): *The Million Eyes Of Sumuru*

Gray, Lorna (act): *The Lone Wolf Spy Hunt; The Man They Could Not Hang; Nyoka And The Lost Secrets Of Hippocrates*

Gray, Lorraine (act): *Offerings*

Gray, Mike (dir): *Wavelength*

Gray, Mike (wri): *The China Syndrome; Wavelength*

Gray, Nadia (act, b. 1923, nee Nadia Kujnir-Herescu): *Adventurer Of Tortuga; Les Femmes S'en Balancent; The Golden Falcon; Maniac (1963); Night Without Stars; The Spider And The Fly; Top Secret (1952); Valley Of The Eagles*

Gray, Paul (act): *Around The World Under The Sea*

Gray, Peter (cin): *Endgame*

Gray, Roger (act): *The Lone Wolf Returns (1935)*

Gray, Sally (Can act): *The Keeper*

Gray, Sally (GB act, b. 1916, nee Constance Stevens): *Green For Danger; I'll Get You; The Mark Of Cain; Mr. Reeder In Room 13; Obsession (1949); The Saint In London; The Saint's Vacation; They Made Me A Fugitive*

Gray, Sam (act): *Wolfen*

Gray, Sherman (wri): *Hitler's Daughter*

Gray, Spalding (act): *Diabolique (1996); To Save A Child*

Gray, Vivean (act): *The Last Wave; Picnic At Hanging Rock*

Gray, William (wri): *The Changeling; Humongous; The Philadelphia Experiment; Prom Night*

Gray, Willoughby (act): *The Man Outside (1967); Richard III (1955); Stranger From Venus; A View To A Kill*

Graydon, Richard (act): *Deja Vu; Octopussy*

Graydon, W. Murray (wri): *Sexton Blake*

Grayling, Richard Ford (act): *Simon, King Of The Witches*

Grayson, Ambrose (wri): *Dick Barton At Bay; Dick Barton Strikes Back*

Grayson, Barry (act): *Writer's Block*

Grayson, Brian (act): *The Power (1980)*

Grayson, Charles (wri): *The Boys From Syracuse*

Grayson, Diane (act): *Blind Terror*

Grayson, Garth (wri): *The Girl From Downing Street*

Grayson, Godfrey (dir): *Date At Midnight; Dick Barton At Bay; Dick Barton Strikes Back; Room To Let; The Spider's Web*

Grayson, Godfrey (wri): *Room To Let*

Grayson, Kurt (act): *The Octagon; Ravagers*

Grayson, Richard (act): *Chain Of Circumstance*

Grayson, Wendell (act): *Death Dreams*

Grdnic, Joy (act): *Time Walker*

Greatbatch, Paul (act): *Vice Versa (1988)*

Greatorex, Christina (act): *Murder In Mind*

Greaves, Kristoffer (act): *Something Is Out There*

Greaves, Paul (act): *Burke And Hare*

Greci, Jose (act): *Hercules Against The Barbarians; Sins Of Babylon*

Greco, Joe (act): *The Nutty Professor (1996)*

Greco, Jose (act, b. 1918): *Around The World In 80 Days*

Greco, Juliette (act, b. 1927): *The Green Glove; The Night Of The Generals; Orphee*

Greek, Janet (dir): *Spellbinder*

Greely, Evelyn (act): *Bulldog Drummond (1923)*

Green, Adolph (act): *Simon*

Green, Adolph (mus & wri, b. 1915): *It's Always Fair Weather*

Green, Alan (wri): *The Long Wait*

Green, Alfred E. (dir, 1889-1960): *The Gracie Allen Murder Case; The Green Goddess (1929); Invasion U.S.A.; League Of Frightened Men; A Thousand And One Nights (1945)*

Green, Amy (act): *An Inspector Calls*

Green, Austin (act): *Journey To The Center Of Time; Ring Of Terror; The Story Of Mankind*

Green, Bernard (mus): *The Brass Bottle (1964); Zotz!*

Green, Billy (act): *Midnight (1980)*

Green, Bruce Seth (dir): *Running Against Time*

Green, Carlotta (act): *The Adventures Of Hercules*

Green, Cathy (act): *I, Desire*

Green, Cliff(ord) (wri): *Baby: Secret Of The Lost Legend; Picnic At Hanging Rock; Three Wishes (1995)*

Green, Danny (act, b. 1903): *Fiddlers Three; A Kid For Two Farthings; The Lady Killers (1956); Man In The Moon (1960); The Old Dark House (1963); The 7th Voyage Of Sinbad; The Silent House; Whispering Smith Hits London*

Green, Dennis (1930s & 1940s act): *The Hound Of The Baskervilles (1939); The Lone Wolf In London; Mighty Joe Young*

Green, Dennis (1990s act): *Jacob's Ladder*

Green, Donald (cin): see Masciocchi, Raffaele

Green, Donna (act): *Frankenstein Island*

Green, Dorothy (act): *The Six Million Dollar Man*

Green, Eileen (wri): *Baby: Secret Of The Lost Legend*

Green, Ellen (wri): *Three Wishes (1995)*

Green, G. (wri): *La Vergine Di Norimberga*

Green, Garard (act): *The Flesh And The Fiends; Hour Of Decision; The Trollenberg Terror*

Green, Gilbert (act): *Dark Intruder; Experiment In Terror; Homicidal*

Green, Gladys (act): see Arthur, Jean

Green, Guy (cin, b. 1913): *Great Expectations (1946); The Hour Of 13; The Story Of Robin Hood; Take My Life*

Green, Guy (dir, b. 1913): *The Magus; The Snorkel*

Green, Heather (act): *Bloodspell*

Green, Howard J. (wri): *After Midnight With Boston Blackie; The Mad Doctor; Meet Nero Wolfe*

Green, J.R. (act): *The Alien's Return*

Green, Jack N. (cin): *Twister*

Green, Jane (act): *The Cockeyed Miracle*

Green, Janet (wri, b. 1914): *Life For Ruth; Midnight Lace (1960 & 1981); Sapphire*

Green, Joey (act): *Exorcist II: The Heretic*

Green, John Martin (act): [illegible]

Green, Joseph (act): *The Baron Of Arizona*

Green, Joseph (dir & wri): *The Brain That Wouldn't Die*

Green, Judd (act): *Called Back; Chu Chin Chow* (1923); *High Treason* (1929); *The Man In Motley; Maria Marten* (1928); *The Pied Piper Of Hamelin; A Smart Set; Sweeney Todd*

Green, Karen (act): *Lizzie*

Green, Katie (act): *Revenge Of The Teenage Vixens From Outer Space*

Green, Kerri (act): *The Goonies*

Green, Lewis (wri): *Never Talk To Strangers*

Green, Lynda Mason (act): *The Intruder Within*

Green, Lynn (act): *The Shape Of Things To Come* (1979)

Green, Mae (act): see Parker, Jean

Green, Michael (act): *Creator*

Green, Mike (act): *This Is Not A Test*

Green, Nan (act): *Teenage Zombies*

Green, Nigel (act, 1923-1972): *Countess Dracula; Deadlier Than The Male; Doctor Of Seven Dials; The Face Of Fu Manchu; Gawain And The Green Knight; The Ipcress File; Jason And The Argonauts; The Kremlin Letter; Let's Kill Uncle; Man At Carlton Tower; The Man Who Finally Died; The Masque Of The Red Death* (1964); *Mysterious Island* (1961); *Playback; The Ruling Class; The Skull; Sword Of Sherwood Forest; Witness In The Dark; The Wrecking Crew*

Green, Pamela (act): *Legend Of The Werewolf; Peeping Tom*

Green, Philip (act): *The Frozen Dead*

Green, Phil(ip) (mus, b. 1917): *Bobbikins; The Girl Hunters; Man In The Moon* (1960); *The Man Who Finally Died; Masquerade; Sapphire; Who Done It?* (1956); *The Yellow Balloon*

Green, Reg (act): *At The Stroke Of Nine*

Green, Rita (act): *Daughter Of Dr. Jekyll; Indestructible Man*

Green, Rocky (act): *King Solomon's Mines* (1985)

Green, Seth (act): *It* (1990); *My Stepmother Is An Alien*

Green, Seymour (act): *The Diamond*

Green, Steven Alan (act): *It's Alive III: Island Of The Alive*

Green, Tom (act): *Mother Goose Nursery Rhymes; X-Rays*

Green, Tom (dir): *Natural Laws Reversed; Shamus O'Brien: or, Saved From The Scaffold*

Green, Wallace (dir & cin): *The Hellstrom Chronicle*

Green, Walon (wri): *Eraser; RoboCop 2; Solarbabies; Strange New World*

Green, Wanya (act): *Heart And Souls*

Green, Wilhelmina (act): *The Godsend*

Green, William E. (act): *It Happens Every Spring*

Greenan, David (E.) (act): *Battlestar Galactica; The Man In The Santa Claus Suit*

Greenaway, David (act): *Return To Oz*

Greenaway, Peter (dir): *Prospero's Books*

Greenaway, Peter (wri): *The Medusa Touch; Prospero's Books*

Greenawdt, Debi (act): *The Reflecting Skin*

Greenbaum, Everett (wri): *The Ghost And Mr. Chicken; The Reluctant Astronaut*

Greenbaum, Mutz (cin & dir): see Greene, Max

Greenberg, Adam (cin): *Alien Nation; Eraser; First Knight; Ghost* (1990); *Near Dark; Once Bitten; Spellbinder; The Terminator; Terminator 2: Judgment Day*

Greenberg, Barry (act): *Slaughter*

Greenberg, Bob (cin): *Dark Star*

Greenberg, Ed (act): *Caveman* (1981)

Greenberg, Glen (act): *Slugs*

Greenberg, Helen (act): *Ghost In The Machine*

Greenberg, Henry F. (wri): *The Caretakers*

Greenberg, Joel (act): *Mother's Day*

Greenberg, Marti (act): *Edward Scissorhands*

Greenberg, Mitchell (act): *Thinner*

Greenberg, Richard Alan (dir): *Little Monsters*

Greenberg, Robbie (cin): *Creator; Dr. Dracula; Time Walker*

Greenberg, Robert (act): *Chopping Mall*

Greenberg, Stanley (R.) (wri): *Logan's Run; Soylent Green*

Greenblatt, Shon (act): *Freddy's Dead: The Final Nightmare*

Greenburg, Dan (wri): *A Deadly Vision; The Guardian*

Greene, Addison (act): *Naked Evil*

Greene, Al (mus): *Death Curse Of Tartu*

Greene, Angela (act, 1921-1978): *The Cosmic Man; Futureworld; Jungle Jim In The Forbidden Land; Night Of The Blood-Beast*

Greene, Barbara (act): *Blind Man's Bluff* (1936)

Greene, Bob (act): *Copycat*

Greene, Clarence (wri): *Color Me Dead; D.O.A.* (1949 & 1988); *The Thief*

Greene, Craig (cin): *The Offspring*

Greene, Daniel (act): *Elvira, Mistress Of The Dark*

Greene, David (act): *Daughter Of Darkness* (1948)

Greene, David (dir, b. 1924): *The Count Of Monte Cristo* (1975); *Ellery Queen; I Start Counting; Madame Sin; Night Of The Hunter* (1991); *Prototype; The Shuttered Room; A Vacation In Hell; What Ever Happened To Baby Jane?* (1991); *World War III*

Greene, David (wri, b. 1924): *Madame Sin*

Greene, David Plunkett (wri): *The Tell-Tale Heart* (1934)

Greene, Deborah (act): *Beyond The Universe*

Greene, Elizabeth (act): *Offerings*

Greene, Ellen (act): *Little Shop Of Horrors* (1986); *Me And Him*

Greene, Eric (act): *Through The Magic Pyramid*

Greene, Eve (wri): *The Great Impersonation* (1935)

Greene, Graham (wri, 1904-1991): *Confidential Agent; The Fallen Idol; Ministry Of Fear; The Stranger's Hand; The Third Man*

Greene, Harold (wri): *Hide And Seek*

Greene, Harrison (act): *Dick Tracy* (1937); *Dick Tracy's G-Men; International House; Mr. Moto's Gamble; The Vampire Bat*

Greene, Herbert (dir): *The Cosmic Man*

Greene, Howard (act): *Horrors Of The Black Museum*

Greene, James (act): *Bug; Philadelphia Experiment Ii; The Spell*

Greene, Jon (act): *New Year's Evil; Schizoid* (1980)

Greene, Juliana (act): *Phoenix The Warrior*

Greene, Kim Morgan (act): *Dr. Jekyll And Ms. Hyde*

Greene, Leon (act): *Assignment To Kill; A Challenge For Robin Hood; The Devil Rides Out; Flash Gordon; Royal Flash; The Seven-Per-Cent Solution; The Thief Of Baghdad* (1978)

Greene, Lorne (act, 1915-1987, nee Chaim Leib): *Battlestar Galactica; Earthquake; The Submersion Of Japan*

Greene, Max (cin, a.k.a. Mutz Greenbaum): *Thunder Rock; Trent's Last Case* (1952); *Wanted For Murder*

Greene, Max (dir, a.k.a. Mutz Greenbaum): *Escape To Danger*

Greene, Melissa (act): *Crackle Of Death*

Greene, Michael (act): **Batteries Not Included; The Clones; Eve Of Destruction; Not Of This World; The Unborn II; White Of The Eye*

Greene, Michele (act): *Nightmare On The 13th Floor*

Greene, Otis (act): *The Disembodied; Voodoo Woman*

Greene, Peter (act): *The Mask* (1994); *The Rich Man's Wife*

Greene, Richard (act, 1918-1985): *The Bandits Of Corsica; The Black Castle; The Blood Of Fu Manchu; Captain Scarlett; The Castle Of Fu Manchu; The Hound Of The Baskervilles* (1939); *My Daughter Joy; Shadow Of The Eagle; Sword Of Sherwood Forest; Tales From The Crypt*

Greene, Russ (act): *A Nymphoid Barbarian In Dinosaur Hell*

Greene, Shecky (act): *Midnight Lace* (1981); *Splash*

Greene, Stanley (act): *The Wiz*

Greene, Victor M. (wri): *The Spider* (1939)

Greene, (W.) Howard (cin): *Cobra Woman; Gypsy Wildcat; The Jungle Book* (1942); *Phantom Of The Opera* (1943); *Raiders Of The Seven Seas; When Worlds Collide*

Greene, Walter (mus): *The Brain From Planet Arous; Teenage Monster; War Of The Satellites*

Greener, Dorothy (act): *They Might Be Giants*

Greenewalt, Mark (act): *Princess Warrior*

Greenfeld, Josh (wri): *Oh, God! Book II*

Greenfield, Debbie (act): *Prom Night*

Greenfield, Kate (act): *Willow*

Greenfield, Ruth (act): *Willow*

Greenfield, Stephen (cin): *The Strangeness*

Greenhalgh, Jack (cin): *Adventure Island; Blonde For A Day; Buried Alive* (1940); *Dead Men Walk; Fear In The Night* (1947); *Larceny In Her Heart; Lost Continent* (1951); *The Mad Monster; Murder Is My Business; Three On A Ticket; Too Many Winners; White Pongo*

Greenhut, Jennifer (act): *The Craft; Virtuosity*

Greenidge, Terence (act): *Richard III* (1955)

Greenison, Amy (act): *Mutants In Paradise*

Greenlaw, Verina (act): *The Haunting; The Masque Of The Red Death* (1964)

Greenleaf, Jim (act): *Evilspeak*

Greenleaf, Raymond (act, 1892-1963): *The Bandits Of Corsica; The Night The World Exploded; Son Of Sinbad; The Vampire* (1957)

Greenman, Alvin (act): *The Beast From 20,000 Fathoms*

Greeno, Paul (act): *Tales From The Darkside*

Greenquist, Brad (act): *Mutants In Paradise; Pet Sematary*

Greenspan, David (act): *The Toxic Avenger, Part II*

Greenspon, Sis (act): *Jack's Back*

Greenstreet, Sydney (act, 1879-1954): *Background To Danger; Between Two Worlds; The Conspirators; Devotion; The Maltese Falcon* (1941); *The Mask Of Dimitrios; Three Strangers; The Velvet Touch; The Woman In White* (1948)

Greenwald, Robert (dir): *Xanadu*

Greenwald, Virginia (act): *Jack's Wife*

Greenway, Tom (act, 1909-1985): *North By Northwest*

Greenwood, Bobbie/Bobby (act): *Daughters Of Satan; Equalizer 2000*

Greenwood, Bruce (act): *The Companion* (1994); *Dream Man; The Servants Of Twilight*

Greenwood, Charlotte (act, 1893-1978): *Cheaters At Play*

Greenwood, Edwin (act): *Jamaica Inn* (1939)

Greenwood, Edwin (dir): *The Bells* (1923); *Lucrezia Borgia: Or, Plaything Of Power; Scrooge* (1923)

Greenwood, Edwin (wri): *The Man Who Knew Too Much* (1934); *Young And Innocent*

Greenwood, Joan (act, 1919-1987): *The Bad Lord Byron; The Hound Of The Baskervilles* (1978); *Kind Hearts And Coronets; The Man In The White Suit; Mr. Peek-A-Boo; The Moon-Spinners; Mysterious Island* (1961); *The October Man; The Uncanny; The Water Babies*

Greenwood, John (mus, b. 1889): *Elephant Boy; Pimpernel Smith*

Greenwood, Miles (act): *Psychomania* (1972)

Greenwood, Patrick (act): *Short Circuit 2*

Greenwood, Paul (act): *Captain Kronos: Vampire Hunter; Frightmare* (1974)

Greenwood, Rochelle (act): *The Stepfather*

Greenwood, Rosamund (act): *Night Of The Demon* (1972); *The Village Of The Damned* (1960); *The Witches* (1990)

Greer, Bob (act): *King Solomon's Mines* (1985)

Greer, Dabbs (act): *House Of Wax; Invasion Of The Body Snatchers* (1956); *It!—The Terror From Beyond Space; Monkey Business; The Vampire* (1957)

Greer, Jane (act, b. 1924): *Dick Tracy* (1945); *The Falcon's Alibi; Man Of A Thousand Faces; The Prisoner Of Zenda* (1952); *Run For The Sun; Sinbad The Sailor*

Greer, Johnny (act): *Scared To Death* (1980)

Greer, Lennie (act): *Billy The Kid vs. Dracula*

Greer, Luanshya (act): *They Came From Beyond Space*

Greer, Michael (act): *Dead People*

Greer, Robin (act): *Satan's Cheerleaders*

Greet, Clare (act): *Maria Marten: or, The Murder In The Red Barn* (1935); *The Pointing Finger; The Ring; The Sign Of Four* (1932)

Greeves, Vernon (act): *The Intimate Stranger; Lady Of Vengeance*

Grefe, William (dir): *The Checkered Flag; Death Curse Of Tartu; Impulse!* (1974); *The Naked Zoo; Stanley; Sting Of Death*

Grefe, William (wri): *The Checkered Flag; Death Curse Of Tartu; Stanley*

Greger, Freddy (wri): *The Ape Creature*

Gregg, Alan (act): *Dick Tracy Returns*

Gregg, Bradley (act): *Class Of 1999; Explorers; Fire In The Sky* (1993); *A Nightamre On Elm Street 3: Dream Warriors*

Gregg, Christina (act): *Cover Girl Killer*

Gregg, Dave (act): *Empire Of Ash III*

Gregg, Everley (act): *Deadly Record; The Ghost Goes West; Great Expectations* (1946); *The Night Of The Full Moon; A Stolen Face*

Gregg, Hubert (act): *The Story Of Robin Hood; Svengali* (1954)

Gregg, Joyce (act): *The Woman Eater*

Gregg, Olive (act): *The Water Babies*

Gregg, Virginia (act, 1916-1986): *The Amazing Mr. X; The Bubble; Crowhaven Farm; The Night Stalker* (1971); *The Stranger; Two On A Guillotine*

Gregor, Nora (act): *The Rules Of The Game*

Gregoretti, Ugo (dir & wri, b. 1930): *Omicron*

Gregorio, Darnelle (act): *Tarzan In Manhattan*

Gregoris, Jerry (act): *Rana: The Legend Of Shadow Lake*

Gregory, A. (act): *The Glittering Sword*

Gregory, Andre (act): *Demolition Man*

Gregory, Celia (act): *Agatha*

Gregory, Constantine (act): *Goldeneye*

Gregory, Dick (act): *The Wrong Box*

Gregory, Edna (act): *The Great Gabbo; In The Palace Of The King*

Gregory, Erna (act): *Repossessed*

Gregory, Iain (act): *Lancelot And Guinevere*

Gregory, James (act, b. 1911): *The Ambushers; Beneath The Planet Of The Apes; The Manchurian Candidate; Miracle On 34th Street* (1973); *Murderers' Row; Nightfall* (1956); *The Silencers* (1966); *The Strongest Man In The World; A Very Missing Person; X-15*

Gregory, Joy E. (act): *Blink*

Gregory, Kathleen Jordon (act): *The Curse*

Gregory, Laura (act): *Surf Nazis Must Die*

Gregory, Lee (act): *The Godsend*

Gregory, Mark (act): *Escape From The Bronx*

Gregory, Mary (act): *Sleeper*

Gregory, Michael (USA act): *Eraser; The Lawnmower Man; Robocop; Total Recall*

Gregory, Michael (W. Ger act): *Making Contact*

Gregory, Natalie (act): *Alice In Wonderland* (1985)

Gregory, Nigel (act): *Killer's Moon*

Gregory, Paul (act): *Mary Shelley's 'Frankenstein'*

Gregory, Sharee (act): *Alice In Wonderland* (1985)

Gregory, Thea (act): *The Golden Link; Satellite In The Sky; Solution By Phone*

Gregson, Joan (act): *The Neptune Factor*

Gregson, John (act, 1919-1975): *Faces In The Dark; Fright* (1971); *The Frightened City; The Lavender Hill Mob; The Night Of The Generals; Treasure Island* (1950); *The Treasure Of Monte Cristo* (1961); *Three Cases Of Murder; Venetian Bird*

Gregson, Michael (act): see Craig, Michael

Grei, Robyn (act): *The Brotherhood Of Satan*

Greif, Stephen (act): *Cry Wolf* (1980); *A Distant Scream; The Savage Curse*

Greifer, Lewis (wri): *Cash On Demand; The Man Who Finally Died*

Greig, Clive (act): see Clive, Colin

Greig, Robert (act, 1880-1958): *Arabian Nights; Devil Doll* (1936); *Love Me Tonight; The Picture Of Dorian Gray* (1945); *Trouble For Two*

Greig, Virginia (act): *Supergirl* (1984)

Greist, Kim (act): *Brazil; C.H.U.D.; Roswell*

Grell, Dean (act): *Attack Of The Killer Tomatoes*

Grellier, Michelle (act): *Act Of Aggression*

Grellis, Brian (act): *Fear In The Night* (1972); *Threads; Trog*

Grelson, Ankie (act): *Blind Date*

Gremillon, Jean (dir, 1901-1959): *Astrologie*

Grenfell, Joyce (act, 1910-1979, nee Joyce Phipps): *The Old Dark House* (1963); *Stage Fright*

Grenham, Jami Lynn (act): *C.H.U.D. II*

Grenier, Zach (act): *Twister*

Grenrock, Joshua (act): *Nightmares* (1983)

Grenville-Taylor, H. (wri): *Abide With Me*

Gresak, Beryl (act): *Howling IV*

Gresham, Velma (act): *White Zombie*

Gresham, William Lindsay (wri): *Nightmare Alley*

Gresley, Margery (act): *The Revenge Of Frankenstein*

Gress, Googy (act): *Babes In Toyland* (1986); *Vibes*

Gretter, Heinrich (act): *The Invisible Terror*

Greve, Gunther (act): *The Green Slime*

Greville, Edmond T. (dir, b. 1906): *The Accident; The Hands Of Orlac* (1959); *Secret Lives*

Greville, Edmond T. (wri, b. 1906): *The Hands Of Orlac* (1959); *La Vergine Di Norimberga*

Greville, Margot (act): *Moonbeam Magic*

Greville-Bell, Anthony (wri): *The God King; Theater Of Blood*

Grevioux, Kevin (act): *Congo*

Grewald, Helmut (cin): *Milczaca Gwiazda*

Grey, Alexis (act): *The Toxic Avenger, Part II*

Grey, Anne (act): *Dr. Sin Fang; The Lure; The Man At Six; Murder At Covent Garden; Number 17; The Old Man; The Squeaker* (1930); *The Wandering Jew* (1933)

Grey, Arnold (act): *The Mummy* (1932)

Grey, Clifford (wri): *Sleeping Car To Trieste*

Grey, David (act): *The Asphyx*

Grey, Eunice (act): *Dungeons Of Horror*

Grey, Gloria (act): *Dante's Inferno* (1924)

Grey, Harold (wri): The Man Who Stayed At Home
Grey, Harry (mus): Dick Tracy (1937); Sharad Of Atlantis
Grey, Jennifer (act): Light Years
Grey, Joel (act, b. 1932): Man On A Swing; Remo Williams: The Adventure Begins; The Seven-Per-Cent Solution
Grey, Lorraine (act): Sexton Blake And The Mademoiselle
Grey, Minna (act): Altar Chains; Paul Sleuth, Crime Investigator: The Burglary Syndicate; The Sorrows Of Satan (1917); The Woman In White (1929)
Grey, Monica (act): Undercover Girl (1958)
Grey, Nan (act, 1918-1993, nee Eschal Miller): The Black Doll; Dracula's Daughter; The House Of The Seven Gables; The Invisible Man Returns; Tower Of London (1939)
Grey, Richard (act): The Two-Headed Spy
Grey, Richard M. (dir): The Man With The Twisted Lip
Grey, Ronald (act): Scream Of The Demon Lover
Grey, Samantha (act): Night Of The Zombies (1981)
Grey, Shirley (act): Green Eyes; The Mystery Of The Mary Celeste
Grey, Virginia (act, b. 1917): Another Thin Man; Black Zoo; House Of Horrors (1946); Jungle Jim; Strangers In The Night; Swamp Fire; Target Earth; Tarzan's New York Adventure; The Threat (1949); Unknown Island
Greybe, Valerie (act): Cavegirl (1985)
Grey Shadow (act): The Invisible Man's Revenge
Greytak, Eugene (act): Repossessed
Gribbin, Katherine Houston (act): see Houston, Renee
Gribble, William (act): Secrets Of The Phantom Caverns
Gribbon, Eddie (act): The Bat (1926)
Gribbon, Harry (act): The Gorilla (1931); The Mysterious Island (1929)
Grice, Grimes (wri): The Beguiled; The Possession Of Joel Delaney
Gricius, Jonas (cin): Korol Lir
Grieco, Richard (act, b. 1964): The Demolitionist; Inhumanoid; Tomcat: Dangerous Desires; A Vow To A Kill; When Time Expires
Grieco, Sergio (dir): The Nights Of Lucretia Borgia
Griego, Tony (act): The Resurrection Of Zachary Wheeler
Grier, David Alan (act): Amazon Women On The Moon; Blankman; Jumanji; Tales From The Hood
Grier, Pam (act, b. 1949): The Arena (1973); Bill & Ted's Bogus Journey; Class Of 1999; Escape From L.A.; Mars Attacks!; Scream, Blacula, Scream; Something Wicked This Way Comes; Twilight People; The Vindicator
Grier, Roosevelt "Rosey" (act, b. 1932): Evil In The Deep; The Thing With Two Heads
Gries, Jonathan (act): Fright Night II; The Monster Squad; Terrorvision
Gries, Tom (dir, b. 1922): _Earth II
Gries, Tom (wri, b. 1922): King Dinosaur
Griesemer, John (act): The Brother From Another Planet
Grieve, John (act): The 39 Steps (1978)
Grieve, Oriane (act): The Mirror Crack'd
Grieve, Russ (act): The Hills Have Eyes
Grifasi, Joe (act): Batman Forever; Still Of The Night
Griffen, Garett (cin): Ice Cream Man
Griffeth, Simone (act): Death Race 2000; Mandrake
Griffi, Peppino Patroni (wri): C'era Una Volta
Griffies, Ethel (act, 1878-1975): Alice In Wonderland (1933); The Birds; Bulldog Drummond Strikes Back (1934); Castle In The Desert; Dead Men Tell; Devotion; Four Frightened People; The Horn Blows At Midnight; Jane Eyre (1944); Love Me Tonight; Stranger On The Third Floor; Time To Kill (1942); Werewolf Of London
Griffin, Celine (act): Encounter At Raven's Gate
Griffin, David (act): The Deathshead Vampire; Trog
Griffin, Debralee (act): see Paget, Debra
Griffin, Eddie (act): The Meteor Man
Griffin, Jack (act): Charley And The Angel; Mind Over Murder
Griffin, Josephine (act): The House Of The Arrow (1953)
Griffin, Katie (act): Electra (1995)
Griffin, Lorie (act): Teen Wolf
Griffin, Lynne (act): Curtains; Silent Night, Evil Night
Griffin, Merv (act, b. 1925): Alice In Wonderland (1985); Hello Down There; The Man With Two Brains; Phantom Of The Rue Morgue
Griffin, Renee (act): Cyborg 2: Glass Shadow
Griffin, Robert (E.) (act): I Was A Teenage Werewolf; The Monster From Green Hell; Please Murder Me
Griffin, Sean (act): The Aliens Are Coming
Griffin, Tod (act): She Demons; She-Devil
Griffin, Tom (act): Ice
Griffis, Robert (act): Offerings
Griffis, William (act): It Came Upon The Midnight Clear; Mr. Destiny
Griffith, Andy (act, b. 1926): The Demon Murder Case; Salvage
Griffith, Anthony (act): Tales From The Hood
Griffith, Benjamin (act): Those Dear Departed
Griffith, Billy (act): The Devil Bat
Griffith, Charles B. (act): It Conquered The World
Griffith, Charles (B.) (dir): Dr. Heckyl & Mr. Hype; Up From The Depths
Griffith, Charles (B.) (wri): Atlas; Attack Of The Crab Monsters; Beast From Haunted Cave; A Bucket Of Blood (1959); Creature From The Haunted Sea; Death Race 2000; Dr. Heckyl & Mr. Hype; The Little Shop Of Horrors (1960 & 1986); Not Of This Earth (1957 & 1988); The Undead
Griffith, Cindi (act): Shadow Of The Hawk
Griffith, D.W. (act, 1875-1948, nee Lawrence Griffith): Rescued From An Eagle's Nest
Griffith, D.W. (dir, 1875-1948): The Avenging Conscience; Edgar Allan Poe; In Prehistoric Days; The Lesser Evil; One Exciting Night; One Million B.C.; Richelieu, Or The Cardinal's Conspiracy; The Sorrows Of Satan (1925)
Griffith, D.W. (wri, 1875-1948): The Avenging Conscience; The Flying Torpedo; One Exciting Night
Griffith, Edward H. (dir & wri): Alias The Lone Wolf
Griffith, Eva (act): Voices; The Witches And The Grinnygog
Griffith, Fred (act): 23 Paces To Baker Street
Griffith, Gordon (S.) (act): The Clutching Hand; Jungle Trail Of The Son Of Tarzan; Tarzan Of The Apes
Griffith, Hugh (act, b. 1912): The Abominable Dr. Phibes; Craze; Cry Of The Banshee; Dr. Phibes Rises Again; Hide And Seek; The Hound Of The Baskervilles (1978); Kind Hearts And Coronets; The Last Days Of Man On Earth; Legend Of The Werewolf; Oh Dad Poor Dad, Mamma's Hung You In The Closet And I'm Feelin' So Sad; The Three Weird Sisters; Who Slew Auntie Roo?; Wuthering Heights (1970)
Griffith, James (act): The Amazing Transparent Man; Flood; The Legend Of Sleepy Hollow; Omar Khayyam; Phantom Of The Jungle; Search For Danger; The Vampire (1957)
Griffith, Jay (act): Appointment With Murder
Griffith, Kenneth (act, b. 1921): The Assassination Bureau; Circus Of Horrors; Forbidden; The Frightened City; The Green Buddha; High Treason (1951); The House In Nightmare Park; Jane Eyre (1970); Koroshi; The Man Upstairs; 1984 (1955); Revenge (1971, Gb); The Shop At Sly Corner; The Starfish; Thirty-Six Hours; The Two-Headed Spy; The Zany Adventures Of Robin Hood
Griffith, Lawrence (act): see Griffith, D.W.
Griffith, Mark (act): Hamlet (1969)
Griffith, Melanie (act, b. 1957): Alfred Hitchcock Presents; Body Double; Cherry 2000; Pacific Heights
Griffith, Nona (act): The Unseen (1945)
Griffith, Peter (act): Halloween
Griffith, Robert (act): A Night Of Magic
Griffith, Tom (act): Fiend (1980); Nightbeast
Griffith, Tracy (act): The First Power; Skeeter
Griffith, William (act): Devil Goddess; Jaws 2
Griffiths, Charles (dir): La Sorella Di Satan
Griffiths, Lt. Comm. David (act): Virus
Griffiths, Derek (act): Rentadick
Griffiths, Fred (act): Billion Dollar Brain; The Lady Killers (1956)
Griffiths, Georgina (act): Memoirs Of A Survivor
Griffiths, Howard (wri): Licensed To Kill
Griffiths, Jane (act, b. 1920): The Accursed; The Double; The Green Scarf; Shadow Of A Man
Griffiths, Leon (wri): The Flesh And The Fiends; The Hell-Fire Club; The Treasure Of Monte Cristo (1961)
Griffiths, Lucy (act): Frankenstein And The Monster From Hell; The Hound Of The Baskervilles (1978); The Lady Killers (1956)
Griffiths, Richard (act): Greystoke: The Legend Of Tarzan, Lord Of The Apes; Superman II
Griffiths, Robert (act): The Elusive Pimpernel (1950)
Griffiths, S.G. (cin): Animal Farm
Griffo, Joseph S. (act): Night Of The Creeps
Grigg, Dewey G. (cin): Jekyll And Hyde...Together Again
Griggs, Barklie K. (mus): Barb Wire
Griggs, Gene (cin): The Octagon; The Ultimate Warrior
Griggs, Jeff (act): Forbidden Games (1995)
Griggs, Loyal (cin): Visit To A Small Planet
Grigsby, Ele (act): Invasion Of The Girl Snatchers
Grigsby, Garon (act): Watchers II
Grillet, Eugene (act): La Prima Donna
Grilli, Armando (cin): She (1983)
Grimaldi, Dan (act): Don't Go In The House
Grimaldi, gabrielle (act): Johnny Hamlet
Grimaldi, Giovanni (wri): Il Figlio Di Spartacus
Grimaldi, Hugo (dir): Godzilla Raids Again; The Human Duplicators; Mutiny In Outer Space
Grimaud, (Jean) (wri): La Danza Macabra; Horror
Grimes, Barbara (act): Macbeth (1971)
Grimes, Chester (act): Kiss Daddy Goodbye
Grimes, Frank (act): The Funhouse (1981)
Grimes, Karolyn (act): The Bishop's Wife
Grimes, Rosemary (act): Island Of Lost Souls
Grimes, Scott (act): Critters; Critters 2: The Main Course; It Came Upon The Midnight Clear; Night Life (1989, USA); The Night They Saved Christmas; Pinocchio And The Emperor Of The Night
Grimes, Tammy (act, b. 1934): The Borrowers; The Horror At 37,000 Feet; The Other Man
Grimm, The Brothers (wri): The Three Wishes (1954); Tom Thumb; The Wonderful World Of The Brothers Grimm
Grimm, Maria (act): Sherlock Holmes In New York
Grimm, Tim (act): Pandora's Clock
Grimsby, Roger (act): Nothing But Trouble
Grimshaw, Jim (act): The Handmaid's Tale; King Kong Lives
Grimwood, Herbert (act): Kismet (1914)
Grinde, Nick (dir, b. 1894): Before I Hang' The Bishop Murder Case; The Man They Could Not Hang; The Man With Nine Lives
Grinde, Nick (wri, b. 1894): Babes In Toyland (1934)
Grinell, William (act): Carnival Of Blood
Grinko, Nikolai (act): Solaris
Grinling, Amanda (act): Hot Enough For June
Grinn, Sandey (act): The Return Of The Six Million Dollar Man And The Bionic Woman
Grinnage, Jack (act): Crackle Of Death; Demon And The Mummy
Grippe, Peter (act): La Sorella Di Satan
Grippe, Ragnar (mus): Return (1985)
Grippo, Jim (act): Midnight (1980)
Grippo, Lou (act): Midnight (1980)
Grisel, Louis (act): Jane Eyre (1921)
Grisham, John (wri): A Time To Kill (1996)
Grisham, Paul (act): The Pit (1983)
Grisoni, Tony (wri) Dark Water
Grissell, Wallace (dir): Captain Mephisto And The Transformation Machine; Jungle Gold
Grissmer, John (dir): Scalpel
Grissmer, John (wri): The Bride (1973); Scalpel
Grissom, John (act): Dream A Little Dream
Griswold, Grace (act): One Exciting Night
Griswold, Michael (act): Creature; Scared To Death (1980)
Griswold, Tracy (act): The Children
Gritzus, Ionas (cin): The Blue Bird (1976)
Grives, Steven (act): Inseminoid
Grizz, Pam (act): The Ewok Adventure; Ewoks: The Battle For Endor
Grizzard, George (act, b. 1928): The Stranger Within
Grodin, Charles (act, b. 1935): Heart And Souls; Heaven Can Wait (1978); The Incredible Shrinking Woman; King Kong (1976); Rosemary's Baby
Grody, Kathryn (act): Parents
Groenenberg, Ed (act): Starcrossed
Groenenberg, Roland (act): Starcrossed
Grofe, Ferde (mus, 1892-1972): Rocketship X-M
Grohl, David (mus): Touch
Grohmann, Martje (act): Nosferatu, The Vampyre
Gromov, A. (act): Pikovaya Dama (1910)
Gronau, Ernst (act): Genuine
Groom, Alison (act): see Skipworth, Alison
Groom, Sam (act): Betrayal; Beyond The Bermuda Triangle; Deadly Eyes; The Eliminators; Time Travelers (1976)
Groome, Mrs. Sydney (wri): The Mystery Of Mr. Bernard Brown
Gross, Andrew (mus): Bio-Dome
Gross, Arye (act, b. 1960): Hexed; House II: The Second Story
Gross, Charles (mus): Apprentice To Murder; Arthur The King; Brock's Last Case; The Murders In The Rue Morgue (1986); The Night They Saved Christmas
Gross, Edan (act): And You Thought Your Parents Were Weird
Gross, Francis (wri): The Diabolical Invention
Gross, Gene (act): Phantom Of The Paradise
Gross, Greg(g) (mus): Deathrow Gameshow; A Polish Vampire In Burbank
Gross Jr., Jack (wri): Welcome To Arrow Beach
Gross, Jackie (act): The Dungeonmaster
Gross, Joel (wri): No Escape (1994)
Gross, Michael (act, b. 1947): A Connecticut Yankee In King Arthur's Court (1989); Sometimes They Come Back...Again; Tremors; Tremors 2: Aftershocks
Gross, Paul (act): 20,000 Leagues Under The Sea (1997, CBS-TV)
Gross, Richard (act): Phenomenon
Gross, Sol (act): Torchy Plays With Dynamite
Gross, Willard (act): Creature Of The Walking Dead
Gross, Yoram (wri): Dot And The Kangaroo
Grossman, Karen (cin): Shadowzone
Grossman, Ted (act): Always; The Goonies; Raiders Of The Lost Ark; Ssssss
Grossmith, Lawrence (act): The Brass Bottle (1914); The Private Life Of Don Juan; Silver Blaze (1937)
Grossowna, Helena (act): O Dwoch Takich Co Ukradli Ksiezyc
Grote, William (wri): The Man Without A Body
Groth, Jan (act): Nosferatu, The Vampyre
Groth, Robin (act): The Seventh Sign
Grothum, Brigette (act): Curse Of The Yellow Snake
Grottesi, Rosalba (act): Spara Forte, Piu Forte...Non Capisco
Grout, Austin (act): Just Imagine
Grout, James (act): The Abominable Dr. Phibes; File It Under Fear; The Ruling Class
Grove, Ethel (act): The Clutching Hand
Grove, R.L. (wri): The Deathmaster
Grove, Richard (act): Not Of This World
Grove, Sybil (act): The Black Pearl; I'm An Explosive
Grover, Cynthia (act): Jaws 2
Grover, Ed (act): Who?
Grover, Gar (act): Torment (1986)
Grover, George (act): The Frighteners
Grover, Mary (act): The Spectre Of Edgar Allan Poe
Grover, Max (act): The Frighteners
Grovernor, Linda (act): Stunts Unlimited
Groves, Charles (act): The Face At The Window (1932); The Sands Of Time
Groves, Fred (act): Beautiful Jim; The Crimson Circle (1922); The Firm Of Girdlestone; London's Yellow Peril; Maria Marten: Or, The Murder In The Red Barn (1913); Popsy Wopsy; Puppets Of Fate; The Suicide Club (1914); The Two Roads
Groves, Herman (wri): The Strongest Man In The World
Groves, Jerry (act): The Naked Jungle
Groves, John (wri): Biggles: Adventures In Time; Tarantulas: The Deadly Cargo
Groves, Phil (wri): Cavegirl (1985)
Groves, Robin (act): The Nesting; Silver Bullet
Growcott, Frank R. (act): The Underworld Of London
Gruault, Jean (wri): L'enfant Sauvage
Grubb, Davis (wri): The Night Of The Hunter (1955 & 1991)
Grubb, Robert (act): Mad Max Beyond Thunderdome
Grubel, Ilone (act): Jonathan
Gruber, Frank (wri, b. 1904): Bulldog Drummond At Bay (1947): The Challenge; The Mask Of Dimitrios; Terror By Night
Gruber, John (act): Gargoyles
Grubman, Carol (act): The Horror Of Party Beach
Grueber, Charles (act): The Kindred
Gruen, Barbara (act): Jacob's Ladder
Gruendgens, Gustaf (act): Faust (1963); M (1931)
Grumbach, Jean-Pierre (dir): see Melville, Jean-Pierre
Grumbar, Dorothy (act): Secrets Of Sex
Grummette, Steve (act): Flesh Gordon
Grundy, Sam (act): see Ford, Wallace

Grune, Karl (dir, 1890-1962): *Am Rande Der Welt; Arabella*
Gruner, Mark (act): *Jaws 2; The Tribe*
Gruner, Olivier (act): *Automatic; Nemesis*
Gruning, Ilka (act): *Temptation (1946)*
Grunwald, Cheryl (act): *A Clockwork Orange*
Grunwald, Morten (act): *Operation: Lovebirds; Relax, Freddie*
Grushko, Nicolai (act): *Rocket Attack U.S.A.*
Grusin, David/Dave (mus): *Dead Men Tell No Tales; The Goonies; Heaven Can Wait (1978); A Howling In The Woods; The Mad Room; Murder By Death; 3 Days Of The Condor*
Gruska, Jay (mus): *Child Of Darkness, Child Of Light; Nightmare On The 13th Floor; Wheels Of Terror*
Gruska, Michele (act): *Return Of The Jedi*
Gruskin, Jerry (wri): *Tarzan And The Huntress*
Gruszynski, Alexander (cin): *Bad Dreams; Cast A Deadly Spell; The Craft; Tremors; Twisted*
Gryff, Stefan (act): *Legend Of The Werewolf*
Gual, Pamela (act): *Caveman (1981)*
Guard, Barrie (mus): *Monster In The Closet; The Toxic Avenger, Part II*
Guard, Christopher (act): *Dead Man's Folly; Memoirs Of A Survivor*
Guard, Dominic (act): *The Count Of Monte Cristo (1975); Picnic At Hanging Rock*
Guard, Kit (act): *Torchy Runs For Mayor*
Guard, Philip (act): *The Angel Who Pawned Her Harp*
Guardino, Harry (act, 1925-1995): *Hold Back Tomorrow; The Last Child; Rollercoaster*
Guardino, Jerome (act): *Octaman; Tarantulas: The Deadly Cargo*
Guarino, Gustavo (act): *Anguish*
Guarneri, Miles (act): *Surf Nazis Must Die*
Guarnieri, Ennio (cin): *The Flower In His Mouth; Hitler: The Last Ten Days; Marta*
Guash, Sara (act): *Survive!*
Guastaferro, Joe (act): *Vice Versa (1988)*
Guastaferro, Vincent (act): *Shocker*
Guay, Paul (wri): *Liar Liar*
Guber, Elizabeth (act): *The Craft*
Guderman, Linda (act): *Macabre (1958)*
Gudrun, Ann (act): *The Diamond; Thirty-Six Hours*
Guedes, Luis (act): *The 7th Voyage Of Sinbad*
Guefen, Anthony (mus): *Assassin (1986); Deadly Eyes; The Stuff*
Guenette, Robert (dir & wri): *The Man Who Saw Tomorrow; The Mysterious Monsters*
Guerin, Francois (act): *The Spy Is A Girl; Les Yeux Sans Visage*
Guerin, Lenmana (act): *From Hell It Came*
Guerner, Enrique (cin): *Cuento De Hadas*
Guerney, Claude (wri): *Green For Danger*
Guernsey Jr., Otis (wri): *13 Frightened Girls*
Gueron, Ivan (act): *I'm Dangerous Tonight*
Guerra, Blanca (act): *Robbers Of The Sacred Mountain*
Guerra, Luigi Antonio (act): *Deborah*
Guerra, Ruy (dir, b. 1931): *Os Deuses E Os Mortos*
Guerra, Ruy (wri, b. 1931): *L'assassino; Os Deuses E Os Mortos*
Guerra, Tonino (wri): *Amarcord; C'era Una Volta; La Decima Vittima; Ghosts-Italian Style; Perseus The Invincible*
Guerrero, Carmen (act): *Dracula (1931, Spanish-Speaking Version)*
Guerrero, Evelyn (act): *The Toolbox Murders*
Guerrini, Mino (wri): *La Ragazza Che Sapeva Troppo*
Guest, Christopher (act, b. 1948): *Heartbeeps; It Happened One Christmas; Little Shop Of Horrors (1986); The Princess Bride*
Guest, Christopher (dir, b. 1948): *Attack Of The 50-Foot Woman (1993)*
Guest, Lance (act): *Halloween II; Jaws: The Revenge*
Guest, Nicholas (act): *The Return Of Sherlock Holmes (1986)*
Guest, Val (dir, b. 1911): *The Abominable Snowman Of The Himalayas; Assignment K; The Camp On Blood Island; Casino Royale; The Day The Earth Caught Fire; The Full Treatment; Just William's Luck; Life Is A Circus; Mark Of The Devil (1985); Men Of Sherwood Forest; Mr. Drake's Duck; Murders At The Windmill; The Quatermass Experiment; Quatermass II; They Can't Hang Me; When Dinosaurs Ruled The Earth; Where The Spies Are*
Guest, Val (wri, b. 1911): *Alf's Button Afloat; Another Man's Poison; Assignment K; The Camp On Blood Island; The Day The Earth Caught Fire; The Full Treatment; The Ghost Train (1941); Just William's Luck; King Arthur Was A Gentleman; Life Is A Circus; Mr. Drake's Duck; Murder At The Windmill; The Quatermass Experiment; Quatermass II; They Can't Hang Me; When Dinosaurs Ruled The Earth; Where The Spies Are*
Guetzkow, Scott (act): *Neon Maniacs*
Guffey, Burnett (cin, 1905-1983): *The Ambushers; A Close Call For Boston Blackie; Homicidal; I Love A Mystery (1945); Mr. Sardonicus; Nightfall (1956); Screaming Mimi; The Silencers (1966); The Sniper*
Guffey, Carl (act): *Close Encounters Of The Third Kind; The Sheriff And The Satellite Kid*
Guffey, Cary (act): *Mutant*
Guggenheim, Lisa (act): *Blood Diner*
Guggenheim, Ted (act): *Blood Diner*
Gugino, Roslyn (act): *Fear No Evil (1981)*
Gugolka, John (act): *Our Mother's House*
Guhl, George (act): *The Adventurous Blonde; After The Thin Man; Blondes At Work; Charlie Chan On Broadway; Fly-Away Baby; Nancy Drew And The Hidden Staircase; Torchy Blane In Chinatown; Torchy Blane In Panama; Torchy Gets Her Man; Torchy Runs For Mayor*
Guhl, William (act): *Grave Of The Vampire*
Guichard, Paul (cin): *Paris Qui Dort*
Guida, Wandisa (act): *Ercole Contro Roma; Killers Are Challenged; Machiste In King Solomon's Mines; The Prisoner Of The Iron Mask; I Vampiri*
Guidall, George (act): *Tales From The Darkside*
Guidera, Anthony (act): *Species*
Guidry, Cindy (act): *Wes Craven's New Nightmare*
Guilbert, Yvette (act): *Faust (1926)*
Guild, Leo (wri): *The Devil's Messenger*
Guild, Nancy (act, b. 1926): *Abbott And Costello Meet The Invisible Man; Black Magic (1949); The Brasher Doubloon; Francis Covers The Big Town; Somewhere In The Night*
Guilfoyle, Paul (act, 1902-1961): *Bomba And The Hidden City; The Boy And The Pirates; The Diamond Queen; The Golden Idol; It Happened Tomorrow; Mighty Joe Young; The Millerson Case; The Saint In New York; The Saint In Palm Springs; The Saint Takes Over; Time To Kill (1942); White Savage*
Guilfoyle, Paul (1980's & 1990's act): *Extreme Measures; Howard The Duck; Notorious (1992); The Serpent And The Rainbow*
Guillaume, Robert (act, b. 1937): *The Kid With The Broken Halo; The Meteor Man; Pandora's Clock*
Guillen, Victor (act): *Anguish*
Guillermin, John (dir, b. 1925): *Death On The Nile; King Kong (1976); King Kong Lives; Sheena; Tarzan Goes To India; Tarzan's Greatest Adventure; Torment (1949); The Towering Inferno*
Guillermin, John (wri, b. 1925): *Tarzan Goes To India; Tarzan's Greatest Adventure; Torment (1949)*
Guillory, Bennet (act): *Maid To Order*
Guillory, Donahue (act): *Shock Waves*
Guillot, Alvaro (act): *Pharaoh's Curse*
Guillot, Claudia (act): *The King Of Crime*
Guilmain, Ofelia (act): *El Baron Del Terror; El Hombre Y El Monstruo*
Guinan, Francis (act): *Mortal Sins*
Guindon, Ian (act): *The Lost Boys*
Guinle, Armande (act): *Zex*
Guinness, (Sir) Alec (act, b. 1914): *The Empire Strikes Back; Great Expectations (1946); Hitler: The Last Ten Days; Kind Hearts And Coronets; The Lady Killers (1956); Last Holiday; The Lavender Hill Mob; The Man In The White Suit; Murder By Death; The Quiller Memorandum; Return Of The Jedi; Scrooge (1970); Star Wars*
Guinness, Lindus (act): *Grave Of The Vampire*
Guinness, Matthew (act): *The Bride (1985)*
Guion, Raymond (act): see Raymond, Gene
Guiot, Fernand (act): *The Murders In The Rue Morgue (1986)*
Guise, Tom S. (act): *Crooked Alley; Secrets Of The Night*
Guise, Windham/Wyndham (act): *A Christmas Carol (1914); The Firm Of Girdlestone; The Lyons Mail; The Sons Of Satan; Trilby (1914)*
Guisol, Henri (act): *Le Comte De Monte Cristo; Lola Montes; Teodora, Imperatrice Di Bisanzio*
Guissart, Rene (cin): *While Paris Sleeps*
Guitry, Sacha (act, dir & wri, 1885-1957): *Poison (1951)*
Guittard, Laurence (act): *Covenant*
Gulager, Clu (act): *Bridge Across Time; A Force Of One; The Hidden; Houston, We've Got A Problem; The Initiation; A Nightmare On Elm Street, Part 2: Freddy's Revenge; The Off-Spring; The Return Of The Living Dead (1985); Smile, Jenny, You're Dead; Uninvited (1987)*
Gulino, Mary (act): *Tuck Everlasting*
Gulla, Jonathan (act): *Deadly Blessing*
Gullan, Campbell (act): *The Black Tulip (1937); The Claydon Treasure Mystery*
Gulliton, Patrick (act): *Time Travelers (1976)*
Gulliver, Clifford (dir): *Museum Mystery*
Gulliver, Tony (act): *Around The World Under The Sea*
Gullotta, Leo (act): *Sinbad And The Seven Seas*
Gulpilil (act): *Dark Age; The Last Wave*
Gumbert, Steve (act): *Empire Of Ash III*
Gumm, Frances (act): see Garland, Judy
Gummer, Chris (act): *Nightbeast*
Gummersbach, Florence (act): *The Toxic Avenger, Part II*
Gunderman, Ralph (act): *Making Mr. Right*
Gundrey, V. Gareth (dir & wri): *The Hound Of The Baskervilles (1931)*
Gunn, Andrew (act): *The Gate*
Gunn, Bill (act & dir): *Ganja And Hess*
Gunn, Bill (wri): *The Angel Levine; Ganja And Hess*
Gunn, Gilbert (dir, b. 1912): *The Strange World Of Planet X*
Gunn, Gilbert (wri, b. 1912): *The Door With Seven Locks (1940)*
Gunn, Gladys (act): see Henson, Gladys
Gunn, James (wri, b. 1923): *The Immortal; Lady Of Burlesque; Tromeo And Juliet*
Gunn, Janet (act): *Marquis De Sade*
Gunn, Judy (act): *Silver Blaze (1937); White Lilac*
Gunn, Moses (act, 1929-1993): *Amityville II: The Possession; Bates Motel; Firestarter; Haunts Of The Very Rich; The Neverending Story; Rollerball*
Gunn, Nicholas (act): *Charlie Chan And The Curse Of The Dragon Queen*
Gunn, Rocky (act): *Charlie Chan: Happiness Is A Warm Clue*
Gunn, Vincenetta (act): *Copycat*
Gunnell, Frank (act): *Picnic At Hanging Rock*
Gunner, Robert (act): *Planet Of The Apes*
Gunning, Christopher (mus): *Hands Of The Ripper*
Gunsburg, Roy S. (act): *Death Valley*
Gunter, Bob (act): *Maximum Overdrive*
Gunther, Hilda (act): *The Night Porter*
Gunther, Ted (act): *The Green Slime*
Gunther, Ulrich (act): *Enemy Mine*
Gunton, Bob (act): *Demolition Man; Dolores Claiborne*
Gunzburg, Milton (wri): *The Devil Commands*
Gupta, Sneh (act): *The Return Of Sherlock Holmes (1986)*
Gur, Aliza (act): *Agent For H.A.R.M.; From Russia With Love; The Hand Of Night; Tarzan And The Jungle Boy*
Gurdin, Natasha (act): see Wood, Natalie
Gurfinkel, David (cin): *Mata Hari (1985)*
Gurie, Sigrid (act, 1911-1969, nee Sigrid Gurie Haukelid): *Dark Streets Of Cairo; Sword Of The Avenger*
Gurley, Lisa (act): *The Entity*
Gurney, Kate (act): *At The Villa Rose (1920)*
Gurney, Rachel (act): *Funeral In Berlin*
Gurney Jr., Robert J. (dir, b. 1924): *Edge Of Fury; Terror From The Year 5,000*
Gurney Jr., Robert J. (wri, b. 1924): *Edge Of Fury; Invasion Of The Saucer Men; Terror From The Year 5,000*
Gurney, Sharon (act): *The Corpse; Deathline*
Gurovich, Danko (act): *White Of The Eye*
Gurpinar, Gigi (act): *Captain Kronos: Vampire Hunter*
Gurr, J. (cin): *Animal Farm*
Gurskey, Barbara J. (act): *The Toxic Avenger*
Gurtler, Danny (act): *Der Januskopf*
Gurwitch, Annabelle (act): *Encino Woman*
Guss, Louis (act): *Highlander*
Guss, Peter (act): *Revenge Of The Teenage Vixens From Outer Space*
Guss, Reuben (act): *Class Of Nuke'em High; The Toxic Avenger*
Gustafson, Lori (act): *Flesh-Eating Mothers*
Gustafsson, Greta Louisa (act): see Garbo, Greta
Guthe, Fred (cin): *Curtains; The Pit (1983)*
Guthrie, Carl (E.) (cin): *Bedtime For Bonzo; Between Two Worlds; Bonzo Goes To College; Cry Wolf (1947); Everything's Ducky; Francis Covers The Big Town; Francis Goes To West Point; Francis In The Navy; Frankenstein (1970); House On Haunted Hill; Long John Silver; Macabre (1958); The Woman In White (1948); X-15*
Guthrie, Michelle (act): *Child Of Darkness, Child Of Light*
Guthrie, Richard (act): *Fer-De-Lance*
Guthrie, Tani (Phelps) (act): *Daughters Of Satan; The Thirsty Dead; The Tribe*
Guthrie, Tyrone (dir): *Oedipus Rex*
Gutierez, Eduardo (act): *Tystnaden*
Gutierrez, Armando (act): *The Beast Of Hollow Mountain*
Gutierrez, Ricardo (act): *Shocker*
Gutlich, Georg (act): *Confess, Dr. Corda*
Guttenberg, Steve(n) (act, b. 1958): *Amazon Women On The Moon; The Boys From Brazil; Cocoon; Cocoon: The Return; The Day After; High Spirits; The Man Who Wasn't There; Short Circuit*
Gutteridge, Lucy (act): *Arthur The King; A Christmas Carol (1984)*
Gutteridge, Martin (cin): *A Christmas Carol (1984); Highlander*
Guttierrez, Zaide S. (act): *Firewalker*
Guttman, Ronald (act): *The Beast (1996); Notorious (1992)*
Guy, Jennifer (act): *Persecution; Without A Clue*
Guy, Joyce (act): *Shocker*
Guy, Lawrence (act): *Chopping Mall; Witches' Brew*
Guy, Virginia (act): *Deja Vu*
Guy-Blache, Alice (dir, 1875-1968): *The Pit And The Pendulum (1913)*
Guyer, Cindy (act): *Jack's Back*
Guyler, Deryck (act): *One Of Our Dinosaurs Is Missing*
Guza Jr., Robert (wri): *Curtains; Prom Night*
Guzda, Laurie (act): *Blood Diner*
Guzman, Enrique (act): *Invasion Sinitestra*
Guzman, Linda (act): *Amazons (1986)*
Guzzi, Paul (act): *A Nymphoid Barbarian In Dinosaur Hell*
Guzzinati, Margherita (act): *La Strega In Amore*
Gwaltney, Robert (act): *Cocoon: The Return*
Gwenn, Edmund (act, 1875-1959): *Between Two Worlds; Bewitched; Bonzo Goes To College; Condemned To Death; Foreign Correspondent; For Heaven's Sake; It's A Dog's Life; I Was A Spy; Miracle On 34th Street (1947); Peking Express; Les Miserables (1952); Passing Shadows; A Rocket From Calabuch; Scotland Yard (1941); Them! (1954); The Trouble With Harry; The Walking Dead*
Gwillim, David (act, b. 1948): *The Island At The Top Of The World*
Gwillim, Jack (act): *Circus Of Horrors; Clash Of The Titans; The Curse Of The Mummy's Tomb; In Search Of The Castaways; Jason And The Argonauts; The Monster Squad; Sword Of Sherwood Forest*
Gwilym, Mike (act): *Venom (1982)*
Gwoman, Milton (act): *Charlie Chan At The Opera*
Gwynn, Alfred (mus): *The Devil's Messenger*
Gwynn, Michael (act, 1916-1976): *The Camp On Blood Island; The Deadly Bees; Jason And The Argonauts; The Revenge Of Frankenstein; Scars Of Dracula; The Village Of The Damned (1960); What A Carve Up!*
Gwynne, Anne (act, b. 1918, nee Marguerite Gwynne Trice): *The Black Cat (1941); Black Friday; The Deadly Ray From Mars; Dick Tracy Meets Gruesome; Fear (1946); The Ghost Goes West; The Glass Alibi; House Of Frankenstein; Murder In The Blue Room; Phantom Of The Jungle; Peril From The Planet Mongo; Purple Death From Outer Space; The Strange Case Of Dr. Rx; Teenage Monster; Weird Woman*
Gwynne, Fred (act, 1926-1993): *The Boy Who Could Fly; The Littlest Angel (1969); Munster, Go Home!; The Munsters' Revenge; The Mysterious Stranger; Pet Sematary; Sanctuary Of Fear; Simon*
Gwynne, Michael C. (act): *A Cold Night's Death; Matt Helm; The Terminal Man*
Gwyther, Geoffrey (act): *Red Aces*
Gyalog, Odon (act): *Mata Hari (1985)*
Gyergyay, Stefan (act): see Geray, Steven
Gynt, Greta (act, b. 1916, nee Greta Woxholt): *Bluebeard's Ten Honeymoons; Bulldog Sees It Through; Dark Eyes Of London; Dear Murderer; The Ringer (1952); Sexton Blake And The Hooded Terror; Shadow Of The Eagle; The Strange Case Of Dr. Manning; Take My Life; Whispering Smith Hits London*

Haade, William (act): *The Gracie Allen Murder Case; The Invisible Menace; Just Off Broadway*
Haag, Bob (act): *School Spirit*
Haag, Christina (act): *Lost In The Bermuda Triangle*
Haak, Dianne (dir): *Secrets In The Attic*
Haas, Charles (F.) (dir, b. 1913): *Platinum High School; Tarzan And The Trappers*
Haas, Charlie (act): *Gremlins 2: The New Batch; Matinee*

Haas, Charlie (wri): Gremlins 2: The New Batch; Martians Go Home; Matinee

Haas, Dolly (act): I Confess; Spy Of Napoleon

Haas, Hugo (act, 1901-1968): Bait; The Girl On The Bridge; King Solomon's Mines (1949); Lizzie; One Girl's Confession; Pickup; Strange Fascination; Thy Neighbor's Wife; Vendetta

Haas, Hugo (dir, 1901-1968): Bait; The Girl On The Bridge; Hold Back Tomorrow; Lizzie; One Girl's Confession; Pickup; Strange Fascination; Thy Neighbor's Wife

Haas, Hugo (wri, 1901-1968): Bait; The Girl On The Bridge; Hold Back Tomorrow; One Girl's Confession; Pickup; Strange Fascination; Thy Neighbor's Wife

Haas, Jerrico (wri): Matinee

Haas, Lukas (act, b. 1976): Amazing Stories II; Lady In White; Mars Attacks!; Solarbabies

Haas, Heather (act): The 'Burbs; Gremlins 2: The New Batch

Haas, Victoria (act): Attack Of The 50-Foot Woman (1993)

Haase, Cathy (act): The Kill-Off

Haase, Rod (act): Final Eye

Haba, Bohumil (cin): Cisaruv Pekar, Pekaruv Cisar

Habbema, Cox (act): A Question Of Silence

Habe, Hans (wri): The Devil's Agent

Haber, Joyce (act): Conquest Of The Planet Of The Apes

Haber, Mark (dir): Alien Cargo

Haber, Paul (act): Fear No Evil (1981)

Haber, Sandy (wri): The Mask (1961)

Haberle, Sean (act): The Surgeon

Haberman, Linda (act): The Fan

Haberman, Steve (wri): Dracula: Dead And Loving It

Habermann, Eva (act): I Worship His Shadow

Haberstroh Studios (cin): Mission Mars

Hachey, Sylvie (act): Alien High

Hachford, Rio (act): Strange Days

Hack, Charly (act): Making Contact

Hack, Olivia (act): Star Trek: Generations

Hack, Shelley (act, b. 1949): Blind Fear; The Stepfather; Time After Time; Troll

Kackenberg, Siegrid (act): Confess, Dr. Corda

Hacker, Joseph (act): The Ultimate Impostor

Hacker, Leonard (act): see Hackett, Buddy

Hackett, Albert (wri, 1900-1995): After The Thin Man; Another Thin Man; It's A Wonderful Life; Lady In The Dark; The Thin Man

Hackett, Buddy (act, b. 1924, nee Leonard Hacker): Everything's Ducky; The Little Mermaid; The Love Bug; Scrooged; The Wonderful World Of The Brothers Grimm

Hackett, Gillian (act): The Outcasts

Hackett, Jim (act): I Was A Teenage Sex Mutant

Hackett, Joan (act, 1934-1983): Assignment To Kill; Dead Of Night (1977); How Awful About Allan; The Last Of Sheila; The Other Man; The Possessed (1977); Reflections of Murder; The Terminal Man

Hackett, John (act): Tales Of Terror

Hackett, Jonathan (act): The Lady Vanishes (1979)

Hackett, Karl (act): His Brother's Ghost

Hackett, Martha (act): The Last Man On Planet Earth; Leprechaun 2

Hackett, Raymond (act, 1903-1958): The Cat Creeps (1930)

Hackett, Tod (wri): Popcorn

Hackett, Walter (wri): The Barton Mystery (1920 & 1932); Sorry You've Been Troubled

Hackford, Taylor (dir): Devil's Advocate; Dolores Claiborne

Hackforth, Norman (act): The Twenty Questions Murder

Hackman, Bob (act): Magic

Hackman, Gene (act, b. 1931): Antz; The Domino Principle; Extreme Measures; Lilith; Marooned; Narrow Margin (1990); Night Moves; No Way Out; The Package; The Poseidon Adventure; Shadow On The Land; Superman (1978); Superman II; Superman IV: The Quest For Peace; Target; Young Frankenstein

Hackney, Alan (wri, b. 1924): Sword Of Sherwood Forest

Hackney, Doris (act): Midnight (1980)

Hackney, Pearl (act): The Hound Of The Baskervilles (1978); Schizo (1977); Tiffany Jones

Hada, Michiko (act): The Mystery Of Rampo

Hadden, Connie Lynn (act): Piranha II: The Spawning

Hadden, George (dir): Charlie Chan's Courage

Haddigan, Mark (act): 101 Dalmatians (1996)

Haddock, Jack (act): The Angry Red Planet

Haddon, Dayle (act): Cyborg (1989); The Magic Bubble; Spermula

Haddon, Larry (act): Hands Of A Stranger

Haddon, Laurence (act): The Aliens Are Coming; School Spirit

Haddon, Peter (act): Alf's Button (1930); Death At Broadcasting House; The Secret Of Stamboul; The Silent Passenger

Haden, Oliver (act): Blue Ice

Haden, Sara (act, 1899-1981): Above Suspicion; Betrayed Women; The Bishop's Wife; Crime And Punishment (1935, USA); The Great Rupert; Mad Love; She-Wolf Of London

Hadfield, Mark (act): Mary Shelley's 'Frankenstein'

Hadjidakis, Manos (mus, 1925-1994): Sweet Movie; Topkapi

Hadji-Lazaro, Francos (act): Cemetery Man

Hadley, Brett (act): Maid To Order

Hadley, Don (wri): The Legend Of Blood Mountain

Hadley, Michael (act): Never-Never Land

Hadley, Reed (act, 1911-1974, nee Reed Herring): The Baron Of Arizona; Brain Of Blood; The Brasher Doubloon; Circumstantial Evidence; Leave Her To Heaven; Moro Witch Doctor; Shock (1946)

Hadlow, Mark (act): Meet The Feebles; Strange Behavior

Hadzivageli, Laoura (act): For Your Eyes Only

Haefli, Charles (act): Charlie Chan On Broadway

Hae-Jin, Shim (act): Gesom E Kako Shipta

Haeni, Gaston (act): Babes In Toyland (1986)

Haentzchel, George (mus): Confess, Dr. Corda

Haerter, Gerald (act): Caltiki, Il Mostro Immortale

Haffner, Ingrid (act): Dilemma; Five To One

Haffner, Jack (act): The Incredible Petrified World; Rymdinvasion I Lappland

Hafner, Bob (act): The Hideous Sun Demon

Hafner, Ingrid (act): Bluebeard's Ten Honeymoons

Hagan, Anna (act): Shadow Of The Hawk; The Stepfather

Hagan, Gordon (act): The Boy Who Never Was

Hagan, Laurie (act): Something Evil

Hagan, Marianne (act): Halloween: The Curse Of Michael Myers

Hagan, Molly (act): Justin Case

Hagar, Karol (act): Where Has Poor Mickey Gone?

Hagar, Sammy (mus): Heavy Metal

Hagdahl, Doug (act): The Milpitas Monster

Hageman, Richard (mus): Paris Calling

Hagen, Anna (act): The Groundstar Conspiracy

Hagen, Antje (act): Due To An Act Of God

Hagen, Claire (act): Night Creature; Wonder Women

Hagen, Earle (mus): Forgotten City Of The Planet Of The Apes

Hagen, Edna (act): A Kiss For Cinderella

Hagen, Erica (act): Soylent Green

Hagen, Eve-Maria (act): Milczaca Gwiazda

Hagen, Ira (act): Funeral In Berlin

Hagen, Jean (act, 1925-1977, nee Jean Verhagen): Dead Ringer; Panic In Year Zero; Shadow In The Sky; The Shaggy Dog (1959)

Hagen, Julia (act): Mary Reilly

Hagen, Kevin (act): Dead Men Tell No Tales (1971)

Hagen, Mary Ann (act): Freejack

Hagen, Molly (act): Sometimes They Come Back...Again

Hagen, Paul (act): Crazy Paradise

Hagen, Peter (act): Kil 1

Hagen, Ross (act): Alienator; Angels' Wild Women; Attack Of The 60 Foot Centerfold; Dinosaur Island (1994); Night Creature; The Phantom Empire; Star Slammer; Warlords; Wonder Women

Hagen, Uta (act, b. 1919): The Boys From Brazil; The Other (1972)

Hagen, Victor (act): Dial 999 (1938); Passenger To London; Twin Faces

Hager, Harold (act): Blood Diner

Hagerty, Michael G. (act): Dick Tracy (1990)

Haggar, James (act): The Sign Of The Cross

Haggar, James (wri): The Maid Of Cefn Ydfa (1914)

Haggar, Jenny (act): The Maid Of Cefn Ydfa (1914)

Haggar, Violet (act): The Red Barn Crime: or, Maria Martin

Haggar, Walter (act): The Red Barn Crime: or, Maria Martin

Haggar, William (dir): The Dumb Man Of Manchester; The Maid Of Cefn Ydfa (1908); The Maniac's Guillotine; The Sign Of The Cross; The Wild Man Of Borneo

Haggar Jr., Will(iam) (act): The Dumb Man Of Manchester; The Maid Of Cefn Ydfa (1908 & 1914); The Sign Of The Cross

Haggar Jr., William (dir & wri): The Maid Of Cefn Ydfa (1914)

Haggard, H. Rider (wri, 1856-1925): Allan Quatermain And The Lost City Of Gold; La Danse De Feu; King Solomon's Mines (1937, 1949 & 1985); King Solomon's Treasure; She (1911, 1916, 1917, 1925, 1935, 1965 & 1983); The Vengeance Of She; Watusi

Haggard, Merle (act): Hillbillys In A Haunted House

Haggard, Piers (dir): The Blood On Satan's Claw; The Fiendish Plot Of Dr. Fu Manchu; The Quatermass Conclusion; Venom (1982)

Haggard, Piers (wri): The Blood On Satan's Claw

Haggard, Stephen (act): Jamaica Inn (1939)

Haggart, David (wri): Sinful Davey

Haggart, James (wri): Sinful Davey

Haggarty, John (wri): Murder In Eden

Haggerty, Arthur (act): The Telephone Book

Haggerty, Dan (act): Bury Me An Angel; The Channeler; The Chilling (1989); Elves; Grizzly Mountain; Hex; Terror Out Of The Sky

Haggerty, Don (act): Back From The Dead; Calling Homicide; Cause For Alarm!; Crashing Las Vegas; Footsteps In The Night; Lost Planet Airmen; The Resurrection Of Zachary Wheeler; Rocket Man (1954)

Haggerty, Dylan (act): Grizzly Mountain

Haggerty, Fred (act): From Russia With Love

Haggerty, H.B. (act): Buck Rogers In The 25th Century; Curse Of The Black Widow; Death-Sport; Earthquake

Haggerty, Hardboiled (act): Shadow Of The Thin Man

Hagins, Montrose (act): Critters 2: The Main Course; The Relic

Hagiwara, Michael (act): Prehysteria! 2; Wes Craven's New Nightmare

Hagler, Nik (act): I Come In Peace

Hagleton, Lewis J. (wri): Clegg

Hagman, Larry (act, b. 1931): Beware! The Blob; Fail-Safe; A Howling In The Woods; The Return Of The World's Greatest Detective; Superman (1978)

Hagman, Larry (dir, b. 1931): Beware! The Blob

Hagmann, Stuart (dir): Tarantulas: The Deadly Cargo

Hagney, Frank (act): The Adventures Of Robin Hood; The Mysterious Mr. Moto; The Sea Beast; Too Many Winners; Zombies Of Mora Tau

Hagon, Garrick (act): Batman (1989); The Carnation Killer; Endless Descent; Mission: Impossible

Hagon, Rex (act): Hitler's Daughter; Last Bride of Salem; Short Circuit 2

Hagood, Rick (act): Sugar Hill

Hagopian, Berj (dir): Invasion of the Star Creatures

Hagopian, Dean (act): Brainscan; Scanners

Hague, Albert (act): Nightmares (1983)

Haguet, Andre (wri): Nick Carter Va Tout Casser

Hahn (III), Archie (act): Gremlins 2: The New Batch; Innerspace; It Happened One Christmas; Matinee; Misery; Phantom of the Paradise

Hahn, Eliska (act): Strangest Dreams: Invasion of the Space Preachers

Hahn, Jess (act): The Great Spy Chase; Mama Dracula; The Mysterious Island of Captain Nemo; Secret Agent Super Dragon; Topkapi

Hahn, Lisa (act): Alien Contamination

Hahn, Paul (act): The Amazing Colossal Man

Hahn, Ross (cin): Isle of the Snake People

Hahn, Steven (dir): Starchaser: The Legend of Orin

Hahn-Byrd, Adam (act): Diabolique (1996); Halloween H20

Hai, Farid Abdoul (cin): Dawn of the Mummy

Haid, Charles (act, b. 1943): Altered States; Deathmoon; Nightbreed

Haiduc, Ion (act): Bloodlust: Subspecies III

Haiduk, Stacy (act): The Beneficiary; Steel and Lace

Haig, Jack (act): Kadoyng

Haig, Raoul (dir & wri): The Wacky World of Dr. Morgus

Haig, Sid (act): Aftermath; Beyond Atlantis; Blood Bath (1966); Galaxy of Terror; The Goddess of Love; The Helicopter Spies; The Return of the World's Greatest Detective; Spider Baby; THX 1138; Warlords; Wonder Women

Haig, Terry (act): City On Fire; Happy Birthday to Me

Haig, Tony (act): The Clonus Horror; The Swarm

Haigh, Charles (act): Moon 44

Haigh, Ernest (act & wri): Fight In a Thieves' Kitchen; The Girl Who Came Back; The Lady In Black; Lost, Stolen or Strayed; Mother's Darling; The Prodigal Son

Haigh, Kenneth (act, b. 1932): The Deadly Affair; The Hunchback of Notre Dame (1977); Robin and Marian

Haigh, Michael (act): Dark of the Night

Haigh, Peter (act): Witch-Finder General

Haile, Henri (wri): Paradisio

Haim, Corey (act, b. 1971): Dream a Little Dream; Dream a Little Dream 2; Fever Lake; The Lost Boys; Silver Bullet; Watchers

Haines, Bill (act): I Was a Zombie for the F.B.I.

Haines, Brian (act): The Curse of the Golem; Never Mention Murder; Payment In Kind

Haines, Daniel (act): The Invisible Ray

Haines, Donald (act): Spooks Run Wild

Haines, Francis (mus): Split Second (1992)

Haines, Fred (dir): Steppenwolf

Haines, Jack (act): Strange Behavior

Haines, Jean (wri): Mr. H.C. Andersen

Haines, John (act): Empire of Ash III

Haines, Laurie (act): Starship Invasions

Haines, Lloyd (act): Look What's Happened to Rosemary's Baby

Haines, Loren (act): The Drifter

Haines, Patricia (act): The Fast Kill; The Last Shot You Hear; Night Caller from Outer Space; Virgin Witch

Haines, Paul (cin): The Lawnmower Man

Haines, Randa (dir): Alfred Hitchcock Presents

Haines, Richard (act): Alien from L.A.

Haines, Richard W. (dir): Alien Space Avenger; Class of Nuke 'em High; Splatter University

Haines, Richard W. (wri): Alien Space Avenger; Class of Nuke 'em High

Haines, Robert E. (act): The Lone Wolf (1924)

Haines, Ronald (dir): Deadlock (1943); The Man from Scotland Yard; The Man With the Magnetic Eyes; Mr. H.C. Andersen; The Thirteenth Instant

Haines, Ronald (wri): The Man from Scotland Yard; Mr. H.C. Andersen

Haines, William (act, 1900-1973): The Tower of Lies

Hair, Tom (act): Frankenhooker

Haire, Mary (act): Howling III

Hairston, Jester (act): Tarzan's Hidden Jungle

Haisman, Mervyn (wri): Curse of the Crimson Altar; Jane and the Lost City

Haitkin, Jacques (cin): The Ambulance; Buried Alive II; Galaxy of Terror; The Hidden; The House Where Evil Dwells; Inferno (1998); The Last Man On Planet Earth; The Lost Empire; Mom and Dad Save the World; My Demon Lover; A Nightmare On Elm Street, Part 2: Freddy's Revenge; The Private Eyes (1980); Shocker; The Silence of the Hams; Strays; To Die For

Haje, Khrystyne (act): Bates Motel; Cyborg 3; The Gifted One; Scanners: The Showdown

Haji (act): Bigfoot; Faster, Pussycat! Kill! Kill!; Motor Psycho

Hajmassy, Ilona (act): see Massey, Ilona

Hajnal, Stephen (cin): The Brain That Wouldn't Die

Hajos, Karl (mus): Appointment With Murder; The Devil's Cargo; Fog Island; Four Frightened People; Search for Danger

Hake, Ardell (mus): Scared to Death (1980)

Halain, Jean (wri): Le Comte de Monte Cristo; Fantomas Contro Scotland Yard

Halas, John (dir & wri, b. 1912): Animal Farm (1954)

Halberg, Garry (act): King Kong (1976)

Halbik, Herbert (act): The Third Man

Haldane, Bert (dir): Allan Field's Warning; An' Good In the Worst of Us; The Baby and the Bomb; Beneath the Mask; A Bid for Fortune; The Blind Heroine; A Boy Scout's Dream: or, How Billie Captured the Kaiser; Brigadier Gerard; A Brother's Atonement; A Burglar for a Night; By His Father's Orders; The Child Detective; Circumstantial Evidence (1910); The Convict's Sister; Darkest London: or, The Dancer's Romance; The Debt of Gambling; The Deception (1912); The Disinherited Nephew; A Double Life (1913); The Eccentric Uncle's Will; Ethel's Danger; The Faith Healer; A Flowergirl's Romance; The Foreign Spy (1911); The German Spy Peril; The Grip of Iron; His Honour at Stake; His Sister's Honour; Hunger's Curse; The Irony of Fate; Jane Shore (1915); The Lights o' London; Lust for Gold; The Man Who Kept Silent; A Night of Peril; A Plucky Kiddie; Polly the Girl Scout and the Jewel Thieves; The Price of Deception; Proud Clarissa; The Queen of the May; Right Is Might; The Rogues of London; The Silver Lining; The Thieves' Decoy; The Trail of Sand; The Trail of the Fatal Ruby; When Paths Diverge

Haldane, Bert (wri): The Grip of Iron

Haldane, Don (dir): *The Reincarnate*
Haldeman, Joe (wri): *Robot Jox*
Haldeman, Tim (act): *The Boy Who Cried Werewolf; Dante's Peak; Dark Mirror (1984)*
Hale (Sr.), Alan (act, 1892-1950, nee Rufus Alan McKahan): *The Adventures of Don Juan; The Adventures of Robin Hood; Dick Turpin; The Eleventh Hour (1923); Footsteps In the Dark; Great Expectations (1934); Green Hell; The Killer Is Loose; The Last Days of Pompeii (1935); The Leopard Lady; The Lost Patrol (1934); The Man In the Iron Mask (1939); Pursued; Robin Hood (1922); The Scarlet Letter (1934)*
Hale Jr., Alan (act, 1918-1990): *At Sword's Point; Captain Kidd and the Slave Girl; The Crawling Hand; The Fifth Musketeer; The Giant Spider Invasion; It Happens Every Spring; The Lady In the Iron Mask; Rogues of Sherwood Forest*
Hale, Barbara (act, b. 1922): *The Boy With Green Hair; The Clay Pigeon; The Falcon In Hollywood; The Falcon Out West; The Giant Spider Invasion; Lorna Doone (1951); The Seventh Victim; The Window*
Hale, Binnie (act): *Love from a Stranger (1937); The Phantom Light*
Hale, Bobby/Bobbie (act): *Bulldog Drummond Escapes; Mr. Moto Takes a Vacation*
Hale, Creighton (act, 1882-1965, nee Patrick Fitzgerald): *Bulldog Drummond Strikes Back (1934); Calling Philo Vance; The Cat and the Canary (1927); Charlie Chan On Broadway; Crime by Night; Cry Wolf (1947); Death from a Distance; The Hidden Hand; The Maltese Falcon (1941); Nancy Drew and the Hidden Staircase; One Million B.C.; Possessed (1947); The Return of Dr. X; Seven Footprints to Satan; The She-Creature; The Thin Man; Torchy Plays With Dynamite; Trilby (1923); The Two Mrs. Carrolls*
Hale, Diana (act): *It's Alive (1974)*
Hale, Elvi (act): *Man Detained*
Hale, George (cin): *Crazy House (1943)*
Hale, Georgina (act): *The Devils; The Watcher In the Woods*
Hale, Jean (act): *In Like Flint; Psychomania (1964); The St. Valentine's Day Massacre*
Hale, John (wri): *The Mind of Mr. Soames*
Hale, Jonathan (act, 1892-1966, nee Jonathan Hatley): *The Beginning or the End?; Call Northside 777; The Cat Creeps (1946); Charlie Chan at the Olympics; Charlie Chan at the Race Track; Charlie Chan's Secret; Dead Man's Eyes; Jaguar; League of Frightened Men; Lightning Strikes Twice; The Saint In New York; The Saint In Palm Springs; The Saint's Double Trouble; The Saint Strikes Back; The Saint Takes Over; The Steel Trap; The Strange Mr. Gregory; Strangers On a Train; Till Death*
Hale, Louise Closser (act): *Shanghai Express*
Hale, Mary (act): *Calling Dr. Death*
Hale, Mary (wri): *Multiplicity*
Hale, Michael (act): *Devil Bat's Daughter*
Hale, Nancy (act): *Lord of the Jungle; The War of the Worlds*
Hale, Richard (act): *The Diamond Queen; The Man With a Cloak; Night Gallery; Tower of London (1962)*
Hale, Robert (act): *Counter-Espionage*
Hale, Sonnie (act, 1902-1959, nee Robert Hale Munro): *Fiddlers Three; The Gaunt Stranger*
Hale, William/Billy (dir): *The Demon Murder Case; Red Alert*
Haler, Ted (act): *Deadly Messages; Uninvited (1993)*
Hales, Eric (act): *Double Alibi; The Secret of the Loch (1934)*
Hales, Gordon (dir): *Evidence In Concrete; Return to Sender; The Undesirable Neighbour*
Hales, Jonathan (wri): *Loophole; The Mirror Crack'd*
Halevy, Julian (wri): *Crack In the World; Horror Express; Psyche 59*
Haley, Bill (act): *The Fairy Bottle*
Haley, Brian (act): *Always; Mars Attacks!*
Haley, Haven Earle (act): *The Octagon*
Haley, Jack (act, 1900-1979): *Beyond the Blue Horizon; One Body Too Many; Scared Stiff (1945); The Wizard of Oz (1939)*
Haley, Jackie Earle (act): *Damnation Alley; Dollman; Forgotten City of the Planet of the Apes; Nemesis*
Haley, Janet (act): *Writer's Block*
Haley, Paul (act): *Killer Klowns from Outer Space*
Haley, W. Gladstone (act): *The Adventures of Dick Turpin-The Gunpowder Plot; Don Q-How He Outwitted Don Luis; Lieutenant Daring and the Photographing Pigeon*
Halffter, Cristobal (mus): *El Principe Encadenado*
Halffter, Rudolfo (mus): *The Living Idol*
Halford, Michael Craig (act): *Cyborg (1989)*
Halfpenny, Jim (mus): *The Power Within (1995)*
Halfpenny, Tony (act): *Eyes of Fate*
Halin, Jean (wri): *OSS 117-Mission for a Killer*
Hall, Adam (wri): *The Quiller Memorandum; Quiller: The Price of Violence*
Hall, Adelaide (act): *The Thief of Bagdad (1940)*
Hall, Adrian (act): *Chitty Chitty Bang Bang; Kadoyng*
Hall, Alaina Reed (act): *Death Becomes Her*
Hall, Alan (cin): *The Glitterball*
Hall, Albert (act): *The Bermuda Traingle; The Night They Saved Christmas*
Hall, Alexander (dir, 1894-1968): *Down to Earth; Here Comes Mr. Jordan; Once Upon a Time (1944)*
Hall, Amelia (act): *Iceman*
Hall, Andria (act): *The Good Son*
Hall, Angus (wri): *Madhouse*
Hall, Anthony (act): *Atlantis, the Lost Continent*
Hall, Anthony C. (act): *Virtuosity*
Hall, Anthony Michael (act, b. 1968): *A Bucket of Blood (1995); Edward Scissorhands; A Gnome Named Gnorm; Upworld; Weird Science*
Hall Sr., Arch (act, b. 1908): *The Nasty Rabbit*
Hall Sr., Arch (wri, b. 1908): *Magic Spectacles; The Nasty Rabbit*
Hall Jr., Arch (act, b. 1943): *Eegah!; The Nasty Rabbit; The Sadist*
Hall (Jr.), Arch (wri, b. 1943): *The Corpse Grinders*
Hall, Archie (act): *His Brother's Ghost*
Hall, Arsenio (act): *Amazon Women On the Moon*
Hall, Betty Lynn (act): *Sling Blade*
Hall, Brad (act): *The Guardian; Limit Up; Troll*
Hall, Brian (act): *The Land That Time Forgot*
Hall, Bug (act): *The Munsters' Scary Little Christmas*
Hall, Cameron (act): *Blood of the Vampire; East of Piccadilly; Footsteps In the Fog; Impulse (1955); Stormy Crossing; The Stranger Left No Card*
Hall, Carrie (act): *Darkman (1990)*
Hall, Catherine (act): *A Christmas Carol (1984)*
Hall, Cheryl (act): *Rentadick*
Hall, Claude (wri): *The Devil's Bedroom*
Hall, Cleve (A.) (act): *The Dungeonmaster; Roller Blade Warriors: Taken by Force*
Hall, Conrad (L.) (cin): *Black Widow (1987); Jennifer 8; Marathon Man*
Hall, Daisy (act): *I'm Dangerous Tonight*
Hall, David (act): *Attack of the Killer Tomatoes*
Hall, Dickie (act): *Shadow of the Thin Man*
Hall, Dolly (act): *The Toxic Avenger*
Hall, Don (act): *Invasion of the Bee Girls*
Hall, Don Ray (act): *Mind Over Murder*
Hall, Elizabeth (act): *Boarding House*
Hall, Ella (act): *The Flying Dutchman*
Hall, Ellen (act): *Voodoo Man*
Hall, Evan (act): *The Reflecting Skin*
Hall, Evelyn (act): *The Return of Dr. Fu Manchu*
Hall, Frank (wri): *The Astounding She-Monster*
Hall, Gabriella (act): *O Lita 2000*
Hall, George Edwards (dir): *Desire*
Hall, George Edwards (wri): *Desire; The Lone Wolf (1917); 12-10*
Hall, Geraldine (act, 1905-1970): *Secret of the Incas*
Hall, Grayson (act, 1926-1985): *Gargoyles; House of Dark Shadows; Night of Dark Shadows*
Hall, Harriet (act): *The Witching of Ben Wagner*
Hall, Harvey (act): *The Masque of the Red Death (1964); Twins of Evil; The Vampire Lovers; Yellow Dog*
Hall, Henry (act): *The Ape (1940); The Ape Man; The Beginning or the End?; The Clutching Hand; The Jade Mask; Larceny In Her Heart; The Mad Monster; Midnight Warning; Murder by Television; Nightmare Alley; Voodoo Man*
Hall, Huntz (act, b. 1920): *Auntie Lee's Meat Pies; The Bowery Boys Meet the Monsters; Bowery to Bagdad; Crashing Las Vegas; Cyclone; Dig That Uranium!; Escape; Ghost Chasers; Ghosts On the Loose; Hold That Hypnotist; Hold That Line; Jalopy; Jungle Gents; Master Minds (1950); Mr. Hex; No Holds Barred; Paris Playboys; Private Eyes (1953); The Return of Mr. X; Smuggler's Cove; Spook Busters; Spook Chasers; Spooks Run Wild; Spy Chasers; Up In Smoke*
Hall, Irma (act): *In the Company of Darkness*
Hall, Ivan (dir): *Kill and Kill Again; Kill or Be Killed (1980)*
Hall, J.D. (act): *Final Eye*
Hall, James (1920s act): *The Canary Murder Case*
Hall, James (1970s act): *The China Syndrome; A Force of One*
Hall, jenni (wri): *Twinsanity*
Hall, Jerry (USA act): *Batman (1989); Freejack; Vampire In Brooklyn*
Hall, Jerry (W. Ger act): *Making Contact*
Hall, Joanna (act): *Futureworld*
Hall, John (act): *Midnight (1980); Surf Nazis Must Die*
Hall, Jon (act, 1913-1979, nee Charles Loeher): *Ali Baba and the Forty Thieves (1943); Aloma of the South Seas (941); Arabian Nights (1942); Beach Girls and the Monster; Charlie Chan In Shanghai; Cobra Woman; Eyes of the Jungle; Forbidden Island; Gypsy Wildcat; Hell Ship Mutiny; Hurricane Island; Invisible Agent; The Invisible Man's Revenge; Lady In the Dark; Last Train from Bombay; Lion Man (1938); The Mutineers; On the Isle of Samoa; Phantom of the Jungle; The Prince of Thieves; Ramar and the Burning Barrier; Ramar and the Deadly Females; Ramar and the Jungle Secrets; Ramar and the Savage Challengers; Ramar and the Unknown Terror; Ramar of the Jungle; Ramar's Mission to India; Sudan; Thunder Over Sangoland; The White Goddess; White Savage; Zamba*
Hall, Jon (dir, 1913-1979): *Beach Girls and the Monster*
Hall, Ken (act): *The Dungeonmaster*
Hall, Kenneth J. (dir): *Ghost Writer*
Hall, Kenneth J. (wri): *Ghost Writer; I Was a Teenage Sex Mutant; Nightmare Sisters; Puppet Master; Test Tube Teens from the Year 2000; The Tomb*
Hall, Kevin Peter (act, 1955-1991): *Harry and the Hendersons; Highway to Hell; Misfits of Science; Monster In the Closet; One Dark Night; Predator; Predator 2*
Hall, Landon (act): *The Escort*
Hall, Lani (act): *Never Say Never Again*
Hall, Laurence (act): *I Was a Zombie for the F.B.I.*
Hall, Lena (act): *Witchcraft 3: The Kiss of Death*
Hall, Lois (act): *Daughter of the Jungle; Dead Again; Secrets of Monte Carlo*
Hall, Manly P. (act): *Black Friday*
Hall, Matt (cin): *Strays*
Hall, Michael (act): *Blood of Dracula*
Hall, Michael Keys (act): *Blackout (1988); Flight of Black Angel; Sphere*
Hall, Misty (act): *Amazons (1984)*
Hall, Norman S. (wri): *The Adventures of Captain Marvel; Destination Saturn; Dick Tracy vs. Crime, Inc.; Dr. Satan's Robot; Nyoka and the Lost Secrets of Hippocrates; Spy Smasher Returns*
Hall, Ollie (act): *Mad Max Beyond Thunderdome*
Hall, Parnell (wri): *C.H.U.D.*
Hall, Peter (dir, b. 1930): *Never Talk to Strangers; Orpheus Descending; Perfect Friday; Work Is a Four Letter Word*
Hall, Peter (wri, b. 1930): *Orpheus Descending*
Hall, Phil(l)ip Baker (act): *Ghostbusters II; The Goddess of Love; Tempting Fate*
Hall, Porter (act, 1888-1953): *Bulldog Drummond Escapes; Bulldog Drummond's Peril; Double Indemnity (1944); Mark of the Whistler; Miracle On 34th Street (1947); The Remarkable Andrew; Return to Treasure Island; Satan Met a Lady; The Thin Man*
Hall, Randy (act): *Eve of Destruction*
Hall, Rich (act): *C.H.U.D. II*
Hall, Rick (act): *Vice Versa (1988)*
Hall, Robert (wri): *You Can't Escape*
Hall, Ronnie (act): *Pit of Darkness*
Hall, Ruth (act): *Miss Pinkerton*
Hall, Sam (wri): *House of Dark Shadows; Night of Dark Shadows*
Hall, Scott H. (act): *Blood Feast*
Hall, Shannah (act): *Boogeyman II*
Hall, Shashawnee (act): *Pet Shop*
Hall, Sherry (act): *Charlie Chan On Broadway; Isle of the Dead (1945); The Thin Man*
Hall, Terri (act): *The Amazing Dr. Jekyll*
Hall, Thurston (act, 1883-1958): *The Black Room; Counter-Espionage; The Invisible Woman (1941); The Lone Wolf Keeps a Date; The Lone Wolf Meets a Lady; The Lone Wolf Returns (1935); The Lone Wolf Takes a Chance; The Man Who Lived Twice; One Dangerous Night; The Secret Life of Walter Mitty; Secrets of the Lone Wolf; Sherlock Holmes In Washington*
Hall, Virginia (act): *The War of the Worlds*
Hall, Willard Lee (act): *The Conquering Power*
Hall, William (act): *Howard the Duck; The Time of Their Lives*
Hall, Willis (wri): *West 11*
Hall, Winter (act): *The Invisible Ray; The Lost Zeppelin*
Hall, Zooey (act): *I Dismember Mama*
Hallahan, Charles (act): *Cast a Deadly Spell; Dante's Peak; Margin for Murder; Nightwing; Terror Out of the Sky; Twilight Zone; Warlock: The Armageddon*
Hallam, John (act): *A Choice of Weapons; Dragonslayer; Flash Gordon (1980); Hitler: The Last Ten Days; Lifeforce; Murder Motel; The Offence; The People That Time Forgot; Quest for Love; Robin Hood: Prince of Thieves; The Saint and the Brave Goose; Santa Claus (1985); The Wicker Man*
Hallard, C.M. (act): *The Case of Lady Camber; On Secret Service; The Third Clue*
Hallaren, Jane (act): *Body Heat*
Hallatt, May (act, b. 1882): *Black Narcissus; Dangerous Afternoon; Dark Eyes of London; The Gold Express; The Spider and the Fly (1949); The Stateless Man*
Hallenbeck, Bruce (dir): *Vampyre*
Hallenbeck, E. Darrel (dir): *One of Our Spies Is Missing*
Haller, Daniel (dir, b. 1929): *Buck Rogers In the 25th Century; The Dunwich Horror; Margin for Murder; Monster of Terror*
Haller, Ernest (cin, 1896-1970): *Back from the Dead; The Boy and the Pirates; British Agent; Dead Ringer; Devotion; The Flame and the Arrow; Footsteps In the Dark; The House of Horror (1929); International House; Journal of a Crime; The Lash; The Miracle (1959); The Verdict (1946); What Ever Happened to Baby Jane? (1962)*
Haller, Hans J. (wri): *Making Contact*
Haller, Richard/Ty (act): *The Babysitter; The Groundstar Conspiracy*
Hallett, Henry (act): *The Hound of the Baskervilles (1931); The Ringer (1931)*
Hallett, Neil (act): *The Brain Machine; Model for Murder; Transatlantic; Virgin Witch; A Woman's Temptation; The Zany Adventures of Robin Hood*
Halley, Edmund (act): *Midnight Tease*
Hallick, Tom (act): *The Amazing Captain Nemo; Hangar 18; The Last Man On Planet Earth; Time Travelers (1976)*
Halliday, Brett (wri): *Blonde for a Day; Blue, White and Perfect; Dressed to Kill (1941); Just Off Broadway; Larceny In Her Heart; The Man Who Wouldn't Die; Michael Shayne, Private Detective; Murder Is My Business; Sleepers West; Three Cases of Murder; Three On a Ticket; Time to Kill (1942); Too Many Winners*
Halliday, Bryant (act): *Curse of Simba; Devil Doll (1963); The Projected Man; Tower of Evil*
Halliday, Clive (act): *The Premature Burial*
Halliday, John (act, 1880-1947): *Peter Ibbetson; Return of the Terror*
Halliday, Lena (act): *When Knights Were Bold (1929)*
Halliday, Michael (wri): *Cat and Mouse (1958)*
Halliday, Peter (act): *The Black Windmill; Captain Clegg; Dilemma; The fast Kill; Madhouse; The Swordsman*
Hallier, Lori (act): *My Bloody Valentine; Night of the Twisters; Warning Sign*
Halligan, Derek (act): *Rawhead Rex*
Halligan, Dick (mus): *A Force of One; The Octagon*
Halligan, Liam (act): *Robin Hood: Prince of Thieves*
Halligan, Tim (act): *When the Bough Breaks*
Halligan, William (act): *The Dark Mirror (1946); Dick Tracy (1945)*
Hallinan, Susan (act): *Enter Inspector Duval*
Halliwell, Steve (act): *Threads*
Hallor, Ray (act): *The Black Pearl*
Halloran, John (act): *Kronos (1957)*
Hallowell, Lynn (act): *Eyes of a Stranger*
Hallows, Lillian (act): *For Love and the Crown*
Hallward, Gloria Grahame (act): see Grahame, Gloria
Hallward, Joy (act): *Witness to Murder*
Hallyday, Johnny (act): *Terminus*
Halmagyi, Sandor (act): *Phantom of the Opera (1983)*
Halmos, Rozsika (act): *Human Feelings*
Halop, Florence (act, 1926-1986): *Nancy Drew, Reporter*
Halperin, Victor (dir, b. 1895): *Buried Alive (1940); Revolt of the Zombies; Supernatural (1933); White Zombie*
Halperin, Victor (wri, b. 1895): *Revolt of the Zombies*
Halpern, Dina (act): *The Dybbuk*

Halpern, Lisa (act): The Nutty Professor (1996)
Halpern, Richard (act): Repossessed
Halphie, Michael (act): The Awakening; Octopussy
Halpin, Luke (act): Eyes of a Stranger; Matinee; Shock Waves
Halpin, Michael (act): Black Magic Woman
Halprin, Daria (act): The Jerusalem File
Halsey, Betty (act): Just Imagine
Halsey, Brett (act): The Atomic Submarine; Berlino Appuntamento per le Spie; The Black Cat (1990); The Cry Baby Killer; The Girl In Lover's Lane; Jet Over the Atlantic; Return of the Fly; Revenge of the Creature; The Seventh Sword; Three Bad Sisters; Twice-Told Tales
Halsey, Forrest (wri): The Green Goddess (1923); The Sorrows of Satan (1925)
Halsey, Genitha (act): The Angel Who Pawned Her Harp
Halsey, Mary (Jane) (act): Cat People (1942); The Falcon Out West; The Falcon's Brother
Halsey, Michael (act): Dollman; Monolith; Postmortem; Treasure Island (1990)
Halstead, Henry (wri): Escape to Justice
Halstead, Rodger (act): Alien Terminator
Halsted, Christopher (act): The Haunting of Morella
Halston, Julie (act): Addams Family Values
Halston, Rodger (act): Alien Terminator
Halton, Charles (act, 1876-1959): Charlie Chan at Treasure Island; Dr. Cyclops; Nancy Drew, Reporter; The Saint In New York; Shadows In the Night; Stranger On the Third Floor; The Thin Man Goes Home
Halton, Michael (act): Heart and Souls; Killer Klowns from Outer Space
Halverstadt, Constance (act): see Cummings, Constance
Halvick, James (wri): Beat the Devil
Halward, Chris (act): Johnny, You're Wanted
Ham, Eben (act): The Unnamable
Ham, Gary (act): The Howling: New Moon Rising
Ham, Harry (act): Blood Money
Hama, Mie (act): King Kong Escapes; King Kong vs. Godzilla; Samurai Pirate; You Only Live Twice
Hamada, Torahiko (act): Kwaidan; The X from Outer Space
Hamaguchi, Ted (act): Vampire at Midnight
Hamama, Faten (act): Cairo
Hamamura, Jun (act): Kwaidan
Haman, Abby (act): Sparkling Cyanide
Hamann, Craig (act): The Tomb
Hamann, Craig (wri): Dollman vs. Demonic Toys
Hamans, Robert (act): Beyond Tomorrow
Hamaoa, Kiku (act): Beyond Evil
Hamaty, Emile (act): The Man Who Saw Tomorrow
Hambleton, Harry (act): Long John Silver
Hambleton, Peter (act): Night of the Red Hunter
Hambling, Arthur (act): Bulldog Sees It Through; Daughter of Darkness (1948); Death at Broadcasting House; The Gaunt Stranger; A Night in Montmartre; The Saint Meets the Tiger; Three Silent Men
Hambrick, John (act): Making Mr. Right
Hamby, Walter (act): I Was a Zombie for the F.B.I.
Hameister, Willy (cin): Genuine; Das Kabinett des Dr. Caligari
Hamel, Gustav (act): The Secret of the Air
Hamel, Veronica (act, b. 1943): Beyond the Poseidon Adventure; The Disappearance of Nora; When Time Ran Out
Hamel, William (act): The Unknown Terror
Hamer, Gerald (act): Bulldog Drummond's Bride; Pursuit to Algiers; The Scarlet Claw; Sherlock Holmes Faces Death; Sherlock Holmes In Washington
Hamer, Gladys (act): Alf's Carpet; The Magician (1926)
Hamer, Jason (cin): The Fear (1994)
Hamer, Robert (dir, 1911-1963): Dead of Night (1945); Father Brown; Kind Hearts and Coronets; The Scapegoat; The Spider and the Fly (1949)
Hamer, Robert (wri, 1911-1963): Father Brown; A Jolly Bad Fellow; The Scapegoat
Hamerton, May (act): Signals In the Night
Hamil, Tom (act): Cavegirl (1985)
Hamill, Alanna (wri): The Spider and the Fly (1994)
Hamill, John (act): Are You Dying Young Man?; No Blade of Grass; Tower of Evil; Trog
Hamill, Mark (act, b. 1951): Amazing Stories: The Movie VI; Batman: Mask of the Phantasm; Black Magic Woman; Body Bags; Earth Angel; The Empire Strikes Back; The Flash 2: Revenge of the Trickster; The Guyver; Midnight Ride; Return of the Jedi; Silk Degrees; Slipstream; Star Wars; Time Runner; Village of the Damned (1995); Watchers Reborn; When Time Expires; Wizards
Hamilton, Alana (act): Ravagers
Hamilton, Alexa (act): The Invisible Woman (1983)
Hamilton, Allen (act): The Fugitive (1993); The Package
Hamilton, Anthony Fife (act): Contact
Hamilton, Antony (act, 1953-1995): Howling IV
Hamilton, Archie (act): Fire and Ice
Hamilton, Barbara (act): Clarence
Hamilton, Barry (act): Human Feelings
Hamilton, Bernard/Bernie (act): Captain Sinbad; Jungle Man-Eaters; Scream, Blacula, Scream
Hamilton, Carrie (act): Cool World
Hamilton, Chico (mus): Repulsion
Hamilton, Claire (act): Hotel Reserve
Hamilton, David (act): Tiffany Jones
Hamilton, David (cin): see Terzano, Ubaldo
Hamilton, Dean (act): Rush Week
Hamilton, Donald (wri): The Ambushers; Matt Helm; Murderers' Row; The Silencers (1966); The Wrecking Crew
Hamilton, Dorothy (act): Murder by Rope
Hamilton, Emily (act): The Ruby Ring
Hamilton, Fenton (cin): It's Alive (1974); It Lives Again
Hamilton, Frank (act, 1924-1991): The Demon Murder Case; A Stranger Is Watching
Hamilton, Fred (act): Dick Tracy (1937)
Hamilton, Gabrielle (act): The Man from Nowhere
Hamilton, Gary (act): Tower of Evil
Hamilton, Gay (act): A Challenge for Robin Hood; Eclipse (1977); The Hunchback of Notre Dame (1965); Journey to the Unknown
Hamilton, George (act, b. 1939): Crime and Punishment U.S.A.; The Dead Don't Die; Love at First Bite; The Power (1967); The Strange Possession of Mrs. Oliver; Zorro, the Gay Blade
Hamilton, Guy (dir, b. 1922): Diamonds Are Forever; Evil Under the Sun; Funeral In Berlin; Goldfinger; An Inspector Calls; Live and Let Die; The Man With the Golden Gun; The Mirror Crack'd; Remo Williams: The Adventure Begins; The Ringer (1952)
Hamilton, Hale (act): Drums of Jeopardy (1931); The Most Dangerous Game; Murder at Midnight
Hamilton, Jane (act): Deranged (1987); Picking Up the Pieces; Wildest Dreams
Hamilton, Jennifer (act): Twister
Hamilton, Jill (act): The Million Eyes of Sumuru
Hamilton, John (Euro act): Fangs of the Living Dead
Hamilton, John (GB act): The Ringer (1928)
Hamilton, John (F.) (USA act): The Beginning or the End?; The Deadly Ray from Mars; Donovan's Brain; Enemy Agents Meet Ellery Queen; The Fatal Hour (1940); The Maltese Falcon (1941); Mr. Moto's Gamble; Mr. Wong, Detective; Peril from the Planet Mongo; Phantom Killer; Purple Death from Outer Space; The Saint's Double Trouble; The Shadow of Egypt; Shadows Over Chinatown; Too Many Winners
Hamilton, Joseph (act): Teenage Cave Man
Hamilton, Judd (act): The Last Horror Film; Star Crash
Hamilton, Julie (act): Rawhead Rex
Hamilton, Kenneth (act): Forever Evil
Hamilton, Kim (act): Heavy Traffic; The Leech Woman; The Wizard of Baghdad
Hamilton, Kipp (act): The War of the Gargantuas
Hamilton, Linda (act): Children of the Corn; Dante's Peak; King Kong Lives; Mr. Destiny; Secret Weapons; Separate Lives; Shadow Conspiracy; TAG: The Assassination Game; The Terminator; Terminator 2: Judgment Day
Hamilton, Lisa Gay (act, b. 1964): Beloved; 12 Monkeys
Hamilton, Lloyd (act): Black Waters
Hamilton, Lois (act): Invitation to Hell
Hamilton, Lynn (act): The Vanishing (1993)
Hamilton, Mae (act): Riches and Rogues
Hamilton, Mahlon (act): The Clutching Hand
Hamilton, Margaret (act, 1902-1985): Guest In the House; The Invisible Woman (1941); Journey Back to Oz; The Night Strangler; 13 Ghosts; The Villain Still Pursued Her; The Wizard of Oz (1939)
Hamilton, Mark (act): Zarkorr! The Invader
Hamilton, Michael (dir): see Scardamaglia, Elio
Hamilton, Murray (act, 1923-1986): The Amityville Horror; The Boston Strangler; Damnation Alley; Hysterical; Jaws; Jaws 2; No Way to Treat a Lady; Rona Jaffe's Mazes and Monsters; Seconds; Summer Girl; 13 Frightened Girls; Too Scared to Scream
Hamilton, Neil (act, 1899-1984): Batman (1966); The Cat Creeps (1930); Darkened Rooms; The Devil's Hand (1961); The Mysterious Dr. Fu Manchu; The Return of Dr. Fu Manchu; The Saint Strikes Back; Secret Lives; Strategy of Terror; Tarzan and His Mate
Hamilton, Dr. Nikola (act & wri): Guarding Britain's Secrets
Hamilton, Ord (act): Death at Broadcasting House
Hamilton, Patricia (act): Last Bride of Salem; My Bloody Valentine
Hamilton, Patrick (wri): Gaslight (1940 & 1944); Hangover Square; Rope
Hamilton, Penny (act): Beverly Hills Bodysnatchers
Hamilton, Reggie (act): I Was a Zombie for the F.B.I.
Hamilton, Richard (act): Plymouth
Hamilton, Robert (wri): Panic In the Skies!
Hamilton, Roy (wri): Cat-Women of the Moon
Hamilton, Rusty (act): The Edge of Hell
Hamilton, Sue (act): Dr. Goldfoot and the Bikini Machine; How to Stuff a Wild Bikini; Sergeant Deadhead the Astronut!
Hamilton, Suzanna (act): Brimstone & Treacle; 1984 (1984); Tale of a Vampire
Hamilton, Suzanne (act): Scream Bloody Murder
Hamilton, Suzette (act): Scream Bloody Murder
Hamilton, Trip (act): Making Mr. Right
Hamilton Jr., Warren (wri): Kiss of the Tarantula
Hamilton, Wendy (act): Scars of Dracula
Hamilton, William (dir): Murder On a Bridle Path
Hamler, Brad (act): Jacob's Ladder
Hamlett, Dexter (act): Return to Horror High
Hamlett, Dilys (act): Diagnosis: Murder; In the Devil's Garden; Mix Me a Person
Hamley-Clifford, Molly (act): The Cobweb; Deadlock (1943); Miracles Do Happen; Murder Tomorrow; Street of Shadows; What a Night!
Hamlin, Harry (act, b. 1951): Clash of the Titans; Her Deadly Rival; The Hunted (1998); Like Father, Like Santa; A Stranger In Town (1998)
Hamlin, Phyllis (act): Heart Condition
Hamlisch, Marvin (mus, b. 1944): D.A.R.Y.L.; The Devil and Max Devlin; The Fan; The Return of the Six Million Dollar Man and the Bionic Woman; The Spy Who Loved Me; The Swimmer
Hamlon, Dan (act): 20,000 Leagues Under the Sea (1916, USA)
Hamm, Al (cin): Beware! The Blob
Hamm, James (act): Lord of the Flies (1990)
Hamm, Sam (wri): Batman (1989); Batman Returns; Mantis
Hammack, Warren (act): The Eye Creatures; Mars Needs Women; Zontar: The Thing from Venus
Hammat, Richard (act): Outland
Hammer, Achim (act): The Erotic Adventures of the Three Musketeers
Hammer, Ben (act): Haunts; Invasion of the Bee Girls
Hammer Jr., Earl (wri): The Last Generation
Hammer, Elinor (act): The Blob (1958)
Hammer, Heidi (act): 2069: A Sex Odyssey
Hammer, Jan (mus): Beastmaster III: The Eye of Braxus; I Come In Peace
Hammer, Richard (wri): Beyond Obsession
Hammer, Robert (dir & wri): Don't Answer the Phone!
Hammeras, Ralph (cin): The Giant Gila Monster; Just Imagine
Hammerstein, Elaine (act): The Drums of Jeopardy (1923); Rupert of Hentzau (1923)
Hammerstein, Oscar (wri, 1895-1960): Carousel
Hammerstein II, Oscar (mus): Cinderella (1997)
Hammett, Dashiell (wri, 1894-1961): After the Thin Man; Another Thin Man; The Dain Curse; The Maltese Falcon (1931 & 1941); Satan Met a Lady; Shadow of the Thin Man; Song of the Thin Man; The Thin Man Goes Home
Hammil, John (act): Ghostbusters II
Hammill, Ellen (wri): Don't Go In the House
Hammond, Adel C. (act): The Clan of the Cave Bear
Hammond, Barbara (act): Vampire at Midnight
Hammond, Bill (act): Radar Secret Service
Hammond, Brandon (act): Mars Attacks!; Strange Days; Tales from the Hood
Hammond, Edward (wri): The Ghost Talks
Hammond, Harriet (act): Bits of Life
Hammond, Joel Steven (act): Neon Maniacs
Hammond, Kay (act, 1909-1980, nee Dorothy Standing): Blithe Spirit; A Night In Montmartre
Hammond, Marcus (act): The Plague of the Zombies
Hammond, Mark (act): The Purple Rose of Cairo
Hammond, Michael (act): Strange Behavior
Hammond, Nancy (act): The Pink Chiquitas
Hammond, Nicholas (act): The Chinese Web; Con Caper/Curse of Rava; Deadly Dust; Lord of the Flies (1963); Spider-Man
Hammond, Norah (act): The House In the Woods
Hammond, Patricia Lee (act): Last Rites (1980)
Hammond, Peter (act, b. 1923): Confession (1955); Model for Murder; The Secret Tent; Soho Incident; X...The Unknown
Hammond, Peter (dir): The Dark Angel (1991)
Hammond, Peter (wri): Jack the Ripper (1958)
Hammond, Phyllis (act): Nightbeast
Hammond, Roger (act): Game for Three Losers; Morons from Outer Space
Hammond, Ronald (act): The Queen Mother
Hammond, Vincent (act): Frankenstein: The College Years; Full Eclipse
Hammond, Virginia (act): Charlie Chan's Courage
Hammontree, Rick (act): Nightbeast
Hamner Jr., Earl (wri): Charlotte's Web
Hamner, Richard (act): Forever Evil
Hamner, Robert (wri): Forgotten City of the Planet of the Apes
Hamnet, Bryce (act): A Connecticut Yankee In King Arthur's Court (1989)
Hamnett, Olivia (act): The Last Wave
Hamos, Christine (act): Bloodhounds
Hamp, Volker (act): Making Contact
Hampden, Walter (act, 1879-1955, nee Walter Hampden Dougherty): 5 Fingers; The Hunchback of Notre Dame (1939)
Hampford, Anne (act): Mutants In Paradise
Hampford, Marty (act): Mutants In Paradise
Hampshire, Melanie (act): Blow-Up
Hampshire, Susan (act, b. 1941): Baffled!; Neither the Sea Nor the Sand; Night Must Fall (1964); The Three Lives of Thomasina; The Trygon Factor
Hampson, T. (act): The Glittering Sword
Hampton, Bill (act): The Hideous Sun Demon; The Human Duplicators
Hampton, Ret., Col. Bruce (act): Sling Blade
Hampton, Chase (act): Offerings
Hampton, Chasiti (act): Heart and Souls
Hampton, Christopher (dir): The Secret Agent (1996)
Hampton, Christopher (wri): Mary Reilly; The Secret Agent (1996)
Hampton, Grayce (act): The Bat Whispers
Hampton, Hope (act): The Light of Faith
Hampton, James (act, b. 1936): The Cat from Outer Space; The China Syndrome; Condorman; Hangar 18; Teen Wolf; Teen Wolf Too; Through the Magic Pyramid; World War III
Hampton, John (act): I Was a Zombie for the F.B.I.
Hampton, Lawrence (cin): The Birds
Hampton, Louise (act): Bedelia; Busman's Honeymoon; The House of the Arrow (1940); The Oracle (1952); The Saint Meetsthe Tiger; The Story of Robin Hood
Hampton, Melvin (act): Earthbound (1981)
Hampton, Orville H. (wri, b. 1917): The Alligator People; The Atomic Submarine; Beauty and the Beast (1962); Follow the Hunter; The Four Skulls of Jonathan Drake; Jack the Giant Killer; Lady In the Fog; The Snake Woman
Hampton, Paul (act): Babylon 5: The Gathering; Shivers; Waxwork II: Lost In Time; Wild Is My Love
Hampton, Richard (act): Yellow Dog
Hampton, Robert (dir & wri): see Freda, Riccardo
Hampton, Roger (act): The Alien's Return; Chiller; In Self Defense; Vamp
Hampton, Ruth (act): Abbott and Costello Go to Mars
Hampton, Susie (act): The Fast Kill
Hamra, Skip (act): The Toxic Avenger
Hamshere, Keith (act): In Search of the Castaways
Hanan, Ahmed (act): A Story of Tutankhamun
Hanau, Sasha (act): Mary Reilly; Mary Shelley's 'Frankenstein'
Hanawalt, Charles (cin): Dementia 13
Hanazawa, Tokue (act): Kwaidan

Hanbury, Victor (dir): The Avenging Hand (1943); Return of a Stranger
Hancock, Barbara (act): Finian's Rainbow
Hancock, Dick (act): Phantom of the Mall: Eric's Revenge
Hancock, Eleanor (act): The Cave Girl (1921)
Hancock, John (act, 1941-1992): Collision Course (1990); Fugitive from the Empire; Sundown: The Vampire In Retreat
Hancock, John (dir): Let's Scare Jessica to Death
Hancock, Lou (act): Miracle Mile
Hancock, Lynn (act): Evilspeak
Hancock, Prentis (act): Jekyll and Hyde; The Saint and the Brave Goose; The 39 Steps (1978)
Hancock, Sheila (act, b. 1933): The Anniversary; The Moon-Spinners; Night Must Fall (1964)
Hancock, Tony (act, 1924-1968): The Wrong Box
Hand, Danelle (act): Cat People (1982)
Hand, David (dir): Bambi
Handfuss, Tracy (act): Prison Girls
Handke, Peter (wri): Wings of Desire
Handl, Irene (act, 1902-1987): Burnt Evidence; Dark Secret; For Them That Trespass; Gestapo; The Girl In the News; The Hills of Donegal; The Hound Of The Baskervilles (1978); The Key; A Kid for Two Farthings; Mad About Men; Mrs. Pym of Scotland Yard; On a Clear Day You Can See Forever; The Perfect Woman; The Private Life of Sherlock Holmes; The Shop at Sly Corner; Strange Boarders; The Terror (1938); Top Secret (1952); The Wrong Box
Handley, Colin (act): The Punisher
Handley, Tom (act): Unknown World
Handley, Tommy (act, 1902-1949): Elstree Calling; Time Flies (1944)
Handley, Tres (act): Grim
Handy, Bill (act): To Die For; Windows
Handy, James (act): Arachnophobia; Obsessed (1992); Point of No Return
Handy, Philip (act): Outbreak
Haneke, Michael (dir): Funny Games
Hanemann, Danny (act): Matinee
Haner, Gladys (act): The Magician (1926)
Hanes, James (act): Witchery
Hanet, Josef (act): Revenge (1986)
Haney, Anne (act): The Bad Seed (1985); Impulse (1984); The Invisible Woman (1983); Liar Liar; The Night They Saved Christmas; Plymouth
Haney, Daryl (act): Watchers II
Haney, Daryl (wri): Crime Zone; Friday the 13th, Part VII-The New Blood
Haney, Dorothy (act): Terror of the Bloodhunters
Haney, Paul (act): The Curse of the Living Corpse
Haney, Tony (act): Copycat
Hanford, Ray (act): Wolf Blood
Hang, Tham Thuy (act): S.T.A.B.
Hanganu, Patricia (act): Wild Thing
Hanich, Davos (act): La Jetee
Hanin, Rofer (act): The Blue Panther; The Brides of Fu Manchu; Code Name: Tiger
Hanis, Raymond (act): Flatliners
Hanke, Robert L. (act): see Lowery, Robert
Hankey, Anthony (act): Matinee Idol
Hankey, Anthony (dir): Too Dangerous to Live
Hankey, Anthony (wri): The Man Who Made Diamonds
Hankin, Larry (act): Black Magic Woman; Dr. Dracula; Prehysteria! 2
Hankins, Carol (act): Addams Family Values
Hankinson, Michael (dir): The Scarab Murder Case
Hankinson, Michael (wri): Crime On the Hill; Ten Minute Alibi
Hanks, Brad (act): HauntedWeen
Hanks, Jim (act): Xtro 3: Watch the Skies
Hanks, Michael (act): Night of the Comet
Hanks, Steve (act): The Night of the Claw
Hanks, Tom (act, b. 1956): Apollo 13; Big; The 'Burbs; The Green Mile; He Knows You're Alone; Rona Jaffe's Mazes and Monsters; Splash; Toy Story; Toy Story II
Hanks, Wade (cin): Eyes of Fire
Hanley, Jenny (act): The Flesh and Blood Show; On Her Majesty's Secret Service; Scars of Dracula; Tam Lin
Hanley, Jimmy (act, 1918-1970): The Black Rider; Gaslight (1940); Landslide (1937); Murder In Reverse; Radio Cab Murder; Room to Let; Satellite In the Sky; The Tunnel; Uncharted Seas
Hanley, Katie (act): Xanadu
Hanlon, Bert (act): The Decision of Christopher Blake
Hanlon, Kevin (act): Toxic Zombies
Hanlon, Peter (act): Deadly Sins
Hanlon, Tom (act): Jalopy
Hanly, Mike (act): Making Mr. Right
Hann, Don (act): Rearview Mirror
Hanna, Brian (act): The Bees
Hanna, Elizabeth (act): Babar: The Movie
Hanna, Mark (wri): The Amazing Colossal Man; Attack of the 50-Foot Woman (1958); Not of This Earth (1957); The Undead
Hanna, Robert (act): Legend of the Seven Golden Vampires
Hanna, Walter (act): The Bees
Hanna, William (act): The Flintstones
Hanna, William (dir): Jetsons: The Movie
Hannaford, David (act): The Dragon of Pendragon Castle; One Jump Ahead
Hannah, Bob (act): Jaws of Satan; The Offspring
Hannah, Daryl (act, b. 1961): Addams Family Reunion; Attack of the 50-Foot Woman (1993); Blade Runner; The Clan of the Cave Bear; The Final Terror; High Spirits; Memoirs of an Invisible Man; Rear Window (1998); Splash
Hannah, Jo-Anne (act): Curtains
Hannah, Mark (act): The Offspring
Hannah, Page (act): Gremlins 2: The New Batch
Hannaman, Kim (act): Princess Warrior
Hannan, Peter (cin): Brimstone & Treacle; Full Circle; Sredni Vashtar
Hannant, Brian (dir): The Time Guardian
Hannant, Brian (wri): The Road Warrior; The Time Guardian
Hannauer, Terri (act): Communion
Hannay, Barbara (act): Her Greatest Performance
Hannen, Athene (act): see Seyler, Athene
Hannen, Nicholas (act): F.P. 1 Antwortet Nicht; Family Doctor; The Man They Could Not Arrest; Murder at the Inn; Richard III (1955); 3 Steps In the Dark; Who Killed John Savage?
Hannen, Peter (act): A Honeymoon Adventure
Hannibal, Linda (act): Attack of the Killer Tomatoes
Hannigan, Alyson (act): My Stepmother Is an Alien
Hannon, Kevin (act): Deadtime Stories
Hannon, Sean (act): Fire and Ice
Hannon, Tim (act): Night of the Comet
Hanold, Marilyn (act): Frankenstein Meets the Space Monster
Hanrahan, Jack (act): Repossessed
Hanray, Lawrence (act): Chu Chin Chow (1934); A Dickensian Fantasy; Hotel Reserve; Knight Without Armour; The Last Chance; Lorna Doone (1934); The Man Who Could Work Miracles; Murder at Monte Carlo; Someone at the Door; What Happened Then?
Hansa, Kali (act): Night of the Sorcerers
Hansard, Paul (act): Trog
Hansel, Arthur (act): Dr. Tarr's Torture Dungeon
Hansel, George E. (act): Raiders of the Living Dead
Hansen, Al (act): Death at Love House; The Hearse
Hansen, Andy (act): Jaws 3-D
Hansen, Bibi (act): Phantom of the Paradise
Hansen, Carl (act): The Last Dinosaur
Hansen, Danna (act): Werewolf of Washington
Hansen, Ed (dir): Cyber-Chic
Hansen, Ellen (act): see Corby, Ellen
Hansen, Erik (wri): Heart and Souls
Hansen, Erika (act): Tales from the Hood
Hansen, Gail (act): Wonder Women
Hansen, Gary (cin): Next of Kin
Hansen, Geoff (act): Appointment for a Killing
Hansen, Gregory (wri): Heart and Souls
Hansen, Grethe (act): After Dark
Hansen, Gunnar (act, b. 1947): The Demon Lover; Freakshow; Hollywood Chainsaw Hookers; Mosquito; The Texas Chainsaw Massacre
Hansen, Heidi (act): Superbug, Super Agent
Hansen, Holger Juul (act): The Kingdom
Hansen, James (act): Night Ripper
Hansen, Janis (act): Angel On My Shoulder (1980); Oh Dad Poor Dad, Mamma's Hung You In the Closet and I'm Feelin' So Sad
Hansen, Jeff (act): Silent Night, Deadly Night
Hansen, Joachim (act): The Boys from Brazil; Frozen Alive; The Secret of the Black Trunk
Hansen, John (act): Earthbound (1981); The Time Machine (1978)
Hansen, Judith (act): Creator
Hansen, Lory (act): Point of Terror
Hansen, Monika (act): I Love You, I Kill You
Hansen, Myrna (act): Cult of the Cobra; Francis In the Navy; Goodbye Charlie; The Purple Mask
Hansen, Nicole (act): American Cyborg: Steel Warrior
Hansen, Nina (act): The Exorcist III
Hansen, Paul (act): Count Yorga, Vampire; The Return of Count Yorga
Hansen, Peter (act): When Worlds Collide
Hansen, Valda (act): Night of the Ghouls
Hansen, William (act): Fail-Safe; Sandcastles; The Terminal Man; Willard
Hanslip, Ann (act): Face the Music; Knights of the Round Table; Three Cases of Murder
Hansner, Jerry (act): The Atomic City
Hanson, Carl (act): Dick Tracy (1945)
Hanson, Curt(is) (act): The Goonies; Praying Mantis
Hanson, Curtis (dir, b. 1945): The Hand That Rocks the Cradle; Sweet Kill
Hanson, Curtis (wri, b. 1945): Sweet Kill
Hanson, Curtis Lee (wri): The Dunwich Horror
Hanson, Dorothy (act): The Elusive Pimpernel (1919)
Hanson, Heather (act): Roswell: The Aliens Attack
Hanson, Jonathan (act): Maroc 7
Hanson, Judy (act): Sugar Hill
Hanson, Karan (act): Surf Nazis Must Die
Hanson, Kathy (act): Spacecamp
Hanson, Kristina (act): Dinosaurus!
Hanson, Lars (act, 1887-1965): The Scarlet Letter (1926); The Story of Gosta Berling
Hanson, Lorna (act): Mr. Sardonicus
Hanson, Luke (act): The Quatermass Conclusion
Hanson, Paul (act): The Lost Patrol (1934)
Hanson, Preston (act): The Loch Ness Horror
Hanson, Ray (cin): Prisoners of the Lost Universe
Hanson, Shirley (act): Howling II
Hanson, Steve (act): Raiders of the Lost Ark
Hanson, Valerie (act): The Black Rider
Hansson, Erling (act): Blade af Satans Bog
Hansson, Maud (act): Det Sjunde Inseglet
Hao, William (act): Vampire On Bikini Beach
Hapner, Ken (act): Hangar 18
Hara, Kazutami (cin): Godzilla 1985
Hara, Setsuko (act): Chusingura (1963)
Harada, Daijiro (act): Live Today, Die Tomorrow
Harada, Ernest (act): Charlie Chan: Happiness Is a Warm Clue; Wicked Stepmother
Harada, Itoko (act): The X from Outer Space
Harada, Masato (dir): Gunhed
Harada, Mieko (act): Ran
Harapes, Vlastimil (act): Beauty and the Beast (1985)
Harareet, Haya (act, b. 1934): Antinea, l'Amante della Citta Sepopolta; The Secret Partner
Harareet, Haya (wri, b. 1934): Our Mother's House
Harari, Clement (act): The Fiendish Plot of Dr. Fu Manchu; Le Saint Mene la Dance; Who Stole the Body?
Harata, Akihiko (act): Mothra
Harben, Hubert (act) The Secret of the Loch (1934)
Harben, Joan (act): The Man In the White Suit
Harben, Philip (act): Meet Mr. Lucifer
Harben, Robert (act): The Limping Man (1953)
Harber, Harry Paul (wri): Terror Is a Man
Harbin, Suzette (act): The Jungle Girl; The Sky Dragon
Harbor, Paul (act): It Conquered the World
Harbord, Carl (act): Bulldog Drummond Strikes Back (1947); The Cavalier of the Streets; Dressed to Kill (1946)
Harbord, Rebecca (act): Strange Behaviour
Harbott, Sandy (act): Color Me Dead
Harburg, E.Y. "Yip" (mus, 1896-1981): Cabin In the Sky; Finian's Rainbow; The Wizard of Oz (1939)
Harcourt, James (act): The Avenging Hand (1943); Gestapo; The House of the Arrow (1940); I Met a Murderer; Obsession (1949); Paris Plane; Return of a Stranger; Seven Sinners
Harcourt, Kate (act): Dark of the Night; Night of the Red Hunter
Hard, Tyler (act): Child's Play (1988)
Harden Jr., Ernest (act): The Final Terror
Harden, Jack (act): Satan's Satellites
Harden, Marcia Gay (act): Flubber; Late for Dinner; Meet Joe Black
Harden, Mark (act): Project X (1987)
Harden, Robert (act): Surf Nazis Must Die
Harder, James (act): The Telephone Book
Hardester, Crofton (act): Android; Death at Love House
Hardie, Kate (act): Tree of Hands
Hardie, Russell (act): Meet Nero Wolfe
Hardiman, Hilary (act): Possession (1973)
Hardiman, James (wri): The House Where Evil Dwells
Hardiman, Marguerite (act): Disciple of Death
Hardiman, Terence (act): Loophole
Hardin, Jerry (act): Bermuda Triangle (1996); Cujo; Murder of Innocence; Pandora's Clock; Plymouth; Warning Sign
Hardin, Joseph (act): The Ultimate Impostor; Watchers II
Hardin, Michael (act): End of the World (1977)
Hardin, Ty (act, b. 1930, nee Ty Hungerford): Berserk; Fire; I Married a Monster from Outer Space; The Space Children
Harding, Ann (act, 1902-1981, nee Dorothy Walton Gatley): Condemned; Eyes In the Night; I've Lived Before; Love from a Stranger (1937); Peter Ibbetson
Harding, D. Garnet (act): Escape Clause
Harding, David Llewellyn (act): see Harding, Lyn
Harding, Evelyn (act): Whosoever Shall Offend
Harding, Gilbert (act): Meet Mr. Lucifer; The Oracle (1952)
Harding, Harry (wri): Hutch Stirs 'em Up
Harding, Jackie Lou (act): Weird Woman
Harding, Jeff (act): Blood Tracks
Harding, John (act): Crime and Punishment, U.S.A.
Harding, Kay (act): The Mummy's Curse; The Scarlet Claw
Harding, Lorraine (act): Annabel Lee
Harding, Lyn (act, 1867-1952, nee David Llewellyn Harding): The Barton Mystery (1920 & 1932); Knight Without Armour; The Man Who Changed His Mind; The Man Who Changed His Name; Les Miserables (1922); The Missing People; Silver Blaze (1937); The Speckled Band (1931); Spy of Napoleon; The Triumph of Sherlock Holmes
Harding, Paul (act): Last Bride of Salem
Harding, Reg (act): Blind Terror; The Legacy
Harding, Rudge (act): The Brass Bottle (1914)
Harding, Shirley (act): Dr. Black Mr. Hyde
Harding Stewart (wri): Spacehunter: Adventures In the Forbidden Zone
Harding, Thomas (act): The Toxic Avenger, Part II
Harding, Vincent (act): Captain Nemo and the Underwater City
Hardinge, Rex (wri): Sexton Blake and the Bearded Doctor
Hardison, Kadeem (act): Def by Temptation; The 6th Man; Vampire In Brooklyn
Hardisty, Linda (act): The Green Slime
Hardman, Frank (wri): Moon Zero Two
Hardman, Karl (act): Night of the Living Dead (1968)
Hardstark, Michael (act): Alice, Sweet Alice
Hardt, Eloise (act): Looker
Hardt, Joe (act): Blood Cult
Hardtmuth, Paul (act): The Curse of Frankenstein; The Diamond; Dr. Blood's Coffin; The Gamma People; Highly Dangerous; Street of Shadows; Timeslip
Hardwick, Dana (act): The Coming
Hardwick, Paul (act): The Deadly Affair
Hardwicke, (Sir) Cedric (act, 1893-1964): Bait; Bella Donna (1934); A Connecticut Yankee In King Arthur's Court (1949); Five Weeks In a Balloon; The Ghost of Frankenstein; The Ghoul (1933); The Green Glove; Helen of Troy (1955); The Hunchback of Notre Dame (1939); Invisible Agent; The Invisible Man Returns; King Solomon's Mines (1937); The Lodger (1944); Lured; Les Miserables (1935); On Borrowed Time; The Picture of Dorian Gray (1945); Richard III (1955); Riches and Rogues; Rope; Salome (1953); The Story of Mankind; Suspicion (1941); Things to Come; A Woman's Vengeance
Hardwicke, Edward (act): Baby: Secret of the Lost Legend; The Black Windmill; Full Circle; Men of Sherwood Forest; Not Guilty; Otley; The Scarlet Letter (1995); Venom (1982)
Hardy, Allan (cin): Revenge In the House of Usher
Hardy, Arthur (act): Creeping Shadows; The Vulture (1937)
Hardy, Carla (act): Gebroken Spiegels
Hardy, George (act): Troll II
Hardy, Giana (act): Popcorn
Hardy, Hagood (mus): An American Christmas Carol; Rituals; Rona Jaffe's Mazes and Monsters
Hardy, Henry (act): Oh Heavenly Dog
Hardy, John (act): The Package
Hardy, Jonathan (act): Mad Max
Hardy, Joseph (dir): Great Expectations (1974)
Hardy, Laurence (act): The Man Who Haunted Himself; Woman of Straw
Hardy, Leslie (act): The Mummy Lives
Hardy, Lindsay (wri): Assignment Redhead
Hardy, Mark (act): The Orchard End Murder
Hardy, Martin (wri): see Martino, Luciano
Hardy, Norvell (act): see Hardy, Oliver
Hardy, Oliver (act, 1892-1957, nee Norvell Hardy): A-Haunting We Will Go; Atoll K; Babes In Toyland (1934); A Chump at Oxford; The Wizard of Oz (1925)

Hardy, Richard (act): Wheels of Terror
Hardy, Robert (GB act): Berserk; Dark Places; Demons of the Mind; Gawain and the Green Knight; Gulliver's Travels (1996);Mary Shelley's Frankenstein; Psychomania (1972); Le Silencieux; The Spy Who Came In from the Cold; 10 Rillington Place; Yellow Dog; The Zany Adventures of Robin Hood
Hardy, Robert (USA act): Night of the Lepus
Hardy, Robin (dir): The Fantasist; The Wicker Man
Hardy, Rod (dir): Thirst; 20,000 Leagues Under the Sea (1997, ABC-TV)
Hardy, Ron (dir): Nick Fury: Agent of Shield
Hardy, Russell (act): Fail-Safe
Hardy, Sam (act): King Kong (1933); The Phantom of Crestwood; The Savage
Hardy, Sophie (act): Cartes sur Table; The Mysterious Magician; Taste of Excitement; The Trygon Factor
Hardy, Stephanie (act): To Sleep With a Vampire
Hardy, Trishalee (act): Little Ghost; Murder of Innocence
Hare, Andy (act): Premonition (1972)
Hare, Doris (act): The League of Gentlemen; Luck of the Navy; A Place to Go
Hare, Ken (act): Creatures the World Forgot
Hare, Lumsden (act, 1875-1964): Charlie Chan Carries On; Dr. Jekyll and Mr. Hyde (1941); The Four Skulls of Jonathan Drake; The Great Impersonation (1935); International House; The Lodger (1944); Love Letters; Mr. Peabody and the Mermaid; My Cousin Rachel; Rebecca; Scotland Yard (1930); Shadows On the Stairs; She (1935); Sherlock Holmes (1922); Svengali (1931)
Hare, Philippa (act): The Servant
Hare, Robertson (act, b. 1891): Out of the Shadow; Seven Keys; Thark; Things Happen at Night
Hare, Will (act): Back to the Future; Eyes of Fire; Grim Prairie Tales; Heaven Can Wait (1978); Silent Night, Deadly Night
Harela, Ava (act): Yellowbeard
Harelik, Mark (act): A Gnome Named Gnorm; The Swan Princess; Upworld
Harens, Dean (act): The Suspect
Harewood, Dorian (act): An American Christmas Carol; Gray Lady Down; I, Desire; Looker; Pacific Heights; Solar Crisis
Harford, Alex (act): Houdini (1953)
Harford, Betty (act): The China Syndrome
Harford, Terry (act): Funeral Home
Harger, Scot (act): Vampire On Bikini Beach
Hargitay, Mariska (act): Ghoulies
Hargitay, Mickey (act): Gli Amori di Ercole; Il Boia Scarlatto; La Figlia di Frankenstein
Hargreaves, Amy (act): Brainscan; Remember Me
Hargreaves, David (act): Agatha
Hargreaves, Sir Gerald (wri): Atlantis, the Lost Continent
Hargreaves, Janet (act): Frankenstein and the Monster from Hell
Hargreaves, John (act): Sky Pirates
Hargreaves, L./Lance Z. (wri): Battle Beneath the Earth; The Crooked Sky; Devil Doll (1963); First Man Into Space; West of Suez
Hargreaves, Reginald (wri): The Dead Heart; Jill and the Old Fiddle
Hargreaves, Robert (wri): Forty Winks
Hargrove, Dean (dir): The Return of the World's Greatest Detective
Hargrove, Dean (wri): The Helicopter Spies; One Spy Too Many; The Return of the World's Greatest Detective
Harht, Wayne (act): The Norsemen
Harimoto, Dale (act): The Puppet Masters
Harington, Donald (wri): Return (1985)
Hark, Tsui (dir): Don't Play With Fire; Zu: Warriors of the Magic Mountain
Harker, Charmienne (act): The Chinese Ring
Harker, Gordon (act, 1885-1967): Bang! You're Dead; Blondes for Danger; Champagne; Condemned to Death; Elstree Calling; The Frightened Lady (1932); The Frog; The Man They Could Not Arrest; The Phantom Light; The Return of the Frog; The Ring; The Ringer (1931); The Squeaker (1930); Things Happen at Night; Warn That Man; White Face; Wolf's Clothing (1936)
Harker, Susannah (act): The Crucifer of Blood
Harker, Wiley (act): Trancers
Harkham, Joel (act): The Howling: New Moon Rising
Harkham, Sally (act): The Howling: New Moon Rising
Harkin, Dennis (act): Home to Danger
Harkin, Kathryn (act): Rhinoceros (1974)
Harkins, John (act): Amityville 3-D; City Killer; Good Against Evil; The Return of the Man
from U.N.C.L.E.; Tarantulas: The Deadly Cargo; This Gun for Hire (1991)
Harlacher, Eric (wri): Homewrecker; What We Did That Night
Harlam, Macey (act): Bella Donna (1923); The Face In the Fog (1922)
Harlan, Jane (act): Two Lost Worlds
Harlan, Jeff (act): The Boogens
Harlan, Kenneth (act, 1895-1967): Black Dragons; Blondes at Work; The Corpse Vanishes; Dick Tracy's G-Men; Dick Tracy vs. Crime, Inc.; Doomed to Die; The Penalty; Torchy Runs for Mayor; The Walking Dead
Harlan, Otis (act, 1865-1940): The Brass Bottle (1923); Frankenstein (1931); A Midsummer Night's Dream (1935); Snow White and the Seven Dwarfs
Harlan, Russ(ell) (cin, b. 1903): Land of the Pharaohs; The Last Hunt; Tarzan's Desert Mystery; The Thing from Another World; Witness for the Prosecution
Harley, Eileen (act): The Monster That Challenged the World
Harlin, Renny (dir, b. 1959): Cutthroat Island; The Long Kiss Goodnight; A Nightmare on Elm Street 4: The Dream Master; Prison (1988)
Harline, Leigh (mus, 1907-1969): Black Widow (1954); The Boy With Green Hair; Isle of the Dead (1945); It Happens Every Spring; Pinocchio (1940); The Road to Utopia; 7 Faces of Dr. Lao; Snow White and the Seven Dwarfs; 23 Paces to Baker Street; The Velvet Touch; Visit to a Small Planet; The Wonderful World of the Brothers Grimm
Harling, Laura (act): Lost Souls (1998)
Harlow, April (act): Night After Night After Night
Harlow, Bob (act): For Heaven's Sake
Harlow, John (dir, b. 1896): Appointment With Crime; The Blue Parrot; Candles at Nine; The Dark Tower; The Echo Murders; Meet Sexton Blake; Spellbound (1941); While I Live
Harlow, John (wri, b. 1896): Appointment With Crime; Candles at Nine; The Dark Tower (1943); The Echo Murders; Meet Sexton Blake; While I Live
Harlow, Pamela (act): Pandemonium
Harmer, Juliet (act): Quest for Love
Harmon, Barbara (act): Tuck Everlasting
Harmon, David P. (wri): Murder On Flight 502; The Wonderful World of the Brothers Grimm
Harmon, Jack (act): Brainstorm (1983)
Harmon, Jim (wri): The Lemon Grove Kids Meet the Monsters
Harmon, John (act): After Midnight With Boston Blackie; The Chance of a Lifetime; Dangerous Money; The Monster of Piedras Blancas; Run for the Hills; Secrets of the Lone Wolf
Harmon, Joy (act): The Loved One; Village of the Giants
Harmon, Julian (wri): Shadowed; The Unknown (1946)
Harmon, Marie (act): Larceny In Her Heart
Harmon, Mark (act, b. 1952): Beyond the Poseidon Adventure; Cold Heaven; Goliath Awaits; Magic In the Water; Shadow of a Doubt (1991); Tuareg, the Desert Warrior
Harmon, Pat (act): Behind the Curtain (1924)
Harmon, Renee (act): Night of Terror (1987)
Harmon, Robert (dir): The Hitcher
Harmon, Robin (act): Def by Temptation
Harmstorf, Raimund (act): The Sheriff and the Satellite Kid
Harnell, Jess (act): Aladdin and the King of Thieves; Casper
Harnell, Joe (mus): The Loves of Dracula; V; World of Dracula
Harner, Joe (act): Strange Behavior
Harner, Mary Ruth (act): Strange Behavior
Harney, Carina (act): Vampirella (1996)
Harnois, Elisabeth (act): The Warlord: Battle for the Galaxy
Harnos, Christine (act): Hellraiser 4: Bloodline; Thrill
Haro, Claudia (act): Wes Craven's New Nightmare
Harold, Rex (act): A Smart Set
Harold, Theresa (act): The Galaxy Invader
Harolde, Ralf (act, 1899-1974): Behind Locked Doors; Deluge; Horror Island; Murder, My Sweet; Night Nurse
Harout, Magda (act): Are You In the House Alone?
Haroy, Claude (cin): The Son of Hercules In the Land of Darkness
Harp, Helen (act): Tombs of the Blind Dead
Harp, Kenneth (act): Fear and Desire
Harp, Peter (act): Primal Scream
Harpaz, Udi (mus): Casper: A Spirited Beginning
Harper, Barbara S. (wri): Account Rendered; Captain Clegg; Port of Escape
Harper, Beth (act): The Haunting of Sarah Hardy
Harper, Colin (act): Erik the Viking
Harper, Dianne (act): Crackle of Death
Harper, Don (mus): Houdini (1998)
Harper, Ed(ward) (wri): A Ghost of a Chance (1968)
Harper, Gerald (act): If It's a Man, Hang Up; The Lady Vanishes (1979); Strangler's Web; Trader Horn (1973)
Harper, Giles (act): The Witches and the Grinnygog
Harper, Harriet (act): Return from the Ashes
Harper, Harry (act): The Element of Crime
Harper, Hill (act): Pumpkinhead II: Blood Wings
Harper, James (act): Switch
Harper, Jessica (act): The Evictors; Phantom of the Paradise; Shock Treatment! (1981); Suspiria
Harper, Kate (act): Batman (1989)
Harper, Len (act): Web of Deceit
Harper, Rand (act): Rear Window (1954)
Harper, Ray (act): Trapped by Boston Blackie
Harper, Robert (act): Nick Knight; Not Quite Human; The Motion (1975)
Harper, Ron (act): Back to the Planet of the Apes; Farewell to the Planet of the Apes; Forgotten City of the Planet of the Apes; Life, Liberty and Pursuit On the Planet of the Apes; Treachery and Greed On the Planet of the Apes
Harper, Sarah (act): The Secret Life of Ian Fleming
Harper, Scott (mus): Eat and Run
Harper, Susan (act): Phantasm
Harper, Tess (act): Amityville 3-D; Starflight: The Plane That Couldn't Land
Harper, Toni (act): How to Stuff a Wild Bikini
Harper, Tracy (act): The Sender
Harper, Valerie (act, b. 1940): Dog's Best Friend; Don't Go to Sleep
Harper, Virgil (cin): Secrets of the Phantom Caverns; Tremors 2: Aftershocks
Harragin, Serena (act): The Witches (1990)
Harrell, Cindy (act): The Final Terror
Harrell, Michele (act): The Exterminator
Harrell (III), Peter (act): Brainstorm (1983); Phantom of the Paradise; Sugar Hill
Harrelson, Woody (act, b. 1961): Bay Coven
Harries-Jones, Roy (act): Inn of the Damned
Harrigan, Michael (act): Superman (1978)
Harrigan, Nedda (act, 1899-1989): Charlie Chan at the Opera; Devil's Island; Thank You, Mr. Moto
Harrigan, William (act): Francis Covers the Big Town; The Invisible Man (1933); Roogie's Bump
Harriman, Fawne (act): The Aliens Are Coming
Harrington, Andy (act): Phoenix the Warrior
Harrington, Cleo (act): Dracula's Dog
Harrington, Curtis (dir, b. 1928): The Cat Creature; The Dead Don't Die; Games; How Awful About Allan; Killer Bees; The Killing Kind; Mata Hari (1985); Night Tide; Queen of Blood; Ruby; What's the Matter with Helen?; Who Slew Auntie Roo?
Harrington, Curtis (wri, 1928): Night Tide; Queen of Blood
Harrington, Ed (act): Memories of Murder
Harrington, George (act): The Tiger of San Pedro
Harrington, Hamtree (act): Pocomania
Harrington, Jean (act): The Deadly Females
Harrington, Joe (act): Laughing at Danger
Harrington, Joy (act): The Quatermass Conclusion
Harrington, Laura (act): Dead Air; Maximum Overdrive
Harrington, Lisa Jay (act): Witchcraft 4: Virgin Heart
Harrington (Jr.), Pat (act, b. 1929): The Computer Wore Tennis Shoes (1970); The Nine Lives of Fritz the Cat; The President's Analyst; 2000 Years Later
Harrington, Peter (act): Time Chasers
Harrington, Ramsey (dir): Compelled
Harris, Alan (act): Evilspeak
Harris, Alan M. (wri): The Devil's Wedding Night
Harris, Albert (act): Deathmoon
Harris, Anita (act): Death Is a Woman
Harris, Anthony (wri): Beware! The Blob
Harris, April (act): Popcorn
Harris, Barbara (act, b. 1935, nee Sandra Markowitz): Family Plot; Freaky Friday (1976); Ghost of a Chance (1987); Nice Girls Don't Explode; Oh Dad Poor Dad, Mamma's Hung You In the Closet and I'm Feelin' So Sad; Peggy Sue Got Married
Harris, Betty (act): The Housekeeper
Harris, Brad (act): Black Panther of Ratana; Goliath Against the Giants; Hercules (1983); Kiss Kiss, Kill Kill; Kong Island; The Mad Butcher; The Mutations; Samson; Secret Agent 077-Operation Hong Kong; Spy Today, Die Tomorrow
Harris, Cassandra (act, 1952-1991): For Your Eyes Only
Harris, Chris (act): Bog
Harris, Clare (act): The Jewel
Harris, Clarence (act): Skullduggery
Harris, Craig (cin): Toxic Zombies
Harris, Cynthia (act): Doctor Franken; Mannequin Two: On the Move
Harris, Damian (act): Otley
Harris, Damian (dir): Deceived
Harris, Danielle (act, b. 1977): Daylight; Halloween 4: The Return of Michael Myers; Halloween 5: The Revenge of Michael Myers; Wish Upon a Star
Harris, Darren (act): Weird Science
Harris, Dean (act): Craze; Double Exposure (1977)
Harris, Deidre (act): Heart Condition
Harris, Denny (dir): Silent Scream (1979)
Harris, Derek (act, cin & dir): see Derek, John
Harris, Dina (act): The Horror of Party Beach
Harris III, Dodd (act): Invasion of the Girl Snatchers
Harris, Donald (act): Flesh Gordon
Harris, Ed (act, b. 1951): The Abyss; The Aliens Are Coming; Apollo 13; Creepshow; Knightriders; Needful Things; The Stand; The Truman Show
Harris, Edna Mae (act): Green Pastures
Harris, Eric (act): Tuck Everlasting
Harris, Estelle (act): Perfect Alibi
Harris, Fox (act): Alienator; Dr. Caligari; Forbidden World; Repo Man; Warlords
Harris, Frank (dir): Aftershock
Harris, Fred (act): see Bilbao, Fernando
Harris, Gail (act): Cellblock Sisters: Banished Behind Bars; The Haunting of Morella
Harris, George (act): Flash Gordon (1980); Raiders of the Lost Ark
Harris II, George (act): Superman (1978)
Harris, Greg (act): Jaws 2
Harris, Harriet Sansom (act): Addams Family Values
Harris, Harry (dir): Alice In Wonderland (1985)
Harris, Harry (mus): Snow White and the Three Stooges
Harris, Henry (act): Lady In White
Harris, Henry (cin): A Matter of Life and Death; Quatermass II
Harris, Holly (act): The Hypnotic Eye; Slaughter
Harris, Jack H. (act): Schlock
Harris, Jack H. (dir): Mother Goose A Go-Go
Harris, Jack H. (wri): 4D Man; Mother Goose A Go-Go
Harris, James B. (dir): The Bedford Incident; Some Call It Loving
Harris, James B. (wri): Some Call It Loving
Harris, Jared (act): Lost In Space
Harris, Jeff (act): Blood Diner
Harris, Jo Ann (act): The Beguiled; Cruise into Terror; The Eliminator
Harris, Joel Chandler (wri, 1848-1908): Song of the South
Harris, John (act): Carnival of Blood
Harris, Johnny (mus): The Evil; Fragment of Fear; Not of This World
Harris, Jonathan (act): A Bug's Life; Pinocchio and the Emperor of the Night
Harris, Julie (act, b. 1925): The Dark Half; The Haunting; Home for the Holidays; How Awful About Allan; Journey to Midnight; Reflections In a Golden Eye; Too Good to Be True
Harris, Julius (W.) (act): Darkman (1990); King Kong (1976); Live and Let Die
Harris, June (act): Night of the Creeps
Harris, Karmen (act): Angel Heart
Harris, Lara (act): The Dogfighters; Inhumanoid
Harris, Laura (act): The Faculty
Harris, Leigh (act): Sorceress (1982)
Harris, Lionel (act): Lady In the Fog
Harris, Lionel (dir): The Double; Position of Trust
Harris, Lynette (act, b. 1955): Sorceress (1982)
Harris, Lynn (act): The Erotic Adventures of Zorro
Harris, M.K. (act): Slumber Party Massacre 3
Harris, Marcia (act): The Greene Murder Case; The Sorrows of Satan (1926)
Harris, Marilyn (act): Frankenstein (1931)
Harris, Mark (act): Stanley
Harris, Maurice (act): Dungeons of Horror

Harris, Max (act): One of Our Dinosaurs Is Missing
Harris, Mel (act): Cameron's Closet; Desperate Motove; The Pagemaster; Raising Cain; The Secretary; Sharon's Secret; The Spider and the Fly (1994); Suture
Harris, Michael (amateur act): I Was a Teen-Age Mummy
Harris, Michael (pro act): The Amazing Colossal Man; Babylon 5: A Call to Arms; Dead Air; Mr. Stitch; Shriek of the Mutilated; Sleepstalker; Suture
Harris, Neil Patrick (act): The Man In the Attic (1995); Purple People Eater; Starship Troopers; Too Good to Be True
Harris, Nola (act): The Lost Missile
Harris, Owen (wri): The Flight That Disappeared; The Underwater City
Harris, Paul (act): Road Games
Harris, Phil (act, 1906-1995): The Aristocats; The Last Generation; Robin Hood (1973)
Harris, Richard (act, b. 1933): The Bible; Camelot; Gulliver's Travels (1977); The Hunchback (1997); Maigret; 99 and 44/100% Dead; Orca; Ravagers; Red Desert; Robin and Marian; Tarzan, the Ape Man (1981)
Harris, Richard (wri): Attempt to Kill; I Start Counting; Locker 69; The Main Chance; Man Detained; On the Run (1963); Strongroom
Harris, Ricky (act): Tales from the Hood
Harris, Robert (act, b. 1900): The Bad Lord Byron; The Ghost Train (1941); Girl In the Headlines
Harris, Robert (wri): Werewolf of London
Harris, Robert H. (act, 1911-1981): How Awful About Allan; How to Make a Monster; The Invisible Boy; Mirage (1965)
Harris, Robin/Robyn (act): Hard to Die; Sorority House Massacre 2
Harris, Rochelle (act): Road Games
Harris, Rolf (act): Web of Suspicion
Harris, Ron (act): Spacecamp
Harris, Roseann (act): Vampire On Bikini Beach
Harris, Rosemary (act, b. 1930): The Boys from Brazil
Harris, Ross (act): Night of the Living Dead (1968); Scream, Baby, Scream; Top Kids
Harris, (Maj.) Sam (act): The Gracie Allen Murder Case; Mr. Moto Takes a Vacation; The Mysterious Mr. Moto
Harris, Shirley Jane (act): Stay Awake
Harris, Sid (wri): Stormy Crossing; Varan the Unbelievable
Harris, Stacey (act): Brainstorm (1965)
Harris, Stacy (act): Appointment With Danger; Brainstorm (1965)
Harris, Steve (act): Nightmare Street
Harris, Sue Ann (act): Shocker
Harris, Ted (act): Blacula
Harris, Teresa/Theresa (act): I Walked with a Zombie; The Velvet Touch
Harris, Thomas (wri): Black Sunday (1977); The Silence of the Lambs
Harris, Thurston (act): The Burglar and the Clock; Cinderella (1907); The Ghosts' Holiday; The Man and His Bottle; The Man and the Latchkey; That Fatal Sneeze; A Tramp's Dream of Wealth
Harris, Timothy (wri): My Stepmother Is An Alien; Space Jam; Twins
Harris, Tom (cin): Xtro
Harris, Trent (dir & wri): Plan 10 from Outer Space
Harris, Vernon (act): The Claydon Treasure Mystery
Harris, Vernon (wri): A Case for PC 49; Cosh Boy
Harris, William Bevan (act): see Bevan, Billy
Harris, Winifred (act): The Lone Wolf In Mexico; Night Must Fall (1937)
Harrison, Annalie (act): Demons 2
Harrison, Anthony (act): The Village of the Damned (1960)
Harrison, B.J. (act): Circle of Deceit
Harrison, Cathryn (act): Black Moon (1975); Images; The Pied Piper (1971)
Harrison, Craig (wri): The Quiet Earth
Harrison, Cynthia (act): Outbreak; School Spirit
Harrison, Dan (act): Ali Baba and the Seven Saracens; Machiste In King Solomon's Mines
Harrison, Daniel (act): Tales from the Darkside
Harrison, Emily (act): Curse of the Puppet Master
Harrison, F.E. (act): The Case of a Doped Actress
Harrison, Frieda (act): see Kendall, Suzy
Harrison, George (mus, b. 1943): Time Bandits
Harrison, Gillian (act): Supersonic Saucer
Harrison, Gregory (act, b. 1952): A Dangerous Affair; Razorback; Robin Cook's 'Mortal Fear'; Summer of Fear; Trilogy of Terror
Harrison, Harding (act): High Priestess of Sexual Witchcraft
Harrison, Harry (wri, b. 1925): Soylent Green
Harrison, Harvey (cin): American Gothic; The Burning; Cheech and Chong's The Corsican Brothers; A Connecticut Yankee In King Arthur's Court (1989); The Witches (1990)
Harrison, Henry (act): With Human Instinct
Harrison, Irma (act): One Exciting Night
Harrison, James (act): The Saint In Palm Springs
Harrison, Jenilee (act): Curse III: Blood Sacrifice
Harrison, Jim (wri): Wolf
Harrison, Joan (wri, b. 1911): Dark Waters; Jamaica Inn (1939); Rebecca; Saboteur; Suspicion (1941)
Harrison, Joel (act): My Science Project
Harrison, John (act): Knightriders
Harrison, John (dir): Tales from the Darkside
Harrison, John (mus): Day of the Dead; Tales from the Darkside
Harrison, John (wri): Memories of Murder; Shock Waves
Harrison, John Simco (mus): The Legend of Spider Forest
Harrison, Jules (dir): Exterminators of the Year 3000
Harrison, Kathleen (act, b. 1898): Cast a Dark Shadow; Double Confession; The Flying Squad (1940); The Ghost Train (1941); The Ghoul (1933); The Girl In the News; I Killed the Count; Line Engaged; The London Connection; Meet Sexton Blake; Night Must Fall (1937); Scrooge (1951); Seven Thunders; The Shop at Sly Corner; The Terror (1938); They Came by Night; Turn the Key Softly; Wanted for Murder; West 11
Harrison, Ken (mus): Dark Mansions; I Still Dream of Jeannie
Harrison, Linda (act, a.k.a. Augusta Summerland): Beneath the Planet of the Apes; Cocoon; Cocoon: The Return; Planet of the Apes; Way...Way Out
Harrison, Lindsay (wri): Lovestruck; Turn Back the Clock
Harrison, Lottie (act): Lost In a Harem
Harrison, Maurice (wri): Dead Lucky; The Diplomatic Corpse; Stolen Assignment
Harrison, Nigel (act): Blue Ice
Harrison, Noel (act): Hot Enough for June; Where the Spies Are
Harrison, Norman (dir): Calculated Risk; Incident at Midnight; The Invisible Asset; Locker 69
Harrison, Paul (dir & wri): The House of Seven Corpses
Harrison, Paul Carter (wri): Lord Shango
Harrison, Rex (act, 1908-1990, nee Reginald Carey): Blithe Spirit; Dr. Dolittle (1967); The Fifth Musketeer; Gestapo; The Ghost and Mrs. Muir; Midnight Lace (1960); Ten Days In Paris
Harrison, Richard (act): The Alien Within; The Channeler; Giants of Rome; Gladiators Seven; The Invincible Gladiator; Killers Are Challenged; Kronos (1957); Master of the World; Master Stroke; Messalina Against the Son of Hercules; Perseus the Invincible; Secret Agent Fireball; Temple of a Thousand Lights
Harrison, Robert (act): Amazons (1984)
Harrison, Ron (act): Halloween 4: The Return of Michael Myers
Harrison, Roy (act): Always
Harrison, Sally (act): —And Now the Screaming Starts!
Harrison, Sandra (act): Blood of Dracula; The Couch
Harrison, Schae (act): Magic Island
Harrison, Stephen (act): The Baron of Arizona
Harrison, Tom (act): Amazing Stories
Harrison, William (wri): Rollerball
Harrison, Wordsworth (act): Prehistoric Peeps
Harrold, Kathryn (act): The Companion (1994); Nightwing; The Sender; Vampire (1979)
Harron, Donald (act): I Deal In Danger
Harron, John(ny) (act): Behind the Curtain (1924); The Invisible Menace; Midnight Warning; Torchy Blane In Panama; Torchy Gets Her Man; Torchy Plays With Dynamite; Torchy Runs for Mayor; White Zombie
Harron, Robert (act, 1894-1920): Man's Genesis
Harrow, Lisa (act): The Final Conflict; The Tempter (1973); That Eye, the Sky
Harrow, Richard (act): Ganja and Hess
Harry, Deborah (act, b. 1945): Body Bags; Tales from the Darkside; Videodrome
Harry, Michael (wri): In the Shadow of Kilimanjaro
Harryhausen, Ray (cin, b. 1920): The Animal World; The Beast from 20,000 Fathoms; Clash of the Titans; Earth vs. the Flying Saucers; First Men In the Moon (1964); The Golden Voyage of Sinbad; It Came from Beneath the Sea; Jason and the Argonauts; Mighty Joe Young (1949); Mysterious Island (1961); One Million Years B.C.; The 7th Voyage of Sinbad; Sinbad and the Eye of the Tiger; The Three Worlds of Gulliver; 20 Million Miles to Earth; The Valley of Gwangi
Harryson, Leslie (act): The Curse of the Aztec Mummy
Hart, Albert (act): Crooked Alley
Hart, Barry (act): Agatha
Hart, Beverly (act): Star Trek V: The Final Frontier
Hart, Carolyn G. (wri): Dead Man's Island
Hart, Christa (act): Women and Bloody Terror
Hart, Christina (act): Dead of Night (1977)
Hart, Christopher (act): The Addams Family; Addams Family Values; Lady Terminator
Hart, Christopher (dir & wri): Eat and Run
Hart, Diane (act): Britannia Mews; Dick Turpin-Highwayman; Enter Inspector Duval; One Jump Ahead
Hart, Dorothy (act, b. 1923): I Was a Communist for the F.B.I.; Larceny; Take One False Step; Tarzan's Savage Fury
Hart, Eric (act): Halloween 4: The Return of Michael Myers
Hart, Ferdinand (act): Le Golem (1936)
Hart, George (wri): Blood Song
Hart, Gordon (act): Fly-Away Baby; Lady In the Morgue
Hart, Harvey (dir, b. 1928): The Aliens Are Coming; Dark Intruder
Hart, Henry (act): D.O.A. (1949)
Hart, Jacobsen (dir): Steel Frontier
Hart, Jacobsen (wri): The Power Within (1995); Steel Frontier
Hart, James V. (wri): Bram Stoker's Dracula; Contact
Hart, Joe (act): The Lawnmower Man
Hart, John (act): Blackenstein; Champagne for Caesar; Day of the Nightmare; Simon, King of the Witches; Welcome to Arrow Beach
Hart, John F. (act): Beyond and Back
Hart, John (wri): Atom Age Vampire
Hart, Judith (wri): The Flight That Disappeared
Hart, Kathryn (act): X-The Man with the X-Ray Eyes
Hart, Kenneth J. (act): Raiders of the Living Dead
Hart, Kevin (act): Absolution; Lone Wolf (1988); Mind Killer
Hart, Lorenz (mus, 1895-1943): The Boys from Syracuse; I Married an Angel; Love Me Tonight
Hart, Malcolm (wri): Vanishing Point (1971)
Hart, Melissa Joan (act): Sabrina Goes to Rome; Sabrina the Teenage Witch
Hart, Morgan (act): The Man Who Wasn't There
Hart, Moss (wri, 1904-1961): The Decision of Christopher Blake; Hans Chrstian Andersen; Lady In the Dark
Hart, Nadine (act): Robot Holocaust
Hart, Peggy (act): The Keeper
Hart, Peter (mus): Man In the Dark (1965)
Hart, Ralph (wri): The Flight That Disappeared
Hart, Richard (act, 1915-1951): The Black Book
Hart, Robert Sterling (act): see Sterling, Robert
Hart, Roxanne (act): Highlander; Meteorites!; Oh, God! You Devil; Pulse
Hart, Stan (wri): Eat and Run
Hart, Stephen (act): Magic
Hart, Susan (act, b. 1941): The City Under the Sea; Dr. Goldfoot and the Bikini Machine; The Ghost In the Invisible Bikini; Pajama Party; The Slime People
Hart, Teddy (act): After the Thin Man
Harte, Jennifer (act): Prehysteria! 2
Harte, Jerry (act): The Empire Strikes Back; Loophole
Harte, Michael (act): Magic
Harter, Robert (act): Web of Deceit
Hartford, Alec (act): The Adventures of Robin Hood
Hartford, Andrea (act): Monstroid
Hartford, Eden (act): Invisible Invaders; The Story of Mankind
Hartford, Fiona (act): Rasputin, the Mad Monk
Hartford, Glen (act): Monstroid
Hartford, James (wri): Dr. Goldfoot and the Bikini Machine; Dr. Goldfoot and the Girl Bombs
Hartford, Karen (act): The Spectre of Edgar Allan Poe
Hartford, Kenneth (cin): Monstroid
Hartford, Kenneth (dir & wri): The Lucifer Complex; Monstroid
Hartford-Davis, Robert (act, b. 1923): Dollars for Sale
Hartford-Davis, Robert (dir, b. 1923): Beware, My Brethren; Black Torment; Carry On Spying; A Christmas Carol (1960); Corruption; Crosstrap; Doctors Wear Scarlet; The Fiend (1972); The Man On the Cliff
Hartford-Davis, Robert (wri, b. 1923): Dollars for Sale
Hartigan, Ben (act): Psycho II; Switch (1991)
Hartigan, John C. (cin): Bridge Across Time
Hartill, Willie (act): Dick Turpin's Ride to York
Hartl, Karl (dir): F.P. 1 Antwortet Nicht; Gold (1934, German-speaking version)
Hartley, Clare (act): Trancers 4: Jack of Swords; Trancers 5: Sudden Death
Hartley, Cynthia (act): Alfred Hitchcock Presents
Hartley, Harry (act): The Beggar Girl's Wedding
Hartley, Jennifer (act): Scream of the Demon Lover
Hartley, Mariette (act, b. 1940): Drums of Africa; Earth II; Encino Man; Genesis II; Marooned; No Place to Hide (1981); The Return of Count Yorga; Sandcastles
Hartley, Richard (mus): Alice In Wonderland (1999); The Lady Vanishes (1979); The McGuffin; Midnight's Child; Sheena; Shock Treatment! (1981)
Hartley, Ted (act): Murderers' Row
Hartley, Vivian Mary (act): see Leigh, Vivien
Hartline, Gene (act): Deathsport; Space Rage; Time After Time
Hartling, Lore (act): Confess, Dr. Corda
Hartman, Billy (act): Highlander; Slaughter High
Hartman, David (act, b. 1935): I Love a Mystery (1966); The Island at the Top of the World; Miracle On 34th Street (1973)
Hartman, Don (wri): Down to Earth
Hartman, Elizabeth (act, 1944-1987): The Beguiled; Full Moon High; The Secret of NIMH
Hartman, Ena (act): Terminal Island
Hartman, Karen (act): Houdini (1998)
Hartman, Kenneth (act): My Neighbor Totoro
Hartman, Lee (act): Night of the Living Dead (1968)
Hartman, Lisa (act, b. 1956): Deadly Blessing; Not of This World
Hartman, Margot (act): The Curse of the Living Corpse
Hartman, Margot (wri): Psychomania (1964)
Hartman, Paul (act, 1904-1973): The Reluctant Astronaut
Hartman, Phil (act, 1948-1998): The Brave Little Toaster; Small Soldiers
Hartman, Ron (act): Change of Mind; Escape Clause; The Only Way Out Is Dead; Virus (1980)
Hartman, Steven (act): Candyman: Farewell to the Flesh
Hartman, Victoria (act): Motel Hell
Hartmann, Edmund L. (wri, b. 1911): Ali Baba and the Forty Thieves (1943); Ghost Catchers; The Last Warning (1938); Sherlock Holmes and the Secret Weapon; Sudan
Hartmann, Erhart (act): The Fifth Musketeer
Hartmann, Paul (act): Chronik von Grieshuus; F.P. 1 Antwortet Nicht; Schloss Vogelod
Hartmann, Phil (act): Pandemonium
Hartmann, Sadakichi (act): The Thief of Bagdad (1924)
Hartmann, Tanja (act): Making Contact
Hartnell, Billy (act): see Hartnell William/Billy
Hartnell, Max (act): No Blade of Grass
Hartnell, William/Billy (act, 1908-1975): Appointment With Crime; The Dark Man (1951); The Dark Tower (1943); Date With Disaster; The Desperate Man; Double Confession; Footsteps In the Fog; The Hypnotist (1957); I'm an Explosive; Jackpot; The Lure; Midnight at Madame Tussaud's; The Mouse That Roared; Murder In Reverse; Murder Will Out (1939); On the Run (1958); The Perfect Flaw; Piccadilly Third Stop; The Ringer (1952); Suspected Person; To Have and To Hold; Tomorrow at Ten
Hartnett, Josh (act): The Faculty; Halloween H20
Hartpeng, Lucia (act): The Handmaid's Tale
Hartree, Charles (act): see Hawtrey, Charles
Hartsell, Jimmy Dale (act): Seven
Hartson, Michael (act): Terrorgram
Hartstone, Christopher (act): Captain Nemo and the Underwater City
Hartung, Raymond (wri): Snow Kill
Hartwell, John (wri): The Fan
Hartwell, Taea (act): The Frighteners
Hartz, April (act): Dr. Caligari
Harum, Eivind (act): Frankenhooker; The Shaman

Harvard, Elvenn (act): Fer-de-Lance
Harvest, Rainbow (act): Earth Angel; Mirror, Mirror
Harvey, Anthony (dir, b. 1931): Svengali (1983); They Might Be Giants
Harvey, Bob (act): How to Stuff a Wild Bikini; Sergeant Deadhead the Astronut!
Harvey, David (act): Bay Coven
Harvey, Don (act): Prey of the Chameleon; The Relic; Sawbones; Tank Girl
Harvey, Don (C.) (act): The Beginning of the End; Creature With the Atom Brain; Forbidden Jungle; The Golden Idol; The Lost Volcano
Harvey, Edward (act): Cat Girl
Harvey, Eric LaRay (act): Twister
Harvey, Erwin (act): The Goonies
Harvey, Forrester (act, 1890-1945): Arrest Bulldog Drummond; Bulldog Drummond In Africa; Bulldog Drummond's Secret Police; A Chump at Oxford; Devotion; Great Expectations (1934); The Invisible Man (1933); The Invisible Man Returns; Kongo; The Lodger (1944); The Mysterious Doctor; The Mysterious Mr. Moto; The Mystery of Mr. X; Rebecca; The Ring; Scotland Yard Investigator; Secrets of Scotland Yard; Shanghai Express; Tarzan and His Mate; Tarzan the Ape Man (1932); The Wolf Man (1941)
Harvey, Frank (wri, b. 1912): High Treason (1951); Murder Tomorrow; My Brother's Keeper; Portrait from Life; Seven Days to Noon; Things Happen at Night; The 39 Steps (1959)
Harvey (Sr.), Harry (act): The Falcon's Adventure; The Falcon's Alibi; The Lone Wolf Returns (1935); The Narrow Margin (1952); The Return of Dracula
Harvey Jr., Harry (act): Forbidden Planet; They Won't Believe Me
Harvey, Herk (act & dir): Carnival of Souls (1962)
Harvey, Jack (act): Blue Velvet
Harvey, Jack (wri): City Beneath the Sea (1952); Unknown Island
Harvey, Jean (act): Ambush In Leopard Street; Guns Don't Argue
Harvey, Jim(my) (cin): Murder by Proxy; The Quatermass Experiment; Spy In the Sky
Harvey, Joan (act): Hands of a Stranger
Harvey, John (GB act): Black Widow (1951); The Black Windmill; The Dark Light; The Deadly Bees; Dick Barton Strikes Back; Kiss of the Vampire; Legend of the Werewolf; The Old Dark House (1963); The Psychopath (1965); The Satanic Rites of Dracula; They Came from Beyond Space; X...The Unknown
Harvey, John (USA act): The Spider (1945)
Harvey, Laurence (act, 1928-1973, nee Larushka Mischa Skikne): The Black Rose; A Dandy in Aspic; House of Darkness; A Killer Walks; The Magic Christian; The Manchurian Candidate; The Man from Yesterday (1949); Man On the Run; Night Watch (1973); The Running Man (1963); Scarlet Thread; The Spy With a Cold Nose; Wall of Death (1952); Welcome to Arrow Beach; The Wonderful World of the Brothers Grimm
Harvey, Laurence (dir, 1928-1973): A Dandy in Aspic; Welcome to Arrow Beach
Harvey, Lola (wri): What a Night!
Harvey, Marcus (act): Spawn of the Slithis
Harvey, Marilyn (act): The Astounding She-Monster
Harvey, Mike (mus): Chilling (1981)
Harvey, Morris (act): Scrooge (1935)
Harvey, Nita (act): The Sky Raiders
Harvey, Orwin (act): The Final Countdown; The Prisoner of Zenda (1979)
Harvey, Paul (act, 1884-1955): The Beginning or the End?; Call Northside 777; Charlie Chan In Honolulu; Charlie Chan's Courage; The Gorilla (1939); The Man Who Wouldn't Die; Mr. Moto In Danger Island; Spellbound (1945); Take One False Step
Harvey, Peter (cin): Chinese Boxes; The Face of Darkness
Harvey, Phil (act): The Deadly Mantis; I've Lived Before; The Land Unknown; The Monolith Monsters; Monster On the Campus
Harvey, Richard (mus): House of the Long Shadows; Jane Eyre (1997)
Harvey, Robert (H.) (act): I'm Dangerous Tonight; Murder of Innocence; Point of No Return; Pumpkinhead II: Blood Wings
Harvey, Rupert (dir): Critters 4
Harvey, Russ (act): Dungeons of Horror
Harvey, Terence (act): The Phantom of the Opera (1989)
Harvey, Tom (act): Bay Coven
Harvey, Verna (act): Assassin (1973); Blue Movie Blackmail; The Nightcomers
Harvey, W.F. (wri): The Beast With Five Fingers
Harvey, Walter (J.) (cin): Bulldog Drummond at Bay (1937); Kill Her Gently; Lady In the Fog; The Saint's Return; Tower of Terror
Harvey, William (act): The Midnight Girl
Harwell, David (act): Secrets of the Phantom Caverns
Harwood, Anthony (act): The Adding Machine
Harwood, Bo (mus): Happy Birthday to Me
Harwood, Bobbie (act): The Copper Beeches (1921)
Harwood, Johanna (wri): Call Me Bwana; Dr. No; From Russia With Love
Harwood, Ronald (wri, b. 1934): The Doctor and the Devils; Eyewitness (1970); A High Wind In Jamaica; Sudden Terror
Harwood, Stewart (act): The Quatermass Conclusion; The Squeeze
Harwood, Tony (act): Billion Dollar Brain
Has, Wojciech Jerzy (dir, b. 1925): Rekopis Znaleziony w Saragossie
Hasak, Adi (wri): Shadow Conspiracy
Hasebe, Keiji (wri): The Profound Desire of the Gods
Hasegawa, Hajime (cin): Little Nemo: Adventures In Slumberland
Hasel, Julie (act): Wheels of Terror
Haselden, W.K. (wri): The Adventures of Big and Little Willie
Hasenau, Beate (act): The Ape Creature
Hasenecz, Sergei (wri): Sorority Babes In the Slimeball Bowl-O-Rama
Hasfal, Topaz (act): The Pink Chiquitas
Hash, Joy (act): Horror High
Hashimoto, Izo (wri): Akira
Hashimoto, Koji (dir): Godzilla 1985
Hashimoto, Lonnie (act): The Dungeonmaster
Hashimoto, Shinobu (wri): Catastrophe 1999: The Prophecies of Nostradamus; Throne of Blood; Yellow Dog
Haskell, David (act): Body Double
Haskell, Jimmie (mus): The Dogfighters; Night of the Lepus
Haskell, Peter (act): Child's Play 2; Child's Play 3; The Eyes of Charles Sand; Mandrake; Once You Meet a Stranger; The Phantom of Hollywood; Robot Wars
Haskell, Robert (act): Teenage Mutant Ninja Turtles
Haskell, Susan (act): The Pink Chiquitas
Haskin, Byron (cin, b. 1899): Arsenic and Old Lace; Don Juan (1927); The Sea Beast
Haskin, Byron (dir, b. 1899): Captain Sinbad; Conquest of Space; From the Earth to the Moon; Jet Over the Atlantic; The Little Savage; Long John Silver; Man-Eater of Kumaon; The Naked Jungle; The Power (1967); Robinson Crusoe On Mars; Tarzan's Peril; Treasure Island (1950); The War of the Worlds
Haskin, Paul (act): Bloodeaters
Haskins, Jamie (act): He Knows You're Alone
Haskins, Troy (act): Phantom of the Paradise
Hasler, Joachim (cin): Milczaca Gwiazda
Haslett, Matthew (act): Give Us Tomorrow
Hass, Dean (act): The Reflecting Skin
Hass, Hans (act): Night of the Blood Monster
Hassall, Imogen (act): Doctors Wear Scarlet; Girly; Licensed to Love and Kill; Position of Trust; Toomorrow; When Dinosaurs Ruled the Earth
Hassan, Jamiel (act): Behind That Curtain
Hassani, Linda (dir): Dark Angel: The Ascent
Hasse, O.E. (act, 1903-1978): The Glass Tower; I Confess
Hassel, Danny (act): A Nightmare On Elm Street 4: The Dream Master; A Nightmare On Elm Street 5: The Dream Child; Nick Fury: Agent of Shield
Hasselhoff, David (act, b. 1952): Bridge Across Time; Nick Fury: Agent of Shield; Ring of the Musketeers; Star Crash; Witchery
Hassell, George (act): Think Fast, Mr. Moto
Hasselquist, Jenny (act): The Story of Gosta Berling
Hassen, Alaoui (act): The Jewel of the Nile
Hassen, Lee (act): Goliathon
Hassett, Marilyn (act): Body Count (1987); Shadow of the Hawk
Hassett, Ray (act): The Empire Strikes Back; Superman (1978)
Hasso, Signe (act, b. 1915, nee Signe Larsson): The Black Bird (1975); A Double Life (1947); Heaven Can Wait (1942); The Magician (1973); Picture Mommy Dead; A Reflection of Fear; Sherlock Holmes In New York; Strange Triangle; To the Ends of the Earth
Hastings, Bob (act): see Hastings, Robert/Bob
Hastings, Chad (act): The Bees
Hastings, Hazel (act): Queenie of the Circus
Hastings, Michael (wri): The Nightcomers; Tennis Court
Hastings, Robert/Bob (act): The Bamboo Saucer; Charley and the Angel; Ellery Queen: Don't Look Behind You; The Munsters' Revenge; The Poseidon Adventure; Spider-Man; A Very Missing Person
Hastings, Stephen (act): The Gifted One
Hata, Masami (dir): Little Nemo: Adventures In Slumberland
Hata, Micah (act): Addams Family Values
Hatch, Jim (act): The Silencers (1995)
Hatch, Lee (act): Empire of Ash III
Hatch, Richard (act, b. 1946): Battlestar Galactica; Charlie Chan and the Curse of the Dragon Queen; Party Line; Prisoners of the Lost Universe
Hatch, Riley (act): see Hatch, (William) Riley
Hatch, Tony (mus): The Secret of Seagull Island
Hatch, Wilbur (mus): The Whistler
Hatch, (William) Riley (act): The Lone Wolf (1917); Missing Millions
Hatcher, Mary (act): Tales of Robin Hood
Hatcher, Rick (cin): Blood Song
Hatcher, Teri (act): Tomorrow Never Dies
Hateley, John (act): RoboCop 2
Hatfield, Hurd (act, b. 1918): Amazing Stories: The Movie V; The Beginning or the End?; The Boston Strangler; Chinatown at Midnight; Mickey One; The Norliss Tapes; The Picture of Dorian Gray (1945); Tarzan and the Slave Girl; The Unsuspected
Hatfield, John (act): Spawn of the Slithis
Hatfield, Mert (act): Freejack
Hatfield, Philip (act): Ten Minute Alibi
Hathaway, Henry (dir, 1898-1985): The Black Rose; Call Northside 777; Fourteen Hours; The Legend of the Lost; Niagara; Peter Ibbetson; Prince Valiant (1954); Rampage; 23 Paces to Baker Street
Hathaway, Noah (act): Battlestar Galactica; The Neverending Story; Troll
Hathaway, Robert (act): Troll
Hathcock, Jeff (dir): Night Ripper
Hatley, Carla (act): Scream
Hatley, Jonathan (act): see Hale, Jonathan
Hatosy, Shawn (act): The Faculty
Hatti, Hilo (act): City Beneath the Sea (1952)
Hatton, Charles (act): Lorna Doone (1922)
Hatton, David (act): Mystery On Monster Island
Hatton, Mercy (act): Broken Barrier; The Case of Lady Camber; The Girl Who Didn't Care; The Girl Who Took the Wrong Turning; The Harbour Lights; In the Days of Robin Hood; The Romany Rye; The Sands of Time; When Woman Hates
Hatton, Ray(mond) (act, 1887-1971): The Adventurous Blonde; Day the World Ended (1955); Dig That Uranium!; Fly-Away Baby; Ghost Rifer (1943); Girls In Prison; The Hunchback of Notre Dame (1923); Invasion of the Saucer Men; Male and Female; Midnight Mystery; Sharad of Atlantis; Three Wise Fools; Trent's Last Case (1929)
Hatton, Ronald (act): The Undesirable Neighbour
Hatton, Rondo (act, 1902-1946): The Brute Man; House of Horrors (1946); The Hunchback of Notre Dame (1939); Jungle Captive; The Pearl of Death; The Spider Woman Strikes Back
Hattori, Katsuhisa (mus): Fist of the North Star
Hattori, Mako (act): The House Where Evil Dwells
Hattori, Yoshio (act): Mothra
Hatula, Judy (act): Abbott and Costello Go to Mars
Hauber, Jody (act): Sandcastles
Hauck, Rex (wri): Destroyer
Hauer, Aysha (act): Witchcraft 5: Dance With the Devil
Hauer, Rutger (act, b. 1944): Blade Runner; The Blood of Heroes;Bone Daddy; Buffy the Vampire Slayer; Crossworlds; Deadlock; Flesh & Blood; The Hitcher; Ladyhawke; Merlin (1998); Mr. Stitch; Nostradamus; Omega Doom; Past Midnight; Precious Find; Split Second (1992); Surviving the Game
Hauff, Thomas (act): Millennium
Haufrect, Alan (act): Coma; Eve of Destruction; Halloween II; Nightmare On the 13th Floor; Twilight Zone
Haugen, Alf (act): The Falcon's Alibi
Haughton, David (act & wri): A Midsummer Night's Dream (1985)
Haugk, Charles (act): Ghost in the Machine
Haukelid, Sigrid Gurie (act): see Gurie, Sigrid
Haun, Lindsey (act): Deep Red (1994); Village of the Damned (1995)
Haunted Garage (mus): Nightmare Sisters
Haupt, Ulrich (act): The Greene Murder Case; The Iron Mask
Hauptmann, Gerhardt (wri): Atlantis (1913)
Hause, Jeffrey (wri): Once Bitten
Hausenberger, Mandy (act): Enemy Mine
Hauser, Burford (wri): Creepozoids
Hauser, Fay (act): Candyman: Farewell to the Flesh
Hauser, Gilgi (act): The Day of the Triffids
Hauser, Nancy Locke (act): Dead and Buried
Hauser, Philo (act): The House of the Seven Hawks
Hauser, Robert (B.) (cin): The Brotherhood of the Bell; The Legend of Lizzie Borden; Night Slaves; No Place to Hide (1981); Someone's Watching Me!; Willard
Hauser, Stephen (wri): Sphere
Hauser, Stone (act): Species
Hauser, Wings (act): Beastmaster 2: Through the Portal of Time; Dead Man Walking; In-Between; Mutant; Nightmare at Noon; Tales from the Hood; Victim of Desire; Watchers III
Hausman, David (act): OSA
Hauss, Harold D. (act): Cat People (1982)
Havard, Dafydd (act): Are You Dying Young Man?; La Ragazza Che Sapeva Troppo
Havard, Elven (act): My Science Project
Havelock-Allan, Anthony (wri): Great Expectations (1946)
Haven, Annette (act): Dracula Sucks
Haven, Terri (act): Heavy Traffic
Haver, Phyllis (act): Don Juan (1927); The Temple of Venus
Havers, Nigel (act): Bridge of Time; Full Circle; Who Is Killing the Great Chefs of Europe?
Havet, Martine (act): Les Miserables (1957)
Havez, Jean (wri): Sherlock Jr.
Havins, Hal (act): Night of the Demons; Sorority Babes In the Slimebowl Bowl-O-Rama
Havoc, June (act, b. 1916): Intrigue; A Return to Salem's Lot
Hawbecker, Laura (act): Glen and Randa
Hawdon, Robin (act): Alien Women; Bedazzled; Burke and Hare; When Dinosaurs Ruled the Earth; Zeta One
Hawes, Mary (act): The Scarlet Letter (1926)
Hawes, Michael (wri): One Dark Night
Hawes, Peter (act): Night of the Red Hunter
Hawes, Tony (act): The Unstoppable Man
Hawk, Jay (act): Teenage Zombies
Hawk, Jeremy (act): The Stranger Came Home; The Trygon Factor; Who Done It? (1956)
Hawke, Ethan (act, b. 1970): Explorers; Gattaca; Great Expectations (1998)
Hawkes, Geoffrey (cin): Bobbikins
Hawkes, Graham (act): For Your Eyes Only
Hawkes, John (act): Congo; D.O.A. (1988); From Dusk Till Dawn
Hawkes, Terri (act): The Haunting of Hamilton High
Hawkeye, Ricky (act): Wolfen
Hawkings, Christopher (act): The Black Windmill
Hawkins, Anthony (act): Damien-Omen II
Hawkins, Carol-Anne (act): The Body Stealers; When Dinosaurs Ruled the Earth; Zeta One
Hawkins, Caroline (act): Alien Women
Hawkins, Edward H. (wri): Sasquatch, the Legend of Bigfoot
Hawkins, Frank (act): The Crooked Sky; Escape from Broadmoor (1948); The Hideout; Kill Her Gently; The Mysterious Mr. Nicholson; Shoot to Kill (1961)
Hawkins, Jack (act, 1910-1973): Birds of Prey; The Black Rose; Death at Broadcasting House; The Elusive Pimpernel (1950); The Fallen Idol; The Flying Squad (1940); Fortune Is a Woman; The Frog; Gideon's Day; The Intruder (1955); Jane Eyre (1970); The Jewel; Land of the Pharaohs; The League of Gentlemen; The Lodger (1932); The Long Arm; Murder On Monday; Murder Will Out (1939); No Highway In the Sky; Rampage; The Shot In the Dark; State Secret; Tales That Witness Madness; Theater of Blood; The Third Secret; The Two-Headed Spy
Hawkins, Jimmy (act): Zotz!
Hawkins, John (act): The Two Worlds of Jennie Logan
Hawkins, John (wri): Floods of Fear
Hawkins, Michael (act): The Terror of the Tongs; They Came from Beyond Space
Hawkins, Patricia (act): Man On a Swing
Hawkins, Peter (act): Assassin (1973)
Hawkins, Richard (act): Creepozoids
Hawkins, Robert (act): Last Bride of Salem
Hawkins, Seth Oliver (act): Class of Nuke 'em High
Hawkins, Timothy (act): Eyes of a Stranger
Hawkins, Valerie (act): Sting of Death
Hawkins, Ward (wri): Floods of Fear
Hawkins, Willis (cin): The Worm Eaters
Hawkshaw, Jean (act): Wild Women of Wongo
Hawley, Richard (act): Jane Eyre (1997)

Hawks, Howard (dir, 1896-1977): The Big Sleep (1946); Land of the Pharaohs; Monkey Business; Trent's Last Case (1929)
Hawks, J.G. (wri): A Blind Bargain; The Last Warning (1929)
Hawks, Kenneth (dir): Such Men Are Dangerous
Hawksley, Brian (act): The Witches (1990)
Hawksworth, John (mus): The Penthouse (1967)
Hawley, Lowell S. (wri): Babes In Toyland (1961); In Search of the Castaways; The Sign of Zorro (1960); Zorro, the Avenger
Hawn, Goldie (act, b. 1945): Death Becomes Her; Deceived
Haworth, Jill (act, b. 1945): The Curse of the Golem; The Haunted House of Horror; Home for the Holidays; Light Years; The Mutations; Tower of Evil
Haworth, Vinton (act): The Saint In Palm Springs
Hawthorne, Christopher (wri): Parents
Hawthorne, David (act): Birds of Prey; Creeping Shadows; In His Grip; Silent Evidence
Hawthorne, Elizabeth (act): The Frighteners
Hawthorne, Matt (act): Virus (1980)
Hawthorne, Nathaniel (wri, 1804-1864): The House of the Seven Gables; The Scarlet Letter (1908, 1911, 1913 {GB}, 1913 {USA}, 1917, 1920, 1922, 1926, 1934, 1972 & 1995); Twice-Told Tales
Hawthorne, Nigel (act): Demolition Man; Freddie as F.R.O.7; The Hunchback of Notre Dame (1982); Memoirs of a Survivor; Richard III (1995); Watership Down
Hawtrey, Anthony (act): Latin Quarter; Warn That Man
Hawtrey, Charles (silent-film act): A Message from Mars (1913)
Hawtrey, Charles (act, 1914-1988, nee Charles Hartree): Alien Women; Carry On Screaming; Carry On Spying; Dark Secret; The Ghost at St. Michael's; The March Hare; The Princess and the Pea; Room to Let; Sabotage; The Terrornauts; Timeslip; Who Done It? (1956); Zeta One
Hawtrey, Kay (act): Funeral Home; Haunted by Her Past; The Intruder (1981); Videodrome
Hay, Alan (act): Double Exposure (1977)
Hay, Alexandra (act, b. 1944): A Place to Die; The Screaming Woman
Hay, Charles (act): Ysani the Priestess
Hay, Helen (act): see Haye, Helen
Hay, Ian (wri): The Frog; I Was a Spy; The Man Behind the Mask (1936); The Return of the Frog; Sabotage; The Secret Agent (1936); The 39 Steps (1935 & 1959)
Hay, Keith (act): The Resurrected
Hay, Phil (act): Red Blooded American Girl
Hay, Will (act): The Ghost at St. Michael's
Hay, William (act): Doom Asylum
Hayakawa, Sessue (act, 1889-1973): The Bottle Imp; Daughter of the Dragon; Green Mansions
Hayamizu, Arai (act): Mothra
Hayashi, Marc (act): White of the Eye
Hayashi, Mitsu (mus): Onibaba
Hayashi, Teru (cin): The Prey (1980)
Hayashi, Yoichi (act): Kwaidan
Hayashi, Yutaka (act): Godzilla vs. Megalon
Hayden, Ashley (act): The Mangler
Hayden, Dennis (act): The Man In the Iron Mask (1997); Slam Dance
Hayden, Frank (act): Creatures the World Forgot; Prehistoric Women (1966)
Hayden, Harry (act): Boston Blackie's Rendezvous; The Docks of New Orleans; Sleepers West; The Thin Man Goes Home; The Unknown Guest; The Velvet Touch; Weird Woman
Hayden, James (act): The Intruder Within; The Nesting
Hayden, Jeffrey (dir): World of Dracula
Hayden, Julie (act): Killer's Moon
Hayden, Kathleen (wri): The Clue of the New Pin (1929)
Hayden, Linda (act): The Blood on Satan's Claw; The Boys from Brazil; The House On Straw Hill; Madhouse; Night Watch (1973); Something to Hide; Taste the Blood of Dracula; Vampira
Hayden, Nora (GB act): The Other Person
Hayden, Nora (USA act): The Angry Red Planet
Hayden, Sterling (act, 1916-1986): Crime of Passion; Deadly Strangers; Dr. Strangelove, or: How I Learned to Stop Worrying and Love the Bomb; Five Steps to Danger; Johnny Guitar; The Killing; The Last Days of Man On Earth; Naked Alibi; Prince Valiant (1954); Valerie; Venom (1982); Winter Kills
Hayden, Ted (act): The Prey (1980)
Haydn, Franz Joseph (mus, 1732-1809): Gebroken Spiegels
Haydn, Richard (act, 1905-1985): Alice In Wonderland (1951); And Then There Were None; The Beginning or the End?; Charlie Chan: Happiness Is a Warm Clue; Five Weeks In a Balloon; The Lost World (1960); Young Frankenstein
Haydock, Ron(ald) (act): The Thrill Killers
Haydock, Ronald (wri): The Lemon Grove Kids Meet the Monsters; Rat Pfink & Boo Boo
Haye, Helen (act, 1874-1957, nee Helen Hay): Bleak House; The Case of the Frightened Lady; Fanny by Gaslight; Honour In Pawn; The Man In Grey; A Place of One's Own; Richard III (1955); The Spy In Black; The 39 Steps (1935); Wolf's Clothing (1936)
Hayek, Salma (act, b. 1969): The Faculty; From Dusk Till Dawn; The Hunchback (1997)
Hayen, Todd (mus): The Devil's Gift; Panic In the Skies!
Hayenga, Jeff (act): The Unborn
Hayer, Nicholas (cin, b. 1898): Le Corbeau; Doulos-The Finger Man; L'Or du Cristobal; Orphee
Hayers, Sidney (dir, b. 1921): Circus of Horrors; Deadly Strangers; Diagnosis: Murder; Echo of Barbara; The Firechasers; In the Devil's Garden; King Arthur, the Young Warlord; The Malpas Mystery; Night of the Eagle; Payroll; Revenge (1971,GB); The Southern Star; Violent Moment
Hayes, Alfred (wri): The Double Man
Hayes, Allan (act): Neon Maniacs
Hayes, Allison (act, b. 1930, nee Mary Jane Hayes): Attack of the 50-Foot Woman (1958); Counterplot; The Crawling Hand; Deep Freeze; The Disembodied; Francis Joins the WACs; The Hypnotic Eye; Pier 5, Havana; Sign of the Pagan; The Undead; The Unearthly; Zombies of Mora Tau
Hayes, Bernadene (act): Dick Tracy's Dilemma; The Thirteenth Hour (1947)
Hayes, Billie (act): Li'l Abner (1959)
Hayes, Bruce (act): Miracle Mile
Hayes, Catherine Anne (act): Serial Mom
Hayes, Chester (act): From Hell It Came
Hayes, Christopher (act): Distortions
Hayes, Dallas Edward (act): Eyes of Laura Mars
Hayes, Daryl (act): Runaway
Hayes, Denise (act): Dr. Heckyl & Mr. Hype
Hayes, Donald (act): The Annihilator
Hayes, Elizabeth (act): King Kong Lives
Hayes, Elton (act): The Black Knight; Isabel; The Story of Robin Hood
Hayes, George (F.) (act, 1885-1969): East of Piccadilly; Great Expectations (1946); Inside the Room; The Lost City; The Mind of Mr. Reeder; The Return of the Frog; The Sphinx (1933); Wolf's Clothing (1936)
Hayes, George "Gabby" (act): Mystery Liner; The Phantom Broadcast
Hayes, Gloria (act): Judgment Day
Hayes, Helen (act, 1900-1993, nee Helen Brown): Do Not Fold, Spindle or Mutilate; Murder Is Easy; Murder with Mirrors; One of Our Dinosaurs Is Missing
Hayes, Isaac (act, b. 1942): Acting On Impulse; Backlash: Oblivion 2; Escape from New York; Oblivion; Robin Hood: Men In Tights
Hayes, Jack (act): Monster from the Ocean Floor
Hayes, Jaysen (act): The Prisoner of Zenda (1979)
Hayes, John (act): End of the World (1977); The Shaggy D.A.
Hayes, John (dir): Dream No Evil; End of the World (1977); Garden of the Dead; Grave of the Vampire
Hayes, John Anthony (act): Strait-Jacket
Hayes, John J. (act & dir): The Fatal 30
Hayes, John Michael (wri, b. 1919): It's a Dog's Life; The Man Who Knew Too Much (1956); Rear Window (1954); To Catch a Thief; The Trouble With Harry
Hayes, Kevin (act): Unforgettable
Hayes, Lee (act): The Dark Half
Hayes, Linda (act): Ellery Queen and the Perfect Crime; The Saint In Palm Springs
Hayes, Lucky (act): The Gifted One
Hayes, Margaret (act): Omar Khayyam; One Dangerous Night
Hayes, Mary Jane (act): see Hayes, Allison
Hayes, Maxwell (act): The Climax
Hayes, Melvyn (act): The Curse of Frankenstein; The Flesh and the Fiends; No Trees In the Street; Santa Claus (1985); The Zany Adventures of Robin Hood
Hayes, Patricia (act): Blue Movie Blackmail; Fragment of Fear; A Ghost of a Chance (1968); Hotel Reserve; The Neverending Story; The Terrornauts; Willow; The Witches and the Grinnygog
Hayes, Peter Lind (act, b. 1915): The 5000 Fingers of Dr. T; Once You Kiss a Stranger
Hayes, Philip (act): The Resurrected
Hayes, Philip Maurice (act): Powder
Hayes, Raphael (wri): Have Rocket, Will Travel
Hayes, Robert (dir & wri): Phoenix the Warrior
Hayes, Robert D. (cin): Dead Man's Island
Hayes, Ron (act): Around the World Under the Sea
Hayes, Sam (act): The Hitch-Hiker
Hayes, Sherman (act): Death Curse of Tartu
Hayes, Siobhan (act): Flesh & Blood
Hayes, Steve (wri): Bravestarr-The Movie; Time After Time
Hayes, Terry (act): Flesh-Eating Mothers
Hayes, Terry (wri): Dead Calm; The Road Warrior
Hayes, Trudy (act): Lovespell
Haygarth, Tony (act): The Bride (1985); Dracula (1979); Tree of Hands
Hayland, Lisa (act): Fatal Passion
Hayle, Grace (act): Arrest Bulldog Drummond; The Casino Murder Case; Houdini (1953); Mr. Moto In Danger Island
Hayles, Brian (wri): Arabian Adventure; Nothing But the Night; Warlords of the Deep
Hayles, Kenneth R. (wri): Barbados Quest; Blind Spot (1958) Find the Lady; The Hideout; Passport to Treason; Secret Venture; Stolen Assignment; Suspended Alibi; Track the Man Down
Hayling, Jerry (wri): Case of the Full Moon Murders
Hayman, Cyd (act): The Godsend
Hayman, Damaris/Danarys (act): Bunny Lake Is Missing; Full Circle
Hayman, David (act): Eye of the Needle
Hayman, David (dir): The Hawk
Hayman, James (cin): Buffy the Vampire Slayer
Hayman, James (dir): Her Deadly Rival
Hayman, Joe (act): Terror On Tiptoe
Haymer, Johnny (act): The Magician (1973); Teen-Age Strangler
Haymes, Dick (act, 1918-1980): Betrayal (1974); One Touch of Venus
Hayne, Murray (act): The Rivals
Haynes, Abner (act): Horror High
Haynes, Cal (act): Kemek
Haynes, Clarence (act): Change of Mind
Haynes, Dick (act): The Phantom Planet
Haynes, H. Manning (act): Lady Audley's Secret (1920)
Haynes, Hilda (act): Time After Time
Haynes, Jayne (act): Painted Heart
Haynes, Jerry (act): RoboCop
Haynes, Linda (act): Human Experiments; Latitude Zero
Haynes, Lloyd (act, 1934-1986): The Mad Room
Haynes, Loren (act): Eve of Destruction; The Hidden; Into the Badlands
Haynes, Manning (dir): The Claydon Treasure Mystery; The Monkey's Paw (1923); The Old Man; The Perfect Flaw
Haynes, Michael (act): Maroc 7
Haynes, Patricia (act): Hell Ship Mutiny
Haynes, Randall (act): The Handmaid's Tale
Haynes, Roberta (act): Hell Ship Mutiny
Haynes, Stanley (wri): The Man Behind the Mask (1936); Madeleine
Haynes, Todd (dir): Poison (1990)
Haynes, Tommy (act): Glen or Glenda?
Haynie, Jim (act): Disaster in Time; The Fog; I Come In Peace; Jack's Back; Midnight Lace (1981); Sleepwalkers; Time After Time
Hays, Andrea (act): Twin Peaks: Fire Walk With Me
Hays, Gary (act): The 'Burbs
Hays, Robert (act, b. 1947): Cat's Eye; Christmas Every Day; Cyber Bandits; Deadly Invasion: The Killer Bee Nightmare; The Fall of the House of Usher (1982); The Initiation of Sarah; Murder by the Book; Running Against Time; Scandalous; 30-Years-to-Life
Hays, Sharon (act): Elvira, Mistress of the Dark
Haysbert, Dennis (act): Suture; Widow's Kiss
Haystead, Mercy (act): Crossroads; Death Trap (1962)
Hayt, Maxine (act): The Toxic Avenger
Hayter, David (act): Guyver 2: Dark Hero
Hayter, James (act, b. 1907): The Blood On Satan's Claw; Calling Bulldog Drummond; A Challenge for Robin Hood; The Crimson Pirate; The Fallen Idol; The Firechasers; For Them That Trespass; Four Sided Triangle; The Ghosts of Berkeley Square; Gideon's Day; The Heart Within; I'm a Stranger; Land of the Pharaohs; The Mark of Cain; The October Man; Out of the Fog (1962); Port Afrique; Sail Into Danger; Sensation (1937); The Spider and the Fly (1949); The Story of Robin Hood; Stranger In the House (1967); The 39 Steps (1959); Vice Versa (1947); Woman With No Name; Your Witness
Hayter, John (act): A Christmas Carol (1960)
Haythorne, Joan (act, b. 1915, nee Joan Haythornwaite): Highly Dangerous; The Shakedown; Svengali (1954)
Haythornwaite, Joan (act): see Haythorne, Joan
Hayton, Lennie (mus): Eyes In the Night
Hayward, Brooke (act): The Day of the Dolphin
Hayward, Charles (act): Nightfall (1988)
Hayward, Chuck (act): The Clonus Horror; Night of the Lepus; The Swarm
Hayward, David (act): Delusion; Eve of Destruction; Northstar; Red Alert; Slayground
Hayward, Duke (cin): Black Orchids
Hayward, Frederick (wri): Crimes at the Dark House; The Demon Barber of Fleet Street
Hayward, Jane (act): House of Whipcord
Hayward, Justin (mus): She (1983)
Hayward (III), Leland (act): The Fear (1994); Outbreak
Hayward, Lillie (wri, 1896-1978): The Boy and the Pirates; The Shaggy Dog (1959 & 1994); Tarzan and the Lost Safari; The Undying
Monster; The Walking Dead
Hayward, Louis (act, 1909-1985, nee Seafield Grant): And Then There Were None; Captain Pirate; Fortunes of Captain Blood; House by the River; Ladies In Retirement; The Lady In the Iron Mask; The Man In the Iron Mask (1939); The Man Outside (1933); I Pirati di Capri; Repeat Performance; The Return of Monte Cristo; Ruthless; The Saint In New York; The Saint's Return; The Search for Bridey Murphy; The Son of Dr. Jekyll; The Son of Monte Cristo; Terror In the Wax Museum; The Thirteenth Candle; Trouble for Two
Hayward, Lydia (wri): The Monkey's Paw (1923)
Hayward, Richard (act): Flame In the Heather
Hayward, Sarah (act): Alien High
Hayward, Susan (act, 1918-1975, nee Edythe Marriner): Among the Living; Deadline at Dawn; The Hairy Ape; I Married a Witch; I Thank a Fool; The Lost Moment; They Won't Believe Me
Hayward, William (act): Strange Behavior
Haywood, Chris (act): The Cars That Ate Paris; The Navigator: An Odyssey Across Time; Razorback
Hayworth, Rita (act, 1918-1987, nee Margarita Carmen Cansino, a.k.a. Rita Cansino): Charlie Chan In Egypt; Dante's Inferno (1935); Down to Earth; Gilda; The Lady from Shanghai; The Lone Wolf Spy Hunt; The Loves of Carmen (1948); Meet Nero Wolfe; The Naked Zoo; Salome (1953); Who Killed Gail Preston?
Hazard, Jayne (act): Black Market Babies
Hazard, Richard (mus): Some Call It Loving
Haze, Jonathan (act): Blood Bath (1966); Day the World Ended (1955); Forbidden Island; It Conquered the World; The Little Shop of Horrors (1960); Not of This Earth (1957); Swamp Women; Teenage Cave Man; The Terror (1963); The Viking Women and the Sea Serpent
Haze, Jonathan (wri): Invasion of the Star Creatures
Haze, Stan (act): Don't Answer the Phone!
Hazel, Derna (act): The Dummy Talks
Hazeldine, James (act): The Corsican Brothers (1985); The Medusa Touch; The Ruling Class
Hazell, Hy (act): Celia; Just William's Luck; The Key Man; The Mail Van Murder; The Night Won't Talk; Stolen Assignment; The Whole Truth; The Yellow Balloon
Hazelton, George C. (dir): The Raven (1915)
Hazelwood, Cheryl (act): A Midsummer Night's Dream (1985)
Hazelwood, John (act): Firewalker
Hazelwood, Karen (act): Blood Diner
Hazlegrove, Jane (act): Threads
Hazleton, C. (wri): Sweeney Todd
Hazlett, Bob (act): Mars Needs Women
Hazlewood, Jean (wri): The Secret Ways
Heacock, Gary R. (wri): Gallery of Horror
Head, Bob (act): Captain Clegg; Treasure Island (1950)
Head Marilyn (act): The Private Life of Sherlock Holmes
Head, Murray (act): Gawain and the Green Knight
Head, Peter (act): Dementia 13
Head, Ruby (act): Never-Never Land
Head, Sandra (act): The Stepfather
Headey, Lena (act): The Jungle Book (1994)
Headey, Ted (act): Crime and Punishment (1935, USA)
Headley, Mark (wri): Vampire On Bikini Beach

Headly, Glenne (act, b. 1959): Dick Tracy (1990); Making Mr. Right; Mortal Thoughts; Paperhouse
Headwelles, Richard (act): The Mutagen
Heady, Lena (act): Merlin (1998)
Heagerty, Travers (act): see Travers, Henry
Heal Joan (act): Dead Lucky; Jekyll and Hyde; The Price of Silence; Svengali (1954); Tiger by the Tail
Heald, Anthony (act): Deep Rising; The Silence of the Lambs
Heald, Eva (act): Anguish
Heald, John (act): Anguish
Heald, Margaret (act): Vampyres...Daughters of Dracula
Heale, Patrick K. (dir): Murder at Ten
Healey, Ben (wri): Taste of Excitement
Healey, David (act): Endless Night
Healey, John J. (act): Hello Again
Healey, Myron (act, b. 1923): African Manhunt; Bomba and the Elephant Stampede; Calling Homicide; The Claw Monsters; The Computer Wore Tennis Shoes (1970); Crime Doctor's Manhunt; Dig That Uranium!; Down to Earth; Guns Don't Argue; The Incredible Melting Man; Jungle Moon Men; Private Eyes (1953); Pulse; Shadow On the Land; Storm Over Tibet; Undersea Girl; The Unearthly; V; Varan the Unbelievable
Healy, Annesley (act): The Grip (1913)
Healy, Dave (act): Shock Chamber
Healy, David (act): Assignment K; Embassy; Lust for a Vampire; Madame Sin; The Sign of Four (1983); Supergirl (1984); Twinkle, Twinkle, Killer Kane
Healy, Jim (act): The Resurrection of Zachary Wheeler
Healy, Mary (act, b. 1918): The 5000 Fingers of Dr. T
Healy, Pat (act): Moment of Decision
Healy, Ted (act, 1896-1937): The Casino Murder Case; Mad Love
Healy, Walt (act): The Reflecting Skin
Heams, Darin (act): The Fear (1994)
Heape, Jonathan (act): Lord of the Flies (1963)
Heape, Jonathan (dir): Benefit of the Doubt
Heard, Charles (act): Desk Set
Heard, Ellen (act): Scalpel
Heard, H.F. (wri, 1889-1971): The Deadly Bees
Heard, Howard (dir): Shadows Run Black
Heard, John (act, b. 1945): Big; Cat People (1982); C.H.U.D.; Deceived; The Package; The Seventh Sign; Too Scared to Scream
Heard, Katherine (act): Neon Maniacs
Hearn, Ann (act): Omen IV: The Awakening
Hearn, Chick (act): Heart Condition
Hearn, E. Guy (act): Port Sinister
Hearn, Edward (act): The Lone Wolf Spy Hunt; Shadow of the Thin Man
Hearn, George (act): Barney's Great Adventure; Sanctuary of Fear; The Vanishing (1993)
Hearn, Lafcadio (wri): Kwaidan
Hearn, Mary (act): The Conquering Power
Hearn, Maryann (act): Grizzly
Hearne, Clive (act): Mad Max
Hearne, Reginald (wri): Echo of Diana; Serena
Hearshen, Ira (mus): The Loves of Dracula
Hearst, Patricia (act): Bio-Dome; Serial Mom
Heart, John X. (act): Buddha's Lock
Heasley, John (act): The 5000 Fingers of Dr. T
Heasley, Robert (act): The 5000 Fingers of Dr. T
Heat, Michael (act): Anguish
Heater, Gabriel (act): Champagne for Caesar
Heath, Arch B. (wri): The Adventures of Captain Marvel
Heath, Ariel (act): The Leopard Man
Heath, Brendan (act): Mad Max
Heath, Charlie (act): Leprechaun 2
Heath, Dave (act): The Demon from Devil's Lake
Heath, Dody (act): Dog Eat Dog; Seconds
Heath, Eira (act): Gang War
Heath, Eric (act): Wavelength
Heath, Gordon (act): Sapphire
Heath, Jean (act): Dilemma
Heath, Laurence (wri): The Magician (1973); The Memory of Eva Ryker
Heath, Len (wri): Life Is a Circus
Heath, Mark (act): Paint Me a Murder
Heath, Michael (wri): Death Warmed Up; Next of Kin
Heath, Percy (wri): Dr. Jekyll and Mr. Hyde (1932)
Heath, Scott (act): To Die For II: Son of Darkness
Heathcote, Geoffrey (act): The Man from Scotland Yard
Heathcote, Humphrey (act): Fury at Smugglers' Bay
Heathcote, Roger (act): Island of Terror
Heathcote, Thomas (act): The Abominable Dr. Phibes; Burke and Hare; A Choice of Weapons; Cloudburst; Demons of the Mind; The Large Rope; The Night of the Big Heat; Quatermass and the Pit; Sword of the Valiant; Tiger In the Smoke; Tread Softly Stranger; The Village of the Damned (1960)
Heather, Jean (act): Double Indemnity (1944)
Heatherington, Keith (act): The Amazing Colossal Man
Heatherley, Clifford (act): Bleak House; Boadicea; Champagne; Forging Ahead; High Treason (1929); The Mystery of Mr. Bernard Brown; The Private Life of Don Juan; Yellow Face
Heatherly, May (act): Ella y el Miedo; Los Muertos No Perdonan; Pieces
Heatherton, Joey (act, b. 1944): Bluebeard (1972); My Blood Runs Cold
Heathwood, Julie-Ann (act): The Dead Zone
Heaton, Anthony (act): Are You Dying Young Man?
Heaton, Tom (act): April Fool's Day; The Haunting Passion
Heaton-Grey, R. (act): Love In the Welsh Hills
Heaven 17 (mus): Electric Dreams
Heavener, David (act & dir): Deadly Reactor; Twisted Justice
Heavener, David (wri): Twisted Justice
Hebb, Brian R.R. (cin): Humongous; In the Nick of Time; Running Against Time; The Spider and the Fly (1994)
Hebden, Mark (wri): Eyewitness (1970); Sudden Terror
Hebey, Jean (act): To Catch a Thief
Hebron, Douglas (act): Outbreak
Heche, Anne (act, b. 1969): I Know What You Did Last Summer; Psycho (1998); Volcano
Hecht, Ben (wri, 1894-1964): The Black Swan; The Great Gabbo; Monkey Business; Notorious (1946 & 1992); Queen of Outer Space; Ride the Pink Horse; Le Spectre Vert; Spellbound (1945); Ulysses; The Unholy Night; Wuthering Heights (1939)
Hecht, Donatella (act): Flesh-Eating Mothers
Hecht, Lawrence (act): Scream
Hecht, Paul (act): The Reincarnation of Peter Proud; The Savage Bees
Hecht, Ted (act, 1908-1969): Boston Blackie and the Law; Desert Legion; Just Before Dawn (1946); Man-Eater of Kumaon; Tarzan and the Huntress; Tarzan's Magic Fountain; Time to Kill (1942)
Heck, Stanton (act): The Mystic
Heckart, Eileen (act, b. 1919): The Bad Seed (1956); Burnt Offerings; No Way to Treat a Lady
Heckler, Jonellen (wri): Circumstances Unknown
Hector, Frank (act): A Message from Mars (1913)
Hedahl, Mary (act): The Purple Rose of Cairo
Hedaya, Dan (act, b. 1940): The Addams Family; The Adventures of Buckaroo Banzai; Blood Simple; Daylight; Endangered Species; Freeway; The Hunger; Pacific Heights; The Usual Suspects
Hedberg, John (act): Don't Go In the House
Hedden, Peggy (act): Friday the 13th, Part VIII-Jason Takes Manhattan
Hedden, Rob (dir & wri): The Colony (1995); Friday the 13th, Part VIII-Jason Takes Manhattan
Hedin, June (act): Welcome to Arrow Beach
Hedin, Serene (act): Boggy Creek II-The Legend Continues
Hedison, Al (act): see Hedison, David
Hedison, David (act, b. 1929, nee Ara Heditsian, a.k.a. Al Hedison): Adventures of the Queen; The Cat Creature; The Fly (1958); Kemek; Licence to Kill (1989); Live and Let Die; The Lost World (1960); The Power Within (1979); Son of Robin Hood
Heditsian, Ara (act): see Hedison, David
Hedland, Franciszka (act): Videodrome
Hedley, Jack (act, b. 1933): The Anniversary; For Your Eyes Only; Never Back Losers; New York Ripper; The Scarlet Blade; The Secret of Blood Island; The Very Edge; Witchcraft (1964)
Hedley, Maurice (act): Strangler's Web
Hedloe, John (act): Project Moonbase; Riders to the Stars
Hedren, Tippi (act, b. 1935): Alfred Hitchcock Presents; The Birds; The Birds II: Land's End; Marnie; Pacific Heights; Roar; Shadow of a Doubt (1991)
Hedwall, Deborah (act): Alone in the Dark
Hedy, Helen (act): The Fourth Man
Hee, Dana (act): Species
Heeren, Astrid (act): Castle Keep; Silent Night, Bloody Night
Heerman, Victor (dir): Rupert of Hentzau (1923)
Heermance, Dorothy (act): see Collyer, June
Heesel, Herb (act): 2069: A Sex Odyssey
Heetu (act): When a Stranger Calls
Heffer, Richard (act): Penny Gold
Hefferman, James (act): Making Contact
Heffley, Wayne (act): Crime and Punishment, U.S.A.; King Kong (1976); Mind Over Murder
Heffner, Kyle T. (act): Runaway Train; Spellbinder; Warning Sign
Heffron, Richard (T.) (dir): Futureworld; I, the Jury (1982)
Heflin, Emmett Evan (act): see Heflin, Van
Heflin, Nora (act): The Initiation of Sarah
Heflin, Van (act, 1910-1971, nee Emmett Evan Heflin): Black Widow (1954); The Golden Mask; Kid Glove Killer; The Last Child; The Man Outside (1967); Possessed (1947); The Prowler (1951); The Strange Love of Martha Ivers; The Three Musketeers (1948)
Hefti, Neal (mus): Oh Dad Poor Dad, Mamma's Hung You In the Closet and I'm Feelin' So Sad
Hegan, Campbell (act): Strange Behavior
Hegazi, Ahmed (act): Sphinx (1981)
Hegeman, Timothy (act): The Phoenix and the Magic Carpet
Hegger, Johanna (act): Whirlpool (1970)
Heggie, O.P. (act, 1879-1936): Bride of Frankenstein; The Count of Monte Cristo (1934); The Mysterious Dr. Fu Manchu; The Return of Dr. Fu Manchu
Heiberg, Birgit (act): City of Fear (1965)
Heiden, Ira (act): Dangerous Touch; Elvira, Mistress of the Dark; A Nightmare On Elm Street 3: Dream Warriors
Heider, Patti (act): The Initiation
Heidi (animal act): Man's Best Friend
Heifetz, Luis E. (wri): International House
Heigh, Helene (act): Monsieur Verdoux; Murder Is My Business; What's the Matter With Helen?
Heighley, Bruce (act): Goliath Awaits
Heigl, Katherine (act): The Tempest (1998); Wish Upon a Star
Heil, Ted (act): Something Weird
Heilbron, Lorna (act): The Creeping Flesh; The Girl In a Swing; Symptoms
Heilman, Gloria (act): Hell Night
Heilmayr, Susanna (act): Flaming Ears
Heim, Alan (act): All That Jazz
Heim, Carrie Kei (act): Santa Claus (1985)
Heimberger, Eddie (act): see Albert, Eddie
Heims, Jo (wri): The Devil's Hand (1961); Play Misty for Me; You'll Like My Mother
Hein, Richard (act): Kiss Meets the Phantom of the Park
Heindorf, Ray (mus, b. 1910): Finian's Rainbow; I Confess
Heineman, Alicia (act): Target...Earth?
Heiner, Barta Lee (act): Beyond and Back
Heiner, Thomasine (act): Dreamchild
Heininger, Jan (act): The Manitou
Heinl, Bernd (cin): The Fear (1994); Suburban Commando
Heinle, Amelia (act): Purgatory
Heinlein, Robert A. (wri, 1907-1988): The Brain Eaters; Destination Moon; Project Moonbase; The Puppet Masters
Heinrich, Andre (act): La Jetee
Heinrich, Mimi (act): Journey to the Seventh Planet; Reptilicus
Heinz, Gerard (act, b. 1907): Devils of Darkness; The Fallen Idol; The House of the Seven Hawks; I Aim at the Stars; The Legend of Spider Forest; The Man Inside; Out of the Shadow; Portrait from Life; The Projected Man; Seven Thunders; State Secret; Top Secret (1952); You Pay Your Money
Heinz, Gerhard (mus): Dracula Blows His Cool; Superwheels
Heinz, Wolfgang (act): Nosferatu, eine Symphonie des Grauens
Heinzman, Bill (act): Night of the Living Dead (1968)
Heisler, Stuart (dir, b. 1894): Among the Living; The Lone Ranger; The Monster and the Girl; The Remarkable Andrew; Saturday Island; This Is My Love
Heisler, Stuart (wri, b. 1894): Saturday Island
Heisman, Nahum (mus): Neither the Sea Nor the Sand
Heiss, Carol (act): Snow White and the Three Stooges
Heitmeyer, Jayne (act): Sci-Fighters
Heiberg, Sandy (act): The Granny; Modern Problems
Held, David (act): Alfred Hitchcock Presents
Held, Ingrid (act): The Secret Life of Ian Fleming
Held, Karl (act): Embassy; 36 Hours (1965)
Held, Martin (act): The Serpent (1973); Spy for Germany
Held, Stephen (act): Shocker
Helde, Annette (act): Freeway
Heldebrant, Michael (act): Trancers
Helfend, Dennis (act): Bloodeaters; Toxic Zombies
Helfer-Friedrich, Monika (act): Invisible Adversaries
Helgeland, Brian (act): Highway to Hell
Helgeland, Brian (wri): A Nightmare On Elm Street 4: The Dream Master; 976-EVIL; The Postman (1997)
Helgenberger, Marg (act): After Midnight; Always; Conundrum; Death Dreams; Giving Up the Ghost; Species; Species II; The Tommyknockers
Helia, Jenny (act): Toni
Helkamp, Charlotte (act): Repossessed
Hell, Erik (act): Morianna; La Sorciere
Helland, Eric (act): The Being
Hellen, Marjorie (act): Missile to the Moon
Heller, Abbey (act): Honeymoon of Horror
Heller, Ben (act): It (1990)
Heller, Bill (mus): Deranged (1987)
Heller, Chip (act): White Dwarf
Heller, Jack (act): Uninvited (1987)
Heller, Jane (wri): Infernal Affairs
Heller, John G. (act): Cloak Without Dagger
Heller, Ken (mus): Condor
Heller, Lukas (wri, b. 1930): Candidate for Murder; Hitler's Son; Hot Enough for June; Hush...Hush, Sweet Charlotte; Never Back Losers; What Ever Happened to Baby Jane? (1962)
Heller, Otto (cin, 1896-1970): Alibi (1942); The Crimson Pirate; The Curse of the Mummy's Tomb; Funeral In Berlin; The Ipcress File; The Lady Killers (1956); Masquerade; Paris Express; Peeping Tom; The Queen of Spades (1948); Richard III (1955); Too Hot to Handle; The Vicious Circle (1957); Who Done It? (1956); Woman of Straw
Heller, Paul (wri): A Choice of Weapons
Hellman, George S. (wri): A Night In Paradise
Hellman, Jacqueline (act): Flight to Fury
Hellman, Melissa (act): Silent Night, Deadly Night III
Hellman, Miriam (act): Just Imagine
Hellman, Monte (dir): Beast from Haunted Cave; Flight to Fury; Silent Night, Deadly Night III
Hellman, Monte (wri): Flight to Fury; Silent Night, Deadly Night III
Hellman, Ocean (act): The Haunting Passion
Hellman, Oliver (dir): see Assonitis, Olvidio
Hellman, Sam (wri): The Horn Blows at Midnight; Murder at the Vanities; The Three Musketeers (1939)
Hellmer, Karl (act): Das Kalte Herz; Das Schloss
Hellstrom, Eric (act): La Sorciere
Hellstrom, Gunnar (dir): The Name of the Game Is Kill
Helm, Anne (act): The Couch; The Magic Sword (1962); Mother Goose A Go-Go; Nightmare In Wax
Helm, Brigitte (act, 1907-1996, nee Gisela Eve Schittenheim): Alraune (1928 & 1930); Am Rande der Welt; Gold (German- & French-speaking Versions); Die Herrin von Atlantis; Metropolis (1926)
Helm, Estelle (act): I Was a Zombie for the F.B.I.
Helm Fay (act): Calling Dr. Death; Captive Wild Woman; The Falcon In San Francisco; Lady In the Dark; The Locket; Night Monster; One Body Too Many; Phantom Lady; The Wolf Man (1941)
Helm, Harry (act): Alraune (1952)
Helm, Kathleen (act): Otley
Helm, Stephen Douglas (act): Tomorrow's Child
Helm, Tiffany (act): Friday the 13th-PartV: A New Beginning
Helman, Michael (act): Flesh-Eating Mothers
Helmer, Heidi (act): The Nest
Helmkamp, Charlotte (J.) (act): Frankenhooker; Posed for Murder
Helmond, Katherine (act, b. 1934): Brazil; Family Plot; Lady In White; The Legend of Lizzie Borden; Ms. Scrooge; Shadey; The Spy Within; Time Bandits; World War III
Helmore, Tom (act): The Barton Mystery (1932); The Feathered Serpent (1934); The House of Silence; The House of Unrest; The Riverside Murder; The Secret Agent (1936); [illegible]
Helms, Jim ([illegible]): Night Creature
Helpmann, Robert (act, 1909-1986): Alice's Adventures In Wonderland (1972); Chitty

Chitty Bang Bang; Patrick; The Quiller Memorandum; Puzzle
Helsham, Rita (act): Death On the Set
Helton, Percy (act, 1894-1971): Criss Cross; Hush...Hush, Sweet Charlotte; The Set-Up (1949); Spook Chasers; 20,000 Leagues Under the Sea (1954)
Helvey, Carol (act): The China Syndrome
Hely, Annesley (act): Esmeralda
Hely, Gerald (act): Holocaust 2000
Hemblen, David (act): Brainscan; Short Circuit 2; The Song-Spinner
Hembrow, Mark (act): Out of the Body
Hembruff, Paul (act): The Pink Chiquitas
Hemingway, Carole (act): The Manitou
Hemingway, Chuck (act): My Science Project; Neon Maniacs
Hemingway, Helen (act): Patrick
Hemingway, Margaux (act, b. 1955): Inner Sanctum (1991); Inner Sanctum 2; Killer Fish
Hemingway, Mariel (act, b. 1961): Bad Moon; Creator; The Crying Child; Into the Badlands; The Suicide Club (1988); Superman IV: The Quest for Peace
Hemingway, Pat (act): My Bloody Valentine
Hemingway, Winston (act): King Kong Lives; Teenage Mutant Ninja Turtles
Hemme, Edouard (act): The Hands of Orlac (1959)
Hemmings, David (act, b. 1938): Barbarella; Blood Relatives; Blow-Up; Camelot; The Disappearance; Eye of the Devil; Fragment of Fear; Harlequin; The Heart Within; Murder by Decree; No Trees In the Street; Profundo Rosso; The Squeeze; Survivor (1980); Thirst; The Wind of Change
Hempel, Anoushka (act): Double Exposure (1977); On Her Majesty's Secret Service; Scars of Dracula; Tiffany Jones
Hempel, Elizabeth (act): Chamber of Horrors (1929)
Hemphill, John (act): The Pink Chiquitas
Hemric, Guy (act): How to Stuff a Wild Bikini
Hemsley, Estelle (act): Green Mansions; The Leech Woman
Hemsley, Sherman (act, b. 1938): Alice In Wonderland (1985); Ghost Dance; Ghost Fever; Love at First Bite
Hemson, Joyce (act): Dracula, Prince of Darkness; The Gorgon; Island of Terror
Henaberry, Joseph (dir): Missing Millions
Henaine, Gasper A. (act): The Octagon
Hench, Richard (Alan) (act): Biohazard (1985); Scalps; Slaughterhouse Rock; The Tomb
Hendel, Kenneth (act): Die Screaming, Marianne; Man of Violence; Prisoners of the Lost Universe
Hender, Frederique (act): The Devil's Nightmare
Henderson, Abbi (act): Grave of the Vampire
Henderson, Adam (act): Judge Dredd
Henderson, Albert (act): Trancers II: The Return of Jack Deth
Henderson, Anthony (act): Neon Maniacs
Henderson, Don (act): The Big Sleep (1978); Brazil; The Ghoul (1974); No Escape (1994); White Angel
Henderson, Don (dir): The Touch of Satan
Henderson, Douglas (act): Black Zoo; Invasion of the Saucer Men; King Dinosaur; The Manchurian Candidate
Henderson, Edward (act): Zombies of Mora Tau
Henderson, Ena (act): Fatal Exposure
Henderson, Fred (act): The Death of the Incredible Hulk; Friday the 13th, Part VIII-Jason Takes Manhattan
Henderson, Ivor (act): The Adventures of Robin Hood; Bulldog Drummond Comes Back
Henderson, Jane (act): The Green Scarf
Henderson, John (dir): The Borrowers (1993); Loch Ness
Henderson, Kim (act): Waxwork II: Lost In Time
Henderson, Laurence (wri): Sitting Target
Henderson, Lucius (dir): Dr. Jekyll and Mr. Hyde (1912)
Henderson, Lynn A. (act): The Relic
Henderson, Marcia (act, b. 1932): The Glass Web; The Hypnotic Eye; Naked Alibi
Henderson, Mary (act): Hush...Hush, Sweet Charlotte
Henderson, Meredith (act): The Song Spinner
Henderson, Richard (act): The Last Wave
Henderson, Robert (act): Phase IV; Superman (1978)
Henderson, Robert (cin): Gremlins 2: The New Batch
Henderson, Saffron (act): Friday the 13th, Part VIII-Jason Takes Manhattan
Henderson, Scott A. (act): The Milpitas Monster
Henderson, Susan (act): Roller Blade Warriors: Taken by Force
Henderson, Ty (act): Dark Mirror (1984)
Henderson, Zenna (wri, b. 1917): The People
Hendery, Richard (act): Empire of Ash III
Hendrian, Dutch (act): Bulldog Drummond's Secret Police; The Most Dangerous Game
Hendrian, Oscar (G.) (act): The Gracie Allen Murder Case; Mr. Moto In Danger Island
Hendrick, James Quincey (act): I, Madman
Hendricks, Alan (act): Holocaust 2000
Hendricks (Jr.), Ben (act): Black Waters; The Headless Horseman
Hendricks, Evelyn (act): Night of Bloody Horror
Hendricks, Jan (act): The Devil's Daffodil; Die Tur mit den Sieben Schlossern
Hendricks, Ray (act): Think Fast, Mr. Moto
Hendrickson, Benjamin (act): The Demon Murder Case
Hendrickson, Nancy (act): Mother's Day
Hendrie, Chris (act): Fright Night; Psycho II
Hendrie, Ernest (act): The Blue Bird (1910)
Hendrix, Elaine (act): The Munsters' Scary Little Christmas
Hendrix, Lori Jo (act): Prison Heat
Hendrix, Wanda (act, 1928-1981): Confidential Agent; The Golden Mask; Johnny Cool; Ride the Pink Horse
Hendrixson, Heather (act): Motel Hell
Hendrixson, Shaylin (act): Motel Hell
Hendry, Beverly (act): The Haunting of Hamilton High
Hendry, Gloria (act, b. 1949): Live and Let Die; Pumpkinhead II: Blood Wings
Hendry, Ian (act, 1931-1984): Assassin (1973); Captain Kronos: Vampire Hunter; Children of the Damned; Damien-Omen II; Doppelganger (1969); Get Carter; Girl In the Headlines; The Internecine Project; The Jerusalem File; Killer With Two Faces; The Model Murder Case; The Passenger; Repulsion; The Southern Star; Tales from the Crypt (1971); Theater of Blood; Vendetta for the Saint
Hendry, Len (act): Rear Window (1954); Sunset Boulevard
Heneghan, Patricia (act): Crossroads to Crime
Henenlotter, Frank (dir & wri): Basket Case; Basket Case 2; Brain Damage; Frankenhooker
Henerson, James (wri): The Tempest (1998)
Henesy, David (act): House of Dark Shadows
Hengstler, Dee (act): Dick Tracy (1990)
Henick, Howard (act): Twisted
Henkel, Kim (wri): Leatherface: Texas Chainsaw Massacre III
Henkin, Hilary (wri): Romeo is Bleeding
Henley, Barry "Shabaka" (act): Destiny Turns On the Radio
Henley, Drewe (act): Quest for Love; When Dinosaurs Ruled the Earth
Henley, Jack (wri): Bonzo Goes to College; Rocket Man (1954); Roogie's Bump; A Thousand and One Nights (1945)
Henley, Joan (act): The 39 Steps (1978)
Henley, Susan (act): The Long Kiss Goodnight
Henn, Carie (act): Aliens
Hennen, Paul (act): Macbeth (1971)
Henner, Marilu (act): Batman and Mr. Freeze: Subzero; Hammett; Ladykillers (1988)
Hennessey, Anthony (act): Frightmare (1974)
Hennessey, Dan (act): Starship Invasions
Hennessey, Jill (act): RoboCop 3
Hennessy, Marcus (act): Outbreak
Hennessy, Mary (act): War of the Colossal Beast
Hennessy, Monique (act): Doulos-The Finger Man
Hennessy, Peter (cin): Cat Girl
Henney, Del (act): Straw Dogs
Henniger, Rolf (act): The Nibelungs (1966)
Henning, Carlos (act): Run for the Sun
Henning, Eva (act): The Devil's Wanton
Henning, Gitte (act): The Red Mantle
Henning, Uno (act): A Cottage On Dartmoor
Henninger, Corie (act): Copycat
Henning-Jensen, Astrid (act): The Element of Crime
Hennings, David (cin): Asteroid; Netforce
Hennings, Sam (act): Night Angel; Seedpeople
Henreid, Monika (act): Dead Ringer
Henreid, Paul (act, 1908-1992, nee Paul Julius von Hernreid): Between Two Worlds; The Conspirators; Devotion; Exorcist II: The Heretic; Gestapo; Last of the Buccaneers; Man In Hiding; Mantrap; Operation Crossbow; Pirates of Tripoli; Siren of Bagdad; The Spanish Main; A Stolen Face; Thief of Damascus; A Woman's Devotion
Henreid, Paul (dir, 1908-1992): Dead Ringer; A Woman's Devotion
Henrey, Bobby (act, b. 1939): The Fallen Idol
Henrici, Jacques (wri): Paradisio
Henriksen, Lance (act): Aliens; Alien 3; Color of Night; Damien-Omen II; Deadly Intent; Dusting Cliff Seven; The Horror Show; The Jagged Edge; Jennifer 8; Knights; Man's Best Friend; Mansion of the Doomed; The Nature of the Beast; Near Dark; Nightmares (1983); No Escape (1994); Piranha II: The Spawning; The Pit and the Pendulum (1991, USA); Powder; Pumpkinhead; Super Mario Bros.; The Terminator; Wes Craven Presents Mind Ripper
Henriksson, Anders (act): The Devil's Wanton; Morianna
Henriksson, Ella (act): Morianna
Henriot, Sam (act): Reflections of Murder
Henriques, Sylvana (act): On Her Majesty's Secret Service
Henritze, Bette (act): The Mind Snatchers
Henry, Bernard (act): Nightbreed
Henry, Bill (act): Jungle Moon Men
Henry, Buck (act, b. 1931, nee Buck Zuckerman): Eating Raoul; Heaven Can Wait (1978); Kurt Vonnegut's Harrison Bergeron; The Man Who Fell to Earth (1976)
Henry, Buck (dir, b. 1931): Heaven Can Wait (1978)
Henry, Buck (wri, b. 1931): The Day of the Dolphin; The Nude Bomb
Henry, Carol (act): Maniac (1980)
Henry, Charlotte (act, 1916-1980): Alice In Wonderland (1933); Babes In Toyland (1934); Charlie Chan at the Opera; The Mandarin Mystery
Henry, Cheryl (act): Vampire's Kiss
Henry, Chuck (act): The Tommyknockers
Henry, David (act): Xtro
Henry, Emmaline (act): Marnie; Rosemary's Baby
Henry, Gale (act): Darkened Rooms
Henry, Gloria (act, b. 1923): Bulldog Drummond Strikes Back (1947); Port Said
Henry, Gloria Lynne (act): Phantasm III: Lord of the Dead
Henry, Gregg (act): Bates Motel; Bodily Harm; Body Double; Fair Game (1988); The Gifted One; Just Before Dawn (1980); Raising Cain; Sharon's Secret; Terminal; Tidal Wave: No Escape
Henry, Gustav (act): Our Mother's House
Henry, Hank (act): Johnny Cool
Henry, Joan (wri): Yield to the Night
Henry, Kenneth (act): Dangerous Voyage; Passenger to Tokyo; The Silent Witness (1954)
Henry, Lenny (act): Bernard and the Genie; The Suicide Club (1988)
Henry, Leonard (act): The Face at the Window (1939)
Henry, Louise (act): The Casino Murder Case; Charlie Chan In Reno; Charlie Chan On Broadway; The Gaunt Stranger
Henry, Mary (act): Glen and Randa
Henry, Mike (act): Soylent Green; Tarzan and the Great River; Tarzan and the Jungle Boy; Tarzan and the Valley of Gold
Henry, Norman (act): 10 Rillington Place
Henry, Pam (act): Prom Night
Henry, Peter (cin): The Body Stealers
Henry, Philippe (act): La Prima Donna
Henry, Richard (act): Without a Clue
Henry, Rohan (act): Popcorn
Henry, Terence (act): The Berlin Conspiracy
Henry, Thomas B. (act): The Beginning of the End; Behind Locked Doors; Blood of Dracula; The Brain from Planet Arous; Earth vs. the Flying Saucers; How to Make a Monster; Space Master X-7; 20 Million Miles to Earth
Henry, Tim (act): Eye of the Cat
Henry, Tom Brown(e) (act): see Henry, Thomas B.
Henry, Victor (act): Privilege; The Sorcerers
Henry, William (act, b. 1918): Invisible Informer; The Lone Ranger and the Lost City of Gold; Mysterious Mr. Valentine; Secret of the Incas; Spook Chasers; Tarzan Escapes; The Thin Man
Henschel, Ron (act): Battle Beyond the Stars (1980)
Henschell, Todd (wri): Puppet Master 4
Hensel, Howard (act): The Tragedy of Carmen
Hensel, Kim (wri): The Texas Chainsaw Massacre
Henshaw, Eric (act): Piranha (1978)
Hensleigh, Jonathan (wri): Armageddon; Jumanji; The Saint
Hensley, Craig (act): Natas...The Reflection
Hensley, Lisa (act): The 13th Floor
Hensley, Pamela (act, b. 1950): Buck Rogers in the 25th Century; Doc Savage, the Man of Bronze; Double Exposure; The Nude Bomb; Rollerball
Hensley, Sonya (act): Frankenhooker
Henson, Basil (act): Change Partners; Dr. Crippen; The Double; The Frozen Dead; Inside Information; The Last Days of Man On Earth
Henson, Brian (act): Return to Oz
Henson, Brian (dir): The Muppet Christmas Carol
Henson, Christian (act): Never-Never Land
Henson, Frank (act): The Black Windmill; Dracula (1979); Enemy Mine
Henson, Gladys (act, b. 1897, nee Gladys Gunn): Cage of Gold; Clue of the Twisted Candle; Counterblast; Dangerous Afternoon; Death Trap (1962); First Men In the Moon (1964); Highly Dangerous
Henson, Heather (act): Little Shop of Horrors (1986)
Henson, Jim (dir, 1936-1990): The Dark Crystal; The Great Muppet Caper
Henson, Jim (wri, 1936-1990): The Dark Crystal; The Great Muppet Caper; The Muppet Movie
Henson, Leslie (act): Alf's Button (1920); The Life-guardsman
Henson, Lin (act): Doctor Death: Seeker of Souls
Henson, Nicky (act): No. 1 of the Secret Service; Penny Gold; Psychomania (1972); The Secret of Seagull Island; Vampira; Witch-Finder General
Henstell, Diana (wri): Deadly Friend
Henstridge, Natasha (act, b. 1975): Adrenalin; Species; Species II
Henteloff, Alex (act): The Invisible Man (1975)
Hentschel, David (mus): The Squeeze
Henwood, Peter (act): Tam Lin
Hepburn, Audrey (act, 1929-1993, nee Edda Hepburn van Heemstra): Always; Green Mansions; The Lavender Hill Mob; Paris When It Sizzles; Robin and Marian; Secret People
Hepburn, Barton (act): The Bridge of San Luis Rey (1944)
Hepburn, Katherine (act, b. 1907): Desk Set; Keeper of the Flame; Suddenly Last Summer; The Trojan Women
Hepler, Heather (act): Amazons (1984)
Hepner, Don (act): Final Exam
Heppleston, Peter (act): Virus (1980)
Hepton, Bernard (act): Shadey
Hepworth, Cecil (act, 1874-1953): Alice In Wonderland (1903); Clown and the Policeman; The Conjurer and the Boer; The Explosion of a Motor Car; The Gunpowder Plot; Topsy-Turvy Villa; The Unclean World:The Suburban-Bunkum Microbe-Guyoscope
Hepworth, Cecil (M.) (dir, 1874-1953): Alf's Button (1920); Alice In Wonderland (1903); The American Heiress; Anna the Adventuress; The Basilisk; Be Sure Your Sins; Blind Fate; Boundary House; Clown and the Policeman; The Cobweb; The Conjurer and the Boer; The Eccentric Dancer; Embroidery Extraordinary; The Explosion of a Motor Car; Faust (1911); The Gunpowder Plot; The Indian and the Seidlitz; Invisibility; The Jonah Man: or, The Traveller Bewitched; The Man Who Stayed at Home; A Moment of Darkness; Morphia, the Death Drug; The Passing of a Soul; The Quarry Mystery; The Tinted Venus; Topsy-Turvy Villa
Hepworth, Cecil (M.) (wri, 1874-1953): Alice In Wonderland (1903); The Basilisk; The Passing of a Soul
Hepworth, Mrs. (Cecil) (act): Alice In Wonderland (1903)
Herald, Douglas (act): The Large Rope
Herazo, Tina (act): Hex
Herb, Carla (act): Deathstalker III: Warriors from Hell
Herbeck, Bobby (wri): Teenage Mutant Ninja Turtles
Herbert, A.P. (wri): House by the River
Herbert, B. (act): Dark Eyes of London
Herbert, Bessie (act): Lorna Doone (1920)
Herbert, Bill (dir): Warlock Moon
Herbert, Brian (act): Silver Top
Herbert, Charles (act): The Boy and the Pirates; The Colossus of New York; The Fly (1958); 13 Ghosts
Herbert, Chris (act): The Last Starfighter
Herbert, Don (act): Terror In the Wax Museum
Herbert, (F.) Hugh (wri, 1887-1952): The Dragon Murder Case; The Great Gabbo
Herbert, Frank (wri, 1920-1986): Dune
Herbert, George (act): Horror Hospital; Secrets of Sex; Tales from the Crypt (1971); The Trollenberg Terror
Herbert, Gwynne (act): Alf's Button (1920); Anna the Adventuress; The Ashes of Revenge; Boundary House; Broken Threads; The Firm of Girdlestone; A Garret In Bohemia; The Man In the Attic (1915); The Princess of Happy

Chance; The Tinted Venus; When Knights Were Bold (1916); Whoso Diggeth a Pit

Herbert, Hans (act): *House of Frankenstein; Phantom of the Opera (1943)*

Herbert, Holmes (E.) (act, 1882-1956, nee Edward Sanger): *The Adventures of Robin Hood; British Intelligence; Bulldog Drummond at Bay (1947); Bulldog Drummond Strikes Back (1947); Calling Dr. Death; Daughter of the Dragon; Dr. Jekyll and Mr. Hyde (1932); Dressed to Kill (1946); The Enchanted Cottage (1924); The Ghost of Frankenstein; The House of Fear (1945); The House of Secrets (1937); Invisible Agent; The Invisible Man (1933); The Mark of the Vampire (1935); Miss Pinkerton; Mr. Moto's Last Warning; Mr. Wu (1927); The Mummy's Curse; The Mystery of Mr. Wong; Mystery of the Wax Museum; The Pearl of Death; Sherlock Holmes and the Secret Weapon; Sherlock Holmes In Washington; The Terror (1928); The Thirteenth Chair (1929); The Undying Monster; The Uninvited (1944)*

Herbert, Hugh (act, 1887-1952): *The Black Cat (1941); Cracked Nuts (1941); Hellzapoppin; Kismet (1944); The Lost Squadron; A Midsummer Night's Dream (1935); Sh! The Octopus; The Villain Still Pursued Her*

Herbert, James (wri): *Deadly Eyes; Haunted (1996)*

Herbert, Joe (act): *Seven Keys to Baldpate (1929)*

Herbert, John (act): *Love Slaves of the Amazons*

Herbert, Leon (act): *Batman (1989)*

Herbert, Martin (act): *A Shattered Idyll*

Herbert, Martin (dir): see de Martino, Alberto

Herbert, Murray (wri): *The Angel of the Ward*

Herbert, Paul (mus): *The Shape of Things to Come (1979)*

Herbert, Percy (act, b. 1925): *Bunny Lake Is Missing; Call Me Bwana; Child In the House; Craze; Doomwatch; The Fiend (1972); The Green Buddha; The London Connection; Mysterious Island (1961); The Night of the Big Heat; Night of the Demon (1957); One Million Years B.C.; One of Our Dinosaurs Is Missing; The Viking Queen*

Herbert, Sidney (act): *Missing Millions*

Herbert, Tim (act): *Duel; Ellery Queen: Don't Look Behind You; Soylent Green*

Herbert, Tom (act): *The Casino Murder Case; Think Fast, Mr. Moto*

Herbert, Victor (mus, 1859-1924): *Babes In Toyland (1934, 1961, 1986 & 1997)*

Herbert-Bond, John (act): *Tower of London (1939)*

Herbst, Rick (act): *Brain Damage*

Herbst, Ron (wri): *Warlords 3000*

Herczeg, Dr. Arpad (wri): *Rapture*

Herczeg, Christina (act): *The Gifted One*

Herczeg, Geza (wri): *Rapture*

Herd, Richard (act): *The China Syndrome; Dr. Scorpion; The Judas Project; Schizoid (1980); The Secretary; Terror Out of the Sky; Trancers; V*

Herdegen, Leszek (act): *Faraon*

Herden, Jacques (act): *Nick Carter et le Trefle Rouge*

Herder, Lawrence (act): *First Men in the Moon (1964)*

Herdig, James (act): *Moon 44*

Heredia, Adolfo (act): *Hundra*

Heredia, Luis (act): *Viridiana*

Herek, Stephen (dir): *Bill & Ted's Excellent Adventure; Critters; The Gifted One; 101 Dalmatians (1996); The Three Musketeers (1993)*

Herek, Stephen (wri): *Critters*

Herelle, Johanne (act): *The Kiss (1988)*

Herger, Aukie (act): *The Possession of Joel Delaney*

Hergert, Teresa (act): *Never Talk to Strangers*

Heriat, Philippe (act): *L'Inhumaine*

Heriot, Nan (act): *The Loudwater Mystery*

Heritage, Leslie (act): *The Trollenberg Terror*

Herkert, Richard (act): *Beyond Evil*

Herkomer, S.H. (wri): *The Shuttle of Life; The Temptation of Carlton Earle*

Herley, Richard (wri): *No Escape (1994)*

Herlie, Eileen (act, b. 1919, nee Eileen Herlihy): *Hamlet (1948)*

Herlihy, Eileen (act): see Herlie, Eileen

Herlin, Jacques (act): *La Frusta e il Corpo; Ironmaster*

Herman, Al (act): *The Adventurous Blonde; Boston Blackie Goes Hollywood; The Lone Wolf In Paris*

Herman, Al(bert) (dir): *The Clutching Hand; The Missing Corpse; The Phantom of 42nd Street*

Herman, Christine (act): *Nightbeast*

Herman, Eleanor (act): *Nightbeast*

Herman, Glenn (act): *Hypernauts*

Herman, Jack (act): *The Yesterday Machine*

Herman, Jeffrey (act): *Doctor Death: Seeker of Souls*

Herman, Jerry (mus): *Mrs. Santa Claus*

Herman, Paul (act): *The Purple Rose of Cairo*

Hermano, Joe (act): *The Penguin Pool Murder*

Herman's Hermits (act): *Hold On!*

Hermitage, Doreen (act): *Little Shop of Horrors (1986)*

Hern, Art (act): *The Lost Empire; Simon, King of the Witches*

Hern, Bernie (act): *The Man With Two Brains*

Hernadi, Tibor (dir): *Felix the Cat: The Movie*

Hernandez, Alex (act): *The Fugitive (1993)*

Hernandez, Azucena (act): *Hundra*

Hernendez, Ernesto (act): *Dead Connection*

Hernandez, Felicia (act): *Waxwork II: Lost In Time*

Hernandez, Guillermo (act): *El Ladron de Cadaveres*

Hernandez, Ivan (act): *Vampire On Bikini Beach*

Hernandez, Jesse (act): *Ed Wood*

Hernandez, Johnny Vatos (act): *From Dusk Till Dawn*

Hernandez, Juan (mus): *El Castillo de las Bofetadas*

Hernandez, Juano (act, 1896-1970): *The Extraordinary Seaman*

Hernandez, Manuel (cin): *Ella y el Miedo*

Hernandez, Nicholas (act): *Return of the Living Dead, Part II*

Hernandez, Robert (act): *War of the Colossal Beast*

Hernandez, Roberto (act): *Dr. Tarr's Torture Dungeon*

Hernandez, Tessie (act): *Curse of the Vampires*

Hernandez, Tom (act): *Dead Men Tell No Tales (1971)*

Hernreid, Paul Julius von (act & dir): see Henreid, Paul

Herod Jr., Tom (act): *Silent Night, Deadly Night III*

Herold, Meredyth (act): *Singapore Sling*

Heron, Blake (act): *Trilogy of Terror II*

Heron, Joyce (act): *Beyond This Place; She Shall Have Murder*

Heron, Ken (act): *Night of the Creeps*

Heroux, Denis (dir): *The Uncanny*

Herrand, Marcel (act): *Les Visiteurs du Soir*

Herred, Brandy (act): *Some Call It Loving; Sweet Kill*

Herren, Gill (act): *I Was a Zombie for the F.B.I.*

Herren, Roger (act): *Myra Breckinridge*

Herrera, Anthony (act): *Mandrake; Twisted; Writer's Block*

Herrera, Margarita (act): *Hundra*

Herrera Jr., Rudy (act): *The Stepmother*

Herrera, Victor (cin): *El Ladron de Cadaveres*

Herrero, Gerardo (dir): *Desvio al Paraiso*

Herrick, Fred (act): *Terror from the Year 5,000*

Herrier, Mark (dir): *Popcorn*

Herriman, Damon (act): *Meteorites!*

Herring, Aggie (act): *A Blind Bargain; The Brass Bottle (1923); The Gorilla (1927); In the Next Room*

Herring, Laura (act): *Silent Night, Deadly Night III*

Herring, Lynn (act): *Pandemonium*

Herring, Phil (act): *I Was a Zombie for the F.B.I.*

Herring, Reed (act): see Hadley, Reed

Herrington, David (cin): *Ghost of a Chance (1987); The Housekeeper*

Herrington, John (act): *Billion Dollar Brain; It Happened Here*

Herrington, Katherine (act): *To All a Goodnight*

Herrington, Rowdy (dir & wri): *Jack's Back*

Herrmann, Bernard (mus, 1911-1979): *All That Money Can Buy; Beneath the 12-Mile Reef; Cape Fear (1961 & 1991); The Day the Earth Stood Still; Endless Night; Fahrenheit 451; 5 Fingers; The Ghost and Mrs. Muir; Hangover Square; It Lives Again; It's Alive (1974); It's Alive III: Island of the Alive; Jane Eyre (1944); Jason and the Argonauts; Journey to the Center of the Earth (1959); The Man Who Knew Too Much (1956); La Mariee etait en Noir; Marnie; Mysterious Island (1961); The Night Digger; North by Northwest; Obsession (1976); On Dangerous Ground; Psycho (1960); Psycho IV: The Beginning; The 7th Voyage of Sinbad; Sisters; The Three Worlds of Gulliver; The Trouble With Harry; The Twisted Nerve; Vertigo; The Wrong Man*

Herrmann, Edward (act, b. 1943): *The Day of the Dolphin; Death Valley; Here Come the Munsters; The Lost Boys; My Boyfriend's Back; Pandora's Clock; The Purple Rose of Cairo*

Herron, Bob (act): *Grave Secrets*

Herron, Gordie (act): *The Resurrected*

Herron, Mark (act): *Eye of the Cat*

Herron, Victoria (act): *Boarding House*

Herschel, David (wri): *The Boogey Man*

Hersent, Philippe (act): *The Murder Clinic; Roma Contra Roma; La Vendetta di Ercole*

Hersh, Paul (act): *Raiders of the Living Dead*

Hershberger, Ed (cin): *There's Nothing Out There*

Hershberger, Gary (act): *Twin Peaks: Fire Walk With Me*

Hershey, Barbara (act, b. 1948): *Angel On My Shoulder (1980); A Choice of Weapons; The Entity; Flood; Splitting Heirs*

Hershey, Stephanie (act): *The Goddess of Love*

Hersholt, Jean (act, 1886-1956): *The Cat Creeps (1930); Don Q, Son of Zorro; The Mark of the Vampire (1935); The Mask of Fu Manchu; Mr. Moto In Danger Island; The Phantom of Paris (1931)*

Hersko, Janos (act): *The Element of Crime*

Herskovic, Patricia (wri): *Body Parts (1991)*

Herskowitz,Brian (act): *The Bermuda Triangle*

Hertford, Bruce (act): *Beyond and Back*

Hertford, Carol (act): *Beyond and Back*

Hertford, Whit(by) (act): *In Self Defense; Jurassic Park; The Land Before Time III: The Time of the Great Giving; A Nightmare On Elm Street 5: The Dream Child*

Hertz, Lone (act): *Crazy Paradise*

Hertz, Nathan (dir): *Attack of the 50-Foot Woman (1958); The Brain from Planet Arous*

Hertzog, Lawrence (wri): *Darkman II: The Return of Durant*

Herubel, Michel (act): *Proces de Jeanne d'Arc*

Hervey, Grizelda (act): *Gideon's Day*

Hervey, Harvey (wri): *Peking Express; Shanghai Express*

Hervey, Irene (act, b. 1916, nee Irene Herwick): *The Boys from Syracuse; Charlie Chan In Shanghai; Crash Landing; House of Fear (1939); League of Frightened Men; Mr. Peabody and the Mermaid; Night Monster; Play Misty for Me*

Hervey, Jason (act, b. 1970): *The Monster Squad*

Hervey, Richard (act): *It!—The Terror from Beyond Space*

Herwick, Irene (act): see Hervey, Irene

Hery, Sylvette (act): see Miou-Miou

Herz, Juraj (dir): *Beauty and the Beast (1985); The Cremator*

Herz, Juraj (wri): *Beauty and the Beast (1985)*

Herz, Michael (dir): *The Toxic Avenger; The Toxic Avenger, Part II; The Toxic Avenger,Part III: The Last Temptation of Toxie; Troma's War*

Herz, Sloane (act): *Class of Nuke 'em High; The Toxic Avenger, Part II*

Herzbrun, Bernard (cin): *The Mysterious Mr. Moto*

Herzer, Geoffrey (act): *Grim Prairie Tales*

Herzer, Timmy (act): *Grim Prairie Tales*

Herzfeld (act): *Nosferatu, eine Symphonie des Grauens*

Herzig, Sid (wri): *The Lone Wolf's Daughter (1929)*

Herzinger, Charles W. (act): *The Bat (1926)*

Herzog, Arthur (wri): *The Swarm*

Herzog, Fred (act): *The Scarlet Letter (1926)*

Herzog, John (cin): *The Haunting of Hamilton High*

Herzog, Werner (dir & wri, b. 1932): *Nosferatu, the Vampyre*

Heschong, Gregg (cin): *Heavy Traffic*

Heslewood, Tom (act): *Moonbeam Magic*

Heslop, Charles (act): *The Late Edwina Black*

Heslov, Grant (act): *Congo; Dante's Peak*

Hess, Favid (dir): *To All a Goodnight*

Hess, David (Alexander) (act): *Avalanche Express; The Last House On the Left; Swamp Thing*

Hess, David (dir): *To All a Goodnight*

Hess, David (Alexander) (mus): *The Last House On the Left*

Hess, Eric Nicole (act): *Leapin' Leprechauns!*

Hess, James (act): *Godzilla 1985; Wavelength*

Hess, James Scott (act): *Matinee*

Hess, Jean (act): *La Prima Donna*

Hess, Jim (act): *Attack of the Killer Tomatoes*

Hess, John T. (act): *Beverly Hills Bodysnatchers*

Hess, Jon (Daniel) (dir): *Alligator II: The Mutation; Not of This World; Watchers*

Hess, Judy (act): *To All a Goodnight*

Hess, Laura (act): *Strait-Jacket*

Hess, Leslie (act): *Beverly Hills Bodysnatchers*

Hess, Linda Jean (act): *Edward Scissorhands*

Hess, Sandra (act): *Beastmaster III: The Eye of Braxus; Nick Fury: Agent of Shield*

Hesse, Gregor (act): *Dead Again*

Hesse, Hermann (wri, 1877-1962): *Siddhartha; Steppenwolf*

Hesselberg, Melvyn (act): see Douglas, Melvyn

Hesseman, Howard (act, b. 1940): *Amazon Women On the Moon; Flight of the Navigator; The Ghost of Flight 401; Tarantulas: The Deadly Cargo*

Hessey, B. Russell/Russ (cin): *Deep Red (1994); Invasion of the Body Snatchers (1978)*

Hession, Chris (act): *The Punisher; Razorback*

Hessler, Gordon (dir, b. 1930): *Betrayal (1974); Catacombs (1964); Cry of the Banshee; Embassy; Evil Stalks This House; The Girl In a Swing; The Golden Voyage of Sinbad; Kiss Meets the Phantom of the Park; The Last Shot You Hear; Murders In the Rue Morgue (1971); The Oblong Box; Pray for Death; Puzzle; Scream and Scream Again; Scream, Pretty Peggy; The Strange Possession of Mrs. Oliver*

Hessler, Gordon (wri, b. 1930): *The Girl In a Swing*

Hester, Ashley (act): *Distortions*

Heston, Charlton (act, b. 1924): *The Adventures of Mowgli; The Awakening; Beneath the Planet of the Apes; The Crucifer of Blood; Earthquake; Gray Lady Down; Hamlet (1996); In the Mouth of Madness; The Naked Jungle; The Omega Man; Planet of the Apes; Secret of the Incas; Solar Crisis; SoylentGreen; The Three Musketeers (1974); Treasure Island (1990); The War Lord*

Heston, Fraser C. (dir, b. 1955): *The Crucifer of Blood; Needful Things; Treasure Island (1990)*

Heston, Fraser C. (wri, b. 1955): *Treasure Island (1990)*

Heston, John (act): *Triumph of the Ten Gladiators*

Heston, Joy (act): *Return to Horror High*

Heston, Lauren (act): *The Secret Life of Ian Fleming*

Hetherington, Bob (act): *The Keeper*

Hetfield, Diane (act): *Jaws: The Revenge*

Hetherington, Gary (act): *The Stepfather*

Hetter, Heinz (mus): *I Love You, I Kill You*

Heugly, Archie (act): *Macbeth (1947)*

Heusch, Paolo (dir): *Death Comes from Space*

Hevner, Jerold T. (act): *Horrible Hyde*

Hewer, John (act): *Assassin for Hire; Strip Tease Murder*

Hewett, Christopher (act): *Ratboy*

Hewett, Robert (act): *Endplay*

Hewitt, Alan (act, 1915-1986): *The Barefoot Executive; The Computer Wore Tennis Shoes (1970); The Legend of Lizzie Borden; The Misadventures of Merlin Jones; The Monkey's Uncle; Now You See Him, Now You Don't*

Hewitt, Barbara (act): *Equinox*

Hewitt, Celia (act): *Satan's Slave; The Shuttered Room*

Hewitt, David (L.) (cin): *Doomsday Machine; Horror of the Blood Monsters; The Time Travelers(1964)*

Hewitt, David L. (dir): *Gallery of Horror; Journey to the Center of Time; The Lucifer Complex; The Mighty Gorga; Monsters Crash the Pajama Party; The Wizard of Mars*

Hewitt, Enid (act): *Solution by Phone*

Hewitt, Heather (act): *Mission Mars; Voodoo Blood Bath*

Hewitt, Henry (act): *Betrayal (1932)*

Hewitt, Jennifer Love (act, b. 1979): *I Know What You Did Last Summer*

Hewitt, Jerry (act): *The Nesting*

Hewitt, Jery (act): *Wolfen*

Hewitt, Joan (wri): *The Mighty Gorga*

Hewitt, Lee (wri): *The Golden Mistress*

Hewitt, Martin (act): *Alien Predators; Killer Party; Night Rhythms; Yellowbeard*

Hewitt, Paul (act): *Netforce*

Hewitt, Peter (dir): *Bill & Ted's Bogus Journey; The Borrowers (1998)*

Hewitt, Sean (act): *The Fast Kill; The Sender; Thinner; Wild Thing*

Hewitt, Shawn (act): *The Fly (1986)*

Hewitt, Violet (act): *The Solitary Cyclist*

Hewitt, Virginia (act): *The Flying Saucer (1950)*

Hewland, Philip (act): *Alf's Carpet; Altar Chains; Arsene Lupin; The Ashes of Revenge; The Golden Dawn; The King's Outcast; The Man In Motley; The Man In the Attic (1915); The Missing Rembrandt; Murder by Rope; The Secret of the Moor; The Sleeping Cardinal; Sweeney Todd; When Knights Were Bold (1916); Whosoever Shall Offend*

Hewlett, Arthur (act): *The Night Visitor; The Pied Piper (1971)*

Hewlett, Bob (act): *The Norsemen*

Hewlett, Brian (act): *The Masque of the Red Death (1964)*

Hewlett, David (act): *Desire and Hell at the Sunset Motel; The Penthouse (1989); Pin; Scanners II: The New Order*

Hewlett, Donald (act): Moments
Hewson, Bill (act): Hypnotic Suggestion
Hewson, Sherrie (act): The Slipper and the Rose
Hey, Stan (wri): Cry Wolf (1980)
Hey, Virginia (act): Obsession: A Taste for Fear
Heyburn, Weldon (act): The Chinese Cat; Criminals Within; The Thirteenth Man
Heyde, Dean (wri): Moon 44
Heydt, Louis Jean (act): Charlie Chan at Treasure Island; One Dangerous Night; Sleepers West; Zombies On Broadway
Heyermans, Franulka (act): My Nights With Susan, Sandra, Olga and Julie
Heyes, Herbert (act, 1889-1958): Bedtime for Bonzo; Behind Locked Doors; The Cobra Strikes
Heyking, Werner J. (act): Willy Wonka and the Chocolate Factory
Heyman, Barton (act): The Exorcist; Let's Scare Jessica to Death; Raising Cain
Heyman, Sean (act): The Lost Platoon
Heymann, Werner R. (mus): One Million B.C.
Heynemann, Laurent (dir): Birgitt Haas Must be Killed
Heyns, Alex (act): Steel Dawn
Heyward, Louis M. (wri, b. 1920): The City Under the Sea; Dr. Goldfoot and the Girl Bombs; Evil Stalks This House; The Ghost In the Invisible Bikini; Pajama Party; Sergeant Deadhead the Astronut!; Terrore Nello Spazio
Heywood, Anne (act, b. 1933, nee Violet Pretty): Carthage In Flames; The Depraved; Find the Lady; Floods of Fear; Scenes from a Murder; Secrets of the Phantom Caverns; Trader Horn (1973); Vengeance; The Very Edge; Violent Playground
Heywood, Colin (act): Bloody New Year
Heywood, Pat (act): Girly; 10 Rillington Place; Who Slew Auntie Roo?
Hi, Mae (act): Pandemonium
Hiatt, Philippa (act): Bullet from the Past; Halfway House
Hibbard, Barry (act): Cavegirl (1985)
Hibbard, Robert (act): The Bermuda Triangle
Hibbert, Geoffrey (act): The End of the Line; Gaolbreak (1962); The Great Van Robbery; Links of Justice; Secret People
Hibbert, Judith (act): Slipstream
Hibbert, Sydney (act): Sanctuary of Fear
Hibler, Winston (wri): Alice In Wonderland (1951)
Hice, Fred (act): Avalanche; RoboCop
Hichens, Robert (Smythe) (wri): Bella Donna (1923 & 1934); Flames; Temptation (1946)
Hickenlooper, George (dir): Grey Knight
Hickey, Brendan (act): I Married a Vampire
Hickey, Donna Lee (act): see Wynn, May
Hickey, Michael (wri): Silent Night, Deadly Night
Hickey, Paul (act): Blood Pen
Hickey, Tom (act): Gothic; High Spirits
Hickey, William (act, 1928-1997): The Boston Strangler; The Maddening; The Name of the Rose; The Nightmare Before Christmas; Puppet Master; Remo Williams: The Adventure Begins; The Sentinel; A Stranger Is Watching; Tales from the Darkside; The Telephone Book
Hickford, Suzie (act): Rapunzel Let Down Your Hair
Hickland, Catherine (act): Ghost Town; Witchery
Hickman, Alfred (act): The Enchanted Cottage (1924); The Last of the Lone Wolf; The Lone Wolf (1917)
Hickman, Bill (act): Daughter of the Mind
Hickman, Charles (act): Ten Minute Alibi
Hickman, Cordell (act): Tarzan's Secret Treasure
Hickman, Darryl (act, b. 1933): Alias Nick Beal; Keeper of the Flame; Leave Her to Heaven; Lightning Strikes Twice; Looker; The Set-Up (1949); The Strange Love of Martha Ivers; The Tingler
Hickman, Dwayne (act, b. 1934): The Boy with Green Hair; Dr. Goldfoot and the Bikini Machine; How to Stuff a Wild Bikini; 1,001 Arabian Nights (1959)
Hickman, Gail Morgan (wri): The London Connection
Hickman, George (act): The Gracie Allen Murder Case
Hickman, Howard (act): Charlie Chan at the Olympics; Dick Tracy vs. Crime, Inc.; The Return of Dr. X; Tarzan's New York Adventure
Hickman, Jason (act): Zapped!
Hickman, Julie (act): The Haunted (1991)
Hickman, Myrthas Helen (act): see Westcott, Helen
Hickner, Steve (dir): The Prince of Egypt
Hickox, Anthony (act): Waxwork II: Lost in Time
Hickox, Anthony (dir): Full Eclipse; Hellraiser III: Hell On Earth; Sundown: The Vampire In Retreat; Warlock: The Armageddon; Waxwork; Waxwork II: Lost in Time
Hickox, Anthony (wri): Sundown: The Vampire In Retreat; Waxwork II: Lost In Time
Hickox, Douglas (dir): Blackout (1985); The Phoenix (1981); Sitting Target; Theater of Blood
Hickox, Harry (act): The Ghost and Mr. Chicken
Hickox, James (act): Waxwork II: Lost In Time
Hickox, James D.R. (dir): Children of the Corn III: Urban Sacrifice
Hickox, Sid(ney) (cin, b. 1895): The Big Sleep (1946); Dark Passage; The Gorilla (1931); The Horn Blows at Midnight; Lightning Strikes Twice; The Private Life of Helen of Troy; The Return of Dr. X; Them! (1954)
Hicks, Barbara (act): Brazil; Evil Under the Sun; Memoirs of a Survivor; Morons from Outer Space
Hicks, Bill (act): The Resurrection of Zachary Wheeler
Hicks, Caitlin (act): It (1990)
Hicks, Catherine (act): Child's Play (1988); Death Valley; Peggy Sue Got Married; Running Against Time; Star Trek IV: The Voyage Home
Hicks, Chuck (act): Beyond Evil; Dick Tracy (1990); The Hound Of The Baskervilles (1972)
Hicks, Dan(ny) (act): Darkman (1990); Evil Dead 2: Dead by Dawn
Hicks, David (act): Shadowzone
Hicks, Hilly (act): Gray Lady Down; Spider-Man
Hicks, James (act): The Lair of the White Worm
Hicks, Kevin (act): Blood Relations; Final Notice
Hicks, Leonard (act): Santa Claus Conquers the Martians
Hicks, Marva (act): Virtuosity
Hicks, Neill (wri): Escape 2000; The Final Terror
Hicks, Peter (act): Phobia
Hicks, Russell (act, 1895-1957): The Bandit of Sherwood Forest; The Blue Bird (1940); Charlie Chan In Shanghai; A Close Call for Boston Blackie; Dark Alibi; Ellery Queen's Penthouse Mystery; The Flying Saucer (1950); A Game of Death; Hold That Ghost; Man-Made Monster; Samson and Delilah; The Shanghai Chest; Tarzan's New York Adventure; The Westland Case
Hicks, (Sir) Seymour (act, 1871-1949): Busman's Honeymoon; A Prehistoric Love Story; Scrooge (1913 & 1935); The Secret of the Loch (1934)
Hicks, (Sir) Seymour (wri, 1871-1949): A Prehistoric Love Story; Scrooge (1913 & 1935)
Hicks, William T. (act): Death Screams; Order of the Black Eagle
Hickson, Joan (act, 1906-1998): Child In the House; Deadly Nightshade; High Treason (1951); Love from a Stranger (1937); Mad About Men; The Man Who Could Work Miracles; Murder She Said; No Haunt for a Gentleman; One of Our Dinosaurs Is Missing; Port ofEscape; The Secret of My Success; Seven Days to Noon; Theater of Blood; The Wicked Lady
Hicky, Cathy (act): To All a Goodnight
Hicky, Mary (act): To All a Goodnight
Hidaka, Shigeaki (dir): The Final War
Hidaka, Shigeaki (wri): Godzilla Raids Again
Hidaka, Sumiko (act): Yoru No Tsuzumi
Hideki, Sonoda (act): The Toxic Avenger, Part II
Hiemer, Horst (act): Held for Questioning
Hieronimko, Jan (act): Vampyr
Hiers, Bob (act): Barracuda
Hieu, Joseph (act): Twilight Zone
Higata, Kazuo (act): Mothra
Higby, Mary Jane (act): The Honeymoon Killers
Higgin, Howard (wri): Revolt of the Zombies
Higgings, Edward (act): The Woman Eater
Higgins, Anthony (act): The Bride (1985); The Cold Room; Nostradamus; Raiders of the Lost Ark; Young Sherlock Holmes
Higgins, Claire (act): Hellbound: Hellraiser II; Hellraiser
Higgins, Colin (act, 1941-1988): The Shout
Higgins, Colin (wri): The Devil's Daughter (1972)
Higgins, Deborah (act): End of the World (1977)
Higgins, Fran (act): Squirm
Higgins, Joel (act): Salvage
Higgins, John (act): Chilling (1981)
Higgins, John (C.) (wri): The Black Sleep; Daughters of Satan; The Diamond; The File of the Golden Goose; Robinson Crusoe On Mars
Higgins, John Michael (act): Vampire's Kiss
Higgins, Kenneth (cin): The Spy With a Cold Nose
Higgins, Kenneth (mus): Spookies
Higgins, Kenneth (wri): Ghosts On the Loose; The Unknown Terror
Higgins, Lynn Rose (wri): Mutator
Higgins, Michael (act): Angel Heart; The Cradle Will Fall; Edge of Fury
Higginson, Jane (act): The Silencers (1995)
Higginson, Tom (act): TekWar
Higginson, Torri (act): Storm of the Century; Synapse
Higgon, Dai (cin): Murder in Mind
High, Angela (act): The Zero Boys
Higham, Danny (act): Death Ship
Highsmith, Patricia (wri, 1920-1995): The Glass Cell; Once You Meet a Stranger; Strangers On a Train
Hignett, H.R. (act): The Blue Bird (1910); Silent Evidence
Hignett, Mary (act): The Corpse; Prehistoric Women (1966)
Higuchi, Kanaka (act): Deaths In Tokimeki
Hiken, Gerald (act): Blackout (1985)
Hilario Brothers (cin): The Blood Drinkers
Hilary, Jennifer (act): Journey Into Darkness; Slipstream
Hilbeck, Fernando (act): Flesh & Blood; The Living Dead at the Manchester Morgue; Pyro
Hilbert, Antje (act): Making Contact
Hilbert, Tina Louise (act): Basket Case 3: The Progeny
Hilboldt, Lise (act): The Hunger; Superman (1978)
Hilburn, Percy (cin): The Black Bird (1926); The Mysterious Island (1929); The Unholy Three (1930)
Hild, Jim (act): Contact
Hildebrandt, Charles George (act): The Deadly Spawn
Hildebrandt, Jason (act): The Cyber-Stalking
Hilder, Tony (act): The Hideous Sun Demon
Hildreth, Gary (act): Lifeforce
Hildreth, Mark (act): Past Perfect
Hildyard, Jack (cin, b. 1915): The Beast Must Die; Blue Movie Blackmail; Casino Royale; Cat and Mouse (1974); The Living Idol; Modesty Blaise; Murder On Monday; The Perfect Woman; The Sound Barrier; Suddenly Last Summer; Topaz; The Zany Adventures of Robin Hood
Hile, Joel (act): Surf Nazis Must Die; Visitants
Hill, Al (act): After Midnight With Boston Blackie; The Death Kiss; Lady In the Morgue
Hill, Amy (act): Mountaintop Motel Massacre
Hill, Arthur (GB act): Paul Temple Returns; Scarlet Thread
Hill, Arthur (USA act, b. 1922): The Andromeda Strain; Futureworld; Moment to Moment; Murder In Space; One Magic Christmas; Ordeal; The Other Man; Prototype; Revenge of the Stepford Wives; Something Wicked This Way Comes; Tomorrow's Child Tomorrow's Child
Hill, Benny (act, 1925-1992): Chitty Chitty Bang Bang; Who Done It? (1956)
Hill, Bernard (act): A Choice of Weapons; The Ghost and the Darkness
Hill, Brian Alan (act): Asteroid
Hill, Carole (act): Silent Night, Deadly Night III
Hill, Claudio Guerin (dir): A Bell from Hell
Hill, Clayton D. (act): Lady Beware
Hill, Craig (act): Anguish; The Black Shield of Falworth; The Flight That Disappeared; Top Secret (1978)
Hill, Dana (act): Jetsons: The Movie; Tom and Jerry: The Movie
Hill, Dave (act): Now You See Him, Now You Don't
Hill, Dean (act): Running Against Time
Hill, Debra (wri, b. 1950): Escape from L.A.; The Fog; Halloween; Halloween II
Hill, Doris (act): Darkened Rooms; Tangled Destinies
Hill, Douglas (cin): The Playbirds
Hill, Ed (mus): The Devonsville Terror
Hill, Eddita (act): Mr. Destiny
Hill, Ethel (wri): The Best Man Wins
Hill, Frankie (act): Wargames
Hill, George (dir): Through the Dark
Hill, George A. (wri): The Secret of Stamboul
Hill, George Roy (dir, b. 1922): The Little Drummer Girl; Slaughterhouse-Five
Hill, Gladys (wri): The Kremlin Letter; The Man Who Would Be King; Reflections In a Golden Eye
Hill, Graham (act): Caravan to Vaccares; Threads
Hill, Hallene (act): The Search for Bridey Murphy; The Vampire (1957)
Hill, Harry (act): Oh Heavenly Dog; Rabid
Hill, Howard (act): The Adventures of Robin Hood
Hill, Jack (act): The Brain Eaters; House of Evil (1968)
Hill, Jack (dir): Blood Bath (1966); The Fear Chamber; House of Evil (1968); Invasion Sinitestra; Portrait In Terror; Spider Baby
Hill, Jack (wri): Blood Bath (1966); City On Fire; Death Ship; The Fear Chamber; House of Evil (1968); Isle of the Snake People; Spider Baby; The Terror (1963)
Hill, Jacqueline (act): The Blue Parrot
Hill, James (dir, b. 1919): Captain Nemo and the Underwater City; Journey Into Darkness; The Man from Nowhere; The Stolen Plans (1952); A Study In Terror
Hill, James (wri, b. 1916): Mr. Selkie; The Stolen Plans (1952)
Hill, Jerome (dir & wri): The Sand Castle
Hill, John (act): The Seven-Per-Cent Solution
Hill, John (wri): Heartbeeps
Hill, John Stephen (act): The Hunger; Blood Bath at the House of Death
Hill, Kathy (act): Blind Date
Hill, Ken (act): Killer In the Mirror
Hill, Kimberly (act): The Hand That Rocks the Cradle
Hill, Kristopher Kent (act): The Gifted One
Hill, Mariana/Marianna (act): The Astral Factor; The Baby; Black Zoo; Blood Beach; Dead People; Death at Love House; The Invisible Strangler; Schizoid (1980)
Hill, Marla (act): Sorceress (1982)
Hill, Mary (act): The Beast from 20,000 Fathoms; Mesa of Lost Women
Hill, Matt (act): Watchers
Hill, Maude (act): Puritan Passions
Hill, Phyllis (act): Haunts of the Very Rich
Hill, Richard (act): Deathstalker; Warrior Queen
Hill, Richard (mus): Baffled!; To Kill a Clown
Hill, Rick/Richard (act): Cyborg 2: Glass Shadow; Deathstalker 4: Match of Titans; Dune Warriors
Hill, Riley (act): Radar Secret Service
Hill, Robert (F.) (dir): Blake of Scotland Yard; Crooked Alley; Face In the Fog (1935); Kelly of the Secret Service; Queen of the Jungle; Tarzan the Fearless
Hill, Robert (F.) (wri): The Beast of Hollow Mountain; The Cat and the Canary (1927); Confessions of an Opium Eater; Crooked Alley; Dog Eat Dog; The Last Warning (1929); The Private Lives of Adam and Eve; Sex Kittens Go to College; She-Gods of Shark Reef; A Woman's Devotion
Hill, Roger (act): Doctor Franken
Hill, Rose (act): The Bank Raiders; File It Under Fear; Footsteps; House of Whipcord
Hill, Sinclair (dir): Boadicea; The Mystery of Mr. Bernard Brown; The Secret Kingdom; The Unwritten Law; Widow Twan-Kee
Hill, Sinclair (wri): At the Villa Rose (1920); Boadicea; The Prehistoric Man (1924); Widow Twan-Kee
Hill, Steven (act): Eyewitness (1981)
Hill, Terence (act): see Girotti, Mario
Hill, Teresa (act): Bio-Dome; Puppet Master 4; Puppet Master 5
Hill, Thomas/Tom (act): The Nude Bomb; Revenge of the Stepford Wives; Sanctuary of Fear
Hill, Walter (dir): Streets of Fire; Tales from the Crypt (1989)
Hill, Walter (wri): Alien; Alien 3; Streets of Fire
Hill, William (act): Wolf
Hill, Winfrey Hester (act): Premonition (1972)
Hiller, Arthur (dir, b. 1924): Nightwing
Hiller, Kurt (act): Der Letzte Mann
Hiller, Wendy (act, b. 1912): The Cat and the Canary (1978); The Curse of King Tut's Tomb; How to Murder a Rich Uncle; Miss Morison's Ghosts; Murder On the Orient Express
Hillerman, John (act, b. 1932): Audrey Rose; Ellery Queen; Hands of a Murderer
Hillhouse, Brenda (act): From Dusk Till Dawn
Hilliard, Ernest (act): Annabel Lee; Drums of Jeopardy (1931)
Hilliard, Harriet (act, 1909-1994): Confessions of Boston Blackie; The Falcon Strikes Back
Hilliard, Marshall (act): Getting Lucky
Hilliard, Patricia (act): The Ghost Goes West; The Limping Man (1936); The Missing Million; The Private Life of Don Juan; Things to Come
Hilliard, Richard L. (cin): The Curse of the Living Corpse; The Horror of Party Beach
Hilliard, Richard (L.) (dir): The Lonely Sex; The Playground; Psychomania (1964); Wild Is My Love
Hilliard, Richard L. (wri): The Horror of Party Beach; The Lonely Sex

Hilliard, Ryan (act): Inferno (1979); Night of the Zombies (1981)
Hilliard, Stafford (act): The Man In the Mirror; The Secret of the Loch (1934)
Hilliard, Thomas (act): Evilspeak
Hillier, Erwin (cin, b. 1911): Chase a Crooked Shadow; Eye of the Devil; The Naked Edge; The October Man; Operation Crossbow; The Quiller Memorandum; The Valley of Gwangi
Hillig, Chuck (act): The Cremators
Hilligoss, Candace (act): Carnival of Souls (1962); The Curse of the Living Corpse
Hilling, Jacques (act): The Hunchback of Notre Dame (1957)
Hillinger, Wolfgang (act): Satyricon
Hillis, Verna (act): The House of Mystery (1931)
Hillman, David Michael (dir & wri): The Strangeness
Hillman, William B. (dir): Double Exposure
Hills, (Miss) Beverly (act): Brides of Blood; The Comedy of Terrors; The Power (1967)
Hills, David (dir): Ator: The Fighting Eagle; Quest for the Mighty Sword
Hills, David (wri): Ator: The Fighting Eagle
Hills, Gillian (act): Blow-Up; A Clockwork Orange; Demons of the Mind
Hills, Joan (act): Horror
Hillstead, Mary (act): Explorers
Hillyer, Lambert (dir, b. 1889): The Altar Stairs; Dracula's Daughter; The Invisible Ray; The Shock(1923)
Hilsdon, George (act): An American Werewolf In London; The Fiendish Plot of Dr. Fu Manchu
Hilton, Arthur (dir): Cat-Women of the Moon
Hilton, Cathy (act): Invasion of the Bee Girls
Hilton, Daisy (act, 1908-1969): Chained for Life; Freaks
Hilton, Edward (act): David and Goliath
Hilton, George (act): Blade of the Ripper; Demons of the Dead; The Masked Man Against the Pirates; Lo Strano Caso della Signora Ward
Hilton, James (wri, 1900-1954): Knight Without Armour; Lost Horizon (1937 & 1973); Rage In Heaven
Hilton, Jasmina (act): The Vault of Horror
Hilton, Joseph (cin): Night of Terror (1933)
Hilton, LaSesne (act): The Deathmaster
Hilton, Marjorie (act): Appointment for a Killing; Double Jeopardy
Hilton, Steven (act): It (1990)
Hilton, Tony (wri): The Hand (1960); What a Carve Up!
Hilton, Violet (act, 1908-1969): Chained for Life; Freaks
Himes, John (act): Deathsport
Himmelstein, David (wri): Village of the Damned (1995)
Himmelstein, Howard (act): Full Eclipse
Hinatsu, Tayori (act): Virus (1980)
Hinchcliffe, Stuart (cin): Frankenstein (1984)
Hinchley, Tommy (act): The Terror Within
Hinchman, Bert (act): 976-EVIL
Hinde, Madeleine (act): Doctors Wear Scarlet; The Fiend (1972)
Hindle, Art (act): The Brood; The Clone Master; Into the Fire; Invasion of the Body Snatchers (1978); Let Me Call You Sweetheart; The Man Who Wasn't There; The Octagon; The Power Within (1979); Silent Night, Evil Night
Hinds, Anthony (dir, b. 1922, a.k.a. John Elder): The Reptile
Hinds, Anthony (wri, b. 1922): Captain Clegg; The Curse of the Werewolf; Dracula Has Risen from the Grave; Evil of Frankenstein; Frankenstein and the Monster from Hell; Frankenstein Created Woman; The Ghoul (1974); Kiss of the Vampire; Legend of the Werewolf; The Mummy's Shroud; The Phantom of the Opera (1962); Rasputin, the Mad Monk; The Reptile; Scars of Dracula; Taste the Blood of Dracula
Hinds, Ciarin (act): Excalibur; Jane Eyre (1997); Mary Reilly
Hinds, Cindy (act): The Brood; Deadline
Hinds, Harry (act): Houdini (1953); Talk About a Stranger
Hinds, Samuel S. (act, 1875-1948): The Boy With Green Hair; Cobra Woman; Deluge; Gabriel Over the White House; The Jungle Woman; Kid Glove Killer; Man-Made Monster; The Night Key; The Raven (1935); The Return of October; She (1935); Son of Dracula (1943); The Strange Case of Dr. Rx; Weird Woman
Hindy, Joseph (act): Charlie Chan: Happiness Is a Warm Clue
Hine, Larry (act): Outbreak
Hine, Michele (act): Return to Oz
Hiner, Phil (wri): The Hideous Sun Demon
Hines, Barbara (act): The Three Stooges Meet Hercules
Hines, Barry (dir & wri): Threads
Hines, David (wri): Once Bitten
Hines, Frazer (act): X...The Unknown; Zeppelin
Hines, Grainger (act): The Secretary; Someone's Watching Me!
Hines, Gregory (act, b. 1946): Dead Air; Eve of Destruction; The Muppets Take Manhattan; The Preacher's Wife; Wolfen
Hines, Janear (act): Welcome to Arrow Beach
Hines, Leonard (wri): The Ghoul (1933)
Hines, Milton (act): see Sales, Soupy
Hines, Mimi (act): Fake-Out
Hines, Robert (act): Hellraiser; Mary Shelley's Frankenstein
Hines, Ronald (act): Echo of Barbara; The Laughing Girl Murder; Seance On a Wet Afternoon
Hingle, Pat (act, b. 1913): Batman (1989); Batman and Robin; Batman Forever; Batman Returns; The Land Before Time; Maximum Overdrive; Nightmare Honeymoon; Not of This World; Of Mice and Men (1981); Sweet, Sweet Rachel; Tarantulas: The Deadly Cargo
Hinkley, Brent (act): Ed Wood; Jacob's Ladder; The Silence of the Lambs
Hinkley, Tom(my) (act): Buried Alive II; Her Deadly Rival; Silent Night, Deadly Night 4: Initiation; Star Trek: Generations; Watchers II
Hinn, Michael (act): The Devil's Messenger
Hinnant, Skip (act): Fritz the Cat; The Nine Lives of Fritz the Cat
Hinrich, John (act): Les Miserables (1943)
Hinrichsen, Niels (act): The Island at the Top of the World
Hintermann, Carlo (act): The Eyes Behind the Stars
Hintnaus, Tom (act): Graduation Day
Hinton, Darby (act): The Alien's Return; Mr. Sycamore; Without Warning (1980)
Hinton, Ed (act): Cry Terror!; Devil Goddess; Jungle Moon Men; The 27th Day
Hinton, James David (act): Galaxina
Hinton, James E. (cin): Ganja and Hess
Hinton, Mary (act): Gaslight (1940); Once In a New Moon; Poison Pen
Hinton, Robert (act): The Snow Creature
Hintz, Peter (act): Zone Troopers
Hintze, Naomi A. (wri): You'll Like My Mother
Hinwood, Peter (act): The Rocky Horror Picture Show
Hinz, Edgar (act): Chinese Boxes
Hinzman, Bill (act): Jack's Wife; Revenge of the Living Zombies
Hinzman, Bill (dir): The Majorettes; Revenge of the Living Zombies
Hiona, Sam (act): Invasion of the Body Snatchers (1978)
Hipkins, Chip (act): Nightmare On the 13th Floor
Hipp, Paul (act): Bad Channels
Hipp, Paul (cin): Blood and Lace; The Boogens; Earthbound (1981); Grave of the Vampire; Hangar 18; The Horrible House On the Hill; The Incredible 2-Headed Transplant; The Legend of Sleepy Hollow
Hippard, Robert (act): Brainstorm (1983); Haunts
Hippe, Laura (act): Logan's Run; Mausoleum
Hipple, Hugh (act): see Marlowe, Hugh
Hippodrome Chorus, The (act): The Clue of the New Pin (1929)
Hippolyte, Alexander Gregory (dir): Night Rhythms
Hira, Mikijiro (act): The Mystery of Rampo; Tanin No Kao
Hirai, Kiyoko (act): Uchujin Tokyo No Arawaru
Hiranand, Shanti (act): Siddhartha
Hirata, Akihiko (act): Godzilla vs. the Bionic Monster; Gojira; Gorath; The H-Man; The Mysterians; Rodan, the Flying Monster; The Secret of the Telegian; The War In Space
Hirata, Isao (act): The Punisher
Hird, Robert (dir): Mr. Horatio Knibbles
Hird, Thora (act, b. 1914): The Frightened Man; Lost; The Lost Hours; The Nightcomers; Portrait from Life; The Quatermass Experiment; Tiger by the Tail; Turn the Key Softly; Went the Day Well?
Hirokane, David (act): Charlie Chan and the Curse of the Dragon Queen
Hirose, Shoichi (act): Mothra
Hirsch, Bernard (act): Traitement de Choc
Hirsch, Bettina (dir): Munchies
Hirsch, Daniel (act): The Zero Boys
Hirsch, Emile (act): Gargantua; Houdini (1998)
Hirsch, Judd (act, b. 1935): Independence Day
Hirsch, Lou (act): Superman III; Who Framed Roger Rabbit
Hirsch, Patrick (act): The Zero Boys
Hirsch, Robert (act, b. 1929): The Hunchback of Notre Dame (1957)
Hirsch, Steven (act): The Alien's Return
Hirsch, Wilbert (mus): An American Werewolf In Paris
Hirschfeld, Alec (cin): Space Raiders
Hirschfeld, Gerald (cin): Fail-Safe; Ladybug, Ladubug; Neighbors; The Ultimate Warrior; W; Young Frankenstein
Hirschfield, Robert (act): The Island
Hirschman, Herbert (act): Brainstorm (1983)
Hirschman, Ray (dir): Plutonium Baby
Hirson, Alice (act): Nightwing; Psycho IV: The Beginning
Hirson, Roger O. (wri): A Christmas Carol (1984)
Hirt, Eleanore (act): The Killing Game
Hirvikangas, Jukka (act): Gorky Park
Hisaishi, Joh (mus): Laputa: Castle In the Sky
Hisamune, Hiroshi (act): Varan the Unbelievable
Hiscott, Leslie (dir, 1894-1968): Alibi (1931); Death On the Set; The Face at the Window (1932); Flat No. 3; The House of the Arrow (1930); Inside the Room; The Iron Stair (1933); The Missing Rembrandt; Murder at Covent Garden; A Night In Montmartre; Passing Shadows; The Sleeping Cardinal; The Stickpin; The Stolen Necklace; The Triumph of Sherlock Holmes
Hishimi, Yuriko (act): Godzilla On Monster Island
Hissink, Coen (act): The Black Tulip (1921)
Hitchcock, (Sir) Alfred (dir, 1899-1980): The Birds; Blackmail (1929); Champagne; Dial M for Murder (1954); Downhill; Elstree Calling; Family Plot; Foreign Correspondent; Frenzy; I Confess; Jamaica Inn (1939); The Lady Vanishes (1938); Lifeboat; The Lodger (1926); The Man Who Knew Too Much (1934 & 1956); Marnie; Murder; North by Northwest; Notorious (1946); Number 17; The Paradine Case; Psycho (1960); Rear Window (1954); Rebecca; Rich and Strange; The Ring; Rope; Sabotage; Saboteur; The Secret Agent (1936); Shadow of a Doubt (1943); Spellbound (1945); Stage Fright (1950); Strangers On a Train; Suspicion (1941); The 39 Steps (1935); To Catch a Thief; Topaz; Torn Curtain; The Trouble With Harry; Under Capricorn; Vertigo; The Wrong Man; Young and Innocent
Hitchcock, (Sir) Alfred (wri, 1899-1980): Blackmail (1929); Champagne; Murder; Number 17; The Lodger (1926); Rich and Strange; The Ring; Saboteur
Hitchcock, Bill (act): The Mutilator (1985)
Hitchcock, Keith (act): Counter-Espionage
Hitchcock, Mike (act): Nightmare In Blood
Hitchcock, Pat (act, b. 1928): Psycho (1960); Stage Fright (1950); Strangers On a Train
Hitchcock, Raymond (act): The Monkey Talks
Hite, Henry (act): Monster A Go-Go
Hitt, Robert (act): All That Jazz
Hittleman, Karl (wri): Billy the Kid vs. Dracula
Hitu (act): Tabu
Hively, George (wri): The Altar Stairs
Hively, Jack (dir): The Saint In Palm Springs; The Saint's Double Trouble; The Saint Takes Over
Hixon, Ken (act): Knightriders
Hjortsberg, William (wri): Angel Heart; Legend
Hlubi, Majabalo (act): King Solomon's Mines (1937)
Ho, Don (act): Joe's Apartment
Ho, Lee Kyang (act): Yongary, Monster from the Deep
Ho, Linda (act): Confessions of an Opium Eater; Dimension 5; Hillbillys In a Haunted House
Ho, Michael (act): Riders of the Storm
Ho, Soon-Taik (act): The Man With the Golden Gun
Ho, Yim (dir): Buddha's Lock
Hoag, Judith (act): Acting On Impulse; Halloweentown; Teenage Mutant Ninja Turtles
Hoag, Richard (act): Earthbound (1981)
Hoag, Stephen J. (act): Spawn of the Slithis
Hoagland, Ellsworth (cin): Dr. Cyclops
Hoak, Clare (act): Masque of the Red Death (1989); The Terror Within II
Hoar, Jack (act): Shocker
Hoare, Douglas (wri): A Safe Affair
Hoare, John (wri): Red Planet Mars
Hoath, Florence (act): Fairy Tale: A True Story
Hoban, Russell (wri): The Mouse and His Child
Hobart, Doug (act): Death Curse of Tartu
Hobart, Rose (act, b. 1906, nee Rose Keefer): Bride of Vengeance; The Brighton Strangler; The Cat Creeps (1946); Crime Doctor's Strangest Case; Dr. Jekyll and Mr. Hyde (1932); East of Borneo; Liliom (1930); The Mad Ghoul; Soul of a Monster; Tower of London (1939)
Hobbes, Halliwell (act, 1877-1962): British Agent; Bulldog Drummond's Peril; Bulldog Drummond Strikes Back (1934); Charlie Chan In Shanghai; Dr. Jekyll and Mr. Hyde (1932); Dracula's Daughter; Gaslight (1944); Here Comes Mr. Jordan; The Invisible Man's Revenge; Maid of Salem; The Menace (1932); Scotland Yard (1930); Sherlock Holmes Faces Death; A Study In Scarlet (1933); The Undying Monster
Hobbes, Peter (act): The Adventures of Robin Hood
Hobbs, Carleton (act): Dark Places; Death In the Hand; The House That Dripped Blood; Perfect Friday
Hobbs, Connie (act): Those Dear Departed
Hobbs, Fredric (dir & wri): Alabama's Ghost
Hobbs, Hayford (act): Asthore; Broken Barrier; The Firm of Girdlestone; High Treason (1929); The King's Daughter; The Man In Motley; The Polar Star; The Princess of Happy Chance; The Ringer (1928); The Sons of Satan; When Knights were Bold (1916); Whosoever Shall Offend
Hobbs, Heather (act): The Darker Side of Terror
Hobbs, Jack (act): The Crimson Circle (1922); The Face at the Window (1920); Miracles Do Happen; The Naval Treaty; The Shuttle of Life
Hobbs, Katrina (act): The Boy from Andromeda
Hobbs, Peter (act): The Andromeda Strain; Heavy Traffic; The Man With Two Brains; The Next One; Night of the Demon (1957); Sleeper; The Two Worlds of Jennie Logan
Hobbs, Peter Halliwell (act): Meet Maxwell Archer
Hobbs, Robert (act): Chinatown Nights; Dr. Sin Fang
Hobbs, William (act): Captain Kronos: Vampire Hunter; Macbeth (1971)
Hobel, Mara (act): The Hand (1981)
Hobkins, Dr. (act): Making Contact
Hobl, Pavel (dir): Do You Keep a Lion at Home?; The Lost Face
Hobley, McDonald (act): Meet Mr. Lucifer
Hoblit, Gregory (dir): Fallen; Primal Fear
Hobo, Johan (act): The Lift
Hobson, Gene (mus): Student Bodies
Hobson, I.M. (act): Bram Stoker's 'Dracula'; Hello Again
Hobson, Valerie (act, b. 1917): Blanche Fury; Bride of Frankenstein; The Drum; Eyes of Fate; Great Expectations (1934 & 1946); The Great Impersonation (1935); The Interrupted Journey; Kind Hearts and Coronets; Mad Love; The Mystery of Edwin Drood (1935); Q Planes; Rendezvous at Midnight; The Rocking Horse Winner; The Secret of Stamboul; The Spy In Black; This Man Is News; The Voice of Merrill; Werewolf of London
Hoch, Winton C. (cin, b. 1908): Darby O'Gill and the Little People; Five Weeks In a Balloon; The Lost World (1960); Necromancy; Robinson Crusoe On Mars; Voyage to the Bottom of the Sea
Hochstatter, Zoran (cin): Beverly Hills Bodysnatchers; The Haunting of Morella; Not of This Earth (1988); The Return of Swamp Thing; Twice Dead
Hock, Johnny (act): The Darker Side of Terror
Hock, Peter (act): A Return to Salem's Lot; The Stuff; Vampire's Kiss
Hocke, Bernard (act): Sphere
Hocking, Anne (wri): The Surgeon's Knife
Hocking, Silas K. (wri): The Great Anarchist Mystery; The Shadow Between
Hockley, Andy (act): Robin Hood: Prince of Thieves
Hockman, Ned (dir): Stark Fear
Hockridge, Edmund (act): Bang! You're Dead
Hodder, K. Alan (act): A Nymphoid Barbarian In Dinosaur Hell
Hodder, Kane (act): Friday the 13th, Part VII-The New Blood; Friday the 13th, Part VIII-Jason Takes Manhattan; House II: The Second Story; Jason Goes to Hell: The Final Friday; Pumpkinhead II: Blood Wings; Wishmaster
Hoddinott, Alan (mus): Sword of Sherwood Forest
Hodes, Ryn (act): Primal Scream
Hodge, Bill (act): Death In High Heels
Hodge, Edwin (act): The Long Kiss Goodnight
Hodge, Jim (act): Bridge Across Time
Hodge, Jonathan (mus): Embassy; Z.P.G.
Hodge, Kate (act): The Hidden II; Leatherface: Texas Chainsaw Massacre III; Love Kills; Pandora's Clock
Hodge, Kenneth J. (act): Scalpel

Hodge, Mike (act): Dr. Jekyll and Ms. Hyde
Hodge, Morton (act): Primal Scream
Hodge, Patricia (act): Just Ask for Diamond; The Disappearance; The Secret Life of Ian Fleming
Hodge, Robert (act): Windows
Hodge, Stephanie (act): I, Madman
Hodge, Steve (wri): Mosquito
Hodge, Vicky (act): Mini Weekend
Hodgeman, Edwin (act): Mad Max Beyond Thunderdome
Hodges, Clay (act): The China Syndrome
Hodges, David (act): The Fugitive (1993)
Hodges, Hal (act): Frogs
Hodges, Horace (act): After Dark; Jamaica Inn (1939); A Night In Montmartre
Hodges, Ken(neth) (cin): Assignment K; Baffled!; Behemoth, the Sea Monster; In the Devil's Garden; Negatives; Penny Gold; Revenge (1971, GB); The Ruling Class; The Shuttered Room; The Spiral Staircase (1975); Sword of Sherwood Forest
Hodges, Mike (dir): Black Rainbow; Flash Gordon (1980); Get Carter; Morons from Outer Space; Pulp; The Terminal Man
Hodges, Michael/Mike (wri): Black Rainbow; Damien-Omen II; Pulp; The Terminal Man
Hodges, Steven (act): Twin Peaks: Fire Walk With Me
Hodges, Tom (act): The Baby Doll Murders; Critters 2: The Main Course
Hodgin, Barry (mus): Blood Waters of Dr. Z
Hodgins, Earle (act): Song of the Thin Man
Hodgkinson, Isabel (act): see Dean, Isabel
Hodgson, Brian (mus): The Legend of Hell House; The Tempest (1980)
Hodgson, J.L. (wri): Under the Red Robe (1937)
Hodgson, Leland/Leyland (act): The Adventurous Blonde; Bedlam; The Challenge; Flesh and Fantasy; The Ghost of Frankenstein; The Invisible Man's Revenge; Just Off Broadway; Mr. Moto's Last Warning; Murder Over New York; Sherlock Holmes and the Voice of Terror; Trouble for Two; The Two Mrs. Carrolls
Hodgson, Michael (act): First Knight
Hodgson, Phoebe (act): The Lady Killers (1956)
Hodiak, John (act, 1914-1955): The Arnelo Affair; The Bribe; Lifeboat; Love from a Stranger (1947); On the Threshold of Space; Somewhere In the Night
Hodson, Donal(d) (act): Roger Corman's Frankenstein Unbound; She (1983)
Hoeberg, Albert (act): Vredens Dag
Hoechst, Wolfram (act): Amazons (1986)
Hoeffer, Norman (act, dir & wri): see Foster, Norman
Hoelcher, Philip (act): Flight of the Navigator
Hoelscher, Devin (act): Sorry You've Been Troubled
Hoelscher, Matt (act): My Science Project
Hoenack, Jeremy (dir): The Dark Ride
Hoenig, Michael (mus): The Blob (1988); Class of 1999; The Gate; I, Madman; Thrill; Visions of Murder; The Wraith
Hoerbiger, Paul (act): Spione; The Third Man
Hoerl, Arthur (wri, b. 1892): The Black Pearl; The Drums of Jeopardy (1923); Drums O'Voodoo; Killer Ape; The Lost Tribe; Strange Adventure; The Thirteenth Guest
Hoerter, Dennis (act): Return (1985)
Hoes, Guus (act): The Lift
Hoey, Dennis (act, 1893-1960, nee Samuel David Hyams): Chu Chin Chow (1934); Faust (1936); Frankenstein Meets the Wolf Man; Golden Earrings; The House of Fear (1945); Maria Marten: or, The Murder In the Red Barn (1935); The Mystery of the Mary Celeste; The Pearl of Death; Sherlock Holmes and the Secret Weapon; Sherlock Holmes Faces Death; She-Wolf of London; Spider Woman; Terror by Night; A Thousand and One Nights (1945); The Wandering Jew (1933)
Hoey, Iris (act): The Limping Man (1936); Living Dangerously; The Midas Touch; The Perfect Crime; The Terror (1938)
Hoey, Michael A. (dir & wri): The Navy vs. the Night Monsters
Hofbauer, Ernest (dir): Red Dragon (1965)
Hofer, Johanna (act): Above Suspicion; Der Verlorene
Hoff, Christian (act): Beverly Hills Bodysnatchers
Hoff, Halvard (act): Blade af Satans Bog
Hoff, Robin (act): Charlie Chan and the Curse of the Dragon Queen; The Eliminator
Hoffe, Arthur (wri): Scream, Pretty Peggy
Hoffe, Monckton (wri): Busman's Honeymoon; Daybreak; The Man Without Desire
Hoffenstein, Samuel (wri): Dr. Jekyll and Mr. Hyde (1932); Flesh and Fantasy; Laura; Love Me Tonight; The Miracle Man (1932); Phantom of the Opera (1943); White Woman
Hoffer, Bernard (mus): The Ivory Ape; The Sins of Dorian Gray
Hoffer Sr., Robert (act): The Toxic Avenger, Part II
Hoffer Jr., Robert (act): The Toxic Avenger, Part II
Hoffert, Paul (mus): Firebird 2015 A.D.; The Groundstar Conspiracy
Hoffman, Alice (wri): Practical Magic
Hoffman, Angela (act): Bad Ronald
Hoffman, Basil (act): Communion; Love at First Bite; Switch
Hoffman, Brant (act): The Granny
Hoffman, Bridget (act): Darkman (1990); Time Trackers
Hoffman, Cary (act): The Island
Hoffman, Cecil (act): Stargate
Hoffman, David (act): The Beast With Five Fingers; Flesh and Fantasy; The Mask of Dimitrios; The Shanghai Chest
Hoffman, Dustin (act, b. 1937): Agatha; Dick Tracy (1990); Marathon Man; Outbreak
Hoffman, Elizabeth (act): Dante's Peak; Fear No Evil (1981); Silent Night, Deadly Night III
Hoffman, Gertrude W. (act): The Ape (1940)
Hoffman, Harold (dir): The Black Cat (1965)
Hoffman, Harold (wri): The Black Cat (1965); In the Year 2889
Hoffman, Herman (dir): The Invisible Boy; It's a Dog's Life
Hoffman, Hillary (act): D.O.A. (1988)
Hoffman, Holly (act): Fire In the Sky (1993)
Hoffman, Howard (act): House On Haunted Hill (1958); Macabre (1958)
Hoffman, Jane (act): *Batteries Not Included; Tattoo; They Might Be Giants
Hoffman, Joel (act): Pumpkinhead
Hoffman, John (dir, b. 1905): The Lone Wolf and His Lady; Strange Confession
Hoffman, Joseph (wri, b. 1912): At Sword's Point; Charlie Chan In Shanghai; Charlie Chan's Secret; The Living Ghost (1942)
Hoffman, Leila (act): The Witches (1990)
Hoffman, Leslie (act): Avalanche
Hoffman, Linda (act): The Dentist; The Dentist II
Hoffman, Lori (act): Primal Scream
Hoffman, Lou (act): So Sad About Gloria
Hoffman, Margaret (act): Monsieur Verdoux
Hoffman Jr., Max (act): Black Dragons
Hoffman, Monty (act): Howard the Duck
Hoffman, Nancy (act): Dracula Sucks
Hoffman, Otto (act): Death Takes a Holiday (1934); Kismet (1930); Secrets of the Night; The Terror (1928)
Hoffman, Paul (act): Creature With the Atom Brain; Donovan's Brain; Voodoo Tiger
Hoffman, Philip (act): My Boyfriend's Back
Hoffman, Philip Seymour (act): Twister
Hoffman, Robert (cin): The Magician (1973)
Hoffman, Roswell (A.) (cin): The Brass Bottle (1964); The Land Unknown
Hoffman, Sharon (act): Adventures In Dinosaur City
Hoffman, Shelley (act): Final Eye
Hoffman, Susan Lee (act): Outbreak
Hoffman, Susannah (act): Millennium
Hoffman, Thom (act): The Fourth Man; Orlando
Hoffman, Thurn (act): In the Spirit
Hoffman, Todd (act): Weird Science
Hoffman, V. (act): Sonka Zolotaya Ruchka
Hoffmann, Benno (act): Das Schloss
Hoffmann, Carl/Karl (cin): Doctor Mabuse; Faust (1926); Homunculus; Der Januskopf; Die Niebelungen; Der Steinerne Reiter
Hoffmann, Cecil (act): The Bride In Black
Hoffmann, E.T.A. (wri, 1776-1822): The Nutcracker Prince; Die Puppe; Der Student von Prag (1913)
Hoffmann, Gaby (act): Freaky Friday (1995); Volcano
Hoffmann, Gloria (act): Mars Attacks!
Hoffmann, Pato (act): Meteorites!
Hoffmann, Robert (act): Assignment K; The Eyes Behind the Stars; Spasmo
Hoffmeister, John (act): Blow Out; Ganja and Hess
Hofmann, Isabella (act): The Advanced Guard; Atomic Dog
Hofschneider, Marco (act): The Island of Dr. Moreau (1996)
Hogan, Bill (cin): Strangest Dreams: Invasion of the Space Preachers
Hogan, Bosco (act): Zardoz
Hogan, Brenda (act): The Fatal Night; Saturday Island; Time Is My Enemy
Hogan, Dan (act): The Toxic Avenger
Hogan, David (dir): Barb Wire
Hogan, Heather (act): The Land Before Time III: The Time of the Great Giving; The Land Before Time IV: Journey Through the Mists
Hogan, Helen (act): Dungeons of Horror
Hogan, Hulk (act): Gremlins 2: The New Batch; Suburban Commando
Hogan, Jack (act): The Bonnie Parker Story; Houston, We've Got a Problem
Hogan, James (dir, 1894-1944): Arrest Bulldog Drummond; Bulldog Drummond Escapes; Bulldog Drummond's Bride; Bulldog Drummond's Peril; Bulldog Drummond's Secret Police; Close Call for Ellery Queen; Desperate Chance for Ellery Queen; Ellery Queen and the Murder Ring; Ellery Queen and the Perfect Crime; Ellery Queen's Penthouse Mystery; Enemy Agents Meet Ellery Queen; The Mad Ghoul; The Strange Death of Adolf Hitler
Hogan, James (wri, 1894-1944): Gypsy Wildcat
Hogan, Jason (act): Return of the Living Dead, Part II
Hogan, Mary (act): Poltergeist III
Hogan, Michael (GB act, b. 1899): The Ace of Spades; The Iron Stair (1933); The Man Outside (1933); The Pointing Finger; Puppets of Fate; The Roof; The Safe (1932); Tangled Evidence; They Came by Night
Hogan, Michael (USA act): The Intruder Within; The Peanut Butter Solution
Hogan, Michael (wri): Arabian Nights (1942); Bride of Vengeance; Dr. Syn; King Solomon's Mines (1937); The Mind of Mr. Reeder; The Passing of the Third Floor Back (1935)
Hogan, Pat (act): Sign of the Pagan
Hogan, Paul (act): Empire of Ash III
Hogan, Percy (act): War of the Planets
Hogan, Robert (act): The Memory of Eva Ryker; Westworld
Hogan, Susan (act): An American Christmas Carol; The Brood; Narrow Margin (1990); Phobia
Hogarth, Michael (act): False Evidence; The Sky Raiders
Hogel, Karel (act): Baron Prasil
Hogen, Rand (act): Surf Nazis Must Die
Hogg, Ian (act): King Lear (1971); The Legacy; Macbeth (1971)
Hogman, Jan-Ove (act): Surf Nazis Must Die
Hohimer, Garrett (act): Vice Versa (1988)
Hohl, Arthur (act, b. 1889): Bulldog Drummond Strikes Back (1934); Devil Doll (1936); The Frozen Ghost; The Hunchback of Notre Dame (1939); Island of Lost Souls; The Kennel Murder Case; One Frightened Night; The Scarlet Claw; Shadows In the Night; Spider Woman; The Thin Man Goes Home
Hohman, R.J. (cin): Radioactive Dreams
Hohn, Jean (act): Le Saint Prend l'Affut
Hoit, Michael (act): The Sword and the Sorcerer
Hojo, Makiko (act): Kwaidan
Hokanson, Mary Ann (act): Them! (1954)
Holahan, Philip (cin): Silent Night, Deadly Night 4: Initiation
Holbek, Joachim (mus): The Kingdom
Holbert, Fred (act): Scream Bloody Murder
Holbrook, David (act): A Return to Salem's Lot; Vampire's Kiss
Holbrook, Hal (act, b. 1925): Capricorn One; Creepshow; The Fog; Girl's Nite Out; Hercules (1997); Hush; Jonathan Livingston Seagull; The Kidnapping of the President; Rituals; Sorry, Wrong Number (1989); The Unholy; Wild In the Streets
Holbrook, John (cin): Shadow of the Hawk
Holcomb, Lance (act): Ghost Story (1981); Venom (1982)
Holcomb, Robert (act): Re-Animator
Holcomb, Rod (dir): Captain America (1978); Midnight Offerings
Holcomb, Scott (act): Spacecamp
Holcombe, Harry (act): The Couch; Empire of the Ants; Escape to Witch Mountain (1975); King Kong vs. Godzilla; The Monkey's Uncle; Psychic Killer; The Resurrection of Zachary Wheeler
Hold, Mary (act): The Being
Holden, Amy (dir & wri): The Rich Man's Wife
Holden, Anthony (act): The Gifted One
Holden, Arthur (act): Wild Thing
Holden, Cindy (act): The Brotherhood of Satan
Holden, Diane (act): Grave of the Vampire
Holden, Eddie (act): The Mad Monster
Holden, Fay (act, 1895-1973): Bulldog Drummond Escapes; Samson and Delilah; Whispering Smith
Holden, Gloria (act, b. 1908): The Corsican Brothers (1941); Dracula's Daughter; Miracles for Sale; Seeds of Destruction
Holden, Jack (cin): Devotion
Holden, Jan (act): Assignment Redhead; The Camp On Blood Island; Escort for Hire; The Haunted House of Horror; Links of Justice; The Primitives; The Stranglers of Bombay; A Woman Possessed; Work Is a Four Letter Word
Holden, Joyce (act): Murder Without Tears; Terror from the Year 5,000; You Never Can Tell
Holden, Katrina (act): The Uncanny
Holden, Lansing C. (dir): She (1935)
Holden, Laurie (act): Past Perfect
Holden, Marjean (act): Dr. Caligari; Nemesis; Philadelphia Experiment II; Silent Night, Deadly
Night 4: Initiation
Holden, Michael (act): Uninvited (1987)
Holden, Peter (act): Child of Darkness, Child of Light
Holden, Ruth (act): Threads
Holden, Tommy (act): Magic Spectacles
Holden, William (act, 1918-1981, nee William Franklin Beedle Jr.): Casino Royale; Damien-Omen II; The Dark Past; The Key; Paris When It Sizzles; The Remarkable Andrew; Sunset Boulevard; The Towering Inferno; When Time Ran Out
Holdenreid, Kris (act): Night of the Demons 3
Holder, Chris (act): Deadly Intruder
Holder, Geoffrey (act, b. 1930): Dr. Dolittle (1967); Ghost of a Chance (1987); Live and Let Die
Holder, Ginny (act): The Saint
Holder, Ines (act): Colossus and the Headhunters
Holder, Jack (act): The Howling: New Moon Rising
Holder, Owen (act): Lifeforce
Holder, Roy (act): The Land That Time Forgot; Psychomania (1972)
Holder, Tim (act): Sling Blade
Holding, Thomas (act): The Lone Wolf's Daughter (1919); The Three Musketeers (1921)
Holdings, Protea (cin): House of the Living Dead
Holdren, Judd (act): The Amazing Colossal Man; The Lady In the Iron Mask; Satan's Satellites; Space Master X-7; This Is My Love
Holdridge, Lee (mus): The Beastmaster; Obsessed (1992); The Pack; Splash; Star Command; Transylvania 6-5000
Holdsworth, Godfrey (act): Blind Date
Holdsworth, Rex (act): Jamaica Inn (1985)
Hole Jr., William (dir): The Devil's Hand (1961); The Ghost of Dragstrip Hollow
Holec, Jeff (act): Survival 1990
Holender, Adam (cin): The Boy Who Could Fly; Man On a Swing; Simon
Holender, Adam (dir): Twisted
Holiday, David (act): The Projectionist
Holiday, John E. (act): Witchcraft 6: The Devil's Mistress
Holiday, Lindsay (act): Nightbreed
Holiday, Talmadge (act): Glen and Randa
Holihan, Ryan (act): Addams Family Values; Ed Wood
Holin, Michael (mus): Mark of the Devil (1972)
Holister, Boyd (act): The Clonus Horror
Holl, Milo (wri): The Diabolical Invention
Holland, Agnieszka (act): Przesluchanie
Holland, Anne (act): Great Expectations (1946)
Holland, Anthony (act, 1928-1988): All That Jazz; Fearless Frank; Goldstein; Hammersmith Is Out; Oh, God! Book II
Holland, Bert (act): Tarantula
Holland, Billy/William (act): The Demon Barber of Fleet Street; The Man Without a Face; Murder at Ten; The Vandergilt Diamond Mystery; White Lilac
Holland, Buck (act): Simon, King of the Witches
Holland, Byrd (act): The Creeping Terror
Holland, Dave (act): Missing Link
Holland, Deborah (mus): Circuitry Man; Out There
Holland, Edna (act): Criss Cross; Dark Alibi; The Hunted (1948); The Sky Dragon
Holland, Erik (act): Blood Pen; Ghostbusters II; Maniac Cop; Stargate; Trader Horn (1973)
Holland, Floyd Gale (act): Copycat
Holland, Gerry (wri): Jaws of Satan
Holland, Gladys (act): Stargate
Holland, Gretchen (act): The Thirteenth Chair (1929)
Holland, Harold (act): Riches and Rogues
Holland, Hilary (act): The Man Who Fell to Earth (1976)
Holland, Jack (act): Fear No Evil (1981); Lady In White; The Lost Missile
Holland, John (act): The Girl In Black Stockings; Madman of Mandoras; My Blood Runs Cold; Phantom of Chinatown
Holland, Josh (act): Thinner

Holland, Kristina (act): Demon and the Mummy
Holland, Leslie (act): Chamber of Horrors (1929)
Holland, Mary (act): Tommy
Holland, Nathan (act): Slaughterhouse Rock
Holland, Pamela (act): Pranks
Holland, Randy (act): When a Stranger Calls
Holland, Tom (act): Psycho II
Holland, Tom (dir): Child's Play (1988); Fright Night; The Temp; Thinner
Holland, Tom (wri): The Beast Within; Child's Play (1988); Class of '84; Cloak and Dagger (1984); Fright Night; Fright Night II; Psycho II; Scream for Help; Thinner
Holland, Wim (act): Violated
Hollander, Adam (act): Halloween
Hollander, David (act): The Relic
Hollander, Frederick (mus, 1896-1976): Androcles and the Lion; Background to Danger; Berlin Express; Caught (1948); Footsteps In the Dark; Once Upon a Time (1944); The Verdict (1946)
Hollander, Owen (act): Romeo Is Bleeding
Hollar, Lloyd (act): Code Name Trixie
Holleb, Alan (dir): School Spirit
Hollenbeck, Webb Parmalee (act): see Webb, Clifton
Hollerbach, Kit (act): Batman (1989)
Holles, Antony/Anthony (act, 1901-1950): Dangerous Medicine; Forging Ahead; The Lodger (1932); Miracles Do Happen; The Missing People; The Missing Rembrandt; The Rocking Horse Winner; Seven Sinners; Sorry You've Been Troubled; The Spider (1939); The Star Reporter; Ten Days In Paris; They Drive by Night; They met In the Dark; Things to Come; Warn That Man
Holley, Bernard (act): Come Out, Come Out, Wherever You Are; The Deadly Females
Holliday, Art (act): The Man With Two Brains
Holliday, Bill (act): The Savage Bees
Holliday, Billy (act): Terror In the Swamp
Holliday, Charlie (act): Ed Wood
Holliday, David (act): Sleeping Beauty (1986)
Holliday, Don (wri): Night of the Lepus
Holliday, Kene (act): The Philadelphia Experiment
Holliday, Michael (act): Life Is a Circus
Holliday, Polly (act, b. 1937): Gremlins
Hollier, Emery (act): Cat People (1982)
Holliman, Earl (act, b. 1928, nee Anthony Numkena): East of Sumatra; Forbidden Planet; The Power (1967); Scared Stiff (1953); Secret of the Incas; Visit to a Small Planet
Hollimon, Tina (act): Cave Girl Island; Demon Knight
Hollinghead, Heather (act): Secrets of the Phantom Caverns
Hollingsworth, Harry (act): Torchy Plays With Dynamite
Hollingsworth, John (mus): The Abominable Snowman of the Himalayas; Brides of Dracula; The Man Who Could Cheat Death; The Perfect Woman; The Quatermass Experiment; The Terror of the Tongs; The Two Faces of Dr. Jekyll; X...The Unknown
Hollingsworth, Laura (act): The Pit (1983)
Hollis, Dr. (act): Making Contact
Hollis, Chris (act): Mary Shelley's 'Frankenstein'
Hollis, Glen (act): The Norsemen
Hollis, John (act): Captain Kronos: Vampire Hunter; The Empire Strikes Back; Freelance; Superman (1978); Superman II
Hollis, Suzan (act): Space Raiders
Hollis-Andrews, Sarah (act): The Man from Nowhere
Hollister, Alice (act): The Vampire (1913, USA)
Hollman, Bridget (act): Evils of the Night
Holman, Winnie (act): Eyes of Laura Mars
Holloway, Baliol (act): Under the Red Robe (1937)
Holloway, Julian (act): Sammy's Super T-Shirt
Holloway, Kamau (act): Tales from the Hood
Holloway, Merritt (act): Death Valley
Holloway, Michael (cin): The Devil's Wedding Night
Holloway, Stanley (act, 1890-1982): Hamlet (1948); Journey Into Fear (1975); The Lavender Hill Mob; Meet Mr. Lucifer; Noose; No Trees In the Street; The Perfect Woman; The Private Life of Sherlock Holmes; Target: Harry; Ten Little Indians (1965); Wanted for Murder
Holloway, Sterling (act, 1904-1992): Alakazam the Great; Alice In Wonderland (1951); The Aristocats; Bambi; The Blue Bird (1940); Dumbo; The Gift of Gab; International House; Maid of Salem; Nick Carter, Master Detective; The Three Caballeros
Holloway, W.E. (act): Elephant Boy; Member of the Jury
Holloway, William (act): Haunted Palace (1949)
Hollrah, Gary (act): Primal Scream
Holly, Ruth (act): Sherlock Jr.
Hollyday, Fred (act): Edge of the Axe
Hollyman, Tom (cin): Lord of the Flies (1963)
Hollywood, Lysle (act): see Talbot, Lyle
Holm, Arwen (act): The Final Conflict
Holm, Astrid (act): Haxan
Holm, Barnaby (act): The Final Conflict
Holm, Celeste (act, b. 1919): Champagne for Caesar; Death Cruise; Midnight Lace (1981); Murder by the Book; Once You Meet a Stranger; The Snake Pit (1948)
Holm, Claus (act): The Ape Creature; The Devil Strikes at Night; Journey to the Lost City
Holm, Eleanor (act, b. 1913): Tarzan's Revenge
Holm, (Sir) Ian (act, b. 1932): Alien; The Borrowers (1993); Brazil; Dreamchild; The Fifth Element; Greystoke: The Legend of Tarzan, Lord of the Apes; Hamlet (1990); King Lear (1998); Loch Ness; Mary Shelley's Frankenstein; Robin and Marian; The Thief of Baghdad (1978); Time Bandits
Holm, Sharon (act): Batman (1989)
Holm, Sonia (act): The Bad Lord Byron; Miranda; Radio Cab Murder; Stop Press Girl; 13 East Street
Holman, Clare (act): Afraid of the Dark
Holman, Harry (act): Doctor X; The Lone Wolf Returns (1935)
Holman, Joel (act): Nightmares (1983)
Holman, John (act): Premonition (1972)
Holman, Rex (act): Panic In Year Zero; Star Trek V: The Final Frontier
Holman, Vincent (act): The Feathered Serpent (1934); Sexton Blake and the Mademoiselle; The Sound Barrier; Special Edition
Holman, Winnie (act): Rentadick; Victims
Holmer, Robert (act): Glen and Randa
Holmes, Abbe (act): Road Games
Holmes, Allison (act): The Handmaid's Tale
Holmes, Ben (dir): The Plot Thickens; The Saint In New York
Holmes, Ben (wri): The Saint's Double Trouble
Holmes, Bertha (act): Zontar: The Thing from Venus
Holmes, Bill (mus): The Curse of the Living Corpse; The Horror of Party Beach
Holmes, Brittany Ashton (act): Inhumanoid
Holmes, Brown (wri): The Florentine Dagger; The Maltese Falcon (1931); Satan Met a Lady
Holmes, Catherine (act): Revenge of the Teenage Vixens from Outer Space
Holmes, Chris (act): The Dungeonmaster
Holmes, David (cin): Deja Vu; Sudden Terror
Holmes, Denis (act): Attempt to Kill; The Brides of Fu Manchu; The Partner; The Return of Mr. Moto
Holmes, Ed (act): Howard the Duck
Holmes, Elsie (act): Francis Joins the WACs
Holmes, Ernie (act): Fright Night
Holmes, Geoffrey (wri): Swamp Fire
Holmes, George (act, 1918-1985): Dark Alibi; The Falcon In San Francisco; The Falcon's Alibi
Holmes, Jennifer (act): The Demon (1981)
Holmes, Joe (act): Threads
Holmes, John (act): Dracula Sucks
Holmes, Katie (act): Disturbing Behavior; Killing Mrs. Tingle
Holmes, Kelda (act): An Unsuitable Job for a Woman
Holmes, Leland (act): The Bermuda Triangle
Holmes, Lois (act): Edge of Fury
Holmes, Luree (act): Dr. Goldfoot and the Bikini Machine; How to Stuff a Wild Bikini; Sergeant Deadhead the Astronut!
Holmes, Madeleine Taylor (act): Pumpkinhead
Holmes, Maynard (act): Satan Met a Lady
Holmes, Meredyth (act): Forbidden Zone: Alien Abduction
Holmes, Phillips (act, 1909-1942): Great Expectations (1934); The Secret of Madame Blanche; Ten Minute Alibi
Holmes, Robert (act): Come Into My Parlour; The Rosary
Holmes, Robert (wri): Invasion (1965)
Holmes, Stuart (act, 1884-1971): Daughter of the Gods; Devil's Island; The Man Who Laughs (1928); The Prisoner of Zenda (1922); Satan Met a Lady; The Scarlet Letter (1917); The She-Creature; Torchy Runs for Mayor
Holmes, Taylor (act, 1872-1959): Beware, My Lovely; Nightmare Alley; Sleeping Beauty (1959); Tobor the Great; Woman In Hiding
Holmes, Tracy (act): The Ghost Train (1931); Jury's Evidence
Holmes-Gore, Arthur (act): The Black Spot; His Reformation; The King's Minister; The Prisoner of Zenda (1915); The Ring and the Rajah
Holms, Livingston (act): Prophecy (1979)
Holness, Bob (act): One Deadly Owner
Holohan, Dennis (act): The Fifth Missile
Holosko, John (cin): Giving Up the Ghost
Holotik, Rosie (act): Don't Look In the Basement; Encounter With the Unknown; Horror High
Holoubek, Gustaw (act): Rekopis Znaleziony w Saragossie
Holroyd, Chris (act): Give Us Tomorrow
Holscher, Heinz (cin): Dracula Blows His Cool
Holst (mus): The Birth of the Robot
Holt, Bob (act): Abby; The Nine Lives of Fritz the Cat; Wizards
Holt, Charlene (act, b. 1939): Wonder Woman
Holt, David (1930s act): The Last Days of Pompeii (1935)
Holt, David (1970s act): Grizzly
Holt, Eunice (act): The Fish Men
Holt, Hans (act): Embezzled Heaven
Holt, Henry (wri): The Spider (1939)
Holt, Jack (act, 1888-1951): Behind the Mask; The Best Man Wins; Cat People (1942); The Chase; Dirigible; Flight to Nowhere; The Lone Wolf (1924)
Holt, Jany (act): Le Golem (1936); The Green Glove
Holt, Jim (act): The Time Guardian
Holt, Joel (act): Karate, the Hand of Death
Holt, Larry (act): The Prisoner of Zenda (1979)
Holt, Lester (D.) (act): The Fugitive (1993); Primal Fear
Holt, Marie (act): see Burke, Marie
Holt, Mette (act): The Whispering
Holt, Nick (act): Invasion from Inner Earth
Holt, Patrick (act, b. 1912): Alias John Preston; Circumstantial Evidence (1952); Diamonds On Wheels; Fortune Is a Woman; The Frightened City; The Gelignite Gang; Girl In the Headlines; The Golden Link; Guilt Is My Shadow; Hammerhead; Legend of the Werewolf; The Magic Christian; The Mark of Cain; Men of Sherwood Forest; Murderers' Row; Murder Reported; Night of the Prowler; No Blade of Grass; The October Man; Operation Murder; Portrait from Life; Psychomania (1972); Serena; Stolen Assignment; The Stranger Came Home; Suspended 13 Alibi; 13 East Street; Thunderball; Too Hot to Handle; The Vulture (1966); When Dinosaurs Ruled the Earth
Holt, Paul (wri): The Bad Lord Byron
Holt, Penelope (act): Blood from the Mummy's Tomb
Holt, Robert (act): Bedknobs and Broomsticks; Charlotte's Web; Explorers
Holt, Robert (wri): Rampage
Holt, Sandy (mus): The Monitors
Holt, Seth (dir, 1923-1971): Blood from the Mummy's Tomb; Danger Route; The Nanny; Nowhere to Go; Station Six-Sahara; A Taste of Fear
Holt, Seth (wri, 1923-1971): Nowhere to Go
Holt, Tim (act, 1918-1973): Hitler's Children; The Monster That Challenged the World; The Yesterday Machine
Holt, Ula (act): Tarzan and the Green Goddess; Tarzan's New Adventure
Holter, Chris (act): Westworld
Holton, Bo (mus): The Element of Crime
Holton, Leonard (wri): see Wibberley, Leonard
Holton, Mark (act): Leprechaun; Teen Wolf; Teen Wolf Too
Holton, Nigel (mus): Carnosaur; Naked Souls
Holton, Sean (act): Blood Diner
Holtz, Gary (act): Death Curse of Tartu
Holtz Jr., Lou (wri): The Cable Guy
Holtz, Tenen (act): The House of Horror (1929)
Holtzmann, Thomas (act): Funeral In Berlin
Holub, Diane Clayre (act): Zombie Island Massacre
Holubar, Allen (act): 20,000 Leagues Under the Sea (1916, USA)
Holvoe, Maria (act): Willow
Holyfield, Evander (act): Blood Salvage
Holzbog, Arabella (act): Carnosaur 2
Holzboer, Max (act): Das Blaue Licht
Holzer, Hans (wri): The Amityville Curse; Amityville II: The Possession
Holzer, Ivy (act): L'Ultima Preda del Vampiro
Holzman, Allan (dir): Forbidden World; Programmed to Kill
Holzman, Annyce (act): Re-Animator
Holzman, Catherine (act): see Carlisle, Kitty
Holzman, Daniel (act): It's Alive (1974)
Holzmann, Patty (act): The Capture of Bigfoot
[illegible] The Scarlet Clue; The Thin Man
Homb, David (act): The Channeler
Home, William Douglas (wri): For Them That Trespass; Sleeping Car to Trieste; Your Witness
Homeier, Skip (act, b. 1930): Black Widow (1954); The Ghost and Mr. Chicken; No Road Back; Stark Fear
Homel, Bob (act & wri): The Boy Who Cried Werewolf
Homer (wri, c. 800 B.C.?): The Adventures of Ulysses; L'Ile de Calypso: Ulysse et Polypheme; The Odyssey; Ulysses
Homer, Mark (wri): Free Fall; Sharon's Secret
Homolka, Oscar (act, 1898-1978): Assignment to Kill; Billion Dollar Brain; The Executioner; Funeral In Berlin; The House of the Arrow (1953); The Invisible Woman (1941); The Key; Mr. Sardonicus; Rage In Heaven; Sabotage; Schuss im Morgengrauen; The Shop at Sly Corner; Top Secret (1952); The Wonderful World of the Brothers Grimm
Homrich, Junior (mus): Ghosts Can't Do It
Homsher, Tom (cin): Gremlins 2: The New Batch
Homyak, Louis (act): Flesh-Eating Mothers
Honce, Mimi (act): Scalpel
Honda, Inoshiro/Ishiro (dir, 1912-1993): Atragon; Battle In Outer Space; Destroy All Monsters; Dogora, the Space Monster; Frankenstein vs. the Giant Devil Fish; Ghidrah, the Three-Headed Monster; Godzilla's Revenge; Godzilla vs. Mothra; Gojira; Gorath; Half-Human; The H-Man; The Human Vapor; King Kong Escapes; King Kong vs. Godzilla; Latitude Zero; Matango; Monster Zero; Mothra; The Mysterians; Rodan, the Flying Monster; The Terror of Godzilla; Terror of Mechagodzilla; The War of the Gargantuas; Yog-Monster from Space
Honda, Inoshiro (wri, 1912-1993): Destroy All Monsters; Gojira; The War of the Gargantuas
Hone, Emily (act): Evil Under the Sun
Honegger, Arthur (mus): Crime and Punishment (1935, USA); Storm Over Tibet
Hones, Samantha (act): Mary Reilly
Honeycombe, Gordon (act): The Medusa Touch
Honeycombe, Gordon (wri): Neither the Sea Nor the Sand
Honeywell, Roger (act): Escape Clause
Hong, Alison (act): Charlie Chan and the Curse of the Dragon Queen; Jekyll and Hyde...Together Again
Hong, James (act): Big Trouble In Little China; Black Widow (1987); Blade Runner; Colossus: The Forbin Project; Destination Inner Space; Dr. Scorpion; The Golden Child; The Jitters; Judge Dee and the Monastery Murder; Merlin (1993); One Spy Too Many; The Satan Bug; The Shadow (1994); Shadowzone; Vice Versa (1988); The Vineyard
Hong, James (dir): The Vineyard
Hong, Pearl (act): Charlie Chan: Happiness Is a Warm Clue
Hongo, Kojiro (act): Buddha; Gammera vs. Barugon; Gammera vs. Gyaos; Gammeras vs. Viras; The Return of the Giant Majin; Return of the Giant Monsters
Honig, Peter (act): Blood Diner
Honnold, Nancy (act): The Mad Bomber
Honore, Andree (act): The Slumber Party Massacre
Honour, Tony (act): Spaceflight IC-1
Honthaner, Ron (dir): The House On Skull Mountain The Crimson Circle (1922); The Ghost of Frankenstein; The Girl Who Came Back; House of Frankenstein; The Lodger (1944); The Lone Wolf In Paris; The Lone Wolf Returns (1935); The Notorious Lone Wolf; The Shanghai Chest; Sherlock Holmes and the Voice of Terror; Sherlock Holmes Faces Death; The Spanish Cape Mystery; The Stockbroker's Clerk; Trapped by the Mormons; Trouble for Two
Hoo, Jeff Soo (act): The Golden Child
Hoobler, John (act): Twin Peaks: Fire Walk With Me
Hood, Darla (act, 1931-1979): The Bat (1959)
Hood, Don (act): Alien Nation; Cat People (1982); Dean Koontz' 'Mr. Murder'; Ed Wood; Obsession (1976); The Savage Bees
Hood, Morag (act): Wuthering Heights (1970)
Hood, Noel (act): The Curse of Frankenstein; How to Murder a Rich Uncle
Hood, Thomas (wri): Circumstances Unknown
Hook, Harry (dir): Lord of the Flies (1990)
Hook, Trevor (act): Charlie Chan and the Curse of the Dragon Queen
Hooke, Nina Warner (wri): Deadly Record
Hooker, Buddy Joe (act): The Arrival (1996); The Entity
Hooker, Kathy (act): Neon Maniacs
Hooker, Ken (act): Dark Intruder
Hooker, Lois (act): see Maxwell, Lois

Hooker, Ted (dir & wri): *Crucible of Terror*
Hooks, David (act): *The Clonus Horror; Dr. Strange; V; Vampire (1979)*
Hooks, Ed (act): *Heart and Souls*
Hooks, Jan (act, b. 1957): *Batman Returns; Coneheads*
Hooks, Robert (act, b. 1937): *Crosscurrent; The Flash; Star Trek III: The Search for Spock*
Hool, Brett (act): *Steel Dawn*
Hool, Lance (dir): *Steel Dawn*
Hoole, Michael (act): *Psycho Girls*
Hooper, Ewan (act): *Dracula Has Risen from the Grave*
Hooper, Geoffrey (act): *No Blade of Grass*
Hooper, Joy (act): *Angel Heart*
Hooper, Kaitlin (act): *Addams Family Values*
Hooper, Kristen (act): *Addams Family Values*
Hooper, Peter (act): *Deathsport*
Hooper, Tim (act): *Jamaica Inn (1985)*
Hooper, Tobe (act): *Body Bags*
Hooper, Tobe (dir): *Body Bags; Eaten Alive! (1976); The Funhouse (1981); I'm Dangerous Tonight; Invaders from Mars (1986); Lifeforce; The Mangler; Poltergeist; Salem's Lot; Spontaneius Combustion; The Texas Chainsaw Massacre; The Texas Chainsaw Massacre 2*
Hooper, Tobe (mus): *The Texas Chainsaw Massacre; The Texas Chainsaw Massacre 2*
Hooper, Tobe (wri): *Leatherface: Texas Chainsaw Massacre III; The Texas Chainsaw Massacre*
Hoopes, Melanie (act): *Twister*
Hooten, Peter (act): *Dr. Strange; 2020 Texas Gladiators*
Hootkins, William (act): *American Gothic; Batman (1989); Death Machine; Dreamchild; Dust Devil; Flash Gordon (1980); Hardware; The Island of Dr. Moreau (1996); Like Father, Like Santa; Raiders of the Lost Ark; The Return of Sherlock Holmes (1986); Sphinx (1981)*
Hoover, Elva May (act): *Superman II*
Hoover, Joseph (act): *Astro Zombies*
Hoover, Michael (act): *The Crater Lake Monster*
Hoover, Mike (cin): *Equinox*
Hoover, Phil (act): *Race With the Devil; The Thing With Two Heads*
Hopcraft, Arthur (wri): *Agatha*
Hope, Anna (act): *Bowery at Midnight*
Hope, Anthony (wri, 1863-1933): *The Prisoner of Zenda (1914, 1915, 1922, 1937, 1952 & 1979); Prisoner of Zenda, Inc., Rupert of Hentzau (1915 & 1923)*
Hope, Bob (act, b. 1903, nee Leslie Townes Hope): *Call Me Bwana; Casanova's Big Night; The Cat and the Canary (1939); The Ghost Breakers; The Muppet Movie; The Road to Bali; The Road to Hong Kong; The Road to Utopia; Scared Stiff (1953)*
Hope, Courtney (act): *The Man In Black*
Hope Deborra (act): *The Resurrected*
Hope, Erica (act): *Graduation Day*
Hope, Gary/Garry (GB act): *Clegg; Licensed to Love and Kill*
Hope, Gary (USA act): *Romeo Is Bleeding*
Hope, Harry (dir): *Doomsday Machine*
Hope, Leslie (act): *The Conspiracy of Fear; Fun; Doppelganger: The Evil Within*
Hope, Leslie Townes (act): see Hope, Bob
Hope, Margo (act): *Brain of Blood*
Hope, Margot (act): *Virtuosity*
Hope, Vida (act, 1918-1962): *Double Confession; Family Doctor; For Them That Trespass; The Interrupted Journey; The Man In the White Suit; The Mark of Cain; They Made Me a Fugitive; Vice Versa (1947); The Woman In Question*
Hope, William (act): *Aliens; Hellbound: Hellraiser II; The Saint*
Hopgood, Alan (act): *Road Games*
Hopgood, Alan (wri): *The Man Who Saw Tomorrow*
Hopkins, Albert (dir): *Faust (1936)*
Hopkins, Anthony (act, b. 1937): *Audrey Rose; Bram Stoker's Dracula; The Edge; Freejack; Hamlet (1969); The Hunchback of Notre Dame (1982); Instinct; Magic; The Mask of Zorro (1998); Meet Joe Black; The Silence of the Lambs*
Hopkins, Antony (mus): *The Angel Who Pawned Her Harp*
Hopkins, Art (mus): *Capture That Capsule!*
Hopkins, Bo (act, b. 1942): *Fertilize the Blaspheming Bombshell!; Fever Lake; The Fifth Floor; Mutant; Nightmare at Noon; The Plutonium Incident; Sweet Sixteen; Tentacles; Uncle Sam*
Hopkins, Frances (act): *Just Imagine*
Hopkins, Glen (act): *Bog*
Hopkins, Jack (act): *Life Without Soul*
Hopkins, Jeff (act): *Stalking Laura*
Hopkins, Joan (act): *Double Confession; Man On the Run*
Hopkins, John (dir): *Torment (1986)*
Hopkins, John (GB wri): *Murder by Decree; The Offence; Thunderball*
Hopkins, John (USA wri): *The Power (1980); Torment (1986)*
Hopkins, Katherine (act): *The Capture of Bigfoot*
Hopkins, Kenyon (mus): *The Fugitive Kind; Lilith*
Hopkins, Linda (act): *Leprechaun 2*
Hopkins, Mark (act): *Return to Oz*
Hopkins, Mary (act): *Nightbeast*
Hopkins, Miriam (act, 1902-1972): *Dr. Jekyll and Mr. Hyde (1932)*
Hopkins, Pat (act & mus): *Bog*
Hopkins, Randle (act): *I Was a Zombie for the F.B.I.*
Hopkins, Rhonda Leigh (act): *The Submersion of Japan*
Hopkins, Stephen (dir): *The Ghost and the Darkness; Lost In Space; Nightmare On Elm Street 5: The Dream Child; Predator 2*
Hopkins, Telma (act, b. 1948): *The Kid With the Broken Halo; Trancers; Trancers II: The Return of Jack Deth; Trancers III: Deth Lives*
Hopkins, Tony (act): *The Frighteners*
Hopkirk, Gordon (act): *Faust (1922); Jane Shore (1922)*
Hopman, Gerald (wri): *The Devil's Rain*
Hoppe, Eliana (act): *Demons 2*
Hoppe, Marianne (act): *The Strange Countess; Ten Little Indians (1965)*
Hoppe, Ralf (act): *Three Nuts for Cinderella*
Hopper, Dennis (act, b. 1936): *Black Widow (1987); Eye of the Storm; Blue Velvet; The Heart of Justice; My Science Project; Night Tide; Panic In the City; Queen of Blood; Riders of the Storm; The Story of Mankind; Super Mario Bros.; The Texas Chainsaw Massacre 2; The Trip; Waterworld; Witch Hunt*
Hopper, DeWolf (act, 1858-1935): *Calling Philo Vance; The Return of Dr. X*
Hopper, E. Mason (dir): *Boston Blackie's Little Pal; Held for Murder*
Hopper, Hedda (act, 1890-1966, nee Elda Furry): *As You Desire Me; The Dark Hour; Don Juan (1927); Dracula's Daughter; Murder Will Out (1930); One Frightened Night; Seven Keys to Baldpate (1917); Sherlock Holmes (1922); Such Men Are Dangerous; Sunset Boulevard; Tarzan's Revenge; Topper (1937)*
Hopper, Jerry (dir, b. 1907): *The Atomic City; Naked Alibi; Secret of the Incas*
Hopper, Stephen (act): *The Devil's Wedding Night*
Hopper, Susan (act): *The Good Son*
Hopper, Victoria (act): *Escape from Broadmoor (1948); Lorna Doone (1934)*
Hopper, William (act, 1915-1970): *The Adventurous Blonde; The Bad Seed (1956); Conquest of Space; The Deadly Mantis; The Maltese Falcon (1941); Myra Breckinridge; Nancy Drew and the Hidden Staircase; This Is My Love; Track of the Cat; 20 Million Miles to Earth*
Hopson, Lew (act): *The Hidden*
Hopson, Violet (act): *The American Heiress; Behind the Curtain; Be Sure Your Sins; The Bridge Destroyer; The Case of Lady Camber; The Chimes; The Cobweb; The Cry of the Captive; The Grand Babylon Hotel; The House Opposite (1917); The Hunchback (1914); The Jewel Thieves Outwitted; The Kleptomaniac; The Man Who Stayed at Home; A Moment of Darkness; The Nightbirds of London; The Quarry Mystery; The Schemers: or, The Jewels of Hate; The Stress of Circumstance; The Terror of the Air; The Tragedy of Basil Grieve; The Unseen Witness; The Ware Case*
Hopton, Russell (act): *Death from a Distance; The Saint Strikes Back; Zombies On Broadway*
Hopwood, Avery (wri, 1882-1928): *The Bat (1926 & 1959); The Bat Whispers*
Hora, John (act): *Innerspace*
Hora, John (cin): *Explorers; Gremlins; Gremlins 2: The New Batch; The Howling; Matinee*
Horan, Gerard (act): *Mary Shelley's 'Frankenstein'*
Horan, Hillary (act): *The Munsters' Revenge; Satan's Cheerleaders*
Horan, Kathy (act): *The Green Slime*
Hordern, (Sir) Michael (act, 1911-1995): *Alice's Adventures In Wonderland (1972); The Bed-Sitting Room; Demons of the Mind; Dr. Syn-Alias the Scarecrow; Freddie as F.R.0.7; Grand National Night; Highly Dangerous; The Hour of 13; I Accuse (1958); Man In the Moon (1960); The Medusa Touch; Moment of Danger; The Pied Piper (1971); The Possession of Joel Delaney; Royal Flash; Scrooge (1951); The Slipper and the Rose; The Spaniard's Curse; The Spanish Gardener; The Spy Who Came In from the Cold; The Story of Robin Hood; Suspicion (1987); Theater of Blood; Watership Down; The Zany Adventures of Robin Hood*
Horelick, Stephen (mus): *Madman*
Hori, Shinji (act): *The Return of Giant Majin*
Horinne, Marianne (act): *Ewoks: The Battle for Endor*
Horino, Tad (act): *Dimension 5; Galaxina; Red Sonja; Remote Control (1988)*
Horlan, Cathy (act): *Body Snatcher from Hell*
Horler, Sydney (wri): *The House of Secrets (1929)*
Horman, Arthur T. (wri): *The Lone Wolf In Paris*
Hormann, Nicholas (act): *The Hand (1981); The Incredible Shrinking Woman; It Came Upon the Midnight Clear; The Trial of the Incredible Hulk*
Hormel, Gregory "Smokey" (act): *Twin Peaks: Fire Walk With Me*
Horn, Camilla (act, b. 1907): *Faust (1926); Matinee Idol*
Horn, Holloway (wri): *Eyes of Fate*
Horn, Kirby Grant (act): see Grant, Kirby
Horn, Lanny (act): *Tarantulas: The Deadly Cargo*
Horn, Lanny (wri): *Skeeter*
Horn, Leonard (dir): *The New, Original Wonder Woman*
Horn, Lew (act): *Dick Tracy (1990); I'm Dangerous Tonight; It Came Upon the Midnight Clear; Time Flyer*
Horn, Ruth (act): *Invasion of the Girl Snatchers*
Horna, Alfonso (act): *El Otro Fu Manchu*
Horna, Mario (act): *No Exit*
Hornack, Lucy (act): *The Cold Room*
Hornby, Lesley (act): see Twiggy
Horne, Andrew (act): *Lord of the Flies (1963)*
Horne, Criss (act): *The Fugitive (1993)*
Horne, Carl (act): *Slavegirls from Beyond Infinity*
Horne, David (act, b. 1898): *The Clue of the New Pin (1961); Crimes at the Dark House; The Door With Seven Locks (1940); Gestapo;The Last Man to Hang?; Seven Sinners; Spaceways; Three Cases of Murder*
Horne, Geoffrey (act): *The Corsican Brothers (1960)*
Horne, James W. (dir, 1880-1942): *Laughing at Danger*
Horne, Kenneth (wri): *A Lady Mislaid; The Spider (1939)*
Horne, Lena (act, b. 1917): *Cabin In the Sky; The Wiz*
Horne, Victoria (act, b. 1920): *Abbott and Costello Meet the Killer; The Ghost and Mrs. Muir; Harvey; Pillow of Death; The Scarlet Claw; The Snake Pit (1948)*
Horneff, Wil (act): *Ghost In the Machine*
Horner, Caroline (act): *Holocaust 2000*
Horner, Harry (dir, b. 1910): *Beware, My Lovely; Red Planet Mars; Vicki*
Horner, James (mus, b. 1953): *Aliens; An American Tail; Apollo 13; *Batteries Not Included; Battle Beyond the Stars (1980); Brainstorm Casper; Cocoon; Cocoon: The Return; Deadly Blessing; The Hand (1981); Honey, I Shrunk the Kids; Humanoids from the Deep; Jumanji; Krull; The Land Before Time; The Mask of Zorro (1998); Mighty Joe Young (1998); The Name of the Rose; The Pagemaster; The Rocketeer; Something Wicked This Way Comes; Space Raiders; Star Trek II: The Wrath of Khan; Star Trek III: The Search for Spock; To Gillian On Her 37th Birthday; Vibes; We're Back! A Dinosaur's Story; Willow; Wizards of the Lost Kingdom; Wolfen*
Horner, John (act): *Rocket Attack U.S.A.*
Horner, Lottie (wri): *The Man from Downing Street*
Horner, Penelope (act): *The Devil's Daffodil; Dracula (1973); Holocaust 2000; Locker 69*
Horner, Yvonne (act): *One Million Years B.C.; Prehistoric Women (1966)*
Hornery, Bob (act): *Mad Max Beyond Thunderdome*
Horney, Brigitte (act, b. 1911): *Die Avonturen von Baron Munchhausen; Secret Lives, The Trygon Factor*
Horniak, Maia (act): *Howling III*
Horniman, Roy (wri): *Kind Hearts and Coronets*
Hornish, Krista (act): *High Spirits*
Horntraeger, Justin (act): *Kids of the Round Table*
Horoks, Zbigniew (act): *Docteur Petiot*
Horovitch, David (act): *An Unsuitable Job for a Woman*
Horovitz, Adam (act): *A Kiss Before Dying (1991)*
Horowitz, Anthony (wri): *Just Ask for Diamond*
Horowitz, Morris (act): see Howard, Moe
Horowitz, Samuel (act): see Howard, Shemp
Horowitz, Steve (act): *Buddha's Lock*
Horowitzo, Stefano (act): *Ladyhawke*
Horrall, Craig (wri): *Deranged (1987)*
Horrigan, Jack (wri): *Twisted*
Horrigan, William/Bill (act): *The Fifth Musketeer; The Ivory Ape*
Horrocks, Jane (act): *Deadly Advice; The Witches (1990)*
Horrocks, Peter (act): see Reynolds, Peter
Horruzey, Paul (act): *Bay Coven*
Horsborough, Walter (act): *The Abominable Dr. Phibes; 23 Paces to Baker Street*
Horsburgh, Mike (act): *A Choice of Weapons*
Horse, Michael (act): *Deadly Weapon; The Legend of the Lone Ranger*
Horsey, Lonnie (act): *Serial Mom*
Horsey, Martin (act): *The President's Analyst*
Horsfall, Bernard (act): *A Distant Scream; Man In the Moon (1960); Mr. Horatio Knibbles; On Her Majesty's Secret Service; Quest for Love*
Horsford, Anna Maria (act): *The Fan*
Horsley, David (S.) (cin, b. 1906): *Abbott and Costello Go to Mars; Abbott and Costello Meet Dr. Jekyll and Mr. Hyde; Abbott and Costello Meet Frankenstein; Abbott and Costello Meet the Invisible Man; Abbott and Costello Meet the Killer; Buccaneer's Girl; Criss Cross; It Came from Outer Space; Jack the Giant Killer; Spy Hunt; The Time of Their Lives; You Never Can Tell*
Horsley, John (act): *Barbados Quest; Bond of Fear; Breakaway; Deadly Nightshade; Double Exposure (1954); The Frightened Man; Little Red Monkey; Man In the Shadow; The Material Witness; Meet Mr. Malcolm; Night of the Prowler; Panic (1963); Recoil (1953); Return to Sender; Serena; Stranger In Town (1957); Time Bomb; The Weapon; Wrong Number*
Horsley, Lee (act, b. 1955): *The Sword and the Sorcerer; Thirteen at Dinner*
Horsley, Michael (act): *Mind Over Murder*
Horsley, Stanley (cin): *This Island Earth*
Horton, Edward Everett (act, 1887-1970): *Alice In Wonderland (1933); Arsenic and Old Lace; The Body Disappears; Down to Earth; The Ghost Goes Wild; Here Comes Mr. Jordan; I Married an Angel; Lost Horizon (1937); The Man In the Mirror; The Perils of Pauline; The Story of Mankind; The Terror (1928); 2000 Years Later*
Horton, Helen (act): *Alien; Endless Night; The Last Shot You Hear; Phase IV; Superman III*
Horton, Jamie (act): *Wavelength*
Horton, John (act): *Thinner*
Horton, Juanita (act): see Love, Bessie
Horton, Louisa (act): *Alice, Sweet Alice*
Horton, Peter (act): *Children of the Corn; Death Benefit; Fade to Black; Death Benefit; She's Dressed to Kill*
Horton, Peter (dir): *Amazon Women On the Moon*
Horton, Red (act): *Monolith*
Horton, Robert (GB act): *Inside the Room; Silver Blaze (1937); Sorry You've Been Troubled; When Knights Were Bold (1936)*
Horton, Robert (USA act, b. 1924): *The Green Slime*
Horvath, Charles (act, 1921-1978): *Confessions of an Opium Eater; Francis In the Haunted House; The Thing That Couldn't Die; Voodoo Tiger*
Horvath, Emil (act): *Na Komete*
Horvath, Lou (act): *The Island of Dr. Moreau (1996)*
Horvath, Louis (cin): *Blood of Ghastly Horror; Brain of Blood; Strange Behavior; Strange Invaders*
Horvitz, Richard (act): *The Adventures of Galgameth*
Hose, Tushka (act): *Mad Max Beyond Thunderdome*
Hosea, Bobby (act): *Gargantua; Jack's Back; Mantis; Nightscream*
Hoselton, David (wri): *Clarence; First Knight*
Hoshelle, Marjorie (act): *Blonde for a Day; Cloak and Dagger (1946); The Mask of Dimitrios; The Red Dragon (1945); The Strange Mr. Gregory*
Hoshi, Shizuko (act): *Fer-de-Lance*
Hoshi, Yuriko (act): *Ghidrah, the Three-Headed Monster; Godzilla vs. Mothra*
Hosking, Craig (act): *Darkman (1990)*
Hoskins, Basil (act): *Edge of Sanity*
Hoskins, Bob (act, b. 1942): *Brazil; Heart Condition; Michael; The Secret Agent (1996); Super Mario Bros.; Who Framed Roger Rabbit*

Hoskins, Dan (dir & wri): Chopper Chicks In Zombietown
Hoskins, Percy (wri): The Blue Parrot; Burnt Evidence; The Hand of Fate; The Laughing Girl Murder
Hosoda, Tamiyo (cin): Fist of the North Star
Hosokawa, Masayoshi (act): The Toxic Avenger, Part II
Hossack, Allison (act): White Light
Hossein, Robert (act, b. 1927): The Burglars; Crime and Punishment (1958); The Double Agents; I Killed Rasputin; Shadow of Evil (1964); Le Vampire de Dusseldorf; Le Vice et la Vertu
Hossein, Robert (dir, b. 1927): I Killed Rasputin; La Nuit des Espions; Le Vampire de Dusseldorf
Hossein, Robert (wri, b. 1927): La Nuit des Espions; Le Vampire de Dusseldorf
Hossner, Eve (act): The Devil's Messenger
Host, Agnes (act): The Tragedy of Carmen
Hostetler, Barry (act): The Worm Eaters
Hostetter, Iris Adrian (act): see Adrian, Iris
Hostetter, John (act): The People Under the Stairs; The Stepford Children
Hotaru, Yukihiro (act): Zeram
Hotchkis, John (mus): The Corpse
Hotchkiss, Lt. E.H. (act): Lieutenant Daring and the Plans of the Minefields
Hoth, George (act): The Tomb
Hotta, Yoshie (wri): Mothra
Hotton, Donald (act): Brainstorm (1983); Calendar Girl Murders; The China Syndrome; Deadly Lessons; Freeway Maniac; The Hearse; Invaders from Mars (1986); Nightwing; One Dark Night
Houck, Byron (cin): Sherlock Jr.
Houck, Doris (act): A Close Call for Boston Blackie; Shadowed
Houck, J.N. (act): The Hidden
Houck Jr., Joy N. (dir): Creature from Black Wing; Mind Warp (1972); Night of Bloody Horror; Women and Bloody Terror
Houde, Germain (act): A Scream from Silence
Houde, Joe (act): The Bermuda Triangle
Houde, Serge (act): Empire of Ash III; Midnight In Saint Petersburg; The Resurrected
Houdini, Genie (act): Killer Klowns from Outer Space
Houdini, Harry (act, 1874-1926, nee Ehrich Weiss): The Man from Beyond; Terror Island
Houdini, Harry (wri, 1874-1926): The Man from Beyond
Hough, John (dir, b. 1941): American Gothic; Biggles: Adventures In Time; A Distant Scream; The Dying Truth; Escape to Witch Mountain (1975); Eyewitness (1970); A Ghost In Monte Carlo; Howling IV; Incubus (1982); The Legend of Hell House; Return from Witch Mountain; Sudden Terror; Treasure Island (1971); Twins of Evil; The Watcher In the Woods
Hough, Julian (act): The Shout
Houghston, Walter (act): see Huston, Walter
Houghton, Barrie/Barry (act): Blind Terror; Inseminoid
Houghton, Don (wri): Call Him Mr. Shatter; Dracula A.D. 1972; Legend of the Seven Golden Vampires; The Satanic Rites of Dracula
Houghton, Harold (act): The Adventures of Dick Turpin-The King of Highwaymen
Houghton, Jack (act): The Adventures of Dick Turpin-The Gunpowder Plot; Robin Hood Outlawed
Houghton, James (act): Purple People Eater; Superstition
Houghton, Katharine (act, b. 1945): Seeds of Evil
Houghton, Margaret (wri): The Vandergilt Diamond Mystery
Houghton, Mark (act): Mission: Impossible
Houlihan, Carolyn (act): The Burning
Hourani, Gary (act): The Outing
Houry, Henri (act): The Bloodstained Shoe
House, Ashley (act): The Seven-Per-Cent Solution
House, Billy (act): Bedlam; Inner Sanctum (1949); Rogues of Sherwood Forest; Where Danger Lives
House, Dale (E.) (act): Night of the Comet; Wavelength
House, Eric (act): Oedipus Rex (1956)
House, Gerry (act): The Cradle Will Fall
House, Jane (act): Werewolf of Washington
House, Joey (act): The Last Man On Planet Earth
House, Ron (act): Modern Problems
Household, Geoffrey (wri): Dance of the Dwarfs
Housely, James (act): Redneck Zombies
Houseman, Arthur (act): The Bat (1926)
Houseman, John (act, b. 1902): The Babysitter; Bells (1983); The Fog; Ghost Story (1981); Rollerball; Scrooged; Seven Days In May; 3 Days of the Condor
Houseman, Laurence (wri): Consider Your Verdict
Houser, Christie (act): Joe & the Colonel
Houser, Jerry (act, b. 1952): Magic
Houser, Lionel (wri): The Lone Wolf Returns (1935)
Houser, Patrick (act): Endangered Species
Houston, Anthony (act): Mars Needs Women; Zontar: The Thing from Venus
Houston, Bob (act): Strange Behavior
Houston, Barbara (act): Stalking Laura
Houston, Charles (act): The Devil-Ship Pirates; Hell Is a City; The Man Upstairs; Panic (1963); The Scarlet Blade
Houston, Charles E. (act): The Bermuda Triangle
Houston, Danny (act): The Human Factor
Houston, Donald (act, b. 1923): Clash of the Titans; Crow Hollow; Find the Lady; The Flaw (1955); The Large Rope; Maniac (1963); The Man Upstairs; The Mark; A Study In Terror; The Surgeon's Knife; Tales That Witness Madness; The Viking Queen
Houston, Gary (act): Fargo
Houston, Glyn (act, b. 1926): The Brigand of Kandahar; Invasion (1965); Mix Me a Person; Panic (1963); The Secret of Blood Island; Solo for Sparrow; Turn the Key Softly; The Wind of Change
Houston, James (act): Powder
Houston, Karen (act): The Return of Count Yorga
Houston, Norman (wri): A Game of Death
Houston, Renee (act, b. 1902, nee Katherina Houston Gribbin): Carry On Spying; Come Into My Parlour; Cul-de-Sac; The Flesh and the Fiends; Legend of the Werewolf; Out of the Fog (1962); The Phantom of the Opera (1962); Repulsion; Time Without Pity; Tomorrow at Ten; Track the Man Down
Houston, Robert (act): The Hills Have Eyes; The Hills Have Eyes II
Houston, Tony (act & wri): Curse of the Swamp Creature
Houston, Whitney (act): Cinderella (1997); The Preacher's Wife
Houston, William (act): The Odyssey
Houston-Jones, Ishmael (act): The Brother from Another Planet
Houtchens, Pat (act): Soylent Green
Hovanes, Cecily (act): Ravagers
Hovanessian, Ara (act): Virus (1980)
Hove, Anders (act): Bloodlust: Subspecies III; Bloodstone: Subspecies II; Critters 4; Subspecies; Subspecies 4: Bloodstorm
Hoven, Adrian (act): The Black Cobra; Cave of the Living Dead; I Aim at the Stars; Kiss Me, Monster; Necronomicon; Sadist Erotica; Secret of the Red Orchid
Hoven, Adrian (dir & wri): Mark of the Devil II
Hovey, Helen (act): The Sadist
Hovey, Natasha (act): Demons (1985)
Hovey, Tim (act, b. 1945):Queen Bee
Hovick, Rose Louise (act & wri): see Lee, Gypsy Rose
Howard, Adrienne (act): Too Scared to Scream
Howard, Alan (act): Work Is a Four Letter Word
Howard, Andrea (act): The Nude Bomb
Howard, Ann (act): Peter Rabbit and the Tales of Beatrix Potter
Howard, Anne (GB act): Great Expectations (1934); Night Comes Too Soon
Howard, Anne (USA act): Prince of Darkness
Howard, Arliss (act, b. 1955): The Lost World: Jurassic Park; Wilder Napalm
Howard, Art (act): The Clutching Hand
Howard, Arthur (act): Cage of Gold; Footsteps In the Fog; Full Circle; The Glass Tomb; I Accuse (1958); Kill or Cure; Moonraker; Never Look Back; Nowhere to Go; One of Our Dinosaurs Is Missing; One Way Out; One Wish Too Many; Paradisio; The Prisoner of Zenda (1979)
Howard, Augustus (act): see McNaughton, Gus
Howard, Barbara (act): Friday the 13th-The Final Chapter
Howard, Ben (act): The Land That Time Forgot; The Sex Victims; Zeppelin
Howard, Bert (act): The Clutching Hand
Howard, Boothe (act): Charlie Chan at the Circus; Mystery Liner; Sharad of Atlantis
Howard, Brie (act): Android
Howard, Bruce (act): Secrets of the Phantom Caverns
Howard, Bruce (wri): King Kong vs. Godzilla
Howard, Bus (act): Serial Mom
Howard, Cathy (act): Secrets of Sex
Howard, Charlotte (act): Jekyll and Hyde
Howard, Christopher (act): Ladybug, Ladybug
Howard, Clarence (act): The Green Slime
Howard, Clint (act): Barb Wire; Bigfoot: The Unforgettable Encounter; Body Armor; Carnosaur; Cocoon; Disturbed; Evilspeak; Ice Cream Man; The Jungle Book (1967); Leprechaun 2; Rattled; Silent Night, Deadly Night 4: Initiation; Ticks; The Wraith
Howard, Dan (act): The Eiger Sanction
Howard, David (act): The Demon Lover
Howard, David/Dave (dir): The Lost Jungle
Howard, Duane (act): The Disappearance
Howard, Duke (act): Murderers' Row
Howard, Eldon (wri): The Betrayal (1958); The Child and the Killer; The Great Van Robbery; High Jump; Innocent Meeting; Links of Justice; Moment of Indiscretion; On the Run (1958); Sentenced for Life; The Spider's Web; The Tell-Tale Heart (1960); Three Crooked Men; Two Wives at One Wedding; Web of Suspicion; A Woman of Mystery; A Woman Possessed; A Woman's Temptation
Howard, Elizabeth Jane (wri): Dark of the Night; The Very Edge
Howard, Emma (act): Mad Max Beyond Thunderdome
Howard, Esther (act, 1893-1965): Born to Kill; Dick Tracy vs. Cueball; The Falcon In San Francisco; The Falcon's Alibi; The Gracie Allen Murder Case; Song of the Thin Man; The Velvet Touch
Howard, Gordon (act): Return of the Killer Tomatoes
Howard, Hartley (wri): Assignment K
Howard, James B. (act): The Silence of the Lambs
Howard, James Newton (mus): Dante's Peak; Devil's Advocate; Flatliners; The Fugitive (1993); Junior (1994); Outbreak; The Package; A Perfect Murder; The Postman (1997); Primal Fear; Space Jam; Waterworld
Howard, Jane (act): The Big Switch
Howard, Jean Speegle (act): Apollo 13
Howard, Jennifer (act): To All a Goodnight
Howard, John (Austral act): The Girl from Tomorrow; Razorback; The Sky Bike
Howard, John (USA act, b. 1913, nee John Cox): Arrest Bulldog Drummond; Bulldog Drummond Comes Back; Bulldog Drummond In Africa; Bulldog Drummond's Bride; Bulldog Drummond's Peril; Bulldog Drummond's Revenge; Bulldog Drummond's Secret Police; Destination Inner Space; The Destructors; Four Hours to Kill; Green Hell; The Invisible Woman (1941); Lost Horizon (1937); Love from a Stranger (1947); The Mad Doctor; Make Haste to Live; Radar Secret Service; So Evil, My Sister; The Undying Monster; The Unknown Terror
Howard, Joyce (act, b. 1922): Appointment With Crime; The Night Has Eyes; Shadow of the Past; They Met In the Dark
Howard, Judy (act): Anatomy of a Psycho; The Ghost of Dragstrip Hollow
Howard, Karin (wri): The Neverending Story II: The Next Chapter
Howard, Kate (act): The Great Muppet Caper
Howard, Kathleen (act, 1879-1956): Death Takes a Holiday (1934); Laura
Howard, Kevin (act): I Come In Peace
Howard, Kevyn Major (act): Alien Nation
Howard, Key (act): Ernest Saves Christmas
Howard, Langley (act): False Evidence
Howard, Leigh (wri): Blind Date (1959)
Howard, Leslie (act, 1893-1943, nee Leslie Howard Stainer): Berkeley Square; British Agent; 49th Parallel; Outward Bound; Pimpernel Smith; The Scarlet Pimpernel (1934)
Howard, Leslie (dir, 1893-1943): Pimpernel Smith
Howard, Leslie C. (act): Star Trek
Howard, Lewis (act): Horror Island
Howard, Lionelle (act): The American Heiress; The Breaking Point (1914); The Bridge Destroyer; The Cobweb; The Confession (1915); The Dead Heart; Face to Face; The Failure; A Grain of Sand; The Grand Babylon Hotel; The Grip of Ambition; The Incorruptible Crown; The Man Behind "The Times"; The Man Who Stayed at Home; The Man Who Wasn't; The Man With the Scar; A Moment of Darkness; The Mystery of Mr. Marks; The Nightbirds of London; Old St. Paul's; A Secret Life; The Stress of Circumstance; Things We Want to Know; Widow Twan-Kee
Howard, Lionelle (wri): The Man Who Wasn't; Things We Want to Know
Howard, Lisa (1950s act): Donovan's Brain; Sabaka
Howard, Lisa (1980s act): Rolling Vengeance
Howard, Lydia (wri): The Missing People
Howard, Marc (act): The Resurrected
Howard, Marvin C. (act): The Cremators
Howard, Mary (act): The Loves of Edgar Allan Poe
Howard, Matthew (wri): The Groundstar Conspiracy
Howard, Moe (act, d. 1975, nee Morris Horowitz): Doctor Death: Seeker of Souls; Have Rocket, Will Travel; Snow White and the Three Stooges; Space Master X-7; The Three Stooges In Orbit; The Three Stooges Meet Hercules
Howard, Nora (act): Condemned to Death; The Saint In London
Howard, Norman (act): Guarding Britain's Secrets; His Country's Honour
Howard, Peter (wri): see Koch, Howard
Howard, Rance (act): Bigfoot: The Unforgettable Encounter; The 'Burbs; Creator; Ed Wood; Limit Up; Mars Attacks!; Ticks
Howard, Rance (wri): Through the Magic Pyramid
Howard, Richard (dir): Circle of Iron
Howard, Rick (act): Class of Nuke 'em High
Howard, Rikki (act): Liszt O' Mania
Howard, Robert E. (wri, 1906-1936): Conan the Barbarian; Conan the Destroyer; Kull the Conqueror; Red Sonja
Howard, Ronald (act, b. 1918): Assassin for Hire; Black Orchid; Bomb In the High Street; Compelled; The Curse of the Mummy's Tomb; Double Confession; Gideon's Day; The Hideout; The House In the Woods; I Accuse (1958); Kil 1; Koroshi; The Malpas Mystery; Man Accused; Moment of Indiscretion; The Monster of Highgate Ponds; Murder She Said; The Naked Edge; Night Was Our Friend; Noose for a Lady; No Trees In the Street; Persecution; The Queen of Spades (1948); Siege of the Saxons; The Spider's Web; Wide Boy
Howard, Ron(ny) (act, b. 1953): Happy Mother's Day, Love George; Village of the Giants
Howard, Ron(ny) (dir, b. 1954): Apollo 13; Cocoon; How the Grinch Stole Christmas; Splash; Through the Magic Pyramid; Willow
Howard, Sandy (dir): Tarzan and the Trappers
Howard, Sheila (act): Phoenix the Warrior
Howard, Shemp (act, 1895-1955, nee Samuel Horowitz): Africa Screams; Another Thin Man; Arabian Nights (1942); Crazy House (1943); Ghost Crazy; Hellzapoppin; Hold That Ghost; The Invisible Woman (1941); Murder Over New York; The Strange Case of Dr. Rx
Howard, Sherman (act): I Come In Peace
Howard, Shingzie (act): The Dungeon
Howard, Sidney (wri, 1891-1939): Bulldog Drummond (1929); Condemned
Howard, Susan (act, b. 1944): Lost In Time; The Power Within (1979)
Howard, Ted (act): Moby Dick (1956)
Howard Jr., Thomas J. (act): Scalpel
Howard, Tom(my) (cin): Battle Beneath the Earth; Gorgo; The Haunting; The Man Who Haunted Himself; Tom Thumb; 2001: A Space Odyssey; The Village of the Damned (1960)
Howard, Trevor (act, 1916-1988): Around the World in 80 Days; Catch Me a Spy; The Count of Monte Cristo (1975); Craze; Green for Danger; Interpol; The Key; The Liquidator; Meteor; Moment of Danger; The Night Visitor; The Offence; Operation Crossbow; Persecution; Run for the Sun; The Satanist; The Stranger's Hand; Superman (1978); Sword of the Valiant; They Made Me a Fugitive; The Third Man; The Unholy; Who?
Howard, Vanessa (act): Corruption; The Deathshead Vampire; Girly; Some Girls Do; What Became of Jack and Jill
Howard, Vince (act): The Barefoot Executive
Howard, Walter (wri): The Lifeguardsman; The Prince and the Beggarmaid; The Story of the Rosary
Howard, Wanda (act): The Raven (1915)
Howard, William (act): The Lone Wolf Returns (1935)
Howard, William K. (dir, 1899-1954): The Fourth Musketeer; Scotland Yard (1930); Sherlock Holmes (1932); The Squeaker (1937)
Howard-Carrington, Jane (wri): Kaleidoscope
Howard-Carrington, Robert (wri): Kaleidoscope
Howard-Jones, Pam (act): Memories of Murder
Howarth, Alan (mus): Arcade; Christine; Escape from New York; Halloween III: Season of the Witch; Halloween 4: The Return of Michael Myers; Halloween 5: The Revenge of Michael Myers; Halloween: The Curse of Michael Myers; The Lost Empire; Prince of Darkness; Retribution (1988); They Live
[illegible]
Howarth, Andy (act): Moon 44
Howarth, Betty Jane (act): Francis In the Navy
Howarth, Ian (act): Loophole

Howarth, Kristine (act): *Dracula (1979)*
Howat, Clark (act): *Earth vs. the Flying Saucers; Fu Manchu; The Giant Claw; The Glass Web*
Howatt, Nina (wri): *The Mysterious Mr. Wong*
Howe, Bones (mus): *Serial Mom*
Howe, Caroline (act): *Ghosts That Still Walk*
Howe, Darrell (act): *Anatomy of a Psycho*
Howe, David (cin): *Carnival of Blood*
Howe, Eric (act): *Perfect Alibi*
Howe, James Wong (cin, 1899-1976): *The Baron of Arizona; Bell, Book and Candle; Chandu the Magician; Confidential Agent; Jennifer (1953); Laugh, Clown, Laugh; The Mark of the Vampire (1935); Out of the Fog (1941); Peter Pan (1924); The Prisoner of Zenda (1937); Pursued; Seconds; The Thin Man*
Howe, James Wong (dir, 1899-1976): *The Invisible Avenger*
Howe, Jeanette (act): *How Awful About Allan*
Howe, Lorrie (act): *The Pink Chiquitas*
Howe, Michael (act): *Blind Date; The Hunger*
Howell, C. Thomas (act, b. 1966): *Acting On Impulse; Curiosity Kills; Dark Reflection; Dead Fire; The Hitcher; The Return of the Musketeers; Sleeping Dogs (1998); Suspect Device*
Howell, Cheri (act): *Sisters of Death; Soylent Green*
Howell, Chris (act): *The Entity*
Howell, Dorothy (wri): *Alias the Lone Wolf; Behind the Mask (1932); Dirigible; The Last of the Lone Wolf; The Menace (1932)*
Howell, Edward (act): *The Cars That Ate Paris*
Howell, Erik (act): *The Dark (1979)*
Howell, Hoke (act): *Humanoids from the Deep; Kingdom of the Spiders; Through the Magic Pyramid*
Howell, Jean (act): *Lies*
Howell, Jeffery (act): *The Dark Half*
Howell, Linda (act): *Total Recall*
Howell, Margaret (act): *Candyman: Farewell to the Flesh*
Howell, Norman (act): *They Live*
Howell, Peter (act): *The Corsican Brothers (1985); The Devil-Ship Pirates; The Project; Screamer; Two Letter Alibi*
Howell, Prince (act): *Highlander*
Howell, Shawn (act): *The Entity*
Howell, Virginia (act): *The Scarlet Letter (1934)*
Howell, William (act): *Earthbound (1981)*
Howells, Colin (act): *Terror (1979)*
Howells, Ursula (act, b. 1922): *Account Rendered; Assignment K; The Cold Room; Crossplot; Dr. Terror's House of Horrors (1964); The Gilded Cage; Girly; The Long Arm; The Oracle (1952); They Can't Hang Me; Torture Garden; Track the Man Down; Two Letter Alibi; West of Suez*
Hower, Nancy (act): *The Last Man On Planet Earth*
Howerd, Frankie (act, b. 1921): *The House In Nightmare Park; The Lady Killers (1956); The Mouse On the Moon*
Howerton, Charles (act): *Up from the Depths*
Howes, Reed (act): *The Clutching Hand; Cyclone Cavalier; Destination Saturn; Dick Tracy Returns; The Phantom Creeps; Queen of the Jungle*
Howes, Sally Ann (act, b. 1934): *Chitty Chitty Bang Bang; Dead of Night (1945); Death Ship; Halfway House; The Hound of the Baskervilles (1972); Stop Press Girl*
Howey, David (act): *The Flesh and Blood Show*
Howland, Chris (act): *Formula C-12/Beirut*
Howland, Olin (act): see Howlin, Olin
Howle, Devora (act): *Hundra*
Howlett, Noel (act, b. 1901): *Cloudburst; Corridor of Mirrors; Father Brown; Kiss of the Vampire; Mr. Selkie; The Perfect Woman; Quatermass and the Pit; The Scapegoat; Woman of Straw; Your Witness*
Howley, Janice (act): *The Village of the Damned (1960)*
Howlin, Olin (act, 1896-1959, a.k.a. Olin Howland): *The Blob (1958); Cheaters at Play; Crime Doctor's Manhunt; Ellery Queen and the Murder Ring; The Man Who Wouldn't Die; Mr. Moto's Gamble; Nancy Drew, Reporter; The Return of Dr. X; Satan Met a Lady; Them! (1954)*
Howson, Hazel (act): *Bloodmoon (1990)*
Howze, Perry (wri): *Chances Are; Maid to Order*
Howze, Randy (wri): *Chances Are; Maid to Order*
Hoxby, Derek (act): *Dreamchild; Riders of the Storm*
Hoxie, Richmond (act): *Dr. Scorpion*
Hoy, Drucilla (act): *The Corpse Grinders*
Hoy, Linda (act): *Alfred Hitchcock Presents; My Science Project; Sparkling Cyanide*
Hoy, Renate (act): *Missile to the Moon*
Hoy, Robert F. (act): *Assassin (1986); The Return of the Six Million Dollar Man and the Bionic Woman*
Hoye, Cherron (act): *Dance of the Dwarfs*
Hoye, Stephen (act): *Little Shop of Horrors (1986); Nightbreed*
Hoyer, Edgar (wri): *Blade of Satan's Bog*
Hoyes, Diane (act): *School Spirit*
Hoyes, Richard (act): *Time Walker*
Hoyland, William (act): *For Your Eyes Only; In the Devil's Garden*
Hoyle, Geoff (act): *The Spirit of 76*
Hoyos, Cristina (act): *El Amor Brujo (1986)*
Hoyos (Jr.), Rodolfo (act): *Ghost Diver; The Resurrection of Zachary Wheeler; Second Chance; Secret of the Incas*
Hoysradt, John (act & wri): see Hoyt, John
Hoyt, Arthur (act): *The Lost World (1925); Murder On a Honeymoon; The Raven (1935); A Shriek In the Night;The Westland Case*
Hoyt, Carol (act): *Midnight Confessions*
Hoyt, Erich (mus): *The Keeper*
Hoyt, Harry (O.) (dir): *The Lost World (1925); The Return of Boston Blackie*
Hoyt, Harry O. (wri): *The Wizard*
Hoyt, John (act, 1905-1991, nee John Hoysradt): *Androcles and the Lion; Attack of the Puppet People; The Black Castle; The Bribe; Casanova's Big Night; The Curse of the Undead; The Decision of Christopher Blake; Flesh Gordon; Forgotten City of the Planet of the Apes; The Glass Cage (1961); It Came from Beneath the Sea; Lost Continent (1951); Operation C.I.A.; O.S.S.; Panic In the City; The Purple Mask; Sealed Verdict; Sins of Jezebel; The Time Travelers (1964); Trapped; Treachery and Greed On the Planet of the Apes; Two On a Guillotine; When Worlds Collide; X-The Man With the X-Ray Eyes*
Hoyt, John (wri, 1905-1991): *The Glass Cage (1961)*
Hoyt-Miller, Richard (act): *The Flash*
Hrabetova, Eva (act): *Rocket to Nowhere*
Hrusinsky, Rudolf/Rudolph (act): *Baron Prasil; The Cremator*
Hsieh, Wang (act): *Infra-Man*
Hsien, Wong Tsu (act): *A Chinese Ghost Story; A Chinese Ghost Story II*
Hsiu-Hsien, Li (act): *Infra-Man*
Hsu, Talun (dir): *Witchcraft 5: Dance With the Devil*
Hsueh, Nancy (act): *The Spy With My Face; Targets*
Hu, Kelly (act): *Friday the 13th, Part VIII-Jason Takes Manhattan; Star Command; Strange Days*
Hu, King (dir): *A Touch of Zen*
Huang, Essie (act): *The Million Eyes of Sumuru*
Hua-Shan (dir): *Infra-Man*
Hubbard, Doug (cin): *Weird Science*
Hubbard, Esme (act): *The Red Circle (1922)*
Hubbard, John (act, b. 1914): *The Mummy's Tomb; One Million B.C.; Turnabout*
Hubbard, Lorna (act): *Gaol Break (1936)*
Hubbard, Lucien (dir): *The Mysterious Island (1929)*
Hubbard, Lucien (wri): *The Maltese Falcon (1931); The Mysterious Island (1929); Outside the Law*
Hubbard, P.E. (act): *Trent's Last Case (1920)*
Hubbard, Paul (act): *Funeral Home; Julie Darling*
Hubbard, Tom (act & wri): *Two Lost Worlds*
Hubbard, Valorie (act): *Flesh-Eating Mothers*
Hubbell, Chris (wri): *Night of the Twisters*
Hubbert, Cork (act): *Caveman (1981); Legend; Lifepod*
Hubbs, Gil (cin): *Flowers In the Attic; The Goddess of Love; Starcrossed*
Huber, Bobby (act): *The Good Son*
Huber, Charles (act): *Skyscraper*
Huber, Charly (act): *Enemy Mine*
Huber, Harold (act, 1904-1959): *Charlie Chan at Monte Carlo; Charlie Chan In City In Darkness; Charlie Chan In Rio; Charlie Chan On Broadway; Crime Doctor; Mad Love; Mr. Moto's Gamble; The Mysterious Mr. Moto; The Thin Man*
Huber, Rhys (act): *Circumstances Unknown*
Huber, Robert (act): *Raiders of the Living Dead*
Hubert, Jacques (act): *Shadow of the Hawk*
Hubert, Lucien (act): *Jeux Interdits*
Hubert, Robert (cin): *Le Saint Mene la Dance*
Hubert-Whitten, Janet (act): *New Eden*
Hubley, Faith (dir): *The Cosmic Eye*
Hubley, Season (act): *Black Carrion; Escape from New York; Stepfather III: Father's Day*
Hubley, Whip (act): *A Connecticut Yankee In King Arthur's Court (1989); Desire and Hell at the Sunset Motel; Species*
Hubner, Ronald M. (act): *The Initiation*
Hubschmid, Paul (act, a.k.a. Paul Christian): *Bagdad; The Beast from 20,000 Fathoms; Death Comes from Space; Funeral In Berlin; Journey to the Lost City; Il Ladro di Venezia; The Red Hand; Skullduggery; Taste of Excitement; Tell Me Whom to Kill; Why Would Anyone Want to Kill a Nice Girl Like You?*
Huby, Roberta (act): *Zex*
Huck, Jon (act): *Twin Peaks: Fire Walk With Me*
Huckabee, Cooper (act): *The Curse; The Funhouse (1981)*
Huckle, Annie (act): *A Midsummer Night's Dream (1985)*
Hudd, Roy (act): *The Deathshead Vampire*
Hudd, Walter (act, 1898-1963): *All Hallowe'en; Black Limelight; Cast a Dark Shadow; Cosh Boy; Dead Man's Shoes; Elephant Boy; The Last Man to Hang?; Life for Ruth; The Man Upstairs; Satellite In the Sky; The Two-Headed Spy*
Huddle, Elizabeth (act): *Deadly Messages*
Huddleston, David (act): *Capricorn One; Computercide; Final Eye; Nightmare Honeymoon; Santa Claus (1985); Sherlock Holmes In New York*
Hudgins, Joseph (act): *Flesh Gordon*
Hudis, Norman (wri, b. 1922): *Bond of Fear; Breakaway; The Crooked Sky; Death Over My Shoulder; Face In the Night; The Flying Scot; The High Terrace; Hour of Decision; How to Steal the World; The Karate Killers; Koroshi; Mark of the Phoenix; Passport to Treason; Stranger In Town (1957); West of Suez*
Hudis, Stephen R. (act): *Shocker*
Hudkins, John (act): *The Prisoner of Zenda (1979); Something Evil*
Hudlin, Reginald (act): *Joe's Apartment*
Hudson, Bill (act): see Hudson, William
Hudson, Bob (act): *They Live; Those Dear Departed*
Hudson, Brett (act): *Hysterical*
Hudson, Brooke (act): *Wavelength*
Hudson, David (act): *The Island of Dr. Moreau (1996)*
Hudson, Don (act): *Ladyhawke*
Hudson, Ernie (act, b. 1945): *Collision Course (1990); Congo; The Crow (1994); Ghostbusters; Ghostbusters II; The Hand That Rocks the Cradle; Leviathan; No Escape (1994); The Octagon; Spacehunter: Adventures In the Forbidden Zone; Tornado!*
Hudson, Gary (act): *Cameron's Closet; Mind Twister; Night Angel; Scanner Cop; Serial Killer*
Hudson, Hugh (dir): *Greystoke: The Legend of Tarzan, Lord of the Apes*
Hudson, James W./Jim (act): *Modern Problems; Scalpel*
Hudson, John (act): see Hudson, William
Hudson, Judy (act): *The Golden Child*
Hudson, Kim (act): *Maniac (1980)*
Hudson, Larry (act): *The Creature Walks Among Us*
Hudson, Mark (act): *Hysterical*
Hudson, Michael (act): *Spawn of the Slithis*
Hudson, Pat (act): *Flesh Gordon*
Hudson, Robert (act): *Atlas*
Hudson, Rochelle (act, 1914-1972): *The Devil's Cargo; Gallery of Horror; Island of Doomed Men; Meet Boston Blackie; Les Miserables (1935); Mr. Moto Takes a Chance; The Night Walker; The Penguin Pool Murder; Strait-Jacket*
Hudson, Rock (act, 1925-1985, nee Roy Scherer Fitzgerald Jr.): *Avalanche; Blindfold; Embryo; The Golden Blade; The Mirror Crack'd; Pretty Pretty Maids All In a Row; Seconds; World War III*
Hudson, Stephanie (act): *Cave Girl Island*
Hudson, Tim (act): *Moment of Decision*
Hudson, Tina (act): *Octopussy*
Hudson, Toni (act): *Leatherface: Texas Chainsaw Massacre III; School Spirit; Uninvited (1987)*
Hudson, Valerie (act): *Subterfuge*
Hudson, Vanda (act): *Circus of Horrors; Jungle Street; Strip Tease Murder*
Hudson, W.H. (wri, 1841-1922): *Green Mansions*
Hudson, William/Bill (act, a.k.a. John Hudson): *The Amazing Colossal Man; Attack of the 50-Foot Woman (1958); Kiss Meets the Phantom of the Park; The Man Who Turned to Stone; The Screaming Skull; The She-Creature; The Steel Trap*
Hudson, William (1980s act): *Hysterical*
Huebling, Craig (act): *Marooned*
Huebsch, Edward (wri): *The Son of Dr. Jekyll*
Huemer, Dick (wri): *Dumbo*
Huerta, Rosa (act): *Terror In the Wax Museum*
Huertas, Luisa (act): *The Arrival (1996)*
Hues, Jack (mus): *The Guardian*
Hues, Matthias (act): *Cyberzone; Digital Man; I Come In Peace; TC 2000*
Huey, Garrick (act): *Charlie Chan and the Curse of the Dragon Queen*
Huey Lewis and the News (mus): *Back to the Future*
Huff, Brent (act): *Stormquest*
Huff, John (act): *The Howling: New Moon Rising*
Huff, Shawn (act): *Dead Connection*
Huff, Thomas (J.)/Tom (act): *The Entity; Eraser; Heart Condition*
Huff, Tommy (act): *Brainstorm (1983)*
Huff, William L. (wri): *The Giant Spider Invasion*
Huffaker, Clair (wri): *Tarzan and the Valley of Gold*
Huffman, Alice (act): *Glen and Randa*
Huffman, Charles (act): *Glen and Randa*
Huffman, David (act, 1944-1985): *Blood Beach; Look What's Happened to Rosemary's Baby; Sparkling Cyanide*
Huffman, Franklin (act): *12 Monkeys*
Huffman, Linus (act): *Cyborg 2: Glass Shadow*
Huffman, Rosanna (act): *I Saw What You Did (1988)*
Huffman, Tracey (act): *Forever Evil*
Huffman-Kerr, Ross (act): *The Haunting of Sarah Hardy*
Hufsey, Billy (act): *Graduation Day*
Hug, Mike (mus): *Paroxysmus*
Huggett, Bruce (act): *Empire of Ash III*
Huggett, Richard (act): *Slipstream*
Huggins, Jeremy (act): see Brett, Jeremy
Huggins, Roy (wri, b. 1914): *The Fugitive (1993); State Secret; U.S. Marshals*
Hugh, John (act): *Brainstorm (1983); Charlie Chan and the Curse of the Dragon Queen; Ghost (1990)*
Hughes, Alison (act): *The Wicker Man*
Hughes, Amanda (act): *Vampire On Bikini Beach*
Hughes, Andrew (act): *Destroy All Monsters; Terror Beneath the Sea*
Hughes, Anthony (act): *Charlie Chan at the Opera*
Hughes, Barnard/Barney (act, b. 1915): *The Lost Boys; Oh, God!; Rage; Sanctuary of Fear; Sisters; Tron; The UFO Incident*
Hughes, Barney (act): see Hughes, Barnard/Barney
Hughes, Beulah (act): *Hands of the Ripper*
Hughes, Brendan (act): *Howling VI: The Freaks; Outland; Return to Horror High; Stranded; To Die For*
Hughes, Carol (act): *The Deadly Ray from Mars; Peril from the Planet Mongo; Purple Death from Outer Space; The Red Dragon (1945); The Westland Case*
Hughes, Carol (cin, dir & wri): *Missing Link*
Hughes, Carolyn (act): *The Wasp Woman (1959)*
Hughes, Chuck (wri): *Ed and His Dead Mother*
Hughes, Cooper (mus): *C.H.U.D.*
Hughes, David (1950s act): *The Brain Eaters*
Hughes, David (1990s act): *Storm of the Century*
Hughes, David (cin, dir & wri): *Missing Link*
Hughes, Dorothy (act): *The Sorrows of Satan (1925)*
Hughes, Dorothy B. (wri, b. 1904): *The Hanged Man; Ride the Pink Horse*
Hughes, Doug (act): *Capture That Capsule!*
Hughes, Finola (act): *The Bride In Black; The Crying Child; Generation X; Haunted by Her Past*
Hughes, Gareth (act, 1894-1965): *The Midnight Girl*
Hughes, Gary (mus): *A Challenge for Robin Hood; The Pirates of Blood River; The Scarlet Blade; The Viking Queen*
Hughes, Geoffrey (act): *Revenge (1971, GB); Tiffany Jones*
Hughes, Harry (dir): *The Gables Mystery; The Man at Six*
Hughes, Harry (wri): *Dead Men Are Dangerous; The Gables Mystery; The Last Chance; The Man at Six; Shadow of Evil (1921)*
Hughes, Heather (act): *Flesh Feast*
Hughes, Helen (act): *The Amityville Curse; Evil Stalks This House; Incubus (1982); Moonlight Becomes You; Night of the Twisters; The Peanut Butter Solution; Sorry, Wrong Number (1989); Storm of the Century*
Hughes, J. Anthony (act): *Beyond Tomorrow; The Lost Missile*
Hughes, John (dir, b. 1950): *Weird Science*
Hughes, John (wri, b. 1950): *Flubber; Miracle On 34th Street (1994); 101 Dalmatians (1996); Weird Science*

Hughes, Julie (act):   Stormquest
Hughes, Katherine (act):   Thy Neighbor's Wife
Hughes, Kathleen (act, b. 1928, nee Betty von Gerkan): Cult of the Cobra; The Glass Web; The Golden Blade; It Came from Outer Space; The President's Analyst; Three Bad Sisters
Hughes, Kay (act): Dick Tracy (1937); Dick Tracy vs. the Spider; The Mandarin Mystery
Hughes, Ken (dir, b. 1922): Black 13; The Brain Machine; The Candlelight Murder; Casino Royale; Chitty Chitty Bang Bang; Confession (1955); The House Across the Lake; The Internecine Project; Joe Macbeth; Little Red Monkey; Murder Anonymous; Night Plane to Amsterdam; Passenger to Tokyo; The Strange Case of Blondie; Timeslip; Wide Boy
Hughes, Ken (wri, b. 1922): Black 13; The Brain Machine; The Candlelight Murder; Chitty Chitty Bang Bang; Confession (1955); The House Across the Lake; Little Red Monkey; Timeslip; Town On Trial
Hughes, Kenneth (dir):   Night School
Hughes, Kirsten (act): Jane and the Lost City
Hughes, Kris (dir):   Dying Game
Hughes, Laura Leigh (act):Virtuosity
Hughes, Lawrence (act):   The Altar Stairs
Hughes, Llewellyn (wri): Temple Tower
Hughes, Lloyd (act, 1897-1958): Blake of Scotland Yard; Drums of Jeopardy (1931); Face In the Fog (1935); Kelly of the Secret Service; The Lost World (1925); Moby Dick (1930); The Mysterious Island (1929); Where East Is East
Hughes, Mary (act): Dr. Goldfoot and the Bikini Machine; Sergeant Deadhead the Astronut!
Hughes, Mary Beth (act, b. 1919): Blue, White and Perfect; Caged Fury; Charlie Chan In Rio; The Devil's Henchman; Dig That Uranium!; Dressed to Kill (1941); Inner Sanctum (1949); The Lady Confesses; Sleepers West
Hughes, Megan (act): Adventures In Dinosaur City
Hughes, Michael (act):   Dying Game
Hughes, Miko (act): Apollo 13; Pet Sematary; Wes Craven's New Nightmare
Hughes, Mildred (act): The Funhouse (1981)
Hughes, Peter (act):   The Primitives
Hughes, Prince A. (act): Fright Night; Weird Science
Hughes, Richard (wri, 1900-1976): A High Wind In Jamaica
Hughes, Robert C. (dir): Hunter's Blood; Memorial Valley Massacre
Hughes, Robin (act): Dial M for Murder (1954); The Flame and the Arrow; The Maze; The Mole People; The Road to Hong Kong; The Thing That Couldn't Die
Hughes, Roddy (act, b. 1891): Escape Route; The Ghost at St. Michael's; The House of Silence; The House On Marsh Road; Old Mother Riley's Jungle Treasure; One Jump Ahead; The River House Mystery; The Saint's Vacation; Scrooge (1951); The Spaniard's Curse
Hughes, Sharon (act):   Grotesque
Hughes, Spike (mus):   Fiddlers Three
Hughes, Stacey (act): Scream for Help
Hughes, Terry (dir):   The Butcher's Wife; Mrs. Santa Claus
Hughes, Tony (act): The Lone Wolf Spy Hunt
Hughes, Wendy (act): A Dangerous Summer; Donor; Puzzle
Hughes, Whitey (act): The Bees; Demonoid; Kingdom of the Spiders; She Demons
Hughes, William (act): The Amazing Colossal Man
Hugh-Kelly, Daniel (act): Atomic Dog; Cujo; The Good Son
Hughman, John (act):   Time Bandits
Hugho, Kimo (act):   The Presence
Hughs, Andrew (act):   Destroy All Monsters
Hugo, Francois (act):   The Arp Statue
Hugo, Mauritz (act, 1909-1974): Blonde for a Day; Search for Danger; The Vampire (1957)
Hugo, Michel (cin): Bug; Earth II; The Manitou; The Night Stalker (1971); The Octagon; Terror Out of the Sky
Hugo, Monique (act):   The Arp Statue
Hugo, Robert (wri):   La Frusta e il Corpo
Hugo, Victor (wri, 1802-1885): Esmeralda; The Hunchback (1997); The Hunchback of Notre Dame (1923, 1939, 1957, 1965, 1977, 1982 & 1996); The Man Who Laughs (1928 & 1965); Les Miserables (1918, 1922, 1935, 1935, 1943, 1952, 1957, 1978 & 1995); Notre Dame de Paris
Huguely, Jay (wri): Jason Goes to Hell: The Final Friday
Hui, Ricky (act):   Mr. Vampire
Huie, Karen (act):   Chiller

Huke, Bob (cin): Vengeance; The Very Edge
Hukushi, John (act):   Street Trash
Hulbert, Claude (act, 1900-1963): Bulldog Jack; Champagne; The Dummy Talks; The Face at the Window (1932); The Ghost at St. Michael's; The Ghosts of Berkeley Square; Thark; Under the Frozen Falls; The Vulture (1937); Wolf's Clothing (1936)
Hulbert, Jack (act, 1892-1978): Bulldog Jack; Elstree Calling; The Ghost Train (1931); The Spider's Web
Hulbert, Jack (dir, 1892-1978): Elstree Calling
Hulce, Tom (act, b. 1953): Black Rainbow; The Hunchback of Notre Dame (1996); Mary Shelley's 'Frankenstein'; Slam Dance
Hulcher, Mark (act): The Henderson Monster
Hulcup, Jack (act): Faust (1911); The Jewel Thieves Outwitted; The Mill Girl
Hules, Endre (act): Babylon 5: A Call to Arms; The Craft; Houdini (1998); Seven
Hulett, Otto (act): Francis Goes to West Point
Hulette, Gladys (act):   The Mystic
Hulke, Malcolm (wri): The Man In the Back Seat
Hull, Arthur Steward (act): Meet Nero Wolfe
Hull, Cynthia (act):   The Eye Creatures
Hull, Dianne (act): The Fifth Floor; Man On a Swing; You Better Watch Out
Hull, Henry (act, 1890-1977): The Fool Killer; Great Expectations (1934); Inferno (1953); Lifeboat; Master of the World; Miracles for Sale; Nick Carter, Master Detective; One Exciting Night; Portrait of Jennie; The Treasure of Lost Canyon; Werewolf of London
Hull, Josephine (act, 1884-1957, nee Josephine Sherwood): Arsenic and Old Lace
Hull, Richard (act):   The Dark Dealer
Hull, Warren (act, 1903-1974): Hidden Enemy; The Lone Wolf Meets a Lady; The Night Key; The Walking Dead
Huller, Turk (act):   Primal Fear
Hullett, Steve (wri): The Fox and the Hound
Hulme, Anthony (act): The Body Vanishes; The Mysterious Mr. Nicholson; Send for Paul Temple; They Came by Night; The Three Weird Sisters
Hulme, Georgina (act):   The Magic Toyshop
Hulverschiedt, Manfred (act): Georgette Meunier
Humberstone, (H.) Bruce (dir, 1903-1984): Charlie Chan at the Olympics; Charlie Chan at the Opera; Charlie Chan at the Race Track; Charlie Chan In Honolulu; The Dragon Murder Case; I Wake Up Screaming; King of the Jungle; The Purple Mask; Strangers of the Evening; Tarzan and the Lost Safari; Tarzan's Fight for Life; Wonder Man
Humbert, George (act): Mr. Moto's Last Warning
Humbert, Henri (act):   Diabolique (1955)
Humbert, Humphrey (dir): Ghosthouse
Hume, Alan (cin): Arabian Adventure; At the Earth's Core; Captain Nemo and the Underwater City; Carry On Screaming; Carry On Spying; Caveman (1981); A Choice of Weapons; Dr. Terror's House of Horrors (1964); Eve of Destruction; Eye of the Needle; For Your Eyes Only; From Beyond the Grave; Gulliver's Travels (1977); The Hunchback of Notre Dame (1982); Kiss of the Vampire; The Land That Time Forgot; The Legacy; The Legend of Hell House; Lifeforce; Octopussy; The People That Time Forgot; Return of the Jedi; Supergirl (1984); 20,000 Leagues Under the Sea (1997, CBS-TV); A View to a Kill; Warlords of the Deep; The Watcher In the Woods; Without a Clue; Wombling Free; Zeppelin
Hume, Benita (act, 1906-1967): The Clue of the New Pin (1929); The Flying Fool; The Garden Murder Case; High Treason (1929); A Honeymoon Adventure; The House of the Arrow (1930); The Private Life of Don Juan; Tarzan Escapes
Hume, Brian Kenneth (act): The Hand (1981)
Hume, Cyril (wri, d. 1966): Bride of Vengeance; Forbidden Planet; The Invisible Boy; Tarzan Escapes; Tarzan's Savage Fury; Trader Horn (1931)
Hume, David (wri): Crime Unlimited; The Patient Vanishes; Too Dangerous to Live
Hume, Edward (wri): The Day After; A Reflection of Fear
Hume, Fergus (wri): The Mystery of a Hansom Cab; The Other Person
Hume, Kenneth (dir): Bullet from the Past; Hot Ice; Sail Into Danger
Hume, Kenneth (wri): Hot Ice; Sail Into Danger
Hume, Marjorie (act): Betrayal (1932); Bluff; The Curse of Frankenstein; Deadlock (1931); Member of the Jury; Sexton Blake, Gambler;

Silent Evidence; Silken Threads; The Triumph of the Scarlet Pimpernel; White Lilac
Hume, Maude (act): In the Days of Saint Patrick
Hume, Roger (act):   Anatomy of Terror
Humenick, Nadine (cin): The Music of the Spheres
Hummel, Carrie Starner (act): Ed Wood
Hummel, Lisabeth (act): The Beast (1974)
Hummel, Paul (act):   The Fan
Hummel, Sayra (act):   Star Trek
Hummer, Rick (act): Night of the Lepus
Hummer, Sherry (act): Night of the Lepus
Humphrey, Alf(red) (act): Funeral Home; My Bloody Valentine; Virus (1980)
Humphrey, Andy (act):   Body Parts (1991)
Humphrey, Harry (act): Dick Tracy's G-Men
Humphrey, Steven (wri): Sparkling Cyanide
Humphrey, William J. (dir & wri): The Black Spider
Humphreys, Cecil (act): Accused (1936); The Dying Detective; The Elusive Pimpernel (1919); Her Redemption; The House On the Marsh; Koenigsmark; The Lifeguardsman; The Old Man; The Pleydell Mystery; Shadow of Evil (1921); The Sorrows of Satan (1917); The Woman In White (1929); A Woman's Vengeance; Wuthering Heights (1939)
Humphreys, Griffith (act):Condemned to Death
Humphreys, Renee (act):   Fun
Humphreys, William (act): The Unholy Three (1925)
Humphries, Barry (act): Bedazzled; Howling III; Shock Treatment! (1981)
Humphries, Dave (wri):   Full Circle
Humphries, Dot (act):   Just Imagine
Humphries, Tessa (act): Cassandra; Out of the Body
Humpoletz, Paul (act): The Black Windmill; Murder Motel; Nothing But the Night
Hundar, Robert (act): Terror of Rome Against the Son of Hercules
Hundley, Craig (act):   Planet Earth
Hundley, Craig (mus): Alligator (1981); Schizoid (1980)
Hunebelle, Andre (dir): Fantomas Contro Scotland Yard; Mission a Tangiers; OSS 117-Mission for a Killer; Shadow of Evil (1964)
Hunebelle, Andre (wri): The Devil's Nightmare; OSS 117-Mission for a Killer; Shadow of Evil (1964)
Huneck, John (cin): End of the World (1977); Party Line
Huner, Mary (act):   Slime City
Hung, Samo (act): The Dead and the Deadly
Hungerford, F. Edward (wri): The Devil's Assistant
Hungerford, Michael (act): The Wraith
Hubgerford, Ty (act): see Hardin, Ty
Hunnicutt, Arthur (act, 1910-1979): The Chance of a Lifetime; Split Second (1953)
Hunnicutt, Gayle (act, b. 1943): Color Him Dead; Eye of the Cat; Fragment of Fear; Freelance; The Legend of Hell House; Les Nuits Rouges; The Return of the Man from U.N.C.L.E.; The Saint and the Brave Goose; Scorpio; The Spiral Staircase (1975); Target; Voices
Hunsaker, John (act): Just Before Dawn (1980)
Hunsaker, Lee (act):   Serial Mom
Hunsberger, Vic (act): Charlie Chan and the Curse of the Dragon Queen
Hunsberger Jr., Victor (act): Evilspeak
Hunsicker, Jackson (wri): Ten Little Indians (1989)
Hunsinger, Tom (act):   Nightbreed
Hunt, Bob (wri): The Boogens; The Hidden; The Hidden II
Hunt, Bonnie (act):   Jumanji
Hunt, Caroline (act):   Fahrenheit 451
Hunt, Cecil (act): The Giant Gila Monster
Hunt, Christine (act): Arthur the King
Hunt, Edward (act):   The Invisible Fear
Hunt, Ed(ward) (dir): Alien Warrior; Bloody Birthday; The Brain (1988); Plague; Starship Invasions
Hunt, Ed(ward) (wri): Alien Warrior; Plague; Starship Invasions
Hunt, Eleanor (act): see Compton, Joyce
Hunt, F.J.J. (act):   Old St. Paul's
Hunt, Florence (act): The Black Tulip (1937)
Hunt, Gareth (act): And the Wall Came Tumbling Down; Blood Bath at the House of Death; A Ghost In Monte Carlo; Licensed to Love and Kill
Hunt, Gordon (act): Trancers II: The Return of Jack Deth
Hunt, Helen (act, b. 1963): In the Company of Darkness; Into the Badlands; Peggy Sue Got Married; Project X (1987); The Spell; Trancers; Trancers II: The Return of Jack Deth; Trancers III: Deth Lives; Twister

Hunt, Helene (act):   Octopussy
Hunt, (J.) Roy (cin): The Falcon and the Co-Eds; A Game of Death; I Walked With a Zombie; A Kiss for Cinderella; The Lone Wolf (1917); Mighty Joe Young (1949); The Saint's Double Trouble; Sherlock Holmes (1922)
Hunt, Jim(my) (act): Invaders from Mars (1953 & 1986); Shadow on the Wall; Sorry, Wrong Number (1948)
Hunt, Letitia (act):   Forever Evil
Hunt, Linda (act, b. 1945): Dune; Pocahontas; Rain Without Thunder; The Relic; Teen Agent
Hunt, Lois Kelso (act): The House On Sorority Row
Hunt, Lou (act):   Bog
Hunt, Madge (act):   Queen Kelly
Hunt, Marcia (act): see Hunt, Marsha
Hunt, Marsha (act, b. 1917, nee Marcia Hunt): Back from the Dead; Ellery Queen, Master Detective; Fear No Evil (1969); Kid Glove Killer; Mary Ryan, Detective; None Shall Escape; Take One False Step
Hunt, Marsha (A.) (act): Dracula A.D. 1972; Howling II; The Sender
Hunt, Martita (act, 1900-1969): At the Villa Rose (1939); Brides of Dracula; Bunny Lake Is Missing; The Case of Gabriel Perry; East of Piccadilly; The Ghosts of Berkeley Square; Great Expectations (1946); I Was a Spy; The Man In Grey; The March Hare; The Nursemaid Who Disappeared; Sabotage; So Evil My Love; The Story of Robin Hood; Strange Boarders; When Knights Were Bold (1936); The Wonderful World of the Brothers Grimm
Hunt, Maurice (dir):   The Pagemaster
Hunt, Neil (act): Jekyll and Hyde...Together Again
Hunt, Paul (dir): The Clones; Merlin (1993)
Hunt, Peter (H.) (dir, b. 1928): Dead Man's Island; Gulliver's Travels (1977); Hyper Sapien: People from Another Star; It Came Upon the Midnight Clear; On Her Majesty's Secret Service
Hunt, Ronald Leigh (act): The Hand (1960); Hi-Jack
Hunt, Susan (act):   The Clones
Hunt, Suzanne (act):   Popcorn
Hunt, Tanner (act): Creature from the Haunted Sea
Hunt, Tracy (act):   The Pink Chiquitas
Hunt, William (Dennis) (act): Flesh Gordon; Flesh Gordon 2: Flesh Gordon Meets the Cosmic Cheerleaders
Hunter, A.C. (dir): Marzipan of the Shapes
Hunter, Alastair (act): Castle Sinister (1948); Lady In the Fog; Operation Murder; Satellite In the Sky; Three Steps In the Dark
Hunter, Alberta (mus):   Remember My Name
Hunter, Anne (act):   The Gay Falcon
Hunter, Arline (act): The Angry Red Planet
Hunter, Bill (act): Moby Dick (1998); Sky Pirates
Hunter, Ciara (act):   Dangerous Prey
Hunter, Connie (act):   The Prey (1980)
Hunter, Craig (act): A Clockwork Orange
Hunter, Debra (act):   Nightmare Weekend
Hunter, Dick (act): The Fatal Hour (1937)
Hunter, Drew (wri):   Bridge of Time
Hunter, Evan (wri, b. 1926, a.k.a. Ed McBain): The Birds; Blood Relatives; High and Low
Hunter, Glenn (act, 1893-1945): Puritan Passions
Hunter, Greg (act):   Wavelength
Hunter, Heather (act):   Frankenhooker
Hunter, Henry (act):   Missile to the Moon
Hunter, Holly (act, b. 1958): Always; The Burning; Copycat; Crash (1996)
Hunter, Ian (act, 1900-1975): The Adventures of Robin Hood; Bad Sister; Bedelia; Death at Broadcasting House; Dr. Blood's Coffin; Dr. Jekyll and Mr. Hyde (1941); The Door In the Wall; Downhill; Fortune Is a Woman; A Midsummer Night's Dream (1935); No Escape (1934); Order of the Black Eagle; The Phantom Light; The Ring; The Sign of Four (1932); Tarzan Finds a Son!; Tower of London (1939); The Treasure of Monte Cristo (1961)
Hunter, Ian (wri): The Amazing Mr. X; Your Witness
Hunter, J. Michael (act): The Dark Half; The Handmaid's Tale; King Kong Lives; Time Walker
Hunter, James (act): A Polish Vampire In Burbank
Hunter, Jeffrey (act, 1925-1969, nee Henry H. McKinnies): Brainstorm (1965); Dimension 5; Fourteen Hours; Gold for the

Caesars; A Kiss Before Dying (1956); A Witch Without a Broom
Hunter, John (wri): Never Look Back; The Pirates of Blood River
Hunter, Kathryn (act): Orlando
Hunter, Kenneth (act): The Adventures of Robin Hood; League of Frightened Men
Hunter, Kim (act, b. 1922, nee Janet Cole): Bad Ronald; Beneath the Planet of the Apes; Dark August; Ellery Queen; Escape from the Planet of the Apes; The Kindred; Lilith; The Magician (1973); A Matter of Life and Death; Planet of the Apes; The Seventh Victim; The Swimmer; Two Evil Eyes
Hunter, Lois (act): A Polish Vampire In Burbank
Hunter, Michael (act): RoboCop; Wild Thing
Hunter, Morgan (act): Cyborg Cop II
Hunter, N.C. (wri): Poison Pen
Hunter, Nancy (act): Once Bitten
Hunter, Neith (act): Fright Night II; Silent Night, Deadly Night 4: Initiation
Hunter, Pamela (act): The Secret Life of Ian Fleming
Hunter, Richard (act): House of the Long Shadows; The Project
Hunter, Rion (act): Deadly Messages
Hunter, Robert (act): Men of Sherwood Forest
Hunter, Robin (act): Vampire Circus
Hunter, Russell (act): The Savage Curse; Taste the Blood of Dracula
Hunter, Russell (wri): The Changeling
Hunter, Sheena (act): The Private Life of Sherlock Holmes
Hunter, Steve (mus): The Invisible Kid
Hunter, T. Hayes (dir, b. 1896): The Frightened Lady (1932); The Ghoul (1933); The Man They Could Not Arrest; The Triumph of the Scarlet Pimpernel; Warn London; White Face
Hunter, T. Hayes (wri, b. 1896): The Man They Could Not Arrest
Hunter, Tab (act, b. 1931, nee Arthur Kelm): Birds Do It; Cameron's Closet; The City Under the Sea; Damn Yankees; La Freccia d'Oro; Grotesque; The Loved One; Out of the Dark; Pandemonium; Polyester; Return to Treasure Island; Saturday Island; Sweet Kill; Track of the Cat; Troubled Waters (1964)
Hunter, Tanna (act): Invasion of the Blood Farmers
Hunter, Thomas (wri): The Final Countdown; The Human Factor
Hunter, Tim (dir): Paint It Black
Hunter, Tom (act): The Cassandra Crossing; The Human Factor
Hunter, Tommy (act): Agatha
Hunter, Troy (act): Fortress
Hunter, Virginia (act): The Notorious Lone Wolf
Hunter, William (act): The Other Person
Huntington, Joan (act): What Ever Happened to Aunt Alice?
Huntington, Lawrence (dir, 1900-1968): The Bank Messenger Mystery; Contraband Spain; Deadly Record; Death Drums Along the River; Dial 999 (1938); The Fur Collar; Man On the Run; Passenger to London; The Patient Vanishes; Suspected Person; Tower of Terror; Twin Faces; The Upturned Glass; The Vulture (1966); Wanted for Murder; Warn That Man
Huntington, Lawrence (wri, 1900-1968): Contraband Spain; Deadly Nightshade; Deadly Record; Death Drums Along the River; Dial 999 (1938); The Fur Collar; I Killed the Count; Impulse (1955); Man On the Run; The Oblong Box; A Question of Suspense; Suspected Person; The Vulture (1966); Warn That Man
Huntington, M. (act): A Yell of a Night
Huntington, Terry (act): The Three Stooges Meet Hercules
Huntley, Chet (act): Cry Terror!
Huntley, Chris (act, cin & wri): The Strangeness
Huntley Jr., George P./G.P. (act): Charlie Chan at the Race Track; Death Takes a Holiday (1934); Mr. Moto Takes a Vacation; Tower of London (1939)
Huntley, Hugh (act): The Bat Whispers; The Phantom Creeps
Huntley, Kelly (act): Little Shop of Horrors (1986)
Huntley, Noah (act): The Cyber-Stalking
Huntley, Raymond (act, 1904-1990): The Adding Machine; Black Torment; Gestapo; The Ghost at St. Michael's; The Ghost Train (1941); The Green Man; Hostile Witness; The House In the Square; Innocent Meeting; The Last Man to Hang?; The Last Page; Meet Mr. Lucifer; Mr. Denning Drives North; The Mummy (1959); Pimpernel Smith; So Evil My Love; Symptoms; The Teckman Mystery; They Came to a City; Town On Trial
Huntley, Tim (act): Rogues of Sherwood Forest
Huntley-Wright, Betty (act): Meet Sexton Blake
Huntly, Leslie (act): Demon of Paradise
Hunyadkurthy, Istvan (act): Daughter of Darkness (1990)
Hupp, Tara (act): Trick or Treats
Huppert, Isabelle (act, b. 1955): Violette Noziere
Hurd, Earl (wri): Snow White and the Seven Dwarfs
Hurd, Gale Anne (wri): The Terminator
Hurkos, Peter (act): The Mysterious Monsters
Hurlbut, William (wri): Bride of Frankenstein; The Cat Creeps (1930)
Hurley, Craig (act): Warlock: The Armageddon
Hurley, Elizabeth (act, b. 1965): My Favorite Martian
Hurley, James F. (wri): Something Weird
Hurley, Julia (act): Jane Eyre (1921)
Hurley, Maurice (wri): Firebird 2015 A.D.
Hurndall, Richard (act): Eye of the Devil; Gawain and the Green Knight; Hostile Witness; I, Monster; Royal Flash; Zeppelin
Hurry, David (act): Quarantine
Hurst, Brandon (act): Devotion; Dr. Jekyll and Mr. Hyde (1920, Famous Players/Para); The Greene Murder Case; He Who Gets Slapped; House of Frankenstein; The Hunchback of Notre Dame (1923); The Lost Patrol (1934); The Man In Half Moon Street; The Man Who Laughs (1928); Murder at Midnight; The Murders In the Rue Morgue (1932); The Thief of Bagdad (1924); White Zombie
Hurst, Brian Desmond (dir, b. 1900): Alibi (1942); The Mark of Cain; On the Night of the Fire; Scrooge (1951); Sensation (1937); The Tell-Tale Heart (1934)
Hurst, Brian Desmond (wri, b. 1900): On the Night of the Fire
Hurst, David (act, b. 1925): The Boys from Brazil; The Intimate Stranger; Mad About Men; Mother Riley Meets the Vampire; The Perfect Woman; Venetian Bird
Hurst, Elliott (act): Popcorn
Hurst, Lillian (act): Sleepstalker
Hurst, Michael (act): Death Warmed Up
Hurst, Paul (act, 1889-1953): Ellery Queen and the Murder Ring; Island of Lost Souls; The Sphinx (1933)
Hurst, Peter (cin): Ghost Story (1975)
Hurst, Richard (act): Earth Girls Are Easy
Hurst, Robert (wri): No Safety Ahead
Hurst, Rick (act): The Cat from Outer Space
Hurst, Veronica (act): Bang! You're Dead; The Boy Cried Murder; Dead Man's Evidence; The Gilded Cage; The Girl On the Pier; Licensed to Kill; The Maze; Peeping Tom; The Yellow Balloon
Hurt, John (act, b. 1940): Alien; Contact; The Black Cauldron; Contact; The Disappearance; The Ghoul (1974); Jake Speed; Monolith; 1984 (1984); The Pied Piper (1971); Roger Corman's 'Frankenstein Unbound'; The Shout; Sinful Davey; Spectre (1977); 10 Rillington Place; Thumbelina (1994); Watership Down
Hurt, Keith (act): The Strangeness
Hurt, Mary Beth (act): D.A.R.Y.L.; My Boyfriend's Back; Parents
Hurt, William (act, b. 1950): Altered States; Dark City; Jane Eyre (1996); Lost In Space; Michael; Until the End of the World
Hurtz, Ted (act): Howard the Duck
Hurtz, William T. (dir): Little Nemo: Adventures In Slumberland
Hurwitz, Harvey (act, dir & wri, 1938-1995): The Projectionist
Hurwitz, Victor (cin): The Last House On the Left
Husain, Jory (act): Earth Girls Are Easy
Husebo, Knut (act): Apprentice to Murder
Hush, Lisabeth (act): The Threat (1960); X-15
Husky, Ferlin (act, b. 1927): Hillbillys In a Haunted House
Husky, Rick (wri): Mandrake
Huson, Paul (act): Richard III (1955)
Huson, Paul (wri): The Fury Within
Huss, Jon (act): Premonition (1972)
Hussein, Waris (dir, b. 1938): The Henderson Monster; The Possession of Joel Delaney; She Woke Up
Hussey, Olivia (act, b. 1951): The Cat and the Canary (1978); The Corsican Brothers (1985); Dead Man's Island; Death On the Nile; Distortions; Escape 2000 (1983); Ice Cream Man; It (1990); Lost Horizon (1973); Psycho IV: The Beginning; Quest of the Delta Knights; Silent Night, Evil Night; Virus (1980)
Hussey, Ruth (act, b. 1917): Another Thin Man; The Uninvited (1944)
Hussmann, Larry (act): Blood Pen
Huster, Francis (act): I Married a Shadow
Huston, Anjelica (act, b. 1951): The Addams Family; Addams Family Values; Ever After: A Cinderella Story; Hamlet (1969); The Ice Pirates; The Witches (1990)
Huston, Danny (dir): The Maddening
Huston, James (act): The Outing
Huston, Jimmy (dir): Final Exam; My Best Friend Is a Vampire
Huston, Jimmy (wri): Final Exam
Huston, John (act, 1906-1987): Alfred Hitchcock Presents; Battle for the Planet of the Apes; The Bible; Casino Royale; De Sade; The Hobbit; The Kremlin Letter; Myra Breckinridge; The Return of the King; Sherlock Holmes In New York; Tentacles; The Visitor; Winter Kills
Huston, John (dir, 1906-1987): Beat the Devil; The Bible; Casino Royale; Key Largo; The Kremlin Letter; The List of Adrian Messenger; The Maltese Falcon (1941); The Man Who Would Be King; Moby Dick (1956); Phobia; Reflections In a Golden Eye; Sinful Davey
Huston, John (wri, 1906-1987): Beat the Devil; Key Largo; The Kremlin Letter; The Maltese Falcon (1941); The Man Who Would Be King; Moby Dick (1956); Three Strangers
Huston, Patricia (act): Experiment In Terror
Huston, Virginia (act, b. 1925): Flight to Mars; Nocturne; Sudden Fear; Tarzan's Peril
Huston, Walter (act, 1884-1950, nee Walter Hughston): All That Money Can Buy; And Then There Were None; Dragonwyck; Gabriel Over the White House; Kongo; Love Me Tonight; The Maltese Falcon (1941); The Tunnel
Huston, Will (act): Pumpkinhead II: Blood Wings
Huston, Zandra (act): Lost Prophet
Huszar, Karl (act): Doctor Mabuse
Hutch the Dog (animal act): Attack of the Killer Tomatoes
Hutchence, Michael (act): Roger Corman's 'Frankenstein Unbound'
Hutcheson, Anne (act): Red Blooded American Girl
Hutcheson, David (act, b. 1905): The Abominable Dr. Phibes; The Birthday Present; Bulldog Sees It Through; Circle of Danger; The Elusive Pimpernel (1950); Evil of Frankenstein; The Magic Christian; My Daughter Joy; No Highway In the Sky; Sleeping Car to Trieste; Vice Versa (1947)
Hutchings, Debbie (act): Memoirs of a Survivor
Hutchins, Peter (act): The Orchard End Murder; Puppet On a Chain
Hutchins, Tara (act): Party Line
Hutchins, Will (act): The Horror at 37,000 Feet
Hutchinson, Bill (act): The Adding Machine
Hutchinson, Brenda I. (mus): Liquid Sky
Hutchinson, Charles (dir): Found Alive
Hutchinson, Harry (act): Blow-Up; The Door With Seven Locks (1940); Dublin Nightmare; The Silver Greyhound (1932)
Hutchinson, Jeffery (act): Roller Blade Warriors: Taken by Force
Hutchinson, Josephine (act, b. 1904): North by Northwest; Somewhere In the Night; Son of Frankenstein; Step Down to Terror
Hutchinson, Michelle (act): Fargo
Hutchinson, Peter (cin): Excalibur; Greystoke: The Legend of Tarzan, Lord of the Apes
Hutchinson, Ron (wri): Blue Ice; The Island of Dr. Moreau (1996)
Hutchinson, Tim (act): Tales from the Hood
Hutchinson, vanessa (act): Mirrors
Hutchison, Charles (act): The Hidden Menace; Hutch Stirs 'em Up
Hutchison, Charles (dir): The Hidden Menace
Hutchison, Doug (act): The Lawnmower Man
Hutchison, Fiona (act, b. 1960): American Gothic; Biggles: Adventures In Time
Hutchison, Ken (act): Deadly Strangers; Ladyhawke
Hutchison, Muriel (act): Another Thin Man
Hutchison, Robert (wri): Frogs
Huth, Harold (act, b. 1892): Blackmailed; The Ghoul (1933); A Honeymoon Adventure; The Hostage (1956); The Triumph of the Scarlet Pimpernel
Huth, Harold (dir, b. 1892): Bulldog Sees It Through; East of Piccadilly; The Hostage
Hutsko, Steve (act): Night of the Living Dead (1968)
Hutson, Candace/Candy (act): Hider In the House; The Land Before Time; The Land Before Time III: The Time of the Great Giving; The Land Before Time IV: Journey Through the Mists; The Land Before Time V: The Mysterious Island
Hutson, Lee (wri): Turn Back the Clock
Hutson, Shaun (wri): Slugs
Hutton, Betty (act, b. 1921, nee Betty Thornberg): Dream Girl
Hutton, Beulah (act): Charlie Chan On Broadway
Hutton, Brian G. (dir, b. 1935): The First Deadly Sin; Night Watch (1973)
Hutton, Camilla (act): King Solomon's Treasure
Hutton, Geneve (act): The Great Alligator
Hutton, Ian (act): Return of the Killer Tomatoes
Hutton, Jayne (act): Stay Awake
Hutton, Jim (act, 1938-1979): Don't Be Afraid of the Dark; Ellery Queen; Psychic Killer; They Call It Murder; Whispering Death
Hutton, Lauren (act, b. 1943): The Cradle Will Fall; Fear (1990); Once Bitten; Someone's Watching Me!; Starflight: The Plane That Couldn't Land; Timestalkers; Zorro, the Gay Blade
Hutton, Linda (act): The Man Who Fell to Earth (1976)
Hutton, Lucille (act): The Miracle Man (1919)
Hutton, Marian (act, b. 1920): Crazy House (1943)
Hutton, Nedinia (act): see Merrill, Dina
Hutton, Ric (act): The Ipcress File
Hutton, Rif (act): Star Trek: Generations; Wavelength
Hutton, Robert (act, b. 1920, nee Robert Winne): Casanova's Big Night; Cinderfella; The Colossus of New York; Cry of the Banshee; Invisible Invaders; Man from Tangier; The Man Without a Body; The Secret Door; The Slime People; Tales from the Crypt (1971); They Came from Beyond Space; Torture Garden; Trog; The Vulture (1966); You Only Live Twice
Hutton, Robert (dir, b. 1920): The Slime People
Hutton, Robert B. (wri): Persecution
Hutton, Timothy (act, b. 1960): The Dark Half; Iceman; Made In Heaven; The Temp
Hutton, Timothy (dir, b. 1960): Amazing Stories: The Movie V
Hutton, Tom (act): The Demon Lover
Huu Phu, Nguyen (act): Warriors of the Wasteland
Huxley, Aldous (wri, 1894-1963): Brave New World (1980 & 1998); The Devils; Jane Eyre (1944); A Woman's Vengeance
Huxtable, Judy (act): Die Screaming, Marianne; Licensed to Kill; The Psychopath (1965); Scream and Scream Again
Huy, Renate (act): Abbott and Costello Go to Mars
Huyck, Willard (dir): Dead People; Howard the Duck
Huyck, Willard (wri): Dead People; Howard the Duck; Indiana Jones and the Temple of Doom
Huysmans, Dio (act): The Black Tulip (1921)
Hyams, Joe (act): The Lost Missile
Hyams, Leila (act): The Bishop Murder Case; Freaks; Island of Lost Souls; The Phantom of Paris (1931); The Thirteenth Chair (1929); The Wizard
Hyams, Nick (act): Timecop
Hyams, Peter (cin, b. 1943): Narrow Margin (1990); The Relic; Stay Tuned; Timecop; 2010
Hyams, Peter (dir, b. 1943): Capricorn One; Narrow Margin (1990); Outland; The Relic; Stay Tuned; Timecop; 2010
Hyams, Peter (wri, b. 1943): Capricorn One; Narrow Margin (1990); Outland; 2010
Hyams, Samuel David (act): see Hoey, Dennis
Hyatt, Bobby (act): Les Miserables (1952)
Hyatt, Charles (act): Freelance
Hyatt, Daniel (wri): Gorgo
Hyatt, Gail (act): Time After Time
Hyatt, Pam (act): Care Bears Movie II: A New Generation
Hyde, Cassandra (act): Gargantua
Hyde, David S. (act): I Was a Zombie for the F.B.I.
Hyde, Donald (wri): Please Murder Me
Hyde (Ph.D.), Gordon (act): Ravagers
Hyde, Jacquelyn (act): The Dark (1979); House of Terror (1987); Superstition
Hyde, Jonathan (act): Anaconda; Being Human; Jumanji
Hyde, Kenneth (wri): The Spaniard's Curse
Hyde, Tracy (act): The Orchard End Murder
Hyde, Vernon (cin): The Visitor
Hyden, Walford (act): Great Expectations (1946)
Hyde-White, Alex (act): Biggles: Adventures In Time; Captain America II; Mars; The Phantom of the Opera (1989); Time Trackers
Hyde-White, Wilfrid (act, 1903-1991): Alibi Inn; Appointment With Crime; The Bad Lord Byron; Battlestar Galactica; Blackmailed; Britannia Mews; City After Midnight; Drummond at Bay (1937); The Cat and the Canary (1978); Chamber of Horrors (1966);

Elephant Boy; Fear No Evil (1969); Fragment of Fear; The Ghosts of Berkeley Square; The Great Houdinis; Highly Dangerous; In Search of the Castaways; King Solomon's Treasure; Last Holiday; The Liquidator; The Magic Christian; The March Hare; The Million Eyes of Sumuru; Mr. Denning Drives North; Mr. Drake's Duck; Murder by Rope; My Brother's Keeper; No Highway In the Sky; Oh, God! Book II; Our Man In Marrakesh; Poison Pen; Ritual of Evil; The Scarab Murder Case; Skulldug-gery; Tarzan and the Lost Safari; Tarzan, the Ape Man (1981); Ten Little Indians (1965); The Third Man; Top Secret (1952); The Vicious Circle (1957); Wanted for Murder

Hyem, Jill (act): *Evidence In Concrete*

Hyer, Martha (act, b. 1930): *Abbott and Costello Go to Mars; The Clay Pigeon; Crossplot; Down Three Dark Streets; First Men In the Moon (1964); Francis In the Navy; House of 1,000 Dolls; Mistress of the World (1959); Once You Kiss a Stranger; Picture Mommy Dead; Pyro; Riders to the Stars; The Scarlet Spear; 2267 A.D.-When the Sleeper Wakes (unfinished); The Velvet Touch*

Hyett, Lois (act): *Fragment of Fear*

Hyke, Ray (act): *The Beast from 20,000 Fathoms*

Hyland, Diana (act): *Ritual of Evil*

Hyland, Frances (act): *The Changeling; Evil Stalks This House; Happy Birthday to Me; Moonlight Becomes You; Never Talk to Strangers; When the Dark Man Calls*

Hyland, Frances (wri): *Charlie Chan In Reno; The Lost Zeppelin; The Thirteenth Guest*

Hyland, Peggy (act): *Fetters of Fear; In the Ranks*

Hylands, Scott (act): *Daddy's Gone A-Hunting; Earthquake; Earth II*

Hyler, Tamara (act): *Slaughterhouse Rock*

Hylland, Richard (act): *The Green Slime*

Hylten-Cavallius, Ragnar (wri): *The Story of Gosta Berling*

Hylton, Edgar W. (act): *The Secret of the Moor*

Hylton, Gloria (act): *Sorority Girls and the Creature from Hell*

Hylton, Jane (act, 1926-1979): *Burnt Evidence; Circus of Horrors; Daybreak; Deadly Record; Dear Murderer; The Frightened Bride; House of Mystery (1961); The Manster; My Brother's Keeper; Night Train for Inverness; Secret Venture; The Upturned Glass; Violent Moment; You Pay Your Money*

Hyman, Bob (act): *The Crater Lake Monster*

Hyman, Dick (mus): *The Henderson Monster; The Purple Rose of Cairo*

Hyman, Earle (act, b. 1926): *The Ivory Ape; Light Years; The Possession of Joel Delaney*

Hyman, Phyllis (mus): *Too Scared to Scream*

Hyman, Prudence (act): *The Gorgon*

Hymer, Warren (act, 1906-1948): *Charlie Chan Carries On; Lure of the Islands; Mr. Moto In Danger Island; The Phantom Killer*

Hynek, Joel (cin): *Judge Dredd*

Hynes, Karen (act): *Happy Birthday to Me*

Hyson, Dorothy (act, b. 1915): *The Ghoul (1933)*

Hystad, Bruce (act): *Empire of Ash III*

Hystad, Jeff (act): *Empire of Ash III*

Hytner, Nicholas (dir): *The Crucible (1996)*

Hytner, Steve (act): *The Prophecy (1995)*

Hytower, Roy (act): *Poltergeist III*

Hytten, Olaf (act): *The Adventures of Robin Hood; Arrest Bulldog Drummond; The Brighton Strangler; Chu Chin Chow (1923)*

Iacangelo, Peter (act): *Tattoo*

Iandoli, Dean (act): *Monster High*

Iannaccone, Carmine (act): *Maid to Order; Slaughter High*

Iannini, Lisa (act): *The Fear (1994)*

Iaquinta, Jim (act): *Rana: The Legend of Shadow Lake*

Iasillo (Jr.), Peter (act): *Spookies; Street Trash*

Ibanez (act): *L'Age d'Or*

Ibanez, Juan (dir): *The Fear Chamber; House of Evil (1968); Invasion Sinitestra; Isle of the Snake People*

Ibbetson, Arthur (cin, b. 1921): *Babes In Toyland (1986); Fanatic (1965); Frankenstein: The True Story; The Medusa Touch; The Prisoner of Zenda (1979); Santa Claus (1985); Spectre (1977); Willy Wonka and the Chocolate Factory*

Ibert, Jacques (mus, 1890-1962): *Macbeth (1947)*

Ibn Israel, Mohamed (act): *Devi*

Ibold, Doug (act): *The Capture of Bigfoot*

Ice, Gerald (mus): *Satan's Cheerleaders*

Ice Cube (act): *Anaconda*

Ice-T (act): *Johnny Mnemonic; Surviving the Game; Tank Girl*

Ichac, Pierre (wri): *Die Herrin von Atlantis*

Ichaso, Leon (dir): *A Kiss to Die For*

Ichiha, Kiyohiko (act): *Suna No Onna*

Ichikawa, Chusha (act): *Chusingura (1963)*

Ichikawa, Hiroshi (act): *Godzilla On Monster Island*

Ichikawa, Raizo (act): *Buddha*

Icsey, Rudolfo (cin): *Macumba Love*

Ida, Hiroki (act): *Cyber Ninja*

Ida, Kunihiko (act): *Zeram*

Ide, Masato (wri): *Ran*

Idelson, William (wri): *The Crawling Hand*

Idle, Eric (act, b. 1943): *The Adventures of Baron Munchausen (1989); Casper; Mom and Dad Save the World; Monty Python and the Holy Grail; Quest for Camelot; Splitting Heirs*

Idle, Eric (wri, b. 1943): *Mom and Dad Save the World; Monty Python and the Holy Grail; Splitting Heirs*

Idol, Billy (mus, b. 1955): *Demons (1985)*

Idris, Yusuf (wri): *A Story of Tutankhamun*

Ieda, Yoshiko (act): *Kwaidan*

Ifukube, Akira (mus): *Atragon; Battle In Outer Space; Chusingura (1963); Destroy All Monsters; Godzilla vs. Mothra; Latitude Zero; Majin, Monster of Terror; Monster Zero; The Mysterians; Rodan,the Flying Monster; Terror of Mechagodzilla; Yog-Monster from Space*

Igami, Masaru (wri): *The Magic Serpent*

Igarashi, Tomoko (act): *Virus (1980)*

Igawa, Hisashi (act): *Ran*

Iglesias, Gene (act): *East of Sumatra*

Iglesias, Paulita (act): *The Possession of Joel Delaney*

Iglesias, Ron (act): *The Dark (1979)*

Ignaciuk, Eugeniusz (cin): *Niebezpieczenstwo*

Ignatova, Kyunna (act): *Planeta Bura*

Ignico, Robin (act): *Cry for the Strangers; Don't Go to Sleep*

Ignon, Sandy (act): *Creator; Death Race 2000*

Iguchi, Yoneo (act): *Varan the Unbelievable*

Ihara, Tsuyoshi (act): *Gamera: Guardian of the Universe*

Ihnat, Steve (act): *Countdown; In Like Flint*

Ikebe, Ryo (act): *Battle In Outer Space; Gorath; The War In Space*

Ikeda, Edmund (act): *Freejack*

Ikeda, Hiroshi (cin): *The X from Outer Space*

Ikeuchi, Junko (act): *Atomic Rulers of the World; Evil Brain from Outer Space; Onna Kyuketsuki*

Ikpeama, Emmanuel (act): *Forever Evil*

Ikuta, Yorozu (wri): *Angel Dust*

Ilagan, Jay (act): *Moro Witch Doctor*

Iles, Francis (wri): *Suspicion (1941 & 1987)*

Iles, Gerald (act): *Oh Heavenly Dog*

Ilimaiti, Strong (act): *The Green Slime*

Ilinsky, Igor (act): *Aelita*

Illa, Aron (act): *Blood Diner*

Illescas, Charles (wri): *Dr. Tarr's Torture Dungeon*

Illing, Peter (act, 1899-1966): *Bluebeard's Ten Honeymoons; TheDevil's Daffodil; Devils of Dark-ness; Echo of Diana; The House Across the Lake; I Accuse (1958); Interpol; Man In the Shadow; Moment of Danger; My Daughter Joy; Passport to Treason; The Secret Door; The Secret Partner; State Secret; Svengali (1954); Whirlpool (1959); Zex*

Ilush, Rod Flash (act): *Ali Baba and the Sacred Crown; Vulcan, Son of Jupiter*

Imada, Jeff (act): *Big Trouble In Little China; They Live*

Image, Jean (dir): *Johnny the Giant Killer*

Image Engineering (Inc.) (cin): *The Loch Ness Horror; Neon Maniacs; The People Under the Stairs; Tarzan In Manhattan*

Imai, Hiroshi (cin): *Buddha*

Imai, Kazuo (act): *Mothra*

Imai, Tadashi (dir, b. 1912): *Yoru No Tsuzumi*

Imamura, Hideo (act): *Varan the Unbelievable*

Imamura, Shohei (dir & wri): *The Profound Desire of the Gods*

Iman (act): *Exit to Eden; No Way Out; Star Trek VI: The Undiscovered Country*

Imeson, A.B. (act): *Discipline; The House of Peril; The Monkey's Paw (1923); The Picture of Dorian Gray (1916); The River House Mystery*

Imeson, A.B. (dir): *Discipline; The Strange Case of Mr. Todmorden*

Imhoff, Gary (act): *It Came Upon the Midnight Clear; The Nude Bomb; Thumbelina (1994)*

Imhoff, Roger (act): *Charlie Chan's Greatest Case; Nancy Drew, Troubleshooter*

Imi, Tony (cin): *A Christmas Carol (1984); Enemy Mine; The Return of Swamp Thing (1986); Robin Hood Junior (1975);The Slipper and the Rose*

Imler, J. Ross (act): *The Octagon*

Immel, Jerrold (mus): *The House On Skull Mountain; Megaforce*

Immel/Huxley (mus): *Programmed to Kill*

Imperio, Flavio (wri): *Os Deuses e os Muertos*

Imperio, Liz (act): *Dick Tracy (1990)*

Imperioli, Michael (act): *The Addiction*

Impert, Margie (act): *The Howling*

Impey, Betty (act): *Quatermass II; Stranger In Town (1957)*

Imrie, Celia (act): *The Borrowers (1998); Highlander; House of Whipcord; Mary Shelley's Frankenstein; Murder by Moonlight*

Imrie, Richard (wri): *Operation Crossbow*

Inaba, Yoshio (act): *Harakiri*

Inagaki, Hiroshi (dir & wri): *Chusingura (1963); Secret Scrolls-Parts I & II*

Inagaki, Yozo (cin): *The Ivory Ape*

Ince, John (act): *The Clutching Hand; Moby Dick (1930)*

Ince, John (dir): *Blackie's Redemption*

Ince, Ralph (act, 1887-1937): *Gaol Break (1936); No Escape (1934); The Perfect Crime*

Ince, Ralph (dir, 1887-1937): *Black Mask; Crime Unlimited; Gaol Break (1936); Jury's Evidence; The Lone Wolf Returns (1926); The Man Who Made Diamonds; Murder at Monte Carlo; No Escape (1934); The Perfect Crime; Twelve Good Men; The Vulture (1937)*

Ince, Thomas H. (act): *Richelieu, or The Cardinal's Conspiracy*

Inch, Bonnie (act): *The Incredible Melting Man*

Inciarte, Juan (act): *El Dia de la Bestia*

Incontrera, Annabella (act): *The Assassination Bureau; The Black Belly of the Tarantula; Il Diavolo Innamorato*

Indri, Ross (act): *Hello Again*

Induni, Luis (act): *La Maldicion de la Bestia*

Industrial Light & Magic (cin): **Batteries Not Included; Cocoon:The Return; Dragonheart; Death Becomes Her; Ewoks: The Battle for Endor; Explorers; The Flintstones;The Golden Child; The Goonies;Howard the Duck; The Indian In the Cupboard; Jack Frost (1998);Jumanji; The Lost World: Jurassic Park; The Mask (1994); Mission: Impossible; Spawn; Star Trek III: The Search for Spock; Star Trek: First Contact; Who Framed Roger Rabbit; Young Sherlock Holmes*

Inescort, Frieda (act, 1901-1976): *The Alligator People; Casanova's Big Night; The Garden Murder Case; The Return of the Vampire; Shadows On the Stairs; The She-Creature; Tarzan Finds a Son!*

Ineson, Ralph (act): *First Knight*

Infante, Sonia (act): *Doctor of Doom*

Infanti, Angelo (act): *The Count of Monte Cristo (1975); Fragment of Fear*

Infascelli, Carlo (wri): *Robin Hood and the Pirates*

Infuhr, Teddy (act): *The Bishop's Wife; The Boy With Green Hair*

Ingalls, Don (wri): *Captain America (1978); Flood*

Ingber, Amanda/Mandy (act): *The Relic; Teen Witch*

Ingels, Marty (act, b. 1936): *The Busy Body*

Inger, Melissa (act): *It Lives Again*

Ingersoll, James (act): *The Man With the Power*

Ingersoll, Mary (act): *Watchers II*

Ingerson, Jay R. (act): *Slugs*

Ingham, Barrie (act): *A Challenge for Robin Hood; Company of Fools; Dr. Who and the Daleks; Invasion (1965); Secret Weapons; Sparkling Cyanide*

Ingham, Jill (act): *Superman (1978)*

Ingham, Jonathan (act): *The Bermuda Depths*

Ingham, Nicholas (act): *The Bermuda Depths*

Ingham, Robert (act): *Mutants In Paradise*

Ingle, John (H.) (act): *The Land Before Time V: The Mysterious Island; Repossessed; RoboCop 2; Stepfather III: Father's Day; Suture*

Ingles, Rufino (act): *Tombs of the Blind Dead*

Inglis, Elizabeth (act): *Landslide (1937); Museum Mystery*

Inglis, Margaret (act): *House of the Living Dead*

Ingolia, Concetta Ann (act): see Stevens, Connie

Ingraham, Lloyd (act): *Ghost Rider (1935); The Lost Jungle*

Ingram, Donna Patrice (act): *The Wiz*

Ingram, Fred (act): *The Beggar Girl's Wedding*

Ingram, Jack (act): *Dick Tracy's Returns; The Jade Mask*

Ingram, Jean (act): *Sergeant Deadhead the Astronut!*

Ingram, Joan (act): *The Deathshead Vampire; The Man Outside*

Ingram, Jonathan (wri): *It Happened Here*

Ingram, Rex (act, 1896-1969, aka Rex Fitchcock): *Cabin In the Sky; Congo Crossing; Dark Waters; Green Pastures; Hell On Devil's Island; Tarzan of the Apes; Tarzan's Hidden Jungle; The Thief of Bagdad (1940); A Thousand and One Nights (1945); Watusi*

Ingram, Rex (dir, 1893-1950): *Black Orchids; The Conquering Power; The Flower of Doom; The Magician (1926); The Prisoner of Zenda (1922); Trifling Women*

Ingram, Rex (wri, 1893-1950): *Black Orchids; The Magician (1926);Trifling Women*

Ingram, Terry (dir): *Earthquake In New York*

Ingram, Willie (act): *The Mutations*

Ingrassia, Ciccio (act): *Amarcord; Dr. Goldfoot and the Girl Bombs; Kaos; Two Mafia Guys vs Goldginger*

Ingster, Boris (dir): *Stranger On the Third Floor*

Inigo, Lina (act): *The Omegans*

Inkihinoff, (Vladimir) (act): *Journey to the Lost City; Nick Carter Va Tout Casser*

Inkijinoff, Valery (act): *The Black Rose*

Inman, Mark (act): *Mary Shelley's Frankenstein*

Inneo, Vince (Act): *They Live*

Innes, Alexandra (act): *Alien High*

Innes, Charmian (act): *Dark Interval*

Innes, Edward (act): *The Angry Red Planet*

Innes, George (act): *Fugitive from the Empire; Goliath Awaits; The Medusa Touch; Morons from Outer Space; Ordeal by Innocence; Where's Johnny*

Innes, John (act): *Storm of the Century*

Innes, Margaret (act): *The Mutagen*

Innes, Neil (act & mus): *Erik the Viking; Jabberwocky; Monty Python and the Holy Grail*

Inness, Jean (act): *The Man With a Cloak*

Innocent, Harold (act): *The Canterville Ghost (1986); Robin Hood: Prince of Thieves; Without a Clue; Yellow Dog*

Innocenzi, Carlo (mus): *Gli Amori di Ercole; David and Goliath; Goliath Against the Giants*

Innys, Francis (act): *The Temptation of Carlton Earle*

Inoles, Rufino (act): *Goliath Against the Giants*

Inouye, Julie (act): *Killer In the Mirror*

Insana, Tino (act): *Neighbors*

Inscoe, Joe (act): *Teenage Mutant Ninja Turtles*

Instone, John (act): *The Bermuda Depths*

Insua, Alberto (S.) (wri): *Gran Amore del Conde Dracula; El Jorobado de la Morgue*

Interlenghi, Franco (act): *Ulysses*

Introvision (cin): *Monolith*

Inward, Alice (act): *Detective Finn and the Foreign Spies; Detective Finn: or, In the Heart of London; The Dungeon of Death; The King of Seven Dials;The Port of Missing Women; Vice and Virtue: or, The Tempters of London*

Inwood, Steve (act): *Dark Mansions*

In-Zip, Byon (cin): *Yongary, Monster from the Deep*

Ioannidou, Theano (act): *Electra (1961)*

Iocouvozzi, Kim (act): *Squirm*

Ione (act): *Something Weird*

Ionesco, Eugene (wri, 1912-1994): *Die Nashorner; Rhinoceros (1974)*

Iovieno, Frank (act): *Invasion of the Blood Farmers*

Iovine, Fabrizio (act): *The Secret of Seagull Island*

Ipale, Aharon (act): *A Ghost in Monte Carlo; Invisible: The Chronicles of Benjamin Knight*

Ippoliti, Mimma (act): *Satanik*

Ippoliti, Silvano (cin): *Sodom and Gomorrah; Super Fuzz*

Ipua, Gasphar (act): *Mystery On Monster Island*

Irarte, Miguel A. (act): *No Exit*

Ireland, Anthony (act): *I Accuse (1958); Juggernaut; Mrs.Pym of Scotland Yard; The Night of the Full Moon; Spaceways; Twin Faces*

Ireland, Bob (act): *Shadow of the Thin Man*

Ireland, Ian (act): *The Hound of The Baskervilles (1972)*

Ireland, Jill (act, 1936-1990): *The Desperate Man; The Ghost Train Murder; Jungle Street; The Karate Killers; Passager de la Pluie; Quelqu'un Derriere la Porte*

Ireland, John (act, 1914-1992): *Day of the Nightmare; Faces In the Dark; Farewell, My Lovely; The 49th Man; The Glass Tomb; Guyana, Cult of the Damned; The House of Seven Corpses; Incubus (1982); I Saw What You Did (1965); The Mad Butcher; Miami Golem; Open Secret; The Phantom of Hollywood; Queen Bee; Return of a Stranger (1962); Satan's Cheerleaders; The Scarf; Security Risk; The Shape of Things to Come (1979); Stormy Crossing; Sundown:The Vampire In Retreat; Tomorrow Never Comes; Waxworks II: Lost In Time; Welcome to Arrow Beach*

Ireland, Kathy (act, b. 1963): *Mr. Destiny; Mom and Dad Save the World; The Presence*

Ireland, Kylie (act): *Strange Days*

Ireland, Peter (act): *Myra Breckinridge; Welcome to Arrow Beach*
Irey, Carol (act): *X-The Man With the X-Ray Eyes*
Irie, Miki (act): *Tanin No Kao*
Irish, Beverly (act): *The Toxic Avenger, Part II*
Irish, Mitch (act): *The Capture of Bigfoot*
Irish, William (wri): *Fear In the Night (1947); The House of Horror (1929); La Marieeetait en Noir; Obsession (1954);Phantom Lady*
Irizarry, Gloria (act): *Jacob's Ladder*
Iron Maiden (mus): *Phenomena*
Irons, Jeremy (act, b. 1948): *Dead Ringers; The Man In the Iron Mask (1998)*
Irons, Kathy (act): *The Psychotronic Man*
Irons, Tommy (mus): *The Psychotronic Man*
Ironside, Michael (act, b. 1950): *The Haunting of Hamilton High; Highlander 2: The Quickening; Johnny 2.0; Mardi Gras for the Devil; Mindfield; Murder In Space; Neon City; Portraits of a Killer; Scanners; The Sins of Dorian Gray; Spacehunter: Adventures In the Forbidden Zone; Starship Troopers; Terminal; Total Recall; Visiting Hours; Voyage of Terror; Watchers*
Irrera, Dom (act): *The Silence of the Hams*
Irta, Miss (act): *The Bride (1985)*
Irvin, Barbara (act): *Child of Darkness, Child of Light*
Irvin, John (dir): *Ghost Story (1981); Robin Hood (1991)*
Irvin, Sam (dir): *Acting On Impulse; Backlash: Oblivion 2; Magic Island; Oblivion; Out There*
Irvine, Beth (act): *Queen of the Sea*
Irvine, Irina (act): *Fright Night*
Irvine, Paula (act): *Bates Motel; Phantasm II; Phantasm III: Lord of the Dead*
Irvine, Robin (act): *Downhill; The Secret Kingdom*
Irvine, St. John (wri): *The Man Without a Face*
Irving, Amy (act, b. 1953): *An American Tail: Fievel Goes West; Benefit of the Doubt; Carrie; The Fury; The Rage: Carrie 2; Rumpelstiltskin (1987); Who Framed Roger Rabbit*
Irving, Charles (act): *Project X (1967)*
Irving, David (dir): *C.H.U.D. II; The Emperor's New Clothes (1989); Rumpelstiltskin (1987); Sleeping Beauty (1986)*
Irving, Ellis (act): *Black Mask; Member of the Jury; Murder at Monte Carlo; Murder In Reverse; Pool of London*
Irving, George (act): *Calling Philo Vance; Charlie Chan at the Race Track; Charlie Chan In Egypt; Island of Lost Souls; The Mandarin Mystery; Son of Dracula (1943)*
Irving, Gregg (wri): *Just Before Dawn (1980)*
Irving, H.B. (act): *The Lyons Mail; Princess Clementina*
Irving, Holly (act): *Frogs; The Magician (1973)*
Irving, Jules (act): *It Came from Beneath the Sea*
Irving, Katie (mus): *Carrie*
Irving, Louis (cin): *Communion; Howling III*
Irving, Margaret (act): *Charlie Chan at the Opera; Mr. Moto's Last Warning*
Irving, Paul (act): *Charlie Chan In City in Darkness*
Irving, Penny (act): *The Day the Screaming Stopped; House of Whipcord; Spectre (1977)*
Irving, Richard (act): *Mars Attacks!; Missile Monsters*
Irving, Richard (dir): *Exo-Man; The Six Million Dollar Man*
Irving, Washington (wri, 1783-1859): *The Headless Horseman; La Legendede Rip Van Winkle; The Legend of Sleepy Hollow; Once Upon a Midnight Scary; Rip Van Winkle (1896, 1903, 1910, 1914 & 1921)*
Irwin (Jr.), Boyd (act): *Buried Alive (1940); The Docks of New Orleans; Meet Nero Wolfe; The Three Musketeers (1921)*
Irwin, Carl (act): *Modern Problems*
Irwin, Charles (act): *The Adventures of Robin Hood; Bomba, the Jungle Boy; Bulldog Drummond Strikes Back (1934); The Great Impersonation (1942); League of Frightened Men; The Mystery of Mr.X; Panther Island; Think Fast, Mr. Moto*
Irwin, Coulter (act): *Crime Doctor's Warning*
Irwin, Edward (wri): *The Bargain*
Irwin, James B. (act): *For All Mankind*
Irwin, James G. (act): *Cyborg (1989)*
Irwin, John (act): *Someone at the Door*
Irwin, John (dir): *A Piece of Cake*
Irwin, Mark (cin): *The Blob (1988); The Brood; Class of 1999; The Dead Zone; The Fly (1986); Fright Night II; Funeral Home; I Come In Peace; Man's Best Friend; Night School; Not of This World; RoboCop 2; Scanners; Scream; Starship Invasions; Videodrome;Wes Craven's New Nightmare*
Irwin, May (act, 1862-1938): *The Kiss (1896)*
Irwin, Tom (act): *Deceived*
Irwin, Wynn (act): *It Came Upon the Midnight Clear*
Isaac, Brad (act): *Shock! Shock! Shock!*
Isaac, Gerald (act): *The Pink Chiquitas*
Isaac, James (cin): *Deepstar Six*
Isaac, James (dir): *The Horror Show*
Isaac, Jeffrey (act): *The Hunchback of Notre Dame (1965)*
Isaac, John (act): *Empire of Ash III*
Isaac, Robert (act): *Strange Behaviour*
Isaac, Susan (act): *House II: The Second Story*
Isaac, Vincent J. (act): *Twilight Zone*
Isaacks, Levie (cin): *Children of the Corn II: The Final Sacrifice; The Dogfighters; I'm Dangerous Tonight; Leprechaun; The Nature of the Beast; Sundown: The Vampire In Retreat*
Isaacs, Andy (act): *Matinee*
Isaacs, Charles (wri): *Digby-The Biggest Dog In the World*
Isaacs, David (wri): *Mannequin Two: On the Move*
Isaacs, Frank H. (cin): *Beastmaster 2: Through the Portalof Time*
Isaacs, Jason (act): *Dragonheart*
Isaacs, Susan (act & wri): *Hello Again*
Isaacson, Karin (act): *The Legend of Sleepy Hollow*
Isaak, Chris (act, b. 1956):*The Silence of the Lambs; Twin Peaks: Fire Walk With Me*
Isaak, Nancy (wri): *Terminal*
Isabelle, Katharine (act): *Voyage of Terror*
Isacksen, Peter (act): *Earthbound (1981)*
Isacson, Bruce (act): *Outbreak*
Isar, Karl (wri): *The Magic Voyage of Sinbad*
Isbecque, Doug (act): *The Toxic Avenger*
Isbell, Anthony (act): *I Was a Zombie for the F.B.I.*
Isbell, John C. (act): *Cat People (1982)*
Isbert, Jose (act): *Faustina; Not On Your Life!; A Rocket from Calabuch*
Isbert, Maruja (act): *Not On Your Life!*
Isbert, Tony (act): *Endless Descent; The Saga of the Draculas*
Iscove, Robert (dir): *Cinderella (1997); Dark Angel (1996); The Flash*
Isedal, Tor (act): *Mortanna*
Isfeld, Justin (act): *Ice Cream Man*
Isham, Gyles (act): *Secret Lives*
Isham, Jeffery (act): *Blood Song*
Isham, Mark (mus, b. 1951): *Cool World; Fire In the Sky (1993); The Hitcher; Made In Heaven; Of Mice and Men (1992); Romeo Is Bleeding; Timecop*
Isherwood, Christopher (wri, 1904-1986): *Frankenstein: The True Story; The Loved One; Rage In Heaven*
Ishi, Ryuko Nakan (wri): *Gappa, the Triphibian Monster*
Ishida, Ayumi (act): *The Submersion of Japan*
Ishida, James/Jim (act): *Back to the Future, Part II; The Silencers (1995); Strange Days*
Ishida, Moriyoshi (wri): *The X from Outer Space*
Ishihama, Akira (act): *Harakiri*
Ishii, Leslie (act): *Species*
Ishii, Masahiro (act): *The Toxic Avenger, Part II*
Ishii, Sogo (dir & wri): *Angel Dust; The Crazy Family*
Ishii, Teruo (dir): *Atomic Rulers of the World; Evil Brain from Outer Space*
Ishikawa, Komei (cin): *Alakazam the Great*
Ishikawa, Miko (act): *Ghost Warrior*
Ishiyama, Kenjiro (act): *High and Low; Kwaidan*
Isitt, Kate (act): *The Saint*
Island, Bert F. (wri): *Kiss Kiss, Kill Kill*
Island, Nancy (act): *The Mask (1961)*
Isley, Phyllis (act): see Jones, Jennifer
Ismael, Zoreen (act): *Shoot to Kill (1961)*
Isobe, Saburo (act): *The Toxic Avenger, Part II*
Israel, Al (act): *Body Double*
Israel, Betsy (wri): *Mannequin Two: On the Move*
Israel, Charles (wri): *The Mark*
Israel, David (wri): *Pandora's Clock*
Israel, Neil (dir): *Americathon*
Israel, Victor (act): *The House That Screamed; La Maldicion de la Bestia*
Isreal, Neal (act): *It's Alive III: Island of the Alive*
Issa, Massoud (cin): *Dawn of the Mummy*
Issacs, Frank (cin): *The Alien Within*
Isyanov, Ravil (act): *Goldeneye; The Saint*
Italiano, Anna Maria Luisa (act): see Bancroft, Anne
Italiano, Jennifer (act): *Beyond Evil*
Itard, Jean (wri): *L'Enfant Sauvage*
Itkine, Sylvain (act): *Le Roman de Renard*
Ito, Akjo (act): *Voyage into Space*
Ito, Emi (act): *Godzilla vs. Mothra; Mothra*
Ito, Hiroko (act): *Suna No Onna*
Ito, Jelly (act): *Mothra*
Ito, Jerry (act): *The Manster*
Ito, Jill (act): *Murder of Innocence*
Ito, Keiko (act): *Virus (1980)*
Ito, Kisaya (act): *Battle In Outer Space; The Mysterians*
Ito, Robert (act): *The Adventures of Buckaroo Banzai;Dimension 5; Fer-de-Lance; The Terminal Man*
Ito, Yukari (act): *Five Golden Dragons*
Ito, Yumi (act): *Godzilla vs. Mothra; Mothra*
Itzkowitz, Edward (act): see Cantor, Eddie
Itzkowitz, Howard (act): *Star Trek*
Iures, Marcel (act): *The Peacemaker (1997)*
Ivan, Rosalind (act, 1884-1959): *The Garden Murder Case; Pillow of Death; The Suspect; Three Strangers; The Verdict (1946)*
Ivanek, Zeljko (act, b. 1957): *The Sender*
Ivanhoe, Burl Icle (act): see Ives, Burl
Ivano, Paul (cin, b. 1900):*Black Angel (1946); Captive Women; Champagne for Caesar; Dead Man's Eyes; Flesh and Fantasy; The Frozen Ghost; Lizzie; Pursuit to Algiers; Search for Danger; The Suspect*
Ivanov, Nicolai (act): *The Red Tent*
Ivan-Zadeh, Michele (act): *The Great Muppet Caper*
Ivar, Stan (act): *Creature; The Disappearance of Nora*
Ivens, Terri (act): *Trancers 4: Jack of Swords; Trancers5: Sudden Deth*
Iveria, Miki (act): *Berserk; Billion Dollar Brain*
Ivernel, Daniel (act): *The French Conspiracy; Ulysses*
Ivers, Peter (act): *Jekyll and Hyde...Together Again*
Ivers, Robert (act): *I Married a Monster from Outer Space*
Ives, Anne (act): *The Reincarnation of Peter Proud*
Ives, Burl (act, 1909-1995, nee Burl Icle Ivanhoe): *The Bermuda Depths; The Brass Bottle (1964); Earthbound (1981); The Ewok Adventure; The Only Way Out Is Dead; Those Fantastic Flying Fools;White Dog*
Ives, David (wri): *The Hunted (1998)*
Ives, Douglas (act): *The Big Chance; Two Wives at One Wedding*
Ives, Lisa (act): *Psycho III*
Ives-Cameron, Elaine (act): *Blue Blood; Terror (1979)*
Ivey, Dana (act): *The Addams Family; Addams Family Values; Explorers; Guilty as Sin*
Ivey, Edith (act): *Rearview Mirror; Web of Deceit*
Ivey, Judith (act, b. 1951):*Devil's Advocate; Hello Again; Sister, Sister*
Ivins, Perry (act): *The Benson Murder Case; Charlie Chan In London; Charlie Chan In Paris; Son of Frankenstein*
Ivo, Tom(my) (act): *The Ghost of Dragstrip Hollow; The Lost Volcano; The Treasure of Lost Canyon*
Ivory, James (dir & wri, b. 1928): *Savages*
Ivy, Bob (act): *The Phantom Empire*
Ivy, Joe (act): *Child of Darkness, Child of Light*
Iwamoto, Hiroshi (act): *Mothra*
Iwanaga, Frank (act): *Gojira*
Iwara, Mitsuo (act): *Akira*
Iwashita, Shima (act): *Harakiri*
Iwaskiewicz, Jaroslav (wri): *Matka Joanna od Aniolow*
Iwata, Mitsuo (act): *Akira*
Iwerks, Ub (cin, 1901-1971): *Peter Pan (1953); 20,000 Leagues Under the Sea (1954)*
Iwerks, Ub (dir, 1901-1971): *The Frog Pond*
Izay, Victor (act): *Astro Zombies; Blood Song; Night Slaves; Premonition (1972)*
Izotov, E. (act): *Jack Frost*
Izquierdo, Pat (act): *Hundra*
Izzard, Eddie (act): *The Avengers; The Secret Agent (1996)*

J, Ray (act): *Mars Attacks!*
Jabotinsky, Vladimir (wri): *Samson and Delilah*
Jaboulian, Arch (act): *The Meateater*
Jabour, Gabriel (act): *La Poupee*
Jace, Michael (act): *Strange Days*
Jachino, Alex (act): *Ms. 45*
Jachino, Silvana (act): *Giulietta degli Spiriti*
Jack, Collette (act): *Night Hair Child*
Jack, Stephen (act): *Gulliver's Travels (1977); Treasure Island (1950)*
Jackley, Jolyon (act): *The Sound Barrier*
Jackley, Nat (act): *The Inside Man; Threads*
Jacklin, Martin (mus): *The Face of Darkness*
Jackman (Jr.), Fred (cin): *Creature With the Atom Brain; Earth vs. the Flying Saucers; Julie; One Body Too Many; Phantom of Chinatown; Time Travelers (1976)*
Jackman, Tom (act): *The Cat from Outer Space*
Jacko, David (act): *Secrets of the Phantom Caverns*
Jackos, George (act): *Young Indiana Jones: Travels With Father*
Jackson, Mr. (act): *The Corner House Burglary; The Rajah's Tiara*
Jackson, Andrew (1910s act): *The Mystery of a London Flat*
Jackson, Andrew (act): *The Glitterball; Red Blooded American Girl*
Jackson, Andrew (cin): *The Strongest Man In the World*
Jackson, Anne (act, b. 1926): *The Angel Levine; The Shining*
Jackson, Barry (act): *Diamonds On Wheels; The Glitterball*
Jackson, Billy (act): *The Frighteners*
Jackson, Brad(ford) (act): *The Search for Bridey Murphy; The Viking Women and the Sea Serpent*
Jackson, Brian (act, b. 1931): *The Deadly Females*
Jackson, Charles (act): *Midnight (1980)*
Jackson, Charles (wri): *The Lost Weekend*
Jackson, Clinton (act): *The Wiz*
Jackson, Crane (act): *The Octagon; Something Evil; Time Flyer*
Jackson, Curtis (act): *The Boy With Green Hair*
Jackson, D.J. (act): *I Still Dream of Jeannie*
Jackson, Dan (act): *The Heart Within; A High Wind In Jamaica; The Mind of Mr. Soames; Mysterious Island (1961); Naked Evil; Paul Temple Returns*
Jackson, David (act): *Always; The Big Sleep (1978); Blood from the Mummy's Tomb; Killer's Moon; 10 Rillington Place*
Jackson, David E. (cin): *The Lucifer Complex*
Jackson, Donald (dir & wri): *The Demon Lover*
Jackson, Donald G. (cin): *Roller Blade Warriors: Taken by Force*
Jackson, Donald G. (dir & wri): *The Demon Lover; Hell Comes to Frogtown; Roller Blade Warriors: Taken by Force*
Jackson, Doug(las) (dir): *Deadbolt; Dean R. Koontz' Whispers; Midnight In Saint Petersburg*
Jackson, Elma V. (act): *The Man With Two Brains*
Jackson, Ernest/Ernie (act): *Lunatic; Timecop*
Jackson, Eugene (act): *Arrest Bulldog Drummond*
Jackson, Freda (act, b. 1909): *Attempt to Kill; Boy With a Flute; Brides of Dracula; Clash of the Titans; The Flesh Is Weak; Great Expectations (1946); The Last Man to Hang?; Mr. Denning Drives North; Monster of Terror; The Shadow of the Cat; The Third Secret; The Valley of Gwangi; West 11*
Jackson, Freddie (act): *Def by Temptation*
Jackson, G. Philip (dir): *The Music of the Spheres; Replikator: Cloned to Kill*
Jackson, G. Philip (wri): *The Music of the Spheres*
Jackson, Glenda (act, b. 1936): *The Maids; Negatives; The Persecution and Assassination of Jean-Paul Marat as Performed by the Inmates of the Asylum of Charenton Under the Direction of the Marquis de Sade; The Tempter (1973)*
Jackson, Gordon (act, 1923-1990): *Blind Date (1959); Blind Spot (1958); Danger Route; Death Goes to School; Hamlet (1969); The Ipcress File; Madame Sin; Man In the Shadow; The Medusa Touch; Meet Mr. Lucifer; The Night of the Generals; The Price of Silence; The Quatermass Experiment; Scrooge (1970); Spectre (1977); Stop Press Girl; Three Crooked Men; Two Wives at One Wedding*
Jackson, Harold (act): *The Coming*
Jackson, Harry (act): *The Monolith Monsters*
Jackson, Harry (cin): *Charlie Chan at the Race Track; Charlie Chan On Broadway; Think Fast, Mr. Moto*
Jackson, Howard (mus): *Cry Terror!; Tobor the Great*
Jackson, Inigo (act): *The Brigand of Kandahar; He Who Rides a Tiger; Twins of Evil*
Jackson, Jalil (dir): *Lady Terminator*
Jackson, Jamie Smith (act): *Bug; Satan's School for Girls*
Jackson, Jeanine (act): *The Craft*
Jackson, Jermaine (act): *Voyage of the Rock Aliens*
Jackson, John (act): *The Hitcher*
Jackson, John M. (act): *Eve of Destruction; In Self Defense; Roswell*
Jackson, Jonathan (act): *Prisoner of Zenda, Inc.*
Jackson, Joshua (act, b. 1978): *Magic In the Water; Scream 2; Urban Legend*
Jackson, Kate (act, b. 1948): *Death at Love House; Death Cruise; Homewrecker; Killer Bees; Night of Dark Shadows; Panic In the Skies!;*

Quiet Killer; Satan's School for Girls; Topper (1979)

Jackson, Kendall (act): Haunts

Jackson, Larry E. (wri): The Destructors

Jackson, LaVerne (act): Dr. Black Mr. Hyde

Jackson, Leonard (act): The Brother from Another Planet; Ganja and Hess

Jackson, Lewis (dir): You Better Watch Out

Jackson, Lewis (wri): The Great Office Mystery

Jackson, Lindsay (act): Secrets In the Attic

Jackson, Mark (wri): Eyes of a Stranger

Jackson, Mary (act): Audrey Rose; The Exorcist III; The Folks at Red Wolf Inn; Targets

Jackson, Michael (act, b. 1958): The Wiz

Jackson, Mick (dir): Volcano

Jackson, Mike (dir): Blood Tracks

Jackson, Pat (dir, b. 1916): The Birthday Present; Don't Talk to Strange Men; King Arthur, the Young Warlord; Seven Keys; What a Carve Up!

Jackson, Patrick (dir): Shadow On the Wall

Jackson, Peter (act): Bad Taste

Jackson, Peter (dir): Bad Taste; Dead Alive; The Frighteners; Meet the Feebles

Jackson, Peter (wri): Dead Alive; The Frighteners; Meet the Feebles

Jackson, Philip (dir & wri): Project: Genesis

Jackson, Ray (act): Under the Frozen Falls

Jackson, Roger (act): Scream

Jackson, Roosevelt (act): Blackenstein

Jackson, Samuel L. (act, b. 1949): Def by Temptation; The Exorcist III; Fluke; Jurassic Park; The Long Kiss Goodnight; Sphere; Star Wars: Episode I-The Phantom Menace; A Time to Kill (1996)

Jackson, Sarah Jane (act): To Save a Child

Jackson, Selmer (act): The Ape (1940); The Atomic Submarine; Boston Blackie and the Law; Charlie Chan at the Olympics; Crime Doctor's Diary; Dangerous Money; Devil Goddess; Dick Tracy vs. Crime, Inc.; The Falcon Takes Over; The Lost Missile; Mark of the Gorilla; The Missing Guest; The Thirteenth Man; The Westland Case

Jackson, Sherry (act): The Monitors

Jackson, Shirley (wri, 1920-1965): The Haunting; Lizzie; The Lottery

Jackson, Stanley (act): 7 Surprises

Jackson, Stanley (wri): The Man Who Wouldn't Talk

Jackson, Stephen (act): Strange Behavior

Jackson, Stoney (act): Streets of Fire

Jackson, Tanya (act): Midnight In Saint Petersburg

Jackson, Telford (act): Mad Max

Jackson, Terry (act): 12 Monkeys

Jackson, Thomas/Tommy (E.) (act): Another Thin Man; Blondes at Work; Crime Doctor's Strangest Case; The Hidden Eye; Just Before Dawn (1946); Lady In the Morgue; Nancy Drew, Reporter; The Thin Man; Torchy Gets Her Man; Valley of the Zombies

Jackson, Tom (act): It Conquered the World

Jackson, Travis (dir): The Mountain

Jackson, Valerie (act): Abbott and Costello Go To Mars; The Golden Blade

Jackson, Varerie (act): Angel Heart

Jackson, Veda (act): Jekyll and Hyde...Together Again

Jackson, Victoria (act): Dream a Little Dream

Jackson, Wesley John (act): Scalpel

Jackson, Wilfred (dir): Alice In Wonderland (1951); Song of the South

Jackson, William B. (act): The Annihilator

Jacob, Irene (act): U.S. Marshals

Jacobbi, Ruggero (wri): The Prisoner of the Iron Mask

Jacobi, Derek (act, b. 1938): Blue Blood; Dead Again; Hamlet (1996); The Hunchback of Notre Dame (1982); The Medusa Touch; The Secret of NIMH

Jacobi, Joelle (act): Lady In White

Jacobi, Lou (act, b. 1913): Amazon Women On the Moon; A Kid for Two Farthings; The Last of the Secret Agents?

Jacobs, Al (mus): Death Curse of Tartu

Jacobs, Alexander (wri): Sitting Target

Jacobs, Andre (act): Curse III: Blood Sacrifice; Curse of the Crystal Eye; Prey for the Hunter

Jacobs, Anthony (act): The File of the Golden Goose

Jacobs, Brian (act): Lord of the Flies (1990)

Jacobs, Carl (act): Student Bodies

Jacobs, Claire Rainwater (wri): Mother, May I Sleep with Danger?

Jacobs, David (act): Towers Open Fire

Jacobs, Emma (act): Lifeforce

Jacobs, Herb (act): Project Moonbase

Jacobs, Hilary (act): Distortions

Jacobs, Jack (wri): The Legend of Sleepy Hollow

Jacobs, Jacqueline (act): Galaxina

Jacobs, Jake (act): The Haunted (1991); Phantom of the Mall: Eric's Revenge

Jacobs, Joan Browning (act): Student Bodies

Jacobs, Joey (act): Boston Blackie's Little Pal

Jacobs, Lawrence-Hilton (act): Tidal Wave: No Escape

Jacobs, Linda (act): The Entity

Jacobs, Manny (act): The Seventh Sign

Jacobs, Mark (act): Blood Hook

Jacobs, Martyn (act): Jekyll and Hyde

Jacobs, Matthew (wri): Doctor Who; Lorna Doone (1990); Paperhouse

Jacobs, Michael (act): Halloween 5: The Revenge of Michael Myers

Jacobs, Nicholas A.E. (dir & wri): The Refrigerator

Jacobs, Olu (act): The Witches and the Grinnygog

Jacobs, Paula (act): An American Werewolf In London

Jacobs, Richard (act): The Final Terror

Jacobs, Rosetta (act): see Laurie, Piper

Jacobs, Seaman (wri): Oh, God! Book II

Jacobs, Shirley Spiegler (act): Blink

Jacobs, T.C.H. (wri): Traitor Spy

Jacobs, W.W. (wri, 1863-1943): Deathdream; Footsteps In the Fog; The Monkey's Paw (1915 & 1923); Spiritism

Jacobs, William (wri): Night of Terror (1933)

Jacobsen, Howard (act): Forever Evil

Jacobson, Dean (act): Child's Play 3

Jacobson, Glenn (act): Trick or Treats

Jacobson, Jill (act): Beyond the Living

Jacobson, Paul L. (wri): Santa Claus Conquers the Martians

Jacobson, Rick "The Cheese" (act): Bloodspell

Jacobson, Rick (dir): Night Hunter; Star Quest (1994); Suspect Device; The Unborn II

Jacobson, Todd (act): Always

Jacobsson, Ulla (act, b. 1929): Crime and Punishment (1958); The Double Man; Herr Arnes Pengar (1954); Nattmara

Jacobus, Jay (act): Copycat

Jacoby, Billy (act): Angel On My Shoulder (1980); Bloody Birthday; Cujo; Demonwarp; Dr. Alien; I Was a Teenage Sex Mutant; Nightmares (1983); Superstition

Jacoby, Bobby (act): I Was a Teenage Sex Mutant; Meet the Applegates; Tremors

Jacoby, Hans (wri, b. 1904): Champagne for Caesar; Stranger from Venus; Tarzan's Savage Fury

Jacoby, Laura (act): The Night They Saved Christmas

Jacoby, Michael/Michel (wri): Doomed to Die; The Face of Marble; The Mystery of Marie Roget; The Undying Monster

Jacoby, Scott (act, b. 1956): Bad Ronald; The Little Girl Who Lives Down the Lane; Return to Horror High; To Die For; To Die For II: Son of Darkness

Jacome, Richard (act): Night of the Lepus

Jacox Jr., David (act): Timecop

Jacquemont, Maurice (act): I Married a Shadow

Jacques, Hattie (act, 1924-1980): All Hallowe'en; The Magic Christian; Mother Riley Meets the Vampire; No Haunt for a Gentleman

Jacques, Norbert (wri): Doctor Mabuse; Das Testament des Dr. Mabuse

Jacquet, Dany (act): The Burning Court

Jacquet, Frank (act): Black Magic (1944); Jungle Jim In the Forbidden Land; The Scarf

Jacquet, Gaston (act): Le Golem (1936)

Jacquet, Jeffrey (act): Return from Witch Mountain

Jacquet, Roger (act): Au Coeur de la Vie

Jad-Bal-Ja (animal act): Tarzan and the Golden Lion

Jade, Claude (act): Topaz

Jaden, Donna Mae (act): see Paige, Janis

Jaeckel, Richard (act, 1926-1997): The Awakening of Candra; Blood Song; Chosen Survivors; The Dark (1979); Day of the Animals; The Deadly Dream; The Green Slime; Grizzly; Herbie Goes Bananas; Latitude Zero; The Lineup; Nightmare in the Sun; Platinum High School; Salvage; Starman; Twilight's Last Gleaming

Jaegen, Elizabeth (act): Barbarian Queen II (The Empress Strikes Back)

Jaeger, Claude (act): Perceval

Jaeger, Denny (mus): The Hunger; Secrets of the Phantom Caverns

Jaeger, Ernst (wri): Devil Bat's Daughter

Jaeger, Frederick (act): The Seventh... Solution

Jaenicke, Hannes (act): Free Fall; The Hunted (1998); Out of Order

Jaenzon, Julius (cin): The Story of Gosta Berling

Jaffa, Rick (wri): The Relic

Jaffe, Allen (act): The Love War; The War Lord

Jaffe, Carl/Karl (act, 1902-1974): The Accursed; Battle Beneath the Earth; The Case of the Smiling Widow; Child's Play (1954); Counterblast; Cross Channel; The Double Man; First Man Into Space; The Hostage (1956); House of Secrets; I Accuse (1958); Law and Disorder; Operation Crossbow; The Saint In London; Satellite In the Sky; State Secret; Subway In the Sky; Timeslip; Warn That Man; Zex

Jaffe, Chapelle (act): Millennium

Jaffe, Linda (act): Vice Versa (1988)

Jaffe, Nina (act): Phoenix the Warrior

Jaffe, Robert (act): Creature; Maid to Order

Jaffe, Robert (wri): Motel Hell; Nightflyers

Jaffe, Rona (wri): Rona Jaffe's Mazes and Monsters

Jaffe, S.C. (wri): Motel Hell

Jaffe, Sam (act, 1891-1984): The Accused (1948); Battle Beyond the Stars (1980); Bedknobs and Broomsticks; The Day the Earth Stood Still; The Dunwich Horror; Lost Horizon (1973); Night Gallery; Under the Gun

Jaffe, Seth (act): Beverly Hills Bodysnatchers

Jaffe, Shirley (act): A Clockwork Orange; Taste the Blood of Dracula

Jaffe, Taliesin (act): Explorers; 2010

Jaffers, Melissa (act): The Cars That Ate Paris

Jaffrey, Madhur (act): Wolf

Jaffrey, Saeed (act): The Deceivers; Just Ask for Diamond; The Man Who Would Be King; Sphinx (1981)

Jaffrey, Sakina (act): Daylight

Jager, Angelika (act): Robot Holocaust

Jager, Hanns Ernst (act): Das Schloss

Jagger, Bianca (act): C.H.U.D. II

Jagger, Christopher (act): Lifeforce

Jagger, Dean (act, 1903-1991): Alligator (1981); The Brotherhood of the Bell; End of the World (1977); Evil Town; It Grows On Trees; It's a Dog's Life; The Kremlin Letter; On the Threshold of Space; Private Hell 36; Pursued; Revolt of the Zombies; So Sad About Gloria; The Stranger; Vanishing Point (1971); X...The Unknown

Jagger, Etta (act): So Sad About Gloria

Jagger, Mick (act, b. 1943): Freejack; One Plus One; Performance

Jaglom, Henry (dir): A Safe Place

Jago, Alexa (act): The Puppet Masters

Jago, Jo (cin): Where's Johnny

Jahnberg, Hakan (act): Tystnaden

Jahncke, Herbert G. (act): Crypt of Dark Secrets

Jahnen, Margaret (act): Captain Sinbad

Jahnke, Edward (act): Wargames

Jahoda, Miezyslaw (cin): Rekopis Znaleziony w Saragossie

Jahraus, Donald (cin): The Beginning or the End?

Jai (act): Tarzan Goes to India

Jak, Lisa (act): Hammersmith Is Out

Jake (animal act): The Relic

Jakoby, Don (wri): Arachnophobia; Invaders from Mars (1986); Lifeforce; The Philadelphia Experiment; Philadelphia Experiment II

Jakub, Lisa (act): Bermuda Triangle (1996); Dream House (1998); Matinee

Jakubisko, Juro (dir): The Deserter and the Nomads

Jalil, David (act): Terminus

Jam (act): Bloodspell

James, Adrian (act): Demon (1976)

James, Alan (dir): Dick Tracy (1937); The Phantom (1931)

James, Alan (wri): Captain Mephisto and the Transformation Machine

James, Anne (act): Flatliners

James, Anthony (act): Burnt Offerings; Howling IV; Nightmares (1983); Ravagers; Return from Witch Mountain; Traitor's Gate; Vanishing Point (1971); Wacko

James, Barbara (act): The Adventures of Hajji Baba; The Patient Vanishes; The Strange Case of Blondie

James, Beau (act): Serial Mom

James, Benedict (act): The Case of Lady Camber; Her Greatest Performance; The Lyons Mail; The Other Person

James, Bob (dir): Alien Seed

James, Brion (act, b. 1945): The Annihilator; Assault On Dome 4; Black Magic (1992); Blade Runner; The Companion (1994); The Dark (1994); Dead Man Walking; D.O.A. (1988); Dominion; Enemy Mine; Flesh & Blood; Future Shock; The Horror Show; Plus National Lampoon's Men In White; The Nature of the Beast; Nemesis; Precious Find;

Scanner Cop; Steel Dawn; Steel Frontier; Time Runner; Virtual Assassin; Wishman

James, Carole (act): The Sea Serpent

James, Chick (act): 4D Man

James, Claire (act): Voodoo Man

James, Clare (act): Lady In the Fog

James, Clifton (act, b. 1921): Bon Baisers de Hong Kong; Experiment In Terror; Live and Let Die; The Man With the Golden Gun; The November Plan; Superman II; Werewolf of Washington

James, Curtis (act): Plan 10 from Outer Space

James, Dave (act): Night of the Living Dead (1968)

James, Debbie (act): 976-EVIL II: The Astral Factor

James, Diana (act): Alien Nation; Watchers II

James, Don (act): In the Company of Darkness; The Package; The Puppet Masters

James, Donald (wri): Doppelganger (1969); Limbo Line

James, Eric (act): Solar Crisis

James, Freddie (act): Wild Thing

James, Frederick (wri): Humanoids from the Deep

James, Gerald (act): The Man With the Golden Gun

James, Geraldine (act): Teen Agent

James, Gladden (act): Another Thin Man; Charlie Chan at the Opera

James, Godfrey (act): At the Earth's Core; Cry of the Banshee; The Land That Time Forgot; Leapin' Leprechauns!; Magic In the Mirror; The Oblong Box; The Private Life of Sherlock Holmes; Witch-Finder General

James, Gordon (act): Thark

James, Graham (act): Horror of Frankenstein

James, Harri (act): Pumpkinhead II: Blood Wings

James, Harrison (wri): Abduction

James, Hawthorne (act): Seven

James, Henry (wri, 1843-1916): The Haunting of Helen Walker; The Innocents; The Lost Moment; The Nightcomers; The Turn of the Screw

James, Herb (act): Primal Scream

James, Ida (act): Pocomania

James, Idell (act): Hush...Hush, Sweet Charlotte

James, Jason (wri): The Devil's Cargo

James, Jeri Lou (act): The Glass Web

James, Jessica (act): Alien Nation

James, John (1940s act): Devil Bat's Daughter

James, John (1980s act): Haunted by Her Past

James, Josef (act): Cry for the Strangers

James, Ken (act): City On Fire; Landslide (1992); Ms. Scrooge; Welcome to Blood City

James, Kyle (act): Donovan's Brain

James, Lee (act): Cassandra

James, Lisa (act): Necromancy

James, Lisa (wri): The Gifted One

James, Lonnie (act): Mary Shelley's 'Frankenstein'

James, Mason Armin (act): The Attic

James, Michael (act): Warriors of the Apocalypse

James, Michael (Gaylord) (act): The Fugitive (1993); The Package

James, Milton (act): Dark Angel: The Ascent

James, Montague R. (wri, 1862-1936): Night of the Demon (1957)

James, Oscar (GB act): Hardware; Naked Evil

James, Oscar (USA act): Student Bodies

James, P.D. (wri): An Unsuitable Job for a Woman   James, Peter (cin): Diabolique (1996)

James, Peter (wri): Virtual Obsession

James, Rian (wri): Dead Ringer; The Gift of Gab; The Gorilla (1939); Killer In the Mirror

James, Robert (act): Captain Kronos: Vampire Hunter; The Hand That Rocks the Cradle; The Hidden Face

James, Robin (act): The Creeping Terror

James, Ron (act): The Boogey Man

James, Sally (act): Journey to the Unknown

James, Sidney (act, 1913-1976): Cosh Boy; Escape by Night (1954); Father Brown; The Flanagan Boy; The Glass Tomb; The House Across the Lake; Interpol; Joe Macbeth; A Kid for Two Farthings; Last Holiday; The Lavender Hill Mob; The Man In Black; The Man Inside; Quatermass II; The 39 Steps (1959); Venetian Bird; What a Carve Up!; Where the Bullets Fly; The Yellow Balloon

James, Sonny (act): Hillbillys In a Haunted House

James, Stephen (act): Daylight

James, Steve (GB act): The Land That Time Forgot

James, Steve (USA act): The Brother from Another Planet; Mantis

James, Thomas C. (act): Creature

James, Tim (act): Funny Man

James, Walter (act): The Monster (1925
Jameson, Conrad (act): Pinocchio In Outer Space; The Playground
Jameson, House B. (act): Mirage (1965)
Jameson, Jerry (dir): The Bat People; A Fire In the Sky (1978); Starflight: The Plane That Couldn't Land; Terror on the 40th Floor
Jameson, Joyce (act): The Balcony; The Comedy of Terrors; Death Race 2000; Tales of Terror
Jameson, Louise (act): Disciple of Death
Jameson, Pauline (act): The Black Knight; Full Circle; Night Watch (1973)
Jameson, Susan (act): I, Monster
Jamieson, Harold (act): Treasure Island (1950)
Jamieson, Malcolm (act): Meridian; The Scarlet Pimpernel (1982)
Jamieson, Todd (act): The Hand That Rocks the Cradle
Jamin, Georges (act): Daughters of Darkness
Jamison, Bud (act): Dante's Inferno (1924); The Lone Wolf Spy Hunt
Jamison, Richard (act): Retribution (1988)
Jamrog, Joe (act): You Better Watch Out
Janczak, Andrew (cin): The Creeping Terror
Janczar, Christopher (act): The Hunt for Red October
Janda, Krystyna (act): Przesluchanie
Jane, Sybil (act): The Hound of the Baskervilles (1931)
Janecky, Cheryl (act): Princess Warrior
Jane, Topsy (act): Mix Me a Person
Janes, Tom (act): Nemesis
Janis, Conrad (act, b. 1928): The Brasher Doubloon; Oh, God! Book II
Janis, Ursula (act): House of 1,000 Dolls
Janisch, Michael (act): The Fifth Musketeer
Janiss, Vivi (act): The Phantom from 10,000 Leagues
Jani-Z (act): Octopussy
Jankel, Annabel (dir): D.O.A. (1988); Super Mario Bros.
Jankel, Chaz (mus): D.O.A. (1988); Making Mr. Right; Tales from the Darkside; An Unsuitable Job for a Woman
Jann, Gerald (act): Confessions of an Opium Eater; Dimension 5; Remote Control (1988)
Janney, Allison (act): Wolf
Janney, Leon (act, 1917-1980): Charly
Jannings, Emil (act, 1884-1950): Anna Boleyn; Die Augen der Mumie Ma; Carmen (1918); Faust (1926); Der Letzte Mann; Madame DuBarry (1919); A Night of Horror; Das Wachsfigurenkabinett; Das Weib des Pharao
Jannotta, Toni (act): Scared to Death (1980)
Jannssen, Armond (act): Just Imagine
Jannucci, Robert (act): Exterminators of the Year 3000
Jano, Neal (act): Vampire On Bikini Beach
Janofsky, Murray (act): see Murray, Jan
Janos, Victor (dir): Last House On Dead End Street
Janos, Vilismary (wri): I Married an Angel
Janover, Michael (wri): The Philadelphia Experiment
Janowitz, Hans (wri): Der Januskopf; Das Kabinett des Dr. Caligari
Janowitz, Walter (act): Billy the Kid vs. Dracula; Jekyll and Hyde...Together Again
Jans, Harry (act): Charlie Chan at the Race Track; Murder On a Bridle Path
Jansen, Christine (act): Star Trek: Generations
Jansen, Pierre (mus): Le Boucher
Janson, Gene (act): Blink
Janson, Horst (act): Captain Kronos: Vampire Hunter
Janson, Len (wri): Condor
Jansons, Maris (cin): Bionic Showdown: The Six Million Dollar Man and the Bionic Woman
Janssen, David (act, 1930-1980, nee David Harold Meyer): Bonzo Goes to College; City In Fear; Cult of the Cobra; Fer-de-Lance; Francis In the Haunted House; Francis In the Navy; Marooned; Moon of the Wolf; Ring of Fire; Smile, Jenny, You're Dead; Swamp Fire
Janssen, Eilene (act): The Beginning of the End; Black Zoo; The Boy With Green Hair; The Search
for Bridey Murphy; The Space Children
Janssen, Famke (act, b. 1964): Deep Rising; The Faculty; Goldeneye; The House On Haunted Hill (1999); Lord of Illusions
Janssen, Marlene (act): School Spirit
Janssen, Walter (act): Der Mude Tod
Janssen, Werner (mus): Captain Kidd; Guest In the House
Janti, Azemat (act): The 27th Day
Jantschek, Horst (act): The Secret Life of Ian Fleming
Janus, Samantha (act): Jekyll and Hyde
Janusch, Rod M. (cin): Phenomenon
Janzen, Maureen (act): She Demons
Janzurova, Iva (act): Das Schloss
Jara, Maurice (act): The Lone Ranger and the Lost City of Gold
Jarchow, Bruce (act): Ghost (1990); Outbreak; The Puppet Masters
Jarczyk, Herbert (mus): Cave of the Living Dead
Jardin, Shelly Lynn (act): Red Blooded American Girl
Jardine, Betty (act): The Ghost Train (1941)
Jaregard, Ernst-Hugo (act): The Kingdom
Jaress, Jill (act): The Resurrection of Zachary Wheeler
Jarman, Derek (dir & wri): The Tempest (1980)
Jarman, Jack (act): Black Peter; By the Hand of a Brother; The Counterfeiters; The Crimson Triangle; The Devil to Pay; The Master Crook; Only a Roomer; The Thief (1912); Through the Clouds; Wanderful Will
Jarman, Reginald (act): Zardoz
Jarmen Jr., Claude (act, b. 1934): Fair Wind to Java
Jarmon, Clarenze (act): Street Trash
Jarmusch, Jim (act): Sling Blade
Jarmusch, Jim (cin): Sleepwalk
Jarmyn, Jill (act): Swamp Women
Jarnigan, James (T.) (act): Stranger In Our House; The Sword and the Sorcerer
Jarniou, Solenn (act): I Married a Shadow
Jaroslow, Ruth (act): Eat and Run
Jarratt, John (act): Dark Age; Next of Kin; Picnic at Hanging Rock
Jarre, Kevin (act): Gotham
Jarre, Maurice (mus, b. 1924): After Dark, My Sweet; The Bride (1985); Chances Are; The Collector; Dreamscape; Enemy Mine; The Extraordinary Seaman; Fatal Attraction; Gambit; Ghost (1990); Great Expectations (1974); The Island at the Top of the World; Jacob's Ladder; Judex; The Man Who Would Be King; Mr. Sycamore; The Night of the Generals; No Way Out; La Poursuite; Solarbabies; Solar Crisis; Spotlight On Murder; Topaz; Top Secret! (1984); Les Yeux sans Visage
Jarrell, Stig (act): The Devil's Eye; Hets
Jarret, Jerry (act): Killer's Kiss
Jarrett, Jim (act): Death Dreams
Jarrett, Paul (act): The Resurrected
Jarrett, Phil(lip) (act): Darkman II: The Return of Durant; Escape Clause; Never Talk to Strangers, Short Circuit 2; The Spider and the Fly (1994)
Jarrett, Renne (act): The Cat Creature
Jarrico, Paul (wri, 1915-1997): The Face Behind the Mask
Jarrott, Charles (dir, b. 1927): Condorman; Lost Horizon (1973); Time to Remember
Jarvet, Yuri (act): Korol Lir; Solaris
Jarvis, Al (act): The Twonky
Jarvis, Bill (act): Hamlet (1969)
Jarvis, Bob (act): New Year's Evil
Jarvis, Francesca (act): Night of the Lepus
Jarvis, Graham (act): Misery; Prophecy (1979)
Jarvis, Jeff (cin): Amityville 3-D; Firestarter; Poltergeist
Jarvis, Martin (act): Taste the Blood of Dracula
Jarvis, May (act): Cannibal Girls
Jarvis, Nina (wri): Dead Man's Shoes
Jarvis, Sam (act): Bug
Jarvis, Sidney (act): Kismet (1930); The Unholy Night
Jarvis, Woody (act): The Capture of Bigfoot
Jarvis, Yvette (act): Blind Date
Jasae (act): Cavegirl (1985)
Jasen, Kelly (act): Cocoon: The Return
Jasen, Richard (act): Cocoon: The Return
Jasiukiewicz, Stanislaw (act): Matka Joanna od Aniolow
Jasmer, Brent (act): Leprechaun 4: In Space
Jasmin, Paul (act): Looker
Jasmine, Arthur (act): Salome (1922)
Jasny, Vojtech (dir): The Great Land of Small
Jason, David (act): Royal Flash; The Water Babies; Wombling Free
Jason, Deborah (act): Zombie Island Massacre
Jason, Harvey (act): Genesis II; The Lost World: Jurassic Park; Necromancy
Jason, Peter (act): Alien Nation; The Amazing Captain Nemo; Arachnophobia; Beyond the Universe; Congo; Dante's Peak; Dreamscape; From the Dead of Night; Hyper Sapien: People from Another Star; Impulse (1984); In the Mouth of Madness; Prince of Darkness; They Live; Trick or Treats; Village of the Damned (1995)
Jason, Rick (act, b. 1926): Color Me Dead; Family Doctor; The Saracen Blade; This Is My Love
Jason, Ron (act): Las Vegas Serial Killer
Jason, Sybil (act, b. 1929): The Blue Bird (1940)
Jason, Will (dir, b. 1910): Soul of a Monster; Thief of Damascus
Jaspe, Jose (act): House of 1,000 Dolls; El Otro Fu Manchu
Jasset, Victorin (dir, 1862-1913): Balaoo; La Fin de Don Juan
Jasset, Victorin (wri, 1862-1913): La Fin de Don Juan
Jasso, Nicolas (act): Firewalker
Jastrow, Terry (act): The Phoenix (1981)
Jaubert, Maurice (mus): Le Quai des Brumes
Jaubert, Rosette (act): The Corsican Brothers (1985)
Jauregui, Victor Hugo (act): The Woman Hunter
Javal, Camille (act): see Bardot, Brigitte
Javarone, Franco (act): The Fish Men
Javier, Elmer Davis (act): Rearview Mirror
Javier, Valentin (cin): Carlota; La Corona Negra
Jawdokimov, Alexei (act): Billion Dollar Brain
Jawitz, Louis (act): Maniac (1980)
Jay, Angela (act): The Deadly Females
Jay, Ernest (act, 1894-1957): Blanche Fury; Checkmate; The Curse of Frankenstein; Death In the Hand; On Secret Service; So Evil My Love; Who Done It? (1956)
Jay, Griffin (wri): Captive Wild Woman; Cry of the Werewolf; Devil Bat's Daughter; The Mask of Dijon; The Mummy's Ghost; The Mummy's Hand; The Mummy's Tomb; The Return of the Vampire
Jay, Harriet (wri): Alone In London
Jay, Helen (act): The Deadly Mantis; She-Devil (1957); Simon, King of the Witches; Space Master X-7
Jay, Ivor (wri): The Green Shoes
Jay, Jean (wri): Come Into My Parlour
Jay, Kevin (act): Cafe Flesh
Jay, Lisa (act): Waxwork II: Lost In Time
Jay, Merryl (act): Dracula's Dog
Jay, Susan (act): Bay Coven
Jay, Tony (act): The Hunchback of Notre Dame (1996)
Jayant (act): Simon
Jayne, Jennifer (act): Black Widow (1951); Clash by Night; Dr. Terror's House of Horrors (1964); The End of the Line; Hysteria! The Liquidator; Mark of the Phoenix; The Medusa Touch; They Came from Beyond Space; The Trollenberg Terror; A Woman of Mystery
Jayne, Keith (act): The Glitterball; Robin Hood Junior (1975); Sammy's Super T-Shirt
Jaynes, David (act): Summer of Fear
Jaynes, Jonathan (act): First Knight
Jayston, Michael (act): Alice's Adventures In Wonderland (1972); Craze; Death In Small Doses (1973); Dominique; The Internecine Project; Quiller: The Price of Violence; Tales That Witness Madness; 20,000 Leagues Under the Sea (1997, CBS-TV)
Jazwinski, Peter (act): The Mask (1994)
Jeakins, Adrian (cin): Mr. Horatio Knibbles; Strange Behaviour
Jean (act): Tabu
Jean, Gloria (act, b. 1928, nee Gloria Jean Schoonover): Destiny (1944); Ghost Catchers
Jean, Lorin (act): Rest In Pieces
Jeanmarie, Zizi (act): Hans Christian Andersen
Jean-Phillipe, Michel (act): Stargate
Jeans, Desmond (act): The Six Men
Jeans, Isabel (act, 1891-1985): Downhill; The Magic Christian; Suspicion (1941)
Jeans, Ursula (act, 1906-1973, nee Ursula McMinn): The Barton Mystery (1932); Boy With a Flute; Dark Journey; The Flying Fool; The Man In the Mirror
Jeanson, Henri (wri, 1900-1970): Carmen (1942); Madame DuBarry (1954); Nathalie, Agent Secret; La Nuit Fantastique; Paris When It Sizzles; Le Saint Prend l'Affut
Jeapes, Harold (dir): Jack and Jill; The Ride of the Valkyries
Jeavons, Colin (act): The Devil's Daffodil; Diagnosis: Murder; Schizo (1977)
Jeayes, Allan (act, 1885-1963): Attempt to Kill; Blanche Fury Bulldog Drummond's Third Round;
Dangerous Medicine; Dead of Night (1945); Elephant Boy; Eyes of Fate; The Flying Squad (1940); The Ghost Train (1931); Koenigsmark; Obsession (1949); Paris Plane; Pimpernel Smith; The Return of the Scarlet Pimpernel; The Scarlet Pimpernel (1934); Seven Sinners; The Solitary Cyclist; The Spider (1939); The Squeaker (1937); They Drive by Night; The Thief of Bagdad (1940); Things to Come
Jedryka, Joanna (act): Rekopis Znaleziony w Saragossie
Jedwab, Rusty (act): The Young Magician
Jee, Elizabeth (act): Not of This World
Jeep, Robin (act): Phantom of the Paradise
Jeeves, M. Kane (wri): C.H.U.D. II
Jeeves, McCain (act): Invasion of the Girl Snatchers
Jeferson, Tanya (act): Those Dear Departed
Jeffcoat, Don(nie) (act): Ghoulies II; Wish Upon a Star
Jefferies, Amanda (act): Invasion of the Bee Girls
Jefferies, Peter (dir): Only a Scream Away; A Place to Die
Jeffers, Charles (act): The Ivory Ape
Jefferson, Arthur Stanley (act): see Laurel, Stan
Jefferson, Branden (act): Tales from the Hood
Jefferson, Brenden Richard (act): Zenon: Girl of the 21st Century
Jefferson Jr., Herb(ert) (act): Battlestar Galactica; Outbreak; World War III
Jefferson, Joseph (act): Rip Van Winkle (1896)
Jefferson, Laurie Brooks (act): The Bat People
Jefferson, Marvin (act): Raiders of the Living Dead
Jefferson, Thomas (act): Rip Van Winkle (1921); Tarzan of the Apes
Jefford, Barbara (act): Hitler: The Last Ten Days; Lust for a Vampire; The Saint
Jeffory, Dawn (act): Tourist Trap
Jeffrey, Barney (cin): Hardware
Jeffrey, Doug (act): Deadlock: A Passion for Murder; Shades of Gray
Jeffrey, Howard (act): The Black Bird (1975)
Jeffrey, Peter (act): The Abominable Dr. Phibes; Come Out, Come Out, Wherever You Are; Countess Dracula; Deadly Strangers; Dr. Phibes Rises Again; Hands of a Murderer; Twinsanity; What Became of Jack and Jill
Jeffrey, R.E. (act): Murder
Jeffrey, R.E. (dir): Double Bluff
jeffrey, Vicky (act): The Naked Cell
Jeffrey, William (act): Charlie Chan On Broadway
Jeffreys, Anne (act, b. 1923): Dick Tracy (1945); Dick Tracy vs. Cueball; Genius at Work; I Married an Angel; Panic In the City; Step by Step; Zombies On Broadway
Jeffreys, Chuck (act): Aftershock; 12 Monkeys
Jeffreys, Ellis (act): The Barton Mystery (1932); Birds of Prey; Return of a Stranger
Jeffries, Betty (wri): The Invisible Avenger
Jeffries, Douglas (act): A Safe Affair
Jeffries, Herbert (dir & wri): World of the Depraved
Jeffries, Lang (act): The Becket Affair; Mission Stardust; The Spy Strikes Silently
Jeffries, Lionel (act, b. 1926): The Black Rider; Bobbikins; Call Me Bwana; Camelot; Chitty Chitty Bang Bang; Eyewitness (1970); First Men In the Moon (1964); The High Terrace; Hour of Decision; Jekyll and Hyde; Kill or Cure; Life Is a Circus; Murder Ahoy; Nowhere to Go; Oh Dad Poor Dad, Mamma's Hung You In the Closet and I'm Feelin' So Sad; The Prisoner of Zenda (1979); The Quatermass Experiment; The Revenge of Frankenstein; Royal Flash; The Scarlet Blade; The Secret of My Success; The Spy With a Cold Nose; Sudden Terror; Tarzan the Magnificent; Those Fantastic Flying Fools; The Vicious Circle (1957); Who Slew Auntie Roo?; Wombling Free
Jeffries, Lionel (dir & wri, b. 1926): The Amazing Mr. Blunden; The Water Babies; Wombling Free
Jeffries, Oliver (wri): Dracula's Daughter
Jeffries, Richard (dir): Blood Tide
Jeffries, Todd (act): The Colony (1995); The First Power; Monolith
Jeffries, Will (act): Remo Williams: The Adventure Begins
Jein, Greg (cin): Dark Star
Jelinek, Rudolf (act): Baron Prasil
Jelinek, Tobias (act): Hocus Pocus
Jellinek, Tristram (act): Greystoke: The Legend of Tarzan, Lord of the Apes; Morons from Outer Space; Top Secret! (1984)
Jelmini, Tiziana (act): Georgette Meunier
Jemison, Edward (act): The Relic
Jemison, Kimble (act): Bloodspell
Jemma, Ottavio (act): When Women Had Tails
Jendreyko, Hans Dieter (act): Jonathan
Jenesky, George (act): Alien Nation
Jeni, Richard (act): The Mask (1994)
Jenkins, Allen (act, 1900-1974, nee Al McGonegal): Chained for Life; A Date With the Falcon; Eyes In the Night; The Falcon Takes Over; Footsteps In the Dark; The Gay Falcon; The Mind Reader; Sh! The Octopus; The Spy In the Green Hat; Torchy Plays With Dynamite; Wonder Man
Jenkins, Anthony (act): Bloodspell
Jenkins, Bunker (wri): Swords of the Space Ark

Jenkins, dal (act): The War Lord
Jenkins, David (act): The Invincible Barbarian
Jenkins, Eric (act): Laserblast
Jenkins, Gordon (mus): Bwana Devil
Jenkins, Ken (act): The Stand
Jenkins, Larry Flash (act): Elvira, Mistress of the Dark; Fantasies; Prison (1988)
Jenkins, Mark (act): The Andromeda Strain; The Man from Atlantis
Jenkins, Megs (act, b. 1917): Asylum (1972); Bunny Lake Is Missing; Green for Danger; The Innocents; Jet Storm; Life for Ruth; Murder Most Foul; Secret People; Stranger In the House (1967)
Jenkins, Rebecca (act): A Stranger In Town (1998)
Jenkins, Richard (GB-born act): see Burton, Richard
Jenkins, Richard (USA act): The Indian In the Cupboard; The Manhattan Project; Wolf
Jenkins, Robert (act): Fright Night II
Jenkins, Sam (act): Ed and His Dead Mother
Jenkins, Terence (act): Vampire Cop
Jenkins, Wendy (act): see Barrie, Wendy
Jenkins, Will F. (wri): Murder Will Out (1930)
Jenks, Frank (act, 1902-1962): The Amazing Colossal Man; Blonde Savage; The Falcon In Hollywood; Lady In the Morgue; The Last Warning (1938); The Missing Corpse; The Phantom of 42nd Street; Philo Vance's Gamble; Philo Vance's Secret Mission; The Scarf; Shake Hands With Murder; The She-Creature; Sudden Danger; The Westland Case; Zombies On Broadway
Jenks, Si (act): Charlie Chan's Courage
Jenner, Barry (act): Looker; Popcorn
Jennewein, Jim (wri): The Flintstones; Stay Tuned
Jenney, Lucinda (act): Matinee; Thinner
Jenning, Ernest (act): Whirlpool (1970)
Jennings, Anna (act): The Ghost Train (1927)
Jennings, Brent (act): Children of the Corn IV; The Serpent and the Rainbow
Jennings, Claudia (act, d. 1978): Deathsport; Sisters of Death; The Stepmother
Jennings, DeWitt (C.) (act): The Bat Whispers; Charlie Chan's Courage; In the Next Room; Murder On a Honeymoon; Mystery of the Wax Museum; The Mystic; Secret of the Chateau; Seven Footprints to Satan; Seven Keys to Baldpate (1929)
Jennings, Dominique (act): Seven
Jennings, Ernest C. (act): Tales from the Crypt (1971)
Jennings, Gladys (act): Alibi Inn; The Face at the Window (1920); I'm an Explosive; The Shuttle of Life
Jennings, Gordon (cin): The Atomic City; The Big Clock; Bride of Vengeance; Golden Earrings; Peter Ibbetson; Sorry, Wrong Number (1948); Sunset Boulevard; The War of the Worlds; When Worlds Collide
Jennings, J. Devereaux (cin): The Dark Mirror (1946)
Jennings, Juanita (act): Murder of Innocence; Running Against Time; Spirit Lost
Jennings, Junero (act): Star Trek
Jennings, Kay (act): Beast from Haunted Cave
Jennings, Maxine (act): Mr. Wong, Detective
Jennings, Nolan (act): Never Talk to Strangers
Jennings, Patrice (act): Society
Jennings, Paul Craig (act) Invasion of the Blood Farmers
Jennings, Rory (act): Mary Shelley's Frankenstein
Jennings, S.E. (act): The Bat Whispers
Jennings, Talbot (wri): The Black Rose; Knights of the Round Table
Jennings, Tom (act): Stones of Death
Jenrette, Rita (act): Zombie Island Massacre
Jens, Arnette (act): The Balcony
Jens, Salome (act, b. 1935): The Fool Killer; The Lottery; Savages; Seconds; Tomorrow's Child
Jensen, Arthur (act): Crazy Paradise
Jensen, Beate (act): Chinese Boxes
Jensen, Bing (act): The Keeper
Jensen, Dave (act): Snow Kill
Jensen, David (act): Halloween 4: The Return of Michael Myers; Species; Virtual Obsession
Jensen, Doris (act): see Gray, Coleen
Jensen, Erik (act): The Dark Half
Jensen, Eulalie (act): The Hunchback of Notre Dame (1923)
Jensen, Gail (act): Future Zone
Jensen, Gunther (act): 976-EVIL
Jenson, Howard (cin): Beyond the Poseidon Adventure
Jensen, Irja (act): Operation Manhunt
Jensen, Jan (act): The Last Slumber Party
Jensen, Jane (act): Tromeo and Juliet
Jensen, Jeff (act): Weird Science
Jensen, Johnny (act): The War Lord
Jensen, Johnny E. (cin): Into the Badlands; Three Wishes (1995)
Jensen, Karen (act, b. 1944): I Love a Mystery (1966)
Jensen, Kimberly (act): Schizoid (1980)
Jensen, Lola (act): The Lone Wolf Spy Hunt
Jensen, Maren (act): Battlestar Galactica; Deadly Blessing
Jensen, Peter (wri): Shadow of the Hawk
Jensen, S. (act): Mr. Lyndon at Liberty
Jensen, Sherri (act): Praying Mantis
Jensen, Steve "O" (act): Trancers
Jensen, Wiers (wri): Vredens Dag
Jenson, Jerry (act): Ghosts That Still Walk
Jenson, Roy (Cameron) (act): The Ambushers; Demonoid; Solar Crisis; Soylent Green
Jenson, Sasha (act): Ghoulies II; A Girl to Kill For; Halloween 4: The Return of Michael Myers; The Nature of the Beast
Jenson, Steve (act): Blood Diner
Jenson, Todd (act): Cyborg Cop; Prey for the Hunter
Jephcott, Dominic (act): Inseminoid; The Scarlet Pimpernel (1982)
Jepson, Edgar (wri): The Loudwater Mystery
Jepson, Selwyn (wri): Dark World; The Riverside Murder; The Scarab Murder Case; Stage
Fright (1950)
Jepson, Warner (mus): Luminous Procuress
Jeremias, James (wri): The Lost Boys
Jergens, Adele (act, b. 1922): Abbott and Costello Meet the Invisible Man; Armored Car Robbery; Crime Doctor's Diary; Day the World Ended (1955); Down to Earth; Girls In Prison; The Mutineers; Radar Secret Service; The Sound of Fury; A Thousand and One Nights (1945); Teasure of Monte Cristo (1949)
Jergens, Diane (act): Desk Set; Island of Lost Women
Jernudd, Judy (act): Beverly Hills Bodysnatchers
Jerome, Edwin (act): The Three Faces of Eve; The Tattered Dress
Jerome, Jerome K. (wri): The Passing of the Third Floor Back (1918 & 1935)
Jerome, Jerry (act): Charlie Chan's Courage; Shadow of the Thin Man
Jerrold, Mary (act, 1877-1955, nee Mary Allen): Alibi (1931); Blind Spot (1932); Colonel Bogey; The Ghosts of Berkeley Square; The Queen of Spades (1948); She Shall Have Murder
Jesse, Anita (act): Nomads
Jesse, Tom (act): The Keeper
Jessel, George (act, 1898-1981): The Busy Body
Jessel, Patricia (act, 1921-1968): City of the Dead; The Flesh Is Weak; The Man Upstairs; Model for Murder
Jesson, Marguerita (act): Iron Justice
Jessop, Clytie (act): The Innocents; Nightmare (1963); Torture Garden
Jessop, Jack (act): Ghost of a Chance (1987); Storm of the Century
Jessop, Peter (cin): The Day the Screaming Stopped; The Flesh and Blood Show; Frightmare (1974); House of Mortal Sin; House of Whipcord; The Legend of Spider Forest; The Lifetaker; The Monster Club; The Orchard End Murder; Schizo (1977); Tiffany Jones
Jessua, Alain (dir & wri, b. 1932): The Killing Game; Traitement de Choc
Jessua, Alain (mus, b. 1932): Traitement de Choc
Jessup, George (act): Secrets of the Phantom Caverns
Jessup, Robert (C.) (cin): Deadly Blessing; In the Year 2889; Mars Needs Women; Race With the Devil; Sugar Hill
Jet (animal act): Street Trash
Jeter, Michael (act): Mrs. Santa Claus; Waterworld
Jeunet, Jean-Marie (wri): The City of Lost Children
Jeunet, Jean-Pierre (dir): Alien Resurrection; The City of Lost Children
Jevicky, Mark V. (act): The Majorettes
Jevne, Jack (wri): Topper Takes a Trip
Jewel, Estele (act): Shadow of a Doubt (1943)
Jewell, Austen (dir): Hold That Hypnotist
Jewell, Hollis (act): Nightmare Alley
Jewell, Isabel (act, 1909-1972): The Bishop's Wife; Born to Kill; The Casino Murder Case; The Falcon and the Co-Eds; The Leopard Man; Lost Horizon (1937); Mad Love; Man In the Attic (1953); The Seventh Victim; The Snake Pit (1948)
Jewell, Jefferson (act): The Being
Jewell, Robert (act): Daleks' Invasion Earth 2150 A.D.; The Terrornauts
Jewell, Wendy (act): Phobia
Jewers, Ray (act): Edge of Sanity; The Return of Sherlock Holmes (1986)
Jewesbury, Edward (act): Mary Shelley's 'Frankenstein'
Jewett, Thomas (cin): Peacemaker (1990)
Jewison, Norman (dir, b. 1926): Bogus; Rollerball
Jewkes, Richard (act): Halloween 4: The Return of Michael Myers
Jeyes, Jazzer (act): Batman (1989); Enemy Mine; Jekyll and Hyde
Jianni, Pietro (act): The Corsican Brothers (1985)
Jiliano, Janette (act): The Octagon
Jillette, Penn (act): Light Years
Jillian, Ann (act, b. 1951): Alice In Wonderland (1985); Babes In Toyland (1961); Killer In the Mirror
Jillson, Joyce (act): Crackle of Death; Superchick
Jilot, Yolanda (act): Waxwork II: Lost In Time
Jim Jr. (aninal act): The Raven (1963)
Jimenez, Chrysti (act): Omega Cop
Jimenez, Juan Antonio (act): El Amor Brujo (1986)
Jimenez, Neal (wri): Hideaway
Jimeniz, Jaime (act): Mystery In Mexico
Jim Henson Prods. (cin): Gulliver's Travels (1996)
Jiminez, Jose Luis (act): Macario; Spiritism
Jiminez, Joseph Louis (act): see Jiminez, Jose Luis
Jimmerson, Jim (act): The Resurrection of Zachary Wheeler
Jinzhan, Zhang (act): Life On a String
Jires, Jaromil (dir): Valerie and Her Week of Wonders
Jiri Trnka Puppets (act): The Emperor's Nightingale; The Hand (1966)
Ji-Yung, Kim (act): Village In the Mist
Joachim, Suzy (act): Hideaway; Unforgettable
Joannon, Leo (dir & wri, 1904-1969): Atoll K
Job, Thomas (wri): The Two Mrs. Carrolls
Job, William (act): Anatomy of Terror; Privilege
Jobert, Marlene (act): Catch Me a Spy; The Evil Trap; Passager de la Pluie
Jobin, Peter (act): Gotham
Jobin, Peter (wri): Happy Birthday to Me
Jobling, David (act): Something Is Out There
Jobling, Hugh (act): Howling IV
Jobson, Edward (act): The Brass Bottle (1923)
Jocelyn, June (act): The Amazing Colossal Man; Attack of the Puppet People; The Spider (1958); Teenage Cave Man; War of the Colossal Beast
Jochim, Anthony (act): The Brotherhood of Satan; The Neanderthal Man
Jochim, Keith (act): The Witches of Eastwick
Jochimsen, Gary (act): The Zero Boys
Jockers, Robert (act): Street Trash
Joe, Jeanne (act): The UFO Incident
Joel, Deborah (act): Hellbound: Hellraiser II
Joens, Michael (dir): My Little Pony
Joffe, Kai (mus): Warrior Queen
Joffe, Roland (dir, b. 1945): The Scarlet Letter (1995)
Joffe, Stephen (act): Storm of the Century
Joffin, Jon (cin): I've Been Waiting for You; Lost Souls (1998)
Joffray, Pierre (act): La Jetee
Johan, Louise (act): Runaway
Johann, Zita (act, 1904-1993): The Mummy (1932); Raiders of the Living Dead
Johannsen, Ingemar (act): 48 Hours to Live
Johansen, Aud (act): Macbeth (1971)
Johansen, David (act): Desire and Hell at the Sunset Motel; Freejack; Light Years; Scrooged; Tales from the Darkside
Johansen, Mikhail (wri): Zvenigora
Johansson, Lena Marie (act): Amazons (1986)
Johansson, Ulf (act): Det Sjunde Inseglet
Johar, I.S. (act): Death On the Nile
John, Alexander (act): The Orchard End Murder; Robin Hood Junior (1975)
John, Annette (act): Stalking Laura
John, Elton (act, b. 1947, nee Reginald Kenneth Dwight): Tommy
John, Elton (mus, b. 1947): The Lion King; Oh Heavenly Dog
John, George (act): Doctor Mabuse; Der Letzte Mann; M (1931); Metropolis (1926); Die Nibelungen; Die Spinnen; Der Steinerne Reiter
John, Gottfried (act): Chinese Boxes; Goldeneye; Mata Hari (1985); Wings of Fame
John, H.W. (wri): I Aim at the Stars
John, Karl (act): The Mysterious Magician; Der Verlorene
John III, King (act): Psycho from Texas
John, Maxine (act): Howling IV
John, Robert (act): Creatures the World Forgot
John, Rosamund (act, b. 1913): Green for Danger; Never Look Back; Operation Murder; The Secret of the Loch (1934); She Shall Have Murder; The Upturned Glass
John, Tim (wri): Dr. Jekyll and Ms. Hyde
Johnes, Alexandra (act): The Neverending Story II: The Next Chapter
John-Jules, Danny (act): Little Shop of Horrors (1986)
Johnny, Talib (act): Octopussy
Johns, Bertram (act): The Thirteenth Chair
Johns, Calvin (act): King Solomon's Mines (1985)
Johns, David (act): Halloween With the Addams Family
Johns, Glynis (act, b. 1923): Around the World In 80 Days; The Cabinet of Caligari; 49th Parallel; Halfway House; Mad About Men; Mary Poppins; Miranda; Murder In the Family; No Highway In the Sky; Nukie; On the Night of the Fire; The Spider's Web; State Secret; The Vault of Horror
Johns, Harriet(te) (act): Date at Midnight; Meet Mr. Callaghan; The Never Never Murder; The Two-Headed Spy
Johns, Judith (act): Runaway
Johns, Larry (act): The Beginning or the End?; Project Moonbase
Johns, Margo (act): Konga
Johns, Margot (act): Murder at the Windmill
Johns, Mervyn (act, b. 1899): Counterblast; The Counterfeit Plan; The Day of the Triffids; Dead of Night (1945); Echo of Barbara; Find the Lady; The Frightened Bride; The Girl In the News; Halfway House; House of Mortal Sin; The Intimate Stranger; Jamaica Inn (1939); Moby Dick (1956); Never Let Go; 1984 (1955); The Old Dark House (1963); The Oracle (1952); Scrooge (1951); TheSurgeon's Knife; The Vicious Circle (1957); Went the Day Well?; Who Killed the Cat?
Johns, Milton (act): Baffled!; The House That Bled to Death/Growing Pains
Johns, Stratford (act): The Fiendish Plot of Dr. Fu Manchu; The Lair of the White Worm; The Long Arm; The Professionals; The Saint and the Brave Goose; Splitting Heirs; Those Fantastic Flying Fools; Two Letter Alibi; Who Done It? (1956)
Johns, Capt. W.E. (wri): Biggles: Adventures In Time
Johnson, Adrian (wri): Crooked Alley
Johnson, Alan (act): Iced
Johnson, Alan (dir): Solarbabies
Johnson, Alexandra (act): A Stranger Waits
Johnson, Amy Jo (act): Mighty Morphin Power Rangers; Susie Q; Turbo: A Power Rangers Movie
Johnson, Andrew (act): Blind Date; The Human Duplicators; The Kiss (1988)
Johnson, Anne Marie (act): Asteroid; Robot Jox
Johnson, Arch (act): Double Indemnity (1973); The Invisible Man (1975)
Johnson, Arnold (act): My Demon Lover; The Seventh Sign
Johnson, Arte (act, b. 1934): Alice In Wonderland (1985); Evil Spirits; Evil Toons; Love at First Bite; Munchie; The President's Analyst
Johnson, Barbara (act): Victims
Johnson, Ben (act, 1919-1996): Mighty Joe Young (1949); The Savage Bees; The Swarm; Terror Train; The Town That Dreaded Sundown
Johnson, Bert (act): The Devil's Messenger
Johnson, Beverly (act): The Cover Girl Murders; The Meteor Man
Johnson, Bill (act): The Eliminator; The Texas Chainsaw Massacre 2
Johnson, Bob (act): Midnight (1980)
Johnson, Bobby (act): Lovespell
Johnson, Brad (act): Bedtime for Bonzo
Johnson, Brad (act): Always; The Birds II: Land's End; Dominion; The Philadelphia Experiment II
Johnson, Brian (cin): Assassin (1973); Captain Scarlet vs. the Mysterons; Dragonslayer; The Medusa Touch; The Neverending Story; Slipstream; Thunderbirds In Outer Space
Johnson, Brian (wri): A Place to Die
Johnson, Bruce Douglas (cin): The Prophecy (1995)
Johnson, Cage S. (act): Flatliners
Johnson, Candy (act): Pajama Party
Johnson, Carl (act): Sorority Girls and the Creature from Hell
Johnson, Carl (mus): Aladdin and the King of [illegible]
[illegible]
Johnson, Caroline Lee (act): The Saint
Johnson, Celia (act, 1908-1982): A Kid for Two Farthings; Les Miserables (1978)

Johnson, Charles (wri): *Beyond Atlantis*
Johnson, Charles Van (act): see Johnson, Van
Johnson, Chic (act, 1891-1962, nee Harold Ogden Johnson): *Crazy House (1943); Ghost Catchers; Hellzapoppin*
Johnson, Chip (act): *Battlestar Galactica; Captain America (1978); The Ultimate Impostor*
Johnson, Chubby (act): *The Scarf; The Treasure of Lost Canyon*
Johnson, Clark (act): *Starcrossed; Wild Thing*
Johnson, Claude (act): *Space Raiders*
Johnson, Darlene (act): *Shock Treatment! (1981)*
Johnson, Darrell H. (act): *Princess Warrior*
Johnson, Dasanea (act): *Heart Condition*
Johnson, Dave Alan (act): *Night of the Creeps*
Johnson, Deborah Lee (act): *Nothing But Trouble*
Johnson, Diane (act): *Forver Evil*
Johnson, Diane (wri): *The Shining*
Johnson, Don (act, b. 1950): *A Boy and His Dog; Dead Bang; Guilty as Sin; Revenge of the Stepford Wives*
Johnson, Edna (act): *The Living Ghost (1942)*
Johnson, Elinore Swinburne (act): see Swinburne, Nora
Johnson, Frank (act): see Darro, Frankie
Johnson, Franklin (act): *The Little Match Girl (1987)*
Johnson, Fred (1910s act): *The Failure*
Johnson, Fred (act): *Brides of Dracula; Broken Threads; City of the Dead; The Curse of Frankenstein; Dr. Blood's Coffin; Face the Music; The Saint's Return; Scrooge (1951); A Taste of Fear*
Johnson, Gayle (act): *Curse of the Swamp Creature*
Johnson, Georgann (act): *The Day After; Looker*
Johnson, George Clayton (wri): *Logan's Run; Twilight Zone*
Johnson, Gladys (act): *The Water Rats of London*
Johnson, Gloria (act): *Noddy In Toyland*
Johnson, Gray (act): *The Bees; The Ultimate Warrior*
Johnson, Harold Ogden (act): see Johnson, Chic
Johnson, Harry (act): *Death Dreams; Warlock*
Johnson, Harry "Duke" (act): *Carousel*
Johnson, Holly (act): *Gotham*
Johnson, J. McMillan (cin): *The Power (1967)*
Johnson, Jack (act): *Lost In Space*
Johnson, James E. (act): *Trick or Treats*
Johnson, Janet (act): *Blondes for Danger; Mrs. Pym of Scotland Yard*
Johnson, Janine (act): *Mr. Sycamore*
Johnson, Jason (act): *The Cape Canaveral Monsters; Invasion of the Saucer Men*
Johnson, Jeff (act): *Contact*
Johnson, Jesse (act): *Strangest Dreams: Invasion of the Space Preachers*
Johnson, Jill (act): *Wildest Dreams*
Johnson, Joanna (act): *Killer Party*
Johnson, Joe (act): *The Slumber Party Massacre*
Johnson, John H. (dir): *Curse of the Blue Lights*
Johnson, John Lester (act): *Tarzan's Revenge*
Johnson (III), Johnnie (act): *Heart Condition; Writer's Block*
Johnson, Johouache (act): *Heart Condition*
Johnson, Josie (act): *Stigma*
Johnson, Jude (act): *The Abomination*
Johnson, Karl (GB act): *The Magic Shop; The Tempest (1980)*
Johnson, Karl (USA act): *Night of the Comet*
Johnson, Katie (act, 1878-1957): *Death of an Angel; How to Murder a Rich Uncle; Lady In the Fog; The Lady Killers (1956); Three Steps In the Dark*
Johnson, Ken(neth) (dir): *Alien Nation: Body and Soul; Alien Nation: Dark Horizon; Alien Nation: Millennium; Alien Nation: The Enemy Within; The Incredible Hulk; The Loves of Dracula; Short Circuit 2; Steel; V; World of Dracula; Zenon:Girl of the 21st Century*
Johnson, Ken(neth) (wri): *Alien Nation: Millennium; The Incredible Hulk; Last Bride of Salem; The Loves of Dracula; V; World of Dracula*
Johnson, Kent (act): *Forever Evil*
Johnson, Kurt (act): *The Fan; Ghost Story (1981); Sole Survivor*
Johnson, Lamont (act): *Please Murder Me*
Johnson, Lamont (dir): *The Groundstar Conspiracy; Spacehunter: Adventures In the Forbidden Zone; You'll Like My Mother*
Johnson, Laraine (act): see Day, Laraine
Johnson, Larry (wri): *Dance of the Dwarfs*
Johnson, Larry D. (act): *Sugar Hill*
Johnson, Laura (act): *Awake to Danger; Chiller; Mr. Atlas; Murderous Vision; Nick Fury: Agent of Shield; Trauma (1993)*
Johnson, Laurel (act): *Frankenstein Island*
Johnson, Laurie (mus, b. 1927): *And Soon the Darkness; Captain Kronos: Vampire Hunter; Diagnosis: Murder; Dr. Strangelove, or: How I Learned to Stop Worrying and Love The Bomb; First Men In the Moon (1964); A Ghost In Monte Carlo; I Aim at the Stars; It's Alive III: Island of the Alive; The Maids; Murder In Mind; Murder Motel; Murder On the Midnight Express; Not Guilty; Once the Killing Starts; One Deadly Owner; Only A Scream Away; A Place to Die; Possession (1973); The Savage Curse; Spell of Evil*
Johnson, Lawrence (act): see Naismith, Laurence
Johnson, Leonard (act): *Glen and Randa*
Johnson, Leroy (act): *The Magic Sword (1962)*
Johnson, Sen. Leroy (act): *The House On Skull Mountain*
Johnson, Linda (act): *Jungle Goddess*
Johnson, Lucille (act): *Glen and Randa*
Johnson, Lucy (act): see Garner, Ava
Johnson, Lyell (act): *The Copper Beeches (1921)*
Johnson, Lynn-Holly (act, b. 1958): *Alien Predators; For Your Eyes Only; The Watcher In the Woods*
Johnson, Mae (act): *The Defilers*
Johnson, Marilyn (act): *Boston Blackie's Rendezvous*
Johnson, Mark (act): *The Nature of the Beast*
Johnson, May (act): *A Witch Without a Broom*
Johnson Jr., Mel (act): *Total Recall*
Johnson, Melodie (act): *I Love A Mystery (1966)*
Johnson, Merle (act): see Donahue, Troy
Johnson, Michael (act): *Lust for a Vampire*
Johnson, Michelle (act): *Death Becomes Her; Dr. Giggles; Waxwork; Wishful Thinking*
Johnson, Mike (GB act): *The River House Ghost*
Johnson, Mike (USA act): *Pumpkinhead II: Blood Wings; Through the Magic Pyramid*
Johnson, Monica (wri): *Americathon; Jekyll and Hyde...Together Again*
Johnson, Nancy (act): *Strange Invaders*
Johnson, Nell (act): *12 Monkeys*
Johnson, Noble (act): *Black Waters; A Game of Death; The Ghost Breakers; Green Hell; The Jungle Book (1942); King Kong (1933); Kismet (1930); Lost Island of Kioga; Moby Dick (1930); The Most Dangerous Game; The Mummy (1932); The Murders In the Rue Morgue (1932); The Mysterious Dr. Fu Manchu; She (1935); Son of Kong; The Thief of Bagdad (1924); White Woman*
Johnson, Noel (act): *For Your Eyes Only; Frenzy; Frightmare (1974); Highly Dangerous; Licensed to Love and Kill; Little Red Monkey; The Partner; Royal Flash; The Swordsman*
Johnson, Norris (act): *Lorna Doone (1922)*
Johnson, Nunnally (dir, 1897-1977): *Black Widow (1954); The Three Faces of Eve*
Johnson, Nunnally (wri, 1897-1977): *Black Widow (1954); Bulldog Drummond Strikes Back (1934); The Dark Mirror (1946 & 1984); Mr. Peabody and the Mermaid; My Cousin Rachel; The Prisoner of Shark Island; The Three Faces of Eve; The Woman In the Window*
Johnson, Orin (act): *The Three Musketeers (1916)*
Johnson, Pat (act): *The Ultimate Warrior*
Johnson, Pat (wri): *A Force of One*
Johnson, Patrick Read (wri): *Dragonheart*
Johnson, Penny (act): *The Hills Have Eyes II; Night Visions*
Johnson, Rafer (act, b. 1935): *Tarzan and the Great River; Tarzan and the Jungle Boy*
Johnson, Ralph K. (cin): *Curse of the Swamp Creature; The Eye Creatures*
Johnson, Raymond K. (dir): *Daughter of the Tong*
Johnson, Reginald Vel (act): *Wolfen*
Johnson, Richard (act, b. 1927): *Beyond the Door; Cairo; The Crucifer of Blood; The Cursed Medallion; Danger Route; The Day the Screaming Stopped; Deadlier Than the Male; The Fish Men; The Great Alligator; The Haunting; Lady In the Fog; The Monster Club; Murder In Mind; Operation Crossbow; Saadia; The Secret Life of Ian Fleming; Secrets of the Phantom Caverns; Some Girls Do; La Strega in Amore; Treasure Island (1990); Zombie*
Johnson, Richard (cin): *Final Eye*
Johnson, Rita (act, 1912-1965): *The Big Clock; Here Comes Mr. Jordan; Nick Carter, Master Detective; Sleep, My Love; They Won't Believe Me*
Johnson, Robert Lee (wri): *The Enchanted Forest; Tarzan's Revenge*
Johnson, Robin (act): *D.O.A. (1988)*
Johnson, Rodney (act): *George of the Jungle*
Johnson, Roger (act): *Ewoks: The Battle for Endor*
Johnson, Russell (act): *Adventures of the Queen; Attack of the Crab Monsters; The Ghost of Flight 401; The Horror at 37,000 Feet; It Came from Outer Space; The Space Children; This Island Earth*
Johnson, Ryan Thomas (act): *Carnosaur 2*
Johnson, Sandy (act): *Halloween*
Johnson, Sean (act): *Making Contact*
Johnson, Shauntae (act): *Heart Condition*
Johnson, Shelly (cin): *Alien Nation: Body and Soul; Alien Nation: Millennium; Jack's Back; Maid to Order; Murder of Innocence; Nightflyers; Teenage Mutant Ninja Turtles II: The Secret of the Ooze; Virtual Obsession*
Johnson, Sidney (act): *The Hound of The Baskervilles (1978)*
Johnson, Stephen (act): *The Loves of Dracula; World of Dracula*
Johnson, Steve (act): *Lemora, the Lady Dracula*
Johnson, Sunny (act): *Dr. Heckyl & Mr. Hype*
Johnson, Swede (act): *Project X (1987)*
Johnson, Tasha (act): *Tales from the Hood*
Johnson, Terri (act): *Flesh Gordon*
Johnson, Tony (act): *The Screaming Skull*
Johnson, Tony T. (act): *The Arrival (1996); Shadow Zone: The Undead Express*
Johnson, Tor (act, d. 1971): *The Beast of Yucca Flats; Behind Locked Doors; The Black Sleep; Bride of the Monster; Carousel; Ghost Catchers; The Lady In the Iron Mask; Night of the Ghouls; Plan 9 from Outer Space; Shadow of the Thin Man; The Unearthly*
Johnson, Van (act, b. 1916, nee Charles Van Johnson): *Beyond This Place; Brigadoon; A Guy Named Joe; The Kidnapping of the President; The Purple Rose of Cairo; Scene of the Crime; Scorpion With Two Tails; Subway In the Sky; 23 Paces to Baker Street*
Johnson, Vicki (act): *Grizzly*
Johnson, Victoria (act): *Starship Invasions*
Johnson, Walter (act): *Charlie Chan In London*
Johnson, William (act): *D.O.A. (1988)*
Johnson, William R. (cin): *Dear, Dead Delilah*
Johnson-Miller, Karen (act): *Praying Mantis*
Johnston, Alexander (act): *I Come In Peace*
Johnston, Becky (wri): *Seven Years In Tibet*
Johnston, Bobby (act): *Sinful Intrigue*
Johnston, Christopher (act): *The Annihilator*
Johnston, Clint (wri): *The Sky Dragon*
Johnston, Garry (act): *The Crater Lake Monster*
Johnston, Gerry (cin): *Rawhead Rex*
Johnston, J.J. (act): *Fatal Attraction; 976-EVIL*
Johnston, Jerry (cin): *Zardoz*
Johnston, Jerry-Mac (act): *Cry for the Strangers*
Johnston, Jim (dir): *Star Command*
Johnston, Joe (dir): *Honey, I Shrunk the Kids; Jumanji; The Pagemaster; The Rocketeer*
Johnston, John Dennis (act): *Communion; Flesh & Blood; Jekyll and Hyde...Together Again; Kiss Meets the Phantom of the Park; Purgatory; Twilight Zone*
Johnston, Julianne (act): *The Brass Bottle (1923); The Thief of Bagdad (1924)*
Johnston, Justine (act): *Fatal Attraction*
Johnston, Lionel (act): *Earthquake*
Johnston, Lorimer (act): *The Bells (1926); Dante's Inferno (1924); Son of Frankenstein*
Johnston, Margaret (act, b. 1917): *Girl In the Headlines; A Man About the House; Night of the Eagle; The Psychopath (1965)*
Johnston, Michelle (act): *Dick Tracy (1990)*
Johnston, Moffat (act): *Richard III (1911)*
Johnston, Oliver (act): *Backfire!; The Curse of the Golem; Dr. Crippen; The Hypnotist (1957); The Three Lives of Thomasina; The Tomb of Ligeia*
Johnston, Philip (act): *Outland*
Johnston, Tony (wri): *Replikator: Cloned to Kill*
Johnston, Tucker (dir): *Blood Salavge*
Johnston, Velda (wri): *A Howling In the Woods*
Johnstone, Hope (act): *Agatha*
Johnstone, Paul (act): *Mad Max*
Johnstone, Shane (act): *The Company of Wolves*
Joi, Marilyn (act): *Beyond the Living; Galaxina*
Joint, Alf (act): *Goldfinger; Macbeth (1971); The Sorcerers; Uncharted Seas; Witch-Finder General*
Jolie, Angelina (act): *Cyborg 2: Glass Shadow*
Jolivet, Pierre (act): *Le Dernier Combat*
Jolley, (I.) Stanford (act, 1900-1978): *The Baron of Arizona; Black Dragons; The Black Raven; The Chinese Cat; Cyclotrode X; The Fatal Hour (1940); Lost Planet Airmen; Night of the Lepus; The Scarlet Clue; Valley of the Dragons*
Jollcy, Norman (wri): *I've Lived Before, The Monolith Monsters*
Jolley, William (act): *Atlas*
Jolliffe, Brock (act): *The Pink Chiquitas*
Jolly, Arthur (act): *The Toxic Avenger, Part II*
Jolly, Mike (act): *Creator; Eve of Destruction*
Jolly, Nick (act): *Asylum of Satan*
Jolly, Ross (act): *Dark of the Night; Meet the Feebles*
Jonas, Chad (act): *Bates Motel*
Jonas, Norman (wri): *Let's Scare Jessica to Death*
Jonathan, Robert (act): *Street Trash*
Jonema (wri): *Boarding House*
Jones, Al (act): *The Bees; Demonoid*
Jones, Allan (act, 1908-1992): *The Boys from Syracuse*
Jones, Amanda (act): *The Adventures of Young Robin Hood*
Jones, Amy (dir): *Maid to Order; The Slumber Party Massacre*
Jones, Amy (Holden) (wri): *Maid to Order; The Relic*
Jones, Andras (act): *A Nightmare On Elm Street 4: The Dream Master; Sorority Babes In the Slimeball Bowl-O-Rama*
Jones, Angela (Rosignalo) (act): *Curdled; Lady Beware*
Jones, April Campbell (wri): *Awake to Danger; Prey of the Chameleon*
Jones, Arien (act): *Unforgettable*
Jones, Arthur V. (wri): *Undersea Girl*
Jones, B.J. (act): *The Fugitive (1993)*
Jones, Barbara (act): *Invasion of the Girl Snatchers*
Jones, Barbara O. (act): *Demon Seed*
Jones, Barry (act, b. 1893): *The Bad Lord Byron; Brigadoon; Dancing With Crime; The Glass Slipper; Madeleine; Murder In the Family; Number 17 (1932); Prince Valiant (1954); Seven Days to Noon; A Study In Terror; The 39 Steps (1959)*
Jones, Bertram (act): *The Thirteenth Chair (1929)*
Jones, Billy (wri): *The Falcon Out West*
Jones, Brett (act): *Empire of Ash III*
Jones, Brian (act): *Wombling Free*
Jones, Brian (mus): *A Degree of Murder*
Jones, Brian Thomas (dir): *Posed for Murder; The Rejuvenator*
Jones, Bridget (act): *Mystery Science Theater 3000: The Movie*
Jones, Carolyn (act, 1933-1983): *Color Me Dead; Demon and the Mummy; Eaten Alive! (1976); Halloween With the Addams Family; House of Wax; Invasion of the Body Snatchers (1956); Make Haste to Live; The Man In the Net; The Man Who Knew Too Much (1956); Midnight Lace (1981); The Saracen Blade; Shield for Murder; The War of the Worlds*
Jones, Carolyn (1990s act): *A Ghost In Monte Carlo; Nightbreed*
Jones, Catherine Zeta (act): *The Mask of Zorro (1998); The Phantom (1996); Splitting Heirs*
Jones, Ceri (wri): *Deathline*
Jones, Charles (act): *The Eleventh Hour (1923)*
Jones, Charlie (act): *Return of the Killer Tomatoes*
Jones, Charlotte (act): *The Fool Killer; Twisted*
Jones, Cherry (act, b. 1956): *Murder In a Small Town*
Jones, Chester (act): *The Bubble*
Jones, Chris (dir): *White Angel*
Jones, Christian (act): *Flesh-Eating Mothers*
Jones, Christina (act): *Killer's Moon*
Jones, Christine (act): *Wild Thing*
Jones, Christopher (act, b. 1941): *Wild In the Streets*
Jones, Chuck (act, b. 1912): *Gremlins*
Jones, Chuck (wri, b. 1912): *The Phantom of the Tollbooth*
Jones, Claud (act): *The Haunting*
Jones, Claude Earl (act): *Bride of Re-Animator; Dark Night of the Scarecrow; Evilspeak; Impulse (1984); Miracle Mile*
Jones, Clifton (act): *Sheena*
Jones, Constance (wri): *The Luck of the Irish; Mr. Peabody and the Mermaid*
Jones, D.F. (wri): *Colossus: The Forbin Project*
Jones, Damian (act): *Dead Weekend*
Jones, Dan(iel) (act): *—And Now the Screaming Starts!; Asylum (1972)*
Jones, Daniel L. (act): *Slugs*
Jones, Darby (act): *I Walked With a Zombie; Tarzan Escapes; The White Goddess; Zombies On Broadway*
Jones, Dario O. (act): *Student Bodies*
Jones, Dave (act): *Castle Keep*
Jones, Deacon (act): *Heaven Can Wait (1978)*
Jones, Dean (act, b. 1931): *Blackbeard's Ghost; The Computer Wore Tennis Shoes (1995); Herbie Goes to Monte Carlo; El Invencible Hombre Invisible; The Love Bug; Once Upon a*

Brothers Grimm; The Shaggy D.A.; Two on a Guillotine
Jones, Derrick (act): *An American Christmas Carol*
Jones, Diana (act): *Fake-Out*
Jones, Dick (act): *The Devil's Bedroom*
Jones, Dickie (act): *Heaven Can Wait (1943); Queen of the Jungle*
Jones, Don(ald M.) (dir): *The Forest; Love Butcher; Murderlust; Project: Nightmare*
Jones, Don(ald M.) (wri): *Love Butcher*
Jones, Doug (act): *Hocus Pocus; Night Angel*
Jones, Doug (cin): *Dr. Dracula*
Jones, Douglas (act): *Vampyres...Daughters of Dracula*
Jones, Duane (act, 1937-1988): *Fright House; Ganja and Hess; Night of the Living Dead (1968); To Die For*
Jones, Dylan (wri): *The Horrible House On the Hill*
Jones, Emrys (act): *Dark Secret; Deadly Nightshade; On the Run (1963); Serena; This Was a Woman; Three Cases of Murder*
Jones, Evan (wri): *The Damned; Funeral In Berlin; Modesty Blaise*
Jones, F. Richard (dir): *Bulldog Drummond (1929)*
Jones, Fenton (act): *The Octagon*
Jones, Freddie (act, b. 1927): *Appointment With a Killer; The Black Cauldron; Dune; Erik the Viking; Firestarter; Frankenstein Must Be Destroyed; In the Devil's Garden; Krull; The Man Who Haunted Himself; Mr. Horatio Knibbles; Murder Is Easy; The Mystery of Edwin Drood (1993); Otley; The Persecution and Assassination of Jean-Paul Marat as Performed by the Inmates of the Asylum of Charenton Under the Direction of the Marquis de Sade; The Satanic Rites of Dracula; Sitting Target;Son of Dracula (1974); Twinsanity; Vampira; Young Sherlock Holmes*
Jones, Gary (act): *Angels In the Endzone*
Jones, Gary (cin): *Moontrap*
Jones, Gary (dir & wri): *Mosquito*
Jones, Gemma (act): *The Devils; Dial a Deadly Number; Footsteps; Jane Eyre (1997); Paperhouse*
Jones, Glyn (act): *The Verdict (1964)*
Jones, Gordon (act): *Among the Living; Everything's Ducky; Highways by Night; The Monster That Challenged the World*
Jones, Grace (act, b. 1953): *Conan the Destroyer; Cyber Bandits; Vamp; A View to a Kill*
Jones, Griff Rhys (act & wri): *Morons from Outer Space*
Jones, Griffith (act, b. 1910): *Account Rendered; Face In the Night; Hidden Homicide; Kill Her Gently; Miranda; Return of a Stranger; The Scarlet Web; Strangler's Web; They Made Me a Fugitive*
Jones, Guy (act): *Vampire On Bikini Beach*
Jones, Guy (wri): *The Luck of the Irish; Mr. Peabody and the Mermaid*
Jones, Hank (act): *The Cat from Outer Space; The Shaggy D.A.; Village of the Giants*
Jones, Hannah (act): *Blackmail (1929); Elstree Calling; Murder; Rich and Strange*
Jones, Harmon (dir, b. 1911): *Gorilla at Large*
Jones, Harold Wayne (act): *Code Name Trixie*
Jones, Harry (act): *Clash of the Titans; Erik the Viking*
Jones, Haywood (act): *The Docks of New Orleans*
Jones, Hazel (act): *The Secret of the Moor*
Jones, Helen (act): *The Girl from Tomorrow*
Jones, Henry (act, b. 1912): *Arachnophobia; The Bad Seed (1956); Dick Tracy (1990); Project X (1967); Vertigo*
Jones, Ignatius (act): *Those Dear Departed*
Jones, Ike (act): *Tarzan's Hidden Jungle*
Jones, Ivy (act): *Dark Night of the Scarecrow*
Jones, J.B. (cin): *The Cradle Will Fall; The Man With the Power; The Night of the Claw*
Jones, J. Bill (act): *Ghost Warrior*
Jones, Jack (act): *The Day the Screaming Stopped*
Jones, Jacqueline (act): *Company of Fools; The Fourth Square; Incident at Midnight; The Road to Hong Kong*
Jones, Jake (act): *The Power (1980); Pranks*
Jones, James Cellan (dir): *The Hunchback of Notre Dame (1965)*
Jones, James Earl (act, b. 1931): *Allan Quatermain and the Lost City of Gold; The Ambulance; Blood Tide; By Dawn's Early Light; Casper: A Spirited Beginning; Conan the Barbarian; Demon Island; Dr. Strangelove, or: How I Learned to Stop Worrying and Love the Bomb; The Empire Strikes Back; Exorcist II: The Heretic; The Flight of Dragons; Grim Prairie Tales; The Hunt for Red October; Merlin (1998); The Meteor Man; Pinocchio and the Emperor of the Night; Return of the Jedi; Star Wars; Terrorgram; The UFO Incident*
Jones, Jane (act): *The Hand That Rocks the Cradle; Twin Peaks: Fire Walk With Me*
Jones, Jay Arlen (act): *Night of the Creeps*
Jones, Jeffrey (act, b. 1947): *Beetlejuice; The Crucible (1996); Devil's Advocate; Ed Wood; Howard the Duck; The Hunt for Red October; Mom and Dad Save the World; Stay Tuned; Transylvania 6-5000; Without a Clue*
Jones, Jennifer (act, b. 1919, nee Phyllis Isley): *Angel, Angel, Down We Go; Beat the Devil; Dick Tracy's G-Men; Love Letters; Portrait of Jennie; The Towering Inferno*
Jones, Jessie (act): *Switch (1991)*
Jones, Jo (act): *Hello Again*
Jones, Jocelyn (act): *Tourist Trap*
Jones, John (wri): *Garden of the Dead*
Jones, John Glyn (act): *They Came by Night*
Jones, John Marshall (act): *A Dangerous Affair*
Jones, John Paul (mus): *Scream for Help*
Jones, John Pierce (act): *Brazil*
Jones, Jon Paul (act): *They Live*
Jones, Josephine Jacqueline (act): *Warrior Queen*
Jones, Joy (act): *The Initiation*
Jones, Ken (act): *Phantasm*
Jones, Ken(neth V.) (mus): *Battle Beneath the Earth; City of the Dead; Maroc 7; Psyche 59; Tarzan Goes to India; Tarzan the Magnificent; The Tomb of Ligeia; Tower of Evil; Vengeance; Who Slew Auntie Roo?*
Jones, L.Q. (act): *The Beast Within; The Brotherhood of Satan; The Strange and Deadly Occurrence; Timerider; Tornado!*
Jones, L.Q. (dir): *A Boy and His Dog; The Devil's Bedroom*
Jones, L.Q. (wri): *A Boy and His Dog*
Jones, Laurie (act & wri): *In the Spirit*
Jones, Lee (cin & dir): *Invasion of the Girl Snatchers*
Jones, Lisa Dean (act): *I Was a Zombie for the F.B.I.*
Jones, Mal (act): *Cocoon: The Return; The Night of the Claw*
Jones, Marcia Mae (act, b. 1924): *The Barefoot Boy; Lady In the Death House; The Spectre of Edgar Allan Poe*
Jones, Marian (act): *Mountaintop Motel Massacre*
Jones, Marianne (act): *Shadow of the Hawk*
Jones, Marilyn (act): *I, Desire*
Jones, Mark (act): *Don't Open Till Christmas; The Medusa Touch; Morons from Outer Space; The Persecution and Assassination of Jean-Paul Marat as Performed by the Inmates of the Asylum of Charenton Under the Direction of the Marquis de Sade; The Sexplorer*
Jones, Mark (dir): *Leprechaun*
Jones, Mark (wri): *Leprechaun; Leprechaun 2; Leprechaun 3*
Jones, Mark Lewis (act): *Paper Mask*
Jones, Marshall (act): *Cry of the Banshee; Murders In the Rue Morgue (1971); Scream and Scream Again*
Jones, Martin C. (act): *Waxwork II: Lost In Time*
Jones, Mary (act): *Black Orchid*
Jones, Maurice (act): *The Mountain*
Jones, Melanie (act): *Something Is Out There*
Jones, Melvin (act): *Ghost Warrior*
Jones, Mervyn (act): *The Vicious Circle*
Jones, Michael (act): *Creature; The Dungeonmaster*
Jones, Michael (wri): *Mutant*
Jones, Michael Steve (act): *Always; Arachnophobia*
Jones, Mickey (act): *Sling Blade; Something Is Out There; Total Recall*
Jones, Moon (act): *Tales from the Hood*
Jones, Morgan (act): *The Boy and the Pirates; Forbidden Planet; The Giant Claw; Not of This Earth (1957); Untamed Women*
Jones, Neal (act): *Romeo Is Bleeding*
Jones, Nicholas (act): *The Corpse*
Jones, Noel (act): *Angel Heart*
Jones, Norman (act): *The Abominable Dr. Phibes; The Mind of Mr. Soames*
Jones, Norman (cin): *Mr. Selkie; Sammy's Super T-Shirt*
Jones, O-Lan (act): *Edward Scissorhands; Mars Attacks; Miraclo Milo*
Jones, Paul (GB act): *The Committee; Demons of the Mind; Privilege*
Jones, Paul (USA act): *Waxwork II: Lost In Time*
Jones, Peter (GB act, b. 1920): *Home to Danger; Last Holiday; Never Let Go; Vice Versa (1947); The Yellow Balloon*
Jones, Peter (Mex act): *Dr. Tarr's Torture Dungeon*
Jones, Philip J. (dir): *Wish Me Luck*
Jones, Pirie (act): *The Stepford Children*
Jones, Quincey (mus, b. 1933): *A Dandy In Aspic; The Deadly Affair; Mackenna's Gold; Mirage (1965); The Wiz*
Jones, R.J. (act): *Princess Warrior*
Jones, Ralph (mus): *The Slumber Party Massacre*
Jones, Raymond F. (wri, b. 1915): *This Island Earth*
Jones, Rebunkah (act): *Hide and Go Shriek*
Jones, Reed (act): *The Fan*
Jones, Renee (act): *Friday the 13th, Part VI: Jason Lives*
Jones, Retha (act): *The Nutty Professor (1996)*
Jones, Richard (act): *Mutants In Paradise*
Jones, Rick (GB act): *The Shuttered Room*
Jones, Rick (USA act): *Deadly Game; How to Stuff a Wild Bikini*
Jones, Rick (cin): *Psycho IV: The Beginning*
Jones, Rickie Lee (act): *Pinocchio and the Emperor of the Night*
Jones, Robert (act): *Deadly Sins*
Jones, Robert Earl (act): *Rain Without Thunder*
Jones, Rosie (act): *Ganjasaurus Rex*
Jones, Roy (act): *Macbeth (1971)*
Jones, Ruth (act & wri): see Gordon, Ruth
Jones, Sally (act): *Erik the Viking*
Jones, Sam (1910s act): *Lieutenant Daring and the Ship's Mascot*
Jones, Sam (J.) (act, b. 1954): *Flash Gordon (1980); Jane and the Lost City; Night Rhythms; The Spirit; Stunts Unlimited*
Jones, Sammee Lee (act): *What's the Matter With Helen?*
Jones, Sebastian Graham (act): *Because of the Cats*
Jones, Seth (act): *Madman*
Jones, Sharon Lee (act): *Leapin' Leprechauns!; Princess Warrior*
Jones, Shirleta (act): *Angel Heart*
Jones, Shirley (act, b. 1934): *Beyond the Poseidon Adventure; Black Devil Doll from Hell; Bobbikins; Carousel; Dog's Best Friend; L'Intrigo; The Secret of My Success*
Jones, Simon (act): *Brazil; 12 Monkeys*
Jones, Stanley (act): *Little Shop of Horrors (1986)*
Jones, Stanley G. (act): *The Crawling Hand*
Jones, Steve (act): *Buck Rogers In the 25th Century*
Jones, Steven (act): *Killer Klowns from Outer Space*
Jones, Steven A. (mus): *The Borrower*
Jones, Steven Anthony (act): *Eyes of Terror*
Jones, Susan (act): *Roller Blade Warriors: Taken by Force*
Jones, T.C. (act, 1921-1971): *The Name of the Game Is Kill; The President's Analyst*
Jones, Terry (act, b. 1942): *Erik the Viking; Jabberwocky; Monty Python and the Holy Grail*
Jones, Terry (dir, b. 1942): *Erik the Viking; Monty Python and the Holy Grail*
Jones, Terry (wri, b. 1942): *Erik the Viking; Labyrinth (1986); Monty Python and the Holy Grail*
Jones, Texacala (act): *Dr. Caligari*
Jones, Tom (act): *Hex; Mars Attacks!*
Jones, Tommy Lee (act, b. 1947): *Batman Forever; Eyes of Laura Mars; The Fugitive (1993); Gotham; Men In Black; The Package; Small Soldiers; U.S. Marshals; Volcano*
Jones, Trevor (act): *Big & Hairy Volcano*
Jones, Trevor (mus): *Arachnophobia; Black Angel (1980); The Dark Crystal; Excalibur; Freejack; Gulliver's Travels (1996); Hideaway; Just Ask for Diamond; Labyrinth (1986); Loch Ness; Murder by Moonlight; Richard III (1995); Runaway Train; The Sender*
Jones, Vernon (act): *The Barton Mystery (1920)*
Jones, Virginia (act): see Mayo, Virginia
Jones, Winston (dir): *U.F.O.; Wink of an Eye*
Jones-Moreland, Betsy (act): *Creature from the Haunted Sea; Last Woman On Earth; The St. Valentine's Day Massacre; The Viking Women and the Sea Serpent*
Jonfield, Peter (act): *Mary Shelley's 'Frankenstein'; Murder by Decree*
Jongeneel, William (act): *A Connecticut Yankee In King Arthur's Court (1989)*
Jonnason, Hans (act): *Re-Animator*
Jons, Beverly (act): *The Feathered Serpent (1948)*
Jonson, Bari (act): *Naked Evil; Prehistoric Women (1966)*
Jonson, Brian (cin): *Hunted (1973)*
Jonson, Tom (mus): *The Brain Eaters*
Joo, Chua Kah (act): *Indiana Jones and the Temple of Doom*
Joosten, Kathryn (act): *The Package*
Jordahl, Richard (act): *Capture That Capsule!*
Jordan, Alan (act): *Sorry, Wrong Number (1989)*
Jordan, Alan R. (act): *Cocoon: The Return*
Jordan, Angel (act): *Parsifal*
Jordan, Armand (act): *Perseus the Invincible*
Jordan, Bobby (act, 1923-1965): *The Ghost Creeps; Ghosts On the Loose; Mr. Hex; Spook Busters; Spooks Run Wild*
Jordan, Cecil (act): *Wavelength*
Jordan, Charles (act): *Black Magic (1944); The Scarlet Clue; Shadows Over Chinatown; The Sky Dragon*
Jordan, Don (act): *Brainscan; Deadbolt; Dr. Jekyll and Ms. Hyde*
Jordan, Dorothy (act, 1906-1988): *The Lost Squadron*
Jordan, France (act): *Oasis of the Zombies*
Jordan, George Banito (act): *Halloween With the Addams Family*
Jordan, Gerard (act): *Funeral Home; The Intruder (1981); The Pit (1983)*
Jordan, Glenn (dir): *Frankenstein (1973); Les Miserables (1978)*
Jordan, Harlan (act): *The Texas Chainsaw Massacre 2*
Jordan, Henry (act): *One Mysterious Night*
Jordan, Jack (act): *The Picture of Dorian Gray (1916)*
Jordan, James Carroll (act): *Slashdance*
Jordan, Jeremy (act): *Storm of the Century*
Jordan, Jeri (act): *The Snake Pit (1948)*
Jordan, Jimmy (act): *Dick Tracy (1945); The Falcon In Hollywood*
Jordan, Joanne (Moore) (act): *Bury Me an Angel; The Dunwich Horror; I Cover the Underworld; I Dismember Mama*
Jordan, John (cin): *On Her Majesty's Secret Service*
Jordan, Larry (act): *Jaws of Satan*
Jordan, Leslie (act): *Frankenstein General Hospital; Jason Goes to Hell: The Final Friday*
Jordan, Marsha (act): *Count Yorga, Vampire*
Jordan, Michelle (act): *I, Madman*
Jordan, Miriam (act): *Sherlock Holmes (1932); Six Hours to Live*
Jordan, Neil (dir, b. 1950): *The Company of Wolves; High Spirits; In Dreams; Interview With the Vampire*
Jordan, Neil (wri, b. 1950): *The Company of Wolves; High Spirits; In Dreams*
Jordan, Nick (act): *Reactor*
Jordan, Patrick (act): *Behemoth, the Sea Monster; Bunny Lake Is Missing; Cloak Without Dagger; Dilemma; In the Devil's Garden; Man Detained; The Marked One; Murder Motel; Rag Doll; Robbery; The Slipper and the Rose*
Jordan, Richard (act, 1938-1993): *Dune; The Hunt for Red October; Logan's Run; Les Miserables (1978); Solarbabies*
Jordan, Robert (act): *Primal Fear*
Jordan, Tom (act): *The Outcasts*
Jordan, Troy (act): *Alice In Wonderland (1985)*
Jordan, William (act): *Contact; The Deathmaster; Gray Lady Down; Rage*
Jordine, Merdel (act): *Death May Be Your Santa Claus*
Jordon, Jo (act): *Rattlers*
Jordon, Mike (act): *House of Usher (1960)*
Jorge, Paul (act): *The Passion of Joan of Arc*
Jorge, Victor (act): *Last Rites (1980)*
Jorgensen, Kent (act): *Cavegirl (1985)*
Jorgensen, Ole (act): *Zone Troopers*
Jorgseeberger, Hans (act): *The Green Slime*
Jory, Victor (act, 1902-1982): *Bulldog Drummond at Bay (1937); Cat-Women of the Moon; Charlie Chan In Rio; Devil Dog: The Hound from Hell; The Fugitive Kind; The Lone Wolf Meets a Lady; The Loves of Carmen (1948); Manfish; The Man Who Turned to Stone; Meet Nero Wolfe; A Midsummer Night's Dream (1935); Sabaka; Secrets of the Lone Wolf; Son of Ali Baba; The Unknown Guest*
Jose, Edward (dir): *The Man from Downing Street*
Jose, Leonardo (act): *Women In Fury*
Jose, Paulo (act): *Macunaima*
Jose, Paulo (wri): *Os Deuses e os Mortos*
Joseph, Aaron (act): *Tarzan Goes to India*
Joseph, Allen (act): *Eraserhead; Marathon Man; The Return of Count Yorga*
Joseph, Carrie (act): *Surf Nazis Must Die*
Joseph, Don (act): *Color Me Blood Red*
Joseph, Edmund (wri): *Who Done It? (1942)*
Joseph, Eugenie (dir): *Alien High; Spookies*
Joseph, Felix (act): *Welcome II the Terrordome*
Joseph, Helen (act): *The Hideous Sun Demon*

Joseph, Jackie (act): Gremlins; Gremlins 2: The New Batch; The Little Shop of Horrors (1960)
Joseph, Joanna (act): Child's Play (1985)
Joseph, Joanne (act): The Quatermass Conclusion
Joseph, Julian (mus): Tale of a Vampire
Joseph, Ralph (act): Candyman: Farewell to the Flesh
Joseph, Robert Alan (wri): Outbreak
Joseph, Robert L. (wri): Asylum for a Spy; Strategy of Terror; The Third Secret; World War III
Joseph, Ron (act): Murder of Innocence
Joseph, Todd (act): Midnight Tease
Joseph, Yvonne (act): see Mitchell, Yvonne
Josepher, Wendle (act): Twister
Josephs, Wilfred (mus): Dark Places; The Deadly Bees; Fanatic (1965); Mata Hari (1985); The Uncanny
Josephs, Wilfred (wri): Touch of Death
Josephsen, Rick (cin): Deadly Game; Secrets of the Phantom Caverns; Snow Kill
Josephson, Erland (act, b. 1923): Ansiktet; Prospero's Books; Vargtimmen
Josephson, Jeffrey (act): Retribution (1988)
Josephson, Julian (wri): The Bat (1926); The Green Goddess (1929)
Josephson, Les (act): Heaven Can Wait (1978)
Josephy, Alvin (wri): Operation Secret
Joshi, Bindra (act): The Golden Child
Joshi, Indira (act): Paint Me a Murder
Joshua, Larry (act): The Burning; Romeo Is Bleeding; Svengali (1983)
Joslin, Annis (act): Tennis Court
Joslin, Oliver (act): Secrets In the Attic
Joslyn, Allyn (act, 1901-1981): Heaven Can Wait (1942); The Horn Blows at Midnight; I Wake Up Screaming; Nightmare In the Sun
Jossa, Piero (act): The Great Alligator
Josselyn, Randy (act): Too Good to Be True
Jost, Paul (mus): Last Rites (1980)
Jostin, Darwin (act): Eraserhead; Rattlers; Time Walker
Jostyn, Jennifer (act): Omega Cop; Vampire on Bikini Beach
Jotta, Elio (act): The Mattei Affair; Lo Spettro
Jouanneau, Jacques (act): Judex
Jourdan, Louis (act, b. 1921, nee Louis Gendre): Anne of the Indies; Le Comte de Monte Cristo; The Count of Monte Cristo (1975); Fear No Evil (1969); Julie; Octopussy; The Paradine Case; The Return of Swamp Thing; Ritual of Evil; Swamp Thing; To Commit a Murder
Journeaux, Donald (act): The Brotherhood of Satan
Journet, Marcel (act): Crime Doctor's Gamble
Journey (mus): Heavy Metal
Jovan, Slavitza (act): Ghostbusters
Jove, Angel (act): Anguish
Jovovich, Milla (act): The Fifth Element
Joy, Charlie (act): When Quackel Did Hyde
Joy, Karen (act): Gallery of Horror
Joy, Mark (act): Black Rainbow; Lovestruck
Joy, Nicholas (act): Abbott and Costello Meet the Killer; Bride of Vengeance; Desk Set; The Man With a Cloak
Joy, Robert (act): Amityville 3-D; The Dark Half; Millennium; The Suicide Club (1988); Waterworld
Joyce, Alice (act, 1889-1955): The Green Goddess (1923 & 1929)
Joyce, Brenda (act, b. 1918, nee Betty Leabo): Danger Woman; The Enchanted Forest; Pillow of Death; The Spider Woman Strikes Back; Strange Confession; Tarzan and the Amazons; Tarzan and the Huntress; Tarzan and the Leopard Woman; Tarzan and the Mermaids; Tarzan's Magic Fountain; Whispering Ghosts
Joyce, Eileen (act): Trent's Last Case (1952)
Joyce, Elaine (act): The November Plan; Trick or Treat
Joyce, Emily (act): Jane Eyre (1997)
Joyce, Jimmy (act): Ritual of Evil
Joyce, John (act): Agatha; Morons from Outer Space
Joyce, Kathleen (act): The Ringer (1931)
Joyce, Kathy (act): Stigma
Joyce, Lind (act): The Clouded Crystal
Joyce, Michael P. (cin): The Boy Who Cried Werewolf
Joyce, Paddy (act): Erik the Viking
Joyce, Peggy Hopkins (act): International House
Joyce, Stephen (act): A Stranger Is Watching
Joyce, William (act): Voodoo Blood Bath
Joyce, Yootha (act): Burke and Hare; Fanatic (1965); Fragment of Fear; Frankenstein: The True Story; Kaleidoscope; The Night Digger; Our Mother's House
Joyeux, Odette (act): Sylvia and the Phantom
Joyner, C. Courtney (dir): Lurking Fear; Trancers III: Deth Lives
Joyner, (C.) Courtney (wri): Catacombs (1989); Class of 1999; Lurking Fear; The Offspring; Prison (1988); Trancers III: Deth Lives
Joyner, Kimble (act): Ghost of a Chance (1987)
Joyner, Michelle (act): Grim Prairie Tales; Outbreak; Traces of Red
Joynt, Paul (act): Echoes
Joyzelle (act): Just Imagine
Jozefowicz, Zbigniew (act): O Dwoch Takich Co Ukradli Ksiezyc; Wielka, Wielka I Najwieksza
Jubenvill, Ken (dir): Ebenezer
Jubert, Alice (act): J.D.'s Revenge
Judd, Ashley (act, b. 1968): Eye of the Beholder (1999); Kiss the Girls; A Time to Kill (1996)
Judd, Edward (act, b. 1932): Assassin (1973); The Criminal; The Day the Earth Caught Fire; First Men In the Moon (1964); Frankenstein (1984); Invasion (1965); Island of Terror; The Man Upstairs; Murder Motel; The Shakedown; Subway In the Sky; The Vault of Horror; The Vengeance of She; X...The Unknown
Judd, Lesley (act): Threads
Judel, Charles (act): Close Call for Ellery Queen; The Florentine Dagger; Pinocchio (1940)
Juden, R. (act): Old St. Paul's
Judge, Arline (act, 1912-1974): The Crawling Hand; Girls In Chains; Law of the Jungle; The Mysterious Mr. Wong
Judge, Joel (dir & wri): The Golden Mistress
Judges, Christopher (act): Turn Back the Clock
Judith, Debbie (act): The Brotherhood of Satan
Juditz, Vicki (act): The Toxic Avenger
Judson, Lester (act): The Sand Castle
Jue, Rosalind (act): Point of No Return
Juel, Bente (act): Journey to the Seventh Planet
Juerging, Arno (act): Dracula (1974); Frankenstein (1974)
Juhl, Jerry (wri): The Great Muppet Caper; The Muppet Movie
Juhlin, Nicklas (act): Mystery Island
Juhnke, Harald (act): Red Dragon (1965)
Jul, Christen (wri): Vampyr
Jules (act): Tabu
Jules, Maurice (wri): Scream, Blacula, Scream; The Velvet Vampire
Julia, Raul (act, 1940-1994): The Addams Family; Addams Family Values; Eyes of Laura Mars; Roger Corman's Frankenstein Unbound
Julian, Arthur (act): How to Stuff a Wild Bikini
Julian, Chuck (act): Superman (1978); Spaceflight IC-1; Terror (1979)
Julian, Janet (act): Ghost Warrior; Humongous
Julian, Rupert (act, 1889-1943): The Dumb Girl of Portici
Julian, Rupert (dir, 1889-1943): The Cat Creeps (1930); The Leopard Lady; The Phantom of the Opera (1925)
Juliano, Joe (cin): An American Tail
Juliano, Lenny (act): Chopping Mall; Not of This Earth (1988)
Julianov, Lev (dir): Crime and Punishment (1975)
Julien, Max (act): Psych-Out
Julio, Montserrat (act): The Blood Spattered Bride; Robin and Marian
Julissa (act): Isle of the Snake People
Juma (act): Fury at Smugglers' Bay
Jump, Gordon (act, b. 1932): Conquest of the Planet of the Apes; Justin Case; Midnight Offerings
Junco, Tito (act): La Mort en Ce Jardin
Jundeff, Jake (act): Earth Girls Are Easy
June (act): The Lodger (1926)
June, Ray (cin, 1898-1958): The Bat Whispers; The Beginning or the End?; The Cockeyed Miracle; I Married an Angel; The Last Days of Pompeii (1935); Night Must Fall (1937); This Is My Love; Treasure Island (1934)
Jung, Allan (act): Dimension 5; Murder by Television
Jung, Calvin (act): The Day After; In the Shadow of Kilimanjaro; RoboCop
Jung, David (act): Netforce
Jung, Jurgen (act): Jonathan
Jung, Nathan (act): Darkman (1990); Galaxis
Jung, Shia (act): Charlie Chan at the Circus
Jung-Kun, Chun (mus): Yongary, Monster from the Deep
Junior, Mark Boone (act): Seven
Junkerman, Kelly (act): Time Walker
Junkermann, Hans J. (act): Doctor Mabuse
Junkin, Harry W. (wri): The Fiction-Makers; Vendetta for the Saint
Junkin, John (act): Journey to the Unknown; Kaleidoscope; Licensed to Love and Kill; Vengeance; Wombling Free
Jupp, Julie (act): Victims
Jur, Jeffrey (cin): Unforgettable
Juracek, Pavel (dir, b. 1935): Order and Disorder
Juracek, Oavel (wri, b. 1935): Ikaria XB1; War of the Fools
Jurado, Katy (act): Fearmaker
Juran, Jerry (wri): Dr. Blood's Coffin
Juran, Nathan (H.) (dir, b. 1907): The Black Castle; The Boy Who Cried Werewolf; The Deadly Mantis; First Men In the Moon (1964); Flight of the Lost Balloon; The Golden Blade; Jack the Giant Killer; The 7th Voyage of Sinbad; Siege of the Saxons; 20 Million Miles to Earth
Juran, Nathan (H.) (wri, b. 1907): Flight of the Lost Balloon; Jack the Giant Killer
Jurcec, Rajka (act): Zorro (1975)
Jurgens, Curt (act, 1915-1982): An Affair of State; The Assassination Bureau; Brainwashed; Hide and Seek; I Aim at the Stars; The Karate Killers; The Mephisto Waltz; Orient Express; OSS 117-Double Agent; Psyche 59; Sleep of Death; The Spy Who Loved Me; A Target for Killing; The Vault of Horror
Jurgens, Helen (act): see Twelvetrees, Helen
Jurgensen, Randy (act): Maniac (1980); Superman (1978); Thinner
Jurgensen, William (J.) (cin): Arnold; Human Feelings; The Return of the Six Million Dollar Man and the Bionic Woman; Terror In the Wax Museum
Jurges, Jurgen (cin): Funny Games
Juris, Larry (mus): The Rejuvenator
Jury, Richard (act): Endangered Species
Jury, Rick (act): Earthbound (1981)
Just, Monique (act): Psycosissimo
Just, Philip (wri): see Sanjust, Filippo
Juster, Norman (wri): The Phantom Tollbooth
Justice, Edgar (act): Final Eye; It Came Upon the Midnight Clear; Someone's Watching Me!
Justice, James Robertson (act, 1905-1975): Alien Women; Anne of the Indies; Blackmailed; The Black Rose; Chitty Chitty Bang Bang; Dr. Crippen; The Face of Fu Manchu; Fiddlers Three; Land of the Pharaohs; The Living Idol; Les Miserables (1952); Moby Dick (1956); Murder She Said; My Daughter Joy; Pool of London; Seven Thunders; Spirits of the Dead; Stop Press Girl; The Story of Robin Hood; The Trygon Factor; Vice Versa (1947); The Voice of Merrill; Zeta One
Justice, Katherine (act): Captain America II; The Stepmother
Justice, William (act): see Travis, Richard
Justin, Ed (wri): Pumpkinhead
Justin, Ginger (act): Phoenix the Warrior
Justin, Greer (act): Scared to Death (1980)
Justin, John (act, b. 1917): The Big Sleep (1978); Candidate for Murder; Guilty?; Hot Ice; Liszt O' Mania; The Sound Barrier; The Spider's Web; The Teckman Mystery; The Thief of Bagdad (1940)
Justin, Susan (mus): The Final Terror; Forbidden World
Justine (wri): Alibi (1942)
Justine, William (act): The Bride and the Beast
Justini, Carlo (act): Intent to Kill; The Whole Truth
Jutra, Claude (act, 1930-1986): 7 Surprizes
Juttke, Herbert (wri): On Secret Service
Juttner, Christian (act): Return from Witch Mountain; The Swarm
Juul, Ole (wri): Crazy Paradise
Juvan, Vida (act): Cave of the Living Dead

Kaa, Kuki (act): Inn of the Damned
Ka'Ahea, Ed (act): A Vacation In Hell
Kaapa, Manna (act): Weird Woman
Kaaren, Suzanne (act): Blondes at Work; The Devil Bat
Kaatz, Wayne (act): The Brave Little Toaster
Kabibble, Ish (act, 1909-1995): You'll Find Out
Kac, Isser (act): see Katch, Kurt
Kachler, Robert S. (wri): Megaforce
Kacirkova, Irena (act): Ikaria XB1
Kaczender, George (dir): Agency
Kaczmarek, Jane (act): D.O.A. (1988); The Heavenly Kid; Vice Versa (1988)
Kaczynski, Jaroslaw (act): O Dwoch Takich Co Ukradli Ksiezyc
Kaczynski, Lech (act): O Dwoch Takich Co Ukradli Ksiezyc
Kadamba (act): Mary Reilly
Kadani, Otis (act): Play Misty for Me
Kadanyov, Alexander (act): The Saint
Kadar, Janos (dir, 1918-1979): The Angel Levine
Kaden, Katherine (act): The Offspring
Kadison, Ellis (wri): The Gnome-Mobile; Theatre of Death
Kadler, Karen (act): The Devil's Messenger; Francis Joins the WACs; It Conquered the World
Kadogo, Aku (act): The Punisher
Kadotchnikova, Larisa (act): Shadows of Forgotten Ancestors
Kaell, Ron (act): Copycat
Kaempffert, Waldemar (wri): Un Amour de Poche
Kaethler, Paul (act): Superman III
Kafafian, Eddie (act): Walk the Dark Street
Kafka, Franz (wri, 1883-1924): Das Schloss; The Trial
Kafka, Hans (wri): Dead Man's Shoes
Kafka, John (wri): Woman Who Came Back
Kagan, Diane (act): Jacob's Ladder
Kagan, Elaine (act): Love Can Be Murder
Kagan, Jeremy (Paul) (dir): Judge Dee and the Monastery Murder; Roswell
Kagan, Jeremy Paul (wri): Roswell
Kagan, Marilyn (act): The Initiation
Kagawa, Kyoko (act): High and Low
Kagawa, Teruyuki (act): The Mystery of Rampo
Kagen, David (act): Friday the 13th, Part VI: Jason Lives
Kagure, Brian (act): King Solomon's Mines (1985)
Kagy, Tom (act): Sling Blade
Kahan, Saul (act): Schlock
Kahan, Stephen/Steve (act): Predator 2; Superman (1978); Warlock: The Armageddon
Kahler, Wolf (act): The Boys from Brazil; The Lady Vanishes (1979); Raiders of the Lost Ark
Kahn, Allen (wri): The Wizard of Gore
Kahn, Florence (act): The Secret Agent (1936)
Kahn, Frances (act): The Blood of Fu Manchu
Kahn, Gordon (wri): The Death Kiss
Kahn, Jeff (act): Vice Versa (1988)
Kahn, Karen (act): Village of the Damned (1995)
Kahn, Madeline (act, b. 1942): The Adventures of Sherlock Holmes' Smarter Brother; An American Tail; A Bug's Life; The Muppet Movie; My Little Pony; Simon; Young Frankenstein
Kahn, Richard C. (dir): Son of Ingagi
Kahn, Shanti (act): Dangerous Touch
Kahner, Julie (act): Videodrome
Kahson, Elisabeth (act): The Beast (1974)
Kai, Carole (act): Deathmoon
Kaige, Chen (dir): Life On a String
Kaijo, Hideo (wri): The H-Man
Kaikaka, Gary (act): King Kong Lives
Kaine, Nancy (act): Repossessed
Kairys, Valerie (act): Vanishing Point (1971)
Kaiser, Arnold (act): see Kerry, Norman
Kaiser, Burt (wri): The Female Jungle
Kaiser, Joel (act): Dead Certain
Kaiser, Sid (act): Invasion of the Bee Girls
Kaiser, Suki (act): Virtual Assassin
Kaitan, Elizabeth (act): Aftershock; Necromancer: Satan's Servant; Nightwish; Petticoat Planet; Roller Blade Warriors: Taken by Force
Kaizer, Sandra (act): The Music of the Spheres
Kaji, Kentaro (act): Onibaba
Kajima, Nobuhiro (act): Attack of the Monsters
Kajlicheva, Anita (act): The Man of the First Century
Kal, Harris (act): The Pit (1983)
Kalajian, Berje (mus): Mission Mars
Kalantan (act): Son of Sinbad
Kalashnikov, Leonid (cin): The Red Tent
Kalatozov, Mikhail (dir, 1903-1973): The Red Tent
Kalbus, Terrie (act): Phantasm
Kalcheim, Lee (wri): Is This Trip Really Necessary?
Kalem, Toni (act): Silent Rage
Kalember, Patricia (act, b. 1956): Jacob's Ladder
Kaler, Bernard (act): The Rats Are Coming! The Werewolves Are Here!
Kaler, Berwick (act): Bloodthirsty Butchers
Kaler, Ted (act): Strange Days
Kaley, Vi (act): The Man Without a Face; Vice Versa (1947)
Kalfon, Jean-Pierre (act): Condorman
Kalinski, Edward (act): Frightmare (1974)
Kalipha, Stefan (act): For Your Eyes Only
Kalis, Van (cin): Ikaria XB1
Kalish, Irma (wri): I Dream of Jeannie: Fifteen Years Later
Kalish, Stanley (act, 191801989): House of Wax
Kalli, Maxine (act): Sudden Terror
Kallianiotes, Helena (act): Alfred Hitchcock Presents; Shanks
Kallman, Dick (mus): The Cry Baby Killer
Kalmanowicz, Max (dir): The Children; Dreams Come True
Kalser, Erwin (act): Dressed to Kill (1941)
Kamal, Jon Rashad (act): Star Trek
Kaman, Kristine (act): Mad Max
Kaman, Steve (act): Demolition Man
Kamb, Karl (wri): Tarzan and the She-Devil
Kambes, Ann (act): Midnight (1980)

Kameha, Lahaina (act): Def by Temptation
Kamekona, Danny (act): Robot Jox; Robot Wars
Kamel, Stanley (act): Captain America II
Kamen, Michael (mus): The Adventures of Baron Munchausen (1989); Blue Ice; Brazil; The Dead Zone; Event Horizon; Highlander; Jack; Licence to Kill (1989); Nothing But Trouble; 101 Dalmatians (1960 & 1996); Polyester; Robin Hood: Prince of Thieves; S*H*E (1980); The Three Musketeers (1993); What Dreams May Come; Wilder Napalm; Venom (1982)
Kamen, Robert Mark (wri): The Fifth Element
Kamerer, Dan (act): Midnight (1980)
Kamiat, Bernice (act): see Williams, Cara
Kamier, Piotr (dir): Chronopolis
Kamimura, Yoshiyuki (act): Mothra
Kamini, Susana (act): Dr. Tarr's Torture Dungeon; Sisters of Satan
Kaminka, Didier (act): Nada
Kaminker, Simone-Henriette-Charlotte (act): see Signoret, Simone
Kamins, Laura (act): I Saw What You Did (1988)
Kaminska, Ida (act, 1899-1980): The Angel Levine
Kaminski, Dana (act): Super Mario Bros.
Kaminski, David Daniel (act): see Kaye, Danny
Kaminski, Janusz (cin): Grim Prairie Tales; The Lost World Jurassic Park
Kaminsky, Leon (dir): Dr. Jekyll y el Hombre Lobo
Kaminsky, Stuart M. (wri): When the Dark Man Calls
Kamiyama, Shigeru (act): Kwaidan
Kamm, Kris (act): Elvira, Mistress of the Dark
Kammeren, Torsten (act): The Story of Gosta Berling
Kammesri, Tuantone (act): Vice Versa (1988)
Kamoi, Kip (act): Golden Ivory
Kampe, Susan (act): Brainstorm (1983)
Kampers, Fritz (act): Der Steinerne Reiter
Kampmann, Judith Kahan (act): Twice Upon a Time
Kamps, John (wri): The Borrowers (1998); Mighty Morphin Power Rangers
Kamrath, Laura (act): The Phoenix and the Magic Carpet
Kamreither, Tony (act): Change of Mind
Kamuyu, Andrew (act): Congo
Kanagawa, Hiro (act): Hideaway
Kanakaredes, Melina (act): The Long Kiss Goodnight
Kanakis, Anna (act): After the Fall of New York
Kanaly, Steve (act, b. 1946): Headhunter; Pumpkinhead II: Blood Wings; The Terminal Man
Kanaoko, Nobu (act): Iron Man
Kanayama, Hirofumi (act): The Punisher
Kanbe, Masamori (act): The Toxic Avenger, Part II
Kanbe, Morikazu (act): The Toxic Avenger, Part II
Kandel, Aben (wri, 1896-1993, nee Kenneth Langtry): Berserk; Craze; The Headless Ghost; Horrors of the Black Museum; How to Make a Monster; I Was a Teenage Frankenstein; Konga; Trog
Kandel, Jack (act): The Package
Kandel, Paul (act): The Hunchback of Notre Dame (1996)
Kandel, Stephen (wri): Chamber of Horrors (1966)
Kander, John (mus, b. 1927): Still of the Night
Kane, Alden (act): Prom Night IV: Deliver Us from Evil
Kane, Artie (mus): The Bat People
Kane, Beatrice (act): Dick Barton, Detective; Dick Barton, Special Agent; Nothing But the Night
Kane, Big Daddy (act): The Meteor Man
Kane, Billy (act): Waxwork II: Lost In Time
Kane, Bob (wri, 1915-1998): Batman (1966 & 1989); Batman and Robin; Batman Forever; Batman: Mask of the Phantasm; Batman Returns
Kane, Brad (act): Aladdin (1992); The Return of Jafar
Kane, Byron (act): Gog; The Monster That Challenged the World
Kane, Candye (act): Blood Diner
Kane, Carol (act, b. 1952): Addams Family Values; Dad, the Angel & Me; Freaky Friday (1995); The Games of the Countess Dolingen of Gratz; Is This Trip Really Necessary?; Jawbreaker; The Mafu Cage; The Muppet Movie; Pandemonium; The Princess Bride; [illegible] Stranger Calls; When a Stranger Calls Back
Kane, Eddie (act): The Mummy (1932)
Kane, Emmet (act): Graveyard Shift (1990)
Kane, Fernne (act): Psycho Girls
Kane, Irene (act): Killer's Kiss
Kane, Ivan (act): Prison (1988)
Kane, Jackson D. (act): The Man Who Fell to Earth (1976)
Kane, Janice (act): 23 Paces to Baker Street; Venetian Bird
Kane, Joe (act): Eve of Destruction
Kane, Joseph (dir, b. 1897): Accused of Murder; Darkest Africa; Fair Wind to Java; The Man Who Died Twice
Kane, Lou (act): The Mad Room; What Ever Happened to Aunt Alice?
Kane, Marjorie (act): Dick Tracy vs. Crime, Inc.
Kane, Michael (act): The Bedford Incident; 3 Days of the Condor
Kane, Michael (wri): The Legend of the Lone Ranger
Kane, Robert (act): Child's Play (1988)
Kane, Robert G. (wri): Kisses for My President
Kane, Whitford (act): The Ghost and Mrs. Muir
Kanebako, Kazumi (act): The Toxic Avenger, Part II
Kanedo, Naomi (act): Blood Tracks
Kanefsky, Rolfe (dir & wri): There's Nothing Out There
Kaneko, Mitsundbu (act): Voyage Into Space
Kaneko, Nobuo (act): Godzilla (1985)
Kaneko, Shu (dir): Necronomicon: Book of the Dead
Kaneko, Shusuke (dir): Gamera: Guardian of the Universe
Kanemori, Aimee (act): The Hand That Rocks the Cradle
Kang, Moon (act): Yongary, Monster from the Deep
Kang, Stan (act): 12 Monkeys
Kang, Yu Yung (act): A Terra-Cotta Warrior
Kanghanamat, Rachan (act): Night Creature
Kangrga, Rick (act): The Body Snatchers
Kani, John (act): The Ghost and the Darkness
Kania, Cynthia (act): Murder of Innocence
Kanin, Fay (act): A Double Life (1947)
Kanin, Garson (wri, b. 1912): A Double Life (1947)
Kankura, Taiichi (cin): Destroy All Monsters; Yog-Monster from Space
Kann, Lily (act, b. 1898): Beautiful Stranger; Cat Girl; Escape to Danger; A Kid for Two Farthings; Latin Quarter; No Trees In the Streets; Whirlpool (1959)
Kanner, Alexis (act): Crossplot; Kings and Desperate Men; Nightfall (1988); Twinsanity
Kanner, Alexis (dir): Kings and Desperate Men
Kannon, Mike (act): Rat Pfink & Boo Boo
Kano, Keiko (act): The Toxic Avenger, Part II
Kantenwine, Vicki (act): Mermaids of Tiburon
Kanter, Hal (wri, b. 1918): Casanova's Big Night; The Road to Bali
Kanter, Jennifer (act): Maximum Thrust
Kanter, Marin (act): Endangered Species
Kantor, Igo (mus): Kingdom of the Spiders; Motor Psycho; The Projectionist
Kantor, MacKinlay (wri, b. 1904): The Happy Land
Kants, Ivar (act): The Plumber
Kanturek, Otto (cin): Die Frau im Mond
Kapelos, John (act): Deep Red (1994); Nick Knight; The Relic; Weird Science
Kaper, Bronislau (mus, 1902-1983): Above Suspicion; Alraune (1930); Fingers at the Window; Gaslight (1944); The Glass Slipper; Green Mansions; Keeper of the Flame; Kisses for My President; Saadia; Them! (1954); Three Wise Fools
Kaplan, Cory (act & cin): The Phantom Empire
Kaplan, Don (act): The Toxic Avenger, Part II
Kaplan, Elliot (mus): The Food of the Gods
Kaplan, Ervin L. (cin): Pinocchio and the Emperor of the Night
Kaplan, George (wri): The Seventh Sign
Kaplan, Holly (act): Shocker
Kaplan, Joel (wri): Murder of Innocence
Kaplan, Jonathan (dir, b. 1947): Project X (1987)
Kaplan, Mady (act): Project X (1987)
Kaplan, Marvin (act): Fangs; The Nutty Professor (1963); The Severed Arm
Kaplan, Michael (act): The Toxic Avenger, Part III: The Last Temptation of Toxie
Kaplan, Nelly (act): La Prima Donna
Kaplan, Sol (mus, 1919-1990): The Black Book; Niagara; The Spy Who Came In from the Cold
Kaplan, Vivienne (act): The Frighteners
Kaplan, Wendy (act): Halloween 5: The Revenge of Michael Myers
[illegible]
Kaplanova, Valerie (act): Howling II
Kapler, A. (act): Shinel (1926)
Kapler, Alexei (wri): The Amphibian Man
Kaplowitz, Herbert (act): Galaxina
Kaplowitz, Matt (mus): Night of the Zombies (1981)
Kapner, Nancy (wri): The Worm Eaters
Kapoor, Kunal (act): Siddhartha
Kapoor, Pincho (act): Siddhartha
Kapoor, Shashi (act): The Deceivers; Gulliver's Travels (1996); Siddhartha
Kappelhoff, Doris (act): see Day, Doris
Kaproff, Dana (mus): Chiller; Dead Air; Death Valley; Exo-Man; I Saw What You Did (1988); Nightlife (1989, USA-Mex); Nightmare Street; Pandemonium; The Stepford Husbands; Tainted Blood; The Ultimate Impostor; What We Did That Night; When a Stranger Calls; When a Stranger Calls Back
Kaptan, Atif (act): Drakula Istanbulda
Kapture, Mitzi (act): House II: The Second Story
Karamesinis, Vassili (act): The Secret of Seagull Island
Karanikas, Diana (act): Princess Warrior
Karas, Anton (mus, 1906-1985): The Third Man
Karas, Nick (cin): Strays
Karaski, Nico (mus): Astro Zombies
Karasumaru, Setsuko (act): Twilight of the Cockroaches
Karaszewski, Larry (wri): Ed Wood
Karath, Kym (act): Midnight Offerings
Karay, Selan (act): Night of the Zombies (1983)
Karcher, Annette (act): Dr. Caligari
Kardian, Karin (act): Nightbeast
Kardon, Darlene (act): Running Against Time
Kardos, Leslie (dir): The Man Who Turned to Stone
Karelsen, John (act): Mission Stardust
Karen, James/Jim (act): The China Syndrome; The Companion (1994); Congo; Frankenstein Meets the Space Monster; Future Shock; Girlfriend from Hell; Hercules In New York; Invaders from Mars (1986); The Jagged Edge; Piranha (1995); The Return of the Living Dead (1985); Return of the Living Dead, Part II; Time Walker; Topper (1979); The Unborn; The Willies
Karfo, Robin (act): Echoes
Karger, Fred (mus): Necromancy
Karger, Maxwell (dir): A Message from Mars (1921)
Kargianis, Gregory (act): The Warlord: Battle for the Galaxy
Kargo, Lucky (act): The Projectionist
Karig, Walter (wri): Zotz!
Karin, Anna (act): The Fear (1994)
Karina, Anna (act, b. 1941, nee Hanne Karin Beyer): Alphaville, une Etrange Aventure de Lemmy Caution; The Magus; Le Plus Vieux Metier du Monde; Scheherazade
Karinkov, M. (dir): The Heavens Call
Karis, George (act): The Blob (1958)
Karis, Max (act): War of the Planets
Karita, Toyomi (act): Uchujin Tokyo No Arawaru
Karl, Roger (act): Le Golem (1936)
Karlan, Richard (act): Abbott and Costello Meet the Mummy; Captain Kidd and the Slave Girl
Karlen, John (act): Daughters of Darkness; House of Dark Shadows; Impulse (1984); Nightmare On the 13th Floor; Night of Dark Shadows; Trilogy of Terror
Karlin, Bo Peep (act): Just Imagine
Karlin, Fred (mus): Bad Ronald; Chosen Survivors; Futureworld; The Plutonium Incident; Ravagers; Topper (1979); Vampire (1979); Westworld
Karlin, Miriam (act, b. 1925, nee Miriam Samuels): A Clockwork Orange; Crossroads to Crime; The Fourth Square; I Thank a Fool; Jekyll and Hyde; The Phantom of the Opera (1962)
Karloff, Boris (act, 1887-1969, nee William Henry Pratt): Abbott and Costello Meet Dr. Jekyll and Mr. Hyde; Abbott and Costello Meet the Killer; Alias the Doctor; The Altar Stairs; The Ape (1940); Bedlam; Before I Hang; Behind That Curtain; Behind the Mask (1932); The Bells (1926); The Black Castle; The Black Cat (1934); Black Friday; The Black Room; The Body Snatcher (1945); The Boogie Man Will Get You; Bride of Frankenstein; British Intelligence; Cauldron of Blood; The Cave Girl (1921); Charlie Chan at the Opera; Cisaruv Slavik; The Climax; Colonel March Investigates; Colonel March of Scotland Yard; The Comedy of Terrors; Cracked Nuts (1931); Curse of the Crimson Altar; The Devil Commands; Devil's Island; Dick Tracy Meets Gruesome; Doctor of Seven Dials; Doomed to Die; The Dumb Girl of Portici; The Fatal Hour (1940); The Fear Chamber; Frankenstein (1931); Frankenstein (1970); The Ghost In the Invisible Bikini; The Ghoul (1933); The Gift of Gab; Grip of the Strangler; House of Evil (1968); House of Frankenstein; Invasion Sinitestra; The Invisible Menace; The Invisible Ray; Isle of the Dead (1945); Isle of the Snake People; Juggernaut; The Lost Patrol (1934); Lured; The Mad Genius; Mad Monster Party; The Man from Downing Street; The Man They Could Not Hang; The Man Who Changed His Mind; The Man With Nine Lives; The Mask of Fu Manchu; The Miracle Man (1932); Mr. Wong, Detective; Mr. Wong In Chinatown; Mondo Balordo; Monster of Terror; Il Mostro dell'Isola; The Mummy (1932); The Mystery of Mr. Wong; The Night Key; The Old Dark House (1932); The Raven (1935 & 1963); Sabaka; The Secret Life of Walter Mitty; Son of Frankenstein; The Sorcerers; The Strange Door; Targets; Tarzan and the Golden Lion; The Terror (1963); Tower of London (1939); I Tre Volti della Paura; The Unholy Night; The Venetian Affair; Voodoo Island; The Walking Dead; West of Shanghai; You'll Find Out
Karlsen, John (act): Mission Stardust; Roger Corman's 'Frankenstein Unbound'; Slaughter Hotel (1972); La Sorella di Satan; The Witch's Curse
Karlson, Phil (dir, b. 1908): Behind the Mask (1946); Ben; Dark Alibi; Lorna Doone (1951); Mask of the Avenger; 99 River Street; Rampage; The Secret Ways; The Shanghai Cobra; The Silencers (1966); The Wrecking Crew
Karlweis, Oscar (act): 5 Fingers
Karman, Janice (dir & wri): The Chipmunk Adventure
Karmel, Alex (wri, b. 1931): Something Wild
Karnes, Robert (act, 1917-1979): The Clone Master; Half-Human; One Spy Too Many; Project Moonbase; Riders to the Stars; Storm Over Tibet; Trapped
Karnowski, Tom (wri): The Sword and the Sorcerer
Karns, Roscoe (act, 1893-1970): The Devil's Cargo; Dirigible; Footsteps In the Dark; Four Hours to Kill; The Gorilla (1931); A Night of Mystery (1937)
Karns, Virginia (act): Babes In Toyland (1934)
Karon, Gwyn (act): Dr. Black Mr. Hyde
Karon, Marvin (act): Clarence
Karp, David (act): The Dungeonmaster
Karp, David (wri, b. 1922): The Brotherhood of the Bell
Karpathi, Geza Korvin (act): see Korvin, Charles
Karpf, Elinor (wri): Gargoyles
Karpf, Stephen (wri): Gargoyles
Karpick, Avi (cin): Cutting Class
Karpman, Laura (mus): The Sitter
Karr, Amy Allen (act): Mind Over Murder
Karr, Mabel (act): The Colossus of Rhodes; The Diabolical Dr. Z
Karr, Sarah Rose (act): Homewrecker
Karras, Alex (act, b. 1935): Jacob Two-Two Meets the Hooded Fang
Karroll, Dennis P. (act): Blood Song
Karsian, Tara (act): Single White Female
Karson, Eric (dir): The Octagon
Kartalian, Buck (act): Conquest of the Planet of the Apes; Legacy of Blood; Myra Breckinridge; Octaman; Please Don't Eat My Mother
Kartalos, Olga (act): The Sins of Dorian Gray; Zombie
Kartheiser, Vincent (act): Heaven Sent; The Indian In the Cupboard
Karvitz, Steve (act): Howard the Duck
Karyo, Tcheky (act): La Femme Nikita; Habitat; Nostradamus; Wing Commander
Karz, Lori (act): A Taste for Flesh and Blood
Kasamatsu, Norimichi (cin): Angel Dust
Kasbek Singers, The (act): Elstree Calling
Kasdan, Lawrence (dir): Body Heat
Kasdan, Lawrence (wri): Body Heat; The Empire Strikes Back; Raiders of the Lost Ark; Return of the Jedi
Kasdan, Meg (act): Body Heat
Kasdorf, Lenore (act): Covenant
Kase, Russell (act): Ladyhawke
Kaselonis, Ray (act): Making Contact
Kasem, Casey (act): The Dark (1979); Doomsday Machine; The Incredible 2-Headed Transplant; The Return of the King; 2000 Years Later
Kash, Daniel (act): Nightbreed
Kash, Murray (act): The Crooked Sky; The Girl Hunters; The Secret Man
Kashara, Reiko (act): Return of the Giant Monsters
Kashay, King Kong (act): Crime Doctor's Courage
Kashima, Nobuhiro (act): Gammera vs. Guiron
Kasica, Maryanne (wri): Topper (1979)

Kaske, Scott (act): *The Newlydeads*
Kasket, Harold (act, b. 1916): *The Fourth Square; The House of the Arrow (1953); The Key Man; The Mouse That Roared; The Return of Mr. Moto; Saadia; The 7th Voyage of Sinbad; Whirlpool (1959)*
Kasman, Dale (act): *Wolf*
Kasper, Gary (act): *Joe & the Colonel; Point of No Return*
Kass, Robert (act): *Waxwork II: Lost In Time*
Kassel, Coral (act): *Monstroid*
Kassir, John (act): *Casper; Cybertracker 2; Demon Knight; Encino Woman; Pocahontas; Tales from the Crypt Presents Bordello of Blood*
Kast, Pierre (dir, b. 1920): *Un Amour de Poche; La Brulure de Mille Soleils*
Kast, Pierre (wri, b. 1920): *La Brulure de Mille Soleils*
Kasten, Laura Lee (act): *School Spirit*
Kastle (act): *Phoenix the Warrior*
Kastle, Leonard (dir & wri): *The Honeymoon Killers*
Kastner, Peter (act): *Frightmare (1983)*
Kasyanov, Vladimir (dir): *Sonka Zolotaya Ruchka*
Kasznar, Kurt (act, 1913-1979): *The Ambushers; Casino Royale; The Legend of the Lost; The Perils of Pauline; Talk About a Stranger*
Katarina, Anna (act): *The Blood of Heroes*
Katayanagi, Claudia (cin): *Target...Earth?*
Katch, Kurt (act, 1896-1958, nee Isser Kac): *Abbott and Costello Meet the Mummy; The Adventures of Hajji Baba; Ali Baba and the Forty Thieves (1943); Background to Danger; Counter-Espionage; The Mask of Dimitrios; The Mummy's Curse; Pharaoh's Curse; Secret of the Incas; The Strange Death of Adolf Hitler*
Katcher, Aram (act): *East of Sumatra; Invasion U.S.A.; The Perils of Pauline; The Right Hand of the Devil; Spy Hunt*
Katcher, Aram (dir & wri): *The Right Hand of the Devil*
Katcher, Leo (wri, 1911-1991): *Between Midnight and Dawn; M (1950)*
Katelbach, Andre (act): *Aimez-Vous les Femmes?*
Katerina, Anna (act): *The Death of the Incredible Hulk*
Kates, Bernard (act): *Seedpeople*
Kath, Camilla (act): *Fake-Out*
Kath, Katherine (act): *The Assassination Bureau; Fury at Smugglers' Bay; The Man Who Wouldn't Talk; Seven Thunders; Subway In the Sky*
Katims, David (act): *The First Power*
Katims, Robert (act): *The Bride In Black*
Katleman, Michael (dir): *The Spider and the Fly (1994)*
Kato, Daisuke (act): *The Toxic Avenger, Part II*
Kato, Haruya (act): *Mothra*
Kato, Kazuo (act): *Body Snatcher from Hell*
Kato, Masaya (act): *The Seventh Floor*
Kato, Mieko (act): *The Private Lives of Adam and Eve*
Kato, Shigeo (act): *Mothra*
Kato, Sydney (act): *Blood Diner*
Katoh, Takeshi (act): *Godzilla 1985*
Katon, Rosanne (act): *Zapped!*
Katona, Victor (wri): *The Twenty Questions Murder*
Katrakis, Manos (act): *Electra (1961)*
Katsaros, Andonia (act): *Time After Time*
Katsaros, Doug (mus): *Star Crystal*
Katsu, Shintaro (act): *Buddha; Inn of Evil*
Katsulas, Andreas (act): *Communion; The Death of the Incredible Hulk; The Fugitive (1993)*
Katsuragi, Mayako (act): *The Toxic Avenger, Part II*
Katt, Nick(y) (act): *The Babysitter (1995); The 'Burbs; Strange Days*
Katt, William (act, b. 1950): *Baby: Secret of the Lost Legend; Carrie; Daddy's Girl; Desperate Motive; House; House IV; Piranha (1995); Rattled*
Kattan, Chris (act): *The House On Haunted Hill (1999)*
Katya (act): *Mother's Day*
Katz, A.L. (wri): *Children of the Corn II: The Final Sacrifice; Tales from the Crypt Presents Bordello of Blood*
Katz, Alan (act): *Happy Birthday to Me*
Katz, Carol (act): *Blood Diner*
Katz, Fred (mus): *A Bucket of Blood (1959); Creature from the Haunted Sea; The Little Shop of Horrors (1960); The Monitors; The Wasp Woman (1959)*
Katz, Gloria (dir): *Dead People*
Katz, Gloria (wri): *Dead People; Howard the Duck; Indiana Jones and the Temple of Doom*
Katz, Judah (act): *The Long Kiss Goodnight*
Katz, Lee (wri): *British Intelligence; The Return of Dr. X*
Katz, Marlene (act): *Arachnophobia*
Katz, Omri (act): *Adventures In Dinosaur City; Hocus Pocus; Matinee*
Katz, Paul (act): *Premonition (1972)*
Katz, Robert (wri): *The Cassandra Crossing*
Katz, Shelley (wri): *A Vacation In Hell*
Katz, Stephen M. (cin): *18 Again!; Mrs. Santa Claus; Sister, Sister*
Katz, Steve (wri): *Hex*
Katz, William (wri): *Death Dreams*
Katzakian, Chuck (act): *Omega Cop*
Katzin, Lee H. (dir): *Ordeal; The Stranger; Terror Out of the Sky; What Ever Happened to Aunt Alice?; World Gone Wild*
Katzman, Leonard (dir & wri, 1927-1996): *Space Monster*
Katzman, Lon (act): *Prophecy (1979); Timecop*
Kauer, Gene (mus): see Kauer, Guenther/Gene
Kauer, Guenther/gene (mus): *Agent for H.A.R.M.; The Astounding She-Monster; Monstroid*
Kauffman, Charles (wri): *The Saint In New York*
Kauffman, Cristina (act): see Kaufmann, Christine
Kauffman, Ola (act): *The Cremators*
Kauffman, Timothy (act): *Nightmare Sisters*
Kaufman, Andy (act, 1949-1984): *Demon (1976); Heartbeeps*
Kaufman, Boris (cin, 1906-1980): *The Fugitive Kind*
Kaufman, Charles (act): *Stanley*
Kaufman, Charles (dir & wri): *Mother's Day*
Kaufman, Charlotte (act): *The Toxic Avenger, Part II*
Kaufman, David (act): *Invisible: The Chronicles of Benjamin Knight*
Kaufman, David M. (wri): *Werewolves On Wheels*
Kaufman, George S. (wri, 1889-1961): *The Dark Tower (1943); Roman Scandals*
Kaufman, Joseph (act): *Heavy Traffic*
Kaufman, Leonard (wri): *Birds Do It*
Kaufman, Lily Hayes (act): *Class of Nuke 'em High; The Toxic Avenger, Part II*
Kaufman, Lisbeth (act): *The Toxic Avenger, Part II*
Kaufman, Lloyd (cin): *The Toxic Avenger*
Kaufman, Lloyd (dir): *The Toxic Avenger, Part II; The Toxic Avenger, Part III: The Last Temptation of Toxie; Troma's War; Tromeo and Juliet*
Kaufman, Lloyd (wri): *Class of Nuke 'em High; Class of Nuke'em High, Part 2: Subhumanoid Meltdown; The Toxic Avenger; The Toxic Avenger, Part II; The Toxic Avenger, Part III: The Last Temptation of Toxie; Tromeo and Juliet*
Kaufman, Mark S. (wri): *Toothless*
Kaufman, Michael (act): *Wicked Stepmother*
Kaufman, Mikhail (cin & dir, b. 1897): *The Three Musketeers (1923)*
Kaufman, Millard (wri): *Unknown World; The War Lord*
Kaufman, Patricia (act): *The Toxic Avenger, Part II*
Kaufman, Philip (dir, b. 1936): *Fearless Frank; Goldstein; Invasion of the Body Snatchers (1978)*
Kaufman, Philip (wri, b. 1936): *Fearless Frank; Goldstein; Raiders of the Lost Ark*
Kaufman, Robert (wri, 1931-1991): *Dr. Goldfoot and the Bikini Machine; Dr. Goldfoot and the Girl Bombs; Love at First Bite; The Zany*
Adventures of Robin Hood
Kaufman, Robin (act): *Vamp*
Kaufman, Rose (act): *Invasion of the Body Snatchers (1978)*
Kaufman, Stanley (act): *Mother's Day*
Kaufmann, Charles (wri): *Paris Calling*
Kaufmann, Christine (act, b. 1945): *The Last Days of Pompeii (1959); Murders In the Rue Morgue (1971)*
Kaufmann, Maurice (act): *The Abominable Dr. Phibes; The Angel Who Pawned Her Harp; Behemoth, the Sea Monster; Circus of Fear; Company of Fools; Date With Disaster; Fanatic (1965); Find the Lady; Fright (1971); Gorgo; House of Mystery (1961); Man of Violence; The Man Without a Body; The Quatermass Experiment; Robin Hood Junior (1975); Secret Venture; Three Cases of Murder; We Shall See*
Kaufmann, Todd (act): *Vampire On Bikini Beach*
Kaul, Alan (act): *The China Syndrome*
Kaumeyer, Dorothy (act): see Lamour, Dorothy
Kaurismaki, Aki (dir): *I Hired a Contract Killer*
Kaus, Gina (wri): *Charlie Chan In City In Darkness*
Kautner, Helmut (act): *Hauser's Memory*
Kava, Terrence (act): *Thinner*
Kavanagh, Denis (dir): *Dollars for Sale; Night Comes Too Soon; They Never Learn*
Kavanagh, Denis (wri): *Dollars for Sale; They Never Learn*
Kavanagh, H.T. (wri, 1876-1933): *Darby O'Gill and the Little People*
Kavanagh, Kevin (wri): *Death Drums Along the River; The Million Eyes of Sumuru; A Prize of Arms*
Kavanagh, Michael (cin): *Gotham; Hitler's Daughter*
Kavanagh, Ted (wri): *Time Flies (1944)*
Kavner, Julie (act, b. 1951): *Dr. Dolittle (1998); Revenge of the Stepford Wives*
Kavtzer, Gregory (act): *The People Under the Stairs*
Kawa, Mori (cin): *The Hearse*
Kawada, Clifford (act): *Varan the Unbelievable*
Kawaguchi, Hiroshi (act): *Buddha*
Kawai, Hanbel (act): *Cyber Ninja*
Kawaji, Tamio (act): *Gappa, the Triphibian Monster*
Kawalerowicz, Jerzy (dir, b. 1922): *Faraon; Matka Joanna od Aniolow; Pod Gwiazda Frygijska*
Kawalerowicz, Jerzy (wri, b. 1922): *Faraon; Matka Joanna od Aniolow*
Kawamoto, kayko (act): *The Toxic Avenger, Part II*
Kawarazaki, Choichiro (act): *The Profound Desire of the Gods*
Kawasaki, Keizo (act): *Buddha; Uchujin Tokyo No Arawaru*
Kawase, Hiroyuki (act): *Godzilla vs. Megalon; Godzilla vs. the Smog Monster*
Kawata, Takeshi (wri): *Solar Crisis*
Kawaye, Janice (act): *Night of the Comet*
Kawazu, Seizaburo (act): *Mothra*
Kawazu, Yusuke (act): *Gammera vs. Zigra*
Kay, Arthur (mus): *Just Imagine*
Kay, Bernard (act): *A Ghost In Monte Carlo; The Shuttered Room; Sinbad and the Eye of the Tiger; They Came from Beyond Space; Torture Garden; Trog; Witch-Finder General*
Kay, Charles (act): *Piccadilly Third Stop*
Kay, Edward (J.) (mus, b. 1898): *The Ape (1940); The Ape Man; Bomba, the Jungle Boy; The Chinese Ring; Dangerous Money; Dark Alibi; Ghost Chasers; The Golden Eye; Mr. Hex; Mr. Wong In Chinatown; Panther Island; The Scarlet Clue; The Shanghai Cobra; The Trap; Voodoo Man*
Kay, Gilbert L. (dir): *The Secret Door; Three Bad Sisters*
Kay, Hadley (act): *Care Bears Movie II: A New Generation; Superman II*
Kay, Harold (act): *The Spy Is a Girl*
Kay, Howard (act): *The Mask (1994)*
Kay, James/Jim (H.) (dir & wri): *Seeds of Evil*
Kay, Jody (act): *Death Screams*
Kay, Joyce (act): *The Prisoner of Shark Island*
Kay, Kalassu (act): *Boarding House*
Kay, Louise (act): *No Blade of Grass*
Kay, Mary Ellen (act): *The Long Wait*
Kay, Mike (act): *Threads*
Kay, Patrick (act): *The Priory School*
Kay, Peter (wri): *The Trollenberg Terror*
Kay, Philip (act): *Britain's Secret Treaty; The Kaiser's Spies; The Mystery of the Diamond Belt*
Kay, Richard (act): *Deja Vu*
Kay, Roger (dir): *The Cabinet of Caligari*
Kay, Ron (act): *The Immortalizer*
Kay, Sibylla (act): *The Night Digger*
Kay, Stephen (act): *The Zero Boys*
Kay, Sylvia (act): *Who Is Killing the Great Chefs of Europe?*
Kay, Una (act): *Oh Heavenly Dog; Rabid*
Kayahara, Lydia lei (act): *Deathmoon*
Kayama, Shigem (wri): *Godzilla Raids Again; Gojira*
Kayama, Yuzo (act, b. 1937): *Chusingura (1963)*
Kayara, George (act): *4D Man*
Kayashi, Hikaru (mus): *Live Today, Die Tomorrow*
Kayden, Tony (wri): *Slipstream*
Kaye, Caren (act): *Pumpkinhead II: Blood Wings; Satan's Princess; Teen Witch*
Kaye, Celia (act): *Rattlers; Vampire at Midnight*
Kaye, Clarissa (act): *Frankenstein: The True Story; Salem's Lot*
Kaye, Danny (act, 1913-1987, nee David Daniel Kaminski): *Hans Christian Andersen; Pinocchio (1976); The Secret Life of Walter Mitty; Wonder Man*
Kaye, Davy (act): *Alice's Adventures In Wonderland (1972); Frankenstein: The True Story*
Kaye, Del (act): *The Witchmaker*
Kaye, Gordon (act): *Brazil; Sredni Vashtar*
Kaye, Lila (act): *An American Werewolf In London; The Black Panther; Blind Terror; The Canterville Ghost (1986); Dragonworld; A Place to Die; The Return of Sherlock Holmes (1986); Sredni Vashtar*
Kaye, Linda (act): *Shocker*
Kaye, Mary Ellen (act): *Francis In the Haunted House; Voodoo Woman*
Kaye, Norman (mus): *Journey to the Unknown*
Kaye, Stubby (act, 1918-1997): *Li'l Abner (1959); The Monitors*
Kaye, Suzie (act): *Women of the Prehistoric Planet*
Kaye, Thorsten (act): *The Silencers (1995)*
Kaylen, Marty (wri): *Max Q: Emergency Landing*
Kaylin, Samuel (mus): *Charlie Chan at Monte Carlo; Charlie Chan at the Circus; Charlie Chan at the Olympics; Charlie Chan at the Opera; Charlie Chan at the Race Track; Charlie Chan In Egypt; Charlie Chan In Honolulu; Charlie Chan In London; Charlie Chan In Paris; Charlie Chan's Courage; Charlie Chan's Strangest Case; Mr. Moto's Last Warning; Thank You, Mr. Moto; Think Fast, Mr. Moto*
Kaylor, Arnold (act): *The Magic Voyage of Sinbad*
Kayne, Jan (act): *Ghost Chasers; Radar Secret Service*
Ka Yong, Liu (act): *Shatter*
Kayser, Allan J. (act): *Night of the Creeps*
Kayser, Chris (act): *Freejack*
Kayser, Kay (act & mus, 1906-1985): *You'll Find Out*
Kayser, Manuel (act): *El Otro Fu-Manchu*
Kayssler, Frederich (act): *Gold (German-speaking version)*
Kaza, Elisabeth (act): *Iron Warrior...The Legend!*
Kazakos, Costa (act): *Iphigenia*
Kazan, Lainie (act, b. 1942): *Amazing Stories: The Movie V; Harry and the Hendersons; Out of the Dark*
Kazan, Lainie (mus, b. 1942): *Blood Song*
Kazan, Nicholas (wri): *Fallen*
Kazanjian, Arlene (act): see Francis, Arlene
Kazann, Zitto (act): *Beyond Evil; Dr. Scorpion; Meteor; Satan's Triangle*
Kazanskaya, Alla A. (act): *The Saint*
Kazansky, Gennadi (dir): *The Amphibian Man*
Kazantsev, Alexander (wri): *Planeta Bura*
Kazurinsky, Tim (act, b. 1950): *Neighbors*
Keach, James (act): *Evil Town*
Keach, James (dir): *Praying Mantis; Sunstroke*
Keach Sr., Stacy (act): *Body Bags; Lies; Saturday the 14th; Superstition*
Keach, Stacy (act, b. 1941): *Amanda and the Alien; Batman: Mask of the Phantasm; Class of 1999; The Clone Master; Gray Lady Down; The Killer Inside Me; Legend of the Lost Tomb; Il Montagna di Dio Cannibale; New Crime City: Los Angeles 2020; Prey of the Jaguar; Road Games; The Squeeze; Sunset Grill; Twinkle, Twinkle, Killer Kane*
Kean, Betty (act, 1917-1986): *Murder In the Blue Room*
Kean, Georgina (act): *Killer's Moon*
Kean, Greg (act): *A Gnome Named Gnorm*
Kean, Jane (act): *Explorers; Pete's Dragon*
Kean, Joshua (act): *Emerald of the East*
Kean, Marie (act): *Cul-de-Sac*
Kean, Sidney (act): *Lifeforce*
Keane, Charles (act): *Les Miserables (1952); Project Moonbase; 23 Paces to Baker Street*
Keane, Constance (act): see Lake, Veronica
Keane, Ed(ward) (act): *The Baron of Arizona; Charlie Chan at the Olympics; Charlie Chan In Panama; Devil's Island; It Happens Every Spring; Mr. Moto In Danger Island; Nancy Drew, Detective; The Son of Monte Cristo; Torchy Gets Her Man*
Keane, James (act): *Dick Tracy (1990); Phenomenon*
Keane, John M. (mus): *A Vow to Kill*
Keane, Kerrie (act): *Alien Nation: Millennium; Alien Nation: The Enemy Within; Bates Motel; Incubus (1982); Spasms*
Keane, Lawrence (act): *Scream and Die!*
Keane, Robert Emmett (act, 1885-1981): *The Atomic Kid; The Beginning or the End?; Crazy House (1943); Crime Doctor's Diary; Fear In the Night (1947); The Lone Wolf Meets a Lady; The Man Who Wouldn't Die; The Red Dragon (1945); The Saint Takes Over; Scared Stiff (1953); The Strange Mr. Gregory; The Whistler*
Kearney, Carolyn (act): *The Thing That Couldn't Die*
Kearney, Charles (act): *The Wicker Man*

Kearney, Gene (R.) (wri): *Charlie Chan: Happiness Is a Warm Clue; Games; Night of the Lepus*
Kearney, Patrick (wri): *Darkened Rooms*
Kearney, Philip (wri): *Private Parts*
Kearns, Bernard (act): *Night of the Red Hunter; Sleeping Dogs (1977)*
Kearns, Bill (act, 1923-1992): *The Trial*
Kearns, Sidney (act): *Bernardo's Confession*
Keast, Paul (act): *I Was a Teenage Frankenstein*
Keating, Fred (act): *Firebird 2015 A.D.*
Keating, John (mus): *Innocent Bystanders*
Keating, Larry (act, 1897-1964): *Francis Goes to the Races; The Incredible Mr. Limpet; Inferno (1953); Monkey Business; When Worlds Collide*
Keaton, Buster (act, 1895-1966, nee Joseph Francis Keaton): *Around the World In 80 Days; The Haunted House (1921); How to Stuff a Wild Bikini; Li'l Abner (1940); Pajama Party; Sergeant Deadhead the Astronut!; Sherlock Jr.; Sunset Boulevard; The Villain Still Pursued Her*
Keaton, Buster (dir & wri, 1895-1966): *The Haunted House (1921); Sherlock Jr.*
Keaton, Camille (act): *I Spit On Your Grave*
Keaton, Diane (act, b. 1946): *The Little Drummer Girl; Sleeper*
Keaton, Joe (act): *Sherlock Jr.*
Keaton, Joseph Francis (act, dir & wri): see Keaton, Buster
Keaton, Michael (act, b. 1951): *Batman (1989); Batman Returns; Beetlejuice; Jack Frost (1998); Multiplicity; Pacific Heights*
Keator, Dolores (act): *Dr. No*
Keats, Ele (act): *White Dwarf*
Keats, Richard (act): *A.P.E.X.*
Keats, Steven (act): *Black Sunday (1977); Hangar 18; The Ivory Ape; The Last Dinosaur; Mysterious Island of Beautiful Women; Silent Rage; The Spring*
Keats, Viola (act): *Matinee Idol; Moment of Decision; The Pointing Finger; Two Wives at One Wedding; Witchcraft (1964)*
Keays-Byrne, Hugh (act): *The Chain Reaction (1980); The Day After Halloween; Mad Max; The Man from Hong Kong; Moby Dick (1998)*
Kechler, Charles (act): *Lo Spettro*
Keckey, Jane (act): *Charlie Chan at the Opera*
Kedrova, Lila (act, b. 1918): *Blood Tide; A High Wind In Jamaica; The Kremlin Letter; Sword of the Valiant; The Tenant; Torn Curtain*
Kee, Gordon K. (act): *Twinkle, Twinkle, Killer Kane*
Keefe, Cornelius (act): *Charlie Chan's Greatest Case; Death from a Distance; Mystery Liner*
Keefer, Don (act): *Mirrors; Sleeper*
Keefer, Rose (act): see Hobart, Rose
Keefler, Kathy (act): *Rabid*
Keegan, Barry (act): *Company of Fools; Flat Two; Footsteps In the Fog; Gorgo; Moment of Danger; Payroll; Satellite In the Sky; Wrong Number*
Keegan, Donna (act): *RoboCop*
Keegan, Jimmy E. (act): *Here Come the Littles*
Keegan, John (act): *Lifeforce*
Keegan, Kari (act): *Jason Goes to Hell: The Final Friday*
Keegan, Robert (act): *Endless Night; Frenzy; 10 Rillington Place*
Keegan, Rose (act): *First Knight*
Keehne, Virginya (act): *Ticks*
Keekis, Joanna (act): *Coma*
Keel, Charles (act): *Mirrors*
Keel, Howard (act, b. 1919): *The Day of the Triffids; Floods of Fear*
Keel, Jennifer (act): *Cavegirl (1985)*
Keeler, Brad (act): *Eraserhead*
Keeler, Doddie (act): *Eraserhead*
Keeler, Harry Stephen (wri): *The Mysterious Mr. Wong*
Keeler, Toby (act): *Eraserhead*
Keeley, Eugene (act): *Return from the Ashes*
Keeling, Kenneth (act): *Crucible of Terror*
Keen, Bob (act): *Waxwork II: Lost In Time*
Keen, Bob (cin): *Hellraiser III: Hell on Earth; The Unholy*
Keen, Diane (act): *Jekyll and Hyde; Popdown; Thirteen at Dinner*
Keen, Dorothy (act): *Thelma: or, Saved from the Sea*
Keen, Frederick (act): see Kerr, Frederick
Keen, Geoffrey (act, b. 1918): *Beyond This Place; The Birthday Present; Deadly Record; Dr. Syn-Alias the Scarecrow; Doomwatch; The Dover Road Mystery; Face the Music; The Fallen Idol; Fortune Is a Woman; For Your Eyes Only; The Glass Tomb; High Treason (1951); Holocaust 2000; Horrors of the Black Museum; House of Secrets; Hunted (1952); Lady In the Fog; Licensed to Love and Kill; The Long Arm; The Malpas Mystery; The Mind Benders (1963); Moonraker; Nowhere to Go; No. 1 of the Secret Service; Octopussy; Return to Sender; The Scapegoat; The Secret Place; Seven Days to Noon; The Silent Weapon; The Spanish Gardener; The Spy Who Loved Me; Taste the Blood of Dracula; Thunderbird 6; Town On Trial; Treasure Island (1950); Turn the Key Softly; A View to a Kill; Yield to the Night*
Keen, George (act): *The Dungeon of Death*
Keen, Malcolm (act): *Dangerous Ground; Fortune Is a Woman; The House of Unrest; Life for Ruth; The Lodger (1926); Mr. Reeder In Room 13; Whispering Tongues*
Keen, Noah (act): *Battle for the Planet of the Apes; She's Dressed to Kill*
Keen, Pat (act): *Memoirs of a Survivor; Without a Clue*
Keena, Monica (act, b. 1979): *Snow White: A Tale of Terror*
Keenan, Christy (act): *Blind Date*
Keenan, Frank (act): *Lorna Doone (1922)*
Keenan, Will (act): *Tromeo and Juliet*
Keenan, William J. (wri): *King Kong Escapes*
Keene, Carolyn (wri): *Nancy Drew and the Hidden Staircase; Nancy Drew, Detective; Nancy Drew, Reporter; Nancy Drew, Troubleshooter*
Keene, Christopher (J.) (act): *Ghost (1990); Slam Dance*
Keene, George (act): *The Price He Paid; Through Stormy Waters; The Woman of the Iron Bracelets*
Keene, Hamilton (act): *The Devil's Jest; The Lost Patrol (1929)*
Keene, Maurice (act): *Strange Behavior*
Keene, Ralph (wri): *Double Confession*
Keene, Richard (act): *Charlie Chan's Murder Cruise; Murder Is My Business*
Keene, Tom (act, 1896-1963): *Plan 9 from Outer Space; Red Planet Mars*
Keene, Vincent (act): *Nightbreed*
Keene, William (act): *Heavy Traffic; Tarzan and the Trappers*
Keener, Catherine (act): *Switch*
Keener, Eliott (act): *Angel Heart; The Savage Bees*
Keener, Hazel (act): *The Brass Bottle (1923)*
Keener, Susan (act): *The Ultimate Warrior*
Keenleyside, Eric (act): *Short Circuit 2*
Keep, Stephen (act): *Billion Dollar Threat*
Keesee, Oscar (act): *Terror Is a Man*
Keesee, Peyton (act): *Terror Is a Man*
Keeslar, Don (dir): *Bog*
Keet, Glenn (act): *The Toxic Avenger, Part II*
Keeter, Worth (dir): *Dogs of Hell; Order of the Black Eagle; Snapdragon; Wolfman (1979)*
Keeter, Worth (wri): *Wolfman (1979)*
Keeton, Kathy (act): *The Spy Who Came In from the Cold*
Kehela, Steve (act): *When the Bough Breaks*
Kehler, Jack (act): *Bloodstone; Strange Invaders*
Kehoe, Jack (act): *Dick Tracy (1990); The Servants of Twilight*
Kehoe, Michael (dir & wri): *Dominion*
Kei, Kathie (act): *Charlie Chan and the Curse of the Dragon Queen*
Keifer, Warren (dir): *Castle of the Living Dead*
Keigel, Leonard (dir): *The Queen of Spades (1966)*
Keighley, William (dir, b. 1893): *Green Pastures; Journal of a Crime; The Street With No Name*
Keil, Era (act): *The Pit (1983)*
Keil, George (dir): *2069: A Sex Odyssey*
Keil, Marvin (act): *The Pit (1983)*
Keiler, Courtney (act): *The Punisher*
Keily, Mark (act): *Leprechaun 2*
Keir, Andrew (act, b. 1910): *Absolution; Blood from the Mummy's Tomb; Daleks' Invasion Earth 2150 A.D.; The Devil-Ship Pirates; Dracula, Prince of Darkness; Dragonworld: The Legend Continues; Haunters of the Deep; The Night Visitor; The Pirates of Blood River; Quatermass and the Pit; Suspended Alibi; The 39 Steps (1978); Tread Softly Stranger; The Viking Queen; Zeppelin*
Keir, David (act): *The Ghost Goes West; The Howard Case; Night Comes Too Soon; The Sky Raiders*
Keir, Udo (act, b. 1944): *The Adventures of Pinocchio (1996); Barb Wire; Dracula (1974); Frankenstein (1974); The German Chainsaw Massacre; The House On Straw Hill; Johnny Mnemonic; The Kingdom; Mark of the Devil (1972); Spermula; Suspiria*
Keitel, Harvey (act, b. 19[illegible]): *Deathwatch (1980); Fairy Tale: A True Story; From Dusk Till Dawn; Head Above Water; The Knight of the Dragon; Mortal Thoughts; Point of No Return; Saturn 3; Two Evil Eyes*
Keith, Alan (act): *The Long Knife*
Keith, Anita (act): *Tarantulas: The Deadly Cargo*
Keith, Brian (GB act): *Moonraker*
Keith, Brian (USA act, 1921-1997, nee Robert Keith Jr.): *Appointment With a Shadow; Charlie Chan and the Curse of the Dragon Queen; Cry for the Strangers; Jivaro; Krakatoa-East of Java; Meteor; Moon Pilot; Nightfall (1956); Portrait of Jennie; Reflections In a Golden Eye; Way...Way Out; World War III*
Keith, Carlos (wri): *Bedlam; The Body Snatcher (1945)*
Keith, David (act, b. 1954): *Deadly Sins; Desperate Motive; Firestarter; The Indian In the Cupboard; Judge and Jury; White of the Eye*
Keith, David (dir, b. 1954): *The Curse*
Keith, Deborah (act): *Urban Warriors*
Keith, Donald (act): *The Lone Wolf's Daughter (1929)*
Keith, Hardy (act): *Zapped!*
Keith, Ian (act, 1899-1960, nee Keith Ross): *The Black Shield of Falworth; The Chinese Cat; Dick Tracy's Dilemma; Dick Tracy vs. Cueball; Fog Island; Identity Unknown; It Came from Beneath the Sea; Mr. Hex; Nightmare Alley; The Phantom of Paris (1931); The Three Musketeers (1935 & 1948); Valley of the Zombies*
Keith, Michael (act): *King Kong vs. Godzilla*
Keith, Paul (act): *Space Rage*
Keith, Penelope (act): *Ghost Story (1975); The Hound of the Baskervilles (1978); Rentadick*
Keith, Robert (act): *Just Imagine; The Lineup*
Keith, Robert (1990s act): *The Mask (1994)*
Keith Jr., Robert (act): see Keith, Brian
Keith, Sheila (act): *The Day the Screaming Stopped; Frightmare (1974); House of Mortal Sin; House of the Long Shadows; House of Whipcord*
Keith, Sherwood (act): *Terrified (1963)*
Keith, Warren (act): *Fargo*
Keith, Woody (wri): *Bride of Re-Animator; Silent Night, Deadly Night 4: Initiation*
Keith-Johnson, Colin (act): *Berkeley Square; The Price of Folly*
Kelber, Michel (cin, b. 1908): *La Beaute du Diable; The Hunchback of Notre Dame (1957); Les Parents Terribles*
Kelinman, Dan (wri): *Rage*
Kelland, Clarence Buddington (wri): *Highways by Night*
Kelland, John (act): *Are You Dying Young Man?; Nothing But the Night*
Kellard, Robert (act): *Drums of Fu Manchu; Phantom of Chinatown; Shadow of the Thin Man*
Kellaway, Cecil (act, 1893-1973): *The Beast from 20,000 Fathoms; The Cockeyed Miracle; The Decision of Christopher Blake; Francis Goes to the Races; Half Angel; Harvey; The House of the Seven Gables; Hush...Hush, Sweet Charlotte; I Married a Witch; The Invisible Man Returns; Love Letters; The Luck of the Irish; The Mummy's Hand; Phantom Raiders; Portrait of Jennie; The Private Lives of Adam and Eve; The Shaggy Dog (1959); Wuthering Heights (1939); Zotz!*
Kellaway, Roger (mus): *The Dark (1979); Evilspeak; Jaws of Satan*
Kelleher, Ed (wri): *Invasion of the Blood Farmers; Shriek of the Mutilated*
Kelleher, Tim (act): *Never Talk to Strangers*
Kellem, Jane (act): *The Thing with Two Heads*
Kellems, Suzy J. (act): *Weird Science*
Keller, Almanta (act): *New York Ripper*
Keller, Billie (act): *Bloodsuckers from Outer Space*
Keller, Derek (act): *No Blade of Grass*
Keller, Frank (act): *The Temple of Venus*
Keller, Fred A. (act & wri): *Tuck Everlasting*
Keller, Frederick King (dir & wri): *Tuck Everlasting*
Keller, Harry (dir, b. 1913): *The Brass Bottle (1964); Man Afraid; Step Down to Terror; The Unguarded Moment*
Keller, Hiram (act): *Satyricon; Seven Deaths In the Cat's Eye*
Keller, Joel (act): *Storm of the Century*
Keller, Marthe (act, b. 1945): *Black Sunday (1977); Marathon Man*
Keller, Mary Page (act, b. 1961): *The Colony (1995); Scared Stiff (1987)*
Keller, Max A. (wri): *Stranger In Our House*
Keller, Robert (act): *Wicked Stepmother*
Keller, Sarah (act): *A Kiss Before Dying (1991); 7 Doors of Death; Terror (1979)*
Kellan, William (act): *Invasion of the Bee Girls*
Kellerman, Bernhard (wri): *The Tunnel*
Kellerman, Sally (act, b. 1938): *Boris and Natasha; The Boston Strangler; Doppelganger: The Evil Within; Hands of a Stranger; Limit Up; Lost Horizon (1973); Mirror, Mirror 2: Raven Dance; The Mouse and His Child; A Reflection of Fear; Secret Weapons*
Kellerman(n), Susan (act): *Elvira, Mistress of the Dark; Heart and Souls; I Saw What You Did (1988); Oh Heavenly Dog*
Kellermann, Annette (act, b. 1888): *Daughter of the Gods; Neptune's Daughter; Queen of the Sea*
Kellermann, Barbara (act): *The Monster Club; The Quatermass Conclusion; Satan's Slave*
Kellers, Connie (act): *Strange Invaders*
Kellet, Pete (act): *The Prisoner of Zenda (1979)*
Kelley, Alice (act): *Francis Goes to West Point; The Golden Blade; Son of Ali Baba*
Kelley, Barry (act): *The Extraordinary Seaman; Francis Goes to the Races; Jack the Giant Killer; The Manchurian Candidate; The Well*
Kelley, David E. (wri): *To Gillian On Her 37th Birthday*
Kelley, DeForest (act, b. 1920): *The Brave Little Toaster Goes to Mars; Fear In the Night (1947); Illegal; Night of the Lepus; Star Trek; Star Trek II: The Wrath of Khan; Star Trek III: The Search for Spock; Star Trek IV: The Voyage Home; Star Trek V: The Final Frontier; Star Trek VI: The Undiscovered Country*
Kelley, Hugh (wri): *Warriors of Virtue*
Kelley, John (act): *I Was a Zombie for the F.B.I.*
Kelley, P.J. (act): *Spooks Run Wild*
Kelley, Sheila (act): *Mortal Passions; A Passion to Kill; The Secretary*
Kelley, Ty (act): *Remote Control (1988)*
Kelley, Virginia (act): *Operation Murder*
Kelley, (W.) Wallace (cin): *Dr. Cyclops; It's Only Money; The Nutty Professor (1963); The War of the Worlds*
Kelley, Walter (act): *Night of the Lepus*
Kelley, William (act): *Empire of Ash III*
Kelley, William (wri): *The Demon Murder Case*
Kelli, Dennis (act): *Runaway*
Kellin, Mike (act, 1922-1983): *The Boston Strangler; Demon (1976); Echoes; Just Before Dawn (1980); Sleepaway Camp*
Kelling, Thom (act): *Hunted In Holland*
Kellino, Pamela (act): see Mason, Pamela
Kellino, Roy (cin): *I Met a Murderer*
Kellino, Roy (dir): *Catch as Catch Can; Concerning Mr. Martin; Guilt Is My Shadow; I Met a Murderer*
Kellino, Roy (wri): *Guilt Is My Shadow*
Kellino, W.P. (dir): *Alf's Button (1930); Alf's Carpet; Bumbles' Diminisher; The Dustman's Nightmare; The Fall of a Saint; A Fight for Life; The Green Terror; The Gypsy's Curse; Hamlet (1915); Inventing Trouble; The Jovial Fluid; The Terrible 'Tec; Wishes*
Kelljan, Robert (act): *The Glass Cage (1961); Psych-Out*
Kelljan, Robert/Bob (dir): *Count Yorga, Vampire; The Return of Count Yorga; Scream, Blacula, Scream*
Kelljan, Robert/Bob (wri): *Count Yorga, Vampire; The Return of Count Yorga*
Kelloff, Michael (act): *Fire and Ice*
Kellogg, Bruce (act): *The Golden Eye; Shadows Over Chinatown; Unknown World*
Kellogg, Gayle (act): *Operation Secret; Satan's Satellites*
Kellogg, John (G.) (act): *Bomba and the Elephant Stampede; Gorilla at Large; Night Slaves; The Thirteenth Hour (1947)*
Kellogg, Ray (cin): *Desk Set; Monkey Business; Niagara; River of No Return*
Kellogg, Ray (dir): *The Giant Gila Monster; The Killer Shrews*
Kellogg, Ray (wri): *The Giant Gila Monster*
Kellogg, Sharon (act): *The Human Factor*
Kells, Janie (act): *Macbeth (1971)*
Kelly, April (wri): *I Still Dream of Jeannie*
Kelly, Barbara (act): *Jet Storm*
Kelly, Bebe (act): *Fangs*
Kelly, Bill (act): *Mission Mars*
Kelly, Brian (act): *Around the World Under the Sea*
Kelly, Brian D. (act): *Freakshow*
Kelly, Caron Anne (act): *The Lair of the White Worm*
Kelly, Claire (act): *The Loved One; Straight On Till Morning; What Ever Happened to Aunt Alice?*
Kelly, Clare (act): *And Soon the Darkness*
Kelly, Clyde (act): *The Dead One*
Kelly, Colleen (act): *Buck Rogers In the 25th Century*
Kelly, Craig (act): *Satan's Satellites*
Kelly, David Patrick (act): *The Crow (1994); Dreamscape*
Kelly, Dawn Carver (act): *Dr. Jekyll's Dungeon of Death*

Kelly, Dermot (act): *Breakout; Panic (1963); Subterfuge*
Kelly, Desmond (act): *The Frighteners*
Kelly, Dorothy (act): *Pawns of Mars*
Kelly, Douglas W. (act): *Repossessed*
Kelly, Eamonn (act): *Excalibur*
Kelly, Elizabeth (act): *Without a Clue*
Kelly, Ellen (act): *The Kill-Off*
Kelly, Erica (act): *Strange Days*
Kelly, Eugene Curran (act): see Kelly, Gene
Kelly, Gene (act, b. 1912, nee Eugene Curran Kelly): *Brigadoon; It's Always Fair Weather; The Three Musketeers (1948); Xanadu*
Kelly, Gene (dir, b. 1912): *It's Always Fair Weather*
Kelly, Gerald (act): *Blind Date*
Kelly, Grace (act, 1929-1982): *Dial M for Murder (1954); Fourteen Hours; Rear Window (1954); To Catch a Thief*
Kelly, Graham (cin): *Calling Bulldog Drummond*
Kelly, Jack (act, 1927-1992): *Cult of the Cobra; Forbidden Planet; Julie; The Night Holds Terror; Red Nightmare; She-Devil (1957); Where Danger Lives*
Kelly, Jack (act): *Spawn of the Slithis*
Kelly, James (dir): *Are You Dying Young Man?; Night Hair Child*
Kelly, James (wri): *Are You Dying Young Man?; Blind Corner; Man In the Dark (1965); Tomorrow at Ten; W*
Kelly, Jean Louisa (act): *The Cyber-Stalking*
Kelly, Jim (act): *Death Dimension*
Kelly, Jo Ann (act): *Violent Women*
Kelly, John (GB act): *The Black Knight; The Village of the Damned (1960)*
Kelly, John (USA act): *After the Thin Man*
Kelly, John Thomas (act): *Scalpel*
Kelly, Judy (act, b. 1913): *At the Villa Rose (1939); The Black Abbot (1934); Crime On the Hill; Dancing With Crime; Dead Man's Shoes; Dead of Night (1945); The Last Chance; The Limping Man (1936); Luck of the Navy; The Midas Touch; Premiere; The Price of Folly; Queer Cargo*
Kelly, K.C. (act): *The Frighteners*
Kelly, Kathleen (act): *The Avenging Hand (1936); Dangerous Ground; The Scarab Murder Case; Who Killed John Savage?*
Kelly, Kitty (act): *The Avenging Hand (1943); The Lost Missile; The Man Behind the Mask (1936)*
Kelly, Lee (act): *Bowery at Midnight*
Kelly, Leslie (act): *The Mutagen; School Spirit*
Kelly, Lew (act): *Death from a Distance*
Kelly, Margot (act): *Riches and Rogues*
Kelly, Michael (act): *Links of Justice; Recoil (1953)*
Kelly, Michael T. (act): *Matinee*
Kelly, Moira (act): *Daybreak; The Lion King; Twin Peaks: Fire Walk With Me*
Kelly, Monika (act): *The Corpse Grinders*
Kelly, Nancy (act, 1921-1995): *The Bad Seed (1956); Betrayal from the East; Double Exposure;*
Follow That Woman; Scotland Yard (1941); Tarzan's Desert Mystery; Woman Who Came Back
Kelly, Ned (act): *20th Century Oz*
Kelly, Norman (act): *Invasion of the Blood Farmers*
Kelly, Pamela Dean (act): *Vampire's Kiss*
Kelly, Patrick (J.) (act): *Bulldog Drummond Escapes; The Missing Guest*
Kelly, Patrick Smith (wri): *A Perfect Murder*
Kelly, Patsy (act, 1910-1981): *Freaky Friday (1976); The Ghost In the Invisible Bikini; The Gorilla (1939); Rosemary's Baby; Topper Returns*
Kelly, Paul (act, 1899-1956): *Adventure Island; The Cat Creeps (1946); Crossfire; Deadline for Murder; Dead Man's Eyes; Faces in the Fog; Fear In the Night (1947); The Glass Alibi; The Missing Guest; The Secret Fury; Split Second (1953); Star of Midnight; Tarzan's New York Adventure; Torchy Blane In Panama*
Kelly, Paula (act): *The Andromeda Strain; Soylent Green*
Kelly, P.J. (act): *Devotion*
Kelly, Rachael (act): *Scream for Help*
Kelly, Renee (act): *Scarlet Thread*
Kelly, Robyn (act): *Flesh Gordon 2: Flesh Gordon Meets the Cosmic Cheerleaders*
Kelly, Roz (act): *Curse of the Black Widow; Full Moon High; New Year's Evil*
Kelly, Seamus (act): *Moby Dick (1956)*
Kelly, Sean (act): *First Men In the Moon (1964); Gang War; The Man Inside; 12 Monkeys; West 11*
Kelly, Shane (act): *Cavegirl (1985); Timecop*
Kelly, Simon (act): *Rawhead Rex*
Kelly, Terence (act): *The Hunted (1998); It (1990)*
Kelly, Terry (act): *American Gothic*
Kelly, Tim (wri): *Cry of the Banshee; Sugar Hill*
Kelly, Tom (act): *Tuck Everlasting*
Kelly, Vince (act): *Dracula (The Dirty Old Man)*
Kelly, Virginia (act): *Morning Call*
Kelly-Miller, Lois (act): *Meet Joe Black*
Kelm, Arthur (act): see Hunter, Tab
Kelman, Paul (act): *My Bloody Valentine*
Kelman, Rickey (act): *Step Down to Terror*
Kelpine, Dan (act): *Twister*
Kelsall, Moultrie (act, b. 1901): *Beyond This Place; The Hour of 13; The Lavender Hill Mob; Violent Playground*
Kelsch, Ken (cin): *Driller Killer; Rear Window (1998); Spookies*
Kelsey (act): *Roller Blade Warriors: Taken by Force*
Kelsey, Dick (wri): *Alice In Wonderland (1951)*
Kelsey, Frank (act): *The Gorilla (1927)*
Kelsey, Fred (act): *Charlie Chan at the Opera; Counter-Espionage; The Eleventh Hour (1923); The Invisible Ghost; The Last Warning (1929); The Lone Wolf Keeps a Date; The Lone Wolf Meets a Lady; The Lone Wolf Strikes; The Lone Wolf Takes a Chance; Mr. Moto's Gamble; One Dangerous Night; One Frightened Night; Secrets of the Lone Wolf; Seven Keys to Baldpate (1925); The Thirteenth Hour (1927)*
Kelsey, Gerald (wri): *The Golden Rabbit*
Kelsey, Tamsin (act): *The Little Match Girl (1987)*
Kelso, Edmond (wri): *King of the Zombies; Revenge of the Zombies (1943)*
Kelso, George (act): *Those Dear Departed*
Kelso, James (act): *The Gracie Allen Murder Case*
Kelso, Maym (act): *Seven Keys to Baldpate (1925)*
Kelso, Vernon (act): *Mrs. Pym of Scotland Yard*
Kelt, John (act): *The Tell-Tale Heart (1934)*
Kelton, Richard (act): *The Ultimate Warrior*
Kelton, Roger (act): *Android*
Kemball, Stella (act): *It Happened Here*
Kember, Paul (act): *An American Werewolf In London*
Kemble, Vivian (wri): *Blind Corner; Man In the Dark (1965)*
Kemmer, Ed(ward) (act): *Giant from the Unknown; Mara of the Wilderness; The Spider (1958)*
Kemmerling, Warren (J.) (act): *The Bermuda Triangle; Close Encounters of the Third Kind; The Dark (1979); Family Plot; Godzilla 1985; Trauma (1963)*
Kemp, Brandis (act): *Hexed*
Kemp, Drew (act): *The Hound of London*
Kemp, Edward (act): *Fragment of Fear*
Kemp, Elizabeth (act): *The Clairvoyant (1985); He Knows You're Alone*
Kemp, Gary (act): *Magic Hunter*
Kemp, Gypsy (act): *A Touch of the Other*
Kemp, Heidi (act): *Gremlins 2: The New Batch*
Kemp, Jason (act): *The Swordsman*
Kemp, Jeremy (act, b. 1934, nee Edmund Walker): *Assignment K; Dr. Terror's House of Horrors (1964); Eyewitness (1970); Face of a Stranger; Feet Foremost; Operation Crossbow; Phantom of the Opera (1983); The Prisoner of Zenda (1979); The Seven-Per-Cent Solution; The Strange Affair; Sudden Terror; Top Secret! (1984)*
Kemp, Lindsay (act): *A Midsummer Night's Dream (1985); The Wicker Man*
Kemp, Lindsay (wri): *A Midsummer Night's Dream (1985)*
Kemp, Margaret (act): *Sherlock Holmes (1922)*
Kemp, Martin (act): *Cyber Bandits; The Nosferatu Diaries: Embrace of the Vampire; Waxwork II: Lost In Time*
Kemp, Matty (act): *The Phantom of Crestwood*
Kemp, Paul (act): *M (1931)*
Kemp, Robert Lamar (act): *Ghost In the Machine*
Kemp, Roger (act): *The Awakening; Dragonslayer; Superman II*
Kemp, Sally (act): *Communion; Planet Earth; Spellbinder*
Kemp, Valli (act): *Dr. Phibes Rises Again; The Great Muppet Caper*
Kemp-Blair, Ramona (act): *Ed Wood*
Kempe, Will (act): *Pledge Night*
Kempel, Arthur (mus): *The Arrival (1996); The Coming; Sensation (1994)*
Kemper, Charles (act): *On Dangerous Ground; Where Danger Lives*
Kemper, Doris (act): *Crashing Las Vegas*
Kemper, Terry (act): *People Who Own the Dark*
Kemper, Victor (J.) (cin): *Cloak and Dagger (1984); Coma; The Final Countdown; Magic; Oh. God!; The Reincarnation of Peter Proud; They Might Be Giants; Xanadu*
Kempf, Ruth (act): *Live and Let Die*
Kempinski, Thomas/Tom (act): *The Committee; The Damned*
Kemplen, Ralph (dir): *The Spaniard's Curse*
Kempson, Rachel (act, b. 1910): *Curse of the Fly; Jane Eyre (1970); Lorna Doone (1990); The Third Secret; A Woman's Vengeance*
Kempton, William (act): *Blood Diner*
Kemp-Welch, Joan (act, b. 1906): *Busman's Honeymoon; Pimpernel Smith*
Kenan, Dodi (act): *Remo Williams: The Adventure Begins*
Kenan, Ron (mus): *Turbo: A Power Rangers Movie*
Kendal, Felicity (act): *We're Back! A Dinosaur's Story*
Kendall, Brenda (act): *Dead Alive*
Kendall, Cy (act): *After Midnight With Boston Blackie; Alias Boston Blackie; Blonde for a Day; The Chance of a Lifetime; The Chinese Cat; The Invisible Menace; The Saint Takes Over; Tarzan's New York Adventure*
Kendall, Fiona (act): *Psychomania (1972)*
Kendall, Henry (act, 1897-1962): *Death On the Set; The Flaw (1933); The Flying Fool; The Ghost Camera; The House Opposite (1931); The Iron Stair (1933); The Man Outside (1933); Rich and Strange; The Shadow (1933); The Shadow of the Cat; The Stickpin; Twelve Good Men; The Voice of Merrill*
Kendall, Howard (act): *Monte Cristo*
Kendall, Kay (act, 1927-1959): *Abdullah's Harem; Fiddlers Three; Man In Hiding; Mantrap; Meet Mr. Lucifer; Street of Shadows*
Kendall, Kenneth (act): *Electric Eskimo; Evidence In Concrete; They Came from Beyond Space; Vengeance*
Kendall, Mark (act): *Maid to Order*
Kendall, Merelina (act): *Robin Hood: Prince of Thieves*
Kendall, Suzy (act, b. 1943, nee Frieda Harrison): *Circus of Fear; Craze; Fear Is the Key; In the Devil's Garden; The Liquidator; The Penthouse (1967); Spasmo; Tales That Witness Madness; Torso; L'Uccello delle Piume di Cristallo*
Kendall, Tony (act): *El Ataque de los Muertos sin Ojos; La Frusta e il Corpo; Kiss Kiss, Kill Kill; People Who Own the Dark; When the Screaming Stops; Yeti*
Kendall, Victor (wri): *Dead Men Are Dangerous; The Gables Mystery; The Man at Six; Mr. Reeder In Room 13*
Kendall, William (act): *The Assassination Bureau; The Two Faces of Dr. Jekyll*
Kendrick, Baynard (wri): *Eyes In the Night; The Hidden Eye*
Kendrick, David (act): *School Spirit*
Kendrick, Florina (act): *Bram Stoker's 'Dracula'*
Kendrick, Henry Max (act): *Wheels of Terror*
Kendrick, Lola (act): *Willard*
Kendrick, Tommy (act): *The Bermuda Triangle*
Kenealy, Philip (act): *Fright (1957)*
Kenedy, Karen (act): *Def Con 4*
Kener, David (act): *Alien High*
Kennard, Conover (act): *Scandalous*
Kennard, Graham (act): *The Demon (1981)*
Kennaway, James (wri, 1928-1968): *The Mind Benders (1963); Violent Playground*
Kenneally, John (act): *Garden of the Dead*
Kennedy, Alexandra (act): *Bloodspell*
Kennedy, Alita (act): *Scandalous*
Kennedy, Angela (act): *The Wicked*
Kennedy, Arthur (act, 1914-1990): *L'Anticristo; The Cauldron of Death; Devotion; Fantastic Voyage; The Humanoid; Impulse (1955); The Living Dead at the Manchester Morgue; Murder She Said; The Sentinel; The Sharks' Cave; The Window*
Kennedy, Beth (act): *Phenomenon*
Kennedy, Bill (act): *Red Planet Mars; Web of Danger*
Kennedy, Burt (dir, b. 1923): *The Killer Inside Me; Suburban Commando*
Kennedy, Daun (act): *The Falcon Out West*
Kennedy, David (act): *Mary Shelley's 'Frankenstein'*
Kennedy, Douglas (R.) (act, 1918-1973, a.k.a. Keith Douglas): *The Adventures of Don Juan; The Alligator People; The Amazing Transparent Man; The Bonnie Parker Story; Dark Passage; The Decision of Christopher Blake; The Destructors; Flight of the Lost Balloon; Invaders from Mars (1953); The Land Unknown; The Lion Hunters; The Lone Ranger and the Lost City of Gold; The Next Voice You Hear; Possessed (1947); Safari Drums*
Kennedy, Edgar (act, 1890-1948): *The Black Doll; The Chinese Parrot; Crazy House (1943); The Falcon Strikes Back; Heaven Only Knows; It Happened Tomorrow; Murder On the Blackboard; The Penguin Pool Murder*
Kennedy, Edmund (act): *Castle Sinister (1932)*
Kennedy, Fiona (act): *The Wicker Man*
Kennedy, Frank (act): *Night of the Lepus*
Kennedy, George (act, b. 1925): *The Boston Strangler; Brain Dead; Creepshow 2; Death On the Nile; Death Ship; Demonwarp; Earthquake; The Eiger Sanction; Fugitive from the Empire; The Human Factor; Hush ...Hush, Sweet Charlotte; Just Before Dawn (1980); Lost Horizon (1973); Mirage (1965); National Lampoon's Men In White; Nightmare at Noon; Radioactive Dreams; Small Soldiers; Strait-Jacket; The Terror Within; Uninvited (1987); Virus (1980); Wacko*
Kennedy, Gerald (act): *Puzzle*
Kennedy, Gerard (act): *Body Melt*
Kennedy, Heather (act): *Princess Warrior*
Kennedy, Holly (act): *Jacob's Ladder*
Kennedy, Jack (act): *The Fatal Hour (1940)*
Kennedy, Jamie (act): *Scream; Scream 2*
Kennedy, Jane (act): *Ms. 45*
Kennedy, Jayne (act): *Mysterious Island of Beautiful Women*
Kennedy, Jim (act): *The Night Visitor*
Kennedy, Joyce (act): *Black Mask; Dangerous Ground; The Nursemaid Who Disappeared; The Return of Bulldog Drummond; Seven Sinners; Twelve Good Men*
Kennedy, Karen (act): *The Pink Chiquitas*
Kennedy, Kathy Lee (act): *The Initiation*
Kennedy, Kevin (act): *Pinocchio In Outer Space*
Kennedy, Laurie (act): *Twisted*
Kennedy, Leon Isaac (act): *Too Scared to Scream*
Kennedy, Ludovic (act): *The Lonely House*
Kennedy, Ludovic (wri): *10 Rillington Place*
Kennedy, Madge (act): *Three Bad Sisters*
Kennedy, Mardi (act): *Chilling (1981)*
Kennedy, Margaret (wri): *The Man In Grey; The Midas Touch; Take My Life*
Kennedy, Marklen (act): *Witchcraft 5: Dance With the Devil*
Kennedy, Merle (act): *Nemesis*
Kennedy, Mike (act): *Shock Waves*
Kennedy, Mimi (act): *Bride of Boogedy; Death Becomes Her*
Kennedy, Neil (act): *Tales That Witness Madness*
Kennedy, Nina (act): *Jekyll and Hyde*
Kennedy, Phyllis (act): *Time to Kill (1942)*
Kennedy, Rand (act): *Halloween 4: The Return of Michael Myers*
Kennedy, Ray (mus): *Phantom of the Paradise*
Kennedy, Richard (act): *The Capture of Bigfoot*
Kennedy, Rick (act): *Razorback*
Kennedy, Rigg (act): *Maid to Order*
Kennedy, Ron (act): *Killers from Space*
Kennedy, Ryan (act): *Scream; The Slumber Party Massacre*
Kennedy, Sarah (act): *The Telephone Book*
Kennedy, Tom (act, 1885-1965): *The Adventurous Blonde; Blondes at Work; The Devil's Cargo; Fly-Away Baby; Forty Naughty Girls; Invasion U.S.A.; The Mutineers; Smart Blonde; Torchy Blane In Chinatown; Torchy Blane In Panama; Torchy Gets Her Man; Torchy Plays With Dynamite; Torchy Runs for Mayor*
Kennedy, Tom (dir): *Time Walker*
Kennedy, William (act): *Two Lost Worlds*
Kennedy-Dohrn, Helga (act): *The Last Ten Days of Adolf Hitler*
Kenner, Dawn (act): *Getting Lucky*
Kenner, Devon (act): *Getting Lucky*
Kenner, Jacob (act): *Heart and Souls; Wheels of Terror*
Kenner, Paul G. (act): *Getting Lucky*
Kenner, Warren (act): *Mirrors*
Kennerly, Mark D. (act): *Demon Knight*
Kennett, George (wri): *The Private Lives of Adam and Eve*
Kenney, Bob (act): *Primal Fear*
Kenney, Charlie (act): *Mad Max Beyond Thunderdome*
Kenney, Colin (act): *The Clue of the New Pin (1929)*
Kenney, Flynn (act): *Mad Max Beyond Thunderdome*
Kenney, James (act): *Ambush In Leopard Street; Cosh Boy; The Gelignite Gang: Hidden Homicide; No Safety Ahead; Seven Thunders; No Safety Ahead; Son of a Stranger; Vice Versa (1947)*
Kenney, Joel P. (act): *The Bermuda Triangle*
Kenney, Sean (act): *The Corpse Grinders*

Kennington, Alan (wri): *The Night Has Eyes; You Can't Escape*

Kennington, Jill (act): *Blow-Up*

Kenny, Colin (act): *The Adventures of Robin Hood*

Kenny, Francis (cin): *Coneheads; Dark Angel (1996); Ed and His Dead Mother; Pretty Poison (1996)*

Kenny, Jessica (act): *Strange Behavior*

Kenny, June (act): *Attack of the Puppet People; Bloodlust!; The Spider (1958); The Viking Women and the Sea Serpent*

Kenny, Lee (act): *Just Imagine*

Kenny, Nicholas (act): *Dead Connection*

Kenny, Shannon (act): *Bodily Harm; Purgatory*

Kenny, Simon (act): *Dead Connection*

Kenoi, Harry (act): *The Black Bird (1975)*

Kensit, Patsy (act, b. 1969): *At the Midnight Hour; The Blue Bird (1976); The Corsican Brothers (1985); Dream Man; Full Eclipse; Harlequin's 'At the Midnight Hour'; Tunnel Vision; The Turn of the Screw*

Kent, April (act): *I've Lived Before; The Incredible Shrinking Man*

Kent, Bertha (act): *Jane Eyre (1921)*

Kent, Carl (act): *The Falcon In Hollywood; The Falcon In San Francisco*

Kent, Carol (act): *This Is Not a Test*

Kent, Charles (act): *Pawns of Mars*

Kent, Christopher (Euro act & dir): see Kjellin, Alf

Kent, Christopher (USA act): *Gypsy Fury*

Kent, (J.) Crauford (act, 1880-1953): *The Adventures of Robin Hood; In the Next Room; Jane Eyre (1921); The Lost Jungle; The Menace (1932); Seven Keys to Baldpate (1925 & 1929); The Unholy Three (1930)*

Kent, Dorothea (act): *Behind the Mask (1946)*

Kent, Elizabeth (act): *The Dance of Death (1938); Dial 999 (1938); Mind Warp (1990)*

Kent, Gary (act): *Satan's Sadists; Targets; The Thrill Killers*

Kent, Humphrey (act): *Dick Barton Strikes Back; Horror of Dracula*

Kent, Janice (act): *The Flintstones*

Kent, Jean (act, b. 1921, nee Joan Summerfield): *Before I Wake; Beyond This Place; Bluebeard's Ten Honeymoons; Fanny by Gaslight; Grip of the Strangler; The Lost Hours; Sleeping Car to Trieste; The Woman In Question*

Kent, Jennifer (act): *The Pink Chiquitas*

Kent, Joan-Carol (act): *Retribution (1988)*

Kent, Keneth (act): *At the Villa Rose (1939); Gestapo; The House of the Arrow (1940); Luck of the Navy; Queer Cargo*

Kent, Larry (act): *The Haunted House (1929)*

Kent, Lenny (act): *The 30 Foot Bride of Candy Rock*

Kent, Michael (act): *Dick Tracy Returns*

Kent, Paul (act): *The Astronaut; The Invisible Man (1975); A Nightmare On Elm Street 3: Dream Warriors; Ruby*

Kent, Peter (act): *The Dungeonmaster; Gargantua; Re-Animator*

Kent, Robert (act): *Charlie Chan at Monte Carlo; For Heaven's Sake; The Gladiator; Mr. Moto Takes a Chance; The Phantom Creeps; Radar Secret Service*

Kent, Robert (E.) (wri, b. 1911): *Charlie Chan In Reno; Diary of a Madman; Dick Tracy Meets Gruesome; Dick Tracy vs. Cueball; Drums of Tahiti; The Falcon In San Francisco; The Falcon's Adventure; Genius at Work; Gildersleeve's Ghost; Philo Vance Returns; Thief of Damascus; Twice-Told Tales; The Werewolf (1955); Zombies On Broadway*

Kent, Rolfe (mus): *Dead Connection*

Kent, Stanley (act): *Triumph of the Ten Gladiators*

Kent, Stapleton (act): *Donovan's Brain*

Kent, Suzanne (act): *Amazons (1984); Pandemonium*

Kent, Thomas (act): *Disaster In Time*

Kent, Willard (act): *The Clutching Hand*

Kent, William (act): *The Scarlet Letter (1934)*

Kenter, Musfik (act): *Lebewohl Fremde*

Kentish, Elizabeth (act): *You Can't Escape*

Kenton, Earl (wri): *Invisible: The Chronicles of Benjamin Knight; Mandroid*

Kenton, Erle C. (dir, 1896-1980): *The Best Man Wins; The Cat Creeps (1946); The Ghost of Frankenstein; House of Dracula; House of Frankenstein; Island of Lost Souls; Who Done It? (1942)*

Kenton, Will (act): *Haunted Honeymoon (1986)*

Kenworthy, Michael (act): *The Blob (1988); Return of the Living Dead, Part II*

Kenyatta, Caro (act): *Trader Horn (1973)*

Kenyatta, Stogie (act): *Species*

Kenyon, Albert (wri): *The Monster (1925)*

Kenyon, Charles (act): *The Penalty*

Kenyon, Charles (wri): *Crack-Up; The Lost Zeppelin; The Man In Half Moon Street; A Mid-summer Night's Dream (1935)*

Kenyon, Doris (act, 1897-1979): *The Man In the Iron Mask (1939)*

Kenyon, Gwen (act): *Charlie Chan In the Secret Service; The Corpse Vanishes*

Kenyon, Sandy (act): *The Loch Ness Horror; Sweet Kill; When Time Ran Out*

Kenyon, Taldo (act): *The Magic Sword (1962)*

Kenyon, Tony (act): *The Playbirds; The Sexplorer*

Kenzle, Ken (act): *Sasquatch, the Legend of Bigfoot*

Keogh, Barbara (act): *The Abominable Dr. Phibes; Paperhouse; The Quatermass Conclusion*

Keogh, Garrett (act): *Excalibur*

Keough, Cara (act): *Outbreak*

Keown, Eric (wri): *The Ghost Goes West*

Kepnick, Brad (act): *Fright Night II*

Ker, Lillian (act): *Deathstalker*

Keraudy, Jean (act): *Le Trou*

Kerber, Randy (mus): *Date With an Angel*

Kerbosch, Michiel (act): *The Lift*

Kerby, Bill (wri): *Firepower*

Kerchbron, Jean (dir): *Le Golem (1966)*

Kercheval, Ken (act, b. 1935): *The Demon Murder Case; Devil Dog: The Hound of Hell; I Still Dream of Jeannie; Pretty Poison (1968)*

Kereluk, Cynthia (act): *The Pink Chiquitas*

Keremes, Tomasina (act): *Mutants In Paradise*

Kerien, M. Jean-Pierre (act): *September Storm*

Kerima (act): *Land of the Pharaohs; The She-Wolf (1954)*

Kerin, Jackie (act): *Next of Kin*

Kerjean, Germaine (act): *Le Diable et les Dix Commandements*

Kerlow, Max (act): *Dr. Tarr's Torture Dungeon*

Kerman, David (act): *Frankenstein Meets the Space Monster*

Kerman, Ken (act): *Nightmare On the 13th Floor; Separate Lives*

Kerman, Robert (act): *Cannibal Ferox; Night of the Creeps*

Kern, Daniel (act): *Rocket Attack U.S.A.*

Kern, David J. (wri): *Dracula Sucks*

Kern, James V. (wri): *The Horn Blows at Midnight; You'll Find Out*

Kernan, David (act): *Gaolbreak (1962); Otley*

Kernchan, Roxanne (act): *Phoenix the Warrior*

Kernell, William (mus): *Charlie Chan at the Opera*

Kerner, Diana (act): *Creature With the Blue Hand*

Kernichan, Roxane (act): *Critters 2: The Main Course*

Kernke, Karin (act): *The Naked Woman and Satan*

Kerns (Jr.), Hubie (act): *Beyond the Poseidon Adventure; The Sword and the Sorcerer*

Kerns, Joanna (act, b. 1953): *Captive; Emma's Wish; Robin Cook's 'Mortal Fear'*

Kerns, Sandra (act): *C.H.U.D. II; Dr. Scorpion*

Kerns, Sheree (act): *Beyond the Poseidon Adventure*

Kerns, Zachariah Sage (act): *C.H.U.D. II*

Kershaw, Glenn (cin): *Death Ring*

Kerova, Zora (act): *Cannibal Ferox; The Grim Reaper*

Kerr, Annette (act): *The Private Life of Sherlock Holmes*

Kerr, Bill (act): *House of Mortal Sin; Port of Escape; Razorback; Tiffany Jones*

Kerr, Bruce (act): *The Brain That Wouldn't Die*

Kerr, Cecil (act): *The Empty House; The Priory School*

Kerr, Deborah (act, b. 1921, nee Deborah Jane Kerr-Trimmer): *Black Narcissus; Casino Royale; Eye of the Devil; The Innocents; King Solomon's Mines (1949); The Naked Edge; The Prisoner of Zenda (1952)*

Kerr, Donald (act): *The Devil Bat; Lady In the Morgue; Murder Is My Business; The Saint's Double Trouble; Song of the Thin Man; The Spanish Cape Mystery*

Kerr, Edward (act): *Magic Island*

Kerr, Fred(erick) (act, 1858-1933, nee Frederick Keen): *Frankenstein (1931); The Lifeguardsman; 12-10*

Kerr, Geoffrey (act): *12-10*

Kerr, Geoffrey (wri): *Cottage to Let; The Ghost Goes West; Living Dangerously*

Kerr, John (act, b. 1931): *Men of Sherwood Forest; The Pit and the Pendulum (1961)*

Kerr, Judy (act): *The Hidden*

Kerr, Larry (act): *The Lost Missile*

Kerr, Nancy (act): *The Intruder (1981)*

Kerr, Richard (act): [illegible]

Kerran, David (act): *Mix Me a Person*

Kerridge, Linda (act): *Alien from L.A.; Fade to Black*

Kerridge, Mary (act): *Curse of Simba; Richard III (1955); Under the Frozen Falls*

Kerridge, Roy (wri): *Mix Me a Person*

Kerrigan, J.M. (act, 1885-1965): *The Black Camel; Crime Doctor's Warning; It's a Dog's Life; The Lost Patrol (1934); The Luck of the Irish; My Cousin Rachel; The Spanish Main; A Study In Scarlet (1933); Tarzan and the Amazons; Werewolf of London; The Wolf Man (1941)*

Kerrigan, Lodge (dir & wri): *Clean, Shaven*

Kerrigan, Patricia (act): *The Magic Toyshop*

Kerr-Trimmer, Deborah Jane (act): see Kerr, Deborah

Kerruish, Jessie D. (wri): *The Undying Monster*

Kerry, Evelyn (act): *The Lady Killers (1956)*

Kerry, James (act): *Give Us Tomorrow*

Kerry, John (act): *Memorial Valley Massacre*

Kerry, Norman (act, 1889-1956, nee Arnold Kaiser): *Buried Treasure; The Hunchback of Notre Dame (1923); The Phantom of the Opera (1925); The Unknown (1927)*

Kersch, Robert (act): *Wonder Woman*

Kersey, Yvonne Talton (act): *Too Scared to Scream*

Kershaw, Glenn (wri): *Twisted*

Kershaw, W. (act): *The King's Outcast*

Kershaw, Whitney (act): *Covenant*

Kershner, Irvin (dir, b. 1923): *The Empire Strikes Back; Eyes of Laura Mars; Never Say Never Again; RoboCop 2; The Young Captives*

Kertel, Jason (act): *Shadow of a Doubt (1991)*

Kertes, David C. (cin): *The Unsuspected*

Kerton, Patrick (act): *Alien High*

Kervyn, Emmanuel (dir & wri): *Rabid Grannies*

Kerwin, Brian (act, b. 1949): *Giving Up the Ghost; It Came from Outer Space II; Jack; King Kong Lives; Unlikely Angel; Volcano: Fire On the Mountain*

Kerwin, Harry (act): *Barracuda*

Kerwin, Harry (dir): *Barracuda; God's Bloody Acre*

Kerwin, Lance (act, b. 1960): *Enemy Mine; The Mysterious Stranger; Outbreak; Reflections of Murder; Salem's Lot*

Kerwin, Patrick (wri): *Bulldog Drummond at Bay (1937)*

Kerwin, William (act): *Barracuda; Decoy for Terror*

Kerzner, D.J. (act): *Monster High*

Kerzt, Ludwig (wri): *Orlacs Haende*

Kesler, Henry S. (dir): *Five Steps to Danger*

Kesler, Rick (act): *Beyond Dream's Door*

Kesner, Killian (act): *Trick or Treats*

Kessel, Joseph (wri): *Belle de Jour; The Night of the Generals*

Kesselring, Joseph (wri): *Arsenic and Old Lace*

Kessinger, Carolyn (act): *Ed Wood*

Kessler, Alice (act): *Gli Invasori; Sodom and Gomorrah*

Kessler, Bruce (dir): *Angels from Hell; Cruise Into Terror; Deathmoon; Simon, King of the Witches*

Kessler, Catherine (act): *Murder by Decree*

Kessler, Ellen (act): *Gli Invasori; Sodom and Gomorrah*

Kessler, Kenneth (act): *The Toxic Avenger*

Kessler, Lee (act): *Creator*

Kessler, Quin (act): *She (1983); Wishman*

Kessler, Zale (act): *The Attic; The Clonus Horror*

Kesson, David (cin): *Bits of Life; The Unholy Three (1925)*

Kesson, Frank (cin): *The Sea Beast*

Kestelman, Sara (act): *Lisztomania; Zardoz*

Kesten, Bob (wri): *Kil 1*

Kester, Ernest (act): *The Howling: New Moon Rising*

Kester, Karen (act): *The Baron of Arizona*

Kestermann, Rolf (cin): *Surf Nazis Must Die*

Kestner, Bryan (act): *In Dark Places; The Monster Squad*

Keston, Robin (act): *The Man from Nowhere*

Ketchum, David (act): *Love at First Bite*

Ketchum, Larry (act, 1946-1995): *World Gone Wild*

Ketelsen, Kim Steven (wri): *Philadelphia Experiment II*

Ketoff, Fulvia (act): *The Kremlin Letter*

Kettlewell, Ruth (act): *The Black Panther; The Clue of the New Pin (1961); No Blade of Grass*

Kettley, S.P. Goodyer (act): *In the Grip of Death; The Old Gardener*

Kevan, Jack (cin): *The Land Unknown*

Kevan, John (act): *The Secret Voice*

Key, Alexander (wri, b. 1904): *Escape to Witch Mountain (1975); Return from Witch Mountain*

Key, Alison (act): *The Black Panther*

Key, Janet (act): *—And Now the Screaming Starts!; Dracula A.D. 1972; I Don't Want to Be Born; The Vampire Lovers*

Key, Peter (wri): *The Trollenberg Terror*

Key, Ted (wri): *The Cat from Outer Space; Digby-The Biggest Dog In the World; The $1,000,000 Duck*

Keyes, Christopher (act): *Shocker*

Keyes, Daniel (wri, b. 1927): *Charly*

Keyes, Evelyn (act, b. 1919): *Around the World In 80 Days; Before I Hang; The Face Behind the Mask; Here Comes Mr. Jordan; Ladies In Retirement; The Prowler (1951); A Return to Salem's Lot; Smuggler's Island; A Thousand and One Nights (1945); Wicked Stepmother*

Keyes, Irwin (act): *Backlash: Oblivion 2; Disturbed; The Flintstones; Frankenstein General Hospital; It Came Upon the Midnight Clear; The Private Eyes (1980); The Silence of the Hams; Zapped!*

Keyes, Joanna (act): *976-EVIL*

Keyhoe, Maj. Donald (wri, 1897-1988): *Earth vs. the Flying Saucers*

Keyhoe, Jack (act): *D.O.A. (1988)*

Keyhoe, Mike (act): *Vampire at Midnight*

Keyke, E.M. (wri): *The Incredibly Strange Creatures Who Stopped Living and Became Mixed-Up Zombies*

Keymas, George (act): *Drums of Tahiti*

Keymer, Richard (act): *The Keeper*

Keys, Anthony Nelson (wri, 1910-1985): *Frankenstein Must Be Destroyed*

Keys, Nelson (act): *Drowsy Dick's Dream; The Triumph of the Scarlet Pimpernel; When Knights Were Bold (1929)*

Keys, Robert (act): *Street of Darkness*

Keyser, Chuck (act): *First Man Into Space; Subway In the Sky*

Keyser-Heyl, Willy (act): *Der Januskopf*

Keyser-Korff, Lulu (act): *Schloss Vogelod*

Keys-Hall, Michael (act) *The Night They Saved Christmas*

Keyworth, Ben (act): *Afraid of the Dark*

Kezer, Glenn (act): *Werewolf of Washington*

K'Gong, Kenny (act): *Copycat*

Khachaturian, Aram (mus, 1903-1978): *2001: A Space Odyssey*

Khambatta, Persis (act, b. 1946): *Deadly Intent; The Man With the Power; Megaforce; Phoenix the Warrior; Star Trek; Warriors of the Wasteland*

Khan, Abas (act): *Tarzan Goes to India*

Khan, Alik Akbar (mus): *Devi*

Khan, Feroz (act): *Tarzan Goes to India*

Khan, Ibrahim (act): *Dawn of the Mummy*

Khaner, Julie (act): *Spasms; Videodrome; Virus (1980)*

Khmara, Ed(ward) (wri): *Enemy Mine; Ladyhawke*

Khmelnitsky, Boris (act): *The Savage Hunt of King Stakh*

Khokhlova, Alexandra (act): *Luch Smerti*

Khondji, Darius (cin): *The City of Lost Children; Seven*

Khorsand, Philippe (act): *Les Miserables (1995)*

Khoury, George (act): *Abbott and Costello Meet the Mummy; Sabu and the Magic Ring; 20 Million Miles to Earth*

Khouth, Gabe (act): *It (1990)*

Khrabovitsky, Danily (wri): *Devyat'dney Odnogo Goda*

Khuylya, Alexander (act): *Jack Frost*

Kiara, Yoshiaki (cin): *Buddha*

Kibbe, Gary B. (cin): *In the Mouth of Madness; Prince of Darkness; They Live; Village of the Damned (1995)*

Kibbee, Guy (act, 1882-1956): *The Horn Blows at Midnight*

Kibbee, Milton (act): *Another Thin Man; The Casino Murder Case; Jungle Siren; The Kennel Murder Case; Larceny In Her Heart; The Scarlet Clue; White Pongo*

Kibbee, Roland (wri, 1914-1984): *Angel On My Shoulder (1946); The Crimson Pirate; The Return of the World's Greatest Detective*

Kibler, Belva (act): *The Medium (1951)*

Kibrick, Leonard (act): *The Return of the Six Million Dollar Man and the Bionic Woman*

Kichta, Kathleen (act): *It's Alive III: Island of the Alive; A Return to Salem's Lot*

Kidd, David (wri): *The Love War*

Kidd, Jonathan (act, 1914-1987, nee Kurt Richards): *Macabre (1958); Wink of an Eye*

Kidd, Michael (act, b. 1919): *It's Always Fair Weather*

Kidder, Margot (act, b. 1948): *The Amityville Horror; Beanstalk; Bloodknot; GoBots: Battle of the Rock Lords; The Reincarnation of Peter Proud; Silent Night, Evil Night; Sisters; Superman (1978); Superman II; Superman III; Superman IV: The Quest for Peace; White Room*

Kidman, Nicole (act, b. 1967): *Batman Forever; Dead Calm; Eyes Wide Shut; Malice; The Peacemaker (1997); Practical Magic*
Kidnie, James (act): *Body Parts (1991); Curtains; Gate II; Starcrossed*
Kido, Caroline (act): *Confessions of an Opium Eater*
Ki-Duk, Kim (dir): *Yongary, Monster from the Deep*
Kiebach, Max (act): *De Sade*
Kiekens, Rose (act): *Virgin Among the Living Dead*
Kiel, Richard (act): *Eegah!; House of the Damned (1962); The Human Duplicators; The Humanoid; Hysterical; A Man Called Dagger; Moonraker; The Phantom Planet; The Phoenix (1980); The Spy Who Loved Me; War of the Wizards*
Kiel, Sue (act): *Survivor (1987)*
Kieling, Wolfgang (act): *Amsterdam Affair; House of 1,000 Dolls; Out of Order; Torn Curtain; The Vengeance of Fu Manchu*
Kienzle, William X. (wri): *The Rosary Murders*
Kiernan, David (act): *The Lair of the White Worm*
Kiernan, Harry (act): *Twisted*
Kiernan, J. Edward (wri): *Deadtime Stories*
Kierney, Tyde (act): *I Drink Your Blood*
Kiersch, Fritz (dir): *Children of the Corn*
Kies, Margaret (act): see Lindsay, Margaret
Kieserman, David (act): *The Purple Rose of Cairo*
Kiesler, Hedwig "Hedy" (act): see Lamarr, Hedy
Kieslowski, Krzysztof (dir): *Krotki Film O Zabijaniu*
Kiesouw, Hans (act): *Creatures the World Forgot*
Kiesouw, Josje (act): *Creatures the World Forgot*
Kiesser, Jan (cin): *The Adventures of Captain Zoom In Outer Space; Fright Night; Made In Heaven; Nightmare Street*
Kiger, Bobbi (act): *Ssssss*
Kiger, Robby (act): *Children of the Corn; The Monster Squad*
Kiger, Susan (act): *The Alien's Return; Death Screams; Galaxina; House of Death (1981)*
Kihlstedt, Rya (act): *Brave New World (1998)*
Kihn, Albert (cin): *THX 1138*
Kijima, Ichiro (act): *Virus (1980)*
Kiki (act): *The Golden Mistress*
Kikoine, Gerard (dir): *Buried Alive (1989); Edge of Sanity*
Kikuchi, Hideyuki (wri): *A Wind Named Amnesia*
Kikuchi, Shunsuke (mus): *Attack of the Monsters; Gammera vs. Zigra*
Kikume, Al (act): *Daughter of the Jungle; Mr. Moto In Danger Island; Mr. Moto Takes a Chance*
Kikushima, Riyuzo (wri): *Throne of Blood*
Kilar, Wojciech (mus): *Bram Stoker's 'Dracula'*
Kilbane, Dennis (act): *The Valley of Gwangi*
Kilbert, Tony (act): *Scream*
Kilbertus, Nicholas/Nickolas/Nick (act): *Happy Birthday to Me; The Kiss (1988); Scanners*
Kilbey, Reginald (act): *Agatha*
Kilbourne, Wendy (act, b. 1964): *Condor; Turn Back the Clock*
Kilbride, Percy (act): *Crazy House (1943); Guest In the House; Keeper of the Flame*
Kilbride, Richard (act): *The Playground*
Kilburn, Terence/Terry (act, b. 1927): *Bulldog Drummond at Bay (1947); Bulldog Drummond Strikes Back (1947); The Challenge; A Christmas Carol (1938); Fiend Without a Face; Fortunes of Captain Blood; Slaves of Babylon; 13 Lead Soldiers*
Kiley, Richard (act, b. 1922): *Angel On My Shoulder (1980); The Bad Seed (1985); Howard the Duck; Jurassic Park; The Little Prince; Murder Once Removed; Night Gallery; Phenomenon; The Sniper*
Kilgarriff, Michael (act): *The Dark Crystal*
Kilgas, Nancy (act): *The Spider (1958)*
Kilgore, David (act): *The Henderson Monster*
Kilgour, Joseph (act): *Blackie's Redemption*
Kilgour, Melanie (act): *Empire of Ash III*
Kilian, Kristin L. (act): *Slugs*
Kilian, Victor (act, 1891-1979): *A Date With the Falcon; Dr. Cyclops; Forgotten City of the Planet of the Apes; League of Frightened Men; Secrets of the Lone Wolf; Spellbound (1945); Unknown World*
Killeen, James (act): *Short Circuit 2*
Killian, Dan (act): *Bog*
Killick, Tim (act): *Erik the Viking; Without a Clue*
Killips, Neveda (act): *Slugs*
Killy, Edward (dir): *Murder On a Bridle Path*
Kilman, Buzz (act): *The Silence of the Lambs*
Kilman, Sam (act): *Final Exam*
Kilmer, Val (act, b. 1959) *Batman Forever; The Ghost and the Darkness; The Island of Dr. Moreau (1996); Kill Me Again; The Murders In the Rue Morgue (1986); The Prince of Egypt; The Saint; Top Secret! (1984); Willow*
Kilner, Kevin (act): *Switch (1991)*
Kilpatrick, Erik (act): *Dead Again*
Kilpatrick, Ilsa (act): *Castle Sinister (1932)*
Kilpatrick, Lincoln (act): *Chosen Survivors; Dr. Scorpion; Fortress; The Mask of Sheba; The Omega Man; Prison (1988); Soylent Green*
Kilpatrick Jr., Lincoln (act): *Dead Men Tell No Tales (1971)*
Kilpatrick, Pat (act): *The Toxic Avenger*
Kilpatrick, Patrick (act): *Beastmaster III: The Eye of Braxus; The Cellar (1989); Class of 1999; Eraser; Remo Williams: The Adventure Begins; Scanners: The Showdown*
Kilpatrick, Reid (act): *The Scarlet Clue*
Kilpatrick, Shirley (act): *The Astounding She-Monster*
Kilpatrick, Tom (wri): *Dr. Cyclops*
Kilroy, Mathias (act): *The Legacy*
Kilton, Leigh (act): *Deadtime Stories*
Kim, Derek (act): *Outbreak*
Kim, Evan (C.) (act): *Caveman (1981); V*
Kim, Jacqueline/Jacqui (act): *Star Trek: Generations; Trauma (1993)*
Kim, June (act): *Confessions of an Opium Eater*
Kim, Robert (act): *Donor*
Kimball, Bruce (act): *Brain of Blood; The Thing With Two Heads*
Kimball, Jeffrey L. (cin): *Jacob's Ladder*
Kimball, Jim (act): *Blood Song*
Kimball, Ward (dir): *Peter Pan (1953)*
Kimball, Ward (wri): *Babes In Toyland (1961)*
Kimbell, Anne (act): *The Golden Idol; Monster from the Ocean Floor; Port Sinister*
Kimbell, Glenn (cin): *7 Doors of Death*
Kimberley, Glen (act): *Carnival of Blood*
Kimberley, John (act): *Skullduggery*
Kimberley, Maggie (act): *The Mummy's Shroud; Where the Bullets Fly*
Kimble, Lawrence (wri): *Mystery In Mexico; Zombies On Broadway*
Kimbro, Art (act): *Are You In the House Alone?*
Kimbrough, Andrew (act): *Puppet Master*
Kimbrough, Charles (act): *The Hunchback of Notre Dame (1996)*
Kimler, Kay (act): *Beyond the Poseidon Adventure; Charlie Chan and the Curse of the Dragon Queen*
Kimmel, Bruce (act, dir & wri): *The Creature Wasn't Nice*
Kimmell, Dana (act): *Friday the 13th-Part 3; Midnight Offerings; Sweet Sixteen*
Kimmich, Barbara (act): *The Alien's Return*
Kimmich, Max (wri): *On Secret Service*
Kimmich, Ronald (act): *The Alien's Return*
Kimmins, Anthony (dir, b. 1901): *Mr. Denning Drives North; Night Club Queen; Once In a New Moon*
Kimmins, Kenneth (act): *The Henderson Monster; My Best Friend Is a Vampire*
Kimura, Daisaku (cin): *Virus (1980)*
Kimura, Takeshi (wri): *The Final War; Gorath; The H-Man; The Human Vapor; Matango; The Mysterians; Rodan, the Flying Monster; Samurai Pirate; Secret Scrolls-Parts I & II*
Kimura, Toshie (act): *Godzilla vs. the Smog Monster*
Kimursi (act): *King Solomon's Mines (1949)*
Kinberg, Jud(son) (wri): *Siege of the Saxons; Vampire Circus*
Kincaid, Aron (act, b. 1943, nee Norman Neale Williams III): *Creature of Destruction; Dr. Goldfoot and the Bikini Machine; The Ghost In the Invisible Bikini; Planet Earth; The Wasp Woman (1959)*
Kincaid, Tim (dir): *Breeders; Maximum Thrust; Mutant Hunt; Necropolis; The Occultist; Robot Holocaust*
Kincaid, Tim (wri): *Mutant Hunt; The Occultist; Robot Holocaust*
Kincaide, Mimi (act): *My Best Friend Is a Vampire*
Kincaide, Tina (act): *Mutant*
Kincannon, Kit (act): *Anguish*
Kind, Richard (act): *All-American Murder; A Bug's Life; Stargate; Tom and Jerry: The Movie; Vice Versa (1988)*
Kind, Sophie (act): *The Quatermass Conclusion*
Kindberg, Ann (wri): *The Toolbox Murders*
Kinder, Kurt Christopher (act): *Hider In the House*
Kinder, Sandra (act): *Twin Peaks: Fire Walk With Me*
Kinder, Stuart (dir): *The Adventures of a Football; Belinda's Dream; Black and White; Crime at the Mill; Jack and the Fairies; Japanese Magic; The Kiss of Clay; Marjory's Goldfish; Mirth and Mystery; Mizpah: or, Love's Sacrifice; The Opium Cigarettes; The Palace of Mystery; The Rejuvenation of Dan; Rip Van Winkle (1914); Sports In Toyland; The Stolen Airship Plans*
Kinder, Stuart (wri): *Japanese Magic; Marjory's Goldfish; Mirth and Mystery; The Opium Cigarettes; The Stolen Airship Plans*
Kindermann, Helmo (act): *I Aim at the Stars*
Kindlin, Kevin (act): *Heartstopper; The Majorettes; Revenge of the Living Zombies*
Kiner, Kevin (mus): *Freaked; Leprechaun; Nick Fury: Agent of Shield; Wing Commander*
King, Adrienne (act): *Friday the 13th (1980); Friday the 13th-Part 2*
King, Alan (act, b. 1927): *The Brave Little Toaster Goes to Mars; Cat's Eye; I, the Jury (1982)*
King, Aldine (act): *The Strange and Deadly Occurrence*
King, Andrea (act, b. 1915, nee Georgetta Barry): *The Beast With Five Fingers; Blackenstein; Buccaneer's Girl; Daddy's Gone A-Hunting; Dial 1119; House of the Black Death; Mr. Peabody and the Mermaid; Red Planet Mars; Ride the Pink Horse; Shadow of a Woman*
King, Anna (act): *Inn of the Damned*
King, Arthur (act): *The Hills Have Eyes*
King, Atlas (act): *The Incredibly Strange Creatures Who Stopped Living and Became Mixed-Up Zombies; The Thrill Killers*
King, B.B. (act, b. 1925): *Amazon Women On the Moon; Heart and Souls*
King, Barbara (act): *Night of the Sorcerers*
King, Bradley (wri): *The Mystery of Edwin Drood (1935); The Return of Peter Grimm (1926)*
King, Brenda (act): *Dawn of the Mummy*
King, Burton (dir): *The Man from Beyond*
King, Cammie (act): *Bambi*
King, Casey (act): *Superstition*
King, Charles (1940s act): *His Brother's Ghost; Three On a Ticket*
King, Charles (1980s act): *The Unnamable*
King, Claude (act): *Behind That Curtain; Behind the Mask (1932); Bella Donna (1923); Charlie Chan In London; Charlie Chan's Greatest Case; London After Midnight; Mr. Wu (1927); The Mysterious Dr. Fu Manchu; A Night of Mystery (1928)*
King, David (act): *The Golden Lady*
King, Dean (cin): *Just Before Dawn (1980)*
King, Debra (act): *Empire of Ash III*
King, Dennis (act, 1897-1971): *Between Two Worlds; The Miracle (1959)*
King, Diana (act): *Electric Eskimo; The Man In Grey*
King, Diane (act): *Fanatic (1965); Schizo (1977); Spellbound (1941); They Came from Beyond Space*
King, Don (act): *Devil's Advocate*
King, Donald (act): *The Wiz*
King, Donna (act): *Def Con 4*
King, Elly (act): *War of the Planets*
King, Evelyn (act): *The Checkered Flag*
King, (Dr.) Frank (wri): *Death of an Angel; The Ghoul (1933); What a Carve Up!*
King, George (dir, 1900-1966): *The Case of the Frightened Lady; The Chinese Bungalow; Crimes at the Dark House; The Crimes of Stephen Hawke; Deadlock (1931); The Demon Barber of Fleet Street; The Face at the Window (1939); Forbidden; The Man Without a Face; Maria Marten: or, The Murder In the Red Barn (1935); Matinee; Midnight (1931); Murder at the Inn; Sexton Blake and the Hooded Terror; The Shop at Sly Corner; Silver Top; Two for Danger*
King, Gregory Weston (wri): *Dance of the Dwarfs*
King, Harold (wri): *Red Alert*
King, Henry (dir, 1886-1982): *The Black Swan; Carousel; One Hour Before Dawn; 23 1/2 Hours Leave*
King, Ivy (act): *The Grip of Iron; The Mystery of Mr. Bernard Brown; The Yellow Claw*
King, Jack (act): *The Creeping Terror*
King, Jan (mus): *The Invisible Kid*
King, Janel (act): *Psycho from Texas*
King, Jeff (wri): *Lost In the Bermuda Triangle*
King, Jeffrey (act): *Mars Attacks!*
King, Jennifer (act): *Soylent Green*
King, Jill (act): *Mountaintop Motel Massacre*
King, Joel (cin): *Frightmare (1983); Just Before Dawn (1980)*
King, John (act): *Charlie Chan In Honolulu; The House of the Dead; Law of the Jungle; Mr. Moto Takes a Vacation*
King, Joseph/Joe (act): *Black Friday; Charlie Chan at the Wax Museum; The Face In the Fog (1922); Satan Met a Lady*
King, Karen (act): *The Toxic Avenger, Part II*
King, Kathleen (act): *Ssssss*
King, Ken (act): *Polyester*
King, Kevin (act): *Def Con 4*
King, Kip (act): *Westworld*
King, L.J. (act): *RoboCop*
King, Larry (act, b. 1933): *The Exorcist III; The Long Kiss Goodnight*
King, Leila (act): *Lieutenant Daring, RN, and the Water Rats*
King, Leslie (wri): *To Die For; To Die For II: Son of Darkness*
King, Lorelei (act): *The Saint*
King, Loretta (act): *Bride of the Monster*
King, Louis/Luis (dir): *Bulldog Drummond Comes Back; Bulldog Drummond In Africa; Bulldog Drummond's Revenge; Charlie Chan In Egypt; Dangerous Mission; Special Investigator*
King, Louise (act): *Octopussy*
King, Mabel (act): *Amazing Stories: The Movie V; Dead Men Don't Die; Ganja and Hess; The Wiz*
King, Manuel (act): *Darkest Africa*
King, Mark (act): *Caveman (1981)*
King, Martha Jo (act): *Secrets of the Phantom Caverns*
King, Matt (act): *Barracuda*
King, Matthew (act): *The Lair of the White Worm*
King, Meta (act): *Warlock*
King, Michael (act): *The Mutagen*
King, Pascal (act): *Gothic*
King, Paul Joseph (act): *The Walking Dead*
King, Peggy (act, b. 1931): *Abbott and Costello Meet the Mummy*
King, Perry (act): *City In Fear; The Clairvoyant (1985); Class of '84; The Possession of Joel Delaney; Slaughterhouse-Five; Switch (1991)*
King, Regina (act): *Mighty Joe Young (1998)*
King, Reina (act): *Maid to Order*
King, Rick (dir): *A Passion to Kill*
King, Robert (act): *The Projectionist*
King, Robert (wri): *Cutthroat Island; The Nest; Phantom of the Mall: Eric's Revenge*
King, Robert (L.) (wri): *The Nest; Now You See Him, Now You Don't*
King, Rufus (wri): *Murder by the Clock; Secret Beyond the Door*
King, Ruth (act): *He Who Gets Slapped*
King, Sherwood (wri): *The Lady from Shanghai*
King, Sidney (act): *The Gables Mystery*
King, Sonny H. (act): *Eraser*
King, Stephanie (act): *The Steel Trap*
King, Stephen (act, b. 1947): *Creepshow; Maximum Overdrive; Sleepwalkers; The Stand; Thinner*
King, Stephen (dir, b. 1947): *Maximum Overdrive*
King, Stephen (wri, b. 1947, a.k.a. Richard Bachman): *Apt Pupil; Carrie; Cat's Eye; Children of the Corn; Children of the Corn II: The Final Sacrifice; Children of the Corn III: Urban Sacrifice; Children of the Corn IV; Christine; Creepshow; Creepshow 2; Cujo; The Dark Half; The Dead Zone; Dolores Claiborne; Firestarter; Graveyard Shift (1990); The Green Mile; It (1990); The Lawnmower Man; The Mangler; Maximum Overdrive; Misery; Needful Things; The Night Flier; Pet Sematary; Pet Sematary Two; The Rage: Carrie 2; A Return to Salem's Lot; The Running Man (1987); The Shining; Sleepwalkers; Sometimes They Come Back; Sometimes They Come Back...Again; The Stand; Storm of the Century; Tales from the Darkside; Thinner; The Tommyknockers*
King, Sydni (act): *Cavegirl (1985)*
King, Walter Woolf (act): *House of Fear (1939)*
King, Wright (act): *Finian's Rainbow; Invasion of the Bee Girls; Planet of the Apes; The Spell*
King, Zalman (act): *Blue Sunshine; Endangered Species; Galaxy of Terror; Smile, Jenny, You're Dead; Some Call It Loving*
Kingdon, Edith (act): *After the Thin Man; When Knights Were Bold (1929)*
King-Hall, Magdalen (wri): *The Wicked Lady*
Kinghorn, Sally (act): *Monty Python and the Holy Grail*
Kingi, Henry (act): *The Ultimate Warrior*
Kingkade, Howard (act): *Mr. Destiny*
King-Kelly, John (act): *Ghost Ship (1952); Little Red Monkey*
Kingsbury, Brita (act): *Chilling (1981)*
Kingsbury, Jan (act): *Chilling (1981)*
Kingsford, Guy (act): *Counter-Espionage; The Lone Wolf In London; On the Threshold of Space*
Kingsford, Walter (act, 1882-1959): *Bulldog Drummond Escapes; The Corsican Brothers (1941); Ellery Queen and the Perfect Crime; The Invisible Ray; League of Frightened Men;*

The Lone Wolf In Paris; The Lone Wolf Takes a Chance; The Man In the Iron Mask (1939); Meet Nero Wolfe; The Mystery of Edwin Drood (1935); The Search for Bridey Murphy; Secrets of Scotland Yard; Trouble for Two; The Velvet Touch
Kingsley, Albert (act): *Condemned (1929)*
Kingsley, Arthur (act): *Esmeralda*
Kingsley, Ben (act, b. 1943): *Alice In Wonderland (1999); Crime and Punishment (1998); Fear Is the Key; Freddie as F.R.O.7; Nostradamus; Slipstream; Species; The Tale of Sweeney Todd; Without a Clue*
Kingsley, Charles (wri, 1819-1875): *The Water Babies; The Water Babiesr, The Little Chimney Sweep*
Kingsley, Danitza (act): *Amazons (1986); Jack's Back*
Kingsley, Don (act): *Star Crystal*
Kingsley, Dorothy (wri, 1908-1997): *Angels In the Outfield (1951); Green Mansions*
Kingsley, Edmund (act): *Freddie as F.R.O.7*
Kingsley, Florida (act): *Annabel Lee*
Kingsley, Roxane (act): *Hundra*
Kingsley, Taylor (act): *Star Crystal*
King-Smith, Dick (wri): *Babe; Babe: Pig In the Story*
Kingston, Claude (act): *The Curse of Frankenstein*
Kingston, Kiwi (act): *Evil of Frankenstein*
Kingston, Mark (act): *Hitler: The Last Ten Days; Sphinx (1981)*
Kingston, Phil (act): *Judge Dredd*
Kingston, Stuart (act): *Warriors of Virtue*
Kinkade, Amelia (act): *Night of the Demons 2; Night of the Demons 3*
Kinkade, Chris (act): *I Come In Peace*
Kinkade, Mimi (act): *Night of the Demons*
Kinkel, Dean (act): *I Come In Peace*
Kinlaw, Chuck (act): *The Exorcist III*
Kinmont, Kathleen (act, b. 1965): *Bride of Re-Animator; Dead of Night (1998); Halloween 4: The Return of Michael Myers; Phoenix the Warrior; Roller Blade Warriors: Taken by Force; Rush Week; Stormswept*
Kinn, Donald (act): *To All a Goodnight*
Kinnaman, Melanie (act): *Friday the 13th-Part V: A New Beginning*
Kinnear, Roy (act, 1934-1988): *The Adventures of Sherlock Holmes' Smarter Brother; Alice's Adventures In Wonderland (1972); The Bed-Sitting Room; The Boys; The Deadly* Affair; *Egghead's Robot; The Firechasers; Hammett; Hawk the Slayer; The Hound Of The Baskervilles (1978); The Informers; Just Ask for Diamond; The London Connection; Madame Sin; On a Clear Day You Can See Forever; One of Our Dinosaurs Is Missing; A Place to Go; The Pied Piper (1971); The Princess and the Goblin; The Princess and the Pea; The Return of the Musketeers; Royal Flash; Scrooge (1970); Taste the Blood of Dracula; The Three Musketeers (1974); Willy Wonka and the Chocolate Factory; The Zany Adventures of Robin Hood*
Kinnell, Murray (act): *The Black Camel; Charlie Chan In London; Charlie Chan In Paris; Charlie Chan's Courage; The Last Days of Pompeii (1935); Mad Love; The Menace (1932); Think Fast, Mr.Moto*
Kinner, Jackie (act): *Project X (1987)*
Kinney, Jack (dir): *The Adventures of Ichabod and Mr. Toad; 1,001 Arabian Nights (1959)*
Kinney, Kathy (act, b. 1953): *Arachnophobia*
Kinney, Terry (act): *The Body Snatchers; Don't Look Down*
Kinnoch, Ronald (dir): *The Secret Man*
Kino, Robert (act): *Ghost Warrior; Night of the Creeps; The Snow Creature*
Kinoy, Ernest (wri): *The Henderson Monster*
Kinsey, Lance (act): *The Silence of the Hams*
Kinskey, Leonid (act): *Espionage*
Kinski, Klaus (act, 1926-1991): *Android; Circus of Fear; Count Dracula; Crawlspace; Creature; Creature With the Blue Hand; Death Smiles On a Murderer; Five Golden Dragons; The Inn On the River; Jack the Ripper (1979); The Knight of the Dragon; The Little Drummer Girl; Marquis de Sade: Justine; The Million Eyes of Sumuru; Nosferatu, the Vampyre; Our Man In Marrakesh; Paroxysmus; Der Raecher; Schizoid (1980); Slaughter Hotel (1972); A Target for Killing; Timestalkers; Die Toten Augen von London; Traitor's Gate; Die Tur mit den Sieben Schlossern; The Vatican Affair; Venom (1982); Web of the Spider*
Kinski, Nastassia/Nastassja (act, b. 1960): *Cat People (1982); To the Devil a Daughter*
Kinsler, Jonathan (act): *Chinese Boxes*
Kinugasa, Teinosuke (act, dir & wri, 1896-1982): *Chusingura (1932)*
Kinyon, Bert (act): *Copycat*
Kip, Bob (act): *Dead of Night (1987)*
Kipling, Richard (act): *Calling Philo Vance; Voodoo Tiger*
Kipling, Rudyard (wri, 1865-1936): *The Adventures of Mowgli; The Airship Destroyer; Elephant Boy; The Fool; The Jungle Book (1942, 1967 & 1994); The Man Who Would Be King; The Second Jungle Book: Mowgli and Baloo*
Kipp, Bill (act): *Equalizer 2000*
Kippy, Dan (act): *Virus (1980)*
Kiralee (act): *Fortress*
Kiralfy, A. (dir): *The Arab's Curse*
Kirby, Bruce (act): *Lady In White*
Kirby, Bruno (act, b. 1949): *Flesh & Blood*
Kirby, David (act): *In the Palace of the King*
Kirby, Debbie (act): *Millennium*
Kirby, George (act, 1924-1995): *Oh Dad Poor Dad, Mamma's Hung You In the Closet and I'm Feelin' So Sad; The Shaggy D.A.; Who Killed John Savage?*
Kirby, Grace (act): *Hellraiser*
Kirby, Jack (act): *Captain America (1992)*
Kirby, John (act): *Dracula's Dog*
Kirby, Joyce (act): *The Fire Raisers; The Thirteenth Candle*
Kirby, Max (act): *Billion Dollar Brain*
Kirby, Steve (act): *The Curse of the Golem*
Kirchenbauer, Bill (act): *Full Moon High*
Kirchin, Basil (mus): *The Abominable Dr. Phibes; Assignment K; Freelance; The Mutations; Negatives; The Shuttered Room*
Kirchner, James (act): *Millennium; The Quilt of Hathor*
Kirchner, Kendra (act): *Android*
Kirck, Milow (act): *Never Say Never Again*
Kirek, Milos (act): *The Final Conflict*
Kirgo, Dinah (wri): *I Dream of Jeannie: Fifteen Years Later*
Kirgo, George (wri): *Angel On My Shoulder (1980); Brenda Starr (1976); The Kid With the Broken Halo; The Man In the Santa Claus Suit; Topper (1979); Voices*
Kirgo, Julie (wri): *I Dream of Jeannie: Fifteen Years Later*
Kirk, Alyson (act): *It Came Upon the Midnight Clear*
Kirk, Gary (act): *Impulse (1984)*
Kirk, Joann (act): *The Dark (1979)*
Kirk, Joe (act): *Abbott and Costello Go to Mars; Beyond a Reasonable Doubt*
Kirk, Linda (act): *The Destructors*
Kirk, Phyllis (act, b. 1930, nee Phyllis Kirkegaard): *City After Midnight; House of Wax*
Kirk, Robert (dir): *Destroyer*
Kirk, Stanley (act): *Making Mr. Right*
Kirk, Tommy (act, b. 1941): *The Absent-Minded Professor (1961); Attack of the 60 Foot Centerfold; Babes In Toyland (1961); Blood of Ghastly Horror; The Ghost In the Invisible Bikini; It's Alive (1968); Mars Needs Women; The Misadventures of Merlin Jones; The Monkey's Uncle; Moon Pilot; Mother Goose A Go-Go; Pajama Party; The Shaggy Dog (1959); The Snow Queen; Son of Flubber; Village of the Giants*
Kirk, Vic (act): *Dr. Dracula*
Kirkconnell, Clare (act): *Dead Heat*
Kirkconnell, Kristin (act): *Street Trash*
Kirke, Donald (act): *A Night for Crime*
Kirkegaard, Phyllis (act): see Kirk, Phyllis
Kirkham, Kathleen (act): *Tarzan of the Apes*
Kirkin, Corinne (act): *The Wizard of Gore*
Kirkland, Alexander (act): *Charlie Chan's Chance*
Kirkland, Billie (act): *Endangered Species*
Kirkland, Jimmy (act): *Secrets of the Phantom Caverns*
Kirkland, John (dir): *Curse of the Headless Horseman*
Kirkland, Sally (act, b. 1945): *Brave New World (1998); Double Jeopardy; Forever; The Haunted (1991); Paint It Black*
Kirkpatrick, Amy (act): *The Entity*
Kirkpatrick, Bruce (act): *The Dark Half; 12 Monkeys*
Kirkpatrick, Helen (act): *The Green Slime*
Kirkpatrick, Jess (act): *D.O.A. (1949); On the Threshold of Space; Space Master X-7*
Kirkpatrick, Karey (wri): *The Rescuers Down Under*
Kirkpatrick, Katherine (act): *Dr. Heckyl & Mr. Hype*
Kirkpatrick, Michael Stuart (act): *Blink*
Kirksey, Van (act): *Scream, Blacula, Scream*
Kirkwood, James (act): *Black Waters*
Kirner, Michael (act, b. 1944): [illegible]
[illegible]
Kirschner, David (wri): *The Pagemaster*
Kirschner, William (act): *The Corpse Grinders*
Kirschenbaum, Deborah (act): *Clarence*
Kirsh, Stan (act): *Highlander: The Gathering*
Kirshenbaum, Debra (act): *The Long Kiss Goodnight*
Kirshner, Mia (act): *The Crow: City of Angels; Love and Human Remains*
Kirshoff, Steve (cin): *Friday the 13th-Part 2; Zombie Island Massacre*
Kirst, Hans Helmut (wri, 1914-1989): *The Night of the Generals*
Kirstin, Kristina (act): *Hellhole*
Kirtland, Harden (act): *While Paris Sleeps*
Kirtman, Leonard (dir & wri): *Carnival of Blood*
Kirwin, Patrick (wri): *Dark Eyes of London; The Drum; Escape to Danger; On the Night of the Fire; Queer Cargo; The Twenty Questions Murder*
Kirwin, William (act): *Playgirl Killer*
Kis, Jeno (act): *Phantom of the Opera (1983)*
Kiser, Rodman (cin): *The Package*
Kiser, Terry (act): *Friday the 13th, Part VII-The New Blood; Looker; Mannequin Two: On the Move; The Offspring; Pet Shop; The Return of the Six Million Dollar Man and the Bionic Woman; Starflight: The Plane That Couldn't Land; Tammy and the T-Rex*
Kiser, Virginia (act): *The Babysitter; Space Raiders*
Kishi, Keiko (act): *Kwaidan*
Kishida, Kyoko (act): *Tanin No Kao*
Kishida, Mori (act): *Lake of Dracula*
Kishonti, Billy (act): *Funeral Home*
Kiskella, Kirk I. (act): *Death Valley*
Kisman, Lee (act): *Witchcraft (1988)*
Kiss, Cassia (act): *The Dolphin*
Kissinger, Charles (act): *Abby; Asylum of Satan; Grizzly; Three On a Meathook*
Kissinger, Miriam (wri): *Dangerous Money; The Trap*
Kissling, Van (act): *The Diabolical Invention*
Kitabchi, Kathy (act): *I Was a Zombie for the F.B.I.*
Kitaen, Tawny (act, b. 1961): *Witchboard*
Kitahara, Fumie (act): *Kwaidan*
Kitaj, Lem (act): *The Boy Who Turned Yellow*
Kitakubo, Hiroyuki (dir): *Robot Carnival; Roujin Z*
Kitamura, Eizo (act): *Body Snatcher from Hell*
Kitamura, Kazuo (act): *Kwaidan*
Kitay, David (act): *Always*
Kitazaki, Akira (cin): *Attack of the Monsters*
Kitazume, Kiroyuki (dir): *Robot Carnival*
Kitchen, Kathy (act): *The Mutations*
Kitchen, Lawrence (act): *Pimpernel Smith*
Kitchen, Michael (act): *Doomsday Gun; Dracula A.D. 1972; Goldeneye; Once the Killing Starts; Sleepwalker (1975)*
Kitchin, Laurence (wri): *The Bad Lord Byron*
Kite, barbara (act): *Praying Mantis*
Kite, Joyce (act): *Prom Night*
Kitley, Rhonda (act): *Secrets In the Attic*
Kitrosser, Martin (wri): *Friday the 13th-Part V: A New Beginning*
Kitt, Carl N. (wri): *Bog*
Kitt, Eartha (act, b. 1928): *Erik the Viking; Ernest Scared Stupid; The Pink Chiquitas*
Kittel, Bert (act): *Neighbors*
Kitzmiller, John (act, 1913-1965): *Cave of the Living Dead; Dr. No*
Kivett, Ron (wri): *Blood Waters of Dr. Z*
Kivilo, Alan (cin): *Heads*
Kizer, R.J. (dir): *Death Ring; Godzilla 1985; Hell Comes to Frogtown*
Kizziah, Rodney (act): *Ed Wood*
Kjelle, Mark (act): *Raiders of the Living Dead*
Kjellin, Alf (act, 1920-1988, a.k.a. Christopher Kent): *Hets*
Kjellin, Alf (dir, 1920-1988): *The Deadly Dream; Life, Liberty and Pursuit On the Planet of the Apes*
Klaff, Jack (act): *For Your Eyes Only*
Klaiber, Bill (act): *Tuck Everlasting*
Klan, Matt (act): *The Toxic Avenger*
Klan, William (act): *The Toxic Avenger*
Klangsuwan, Surasri (act): *Vice Versa (1988)*
Klar, G. Howard (act): *Day of the Dead*
Klar, Nick (act): *Neon City*
Klaus, Damian (dir & wri): *Futurekick*
Klass, Eugene (act): see Barry, Gene
Klauber, Gertan (act): *Carry On Spying; The Cold Room; Cry of the Banshee; The Hands of Orlac (1959); The Legend of Spider Forest; Octopussy; The Pied Piper (1971); The Seven-Per-Cent Solution; Top Secret! (1984)*
Klaus, Bert (act): *The Invisible Terror*
Klavun, Walter (act): *Fright (1957); Silent Night, Bloody Night*
[illegible] *The Children*
[illegible] Richard (act): *Ghost (1990)*
Klebroyd, Damon (act): *The Horror of Party Beach*
Klee, Richard (act): *Impact*
Kleeb, Helen (act): *The Curse of the Undead; Hush...Hush, Sweet Charlotte*
Kleeman, Fredi (act): *Os Deuses e os Mortos*
Kleemann, Gunter (act): *I Spit On Your Grave*
Kleg, Peter W. (act): *Making Contact*
Klein, Barbara (act): *Making Contact*
Klein, Ben (cin): *The Chinese Parrot*
Klein, Cameron (act): *Science Crazed*
Klein, Dani (act): *Trancers II: The Return of Jack Deth*
Klein, Dennis (act): *Freejack*
Klein, I.W. (act): *Magic*
Klein, Jaime (wri): *Pandemonium*
Klein, James (act): *The Punisher*
Klein, Mark (wri): *Endless Descent*
Klein, Nick (act): *The Phoenix and the Magic Carpet*
Klein, Peter (cin): *Moontrap*
Klein, Philip (wri): *The Black Camel; Chandu the Magician; Charlie Chan Carries On; Charlie Chan's Chance; Dante's Inferno (1935)*
Klein, Robert (1920s act): *Dante's Inferno (1924); The Temple of Venus*
Klein, Robert (act, b. 1942): *The Last Unicorn; Tales from the Darkside*
Klein, Robin (act): *Midnight Offerings; Once Bitten*
Klein, Rolando (dir): *Chac*
Klein, Sally (act): *Eyes of Fire*
Klein, T.E.D. (wri): *Trauma (1993)*
Klein, William (dir & wri): *Mister Freedom*
Klein, William R. (act): *Voodoo Tiger*
Kleinbach, Henry (act): see Brandon, Henry
Kleinberger, David (act): *The Wacky World of Dr. Morgus*
Kleiner, Harry (wri, b. 1916): *Fantastic Voyage; Salome (1953)*
Kleinholtz, Nick (act): *My Brother Has Bad Dreams*
Kleinman, Joel (act): *Making Contact*
Klein-Rogge, Rudolf (act, 1889-1955): *Doctor Mabuse; Metropolis (1926); Der Mude Tod; Die Nibelungen; Spione; Der Steinerne Reiter; Das Testament des Dr. Mabuse*
Kleiser, Randal (dir): *Flight of the Navigator; Honey, I Blew Up the Kid*
Klement, Otto (wri): *Fantastic Voyage*
Klemme, Brenda Lynn (act): *Cutting Class*
Klemperer, Werner (act, b. 1920): *Dark Intruder; Five Steps to Danger*
Klenhard, Walter (act): *Alfred Hitchcock Presents*
Klenhard, Walter (wri): *Buried Alive II*
Kless, Michael (act): *Pandemonium*
Kletter, Richard (dir): *The Android Affair*
Kletter, Richard (wri): *The Android Affair; The Man Who Fell to Earth (1987)*
Kleven, Max (act): *Billy the Kid vs. Dracula*
Kleven, Max (dir): *The Night Stalker (1987)*
Kleynen, Alex (act): *Howling II*
Kleynen, Ed (act): *Howling II*
Kliedermacher, Morty (act): *Flesh-Eating Mothers*
Klimov, Arkady (cin): *Planeta Bura*
Klimov, Elem (dir): *Rasputin (1985)*
Klimovsky, Leon (dir): *The Devil's Possessed; Dr. Jekyll y el Hombre Lobo; Ella y el Miedo; La Noche de Walpurgis; La Orgia Nocturna de los Vampiros; The Saga of the Draculas; Vengeance of the Zombies*
Klinckerfuss, Ingabor Katrine (act): see Verne, Kaaren
Kline, B. (wri): *Ernest Saves Christmas*
Kline, Ben(jamin H.) (cin): *Before I Hang; The Giant Claw; The Last of the Lone Wolf; The Man They Could Not Hang; The Man Who Turned to Stone; The Man With Nine Lives; Munster, Go Home!; The Night the World Exploded*
Kline, Frank (act): see Latimore, Frank
Kline, Gerald (act): *Eyes of Laura Mars*
Kline, James/Jim (act): *The China Syndrome; Cyborg 2087; The Destructors*
Kline, Kevin (act): *The Hunchback of Notre Dame (1996)*
Kline, Richard (H.) (cin, b. 1926): *All of Me; The Andromeda Strain; Battle for the Planet of the Apes; Body Heat; The Boston Strangler; Camelot; Chamber of Horrors (1966); The Fury; Hammersmith Is Out; Howard the Duck; King Kong (1976); Lovespell; My Stepmother Is an Alien; Soylent Green; Star Trek; The Terminal Man*
Kline, Robert A. (act): *Roller Blade Warriors: Taken by Force*
Kliner, Alex (act): *The Keeper*
Kliner, Gordon (act): *The Housekeeper*
Klinger, Brendan (act): *Something Wicked This Way Comes*
Klinger, James L. (cin): *Night Slaves*
Klinger, Judson (wri): *Endangered Species*
Klinger, Paul (act): *The Inn on Dartmoor*

Klinger, Werner (dir): *The Secret of the Black Trunk; The Testament of Dr. Mabuse (1960)*

Klingher, Michael (act): *Jekyll and Hyde...Together Again*

Klingler, Kevin (mus): *Earth Angel*

Klingler, Rebecca Jane (act): *Copycat*

Klisser, Evan J. (act): *Prey for the Hunter*

Klitsner, Stu (act): *Time After Time; Time Flyer*

Klopp, Julia (act): *Squirm*

Kloren, Georg (wri): *On Secret Service*

Klorer, John (wri): *Atoll K*

Klosinski, J. (act): *Wielka, Wielka I Najwieksza*

Kloss, Marlene (act): *The Cyclops*

Kloss, Thomas (cin): *Fear (1996)*

Klotz, Claude (wri): *Dracula, Pere et Fils*

Kloucowsky, I. (wri): *Atoll K*

Kloufetos, V. (act): *Blind Date*

Kluge, Alexander (dir & wri, b. 1932): *Artists In the Circus Tent/Perplexed*

Kluger, Garry (act): *Getting Lucky*

Kluger, Jeffrey (wri): *Apollo 13*

Klugman, Jack (act, b. 1922): *Cry Terror!; Poor Devil*

Klunis, Tom (act): *The Day the Fish Came Out*

Klushantsev, Pavel (dir & wri): *Planeta Bura*

Kluss, Igor (act): *The Savage Hunt of King Stakh*

Klutznick, Kim (act): *In the Company of Darkness*

Kluzak, Jan (act): *Valerie and Her Week of Wonders*

Klyn, Vince(nt) (act): *Cyborg (1989); Dollman; Knights; Nemesis*

Klys, Steven (act): *Starship Invasions*

Kmelnizki, Boris (act): *The Red Tent*

Knaggs, Skelton (act): *Bedlam; Blackbeard the Pirate; Dick Tracy Meets Gruesome; Dick Tracy vs. Cueball; Ghost Ship (1943); House of Dracula; The Invisible Man's Revenge; Isle of the Dead (1945); The Lodger (1944); Master Minds (1950); The Spy In Black; Terror by Night*

Knapp, Charles (act): *Twilight Zone*

Knapp, David (act): *Something Evil*

Knapp, Douglas (cin): *Dark Star*

Knapp, Evalyn (act): *The Lone Wolf Takes a Chance; One Frightened Night*

Knapp, Gregory (wri): *Virus (1980)*

Knapp, James (act): *The Mutagen*

Knapp, Robert (act): *Mesa of Lost Women; The Threat (1960)*

Knapp, Stanley (act): *Liquid Sky; Mother's Day*

Knapp, Terence (act): *Urge to Kill*

Knatchbull, Melissa (act): *Mission: Impossible; The Saint*

Kneale, Nigel (wri, b. 1922): *The Abominable Snowman of the Himalayas; First Men In the Moon (1964); Halloween III: Season of the Witch; Quatermass and the Pit; The Quatermass Conclusion; The Quatermass Experiment; Quatermass II; The Witches (1966)*

Kneale, Patricia (act): *Spell of Evil*

Knebel, Fletcher (wri, 1912-1993): *Seven Days In May*

Kneebone, Tom (act): *The Housekeeper*

Kneeland, Richard (act): *The Coming*

Kneeland, Ted (dir & wri): *Doctor?? Coppelius!!*

Knef(f), Hildegard(e) (act, b. 1925): *Alraune (1952); Hipnosis; Landru; Subway In the Sky; Svengali (1954); Uncharted Seas*

Knell, Catalaine (act): *Dr. Heckyl & Mr.Hype*

Knell, David (act): *The Devil and Max Devlin; Total Recall*

Knepper, Ron (act): *D.O.A. (1988); When the Bough Breaks; Wild Thing*

Kneubuhl, John (wri): *The Screaming Skull; Two On a Guillotine*

Knickerbocker, Bob (act): *Just Imagine*

Knickerbocker, Thomas (act): *Eve of Destruction*

Knickerbocker, Will(is) (act): *Barracuda; Jaws 3-D; The Night of the Claw; Popcorn*

Knie, Rolf (act): *Babes In Toyland (1986)*

Knieper, Jurgen (mus): *The Scarlet Letter (1972); Wings of Desire*

Kniest, Frank (act): *Return to Horror High*

Knight, Andy (act): *Battle for the Planet of the Apes*

Knight, Andy (dir): *Beauty and the Beast: The Enchanted Christmas*

Knight, Ashley (act): *Treasure Island (1976); Warlords of the Deep*

Knight, Barry (act): *The Secret of the Forest*

Knight, C. Pattinson (dir): *Escape to Justice*

Knight, Castleton (act, dir & wri): *Prelude*

Knight, Charlotte (wri): *20 Million Miles to Earth*

Knight, Damien (act): *The Redeemer*

Knight, David (act, b. 1927, nee David Mintz): *Across the Bridge; Clue of the Twisted Candle; The Devil's Agent; Eyewitness (1956); Lost; Nightmare (1963)*

Knight, David (1980s act): *Demons 2*

Knight, Don (act): *Swamp Thing; Trader Horn (1973)*

Knight, Edward (act): *The Magician (1973)*

Knight, Eric (act): *The Pack*

Knight, Esmond (act, b. 1906): *Black Narcissus; The Boy Who Turned Yellow; Crime Unlimited; Deadlock (1931); The Element of Crime; Halfway House; Hamlet (1948); Peeping Tom; Richard III (1955); The Ringer (1931); Robin and Marian; The Spy Who Came In from the Cold; The Steel Key; Uncle Silas; Yellow Dog*

Knight, Felix (act): *Babes In Toyland (1934)*

Knight, Fuzzy (act, 1901-1976): *Horror Island; Kelly of the Secret Service*

Knight, Harlan (act): *Jane Eyre (1921)*

Knight, Howard (act): *The Village of the Damned (1960)*

Knight, Jack (act): *Houdini (1998)*

Knight, James (act): *Love In the Welsh Hills; Maria Marten (1928); A Safe Affair; Sexton Blake and the Bearded Doctor; The Silver Greyhound (1919); The Splendid Coward*

Knight, Jim (act): *The Devil's Hand (1961)*

Knight, John (dir): *The Mail Van Murder; The Main Chance; Moment of Decision*

Knight, Keith (act): *My Bloody Valentine; Of Unknown Origin*

Knight, Kerry (act): *The Night Brings Charlie*

Knight, Lynda (act): *Octopussy*

Knight, Marcie (act): *Stanley*

Knight, Michael (E.) (act, b. 1959): *Date With an Angel; Hexed*

Knight, Nina (act): *Attack of the Mayan Mummy*

Knight, Norma (act): *The New House On the Left*

Knight, Patricia (act): *Shockproof*

Knight, Percy (act): *Sherlock Holmes (1922)*

Knight, Peter (mus): *Curse of the Crimson Altar*

Knight, Ronald (act): *Galaxina*

Knight, Rosalind (act): *The Lady Vanishes (1979)*

Knight, Sandra (act): *Blood Bath (1966); Frankenstein's Daughter (1958); The Terror (1963); Tower of London (1962)*

Knight, Shirley (act, b. 1936): *Beyond the Poseidon Adventure; Color of Night; The Couch; Dad, the Angel & Me; Diabolique (1996); The Sender; Shadow of a Doubt (1991); The Sweet Scent of Death; To Save a Child; The Uninvited (1996)*

Knight, Ted (act, 1923-1986): *Countdown; Psycho (1960)*

Knight, Tracy (wri): *Sharad of Atlantis*

Knight, Trenton (act): *Invisible Mom*

Knight, Tuesday (act): *The Babysitter (1995); A Nightmare On Elm Street 4: The Dream Master; Wes Craven's New Nightmare*

Knight, Victor (act): *Dr. Jekyll and Ms. Hyde; Happy Birthday to Me; Scanners; Terror Train*

Knight, Vivienne (wri): *Floods of Fear; Girl In the Headlines*

Knight, Wayne (act, b. 1955): *The Brave Little Toaster Goes to Mars; Dead Again; Jurassic Park;*
Space Jam

Knight, William (act): *The Lost Platoon*

Knoblock, Edward (wri): *Chu Chin Chow (1934); Kismet (1914, 1930 & 1944)*

Knoll, Robyn (act): *Vampire's Kiss*

Knopf, Christopher (wri): *A Cold Night's Death; 20 Million Miles to Earth*

Knopfler, Mark (mus): *The Princess Bride*

Knorr, Freda/Frieda (act): *The Haunting; Kadoyng*

Knoth, Fred (cin): *The Land Unknown*

Knott Limited (cin): *Angel On My Shoulder (1980); Dead and Buried; Halloween With the Addams Family*

Knott, Andy (act): *The Housekeeper*

Knott, Frederick (wri): *Dial M for Murder (1954 & 1981); The Last Page; A Perfect Murder*

Knott, Robbie (cin): *Miracle Mile; Pandora's Clock*

Knotts, Don (act, b. 1924): *The Ghost and Mr. Chicken; I Love a Mystery (1966); The Incredible Mr. Limpet; Pinocchio and the Emperor of the Night; Pleasantville; The Private Eyes (1980); The Reluctant Astronaut*

Knotts, John (act): *Praying Mantis*

Knower, Rosemary (act): *Serial Mom*

Knowland, Nic (cin): *Recluse*

Knowles, Bernard (act, b. 1900): *The Perfect Woman*

Knowles, Bernard (cin, b. 1900): *Gaslight (1940); King of the Damned; Sabotage; The Saint's Vacation; The Secret Agent (1936); The 39 Steps (1935)*

Knowles, Bernard (dir, b. 1900): *Barbados Quest; Frozen Alive; The Perfect Woman; A Place of One's Own; Spaceflight IC-1*

Knowles, Bernard (wri, b. 1900): *The Perfect Woman*

Knowles, Cyril (J.) (cin): *King Solomon's Mines (1937); Sodom and Gomorrah*

Knowles, Michael (act): *The Flesh and Blood Show; Vampire's Kiss*

Knowles, Patric (act, b. 1911, nee Reginald Knowles): *The Adventures of Robin Hood; Another Thin Man; Arnold; Crazy House (1943); Dream Girl; Eyes of the Underworld; Frankenstein Meets the Wolf Man; From the Earth to the Moon; Jamaica Run; Mutiny; The Mystery of Marie Roget; O.S.S.; The Strange Case of Dr. Rx; Tarzan's Savage Fury; Terror In the Wax Museum; Torchy Blane In Chinatown; Who Done It? (1942); The Wolf Man (1941); World for Ransom*

Knowles, Patrick (act): *The Brown Wallet*

Knowles, Paula (act): *The Initiation*

Knowles, Reginald (act): see Knowles, Patric

Knowlton, Peter (cin): *The Presence*

Knox, Alexander (act, 1907-1995): *Alias John Preston; Chase a Crooked Shadow; Crack In the World; The Damned; The Gaunt Stranger; Gorky Park; Hidden Fear; Holocaust 2000; Intent to Kill; Modesty Blaise; None Shall Escape; The Psychopath (1965); Puppet On a Chain; The Share Out; Skullduggery; The Son of Dr. Jekyll; The Two-Headed Spy; Woman of Straw; You Only Live Twice*

Knox, Doris (act): *The Servant*

Knox, Elyse (act, b. 1917): *The Mummy's Tomb*

Knox, Jayme (act): *Hideaway*

Knox, Ken (act): *Beyond the Time Barrier; The Giant Gila Monster*

Knox, Mark (mus): *Primal Scream*

Knox, Matthew (act): *Rattlers*

Knox, Mickey (act): *The Accused (1948); La Decima Vittima; Ghoulies II; Roger Corman's 'Frankenstein Unbound'*

Knox, Mona (act): *Escape from Terror; Jalopy*

Knox, Richard Alan (act): *Ritual of Evil*

Knox, Robert (act): *Scream Bloody Murder*

Knox, Teddy (act): *Alf's Button Afloat; Life Is a Circus*

Knox, Terence (act): *Children of the Corn II: The Final Sacrifice; City Killer; Distortions; Forever; Joe & the Colonel; Lies; Snow Kill; The Spy Within*

Knox, Terry (act): *The Offspring*

Knudsen, Peggy (act, 1923-1980): *Betrayed Women; The Big Sleep (1946); Half-Past Midnight*

Knudsen, Poul (wri): *Vredens Dag*

Knudson, Barbara (act): *Son of Ali Baba*

Knudson, Brian (act): *Project Vampire*

Ko, Hideo (act): *Body Snatcher from Hell*

Koba, Alex (act): *Flowers In the Attic*

Kobayashi, Eiji (act): *The Toxic Avenger, Part II*

Kobayashi, K. (wri): *Body Snatcher from Hell*

Kobayashi, Kaoru (act): *Twilight of the Cockroaches*

Kobayashi, Katsuya (act): *The Crazy Family*

Kobayashi, Keiju (act): *Godzilla 1985; The Submersion of Japan*

Kobayashi, Kenji (act): *Catastrophe 1999: The Prophecies of Nostradamus*

Kobayashi, Masaki (dir, b. 1916): *Harakiri; Inn of Evil; Kwaidan*

Kobayashi, Mieko (act): *Ghost Warrior*

Kobayashi, Nenji (act): *Virus (1980)*

Kobayashi, Tsuruko (act): *Varan the Unbelievable*

Kobayashi, Yokiko (act): *Destroy All Monsters; The Vampire Doll; Yog-Monster from Space*

Kobayashi, Yoshinori (wri): *The Crazy Family*

Kobayashi, Yuji (act): *The Toxic Avenger, Part II*

Kobe, Gail (act): *The Legend of Lizzie Borden*

Kober, Jeff (act): *Alien Nation; The Baby Doll Murders; The First Power; Tank Girl*

Kober, Marta (act): *Friday the 13th-Part 2; Neon Maniacs; School Spirit*

Koberidze, Otar (act): *The Red Tent*

Kobi, Michi (act): *12 to the Moon*

Kobiela, Bogumil (act): *Rekopis Znaleziony w Saragossie*

Kobin, Chris (act): *The Alien Within*

Kobler, Flip (wri): *Beauty and the Beast: The Enchanted Christmas*

Koblik, Allison (act): *Making Contact*

Kobori, Akio (act): *Rodan, the Flying Monster*

Kobylt, Deborah Zara (act): *Wes Craven's New Nightmare*

Koc, Laka (act): *Rapunzel Let Down Your Hair*

Koch, Carl (wri): *The Night of the Full Moon*

Koch, Howard (wri, 1902-1995, a.k.a. Peter Howard): *The Intimate Stranger; The Thirteenth Letter; Three Strangers*

Koch, Howard W. (dir, b. 1916): *Frankenstein (1970); The Girl In Black Stockings; Jungle Heat; Shield for Murder*

Koch, Jacqueline (act): *Point of No Return*

Koch, Marianne (act): *Death Drums Along the River; The Devil's Agent; Frozen Alive; The Monster of London (1964)*

Koch, Pete (act): *Adventures In Dinosaur City*

Koch, Willard (act): *Monte Cristo*

Kochi, Momoko (act): *Godzilla vs. Destroyer; Gojira; The Mysterians*

Kochoff, Kristina (act): *Nothing But Trouble*

Koehler, David (cun): *She Demons*

Koenekamp, Fred (J.) (cin): *The Adventures of Buckaroo Banzai; Alice In Wonderland (1985); The Amityville Horror; City Killer; Doc Savage, the Man of Bronze; Embryo; One Spy Too Many; Rage; The Return of the Man from U.N.C.L.E.; The Swarm; The Towering Inferno*

Koenig, Danielle (act): *The Craft*

Koenig, Kip (wri): *Bio-Dome*

Koenig, Laird (wri): *The Little Girl Who Lives Down the Lane*

Koenig, Raymond (wri): *Blacula; Scream, Blacula, Scream*

Koenig, Walter (act, b. 1936): *Moontrap; The Questor Tapes; Star Trek; Star Trek II: The Wrath of Khan; Star Trek III: The Search for Spock; Star Trek IV: The Voyage Home; Star Trek V: The Final Frontier; Star Trek VI: The Undiscovered Country; Star Trek: Generations*

Koepp, David (wri): *Apartment Zero; Death Becomes Her; Jurassic Park; The Lost World: Jurassic Park; Mission: Impossible; The Shadow (1994)*

Koering, Rene (mus): *Traitement de Choc*

Koff, Charles (mus): *Captive Women*

Koford, Helen (act): see Moore, Terry

Kogan, Ephraim (wri): *Faces In the Dark*

Kogan, Milt (act): *Dr. Black Mr. Hyde; Wavelength*

Kogan, Victoria (act): *Oh Heavenly Dog*

Kogen, Arnie (wri): *Birds Do It*

Kohane, Lisa (act): *The Possession of Joel Delaney*

Kohl, Danielle (act): *Vice Versa (1988)*

Kohl, Eric (act): *Revenge of the Teenage Vixens from Outer Space*

Kohlhaase, W. (wri): *Milczaca Gwiazda*

Kohler, Fred (act): *Deluge; The Eleventh Hour (1923); Loves of Carmen (1927)*

Kohler Jr., Fred (act): *The Baron of Arizona; Two Lost Worlds*

Kohler, Jon (act): *Freejack*

Kohler, Manfred (R.) (wri): *Die Schlangengrube und das Pendel; A Target for Killing*

Kohlman, Louis Freddie (act): *Angel Heart*

Kohlmar, Lee (act): *Death from a Distance; Son of Kong*

Kohn, Joan (act): *Chain Reaction (1996); The Fugitive (1993)*

Kohn, John (wri): *The Collector; Siege of the Saxons*

Kohnami, Fumio (wri): *The Crazy Family*

Kohne, Bill (act): *In Self Defense*

Kohner, Eric (act): *Sex and the Single Alien*

Kohner, F. (wri): *Atoll K*

Kohner, Frederick (wri, b. 1905): *The Lady and the Monster*

Kohner, Pancho (dir & wri): *Mr. Sycamore*

Kohnert, Mary (act): *Beyond the Door III*

Kohout, Eduard (act): *Baron Prasil*

Kohout, Jara (act): *The Projectionist*

Kohoutova, Kristyna (act): *Alice*

Kohut, Walter (act): *The Glass Cell*

Koitzsch-Koltzack, Erich (act): *No Mercy, No Future*

Koizumi, Hajime (cin): *Battle In Outer Space; Dogora, the Space Monster; Ghidrah, the Three-Headed Monster; Godzilla vs.Mothra; The H-Man; Mothra; The Mysterians*

Koizumi, Hiroshi (act): *Atragon; Dogora, the Space Monster; Ghidrah, the Three-Headed Monster; Godzilla 1985; Godzilla Raids Again; Godzilla vs. Mothra; Godzilla vs. the Bionic Monster*

Kojucharov, Vasil (mus): *The Devil's Wedding Night*

Kokernot, Larissa (act): *Fargo*

Koko (act): *For Your Eyes Only*

Kokodi, Lily (act): *The Enchantress*

Kokotakis, Nick (act): *The Nutty Professor (1996)*

Kolarova, Anna Maria (act): *Howling II*

Kolb, Clarence (act, 1875-1964): *After the Thin Man; Beware, Spooks!; The Falcon In Danger; Hellzapoppin; Man of a Thousand Faces; Michael Shayne, Private Detective*

Kolb, Kenneth (wri): *The 7th Voyage of Sinbad*

Kolden, Scott (act): *Charley and the Angel; The Day Time Ended*
Kolima, Lee (act): *Dimension 5*
Kolker, Henry (act, 1874-1947): *Blackie's Redemption; The Black Room; Bluebeard (1944); Charlie Chan In Paris; The Florentine Dagger; The Ghost Walks; The Invisible Menace; The Last Days of Pompeii (1935); Mad Love; Marie Antoinette (1938)*
Kolldehoff, Heinhard (act): *Confess, Dr. Corda*
Kollins, Nikki (act): *Don't Go In the House*
Kolman, Allan (act): *Seven*
Kologie, Ron (act): *Iced*
Kolstad, Lasse (act): *The Island at the Top of the World*
Komack, Jimmie (act): *Damn Yankees*
Komai, Tetsu (act): *Bulldog Drummond (1929); Four Frightened People; Island of Lost Souls; Mr. Moto Takes a Chance; The Mysterious Dr. Fu Manchu; The Night Walker; The Return of Dr. Fu Manchu*
Koman, Vanessa (act): *Little Miss Magic*
Komarov, Sergei (act): *Luch Smerti*
Komatsu, Sakyo (wri): *Virus (1980)*
Komatsubara, Kazuo (cin): *Warriors of the Wind*
Komeda(-Trzcinski), Krzysztof/Christopher (mus, 1932-1969): *Bariera; Cul-de-Sac; The Fearless Vampire Killers or: Pardon Me, But Your Teeth Are In My Neck; Rosemary's Baby*
Kominowski, Bogdan (act): *A View to a Kill*
Komorowska, Liliana (act): *Scanners III: The Takeover; Screamers (1996)*
Konchalovsky, Andrei (dir & wri): *The Odyssey; Runaway Train*
Kondazian, Karen (act): *Mortal Sins*
Kondo, Yutaka (act): *The Toxic Avenger, Part II*
Kondrashoff, Kim (act): *It (1990); The Little Match Girl (1987); Quarantine; Timecop*
Kong, Daniel (act): *Surf Nazis Must Die*
Kong, Jackie (dir): *The Being; Blood Diner*
Kong, Jackie (wri): *The Being*
Kong, Queen (act): *Slashdance*
Kongos, John (mus): *Blind Date*
Konigsberg, Allen Stewart (act, dir, mus & wri): see Allen, Woody
Konner, Lawrence (wri): *The Jewel of the Nile; Sometimes They Come Back; Star Trek VI: The Undiscovered Country; Superman IV: The Quest for Peace*
Kono, Aritake (act): *Tora No O O Fumu Otokotachi*
Konopka, Magda (act): *Satanik; When Dinosaurs Ruled the Earth*
Konrad, Dorothy (act): *Futureworld*
Konrad, Volker (act): *Making Contact*
Konstam, Anna (act): *The Midas Touch; They Drive by Night; Too Dangerous to Live*
Konstam, Phyllis (act): *Murder*
Konstantin, madame Leopoldine (act): *Notorious (1946)*
Konstantopoulou, Katina (act): see Paxinou, Katina
Konvitz, Jeffrey (wri): *The Sentinel; Silent Night, Bloody Night*
Konwicki, Tadeusz (wri): *Faraon; Matka Joanna od Aniolow*
Konya Jr., Charles Joseph (act): *Cat People (1982)*
Koock, Guich (act): *Piranha (1978)*
Koons, Edmund (cin): *Modern Problems*
Koons, Robert (act): *The Reflecting Skin*
Koontz, Dean R. (wri, b. 1945): *Dean R. Koontz' Whispers; Demon Seed; Hideaway; Intensity; Phantoms; The Servants of Twilight; Watchers; Watchers II; Watchers III; Watchers Reborn*
Koop, C. Everett (act): *The Exorcist III*
Kooris, Richard (cin): *The Texas Chainsaw Massacre 2*
Kopache, Thomas (act): *Star Trek: Generations; Strange Invaders*
Kopcha, Mike (act): *Simon, King of the Witches*
Kopecky, Milos (act): *Baron Prasil; The Man of the First Century*
Kopell, Bernie (act, b. 1933): *The Loved One*
Kopelow, Michael (act): *The People Under the Stairs*
Kopins, Karen (act): *Creator; Jake Speed; Once Bitten*
Kopit, Arthur (wri): *Oh Dad Poor Dad, Mamma's Hung You In the Closet and I'm Feelin' So Sad; The Phantom of the Opera (1990); Roswell*
Kopp, Frederick (mus): *The Creeping Terror*
Kopp, Lawrence (act): *Alien Nation*
Kopp, Lee (act): *Copycat*
Kopp, Pierre (act): *The Creeping Terror*
Kopp, Rudolph G. (mus): *Calling Bulldog Drummond; Mystery Street*
Koppel, Laura (act): *Poltergeist III*
Koppel, Lynn (act): *Poltergeist III*

Kopriva, Petr (act): *Valerie and Her Week of Wonders*
Kopsa, Michael (act): *The Mutagen*
Kopvc, Frank (act): *Nightmare On the 13th Floor; Total Recall*
Kor, Dobi (act): *La Captive du Desert*
Kora, Belma (act): *Boarding House*
Korangy, Amir (act): *Batman (1989)*
Korb, Michael (act): *2000 Maniacs*
Korbin, Gaetana (act): *Hideaway*
Korcelli, Jacek (cin): *Wielka, Wielka I Najwieksza*
Korda, (Sir) Alexander (dir, 1893-1956): *The Private Life of Don Juan; The Private Life of Helen of Troy*
Korda, Zoltan (dir, 1895-1961): *The Drum; Elephant Boy; The Jungle Book (1942); A Woman's Vengeance*
Korelin, George (act): *The Demon (1981)*
Koren, Avi (cin): *The Mummy Lives*
Koren, William (act): *The Amphibian Man*
Koetsky, Rachel (wri): *The Pebble and the Penguin*
Korff, Arnold (act): *Schloss Vogelod*
Korieniev, K. (act): *The Amphibian Man*
Korkes, Jon (act): *The Day of the Dolphin; Jaws of Satan; Syngenor*
Korman, Harvey (act, b. 1927): *Alice In Wonderland (1985); Americathon; Dracula: Dead and Loving It; The Flintstones; Herbie Goes Bananas; The Invisible Woman (1983);The Last of the Secret Agents?; Munchies*
Korn, Iris (act): *Blood Pen; Tarantulas: The Deadly Cargo*
Korn, Sandi (act): *Exit to Eden*
Kornacki, Steve (act): *Tainted Image*
Korne, Robert (act): *The Disappearance*
Kornel, Helena (act): *L'Annee Derniere a Marienbad*
Korner, Lothar (act): *Der Student von Prag (1913)*
Kornfield, Randy (wri): *Bloodknot*
Korngold, Erich Wolfgang (mus, 1897-1957): *The Adventures of Robin Hood; Between Two Worlds; Devotion; Green Pastures; A Midsummer Night's Dream (1935)*
Kornman, Mary (act): *Queen of the Jungle*
Kornmann, Tony (cin): *The Hunchback of Notre Dame (1923)*
Kornstadt, Grethe Gerda (act): see Parlo, Dita
Korobkin, Len (wri): *Mad Monster Party*
Koroku, Reijiro (mus): *Godzilla 1985*
Korolenko, Agnes (act): *The Ghost Train (1927)*
Koromzay, Alix (act): *Ghost In the Machine; Mimic*
Korotkevich, Vladimir (wri): *The Savage Hunt of King Stakh*
Korrado, George (act): *Seven Deaths In the Cat's Eye*
Korsmo, Charlie (act): *Dick Tracy (1990)*
Kortman, Robert (act): *Bulldog Drummond Strikes Back (1934); The Clutching Hand*
Kortner, Fritz (act, 1892-1970): *Berlin Express; The Brasher Doubloon; Die Buchse der Pandora; Chu Chin Chow (1934); Dr. Hallers; Orlacs Haende; Schatten, eine Nachtliche Halluzination; Somewhere In the Night; The Strange Death of Adolf Hitler; The Vicious Circle (1957)*
Kortner, Fritz (wri, 1892-1970): *The Strange Death of Adolf Hitler*
Korty, John (cin, b. 1936): *The Ewok Adventure*
Korty, John (dir, b. 1936): *The Ewok Adventure; The Haunting Passion; Ms. Scrooge; The People; Twice Upon a Time*
Koruba, Matt (act): *The Incredible Genie*
Korvin, Charles (act, nee Geza Korvin Karpathi): *Berlin Express; Enter Arsene Lupin; Tarzan's Savage Fury; Temptation (1946); Zorro, the Avenger*
Korvin, George (act): *Enter Arsene Lupin*
Kory, Richard (act): *Vampire at Midnight*
Kosa Jr., Emil (cin): *Fantastic Voyage; Five Weeks In a Balloon; Journey to the Center of the Earth (1959); The Lost World (1960); Our Man Flint; Way...Way Out*
Kosala, Joseph/Joe (act): *The Fugitive (1993); Primal Fear*
Kosana, George (act): *Night of the Living Dead (1968)*
Koschka, Julia (act): *Alraune (1952)*
Koscina, Sylva (act, 1933-1994): *Baraka X-77; Deadlier Than the Male; Ercole e la Regina di Lidia; Giulietta degli Spiriti; Hercules (1957); Hot Enough for June; House* [illegible] *Marquis de Sade: Justine; Penetration; Siege of Syracuse; Tempi Duri per i Vampiri*
Koseki, Yuji (mus): *Mothra*

Koski, Maria (act): *The Saga of the Draculas*
Kosleck, Martin (act, b. 1907, nee Nicolai Yoshkin): *Agent for H.A.R.M.; Calling Philo Vance; The Flesh Eaters; Foreign Correspondent; The Frozen Ghost; House of Horrors (1946); Just Before Dawn (1946); The Mad Doctor; The Mummy's Curse; Nazi Agent; Nick Carter, Master Detective; Pursuit to Algiers; Secrets of Scotland Yard; She-Wolf of London; Something Wild; The Spider (1945); 36 Hours (1965); The Wife of Monte Cristo*
Koslo, Elly (act): *Project: Nightmare*
Koslo, Paul (act): *The Omega Man; Project: Shadowchaser; Robot Jox; Solar Crisis; Tomorrow Never Comes; Vanishing Point (1971); Xtro II: The Second Encounter*
Kosloff, Theodore (act, 1881-1956): *Adam's Rib*
Kosma, Joseph (mus, 1905-1969): *The Green Glove; Le Port du Desir; La Poupee; Le Testament du Dr. Cordelier; Torticola Contre Frankensberg*
Kosma, Peter (act): *Making Contact*
Kosow, Sophia (act): see Sidney, Sylvia
Koss, Alan (act): *Fire and Ice; Wavelength*
Koss, Jo (act): *Haunted Honeymoon (1986)*
Kossak, Andreas (cin): *The Howling: New Moon Rising*
Kosslyn, Jack (act): *The Amazing Colossal Man; Attack of the Puppet People; The Magic Sword (1962); Play Misty for Me; The Spider (1958); War of the Colossal Beast*
Kossoff, David (act, b. 1919): *The Angel Who Pawned Her Harp; The Bespoke Overcoat; House of Secrets; The House of the Seven Hawks; Jet Storm; A Kid for Two Farthings; The London Connection; The Mouse On the Moon; The Mouse That Roared; 1984 (1955); Ring of Spies; Svengali (1954); The Two Faces of Dr. Jekyll; Who Done It? (1956)*
Kossoff, Simon (cin): *The Scarlet Pimpernel (1999)*
Kosstrin, Bobbie-Ellyne (act): *Barracuda*
Kostal, Irwin (mus, b. 1915): *The Blue Bird (1976); Chitty Chitty Bang Bang*
Koster, Henry (dir, 1905-1988, nee Hermann Kosterlitz): *The Bishop's Wife; Harvey; The Luck of the Irish; My Cousin Rachel; No Highway In the Sky*
Koster, Nat (act): *Treasure of the Petrified Forest*
Koster, Nicholas (act): *My Cousin Rachel*
Kosterlitz, Hermann (dir): see Koster, Henry
Kosti, Maria (act): *Night of the Sorcerers*
Kostritchkin, Andrei (act): *Shinel (1926)*
Kosugi, Sho (act): *Pray for Death*
Kosugi, Yoshio (act): *Mothra; The Mysterians*
Kotani, Tom (dir): *The Bermuda Depths; The Ivory Ape; The Last Dinosaur*
Kotcheff, Ted (dir, b. 1931): *Who Is Killing the Great Chefs of Europe?*
Koteas, Elias (act): *Apt Pupil; Crash (1996); Cyborg 2: Glass Shadow; Fallen; Lost Souls (1999); The Prophecy (1995); Teenage Mutant Ninja Turtles*
Kotero, Appolonia (act): *Black Magic Woman*
Kotetsu, Nao (act): *The Toxic Avenger, Part II*
Koth, Doug(las) (act): *Critters; Sorority Girls and the Creature from Hell*
Kothawala, Jerbanu (wri): *Emerald of the East*
Kotkin, Edward (act): *Neighbors*
Kotochnev, V. (wri): *Ilya Mourometz*
Kotonski, Wlodzimierz (mus): *Labirynt; Niebezpieczenstwo*
Kotowski, Jerzy (dir): *In an Old Manor House; Niebezpieczenstwo*
Kotsonaros, George (act): *The Private Life of Helen of Troy; The Wizard*
Kotto, Yaphet (act, b. 1937): *Alien; Freddy's Dead: The Final Nightmare; In Self Defense; Live and Let Die; The Puppet Masters; The Running Man (1987); Sharks' Treasure; Terminal Entry; Warning Sign; A Whisper to a Scream*
Kotz, Adam (act): *Without a Clue*
Kouchalakos, Tom (act): *Cocoon: The Return*
Kouerini, E. (act): *Blind Date*
Kouguell, Suzan (wri): *The Suicide Club (1988)*
Koulianou, Vicky (act): *The Enchantress*
Koulolia, Vasco (act): *A Touch of the Other*
Koumani, Maya (act): *The Diplomatic Corpse; Hidden Homicide; The Price of Silence; Son of Robin Hood, Undercover Girl (1958); West of Suez*
Koundouros, Nikos (dir, b. 1929): *Dracos*
Kounelaki, Miranda (act): *Atlas*
Kounnas, Mark (act): *Mad Max Beyond Thunderdome*
Kouprine, Alexander (wri): *La Sorciere*
Kourant, Kurt (cin): *Die Frau im Mond*
Kourkoulos, Alkis (act): *The Enchantress*

Kousi, Katherine (act): *Encino Woman*
Koustik, Art (act): *Attack of the Killer Tomatoes*
Kouzouyan, Jono (act): *Trick or Treats*
Kovac, Roland (mus): *Jonathan*
Kovacic, Chuck (act): *Repossessed*
Kovack, Nancy (act, b. 1940): *Diary of a Madman; Jason and the Argonauts; Marooned; The Silencers (1966); Tarzan and the Valley of Gold*
Kovack, Sandy (act): *The Pit (1983)*
Kovacs, Bela (act): *To Catch a Thief*
Kovacs, Danny (act): *Copycat; Killer Klowns from Outer Space*
Kovacs, Ernie (act, 1919-1962): *Bell, Book and Candle*
Kovacs, Geza (act): *The Dead Zone; Return to the Lost World; Scanners*
Kovacs, Laszlo (act, b. 1933): *The Nasty Rabbit*
Kovacs, Laszlo (cin, b. 1933): *Copycat; Ghostbusters; Hell's Bloody Devils; Kiss Me Quick; The Legend of the Lone Ranger; Mantis In Lace; Multiplicity; The Nasty Rabbit; Psych-Out; Reflection of Fear; Targets*
Kovacs, Leslie (cin): *Blood of Dracula's Castle; A Man Called Dagger*
Kovacs, Pal (act): *Phantom of the Opera (1983)*
Kovacs, Tom (act): *My Bloody Valentine*
Kove, Edna (act): *Murder Reported*
Kove, Kenneth (act): *The Bank Messenger Mystery; Crime On the Hill; The Crimson Candle; The Man at Six; Murder*
Kove, Martin (act): *Blood Tide; Cry for the Strangers; Death Race 2000; Final Equinox;Future Shock; Judge and Jury; The Last House On the Left; Project: Shadowchaser; Savages; White Light*
Kove, Vivienne (act): *To All a Goodnight*
Kowal, Mitchell (act): *Violated*
Kowalchik, Sergei M. (act): *The Final Countdown*
Kowalski, Bernard L. (dir, b. 1933): *Attack of the Giant Leeches; Black Noon; Krakatoa-East of Java; Night of the Blood-Beast; Sssssss; The Woman Hunter*
Kowalski, Frank (act): *Sssssss*
Kowalski, Waclaw (act): *O Dwoch Takich Co Ukradli Ksiezyc*
Kowanko, Pete (act): *Amityville 3-D; Date With an Angel; The Gifted One; Starcrossed; To Save a Child*
Koyama, Mami (act): *Akira*
Koyama, Shigeru (act): *Inn of Evil*
Kozachik, Pete (cin): *James and the Giant Peach*
Kozak, Harley Jane (act): *The Android Affair; Arachnophobia; Emma's Wish*
Kozak, Heidi (act): *Society*
Kozak, John (act): *Millennium*
Kozintsev, Grigori (dir, 1905-1973): *Korol Lir; Hamlet (1964); Shinel (1926)*
Kozintsev, Grigori (wri, 1905-1973): *Korol Lir*
Kozlov, Sergei (cin): *The Odyssey*
Kozlowski, Linda (act): *The Neighbor; Village of the Damned (1995)*
Kozoll, Michael (wri): *Demon and the Mummy; Vampire (1979)*
Kozyr, Alexander (dir): *The Heavens Call*
Krabbe, Jeroen (act, b. 1944): *Code Name: Dancer; The Fourth Man; The Fugitive (1993); The Living Daylights; The Odyssey; The Punisher; Robin Hood (1991); World War III*
Krabbe, Tim (wri): *The Vanishing (1988 & 1993)*
Kracht, Claudius (act): *The Glass Cell*
Krafftowna, Barbara (act): *Rekopis Znaleziony w Saragossie*
Kraft, Evelin/Evelyne (act): *Goliathon; Superwheels*
Kraft, Scott (act): *Enemy Mine; The Return of the Six Million Dollar Man and the Bionic Woman*
Kraft, Tenna (act): *Blade af Satans Bog*
Kraft, William (mus): *Avalanche; Fire and Ice; Psychic Killer*
Kraines, Carl (act): *The Gate*
Krainz, Dee (act): *Ghosts Can't Do It*
Krakowski, Jane (act): *Fatal Attraction*
Kraly, Hans (wri, 1885-1950): *Carmen (1918)*
Kramarov, Savely (act): *2010*
Kramarsky, David (dir): *The Beast With a Million Eyes*
Kramer, David (act): *Hands of a Stranger*
Kramer, Eric (act): *The Incredible Hulk Returns*
Kramer, Eric Allen (act): *Quest for the Mighty Sword*
Kramer, Frank (act): *The Toxic Avenger, Part II*
Kramer, Frank (dir): *Kiss Kiss, Kill Kill; Yeti*
Kramer, George (act): *Poor Devil*
Kramer, Hope (act): *The Flying Serpent*

Kramer, Jeffrey (C.) (act): Halloween II; Heartbeeps; Jaws; Jaws 2; Santa Claus (1985)
Kramer, Joel (J.) (act): Remo Williams: The Adventure Begins; Star Trek
Kramer, Larry (wri): Lost Horizon (1973)
Kramer, Michael (act): The Disappearance
Kramer, Michael Eric (act): Project X (1987); Return to Horror High; To Die For II: Son of Darkness
Kramer, Nicole (act): Earth Girls Are Easy
Kramer, Robert (act & dir): Ice
Kramer, Sharon (act): Ghostbusters II
Kramer, Stanley (dir, b. 1913): The Domino Principle; On the Beach
Kramer, Stepfanie/Stephanie (act): Bridge Across Time; The Man With Two Brains; Thrill
Kramer, Sylvia (act): Watch Me When I Kill
Kramer, Wright (act): Before I Hang
Kramm, Hans (act): Polyester
Krampe, Hugh J. (act): see O'Brian, Hugh
Krampf, Gunther (cin, b. 1899): Die Buchse der Pandora; The Ghoul (1933); The Night Has Eyes; Orlacs Haende; Der Student von Prag (1926); The Tunnel; Der Verlorene Schuh
Kraner, Cissy (act): The Fifth Musketeer
Kranhouse, Jon (R.) (cin): Brainwaves; Friday the 13th, Part VI: Jason Lives; Shadow of Death (1983)
Krantz, Lantza (act): Trancers
Krantz, Steve (wri): Jennifer (1978); Ruby
Kranz, Stanley (cin): see Cortez, Stanley
Krasina, Olga (act): Queen of Spades (1960)
Krasker, Robert/Bob (cin, 1913-1981): Another Man's Poison; The Collector; The Criminal; Cry Wolf (1980); The Running Man (1963); The Saint Meets the Tiger; State Secret; The Third Man
Krasna, Maria (act): Confess, Dr. Corda
Krasna, Norman (wri, b. 1909): Four Hours to Kill
Krasner, Milton (cin, 1904-1988): The Accused (1948); Arabian Nights (1942); Beneath the Planet of the Apes; The Dark Mirror (1946); A Double Life (1947); The Ghost of Frankenstein; Goodbye Charlie; The Great Impersonation (1935); Half Angel; The House of the Seven Gables; The Invisible Man Returns; The Invisible Man's Revenge; The Missing Guest; Monkey Business; Paris Calling; The St. Valentine's Day Massacre; The Set-Up (1949); 23 Paces to Baker Street; The Venetian Affair; Vicki; The Woman In the Window
Krasny, Paul (dir): The Adventures of Nick Carter
Kratina, Richard/Dick (cin): The Angel Levine; Scream for Help; The Sentinel
Kratka, Paul (act): Friday the 13th-Part 3
Kraus, Jan (act): Howling II
Kraus, Mathias (act): Making Contact
Kraus, Robert (dir & wri): The Monster In the Basement
Krause, Bernard (mus): The Last Days of Man On Earth
Krause, Brian (act, b. 1968): Earth Angel; Naked Souls; Sleepwalkers
Krause, Willy (act): The Last Ten Days of Adolf Hitler
Kraushaar, Raoul (mus, b. 1908): Abbott and Costello Meet Captain Kidd; Back from the Dead; Billy the Kid vs. Dracula; The Golden Mistress; Invaders from Mars (1953); Island of Lost Women; Jack and the Beanstalk (1952); The 30 Foot Bride of Candy Rock; The Unknown Terror; Untamed Women
Krauss, Werner (act, 1884-1959): Geheimnisse einer Seele; Das Kabinett des Dr. Caligari; Mensch Ohne Namen; A Night of Horror; Der Student von Prag (1926); Das Wachsfigurenkabinett
Kraussneck, Arthur (act): Chronik von Grieshuus
Krauth, Violet (act): see Marsh, Marion
Krawford, Gary (act): The Housekeeper
Kray, Marilyn (act): Street Trash
Krazna, Suzanne (act): Halloween With the Addams Family
Krebs, Marie Tomlinson (act): see Main, Marjorie
Krebs, Susan (act): Earth Girls Are Easy
Krech, Warren (act): see William, Warren
Krecmer, Ladislav (act): Howling II
Kreidt, Martin (act): Raiders of the Lost Ark
Kreig, Frank (act): The War of the Worlds
Kreindel, Mitch (act): The Goddess of Love; Modern Problems
Kreisel, Nancy (act): The Unnamable
Kreitsek, Howard B. (wri): The Illustrated Man
Kreppel, Paul (act): Jetsons: The Movie
Kresel, Lee (wri): Alakazam the Great
Kreski, Connie (act): The Black Bird (1975)
Kress, Earl (wri): The Fox and the Hound
Kress, Eric (cin): The Kingdom
Kress, Frank (act): The Gore-Gore Girls
Kress, Mitzi (act): The Capture of Bigfoot
Kressing, Harry (wri): Something for Everyone
Krest, Patricia (act): Strait-Jacket
Krestalude, Jim (act): Star Trek: Generations
Kretzmer, Herbert (wri): Too Hot to Handle
Kreuger, Kurt (act, b. 1917): The St. Valentine's Day Massacre; The Spider (1945); Spy Hunt; The Strange Death of Adolf Hitler
Kreusser, Dick (act): Backwoods
Kreuzer, Elisabeth (act): Birgitt Haas Must Be Killed
Kreuzer, Lisa (act): Flight to Berlin
Krevoy, Cecile (act): Pumpkinhead II: Blood Wings
Krick, Howard (act): Short Circuit
Kriegel, David (act): Quest of the Delta Knights
Krieger, Ed (act): Alien Nation
Krieger, Michele (act): Boarding House
Krieger, Nick (act): Obsession (1976)
Krieger, Robby (mus): Freeway Maniac
Krieger, Robin (act): The Goddess of Love
Krieger, Stu (wri): Amazing Stories: The Movie VI; Freaky Friday (1995); The Land Before Time; A Troll In Central Park; Zenon: Girl of the 21st Century
Kriel, Annaline (act): Kill and Kill Again
Kriesa, Chris(topher) (act): Eve of Destruction; I, Madman; Shocker; The Silencers (1995)
Krige, Alice (act): Ghost Story (1981); Habitat; Haunted Summer; Sleepwalkers; Star Trek: First Contact
Krige, Tai (cin): Kill and Kill Again
Krikes, Peter (wri): Star Trek IV: The Voyage Home
Kring, R. Timothy (wri): Bay Coven; Teen Wolf Too
Krish, John (dir, b. 1923): Unearthly Stranger
Krista, Charlene (act): Street Trash
Kristel, Sylvia (act, b. 1952): Because of the Cats; Dracula's Widow; The Fifth Musketeer; Mata Hari (1985); The Nude Bomb
Kristen, Lidia (act): Young Frankenstein
Kristen, Marta (act, b. 1944): Battle Beyond the Stars (1980)
Kristian, Charles (act): The Resurrected
Kristiansen, Henning (cin): King Lear (1970); The Night Visitor
Kristofer, Jason (act): Fear (1996)
Kristofferson, Kris (act, b. 1936): Blade; Knights; Millennium; Netforce
Kritikos, Alkis (act): For Your Eyes Only; Slipstream
Krizman, Dwight (act): Dracula's Dog
Krizsan, Les (cin): I Worship His Shadow
Kroeger, Berry (act, 1912-1991): Atlantis, the Lost Continent; Demon Seed; The Incredible 2-Headed Transplant; The Mephisto Waltz; Nightmare In Wax; The Sword of Monte Cristo
Kroetsch, Neil (act): Wild Thing
Krog, Tim (mus): The Boogey Man
Krohn, Charles (act): Red Alert; Sugar Hill
Krohnke, Erich (wri): Marquis de Sade: Justine
Kroitor, Roman (dir & wri): The Universe
Kroll, John (dir & wri): Amanda and the Alien
Krome, Konnie (act): The Pink Chiquitas
Krone, Fred (act): Hand of Death
Kronen, Ben (act): Bad Dreams; Howling VI: The Freaks; Repossessed
Kronenberg, Adrienne (act): Flash Gordon (1980)
Kronenberg, Bruce (act): The Nesting
Kronert, Max (act): The Golem: How He Came Into the World
Kronos (act): David and Goliath
Krook, Margareta (act): Persona
Kropke, Stephane (act): Revenge (1986)
Kroth, Gene (act): The Edge of Hell
Kroyer, Bill (dir): Ferngully: The Last Rain Forest
Krska, Karol (cin): Sedmi Kontinent
Krueger, Michael (dir): Mind Killer; Night Vision
Kruger, Alma (act, 1872-1960): Crime Doctor's Warning; Saboteur; You'll Find Out
Kruger, Christiane (act): Le Dernier Combat; De Sade; The Internecine Project
Kruger, Franz Otto (act): The Ape Creature
Kruger, Hardy (act, b. 1928): Blind Date (1959); Confess, Dr. Corda; Liane, das Madchen aus dem Urwald; Night Hair Child; The Red Tent
Kruger, Henry (act): La Danza Macabra
Kruger, Kim (act): Dr. Caligari
Kruger, Leo (act): Sei Donne per l'Assassino
Kruger, Mark (wri): Candyman: Farewell to the Flesh
Kruger, Otto (act, 1885-1974): Another Thin Man; Black Widow (1954); The Colossus of New York; Dracula's Daughter; Escape In the Fog; Hitler's Children; Jungle Captive; Living Dangerously; Murder, My Sweet; Saboteur; Tarzan's Desert Mystery; They Live In Fear; Treasure Island (1934); Woman Who Came Back; The Wonderful World of the Brothers Grimm; Wonder Man
Kruger, Paul (act): Castle In the Desert
Kruger, Richard (act): Das Singende Ringende Baumchen
Krugman, Lou (act): Sabaka
Kruize, John C. (wri): Mutant
Kruk, Richard (act): Nothing But Trouble
Krull, Karla Sue (act): Killer Klowns from Outer Space
Krumgold, Joseph (wri): The Lone Wolf Returns (1935)
Krumholtz, David (act): Addams Family Values; The Santa Clause
Krumm, Paul Albert (act): Jonathan
Krunch, M D'Jango (act): Street Trash
Krupa, Olek (act): Eraser
Kruschen, Jack (act, b. 1922): Abbott and Costello Go to Mars; The Angry Red Planet; A Blueprint for Murder; Cape Fear (1961); Cry Terror!; Dark Mirror (1984); The Last Voyage; The $1,000,000 Duck; The November Plan; Satan's Cheerleaders; The Time Machine (1978); The War of the Worlds; Where Danger Lives
Kruse, John (dir): October Moth
Kruse, John (wri): Crossplot; Echo of Barbara; The Fiction-Makers; In the Devil's Garden; October Moth; Revenge (1971, GB); The Saint and the Brave Goose; Vendetta for the Saint
Kruskal, Megan (act): Howling IV
Krutoff, Brian (act): Surf Nazis Must Die
Krutonog, Boris (act): Monolith
Kryeger, Ken (act): Empire of Ash III
Kryll, Eva (act): Making Contact
Krylov, S. (act): My Name Is Ivan
Krystantos, Mitchell (act): Alien High
Krytinar, Jiri (act): Howling II
Kuban, August (act): The Deserter and the Nomads
Kubelsky, Benjamin (act): see Benny, Jack
Kubo, Akiro (act): Destroy All Monsters; Matango; Monster Zero; Son of Godzilla; Throne of Blood; Yog-Monster from Space
Kubrick, Stanley (cin, 1928-1999): Killer's Kiss
Kubrick, Stanley (dir & wri, 1928-1999): A Clockwork Orange; Dr. Strangelove: or, How I Learned to Stop Worrying and Love the Bomb; Eyes Wide Shut; Killer's Kiss; The Killing; The Shining; 2001: A Space Odyssey
Kuby, Bernard/Bernie (act): The Fury; Impulse (1984)
Kucha, Ka'imi (act): Return of the Killer Tomatoes
Kuchar, George (act): Screamplay
Kucowna, Z. (act): Wielka, Wielka I Najwieksza
Kudo, Yuki (act): The Crazy Family
Kueckelmann, Gertrud (act): The Dancing Heart
Kuehn, Andrew J. (dir): Terror In the Aisles
Kuenstle, Charles R. (wri): The Astronaut
Kuether, Steven (dir): Demons of Ludlow
Kuga, Yoshiko (act): Secret Scrolls-Parts I & II
Kugelmass, J. Alvin (wri): The Two-Headed Spy
Kuhle, Walter (act): Metropolis (1926)
Kuhlke, William (act): Sometimes They Come Back
Kuhn, Frederich (act): Homunculus
Kuhn, Irene (wri): The Mask of Fu Manchu
Kuhn, Judy (act): Pocahontas
Kuhn, Kelli (act): Natas...The Reflection
Kuhn, Michael (act): The House on Sorority Row
Kuhn, Mickey (act): Dick Tracy (1945)
Kuhn, Steve (act): The Punisher
Kuhne, Gustav (act): Homunculus
Kuhne(-Adams), Stacey (act): Brainstorm (1983); Fantasies
Kuinzhi, Valentina (act): Aelita
Kujnir-Herescu, Nadia (act): see Gray, Nadia
Kukoricza, Janos (cin): Phantom of the Opera (1983)
Kulas Jr., Chester (act): Deadly Blessing
Kulcsar, Mike (act): The Ultimate Impostor
Kuleshov, Lev (dir, 1899-1970): Luch Smerti
Kulich, Vladimir (act): Pandora's Clock
Kuliev, Djavashir (mus): Ashik Kerib
Kulik, Buzz (dir, b. 1922): Bad Ronald; Matt Helm
Kulik, Jeni (act): The Bat People
Kulik, Mark (act): Zombie Nightmare
Kulik, Tony (act): Witches' Brew
Kulis, Juni (act): Night of the Zombies (1981)
Kulka, Janos (act): Terminus
Kulky, Henry (act, 1921-1965): The 5000 Fingers of Dr. T; No Holds Barred; Tobor the Great
Kull, Edward (dir): Tarzan and the Green Goddess
Kulle, Jarb (act, b. 1927): The Devil's Eye
Kulp, Nancy (act, 1921-1991): The Aristocats; Moon Pilot; The Three Faces of Eve
Kuluva, Will (act, 1917-1990): To Trap a Spy
Kulzer, William J. (act): Shadows Run Black
Kum, Kristopher (act): Koroshi; Rentadick
Kumar, Ashok (act): The McGuffin
Kumar, Dilip (act): Savage Princess
Kumar, Hemanta (mus): Siddhartha
Kumaratunga, Wijaya (act): The God King
Kumel, Harry (dir): Daughters of Darkness
Kumel, Harry (wri): Daughters of Darkness; My Nights With Susan, Sandra, Olga and Julie
Kun, Magda (act): Dead of Night (1945); Meet Sexton Blake
Kunholm, Mai-Lis (act): Arachnophobia
Kunicki, Kelley (act): Gore-Met Zombie Chef from Hell
Kuniholm, Cal (act): Dark Star
Kunis, Mila (act): Piranha (1995)
Kunisawa, Toyoko (act): The Toxic Avenger, Part II
Kunitomi, Darrell (act): In Self Defense
Kunkele, Ilse (act): Jonathan; Das Schloss
Kunstmann, Doris (act, b. 1944): Hitler: The Last Ten Days; Seven Deaths In the Cat's Eye
Kunstmann, Ernst (cin): Milczaca Gwiazda
Kunstmann, Vera (cin): Milczaca Gwiazda
Kuntarich, Jackie (act): Jaws 3-D
Kunz, David A. (act): Outbreak
Kunz, Peter (cin): Echoes; Night of the Zombies (1981)
Kunz, Simon (act): Goldeneye
Kupfer, Margarete (act): Der Januskopf
Kupferman, Meyer (mus): Fearless Frank
Kurado, Kuyomi (cin): Live Today, Die Tomorrow
Kuran, Peter (cin): Dreamscape
Kurant, Willy (cin): Sous le Soleil de Satan
Kuratomi, Lynn (act): Ghost Warrior
Kurcz, Robert (act): Moontrap
Kurihara, Komaki (act): Inn of Evil
Kuriki, Yoko (act): The Toxic Avenger, Part II
Kuriloff, Jason (act): Short Circuit 2
Kurita, N. "Kuri" (cin): Shock Chamber
Kurlander, Tom (act): Flatliners
Kurlick, Daniel (act): Black Zoo
Kurnitz, Harry (wri, 1908-1968): The Adventures of Don Juan; Goodbye Charlie; Land of the Pharaohs; One Touch of Venus; Shadow of the Thin Man; The Thin Man Goes Home; The Web; Witness for the Prosecution
Kuroda, Emily (act): Awake to Danger; Donor; Heartless
Kuroda, Yoshio (dir): Gulliver's Travels Beyond the Moon
Kuroda, Yoshiyuki (cin): Majin, Monster of Terror
Kuroda, Yoshiyuki (dir): The Return of Giant Majin
Kuroki, Hikaru (act): Latitude Zero
Kuronuma, Takashi (wri): Rodan, the Flying Monster
Kurosawa, Akira (dir, 1910-1998): High and Low; Ran; Throne of Blood; Tora No O O Fumu Otokotachi
Kurosawa, Akira (wri, 1910-1998): Ran; Throne of Blood; Tora No O O Fumu Otokotachi
Kurowski, Piotr (act): Profesor Zazul; Przyjaciel
Kurowski, Ron (act): The Creature Wasn't Nice
Kurrie, Robert (B.) (cin): The Invisible Fear; Moby Dick (1930)
Kurtz, David (mus): Alien Nation: Dark Horizon; Alien Nation: Millennium; Journey to the Center of the Earth (1993)
Kurtz, Linda (act): Carnival of Blood
Kurtz, Michael (act): Class of Nuke 'em High, Part 2: Subhumanoid Meltdown
Kurtz, Swoosie (act, b. 1944): Liar Liar; Storybook; Vice Versa (1988)
Krtzman, Harvey (wri, 1925-1993): Mad Monster Party
Kurtzman, Katy (act): Child of Glass
Kurtzman, Robert (act): Night of the Creeps
Kurtzman, Robert (dir): Wishmaster
Kurtzman, Robert (wri): From Dusk Till Dawn
Kurutz, Janos (act): Billion Dollar Brain
Kuryluk, Jadwiga (act): O Dwoch Takich Co Ukradli Ksiezyc
Kurz, Emilie (act): Der Letzte Mann
Kurz, Ron (wri): Friday the 13th-Part 2
Kusakari, Masao (act): Virus (1980)
Kusama, Akio (act): Mothra
Kusano, Daigo (act): Live Today, Die Tomorrow

Kusatsu, Clyde (act): Aladdin and the King of Thieves; Dr. Strange; Meteor; Thirdspace: A Babylon 5 Adventure
Kusenko, Nick (act): The Package
Kushida, Alice (act): Contact
Kushida, Beverly (act): The Manitou
Kusonoki, Yuko (act): Body Snatcher from Hell
Kuss, Richard (act): Warlock
Kusuhara, Eiji (act): Licensed to Love and Kill
Kutches, Todd (act): The Entity
Kuter, Kay E. (act): The Goddess of Love; The Last Starfighter; Warlock; Zombie High
Kuttner, Henry (wri, b. 1915): The Twonky
Kuveiller, Luigi (cin): Dracula (1974); Frankenstein (1974); A Lizard In a Woman's Skin; Profundo Rosso
Kuwa, George (act): The Chinese Parrot; The House Without a Key; The Invisible Fear
Kuwayama, Shoichi (act): Kwaidan
Kuyer, Sydney (act): The Lift
Kuzman, Lis (act): The Toxic Avenger, Part II
Kuzui, Fran Rubel (dir): Buffy the Vampire Slayer
Kuznetzoff, Adia (act): Bulldog Drummond's Bride; Devil's Island
Kuzyk, Mimi (act): The Kiss (1988); The Lifeforce Experiment
Kwan, Nancy (act, b. 1939): Night Creature; Wonder Women; The Wrecking Crew
Kwang-Su, Park (dir): Gesom E Kako Shipta
Kwapis, Ken (dir): Amazing Stories: The Movie VI; Vibes
Kwiatkowski, Tadeusz (wri): Rekopis Znaleziony w Saragossie
Kwitny, Jeff (dir): Beyond the Door III; Iced
Kwong, Kenny (act): Scream
Kwong, Peter (act): The Golden Child
Kwon-Taek, Lim (dir): Village In the Mist
Kwouk, Burt (act): Curse of the Fly; Koroshi; Mark of the Devil (1985); Rollerball; The Terror of the Tongs; Visa to Canton
Kyasht, Lydia (act): The Black Spider
Kydd, Sam (act, b. 1917): The Clue of the Silver Key; Dead Lucky; Death Goes to School; Eye of the Needle; The Glass Tomb; Great Expectations (1974); The Hideout; The Hound of The Baskervilles (1959); The House On Marsh Road; Island of Terror; The Lady Killers (1956); Moon Zero Two; The Projected Man; The Quatermass Experiment; Quatermass II; Quest for Love; Radio Cab Murder; Smokescreen; Soho Incident; 10 Rillington Place; Tiger In the Smoke; Treasure Island (1950); The Treasure of Monte Cristo (1961); Trent's Last Case (1952); Vengeance Is Mine; The Voice of Merrill
Kyle, David (act): Halloween
Kyle, George (act): Heart Condition
Kyle, Gordon (dir): Who Killed Van Loon?
Kyles, Dwania (act): The Brother from Another Planet
Kymlicki, Milan (mus): Deadbolt
Kynman, Paul (act): First Knight
Kyo, Machiko (act, b. 1924): Buddha; Tanin No Kao; Ugetsu Monogatari
Kyper, Al (act): Wavelength
Kyriazi, Paul (dir): Omega Cop
Kyser, Hans (wri): Faust (1926)

L7 (act): Serial Mom
L.A. Effects Group, Inc., The (cin): Creature
Laage, Barbara (act): Guilty?
Laban, Ahmed (act): Dawn of the Mummy
La Barba, Joe (act): The Falcon's Alibi
Labarr, Marta (act): Meet Maxwell Archer; Traitor Spy
La Bassiere, Robert (act): The Boy Who Never Was
LaBeau, Steve (act): Night of the Comet
LaBelle, Michel Rene (act): Happy Birthday to Me
LaBelle, Rob (act): Wes Craven's New Nightmare
Labern, Arthur (wri): Accidental Death; Dead Man's Evidence; Freedom to Die; Frenzy; Incident at Midnight; Time to Remember; The Verdict (1964)
Labine, Claire (wri): The Bride In Black; Lovespell; She Woke Up
Labine, John (act): Lovespell
Labiosa, David (act): The Entity
Laborteaux, Matthew (act): The Aliens Are Coming; Deadly Friend; Tarantulas: The Deadly Cargo
Laborteaux, Patrick (act): Heathers
Labourier, Dominique (act): La Citta delle Donne
Labow, Hilary (act): The Alien's Return; The Rocky Horror Picture Show
Labowskie, Lisa (act): To All a Goodnight
Labra, Alvaro (act): Endless Descent
Labrador, Honey (act): Strange Days
LaBranche, Erin (act): Candyman: Farewell to the Flesh
Labuschagne, Nick (mus): The Demon (1981)
Lacamara, Carlos (act): Zapped!
Lacambre, Daniel (cin): Battle Beyond the Stars (1980);Humanoids from the Deep; Saturday the 14th; Sweet Kill; The Velvet Vampire
La Capria, Raffaele (wri): C'era una Volta
Lacas, Victoria (act): Street Trash
Lacassin, Francis (wri): Judex
Lacatus, Carmen (act): Forbidden Zone: Alien Abduction
LaCause, Sebastian (act): Eraser
LaCava, Gregory (dir, 1892-1952): Gabriel Over the White House
Lace, Lentia (act): Federal Agent
Lacerte, Jacque (dir & wri): Love Me Deadly
Lacey, Aaron Michael (act): 12 Monkeys
Lacey, Catherine (act, b. 1904): Cottage to Let; The House of the Arrow (1940); Journey to Midnight; The Lady Vanishes (1938); The Mummy's Shroud; The October Man; Poison Pen; The Private Life of Sherlock Holmes; The Servant; The Shadow of the Cat; The Solitary Child; The Sorcerers
Lacey, Ingrid (act): Funny Man
Lacey, Jacqueline (act): Accidental Death
Lacey, Joe (act): 101 Dalmatians (1996)
Lacey, Leslee (act): HauntedWeen
Lacey, Margaret (act): Diamonds Are Forever; The Ruling Class
Lacey, Ronald (act): The Adventures of Buckaroo Banzai; The Boys; Crucible of Terror; Disciple of Death; The Fearless Vampire Killers or: Pardon Me, But Your Teeth Are In My Neck; Gawain and the Green Knight; Into the Darkness; Landslide (1992); Last Days of Man On Earth; Otley; Raiders of the Lost Ark; Red Sonja; Sword of the Valiant; Yellowbeard
Lachaumette, Alan (act): Ghost Warrior
Lachelle, Tia (act): Bloodspell
Lacher, Taylor (act): Cry for the Strangers; A Force of One; The Horrible House On the Hill
Lachman (Jr.), Ed(ward) (cin): Making Mr. Right; Scalpel; Touch
Lachman, Harry (dir): Castle In the Desert; Charlie Chan at the Circus; Charlie Chan In Rio;
Dante's Inferno (1935); Dead Men Tell; Dr. Renault's Secret; The Loves of Edgar Allan Poe; The ManWho Lived Twice; Murder Over New York; They Came by Night; The Yellow Mask
Lachman, Stanley (act): The Amazing Colossal Man
Lack, Simon (act): Shadow of Death (1939); Trog;Wings of Death
Lack, Stephen (act): Dead Ringers; Scanners
Lackaye, Wilton (act): The Lone Wolf (1924); Trilby (1915)
Lackey, Doug (mus): Swords of the Space Ark
Lackey, Mike (act): Street Trash
Lackey, Skip (act): Alien High; Once Bitten
Lackie, James (act): Shock Chamber
Lackteen, Frank (act): Above Suspicion; Arrest Bulldog Drummond; Daughter of the Jungle; Devil Goddess; The House Without a Key; Man-Eater of Kumaon; Nyoka and the Lost Secrets of Hippocrates
La Cock, Joanne Letitia (act): see Dru, Joanne
Lacommaro, Cathy (act): Splatter University
Laconi, Bob (act): Night of the Zombies (1981)
Lacouter, Jacques (wri): Frankenstein Island
Lacroix, Denis (act): Rabid; Scanners
Lacroix, Peter (act): The Hunted (1998)
Lacy, Beatriz (act): Graveyard of Horror
Lacy, Jerry (act, b. 1936): Blood Bath (1975); Chiller
Lacy, Joe (dir & wri): see Lorietta, Jose E.
Lacy, Steve (act): Secrets of the Phantom Caverns
Lacy, Tom (act): The Mark of Zorro (1974)
Laczkovich, Geza (act): Mata Hari (1985)
Ladanyi, Andrea (act): Gate II
Ladd, Alan (act, 1913-1964): Appointment With Danger; The Black Cat (1941); The Black Knight; The Blue Dahlia; Desert Legion; The Man In the Net; O.S.S.; 13 West Street; This Gun for Hire (1942); Whispering Smith
Ladd, Aldo (dir): The New House On the Left
Ladd, Cheryl (act, b. 1951): Evil In the Deep; The Haunting of Lisa; Jekyll and Hyde; Millennium; Perfect Little Angels; Poison Ivy (1992)
Ladd, David (act): Beyond the Universe; Deathline
Ladd, Diane (act, b. 1932): Black Widow (1987); Carnosaur; The Devil's Daughter (1972); Embryo; Forever; A Kiss Before Dying (1991); The Lookalike; Mrs. Munck; The November Plan; Shadow of a Doubt (1991); Something Wicked This Way Comes
Ladd, Diane (dir & wri, b. 1932): Mrs. Munck
Ladd, Jim (act): Silent Night, Deadly Night III
Ladd, Jordan (act): The Nosferatu Diaries: Embrace of the Vampire
Ladenburg, Richard (act): Witchery
Ladengast, Walter (act): Nosferatu, the Vampyre
Laderman, Fred (wri): Pinocchio In Outer Space
Ladizinsky, Stefan (act): The Deserter and the Nomads
Ladkin, Michael (act): Deja Vu
Lado, Aldo (wri): The Humanoid
Lado, Jose M. (act): La Corona Negra
Ladue, Lyzanne (act): Sergeant Deadhead the Astronut!
LaFave, Mark (act): Raiders of the Living Dead
Lafayette, Andree (act): Trilby (1923)
LaFayette, John (act): Fright Night II; Neon Maniacs; Remote Control (1988); Switch (1991); The Terror Within; Watchers II
Lafayette, Ruby (act): The Miracle Man (1919)
Laffan, Pat (act): The Saint
Laffan, Patricia (act, b. 1919): Death In High Heels; Devil Girl from Mars; Escape Route; Hidden Homicide; 23 Paces to Baker Street;Who Killed Van Loon?
Lafferty, Marcy (act): The Day Time Ended; Kingdom of the Spiders; Star Trek
Lafferty, Martha Jane (act): see Blair, Janet
Lafferty, Sandra Ellis (act): Wes Craven's New Nightmare
Lafia, John (dir & wri): Child's Play 2; Man's Best Friend
LaFitte, Tommy (act): The Silence of the Lambs
La Fleur, Art (act): The Blob (1988); The Fifth Missile; Forever Young; The Invisible Woman (1983); Jekyll and Hyde...Together Again; Trancers; Trancers II: The Return of Jack Deth; WarGames; Zone Troopers
Lafleur, Jean (wri): Spacehunter: Adventures In the Forbidden Zone
Lafont, Bernadette (act, b. 1938): Catch Me a Spy; Violette Noziere
LaFontaine, Don (act): Time Walker
Laforet, Marie (act): The Blue Panther
Laforteza, Gina (act): Daughters of Satan
La France, LaNetta (act): Blood Diner
La Frenais, Ian (wri): Catch Me a Spy; Otley; The Prisoner of Zenda (1979); Vice Versa (1988)
La Freniere, Celine (wri): City On Fire
LaGassa, Bonnie (act): The Howling: New Moon Rising
LaGassa, Carl (act): The Howling: New Moon Rising
Lager, Martin (wri): The Shape of Things to Come (1979)
Lagerlof, Selma (wri, 1858-1940): Herr Arnes Pengar (1919 & 1954); The Story of Gosta Berling
Lagerwell, Sture (act): The Devil's Eye
Lagneau, Jacques (wri): Amador
Lagnell, Ulla (act): La Sorciere
Lagrange, Louise (act, b. 1896): Cinderella: or, The Glass Slipper
Lagrange, Michele (act): The Phantom of the Opera (1990)
Lagrange, Valerie (act): Morgan the Pirate
LaGravenese, Richard (wri): Beloved
La Guardia, Fiorello (act, 1882-1947): Crazy House (1943)
LaGuardia, Michael (act): Ghost In the Machine; Total Recall
Laguna, Elisa (act): Night Fiend
Lahee, Sally (act): The Flesh and Blood Show; Venom (1982)
Lahr, Bert (act, 1895-1967, nee Irving Lahrheim): The Wizard of Oz (1939)
Lahrheim, Irving (act): see Lahr, Bert
Lahti, Christine (act, b. 1950): Dr. Scorpion; The Fear Inside; The Henderson Monster; Hideaway
Lahti, Gary (act): Knightriders
Lai, Christina (act): Savage Island
Lai, Francis (mus): Les Miserables (1995)
Lai, Leon (act): Wicked City
Lai, Me Me (act): Licensed to Love and Kill
Laight, Virginia (act): Curtains
Laine, Cleo (act): Murder by Proxy; The Third Alibi
Laine, Jimmy (act): Driller Killer; Ms. 45
Laine, Philippe (cin): Asterix In Britain
Laine, Ray (act): Jack's Wife
Laine, Raymond (act): Lady Beware
Laing, C.J. (act): The Amazing Dr. Jekyll
Laing, Hugh (act): Brigadoon
Lainsbury, Helen (act): The Harbour Lights
Lainz, Toby (act): Night of the Red Hunter
Laird, Jack (wri): The Bride In Black; The Hanged Man
Laird, Jenny (act, b. 1917): Black Narcissus; Face In the Night; The House of Silence; The Last Chance; Passenger to London; A Place to Die; The Village of the Damned (1960); Wanted for Murder; Your Witness
Laird, Michael (act): Primal Scream
Laird, Peter (wri): Teenage Mutant Ninja Turtles; Teenage Mutant Ninja Turtles II: The Secret of the Ooze
Laird, Trevor (act): Slipstream
Lajeunesse, Isabelle (act): Rabid
Lajos, Julia (act): Cuento de Hadas; La Torre de los Siete Jorobados
Lakatos, Sandor Deki (act): Phantom of the Opera (1983)
Lake, Alan (act, 1941-1984): Don't Open Till Christmas; Freelance; Paint Me a Murder; The Playbirds; The Swordsman
Lake, Alice (act, 1896-1967): Blackie's Redemption
Lake, Arthur (act, 1905-1987, nee Arthur Silverlake): The Ghost That Walks Alone; Jackand the Beanstalk (1917); 16 Fathoms Deep; Topper (1937)
Lake, Bill (act): Funeral Home; The Shape of Things to Come (1979)
Lake, Don (act): The Pink Chiquitas; Rocketman (1997); Short Circuit 2
Lake, Florence (act, 1904-1980): Drums of Jeopardy (1931); Welcometo Arrow Beach
Lake, Harriette (act): see Sothern, Ann
Lake, Mark (act): The Relic
Lake, Ricki (act, b. 1968): Serial Mom
Lake, Robert (act): Just Imagine
Lake, Veronica (act, 1919-1973, nee Constance Frances Marie Ockleman, a.k.a. Constance Keane): The Blue Dahlia; Flesh Feast; I Married a Witch; This Gun for Hire (1942)
Lakes, Ilona (act): Prison Girls
Lakin, Howard (wri): Northstar
Lakin, Rita (wri): Death Takes a Holiday (1971); Last Bride of Salem
Laks, Bruce (act): Flight of the Navigator
Laks, Lucile (wri): The Black Belly of the Tarantula
Lala (act): Dream a Little Dream; Watchers
Lalande, Francois (act): The Phantom of the Opera (1990)
LaLanne, Jack (act): Repossessed
LaLanne, Louis (act): The Corsican Brothers (1985)
Lalara, Cedric (act): The Last Wave
Lalara, Morris (act): The Last Wave
Laliberte, Eric (act): Oh Heavenly Dog
Lally, Michael (David) (act): Last Rites (1980); The Nesting; The Secret of Roan Inish
Lally, Mick (act): The Outcasts
Lally, Mike (act): The Falcon's Alibi; Nightmare Alley
La Loggia, Danica (act): Satyricon
LaLoggia, Frank (dir, mus & wri, b. 1958): Fear No Evil (1981); Lady In White
Lalonde, Catherine (act): Secret Weapons
Laloux, Rene (dir & wri): Fantastic Planet; Light Years
LaLumia, Drinda (act): The Dark Half
Lam, Chan Yiu (act): The Man With the Golden Gun
Lamac, Karel (dir): They Met In the Dark
La Macchi, Nico (act): Ironmaster
La Mal, Isabel(le) (act): Mr. Moto Takes a Vacation; Think Fast, Mr. Moto
LaMarr, Barbara (act, 1896-1926, nee Reatha Watson): The Brass Bottle (1923); The Prisoner of Zenda (1922); Trifling Women
Lamarr, Hedy (act, b. 1915, nee Hedwig Kiesler): The Conspirators; Die Dreizehn Koffer des Herrn O.F.; The Love of Three Queens; Samson and Delilah; The Story of Mankind
Lamarr, John (act): Monstroid
La Marr, Les (act): The Creeping Terror
La Marr, Margaret (act): Just Imagine
LaMarre, Marie (act): Hellhole
Lamas, Fernando (act, 1915-1982): The Diamond Queen; Jivaro; The Lost World (1960); Murder On Flight 502
Lamas, Lorenzo (act): Gladiator Cop: The Swordsman 2; Mask of Death; The Swordsman; Terminal Justice
Lamay, Charles (act): La Chute de la Maison Usher
Lamb, Charles (act): The Curse of the Werewolf; Hands of the Ripper; Model for Murder; Quatermass and the Pit; The Southern Star; Subterfuge
Lamb, Debra (act): Beverly Hills Vamp; Evil Spirits; The Invisible Maniac
Lamb, Gil (act, b. 1906): Day of the Animals; [illegible]
Lamb, Harold (wri): Samson and Delilah
Lamb, John (dir & wri): Mermaids of Tiburon

Lamb, Larry (act): Shadey; Superman (1978); Transmutations
Lamb, Linda (act): I Was a Zombie for the F.B.I.
Lamb, Mel (act): The Arp Statue
Lamb, Peter (act): Fortress
Lamb, Stuart J. (act): Secrets of the Phantom Caverns
Lambach, Boguslaw (cin): O Dwoch Takich Co Ukradli Ksiezyc
Lamberson, Gregory (dir): Slime City
Lambert, Anne (act): Picnic at Hanging Rock
Lambert, Christopher (act, b. 1957): Adrenalin; Fortress; Greystoke: The Legend of Tarzan, Lord of the Apes; Highlander; Highlander 2: The Quickening; Highlander: The Gathering; Knight Moves; Mortal Kombat; Road Flower; The Road Killers
Lambert, Del (act): Empire of Ash III
Lambert, Diana (act): The Grand Junction Case; Seance On a Wet Afternoon
Lambert, Douglas (act, 1936-1986): The Hunger; Moonraker; Saturn 3
Lambert, Ed (act): Mars Attacks!
Lambert, Henry (act): Oasis of the Zombies
Lambert, Jack (act, b. 1899): Blackbeard the Pirate; Bomb In the High Street; The Candlelight Murder; Dick Tracy's Dilemma;The Ghost Goes West; The Hidden Eye; A Honeymoon Adventure; Kiss Me Deadly; The Lost Hours; Modesty Blaise; Neither the Sea Nor the Sand; Scared Stiff (1953); Son of Robin Hood; The Spider (1939); They Came from Beyond Space; Three Cases of Murder; The Unsuspected
Lambert, Jane (act): Crazy Fat Ethel II; The Fury
Lambert, Jeffrey (act): Twilight Zone
Lambert, Jerry (mus): The Texas Chainsaw Massacre 2
Lambert, Joanna (act): The Punisher
Lambert, Lee J. (act): Simon, King of the Witches
Lambert, Locky (act): Witchboard: The Possession
Lambert, Mary (dir): Pet Sematary; Pet Sematary Two
Lambert, Paul (act, 1922-1997): Planet of the Apes
Lambert, Peter (wri): The Breaking Point (1961)
Lambert, Ryan (act): The Monster Squad
Lambert, Steve (act): Invaders from Mars (1986); Timecop
Lambert, Tracy (act): Switch (1991)
Lamberts, Heath (act): To Kill a Clown
Lambeth, Larry (act): Kidnapped Co-Ed
Lambie, Joe (act): Nightmares (1983)
Lamble, Lloyd (act, b. 1914): —And Now the Screaming Starts!;The Bank Raiders; The Green Buddha; The Gelignite Gang; Lady In the Fog; Mantrap; The Man Who Wouldn't Talk; The Mirror and Markheim; Night of the Demon (1957); Person Unknown; Profile; Quatermass II; Saturday Island; The Straw Man; Suspended Alibi; 3 Steps to the Gallows; Track the Man Down
Lambro, Phillip (mus): Crypt of the Living Dead
Lambton, Anne (act): The Witches (1990)
Lamdo, Mao (dir): Robot Carnival
La Mel, Lisa (act): Dr. Caligari
Lamey, Tommy (act): Timestalkers
Lamielle, Pierre (act): The Clan of the Cave Bear
Lamkin, Ken (cin): Mistress of Paradise
Lamm, Karen (act): It Happened at Lake Wood Manor; The Unseen (1981)
Lammers, Kelly (mus): Planet of the Dinosaurs
Lamond, Andrew (act): Monolith
Lamond, Don (act): The Angry Red Planet; Space Master X-7; The Three Stooges In Orbit
Lamonea, Angelo (act): Avalanche; Through the Magic Pyramid
Lamont, Adele (act): The Brain That Wouldn't Die
La Mont, Alice (act): Satan Met a Lady
Lamont, Charles (dir, b. 1898): Abbott and Costello Go to Mars;Abbott and Costello Meet Captain Kidd; Abbott and Costello Meet Dr. Jekyll and Mr. Hyde; Abbott and Costello Meet the Invisible Man; Abbott and Costello Meet the Mummy; Bagdad; The Dark Hour; Flame of Araby; Francis In the Haunted House; International Crime; Slave Girl
Lamont, Duncan (act, b. 1918): The Brigand of Kandahar; Burnt Evidence; The Creeping Flesh; The Devil-Ship Pirates; Evil of Frankenstein; Frankenstein Created Woman; The Lost Hours; The Man In the White Suit; Meet Mr. Malcolm;Murder at the Gallop; The Murder Game; The Night Won't Talk; Nothing But the Night; Panic (1963); Quatermass and the Pit; The Scarlet Blade; The Teckman Mystery; The 39 Steps (1959); Time Is My Enemy; The Witches (1966); The Woman in Question
Lamont/La Mont, Harry (act): House of Dracula; Robin Hood Jr. (1923)
Lamont, John (dir & wri): The Mirror and Markheim
Lamont, Marten (act): The Adventures of Robin Hood
Lamont, Molly (act): Alibi Inn; The House Opposite (1931); Murder at Monte Carlo; No Escape (1934); Paris Plane; Scared to Death (1947); The Strangler (1932); The Suspect; The Third Clue; What a Night!
Lamont, Robin (act): He Knows You're Alone
Lamont, Syl (act): Mirage (1965)
Lamor, Maria (act): The Knight of the Dragon
Lamoreux, Donald (act): Wild Thing
Lamorisse, Albert (dir, 1922-1970): Circus Angel; The Red Balloon
Lamorisse, Albert (wri, 1922-1970): The Red Balloon
Lamorisse, Pascal (act): The Red Balloon
Lamorisse, Sabine (act): The Red Balloon
LaMoth, Don (act): Mars Attacks!
La Mothe, Ken (act): Tainted Image
La Motta, Jack (act): Firepower
La Motta, John (act): Pet Shop
Lamour, Dorothy (act, 1914-1996, nee Dorothy Kaumeyer): Aloma of the South Seas (1941); Beyond the Blue Horizon; Creepshow 2; Death at Love House; Pajama Party; The Road to Bali; The Road to Hong Kong; The Road to Utopia
Lamoureux, Blaine (act): Quarantine
Lamp, Rebecca (act): The Quilt of Hathor
Lampell, Millard (wri): Blind Date (1959)
Lampert, Zohra (act): The Exorcist III; Let's Scare Jessica to Death
Lampin, Georges (dir, 1895-1979): Crime and Punishment (1958); Killer Spy
Lampkin, Charles (act): Cocoon; Five; Ghost Warrior
Lampley, Morey (act): The Mutilator (1985)
Lampley, William (act): The Dark (1979)
Lamplugh, Ken (wri): Midnight Kiss
Lamprell, Mark (wri): Babe: Pig In the City
Lampson, David (act): Murder In Mind; The Return of Count Yorga
LaNasa, Katherine (act): Nothing But the Truth; Robin Cook's 'Mortal Fear'
Lancaster, Ann (act): Fathom
Lancaster, Bill (wri): The Thing (1982)
Lancaster, Burt (act, 1913-1994): Castle Keep; The Crimson Pirate; Criss Cross; The Flame and the Arrow; The Island of Dr. Moreau (1977); Kiss the Blood Off My Hands; The List of Adrian Messenger; The Phantom of the Opera (1990); Scorpio; Seven Days In May; Sorry, Wrong Number (1948); The Swimmer; Twilight's Last Gleaming
Lancaster, G.B. (wri): The Altar Stairs
Lancaster, James (act): Leprechaun 2
Lancaster, Karen (act): Morons from Outer Space
Lancaster, Kate (act): Unforgettable
Lancaster, Lucie (act): 23 Paces to Baker Street
Lancaster, Pete (act): The Name of the Rose
Lancaster, Stuart (act): Edward Scissorhands; Faster, Pussycat! Kill! Kill!; The Loch Ness Horror; Mistress of the Apes
Lance, Henri (mus): Au Coeur de la Vie
Lanchberry, John (mus): Peter Rabbit and the Tales of Beatrix Potter
Lanchbury, Karl (act): Scream and Die!; Vampyres...Daughters of Dracula; Whirlpool (1970)
Lanchester, Elsa (act, 1902-1986, nee Elizabeth Sullivan): Androcles and the Lion; Arnold;Ashes; Bell, Book and Candle; The Big Clock; The Bishop's Wife;Blackbeard's Ghost; Bride of Frankenstein; Buccaneer's Girl; The Ghost Goes West; The Glass Slipper; Ladies In Retirement; Mary Poppins; Les Miserables (1952); Murder by Death; Mystery Street; Pajama Party; The Spiral Staircase (1946); Terror In the Wax Museum; Willard; Witness for the Prosecution
Lanci, Giuseppe (cin): Kaos
Lanctot, Micheline (act): Blood Relatives; A Scream from Silence
Land, Deborah Leah (act): Don't Answer the Phone!
Land, Geoffrey (act): Beyond the Living; Dr. Dracula
Land, Ian (act): Never-Never Land
Land, Kena (act): Prison Heat
Land, Mary (act): The Twisted Nerve
Landa, Rodolfo (act): Neutron vs. the Maniac
Landau, Juliet (act, b. 1971): Ed Wood; Neon City; Theodore Rex
Landau, Les (dir): The Last Man On Planet Earth
Landau, Leslie (wri): Dark World; The Riverside Murder
Landau, Martin (act, b. 1933): The Adventures of Pinocchio (1996); The Alien's Return; Alone In the Dark; The Being; By Dawn's Early Light; Cyclone; Destination MoonbaseAlpha; Ed Wood; The Fall of the House of Usher (1982); Firehead; The Gazebo; Meteor; North by Northwest; Paint It Black; The Return of the Six Million Dollar Man and the Bionic Woman; Sliver; Strange Shadows In an Empty Room; 12:01;Without Warning (1980); The X-Files
Landau, Richard (H.) (wri, b. 1914): The Black Hole; The Flanagan Boy; Frankenstein (1970); The Girl In Black Stockings; The Glass Tomb;Lost Continent (1951); Murder by Proxy; Pharaoh's Curse; The Quatermass Experiment; Spaceways; A Stolen Face
Landay, David (act): Gabriel Over the White House
Landberg, Karen (act): Slugs
Landeau, Gerald (wri): The Voice of Merrill
Landeck, Ben (wri): Broken Barrier; The Two Roads
Landen, Dinsdale (act): Digby-The Biggest Dog In the World; Morons from Outer Space; Not Guilty; Playback; Rasputin, the Mad Monk
Lander, David (act): The Tell-Tale Heart (1960)
Lander, David L. (act): Pandemonium; Steel and Lace
Lander, Eric (act): One Deadly Owner
Landerer, Greg(ory C.) (cin): Cavegirl (1985); The Goddess of Love
Landers, Audrey (act): Ghost Writer
Landers, Harry (act): Phantom from Space; Rear Window
Landers, Judy (act, b. 1959): Dr. Alien; Ghost Writer; Hellhole; I Was a Teenage Sex Mutant
Landers, Lew (dir, 1901-1962, nee Louis Friedlander): After Midnight With Boston Blackie; Alias Boston Blackie; The Boogie Man Will Get You; Captain Kidd and the Slave Girl; A Close Call for Boston Blackie; The Enchanted Forest; Hurricane Island; Inner Sanctum (1948); Jungle Jim In the Forbidden Land; Jungle Manhunt; The Magic Carpet (1951); Man In the Dark (1953); The Mask of Dijon; Power of the Whistler; The Raven (1935); The Return of the Vampire; Run for the Hills; Seven Keys to Baldpate (1947); Shadow of Terror; Terrified (1963); U-Boat Prisoner
Landers, Matt (act): Fright Night II
Landers, Muriel (act): The Boys from Brooklyn; Dr. Dolittle (1967)
Landesburg, Steve (act, b. 1945): Final Notice
Landey, Clayton (act): Eraser; The First Power; Ghost In the Machine; Heart Condition; A Nightmare On Elm Street 3: Dream Warriors
Landfield, David (act): The Nutty Professor (1963)
Landfield, Timothy (act): Ticks
Landgaard, Janet (act): Moonchild; The Swimmer
Landgre, Inga (act): Det Sjunde Inseglet
Landgren, Karl (act): Urban Warriors
Landgut, Inge (act): M (1931)
Landham, Sonny (act): Firewalker; Northstar; Predator
Landi, Aldo Bufi (act): Last of the Vikings
Landi, Elissa (act, 1904-1948): After the Thin Man; By Candlelight; The Count of Monte Cristo (1934); Koenigsmark; The 13th Chair (1937)
Landi, Marla (act, b. 1937): Across the Bridge; Dublin Nightmare; First Man Into Space; The Hound of the Baskervilles (1959); The Murder Game; The Pirates of Blood River
Landi, Sal (act): The Silence of the Hams; Xtro 3:Watch the Skies
Landingham, D.W. (act): Omega Cop
Landis, Bernie (act): Vice Versa (1988)
Landis, Carole (act, 1919-1948, nee Frances Ridste): Blondes at Work; I Wake Up Screaming; One Million B.C.; The Silk Noose; Topper Returns; Turnabout
Landis, Elizabeth (act): Heartless
Landis, Harry (act): Edge of Sanity
Landis, James (dir): The Nasty Rabbit; The Sadist
Landis, James (wri): The Sadist
Landis, Jeanette (act): The Persecution and Assassination of Jean-Paul Marat as Performed by the Inmates of the Asylum of Charenton Under the Direction of the Marquis de Sade
Landis, Jerry (act): Time Flyer
Landis, Jessie Royce (act, 1904-1972): It Happens Every Spring; North by Northwest; To Catch a Thief
Landis, Jim (act): The Lawnmower Man; 976-EVIL
Landis, John (act, b. 1950): Battle for the Planet of the Apes;Darkman (1990); Death Race 2000;Psycho IV: The Beginning; Schlock;The Silence of the Hams; Spontaneous Combustion
Landis, John (dir, b. 1950): Amazon Women On the Moon; An American Werewolf In London; Innocent Blood; Schlock; Twilight Zone
Landis, John (wri, b. 1950): An American Werewolf In London; Schlock; Twilight Zone
Landis, Margaret (act): The Confession (1920)
Landis, Monte (act): Heart Condition; Yellowbeard
Landis, Monty (act): The Mouse That Roared; Myra Breckinridge; Targets; The Vulture (1966); Young Frankenstein
Landis, Winifred (act): Dante's Inferno (1924)
Landiss, Brent (act): The Visitors (1989)
Landless, Larry (act): Always
Landman, Hannie (act): Billy the Kid vs. Dracula
Landman, Jeffrey (act): Halloween 5: The Revenge of Michael Myers
Lando, Brian (act): Alien Nation
Lando, Joe (act): Alien Nation: The Enemy Within
Landon, Avice (act, b. 1910): The Blood on Satan's Claw; Escap by Night (1954); Eyewitness (1956); Family Doctor; Gaolbreak (1962); Guilt Is My Shadow
Landon Jr., Hal (act): Bill & Ted's Bogus Journey; Eraserhead; Prison (1988)
Landon, John (act): Rattlers
Landon, Joseph (wri): Johnny Cool
Landon, Judy (act): Prehistoric Women (1950)
Landon, Laurene (act): The Ambulance; America 3000; Hundra; It's Alive III: Island of the Alive; I, the Jury (1982); Maniac Cop; Maniac Cop 2; Wicked Stepmother
Landon, Michael (act, 1936-1991, nee Eugene Orowitz): I Was a Teenage Werewolf
Landon, Patricia (act): Kiss of the Tarantula
Landon, Percival (wri): The House Opposite (1917)
Landon, Ross (act): The Door With Seven Locks (1940); Who Killed John Savage?
Landon, Ruth (wri): The Price of Folly
Landon, Ted (act & wri): Slaughterhouse Rock
Landon-Smith, Kristine (act): Gothic
Landor, Jenifer (act): Supergirl (1984)
Landor, Rosalyn (act): The Amazing Mr. Blunden; Arthur the King; The Devil Rides Out; Guardian of the Abyss
Landres, Paul (dir, b. 1912): Chain of Evidence; Eyes of the Jungle; The Flame Barrier; The Return of Dracula
Landrum, Teri (act): Pandemonium
Landry, Aude (act): Blood Relatives
Landry, Clarence (act): Alien Nation; Dead Connection
Landry, Gerard (act): The Black Devil (1963); Night Without Stars; Pirate of the Black Hawk
Landry, Jeanette (act): Transmutations
Landry, Margaret (act): The Leopard Man
Landry, Tim (cin): Dr. Jekyll and Ms. Hyde; George of the Jungle
Landsdowna, Howard (act): The Invincible Barbarian
Landshoff, Ruth (act): Nosferatu, eine Symphonie des Grauens
Landsman, Stephen A. (act): The Fugitive (1993)
Landson, Muriel (act): Oasis of the Zombies
Landy, Hannah (act): In Like Flint; Rosemary's Baby
Landy, Michael (act): No Blade of Grass
Lane, Abbe (act, b. 1932): My Friend, Dr. Jekyll; Twilight Zone
Lane, Allan (act, 1901-1973, nee Albert Albershart): Charlie Chan at the Olympics; Jungle Gold; Night Nurse
Lane, Andrew (dir): Jake Speed; Mortal Passions; The Secretary
Lane, Andrew (wri): Jake Speed
Lane, Art (act): Kiss of the Tarantula
Lane, Arthur (act): Face the Music; Secret Venture
Lane, Billie (act): The Man On the Cliff
Lane, Burton (mus, b. 1912): On a Clear Day You Can See Forever
Lane, Charles (act, b. 1899): Arsenic and Old Lace; Call Northside 777; The Canary Murder Case; A Close Call for Boston Blackie; Dr. Jekyll and Mr. Hyde (1920, Famous

Players/Para); Ellery Queen and the Perfect Crime;Ellery Queen, Master Detective; Ellery Queen's Penthouse Mystery; For Heaven's Sake; The Gnome-Mobile; I Wake Up Screaming; Just Before Dawn (1946); Tarzan's NewYork Adventure; The 30 Foot Bride of Candy Rock

Lane, Charles (1980s act): *Strange Behavior; Strange Invaders*

Lane, Christina Marie (act): *Edge of the Axe*

Lane, Dave (act): *The Edge of Hell*

Lane, David (act): *Trick or Treats*

Lane, David (dir): *Thunderbirds Are Go; Thunderbird 6*

Lane, Diane (act, b. 1965): *Jack; Judge Dredd; Lady Beware; Streets of Fire*

Lane, Dick (act): *The Shaggy D.A.*

Lane, Dickson (act): *Echoes*

Lane, Don (act): *Razorback*

Lane, Fredric (act): *Inferno (1998)*

Lane, Guy Rupert (act): *The Underworld of London*

Lane, Iva (act): *Star Trek*

Lane, Jackie (act): *The Gamma People; Jet Storm; Marte, Dio della Guerra; Men of Sherwood Forest; Robin Hood and the Pirates; Venus Against the Son of Hercules; War Gods of Babylon*

Lane, Jeffrey (act): *Forever Evil*

Lane, Jeffrie (act): *The Silence of the Lambs*

Lane, Joycelyn (act): *The Sword of Ali Baba*

Lane, Laura (act): *Interface*

Lane, Lenita (act): *The Bat (1959); Castle In the Desert; Dead Men Tell; The Mad Magician*

Lane, Lola (act, 1909-1981): *Deadline at Dawn; Death from a Distance; Identity Unknown; Murder On a Honeymoon; Torchy Blane In Panama*

Lane, Lupino (act, 1892-1959): *A Dreamland Frolic; The Yellow Mask*

Lane, Marc (cin): *The Murder Clinic*

Lane, Mark S. (act): *C.H.U.D. II*

Lane, Michael (Euro act): *Beast of Babylon Against the Son of Hercules; Ulysses Against the Son of Hercules*

Lane, Michael (USA act): *Code Name: Minus One*

Lane, Mike (act): *Curse of the Crystal Eye;Frankenstein (1970); Grotesque; A Name for Evil; Valley of the Dragons*

Lane, Nathan (act, b. 1956): *Addams Family Values; The LionKing; The Lion King II: Simba's Pride*

Lane, Nicholas (act): *Threads*

Lane, Nora (act): *Dick Tracy vs. Crime, Inc.; A Night of Mystery (1928)*

Lane, Pat (act): *Appointment With Murder*

Lane, Priscilla (act, 1917-1995): *Arsenic and Old Lace; Saboteur*

Lane, Richard (act, b. 1898): *After Midnight With Boston Blackie; Alias Boston Blackie; Arabian Nights (1942); Boston Blackie and the Law; Boston Blackie Booked On Suspicion; Boston Blackie Goes Hollywood; Boston Blackie's Appointment With Death; Boston Blackie's Chinese Venture; Boston Blackie's Rendezvous; The Chance of a Lifetime; Charlie Chan In Honolulu; A Close Call for Boston Blackie; Confessions of Boston Blackie; Hellzapoppin; The Last Warning (1938); Meet Boston Blackie; Mr. Moto In Danger Island; One Mysterious Night; The Phantom Thief; Song of Scheherazade; Time to Kill (1942); Trapped by Boston Blackie*

Lane, Robert (mus): *The Young Poisoner's Handbook*

Lane, Rosemary (act, 1913-1974): *The Boys from Syracuse; The Return of Dr. X*

Lane, Rusdi (act): *Damien-Omen II*

Lane, Rusty (act): *Beyond a Reasonable Doubt*

Lane, Sarah (act): *I Saw What You Did (1965)*

Lane, Scott (act): *Phantom of the Paradise*

Lane, Sheila (act): *Howling VI: The Freaks*

Lane, Sirpa (act): *The Beast (1974)*

Lane, Stewart (act): *Puppet On a Chain*

Lane, Tim (act): *Iron Warrior...The Legend!*

Lane, Tommy (act): *Ganja and Hess; Live and Let Die*

Lane, Trudy (act): *The China Syndrome*

Lane, Vicky (act): *Jungle Captive*

Laneuville, Eric (act): *A Force of One; The Omega Man*

Laneuville, Eric (dir): *Pandora's Clock*

Laney, Lanier (wri): *Love at Stake*

Lanfield, Sidney (dir, 1898-1972): *The Hound of the Baskervilles (1939)*

Lang, Arthur (mus): *The Woman In the Window*

Lang, Barbara (act): *Weird Science*

Lang, Carl (act): *Creature With the Blue Hand*

Lang (Jr.), Charles (B.) (cin, b. 1902): *The Atomic City; The Cat and the Canary (1939); Death Takes a Holiday (1934); The Ghost and Mrs.Muir; The Ghost Breakers; The Gracie Allen Murder Case; Paris When It Sizzles; Peking Express;Peter Ibbetson; Queen Bee; Salome (1953); Sudden Fear; The Uninvited (1944)*

Lang, Charles (act): *War of the Wizards*

Lang, Charley (act): *Fire In the Sky (1993)*

Lang, Christa (act): *Dead Pigeon On Beethoven Street;White Dog*

Lang, Doreen (act): *The Birds; The Cabinet of Caligari; The House That Wouldn't Die*

Lang, Fritz (act, 1890-1976): *Le Mepris*

Lang, Fritz (dir, 1890-1976): *Beyond a Reasonable Doubt; Cloak and Dagger (1946); Doctor Mabuse;Die Frau im Mond; House by the River; Journey to the Lost City; Liliom (1933); M (1931);Metropolis (1926); Ministry of Fear; Der Mude Tod; Die Nibelungen; Secret Beyond the Door; The Secret of Dr. Mabuse; Die Spinnen; Spione;Die Tausend Augen des Dr. Mabuse;Das Testament des Dr. Mabuse; While the City Sleeps; The Woman In the Window*

Lang, Fritz (wri, 1890-1976): *Doctor Mabuse; Die Frau im Mond; Liliom (1933); M (1931); Der Mude Tod; Die Nibelungen; Die Spinnen; Spione; Die Tausend Augen des Dr. Mabuse; Das Testament des Dr. Mabuse*

Lang, Harold (act, b. 1923): *The Betryal (1958); Calling Bulldog Drummond; Chain of Events; Cloudburst; Dr. Terror's House of Horrors (1964); The Flesh Is Weak; Man With a Gun; Men of Sherwood Forest; Murder by Proxy; Paranoiac; The Quatermass Experiment; The Saint's Return; The Spider and the Fly (1949); Thirty-Six Hours (1954); West 11*

Lang, Howard (act): *Date at Midnight; The Haunting; The Hideout; Innocent Meeting; Macbeth (1971); Men of Sherwood Forest; The Mysterious Bullet; Night Train for Inverness; Personal and Confidential; 23 Paces to Baker Street*

Lang, Iris (act): *Time Flies (1944)*

Lang, Jim (mus): *In the Mouth of Madness*

Lang, Judith (act): *Count Yorga, Vampire*

Lang, Julia (act): *Dr. Morelle-The Case of the Missing Heiress; Stop Press Girl*

Lang, June (act, b. 1917, nee June Vlasek): *Ali Baba Goes to Town; Chandu the Magician; Flesh and Fantasy*

lang, k.d. (act): *Eye of the Beholder (1999)*

Lang, Katherine Kelly (act): *Evilspeak; The Night Stalker (1987)*

Lang, Lester (cin): *The House of Secrets (1929)*

Lang, Marion (act): *The Invincible Barbarian*

Lang, Mary (act): *Raiders of the Living Dead*

Lang, Matheson (act, 1879-1948): *The Chinese Bungalow; The House Opposite (1917); Mr. Wu (1919); The Secret Kingdom; The Triumph of the Scarlet Pimpernel; The Ware Case*

Lang, Melvin (act): *Doomed to Die*

Lang, Perry (act): *Alligator (1981); Greedy Terror; The Hearse; Jacob's Ladder; Jennifer 8; TAG: The Assassination Game*

Lang, Richard (dir): *Dark Mirror (1984); Dr. Scorpion;Don't Go to Sleep; Fantasy Island*

Lang, Robert (act): *The House That Dripped Blood; The Medusa Touch; Night Watch (1973)*

Lang, Sophie (act): *Let Me Call You Sweetheart*

Lang, Stephen (act): *Guilty as Sin; Project X (1987); Shadow Conspiracy; A Town Has Turned to Dust*

Lang, Stevenson (act): *The Snake Woman*

Lang, Veronica (act): *Mini Weekend*

Lang, Walter (dir, 1898-1972): *The Blue Bird (1940); Desk Set; Snow White and the Three Stooges*

Langan, Glenn (act, 1917-1991): *The Amazing Colossal Man; Dragonwyck; Hangover Square; Mutiny In Outer Space; One Girl's Confession; Rapture; The Return of Dr.X; The Snake Pit (1948); Treasure of Monte Cristo (1949)*

Langdon, Dorian (act): *Waxwork II: Lost In Time*

Langdon, Harry (wri, 1884-1944): *A Chump at Oxford*

Langdon, Rose (act): *The Road to Mandalay*

Langdon, Sue Ane (act, b. 1936): *The Evictors; Hold On!; A Man Called Dagger; Without Warning (1980); Zapped!; Zapped Again*

Langdon, Terrence (act): *Mr. Arkadin*

Langdon, Tracy-Marie (act): *Happy Birthday to Me*

Lange, Arthur (mus): *Lady of Burlesque; Lancer Spy; The Mad Magician; The Mysterious Island (1929); Ring of Fear*

Lange, Carl (act): *Fellowship of the Frog; The Mysterious Magician; Die Schlangengrube und das Pendel*

Lange, Christina (act): *Alfred Hitchcock Presents*

Lange, Claudia (act): *Crossplot; The Invincible Brothers Maciste*

Lange, Elaine (act): *Dangerous Money*

Lange, Hellmut (act): *Forger of London*

Lange, Hope (act, b. 1933): *Blue Velvet; Crowhaven Farm; Ferde-Lance; A Nightmare On Elm Street, Part 2: Freddy's Revenge*

Lange, Jean (act): *Eraserhead*

Lange, Jessica (act, b. 1949): *All That Jazz; Cape Fear (1991); Hush; King Kong (1976)*

Lange, Kelly (act): *Chosen Survivors*

Lange, Richard (act): *Rana: The Legend of Shadow Lake*

Langedijk, Jack (act): *Blind Fear; Darkman II: The Return of Durant*

Langelaan, George (wri): *The Fly (1958 & 1986); Return of the Fly*

Langella, Frank (act, b. 1946): *Brainscan; Cutthroat Island; The Deadly Trap; Doomsday Gun; Dracula(1979); Junior; The Mark of Zorro (1974); Masters of the Universe; Small Soldiers; Sphinx (1981)*

Langen, Inge (act): *The Ape Creature*

Langen, Todd W. (wri): *Teenage Mutant Ninja Turtles; Teenage Mutant Ninja Turtles II: The Secret of the Ooze*

Langenfeld, Sarah (act): *Blood Link*

Langenkamp, Heather (act): *A Nightmare On Elm Street; A Nightmare On Elm Street 3: Dream Warriors; Shocker; Wes Craven's New Nightmare*

Langer, A.J. (act, b. 1974): *Escape from L.A.; The People Under the Stairs*

Langford, Bonnie (act): *Wombling Free*

Langford, Judy (act): *The Savage Bees*

Langham, Chris (act): *The McGuffin*

Langhanke, Lucile (act): see Astor, Mary

Langker, Bibi (act): *Those Dear Departed*

L'Anglaise, Kevin (act): *A Midsummer Night's Dream (1985)*

Langland, Liane (act): *The Demon Murder Case; Murder With Mirrors*

Langlen, Paula (act): *Just Imagine*

Langley, Faith (act): *Donovan's Brain*

Langley, Herbert (act): *Chu Chin Chow (1923); Number 17*

Langley, John (wri): *Deadly Sins*

Langley, Noel (dir, b. 1911): *The Search for Bridey Murphy; Svengali (1954)*

Langley, Noel (wri, b. 1911): *Androcles and the Lion; Knights of the Round Table; The Prisoner of Zenda (1952); Queer Cargo; Scrooge (1951); The Search for Bridey Murphy; The Secret of Stamboul; Snow White and the Three Stooges; Svengali (1954); They Made Me a Fugitive; The Wizard of Oz (1939)*

Langley, Norman (cin): *Freelance; House of the Long Shadows; Jekyll and Hyde*

Langley, Peter (act): *Escape Clause; The Spider and the Fly (1994)*

Langley, Victor (act): *Mata Hari (1985); Murder by Decree*

Langlois, Eric (act): *Greystoke: The Legend of Tarzan, Lord of the Apes*

Langlois, Lisa (act): *Blood Relatives; Deadly Eyes; Happy Birthday to Me; The Man Who Wasn't There; Mindfield; The Nest; Phobia; Transformations (1989); Violette Noziere*

Langlois, Yves (act): *Quest for Fire*

Langly, Bryan (cin): *Dark Eyes of London*

Langone, Steve (act): *Primal Scream*

Langone, Vincent (act): *Primal Scream*

Langova, Sylva (act): *Avalanche Express; Incident at Midnight; Little Red Monkey*

Langrick, Margaret (act): *Cold Comfort; Harry and the Hendersons*

Langrishe, Caroline (act): *A Christmas Carol (1984); Dead Man's Folly; Who Is Killing the Great Chefs of Europe?*

Langsdale, Keith (act): *The Clonus Horror*

Langston, Murray (act): *The Being; Repossessed; Wishful Thinking*

Langston, Murray (dir): *Wishful Thinking*

Langton, David (act, 1911-1994): *Last Video and Testament; The Liquidator*

Langton, Diane (act): *A Choice of Weapons*

Langton, Paul (act, 1913-1980): *The Cosmic Man; For You I Die; The Hidden Eye; The Incredible Shrinking Man; Invisible Invaders; It!—The Terror from Beyond Space; Murder Is My Beat; Shock Treatment(1964); The Snow Creature*

Langtry, Kenneth (wri) see Kandel, Aben

Lanier, Bob (act): *Blink*

Lanier, Didi (act): *The Offspring*

Lanier, Jean (act): *L'Annee Derniere a Marienbad*

Lanier, Phil (act): *The Psychotronic Man*

Lanier, Stephen H. (cin): *The [illegible] of Karen*

Lanier, Susan (act): *The Hills Have Eyes; The Hills Have Eyes II*

Laning, Robert (wri): *The Hostage (1966)*

Lankford, Kim (act): *Cameron's Closet; The Octagon*

Lankford, T.L. (wri): *Deep Space; The Phantom Empire*

Lanko, Vivian (act): *The Rejuvenator*

Lanner, Margarete (act): *Metropolis (1926)*

Lanning, Frank (act): *Temple Tower; The Unknown (1927)*

Lanning, Reggie (cin): *The Catman of Paris; Dick Tracy vs. Crime, Inc.*

Lanning, William (act): *The Lucifer Complex*

Lannom, Les (act): *Purgatory; The Spirit*

Lanoe, J.J. (act): *The Altar Stairs*

Lanoff, Lawrence (dir): *Temptress (1995)*

La Noire, Rosetta (act): *Fritz the Cat*

Lanois, Dan(iel) (mus): *For All Mankind; Sling Blade*

Lanoux, Victor (act): *The Evil Trap*

Lanphier, James (act, 1920-1969): *Experiment In Terror; Flight of the Lost Balloon*

Lansbury, Angela (act, b. 1925): *Anastasia; Beauty and the Beast (1991); Beauty and the Beast: The Enchanted Christmas; Bedknobs and Broomsticks; The Company of Wolves; Death On the Nile; Gaslight (1944); Kind Lady (1951); The Lady Vanishes (1979); The Last Unicorn; A Life at Stake; The Manchurian Candidate; The Mirror Crack'd; Mrs. Santa Claus; Mutiny; The Picture of Dorian Gray (1945); Please Murder Me; The Purple Mask; Samson and Delilah; Something for Everyone;The Three Musketeers (1948)*

Lansbury, Bruce (wri): *I'm Dangerous Tonight; The Return of the Six Million Dollar Man and the Bionic Woman*

Lansbury, Felicia (act): *I'm Dangerous Tonight*

Lanser, Roger (cin): *The Munsters' Scary Little Christmas*

Lansford, Roy (act): *Murder by Decree*

Lansford, William Douglas (wri): *The Big Cube*

Lansing, Joe (act): *Big Foot*

Lansing, Joi (act, 1929-1972): *The Atomic Submarine; Hillbillys In a Haunted House; Pier 23*

Lansing, Mary (act): *Just Imagine*

Lansing, Robert (act, 1926-1994, nee Robert Howell Brown): *The Astronaut; Bionic Showdown: The Six Million Dollar Man and the Bionic Woman; Empire of the Ants; 4D Man; The Nest; The Night of the Claw; Scalpel; S*H*E (1980)*

Lanson, Len (act): *Wargames*

Lanteau, William (act, 1923-1993): *Shadow of a Doubt (1991)*

Lanter, Mieke (act): *Zapped!*

Lanthier, Steven (act): *Oh Heavenly Dog*

Lantieri, Louie (cin): *Nothing But Trouble*

Lantieri, Michael (cin): *The Flintstones; Jurassic Park; The Lost World: Jurassic Park*

Lantz, Louis (wri): *Crime Doctor; River of No Return*

Lanvin, Gerard (act): *The Prize of Peril*

Lanyer, Charles (act): *The Stepfather*

Lanyon, Annabelle (act): *Legend; The Quatermass Conclusion*

Lanza, Anthony M. (dir): *The Incredible 2-Headed Transplant*

Lanza, Laura (act): *The Incredible 2-Headed Transplant*

Lanza, Sophie (act): *Alien High*

LaPage, Roger (act): *I, Madman*

LaPaglia, Anthony (act, b. 1959): *Black Magic (1992); Innocent Blood; Past Tense*

LaPaglia, Jonathan (act): *Inferno (1998)*

Lapenieks (Jr.), Vilis (cin): *Capture That Capsule!; Night Tide; Queen of Blood*

la Penna, J. Anthony (act): *Room to Let*

Lapensee, Francine (act): *Demon Wind; Rape of Eden*

Lapidus, Esther (act): *Jack's Wife*

Lapidus, Lily (act): *The Dragon of Pendragon Castle*

LaPiere, Georganne (act): *Jennifer (1978)*

La Pillina (act): *Pandora and the Flying Dutchman*

Lapin, Jeanne (act): *L'Ours*

Lapinski, Laurie (act): *Pranks*

La Placa, Alison (act): *In the Nick of Time*

LaPlanche, Rosemary (act): *Devil Bat's Daughter; The Falcon Out West; Strangler of the Swamp*

LaPlante, Ed (act): *The Intruder Within*

La Plante, Laura (act, b. 1904): *The Cat and the Canary (1927); Crooked Alley; The Last Warning(1929)*

La Paloma (act): *El Amor Brujo (1973 & 1986)*

La Porta, Fred (act): *The Hideous Sun Demon*

Laporta, Jeanne (act): *Street Trash*

La Porte, Eliza (act): Der Student von Prag (1926)
Lapotaire, Jane (act, b. 1944): The Asphyx; Crescendo; The Dark Angel (1991); Murder by Moonlight; One of Our Dinosaurs Is Missing
Lapp, Richard (act): The Clone Master
La Presle, Kevin (act): Virtuosity
Lara, Jean (act): The Man In the Iron Mask (1962)
Lara, Joann (act): It's Alive III: Island of the Alive
Lara, Joe (act, b. 1962): American Cyborg: Steel Warrior;Final Equinox; Human Timebomb; The Presence; Steel Frontier; Tarzan In Manhat-tan; Warhead
Laraia, Carol (act): see Lawrence, Carol
Laramy, Grant (act): The Murder Clinic
Larange, Stewart (act): Return to Oz
Larbi, Doghmi (act): The Man Who Would Be King
Larch, John (act): The Amityville Horror; Bad Ronald; Ellery Queen; A Fire In the Sky (1978); Future Cop; Play Misty for Me; The Wrecking Crew
Lardie, Michael (act): Maid to Order
Lardner Jr., Ring (wri, b. 1915): Britannia Mews
Laren, Michael (act): The Manitou
Laretta, August (act): Wizards of the Lost Kingdom
Larew, Lee O. (wri): Blood Waters of Dr. Z
Largay, Ray (act): The Hidden Eye
Large, Norman (act): Repossessed
Large, Rob (act): Earth Girls Are Easy
La Riana (act): The Wolf Man (1941)
Larimer, Linda (act): Phantom of the Paradise
Larimore, Lois (act): The Punisher
Larinaga, Forster (act): Doctor Mabuse
Larion, Anna (act): The Magic Voyage of Sinbad
Larive, L. (act): The Passion of Joan of Arc
Larken, Sheila (act): The Midnight Hour
Larkey, Caren (act): Sole Survivor
Larkin, Bob (act): Prey of the Chameleon
Larkin, Bryan (act): Edward Scissorhands; Jacob's Ladder; Jennifer 8
Larkin, John (act, 1912-1965): The Satan Bug
Larkin, John (dir): Circumstantial Evidence
Larkin, John (F.) (wri): Castle In the Desert; Charlie Chan at the Wax Museum; Charlie Chan at Treasure Island; Charlie Chan In Panama; Dead Men Tell; The LoneWolf Meets a Lady; The Mandarin Mystery
Larkin, Kirsten (act): When a Stranger Calls
Larkin, Laure (act): The Silencers (1995)
Larkin, Linda (act): Aladdin (1992); Aladdin and the King of Thieves; The Return of Jafar
Larkin, Mary (act): Midnight's Child; Psychomania (1972)
Larkin, Sheena (act): Dr. Jekyll and Ms. Hyde
Larner, Elizabeth (act): Royal Flash
Larner, Stevan (cin): Gray Lady Down; Heartless; What Ever Happened to Baby Jane? (1991); World War III
LaRocca, Sonny (act): Midnight Lace (1981)
LaRocco, Carl (act): Amazons (1984)
La Roche, Mary (act): The Lineup
La Rocque, Rod (act, 1896-1969): Beyond Tomorrow; The Hunchback of Notre Dame (1939); International Crime; The Shadow Strikes
LaRosa, Kevin (act): The Fugitive (1993)
LaRossa, Adrienne (act): The Conspiracy of Torture
La Roy, Rita (act): Midnight Mystery
Larquey, Pierre (act): Le Corbeau; Diabolique (1955); La Main du Diable; Les Sorcieres de Salem
Larrabeiti, Mariana (act): Cuento de Hadas
Larranga, Fernando (act): Survive!
Larrath, J.R. (dir & wri): Whirlpool (1970)
Larraz, Jose(ph) (dir): The Golden Lady; Scream and Die!; Symptoms; Vampyres; Daughters of Dracula
Larraz, Jose (wri): Symptoms
Larri (act): Hundra
Larrimore, George (act): I Was a Zombie for the F.B.I.
Larriva, Tito (act): From Dusk Till Dawn
Larriva, Tito (mus): Freeway; Repo Man
Larronde, Annie (act): Amazons (1986)
Larroquette, John (act, b. 1947): Altered States; Cat People (1982); Demon Knight; Second Sight; Star Trek III: The Search for Spock; Twilight Zone
Larsen, Barbara (act): Akira
Larsen, Bob (act): The Grim Reaper
Larsen, Chris (act): Vampire On Bikini Beach
Larsen, Craig R. (act): Earthbound (1981)
Larsen, Elsebeth (act): Crazy Paradise
Larsen, Gerd (act): Stories from a Flying Trunk
Larsen, Gerda (act): The Man Who Could Cheat Death
Larsen, Gregg R. (act): Earthbound (1981)
Larsen, Grey (mus): Tuck Everlasting
Larsen, Keith (act): Dial Red O; Hiawatha (1952); Night of the Witches; The Omegans; Security Risk; Women of the Prehistoric Planet
Larsen, Lance (act): Flesh Gordon
Larsen, Louis (cin): Himmelskibet
Larsen, Suzan (act): see Foster, Susanna
Larsen, Trygve (wri): Die Toten Augen von London
Larsen, William (act): Heaven Can Wait (1978)
Larsen, Wolf (act): Tracks of a Killer
Larson, Bob (act): Toxic Zombies
Larson, Christine (act): Valley of the Headhunters; The Well
Larson, Darrell (act): Android; Brainstorm (1983); The China Syndrome; Futureworld; When Time Ran Out
Larson, Dennis (act): The Borrowers (1973)
Larson, Eric (act): Demon Wind; Uninvited (1987)
Larson, Eric (dir): Peter Pan (1953); Sleeping Beauty (1959)
Larson, George (cin): Rip Van Winkle (1921)
Larson, Glen A. (wri): Battlestar Galactica; Buck Rogers In the 25th Century
Larson, Jay B. (act): Cinderella 2000
Larson, John (cin): 2020 Texas Gladiators
Larson, Lisa (act): Empire of Ash III
Larson, Liz (act): Dr. Jekyll and Ms. Hyde
Larson, Paul (act): Altered States; The China Syndrome; The Intruder Within
Larson, Scott Alan (act): Heartless
Larson, Wolf (act): Storm Chasers: Revenge of the Twister
Larsson, Signe (act): see Hasso, Signe
Larsson, Stig (act): The Element of Crime
la Rubia, Marga (act): Arsene Lupin
La Rue, Eva (act): The Barbarians (1987); Crash and Burn; Heart Condition
La Rue, Fontaine (act): A Blind Bargain
LaRue, Jack (act, 1903-1984, nee Gaspare Biondolillo): Charlie Chan In Panama; Desperate Chance for Ellery Queen; Footsteps In the Dark; For Heaven's Sake; The Kennel Murder Case; No Orchids for Miss Blandish; The Road to Utopia; Secret of the Chateau; The Spanish Cape Mystery; The Spy In the Green Hat
La Rue Jr., Jack (act): Crypt of the Living Dead
LaRue, Rodger (act): The Annihilator
LaRussa, Adrienne (act): The Man Who Fell to Earth (1976); Psychout for Murder
Lary, Pierre (cin): The Discreet Charm of the Bourgeoisie
La Salle, Eriq (act, b. 1962): Color of Night; Jacob's Ladder
LaSalle, Martin (act): Dr. Tarr's Torture Dungeon; Nightlife (1989, USA-Mex); Sorceress (1982)
LaSalle, Richard (mus): The Amazing Captain Nemo; City Beneath the Sea (1970); Daughters of Satan; The Day Mars Invaded Earth;Diary of a Madman; Doctor Death: Seeker of Souls; The Flight That Disappeared; Hands of a Stranger; Mermaids of Tiburon; The Thirsty Dead; The Time Travelers (1964)
LaSane, James (act): Ritual of Evil
LaSardo, Robert (act): Short Circuit 2
Lascelle, Ward (dir): Rip Van Winkle (1921)
Lascelles, Andrea (act): House of 1,000 Dolls
Lasdun, Gary (act): Crack In the World
Lasell, John (act): The Deathmaster
Laser, Dieter (act): The Glass Cell
Laser, J.A. (dir): Zombies Lake
Laseur, Cees (act): They Came by Night
La Shelle, Joseph (cin, b. 1905): The Anductors; Crime of Passion; Hangover Square; The Happy Land; I Was a Teenage Werewolf; Laura; The Luck of the Irish; Les Miserables (1952); My Cousin Rachel; River of No Return; Run for the Sun; The Thirteenth Letter
Lashley, Steve (act): Ravagers
Lashly, James (act): Always; Howard the Duck
Laska, Ray (act): The Man Who Saw Tomorrow
Laskay, Jason (act): Secrets of the Phantom Caverns
Lasker, Lawrence (wri): Project X (1987); WarGames
Laskin, Michael (act): It Came Upon the Midnight Clear; The Seventh Sign
Lasko, Diane (act): Phobia; Virus (1980)
Laskos, Andrew (wri): Daughter of Darkness (1990); House of Secrets (1993)
Laskowski, Jan (cin): Bariera
Laskus, Jacek (cin): Stepfather II
Lasky, Betty (wri): This Is Not a Test
Lasky, Gil (wri): Blood and Lace; The Night God Screamed
Lasky Jr., Jesse (L.) (wri, b. 1910): Il Ladro di Venezia; Mask of the Avenger; Paint Me a Murder; Pearl of the South Pacific; Salome (1953); Samson and Delilah; The Secret Agent (1936); The Wizard of Baghdad
Lasky, Mark (act): Deathrow Gameshow
Lass, Barbara (act): Hauser's Memory; Lycanthropus
Lass, Jeanne (act): Pulp
Lass, Jeff (mus): The Magic Bubble
Lassally, Walter (cin, b. 1926): The Adding Machine; The Day the Fish Came Out; Electra (1961); Memoirs of a Survivor; Psyche 59; Savages; Something for Everyone;To Kill a Clown
Lassander, Dagmar (act): The Black Cat (1980); Hatchet for a Honeymoon; The House by the Cemetery
Lasser, Louise (act, b. 1939): Blood Rage; Frankenhooker; Isn't It Shocking?
Lasseter, John (dir): Toy Story
Lassick, Sydney/Sidney (act): Alligator (1981); Carrie; Committed;Curse II: The Bite; Freeway; Future Shock; Lady In White; Pandemonium; Silent Madness; The Unseen (1981)
Lasswell, Tom (act): Don't Answer the Phone!
Last, Brenda (act): Peter Rabbit and the Tales of Beatrix Potter
Last, Simon (wri): Charlie Chan: Happiness Is a Warm Clue
Laster, Debbie (act): Nightmare Weekend
Lastimoso, Frankie (act): The Blood Drinkers
Laszlo, Alexander (mus): Amazon Quest; Beast from Haunted Cave; Black Magic (1944); Night ofthe Blood-Beast; One Body Too Many; Tarzan's Magic Fountain
Laszlo, Andrew (cin): The Funhouse (1981); Ghost Dad; Innerspace; Poltergeist II: The Other Side; Remo Williams: The Adventure Begins; Star Trek V: The Final Frontier; Streets of Fire
Laszlo, Carlos (wri): Silent Night, Deadly Night III
Laszlo, Ernest (cin, 1906-1984): Attack of the Puppet People; Daddy's Gone A-Hunting; D.O.A. (1949); Fantastic Voyage; Houdini (1953); Kiss Me Deadly; The Lady In the Iron Mask; Logan's Run;M (1950); The Naked Jungle; Omar Khayyam; Scared Stiff (1953);The Space Children; The Steel Trap; Tormented (1960); The Well
Late, Jason (act): Vice Versa (1988)
Latell, Lyle (act): Dick Tracy (1945); Dick Tracy Meets Gruesome; Dick Tracy's Dilemma; Dick Tracy vs. Cueball; One Mysterious Night; Shadows Over Chinatown; The Sky Dragon
Latella, Phil (act): Mannequin Two: On the Move
LaTesta, Pam (act): The Oracle (1985)
Latham, Anne (act): Mind Warp (1972)
Latham, John (act): We Do Believe In Ghosts
Latham, Larry (act): Aftermath
Latham, Louise (act): Dying Room Only; The Haunted (1991); Marnie; The Philadelphia Experiment
Latham, Lynn (act): Xanadu
Latham, Patricia (wri): A Ghost of a Chance (1968)
Latham, Philip (act): The Devil-Ship Pirates; Dracula, Prince of Darkness; The Invisible Asset; The Rivals; The Secret of Blood Island; Spy Story
Latham, Stuart (act): The Ghost Train (1941); The Man In the White Suit
Latham, Tony (act): Wolfen
Lathan, Bobbi Jo (act): The Man Who Fell to Earth (1987)
Lathbury, Stanley (act): The Speckled Band (1931); The Terror (1938)
Lathouris, Nico/Nick (act): Death In Brunswick; Mad Max
Lathrop, Philip (H.) (cin, b. 1916): The Black Bird (1975); Deadly Friend; Earthquake; Experiment In Terror; Finian's Rainbow; Hammett; The Illustrated Man; Jekyll and Hyde...Together Again; The Monster of Piedras Blancas; The Private Lives of Adam and Eve; 36 Hours (1965)
Latifah, Queen (act, b. 1970): Sphere
Latimer, Cherie (act): Sweet Kill
Latimer, Harry (act): Fatal Fingers
Latimer, Hugh (act): Counterspy; The Gentle Trap; Ghost Ship (1952); Jane Eyre (1970); The Last Man to Hang?; Night Train to Paris; Rogue's Yarn; The Strange World of Planet X; Talk of the Devil
Latimer, Jonathan (wri, 1907-1983): Alias Nick Beal; The Big Clock; Lady In the Morgue; The Last Warning(1938); The Lone Wolf Spy Hunt;Night Has a Thousand Eyes; Nocturne; Phantom Raiders; They Won't Believe Me; Topper Returns; The Westland Case; The Whole Truth
Latimer, Louise (act): Murder On a Bridle Path; The Plot Thickens
Latimer, Michael (act): Man of Violence; Prehistoric Women (1966); Spectre (1977)
Latimer, Robert (act): Shock Chamber
Latimore, Frank (act, b. 1925, nee Frank Kline): Black Magic (1949); The Golden Falcon; Mata Hari's Daughter; The Shadow of Zorro; Shock (1946)
Latimore, Joseph (act): Outbreak
Lating, Manfred (act): Bedknobs and Broomsticks
Latino, Nino (wri): Slaughter Hotel (1972)
Latinopoulos, Dede (act): Flatliners
Latler, Gregg (act): Howling IV
Latorraca, Ney (act): The Dolphin
La Torre, Charles (act, b. 1900): Bomba and the Hidden City; A Double Life (1947)
La Torre, Tony (act): The Man In the Santa Claus Suit
LaTouche, Richard (act): Shadow of a Doubt (1991)
Latremouile, Fred (act): The Plutonium Incident
Latshaw, Ryan (act): Jack-O
Latshaw, Steve (dir): Biohazard: The Alien Force; Jack-O; Dark Universe
Lattanzi, Michael (mus): Class of Nuke 'em High
Lattanzi, Tina (act): The Minotaur
Latter, Greg (wri): Cyborg Cop
Latter, Travis (act): Mad Max Beyond Thunderdome
Lattuada, Alberto (dir, b. 1914): Il Cappotto; Matchless
Lattuada, Alberto (wri, b. 1914): Il Cappotto
Latty, Beth (act): Def by Temptation
Latur, Susana (act): Gran Amore del Conde Dracula
Latzen, Ellen Hamilton (act):Fatal Attraction
Lau, Damian (act): The Heroic Trio
Lau, Laurence (act): Fantasies
Lau, Patrick (dir): The Scarlet Pimpernel (1999)
Lau, Wesley (act): The Venetian Affair
Laube, Mildred (act): Just Imagine
Laubenthal, Georg (act): Das Kalte Herz
Lauchlan, Agnes (act): Alf's Button Afloat; The Spy In Black; Time Is My Enemy
Lauchu, Carlos (act): The Silencers (1995); Stargate
Lauck, Joe D. (act): The Package
Lauda, Niki (act): Top Kids
Laudenbach, Philippe (act): Confidentially Yours
Laudenbach, Pierre (act): see Fresnay, Pierre
Lauer, Andy (act): Screamers (1996)
Lauer, William (act): To All a Goodnight
Laufer, Jack (act): Ghost In the Machine
Laufer, Jacob (act): The Fan
Laufglin, Candace (act): Critters 2: The Main Course
Laughinghouse, John (act): Operation C.I.A.
Laughlin, John (act): The Hills Have Eyes II; The Lawnmower Man; Murder With Mirrors; Space Rage
Laughlin, Michael (dir & wri): Strange Behavior; Strange Invaders
Laughton, Charles (act, 1899-1962): Abbott and Costello Meet Captain Kidd; The Big Clock; The Bribe; The Canterville Ghost (1944); Captain Kidd; The Hunchback of Notre Dame (1939); Island of Lost Souls; Jamaica Inn (1939); Les Miserables (1935); The Old Dark House (1932); The Paradine Case; Salome (1953);The Strange Door; The Suspect;White Woman; Witness for the Prosecution
Laughton, Charles (dir, 1899-1962): The Night of the Hunter (1955)
Laughton, Eddie (act): Confessions of Boston Blackie; Counter-Espionage; The Lone Wolf Keeps a Date; The Lone Wolf Spy Hunt; Meet Boston Blackie; One Dangerous Night
Laumer, Keith (wri, 1926-1993): The Monitors
Launder, Frank (wri, 1907-1997): Black Mask; Fortune Is a Woman; Gestapo; The Girl In the News; The Green Man; The Lady Vanishes (1938 & 1979); Ring of Spies; Seven Sinners; They Came by Night; Twelve Good Men
Launders, Perc (act): The Falcon In Hollywood; The Falcon Out West; For Heaven's Sake
Laundy, George (act): The Old Gardener
Launer, Dale (dir & wri): Love Potion No. 9
Launer, (S.) John (act): I Was a Teenage Werewolf; The Werewolf (1955)
Lauper, Cyndi (act): Vibes
Laurance, Judd (act): The Man With the Power; Wavelength
Laurance, Matthew (act): Tales from the Darkside

Laurance, Mitchell (act): The Hand That Rocks the Cradle; Syngenor
Laure, Carole (act, b. 1951): Sweet Movie
Laurel, Allen (act): The Horror of Party Beach
Laurel, Bobby (mus): The Rosary Murders
Laurel, Emily (act): The Horror of Party Beach
Laurel, Stan (act, 1890-1965, nee Arthur Stanley Jefferson): A-Haunting We Will Go; Atoll K; Babes In Toyland (1934); A Chump at Oxford
Lauren, Ashley (act): Lurking Fear
Lauren, Elizabeth (act): Neon Maniacs
Lauren, Honey (act): Bram Stoker's 'Dracula'
Lauren, Jeanne (act): Howard the Duck
Lauren, Rod (act): Black Zoo; The Crawling Hand; Terrified (1963)
Lauren, S.K. (wri): Crime and Punishment (1935, USA)
Lauren, Tammy (act): Bride of Boogedy; I Saw What You Did (1988); The Kid With the Broken Halo; The Stepford Children; Wishmaster
Lauren, Veronica (act): Forever Young
Laurence, Andrew (act): The Curse of the Wraydons; Macbeth (1971); The Mysterious Mr. Nicholson
Laurence, Ashley (act): Blood Run; Cupid; Hellbound: Hellraiser II; Hellraiser; Hellraiser III: Hell On Earth
Laurence, Charles (act): Cross Channel
Laurence, Michael (GB act): For Them That Trespass
Laurence, Michael (USA act): Someone's Watching Me!; Syngenor
Laurence, Paul (act): Death Race 2000
Laurence, Paul (mus): Def by Temptation
Laurence, Zack (mus): Assassin (1973)
Laurensen, Phil (act): The Wizard of Gore
Laurenson, James (act): In the Devil's Garden; The Man Who Fell to Earth (1987); The Monster Club; Paint Me a Murder
Laurent, Agnes (act): Un Amour de Poche; The Night of the Great Attack
Laurent, Lilian S. (act): Kemek
Laurent, Marie (wri): Curse of the Stone Hand
Laurent, Michele (act): Hellhole
Laurent, Patrick (wri): I Married a Shadow
Laurenti, Fabrizio (dir, a.k.a. Martin Newlin): The Crawlers; Witchery
Laurenti, Fabrizio (wri): The Crawlers
Laurents, Arthur (wri, b. 1918): Caught (1948); Rope
Lauria, Dan (act): Dean Koontz' 'Mr. Murder'
Lauria, Mary Dean (act): Heavy Traffic
Laurie, Edward (act): Jaws 3-D
Laurie, Hugh (act): 101 Dalmatians (1996)
Laurie, James (act): The Haunted School
Laurie, John (act, 1897-1980): The Abominable Dr. Phibes; The Black Knight; Devil Girl from Mars; Fanny by Gaslight; The Ghost at St. Michael's; Hamlet (1948); Madeleine; Murder Reported; No Trace; Old Mother Riley's Ghosts; One of Our Dinosaurs Is Missing; Pandora and the Flying Dutchman; Potter of the Yard; The Prisoner of Zenda (1979); Q Planes; The Reptile; Richard III (1955); Saturday Island; Siege of the Saxons; The 39 Steps (1935); Too Many Detectives; Tread Softly; Treasure Island (1950); Uncle Silas
Laurie, Hugh (act): The Borrowers (1998); 101 Dalmatians (1996)
Laurie, John (act): The Hand of Fate
Laurie, Piper (act, b. 1932, nee Rosetta Jacobs): Carrie; Dangerous Mission; Distortions; Dream a Little Dream; The Faculty; Francis Goes to the Races; The Golden Blade; Intensity; Return to Oz; Ruby; Son of Ali Baba; Trauma (1993)
Laurier, Jay (act): The Black Tulip (1937)
Laurin, Marie (act): Creature
Lauris, George (act): Sasquatch, the Legend of Bigfoot
Laurita, Dana (act): Demon Seed
Laustsen, Dan (cin): Mimic
Lauter, Ed (act): The Clone Master; Cujo; Digital Man; Family Plot; King Kong (1976); Magic; Rattled; The Rocketeer; Satan's Triangle; Timerider; Under Wraps
Lauter, Harry (act): Creature with the Atom Brain; The Cry Baby Killer; A Date With Death; Dig That Uranium!; Earth vs. the Flying Saucers; Escape from the Planet of the Apes; It Came from Beneath the Sea; Missile Monsters; Return to Treasure Island; The Satan Bug; Tarzan's Fight for Life; The Werewolf (1955)
Lauterer, Maggie (act): Wolfman (1979)
Lautner, Georges (dir, b. 1926): Icy Breasts; The Monocle
Lautore, Ronald (cin): Sanctuary of Fear
Lava, Tiva (act): The Blood Drinkers
Lava, William (mus): Assignment to Kill; Chamber of Horrors (1966); Dick Tracy's G-Men; Phantom from Space; The Sign of Zorro (1960); Zorro, the Avenger
Lavachielle, John (act): Time Walker
Lavagnino, Angelo (Francisco) (mus, b. 1909): The Colossus of Rhodes; I Criminali della Galassia; Gorgo; Hot Enough for June; The Last Days of Pompeii (1959); The Wonders of Aladdin
Lavalle, David (wri): Gray Lady Down
LaValley, Mara (act): Secrets In the Attic
Lavanant, Dominique (act): Monster (1994)
Lavelle, Bradley (act): Hellbound: Hellraiser II; Nightbreed
Laven, Arnold (dir, b. 1922): Down Three Dark Streets; Life, Liberty and Pursuit On the Planet of the Apes; The Monster That Challenged the World
Lavender, Peter (act): The Groundstar Conspiracy
Laverick, June (act, b. 1932): The Flesh and the Fiends; Son of Robin Hood
LaVerne, Lucille (act): Snow White and the Seven Dwarfs
Lavery, Emmet (wri): A Night In Paradise
Lavi, Daliah (act, b. 1940): Casino Royale; Il Demonio; La Frusta e il Corpo; In the Steel Net of Dr. Mabuse; Nobody Runs Forever; The Silencers (1966); Some Girls Do; The Spy With a Cold Nose; Ten Little Indians (1965); Those Fantastic Flying Fools
Lavia, Gabriele (act): Beyond the Door; Inferno (1979); Profundo Rosso; Revenge of the Dead (1984)
La Vigne, Michelle (act): My Best Friend Is a Vampire
Lavil, Denny (cin): The Creature Wasn't Nice
Lavin, Linda (act, b. 1937): The Muppets Take Manhattan
Lavis, Arthur (cin): Catacombs (1964); The Earth Dies Screaming; Journey Into Darkness; Journey to the Unknown; Killer's Moon; The Penthouse (1967); Ten Little Indians (1989); Witchcraft (1964)
Lavista, Raul (mus): Enchanted Island; The Little Savage; Robinson Crusoe and the Tiger; El Santo Contra las Vampiras
Lavitan, Gladys (act): Kidnapped Co-Ed
Lavogez, Yvette (act): Sous le Soleil de Satan
Lavoine, Marc (act): Torment (1993)
Lavrov, German (cin): Devyat'dney Odnogo Goda
Lavrova, Tamara (act): Dvyat'dney Odnogo Goda
Lavut, Martin (act): Heavy Metal; The Mask (1961)
Law, Don (act): King Kong Lives
Law, John (wri): Casino Royale
Law, John Phillip (act, b. 1937): Alienator; Barbarella; The Cassandra Crossing; Diabolik; The Golden Voyage of Sinbad; Space Mutiny; The Spiral Staircase (1975); Tarzan, the Ape Man (1981)
Law, Jude (act): eXistenZ; Gattaca
Law, Michael (dir & wri): The Six Men
Law, Phyllida (act): Hitler: The Last Ten Days; Otley; Tree of Hands
Law, Russell (act): Party Line
Law, Walter (act): The Flying Dutchman
Law, William (act): After the Thin Man; Think Fast, Mr. Moto
Lawden, Andrew (act): Robin Hood: Prince of Thieves
Lawford, Christopher (act): Spellbinder
Lawford, Peter (act, 1923-1984): Above Suspicion; The Canterville Ghost (1944); Dead Ringer; Ellery Queen: Don't Look Behind You; Fantasy Island; Flesh and Fantasy; The Hour of 13; Mysterious Island of Beautiful Women; The Phantom of Hollywood; The Picture of Dorian Gray (1945)
Lawhon, Woody (cin): Timecop
Lawler, Bill (act): The Norsemen
Lawler, Patti (act): Invasion of the Saucer Men
Lawless, Blackie (act): The Dungeonmaster
Lawless, Eddie (act): In the Days of Saint Patrick
Lawless, James (act): Satan's Touch
Lawless, Louie (act): Planet of Dinosaurs
Lawley, Henry (act): The Explosion of a Motor Car
Lawley, Yvonne (act): Death In Brunswick
Lawlor, Anderson (act): The Adventurous Blonde; Fly-Away Baby; The Invisible Menace; Torchy Blane In Chinatown
Lawlor, Harold (wri): Dominique
Lawlor, Ray (act): The Mask (1961)
Lawlor, Tom (act): Rawhead Rex
Lawner, Damon (act): Copycat
Lawner, Hadria (act): Waxwork II: Lost In Time
Lawner, Mordecai (act): Ghostbusters II
Lawrence, Adam (act): Drive-In Massacre
Lawrence, Alison (act): Curtains
Lawrence, Andrea (act): Countess Dracula; Frankenstein and the Monster from Hell
Lawrence, Andrew (act): Deadly Web
Lawrence, Anthony (wri): Dark Mansions; The Phoenix (1981); Sweet, Sweet Rachel
Lawrence, Barbara (act, b. 1930): Kronos (1957); The Street With No Name
Lawrence, Bert (wri): Dig That Uranium!; Jalopy; No Holds Barred; Spy Chasers
Lawrence, Billy (act): The Village of the Damned (1960)
Lawrence, Brian (wri): Last House on Dead End Street
Lawrence, Bruno (act): The Bridge to Nowhere; Death Warmed Up; The Quiet Earth
Lawrence, Bruno (wri): The Quiet Earth
Lawrence, Carol (act, b. 1935, nee Carol Laraia): Stranger In Our House
Lawrence, Christopher (act): The House On Sorority Row
Lawrence, D.H. (wri, 1885-1930): The Rocking Horse Winner
Lawrence, David (wri): Escape 2000
Lawrence, David (mus): Dog's Best Friend; Skeeter
Lawrence, Dean (act): Robin Hood Junior (1975)
Lawrence, Delphi (act, b. 1927): Barbados Quest; Blind Spot (1958); Bunny Lake Is Missing; The Fourth Square; Frozen Alive; The Gold Express; The Man Who Could Cheat Death; Meet Mr. Callaghan; Murder by Proxy; On the Run (1963); Seven Keys; Son of Robin Hood; The Square Mile Murder; Strangers' Meeting
Lawrence, Diarmuid (dir): The Witches and the Grinnygog
Lawrence, Dorothy (act): The Climax
Lawrence, Edmund (dir): The House of Secrets (1929)
Lawrence, Edwin (act): Seven Sinners
Lawrence, Elliot (mus): The Cradle Will Fall
Lawrence, Eric (act): Buck Rogers In the 25th Century
Lawrence, Gail (act): Maniac (1980)
Lawrence, Gerald (act): The Fall of a Saint; The Grand Babylon Hotel; The Harbour Lights; The Romany Rye
Lawrence, Gerald (dir & wri): His Just Desserts
Lawrence, Glen (act): The Funhouse (1981)
Lawrence, H.L. (wri): The Damned
Lawrence, Hank (act): The Gifted One
Lawrence, Hap (act): Altered States; Fantasies
Lawrence, James C. (act): The Final Countdown
Lawrence, Jay (act): The Dark (1979); Heavy Traffic; Kingdom of the Spiders
Lawrence, Jeremy (act): Critters
Lawrence, Jessie (act): Darkman (1990)
Lawrence, Jody (act, b. 1930): Capt. John Smith and Pocahontas; Mask of the Avenger; The Scarlet Hour; The Son of Dr. Jekyll
Lawrence, Joel (act): The Clonus Horror
Lawrence, Joey (act, b. 1976): Oliver & Company; Pulse
Lawrence, John (GB act): The Asphyx
Lawrence, John (USA act): The Destructors; Seconds; They Live
Lawrence, John (dir): Cycle Psycho
Lawrence, John (wri): Cycle Psycho; The Incredible 2-Headed Transplant
Lawrence, Joyce (act): see Carey, Joyce
Lawrence, Kenneth (act): How Awful About Allan
Lawrence, Kiva (act): Schizoid (1980)
Lawrence, Linda (act): I, Desire
Lawrence, Marc (act, b. 1910): Beware, Spooks!; Blind Alley; Blood Pen; Cataclysm; Charlie Chan at the Wax Museum; Charle Chan In Honolulu; Charlie Chan OnBroadway; Cloak and Dagger (1946); Diamonds Are Forever; Donor; Dream No Evil; Eyes of the Underworld; From Dusk Till Dawn; Hold That Ghost; Kill Her Gently; Kong Island; The Kremlin Letter; The Lone Wolf Spy Hunt; The Man With the Golden Gun; Marathon Man; The Monster and the Girl; Nazi Agent; Super Fuzz; This Gun for Hire (1942); Who Killed Gail Preston?
Lawrence, Marc (dir, b. 1910): Blood Pen; Nightmare In the Sun
Lawrence, Marjie/Marjy (act): Hands of the Ripper; I, Monster; Moment of Decision; Stranger In the House (1967)
Lawrence, Mark (act): Johnny Cool
Lawrence, Mark Christopher (act): Tales from the Hood
Lawrence, Matthew (act, b. 1980): With a Vengeance
Lawrence, Max (act): Operazione Paura
Lawrence, Michael (act): Color Me Dead
Lawrence, Nancy (wri): Dark Mansions; The Phoenix (1981)
Lawrence, Paula (act): Eyes of Laura Mars
Lawrence, Peter (wri): The Burning; The Sins of Dorian Gray
Lawrence, Quentin (dir, b. 1923): Cash On Demand; The Man Who Finally Died; Playback; The Secret of Blood Island; The Trollenberg Terror; We Shall See
Lawrence, Ronald William (act): Eve of Destruction
Lawrence, Rosina (act): Charlie Chan's Secret
Lawrence, Scott (act): The First Power; God's Bloody Acre; Timecop; When the Bough Breaks
Lawrence, Sharon (act, b. 1961): The Shaggy Dog (1994); The Uninvited (1996)
Lawrence, Shawn (act): Clarence; Escape Clause
Lawrence, Sheldon (act): Bluebeard's Ten Honeymoons; The Crooked Sky; The Long Knife; The Man Without a Body; Mark of the Phoenix; The Pursuers; Stormy Crossing; Too Hot to Handle; Transatlantic; West of Suez
Lawrence, Shirley (act): Satellite In the Sky; Willard
Lawrence, Stanley (act): Ghost (1990)
Lawrence, Stephanie (act): The Phantom of the Opera (1989)
Lawrence, Stephen (mus): Alice, Sweet Alice; Mirrors
Lawrence, Steve (act, b. 1935): Alice In Wonderland (1985)
Lawrence, Tom (act): Wargames
Lawrence, Toni (act): Blood Pen; Donor
Lawrence, Trevor (act): Captain Kronos: Vampire Hunter; The Quatermass Conclusion
Lawrence, Vincent (wri): Peter Ibbetson
Lawrence, Wingold (act): Eugene Aram; For East Is East; The Girl Who Took the Wrong Turning; The Mysteries of London; The Price He Paid; The Rajah's Revenge
Lawrence, Wood (wri): Mizpah: or, Love's Sacrifice
Lawrie, Dean (act): Bad Taste
Laws, Maury (mus): The Bermuda Depths; The Flight of Dragons; The Hobbit; The Ivory Ape; The Last Dinosaur; The Return of the King
Laws, Sam (act): Dr. Black Mr. Hyde; The Fury; Project X (1987)
Lawson, Adam (act): A.P.E.X.
Lawson, Anne (act): The Double
Lawson, Barbara (act): Visit to a Small Planet
Lawson, Cheryl (act): Virtuosity
Lawson, David (mus): Victims
Lawson, Denis (act): Holocaust 2000; The Empire Strikes Back; Return of the Jedi
Lawson, Eric (act): Rattlers
Lawson, Gerald (C.) (act): Dr. Blood's Coffin; The Mummy (1959); The Vengeance of She
Lawson, John (act): The King of Crime; The Monkey's Paw (1915)
Lawson, Kate (act): Phantom of the Opera (1943); Torchy Plays With Dynamite
Lawson, Leigh (act, b. 1945): Black Carrion; Charlie Boy/The Thirteenth Reunion; Fire & Sword; Ghost Story (1975); The God King; Murder Is Easy; Sword of the Valiant
Lawson, Lewis (act): The Creeping Terror
Lawson, Linda (act): Let's Kill Uncle; Night Tide; The Threat (1960)
Lawson, Louise (act): The Creeping Terror
Lawson, Maggie (act): I've Been Waiting for You
Lawson, Mary (act): Scrooge (1935)
Lawson, Mindy (act): Switch (1991)
Lawson, Oscar (act): Zombie Island Massacre
Lawson, Richard (act): Audrey Rose; Pandora's Clock; Scream, Blacula, Scream; Streets of Fire; Sugar Hill; V
Lawson, Sandra (act): The Medium (1934)
Lawson, Sarah (act, b. 1928): The Devil Rides Out; Links of Justice; Meet Mr. Malcolm; The Night of the Big Heat; Night Without Pity; The Night Won't Talk; On the Run (1963); The Solitary Child; Three Crooked Men; Three Steps In the Dark
Lawson, Wilfrid (act, 1900-1966, nee Wilfrid Worsnop): Dead Man's Shoes; Fanny by Gaslight; The Gaunt Stranger; The Ghost Train (1941); The Man Who Made Diamonds; The Naked Edge; The Night Has Eyes; The Terror (1938); Tower of Terror; Tread Softly Stranger; The Viking Queen; The Wrong Box
Lawton, Alma (act): My Cousin Rachel
Lawton (Jr.), Charles (cin, 1904-1965): Eyes In the Night; The Lady from Shanghai; Mask of the Avenger; Miracles for Sale; Nick Carter, Master Detective; The Return of Monte Cristo; [illegible]
Lawton, David (act): Kill Her Gently
Lawton, Frank (act, 1904-1969): Birds of Prey; Devil Doll (1936); Gideon's Day; The Invisible Ray; Went the Day Well?

Lawton, J.F. (wri): Blankman; Chain Reaction (1996)
Lay, Mei Mei (act): Cannibal; Crucible of Terror; Eaten Alive (1980)
Lay, Robert (wri): Atlantis (1948)
Laye, Dilys (act): Carry On Spying; Torment (1949)
Laye, Evelyn (act, b. 1900): Never-Never Land; Theatre of Death
Layne, G. Cornell (wri): Abby
Layne, Randi (act): Web of Deceit
Layng, Lissa (act): Night of the Comet
Layton, Marcia (act): Cthulhu Mansion
Layton, Vernon (cin): Panic (1979)
Layton, William (act): The Scarlet Letter (1972)
Lazaga, Pedro (dir): Gladiators Seven
Lazar, Ava (act): The Nature of the Beast
La Zar, John (act): Attack of the 60 Foot Centerfold; Deathstalker II: Duel of the Titans
Lazar, Paul (act): The Silence of the Lambs
Lazar, Veronica (act): Inferno (1979); 7 Doors of Death
Lazard, Justin (act): Species II
Lazard, Isabelle (act): Notorious (1992)
Lazare, Carol (act): The Fly (1986)
Lazareff, Vladovia (act): Rocket Attack U.S.A.
Lazaren, Norma (act): Survive!
Lazarev, Evgeny (act): The Saint
Lazaro, Eusebio (act): The Return of the Musketeers
Lazarus, Frank (act): Superman (1978)
Lazarus, Jerry (wri): Treasure of the Four Crowns
Lazarus, Tom (wri): The Awakening of Candra; Rona Jaffe's Mazes and Monsters
Lazarus, Zack (act): Spookies
Lazauer, Jeff (act): Twister
LaZebnik, Philip (wri): Pocahontas
Lazenby, George (act, b. 1939): Death Dimension; Fatally Yours; The Man from Hong Kong; On Her Majesty's Secret Service; The Return of the Man from U.N.C.L.E.; Stoner
Lazer, Peter (act): Pinocchio In Outer Space
Lazzarino, Tony (wri): X-15
Lea, Andrea (act): The House of the Arrow (1953)
Lea, Daphne (act): Scream and Die!
Lea, Nicholas (act): Xtro II: The Second Encounter
Lea, Ron (act): Giving Up the Ghost; Happy Birthday to Me; The Neighbor; Wild Thing
Lea, Sharan (act): Something Wicked This Way Comes
Leabo, Betty (act): see Joyce, Brenda
Leach, Alan (act): Tattoo
Leach, Alexander Archibald (act): see Grant, Cary
Leach, Britt (act): Silent Night, Deadly Night; Weird Science
Leach, Geoff (mus): Panic (1979)
Leach, Nicole (act): Tales from the Darkside
Leach, Robert (wri): Tarzan and the Trappers
Leach, Rosemary (act): Face of a Stranger; The Hawk; The Mystery of Edwin Drood (1993)
Leach, Sheryl (wri): Barney's Great Adventure
Leachman, Cloris (act, b. 1926): Charley and the Angel; The Demon Murder Case; Double, Double, Toil and Trouble; Dying Room Only; Happy Mother's Day, Love George; Haunts of the Very Rich; Herbie Goes Bananas; It Happened One Christmas; Kiss Me Deadly; The Mouse and His Child; The Muppet Movie; My Boyfriend's Back; My Little Pony; The New, Original Wonder Woman; A Troll In Central Park; Young Frankenstein
Leacock, Philip (dir, 1917-1990): Baffled!; The Curse of King Tut's Tomb; Dying Room Only; The Spanish Gardener; 13 West Street; When Michael Calls
Lead, Shannon (act): Witchcraft 6: The Devil's Mistress
Leadbetter, Cindy (act): The Adventures of Hercules
Leader, Anton M. (dir, 1914-1988): Children of the Damned
Leaf, Hillary (act): The Human Factor
Leaf, Paul (act): Top Secret (1978)
Leaf, Richard (act): Mary Reilly
Leahey, Nicholas (act): Never-Never Land
Leahy, Brian (mus): Distortions
Leahy, Eugene (act): The Crimson Candle
Leak, Jennifer (act): Eye of the Cat
Leake, Cynthia (act): Fire and Ice
Leake, Damien (act): Highlander
Leakey, Barbara (act): Dead of Night (1945); Kind Hearts and Coronets
Leal, Amparo Soler (act): Amador
Leal, Jack (act): Shadowzone
Lealand, David (act): Scars of Dracula
Leamer, John (act): The Fifth Missile; From Beyond; Terrorvision; Zone Troopers
Lean, David (dir, 1908-1991): Blithe Spirit; Great Expectations (1946); Madeleine; The Sound Barrier
Lean, David (wri, 1908-1991): Great Expectations (1946)
Leander, Mike (mus): The Adding Machine; Privilege
Learned, Jane (act): The Handmaid's Tale
Leary, Craig S. (act): Cavegirl (1985)
Leary, Denis (act): A Bug's Life; Demolition Man
Leary, Nolan (act): Man of a Thousand Faces
Leary, O'Mara (act): Don't Go In the House
Leary, (Dr.) Timothy (act): Night Visions; Shocker
Lease, Maria (dir & wri): Dolly Dearest
Lease, Rex (act, 1901-1966): The Clutching Hand; Cyclotrode X; Ghost Rider (1935); The Monster Walks; On the Threshold of Space; The Time of Their Lives
Leask, Don B. (cin): Timecop
Leasor, James (wri): Where the Spies Are
Leather, Frank (act): Making Contact
Leaud, Jean-Pierre (act, b. 1944): I Hired a Contract Killer; Le Plus Vieux Metier du Monde; Le Testament d'Orphee
Leavengood, Joe (act): Lurking Fear
Leaver, Philip (act): Dr. Morelle-The case of the Missing Heiress; The Flesh and the Fiends; The Gamma People; Jack the Ripper (1958); The Key Man; The Lady Vanishes (1938); Mother Riley Meets the Vampire; Spaceways; This Man Is News
Leavitt, Lane (act): Timestalkers
Leavitt, Norman (act): The Three Stooges in Orbit
Leavitt, Sam (cin): Brainstorm (1965); Cape Fear (1961); Dr. Goldfoot and the Bikini Machine; I Deal In Danger; Johnny Cool; Murderers' Row; My Blood Runs Cold; The Screaming Woman; Shock Treatment (1964); The Thief (1952); Two On a Guillotine
Leavitt, Stanley (act): Carnival of Souls (1962)
Leavy, Jack (act): The Keeper
Leavy, Leo (act): The Keeper
Le Ballister, Renee (act): Dr. Caligari
Lebar, Bob (cin): Raiders of the Living Dead
Le Bar John (wri): The Enchanted Forest
LeBeau, Becky (act): The Malibu Beach Vampires; Not of This Earth (1988); School Spirit
le Beau, Betty (act): The Trunk
Lebeau, Madeleine (act): Cage of Gold; 8 1/2; Paris After Dark
Lebeau, Mikey (act): Ice Cream Man
Lebedeff, Ivan (act, 1899-1953): Blue, White and Perfect; Midnight Mystery; The Mystery of Mr. Wong; The Sorrows of Satan (1925); TheWar of the Worlds
LeBell, (David) Gene (act): Ed Wood; Heartbeeps; Remo Williams: The Adventure Begins
Le Berthon, Helene (act): Mystery Circle Murder
LeBlanc, Carl (act): Candyman: Farewell to the Flesh
Leblanc, Georgette (act & wri): L'Inhumaine
LeBlanc, Matt (act, b. 1967): Lost In Space
le Blanc, Maurice (wri): Arsene Lupin
Leblanc, Paul (act): Alien High
Leblanc, Tony (act): Faustina
Lebo, Henry (cin): Ebenezer
Lebon, Yvette (act): Baraka X-77
Lebor, Stanley (act): The Deadly Affair; Flash Gordon (1980); I Don't Want to Be Born; The Medusa Touch; Nothing But the Night
LeBorg, Reginald (dir, b. 1902): The Black Sleep; Calling Dr. Death; Dead Man's Eyes; Destiny (1944);Diary of a Madman; The Eyes of Annie Jones; The Flanagan Boy; The Flight That Disappeared; House of the Black Death; The Jungle Woman;The Mummy's Ghost; Philo Vance's Secret Mission; Sins of Jezebel; So Evil, My Sister; Voodoo Island; Weird Woman; The White Orchid
LeBorg, Reginald (wri, b. 1902): The White Orchid
Le Bouvier, Jean (act): Someone's Watching Me!
LeBow, Hilary (act): City On Fire
Lebowitz, Leo (cin): Hercules In New York
le Breton, Flora (act): The Crimson Circle (1922); The House of Peril
LeBrock, Gene (act): Beyond Darkness; Fortress of Amerika; Metamorphosis
LeBrock, Kelly (act, b. 1960): Tracks of a Killer; Weird Science
LeBron, Larry (wri): Dr. Black Mr. Hyde
LeBrun, George T. (wri): Death Ring
Lebrun, Michel (wri): Shadow of Evil (1964)
le Carpentier, Jacques (act): Perceval
Le Carre, John (wri, b. 1931): The Deadly Affair; The Little Drummer Girl; The Spy Who Came In from the Cold
Lecavalier, Louise (act): Strange Days
Lech, Zygmunt (dir): Sarah's House
Le Chanois, Jean-Paul (dir, b. 1909, nee Jean-Paul Dreyfus): Les Miserables (1957)
Le Chanois, Jean-Paul (wri, b. 1909): La Main du Diable; Les Miserables (1957)
Lechner, Thomas (wri): Making Contact
LeClair, Paul (act): Nothing But Trouble
Le Claire, Tokeli (act): Writer's Block
Leclerc, Georges (cin & mus): Le Testament du Dr. Cordelier
Leclerc, Ginette (act, 1912-1992): Le Corbeau
Leclerc, Jean (act): Dean R. Koontz' 'Whispers'; The Uncanny
Leclerc, Srance (act): Howling II
Leclerq, Arthur (wri): Alf's Carpet
Lecocq, Charles (wri): The Devil's Nightmare
Lecompte, Yvon (act): Rabid
Lecourtois, Daniel (act): L'Ours
Lecoutier, Jacques (wri): Teenage Zombies; Terror of the Bloodhunters
Le Cover, Lisa (act): Zapped!
Led & Silver (mus): The Galaxy Invader
Ledden, Edward (act): Anguish
Ledebur, Friedrich von/Frederick (act): Assignment K; Enchanted Island; Giulietta degli Spiriti; The Man Who Turned to Stone; Moby Dick (1956); Slaughterhouse-Five; The 27th Day; Voodoo Island
Leder, Herbert J. (dir, 1922-1983): The Curse of the Golem; The Frozen Dead
Leder, Herbert J. (wri, 1922-1983): The Curse of the Golem; Fiend Without a Face; The Frozen Dead
Leder, Mimi (dir): Deep Impact; House of Secrets (1993); The Peacemaker (1997)
Leder, Paul (dir): A*P*E*; The Baby Doll Murders; Body Count (1987); I Dismember Mama; Killing Obsession; Sketches of a Strangler
Leder, Paul (wri): A*P*E*; The Baby Doll Murders; Killing Obsession
Leder, Reuben (wri): A*P*E*
Lederer, Charles (dir, 1911-1976): Fingers at the Window
Lederer, Charles (wri, 1911-1976): Monkey Business; Ride the Pink Horse; The Thing from Another World
Lederer, Francis (act, 1906-1976): The Bridge of San Luis Rey (1944); The Lone Wolf In Paris; The Madonna's Secret; The Return of Dracula; Terror Is a Man
Lederer, Franz (act): Die Buchse der Pandora
Lederer, Otto (act): The Bells (1926)
Lederman, (D.) Ross (dir, 1895-1972): The Body Disappears; Boston Blackie and the Law; The Lone Wolf In Mexico; The Notorious Lone Wolf; The Phantom Thief; Shadows On the Stairs; Tarzan's Revenge
Ledford, Brandy (act): Panic In the Skies!
Ledford, Jonathan (act): The Amazing Transparent Man; Zontar: The Thing from Venus
Ledoux, Fernand (act, b. 1897): The Trial; Les Visiteurs du Soir
Ledoux, Jacques (act): La Jetee
LeDoux, Michelle Suzanne (act): Fargo
Ledrov, D.B. (wri): The Shuttered Room; A Vacation In Hell
Leduke, Harrison (act): Laser Moon
Ledyakh, Gennady (act): Cinderella (1961)
Lee, Madame (act): She Freak
Lee, Adriane (act): Breeders
Lee, Alan (act): Eyes of a Stranger; Hell On Devil's Island; Rear Window (1954)
Lee, Angela (GB act): Countdown to Danger
Lee, Angela (USA act): Explorers
Lee, Anna (act, b. 1914, nee Joanna Winnifrith): Bedlam; Flesh and Fantasy; The Ghost and Mrs. Muir; Gideon's Day;In Like Flint; Jack the Giant Killer; Jet Over the Atlantic; King Solomon's Mines (1937); The Man Who Changed His Mind; The Passing of the Third Floor Back (1935); Picture Mommy Dead; What Ever Happened to Baby Jane? (1962)
Lee, Anne Marie (act): The Fly II
Lee, Ariol (act): Suspicion (1941)
Lee, Arnold (act): Hardware; The Sinister Man
Lee, Barbara (GB act): The Camp On Blood Island
Lee, Barbara (USA act): Praying Mantis
Lee, Belinda (act, 1935-1961): Eyewitness (1956); Footsteps In the Fog; Meet Mr. Callaghan; Murder by Proxy; The Nights of Lucretia Borgia; The Secret Place; Who Done It? (1956)
Lee, Benny (act): The Girl Hunters; Night of the Prowler
Lee, Bernard (act, 1907-1981): Across the Bridge; Beat the Devil; Beyond This Place; The Black Tulip (1937); Cage of Gold; Calling Bulldog Drummond; The Clue of the Silver Key; Clue of the Twisted Candle; Crossplot; Diamonds Are Forever; Dr. No; Dr. Terror's House of Horrors (1964); The Fallen Idol; Father Brown; Frankenstein and the Monster from Hell; From Russia With Love; Fury at Smugglers' Bay; Goldfinger; Journey to Midnight; The Key; Last Holiday; Live and Let Die; The Man Upstairs; The Man With the Golden Gun; Mr. Denning Drives North; Moonraker; Nowhere to Go; On Her majesty's Secret Service; Operation Kid Brother; Partners In Crime (1961); A Place to Go; Ring of Spies; The River House Mystery (1935); The Secret Partner; The Share Out; The Spanish Gardener; The Spy Who Came In from the Cold; The Spy Who Loved Me; The Spy With a Cold Nose; 10 Rillington Place; The Terror (1938); The Third Man; Thunderball; Vengeance; Who Was Maddox?; The Yellow Balloon; You Only Live Twice
Lee, Billy (act): Eyes of the Underworld; Secrets of the Phantom Caverns
Lee, Brandon (act, 1964-1993): The Crow (1994)
Lee, Bruce (act, 1940-1973): The Green Hornet
Lee, Bruce A. (act): Body Heat
Lee, Bryarly (act): The Naked Witch
Lee, Canada (act, 1907-1952, nee Leonard Canegata): Lifeboat
Lee, Carl (cin): Africa Screams
Lee, Celeste (act): The Temple of Venus
Lee, Chai (act): For Your Eyes Only
Lee Jr., Charles (act): The Toxic Avenger
Lee, China (act): Dr. Goldfoot and the Bikini Machine
Lee, Christian (act): Invasion Earth: The Aliens Are Here!
Lee, Christopher (act, b. 1922): The Accursed; Alias John Preston; Arabian Adventure; Babes In Bagdad; Bear Island; The Blood of Fu Manchu; The Brides of Fu Manchu; Captain America II; Castle of the Living Dead; Circle of Iron; Corridor of Mirrors; Count Dracula; The Creeping Flesh; The Crimson Pirate; Crossroads; Curse III: Blood Sacrifice; The Curse of Frankenstein; Curse of the Crimson Altar; Dark Places; Death Line; The Devil Rides Out; The Devil's Agent; The Devil's Daffodil; The Devil-Ship Pirates; Diagnosis: Murder; The Diamond Mercenaries;Doctor of Seven Dials; Dr.Terror's House of Horrors (1964); Dracula A.D. 1972; Dracula Has Risen from the Grave; Dracula, Pere et Fils; Dracula, Prince of Darkness; End of the World (1977); Ercole al Centro della Terra; Eugenie...The Story of Her Journey into Perversion; The Face of Eve; The Face of Fu Manchu; Five Golden Dragons; Fortune Is a Woman; La Frusta e il Corpo; Funny Man; Goliath Awaits; The Gorgon; Gremlins 2: The New Batch; Hamlet (1948); The Hands of Orlac (1959); Horror Express; Horror of Dracula; The Hound Of The Baskervilles (1959); House of the Long Shadows; The House That Dripped Blood; Howling II; I, Monster; Innocent Blood; In Search of Dracula; Katharsis; The Keeper; The Last Unicorn; Long Distance; The Magic Christian; La Maldicion de los Karnsteins; The Man Who Could Cheat Death; The Man With the Golden Gun; Meat Cleaver Massacre; The Mirror and Markheim; The Mummy (1959); My Brother's Keeper; The Night of the Big Heat; Night of the Blood Monster; Nothing But the Night; The Oblong Box; The Odyssey; Once Upon a Spy; Paul Temple Returns; The Pirates of Blood River; Police Dog; Poor Devil; Port Afrique; The Private Life of Sherlock Holmes; Rasputin, the Mad Monk; Return from Witch Mountain; The Return of Captain Invincible; The Return of the Musketeers; The Satanic Rites of Dracula; Scars of Dracula; Die Schlangengrube und das Pendel; Scream and Scream Again; Secret of the Red Orchid; She (1965); Sherlock Holmes and the Deadly Necklace; Sherlock Holmes and the Incident at Victoria Falls; The Skull; Starship Invasions; A Taste of Fear; Taste the Blood of Dracula; Tempi Duri per i Vampiri; The Terror of the Tongs; Theatre of Death; The Three Musketeers (1974); Too Hot to Handle; To the Devil a Daughter; Treasure Island (1990); The Two Faces of Dr. Jekyll; Valley of Fear (1964); Valley of the Eagles;

The Vengeance of Fu Manchu; La Vergine di Norimberga; The Wicker Man
Lee, Conan (act): *Eliminators*
Lee, Cosette (act): *Change of Mind; Deranged (1974)*
Lee, Damian (dir): *The Food of the Gods II*
Lee, Damian (wri): *Watchers*
Lee, Dana (act): *Futureworld*
Lee, Danny (cin): *The Ambushers; Bedknobs and Broomsticks; Escape to Witch Mountain (1975); The Island at the Top of the World; Murderers' Row*
Lee, Darrin (act): *The Octagon*
Lee, David (mus): *The Masque of the Red Death (1964); The Very Edge*
Lee, Dexter (act): *Sleepwalk*
Lee, Dick (act): *The Devil's Hand (1961)*
Lee, Dickie (act): *Nancy Drew, Reporter*
Lee, Dino (act): *Blood Diner*
Lee, Donna (act): *The Body Snatcher (1945)*
Lee, Dorothy (act): *Cracked Nuts (1931)*
Lee, Earl (act): *Five*
Lee, Edgy (act): *Deadly Messages; The Sword and the Sorcerer*
Lee, Elizabeth (act): *Something Weird*
Lee, Etta (act): *The Chinese Parrot; The Mysterious Mr. Wong; The Thief of Bagdad (1924)*
Lee, Evan (dir): *Meat Cleaver Massacre*
Lee, Frankie (act): *The Miracle Man (1919); Robin Hood Jr. (1923)*
Lee, Fred (act): *Starcrossed*
Lee, Gavin (act): *The Fall of the House of Usher (1950)*
Lee, George (GB act): *Eye of the Needle; Quarantine; 10 Rillington Place*
Lee, George (USA act): *Dracula Sucks*
Lee, Gertrude (act): *Day of the Animals*
Lee, Glen (act): *Brainstorm (1983); Fire In the Sky (1993)*
Lee, Gloria (act): *The Clan of the Cave Bear*
Lee, Gracia (act): *Schizoid (1980)*
Lee, Gwen (act): *Laugh, Clown, Laugh; The Lone Wolf Returns (1926)*
Lee, Gypsy Rose (act, 1914-1970, nee Rose Louise Hovick): *Ali Baba Goes to Town; Babes In Bagdad; Screaming Mimi*
Lee, Gypsy Rose (wri, 1914-1970): *Lady of Burlesque*
Lee, Harry (wri): *Too Hot to Handle*
Lee, Ida (act): *Grandma's House*
Lee, J.V. (act): *Curse of the Swamp Creature*
Lee, Jack (dir, b. 1913): *The Golden Mask; Turn the Key Softly*
Lee, Jack (M.) (act): *Crime Doctor's Manhunt; Desk Set*
Lee, Jae Woo (act): *Outbreak*
Lee, James (act): *The Kennel Murder Case*
Lee, Jason Scott (act): *Back to the Future, Part II; The Jungle Book (1994); The Lookalike; Soldier*
Lee, Jesse (act): *Matinee*
Lee, Joanna (act): *The Brain Eaters; Plan 9 from Outer Space*
Lee, John (act, b. 1928): *Cat Girl; The Secret Partner; Seven Keys; Spaceflight IC-1*
Lee, Johnny (act): *The Fugitive (1993); School Spirit*
Lee, Jonna (act): *The Midnight Hour*
Lee, Joy (act): *Dr. Black Mr. Hyde; A Kiss Before Dying (1991)*
Lee, Kaaren (act): *Remote Control (1988)*
Lee, Karen (act): *Blind Date*
Lee, Kathryn (act): *Vampire at Midnight*
Lee, Kauilani (act): *Cujo; The Fan; Hello Again*
Lee, Kieron (act): *Stargate*
Lee, Larry (wri): *Anatomy of a Psycho*
Lee, Leo (act): *Contact*
Lee, Leonard (wri): *Dressed to Kill (1946); The Glass Web; Pursuit to Algiers; Spy Hunt*
Lee, Lesa (act): *Memorial Valley Massacre*
Lee, Lila (act, 1905-1973): *The Black Pearl; The Gorilla (1931); Male and Female; The Midnight Girl; Murder Will Out (1930); The Unholy Three (1930)*
Lee, Linda (act): *Maniac (1980)*
Lee, Lisa (act): *Circumstantial Evidence (1952); Lady In the Fog*
Lee, Lois (act): *The Prisoner of Zenda (1922)*
Lee, Louise (act): *The Million Eyes of Sumuru*
Lee, Madeline (act): *Cocoon: The Return*
Lee, Margaret (act): *Circus of Fear; Dorian Gray; Fire Monsters vs. the Son of Hercules; Five Golden Dragons; Ghosts-Italian Style; Kiss the Girls and Make Them Die; Master Stroke; Night of the Blood Monster; OSS 117-Double Agent; Our Man In Marrakesh; Paroxismus; Samson and the Sea Beasts; Secret Agent Superdragon; Slaughter Hotel (1972)*
Lee, Mary (act): *Nancy Drew, Reporter*
Lee, Michele (act, b. 1942): *Color Me Perfect; The Love Bug*
Lee, Michele (dir & wri, b. 1942): *Color Me Perfect*
Lee, Myra (act): *The Creeping Terror*
Lee, Myron Bruce (act): *Death Dimension*
Lee, Norman (dir): *Bulldog Drummond at Bay (1937); Dangerous Fingers; The Door With Seven Locks (1940); Luck of the Navy; Mr. Reeder In Room 13; The Strangler (1932)*
Lee, Norman (wri): *The Door With Seven Locks (1940); The Strangler (1932)*
Lee, Olive Joyce (act): *Endangered Species*
Lee, Owen (act): *Zorro, the Gay Blade*
Lee, Paige (act): *Voyage to a Prehistoric Planet*
Lee, Palmer (act): see Palmer, Gregg
Lee, Pamela Anderson (act): *Barb Wire; Naked Souls; Snapdragon*
Lee, Peggy (act, b. 1920): *Lady and the Tramp*
Lee, Peggy (mus, b. 1920): *Johnny Guitar*
Lee, Penelope (act): *Superman (1978); The Tomb of Ligeia*
Lee, Pinky (act, d. 1993): *Lady of Burlesque*
Lee, Piu Fan (act): *Mary Reilly*
Lee, Robert (GB act): *Koroshi; Mark of the Devil (1985)*
Lee, Robert (USA act): *The Projectionist*
Lee, Robert (dir): *Virtual Assassin*
Lee, Robert N. (wri): *Captain Kidd; The Dragon Murder Case; The Kennel Murder Case; Tower of London (1939)*
Lee, Rose (act): *Just Imagine*
Lee, Rowland V. (dir, 1891-1975): *The Bridge of San Luis Rey (1944); Captain Kidd; The Count of Monte Cristo (1934); Love from a Stranger (1937); The Mysterious Dr. Fu Manchu; The Return of Dr. Fu Manchu; The Sign of Four (1932); Son of Frankenstein; The Son of Monte Cristo; The Three Musketeers (1935); Tower of London (1939)*
Lee, Rowland V. (wri, 1891-1975): *The Count of Monte Cristo (1934)*
Lee, Ruta (act, b. 1936): *Doomsday machine; A Howling In the Woods; Witness for the Prosecution*
Lee, Sam (act): *The Gracie Allen Murder Case; Panic at Madam Tussaud's; A Yell of a Night*
Lee, Sam (wri): *Panic at Madam Tussaud's*
Lee, Sandra (act): *Psyche 59*
Lee, Sharron (act): *Motor Psycho*
Lee, Sherry (act): *The Pink Chiquitas*
Lee, Sheryl (act): *Guinevere; Twin Peaks: Fire Walk With Me; Vampires (1998)*
Lee, Soonjai (act): *Yongary, Monster from the Deep*
Lee, Stan (act): *The Ambulance*
Lee, Stephen (act): *Dolls; Prehysteria; RoboCop 2; Wargames*
Lee, Stevie (act): *The Carrier*
Lee, Suzanne (act): *Dark of the Night*
Lee, Swin (act): *Return of the Jedi*
Lee, Tammy (act): *What's the Matter With Helen?*
Lee, Teri (act): *Body Parts (1990)*
Lee, Terry (act): *Queen of Blood; Surf Nazis Must Die*
Lee, Thelma (act): *They Live*
Lee, Tiger Chung (act): *The Golden Child*
Lee, Tom (act): *Maroc 7*
Lee, Vicki (act): *X—The Man With the X-Ray Eyes*
Lee, Virginia (act): *Charlie Chan: Happiness Is a Warm Clue; Dimension 5; D.O.A. (1949)*
Lee, Waveney (act): *Konga*
Lee, Winifred (act): see Gombell, Minna
Leech, Richard (act, b. 1922): *The Birthday Present; Dublin Nightmare; A Lady Mislaid; The Laughing Girl Murder; The LongArm; Night of the Demon (1957);Ricochet; The Terror of the Tongs; Walk a Tightrope*
Leeds, Andrea (act, 1914-1984, nee Antoinette Lees): *Earthbound (1940)*
Leeds, Charles (wri): *No Road Back; The Twenty Questions Murder*
Leeds, Elissa (act): *Earthbound (1981)*
Leeds, Herbert I. (dir): *Blue, White and Perfect; Charlie Chan In City In Darkness; Just Off Broadway; The Man Who Wouldn't Die; Mr. Moto In Danger Island; Time to Kill (1942)*
Leeds, Howard (act): *Sherlock Holmes (1932)*
Leeds, Lila (act): *Lady In the Lake*
Leeds, Marcie (act): *Near Dark; Wheels of Terror*
Leeds, Peter (act): *The Atomic Kid; The 30 Foot Bride of Candy Rock*
Leeds, Phil(ip) (act, 1916-1998): *Ghost (1990); Rosemary's Baby*
Leegant, Dan (act): *Grim Prairie Tales; I'm Dangerous Tonight*
Leek, Tiiu (act): *The First Power; Starship Invasions*
Leekley, John (wri): *Buried Secrets; In the Company of Darkness*
Leeming, Peter (act): *The Slipper and the Rose*
Leendeerts, Rolf (act): *Gebroken Spiegels*
Leeown, Fred (act): *Hardware*
Leerdorff-Rye, Preben (act): *The Element of Crime*
Lees, Antoinette (act): see Leeds, Andrea
Lees, John (act): *Daylight*
Lees, Robert (wri): *Abbott and Costello Meet Frankenstein; Abbott and Costello Meet The Invisible Man; The Black Cat (1941); Crazy House (1943); Hold That Ghost; The Invisible Woman (1941)*
Lees, Tamara (act): *A Piece of Cake; The Queen of Babylon*
Leese, Sarah S. (act): *Species*
Leeson, Michael (wri): *Jekyll and Hyde...Together Again*
Lee-Sung, Richard (act): *Firewalker*
Lee-Thompson, John (wri): *The Price of Folly*
Leeves, Jane (act): *James and the Giant Peach; Pandora's Clock*
Le Faber, Eleanor (act): *House of Usher (1960)*
LeFanu, Sheridan (wri, 1814-1873): *The Blood Spattered Bride; The Dark Angel (1991); Et Mourir de Plaisir; Lust for a Vampire; La Maldicion de los Karnsteins; Shamus O'Brien: or, Saved from the Scaffold; Twins of Evil; Uncle Silas; The Vampire Lovers; Vampyr*
Lefcourt, Carolyn (wri): *The Stepfather; Stepfather II; Stepfather III: Father's Day*
Lefeaux, Charles (act): *The Return of the Frog*
Lefebvre, Germaine (act): see Capucine
Lefebvre, Jean (act): *Bluebeard (1972); Treasure Island (1971)*
Lefebvre, John (act): *Oh Heavenly Dog*
Lefebvre, Stephane (act): *Dr. Jekyll and Ms. Hyde*
LeFevor/Lefevour, Rick (act): *Blink; Weird Science*
LeFevre, Adam (act): *Storm of the Century*
le Fevre, Michael (wri): *Counterspy*
Lefevre, Ned (act): *Creature from the Black Lagoon*
le Fevre, Pierre (act): *The House of the Arrow (1953)*
Lefevre, Rene (act): *The Crime of Monsieur Lange; Doulos-The Finger Man*
Leff, Adam (wri): *Bio-Dome*
Lefferts, George (wri): *She's Dressed to Kill*
Lefkowitz, Steve (act): *Invasion of the Bee Girls*
Lefler, Doug (wri): *Steel Dawn*
LeFlore, Julius (act): *The Monster Squad; Vamp*
LeForet, Nathalie (act): *Et Mourir de Plaisir*
Le Fre, James (act): *A Study In Scarlet (1914)*
Legare, Ovila (act): *I Confess*
LeGate, Penny (act): *The Hand That Rocks the Cradle*
LeGault, Lance (act): *Captain America (1978); Coma; Dark Breed; The Silencers (1995)*
Legendre, Brigitte (act): *Sous le Soleil de Satan*
Leger, Fernand (dir & wri, 1881-1955): *Dreams That Money Can Buy*
Legere, Phoebe (act): *The Toxic Avenger, Part II; The Toxic Avenger, Part III: The Last Temptation of Toxie*
Leggatt, Alison (act, 1904-1990): *The Day of the Triffids; Noose for a Lady; The Seven-Per-Cent Solution; A Woman Possessed*
Legge, Joan (act): *The Blackmailers; Queenie of the Circus; The Splendid Coward; The Third Witness; The Wheel of Death*
Legler, Cindy (act): *Vice Versa (1988)*
LeGon, Jeni (act): *Arabian Nights (1942); Cat People (1942); I Walked with a Zombie; The Velvet Touch*
Legrand, Andre (wri): *Nick Carter Va Tout Casser*
Legrand, Michel (mus, b. 1932): *Castle Keep; La Dame dans l'Auto Avec des Lunettes et un Fusil; Gulliver's Travels (1977); Les Parapluies de Cherbourg; Peau d'Ane; Le Plus Vieux Metier du Monde; The Smurfs and the Magic Flute; The Three Musketeers (1974); Wuthering Heights (1970)*
LeGrand, Richard (act): *Gildersleeve's Ghost*
Le Grice, Marcus (act): *Strange Behavior*
LeGros, James (act): *Blood and Concrete; Destiny Turns On the Radio; Phantasm II*
Le Guere, George (act): *Missing Millions*
Le Guin, Ursula K. (wri, b. 1929): *The Lathe of Heaven*
Leguizamo, John (act): *Dr. Dolittle (1998); Spawn; Super Mario Bros.*
Lehman, Ernest (dir, b. 1920): *Portnoy's Complaint*
Lehman, Ernest (wri, b. 1920): *Family Plot; North by Northwest; Portnoy's Complaint*
Lehman, Gladys (wri): *The Cat Creeps (1930); Death Takes a Holiday (1934); White Woman*
Lehman, Jennifer (act): *The Pit (1983)*
Lehman, John Paul (act): *Matinee*
Lehman, Lew (dir): *The Pit (1983)*
Lehman, Lew (mus): *King Solomon's Treasure*
Lehman, Lew (wri): *Phobia*
Lehman, Ted (act): *One Dark Night*
Lehmann, Beatrix (act): *Candles at Nine; The Cat and the Canary (1978); The Hunchback of Notre Dame (1965); The Key; The Passing of the Third Floor Back (1935); Psyche 59; The Rat; The Spy Who Came In from the Cold*
Lehmann, Carla (act): *Cottage to Let*
Lehmann, Michael (dir): *Heathers; Meet the Applegates*
Lehmann, Michael (wri): *Meet the Applegates*
Lehn, Georg (act): *Das Schloss*
Lehne, Fredric (act): *Amityville: The Evil Escapes; Deadly Game; Man's Best Friend; This Gun for Hire (1991)*
Lehne, John (act): *The Darker Side of Terror; Family Plot; Who?*
Lehner, Helga (act): *24 Hours to Kill*
Lehner, Peter (dir & wri): *Megaville*
Lei, Chao (act): *Madam White Snake*
Lei, Huang (act): *Life On a String*
Lei, Lydia (act): *Hammett*
Lei, Meme (act): *The Element of Crime*
Leiataua, Kuinise (act): *Beyond Evil*
Leiataua, Lisona (act): *Beyond Evil*
Leib, Chaim (act): see Greene, Lorne
Leiber (Sr.), Fritz (act, 1883-1949): *Bride of Vengeance; Cry of theWerewolf; The Hunchback of Notre Dame (1939); Inner Sanctum (1949); Phantom of the Opera (1943); Samson and Delilah; The Spanish Main; The Web*
Leiber Jr., Fritz (act, 1910-1992): *Baghdad; The Bermuda Triangle; Equinox*
Leiber (Jr.), Fritz (wri, 1910-1992): *Night of the Eagle; Weird Woman;Witches' Brew*
Leiber, Jed (mus): *Love Potion No. 9*
Leiberman, Jeff (dir & wri): *Squirm*
Leibman, Ron (act, b. 1937): *Slaughterhouse-Five; Zorro, the Gay Blade*
Leicester, James (wri): *Enchanted Island; Most Dangerous Man Alive*
Leicester, William (act): *Beyond a Reasonable Doubt; Operation Secret*
Leicester, William F. (wri): *The Last Man On Earth*
Leichtling, Jerry (wri): *Peggy Sue Got Married*
Leider, Linda (act): *Sweet Kill*
Leider, R. Allen (wri): *The Oracle (1985)*
Leifert, Don (act): *Fiend (1980); The Galaxy Invader; Nightbeast*
Leigh, Andrew (act): *The Curse of Frankenstein; Paut Temple's Triumph*
Leigh, Austin (act): *Brigadier Gerard; Bulldog Drummond's Third Round; Desire; Old Bill Through the Ages*
Leigh, B. Courtenay (act): *Strange Behavior*
Leigh, Barbara (act): *Mistress of the Apes; Pretty Maids All In a Row; Terminal Island; Vampirella (1978, unfinished)*
Leigh, Brenda (act): *The Companion (1994)*
Leigh, Casey (act): *The Mutagen*
Leigh, Cassandra (act): *Alien Terminator; Dream Master: The Erotic Invader; Midnight Tease*
Leigh, Charlotte (act): *The Brown Wallet*
Leigh, Coco (act): *Mars Attacks!*
Leigh, Constance (act): *Stolen Time*
Leigh, Frank (act): *The Clutching Hand; A Night of Mystery (1928); The Spanish Cape Mystery; The Thirteenth Chair (1929)*
Leigh, George (act): *Champagne for Caesar; Dial M for Murder (1954); The Fatal Witness*
Leigh, J.L.V. (act): *The Jailbird; Ultus and the Grey Lady; Ultus and the Secret of the Night; Ultus, the Man from the Dead*
Leigh, J.L.V. (dir): *Fetters of Fear; First Men In the Moon (1919); Quicksands of Life*
Leigh, Jack (act): *A Daughter of Satan (1914); Eugene Aram; The Foreign Spy (1913); His Wonderful Lamp; The Rajah's Revenge; Temptation (1914); The Vengeance of Daniel Whidden; The Wrecker of Lives*
Leigh, Janet (act, b. 1927, nee Jeanette Helen Morrison): *Angels In the Outfield (1951); The Black Shield of Falworth; The Deadly Dream; The Fog; Halloween H20; Hello Down There; Houdini (1953); The Manchurian Candidate; Night of the Lepus; Prince Valiant (1954); Psycho (1960); Safari; The Spy In the Green Hat*
Leigh, Jennifer Jason (act, b. 1961): *Dolores Claiborne; Eyes of a Stranger; eXistenZ; Flesh*

& Blood; The Hitcher; The Love Letter; Single White Female; Sister, Sister

Leigh, John (act): The Frighteners

Leigh, Laurie (act): Freedom to Die; The Marked One; Paranoiac

Leigh, Louise (act): Talk of the Devil

Leigh, Malcolm (dir & wri): Legend of the Witches

Leigh, Nadia (act): Circle of Deceit

Leigh, Nelson (act): Captive Girl; Creature With theAtom Brain; The Lost Tribe; Prisoners of the Casbah; The Saracen Blade; Savage Mutiny; Thief of Damascus; Valley of the Headhunters; World Without End

Leigh, Norman (cin): Schizoid (1980)

Leigh, Roland (wri): Atalntis (1948)

Leigh, Rowland (wri): Heaven Only Knows; Tarzan and the Huntress

Leigh, Steven (act): Deadly Game

Leigh, Suzanna (act, b. 1945): Deadlier Than the Male; The Deadly Bees; The Fiend (1972); Lust for a Vampire; Son of Dracula (1974); Subterfuge; Uncharted Seas

Leigh, Suzanne (act): Bomb In the High Street

Leigh, Tara (act): Metamorphosis: The Alien Factor

Leigh, Taylor (act): Under Lock and Key

Leigh, Vivien (act, 1913-1967, nee Vivian Mary Hartley): Dark Journey

Leigh, Wandisa (act): Lightning Bolt

Leigh-Hunt, Barbara (act): Frenzy; Oh Heavenly Dog; Paper Mask

Leigh-Hunt, Ronald (act, b. 1916): Clegg; Curse of Simba; Frankenstein (1993); Hostile Witness; The Invisible Asset; The Liquidator; The Man On the Cliff; Melody of Hate; The Omen; Paul Temple Returns; Shadow of a Man; Where the Bullets Fly

Leight, Timmie (act): Mother's Day

Leight, Warren D. (wri): Mother's Day

Leighton, Fran (act): The Hideous Sun Demon

Leighton, Frank (act): The Last Chance; The Stateless Man

Leighton, Jan (act): Zapped!

Leighton, Joanne (wri): The Black Panther

Leighton, Lillian (act): Cinderella (1911, Selig); The Sphinx (1933)

Leighton, Margaret (act, 1922-1976): Calling Bulldog Drummond; A Choice of Weapons; The Elusive Pimpernel (1950); Frankenstein: The True Story; From Beyond the Grave; Great Expectations (1974), The Loved One; Murder On Monday; The Teckman Mystery; Under Capricorn

Leighton, Michael (wri): Appointment With Crime; Johnny,You're Wanted

Leighton, Roberta (act): Barracuda

Leighton, Sara (act): The Woman Eater

Leighton, Ted (wri): Ellery Queen: Don't Look Behind You

Leighton, Will (act): An American Werewolf In London

Leim, Sandy (act): My Bloody Valentine

Leinberger, Jefferson (act): Maxim Xul

Leinster, Murray (wri, 1896-1975): The Navy vs. the Night Monsters;The Terrornauts

Leipnitz, Harald (act): The Brides of Fu Manchu; Creature With the Blue Hand

Leipzig, Dina (act): Georgette Meunier

Leisen, Mitchell (act, 1898-1972): Four Hours to Kill

Leisen, Mitchell (dir, 1898-1972): Death Takes a Holiday (1934); Dream Girl; Four Hours to Kill;Golden Earrings; Lady In the Dark; Murder at the Vanities

Leisen, Richard (dir): Bride of Vengeance

Leisenring, John (act): Shadow Conspiracy

Leister, Frederick (act): Before I Wake; Circumstantial Evidence (1952); The Crimson Pirate;Dinner at the Ritz; Family Doctor; Footsteps In the Fog; Forbidden For Them That Trespass; King Solomon's Mines (1937); On the Night of the Fire; Spellbound (1941); Top Secret (1952); The Twenty Questions Murder

Leisure, David (act, b. 1950): The Goddess of Love

Leitch, Christopher (dir): I've Been Waiting for You; Teen Wolf Too

Leitch, Christopher (wri): Universal Soldier

Leitch, Donovan (act): The Blob (1988); Cutting Class

Leitch, Megan (act): Omen IV: The Awakening; The Resurrected

Leite, Sonya (act): Supergirl (1984)

Leiterman, Richard (cin): Beyond Obsession; It (1990);Memories of Murder; Watchers

Leith, James (act): The Quatermass Conclusion

Leith, Virginia (act): Black Widow (1954); The Brain That Wouldn't Die; A Kiss Before Dying (1956); On the Threshold of Space

Leitl, Bruce (mus): Ebenezer

Leitterboom, Jerrol (act): The Cyber-Stalking

Leitzbach, Adeline (wri): The House of Secrets

Lekand, Beau (act): Nail Gun Massacre

Leland, David (act): Gawain and the Green Knight

Leland, Jack (act): Rearview Mirror

Leland, Fiona (act): It Happened Here

Leland, Nicholas (act): The Haunting of Sarah Hardy

Leland-St. John, Sharmagne (act): Dick Tracy (1990)

Lelong, Suzanne (act): The Dungeonmaster

Lelouch, Claude (cin & wri, b. 1937): Les Miserables (1995)

Lelouch, Claude (dir, b. 1937): Cat and Mouse (1978); Les Miserables (1995)

Lelouch, Salome (act): Les Miserables (1995)

Lem, Bob (act): The Intruder (1981)

Lem, Stanislaw (wri): Bezludna Planeta; Milczaca Gwiazda; Profesor Zazul; Przyjaciel; Solaris; Wycieczka w Kosmos

Lemaire, Ken (act): The Music of the Spheres

Lemaire, Philippe (act): A Toi de Faire, Migonne; The Blood Rose; Cartouche (1962); Spirits of the Dead; Le Vice et la Vertu

Le Maire, William (act): The Penguin Pool Murder

Lemarchand, Lucienne (act): Crime and Punishment (1935, Fr)

Le Massena, William (act): All That Jazz; Carousel

LeMat, Paul (act): Death Valley; Grave Secrets; The Night They Saved Christmas; Puppet Master; Sensation (1994); Strange Invaders; Wishman

LeMay, Alan (wri, b. 1899): Blackbeard the Pirate

Le May, Greg (act): I Was a Zombie for the F.B.I.

LeMay, John D. (act): Jason Goes to Hell: The Final Friday; The Quilt of Hathor

Lemay, Lewis (act): Akira

Lemay-Thivierge, Guillaume (act): Wild Thing

Lembeck, Harvey (act, 1923-1982): Dr. Goldfoot and the Bikini Machine; The Ghost In the Invisible Bikini; Hello Down There; How to Stuff a Wild Bikini; Pajama Party; Sergeant Deadhead the Astronut!

Lembeck, Michael (act): Haunts of the Very Rich

Le Mener, Jean-Yves (cin): The Visitors (1993)

Lemercier, valerie (act): The Visitors (1993)

LeMesurier, John (act, 1912-1983): Black 13; Blind Man's Bluff (1952); Blind Spot (1958); Blood of the Vampire; The Blue Parrot; Casino Royale; City Under the Sea; Dark Interval; Dead Lucky; Death In the Hand; Escape from Broadmoor (1948); Eye of the Devil; The Fiendish Plot of Dr. Fu Manchu; Flat Two; Hot Enough for June; The Hound of the Baskervilles (1959); Jabberwocky; Jack the Ripper (1958); Jigsaw; The Liquidator; The Magic Christian; The Man Who Wouldn't Talk; Man With a Gun; Masquerade; A Matter of Murder;The Moon-Spinners; The Mouse On the Moon; Never Let Go; On a Clear Day You Can See Forever; Our Man In Marrakesh; Police Dog; The Spaceman and King Arthur; Where the Spies Are; Who Is Killing the Great Chefs of Europe?; The Wrong Box

Lemkin, Jonathan (wri): Devil's Advocate

Lemkow, Tutte (act): Fathom; Masquerade; Mata Hari (1985); Raiders of the Lost Ark; Red Sonja; Sphinx (1981); The Stranglers of Bombay; Theater of Blood; The Treasure of Monte Cristo (1961); The Wrong Box

Lemley, Ned (act): The Hound of London

Lemming, Otto (wri): Wild Is My Love

Lemmo, James (act): Dream a Little Dream 2

Lemmo, James (cin): Dangerous Touch

Lemmo, James (dir & wri): Bodily Harm

Lemmo, Joan (act): Grim Prairie Tales

Lemmon, Chris (act): Just Before Dawn (1980)

Lemmon, Jack (act, b. 1925, nee John Uhler Lemmon III): Bell, Book and Candle; The China Syndrome; Hamlet (1996)

Lemmons, Kasi (act): Candyman; The Silence of the Lambs; Vampire's Kiss

Lemmy (act): Hardware; Tromeo and Juliet

LeMoigne, Ray (cin): To Commit a Murder

Lemoine, Michel (act): The Conquest of Mycenae; Necronomicon; Planets Against Us; The Prisoner of the Iron Mask

Le Moire, Rosetta (act): The Brother from Another Planet

Lemon, Rev. Lynn (act): Plan 9 from Outer Space

Lemonnier, Meg (act): The Green Glove

Lemont, John (dir): And Women Shall Weep; The Frightened City; The Green Buddha; Konga; The Shakedown

Lemont, John (wri): And Women Shall Weep; The Frightened City; The Shakedown; Witness In the Dark

Lemorande, Rusty (dir): Journey to the Center of the Earth (1989); The Turn of the Screw

Lemorande, Rusty (wri): Electric Dreams; Journey to the Center of the Earth (1989)

Lemore, George (act): Candyman: Farewell to the Flesh

Lemos, Toni (act): Haunts

LeMothe, Michelle (act): The Children

Lempert, Debbie (act): Something Evil

Lempert, Sandy (act): Something Evil

Lemus, Luis (act): I Come In Peace

Lemvigh, Gunnar (act): Crazy Paradise

Lenahan, Jim (wri): Space Rage

Lenard, Mark (act, 1928-1996): Forgotten City of the Planet of the Apes; Star Trek; Star Trek III:

The Search for Spock; Star Trek IV: The Voyage Home; Star Trek VI: The Undiscovered Country; Treachery and Greed on the Planet of the Apes

Lenard, Melvyn (mus): Daughter of Dr. Jekyll

Lenders, Armand (act): At the Villa Rose (1920)

Lendon, Alexandra (act): 13 Frightened Girls

Lenehan, Nancy (act): Assassin (1986); Jekyll and Hyde...Together Again

Leng, Deborah (act): Slipstream

Lenhart, Heidi (act): Deadly Sins

Lenhart, Lane (act): Prototype X29A

Leni, Paul (dir, 1885-1929): The Cat and the Canary (1927); The Chinese Parrot; The Last Warning (1929); The Man Who Laughs (1928);

Das Wachsfigurenkabinett

Lenica, Jan (dir, b. 1928): Labirynt; Die Nashorner

Lenica, Jan (wri, b. 1928): Labirynt

Leningrad Kirov Ballet, The (act): The Blue Bord (1976); The Sleeping Beauty (1965, Russ)

Lenkov, Peter M. (wri): Demolition Man

Lenkowsky, Philip (act): Tales from the Darkside

Lennard, Arthur (act): A Man's Shadow

Lennard, Philip (act): The Case of the Old Rope Man

Lennert, LeRoy (act): Trauma (1963)

Lennertz, Christopher (mus): Piranha (1995); Suspect Device

Lenney, Dinah (act): The Puppet Masters

Lennie, Angus (act): The Zany Adventures of Robin Hood

Lennix, Harry (act): Nothing But the Truth; The Package

Lennon, Jarrett (act): Amityville Dollhouse; The Servants of Twilight

Lennon, Paul (act): Howling III

Lennon, Thomas (wri): Murder On a Bridle Path

Lennon, Toby (act): The Mutations

Lennox, Doug (act): Pretty Poison (1996)

Lennox, Michael (act): Dr. Who and the Daleks

Lennox, Richard (cin): Wizards of the Lost Kingdom

Leno, Jay (act, b. 1950): Collision Course (1990); The Flintstones; We're Back! A Dinosaur's Story

Lenoir, Denis (cin): The Secret Agent (1996)

Lenoir, Leon (act): Crime Doctor's Gamble; Crime Doctor's Manhunt

Lenoir, Marie (act): The Phantom of the Opera (1990)

Lenrot, Elias (wri): Sampa

Lenska, Rula (act, b. 1948): The Deadly Females; Robin Hood: Swords of Wayland; Royal Flash

Lenski, Robert (wri): The Aliens Are Coming

Lensky, Leib (act): Echoes; The Silence of the Lambs

Lente, Miklos (cin): Happy Birthday to Me; Storm Chasers: Revenge of the Twister

Lenti, Lara (act): House of 1,000 Dolls

Lenya, Lotte (act, 1898-1981, nee Karoline Blamauer): From Russia With Love

Lenz, Abigail (act): Dead of Night (1987)

Lenz, Cliff (act): The Hand That Rocks the Cradle

Lenz, Jerry (act): Getting Lucky

Lenz, Joy (act): Thinner

Lenz, Kay (act, b. 1951): Fear (1988); Headhunter; Hitler's Daughter; House; The Initiation of Sarah; Murder by Night; Prisoners of the Lost Universe; Sanctuary of Fear; Trapped In Space

Lenz, Rick (act, b. 1939): In Self Defense; Shadow of a Doubt (1991)

Lenzey, Margaret (act): Quest for the Mighty Sword

Lenzi, Bruno (act): Amarcord

Lenzi, Laura (act): The Adventures of Hercules

Lenzi, Paul (act): Invasion of the Girl Snatchers

Lenzi, Umberto (dir): Cannibal Ferox; City of the Walking Dead; Eaten Alive (1980); Eyeball; Ghosthouse; Ironmaster; Orgasmo; A Quiet Place to Kill; Samson and the Slave Queen; Sandokan the Great; Spasmo; Zorro Contro Maciste

Lenzi, Umberto (wri): Cannibal Ferox; Orgasmo; Sandokan the Great; Zorro Contro Maciste

Leo, Frank (act): End of the World (1977)

Leo, Melissa (act, b. 1960): The Bride In Black; Deadtime Stories

Leoce, Michael (act): The Toxic Avenger, Part II

Leon (act): Spirit Lost

Leon, Alesia (act): Crime and the Penalty; The Devil's Profession; Her Life In London

Leon, Bob (act): Grotesque

Leon, Connie (act): The Adventures of Robin Hood

Leon, Daniel (act): Through the Magic Pyramid

Leon, David (act): Are You In the House Alone?

Leon, David Ari (mus): Turbo: A Power Rangers Movie

Leon, Eva (act): House of Doom (1973)

Leon, Gary (act): Dante's Inferno (1935)

Leon, Jean (dir & wri): Aimez-Vous les Femmes?

Leon, Joseph (act): He Knows You're Alone

Leon, Kenny (act): Web of Deceit

Leon, Madeline (act): The Tell-Tale Heart (1960)

Leon, Valerie (act): Alien Women; Blood from the Mummy's Tomb; Never Say Never Again; The Spy Who Loved Me; Zeta One

Leon, William (act): The Magic Voyage of Sinbad

Leonard, Ada (act): Forty Naughty Girls

Leonard, Arthur (dir): Pocomania

Leonard, Barbara (act): Charlie Chan In City In Darkness; Scotland Yard (1930)

Leonard, Brett (dir): Dead Pit; Hideaway; The Lawnmower Man; Virtuosity

Leonard, Brett (wri): The Lawnmower Man

Leonard, Carl (act): Horror of the Zombies

Leonard, Courtney (act): Howling II

Leonard, David (act): Philo Vance's Secret Mission

Leonard, Don (act): Creatures the World Forgot

Leonard, Douglas (act): Lies

Leonard, Elmore (wri): The Rosary Murders; Touch

Leonard, Grace (act): Red Planet Mars

Leonard, Herbert B. (dir): The Perils of Pauline

Leonard, Hugh (wri): Percy

Leonard, J. (act): Robin Hood Outlawed

Leonard, Jack (wri): Man In the Dark (1953); The Narrow Margin (1952 & 1990)

Leonard, Jack E. (act): The Fat Spy; Journey Back to Oz

Leonard, John (act): Howling II

Leonard Sr., John R. (act): Nightwing

Leonard, Lawrence (act): Shadow Conspiracy

Leonard, Leo (dir): Omoo Omoo, the Shark God

Leonard, Lu (act): Circuitry Man; Shadowzone; Starman

Leonard, Michelle (act): Howling II

Leonard, Patrick (mus): Heart Condition

Leonard, Paul (act): Howling II

Leonard, Phillip (act): Deadline

Leonard, Queenie (act): Alice In Wonderland (1951); And Then There Were None; The Locket;

The Lodger (1944); The Lone Wolf In London; Les Miserables (1952); The Narrow Margin (1952); 23 Paces to Baker Street

Leonard, Robert (act): The Primeval Test

Leonard, Robert E. (act): Heaven Can Wait (1978)

Leonard, Robert Sean (act, b. 1969): My Best Friend Is a Vampire

Leonard, Robert Z. (dir, 1889-1968): The Bribe; The Scarlet Shadow

Leonard, Ron (act): Howling II

Leonard, Sheldon (act, 1907-1996, nee Sheldon Bershad): Abbott and Costello Meet the Invisible Man; Another Thin Man; Captain Kidd; Daughter of the Jungle; The Diamond Queen; The Falcon In Hollywood; Passport to Suez; Sinbad the Sailor; Somewhere In the Night; Take One False Step; Top Secret (1978); Zombies On Broadway

Leonard, Susan (act): Mad Max Beyond Thunderdome

Leonardi, Anthony (act): Ghost Warrior

Leonardi, Lisa (act): Demons of the Dead
Leone, Alfred (wri): House of Exorcism
Leone, Joan (act): Dracula's Dog
Leone, Kathy (act): House of Exorcism
Leone, Sergio (dir, 1921-1989): The Colossus of Rhodes; Sodom and Gomorrah
Leone, Sergio (wri, 1921-1989): The Last Days of Pompeii (1959); Romolo e Remo
Leone, William (act): The Toxic Avenger, Part II
Leonetti, John R. (cin): Child's Play 3; The Mask (1994); Mortal Kombat
Leonetti, Matthew F./Matt (cin): The Bat People; Dead Again; Eyewitness (1981); A Fire In the Sky (1978); The Ice Pirates; Poltergeist; Search for the Gods; Species II; Star Trek: First Contact; Strange Days; Weird Science
Leonetti, Tommy (act): The Human Duplicators
Leong, Al(bert) (act): Big Trouble In Little China; I Come In Peace; Twilight Zone
Leong, Colin (act): The Punisher
Leong, James (B.) (act): Mr. Moto Takes a Chance; Thank You, Mr. Moto
Leong, Page (act): Ghostbusters II
Leong, Susan (act): Slipstream
Leoni, Gene (act): Distortions
Leoni, Tea (act, b. 1966): Deep Impact; Switch (1991)
Leontovich, Eugenie (act, b. 1894): Homicidal
Leopardi, Chauncey (act): Casper; Shadow Zone: The Undead Express
Leopold, Douglas (act): Wild Thing
Leopold, Frank (act): see Wynn, Keenan
Leopold, Glenn (wri): The Prowler (1981); Too Scared to Scream
Leopold, Harold (act): Creature With the Blue Hand
Leopold, Isaiah Edwin (act): see Wynn, Ed
Leopold, Stratton (act): Kiss of the Tarantula; They Live
Leos, Virgilio (act): Dr. Tarr's Torture Dungeon
Leotard, Philippe (act): Les Miserables (1995); Le Paltoquet
Leoville, Charles (act): Forty Winks
LePage, Brent (act): Halloween
Leparmentier, Richard (act): The Berlin Conspiracy
Lepe, Ana Bertha (act): La Nave de los Monstruos
LePicard, Marcel (cin): The Enchanted Forest; Flight to Nowhere; Ghost Chasers; The Invisible Ghost; The Lost Volcano; Spooks Run Wild; Voodoo Man
Leplat, Rene (act): The Golden Mask
Leplat, Ted (act): The Kirlian Witness
Lepler, Robert (act): Murder In Eden
Le Pore, Richard (act): Fer-de-Lance
Leppanen, Hekki (act): Gorky Park
Leppard, Alex (act): Scream and Die!
Leppard, Raymond (mus): Lord of the Flies (1963)
Leppell, Jonathan J. (act): Twin Peaks: Fire Walk With Me
Le Prevost, Nicholas (act): The Girl In a Swing
LePrince de Beaumont, Mme. (wri): La Belle et la Bete
le Queux, William (wri): The Sons of Satan
Lerdorff, Preben (act): Vredens Dag
Lerin, Hans (cin): The Visitors (1989)
Lerios, Cory (mus): Child's Play 3; Night Angel
Lerman, Steve (act): Retribution (1988)
Lermontov, Mikhail (wri): Ashik Kerib
Lerner, Alan Jay (mus, 1918-1986): Brigadoon; The Little Prince; On a Clear Day You Can See Forever
Lerner, Alan Jay (wri, 1918-1986): Camelot; The Little Prince; On a Clear Day You Can See Forever
Lerner, Allen Michael (act): Remote Control (1988)
Lerner, Fred (act): Covenant; Endangered Species; Switch (1991)
Lerner, Irving (dir): City of Fear (1959); Edge of Fury; Murder by Contract
Lerner, Jacques (act): The Monkey Talks
Lerner, Joseph (dir): Guilty Bystander
Lerner, Ken (act): Bodily Harm; The Exorcist III; Project X (1987); RoboCop 2
Lerner, Michael (act): Anguish; Maniac Cop 2; Godzilla (1998); Maniac Cop 2; No Escape (1994); Omen IV: The Awakening; Reflections of Murder; Strange Invaders; Vibes
Lerner, Scott (act): Flesh-Eating Mothers
Leroux, Gaston (wri, 1868-1927): Balaoo; The Phantom of Paris (1931); The Phantom of the Opera (1925, 1943, 1962, 1983, 1989,1990 & 1999); The Wizard
Leroux, Maxime (act): Mr. Frost
Leroy (act): Offerings
LeRoy, Eddie (act): Up In Smoke
Leroy, Frank (act): Colossus and the Headhunters
LeRoy, Gloria (act): The Strange Possession of Mrs.Oliver; Topper (1979); Welcome to Arrow Beach
LeRoy, Mervyn (dir, 1900-1987): The Bad Seed (1956); Moment to Moment
Leroy, Philippe (act, b. 1930): Castle of the Living Dead; The Night Porter; Le Trou
Le Roy, Rita (act): The Mandarin Mystery
LeRoy, Zoaunne (act): Flatliners
le Royer, Michel (act): Agents of Doom
Lerpae, Paul (cin): Conquest of Space; The Dark Mirror (1946); Project X (1967); The War of the Worlds
Lerski, Helmar (cin): Das Wachsfigurenkabinett
Le Sache, Bernadette (act): The Vanishing (1988)
Lesaffre, Roland (act): The Tartar Invasion; To Catch a Thief
LeSage, Bill (mus): The Tell-Tale Heart (1960)
Le Saint, Edward (act): The Lost Jungle
Lesco, Ken (act): The Octagon
Lescot, Raymond (act): Rabid Grannies
Leskin, Boris (act): The Package; Vampire's Kiss
Lesley, Bill (dir): Nail Gun Massacre
Lesley, Carole (act): No Trees In the Street
Lesley, Mick (act): King Solomon's Mines (1985)
Leslie, Avril (act): The Revenge of Frankenstein
Leslie, Bethel (act, b. 1929): Dr. Cook's Garden
Leslie, Brian (act): The Door In the Wall
Leslie, Colin (act): The Ghost Goes West
Leslie, Desmond (wri): Stranger from Venus
Leslie, Dudley (wri): Black Limelight; The Frightened Bride; Living Dangerously; Sensation (1937); Three Silent Men
Leslie, Edward/Eddie (act): The Devil's Jest; Echo of Barbara; Saadia
Leslie, J. Hubert (act): Doss House; The Dragon of Pendragon Castle; Menace (1934)
Leslie, Joan (act, b. 1925, nee Joan Brodell): Nancy Drew, Reporter; Repeat Performance; Turn Back the Clock
Leslie, John (act): Dracula Sucks
Leslie, Karen (act): Mini Weekend
Leslie, Laurie (act): The Prehistoric Man (1924)
Leslie, Nan (act): The Bamboo Saucer; The Devil Thumbs a Ride; The Falcon's Alibi
Leslie, Noel (act): The Search for Bridey Murphy
Leslie, Rolf(e) (act): The Beetle; In the Toils of the Blackmailer; Jane Shore (1915); The Lights O' London; The Tube of Death
Leslie, Vilma Ann (act): The Professionals
Leslie, William (act): The Couch; The Lineup; Mutiny In Outer Space; The Night the World Exploded
Lesnie, Andrew (cin): Babe; Babe: Pig In the City
Lessane, Leroy (act): Silent Night, Bloody Night
Lessard, Bob (act): Empire of Ash III
Lesser, Bob (act): Space Rage
Lesser, Bobby (act): Christmas Evil
Lesser, Len (act): Blood and Lace; How to Stuff a Wild Bikini; Ruby; Someone's Watching Me!; Sorority Girls and the Creature from Hell; Through the Magic Pyramid
Lesser, Robert (act): Ernest Saves Christmas; The Monster Squad; The Relic
Lessing, Arnold (act): Beach Girls and the Monster
Lessing, Doris (wri): Memoirs of a Survivor
Lessley, Elgin (cin): Sherlock Jr.
Lessy, Ben (act): Pajama Party
Lessy, George (act): Charlie Chan In the Secret Service; Sky Murder
Lester, Bruce (act, b. 1912, nee Bruce Lister): Above Suspicion; British Intelligence; Celia; Crime Over London; Death at Broadcasting House; Golden Earrings; The Mysterious Doctor; Shadows On the Stairs; Tarzan and the Trappers; The Third Clue
Lester, Buddy (act): Ellery Queen: Don't Look Behind You; Fake-Out; The Nutty Professor (1963); Poor Devil
Lester, Carl (act): The Henderson Monster
Lester, Dan (cin): Gremlins 2: The New Batch; Houdini (1998)
Lester, Jack (act): The Incredible 2-Headed Transplant
Lester, Jane (act): Killer's Moon
Lester, Kat (act): Phantasm III: Lord of the Dead
Lester, Kate (act): Crooked Alley; The Hunchback of Notre Dame (1923)
Lester, Katherine (act): see DeMille, Katherine
Lester, Kathy (act): Phantasm
Lester, Ken (act): Empire of Ash III
Lester, Ketty (act): Blacula
Lester, Loren (act): Evilspeak
Lester, Mark (1930s act): Seven Sinners
Lester, Mark (act, b. 1958): Eyewitness (1970); Night Hair Child; Our Mother's House; Spaceflight IC-1; Sudden Terror; Who Slew Auntie Roo?
Lester, Mark (L.) (dir): Class of '84; Class of 1999; Firestarter; Gold of the Amazon Women
Lester, Mark L. (wri): Class of 1999
Lester, Neil (act): The Ghost Goes West
Lester, Renny (act): The Curse of the Werewolf
Lester, Richard (dir, b. 1932): The Bed-Sitting Room; The Mouse On the Moon; The Return of the Musketeers; Robin and Marian; Royal Flash; Superman II; Superman III; The Three Musketeers (1974)
Lester, Seeleg (wri): Change of Mind; The Reincarnate
Lester, Stephen (act): The Corpse Grinders
Lester, Terry (act): In Self Defense; Kiss Meets the Phantom of the Park; Once Upon a Spy
Lestocq, Humphrey (act): Bomb In the High Street; The Golden Rabbit; Meet Mr. Lucifer; Pit of Darkness; Son of Robin Hood; Stop Press Girl; The Third Alibi; Two Wives at One Wedding; The Unstoppable Man
Le Sueur, Hal (act): Shadow of the Thin Man
Letch, David (act): Dark of the Night; Death Warmed Up
Letch, Joan (act): Mad Max
Leterrier, Francois (dir, b. 1929): La Poursuite
Letham, Ronnie (act): The Saint
Lethin, Lori (act): Bloody Birthday; The Day After; The Prey (1980); Return to Horror High
Leto, Jared (act, b. 1971): Urban Legend
Letondal, Henri (act): The Big Clock; Crime Doctor's Gamble; Desert Legion
Letourneau, Gil (dir): The Hound of London
Letterman, Richard (cin): It (1990)
Lettieri, Al (act): Pulp
Lettinger, Bruno (act): Die Spinnen
Letts, Pauline (act): Gawain and the Green Knight
Letz, George (act): see Montgomery, George
Leubner, Marilyn (act): Dante's Peak
Leuvrais, Jean (act): He Died With His Eyes Open
Levant, Brian (dir): The Flintstones
Levant, Mark (mus): The Woman In Green
Levant, Oscar (mus, 1906-1972): Charlie Chan at the Opera
LeVant, Rene (act): We're Back! A Dinosaur's Story
LeVay, Sylvester (mus): The Annihilator; Creator; Invitation to Hell; Snow Kill; Something Is Out There; Stalking Laura
Levels, Calvin (act): Hellbound; Point of No Return
Leven, Boris (mus): The Andromeda Strain
Leven, Jeremy (wri): Creator
Levenbrown, Brittany (act): The Silencers (1995)
Levene, John (act): Dark Places
Levene, Philip (wri): Deadly Strangers; Diagnosis: Murder
Levene, Sam (act, 1905-1980): After the Thin Man; Crossfire; Demon (1976); Dial 1119; Guilty Bystander; Last Embrace; Shadow of the Thin Man
Levenson, Dode (wri): Children of the Corn III: Urban Sacrifice
Levenson, Lew (wri): The Mysterious Mr. Wong
Levent, Alan (cin): Dracula, Pere et Fils
Lever, Huggy (act): Judge Dredd
Lever, Reg (act): Are You Dying Young Man?; Scrooge (1970)
Levering, Frank (wri): Parasite
Levering, Joseph (dir): Finger Prints
Leversee, Loretta (act): The Astronaut; The Other (1972); The Playground; Sandcastles
Leversuch, Ted (dir & wri): Tangier Assignment
Levesque, Marcel (act): The Crime of Monsieur Lange
Levesque, Mariette (act): Tanya's Island
Levesque, Michel (dir & wri): Werewolves On Wheels
Levesque, Stephanie (act): Alien High
Levey, Charles (act): The Shadow of Egypt
Levey, William A. (dir): Committed; Hellgate
Levi, Alan (J.) (dir): Bionic Showdown: The Six Million Dollar Man and the Bionic Woman;Blood Song; Code Name: Minus One; The Incredible Hulk, Part 2; The Invisible Woman (1983); The Stepford Children
Levi, Eric (mus): The Visitors (1995)
Levi, Nili (act): Flatliners
Levi, Nur Al (act): Zorro: The Legend Begins
Levien, Sonya (wri, 1888-1960): Behind That Curtain; Berkeley Square; The Hunchback of Notre Dame (1939); Liliom (1930)
Le Vigan, Robert (act): Le Quai des Brumes
Levignac, Sylvain (act): Perceval
Levin, Alvin (mus): Too Many Winners
Levin, Charles (act): The Golden Child
Levin, Darlene (act): Addams Family Values
Levin, Deborah (act): Timestalkers
Levin, Erma E. (mus): The Projectionist
Levin, Henry (dir, 1909-1980): The Ambushers; Cry of the Werewolf; The Devil's Mask; I Love a Mystery (1945); Journey to the Center of the Earth (1959); Kiss the Girls and Make Them Die; Murderers' Row; The Return of Monte Cristo; The Unknown (1946); The Wonderful World of the Brothers Grimm; The Wonders of Aladdin
Levin, Ira (wri, b. 1929): The Boys from Brazil; Dr. Cook's Garden; Revenge of the Stepford
Wives; Rosemary's Baby; Sliver; The Stepford Children; The Stepford Husbands; The Stepford Wives
Levin, John (act): Dracula's Dog; Reflections of Murder
Levin, Larry (wri): Dr. Dolittle (1998)
Levin, Maureen Sue (act): Addams Family Values
Levin, Peter (dir): Northstar
Levin, Sam (cin): The Rules of the Game
Levine, Anna (act): Warlock
Levine, Floyd (act): Cellar Dweller; Repossessed
Levine, Hank (mus): So Sad About Gloria
Levine, Jack (dir): Ghost Rider (1935)
Levine, Jason (act): RoboCop
Lavine, Jay (act): The Fugitive (1993)
Levine, Jean (act): The Newlydeads
Levine, Jeff (act): The Hidden
Levine, Jerry (act, b. 1957): Teen Wolf
Levine, Joe (mus): Target...Earth?
Levine, Joel (act): Night of the Comet
Levine, Ken (wri): Mannequin Two: On the Move
Levine, Marcia (act): The Pink Chiquitas
Levine, Matthew (act): Glen and Randa
Levine, Mike (act): Don't Answer the Phone!
Levine, Minnie (act): With Human Instinct
Levine, Philip (wri): The Firechasers
Levine, Ron (act): The Nesting
Levine, Ted (act): Flubber; The Mangler; Moby Dick (1998); The Silence of the Lambs
Levingston, Javar David (act): Heart and Souls
Le Vino, Albert S(helby) (wri): Boston Blackie's Little Pal; The Canary Murder Case; Missing Millions
Levinson, Barry (dir, b. 1942): The Internecine Project; Sphere; Young Sherlock Holmes
Levinson, David (wri): Fantasies
Levinson, Gary (J.) (act): The Alien Within; The Phantom Empire; Shock Waves; Surf Nazis Must Die
Levinson, Gregory (act): Alfred Hitchcock Presents; Lady In White
Levinson, Janice (act): Sergeant Deadhead the Astronut!
Levinson, Richard (wri, 1934-1987): Ellery Queen; Prototype; Rollercoaster
Levinson, Sarabel (act): The Toxic Avenger
Levis, Carroll (act): The Depraved
Levis, Dora (act): Chu Chin Chow (1923)
Levisetti, Emile (act): Alien Terminator
Levison, Nat (act): Inn of the Damned
Levit, Aric (act): Blood Diner
Levitan, Charan (act): Beyond and Back
Levitch, Joel (act): Werewolf of Washington
Levitch, Joseph (act): see Lewis, Jerry
Leviton, Eric (act): Vampire at Midnight
Levitsky, Al (act): Martin
Levitsky, Alexander (cin): Luch Smerti; Portret Doriana Greya
Levitt, Alfred Lewis (wri): The Boy With Green Hair
Levitt, Gene (dir): The Phantom of Hollywood
Levitt, Gene (wri): Fantasy Island
Levitt, Judy (act): Moontrap; Star Trek: Generations
Levitt, Karen (wri): Time Walker
Levitt, Paul (act): Cape Fear (1961)
Levitt, Stan (act): Carnival of Souls
Levitt, Steve (act): Hunk; The Incredible Hulk Returns
Levitt, Zane W. (wri): Out of the Dark
Levka, Uta (act): De Sade; The Oblong Box; Scream and Scream Again
Levy, Annabella (act): Moebius
Levy, Barry W. (act): Time Runner
Levy, Benn W. (wri): Blackmail (1929); The Old Dark House (1932)
Levy, Don (act): The Pirates of Blood River
Levy, Edward (wri): The Beast Within
Levy, Eric Louis (act): Watchers II
Levy, Eugene (act, b. 1946): Bride of Boogedy; Cannibal Girls; Heavy Metal; Kurt Vonnegut's Harrison Bergeron; Multiplicity; Splash; Stay Tuned
Levy, Frederick (act): see Tearle, Conway

Levy, Gerry (dir): The Body Stealors; Where Has Poor Mickey Gone?
Levy, J. (wri): The Traitors
Levy, Jefery (wri): Ghoulies
Levy, Joan (act): Dawn of the Mummy
Levy, Julius (wri): The Hairy Ape
Levy, Julien (act): Dreams That Money Can Buy
Levy, Katherine (act): The Watcher In the Woods
Levy, Louis (mus, b. 1893): The Clairvoyant (1934); The Lady Vanishes (1938); Moby Dick (1956); 1984 (1955); A Place of One's Own; Sabotage; The Secret Agent (1936); The 39 Steps (1935); The Tunnel
Levy, Marty (act): I, Madman; Slam Dance
Levy, Melvin (wri): The Bandit of Sherwood Forest; Who Fears the Devil?
Levy, Ori (act): The Jerusalem File; Moon Zero Two
Levy, Paulette (act): see Goddard, Paulette
Levy, Peter (cin): Cutthroat Island; Lost In Space; A Nightmare On Elm Street 5: The Dream Child; Predator 2
Levy, Robert L. (wri): A Kid In King Arthur's Court
Levy, Scott (dir): Midnight Tease; National Lampoon's Men In White; Piranha (1995)
Levy, Shawn (act): The Kiss (1988); Wild Thing
Levy, Shuki (dir): Perfect Victims; Turbo: A Power Rangers Movie
Levy, Shuki (wri): Turbi: A Power Rangers Movie
Levy, Shuki (Y.) (mus): Bay Coven; Dawn of the Mummy; Prey of the Chameleon; Turbo: A Power Rangers Movie
Levy, Simon (act): The Road to Hong Kong
Levy, Stephen (act): see Young, Stephen
Levy, Weaver (act): The Wrecking Crew
Lew, James (act): Timecop
Lewallen, Raymond (act): Sling Blade
LeWars, Margaret (act): Dr. No
Lewellyn, Mr. (act): The Harper Mystery
Lewes, Fred (act): The Kidnapped King
Lewgoy, Jose (act): Terra em Transe
Le White, Jack (act): Blood Bath at the House of Death
Lewin, Albert (dir & wri, 1894-1968): The Living Idol; Pandora and the Flying Dutchman; The Picture of Dorian Gray (1945); Saadia
Lewin, David (act): Deja Vu
Lewin, Irwin (act): The Psychotronic Man
Lewis, Abby (act): Dr. Cook's Garden
Lewis, Al (act, b. 1923): Munster, Go Home!; The Munsters'Revenge; They Might Be Giants
Lewis, Al (act): The Creeping Terror; Fright House
Lewis, Alyce (act): Eyes of the Jungle
Lewis, Bernard (wri): Undercover Girl (1958)
Lewis, Bobo (act): The Nesting; Way...Way Out
Lewis, Cecil (dir & wri): Gipsy Blood
Lewis, Charlotte (act): Dial Help; The Golden Child; The Nosferatu Diaries: Embrace of the Vampire
Lewis, Christopher (dir): Blood Cult; Revenge (1986); The Ripper (1985)
Lewis, Clea (act): Diabolique (1996); The Rich Man's Wife
Lewis, Constance (act): Mr. H.C. Andersen
Lewis, D. David (act): The Fan
Lewis, David (act): The Absent-Minded Professor (1961); Voyage of Terror
Lewis, David (cin): Atomic Dog; The Hills Have Eyes II; Leprechaun 3; Night Angel; Night of the Demons
Lewis, David P. (act): I, Madman
Lewis, David P. (wri): City On Fire; Death Ship
Lewis, Diana (act): The Monster Squad
Lewis, Diane (act): Body Heat
Lewis, Duncan (act): Act of Murder (1964)
Lewis, Eddie (act): Mr. Sycamore
Lewis, Emma (act): Merlin (1998)
Lewis, Fiona (act, b. 1946): Blue Blood; Dr. Phibes Rises Again; Dracula (1973); The Fearless Vampire Killers or: Pardon Me, ButYour Teeth Are In My Neck; The Fury; Innerspace; Liszt O' Mania; Otley; Strange Behavior; Strange Invaders; Tintorera...Bloody Waters
Lewis, Forrest (act): The Absent-Minded Professor (1961); It Grows On Trees; The Monster of Piedras Blancas; The Shaggy Dog (1959); Son of Flubber
Lewis, Garrett (act): Oh Heavenly Dog
Lewis, Gene (wri): Cobra Woman; Gypsy Wildcat
Lewis, Geoffrey (act): The Annihilator; Disturbed; Human Experiments; The Lawnmower Man; Moon of the Wolf; Night of the Comet; Out of the Dark; Point of No Return; The Return of the Man from U.N.C.L.E.; Salem's Lot; Trilogy of Terror II; When the Dark Man Calls; Wishman
Lewis, George (J.) (act): The Bandits of Corsica; Charlie Chan In the Secret Service; Desert Legion; The Docks of New Orleans; The Falcon In Mexico; The Falcon's Brother; The Feathered Serpent (1948); Flesh and Fantasy; Ghost of Zorro; The Sign of Zorro (1960); Zorro, the Avenger
Lewis, George (dir): The Humanoid
Lewis, Gerry (act): An American Werewolf In London
Lewis, Gilbert (act): Grave Secrets
Lewis, Gillian (act): Ring of Spies
Lewis, Glenn Charles (act): The Swarm
Lewis, Greg (act): Prehysteria! 2; Repossessed; Vamp
Lewis, Gwen (act): Eyes of a Stranger
Lewis, Harry (act): Panther Island; The Unsuspected
Lewis, Helen Prothero (wri): The Silver Bridge
Lewis, Henry (act): Night of Terror (1987)
Lewis, Herschell Gordon (act, b. 1926): A Taste of Blood
Lewis, Herschell Gordon (cin, b. 1926): Color Me Blood Red; The Gruesome Twosome
Lewis, Herschell Gordon/G. (dir, b. 1926): Blood Feast; Color Me Blood Red; The Gore-Gore Girls; The Gruesome Twosome; How to Make a Doll; Monster A-Go-Go; She-Devils On Wheels; Something Weird; A Taste of Blood; 2000 Maniacs; The Wizard of Gore
Lewis, Herschell Gordon (wri, b. 1926): Color Me Blood Red; How to Make a Doll
Lewis, Howard Lew (act): Brazil; Robin Hood: Prince of Thieves
Lewis, Huey (act): Sphere
Lewis, Jack (wri): The Amazing Transparent Man; The Naked Gun
Lewis, Jarma (act): It's a Dog's Life; The Magnetic Monster; Prince Valiant (1954)
Lewis, Jean Ann (act) The Bride and the Beast
Lewis, Jeff (act): Freejack
Lewis, Jennifer (act, b. 1957): The Meteor Man; The Preacher's Wife
Lewis, Jerry (act, b. 1926, nee Joseph Levitch): Cinderfella; It's Only Money; Li'l Abner (1959); The Nutty Professor (1963); The Road to Bali; Scared Stiff (1953); Visit to a Small Planet; Way...Way Out
Lewis, Jerry (wri & dir, b. 1926): The Nutty Professor (1963 & 1996)
Lewis, John (act): No Blade of Grass
Lewis, John Martin (act): Robbery With Violence
Lewis, John (mus): Kemek; The Tempest (1979)
Lewis, Joseph H. (dir, b. 1900): Criminals Within; The Falcon In San Francisco; The Ghost Creeps; The Invisible Ghost; The Mad Doctor of Market Street; My Name Is Julia Ross; The Return of October; So Dark the Night; The Spy Ring
Lewis, Julia (act): Supergirl (1984)
Lewis, Juliette (act, b. 1973): Cape Fear (1991); From Dusk Till Dawn; Romeo Is Bleeding; Strange Days
Lewis, Kay (act): The Face at the Window (1939)
Lewis, Kim (act): Party Line
Lewis, Kit (act): Blood Song
Lewis, Leo (act): Time After Time
Lewis, Leopold (wri): The Bells (1923)
Lewis, Linda (act): It Fell from the Sky
Lewis, Lori (act): Nightmare Weekend
Lewis, Louise (act): Blood of Dracula; I Was a Teenage Werewolf; The Vampire (1957)
Lewis, Marcia (act): The Ice Pirates; Orpheus Descending
Lewis, Martin (act): Dangerous Ground; The Riverside Murder
Lewis, Mical Shannon (act): Fire In the Sky (1993)
Lewis, Michael (act): Blood Beach
Lewis, Michael (J.) (mus, b. 1939): The Legacy; The Man Who Haunted Himself; The Medusa Touch; Sphinx (1981); Theater of Blood; The Unseen (1981)
Lewis, Milo (dir): Egghead's Robot
Lewis, Mitchell (act, 1880-1956): The Bridge of San Luis Rey (1929); Kongo; The Man With a Cloak; The Mysterious Mr. Moto; The Mystic; Rupert of Hentzau (1923); Salome (1922); Talk About a Stranger; The Thin Man Goes Home
Lewis, Monica (act): Earthquake
Lewis, Morton (act): Heavy Traffic
Lewis, Nathan (act): The Phantom of the Opera (1989)
Lewis, Oliver (act): First Knight
Lewis, Pauline (wri): Fairyland
Lewis, Peter (act): A Shattered Idyll
Lewis, Phill (act): Brother Future
Lewis, Raan (act): The Outing
Lewis, Ralph (act): The Avenging Conscience; The Conquering Power; Dante's Inferno (1924); The Flying Serpent; The Jade Mask; The Lost City; Mystery Liner; Outside the Law
Lewis, Reg (act): Fire Monsters vs. the Son of Hercules
Lewis, Richard (act, b. 1947): Robin Hood: Men In Tights
Lewis, Robert (1940s & 1950s act): The Hidden Eye; The Lost Volcano; Monsieur Verdoux; Paris After Dark
Lewis, Robert (1980s & 1990s act): The Haunting of Hamilton High; Hello Again
Lewis, Robert (Michael) (dir, b. 1909): The Astronaut; Circumstances Unknown; City Killer; Final Eye; The Invisible Man (1975); Ladykillers (1988); Memories of Murder; S*H*E (1980); Sparkling Cyanide; A Stranger Waits
Lewis, Ronald (act, b. 1928): The Brigand of Kandahar; The Full Treatment; Helen of Troy (1955); Jigsaw; Mr. Sardonicus; The Secret Place; Siege of the Saxons; A Taste of Fear
Lewis, Rosalie V. (act): Primal Fear
Lewis, Roy H. (wri): Murder Anonymous
Lewis, Russell (act): Tales That Witness Madness; Voices
Lewis, Sheldon (act, 1868-1958): Dr. Jekyll and Mr. Hyde (1919); Don Juan (1927); The Monster Walks; The Phantom (1931); Seven Footprints to Satan
Lewis, Sheryl Mary (act): Cyborg 2: Glass Shadow
Lewis, Stephanie (act): The Outing
Lewis, Stephen (act): The McGuffin
Lewis, Steven (act): Negatives
Lewis, Suzanne (act): The Crater Lake Monster
Lewis, Sylvia (act): Drums of Tahiti
Lewis, Ted (wri): Get Carter
Lewis, Trey (act): The Outing
Lewis, Vera (act): The Cat Creeps (1946); The Iron Mask; Nancy Drew and the Hidden Staircase; Nancy Drew, Detective; The Return of Dr. X; Spook Busters; Torchy Plays With Dynamite
Lewis, W. Michael (mus): New Year's Evil
Lewis, Warren (wri): Eaters of the Dead
Lewis, Webster (mus): The Hearse
Lewiston, Denis (cin): Appointment for a Killing; Arthur the King; The Canterville Ghost (1996); The Squeeze; The Thief of Baghdad (1978)
Lewk, Daniel (act): The China Syndrome
Lewman, Lance (act): Breeders; Netforce
Lewnes, Pericles (act): Redneck Zombies
Lewnes, Peter (cin): I Was a Teenage Zombie
Lexy, Edward (act): Blanche Fury; Cloudburst; The Drum; Ghosts of Berkeley Square; The ManWho Wouldn't Talk; The Mark of Cain; Mrs. Pym of Scotland Yard; Night Was Our Friend; The Spider (1939); The Terror (1938); This Man Is News; Too Dangerous to Live; Traitor Spy; The Twenty Questions Murder; While I Live
Ley, John (act): Escape 2000; Mad Max
Ley, Margot (act): Captain Nemo and the Underwater City
Ley, Willy (wri, 1906-1969): Conquest of Space
Leycester, Laura (wri): The Five Wishes
Leyden, Leo (act): The Mask (1961)
Leyes, Landy (act): Gunhed
Leyh, Blake (mus): True Crime
Leyrado, Juan (act): Times to Come
Leyssen, Johan (act): Gebroken Spiegels
Leyton, Drue (act): Charlie Chan at the Circus; Charlie Chan In London; Charlie Chan's Courage
Leyton, John (act): Krakatoa-East of Java; Schizo (1977)
Leyva, Frank (act): The Feathered Serpent (1948)
L'Herbier, Marcel (dir, 1890-1979): Don Juan et Faust; L'Inhumaine; Le Mystere de la Chambre Jaune
L'Herbier, Marcel (wri, 1890-1979): Les Derniers Jours de Pompeii; L'Inhumaine
Lhoest, Anita (act): Captive Girl
Lhomme, Pierre (cin, b. 1930): Quelqu'un Derriere la Porte
Li, Alicia (act): Confessions of an Opium Eater
Li, Bernadette (act): Deadbolt
Li, Donald (act): Big Trouble In Little China
Li, Gong (act): A Terra-Cotta Warrior
Li, Lily (act): Call Him Mr. Shatter
Li, Michelle (act): A Chinese Ghost Story II; Wicked City
Liakakis, Peter (act): Hangar 18
Liano, Chris (act): The Toxic Avenger
Liapis, Peter (act): Ghost Warrior; Ghoulies; Ghoulies IV
Libaire, Dorothy (act): Murder On a Honeymoon
Libby, Brian (act): Buried Alive II; Chiller; Eraser; The First Power; The Octagon
Libby Sr., Robert (act): The Toxic Avenger, Part II
Liberace (act, 1919-1987): The Loved One
Liberati, Alberto (wri): Knives of the Avenger
Liberati, Lisa (act): Species
Liberatore, Ugo (wri): La Leggendi di Enea; Il Mulino delle Donne di Pietra; Nights of Rasputin; La Strega In Amore; The Trojan Horse
Libert, Anne (act): The Demons (1974); Virgin Among the Living Dead
Libert, Beatrice (act): Moonraker
Libertini, Richard (act): All of Me; And You Thought Your Parents Were Weird
Liberty, Richard (act): Code Name Trixie; Day of the Dead; The Final Countdown; Flight of the Navigator
Libman, Andrea (act): Susie Q; Them (1996)
Libman, Bryn-Erin (act): Mother, May I Sleep With Danger?
Libman, Syd (act): Millennium
Libra (mus): Shock (1978)
Licasi, Peter (act): Killer Klowns from Outer Space
Licht, Daniel (mus): Bad Moon; Hellraiser: Bloodline; Children of the Corn III: Urban Sacrifice; Hellraiser 4: Bloodline; Legion of Fire: Killer Ants; Thinner
Licht, Jeremy (act): The Next One; Twilight Zone
Lichtenfield, Louis (cin): Helen of Troy (1955)
Lichter, Michelle (wri): Revenge of the Teenage Vixens from Outer Space
Lichtman, Myla (wri): The Loves of Dracula; World of Dracula
Lichtman, Susan (act): Making Mr. Right
Licudi, Gabriella (act, b. 1943): Casino Royale; The Invisible Asset; The Liquidator; Unearthly Stranger
Liddell, Alvar (act): The Counterfeit Plan; They Met In the Dark; The Voice of Merrill
Liddy, James (act): The Last of the Lone Wolf
Lide, Kendell (act): Raiders of the Living Dead
Lidington, Bruce (act): Sword of the Valiant
Lido, Pini (act): La Ragazza Che Sapeva Troppo
Lidstone, Gail (act): Are You Dying Young Man?
Lieb, Daniel (act): Raiders of the Living Dead
Lieb, Harald (act): The Curse of the Hidden Vault
Lieb, Robert (act): Myra Breckinridge
Liebeneiner, Wolfgang (dir): The Dancing Heart
Lieber, Marvin (act): Jack's Wife
Lieber, Mimi (act): Ghost In the Machine; White of the Eye; Wilder Napalm
Lieber, Shawn (act): Neon Maniacs
Lieberman, Bradley (act): Pandemonium
Lieberman, Jeff (dir): Blue Sunshine; Just Before Dawn (1980); Remote Control (1988)
Lieberman, Jeff (wri): Blade (1973); Blue Sunshine; Doctor Franken; Remote Control (1988)
Lieberman, Leo (wri): Bonzo Goes to College
Lieberman, Rick (act): Bates Motel; The Hidden; RoboCop; Snow Kill
Lieberman, Robert (dir): Fire In the Sky (1993); Netforce
Liebgold, Leon (act): The Dybbuk
Liebing, Franziska (act): Willy Wonka and the Chocolate Factory
Liebman, Cecile (act): The Nesting
Liebmann, Robert (wri): Liliom (1930)
Liedtke, Harry (act): Die Augen der Mumie Ma; Carmen (1918)
Lieh, Lo (act): Don't Play With Fire
Lien, Nancy (act): Blood Waters of Dr. Z
Lienas, Silvia (act): Hatchet for a Honeymoon
Liessen, Vera (act): Das Testament des Dr. Mabuse
Lietot, Christine (act): Perceval
Lieven, Albert (act, 1906-1971): The Ape Creature; City of Fear (1965); The Dark Light; Death Drums Along the River; Death Trap (1962); The Devil Agent; The Devil's Daffodil; Gestapo; Sleeping Car to Trieste; Subway In the Sky; Traitor's Gate
Liew, Wan Thye (act): The Time Guardian
Lifchitz, Philippe (dir & wri): La Prima Donna
Lifschitz, Gabriel (wri): Moebius
Lifsey, Roger (cin): Weird Science
Lifton, Jimmy (dir & wri): Mirror, Mirror 2: Raven Dance

Ligarde, Sebastian (act): Remo Williams: The Adventure Begins
Ligeti, Gyorgy (mus, b. 1923): 2001: A Space Odyssey
Liggatt, James (act): Castle Sinister (1948); Fury at Smugglers' Bay
Liggett, Agnieszka (act): The Saint
Light, Karl (act): The Lonely Sex
Lightning, Suzie (act): I Don't Want to Be Born
Lightstone, Marilyn (act): Disaster In Time; Heavy Metal; Spasms
Lightsy, Jack (act): Night of the Creeps
Ligier, Teresa (act): Deadly Messages
Ligman, Paul (act): Willy McBean and His Magic Machine
Ligon, Tom (act, b. 1945): Cutting Class; The Demon Murder Case
Lijer, Fernando (act): Perseus the Invincible
Liles, Linda (act): Devil's Web
Liles, Ronald (C.) (wri): Danger by My Side; The Night of the Big Heat
Liliana, Lili (act): The Dybbuk
Lilitts, Martha Maria (act): see Dagover, Lil
Liljencrantz, Ottilie A. (wri):The Viking
Liljedahl, Marie (act): Dorian Gray; Eugenie...The Story of Her Journey into Perversion;
Grimm's Fairy Tales for Adults
Lill, Den(n)is (act): Arthur the King; Batman (1989); The Scarlet Pimpernel (1982)
Lillard, Matthew (act): Scream; Serial Mom; Senseless (1998); Wing Commander
Lilley, Heather (act): Strays
Lilley, Jessica (act): Strays
Lilley, Joseph J. (mus): The Road to Bali; Scared Stiff (1953)
Lilley, Merv (act): The Last Wave
Lilley, Peter (act): The Man With the Magnetic Eyes
Lillie, Beatrice (act, 1894-1989): Around the World In 80 Days
Lillig, Jane (act): Lies
Lillingston, Sandie (act): Mad Max Beyond Thunderdome
Lillitsch, Georg (act): The Arrival (1996)
Lillo, George (wri): George Barnwell, the London Apprentice
Lillo, Marie (act): Beyond and Back
Lilly, Anne (act): Revenge of the Teenage Vixens from Outer Space
Lilly, Sarah (act): Gremlins 2: The New Batch
Lim, Pik-sen (act): Madame Sin
Lim, Swee (act): Return to Oz
Lima, Elyane (act): Devotion
Lima Jr., Walter (dir & wri): The Dolphin
Lime, Yvonne (act): I Was a Teenage Werewolf
Lin, F. Kenneth (wri): The Phoenix (1980); War of the Wizards
Lin, Traci (act): Class of 1999; Fright Night II
Linaker, Kay (act): Charlie Chan at Monte Carlo; Charlie Chan In Reno; Charlie Chan In Rio; Charlie Chan's Murder Cruise; Close Call for Ellery Queen; Hidden Enemy; Lady In the Dark; The Last Warning (1938)
Lincoln, Andrew (act): The Woman In White (1998)
Lincoln, Ann (act): Brainstorm (1983)
Lincoln, Elmo (act, 1889-1952, nee Otto Elmo Linkenhelter): Romance of Tarzan; Rupert of Hentzau (1923); Tarzan of the Apes
Lincoln, Fred (act): The Last House On the Left
Lincoln, Henry (wri): Curse of the Crimson Altar
Lincoln, Lar Park (act): Friday the 13th, Part VII—The New Blood; House II: The Second Story
Lincoln, Pamela (act): Anatomy of a Psycho; The Tingler
Lincoln, Scott (act): Assassin (1986)
Lincoln, Warren (act): The Power (1980); Torment (1986)
Lind, Brit (act): Play Misty for Me
Lind, Charles (act): On the Threshold of Space
Lind, Gillian (act): —And Now the Screaming Starts!;Don't Talk to Strange Men; Fear In the Night (1972); The Man Outside (1933); The Oracle (1952)
Lind, Jane (act): Wolfen
Lind, Lars (act): Det Sjunde Inseglet
Lind, Ragnar (act): see Lynn, Jeffrey
Lind, Traci (act): The Handmaid's Tale
Lindau, Paul (wri): Der Andere
Linday-Gray, Jayne (act): King Kong Lives
Lindberg, Donna (act): Mars Needs Women
Lindberg, Lasse (act): Gorky Park
Lindbjerg, Lalainia (act): Sabrina the Teenage Witch
Lindblom, Gunnel (act, b. 1931): Det Sjunde Inseglet; Smultronstallet; Tystnaden
Linde, Bette (act): I Still Dream of Jeannie
Lindell, Carrie (act): Cannibal Campout
Lindeman, Susie (act): Nightfall (1988)
Linden, Debbie (act): Blood Bath at the House of Death
Linden (Jr.), Edward/Eddie (cin): King Kong (1933); The Last Days of Pompeii (1935); The Lost City; Son of Kong
Linden, Eric (act): Criminals Within
Linden, Hal (act, b. 1931): The Colony (1995); Starflight: The Plane That Couldn't Land
Linden, Jenny (act): The Dumb Man of Manchester; The Maid of Cefn Ydfa (1908); The
Sign of the Cross
Linden, Jennie/Jenny (act): The Corsican Brothers(1985); Dr. Who and the Daleks; Murder Is a One-Act Play; Nightmare (1963); Vampira
Linden, Joyce (act): Dick Barton at Bay
Linden, Penny (act): Howling III
Linden, Warris (act): A Man's Shadow
Lindenlaub, Karl Walter (cin): Eye of the Storm; Independence Day; Moon 44; Stargate; Universal Soldier
Lindenmuth, Kevin J. (dir): Beyond Sanity
Linder, Alfred (act): The Invisible Boy
Linder, Cec (act): An American Christmas Carol; Blue Movie Blackmail; City On Fire; Deadly Eyes; Goldfinger; Hitler's Daughter; Jet Storm; Subway In the Sky; Tomorrow Never Comes; The Verdict (1964); Virus (1980)
Linder, Christa (act): Kiss Kiss, Kill Kill; The Night of a Thousand Cats
Linder, Emilio (act): Endless Descent; Slugs
Linder, Leslie (act): The Green Buddha; Men of Sherwood Forest; Star of India
Linder, Michael (act): Frightmare (1983)
Linder, Slawomir (act): Rekopis Znaleziony w Saragossie
Linderman, Maggie (act): The Vanishing (1993)
Lindert, Christoph (act): Making Contact
Lindfors, Viveca (act, 1920-1995, nee Elsa Viveca Torstens-dotter):The Adventures of Don Juan; A Bell from Hell; Brainstorm (1965); Cauldron of Blood; Child of Darkness, Child of Light; Creepshow; The Damned; The Exorcist III; Gypsy Fury; The Hand (1981); I Accuse (1958); Night Unto Night; No Exit; Secret Weapons; Silent
Madness; Stargate; This Side of the Law
Lindgren, Astrid (wri): Pippi Longstocking
Lindgren, Orley (act): Red Planet Mars
Lindgren, Peter (act): I Am Curious (Yellow)
Lindholm, Kirsten (act): Twins of Evil
Lindholm, Marita (act): The Possession of Joel Delaney
Lindig, Jillian (act): Eyes of a Stranger
Lindley, Audra (act): The Relic; Revenge of the Stepford Wives; Spellbinder
Lindley, Barbara (act): Dracula (1973)
Lindley, John (W.) (cin): The Demon Murder Case; The Good Son; Michael; The Serpent and the
Rainbow; The Stepfather; A Stranger Waits
Lindley Jr., Louis Bert (act): see Pickens, Slim
Lindley, Virginia (act): Sombra the Spider Woman
Lindo, Delroy (act): The Blood of Heroes
Lindo, Olga (act, 1898-1968): Alibi (1942); Bedelia; The Case of Gabriel Perry; Dark World; Dr. Crippen; An Inspector Calls; Luck of the Navy; Obsession (1949); Out of the Fog (1962); Things
Happen at Night; Time Flies (1944); The Twenty Questions Murder; Yield to the Night
Lindon, Lionel (cin, 1905-1971): Alias Nick Beal; Around the World In 80 Days; The Black Scorpion (1957); The Blue Dahlia; Casanova's Big Night; Conquest of Space; Destination Moon; The Extraordinary Seaman; The Great Rupert; Jamaica Run; The Manchurian Candidate; Ritual of Evil; The Road to Utopia; The Scarlet Hour; Secret of the Incas; The Werewolf (1955)
Lindon, Luna (act): Spiritualism Exposed (1913)
Lindon-Travers, Florence (act): see Travers, Linden
Lindop, Audrey Erskine (wri): Blanche Fury; The Frightened Bride; I Start Counting; I Thank a Fool
Lindsay, Barbara (act): Eye of the Storm
Lindsay, Carol (act): She-Gods of Shark Reef
Lindsay, Delia (act): Scars of Dracula
Lindsay, Helen (act): Mission: Impossible; The Partner
Lindsay, J. Dean (act): Twister
Lindsay, James (act): Alone In London; The Cry of the Captive; The Dead Heart; The Disappearance of the Judge; The Dungeon of Death; The Grip of Iron; Her Greatest Performance; In the Ranks; The Lyons Mail; The Port of Missing Women; The Temptation of Carlton Earle
Lindsay, Joan (wri): Picnic at Hanging Rock
Lindsay, Lance (dir & wri): Star Crystal
Lindsay, Lara (act): Logan's Run
Lindsay, Margaret (act, 1910-1981, nee Margaret Kies): British Intelligence; Close Call for Ellery Queen; Crime Doctor; Desperate Chance for Ellery Queen; The Dragon Murder Case; Ellery Queen and the Murder Ring; Ellery Queen and the Perfect Crime; Ellery Queen, Master Detective; Ellery Queen's Penthouse Mystery; Enemy Agents Meet Ellery Queen; The Florentine Dagger; The House of the Seven Gables; Jet Over the Atlantic; Seven Keys to Baldpate (1947)
Lindsay, Marisa (act): A Connecticut Yankee In King Arthur's Court (1989)
Lindsay, Mark (act): Assassin (1986)
Lindsay, Minnie (act): Trancers
Lindsay, Philip (wri): Under the Red Robe (1937)
Lindsay, Richard (act): The Pleydell Mystery
Lindsay, Robert (cin): Maniac (1980)
Lindsay, Vera (act): Spellbound (1941)
Lindsay, William (act): Lifeforce
Lindsay-Hogg, Michael (dir): The Little Match Girl (1987); Murder by Moonlight
Lindsell, Stuart (act): Fanny by Gaslight; Profile
Lindsey, George (act): Charley and the Angel; Robin Hood (1973)
Lindsey, George T. (wri): The Devonsville Terror
Lindsey, John (act): Asteroid
Lindsey, Lois (act): The Black Room
Lindsey, Minnie (act): Ghost (1990)
Lindsley, Clarke (act): The Immortalizer
Lindstedt, Carl-Gustaf (act): Man On the Roof
Lindstrom, Jorgen (act): Persona; Tystnaden
Lindstrom, Rune (act): La Sorciere
Lindt, Karl L. (act): This Island Earth
Lindup, David (mus): Call Him Mr. Shatter; Journey to the Unknown; The Spiral Staircase (1975)
Line, Helga (act): Ercole Contro i Tiranni di Babilonia; Goliath at the Conquest of Damascus; Horror; Horror Express; Horror Rises from the Tomb; The Mummy's Revenge; The Saga of the Draculas; Triumph of the Ten Gladiators; When the Screaming Stops
Lineback, Richard (act): Alfred Hitchcock Presents; Friday the 13th-Part V: A New Beginning; Twister
Lineburg, Stephi (act): Dad, the Angel & Me
Linehan, Barry (act): Dark Places; The Devil-Ship Pirates; The Rivals
Lineham, Danny (act): The Frighteners
Lineham, Hardee T. (act): Storm of the Century
Linei, Velta (act): Rasputin (1985)
Linero, Jeannie (act): Heaven Can Wait (1978)
Lines, Graham (act): Subterfuge
Ling, Bai (act): The Crow (1994)
Ling, Bo (act): Calling Philo Vance
Ling, Eugene (wri, b. 1915): Behind Locked Doors; Between Midnight and Dawn; Hand of Death; Shock (1946)
Ling, Ma (act): Life On a String
Ling, Mai (act): Goldfinger; The Road to Hong Kong; Taste the Blood of Dracula
Ling, Suzanne (act): Kiss of the Tarantula
Ling, Van (act): Alien Nation
Ling, Zhong (act): Life On a String
Lingard, Edward (act): Alone In London; The Cry of the Captive; The Dead Heart; His Great Opportunity
Lingen, Theo (act): M (1931)
Lingham, Wendy (act): Alien Women; The Private Life of Sherlock Holmes; Zeta One
Linhart, Buzzy (act): Modern Problems
Link, John F. (dir): The Devil's Cargo
Link, Michael (act): Stowaway to the Moon
Link, Ron (dir): Zombie High
Link, William (wri): Ellery Queen; Prototype; Rollercoaster
Linke, Don (act): Dark of the Night
Linke, Paul (act): Awake to Danger; Motel Hell; Space Rage
Linkenhelter, Otto Elmo (act): see Lincoln, Elmo
Linker, Amy (act): D.A.R.Y.L.
Linkletter, Art (act, b. 1912): Champagne for Caesar
Linn, Marcia (act): Star Crystal
Linn, Michael (mus): Allan Quatermain and the Lost City of Gold
Linn, Rex (act): Cutthroat Island; The Long Kiss Goodnight; Perfect Alibi
Linnane, Joe (act): The Angel Who Pawned Her Harp; Hunted (1952); The Woman In Question
Linn-Baker, Mark (act): Me and Him
Linne, Velta (act): Rasputin (1985)
Linney, Laura (act, b. 1964): Congo; Primal Fear; The Truman Show
Linow, Ivan (act): Just Imagine; Temple Tower; The Unholy Three (1930)
Linschoten, Rudi (act): The Mask (1961)
Linscott, Glenda (act): Howling III
Linskey, Melanie (act): The Frighteners
Lintern, Richard (act): Lost Souls (1998)
Linton, Betty Hyatt (act): Voodoo Blood Bath
Linton, Donald (act): Around the World Under the Sea
Linton, John K. (act): Watchers 3
Linton, Mildred (act): see Morley, Karen
Linton, Philip (act): Once Bitten
Linville, Albert (act): Damn Yankees
Linville, Joanne (act): From the Dead of Night; Scorpio; The Seduction
Linville, Larry (act, b. 1939): C.H.U.D. II; Earth Girls Are Easy; The Night Stalker (1971); School Spirit; The Stepmother
Linz, Alex D. (act): The Uninvited (1996)
Linza, Charles (act): Star Crystal
Linzey, Philip (cin): Bloodknot; Mother, May I Sleep With Danger?; Night Visitors
Liofredi, Marco (act): Frankenstein (1974)
Lion, Leon M. (act): Chin Chin Chinaman; The Chinese Puzzle; The Grip (1915); Number 17 (1932); Strange Boarders; The Woman Who Was Nothing
Lion, Leon M. (wri): The Chinese Puzzle; The Cobweb
Lion, Margo (act): La Rupture
Lionheart, Roselyn (act): Angel Heart
Lioni, Sal (act): The Toxic Avenger, Part II
Liotard, Therese (act): Deathwatch (1980)
Liotta, Ray (act, b. 1955): No Escape (1994); Unforgettable
Lipari, Joanna (act): Awake to Danger; Laserblast
Lipin, Arnold (act): Red Alert
Lipinski, Eugene (act): Never Talk to Strangers; Outland; Riders of the Storm; Shock Treatment! (1981); Superman II
Lipman, David (act): The Exterminator; Frankenhooker
Lipman, Maureen (act): File It Under Fear
Lipman, Moshe (act): The Dybbuk
Lipman, William P. (wri): Phantom Raiders; Sky Murder; Tarzan's New York Adventure
Lipovsky, Zach (act): Zenon: Girl of the 21st Century
Lippman, Irving (cin): Tarzan and the Great River; Tarzan and the Valley of Gold; 20 Million Miles to Earth
Lippman, Paul E. (act): Play Misty for Me
Lippold, Nancy (act): Supergirl (1984)
Lipscomb, Dennis (act): The Day After; Eyes of Fire; The First Power; Retribution (1988); Sister, Sister; Time Flyer;WarGames
Lipscomb, Gwen (act): The Witchmaker
Lipscomb, W.P. (wri, 1887-1958): I Was a Spy; The Mark of Cain; Les Miserables (1935); The Safe (1930 & 1932); The Sign of Four (1932); The Speckled Band (1931);Troubled Waters (1936)
Lipsius, Dhani (wri): Halloween 4: The Return of Michael Myers
Lipsky, Oldrich (dir, b. 1924): Gentleman, I Have Killed Einstein; The Man of the First Century
Lipson, Doreen (act): Starship Invasions
Lipstadt, Aaron (act): The Slumber Party Massacre
Lipstadt, Aaron (dir): Android
Lipstein, Harold (cin): The Adventures of Hajji Baba; Assignment to Kill; Damn Yankees; Let's Kill Uncle; Rampage
Lipton, Celia (act): The Frightened Bride; This Was a Woman
Lipton, Evelyn (act): End of the World (1977)
Lipton, Lawrence (act): The Hypnotic Eye
Lipton, Lynn (act): The Monitors
Lipton, Michael (act): Windows
Lipton, Michael (mus): Strangest Dreams: Invasion of the Space Preachers
Lipton, Peggy (act): Purple People Eater; The Spider and the Fly (1994); Twin Peaks: Fire Walk With Me
Lisberger, Steven (M.) (dir): Slipstream; Tron
Lisberger, Steven (M.) (wri): Tron
Lish, Fran (act): Shadow of a Doubt (1991)
Li Shiu, Paula (act): Koroshi
Lisi, Gaetano (act): Too Scared to Scream
Lisi, Joe (act): Traces of Red
Lisi, Virna (act, b. 1938, nee Virna Pieralisi): Bluebeard (1972); Romolo e Remo; The Serpent (1973); The Spy I Love; La Tulipe Noire
Liska, Stephen (act): The Bride In Black; Star Trek III: The Search for Spock

Liska, Zdenek (mus): The Angel Levine; Baron Prasil
Lisker, Holly (act): Jaws 3-D
Liskum, Phil (act): A Polish Vampire In Burbank
Lisle, Lucille (act): After Dark; Midnight at Madame Tussaud's; Special Edition
Lison, Elie (act): Rabid Grannies
Liss, Bennett (act): Evilspeak; Superstition; Zapped!
Liss, Ted (act): Child's Play (1988)
Lissek, Leon (act): Bloodmoon (1990); Countess Dracula; Journey to the Unknown; The Saint and the Brave Goose; Tales That Witness Madness
Lisson, Mark (wri): Return to Horror High
List, Joe (act): Let Me Call You Sweetheart
Lister, Bruce (act): see Lester, Bruce
Lister, Eve (act): The Demon Barber of Fleet Street
Lister, Francis (act, 1899-1951): Home to Danger; Living Dangerously; The Return of the Scarlet Pimpernel; Sensation (1937)
Lister, Loren (act): Midnight Offerings
Lister, Moira (act): The Double Man; Grand National Night; The Limping Man (1953); Pool of London; So Evil My Love; Stranger In the House (1967); Ten Little Indians (1989); Wanted for Murder
Lister, Renny (act): A Touch of the Other
Lister, Stephen (wri): Monolith
Lister Jr., Tom "Tiny" (act): Prison (1988)
Liston, Ian (act): The Empire Strikes Back
Liszewski, Janie (act): Princess Warrior
Litefoot (act): The Indian In the Cupboard; Kull the Conqueror
Litel, John (act, 1894-1972): The Beginning or the End?; Crime Doctor; Crime Doctor's Warning; Desperate Chance for Ellery Queen; Flight to Mars; Heaven Only Knows; Henry Aldrich Haunts a House; Invisible Agent; The Madonna's Secret; Mary Ryan, Detective; Murder In the Air (1940); Murder In the Blue Room; The Mystery of Marie Roget; Nancy Drew and the Hidden Staircase; Nancy Drew, Detective; Nancy Drew, Reporter; Nancy Drew, Troubleshooter;A Night In Paradise; Pitfall; The Return of Dr. X; Voyage to the Bottom of the Sea; Woman In Hiding
Lithgow, John (act, b. 1946): The Adventures of Buckaroo Banzai; All That Jazz; Amazing Stories II;Blow Out; The Day After; Harry and the Hendersons; The Manhattan Project; Obsession (1976); Raising Cain; Santa Claus (1985); Twilight Zone; 2010
Lithgow, Tom (act): Golden Ivory
Liti, Massimo (act): Warriors of the Wasteland
Litt, Andrea (act): American Cyborg: Steel Warrior
Litten, Peter (dir & wri): Slaughter High
Littinger, Rudolf (act): Das Kabinett des Dr. Caligari
Little Alan (act): Fairyland
Little Nell (act): see Campbell, Nell
Little Richard (act, b. 1935): The Goddess of Love; Purple People Eater
Little, Cleavon (act, 1939-1992): Double Exposure; In the Nick of Time; Once Bitten; Once Upon aBrothers Grimm; Vanishing Point (1971)
Little, Constance (act): The Vengeance of the Air
Little, Dwight (H.) (dir): Bloodstone; Halloween 4: The Returnof Michael Myers; The Phantom of the Opera (1989)
Little, George (act): Tennis Court
Little, Little Jack (act): The Nasty Rabbit
Little, Michelle (act): My Demon Lover; Radioactive Dreams
Little, Stanley (act): The Glass Tomb
Little, Steven E. (act): Prison (1988)
Little, Treasure (act): Waxwork II: Lost In Time
Littledale, Anabel (act): Are You Dying Young Man?; In the Devil's Garden
Littledale, Richard (act): The Medium (1934)
Littlefield, Jack (act): It Came from Beneath the Sea
Littlefield, L.D. (cin): The Man from Beyond
Littlefield, Lucien (act, 1895-1959): Bulldog Drummond's Revenge; Castle in the Desert; The Cat and the Canary (1927); The Gladiator; Henry Aldrich Haunts a House; In the Palace of the King; Li'l Abner (1940); One Body Too Many; One Frightened Night; Seven Keys to Baldpate (1929); Strangers of the Evening; Sudden Danger
Littlefield, Ralph (act): The Ape Man
Little John (act): High Spirits
Littlejohn, Gary (act): Bury Me an Angel; Howard the Duck
Littler, Tiny (act): Shamus
Littleton, Twyla (act): Frightmare (1983)
Littlewood, Harry (act): The Final Conflict; Personal and Confidential
Littman, Greg (act): The Fear (1994)
Litto, Maria (act): The Ape Creature; Der Raecher
Litton, Foster (act): Mountaintop Motel Massacre
Litvak, Anatole (dir, 1902-1974): Confessions of a Nazi Spy; La Damedans l'Auto Avec des Lunettes et un Fusil; The Night of the Generals; Out of the Fog (1941); The Snake Pit (1948); Sorry, Wrong Number (1948)
Litwak, Ezra (wri): The Butcher's Wife
Litwin, Krzysztof (act): Rekopis Znaleziony w Saragossie
Lium Alice (act): Wolf
Liu, Ernest (act): From Dusk Till Dawn
Liu, Robert F. (cin): The Loves of Dracula; World of Dracula
Liu, Terry (act): Infra-Man
Lively, Ernie (act): Past Midnight; Shocker
Lively, Gerry (act): Waxwork II: Lost In Time
Lively, Gerry (cin): Children of the Corn III: Urban Sacrifice; Girlfriend from Hell; Hellraiser III: Hell On Earth; Hellraiser 4: Bloodline; To Die For II: Son of Darkness; Warlock: The Armageddon; Waxwork II: Lost In Time
Lively, Jason (act): Brainstorm (1983); Night of the Creeps
Lively, Lori (act): Disaster In Time
Lively, Robyn (act): Not Quite Human; Not Quite Human II; Teen Witch
Lively, William (wri): Daughter of the Jungle; Dick Tracy vs. Crime, Inc.; The Ghost Creeps; Lost Planet Airmen; Nyoka and the Lost Secrets of Hippocrates; Phantom of the Jungle; Spy Smasher Returns; Tarzan's Hidden Jungle
Livermore, Rick (act): High Priestess of Sexual Witchcraft
Livesey, Barrie (act): Paris Plane
Livesey, Jack (act): The Howard Case; Murder at theWindmill; Murder Tomorrow; The Passing of the Third Floor Back (1935); Paul Temple's Triumph; The Wandering Jew (1933)
Livesey, John (act): Threads
Livesey, Roger (act, 1906-1976): The Drum; The Girl In the News; Hamlet (1969); The Intimate Stranger; It Happened In Broad Daylight; The League of Gentlemen; Lorna Doone (1934); A Matter of Life and Death; Spies of the Air; Vice Versa (1947); Where the Rainbow Ends
Livesey, Sam (act, 1873-1936): The Black Spider; The Chinese Puzzle; Dark Journey; The Hound ofthe Baskervilles (1931); The Lifeguardsman; The Shadow (1933); Tangled Evidence; The Wickham Mystery
Livi, Ivo (act): see Montand, Yves
Livings, Henry (wri): Work Is a Four Letter Word
Livingston, Barry (act): Invisible Mom; Masters of the Universe
Livingston, Bob (act, a.k.a. Bob Randall): The Black Raven
Livingston, Doc (act): The Loch Ness Horror
Livingston, Elizabeth (wri): Drop Dead Fred
Livingston, Harold (wri): Star Trek
Livingston, Jay (act): Sunset Boulevard
Livingston, Jo (act): RoboCop
Livingston, Margaret (act, b. 1900): The Last Warning (1929); Seven Keys to Baldpate (1929)
Livingston, Paul (act): The Navigator: An Odyssey Across Time
Livingston, Robert (act, 1904-1988): The Black Raven; The Bold Caballero; The Feathered Serpent (1948);Undercover Woman; Valley of the Zombies
Livingston, Shelby (act): 2000 Maniacs
Livingston, Stanley (act, b. 1950): Attack of the 60 Foot Centerfold; The Bonnie Parker Story; Private Parts; X-15
Livingstone, Russell (act): Dream a Little Dream
Livingstone, Sydney (act): Lifeforce
Livneh, Samuel (act): Dr. Heckyl & Mr. Hype
Liwanage, Vicente (act): The Horror from Beyond
Ljung, Oscar (act): Ansiktet
Llamas, Roberto (act): Amador
Llanes, Juan Antonio (act): Nightlife (1989, USA-Mex)
Llewellyn, Fewlass (act): The Phantom Light; The Secret of the Loch (1934); Special Edition
Llewellyn, Josephine (act): The Curse of the Werewolf
Llewellyn, Ray (act): The Secret Life of Ian Fleming
Llewellyn, Richard (wri, 1906-1983): Catch as Catch Can; Noose; Poison Pen
Llewellyn, Suzette (act): Welcome II the Terrordome
Llewellyn, Sylvia (act): An American Christmas Carol
Llewelyn, Desmond (act): The Curse of the Werewolf; Diamonds Are Forever; For Your Eyes Only; From Russia With Love; Goldeneye; The Golden Lady; Goldfinger; Licence to Kill (1989); The Living Daylights; The Man With the Golden Gun; Merlin (1993); Moonraker; Octopussy; The Pirates of Blood River; The Spy Who Loved Me; Thunderball; Tomorrow Never Dies; A View to a Kill; You Only Live Twice
Llimera, Veronica (act): Hatchet for a Honeymoon; Tombs of the Blind Dead
Llorens, Ruth Ann (act): Graduation Day
Llosa, Luis (dir): Anaconda; Crime Zone
Lloveras, Joan (act): Anguish
Lloyd, Art (cin): Babes In Toyland (1934); A Chump at Oxford
Lloyd, Christopher (act, b. 1938): The Addams Family; Addams Family Values; The Adventures of Buckaroo Banzai; Alice In Wonderland (1999); Amazing Stories; Anastasia; Angels In the Endzone; Angels In the Outfield (1994); Back to the Future; Back to the Future, Part II; Back to the Future, Part III; The Legend of the Lone Ranger; Legend of the White Horse; My Favorite Martian; The Pagemaster; Schizoid (1980); Star Trek III: The Search for Spock; Suburban Commando; Track 29; Who Framed Roger Rabbit
Lloyd, Danny (act): The Shining
Lloyd, Dian (act): Sin You Sinners
Lloyd, Doris (act, 1899-1968): Alice In Wonderland (1951); The Black Bird (1926); Bulldog Drummond Escapes; Devotion; Flesh and Fantasy; Frankenstein Meets the Wolf Man; The House of Fear (1945); House of Menace; The Invisible Man's Revenge; Kind Lady (1951); The Lodger (1944); Midnight Lace (1960); Peter Ibbetson;Phantom Lady; Scotland Yard Investigator; The Secret Life of Walter Mitty; The Shadow Between; A Study In Scarlet (1933); Tarzan the Ape Man (1932); Three Strangers; The Time Machine (1960); The Wolf Man (1941)
Lloyd, Emily Ann (act): Apollo 13
Lloyd, Eric (act, b. 1986, nee Eric Morelli): Batman and Robin; Chameleon; Heart and Souls; The Santa Clause
Lloyd, Esther (act): Surf Nazis Must Die
Lloyd, Frank (act): Those Dear Departed
Lloyd, Frank (dir, 1889-1960): Berkeley Square; The Lash; Maid of Salem; Les Miserables (1918); The Silent Watcher
Lloyd, Frederick (act): The Crime at Blossoms; The Hound of the Baskervilles (1931); Princess Clementina; Secret Lives
Lloyd, George (act): Boston Blackie Booked on Suspicion; Boston Blackie's Chinese Venture; Fog Island; Mr. Wong, Detective; Nightmare Alley; Smart Blonde; Torchy Blane In Panama; Torchy Plays With Dynamite; White Pongo
Lloyd (Sr.), Harold (act, 1894-1971): Haunted Spooks
Lloyd Jr., Harold (act, b. 1932): The Flaming Urge; Frankenstein's Daughter (1958); Mutiny In Outer Space; Platinum High School; Sex Kittens Go to College
Lloyd, Hugh (act): The Mouse On the Moon; Venom (1982)
Lloyd, Ian (dir & wri): The Face of Darkness
Lloyd, Jake (act, b. 1989): Star Wars: Episode I- The Phantom Menace; Virtual Obsession
Lloyd, Jeremy (act): Death Drums Along the River; The Liquidator; Murder On the Orient Express; The Wrong Box
Lloyd, Jeremy (wri): Vampira
Lloyd, John Bedford (act): The Abyss
Lloyd, Kathleen (act): The Car; It Lives Again; The Uninvited (1996)
Lloyd, Kevin (act): A Choice of Weapons; Link
Lloyd, Lola (act): The Adding Machine; Fiend Without a Face
Lloyd, M.J. (act): Jaws 3-D
Lloyd, Mary (act): see Merrall, Mary
Lloyd, May (act): The Punisher
Lloyd, Norman (act, b. 1910): Amityville: The Evil Escapes; Audrey Rose; The Beginning or the End?; The Black Book; The Dark Secret of Harvest Home; The Flame and the Arrow; Jaws of Satan; M (1950); The Nude Bomb; Saboteur; Spellbound (1945)
Lloyd, Richard (act): Hercules, Samson and Ulysses; The Invincible Brothers Maciste
Lloyd, Robert (act): The Committee; King Lear (1970); The Persecution and Assassination of Jean-Paul Marat as Performed by the Inmates of the Asylum of Charenton Under the Direction of the Marquis de Sade
Lloyd, Robin (act): Mary Shelley's 'Frankenstein'
Lloyd, Rollo (act): Bride of Frankenstein; Bulldog Drummond In Africa; Devil Doll (1936); Lady In the Morgue; Mad Love; Murder On a Honeymoon; The Westland Case
Lloyd, Rollo (wri): Revolt of the Zombies
Lloyd, Rosalind (act): Inseminoid
Lloyd, Sherman (act): Neighbors
Lloyd, Sue (act): Corruption; Hysteria!; Innocent Bystanders; The Ipcress File; No. 1 of the Secret Service; Penny Gold
Lloyd, Suzanne (act): Cat and Mouse (1974); The Return of Mr. Moto; Le Scandale; Who Was Maddox?
Lloyd, Tricia (act): Edward Scissorhands
Lloyd, Walter (act): Cannibal Ferox
Lloyd-Pack, Charles (act, b. 1901): Bobbikins; Cover Girl Killer; Flat Two; Frankenstein and the Monster from Hell; High Treason (1951); Horror of Dracula; I'm a Stranger; Madame Sin; The ManWho Haunted Himself; The Mirror Crack'd; Night of the Demon (1957); Noose for a Lady; Quatermass II; The Reptile; The Revenge of Frankenstein; The Shuttered Room; Siege of the Saxons; Stranger In Town (1957); The Terror of the Tongs; The Third Secret; The Three Worlds of Gulliver
Lloyd-Pack, Roger (act): Fright (1971); Hamlet (1969); The Magus; The McGuffin; 1984 (1984); The Young Poisoner's Handbook
Lo, Chi Muoi (act): The Relic
Loader, Jayne (dir): The Atomic Cafe
Lobanov, L. (act): The Heavens Call
Lobato, Ebar (dir): Scream of the Butterfly
Lobato, Nelida (act): Scream of the Butterfly
Lobban, Deborah (act): Hitler's Daughter
Lo Bianco, Tony (act): Demon (1976); The Honeymoon Killers; Let Me Call You Sweetheart
Lobinger, Lotte (act): Das Kalte Herz
Lobos, Los (mus): I Was a Teenage Zombie
Loc, Tone (act): Ferngully: The Last Rain Forest
Locane, Amy (act): Bram Stoker's 'The Mummy'; Ebenezer
Locatell, Carol (act): The Bad Seed (1985); Friday the 13th Part V: A New Beginning
Lochary, David (act): Multiple Maniacs
Locher, Felix (act): Curse of the Faceless Man; Frankenstein's Daughter (1958)
Lochner, Charles (act): The Clutching Hand
Lochner, Hayley (act): Mind Games
Lock, Stuart (act): The Amazing Mr. Blunden
Locke, Bruce (act): RoboCop 3
Locke, Donna (act): Neon Maniacs
Locke, Edward (wri): The Climax
Locke, Harry (act): The Creeping Flesh; The Devil-Ship Pirates; Kill or Cure; The Man In the Back Seat; The Material Witness; Never Back Losers, Nowhere to Go; Panic at Madam Tussaud's; The Sky Bike; Subterfuge; Tales from the Crypt (1971); The Teckman Mystery; Town On Trial; Tread Softly; Treasure island (1950);Yield to the Night
Locke, Joe (act): On the Threshold of Space
Locke, Katherine (act): The Snake Pit (1948); The Sound of Fury
Locke, Martin (wri): Secrets of Sex
Locke, Nancy (act): Eve of Destruction
Locke, Philip (act): Face of a Stranger; The Fiction-Makers; Hitler: The Last Ten Days; Incident at Midnight; Jekyll and Hyde; On the Run (1963); Thunderball
Locke, Rosanna (act): Curse of the Black Widow
Locke, Sharyl (act): I Saw What You Did (1965)
Locke, Sondra (act, b. 1947): Ratboy; A Reflection of Fear; Willard
Locke, Sondra (dir, b. 1947): Ratboy
Locke, Tembi (act): Star Command
Locke, Terrence (act): The Incredible Hulk
Locken, Lee Anne (act): My Best Friend Is a Vampire
Locker, Phil (act): Poltergeist III
Lockett-Lawson, Renee (act): Blink
Lockhart, Anne (act): Dark Tower (1987); The Magician (1973); Troll
Lockhart, Araby (act): The Quilt of Hathor
Lockhart, Calvin (act): The Beast Must Die; Myra Breckinridge; Nobody Runs Forever; Predator 2; Twin Peaks: Fire Walk With Me
Lockhart, Craig (act): The Body Snatchers
Lockhart, Gene (act, 1891-1957): All That Money Can Buy; Androcles and the Lion; Bonzo Goes to College; Carousel; A Christmas Carol (1938); Crime and Punishment (1935, USA); Francis Covers the Big Town; The Garden Murder Case; Leave Her to Heaven;

Miracle On 34th Street (1947); Seeds of Destruction; Star of Midnight; World for Ransom
Lockhart, H. Bruce (wri): *British Agent*
Lockhart, June (act, b. 1925): *Bury Me Dead; A Christmas Carol (1938); C.H.U.D. II; The Colony (1995); Curse of the Black Widow; Dead Women In Lingerie; The Eliminator; The Night They Saved Christmas; Out There; The Presence; She-Wolf of London; Strange Invaders; T-Men; Troll*
Lockhart, Kathleen (act, 1893-1978): *Bewitched (1944); A Christmas Carol (1938); Lady In the Lake*
Lockhart, Laurel (act): *Silent Night, Deadly Night 4: Initiation*
Locklear, Heather (act, b. 1961): *City Killer; Firestarter; Illusions; The Return of Swamp Thing*
Locklin, Loryn (act): *Fortress; Night Visions*
Lockmiller, Richard (act): *The Aliens Are Coming; Rattlers*
Lockney, John P./J.P. (act): *The Return of Boston Blackie; Seven Keys to Baldpate (1925)*
Lockridge, Mabel (act): *Ghost (1990)*
Locks, Shamus (act): *It's Alive (1974)*
Lockton, Joan (act): *The Disappearance of the Judge; The Girl Who Came Back*
Lockwood, Alexander (act): *Duel; Family Plot; The Invisible Boy; Just Off Broadway; The Monkey's Uncle; Monster On the Campus; The Story of Mankind; The Tattered Dress*
Lockwood, Gary (act, b. 1940, nee J. Gary Yusolfsky): *Earth II; The Ghost of Flight 401; The Magic Sword (1962); The Return of the Six Million Dollar Man and the Bionic Woman; Survival Zone; 2001: A Space Odyssey*
Lockwood, J.H. (act): *The Fatal Hour (1937)*
Lockwood, Jale (wri): *The Female Bunch*
Lockwood, Julia (act, b. 1941): *The Solitary Child*
Lockwood, Lyn (wri): *A Piece of Cake*
Lockwood, Margaret (act, 1916-1990, nee Margaret Day): *Alibi (1942); Bad Sister; Bedelia; The Case of Gabriel Perry; Cast a Dark Shadow; Dr. Syn; Gestapo; The Girl In the News; Highly Dangerous; Jury's Evidence; The Lady Vanishes (1938); Lorna Doone (1934); The Man In Grey; A Place of One's Own; The Slipper and the Rose; Trent's Last Case (1952)*
Lockwood, Preston (act): *Absolution; The Black Windmill; High Spirits; Scandalous; Time Bandits*
Lockyear, Tom (act): *Teenagers from Outer Space*
Lockyer, Malcolm (mus): *Deadlier Than the Male; Dr. Who and the Daleks; Five Golden Dragons; Island of Terror; Ten Little Indians (1965); The Vengeance of Fu Manchu*
Locricchio, Matthew (act): *Robot In the Family*
Locust, Jimmy (act): *Killer Klowns from Outer Space*
Loddi, Loris (act): *Ladyhawke*
Loder, Anne Marie (act): *Darkman II: The Return of Durant*
Loder, Anthony (act): *Doomsday Machine*
Loder, John (act, 1898-1988, nee John Lowe): *Anything to Declare?; Black Waters; The Brighton Strangler; Dead On Time; Dr. Syn; The Firechasers; A Game of Death; Gideon's Day; The Hairy Ape; King Solomon's Mines (1937); Lorna Doone (1934); The Man Who Changed His Mind; Meet Maxwell Archer; Murder Will Out (1939); The Mysterious Doctor; Paris Plane; Sabotage; Scotland Yard (1941); The Secret Man; The Silent Passenger; Under Secret Orders; The Unholy Night; Warn London; The Wife of Monte Cristo; Woman Who Came Back*
Loder, Pegi (act): *Willy McBean and His Magic Machine*
Lodestone (mus): *The Wicker Man*
Lodge, Andrew (act): *Assassin (1973); The Beast Must Die; The Land That Time Forgot*
Lodge, David (act, b. 1922): *The Amazing Mr. Blunden; Blood Bath at the House of Death; Captain Clegg; Corruption; The Counterfeit Plan; The Crossroad Gallows; Doctors Wear Scarlet; Edge of Sanity; The Fiend (1972); The Hell-Fire Club; The Intimate Stranger; Killer With Two Faces; Kill or Cure; The League of Gentlemen; Mr. Horatio Knibbles; Never Let Go; The Pirates of Blood River; Scream and Scream Again; The Sky Bike; Strangers' [illegible] Time to Remember; The Ugly Duckling*
Lodge, Jean (act): *Accidental Death; The Black Knight; Curse of Simba; Dangerous Voyage; Death of an Angel; Dick Barton Strikes Back; Dr. Morelle-The Case of the Missing Heiress; The Eyes of Annie Jones; The Hell-Fire Club; Invasion (1965); The Masque of the Red Death (1964); The Silent Witness (1954)*
Lodge, Jimmy (act): *When Dinosaurs Ruled the Earth*
Lodge, John (GB act): *Bulldog Drummond at Bay (1937); Koenigsmark; Premiere; Queer Cargo; Sensation (1937)*
Lodge, John (1930s USA act): *Murders In the Zoo*
Lodge, John (1960s USA act): *The Witchmaker*
Lodge, Roger (act): *Not of This Earth (1988)*
Lodge, Stephen (wri): *Kingdom of the Spiders*
Lodge, Terence (act): *Hands of a Murderer*
Lodi, Rodolfo (act): *Inferno (1979)*
Lodoli, Luigi (act): *Inferno (1979)*
Lodolini, Mario (act): *The Conquest of Mycenae*
Lo Duca, Joseph/Joe (mus): *Army of Darkness; The Evil Dead; Evil Dead 2: Dead by Dawn; Mantis; Moontrap; Young Hercules*
Loeb III, Joseph (wri): *Teen Wolf; Teen Wolf Too*
Loeb, Leo (wri): *Abbott and Costello Meet Dr. Jekyll and Mr. Hyde; Abbott and Costello Meet the Mummy*
Loeb, Philip (act): *A Double Life (1947)*
Loeher, Charles (act): see Hall, Jon
Loehr, Dolly (act): see Lynn, Diana
Loeschke, Paul E. (cin): *The Galaxy Invader*
Loesser, Frank (mus): *The Gracie Allen Murder Case; Hans Christian Andersen; Hoppity Goes to Town*
Loew, Kevin (act): *Mother's Day*
Loewe, Frederick (mus, 1901-1988): *Brigadoon; The Little Prince*
Loewe, Frederick (wri, 1901-1988): *Camelot*
Loewen, Dale (act): *Empire of Ash III*
Loewenstein, Laszlo (act): see Lorre, Peter
Loffler, Gianin (act): *Stargate*
Loffrey, Johnny (act): *La Figlia di Frankenstein*
Lofgren, Marianne (act): *The Devil's Wanton*
Loft, Arthur (act): *Blue, White and Perfect; Charlie Chan In the Secret Service; The Lone Wolf Returns (1935); The Shanghai Cobra; Who Killed Gail Preston?*
Lofthouse, Christopher (act): *No Blade of Grass*
Loftin, Cary (act): *Duel*
Loftin, Lennie (act): *Seven*
Loftin, Zoe (act): *The Witches and the Grinnygog*
Lofting, Harry (act): *Her Greatest Performance*
Lofting, Hugh (wri, 1886-1947): *Dr. Dolittle (1967 & 1998)*
Lofting, Maud (act): *Forty Winks*
Lofting, Morgan (act): *Amazons (1984)*
Lofton, Christopher (wri): *Let Me Call You Sweetheart*
Loftus, Brian (cin): *The Company of Wolves; Jake Speed*
Loftus, Cecilia (act, 1876-1943): *The Black Cat (1941); The Blue Bird (1940)*
Loftus, Jimmy (act): *Haunted by Her Past*
Lofven, Chris (dir & wri): *20th Century Oz*
Logan, Bellina (act): *Jacob's Ladder*
Logan, Bob (dir & wri): *Repossessed*
Logan, Brad (act): *Trancers; Vamp*
Logan, Bruce (cin): *Dracula's Dog*
Logan, Dennis (act): *Blood Diner*
Logan, Frank (act): *Around the World Under the Sea; Barracuda; Black Sunday (1977)*
Logan, Helen (wri, b. 1906): *Charlie Chan at Monte Carlo; Charlie Chan at the Circus; Charlie Chan at the Olympics; Charlie Chan at the Race Track; Charlie Chan In City In Darkness; Charlie Chan In Egypt; Charlie Chan In Shanghai; Charlie Chan's Secret*
Logan, Jacqueline (act, 1901-1983): *A Blind Bargain; The Leopard Lady*
Logan, James (act): *The Man With a Cloak*
Logan, James (act): *The Bermuda Triangle*
Logan, Janice (act): *Dr. Cyclops*
Logan, Jennifer (act): *Vampire On Bikini Beach*
Logan, Jesse (act): *Looker*
Logan, John (act): *The Boy Who Cried Werewolf*
Logan, John (wri): *Tornado!*
Logan, Joshua (dir, 1908-1988): *Camelot*
Logan, Kristopher (act): *Crash and Burn; Howard the Duck; Star Trek: Generations*
Logan, Laurie V. (act): *Poltergeist III*
Logan, Lillian (act): *The Cage*
Logan, Mark (act): *The Grim Reaper*
Logan, Michael (act): *The Snake Woman*
Logan, Pat (act): *Picking Up the Pieces*
Logan, Phyllis (act): *Freddie as F.R.O.7; The McGuffin; 1984 (1984)*
Logan, Ricky Dean (act): *Back to the Future, Part II; The Flash; Freddy's Dead: The Final Nightmare*
Logan, Robert (act): *Snowbeast*
Logan, Stanley (act): *The Challenge; Counter-Espionage*
Logan, Stanley (dir): *The Falcon's Brother*
Logan, Tom (dir): *The Night Brings Charlie*
Loggia, Kristina (act): *Bad Dreams; Chopper Chicks In Zombietown*
Loggia, Robert (act, b. 1930): *The Believers; Big; Independence Day; Innocent Blood; The Jagged Edge; Lifepod; The Lost Missile; Oliver & Company; Pandora's Clock; Psycho II; Twinkle, Twinkle, Killer Kane*
Logineva, Tatyana (cin): *The Savage Hunt of King Stakh*
Logo, Tau (act): *The Golden Child*
Logothetis, Dimitri (act): *Dracula's Dog*
Logothetis, Dimitri (dir): *Slaughterhouse Rock*
Logue, Charles (wri): *The Menace (1932)*
Logue, Christopher (act): *The Devils; Jabberwocky*
Logue, Donal (act): *The Crew; Diabolique (1996); The Grave*
Lohman, Augie (cin): *Lost Continent (1951)*
Lohman, Lenore (act): *Daylight*
Lohmann, Paul (cin): *Charlie Chan and the Curse of the Dragon Queen; Curse of the Black Widow; Dark Mansions; Endangered Species; Looker; Meteor; Time After Time; Trilogy of Terror*
Lohmeyer, Peter (act): *Kondom des Grauens*
Lohr, Marie (act, b. 1890): *Counterblast; The Ghosts of Berkeley Square; Went the Day Well?*
Loi, Marina (act): *Demons 2*
Loiselle, Rachel (act): *Mosquito*
Lok, Christine (act): *The Million Eyes of Sumuru*
Lolich, Mickey (act): *The Incredible Melting Man*
Lollobrigida, Gina (act, b. 1927): *Beat the Devil; La Beaute du Diable; The Hunchback of Notre Dame (1957); Plucked; Woman of Straw*
Lollobrigida, Guido (act): *Operation Kid Brother*
Lom, Herbert (act, b. 1917): *—And Now the Screaming Starts!; Appointment With Crime; Assignment to Kill; Asylum (1972); Beautiful Stranger; The Black Rose; Cage of Gold; Chase a Crooked Shadow; Count Dracula; Dark Places; The Dark Tower (1943); The Dead Zone; The Devil's Daughter (1995);Doppelganger (1969); Dorian Gray; Dual Alibi; The Face of Eve; The Frightened City; Gambit; Hotel Reserve; I Accuse (1958); I Aim at the Stars; Intent to Kill; Island of Despair; I Spy, You Spy; The Karate Killers; King Solomon's Mines (1985); The Lady Killers (1956); The Lady Vanishes (1979); Mark of the Devil (1972); Masque of the Red Death (1989, 21st Century); Mr. Denning Drives North; Murders In the Rue Morgue (1971); Mysterious Island (1961); The Net; No Trees In the Street; Our Man In Marrakesh; Paris Express; Passport to Shame; The Phantom of the Opera (1962); Portrait from Life; Return from the Ashes; The Ringer (1952); La Setta; Star of India; State Secret; Ten Little Indians (1974 & 1989); Treasure of Silver Lake; Whispering Smith Hits London*
Lomas, Herbert (act, 1887-1961): *Black Mask; The Ghost Goes West; The Ghost Train (1941); Inquest (1939); Jamaica Inn (1939); Knight Without Armour; Lorna Doone (1934); The Net; The Phantom Light; The Sign of Four (1932); They Met In the Dark*
Lomas, Pauline (act): *The Entity*
Lomas, Raoul (cin): *Children of the Corn; The Prowler (1981)*
Lomax, David (act): *Fargo*
Lomazow, Michael (act): *Psycho II*
Lombard, Carole (act, 1908-1942, nee Jane Alice Peters): *Supernatural (1933); White Woman*
Lombard, Karina (act): *Kull the Conqueror; Wide Sargasso Sea*
Lombard, Michael (act): *Who?*
Lombard, Paty (act): *Poltergeist III*
Lombard, Peter (wri): *The Invincible Barbarian*
Lombard, Ron (act): *The China Syndrome*
Lombardi, Joe (cin): *The Entity; How Awful About Allan; Invasion of the Bee Girls*
Lombardi, John R. (act): *Poison (1990)*
Lombardi, Leigh (act): *Moontrap*
Lombardi, Louis (act): *Ed Wood*
Lombardi, Paul (cin): *Super Mario Bros.*
Lombardo, Bob (act): *Planet of the Apes*
Lombardo, Miroslawa (act): *Rekopis Znaleziony w Saragossie*
Lombarte, Angel (act): *The Blood Spattered Bride*
Lomez, Celine (act, b. 1953): *The Ivory Ape; The Kiss (1988); Plague*
[illegible]
Lommel, Ulli (act): *Boogeyman II*
Lommel, Ulli (cin): *The Devonsville Terror*
Lommel, Ulli (dir & wri): *The Boogeyman; Boogeyman II; Brainwaves; The Devonsville Terror; Shadow of Death (1983)*
Lomnicki, Tadeusz (act): *Bariera*
Lomond, Britt (act): *The Sign of Zorro (1960)*
Loncar, Beba (act): *The Boy Cried Murder; Some Girls Do*
Loncraine, Richard (dir): *Brimstone & Treacle; Full Circle Rentadick; Richard III (1995)*
Loncraine, Richard (wri): *Richard III (1995)*
London, Arthur (wri): *L'Aveu*
London, Jack (wri, 1876-1916): *The Assassination Bureau*
London, James (cin): *The Toxic Avenger; The Toxic Avenger, Part II; The Toxic Avenger, Part III: The Last Temptation of Toxie*
London, Jason (act): *Alien Cargo*
London, Jeremy (act, b. 1971): *The Babysitter (1995)*
London, Jerry (dir): *Dark Mansions; The Haunting of Sarah Hardy; Killdozer*
London, Julie (act, b. 1926, nee Julie Peck): *The Helicopter Spies; Nabonga; The Red House*
London, Linda (act): *The Resurrection of Zachary Wheeler*
London, Lise (wri): *L'Aveu*
London, Maggie (act): *Maroc 7*
London, Mark (act): *Privilege*
London, Mark (mus): *Blood Bath at the House of Death*
London, Michael J. (act): *Snowbeast*
London, Robby (wri): *Pinocchio and the Emperor of the Night*
London, Steve (act): *I Married a Monster from Outer Space*
London, Tom (act): *The Clutching Hand; The Lone Wolf Takes a Chance; Spy Smasher Returns*
London, Vicki (act): *Village of the Giants*
Lone, John (act, b. 1952): *Iceman; King Kong (1976); The Shadow (1994)*
Lonehill, Ed (act): *The Last Hunt*
Long, Amelia Reynolds (wri): *Fiend Without a Face*
Long, Andrew (act): *Empire of Ash III*
Long, Ann (act): *The Nest of the Cuckoo Birds*
Long, Audrey (act, b. 1924): *Born to Kill; David Harding, Counterspy; Desperate; A Game of Death; In Self Defense; Insurance Investigator; Perilous Waters; Post Office Investigator*
Long, Danny (act): *Murder by Decree*
Long, Doris (act): *The Lure*
Long, Frederick (act): *The Lost Patrol (1929)*
Long, Jodi (act): *The Exorcist III*
Long, Johnny (act): *Beast of Blood; Twilight People*
Long, Kathy (act): *Knights*
Long, Keny (act): *King Lear (1976)*
Long, Kevin (act): *Raiders of the Living Dead*
Long, Lionel (act): *Inn of the Damned*
Long, Lisa (act): *The Last man On Planet Earth*
Long, Lotus (act): *Mr. Wong In Chinatown; The Mysterious Mr. Wong; The Mystery of Mr. Wong; Phantom of Chinatown; Think Fast, Mr. Moto*
Long, Louise (wri): *The Greene Murder Case*
Long, Matthew (act): *The Medusa Touch*
Long, Melissa (act): *Reactor; War of the Robots*
Long, Nathan (wri): *Guyver 2: Dark Hero*
Long, Nia (act): *Buried Alive (1989)*
Long, Reginald (act): *The Avenging Hand (1936)*
Long, Reginald (wri): *The Avenging Hand (1936); Death of an Angel; The Limping Man (1953); Return of a Stranger; The Spider (1939)*
Long, Richard (act, 1927-1974): *Criss Cross; Cult of the Cobra; The Dark Mirror (1946); Death Cruise; House On Haunted Hill (1958)*
Long, Ricky (act): *Ghostriders*
Long, Robert (Euro act): *Anguish*
Long, Robert (USA act): *Captain Kidd and the Slave Girl; Death Goes to School; The Neanderthal Man; Return to Treasure Island*
Long, Ronald (act): *Wonder Woman*
Long, Sarah (act): *The Village of the Damned (1960)*
Long, Shelley (act, b. 1949): *Caveman (1981); Freaky Friday (1995); Hello Again; Susie Q*
Long, Stanley A. (cin): *The Sorcerers*
Long, Stephen (act): *On Her Bed of Roses*
Long, Sue (act): *Mary Shelley's 'Frankenstein'*
Long, Tony (act): *Eraser*
Long, Walter (act, 1882-1952): *The Maltese Falcon (1931); Moby Dick (1930); Queen of the Sea; The Road to Yesterday; The Shock* [illegible]
Long Jr., William (act): *Sandcastles*
Longden, John (act, 1900-1971): *Alias John Preston; Blackmail (1929); Black Widow*

(1951); The Dark Light; Dial 999 (1938); Elstree Calling; The Elusive Pimpernel (1950); Frozen Alive; The Gaunt Stranger; The Ghosts of Berkeley Square; Jamaica Inn (1939); Jenifer Hale; Lancelot and Guinevere; The Man With the Twisted Lip; Meet Mr. Callaghan; Murder On the Second Floor; Pool of London; Q Planes; Quatermass II; The Ringer (1931); Three Sundays to Live; Tower of Terror; The Wickham Mystery; A Woman's Temptation; Young and Innocent

Longden, John (dir & wri): Come Into My Parlour

Longden, Robert (act): Agatha; The Secret Life of Ian Fleming

Longden, Terence (cin): Helen of Troy (1955)

Longdon, Terence (act): Clash by Night; Helen of Troy (1955); Murder On the Campus; Never Look Back; Out of the Shadow; The Return of Mr. Moto

Longfellow, Henry Wadsworth (wri, 1807-1882): Hiawatha (1903 & 1952); King Robert of Sicily

Longfellow, Malvina (act): For All Eternity; The Grip of Iron; The Story of the Rosary

Longhi, Carlo (act): Il Montagna di Dio Cannibale

Longhurst, Graham (cin): Frankenstein (1993)

Longhurst, Henry (B.) (act): Dangerous Ground; Old Mother Riley's Ghosts; The Vandergilt Diamond Mystery

Longhurst, Jeremy (act): The Gorgon; Koroshi; Spaceflight IC-1; Spell of Evil; The Trollenberg Terror

Longo, Germano (act): Revenge of the Gladiators; Seven Slaves Against the World

Longo, Malisa/Melisa (act): The Cauldron of Death; War of the Planets

Longo, Robert (dir): Johnny Mnemonic

Longo, Tony (act): Mr. Destiny; Prehysteria; Suburban Commando

Longstreet, Harry (wri & dir): A Vow to Kill; World of Dracula

Longstreet, Renee (wri): A Vow to Kill; World of Dracula

Longstreth, Emily (act): Star Crystal; Wired to Kill

Longworth, Adam (act): Empire of Ash III

Longworth, David (act): Friday the 13th, Part VIII-Jason Takes Manhattan; The Reflecting Skin; Runaway

Longyear, Barry (wri): Enemy Mine

Longyear, Nancy (act): Ed Wood

Lonnberg, Anne (act): Moonraker

Lonnen, Ray (act): Guardian of the Abyss

Lonsdale, Frederick (wri): The Private Life of Don Juan

Lonsdale, Gordon C. (cin): Houdini (1998)

Lonsdale, Harry (act): Monte Cristo

Lonsdale, Henry (act): The Beggar Girl's Wedding; The Female Swindler; The Girl Who Took the Wrong Turning; The Girl Who Wrecked His Home; The Phantom Picture; Queen of the Wicked; When Woman Hates

Lonsdale, Michel/Michael (act, b. 1931): Caravan to Vaccares; The Evil Trap; La Mariee etait en Noir; Moonraker; The Name of the Rose

Lontoc, Leon (act): The Adventures of Nick Carter; City Beneath the Sea (1952); The Naked Jungle; One Spy Too Many

Lonzo, Michael (cin): Die Sister, Die!

Loo, Bessie (act): Mr. Wong In Chinatown

Loo, Jerry (act): Charlie Chan and the Curse of the Dragon Queen

Loo, Richard (act, 1903-1983): After the Thin Man; Betrayal from the East; The Clay Pigeon; Confessions of an Opium Eater; Dirigible; Golden Eye; The Man With the Golden Gun; Mr. Wong In Chinatown; West of Shanghai

Loof, Claus (cin): The Girl In a Swing

Lookinland, Mike (act, b. 1960): Dead Men Tell No Tales (1971)

Lookinland, Todd (act): The Blue Bird (1976)

Loomis, Christopher (act): The Nesting

Loomis, Deborah (act): Hercules In New York

Loomis, Frank (act): Making Contact

Loomis, Nancy (act): The Fog; Halloween

Loomis, Rod (act): The Beastmaster; Jack's Back

Looney, Peter (act): Outbreak

Loong, Blaise (act): Cyborg (1989)

Loos, Anita (wri, 1893-1981): I Married an Angel

Loos, Ann (act): One Mysterious Night

Loos, Anne (act): The God King

Loos, Theodor (act): Homunculus; M (1931); Metropolis (1926); Die Nibelungen

Loose, William/Bill (mus): Grotesque; The Horrible House On the Hill; The Lucifer Complex; The Man Who Saw Tomorrow; Tarzan and the Great River; Tarzan and the Jungle Boy

Lootens, Jinx (act): Razorback

Lopate, Fran (act): Deadtime Stories

Loper, Don (act): Lady In the Dark

Lopert, Tanya (act): Satyricon

Lopez (act): I Don't Want to Be Born

Lopez, Atilio (act): A Midsummer Night's Dream (1985)

Lopez, Candida (act): El Otro Fu Manchu

Lopez, Carlos (act): Neutron Battles the Karate Assassins

Lopez, Chel (act): The Adventures of Robinson Crusoe (1952)

Lopez, Elena (act): Grim Prairie Tales

Lopez, Elisio (act): Creature from the Haunted Sea

Lopez, Fritz (act): Princess Warrior

Lopez, Gerry (act): Conan the Barbarian

Lopez, Gretchen (act): Tuck Everlasting

Lopez, J. Victor (act): Fantasies

Lopez, Jean (act): Ator: The Fighting Eagle

Lopez, Jennifer (act): Anaconda; Antz; The Hollow Man; Jack

Lopez, Joe (act): The Norsemen

Lopez, Julio (act): Creature from the Black Lagoon

Lopez, Kamala (act): Dollman

Lopez, Manny (act): The Fugitive (1993)

Lopez, Manuel (act): The Cyclops

Lopez, Mario (act): Fever Lake

Lopez, Miguel (act): The Island of Dr. Moreau (1996); Mad Max Beyond Thunderdome

Lopez, Perry (act, b. 1931): The Lone Ranger; Omar Khayyam

Lopez, Ricardo T. (act): Wavelength

Lopez, Sylvia (act): Ercole e la Regina di Lidia

Lopez, Tony (act): Hellhole

Lopez-Cal, Sergio (act): The Fan

Lopinto, Dorian (act): He Knows You're Alone

Loraine, Robert (act): Birds of Prey

Lorca, Isabel Garcia (act): Anguish

Lorch, Theodore (act): Dick Tracy (1937)

Lord, Annabel (act): Yellow Dog

Lord, Basil (act): Revenge (1971, GB)

Lord, Byron (act): In the Year 2889; Mars Needs Women

Lord, Derek (act): The Black Windmill

Lord, H.J. (act): What's Bred...Comes Out In the Flesh

Lord, Jack (act, 1928-1998, nee John Joseph Ryan): Cry Murder; Dr. No; The Name of the Game Is Kill

Lord, Jean-Claude (dir): Landslide (1992); Mindfield; The Vindicator; Visiting Hours

Lord, Justine (act): Act of Murder (1964); Deadlier Than the Male; The Fiction-Makers; Incident at Midnight; Maniac (1963); Night After Night After Night; Payment In Kind

Lord, Lonnie (act): The Thrill Killers

Lord, Marjorie (act, b. 1921): The Argyle Secrets; Flesh and Fantasy; Forty Naughty Girls; The Lost Volcano; Sherlock Holmes In Washington; Thunder Over Sangoland

Lord, Mindret (wri): Alias Nick Beal

Lord, Robert (wri, 1902-1976): The Mind Reader

Lord, Rosemary (act): Dr. Jekyll and Sister Hyde

Lord, Rupert (act): Yellow Dog

Lord, Stephen (act): Judge Dredd

Lord, Stephen (wri): The Bermuda Triangle; Beyond and Back; Demon and the Mummy; The Fall of the House of Usher (1982); Tarzan and the Jungle Boy

Lorde, Athena (act, 1915-1973): Doctor Death: Seeker of Souls

Lords, Traci (act, b. 1968): Blade; Dead Man's Island; Laser Moon; Not of This Earth (1988); Raw Nerve; Serial Mom; Shock 'em Dead; The Tommyknockers; Virtuosity

Lorea, Tony (act): Midnight Lace (1981); The Phantom Empire; Wonder Women

Loree, Brad (act): Timecop

Loren, Frank (act): Missing Millions

Loren, Donna (act): Pajama Party; Sergeant Deadhead the Astronut!

Loren, Eric (act): Nightbreed; The Saint

Loren, James (act): Zapped!

Loren, Sophia (act, b. 1934, nee Sophia Villani Scicolone): C'era una Volta; Firepower; Ghosts-Italian Style; The Key; Legend of the Lost; Operation Crossbow; Il Sogno di Zorro

Loren, Tray (act): Rocktober Blood

Lorentowicz, Malgorzata (act): Bariera

Lorenz, Arthur (act): Class of Nuke 'em High

Lorenz, Bob (act): Mars Needs Women

Lorenz, Howard (act): The Black Pearl

Lorenz, Jerry (act): The Texas Chainsaw Massacre

Lorenz, Lee (act): The Monster In the Basement

Lorenz, Robert (act): Ghost Diver

Lorenzelli, Ulisse (act): Seven Dwarfs to the Rescue

Lorenzen, Kenneth (act): The Savage Bees

Lorenzo, Luis (act): Endless Descent; Hundra; Zorro: The Legend Begins

Lorenzon, Livio (act): Fury of the Pagans; Gladiators Seven; The Invincible Gladiator

Loreque, Kevin (act): Virtuosity

Loret, Susanne (act): Atom Age Vampire; The Minotaur

Lorey, Dean (act): Jason Goes to Hell: The Final Friday

Lorey, Dean (wri): Jason Goes to Hell: The Final Friday; My Boyfriend's Back

Loridans, Virginia (act): Mountaintop Motel Massacre

Lorietta, Jose E. (dir, a.k.a. Joe Lacy): The Emerald of Artatama; A Thousand and One Nights (1968); A Witch Without a Broom

Lorietta, Jose E. (wri, a.k.a. Joe Lacy): The Emerald of Artatama; A Thousand and One Nights (1968)

Lorimer, Al (cin): I, Desire

Lorimer, Enid (act): Witness In the Dark

Lorimer, Enid (wri): Her Greatest Performance; The House Opposite (1917)

Lorimer, Glennis (act): Alf's Button Afloat

Lorimer, Nora (wri): The Shadow of Egypt

Lorin, Gerard (act): L'Annee Derniere a Marienbad

Loring, John (wri): Gorgo

Loring, Lisa (act): Blood Frenzy; Halloween With the Addams Family

Loring, Lyn (act): Black Noon; Doppelganger (1969); The Horror at 37,000 Feet

Loring, Robert B. (act): The Octagon

Loring, Teala (act): Bluebeard (1944); Dark Alibi

Loring, Val (act): Dr. Black Mr. Hyde

Lorinz, James (act): Frankenhooker; Street Trash

Loritz, Katia (act): El Principe Encadenado

Lormer, John/Jon (act): Dimension 5; Forgotten City of the Planet of the Apes

Lorne, Marion (act, 1886-1968): Strangers On a Train

Lornie, Hedda (act): The Fourth Man

LoRosa, Kevin (act): The Silencers (1995)

Lorraine, Amy (act): Alone In London

Lorraine, Carrie (act): Dolls

Lorraine, Guido (act): City After Midnight; Port Afrique; State Secret; They Can't Hang Me

Lorraine, Harry (act): The Counterfeiters; Detective Daring and the Thames Coiners; The Great Cheque Fraud; The Great Spy Raid; Lieutenant Daring, Aerial Scout; Lieutenant Daring and the Mystery of Room 41;Lieutenant Rose and the Sealed Orders; Lieutenant Rose and the Train Wreckers; The Master Crook;London's Underworld; Queenie of the Circus; Robin Hood Outlawed; Signals In the Night; The Stolen Heirlooms; Sweeney Todd; The Thornton Jewel Mystery; Through the Clouds

Lorraine, Harry (dir): Further Exploits of Sexton Blake—The Mystery of the S.S. Olympic

Lorraine, Louise (act): The Altar Stairs

Lorraine, Nita (act): The Viking Queen

Lorraine, Ola (act): My Cousin Rachel

Lorraine, Philip (wri): Eye of the Devil

Lorraine, Tui (act): The Thin Man

Lorrayne, Vyvyan (act): Top Secret! (1984)

Lorre, Lolita (act): Scream for Help

Lorre, Peter (act, 1904-1964, nee Laszlo Loewenstein): Around the World In 80 Days; Arsenic and Old Lace; Background to Danger; The Beast With Five Fingers; Beat the Devil; Black Angel (1946); The Boogie Man Will Get You; The Chase; The Comedy of Terrors; Confidential Agent; Congo Crossing; The Conspirators; Crack Up; Crime and Punishment (1935,USA); Double Confession; Die Dreizehn Koffer des Herrn O.F.; The Face Behind the Mask; Five Weeks In a Balloon; F.P. 1 Antwortet Nicht; Hell Ship Mutiny; Invisible Agent; Island of Doomed Men; Lancer Spy; M (1931); Mad Love; The Maltese Falcon (1941); The Man Who Knew Too Much (1934); The Mask of Dimitrios; Mr. District Attorney Mr. Moto In Danger Island; Mr. Moto's Gamble; Mr. Moto's Last Warning; Mr. Moto Takes a Chance; Mr. Moto Takes a Vacation; The Mysterious Mr. Moto; The Raven (1963); Schuss im Morgengrauen; The Secret Agent (1936); The Story of Mankind; Stranger On the Third Floor; Tales of Terror; Thank You, Mr. Moto; Think Fast, Mr. Moto; Three Strangers; 20,000 Leagues Under the Sea (1954); The Verdict (1946); Der Verlorene; Voyage to the Bottom of the Sea; You'll Find Out

Lorre, Peter (wri, 1904-1964): Der Verlorene

Lorre Jr., Peter (act): The Cat Creature

Lorring, Joan (act, b. 1926, nee Magdalen Ellis): The Bridge of San Luis Rey (1944); The Lost Moment; Stranger On the Prowl; Three Strangers; The Verdict (1946)

Lortz, Richard (wri): Voices

Lory, Jacques (act): Bulldog Drummond's Bride; The Falcon In Hollywood; Mr. Moto's Last Warning

Lorys, Diana (act): The Awful Dr. Orlof; Fangs of the Living Dead; House of Doom (1973); Lightning Bolt; Superargo e i Giganti Senzo Volto

Losada, Candida (act): The House That Screamed; Tristana

Losby, Donald (act): Tower of London (1962)

Losey, Joseph (act, b. 1909): The Intimate Stranger

Losey, Joseph (dir, b. 1909, a.k.a. J. Walton): Blind Date (1959); Boom; The Boy With Green Hair; The Criminal; The Damned; The Intimate Stranger; M (1950); A Man On the Beach; Modesty Blaise; The Prowler (1951); Secret Ceremony; The Servant; Time Without Pity

Loskowski, Marcia (act): Storm of the Century

Lothar, Ernst (wri): An Act of Murder (1948); The Clairvoyant (1934)

Lothar, Rudolph (wri): Return of a Stranger

Lothar, Susanne (act): Funny Games

Loti, Gianni (act): Gli Amori di Ercole

Lotinga, R.W. (dir): The Dream Doctor; The Unholy Quest

Lotis, Dennis (act): City of the Dead; Sword of Sherwood Forest

Lotorto Jr., Louis A. (act): Fire In the Sky (1993)

Lotosky, Michael (cin): Cannibal Girls

Lott, Dale (act): Zapped!

Lott, Milton (wri): The Last Hunt

Lott, Mona (wri): The Erotic Adventures of Zorro

Lotterman, Beau (act): The Mask (1994); Phantasm III: Lord of the Dead

Lotti, Angelo (cin): The Lion of Thebes

Lotti, Mariella (act): His Last 12 Hours

Lottimer, Eb (act): Futurekick

Louanne (act): Oh, God! Book II

Loud, Grant (act): Graduation Day

Loudon, Carolyn (act): Friday the 13th-Part 2

Lough, John (act): The Ivory Ape

Loughery, David (wri): Dreamscape; Star Trek V: The Final Frontier; The Three Musketeers (1993)

Loughery, Jackie (act): Abbott and Costello Go to Mars;The Veils of Baghdad

Loughlin, Lori (act): Amityville 3-D; Casper: A Spirited Beginning

Loughlin, Terry (act): Mr. Destiny

Loughran, Derek (act): Return of the Living Dead, Part II

Loughridge, Graham (act):Mary Shelley's 'Frankenstein'

Louie, John (act): Gremlins; Oh, God! Book II

Louis, Alyce (act): Forbidden Jungle

Louis, Justin (act): Blood & Donuts; The Haunting of Hamilton High

Louis, Lee (act): Q

Louis, Marilyn (act): see Fleming, Rhonda

Louis, Pira (act): Ghost Diver

Louis, Willard (act): Don Juan (1927); Robin Hood (1922)

Louis-Dreyfus, Julia (act, b. 1961): A Bug's Life; Troll

Louise, Anita (act, 1916-1970, nee Anita Fremault): The Bandit of Sherwood Forest; Bulldog Drummond at Bay (1947);The Devil's Mask; The Gorilla (1939); Love Letters; Marie Antoinette (1938); A Midsummer Night's Dream (1935); The Phantom of Crestwood; Shadowed; The Villain Still Pursued Her

Louise, Anna (act): Beyond and Back

Louise, Jenna (act): Curtains

Louise, Theodora (act): Bloodspell

Louise, Tina (act, b. 1934, nee Tina Blacker): Evils of the Night; Look What's Happened to Rosemary's Baby; Siege of Syracuse; The Stepford Wives; The Wrecking Crew

Lounsbery, Dan (act): Twisted

Lounsbery, John (dir): The Rescuers

Lourie, Eugene (cin, 1903-1991): Crack in the World

Lourie, Eugene (dir, 1903-1991): The Beast from 20,000 Fathoms; Behemoth, the Sea Monster; The Colossus of New York; Gorgo

Lourie, Eugene (wri, 1903-1991): *Behemoth, the Sea Monster*
Lourie, Michele (act): *The Deadly Trap*
Loussier, Jacques (mus): *The Killing Game*
Louthan, Guy J. (act): *Full Eclipse*
Louzil, Eric (dir & wri): *Class of Nuke 'em High, Part 2: Subhumanoid Meltdown*
Lovatt, Jack (act): *Crime and Penalty*
Love, Bessie (act, b. 1898, nee Juanita Horton): *Battle Beneath the Earth; Cat and Mouse (1974); Children of the Damned; The Flying Torpedo; Gulliver's Travels (1977); The Hunger; The Lost World (1925); Nowhere to Go; On Her Majesty's Secret Service; Vampyres...Daughters of Dracula*
Love, Charles (act): *Train Ride to Hollywood*
Love, David (act): *Teenagers from Outer Space*
Love, Dorothy (act): *The Incredible Melting Man*
Love, Ed (act): *The Day It Came to Earth*
Love, Lewis (act): *Silent Night, Bloody Night*
Love, Lucretia (act): *Battle of the Amazons; Deborah; Dr. Hecklyl & Mr. Hype; The Tormented (1977); Zenabel*
Love, Marilyn (act): *The Bank Messenger Mystery*
Love, Mary (act): *The Greed of William Hart*
Love, Montagu (act, 1877-1943): *The Adventures of Robin Hood; Bulldog Drummond (1929); The Cat Creeps (1930); Devotion; Don Juan (1927); The Haunted House (1929); Kismet (1930); The Last Warning (1929); The Lone Wolf Strikes; The Man In the Iron Mask (1939);The Mark of Zorro (1940); The Mysterious Island (1929); Outward Bound; The Prisoner of Zenda (1937); The Remarkable Andrew;Sherlock Holmes and the Voice of Terror; The Son of Monte Cristo; The Suicide Club (1914); The Torpedo of Doom*
Love, Mother (act): *The Surgeon*
Love, Nicholas (act): *The Boogeyman; Brainwaves; Shadow of Death (1983)*
Love, Patti (act): *Terror (1979)*
Love, Reginald (act): *Evil Stalks This House*
Love, Steve (act): *Party Line*
Love, Suzanna (act): *The Boogeyman; Boogeyman II; The Devonsville Terror; Shadow of Death (1983)*
Love, Suzanna (wri): *The Boogey Man; The Devonsville Terror*
Lovecraft, H.P. (wri, 1890-1937): *Bride of Re-Animator; The Curse; Curse II: The Bite; Curse of the Crimson Altar; The Dunwich Horror; From Beyond; The Haunted Palace (1963); Lurking Fear; Monster of Terror; Necronomicon: Book of the Dead; Re-Animator; The Resurrected; The Shuttered Room; The Unnamable*
Loveface, Tim (act): *Mosquito*
Lovegrove, Arthur (act): *Clash by Night; Dial 999 (1955); Eye of the Needle; The Marked One; Memoirs of a Survivor; Naked Fury; The Secret of the Forest; The Steel Key*
Lovejoy, Frank (act, 1912-1962): *The Crooked Web; The Finger Man; The Hitchhiker; House of Wax; I Was a Communist for the F.B.I.; Julie; The Sound of Fury*
Lovejoy, Harry (act): *The Corpse Grinders*
Lovelett, Jim (act): *It Happened One Christmas; Phantom of the Paradise; Switch (1991)*
Lovell, Dyson (act): *Panic (1963)*
Lovell, Jacqueline (act): *Head of the Family; O Lita 2000*
Lovell, Capt. James (act): *The Man Who Fell to Earth (1976)*
Lovell (Jr.), James (A.) (act): *Apollo 13; For All Mankind*
Lovell, Raymond (act, 1900-1953): *Alibi (1942); Appointment With Crime; The Bad Lord Byron; The Case of Gabriel Perry; Crime Unlimited; 49th Parallel; Gaol Break (1936); Hotel Reserve; King of the Damned; The Man In Grey; Murder Tomorrow; My Brother's Keeper; Sexton Lives; Sexton Blake and the Mademoiselle; So Evil My Love; The Steel Key; The Third Clue; The Three Weird Sisters; Troubled Waters (1936); Warn London; Warn That Man; Who Killed Van Loon?*
Lovell, Roderick (act): *Mother Riley Meets the Vampire; So Evil My Love*
Lovelock, Ray (act): *Autopsy; The Cassandra Crossing; The Living Dead at the Manchester Morgue*
Lovely, Louise (act): *Sirens of the Sea*
Loventhal, Charles (dir): *My Demon Lover*
Lo Verde, Rita (act): *Deborah*
Loveridge, George (wri): *The Next Voice You Hear*
Loveridge, Larry (act): *Premonition (1972)*
Lovett, Josephine (wri): *The Enchanted Cottage (1924)*
Lovi, Regine (act): *Un Amour de Poche*
Lovitz, Jon (act, b. 1957): *An American Tail: Fievel Goes West; Big; The Brave Little Toaster; Coneheads; Mr. Destiny; Mom and Dad Save the World; My Stepmother Is an Alien*
Lovsky, Celia (act): *Man of a Thousand Faces; The Power (1967); The St. Valentine's Day Massacre; The Scarf; Soylent Green; 36 Hours (1965)*
Lovstrom, Peter (act): *Haunters of the Deep; Lifeforce*
Lovy, Steven (dir & wri): *Circuitry Man*
Low, Georgia (act): *Vampire On Bikini Beach*
Low, Roger (act): *Hamlet (1990)*
Lowden, Susan (act): *Graveyard Shift (1990)*
Lowe, Alex (act): *Mary Shelley's 'Frankenstein'*
Lowe, Alison Carole (act): *Weird Science*
Lowe, Arthur (act, 1915-1982): *The Bed-Sitting Room; Fragment Of Fear; Hour Of Decision; Kind Hearts And Coronets; The Lady Vanishes (1979); The Mirror And Markheim; The Ruling Class; Theater Of Blood*
Lowe, Barry (act): *The Camp On Blood Island; Cash On Demand; Hands Of The Ripper*
Lowe, Beverly (act): *Alien High*
Lowe, Chad (act): *Apprentice To Murder; Highway To Hell*
Lowe, Edmund (act, 1890-1971): *Around The World In 80 Days; The Best Man Wins; Chandu The Magician; The Devil (1921); The Enchanted Forest; The Garden Murder Case; The Gift Of Gab; The Girl In The Case; The Great Impersonation (1935); In The Palace Of The King; Scotland Yard (1930); The Spider (1932); The Squeaker (1937); Strange Mr. Gregory; The Wizard; Women Of All Nations*
Lowe (Jr.), Edward T. (wri, 1889-1973): *Bulldog Drummond Comes Back; Bulldog Drummond Escapes; Bulldog Drummond's Revenge; Charlie Chan At The Race Track; Charlie Chan In Paris; House Of Dracula; House Of Frankenstein; The Hunchback Of Notre Dame (1923); Sherlock Holmes And The Secret Weapon; Tarzan's Desert Mystery; The Vampire Bat*
Lowe, Ellen (act): *The Snake Pit (1948)*
Lowe, Grant (act): *Rabid*
Lowe, Heather (act): *Battle For The Planet Of The Apes; The Spiral Staircase (1975)*
Lowe, J. (act): *The Kidnapped King*
Lowe, John (act): see Loder, John
Lowe, Kevin (act): *Mother's Day*
Lowe, Lawrence (act): *Re-Animator*
Lowe, Mignon (act): *Zombie Island Massacre*
Lowe, Mudell (mus): *Tarantulas: The Deadly Cargo*
Lowe, Rob (act): *Contact*
Lowe, Sherman (L.) (wri, b. 1894): *The Catman Of Paris; Eyes Of The Jungle; The Lost Jungle; Phantom Of The Jungle; Valley Of The Zombies; The White Goddess*
Lowe, Skip E. (act): *Cameron's Closet*
Lowe, Stranja (act): *Doctor Franken*
Lowe, Susan (act): *Serial Mom*
Lowell, Carey (act): *The Guardian; Licence To Kill (1989)*
Lowell, Helen (act): *The Dragon Murder Case*
Lowell, Margot (act): *Haunts*
Lowell, Mark (act): *Attack Of The Puppet People; Donovan's Brain; Untamed Women*
Lowell, Robert (act): *The Human Factor*
Lowell, Tom (act): *The Aliens Are Coming; Escape From The Planet Of The Apes; The Gnomemobile*
Lowenadler, Holger (act): *I Am Curious (Yellow)*
Lowenberg, B. (act): *The Lost Boys*
Lowens, Curt (act): *The Entity; Lycanthropus; The Mephisto Waltz; V*
Lowensohn, Elina (act): *Nadja*
Lowenthal, A.J. (act): *Spookies*
Lowenthal, Mark (act): *I Come In Peace*
Lowery, Andrew (act): *The Conspiracy Of Fear; My Boyfriend's Back*
Lowery, Edward (act): *The House Of Mystery (1931)*
Lowery, Robert (act, 1914-1971, nee Robert L. Hanke): *Charlie Chan In Reno; Charlie Chan's Murder Cruise; Danger Street; Highway 13; House Of Horrors (1946); Jalopy; Killer At Large; The Mark Of Zorro (1940); Mr. Moto In Danger Island; The Mummy's Ghost; Murder Over New York; Queen Of The Amazons (1947); Revenge Of The Zombies (1943); Tarzan's Desert Mystery; They Made Me A Killer; The Undertaker And His Pals*
Lowery, William (act): *Robin Hood (1922)*
Lowitz, Siegfried (act): *Confess, Dr. Corda; The Invisible Dr. Mabuse; The Mysterious Magician; Vengeance*
Lowndes, Marie Belloc (wri, 1868-1947): *The House Of Peril; The Lodger (1926, 1932 & 1944); Man In The Attic (1953)*
Lowry, Dick (dir): *Murder With Mirrors; Project: Alf*
Lowry, Jane (act): *Alice, Sweet Alice*
Lowry, Jennifer (act): *Brain Damage*
Lowry, Joe (act): *The China Syndrome*
Lowry, Judith (act, 1890-1976): *Ladybug, Ladybug; On A Clear Day You Can See Forever*
Lowry, Lynn (act): *Cat People (1982); Code Name Trixie; I Drink Your Blood; Shivers*
Lowry, Morton (act): *Counter-Espionage; The Hound Of The Baskervilles (1939); The Picture Of Dorian Gray (1945); Pursuit To Algiers; The Verdict*
Lowry, Murray (act): *Shadow Of The Hawk*
Lowry, Roger (wri): *Negatives*
Loxton, David R. (dir): *The Lathe Of Heaven*
Loy, Myrna (act, 1905-1993, nee Myrna Williams): *After The Thin Man; Another Thin Man; A Connecticut Yankee; Death Takes A Holiday (1971); Don Juan (1927); Do Not Fold, Spindle Or Mutilate; It Happened At Lake Wood Manor; Love Me Tonight; The Mask Of Fu Manchu; Midnight Lace (1960); Shadow Of The Thin Man; Song Of The Thin Man; The Thin Man; The Thin Man Goes Home*
Loy, Sonny (act): *Mr. Wu (1927)*
Loya, Bob (act): *Blood Diner*
Loyer, Raymond (act): *The Gentle Art Of Murder*
Loyola, Javier (act): *El Principe Encadenado; El Santo Contra Las Vampiras*
Lozito, Allan (act): *Street Trash*
Lozoff, Joshua Bo (act): *Teenage Mutant Ninja Turtles*
Lu, Lisa (act): *Demon Seed; Terror In The Wax Museum*
Lualdi, Antonella (act, b. 1931): *His Last 12 Hours; Leda*
Lubin, Arthur (dir, 1901-1995): *Ali Baba And The Forty Thieves (1943); Black Friday; Footsteps In The Fog; Francis; Francis Covers The Big Town; Francis Goes To The Races; Francis Goes To West Point; Francis In The Navy; Francis Joins The Wacs; Hold On!; Hold That Ghost; The Incredible Mr. Limpet; It Grows On Trees; A Night In Paradise; Phantom Of The Opera (1943); The Thief Of Baghdad (1960); White Savage*
Lubin, Hedda (act): *The Gore-Gore Girls*
Lubin, Lou (act): *Shadow Of The Thin Man*
Lubitsch, Ernst (act, 1892-1947): *Sumurun*
Lubitsch, Ernst (dir, 1892-1947): *Anna Boleyn; Die Augen Der Mumie Ma; Carmen (1918); Heaven Can Wait (1942); Madame Dubarry (1919); Die Puppe; Sumurun; Das Weib Des Pharao*
Lubow-Bellamy, Keith Anthony (act): *Shocker*
Lucan, Arthur (act, 1887-1954): *Mother Riley Meets The Vampire; Old Mother Riley's Ghosts; Old Mother Riley's Jungle Treasure*
Lucan, Arthur (wri, 1887-1954): *Old Mother Riley's Ghosts*
Lucarda, Toni (act): *Venetian Bird*
Lucas (cin): *La Chute De La Maison Usher*
Lucas, Bryon (act): *Quarantine*
Lucas, Craig (wri): *Prelude To A Kiss*
Lucas, Drew (act): *Moon 44*
Lucas (Jr.), George (dir, b. 1944): *Star Wars; Thx 1138; Thx 1138 4eb*
Lucas (Jr.), George (wri, b. 1944): *The Empire Strikes Back; The Ewok Adventure; Ewoks: The Battle For Endor; Indiana Jones And The Last Crusade; Indiana Jones And The Temple Of Doom; Raiders Of The Lost Ark; Return Of The Jedi; Star Wars; Thx 1138; Thx 1138 4eb; Willow*
Lucas, Isabelle (act, 1920-1997): *Outland*
Lucas, J. Frank (act): *The Curse Of The Living Corpse*
Lucas, Jack (act): *The Boy Who Cried Werewolf*
Lucas, Jan (cin): *Boarding House*
Lucas, John Meredyth (wri): *City Beneath The Sea (1970); Peking Express; The Sign Of Zorro*
Lucas, Joshua (act): *Child Of Darkness, Child Of Light*
Lucas, Leighton (mus, b. 1903): *Son Of Robin Hood; Stage Fright*
Lucas, Lisa (act): *Heart And Souls*
Lucas, Ralph (wri): *The Child; Planet Of Dinosaurs*
Lucas, Scott (act): *Mother's Day*
Lucas, Tom (act): *Treasure Island (1950)*
Lucas, Wilfred (act): *A Chump At Oxford; Just Imagine; Modern Times; The Sphinx (1933); Trilby (1923)*
Lucas, William (act, b. 1926): *The Devil's Daffodil; The Night Of The Big Heat; The Shadow Of The Cat; The Sky Bike; Tower Of Evil; The Very Edge; X...The Unknown*
Luccetti, Monica (act): *Flesh & Blood*
Lucchesi, Vincent (act): *The Goddess Of Love*
Lucchini, Walter (act): *Ironmaster*
Lucci, Susan (act, b. 1948): *Ebbie; Haunted By Her Past; Invitation To Hell*
Luce, Deborah (act): *Mother's Day*
Luce, Ron (act): *The Attic*
Lucero, Enrique (act): *Macario; The Octagon; El Vampiro Sangriento; The Woman Hunter*
Luchini, Fabrice (act): *Perceval*
Lucht, Darlene (act): *The Haunted Palace (1963)*
Lucia, Chip (act): *The Hand That Rocks The Cradle; Vice Versa (1988)*
Lucia, Luis (dir): *El Principe Encadenado*
Lucie, Michael (act): *Blood Diner*
Lucien, Joseph (act): *The City Of Lost Children*
Lucker, Michael (wri): *Vampire In Brooklyn*
Luckey, Susan (act): *Carousel*
Luckham, Cyril (act): *The Alphabet Murders; How To Murder A Rich Uncle; The Saint And The Brave Goose; Stranger From Venus*
Luckinbill, Laurence (act, b. 1934): *Moonwalk One; Star Trek V: The Final Frontier*
Lucking, William/Bill (act): *Captain America Ii; Doc Savage, The Man Of Bronze; Dr. Scorpion; Ellery Queen: Don't Look Behind You; Joe & The Colonel; Sleepstalker*
Luckwell, Bill (wri): *Hidden Homicide; Undercover Girl (1958)*
Lucoque, H. Lisle (dir): *Fairyland; Lorna Doone (1920); She (1916); Where The Rainbow Ends*
Lucoque, Nellie E. (wri): *Lorna Doone (1920); She (1916)*
Lucy, Arnold (act): *Dr. Jekyll And Mr. Hyde (1932); The Ghost Talks; Scotland Yard (1930); The Wandering Jew (1933)*
Lucy, Tom (act): *First Knight*
Ludden, Allen (act, 1918-1981): *Futureworld*
Luddy, Barbara (act): *Terrified*
Luddy, Tom (act): *Invasion Of The Body Snatchers (1978)*
Luders, Gunther (act): *Hi, Here's Eddie*
Ludlow, John (act): *Agatha*
Ludovitch, Clayton (act): *Making Mr. Right*
Ludvikova, Hana (act): *Howling II*
Ludwig, Adam (act): *Scanners; Short Circuit 2*
Ludwig, Edward (dir, 1900-1982): *The Black Scorpion; Jivaro; The Man Who Reclaimed His Head*
Ludwig, Jerry (wri): *Midnight Lace (1981)*
Ludwig, Julian (act): *Gog*
Ludwig, Pamela (act): *Project X (1987)*
Ludwig, William (wri, b. 1912): *Shadow On The Wall*
Luedecke, Werner Joerg (wri): *Journey To The Lost City*
Luez, Laurette (act): *The Adventures Of Hajji Baba; African Treasure; D.O.A. (1949); Jungle Gents; Killer Shark; Prehistoric Women (1950)*
Luff, William (cin): *Scrooge (1935); The Triumph Of Sherlock Holmes*
Luft, Liesel (act): *Making Contact*
Luft, Sacha (act): *Making Contact*
Luft, William (act): *The Stolen Plans*
Lugagne, Francoise (act): *Landru; Les Sorcieres De Salem*
Lugerova, Miriam (act): *Howling II*
Luget, Andre (act): *Comment Qu'ella Est!; The Mad Genius; The Queen Of Spades (1937); Le Spectre Vert*
Lugg, Alfred (act): *Queen Of My Heart*
Lugg, William (act): *Scrooge (1913)*
Lugosi, Bela (act, 1882-1956, nee Bela Blasko): *Abbott And Costello Meet Frankenstein; The Ape Man; The Best Man Wins; The Black Camel; The Black Cat (1934 & 1941); Black Dragons; Black Friday; The Black Parachute; The Black Sleep; The Body Snatcher (1945); Bowery At Midnight; The Boys From Brooklyn; Bride Of The Monster; Chandu; Chandu The Magician; The Corpse*

Vanishes; Dark Eyes Of London; The Death Kiss; The Devil Bat; Dracula (1931, English-Speaking Version); Eyes Of The Underworld; Frankenstein Meets The Wolf Man; Genius At Work; The Ghost Of Frankenstein; Ghosts On The Loose; The Gift Of Gab; Glen Or Glenda?; The Gorilla (1939); Hamlet (1920); International House; The Invisible Ghost; The Invisible Ray; Island Of Lost Souls; Der Januskopf; King Robot (Unfinished); Lock Up Your Daughters; The Mark Of The Vampire (1935); The Master Minds (1949); The Midnight Girl; Mother Riley Meets The Vampire; Murder By Television; The Murders In The Rue Morgue (1932); The Mysterious Mr. Wong; The Mystery Of The Mary Celeste; The Necklace Of Death; Night Monster; Night Of Terror (1933); One Body Too Many; The Phantom Creeps; The Phantom Killer; Plan 9 From Outer Space; The Raven (1935); Return Of The Ape Man; The Return Of The Vampire; The Saint's Double Trouble; Scared To Death (1947); Son Of Frankenstein; S.O.S. Coast Guard; Spooks Run Wild; Such Men Are Dangerous; Die Teufelsanbeter; The Thirteenth Chair (1929); Voodoo Man; White Zombie; The Wolf Man (1941); Women Of All Nations; You'll Find Out; Zombies On Broadway
Lugosi, Boris (act): El Castello Dell'orrore
Luis, Jose Miguel (act): Wild Thing
Luis, Madina (act): Blood From The Mummy's Tomb
Luisi, James (act): Ben; Fade To Black; Future Cop; The Hidden
Luiz, Linda (act): The Silence Of The Hams
Lujan, Bob/Robert (act, b. 1959): Vampire's Kiss
Lujan, Crystal (act): Earth Girls Are Easy
Lukacs, Pal (act): see Lukas, Paul
Lukas, Karl (act): The Shaggy D.A.
Lukas, Paul (act, 1895-1971, nee Pal Lukacs): Address Unknown; The Benson Murder Case; Berlin Express; The Casino Murder Case; The Ghost Breakers; The Gift Of Gab; The Lady Vanishes (1938); The Monster And The Girl; The Secret Of The Blue Room; Temptation (1946); 20,000 Leagues Under The Sea (1954)
Lukather, Dorys (wri): The Phantom From 10,000 Leagues
Lukather, Paul (act): Dinosaurus!; Hands Of A Stranger; Mind Over Murder
Lukavsky, Radevan (act): Ikaria Xb1; The Man Of The First Century
Luke, Edwin (act): The Jade Mask
Luke, Eric (act & wri): Explorers
Luke, Jayne (act): Species
Luke, Keye (act, 1904-1991): The Casino Murder Case; The Cat Creature; Charlie Chan At Monte Carlo; Charlie Chan At The Circus; Charlie Chan At The Olympics; Charlie Chan At The Opera; Charlie Chan At The Race Track; Charlie Chan In Paris; Charlie Chan In Shanghai; Charlie Chan On Broadway; Dead Heat; The Falcon's Brother; The Feathered Serpent (1948); Gremlins; Gremlins 2: The New Batch; Invisible Agent; Mad Love; Mr. Moto's Gamble; Phantom Of Chinatown; Project X (1967); The Sky Dragon; Sleep, My Love
Lukes, Oldrich (act): Milczaca Gwiazda
Lukschy, Wolfgang (act): Frozen Alive; 24 Hours To Kill
Lulli, Folco (act): Duel At The Rio Grande; Le Salaire De La Peur; The Tartars
Lulli, Piero (act): Beast Of Babylon Against The Son Of Hercules; Il Trionfo Di Ercole; Ulysses
Lum, Joanie (act): Primal Fear
Lumbly, Carl (act): Brother Future; Caveman (1981); Mantis; Pacific Heights
Lumet, Baruch (act): The Killer Shrews
Lumet, Sidney (dir, b. 1924): The Deadly Affair; Fail-Safe; The Fugitive Kind; Murder On The Orient Express; The Wiz
Lumley, Joanna (act, b. 1946): A Ghost In Monte Carlo; James And The Giant Peach; On Her Majesty's Secret Service; The Satanic Rites Of Dracula; Tam Lin
Lumley, Terry (act): Satan's School For Girls
Lummis, Dayton (act): Beauty And The Beast (1962); The Flight That Disappeared; Jack The Giant Killer; Port Sinister; Return To Treasure Island
Lummiss, John (act): Wombling Free
Lumont, Roger (act): The Black Windmill; The Murders In The Rue Morgue (1986)
Lumsden, Norman (act): The Big Sleep (1978)
Luna, Barbara (act, b. 1937): Brenda Starr (1976); Five Weeks In A Balloon
Luna, Bigas (dir & wri): Anguish
Luna, Donyale (act): Satyricon
Luna, Margarita (act): The Beast Of Hollow Mountain; Run For The Sun
Lund, Art (act, 1915-1990): It's Alive III: Island Of The Alive; The Man From Atlantis
Lund, Camille (act): Vampire At Midnight
Lund, Caroline Christina (act): Demons 2
Lund, Deanna (act): Dimension 5; I Love A Mystery (1966)
Lund, Jana (act): Frankenstein—1970
Lund, John (act, 1911-1992): Bride Of Vengeance; Night Has A Thousand Eyes
Lund, Jordan (act): Species
Lund, Lucille (act): The Black Cat (1934)
Lund, Marcus (act): Threads
Lund, Margaret (act): 7 Doors Of Death
Lundberg, Otto Elg (act): The Story Of Gosta Berling
Lundequist, Gerda (act): The Story Of Gosta Berling
Lundgren, Dolph (act, b. 1959): I Come In Peace; Johnny Mnemonic; Masters Of The Universe; The Punisher; Universal Soldier
Lundgren, Lyn (act): Strait-Jacket
Lundigan, William (act, b. 1914): The Black Doll; Follow Me Quietly; The Missing Guest; Mystery In Mexico; Riders To The Stars; State Department-File 649; Terror Ship; The Underwater City; The White Orchid
Lundin, Justin (act): Grim Prairie Tales
Lundin, Robyn (act): Endangered Species
Lundin, Victor (act): Robinson Crusoe On Mars
Lundquist, Peter (act): Flight Of The Navigator
Lundquist, Steve (act): Earth Girls Are Easy; Return Of The Killer Tomatoes
Lundy, Burke (act): The Keeper
Lundy, Jessica (act): Single White Female; Vampire's Kiss
Lune, Ted (act): Berserk
Lung, Ti (act): Revenge Of The Zombies (1981)
Lung, Tong (act): Unforgettable; Watchers
Lunge, Romilly (act): The Door With Seven Locks (1940); The Mind Of Mr. Reeder
Lunghi, Cherie (act): Excalibur; Mary Shelley's 'Frankenstein'
Lunghin, Semyon (wri): Rasputin (1985)
Lunham, Dan (act): The Strangeness
Lunnon, Bernard (act): Street Trash
Lunny, Cora (act): Rawhead Rex
Lunt, Susan (act): Forever Evil
Luotto, Steven (wri): Iron Warrior...The Legend!
Lupe, Kendall (act): Angel Heart
Lupi, Rolando (act): Il Gigante Di Metropolis; The Queen Of Babylon
Lupino, Barry (act): Wishes
Lupino, Ida (act, 1918-1995): The Adventures Of Sherlock Holmes (1939); Beware, My Lovely; The Devil's Rain; Devotion; The Food Of The Gods; The Ghost Camera; I Love A Mystery (1966); Jennifer (1953); Ladies In Retirement; The Lone Wolf Spy Hunt; On Dangerous Ground; Out Of The Fog (1941); Peter Ibbetson; Strange Intruder; While The City Sleeps; Woman In Hiding
Lupino, Richard (act): Midnight Lace (1960)
Lupino, Rita (act): Time Travelers (1976)
Lupino, Wallace/Wally (act): Forging Ahead; The Man Who Could Work Miracles; The Stolen Necklace; Wishes; The Yellow Mask
Lupino, Wallace (wri): Wishes
Lupinski, Ed (act): Barracuda
Lupo, Alberto (act): Atom Age Vampire; The Bacchantes; The Lion Of Thebes; The Masked Conqueror; The Minotaur
Lupo, Frank (wri): Something Is Out There
Lupo, Michele (dir, 1932-1989): Maciste, L'eroe Piu Grande Del Mondo; Master Stroke
Lupo, Thomas (act): Eve Of Destruction
Lupoff, Richard A. (wri): 12:01
Lupone, Dolly (act): Cinderella (1907); The Magic Ring (1906)
Lupone, Patti (act): The Song Spinner
Luppi, Federico (act): Cronos
Lupton, John (act): The Astronaut; Jesse James Meets Frankenstein's Daughter; The Man In The Net; The Phantom Of Hollywood; Three Came To Kill
Lupus, Peter (act): Pumpkinhead II: Blood Wings
Luque, Isabelle (act): Pieces
Lush Jr., R.K. (act): Secrets Of The Phantom Caverns
Lusicic, Andro (dir): Sedmi Kontinent
Lusk, Victor (act): The Cry For Justice
Luske, Hamilton (dir): 101 Dalmatians (1960)
Lussier, Dane (wri, b. 1909): Dick Tracy vs. Cueball; The Falcon's Alibi; The Lady And The Monster
Lussier, Marcel (act): The Unnamable
Lussier, Robert (act): Salem's Lot; Welcome To Arrow Beach
Lustgarten, Edgar (wri): The Candlelight Murder; Person Unknown
Lustig, Aaron (act): Darkman (1990); Edward Scissorhands; Ghostbusters II; The Relic
Lustig, Jan (wri, b. 1902): Knights Of The Round Table
Lustig, William (act): Darkman (1990)
Lustig, William (dir): Maniac (1980); Maniac Cop; Maniac Cop 2
Lute, Attila (act): Daughter Of Darkness (1990)
Lutfi, Dib (cin): Os Deuses E Os Mortos
Luthan, Guy (act): Waxwork II: Lost In Time
Luther, Igor (cin): The Handmaid's Tale
Lutong, Zhang (act): Buddha's Lock
Luty, Paul (act): The Water Babies
Lutyens, Elisabeth (mus): Dr. Terror's House Of Horrors (1964); The Earth Dies Screaming; Paranoiac; The Psychopath (1965); The Skull; Spaceflight Ic-1; The Terrornauts
Lutz, Adelle (act): The Silence Of The Lambs
Lutz, John (wri): Single White Female
Lutz, Pieter (act): The Lift
Lutze, Rick (act): Flesh Gordon
Luv Johnsons, The (act & mus): Blood Diner
Luxford, Nola (act): The Flying Dutchman
Luz, Franc/Frank (act): Ghost Town; The Nest; Turn Back The Clock
Luzi, Maria Pia (act): Planets Against Us
Lyall, Gavin (wri): Moon Zero Two
Lyberten, Eva (act): Hundra
Lycett, Eustace (cin): Bedknobs And Broomsticks; The Love Bug; Mary Poppins
Lydecker, Howard (cin): The Catman Of Paris; Cyclotrode X; Daughter Of The Jungle; Dick Tracy vs. Crime, Inc.; Our Man Flint; Spy Smasher Returns; Way...Way Out
Lydecker, Theodore (cin): The Catman Of Paris; Cyclotrode X; Daughter Of The Jungle
Lyden, Pierce (act): Mark Of The Gorilla; The Phantom From 10,000 Leagues; Pygmy Island
Lyden, Robert (act): The Forbidden Moon; Man Of A Thousand Faces
Lydon, James (act, b. 1923): Brainstorm (1965); Chain Of Evidence; Ellery Queen; Hnery Aldrich Haunts A House; The Hypnotic Eye; Out Of The Storm
Lye, Len (dir, 1901-1980): The Birth Of The Robot
Lye, Reg (act): A Challenge For Robin Hood; Dracula (1973); Fathom; The Spaceman And King Arthur; Spell Of Evil; 10 Rillington Place; Uncharted Seas; Wombling Free
Lyel, Viola (act, b. 1900, nee Violet Watson): Black 13; Passing Shadows; Wanted For Murder
Lygizos, Danos (act): Blind Date; The Next One
Lykins, Ray (act): The Lawnmower Man
Lyle, Lyston (act): A Vagabond's Revenge; The Woman Who Was Nothing
Lymington, John (wri): The Night Of The Big Heat
Lyn, Dawn (act): The Horrible House On The Hill
Lyn, Keri (act): Sorry, Wrong Number (1989)
Lynch, Barry (act): Rawhead Rex; Sleepstalker
Lynch, Christopher (act): Trancers II: The Return Of Jack Deth
Lynch, David (dir & wri): Blue Velvet; Dune; Eraserhead; Lost Highway; Twin Peaks: Fire Walk With Me
Lynch, Edward (act): The Exorcist III
Lynch, Heather (act): Mr. Destiny
Lynch, Jane (act): Vice Versa (1988)
Lynch, Jennifer (act, b. 1968): Eraserhead
Lynch, Joe (act): The Saint And The Brave Goose
Lynch, John (act): Hardware; The Secret Of Roan Inish
Lynch, John (wri): The Face In The Fog (1922)
Lynch, John Carroll (act): Fargo
Lynch, Kara (act): Witchery
Lynch, Kate (act): Curtains; Def Con 4
Lynch, Kelly (act, b. 1960): Virtuosity
Lynch, Ken (act): Dead Ringer; I Married A Monster From Outer Space; Poor Devil; W
Lynch, Kenny (act): Dr. Terror's House Of Horrors (1964); The Playbirds
Lynch, Kevin (act): Mutants In Paradise
Lynch, Paul (dir): Humongous; Prom Night
Lynch, Peggy (act): Eraserhead
Lynch, Raymond (act): Night Of The Comet
Lynch, Richard (act): Bad Dreams; Cyborg 3; Deathsport; Demon (1976); Good Against Evil; Merlin; The Premonition (1975); Puppet Master Iii: Toulon's Revenge; The Sword And The Sorcerer; Trancers II: The Return Of Jack Deth; Vampire (1979)
Lynch, Sean (act): At The Earth's Core; The Brigand Of Kandahar; Cosh Boy
Lynch, Susie (act): Cavegirl (1985)
Lynch Jr., Vernon (wri): Vampire In Brooklyn
Lynch, Warren (cin): Blondes At Work; Fly-Away Baby; Smart Blonde; Torchy Blane In Chinatown; Torchy Gets Her Man; Torchy Runs For Mayor
Lynd, Helen (act): The Lone Wolf Spy Hunt
Lynd, Moira (act): The Spider (1939); The Strangler (1932)
Lynde, Janice (act): Beyond Evil
Lynde, Paul (act, 1926-1982): Son Of Flubber
Lyndhurst, F.L. (dir): The Showman's Dream
Lyndon, Barre (wri, 1896-1972): Dark Intruder; Hangover Square; The Lodger (1944); The Man In Half Moon Street; Man In The Attic (1953); The Man Who Could Cheat Death; Night Has A Thousand Eyes; Omar Khayyam; The War Of The Worlds
Lyne, Adrian (dir): Jacob's Ladder
Lynes, Kristi (act): Alice In Wonderland (1985)
Lynley, Carol (act, b. 1942): Beware! The Blob; Bunny Lake Is Missing; The Cat And The Canary (1978); Crosscurrent; Danger route; Fantasy Island; Flood; The Helicopter Spies; If It's A Man, Hang Up; The immortal; the Maltese Bippy; The Night Stalker (1971); The Poseidon Adventure; Shadow On the land; The Shape Of Things To Come (1979); Shock Treatmenmt (1964); The Shuttered Room
Lynn, Alison (act): Return To Oz
Lynn, Ann (act, b. 1939): Black Torment; Hitler: The Last Ten Days
Lynn, April (act): The Sinister Urge
Lynn, Billy (act): The Twonky
Lynn, Carole (act): The Ghost Train (1941)
Lynn, Dani (act): Black Zoo; Madman Of Mandoras
Lynn, Diana (act, 1926-1971, nee Dolly Loehr): Bedtime For Bonzo; Rogues Of Sherwood Forest
Lynn, Emmett (act, b. 1897): Nightmare Alley; Ring Of Fear; The Scarf
Lynn, George (E.) (act): The Atomic City; Charlie Chan At Monte Carlo; Crime Doctor's Strangest Case; House Of Frankenstein; I Was A Teenage Frankenstein; The Man Who Turned To Stone; Sudan; The Werewolf (1955)
Lynn, Janet (act): In The Devil's Garden
Lynn, Janis Eve (act): Phantom Of The Paradise
Lynn, Jeffrey (act, 1909-1995, nee Ragnar Lind): The Body Disappears
Lynn, Jenny (act): The Greed Of William Hart
Lynn, Joe (act): The Wiz
Lynn, Jonathan (act): The House That Dripped Blood
Lynn, Kane W. (wri): Brain Of Blood
Lynn, Kathy (act): The Witchmaker
Lynn, Mara (act): Prehistoric Women (1950)
Lynn, Mari (act): Experiment In Terror
Lynn, May (act): The Devil's Profession; The Harbour Lights
Lynn, Nina (act): The Beggar Girl's Wedding; The Girl Who Took The Wrong Turning; Her Life In London; Queen Of The Wicked
Lynn, Peter (George) (act): Buried Alive (1940); The Lone Wolf Strikes; Mr. Wong In Chinatown; The Saint In Palm Springs
Lynn, Ralph (act): Thark
Lynn, Robert (act): The Return Of Dracula
Lynn, Robert (dir): Dr. Crippen; The Face Of Eve; Information Received; Victim Five
Lynn, Sandra (act): On Her Bed Of Roses
Lynn, Stacy (act): Sorority Girls And The Creature From Hell
Lynne, Amy (act): The Stepford Children
Lynne, Betty (act): The Bad Lord Byron; Dangerous Fingers; Dead Men Are Dangerous
Lynne, Donna (act): The Private Lives Of Adam And Eve
Lynne, Jeff (mus): Electric Dreams
Lynne, Virginia (act): Dr. Black Mr. Hyde
Lynton, Maggie (act): When Dinosaurs Ruled The Earth
Lyon, Alice (act): The Horror Of Party Beach
Lyon, Ben (act, 1901-1979): The Dark Tower; I Killed The Count; The Savage
Lyon, Francis D. (dir, b. 1905): Castle Of Evil; Cult Of The Cobra; Destination Inner Space; The Destructors
Lyon, Lisa (act): Vamp
Lyon, M.D. (act & wri): Ashes
Lyon, Richard (GB act): The Headless Ghost
Lyon, Richard (USA act): The Boy With Green Hair; The Unseen (1945)
Lyon, Sue (act, b. 1946): Alligator (1981); Death Ride; End Of The World (1977)
Lyon, Ted (act): The Toxic Avenger, Part II
Lyon, Theresa (act): The Snake Pit (1948)
Lyon, Wendy (act): The Haunting Of Hamilton High

Lyons, Bruce (act): The Navigator: An Odyssey Across Time
Lyons, Chester (cin): Liliom (1930); Mad Love
Lyons, Collette (act): The Lone Wolf And His Lady
Lyons, Edgar (cin): Dick Tracy (1937)
Lyons, Gene (act): Daddy's Gone A-Hunting
Lyons, H. Agar (act): Dr. Sin Fang; The Fish And The Ring; In The Days Of Robin Hood; Melody Of Death; The Prehistoric Man (1924); The Tempter (1913); Widow Twan-Kee
Lyons, Kely (wri): The Navigator: An Odyssey Across Time
Lyons, James (act): Poison (1990)
Lyons, Lori (act): The Human Duplicators
Lyons, Marty (act): The Body Snatchers
Lyons, Robert F. (act): Dark Night Of The Scarecrow; The Disappearance Of Flight 412; The Ghost Of Flight 401; The Strange Possession Of Mrs. Oliver
Lyons, Tony (act): Supersonic Saucer
Lys, Lya (act, 1908-1986): L'age D'or; Murder In The Air (1940); The Return Of Dr. X
Lysons, Fotheringham (act): The Elusive Pimpernel (1919); The Yellow Claw
Lytell, Bert (act, 1885-1954): Alias The Lone Wolf; Blackie's Redemption; Boston Blackie's Little Pal; The Last Of The Lone Wolf; The Lone Wolf (1917); The Lone Wolf Returns (1926); The Lone Wolf's Daughter (1929); A Message From Mars (1921); Rupert Of Hentzau (1923)
Lythgow, Gene (act): When A Stranger Calls Back
Lyttkens, Ulla (act): I Am Curious (Yellow)
Lytton, Lord (wri): Night Comes Too Soon
Lytton, Debbie (act): The Man In The Santa Claus Suit
Lytton, Doris (act): The Blue Bird (1910); The Brass Bottle (1914)
Lytton, Herbert (act): Champagne For Caesar; The Cosmic Man; The Glass Web

M, Johnny (act): Dreamchild
M, Josh (act): Surf Nazis Must Die
Ma, James (act): Legend Of The Seven Golden Vampires
Ma, Tzi (act): Chain Reaction (1996); RoboCop 2
Ma, Wu (act): A Chinese Ghost Story; A Chinese Ghost Story II
Ma, Wu (dir): The Dead And The Deadly
Maar, Pons (act): Return To Oz
Maas, Dick (dir, mus & wri): The Lift
Maas Jr., Leonard (wri): I Come In Peace
Maass, John (wri): Curdled
Maassri, Mounir (act): Embassy
Maasz, Ronald (cin): Haunters Of The Deep
Maat, Mathias (act): The Lift
Maazel, Lincoln (act): Martin
Mabe, Byron (dir): She Freak
Maben, Alvis/Alvys (act): Murder By Proxy; The Stranger Came Home
Mabhikwa, Isaac (act): King Solomon's Mines (1985)
Mabray, Stuart (act): The Goddess Of Love
Mabuchi, Kaoru (wri): Destroy All Monsters; Godzilla Vs. The Smog Monster; War Of The Gargantuas
Mabuto, Romeo (act): Twilight People
Mac (act): Shadowzone
Macadams, Annabelle (act): It's Alive! (1968)
Macallister, Patrick (act): It's Alive (1974)
Macaluso, Dee (act): Powder
MacAndrews, John (act): The American Heiress; Boundary House; The Cobweb; A Grain Of Sand; The Man Behind "The Times"; The Quarry Mystery; The Tragedy Of Basil Grieve
Macardle, Dorothy (act): The Uninvited (1944)
MacArthur, Charles (wri, 1895-1956): Rasputin And The Empress; Wuthering Heights (1939)
MacArthur, James (act, b. 1937): The Bedford Incident
Macartney, Sydney (cin): Transmutations
Macasoli, Anthony (cin): The Bang-Bang Kid
Macat, Julio (cin): The Borrower; Miracle On 34th Street (1994); The Nutty Professor (1996); Out Of The Dark
Macaulay, Charles (act): Blacula, The Bloodless Vampire; The Munsters' Revenge; The Return Of The World's Greatest Detective; Splash; Tower Of London (1962); Twilight People
Macaulay, Jack (act): The Valley Of Fear (1916)
Macaulay, Marc (act): Edward Scissorhands; Matinee
Macaulay, Tony (mus): Are You Dying Young Man?
Macauley, Nancy (act): Galaxina
Macauley, Tom (act): Murder At Scotland Yard
MacBean, L.C. (dir): Trapped By The London Sharks
MacBean, L.C. (wri): The Clue Of The Cigar Band; The Corner House Burglary; The False Wireless; The Hidden Witness; In The Grip Of Spies; The Live Wire; The Mystery Of The Old Mill; The Rajah's Tiara; The Stolen Masterpiece
MacBird, Bonnie (wri): Tron
MacBride, Donald (act, 1894-1957): The Brute Man; Charlie Chan At Treasure Island; The Gracie Allen Murder Case; Here Comes Mr. Jordan; The Invisible Woman (1941); Michael Shayne, Private Detective; Murder Over New York; The Saint's Double Trouble; The Thin Man Goes Home; The Time Of Their Lives; Topper Returns
MacBurnie, John (cin): Daughter Of The Jungle
Maccari, Giuseppe (cin): Shock (1978)
Maccari, Ruggero (wri): Il Diavolo Innamorato
Maccarone, Stefania (act): The Secret Of Seagull Island
MacCarron, Lauretta (act): Empire Of Ash III
MacCloskey, Ysabel (act): The Brotherhood Of Satan
MacColl, Catriona/Katherine (act): The Gates Of Hell; Hawk The Slayer; The House By The Cemetery; 7 Doors Of Death
MacConnachie, Boyd (act): Watchers
MacCorkindale, Simon (act): At The Midnight Hour; Death On The Nile; Jaws 3-D; The Quatermass Conclusion; Robbers Of The Sacred Mountain; The Sword And The Sorcerer
MacDermot, Galt (mus): Rhinoceros (1974)
MacDermott, Marc (act): He Who Gets Slapped
MacDonald, Aimi (act): No. 1 Of The Secret Service; Vampira; Vendetta For The Saint
MacDonald, Bill (act): The Long Kiss Goodnight; Millennium
MacDonald, Braden (act): Lord Of The Flies (1990)
MacDonald, Dan (act): Change Of Mind; The Neptune Factor
MacDonald, David (dir, b. 1905): Alias John Preston; The Bad Lord Byron; Devil Girl From Mars; Double Alibi; The Golden Rabbit; A Lady Mislaid; Law And Disorder; The Lost Hours; The Midas Touch; Tread Softly
MacDonald, Don (mus): Kissed
MacDonald, Donald (act): Lorna Doone (1922)
MacDonald, Edmund (act): Black Friday; Castle In The Desert; Sherlock Holmes In Washington
Macdonald, Glenn (cin): A-Haunting We Will Go
Macdonald, Gordon (act): Brain Damage
MacDonald, Ian (act): Son Of Sinbad
MacDonald, J. Farrell (act, 1875-1952): The Ape Man; The Living Ghost (1942); The Maltese Falcon (1931); Pillow Of Death; Superman And The Mole Men; The Thirteenth Guest; Topper (1937); While Paris Sleeps; Woman Who Came Back
MacDonald, Jeanette (act, 1907-1965): I Married An Angel; Love Me Tonight
MacDonald, John (act): My Bloody Valentine
MacDonald, John D. (wri): Cape Fear (1961 & 1991)
MacDonald, Joseph P./Joe (cin, 1906-1968): Charlie Chan In Rio; It Happens Every Spring; The List Of Adrian Messenger; The Man Who Wouldn't Die; Niagara; On The Threshold Of Space
MacDonald, Kenneth (act): Before I Hang; Confessions Of Boston Blackie; The Devil Commands; Phantom Of The Jungle; The She-Creature
MacDonald, Mac (act): Hardware
MacDonald, Marie (act, 1923-1965, nee Marie Frye): Guest In The House
Macdonald, Nesta (wri): Johnny The Giant Killer
MacDonald, Peter (cin): Solarbabies
MacDonald, Philip (wri): Blind Alley; The Body Snatcher (1945); Charlie Chan In London; Charlie Chan In Paris; Circle Of Danger; The Hour Of 13; The Lost Patrol (1929 & 1934); Love From A Stranger (1947); Mr. Moto's Last Warning; Mr. Moto Takes A Vacation; The Mysterious Mr. Moto; The Mystery Of Mr. X; Ring Of Fear; Tobor The Great; 23 Paces To Baker Street
MacDonald, Robert (cin): Heaven Can Wait (1978); The Night Of The Claw
Macdonald, Roger (wri): Law And Disorder
MacDonald, Scott (act): Fire In The Sky (1993)
MacDonald, Thomas H./Tom (act): Jane Shore (1915); The Lights O' London; London By Night (1913)
MacDonald, Wallace (act, 1891-1978): Darkened Rooms; Drums Of Jeopardy (1931)
MacDonnell, A.G. (wri): Pimpernel Smith
MacDougall, Ranald (dir, b. 1915): The World, The Flesh And The Devil
MacDougall, Ranald (wri, b. 1915): The Decision Of Christopher Blake; The House In The Square; The Naked Jungle; Possessed (1947); Secret Of The Incas; The World, The Flesh And The Devil; The Unsuspected
MacDougall, Robin (act): The Blue Bird (1918)
MacDougall, Roger (wri, b. 1910): The Man In The White Suit; Midnight At Madame Tussaud's; The Mouse That Roared
MacDowell, Andie (act, b. 1958): Greystoke: The Legend Of Tarzan, Lord Of The Apes; Groundhog Day; Michael; Multiplicity
MacDowell, Melbourne (act): Outside The Law
Mace, Borden (wri): Animal Farm
Mace, Glenda (act): I Was A Zombie For The F.B.I.
Mace, Terry (act): Bury Me An Angel
MacEachern, Malcolm (act): Chu Chin Chow (1934)
Macedo, Rita (act): La Maldicion De La Llorona
Macer Jr., Sterling (act): The Beast (1996)
Macero, Teo (mus): Top Secret (1978); Virus
MacFadden, Hamilton (act): The Black Camel; Charlie Chan In Reno; Charlie Chan In Rio; Dressed To Kill (1941); Sleepers West
MacFadden, Hamilton (dir): The Black Camel; Charlie Chan Carries On; Charlie Chan's Greatest Case; Cheaters At Play
MacFarlane, Bruce (act): Totchy Plays With Dynamite
Macfarlane, Peter (wri): F.P. 1 Antwortet Nicht
MacFarquhar, Maisie (act): Macbeth (1971)
Macfayden, Angus (act): Warriors Of Virtue
MacGill, Moyna (act): The Picture Of Dorian Gray (1945)
MacGinnis, Niall (act, b. 1913): The Crimson Circle (1936); The Devil's Agent; East Of Piccadilly; 49th Parallel; Hamlet (1948); Island Of Terror; Jason And The Argonauts; Knights Of The Round Table; The Kremlin Letter; The Man Who Finally Died; Night Of The Demon (1957); The Spy Who Came In From The Cold; Sword Of Sherwood Forest; Tarzan's Greatest Adventure; Torture Garden; The Viking Queen
MacGowan, George (dir): Murder On Flight 502
MacGowran, Jack (act, 1918-1973): Behemoth, The Sea Monster; Captain Clegg; Cul-De-Sac; Darby O'Gill And The Little People; The Exorcist; The Fearless Vampire Killers: or, Pardon Me, But Your Teeth Are In My Neck; King Lear (1970); Vengeance
MacGowran, Tara (act): Memoirs Of A Survivor
MacGrath, Harold (wri): Drums Of Jeopardy (1923 & 1931)
MacGrath, Leueen (act, 1914-1992): The Saint's Vacation
MacGreevy, Oliver (act): The Ipcress File; No. 1 Of The Secret Service; Tales From The Crypt
MacGregor, Andrew (act): Empire Of Ash III
MacGregor, Brian (act): Night Of The Creeps
MacGregor, Hector (act): Stage Fright
MacGregor, John (act): The Wicker Man
MacGregor, Sean (dir): The Horrible House On The Hill
MacGregor, Stacy (act): I, Desire
Machado, Mario (act): Jack's Back; RoboCop; RoboCop 2
Machado, Ricker (act): Vampire On Bikini Beach
Machale, Philip (act): Slugs
Machione, John (act): The Dark Half
Machitani, Masao (act): The Toxic Avenger, Part II
Machowski, Ignacy (act): Milczaca Gwiazda
Macht, Stephen (act): Amityville 1992: It's About Time; Graveyard Shift (1990); The Monster Squad; Nightwing
MacHugh, Doug (act): Alien Nation; House II: The Second Story; Something Is Out There; Weird Science
MacInnes, Angus (act): Judge Dredd; Outland; Spasms
MacInnes, Helen (wri, 1907-1985): Above Suspicion; The Venetian Affair
MacIntosh, Alex (act): The Hidden Face
MacIntosh, Fraser (act): The Boy Cried Murder
MacIntosh, Jay W. (act): Where Have All The People Gone?
MacIntyre, Gandhi (act): The Blood Of Heroes
MacIntyre, Polly (act): Forever Evil
Maciste (act, 1878-1947, nee Bartolomeo Pagano): Maciste
Mack, Allison (act): Unlikely Angel
Mack, Baby (act): The Ghost Talks
Mack, Billy (act): The Black Bird (1926)
Mack, Bob (act): Seven
Mack, Brice (cin): Ruby
Mack, Brice (dir): Jennifer (1978)
Mack, Charles E. (act): One Exciting Night
Mack, Gene (act): Body Parts
Mack, Helen (act, 1913-1986): Mystery Of The White Room; The Return Of Peter Grimm (1934); She (1935); Son Of Kong
Mack, James T. (act): Charlie Chan's Secret
Mack, L.E. (act): Terror (1979)
Mack, Max (dir): Der Andere
Mack, Michael (act): Star Trek: Generations
Mack, Patrick Kelly (act): Blood Diner
Mack, Patty (act): Freejack
Mack, Shelton (act): Congo
Mack, Wayne "V" (act): The Savage Bees
Mack, Wilbur (act): Dick Tracy (1945); Doomed To Die; Mr. Wong, Detective
Mack, Willard (wri): The Monster (1925); Night Of Terror (1933)
Mackay, Angus (act): Quest For Love; Revenge (1971, Gb)
Mackay, Barry (act, b. 1906): A Christmas Carol (1938); Grand National Night; Passing Shadows; The Private Life Of Don Juan; Timeslip
MacKay, Don (act): The Plutonium Incident; The Stepfather
Mackay, Fulton (act, 1922-1987): Nothing But The Night
MacKay, Jeff (act): Midnight Offerings
MacKay, John (act): The Rejuvenator
MacKay, Josie (act): Inn Of The Damned
MacKay, Mark (cin): The Edge Of Hell
MacKay, Michael (act): The Monster Squad
MacKay, Michael Reid (act): Seven
Mackay, Ruth (act): The Woman Who Was Nothing
MacKaye, Norman (act): Fright (1957)
MacKaye, Percy (wri): Puritan Passions
MacKellar, Helen (act): The Gracie Allen Murder Case
Mackendrick, Alexander (dir, b. 1912): A High Wind In Jamaica; The Lady Killers (1956); The Man In The White Suit
Mackendrick, Alexander (wri, b. 1912): The Man In The White Suit
MacKenna, Kenneth (act, 1899-1962): Temple Tower
Mackenzie, Aeneas (wri): The Black Book
Mackenzie, Alastair (act): The Man Who Haunted Himself
Mackenzie, Alex (act): The Three Lives Of Thomasina
MacKenzie, Donald (act): The Mysterious Dr. Fu Manchu
MacKenzie, Evan (act): Children Of The Night
Mackenzie, Hugh (act): The Man Who Haunted Himself
MacKenzie, Jack (cin): Isle Of The Dead (1945); The Jungle Woman; The Return Of Dracula; Zombies On Broadway
MacKenzie, Jimmy (act): The Wicker Man
MacKenzie, Joyce (act): Destination Murder; Tarzan And The She-Devil
Mackenzie, Mary (act): Cloak Without Dagger; Lady In The Fog; Maria Marten: Or, The Murder In The Red Barn (1913); Paris Express; A Stolen Face; Track The Man Down
MacKenzie, Patch (act): Graduation Day; It's Alive III: Island Of The Alive
MacKenzie, Paul (act): The Mcguffin
Mackenzie, Robert (act): Fiend Without A Face; The Woman Eater
Mackenzie, Sam (act): Dragonworld
MacKerall, Vivian (act): Ghost Story (1975)
Mackey, Cynthia (act): RoboCop 2
Mackey, John (cin): The Corpse
Mackhaill, Dorothy (act, 1903-1990): Bits Of Life; Bulldog Drummond At Bay (1937); The Face At The Window (1939)
Mackie, Don (act): Quarantine
Mackie, Iris (act): A Smart Set
Mackie, Lesley (act): The Wicker Man
Mackie, Philip (wri): The Clue Of The New Pin (1961); The Clue Of The Silver Key; Clue Of The Twisted Candle; Man At Carlton Tower; Number Six; Vengeance
MacKillop, Ed (wri): Killdozer
Mackinnon, Allan (wri): The Golden Link; House Of Blackmail; The March Hare; Men Of Sherwood Forest; The Saint's Return; She Shall Have Murder; [illegible] My Enemy
MacKinnon, Derek (act): Terror Train
Mackintosh, Louise (act): The Black Camel

Mackintosh, Mary (act): Discipline
Mackintosh, Steven (act): Treasure Island (1990)
Macklin, Albert (act): Date With An Angel; Daylight
Macklin, David (act): Welcome To Arrow Beach
MacKriel, Peter (act): Murder Motel
MacLachlan, Annie (act): The Presence
MacLachlan, Janet (act): The Boy Who Could Fly; Change Of Mind; Heart And Souls
MacLachlan, Kyle (act, b. 1959): Blue Velvet; Dune; The Flintstones; The Hidden; Roswell; Twin Peaks: Fire Walk With Me
MacLachlan, Ron (act): The Garbage Pail Kids
MacLaine, Marcia (act): Fire In The Sky (1993)
MacLaine, Shirley (act, b. 1934): Around The World In 80 Days; The Possession Of Joel Delaney; The Trouble With Harry
MacLane, Barton (act, 1900-1969): The Adventurous Blonde; Blondes At Work; Crime Doctor's Strangest Case; Cry Of The Werewolf; Dr. Jekyll And Mr. Hyde (1941); Flyaway Baby; The Maltese Falcon (1941); The Mummy's Ghost; Nabonga; The Naked Gun; Smart Blonde; Tarzan And The Amazons; Tarzan And The Huntress; Torchy Blane In Chinatown; Torchy Gets Her Man; Torchy Runs For Mayor; Unknown Island; The Walking Dead
MacLaren, Ivan (act): The Hound Of The Baskervilles (1939)
MacLaren, Mary (act, 1900-1985): The Face In The Fog (1922); The Saint In Palm Springs; The Three Musketeers (1921)
MacLaverty, E. (act): see Breon, Edmond
MacLean, Alistair (wri, 1922-1987): Bear Island; Caravan To Vaccares; Fear Is The Key; The Satan Bug
MacLean, Douglas (act, 1890-1967): Seven Keys To Baldpate (1925)
MacLean, Janet (wri): The Quilt Of Hathor
MacLean, Monica (act): Demon Seed
MacLean, Peter (act): Angel On My Shoulder (1980); Fantasy Island; Midnight Offerings; Squirm
MacLellan, Don (act): The Relic
MacLellan, Elizabeth (act): Crash And Burn; Puppet Master Ii
MacLennan, Andy (act): The Black Bird (1926)
MacLennan, Elizabeth (act): Hands Of The Ripper; The House In Nightmare Park
MacLeod, Robert (act): The Omen; Superman (1978)
MacLiammoir, Michael (act): The Kremlin Letter; What's The Matter With Helen?
MacLise, Hettie (act): Silent Night, Bloody Night
MacMahon, Aline (act, 1899-1991): Guest In The House; House Of Menace; Out Of The Fog (1941)
MacMahon, Paul (act): see Gilbert, Paul
MacManus, Matt (wri): Flight Of The Navigator
MacMillan, Andrew (act): Remo Williams: The Adventure Begins
MacMillan, Kenneth (cin): The Little Match Girl (1987); Of Mice And Men (1992)
MacMillan, Norma (act): The Little Match Girl (1987); Nightmare On The 13th Floor
MacMillan, Violet (act): The Patchwork Girl Of Oz
MacMillan, J.C. (act): The Beggar Girl's Wedding
MacMurray, Fred (act, 1908-1991): Above Suspicion; The Absent-Minded Professor (1961); Beyond The Bermuda Triangle; Charley And The Angel; Fair Wind To Java; Kisses For My President; The Shaggy Dog; Son Of Flubber; The Swarm
MacNamara, Pat (act): Orpheus Descending
MacNaughton, Alan (act): The Double; Frankenstein Created Woman
Macnaughton, Robert (act): E.T-The Extra-Terrestrial
Macnee, Patrick (act, b. 1922): Billion Dollar Threat; The Creature Wasn't Nice; Dead Of Night (1977); Doctors Wear Scarlet; The Elusive Pimpernel (1950); The Fatal Night; Hamlet (1948); The Howling; Jane Eyre (1957); King Solomon's Treasure; The Masque Of The Red Death (1989, Roger Corman/ New World); Matt Helm; The Return Of The Man From U.N.C.L.E.; Sherlock Holmes In New York; Sorry, Wrong Number (1989); Sweet Sixteen; A View To A Kill; Waxwork; Waxwork II: Lost In Time
MacNeil, Carole (act): Shock Chamber
MacNeil, Claudia (act, 1916-1993): Moon Of The Wolf
MacNeill, Peter (act): Body Parts; The Housekeeper
MacNeille, Tress (act): Elvira, Mistress Of The Dark
MacNicol, Peter (act): Addams Family Values; Dracula: Dead And Loving It; Dragon-slayer; Ghostbusters II
Macnow, Marvin (act): Tuck Everlasting
Macollum, Barry (act): Bulldog Drummond Escapes; The Trouble With Harry
Macowan, Norman (act, 1877-1961): City Of The Dead; Footsteps In The Fog; Valley Of The Eagles
Macphail, Angus (wri, b. 1903): Ashes; Busman's Honeymoon; Dead Of Night (1945); Fiddlers Three; The Frightened Lady (1932); The Ghost At St. Michael's; The Ghost Train (1931); Halfway House; The Man They Could Not Arrest; The Man Who Knew Too Much (1956); The Ringer (1931); Spellbound (1945); The Triumph Of The Scarlet Pimpernel; The Wrong Man
Macpherson, Elle (act, b. 1964): Batman And Robin; Jane Eyre (1996)
MacPherson, Glen (cin): Clarence; Doctor Who
Macpherson, Jeannie (wri, 1884-1946): The Road To Yesterday
MacPherson, Stewart (act): The Twenty Questions Murder
MacPherson, Walt (act): The Exorcist III; Serial Mom
MacQuarrie, Albert (act): Don Q, Son Of Zorro
MacQuarrie, Melanie Morse (act): Prom Night
Macrae, Arthur (act): The House Of Opposite (1931); The Oracle (1952); The Saint's Vacation; Silver Blaze (1937)
Macrae, Arthur (wri): Silver Blaze (1937)
MacRae, Bruce (mus): A*P*E*
Macrae, Duncan (act, 1905-1967): Casino Royale; The Woman In Question
MacRae, Elizabeth (act): Everything's Ducky; The House Of The Dead
MacRae, Gordon (act, 1921-1986): Carousel
MacRae, Meredith (act, b. 1945): Earthbound (1981)
MacRae, Michael (act): Coma
MacRauch, Earl 9wri): A Stranger Is Watching
Macready, Erica (act): Count Yorga, Vampire
Macready, George (act, 1909-1973): Alias Nick Beal; The Alligator People; Asylum For A Spy; The Bandit Of Sherwood Forest; The Big Clock; Count Yorga, Vampire; Daughter Of The Mind; Dead Ringer; Down To Earth; Gilda; The Golden Blade; The Green Glove; The Human Duplicators; I Love A Mystery (1945); Night Gallery; The Return Of Count Yorga; The Return Of Monte Cristo; Rogues Of Sherwood Forest; Seven Days In May; Soul Of A Monster; Tarzan's Peril
Macready, Michael (act): Count Yorga, Vampire; The Folks At Red Wolf Inn; Something Evil
Macready, Rene (act): The House Opposite (1931)
Macrenaris, George (act): Scalpel
Maculani, Giulio (act): The Trojan Horse
MacVicar, Martha (act): see Vickers, Martha
MacVittie, Bruce (act): Night Visions
MacWilliams, Bill (act): see Williams, Bill
MacWilliams, Glen (cin): Blue, White And Perfect; Dressed To Kill (1941); Lifeboat; The Return Of Peter Grimm (1926); Rupert Of Hentzau (1923); Shock (1946)
MacWilliams, Paul (act): The Unearthly
Macy, Bill (act, b. 1922): Death At Love House
Macy, Carleton (act): Seven Keys To Baldpate (1929)
Macy, William/W.H. (act): The Cradle Will Fall; Fargo
Madaras, Joszef (act): Howling V: The Rebirth
Maddalena, Julie (act): To Die For
Maddalena, Marianne (act): Wes Craven's New Nightmare
Maddalena, Renato (act): Robin Hood And The Pirates
Madden, Bill (act): I'm Dangerous Tonight
Madden, Cassie (act): I Was A Teenage Zombie
Madden, Ciaran (act): The Beast Must Die; Gawain And The Green Knight
Madden, Doreen (act): Gideon's Day
Madden, Harry (act): Goodbye Charlie
Madden, Lee (dir): Night Creature; The Night God Screamed
Madden, Lee (wri): Night Creature
Madden, Peter (act, b. 1910): Counterblast; Dr. Terror's House Of Horrors (1964); Fiend Without A Face; Floods Of Fear; Frankenstein And The Monster From Hell; Frankenstein Created Woman; From Russia With Love; Kiss Of The Vampire; One Of Our Dinosaurs Is Missing; The Private Life Of Sherlock Holmes; The Road To Hong Kong; Woman Of Straw
Madden, Tom(my) (act): The Majorettes; Swamp Thing
Maddern, Victor (act, b. 1926): Blood Of The Vampire; Bunny Lake Is Missing; Carry On Spying; Chitty Chitty Bang Bang; Circus Of Fear; Digby-The Biggest Dog In The World; Face In The Night; Footsteps In The Fog; The Last Man To Hang?; Pool Of London; Street Of Shadows; Talk Of The Devil; Uncharted Seas
Maddin, Guy (dir): Careful
Maddock, Brent (wri): *Batteries Not Included; Ghost Dad; Heart And Souls; Short Circuit; Short Circuit 2; Tremors
Maddow, Ben (wri, 1909-1992): The Balcony; The Mephisto Waltz; Shadow In The Sky
Maddox Jr., Dean (act): It Came From Beneath The Sea
Maddox, Diana (wri): The Changeling
Madero, Robert (wru): Mausoleum
Madigan, Amy (act): The Dark Half; The Day After
Madigan, Paul (act): Waxwork II: Lost In Time
Madigan, Sharon (act): Invasion Of The Bee Girls
Madison (act): Daylight
Madison, Cleo (act): Black Orchids
Madison, Ellen (act): Goldstein
Madison, Guy (act, 1922-1996, nee Robert Moseley): Adventurer Of Tortuga; The Bang-Bang Kid; The Beast Of Hollow Mountain; The Mystery Of Thug Island; On The Threshold Of Space; Sandokan Against The Leopard Of Sarawak; Sandokan Fights Back; Superargo E I Giganti Senza Volto; Sword Of The Conqueror; Women Of Devil's Island
Madison, John (act): Young Frankenstein
Madison, Julian (act): Dick Tracy's G-Men
Madison, Leigh (act): Behemoth, The Sea Monster
Madison, Mae (act): The Mad Genius
Madison, Noel (act, 1898-1975, nee Noel Moscovitch): The Black Raven; Charlie Chan In City In Darkness; Desperate Chance For Ellery Queen; Ellery Queen's Penthouse Mystery; The Gentleman From Nowhere; The Man Who Made Diamonds; Secret Agent Of Japan
Madison, Rock (act): Creature Of The Walking Dead; Man Beast
Madison, Virginia (act): A Blind Bargain
Madoc, Philip (act): Berserk; Daleks' Invasion Earth 2150 A.D.; Dr. Jekyll And Sister Hyde; The Quiller Memorandum
Madonna (act, b. 1960): Dick Tracy (1990)
Madorsky, Bryan (act): Parents
Madrid, Jose Luis (dir): El Vampiro De La Utopista
Madrid, Miguel (dir & wri): Necrophagus
Madsen, David (wri): Copycat
Madsen, Forrest Holger (act & wri, 1878-1943): Sherlock Holmes (1909)
Madsen, Forrest Holger (dir, 1878-1943): Himmelskibet; Sherlock Holmes (1909); Spirits
Madsen, Harry (act): Too Scared To Scream; The Wiz
Madsen, Michael (act): A House In The Hills; Species
Madsen, Virginia (act, b. 1961): Candyman; Creator; Dune; Electric Dreams; Gotham; Highlander 2: The Quickening; The Prophecy (1995); Zombie High
Maduzia, Brenda (act): Student Bodies
Maeba, Berbay (act): Son Of Godzilla
Maeder, Jay (act): Shock Waves
Maesso, Joe (wri): The Cauldron Of Death
Maeterlinck, Maurice (wri, 1862-1949): The Blue Bird (1910, 1918, 1940 & 1976)
Maetzig, Kurt (dir & wri, b. 1911): Milczaca Gwiazda
Maffei, Buck (act): Atlantis, The Lost Continent
Maffei, Joe (act): Empire Of Ash III
Maffia, Roma (act): Eraser
Magar, Guy (act & wri): Retribution (1988)
Magar, Guy (dir): Retribution (1988); Stepfather III: Father's Day
Magder, Zale (cin): The Sins Of Dorian Gray
Magee, Ken (act): The Relic
Magee, Patrick (act, 1924-1982): —And Now The Screaming Starts!; Asylum; Beware, My Brethren; The Black Cat (1980); A Clockwork Orange; Dementia 13; Demons Of The Mind; The Fiend (1972); Hawk The Slayer; King Lear (1970); The Last Days Of Man On Earth; The Masque Of The Red Death (1964); The Monster Club; Monster Of Terror; The Persecution And Assassination Of Jean-Paul Marat As Performed By The Inmates Of The Asylum Of Charenton Under The Direction Of The Marquis De Sade; Portrait In Terror; Seance On A Wet Afternoon; The Servant; The Skull; Sleep Of Death; Tales From The Crypt; The Trojan Women; The Very Edge
Magerman, William (act): Stigma
Magestretti, Adriano (act): Quelqu'un Derriere La Porte
Maggart, Brandon (act): Dressed To Kill (1980)
Maggi, Luigi (dir, 1867-1946): Gli Ultimi Giorni Di Pompei
Maggio, Dante (act): David And Goliath
Maggio, Nicole (act): Pumpkinhead II: Blood Wings
Maggio, Pupella (act): Amarcord; The Bible
Magid, Paul David (act): The Jewel Of The Nile
Magidow, Aaron (act): Seconds
Magliochetti, Al (act): Spookies
Magliochetti, Al (cin): Frankenhooker; Jason Goes To Hell: The Final Friday
Magnani, Anna (act, 1908-1973): The Fugitive Kind; Il Miracolo
Magner, Jack (act): Amityville II: The Possession; Firestarter
Magness, Kerry (wri): Night Of The Cobra Woman
Magnus, Edythe (act): The Alien's Return
Magnus, Robert M. (act): The Alien's Return
Magnuson, Ann (act): Making Mr. Right; The Munsters' Scary Little Christmas; Sleepwalk
Magoon, Brian (act): Raiders Of The Living Dead
Magoon, Greg (act): Raiders Of The Living Dead
Magrill, George (act): The Chance Of A Lifetime; Dick Tracy (1945); Meet Boston Blackie; Mr. Moto In Danger Island; The Phantom Thief
Maguire, Charles H. (cin): Audrey Rose
Maguire, George (act): Heart And Souls
Maguire, Jack (act): Theater Of Blood
Maguire, Leo (act): Kadoyng
Maguire, Leo (wri): The Flying Sorceror; Kadoyng
Maguire, Leonard (act): The Awakening
Maguire, Mary (act): The Mysterious Mr. Moto
Maguire, Rick (cin): The Lottery
Maguire, Thomas F. (act): Spellbinder
Maguire, Tom (act): The Savage
Magwili, Dom (act): Ghost In The Machine
Mahaffy, Blanche (act): Devil Monster
Mahal, Camillia (act): Empire Of Ash III
Mahaney, Matthew (act): Eraser
Maharis, George (act, b. 1928): Look What's Happened To Rosemary's Baby; Murder Is A One-Act Play; Murder On Flight 502; Return To Fantasy Island; The Satan Bug; The Sword And The Sorcerer
Maher, Bill (act): House II: The Second Story
Maher, Christopher (act): Mannequin
Maher, Joseph (act): Heaven Can Wait (1978); Mars Attacks!; My Stepmother Is An Alien; The Shadow (1994); Time After Time
Maher, Nora (act): Street Trash
Maher, Terry (cin): Licensed To Kill
Maher, Wally (act): Mystery Street; Nick Carter, Master Detective
Mahin, John Lee (wri, b. 1902): The Bad Seed (1956); Dr. Jekyll And Mr. Hyde (1941); Moment To Moment; Treasure Island (1934)
Mahl, Fiona (act): The Island Of Dr. Moreau (1996)
Mahmoud, Abdullah (act): Sphinx (1981)
Mahn, Paul (act): The Angry Red Planet
Mahon, Anthony (wri): The Premonition (1975)
Mahon, Barry (dir, b. 1921): The Beast That Killed Women; Rocket Attack U.S.A.; The Wonderful Land Of Oz
Mahon, Barry (wri, b. 1921): The Beast That Killed Women
Mahon, John (act): The People Under The Stairs; Someone's Watching Me!
Mahon, Peggy (act): Funeral Home
Mahoney, Jock (act, 1919-1989, nee Jacques O'Mahoney): I've Lived Before; The Land Unknown; Moro Witch Doctor; Tarzan Goes To India; Tarzan's Deadly Silence; Tarzan's Three Challenges; Tarzan The Magnificent
Mahoney, John (act): The Manhattan Project; Primal Fear
Mahoney, Louis (act): The Final Conflict; The Plague Of The Zombies; Prehistoric Women (1966)
Mahoney, Mike (act): Rear Window
Mahoney, Pat (act): Endangered Species
Mahoney, Richard (wri): House Of The Black Death
Mahoney, Victoria (act): Switch
Mahor, Maria (act): El Principe Encadenado
Mahree, Diane (act): Manos, The Hands Of Fate

Mai, Anna (act): Koroshi
Mai, Larissa (act): Empire Of Ash III
Maibaum, Paul (cin): Phoenix The Warrior
Maibaum, Richard (wri, 1909-1991): Diamonds Are Forever; Dr. No; For Your Eyes Only; From Russia With Love; Goldfinger; Licence To Kill (1989); The Living Daylights; The Man Inside; The Man With The Golden Gun; Octopussy; On Her Majesty's Secret Service; S*H*E (1980); The Spy Who Loved Me; Thunderball; A View To A Kill
Maiden, Cecil (wri): Blind Man's Bluff (1936); Cult Of The Cobra
Maiden, Tony (act): Outer Touch
Maidera, Roberto (act): The Night Evelyn Came Out Of The Grave
Maiello, Dana (act): The Majorettes
Maien, Michael (act): Mark Of The Devil (1972)
Maier, Tim (act): Psycho II
Maierhouser, Joe (act): The Incredible Petrified World
Mailes, Charles H./Hill (act): The Man From Downing Street; The Mark Of Zorro (1920); Murder By Television
Mailfort, Maxence (act): The Murders In The Rue Morgue (1986)
Maillet, Jacques (cin): La Brulure De Mille Soleils
Mailleux, Marie-Paul (act): Symptoms
Main, Laurie (act): On A Clear Day You Can See Forever; Time After Time; Wicked Stepmother
Main, Marjorie (act, 1890-1975, nee Marie Tomlinson Krebs): Another Thin Man; Heaven Can Wait (1942)
Main, Natalie (act): Hellhole
Mainardi, Elisa (act): Satyricon
Maine, Charles Eric (wri, b. 1921): The Mind Of Mr. Soames; Spaceways; Timeslip; Zex
Maini, Al (act): Spasms
Mainprize, James (act): Hitler's Daughter; Millennium
Mains, Laurie (act): Tarzan, The Ape Man (1981)
Mainwaring, Bernerd (dir): The Crimson Candle
Mainwaring, Bernerd (wri): Whispering Tongues
Mainwaring, Daniel (wri): Atlantis, The Lost Continent; Catacombs; Invasion Of The Body Snatchers (1956); The Minotaur; Space Master X-7
Maio, John (act): The Last Starfighter
Maioletti, Gianfranco (cin): Burial Ground
Mair, Jimmy (act): The Phoenix (1981)
Mair, Karen (act): The Pink Chiquitas
Maitland, Christine (act): Desire
Maitland, Colin (act): The Bedford Incident
Maitland, Lauderdale (act): The Beggar Girl's Wedding; What's Bred...Comes Out In The Flesh
Maitland, Marne (act, b. 1920): The Camp On Blood Island; First Men In The Moon (1964); The Golden Mask; Hour Of Decision; Journey To Midnight; The Man With The Golden Gun; Master Spy; The Phantom Of The Opera (1962); The Reptile; The Return Of Mr. Moto; Saadia; The Stranglers Of Bombay; Svengali (1954); The Terror Of The Tongs
Maitland, Ruth (act): At The Villa Rose (1939); Where The Rainbow Ends
Maiuri, Dino (wri): Diabolik; Kiss The Girls And Make Them Die
Majan, Juan (act): Slugs
Majano, Anton Giulio (dir): Atom Age Vampire
Majano, A.G. (Anton Giulio) (wri): Atom Age Vampire
Majer, peter (act): Goldeneye
Majeroni, Mario (act): The Face In The Fog (1922)
Majewski, Hans-Martin (mus): Brainwashed
Majlioni, Mario (act): The Face In The Fog (1922)
Major, Bessie (act): Kismet (1914)
Major, Carl (act): Alien Contamination
Major, David (act): The Plutonium Incident; Threads
Majorino, Tina (act): Waterworld
Majors, lee (act, b. 1940): Bionic Showdown: The Six Million Dollar Man And The Bionic Woman; Killer Fish; The Last Chase; The Norsemen; The Return Of The Six Million Dollar Man And The Bionic Woman; The Six Million Dollar Man; Starflight: The Plane That Couldn't Land
Majors II, Lee (act): Bionic Showdown: The Six Million Dollar Man And The Bionic Woman; Ice Cream Man; The Return Of The Six Million Dollar Man And The Bionic Woman
Majos, Karl (mus): Charlie Chan In The Secret Service
Makaj, Stephen (act): It (1990)
Makan, Moti (act): Venom (1982)
Makaro, J.J. (act): Timecop
Makavejev, Dusan (dir & wri, b. 1932): Sweet Movie
Makeham, Eliot (act, 1882-1956): Busman's Honeymoon; Candles At Nine; The Clairvoyant (1934); The Crimson Candle; The Crimson Pirate; Dark Journey; Forbidden; Forging Ahead; Gestapo; Halfway House; I'm An Explosive; I Was A Spy; Murder At The Windmill; Once In A New Moon; Scarlet Thread; Scrooge (1951); The Yellow Balloon
Makel, Joseph F. (act): Heaven Can Wait (1978)
Makepeace, Chris(topher) (act, b. 1964): The Last Chase; The Mysterious Stranger; Rona Jaffe's Mazes And Monsters; Vamp
Makichuk, James (dir & wri): The Tower
Makin, Harry (cin): The Neptune Factor
Makin, William J./W.J. (wri): Murder At Covent Garden; The Return Of Dr. X
Maklakiewicz, Zdzislaw (act): Rekopis Znaleziony W Saragossie
Mako (act): Conan The Barbarian; Conan The Destroyer; Highlander: The Final Dimension; The Island At The Top Of The World; Pacific Heights
Maksimovich, Alec (act): Howling III
Makuszynski, K. (wri): O Dwoch Takich Co Ukradli Ksiezyc
Maky, Thony (act): Tomb Of Torture
Mala, (Ray) (act, 1906-1952): Lost Island Of Kioga; The Mad Doctor Of Market Street
Malacrida, Dino (act): Morgan The Pirate
Malahide, Patrick (act): Cutthroat Island; The Long Kiss Goodnight
Malakian, Achod (dir): see Verneuil, Henri
Malamud, Bernard (wri, 1914-1986): The Angel Levine
Malandrinos, Andreas (act): The Fearless Vampire Killers Or: Pardon Me, But Your Teeth Are In My Neck; The Magus; The Mummy's Shroud; On Secret Service; The Secret Agent (1936)
Malang (act): Congo
Malanga, Gerard (act): The Iliac Passion
Malatesta, Fred (act): The Thin Man
Malatesta, Guido (dir): Colossus And The Headhunters; Goliath Against The Giants
Malatesta, Guido (wri): Zorro Contro Maciste
Malatesta, Luigi (mus): Scream Of The Demon Lover
Malave, Chu Chu (act): A Force Of One
Malawski, Z. (act): Wielka, Wielka I Najwieksza
Malco, Paolo (act): Escape From The Bronx; The House By The Cemetery
Malcolm, Chris(topher) (act): Highlander; Shock Treatment! (1981); The Spiral Staircase (1975)
Malcolm, Doris (act): Oh Heavenly Dog
Malcolm, John (act): The House That Dripped Blood; Where Has Poor Mickey Gone?
Malczewska, Phillips (act): The Keeper
Malden, Karl (act, b. 1912, nee Mladen Sekulovich): Alice In Wonderland (1985); Beyond The Poseidon Adventure; Billion Dollar Brain; The Cat O' Nine Tails; Dead Ringer; I Confess; Meteor; Murderers' Row; Operation Secret; Phantom Of The Rue Morgue
Maldonado, Guillermo (act): Dr. Tarr's Torture Dungeon
Malet, Arthur (act): Beastmaster 2: Through The Portal Of Time; Dick Tracy (1990); Halloween; Heaven Can Wait (1978); The Hound Of The Baskervilles (1972); Mary Poppins; Oh, God! You Devil; The Secret Of Nimh; Vanishing Point; Young Frankenstein
Maley, Alan (cin): Bedknobs And Broomsticks
Maley, Gloria (wri): Inseminoid
Maley, Nick (wri): Inseminoid
Maley, Peggy (act): Indestructible Man
Malfatti, Marina (act): C'era Una Volta; Deborah; Demons Of The Dead; The Night Evelyn Came Out Of The Grave
Maliaros, Vasiliki (act): The Exorcist
Maligny, H. (act): The Corner House Burglary
Malik, Art (act): A Kid In King Arthur's Court; The Living Daylights; Transmutations
Malik, Athar (act): Arabian Adventure
Malik, Roger (act): The Village Of The Damned (1960)
Malikyan, Kevork (act): Indiana Jones And The Last Crusade; The Man Who Haunted Himself; Sphinx (1981)
Malin, Bill (act): Lifeforce
Malin, Emma Griffiths (act): Mary Reilly
Malin, Kym (act): Weird Science
Malina, Judith (act): The Addams Family
Malinda, Jim (act): Party Line
Malinger, Ross (act): Eve Of Destruction; Late For Dinner
Malins, Geoffrey H. (dir): Bluff; The Girl From Downing Street; The Golden Web
Malins, Geoffrey H. (wri): The Girl From Downing Street
Malis, Adele (act): Kingdom Of The Spiders
Malis, Claire (act): Cry For The Strangers
Malivoire Productions (cin): Deadly Eyes
Malken, Jack (mus): The Nesting
Malkiewicz, Lisa (act): Ed Wood
Malkin, Sam (act): Dead Of Winter
Malkovich, John (act, b. 1954): The Convent; Making Mr. Right; The Man In The Iron Mask (1998); Mary Reilly; Of Mice And Men (1992)
Mall, Paul (act): Flight Of The Navigator
Mallaber, Gary (act): Phantom Of The Paradise
Mallalieu, Aubrey (act): The Bad Lord Byron; The Black Tulip (1937); Bulldog Sees It Through; Busman's Honeymoon; The Claydon Treasure Mystery; Dead Men Are Dangerous; The Demon Barber Of Fleet Street; The Door With Seven Locks (1940); The Face At The Window (1939); The Fatal Night; The Gables Mystery; I Killed The Count; Miracles Do Happen; Murder In Reverse; Pimpernel Smith; A Place Of One's Own; The Return Of The Frog
Mallard, Bart (act): I Was A Zombie For The F.B.I.
Malle, Louis (dir & wri, 1932-1995): Black Moon (1975); Frantic; Spirits Of The Dead
Malleson, Miles (act, 1888-1969): Brides Of Dracula; Dead Of Night (1945); First Men In The Moon (1964); Fury At Smugglers' Bay; Gideon's Day; The Hell-Fire Club; Horror Of Dracula; The Hound Of The Baskervilles (1959); Kind Hearts And Coronets; Knight Without Armour; The Man In The White Suit; The Mark Of Cain; Peeping Tom; The Perfect Woman; The Phantom Of The Opera (1962); The Queen Of Spades (1948); Scrooge (1951); The Sign Of Four (1932); Stage Fright; The Thief Of Bagdad (1940); The 39 Steps (1935); Thunder Rock; Trent's Last Case (1952); Venetian Bird; Vengeance
Malleson, Miles (wri, 1888-1969): Spellbound (1941); Strange Evidence; The Thief Of Bagdad (1940); The Yellow Mask
Mallet, Jane (act): Sweet Movie
Mallet, Odile (act): The City Of Lost Children
Mallett, Tania (act): Goldfinger
Mallia, Victor (act): The Keeper
Mallinger, Dan (act): Jack's Wife
Mallinson, Rory (act): Cry Wolf (1947); The Docks Of New Orleans; Killer Ape; Killer Leopard; Possessed (1947); Safari Drums
Mallo, Santiago (act): Amazons (1986)
Mallon, Dan (act): The Baby
Mallon, Jim (act & dir): Mystery Science Theater 3000: The Movie
Mallone, Wil (mus): Deathline
Mallory, Barbara (act): Is This Trip Really Necessary?
Mallory, Carole (act): The Stepford Wives
Mallory, Edward (act): The Underwater City
Mallory, Shawn (act): Sherlock Holmes In New York
Mallott, Yolande (act): The Devil Bat
Malloy, Dan (act): The Phantom Empire
Mally, Leo (act): Das Schloss
Malmerfelt, Sixten (act): The Story Of Gosta Berling
Malmsten, Birger (act, b. 1920): The Devil's Wanton; Tystnaden
Malmuth, Bruce (dir): The Man Who Wasn't There
Malneck, Matty (mus): The Gracie Allen Murder Case
Malnik, Susie (act): The Funhouse (1981)
Malo, Gina (act, 1909-1963, nee Janet Flynn): The Door With Seven Locks (1940); The Private Life Of Don Juan
Malof, Peter (act): The Initiation
Malolepsy, Jennifer (act): I Was A Zombie For The F.B.I.
Melolepsy, Paul (act): I Was A Zombie For The F.B.I.
Malone, Angus (act): Razorback
Malone, Bill (dir & wri): see Malone, William/Bill
Malone, Dorothy (act, b. 1925, a.k.a. Dorothy Maloney): The Being; The Big Sleep (1946); The Falcon And The Co-Eds; Man Of A Thousand Faces; One Mysterious Night; Rest In Pieces; Scared Stiff (1953); [illegible]
Malone, Joel (wri): Appointment With Murder
Malone, Mark (act & wri): Dead Of Winter
Malone, Micki (act): Weekend Of Fear
Malone, Mike (act): Schizopolis
Malone, Nancy (act): Fright (1957)
Malone, Tony (act): Trancers
Malone, William (act): The Incredible Hulk Returns; Scared To Death (1980)
Malone, William/Bill (dir & wri): Creature; Scared To Death (1980)
Maloney, Coleen (act): Eve Of Destruction
Maloney, Dorothy (act): see Malone, Dorothy
Maloney, Jack (act): King Kong Lives
Maloney, Marc (act): Anguish
Maloney, Michael (act): Hamlet (1990)
Maloney, Peter (act): The Children; Revenge Of The Stepford Wives; Sanctuary Of Fear; Thinner
Malory, Sir Thomas (wri, fl. 1470): Knights Of The Round Table
Malotte, Albert Hay (mus): Dr. Cyclops; The Enchanted Forest
Malovic, Steve (act): America 3000
Malpas, Howard (act): Killer Klowns From Outer Space
Malson, Linda (act): The Green Slime
Maltagliati, Evi (act): Ulysses
Maltby, David (act): Oh Heavenly Dog
Maltby, H.F. (act): Young And Innocent
Maltby, H.F. (wri): Crimes At The Dark House; The Crimes Of Stephen Hawke; The Demon Barber Of Fleet Street; The Howard Case
Maltin, Leonard (act): Gremlins 2: The New Batch
Maltz, Albert (wri, 1908-1985): Cloak And Dagger (1946)
Malvern, Paul (dir): The House Of Mystery (1931)
Malwee, Steve (act): I Was A Zombie For The F.B.I.
Malyon, Eily (act): Above Suspicion; The Challenge; Dracula's Daughter; The Florentine Dagger; Great Expectations (1934); The Hound Of The Baskervilles (1939); Night Must Fall (1937); On Borrowed Time; She-Wolf Of London; The Undying Monster
Mamakos, Peter (act): The Adventures Of Hajji Baba; The Bandits Of Corsica; Between Midnight And Dawn; I Love A Mystery (1966); The Resurrection Of Zachary Wheeler; Sabu And The Magic Ring
Mamches, Valerie (act): Children Shouldn't Play With Dead Things
Mamo, John (act): Confessions Of An Opium Eater
Mamoulian, Rouben (dir, 1897-1987): Dr. Jekyll And Mr. Hyde (1932); Love Me Tonight; The Mark Of Zorro (1940)
Man, David (act): The Ivory Ape; Westworld
Man, Frankie (act): All That Jazz
Manabe, Riichiro (mus): Godzilla vs. The Smog Monster
Manahan, Anna (act): Clash Of The Titans; The Viking Queen
Manahan, Sheila (act): Footsteps In The Fog; Seven Days To Noon
Manakaze, Yoko (act): The Vampire Doll
Manard, Biff (act): The Flash; Shanks; Trancers; Trancers II: The Return Of Jack Deth; Zone Troopers
Manaster, Benjamin (dir & wri): Goldstein
Manca, Alberto (wri): Gli Amori Di Ercole
Manceri, Patricia (act): Target...Earth?
Manchester, Michael (act): Witchery
Mancina, Mark (mus): Twister
Mancini, Al (act): Baffled!; Madame Sin
Mancini, Carla (act): The Black Belly Of The Tarantula; Demons Of The Dead; Frankenstein (1974)
Mancini, Don (wri): Child's Play (1988); Child's Play 2; Child's Play 3
Mancini, Henry (mus, 1924-1994): Condorman; Experiment In Terror; Ghost Dad; Lifeforce; Moment To Moment; The Night Visitor; Nightwing; The Prisoner Of Zenda (1979); Santa Claus (1985); Switch; Without A Clue
Mancini, Mario (cin): El Castello Dell'orrore
Mancini, Michael (act): The Gifted One
Mancini, Ray "Boom Boom" (act): Mutants In Paradise
Mancini, Ric (act): Ed Wood; Friday The 13th-Part V: A New Beginning
Mancori, Alvaro (cin): Ulysses Against The Son Of Hercules
Mancori, Guglielmo (cin): Manhattan Baby; Murder Mansion
Mancori, Sandro (cin): Hunters Of The Golden Cobra; She (1983); Yeti
Mancuso, Didi (act): The Toxic Avenger, Part II
Mancuso, Kevin (dir): 2020 Texas Gladiators

Mancuso, Nick (act): Death Ship; Dr. Scorpion; The Ex; Marquis De Sade; Nightwing; Once You Meet A Stranger; Past Perfect
Mandan, Robert (act): The Magician (1973); Zapped!
Mandaville, Michael (act): Pumpkinhead II: Blood Wings
Mandel, Babaloo (wri): Multiplicity; Splash; Vibes
Mandel, Howie (act): Gremlins 2: The New Batch; Little Monsters
Mandel, Johnny (mus): Agatha; Brenda Starr (1992); Escape To Witch Mountain; Pretty Poison (1968); W
Mandel, Joseph (dir): see May, Joe
Mandel, Loring (wri): Countdown
Mandel, Rena (act): Vampyr
Mandel, Robert (dir): The Haunted (1991)
Mandel, Suzy (act): The Playbirds
Mandelik, Gil (act): Project X (1987)
Mandell, Pamela (act): Superman Ii
Mandell, Peter (act): Xtro
Mandell, Robyn (act): Supergirl (1984)
Mander, Lionel (act): see Mander, Miles
Mander, Miles (act, 1888-1946, nee Lionel Mander): The Bandit Of Sherwood Forest; The Brighton Strangler; Crime Doctor's Warning; The House Of The Seven Gables; The Man In The Iron Mask (1939); The Missing Rembrandt; Murder, My Sweet; The Pearl Of Death; Phantom Of The Opera (1943); The Picture Of Dorian Gray (1945); The Return Of The Vampire; The Scarlet Claw; Tarzan's New York Adventure; The Three Musketeers (1939); Tower Of London (1939); Wuthering Heights (1939)
Mander, Miles (wri, 1888-1946): The Lodger (1932)
Mander, Tony (cin): Only A Scream Away
Manderville, Mike (act): Zone Troopers
Mandon, Jeff (act): Serial Mom
Mandre, Joyce (act): Cry Of The Banshee
Mandylor, Costas (act): Last Exit To Earth; Virtuosity
Manesh, Marshall (act): Kazaam
Maness, Sherman (act): Rabid
Manette (mus): Fright (1971)
Maney, Virginia P. (act): Nightwing
Manfredi, Nino (act, b. 1921): Italian Secret Service; Not On Your Life!
Manfredini, Harry (mus): Cameron's Closet; The Children; Deepstar Six; Friday The 13th (1980); Friday The 13th-Part 2; Friday The 13th-Part 3; Friday The 13th-The Final Chapter; Friday The 13th-Part V: A New Beginning; Friday The 13th, Part Vi: Jason Lives; Friday The 13th, Part VII-The New Blood; The Hills Have Eyes II; House; House Ii: The Second Story; Jason Goes To Hell: The Final Friday; The Kirlian Witness; Slaughter High; Swamp Thing; Zombie Island Massacre
Mangan, Kevin (act): Mars Attacks!
Mangano, Silvana (act, 1930-1989): Black Magic (1949); Il Disco Volante; Dune; Edipo Re; Ulysses
Mangano, Vittorio (act): Deborah
Manget, Patricia (act): Anguish
Mangine, Joseph/Joe (cin): Alligator (1981); Alone In The Dark; Mother's Day; Neon Maniacs; Squirm; The Sword And The Sorcerer
Mangine, Joseph (dir): Neon Maniacs
Mangini, Alda (act): Ok, Nero!
Mangini, Gino (wri): David And Goliath; Il Terror Dei Barberi
Mangione, Giuseppe (wri): Hipnosis; The Queen Of Babylon
Mango, Alec (act): The Golden Mask; Gothic; The Man Inside; The Playbirds; The 7th Voyage Of Sinbad; The Strange World Of Planet X; The Three Worlds Of Gulliver
Mangon, Alf (act): Dragonslayer
Mangrane, Daniel (dir & wri): Parsifal
Manheim, Camryn (act): Eraser
Maniaci, Jim (act): Cyber-Tracker; Cybertracker 2; The Silence Of The Hams
Manikum, Phillip (act): Corruption
Maning, Monroe (wri): La Cara Del Terror
Manion, Cindy (act): The Toxic Avenger
Mankerius, James (act): Glen And Randa
Mankiewicz, Christopher (act): Eraser
Mankiewicz, Don (M.) (wri): The Black Bird (1975); Sanctuary Of Fear
Mankiewicz, Herman J. (wri, 1897-1953): The Enchanted Cottage (1945); The Lost Squadron; The Road To Mandalay
Mankiewicz, Joseph L. (dir, 1909-1993): Dragonwyck; The Ghost And Mrs. Muir; Sleuth; Suddenly Last Summer
Mankiewicz, Joseph L. (wri, 1909-1993): Alice In Wonderland (1933)
Mankiewicz, Tom (wri): Diamonds Are Forever; Ladyhawke; Live And Let Die; The Man With The Golden Gun
Mankofsky, Isidore (cin): Ewoks: The Battle For Endor; Midnight Lace (1981); Scream, Blacula, Scream
Mankowitz, Wolf (wri, b. 1924): The Bespoke Overcoat; Casino Royale; The Day The Earth Caught Fire; A Kid For Two Farthings; Treasure Island (1971); The Two Faces Of Dr. Jekyll; Where The Spies Are
Manku, Vivianne (act): Confessions Of An Opium Eater
Mankuma, Bill (act): The Little Match Girl (1987)
Mankuma, Blu (act): Mortal Sins; The Plutonium Incident; The Stepfather; Watchers
Manley, Stephen (act): Star Trek III: The Search For Spock
Manlove, Dudley (act): Plan 9 From Outer Space
Mann, Alex (act): I Drink Your Blood
Mann, Andrew (act): Not Guilty
Mann, Anthony (dir, 1906-1967): The Black Book; A Dandy In Aspic
Mann, Brian (act): School Spirit
Mann, Chris (act): Hitler's Daughter
Mann, Colin (act): Quelqu'un Derriere La Porte
Mann, Daniel (dir, 1912-1991): Journey Into Fear (1975); Our Man Flint; Willard
Mann, Danny (act): Little Nemo: Adventures In Slumberland
Mann, Dave (act): The Neptune Factor
Mann, Delbert (dir, b. 1920): Jane Eyre (1970); She Waits
Mann, Dolores (act): The Munsters' Revenge
Mann, Edward (dir): see Alcocer, S.
Mann, Ed(ward) (Andrew) (wri): Cauldron Of Blood; Island Of Terror; The Killer Inside Me; The Mutations; Seizure
Mann, Eric (act): El Castello Dell'orrore
Mann, Farhad (dir & wri): Lawnmower Man 2: Beyond Cyberspace
Mann, Hank (act, 1887-1971): Dr. Jekyll And Mr. Hyde (1920, Arrow); The Maltese Falcon (1941); Man Of A Thousand Faces; Modern Times; Two Lost Worlds
Mann, Helen (act): Just Imagine
Mann, Hummie (mus): Dracula: Dead And Loving It; Robin Hood: Men In Tights
Mann, Jane (wri): Anatomy Of A Psycho
Mann, Kris (act): Slugs
Mann, Larry (D.) (act): Charley And The Angel; Dead Men Tell No Tales; Do Not Fold, Spindle Or Mutilate; The Octagon; Willy Mcbean And His Magic Machine
Mann, Laura (act): Phantasm
Mann, Leonard (act): Flowers In The Attic; The Humanoid; Night School; Silent Night, Deadly Night Ii
Mann, Leslie (act): The Cable Guy; George Of The Jungle
Mann, Manfred (mus): Paroxysmus
Mann, Margaret (act): Charlie Chan In London
Mann, Maryke (act): Strange Behavior
Mann, Michael (act): The China Syndrome
Mann, Michael (dir & wri): The Keep
Mann, Ned (cin, 1893-1967):. Beyond Tomorrow; The Man Who Could Work Miracles; Things To Come
Mann, Norman (act): The Plague Of The Zombies; Venom (1982)
Mann, Peter (act): The Sword Of Ali Baba
Mann, Sam (act): Hard Rock Zombies; Roller Blade Warriors: Taken By Force
Mann, Sheri (act): Mausoleum
Mann, Stanley (wri): Circle Of Iron; The Collector; Conan The Destroyer; Damien-Omen II; Firestarter; A High Wind In Jamaica; Meteor; The Mouse That Roared; Woman Of Straw
Mann, Terrence (act): Critters; Critters 2: The Main Course; Light Years; Mrs. Santa ClausMann, Traci (act): The Toxic Avenger, Part II
Mann, Wesley (act): My Stepmother Is An Alien
Mann, Yanka (act): Flesh Feast
Mannen, Monique (act): The Fear (1994)
Mannering, Cecil (act): The Valley Of Fear (1916)
Mannering, Lewin (act): Gipsy Blood
Manners, David (act, b. 1902, nee Rauff de Ryther Duan Acklom): The Black Cat (1934); The Death Kiss; Dracula (1931, English-Speaking Version); Kismet (1930); The Mummy (1932); The Mystery Of Edwin Drood (1935); Roman Scandals
Manners, John (act): The Ghost Train (1927)
Manners, Marjorie (act): The Fairy Doll
Manners, Mary (act): Eugene Aram; The Smugglers' Cave
Mannheim, Lucie (act, b. 1905): Bunny Lake Is Missing; Confess, Dr. Corda; Paris Express; Der Steinerne Reiter; The 39 Steps (1935)
Manni, Ettore (act, 1927-1979): Il Diavolo Innamorato; Ercole Alla Conquista Della Atlantide; Hercules And The Masked Rider; Hercules-Prisoner Of Evil; Roma Contra Roma
Manning, Bruce (wri): The Best Man Wins; The Lone Wolf Returns (1935); Meet Nero Wolfe
Manning, Hugh (act): The House That Dripped Blood
Manning, Larry (act): The Clonus Horror
Manning, Marcia (act): The House Of Secrets (1929)
Manning, Marilyn (act): Eegah!; The Sadist
Manning, Mark (act): The Gifted One
Manning, Mildred (act): While Paris Sleeps
Manning, Monroe (wri): They Ran For Their Lives
Manning, Ned (act): Dead End Drive-In
Manning, Patricia (act): The Hideous Sun Demon
Manning, Roger (act): The Day It Came To Earth
Manning, Ruth (act): The Devil And Max Devlin; Grave Secrets
Manning, William (act): Mad Max Beyond Thunderdome
Mannino, Anthony (act): Highlander; Tattoo
Mannino, Franco (mus): Beat The Devil; Morgan The Pirate; I Vampiri
Mannino, Vincenzo (wri): Anticristo
Mannion, Michael (act): Mr. Selkie
Mannion, Tom (act): Return Of The Jedi
Mannis, Kevin (act): Student Bodies
Mannock, Patrick/P.L. (wri): The Crimson Circle (1922); Trent's Last Case (1920)
Manoda, Yoichi/Yukio (cin): Godzilla vs. The Smog Monster; The Green Slime
Manoff, Dinah (act): Child's Play (1988)
Manolukas, John (act): Mutants In Paradise
Manon, Christian (act): The Punisher
Manon, Gloria (act): The Mad Room
Manoogian, Michael (act): Neighbors
Manoogian, Peter (dir): The Dungeonmaster; Eliminators
Manoogian, Peter (wri): The Dungeonmaster
Manos, George J. (act): Heaven Can Wait (1978)
Manouk, Edward (act): To Catch A Thief
Manoux, Jean-Paul (act): Pumpkinhead II: Blood Wings
Manquero, Albert (act): Running Against Time
Mans, Lorenzo (wri): Glen And Randa
Mansaray, Sam (act): The Beast Must Die
Mansell, Janet (act): The Haunting
Mansell, Tony (act): Dreamchild
Mansfield, David (mus): Late For Dinner
Mansfield, Elizabeth (act): The Slipper And The Rose
Mansfield, Jayne (act, 1934-1967, nee Jayne Palmer): Gli Amori Di Ercole; The Burglar; Dog Eat Dog; The Fat Spy; The Female Jungle
Mansfield, John (act): Man-Eater Of Kumaon; The Naked Jungle; Prisoners Of The Casbah
Mansfield, Martha (act): Dr. Jekyll And Mr. Hyde (1920, Famous Players/Para)
Mansfield, Rankin (act): World Without End
Mansfield, Sally (act): Beyond The Moon; Manhunt In Space
Mansfield, Scott (dir & wri): The Eliminator
Mansker, Eric (act): Prophecy (1979); Timestalkers
Mansl, Louis (act): Tales From The Crypt
Manson, Alan (act): Let's Scare Jessica To Death; Poor Devil
Manson, Helena (act): The Burning Court; Le Corbeau; Torticola Contre Frankensberg
Manson, Jean (act): Bon Baisers De Hong Kong
Manson, Mary (act): Curse Of The Fly
Manson, Maurice (act): The Creature Walks Among Us; The Girl In The Kremlin
Mantee, Ann (act): The Manitou
Mantee, Paul (act): The Adventures Of Nick Carter; Day Of The Animals; A Man Called Dagger; The Manitou; Robinson Crusoe On Mars
Mantegna, Joe (act): Thinner
Mantel, Bronwen (act): City On Fire; Of Unknown Origin
Mantel, Michael Albert (act): The Brother From Another Planet
Mantell, James (act): The Clonus Horror
Mantell, Joe (act): The Birds
Mantia, Buddy (act): Street Trash
Mantle, Clive (act): The Orchard End Murder; The Secret Life Of Ian Fleming; Without A Clue
Mantley, John (wri): My Blood Runs Cold; The 27th Day
Manton, Percy (act): The Fairies' Revenge
Manton, Percy (wri): The Cry Of The Captive; The Man Behind "The Times"
Mantooth, Donald (act): Demon And The Mummy; Earthquake
Mantooth, Randolph (act): Bridge Across Time
Manuska (act): Zombie Nightmare
Manx, Kate (act): Private Property
Manza, Ralph (act): The Cat From Outer Space; The Philadelphia Experiment; Retribution (1988); This Is Not A Test
Manzel, Michael (cin): The Night They Saved Christmas
Manzie, Jim (mus): Leatherface: Texas Chainsaw Massacre III; The Offspring; Pumpkinhead II: Blood Wings; Red Blooded American Girl; The Servants Of Twilight; Sleepstalker; Stepfather II; Tales From The Darkside
Manzy, David (act): The Baby
Mao, Angela (act): Stoner
Mapes, Ted (act): Dick Tracy's G-Men
Maples, Marla (act, b. 1963): Maximum Overdrive
Maples, Tammy (act): Solar Crisis
Maples, Virginia (act): Black Widow (1954)
Mapp, Jamilah Adams (act): Heart And Souls
Mapp, Jim (act): Enemy Mine
Mappin, Jeff(erson) (act): City On Fire; Virus
Mappin, John Mushroom (act): Waxwork II: Lost In Time
Maqsood, Tasneem (act): Stories From A Flying Trunk
Mara, Adele (act, b. 1923, nee Adelaida Delgado): Alias Boston Blackie; Blackmail (1947); The Catman Of Paris; Curse Of The Faceless Man; Exposed; The Tiger Woman; Traffic In Crime; The Vampire's Ghost; Web Of Danger
Mara, Mary (act): Love Potion No. 9
Marachuk, Steve (act): Piranha II: The Spawning
Maraden, Frank (act): King Kong Lives
Marais, Jean (act, b. 1913, nee Jean Villain-Marais): L'aigle A Deux Tetes; Un Amour De Poche; La Belle Et La Bete; Blood On His Sword; Carmen (1942); L'eternel Retour; Fantomas Contro Scotland Yard; Killer Spy; The King's Avenger; The Man In The Iron Mask (1962); Operation Double Cross; Orphee; Peau D'ane; Le Saint Prend L'affut; Le Testament D'orphee
Marais, Marc (wri): Death Ride
Maranda, Andree (act): The Toxic Avenger
Maranda, Roxanne (act): The Toxic Avenger
Marandi, Evi (act): Terrore Nello Spazio
Maranne, Andre (act): Morons From Outer Space; The Terrornauts
Marano, Ezio (act): The Black Belly Of A Tarantula
Maranzana, Mario (act): The Dead Are Alive
Marascalchi, Pietro (act): The Conquest Of Mycenae
Maraschal, Launce (act): Barbados Quest; Fiend Without A Face; Timeslip
Marasco, Robert (wri): Burnt Offerings
Maraszek, Natasza (act): The Young Magician
Maravidi, Mirella (act): Behind The Mask Of Zorro
Marbrugh, Bertram (act): Before I Hang
Marc, Jean (act): Return From The Ashes
Marc, Nina (act): The Secret Life Of Ian Fleming
Marcaccini, Consuelo (act): Warriors Of The Wasteland
Marcaccini, Goffredo (act): Warriors Of The Wasteland
Marcano, Scott (wri): Bio-Dome
Marceau, Marcel (act, b. 1923): Barbarella; Shanks
Marcel, Leonard (mus): The Video Dead
Marcel, Nino (act): Sabaka
Marcel, Terence/Terry (dir & wri): Hawk The Slayer; Prey (1978); Prisoners Of The Lost Universe
Marcelino, Mario (act): Star Trek III: The Search For Spock
Marcellini, Romolo (dir & wri): Taboos Of The World
Marcellini, Siro (dir): The Secret Mark Of D'artagnan
March, Alex (dir): The Amazing Captain Nemo
March, Anita (act): Scouts To The Rescue
March, Barbara (act): Star Trek: Generations
March, Elspeth (act): Dr. Crippen; Midnight Lace (1960); Psyche 59; The Three Lives Of Thomasina
March, Eve (act, d. 1974): Curse Of The Cat People
March, Fredric (act, 1897-1975, nee Frederick McIntyre Bickel): An Act Of Murder (1948); Death Takes A Holiday (1934); Dr.

Jekyll And Mr. Hyde (1932); I Married A Witch; Les Miserables (1935); Seven Days In May; The Studio Murder Mystery
March, Hal (act, 1920-1970, nee Hal Mendelsohn): The Atomic Kid
March, Jane (act): Color Of Night
March, John (act): Moon 44
March, Keith (act): Scrooge (1970)
March, Nadine (act): Bulldog Sees It Through; Dangerous Fingers
March, William (wri): The Bad Seed (1956 & 1985)
Marchal, Arlette (act, b. 1903): The Elusive Pimpernel (1950)
Marchal, Georges (act): Affairs Of Messalina; Belle De Jour; The Colossus Of Rhodes; The Last Musketeer; The Seven Dwarfs To The Rescue; Sins Of Pompeii; Teodora, Imperatrice Di Bisanzio; Ulysses Against The Son Of Hercules
Marchall, Robin (act): Murder By Decree
Marchand, Leopold (wri): Faust And The Devil; Love Me Tonight
Marchand, Nancy (act, b. 1928): Ladybug, Ladybug; Sparkling Cyanide
Marchant, Shirley (act): Time After Time
Marchant, William (wri): Desk Set
Marchesi, Marcello (wri): Hercules In The Vale Of Woe
Marchesini, Emilio (act): The Cat O' Nine Tails
Marchetti, Nino (act): Il Trionfo Di Ercole
Marchetti, Will (act): Cocoon: The Return
Marchevsky, Alex (act): Billion Dollar Brain
Marchew, Eve (act): I Hear You Calling Me
Marchiano, Bruce (act): Curse II: The Bite
Marchick, David (act): Midnight (1980)
Marchman, Joe (act): Powder
Marciano, David (act): Eyes Of Terror
Marcillac, Jean (wri): Nick Carter Va Tout Casser
Marcin, Max (dir): King Of The Jungle
Marcin, Max (wri): Crime Doctor; Crime Doctor's Courage; Crime Doctor's Diary; Crime Doctor's Gamble; Crime Doctor's Manhunt; Crime Doctor's Strangest Case; Crime Doctor's Warning; The Ghost Talks; Just Before Dawn (1946); The Millerson Case; Secrets Of The Night; Shadows In The Night
Marco, Luis (act): Goliath Against The Giants
Marco, Paul (act): Bride Of The Monster; Plan 9 From Outer Space
Marco, Senor (act): Blood Simple
Marco, Silvia (act): The Man Who Wagged His Tail
Marcos, Joseph P. (act): The Adventures Of Nick Carter
Marcoux, Ted (act): Eyes Of Terror; Ghost In The Machine
Marcovicci, Andrea (act): The Canterville Ghost (1986); Devil's Web; The Hand (1981); Smile, Jenny, You're Dead; Spacehunter: Adventures In The Forbidden Zone; The Stuff; A Vacation In Hell
Marcucella, Leslie (act): Roller Blade Warriors: Taken By Force
Marcus, Adam (act, dir & wri): Jason Goes To Hell: The Final Friday
Marcus, Alan (act): The Hidden; The Octagon
Marcus, Bill (act): Babes In Toyland (1986); Death Curse Of Tartu
Marcus, DeVera (act): Hellhole
Marcus, Dominic (act): Eraser; Frankenhooker
Marcus, James (act): A Clockwork Orange; Never-Never Land
Marcus, James A. (act): Liliom (1930); The Scarlet Letter (1926)
Marcus, Jeff (act): Alien Nation: Body And Soul; Alien Nation: Millennium; Alien Nation: The Enemy Within; Nightmare On The 13th Floor
Marcus, Joe David (act): Search For The Gods
Marcus, Julie (act): Westworld
Marcus, Kipp (act): Jason Goes To Hell: The Final Friday
Marcus, Larry (wri): Brainstorm (1965); The Unguarded Moment
Marcus, Peter (wri): The Body Stealers; The Haunted House Of Horror; Where Has Poor Mickey Gone?
Marcus, Raymond T. (wri): Earth Vs. The Flying Saucers; The Man Who Turned To Stone; Voodoo Island, Zombies Of Mora Tau
Marcus, Richard (act): The Being; Deadly Friend; Enemy Mine; Tremors
Marcus, Vitina (act): The Lost World (1960)
[illegible] (1930-1967): [illegible]
Mardany, Larry (act): The Toxic Avenger, Part II
Marder, Jordan (act): Virtuosity
Mardirosian, Tom (act): The Dark Half; Eat And Run
Maree, Lynne (act): House Of The Living Dead
Maree, Tanya (act): Blood Of Ghastly Horror
Maren, Jerry (act): It Came Upon The Midnight Clear
Mareth, Glenville (wri): Santa Claus Conquers The Martians
Maretti, Sandro (act): La Vendetta Di Ercole
Mareuil, Philippe (act): Judex
Marfield, Dwight (act): Shriek Of The Mutilated; The Trouble With Harry
Margaral, Michael (act): Galaxina
Margarian, Andrew (act): Communion
Margetson, Arthur (act, 1897-1951): Juggernaut; The Mystery Of The Mary Celeste; Sherlock Holmes Faces Death
Margheriti, Antonio (dir, a.k.a. Anthony M. Dawson): Assignment-Outer Space; Cannibal In The Streets; I Criminali Della Galassia; La Danza Macabra; The Deadly Diaphanoids; Death Rage; I Diavoli Della Spazio; La Freccia D'oro; Hercules-Prisoner Of Evil; Hunters Of The Golden Cobra; El Invencible Hombre Invisible; Killer Fish; Lightning Bolt; I Lunghi Capelli Della Morte; Il Planeta Degli Uomini Spenti; Planet On The Prowl; Seven Deaths In The Cat's Eye; La Vergine Di Norimberga; Web Of The Spider; Yor, The Hunter From The Future
Margheriti, Antonio (wri): Cannibal In The Streets; I Lunghi Capelli Della Morte; Seven Deaths In The Cat's Eye; La Vergine Di Norimberga; Yor, The Hunter From The Future
Margheriti, Edward (cin): Yor, The Hunter From The Future
Margheriti, Tony (cin): Yor, The Hunter From The Future
Margo (act, 1917-1985, nee Marguerita Guadalupe Boldoay y Castilla): The Leopard Man; Lost Horizon (1937)
Margo, George (act): The Adding Machine; Mark Of The Phoenix; The Mouse That Roared; Who Done It? (1956)
Margo, Mitch (mus): The Goddess Of Love
Margo, Phil (act & wri): The Goddess Of Love
Margolin, Janet (act, b. 1943): Ghostbusters II, The Last Child; Last Embrace; Planet Earth; The Plutonium Incident
Margolin, Stuart (act): Futureworld; Women Of The Prehistoric Planet
Margolis, Herbert (wri): Francis In The Haunted House
Margolis, Ilona (act): Flatliners; Graveyard Shift (1990); Waxwork II: Lost In Time
Margolis, Mark (act): The Pit And The Pendulum (1990); Tales From The Darkside
Margolyes, Miriam (act): The Awakening; Electric Dreams; James And The Giant Peach; Little Shop Of Horrors (1986); Morons From Outer Space; Orpheus Descending; Pacific Heights
Margulies, David (act): All That Jazz; Dressed To Kill (1980); Ghostbusters; Ghostbusters II
Margulies, Michael (D.) (cin): The Baby; The Haunted (1991); Northstar; The Questor Tapes; Repossessed; Sherlock Holmes In New York; Strange New World; The Stranger Within; Too Good To Be True; Where Have All The People Gone?
Margulies, William (cin): The Ghost And Mr. Chicken; Night Gallery; The Sword Of Ali Baba
Mari, Fiorella (act): Death Comes From Space
Mari, Gina (act): The Slumber Party Massacre
Mari, Keiko (act): Godzilla Vs. The Smog Monster
Mari, Paul (act): Transmutations
Mari, Sergio (act): The Man Without Desire
Marian, Marc (act): Le Manoir Maudit; Tomb Of Torture
Mariano, Detto (mus): Exterminators Of The Year 3000
Mariaux, A.L. (wri): Zombies Lake
Marichal, Julia/July (act): Dr. Tarr's Torture Dungeon; Isle Of The Snake People
Maricle, Leona (act): The Lone Wolf In Paris
Marie, Kim (act): Superstition
Marie, Lisa (act): Dead And Buried; Ed Wood; Mars Attacks!
Marie-France (act): The Golden Mask
Marielle, Catherine (act): Starship Invasions
Marielle, Jean Pierre (act): Quatro Mosche Di Velluto Gris
Marienthal, Ely (act): Unlikely Angel
Marier, Paula (act): Forever Evil
Marin, Andrew Peter (wri): Bad Ronald
Marin, Cheech (act): Charlie's Ghost Story; From Dusk Till Dawn; Ghostbusters II; Ring Of The Musketeers
Marin, Edwin L. (dir, 1901-1951): The Casino Murder Case; A Christmas Carol (1938); The Death Kiss; The Garden Murder Case; Invisible Agent; Paris Calling; A Study In Scarlet (1933)
Marin, Guglielmo (act): The Last Days Of Pompeii (1959)
Marin, Guillermo (act): La Torre De Los Siete Jorobados
Marin, Jacques (act, b. 1919): The Island At The Top Of The World; Jeux Interdits; Marathon Man
Marin, Jerry (act): The Being
Marin, Luciano (act): Ercole Alla Conquista Della Atlantide; Siege Of Syracuse; The Tartars; War Gods Of Babylon
Marin, Luis (act): Ella Y El Miedo; Voodoo Black Exorcist
Marin, Russ (act): Chiller; The Dark (1979); Deadly Friend; Running Against Time; The Sword And The Sorcerer
Marinan, Terence (act): The Fan
Marinaro, Ed (act): Deadly Web
Marine, Juan/John (cin): Las Cuatro Noches De La Luna Llena; Endless Descent; Pieces
Marinelli, Anthony (mus): Graveyard Shift (1990)
Marinelli, Maria (act): Blind Date
Marini, Alessandra (act): see Milo, Sandra
Marinker, Peter (act): Fear Is The Key; Nightbreed
Marino, Ralph (act): The Funhouse (1981)
Marinoff, Brenda (act): The Hills Have Eyes
Marinuzzi, Gino (mus): Terrore Nello Spazio
Marion, Blake (act): Dr. Strange
Marion, Charles (R.) (wri, b. 1914): Ghost Chasers; Hold That Line; Master Minds (1950); The Mystery Of The 13th Guest; Trapped By Boston Blackie
Marion, Frances (wri, 1888-1973): Green Hell; Knight Without Armour; Love From A Stranger (1937); The Scarlet Letter (1926); Through The Dark
Marion, George (act): The Bishop Murder Case
Marion Jr., George (wri): Love Me Tonight; The Mysterious Dr. Fu Manchu
Marion, Joan (act): Black Limelight; The River House Ghost; The Stolen Necklace; Tangled Evidence
Marion, Paul (act): Bowery To Bagdad; The Devil's Cargo; Killer Ape; The Lost Tribe; Phantom Of The Opera (1943); Sabaka; Safari Drums; Savage Mutiny; Scared Stiff (1953)
Marion-Crawford, Howard (act, b. 1914): The Blood Of Fu Manchu; The Brides Of Fu Manchu; The Castle Of Fu Manchu; The Face Of Fu Manchu; Gideon's Day; The Man In The White Suit; Mr. Drake's Duck; Model For Murder; The Secret Agent (1936); The Vengeance Of Fu Manchu
Marioni, Roy (act): One Deadly Owner
Maris, Mona (act, b. 1903, nee Maria Capdevielle): A Date With The Falcon; The Death Kiss; The Falcon In Mexico; I Married An Angel
Maris, Stella (act): Electric Dreams
Mariscal, Ana (act): Carlota
Marischka, Ernest (dir & wri): Embezzled Heaven
Marischka, George (act): The Boys From Brazil
Marisenka (act): Pyro
Marisini, Maresco (act): My Lord Conceit
Marisse, Anne (act): Beyond Evil
Marisse, Anne (wri): Graduation Day; Haunts
Mariye, Lily (act): Switch
Marjanovic, Dragana (act): The Magic Snowman
Mark, Ivan (cin): Daughter Of Darkness (1990)
Mark, Michael (act): Appointment With Murder; Attack Of The Puppet People; Charlie Chan In City In Darkness; House Of Frankenstein; Lizzie; Mad Love; The Mummy's Hand; Peril From The Planet Mongo; Phantom From Space; Purple Death From Outer Space; Return Of The Fly; Search For Danger; Son Of Frankenstein; The Son Of Monte Cristo; The Wasp Woman
Mark, Neil D. (act): I Still Dream Of Jeannie
Mark, Robert (act): Superbug; Superbug, Super Agent; Superwheels
Mark, Solly (act): Neon Maniacs
Mark, Tamara (act): Wes Craven's New Nightmare
Markel, Daniel (act): Dark Angel: The Ascent
Markell, Douglas (act): Neon Maniacs
Markell, Jodie (act): Vampire's Kiss
Marker, Chris (dir & wri, b. 1921): La Jetee
Marker, Russ (dir & wri): The Demon From Devil's Lake
Markey, Andrew (act): Watchers
Markey, Enid (act, 1886-1981): Tarzan Of The Apes
Markey, Gene (wri, 1895-1980): As You Desire Me
Markey, Melinda (act): The Adventures Of Hajji Baba
Markey, Zoli (act): The Demon (1981)
Markham, Barbara (act): House Of Whipcord; The Lady Vanishes (1979)
Markham, David (act): Blood From The Mummy's Tomb; Tales From The Crypt
Markham, Kika (act): Outland
Markham, Monte (act, b. 1935): The Astronaut; Death Takes A Holiday (1971); Ellery Queen; Project X (1967)
Markham, Petra (act): Fragment Of Fear
Markinson, Brian (act): Alien Nation: Millennium; Wolf
Markland, Ted (act): Doomsday Machine
Markle, Fletcher (dir, 1921-1991): The Man With A Cloak
Markle, Peter (dir): White Dwarf
Markle, Stephen (act): The Haunted (1991)
Markofsky, Isidore (cin): Somewhere In Time
Markopoulos, Gregory J. (cin, dir & wri, 1928-1992): Galaxie; The Iliac Passion
Markota, Ivan S. (act): Waxwork II: Lost In Time
Markov, Margaret (act): The Arena (1973)
Markova, Nadine (act): Dr. Tarr's Torture Dungeon
Markowitz, Alan G. (cin): Dolly Dearest
Markowitz, Barry (cin): Sling Blade
Markowitz, Richard (mus): The Magic Sword (1962)
Markowitz, Robert (dir): Phantom Of The Opera (1983)
Markowitz, Sandra (act): see Harris, Barbara
Markowski, Andrzej (mus): Milczaca Gwiazda; Wielka, Wielka I Najwieksza
Marks, Alfred (act, b. 1921): The Frightened City; Scream And Scream Again
Marks, Arthur (dir): J.D.'s Revenge
Marks, Aub (act): Castle Of Terrors
Marks, Bridget (act): Thinner
Marks, Elaine (act): Demon Knight
Marks, Garnett (act): Philo Vance's Gamble
Marks, Harlow (act): Halloween 4: The Return Of Michael Myers
Marks, Harry S. (dir): Shadow Of Death (1939)
Marks, Jack (act): Friday The 13th-Part 2
Marks, Jack (wri): Miracles Do Happen
Marks, Jack R. (act): The Fan
Marks, Leo (wri): Cloudburst; Peeping Tom; The Twisted Nerve
Marks, Louis (wri): The Man Who Finally Died
Marks, Robert (act): The Village Of The Damned (1960)
Marks, Sherry (act): Satan's Cheerleaders
Marks, Slash (act): Night Of The Cobra Woman
Marksen, Edward (act): The Company Of Wolves
Markson, Ben (wri): A Close Call For Boston Blackie; The Falcon In San Francisco
Markwald, Daniel (act): Making Contact
Marla, Norma (act): The Two Faces Of Dr. Jekyll
Marlborough, Leah (act): The Madman's Fate
Marle, Arnold (act): The Abominable Snowman Of The Himalayas; The Glass Tomb; The Green Buddha; Little Red Monkey; The Man Who Could Cheat Death; Portrait From Life; The Snake Woman
Marley, Ben (act): Fantasies; Jaws 2
Marley, J. Peverell (cin, 1899-1964): Bulldog Drummond Strikes Back (1934); The Count Of Monte Cristo (1934); The Hound Of The Baskervilles (1939); Phantom Of The Rue Morgue; The Road To Yesterday; Sleepers West; The Three Musketeers (1939); The Two Mrs. Carrolls
Marley, John (act, 1908-1984): Blade; The Car; The Dead Are Alive; Deathdream; It Lives Again; Nightmare In The Sun; Robbers Of The Sacred Mountain
Marlier, Carla (act): La Leggendi Di Enea; Spirits Of The Dead
Marlo, Steve(n) (act): Arnold; The Swarm; Terror In The Wax Museum; The Young Captives
Marlow, Anna (act): Beyond Evil
Marlow, Charles (wri): When Knights Were Bold (1916, 1929 & 1936)
Marlow, June (act): Jamaica Inn (1985)
Marlow, Nancy (act): The Falcon In Hollywood
Marlow, Tony (act): The Black Cat (1934); The Mummy (1932)
Marlow, William (act): Zeppelin
Marlowe, Anthony (act): Saadia
Marlowe, Brian (wri): Supernatural (1933)
Marlowe, Christopher (wri, 1564-1593): Dr. Faustus; Faust (1963)
Marlowe, Derek (wri): A Dandy In Aspic; Jamaica Inn (1985)
Marlowe, Faye (act): [illegible]
Marlowe, Frank (act): Dark Alibi
Marlowe, Hugh (act, 1911-1982, nee Hugh Hipple): Castle Of Evil; The

Day The Earth Stood Still; Earth vs. The Flying Saucers; How To Steal The World; Monkey Business; Seven Days In May; 13 Frightened Girls; World Without End

Marlowe, Jonas (act): Children Of The Corn

Marlowe, June (act, 1903-1984): Don Juan (1927)

Marlowe, Katherine/Kathy (act): Queen Of Outer Space; Rocketship X-M

Marlowe, Linda (act): The Man Outside (1967); Spaceflight IC-1

Marlowe, Nora (act): Westworld

Marlowe, Scott (act): Journey Into Fear (1975); Night Slaves

Marly, Florence (act, 1919-1978, nee Hana Smekalova): Doctor Death: Seeker Of Souls; Games; Queen Of Blood; Sealed Verdict

Marmont, Patricia (act): Suddenly Last Summer

Marmont, Percy (act, 1883-1977): Dark Secret; Footsteps In The Fog; Four Sided Triangle; Rich And Strange; The Secret Agent (1936); The Silver Greyhound (1932); The Squeaker (1930); White Lilac; Young And Innocent

Marmorstein, Malcolm (wri): Mary, Mary, Bloody Mary; Return From Witch Mountain

Marner, Carmela (act): Mission: Impossible

Marner, Richard (act): The Boys From Brazil

Marner-Brooks, Elizabeth (act): I Drink Your Blood

Marnham, Christian (dir & wri): The Orchard End Murder

Maron, Alfred (act): The Man In The Road

Maroney, Kelli (act): Chopping Mall; Night Of The Comet; Not Of This Earth (1988); The Zero Boys

Maros, Basil (cin): Atlas

Marotta, Davide (act): Demons 2

Marotte, Carl (act): My Bloody Valentine

Marquand, Christian (act, b. 1927): La Belle Et La Bete; The Gentle Art Of Murder; Lucrezia Borgia (1952)

Marquand, John P. (wri, 1893-1960): Mr. Moto In Danger Island; Mr. Moto's Gamble; Mr. Moto's Last Warning; Mr. Moto Takes A Chance; Mr. Moto Takes A Vacation; The Mysterious Mr. Moto; The Return Of Mr. Moto; Thank You, Mr. Moto; Think Fast, Mr. Moto

Marquand, Richard (dir, 1938-1987): The Legacy; Return Of The Jedi

Marquand, Serge (act): Caravan To Vaccares; Et Mourir De Plaisir; Spirits Of The Dead; Le Vice Et La Vertu

Marquand, Tina (act): Modesty Blaise

Marquard, Brick (cin): Destination Inner Space; This Is Not A Test

Marques, Ed (act): Virtuosity

Marques-Riviere, Jean (wri): Forces Occultes

Marquet, Mary (act): Landru

Marquette, Jacques/Jack (R.) (cin): The Aliens Are Coming; Attack Of The 50-Foot Woman (1958); A Bucket Of Blood (1959); Burnt Offerings; Creature From The Haunted Sea; Flight Of The Lost Balloon; Halloween With The Addams Family; Last Woman On Earth; The Strangler (1963); Teenage Monster; Varan The Unbelievable

Marquette, Jacques (dir): Teenage Monster

Marquette, Jacques (wri): The Brain From Planet Arous

Marquette, Ron (act, d. 1994): Past Tense

Marquetti, Laura (act): El Santo Contra Las Vampiras

Marquez, Bill (act): Stanley

Marquez, Gabriel Garcia (wri): A Very Old Man With Enormous Wings

Marquez, William (act): Midnight Lace (1981)

Marquina, Luis (wri): El Invencible Hombre Invisible

Marquis, Don (act): The Incredibly Strange Creatures Who Stopped Living And Became Mixed-Up Zombies

Marquis, Ken (act): Halloween With The Addams Family

Marr, Edward/Eddie (act): Charlie Chan At The Wax Museum; Forty Naughty Girls; How To Make A Monster; I Was A Teenage Werewolf; Mr. Moto In Danger Island; Mr. Moto's Gamble; One Dangerous Night; The Steel Trap; Torchy Plays With Dynamite

Marr, Richard (act): Werewolf Of Washington

Marr, Sally (K.) (act): The Devil And Max Devlin; Dracula's Dog

Marrero, Ralph (act): Tales From The Darkside

Marriner, Edythe (act): see Hayward, Susan

Marriner, Peter (act): Judge Dredd

Marriot, Robert (act): Roogie's Bump

Marriott, Anthony (wri): The Deadly Bees

Marriott, John (act): Dear, Dead Delilah

Marriott, Moore (act, 1885-1949, nee George Thomas Moore-Marriott): The Crime At Blossoms; The Fatal Hour (1937); The Feathered Serpent (1934); Green For Danger; The Grip Of Iron; The Hills Of Donegal; His Sister's Honour; The Monkey's Paw (1923); A Place Of One's Own; The Sign Of Four (1932); Sweeney Todd; Time Flies (1944); When Knights Were Bold (1936)

Marriott, Ronald Lee (act): Fire In The Sky (1993)

Marriott, Sylvia (act): Asylum; Crimes At The Dark House; The Hand Of Night

Marriott, Violet (act): Asthore

Marriot-Watson, Elsie (act): The Prehistoric Man (1924)

Marrottax, Franco (wri): The Cursed Medallion

Marrow, Hyla (act): Maniac (1980)

Marryat, Frederick (wri): The Little Savage

Mars, Douglas (act): When London Sleeps

Mars, Jacques (act): The Phantom Of The Opera (1990)

Mars, Kenneth (act, b. 1936): Full Moon High; The New, Original Wonder Woman; We're Back! A Dinosaur's Story; Young Frankenstein

Mars, Lani (act): The Wasp Woman

Mars, Marjorie (act): Take My Life

Mars, Michele (act): Deadtime Stories

Marsac, Laure (act): Interview With The Vampire

Marsac, Maurice (act): Captain Sinbad; Crime Doctor's Gamble; Lycanthropus; Tarzan And The Trappers

Marsden, Beatrice (act): Night Comes Too Soon

Marsden, Betty (act): Sudden Terror

Marsden, Roy (act): Toomorrow

Marsell, Tita (act): Dimension 5

Marsh, Carol(e) (act, b. 1926, nee Norma Simpson): Alice In Wonderland (1950); Horror Of Dracula; Scrooge (1951)

Marsh, Eve (act): Making Mr. Right

Marsh, Garry (act, b. 1902, nee Leslie March Geraghty): The Claydon Treasure Mystery; The Dark Stairway; Dead Of Night (1945); Forbidden; Forging Ahead; The Haunted Castle (1948); Inside The Room; Just William's Luck; The Lost Hours; The Man In The Mirror; The Man They Could Not Arrest; Murder At The Windmill; Number 17; Old Mother Riley's Jungle Treasure; Scrooge (1935); The Shop At Sly Corner; Things Happen At Night; The Voice Of Merrill; When Knights Were Bold (1936); Where The Bullets Fly; Who Done It? (1956)

Marsh, Gene (act): His Prehistoric Past

Marsh, Isabella (act): Mary Reilly

Marsh, Jamie (act): Brainscan

Marsh, Jean (act, b. 1934): The Changeling; A Connecticut Yankee In King Arthur's Court (1989); Dark Places; Frenzy; Goliath Awaits; Jane Eyre (1970); Limbo Line; Return To Oz; Unearthly Stranger; Willow

Marsh, Joan (act, b. 1913): Charlie Chan On Broadway

Marsh, Keith (act): Daleks' Invasion Earth 2150 A.D.

Marsh, Linda (act): The Dark Secret Of Harvest Home

Marsh, Mae (act, 1895-1968, nee Mary Warne Marsh): The Avenging Conscience; Blue, White And Perfect; Cry Terror!; Girls In Prison; Jane Eyre (1944); Julie; The Lesser Evil; Man's Genesis; The Snake Pit (1948)

Marsh, Marian (act, b. 1913, nee Violet Krauth): The Black Room; Crime And Punishment (1935); The Great Gambini; The Mad Genius; The Man Who Lived Twice; Svengali (1931)

Marsh, Mary (act): Child Of Darkness, Child Of Light

Marsh, Mary Warne (act): see Marsh, Mae

Marsh, Myra (act): A Night Of Mystery (1937)

Marsh, Nicole (act): The Bermuda Depths

Marsh, Oliver T. (cin): After The Thin Man; Another Thin Man; The Mystery Of Mr. X

Marsh, Raymond (dir): Lord Shango

Marsh, Reginald (act): Berserk; It Happened Here; Mark Of The Devil (1985)

Marsh, Richard (wri): The Beetle

Marsh, Tani (act): From Hell It Came

Marsh, Terence (wri): Haunted Honeymoon (1986)

Marsh, Tiger Joe (act): The Cat From Outer Space

Marshak, Jack (act): The Quilt Of Hathor

Marshal, Alan (act, 1909-1961): The Adventures Of Sherlock Holmes (1939); After The Thin Man; Exile Express; House On Haunted Hill; The Hunchback Of Notre Dame (1939); Night Must Fall (1937)

Marshal, Gary (act): Camelot

Marshal, Stephen (act): Cat People (1982)

Marshall, Annie (act): Return Of The Living Dead, Part II

Marshall, Bill (wri): Dr. Frankenstein On Campus

Marshall, Brenda (act, b. 1915, nee Ardis Anderson Gaines): Background To Danger; The Smiling Ghost; Whispering Smith

Marshall, Bryan (act): I Start Counting; A Place To Die; The Punisher; Quatermass And The Pit; Rasputin, The Mad Monk; The Spy Who Loved Me

Marshall, Burt (act): Buck Rogers In The 25th Century

Marshall, Clive (act): Koroshi

Marshall, Connie (act): Dragonwyck

Marshall, Darah (act): Teenage Cave Man

Marshall, Don (act): Terminal Island; The Thing With Two Heads

Marshall, E.G. (act, b. 1910): Creepshow; Ellery Queen: Don't Look Behind You; The Littlest Angel (1969); The Phoenix (1981); Pursuit (1972); Superman II; Two Evil Eyes; Vampire (1979)

Marshall, Ellye (act): Champagne For Caesar

Marshall, Frank (act): Raiders Of The Lost Ark; Targets

Marshall, Frank (dir): Arachnophobia; Congo

Marshall, Fred (act): Cheldsea Bird

Marshall, Garry (dir): Exit To Eden

Marshall, George (dir, 1891-1975): The Gazebo; The Ghost Breakers; Houdini; L'intrigo; Scared Stiff (1953)

Marshall, Helene (act): The Incredible Shrinking Man

Marshall, Henry (act): Star Trek: Generations

Marshall, Herbert (act, 1890-1966): The Black Shield Of Falworth; The Caretakers; The Enchanted Cottage (1945); Five Weeks In A Balloon; The Fly (1958); Foreign Correspondent; Four Frightened People; Gog; I Was A Spy; The List Of Adrian Messenger; Midnight Lace (1960); Murder; Riders To The Stars; The Unseen (1945)

Marshall, Jack (mus): The Giant Gila Monster; Munster, Go Home!

Marshall, Joanne (act): see Dru, Joanne

Marshall, Joe (act): Tuck Everlasting

Marshall, John (act): Prisoners Of The Casbah; Secret Of The Incas

Marshall, Ken (act): Krull

Marshall, Lyn (act): Subterfuge

Marshall, Michael (GB act): Moonraker

Marshall, Michael (USA act): The Phantom Planet

Marshall, Mort (act): Skullduggery; Target Earth

Marshall, Nancy (act): Frankenstein Meets The Space Monster

Marshall, Nicholas H. (act): Outbreak

Marshall, Paula (act): The Flash; Full Eclipse; Hellraiser Iii: Hell On Earth

Marshall, Penny (dir, b. 1943): Big; The Preacher's Wife

Marshall, Peter (act): Fortress

Marshall, Phil (mus): Rolling Vengeance

Marshall, Roger (wri): —And Now The Screaming Starts!; Invasion (1965); The Man Outside (1967); Theatre Of Death; What Became Of Jack And Jill

Marshall, Sara (act): Embassy

Marshall, Sean (act): Pete's Dragon

Marshall III, Seth (wri): Beyond The Universe

Marshall, Shary (act): Panic In Year Zero

Marshall, Steve (act): Night Of The Creeps

Marshall, Tom (act): Killer's Moon; Revenge (1971, Gb)

Marshall, Tony (act): I Was A Teenage Werewolf

Marshall, Trudy (act, b. 1922): Boston Blackie And The Law; Key Witness; Mark Of The Gorilla; Secret Agent Of Japan; Too Many Winners

Marshall, Tully (act, 1864-1943): The Brass Bottle (1923); The Bridge Of San Luis Rey (1929); The Cat And The Canary (1927); The Gorilla (1927); He Who Gets Slapped; The Hunchback Of Notre Dame (1923); Murder On The Blackboard; Murder Will Out (1930); The Mysterious Dr. Fu Manchu; Night Of Terror (1933)

Marshall, William (1940s act): Blackmail (1947); Murder In The Music Hall

Marshall, William (act, b. 1924): Abby; Blacula; The Mask Of Sheba; Sabu And The Magic Ring; Scream, Blacula, Scream; Skullduggery; To Trap A Spy

Marshall, William (dir): Adventures Of Captain Fabian; The Phantom Planet

Marshall, Zena (act, b. 1926): The Bad Lord Byron; Dark Interval; Dr. No; Miranda; Sleeping Car To Trieste; So Long At The Fair; The Terrornauts; Three Cases Of Murder

Marshe, Sheena (act): Act Of Murder (1964)

Marshe, Vera (act): The Space Children; Tormented (1960)

Marshman Jr., D.M. (wri): Second Chance; Sunset Boulevard

Marsillach, Blanca (act): Flesh & Blood

Marsillach, Christina (act): Terror At The Opera

Marsina, Antonio (act): Il Montagna Di Dio Cannibale

Marson, Aileen (act): The Merry Men Of Sherwood Forest; Passing Shadows; Someone At The Door

Marston, Jack (act): Frightmare (1983)

Marston, Joel (act): The Disembodied; Heaven Can Wait (1978); The Sky Dragon

Marston, John (act): Son Of Kong

Marston, Nathaniel (act): The Craft

Marston, Theodore (dir): Pawns Of Mars

Mart, Gin (act): Il Mostro Di Venezia

Marta, Jack (A.) (cin, b. 1905): The Beginning Of The End; Fair Wind To Java; A Howling In The Woods; The Mandarin Mystery; The Perils Of Pauline; The Spider (1958); War Of The Colossal Beast; You'll Like My Mother

Marta, John (cin): Loves Of Carmen

Marta, Lynn(e) (act): Blood Beach; The First Power

Martans, Manilla (act): Jungle Trail Of The Son Of Tarzan

Martel, Christine (act): Adam And Eve; The Little Savage

Martel, June (act): A Night Of Mystery (1937)

Martel, K.C. (act): The Amityville Horror; The Munsters' Revenge

Martel, Paul (act): La Venganza De Don Mendo

Martel, Wendy (act): Sorority House Massacre

Martel, William (act): Simon, King Of The Witches; Violated

Martell, Alphonse (act): The Black Cat (1934); Charlie Chan In City In Darkness; Dick Tracy (1945); The Falcon's Alibi; Satan Met A Lady

Martell, Arlene (act): The Adventures Of Nick Carter; Dracula's Dog

Martell, Carlo (mus): The Curse Of The Golem

Martell, Chris (act): Flesh Feast; The Gruesome Twosome

Martell, Donna (act): Abbott And Costello Meet The Killer; Bomba And The Elephant Stampede; Project Moonbase

Martell, Gillian (act): Dark Water

Martell, Gregg (act): Dinosaurus!; Return Of The Fly; Space Master X-7; The Three Stooges Meet Hercules; Valley Of The Dragons

Martell, Kurt (act): The Steel Trap

Martell, Peter (act): The Cobra; Night Of The Blood Monster

Martell, Philip (mus): The Anniversary; Captain Kronos: Vampire Hunter; The Curse Of The Golem; The Devil Rides Out; A Distant Scream; Frankenstein And The Monster From Hell; The Frozen Dead; The Ghoul (1974); Journey To The Unknown; Mark Of The Devil (1985); Paint Me A Murder; Tennis Court; The Terrornauts; They Came From Beyond Space; The Uncanny; Uncharted Seas; The Vengeance Of She; The Viking Queen

Martelli, Carlo(s) (mus): Catacombs; The Curse Of The Mummy's Tomb; Prehistoric Women (1966); Witchcraft (1964)

Martelli, Tony (act): Mr. Moto In Danger Island

Marten, Felix (act): Atomic Agent; Le Saint Mene La Dance

Marten, Nina (act): The Coming

Marten, Seth (act): Alien Nation

Martenson, Mona (act): The Story Of Gosta Berling

Marter, Ian (act): Dr. Faustus

Marth, Frank (act): Captain America (1978); Fright (1957)

Martha the Armless Wonder (act): Freaks

Martin, A.E. (wri): The Glass Tomb

Martin, A.Z. (wri): The Mad Room

Martin, Al (wri): Amazon Quest; Invasion Of The Saucer Men; The Invisible Ghost; The Lost Jungle; The Mad Doctor Of Market Street

Martin, Alan (act): Ed Wood

Martin, Alviero (act): Zone Troopers

Martin, Andra (act): The Thing That Couldn't Die

Martin, Andrea (act): Boris And Natasha; Cannibal Girls; Innerspace; Silent Night, Evil Night

Martin, Anne-Marie (act): The Boogens; Runaway

Martin, Anne-Marie (wri): Twister

Martin, Armand (act): The Bees; Midnight (1980)

Martin, Ashlyn (act): Blood Feast (1963)
Martin, Aubrey (act): This Is Not A Test
Martin, Barney (act): Charly; It Happened One Christmas; Killer In The Mirror
Martin, Barry (act): House Of Whipcord
Martin, Charles (cin): Rich And Strange
Martin, Charles (wri): The Missing Guest
Martin, Charles G. (act): The Checkered Flag
Martin, Chris-Pin (act, 1894-1953): Charlie Chan In Panama; Four Frightened People
Martin, Claude (wri): Et Mourir De Plaisir
Martin, Claudia (act): The Ghost In The Invisible Bikini
Martin, Colin (act): The Majorettes
Martin, Dale (cin): RoboCop
Martin, Damon (act): Ghoulies II
Martin, Dan (act): Sleepwalkers
Martin, Daniel (act): Mystery On Monster Island
Martin, Danny R. (act): Secrets Of The Phantom Caverns
Martin, Dean (act, 1917-1995, nee Dino Crocetti): The Ambushers; Murderers' Row; The Road To Bali; The Road To Hong Kong; Scared Stiff (1953); The Silencers (1966); The Wrecking Crew
Martin, Derek (act): Dark Water
Martin, Dewey (act, b. 1923): Land Of The Pharaohs; The Thing From Another World
Martin, Diana (act): Brazil; The Hyena Of London
Martin, Dick (act): The Maltese Bippy
Martin, Don (dir, b. 1911): Search For Danger
Martin, Don (wri, b. 1911): The Devil's Cargo; The Lost Tribe; Search For Danger
Martin, Douglas Brian (act): Addams Family Values
Martin, Duane (act): Scream II
Martin, Duke (act): The Lost Zeppelin
Martin, Eddie (act): Great Expectations (1946)
Martin, Edie (act, 1880-1964): The Lady Killers (1956); The Lavender Hill Mob; The Man In The White Suit; A Place Of One's Own
Martin, Eugene (act): Tower Of London (1962)
Martin, Eugenio/Gene (dir & wri): Hipnosis; Horror Express
Martin, Francis (wri): International House; U.F.O.
Martin, Frank (act): Marooned
Martin, Gary (act): Slaughter High
Martin, Gene (dir & wri): see Martin, Eugenio/Gene
Martin, George (act): La Isla De La Muerte
Martin, George (mus): Live And Let Die
Martin, George R.R. (wri): Nightflyers
Martin, Grady (cin): Sisters Of Death
Martin, Helen (act): Night Angel
Martin, Helen (wri): The Invisible Ghost
Martin, Hilary (act): —And Now The Screaming Starts!
Martin, J.H. (cin): The Pirates Of 1920
Martin, J.H. (dir): The Chef's Revenge; A Christmas Card: Or, The Story Of Three Homes; The Cook's Dream; The Dancer's Dream; The Fatal Hand; The Freak Barber; How To Make Time Fly; Introductions Extraordinary; A Lively Quarter Day; The Madman's Fate; The Medium Exposed; My Lady's Revenge; The Phantom Ship (1908); The Pierrot And The Devil's Dice; The Visions Of An Opium Smoker; The World's Wizard
Martin Jr., James G. (act): The Handmaid's Tale
Martin, James Aviles (dir & wri): Flesh-Eating Mothers
Martin, Jared (act, b. 1947): Westworld
Martin, Jayne Lyn (act): Are You In The House Alone?
Martin, Jennifer (act): The Wicker Man
Martin, John (GB act): The Tell-Tale Heart (1960); Web Of Suspicion
Martin, John (USA act): Black Roses; Night Visions; Red Alert
Martin, John Ara (act): Return Of The Killer Tomatoes
Martin, John Benjamin (act): Flatliners
Martin, John Scott (act): Little Shop Of Horrors (1986)
Martin, Jose manuel (act): The Castle Of Fu Manchu; Gran Amore Del Conde Dracula
Martin, Julie (act): Octopussy; Where The Bullets Fly
Martin, Keith (act): Peter Rabbit And The Tales Of Beatrix Potter
Martin, Kellie (act, b. 1975): Doin' [illegible]
Martin, Laurie (act): Empire Of Ash III
Martin, Leila (act): Santa Claus Conquers The Martians
Martin, Lew (act): Dark Of The Night
Martin, Lewis (act): Diary Of A Madman; The Frighteners; Houdini; The Man Who Knew Too Much (1956); Red Planet Mars; The War Of The Worlds; Witness To Murder
Martin, Lock (act): The Day The Earth Stood Still
Martin, Lori (act): Cape Fear (1961)
Martin, Lottie (act): Prehistoric Peeps
Martin, M. (wri): The Emerald Of Artatama
Martin, Maggie (act): The Phantom Empire
Martin, Malaika (act): Taste The Blood Of Dracula
Martin, Margaret (act): The Plutonium Incident
Martin, Maribel (act): A Bell From Hell; The Blood Spattered Bride; The House That Screamed
Martin, Marion (act, 1916-1985): Angel On My Shoulder (1946); Ellery Queen, Master Detective; Gildersleeve's Ghost; Lady Of Burlesque; The Man In The Iron Mask (1939)
Martin, Marji (act): Shocker
Martin, Mary (act): The Scarlet Letter (1917)
Martin, Melvyn (act): Les Enfants Terribles
Martin, Mia (act): The Satanic Rites Of Dracula
Martin, Nan (act): The Mugger; A Nightmare On Elm Street 3: Dream Warriors
Martin, P.J. (act): Zapped!
Martin, Pamela (act): Timecop
Martin, Pamela Sue (act, b. 1952): Bay Coven; Human Feelings; The Poseidon Adventure
Martin, Paul (act): The Pit (1983); Uninvited (1987)
Martin, Pepper (act): Ghost Fever; Return To Horror High; Superman II; The Wrecking Crew
Martin, Percy (act): Angel Heart
Martin, Philip (act): Haunters Of The Deep
Martin, Richard (act): The Falcon In Danger; The Falcon's Brother; The Leopard Man
Martin, Robert (wri): Frankenhooker
Martin, Ron (act): Quarantine
Martin, Ross (act, 1920-1981, nee Martin Rosenblatt): Charlie Chan: Happiness Is A Warm Clue; The Colossus Of New York; Conquest Of Space; Dying Room Only; Experiment In Terror
Martin, Russ (act): She's Dressed To Kill
Martin, Sandra (act): Supergirl (1984)
Martin, Sandy (act): Scalpel
Martin, Sharlene (act): Friday The 13th, Part VIII-Jason Takes Manhattan
Martin, Skip (act): Circus Of Fear; Horror Hospital; The Masque Of The Red Death (1964); Vampire Circus
Martin, Sobey (dir, b. 1909): Las Cuatro Noches De La Luna Llena
Martin, Steve (act, b. 1945): All Of Me; Little Shop Of Horrors (1986); The Man With Two Brains
Martin, Steven M. (act): Addams Family Values
Martin, Strother (act, 1919-1980): Brainstorm (1965); The Brotherhood Of Satan; Kiss Me Deadly; The Magnetic Monster; Nightwing; The Shaggy Dog; Sssssss; Storm Over Tibet
Martin, Sylvia (act): Prom Night
Martin, Teddy (act): Sleuth
Martin, Terry (act): Cry Of The Banshee; Phobia; Virus
Martin, Todd (act): Crack In The World; Haunts Of The Very Rich
Martin, Tom (act): The Pit (1983)
Martin, Tony (act, b. 1913, nee Alfred Norris): Ali Baba Goes To Town
Martin, Townsend (wri): A Kiss For Cinderella
Martin, Tracy (act): Fortress
Martin, Troy Kennedy (wri): The Jerusalem File
Martin, Valerie (wri): Mary Reilly
Martin, Wally (act): Wild Thing
Martin, William E. (act): Little Nemo: Adventures In Slumberland
Martin, William E. (wri): Harry And The Hendersons
Martin, Yves Andre (act): Dark Mansions
Martinek, H.O. (act): The Clue Of The Cigar Band; The False Wireless; Her Lover's Honour; The Hidden Witness; In The Grip Of Spies; The Mystery Of The Old Mill; The Stolen Masterpiece
Martinek, H.O. (dir): The Clue Of The Cigar Band; The Corner House Burglary; Drowsy Dick's Dream; The False Wireless; Her Lover's Honour; The Hidden Witness; In The Grip Of Spies; Jim The Scorpion; The King's Peril; The Mystery Of The Old Mill; The Octopus Gang; The Prehistoric Man (1911); The Professor's Twirly-Whirly Cigarettes; The Rajah's Tiara; The Stolen Masterpiece
Martinek, H.O. (wri): Her Lover's Honour
Martinek, Ivy (act): Drowsy Dick's Dream; Her Lover's Honour; Jim The Scorpion; The Octopus Gang; Robin Hood Outlawed
Martinelli (act): Paris Qui Dort
Martinelli, Arthur (cin): Black Magic (1944); The Devil Bat; A Message From Mars (1921); Supernatural (1933); White Zombie
Martinelli, Elsa (act, b. 1935): La Decima Vittima; Et Mourir De Plaisir; Maroc 7; Le Plus Vieux Metier Du Monde; Rampage; The Trial
Martinelli, Enzo A. (cin): Code Name: Minus One; Dr. Strange; Exo-Man
Martinelli, Frank (act): A Date With The Falcon
Martinelli, Greg (wri): Mortal Sins
Martinelli, Jean (act): Le Comte De Monte Cristo; To Catch A Thief
Martinelli, Vincent (A.) (cin): Captain America II; Dark Night Of The Scarecrow; The Ultimate Impostor
Martines, Alessandra (act): Les Miserables (1995)
Martinez, A (act): Exo-Man; Not Of This World
Martinez, Adalberto (act): Flying Saucers
Martinez, Antonio (act): El Castillo De Las Bofetadas
Martinez, Arturo (act): The Black Scorpion; El Ladron De Cadaveres
Martinez, Benito (act): Outbreak
Martinez, Chico (act): The Howling
Martinez, Edward (act): Dance Of The Dwarfs
Martinez, Feiga (act): The Fan
Martinez, Fernando (act): Hundra
Martinez III, Flavio (act): Nightwing
Martinez, George (act): 100 Cries Of Terror
Martinez, Joaquin (act): The Lightning Incident
Martinez, Maribel (act): Anguish
Martinez, Mary (act): Voodoo Heartbeat
Martinez, Raoul (act): The Phantom Of The Red House
Martinez, Roberto (act): Monstroid
Martinez, Ruth (act): The Mutilator
Martinez, Terc (act): Cat People (1982)
Martin-Harvey, Michael (act): Torment (1949)
Martin-Harvey, Muriel (act): The Answer
Martini, Ettore (act): Ghoulies II
Martinique (act): Isle Of The Snake People
Martino, Al (mus, b. 1927): Hush...Hush, Sweet Charlotte
Martino, Chris (wri): Blood Of Ghastly Horror
Martino, Francesco (dir & wri): Queen Of The Cannibals
Martino, L. (wri): Ercole Contro I Tiranni Di Babilonia
Martino, Lea (wri): Ironmaster
Martino, Luciano (wri, a.k.a. Martin Hardy): The Fish Men; La Frusta E Il Corpo; Ironmaster; The Murder Clinic; Romolo E Remo
Martino, Ray (act): Goliath Against The Giants
Martino, Rik (act): A Polish Vampire In Burbank
Martino, Sergio (dir): Demons Of The Dead; The Fish Men; The Great Alligator; Il Montagna Di Dio Cannibale; Lo Strano Caso Della Signora Ward; Torso
Martino, Sergio (wri): The Fish Men; The Great Alligator; Il Montagna Di Dio Cannibale; Perseus The Invincible; Torso
Martinon, Jean (mus): Forces Occultes
Martinov, Peter (act): La Figlia Di Frankenstein
Martinovic, Mise (act): Arthur The King
Martins, Bill (act): To All A Goodnight
Martins, Orlando (act, b. 1899): Call Me Bwana; Sapphire; Tarzan And The Lost Safari
Martinsen, Britt (act): The Toxic Avenger
Martinsen, Dick (act): The Toxic Avenger
Martinsen, Kristen (act): The Toxic Avenger
Martinsen, Lisa (act): The Toxic Avenger
Martinson, Leslie (H.) (dir): The Atomic Kid; Batman (1966); Fathom; The Kid With The Broken Halo
Martitza, Sari (act): International House
Marton, Andrew (dir, 1908-1992): Around The World Under The Sea; Birds Do It; Crack In The World; King Solomon's Mines (1949); The Secret Of Stamboul; Storm Over Tibet; Wolf's Clothing (1936)
Marton, George (wri): Catch Me A Spy
Marton, jarmila (act): Storm Over Tibet
Martone, Elaine (act): Hands Of A Stranger; Zotz!
Marturano, Luigi (act): Goliath Against The Giants
Marty, Albert (act): Amazons (1986)
Martyn, Debbie (act): Killer's Moon
Martyn, Dickie (act): Macbeth (1971)
Martyn, Larry (act): The Final Conflict
Martyn, Peter (act): Child's Play (1954); Mad About Men
Maruna, Chris (wri): Empire Of Ash III
Maruzzi, Tom (act): Man Beast
Marvel, Holt (wri): Death At Broadcasting House
Marvel, Paul (act): The Psychotronic Man
Marvin, Grace (act): The Phantom Of The Opera (1925)
Marvin, Lee (act, 1924-1987): Gorilla At Large
Marvin, Mike (dir & wri): The Wraith
Marvin, Michelle (act): A Reflection Of Fear
Marx, Adolph Arthur (act): see Marx, Harpo
Marx, Chico (act, 1887-1961, nee Leonard Marx): The Story Of Mankind
Marx, Christy (wri): Secrets Of The Phantom Caverns
Marx, Groucho (act, 1890-1977, nee Julius Henry Marx): The Story Of Mankind
Marx, Harpo (act, 1888-1964, nee Adolph Arthur Marx): The Story Of Mankind
Marx, Julius Henry (act): see Marx, Groucho
Marx, Leonard (act): see Marx, Chico
Marx, Melinda (act): The Story Of Mankind
Marx, Rick (wri): Warrior Queen
Marx, Robert (act): El Castello Dell'orrore
Marx, William "Bill" (mus): Count Yorga, Vampire; The Deathmaster; The Folks At Red Wolf Inn; The Return Of Count Yorga; Scream, Blacula, Scream
Marxuach, A.M. (act): Jacob's Ladder
Mary, Joan (act): Dr. Tarr's Torture Dungeon
Mary, Renaud (act): Comment Qu'ella Est!
Marz, Carolyn (act): Driller Killer
Marzac, Mario (wri): The Night Of A Thousand Cats
Marzan, Rick (act): Eraser
Marzello, Vincent (act): Never Say Never Again; Superman (1978); The Witches (1990)
Marzevuc, Edward (act): The Red Tent
Marzi, Franca (act): Il Mostro Dell'isola; Psycosissimo
Marzorati, Harold J. (cin): The World, The Flesh And The Devil
Mas, Antonia (act): Hatchet For A Honeymoon
Masaaki, Fukawa (act): The Toxic Avenger, Part II
Masak, Ron (act): The Aliens Are Coming; Daddy's Gone A-Hunting; Laserblast
Mascaras, Mils (act): Las Vampiras (1969)`
Mascelli, Joseph (dir): Monstrosity
Masche, Jacquelyn (act): Repossessed
Maschinski, Shirl (act): The Psychotronic Man
Maschwitz, Eric (wri): Little Red Monkey
Mascia, Tony (act): The Man Who Fell To Earth (1976)
Mascini, Peer (act): The Lift
Masciocchi, Marcello (cin): Il Planeta Degli Uomini Spenti; Yor, The Hunter From The Future
Masciocchi, Raffaele (cin, a.k.a. Donald Green): Queen Of The Pirates; Raptus; Lo Spettro
Mascolo, Joseph (act): Jaws 2; The Trial Of The Incredible Hulk
Mascot, Jerry (act): Blood Diner
Mascutto, Steve (act): Raiders Of The Living Dead
Mase, Marino (act, a.k.a. Martin Mase): Alien Contamination; The Night Porter; The Vatican Affair; Zorro (1975)
Mase, Martin (act): see Mase, Marino
Masefield, Joseph R. (wri): Don't Go In The House
Mashaw, Sue (act): The Alien Within
Mashita, Nelson (act): Darkman (1990); Eve Of Destruction
Masina, Giuletta (act, 1920-1994): Giulietta Degli Spiriti; Lo Sceicco Bianco
Masino, Steve (act): Master Of The World
Mask, Ace (act): Chopping Mall; Not Of This Earth (1988)
Maskell, Tina (act): Transmutations
Maskell, Virginia (act, 1936-1968): The Man Upstairs
Maslansky, Paul (dir): Sugar Hill
Maslow, Walter (act): Atlas; The Cosmic Man; The Human Duplicators
Mason, A.E.W. (wri): At The Villa Rose (1920 & 1939); The Drum; The House Of The Arrow (1930, 1940 & 1953); Princess Clementina
Mason, B.J. (act): Whispering Death
Mason, Basil (wri): Candles At Nine; Death At Broadcasting House; Secret Lives; The Silent Passenger
Mason, Bert (cin): Zex
Mason, Bob (act): Mary Reilly
Mason, Brewster (act): The Quatermass Conclusion
Mason, Buddy (wri): The Comedy Of Terrors; Invasion Of The Saucer Men
Mason, Connie (act): Blood Feast; 2000 Maniacs

Mason, Curt (act): The Corpse Grinders
Mason, Dan (act): The Last Starfighter
Mason, Edward J. (wri): Celia; Dick Barton At Bay; Dick Barton, Detective; Dick Barton, Special Agent; Dick Barton Strikes Back
Mason, Eliot (act, 1897-1949): Black Limelight; The Ghost At St. Michael's; The Ghost Goes West
Mason, Eric (GB act): Jekyll And Hyde
Mason, Eric (USA act): Kiss Of The Tarantula
Mason, Frank (mus): The Murder Clinic
Mason, Gabby (act): Chilling
Mason, Gladys (act): The Amazing Partnership; Her Greatest Performance; A Man's Shadow; The Queen Mother; Shadow Of Evil (1921)
Mason, Haddon (act): Castle Sinister (1932); The Triumph Of The Scarlet Pimpernel; The Woman In White (1929); The Yellow Mask
Mason, Henry (act): The Invincible Barbarian
Mason, Hilary (act): Dolls; Don't Look Now; I Don't Want To Be Born; Meridian; Robot Jox
Mason, Ingrid (act): Picnic At Hanging Rock
Mason, James (act, 1909-1984): Alias The Lone Wolf; Alibi (1942); Blind Man's Bluff (1936); The Boys From Brazil; Caught; Cry Terror!; The Deadly Affair; Evil Under The Sun; Fanny By Gaslight; The Flower In His Mouth; Frankenstein: The True Story; Great Expectations (1974); Heaven Can Wait (1978); I Met A Murderer; Journey To The Center Of The Earth (1959); The Man In Grey; Murder By Decree; The Night Has Eyes; North By Northwest; Pandora And The Flying Dutchman; The Patient Vanishes; A Place Of One's Own; Prince Valiant; The Prisoner Of Zenda (1952); The Return Of The Scarlet Pimpernel; Salem's Lot; The Secret Of Stamboul; Stranger In The House (1967); The Tell-Tale Heart (1953, Usa); Thunder Rock; 20,000 Leagues Under The Sea (1954); The Water Babies
Mason, James (wri, 1909-1984): I Met A Murderer
Mason, Kathleen (act): My Cousin Rachel
Mason, Kaye (wri): Dr. Sin Fang
Mason, Laura (act): The Bowery Boys Meet The Monsters; Queen Of Outer Space
Mason, LeRoy (act): The Man Who Wouldn't Die; Time To Kill (1942)
Mason, Lola (act): The Brain That Wouldn't Die
Mason, Louis (act): The Shanghai Chest; The Velvet Touch
Mason, Madison (act): Omen IV: The Awakening
Mason, Maria (act): Candyman: Farewell To The Flesh
Mason, Marsha (act, b. 1942): Audrey Rose
Mason, Max (act): The Next Victim (1975)
Mason, May (act): The Penguin Pool Murder
Mason, Nick (mus): White Of The Eye
Mason, Pamela (act, b. 1918, nee Pamela Kellino): I Met A Murderer; The Navy Vs. The Night Monsters; Pandora And The Flying Dutchman; Sex Kittens Go To College
Mason, Pamela (wri, b. 1918): I Met A Murderer
Mason, Patricia (act): Macbeth (1971)
Mason, Paul (wri): King Kong vs. Godzilla
Mason, Portland (act): Cry Terror!
Mason, Reginald (act): Charlie Chan's Courage
Mason, Renee (act): Trauma (1963)
Mason, Robert (wri): Solo
Mason, Roy (act): Man On A Swing
Mason, Sharon (act): Primal Scream
Mason, Shirley (act, 1900-1979, nee Leona Flugrath): The Eleventh Hour (1923); Treasure Island (1920)
Mason, Stan (act): Voodoo Heartbeat
Mason, Sydney (act): Creature From The Black Lagoon
Mason, Tom (act): The Aliens Are Coming; Nero Wolfe; The Puppet Masters; The Return Of The Man From U.N.C.L.E.
Mason, Dr. Tom (act): Night Of The Ghouls; Plan 9 From Outer Space
Masreliez, Curt (act): The Devil's Wanton
Massa, Bernie (act): Heaven Can Wait (1978)
Massaccesi, Aristide (dir): Death Smiles On A Murderer
Massaccesi, Aristide (wri): The Grim Reaper
Massara, Natale (mus): The Black Cat (1980); Piranha (1978); Treasure Island (1971)
Massari, John (mus): Killer Klowns From Outer Space
Massari, Lea (act, b. 1933): The Colossus Of Rhodes; The Great Manhunt (1974); The Night Caller
Massart, Mary (act): The Yellow Claw
Massasso, Aldo (act): The Living Dead At Manchester Morgue
Massee, Michael (act): Seven; Tales From The Hood
Massen, Osa (act, b. 1916): Background To Danger; Cry Of The Werewolf; Rocketship X-M
Massey, Achena (act): Waxwork II: Lost In Time
Massey, Anna (act): Bunny Lake Is Missing; De Sade; Frenzy; Gideon's Day; The Mcguffin; Peeping Tom; The Vault Of Horror
Massey, Athena (act): The Nutty Professor (1996)
Massey, Daniel (act, b. 1933): The Cat And The Canary (1978); Fragment Of Fear; The Vault Of Horror; Warlords Of The Deep
Massey, Daria (act): The Miracle (1959); Sabu And The Magic Ring
Massey, Edith (act): Mutants In Paradise; Polyester
Massey, Gene (act): Dr. Black Mr. Hyde
Massey, Ilona (act, 1912-1974, nee Ilona Hajmassy): Frankenstein Meets The Wolf Man; Invisible Agent
Massey, Jayne (act): The Destructors
Massey, Mark (act): Offerings
Massey, Raymond (act, 1896-1983): Arsenic And Old Lace; Black Limelight; The Drum; The Face At The Window (1932); 49th Parallel; High Treason (1929); A Matter Of Life And Death; The Old Dark House (1932); Omar Khayyam; Possessed (1947); The Prisoner Of Zenda (1937); The Scarlet Pimpernel (1934); The Speckled Band (1931); Things To Come; The Woman In The Window
Massey, Walter (act): Happy Birthday To Me
Massie, Chris (wri): Corridor Of Mirrors; Love Letters
Massie, Elizabeth (act): Wolf
Massie, Paul (act, b. 1932): Sapphire; The Two Faces Of Dr. Jekyll
Mass Illusion (cin): Judge Dredd
Massimi, Massimilio (act): Captain America (1992)
Massingham, Richard (act): Turn The Key Softly
Masso, Sylvain (act): Screamers (1996)
Masson, Diego (mus): Spirits Of The Dead
Mastandrea, Nick (act): Martin
Mastantuono, Marco (act): The Great Alligator; The Secret Of Seagull Island
Mastelloni, Leopoldo (act): Inferno (1979)
Mastellos, Katherine (act): Phantom Of The Paradise
Master, Ian (act): The Medusa Touch
Masters, Ben (act): All That Jazz; Demon And The Mummy; Dream Lover; Making Mr. Right
Masters, Michael (act): Ssssss
Masters, Natalie (act): The Vampire (1957)
Masters, Todd (act & cin): The Resurrected
Masterson, Mary Stuart (act, b. 1966): Chances Are
Masterson, Peter (act, b. 1934): The Exorcist; Man On A Swing; The Stepford Wives
Masterton, Graham (wri, b. 1946): The Manitou
Mastorakis, Nico (dir & wri): Blind Date; The Next One; The Zero Boys
Mastrantonio, Mary Elizabeth (act, b. 1958): The Abyss; Robin Hood: Prince Of Thieves; Three Wishes (1995)
Mastrianna, Domenick (act): The Toxic Avenger, Part II
Mastrianni, Federica (act): Phenomena
Mastrocinque, Camillo (dir): La Maldicion De Los Karnsteins
Mastroianni, Armand (dir): Cameron's Closet; The Clairvoyant (1985); Distortions; He Knows You're Alone; Robin Cook's Invasion; The Supernaturals
Mastroianni, Marcello (act, 1924-1996): L'assassino; City Of Women; La Decima Vittima; 8 1/2; Spara Forte, Piu Forte...Non Capisco
Mastropietro, Eugenio (act): Satyricon
Masur, Richard (act): The Believers; Bride Of Boogedy; The Demon Murder Case; Encino Man; It (1990); Multiplicity; My Science Project; Nightmares (1983); The Thing (1982); Timerider
Mata, Cosme T. (act): Surf Nazis Must Die
Matalon, Eddy (dir): Blackout (1978); Cauchemares
Matalon, Eddy (wri): Cauchemares
Matamoros, Diego (act): The Quilt Of Hathor
Matania, Clelia (act): Don't Look Now
Mataras, Krystle (act): Single White Female
Mataras, Tiffany (act): Single White Female
Matas, Fabia (act): Anguish
Matchett, Christopher (act): The Illustrated Man
Mate, Rudolph (cin, 1898-1964): Address Unknown; Charlie Chan In Shanghai; Charlie Chan's Secret; Dante's Inferno (1935); Down To Earth; Foreign Correspondent; Gilda; Liliom (1933); Vampyr
Mate, Rudolph (dir, 1898-1964): The Black Shield Of Falworth; D.O.A. (1949); The Green Glove; Revak, Lo Schiavo Di Cartagine; Second Chance; When Worlds Collide
Materassi, Giovanni (act): The Prisoner Of The Iron Mask
Mathen, Mahdu (act): Children Of The Damned
Mather, Anna (act): The Charlatan
Mather, Aubrey (act, 1885-1958): The Adventures Of Don Juan; The Golden Mask; The Great Impersonation (1942); Heaven Can Wait (1942); The House Of Fear (1945); Jamaica Inn (1939); Jane Eyre (1944); The Lodger (1944); The Man In The Mirror; The Man Who Changed His Name; Sabotage; The Silent Passenger; The Undying Monster; When Knights Were Bold (1936)
Mather, Berkeley (wri): Dr. No; Information Received
Mather, George (act): Galaxina; Pattern For Murder; Ring Of Terror
Mather, Jack (act): Deranged (1974)
Mather, John (act): The Jungle Book (1942)
Mather, John (C.) (wri): Devil Girl From Mars; Satellite In The Sky
Mathers, James (wri): Dr. Jekyll's Dungeon Of Death
Mathers, Jerry (act, b. 1948): This Is My Love; The Trouble With Harry
Mathers, Susie (act): This Is My Love
Mathes, Marissa (act): Blood Bath (1966)
Matheson, Bryan (act): Memoirs Of A Survivor
Matheson, Chris (wri): Bill & Ted's Bogus Journey; Bill & Ted's Excellent Adventure; Mom And Dad Save The World
Matheson, Don (act): Alice In Wonderland (1985)
Matheson, Judy (act): Crucible Of Terror; The Flesh And Blood Show; Scream And Die!; Twins Of Evil
Matheson, Lee (act): The Resurrected
Matheson, Richard (wri, b. 1926): The Comedy Of Terrors; Dead Of Night (1977); De Sade; The Devil Rides Out; Dracula (1973); Dying Room Only; Fanatic; House Of Usher; The Incredible Shrinking Man; The Incredible Shrinking Woman; Jaws 3-D; The Last Man On Earth; The Legend Of Hell House; Master Of The World; Night Of The Eagle; The Night Stalker (1971); The Night Strangler; The Omega Man; The Pit And The Pendulum (1961); The Raven (1963); Scream Of The Wolf; Somewhere In Time; The Strange Possession Of Mrs. Oliver; The Stranger Within; Tales Of Terror; Trilogy Of Terror; Twilight Zone
Matheson, Richard Christian (wri): Full Eclipse
Matheson, Tim (act, b. 1947): Bay Coven; Buried Secrets; Impulse (1984); A Kiss To Die For; Robin Cook's Harmful Intent; Solar Crisis; Sometimes They Come Back
Mathews, Carmen (act): They Call It Murder
Mathews, David (wri): Hurricane Island; The Magic Carpet
Mathews, George (act): City Beneath The Sea (1952)
Mathews, Grace (act): The Flame Barrier; From Hell It Came; She Demons
Mathews, Jeremy (act): Quarantine
Mathews, John (act): Shock Corridor
Mathews, Joyce (act): Arrest Bulldog Drummond
Mathews, Kerwin (act, b. 1926): Battle Beneath The Earth; The Boy Who Cried Werewolf; Death Takes A Holiday (1971); Jack The Giant Killer; Maniac (1963); Nightmare In Blood; Octaman; The Pirates Of Blood River; The 7th Voyage Of Sinbad; Shadow Of Evil (1964); The Three Worlds Of Gulliver
Mathews, Laura J. (wri): The Devil's Partner
Mathews, Michael G. (cin): Tuck Everlasting
Mathews, Richard (act): The Satanic Rites Of Dracula
Mathews, Sheila (act): The Poseidon Adventure; The Towering Inferno
Mathews, Stephen (act): Vampire On Bikini Beach
Mathews, Thom (act): Friday The 13th, Part Vi: Jason Lives; The Return Of The Living Dead (1985); Return Of The Living Dead, Part Ii
Mathias, Anna (act): Night Of The Comet; Once Bitten
Mathias, Bob (act, b. 1930): The Minotaur
Mathias, Harry (cin): Creature; Phantom Of The Mall: Eric's Revenge; Timestalkers
Mathias, Liat (act): The Phantom Empire
Mathie, Marion (act): Dracula Has Risen From The Grave
Mathieson, Muir (mus, 1911-1975): Circus Of Horrors; The House In The Square; How To Murder A Rich Uncle; The Man Inside; The Man Who Could Work Miracles; The October Man; Saturday Island; The Sound Barrier; Svengali (1954); Tom Thumb; Woman Of Straw
Mathieson, Murray (act, 1912-1985): Angel On My Shoulder (1980); Jamaica Run; Twilight Zone
Mathis, Johnny (act, b. 1935): Lizzie
Mathis, June (wri, 1892-1927): The Conquering Power; In The Palace Of The King
Mathison, Melissa (wri): E.T.-The Extra-Terrestrial; The Indian In The Cupboard
Mathison, Vern (act): Sisters Of Death
Mathot, Jenny (act): Paul Temple's Triumph
Matias, Emi (act): Anguish
Matieson, Otto (act): Boston Blackie; The Last Of The Lone Wolf; The Maltese Falcon (1931)
Matisse, Anna (act): The Private Life Of Sherlock Holmes
Matlen, Patty (act): Silent Night, Deadly Night III
Matlovsky, Samuel (mus): Birds Do It; Games
Matmor, Daniel (act): The Mangler
Mato, Oliver (act): Revenge In The House Of Usher
Maton, Andy (act): Starcrossed
Matos, Paola (act): Hundra
Matou, Michael (act): A Midsummer Night's Dream (1985)
Matras, Christian (cin, b. 1903): L'aigle A Deux Tetes; Cartouche (1962); Lola Montes; Lucrezia Borgia (1952); Madame Dubarry (1954)
Matson, Ericka (act): The Hand That Rocks The Cradle
Matsuda, Hiroo (wri): Message From Space
Matsuda, Shozo (wri): Live Today, Die Tomorrow
Matsuda, Yusaka (act): Murder In The Doll House
Matsukata, Hiroki (act): The Magic Serpent
Matsumoto, Katsuhei (act): Kwaidan
Matsumoto, Koshiro (act): Chusingura (1963)
Matsumoto, Mitsuo (act): Mothra
Matsumura, Tatsuo (act): King Kong Vs. Godzilla
Matsuya, Hiroaki (act): The Toxic Avenger, Part II
Matsuyama, Keisuke (act): Mothra
Mattei, Bruno (dir, a.k.a. Vincent Dawn): Night Of The Zombies (1983)
Mattei, Pino (act): Kiss Kiss, Kill Kill
Mattera, Gino (act): Faust And The Devil
Matters, Graham (act): 20th Century Oz
Matteucci, Steve (act): Waxwork II: Lost In Time
Mattey, Robert A. (cin): Mary Poppins
Matthau, Charlie (dir): Doin' Time On Planet Earth
Matthau, David (act): Battlestar Galactica
Matthau, Walter (act, b. 1923, nee Walter Matuschanskayasky): Earthquake; Fail-Safe; Goodbye Charlie
Matthews, A.E. (act, 1869-1960): Around The World In 80 Days; Escape To Danger; The Ghosts Of Berkeley Square; Just William's Luck; The Lifeguardsman; The Man In Grey; Mr. Drake's Duck; Pimpernel Smith; They Came To A City; Thunder Rock
Matthews, Al (act): Aliens; The Final Conflict; Meet Nero Wolfe; Riders Of The Storm
Matthews, Brendan (act): The Viking Queen
Matthews, Brian (act): The Burning; Lord Of The Flies (1990)
Matthews, Carole (act): Amazon Quest; Betrayed Women; Cry Murder; I Love A Mystery (1945); The Man With My Face; The Strange Awakening; Swamp Women
Matthews, Christopher (act): Blind Terror; Scars Of Dracula; Scream And Scream Again
Matthews, Dakin (act): Eve Of Destruction
Matthews, Ed (act): Eve Of Destruction
Matthews, Forrest (act): The Docks Of New Orleans
Matthews, Francis (act): Doctor Of Seven Dials; Dracula, Prince Of Darkness; The Hell-Fire Club; The Mcguffin; Rasputin, The Mad Monk; The Revenge Of Frankenstein; The Treasure Of Monte Cristo (1961)
Matthews, Geoffrey (act): The Day Of The Triffids
Matthews, James (wri): The Teckman Mystery

Matthews, Jessie (act, 1907-1981): Candles At Nine; The Hound Of The Baskervilles (1978); Tom Thumb
Matthews, John (act): Sleuth
Matthews, Kevin (act): Pumpkinhead II: Blood Wings
Matthews, Lester (act, b. 1900) The Adventures Of Robin Hood; Between Two Worlds; Bulldog Drummond At Bay (1947); Creeping Shadows; Gaslight (1944); Gipsy Blood; The Invisible Man's Revenge; Jamaica Run; Jungle Jim In The Forbidden Land; Jungle Man-Eaters; The Lady In The Iron Mask; The Lone Wolf Keeps A Date; The Man At Six; The Miracle (1959); The Mysterious Doctor; The Mysterious Mr. Moto; The Old Man; On Secret Service; Operation Secret; The Raven (1935); Rogues Of Sherwood Forest; Savage Mutiny; Shadows In The Night; The Son Of Dr. Jekyll; The Stolen Necklace; Werewolf Of London; The Wickham Mystery
Matthews, M.J. (act): No Blade Of Grass
Matthews, Michael (act): Donor; Shocker
Matthews, Thom (act): Heatseeker
Mattick, Pattye (act): The Beguiled
Matticola, C.M. (act): Flesh-Eating Mothers
Mattingly, Hedley (act): Goliath Awaits
Mattingly 2nd, T. Kenneth (act): For All Mankind
Matton, Charles (dir & wri): Spermula
Mattos, Laure (act): C.H.U.D.
Mattos, Tony A. (act): Phenomenon
Mattox, Martha (act): The Cat And The Canary (1927); The Monster Walks
Mattraw, Scotty (act): The Thief Of Bagdad (1924)
Mattson, Bart (act): The Story Of Mankind
Mattson, Denver (act): The Monster Squad
Mattson, Robin (act): Are You In The House Alone?; Captain America (1978); Fantasies; Phantom Of The Paradise
Mattsson, Arne (dir, b. 1919): The Doll (1963); Morianna; Nattmara
Mattsson, Arne (wri, b. 1919): Morianna
Matty (act): Dark Of The Night
Mature, Victor (act, b. 1916): Affair With A Stranger; Androcles And The Lion; Dangerous Mission; I Wake Up Screaming; Moss Rose; One Million B.C.; Samson And Delilah; The Tartars; The Veils Of Bagdad
Maturin, Eric (act): The Face At The Window (1932); The Flaw; The Squeaker (1930)
Matus, Charlene (act): Night Of The Zombies (1981)
Matuschanskayasky, Walter (act): see Matthau, Walter
Matuszak, John (act, 1950-1989): Caveman (1981); Ghost Writer; The Goonies; The Ice Pirates
Matz, Peter (mus): The Man In The Santa Claus Suit
Matzenauer, Robert (act): Attack Of The Killer Tomatoes
Matzo, Emma (act): see Scott, Lizabeth
Mauban, Maria (act): Cage Of Gold
Maude, Arthur (act): The Man From Beyond; The Thirteenth Candle
Maude, Arthur (dir): The Clue Of The New Pin (1929); The Lure; The Ringer (1928)
Maude, Arthur (wri): A Message From Mars (1921)
Maude, Beatrice (act): Invasion Of The Body Snatchers (1956)
Maude, Edna (act): The Princess Of Happy Chance; When Knights Were Bold (1916)
Maude, Evelyn (act): The Romany Rye
Maude, Gillian (act): Dick Barton, Special Agent; Sexton Blake And The Bearded Doctor
Maude, Joan (act): Chamber Of Horrors (1929); Corridor Of Mirrors; A Matter Of Life And Death; Menace (1934); The Wandering Jew (1933)
Maude, Joan (wri): All Hallowe'en
Maude, Mary (act): Crucible Of Terror; The House That Screamed; Terror (1979)
Maude-Roxby, Roddy (act): Greystoke: The Legend Of Tarzan, Lord Of The Apes
Maudet, Christian (dir & wri): see Christian-Jaque
Mauge, Roger (wri): L'ours
Maugham, Robert (wri): The Servant
Maugham, Somerset (wri, 1874-1965): The Magician (1926); The Secret Agent (1936); Three Cases Of Murder
Mauldin, John (act): The Magic Sword (1962)
Mauldin, Nat (wri): The Preacher's Wife
Maule, Annabel (act): Danger Tomorrow; Model For Murder

Maur, Meinhart (act): Dick Barton At Bay; Dr. Syn; The Return Of The Frog; Three Silent Men
Mauras, Felix (act): Angel Heart
Maureen, Mollie/Molly (act): The Hound Of The Baskervilles (1978); Jabberwocky; The Orchard End Murder; The Private Life Of Sherlock Holmes
Maurer, Friedrich (act): Das Schloss
Maurer, Michael (act): Street Trash
Maurer, Norman (wri, d. 1986): The Three Stooges In Orbit; The Three Stooges Meet Hercules
Maurer, Peggy (act): I Bury The Living
Maurey, Nicole (act, b. 1925): The Day Of The Triffids; Secret Of The Incas; The Very Edge
Mauri, Francisco (act): Zorro, The Gay Blade
Mauri, Glauco (act): Profundo Rosso
Mauri, Roberto (dir & wri): La Strage Dei Vampiri
Maurice, Clement (dir): Le Duel D'hamlet
Maurice, Jon (act): Primal Scream
Maurice, Paula (act): The Brain That Wouldn't Die
Maurice, Rex (act): The Silent House
Maurin, Delphine (act): The Murder Clinic
Mauro, David (act): The Ambushers
Mauro, Gary (act): Once Bitten
Mauro, Glen (act): Once Bitten
Maurstad, Alfred (act): Valley Of The Eagles
Maur-Thorp, Sarah (act): Edge Of Sanity; Ten Little Indians (1989)
Maurus, Gerda (act): Die Frau Im Mond; Spione
Maury, Darrel (act): Looker
Mavity, Arthur (D.) (act): Detective Daring And The Thames Coiners; Thelma: Or, Saved From The Sea
Max (animal act): Man's Best Friend
Max, Ed(win) (act): Follow Me Quietly; The Incredible Melting Man; A Matter Of Life And Death; The Twonky
Max, Jean (act): J'accuse (1937)
Max, Jerome (wri): Tentacles
Maxey, Paul (act): Bride Of The Gorilla; Philo Vance's Secret Mission; The Sky Dragon
Maxfield, Henry S. (wri): The Double Man
Maxie, Judith (act): The Death Of The Incredible Hulk; The Resurrected
Maxim, John (act): Frankenstein Created Woman; She (1965)
Maxon, Dan (act): The Chinese Parrot
Maxon, Eric (act): Richard III (1911)
Maxt, David (act): Superman (1978)
Maxted, Stanley (act): Fiend Without A Face
Maxwell, Charles (act): The Search For Bridey Murphy
Maxwell, Chet (act): Vampire On Bikini Beach
Maxwell, Don (act): The Bees; Humanoids From The Deep; Return Of The Living Dead, Part II
Maxwell, Edwin (act): The Gorilla (1931); Mystery Of The Wax Museum; The Night Key; Night Of Terror (1933)
Maxwell, Frank (act): Daughter Of The Mind; The Haunted Palace (1963)
Maxwell, Geraldine (act): Pearls Of Death
Maxwell, James (act): The Damned; Evil Of Frankenstein; The Hunchback Of Notre Dame (1965); Mirror Of Deception; Otley
Maxwell, Jane (act): Black Devils Of Kali
Maxwell, John (act): The Prowler (1951); The War Of The Worlds
Maxwell, Larry (act): Poison (1990)
Maxwell, Lily (act): The Mystery Of The Diamond Belt
Maxwell, Lisa (act): The Dark Crystal
Maxwell, Lois (act, b. 1927, nee Lois Hooker): Corridor Of Mirrors; Crime Doctor's Diary; The Decision Of Christopher Blake; Diamonds Are Forever; Dr. No; Endless Night; Eternal Evil; Face Of Fire; For Your Eyes Only; From Russia With Love; Goldfinger; The Haunting; Kill Me Tomorrow; Lady In The Fog; Live And Let Die; Love And Poison; Man In Hiding; The Man With The Golden Gun; Moonraker; Octopussy; On Her Majesty's Secret Service; Operation Kid Brother; Passport To Treason; Satellite In The Sky; The Spy Who Loved Me; Thunderball; A View To A Kill; You Only Live Twice
Maxwell, Marilyn (act, 1922-1972, nee Marvel Maxwell): Lost In A Harem
Maxwell, Marvel (act): see Maxwell, Marilyn
Maxwell, Max (act): I Was A Zombie For The F.B.I.
Maxwell, Paul (GB act): Cry Wolf (1980); The Curse Of The Golem; The Haunting; Madame Sin; The Man Outside (1967); The Return Of Sherlock Holmes (1986)
Maxwell, Paul (USA act): Blood Of Dracula; How To Make A Monster
Maxwell, Paula (act): 20th Century Oz
Maxwell, Peter (dir): The Ghost Train Murder

Maxwell, Richard (wri): The Serpent And The Rainbow
Maxwell, Robert (cin): Astro Zombies
Maxwell, Roberta (act): Psycho III
Maxwell, W.B. (wri): Honour In Pawn
May, Ackerman (act): Called Back
May, Alice (act): Missing Millions
May, Anthony (act): No Blade Of Grass
May, Betty (act): see Adams, Julie
May, Billy (mus): Johnny Cool
May, Bradford (cin): Darkman II: The Return Of Durant; The Monster Squad
May, Bradford (dir): Asteroid; Darkman Ii: The Return Of Durant; Mortal Sins
May, Brian (mus, b. 1947): Cloak And Dagger (1984); The Day After Halloween; Dr. Giggles; Freddy's Dead: The Final Nightmare; Harlequin; Mad Max; Patrick; Road Games; The Road Warrior; Steel Dawn; Thirst
May, Bunny (act): Frenzy
May, Curt (act): Blow Out
May, Daniel (mus): Zombie High
May, Dinah (act): Mark Of The Devil (1985)
May, Donald (act): Kisses For My President
May, Elaine (act, b. 1932):In The Spirit
May, Elaine (wri, b. 1932): Heaven Can Wait (1978)
May, Hans (mus): Thunder Rock
May, Harry (cin): The Plutonium Incident; A Vacation In Hell
May, Jack (act): Cat Girl; The Man Who Would Be King; The Seven-Per-Cent Solution; Trog
May, Jay (act): Schizoid (1980)
May, Joe (dir, 1880-1954, nee Joseph Mandel): Die Herrin Der Welt; House Of Fear (1939); The House Of The Seven Gables; The Invisible Man Returns
May, Joe (wri, 1880-1954): The Invisible Man Returns; The Invisible Woman (1941); The Strange Death Of Adolf Hitler
May, Julie (act): Work Is A Four Letter Word
May, Kathleen (act): Jungle Trail Of The Son Of Tarzan
May, Lenora (act): Fantasies; House II, The Second Story; When A Stranger Calls
May, Mary (act): Phoenix The Warrior
May, Mathilda (act): Lifeforce
May, Peter (act): Countess Dracula; Taste The Blood Of Dracula
May, Rita (act): Threads
Mayall, Rik (act): An American Werewolf In London; Shock Treatment! (1981)
Mayans, Anthony (act): Zombies Lake
Maybach, Christiane (act): The Naked Woman And Satan
Maybanke, Laon (act): Night Watch
Mayberg, Katharina (act): The Dragon's Blood
Mayberry, James (act): Freejack
Mayberry, Russ(ell) (dir): Fer-De-Lance; Probe; The Spaceman And King Arthur; A Very Missing Person
Mayer, Carl (wri, 1894-1944): Genuine; Das Kabinett Des Dr. Caligari; Der Letzte Mann; Schloss Vogelod
Mayer, Chip (act): Stunts Unlimited; Survivor
Mayer, Edwin Justus 9wri, b. 1896): Peter Ibbetson; The Unholy Night
Mayer, Jerry (act): Single White Female
Mayer, Ken (act): Jack The Giant Killer
Mayer, Lawrence (act): Mother's Day
Mayer, Ronald (act): Only A Scream Away
Mayer, Sam (wri): Storm Over Tibet
Maverick, Val (act): The Demon Lover
Mayers, Michael (cin): Class Of Nuke'em High
Mayersberg, Paul (dir): Nightfall (1988)
Mayersberg, Paul (wri): The Man Who Fell To Earth (1976); Nightfall (1988)
Mayes, Norman (act): The Falcon Out West; The Saint In Palm Springs
Mayes, Richard (act): Top Secret! (1984)
Mayes, Wendell (wri, b. 1918): The Poseidon Adventure
Mayeux, Rosalee (act): The Lawnmower Man
Mayfield, Ann Todd (act): see Todd, Ann (USA act)
Mayfield, Katherine (act): Flesh-Eating Mothers
Mayfield, Les (dir): Encino Man; Miracle On 34th Street (1994)
Mayhew, Peter (act): The Empire Strikes Back; Return Of The Jedi; Star Wars; Terror (1979)
Maylam, Tony (dir): The Burning; The Sins Of Dorian Gray; Split Second (1992)
Maylia (act): Boston Blackie's Chinese Venture
Maynard, Amanda (act): Murder With Mirrors
Maynard, Bill (act): Robin And Marian
Maynard, Earl (act): The Deep; The Sword And The Sorcerer
[illegible]: Big Foot
Maynard, Kermit (act): Girls In Prison
Maynard, Ted (act): Highlander; Nightbreed

Mayne, Belinda (act): Goliath Awaits; Krull; Not Guilty; The Strangers
Mayne, Eric (act): Beyond The Curtain (1924); The Black Bird (1926); The Conquering Power; The Drums Of Jeopardy (1923)
Mayne, Ferdinand/Ferdy/Ferdi (act, b. 1917): All Hallowe'en; Conan The Destroyer; Deadly Record; The Echo Murders; The End Of The Line; The Fearless Vampire Killers Or: Pardon Me, But Your Teeth Are In My Neck; Find The Lady; Frightmare (1983); The Glass Tomb; Hawk The Slayer; Howling Ii; Limbo Line; The Magic Christian; Meet Sexton Blake; Operation Crossbow; Paris Express; The Spider's Web; The Vampire Happening; The Vampire Lovers; A Woman Of Mystery
Mayne, G.E.R. (wri): A Garret In Bohemia
Mayne, Margo (act): Spaceflight IC-1
Mayne, Tony (act): The Mutations
Mayniel, Juliette (act): The Trojan Horse; Les Yeux Sans Visage
Maynor, Asa (act): Conquest Of The Planet Of The Apes; The Loved One
Maynor, Virginia (act): Man Beast
Mayo, Alfredo (act): A Bell From Hell
Mayo, Archie (dir, 1891-1968): Angel On My Shoulder (1946); Svengali (1931)
Mayo, Christine (act): The Shock (1923)
Mayo, David (act): I Was A Zombie For The F.B.I.
Mayo, Frank (act): The Altair Stairs; Nancy Drew And The Hidden Staircase; The Phantom Creeps; Think Fast, Mr. Moto; Torchy Plays With Dynamite
Mayo, Heidi (act): The Witches And The Grinnygog
Mayo, Raymond (act): Doomsday Machine; Night Slaves
Mayo, Susana (act): No Exit
Mayo, Tobar (act): Schizoid (1980)
Mayo, Virginia (act, b. 1920, nee Virginia Jones): Castle Of Evil; Congo Crossing; Pearl Of The South Pacific; The Secret Life Of Walter Mitty; The Story Of Mankind
Mayo, Whitman (act): Of Mice And Men (1981)
Mayo-Chandler, Karen (act): Explorers
Mayoff, Steven (act): Happy Birthday To Me
Mayol, Gerardo (act): Nightlife (1989, USA-Mex)
Mayr, K. (act): Twisted
Mayron, Gale (act): Donor
Mayron, Melanie (act, b. 1956): Heartbeeps
Mays, Ralph E. (act): Scalpel
Mays, Rod (act): The Power (1980)
Mays, Walter R. (act): Scalpel
Mayuzumi, Toshiro (mus, 1929-1997): The Bible; Reflections In A Golden Eye
Mayweather, Joshua Gibran (act): Candyman: Farewell To The Flesh
Maywood, Patricia (act): Empire Of Ash III
Mazar, Debi (act, b. 1964):Batman Forever
Maze, Gertrude (act): Forever Evil
Mazur, Heather (act): Night Of The Living Dead (1990)
Mazur, Monet (act):Addams Family Values
Mazur, Stephen (wri): Liar Liar
Mazure, Alfred (wri): Secrets Of Sex
Mazurki, Mike (act, 1908-1990): Around The World In 80 Days; The Canterville Ghost (1944); Dick Tracy (1945 & 1990); Dr. Renault's Secret; Five Weeks In A Balloon; Hell Ship Mutiny; The Horn Blows At Midnight; Murder, My Sweet; Nightmare Alley; Samson And Delilah; Sinbad The Sailor; The Thin Man Goes Home; Zotz!
Mazursky, Paul (act, b. 1930): Deathwatch; Touch
Mazzei, Cariann (act): The Toxic Avenger, Part II
Mazzei, Carol (act): The Toxic Avenger, Part II
Mazzella, Dawn (act): Repossessed; Wicked Stepmother
Mazzello, Joseph (act): Jurassic Park; Three Wishes (1995)
Mazzieri, Francesco (act): The Fish Men
Mazzinghi, Piero (act): The Night Porter; Profundo Rosso
Mazziotti, Julianne (act): Puppet Master II
Mazzola, Leonard A. (act): Assassin (1986)
Mazzone-Abbott Dancers (act): Abbott And Costello Meet The Mummy
Mazzoni, Frances (act): Martin
Mazzuca, Joseph A. (dir): Sisters Of Death
M'Bia, Ambroise (act): The Mysterious Island Of Captain Nemo
McAboy, Scott (wri): The Power Within
McAdam, Heather (act): Starflight: The Plane That Couldn't Land
McAdams, Ann (act): Don't Look In The Basement

McAdams, Bob (act): Blood Simple

McAdams, Brett (act): Funeral Home

McAlee, Anndi (act): Ice Cream Man

McAlinney, Patrick (act): The Boy Who Turned Yellow; The Insect Play; The Omen; Return Of A Stranger; Revenge (1971, Gb)

McAllen, Kathleen Rowe (act): Fear No Evil (1981)

McAllister, Guy (act): Secrets Of The Phantom Caverns

McAllister, Lon (act): The Red House

McAllister, Paul (act): The Lone Wolf (1924); Trilby (1915)

McAllister, Shawn (act):The Funhouse (1981)

McAlpine, Donald (cin): Predator

McAlpine, James (act):Someone's Watching Me!

McAmish, Chuck (act): Galaxina

McAnally, Ray (act): Fear Is The Key; High Spirits; Murder In Eden; Quest For Love

McAndrew, Marianne (act): The Bat People; She's Dressed To Kill

McAndrew, Robert (act): Planet Earth

McAndrews, John (act): Alf's Button (1920); The Bargain; The Chimes; The Dead Heart; On The Brink Of The Precipice

McAnnan, George Burr (act): Supernatural (1933); White Zombie

McAuley, Nichole (act): The Nutty Professor (1996)

McAvoy, Charles (act): The Dark Mirror (1946)

McAvoy, May (act, b. 1901): The Enchanted Cottage (1924); The Savage; The Terror (1928)

McBain, Diane (act): The Karate Killers; Wicked, Wicked

McBain, Ed (wri): see Hunter, Evan

McBan, Mickey (act): The Return Of Peter Grimm (1926); The Temple Of Venus

McBeath, Tom (act): Hideaway; Quarantine; Timecop

McBrearty, John (dir & wri): Sorority Girls And The Creature From Hell

McBrearty, Lynette (wri): Sorority Girls And The Creature From Hell

McBride, Chi (act): The Frighteners

McBride, Jeri (act): Star Trek

McBride, Jim (dir & wri): Glen And Randa

McBride, Katherine (act): School Spirit

McBride, Mark (act): Enemy Mine; Tower Of Evil

McBride, Michelle (act): Subspecies

McBride, Norm (act): The Gifted One

McBride, Suzanne (act): Echoes

McBride, Tom (act): Friday The 13th-Part 2; Remo Williams: The Adventure Begins

McBroom, Marden (act): see Bruce, David

McBurnie, Peter (act): The Pink Chiquitas

McCabe, John (act): Wheels Of Terror

McCabe, John (mus): Fear In The Night (1972)

McCabe, Michael (act): Raiders Of The Living Dead

McCabe, Tony (act): Something Weird

McCaddon, Wanda (act): Howard The Duck

McCafferty, Dee (act): Short Circuit 2

McCafferty, John (act): Deathrow Gameshow; A Polish Vampire In Burbank

McCaffery, Anthony (act): The Man From Nowhere

McCain, Deanne (act): Blood Diner

McCain, Frances Lee (act): Gremlins

McCall, Joan (act): The Horrible House On The Hill

McCall Jr., Mary C. (wri): A Midsummer Night's Dream (1935)

McCall, Mitzi (act): The Cry Baby Killer; War Of The Satellites

McCall, Ross (act): Jekyll And Hyde

McCalla, Irish (act): Hands Of A Stranger; She Demons

McCallin, Clement (act): The Story Of Robin Hood

McCallion, James (act, 1919-1991): North By Northwest; The Strange And Deadly Occurrence

McCallum, Charles (act): Next Of Kin

McCallum, David (GB act): Last Holiday

McCallum, David (USA act, b. 1933): Around The World Under The Sea; Casino Royale; Frankenstein: The True Story; The Haunting Of Morella; Hauser's Memory; The Helicopter Spies; How To Steal The World; The Invisible Man (1975); The Karate Killers; King Solomon's Treasure; One Of Our Spies Is Missing; One Spy Too Many; The Return Of The Man From U.N.C.L.E.; She Waits; Slaughter; The Spy In The Green Hat; The Spy With My Face; To Trap A Spy; The Watcher In The Woods

McCallum, John (act, b. 1917): Miranda; Trent's Last Case (1952); Valley Of The Eagles; The Woman In Question

McCallum, Jon (mus): Surf Nazis Must Die

McCallum, Kary (act): Kemek

McCallum, Neil (act): Catacombs; Dr. Terror's House Of Horrors (1964); Moon Zero Two; Quest For Love; Thunderbirds Are Go; Uncharted Seas

McCallum, Sandy (act): Death Race 2000

McCallum, Sherry (act): Kemek

McCalman, Macon (act): Dead And Buried; Topper (1979); The Ultimate Impostor

McCambridge, Mercedes (act, b. 1918):Echoes; The Exorcist; Island Of Despair; The Last Generation; Lightning Strikes Twice; Marquis De Sade; Justine; The Scarf; Suddenly Last Summer

McCann, Chuck (act): Cameron's Closet; Chomps; The Projectionist

McCann, Chuck (dir & wri):Bloodeaters

McCann, Donal (act): High Spirits; Rawhead Rex; Screamer

McCann, Frances (act): Creation Of The Humanoids

McCann, Henry (act): The Ghost Of Dragstrip Hollow

McCann, John (act): The Hidden

McCann, Sean (act): Ghost Of A Chance (1987); Starship Invasions; The Uncanny

McCants, Reed R. (act): Project X (1987)

McCard, Mollie (act): Daughter Of Dr. Jekyll

McCardie, Brian (act): The Ghost And The Darkness

McCarey, Ray(mond) (dir): The Falcon's Alibi; Torchy Runs For Mayor

McCarren, Fred (act): The Boogens; Xanadu

McCarroll, Joanna (act): Mad Max Beyond Thunderdome

McCarron, Bob (act): Howling III

McCarron, Bob (cin): Razorback

McCarten, Hugh (act): Gotham

McCarter, Brooke (act): The Lost Boys

McCarter, Scott (act): Rattlers

McCarthur, Avis (act): Lord Shango

McCarthy, Andrew (act, b. 1963): The Courtyard; Dr. M; Dream Man; Mannequin

McCarthy, Annette (act): Creature

McCarthy, Dennis (act): The Invisible Boy; The Monster That Challenged The World

McCarthy, Dennis (mus): Star Trek: Generations

McCarthy, Francis X. (act): Night Visions; The Relic

McCarthy, Francis X. (wri): Bogus

McCarthy, Frank (act): Alien Nation

McCarthy, Gerald (act): The Black Tulip (1921)

McCarthy, Helena (act): The Hound Of The Baskervilles (1978)

McCarthy, Henry (wri): The Gorilla (1927)

McCarthy, Jeff (act): Eve Of Destruction; RoboCop 2

McCarthy, John (act): Dr. Strangelove: or, How I Learned To Stop Worrying And Love The Bomb; The Road To Hong Kong; The Snake Woman; Zex

McCarthy, Julia (act): House Of Mortal Sin

McCarthy, Julianna (act): The First Power; The Frighteners; Maid To Order; When The Bough Breaks

McCarthy, Kenneth (cin): Slaughterhouse Rock

McCarthy, Kevin (act, b. 1914): Exo-Man; The Howling; Innerspace; Invasion Of The Body Snatchers (1956 & 1978); Invitation To Hell; Matinee; The Midnight Hour; Nightmare (1956); Piranha (1978); The Sleeping Car; Twilight Zone

McCarthy, Kevin (cin): Phantasm III: Lord Of The Dead

McCarthy, Leo T. (wri): Devil Bat's Daughter

McCarthy, Lillah (act): Mr. Wu (1919)

McCarthy, Lin (act): The Day After

McCarthy, Matt (dir & wri): Robin Hood Junior (1975)

McCarthy, Michael (dir, 1917-1959): The Accursed; Crow Hollow; Mystery Junction; Shadow Of A Man

McCarthy, Michael (wri, 1917-1959): The Accursed; Hunted (1952); Mystery Junction; Shadow Of A Man

McCarthy, Neil (act): Clash Of The Titans; The Monster Club; Ten Little Indians (1989); The Thief Of Baghdad (1978)

McCarthy, Nobu (act): Pacific Heights

McCarthy, Sheila (act): Pacific Heights; White Room

McCarthy, Tom (act): Blow Out

McCartney, (Sir) Paul (mus. b. 1942): Live And Let Die; Oh Heavenly Dog

McCarty, David Ross (act): Cat People (1982)

McCarty, Mary (act): Babes In Toyland (1961)

McCarty, Michael (act): Orpheus Descending

McCarty, Norma (act): Plan 9 From Outer Space

McCarver, Holly (act): I, Desire

McCashin, Constance (act): The Two Worlds Of Jennie Logan

McCaslin, Maylo (act): Superstition

McCauley, Chris (act): The Outing

McCauley, John (dir): Rattlers

McCauley, William (mus):City On Fire

McCausland, James (wri): Mad Max

McCay, Peggy (act): Good Against Evil

McCay, Winsor (wri, 1869-1934): The Dream Of A Rarebit Fiend; Little Nemo; Little Nemo: Adventures In Slumberland

McCharen, David (act): Pandemonium

McClain, Joedda (act): Jack's Wife

McClain, Lee (act): The Deep

McClanahan, Rue (act): The Little Match Girl (1987); They Might Be Giants; Topper (1979)

McClaren, Vincent (act): The Company Of Wolves

McClarty, Edward (act): Trancers

McClary, Dwayne (act): Wolf

McClatchy, Gregory (dir): Vampire At Midnight

McClellan, Charlie (act): The Frighteners

McClellan, Michelle (act): Nightmare Sisters; Sorority Babes In The Slimeball Bowl-O-Rama

McClelland, Allan (act): Murder Motel

McClelland, Sam David (act): The Video Dead

McCleod, Mary (act): London Blackout Murders

McCleod, Norman Z. (dir, 1898-1964): The Secret Life Of Walter Mitty; Topper Takes A Trip

McClaerkins, Bufort (act): Angel Heart

McClory, Kevin (wri, b. 1926): Never Say Never Again; Thunderball

McClory, Sean (act, b. 1924): Dick Tracy Meets Gruesome; The Gnome-Mobile; I Cover The Underworld; Mara Of The Wilderness; Les Miserables (1952); Niagara; Ring Of Fear; Them! (1954); Valley Of The Dragons

McCloskey, Carol (act): Martin

McCloskey, Leigh (act): The Bermuda Depths; Cameron's Closet; Inferno (1979)

McCloud, Charlene (act): Phoenix The Warrior

McCloud, Duncan (act): Garden Of The Dead

McClure, Doug (act, 1935-1995): At The Earth's Core; Firebird 2015 A.D.; The House Where Evil Dwells; Humanoids From The Deep; The Land That Time Forgot; The People That Time Forgot; Satan's Triangle; Warlords Of The Deep

McClure, Ernest (act): Blow Out

McClure, Marc (act): Back To The Future; Grim Prairie Tales; Pandemonium; Sleepstalker; Strange Behavior; Supergirl (1984); Superman (1978); Superman Ii; Superman III; Superman IV: The Quest For Peace

McClure, Melissa (act): The White Goddess

McClure, Paula (act): The First Power; Total Recall

McClure, Tipp (act): Rattlers

McClurg, Edie (act): Carrie; Elvira, Mistress Of The Dark; Pandemonium

McCoin, Roger (act): The Alien Within

McColl, J.J. (act): I Still Dream Of Jeannie

McColl, Kirk (act): Rabid

McCollough, David (act): Midnight (1980)

McCollough, Paul (act): Jack's Wife

McCollough, Paul (cin): The Majorettes; Midnight (1980)

McCollough, Paul (mus): The Majorettes; Night Of The Living Dead (1990)

McComas, Carroll (act): Jamaica Run

McComb, Heather (act): Generation X; Stay Tuned

McConaughey, Matthew (act): Contact; Return Of The Texas Chainsaw Massacre; A Time To Kill (1996)

McConkey, Larry (cin): White Of The Eye

McConnell, Joe (act): Blink

McConnell, Judith (act): The Thirsty Dead

McConnell, Judy (act): The Brotherhood Of Satan

McConnell, Keith (act): Time After Time; The Vulture (1966)

McConnell, Peter (act): Spasms

McConnohie, Michael (act): Fist Of The North Star; Vampire Hunter D

McConville, Bernard (wri): Monte Cristo

McCord, Cal (act): The Adding Machine

McCord, Kent (act, b. 1942): Predator 2

McCord, Pat (act): Deadtime Stories

McCord, Ted (cin): Operation Secret; Private Property

McCorkindale, Christine (act): Nightbreed

McCormack, Colin (act): Deathline; First Knight

McCormack, Eric (act): Island City; Night Visitors

McCormack, John (wri): Life For Ruth

McCormack, Lynne (act): Synapse

McCormack, Patricia (act): Invitation To Hell

McCormack, Patty (act, b. 1945): The Bad Seed (1956); Bug

McCormick, Alan (act): Secrets Of The Phantom Caverns

McCormick, Carolyn (act): Enemy Mine

McCormick, Gilmer (act): Silent Night, Deadly Night; Slaughterhouse-Five

McCormick, Kevin (act): Dr. Tarr's Torture Dungeon

McCormick, Larry (act): The Punisher

McCormick, Maureen (act): Return To Horror High; A Vacation In Hell

McCormick, Merrill (act): Eyes Of The Jungle; Robin Hood (1922)

McCormick, Michael (act): Return Of The Jedi

McCormick, Parker (act): The Fan

McCormick, Pat (act): Scrooged; The Shaggy D.A.

McCowan, George (dir): Frogs; The Love War; Return To Fantasy Island; Shadow Of The Hawk; The Shape Of Things To Come (1979)

McCowen, Alec (act, b. 1925): Frenzy; Never Say Never Again; The Witches (1966)

McCoy, Carl (act): Hardware

McCoy, Gertrude (act): The Blue Bird (1918); The Golden Dawn

McCoy, Horace (wri): Dangerous Mission

McCoy, Matt (act): The Apocalypse; Dead On; Deepstar Six; Eyes Of The Beholder; The Hand That Rocks The Cradle; Synapse

McCoy, Peter (act): The Invincible Barbarian

McCoy, Sid (act): Colossus: The Forbin Project

McCoy, Steve (act): I Was A Teenage Zombie

McCoy, Sylvester (act): Doctor Who; Dracula (1979)

McCoy, Tim (act, 1891-1978): Around The World In 80 Days

McCoy, Tim (dir): The Amazing Dr. Jekyll

McCoy, Tony (act): Bride Of The Monster

McCoy, William (act): Howard The Duck

McCracken, Bob (act): Spellbinder

McCracken, Esther (wri): Poison Pen

McCracken, Jeffrey (act): Stranger In Our House

McCracken, Jenny (act): The Night Digger

McCracken, Mark (act): Matinee; Pumpkinhead II Blood Wings

McCrane, Paul (act): The Blob (1988); RoboCop

McCrann, Charles (dir & wri): Toxic Zombies

McCraw, Lezlie Z. (act): Getting Lucky

McCrea, Jody (act): How To Stuff A Wild Bikini; The Monster That Challenged The World; The Naked Gun; Pajama Party

McCrea, Joel (act, 1905-1990): Foreign Correspondent; The Lost Squadron; The Most Dangerous Game; The Unseen (1945)

McCreadie, Adan (act): Mad Max Beyond Thunderdome

McCready, Ed (act): Dick Tracy (1990); Sssssss; Wonder Woman

McCrindle, Alex (act): The House In The Square; The Private Life Of Sherlock Holmes; Star Wars

McCrory, Tom (act): I Was A Zombie For The F.B.I.

McCrossin, Joseph (act): Always

McCuaig, Alison (act): The Pit (1983)

McCullen, Kathy (act): Evilspeak

McCullers, Carson (wri, 1917-1967): Reflections In A Golden Eye

McCulley, Johnston (wri): The Mark Of Zorro (1920, 1940 & 1974); The Mask Of Zorro; The Sign Of Zorro; Zorro (1975); Zorro, The Gay Blade; Zorro: The Legend Begins

McCulley, Sandra Walker (act): The Dark (1979)

McCulloch, Andrew (act): Cry Of The Banshee; The Land That Time Forgot; Macbeth (1971); Nothing But The Night

McCulloch, Ian (act, b. 1940): Alien Contamination; The Curse Of The Golem; The Ghoul (1974); Queen Of The Cannibals; Zombie

McCullock, Arthur (act): Just Imagine

McCullock, Allen (act): Vampire's Kiss

McCullough Sr., Jim (dir):Aurora Encounter; Mountaintop Motel Massacre

McCullough Jr., Jim (wri): Creature From Black Lake; Mountaintop Motel Massacre

McCullough, Lisa (act): Daylight

McCullough, Patrick (act): Magic

McCullough, Philo (act, 1894-1981): Possessed (1947); The Savage; Tarzan The Fearless; Trilby (1923)

McCullough, Robert L. (wri): Dark Mansions; Zorro: The Legend Begins

McCullum, Nancy (act): The Falcon And The Co-Eds

McCune, Judson (act): Lord Of The Flies (1990)
McCune, Lynn (act): Mutants In Paradise
McCurdy, Bill (act): Freejack
McCurley, Doyle (act): Neon Maniacs
McCurry, John (act): They Might Be Giants; Wolfen
McCurry, Michael (cin): The Hotel Manor Inn
McCurry, Natalie (act): Dead End Drive-In
McCusker, Mary (act): Jekyll And Hyde...Together Again
McCutcheon, Bill (act): Mr. Destiny; Santa Claus Conquers The Martians
McCutcheon, Gillian (act): Murder Motel
McDade, Valla Rae (act): The Dark (1979); Kingdom Of The Spiders
McDancer, Buck (act): Time Flyer
McDaniel, Charles (act): The Goonies
McDaniel, Charles A. (wri): Beyond The Bermuda Triangle
McDaniel, Donna (act): Frightmare (1983)
McDaniel, Etta (act): The Invisible Ray; Son Of Dracula (1943)
McDaniel, George (act): The Last Starfighter
McDaniel, Hattie (act, 1895-1952): Murder By Television
McDaniel, James (act): A Deadly Vision
McDermott, Brian (act): The Punisher; The Sinister Man
McDermott, Dylan (act): Hardware; Into The Badlands; Miracle On 34th Street (1994)
McDermott, Hugh (act, b. 1908): The Adding Machine; Devil Girl From Mars; First Men In The Moon (1964); Pimpernel Smith; The Saint In London; Trent's Last Case (1952)
McDermott, Jack (act): Cocoon: The Return; The Funhouse (1981)
McDermott, Keith (act): Tourist Trap
McDermott, Marc (act): The Antique Brooch; The Daughter Of Romany; A Letter To The Princess; The Stolen Plans
McDevitt, Ruth (act, 1895-1976): The Birds; Crackle Of Death; Demon And The Mummy; Homebodies
McDiarmid, Ian (act): The Awakening; Dragonslayer; Return Of The Jedi
McDiarmid, Karen (act): Rana: The Legend Of Shadow Lake
McDonald, A.C. (act): Night Of The Living Dead (1968)
McDonald, Bob (act): The Psychotronic Man
McDonald, Christopher (act): The Hearse; The Rich Man's Wife; Unforgettable
McDonald, David (cin): Horror Hospital
McDonald, Doug (act): The Toxic Avenger, Part II
McDonald, Durwood (act): The Capture Of Bigfoot
McDonald, Francis (J.) (act, 1891-1968): The Bandits Of Corsica; Black Orchids; Daughter Of The Jungle; The Lone Wolf Keeps A Date; Monte Cristo; Samson And Delilah; Strange Confession; Trilby (1923)
McDonald, Frank (act): The Tomb
McDonald, Frank (dir, b. 1899): The Adventurous Blonde; Blondes At Work; Bulldog Drummond Strikes Back (1947); Fly-Away Baby; Mara Of The Wilderness; One Body Too Many; Smart Blonde; 13 Lead Soldiers; The Underwater City
McDonald, Garry (act): Picnic At Hanging Rock; Those Dear Departed
McDonald, Grace (act): Destiny (1944); Flesh And Fantasy; Murder In The Blue Room
McDonald, Jack (act): Don Q, Son Of Zorro; Lorna Doone (1922)
McDonald, Joe (act): Mind Killer
McDonald, Joshua (act): Zone Troopers
McDonald, Kate (act): Funeral Home
McDonald, Ken (act): A Hitch In Time
McDonald, Lana (act): Rawhead Rex
McDonald, Lisa (act): The Right Hand Of The Devil
McDonald, Mac (act): Electric Dreams; Nightbreed
McDonald, Mark (cin): Kadoyng
McDonald, Mary Ann (act): The Intruder Within
McDonald, Michael (act): Hideaway
McDonald, Michael James (act): Leprechaun 2
McDonald, Mike (act): Watchers II
McDonald, Pat (act): Empire Of Ash III
McDonald, Samantha (act): Twister
McDonald, Scott (act): Empire Of Ash III
McDonald, Teru (act): Pandora's Clock
McDonald, Tommy (act): The Destructors
McDonell, Darla (act): Death Race 2000
McDonell, Gordon (wri): Shadow Of A Doubt (1943 & 1991)
McDonnell, Jo (act): The Munsters' Revenge; The Night Of The Claw; The Octagon; Once Upon A Spy
McDonnell, M.J. (act): Halloween 4: The Return Of Michael Myers
McDonnell, Mary (act): Independence Day
McDonnell, Renee (act): Dead And Buried
McDonnell, Robert (wri): Twice Dead
McDonough, Glenn (mus): Babes In Toyland (1934, 1961 & 1986)
McDonough, Kit (act): Deadly Messages
McDonough, Mary (act): Midnight Offerings; Mortuary
McDonough, Neal (act): Darkman (1990); White Dwarf
McDonough, Shannon (act): The Kiss (1988)
McDormand, Frances (act, b. 1957): Blood Simple; The Butcher's Wife; Darkman (1990); Fargo; Primal Fear
McDougall, Don (dir): The Aquarians; Demon And The Mummy; Forgotten City Of The Planet Of The Apes; The Mark Of Zorro (1974)
McDougall, Martin (act): Judge Dredd
McDougall, Rex (act): The Bargain; The Hound Of The Baskervilles (1921)
McDowall, Betty (act): First Men In The Moon (1964); Jack The Ripper (1958); The Liquidator; The Omen
McDowall, Roddy (act, b. 1928): Alice In Wonderland (1985); Angel, Angel, Down We Go; Arnold; Back To The Planet Of The Apes; Battle For The Planet Of The Apes; Bedknobs And Broomsticks; Black Midnight; The Cat From Outer Space; Charlie Chan And The Curse Of The Dragon Queen; Circle Of Iron; Class Of '84; Conquest Of The Planet Of The Apes; The Curse Of The Golem; Deadly Game; Dead Man's Island; Dead Of Winter; Earth Angel; Embryo; Escape From The Planet Of The Apes; Evil Under The Sun; Farewell To The Planet Of The Apes; Flood; Forgotten City Of The Planet Of The Apes; Fright Night; Fright Night II; Hello Down There; Killer Shark; Laserblast; The Legend Of Hell House; Life, Liberty And Pursuit On The Planet Of The Apes; The Loved One; Macbeth (1947); The Memory Of Eva Ryker; Midnight Lace (1960); Miracle On 34th Street (1973); Mirror, Mirror 2: Raven Dance; Night Gallery; Planet Of The Apes; The Poseidon Adventure; The Return Of The King; Shakma; Shock Treatment (1964); A Taste Of Evil; The Thief Of Baghdad (1978); Treachery And Greed On The Planet Of The Apes; Unlikely Angel; The Zany Adventures Of Robin Hood
McDowall, Roddy (dir, b. 1928): Tam Lin
McDowell, Claire (act, 1877-1966): The Mark Of Zorro (1920); Murder By Television
McDowell, Malcolm (act, b. 1943, nee Malcolm Taylor): Arthur The King; Cat People (1982); Class Of 1999; A Clockwork Orange; Disturbed; Kids Of The Round Table; Moon 44; Royal Flash; Star Trek: Generations; Tank Girl; Time After Time; Yesterday's Target
McDowell, Michael (wri): Beetlejuice; Tales From The Darkside; Thinner
McDowell, Paul (act): The 39 Steps (1978)
McDowell, Rick (act): Getting Lucky
McDowell, Trevyn (act): Mary Shelley's 'Frankenstein'
McEachin, James (act): The Dead Don't Die; The Groundstar Conspiracy; Guess Who's Coming For Christmas?; Play Misty For Me; 2010
McElduff, Ellen (act): Maximum Overdrive
McElheney, Carol (act): Howard The Duck
McElhone, Catherine (act): Flesh-Eating Mothers
McElroy, Alan B. (wri): Halloween 4: The Return Of Michael Myers; Wheels Of Terror
McEncore, Anne (act): Snowbeast
McEnery, Donald (wri): Hercules (1997)
McEnery, John (act): Hamlet (1990); Jamaica Inn (1985); The Land That Time Forgot; Schizo (1977)
McEnery, Peter (act, b. 1940): The Cat And The Canary (1978); I Killed Rasputin; The Moonspinners; Negatives; Tales That Witness Madness
McEnnan, Jaime (act): Remote Control (1988)
McEnroe, Annie (act): The Hand (1981); Howling II
McEntire, Reba (act, b. 1955): Tremors
McEveety, Bernard (dir): The Brotherhood Of Satan; Forgotten City Of The Planet Of The Apes
McEveety, Brian (act): The Brotherhood Of Satan
McEveety, Joseph (L.) (wri): The Barefoot Executive; The Computer Wore Tennis Shoes; Now You See Him, Now You Don't; The Strongest Man In The World
McEveety, Kevin (act): The Brotherhood Of Satan
McEveety, Sheila (act): The Brotherhood Of Satan
McEveety, Vincent (dir): Charley And The Angel; The Strongest Man In The World; Wonder Woman
McEvoy, Annemarie (act): Children Of The Corn; Invitation To Hell
McEvoy, Charles (wri): The Man In The Attic (1915)
McEvoy, Renny (act): Desk Set
McEwan, Geraldine (act): Robin Hood: Prince Of Thieves
McEwan, Hamish (act): Secret Weapons
McEwan, Ian (wri): The Good Son
McFadden, Barney (act): Salem's Lot
McFadden, Davenia (act): Remo Williams: The Adventure Begins
McFadden, Gates (act): Star Trek: First Contact; Star Trek: Generations
McFadden, Reggie (act): Jacob's Ladder
McFadden, Thom (act): A Nightmare On Elm Street, Part 2: Freddy's Revenge; 976-Evil
McFadden, Tom (act): Warning Sign
McFarland, Anthony (act): Blood Diner
McFarland, Connie (act): Troll II
McFarland, Garry (mus): Eye Of The Devil
McFarland, Megan (act): The Offspring
McFarland, Olive (act): The Frightened City
McFarland, Stephen (act): Making Mr. Right
McFarlane, Hamish (act): The Navigator: An Odyssey Across Time
McFaul, Harriet (act): Shriek Of The Mutilated
McFayden, John (act): Humongous
McFee, Bruce (act): Clarence; Sorry, Wrong Number (1989)
McFee, Dwight (act): The Death Of The Incredible Hulk; Unforgettable
McGann, Marlon (act): Vamp
McGann, Paul (act): Afraid Of The Dark; Alien 3; Doctor Who
McGann, William (cin): Possessed (1947)
McGann, William (dir, 1895-1977): Sh! The Octopus; The Silver Greyhound (1932); A Voice Said Goodnight
McGarrigle, Pat (act): Empire Of Ash III
McGarry, Garry (act): The False Faces
McGarry, Parnell (act): Bedazzled
McGavin, Darren (act, b. 1922): Blood And Concrete; Captain America (1992); Crackle Of Death; Dead Heat; Demon And The Mummy; Firebird 2015 A.D.; Hangar 18; Mission Mars; The Night Stalker (1971); The Night Strangler; The Six Million Dollar Man; Something Evil
McGavin, Darren (dir, b. 1922): Happy Mother's Day, Love George
McGee, Bill (act): Curse Of The Swamp Creature
McGee, Bobby (act): Tales From The Hood
McGee, Henry (act): Digby-The Biggest Dog In The World
McGee, Jack (act): Crash And Burn; The Hidden; I'm Dangerous Tonight
McGee, Katie (act): Revenge Of The Teenage Vixens From Outer Space
McGee, Mark Thomas (wri): Equinox
McGee, Mike (cin): The Odyssey
McGee, Roger (act): Forbidden Planet
McGee, Vic (act): Gallery Of Horror; The Wizard Of Mars
McGee, Vonetta (act): Blacula; The Eiger Sanction; The Kremlin Letter
McGee-Davis, Trina (act): Daylight
McGeehan, Dennis (act): Nightbeast
McGellin, Debbie (act): Happy Birthday To Me
McGhee, Brownie (act): Angel Heart
McGhee, Johnny Ray (act): Project X (1987)
McGhee, Michael (act): The Brood
McGhee, Scott (dir & wri): Suture
McGhee, William Bill (act): Don't Look In The Basement
McGibbon, Clayton Ed (act): Hitler's Daughter
McGibbon, Ed (act): The Neptune Factor
McGibbon, Jeff (act): Clarence
McGill, Barney (cin): Lancer Spy; The Lone Wolf Keeps A Date; The Mad Genius; Svengali (1931); The Terror (1928)
McGill, Bruce (act): The Hand (1981); The Man Who Fell To Earth (1987); Timecop
McGill, Everett (act): Dune; The People Under The Stairs; Quest For Fire; Silver Bullet
McGill, Gordon (act): Dracula's Dog; End Of The World (1977)
McGillis, Kelly (act): Made In Heaven; Remember Me
McGillivray, David (act): Frightmare (1974); House Of Whipcord; Satan's Slave; Schizo (1977); Terror (1979)
McGillivray, David (wri): Frightmare (1974); House Of Mortal Sin; House Of Whipcord; Satan's Slave; Schizo (1977); Terror (1979)
McGinley, John C. (act): Highlander 2: The Quickening; Seven
McGinley, Ted (act): Deadly Web
McGinn, Walter 9act): The Night That Panicked America; 3 Days Of The Condor
McGinnis, Don (mus): Blood Of Ghastly Horror
McGinnis, Scott (act): Star Trek III: The Search For Spock
McGinnis, Tom (act): Carnival Of Souls
McGiveney, Owen (act): The Maze
McGiver, John (act, b. 1915): Arnold; The Gazebo; Johnny Cool; The Manchurian Candidate; The Spirit Is Willing
McGivern, Cecil (wri): Great Expectations (1946)
McGivern, William (P.) (wri, 1922-1982): I Saw What You Did (1965); The Wrecking Crew
McGlade, Agnes (act): see O'Connor, Una
McGlynn Jr., Frank (act): Trouble For Two
McGonegal, Al (act): see Jenkins, Allen
McGonagle, Richard (act): Howard The Duck
McGoohan, Catherine (act): The Return Of The Six Million Dollar Man And The Bionic Woman
McGoohan, Patrick (act, b. 1928): Baby: Secret Of The Lost Legend; Dr. Syn-Alias The Scarecrow; Jamaica Inn (1985); Journey Into Darkness; Koroshi; Life For Ruth; The Phantom (1996); Scanners; The Three Lives Of Thomasina; A Time To Kill (1996)
McGovern, Don (act): Killer Bees
McGovern, Elizabeth (act): The Handmaid's Tale
McGovern, John (act): The Birds
McGovern, Maureen (mus, b. 1949): The Poseidon Adventure
McGovern, Michael (act): Captain Nemo And The Underwater City
McGovern, Terrence (act): Party Line
McGovern, Tim (cin): Hideaway
McGovern, Tom (act): The Handmaid's Tale
McGowan, Darrell (wri): Valley Of The Zombies
McGowan, Dorothy (act): The Ghost Talks
McGowan, J.P. (dir, 1880-1952): Tarzan And The Golden Lion
McGowan, Jack (cin): Blood Waters Of Dr. Z; Children Shouldn't Play With Dead Things; Deranged (1974)
McGowan, Oliver (act): Screaming Mimi
McGowan, Rose (act): Scream
McGowan, Stuart (wri): Valley Of The Zombies
McGowan, Stuart E. (dir): The Ice House
McGowran, Tara (act): The Secret Life Of Ian Fleming
McGoy, Kevin (act): Flight Of The Navigator
McGrady, Michael (act): Creator; Project X (1987); Trancers
McGrail, Jeffrey (act): Galaxina
McGrail, Walter (act, 1888-1970): Dick Tracy Vs. Crime, Inc.; The Eleventh Hour (1923); The Invisible Fear; Murder By The Clock
McGranahan Sr., Tom (act): Fire In The Sky (1993)
McGrath, Doug (act): Always
McGrath, Frank (act, 1903-1967): The Reluctant Astronaut; The Sword Of Ali Baba
McGrath, Graham (act): Frankenstein (1984); Krull
McGrath, Greg (act): Raiders Of The Living Dead
McGrath, John (wri): Billion Dollar Brain; Robin Hood (1991)
McGrath, Joseph/Joe (dir, b. 1930): Casino Royale; Digby-The Biggest Dog In The World; The Magic Christian
McGrath, Joseph (wri, b. 1930): The Magic Christian
McGrath, Lucy (act): The Monsters Christmas
McGrath, Leueen (act): Three Cases Of Murder
McGrath, Margaret (act): 23 Paces To Baker Street
McGrath, Pat (act): Ghost Ship (1952); Halfway House
McGrath, Paul (act, 1903-1978): Dead Men Tell
McGraw, Charles (act, 1914-1980): The Birds; A Boy And His Dog; The Busy Body; The Night Stalker (1971)
McGreevey, John (wri): Crowhaven Farm; Hello Down There
McGreevey, Michael (act): The Computer Wore Tennis Shoes; Now You See Him, Now You Don't; The Shaggy D.A.; The Strongest Man In The World
McGreevey, Tom (act): Killer In The Mirror
McGregor, Angela Punch (act): The Island

McGregor, Grant (act): The Brotherhood Of The Bell
McGregor, Johnnie (act): Murder At The Windmill
McGregor, Kenneth J. (act): Primal Scream
McGregor, Lisa (act): Revenge Of The Teenage Vixens From Outer Space
McGregor, Malcolm (act): The Dancer Of The Nile; Murder Will Out (1930); The Prisoner Of Zenda (1922)
McGuffie, Bill (mus): The Asphyx; Corruption
McGuinn, Joe (act): Dick Tracy's G-Men
McGuinness, James Kevin (wri): Tarzan And His Mate
McGuire, Barry (act): The President's Analyst; Werewolves On Wheels
McGuire, Betty (act): Coma
McGuire, Biff (act, b. 1926): Child Of Glass; Nero Wolfe; Werewolf Of Washington
McGuire, Biff (wri, b. 1926): Firebird 2015 A.D.
McGuire, Bruce (act): Batman (1989); From Beyond; Roger Corman's Frankenstein Unbound; Zone Troopers
McGuire, Bryan (act): Vamp
McGuire, Don (act, b. 1919): Boston Blackie's Chinese Venture; Possessed (1947); Sideshow
McGuire, Dorothy (act, b. 1919): The Enchanted Cottage (1945); Make Haste To Live; She Waits; The Spiral Staircase (1946)
McGuire, Gary (act): Howling III
McGuire, Harp (act): On The Beach
McGuire, Holden (act): Mother's Day
McGuire, James (act): Tuck Everlasting
McGuire, Jason (act): Pet Sematary Two
McGuire, John (act): Charlie Chan At The Circus; The Invisible Ghost; Stranger On The Third Floor
McGuire, John B. (act): Secrets Of The Phantom Caverns
McGuire, Kathryn (act, 1897-1978): The Lost Zeppelin; Sherlock Jr.
McGuire, Kim (act): Disturbed
McGuire, Michael (act): Dead Of Night (1987); Jekyll And Hyde...Together Again; Sanctuary Of Fear; They Might Be Giants
McGuire, Mickey (act): see Rooney, Mickey
McGuire, Tom (act): Charlie Chan At The Opera
McGuire, Tucker (GB act): A Ghost For Sale; Murder At Scotland Yard; The Net; The Night Has Eyes
McGuire, Tucker (USA act): D.A.R.Y.L.
McGuire, William Anthony (wri): Roman Scandals
McGunn, Joe (act): Secrets Of The Lone Wolf
McGurk, Gary (act): Phantom Of The Mall: Eric's Revenge
McHallem, Chris (act): Hardware
McHattie, Stephen (act): The Dark (1994); Death Valley; Deadly Love; Look What's Happened To Rosemary's Baby; Remember Me; Search For The Gods; The Ultimate Warrior
McHeady, Robert/Bob (act): Cannibal Girls; Deranged (1974)
McHugh, Brian (act): Clownhouse
McHugh, David (mus): Mannequin Two: On The Move
McHugh, Frank (act, 1899-1981): A Midsummer Night's Dream (1935); Mighty Joe Young; Mystery Of The Wax Museum; Return Of The Terror; The Velvet Touch
McHugh, Jimmy (mus, 1894-1969): You'll Find Out
McHugh, Kitty (act): Jennifer (1953)
McHugh, Matt (act): Freaks; Murder On A Honeymoon; Night Of Terror (1933); Song Of The Thin Man
McIlwraith, Bill (wri): The Anniversary
McIlwraith, David (act): Millennium; The Vindicator
McInnerny, Tim (act): Erik The Viking
McInnes, Angus (act): Hellbound: Hellraiser II, Superman II
McIntire, James (act): Return Of The Living Dead, Part II
McIntire, John (act, 1907-1991): Cloak And Dagger (1984); Francis; Goliath Awaits; I've Lived Before; Psycho; Shadow On The Wall
McIntire, Tim (act & mus): A Boy And His Dog
McIntosh, Blanche (wri): Alf's Button (1920); The American Heiress; The Cobweb; The Failure; Morphia, The Death Drug; The Tinted Venus
McIntosh, Burr (act): The Last Warning (1929)
McIntosh, David (act): Dr. Faustus
McIntosh, Douglas Lloyd (wri): Notorious (1992)
McIntosh, Ellen (act): Downfall; The Sky Bike
McIntosh, J.T. (wri, b. 1925): Satellite In The Sky
McIntosh, Tim (act): Incubus (1982)
McIntyre, Andrew J. (cin): Fear No Evil (1969)
McIntyre, Clare (act): Krull
McIntyre, Lucile (act): The Handmaid's Tale
McIntyre, (Mr.) Marvin (J.) (act): C.H.U.D. II, Project X (1987); Return To Horror High
McIver, Elliot (act): Sorry, Wrong Number (1989)
McIver, Susan (act): Dr. Dracula
McKahan, Rufus Alan (act): see Hale (Sr.), Alan
McKamy, Kim (act): Creepozoids
McKay, Allison (act): Matinee
McKay, Doug (cin): The Keeper
McKay, George (act): After Midnight With Boston Blackie; Alias Boston Blackie; The Lone Wolf Returns (1935); One Mysterious Night
McKay, Jock (act): Museum Mystery
McKay, John (act): The Dead One; Rocket Attack U.S.A.
McKay, Rodney (act): Sometimes They Come Back
McKay, Scott (act): Guest In The House
McKay, Steven (wri): Darkman II: The Return Of Durant
Mckay, Wanda (act): The Black Raven; Bowery At Midnight; The Golden Eye; Jungle Goddess; The Monster Maker (1943); Voodoo Man
McKeag, Michael (act): Cosh Boy
McKean, Michael (act): D.A.R.Y.L.; Earth Girls Are Easy; Memoirs Of An Invisible Man; Short Circuit 2
McKeand, Nigel (wri): Don't Be Afraid Of The Dark
McKechnie, Donna (act): The Little Prince
McKee, Elodie (act): Alien Warrior
McKee, Gina (act): The Lair Of The White Worm
McKee, John (act): Cape Fear (1961); Dimension 5; Radar Secret Service
McKee, Michelle (act): Flatliners
McKee, Pat (act): Voodoo Man
McKee, Raymond (act): A Blind Bargain
McKee, Tom (act): The Search For Bridey Murphy
McKee, Vivienne (act): The Slipper And The Rose
McKeehan, Gary (act): The Brood; Rabid
McKeekan, Wayne (act): see Wayne, David
McKeever, Kimberly (act): Scanners
McKeever, Marlon (act): The Three Stooges Meet Hercules
McKeever, Mike (act): The Three Stooges Meet Hercules
McKellen, Ian (act, b. 1939): The Keep; Rasputin (1996); Richard III (1995); The Scarlet Pimpernel (1982); The Shadow (1994)
McKellen, Ian (wri, b. 1939): Richard III (1995)
McKendry, Maxime (act): Dracula (1974)
McKenna, Bernard (act): A Connecticut Yankee In King Arthur's Court (1989)
McKenna, James (act): Highlander
McKenna, Joseph (act): The Long Kiss Goodnight; 12 Monkeys
McKenna, Marthe (Cnockhaert) (wri): I Was A Spy; Lancer Spy
McKenna, Scott (act): Neon Maniacs; Species
McKenna, Siobhan (act, 1923-1986): Daughter Of Darkness (1948)
McKenna, T.P. (act): Are You Dying Young Man?; Downfall
McKenna, Virginia (act, b. 1931): Holocaust 2000; The Oracle (1952)
McKennon, Dallas (act): The Cat From Outer Space
McKeny, Jim (act): Creature; Haunts
McKenzie, Alastair (wri): Zeta One
McKenzie, Bob (act): Buried Alive (1940)
McKenzie, Ella (act): The Last Warning (1929)
McKenzie, Jack (cin): The Falcon Strikes Back
McKenzie, Mark (mus): Dr. Jekyll And Ms. Hyde; To Die For II: Son Of Darkness
McKenzie, Melanie (act): The Rocking Horse Winner
McKenzie, Miki (act): The Loch Ness Horror
Mckenzie, Paul (act): Hardware
McKenzie, Richard (act): Child Of Darkness, Child Of Light; Dark Night Of The Scarecrow; Ghost In The Machine; Man On A Swing
McKeon, Nancy (act): The Lightning Incident
McKeon, Philip (act): Return To Horror High
McKeown, Charles (act & wri): The Adventures Of Baron Munchausen (1989); Brazil
McKern, Leo (act, b. 1925): The Adventures Of Sherlock Holmes' Smarter Brother; Assignment K; Beyond This Place; Damien-Omen II; The Day The Earth Caught Fire; Hot Enough For June; Ladyhawke; The Mouse That Roared; Murder With Mirrors; The Omen; X...The Unknown
McKevitt, Michael (act): Paint Me A Murder
McKewan, Marny (act): Empire Of Ash III
McKewin, Vince (act): Communion
McKie, Angus (wri): Heavy Metal
McKillop, Don(ald) (act): An American Werewolf In London; Otley
McKim, Anna (act): see Dvorak, Ann
McKim, Robert (act): The Bat (1926); The Mark Of Zorro (1920); Monte Cristo
McKinley, Anthony Roy (act): The Keeper
McKinley, J. Edward (act): The Angry Red Planet
McKinley, Mary (act): Boarding House
McKinnel, Norman (act): Downhill; The Frightened Lady (1932); The Sleeping Cardinal
McKinney, Austin (cin): Gallery Of Horror; Isle Of The Snake People; The Wizard Of Mars
McKinney, Bill (act): Strange New World
McKinney, Gregory (act): Eraser
McKinney, Jennifer (act): Death Ship
McKinney, John (act): Meteor
McKinney, Nina Mae (act): Pocomania
McKinnies, Henry H. (act): see Hunter, Jeff(rey)
McKinnon, Clayton (act): Martin
McKinnon, Jeanie (act): The Keeper
McKinnon, Mona (act): Mesa Of Lost Women; Plan 9 From Outer Space
McKinnon, Myra (act): Shadows Over Chinatown
McKinnon, Ray (act): Night Of The Hunter (1991)
McKinsey, Beverlee (act): The Demon Murder Case
McKizzick, Carla (act): Blood Song
McKnight, Charles E. (act): Secrets Of The Phantom Caverns
McKnight, Chuck (act): Secrets Of The Phantom Caverns
McKnight, Thomas F. (act): Secrets In The Attic
McKrell, James/Jim (act): The Howling; I Saw What You Did (1988); Pandemonium; Revenge Of The Stepford Wives; Teen Wolf
McLachlan, Duncan (dir): The Second Jungle Book: Mowgli And Baloo
McLachlan, Neil (act): Strange Behavior
McLaglen, Andrew V. (dir): Stowaway To The Moon
McLaglen, Clifford) (act): Boadicea; The Mystery Of The Mary Celeste
McLaglen, Cyril (act): Alf's Button (1930); Boadicea; The Lost Patrol (1929); The Secret Of The Loch (1934)
McLaglen, Victor (act, 1886-1959): Around The World In 80 Days; City Of Shadows; The Crimson Circle (1922); Fair Wind To Java; The Lost Patrol (1934); Loves Of Carmen; Murder At The Vanities; Prince Valiant; The Unholy Three (1925); Women Of All Nations
McLain, Joali (act): Howard The Duck
McLaine, Marilyn (act): A Kiss For Cinderella
McLaren, Anne (act): Things To Come
McLaren, Hollis (act): Welcome To Blood City
McLaren, Ivor (act): Elstree Calling
McLaren, John (act): First Man Into Space
McLaren, Kay (act): Excalibur
McLarty, Gary (act): The Entity
McLarty, James E. (wri): The Touch Of Satan
McLarty, Jim (act): The Frighteners
McLaughlin, Bobby Travis (act): The Incredible Hulk Returns
McLaughlin, Bruce (act): Cocoon: The Return
McLaughlin, Gibb (act, b. 1884): The Black Rose; The Brain Machine; Bulldog Jack; Grand National Night; The House In The Square; Juggernaut; Mr. Reeder In Room 13; Paris Express; The Queen Of Spades (1948); The Scarlet Pimpernel (1934); The Silent House; Spellbound (1941); The Thirteenth Candle; Who Done It? (1956)
McLaughlin, Jeffrey (act): The Nesting
McLaughlin, John (act): Mission: Impossible; Vampire's Kiss
McLaughlin, John Patrick (act): Jacob's Ladder
McLaughlin, Lee (act): Elvira, Mistress Of The Dark
McLaughlin, Maya (act): Children Of The Night (1992)
McLaughlin, Rebecca (act): The Craft
McLean, Bill (act): The Love War
McLean, Bob (act): Wavelength
McLean, Coll Red (act): Jaws 2
McLean, David (act, 1922-1995): Deathsport; Kingdom Of The Spiders; The Strangler (1963); X-15
McLean, Diana (act): Chilling
McLean, Dwayne (act): Haunted By Her Past
McLean, Eddie (act): Nightfall (1956)
McLean, George Nicholas (act): The Goonies
McLean, Larry (act): Body Parts
McLean, May (wri): The Man Who Laughs (1927)
McLean, Nick (cin): The Goonies; Mac And Me; Short Circuit; Spaceballs
McLean, Paul (act): I Still Dream Of Jeannie
McLean, Warren (act): Equalizer 2000
McLeay, Andrew (act): She (1983)
McLeish, Ronald W. (cin): Monster In The Closet
McLellan, Pheona (act): A Hitch In Time
McLendon, Gay (act): The Giant Gila Monster
McLendon, Gordon (act): The Killer Shrews
McLendon, Michael (act): King Kong Lives
McLeod, Catherine (act, b. 1924): A Blueprint For Murder; The Thin Man Goes Home
McLeod, Debbie (act): King Kong Lives
McLeod, Don (act): The Howling; Pandemonium; Tarzan In Manhattan
McLeod, Duncan (act): Sometimes They Come Back
McLeod, Gordon (act): Busman's Honeymoon; The Crimson Circle (1936); Death At Broadcasting House; The Frog; Meet Sexton Blake; The Patient Vanishes; The Saint In London; The Saint Meets The Tiger; The Saint's Vacation; A Smart Set; The Squeaker (1937)
McLeod, Janell (act): The Handmaid's Tale
McLeod, Lewis (cin): A Story Of Tutankhamun
McLeod, Mary (act): The Last Days Of Man On Earth
McLeod, Norman Z. (dir, 1898-1964): Alice In Wonderland (1933); The Miracle Man (1932); The Secret Life Of Walter Mitty; Topper (1937)
McLeod, Randolph (act): Lady Audley's Secret (1920)
McLeod, Victor (wri): Horror Island
McLerie, Allyn (Ann) (act, b. 1926): Fantasies; Phantom Of The Rue Morgue
McLiam, Don (act): Sleeper
McLiam, John (act): The Food Of The Gods; The Incredible Hulk, Part 2; The Invisible Man (1975); Mistress Of Paradise
McLine, Charles (act): Curse Of The Swamp Creature
McLine, Shirley (act): Curse Of The Swamp Creature
McLinn, Lloyd (act): Invasion Of The Bee Girls
McLinton, Calvin A. (act): Raiders Of The Living Dead
McLoughlin, Bronco (act): Krull
McLoughlin, Nancy (act): Sometimes They Come Back
McLoughlin, Tom (act): Critters 2: The Main Course
McLoughlin, Tom (dir): Date With An Angel; Friday The 13th, Part VI: Jason Lives; One Dark Night; Sometimes They Come Back
McLoughlin, Tom (wri): Date With An Angel; Friday The 13th, Part VI: Jason Lives; One Dark Night
McLoughlin, Tom(my) (act): Alice In Wonderland (1985); The Black Hole
McLuhan, Marshall (act): Gas-S-S-S!
McMahan, Heather (act): Class Of Nuke'em High
McMahon, David/Dave (act): The Creature Walks Among Us; The Scarf
McMahon, Ed (act): Dementia; Full Moon High
McMahon, Elaine Cohen (act): The Goonies
McMahon, Horace (act, 1906-1971): Abbott And Costello Go To Mars; Another Thin Man; The Gracie Allen Murder Case; Man In The Dark (1953); The Return Of October
McMahon, John (act): Edward Scissorhands
McMahon, Kevin (mus): The Video Dead
McMahon, Pat (act): Anatomy Of A Psycho
McMahon, Phyllis (act): I Don't Want To Be Born; 10 Rillington Place
McMains, Mick (act): Hard Rock Zombies
McMann, Dannete (act): Powder
McMann, Martin Scott (act): The Toxic Avenger
McMannis, Cheryl (act): The Return Of The Six Million Dollar Man And The Bionic Woman
McManus, Michael (act): The Munsters' Revenge
McMartin, John (act): Ritual Of Evil
McMartin, Kathleen (act): Sleepstalker
McMaster, Anew (act): The Lost Patrol (1929)
McMaster, Niles (act): Alice, Sweet Alice; The Incredible Torture Show
McMath, Virginia Katherine (act): see Rogers, Ginger
McMillan, Gary A. (act): I, Desire
McMillan, Ian (act): Zombie Island Massacre
McMillan, Julia (act): Larceny In Her Heart; Murder Is My Business

McMillan, Kenneth (act, 1932-1989): *Cat's Eye; The Clairvoyant (1985); Dune; Heartbeeps; Salem's Lot*
McMillan, Roddy (act): *The Mouse On The Moon*
McMillan, Susan O. (act): *Jaws 2*
McMillan, W.G. (act): *Code Name Trixie*
McMillin, Steven B. (act): *Getting Lucky*
McMinn, Teri (act): *The Texas Chainsaw Massacre*
McMinn, Ursula (act): see Jeans, Ursula
McMullen, Dennis (act): *The China Syndrome; Werewolf Of Washington; When A Stranger Calls*
McMullen, James/Jim (act): *The Incredible Shrinking Woman; Pursuit (1972); She's Dressed To Kill; Stowaway To The Moon*
McMullen, Virginia (act): *Beyond Tomorrow*
McMullin, Robert (mus): *Shadow Of The Hawk*
McMurdo-Wallis, Cristine (act): *The Hand That Rocks The Cradle*
McMurphy, Charles (act): *The Benson Murder Case*
McMurray, Sam (act): *Addams Family Values; The Munsters' Scary Little Christmas*
McMurry, Gregory L. (cin): *The Relic*
McMyler, Pamela (act): *Blood Beach*
McNab, Bernard (wri): *A Piece Of Cake*
McNab, Mercedes (act): *Addams Family Values*
McNab, Michael (act): *The First Power; Nightmare On The 13th Floor*
McNabb, Tracy (act): *Secrets Of The Phantom Caverns*
McNair, Barbara (act, b. 1939): *Paroxysmus*
McNair, Sue (wri): *Horror Of The Blood Monsters*
McNally, Edward (act): *Space Master X-7*
McNally, Horace (act): see McNally, Stephen
McNally, John (wri): *The Wickham Mystery*
McNally, Kevin (act): *Jekyll And Hyde*
McNally, Loretta (act): *Serial Mom*
McNally, Stephen (act, b. 1913, nee Horace McNally): *The Black Castle; Eyes In The Night; Make Haste To Live; Panic In The City; Split Second (1953)*
McNally, Terrence (act): *Looker*
McNally, Terrence E. (act & wri): *Earth Girls Are Easy*
McNalty, Frank (act): *Shock Chamber*
McNamara, Brian (act): *Arachnophobia*
McNamara, Ed(ward) (act): *Arsenic And Old Lace; Last Bride Of Salem; League Of Frightened Men*
McNamara, J. Patrick (act): *Close Encounters Of The Third Kind; The First Power; The Fury; Warning Sign*
McNamara, John (act): *From Hell It Came; The Lost Missile; The Return Of Dracula; War Of The Colossal Beast*
McNamara, Miles (act): *The Philadelphia Experiment*
McNamara, Pat(rick) (act): *Blow Out; Obsession (1976); The Silence Of The Lambs*
McNamara, Rosemary (act): *The Premonition (1975)*
McNamara, Ted (act): *The Monkey Talks*
McNamara, William (act, b. 1966): *Copycat; Dream A Little Dream; Storybook*
McNamee, Chris (act): *Class Of Nuke'em High; Street Trash; The Toxic Avenger, Part II*
McNarland, Laura (act): *Empire Of Ash III*
McNarland, Robert (act): *Empire Of Ash III*
McNaught, Bob (dir): *Grand National Night*
McNaughton, Charles (act): *The Adventures Of Robin Hood; Bulldog Drummond Escapes; Charlie Chan's Chance*
McNaughton, Gus (act, 1884-1969, nee Augustus Howard): *Crime On The Hill; I Killed The Count; Murder; A Place Of One's Own; The 39 Steps (1935); Wishes*
McNaughton, Ian (act): *X...The Unknown*
McNaughton, Jack (act): *The Camp On Blood Island; The Hour Of 13; Men Of Sherwood Forest; No Haunt For A Gentleman; They Made Me A Fugitive; Trent's Last Case (1952)*
McNaughton, John (dir): *The Borrower*
McNaughton, Robert (mus): *The Borrower*
McNeal, Heidi (act): *From Dusk Till Dawn*
McNeal, Joyce (act): *Witches' Brew*
McNeal, Julia (act): *The Refrigerator*
McNear, Howard (act, 1904-1969): *Bell, Book And Candle; Voyage To The Bottom Of The Sea*
McNeely, Jerry (act & wri): *Tomorrow's Child*
McNeely, Joel (mus): *Hitler's Daughter*
M[illegible], Mary (act): *Lycanthropus*
McNeice, Ian (act): *No Escape (1994)*
McNeil, Kate (act): *Monkey Shines*
McNeil, Kathryn (act): *The House On Sorority Row*
McNeil, Marguerite (act): *My Bloody Valentine*
McNeil, Thelma (act): *Seven Footprints To Satan*
McNeile, H.C. (wri): see Sapper
McNeill, Peter (act): *Rabid*
McNeill, Robert (act): *The Frighteners*
McNeill, Robert Duncan (act): *Masters Of The Universe*
McNichol, Jimmy (act): *Butcher, Baker (Nightmare Maker)*
McNichol, John (cin): *The Folks At Red Wolf Inn*
McNichol, Kristy (act, b. 1962): *Dream Lover*
McNicol, Douglas (act): *A Midsummer Night's Dream (1985)*
McNulty, Bill (act): *Dungeons Of Horror*
McNulty, Dorothy (act): see Singleton, Penny
McNulty, Kevin (act): *Generation X; Mother, May I Sleep With Danger?; Timecop; When A Stranger Calls Back*
McOmie, Maggie (act): *Thx 1138*
McPartland, Joe (act): *The Mind Of Mr. Soames*
McPartland, John (wri): *Johnny Cool; The Lost Missile*
McPeak, Sandy (act): *No Place To Hide (1981); Solar Crisis; Tarantulas: The Deadly Cargo*
McPhee, Peisha (act): *The Incredible Hulk Returns*
McPherson, Graham (act): *The Long Kiss Goodnight; Superman (1978)*
McPherson, John (cin): **Batteries Not Included; Fugitive From The Empire; Jaws: The Revenge; Short Circuit 2; V*
McPherson, Mark (act): *The Nutty Professor (1996)*
McPherson, Quinton (act): *Maria Marten: Or, The Murder In The Red Barn (1935); The Third Clue*
McPherson, Stephen (wri): *Cocoon: The Return*
McQuade, Billy Ray (act): *Mother's Day*
McQuain, Julie (act): *Street Trash*
McQueen, Armelia (act): *Ghost (1990)*
McQueen, B.J. (act): *Clarence*
McQueen, Butterfly (act, 1911-1995, nee Thelma McQueen): *Cabin In The Sky*
McQueen, James (act): *Robocop 2*
McQueen, Neile (act): *Nightmare On The 13th Floor*
McQueen, Steve (act, 1930-1980): *The Blob (1958); The Towering Inferno*
McQueen, Thelma (act): *see McQueen, Butterfly*
McRae, Alan (act): *Once Bitten; When Michael Calls*
McRae, Ellen (act): *Goodbye Charlie*
McRae, Frank (act): **Batteries Not Included*
McRae, Henry (dir): *The Werewolf (1913)*
McRaney, Gerald (act, b. 1947): *The Aliens Are Coming; Easy Prey; The Haunting Passion; The Incredible Hulk, Part 2; Murder By Moonlight; The Neverending Story; Night Of Bloody Horror; Women And Bloody Terror*
McRay, Leslie (act): *Death Race 2000*
McRitchie, Greig (mus): *This Is Not A Test*
McRoberts, Briony (act): *Edge Of Sanity*
McShane, Ian (act, b. 1942): *The Fifth Musketeer; Journey Into Fear (1975); The Murders In The Rue Morgue (1986); Tam Lin; Too Scared To Scream*
McShane, Kitty (act): *Old Mother Riley's Ghosts; Old Mother Riley's Jungle Treasure*
McShane, Mark (wri): *Seance On A Wet Afternoon*
McShane, Michael (act): *Robin Hood: Prince Of Thieves*
McSkimming, Jason (act): *Clarence*
McStay, Michael (act): *The Curse Of The Mummy's Tomb*
McSwain, Faith (act): *The Toolbox Murders*
McThuzen, Bishop (act): *King Solomon's Mines (1985)*
McTiernan, John (dir): *Eaters Of The Dead; Nomads; Predator*
McTiernan, John (wri): *Nomads*
McTosh, Bill (act): *Star Trek*
McVeigh, Eve (act): *Creator; The Glass Web*
McVeigh, Lee (act): *Invasion Of The Body Snatchers (1978)*
McVey, Michael (act): *A Hitch In Time*
McVey, Paul (act): *Buried Alive (1940); The Living Ghost (1942); The Mysterious Mr. Moto; Phantom Of Chinatown*
McVey, Tyler (act): *Attack Of The Giant Leeches; Creature With The Atom Brain; The Day The Earth Stood Still; Night Of The Blood-Beast; The Resurrection Of Zachary Wheeler*
McVicar, Daniel (act): *The Silence Of The Hams*
McWade, Edward (act): *Arsenic And Old Lace; The Monster (1925); Satan Met A Lady*
McWade, Margaret (act): *The Lost World (1925)*
McWade, Robert (act): *The Dragon Murder Case; The Kennel Murder Case; The Phantom Of Crestwood*
McWhirter, Jillian (act): *After Midnight; Dune Warriors*
McWilliams, Caroline (act): *The Aliens Are Coming*
McWilliams, Daphne (act): *The Wiz*
Meacham, Anne (act): *Dear, Dead Delilah; Lilith; Seizure*
Meacham, Michael (act): *Lancelot And Guinevere*
Mead, Phil(ip) (act): *The Resurrection Of Zachary Wheeler; To Save A Child*
Mead, Robert (act): *Peter Rabbit And The Tales Of Beatrix Potter*
Meade, Harold (act): *The Face At The Window (1932)*
Meade, Julia (act): *Zotz!*
Meade, Michael (act): *The Keeper*
Meade, Taylor (act): *The Iliac Passion*
Meade, Terry (cin): *Future Cop*
Meaden, Dan (act): *Baffled!; Dr. Jekyll And Sister Hyde; The Ghoul (1974)*
Meader, George (act): *Boston Blackie Booked On Suspicion; Champagne For Caesar; Man-Made Monster; Too Many Winners*
Meador, James H. (act): see Craig, James
Meador, Joshua (cin): *Forbidden Planet*
Meadow, Herb (wri): *The Curse Of King Tut's Tomb; The Lone Ranger; The Unguarded Moment*
Meadows, jayne (act, b. 1923): *Alice In Wonderland (1985); Lady In The Lake; The Luck Of The Irish; Song Of The Thin Man*
Meadows, Joyce (act): *The Brain From Planet Arous; I Saw What You Did (1965)*
Meadows, Stanley (act): *Night Caller From Outer Space; The Terrornauts*
Meadows, Stormy (act): *The Giant Gila Monster*
Meadway, Heather (act): *Serpent's Lair*
Meagher, John (act): *The Last Wave*
Meagher, Karen (act): *Threads*
Meakin, Jack (mus): *The Twonky*
Meaney, Colm (act): *Dick Tracy (1990)*
Means, G. Neal (act & cin): *Mutants In Paradise*
Means, Renee (act): *Mutants In Paradise*
Mear, H. Fowler (wri): *Alibi (1931); Bella Donna (1934); The Black Abbot (1934); Condemned To Death; The Face At The Window (1932); The Ghost Camera; Inside The Room; Juggernaut; The Last Hour; The Lodger (1932); The Man Outside (1933); The Man Who Changed His Name; The Missing Rembrandt; Murder At Covent Garden; The Pointing Finger; Puppets Of Fate; Scrooge (1935); The Shadow (1933); The Shot In The Dark; The Silent House; Silver Blaze (1937); The Sleeping Cardinal; Tangled Evidence; The Triumph Of Sherlock Holmes; The Wandering Jew (1933); Whispering Tongues*
Meara, Anne (act, b. 1929): *The Boys From Brazil*
Measor, Adela (act): *Scrooge (1913)*
Measor, Beryl (act): *Dual Albi*
Meatloaf/Meat Loaf (act): *The Rocky Horror Picture Show; To Catch A Yeti*
Mecchi, Irene (wri): *Hercules (1997); The Hunchback Of Notre Dame (1996)*
Mechoso, Julio (act): *Flight Of The Navigator*
Medak, Karen (act): *Switch*
Medak, Peter (dir): *The Babysitter; The Changeling; Cry For The Strangers; Funeral In Berlin; The Hunchback (1997); Mistress Of Paradise; Negatives; Romeo Is Bleeding; The Ruling Class; Zorro, The Gay Blade*
Medalis, Joseph/Joe (G.) (act): *The Cat From Outer Space; Dead And Buried; Deadly Messages; Endangered Species; Looker; Revenge Of The Stepford Wives*
Meddick, Lane (act): *Psychomania (1972); Richard III (1995)*
Meddings, Derek (cin): *Batman (1989); Captain Scarlet vs. The Mysterons; Doppleganger; High Spirits; Krull; The Land That Time Forgot; Moonraker; The Neverending Story II: The Next Chapter; Santa Claus (1985); The Spy Who Loved Me; Supergirl (1984); Thunderbirds In Outer Space; Z.P.G.*
Meddings, Jonathan (act): *Kill Her Gently*
Medeiros, Michael (act): *RoboCop 2*
Medel, Isana (act): *Tenemos 18 Anos*
Medford, Don (dir): *The Clone Master; To Trap A Spy*
Medford, Harold (wri): *Berlin Express; Brainwashed; Operation Secret; Phantom Of The Rue Morgue*
Medford, Jody (act): *Mutant*
Medford, Kay (act, b. 1920, nee Maggie O'Regin): *The Busy Body*
Medhurst, Stafford (act): *Tales From The Crypt*
Medici, John (act): *Tarantulas: The Deadly Cargo*
Medin, Harriet (act): *Blood Beach; Death Race 2000*
Medina, Jimmy (act): *When The Bough Breaks*
Medina, Luis (cin): *Robinson Crusoe And The Tiger*
Medina, Patricia (act, b. 1920): *Aladdin And His Lamp; The Beast Of Hollow Mountain; The Black Knight; Captain Pirate; Fortunes Of Captain Blood; Francis; The Lady In The Iron Mask; Latitude Zero; The Magic Carpet; Mr. Arkadin; Moss Rose; Phantom Of The Rue Morgue; Pirates Of Tripoli; The Red Cloak; Siren Of Baghdad; Snow White And The Three Stooges; Stranger At My Door; The Three Musketeers (1948)*
Medlin, Victoria (act): *Vanishing Point*
Medora, Rustum (act): *The Scarab Murder Case*
Medricka, Dana (act): *Ikaria Xb1*
Medvedeva, Natalia (act): *Ilya Mourometz*
Medway, Heather (act): *The Fear (1994)*
Medwid, Patti (act): *Strange Invaders*
Medwin, Michael (act, b. 1925): *Forbidden; For Them That Trespass; The Green Scarf; Just William's Luck; Never Say Never Again; Night Must Fall (1964); The Oracle (1952); The Queen Of Spades (1948); Scrooge (1970); Shadow Of The Past; Spaceways; The Teckman Mystery; Top Secret (1952); 24 Hours To Kill*
Meehan, Elizabeth (wri): *Laugh, Clown, Laugh; Mr. Reeder In Room 13*
Meehan (Jr.), George (B.) (cin): *The Bandit Of Sherwood Forest; Boston Blackie And The Law; Boston Blackie Booked On Suspicion; Boston Blackie's Rendezvous; The Ghost Talks; The Phantom Thief; Tarzan's Revenge*
Meehan (Jr.), John (wri, b. 1890): *Kismet (1944); Nazi Agent; Peter Ibbetson*
Meehan, Lou (act): *The Lost Jungle*
Meehan, Thomas (wri): *Spaceballs*
Meek, Donald (act, 1880-1946): *The Mark Of The Vampire (1935); Nick Carter, Master Detective; Peter Ibbetson; Phantom Raiders; The Return Of Peter Grimm (1934); Sky Murder*
Meek, Jeffrey (act): *Heart Condition*
Meeker, George (act): *Crime Doctor's Diary; Dead Man's Eyes; The Dragon Murder Case; Michael Shayne, Private Detective; Murder By Television; Murder Is My Business; Murder On A Honeymoon; Night Of Terror (1933); The Red Dragon (1945); Tarzan's Revenge; The Westland Case*
Meeker, Ralph (act, 1920-1988, nee Ralph Rathgeber): *The Alpha Incident; The Dead Don't Die; The Food Of The Gods; Kiss Me Deadly; The Mind Snatchers; The Night Stalker (1971); The St. Valentine's Day Massacre; Shadow In The Sky; Something Wild; A Woman's Devotion*
Meeks, Edith (act): *Poison (1990)*
Meeks, Edward (act): *Bluebeard (1972)*
Meersman, Peter (act): *Death Comes From Space*
Meerson, Steve (wri): *Star Trek IV The Voyage Home*
Megill, Sheelah (act): *It (1990)*
Megna, John (act, 1953-1995): *Hush...Hush, Sweet Charlotte*
Megowan, Don (act): *Creation Of The Humanoids; The Creature Walks Among Us; Prince Valiant; Scream Of The Wolf; The Story Of Mankind; Tarzan And The Valley Of Gold; To Catch A Thief; The Werewolf (1956)*
Meheux, Phil (cin): *The Final Conflict; Ghost In The Machine; Goldeneye; Highlander 2: The Quickening; Morons From Outer Space; No Escape (1994); The Saint*
Mehling, Kathy (act): *Cavegirl (1985)*
Mehra, Lal Chand (act): *Man-Eater Of Kumaon; Mr. Moto's Last Warning; Murder Over New York; The Thirteenth Chair (1929)*
Mehri, Jalal (act): *Tiger Claws*
Mehta, Nancy (act): *Ellery Queen*
Meibes, Joseph (act): see Ericson, John
Meichsner, Rudiger (cin): *Superwheels*
Meier, Barry (act): *Millennium*
Meighan, Thomas (act, 1879-1936): *Cheaters At Play; Male And Female; The Miracle Man (1919)*
Meigs, Leslie (act): *Monstroid*
Meikle, Richard (act): *On The Beach*
Meillon, John (act, 1933-1989): *The Cars That Ate Paris; Dead Man's Chest; Death Trap (1962); Inn Of The Damned; On The Beach*
Meinati, Umberto (act): *La Freccia D'oro*

Meineke, Eva-Marie (act): To The Devil A Daughter
Meisel, Kurt (act): Embezzled Heaven
Meiser, Edith (act): It Grows On Trees
Meisle, Kathryn (act): Basket Case 2
Meisner, Gunter/Gunther (act): The Boys From Brazil; Funeral In Berlin; Hauser's Memory; The Quiller Memorandum; Willy Wonka And The Chocolate Factory
Meixner, Karl (act): Das Testament Des Dr. Mabuse
Mekas, Jonas (act, b. 1922): Galaxie
Mekin, Ahmet (act): The Devil's Castle (1963)
Melachrino, George (act): House Of Darkness
Melachrino, George (mus): The Gamma People
Melander, Ashley (act): The Hand That Rocks The Cradle
Melander, Eric (act): The Hand That Rocks The Cradle
Melander, Jennifer (act): The Hand That Rocks The Cradle
Melato, Mariangela (act): Flash Gordon
Melbe, Lisa (act): Vampire On Bikini Beach
Melchior, Georges (act): L'atlantide (1920)
Melchior, Ib (dir, b. 1917): The Angry Red Planet; The Time Travelers (1964)
Melchior, Ib (wri, b. 1917): The Angry Red Planet; Death Race 2000; Journey To The Seveth Planet; Reptilicus; Robinson Crusoe On Mars; Terrore Nello Spazio; The Time Travelers (1964)
Meldal-Johnsen, Trevor (wri): Deja Vu
Meldegg, Stephane (act): Notorious (1992)
Mele, Nicholas/Nick (act): A Nightmare On Elm Street 4: The Dream Master; A Nightmare On Elm Street 5: The Dream Child
Melendez, Ron (act): Children Of The Corn III: Urban Sacrifice
Melesh, Alex (act): Beyond Tomorrow
Melford, Austin (act): Dream Paintings
Melford, Austin (wri): The Phantom Light
Melford, Berenice (act): Lady Audley's Secret (1920)
Melford, George (dir, 1889-1961): Dracula (1931, Spanish-Speaking Version)
Melford, Jack (act): Bluebeard's Ten Honeymoons; The End Of The Line; Fatal Journey; The Lady Killers (1956); The Laughing Lady; Lust For A Vampire; The October Man; The Spider (1939)
Melford, Jakidawdra (act): The Herncrake Witch; The Land Of The Nursery Rhymes
Melford, Jill (act): Bunny Lake Is Missing; Edge Of Sanity; Murder At Site Three; Murder By Proxy; The Servant; The Vengeance Of She
Melford, Mark (act): The Disappearance Of The Judge; The Herncrake Witch; The Land Of The Nursery Rhymes
Melford, Mark (dir): The Herncrake Witch; The Land Of The Nursery Rhymes
Melford, Mark (wri): Flying From Justice; The Herncrake Witch; The Land Of The Nursery Rhymes
Melhem, Alfred (act): The Bees
Melhuse, Peder (act): The Wraith
Melia, Frank (act): Rawhead Rex
Melia, Joe (act): Modesty Blaise; The Sign Of Four (1983)
Melies, Georges (act, 1861-1938): L'ange De Noel; L'armoire Des Freres Davenport' Les Aventures De Robinson Crusoe; The Brahmin And The Butterfly; Le Diable Au Couvent; Le Diable Geant Ou Le Miracle De La Madonne; Extraordinary Illusions; Les Filles Du Diable; The Infernal Cakewalk; The Magical Box; The Man With The Rubber Head; The One Man Band; Punch And Judy; The Temptation Of Saint Anthony; Les Tresors De Satan; Le Voyage A Travers L'impossible; Le Voyage Dans La Lune
Melies, Georges (dir, 1861-1938): The Adventures Of William Tell; A La Conquete Du Pole; L'ange De Noel; An Angelic Servant; The Apparition; Les Apparitions Fugitives; L'armoire Des Freres Davenport; L'auberge Ensorcelee; Les Aventures De Don Quichotte; Les Aventures De Robinson Crusoe; Barbe-Bleue; Le Bataillon Elastique; The Bewildering Cabinet; The Brahmin And The Butterfly; Le Cabinet De Mephistopheles; Les Cartes Vivantes; Le Carton Fantastique; Le Cauchemar; La Caverne Maudite; Cendrillon; La Chaise A Porteurs Enchantee; Le Chapeau A Surprises; Le Chateau Hante; Le Chaudron Infernal; Le Chevalier Mystere; La Cigale Et La Fourmi; Cinderella: Or, The Glass Slipper; Cinderella Up-To-Date; Cleopatre; La Clownesse Fantome; Le Coffre Enchantee; Le Compositeur Toque; Coppelia Ou La Poupee Animee; La Corbeille Enchantee; Les Costumes Animes; Creations Spontanees; La Cremation; La Cuisine De L'ogre; D. Devant, Conjurer; La Dame Fantome; Damnation Of Doctor Faust; The Damnation Of Faust; La Danse De Feu; La Danseuse Microscopique; Delerium In A Studio; Le Deshabille Impossible; Deux Cent Mille Lieues Sous Les Mers; Le Diable Au Couvent; Le Diable Geant Ou Le Miracle De La Madonne; Le Diable Noir; Le Diner Impossible; Le Dirigeable Fantastique Ou Le Cauchemar D'un Inventeur; Dislocation Mysterieuse; Dix Chapeaux En 60 Secondes; The Dwarf And The Giant; The Eclipse (1907); The Enchanted Well; L'enchanteur Alcofrisbas; L'equilibre Impossible; The Eruption Of Mont-Pele; Evocation Spirite; Excelsior!; L'execution D'un Espion; Extraordinary Illusions; The Fakir; Le Fakir De Singapoure; Le Fantome D'alger; Faust And Marguerite; Faust Aux Enfers; La Femme Volante; Les Filles Du Diable; La Flamme Merveilleuse; La Fontaine Merveilleuse; La Fontaine Sacree Ou La Vengeance De Boudha; Le Fou Assassin; Les 400 Farces Du Diable; The Four Troublesome Heads; Les Fromages Automobiles; Galathee; La Genie De Feu; Grandmother's Story; La Grotte Aux Surprises; Guguste Et Belzebuth; La Guirlande Merveilleuse; L'hallucination De L'alchemiste; Les Hallucinations Du Baron De Munchausen; Hamlet (1907); The Haunted Castle (1896); The Haunted Cave; L'homme Aux Cent Trucs; L'homme Aux Mille Inventions; L'homme Dans La Lune; L'homme-Mouche; The Hypnotist's Revenge; L'ile De Calypso; Ulysse Et Polypheme; L'illusioniste Double Et La Tete Vivante; Les Illusions Fantaisistes; Illusions Phantasmagoriques; L'impressioniste Fin De Siecle; Les Incendiaires; Une Indigestion; The Infernal Cakewalk; Jack Et Jim; Jack Le Ramoneur; Jeanne D'arc; Le Juif Errant; The Knight Of Black Art; The Laboratory Of Mephistopheles; La Lanterne Magique; La Legende De Rip Van Winkle; The Lightning Change Artist; Le Livre Magique; Le Locataire Diabolique; Long-Distance Wireless Photography; The Magical Box; The Magician's Cavern; Le Magicien; La Magie A Travers Les Ages; Magie Diabolique; Le Magnetiseur; Le Malade Hydrophobe; Le Manoir Du Diable; The Man With The Rubber Head; Le Melomane; Le Menuet Lilliputien; Le Merveilleux Eventail Vivant; A Mesmerian Experiment; Les Miracles Du Brahmane; Un Miracle Sous L'inquisition; Le Miroir De Cagliostro; Le Monstre; Le Mousquetaire De La Reine; Les Mousquetaires De La Reine; The Mysterious Paper; The Mysterious Retort; Neptune Et Amphitrite; La Nouvelle Peine De Mort; Une Nuit Terrible; L'oeuf Du Sorcier; Off To Bloomington Asylum; The One Man Band; L'oracle De Delphe; Oriental Black Art; Le Palais Des Mille Et Une Nuits; Le Papillon Fantastique; Le Petit Chaperon Rouge; Un Petit Diable; Un Peu De Feu, S.V.P.; La Phrenologie Burlesque; Le Phenix Ou Le Coffret De Cristal; La Pierre Philosophale; Le Portrait Mysterieux; Le Portrait Spirite; La Poupee Vivante; La Prophetesse De Thebes; Punch And Judy; Pygmalion Et Galathee; Le Repas Fantastique; Le Reve D'artiste; Le Reve De L'horloger; Le Reve De Noel; Le Reve De Shakespeare; Le Reve Du Maitre De Ballet; Le Reve D'un Fumeur D'opium; Le Reve Du Pariah; Le Reve Du Pauvre; Le Reve Du Rajah Ou La Foret Enchantee; Le Revenant; Le Roi Des Mediums; Le Rosier Miraculeux; Le Royaume Des Fees; Satan En Prison; Le Secret Du Medecin; Les Sept Peches Capitaux; La Sirene; Siva, L'invisible; Soap Bubbles; Sorcellerie Culinaire; Le Sorcier; Le Sorcier, Le Prince Et Le Bon Genie; Le Spectre (1899); Spiritisme Abracadabrant; La Statue Animee; La Statue De Neige; Le Systeme Du Docteur Sonflamort; Rchin Chao, The Chinese Conjurer; Le Temple De La Magie; The Temptation Of Saint Anthony; Tom Old Boot; Tom Tight Et Dum Dum; Le Tonnerre De Jupiter; Les Torches Humaines; La Tour De Londres Et Les Derniers Moments D'anne De Boleyn; La Tour Maudite; Les Transmutations Imperceptibles; Les Tresors De Satan; The Triple Lady; Les Trois Bacchantes; Le Tunnel Sous La Manche Ou Le Cauchemar Franco-Anglais; The Vanishing Lady (1896); Le Voyage A Travers L'impossible; Le Voyage Dans La Lune; Les Voyages De Gulliver; The Witch (1906)
Melies, Georges (wri, 1861-1938): The Adventures Of William Tell; Le Chateau Hante; Le Diable Au Couvent; Dix Chapeaux En 60 Secondes; The Haunted Castle (1896); The Magical Box; Le Manoir Du Diable; Le Sorcier; The Vanishing Lady (1896); Le Voyage A Travers L'impossible; Le Voyage Dans La Lune; The Witch (1906)
Melies, Georgette (act): Un Petit Diable
Melische, Judich (act): The Cold Room
Melissis, Tom (act): Sorry, Wrong Number (1989)
Melito, Joseph (act): 12 Monkeys
Melkent, Eric (act): I Was A Zombie For The F.B.I.
Mell, Joseph (act): I Was A Teenage Werewolf
Mell, Marisa (act, 1939-1992): Diabolik; Marta; Masquerade; Night Fiend; Operation Double Cross; Secret Agent Superdragon; Secret Of The Red Orchid
Mella, Eloy (cin): Perseus The Invincible; Tenemos 18 Anos
Mellaney, Victor (act): Cyborg Cop II
Mellay, Emby (act): The Touch Of Satan
Melle, Gil (mus): The Andromeda Strain; Blood Beach; A Cold Night's Death; Crackle Of Death; The Curse Of King Tut's Tomb; Demon And The Mummy; Embryo; Frankenstein: The True Story; Gold Of The Amazon Women; The Intruder Within; Killer In The Mirror; The Questor Tapes; The Sentinel; Star-Crossed; Starship Invasions; The Ultimate Warrior; A Vacation In Hell; World War III; You'll Like My Mother
Meller, Douglas (act): The Beast Of Yucca Flats
Mellinger, Leonie (act): Memoirs Of A Survivor
Mellinger, Michael (act): The Awakening; The Golden Mask; The Secret Man
Mello, Breno (act): Black Orpheus
Mello, Jay (act): Jaws: The Revenge
Mellon, Leonard (act): Charlie Chan At The Opera
Mellon, Lydia (act): El Vampiro
Mellor, William C. (cin, 1904-1963): Beyond The Blue Horizon; Bulldog Drummond Comes Back; Maneater Of Kumaon; The Next Voice You Hear
Mellot, Bud (act): Midnight (1980)
Mellot, Gayle (act): The Saint In Palm Springs
Melly, Andree (act): Brides Of Dracula; The Horror Of It All
Melniker, Janet Scott (wri): Batman Forever
Melocco, Marta (act): La Ragazza Che Sapeva Troppo
Melody, Tom (act): 2000 Years Later
Melon, Christopher (act): 12 Monkeys
Meloy, Robin (act): The House On Sorority Row
Melrose, Frank (act): Eugene Aram; Jane Shore (1915)
Melson, John (wri): Cauldron Of Blood; Viaje Al Centro De La Tierra
Melson, Sara (act): Dr. Giggles
Melton, Frank (act): Black Dragons
Melton, Sid (act): The Atomic Submarine; Ellery Queen: Don't Look Behind You; Lost Continent (1951); Radar Secret Service; Savage Drums; Shadow Of The Thin Man
Melton, Troy (act): Cyborg 2087; The Day Mars Invaded Earth
Meltzer, Douglas (cin): Raiders Of The Living Dead
Meltzer, Lewis (wri, b. 1911): Desert Legion; Man-Eater Of Kumaon; Once Upon A Time (1944)
Melville, Herman (wri, 1819-1891): Enchanted Island; Moby Dick (1930 & 1956); The Sea Beast
Melville, Jean-Pierre (dir, 1917-1973, nee Jean-Pierre Grumbach): Les Enfants Terribles
Melville, Olive (act): The Howard Case
Melville, Sam (act): Twice Dead
Melville, Walter (wri): The Beggar Girl's Wedding; The Girl Who Took The Wrong Turning; The Girl Who Wrecked His Home
Melville, Winifred (act): The Greed Of William Hart
Melvin (act): Frankenstein Island
Melvin, Michael (act): Nightmare On The 13th Floor
Melvin, Murray (act): The Devils; Gawain And The Green Knight; Ghost Story (1975); Gulliver's Travels (1977); Liszt O' Mania; Slipstream; Stories From A Flying Trunk
Memmoli, George (act): Phantom Of The Paradise
Menard, Tina (act): Devil Dog: The Hound Of Hell
Menczer, Enrico (cin): The Cat O' Nine Tails; The Dead Are Alive; Eyes Behind The Stars; Holocaust 2000
Mende, Lisa (act): Gremlins 2: The New Batch
Mendelsohn, Hal (act): see March, Hal
Mendelson, Robert (act): Species
Mendelssohn, Jakob Ludwig Felix (mus, 1809-1847): A Midsummer Night's Dream (1935)
Mendeluk, George (dir): The Kidnapping Of The President; Stone Cold Dead
Mendeluk, George (wri): Stone Cold Dead
Mendenhall, David (act): Space Raiders
Mendenhall, James (act): Space Raiders
Mendenhall, Jennifer (act): Serial Mom
Mendenhall, William (cin): The Return Of The World's Greatest Detective
Mendes, Hercules (act): Arrest Bulldog Drummond
Mendes, Julie (act): Devils Of Darkness; She (1965)
Mendes, Lothar (dir, 1894-1974): The Man Who Could Work Miracles; A Night Of Mystery (1928)
Mendez, Fernando (dir): El Ataud Del Vampiro; El Ladron De Cadaveres; The Living Coffin; Misterios Del Ultratumba; El Vampiro
Mendez, Fernando (wri): El Ladron De Cadaveres
Mendez, Johnny (act): Beyond Evil
Mendez, Ned (act): Hamlet (1990)
Mendez, Racho (mus): Dr. Tarr's Torture Dungeon
Mendis, Nimal (mus): The God King
Mendizabal, Sergio (act): Tristana
Mendlesohn, Bob (act): The Devil's Gift
Mendoza, Quiel (act): Curse Of The Vampires
Mendoza, Ray (act): El Santo Contra Las Vampiras
Mendoza-Nava, Jaime/Jamie (mus): A Boy And His Dog; The Brotherhood Of Satan; Creature From Black Lake; Grave Of The Vampire; The Legend Of Boggy Creek; Mausoleum; The Vampire Girls; The Witchmaker
Menendez, Francis (act): The Slumber Party Massacre
Menendez, Juanjo (act): Tristana
Menendez, Juan Jose (act): Carlota; La Venganza de Don Mendo
Meneray, Bob (act): Funeral Home; The Groundstar Conspiracy
Meneses, Alex (act): Amanda and the Alien
Menez, Bernard (act): Dracula, Pere et Fils
Menga, Horace (dir): Revenge of the Zombies (1981)
Menges, Chris (cin): Warlords of the 21st Century
Menges, Joyce (act): Now You See Him, Now You Don't
Meniconi, Furio (act): David and Goliath; The Tartars; Vulcan, Son of Jupiter
Menik (act): The God King
Menjou, Adolphe (act, 1890-1963): Bella Donna (1923); Journal of a Crime; A Night of Mystery (1928); Rupert of Hentzau (1923); The Sniper; The Sorrows of Satan (1925): The Three Musketeers (1921); Turnabout
Menken, Alan (mus): Hercules (1997); The Hunchback of Notre Dame (1996); The Little Mermaid; Little Shop of Horrors (1986); Pocahontas
Menken, Robin (wri): Teen Witch
Menken, Shep (act): Killers from Space
Mennard, Tom (act): The Flesh and Blood Show; Tiffany Jones
Mennebhi, Abdullah (act): Saadia
Meno, Ian (act); Surf Nazis Must Die
Menotti, Gian-Carlo (dir, b. 1911): The Medium (1951)
Menschik, Josef (act): The Invisible Terror
Menta, Narciso (Ibanez) (act): Master of Horror; The Saga of the Draculas
Mentgosrani, Anna (act): The Devil's Men
Mention, Michel (mus): The Mad Bomber
Mention III, Richard A. (act): Shadow Conspiracy
Mentley, Nelson (act): Psychophobia
Menuez, Stephanie (act): Gremlins 2: The New Batch
Menville, Chuck (wri): Condor
Menyard, Ken (act): The Dark (1979)
Menyert, Balog (act): Enemy Mine
Menyuk, Eric (act): The Babysitter (1995)
Menza, Gina (act): Outbreak; Street Trash
Menzel, Mike (cin): Wavelength
Menzel, Paul (act): The Bermuda Triangle
Menzer, Ernest (act): Aimez-Vous les Femmes?
Menzies, Hamish (act): Dancing With Crime
Menzies, Heather (act, b. 1949): Captain America (1978); Endangered Species; Piranha (1978); Sssssss
Menzies, Mary (act): The Pit and the Pendulum (1961)
Menzies, Nathaniel (act): Dick Turpin's Ride to York
Menzies Jr., Peter (cin): A Time to Kill (1996)
Menzies, William Cameron (dir, 1896- 1957): Address Unknown; Chandu the Magician; Invaders from Mars (1953); The Maze; The

Spider (1932); Things to Come; The Whip Hand

Menzies, William Cameron (wri, 1896-1957): *Alice In Wonderland (1933); The Whip Hand*

Meola, Mike (act): *Seizure*

Merande, Doro (act): *The Gazebo*

Meray, Tibor (wri): *Catch Me a Spy*

Mercado, Hector (act): *Something Is Out There*

Mercado, Jose (act): *Miracle Mile*

Mercedes, Maria (act): *Grand National Night; Mother Riley Meets the Vampire; Patrick*

Mercer, Beryl (act, 1882-1939): *Berkeley Square; The Hound Of The Baskervilles (1939); Jane Eyre (1934); Night Must Fall (1937); Outward Bound; Six Hours to Live; Supernatural (1933)*

Mercer, Bryan (act): *Freejack*

Mercer, Darren Peter (act): *The Lost World (1993); Return to the Lost World*

Mercer, Ernestine (act): *Casper; The Sleeping Car*

Mercer, Freddie (act): *Gildersleeve's Ghost*

Mercer, Johnny (mus, 1909-1976): *Li'l Abner (1959); Robin Hood (1973)*

Mercer, Mabel (act): *The Sand Castle*

Mercer, Mae (act): *The Beguiled; Frogs*

Mercer, Marian (act): *Oh, God! Book II*

Mercer, Martin (act): *Waxwork II: Lost In Time*

Mercer, Ray (cin): *The Baron of Arizona; The Golden Idol; House of Usher (1960); The Lucifer Complex; Tarzan and the Green Goddess*

Mercer, William (wri): *The Velvet Touch*

Merchant, Cathy (act): *The Haunted Palace (1963)*

Merchant, Vivien (act, 1929-1982, nee Ada Thompson): *Frenzy; The Maids; The Offence*

Mercieca, Victor (act): *Pulp*

Mercier, Denis (act): *Bogus*

Mercier, Louis (act): *Bulldog Drummond's Bride; Charlie Chan at Monte Carlo; Charlie Chan In City In Darkness; The Man Who Knew Too Much (1956)*

Mercier, Michele (act, b. 1942): *Fury at Smugglers' Bay; The Nights of Lucretia Borgia; Le Saint Mene la Dance; I Tre Volti della Paura; Web of the Spider; Women of Devil's Island; The Wonders of Aladdin*

Mercier, Robert (act): *Alien High*

Merck, Wallace (act): *Brainstorm (1983); King Kong Lives; RoboCop 2*

Mercouri, Melina (act, 1923-1994): *Topkapi*

Mercure, Monique (act): *Stone Cold Dead*

Mercurio, Gus (act): *Escape 2000*

Mercurio, Joe (cin): *The Clone Master; Look What's Happened to Rosemary's Baby*

Mercurio, Paul (act): *Back of Beyond; Exit to Eden*

Meredith, Burgess (act, b. 1909): *The Amazing Captain Nemo; Batman (1966); Beware! The Blob; Burnt Offerings; Clash of the Titans; King Lear (1987); The Last Chase; Mackenna's Gold; Magic; The Manitou; Night of the Hunter (1991); Of Mice and Men (1939); Probe; Santa Claus (1985); The Sentinel; Torture Garden; When Time Ran Out*

Meredith, Charles (act): *The Boy With Green Hair; The Cave Girl (1921); Francis; The Incredible Mr. Limpet; The Lone Ranger*

Meredith, Frank (act): *Dick Tracy (1945); The Gracie Allen Murder Case*

Meredith, Jill Mai (act): *Billion Dollar Brain; Carry On Spying; The Curse of the Mummy's Tomb*

Meredith, Joanne (act): *The Psycho Lover*

Meredith, John (act): *Devotion*

Meredith, Judi(th) (act): *Dark Intruder; Jack the Giant Killer; The Night Walker; Queen of Blood*

Meredith, Lois (act): *The Headless Horseman*

Meredith, Lucille (act): *They Live*

Meredith, Madeleine (act): *The Silver Bridge*

Meredith, Madge (act): *The Falcon's Adventure*

Meredith, Penny (act): *The Flesh and Blood Show*

Meredith, Olga (act): *The Brother from Another Planet*

Meredyth, Bess (wri, 1890-1969): *Charlie Chan at the Opera; Don Juan (1927); The Mark of Zorro (1940); The Sea Beast*

Merehon, Bob (act): *Rattlers*

Merelles, Alberto (act): *Anguish*

Merenda, Charlotte (act): *Nightbeast*

Merenda, John (act): *Nightbeast*

Merenda, Luc (act): *Torso*

Merenda, Pam (act): *Fiend (1980)*

Merendino, James (dir): *Witchboard 4: Virgin Heart*

Mergey, Marie (act): *Le Comte de Monte Cristo*

Merhi, Jalil (act): *TC 2000*

Merhi, Joseph (dir): *Epitaph; The Newlydeads*

Meril, Macha (act): *Belle de Jour; Profundo Rosso*

Merimee, Prosper (wri, 1803-1870): *Loves of Carmen (1927 & 1948); The Tragedy of Carmen*

Merino, J.L. (dir, a.k.a. John Richardson): *La Orgia de los Muertos; Scream of the Demon Lover*

Merino, J.L. (wri): *Scream of the Demon Lover*

Merino, Manuel (cin): *The Blood of Fu Manchu; The Castle of Fu Manchu; Count Dracula; Future Women; Horror Rises from the Tomb; House of 1,000 Dolls*

Merino, Rick (act): *The Norsemen*

Merius, Renzo (dir): *Mata Hari's Daughter*

Merivale, Bernard (wri): *Condemned to Death; The Flying Fool; Footsteps In the Dark; Seven Sinners*

Merivale, John (act, 1917-1990): *Caltiki, il Mostro Immortale; Circus of Horrors; House of Mystery (1961); The List of Adrian Messenger*

Merivale, Phillip (act): *Trilby (1914)*

Meriwether, Lee (act, b. 1935): *Batman (1966); Cruise Into Terror; 4D Man*

Merkel, Una (act, 1903-1986): *The Bat Whispers; Bulldog Drummond Strikes Back (1934); Cracked Nuts (1941); The Mad Doctor of Market Street; The Maltese Falcon (1931);On Borrowed Time; The Secret of Madame Blanche*

Merkerson, S. Epatha (act, b. 1952): *Jacob's Ladder; Terminator 2:Judgment Day*

Merkyl, John (act): *The Unholy Three (1925)*

Merle, Robert (wri): *The Day of the Dolphin*

Merli, Franco (act): *Arabian Nights (1974)*

Merlin, Jan (act): *Covenant; The St. Valentine's Day Massacre; Strategy of Terror; Twilight People*

Merlin, Joanna (act): *Prince of Darkness*

Merlin, Monica (act): *Repulsion*

Merlini, Marisa (act): *Top Secret (1978)*

Merlo, Ismael (act): *Cuento de Hadas*

Merlo, Tony (act): *Charlie Chan at the Opera*

Merman, Ethel (act): *Journey Back to Oz*

Merolly, Rino (dir): *Queen of the Pirates*

Merovitz, Shirley (act): *Deadbolt*

Merrall, Mary (act, b. 1890, nee Mary Lloyd): *The Camp On Blood Island; Dead of Night (1945); Family Doctor; Fatal Fingers; For Them That Trespass; The Green Buddha; The Late Edwina Black; They Made Me a Fugitive; The Three Weird Sisters; Who Killed the Cat?*

Merriam, Charlotte (act): *The Brass Bottle (1923); Night Nurse*

Merrick, Doris (act): *The Neanderthal Man; Untamed Women*

Merrick, Frederick (wri): *Spy of Napoleon*

Merrick, George W. (wri): *King Tut-Ankh-Amen's Eighth Wife; The Lost City*

Merrick, Ian (dir): *The Black Panther*

Merrick, John (act): *The Alligator People; Killers from Space; The Scarf*

Merrick, Laurence (dir & wri): *Guess What Happened to Count Dracula*

Merrick, Lynn (act): *Boston Blackie Booked On Suspicion; A Close Call for Boston Blackie; Crime Doctor's Strangest Case; Dangerous Business; Down to Earth*

Merrick, Mahlon (mus): *Red Planet Mars*

Merrick, Simon (act): *No Blade of Grass; Not Guilty*

Merrick, T.J. (act): *Slime City*

Merril, Frank (act): *Perils of the Jungle (1927)*

Merrill, Anthony (act): *The Mandarin Mystery*

Merrill, Barbara (act, b. 1947): *What Ever Happened to Baby Jane? (1962)*

Merrill, C.J. (act): *Getting Lucky*

Merrill, Concordia (act): *A Smart Set*

Merrill, Damon (act): *The Outing*

Merrill, Dina (act, b. 1925, nee Nedinia Hutton): *Desk Set; Fear (1990); Suture; Turn Back the Clock; Twisted*

Merrill, Gary (act, 1915-1990): *Another Man's Poison; Around the World Under the Sea; A Blueprint for Murder; Catacombs (1964); Crash Landing; Destination Inner Space; Earth II; Mysterious Island (1961); The Power (1967); Run,Psycho, Run; Witness to Murder*

Merrill, Julie (act): *Dead of Night (1987); The Monster Squad*

Merrill, Kim (act): *Spookies*

Merrill, Lou(is D.) (act): *The Giant Claw; The Lady from Shanghai; Passport to Suez; Sabaka*

Merrill Jr., Norman (act): *Eve of Destruction*

Merrill, Peter (act): *The Time Guardian*

Merrill, Tony (act): *Donovan's Brain*

Merrill, [illegible]

Merrin, Billy (act): *The Dance of Death (1938)*

Merrins, Michael (act): *Posed for Murder*

Merrithew, Lindsay (act): *Body Parts (1991); Hitler's Daughter*

Merritt, A. (wri, 1884-1943): *Devil Doll (1936); Seven Footprints to Satan*

Merritt, George (act, b. 1890): *Alibi (1942); Blind Spot (1932); The Case of the Frightened Lady; The Clairvoyant (1934); Crime On the Hill; Crime Unlimited; Dark Secret; Dangerous Fingers; Dr. Syn; Double Bluff; The Fire Chasers; F.P. 1 Antwortet Nicht; The Full Treatment; The Gaunt Stranger; Gawain and the Green Knight; The Ghost Camera; The Ghost Train (1941); The Green Scarf; Horror of Dracula; I Was a Spy; I, Monster; Line Engaged; The Lodger (1932); The Man Behind the Mask (1936); Meet Maxwell Archer; Mr. Reeder In Room 13;My Brother's Keeper; The Night of the Full Moon; No Escape (1934); Noose for a Lady; Pool of London; Q Planes; Quatermass II; The Rat; The Return of the Scarlet Pimpernel; Ten Minute Alibi; They Came by Night; Two for Danger; The Vulture (1937); Young and Innocent*

Merritt, Juanita (act): *Kingdom of the Spiders*

Merritt, Max (mus): *Vampire On Bikini Beach*

Merritt, Theresa (act, 1922-1998): *The Serpent and the Rainbow; They Might Be Giants; Voodoo Dawn; The Wiz*

Merriweather, Nicholas (dir & wri): *Eegah!*

Merrow, Jane (act, b. 1941): *Assignment K; Catacombs (1964); Diagnosis: Murder; Hands of the Ripper; The Horror at 37,000 Feet; The Hound of the Baskervilles (1972); The Night of the Big Heat*

Merrow, William (act): *Eye of the Needle*

Mersman, Linda (act): *To All a Goodnight*

Merson, Billy (act): *The Terrible 'Tec*

Merson, Susan (act): *Phenomenon*

Mertes, Raffaele (cin): *Fluke; Trauma (1993)*

Merton, John (act): *Dick Tracy Returns; The GoldenEye*

Merton, Roger (wri): *Queen of the Amazons (1947)*

Mertz, Doug (act): *Midnight (1980)*

Mervyn, William (act): *Doctors Wear Scarlet; Hammerhead; Murder Ahoy; The Ruling Class*

Merwin, Anne (wri): *The Daughter of Romany; The Foreman's Treachery; The Ring and the Rajah*

Merwin, (S.) Bannister (dir): *Altar Chains; Her Heritage; The Silver Greyhound (1919)*

Merwin, Bannister (wri): *Altar Chains; The Antique Brooch; The Ashes of Revenge; The Black Spot; The Cage; The Daughter of Romany; The Firm of Girdlestone; The Foreman's Treachery; The Golden Dawn; The King's Minister; The King's Outcast; A Letter to the Princess; Paste; Trilby (1914)*

Merzin, Eduard (act): *Korol Lir*

Mesa, Arthur (act): *Galaxis*

Mesa, William (dir): *Galaxis*

Mescall, John (D.) (cin, b. 1899): *The Black Cat (1934); Bride of Frankenstein; Dark Waters; The Invisible Man (1933); The Leopard Lady; Not of This Earth (1957)*

Mescherin, Enio (act): *Shock Chamber*

Mese, John (act): *Night of the Scarecrow*

Mesmer, Michael (act): *Deadtime Stories*

Mesquita, Theresa (act): *School Spirit*

Mesritz, Andre (act): see Morell, Andre

Messaoud (act): *The Golden Mask*

Messaoudi, Souad (act): *Raiders of the Lost Ark*

Messemer, Hannes (act): *The Red Hand*

Messenger, Charlie (act): *The Sword and the Sorcerer*

Messer, Samuel G. (act): see Middleton, Robert

Messervey, Robert Preston (act): see Preston, Robert

Messick, Dale (wri): *Brenda Starr (1976 & 1992)*

Messick, Don (act): *Charlotte's Web; The Flight of Dragons; The Hobbit; Jetsons: The Movie*

Messina, Emile/Emilio (act): *The Invincible Barbarian; Sodom and Gomorrah*

Messina, Francesco (act): *Point of No Return*

Messina, Giovanni (act): *The Lion of Thebes*

Messina, Philip Frank (wri): *Brainstorm (1983)*

Messina, Roberto (act): *Sodom and Gomorrah*

Messina, Terri (act): *Blood and Lace*

Messinger, Buddy (act): *Aladdin and His Wonderful Lamp*

Messinger, Gertrude (act): *Aladdin and His Wonderful Lamp; Rip Van Winkle (1921); Sunset Boulevard*

Messinger, Jack (act): *Rabid; Scanners*

Messiter, Ian (wri): *Mr. Drake's Duck*

Messiter, Toby (act): *Mad Max Beyond Thunderdome*

Mestral, Armand (act): *Morgan the Pirate*

Metalli, Giuseppe (cin): *La Strega In Amore*

Metanee, Sombat (act): *S.T.A.B.*

Metas, Christopher (act): *976-EVIL*

Metaxa, Georges (act): *The Mask of Dimitrios*

Metcalf, Audrey (act): *The Blob (1958)*

Metcalf, David (act): *The Blob (1958)*

Metcalf, Laurie (act, b. 1955): *Blink; Making Mr. Right; Pacific Heights; Scream 2; Toy Story*

Metcalf, Mark (act): *The Final Terror; The Heavenly Kid*

Metcalfe, Blanche (wri): *Alf's Carpet*

Metcalfe, John (cin): *Inseminoid; Outer Touch; Rawhead Rex; Riders of the Storm; Xtro*

Metcalfe, Ken (act): *Beast of the Yellow Night; Twilight People; Warriors of the Apocalypse*

Metcalfe, Michael (act): *Empire of Ash III*

Metcalfe, Robert/Bob (act): *I Still Dream of Jeannie; Runaway; Unforgettable*

Metcalfe, Tim (wri): *Fright Night II*

Metcalfe, Vince (act): *Beyond Obsession*

Metelkine, Helen (act): *Humanoid Woman*

Methot, Mayo (act): *The Mind Reader*

Metonidze, Veronika (act): *Ashik Kerib*

Metrano, Art(hur) (act): *Beverly Hills Bodysnatchers; Rocket Attack U.S.A.*

Metrov, Douglas Anthony (wri): *Solarbabies*

Metty, Russell (cin, 1906-1978): *Bagdad; Ben; Cult of the Cobra; Eye of the Cat; The Falcon's Brother; Flame of Araby; Forty Naughty Girls; Hitler's Children; Man of a Thousand Faces; Midnight Lace (1960); Mr. Peabody and the Mermaid; Monster on the Campus; The Omega Man; Platinum High School; Portrait In Black; Ride the Pink Horse; Sign of the Pagan; Step Down to Terror; The Thing That Couldn't Die; The Treasure of Lost Canyon; The War Lord; A Woman's Vengeance*

Metwalli, Mohamed (act): *Sphinx (1981)*

Metz, Hans (cin): *Flatliners; Misery*

Metz, Rexford (cin): *The Babysitter; Deadly Messages; The Midnight Hour; The Tribe; The UFO Incident*

Metz, Vittorio (wri): *Hercules In the Vale of Woe; Psycosissimo*

Metzetti, Sylvester (dir): see Talmadge, Richard

Metzger, Alan (cin): *Circle of Deceit; Doctor Franken*

Metzger, Alan (dir): *A Dangerous Affair; New Eden*

Metzger, Michael J. (act): *Into the Badlands*

Metzger, Radley (dir & wri): *The Cat and the Canary (1978)*

Metzler, Jim (act): *Children of the Corn III: Urban Sacrifice; Circuitry Man; The Little Match Girl (1987); Love Kills; Murder by Night; 976-EVIL; Sundown: The Vampire In Retreat; Waxwork II: Lost In Time*

Metzler, Rick (act): *Blacula*

Metzler, Robert F. (wri, b. 1914): *Dr. Renault's Secret*

Metzman, Irving (act): *The Purple Rose of Cairo; Wargames*

Metzner, Jordan (act): *A Troll In Central Park*

Meunich, Ray (act): *Jaws 3-D*

Meunier, Raymond (act): *Le Trou*

Meurer, Eileen (act): *Edward Scissorhands*

Meurer, Thomas (act): *Black Magic Woman*

Meurisse, Paul (act, 1912-1979): *Le Deuxieme Souffle; Diabolique (1955); The Monocle*

Meury, Anne-Laure (act): *Perceval*

Meuthal, Lothar (act): *The Golem: How He Came Into the World*

Meyer, Abe (mus): *Condemned to Live; White Zombie*

Meyer, Andrew (dir): *Night of the Cobra Woman; The Submersion of Japan*

Meyer, Andrew (wri): *Night of the Cobra Woman*

Meyer, Anthony (act): *Octopussy*

Meyer, Art (mus): *Mr. Wong, Detective*

Meyer, Breckin (act): *The Craft; Freddy's Dead: The Final Nightmare*

Meyer, David (act): *A Midsummer Night's Dream (1985);Octopussy; The Tempest (1980)*

Meyer, David Harold (act): see Janssen, David

Meyer, Dina (act): *Dragonheart; Johnny Mnemonic; Starship Troopers*

Meyer, Douglas D. (act): *Surf Nazis Must Die*

Meyer, E.E. (act): *Motor Psycho*

Meyer, Emile (act): *The Lineup*

Meyer, Emmy (act): *The Toxic Avenger, Part II*

Meyer, Greta (act): *A Night of Mystery (1937); Torchy Gets Her Man*

Meyer, Hans (act): *Not Guilty; Red Sonja*

Meyer, Harry (act): *Alraune (1952)*

Meyer, Irwin (dir): *Honeymoon of Horror*

Meyer, Johannes (act): *The Red Mantle*

Meyer, John (wri): *Amazing Stories: The Movie V*
Meyer, Kevin (dir & wri): *Perfect Alibi*
Meyer, Michelle (act): *Nail Gun Massacre*
Meyer, Mimi (act): *Chiller; Swamp Thing*
Meyer, Nancy (act): *The Last Slumber Party*
Meyer, Nicholas (dir): *The Day After; The Deceivers Star Trek II: The Wrath of Khan; Star Trek VI: The Undiscovered Country; Time After Time*
Meyer, Nicholas (wri): *Invasion of the Bee Girls; Judge Dee and the Monastery Murder; The Night That Panicked America; The Seven-per-Cent Solution; Star Trek IV: The Voyage Home; Star Trek VI: The Undiscovered Country; Time After Time*
Meyer, Russ (act, b. 1922): *Amazon Women on the Moon*
Meyer, Russ (dir, b. 1922): *Faster, Pusscat! Kill! Kill! Kiss Me Quick; Motor Psycho*
Meyer, Russ (wri, b. 1922): *Kiss Me Quick; Motor Psycho*
Meyer, Suzy (act): *The Abomination*
Meyer, Thom (act): *Bloodsuckers from Outer Space*
Meyer, Tony (act): *Venom (1982)*
Meyer, Torben (act): *The Black Room; The Fly (1958); The Last Warning (1929); The Man Who Laughs (1928); The Viking*
Meyer, Turi (dir): *Sleepstalker*
Meyer, Turi (wri): *Leprechaun 2; Sleepstalker*
Meyer-Craven, Mimi (act): see Meyer, Mimi
Meyerhold, Vsevolod (act, dir & wri, 1874-1942): *Portret Doriana Greya*
Meyerink, Victoria (act): *Brainstorm (1965); Time Travelers (1976)*
Meyers, Adrian (act): *Batman (1989)*
Meyers, Al (act): *Wolfman (1979)*
Meyers, Bess (act): *Torchy Plays With Dynamite*
Meyers, Bruce (act): *Nostradamus*
Meyers, Dave (cin): *THX 1138*
Meyers, Ernie (act): *Attack of the Killer Tomatoes*
Meyers, Fred (act): *Horror of the Blood Monsters*
Meyers, Gayanne (act): *Revenge of the Stepford Wives*
Meyers, Henry (wri): *The Black Room*
Meyers, Jon (act): *Spookies*
Meyers, Larry (John) (act): *Battle Beyond the Stars (1980); The Dark Half*
Meyers, Lawrence Steven (act): *Dick Tracy (1990)*
Meyers, Marilyn (act): *Eyes of Laura Mars*
Meyers, Marius (act): *Deepstar Six*
Meyers, Mike (act): *Voodoo Heartbeat*
Meyers, Rusty (act): *The Initiation*
Meyers, Ruth (act): *Partners In Crime (1961)*
Meyers, W. Ray (act): *The Hunchback of Notre Dame (1923)*
Meyers, William (act): *Invisible Dad; Twisted*
Meyers, Willie (act): *The Day of the Dolphin*
Meyerson, Ben (act): *Society*
Meyjes, Menno (wri): *Indiana Jones and the Last Crusade*
Meyler, Tony (act): *Never Talk to Strangers*
Meynell, Laurence (wri): *The Breaking Point (1961); The House On Marsh Road; The Price of Silence; Street of Shadows*
Meyrink, Gustav (wri): *The Golem: How He Came Into the World*
Meyrink, Michelle (act): *Nice Girls Don't Explode*
Mezendez, Mark (act): *Werewolf of Washington*
Mezey, Lajos (act): *Mata Hari (1985); Phantom of the Opera (1983)*
Mgoyan, Yiur (act): *Ashik Kerib*
Miake, Bontaro (act): *Uchujin Tokyo No Arawaru*
Micale, Paul (act): *Something Evil*
Micalizzi, Franco (mus): *Battle of the Amazons*
Micantoni, Adriano (act): *Ursus In the Land of Fire*
Michael, Christopher (act): *The Gifted One; Guyver 2: Dark Hero*
Michael, Dennis (act): *They Live*
Michael, Erin (act): *Roller Blade Warriors: Taken by Force*
Michael, Frank (act): *Charlie Chan and the Curse of the Dragon Queen*
Michael, George (act): *The Silence of the Lambs*
Michael, Gertrude (act, 1911-1964): *Four Hours to Kill; Murder at the Vanities; Murder On the Blackboard; Night of Terror (1933)*
Michael, Marion (act): *Liane, das Madchen aus dem Urwald*
Michael, Namara (act): *The Silent Witness (1954)*
Michael, Paul (act): *Batman (1989)*
Michael, Peter (act): *Search for Danger*
Michael, Ralph (act, b. 1907, nee Ralph Champion Shotter): *The Assassination Bureau; TheBirthday Present; Children of the Damned; The Count of Monte Cristo (1975); Date at Midnight; Dead of Night (1945); False Evidence; He Who Rides a Tiger; Murder Most Foul; The Sound Barrier; They Came to a City; Women Without Men*
Michael, Robert (act): *The People Under the Stairs*
Michael, Ryan (act): *It (1990)*
Michael, William (act): *Blood Pen*
Michaelis, Dario (act): *Death Comes from Space; I Vampiri*
Michaelis, Sophus (wri): *Himmelskibet*
Michaels, Alan (act): *The Silver Bridge*
Michaels, Barbara (wri): *The House That Wouldn't Die*
Michaels, Beverly (act): *Betrayed Women; Blonde Bait; The Girl On the Bridge; Pickup*
Michaels, Corinne (act): *Laboratory*
Michaels, David (act): *Jekyll and Hyde*
Michaels, Dolores (act): *Wizards of the Lost Kingdom*
Michaels, Don (act): *Nightbeast*
Michaels, Drake (act): *The Mummy and the Curse of the Jackals*
Michaels, Gordon (act): *Outbreak*
Michaels, Greg (act): *Logan's Run; Pumpkinhead*
Michaels, Irene (act): *Killer Klowns from Outer Space*
Michaels, Joann (act): *Night of the Living Dead (1968)*
Michaels, John (act): *The Zero Boys*
Michaels, Julie (act): *Jason Goes to Hell: The Final Friday*
Michaels, Kay (act): *Dimension 5; Dr. Goldfoot and the Bikini Machine*
Michaels, Ken (act): *Dracula Sucks*
Michaels, Lori (act): *Something Is Out There*
Michaels, Lou (act): *Enemy Mine*
Michaels, Marie (act): *Flesh-Eating Mothers*
Michaels, Michele (act): *The Slumber Party Massacre*
Michaels, Rhino (act): *Nemesis; Trancers II: The Return of Jack Deth; The Warlord: Battle for the Galaxy*
Michaels, Richard (dir): *The Plutonium Incident*
Michaels, Roger (cin): *Beyond the Living*
Michaels, Roxanna (act): *Night Visions*
Michaels, Shawn (act): *Condor*
Michaels, Steve (act): *Oh Heavenly Dog; Scanners; Terror Train*
Michaels, Sue (act): *Jack's Wife*
Michaels, T.J. (act): *Igor and the Lunatics*
Michaels, Toby (act): *The Little Shop of Horrors (1960)*
Michaels, Tommy (act): *Aaron's Magic Village*
Michaels, Wayne (act): *Batman (1989)*
Michaelsen, Kari (act): *Saturday the 14th*
Michaelsen, Melissa (act): *The Lightning Incident*
Michaelson, Brad (act): *The Lightning Incident*
Michaelson, Christian (act): *A Midsummer Night's Dream (1985)*
Michaelson, Lisa (act): *My Neighbor Totoro*
Michalak, Richard (cin): *Children of the Night; Encounter at Raven's Gate*
Michalakias, John Elias (dir): *I Was a Teenage Zombie*
Michalski, Jeff (act): *Pet Shop*
Michas, Jennifer (act): *The Boy Who Could Fly*
Michas, Peter (act): *Charlie Chan and the Curse of the Dragon Queen*
Michaud, Jean (act): *The Black Windmill*
Michel, Andre (dir, b. 1910): *La Sorciere*
Michel, Elizabeth (act): *Barracuda*
Michel, Elmo (act): *The Queen's Swordsman*
Michel, Franny (act): *Ellery Queen*
Michel, Jean-Claude (act): *Le Comte de Monte Cristo*
Michel, Lora Lee (act): *Between Midnight and Dawn; Mighty Joe Young (1949); The Snake Pit (1948)*
Michel, Marc (act): *Les Parapluies de Cherbourg; Le Trou*
Michel, Ray (act): *Barracuda*
Michele, Ann (act): *Psychomania (1972)*
Michele, Michael (act): *The 6th Man*
Michelet, Michel (mus, b. 1894): *Captain Sinbad; The Chase; The Hairy Ape; Lured; M (1950); Tarzan's Peril*
Michelini, Luciano (mus): *The Fish Men*
Michell, Helena (act): *Moments*
Michell, Keith (act, b. 1926): *The Deceivers; The Executioner; Grendel, Grendel, Grendel; The Hell-Fire Club; Moments*
Michell, Paul (act): *Moments*
Michelle, Ann (act): *House of Whipcord; Virgin Witch*
Michelle, Charlotte (act): *Kill or Be Killed (1980)*
Michelle, Donna (act): *Agent for H.A.R.M.; Goodbye Charlie; One Spy Too Many*
Michelle, Janee (act): *The House On Skull Mountain; The Mephisto Waltz; Scream, Blacula, Scream*
Michelle, Lori (act): *Cyborg 2: Glass Shadow*
Michelle, Michael (act): *Def by Temptation*
Michelle, Olivia (act): *Altered States*
Michelle, Vicki/Vicky (act): *Spectre (1977); Virgin Witch*
Michelman, Tony (wri): *Phantom of the Mall: Eric's Revenge*
Michelson, Dennis (cin): *Gremlins 2: The New Batch*
Michelson, Ethel (act): *The Deadly Spawn*
Michener, Dave (dir): *The Great Mouse Detective*
Michener, Dave (wri): *The Fox and the Hound; The Great Mouse Detective*
Michi (act): *Phoenix the Warrior*
Michie, Judy (act): *Pretty Maids All In a Row*
Michl, Keith (act): *The Incredible Melting Man*
Michonne, Danielle (act): *Amazons (1984)*
Micklesen, Elaine (act): *The Hand That Rocks the Cradle*
Micklewhite, Maurice (act): see Caine, Michael
Mickus, E.B. (act): *Wielka, Wielka I Najwieksza*
Micula, Stasia (act): *Warrior Queen*
Middendorf, Tracy (act): *Wes Craven's New Nightmare*
Middlebrooks, Eulan (act): *Matinee*
Middleham, Ken (cin): *The Hellstrom Chronicle*
Middlekoop, George (act): *The Ghost and the Darkness*
Middlemass, Frank (act): *Frankenstein Must Be Destroyed; Madame Sin; Otley*
Middlemass, Robert (act): *Blondes at Work; Charlie Chan On Broadway; The Lone Wolf Returns (1935); The Saint Takes Over*
Middleton, Burr (act): *Not of This World*
Middleton, Charles (act, 1879-1949): *The Black Raven; Charlie Chan's Murder Cruise; The Deadly Ray from Mars; Dick Tracy Returns; Island of Doomed Men; Jungle Man; Mars Attacks the World; Nyoka and the Lost Secrets of Hippocrates; Peril from the Planet Mongo; Purple Death from Outer Space; Spaceship to the Unknown; Spook Busters; Strangler of the Swamp, White Woman*
Middleton, Fran (act): *Martin*
Middleton, George (wri): *The Cave Girl (1921)*
Middleton, Gregory (cin): *Kissed*
Middleton, Guy (act, 1908-1973): *Escort for Hire; The Fur Collar Halfway House; The Magic Christian; A Man About the House; Never Look Back; The Third Visitor*
Middleton, H.S. (wri): *A Modern Dick Whittington*
Middleton, Joseph (wri): *Just Before Dawn (1980)*
Middleton, Josephine (act): *Before I Wake*
Middleton, June (act): *I Was a Zombie for the F.B.I.*
Middleton, Nancy (act): *Dr. Black Mr. Hyde*
Middleton, Noelle (act): *The Golden Mask; A Question of Suspense; The Vicious Circle (1957); You Can't Escape*
Middleton, Peggy (act): see DeCarlo, Yvonne
Middleton, Peter (cin): *A Midsummer Night's Dream (1985); The Tempest (1979)*
Middleton, Robert (act, b. 1911, nee Samuel G. Messer): *The Mark of Zorro (1974)*
Middleton, Stewart (act): *Spaceflight IC-1*
Middleton, Thomas H. (act): *Turn Back the Clock*
Midkiff, Dale (act, b. 1959): *Love Potion No. 9; Nightmare Weekend; Pet Sematary; Plymouth; Toothless*
Midkiff Jr., J. Williams (act): *Shadow Conspiracy*
Midler, Bette (act, b. 1945): *Hocus Pocus; Oliver & Company*
Midway, Reg (act): *Inn of the Damned*
Miekhe, Paulmichel (dir): *Murderer's Keep*
Miele, Valentine (act): *Tromeo and Juliet*
Mielke, Sandy (act): *The Funhouse (1981)*
Mier, Karl (act): *Castle Sinister (1948)*
Mierisch, Susan (act): *Neon Maniacs*
Mierisch, Susanne (act): *Cavegirl (1985)*
Mifune, Toshiro (act, 1920-1997): *Chusingura (1963); High and Low; I Live In Fear; Samurai Pirate; Secret Scrolls-Parts I & II; Throne of Blood; Winter Kills*
Migel, Ivan (act): *The Handmaid's Tale*
Migicovsky, Alan (act): *Shivers*
Migliano, Adriano Amidei (act): *Deborah*
Migliar, Adelqui (act): *Blood Money; The Other Person*
Migliarese, Anna (act): *Curtains*
Migliori, Ralph (cin): *An American Tail; Charlotte's Web*
Migliorini, Romano (wri): *Il Boia Scarlatto; Cinque Tombeper un Medium*
Mignacco, Darlene (act): *Psycho Girls*
Mignone, Jose Luis (cin): *Beyond the Universe*
Mihailoff, R.A. (act): *Leatherface: Texas Chainsaw Massacre III; Pumpkinhead II: Blood Wings*
Mihalka, George (dir): *Eternal Evil; My Bloody Valentine; Relative Fear*
Mihara, Yoko (act): *Onna Kyuketsuki*
Mihashi, Tatsuya (act): *Chusingura (1963); The Human Vapor*
Mihura, Jeronimo (dir): *Babes In Bagdad*
Mihura, Miguel (wri): *Carlota; La Corona Negra*
Mikell, George (act): *The Double Man; Jackpot; Kill Her Gently; The Primitives; Where the Spies Are; Zeppelin*
Mikels, Ted V. (cin): *Day of the Nightmare; The Hostage (1966)*
Mikels, Ted V. (dir): *Aftermath; Astro Zombies; Blood Orgy of the She-Devils; The Corpse Grinders; The Doll Squad*
Mikels, Ted V. (wri): *Astro Zombies; Blood Orgy of the She-Devils*
Mikhailov, Viktor (act): *Window to Paris*
Mikhailov, Yevgeni (cin): *Shinel (1926)*
Mikhalkov, Nikita (act): *The Red Tent*
Mikhelson, Andre (act): *Children of the Damned; The Diplomatic Corpse; The Intimate Stranger*
Mikita, Mori (act): *Godzilla vs. Megalon*
Miler, Michael (act): *Westworld*
Miko, Andras (act): *Phantom of the Opera (1983)*
Miko, Beverly (act): *The Dungeonmaster*
Mikolaitchouk, Ivan (act): *The Shadows of Forgotten Ancestors*
Mikolajewska, Krystyna (act): *Faraon*
Mikouyama, Hiroshi (cin): *Mothra*
Mikulic, Voya (cin): *Nightmare Sisters*
Mikuni, Rentaro (act): *Harakiri; Kwaidan; The Profound Desire of the Gods; Yoru No Tsuzumi*
Mila, Bela (act): *The Avenging Hand (1936)*
Milan, George (act): *Creation of the Humanoids; Merlin's Shop of Mystical Wonders; War of the Colossal Beast*
Milani, Chef (act): *The Falcon Out West; The Seventh Victim*
Milani, Frederica (act): *The Magic World of Topo Gigio*
Milano, Alyssa (act, b. 1972): *The Canterville Ghost (1986); Deadly Sins; Fear (1996); The Nosferatu Diaries: Embrace of the Vampire*
Milano, Lisa (act): *Satan's Black Wedding*
Milano, Mario (act): *Beyond Evil; The Spectre of Edgar Allan Poe*
Milanovich, Vladimir (act): *Goldeneye*
Milas, Tom (act): *Midnight (1980)*
Milashkina, Tamara (act): *Queen of Spades (1960)*
Milasinovic, Vladan (act): *The Dead Are Alive*
Milbourne, Olive (act): *One Way Out*
Milbrook, Leo (act): *My Magic Dog*
Mildfelt, Robert J. (act): *The House of the Dead*
Mileham, Mark (act): *The Village of the Damned (1960)*
Miler, Annie (act): *L'Enfant Sauvage*
Miler, Claude (act): *L'Enfant Sauvage*
Miles, Art (act): *Charlie Chan On Broadway; The Gorilla (1939)*
Miles, Bernard (act, 1907-1991): *Fortune Is a Woman; Great Expectations (1946); The Man Who Knew Too Much (1956); Midnight at Madame Tussaud's; Moby Dick (1956); Sapphire; Tiger In the Smoke; Tom Thumb; Twelve Good Men*
Miles, Bernard (wri): *Thunder Rock*
Miles, Christopher (dir & wri, b. 1939): *The Maids*
Miles, David (act): *Vampire's Kiss*
Miles, Dido (act): *First Knight*
Miles, Ewing (act): *Giant from the Unknown*
Miles, Helen (act): *Jane Eyre (1921)*
Miles, Joanna (act): *Blackout (1988); Bug; The Dark Secret of Harvest Home; A Fire In the Sky (1978); Friday the 13th: The Orphan; Judge Dredd; The Ultimate Warrior*
Miles, John (act): *The Tattooed Stranger*
Miles, Kevin (act): *The Cars That Ate Paris; Endplay*
Miles, Ray (act): *Satan's Black Wedding*
Miles, Richard (act): *Possessed (1947)*
Miles, Richard (wri): *Madman of Mandoras*
Miles, Sarah (act, b. 1943): *The Big Sleep (1978); Blow-Up; A Ghost In Monte Carlo; Great Expectations (1974); Ordeal by Innocence; The Servant; Venom (1982)*

Miles, Sherry (act): The Pack; The Todd Killings; The Velvet Vampire
Miles, Sylvia (act, b. 1932): Evil Under the Sun; Farewell, My Lovely; The Funhouse (1981); Psychomania (1964); The Sentinel; Sleeping Beauty (1986)
Miles, Vera (act, b. 1929): Baffled!; Beyond This Place; Fire; The Hanged Man; A Howling In the Woods; The Initiation; Journey to the Unknown; The Last Generation; Live Again, Die Again; One of Our Spies Is Missing; Psycho (1960); Psycho II; Rona Jaffe's Mazes and Monsters; Separate Lives; Shadow of Death (1983); The Spirit Is Willing; The Strange and Deadly Occurrence; Tarzan's Hidden Jungle; 23 Paces to Baker Street; The Wrong Man
Milestone, Lewis (dir, 1895-1980, nee Lewis Milstein): Les Miserables (1952); Of Mice and Men (1939)
Miley, Jerry (act): Charlie Chan's Secret
Milford, John (act): The Aliens Are Coming
Milford, Kim (act): Laserblast
Milford, Penelope (act): Blood Link; Heathers; Man On a Swing
Milford, Ted (act): Cocoon: The Return
Milgrom, Michael (act): Project X (1987); Twilight Zone
Milhaud, Darius (act, b. 1892): Dreams That Money Can Buy
Milhoan, Michael (act): Phenomenon
Milholland, Richard (act): Looker
Milhollin, James (act, b. 1920): Everything's Ducky; Zotz!
Milian, Tomas/Thomas (act): The Conspiracy of Torture; The Evil Trap; Winter Kills
Milinaire, Catherine (act): La Poupee
Milinaire, Gilles (act): The Last Days of Man On Earth
Military, Frank (act): Dead Bang
Militi, Rick (act): Metalstorm: The Destruction of Jared-Syn
Milius, John (dir & wri, b. 1944): Conan the Barbarian; Red Dawn
Miliutenko, D. (act): My Name Is Ivan
Miljan, John (act, 1893-1960): Bonzo Goes to College; Charlie Chan In Paris; The Ghost Walks (1934); The Lone Ranger and the Lost City of Gold; The Phantom of the Opera (1925); Queen of the Amazons (1947); Samson and Delilah; The Terror (1928); Torchy Runs for Mayor; The Unholy Night; The Unholy Three (1930)
Milkie, Ron (act): A Return to Salem's Lot
Mill, Robert (act): Maroc 7; Schizo (1977)
Millais, Hugh (act): Images; The Wicked Lady
Millais, Ida (act): Lady Audley's Secret (1920)
Millais, Ivy (act): A Grain of Sand
Millan, Al (act): The Video Dead
Millan, Juan Jose Alonso (wri): Marta
Millan, Robyn (act): Murder Motel; The Witchmaker
Millan, Victor (act): Eyes of the Jungle
Milland, Gloria (act): Atlas Against the Czar; Challenge of the Gladiators; Goliath Against the Giants; The Three Swords of Zorro
Milland, Ray (act, 1907-1986, nee Reginald Truscott-Jones): Alias Nick Beal; The Attic; Battlestar Galactica; The Big Clock; The Big Game; Black Noon; Blackout (1978); Bulldog Drummond Escapes; Charlie Chan In London; Circle of Danger; Cruise Into Terror; The Darker Side of Terror; Daughter of the Mind; The Dead Don't Die; Dial M for Murder (1954); Ellery Queen; Embassy; Escape to Witch Mountain (1975); Four Hours to Kill; Frogs; Golden Earrings; Hostile Witness; The House In Nightmare Park; It Happens Every Spring; Jamaica Run; Lady In the Dark; Look What's Happened to Rosemary's Baby; The Lost Weekend; Masks of Death; Ministry of Fear; Night Into Morning; Panic In Year Zero; The Premature Burial; Sealed Verdict; The Sea Serpent;So Evil My Love; Starflight: The Plane That Couldn't Land; Terror In the Wax Museum; The Thief (1952); The Thing With Two Heads; The Uncanny; The Uninvited (1944); X—The Man With the X-Ray Eyes
Milland, Ray (dir, 1907-1986): Hostile Witness; Panic In Year Zero; The Thief (1952)
Millar, Bill (cin): Metamorphoses
Millar, Cynthia (mus): Three Wishes (1995)
Millar, Gavin (dir): Dreamchild
Millar, Hal (cin): Young Frankenstein
Millar (Jr.), Henry (cin): Jaws: The Revenge; Weird Science; Young Frankenstein
Millar, Jeff (wri): Dead and Buried
Millar, Lee (act): Lady and the Tramp
Millar, Mike (cin): Weird Science
Millar, Ronald (wri): So Evil My Love
Millard, Harry (wri): Kemek
Millard, Helene (act): The Thirteenth Chair (1929)
Millard, John (wri): Member of the Jury
Millard, Joseph (wri): They Came from Beyond Space
Millard, Oscar (wri, b. 1908): Dead Ringer; Journey Into Darkness; No Highway In the Sky; Second Chance
Millarde, Harry (act): The Vampire (1913, USA)
Millay, Diana (act): Night of Dark Shadows; Tarzan and the Great River
Millbern, David (act): Amanda and the Alien; Midnight Confessions; The Slumber Party Massacre; Sorceress (1982);Storm Chasers: Revenge of the Twister
Miller, Adolph (act): Bulldog Drummond (1929)
Miller, Albert G. (wri): The Spider's Web
Miller, Alice Duer (wri): On Borrowed Time
Miller, Alice D.G. (wri): The Bridge of San Luis Rey (1929)
Miller, Allan (act): The Ghost of Flight 401; Joe & the Colonel; Star Trek III: The Search for Spock; Warlock
Miller, Allen C. (wri): Doctor X
Miller, Andy (act): From Beyond
Miller, Angela (act): Scream
Miller, Arnold Louis (dir): Kil 1; A Touch of the Other
Miller, Arthur (C.) (cin, 1895-1970): Bella Donna (1923); The Blue Bird (1940); Dragonwyck; The Mark of Zorro (1940); The Prowler (1951)
Miller, Arthur (wri, b. 1915): The Crucible (1996); Les Sorcieres de Salem
Miller, Ashley (dir): A Letter to the Princess
Miller, Aubree (act, b. 1980): The Ewok Adventure; Ewoks: The Battle for Endor
Miller, Balerie (act): I Was a Zombie for the F.B.I.
Miller, Barry (act, b. 1958): Peggy Sue Got Married
Miller, Beth Ann (act): Teen Wolf Too
Miller, Beverly (act & wri): Beast of Blood
Miller, Big (act): Big Meat Eater
Miller, Bill (act): The Silence of the Lambs
Miller, Bob (act): Dracula's Dog
Miller, Bodil (act): Reptilicus
Miller, Brian (act): Brazil
Miller, Bruce (mus): The Outing
Miller, Burt (act): Attack of the Killer Tomatoes
Miller, Candace (act): Daylight
Miller, Carol (act): Just Imagine
Miller, Charles (act): Call Northside 777; House of Frankenstein; Phantom of Chinatown
Miller, Cheryl (act, b. 1943): Code Name: Minus One; Doctor Death: Seeker of Souls; The Monkey's Uncle
Miller, Chris (act): The Cellar (1989)
Miller, Chris (wri): Multiplicity
Miller, Christopher James (act): Star Trek: Generations
Miller, Claude (dir): The Inquisitor
Miller, Colleen (act, b. 1932): The Purple Mask; Step Down to Terror
Miller, Court (act): Cat's Eye
Miller, David (GB act): Meet Mr. Lucifer
Miller, David (USA act): Attack of the Killer Tomatoes
Miller, David (dir, b. 1909): Beautiful Stranger; Hammerhead; Midnight Lace (1960); Sudden Fear
Miller, David (wri, b. 1909):Beautiful Stranger
Miller, David B. (act): Night of the Creeps
Miller, Dean (cin): Purgatory
Miller, Dennis (USA act, b. 1953): Never Talk to Strangers; Tales from the Crypt Presents Bordello of Blood
Miller, Dennis (Austal act): Stir
Miller, Dennis (cin): Stone Cold Dead
Miller, Denny (act): Dr. Scorpion; Doomsday Machine; The Island at the Top of the World; The Norsemen; Tarzan, the Ape Man (1959)
Miller, Diana (act): Dante's Inferno (1924)
Miller, Dick/Richard (act, b. 1931): Amityville 1992: It's About Time; Batman: Mask of the Phantasm; A Bucket of Blood (1959); The 'Burbs; Capture That Capsule!; Chopping Mall; Demon Knight; Dr. Heckyl & Mr. Hype; Evil Toons;Explorers; Ghost Writer; Gremlins; Gremlins 2: The New Batch; Heartbeeps; The Howling; Innerspace; It Conquered the World; Lies; The Little Shop of Horrors (1960); Matinee; Night of the Creeps; Not of This Earth (1957); Piranha (1978); The Premature Burial; Project X (1987); The St. Valentine's Day Massacre; Small Soldiers; Sorority Girl (1957); Space Raiders; The Terminator; The Terror (1963); The Trip; Twilight Zone; The Undead; The Warlord: Battle for the Galaxy; War of the Satellites; X—The Man With the X-Ray Eyes
Miller, Dusty (cin): Blood Bath at the House of Death
Miller, E.K. (act): Black Roses
Miller, (Elizabeth) Lee (act): Please Murder Me; Le Sang d'un Poete
Miller, Ernest/Ernie (cin): The Chance of a Lifetime; One Frightened Night; Radio Ranch
Miller, Eschal (act): see Grey, Nan
Miller, Francis (wri): Consider Your Verdict; Inquest(1939); The Mysterious Mr. Nicholson; Trunk Crime
Miller, Frank (GB wri): Esmeralda; Faust (1922 & 1923); Fight In a Thieves' Kitchen; The Girl Who Came Back; Her Redemption; Jane Shore (1922); The Lady In Black; Macbeth (1922); Lost, Stolen or Strayed; Mother's Darling; The Prodigal Son; The Scarlet Letter (1922); The Scotland Yard Mystery; Trapped by the Mormons; Tut-Tut and His Terrible Tomb; When Knights Were Bold (1916)
Miller, Frank (USA wri): RoboCop 2; RoboCop 3
Miller, Frank (A.) (act): Beyond the Universe; 2001: A Space Odyssey
Miller, Fred (act): The Docks of New Orleans
Miller, Gabrielle (act): Mother, May I Sleep With Danger?
Miller, Garry (act): The Amazing Mr. Blunden
Miller, Gary Neil (act): see Dunn, Michael
Miller, Geof (wri): Deepstar Six
Miller, George (dir): Babe: Pig In the City; In the Nick of Time; Mad Max; The Neverending Story: The Next Chapter; The Road Warrior; Tidal Wave: No Escape; Twilight Zone; The Witches of Eastwick
Miller, George (wri): Babe; Babe: Pig In the City; Mad Max; The Road Warrior
Miller, Geri (act): The Telephone Book
Miller, Greg (act): Roller Blade Warriors: Taken by Force
Miller, Harry (act): White Angel
Miller, Harvey (wri): Jekyll and Hyde...Together Again
Miller, Heather (act): Never-Never Land
Miller, Herman (wri): Crosscurrent; Search for the Gods
Miller, Hugh (act): Before I Wake; Bulldog Drummond at Bay (1937); The Gelignite Gang; In His Grip; The Rat; The Return of the Scarlet Pimpernel
Miller, Irene (wri): The Striped Stocking Gang
Miller, Ivan "Dusty" (act): Charlie Chan's Secret; Man-Made Monster
Miller, Jack (act): The Devoted Ape; The Jailbird
Miller, James (M.) (wri): Betrayal (1974); The People
Miller, Jan (act): The Body Stealers; The Secret
Miller, Jason (act, b. 1939): The Dain Curse; The Exorcist; The Exorcist III; The Henderson Monster; Twinkle, Twinkle, Killer Kane; Vampire (1979)
Miller, Jennifer (wri): The Babysitter; Deadly Lessons
Miller, Jeremy (act, b. 1976):The Willies
Miller, Jeri (act): Abbott and Costello Go to Mars
Miller, Joan (act): Criss Cross; Face In the Night; No Trees In the Street; Yield to the Night
Miller, Joel McKinnon (act):The Swan Princess
Miller, John (act): Young and Innocent
Miller, John "Skins" (act): Torchy Plays With Dynamite
Miller, Jonty (act): First Knight
Miller, Josephine (act): Cinderella (1911, Selig)
Miller, Joshua (act): And You Thought Your Parents Were Weird; Near Dark; Teen Witch
Miller, Joshua John (act): Communion
Miller, Julie (act): Primal Scream
Miller, Karl (cin): Cat People (1982)
Miller, Kate (act): King Lear (1987)
Miller, Kathleen (act): Strange New World
Miller, Kathryn (act): Pumpkinhead II: Blood Wings
Miller, Kelly (act): George of the Jungle
Miller, Ken (act): Attack of the Puppet People; I Was a Teenage Werewolf
Miller, Kenny (act): Bloodstalkers
Miller, Kerry (act): Mad Max
Miller, Kristine (act): Sorry, Wrong Number (1948)
Miller, Larry (act): Carnival of Souls (1998); The Computer Wore Tennis Shoes (1995); Frankenstein: The College Years; The Nutty Professor (1996); Suburban Commando
Miller, Leslie (act): Chelsea Bird
Miller, Linda (act): Alice, Sweet Alice; The Green Slime; King Kong Escapes
Miller, Lorraine (act): Rapture; White Gorilla
Miller, Lucille (act): Just Imagine
Miller, Lynn (act): Murder Motel
Miller, Magda (act): Dollars for Sale; The Secret Man; Town On Trial; The Two Faces of Dr. Jekyll
Miller, Mandy (act, b. 1944): Child In the House; Kill or Cure; The Man In the White Suit; The Secret; The Snorkel
Miller, Marcus (mus): The 6th Man
Miller, Marian (act): Just Before Dawn (1946)
Miller, Mark (act): Mr. Sycamore
Miller, Mark Jeffrey (act): Teenage Mutant Ninja Turtles
Miller, Mark Thomas (act): Misfits of Science; Mom
Miller, Martin (act, b. 1899, nee Rudolph Miller): Child In the House; Children of the Damned; Counterblast; The Gamma People; The Ghosts of Berkeley Square; Hotel Reserve; Incident at Midnight; Latin Quarter; Mad About Men; Mark of the Phoenix; Peeping Tom; The Phantom of the Opera (1962); Seven Thunders; Violent Moment
Miller, Martyn (act): Man On the Run
Miller, Marvin (act, 1913-1985, nee Marvin Mueller): Deadline at Dawn; Dead Reckoning; Intrigue (1947); Is This Trip Really Necessary?; Kiss Daddy Goodbye; The Naked Ape; Peking Express; The Phantom Thief; Red Planet Mars; Sleeping Beauty (1959); The Story of Mankind; The Submersion of Japan
Miller, Matt (act): The Toxic Avenger, Part II
Miller, Maxine (act): Care Bears Movie II: A New Generation
Miller, Melissa (wri): Oh, God! Book II
Miller, Michael/Mike (act): Deadly Messages; Doc Savage, the Man of Bronze; The Invisible Boy; Saturday the 14th; School Spirit; Space Raiders
Miller, Michael (dir): Silent Rage
Miller, Michelle M. (act): Outbreak
Miller, Mindy (act): Slaughterhouse Rock
Miller, Mirt(h)a (act): Battle of the Amazons; Gran Amore del Conde Dracula; No Exit; Vengeance of the Zombies
Miller, Monique (act):A Scream from Silence
Miller, Nancy (act):The Story of Mankind
Miller, P.J. (act): The Dungeonmaster
Miller, Pamela (act): Human Feelings
Miller, Pat (act): I Was a Teenage Frankenstein; Maximum Overdrive
Miller, Patsy Ruth (act, 1904-1995): The Hunchback of Notre Dame (1923); The Last of the Lone Wolf; Wolf's Clothing (1927)
Miller, Paul (act): Amanti d'Oltretomba; Queen of the Pirates
Miller, Penelope Ann (act, b. 1964): Dead Bang; The Relic; The Shadow (1994); Witch Hunt
Miller, Peter (act): Forbidden Planet
Miller, Peter (wri): Blind Corner; Man In the Dark (1965); Tomorrow at Ten
Miller, Philip (act): Dracula A.D. 1972
Miller, Pip (act): Return of the Jedi
Miller, Pola (act): Brenda Starr (1992)
Miller, R.J. (act): Communion
Miller, Ralph (act): Mission Mars; Outbreak
Miller, Randall (dir): The 6th Man
Miller, Randy (mus): And You Thought Your Parents Were Weird; Black Magic Woman; Bloodspell; Darkman II: The Return of Durant; Darkman III: Die Darkman Die; Hellraiser III: Hell On Earth
Miller, Ray (act): Bowery at Midnight
Miller, Robert (act): The Incredible 2-Headed Transplant; Shock Waves; Trader Horn (1973)
Miller, Robert Ellis (dir): Brenda Starr (1992)
Miller, Robin (wri): The Corsican Brothers (1985); Psychomania (1964)
Miller, Roger (act): Robin Hood (1973)
Miller, Ruby (act): Law and Disorder; The Mystery of Mr. Bernard Brown
Miller, Ruth (act): Barracuda; Thinner
Miller, Scott (act): Doomsday Machine
Miller, Selwyn Emerson (act): Jekyll and Hyde...Together Again
Miller, Seton I. (wri, 1902-1974): The Adventures of Robin Hood; The Black Swan; Charlie Chan's Courage; Here Comes Mr. Jordan; Istanbul; Ministry of Fear; Murder On a Honeymoon; Murders In the Zoo; Star of India
Miller, Sharron (dir): The House of the Dead
Miller, Sherry (act): Sabrina the Teenage Witch
Miller, Sidney (act): Alias Boston Blackie; Experiment In Terror; The Sniper
Miller, Sidney (dir): The 30 Foot Bride of Candy Rock
Miller, Sigmund (wri): Jet Storm
Miller, Stan (cin): An American Tail

Miller, Stanley (wri): *Son of a Stranger; Symptoms*
Miller, Stephanie (act): *Happy Birthday to Me*
Miller, Stephen (act): *Funeral Home; The Plutonium Incident; Runaway*
Miller, Stephen (wri): *My Bloody Valentine*
Miller, Stephen E. (act): *The Little Match Girl (1987);The Stepfather*
Miller, Susan (act): *Sleeper*
Miller, Susan (wri): *Lady Beware*
Miller, Tallulah (act): *Hands of the Ripper*
Miller, Terry (act): *Halloween With the Addams Family*
Miller, Tony (act): *Attack of the Crab Monsters; Lies*
Miller, Troy (dir): *Jack Frost (1998)*
Miller, Ty (act): *Slaughterhouse Rock; Trancers 4: Jack of Swords; Trancers 5: Sudden Deth*
Miller, Tyler (act): *Not Quite Human II; Virus (1980)*
Miller, Valerie (act): *The Pink Chiquitas*
Miller, Victor (wri): *Friday the 13th (1980); Friday the 13th—Part 2; A Stranger is Watching*
Miller, Virgil (cin, b. 1886): *Calling Dr. Death; Castle In the Desert; Charlie Chan at the Wax Museum; Charlie Chan at Treasure Island; Charlie Chan In City In Darkness; Charlie Chan In Panama; Charlie Chan In Reno; Charlie Chan's Murder Cruise; Dr. Renault's Secret; The Falcon In San Francisco; The House of Fear (1945); Mr. Moto's Last Warning; Mr. Moto Takes a Chance; The Mummy's Curse; Murder Over New York; The Pearl of Death; The Phantom of the Opera (1925); Scotland Yard (1941); Thank You, Mr. Moto; Weird Woman; The Woman In Green*
Miller, Walter (act): *Charlie Chan's Murder Cruise; Dick Tracy's G-Men; Ghost Patrol; The House Without a Key*
Miller, Wendy (act): *Electric Dreams*
Miller, William (act): see Boyd, Stephen
Miller, Winston (wri): *The Aquarians; Dick Tracy (1937); Jivaro; One Body Too Many*
Milles, Adriana (act): *Nemesis*
Milletaire, Carl (act): *The Adventures of Hajji Baba*
Millett, David (act): *Paint Me a Murder*
Millhauser, Bertram (wri, 1892-1958): *The Garden Murder Case; The Invisible Man's Revenge; Nick Carter, Master Detective; The Pearl of Death; Sherlock Holmes (1932); Sherlock Holmes Faces Death; Spider Woman; The Suspect; The Woman In Green*
Millhouse, Jody (act): *Journey to the Center of Time*
Milli, Robert (act): *The Curse of the Living Corpse*
Millian, Andra (act): *Nightfall (1988)*
Millican, James (act, 1910-1955): *I Was a Communist for the FBI; The Lone Wolf Spy Hunt; Missing Women; The Remarkable Andrew*
Millican, Jane (act): *Crimes Unlimited; The Girl In the Flat; Jury's Evidence*
Millicevic, Djordje (wri): *Runaway Train*
Millichamp, Stephen/Steve (act): *Mad Max; Road Games*
Milligan, Andy (cin): *Bloodthirsty Butchers; The Body Beneath; The Ghastly Ones; Legacy of Horror (1978); The ManWith Two Heads*
Milligan, Andy (dir): *Blood!; Bloodthirsty Butchers; The Body Beneath; Carnage; The Ghastly Ones; Guru, the Mad Monk; Legacy of Horror (1978); The ManWith Two Heads; The Naked Witch; The Rats Are Coming!—The Werewolves Are Here!; Torture Dungeon*
Milligan, Andy (wri): *Blood!; Bloodthirsty Butchers; The Body Beneath; The Ghastly Ones; Guru, the Mad Momnk; Legacy of Horror (1978); The Man With Two Heads; The Rats Are Coming!-The Werewolves Are Here!; Torture Dungeon*
Milligan, Deanna (act): *Intensity*
Milligan, Spencer (act): *Sleeper*
Milligan, Spike (act, b. 1918, nee Terence Alan Milligan): *Alice's Adventures In Wonderland (1972); The Bed-Sitting Room; Digby-The Biggest Dog In the World; Dot and the Kangaroo; The Hound Of The Baskervilles (1978);The Magic Christian; Rentadick; The Three Musketeers (1974); Yellowbeard*
Milligan, Soike (wri, b. 1918): *The Bed-Sitting Room*
Milligan, Stuart (act): *Outland*
Milligan, Terence Alan (act & wri): see Milligan, Spike
Millines, Terry (act): *Tarzan In Manhattan*
Millington, James (act): *Darkman II: The Return of Durant*
Millington, Mary (act): *The Playbirds*
Millington, Rodney (act): *Bella Donna (1934)*
Millner, Jonathan (act): *Schizoid (1980)*
Millot, Charles (act): *The Great Spy Chase*
Mills, Alec (cin): *King Kong Lives; Licence to Kill (1989)*
Mills, Alec (dir): *Bloodmoon (1990); Dead Sleep*
Mills, Alley (act): *Tainted Blood*
Mills, Bill (act): *Teen-Age Strangler*
Mills, Brooke (act): *Dream No Evil; Twilight People*
Mills, Clifford (wri): *Luck of the Navy; Where the Rainbow Ends*
Mills, Donna (act, b. 1943): *Alice In Wonderland (1985); Beyond the Bermuda Triangle; Curse of the Black Widow; Fire; Haunts of the Very Rich; Killer With Two Faces; Live Again, Die Again;Look What's Happened to Rosemary's Baby; Moonlight Becomes You; Night of Terror (1972); One Deadly Owner; Play Misty for Me; Someone at the Top of the Stairs; The Stepford Husbands*
Mills, Eddie (act): *Sabrina Goes to Rome; The Tempest (1998)*
Mills, Edwin (act): *Monsieur Verdoux; Stigma*
Mills, Freddie (act): *Breakaway; Chain of Events; Kill Me Tomorrow; One Jump Ahead*
Mills, Frederic (act): *Moon 44*
Mills, Gordon (act): *Kronos (1957)*
Mills, Grace (act): *La Maldicion de la Bestia*
Mills, Guy (act): *Horror of Dracula*
Mills, Hayley (act, b. 1946): *Deadly Strangers; Endless Night; In Search of the Castaways; The Moon-Spinners; Only a Scream Away; A Troll In Central Park; The Twisted Nerve*
Mills, Heather Lee (act): *The Mutagen*
Mills, Hugh (wri): *Blackmailed; Blanche Fury; The Man In the Mirror; So Long at the Fair*
Mills, Jacqueline (act): *Heavy Traffic*
Mills, James (act): *Cloudburst*
Mills, Jed (act): *Kiss Daddy Goodbye; New Year's Evil*
Mills, Joey R. (act): *Eyes of Laura Mars*
Mills, (Sir) John (act, b. 1908): *Around the World In 80 Days; The Big Sleep (1978); A Choice of Weapons; Cottage to Let; Dr. Strange; Frankenstein (1993); The Ghost Camera; Great Expectations (1946); The Human Factor; Masks of Death; Mr. Denning Drives North; Murder With Mirrors; The October Man; Operation Crossbow;The Quatermass Conclusion; The Rocking Horse Winner; The 39 Steps (1978); Town On Trial; The Vicious Circle (1957); When the Wind Blows; The Wrong Box*
Mills, Juliet (act, b. 1941): *Beyond the Door; Jonathan Livingston Seagull; The October Man; Waxwork II: Lost In Time*
Mills, Kaly (act): *Carnival of Blood*
Mills, Kim (act): *For Your Eyes Only*
Mills, M. (act): *The Queen Mother*
Mills, Mort (act): *Crashing Las Vegas; Psycho (1960)*
Mills, Peggy (act): *A Shattered Idyll*
Mills, Penny Anne (act): *13 Frightened Girls*
Mills, Phillip (act): *Dark of the Night*
Mills, Pierre (wri): *House of Mystery (1961); Latin Quarter; The Medium (1934)*
Mills, Reginald (dir): *Peter Rabbit and the Tales of Beatrix Potter*
Mills, Richard M. (act): *The Bermuda Triangle*
Mills, Riley (act): *I Drink Your Blood*
Mills, Rob (act): *Labyrinth (1986)*
Mills, Samantha (act): *Prehysteria*
Mills, Sherry (wri): *The Adventures of Pinocchio (1996)*
Mills, Slaine (act): *The Call of the Drum*
Mills, Thomas R. (act): *The Adventures of Robin Hood*
Mills, Tom (act): *Luther the Geek*
Mills-Cockrell, John (mus): *Terror Train*
Mills-Cockrell, Juno (act): *Parents*
Millward, Dawson (act): *Altar Chains; The Recoil (1922)*
Milmeister, Jared (act): *Flatliners*
Milmoe, Caroline (act): *The Magic Toyshop; Without a Clue*
Milne, A.A. (wri, 1882-1956): *Birds of Prey; Pooh's Grand Adventure: The Search for Christopher Robin*
Milne, Bernadette (act): *Cover Girl Killer*
Milne, Chris (act): *Thirst*
Milne, Ella (act): *The Green Scarf*
Milne, Lennox (act): *The Quatermass Conclusion*
Milne, Lesley (act): *Vampire at Midnight*
Milne, Murray (cin): *Dead Alive; Meet the Feebles*
Milne, Peter (wri): *House of Fear (1939); The Kennel Murder Case; Mr. Moto In Danger Island; Return of the Terror; The Verdict (1946); The Walking Dead*
Milner, Anthony (act): *Hawk the Slayer; Superman II*
Milner, Dan (dir): *From Hell It Came; The Phantom from 10,000 Leagues*
Milner, Jack (wri): *From Hell It Came*
Milner, Mariah (act): *Praying Mantis*
Milner, Martin "Marty" (act, b. 1927): *Asylum for a Spy; Flood; Francis In the Navy; On the Threshold of Space; The Private Lives of Adam and Eve; Sex Kittens Go to College; 13 Ghosts*
Milner, Roger (act): *Mark of the Devil (1985)*
Milner, Victor (cin, b. 1893): *Bulldog Drummond Escapes; The Cave Girl (1921); Love Me Tonight; The Monster and the Girl; The Strange Love of Martha Ivers; The Studio Murder Mystery*
Milnes, Bernardette (act): *The Man Who Wouldn't Talk*
Milo, Jana (act): *The Cat from Outer Space*
Milo, Sandra (act, b. 1935, nee Alessandra Marini): *The Bang-Bang Kid; 8 1/2; Giulietta degli Spiriti*
Milovan & Serena (act): *Vampire Circus*
Milrad, Josh (act): *The Beastmaster*
Milroy, Vivian (wri): *Crow Hollow*
Milski, Stanislaw (act): *Profesor Zazul*
Milsome, Douglas (cin): *Robin Hood: Prince of Thieves; Sunset Grill*
Milstein, Lewis (dir): see Milestone, Lewis
Milt, Victor C. (cin):*The Premonition (1975)*
Miltern, John (act):*Murder On a Bridle Path*
Milton, Billy (act): *The Black Windmill; The Last Chance; Licensed to Kill; Monster of Terror; Personal and Confidential; The Set-Up (1963); Someone at the Door; Who Was Maddox?*
Milton, Ernest (act, b. 1890): *Cat Girl; Fiddlers Three; The Scarlet Pimpernel (1934)*
Milton, Gerald (act): *The Man Who Died Twice; The Unknown Terror*
Milton, H.A. (wri): *Piranha II: The Spawning*
Milton, John (act): *The Merry Men of Sherwood; The Unholy Quest*
Milton, John (wri, 1608-1674): *Satan-or, The Drama of Humanity*
Milton, Maude (act): *A Message from Mars (1921)*
Milton, Richard (dir): *The Loves of Dracula*
Milton, Robert (dir, b. 1890): *Bella Donna (1934); Outward Bound; Strange Evidence*
Milton, Troy (act): *Dr. Goldfoot and the Bikini Machine*
Miltsakakis, Stefanos (act): *Cyborg (1989); Waxwork II: Lost In Time*
Milzer, Cameron (act): *Bridge Across Time*
Mimaroglu, Ilhan (mus): *Satyricon*
Mimieux, Yvette (act, b. 1941): *The Black Hole; Black Noon;Death Takes a Holiday (1971); Devil Dog: The Hound of Hell; The Fifth Missile; Journey into Fear (1975); The Neptune Factor; Platinum High School; Snowbeast; The Time Machine (1960); The Wonderful World of the Brothers Grimm*
Mimmi (act): *Savage Princess*
Mims, Mavis (act): *Pinocchio In Outer Space*
Mims, William/Bill (act): *Captain America II; The Day Mars Invaded Earth; Fer-de-Lance*
Mina, Mina E. (act): *The Death of the Incredible Hulk*
Minailo, Michele (act): *The Return of the Six Million Dollar Man and the Bionic Woman*
Minami, Kaho (act): *Angel Dust*
Minard, Michael (mus): *The Mutilator (1985); A Return to Salem's Lot*
Minardos, Nico (act): *Ghost Diver*
Minazzoli, Christiane (act): *A Toi de Faire, Migonne*
Mincey, John Wilder (cin): *Monstroid*
Minchenberg, Richard (act): *Wolfen*
Minciotti, Silvio (act): *Francis Covers the Big Town*
Mincks, Jonathan (act): *The Lightning Incident*
Mine, Monnie (act): *Mercia the Flower Girl*
Mine, Shinichi (act): *Fire In the Sky (1993)*
Mineo, Sal (act, 1939-1976): *Escape from the Planet of the Apes; Krakatoa-East of Java; Who Killed Teddy Bear?*
Miner, Allen H. (dir): *The Black Pirates*
Miner, Michael (dir): *Deadly Weapon*
Miner, Michael (wri): *Deadly Weapon; Lawnmower Man 2: Beyond Cyberspace; RoboCop; RoboCop 2; RoboCop 3*
Miner, Steve (dir): *Forever Young; Friday the 13th-Part 2; Friday the 13th-Part 3; Halloween H20; House; Warlock*
Miner, Worthington (act): *They Might Be Giants*
Minerva (mus): *Flesh-Eating Mothers*
Minervini, Angela (act): *La Maldicion de los Karnsteins*
Mines, Gus (dir): *Babes In Toyland (1934)*
Mines, Lee (act): *Invasion of the Body Snatchers (1978)*
Minett, Mike (act): *Bad Taste*
Minetti, Maria (act): *The Second Stain*
Mingaye, Don (mus): *The Devil-Ship Pirates*
Minger, Lynnea (act): *Making Contact*
Mingozzi, Fulvio (act): *The Black Belly of the Tarantula;Inferno (1979)*
Minguillon, Margarita (act): *Robin and Marian*
Minicotti, Esther (act): *Shockproof*
Minifie, Val (act): *Moments*
Minion, Joseph (wri): *Vampire's Kiss*
Miniovich, Margaret (act): *Shock Chamber*
Minitello, Frank (act): *Eraser*
Minjir, Harold (act): *The Death Kiss*
Minkin (dir): *Lunnyi Kamen*
Minkoff, Ron (dir): *The Lion King*
Minkus, Bruce (cin): *Nothing But Trouble*
Minkus-Barron, Barbara (act):*Witches' Brew*
Minn, Haunani (act): *Ghost In the Machine; The Man With Two Brains*
Minnelli, Liza (act): *Journey Back to Oz*
Minnelli, Vincente (dir, 1903-1986): *Brigadoon; Cabin In the Sky; Goodbye Charlie; On a Clear Day You Can See Forever*
Minnick, Dani (act): *The Sleeping Car*
Minns, Byron Keith (act): *Jacob's Ladder*
Minogue, Kylie (act): *Bio-Dome*
Minor, Chris (act): *Wolfen*
Minor, Mike (cin): *Spacehunter: Adventures In the Forbidden Zone*
Minor, Robert/Bob (act): *Death Dimension; The Deep; Dr. Black Mr. Hyde; Dr. Scorpion; Gold of the Amazon Women; Project X (1987)*
Minor, Royce (act): *Strange Days*
Minor, Sue (act): *Shock Chamber*
Minor, Willie (act): *I Come In Peace*
Minot, Dominique (act): *Charade*
Minot, Muriel (act): *Retribution (1988)*
Minotis, Alexis (act, 1906-1990): *Land of the Pharaohs*
Minsky, Charles (cin): *April Fool's Day; Kazaam; Radioactive Dreams*
Minster, Hilary (act): *The Godsend*
Minteer, Maura (act): *Midnight (1980)*
Minter, George (wri): *Tread Softly Stranger*
Minter, Jelly (Jo) (act): *The Lost Boys; Miracle Mile; The People Under the Stairs; Popcorn*
Minter, Kristin (act, b. 1966): *Savage*
Minto, Dorothy (act): *Inside the Room*
Minton, Faith (act): *Switch*
Minty, Emil (act): *The Haunted School; The Road Warrior*
Mintz, David (act): see Knight, David
Mintz, Larry (act): *Remote Control (1988)*
Mintz, Murray (dir): *Cardiac Arrest*
Mintz, Sam (wri): *Crack-Up*
Minuzzi, Nerio (wri): *The Mattei Affair*
Minyard, Ken (act): *The Alien's Return*
Minzenty, Gustave (dir & wri): *A Yell of a Night*
Mioni, Fabrizio (act): *Hercules (1957); The Venetian Affair*
Mioni, Riccardo (act): *Exterminators of the Year 3000*
Mioni, Sergio (act): *Exterminators of the Year 3000*
Mioni, Stefanao (act): *Red Sonja*
Mior, Stefano (act): *Warrors of the Wasteland*
Miou-Miou (act, b. 1950, nee Sylvette Hery): *Tender Dracula*
Mira, Maria Angeles (wri): *Moebius*
Mirabella, Michele (act): *Demons 2*
Miracle, Irene (act): *Inferno (1979); In the Shadow of Kilimanjaro; Puppet Master; Watchers II*
Miraglia, Emilio (P.) (dir): *Halloween Night; The Night Evelyn Came Out of the Grave; The Vatican Affair*
Miraglia, Emilio (P.) (wri):*The Night Evelyn Came Out of the Grave*
Mirand, Evan (act): *My Best Friend Is a Vampire*
Miranda, Aurora (act): *Phantom Lady; The Three Caballeros*
Miranda, Carlos (act & mus): *A Midsummer Night's Dream (1985)*
Miranda, Carmen (act, 1913-1955, nee Maria do Carmo Miranda da Cunha): *Scared Stiff (1953)*
Miranda, Evan (act): *Seven*
Miranda, Isa (act, 1909-1982, nee Ines Isabella Sampietro): *Dog Eat Dog; Dorian Gray; Do You Know This Voice?; Marta; The Night Porter; What Price Murder*
Miranda, John (act): *Bloodthirsty Butchers*
Miranda, Robert (act): *Eraser*
Miranda, Soledad (act): *Count Dracula; Mighty Ursus; Pyro; Sound of Horror*

Miranda, Susana (act): *City Beneath the Sea (1970)*
Mirande, Yves (wri): *Le Spectre Vert*
Mirasol, Letty (act): *Twilight People*
Miravilles, Jaime (act): *Un Chien Andalou*
Mirel, Nicole (act): *Le Saint Mene la Dance*
Mirkovich, Timothy Burr (act): *Friday the 13th, Part VIII-Jason Takes Manhattan*
Mirmer, Tracey (act): *Dr. Caligari*
Miro, Jennifer (act): *Dr. Caligari; The Video Dead*
Mirren, Helen (act, b. 1945): *The Comfort of Strangers; Excalibur; The Fiendish Plot of Dr. Fu Manchu; The Hawk; The Prince of Egypt; 2010*
Misar, Franz (act): *Das Schloss*
Misar, Johann (act): *Das Schloss*
Misawa, Katsuji (cin): *Akira*
Misch, Laura (act): *Mardi Gras Massacre*
Mischon, Martha (act): *Flesh Feast*
Miserlis, George (act): *The Incredible Genie*
Misery the Pig (animal act): *Misery*
Mishima, Ko (act): *Mothra*
Mishima, Masao (act): *Harakiri*
Mishkin, William (cin): *The Rats Are Comin!—The Werewolves Are Here!*
Mishkin, William Paul (wri): *Violated*
Mishler, Tom (act): *Jurassic Park*
Mislove, Michael (wri): *Americathon*
Misraki, Paul (mus, b. 1908): *Ali-Baba et les Quarante Voleurs; Alphaville, une Etrange Aventure de Lemmy Caution; Atoll K; Doulos-The Finger Man; Leda; Mr. Arkadin; La Mort en ce Jardin; Obsession (1954)*
Miss Holly (act): *Retribution (1988)*
Missouri, Harry (act): *The Adventures of Dick Turpin-A Deadly Foe, A Pack of Hounds, and Some Merry Monks; The Adventures of Dick Turpin-The King of Highwaymen; The Adventures of Dick Turpin-200 Guineas Reward, Dead or Alive*
Mistal, Karen (act): *Return of the Killer Tomatoes*
Mistral, Jorge (act): *Cumbres Borrascosas*
Misul, Mauro (act): *Amarcord*
Misumi, Kenji (dir): *Buddha; The Return of Giant Majin*
Mita, Teruko (act): *Mothra*
Mitamura, Kunihiko (act): *Godzilla vs. Biollante*
Mitchel, Mary (act): *Dementia 13; Panic In Year Zero*
Mitchell, Adrian (wri): *The Persecution and Assassination of Jean-Paul Marat as Performed by the Inmates of the Asylum of Charenton Under the Direction of the Marquis de Sade*
Mitchell, Aleta (act): *The Serpent and the Rainbow*
Mitchell, Ann (act): *Full Circle*
Mitchell, Anna (act): *Secrets of the Phantom Caverns*
Mitchell, Basil John (wri): *The Perfect Woman*
Mitchell, Belle (act): *The Beast With Five Fingers; Crazed; The Lone Ranger and the Lost City of Gold; Soylent Green; The War Lord*
Mitchell, Bentley (act): *Hell Mountain*
Mitchell, Beth (act): *Timestalkers*
Mitchell, Betty (act): *Just Imagine*
Mitchell, Beverly (act): *White Dwarf*
Mitchell, Bill (act): *Billion Dollar Brain; Night of the Eagle*
Mitchell, Bill(y J.) (act): *Goldeneye; Morons from Outer Space; Never Say Never Again;Outer Touch; Superman (1978) Top Secret! (1984)*
Mitchell, Bob (act): *Fake-Out*
Mitchell, Cameron (act, 1918-1994): *Autopsia de un Fantasma; The Big Game; Blood Link; Carousel;Cataclysm; The Demon (1981); Dog Eat Dog; Face of Fire; The Fish Men; Flight to Mars; Flood; Frankenstein Island; Gorilla at Large; Haunts; Gli Invasori; La Isla de la Muerte; Jack-O; Knives of the Avenger; Last of the Vikings; Memorial Valley Massacre; Les Miserables (1952); Nightmare In Wax; The Offspring; Pier 5, Havana; Return to Fantasy Island; Sei Donne per l'Assassino; Silent Scream (1979); Smuggler's Gold; Space Mutiny; The Stranger;Supersonic Man; The Swarm; Three Came to Kill; Three Wise Fools; The Tomb; The Toolbox Murders; The Unstoppable Man; Without Warning (1980)*
Mitchell, Camille (act): *Laboratory*
Mitchell, Carlyle (act): *Blood of Dracula; On the Threshold of Space*
Mitchell, Carolyn (act): *The Cry Baby Killer*
Mitchell, Casey T. (wri): *Spacecamp*
Mitchell, Charles (Euro act): *Kemek*
Mitchell, Charles (1940s USA act): *Enter Inspector Duval; Philo Vance's Gamble; Too Many Winners*
Mitchell, Charles (1980s USA act): *Cavegirl (1985)*
Mitchell, Charlotte (act): *The Blood on Satan's Claw; The Village of the Damned (1960)*
Mitchell, Chip (act): *The Brother from Another Planet*
Mitchell, Chuck (act): *Don't Answer the Phone!; Frightmare (1983); The Hearse*
Mitchell, Daryl "Chill" (act): *Toothless*
Mitchell, David (dir): *City of Shadows*
Mitchell, Don (act): *Scream, Blacula, Scream; Short Walk to Daylight*
Mitchell, Donna (act): *The Fan; Psycho IV: The Beginning*
Mitchell, Douglas (act): *A Challenge for Robin Hood*
Mitchell, Duke (act): *The Boys from Brooklyn*
Mitchell, Frank (act): *Flesh and Fantasy*
Mitchell, Gene (act): *Surf Nazis Must Die*
Mitchell, George (GB act): *The Beggar Girl's Wedding*
Mitchell, George (USA act): *The Andromeda Strain; Frankenstein Island*
Mitchell, George (dir): *Wolf Blood*
Mitchell, Gordon (act): *Ali Baba and the Seven Saracens;The Alien Within; Atlas in the Land of Cyclops; El Castello dell'Orrore; Endgame; Frankenstein 1980; Fury of Achilles; Il Gigante di Metropolis; Revenge of the Gladiators; Rush; Satyricon; Seven Slaves Against the World; She (1983); Star Pilot; Treasure of the Petrified Forest; Vulcan, Son of Jupiter*
Mitchell, Grant (act, 1874-1957): *Arsenic and Old Lace; Footsteps In the Dark; The Garden Murder Case; A Midsummer Night's Dream (1935); On Borrowed Time*
Mitchell, Gwen (act): *Chosen Survivors*
Mitchell, H. (act): *The Glittering Sword*
Mitchell, Hamilton (act): *Beyond the Universe*
Mitchell, Helena (act): *The Deceivers*
Mitchell, Herb L. (act): *I, Desire*
Mitchell, Irving (act): *Black Dragons; Secrets of the Lone Wolf*
Mitchell, James (act): *Secrets of the Phantom Caverns*
Mitchell, James (wri): *Innocent Bystanders*
Mitchell, John (act): *The Groundstar Conspiracy*
Mitchell, John Cameron (act): *The Stepford Children*
Mitchell, Joseph (wri): *Sherlock Jr.*
Mitchell, Julien (act, 1888-1954): *Bedelia; The Drum; The Echo Murders; The Frog; Hotel Reserve*
Mitchell, Katharine (act): *The Relic*
Mitchell, Keith (act): *The Fox and the Hound; The Kid With the Broken Halo*
Mitchell, Kirby (act): *Wolf*
Mitchell, Laurie (act): *Attack of the Puppet People; Girls In Prison; Missile to the Moon; Queen of Outer Space*
Mitchell, Leigh (act): *The Incredible Melting Man; Scream Bloody Murder*
Mitchell, Leslie (act): *Grand National Night*
Mitchell, Lisa (act): *Snow White and the Three Stooges*
Mitchell, Marilyn (act): *Cinque Tombe per un Medium*
Mitchell, Mark (act): *The Munsters' Scary Little Christmas; The Outing*
Mitchell, Melissa (wri): *Temptress (1995)*
Mitchell, Mike (act): *Timecop*
Mitchell, Mike (wri): *Super Agent Superdragon*
Mitchell, Millard (act, 1895-1953): *A Double Life (1947)*
Mitchell, Mitch (act): *Deathmoon*
Mitchell, Norman (act): *—And Now the Screaming Starts!; Carry On Screaming; Carry On Spying; Dick Turpin-Highwayman; Electric Eskimo; Frankenstein and the Monster from Hell; A Hitch In Time; The Hunchback of Notre Dame (1965); Legend of the Werewolf*
Mitchell, Oswald (dir, 1890-1949): *The Dummy Talks; The Greed of William Hart; House of Darkness; The Man from Yesterday (1949); The Mysterious Mr. Nicholson; The Temptress (1949)*
Mitchell, Oswald (wri, 1890-1949): *The Mysterious Mr. Nicholson*
Mitchell, P.J. (wri): *Moon 44*
Mitchell, Paula (act): *Point of Terror*
Mitchell, Red (act): *Forever Evil*
Mitchell, Rhea (act): *Boston Blackie's Little Pal*
Mitchell, Rick (act): *Twister*
Mitchell, Sandford (act): *The Corpse Grinders*
Mitchell, Sasha (act): *Class of 1999 II: The Substitute*
Mitchell, Sharon (act): *[illegible] (1980)*
Mitchell, Shirley (act): *Desk Set; My Blood Runs Cold*
Mitchell, Steve (act): *Most Dangerous Man Alive; So Evil, My Sister; Wonder Woman*
Mitchell, Steve (wri): *Chopping Mall*
Mitchell, Ted (act): *Curse of the Swamp Creature*
Mitchell, Thomas (act, 1892-1962): *Alias Nick Beal; The Black Swan; The Dark Mirror (1946); Dark Waters; Flesh and Fantasy; The Hunchback of Notre Dame (1939); It's a Wonderful Life; Lost Horizon (1937); Out of the Fog (1941); Secret of the Incas; Three Wise Fools; While the City Sleeps*
Mitchell, Ty (act): *The Fog*
Mitchell, Warren (act, b. 1926): *The Assassination Bureau; Calculated Risk; The Curse of the Werewolf; Incident at Midnight; Innocent Bystanders; Jabberwocky; Man With a Gun; Moon Zero Two; Night Caller from Outer Space; The Spy Who Came In from the Cold; Three Crooked Men; The Trollenberg Terror; Unearthly Stranger; Where Has Poor Mickey Gone?*
Mitchell, Will (act): *Mountaintop Motel Massacre*
Mitchell, William (act): see Finch, Peter
Mitchell, Yvonne (act, 1925-1979, nee Yvonne Joseph): *The Corpse; Demons of the Mind;The Queen of Spades (1948); Sapphire; Turn the Key Softly; Yield to the Night*
Mitchell-Smith, Ilan (act): *Weird Science*
Mitchnick, Paul (cin): *Black Roses*
Mitchum, Bentley (act): *Demonic Toys; Markus 4; Sometimes They Come Back; Susie Q*
Mitchum, Chris (act): *Aftershock; Big Foot; Biohazard: The Alien Force; The Cauldron of Death*
Mitchum, Jim (act, b. 1941): *Blackout (1978); Monstroid*
Mitchum, John (act): *Bigfoot; Crackle of Death; Escapes*
Mitchum, Julie (act): *House On Haunted Hill (1958)*
Mitchum, Robert (act, 1917-1997): *Agency; The Amsterdam Kill; Angel Face; The Big Sleep (1978); Cape Fear (1961 & 1991); Crossfire; Farewell, My Lovely; Foreign Intrigue; The List of Adrian Messenger; The Locket; Midnight Ride; The Night of the Hunter (1955); Out of the Past (1947); Pursued; Rampage; River of No Return; Scrooged; Second Chance; Secret Ceremony; Track of the Cat; Where Danger Lives*
Mithoff, Bob (mus): *Class of Nuke 'em High, Part 2:Subhumaniod Meltdown; Seedpeople*
Mitler, Matt (act): *Deadtime Stories; The Mutilator (1985)*
Mitman, Thomas (act): *The Resurrection of Zachary Wheeler*
Mito, Mitsuko (act): *Ugetsu Monogatari*
Mito, Yoshiko (act): *The Final War*
Mitra, Subrata (cin, b. 1931): *Devi; Paras Pathar*
Mitrovich, Marta (act): *The Dark Mirror (1946)*
Mitsui, Hiroshi (act): *The Toxic Avenger, Part II*
Mitsui, Koji (act): *Suna No Onna*
Mitsui, Shinpei (act): *Mothra*
Mitsuwa, Akira (dir): *Atomic Rulers of the World; Evil Brain from Outer Space*
Mittelman, Rachel (act): *Beetlejuice*
Mittleman, Phil (wri): *Wes Craven Presents Mind Ripper*
Miura, Toshio (act): *Mothra*
Mix, Ruth (act): *The Clutching Hand*
Mix, Tom (act, 1880-1940): *Dick Turpin*
Mixon, Jamal (act): *The Nutty Professor (1996)*
Miya (act): *Charlie Chan and the Curse of the Dragon Queen*
Miyagawa, Ichiro (wri): *Atomic Rulers of the World; Evil Brain from Outer Space*
Miyagawa, Kazuo (cin, b. 1908): *Ugetsu Monogatari*
Miyaguchi, Seiji (act): *Kwaidan*
Miyajima, Yoshio (cin): *Kwaidan*
Miyazaki, Hayao (dir): *Laputa: Castle In the Sky; My Neighbor Totoro; Warriors of the Wind*
Miyazaki, Hayao (wri): *Laputa: Castle In the Sky; Warriors of the Wind*
Miyazaki, Yoshiko (act): *Ran*
Miyori, Kim (act): *Journey to the Center of the Earth (1993); The Punisher*
Miyoshi, Eiko (act): *I Live In Fear*
Mizak, Zoshka (act): *The Punisher*
Mize, Buddy (act): *The Creeping Terror*
Mizner, Wilson (wri): *The Mind Reader*
Mizoguchi, Kenji (dir, 1898-1956): *Ugetsu Monogatari*
Mizrahi, Stephanie (act): *Pretty Maids All In a Row*
Mizuki, Yoko (wri): *Kwaidan*
Mizuno, Kumi (act): *Ebirah, Horror of The Deep;Frankenstein vs. the Giant Devil Fish; Matango; Monster Zero; The War of the Gargantuas*
Mizurski, Barie (act): *Cocoon: The Return*
Mizzy, Vic (mus): *The Busy Body; The Ghost and Mr. Chicken; Halloween With the Addams Family; The Munsters' Revenge; The Night Walker; The Perils of Pauline; The Reluctant Astronaut; The Spirit Is Willing*
Mladova, Milada (act): *Son of Ali Baba*
Mlodzik, Ron(ald) (act): *Rabid; Shivers*
Moake, Jean (act): *Babes In Toyland (1986)*
Moase, Robyn (act): *Those Dear Departed*
Moatti, Edwin (act): *Au Coeur de la Vie*
Mobley, Roger (act): *Jack the Giant Killer*
Mochizuki, Yuko (act): *Kwaidan*
Mockingbird, Tequila (act): *Dr. Caligari*
Mockler, Denise (act): *No Blade of Grass*
Mockridge, Cyril (J.) (mus, 1896-1979): *The Adventures of Sherlock Holmes (1939); Half Angel; The Happyland; The Hound of the Baskervilles (1939); I Wake Up Screaming; The Luck of the Irish; Miracle On 34th Street (1947); Nightmare Alley; River of No Return*
Mockus Jr., Tony (act): *In the Company of Darkness*
Mocky, Jean-Pierre (act, b. 1929, nee Jean Mokiejewski): *Orphee*
Moctezuma, Juan (Lopez) (dir): *Dr. Tarr's Torture Dungeon; Mary, Mary, Bloody Mary; Sisters of Satan*
Modean, Jayne (act): *House II: The Second Story*
Moder, Richard (dir): *The Bionic Woman*
Modern Film Effects (cin): *Tower of London (1962)*
Modine, Matthew (act, b. 1959): *Cutthroat Island; Fluke; Pacific Heights*
Modot, Gaston (act, 1887-1970): *L'Age d'Or; La Beaute du Diable;Le Diable el les Dix Commandements; La Mome Vert-de-Gris; The Rules of the Game; Le Testament du Dr. Cordelier*
Modrzynska, U. (act): *Wielka, Wielka I Najwieksza*
Modugno, Domenico (act): *The Red Cloak*
Modugno, Enrica Maria (act): *Kaos*
Modugno, Lucia (act): *La Ragazza Che Sapeva Troppo*
Modugno, Marcello (act): *Dial Help*
Modupe, Prince (act): *Nabonga*
Moede, Titus (act): *Rat Pfink & Boo Boo; The Thrill Killers; The World's Greatest Sinner*
Moehl, Brian (act): *Getting Lucky*
Moeller, Ralph (act): *Universal Soldier*
Moen, Jacqulyn (act): *Switch (1991)*
Moffat, Donald (act, b. 1930): *Earthquake; Exo-Man; Monster In the Closet; The Terminal Man; The Thing (1982); Winter Kills*
Moffat, Ivan (wri): *Hitler: The Last Ten Days*
Moffat, Kitty (act): *The Beast Within*
Moffatt, Alice (act): *The Six Napoleons*
Moffatt, Geraldine (act): *Get Carter; Quest for Love*
Moffatt, Graham (act, 1919-1965): *The Clairvoyant (1934); The Dragon of Pendragon Castle; Dr. Syn; Mother Riley Meets the Vampire; Time Flies (1944)*
Moffatt, John (act): *Murder On the Orient Express*
Moffet, Ky (act): *Dr. Caligari*
Moffett, Michelle (act): *Deathstalker 4: Match of Titans*
Moffett, Sharyn (act, b. 1936): *The Body Snatcher (1945); The Falcon In San Francisco; The Locket*
Moffit, John C. (wri): *The Night Key*
Moffit, Peggy (act): *Blow-Up*
Moffitt, Elliott (act): *Abby*
Moffitt, John (dir): *Love at Stake*
Moffly, Joe Reb (wri): *Chosen Survivors*
Mogush, William (act): *Night of the Living Dead (1968)*
Moguy, Leonide (dir): *Paris After Dark*
Mohamed, Abdel Salem (act): *Sphinx (1981)*
Mohamed, Akasby (act): *The Jewel of the Nile*
Mohammed, Attif (act): *The Jewel of the Nile*
Mohammed, Kachela (act): *The Jewel of the Nile*
Mohica, Vic(tor) (act): *Don't Answer the Phone!; Ellery Queen; The Final Countdown; The Incredible Hulk, Part 2*
Mohler, Orv (act): *Invasion of the Saucer Men*
Mohner, Carl (act, b. 1921): *Assignment K; The Camp On Blood Island; Cave of the Living Dead; The Key; Killer With a Silk Scarf*
Mohr, Gerald (act, 1914-1968): *The Angry Red Planet; The Catman of Paris; Charlie Chan at Treasure Island; A Date With*

Death; Deep Freeze; Gilda; Hunt the Man Down; Invasion U.S.A.; The Lone Wolf In London; The Lone Wolf In Mexico; The Monster and the Girl; The Notorious Lone Wolf; One Dangerous Night; Raiders of the Seven Seas; The Sniper; Son of Ali Baba; Terror In the Haunted House; Undercover Girl (1950)

Mohr, Hal (cin, 1894-1974): An Act of Murder (1948); The Cat Creeps (1930; Charlie Chan's Courage; The Climax; Creation of the Humanoids; Green Pastures; The Last Warning (1929); The Last Voyage; The Lineup; The Lost Moment; A Midsummer Night's Dream (1935); The Monster (1925); A Night In Paradise; Outward Bound; Phantom of the Opera (1943); The Walking Dead

Mohrbach, Jo (act): Time Flyer

Mohun, Susan (act): Virtuosity

Moi, Sebastian (wri): Supersonic Man

Moio, John (act): The Alien's Return; Eve of Destruction; Exo-Man; The Prisoner of Zenda (1979)

Moir, Gunner (act): The Mystery of the Mary Celeste

Mojave, King (act): Desk Set

Mok, Michel (act): Dr. No

Mokae, Zakes (act): Body Parts (1991); Dust Devil; The Island; Outbreak; The Serpent and the Rainbow; Vampire In Brooklyn

Mokhtar, Seif Allah (act): Sphinx (1981)

Mokri, Amir (cin): Freejack

Molander, Gustav (dir, 1888-1973): Herr Arnes Pengar (1954)

Molander, Gustav (wri, 1888-1973): Herr Arnes Pengar (1919)

Molant, Jacques (act): The Golden Mistress

Moldovan, Jeff (act): Trancers 5: Sudden Deth

Molen, Jerry (act): Jurassic Park

Molenkamp, Onno (act): The Lift

Molieri, Lillian (act): The Creature Walks Among Us; Tarzan and the She-Devil

Molina, Alfred (act): Hideaway; Ladyhawke; Raiders of the Lost Ark; Species; When Pigs Fly

Molina, Antonio/A. (cin): The Blood Spattered Bride; Crypt of the Living Dead

Molina, Anya (act): Bloodmoon (1990)

Molina, Jacinto/Jack (dir): The Craving

Molina, Jacinto (wri): Dr. Jekyll y el Hombre Lobo; The Fury of the Wolfman; Gran Amoredel Conde Dracula; Horror Rises from the Tomb; House of Doom (1973); El Jorobado de la Morgue; La Maldicion de la Bestia; La Marca del Hombre Lobo; Las Noches del Hombre Lobo; The Mummy's Revenge; La Noche de Walpurgis

Molina, Manny (act): The Silence of the Hams

Molina, (Mariano) Vidal (act): The Mysterious Island of Captain Nemo; Scream of the Demon Lover

Molina, Ray (act): Voodoo Heartbeat

Molina Jr., Ray (act): Voodoo Heartbeat

Molina, Rolando (act): Virtuosity

Molinari, Stefano (act): Demons 2; Evil Clutch

Molinaro, Edouard (dir, b. 1928): Arsene Lupin Contre Arsene Lupin; Dracula, Pere et Fils; To Commit a Murder

Molinaro, Edouard (wri, b. 1928): Dracula, Pere et Fils; To Commit a Murder

Molinaro, Matteo (act): The Silence of the Hams

Molinaro, Richard (act): Are You In the House Alone?

Molinas, Richard (act): The Whole Truth

Molino, Antonio (act): Los Muertos No Perdonan

Molk, Lutz (act): Das Kalte Herz

Moll, Charles (act): Cataclysm

Moll, Georgia/Giorgia (act): Il Diavolo Innamorata; Lipstick; Le Mepris; Requiem for a Secret Agent; The Thief of Bagdad (1960)

Moll, Richard (act, b. 1943): Beanstalk; Casper: A Spirited Beginning; Caveman (1981); The Dungeonmaster; Evilspeak; The Flintstones; Fugitive from the Empire; Galaxis; Highlander: The Gathering; House; Metalstorm: The Destruction of Jared-Syn; Storybook; Survivor (1987); The Sword and the Sorcerer; Through the Magic Pyramid; Wicked Stepmother

Molla, Jose Luis Martinez (wri): A Lizard In a Woman's Skin

Mollica, John (act): The Toxic Avenger, Part II

Mollica, Laura (act): Kaos

Mollicone, Henry (mus): The Premonition (1975)

Mollin, Fred (mus): Friday the 13th, Part VII-The New Blood; Friday the 13th, Part VIII-Jason Takes Manhattan; The Quilt of Hathor; Roswell: The Aliens Attack

Mollison, Clifford (act): Frankenstein and the Monster from Hell; Scrooge (1951)

Mollison, Henry (act): The Bad Lord Byron; The Face at the Window (1932); The Great Impersonation (1935); The LoneWolf Returns (1935); The Man In the White Suit

Mollo, Andrew (dir & wri): It Happened Here

Molloy, Michael/Mike (cin): The Kidnapping of the President; Link; Shock Treatment! (1981); The Shout

Molloy, Patrick (act): Plutonium Baby

Molnar, Ferenc (wri, 1878-1952): Carousel; The Devil (1921); Liliom (1930 & 1933)

Molner, Lily (act): No Orchids for Miss Blandish

Molner, Julius (act): The Man Who Laughs (1928)

Moloney, Janel (act): To Save a Child

Moloney, Jim (wri): The Fiendish Plot of Dr. Fu Manchu; The Night They Saved Christmas

Moloney, Paddy (mus): Treasure Island (1990)

Molteni, Ambrogio (wri): David and Goliath; Il Gigante di Metropolis; The Tartars

Momel, James (cin): Madman; Ms. 45

Momura, Akiko (act): Kwaidan

Mona (act): Cairo

Mona the Woolly Monkey (animal act): Robinson Crusoe On Mars

Monaco, Lea (act): Terror of Rome Against the Son of Hercules

Monaco, Ralph (act): Ed Wood; Ghostbusters II; Zombie Island Massacre

Monaghan, Greg (act): Amazons (1984); Invitation to Hell

Monaghan, Jno P. (act & wri): The Upturned Glass

Monaghan, Marjorie (act: Nemesis; The Warlord: Battle for the Galaxy

Monahan, David (dir): The Phantom Tollbooth

Monahan, Jeff (act): The Dark Half

Monahan, Tom (act):The Night of the Claw

Monash, Paul (wri): Salem's Lot

Monaster, Nate (wri, 1915-1990): Call Me Bwana

Moncada, Santiago (wri): A Bell from Hell; Hatchet for a Honeymoon

Monch, Peter (act): Journey to the Seventh Planet

Monckton, Sydney (act): The Dream Doctor; The Late Edwina Black

Moncorge, Alexis (act): see Gabin, Jean

Moncrieff, Karen (act): Xtro 3: Watch the Skies

Monda, Dick (act): Body Parts (1991); Getting Lucky

Monda, Luci (act): Getting Lucky

Mondi, Bruno (cin): Embezzled Heaven

Mondo (act): Shanks

Mondragon, Jorge (act): La Momia Contra el Robot Humano

Mondy, Pierre (act):Le Comte de Monte Cristo

Mones, Tom (act): Boarding House

Monet, Angie (act): Prison Girls

Monet, Monica (act): Spasmo

Monet, Natalie (act): Oh Heavenly Dog

Moneta, Tullio (act): Howling IV; Steel Dawn

Monette, Richard (act): The Haunting of Hamilton High; Murder by Night

Money, Bo (act): Phoenix the Warrior

Money, Carl (act): Alien Contamination

Money, Zoot (act): Popdown; Scandalous; Supergirl (1984)

Monez, John (act): Eraserhead

Mong, William V. (act): Alias the Lone Wolf; The Haunted House (1929); The House of Horror (1929); In the Palace of the King; The Last Days of Pompeii (1935); Monte Cristo; Seven Footprints to Satan; The Vampire Bat

Monger, Chris (dir): Voice Over

Mongol, Vincent (wri): Chained Heat; Hellhole

Mongriello, Americo (act):Romeo Is Bleeding

Mongriello, James (act): Romeo Is Bleeding

Monica, Monica I. (act): Candyman: Farewell to the Flesh

Monicelli, Mario (dir, b. 1915): One Night of Fame

Monicelli, (Mario) (wri, b. 1915): Il Conte Ugolino; OK, Nero!

Monje, Julio (act): Firewalker

Monjo, Justin (act): The Blood of Heroes

Monk, Debra (act): Extreme Measures

Monk, Isabell (act): Trauma (1993)

Monk, Thomas (act): Peter Ibbetson

Monkhouse, Bob (act, b. 1928): Secret People; Thunderbirds Are Go

Monkman, Phyllis (act): Blackmail (1929); Her Heritage

Monlaur, Yvonne (act): Brides of Dracula; Circus of Horrors; Lemmy pour les Dames; Nick Carter Va Tout Casser; The Terror of the Tongs; Time to Remember

Monne, Jose (act): The Mummy's Revenge

Monnier, Valentine (act): After the Fall of New York

Monod, Jacques (act): The Tenant

Monoghan, James P. (act): The Body Snatchers

Monohan, Richard (act): Untamed Women

Monolescu, Marcia (act): Supersonic Saucer

Monreale, Cinzia (act): Buried Alive (1981)

Monro, Matt (mus): From Russia With Love; The Quiller Memorandum

Monroe, Delbert (act): Voyage to the Bottom of the Sea

Monroe, Denise (act): Two On a Guillotine

Monroe, Doreen (act): Bulldog Drummond Strkes Back (1934)

Monroe, Jack (cin): The Midnight Hour

Monroe, Louise (act): Alien Contamination

Monroe, Marilyn (act, 1926-1962, nee Norma Jean Baker): Don't Bother to Knock; Monkey Business; Niagara; River of No Return

Monroe Jr., Samuel (act): Tales from the Hood

Monroe, Steve (act): The Kill-Off; The Nutty Professor (1996)

Monroe, Tim (act): Two Lost Worlds

Monroy, Alejandro (mus): Mystery on Monster Island

Monsarrat, Nicholas (wri):Something to Hide

Monseau, Jacques (act): The Devil's Nightmare

Monserrat, Garcia (act): Exterminators of the Year 3000

Monsion, Tim (act): Blink

Monson, Carl (dir): Legacy of Blood; Please Don't Eat My Mother

Monson, Lex (act): Tattoo

Monsour, Nyra (act): The Saracen Blade

Montagne, Edward J. (dir): The Reluctant Astronaut

Montagne, Edward J. (wri): Rupert of Hentzau (1923); Secrets of the Night

Montagu, Ivor (wri, b. 1904): The Last Man to Hang?

Montague, Lee (act): The Camp On Blood Island; Deadlier Than the Male; Five to One; Jekyll and Hyde; The Legacy; The London Connection; Man at the Carlton Tower; Nobody Runs Forever; The Secret of Blood Island; The Secret Partner

Montague, Lyrica (act): Serial Mom

Montaigne, Lawrence (act): Captain Sinbad; Deadly Blessing; Escape to Witch Mountain (1975); The Psycho Lover

Montalban, Paolo (act): Cinderella (1997)

Montalban, Ricardo (act, b. 1920): The Aquarians; Conquest of the Planet of the Apes; Escape from the Planet of the Apes; Fantasy Island; The Mark of Zorro (1974); Mystery Street; The Queen of Babylon; Rage of the Buccaneers;The Reluctant Saint; Return to Fantasy Island; The Saracen Blade; Star Trek II: The Wrath of Khan; Wonder Woman

Montalvan, Celia (act): Toni

Montalvo, Mike (act): The Funhouse (1981)

Montama, Jean-Luc (act): Terminus

Montana, Bull (act): see Montana, (Lewis) Bull

Montana, Chris (act): Poltergeist III

Montana, Debra (act): Vampire On Bikini Beach

Montana, Hombre (act): No Holds Barred

Montana, Jody (act): A Nightmare On Elm Street 4: The Dream Master

Montana, Karla (act): Dangerous Touch

Montana, Lenny (act): Evilspeak

Montana, Lenny (wri): Blood Song

Montana (Jr.), Lenny (act): Blood Song; Pandemonium

Montana, (Lewis) Bull (act, 1886-1950): The Clutching Hand; Dick Turpin; The Lost World (1925); Secrets of the Night

Montanaro, Jovin (act): The Hidden II

Montanaro, Susan (act): Felix the Cat: The Movie

Montanaro, Tony (act): The Clan of the Cave Bear

Montand, Yves (act, 1921-1991, nee Ivo Livi): L'Aveu; Mister Freedom; On a Clear Day You Can See Forever; La Salaire de la Peur; The Sleeping Car Murders; Les Sorcieres de Salem

Montaner, Ana Maria (act): Hipnosis

Montano, Felix (act): Earth Girls Are Easy

Montau, Michele (act): A Reflection of Fear

Monte, Rickie (act): Angel Heart

Monte, Ted (act): Attack of the 60 Foot Centerfold

Monte-Britton, Barbara (act): Echoes

Montefiore, Lewis (wri): The Grim Reaper

Montefiore, Victor (wri): A Grain of Sand

Montefiori, Luigi (act): Satyricon

Montefiori, Luigi (wri): The Great Alligator

Monteiro, Johnny (act): Curse of the Vampires

Montejo, Carmen (act): El Vampiro

Montell, Lisa (act): The Lone Ranger and the Lost City of Gold; Pearl of the South Pacific; She-Gods of Shark Reef; World Without End

Montemuri, Davide (act): L'Annee Derniere a Marienbad

Montenegro, Hugo (mus, 1925-1981): The Ambushers; The Wrecking Crew

Montenegro, Mario (act): Brides of Blood

Montero, Roberto (Bianchi) (dir): Mondo Balordo; Il Mostro dell'Isola; Penetration

Montero, John (act): Blood Frenzy

Montero, Roberto (wri): Il Mostro dell'Isola

Monteros, Rosenda (act): Cauldron of Blood; The Face of Eve; She (1965); The White Orchid; A Woman's Devotion

Montes, Elisa/Eliza (act): The Cobra; Faustina; Future Women; La Isla de la Muerte; Island of Despair

Montes, Eva (act): The Blood Drinkers

Montes, Fernando (act): The Diabolical Dr. Z

Montes, Patrick (act): Dead Again

Montes, Richard (act): The Mask (1994)

Montesco, Ofelia (act): El Santo Contra las Vampiras

Montesi, Jorge (dir): Bloodknot; Bridge of Time; Mother, May I Sleep With Danger?; Night Visitors; Omen IV: The Awakening;Visitors of the Night

Monteux, Jacques (wri): Enter Inspector Duval

Montevecchi, Liliane (act):The Glass Slipper; The Living Idol

Montez, Conchita (act): Cuento de Hadas; Night Hair Child

Montez, Maria (act, 1918-1951): Ali Baba and the Forty Thieves (1943); Arabian Nights (1942); Atlantis (1948); Cobra Woman;

Gypsy Wildcat; The Invisible Woman (1941); Il Ladro di Venezia; The Mystery of Marie Roget; Pirates of Monterey; Revenge of the Pirates;South of Tahiti; Tangier; Sudan; White Savage

Montez, Paul-Felix (act): Frankenhooker

Montez, Richard (act): Maroc 7

Montford, Ivy (act): The Clue of the Cigar Band; The Corner House Burglary; The Deadly Model; A Desperate Stratagem; The False Wireless; The Hidden Witness; In the Grip of Spies; The Mystery of the Old Mill; The Rajah's Tiara; The Stolen Masterpiece

Montfort, Miguel (act): Anguish

Montgomery, Belinda (J.) (act, b. 1950): Blackout (1978); The Devil's Daughter (1972); The Man from Atlantis; Ritual of Evil; Silent Madness; Stone Cold Dead; The Todd Killings

Montgomery, Bob (act): Secrets of the Phantom Caverns

Montgomery, Daryl (act): Jack's Wife

Montgomery, Doreen (wri): At the Villa Rose (1939); Bulldog Sees It Through; Dead Men Tell No Tales (1938); Fanny by Gaslight; The Flying Squad (1940); The House of the Arrow (1940); The Man In Grey; Mr. Reeder In Room 13; Murder Reported; The Narrowing Circle; One Jump Ahead; Poison Pen; The Scarlet Web; Shadow of the Eagle; While I Live; You Can't Escape

Montgomery, Douglass (act, 1908-1966, nee Robert Douglass Montgomery): The Cat and the Canary (1939); Forbidden; The Mystery of Edwin Drood (1935)

Montgomery, Earl (act, 1921-1987): Heaven Can Wait (1978)

Montgomery, Elizabeth (act, 1933-1995): Johnny Cool; The Legend of Lizzie Borden

Montgomery, Frank (act): The Man from Beyond

Montgomery, George (act, b. 1916, nee George Letz): The Brasher Doubloon; Daredevil; The Sword of Monte Cristo; Watusi

Montgomery, Goodee (act, 1906-1978): Charlie Chan Carries On

Montgomery, James (act): Beyond and Back

Montgomery, Jeff (act): Oasis of the Zombies

Montgomery, Julia (act): The Kindred

Montgomery, Karen (act): Condor

Montgomery, Lee (Harcourt) (act): Ben; Burnt Offerings; Dead of Night (1977); The Midnight Hour; The $1,000,000 Duck; Mutant

Montgomery, Lionel (act): Concerning Mr. Martin

Montgomery, Mark (act): The Loves of Dracula; World of Dracula

Montgomery, Michael (wri): Rolling Vengeance

Montgomery, Peter (cin): Hocus Pocus; The Puppet Masters

Montgomery, Phil(lip) (act): Fer-de-Lance; The Swarm

Montgomery, Poppy (act): The Cold Equations

Montgomery, Ralph (act): Ssssss

Montgomery, Ray (act): Eyes of the Jungle; Phantom of the Jungle; The Screaming Woman;The White Goddess

Montgomery, Robert (act, 1904-1981): Busman's Honeymoon; Eye Witness (1950); Here Comes Mr. Jordan; Lady In the Lake; The Mystery of Mr. X; Night Must Fall (1937);

Rage In Heaven; Ride the Pink Horse; Trouble for Two; Your Witness

Montgomery, Robert (dir, 1904-1981): Eye Witness (1950); Lady In the Lake; Ride the Pink Horse; Your Witness

Montgomery Jr., Robert (act): 12 to the Moon

Montgomery, Robert Douglass (act): see Montgomery, Douglass

Month, Chris (act); Santa Claus Conquers the Martians

Monti, Maura (act): Bat Woman; Invasion Sinitestra

Monti, Milly (act): I Tre Volti della Paura

Monti, Silvia (act): A Lizard In a Woman's Skin

Montian, Nini (act): Las Cuatro Noches de la Luna Llena

Monticelli, Anna-Maria (act):Nomads

Montiel, Sarita (act): Circle of Death

Montifiere, Phyllis (act): 23 Paces to Baker Street

Montinaro, Brizio (act): Lo Strano Case della Signora Ward

Montini, Luigi (act): Satanik

Monton, Vincent (cin): The Day After Halloween; Road Games; Thirst

Montone, Rita (act): The Children; Maniac (1980)

Montoya, Alex (act): Daughter of the Jungle; Voodoo Tiger

Montoya, Alicia (act): El Ataud del Vampiro

Montoya, Diego (act): Contact

Montoya, Matthew (act): Moby Dick (1998)

Montparnasse Ballet, The (act): Jack the Ripper (1958)

Montresor, Dave (act): Assignment-Outer Space

Montrose, Belle (act): The Absent-Minded Professor (1961)

Montuori, Mario (cin): Sodom and Gomorrah

Monty, Mike (act): El Castello dell'Orrore

Monviso, Piero (wri): Atom Age Vampire

Moodnick, Ronald (act): see Moody, Ron

Moody, Cecil E. (act): Secrets of the Phantom Caverns

Moody, Elizabeth (act): Dead Alive

Moody, Jeanne (act): A Matter of Choice

Moody, King (act): The Dark Backward; The Destructors; Teenagers from Outer Space

Moody, Laurence (wri): What Became of Jack and Jill

Moody, Lynn(e) (act): Escape to Witch Mountain (1995); The Evil; Scream, Blacula, Scream; White Dog

Moody, Ralph (act): Homicidal; The Last Hunt; The Lone Ranger and the Lost City of Gold; Man-Eater of Kumaon; The Monster That Challenged the World; The Road to Bali

Moody, Ron (act, b. 1924, nee Ronald Moodnick): The Bed-Sitting Room; Dial M for Murder (1981); Dominique; A Ghost In Monte Carlo; A Kid In King Arthur's Court; Legend of the Werewolf; The Mouse On the Moon; Murder Most Foul; The Spaceman and King Arthur

Mooers, Randy (act): Blood Sisters

Moog, Heinz (act): The Secret Ways

Moon, Apache (act): Dead Cold

Moon, Ena (act): The River House Mystery (1935)

Moon, Geoffrey (act): The Hound of the Baskervilles (1978)

Moon, George (act): A Guy Called Caesar; A Matter of Choice; Time Flies (1944)

Moon, Georgina (act): Fragment of Fear

Moon, Guy (mus): Creepozoids; The Howling: New Moon Rising; Sorority Babes In the Slimeball Bowl-O-Rama

Moon, Keith (act, 1947-1978): Son of Dracula (1974); Tommy

Moon, Keith (wri, 1947-1978): Tommy

Moon, Lorna (wri): Mr. Wu (1927)

Moon, Lynne Sue (act): 13 Frightened Girls

Moon, Philip (act): Batman Forever; The Warlord: Battle for the Galaxy

Moon, Wally (act): Astro Zombies

Mooney, Debra (act): The Cradle Will Fall; Doctor Franken

Mooney, Dennis (act): Death Row Diner; Hollywood Chainsaw Hookers

Mooney, Laura (act): Little Nemo: Adventures In Slumberland; Suburban Commando;Twilight Zone

Mooney, Martin (wri): The Monster Maker (1943)

Moonves, Nancy (act): Seduced by Evil

Moor, Michael (act): Octopussy

Moor, Saba (act): Cavegirl (1985)

Mooradian, George (cin): Knights; Nemesis; Nemesis 3: Time Lapse

Moorcock, Michael (wri, b. 1939): The Land That Time Forgot; The Last Days of Man On Earth

Moordigan, Dave (act): Star Trek

Moore, Alvy (act, 1921-1997): A Boy and His Dog; The Brotherhood of Satan; The Devil's Bedroom; The Horror Show; Intruder (1988); Mortuary; Secret of the Incas; The War of the Worlds; The Witchmaker

Moore, Alyson (act): The Brotherhood of Satan

Moore, Angela (act): Don't Look Down; The Spider and the Fly (1994)

Moore, Anthony (act): Copycat

Moore, Archie (act): The Hanged Man

Moore, Ben (act): The Mutilator (1985); 2000 Maniacs

Moore, Bonnie (act): To Die For II: Son of Darkness

Moore, Brian (wri): Cold Heaven; Torn Curtain

Moore, Brian Joseph (act): Candyman: Farewell to the Flesh

Moore, C.L. (wri): Disaster In Time

Moore, Charles Philip (act): Demon Wind

Moore, Christine (act): Prime Evil

Moore, Clayton (act, b. 1914): The Bandits of Corsica; Black Dragons; Cyclotrode X; Ghost of Zorro; The Lone Ranger; The Lone Ranger and the Lost City of Gold; Nyoka and the Lost Secrets of Hippocrates; Retik, the Moon Menace; The Son of Monte Cristo; U-238 and the Witch Doctor

Moore, Christine (act): Lurkers

Moore, Clement Clarke (wri, 1779-1863): The Night Before Christmas

Moore, Cleo (act, 1930-1973): Bait; Hold Back Tomorrow; On Dangerous Ground; One Girl's Confession; Strange Fascination; Thy Neighbor's Wife

Moore, Colleen (act, 1900-1988, nee Kathleen Morrison): The Scarlet Letter (1934);Through the Dark

Moore, Connie (act): Monstroid

Moore, Constance (act, b. 1919): Destination Saturn; The Missing Guest

Moore, Deacon John (act): Angel Heart

Moore, Deborah Kim (act):Witches' Brew

Moore, Debrah (act): Warriors of the Apocalypse

Moore, Del (act, 1916-1970): The Nutty Professor (1963)

Moore, Demi (act, b. 1964): The Butcher's Wife; Ghost (1990);The Hunchback of Notre Dame (1996); Mortal Thoughts; Nothing But Trouble; Parasite; The Scarlet Letter (1995); The Seventh Sign

Moore, Dennis (act): Crime Doctor's Courage; Ellery Queen and the Murder Ring; Meet Nero Wolfe; The Mummy's Curse; Spooks Run Wild

Moore, Diana (act): Who Killed Teddy Bear?

Moore, Dickie (act, b. 1925): Gabriel Over the White House; The Gladiator; The Happy Land; Heaven Can Wait (1943); Out of the Past (1947); Peter Ibbetson

Moore, Doreen (act): Return from the Ashes

Moore, Dudley (act, b. 1935): Alice's Adventures In Wonderland (1972); Bedazzled; The Bed-Sitting Room; The Hound of the Baskervilles (1978); Santa Claus (1985); The Wrong Box

Moore, Dudley (mus & wri, b. 1935): Bedazzled; The Hound Of The Baskervilles (1978)

Moore, Duke (act): Plan 9 from Outer Space; The Sinister Urge

Moore, Edwina (act): Elvira, Mistress of the Dark; Ghost In the Machine; Nightmare On the 13th Floor

Moore, Eileen (act): The Girl On the Pier; The Green Man; An Inspector Calls; Men of Sherwood Forest; Mr. Denning Drives North

Moore, Eira (act): Voice Over

Moore, Elsie (act): The Brotherhood of Satan

Moore, Eulabelle (act): The Horror of Party Beach

Moore, Eva (act, 1870-1955): The Bandits of Sherwood Forest; Chu Chin Chow (1923); The Crimson Circle (1922); I Was a Spy; The Old Dark House (1932); Scotland Yard Investigator

Moore, Evadne (act): For Mother's Sake

Moore, Frank (act): The Long Kiss Goodnight; Rabid; Stone Cold Dead

Moore, Frederick (cin): The Man Who Fell to Earth (1987); The Man Who Wasn't There

Moore, Gar (act): Abbott and Costello Meet the Killer; Curse of the Faceless Man; Illegal

Moore, Gene (mus): Carnival of Souls (1962)

Moore, Geoffrey Robert (act): Sherlock Holmes In New York

Moore, H_____ (act): The Day Mars Invaded Earth

Moore, Ian (act): Sling Blade

Moore, Ida (act, 1883-1964): The Dark Mirror (1946); Desk Set

Moore, Jack (act): Stargate

Moore, James (act): Dark Side of Midnight; The Sinister Urge

Moore, Jean (act): Atlas

Moore, Jeanie (act): Vampire at Midnight

Moore, Joanna (act): Appointment With a Shadow; Countdown; Monster On the Campus; Son of Flubber

Moore, John (act): Deadly; I Don't Want to Be Born

Moore, John Rixey (act): Philadelphia Experiment II

Moore, Joyce (act): The Speckled Band (1931)

Moore, Juanita (act): Abby; Lord of the Jungle; Witness to Murder

Moore, Julianne (act, b. 1960): Cast a Deadly Spell; The Fugitive (1993); The Hand That Rocks the Cradle; The Lost World: Jurassic Park; Psycho (1998); Tales from the Darkside

Moore, Kenneth (act): Werewolf of Washington

Moore, Kenny (act): Secrets of the Phantom Caverns

Moore, Kieron (act, b. 1925, nee Kieron O'Hanrahan): Crack In the World; Darby O'Gill and the Little People; The Day of the Triffids; Dr. Blood's Coffin; Girl In the Headlines; The Green Scarf; Hide and Seek; I Thank a Fool; The Key; The League of Gentlemen; A Man About the House; Mantrap; Recoil (1953); Satellite In the Sky; Three Sundays to Live

Moore, Lee (1930s act): The Gracie Allen Murder Case

Moore, Lee (1970s & 1980s act): Blood Bath (1975); Night of the Zombies (1981)

Moore, Linda (act): My Best Friend Is a Vampire

Moore, Maggie (act): Darkman (1990)

Moore, Margaret (act): Gallery of Horror

Moore, Martin (act): The Groundstar Conspiracy

Moore, Mary Tyler (act, b. 1937): X-15

Moore, Matt (act, 1888-1960): Deluge; 20,000 Leagues Under the Sea (1916, USA)

Moore, Maureen (act): Life Is a Circus

Moore, Mavor (act): City On Fire; Mortal Sins; Scanners

Moore, Melba (act, b. 1945): Def by Temptation

Moore, Melissa (act): The Alien Within; Hard to Die; The Invisible Maniac; Repossessed; Scream Dream; Sorority House Massacre 2; Stormswept; Vampire Cop

Moore, Michael (GB act): Booby Trap; Jamaica Run

Moore, Michael (USA act):The Atomic City

Moore, Micki (act): Deranged (1974); Short Circuit 2

Moore, Milton (cin): He Who Gets Slapped

Moore, Muriel (act): Scalpel

Moore, Owen (act, 1886-1939): As You Desire Me; The Black Bird (1926); The Road to Mandalay

Moore, Pauline (act): Charlie Chan at the Olympics; Charlie Chan at Treasure Island; Charlie Chan In Reno; The Three Musketeers (1939)

Moore, Peter (act): Captain America II; Trauma (1993)

Moore, Ray (act): Secrets In the Attic

Moore, Renato (act): Prophecy (1979)

Moore, Richard (GB act): The Offence

Moore, Richard (USA act): Return of the Living Dead, Part II; Strange Behavior

Moore, Richard (cin): Myra Breckinridge; Wild In the Streets

Moore, Robert (act): The Lady Killers (1956)

Moore, Robert (dir): Murder by Death

Moore, Robyn (act): The Magic Riddle

Moore, Roger (act, b. 1927): Crossplot; The Fiction-Makers; For Your Eyes Only; Live and Let Die;The Magic Snowman; The Man Who Haunted Himself; The Man With the Golden Gun; The Miracle (1959); Monkey Business; Moonraker; Octopussy; Romulus and the Sabines; The Saint; Sherlock Holmes In New York; The Spy Who Loved Me; Vendetta for the Saint; A View to a Kill

Moore, Ronald D. (wri): Star Trek: First Contact; Star Trek: Generations

Moore, Ronald (W.) (dir & wri): Future Kill; Splatter

Moore, Rowland (act): The Bishop's Silence; The Master Spy (1914); The Underworld of London; Vice and Virtue: or, The Tempters of London

Moore, Roy (wri): The Last Chase; Silent Night, Evil Night

Moore, Rudy Ray (act): Devil's Son-in-Law

Moore, Sheila (act): Circumstances Unknown; It (1990); The Reflecting Skin

Moore, Simon (wri):Gulliver's Travels (1996)

Moore, Sue (act): The Gracie Allen Murder Case

Moore, Susan (act): Flesh Gordon

Moore, Susanna (act): Strange Behavior

Moore, Ted (cin, b. 1914): Call Me Bwana; Clash of the Titans; The Day of the Triffids; Diamonds Are Forever; Dr. No;Dominique; From Russia With Love;The Gamma People; The Golden Voyage of Sinbad; Goldfinger; How to Murder a Rich Uncle; Live and Let Die; The Man Inside; The Man With the Golden Gun; A Prize of Gold; Psychomania (1972); Sinbad and the Eye of the Tiger; Thunderball

Moore, Teddi (act): Murder by Decree

Moore, Terry (act, b. 1929, nee Helen Koford): Beneath the 12-Mile Reef; City of Fear (1965); Daredevil; Death Dimension; The Great Rupert; Hellhole; A Man Called Dagger; Mighty Joe Young (1949 & 1998); Platinum High School; Postmark for Danger; The Return of October; Shadowed; Why Must I Die?

Moore, Thomas (GB act): The Angel Who Pawned Her Harp; The Black Knight

Moore, Thomas (It act): Escape from the Bronx

Moore, Tom (act, 1883-1955): A Kiss for Cinderella; Trouble for Two

Moore, Tom (dir): Return to Boggy Creek

Moore, Tony (act): Enemy Mine

Moore, Tracey (act): Those Dear Departed

Moore, Ward (wri, 1903-1978): Panic In Year Zero

Moore, Wesley (act): Apprentice to Murder; Are You Lonesome Tonight?

Moore, William (act): Radio Ranch

Moore, William I. (wri): The Philadelphia Experiment

Moorehead, Agnes (act, 1906-1974): Adventures of Captain Fabian; The Bat (1959); Charlotte's Web; Dark Passage; Dear, Dead Delilah; Fourteen Hours; Frankenstein: The True Story; Hush...Hush, Sweet Charlotte; Jane Eyre (1944); Journey Into Fear (1942); The Lost Moment; Night of Terror (1972); The Story of Mankind; What's the Matter With Helen?; The Woman In White (1948)

Moor(e)head, Natalie/Nathalie (act): The Adventurous Blonde; The Benson Murder Case; The Menace (1932); The Mind Reader; The Phantom of Paris (1931); The Thin Man; The Unholy Night

Moore-Marriott, George Thomas (act): see Marriott, Moore

Moorer, Margo (act): Dark Angel (1996)

Moores, Merle (act): Stalking Laura

Moorhead, Barbara (act): see Eden, Barbara

Moorhead, Jean (act): The Amazing Colossal Man; The Atomic Submarine; Attack of the Puppet People

Moorhouse, Bert (act): The Falcon In Hollywood; Sunset Boulevard

Mooring, Jeff (act): The First Power

Moorman, George (act): Zotz!

Mooy, Nancy (act): The Corsican Brothers (1985)

Moppert, Gabrielle (act): see Dorziat, Gabrielle

Mora, Madeleine (act): Communion

Mora, Norma (act): The Saint In the Wax Museum

Mora, Philippe (dir): The Beast Within; Communion; Howling II; Howling III; Precious Find; The Return of Captain Invincible

Mora, Philippe (wri): Howling III

Morahan, Andy (dir): Highlander: The Final Dimension

Morahan, Christopher (dir): After Pilkington; Paper Mask

Morahan, Jim (mus): Witch-Finder General

Moraldi, Franco (act): Scream of the Demon Lover

Morales, Esai (act): Circle of Deceit; Deadlock 2; Freejack; Ultraviolet

Morales, Esy (act): Criss Cross

Morales, Hector (act): Herbie Goes Bananas; Out of the Dark

Morales, Ines (act): House of Doom (1973)

Morales, Julio (act): Night Fiend

Morales, Mario (act): The Last Days of Pompeii (1959); Terrore Nello Spazio

Morales, Maritza (act): Blood Diner

Morales, Santos (act): The Relic

Moran, Dolores (act, b. 1926): The Horn Blows at Midnight

Moran, Eddie (act): Treasure Island (1950)

Moran, Eddie (wri): Topper Takes a Trip

Moran, Erin (act, b. 1961): Galaxy of Terror

Moran, Eve (act): James Tont: Operation Goldsinger

Moran, Francisco (1920s act): The Last Warning (1929)

Moran, Francisco (1920s act): Horror; Los Muertos No Perdonan; Pyro

Moran, Frank (act): *The Corpse Vanishes; A Date With the Falcon; Ghosts On the Loose; Return of the Ape Man; Torchy Plays With Dynamite*
Moran, Jack (wri): *Faster, Pussycat! Kill! Kill!*
Moran, Jackie (act, 1923-1990): *The Barefoot Boy; Destination Saturn; Henry Aldrich Haunts a House*
Moran, Jackie (1990s act): *Blink*
Moran, Jim (act): *The Mask (1961)*
Moran, Lee (act, 1888-1961): *The Death Kiss*
Moran, Leslie (act): *Max Q: Emergency Landing*
Moran, Lois (act, 1909-1990): *Behind That Curtain; The Road to Mandalay; The Spider (1932)*
Moran, Malcolm (act): *Play Misty for Me*
Moran, Manolita (act): *La Torre de los Siete Jorobados*
Moran, Michael (act): *Knightriders*
Moran, Michael P. (act): *Ghostbusters II*
Moran, Mike (mus): *Blood Bath at the House of Death; Time Bandits*
Moran, Nancy (act): *Flatliners*
Moran, Neil (act): *Eraserhead*
Moran, Pat(rick) (act): *Biohazard: The Alien Force; Dark Universe*
Moran, Pat(rick) (wri): *Dark Universe*
Moran, Peggy (act, b. 1918): *Drums of the Congo; Horror Island; The Mummy's Hand*
Moran, Percy (act): *The Adventures of Dick Turpin-A Deadly Foe, A Pack of Hounds, and Some Merry Monks; The Adventures of Dick Turpin-The Gunpowder Plot; The Adventures of Dick Turpin-The King of Highwaymen; The Adventures of Dick Turpin-200 Guineas Reward, Dead or Alive; Britain's Naval Secret; Dick Turpin's Ride to York (1913, B&C/Walturdaw); Don Q-HowHe Outwitted Don Luis; The Great Anarchist Mystery; The Houseboat Mystery; Lieutenant Daring and the Dancing Girl; Lieutenant Daring and the Labour Riots; Lieutenant daring and the Photographing Pigeon; Lieutenant Daring and the Plans of the Minefields; Lieutenant Daring and the Ship's Mascot; Lieutenant Daring Avenges an Insult to the Union Jack;Lieutenant Daring, RN, and theWater Rats; The Live Wire; London Nighthawks; London's Enemies; The Mystery of the Diamond Belt; OHMS-Our Helpless Millions Saved; The Planter's Daughter; Slavers of the Thames*
Moran, Percy (dir): *Britain's Naval Secret; Lieutenant Daring, RN, and the Water Rats; London Nighthawks; London's Enemies; OHMS-Our Helpless Millions Saved; Slavers of the Thames*
Moran, Percy (wri): *Lieutenant Daring, RN, and the Water Rats; OHMS-Our Helpless Millions Saved; Slavers of the Thames*
Moran, Polly (act, 1885-1952): *Alice In Wonderland (1933); London After Midnight; The Scarlet Letter (1926); The Thirteenth Hour (1927); The Unholy Night*
Moran, Sean (act): *True Crime*
Moran, Tony (act): *Halloween*
Morand, Leonard (mus): *Queen of Blood*
Morand, Linda (act): *Pretty Maids All In a Row*
Morand, Sylvester (act): *—And Now the Screaming Starts!*
Morane, Jacqueline (act): *Le Testament du Dr. Cordelier*
Moranis, Rick (act, b. 1953): *The Flintstones; Ghostbusters; Ghostbusters II; Honey, I Blew Up the Kid; Honey, I Shrunk the Kids; Honey, We Shrunk Ourselves; Little Shop of Horrors (1986);Spaceballs; Splitting Heirs; Streets of Fire*
Morano, Carl (wri): *Class of Nuke 'em High, Part 2: Subhumanoid Meltdown*
Morant, Angela (act): *Victims*
Morant, Richard (act): *The Company of Wolves; The Hunchback of Notre Dame (1977); The Scarlet Pimpernel (1982)*
Morante, Mark Edward (act): *The Hidden*
Moranti, Milburn (act, 1887-1964): *The Clutching Hand; Ghost Rider (1943); The Lost City; Wolf Blood*
Moravia, Albert (wri): *Le Mepris*
Moraweck, Lucien (mus): *The Man In the Iron Mask (1939); The Return of Monte Cristo*
Moray, Yvonne (act): *Confessions of an Opium Eater*
Morayta, Francisco (act): *Zorro, the Gay Blade*
Morayta, Miguel (dir & wri): *La Invasion de los Vampiros; El Vampiro Sangriento*
Morayta, Paco (act): *Caveman (1981)*
Moraz, Patrick (mus): *The Stepfather*
Morcillo, Fernando G./Garcia (mus): *The Emerald of Artatama; Night of the Sorcerers; A Witch Without a Broom*
More, Camilla (act): *Dark Side of the Moon*
More, Carey (act): *Once Bitten*
More, Carmen (act): *Black Magic Woman*
More, J. Neil (act): *The Ghost Goes West; A Safe Affair*
More, Julian (wri): *Doctors Wear Scarlet; The Valley of Gwangi*
More, Kenneth (act, 1914-1982, nee Gerrards Cross): *Man In the Moon (1960); Man On the Run; No Highway In the Sky; Scrooge (1970); The Slipper and the Rose; The Spaceman and King Arthur; Stop Press Girl; The 39 Steps (1959); Where Time Began; The Yellow Balloon*
Moreau, Jeanne (act, b. 1928): *Banana Peel; Demoniac; Ever After: A Cinderella Story; La Femme Nikita; Frantic; Mademoiselle; La Mariee etait en Noir; Mata Hari, Agent H21; Le Paltoquet; Le Plus Vieux Metier du Monde; The Trial; Until the End of the World*
Moreau, Marsha (act): *Babar: The Movie; Bay Coven*
Moreau, Nathaniel (act): *Body Parts (1991)*
Moree, Sam (act): *God's Bloody Acre*
Morehart, Deborah (act): *The Initiation*
Moreira, Hernani (act): *Warriors of the Wasteland*
Moreland David (act): *Houdini (1998)*
Moreland, Mantan (act, 1901-1973): *Black Magic (1944); Charlie Chan In the Secret Service; The Chinese Cat; The Chinese Ring; Dark Alibi; The Docks of New Orleans; Dressed to Kill (1941); Ellery Queen's Penthouse Mystery; Eyes In the Night; The Feathered Serpent (1948); The Flying Serpent;The Golden Eye; The Jade Mask; King of the Zombies; Law of the Jungle; Mexican Spitfire Sees a Ghost; Revenge of the Zombies (1943); The Scarlet Clue; Shadows Over Chinatown; The Shanghai Chest; The Shanghai Cobra; The Sky Dragon; The Spider (1945);Spider Baby; The Strange Case of Dr. Rx; The Trap*
Moreland, Sherry (act): *Fury of the Congo; Pyro; Rocketship X-M*
Morell, Andre (act, 1909-1978, nee Andre Mesritz): *Behemoth, the Sea Monster; The Black Knight; The Camp On Blood Island; Cash On Demand; The Frightened Bride; The Golden Link; High Treason (1951); The Hound of the Baskervilles (1959);Interpol; Madeleine; The Moon-Spinners; The Mummy's Shroud; Mysterious Island (1961); The Plague of the Zombies; The Secret; Seven Days to Noon; The Shadow of the Cat; She (1965); The Slipper and the Rose; So Long at the Fair; Stage Fright (1950); A Stolen Face; Ten Days In Paris;10 Rillington Place; They Can't Hang Me; Three Cases of Murder;Three Silent Men; The Vengeance of She; Woman of Straw; TheWrong Box*
Morell, David (act): *Personal and Confidential*
Morell, Penny (act): *A Matter of Choice; Smokescreen*
Morelli, Eric (act): see Lloyd, Eric
Morelli, Tony (act): *Timecop*
Morello, Joe (act): *Sasquatch, the Legend of Bigfoot*
Morello, John (cin): *Just Before Dawn (1980)*
Morena, Mona (act): *Twilight People*
Moreno, Antonio (act, 1886-1967): *The Cat Creeps (1930); Creature from the Black Lagoon; El Cuerpo del Lito; The Dust of Egypt*
Moreno, Belita (act): *Jekyll and Hyde...Together Again; Oh, God! You Devil*
Moreno, Christina (act): *Chosen Survivors*
Moreno, Dario (act): *Les Femmes s'en Blancent; La Mome Vert-de-Gris; Le Saint Prend l'Affut*
Moreno, Gerardo (act): *Nightlife (1989, USA-Mex)*
Moreno, Hector (act): *Caveman (1981)*
Moreno, Inez (act): *Master of Horror*
Moreno, John (act): *For Your Eyes Only*
Moreno, Jorge (act): *Herbie Goes Bananas; King Kong (1976)*
Moreno, Jose Elias (act): see Quezada, Jose Elias Moreno y Cesareo
Moreno, Juan (act): *A Place to Die*
Moreno, Lea (act): *Doom Runners*
Moreno, Marguerite (act): *The Queen of Spades (1937)*
Moreno, Mario (act): see Cantinflas
Moreno, Rita (act, b. 1931): *Jivaro*
Moreno, Robert (cin): *Skullduggery*
Moreno, Ruben (act): *Cruise Into Terror; Herbie Goes Bananas; The Resurrection of Zachary Wheeler; Tarantulas: The Deadly Cargo*
Moreno, Servio T. (act): *Body Heat*
Moretti, Mario (act): *Manhattan Baby*
Moretti, Nadir (act): *Giulietta degli Spiriti*
Moretti, Renato (wri): *I Criminali della Galassia*
Moretti, Ugo (wri): *Orgasmo*
Morevsky, Abraham (act): *The Dybbuk*
Morey, Bill (act): *Brainstorm (1983); Death Race 2000; Elvira, Mistress of the Dark; Ghost Warrior*
Morey, Harry T. (act): *The Green Goddess (1923)*
Morey, Larry (wri): *Bambi*
Morfogen, George (act): *V*
Morga, Javier (act): *The Arrival (1996)*
Morga, Tom (act): *Alien Nation; Eve of Destruction;*
Friday the 13th-Part V: A New Beginning; Star Trek
Morgan, Alexandra (act): *The Eliminator; Spellbinder*
Morgan, Allan (act): *Susie Q*
Morgan, Andre (act): *Twisted*
Morgan, Andre (wri): *Megaforce*
Morgan, Bill (act): *On Her Majesty's Secret Service*
Morgan, C.W. (act): *Scream*
Morgan, Charles (act): *Cash On Demand*
Morgan, Charley M. (act): *Hellhole*
Morgan, Charly (act): *The Monster Squad*
Morgan, Cindy (act): *Galaxis; The Midnight Hour; Tron*
Morgan, Claude (act): *White Zombie*
Morgan, Clive (act): *The Black Sleep*
Morgan, Corney (act): *Damien-Omen II; The Psychotronic Man*
Morgan, David (mus): *Distortions*
Morgan, Dennis (act, 1909-1994, nee Stanley Morner): *Pearl of the South Pacific; The Return of Dr. X*
Morgan, Diana (act): *Eraser*
Morgan, Diana (wri): *Fiddlers Three; Halfway House*
Morgan, Dick (act): *Horror of Dracula*
Morgan, Donald (act): *The Medium (1951)*
Morgan, Donald M. (cin): *Christine, The Darker Side of Terror*
Morgan, Eula (act): *Monsieur Verdoux*
Morgan, Felicite (act): *The Boogey Man*
Morgan, Francine (act): *Mary Shelley's 'Frankenstein'*
Morgan, Frank (act, 1890-1949, nee Francis Wupperman): *The Cockeyed Miracle; The Three Musketeers (1948); Trouble for Two; The Wizard of Oz (1939)*
Morgan, Fred (act): *The Beetle; The Black Cross Gang; Flying from Justice; The Harbour Lights; Her Life In London; The King's Romance; The Man In Motley; Queen of the London Counterfeiters; Through Stormy Waters; Ultus and the Three-Button Mystery; The Water Rats of London;The Wrecker of Lives*
Morgan, Garfield (act): *Catch Me a Spy; Company of Fools; Digby-The Biggest Dog In the World*
Morgan, Gary (act): *Storybook*
Morgan, Gary (act): *The Final Countdown; Logan's Run*
Morgan, Gene (act): *Meet Nero Wolfe; Who Killed Gail Preston?*
Morgan, George (J.) (act): *The Incredibly Strange CreaturesWho Stopped Living and Became*
Mixed-Up Zombies; The Thrill Killers
Morgan, George (wri): *Dick Tracy (1937)*
Morgan, Glen (act): *Trick or Treat*
Morgan, Guy (wri): *Counterblast; The Girl On the Pier; The Man In the Road; Never Look Back; The Woman With No Name*
Morgan, Harry/Henry (Hays) (act, b. 1915): *A-Haunting We Will Go; Appointment With Danger; The Barefoot Executive; The Big Clock; The Cat from Outer Space; Charley and the Angel; Ellery Queen:Don't Look Behind You; Exo-Man; Dragonwyck; The Flight of Dragons; The Happy Land; The Loves of Edgar Allan Poe; Nightmare Alley; Sparkling Cyanide; The Well*
Morgan, Horace (act): *Sherlock Jr.*
Morgan, Ira (H.) (cin, b. 1892): *Charlie Chan In the Secret Service; The Chinese Cat; The Cyclops; The Face In the Fog (1922); Fog Island; The Great Gabbo; The Lost Tribe; Mark of the Gorilla; Modern Times; The Mystic; Pygmy Island; The Unholy Night; The Vampire Bat*
Morgan, Jaye P. (act, b. 1931): *The Adventures of Nick Carter*
Morgan, Jeanne (act): *The Sorrows of Satan (1925)*
Morgan, Jewell (act): *Revenge of the Virgins*
Morgan, Jim (act): *Raiders of the Living Dead*
Morgan, Joan (act): *The Crimson Circle (1922); The Great Spy Raid; Her Greatest Performance; Iron Justice; Queenie of the Circus; The Shadow of Egypt*
Morgan, Joan (wri): *This Was a Woman*
Morgan, Julie H. (act): *The Return of the Six Million Dollar Man and the Bionic Woman*
Morgan, Ken (cin): *The Magic Toyshop*
Morgan, Lee (act): *Dungeons of Horror; The Neanderthal Man; The Weird Ones*
Morgan, Luce (act): *The Hidden*
Morgan, Lynne (act): *Killer's Moon*
Morgan, Melissa (act): *The Nasty Rabbit*
Morgan, Michael (act): *Midnight Offerings*
Morgan, Michele (act, b. 1920, nee Simone Roussel): *Cat and Mouse (1978); The Chase; The Fallen Idol; The Gentle Art of Murder; Landru; Marie Antoinette (1953); Obsession (1954); Le Quai des Brumes; Seven Deadly Sins; Tell Me Whom to Kill*
Morgan, Molly (act): *Nightmare On the 13th Floor*
Morgan, Nancy (act): *The Nest*
Morgan, Nicky (cin): *Deathstalker II: Duel of the Titans*
Morgan, Nicole (act): *The Phantom Empire*
Morgan, Nori/Norri (act): *The Lost Boys; Outland*
Morgan, Olive (act): *Peter Ibbetson*
Morgan, Olwen (act): *The Devil's Gift*
Morgan, Patti (act): *Booby Trap*
Morgan, Paul (act): *Die Spinnen*
Morgan, Ralph (act, 1882-1956, nee Ralph Wupperman): *Black Market Babies; Charlie Chan's Chance; Cheaters at Play; Close Call for Ellery Queen; Condemned to Live; Crack-Up; The Creeper (1948); Dick Tracy vs. Crime, Inc.; The Kennel Murder Case; The Lone Wolf Spy Hunt;The Mad Doctor; The Monster Maker (1943); Night Monster;Rasputin and the Empress; Sleep, My Love; Song of the Thin Man; Weird Woman*
Morgan, Read (act): *The Adventures of Buckaroo Banzai; The Amazing Transparent Man; Back to the Future; Beach Girls and the Monster; Beyond the Time Barrier; Blood Beach; The Munsters' Revenge; A Stranger Is Watching; Time After Time*
Morgan, Richard (act): *The Wicked*
Morgan, Robbi (act): *Friday the 13th (1980); What's the Matter With Helen?*
Morgan, Robert W. (dir): *Bloodstalkers*
Morgan, Roy (act): *The Outing*
Morgan, Sandra (act): *Flesh and Fantasy*
Morgan, Scott Wesley (act): *Serial Mom; Shadow Conspiracy*
Morgan, Shelley Taylor (act): *The Sword and the Sorcerer*
Morgan, Sidney (dir, 1873-1946): *A Bid for Fortune; The Brass Bottle (1914); Bulldog Drummond's Third Round; The Charlatan; Dr. Paxton's Last Crime; The Great Spy Raid; Iron Justice; A Man's Shadow; The Shadow of Egypt; The Stolen Sacrifice; What's Bred...Comes Out In the Flesh; The Woman of the Iron Bracelets*
Morgan, Sidney (wri, 1873-1946): *The Brass Bottle (1914); Bulldog Drummond's Third Round; Dr. Paxton's Last Crime; The Great Spy Raid; Iron Justice; A Man's Shadow; The Stolen Sacrifice; What's Bred...Comes Out In the Flesh; The Woman of the Iron Bracelets*
Morgan, Stafford (act): *The Alpha Incident; The Capture of Bigfoot; Targets*
Morgan, Stanley (act): *The Clue of the Silver Key; Clue of the Twisted Candle; Konga; Partners In Crime (1961); The Return of Mr. Moto; The Silent Weapon; The Square Mile Murder*
Morgan, Tanya (act): *Targets*
Morgan, Terence (act, b. 1921): *The Curse of the Mummy's Tomb; Hamlet (1948); The Lifetaker; The Love of Three Queens; The March Hare; The Penthouse (1967); Piccadilly Third Stop; The Sea Pirate; Shadow of the Past; The Shakedown; The Steel Key; Svengali (1954); They Can't Hang Me; Tread Softly Stranger; Turn the Key Softly*
Morgan, Tim R. (act): *Winterbeast*
Morgan, Trevor (act): *Barney's Great Adventure*
Morgan, Wendy (act): *The Mirror Crack'd*
Morgan, William (dir): *Mr. District Attorney*
Morganfield, DeMarious T. (act): *Always*
Morgenstern, Janusz (act): *Legend of the White Horse*
Morgenstern, Maja (act): *Nostradamus*
Morghan, Mark (act): *Judge Dredd*
Morghen, John (act): *Cannibal Ferox*

Morhaim, Joe (wri): Doc Savage, the Man of Bronze
Morheim, Lou (wri): The Beast from 20,000 Fathoms; Madame Sin
Mori, Claudia (act): Sodom and Gomorrah; Son of Hercules In the Land of Fire
Mori, Jeanne (act): Mars Attacks!; Star Trek III: The Search for Spock
Mori, Masayuki (act, b. 1911): Tora No O O Fumu Otokotachi; Ugetsu Monogatari; Yoru No Tsuzumi
Mori, Mikita (act): Godzilla 1985
Mori, Paola (act): Mr. Arkadin
Mori, Toshia (act): Charlie Chan On Broadway
Moriarity, Patrick (act): Son of Dracula (1943)
Moriarty, Cathy (act): Casper; Matinee; Neighbors;White of the Eye
Moriarty, Daniel (act): Something Is Out There
Moriarty, Don (wri): Zorro, the Gay Blade
Moriarty, Mary (act): Matinee
Moriarty, Michael (act, b. 1941): Blood Link; Dark Tower (1987); Earthquake In New York; It's Alive III: Island of the Alive; Q; A Return to Salem's Lot; The Stuff; Troll
Moriarty, P.H. (act): The Inside Man; Jaws 3-D; Outland
Morici, Franco (act): La Ragazza Che Sapeva Troppo
Morick, Dave (act): Earthquake; W
Morier, James (wri): The Adventures of Hajji Baba
Morier-Genoud, Philippe (act): Confidentially Yours
Morimoto, Kouji (dir): Robot Carnival
Morin, Alberto (act): The Mephisto Waltz
Morin, Victor (cin): L'Atlantide (1920)
Morina, Johnny (act): Kids of the Round Table
Morioka, Ken-Ichiro (mus):Message from Space
Morioka, Satoshi (act): The Toxic Avenger, Part II
Morison, Patricia (act, b. 1919, nee Eileen Morrison): Beyond the Blue Horizon; Calling Dr. Death; Danger Woman; Dressed to Kill (1946); The Prince of Thieves; Queen of the Amazons (1947); Song of the Thin Man;Tarzan and the Huntress
Morissey, Nani (act): Mermaids of Tiburon
Morita, Kansaku (act): Virus (1980); The War In Space
Morita, Miki (act): Bulldog Drummond's Revenge; The Walking Dead
Morita, (Noruhiko) Pat (act): Alice In Wonderland (1985); Auntie Lee's Meat Pies; Babes In Toyland (1986); Collision Course (1990); Human Feelings; Miracle Beach; Mulan; Timemaster; A Very Missing Person; When Time Ran Out
Morita, Rhett (cin): Free Fall
Morita, Shin (wri): Invasion of the Neptune Men
Morita, Yoshimitsu (dir): Deaths In Tokimeki
Moritani, Shiro (dir): Catastrophe 1999: The Prophecies of Nostradamus; The Submersion of Japan
Moritz, Louisa/Louise (act): Chained Heat; Death Race 2000; Galaxis; New Year's Evil
Moritz, Ulla (act): Journey to the Seventh Planet
Moriwaki, Yosh (act): Remote Control (1988)
Moriyama, Rollin (act): The Snow Creature; 20 Million Miles to Earth
Moriyama, Yuko (act): Zeram
Morland, Nigel (wri): Mrs. Pym of Scotland Yard
Morlas, Mary (act): This Is Not a Test
Morley, Angela (mus): Watership Down
Morley, Carol (act): Dr. Cook's Garden
Morley, Christopher (act): Howling VI: The Freaks
Morley, Donald (act): The Man Without a Body; Revenge (1971, GB); Where's Johnny
Morley, John (act): Images
Morley, Karen (act, b. 1905, nee Mildred Linton): Framed; Gabriel Over the White House; The Girl from Scotland Yard; M (1950); The Mask of Fu Manchu; Mata Hari (1932); The Phantom of Crestwood; The Thirteenth Hour (1947); The Unknown (1946)
Morley, Malcolm (act): Inquest (1939)
Morley, Natasha (act): Hideaway; Kissed
Morley, Rita (act): The Flesh Eaters
Morley, Robert (act, 1908-1992): Alice In Wonderland (1985); The Alphabet Murders; Around the World In 80 Days; Beat the Devil; The Blue Bird (1976); The Boys; The Ghosts of Berkeley Square; Great Expectations (1974); The Great Muppet Caper; Hot Enough for June; Hugo the Hippo; Loophole; The Loved One; Marie Antoinette [illegible] Dog; The Old Dark House (1963); The Road to Hong Kong; Sinful Davey; Some Girls Do; A Study In Terror; Theater of Blood; Topkapi; A Troll In Central Park; The Trygon Factor; Way...Way Out; Who Is Killing the Great Chefs of Europe?
Morley, Royston (dir): Attempt to Kill
Mormino, Carmen (act): Sleepstalker
Morne, Maryland (act): The Last of the Lone Wolf
Morneau, Louis (dir): Carnosaur 2
Morner, Stanley (act): see Morgan, Dennis
Moro, Alicia (act): Exterminators of the Year 3000; Slugs
Morocco (act): The Projectionist
Morocco, Beans (act): Wes Craven's New Nightmare
Moroder, Giorgio (act): Electric Dreams
Moroder, Giorgio (mus): Cat People (1982); Electric Dreams; The Neverending Story; Superman III
Moroff, Madeline (act): The Fan
Moroff, Mike (act): From Dusk Till Dawn; RoboCop
Morone, Drew (act & wri): Lost Prophet
Moroni, Mario (wri): Maciste alla Corte della Zar
Moross, Jerome (mus): The Valley of Gwangi; The War Lord
Morphett, Jim (cin): Razorback
Morphett, Tony (wri): The Last Wave
Morphew, Bill (act): Vamp
Morra, Pia (act): Spara Forte, Piu Forte...Non Capisco
Morrell, Berit (act): Making Contact
Morrell, Chuck (act): Grotesque
Morrell, David (act): The Adventures of Hal 5
Morrell, Diandra (act): The China Syndrome
Morrell, Frank (act): Jungle Trail of the Son of Tarzan
Morrell, George (act): The Clutching Hand
Morrell, Holly (act): Grotesque
Morrell, Joshua (act): Making Contact
Morrell, Reid (act): Making Contact
Morrell, Russell (act): Night of the Lepus
Morrell, Stephen (act): Galaxina
Morren, Christopher (act): Storm of the Century
Morricone, Ennio (mus, b. 1928): L'Anticristo; Arabian Nights (1974); Autopsy; The Black Belly of the Tarantula; Bluebeard (1972); The Cat O' Nine Tails; Diabolik; Exorcist II: The Heretic; The Flower In His Mouth; The French Conspiracy; Hamlet (1990); Holocaust 2000; The Human Factor; The Humanoid; Hundra; The Island; A Lizard In a Woman's Skin; Operation Kid Brother; Orca; Quatro Mosche di Velluto Gris; Red Sonja; The Red Tent; Salo, o le Centoventi Giornate di Sodoma;The Serpent (1973); Spasmo; The Thing (1982); Treasure of the Four Crowns; Le Trio Infernal; L'Uccello delle Piume di Cristallo; When Women Had Tails; White Dog; Windows; Wolf
Morrill, Chris (act): Night of the Lepus; The Power (1980); Pranks
Morrill, John A./Arthur (cin): A Boy and His Dog; The Brotherhood of Satan; The Dark (1979); Kingdom of the Spiders; Mr. Sycamore; The Witchmaker
Morrill, Mitch (act): Dracula Sucks
Morris, Adrian (act): Michael Shayne, Private Detective; One Frightened Night
Morris, Alex (Allen) (act): I Come In Peace; Powder
Morris, Anita (act): 18 Again!; Martians Go Home
Morris, Artro (act): The Godsend; The Strange Affair; The 39 Steps (1978)
Morris, Aubrey (act): Blood from the Mummy's Tomb; A Clockwork Orange; Lifeforce; Liszt O' Mania; The Wicker Man; The Zany Adventures of Robin Hood
Morris, Barboura (act): Atlas; A Bucket of Blood (1959); De Sade; The Dunwich Horror; The Haunted Palace (1963); The St.Valentine's Day Massacre; The Wasp Woman (1959); X—The Man With the X-Ray Eyes
Morris, Bert de Wayne (act): see Morris, Wayne
Morris, Beth (act): Crucible of Terror; Tales That Witness Madness
Morris, Bob (act): The Green Slime
Morris, Brad (act): Steel Dawn
Morris, Buckley (act): The Hidden
Morris, Chester (act, 1901-1970): After Midnight With Boston Blackie; Alias Boston Blackie; The Bat Whispers; Blind Alley;Blind Spot (1947); Boston Blackie and the Law; Boston Blackie Booked On Suspicion; Boston Blackie Goes Hollywood; Boston Blackie's Appointment With Death; Boston Blackie's Chinese Venture; Boston Blackie's Rendezvous; The Chance of a Lifetime; A Close Call for Boston Blackie; Confessions of Boston Blackie; Double Exposure; The Gift of Gab; Meet Boston Blackie; The Miracle Man (1932); One Mysterious Night; The Phantom Thief; The Road to Yesterday; The She-Creature; Trapped by Boston Blackie
Morris, Christian (act): Wavelength
Morris, Colleen (act): Prehysteria
Morris, Corbet (act): Tarzan's Revenge
Morris, David (act): The Punisher
Morris, David Burton (dir): Pretty Poison (1996); The Three Lives of Karen
Morris, Desmond (wri): The Naked Ape
Morris, Dorothy (act): Macabre (1958); None Shall Escape; Seconds
Morris, Edmund (wri): Project X (1967)
Morris, Edna (act): Another Man's Poison
Morris, Eric (act): Battle Beyond the Stars (1980); Wavelength
Morris, Ernest (dir, b. 1915): The Betrayal (1958); Echo of Diana; Night Train for Inverness; On the Run (1958); Operation Murder; The Return of Mr. Moto; Son of a Stranger; Strip Tease Murder; The Tell-Tale Heart (1960); Three Crooked Men; Three Sundays to Live; Transatlantic; A Woman of Mystery
Morris, Evan C. (act): The Puppet Masters
Morris, Flora (act): A Burglar for a Night; The Cat and the Chestnuts; The Convict's Sister; A Double Life (1912); A Flowergirl's Romance; The Foreign Spy (1911); The Forsaken; George Barnwell, the London Apprentice; The Heart of a Woman; His Evil Genius; The Man Behind the Mask (1914); The Mysteries of London; Partners In Crime (1913); The Silence of Richard Wilton; The Silver Lining; The Trail of Sand
Morris, Frances (act): Between Midnight and Dawn; The Big Clock; The Millerson Case
Morris, Garrett (act, b. 1937): Black Scorpion (1995); Children of the Night; Coneheads; The Invisible Woman (1983); Severed Ties; The Stuff
Morris, Glenn (act, 1911-1974): Tarzan's Revenge
Morris, Grant (wri): The Return of Swamp Thing
Morris, Greg (act): S.T.A.B.; The Sword of Ali Baba
Morris, Haviland (act): Gremlins 2: The New Batch
Morris, Howard (act, b. 1919): The Munsters' Revenge; The Nutty Professor (1963); Splash; Way....Way Out
Morris, Iona (act): Rain Without Thunder
Morris, Jack (act): The Green Slime
Morris, James (act): Targets
Morris, Jane (act): Pet Shop
Morris, Jeff (act):The Magician (1973)
Morris, Joan Stuart (act): Heart and Souls
Morris, John (act): Inn of the Damned; Toy Story
Morris, John (mus): Doctor Franken; Haunted Honeymoon (1986); The Little Match Girl (1987); Murder In a Small Town; Second Sight; Spaceballs; Yellowbeard; Young Frankenstein
Morris, John Charles (act):Copycat
Morris, Johnnie (act): Li'l Abner (1940)
Morris, Jonathan (act): The Vampire Journals
Morris, Judy (act): The Plumber; Razorback
Morris, Judy (wri): Babe: Pig In the City
Morris, Kathryn (act): Inferno (1998); Sleepstalker
Morris, Kirk (act): Atlas Against the Czar; Colossus and the Headhunters; Conqueror of Atlantis; Devil of the Desert Against the Son of Hercules; Hercules In the Vale of Woe; Hercules of the Desert; Hercules, Samson and Ulysses; Maciste al Inferno; Maciste alla Corte della Zar; Samson and the Sea Beasts; Star Pilot; Triumph of the Son of Hercules
Morris, Lana (act): Black 13; Guilt Is My Shadow; I Start Counting; Jet Storm; Moment of Indiscretion; No Trees In the Street; October Moth; Passport to Shame; Radio Cab Murder; The Straw Man; The Woman In Question
Morris, Leslie (act): Earth Girls Are Easy
Morris, Libby (act): The Adding Machine
Morris, Lily (act): Elstree Calling
Morris, Lisa (act): The Mangler
Morris, Liz (act): Jaws 3-D
Morris, Luis (act): El Principe Encadenado
Morris, Maria (act): Nightbeast
Morris, Marianne (act): Vampyres...Daughters of Dracula
Morris, Marie (act): Fake-Out
Morris, Mary (act, b. 1915): The Double Door; Full Circle; High Treason (1951); Pimpernel Smith; The Spy In Black; The Thief of Bagdad (1940)
Morris, Max (act): Blood Diner
Morris, Michael (act): Notorious (1992)
Morris, Oswald (cin, b. 1915): Beat the Devil; Circle of Danger; The Dark Crystal; Dracula (1973); Fragment of Fear; The Golden Mask; The Great Muppet Caper; The Key; The Man Who Would Be King; Moby Dick (1956); Saturday Island; Scrooge (1970); The Seven-per-Cent Solution; Sleuth; The Spy Who Came In from the Cold; The Wiz
Morris, Paul (cin): Threads
Morris, Phil (act): Devil In the Flesh; Star Trek III: The Search for Spock
Morris, Philip (act): Charlie Chan On Broadway; The Flying Saucer (1950); The Gracie Allen Murder Case
Morris, Phyllis (act): The Angel Who Pawned Her Harp
Morris, Reg(inald H.) (cin): The Food of the Gods; Murder by Decree; Phobia; Shadow of the Hawk; The Shape of Things to Come (1979); Silent Night, Evil Night; Welcome to Blood City
Morris, Robert (act): Frankenstein Created Woman; One Deadly Owner; Quatermass and the Pit
Morris, Robert (dir): Kong Island
Morris, Scott (act): Elvira, Mistress of the Dark; I Was a Teenage Sex Mutant
Morris, Shona (act): Sredni Vashtar
Morris, Suzanne (act): Fight In a Thieves' Kitchen; The Girl Who Came Back; The Lady In Black; Lost, Stolen or Strayed; Mother's Darling; The Prodigal Son
Morris, Tweed (act): Dr. Dracula
Morris, Vernon (act): Koroshi
Morris, Victor (act): Praying Mantis
Morris, Virginia (act): The Flash; Species; Switch
Morris, Wayne (act, 1914-1959, nee Bert de Wayne Morris): The Crooked Sky; Cross Channel;The Gelignite Gang; The Green Buddha; Lord of the Jungle; The Master Plan; The Return of Dr. X; The Smiling Ghost
Morris, Wolfe (act): The Abominable Snowman of the Himalayas; The Camp On Blood Island; The Clue of the New Pin (1961); The House That Dripped Blood; The London Connection
Morrisey, David (act): Robin Hood (1991)
Morrison, Alexander (act): Eye of the Alien
Morrison, Barbara (act, 1907-1992): City Beneath the Sea (1952); Project Moonbase
Morrison, Bill (act): Cyborg (1989)
Morrison, Carl (act): Dracula's Dog
Morrison, Chuck (act): Dick Tracy vs. Crime, Inc.
Morrison, Doug (act): Time Flyer
Morrison, Eileen (act): see Morison, Patricia
Morrison, Frank (wri): see Spillane, Mickey
Morrison, Greg (wri): Madhouse
Morrison, Hollis (act): How to Stuff a Wild Bikini
Morrison, Jack (act): The Strangler (1932); A Vagabond's Revenge
Morrison, Jack L. (act): The Savage Bees
Morrison, James (act): Pawns of Mars
Morrison, Jeanette Helen (act): see Leigh, Janet
Morrison, J.L.D. (act): Teenage Zombies
Morrison, Joe (act): The Checkered Flag; Four Hours to Kill; Sting of Death
Morrison, Jon (act): Slayground
Morrison, Kathleen (act): see Moore, Colleen
Morrison, Kenny (act): The Neverending Story II: The Next Chapter
Morrison, Lou (act): The Unholy Three (1925)
Morrison, Phil (act): Prom Night IV: Deliver Us from Evil; Red Blooded American Girl
Morrison, Richard (act): Death Dreams; When the Bough Breaks
Morrison, Robert (L.) (cin): I, Desire; Tarantulas: The Deadly Cargo
Morrison, Shelley (act): The Horrible House On the Hill; The Night That Panicked America
Morrison, Sue (act): Shock Chamber
Morrison, Sunshine Sammy (act): Ghosts On the Loose; Spooks RunWild
Morrison, T.J. (wri): Stop Press Girl
Morrison, Temeura (act): Barb Wire; The Island of Dr. Moreau (1996)
Morrison, Toni (wri, b. 1931): Beloved
Morriss, Tom (act): Maria Marten (1928); Mike and the Miser
Morrissette, Billy (act): Severed Ties
Morrissey, Carol (act): The Toxic Avenger, Part II
Morrissey, David (act): Robin Hood (1991)
Morrissey, Kevin (act): Primal Scream
Morrissey, Neil (act): Paint Me a Murder
Morrissey, Paul (dir, b. 1939): Frankenstein (1974); The Hound Of The Baskervilles (1978)

Morrissey, Paul (wri, b. 1939): Dracula (1974); Frankenstein (1974); The Hound of the Baskervilles (1978)
Morrisson, Doug (act): Copycat
Morrone, Dina (act): Quest for the Mighty Sword
Morros, Boris (mus): Bulldog Drummond Comes Back
Morrow, Brad (act): I've Lived Before; The Vampire (1957)
Morrow, Byron (act): Black Zoo; Colossus: The Forbin Project; Dark Mansions; The Ghost of Flight 401; Night Gallery; Panic In Year Zero; The Resurrection of Zachary Wheeler
Morrow, "Cousin" Bruce (act): Stigma
Morrow, Douglas (wri): Beyond a Reasonable Doubt
Morrow, Edward (act): Wizards of the Lost Kingdom
Morrow, Jeff (act, 1907-1993): The Creature Walks Among Us; The Giant Claw; Hour of Decision;Kronos (1957); Legacy of Blood;
Octaman; Sign of the Pagan; This Island Earth
Morrow, Jo (act): Doctor Death: Seeker of Souls;13 Ghosts; The Three Worlds of Gulliver
Morrow, Mari (act): Bodily Harm; Children of the Corn III: Urban Sacrifice; Virtuosity
Morrow, Neyle (act): Man-Eater of Kumaon; Mark of the Gorilla; Shock Corridor; Valley of the Headhunters
Morrow, Rob (act, b. 1962): The Island of Dr. Moreau (1996)
Morrow, Scotty (act): The Cosmic Man
Morrow, Sharonlyn (act): Twister
Morrow, Susan (act): Cat-Women of the Moon; Macabre (1958)
Morrow, Vic (act, 1932-1982): Curse of the Black Widow; The Evictors; Great White; Humanoids from the Deep; The Man With the Power; Message from Space; The Night That Panicked America; Target: Harry; Twilight Zone
Morrow, Vic (dir, 1932-1982): Deathwatch (1967)
Morrow, William (wri): The Road to Bali
Morse, Barry (act, b. 1919): Asylum (1972); The Changeling; Covenant; Daughter of Darkness (1948); Destination Moonbase Alpha; Funeral Home; No Trace; The Return of Sherlock Holmes (1986); The Shape of Things to Come (1979); The Telephone Book; Thunder Rock; Welcome to Blood City
Morse, Carlton E. (wri): I Love a Mystery (1966)
Morse, David (act): Contact; Extreme Measures; The Good Son; The Long Kiss Goodnight; Prototype; 12 Monkeys
Morse, Fuzzbee (mus): Dark Angel: The Ascent; Dolls; Ghoulies II
Morse, Hamilton (act): The Invisible Fear
Morse, Helen (act, b. 1948): Agatha; Picnic at Hanging Rock
Morse, Heyward (act): Tam Lin
Morse, Hilary (act): Girlfriend from Hell
Morse, Hollingsworth (dir):Daughters of Satan
Morse, Judith (act): Little Shop of Horrors (1986); Santa Claus (1985)
Morse, Mary Kay (act): Kiss Meets the Phantom of the Park
Morse, Melanie (act): Prom Night
Morse, Richardson (act): Contact
Morse, Robert (act, b. 1931): Calendar Girl Murders; The Loved One; Oh Dad Poor Dad, Mamma's Hung You In the Closet and I'm Feelin' So Sad
Morse, Robin (act):Sabu and the Magic Ring
Morse, Terrell/Terry (O.) (dir, b. 1906): British Intelligence; Dangerous Money; Fog Island; Gojira; Shadows Over Chinatown; Unknown World
Morshower, Glenn (act): The Bermuda Triangle; Dead and Buried; Dominion; The Philadelphia Experiment; Star Trek: Generations
Mort, Patricia (act): Attempt to Kill; Time to Remember
Morten, Gregory (act): The Destructors
Mortensen, Lia D. (act): Blink
Mortensen, Viggo (act, b. 1958): The Crew; Daylight; Leatherface:Texas Chainsaw Massacre III; A Perfect Murder; The Prophecy (1995); Prison (1988); Psycho (1998); The Reflecting Skin; Vanishing Point (1997)
Mortil, Janne (act): The Clan of the Cave Bear
Mortimer, Chapman (wri):Reflections In a Golden Eye
Mortimer, Charles (act): Dial 999 (1955); Discipline; Living dangerously; The Return of Bulldog Drummond; Someone at the Door; Triumph of Sherlock Holmes
Mortimer, Douglas (act): Deathstalker II: Duel of the Titans
Mortimer, Edward (act): The Devil Bat
Mortimer, Emily (act): The Ghost and the Darkness; The Saint
Mortimer, Ian (act): Something Is Out There
Mortimer, Joan (act): Henry Aldrich Haunts a House
Mortimer, John (wri, b. 1923): Bunny Lake Is Missing; The Running Man (1963)
Mortimer, Malcolm (act): Quicksands of Life
Mortimer, Penelope (wri): Bunny Lake Is Missing
Mortimer, Tricia/Trisha (act): Frightmare (1974); Perfect Friday; Schizo (1977)
Morton, Antony (act): Performance
Morton, Arthur (mus, b. 1908): Topper (1937)
Morton, Bruce (act): The Toxic Avenger
Morton, Clive (act, b. 1904): All Hallowe'en; The Alphabet Murders; The Clue of the New Pin (1961); Dead men Tell No Tales (1938); I Thank a Fool; Jane Eyre (1970); Kind Hearts and Coronets; The Lavender Hill Mob; Night Without Stars; Richard III (1955); Stranger In the House (1967); Turn the Key Softly; Zeppelin
Morton, Cyril (act): The Basilisk; The Cat and the Chestnuts; The Curtain; The Guest of the Evening; The Strange Case of Philip Kent; The Tragedy of Basil Grieve;Winning His Stripes
Morton, Elizabeth (act): Lifeforce
Morton, Gabrielle (act): The Clue of the Second Goblet; The Great Office Mystery
Morton, Gregory (act): The Flight That Disappeared; Johnny Cool; The Mephisto Waltz
Morton, Howard (act, 1925-1997): Rhinoceros (1974)
Morton, Hugh (act): Assignment Redhead; Deadlock (1943); The Floating Dutchman;Mark of the Devil (1985)
Morton, Joe (act): The Brother from Another Planet;The Clairvoyant (1985); Forever Young; Of Mice and Men (1992); Stranded; Terminator 2: Judgment Day
Morton, John (act): The Empire Strikes Back; Flash Gordon (1980)
Morton, John (wri): Panic In Year Zero
Morton, Judee (act): The Slime People; Zotz!
Morton, Julian (act): Wolfman (1979)
Morton, Lisa (wri): Adventures In Dinosaur City
Morton, Marjorie (act): The Unholy Three (1925)
Morton, Mary (act): The English Rose
Morton, May (act): The Debt of Gambling; In the Toils of the Blackmailer; Polly the Girl Scout and the Jewel Thieves
Morton, Michael (wri): Alibi (1931)
Morton, Mickey (act): Fire and Ice
Morton, Phil (act): Monster A Go-Go
Morton, Rob (act): Quarantine
Morton, Rocky (dir): D.O.A. (1988); Super Mario Bros.
Morton, Roy (act): Blood of Ghastly Horror
Morton, Sally (act): Mad Max Beyond Thunderdome
Morton, Sam (act): Storm of the Century
Morton, Samantha (act): Jane Eyre (1997)
Mortorff, Larry (act): Full Eclipse
Morucha (act): El Amor Brujo (1972)
Morum, William (wri): The Late Edwina Black
Morwell, Robert (act): The Howling: New Moon Rising
Moscartolo, Jonas (act): Ernest Scared Stupid
Moscati, Italo (wri): The Night Porter
Moschin, Gastone (act): El Invencible Hombre Invisible
Moschitta Jr., John (act): Dick Tracy (1990)
Mosco, maisie (wri): Girly
Moscovenko, Anne Marie (act): Castle Keep
Moscovich, Maurice (act): Lancer Spy
Moscovitch, Noel (act): see Madison, Noel
Moscow, David (act): Big
Moseiwitsch, Pamela (act):The Mind of Mr. Soames
Moseley, Alice (act): Flying from Justice; With Human Instinct
Moseley, Bill (act): Crash and Burn; Endangered Species; Fair Game (1988); The First Power; OSA; Silent Night, Deadly Night III
Moseley Jr., Irwin (act): Trancers II: The Return of Jack Deth
Moseley, Jerry (mus): Frightmare (1983)
Moseley, Leonard (wri): They Can't Hang Me
Moseley, Page (act): Edge of the Axe
Moseley, Robert (act): see Madison, Guy
Mosely, Bill (act): The Texas Chainsaw Massacre 2
Moseng, Eric (act): Star Crystal
Moser, Hans (act): State Secret
Moser, Margot (act): There Goes the Bride
Moser, Sonia (act): Legend of the Lost
Moses, Albert (act): An American Werewolf In London;Octopussy
Moses, Christina (act): Secrets In the Attic
Moses, David (act): see Moses, (Jonathan) David
Moses, (Jonathan) David (act): Creature; The Magician (1973); Scared to Death (1980)
Moses, Jared (act): The Zero Boys
Moses, Mark (act): Dead Men Don't Die
Moses, Nancy (act): Phantom of the Paradise
Moses, Norman (act): The Unearthing
Moses, Sam (act): Short Circuit 2
Moses, William (R.) (act): Alien from L.A.; Almost Dead; Circumstances Unknown; Emma's Wish; The Fiance; Fun; The Haunting of Seacliff Inn
Moses Jr., William (act & mus): Mutants In Paradise
Mosher, Bob (wri): Munster, Go Home!
Moskau, Shari (act): Neon Maniacs
Moskel Jr., John (act): Scared to Death (1980)
Moskoff, John (act): The Goddess of Love
Moskvin, Andrei (cin, 1901-1961): Shinel (1926)
Mosley, Bill (act): Night of the Living Dead (1990)
Mosley, Lucky (act): Deadly Blessing
Mosley, Roger E. (act): Cruise Into Terror; Heart Condition
Mosley, Bryan (act): Get Carter
Mosquera, Gustavo (dir): Moebius; Times to Come
Mosquera, Gustavo (wri): Moebius
Moss, Arnold (act, 1909-1989): The Black Book; The Fool Killer; Gambit; The Loves of Carmen (1948);Mask of the Avenger; Salome (1953); Temptation (1945); The 27th Day
Moss, Bertha (act): El Vampiro Sangriento
Moss, Carrie-Anne (act): The Matrix
Moss, Delbert (act): The New House On the Left
Moss, Don (act): The Dungeonmaster
Moss, Elisabeth (act): Escape to Witch Mountain (1995); Midnight's Child; Once Upon aForest; Separate Lives
Moss, Gerald (cin): Virgin Witch
Moss, Harry (act): For Mother's Sake
Moss, Hugh (dir): Sexton Blake v. Baron Kettler
Moss, Jack (act): Journey Into Fear (1942)
Moss, James (Austral act): Inn of the Damned
Moss, James (USA act): Man-Eater of Kumaon
Moss, Maitland (act): Fury at Smugglers' Bay
Moss, Mark (act): Billion Dollar Brain
Moss, Michael H. (act): The Night Flier
Moss, Mireille (act): The City of Lost Children
Moss, Pat (act): Mutant
Moss, Paul (act): The Black Windmill
Moss, Russell (act): Night of the Creeps
Moss, Stewart (act): The Bat People; Doctor Death: Seeker of Souls; Live Again, Die Again; The Tribe
Moss, Stirling (act): Casino Royale
Mossbacher, Peter (act): The Face of Fu Manchu
Mossberg, Karin (act): The Big Cube
Mossman, James (act): Masquerade
Mossman, John (act): Horror of Dracula
Most, Don (act): Acting On Impulse; Dead Man's Island
Mostel, Josh (act): The Brother from Another Planet; The Maddening
Mostel, Zero (act, 1915-1977): The Angel Levine; Journey into Fear (1975); Rhinoceros (1974);Watership Down
Mostovoy, Leo (act): The Adventures of Hajji Baba
Mostow, Jon (act & wri): Beverly Hills Bodysnatchers
Mostow, Jon (dir): Beverly Hills Bodysnatchers; Flight of Black Angel
Moszkowicz, Roman (act):The Element of Crime
Mote, D. Brent (wri): Earthquake In New York; Night Visitors
Motheny, Andi (act):What We Did That Night
Mothersbaugh, Mark (mus): Slaughterhouse Rock
Motherwell, Phil (act): Mad Max; Stir
Motley Crue (mus): Demons (1985)
Motli, Nasser Malak (act): Ten Little Indians (1974)
Motomochi, Eibi (act): The X from Outer Space
Motoki, Masahiro (act): The Mystery of Rampo
Motorhead (mus): Phenomena; She (1983); Zombie Nightmare
Motoyoshi (dir): Godzilla Raids Again
Mott, Nancy (act): One Dark Night
Mott, Zachary/Zack (Bill) (act): The Dark Half; Lady Beware
Motta, Bess (act): The Terminator
Mottershaw, Frank (dir): The Blackmailer; The Coiners; The Dodgers Dodged; An Eccentric Burglary; The Eccentric Thief; The Impossible Lovers; Willie's Dream
Mottola, Tony (mus): Violated
Mottram, Anna (act): The Lifetaker; Xtro
Motulsky, Judy (act): Spawn of the Slithis
Moulan, Rosita (act): Creatures the World Forgot
Moulden, Prentiss (act): Beyond the Living
Moulder-Brown, John (act): The House That Screamed; Night Without Pity; Operation Third Form; Rumpelstiltskin (1987); Vampire Circus
Moulton, Charles (wri): The New, Original Wonder Woman;Wonder Woman
Moundroukas, Tony (act): Eat and Run
Mount, David (act): Dragonslayer; Silent Night,Deadly Night III
Mount, Sheri (act): Silent Night, Deadly Night III
Mountain, Charles (act): Damien-Omen II
Mountain, Terence "Terry" (act): Macbeth (1971); On Her Majesty's Secret Service
Mourer, Maryse (act): see Carol, Martine
Mousswau, Steve (act): Darkman II: The Return of Durant
Moustache (act): Zorro (1975)
Moustafa, Amira (act): Dangerous Money; Queen of the Amazons (1947)
Mouton, Benjamin (act): Flatliners; The Puppet Masters; Sister, Sister
Mouton, Kufaru Aaron (act):Angel Heart
Mouzakiotis, Priscilla (act):The Kiss (1988)
Movar, Dunja (act): Hamlet (1960)
Movila, Irina (act): Subspecies
Movin, Lisben (act): The Red Mantle
Movin, Lisbeth (act): Vredens Dag
Movita (act): Tower of Terror
Mowbray, Alan (act, 1896-1969): Abbott and Costello Meet the Killer; Androcles and the Lion; Around the World In 80 Days;Berkeley Square; Blackbeard the Pirate; The Boys from Syracuse; Charlie Chan In London; I Wake Up Screaming; The Lone Wolf and His Lady; Lured; The Man WhoKnew Too Much (1956); The Phantom of 42nd Street; Roman Scandals; Sherlock Holmes (1932); A Study In Scarlet (1933); Terror by Night; Topper (1937); Topper Takes a Trip; The Villain Still Pursued Her
Mowbray, Daphne (act): The Callbox Mystery
Mowbray, Henry (act): Murder by Television
Mowbray, Tom (act): The Brass Bottle (1914); Dick Turpin's Ride to York
Mower, Jack (act): Cry Wolf (1947); The Devil's Assistant; The Invisible Menace; The Maltese Falcon (1941); The Return of Dr. X; The Shock (1923); Torchy Plays With Dynamite; Torchy Runs for Mayor
Mower, Patrick (act): Catch Me a Spy; Cry of the Banshee; The Devil Rides Out; Doctors Wear Scarlet
Mowod, John (act): Revenge of the Living Zombies
Mowry, Pat (act): Missile to the Moon
Moxey, Hugh (act): The Case of the River Morgue; The Final Conflict; The SnakeWoman; Spaceways; You Pay Your Money
Moxey, John (Llewellyn) (dir, b. 1920): Circus of Fear; City of the Dead; The Cradle Will Fall; Death Trap (1962); Downfall; Escape; Face of a Stranger; Genesis II; Home for the Holidays; The House That Wouldn't Die; I, Desire; The Last Child; The Night Stalker (1971); No Place to Hide (1981); The Power Within (1979); Ricochet; Sanctuary of Fear; The Strange and Deadly Occurrence; Strangler's Web; A Taste of Evil; Through Naked Eyes; Where Have All the People Gone?
Moxon, Henry (act): Threads
Moy, Wood (act): Howard the Duck; Invasion of the Body Snatchers (1978)
Moya, Javier (act): Anguish
Moya, Stella (act): The Scarab Murder Case
Moya, Victoria (act): see Cristal, Linda
Moyens, Judi (act): The Hound of the Baskervilles (1959)
Moyer, Betty (act): Child of Darkness, Child of Light
Moyer, Tawny (act): Halloween II; Looker
Moyheddin, Zia (act): Deadlier Than the Male; They Came from Beyond Space; Work Is a Four Letter Word
Moyle, Allan (act): Rabid
Moyle, Allan (wri): Red Blooded American Girl
Moynihan, Joseph Patrick (act): Mars Attacks!
Moyse, Mr. (act): The Beryl Coronet; The Copper Beeches; The Musgrave Ritual (1912); The Mystery of Boscombe Vale; The Reigate Squires (1912); Silver Blaze (1912); The Speckled Band (1912); The Stolen Papers

Mozart, George (act): The Bank Messenger Mystery; Dr. Sin Fang; The Mystery of the Mary Celeste; Overcoat Sam
Mozart, Wolfgang Amadeus (mus, 1756-1791): I Love You, I Kill You; Kind Hearts and Coronets
Moze, Doreen (act): Rana: The Legend of Shadow Lake
Mozelle, Maurice B. (act): Too Many Winners
Mozerolle, Arlene (act): Storm of the Century
Mozhukhin, Ivan (act, 1889-1939): Pikovaya Dama (1916)
Mozzato, Umberto (act): Cabiria
Mruwka, Gunther (act): I Aim at the Stars
Mucari, Carlo (act): Obsession: A Taste for Fear
Mucci, David (act): Prom Night
Much, Richard (act): The Inn On the River
Mudie, Leonard (act, 1882-1965): The Adventures of Robin Hood; African Treasure; Arrest Bulldog Drummond; British Intelligence; Bulldog Drummond at Bay (1947); Charlie Chan's Murder Cruise; The Golden Idol; The Jungle Girl; Killer Leopard; League of Frightened Men; Lord of the Jungle; The Magnetic Monster; A Message from Mars (1921); The Mummy (1932); The Mysterious Mr. Moto; The Mystery of Mr. X; Safari Drums; The Scarlet Clue; The Story of Mankind
Mudry, Elizabeth (act): Scanners
Mueck, Ron (act): Labyrinth (1986)
Muehl, Brian (act): The Dark Crystal
Mueller, Barbara (act): The Dungeonmaster
Mueller, Carl (act): Dead Connection
Mueller, Cat (act): Seven
Mueller, Charles (act): The Package
Mueller, Dick (act): Stalking Laura
Mueller, John (act): Return to Horror High; Shocker
Mueller, Marvin (act): see Miller, Marvin
Mueller, Maureen (act): Poltergeist III; She Woke Up
Mueller, Merrill (act): Seven Days to Noon
Mueller, Paul (act): The Secret of Seagull Island
Mueller, Robby (cin): The Glass Cell
Muellerleile, Marianne (act): Curse II: The Bite
Mueller-Stahl, Armin (act, b. 1930): The Game; The Peacemaker (1997); Theodore Rex; The X-Files
Muenster, Klaus (act): The Glass Cell
Muffly, Anne (act): Jack's Wife
Mugavero, Frank (act): School Spirit
Muggleton, Amanda (act): Thirst
Muggli, Debbie (act): Nemesis 3: Time Lapse
Muhe, Ulrich (act): Funny Games
Muhoro, Kahara (act): Congo
Muhtar, Mehmet (dir): Drakula Istanbulda
Mui, Anita (act): The Heroic Trio
Muir, Brian Dominic (wri): Critters
Muir, Darren (act): Impulse (1984)
Muir, David (act): Neon Maniacs
Muir, David (cin): Lust for a Vampire
Muir, Douglas (act): The Sound Barrier
Muir, Frank (act): The Clouded Crystal
Muir, Gavin (act, 1909-1972): Abbott and Costello Meet the Invisible Man; The Abductors; Charlie Chan at the Race Track; The House of Fear (1945); Island of Lost Women; Night Tide; Passport to Suez; Rogues of Sherwood Forest; Sherlock Holmes Faces Death; The Son of Dr. Jekyll; Temptation (1946)
Muir, Jean (act, b. 1911): The Lone Wolf Meets a Lady; A Midsummer Night's Dream (1935); Strip Tease Murder; The Ugly Duckling; The White Cockatoo
Muirhead, Oliver (act): Tarzan In Manhattan
Mukai, Marcus (act): When Time Ran Out
Mukai, Shizuka (act): The Toxic Avenger, Part II
Mukherjee, Prabhat Kumer (wri): Devi
Mukherjee, Purnendu (act): Devi
Mulcahy, Jacinta (act): Frankenstein (1993)
Mulcahy, Russell (dir): Blue Ice; Highlander; Highlander 2: The Quickening; Razorback; The Shadow (1994)
Mulcaster, G.H. (act): Contraband Spain; Downfall; The Dummy Talks; Lady of Vengeance; Overcoat Sam; The Patient Vanishes; The River House Mystery (1935); Under Capricorn
Mulcaster, Michael (act): Brides of Dracula; The Curse of Frankenstein; The Hound of the Baskervilles (1959); The Pirates of Blood River
Muldaur, Diana (act, b. 1938): Chosen Survivors; Hercules and the Princess of Troy; Ordeal; The Other (1972); Planet Earth; The Swimmer
Muldoon, Michael (act): Excalibur
Muldoon, Patrick (act): Starship Troopers
Muldowney, Dominic (mus): 1984 (1984)
Mule, Francesco (act): Dr. Goldfoot and the Girl Bombs; Psycosissimo
Mulgrew, Kate (act, b. 1955): Lovespell; Remo Williams: The Adventure Begins; Riddler's Moon; A Stranger Is Watching
Mulhall, Jack (act, 1888-1979): The Ape Man; The Atomic Submarine; Black Friday; Charlie Chan at the Race Track; The Clutching Hand; Destination Saturn; Dick Tracy vs. Crime, Inc.; The Drums of Jeopardy (1923); Face In the Fog (1935); The Falcon In Danger; Hell's Headquarters; In the Next Room; The Invisible Ghost; Kelly of the Secret Service; Murder Will Out (1930); The She-Creature; Sirens of the Sea; The Son of Monte Cristo; Up In Smoke
Mulhare, Edward (act, 1923-1997): Eye of the Devil; Megaforce; Our Man Flint; Signpost to Murder
Mulhern, Scott (act): Looker
Mulheron, Danny (act): Dark of the Night; Meet the Feebles
Mulheron, Danny (wri): Meet the Feebles
Mulholland, Declan (act): Double Exposure (1977); Hawk the Slayer; The Land That Time Forgot; The Quatermass Conclusion; Theater of Blood
Mulholland, Gordon (act): A Christmas Carol (1960); Treasure Island (1950)
Mulholland, Jim (wri): Amazon Women On the Moon
Muliawan, Fabian (act): Making Contact
Mulin, Sidney (cin): The Magic Voyage of Sinbad
Mulkey, Chris (act): Deadbolt; Dead Cold; Dreamscape; Ghost In the Machine; Jack's Back; Runaway (1984); Timerider
Mulkey, Randy (act): Natas...The Reflection
Mull, Martin (act): Cutting Class; Miracle Beach
Mullally, Megan (act): Once Bitten
Mullane, Liz (act): The Frighteners
Mullaney, Jack (act): The Absent-Minded Professor (1961); Dr. Goldfoot and the Bikini Machine
Mullany, Don (wri): Mystery of the Wax Museum
Mullard, Arthur (act): The Bank Raiders; The Vault of Horror
Mullavey, Greg (act, b. 1939): Body Count (1987); The Disappearance of Flight 412; I Dismember Mama; Not Quite Human II
Mullen, Barbara (act, 1914-1979): Corridor of Mirrors; A Place of One's Own; Thunder Rock; The Very Edge
Mullen, Beckie (act): Sinful Intrigue
Mullen, Jeremy (act): Surf Nazis Must Die
Mullen, Jessica (act): Surf Nazis Must Die
Mullen, Kathryn (act): The Empire Strikes Back
Mullen, Patty (act): Doom Asylum; Frankenhooker
Mullen, Ruth (act): Making Mr. Right
Mullen, Sadie (act): Jane Eyre (1921)
Mullen, Stuart (act): Judge Dredd
Mullenger, Donna (act): see Reed, Donna
Muller, Christiane (act): Jo
Muller, Edward (dir): Savage Island
Muller, Elizabeth (act): Confess, Dr. Corda
Muller, Endre (act): Jack the Ripper (1958)
Muller, Geoffrey (dir): The Last Train; The Unseeing Eye; The Witness
Muller, Harrison (act): The Final Executioner; She (1983); 2020 Texas Gladiators; Warriors of the Wasteland
Muller Jr., Harrison (act): Warriors of the Wasteland
Muller, Herb (act): Jaws 2
Muller, Hero (act): The Fourth Man
Muller, Jo Maxwell (act): A Hitch In Time
Muller, Lillian (act): The Devil and Max Devlin
Muller, Marti (act): Switch (1991)
Muller, Martin (act): Chinese Boxes
Muller, Paul (act): Black Devils of Kali; Count Dracula; La Figlia di Frankenstein; The Minotaur; Revenge of the Pirates; Treasure Island (1971); I Vampiri; Virgin Among the Living Dead; Women of Devil's Island
Muller, Robby (cin): The Believers; Jonathan; Repo Man
Muller, Robert (wri): The Hunchback of Notre Dame (1977); Woman of Straw
Muller, Roby (cin): When Pigs Fly
Muller, Rolf (act): Cyborg (1989)
Muller, Romeo (wri): The Flight of Dragons; The Hobbit; The Return of the King
Muller, Rudolph (act): see Miller, Martin
[illegible]
Muller-Grad, Kurt (act): The Naked Woman and Satan
Mulligan, Barret (act): Slayground
Mulligan, Pat (act): Kill Me Again
Mulligan, Richard (act, b. 1932): Babes In Toyland (1986); Dog's Best Friend; Guess Who's Coming for Christmas?; The Heavenly Kid; Oliver & Company
Mulligan, Robert (dir, b. 1925): The Other (1972)
Mulligan, Terry David (act): Deadly Sins; The Haunting Passion
Mullin, Donna (act): Darkman II: The Return of Durant
Mullin, Jeff (act): I Was a Teen-Age Mummy
Mullin, Scott (act): I Was a Teen-Age Mummy
Mullinar, Rod (act): Patrick; Thirst
Mullings, Sharon (act): To Die For
Mullins, Bartlett (act): Frankenstein Created Woman; Peeping Tom; Tales from the Crypt (1971); Trog
Mullins, Ray (act): Dr. Caligari
Mullion, Annabel (act): Mission: Impossible
Mullowney, Debrah (act): Cellar Dweller
Muloc(k), Al (act): Battle Beneath the Earth; Call Me Bwana; Death Over My Shoulder; Game for Three Losers; Tarzan's Greatest Adventure; Tarzan the Magnificent; A Witch Without a Broom
Mulot, Claude (dir & wri): The Blood Rose
Mulqueen, Kathleen (act): The Night Walker
Mulroney, Dermot (act): Copycat; Point of No Return; The Trigger Effect
Mulroney, Kieran (act): Heart Condition; Sensation (1994)
Mulvey, Anne (act): A Question of Suspense
Mulville, Jimmy (act): Morons from Outer Space
Mumford, Cecil G. (wri): Lorna Doone (1922)
Mumy, Bill(y) (act, b. 1954): Alfred Hitchcock Presents; Captain America (1992); Twilight Zone
Mumy, Seth (act): Three Wishes (1995)
Munafo, Tony (act): Daylight
Muncke, Christopher (act): Saturn 3
Munday, Mary (act): Magic; Serpent Island
Munday, Olivia (act): The Deadly Females
Mundell, Michael (act): Maroc 7; Straw Dogs
Munden, Elizabeth (act): The Village of the Damned (1960)
Munden, Maxwell (dir): The Bank Raiders; The House In the Woods
Munden, Maxwell (wri): The House In the Woods; The Man On the Cliff
Mundin, Herbert (act, 1898-1939): The Adventures of Robin Hood; Ashes; Chandu the Magician; Charlie Chan's Secrets; Sherlock Holmes (1932); Tarzan Escapes
Mundy, Ed (act): Carousel
Mundy, Meg (act): Eyes of Laura Mars; Fatal Attraction
Mundy, Robert (wri): The Visitor
Mune, Ian (act): Sleeping Dogs (1977)
Mune, Ian (dir): The Bridge to Nowhere
Mung, Dennis (act): Warriors of Virtue
Mungai, David (act): Congo
Munger, Chris (dir): Kiss of the Tarantula
Mungle, Matthew (cin): Pranks
Muni (act): Belle de Jour; The Discreet Charm of the Bourgeoisie
Muni, Paul (act, 1895-1967, nee Muni Weisenfreund): Angel On My Shoulder (1946); Stranger On the Prowl
Munier, Ferdinand (act): Arrest Bulldog Drummond
Munkell, Hans (wri): La Noche de Walpurgis
Munn, Alecia (act): Alien High
Munna, T.M. (act): Il Montagna di Dio Cannibale
Munne, Pep (act): Where Time Began
Munos, Carlos (act): El Otro Fu-Manchu
Munoz, Anais (act): Strange Days
Munoz, Loli (act): House of 1,000 Dolls
Munoz, Maybelle (act): Target...Earth?
Munoz, Michael (act): Like Father, Like Santa
Munro, Alan (cin): Addams Family Values; Beetlejuice; A Nightmare On Elm Street 5: The Dream Child
Munro, Caroline (act, b. 1951): The Abominable Dr. Phibes; At the Earth's Core; The Black Cat (1990); Captain Kronos: Vampire Hunter; Don't Open Till Christmas; Dracula A.D. 1972; The Golden Voyage of Sinbad; I Don't Want to Be Born; The Last Horror Film; Maigret; Maniac (1980); Slaughter High; The Spy Who Loved Me; Star Crash
Munro, Douglas (act): Arsene Lupin; Broken Barrier; Flames; The Foreman's Treachery; The Game of Liberty; The King's Outcast; On His Majesty's Service; The Princess of Happy Chance; Rupert of Hentzau (1915); The Sons of Satan; Trilby (1914); The Two Roads; Vice Versa (1916); The Woman Who Was Nothing
Munro, Eileen (act): The Crime at Blossoms; Paris Plane
Munro, George (wri): Sensation (1937)
Munro, James (wri): Innocent Bystanders
Munro, Janet (act, 1934-1972): Darby O'Gill and the Little People; The Day the Earth Caught Fire; Hide and Seek; A Jolly Bad Fellow; Life for Ruth; The Trollenberg Terror
Munro, Lochlyn (act): Mother, May I Sleep With Danger?; Them (1996); Trancers 5: Sudden Deth
Munro, Neil (act): Gate II
Munro, Nina (act): The Golden Web
Munro, Pauline (act): The Committee; Strangler's Web
Munro, Robert Hale (act): see Hale, Sonnie
Munro, Stanley (wri): The Trygon Factor
Munroe, Carmen (act): Naked Evil
Munrow, David (mus): Zardoz
Munson, Art (act): Phantom of the Paradise
Munson, Chris (act): Bloodspell
Munson, Ona (act, 1906-1955, nee Ona Wolcott): Drums of the Congo; The Red House
Munson (III), Warren (A.) (act): The Bermuda Triangle; Friday the 13th, Part VIII-Jason Takes Manhattan
Munt, Peter (act): Hands of the Ripper; The House In Nightmare Park
Muntz, Kelly Jo (act): A Nightmare On Elm Street 5: The Dream Child
Munzar, Ludek (act): Ikaria XB1
Murad (act): Tarzan Goes to India
Murado Jr., Renato (act): The Blood Drinkers
Muraire, Jules (act): see Raimu
Murakami, Fuyuki (act): Battle In Outer Space; Gojira; The Mysterians
Murakami, Ioshio (act): Mystery On Monster Island
Murakami, Jimmy T. (dir): Battle Beyond the Stars (1980); When the Wind Blows
Muramatsu, Hideko (act): Kwaidan
Murari, Kamal (act): Never-Never Land
Murata, Takeo (wri): Godzilla Raids Again; Gojira; Half-Human; Rodan, the Flying Monster
Murcell, George (act): Blood of the Vampire; Crossroads to Crime; Kaleidoscope; Penny Gold; The Pursuers
Murch, Walter (dir): Return to Oz
Murch, Walter (wri): Return to Oz; THX 1138
Murchison, Jim (act): My Bloody Valentine
Murcott, Derek (act): Eat and Run; Sin You Sinners
Murcott, Joel (wri): Dick Turpin-Highwayman; Manfish
Murdocco, Vince (act): Flesh Gordon 2: Flesh Gordon Meets the Cosmic Cheerleaders
Murdoch, Laura (act): Timecop
Murdoch, Richard (act, 1907-1990): The Ghost Train (1941); It Happened In Soho; The Terror (1938)
Murdock, Alec (act): Moon 44
Murdock, George (act): Disaster In Time; Earthquake; A Howling In the Woods; Night Gallery; Retribution (1988); Star Trek V: The Final Frontier; The Sword and the Sorcerer
Murdock, Jack (act): Altered States
Murdock, Kermit (act): The Andromeda Strain; On a Clear Day You Can See Forever
Murdock, Rod (act): The Night Evelyn Came Out of the Grave
Murdock, Tim (act): Philo Vance Returns
Muren, Dennis (cin): Dragonslayer; Equinox; Ghostbusters II; Return of the Jedi
Murert, Isiah (act): King Solomon's Mines (1985)
Muretta, G. (wri): Il Mostro di Venezia
Murfin, Jane (wri): The Savage; Seven Keys to Baldpate (1929)
Murgia, Antonella (act): Anguish
Muri, David (cin): Neither the Sea Nor the Sand
Murill, John (cin): The Day Time Ended
Murlowski, John (dir): Amityville: A New Generation
Murnane, Mary (act): In the Days of Saint Patrick
Murnau, F.W. (dir, 1889-1931): Faust (1926); Der Januskopf; Der Letzte Mann; Nosferatu, eine Symphonie des Grauens; Phantom (1922); Satanas; Schloss Vogelod; Tabu
Murney, Christopher (act): Maximum Overdrive; Murder by the Book
Murnik, Peter (act): Body Parts (1991); Disturbed
Muro, James (act): Strange Days
Muro, Jim (dir, b. 1965): Street Trash
Murphey, Mark (act): Alien Nation
Murphey, Michael S. (wri): The Supernaturals; Trick or Treat

Murphy, Alex (act): *Madman*

Murphy, Allen (act): *Scalpel*

Murphy, Antonia (act): *Those Dear Departed*

Murphy, Ben (act, b. 1942): *Code Name: Minus One; The CradleWill Fall; Time Walker*

Murphy, Bill (act): *It Happens Every Spring*

Murphy, Bri (act): *Teenage Zombies*

Murphy, Brian (act): *The Devils*

Murphy, Brittany (act): *Freeway*

Murphy, Cathy (act): *Edge of Sanity*

Murphy, Charles (act): *Nightmare In Blood*

Murphy, Charles (wri): *Vampire In Brooklyn*

Murphy, Charles Thomas (act): *The Two Worlds of Jennie Logan*

Murphy, Chris(topher) (act): *Asteroid; The Hidden II; Jacob's Ladder; Poltergeist III; Quest for the Mighty Sword*

Murphy, Christopher (act): *Attack of the Monsters; Gammera vs. Guiron*

Murphy, David (act): *Jekyll and Hyde...Together Again*

Murphy, Dennis (wri): *Eye of the Devil*

Murphy, Dick (act): *Invasion of the Bee Girls*

Murphy, Donald (act): *Dracula (1931, English-speaking version); Frankenstein's Daughter (1958); Killer Leopard; On the Threshold of Space*

Murphy, E. Danny (act): *Graduation Day*

Murphy, Donna (act): *Star Trek: Insurrection*

Murphy, Eddie (act, b. 1961): *Dr. Dolittle (1998); The Golden Child; Mulan; The Nutty Professor (1996); Vampire in Brooklyn*

Murphy, Eddie (wri, b. 1961): *Vampire In Brooklyn*

Murphy, Edna (act): *Tarzan and the Golden Lion*

Murphy, Emmett (act): *Zombie Island Massacre*

Murphy, Eric (act): *Bay Coven*

Murphy, Fidela (act): *Sinful Davey*

Murphy (II), Fred(erick V.) (cin): *Babylon 5: A Call to Arms; Q; River of Souls*

Murphy, Gary (wri): *Without a Clue*

Murphy, Geoff (dir): *Freejack; The Quiet Earth*

Murphy, Geoff (wri): *Dark of the Night*

Murphy, George (act, 1902-1992): *The Arnelo Affair; London by Night (1937); Talk About a Stranger*

Murphy, Gerard (act): *Waterworld*

Murphy, Gerry (act): *The Formula*

Murphy, Gloria (wri): *Summer of Fear*

Murphy, Harry (act): *Appointment for a Killing; Return (1985); Vice Versa (1988)*

Murphy, Jack (act): *Peter Pan (1924)*

Murphy, James (act): *Angels from Hell*

Murphy, Jane (act): *The Deadly Affair*

Murphy, Jimmy (act): *Crashing Las Vegas; The Curse of the Undead; Hold That Hypnotist; Spook Chasers*

Murphy, Joe (act): *The Cat and the Canary (1927)*

Murphy, John (Austral act): *Road Games*

Murphy, John (USA act): *The Hideous Sun Demon*

Murphy, June (act): *Ricochet*

Murphy, Kevin (act): *Mystery Science Theater 3000: The Movie*

Murphy, Kevin (wri): *The Munsters' Scary Little Christmas; Mystery Science Theater 3000: The Movie*

Murphy, Krista (act): *The Haunted (1991)*

Murphy, M.R. (act): *Stuff Stephanie In the Incinerator*

Murphy, Mark (act): *Meteorites!*

Murphy, Mary (act, b. 1931): *Crime and Punishment, U.S.A.; Hell's Island; Houdini (1953);The Intimate Stranger; The Mad Magician; Make Haste to Live; Two Before Zero; When Worlds Collide; Zex*

Murphy, Maurice (act): *Found Alive*

Murphy, Michael (act, b. 1938): *Batman Returns; Cloak and Dagger (1984); Countdown; Count Yorga,Vampire; Phase IV; Shocker; Strange Behavior*

Murphy, Michael D. (cin): *Mirrors*

Murphy, Paul (act): *The Viking Queen*

Murphy, Paul (cin): *Dead End Drive-In; Mighty Morphin Power Rangers*

Murphy, Peter (mus): *Demons 2*

Murphy, Ralph (dir, 1895-1967): *Black Devils of Kali; The Lady In the Iron Mask; The Man In Half Moon Street*

Murphy, Ralph (wri, 1895-1967): *Black Devils of Kali*

Murphy, Reilly (act): *The Body Snatchers*

Murphy, Richard (act): *Eyewitness (1981)*

Murphy, Richard (wri, b. 1912): *The Kidnapping of the President; Les Miserables (1952)*

Murphy, Rosemary (act, b. 1927): *The Attic; Ben; The Hand (1981);You'll Like My Mother*

Murphy, Sharon (act): *The Horror of Party Beach*

Murphy, Steve (act): *Tempting Fate*

Murphy, Tab (wri): *The Hunchback of Notre Dame (1996); My Best Friend Is a Vampire*

Murphy, Terry (act): *Casper*

Murphy, Timothy Patrick (act): *Doin' Time On Planet Earth*

Murphy, Walter (mus): *The Savage Bees*

Murphy, Warren B. (wri): *The Eiger Sanction*

Murphy, William (act): *Fair Wind to Java*

Murphy, William John (act): *Congo*

Murray, Alena (act): *The Three Faces of Eve*

Murray, Andrew (wri): *Britain's Secret Treaty*

Murray, Barbara (GB act, b. 1929): *Another Man's Poison; The Curse of King Tut's Tomb; A Dandy In Aspic; The Dark Man (1951); Death Goes to School; The Frightened Man; Hot Ice; Meet Mr. Lucifer; Mystery Junction; Tales from the Crypt (1971); The Teckman Mystery*

Murray, Barbara (USA act): *The Power (1980)*

Murray, Bernard (act): *The Wicker Man*

Murray, Bert (act): *The Adventures of Dick Turpin-The King of Highwaymen; The Adventures of Dick Turpin-200 Guineas Reward, Dead or Alive*

Murray, Beverly (act): *Cauchemares*

Murray, Bill (Can act): *Empire of Ash III*

Murray, Bill (USA act, b. 1950): *Ed Wood; Ghostbusters; Ghostbusters II; Groundhog Day; Jungle Burger; Little Shop of Horrors (1986); Scrooged; Space Jam*

Murray, Billy (act): *Corruption*

Murray, Brendan (act): *Jaws 3-D*

Murray, Brian Doyle (act): *Ghostbusters II*

Murray, Bryan (act): *Mrs. Santa Claus*

Murray, C.A. (act): *Nightbeast*

Murray, Charlie (act, 1872-1941): *The Gorilla (1927)*

Murray, Chris (cin): *Mad Max; Thirst*

Murray, Christopher (act): *Dante's Peak; She Woke Up;Virtuosity*

Murray, Clayton (act): *Amityville Dollhouse*

Murray, David Christie (wri): *In His Grip*

Murray, Del (act): *The Resurrection of Zachary Wheeler*

Murray, Don (act, b. 1929): *Conquest of the Planet of the Apes; Daughter of the Mind; Ghosts Can't Do It; Made In Heaven; Peggy Sue Got Married;Radioactive Dreams; The Stepford Children; The Viking Queen*

Murray, E.J. (act): *Poltergeist III*

Murray, Forbes (act): *The Falcon's Alibi; The Lone Wolf Spy Hunt; The Phantom Thief*

Murray, Guillermo (act): *Neutron Traps the Invisible Killers*

Murray, Jan (act, b. 1916, nee Murray Janofsky): *The Busy Body; A Man Called Dagger; Tarzan and the Great River;*
Who Killed Teddy Bear?

Murray, Joel (act): *Encino Woman*

Murray, John Fenton (wri): *Arnold; The Atomic Kid; Everything's Ducky; It's Only Money; Sabu and the Magic Ring*

Murray, John T. (act): *After the Thin Man; Charlie Chan Carries On*

Murray, Julie Christy (act):*Mausoleum*

Murray, Kate (wri): *Behind the Curtain*

Murray, Kathleen (act): *Lady Beware*

Murray, Ken (act, 1903-1988, nee Don Court): *The Power (1967); Son of Flubber*

Murray, Lee (act): *City On Fire; Death Ship; Scanners*

Murray, Lyn (mus, 1910-1989): *Casanova's Big Night; Signpost to Murder; Strategy of Terror; To Catch a Thief*

Murray, M. Gray (act): *Beautiful Jim; The Courage of a Coward; Grip (1915); Her Luck In London; In the Grip of Death; London's Yellow Peril; Signal In the Night; Strategy; The Suicide Club (1914)*

Murray, Margaret (act): *The Blue Bird (1910)*

Murray, Max (wri): *Jamaica Run*

Murray, Michael (act): *The Falls; The Ipcress Files; The Stepford Children*

Murray, Michael (wri): *The Lightning Incident*

Murray, Mike (act): *Baffled!*

Murray, Patrick (act): *Haunters of the Deep*

Murray, Paul (dir): *Elstree Calling*

Murray, Pauline (act): *It Happened Here*

Murray, Percy (act): *An Affair of Honour*

Murray, Pete (act): *Otley*

Murray, Peter (act): *Escort for Hire; No Highway In the Sky; The Princess and the Goblin; Transatlantic*

Murray, Rosaleen (act): *Blow-Up*

Murray, Ross (act): *The Lair of the White Worm*

Murray, Ryan (act): *Flight of the Navigator*

Murray, Sean (act): *Hamlet (1990); Hocus Pocus; The Lottery*

Murray, Stephen (act, 1912-1983): *At the Stroke of Nine; The Door In the Wall; For Them That Trespass; Four Sided Triangle; Guilty?; Master Spy (1963); The Stranger's Hand*

Murray, Thelma (act): *Blake the Lawbreaker; The BoscombeValley Mystery (1922); The Mystery of the Silent Death*

Murray, William (dir & wri): *Primal Scream*

Murray, Yvonne (act): *The Dream Doctor*

Murray, Zon (act): *The Lone Ranger*

Murray-Hill, Peter (act, 1908-1957): *At the Villa Rose (1939); The Ghost Train (1941); The Houseof the Arrow (1940); Mr. Reeder In Room 13*

Murrill, Milton Raphiel (act):*Mutator*

Murtagh, Kate (act): *The Night Strangler; Waxwork II:Lost In Time*

Murtaugh, James (F.) (act): *Dr. Scorpion; The Howling; Making Mr. Right; Romeo Is Bleeding; The Rosary Murders; Someone's Watching Me!*

Murton, Lionel (act): *Interpol; The Last Shot You Hear; Zeta One*

Murzynski, Antoni (cin): *Labirynt*

Musante, Tony (act, b. 1936): *Rearview Mirror; L'Uccello delle Piume di Cristallo*

Muscat, Michael/Mike (act): *The Clan of the Cave Bear; Retribution (1988); Scared to Death (1980)*

Muse, Clarence (act, 1889-1979): *An Act of Murder (1948); Flesh and Fantasy; Heaven Can Wait (1943); The Invisible Ghost; The Mind Reader; Murder Over NewYork; Shadow of a Doubt (1943); The Thin Man Goes Home; White Zombie*

Muse, Margaret (act): *Something Evil*

Muse, Robert (act):*The Silence of the Hams*

Musetti, Valentino (act): *Batman (1989)*

Musgrave, Dave (act): *Starship Invasions*

Musgrave, William (act): *Blackie's Redemption*

Musgrove, Gertrude (act): *On the Night of the Fire; The Scarlet Pimpernel (1934)*

Mushroom (act): *Pumpkinhead*

Music, Lorenzo (act): *Oh Heavenly Dog; Twice Upon a Time*

Musik, Pat (act): *An American Tail; The Loch Ness Horror*

Musil, Robert (wri): *Der Junge Torless*

Musker, John (dir): *Aladdin (1992); The Great Mouse Detective; Hercules (1997); The*
Little Mermaid

Musker, John (wri): *Aladdin (1992); Hercules (1997)*

Musmanno, M.A. (wri): *The Last Ten Days of Adolf Hitler*

Mussell, Andrew (act): *Kadoyng*

Musselman, M.M. (wri): *The Three Musketeers (1939)*

Mussenden, Isis (act): *Daylight*

Musser, Larry (act):*The Plutonium Incident*

Mustapha, Ziraoui (act): *The Jewel of the Nile*

Mustari, Anna Maria (act):*Il Trionfo di Ercole*

Mustin, Burt (act): *The Strongest Man In the World; The Witchmaker*

Mustin, Tom (act): *Death Dreams*

Musuraca, Nicholas/Nick (cin, b. 1908): *Bedlam; The Blue Dahlia; Cat People (1942); Cracked Nuts (1931); Curse of the Cat People; Deadline at Dawn; The Falcon In Hollywood; The Gay Falcon; The Hitch-Hiker; I Married a Communist; The Locket; Murder On a Bridle Path; Murder On the Blackboard; Out of the Past*
(1947); The Plot Thickens; The Seventh Victim; The Spiral Staircase (1946); Split Second (1953); The Story of Mankind; Stranger On the Third Floor; Where Danger Lives;The Whip Hand

Musy, Mascia (act): *The Secret of Seagull Island*

Musyka, William (act): *The Package*

Muszynski, Jan (act): *Virus (1980)*

Muth, Ellen (act): *Dolores Claiborne*

Muti, Ornella (act): *Chronicle of a Death Foretold; Flash Gordon (1980); Leonor*

Muzquiz, Carlos (act): *The Black Scorpion (1957)*

Mwangi, Sylvester (act): *Congo*

Myatt, Soren (act): *Offerings*

Mycroft, Walter C. (wri): *Champagne; Elstree Calling; Gipsy Blood; Murder; The Yellow Mask*

Myer, Bess (act): *Necronomicon: Book of the Dead*

Myers, Andy (act): *Curse of Simba; Troubled Waters (1964)*

Myers, Bruce (act): *The Awakening; No Blade of Grass*

Myers, Carmel (act, 1899-1980): *The Dancer of the Nile; The Ghost Talks; The Mad Genius; Sirens of the Sea; Svengali (1931)*

Myers, David (cin): *The Mysterious Monsters*

Myers, Elizabeth (wri): *Blackmailed*

Myers, Fredricka (act): *Pretty Maids All In a Row; The Thirsty Dead*

Myers, Harry (C.) (act, 1882-1938): *The Brass Bottle (1923); A Connecticut Yankee In King Arthur's Court (1921); Convicted*

Myers, Henry (wri): *Murder by the Clock*

Myers, James T. (act): *Burnt Offerings*

Myers, Jennifer (act): *The Slumber Party Massacre*

Myers, Kathleen (act): *Dick Turpin*

Myers, Kevin (act): *The Norsemen*

Myers, Kim (act): *Hellraiser 4: Bloodline; A Nightmare On Elm Street, Part 2: Freddy's Revenge*

Myers, Matt (act): *Mannequin Two: On the Move*

Myers, Monroe (act): *Mission Mars*

Myers, Pauline (act): *How to Make a Monster*

Myers, Peter (wri): *Meet Mr. Lucifer; The Snorkel*

Myers, Stanley (mus): *Blind Date; Caravan to Vaccares; The Day the Screaming Stopped; Dream Child; Frightmare (1974); House of Mortal Sin; House of Whipcord; Incubus (1982); No Way to Treat a Lady; Otley; Paperhouse; Schizo (1977); Sitting Target; Tam Lin; The Watcher In the Woods; The Witches (1990); The Zany Adventures of Robin Hood; The Zero Boys*

Myers, Stevie (act): *The Ultimate Warrior*

Myers, Susan (act): *The Spell*

Myers, Virginia (wri): *Jennifer (1953)*

Mygind, Peter (act): *The Kingdom*

Myhers, John (act): *Now You See Him, Now You Don't; The Shaggy D.A.; 2000 Years Later; Willard*

Myhers, John (wri): *The Private Eyes (1980)*

Myler, Jody (act): *Tomorrow's Child*

Myles, Bruce (act): *The Night Digger*

Myles, Kimberley (act): *Secret Weapons*

Myles, Patrick (act): *The Mutagen*

Myles, Rowland (act): *My Lord Conceit*

Mylong, John (act): *The Falcon In San Francisco; Mermaids of Tiburon; Robot Monster; The Strange Death of Adolf Hitler*

Myres (act): *Making Contact*

Myrow, Fred(ric) (mus): *Phantasm; Phantasm II; Phantasm III: Lord of the Dead; Plan 10 from Outer Space; A Reflection of Fear; Soylent Green*

Myrtetus, J. Dinan (act): *The Lost Boys; The Power (1980)*

Myrtil, Odette (act, 1898-1978): *Dark Waters; Devotion*

Myshkova, Ninel (act): *Ilya Mourometz*

Myshrall, Don (act): *The Loch Ness Horror*

Mytnyk, Mariafae (act): *Moontrap*

Myton, Frank (wri): *Dead Men Walk*

Myton, Fred (Kennedy) (wri): *The Black Raven; Blonde for a Day; The Brass Bottle (1923);The Mad Monster; Murder Is My Business; Nabonga; Three on a Ticket; Too Many Winners*

Naboneal, Jed (act): *Timestalkers*

Nabuco, Anne Marie (act): *Love Slaves of the Amazons*

Nachman, K. (wri): *Queen of the Pirates*

Nadajan (act): *House of Usher (1960)*

Nadder, Robert (act): *Fantasies; The Two Worlds of Jennie Logan*

Nadeau, Diana (act): *Wes Craven's New Nightmare*

Nadeau, Elyane (act): *Martin*

Nadeau, Gary (wri): *Jack*

Nadell, Robert (act): *Appointment With Murder*

Nademsky, Mikola (act): *Zvenigora*

Nader, George (act, b. 1921): *Appointment With a Shadow; Beyond Atlantis; Congo Crossing;*
House of 1,000 Dolls; The Human Duplicators; Lady Godiva; The Million Eyes of Sumuru; Nowhere to Go; Robot Monster; The Secret Mark of D'Artagnan; Sins of Jezebel; The Unguarded Moment

Nader, Michael/Mike (act, b. 1945): *The Flash; How to Stuff a Wild Bikini; Nick Knight; Sergeant Deadhead the Astronut!*

Nader, Saladin (act): *Embassy*

Nader, Stephanie (act): *Sergeant Deadhead the Astronut!*

Nadiuska (act): *Guyana, Cult of the Damned*

Naebig, Kurt (act): *The Relic*

Naff, Lycia (act): *Chopper Chicks In Zombietown; The Clan of the Cave Bear; The Flash; Total Recall*

Nagahara, Shuichi (wri): *Godzilla 1985*

Nagai, Go (act): *The Toxic Avenger, Part II*

Nagai, Mieko (act): *Uchujin Tokyo No Arawaru*
Nagashima, Hiroyuki (mus): *Angel Dust*
Nagashima, Takeo (act): *Mothra*
Nagashima, Toshiyuki (act): *Virus (1980)*
Nagashima, Yoshiko (act): *The Toxic Avenger, Part II*
Nagazumi, Yasuko (act): *Deadlier Than the Male; Wombling Free*
Nage, Mason (wri): *The Borrower*
Nagel, Anne (act, 1912-1966): *The Adventurous Blonde; Black Friday; The Invisible Woman (1941); The Mad Doctor of Market Street; The Mad Monster; Man-Made Monster; Mystery House; The Trap*
Nagel, Conrad (act, 1896-1970): *Bella Donna (1923); Hidden Fear; Kongo; London After Midnight; The Thirteenth Chair (1929); Vicious Circle (1948)*
Nagel, Don (act): *Bride of the Monster*
Nagel, Mark (act): *Blink*
Nagle, Steve (act): *The Power (1980)*
Nagler, Austin (act): *Ernest Scared Stupid*
Nagy, Bill (act): *Across the Bridge; The Adding Machine; Battle Beneath the Earth; Boy With a Flute; The Brain Machine; Cloak Without Dagger; Crosstrap; Danger by My Side; Eye of the Needle; First Man Into Space; The Girl Hunters; Goldfinger; The Man Outside (1967); Night of the Prowler; Person Unknown; The Road to Hong Kong; Subterfuge; Transatlantic; Z.P.G.*
Nagy, Christina (act): *Formula for a Murder*
Nagy, Gabor (act): *Mata Hari (1985)*
Nagy, Ivan (dir): *Captain America II; Midnight Lace (1981); Mind Over Murder; Once Upon a Spy*
Naha, Ed (wri): *Dolls; Honey, I Blew Up the Kid; Honey, I Shrunk the Kids; Troll*
Naha, Suzanne Glazener (wri): *Dragonworld*
Nahum, Jacques (dir & wri): *Le Saint Mene la Dance*
Naidu, Ajay (act): *Vice Versa (1988)*
Nail, Jimmy (act): *Crusoe; Dream Demon; Howling II; Just Ask for Diamond; Morons from Outer Space*
Nail, Joanne (act): *Full Moon High; Midnight Lace (1981)*
Nainby, Robert (act): *Death On the Set; When Knights Were Bold (1936)*
Naish, J. Carrol (act, 1900-1973): *The Beast With Five Fingers; Beneath the 12-Mile Reef; British Agent; Bulldog Drummond Comes Back; Bulldog Drummond In Africa; Calling Dr. Death; Charlie Chan at the Circus; The Corsican Brothers (1941); Crack-Up; Dr. Renault's Secret; Dracula vs. Frankenstein; Enter Arsene Lupin; The Fugitive (1947); The Island of Lost Men; The Jungle Woman; The Monster Maker (1943); Return of the Terror; Scotland Yard (1930); Special Investigator; Strange Confession; Think Fast, Mr. Moto; The Whistler*
Naismith, Laurence (act, b. 1908, nee Lawrence Johnson): *The Amazing Mr. Blunden; The Black Knight; Camelot; Cosh Boy; The Criminal; Deadlier Than the Male; Diamonds Are Forever; Eye of the Cat; Gideon's Day; High*
Treason (1951); I Accuse (1958); I Thank a Fool; Jason and the Argonauts; A Killer Walks; A
Piece of Cake; Quest for Love; Richard III (1955); The Scorpio Letters; Scrooge (1970); The Three Lives of Thomasina; Tiger In the Smoke; The Two-Headed Spy; The Valley of Gwangi; The Village of the Damned (1960); The Weapon
Naito, Taketoshi (act): *Godzilla 1985*
Najee (act): *Def by Temptation*
Najera, Miguel (act): *Virtuosity*
Najimy, Kathy (act, b. 1957): *Hocus Pocus*
Naka, Machiko (act): *Godzilla's Revenge*
Nakada, Kei (act): *The Toxic Avenger, Part II*
Nakadai, Tatsuya (act, b. 1930): *Harakiri; High and Low; Inn of Evil; Kwaidan; Phoenix (1978); Ran; Tanin No Kao*
Nakagawa, Kerry (act): *Cameron's Closet*
Nakagawa, Nobuo (dir): *Onna Kyuketsuki*
Nakahara, Sanae (act): *Virus (1980)*
Nakai, Asaishi (cin): *Ran*
Nakajima, Haruo (act): *Mothra*
Nakajima, Kenji (act): *The Toxic Avenger, Part II*
Nakajima, Toro (cin): *Message from Space*
Nakamura, Ganemon (act): *Inn of Evil*
Nakamura, Ganjiro (act): *Kwaidan*
Nakamura, Kan-Emon (act): *Kwaidan*
Nakamura, Katsuo (act): *Kwaidan*
Nakamura, Kichiemon (act): [illegible]
Nakamura, Saemi (act): [illegible]
Nakamura, Satoshi (act): *The Manster*
Nakamura, Shinichiro (wri): *Mothra*
Nakamura, Tadao (act): *The Secret of the Telegian*
Nakamura, Takashi (dir): *Robot Carnival*
Nakamura, Tatsu (act): *The Last Dinosaur*
Nakamura, Tetsu (act): *Mothra*
Nakamura, Wasaburo (act): *The Toxic Avenger, Part II*
Nakano, Kiyoshi (act): *Kwaidan*
Nakano, Teruyoshi (cin): *Godzilla 1985; Terror of Mechagodzilla*
Nakata, Yasulo (act): *Rodan, the Flying Monster*
Nakatani, Ichiro (act): *Kwaidan*
Nakaya, Ichido (act): *Inn of Evil*
Nakaya, Noboru (act): *Kwaidan*
Nakayama, Shunsako (act): *The Toxic Avenger, Part II*
Nakayama, Yutara (act): *Mothra*
Nalbandian, Albert (act): *Invasion of the Body Snatchers (1978)*
Nalder, Reggie (act): *Adventures of Captain Fabian; The Dead Don't Die; The Devil and Max Devlin; Dracula's Dog; Dracula Sucks; The Manchurian Candidate; The Man Who Knew Too*
Much (1956); Mark of the Devil (1972); Mark of the Devil II; Salem's Lot; L'Uccello delle Piume di Cristallo; What's the Matter With Helen?
Naldi, Nita (act, 1899-1961, nee Anita Donna Dooley): *Dr. Jekyll and Mr. Hyde (1920), Famous Players/Para); The Man from Beyond*
Nalevansky, Steven (wri): *Blood Beach*
Nalewicki, Stephen (act): *Daylight*
Nam, Chung-Im (act): *Yongary, Monster from the Deep*
Namara, Marguerite (act): *Gipsy Blood*
Namath, Joe (act): *Avalanche Express*
Nambiar, M.N. (act): *The Jungle*
Nambu, K. (act): *The Thief of Bagdad (1924)*
Nanaki, Satoe (act): *The Toxic Avenger, Part II*
Nanayakkara, D.R. (act): *Indiana Jones and the Temple of Doom*
Nanbu, Shozo (act): *Uchujin Tokyo No Arawaru*
Nance, Jack (act, 1943-1996): *Dune; Eraserhead; Ghoulies; Little Witches; Lost Highway; Voodoo*
Nance, John J. (wri): *Pandora's Clock*
Nandi, Itala (act): *Os Deuses e os Mortos*
Nankerius, James (act): *Glen and Randa*
Nankin, Michael (wri): *The Gate; Gate II*
Nann, Erica (act): *Mind Twister*
Nannuzzi, Armando (cin, b. 1925): *Maximum Overdrive; Roger Corman's 'Frankenstein Unbound'; The Secret of Seagull Island; Silver Bullet*
Nansel, Carla (act): *Boarding House*
Nantel, Monik (act): *Of Unknown Origin*
Nanten, Louis (act): *Crime and the Penalty*
Nanty, Isabelle (act): *The Visitors (1993)*
Napier, Alan (act, 1903-1988, nee Alan Napier-Clavering): *Adventure Island; Batman (1966); Cat People (1942); A Connecticut Yankee In King Arthur's Court (1949); Criss Cross; The Hairy Ape; Hangover Square; House of Horrors (1946); The House of the Seven Gables; The Invisible Man Returns; Island of Lost Women; Isle of the Dead (1945); Journey to the Center of the Earth (1959); The Lone Wolf In London; The Loved One; Lured; Macbeth (1947); Marnie; Master Minds (1950); Ministry of Fear; The Mole People; The Premature Burial; Signpost to Murder; The Strange Door; The Sword In the Stone; Tarzan's Magic Fountain; Tarzan's Peril; 36 Hours (1965); Three Strangers; The Uninvited (1944)*
Napier, Charles (act, b. 1936): *Deep Space; Future Zone; The Incredible Hulk Returns; Last Embrace; The Night Stalker 1987); The Silence of the Lambs; Skeeter*
Napier, Diana (act): *The Private Life of Don Juan; Strange Evidence; The Warren Case*
Napier, Marshall (act): *The Navigator: An Odyssey Across Time*
Napier, Patricia (act): *Stories from a Flying Trunk*
Napier, Russell (act, b. 1910): *Black Orchid; The Black Windmill; Blind Man's Bluff (1952); The Brain Machine; The Case of the Smiling Widow; The Curse of the Golem; Death of an Angel; The Deathshead Vampire; Destination Death; Evidence In Concrete; The Ghost*
Train Murder; The Grand Junction Case; Guilty?; Hell Is a City; The Last Man to Hang; The Last Train; Little Red Monkey; The Lonely House; The Man In the Road; The Mark; The Narrowing Circle; The Never Never Murder; Night Crossing; Nobody Runs Forever; Person Unknown; The Strange Case of
Blondie; The Stranger Came Home; Tread Softly Stranger; The Twisted Nerve; The Unseeing Eye; Where the Spies Are; The White Cliffs Mystery; The Witness
Napier-Clavering, Alan (act): see Napier, Alan
Napierkowska, Stacia (act): *L'Atlantide (1920)*
Napio, David (act): *Empire of Ash III*
Naples, Toni (act): *Chopping Mall; Deathstalker II: Duel of the Titans; Dinosaur Island (1994)*
Naplock, Norman (mus): *The Galaxy Invader*
Napoleon (animal act): *The Thirteenth Hour (1927)*
Napoleon, Titus (act): *The Black Bird (1975)*
Napolitano, Joe (dir): *Earth Angel*
Nappi, Malya (act): *One Million Years B.C.*
Naprous, Daniel (act): *First Knight*
Naprous, Gerard (act): *Krull*
Nara, Kenji (act): *The Toxic Avenger, Part II*
Naranjo, Ivan (act): *Wavelength*
Naraoka, Tomoko (act): *Kwaidan*
Narbaez, Rafael (act): *Distortions*
Narcejac, Thomas (wri, b. 1908): *Body Parts (1991); Diabolique (1955 & 1996); Faces in the Dark; House of Secrets (1993); Letters to an Unknown Lover; Reflections of Murder; Vertigo; Les Yeux sans Visage*
Narciso, Grazia (act): *Between Midnight and Dawn*
Narcisse, Andre (act): *The Golden Mistress*
Narcisse, Jarrett (act): *Angel Heart*
Nardi, Anna Lisa (act): *Murder Mansion*
Nardini, James (act): *Nice Girls Don't Explode*
Nardo, Don (dir): *Stuff Stephanie In the Incinerator*
Narelle, Brian (act): *Dark Star*
Narens, Sherry (act): *Poltergeist III*
Nares, Owen (act, 1888-1943): *Flames; The Private Life of Don Juan; The Sorrows of Satan (1917)*
Narita, Hiro (cin): *The Arrival (1996); The Haunting Passion; Honey, I Shrunk the Kids; James and the Giant Peach; Plymouth; The Rocketeer; Star Trek VI: The Undiscovered Country; Time Flyer*
Narita, Mikio (act): *Message from Space*
Narita, Richard (act): *Exo-Man; Galaxis; Murder by Death*
Narita, Rob (act): *Ghost Warrior*
Narizzano, Dino (act): *The Curse of the Living Corpse*
Narrizano, Silvio (dir, b. 1927): *Fanatic (1965)*
Narke, Rob (act): *The Pack*
Nark-Orn, Willie (act): *Magic In the Water*
Narlay, R. (act): *The Passion of Joan of Arc*
Narvy, Jason (act): *Mighty Morphin Power Rangers; Turbo: A Power Rangers Movie*
Naschy, Paul (act, nee Jacinto Molina): *The Craving; The Devil's Possessed; Dr. Jekyll y el Hombre Lobo; The Fury of the Wolfman; Gran Amore del Conde Dracula; Horror Rises from the Tomb; House of Doom (1973); Inquisition; El Jorobado de la Morgue; La Maldicion de la Bestia; La Marca del Hombre Lobo; The Mummy's Revenge; Mystery On Monster Island; La Noche de Walpurgis; Las Noches del Hombre Lobo; La Orgia de los Muertos; People Who Own the Dark; El Retorno de la Walpurgis;Vengeance of the Zombies*
Naschy, Paul (dir): *Inquisition*
Naschy, Paul (wri): *Inquisition; El Retorno de la Walpurgis*
Nascimbene, Mario (mus): *Carthage In Flames; Creatures the World Forgot; Dr. Faustus; OK, Nero!; One Million Years B.C.; The Vengeance of She; When Dinosaurs Ruled the Earth*
Nascimento, Milton (mus): *Os Deuses e os Mortos*
Nash, Alan (act): *Beyond and Back*
Nash, Alden (wri): *Passport to Suez*
Nash, Anthony (act): *Murder On the Midnight Express*
Nash, Chris (act): *The Wraith*
Nash, Clarence (act): *The Three Caballeros*
Nash, George (act): *The Face In the Fog (1922)*
Nash, Jennifer (act): *Invisible: The Chronicles of Benjamin Knight*
Nash, Joel (act): *The Rosary Murders*
Nash, John (act): *Inn of the Damned*
Nash, Mary (act, 1884-1976): *Charlie Chan In Panama; Cobra Woman; The Lady and the Monster*
Nash, Marilyn (act): *Monsieur Verdoux; Unknown World*
Nash, Maybelle (act): *The Sand Castle*
Nash, Michael (wri): *Uncharted Seas*
Nash, Nancy (act): *Loves of Carmen (1927)*
Nash, Noreen (act): *Aladdin and His Lamp (1952); Assigned to Danger; The Lone Ranger and the Lost City of Gold; Phantom from Space*
Nash, Ogden (mus & wri, 1902-1971): *One Touch of Venus*
Nash, Percy (dir): *The Devil's Bondman; Flying from Justice; The Harbour Lights; In the Ranks; In the Shadow of the Rope; Jack Sheppard; The Little Match Girl (1914); The Mesmerist (1915); A Rogue's Wife; The Romany Rye; Royal Love; The Story of the Rosary*
Nash, Simon (act): *Brazil; Xtro*
Nasr, Laila (act): *Dawn of the Mummy*
Nasar, Deborah Ann (act): *Dance of the Damned*
Nassiet, Henri (act): *Le Saint Mene la Dance*
Nassour, Edward (dir): *The Beast of Hollow Mountain*
Nastasi, Frank (act): *Eat and Run*
Nastro, Nick (dir): *Superargo vs. Diabolicus*
Natroshvoli, Levan (act): *Ashik Kerib*
Naszkinsky, Lara (act): *Red Sonja*
Nat, Marie-Jose (act, b. 1940): *Embassy*
Natale, Greg (act): *Not of This World; The Nutty Professor (1996)*
Natale, Louis (mus): *Clarence*
Natale, Nazareno (act): *Slugs*
Natale, Roberto (wri): *Il Boia Scarlatto; Cinque Tombe per un Medium*
Natali, Edmondo (cin): *Exterminators of the Year 3000*
Natali, Germano (cin): *Inferno (1979); Profundo Rosso; The Secret of Seagull Island*
Natanson, Agathe (act): *Quelqu'un Derriere la Porte*
Natase, Tsunehiko (act): *Virus (1980)*
Nath, Nagendra (act): *Devi*
Nathan, Jack (mus): *The Abominable Dr. Phibes; The Shuttered Room*
Nathan, Peggy (act): *La Ragazza Che Sapeva Troppo*
Nathan, Robert (wri, 1894-1985): *The Bishop's Wife; Portrait of Jennie; The Preacher's Wife*
Nathenson, Stephen D. (act): *Nightfall (1988)*
Natheux, Louis (act): *Modern Times*
Nation, E. Lee (act): *The Dungeonmaster*
Nation, Terry (wri): *And Soon the Darkness; Daleks' Invasion Earth 2150 A.D.; Doctor Who; Dr. Who and the Daleks; The House In Nightmare Park*
National Dance Company of Senegal (act): *The Jewel of the Nile*
National Folklore Theatre of Haiti (act): *The Golden Mistress*
National Music (mus): *War of the Planets*
Natividad, Kitten (act): *The Tomb*
Natole, Steve (act): *The Man Who Fell to Earth (1987)*
Natsukawa, Shizue (act): *Kwaidan*
Natsuki, Akira (act): *Gammera vs. Barugon*
Natsuki, Isao (act): *Virus (1980)*
Natsuki, Yosuke (act): *Dogora; Ghidrah, the Three-Headed Monster; Godzilla 1985*
Natteau, Jacques (cin): *Les Miserables (1957)*
Natteford, Jack (wri, b. 1894): *The Night the World Exploded*
Natteford, John F. (wri): *The Hidden Menace; The Lost Zeppelin*
Natwick, Mildred (act, 1908-1994): *Do Not Fold, Spindle or Mutilate; The Enchanted Cottage (1945); The Trouble With Harry; A Woman's Vengeance*
Natwick, Myron (act): *Mistress of Paradise; Project Vampire*
Natzler, Grete (act): *The Scotland Yard Mystery*
Naud, Bill (dir): *Whodunit*
Naud, Jennifer (act): *Monolith*
Naughton, Charlie (act): *Alf's Button Afloat; Life Is a Circus*
Naughton, David (act, b. 1951): *An American Werewolf In London; Amityville: A New Generation; Beanstalk; Body Bags; The Goddess of Love; Ice Cream Man; I, Desire; The Sleeping Car; Steel and Lace*
Naughton, James (act, b. 1945): *Back to the Planet of the Apes; Cat's Eye; Farewell to the Planet of the Apes; Forgotten City of the Planet of the Apes; Life, Liberty and Pursuit On the Planet of the Apes; A Stranger Is Watching; Treachery and Greed On the Planet of the Apes*
Naukoff, Ralph (act): *La Isla de la Muerte*
Naulin, John (cin): *From Beyond; Re-Animator*
Nauman, Jennie (act): *A Deadly Vision; Switch (1991)*
Navara, Ernest (act): *The Diabolical Invention*
NaVarre, Catherine (act): *Just Imagine*
Navarre, J.L. (wri): *A Thousand and One Nights (1968)*
NaVarre, Joan (act): *Just Imagine*
Navarreta, Roman Ariz (act): *Exterminators of the Year 3000*
Navarrini, Renato (act): *Terror of Rome Against the Son of Hercules*
Navarro, Augustin (wri): [illegible]
Navarro, George (act): *War of the Colossal Beast*

Navarro, Guillermo (cin): *From Dusk Till Dawn; The Long Kiss Goodnight; Spawn*
Navarro, Jose Luis (wri): *A Witch Without a Broom*
Navarro, Julian (act): *Night Fiend*
Navarro, Mario (act): *The Black Scorpion (1957)*
Navarro, Maurice (act): *Nightmare Alley*
Navas, Eddy (act): *Wolfen*
Nave, Rod (wri): *Dolly Dearest*
Navin, Grant (act): *The Haunted School*
Navin Jr., John P. (act): *Explorers*
Nay, A.J. (act): *Eraser*
Naylor, Tom (act): *City of the Dead; Danger by My Side*
Nayyar, Harsh (act): *Freejack; Making Mr. Right*
Nazareth (mus): *Heavy Metal*
Nazareth, Christine (act): *Modern Problems*
Nazaro, Rafael (act): *I, Madman*
Nazarov, Anatoli (cin): *The Sleeping Beauty (1965, Russ)*
Nazarow, Beverly (act): *Sin You Sinners*
Nazarro, Ray (dir, b. 1902): *The Bandits of Corsica; Dog Eat Dog*
Nazimova, (Alla) (act, 1879-1945): *The Bridge of San Luis Rey (1944); Salome (1922)*
Nazir, Phoroze (act): *Man-Eater of Kumaon*
Nazvanov, Mikhail (act): *Hamlet (1966)*
Nazzani, Gregor V. (wri): *Superwheels*
Nazzari, Amedeo (act, 1907-1979, nee Salvatore Amedeo Buffa): *Love and Poison*
N'Daiye, Dialy (act): *Stargate*
Neagle, Anna (act, b. 1904): *The Man Who Wouldn't Talk*
Neal, Billie (act): *Jacob's Ladder; Mortal Thoughts*
Neal, Braedy (mus): *Doom Runners*
Neal, Cooper (act): *Neon Maniacs*
Neal, David (act): *Superman (1978)*
Neal, Dennis (act): *Matinee*
Neal, Edwin (act): *Future Kill; Splatter; The Texas Chainsaw Massacre*
Neal, Elise (act) *Scream 2*
Neal, Ella (act): *Doctor Satan's Robot*
Neal, Jay Scott (act): *Kiss of the Tarantula*
Neal, Pat (act): *An Inspector Calls*
Neal, Patricia (act, b. 1926, nee Patsy Louise Neal): *The Day the Earth Stood Still; Ghost Story (1981); Happy Mother's Day, Love George; The Night Digger; Psyche 59; Stranger from Venus*
Neal, Patsy Louise (act): see Neal, Patricia
Neal, Peggy (act): *Terror Beneath the Sea; The X from Outer Space*
Neal, Roy (act): *Cry Terror!*
Neal, Tom (act, 1915-1972): *Amazon Quest; Another Thin Man; Bowery at Midnight; The Brute Man; Danger Zone; Detour; The Hat Box Mystery; Radar Secret Service; Sky Murder; The Unwritten Code*
Neal, Willer (act): *Old Mother Riley's Jungle Treasure*
Neale, Leslie (act): *Gremlins 2: The New Batch*
Neale, Ralph (wri): *The Cavalier of the Streets; The Fatal Hour (1937); Murder by Rope; Wednesday's Luck*
Nealon, Kevin (act): *Coneheads*
Nealy, Frances (act): *Schizoid (1980); WarGames*
Neame, Christopher (act): *Bloodstone; Boris and Natasha; D.O.A. (1988); Dracula A.D. 1972; Ghostbusters II; Hellbound; No Blade of Grass; Project Shadowchaser III; Steel Dawn; Still Not Quite Human*
Neame, Derek (wri): *Special Edition*
Neame, Elwin (dir): *Dream Paintings; Ghosts (1914); The Haunting of Silas P. Gould; The Lady of Shallot; The Legend of King Cophetua; Mifanwy-A Tragedy; Pygmalion and Galatea (1912); The Sleeping Beauty (1912)*
Neame, Elwin (wri): *Dream Paintings; The Lady of Shallot; The Legend of King Cophetua; Mifanwy-A Tragedy; Pygmalion and Galatea (1912); The Sleeping Beauty (1912)*
Neame, Grace (act): *Lycanthropus*
Neame, Ronald (cin, b. 1911): *Blithe Spirit; The Gaunt Stranger*
Neame, Ronald (dir, b. 1911): *Gambit; Meteor; The Poseidon Adventure; Scrooge (1970); Take My Life*
Neame, Ronald (wri, b. 1911): *Great Expectations (1946)*
Near, Holly (act): *Angel, Angel, Down We Go; Slaughterhouse-Five*
Near, Laurel (act): *Eraserhead*
Naery, Robert (act): *Teen Wolf Too*
Nebel, Frederick (wri): *The Adventurous Blonde; Blondes at Work; Fly-Away Baby; Sleepers West; Smart Blonde; Torchy Blane In Chinatown; Torchy Blane In Panama; Torchy Gets Her Man; Torchy Plays With Dynamite; Torchy Runs for Mayor*
Neberroth, Harold (act): see Curtis, Alan
Necakov, Eli (dir & wri): *The Mutagen*
Neckels, Bruce (act): *Flowers In the Attic*
Nedell, Bernard (J.) (act): *Crime Doctor's Manhunt; The Lone Wolf In Mexico; Mr. Moto's Gamble; Monsieur Verdoux; One Body Too Many; Terror On Tiptoe*
Nedeva, Madlena (act): *The Lady Vanishes (1979)*
Nedobrovo, V. (wri): *Lunnyi Kamen*
Nedwell, Robin (act): *The Vault of Horror; The Zany Adventures of Robin Hood*
Nee, Louis (cin): *Liliom (1933)*
Needham, Gordon (act): *The Case of the River Morgue; The Ghost Train Murder; The Hypnotist (1957); The Lonely House; The Mail Van Murder; No Safety Ahead*
Needham, Hal (dir & wri, b. 1930): *Megaforce*
Needham, Tracey (act): *Buried Alive II; Sensation (1994)*
Needles, William (act): *Spasms*
Neeiendam, Sigrid (act): *Vredens Dag*
Neeley, Ted (act): *Of Mice and Men (1981)*
Neely, Gail (act): *Earth Girls Are Easy; Surf Nazis Must Die*
Neeman, Isaac (act): *The Jerusalem File*
Neer, Kay (act): *Love Butcher*
Neesam, Julie (act): *Panic (1979)*
Neeson, Liam (act, b. 1952): *Arthur the King; Darkman (1990); Excalibur; High Spirits; Krull; Les Miserables (1998); Star Wars: Episode I-The Phantom Menace*
Neff, Hildegarde (act): see Knef(f), Hildegard(e)
Neff, Monica (act): *Nightbeast*
Negami, Jun (act): *The Golden Demon*
Negin, Louis (act): *Rabid*
Negley, Howard (act): *The Docks of New Orleans; Song of the Thin Man; Sunset Boulevard; The Trap*
Negre, Mirielle (act): *Circus Angel*
Negret, Francois (act): *Mr. Frost*
Negretl, Rudy (act): *Nightmares (1983)*
Negri, Pola (act, 1897-1987, nee Apollonia Chalupetz): *Die Augen der Mumie Ma; Bella Donna (1923); Carmen (1918); Madame DuBarry (1919); The Moon-Spinners; Sumurun*
Negro, Lobo (act): *The Beast of Hollow Mountain; El Santo Contra las Vampiras*
Negron, Taylor (act): *Angels In the Outfield (1994); Freaky Friday (1995); Mr. Stitch; Nothing But Trouble*
Negroponte, John (act): *The Punisher*
Negulesco, Jean (dir, b. 1900): *Britannia Mews; The Conspirators; The Mask of Dimitrios; Three Strangers*
Neicher, Ernst (act): *Number Seventeen (1928)*
Neiderman, Andrew (wri): *The Maddening*
Neifert, Nancy (act): *Fire In the Sky (1993)*
Neighbors, Connie (act): *I Was a Zombie for the F.B.I.*
Neighbors, Troy (wri): *Fortress*
Neiiendam, Nicolai (act): *Himmelskibet*
Neiiendam, Sigrid (act): *Vredens Dag*
Neil, Bob (act): *Logan's Run*
Neil, Elissa (act): *The Deadly Spawn*
Neil, Gloria (act): *Beach Girls and the Monster*
Neil, Hildegard (act): *The Legacy; The Man Who Haunted Himself; The Mirror Crack'd*
Neil, Peter (act): *Meet Mr. Callaghan; Satellite In the Sky; The Stolen Plans (1952)*
Neil, Roger (act): *The Oracle (1985)*
Neil, Susan (act): *Kill Her Gently*
Neil, William (cin): *Masters of the Universe*
Neilan, Marshall (a.) (dir, 1891-1958): *Bits of Life; Black Waters; The Bottle Imp*
Neill, Anna (act): *Disaster In Time*
Neill, Beverly Louise (act): *see Blake, Amanda*
Neill, Bob (act): *The Man With the Power*
Neill, James (act): *Bits of Life; The Bottle Imp*
Neill, Noel (act, b. 1921): *Atom Man vs. Superman; The Big Clock; A Dog, a Mouse and a Sputnik; Invasion U.S.A.; The Sky Dragon; Superman (1978)*
Neill, Roy William (dir, 1890-1946, nee Roland de Gostrie): *Black Angel (1946); The Black Room; Dr. Syn; Dressed to Kill (1946); Eyes of the Underworld; Frankenstein Meets the Wolf Man; Gypsy Wildcat; The House of Fear (1945); The Lone Wolf Returns (1935); The Menace (1932); Murder Will Out (1939); The Pearl of Death; Pursuit to Algiers; The Scarlet Claw; Sherlock Holmes and the Secret Weapon; Sherlock Holmes Faces Death; Sherlock Holmes In Washington; Spider Woman; Terror by Night; The Viking; The Woman In Green*
Neill, Roy Will (wri, 1890-1946): *Murder Will Out (1939)*
Neill, Sam (act, b. 1947): *Dead Calm; Death In Brunswick; Event Horizon; The Final Conflict; The Hunt for Red October; In the Mouth of Madness; The Jungle Book (1994); Jurassic Park; Memoirs of an Invisible Man; Merlin (1998); Possession (1981); Sleeping Dogs (1977); Snow White: A Tale of Terror; Until the End of the World*
Neill, Steve (wri): *The Day Time Ended*
Neilsen, Hans (act): *The Monster of London*
Neilsen, Inga (act): *Grave of the Vampire*
Neilson, Bonnie (act): *Cannibal Girls*
Neilson, Caroline (act): *The Pink Chiquitas*
Neilson, James (dir, 1910-1979): *Dr. Syn-Alias the Scarecrow; The Legend of Young Dick Turpin; Moon Pilot; The Moon-Spinners*
Neilson, John (act): *The Folks at Red Wolf Inn*
Neilson, Phil (act): *The Body Snatchers; Remo Williams: The Adventure Begins*
Neilson, Rob (act): *The Man Who Fell to Earth (1987)*
Neilson-Baxter, R.K. (dir): *The House of Silence*
Neilson-Terry, Dennis (act): *Desire; Her Greatest Performance; The House of the Arrow (1930); Murder at Covent Garden*
Neilson-Terry, Phyllis (act): *Boadicea; Family Doctor; Trilby (1922)*
Neiman, Harold (act): *Houdini (1953)*
Neiman, L.E. (dir): *Morgen Grauen*
Neimark, Renee (act): *The Entity*
Neinrad, Josef (act): *Don Juan (1956)*
Neise, George (N.) (act): *The Barefoot Executive; On a Clear Day You Can See Forever; Pharaoh's Curse; The Three Stooges In Orbit; The Three Stooges Meet Hercules*
Nel, Kristine (act): *Avalanche Express*
Nelkin, Stacey (act): *Halloween III: Season of the Witch; Yellowbeard*
Nell, Carlo (act): *Jo*
Nell, Krista (act): *The Million Eyes of Sumuru*
Nell, Mary (act): *Night of the Hunter (1991)*
Nell, Nathalie (act): *Echoes*
Nell, Scott (act): *Not Quite Human II*
Nelligan, Kate (act, b. 1951): *The Count of Monte Cristo (1975); Dracula (1979); Eye of the Needle; U.S. Marshals; White Room; Wolf*
Nellson, John (act): *Sharks' Treasure*
Nelmes, Judith (act): *Horror of Dracula*
Nelms, Aaron (act): *Ed Wood*
Nelsen, Herman (act): *La Isla de la Muerte*
Nelson, A.J. (dir): *The Creeping Terror*
Nelson, Albert (act): *The Man Who Fell to Earth (1976)*
Nelson, Alberta (act): *Dr. Goldfoot and the Bikini Machine; How to Stuff a Wild Bikini; Sergeant Deadhead the Astronut!*
Nelson, Ann (act): *Ghosts That Still Walk*
Nelson, Ann M. (act): *Jekyll and Hyde...Together Again*
Nelson, B.J. (wri): *Scanners II: The New Order*
Nelson, Barry (act, b. 1925, nee Robert Nielsen): *The Beginning or the End?; Death In Small Doses (1973); Eyes In the Night; A Guy Named Joe; The Man With My Face; The Night of the Claw; Shadow of the Thin Man; The Shining*
Nelson, Bek (act): *Bell, Book and Candle*
Nelson, Billy (act): *Search for Danger*
Nelson, Bob (act): *Sorceress (1982)*
Nelson, Bobby (act): *Ghost Rider (1935)*
Nelson, Brian (wri): *20,000 Leagues Under the Sea (1997, ABC-TV)*
Nelson, Burt (act): *The Story of Mankind*
Nelson, Charlene (act): *The Last Starfighter*
Nelson, Christopher S. (act): *Without Warning (1980)*
Nelson, Clay (act): *The Frighteners*
Nelson, Craig Richard (act): *Chiller*
Nelson, Craig (T.) (act, b. 1944): *Devil's Advocate; Me and Him; Peter Benchley's 'Creature'; Poltergeist; Poltergeist II: The Other Side; Red Riding Hood; The Return of Count Yorga*
Nelson, Danny (act): *Blood Salvage; Mutant*
Nelson, Dick (act): *The Amazing Colossal Man*
Nelson, Dixie Kay (act): see Nelson, Lori
Nelson, Don (wri): *The Munsters' Revenge*
Nelson, Dusty (dir): *Effects; Necromancer: Satan's Servant*
Nelson, Dusty (wri): *Effects*
Nelson, Ed(win) (act, b. 1928): *Attack of the Crab Monsters; The Bone Yard; The Brain Eaters; Brenda Starr (1992); A Bucket of Blood (1959); The Cry Baby Killer; Deadly Weapon; The Devil's Partner; Houston, We've Got a Problem; Invasion of the Saucer Men; Night of the Blood-Beast; The Screaming Woman; Teenage Cave Man; The Young Captives*
Nelson, Erik (act): *The Poseidon Adventure*
Nelson, Florence (act): *The Disappearance of the Judge; Love In the Welsh Hills; The Two Roads*
Nelson, Frank (act): *Bonzo Goes to College; The Sea Beast; You Never Can Tell*
Nelson, Gary (dir): *Allan Quatermain and the Lost City of Gold; The Black Hole; Freaky Friday (1976); The Lookalike*
Nelson, Gaye (act): *Witches' Brew*
Nelson, Gene (act, 1920-1996, nee Gene Berg): *Dial 999 (1955); Timeslip*
Nelson, Gene (dir, 1920-1996): *Hand of Death*
Nelson, Gordon (act): *Champagne for Caesar*
Nelson, Grant (wri): *Captain Mephisto and the Transformation Machine*
Nelson, Guy (act): *Strangest Dreams: Invasion of the Space Preachers*
Nelson, Gwen (act): *Don't Talk to Strange Men*
Nelson, Haywood (act): *Evilspeak*
Nelson, Herbert (act, 1914-1990): *Future Cop*
Nelson, Herbie (act): *The Cars That Ate Paris*
Nelson, Ida (wri): *Funeral Home*
Nelson, Jerry (act): *The Dark Crystal; RoboCop 2*
Nelson, Jessica (act): *Assassin (1986); Jekyll and Hyde...Together Again; Masters of the Universe*
Nelson, John (act): *Invasion of the Bee Girls*
Nelson, John (cin): *Anaconda*
Nelson, John Allen (act): *Deathstalker III: Warriors from Hell; Killer Klowns from Outer Space*
Nelson, Judd (act, b. 1960): *Blackwater Trail; Circumstances Unknown; The Dark Backward; Steel*
Nelson, Kenneth (act): *Hellraiser; Nightbreed*
Nelson, Kirk (act): *Wheels of Terror*
Nelson, Lela (act): *Phantom from Space*
Nelson, Lloyd (act): *Creature of the Walking Dead; Curse of the Stone Hand; The Incredible Petrified World; The Wild World of Batwoman*
Nelson, Lori (act, b. 1933, nee Dixie Kay Nelson): *Day the World Ended (1955); Francis Goes to West Point; Revenge of the Creature*
Nelson, Louise (act): *Nothing But the Night*
Nelson, Margaret (act): *Picnic at Hanging Rock*
Nelson, Marion (wri): *Secrets In the Attic*
Nelson, Mark (act): *Friday the 13th (1980)*
Nelson, Matthew (act): *Ed Wood*
Nelson, Mervyn (act): *The Boys from Brazil*
Nelson, Mike J. (act & wri): *Mystery Science Theater 3000: The Movie*
Nelson, Noelle(act): *Fake-Out*
Nelson, Oliver (mus): *I Love a Mystery (1966); Skullduggery*
Nelson, Peter (act): *Crime Zone; V*
Nelson, Portia (act): *Dr. Dolittle (1967); The Other (1972)*
Nelson, Ralph (act, 1916-1987): *Charly*
Nelson, Ralph (dir, 1916-1987): *Charly; Embryo*
Nelson, Randall Edwin (act): *The Jewel of the Nile*
Nelson, Ray (wri): *They Live*
Nelson, Richard (act): *Fiend (1980); Nightbeast*
Nelson, Richard (wri): *Houston, We've Got a Problem*
Nelson, Ruth (act, 1905-1992): *The Haunting Passion*
Nelson, Sam (act): *The Lady from Shanghai*
Nelson, Sandra (act): *Dying to Remember*
Nelson, Shawn (act): *Gremlins 2: The New Batch; Piranha (1978)*
Nelson, Sidney (wri): *Dead Lucky; The Diplomatic Corpse; The Stolen Assignment*
Nelson, Willie (act): *Amazons (1986)*
Nelson, Winifred (act): *Silent Evidence*
Nelthorpe, Malcolm (act): *Rabid; Scanners*
Nemec, Corin (act): *The Lifeforce Experiment; Solar Crisis; The Stand; Summer of Fear*
Nemes, Scott (act): *Twilight Zone*
Nemeth, Chris (act): *The Guardian*
Nemeth, Craig (act): *The Guardian*
Nemeth, Laszlo (act): *Phantom of the Opera (1983)*
Nemeth, Nora (act): *Phantom of the Opera (1983)*
Nemeth, S.D. (act): *RoboCop*
Nemetz, Max (act): *Nosferatu, eine Symphonie des Grauens*
Nemirowsky, Irene (wri): *My Daughter Joy*
Nemser, Alec (act): *Spookies*
Neogy, Chitra (act): *The Premonition (1975)*
Nephew, Neil (wri): *Panic In Year Zero*
Nepomniaschy, Alex (cin): *Poltergeist III*
Neri, Francesca (act): *Captain America (1992)*
Neri, Rosalba (act): *The Castle of Fu Manchu; The Conquest of Mycenae; Island of Despair;*

Kindar the Invulnerable; The Lion of Thebes; Slaughter Hotel (1972); The Three Avengers

Nerman, David (act): Witchboard: The Possession

Nero, Curtis (act): Kongo

Nero, Franco (act, b. 1942): The Bible; Camelot; I Criminali della Galassia; Detective Belli; The Flower In His Mouth; Un Tranquillo Posto di Campagna; Tristana

Nero, Toni (act): Silent Night, Deadly Night

Nervo, Jimmy (act): Alf's Button Afloat; Life Is a Circus

Nery, Gerard (act): The Elusive Pimpernel (1950)

Nery, Gilda (act): Love Slaves of the Amazons

Nesbeth, Vernon (act): Mark of the Devil (1985)

Nesbit, Edith (wri): The Phoenix and the Magic Carpet

Nesbitt, Cathleen (act, 1889-1982): Black Widow (1954); The Door With Seven Locks (1940); Family Plot; Fanny by Gaslight; The Frightened Lady (1932); Full Circle; Law and Disorder; Never-Never Land; The Passing of the Third Floor Back (1935); So Long at the Fair; The Trygon Factor

Nesbitt, Derren (act): Burke and Hare; Fatal Sky; Give Us Tomorrow; The Informers; Innocent Bystanders; Kill or Cure; The Man In the Back Seat; The Naked Runner; Nobody Runs Forever; Operation Third Form; The Playbirds; The Saint and the Brave Goose; Spy Story; Strongroom;Sword of Sherwood Forest

Nesbitt, Derren (wri): A Matter of Choice

Nesbitt, Frank (dir): Do You Know This Voice?; Walk a Tightrope

Nesbitt, Miriam (act): The Antique Brooch; The Daughter of Romany; The Floodtide; The Foreman's Treachery; A Letter to the Princess; The Stolen Plans (1914)

Nesbitt, Sally (act): The Gorgon; The Material Witness

Nesbitt, Simon (act): Strange Behavior

Nesbitt, Stuart (act): Shadow of Evil

Nesbitt, Thomas (act): The Sword of Damocles

Nesbitt, Vickie (act): La Orgia de los Muertos

Nesher, Avi (dir): Doppelganger: The Evil Within; She (1983)

Nesher, Avi (wri): She (1983)

Nesmith, Jason (act): The Man Who Saw Tomorrow

Nesmith, Michael (dir, mus & wri): Timerider

Nesmith, Ottola (act): The Invisible Ghost; The Return of the Vampire; Witness for the Prosecution

Nesor, Al (act): Santa Claus Conquers the Martians

Ness, Debbie (act): Scalpel

Ness, Ed (act): Time Travelers (1976)

Nestell, William (act): The Falcon Out West

Netheim, David (act): The Pied Piper (1971)

Nethercote, Bish (act): Voice Over

Nethercott, Geoffrey (dir): Accidental Death; The Material Witness; Personal and Confidential; Who Was Maddox?

Netsch, Christa-Maria (act): The Glass Cell

Netscher, Robin (act): The Dragon of Pendragon Castle

Nett, Ben (wri): Without Warning (1980)

Netterville, Ned (act): Contact

Nettleton, John (act): And Soon the Darkness; The Last Shot You Hear

Nettleton, Lois (act, b. 1929): The Bamboo Saucer; Deadly Blessing; Last Bride of Salem; Mirror, Mirror 2: Raven Dance

Neubauer, Leonard (wri): New Year's Evil

Neubeck, Jack (act): Invasion of the Blood Farmers; Shriek of the Mutilated

Neuberger, Jan (act): The Exorcist III

Neufeld, Martin (act): Relative Fear

Neuhaus, Ingo (act): Netforce

Neuman, E. Jack (wri): The Venetian Affair

Neuman, Peter (act): Felix the Cat: The Movie

Neuman, Ruth (act): Basket Case

Neumann, Alfred (wri): The Return of Monte Cristo

Neumann, Dorothy (act): The Day the Earth Stood Still; Donor; For Heaven's Sake; The Ghost of Dragstrip Hollow; The Luck of the Irish; Sorry, Wrong Number (1948); The Terror (1963); The Undead

Neumann, Drew (mus): Scalps; The Tomb

Neumann/Newman, Harry (C.) (cin): The Ape (1940); Bowery to Bagdad; The Disembodied; Doomed to Die; The Fatal Hour (1940); Flight to Mars; The Golden Idol; Hold That Hypnotist; The Jade Mask; Jungle Gents; The Maze; Mr. Wong, Detective; Mr. Wong In Chinatown; The Mysterious Mr. Wong; Spook Busters; Spook Chasers; Tarzan the Fearless; The Thirteenth Guest; Up in Smoke; The Wasp Woman (1959)

Neumann, James (act): You'll Like My Mother

Neumann, Jenny (act): Hell Night; Mistress of the Apes; Stage Fright (1983)

Neumann, Kurt/Curt (dir, 1908-1958): Ellery Queen, Master Detective; Espionage; The Fly (1958); Hiawatha (1952); The Island of Lost Men; Kronos (1957); Rocketship X-M; Secret of the Blue Room; She-Devil (1957); Son of Ali Baba; Tarzan and the Amazons; Tarzan and the Huntress; Tarzan and the Leopard Woman; Tarzan and the She-Devil; The Unknown Guest; Watusi

Neumann, Kurt/Curt (wri, 1908-1958): The Return of the Vampire; Rocketship X-M; She-Devil (1957)

Neumann, Margarethe (act): Flaming Ears

Neumann-Viertel, Elizabeth (act): The Fifth Musketeer

Neumeier, Ed(ward) (wri): RoboCop; RoboCop 2; RoboCop 3; Roger Corman's 'Frankenstein Unbound'

Neumeyer, Ingrid (wri): The Capture of Bigfoot

Neuner, Willi (cin): Babes In Toyland (1986)

Neunreuther, Roland (act): The Black Windmill

Neuss, Alwin (act): Dr. Jekyll and Mr. Hyde (1910)

Neuss, Robert (wri): Homunculus

Neuvenheim, Steve (act): Return of the Living Dead, Part II

Neuwirth, Bebe (act): The Adventures of Pinocchio (1996); The Faculty; Jumanji; Malice; Painted Heart

Neuwirth, Thomas/Thom/Tom (cin): Condor; Lady Beware; Shadow of a Doubt (1991)

Nevargic, Peter (act): Lady Beware

Neve, Suzanne (act): Backfire!; Bunny Lake Is Missing; The Hunchback of Notre Dame (1965);Naked Evil; Not Guilty; Scrooge (1970); Terror from Within

Neve, Vivien (act): The Hound of the Baskervilles (1978)

Nevedomsky, Leonid (act): The Blue Bird (1976)

Neves, Vivian (act): Whirlpool (1970)

Nevil, Steve (act): The Howling

Neville, Babs (act): The Great Gold Robbery; Ju-Jitsu to the Rescue

Neville, Daphne (act): Diagnosis: Murder

Neville, Dean (act): Invasion of the Saucer Men

Neville, Edgar (dir): Cuento de Hadas; La Torre de los Siete Jorobados

Neville, Edgar (wri): Cuento de Hadas

Neville, John (act, b. 1925): The Adventures of Baron Munchausen (1989); Journey to the Center of the Earth (1993); A Study In Terror; Unearthly Stranger; Urban Legend; The X-Files

Neville, John Thomas/T. (wri): The Flying Serpent; The Last of the Lone Wolf; Trader Horn (1931)

Neville, Paul (act): The Bank Messenger Mystery; Dial 999 (1938); Double Alibi; Passenger to London; Twin Faces; Wednesday's Luck

Neville, Robert (wri): The Black Cat (1941)

Nevin, Rosa (act): Still Not Quite Human

Nevin, Terry (act): Creature from the Haunted Sea

Nevins, Claudette (act): Child of Darkness, Child of Light; Don't Go to Sleep; The Mask (1961); The Possessed (1977)

Nevinson, Nancy (act): Gulliver's Travels (1977); Infamous Conduct; Ring of Spies; Symptoms

Nevison, Gennie (act): The Deadly Females

Nevman, Yuri (cin): D.O.A. (1988)

New, Robert (C.) (cin): The Borrower; Galaxis; Night of the Creeps; Prom Night

Newall, Guy (act, 1885-1937): The Ghost Train (1927); Number Seventeen (1928); Vice Versa (1916)

Newall, Guy (dir, 1885-1937): Chin Chin Chinaman; The Rosary

Newall, Guy (wri, 1885-1937): Chin Chin Chinaman

Newark, Derek (act): The Black Windmill; The City Under the Sea; Diamonds On Wheels; Fragment of Fear; The Legend of Spider Forest; The Offence

Newbern, George (act): Doppelganger: The Evil Within; Twice Upon a Time; Witness to the Execution

Newberry, Kymberly (act): Heart and Souls

Newbigin, Flora (act): The Borrowers (1998)

Newbold, Sarah (act): Paperhouse

Newborn, Ira (mus): Innocent Blood; Weird Science

Newbrook, Peter (cin): Corruption; Crucible of Terror

Newbrook, Peter (dir): The Asphyx

Newby, Ian (act): The Keeper

Newcastle, Anthony (act): Captive Planet; Metallica

Newcomb, Jamie (act): Lone Wolf (1988)

Newcomb, Mary (act): Strange Experiment

Newcombe, Clovissa (act): Digby-The Biggest Dog In the World

Newcombe, James A. (act): Reflections of Murder

Newcombe, John J. (act): Damien-Omen II

Newcombe, Warren (cin): Above Suspicion; The Beginning or the End?; Dr. Jekyll and Mr. Hyde (1941); Forbidden Planet; Gaslight (1944); The Glass Slipper; Kismet (1944); The Prisoner of Zenda (1952); Tarzan's New York Adventure; Tarzan's Secret Treasure

Newcomer, Jim (act): The Gifted One

Newell, Carol Irene (act): The Alpha Incident

Newell, Chuck (act): The Hideous Sun Demon

Newell, David (act): Darkened Rooms

Newell, Douglas (act): I Still Dream of Jeannie

Newell, Joan (act): Journey to the Unknown

Newell, Michael (act): Saturday Island

Newell, Michelle (act): The Hunchback of Notre Dame (1977); The Saint and the Brave Goose; The Zany Adventures of Robin Hood

Newell, Mike (dir): The Awakening

Newell, Patrick (act): The Golden Lady; Night Without Pity; Unearthly Stranger; Vampira; Where's Johnny; Young Sherlock Holmes

Newell, William (act): Doctor Satan's Robot; The Lone Wolf and His Lady; The Mandarin Mystery

Newfield, Jackie (act): Nabonga

Newfield, Sam (dir, 1900-1964, a.k.a. Sherman Scott & Peter Stewart): Adventure Island; The Black Raven; Blonde for a Day; Dead Men Walk; Federal Agent; The Flying Serpent; Ghost Patrol; The Invisible Killer; His Brother's Ghost; Jungle Siren; The Lady Confesses; Lady In the Fog; Larceny In Her Heart; Lost Continent (1951); The Mad Monster; The Monster Maker (1943); Murder Is My Business; Nabonga; Radar Secret Service; State Department-File 649; Three On a Ticket; White Pongo

Newhard, Robert S. (cin): The Hunchback of Notre Dame (1923)

Newhart, Bob (act, b. 1929): On a Clear Day You Can See Forever; The Rescuers; The Rescuers Down Under

Newhart, Robert William (act): Heart and Souls

Newill, James (act): The Falcon's Brother

Newill, William (act): Invisible Killer

Newirth, Robert (act): Blood Beach

Newkirk, Toy (act): A Nightmare On Elm Street 4: The Dream Master

Newlan, Paul (act): The Gracie Allen Murder Case; Prisoners of the Casbah; To Catch a Thief

Newland, John (act, b. 1916): The Challenge; 13 Lead Soldiers

Newland, John (dir, b. 1916): Don't Be Afraid of the Dark; The Spy With My Face; Who Fears the Devil?

Newland, Mary (act): Death at Broadcasting House; The Jewel; The Silent Passenger

Newlander, Jamison (act): The Lost Boys

Newlands, Anthony (act, b. 1926): Circus of Fear; The Fourth Square; Hysteria!; The Magus; Mata Hari (1985); Scream and Scream Again; Solo for Sparrow; The Undesirable Neighbour; Vendetta for the Saint

Newley, Anthony (act, 1931-1999): Alice In Wonderland (1985); Boris and Natasha; Dr. Dolittle (1967); The Garbage Pail Kids; Highly

Dangerous; How to Murder a Rich Uncle; The Last Man to Hang?; The Man Inside; Port Afrique; Vice Versa (1947); X...The Unknown

Newley, Anthony (mus, 1931-1999): Willy Wonka and the Chocolate Factory

Newlin, Martin (dir & wri): see Laurenti, Fabrizio

Newlon, Neil (act): Angel Heart

Newman, Alfred (mus, 1901-1970): The Black Swan; The Blue Bird (1940); Bulldog Drummond Strikes Back (1934); Call Northside 777; Carousel; The Count of Monte Cristo (1934); Dragonwyck; Earthbound (1940); Foreign Correspondent; For Heaven's Sake; Fourteen Hours; Heaven Can Wait (1942); Leave Her to Heaven; The Mark of Zorro (1940); Les Miserables (1935); The Prisoner of Zenda (1937 & 1952); The Snake Pit (1948)

Newman, Amy (act): Quarantine

Newman, Andrew Hill (act): Mannequin Two: On the Move

Newman, Barry (act, b. 1938): City On Fire; Daylight; Fantasies; Fear Is the Key; Vanishing Point (1971)

Newman, Charles (wri): Zombies On Broadway

Newman, Daniel (act): Bram Stoker's Dracula; Riddler's Moon; Robin Hood: Prince of Thieves

Newman, David (mus): Bill & Ted's Bogus Journey; Bill & Ted's Excellent Adventure; The Brave Little Toaster; Coneheads; Critters; The Flintstones; Frankenweenie; Heathers; The Kindred; Little Monsters; Meet the Applegates; Mr. Destiny; The Nutty Professor (1996); The Phantom (1996)

Newman, David (wri, b. 1937): Santa Claus (1985); Sheena; Superman (1978); Superman II; Superman III

Newman, Dean (act): 4D Man

Newman, Emil (mus): Blue, White and Perfect; Dead Men Tell; Just Off Broadway; Lifeboat; The Mad Magician; The Man Who Wouldn't Die; Michael Shayne, Private Detective; Ring of Fear; Shock (1946); Time to Kill (1942); The Undying Monster

Newman, Frank (dir): The Fakir's Spell; The Great German North Sea Tunnel

Newman, Fred (act): Explorers

Newman, Harry (act): The Sky Raiders

Newman, Harry C. (cin): see Neumann/Newman, Harry (C.)

Newman, Ildeton (act): The Fakir's Spell

Newman, Jack (act): Clarence

Newman, Janice (act): Flesh-Eating Mothers

Newman, Johnny (act): Shadow Conspiracy

Newman, Joseph (dir, b. 1909): Tarzan, the Ape Man (1959); This Island Earth

Newman, Ken (cin): The Premonition (1975)

Newman, Laraine (act, b. 1952): Coneheads; The Flintstones; Invaders from Mars (1986); Witchboard 2: The Devil's Doorway

Newman, Leslie (wri): Superman (1978); Superman II; Superman III

Newman, Lionel (mus): A Blueprint for Murder; The Boston Strangler; Daughter of the Mind; Dead Men Tell No Tales (1971); Desk Set; Forgotten City of the Planet of the Apes; Good Against Evil; Gorilla at Large; Inferno (1953); Man in the Attic (1953); Les Miserables (1952); Monkey Business; Myra Breckinridge; Nightmare Alley; On the Threshold of Space; The St. Valentine's Day Massacre; Time Travelers (1976); Tomorrow's Child; When Michael Calls

Newman, Melissa (act): One Dark Night; Revenge of the Stepford Wives

Newman, Nanette (act, b. 1934): Captain Nemo and the Underwater City; Deadfall; Faces In the Dark; House of Mystery (1961); Journey Into Darkness; The League of Gentlemen; The Mystery of Edwin Drood (1993); The Painted Smile; Pit of Darkness; Seance on a Wet Afternoon; The Stepford Wives; The Wrong Box

Newman, Neal (act): I Was a Zombie for the F.B.I.

Newman, Pamela (act): The Stepford Children

Newman, Paul (act, b. 1925): Quintet; Torn Curtain; The Towering Inferno; When Time Ran Out

Newman, Phyllis (act, b. 1935): Mannequin

Newman, Randy (mus, b. 1943): A Bug's Life; James and the Giant Peach; Michael; Toy Story

Newman, Sam(uel) (wri, b. 1919): The Giant Claw; Invisible Invaders; Jungle Jim In the Forbidden Land; Jungle Man-Eaters; Jungle Manhunt; The Shanghai Chest; Valley of the Headhunters; Voodoo Tiger; The Wizard of Baghdad

Newman, Thomas (act): Cape Fear (1961); Saturday the 14th

Newman, Thomas (mus): The Lost Boys; Meet Joe Black; Phenomenon

Newman, Tom (act): The Munsters' Revenge

Newman, Walter (wri): Crime and Punishment, U.S.A.

Newman, Widgey R. (dir): Castle Sinister (1932); The Merry Men of Sherwood

Newman, Widgey (wri): The Unholy Quest

Newman, William (act): The Craft; Squirm

Newmann, Birthe (act): The Mind Snatchers

Newmar, Julie (act, b. 1935, nee Julie Newmeyer): Backlash: Oblivion 2; Deep Space; Evils of the Night; Ghosts Can't Do It; Hysterical; Li'l Abner (1959); Mackenna's Gold; The Maltese Bippy; Oblivion; Serpent of the Nile; A Very Missing Person

Newmara, Tammy (act): The Devil's Messenger

Newmark, Charles (act): Lord of the Flies (1990)

Newmark, Matthew (act): Retribution (1988)

Newmeyer, Fred (dir, b. 1888): The Savage; Seven Keys to Baldpate (1925)

Newmeyer, Julie (act): see Newmar, Julie

Newney, Raul (act): Hellraiser

Newport, Michael (act): The Devil-Ship Pirates; The Naked Runner

Newson, Lloyd (act): The Magic Toyshop

Newsom, David (act): Wes Craven's New Nightmare
Newsom, Mary (act): Crime Doctor's Manhunt
Newsome, Herbert (act): The Brother from Another Planet
Newson, Jeremy (act): The Rocky Horror Picture Show; Shock Treatment! (1981)
Newth, Jonathan (act): Tennis Court; Yellow Dog
Newton, Andrew (act): Roger Corman's 'Frankenstein Unbound'
Newton, Charles (act): In the Palace of the King
Newton, Daphne (act): The Voice of Merrill
Newton, David (act): Grizzly
Newton, Dodo (act): Charlie Chan at the Opera
Newton, Eric (act): The Resurrected
Newton, Fred W.S. (act): Death Valley
Newton, Joan (act): Bedlam
Newton, Joel (dir): Jennifer (1953)
Newton, Margi (act): The Adventures of Hercules
Newton, Margit Evelyn (act): Night of the Zombies (1983)
Newton, Mary (act): The Seventh Victim
Newton, Mike (act): Secrets of the Phantom Caverns
Newton, Richard (act): Assassin (1986)
Newton, Robert (act, 1905-1956): Androcles and the Lion; Around the World In 80 Days; Blackbeard the Pirate; Bulldog Sees It Through; Busman's Honeymoon; Dark Journey; Dead Men Are Dangerous; Dr. Syn; Gaslight (1940); Jamaica Inn (1939); Long John Silver; Les Miserables (1952); Obsession (1949); Poison Pen;The Squeaker (1937); Treasure Island (1950)
Newton, Robin (act): The Psychotronic Man
Newton, Sally (act): The Armchair Detective; No Haunt for a Gentleman
Newton, Sally Anne (act): Blue Blood; Zardoz
Newton, Thandie (act, b. 1973): Beloved; Interview With the Vampire
Newton, Theodore (act): The Hidden Eye; The Sphinx (1933)
Newton, Wayne (act, b. 1942): The Dark Backward; Licence to Kill (1989)
Newton-John, Olivia (act, b. 1948): A Mom for Christmas; Toomorrow; Xanadu
Newton-John, Rona (act): Trog
New World Effects (cin): Android
Ney, Henry (wri): Voyage to a Prehistoric Planet
Ney, Marie (act): Jamaica Inn (1939); Night Was Our Friend; Scrooge (1935); Seven Days to Noon; Shadow of the Past; The Surgeon's Knife; The Wandering Jew (1933); West 11; Witchcraft (1964); Yield to the Night
Ney, Richard (act, b. 1916): Babes In Bagdad; Midnight Lace (1960); The Premature Burial; Secret of St. Ives
Neylin, James (act): A Question of Suspense
Neyman, Tom (act): Manos, the Hands of Fate
Neyman, Yuri (cin): Liquid Sky
Nezu, Jinpachi (act): Ran
Ng, Richard (act): Mr. Vampire III
Ng, Susie (act): Hardware
Ngakane, Lionel (act): The Squeeze
Ngui, Rex (act): Indiana Jones and the Temple of Doom
Nguyen, Dustin (act): Earth Angel; Virtuosity
N'Iaye, Hyacinthe (act): The Jewel of the Nile
Nibbelink, Phil (dir): An American Tail: Fievel Goes West; We're Back! A Dinosaur's Story
Niblack, Nicole (act): Flatliners
Nibley, Chris (cin): Grave Secrets
Nibley, Tom (act): Virtual Obsession
Niblo, Fred (act, 1874-1948, nee Federico Nobile): Ellery Queen, Master Detective
Niblo, Fred (dir, 1874-1948): The Mark of Zorro (1940); The Three Musketeers (1921)
Niblo Jr., Fred (wri, b. 1903): The Falcon In Danger; King of the Jungle; The Man Who Lived Twice
Nicastro, Michelle (act): The Swan Princess; The Swan Princess: Escape from Castle Mountain
Nicaud, Philippe (act, b. 1926): The Mysterious Island of Captain Nemo
Ni Chaoimh, Bairbre (act): The Outcasts; Rawhead Rex
Niccol, Andrew (dir): Gattaca
Niccol, Andrew (wri): Gattaca; The Truman Show
Nichol, Emilie (act): My Lord Conceit
Nichol, Stuart (act): Lady In the Fog
Nicholas, Allan (wri): It Fell from the Sky
Nicholas, Angela (act): Alien Space Avenger; Galactic Gigolo
Nicholas, Anna (act): Mutants In Paradise
Nicholas, Denise (act): Blacula; Capricorn One; Ghost Dad
Nicholas, Kim (act): Impulse! (1974)
Nicholas, Jonathan (act): Eye of the Needle
Nicholas, Larry (act): Return of the Living Dead, Part II
Nicholas, Mark (mus): Death Warmed Up
Nicholas, Martin (act): The Tomb
Nicholas, P.J. (act): 1984 (1984)
Nicholas, Paul (act): Blind Terror; Liszt O' Mania; Tommy; What Became of Jack and Jill
Nicholas, Paul (dir): Julie Darling; Naked Cage
Nicholas, Thomas Ian (act): A Kid In King Arthur's Court
Nicholl, David (wri): The Pursuers
Nicholl, Lee (act): Party Line
Nicholls, Anthony (act, b. 1902): The Green Scarf; High Treason (1951); The House of the Arrow (1953); The Laughing Lady; Man On the Run; The Man Who Haunted Himself; Night of the Eagle; Our Mother's House; Seven Keys; The Woman With No Name
Nicholls, Phoebe (act): Gulliver's Travels (1996)
Nicholls, Sarah (act): Dr. Terror's House of Horrors (1964); Our Mother's House
Nichols, Andrew (act): Cafe Flesh
Nichols, Anthony (act): I Spit On Your Grave
Nichols, Barbara (act, 1928-1976, nee Barbara Nickerauer): Beyond a Reasonable Doubt; Charley and the Angel; The Human Duplicators; The Loved One; Manfish; The Power (1967)
Nichols, Britt (act): The Demons (1974); Virgin Among the Living Dead
Nichols, Charles A. (dir): Charlotte's Web
Nichols, Conrad (act): Rush
Nichols, Dandy (act, 1906-1985): Act of Murder (1964); The Bed-Sitting Room; Don't Talk to Strange Men; The Fallen Idol
Nichols, David (act): The Hills Have Eyes II
Nichols, Dudley (wri, 1895-1960): And Then There Were None; The Fugitive (1947); It Happened Tomorrow; The Lost Patrol (1934); Prince Valiant (1954); The Prisoner of Shark Island; Run for the Sun
Nichols Jr., George (dir): The Return of Peter Grimm (1934)
Nichols, Joseph (act): The Glass Cage (1996)
Nichols, Kelly (act): The Toolbox Murders
Nichols, Kim (act): Barracuda
Nichols, Lance (act): Project X (1987)
Nichols, Leo (act): Deathstalker II: Duel of the Titans
Nichols, Lisa (act): Murderlust
Nichols, Mike (dir, b. 1931, nee Michael Igor Peschkowsky): The Day of the Dolphin; Wolf
Nichols, Nellie V. (act): Another Thin Man
Nichols, Nichelle (act): Star Trek; Star Trek II: The Wrath of Khan; Star Trek III: The Search for Spock; Star Trek IV: The Voyage Home; Star Trek V: The Final Frontier; Star Trek VI: The Undiscovered Country; The Supernaturals; Tarzan's Deadly Silence
Nichols, Nick (act): Dead Ringers
Nichols, Paunita (act): Vamp
Nichols, Peggy (act): Patrick
Nichols, Perry (act): Angel Heart
Nichols, Phoebe (act): Ordeal by Innocence
Nichols, Robert (act): Jennifer (1953); The Thing from Another World; The 30 Foot Bride of Candy Rock; This Island Earth
Nichols, Sheldon (act): Never-Never land
Nichols, Stephen (act): Phoenix (1995); Witchboard
Nichols, Taylor (act): Congo
Nicholson, Arch (dir): Dark Age
Nicholson, Audrey (act): Where's Johnny
Nicholson, Bruce (cin): Always; Memoirs of an Invisible Man
Nicholson, Gerda (act): Next of Kin (1992)
Nicholson, High/H. (act): The Corner House Burglary; Trapped by the London Sharks
Nicholson, Jack (act, b. 1937): Batman (1989); The Cry Baby Killer; Flight to Fury; The Little Shop of Horrors (1960); Mars Attacks!; On a Clear Day You Can See Forever; The Passenger; Psych-Out; The Raven (1963); A Safe Place; The Shining; The Terror (1963); Tommy; The Witches of Eastwick; Wolf
Nicholson, Jack (wri, b. 1937): Flight to Fury; The Trip
Nicholson, Janie (act): Curtains
Nicholson, Jennifer (act): Wolf
Nicholson, Julianne (act): Storm of the Century
Nicholson, Laura (act): Dr. Goldfoot and the Bikini Machine
Nicholson, Luree (act): The Comedy of Terrors
Nicholson, Marcia (act): The Swarm; When Time Ran Out
Nicholson, Meredith (cin): The Devil's Hand (1961); Frankenstein's Daughter (1958); She Demons
Nicholson, Nora (act, b. 1892): Crow Hollow; Dangerous Afternoon; Devil Doll (1963); Tread Softly
Nicholson, Paul (act): Jamaica Inn (1985)
Nicholson, Robert (act): Earthquake In New York
Nicholson, Sally (act): Flash Gordon (1980)
Nicholson, Scott (act): Timecop
Nicholson, William (wri): First Knight
Nicholson, Yvonne (act): Dreamhouse (1981)
Nick, Bill (act): First Man Into Space
Nick, Heinz (act): The Fifth Musketeer
Nickel, Bernhard (act): Moon 44
Nickel, Jochen (act): Moon 44
Nickel, Thomas (act): Moon 44
Nickerauer, Barbara (act): see Nichols, Barbara
Nickerson, Denise (act, b. 1959): Willy Wonka and the Chocolate
Nickerson, Jim (act): They Live Factory
Nickerson, Susan (act): Witchboard
Nickles, Michael A. (act): The Hidden II
Nicklin, Charles (act): Blind Date
Nickolaus (Jr.), John (M.) (cin): The Day Mars Invaded Earth; Ghost Diver; House of the Damned
(1962); The Terror (1963)
Nicks, Stevie (mus): Heavy Metal
Nickson-Soul, Julia (act): Amityville: A New Generation
Nicodemi, Aldo (act): Les Miserables (1943)
Nicol, Alex (act, b. 1919): A*P*E*; The Black Glove; Face the Music; The Gilded Cage; The House Across the Lake; The Night God Screamed; The Screaming Skull; Stranger In Town (1957)
Nicol, Alex (dir, b. 1919): Point of Terror; The Screaming Skull
Nicol, Emily (act): The Punisher
Nicola, Palumbo (act): El Castello dell'Orrore
Nicolai, Bruno (mus): Count Dracula; The Night Evelyn Came Out of the Grave; Ten Little Indians (1974)
Nicolai, Sergio (act): Yor, the Hunter from the Future
Nicolaides, Daniel (act): Koroshi
Nicolaides, Dimitris (act): The Day the Fish Came Out
Nicolaides, Nicos (dir): Singapore Sling
Nicolaou, Ted (dir): Bad Channels; Bloodlust: Subspecies III; Dragonworld; The Dungeonmaster; Leapin' Leprechauns!; Magic In the Mirror; Subspecies; Terrorvision
Nicolaou, Ted (wri): Bloodlust: Subspecies III; Dragonworld; The Dungeonmaster; Leapin' Leprechauns!; Terrorvision
Nicolas, Paul (dir & wri): Chained Heat
Nicole, Andrea (act): The Adventures of Hercules
Nicolelle, John (dir): Kull the Conqueror
Nicoll, Jackie (act): Midnight (1980)
Nicolodi, Daria (act): Inferno (1979); Phenomena; Profundo Rosso; Shock (1978); Tenebrae; Terror at the Opera
Nicolosi, Michael (act): Dream a Little Dream 2
Nicolosi, Roberto (mus): La Battaglia di Maratona; La Ragazza Che Sapeva Troppo
Nicols, Earl (act): Time After Time
Nicolson, Dave (act): Total Recall
Nicos, Antoine (act): L'Ultima Preda del Vampiro
Nicosia, Joseph A. (act): Phenomenon
Nicotero, Greg (act): From Dusk Till Dawn
Niebel, Gregory (act): Trancers II: The Return of Jack Deth
Niederle, Ivo (act): Howling II
Niederman, Mike (act): Attack of the Killer Tomatoes
Niehaus, Lennie (mus): Ratboy
Nielsen, Asta (act, 1883-1972): Hamlet (1920)
Nielsen, Brigitte (act, b. 1962): Galaxis; Murder by Moonlight; Red Sonja
Nielsen, Christiane (act): The Invisible Terror
Nielsen, Connie (act): Soldier
Nielsen, Hans (act): Confess, Dr. Corda; Legacy of Horror (1964); The Monster of London (1964); Die Tur mit den Sieben Schlossern; The Valley of Fear (1964); Vengeance
Nielsen, Helen (wri): Murder by Proxy
Nielsen, Jamie (act): To All a Goodnight
Nielsen, Leslie (act, b. 1926): The Amsterdam Kill; The Aquarians; Change of Mind; Charlie Chan: Happiness Is a Warm Clue; City On Fire; The Creature Wasn't Nice; Creepshow; Dark Intruder; Day of the Animals; Dracula: Dead and Loving It; Forbidden Planet; Hauser's Memory; How to Steal the World; Night Slaves; Night Train to Paris; The Poseidon Adventure; Prom Night; The Reluctant Astronaut; Repossessed; The Resurrection of Zachary Wheeler; Spaceship (1983); They Call It Murder
Nielsen, Robert (act): see Nelson, Barry
Nielson, Lester (wri): A Night of Terror (1933)
Nielson, Thor (act): The Man Who Saw Tomorrow
Niemczyk, Leon (act): Rekopis Znaleziony w Saragossie
Niemi, Lisa (act): Slam Dance; Steel Dawn
Nieth, Nicole (act): Hell Mountain
Nieto, Jose (act): Contraband Spain
Nietzchmann, Erich (cin): Chronik von Grieshuus; Der Mude Tod; Der Student von Prag (1926)
Nieva, Al(fonso) (cin): The Emerald of Artatama; A Witch Without a Broom
Nieves, Benny (act): The Toxic Avenger, Part II
Nieves, Robaire (act): Secrets In the Attic
Nieves-Conde, (Jose) Antonio (dir & wri): Marta; Sound of Horror
Niewel, Francis (wri): Hipnosis
Nigam, Anjul (act): Netforce
Nigh, Alison (wri): Out There
Nigh, Jane (act, b. 1926): Hold That Hypnotist; Zamba
Nigh, William (dir, b. 1881): The Ape (1940); Black Dragons; Doomed to Die; The Fatal Hour (1940); The Ghost and the Guest; Mr. Wong, Detective; Mr. Wong In Chinatown; Mr. Wu (1927); The Mysterious Mr. Wong; Mystery Liner; The Mystery of Mr. Wong; The Strange Case of Dr. Rx; The Thirteenth Man
Nightingale, Ben (act): Thirst
Nightingale, John (act): File It Under Fear
Nightingale, Michael (act): Clegg; Paris Express
Nightriders, The (mus): Satan's Sadists
Nighy, Bill (act): The Phantom of the Opera (1989)
Nigolian, Artemus (act): The Clutching Hand
Nigra, Christina (act): Cloak and Dagger (1984); Goliath Awaits; The Sword and the Sorcerer; Twilight Zone
Nihomatsu, Kazui (dir & wri): The X from Outer Space
Niida, Sayuri (act): The Toxic Avenger, Part II
Nijo, Eiko (act): Virtuosity
Niki, Jeff (act): Eyes of Laura Mars
Nikkinen, Amanda (act): Mad Max Beyond Thunderdome
Nikkinen, Liam (act): Mad Max Beyond Thunderdome
Niklas, Jan (act): The Formula
Nikola, Louis (act): Spiritualism Exposed (1913)
Nikola, Louis (dir & wri): Magic Squares
Nikolaev, Valery (act): The Saint
Nikolayev, Andrian (act): Stellar Brothers-From the Kremlin to the Cosmos
Nikonenko, Sergei (act): Parad Planyet
Niland, John (act): Horror High
Niles, Blair (wri): Condemned
Niles, Chuck (act): Hand of Death; Teenage Zombies
Niles, Jason (act): Violated
Niles, Ken (act): Out of the Past (1947)
Niles, Richard (act): Blood Bath (1975); Destination Inner Space
Niles, Wendell (act): Beyond a Reasonable Doubt
Nillson, Harry (act & mus): The Point; Son of Dracula (1974)
Nillson, Magnus (act): I Am Curious (Yellow)
Nilssen, Sigurd (act): Peril from the Planet Mongo; Purple Death from Outer Space
Nilsson, Anna Q. (act, 1888-1974): Adam's Rib; Seven Keys to Baldpate (1917); Sunset Boulevard
Nilsson, Britt (act): The Thing With Two Heads
Nilsson, Kjell (act): The Road Warrior
Nimier, Roger (wri): Frantic
Nimmo, Derek (act, b. 1931): Casino Royale; Hot Enough for June; The Liquidator; Murder Ahoy; One of Our Dinosaurs Is Missing
Nimoy, Leonard (act, b. 1931): Baffled!; The Balcony; The Brain Eaters; Brave New World (1998); Deathwatch (1967); Invasion of The Body Snatchers (1978); The Pagemaster; Satan's Satellites; Star Trek; Star Trek II: The Wrath of Khan; Star Trek III: The Search for Spock; Star Trek IV: The Voyage Home; Star Trek V: The Final Frontier; Star Trek VI: The Undiscovered Country; Them! (1954)
Nimoy, Leonard (dir, b. 1931): Star Trek III: The Search for Spock; Star Trek IV: The Voyage Home
Nimoy, Leonard (wri, b. 1931): Star Trek IV: The Voyage Home; Star Trek VI: The Undiscovered
Country
Nimrod, Brent (wri): The Female Bunch
Ninaus, Miguel (act): Making Contact

Nincheri, Rolland/Rollie (act): *Happy Birthday to Me; Scanners*
Ninchi, Ave (act): *Pulp; Seven Dwarfs to the Rescue*
Ninchi, Carlo (act): *La Beaute du Diable; The Queen of Babylon*
Ninestein, Alley (act): *Flesh-Eating Mothers*
Nino, Miguel (act): *The Package*
Niola, Joe (act): *Igor and the Lunatics*
Nipar, Yvette (act): *Doctor Mordrid*
Nipote, Joe (act): *Casper*
Nisbet, Jack (act): *Wolf*
Nishigaki, Rokuro (cin): *Lake of Dracula*
Nissen, (Aud) Egede (act): *Doctor Mabuse; Homunculus*
Nissen, Brian (act): *The Fur Collar; Man Accused; The Marked One; Richard III (1955); Ring of Spies*
Nissen, Brian (wri): *The Swan Princess*
Nissen, Claus (act): *The Mind Snatchers*
Nissen, Greta (act, 1906-1988): *On Secret Service; Women of All Nations*
Nissen, Helge (act): *Blade af Satans Bog*
Nissim, Nitcho Lion (cin): *Programmed to Kill*
Nissinen, Marjatta (act): *Gorky Park*
Nisson, Rob (act): *Copycat*
Nithsdale, Donald (act): *Agatha*
Nitschke, Mathias (act): *Due to an Act of God*
Nitties, Aaron (act): *Chilling (1981)*
Nitzsche, Jack (mus): *The Jewel of the Nile; Performance; The Seventh Sign; Starman; Village of the Giants*
Niven, Barbara (act): *Under Lock and Key*
Niven, David (act, 1910-1983): *Around the World In 80 Days; The Bishop's Wife; Casino Royale; Death On the Nile; Dinner at the Ritz; The Elusive Pimpernel (1950); The Extraordinary Seaman; Eye of the Devil; Eyes of Fate; A Matter of Life and Death; Murder by Death; The Prisoner of Zenda (1937); Vampira; Where the Spies Are; Wuthering Heights (1939)*
Niven Jr., David (wri): *The Night They Saved Christmas*
Niven, Kip (act): *Damnation Alley; Earthquake; A Fire In the Sky (1978); New Year's Evil*
Nix, Stacy (act): *Evil Toons*
Nix, Taylor (act): *Murder of Innocence*
Nixon, Allan (act): *Atlantis (1948); Mesa of Lost Women; Pickup; Prehistoric Women (1950); Untamed Mistress*
Nixon, Cynthia (act): *Addams Family Values; The Manhattan Project; Tattoo*
Nixon, David (act): *The Spider's Web*
Nixon, Jim (act): *The Nesting*
Nixon, John P. (act): *The Legend of Boggy Creek*
Nixon, Marian (act, 1904-1983): *Charlie Chan's Chance; The Chinese Parrot; The Lash*
Nixon, Mojo (act): *Super Mario Bros.*
Nixon, Ruth (act): *Noose*
Nizet, Charles (dir & wri): *Voodoo Heartbeat*
Niznick, Stephanie (act): *Inferno (1998)*
Nizza, Michael (cin): *Zombies Lake*
Nizzica, Cesare (act): *The Eyes Behind the Stars*
Nobile, Federico (act & dir): see Niblo, Fred
Noble, Alison (act): *Return to Horror High*
Noble, Ann (act): *The Corpse Grinders*
Noble, Chris (act): *Cavegirl (1985)*
Noble, Erin (act): *Uninvited (1993)*
Noble, James (act, b. 1922): *Who?*
Noble, Jim (act): *Beverly Hills Bodysnatchers*
Noble, Larry (act): *The Quatermass Conclusion*
Noble, Maurice (cin): *The Phantom Tollbooth*
Noble, Patsy Ann (act): *Death Is a Woman*
Noble, Robert (act): *The Adventures of Robin Hood*
Noble, Shaun (act): *Black Narcissus*
Noble, Terence (act): *Mr. H.C. Andersen*
Noble, Tom (act): *Neon Maniacs*
Noble, Trisha (act): *The Private Eyes (1980)*
Nobles, William (cin): *Dick Tracy (1937); Dick Tracy Returns; Dick Tracy's G-Men; The Lost Jungle; One Frightened Night; Radio Ranch*
Nobrega, Renata (act): *The Pink Chiquitas*
Nocell, Jim (act): *Deadtime Stories*
Nocquet, Andre (act): *Terminus*
Noe, Anna Maria (act): *Operation Kid Brother*
Noe, Robert G. (act): *Barracuda*
Noel, Daniele (act): *Bedazzled; The Magus; Return from the Ashes; The Vengeance of She*
Noel, Hubert (act): *Devils of Darkness; The Little Girl Who Lives Down the Lane*
Noel, Magali (act, b. 1932): *The Accident; Amarcord; The Death of Mario Ricci; Rope Around the Neck; Satyricon; The Secret Mark of D'Artagnan*
Noel, Mark (cin): *Nothing But Trouble*
Noel, Sid (act & wri): *The Wacky World of Dr. Morgus*
Noel, Sterling (wri): *House of Secrets*
Noelle, Lesa (act): *Virtuosity*
Noel-Noel (act): *A Dog, a Mouse and a Sputnik*
Noelte, Rudolf (dir & wri): *Das Schloss*
Noguchi, Haruyasu (dir): *Gappa, the Triphibian Monster*
Noguchi, Takashi (cin): *Virus (1980)*
Nogulich, Natalia/Natalija (act): *The Guardian; Mind Over Murder*
Noh, Lorene (act): *Congo*
Nohr, Susan (act): *Haunts*
Noice, J. Gordon (act): *Virtuosity*
Noiret, Philippe (act, b. 1931): *The Assassination Bureau; Birgitt Haas Must Be Killed; Dear Detective; The French Conspiracy; Mister Freedom; The Night of the Generals; The Return of the Musketeers; The Serpent (1973); Topaz; Who Is Killing the Great Chefs of Europe?*
Noizet, Madame (act): *L'Age d'Or*
Nokes, Jeff (act): *Dangerous Touch*
Nolan, Barry (cin): *Dune; King Kong Lives*
Nolan, Dani Sue (act): *The Sniper*
Nolan, David (act): *Rawhead Rex*
Nolan, James/Jim (USA act): *The Darker Side of Terror; Daughter of the Jungle; Dick Tracy Meets Gruesome; Torchy Blane In Panama*
Nolan, Jeanette (act, 1911-1998): *Avalanche; Chamber of Horrors (1966); Cloak and Dagger (1984); The Fox and the Hound; Goliath Awaits; Macbeth (1947); The Manitou; My Blood Runs Cold; Nightmare Honeymoon; The Reluctant Astronaut; The Rescuers*
Nolan, Jim (Euro act): *La Vergine di Norimberga*
Nolan, John (GB act): *Terror (1979)*
Nolan, John (USA act): *Something Evil*
Nolan, Lloyd (act, 1902-1985): *Blue, White and Perfect; Circumstantial Evidence (1945); The Double Man; Dressed to Kill (1941); Earthquake; Fire; The Girl Hunters; Isn't It Shocking?; It Came Upon the Midnight Clear; Just Off Broadway; Lady In the Lake; The Last Hunt; The Man Who Wouldn't Die; Michael Shayne, Private Detective; The November Plan; Portrait In Black; Sleepers West; Somewhere In the Night; The Street With No Name; Time to Kill (1942)*
Nolan, Margaret (act): *Goldfinger; Toomorrow*
Nolan, Mary (act, 1906-1948): *West of Zanzibar*
Nolan, Matt (act): *Sometimes They Come Back*
Nolan, Riba (act): *Attack of the Killer Tomatoes*
Nolan, Tom (act): *School Spirit; Voyage of the Rock Aliens*
Nolan, William F. (wri, b. 1928): *Bridge Across Time; Burnt Offerings; Logan's Run; The Norliss Tapes; Trilogy of Terror*
Noland, Robert (act): *Revolt of the Zombies*
Nolen, Jack (act): *Attack of the Killer Tomatoes*
Nolin, Maggie (mus): *Night of the Zombies (1981)*
Nolte, Nick (act, b. 1941): *Cape Fear (1991); The Deep; Nightwatch (1998)*
Nomad, Mike (act): *Cocoon; Cocoon: The Return*
Noman, Eric Van Haren (cin): *Terminal*
Nomura, Kozo (act): *Battle In Outer Space*
Nono, Clare (act): *Chiller; Fire and Ice; Nightmares (1983)*
Nonyela, Valentine (act): *Welcome II the Terrordome*
Noon, Frank (act): *The Guardian*
Noonan, Betty (act): *War of the Wizards*
Noonan, Chris (dir): *Babe*
Noonan, Greg (act): *Blink; The Package*
Noonan, Kerry (act): *Friday the 13th, Part VI: Jason Lives; Nightmare On the 13th Floor*
Noonan, Patrick (act): *Royal Love*
Noonan, Sheila (act): *The Incredible Petrified World*
Noonan, Tom (act): *The Monster Squad; RoboCop 2; Wolfen*
Noonan, Tom(my) (act): *Born to Kill; Dick Tracy (1945)*
Noone, Peter (act): *Hold On!*
Noose, Ted (act): *A Return to Salem's Lot*
Noozaki, Fumito (act): *Popcorn*
Nop, Chantara (act): *The Golden Child*
Norbeck, Dana (act): *Frankenstein Island*
Norbert, Frederic (act): *Perceval*
Norbert, Patrick (act): *Ils Appelleny Ca un Accident*
Norby, Ghita (act): *Crazy Paradise; The Kingdom*
Norcia, Joe (act): *Midnight 2: Sex, Death, and Videotape*
Norcross, Van (wri): *Revenge of the Zombies (1943)*
Nord, Eric "Big Daddy" (act): *The Hypnotic Eye*
Nord, Nathalie (act): *Necronomicon*
Nord, Pierre (wri): *The Serpent (1973)*
Nordell, Phil (act): *The Return of the Six Million Dollar Man and the Bionic Woman; 2002: Rape of Eden; Watchers II*
Norden, Christine (act, b. 1923): *Black Widow (1951); A Case for PC 49; The Interrupted Journey*
Norden, Denis (wri): *The Water Babies*
Norden, Eric (wri): *Legacy of Blood; The Little Savage*
Norden, Erika (act): *The Golden Blade*
Nordenhold, Ralph (act): *Making Contact*
Nordgren, Erik (mus): *Face of Fire; Det Sjunde Inseglet*
Nordike, Mark (act): *Vampire at Midnight*
Nordine, Ken (act): *Fearless Frank*
Nordli, Stephanie (wri): *Saturday Island*
Nordling, Jeffrey (act): *Journey to the Center of the Earth (1993)*
Nordra, Greta (act): *The Witches (1990)*
Nordstrom, Kim (act): *Jaws 3-D*
Nored, Don (act): *Secrets in the Attic*
Norero, Matt (act): *Mind Games (1989)*
Norfolk, Edgar (act): *The Black Abbot (1934); Forging Ahead; Sexton Blake and the Mademoiselle; The Sign of Four (1932); Tangled Evidence*
Norgaard, Carsten (act): *Out of Annie's Past*
Norgaard, Per (mus): *The Red Mantle*
Norgard, Lindsay (dir): *Princess Warrior*
Norgate, P.G. (act): *Lieutenant Rose and the Boxers; Lieutenant Rose and the Chinese Pirates; Lieutenant Rose and the Foreign Spy; Lieutenant Rose and the Gun-Runners; Lieutenant Rose and the Hidden Treasure; Lieutenant Rose and the Moorish Raiders; Lieutenant Rose and the Patent Aeroplane; Lieutenant Rose and the Stolen Code; Lieutenant Rose and the Stolen Ship*
Noriega, Eduardo (act): *The Beast of Hollow Mountain; Captain Scarlett; The Living Idol; Zorro, the Gay Blade*
Noriega, Richard (act): *Final Eye*
Norland, Tom Misha (dir & wri): *The Commuter*
Norlie, Richard E. (act): *Impulse (1984)*
Norman, Andy (act): *The Lair of the White Worm*
Norman, Ann (act): *Blow-Up; Maroc 7*
Norman, B.G. (act): *The Big Clock*
Norman, Eva (act): *The Great Spy Raid*
Norman, Gertrude (act): *The Greene Murder Case*
Norman, Helen (act): *The Wicker Man*
Norman, Henry (act): *The Man With the Magnetic Eyes*
Norman, Jett (act): see Walker, Clint
Norman, John (wri, b. 1931): *Gor; Outlaw of Gor*
Norman, Josephine (act): *The Road to Yesterday*
Norman, Leslie (dir, b. 1911): *Mix Me a Person; Too Dangerous to Live; X...The Unknown*
Norman, Lon E. (mus): *Voodoo Blood Bath*
Norman, Maidie (act): *Tarzan's Hidden Jungle; The Well; What Ever Happened to Baby Jane?(1962)*
Norman, Marc (wri): *Cutthroat Island*
Norman, Michel (act): *The Black Windmill*
Norman, Monty (mus): *Call Me Bwana; Dr. No*
Norman, Oliver (act): *Tam Lin*
Norman, Paul (act): *The Village of the Damned (1960)*
Norman, Susan (act): *Poison (1990)*
Norman, Valter (act): *Morianna*
Norman, Vera (act): *Torticola Contre Frankensberg*
Norman, Zack (act): *Romancing the Stone*
Norment, Elizabeth (act): *Runaway; Too Good to Be True*
Normington, John (act): *The Medusa Touch; Rollerball; The 39 Steps (1978)*
Noro, Line (act): *Gold (French-speaking version)*
Norona, David (act): *Mrs. Santa Claus*
Norrington, Malcolm (act): *Strange Days*
Norrington, Stephen (dir & wri): *Death Machine*
Norrington, Steve (act): *Return to Oz*
Norris, Aaron (act): *The Octagon*
Norris, Aaron (dir): *Hellbound*
Norris, Alfred (act): see Martin, Tony
Norris, Buckley (act): *Creature; Highlander; Slam Dance; The Sword and the Sorcerer; Waxwork II: Lost In Time*
Norris, Chet (act): *Hangar 18*
Norris, Chuck (act, b. 1940): *Firewalker; A Force of One; Hellbound; The Octagon; Silent Rage*
[illegible]
Norris, Dean (act): *Dean Koontz's 'Mr. Murder'; Full Eclipse; Gremlins 2: The New Batch; The Lawnmower Man; Total Recall*
Norris, Edward (act, b. 1910): *Close Call for Ellery Queen; Decoy; The Gorilla (1939); The Great Impersonation (1942); The Mystery of Marie Roget; Shadows In the Night; Trapped by Boston Blackie*
Norris, Fred (act): *The Hotel Manor Inn*
Norris, Hermione (act): *The Pale Horse*
Norris, Karen (act): *The Destructors; The Underwater City*
Norris, Ken (act): *Octopussy; Too Scared to Scream*
Norris, Michael/Mike (act): *Death Ring; The Octagon*
Norris, Richard (act): *The Destructors*
Norris, Rufus (act): *Demon Wind*
Norris, Stanley (act): *King Solomon's Mines (1985)*
Norris, Virginia (act): *Shocker*
Norris, William J. (wri): *Re-Animator*
North, Alan (act): *The Formula; Highlander; The Long Kiss Goodnight*
North, Alex (mus, 1910-1991): *The Bad Seed (1956); Dragonslayer; Journey Into Fear (1975); Shanks; The Thirteenth Letter; Willard*
North, Edmund (H.) (wri, 1911-1990): *The Day the Earth Stood Still; Meteor; Murder On a Bridle Path*
North, Heather (act, b. 1950): *The Barefoot Executive*
North, Hope (act): *The Curse; Something Is Out There*
North, J.J. (act): *Attack of the 60 Foot Centerfold*
North, Jack (act): *Appointment for a Killing*
North, Joe (act): *The Adventures of Robin Hood*
North, Michael (act): *The Unsuspected*
North, Neil (act): *Britannia Mews*
North, Noelle (act): *Blood Song; Carrie; Jekyll and Hyde...Together Again; Tarantulas: The Deadly Cargo*
North, Robert (act): *Blades*
North, Rojay (act): *Bog*
North, Sheree (act, b. 1933, nee Dawn Bethel): *Destination Inner Space; Maniac Cop*
North, Ted (act): *Charlie Chan In Rio*
North, Virginia (act): *The Abominable Dr. Phibes; Deadlier Than the Male; On Her Majesty's Secret Service; Some Girls Do*
North, Zeme (act): *Zotz!*
Northam, Jeremy (act): *Mimic*
Northcote, Charles (act): *Virus (1980)*
Northcote, Peter (act): *The Strange Case of Mr. Todmorden*
Northcote, Sidney (act): *A Cornish Romance; A Tragedy of the Cornish Coast*
Northcote, Sidney (dir): *A Cornish Romance; Detective Daring and the Thames Coiners; The King of Crime; The Monkey's Paw (1915); A Tragedy of the Cornish Coast; The Witch of the Welsh Mountains*
Northern, Mark (act): *Secrets of the Phantom Caverns*
Northey, Christopher (act): *Morons from Outer Space*
Northover, Mark (act): *Hardware; Willow*
Northrup, Harry (act): *The Last Warning (1929)*
Northrup, Harry (E.) (act): *Project X (1987); The Silence of the Lambs*
Norton, B.W.L. (dir): *Baby: Secret of the Lost Legend; Gargoyles*
Norton, Barry (act, 1904-1956): *El Cuerpo del Lito; Devil Monster; Dracula (1931, Spanish-speaking version); The Wizard*
Norton, Betty (act): *The Dance of Death (1938)*
Norton, Bill L. (dir): *A Deadly Vision; Them (1996)*
Norton, Christopher (act): *Mad Max Beyond Thunderdome*
Norton, Cliff (act): *Ghost Catchers*
Norton, Edgar (act): *Dr. Jekyll and Mr. Hyde (1932); Dracula's Daughter; Son of Frankenstein; Trouble for Two*
Norton, Edward (act): *Primal Fear*
Norton, Eleanor (wri): *Day of the Animals*
Norton, Frederick (wri): *Chu Chin Chow (1923 & 1934)*
Norton, Jack (act, 1889-1958): *After the Thin Man; The Chinese Cat; Dr. Renault's Secret; The Falcon Strikes Back; The Lone Wolf Spy Hunt; The Scarlet Clue; Shadows Over Chinatown, Strange Confession*
Norton, Jan (act): *Screams of a Winter Night*
Norton, Jim (act): *Memoirs of an Invisible Man; Midnight's Child; Screamer; Straw Dogs*
Norton, John (act): *Superman II*
[illegible]
Norton, Laura Lee (act): *Dream a Little Dream*
Norton, Mary (wri): *Bedknobs and Broomsticks; The Borrowers (1973 & 1998)*

Norton, Randy (act): *Fire and Ice*
Norton, Richard (1910s & 1920s act): *The Murdock Trial; The Mystery of a London Flat; Trent's Last Case (1920); What's Bred...Comes Out In the Flesh*
Norton, Richard (1980s act): *Cyber-Tracker; Equalizer 2000; The Octagon; Raiders of the Sun*
Norton, William (wri): *Day of the Animals; I Dismember Mama; Trader Horn (1973)*
Norvo, Red (act & mus): see Red Norvo and Trio
Norwick, Natalie (act): *Hidden Fear; 23 Paces to Baker Street*
Norwood, Eille (act): *The Abbey Grange; The Beryl Coronet (1921); Black Peter; The Boscombe Valley Mystery (1922); The Bruce Partington Plans; A Case of Identity; The Charlatan; Charles Augustus Milverton; The Copper Beeches (1921); The Crimson Circle (1922); The Devil's Foot; The Dying Detective; The Empty House; The Golden Pince-Nez; The Greek Interpreter; The Hound of the Baskervilles (1921); The Man With the Twisted Lip (1921); The Musgrave Ritual (1922); The Naval Treaty; The Noble Bachelor; The Norwood Builder; Princess Clementina; The Priory School; The Recoil (1922); The Red Circle (1922); The Red-Headed League; The Reigate Squires (1922); The Resident Patient; A Scandal In Bohemia; The Second Stain; The Sign of Four (1923); The Six Napoleons; The Solitary Cyclist; The Stockbroker's Clerk; The Tiger of San Pedro; Yellow Face*
Norwood, Frank (wri): *Past Midnight*
Nosaki, Yoko (act): *Murder In the Doll House*
Nosalt, Margarita (act): *Hellhole*
Noseworthy, Jack (act): *Barb Wire; What We Did That Night*
Nosseck, Martin (act): *One Dark Night*
Nosseck, Max (dir, 1902-1972): *The Brighton Strangler*
Nosseck, Max (wri, 1902-1972): *The Brighton Strangler; One Dangerous Night*
Nosseck, Noel (dir): *The Fury Within; Nightscream; The Sister-In-Law; Tornado!*
Nosseck, Ralph (act): *Captain Nemo and the Underwater City*
Nostro, Nick (dir): *Triumph of the Ten Gladiators*
Notario, Laura (act): *Slugs*
Noth, Christopher (act, b. 1957): *Killer In the Mirror*
Nothaft, Vivian (act): *Primal Scream*
Noto, Vic (act): *Street Trash*
Nott, James (act): *Grip (1915)*
Notteli, Elizabeth (act): *Waxwork II: Lost In Time*
Nottingham, Susie (act): *Baby: Secret of the Lost Legend*
Nottingham, Wendy (act): *Mary Reilly*
Notz, Thierry (dir): *The Terror Within; Watchers II*
Nouri, Michael (act, b. 1946): *Captain America (1992); Eyes of Terror; Fatal Sky; GoBots: Battle of the Rock Lords; The Hidden; The Hidden II; Inner Sanctum 2; The Loves of Dracula; Project:Alien; World of Dracula*
Nourse, Dorothy (act): *The Sorrows of Satan (1925)*
Nova, Lou (act): *Prince Valiant (1954)*
Nova, Ludmilla (act): *The Slipper and the Rose*
Nova, Natalie (act): *Discipline*
Novak (cin): *Do You Keep a Lion at Home?*
Novak, Debbie (act): *He Knows You're Alone*
Novak, Eva (act, 1897-1988): *Boston Blackie; Laughing at Danger; Red Signals*
Novak, Frank (act): *A Dangerous Affair; Murder of Innocence; The Nature of the Beast; Watchers 3*
Novak, George (act): *Mad Max*
Novak, Ivana (act): *The Devil's Nightmare*
Novak, John (act): *The Death of the Incredible Hulk; Doctor Who; Eternal Evil; Volcano: Fire On the Mountain*
Novak, Kim (act, b. 1933, nee Marilyn Novak): *Alfred Hitchcock Presents; Bell, Book and Candle; The Mirror Crack'd; Satan's Triangle; Son of Sinbad; Tales That Witness Madness; Vertigo*
Novak, Lenka (act): *Slaughterhouse Rock; The Vampire Girls*
Novak, Lindsey (act): *The Psychotronic Man*
Novak, Marilyn (act): see Novak, Kim
Novak, Mel (act): *The Ultimate Warrior*
Novak, Mickell (wri): *One Million B.C.; One Million Years B.C.*
Novak, Nardi (act): *The Dark Half*
Novak, Richard (act): *Endgame*
Novak, Ted (act): *The Power (1980)*
Novarro, Mario (act): *The Beast of Hollow Mountain; The Black Scorpion (1957)*
Novarro, Nick (act): *Scream of the Butterfly*
Novarro, Ramon (act, 1899-1968, nee Ramon Samaniegos): *Mata Hari (1932); The Prisoner of Zenda (1922); Trifling Women*
Novella, Rita (act): see Drake, Dona
Novello, Don (act, b. 1943): *Casper*
Novello, Ivor (act, 1893-1951, nee Ivor Davies): *Downhill; The Lodger (1926 & 1932); The Man Without Desire*
Novello, Ivor (wri, 1893-1951): *Downhill; The Lodger (1932); The Rat*
Novello, Jay (act, 1904-1982): *Atlantis, the Lost Continent; The Diamond Queen; The Lost World (1960); The Mad Magician; Operation Secret; Passport to Suez; Sabaka; Salome (1953); The Sniper; Son of Sinbad; Zorro, the Avenger*
Novgrod, Judith (act): *The House of the Dead; Nightwing*
Novis, Donald (act): *Bulldog Drummond (1929)*
Novo, Nancho (act): *La Ardilla Roja*
Novotny, Paul (mus): *Blue Monkey*
Novros, Paul (mus): *Voyage to the Outer Planets*
Nowak, Danny (cin): *Empire of Ash III; Time Runner*
Nowell, Justin (act): *The Offspring*
Nowell, Tommy (act): *The Offspring*
Nowell, Wedgewood (act): *Black Orchids; Calling Philo Vance; Dick Tracy (1937); Torchy Runs for Mayor*
Nowicki, Jan (act): *Bariera*
Nowicki, Marek (cin): *Profesor Zazul*
Nowicki, Marek (dir & wri): *Profesor Zazul; Przyjaciel*
Nowicki, Tom (act): *Web of Deceit*
Noy, Wilfred (act): *The Body Vanishes; Menace (1934)*
Noy, Wilfred (dir): *An Adventuress Outwitted; An Ape's Devotion; Asthore; At the Hour of Three; The Barton Mystery (1932); Behind the Scenes; Dr. Brian Pellie and the Bank Robbery; Dr. Brian Pellie and the Baronet's Bride; Dr. Brian Pellie and the Secret Despatch; Dr. Brian Pellie and the Spanish Grandees; Dr. Brian Pellie and the Wedding Gifts; Dr. Brian Pellie Escapes from Prison; Dr. Brian Pellie, Thief and Coiner; The Enemy In Our Midst; The Eye of the Idol; The Face at the Window (1920); The Family Solicitor; A False Friend; The Five Wishes; The Flooded Mine; Foiled by a Girl; The Forced Confession; The House of Mystery (1913); The Ivory Hand; Kind Hearts Are More Than Coronets; Lorna Doone (1912); The Master of Merripit; The Midnight Girl; Borah's Debt of Honour; Old St. Paul's; A Princess of the Blood; The Queen Mother; A Secret Life; The Seventh Word; A Strong Man's Love; The Temptation of Carlton Earle; Under the Red Robe (1915); When East Meets West; When Passions Rise*
Noy, Wilfred (wri): *The Midnight Girl*
Noyce, Phillip (dir, b. 1950): *Dead Calm; The Saint; Sliver*
Noyes, Jan (act): *Beyond and Back*
Noyons, Ad (act): *The Lift*
Nucci, Danny (act): *Eraser*
Nucci, Laura (act): *Warriors of the Wasteland*
Nuchtern, Simon (wri): *The Rejuvenator; Silent Madness*
Nudell, Noah (act): *The Last Man On Planet Earth*
Nudell, Sam (act): *Dr. Black Mr. Hyde*
Nuffer, Robert (act): *Ed Wood*
Nugent, Eddie (act): *Lost In the Stratosphere; Night Nurse*
Nugent, Elliott (act & wri, 1899-1980): *The Unholy Three (1930)*
Nugent, Elliott (dir, 1899-1980): *The Cat and the Canary (1939)*
Nugent, Frank S. (wri, 1908-1965): *Angel Face*
Nugent, J.C. (wri): *The Unholy Three (1930)*
Nugent, Richard (act): *The Pearl of Death*
Nugent, Tawna (act): *Mr. Sycamore*
Nugget (animal act): *Wavelength*
Numkena, Anthony (act): see Holliman, Earl
Numkena, Ronald Alan (act): *The Naked Jungle*
Nunamaker, Deborah (act): *The Henderson Monster*
Nunes, Mizan (act): *Maximum Thrust*
Nunez, Daniel (act): *The Howling*
Nunez (Jr.), Miguel (A.) (act): *Carnosaur 2; Friday the 13th-Part V: A New Beginning; The Return of the Living Dead (1985); Shadowzone; Slam Dunk Ernest*
Nunez, Tito (act): *Short Circuit 2*
Nunley, Joe (act): *Secrets of the Phantom Caverns*
Nunn, Alice (act): *Dark Night of the Scarecrow; Fangs; The Fury*
Nunn, Bill (act): *Candyman: Farewell to the Flesh; Def by Temptation; Extreme Measures; Kiss the Girls; True Crime*
Nunn, David (act): *I Was a Zombie for the F.B.I.*
Nunn, William (act): *A Connecticut Yankee In King Arthur's Court (1989); The Groundstar Conspiracy*
Nunnerley, Lesley (act): *Tales That Witness Madness*
Nunnery, Hope (act): *King Kong Lives*
Nunziato, Elisabeth (act): *Phenomenon*
Nuridsany, Michel (dir): *Un Peu de Votre Sang*
Nurmi, Harry (act): *Fortress*
Nurmi, Maila (act): see Vampira
Nurse, Catriona (act): *The Sexplorer*
Nusciak, Lordana (act): *Gladiators Seven*
Nuse, Deland (dir): *The Chilling (1989)*
Nusinov, Ilya (wri): *Rasputin (1985)*
Nussbaum, Mike (act): *Fatal Attraction*
Nussbaum, Raphael (dir & wri): *The Invisible Terror*
Nutley, Zara (act): *Mr. Selkie*
Nuttal, Jeff (act): *Robin Hood (1991)*
Nutter, Bryan (act) *Witchcraft 6: The Devil's Mistress*
Nutter, David (act): *Trancers 4: Jack of Swords*
Nutter, David (dir): *Disturbing Behavior; Trancers 5: Sudden Deth*
Nutter, Edna May (act): see Oliver, Edna May
Nutter, Mayf (act): *Hunter's Blood*
Nutter, Tarah (act): *Without Warning (1980)*
Nuttgens, Giles (cin): *Alice In Wonderland (1999)*
Nuyen, France (act, b. 1939): *Battle for the Planet of the Apes; The Big Game; Deathmoon; Dimension 5; The Horror at 37,000 Feet; A Passion to Kill; Return to Fantasy Island*
Nuyen, Laureen (act): *I Lunghi Capelli della Morte*
Nyby, Christian (dir, 1913-1993): *Hell On Devil's Island; Operation C.I.A.; The Thing from Another World*
Nyby II, Christian I. (dir): *Too Good to Be True*
Nye, Carrie (act): *Creepshow; Hello Again; Too Scared to Scream*
Nye, Carroll (act, 1901-1974): *The Bishop Murder Case*
Nye, Louis (act): *Full Moon High; Sex Kittens Go to College; Zotz!*
Nye, Pat (act): *The Mirror Crack'd*
Nye, Will (act): *Heart and Souls; Remote Control (1988)*
Nyerges, Chadd (act): *Sometimes They Come Back*
Nygaard, Paul (act): *The Fourth Man*
Nygaard, Richard (act): *Bog*
Nykvist, Sven (cin, b. 1922): *Black Moon (1975); Dream Lover; Persona; Siddhartha; The Tenant; Through a Glass Darkly; The Tragedy of Carmen; Tystnaden; Vargtimmen*
Nylander, Olov (cin): *The Visitors (1989)*
Nyman, Lena (act): *I Am Curious (Yellow)*
Nyman, Michael (mus): *The Cold Room; The Falls; Prospero's Books*
Nype, Russell (act): *The Stuff*
Nystrom, Carl (wri): *Beautiful Stranger; Impulse (1955)*

Oakes, Harry (cin): *Doppelganger (1969)*
Oakes, Lee (act): *Daylight*
Oakes, Randi (act): *Battlestar Galactica*
Oakey, Philip (mus): *Electric Dreams*
Oakie, Jack (act, 1903-1978, nee Lewis D. Offield): *Alice In Wonderland (1933); Around the World In 80 Days; It Happened Tomorrow; Last of the Buccaneers; Murder at the Vanities*
Oakie, Jack (cin): *Devotion*
Oakie, Joe (act): *Shadow of the Thin Man*
Oakland, Simon (act, 1922-1983): *Crackle of Death; Crosscurrent; Demon and the Mummy; Happy Mother's Day, Love George; The Night Stalker (1971); The Night Strangler; On a Clear Day You Can See Forever; Psycho (1960); The Satan Bug*
Oakman, Wheeler (act): *The Ape Man; Bowery at Midnight; Buried Alive (1940); Death from a Distance; Destination Saturn; Ghost Patrol; The Long Ago; The Lost Jungle; Outside the Law; Radio Ranch*
Oaks, Connie (act): *Don't Go In the House*
Oates, Chubby (act): *Killer's Moon*
Oates, Cicely (act): *The Man Who Knew Too Much (1934); The Wandering Jew (1933)*
Oates, Mark (act): *Vampire's Kiss*
Oates, Robert (act): *Mark of the Devil (1985)*
Oates, Simon (act): *Doomwatch; The Terrornauts*
Oates, Warren (act, 1929-1982): *Private Property; Race With the Devil; Sleeping Dogs (1977)*
Oates, William (act): *Copycat*
Oatman, Doney (act): *The Spell*
Oatway, Devin (act): *The Adventures of Galgameth*
O'Banion, John (act): *The Judas Project*
O'Bannon, Dan (act): *Dark Star*
O'Bannon, Dan (dir): *The Resurrected; The Return of the Living Dead (1985)*
O'Bannon, Dan (wri): *Alien; Aliens; Alien 3; Dark Star; Dead and Buried; Heavy Metal; Invaders from Mars (1986); Lifeforce; The Return of the Living Dead (1985); Screamers (1996); Total Recall*
O'Bannon, Rockne S. (dir): *Fear (1990)*
O'Bannon, Rockne S. (wri): *Alien Nation; Peter Benchley's 'Creature'; Robin Cook's 'Invasion'*
O'Barr, James (wri): *The Crow (1994); The Crow: City of Angels*
Obata, Toshiji (act): *Ghost Warrior*
Obata, Toshishiro (act): *Teenage Mutant Ninja Turtles*
Obedzinski, Shane (act): *Matinee*
Obee, Lois (act): see Dresdel, Sonia
Ober, Arlon (mus): *The Incredible Melting Man; In the Shadow of Kilimanjaro*
Ober, Philip (act, 1902-1982): *Assignment to Kill; The Brass Bottle (1964); The Ghost and Mr. Chicken; North by Northwest; The Secret Fury*
Ober, Robert (act): *The Mystic*
Oberon, Isli (act): *La Frusta e il Corpo*
Oberon, Merle (act, 1911-1979, nee Estelle Merle O'Brien Thompson): *Berlin Express; Dark Waters; The Lodger (1944); A Night In Paradise; The Price of Fear; The Private Life of Don Juan; The Scarlet Pimpernel (1934); Temptation (1946); Wuthering Heights (1939)*
Oblong, Harold (act): *Brenda Starr (1976); Demon Seed; Phantom of the Paradise*
Oblowsky, Stefan (dir): *Other Hell*
Obney, Jack Ross (act): *Bates Motel*
Obolensky, Leonid (act): *Luch Smerti*
Oboler, Arch (dir & wri, 1909-1987): *The Arnelo Affair; Bewitched (1944); The Bubble; Bwana Devil; Five; The Twonky*
Oboler, Edmund (dir): *Bewitched (1985)*
Obon (Jr.), Ramon (wri): *El Ataud del Vampiro; The Living Coffin; Misterios de Ultratumba; El Mundo de los Vampiros; Pacto Diabolico; La Senora Muerte; Swamp of the Lost Souls; El Vampiro*
Oboukhoff, Maurice (act): *The Killing*
O'Brady, Frederick (act): *Foreign Intrigue*
Obrecht, Kathi (act): *Sorority Babes In the Slimeball Bowl-O-Rama*
Obregon, Ana (act): *Mystery On Monster Island*
O'Brian, Hugh (act, b. 1928, nee Hugh J. Krampe): *Cruise Into Terror; The Diamond Mercenaries; Doin' Time On Planet Earth; Fantasy Island; Murder On Flight 502; Probe; Rocketship X-M; Son of Ali Baba; Strategy of Terror; Ten Little Indians (1965)*
O'Brian, Melody (act): *Kil 1*
O'Brian, Tracy (act): *Boarding House*
O'Brien, Angela Maxine (act): see O'Brien, Margaret
O'Brien, Austin (act): *The Lawnmower Man; Lawnmower Man 2: Beyond Cyberspace; Prehysteria*
O'Brien, Barry (wri): *Pinocchio and the Emperor of the Night*
O'Brien, Bill (act): *Trouble for Two*
O'Brien, Brendan (act): *The Adventures of Galgameth*
O'Brien, Chris (act): *The Aliens Are Coming*
O'Brien, Dave (act, 1912-1969, nee David Barclay): *Buried Alive (1940); Daughter of the Tong; The Devil Bat; The Phantom of 42nd Street; Spooks Run Wild*
O'Brien, Dayna (act): *Vice Versa (1988)*
O'Brien, Donal (act): *Quest for the Mighty Sword; 2020 Texas Gladiators*
O'Brien, Donald (act): *Emanuelle e gli Ultimi Cannibali*
O'Brien, Edmond (act, 1915-1985): *An Act of Murder (1948); Between Midnight and Dawn; A Cry In the Night (1956); D.O.A. (1949); A Double Life (1947); Dream No Evil; Fantastic Voyage; The Hanged Man; The Hitch-Hiker; The Hunchback of Notre Dame (1939); Isn't It Shocking?; L.A. 2017; The Last Voyage; Man In the Dark (1953); Moon Pilot; 1984 (1955); 99 and 44/100% Dead; Seven Days In May; Shield for Murder; To Commit a Murder; The Web*
O'Brien, Edmond (dir, 1915-1985): *Shield for Murder*
O'Brien, Eugene (act, 1882-1966): *The Moonstone (1915)*

O'Brien, Glenys (act): *Thirst*

O'Brien, Gypsy (act): *Young Diana*

O'Brien, Jack (act): *Annabel Lee*

O'Brien, Jack (dir): *The Flying Torpedo*

O'Brien, Joan (act): *It's Only Money*

O'Brien, Kevin (act): *Warlock*

O'Brien, Kevin (cin): *The Strangeness*

O'Brien, Laurie (act): *Appointment for a Killing; Timerider*

O'Brien, Margaret (act, b. 1937, nee Angela Maxine O'Brien): *The Canterville Ghost (1944); Jane Eyre (1944); Three Wise Fools*

O'Brien, Maria (act): *Tomorrow; When Dinosaurs Ruled the Earth*

O'Brien, Mariah (act): *Halloween: The Curse of Michael Myers*

O'Brien, Marlane (act): *The Death of the Incredible Hulk*

O'Brien, Niall (act): *Excalibur; Gorky Park; Lovespell; Rawhead Rex*

O'Brien, Pat (act, 1899-1983): *The Adventures of Nick Carter; The Boy With Green Hair; Kill Me Tomorrow; Ring of Fear*

O'Brien, Philip (act): *Batman (1989)*

O'Brien, Richard (act, 1917-1983): *The Andromeda Strain; Dead Men Tell No Tales (1971); Flash Gordon (1980); Heaven Can Wait (1978); The Pack; The Rocky Horror Picture Show; The Shaggy D.A.; Shock Treatment! (1981)*

O'Brien, Richard (1990s act): *Dark City*

O'Brien, Richard (mus & wri, 1917-1983): *The Rocky Horror Picture Show; Shock Treatment! (1981)*

O'Brien, Robert (wri): *The Secret of NIMH*

O'Brien, Seamus (act): *The Incredible Torture Show*

O'Brien, Shauna (act): *Deadlock: A Passion for Murder; The Escort*

O'Brien, Terence (act): *The House Opposite (1917)*

O'Brien, Tom (act): *The Last Warning (1929); Moby Dick (1930); The Phantom (1931); The Private Life of Helen of Troy*

O'Brien, Valerie (act): *Ladyhawke*

O'Brien, Vana (act): *Child of Darkness, Child of Light; The Haunting of Sarah Hardy*

O'Brien, William (act): *Bulldog Drummond Strikes Back (1934)*

O'Brien, Willis (cin, 1886-1962): *The Animal World; Behemoth, the Sea Monster; The Black Scorpion (1957); Creation (unfinished); The Dinosaur and the Missing Link; The Ghost of Slumber Mountain; Gwangi (unfinished); King Kong (1933); The Lost World (1925 & 1960); Mighty Joe Young (1949); Million B.C.; Son of Kong; The War Eagle (unfinished)*

O'Brien, Willis (wri, 1886-1962): *The Beast of Hollow Mountain; The Land Unknown*

O'Brien-Moore, Erin (act, 1902-1979): *Destination Moon; Phantom of the Rue Morgue*

O'Brine, (P.) Manning (wri): *Breakaway; Kill Me Tomorrow; Man from Tangier; Murder at Site Three; Passport to Treason; The Unstoppable Man*

Obrow, Jeff(rey) (dir & wri): *The Kindred; The Power (1980); Pranks; The Servants of Twilight*

O'Bryan, Patrick (act): *I Saw What You Did (1988); 976-EVIL; 976-EVIL: The Astral Factor*

O'Bryan, Sean (act): *Heart and Souls; Phenomenon*

O'Byrne, Bryan (act): *Love at First Bite; The $1,000,000 Duck; Repossessed; Zapped!*

O'Byrne, Kehli (act): *Piranha (1995)*

O'Byrne, Sean (act): *Timecop*

O'Callaghan, Cindy (act): *Bedknobs and Broomsticks*

O'Callaghan, Edward G. (wri): *This Island Earth*

O'Callaghan, Liam (act): *Excalibur*

O'Callaghan, Richard (act): *File It Under Fear; Watership Down*

Ocampo, Roger (act): *Twilight People*

Ocampo, Yvonne (act): *The Man Who Would Be King*

O'Carroll, Marie-Madeleine Bernadette (act): see Carroll, Madeleine

Ocasek, Ric (act, b. 1949): *Made In Heaven*

O'Casey, Ronan (act): *Barbados Quest; Blind Spot (1958); 1984 (1955); Satellite In the Sky; Tiger by the Tail*

Occhini, Ilaria (act): *The Man Who Laughs (1965)*

Occhipinti, Andrea/Andrew (act): *El Barbaro; A Blade In the Dark; Conquest*

Ocean, Ivory (act): *The Mask (1994); Not of This World; The Package*

Ocenasek, Ladislav (act): *Do You Keep a Lion at Home?*

Ochoa, Robert (cin): *Voodoo Black Exorcist*

Ochova, Sheila (wri): *Do You Keep a Lion at Home?*

O'Christopher, C.R. (wri): *The Last Chase*

Ockleman, Constance Frances Marie (act): see Lake, Veronica

O'Connell, Arthur (act, 1908-1981): *Ben; Birds Do It; Fantastic Voyage; Law of the Jungle; The Monkey's Uncle; Nightmare In the Sun; The Poseidon Adventure; The Power (1967); The Reluctant Astronaut; 7 Faces of Dr. Lao; The Silencers (1966); A Taste of Evil; Wicked, Wicked*

O'Connell, Deirdre (act): *Cool World; A Deadly Vision; Murder In a Small Town*

O'Connell, Elinore (act): *Flatliners*

O'Connell, Heather (act): *Galaxina*

O'Connell, Hugh (act): *Fly-Away Baby; Torchy Blane In Panama*

O'Connell, James (act): *The Clone Master*

O'Connell, Jerry (act, b. 1973): *Joe's Apartment; Scream 2*

O'Connell, L.W./William (cin. b. 1890): *After Midnight With Boston Blackie; Assigned to Danger; The Bells (1926); Charlie Chan In London; Crime Doctor's Courage; Crime Doctor's Warning; The Fourth Musketeer; The Invisible Menace; The Menace (1932); The Monkey Talks; One Dangerous Night; One Mysterious Night; Passport to Suez; The Return of the Vampire; Such Men Are Dangerous; Through the Dark; West of Shanghai*

O'Connell, Lew (cin): *Calling Philo Vance; Repeat Performance*

O'Connell, Maureen (act): *Felix the Cat: The Movie*

O'Connell, Maurice (act): *The Medusa Touch; The Satanic Rites of Dracula*

O'Connell, Patrick (act): *Cyborg 2: Glass Shadow*

O'Connell, Robert (wri): *The Lone Wolf Returns (1935)*

O'Connell, Susan (act): *Cardiac Arrest*

O'Connell, Taafe (act): *Galaxy of Terror; New Year's Evil*

O'Connell, Tom (wri): *The Face Behind the Mask*

O'Connell, William (act): *The Dead Don't Die; The Haunted (1991); Way...Way Out*

O'Conner, Fiona (act): *The Lair of the White Worm*

O'Conner, Kevin (act): *It's Alive III: Island of the Alive*

O'Connolly, James/Jim (dir, b. 1926): *Berserk; The Hi-Jackers; Smokescreen; Tower of Evil; The Valley of Gwangi; Vendetta for the Saint*

O'Connolly, James/Jim/J.P. (wri, b. 1926): *The Hi-Jackers; Night Caller from Outer Space; Smokescreen; Tower of Evil; The Traitors*

O'Connor, Alma (act): see Gillis, Ann

O'Connor, Boardman (act): *The Savage Bees*

O'Connor, Carroll (act, b. 1924): *Fear No Evil (1969)*

O'Connor, Candace (act): *Bear Island*

O'Connor, Dennis (act): *Trilogy of Terror II*

O'Connor, Derrick (act): *Brazil; Deep Rising; Hawk the Slayer; The Last Days of Man On Earth*

O'Connor, Donald (act, b. 1925): *Alice In Wonderland (1985); Double Crossbones; Francis; Francis Covers the Big Town; Francis Goes to the Races; Francis Goes to West Point; Francis In the Navy; Francis Joins the WACs; Pandemonium; The Wonders of Aladdin*

O'Connor, Doreen (act): *The Debt of Gambling; London by Night (1913); O.H.M.S.*

O'Connor, Frank (act): *Boston Blackie and the Law; The Chance of a Lifetime; Man-Made Monster; Passport to Suez; The Saint In Palm Springs*

O'Connor, Frank (dir & wri): *Mystery Circle Murder*

O'Connor, Gladys (act): *The Long Kiss Goodnight*

O'Connor, Glynnis (act, b. 1955): *Summer of Fear; Too Good to Be True*

O'Connor, Hazel (act): *Double Exposure (1977)*

O'Connor, Kevin (act, 1935-1991): *Let's Scare Jessica to Death; Peggy Sue Got Married; Special Effects*

O'Connor, Kevin J. (act): *Color of Night; Deep Rising; Lord of Illusions; No Escape (1994); Virtuosity*

O'Connor, Manning (wri): *Dressed to Kill (1946); Michael Shayne, Private Detective*

O'Connor, Marlyn (cin): *An American Tail*

O'Connor, Patrick (wri): see Wibberley, Leonard

O'Connor, Ray (act): *The Goddess of Love*

O'Connor, Raymond (act): *Child's Play (1988); Specimen; Dr. Alien; Halloween 4: The Return of Michael Myers; I Was a Teenage Sex Mutant*

O'Connor, Renee (act, b. 1971): *Darkman II: The Return of Durant*

O'Connor, Robert Emmet/E. (act): *In the Next One; The Lone Wolf Returns (1935); The Mysterious Mr. Wong*

O'Connor, Robin (wri): *The Playbirds*

O'Connor, Terrence (act): *Star Trek; The UFO Incident*

O'Connor, Terry (wri): *Chilling (1981)*

O'Connor, Tim (act): *Buck Rogers In the 25th Century; Ellery Queen; The Groundstar Conspiracy; The Man With the Power; Sssssss; The Stranger*

O'Connor, Una (act, 1893-1959, nee Agnes McGlade): *The Adventures of Don Juan; The Adventures of Robin Hood; Bride of Frankenstein; The Canterville Ghost (1944); The Invisible Man (1933); Murder; The Return of Monte Cristo; The Return of the Frog; Witness for the Prosecution*

O'Conor, Hugh (act): *Rawhead Rex; The Three Musketeers (1993); The Young Poisoner's Handbook*

O'Conor, Joseph (act, b. 1910): *The Black Windmill; The Dark Crystal; The Devil-Ship Pirates; Doomwatch; Gorgo; The Gorgon; Penny Gold; Yellow Dog*

O'Crotty, Peter (act): *Night of the Lepus*

Oda, Akira (act): *The Bullet Train*

Odaka, Yuji (act): *Gappa, the Triphibian Monster*

Odalys, Liana (act): *Donor*

O'Day, Alice (act): *The Phantom Light*

O'Day, Dawn (act): see Shirley, Anne

Ode, David (act): *Curse II: The Bite*

O'Dea, Denis (act, 1905-1978): *The Bad Lord Byron; Darby O'Gill and the Little People; The Fallen Idol; The Mark of Cain; Niagara; Treasure Island (1950); Under Capricorn*

O'Dea, Jimmy (act): *Darby O'Gill and the Little People*

O'Dea, Judith (act): *Night of the Living Dead (1968)*

Odell, David (dir): *Martians Go Home*

Odell, David (wri): *The Dark Crystal; Masters of the Universe; Supergirl*

O'Dell, Denis (wri): *Tread Softly Stranger*

O'Dell, Ron (act): *Steps from Hell*

O'Dell, Tony (act): *Chopping Mall*

Odemar, Fritz (act): *M (1931)*

Oden, Elisabet (act): *Morianna*

O'Den, Jeffrey Allen (act): *Wolf*

Odendal, Sias (dir): *Nukie*

Odessa, Devon (act): *Pumpkinhead*

Odets, Clifford (wri, 1906-1963): *Deadline at Dawn*

Odetta (mus): *The Monitors*

Odette, Mary (act, b. 1901): *The Crimson Circle (1922); Emerald of the East; She (1925)*

O'Doherty, Jim (act): *Basket Case 3: The Progeny*

O'Doherty, Mignon (act): *Ghost Ship (1952)*

Odom, Traci (act): *The Initiation; Outbreak*

O'Donahue, James T. (wri): *The Gorilla (1927)*

O'Donahue, Joan (act): *Quarantine; The Resurrected*

O'Donavan, Derry (act): *Dementia 13*

O'Donnell, Annie (act): *Saturday the 14th*

O'Donnell, Anthony (act): *Santa Claus (1985)*

O'Donnell, Cathy (act, 1924-1970, nee Ann Steely): *The Amazing Mr. X; The Love of Three Queens; The Story of Mankind; Terror In the Haunted House*

O'Donnell, Chris (act, b. 1970): *Batman and Robin; Batman Forever; The Three Musketeers (1993)*

O'Donnell, Gene (act): *The Ape (1940); The Devil Bat*

O'Donnell, James (wri): *The Two-Headed Spy*

O'Donnell, Joseph (wri): *Dick Tracy vs. Crime, Inc.; The Invisible Killer; Murder by Television; Nyoka and the Lost Secrets of Hippocrates; Spy Smasher Returns*

O'Donnell, Lawrence (wri): *Disaster In Time*

O'Donnell, Michael Donovan (act): *Dick Tracy (1990); Satan's Cheerleaders*

O'Donnell, Peter (wri): *Modesty Blaise; The Vengeance of She*

O'Donnell, Rosie (act, b. 1962): *Exit to Eden; The Flintstones; Tarzan*

O'Donnell, Royce (act): *Into the Badlands*

O'Donnell, Steven (act): *Paperhouse; Without a Clue*

O'Donnell, Sylvia (act): *The Black Panther*

O'Donnell, Tara (act): *Of Unknown Origin*

O'Donoghue, Michael (act): *The Suicide Club (1988)*

O'Donoghue, Michael (wri): *Savages; Scrooged*

O'Donohue, Ryan Sean (act): *Demon Knight*

O'Donovan, Noel (act): *Rawhead Rex*

O'Dowd, Dan (act): *Watchers*

O'Driscoll, Martha (act, b. 1922): *Crazy House (1943); Ghost Catchers; House of Dracula; Li'l Abner (1940)*

Odums, Lynda (act): *Flatliners*

O'Dwyer, Michael (act): *The Howling*

Odyssey (mus): *Scream, Baby, Scream*

Oedekerk, Steve (wri): *The Nutty Professor (1996)*

Oehler, Gretchen (act): *Wes Craven's New Nightmare*

Oertel, Curt (cin): *Geheimnisse einer Seele*

Oestreich, Lisa (act): *Waxwork II: Lost In Time*

O'Farrell, Bernadette (act, b. 1926): *Lady In the Fog*

O'Farrell, Broderick (act): *Murder Is My Business*

O'Farrell, Conor (act): *Death Dreams*

O'Farrell, Michael (act): *The Pink Chiquitas*

O'Farrell, Peter (act): *Hawk the Slayer; Legend; Prisoner of the Lost Universe; Santa Claus (1985)*

O'Farrell, Tralle (act): *The Edge of Hell*

O'Farrell, William (wri): *Repeat Performance; Turn Back the Clock*

O'Feldman, Ric (act): *Beyond the Bermuda Triangle; The Night of the Claw*

O'Ferrall, George More (dir): *The Green Scarf; The March Hare; Three Cases of Murder; The Woman With No Name*

Offenheiser, Mike (act): *Serial Mom*

Offerman Jr., George (act): *Meet Nero Wolfe*

Offield, Lewis D. (act): see Oakie, Jack

Offner, Deborah (act): *Project X (1987)*

Offner, Mortimer (wri): *The Saint In New York*

Offord, Dick (act): *No Blade of Grass*

O'Flaherty, Dennis (act): *It Lives Again*

O'Flaherty, Dennis (wri): *Hammett; Pinocchio and the Emperor of the Night*

O'Flathearta, Martin (act): *The Outcasts*

O'Flynn, Damian (act): *The Beginning or the End?; Black Midnight; Bomba and the Hidden City; The Gay Falcon; Philo Vance Returns; The Snake Pit (1948)*

O'Flynn, Joseph Roy (act): *Shocker*

O'Flynn, Paddy (act): *Charlie Chan On Broadway*

O'Flynn, Philip (act): *A Guy Called Caesar; The Viking Queen; What a Carve Up!*

O'Fredericks, Alice (act): *Haxan*

Ogata, Ken (act): *Virus (1980)*

Ogata, Mildred T. (act): *Pandemonium*

Ogata, Rinsaku (act): *Mothra*

Ogata, Roy K. (act): *Varan the Unbelievable*

O'Gatty, Jimmy (act): *Missile Monsters*

Ogawa, Eiji/Ei (wri): *Lake of Dracula; Yog-Monster from Space*

Ogawa, Tomoko (act): *The Magic Serpent*

Ogawa, Toranosuke (act): *Gojira*

Ogden, A.G. (act): *Maria Marten: or, The Murder In the Red Barn (1913)*

Ogden, Denis (wri): *Halfway House*

Ogden, Edward (act): *Island of Terror; Koroshi; The Marked One*

Ogden, James (act): *The Fan*

Ogden, Janine (act): *Mad Max*

Ogden, Joan (act): *The Rats Are Coming! The Werewolves Are Here!*

Ogden, Kay (act): *Student Bodies*

Ogden, Robert (act): *Martin*

Ogden, Tom (act): *The Blob (1958)*

Ogg, James (act): *Blood Beach*

Ogg, Sammy (act): *Desk Set; Prince Valiant (1954)*

Ogier, Bulle (act, b. 1939): *The Discreet Charm of the Bourgeoisie*

Ogilvy, Ian (act, b. 1943): *—And Now the Screaming Starts!; Beyond the Grave; The Day the ish Came Out; Death Becomes Her; Maigret; Puppet Master 5; The Saint and the Brave Goose; The Sorcerers; La Sorella di Satan; Stranger In the House (1967); Witch-Finder General; Wuthering Heights (1970)*

Oginski, Kathrin (act): *Superwheels*

Ogle, Charles (act): *Frankenstein (1910); Treasure Island (1920)*

Oglesby, Randy (act): *Candyman: Farewell to the Flesh*

O'Gorman, Dean (act): *Doom Runners; Young Hercules*

O'Grady, Gail (act, b. 1963): *Blackout (1988); Spellcaster; The Three Lives of Karen*

O'Grady, Lani (act): *The Kid With the Broken Halo*

O'Grady, Tom (act): *Mr. Moto Takes a Vacation*

O'Grady, Tony (wri): *At the Stroke of Nine; Curse of Simba; The Secret Man*

Oguni, Jason (act): *Witchcraft 4: Virgin Heart*

Oguni, Hideo (wri): *Throne of Blood; Uchujin Tokyo No Arawaru*

O'Gunn, Terry (act): Spacecamp

Oh, Andrew (act): Mad Max Beyond Thunderdome

Oh, Soon-Taik/Soon-Teck (act): Charlie Chan: Happiness Is a Warm Clue; Cillision Course (1990); Deadly Game; The Final Countdown; Judge Dee and the Monastery Murder; Legend of the White Horse

Oh, Yungil (act): Yongary, Monster from the Deep

O'Haco, Daniel/Danny (act): Eve of Destruction; The Lightning Incident

O'Haco, Jeff (act): Back to the Future; Killer In the Mirror

O'Hagan, Michael (act): Threads; Without a Clue

O'Halloran, Jack (act): The Flintstones; King Kong (1976); Superman (1978); Superman II

Ohama, Natsuko (act): Flatliners

Ohanian, Kreker (act): see Connors, Michael

O'Hanlon, George (act, 1917-1989, nee George Rice): Charley and the Angel; Jetsons: The Movie; Kronos (1957); The $1,000,000 Duck; Now You See Him, Now You Don't; Zamba

O'Hanlon Jr., George (act): The Evil; Where Have All the People Gone?

O'Hanlon, James (wri): Conquest of Space; Destination Moon; Song of the Thin Man

O'Hanrahan, Kieron (act): see Moore, Kieron

O'Hara, Brett (act): The Incredibly Strange Creatures Who Stopped Living and Became Mixed-Up Zombies

O'Hara, Brian (act): Champagne for Caesar

O'Hara, Buddy (act): Boston Blackie and the Law

O'Hara, Catherine (act, b. 1954): Beetlejuice; Dick Tracy (1990); The Nightmare Before Christmas; Pippi Longstocking; Really Weird Tales

O'Hara, David (act): Link

O'Hara, Frank (act): Tuck Everlasting

O'Hara, George (act): The Sea Beast

O'Hara, Gerry (dir, b. 1924): Amsterdam Affair; Game for Three Losers; Maroc 7; The Mummy Lives

O'Hara, Gerry (wri, b. 1924): The Phantom of the Opera (1989); Ten Little Indians (1989)

O'Hara, Hayden (wri): The Devil's Gift

O'Hara, Jack (act): Backwoods

O'Hara, Jenny (act): A Fire In the Sky (1978); Good Against Evil; The Return of the World's Greatest Detective; Terminal

O'Hara, Kevin (act): Trancers II: The Return of Jack Deth

O'Hara, Mary (wri): The Prisoner of Zenda (1922)

O'Hara, Maureen (act, b. 1920, nee Maureen Fitzsimmons): At Sword's Point; Bagdad; The Black Swan; Britannia Mews; Flame of Araby; The Forbidden Street; The Hunchback of Notre Dame (1939); Jamaica Inn (1939); Lady Godiva; Miracle On 34th Street (1947); Sinbad the Sailor; The Spanish Main

O'Hara, Paige (act): Beauty and the Beast (1991); Beauty and the Beast: The Enchanted Christmas

O'Hara, Pat (act): Return of the Fly

O'Hara, Quinn (act): Cry of the Banshee; The Ghost In the Invisible Bikini; In the Year 2889

Ohara, Reiko (act): Phoenix (1978)

O'Hara, Shirley (act, 1911-1979): Duel; The Falcon Out West; Miracle On 34th Street (1947); Tarzan and the Amazons

O'Hare, Michael (act): Babylon 5: The Gathering

O'Hare, Tim (act): Babylon 5: A Call to Arms

Ohashi, Rene (cin): Millennium

Ohashi, Wataru (act): The Toxic Avenger, Part II

O'Hearn, Patrick (mus): Alien Cargo

O'Heaney, Caitlin (act): He Knows You're Alone

O'Hearn, Patrick (mus): Destroyer

O'Henry, Marie (act): Dr. Black Mr. Hyde; Human Experiments

O'Herlihy, Dan(iel) (act, b. 1919): The Adventures of Robinson Crusoe (1952); At Sword's Point; The Big Cube; The Black Shield of Falworth; The Cabinet of Caligari; City After Midnight; Dark Mansions; Fail-Safe; Good Against Evil; Halloween III: Season of the Witch; How to Steal the World; Invasion U.S.A.; The Last Starfighter; Macbeth (1947); Operation Secret; The People; The Purple Mask; RoboCop; RoboCop 2; Sword of Venus

O'Herlihy, Gavan (act): Never Say Never Again; Superman III; Willow

O'Herne, Pete (act): Bad Taste

Ohlund, Gunnar (act): The Island at the Top of the World

Ohmae, Wataru (act): Mothra

Ohman, Phil (mus): Dick Tracy vs. Cueball

Ohmart, Carol (act, b. 1931): House On Haunted Hill (1958); The Scarlet Hour; The Scavengers; The Spectre of Edgar Allan Poe; Spider Baby

Ohmori, Hidetoshi (dir): Robot Carnival

Ohmori, Kazuki (act & dir): Godzilla vs. Biollante

Ohnaka, Kiyoharu (act): Rodan, the Flying Monster

O'Horgan, Tom (dir): Rhinoceros (1974)

Ohshima, Yoko (act): The Toxic Avenger, Part II

Ohta, Bennett (act): Charlie Chan and the Curse of the Dragon Queen; The Golden Child

Ohun, Jeffrey (cin): Suburban Commando

O'Hurley, John (act): The Power Within (1995); Something Is Out There

O'Hurley, Shannon (act): Copycat

Oja, Kimberly (act): Switch (1991)

Oja, Patty (act): Eyes of Laura Mars

Ojeda, Manuel (act): Romancing the Stone

Ojeda, Manuel (wri): The Queen's Swordsman

Ojena, Louis (act): Orgy of the Dead (1965)

O'John, Leonard (act): Evilspeak

Ok, Phok (act): The Golden Child

Okabe, Tadashi (act): Gojira; Mothra

Okada, Daryn (cin): Phantasm II

Okada, Eiji (act, 1920-1995): Godzilla vs. Mothra; Suna No Onna; Tanin No Kao

Okada, Masumi (act): Latitude Zero

Okada, Reiko (act): Karate, the Hand of Death

Okada, Yutaka (act): Mothra

Okami, Jotaro (wri): Battle In Outer Space; The Mysterians

Okamura, Gerald (act): Charlie Chan and the Curse of the Dragon Queen; The Octagon

Okamura, Seiji (act): Contact

O'Kane, Sean (act): Magic Island; The Saint

Okawara, Takao (dir): Godzilla vs. Destroyer

Okazaki, Kozo (cin): Inn of Evil

O'Keefe, Dennis (act, 1908-1968, nee Edward Flanagan): Atlantis (1948); The Diamond; Drums of Tahiti; Lady of Vengeance; The Leopard Man; Mr. District Attorney; Sail Into Danger; T-Men; Topper Returns; Woman On the Run; You'll Find Out

O'Keefe, Dennis (wri, 1908-1968): The Black Knight

O'Keefe, Jodi Lyn (act): Halloween H20

O'Keefe, Liza (act): Target...Earth?

O'Keefe, Michael (act): The Dark Secret of Harvest Home; Fear (1990); Gray Lady Down; Three Wishes (1995)

O'Keefe, Victoria (act): Threads

O'Keeffe, Miles (act, b. 1955): Acting On Impulse; Ator, the Blademaster; Ator: The Fighting Eagle; The Drifter; Iron Warrior...The Legend!; Sword of the Valiant; Tarzan, the Ape Man (1981); Waxwork

O'Kelly, Don (act): The Hostage (1966)

O'Kelly, Tim (act): Targets

Okerlund, Gene (act): Repossessed

Oki, Masaya (act): The War In Space

Okiyama, Hideko (act): The Profound Desire of the Gods

Oklander, Ruth (act): House of Usher (1960)

O'Klein, Denis Boutin (cin): Johnny the Giant Killer

Okochi, Denjiro (act): Tora No O O Fumu Otokotachi

Okuma, Enuka (act): The Hunted (1998)

Okumoto, Yuji (act): Contact; Nemesis; Robot Wars

Okun, Jeffrey A. (cin): The Long Kiss Goodnight; Stargate; Suburban Commando

Okuneff, Molly (act): Switch

Okuten, Yoshiaki (act): The Toxic Avenger, Part II

Okuyama, Kazuyoshi (dir & wri): The Mystery of Rampo

Olaf, Pierre (act): Camelot

Olaguivel, Juan (act): House of 1,000 Dolls

Olan, Jeff (act): Donor

Oland, Bill (act): Special Effects

Oland, Warner (act, 1880-1938): Before Dawn; The Black Camel; Bulldog Drummond Strikes Back (1934); Charlie Chan at Monte Carlo; Charlie Chan at the Circus; Charlie Chan at the Olympics; Charlie Chan at the Opera; Charlie Chan at the Race Track; Charlie Chan Carries On; Charlie Chan In Egypt; Charlie Chan In London; Charlie Chan In Paris; Charlie Chan In Shanghai; Charlie Chan On Broadway; Charlie Chan's Chance; Charlie Chan's Courage; Charlie Chan's Greatest Case; Charlie Chan's Secret; Daughter of the Dragon; Don Juan (1927); Don Q, Son of Zorro; Drums of Jeopardy (1931); The Mysterious Dr. Fu Manchu; The Return of Dr. Fu Manchu; Shanghai Express; Werewolf of London

Olander, Joan Lucille (act): see Van Doren, Mamie

Olandt, Ken (act): April Fool's Day; Digital Man; Leprechaun

Olanf, Kid (mus): I Love You, I Kill You

Olausson, Anders (act): Surf Nazis Must Die

Olazabal, Angeles (act): The Devil's Gift

Olbrychowski, Mariusz (act): Vampire On Bikini Beach

Olcott, Chip (act): Twisted

Olcott, Nick (act): Shadow Conspiracy

Olcott, Sidney (dir, 1873-1949): The Green Goddess (1923)

Old, John M. (dir): see Bava, Mario

Olden, Charles (act): see Ray, Ted

Olden, George (act): Explorers

Oldfather, Craig (act): Eve of Destruction

Oldfield, Alan (mus): Slaughter

Oldfield, Eric (act): Stones of Death

Oldfield, Richard (act): The Empire Strikes Back; The Final Conflict; The Golden Lady; Lifeforce

Oldland, Lillian (act): The Secret Kingdom

Oldman, Gary (act, b. 1958): Bram Stoker's 'Dracula'; The Fifth Element; Lost In Space; Quest for Camelot; Romeo Is Bleeding; The Scarlet Letter (1995); Track 29

Olds, Ella Wallace Rains (act): see Raines, Ella

Oldziej, Stephanie (act): Cocoon: The Return

Olea, Antonio Perez (mus): The Blood Spattered Bride; Night Fiend

Olea, Emanuele (act): Dr. Tarr's Torture Dungeon

Olea, Pedro (dir): El Fabricante de Monstruos

O'Leary, Alan (act): The Frighteners

O'Leary, Carol (act): Phantom of the Paradise

O'Leary, Jack (act): Death Valley; The Goonies; My Science Project

O'Leary, John (act): Demon Seed; The Haunted (1991); The Haunting of Morella; The Island; The Last Starfighter; Waxwork II: Lost In Time

O'Leary, Liam (act): Towers Open Fire

O'Leary, William (act): Candyman: Farewell to the Flesh; Flight of Black Angel; Nice Girls Don't Explode; Project: Alf

Olejiniczak, Jan (cin): Milczaca Gwiazda

Olek, Henry (wri): All of Me

Oleson, John (act): see Qualen, John

Ole-Thorsen, Sven (act): Abraxas: Guardian of the Universe

Oliansky, Joel (dir): Alfred Hitchcock Presents

Oliansky, Joel (wri): Alfred Hitchcock Presents; The Todd Killings

Olin, Ken (act, b. 1955): Ghost Story (1981); Nothing But the Truth

Olin, Lena (act, b. 1955): Romeo Is Bleeding

Olin, Stig (act): The Devil's Wanton

Oliu, Ingrid (act): Flatliners; Hellhole

Olive, Marian (act): A Night of Magic

Oliveira, Jose (act): The Three Caballeros

Oliveiro, Silvio (act): Graveyard Shift (1987); Psycho Girls; The Understudy: Graveyard Shift II; A Whisper to a Scream

Oliver, Anthony (act): Crossroads to Crime; Danger by My Side; Lost; Out of the Fog (1962);

They Can't Hang Me; Transatlantic

Oliver, Barret (act): Cocoon; Cocoon: The Return; D.A.R.Y.L.; Frankenweenie; Invitation to Hell; Jekyll and Hyde...Together Again; The Neverending Story

Oliver, Brett (act): Outbreak

Oliver, Charles (act): The Avenging Hand (1943); The Drum; The Lady Vanishes (1938); Midnight at Madame Tussaud's; The Saint In London; Sexton Blake and the Hooded Terror

Oliver, David (act): Night of the Creeps

Oliver, David (cin, dir & wri): Cavegirl (1985)

Oliver, Deanna (act): The Brave Little Toaster; The Brave Little Toaster Goes to Mars

Oliver, Deanna (wri): Casper

Oliver, Edna May (act, 1883-1942, nee Edna May Nutter): Alice In Wonderland (1933); Cracked Nuts (1931); Murder On a Honeymoon; Murder On the Blackboard; The Penguin Pool Murder

Oliver, Gene (act): Charlie Chan In the Secret Service

Oliver, Gordon (act, b. 1910): Fly-Away Baby; The Spiral Staircase (1946); West of Shanghai

Oliver, Greg (act): Scalpel

Oliver, Guy (act): Robin Hood (1912)

Oliver, James (act): I, Desire

Oliver, John (act): Fear (1996)

Oliver, Jonathan (act): Return of the Jedi

Oliver, Margaret (act): El Castello dell'Orrore

Oliver, Pita (act): The Intruder (1981); Prom Night

Oliver, Prudence (act): Brazil

Oliver, Ramsey (act): Psychophobia

Oliver, Ray (act): Fire and Ice

Oliver, Raymond (act): Child's Play (1988); Forbidden World

Oliver, Richard (dir): A Girl to Kill For

Oliver, Robert H. (dir): El Castello dell'Orrore

Oliver, Robert Lee (act): Flesh-Eating Mothers

Oliver, Ron (wri): The Hamilton of Hamilton High

Oliver, Stephen (act): Angels from Hell; Cycle Psycho; Motor Psycho; The Naked Zoo; Werewolves On Wheels

Oliver, Susan (act, 1937-1990): The Caretakers; Change of Mind; The Monitors; Tomorrow's Child

Oliver, Ted (act): The Gracie Allen Murder Case; The Son of Monte Cristo

Oliver, Tony (act): Fist of the North Star

Oliver, V.P. (act): Dark Angel (1996)

Olivera, Don (act): Forbidden World

Oliver Onions, The (mus): The Strangers

Olivera, Hector (dir): Barbarian Queen; Wizards of the Lost Kingdom

Oliveri, Robert (act): Edward Scissorhands; Honey, I Blew Up the Kid; Honey, I Shrunk the Kids

Oliveros, Ramiro (act): Hundra

Olivette (act): What a Night!

Olivia, Marie Claire (act): L'Auberge Rouge

Olivier, (Sir) Laurence (act, 1907-1989): The Boys from Brazil; Bunny Lake Is Missing; Clash of the Titans; Dracula (1979); 49th Parallel; Hamlet (1948); Marathon Man; Q Planes; Rebecca; Richard III (1955); The Seven-per-Cent Solution; Sleuth; Wuthering Heights (1939)

Olivier, (Sir) Laurence (dir, 1907-1989): Hamlet (1948); Richard III (1955)

Olivieri, Dennis (act): Phantom of the Paradise

Olivieri, Enrico (act): La Maschera del Demonio

Olkewicz, Walter (act): Twin Peaks: Fire Walk With Me

Olkowski, Roger (cin): Tammy and the T-Rex

Olmar, Maud (act): The Female Swindler; The Girl Who Wrecked His Home

Olmer, Vit (act): The Devil's Trap

Olmi, Corrado (act): The Cat O' Nine Tails

Olmos, Edward James (act, b. 1947): Blade Runner, Caught (1996); The Limbic Region; Mirage (1995); Virus (1980); Wolfen

Olmstead, Edwin (wri): The Crime of Dr. Crespi

Olmstead, Gertrude (act): The Lone Wolf's Daughter (1929); Mr. Wu (1927); The Monster (1925)

Olmsted, Nelson (act): Diary of a Madman; She Waits

Olofson, Ingrid (act): The Fifth Musketeer

Olohan, John (act): Rawhead Rex

O'Loughlin, Gerald S. (act, b. 1921): Twilight's Last Gleaming

Olrich, April (act): Deadly Record; Kill Me Tomorrow; The Skull

Olsen, Arne (wri): Mighty Morphin Power Rangers

Olsen, Ashley (act): Double, Double, Toil and Trouble

Olsen, Chris (act): The Man Who Knew Too Much (1956)

Olsen, Dana (act): The 'Burbs

Olsen, Dana (wri): The 'Burbs; George of the Jungle; Memoirs of an Invisible Man

Olsen, Gary (act): Outland; Transmutations

Olsen, John (act): The Haunting of Hamilton High

Olsen, John Sigurd (act): see Olsen, Ole

Olsen, John T. (act): Party Line

Olsen, Leila Hee (act): Child's Play (1988); Vamp

Olsen, Mary-Kate (act): Double, Double, Toil and Trouble

Olsen, Merlin (act): A Fire In the Sky (1978)

Olsen, Moroni (act, 1889-1954): The Beginning or the End?; Call Northside 777; Cobra Woman; Notorious (1946); Possessed (1947); Samson and Delilah; Sign of the Pagan; Snow White and the Seven Dwarfs; The Three Musketeers (1935 & 1939)

Olsen, Olaf (act): The Man In the White Suit; Tread Softly

Olsen, Ole (act, 1892-1963, nee John Sigurd Olsen): Crazy House (1943); Ghost Catchers; Hellzapoppin

Olsen, Ole (wri, 1892-1963): Himmelskibet

Olsen, R. (wri): Queen of the Pirates

Olsen, Robin (act): To All a Goodnight

Olsen, Rolf (dir): Journey Into Beyond

Olsen, Tracy (act, b. 1940): The Couch; Journey to the Center of Time; Terrified (1963)

Olsen, Wes (act): *Dark Side of Midnight*
Olson, Carla (act): *Magic Spectacles*
Olson, Carlene (act): *Frightmare (1983)*
Olson, Eric (act): *Flood*
Olson, Jack (act): *Time Walker*
Olson, James (act, b. 1930): *Amityville II: The Possession; The Andromeda Strain; Crescendo; The Groundstar Conspiracy; The Mafu Cage; Moon Zero Two; The Spell; Strange New World*
Olson, Jeff (act): *Halloween 4: The Return of Michael Myers; Robin Cook's 'Mortal Fear'*
Olson, John (act): *The Visitors (1989)*
Olson, Ken (act): *Jaws 3-D*
Olson, Larry Joe (act): *The Chance of a Lifetime*
Olson, Nancy (act, b. 1928): *The Absent-Minded Professor (1961); Son of Flubber; Sunset Boulevard*
Olson, Reid (act): *Modern Problems*
Olson, Ronald B. (wri): *Sasquatch, the Legend of Bigfoot*
Olsson, Gunnar (act): *Det Sjunde Inseglet*
Olthof, Dirk (act): *The Aliens Are Coming*
Olvis, William (mus): *Separate Lives*
Olyphant, Timothy (act): *Scream 2*
O'Madden, Laurence (act): *Guilt Is My Shadow*
Omagap, Rico Bello (wri): *The Blood Drinkers*
Omaggio, Maria Rosario (act): *The Adventures of Hercules; City of the Walking Dead*
O'Mahoney, Jacques (act): see Mahoney, Jock
O'Mahoney, Sharon (act): *Killer Klowns from Outer Space*
O'Mahony, Nora (act): *Darby O'Gill and the Little People*
O'Malley, Bingo (act): *Lady Beware*
O'Malley, David (act): *The House of the Dead*
O'Malley, David (wri): *The Boogens; The House of the Dead*
O'Malley, (J.) Pat (act, 1891-1966): *The Adventures of Ichabod and Mr. Toad; Alice In Wonderland (1951); Boston Blackie's Chinese Venture; The Cabinet of Caligari; Charlie Chan In Shanghai; Invasion of the Body Snatchers (1956); The Jungle Book (1967); Mr. Moto Takes a Vacation; Mystery of the Wax Museum; 101 Dalmatians (1961); Paris Calling; The Saint's Double Trouble; Trouble for Two; Willard*
O'Malley, Jack (act): *Confessions of Boston Blackie; Meet Boston Blackie*
O'Malley, Janice E. (act): *Student Bodies*
O'Malley, John (act): *The Invisible Boy; Kind Lady (1951)*
O'Malley, Michael (act): *The Swordsman*
O'Malley, Mike (act): *Terror (1979)*
O'Malley, Pat (act): *The Picture of Dorian Gray (1916)*
O'Malley, Rex (act): *The Thief (1952)*
O'Malley, Rev. William (act): *The Exorcist*
Oman, Bernarda (act): *Captain America (1992)*
Oman, Chad (act): *Pumpkinhead II: Blood Wings*
O'Mara, Kate (act, b. 1939): *Corruption; Horror of Frankenstein; Limbo Line; The Vampire Lovers*
O'Mara, Mollie (act): *Girls School Screamers*
Ombra, Carlo (dir): *Dracula Blows His Cool*
Ombra, Gennaro (act): *Amarcord*
Ombuen, Gianfranco (act): *The Mattei Affair*
O'Meara, Evan (act): *Jacob's Ladder*
Omega the Robot (act): *Milczaca Gwiazda*
Omen, Judd (act): *C.H.U.D. II; Dollman; Dune; Howling II*
Omens, Estelle (act, 1928-1983): *Dead and Buried; Looker*
Omens, Woody (cin): *I Saw What You Did (1988); The Man In the Santa Claus Suit*
Omeze, Tita (act): *Earth Girls Are Easy*
Omicciolí, Palmina (act): see Rossi-Drago, Eleonora
Omilami, Afemo (act): *Web of Deceit*
Omilami, Elizabeth (act): *Web of Deceit*
Omoolu, Mutia (act): *Trader Horn (1931)*
O'Moor, Maureen (act): *Castle Sinister (1948)*
O'Moore, Pat(rick) (act, 1909-1983): *Bulldog Drummond at Bay (1947); Bulldog Drummond Strikes Back (1947); Jungle Gents; The Resurrection of Zachary Wheeler; The Sword and the Sorcerer; The Two Mrs. Carrolls; The Unknown Terror*
Omura, Senkichi (act): *King Kong vs. Godzilla*
On, Ley (act): *49th Parallel*
Onativia, Arturo (wri): *Moebius*
Ondine (act): *Silent Night, Bloody Night; The Telephone Book*
Ondra, Anny (act, 1907-1987, nee Anny Sophie Ondrakova): *Blackmail (1929)*
Ondrakova, Anny Sophie (act): see Ondra, Anny
[illegible]: *The Preacher's Wife; Slaughterhouse-Five*
O'Neal, Anne (act): *The Vampire (1957)*
O'Neal, Carol (act): *When a Stranger Calls*
O'Neal, Charles (wri, 1904-1996): *The Alligator People; Cry of the Werewolf; The Devil's Mask; I Love a Mystery (1945); The Seventh Victim*
O'Neal, Cynthia (act): *Wolf*
O'Neal, Dink (act): *My Uncle the Alien*
O'Neal, Frederick (act, 1905-1992): *Strategy of Terror; Tarzan's Peril*
O'Neal, Griffin (act): *April Fool's Day; Ghoulies 3: Ghoulies Go to College; The Wraith*
O'Neal, Kevin (act): *Village of the Giants*
O'Neal, Mike (act): *Always*
O'Neal, Patrick (act, b. 1927): *Assignment to Kill; The Black Shield of Falworth; Castle Keep; Chamber of Horrors (1966); Fantasies; The Kremlin Letter; The Mad Magician; Maigret; Matchless; Once the Killing Starts; Silent Night, Bloody Night; The Stepford Wives; The Stuff*
O'Neal, Peggy (act): *Matinee; Psycho IV: The Beginning*
O'Neal, Ron (act): *Brave New World (1980); The Final Countdown; A Force of One; Red Dawn; When a Stranger Calls*
O'Neal, Ryan (act, b. 1941): *Chances Are*
O'Neal, Shaquille (act, b. 1972): *Kazaam; Steel*
O'Neil, Barbara (act, 1909-1980): *Angel Face; Secret Beyond the Door; Tower of London (1939)*
O'Neil, Colette (act): *Come Out, Come Out, Wherever You Are; Frankenstein Must Be Destroyed*
O'Neil, Eileen (act): *A Man Called Dagger*
O'Neil, Johnny (act): *Wild Thing*
O'Neil, Larry (act & wri): *Lost Prophet*
O'Neil, Logan (wri): *Zombie Island Massacre*
O'Neil, Nancy (act): *The Angelus; The Brown Wallet; The Medium (1934); The Secret of the Loch (1934); Solo for Sparrow; Twelve Good Men*
O'Neil, Paddie (act): *The Adding Machine*
O'Neil, Patrick (act): *Frankenstein Island*
O'Neil, Peggy (act): *Devil's Angel*
O'Neil, Robert (GB act): *Dr. Strangelove; or, How I Learned to Stop Worrying and Love the Bomb; Satellite In the Sky*
O'Neil, Robert (USA act): *The Baron of Arizona*
O'Neil, Robert (dir): *Blood Mania; The Psycho Lover; Wonder Women*
O'Neil, Robert (wri): *Wonder Women*
O'Neil, Robert Vincent (wri): *The Psycho Lover; Secrets of the Phantom Caverns*
O'Neil, Ronald (act): *Symptoms*
O'Neil, Sean (act): *Asterix In Britain*
O'Neil, Shannon (act): *The Creeping Terror*
O'Neil, Shelly (act): *Tomorrow's Child*
O'Neil, Sherry (act): *Experiment In Terror*
O'Neil, Tricia/Trish (act, b. 1955): *Are You In the House Alone?; Brave New World (1980); Piranha II: The Spawning*
O'Neill, Amy (act): *Honey, I Shrunk the Kids*
O'Neill, Angela (act): *Alien Nation; Sorority House Massacre*
O'Neill, Annie (act): *The Man Who Fell to Earth (1987)*
O'Neill, Barry (act): *The Curse of the Wraydons*
O'Neill, David Michael (act): *Demonwarp*
O'Neill, Dick (act, 1928-1998): *Capture That Capsule!; Chiller; Gammera, the Invincible; It Happened One Christmas; Pretty Poison (1968); The UFO Incident; Wolfen*
O'Neill, Edward (act): *Alf's Carpet; Altar Chains; The Barton Mystery (1920); Boadicea; A Christmas Carol (1914); Flames; Her Heritage; The King's Daughter; The Man Without a Soul; On His Majesty's Service; The Reigate Squires (1922); The Ring and the Rajah; Vice Versa (1916); Widow Twan-Kee*
O'Neill, Elleen (act): *Fire and Ice*
O'Neill, Eugene (wri, 1888-1953): *The Hairy Ape*
O'Neill, Frank (wri): *On Borrowed Time*
O'Neill, Garry (act): *Yellowbeard*
O'Neill, Gene (act): *The Stuff*
O'Neill, Henry (act, 1891-1964): *The Beginning or the End?; Calling Philo Vance; Confessions of a Nazi Spy; The Florentine Dagger;*
The Kennel Murder Case; The Man Who Reclaimed His Head; The Reckless Moment; The Return of October; Shadow of the Thin Man; Three Wise Fools; Torchy Blane In Chinatown; The Walking Dead
O'Neill, James (act, 1849-1920): *The Count of Monte Cristo (1912)*
O'Neill, Jennifer (act, b. 1949): *Committed; The Cover Girl Murders; The Flower In His Mouth; A Force of One; Lady Ice; The Psychic; The Reincarnation of Peter Proud; Scanners*
O'Neill, Kevin (act): *D.A.R.Y.L.*
O'Neill, Maggie (act): *When Pigs Fly*
O'Neill, Maire (act): *Murder In Reverse; Send for Paul Temple*
O'Neill, Mary Ellen (act): *Beyond the Universe; Galaxy of Terror*
O'Neill, Michael (act): *Awake to Danger; Gore-Met Zombie Chef from Hell; Virtual Obsession*
O'Neill, Raymond (act): *Millennium; Starship Invasions*
O'Neill, Remy (act): *Return to Horror High; To Die For; To Die For II: Son of Darkness*
O'Neill, Robert (act): *Shadow of a Man; Superman (1978)*
O'Neill, Robert (dir): *Wonder Women*
O'Neill, Sally (act): *Hundra*
O'Neill, Terry (act): *Dragonheart*
Ones, Arvid (act): *The Witches (1990)*
Onffrey, Roland (act): *The Being*
Ong, Lance (mus): *The Initiation*
Ongewe, Julius (act): *Milczaca Gwiazda*
Onodera, Akira (act): *Gamera: Guardian of the Universe*
Onomatopoeia Inc. (mus): *Night of the Zombies (1981)*
Onorati, Peter (act): *Rocketman (1997)*
Onorato, Paul (cin): *In Self Defense*
Onrust, Emma (act): *The Lift*
Ontanon, Santiago (act): *Faustina*
Ontiveros, Bill (act): *A Stranger Waits*
Ontiveros, Lupe (act): *The Goonies*
Ontkean, Michael (act): *Maid to Order; Necromancy; The Stepford Husbands*
Onwurah, Ngozi (dir): *Welcome II the Terrordome*
Onyx, Narda (act): *Jesse James Meets Frankenstein's Daughter*
Oorthuis, Dity (act): *Spy In the Sky*
O'Pace, Les (act): *Talk About a Stranger*
Opalinski, Kazimierz (act): *Rekopis Znaleziony w Saragossie*
Opatoshu, David (act, 1919-1996): *Beyond Evil; One Spy Too Many; Tarzan and the Valley of Gold; Torn Curtain*
Opert, Sylvia (act): *Devotion*
Ophir, Shai K. (act): *King Solomon's Mines (1985)*
Ophuls, Marcel (dir & wri): *Banana Peel*
Ophuls, Max (dir, 1902-1957, nee Max Oppenheimer): *Caught (1948); Lola Montes; The Reckless Moment*
Oppenheim, E. Phillips (wri): *The Amazing Partnership; Anna the Adventuress; The Game of Liberty; The Golden Web; The Great Impersonation (1935 & 1942); The Master of Merripit; The Mystery of Mr. Bernard Brown; Strange Boarders*
Oppenheim, Jill (act): see St. John, Jill
Oppenheim, Marella (act): *The Mirror Crack'd*
Oppenheim, Tom (act): *Wolf*
Oppenheimer, Alan (act, b. 1930): *The Bionic Woman; Child of Darkness, Child of Light; Freaky Friday (1976); The Ghost of Flight 401;*
The Groundstar Conspiracy; Invisible: The Chronicles of Benjamin Knight; The Neverending Story; Trancers 4: Jack of Swords; Trancers 5: Sudden Death; Westworld
Oppenheimer, Edgar (wri): *The Blood Rose*
Oppenheimer, George (wri, b. 1900): *The Adventures of Don Juan; Roman Scandals*
Oppenheimer, Max (dir): see Ophuls, Max
Oppenheimer, Peer J. (wri): *Operation C.I.A.*
Opper, Don (Keith) (act): *Android; Critters; Critters 2: The Main Course; Critters 3; Critters 4; Ghost In the Machine; Slam Dance*
Opper, Don (wri): *Android; Slam Dance*
Opunui, Charles (act): *She Demons*
O'Quinn, Terry (act, b. 1952): *Amityville: A New Generation; Black Widow (1987); Murder In a Small Town; Pin; Primal Fear; The Rocketeer; Shadow Conspiracy; Shadow Warriors; Silver Bullet; The Stepfather; Stepfather II; Visions of Murder*
Oquino, Hideo (wri): *Ran*
Oraa, Guillermo (act): *El Ataud del Vampiro*
Orain, Marie-Therese (act): *The Phantom of the Opera (1990)*
Oran, Kaz (act): *The Flame Barrier*
Orange, Gerald L. (act): *Angel Heart*
Orano, Alessio (act): *The Count of Monte Cristo (1975); House of Exorcism*
Orbach, Jerry (act, b. 1935): *Aladdin and the King of Thieves; Beauty and the Beast (1991); Dead Women In Lingerie; The Sentinel; Universal Soldier; Upworld*
Orban, Judith (act): *The Quilt of Hathor*
Orchard, Imbert (act): *The Little Match Girl (1997)*
Orchard, John (act): *Bedknobs and Broomsticks*
Orchard, Julian (act, 1930-1979): *Kill or Cure; The London Connection; Perfect Friday; The Slipper and the Rose; The Spy With a Cold Nose*
Orcutt, Janet Lee (act): *Frightmare (1983)*
Orczy, Baroness (wri, 1865-1947): *The Elusive Pimpernel (1919 & 1950); The Return of the Scarlet Pimpernel; The Scarlet Pimpernel (1934, 1982 & 1999); Spy of Napoleon; The Triumph of the Scarlet Pimpernel*
Ord, Murray (act): *Ghost Keeper; Runaway (1984)*
Ord, Robert (wri): *The King's Outcast*
Orde, Beryl (act): *The Dummy Talks*
Ordung, Wyott (act, b. 1922): *Monster from the Ocean Floor*
Ordung, Wyott (dir, b. 1922): *Monster from the Ocean Floor; Walk the Dark Street*
Ordung, Wyott (wri, b. 1922): *First Man Into Space; Walk the Dark Street*
Oreb, Tom (wri): *Alice In Wonderland (1951)*
Oreck, Joshua (act): *Wavelength*
O'Ree, Robert (act): *Phobia; Rabid; Starship Invasions*
O'Regan, James (act): *Clarence*
O'Regin, Maggie (act): see Medford, Kay
O'Reilly, Cyril (act): *Dance of the Damned; Philadelphia Experiment II*
O'Reilly, Erin (act): *The Baby*
O'Reilly, Kathryn (act): *Jack's Back; Puppet Master*
O'Reilly, Robert (act): *The Mask (1994)*
Orellana, Antonio (wri): *El Santo Contra las Vampiras*
Orengo, Antonio (act): *Tombs of the Blind Dead*
Orent, Ernest (cin): *The Land Unknown*
Orfei, Liana (act): *Il Diavolo Innamorata; Hercules, Samson and Ulysses; La Leggendi di Enea; The Tartars*
Orfei, Moira (act): *Gli Amori di Ercole; Beast of Babylon Against the Son of Hercules; Maciste, l'Eroe Piu Grande del Mondo; Mighty Ursus; Molemen Against the Son of Hercules; Il Trionfo di Ercole; Ursus nella Valle dei Leoni; Zorro Contro Maciste*
Orfei, Nando (act): *Amarcord*
Orff, Carl (mus): *Sredni Vashtar*
Orgolini, Lisa (act): *Trick or Treat*
Oriel, Ray (act): *Point of No Return; Ticks*
Orieux, Ron (cin): *Zenon: Girl of the 21st Century*
Oringer, Barry (wri): *The Deadly Dream; Madame Sin*
O'Rinn, Sean (act): *Dressed to Kill (1980)*
Orkow, B. Harrison (wri): *The Gorilla (1931)*
Orla, Ressel (act): *Die Spinnen*
Orlamond, William (act): *The House of Horror (1929); Seven Keys to Baldpate (1925)*
Orlandi, Felice (act): *Killer's Kiss*
Orlandi, Nora (mus): *Lo Strano Caso della Signora Ward*
Orlando, Don (act): *20 Million Miles to Earth*
Orlando, Incredible (act): *A Midsummer Night's Dream (1985)*
Orlando, Joe (wri): *Swamp Thing*
Orloff, Arthur E. (wri): *The Lone Wolf In London*
Orlova, Vera/V. (act): *Aelita; Pikovaya Dama (1916)*
Orman, Felix (dir & wri): *Moonbeam Magic*
Orme, Geoffrey (wri): *The Heart Within; Nothing Venture; Old Mother Riley's Ghosts*
Orme, Gordon (act): *Just Imagine*
Orme, Stuart (dir): *Hands of a Murderer; The Puppet Masters*
Ormerod, James (dir): *Frankenstein (1984)*
Ormond, Julia (act): *First Knight; Nostradamus*
Ormond, June (act): *The Exotic Ones*
Ormond, Linda (act): *The Dead One*
Ormond, Ron (act): *The Exotic Ones*
Ormond, Ron (dir): *The Exotic Ones; Mesa of Lost Women; Untamed Mistress*
Ormond, Ron (wri): *The Exotic Ones; The Naked Gun; Untamed Mistress*
Ormonde, Czenzi (wri): *Strangers On a Train*
Ormont, David (act): *The Man from Planet X*
Ormsby, Adam (act): *Popcorn*
Ormsby, Alan (act): *Children Shouldn't Play With Dead Things*
Ormsby, Alan (dir): *Deranged (1974)*
Ormsby, Alan (wri): *Cat People (1982); Children Shouldn't Play With Dead Things; Deathdream; Deranged (1974)*
Ormsby, Anya (act): *Children Shouldn't Play With Dead Things*
Ormsby, Ethan (act): *Popcorn*
Ornandel, Cyril (mus): *The Flesh and Blood Show; Subterfuge; Tiffany Jones*
Ornelas, Adolfo (act): *The Baron of Arizona*
[illegible] (cin): *Change of Mind; Charly; House of Dark Shadows; The Possession of Joel Delaney; Tattoo*
Ornitz, Samuel (wri): *The Man Who Reclaimed His Head*

Ornstein, Max (act): *Perfect Alibi*
Ornstein, Richard (dir & wri): see Oswald, Richard
O'Rorke, Brefni (act): *Cottage to Let; Escape to Danger; The Ghost at St. Michael's; King Arthur was a Gentleman; The Missing Million; Murder In Reverse; The Patient Vanishes; They Met In the Dark; The Upturned Glass*
O'Ross, Ed (act): *Dick Tracy (1990); The Hidden; The Power Within (1995); Universal Soldier*
O'Rourke, Charles (act): *The Vengeance of She*
O'Rourke, Heather (act, 1975-1988): *Poltergeist; Poltergeist II: The Other Side; Poltergeist III*
O'Rourke, J.A. (act): *Menace (1934); The Silver Greyhound (1932)*
O'Rourke, Kevin (act): *Vice Versa (1988)*
O'Rourke, Patricia (act): *The Jungle Book (1942)*
Orowitz, Eugene (act): see Landon, Michael
Orozco, Mary (act): *Carousel*
Orozco, Russell (act): *The Man With Two Brains*
Orpin, Susan (act): *Grizzly*
Orr, Buxton (mus): *Dr. Blood's Coffin; Doctor of Seven Dials; Fiend Without a Face; First Man Into Space; Grip of the Strangler; The Snake Woman; Suddenly Last Summer*
Orr, Christopher (act): *Robin Cook's 'Invasion'*
Orr, Gertrude (wri): *Loves of Carmen (1927); The Mandarin Mystery*
Orr, James (dir & wri): *Mr. Destiny*
Orr, Owen (act): *Trick or Treats; Werewolves On Wheels*
Orr, Pat (act): *Deranged (1974)*
Orri, Henni (act): *Puppet On a Chain*
Orrico, Carmen (act): see Saxon, John
Orrison, Jack (act): *I Married a Monster from Outer Space*
Orrock, Shannon (act): *Heart and Souls*
Orsatti, Ernie (act): *Alice In Wonderland (1985); The Entity; The Swarm; The Towering Inferno*
Orsatti, Noon (act): *Uninvited (1987)*
Orser, Leland (act b. 1962): *Alien Resurrection; Escape from L.A.; Independence Day; Piranha (1995); Seven*
Orsi, Leigh Ann (act): *Pet Shop*
Orsini, Candy (act): *The Body Snatchers*
Orsini, Maria Teresa (act): *Hercules-Prisoner of Evil*
Orsini, Umberto (act): *L'Anticristo; Mademoiselle; Il Planeta degli Uomini Spenti*
Orso, Anna (act): *Exterminators of the Year 3000*
Ortaz, Julio (cin): *The Mysterious Island of Captain Nemo*
Ortega, Enrique (act): *El Amor Brujo (1986)*
Ortega, Jimmy (act): *Dead Connection; Freejack*
Ortega, Karyne (act): *Dick Tracy (1990)*
Ortega, Kenny (dir): *Hocus Pocus*
Ortega, Miguel (act): *Seduced by Evil*
Ortelli, Dyana (act): *Alienator*
Orth, Frank (act, 1880-1962): *The Big Clock; Blue, White and Perfect; The Great Rupert; Houdini (1953); I Wake Up Screaming; The Lost Weekend; Nancy Drew and the Hidden Staircase; Nancy Drew, Detective; Nancy Drew, Reporter*
Orth, Marion (wri): *Charlie Chan's Greatest Case*
Ortiz, Angel (act): *Goliath Against the Giants; The Last Days of Pompeii (1959)*
Ortiz, Fernando Morales (wri): *Little Red Riding Hood vs. the Monsters*
Ortiz, Humberto (act): *Arcade; Dollman*
Ortiz, Juan Omar (act): *Caveman (1981)*
Ortiz, Louie (act): *The Mask (1994); The Toxic Avenger, Part II*
Ortiz, Lt. Col. Peter (wri): *Operation Secret*
Ortlieb, Jim (act): *Flatliners*
Ortmanns, Pauline Ronacher (act): see Romance, Viviane
Ortolani, Riz (mus): *Blue Movie Blackmail; The Dead Are Alive; The Fifth Musketeer; Seven Deaths In the Cat's Eye; The Spy With a Cold Nose; Web of the Spider*
Orton, J.O.C. (wri): *Bulldog Jack; Cottage to Let; The Ghost Train (1941); Time Flies (1944)*
Orton, John (dir & wri): *Creeping Shadows*
Orton, Peter Z. (wri): *Mutant*
Orton, Ray (cin): *The Boy Who Never Was; Electric Eskimo*
Orton, Tanya (act): *Empire of Ash III*
Orton, Wallace (dir): *Overcoat Sam*
Orwell, George (wri, 1903-1950): *Animal Farm (1954 & 1999); 1984 (1955 & 1984)*
Osborn, Andrew (act, b. 1912): *Dark Interval; Murder by Proxy; Shadow of the Past; Spaceways; The Woman With No Name*
Osborn, Bill (act): *Legion of Fire: Killer Ants*
Osborn, David (wri): *Chase a Crooked Shadow; Deadlier Than the Male; Maroc 7; Moment of Danger; Murder She Said; Some Girls Do; Who Slew Auntie Roo?*
Osborn, Jane (act): *To All a Goodnight*
Osborn, Jason (mus): *Afraid of the Dark*
Osborn, Lyn (act): *The Amazing Colossal Man; The Cosmic Man; Invasion of the Saucer Men*
Osborn, Paul (wri, 1901-1988): *On Borrowed Time; Portrait of Jennie*
Osborn, Ron (wri): *Meet Joe Black*
Osborn, Rupert (act): *Captain Clegg; Konga*
Osborn, Ted (act): *Buried Alive (1940); Charlie Chan at the Wax Museum*
Osborn, William (act): *Rocket Attack U.S.A.*
Osborne, Aaron (act): *Child's Play (1988)*
Osborne, Aaron (dir): *Zarkorr! The Invader*
Osborne, Alan (wri): *The Gentle Trap*
Osborne, Brian (act): *Haunters of the Deep*
Osborne, Bud (act): *Bride of the Monster; His Brother's Ghost*
Osborne, David (wri): *Penny Gold; Stopover Forever*
Osborne, Derek (act): *Oh Heavenly Dog*
Osborne, Gary (mus): *Oh Heavenly Dog*
Osborne, Hubert (wri): *Strange Experiment*
Osborne, John (act): *Flash Gordon (1980); Get Carter; Tomorrow Never Comes*
Osborne, Ken (act): *Blood of Dracula's Castle*
Osborne, Melissa (act): *The Toxic Avenger, Part II*
Osborne, Michael (act): *The Man with the Golden Gun*
Osborne, Tony (mus): *The Fiend (1972)*
Osborne, Vivienne (act, 1896-1961): *Dragonwyck; The Phantom Broadcast; Supernatural (1933)*
Osborne, William (wri): *Dr. Jekyll and Ms. Hyde; Ghost In the Machine; Twins*
Osbourne, Lloyd (wri): *The Wrong Box*
Osbourne, Ozzy (act, b. 1948): *Trick or Treat*
Oscar, Billy (act): *Heart Condition*
Oscar, Henry (act, b. 1891, nee Henry Wale): *After Dark; The Bad Lord Byron; Beyond This Place; Black Limelight; The Black Rose; Brides of Dracula; City Under the Sea; The Case of Gabriel Perry; Dark Journey; Dead Man's Shoes; The Flying Squad (1940); The Greed of William Hart; House of Darkness; It Happened In Soho; I Was a Spy; Luck of the Navy; The Man Behind the Mask (1936); The Man from Yesterday (1949); The Man Who Knew Too Much (1934); Murder Ahoy; On the Night of the Fire; The Return of the Scarlet Pimpernel; The Saint In London; The Secret Man; Sensation (1937); Seven Sinners; Sexton Blake and the Bearded Doctor; The Spaniard's Curse; Spies of the Air; Spy of Napoleon; The Terror (1938); Three Cases of Murder; The Tunnel; Two for Danger; The Upturned Glass; Who Killed John Savage?*
Oscard, Miko (act): *Face of Fire*
Oscarsson, Per (act): *A Dandy In Aspic; The Doll (1963, Swed); Endless Night; Honeycomb; The Night Visitor; Sleep of Death; Terror of Frankenstein*
Oschonneck, Erwin (act): *Das Kalte Herz*
Osco, Nancy (act): *The Being*
Osco, Roxanne Cybelle (act): *The Being*
Osgood, Nathan (act): *Mission: Impossible*
O'Shane, Gene (act): *Blood of Dracula's Castle*
O'Shannon, Finnuala (act): *The Satanic Rites of Dracula*
O'Shaughnessy, Brian (act): *Claws; Creatures the World Forgot*
O'Shaughnessy, Maureen (act): *Those Dear Departed*
O'Shaughnessy, Mickey (act): *The Burglar*
O'Shea, David (act): *Sleepstalker*
O'Shea, Ethel (act): *Recoil (1953)*
O'Shea, Kevin (act): *Inseminoid*
O'Shea, Michael (act, 1906-1973): *Circumstantial Evidence (1945); The Threat (1949); Violence*
O'Shea, Michael D. (cin): *Dracula: Dead and Loving It; Robin Hood: Men in Tights*
O'Shea, Milo (act, b. 1923): *The Adding Machine; The Angel Levine; Arabian Adventure; Barbarella; Circumstantial Evidence; Digby-The Biggest Dog In the World; It's Not the Size That Counts; Journey Into Darkness; Lady of Burlesque; The Purple Rose of Cairo; Theater of Blood; The Threat (1949)*
O'Shea, Oscar (act): *Just Off Broadway; The Mummy's Ghost; Of Mice and Men (1939); Sleepers West*
O'Shea, Tessie (act, 1913-1995): *Bedknobs and Broomsticks*
Oshii, Mamoru (dir): *Ghost In the Shell*
Oshima, Akito (act): *The Toxic Avenger, Part II*
Oslund, Hap (act): *Just Before Dawn (1980)*
Osman, Ahmed (act): *The Awakening*
Osman, Shera (act): *Crypt of the Living Dead*
Osmanoglu, Jem (act): *Crypt of the Living Dead*
Osmond, Cliff (act): *Hangar 18; Invasion of the Bee Girls; Sharks' Treasure*
Osmond, Donnie (act): *Mulan*
Osmond, Hal (act): *Dick Turpin-Highwayman; Murder Reported; The Story of Robin Hood; Web of Suspicion*
Osmond, Lesley (act): *Death Is a Number; House of Darkness; The Mysterious Mr. Nicholson; The Story of Shirley Yorke; This Was a Woman*
Osmond, Marian (wri): *The Chinese Bungalow*
Osmont, Haley Joel (act): *Bogus*
Osorio, Hector (act): *The Fan*
Ospina, Sebastian (act): *Tiempo de Morir*
Oss, Eniko (act): *Bram Stoker's 'Dracula'*
Ossello, Daniel (cin): *Nothing But Trouble*
Osses, Fernando (wri): *El Santo Contra las Vampiras*
O'Steen, Sam (dir): *Look What's Happened to Rosemary's Baby*
Oster, Emil (cin): *Doctor Death: Seeker of Souls*
Osterbuhr, Donna (act): *Red Sonja*
Osterhage, Jeff (act): *Masque of the Red Death (1989)*
Osterhout, David (act): *Mr. Sycamore*
Osterloh, Robert (act): *The Day the Earth Stood Still; I Bury the Living*
Osterloh, Shelley (act): *Beyond and Back*
Osth, Robert (act): *Don't Go In the House*
Ostrander, Jim (act): *I Was a Zombie for the F.B.I.*
Ostrander, John (act): *Christine*
Ostrander, William (act): *Christine; Fire and Ice*
Ostroff, Maggie (act): *Cavegirl (1985)*
Ostrow, Philip (act): *7 Doors of Death*
Ostrum, Peter (act): *Willy Wonka and the Chocolate Factory*
Ostry, Samantha (act): *The Clan of the Cave Bear*
O'Sullivan, Archie (act): *The Face of Fu Manchu*
O'Sullivan, Arthur (act): *The Viking Queen*
O'Sullivan, James (act): *Flight of Black Angel; Party Line*
O'Sullivan, Maureen (act, 1911-1998): *The Big Clock; Bonzo Goes to College; A Connecticut Yankee; Devil Doll (1936); The Great Houdinis; Just Imagine; Peggy Sue Got Married; Stranded; Tarzan and His Mate; Tarzan Escapes; Tarzan Finds a Son!; Tarzan's New York Adventure; Tarzan's Secret Treasure; Tarzan the Ape Man (1932); The Thin Man; Too Scared to Scream; Where Danger Lives*
O'Sullivan, Pat (act): *Dublin Nightmare*
O'Sullivan, Paul (act): *High Spirits*
O'Sullivan, Richard (act): *And Women Shall Weep; A Dandy In Aspic; Dr. Syn-Alias the Scarecrow; The Green Scarf; The Haunted House of Horror; The Secret; The Stranger's Hand; Witness in the Dark*
O'Sullivan, Sean (act, 1961-1995): *The Kill-Off; The Witches of Eastwick*
Oswald, Gerd (dir, b. 1919): *Brainwashed; Crime of Passion; A Kiss Before Dying (1956); Screaming Mimi; Valerie*
Oswald, Gerd (wri, b. 1919): *Brainwashed*
Oswald, Jean Stringham (act): *Beyond and Back*
Oswald, Marianne (act): *The Hunchback of Notre Dame (1957)*
Oswald, Richard (dir, 1880-1963, nee Richard Ornstein): *Alraune (1930); The Arc; Cagliostro; Cesare Borgia; Living Dead (1932); Lucrezia Borgia (1922)*
Oswald, Richard (wri, 1880-1963): *Lucrezia Borgia (1922)*
Ota, Koji (dir): *Invasion of the Neptune Men*
Otaka, Shuji (act): *The War In Space*
Otelo, Grande (act): *Macunaima*
Othenin-Girard, Dominique (dir): *Halloween 5: The Revenge of Michael Myers; Night Angel*
Othenin-Girard, Dominique (wri): *Halloween 5: The Revenge of Michael Myers*
Other Three (mus): *Monster A-Go-Go*
Otis, Ted (act): *Hands of a Stranger*
Otnes, Ola (act): *The Witches (1990)*
Otomo, Katsuhiro (dir): *Akira; Robot Carnival*
Otomo, Katsuhiro (wri): *Akira*
Otomo, Ryutaro (act): *The Magic Serpent*
O'Toole, Annette (act, b. 1952): *Alfred Hitchcock Presents; Cat People (1982); Final Descent; It (1990); Superman III*
O'Toole, Donald (act): *Class of Nuke 'em High*
O'Toole, Elsa (act): *Jane and the Lost City*
O'Toole, Harry (act): *12 Monkeys*
O'Toole, Ollie (act): *It Came Upon the Midnight Clear*
O'Toole, Peter (act, b. 1933): *The Bible; Casino Royale; Creator; The Dark Angel (1991); Fairy Tale: A True Story; Gulliver's Travels (1996); High Spirits; The Night of the Generals; The Nutcracker Prince; Phantoms; The Ruling Class; Supergirl (1984); Svengali (1983); Wings of Fame*
Otowa, Nobuko (act): *Kuroneko; Live Today, Die Tomorrow; Onibaba*
Ott, Dennis (C.) (act, 1958-1994): *Bill & Ted's Bogus Journey; Star Trek III: The Search for Spock; Star Trek VI: The Undiscovered Country; The Zero Boys*
Ott, Warene (act): *Black Zoo; The Witchmaker*
Ottaway, James (act): *Absolution; The Quatermass Conclusion*
Ottesen, Ronnie (cin): *Wolfen*
Ottiano, Rafaela (act, 1894-1942): *As You Desire Me; Devil Doll (1936); The Florentine Dagger; Great Expectations (1934); League of Frightened Men; One Frightened Night; Topper Returns*
Ottman, John (mus): *Apt Pupil; The Cable Guy; Halloween H20; Snow White: A Tale of Terror*
Otto, Barry (act): *Howling III; The Punisher*
Otto, Gotz (act): *Earthquake In New York; Tomorrow Never Dies*
Otto, Henry (act): *The Iron Mask*
Otto, Henry (dir): *Dante's Inferno (1924); The Temple of Venus*
Otto, Henry (wri): *The Temple of Venus*
Otto, Miranda (act): *The 13th Floor*
Ottolina, Rina (act): *The Mummy's Revenge*
Ottosen, Carl (act): *Journey to the Seventh Planet; Reptilicus*
Ottwell, Taleena (act): *Always*
Otzep, Fyodor (dir, 1895-1949): *The Queen of Spades (1937)*
Otzep, Fyodor (wri, 1895-1949): *Aelita; Pikovaya Dama (1916)*
Ouellette, Jean-Paul (dir & wri): *The Unnamable*
Ouester, Hugues (act): *City of Pirates*
Oughton, Frederick (wri): *Breakout*
Oughton, Winifred (act): *The Thirteenth Candle*
Ouimet, Daniele (act): *Daughters of Darkness*
Oulton, Brian (act, b. 1908): *The Damned; Devils of Darkness; Jigsaw; Kiss of the Vampire; Last Holiday; Miranda; Panic at Madam Tussaud's; The Spaniard's Curse; Young Sherlock Holmes*
Ounskowsky, Misha (act): see Auer, Mischa
Oury, Gerard (dir, b. 1919, nee Max-Gerard Tannenbaum): *Father Brown; The Gentle Art of Murder; House of Secrets*
Ousatova, Nina (act): *Window to Paris*
Ousdal, Sverre (Anker) (act): *Insomnia (1998); The Island at the Top of the World*
Ouspenskaya, Maria (act, 1876-1949): *Beyond Tomorrow; Frankenstein Meets the Wolf Man; The Mystery of Marie Roget; Tarzan and the Amazons; The Wolf Man (1941)*
Ousterhouse, Corveth (act): *It's Alive! (1968)*
Outerbridge, Peter (act): *The Android Affair; Escape from Mars; Kissed*
Outin, Nick (act): *Heaven Can Wait (1978)*
Outten, Richard (wri): *Little Nemo: Adventures in Slumberland; Pet Sematary Two*
Ove, Indra (act): *The Cyber-Stalking; Interview With the Vampire*
Overall, Park (act): *The Vanishing (1993)*
Overbaugh, Roy (cin): *The Bishop Murder Case; Dr. Jekyll and Mr. Hyde (1920, Famous Players/Para)*
Overbey, Kellie (act): *Outbreak; The Stand*
Overbye, Camilla (act): *The Element of Crime*
Overdorff, Charlie (act): *The Blob (1958)*
Overgard, William (wri): *The Bermuda Depths; The Ivory Ape; The Last Dinosaur*
Overgon, Rick (act): *Willow*
O'Verlin, John (mus): *Planet of Dinosaurs*
Overman, Jack (act): *The Lone Wolf and His Lady*
Overman, Lynne (act): *Aloma of the South Seas (1941)*
Overman, Susan (act): *Phoenix the Warrior*
Overmyer, Eric (wri): *Rear Window (1998)*
Overton, Frank (act): *Fail-Safe*
Overton, Rick (act): *Earth Girls Are Easy; Encino Woman; Groundhog Day; Target...Earth?*
Ovid (wri, 43 B.C.-A.D. ?17): *Metamorphoses*
Ovington, Joy (act): *Fatal Exposure*
Ovitz, Judy (act): *Ghostbusters II*
Owe, Baard (act): *The Kingdom*
Owen, Alun (act, b. 1926): *In the Wake of a Stranger; The Servant*

Owen, Alun (wri): The Criminal
Owen, Beth (act): —And Now the Screaming Starts!; Macbeth (1971)
Owen, Bill (act, b. 1914, nee Bill Rowbotham): Daybreak; The Day the Screaming Stopped; The Handmaid's Tale; The Hell-Fire Club; Kadoyng; My Brother's Keeper; The Secret of
Blood Island; The Shakedown; The Story of Robin Hood
Owen, Carol (act): Voice Over
Owen, Carol (wri): Robin Hood Jr. (1923)
Owen, Catherine Dale (act, 1903-1965): Such Men Are Dangerous
Owen, Clare (act): Echo of Diana
Owen, Cliff (dir, b. 1919): Offbeat; A Prize of Arms; The Vengeance of She
Owen, Clive (act): Lorna Doone (1990); The Rich Man's Wife
Owen, Dickie (act): The Curse of the Mummy's Tomb; The Mummy's Shroud
Owen, Garry (act): Arsenic and Old Lace; The Dark Mirror (1946); The Thin Man; The Thin Man Goes Home
Owen, Gerry (act): The Flying Saucer (1950)
Owen, Gillian (act): A Lady Mislaid
Owen, Granville (act): The Adventurous Blonde; Li'l Abner (1940)
Owen, Gwyneth (act): Blue Blood
Owen, Harold (wri): Mr. Wu (1919 & 1927)
Owen, Jay (act): Meet Nero Wolfe
Owen, Lloyd (act): Young Indiana Jones: Travels With Father
Owen, Lyla Hay (act): The Savage Bees
Owen, Mary Anne (act): The Hand That Rocks the Cradle
Owen, Maureen (wri): Secrets of Sex
Owen, Megan (act): Clean, Shaven
Owen, Meg Wynn (act): Blue Blood
Owen, Michael (act): Dick Tracy vs. Crime, Inc.
Owen, Milton (act): Blondes at Work
Owen, Nancy Lee (act): Abby
Owen, Reginald (act, 1887-1972): Above Suspicion; Bedknobs and Broomsticks; The Canterville Ghost (1944); Captain Kidd; A Christmas Carol (1938); Five Weeks in a Balloon; I Married an Angel; Mary Poppins; Sherlock Holmes (1932); A Study In Scarlet (1933); Tarzan's Secret Treasure; The Three Musketeers (1948); Trouble for Two
Owen, Ron (act): Otley
Owen, Seena (act, 1894-1966, nee Signe Auen): The Face In the Fog (1922); Queen Kelly
Owen, Sion Tudor (act): Highlander
Owen, Tudor (act): The Black Castle; Congo Crossing; Houdini (1953); Jack the Giant Killer; Most Dangerous Man Alive; My Cousin Rachel; The Story of Mankind; Talk About a Stranger
Owen, Yvonne (act): Miranda; My Brother's Keeper; Portrait from Life
Owens, Albert (act): The Man Who Fell to Earth (1987); Outbreak
Owens, Brett (act): The Howling: New Moon Rising
Owens, Brian (wri): Brainscan
Owens, C. Wayne (act): Mars Attacks!
Owens, Carol Jean (act): Squirm
Owens, Chris (act, b. 1961): Haunted by Her Past
Owens, Cliff (act): Pinocchio In Outer Space
Owens, Edwin (act): Tarantulas: The Deadly Cargo
Owens, F. Rufus (act): Motor Psycho
Owens, Garry (act): Hysterical
Owens, Gerald (act): Making Mr. Right
Owens, Grant (act): Fright Night II; Scream of the Wolf
Owens, Hugh (act): The Ruling Class
Owens, Mark (act): Friday the 13th...The Orphan
Owens, Michael (cin): 101 Dalmatians (1996)
Owens, Michelle (act): Midnight Kiss
Owens, Pat(ricia) (GB act): Crow Hollow; Ghost Ship (1952); House of Blackmail; Mystery
Junction; Panic at Madam Tussaud's; The Stranger Came Home; Walk a Tightrope
Owens, Patricia (USA act, b. 1925): The Destructors; The Fly (1958); X-15
Owens, Richard (act): Vampire Circus
Owens, Robert F. (act): Mr. Moto's Last Warning
Owens, Sky (act): Street Trash
Owens, Thom (act): Return of the Killer Tomatoes
[illegible] (act): Moby Dick (1998)
[illegible] (act): Dogs of Hell; Wolfman (1979)
Owings, Rick (act): I Was a Zombie for the F.B.I.

Owne, A.E. (act): Dark Eyes of London
Owsley, David (act): Jaws 2
Oxenberg, Catherine (act): The Lair of the White Worm
Oxford Scientific Films (cin): Inseminoid
Oxley, David (act, b. 1929): The Armchair Detective; Bunny Lake Is Missing; The Hound of the Baskervilles (1959); House of the Living Dead; Svengali (1954)
Oya, Paul (act): Attack of the Killer Tomatoes
Oz, Frank (act, b. 1944): An American Werewolf In London; The Empire Strikes Back; Labyrinth (1986); The Muppets Take Manhattan; Return of the Jedi
Oz, Frank (dir, b. 1944): The Dark Crystal; The Indian In the Cupboard; Little Shop of Horrors (1986); The Muppets Take Manhattan
Oz, Frank (wri, b. 1944): The Great Muppet Caper; The Muppet Movie; The Muppets Take Manhattan
Ozanne, Christine (act): Mr. Selkie
Ozasky, Robert (act): Fargo
Ozawa, Eitaro (act): Godzilla (1985); The H-Man
Ozawa, Sakae (act): Ugetsu Monogatari
Ozenne, Jean (act): Nick Carter et le Trefle Rouge
Ozeray, Madeleine (act): Crime and Punishment (1935, Fr); Liliom (1933); The Queen of Spades (1937)
Ozerdem, Mahir (act): The Devil's Castle (1963)
Ozier, Michael (cin): The 6th Man
Ozores, Antonio (act): Tenemos 18 Anos
Ozores, Jose Luis (act): A Rocket from Calabuch
Ozores, Robert (act): Wild Thing
Ozorio, Cecile (act): Daughter of the Mind
Ozory, Armand (act): Das Schloss

Paal, Alexander (wri): Countess Dracula
Pabian, David (wri): Puppet Master II; Subspecies
Pabst, G.W. (dir, 1885-1967): Die Buchse der Pandora; Geheimnisse einer Seele; Die Herrin von Atlantis; The Last Ten Days of Adolf Hitler
Pace, Anna Maria (act): Ercole Contro i Figli del Sole
Pace, Judy (act): Frogs; 13 Frightened Girls
Pace, Lloyd (act): Basket Case
Pace, Melissa (act): Appointment for a Killing
Pace, Ralph (act): Mutant
Pace, Richard (act): I Spit On Your Grave
Pace, Roger (act): War of the Colossal Beast
Pace, Tom (act): Astro Zombies; Blood Orgy of the She-Devils
Pacheco, Herb (act): Phantom of the Paradise
Pachelo, Julia (act): La Torre de los Siete Jorobados
Pachis, Stratos (act): The Enchantress
Pachosa, Steven Clark (act): Child of Darkness, Child of Light; The Haunting of Sarah Hardy
Pacific, Mark (act): Princess Warrior
Pacific, Stella (act): Black Magic Woman
Pacifici, Frederico (act): Fluke
Pacino, Al (act, b. 1940): Devil's Advocate; Dick Tracy (1990)
Pack, Roger Lloyd (act): The Young Poisoner's Handbook
Packard, Dana (act): Graveyard Shift (1990)
Packard, Frank (act): The Spectre of Edgar Allan Poe
Packer, David (act): Heartless; RoboCop; Strange Days; V
Packer, Doris (act): The Perils of Pauline
Packer, Eve (act): Carnival of Blood
Packham, Ron (act): The Golden Child
Pacula, Joanna (act, b. 1959): Deep Red (1994); Eyes of the Beholder; Gorky Park; The Haunted Sea; The Kiss (1988); Last Gasp; The Silence of the Hams; Timemaster; Warlock: The Armageddon
Padalewsky, Erich (act): The Seven-Per-Cent Solution
Padbury, Debbie (act): Electric Eskimo
Padbury, Wendy (act): The Blood On Satan's Claw
Paddack, Allan L. (act): Jaws 2
Padden, Bernard (act): Erik the Viking
Padden, Sarah (act): Cross Examination; Identity Unknown; The Mad Monster; The Millerson Case; Possessed (1947)
Paddick, Hugh (act): We Shall See
Paddison, Gordon (act): The Offspring
Paddock, Deborah A. (act): Explorers
Paddock, Joshua (act): My Uncle the Alien
Padel, Daphne (act): The Twenty Questions Murder
Padgett, Calvin Jackson (dir & wri): Secret Agent Superdragon

Padilla Jr., Manuel (act): Tarzan and the Great River; Tarzan and the Valley of Gold; Tarzan's Deadly Silence; Tarzan's Jungle Rebellion
Padilla, Valerie (act): The Outing
Padmus, Rod (act): The Keeper
Padovani, Lea (act, b. 1920): Angels of Darkness; The Reluctant Saint
Padron, Mari (act): Fire In the Sky (1993)
Padrone, Juan (wri): Vampires In Havana
Padula, Vincent(e) (act): El Cuerpo del Lito; The Cyclops; The Flame Barrier
Padwick, Anne (act): Maroc 7
Paek, Soo (act): Spookies
Paetzold, Dore (act): The Golem: How He Came Into the World
Pagan, Antone (act): The Clairvoyant (1985)
Pagan, J.M. (mus): Anguish
Pagan, Jose (mus): Ella y el Miedo
Pagani, Amedeo (wri): The Night Porter
Pagani, Ernesto (act): Salammbo
Pagano, Bartolomeo (act): see Maciste
Pagano, Jo (wri, b. 1906): Jungle Goddess; Jungle Moon Men
Page Cavanaugh & His Trio (act & mus): Frankenstein's Daughter (1958)
Page, Anita (act): Jungle Bride
Page, Anthony (dir): Absolution; The Lady Vanishes (1979)
Page, Betty (act): That Darn Sorceress
Page, Bradley (act): Shadow of Doubt; Sherlock Holmes In Washington
Page, Diane (act): The Initiation
Page, Gene (mus): Blacula
Page, Genevieve (act, b. 1930): Un Amour de Poche; Belle de Jour; Buffet Froid; Foreign Intrigue; The Private Life of Sherlock Holmes; The Reluctant Spy
Page, Geraldine (act, 1924-1987): The Beguiled; The Bride (1985); Live Again, Die Again; The Rescuers; What Ever Happened to Aunt Alice?
Page, Grant (act): Road Games
Page, Harrison (act): Carnosaur
Page, Ilse (act): The Ape Creature; Creature With the Blue Hand
Page, Jean-Claude (act): Dr. Jekyll and Ms. Hyde
Page, Joanne/Joy Ann (act): Kismet (1944); Man-Eater of Kumaon
Page, John Arthur (act): see Paige, Robert
Page, Joy Ann (act): see Page, Joanne
Page, Kari (act): Eyes of Laura Mars
Page, Ken (act): The Nightmare Before Christmas; RoboCop
Page, Kevin (act): Death Dreams; Deep Red (1994); I Come In Peace
Page, LaWanda (act, b. 1920): Mausoleum; The Meteor Man; Zapped!
Page, Marel (act): Daughter of Dr. Jekyll
Page, Norma (act): The Blue Bird (1910)
Page, Norman (act): At the Villa Rose (1920); Bleak House; The Cry for Justice; The Elusive Pimpernel (1919); The Sign of Four (1923); The Yellow Claw
Page, Olga (act): I Was a Zombie for the F.B.I.
Page, Robert (act): I Was a Zombie for the F.B.I.
Page, Susan (act): Planet Earth
Page, Thomas (wri, b. 1942): Bug
Page, Tony (act, b. 1940): Q
Pageau, Madeline (act): Rabid
Paget, Alfred (act): The Lesser Evil
Paget, Debra (act, b. 1933, nee Debralee Griffin): Anne of the Indies; From the Earth to the Moon; The Haunted Palace (1963); Journey to the
Lost City; The Last Hunt; Les Miserables (1952); Most Dangerous Man Alive; Omar Khayyam; Prince Valiant (1954); Tales of Terror; Why Must I Die?
Paget, Doriel (act): A Smart Set
Paget, Elizabeth (act): The Tell-Tale Heart (1960)
Pagett, Nicola (act): Frankenstein: The True Story; The Viking Queen
Pagliero, Marcel (act): Nick Carter ey le Trefle Rouge
Pagnani, Gino (act): The Flower In His Mouth
Pagni, Eros (act): Profundo Rosso
Pagnozzi, Elaine (act): Explorers
Pahernik, Albin (act): Oh Heavenly Dog; The Sexplorer
Pahich, Dre (act): Dark Star
Pahk, Tom (cin): Nothing But Trouble
Pai, Suzee (act): Big Trouble In Little China
Paice, Eric (wri): The Man In the Back Seat
[illegible] (act): Lost; Stranger In Town ([illegible])
Paige, Janis (act, b. 1922, nee Donna Mae Jaden): Angel On My Shoulder (1980); The Caretakers

Paige, Mabel (act, 1880-1953): Houdini (1953); Nocturne; The Sniper
Paige, Robert (act, b. 1910, nee John Arthur Page): Abbott and Costello Go to Mars; Hellzapoppin; The Last Warning (1938); The Monster and them Girl; Son of Dracula (1943); Split Second (1953); Who Killed Gail Preston?
Pain, Barry (wri): A Blind Bargain
Pain, Carolyn (act): Wheels of Terror
Pain, Didier (act): The Visitors (1993)
Pain, Frankie (act): The Phantom of the Opera (1990)
Paine, Cathey (act): Avalanche
Paine, Debbie (act): The Computer Wore Tennis Shoes (1970)
Paine, Heidi (act): Alien Seed; Wildest Dreams
Paine, Nick (wri): Philadelphia Experiment II
Paine, Richard (act): Zapped!
Painter, Steve (act): Waxwork II: Lost In Time
Pais, Josh (act): Teenage Mutant Ninja Turtles
Paisley, Ray (act): The Tower
Paiva, Nestor (act, 1905-1966): Another Thin Man; The Bandits of Corsica; Creature from the Black Lagoon; The Falcon In Mexico; Fear (1946); Killer Ape; Let's Kill Uncle; The Lone Wolf In Mexico; Madman of Mandoras; Mighty Joe Young (1949); The Mole People; Prisoners of the Casbah; Revenge of the Creature; Shoot to Kill; The Spirit Is Willing; Split Second (1953); Tarantula; A Thousand and One Nights (1945);
The Three Stooges In Orbit
Pajor, Paul (act): The Unnamable
Pak, Tae (act): Teenage Mutant Ninja Turtles
Pakdivijt, Chalong (dir): S.T.A.B.
Pako, Martin (wri): Batman: mask of the Phantasm
Pakula, Alan J. (dir, 1928-1998): Dream Lover
Pal, George (dir, 1908-1980): Atlantis, the Lost Continent; 7 Faces of Dr. Lao; The Time Machine (1960); Tom Thumb
Pal, George (wri, 1908-1980): Doc Savage, the Man of Bronze
Palacio, Riccardo (act): Ark of the Sun God
Palacios, Banca (act): Vampire On Bikini Beach
Palacios, Begona (act): El Vampiro Sangriento
Palacios, Ricardo/Richard (act): The Blood of Fu Manchu; A Thousand and One Nights (1968)
Paladino, Dennis (act): Switch (1991); Turn Back the Clock
Palance, Brooke (act, b. 1952): Empire of the Ants
Palance, Holly (act, b. 1950): The Day the Screaming Stopped; The Omen
Palance, Ivan (act): Sword of the Conqueror
Palance, Jack (act, b. 1920, nee Walter Palanuik): Alone In the Dark; Batman (1989); Craze; Cyborg 2: Glass Shadow; Dracula (1973); Ebenezer; Evil Stalks This House; Fligh to Tangier; Gor; Hawk the Slayer; The Ivory Ape; The Man Inside; Man In the Attic (1953); Marquis de Sade: Justine; Le Mepris; Outlaw of Gor; Revak, lo Schiavo di Cartagine; Second Chance; The Shape of Things to Come (1979); Sign of the Pagan; Solar Crisis; The Spy In the Green Hat; Sudden Fear; The Swan Princess; Sword of the Conqueror; Torture Garden; Unknown Powers; Welcome to Blood City; Without Warning (1980)
Palange, Inez (act): One Million B.C.
Palange, Louis (mus): King Dinosaur
Palanuik, Walter (act): see Palance, Jack
Palau (act): La Main du Diable
Palau, Jose Gras (act): Conquest
Palaviccini, Fernando (act): Survive!
Palazzolo, Michael (act): Curse of the Queerwolf
Palella, Oreste (wri): Il Gigante di Metropolis; The Tartars
Palermini, Piero (act): OK, Nero!
Palermo, Anthony (act): Serpent's Lair
Palermo, Michele (act): Not of This World
Paley, Natalie (act): The Private Life of Don Juan
Paley, Richard (act): Wizards of the Lost Kingdom
Palfi, Lotte (act): Above Suspicion
Palfrey, Yolanda (act): Dragonslayer
Pali, Jeanne (act): The House of the Arrow (1953)
Palillo, Ron (act, b. 1954): Committed; Friday the 13th, Part VI: Jason Lives; Hellgate; The Invisible Woman (1983)
Palin, Michael (act, b. 1943): Brazil; Jabberwocky; Monty Python and the Holy Grail; Time Bandits
Palin, Michael (wri, b. 1943): Monty Python and the Holy Grail; Time Bandits
Paliotti, Michael John (act): Lifeforce

Palk, Anna (act): The Earth Dies Screaming; Fahrenheit 451; Mini Weekend; The Nightcomers; The Skull; Tower of Evil
Pallas, Laura (act): Houdini (1998)
Pallascio, Aubert (act): The Kidnapping of the President
Pallasz, Edward (mus): Profesor Zazul
Pallenberg, Anita (act, b. 1943): Barbarella; A Degree of Murder; Performance
Pakkenberg, Rospo (dir): Cutting Class
Pallenberg, Rospo (wri): Excalibur
Paller, Gary (act): Firebird 2015 A.D.
Pallette, Eugene (act, 1889-1954): The Adventures of Robin Hood; The Benson Murder Case; The Canary Murder Case; The Dragon Murder Case; The Ghost Goes West; The Greene Murder Case; Heaven Can Wait (1942); The Kennel Murder Case; The Mark of Zorro (1940); Shanghai Express; Strangers of the Evening; Suspense; The Three Musketeers (1921); Topper (1937)
Pallot, Martin (act): Without a Clue
Pallottini, Riccardo (cin, a.k.a. Richard Pallotin): I Criminali della Galassia; La Figlia di Frankenstein; Mission Stardust
Pallut, Philippe (act): Sous le Soleil de Satan
Palm, Anders (dir & wri): Dead Certain
Palm, Caris (act & cin): The Devil's Gift
Palm, Liselote (act): The Corsican Brothers (1985)
Palma, Andrea (act): Tarzan and the Mermaids
Palma, Joseph (act): Boston Blackie Booked On Suspicion; Boston Blackie's Rendezvous
Palma, Loretta (act): Deranged (1987)
Palma, Pamela (act): Black Devils of Kali
Palmara, Mimmo (act): The Colossus of Rhodes; Ercole e la Regina di Lidia; Hercules (1957); The Last Days of Pompeii (1959); Sodom and Gomorrah; The Three Avengers; The Trojan Horse
Palmaro, Chris (mus): Target...Earth?
Palme, Ulf (act): La Sorciere
Palmer, Adam James (act): Empire of Ash III
Palmer, Ann (act): Mars Needs Women
Palmer, Arnold (act, b. 1929): Call Me Bwana
Palmer, Bert (act): Tales from the Crypt (1971)
Palmer, Betsy (act, b. 1929): Friday the 13th (1980); Friday the 13th-Part 2; The Goddess of Love; Still Not Quite Human
Palmer, Byron (act): Man In the Attic (1953)
Palmer, Charles (wri): The Land Unknown
Palmer, Claud (act): see Allister, Claud
Palmer, Corliss (act): The Return of Boston Blackie
Palmer, David (act): The Damned
Palmer, Dermot (wri): Find the Lady
Palmer, Donna (act): Eyes of Laura Mars
Palmer, Dot (act): Just Imagine
Palmer, Ernest (cin): Ali Baba Goes to Town; Berkeley Square; Charlie Chan In Paris; Charlie Chan's Greatest Case; A Connecticut Yankee; Just Imagine
Palmer, Gary (act): Little Shop of Horrors (1986)
Palmer, Gregg (act, b. 1927, nee Palmer Lee): Billion Dollar Brain; The Creature Walks Among Us; Francis Goes to West Point; From Hell It Came; Most Dangerous Man Alive; Son of Ali Baba; The Veils of Bagdad; Zombies of Mora Tau
Palmer, Henning (act): The Red Mantle
Palmer, Jayne (act): see Mansfield, Jayne
Palmer, Jean (act): High Priestess of Sexual Witchcraft
Palmer, John (act): The Curse of King Tut's Tomb
Palmer, John (wri): Dot and the Kangaroo
Palmer, Jo Lynn (act): I Was a Zombie for the F.B.I.
Palmer, Joni (act): Coma
Palmer, Leland (act): All That Jazz
Palmer, Lilli (act, 1914-1986, nee Lilli Peiser): An Affair of State; The Boys from Brazil; Cloak and Dagger (1946); Crime Unlimited; De Sade; The Door With Seven Locks (1940); The Glass Tower; Hauser's Memory; The House That Screamed; Murders In the Rue Morgue (1971); Night Hair Child; Nobody Runs Forever; Operation Crossbow; The Secret Agent (1936); Thunder Rock; Wolf's Clothing (1936)
Palmer, Linda (wri): Legion of Fire: Killer Ants
Palmer, Maria (act, 1924-1981): 13 Lead Soldiers; The Web
Palmer, Max (act): Killer Ape; The Sniper
Palmer, Melinda (wri): The Garbage Pail Kids
Palmer, Michael (wri): Extreme Measures
Palmer, Peter (act, b. 1931): Deep Space; Edward Scissorhands; Li'l Abner (1959)
Palmer, Renzo (act): Il Planeta degli Uomini Spenti; Spirits of the Dead
Palmer, Richard (act): Treasure at the Mill; Whirlpool (1959)
Palmer, Stuart (wri, b. 1905): Arrest Bulldog Drummond; Bulldog Drummond's Bride; Bulldog Drummond's Peril; The Falcon's Brother; The Falcon Strikes Back; Forty Naughty Girls; Murder On a Bridle Path; Murder On a Honeymoon; Murder On the Blackboard; One Frightened Night; The Penguin Pool Murder; The Plot Thickens; Secrets of the Lone Wolf; A Very Missing Person
Palmer, Sue (act): Final Eye
Palmer, Terry (act): Bomb In the High Street; The Mind Benders (1963)
Palmer Jr., Thomas (dir & wri): Forever
Palmer, Violet (act): Finger Prints; The Return of Boston Blackie
Palmer, Zoe (act): The Black Tulip (1921); The Other Person; Sweeney Todd
Palminteri, Chazz (act): Diabolique (1996); Innocent Blood; Jade; The Usual Suspects
Palmisano, Conrad S. (dir): Space Rage
Palmisano, Esther (act): Space Rage
Palmisano, Nick (act): Piranha (1978); Space Rage
Palmisano, Victory (act): Space Rage
Palo, Alan (act): Prehysteria! 2
Palomino, Carlos (act): Dance of the Dwarfs; It's Alive III: Island of the Alive; Silent Night, Deadly Night III
Palomo, Yolanda (act): Alien Predators
Palovich, Shano (act): The Gifted One
Paltenghi, David (act): The Black Knight
Paltenghi, David (dir): Dick Turpin-Highwayman; The Tyburn Case
Paltrow, Gwyneth (act, b. 1972): Great Expectations (1998); Hush; A Perfect Murder; Seven
Paluzzi, Luciana (act, b. 1939): Captain Nemo and the Underwater City; The Green Slime; Island of Despair; Journey to the Lost City; Manhunt In Milan; OSS 117-Double Agent; A Thousand and One Nights (1968); Thunderball; To Trap a Spy; The Venetian Affair; Le Vice et la Vertu
Palzis, Kelly (act): Metalstorm: The Destruction of Jared-Syn
Pampanini, Silvana (act): The Adventures of Mandrin; Don Juan's Night of Love; OK, Nero!; Orient Express
Pamphili, Mirella (act): Satanik
Pan (wri): see Beresford, Leslie
Pan, George (act): Fer-de-Lance
Pan, Lucien (act): The Omegans
Panama, Norman (dir, b. 1914): The Maltese Bippy; The Road to Hong Kong
Panama, Norman (wri, b. 1914): Li'l Abner (1959); The Return of October; The Road to Hong Kong; The Road to Utopia
Panaro, Alessandra (act): The Bacchantes; The Conquest of Mycenae
Panas, Alexander (wri): Honeymoon of Horror
Pancake, Roger (act): The Cat from Outer Space; The China Syndrome; Dracula's Dog
Pandalfi, Inez (act): The Lost Boys
Pandit, Korla (act): Ed Wood
Pandoliano, Vincent (act): Dark Mansions
Pandora (act): Luminous Procuress
Panelli, Alessandra (act): La Citta delle Donne
Pangborn, Franklin (act, 1894-1958): Crazy House (1943); The Horn Blows at Midnight; International House; The Mandarin Mystery; The Story of Mankind; Topper Takes a Trip
Paniagua, Cecilio (cin): Doctor?? Coppelius!!; Treasure Island (1971)
Panic, Luke (act): Mad Max Beyond Thunderdome
Pankhurst, Patrick (act): The Return of the Six Million Dollar Man and the Bionic Woman
Pankin, Stuart (act): Arachnophobia; Beanstalk; Congo; Earthbound (1981); Fatal Attraction; Hangar 18; Like Father, Like Santa; Love at Stake; Mannequin Two: On the Move; Second Sight; The Silence of the Hams; Zenon: Girl of the 21st Century
Pankiw, Alex (act): Empire of Ash III
Pankow, John (act, b. 1955): *Batteries Not Included; The Hunger; Monkey Shines; Mortal Thoughts
Pankowsky, Raquel (act): Amityville 3-D
Pann, Sandra (act): Kiss Meets the Phantom of the Park
Pansullo, Eddie (act): Space Rage
Pantanella, Tony (act): Martin
Pantera, Malou (act): Horrors of the Black Museum; The Strange Awakening; Transatlantic; Zex
Panto, Clive (act): Transmutations
Pantoja, Diego (act): El Amor Brujo (1986)
Pantoliano, Joe (act): Amazon Women On the Moon; The Final Terror; The Fugitive (1993); The Goonies; Robot In the Family; The Spy Within; Tales from the Crypt (1989); U.S. Marshals
Panzarella, John (act): 12 Monkeys
Panzer, Paul (act, 1872-1958): Cry Wolf (1947)
Panzer, William (wri): Highlander 2: The Quickening
Paola, James (act): Hellhole
Paolella, Domenico (dir & wri): Ercole Contro i Tiranni di Babilonia
Paoletti, Robert (act): Behind the Mask of Zorro
Paoli, Dennis (wri): The Body Snatchers; Castle Freak; From Beyond; Ghoulies II; Meridian; Mortal Sins; Re-Animator
Paoli, Raoul (act): A Night of Mystery (1928)
Paolo, Zane (act): Uninvited (1993)
Paolone, Catherine (act): Project X (1987)
Paoloni, Paolo (act): Inferno (1979)
Papa, Anny (act): A Blade In the Dark; The Great Alligator
Papaconstantinou, Costas (act): The Day the Fish Came Out
Papaconstantinou, Nicols (act): The Enchantress
Papademetriou, Nicholas (act): Death In Brunswick
Papadopoulou, V. (act): Blind Date
Papafrantzis, Spyros (act): Blind Date
Papageorgiou, S. (act): Blind Date
Papajohn, George (wri): Murder of Innocence
Papajohn, Michael (act): Eraser
Papaleo, Anthony (act): see Franciosa, Anthony
Papalimu, Joe (act): When Time Ran Out
Papamichael, Phaedon (cin): Bio-Dome; Phenomenon; White Dwarf
Papamoskou, Tatiana (act): Iphigenia
Papana, Alex (act): Above Suspicion
Papanicolas, Tanya (act): Blood Diner; Vamp
Paparone, Joe (act): Romeo Is Bleeding
Papas, Ciro (act): The Devil's Wedding Night
Papas, Helen (act): Graveyard Shift (1987)
Papas, Irene (act, b. 1923): Chronicle of a Death Foretold; Electra (1961); Iphigenia; The Moon-Spinners; The Odyssey; Teodora, Imperatrice di Bisanzio; The Trojan Women
Papas, Laslo (act): Bloodshed; Crazed
Papas, Michael (dir & wri): The Lifetaker
Papas, Xiro (act): El Castello dell'Orrore
Papatakis, Nico (dir, b. 1918): Les Abysses
Pape, Mel(vin) (act): Eyes of a Stranger; Stanley
Papetti, Nicolina (act): Ladyhawke
Papillon, Mlle. Zizi (act): Le Reve du Maitre de Ballet
Papmoskou, Tatiana (act, b. 1963): Iphigenia
Papp, Melissa (act): The Dark Half
Pappageorge, Demetrios (act): The Exorcist III
Pappas, Ike (act): Matinee; The Package
Pappas, John (act): Tremors
Pappas, Lucia (act): Beyond and Back
Pappas, Robin (act): The Shining; Superman II
Pappas, Valery (act): Ghostbusters II
Pappone, Nicholas (act): Outbreak
Paps, Chris (act): Blind Date
Paquet, Lucina (act): Pumpkinhead II: Blood Wings
Paquin, Anna (act, b. 1982): Jane Eyre (1996)
Parada, Manuel (mus): Satanik
Paradise, James (R.) (act): Congo; Party Line
Paradise, Michael J. (dir): The Visitor
Paradjanov, Sergei (dir & wri, 1924-1990): Ashik Kerib; The Shadows of Forgotten Ancestors
Parady, Hersha (act): The Phoenix (1981)
Paragon, John (act): Elvira, Mistress of the Dark; Pandemonium
Paragon, John (dir): Ring of the Musketeers
Paragon, John (wri): Elvira, Mistress of the Dark
Paraluman (act): Daughters of Satan; Moro Witch Doctor
Param, Fred (act): The Blood Drinkers
Paramor, Norrie (act): The Frightened City
Paramore Jr., Edward E. (wri): Trouble for Two
Parapetti, Mario (cin): Treasure of the Petrified Forest; Vulcan, Son of Jupiter
Pardalis, Gus (mus): Mission Mars
Pardo, Etela (act): The Saint
Pardue, William (act): Old Bill Through the Ages
Pare, Irving (cin): Shock Waves
Pare, Michael (act, b. 1959): Bad Moon; Blink of an Eye; Falling Fire; Lunar Cop; Moon 44; The Philadelphia Experiment; Space Rage; Streets of Fire; Village of the Damned (1995); World Gone Wild
Paredes, Conchita (act): The House That Screamed
Paredes, Jean (act): Who Is Killing the Great Chefs of Europe?
Parely, Mila (act): La Belle et la Bete; Liliom (1933); The Rules of the Game
Parent, Monique (act): Dangerous Touch; Heartless; Midnight Confessions
Parenti, Franco (act): Spara Forte, Piu Forte...Non Capisco
Parenti, Mauro (act): Zenabel
Parenti, Rose (act): Wicked Stepmother
Pares, Mildred (wri): The House On Skull Mountain
Parfitt, Judy (act): Covenant; Dolores Claiborne; Hamlet (1969); Midnight's Child; The Mind of Mr. Soames
Parfrey, Woodrow (act, 1923-1984): The Return of the World's Greatest Detective; A Very Missing Person; The War Lord
Pargiter, Edith (wri): The Spaniard's Curse
Parhm, Sean (act): Lawnmower Man 2: Beyond Cyberspace
Pariente, Albert (act): Notorious (1992)
Parillaud, Anne (act): La Femme Nikita; Innocent Blood; The Man In the Iron Mask (1998)
Paris, Ann (act): Making Contact
Paris, Daniele (mus): The Night Porter
Paris, Dany (act): Giulietta degli Spiriti
Paris, David W. (act): Outbreak
Paris, Dawn (act): see Shirley, Anne
Paris, Dolores (act): El Castillo de las Bofetadas
Paris, Domonic (dir, cin & wri): Last Rites (1980)
Paris, Gerald (act): 101 Dalmatians (1996); The Village of the Damned (1960)
Paris, Jerry (act, 1925-1986): Bonzo Goes to College; The Caretakers; I've Lived Before; Monkey Business
Paris, Judith (act): The Devils
Paris, Nichol (act): Blood Diner
Paris, Robin Mary (act): Sanctuary of Fear
Parisi, Cliff (act): The Saint
Parisi, Franca (act): Atom Age Vampire
Park, Dale (act): Fire and Ice
Park, E.L. (act): Behind That Curtain
Park, Peyton (act): The Lathe of Heaven
Park, Reg (act): Ercole al Centro della Terra; Ercole all Conquista della Atlantide; Hercules-Prisoner of Evil; Hercules, the Avenger; Machiste In King Solomon's Mines
Park, Sherry (act): The Toxic Avenger
Park, Steve (act): Fargo
Park, Tamarah (act): Fire and Ice
Park, Tammy (act): Attack of the 60 Foot Centerfold
Parke, Macdonald (act): Babes In Bagdad; The March Hare; The Mouse That Roared; No Orchids for Miss Blandish; Paris Express; Saturday Island
Parke Sr., William (act): The Hunchback of Notre Dame (1923)
Parker, Alan (dir & wri): Angel Heart; Footsteps
Parker, Alan (mus): American Gothic; Frankenstein (1984); Jaws 3-D; The Phoenix and the Magic Carpet
Parker, Albert (dir, 1887-1974): After Dark; The Black Pirate; Blind Man's Bluff (1936); Murder In the Family; The Right to Live; The Riverside Murder; Sherlock Holmes (1922); Strange Experiment; The Third Clue; Troubled Waters (1936); White Lilac
Parker, Anthony (act): The Trollenberg Terror
Parker, Anthony Ray (act): The Frighteners
Parker, Austin (cin): The Deadly Females
Parker, Austin (wri): When Knights Were Bold (1936)
Parker, Barnett (act): Marie Antoinette (1938)
Parker, Brook Susan (act): Strange Days
Parker, Carl (act): The Man Who Fell to Earth (1987); Phenomenon
Parker, Cecelia (1930s act): The Lost Jungle
Parker, Cecelia (1950s+ act): see Parker, Suzy
Parker, Cecil (act, 1897-1971, nee Cecil Schwabe): Circus of Fear; Crime Unlimited; Dark Journey; Father Brown; Flat No. 3; The Lady Killers (1956); The Lady Vanishes (1938); The Man In the White Suit; The Man Who Changed His Mind; The Saint's Vacation; The Spider(1939); A Study In Terror; 23 Paces to Baker Street; Two for Danger; Under Capricorn; Vengeance
Parker III, Chauncey G. (wri): Of Unknown Origin
Parker, Chris (wri): Vampire In Brooklyn
Parker, Clifton (mus, b. 1905): The Hell-Fire Club; Night of the Demon (1957); The Story of Robin Hood; Tarzan and the Lost Safari; A Taste of Fear; The 39 Steps (1959); Treasure Island (1950); The Treasure of Monte Cristo (1961)
Parker, Corey (act, b. 1965): Encino Woman; Friday the 13th-Part V: A New Beginning; I'm Dangerous Tonight; Scream for Help
Parker, Dan (act): Fake-Out
Parker, David (act): Embassy

Parker, Don (act): *Charlie Chan and the Curse of the Dragon Queen*
Parker, Dorothy (wri, 1893-1967, nee Dorothy Rothschild): *Saboteur*
Parker, Earl (act): *The Folks at Red Wolf Inn*
Parker, Edwin/Eddie/Ed (act): *Abbott and Costello Meet Dr. Jekyll and Mr. Hyde; Abbott and Costello Meet the Mummy; Another Thin Man; Charlie Chan at the Opera; The Curse of the Undead; Dimension 5; Ghost Rider (1935); The Millerson Case; Rear Window (1954); Tarantula*
Parker, Eleanor (act, b. 1922, nee Ellen Friedlob): *Between Two Worlds; Crime by Night; Eye of the Cat; Fantasy Island; Home for the Holidays; How to Steal the World; Lizzie; The Mysterious Doctor; The Naked Jungle; Once Upon a Spy; She's Dressed to Kill; The Woman In White (1948)*
Parker, Elizabeth (act): *The Dark Half*
Parker, Ellen (act): *The Lost Missile*
Parker, F. William (act): *Jack Frost (1997); Switch (1991)*
Parker, Fess (act, b. 1925): *Them! (1954)*
Parker, Franklin (act): *Charlie Chan On Broadway*
Parker, George R. (act): *The People Under the Stairs*
Parker, Jack (cin): *Dead of Night (1945); The Demon Barber of Fleet Street*
Parker, Jacob (act): *The Power Within (1995)*
Parker, Jameson (act, b. 1948): *Curse of the Crystal Eye; Dead Man's Island; Prince of Darkness; White Dog*
Parker, Jarrett (act): *Lords of Magick*
Parker, Jasmine (act): *Anguish*
Parker, Jean (act, b. 1918, nee Mae Green): *Adventures of Kitty O'Day; Beyond Tomorrow; Bluebeard (1944); Dead Man's Eyes; Detective Kitty O'Day; Flying Blind; Gabriel Over the White House; The Ghost Goes West; Lady In the Death House; One Body Too Many; Rasputin and the Empress; The Secret of Madame Blanche*
Parker, John (dir & wri): *Dementia*
Parker, John (mus): *Witches' Brew*
Parker, John F. (act): *Superman (1978)*
Parker, Judith (wri): *Are You In the House Alone?*
Parker, Kay (act): *Dracula Sucks*
Parker, Kim (act): *Fiend Without a Face; The Man Without a Body; Undercover Girl (1958)*
Parker, Lara (act): *Night of Dark Shadows; Race With the Devil*
Parker, Leila (act): *Frankenstein 1980*
Parker, Leni (act): *Screamers (1996)*
Parker, Lindsay (act): *Critters 2: The Main Course; Flowers In the Attic; Shocker*
Parker, Mark (act): *Anguish*
Parker, Mary (GB act): *The Hostage (1956); Third Party Risk*
Parker, Mary (USA act): *Lady In the Dark*
Parker, Mim (act): *Demon Knight*
Parker, Molly (act): *Intensity; Kissed*
Parker, Nathaniel (act): *Hamlet (1990); Wide Sargasso Sea*
Parker, Noelle (act): *Ernest Save Christmas; Twisted*
Parker, Norman (act): *The Clairvoyant (1985)*
Parker, Oliver (act): *Hellbound: Hellraiser; Hellraiser II; Nightbreed*
Parker, Patricia Ann (act): *Hex*
Parker, Paula Jai (act): *Tales from the Hood*
Parker, Raymond (act): *The Last Warning (1938)*
Parker, Richard (act): *Jack's Back*
Parker, Ronald (wri): *Gargantua*
Parker, Sachi (act): *Peggy Sue Got Married*
Parker, Sage (act): *RoboCop*
Parker, Sarah (act): *The Dark Half*
Parker, Sarah Jessica (act, b. 1965): *Ed Wood; Extreme Measures; Flight of the Navigator; Hocus Pocus; Mars Attacks!; Somewhere Tomorrow*
Parker, Scott (act): *The Milpitas Monster*
Parker, Scott (wri): *He Knows You're Alone*
Parker, Shirley (act): *Mission Mars*
Parker, Stephen (act): *Teenage Monster*
Parker, Sunshine (act): *Tremors*
Parker, Suzy (act, b. 1933, nee Cecelia Parker): *Chamber of Horrors (1966)*
Parker, Tom (act): *Howard the Duck*
Parker, Tom S. (wri): *The Flintstones; Stay Tuned*
Parker, Trey (act, dir, mus & wri): *Alferd Packer: The Musical*
Parker, Ursula (act): *Lightning Bolt*
Parker, Willard (act, b. 1912, nee Worster Van Eps): *David Harding, Counterspy; The Earth Dies Screaming; Hunt the Man Down; The Naked Gun*
Parker, William (wri): *The Cave Girl (1921)*
Parker, Zane (act): *Earthbound (1981)*
Parkes, Gerard (act): *An American Christmas Carol; Spasms; Storm of the Century*
Parkes, Gerry (act): *Short Circuit 2*
Parkes, James (act): *The Annihilator*
Parkes, Penelope (act): *The Avenging Hand (1936)*
Parkes, Walter F. (wri): *Wargames*
Parkhill, Tom (act): *King Kong Lives*
Parkhurst, Heather Elizabeth (act): *The Silence of the Hams*
Parkhurst, Rod (cin): *Dog's Best Friend; Doomsday Rock; Panic In the Skies!*
Parkin, Dean (act): *War of the Colossal Beast*
Parkin, Duncan (act): *The Cyclops*
Parkins, Barbara (act, b. 1945): *Asylum (1972); Bear Island; Calendar Girl Murders; The Deadly Trap; The Kremlin Letter; The Mephisto Waltz; Puppet On a Chain; A Taste of Evil*
Parkinson, Austin (cin): *Give Us Tomorrow*
Parkinson, Don (act): *The Strangers*
Parkinson, Eric (dir): *Future Shock*
Parkinson, H.B. (dir): *Macbeth (1922); Trapped by the Mormons*
Parkinson, Michael (act): *Madhouse*
Parkinson, Robin (act): *They Came from Beyond Space*
Parkinson, Tom (dir): *Disciple of Death*
Parkinson, Tom (wri): *Crucible of Terror; Disciple of Death*
Parks, Catherine (act): *Looker*
Parks, Eddie (act): *The Sky Dragon*
Parks, Hildy (act): *The Night Holds Terror*
Parks, Larry (act, 1914-1975): *Alias Boston Blackie; The Boogie Man Will Get You; Down to Earth; Tiger by the Tail*
Parks, Michael (act, b. 1938): *The Bible; Dial M for Murder (1981); The Evictors; From Dusk Till Dawn; The Savage Bees*
Parks, Ronnie (act): *Jaws 3-D*
Parks, Tammy (act): *Attack of the 60 Foot Centerfold*
Parks, Trina (act): *Diamonds Are Forever*
Parks, Wally (act): *Strange Behavior*
Parkyn, Brittany (act): *Star Trek: Generations*
Parlo, Dita (act, 1906-1972, nee Grethe Gerda Kornstadt): *L'Or du Cristobal; The Queen of Spades (1966); Ultimatum; Under Secret Orders*
Parlour, Fairfield (mus): *Sudden Terror*
Parma, Tula (act): *The Leopard Man*
Parmalee, Ted (dir): *The Tell-Tale Heart (1953, USA)*
Parmeggiani, Bernard (mus): *La Brulure de Mille Soleils*
Parmentier, Richard (act): *Paint Me a Murder; The People That Time Forgot; Superman II*
Parnell, Emory (act, 1893-1979): *Arabian Nights (1942); Crime Doctor's Courage; Crime Doctor's Gamble; The Falcon In Hollywood; The Falcon In Mexico; The Falcon's Alibi; Gildersleeve's Ghost; I Married a Witch; The Maltese Falcon (1941); Rocket Man (1954); Safari Drums; The Unknown Guest*
Parnell, Norma (act): *The Silent Weapon*
Parnell, Robert (act): *Heart and Souls*
Parnes, Mitchell R. (act): *Ghost In the Machine*
Parness, Debbie (act): *Silent Night, Bloody Night*
Parolini, Billy (dir & wri): *Igor and the Lunatics*
Parolini, Gianfranco (dir): *The Three Avengers*
Parolini, Gianfranco (wri): *Goliath Against the Giants*
Parr, Anthony (act): *Agency*
Parr, Bobby (act): *At the Earth's Core; The Land That Time Forgot; Robin Hood: Prince of Thieves*
Parr, John H. (dir): *Prey for the Hunter*
Parr, June (act): *Magic Spectacles*
Parr, Kate (act): *Starship Invasions*
Parr, Katherine (act): *Otley*
Parr, Kevin (act): *Earthbound (1981)*
Parra, Mark (act): *The Unnamable*
Parra, Vincent (act): *Apartment On the Thirteenth Floor*
Parracino, Armando (act): *La Citta delle Donne*
Parras, Wendy (act): *The Outing*
Parr-Byrne, Sarah (act): *Without a Clue*
Parres, Berengueia (act): *Hundra*
Parriott, James D. (dir & wri): *Heart Condition*
Parris, Carl (act): *Superman II*
Parrish, Amy (act): *Lovestruck*
Parrish, George (act): *Timestalkers*
Parrish, Helen (act, 1922-1959): *The Mystery of the 13th Guest; You'll Find Out*
Parrish, James (wri): *Bulldog Drummond at Bay (1937)*
Parrish, John (act): *Kronos (1957); Prisoners of the Casbah; Samson and Delilah*
Parrish, Julie (act): *The Devil and Max Devlin*
Parrish, Leslie (act): *The Astral Factor; Deathride; The Giant Spider Invasion; The Invisible Strangler; Li'l Abner (1959); The Manchurian Candidate*
Parrish, Robert (act): *The Prisoner of Shark Island*
Parrish, Robert (dir, b. 1916): *Assignment Paris; Casino Royale; Cry Danger; Doppelganger (1969)*
Parrish, Steve (act): *Midnight (1989); Scanners III: The Takeover*
Parrow, Neal (act): *Trancers II: The Return of Jack Deth*
Parry, Bruce (act): *The Devil's Gift*
Parry, David (act): *Auntie Lee's Meat Pies; Dr. Caligari; The Lost Platoon; The Silencers (1995)*
Parry, Geoff (act): *Mad Max*
Parry, Gisele (act): *Forces Occultes*
Parry, Gordon (dir, b. 1908): *The Surgeon's Knife; Tread Softly Stranger*
Parry, Ken (act): *Hawk the Slayer; Lifeforce; Liszt O' Mania; Otley*
Parry, Michel (wri): *The Uncanny; Xtro*
Parry, Natasha (act, b. 1930): *Crow Hollow; The Dark Man (1951); The Fourth Square; Girl In the Headlines; Midnight Lace (1960)*
Parry, Richard (act): *Jenifer Hale*
Parselow, Frederick (act): *The Last Wave*
Parslow, Ray (cin): *Madhouse*
Parslow, Robert (cin): *The House That Dripped Blood*
Parson, Dave (act): *Nightbeast*
Parson, Ron O.J. (act): *Primal Fear*
Parsonnet, Marion (wri): *Miracles for Sale; The 13th Chair (1937)*
Parsons, Agnes (wri): *Rip Van Winkle (1921)*
Parsons, Alibe (act): *Mark of the Devil (1985)*
Parsons, Anthony (wri): *Meet Sexton Blake*
Parsons, Bonita (act): *Trauma (1993)*
Parsons, Estelle (act, b. 1927): *Dick Tracy (1990); Ladybug, Ladybug; The Love Letter; Terror On the Beach; The UFO Incident*
Parsons, Karyn (act): *Gulliver's Travels (1996)*
Parsons, Mike (act): *Moro Witch Doctor*
Parsons, Milton (act): *Another Thin Man; Castle In the Desert; The Cat Creature; Close Call for Ellery Queen; Cry of the Werewolf; Dark Alibi; The Dead Don't Die; Dead Men Tell; Dick Tracy (1945); Dick Tracy Meets Gruesome; Dick Tracy vs. Cueball; Dressed to Kill (1941); The Haunted Palace (1963); The Hidden Hand; Marnie; The Monster That Challenged the World; The Shanghai Chest; Whispering Ghosts*
Parsons, Nancy (act): *Motel Hell; Wishman*
Parsons, Nicholas (act): *Eyewitness (1956); The Long Arm; Murder Ahoy; Spy Story; The Wrong Box*
Parsons, Paul (act): *Killer Klowns from Outer Space*
Parsons, Percy (act): *Blackmail (1929); Blondes for Danger; The Clairvoyant (1934); Creeping Shadows; The Frightened Lady (1932); King of the Damned; The Tunnel; Twelve Good Men*
Parsons, Robert (act): *Honeymoon of Horror*
Parsons, Shannon Michelle (act): *Freakshow*
Parsons, Stephen (mus): *Split Second (1992)*
Parsons, Steve (mus): *Howling II*
Parsons, Ted (wri): *Darkest Africa*
Parsons, Willy (act): *The Guardian; Trancers II: The Return of Jack Deth*
Parsonson, John (act): *The Demon (1981)*
Part, Michael (wri): *A Kid In King Arthur's Court*
Partain, Dan (act): *Phenomenon*
Partain, Paul A. (act): *The Texas Chainsaw Massacre*
Partin, Stan (act): *Galaxina*
Partington, David (J.) (act): *The First Power; Writer's Block*
Partlow, Richard (act): *The Annihilator; Killer In the Mirror*
Partnow, Elaine (act): *Targets*
Partnow, Richard (act): *Seven*
Parton, Dolly (act & mus): *Unlikely Angel*
Parton, Julia (act): *The Naked Detective*
Parton, Reggie (act): *Alien Nation; The Ultimate Warrior*
Parton, Regis (act): *This Island Earth*
Partos, Frank (wri): *A Night of Mystery (1937); Port Afrique; The Snake Pit (1948); Stranger On the Third Floor; The Uninvited (1944)*
Partos, Gus (act): *The Private Life of Helen of Troy*
Partridge, Derek (act, b. 1935): *The Ivory Ape; The Murder Game; The Verdict (1964)*
Partridge, Ross (act): *Amityville: A New Generation*
Parvianen, Jussi (act): *Gorky Park*
Paryla, Stephan (act): *The Fifth Musketeer*
Pascal, Ernest (wri): *The Blue Bird (1940); Flesh and Fantasy; The Hound of the Baskervilles (1939); A Night In Paradise; The Savage*
Pascal, Francoise (act): *Burke and Hare; One Plus One*
Pascal, Giselle (act): *The Man In the Iron Mask (1962)*
Pascal, Jean Claude (act): *The Lebanese Mission*
Pascal, Jefferson (wri): *Lancelot and Guinevere; No Blade of Grass*
Pascal, Leslie (act): *Street Trash*
Pascal, Marianna (act): *The Mutagen*
Pascal, Mary Ann (act): *Writer's Block*
Pascal, Olivia (act): *Bloody Moon*
Pascale, Nadine (act): *Zombies Lake*
Pasco, Isabelle (act): *High Frequency; Prospero's Books*
Pasco, Richard (act, b. 1926): *The Gorgon; Hot Enough for June; Kill Me Tomorrow; Rasputin, the Mad Monk; Sword of Sherwood Forest; The Watcher In the Woods*
Pasco, Sam (act): *Ironmaster*
Pascuale, Fortunato (act): *Hatchet for a Honeymoon*
Pasdar, Adrian (act, b. 1965): *Grey Knight; House of Frankenstein 1997; Near Dark*
Pasha, Kalla (act): *Seven Footprints to Satan*
Pasolini, Pier Paolo (act, 1922-1975): *Edipo Re*
Pasolini, Pier Paolo (dir, 1922-1975): *Arabian Nights (1974); Edipo Re; Salo, o le Centoventi Giornate di Sodoma; Teorema*
Pasolini, Pier Paolo (wri, 1922-1975): *Arabian Nights (1974); Edipo Re; Teorema*
Pasquale, James D. (mus): *Fantasies*
Pasque, Ernest (act): *The False Faces*
Pasquesi, David (act): *The Puppet Masters*
Pasquin, John (dir): *The Santa Clause*
Pass, Cyndi (act): *Deadbolt; Scanner Cop*
Pass, Mary Kay (act): *Beyond the Living*
Passallia, Antonio (act): *Le Boucher*
Passega, Luisa (act): *Demons 2*
Passer, Dirch/Dirk (act): *Crazy Paradise; Reptilicus*
Passer, Ivan (dir, b. 1933): *Creator; Haunted Summer*
Passerelli, Elizabeth (wri): *Zombie High*
Passgard, Lars (act): *Through a Glass Darkly*
Passingham, Frank (act): *The Secret Adventures of Tom Thumb*
Pastell, George (act): *Blind Spot (1958); The Curse of the Mummy's Tomb; Deadlier Than the Male; Deadly Record; The Frightened City; From Russia With Love; The Golden Mask; Impact; Konga; Licensed to Kill; The Magus; Maniac (1963); The Moon-Spinners; The Mummy (1959); The Stranglers of Bombay; Vendetta for the Saint*
Pastor, Clara (act): *Anguish*
Pastor, Julian (act): *Extranos Caminos*
Pastorelli, Robert (act, b. 1955): *Eraser; Michael; Painted Heart; Robin Cook's Harmful Intent; A Simple Wish*
Pastorini, Dan (act): *Killer Fish; Trick or Treats*
Pastrano, Willie (act): *The Naked Zoo*
Pastrone, Giovanni (dir, 1883-1959): *Cabiria; La Caduta di Troia; Maciste; Salammbo*
Pastrone, Giovanni (wri, 1883-1959): *Cabiria*
Pat (act): *Alf's Carpet*
Patachon (act): *Alf's Carpet*
Pataki, Michael/Mike (act): *The Baby; The Bat People; Dead and Buried; Dracula's Dog; Graduation Day; Grave of the Vampire; Halloween 4: The Return of Michael Myers; Love at First Bite; Remo Williams: The Adventure Begins; The Return of Count Yorga; Spider-Man; Sweet Sixteen*
Pataki, Michael (dir): *Mansion of the Doomed*
Pataki, Nancy (act): *Empire of Ash III*
Pataky, Veronika (act): *The Adventures of Hajji Baba*
Patch, Wally (act, b. 1888, nee Walter Vinicombe): *Alf's Button Afloat; Appointment With Crime; Castle Sinister (1932); Cottage to Let; The Crime at Blossoms; Danger by My Side; Death On the Set; Dr. Syn; Gestapo; The Ghosts of Berkeley Square; High Treason (1929); The Man Who Could Work Miracles; The Mind of Mr. Reeder; Morning Call; Once In a New Moon; Passing Shadows; The Perfect Flaw; Poison Pen; The Price of Folly; The Scarab Murder Case; Serena; The Scotland Yard Mystery; They Came by Night; The Twenty Questions Murder; Wanted for Murder*
Patchett, Tom (wri): *The Great Muppet Caper; Project: Alf*
Pate, Christopher (act): *Howling III*
Pate, Johnny (mus): *Dr. Black Mr. Hyde*
Pate, Michael (act, b. 1920): *Beauty and the Beast (1962); The Black Castle; Brainstorm (1965); Congo Crossing; The Curse of the*

Undead; 5 Fingers; Green Mansions; Houdini (1953); Howling III; The Killer Is Loose; The Maze; The Return of Captain Invincible; Secret of the Incas; The Strange Door; Tower of London (1962); Zorro, the Avenger
Pate, Michael (wri, b. 1920): Most Dangerous Man Alive
Patel, Raju (dir): In the Shadow of Kilimanjaro
Pater, Clara (act): The Edge of Hell
Paternoster, Sydney (wri): In the Hands of the Spoilers
Paterson, Bill (act): The Adventures of Baron Munchausen (1989); Just Ask for Diamond; The Witches (1990)
Paterson, Bill (cin): Licensed to Love and Kill
Paterson, Jayne (act): Pretty Poison (1996)
Paterson, Pat (act): Murder On the Second Floor; The Right to Live
Paterson, Sheila (act): Quarantine; The Stepfather
Patillo, Jerome (act): Howling III
Patinkin, Mandy (act, b. 1952): Alien Nation; Dick Tracy (1990); The Hunchback (1997); Last Embrace; The Princess Bride
Patisson, Danik (act): The Accident; Too Hot to Handle
Paton, Angela (act): Flatliners; Groundhog Day
Paton, Charles (act): Blackmail (1929); The Iron Stair (1933); Jury's Evidence; Museum Mystery; Old Mother Riley's Ghosts; Pimpernel Smith; The Saint In London; The Sleeping Cardinal; The Speckled Band (1931); The Vandergilt Diamond Mystery; What a Night!
Paton, Delia (act): The Black Panther
Paton, Laurie (act): Norman's Awesome Experience
Paton, Stuart (dir & wri): 20,000 Leagues Under the Sea (1916, USA)
Patric, Jason (act): After Dark, My Sweet; The Lost Boys; Roger Corman's Frankenstein Unbound; Solarbabies
Patrice, Ann (act): Captain Nemo and the Underwater City
Patrice, Francois (act): Torticola Contre Frankensberg
Patrick, Alain (act): Fer de Lance; Wonder Woman
Patrick, Butch (act): Hand of Death; Munster, Go Home!; The Phantom Tollbooth
Patrick, Cynthia (act): The Mole People
Patrick, Dennis (act): Daddy's Gone A-Hunting; Dear, Dead Delilah; House of the Dark Shadows; The Time Travelers (1964)
Patrick, Diana (act): The Night Digger
Patrick, Dorothy (act): Federal Agent at Large; Follow Me Quietly; House by the River
Patrick, Gail (act, 1911-1980, nee Margaret Fitzpatrick): Death Takes a Holiday (1934); The Lone Wolf Returns (1935); The Madonna's Secret; Murder at the Vanities; Murders In the Zoo; The Phantom Broadcast
Patrick, Gavin (act): Secret Weapons
Patrick, Gil (act): The Clutching Hand; The Mad Monster
Patrick, Gregory (act): Critters 2: The Main Course
Patrick, Joan (act): Astro Zombies
Patrick, John (act): Sherlock Jr.
Patrick, John (wri): Mr. Moto Takes a Chance
Patrick, Lee (act, b. 1911): The Black Bird (1975); Footsteps In the Dark; Inner Sanctum (1948); The Maltese Falcon (1941); 7 Faces of Dr. Lao; The Smiling Ghost; Vertigo; Visit to a Small Planet
Patrick, Matthew (dir): Tainted Blood
Patrick, Mervyn (act): No Blade of Grass
Patrick, Michael (dir): Hider In the House
Patrick, Millicent (act): The White Goddess
Patrick, Nigel (act, 1913-1981): The Executioner; How to Murder a Rich Uncle; The Informers; The League of Gentlemen; The Man Inside; Mrs. Pym of Scotland Yard; Noose; Pandora and the Flying Dutchman; The Perfect Woman; A Prize of Gold; Sapphire; The Sound Barrier; Tales from the Crypt (1971)
Patrick, Nigel (dir, 1913-1981): Grand National Night; How to Murder a Rich Uncle; Underworld Informers
Patrick, Randal (act): Project X (1987)
Patrick, Randy (act): Zapped!
Patrick, Robert (act): Asylum (1996); Double Dragon; Equalizer 2000; The Faculty; Fire In the Sky (1993); Future Hunters; Last Gasp; Terminator 2: Judgment Day
Patrick, Roy (act): The City Under the Sea; The Road to Hong Kong
Patridge, Joe (act): The Hypnotic Eye
Patrie-Allen (act): The Flash
Patten, Dennis (act): Jamaica Inn (1985)
Patten, Luana (act): Fun and Fancy Free; Grotesque; Song of the South; They Ran for Their Lives; The Young Captives
Patten, Peggy Lloyd (act): What's the Matter With Helen?
Patten, Robert (act): Westworld
Patterly, Donald (cin): The Strangers
Patterson, Barbara (act): Raiders of the Living Dead
Patterson, Don Rene (dir & wri): Kemek
Patterson, Eddie (act): Premonition (1972)
Patterson, Elizabeth (act, 1876-1966): Beyond the Blue Horizon; Bulldog Drummond's Bride; Bulldog Drummond's Peril; Bulldog Drummond's Secret Police; The Cat and the Canary (1939); The Cat Creeps (1930); I Married a Witch; Love Me Tonight; Michael Shayne, Private Detective; Miss Pinkerton; A Night of Mystery (1937); The Return of Peter Grimm (1926)
Patterson, George (act): I Drink Your Blood
Patterson, Ginna (act): Play Misty for Me
Patterson, Hank (act): The Amazing Colossal Man; Attack of the Puppet People; The Beginning of the End; The Spider (1958)
Patterson, Herbert (act): Voodoo Island
Patterson, James (act): Castle Keep; Lilith; Silent Night, Bloody Night
Patterson, James (wri): Child of Darkness, Child of Light; Kiss the Girls
Patterson, Jamie (act): The Fan
Patterson, Jay (act): D.O.A. (1988); Double Jeopardy; Teenage Mutant Ninja Turtles
Patterson, Jerry (act): The Incredible 2-Headed Transplant
Patterson, John D. (dir): The Spring
Patterson, Judith (act): Premonition (1972)
Patterson, Kenneth (act): Invasion of the Body Snatchers (1956); Operation Secret
Patterson, Lee (act, b. 1929): Breakout; Cat and Mouse (1958); The Counterfeit Plan; Deadly Record; The Flying Scot; Jack the Ripper (1958); The Key Man; Man With a Gun; October Moth; Soho Incident; The Spaniard's Curse; Thirty-Six Hours (1954); The Three Worlds of Gulliver
Patterson, Melody (act, b. 1950): Blood and Lace; The Immortalizer
Patterson, Neva (act): All of Me; Desk Set; V
Patterson, Pat (act, 1910-1978): Charlie Chan In Egypt
Patterson, Pat (act & dir): The Body Shop
Patterson, Patrick (act): The Pit (1983)
Patterson, Paul (mus): A Distant Scream
Patterson, Paulette (act): Scream 2
Patterson, Peggy (act): The House On the Marsh; The Polar Star; To Let
Patterson, Raymond (act): Cameron's Closet
Patterson, Richard (dir): J-Men Forever!
Patterson, Rick (mus): Return of the Killer Tomatoes
Patterson, Robert (act): Werewolf of Washington
Patterson, Rocky (act): The Dark Dealer; Nail Gun Massacre
Patterson, Sarah (act): The Company of Wolves; Snow White (1989)
Patterson, Scott (act): Alien Nation: Dark Horizon; Them (1996)
Patterson, Shirley (act): Boston Blackie Goes Hollywood
Patterson, Stephen (act): Street Trash
Patterson, Stewart (act): Eugene Aram
Patterson, Troy (act): Attack of the Puppet People; The Spider (1958)
Patterson, Ytossie (act): Vamp
Patti, Toni (act): Nightbeast
Pattison, Barrie (act): It Happened Here
Patton, Alton (act): Secrets of the Phantom Caverns
Patton, Anna (act): The Slumber Party Massacre
Patton, Bart (act): Dementia 13; Zotz!
Patton, Joshua Lee (act): Freejack; Mutant
Patton, Mark (act): A Nightmare On Elm Street, Part 2: Freddy's Revenge
Patton, Tom (act): The Whispering
Patton, Will (act): Armageddon; Chinese Boxes; Cold Heaven; Copycat; No Way Out; Painted Heart; The Paint Job; The Postman (1997); The Puppet Masters; Romeo Is Bleeding
Patts, Mary Margaret (act): C.H.U.D. II
Patts, Patricia (act): Party Line
Patucchi, Daniele (mus): Warriors of the Wasteland
Paturel, Dominique (act): The Spy I Love
Pau, Peter (cin): Warriors of Virtue
Paukstelis, Tina Ona (act): The Unearthing
Paul, Adrian (act): Highlander: The Gathering; Love Potion No. 9; Masque of the Red Death (1989, Roger Corman/New World)
Paul, Alexandra (act, b. 1963): Christine; Cyber Bandits; House of the Damned (1996); In-Between; Piranha (1995); Prey of the Chameleon; Sunset Grill
Paul, Christina (act): Macbeth (1971); Vampire Circus
Paul, David (act): The Barbarians (1987); Ghost Writer
Paul, Don Michael (act): Alien from L.A.; Robot Wars; Rolling Vengeance
Paul, Eugenia (act): The Adventures of Hajji Baba; The Disembodied
Paul, Fred (act): The Adventures of Lieutenant Daring, RN-In a South American Port; Allan Field's Warning; Black Peter; Buttons; A Double Life (1913); The English Rose; The Great Bullion Robbery; In London's Toils; In the Hands of the London Crooks; Lieutenant Daring Avenges an Insult to the Union Jack; The Lights O' London; O.H.M.S.; The Price of Deception; The Rogues of London; The Sixth Commandment; A Study In Scarlet (1914); The Tube of Death; When Paths Diverge
Paul, Fred (dir): The English Rose; Her Greatest Performance; The House On the Marsh; The Lyons Mail; The Spirit of the Heath; Still Waters Run Deep
Paul, George (act): House of Usher (1960)
Paul, Georgie (act): Demon Seed
Paul, Gloria (act): Two Mafia Guys vs. Goldginger
Paul, Jennie (act): Eclipse (1977)
Paul, Jeremy (wri): Countess Dracula; Journey to Midnight
Paul, John (act): Breakout; The Curse of the Mummy's Tomb; Deadly Record; The Deathshead Vampire; Doomwatch; The Flesh Is Weak; The Man Who Wouldn't Talk; Mark of the Devil (1985); Violent Moment
Paul, Kurt (act): Bates Motel; Psycho IV: The Beginning
Paul, Lee (act): Ben; Deadly Friend; The Island at the Top of the World; Scream of the Wolf
Paul, Nancy (act): Lifeforce; The Return of Sherlock Holmes (1986)
Paul, P.R. (act): Neon Maniacs
Paul, Peter (act): The Barbarians (1987); Ghost Writer
Paul, Randall (act): Mission: Impossible
Paul, Richard (act): Beanstalk; Eating Raoul
Paul, Richard Joseph (act): Oblivion
Paul, Ricky (G.) (act): Echoes; Piranha II: The Spawning
Paul, Sue (act): All That Jazz
Paul, Talia (act): Anguish
Paul, Tori (act): Intensity
Paul, Victor (act): The Prisoner of Zenda (1979)
Paul, William (act): Twinkle, Twinkle, Killer Kane
Paul, Winston R. (wri): The Curious Female
Paulette, Geraldine (act): House of Usher (1960)
Paulin, Scott (act): Captain America (1992); Cat People (1982); Deadly Messages; Deceit (1993); Forbidden World; Full Eclipse; Grim Prairie Tales; Knights; The Quilt of Hathor; Teen Wolf; Warning Sign
Paulino, Justo (cin): Beast of Blood; Beyond Atlantis
Paulino, Ric (act): The Blood Drinkers
Paull, Morgan (act): Blade Runner; Fade to Black; Stowaway to the Moon; The Swarm
Paulo, Harry (act): The Adventures of Dick Turpin-200 Guineas Reward, Dead or Alive; A Study In Scarlet (1914)
Paulsen, Albert (act): Eyewitness (1981); The Manchurian Candidate; Search for the Gods
Paulsen, David (dir & wri): Schizoid (1980)
Paulsen, Duane (act): Flesh Gordon
Paulsen, Harald (act): Genuine
Paulsen, Pat (act, b. 1927): Auntie Lee's Meat Pies
Paulsen, Rob (act): Aladdin and the King of Thieves; Eyes of Fire; The Land Before Time II: The Great Valley Adventure; The Land Before Time III: The Time of the Great Giving; Warlock
Paulsen, Tiffany (act): Friday the 13th, Part VIII-Jason Takes Manhattan
Paulseon, Jack (act): Piranha (1978)
Paulsin, George (act): The Bat People; Simon, King of the Witches
Paulson, William (act): Terrorvision; Zone Troopers
Paulton, Agnes (act): The Girl Who Didn't Care
Pauly, Edgar (act): Die Spinnen
Paumier, Alfred (act): The Lifeguardsman
Pavan, Marisa (act): Down Three Dark Streets
Pavane, Anna (act): Portrait In Terror
Pavel, Anika (act): The Golden Lady; The Spy Who Loved Me
Pavey, Anthony (act): Bond of Fear
Pavel, Paul (act): Les Parapluies de Cherbourg
Pavey, Lucy (act): The Fall of the House of Usher (1950)
Pavey, Stan(ley) (cin): Hour of Decision; Mother Riley Meets the Vampire
Pavez, Terele (act): El Dia de la Bestia
Pavia, Ria (act): Dream a Little Dream
Pavicevac, Ivan (act): The Dead Are Alive
Paviot, Paul (dir & wri): Torticola Contre Frankensberg
Pavlicek, Michal (mus): The Scarlet Pimpernel (1999)
Pavlon, Jerry (act): Friday the 13th-Part V: A New Beginning
Pavlou, George (dir): Rawhead Rex; Transmutations
Pavlova, Anna (act, 1882-1931): The Dumb Girl of Portici
Pavlova, Nadezda (act): The Blue Bird (1976)
Pavlovitch, Robert (act): Cat People (1982)
Pavlow, Muriel (act, b. 1921): Eyewitness (1956); Murder She Said; The Net; The Shop at Sly Corner; Tiger In the Smoke; Whirlpool (1959)
Pavon, Benito (act): Gran Amore del Conde Dracula
Pavoni, Pier Ludovico (cin): Terror of Rome Against the Son of Hercules; Il Trionfo di Ercole
Pawley, William (act): Cheaters at Play; Gabriel Over the White House; Time to Kill (1942)
Pawlick, Amber (act): Friday the 13th, Part VIII-Jason Takes Manhattan
Pawlik, B. (act): Wielka, Wielka I Najwieksza
Pawlikowski, Adam (act): Rekopis Znaleziony w Saragossie
Pawlo, Toivo (act): Ansiktet
Pawloski, Piotr (act): Faraon
Pawluck, Jade (act): Perfect Little Angels
Pawluk, Mira (act): Cannibal Girls
Paxinou, Katina (act, 1900-1973, nee Katina Konstantopoulou): The Miracle (1959); Mr. Arkadin; Uncle Silas
Paxton, Bill (act, b. 1954): Aliens; Apollo 13; Boxing Helena; Brain Dead; The Dark Backward; Future Shock; Impulse (1984); Mighty Joe Young (1998); Monolith; Mortuary; Near Dark; Predator 2; Slipstream; Streets of Fire; Twister; Weird Science
Paxton, Collin Wilcox (act): Fluke
Paxton, Dick (act): Lizzie
Paxton, Glenn (mus): The Clone Master; The Two Worlds of Jennie Logan
Paxton, John (wri, b. 1911): Cornered; Crossfire; Fourteen Hours; How to Murder a Rich Uncle; Interpol; Murder My Sweet; On the Beach; A Prize of Gold
Paxton, Leslie (act): The House of the Dead
Paxton, Letty (act): The Price He Paid
Paxton, Richard (act): It Came Upon the Midnight Clear
Paxton, Sydney (act): Bluff; The Crimson Circle (1922); The Girl from Downing Street; A Man's Shadow; The Midnight Girl; The Prince and the Beggarmaid; A Vagabond's Revenge
Payer, Ivo (act): David and Goliath; Treasure of the Petrified Forest
Paylow, Clark (dir): Ring of Terror
Paylow, Janel (act): Bog
Paymer, David (act): Heart and Souls; Howard the Duck; Might Joe Young (1998); Night of the Creeps; The 6th Man; Unforgettable
Payne, Allen (act): Vampire In Brooklyn
Payne, Andrew (wri): Outer Touch
Payne, Anthony (mus): Tennis Court
Payne, Bruce (act): My Cousin Rachel
Payne, Bruce (Martyn) (act): Full Eclipse; Howling VI: The Freaks; Necronomicon: Book of the Dead; Switch (1991)
Payne, Bunty (act): East of Piccadilly
Payne, Dave (dir): Alien Terminator
Payne, Douglas (act): The Adventures of Dick Turpin-The Gunpowder Plot; The Airman's Children; The Devil's Bondman; The Flaw (1933); Flying from Justice; Further Exploits of Sexton Blake-The Mystery of the S.S. Olympic; The Great Cheque Fraud; The Great Gold Robbery; Guarding Britain's Secrets; The Harbour Lights; His Country's Honour; The Houseboat Mystery; In the Ranks; Ju-Jitsu to the Rescue; Maria Marten: or, The Murder In the Red Barn (1913); The Mesmerist (1915); The Mystery of the Diamond Belt; Old Bill Through the Ages; Red Aces; The Romany Rye; A Rogue's Wife; Royal Love; Spiritualism Exposed (1913); The Stolen Masterpiece; The Triumph of the Scarlet Pimpernel; The Wraith of the Tomb
Payne, Elvis (act): Crusoe
Payne, Graham (act): Jigsaw; Koroshi
Payne, James (act): Dragonslayer
Payne, John (act, 1912-1989): Hell's Island; Hidden Fear; Larceny; Miracle On 34th Street (1947); 99 River Street; Raiders of the Seven Seas; They Ran for Their Lives
Payne, John (dir, 1912-1989): They Ran for Their Lives

Payne, John M. (act): *Iron Justice*

Payne, Julie (act): *The Haunted* (1991); *Misery; Twice Upon a Time*

Payne, Laurence (act, b. 1919): *Crosstrap; One Deadly Owner; The Tell-Tale Heart* (1960); *The Third Alibi; The Trollenberg Terror; Vampire Circus*

Payne, Laurence (wri): *Girl In the Headlines*

Payne, Patricia (wri): *Captain America II*

Payne, Richard (act): *Angel Heart*

Payne, Tom (act): *Curucu, Beast of the Amazon; Love Slaves of the Amazons*

Payne, Wilfred (act): *The Beggar Girl's Wedding*

Paynter, Guy Kingsley (act): *The Girl Hunters*

Paynter, Robert (K.) (cin): *An American Werewolf In London; The Big Sleep* (1978); *Curtains; The Final Conflict; Firepower; Little Shop of Horrors* (1986); *The Muppets Take Manhattan; The Nightcomers; Scream for Help; Superman II; Superman III*

Pays, Amanda (act, b. 1959): *The Cold Room; The Flash; The Flash 2: Revenge of the Trickster; The Kindred; Leviathan; Spacejacked; Thirteen at Dinner*

Pays, Howard (act): *Dangerous Afternoon; Evidence In Concrete; The Grand Junction Case; Jungle Street; The Undesirable Neighbour; Urge to Kill*

Payson, John (dir & wri): *Joe's Apartment*

Payson, Keith (wri): *Puppet Master 4*

Payton, Barbara (act, 1927-1967): *Bride of the Gorilla; The Flanagan Boy; Four Sided Triangle; Kiss Tomorrow Goodbye; Murder Is My Beat; Run for the Hills; Trapped*

Payton, Douglas (act): *Fire and Ice*

Payton, Lee (act): *The Blob* (1958)

Paz, Gerardo (act): *Nightlife* (1989, USA-Mex)

Paz, Jeni (act): *Maniac* (1980)

Pazzafini, Giovanni (act): *The Conquest of Mycenae; The Trojan Horse*

Pazzafini, Nello (act): *Goliath Against the Giants; Ironmaster; The Lion of Thebes*

Peabody, Dick (act): *Mackenna's Gold*

Peabody, Dixie (act): *Bury Me an Angel*

Peace, Brett (act): *Return of the Killer Tomatoes*

Peace, Caesar (cin): *Assignment-Outer Space*

Peace, Chad (act): *Return of the Killer Tomatoes*

Peace, Clint (act): *Return of the Killer Tomatoes*

Peace, Rock (act): *Attack of the Killer Tomatoes; Return of the Killer Tomatoes*

Peach, Kenneth (cin): *City Beneath the Sea* (1970); *Curse of the Faceless Man; It!—The Terror from Beyond Space; The Lone Ranger and the Lost City of Gold; The Lost Missile*

Peach, L. DuGarde (wri): *The Case of Gabriel Perry; Chu Chin Chow* (1934); *The Ghoul* (1933); *The Man Who Changed His Mind; Seven Sinners; Spy of Napoleon; The Tunnel*

Peach, Mary (act, b. 1934): *The Projected Man; Scrooge* (1970)

Peacock, Daniel (act): *The Jewel of the Nile; Robin Hood: Prince of Thieves*

Peacock, John (wri): *Cat and Mouse* (1974); *To the Devil a Daughter*

Peacock, Keith (act): *Our Man In Marrakesh*

Peacock, Kim (act): *The Clue of the New Pin* (1929); *Midnight at Madame Tussaud's*

Peacock, Kim (act): *Midnight at Madame Tussaud's*

Peacock, Marjorie (act): *Concerning Mr. Martin*

Peacock, Michael (wri): *Straight On Till Morning*

Peacock, Sue (act): *The McGuffin*

Peacock, Trevor (act): *Catch Me a Spy; Hamlet* (1990); *He Who Rides a Tiger*

Peacock, Walter (wri): *A Night In Montmartre*

Peacock, William (act): *Payroll*

Peacocke, Thomas (act): *Mortal Sins*

Peake, Don (mus): *The Hills Have Eyes; I, Desire; The People Under the Stairs; The Prey* (1980)

Peake, Lisa (act): *A Matter of Choice; She* (1965)

Peake, Michael (act): *The Devil-Ship Pirates; The Gorgon; High Jump; Mark of the Phoenix; The Pirates of Blood River; Strip Tease Murder*

Peaker, E.J. (act): *Graduation Day*

Peanuts, The (act): *Ghidrah, the Three-Headed Monster*

Pearce, Alice (act): *The Glass-Bottom Boat*

Pearce, Craig (act): *The Seventh Floor*

Pearce, Dale (act): *I Was a Zombie for the F.B.I.*

Pearce, Damon (act): *The Wiz*

Pearce, David (act): *Voice Over*

Pearce, Hen (act): *Queenie of the Circus*

Pearce, Jacqueline (act): *The Plague of the Zombies; The Reptile*

Pearce, Joanne (act): *Morons from Outer Space*

Pearce, John (act): *THX 1138*

Pearce, Leonard (act): *The Face of Darkness*

Pearce, Mary Vivian (act): *Multiple Maniacs; Serial Mom*

Pearce, Perce (act): *Bambi*

Pearce, Vera (act): *Men of Sherwood Forest; Three Cases of Murder*

Pearcy, Patricia (act): *Delusion; Squirm*

Pearl, Aaron (act): *Ebenezer*

Pearl, Alfie (act): *A Polish Vampire In Burbank*

Pearl, Barry (act): *The Annihilator; The Munsters' Revenge*

Pearl, Daniel (cin): *The Alien's Return; The Fifth Floor; Invaders from Mars* (1986); *It's Alive III: Island of the Alive; A Return to Salem's Lot; The Texas Chainsaw Massacre; Zapped!*

Pearl, Herb (cin): *Pandemonium*

Pearl, Julie R. (act): *Chain Reaction* (1996)

Pearlman, Gilbert (wri): *Murder In a Small Town*

Pearlstein, Randy (act): *Revenge of the Radioactive Reporter*

Pearson, Barry (wri): *Alien Warrior; Firebird 2015 A.D.; Plague*

Pearson, Brett (act): *Eyes of Fire; Never Talk to Strangers*

Pearson, Clive (act): *Witchcraft 4: Virgin Heart*

Pearson, Colin (act): *The Swordsman*

Pearson, David (act): *The Tomb*

Pearson, Derek (act): *King Kong Lives*

Pearson, Drew (act): *Betrayal from the East*

Pearson, George (dir, b. 1875-1973): *The Ace of Spades; Buttons; Checkmate; The Fatal Hour* (1937); *The Fool; The Live Wire; Midnight at Madame Tussaud's; Murder by Rope; The Pointing Finger; The Secret Voice; The Shot In the Dark; A Study In Scarlet* (1914); *Wednesday's Luck; Ultus and the Grey Lady; Ultus and the Secret of the Night; Ultus and the Three-Button Mystery; Ultus, the Man from the Dead; Whispering Tongues*

Pearson, George (wri, 1875-1973): *The Fool; Ultus and the Grey Lady; Ultus and the secret of the Night; Ultus and the Three-Button Mystery; Ultus, the Man from the Dead*

Pearson, Hesketh (wri): *The Cage; Don Q and the Artist; Don Q-How He Outwitted Don Luis; Don Q-How He Treated the Parole of Gevil Hay*

Pearson, Jake (act): *Dr. Jekyll's Dungeon of Death*

Pearson, James (act): *The Puppet Masters*

Pearson, Jerold (act): *Remote Control* (1988)

Pearson, Jill (act): *Edge of Sanity; Howling V: The Rebirth; Jekyll and Hyde*

Pearson, Johnny (mus): *Scream for Help; When Michael Calls*

Pearson, Karen (act): *The Borrowers* (1973); *When Michael Calls*

Pearson, Lloyd (act): *Time Flies* (1944)

Pearson, Lora (act): *The Hand* (1981)

Pearson, Malachi (act): *Casper*

Pearson, Richard (act): *Attempt to Kill; The Blue Bird* (1976); *The Blue Parrot; Catch Me a Spy; Macbeth* (1971); *The Mirror Crack'd; Model for Murder; One of Our Dinosaurs Is Missing; Royal Flash; Svengali* (1954)

Pearson, Richard (mus): *The Strange Affair*

Pearson, Ted (act): *Dick Tracy's G-Men*

Pearson, Virginia (act, 1888-1958): *The Phantom of the Opera* (1925); *The Taxi Mystery; The Wizard of Oz* (1925)

Pearson, Winifred (act): *A Study In Scarlet* (1914)

Peart, Joan (act): *The Tell-Tale Heart* (1960)

Peart, Pauline (act): *The Satanic Rites of Dracula*

Pearthree, Pippa (act): *Village of the Damned* (1995)

Peary, Harold (act, 1908-1985): *Gildersleeve's Ghost*

Pease, Chris (act): *Secrets of the Phantom Caverns*

Pease, Fred (act): *Murder at Covent Garden*

Pease, Patsy (act): *He Knows You're Alone; Space Raiders*

Peasgood, Julie (act): *House of the Long Shadows; The Lake*

Peaslee, Richard (mus): *The Persecution and Assassination of Jean-Paul Marat as Performed by the Inmates of the Asylum of Charenton Under the Direction of the Marquis de Sade*

Pechan, Rudolf (act): *Mission: Impossible*

Pechukas, Maria (act): *Spookies*

Peck, Anthony (act): *Creator; The Hunt for Red October; The Magic Bubble*

Peck, Bob (act): *After Pilkington; Jurassic Park; Lord of the Flies* (1990); *Slipstream; A TV Dante: Cantos I-VIII*

Peck, Brian (CD ...): *Return of the Living Dead* ...; *Quantum ... Dead; My Best ... 1963); The Twisted Nerve*

Peck, Brian (USA act): *Return of the Living Dead, Part II*

Peck, Brian (dir): *The Willies*

Peck, Cecilia (act): *Blue Flame; My Best Friend Is a Vampire*

Peck, Clare (C.) (act): *Beyond the Universe; Flowers In the Attic; My Science Project; Retribution* (1988)

Peck, Craig (act): *There's Nothing Out There*

Peck, Ed (V.) (act): *The Flight of Dragons; Heaven Can Wait* (1978)

Peck, George (act): *Curse of the Puppet Master; Dawn of the Mummy*

Peck, Gregory (act, b. 1916): *The Boys from Brazil; Cape Fear* (1961 & 1991); *Mackenna's Gold; Marooned; Moby Dick* (1956 & 1998); *The Omen; On the Beach; The Paradine Case; Spellbound* (1945)

Peck, J. Eddie (act): *Curse II: The Bite*

Peck, Julie (act): see London, Julie

Peck, Kevin (act): *Making Contact*

Peck, Mitchell (wri): *Bio-Dome*

Peck, Richard (wri): *Are You In the House Alone?*

Peck, Tony (act): *Brenda Starr* (1992)

Peckham, George (cin): *Gargoyles*

Peckinpah, David (wri): *In Self Defense; Obsessed* (1992)

Peckinpah, Sam (act, 1925-1984): *Invasion of the Body Snatchers* (1956)

Peckinpah, Sam (wri, 1925-1984): *Straw Dogs*

Pedachini, Peter (act): *Those Dear Departed*

Pedbrey, Maurice (act): *Happy Birthday to Me*

Pedelty, Donovan (dir & wri): *False Evidence; Flame In the Heather; Landslide* (1937); *Murder Tomorrow*

Pedersen, Carl (act): see Brisson, Carl

Pedersen, Chris (act): *Night of the Comet; Twin Peaks: Fire Walk With Me*

Pedersen, Maren (act): *Haxan*

Pederson, Con (cin): *2001: A Space Odyssey*

Pedi, Tom (act): *The Cat from Outer Space; Criss Cross; Human Feelings*

Pedler, Dr. Kit (wri): *Doomwatch*

Pedley, Anthony (act): *The Corsican Brothers* (1985)

Pedley, Ethel (wri): *Dot and the Kangaroo*

Pedone, Mario (act): *Endgame; She* (1983)

Pedro, Illario (act): *One Plus One*

Pedroza, Inez (act): *Dr. Strange; Earthquake*

Peek, Denys (act): *Curse of the Crimson Altar*

Peel, David (act, b. 1920): *Brides of Dracula; Escape to Danger; The Hands of Orlac* (1959)

Peel, Edward (act): *A Distant Scream*

Peel, Eileen (act): *Lost*

Peel, Haley (act): *Addams Family Values*

Peel, Richard (act): *Pharaoh's Curse*

Peelaert, Guy (cin): *The Killing Game*

Peelen, Mara (act): *Gebroken Spiegels*

Peeples, Nia (act, b. 1962): *Deadlock 2; Deepstar Six; Mr. Stitch; Terminal*

Peeples, Samuel A. (wri): *Spectre* (1977)

Peer, Kenneth (act): *Desert Warrior*

Peer, Salmaan (act): *The Twisted Nerve*

Peerce, Larry (dir): *Christmas Every Day; Lovestruck*

Peerless, Donna (act): *It* (1990)

Peet, Bill (wri): *Alice In Wonderland* (1951)

Peeters, Barbara (dir): *Bury Me an Angel*

Peets, Remus (act): *Twilight Zone*

Pegram, Nigel (act): *Riders of the Storm*

Peguri, Gino (mus): *Supersonic Man*

Pehl, Mary Jo (wri): *Mystery Science Theater 3000: The Movie*

Pehlke, Heinz (cin): *De Sade*

Pei, Betty Ting (act): *Stoner*

Pei, Edward (cin): *Howling VI: The Freaks; The Sitter; The Stand; Watchers II*

Peihopa, Len (act): *Those Dear Departed*

Peile, Kinsey (act): *The Face at the Window* (1920)

Peine, Josh (act): *Doomsday Machine*

Peiser, Maria Lilli (act): see Palmer, Lilli

Peisley, Fred(erick) (act): *Hide and Seek; Overcoat Sam; The Secret of the Loch* (1934); *Subterfuge*

Peitch, Monika (act): *The Hunchback of Soho*

Peking Opera (act & mus): *Uproar In Heaven*

Peldon, Ashley (act): *Deceived; Drop Dead Fred; The Secretary*

Pelekis, Fotis (act): *The Punisher*

Pelgrom, Elja (act): *Gebroken Spiegels*

Pelham, David M. (wri): *Rapture*

Pelikan, Lisa (act): *Ghoulies; Into the Badlands; Jennifer* (1978)

Pelish, Andy (act): *C.H.U.D. II*

Pelish, Randy (act): *Howling VI: The Freaks*

Pelissier, Jean-Marie (dir & wri): *The Bride* (1973)

Pelissier, Anthony (dir, 1912-1988): *Meet Mr. Lucifer; Night Without Stars; The Rocking Horse Winner*

Pelissier, Anthony (wri, 1912-1988): *Tiger In the Smoke*

Pelka, Valentine (act): *Time Flies*

Pelky, Sanita (act): *The Ghost of Dragstrip Hollow; Missile to the Moon*

Pellati, Teresa (act): *Ulysses*

Pellegrin, Raymond (act): *Le Deuxieme Souffle*

Pellegrini, Giuseppe (wri): *L'Amante del Vampiri*

Pellegrini, Ines (act): *Arabian Nights* (1974); *Eyeball*

Pellegrino, Frank (act): *Firebird 2015 A.D.*

Pellegrino, Nick (act): *The China Syndrome*

Pelletier, Denis (act): *The Music of the Spheres*

Pelletier, Gilles (act): *I Confess*

Pelletier, Michele-Barbara (act): *Brainscan*

Pellett, Christopher (act): *When Michael Calls*

Pellicer, Coral (act): *Amador*

Pellicer, Pilar (act): *Zorro, the Gay Blade*

Pellicer, Pina (act): *Macario*

Pelligra, Biagio (act): *Spara Forte, Piu Forte...Non Capisco*

Pelling, George (act): *Brainstorm* (1965); *20 Million Miles to Earth*

Pelly, Charles (act): *The Golden Dawn*

Pelly, Farrell (act): *Darby O'Gill and the Little People*

Peloso, Samuel (act): *Octaman*

Peltz, Roger (act): *Explorers*

Peluffo, Ana Luisa (act): *La Cabeza Viviente; H.G. Wells' The New Invisible Man; Sail Into Danger*

Pelusi, Richard (wri): *Mad at the Moon*

Pelzman, Richard (act): *Serial Mom*

Pember, Ron (act): *Deathline; The Glitterball; The Land That Time Forgot; Murder by Decree; Ordeal by Innocence; Subterfuge*

Pemberton, Charles (act): *Electric Eskimo*

Pemberton-Billing, Noel (wri): *High Treason* (1929 & 1951)

Pembroke, Clifford (act): *The Silver Greyhound* (1919); *The Splendid Coward*

Pembroke, George (act): *Black Dragons; Bluebeard* (1944); *Buried Alive* (1940); *False Evidence; The Invisible Ghost*

Pembroke, Scott (dir): *The Black Pearl*

Pen, Howard (wri): *Sword of the Valiant*

Pena, Elizabeth (act, b. 1961): **Batteries Not Included; It Came from Outer Space II; Jacob's Ladder; Vibes*

Pena, Julia (act): *Gran Amore del Conde Dracula*

Pena, Julio (act): *Honeycomb; Horror Express; La Noche de Walpurgis; Satanik*

Pena, Luis (act): *Tenemos 18 Anos*

Pena, Nettie (dir): *Home Sweet Home*

Pena, Pascual Garcia (act): *The Beast of Hollow Mountain; The Black Scorpion* (1957)

Penafiel, Luis (Verna) (wri): *The House That Screamed; Island of the Damned; Master of Horror*

Penalba, Abel (wri): *Moebius*

Penalver, Diana (act): *Dead Alive*

Penberthy, Beverly (act): *Picking Up the Pieces*

Pence, Glen A. (act): *Night of the Zombies* (1981)

Penczner, Jolanda (act): *I Was a Zombie for the F.B.I.*

Penczner, Marius (dir & wri): *I Was a Zombie for the F.B.I.*

Penczner, Paul (act): *I Was a Zombie for the F.B.I.*

Pender, Tommy (act): *The Water Babies*

Penderecki, Krzysztof (mus, b. 1933): *The Exorcist; Rekopis Znaleziony w Saragossie*

Pendergast, Frank (act): *End of the World* (1977)

Pendleton, Austin (act, b. 1940): *Hello Again; The Muppet Movie; My Boyfriend's Back; Rain Without Thunder; Short Circuit; Simon*

Pendleton, David (act): *Abduction*

Pendleton, Derek (act): *Re-Animator*

Pendleton, Nat (act, 1895-1967): *Another Thin Man; The Garden Murder Case; The Mad Doctor of Market Street; On Borrowed Time; Phantom Raiders; Scared to Death* (1947); *The Thin Man*

Pendleton, Steve (act): *Killers from Space; The Sky Dragon; Target Earth*

Pendrell, Anthony (act): *Blind Man's Bluff* (1952); *Hot Ice; No Haunt for a Gentleman*

Pendrey, Michael (act): *Silent Night, Bloody Night*

Pendrey, Richard (act): *File It Under Fear; Yellow Dog*

Penella, Emma (act): *El Amor Brujo* (1986); *Not On Your Life!*

Penella, Terele (act): *Tenemos 18 Anos*

Penfield, Derek (act): *Nightfall* (1988)

Peng, Tien (act): *A Touch of Zen*

Penghlis, Thaao (act): *Altered States; The Bookfair*

Penhaligon, Susan (act): *House of Mortal Sin; The Land That Time Forgot; Patrick; The Uncanny*

Penland, Charles R. (act): *Nightmare On the 13th Floor*
Penn, Arthur (dir, b. 1922): *Dead of Winter; Mickey One; Night Moves; Target*
Penn, Chris(topher) (act): *Futurekick; Josh and S.A.M.*
Penn, Edward (act): *Lady Beware*
Penn, Leo (dir, 1921-1998): *The Dark Secret of Harvest Home*
Penn, Leonard (act): *Eyes of the Jungle; On the Threshold of Space; The Saracen Blade; Savage Mutiny; Thief of Damascus*
Penn, Peter (act): *Passenger to Tokyo*
Penn, Richard (act): *I'm Dangerous Tonight*
Penn, Sean (act): *The Game*
Penna, Tarver (act): *The Avenging Hand (1936)*
Pennell, Jon Maynard (act): *Ghoulies II*
Pennell, Larry (act): *The Borrower; City Beneath the Sea (1970); Metalstorm: The Destruction of Jared-Syn; The Space Children; Superstition*
Pennell, Nicholas (act): *Rasputin, the Mad Monk*
Pennella, Joe (cin): *Alien Warrior*
Penner, Erdman (wri): *Alice In Wonderland (1951); Pinocchio (1940)*
Penner, Janet (act): *The Haunting of Sarah Hardy*
Penner, Joe (act, 1904-1941, nee Joe Pinter): *The Boys from Syracuse*
Penney, John (wri): *The Kindred; The Power (1980)*
Penney, Ralph (act): *The Devil Commands*
Pennick, Jack (act): *The Beast from 20,000 Fathoms*
Pennington, Chuck (act): *Planet of Dinosaurs*
Pennington, Earl (act): *City On Fire; Happy Birthday to Me; Of Unknown Origin*
Pennington, Laura (act): *Virus (1980)*
Pennington, Laurie (act): *Chillers*
Pennington, Michael (act): *Hamlet (1969); The Return of Sherlock Holmes (1986); Return of the Jedi*
Pennington-Richards, C. (cin): *1984 (1955); Obsession (1949); Scrooge (1951); Tarzan and the Lost Safari*
Pennington-Richards, C. (dir): *A Challenge for Robin Hood; Hour of Decision; The Oracle (1952)*
Pennock, Christopher (act): *Night of Dark Shadows*
Penny, Alan (act): *Howling III*
Penny, Allan (act): *Mystery Island*
Penny, Joe (act, b. 1957): *Bloody Birthday; Deathmoon; Whisper Kill*
Penny, Richard (act): *No Blade of Grass*
Penny, Sydney (act): *Child of Darkness, Child of Light; Hyper Sapien: People from Another Star; Through the Magic Pyramid*
Peno, Lola (act): *Hundra*
Penrod, A.G. (wri): *The Man from Beyond*
Penrod, Judy (act): *The Plutonium Incident*
Penrose, Anthony (dir & wri): *Strange Behaviour*
Penrose, Charles (act): *The Crimes of Stephen Hawke; Dark Eyes of London; The Man With the Magnetic Eyes; Miranda*
Penrose, John (act): *Hot Ice; Kind Hearts and Coronets; Mantrap; Street of Shadows*
Penrose, Roland (act): *L'Age d'Or*
Pentecost, George (act): *It Came Upon the Midnight Clear*
Pentelow, Arthur (act): *The Gladiators; Privilege*
Penty, Doug (act): *Gargantua*
Pentz, Robert (act): *Cyborg (1989); The Handmaid's Tale*
Penvern, Andre (act): *Quelqu'un Derriere la Porte*
Penwarden, Hazel (act): *The Man In Black*
Penya, Anthony (act): *Humanoids from the Deep*
Penz, Alena (act): *2069: A Sex Odyssey*
Peoples, David (dir): *The Blood of Heroes*
Peoples, David (wri): *Blade Runner; The Blood of Heroes; Leviathan; 12 Monkeys*
Peoples, Don (act): *Robot In the Family*
Peoples, Janet (wri): *12 Monkeys*
Pepe, Nico (act): *The Minotaur*
Pepin, Richard (dir): *Cyber-Tracker; The Silencers (1995)*
Pepiot, Ken (cin): *The 'Burbs; Chiller; Gremlins 2: The New Batch*
Peploe, Mark (dir): *Afraid of the Dark*
Peploe, Mark (wri): *Afraid of the Dark; The Passenger; The Pied Piper (1971)*
Peppard, George (act, 1933-1994): *Battle Beyond the Stars (1980); Damnation Alley; The Executioner; The Groundstar Conspiracy; Operation Crossbow*
Pepper, Anna (mus): *Outer Touch*
Pepper, Barbara (act, b. 1916): *Foreign Correspondent; Forty Naughty Girls; Girls In Chains; It's Only Money; Lady In the Morgue; The Millerson Case; The Westland Case*
Pepper, Bob (act): *The Hidden Eye*
Pepper, Dan (wri): *Hold That Hypnotist*
Pepper, Dick (wri): *A Piece of Cake*
Pepper, Florence (act): *Dick Tracy (1945)*
Pepper, John (act): *Spettri*
Pepper, Paul (act): *Teenage Zombies*
Pepperman, Paul (wri): *The Beastmaster; Beastmaster 2: Through the Portal of Time; Beastmaster III: The Eye of Braxus*
Peppiatt, Marilyn (act): *Sorry, Wromg Number (1989)*
Perada, Allen (act): *The Body Snatchers; Philadelphia Experiment II*
Peralta, Cesar A. (act): *Zorro: The Legend Begins*
Peralta, Isibella (act): *Princess Warrior*
Peratta, Mike (act): *The Erotic Adventures of Zorro*
Perault, Robert (act): *Doctor Franken*
Perce, Joe (act): *The Hidden*
Percival Mackey & His Band (act & mus): *Death at Broadcasting House*
Percival, Cyril (act): *The Noble Bachelor; The Princess of Happy Chance; The Yellow Claw*
Percival, Lance (act, b. 1933): *The Devil's Daffodil; Hide and Seek; Jekyll and Hyde; The Water Babies*
Percival, Michael (act): *No Blade of Grass; 101 Dalmatians (1996)*
Percival, Robert (act): *The Scarlet Web*
Percy, Edward (wri): *Brides of Dracula; Ladies In Retirement; The Mad Room; The Shop at Sly Corner; Trunk Crime*
Percy, Esme (act, 1887-1957): *Accused (1936); Dead of Night (1945); Death In the Hand; The Frog; The Ghosts of Berkeley Square; Murder; On Secret Service; The Return of the Scarlet Pimpernel*
Percy, Fred (act): *A Cornish Romance*
Percy, Neville (act & wri): *A Smart Set*
Pere, Wayne (act): *Alien Nation: The Enemy Within; Dark Angel (1996); The Flash*
Pereda, Ramon (act): *El Cuerpo del Lito*
Perego, Didi (act, a.k.a. Didi Sullivan): *Caltiki, il Mostro Immortale*
Peregudov, A. (wri): *Zolotoye Ozero*
Pereira, Nelly (act): *Vampire On Bikini Beach*
Pereira, Zeni (act): *Women In Fury*
Pereiro, Manuel (act): *Mystery On Monster Island*
Perella, Marco (act): *D.O.A. (1988)*
Perello, Hope (dir): *Howling VI: The Freaks; Pet Shop*
Perelman, S.J. (wri, 1904-1979): *Around the World In 80 Days; One Touch of Venus*
Pereno, Robert (act): *The Little Drummer Girl; Xtro*
Perer, Leon (cin): *The Telephone Book*
Peres, Marcel (act): *Le Quai des Brumes*
Peretti, Pio (act): *The Lone Wolf In Paris*
Peretz, Susan (act): *Retribution (1988)*
Perev, Irving (act): *The Magic Voyage of Sinbad*
Pereverzev, Ivan (act): *The Heavens Call*
Perez, George (mus): *Nostradamus y el Destructor de Monstruos*
Perez, Inez (act): *Night of the Lepus*
Perez, Louis A. (act): *Project X (1987)*
Perez, Pablo (cin): *Marta*
Perez, Paul (wri): *The Missing Guest*
Perez, Tony (act): *Alien Nation*
Perez, Vincent (act): *The Crow: City of Angels*
Perfit, Tony (act): *Sweet Sixteen*
Perfitt, Frank (act): *Alf's Carpet; Maria Marten (1928); The Silent House; The Woman In White (1929)*
Pergola, James (cin): *The Intruder Within; The Night of the Claw*
Perham, Joe (act): *Graveyard Shift (1990)*
Peri, Jillian (act): *The Edge of Hell*
Periard, J. Roger (act): *Rabid; Starship Invasions; Virus (1980)*
Perier, Etienne (dir): *Zeppelin*
Perier, Francois (act, b. 1919, nee Francois-Gabriel-Marie Pilu): *Demoniac; The French Conspiracy; Orphee*
Peries, Lester James (dir, b. 1921): *The God King*
Perilli, Frank Ray (act): *End of the World (1977); The Fugitive (1993)*
Perilli, Frank Ray (wri): *Dracula's Dog; End of the World (1977); Laserblast; Mansion of the Doomed*
Perilli, Ivo (wri): *Ulysses*
Perilli, Marc (act): *End of the World (1977)*
Perillo, Joey (act): *12 Monkeys*
Perilstein, Michael (mus): *The Deadly Spawn*
Perin, David (act): *The War In Space*
Perinal, Georges (cin, 1897-1965): *Dark Journey; The Fallen Idol; The House In the Square; The Private Life of Don Juan; Le Sang d'un Poete; The Squeaker (1937); The Thief of Bagdad (1940); Things to Come; Tom Thumb*
Periolat, George (act): *The Mark of Zorro (1920)*
Perischini, Robert (act): *Shock Chamber*
Perisic, Zoran (dir): *The Phoenix and the Magic Carpet*
Perkins, Anthony (act, 1932-1992): *The Black Hole; Daughter of Darkness (1990); Destroyer; Edge of Sanity; The Fool Killer; Green Mansions; How Awful About Allan; I'm Dangerous Tonight; Les Miserables (1978); Murder On the Orient Express; On the Beach; Pretty Poison (1968); Psycho (1960); Psycho II; Psycho III; Psycho IV: The Beginning; Quelqu'un Derriere la Porte; Remember My Name; Le Scandale; The Sins of Dorian Gray; The Trial; Winter Kills*
Perkins, Anthony (dir, 1932-1992): *Psycho III*
Perkins, Anthony (wri, 1932-1992): *Double Negative; The Last of Sheila*
Perkins, Bryan (act): *The Toxic Avenger, Part II*
Perkins, Elizabeth (act, b. 1960): *Big; The Flintstones; Miracle On 34th Street (1994)*
Perkins, Emily (act): *It (1990)*
Perkins, Francis/Frank (mus): *The Couch; The Incredible Mr. Limpet*
Perkins, Gil(bert) (act, 1907-1999): *The Prisoner of Zenda (1979); Sherlock Holmes In New York; Teenage Monster; Valley of the Dragons*
Perkins, Jack (act): *Herbie Goes Bananas; Invasion of the Bee Girls*
Perkins, Jessica (act): *The Toxic Avenger*
Perkins, Jo (act): *RoboCop 2*
Perkins, Jonathan P. (act): *Leprechaun 2*
Perkins, Kent (act): *The Being*
Perkins, Millie (act, b. 1939): *Bodily Harm; The Haunting Passion; Murder of Innocence; Necronomicon: Book of the Dead; Slam Dance; Wild In the Streets*
Perkins, Osgood (act, 1893-1937): *Puritan Passions; Secret of the Chateau*
Perkins, Osgood (1980s & 1990s act): *Psycho II; Wolf*
Perkins, Patricia (act): *Cat People (1982)*
Perkins, Pinetop (act): *Angel Heart*
Perkins, Ron (act): *Storm of the Century*
Perkins, Terry (act): *Trauma (1993)*
Perkins, Voltaire (act): *Blood of Dracula; Frankenstein's Daughter (1958); How to Make a Monster; Macabre (1958)*
Perle, Rebecca (act): *Not of This Earth (1988)*
Perlich, Max (act): *The Butcher's Wife*
Perlifi, Virginia (wri): *Mirror, Mirror 2: Raven Dance*
Perlin, Monte R. (act): *Pumpkinhead II: Blood Wings*
Perlman, Bernard (act): *Street Trash*
Perlman, Rhea (act, b. 1948): *Amazing Stories II; Houdini (1998); My Little Pony; We're Back! A Dinosaur's Story*
Perlman, Ron (act, b. 1950): *The Adventures of Captain Zoom In Outer Space; Alien Resurrection; Body Armor; The City of Lost Children; Cronos; Fluke; Houdini (1998); The Ice Pirates; The Island of Dr. Moreau (1996); Mr. Stitch; The Name of the Rose; Quest for Fire; Romeo Is Bleeding; Sensation (1994); Sleepwalkers; A Town Has Turned to Dust; When the Bough Breaks*
Perlman, Stephen (act): *Future Cop*
Perlow, Bob (act): *Night of the Comet*
Perlsten, Michael (mus): *Hollywood Chainsaw Hookers*
Peronne, Denise (act): *Jeux Interdits; Quelqu'un Derriere la Porte*
Peronti, Gino (act): *End of the World (1977)*
Perpiche, Cindy (act): *Avalanche*
Perrault, Charles (wri, 1628-1703): *Cendrillon; Cinderella (1911 {Selig & Thanhouser} & 1961); Cinderella and the Fairy Godmother; A Kiss for Cinderella; Peau d'Ane; Puss In Boots*
Perrault, Gilles (wri): *The Serpent (1973)*
Perrault, Dominique (act): *Deadbolt*
Perreau, Gigi (act, b. 1941, nee Ghislaine Perreau-Saussine): *Bonzo Goes to College; For Heaven's Sake; Journey to the Center of Time; Shadow On the Wall*
Perreau, Janine (act): *Invaders from Mars (1953)*
Perreau-Saussine, Ghislaine (act): see Perreau, Gigi
Perret, Leonce (dir & wri, 1880-1935): *A Modern Salome; The Twin Pawns*
Perrey, Mireille (act): *The Hands of Orlac (1959); Les Parapluies de Cherbourg*
Perri, Paul (act): *Hellraiser 4: Bloodline; She Woke Up*
Perri, Paul (dir): *Revenge of the Virgins*
Perriam, Ron (act): *Murder at the Windmill*
Perrier, Don (act): *Empire of Ash III*
Perriguey, Thelma (act): *Just Imagine*
Perrin, Jack (act): *Midnight Faces*
Perrin, Jacques (act): *Peau d'Ane; The Sleeping Car Murders*
Perrin, Judy (act): *The Strangers*
Perrin, Nat (wri): *The Gracie Allen Murder Case; Hellzapoppin; Roman Scandals; Song of the Thin Man*
Perrine, Valerie (act, b. 1943): *Agency; Maid to Order; Slaughterhouse-Five; Superman (1978); Superman II*
Perrineau, Harold (act): *The Edge; The Tempest (1998)*
Perrinoz, Roger (act): *Les Parapluies de Cherbourg*
Perrins, Leslie (act): *Betrayal (1932); Blake the Lawbreaker; Bulldog Drummond at Bay (1937); The Clue of the Second Goblet; Dangerous Fingers; The Gables Mystery; Grip of the Strangler; Guilty?; The House of Unrest; I Killed the Count; The Limping Man (1936); Line Engaged; The Lost Hours; Luck of the Navy; Man On the Run; The Man Who Changed His Name; Mr. Reeder In Room 13; The Pointing Finger; The Price of Folly; The Roof; The Rosary; The Scotland Yard Mystery; Secret Lives; Sensation (1937); The Silent Passenger; Silken Threads; Suspected Person; The Triumph of Sherlock Holmes; White Face; White Lilac*
Perroni, Marrio (act): *Beat the Devil*
Perrot, Francoise (act): *Women's Prison Massacre*
Perrott, Ruth (act): *The 30 Foot Bride of Candy Rock*
Perry, Barbara (act): *Trancers*
Perry, Ben (act): *The Kindred; The Octagon*
Perry, Betty (act): *The Silencers (1995)*
Perry, Bob (act): *Torchy Plays With Dynamite*
Perry, Bob (act): *Jungle Burger*
Perry, Carol (act): *Demons of Ludlow*
Perry, Christopher (act): *Street Trash*
Perry, Daniel (act): *Jekyll and Hyde*
Perry, Deanna (act): *Road Kill USA*
Perry, Desmond (act): *A Guy Called Caesar*
Perry, Don (act): *Blood Song*
Perry, Eleanor (wri, 1914-1981): *The Swimmer*
Perry, Felton (act): *RoboCop; RoboCop 2; RoboCop 3; The Towering Inferno*
Perry, Frank (act): *The Neptune Factor*
Perry, Frank (dir, 1930-1995): *Hello Again; Ladybug, Ladybug; Man On a Swing; The Swimmer*
Perry, Fred C. (wri): *Blind Date, The Zero Boys*
Perry, Freda (act): *Watchers*
Perry, George (act): *Monster A-Go-Go*
Perry, Harry (act): *Point of No Return*
Perry, Harvey (act): *Sherlock Holmes In New York*
Perry, Helen (act): *The Velvet Touch*
Perry, Jack (act): *Mr. Moto's Last Warning*
Perry, Jaime (act): *Friday the 13th-Part 2; Jacob's Ladder; The Wiz*
Perry, Jessie (act): *Torchy Plays With Dynamite*
Perry, Joan (act): *Blind Alley; The Lone Wolf Strikes; Meet Nero Wolfe; Nine Lives Are Not Enough*
Perry, John (wri): *A Man About the House*
Perry, John Bennett (act): *George of the Jungle; I Dream of Jeannie: Fifteen Years Later; The Legend of the Lone Ranger*
Perry, Joseph V. (act): *Repossessed*
Perry, Julyan (wri): *Raptus*
Perry, Lincoln (act): see Fetchit, Stepin
Perry, Linda (act): *Edward Scissorhands*
Perry, Linette (wri): *The Secret Place*
Perry, Luke (act, b. 1966): *Buffy the Vampire Slayer; Robin Cook's 'Invasion'*
Perry, Morris (act): *Nothing But the Night*
Perry, Navarre (act): *Bloody Wednesday*
Perry, Pamela (act): *Deadly Sins; Violent Women*
Perry, Roger (act): *Count Yorga, the Vampire; The Return of Count Yorga; Revenge (1971, USA); The Thing With Two Heads*
Perry, Ron (act): *Dementia 13*
Perry, Simon (dir & wri): *Eclipse (1977)*
Perry, Vic (act): *Timeslip*
Perry, Walter (act): *The Unholy Three (1925)*
Perry, Wolfe (act): *Space Rage*
Persaud, Toolsie (act): *The Mummy's Shroud*
Perschy, Maria (act, b. 1940): *The Castle of Fu Manchu; Five Golden Dragons; Der Henker von London; Horror of the Zombies; House of Doom (1973); El Jorobado de la Morgue; Kiss Kiss, Kill Kill; Murders In the Rue Morgue (1971); No Survivors, Please; People Who Own the Dark; Secret Agent 077-Operation Hong Kong; Secret of the Sphinx; A Witch Without a Broom*
Persiano, Pascal (act): *Demons 2*
Perske, Betty Jean (act): see Bacall, Lauren

Perske, Lisa Jane (act): *Amazing Stories: The Movie VI; Coneheads; Destiny Turns On the Radio; Kiss Meets the Phantom of the Park; Peggy Sue Got Married*
Persoff, Nehemiah (act, b. 1920): *An American Tail; An American Tail: Fievel Goes West; Deadly Harvest; Green Mansions; The Henderson Monster; Panic In the City; The Power (1967); Psychic Killer; The Stranger Within; TheWrong Man*
Person, Karen (act): *Repossessed*
Person, Maurice (act): *The Fugitive (1993)*
Persons, Mark (act): *Silent Running*
Persson, Essy (act): *Cry of the Banshee; Mission Stardust; Operation: Lovebirds*
Persson, Gene (act): *Bloodlust!; The Spider (1958)*
Pertica, Domenico (act): *Amarcord*
Pertwee, Bill (act): *Psychomania (1972)*
Pertwee, Jon (act, b. 1919): *Carry On Screaming; The House That Dripped Blood; Mr. Drake's Duck; Murder at the Windmill; No. 1 of the Secret Service; One of Our Dinosaurs Is Missing; A Piece of Cake; The Ugly Duckling; The Water Babies; Wombling Free*
Pertwee, Michael (act, b. 1916): *Night Was Our Friend*
Pertwee, Michael (wri, b. 1916): *Digby-The Biggest Dog In the World; The Interrupted Journey; Il Ladro di Venezia; The Mouse On the Moon; Night Was Our Friend; Top Secret (1952)*
Pertwee, Roland (act): *Halfway House; Pimpernel Smith*
Pertwee, Roland (wri): *Blind Spot (1932); Dinner at the Ritz; The Ghoul (1933); Halfway House; King Solomon's Mines (1937); Murder On the Second Floor; Pimpernel Smith; The Silver Greyhound (1932); The Spy In Black; They Came by Night; A Voice Said Goodnight*
Perusse, Jean-Pierre (act): *Highlander: The Final Dimension*
Peryalis, Notis (act): *Electra (1961)*
Pes, Carlo (mus): *Dorian Gray*
Pesce, Albert (mus): *One Exciting Night*
Pesce, Frank (act): *Cameron's Closet; Killer Fish; Maniac (1980)*
Peschka, Egon (act): *The Invisible Terror*
Peschkowsky, Michael Igor (dir): see Nichols, Mike
Peschl, Joey (act): *Don't Go In the House*
Pescia, Lisa (act): *The Dark Dancer*
Pesco, Frank (act): *Maniac (1980)*
Pescow, Donna (act, b. 1954): *Human Feelings*
Peskanov, Alexander (mus): *The Clairvoyant (1985); He Knows You're Alone*
Peskanov, Mark (mus): *He Knows You're Alone*
Pestriniero, Renato (wri): *Terrore Nello Spazio*
Pete, Teresa K. (act): *Serial Mom*
Pete, Zachary S. (act): *Serial Mom*
Peterkofsky, Don (mus): *The Refrigerator*
Peterman, Don(ald) (cin): *Addams Family Values; Cocoon; Splash; Star Trek IV: The Voyage Home; When a Stranger Calls*
Peterman, Melissa (act): *Fargo*
Peters, Arnold (act): *Frankenstein (1984)*
Peters, Barbara (dir): *Bury Me an Angel; Humanoids from the Deep*
Peters, Barbara (wri): *Humanoids from the Deep*
Peters, Bernadette (act, b. 1948): *Beauty and the Beast: The Enchanted Christmas; Cinderella (1997); Heartbeeps; The Odyssey*
Peters, Brock (act, b. 1927): *Alligator II: The Mutation; Soylent Green; Star Trek IV: The Voyage Home; Star Trek VI: The Undiscovered Country*
Peters, Brooke L. (dir): *Anatomy of a Psycho; The Unearthly*
Peters, Carol (act): *Prison Girls*
Peters, Christine (act): *Empire of Ash III*
Peters, Christopher (act): *The Lost Boys*
Peters, Clarke (act): *Outland*
Peters, Dennis (cin): *Primal Scream*
Peters, Dennis Alaba (act): *Curse of Simba*
Peters, Elizabeth (act): see Peters, Jean
Peters, Erica/Erika (act): *House of the Damned (1962); Mr. Sardonicus*
Peters, Faith (act): *Ms. 45*
Peters, Frederic(k) (act): *Salome (1922); Tarzan and the Golden Lion; White Zombie*
Peters, George (act): *The Fan; Zombie Island Massacre*
Peters, George (cin): *The House of Secrets (1929)*
Peters, Gerald Saunderson (act): *Jekyll and Hyde...Together Again; The Questor Tapes*
Peters, Gus (act): *Brain of Blood; Flowers In the Attic*
Peters, Helmut (act): *Empire of Ash III*
Peters Jr., House (act, 1879-1967): *Lost Planet Airmen; Port Sinister; Red Planet Mars; Target Earth (1954)*
Peters, Jane Alice (act): see Lombard, Carole
Peters, Janne K. (act): *Shocker*
Peters, Jean (act, b. 1926, nee Elizabeth Peters): *Anne of the Indies; A Blueprint for Murder; It Happens Every Spring; Niagara; Vicki*
Peters, Jim (act): *Ghostriders*
Peters, John (1930s act): *White Zombie*
Peters, John (1980s & 1990s act): *The Coming; 101 Dalmatians (1996)*
Peters, Julie (act): *Willow*
Peters, Kelly Jean (act): *Witches' Brew*
Peters, Ken (act): *Jack's Wife*
Peters, Lloyd (act): *The Lair of the White Worm*
Peters, Lorraine (act): *More Deadly Than the Male; The Wicker Man*
Peters, Luan (act): *The Devil's Men; The Flesh and Blood Show; Freelance; Man of Violence; Twins of Evil; Vampira*
Peters, Lynn (act): *Grave of the Vampire*
Peters, Mark (act): *Wizards of the Lost Kingdom*
Peters, Matthew (act): *Scream for Help*
Peters, Molly (act): *A Target for Killing; Thunderball*
Peters, Noel (act): *The Invisible Maniac*
Peters, Pauline (act): *By the Hand of a Brother; Deadlock (1931); The Loudwater Mystery; Trent's Last Case (1920)*
Peters, Ralph (act): *Black Magic (1944); The Dark Mirror (1946); The Sniper*
Peters, Scott (act): *The Amazing Colossal Man; Attack of the Puppet People; The Cape Canaveral Monsters; The Girl Hunters; Invasion of the Saucer Men; Madman of Mandoras*
Peters, Scott (wri): *Lost Souls (1998)*
Peters, Steve (act): *Daleks' Invasion 2150 A.D.*
Peters, Svi (act): *Impulse (1984)*
Peters, Tom (act): *The Resurrection of Zachary Wheeler*
Peters, Tony (act): *The Toxic Avenger, Part II*
Peters, Vicki (act): *Blood Mania*
Peters, Warren (act): *Haunts*
Peters, Werner (act): *Assignment K; Curse of the Yellow Snake; Dog Eat Dog; Hipnosis; I Deal In Danger; In the Steel Net of Dr. Mabuse; 36 Hours (1965)*
Peters, Wilma (act): *The Night Strangler*
Petersen, Chris (act): *The Swarm*
Petersen, Curtis (cin): *The Hunted (1998)*
Petersen, Hans W. (act): *Crazy Paradise*
Petersen, Kjeld (act): *Crazy Paradise*
Petersen, Mark (act): *Dr. Who and the Daleks*
Petersen, Pat (act): *Alligator (1981); The Man In the Santa Claus Suit*
Petersen, Paul (act): *In the Year 2889*
Petersen, William (act, b. 1953): *The Beast (1996); Fear (1996)*
Petersen, Wolfgang (dir): *Enemy Mine; The Neverending Story; Outbreak*
Petersen, Wolfgang (wri): *The Neverending Story*
Petersen, Zanny (act): *Himmelskibet*
Peterson, Amanda (act): *Explorers*
Peterson, Arthur (act): *Targets*
Peterson, Bill (act): *Mutant Hunt*
Peterson, Cassandra (act, b. 1951): *Acting On Impulse; Elvira, Mistress of the Dark; Jekyll and Hyde...Together Again*
Peterson, Cassandra (wri, b. 1951): *Elvira, Mistress of the Dark*
Peterson, Daniel James (act): *The Mask (1994)*
Peterson, Daniel M. (dir & wri): *Girlfriend from Hell*
Peterson, Diane (act): *The Man With Two Brains*
Peterson, Frances (act): *The Initiation*
Peterson, Gil (act): *Mind Warp (1972)*
Peterson, Haley (act): *Cyborg (1989)*
Peterson, Hans (act): *Crazy Paradise*
Peterson, Janie (act): *Contact*
Peterson, Jock (act): *Bloodspell*
Peterson, Jodi (act): *Beverly Hills Bodysnatchers*
Peterson, Kathryn (act): *Princess Warrior*
Peterson, Kimberlee (act): *The Last Man On Planet Earth; Legend of the Lost Tomb*
Peterson, Kristine (dir): *Critters 3; Deadly Dreams*
Peterson, Lenka (act): *Werewolf of Washington*
Peterson, Monica (act): *The Dark (1979)*
Peterson, Nan (act): *The Hideous Sun Demon*
Peterson, Peter (act): *Beyond the Poseidon Adventure*
Peterson, Robyn (act): *Flight of the Navigator*
Peterson, Roger (act): [illegible]
Peterson, Ruth (act): *Charlie Chan In Paris*
Peterson, Shelley (act): *The Housekeeper*
Peterson, Sherry (act): *Hellhole*
Peterson, Vidal (act): *Something Wicked This Way Comes; Wizards of the Lost Kingdom*
Peterson, Wally (act): *The Crooked Sky*
Petersson, Harald (wri): *The Nibelungs (1966)*
Petersson, M.G. (wri): *Mistress of the World (1959)*
Petherbridge, Edward (act): *Gulliver's Travels (1996)*
Pethley, Don (act): *The Lost Missile*
Petit, Anne-Marie (act): see Petit, Pascale
Petit, Christopher (act): *Chinese Boxes*
Petit, Christopher (dir): *Chinese Boxes; Flight to Berlin; An Unsuitable Job for a Woman*
Petit, Christopher (wri): *Chinese Boxes; An Unsuitable Job for a Woman*
Petit, Lenard (act): *Eyes of Fire*
Petit, Michael (act): *Hush...Hush, Sweet Charlotte*
Petit, Pascale (act, b. 1938, nee Anne-Marie Petit): *Code Name: Jaguar; Les Sorcieres de Salem*
Petit, Pierre (cin): *Le Saint Prend l'Affut*
Petit, Roland (act): *Hans Christian Andersen*
Petit, Wilfred H. (wri): *A Thousand and One Nights (1945)*
Petit, Yvette (act): *The Murders In the Rue Morgue (1986)*
Petitjean, David (act): *Angel Heart*
Petkoff, Robert (act): *Vice Versa (1988)*
Petley, Frank (E.) (act): *Flying from Justice; The Golden Dawn; The Grip of Iron; The Iron Stair (1920); Melody of Death; Mercia the Flower Girl; My Lord Conceit; The Mystery of Mr. Bernard Brown; The Silver Greyhound (1919)*
Petley, Kate (act): *Beyond and Back*
Petr, Daniela (act): *Jack's Back*
Petracca, Joseph (wri): *The Reluctant Saint*
Petraglia, Sandro (wri): *Fiorile*
Petrashevic, Victor (cin): *The Projectionist*
Petre, Gio (act, b. 1937): *The Doll (1963, Swed)*
Petrelli, Sandra (act): *House of 1,000 Dolls*
Petrenko, Alexi (act): *Rasputin (1985)*
Petretto, Renzo (act): *Psychout for Murder*
Petri, Elio (dir, 1929-1982): *L'Assassino; La Decima Vittima; Un Tranquillo Posto di Campagna*
Petri, Elio (wri, 1929-1982): *L'Assassino; La Decima Vittima*
Petri, Mario (act): *Ercole alla Conquista della Atlantide; Ercole Contro i Tiranni di Babilonia; Goliath at the Conquest of Damascus; Lost Treasure of the Aztecs; Sandokan and the Leopard of Sarawak*
Petrie, Daniel (dir, b. 1920): *Cat and Mouse (1974); Cocoon: The Return; A Howling In the Woods; Moon of the Wolf; The Neptune Factor; The Spy With a Cold Nose*
Petrie, Donald (act): *The Hearse*
Petrie, Doris (act): *Funeral Home*
Petrie, George (O.) (act): *A Fire In the Sky (1978); Wavelength*
Petrie, Gordon (act): *Deathline*
Petrie, (D.) Hay (act, 1895-1948): *Consider Your Verdict; Cottage to Let; Crime on the Hill; Crimes at the Dark House; The Ghost at St. Michael's; The Ghost Goes West; Gipsy Blood; Great Expectations (1946); Inquest (1939); Jamaica Inn (1939); Knight Without Armour; The Laughing Lady; Matinee Idol; Noose; The Private Life of Don Juan; Q Planes; Secret Lives; Spellbound (1941); The Spy In Black; Ten Days In Paris; The Thief of Bagdad (1940); Trunk Crime*
Petrie, Howard (act): *Fair Wind to Java; Sign of the Pagan; The Veils of Bagdad*
Petrie, June (act): *Salem's Lot*
Petrie, Mary (act): *The Hidden*
Petrie, Susan (act): *Shivers*
Petrilli, Vittoriano (wri): *Operation Crossbow*
Petrillo, Sammy (act): *The Boys from Brooklyn*
Petroff, B. (wri): *Two Lost Worlds*
Petroff, Gloria (act): *Two Lost Worlds*
Petronijevic, Daniel (act): *Dream House (1998)*
Petronio, Brigitte (act): *La Citta delle Donne*
Petronio, Tatiana (act): *La Citta delle Donne*
Petrou, David (act): *Superman (1978)*
Petrov, Vassiliz/Vasily (wri): *Assignment-Outer Space; Il Planeta degli Uomini Spenti*
Petrov, Yuri (act): *Yolanta*
Petrovana, Natasha (act): see Pitt, Ingrid
Petrovic, Aleksandar (dir): *Majstori i Margarita*
Petrovich, Ivan (act): *The Magician (1926)*
Petrovitch, Michael (act): *Escape 2000; Neither the Sea Nor the Sand; Spy Story; Tales That Witness Madness*
Petrucelli, Rick (act): *The Purple Rose of Cairo; Windows*
Petters III, Stanley D. (act): *The Nutty Professor (1996)*
Pettersen, Bob (act): *Beetlejuice*
Petterson, Howard Jay (act): *The Jewel of the Nile*
Pettersson, Birgitta (act): *Ansiktet*
Pettet, Joanna (act, b. 1944): *Appointment With a Killer; Casino Royale; Double Exposure; The Evil; The Night of the Generals; Robbery; Welcome to Arrow Beach*
Pettiet, Christopher (act): *The Presence*
Pettiette, P.J. (wri): *Bad Dreams*
Pettifer, Brian (act): *A Christmas Carol (1984)*
Pettijohn, Grace (act): *Flesh-Eating Mothers*
Pettingell, Frank (act, 1891-1966): *Busman's Honeymoon; The Crimson Pirate; Doctor of Seven Dials; Gaslight (1940); Meet Mr. Lucifer; Queer Cargo*
Pettinger, Gary (act): *Electric Dreams*
Pettit Family, The (act): *Treasure at the Mill*
Pettit, Wilfrid H. (wri): *The Bandit of Sherwood Forest*
Pettitt, Henry (wri): *The Harbour Lights; In the Ranks*
Pettus, Ken (wri): *Search for the Gods*
Petty, Kevin (act): *The Bermuda Depths*
Petty, Lori (act): *Bates Motel; Tank Girl*
Petty, Ross (act): *The Housekeeper*
Petty, Tom (act): *Made in Heaven; The Postman (1997)*
Pettyjohn, Angelique (act): *Biohazard (1985); The Curious Female; The Lost Empire; Mad Doctor of Blood Island*
Peturrson, Johann (act): *Prehistoric Women (1950)*
Pevney, Joseph (act, b. 1913): *Mysterious Island of Beautiful Women; Nocturne; The Street With No Name*
Pevney, Joseph (dir, b. 1913): *Congo Crossing; Desert Legion; Istanbul; Man of a Thousand Faces; The Strange Door; Undercover Girl (1950)*
Peyser, John (dir, b. 1916): *Undersea Girl*
Peyser, Penny (act): *Under Wraps*
Peyton, R. (act): *Riches and Rogues*
Pezet, A. Washington (dir): *El Cuerpo del Lito*
Pfaff, Brent (act): *Galaxis*
Pfarrer, Chuck (wri): *Barb Wire; Darkman (1990)*
Pfeiffer, David (act): *The China Syndrome*
Pfeiffer, Deedee/Dedee (act, b. 1964): *The Horror Show; The Midnight Hour; Vamp*
Pfeiffer, Frank (cin): *Monster A Go-Go*
Pfeiffer, James (act): *Firefight*
Pfeiffer, Michelle (act): *Amazon Women On the Moon; Batman Returns; Charlie Chan and the Curse of the Dragon Queen; Ladyhawke; AMidsummer Night's Dream (1999); The Prince of Egypt; To Gillian On Her 37th Birthday; What Lies Beneath; The Witches of Eastwick; Wolf*
Pfeiffer, Miro (act): *Arthur the King*
Pfeiffer, Scott (dir): *Firefight*
Pflug, Eva (act): *Confess, Dr. Corda*
Pflug, Jo Ann (act): *Cyborg 2087; The Night Strangler; Scream of the Wolf*
Phair, Douglas (act): *The Rats Are Coming! The Werewolves Are Here!*
Phalen, Robert (act): *Halloween; Someone's Watching Me!*
Pharrez, Paco (act): *Amityville 3-D; Nightlife (1989, USA-Mex)*
Phelan, Brian (act): *A High Wind In Jamaica; The Servant*
Phelan, David (act): *Mission: Impossible*
Phelan, Gregory (act): *C.H.U.D. II*
Phelan, Jim (act): *Murder of Innocence*
Phelan, Joe (act): *Fatal Pulse; The Zero Boys*
Phelan, Mark (act): *The Hidden; Monolith; Running Against Time*
Pheloung, Barrington (mus): *The Mangler; Nostradamus*
Phelps, Brian (act): *Jason Goes to Hell: The Final Friday*
Phelps, Bud (act): *The Last Warning (1929)*
Phelps, Eleanor (act): *A Stranger Is Watching*
Phelps, Gayle (act): *To Die For II: Son of Darkness*
Phelps, Kate (act): *The Shining*
Phelps, Lee (act): *Ellery Queen, Master Detective; The Hidden Eye; The Lone Wolf and His Lady; The Lone Wolf Spy Hunt; The Magnetic Monster; Mr. Moto Takes a Vacation; The Sky Dragon*
Phelps, Matthew (act): *Nightmare Sisters*
Phelps, Melinda (act): *Xanadu*
Phelps, Peter (act): *Merlin (1993)*
Phelps, Robert (act): *Nightmares (1983)*
Phenicie, Michael (act): [illegible]
Phifer, Mekhi (act): *I Still Know What You Did Last Summer*
Phifer, Zack (act): *Addams Family Values; Ghost In the Machine*

Philbin, John (act): Children of the Corn; The Crew; Martians Go Home; The Return of the Living Dead (1985)
Philbin, Mary (act, 1903-1993): The Man Who Laughs (1928); The Phantom of the Opera (1925); The Temple of Venus
Philbin, Phil (act): The Final Countdown; Flesh Feast
Philbrick, William H. (act): The Gorilla (1931)
Philbrook, James (act): The Emerald of Artatama; Sound of Horror
Philip, J.D. (act): Shock Chamber
Philip, Robert (act): Children Shouldn't Play With Dead Things
Philipe, Gerard (act, 1922-1959): La Beaute du Diable; Seven Deadly Sins
Philippe, D. (act & wri): Remorse
Philippi, Erich (wri): The Missing Guest
Philips, Bill (act): Spacecamp
Philips, Julie (act): Lies
Philips, Lee (act): Psychomania (1964)
Philips, Lee (dir): The Spell; The Stranger Within
Philips, Mary (act): Lady In the Dark; Prince Valiant (1954)
Philipson, Adam (act): Still Not Quite Human
Philliber, John (act): It Happened Tomorrow
Phillipi (act): Bumbles' Diminisher
Phillippe, Andre (act): I Love a Mystery (1966); Invasion of the Bee Girls
Phillippe, Jean Lou (act): What Price Murder
Phillippe, Ryan (act): Deadly Invasion: The Killer Bee Nightmare; I Know What You Did Last Summer
Phillips Sr., Alex (cin): Adam and Eve; The Adventures of Robinson Crusoe (1952); The Night of a Thousand Cats
Phillips (Jr.), Alex (cin): Allan Quatermain and the Lost City of Gold; Demonoid; The Devil's Rain; Fade to Black; Firewalker; The Fool Killer;
King Solomon's Mines (1985); The Queen's Swordsman; Sorceress (1982)
Phillips, Alfred (act): The Murdock Trial
Phillips, Arnold (wri): The Brighton Strangler; One Dangerous Night; The Return of Monte Cristo
Phillips, Barney (act): Cry Terror!; I Was a Teenage Werewolf; The Threat (1960)
Phillips, Barry (act): Dr. Caligari
Phillips, Bertram (dir): Faust (1923); Her Redemption; Tut-Tut and His Terrible Tomb
Phillips, Betty (act): Runaway (1984)
Phillips, Bill (act): The Last Hunt
Phillips, Bill (wri): Christine
Phillips, Bobbie (act): Carnival of Souls (1998); Chameleon; TC 2000
Phillips, Brian (act): Empire of Ash III
Phillips, Chris (act): Felix the Cat: The Movie
Phillips, Chynna (act): The Invisible Kid
Phillips, Conrad (act): Circus of Horrors; Dead Man's Evidence; The Desperate Man; Don't Talk to Strange Men; The Fourth Square; A Guy Called Caesar; Impact; The Last Page; The Murder Game; Murder She Said; The Secret Partner; The Secret Tent; The Shadow of the Cat; Stopover Forever; Strangers' Meeting; The Temptress (1949); Who Killed the Cat?; Witness In the Dark
Phillips, Conrad (wri): Impact
Phillips, Cynthia (act): Miracle Mile
Phillips, David Lee (act): Outbreak
Phillips, Debb Lee (act): Monolith
Phillips, Demetre (act): The Mangler; 976-EVIL; Zapped!
Phillips, Dorothea (act): Santa Claus (1985)
Phillips, Douglas (act): The Strange Case of Mr. Todmorden
Phillips, Edward/Eddie (act): The Bells (1926); The Thirteenth Guest; Through the Dark
Phillips, Ethan (act): Critters
Phillips, Fatty (act): Faust (1923); Tut-Tut and His Terrible Tomb
Phillips, Frank (act): The Quatermass Experiment
Phillips, Frank (cin): Bedknobs and Broomsticks; The Black Hole; The Computer Wore Tennis Shoes (1970); Escape to Witch Mountain (1975); Herbie Rides Again; The Island at the Top of the World; Now You See Him, Now You Don't; Return from Witch Mountain; The Shaggy D.A.
Phillips, G. Elvis (act): The Body Snatchers
Phillips, Gary (act): Whodunit
Phillips, Gina (act): Deadly Invasion: The Killer Bee Nightmare; When the Bough Breaks
Phillips, Gordon (wri): I'm an Explosive
Phillips, Grace (act): Tempting Fate
Phillips, Gregory (act): I Start Counting; Who Killed the Cat?
Phillips, Greigh (act): The Brain Eaters; Forbidden Island
Phillips, Helena (act): The Greene Murder Case
Phillips, James (act): Prison Planet
Phillips, Jean (act): Among the Living
Phillips, Jeff (act): To Die For II: Son of Darkness
Phillips, Jim (act): Equinox
Phillips, Joe (act): After the Thin Man
Phillips, John (GB act): Floods of Fear; I Accuse (1958); Man In the Moon (1960); The Mouse On the Moon; The Mummy's Shroud; Offbeat; A Prize of Arms; Richard III (1955); Torture Garden; The Village of the Damned (1960)
Phillips, John (USA act): How to Make a Monster
Phillips, John (mus): The Man Who Fell to Earth (1976)
Phillips, Jonathan (act): The Mystery of Edwin Drood (1993)
Phillips, Julianne (act): Tidal Wave: No Escape; A Vow to Kill
Phillips, Kate (act): The Sands of Time
Phillips, Kate (wri): The Blob (1958)
Phillips, Keith (act): Copycat
Phillips, Leo (act): Spaceways; Treasure Island (1950)
Phillips, Leslie (act, b. 1924): The Canterville Ghost (1996); The Gamma People; The Limping Man (1953); Maroc 7; The Pale Horse; Pool of London; The Sound Barrier
Phillips, Lou Diamond (act, b. 1962): The First Power; Dangerous Touch; Undertow
Phillips, Lou Diamond (dir & wri, b. 1962): Dangerous Touch
Phillips, Madelon (act): The Devil's Gift
Phillips, Margaret (act): Castle Rock
Phillips, Mary (act): Lady In the Dark; Leave Her to Heaven
Phillips, Maurice (dir): Riders of the Storm
Phillips, Meredith (act): Sky Pirates
Phillips, Michelle (act, b. 1944): Covenant; Paint Me a Murder; Pretty Poison (1996); Scissors
Phillips, Minna (act): Sherlock Holmes Faces Death
Phillips, Miriam (act): The Fan
Phillips, N. Watts (act): Lieutenant Daring, RN, and the Water Rats
Phillips, Nelson (act): Jane Shore (1915)
Phillips, Neville (act): First Knight; The McGuffin; 101 Dalmatians (1996); Svengali (1954)
Phillips, Nick (dir): Crazy Fat Ethel II; Criminally Insane; Death Nurse
Phillips Jr., Norman (act): The Gracie Allen Murder Case
Phillips, Penny Ann (act): The Dark (1979)
Phillips, Randy (act): Werewolf of Washington
Phillips, Redmond (act): The Gorgon; Razorback
Phillips, Robert (act): Dimension 5; Forgotten City of the Planet of the Apes; The Incredible Hulk, Part 2; Moon of the Wolf; The Silencers (1966); U.F.O.; The Ultimate Impostor
Phillips, Robin (act): Tales from the Crypt (1971)
Phillips, Samantha (act): Deceit (1993); Phantasm II; Phantasm III: Lord of the Dead
Phillips, Sarah (act): Hamlet (1990)
Phillips, Sian (act): Clash of the Titans; The Doctor and the Devils; Dune; Ewoks: The Battle for Endor
Phillips, Stephen (act): The Projectionist
Phillips, Stu (mus): Battlestar Galactica; Buck Rogers In the 25th Century; Midnight Lace (1981); Simon, King of the Witches; 2000 Years Later
Phillips, Sydney Coale (act): Princess Warrior
Phillips, Thomas Hal (wri): Tarzan's Fight for Life
Phillips, Tom (dir): A TV Dante: Cantos I-VIII
Phillips, Watts (wri): The Dead Heart
Phillips, Wendell (K.) (act, 1908-1991): The Fool Killer
Phillips, Wendy (act): Amazing Stories: The Movie V; The Gifted One
Phillips, William (act): Attack of the Jungle Women
Phillpotts, Ambrosine (act, b. 1912): Berserk; Diamonds On Wheels
Philoe, Maxime (act): Tarzan, the Ape Man (1981)
Philon, Jon (act): Getting Lucky
Philpot, Michelle (act): Vice Versa (1988)
Philpott, Toby (act): Return of the Jedi
Phippeny, Robert (wri): Simon, King of the Witches
Phipps, Bill (act): see Phipps, William/Bill
Phipps, Joyce (act): see Grenfell, Joyce
Phipps, Max (act): The Cars That Ate Paris; The Road Warrior; Sky Pirates; Stir; Thirst
Phipps, Nicholas (act): Mad About Men; Some Girls Do; Who Done It? (1956)
Phipps, Nicholas (wri): Escape Route; Madeleine
Phipps, William/Bill (act): Cat-Women of the Moon; Cinderella (1950); Five; The Hidden Eye; Invaders from Mars (1953); Lord of the Jungle; The Snow Creature; The Twonky; The War of the Worlds
Phipps-Wilson, V. (act): Eraserhead
Phoenix, Leaf (act): Spacecamp
Phoenix, Rainbow (act): Maid to Order
Phoenix, River (act, 1970-1993): Explorers; Indiana Jones and the Last Crusade
Pia, Al (act): The Toxic Avenger
Pia, Betty (act): The Toxic Avenger
Pialat, Maurice (act & dir, b. 1925): Sous le Soleil de Satan
Piani, Lorenzo (act): Satyricon
Piantadosi, Joseph (act): Schlock
Piat, Jean (act): Tower of Screaming Virgins
Piazza, Ben (act, b. 1934): Fer-de-Lance; Nightwing; No Exit
Piazzi, Giorgio (act): Scenes from a Murder
Piazzoli, Roberto D'Ettore (cin): Curse II: The Bite; Midnight Ride; Piranha II: The Spawning
Pica, Antonio (act): Satanik
Pica, Tony (act): House of Doom (1973)
Picard, Nicole (act): Deadtime Stories
Picardi, Cesarino Miceli (act): Giulietta degli Spiriti
Picardo, Robert (act): Bates Motel; The 'Burbs; Dead Heat; Explorers; Gremlins 2: The New Batch; The Howling; Innerspace; Jack's Back; Legend; The Man Who Fell to Earth (1987); Matinee; Oh, God! You Devil; Total Recall
Picasso, Pablo (act, 1881-1973): Le Testament d'Orphee
Picasso, Paloma (act): Contes Immoraux
Picatto, Alexandra (act): The Colony (1995)
Picavet, Jean-Louis (cin): Enigma
Piccalo, Vince (act): Mother's Day
Piccioni, Piero (mus, b. 1921): L'Assassino; Cadaveri Eccellenti; C'era una Volta; La Decima Vittima; Il Demonio; Il Disco Volante; The Light at the Edge of the World; Marta; The Mattei Affair
Piccoli, Michel (act, b. 1925): Belle de Jour; Diabolik; The Discreet Charm of the Bourgeoisie; Doulos-The Finger Man; The French Conspiracy; Leonor; Marie Antoinette (1953); Masquerade; Le Mepris; La Mort en ce Jardin; Le Paltoquet; The Prize of Peril; The Sleeping Car Murders; Topaz; Torticola Contre Frankensberg; Le Trio Infernal; Wedding In Blood
Piccolo, Marco (wri): La Vendetta di Ercole
Piccolo, Ottavia (act): Zorro (1975)
Piccolo, Rino (act): The Silence of the Hams
Piccori, John (act): Dick Tracy (1937)
Piceau, Colette (act): Matinee
Picerni, Paul (act, b. 1922): The Adventures of Hajji Baba; Beyond the Poseidon Adventure; Capricorn One; Fearmaker; House of Wax; Lord of the Jungle; Omar Khayyam; Operation Secret
Picerni, Steve (act): Candyman: Farewell to the Flesh
Picetti, Lou (act): Mr. Sycamore
Picha (dir): Jungle Burger
Pichel, Irving (act, 1891-1954): British Agent; Dick Tracy's G-Men; Dracula's Daughter; The Great Rupert; King of the Jungle; The Miracle Man (1932); Murder by the Clock; Return of the Terror; Strange Justice
Pichel, Irving (dir, 1891-1954): Before Dawn; Destination Moon; Earthbound (1940); The Great Rupert; The Happy Land; Mr. Peabody and the Mermaid; The Most Dangerous Game; Secret Agent of Japan; She (1935); Temptation (1946); They Won't Believe Me
Pichon, Anne (act): Game for Three Losers
Pick, Debbie (act): Invasion from Inner Earth
Pick, Lupu (act, 1886-1931): Spione
Pickard, Helena (act): The Lodger (1944)
Pickard, John (act): The Bandits of Corsica; The Lone Ranger
Pickard, Margery (act): Dark Journey
Pickard, Raymond (act): The Canterville Ghost (1996)
Pickens Jr., James (act): Rocketman (1997); Sharon's Secret; Sphere
Pickens, Slim (act, 1919-1983, nee Louis Bert Lindley Jr.): Beyond the Poseidon Adventure; The Devil and Miss Sarah; Dr. Strangelove: or, How I Learned to Stop Worrying and Love the Bomb; The Howling; The Swarm; This House Possessed
Pickens Jr., Slim (act): The Uninvited (1996)
Pickering, Betsy (act): Strange Invaders
Pickering, Donald (act): The 39 Steps (1978)
Pickering, Marie (act): The Broken Chisel; The Master Crook; Through the Clouds; What Men Will Do
Pickering, Robert (act): Let's Kill Uncle
Pickets, Jason (act): The Zero Boys
Pickett, Blake (act): Dark Universe; HauntedWeen
Pickett, Bob(by) (act): The Deathmaster; Strange Invaders
Pickett, Cindy (act): Atomic Dog; Cry for the Strangers; Deepstar Six; Evolver; Hysterical; The Ivory Ape; Margin for Murder; Plymouth; Sleepwalkers
Pickett, George (wri): The Silent House
Pickett, James (act): Three On a Meathook
Pickett, Jay (act): Eve of Destruction
Pickford, Jack (act, 1896-1933): The Bat (1926)
Pickford, Jimmy (act): Invasion of the Saucer Men
Pickford, Mary (act, 1893-1979, nee Gladys Mary Smith): Robin Hood (1922)
Pickle, Ashley (act): I Was a Zombie for the F.B.I.
Pickle, Barbara (act): I Was a Zombie for the F.B.I.
Pickles, Carolyn (act): Agatha; The Mirror Crack'd
Pickles, Christina (act): It Came Upon the Midnight Clear; Masters of the Universe; Seizure
Pickles, Vivian (act): Jamaica Inn (1985)
Pickup, Ronald (act): Jekyll and Hyde; Never Say Never Again; The 39 Steps (1978)
Picon, Molly (act, 1898-1992): Murder On Flight 502
Picotte, Lisa (act): Strange Days
Pidgeon, Walter (act, 1897-1984): Calling Bulldog Drummond; Forbidden Planet; The Gorilla (1927 & 1931); Journal of a Crime; Live Again, Die Again; The Mask of Sheba; Murder On Flight 502; The Neptune Factor; Nick Carter, Master Detective; Phantom Raiders; The Screaming Woman; Sky Murder; The Vatican Affair; Voyage to the Bottom of the Sea
Pieczka, Franciszek (act): Rekopis Znaleziony w Saragossie
Pieczynski, Krzysztof (act): Chain Reaction (1996)
Piel, David (act): Killer Klowns from Outer Space
Piel Sr., Edward (J.) (act, 1888-1958): Black Dragons; Charlie Chan's Chance; The Mysterious Mr. Wong; Radio Ranch
Piel, Harry (act & dir, 1882-1963): An Invisible Man Goes On the Town
Pieplu, Claude (act): The Discreet Charm of the Bourgeoisie; Le Paltoquet; The Tenant
Pieracki, Josef (act): Przyjaciel
Pieral (act): La Corona Negra; The Hunchback of Notre Dame (1957)
Pieralisi, Virna (act): see Lisi, Virna
Pierce, Arthur C. (dir): Women of the Prehistoric Planet
Pierce, Arthur C. (wri): The Astral Factor; Beyond the Time Barrier; The Cosmic Man; Cyborg 2087; Destination Inner Space; The Destructors; Dimension 5; The Human Duplicators; Mutiny In Outer Space; Rymdinvasion i Lappland; Women of the Prehistoric Planet
Pierce, Bradley (Michael) (act): Beauty and the Beast (1991); The Borrowers (1998); Doom Runners; Jumanji; The Undercover Kid
Pierce, Brock (act): Legend of the Lost Tomb
Pierce, Burton (act): The People Under the Stairs
Pierce, Charles B. (act): Boggy Creek II-And the Legend Continues; The Town That Dreaded Sundown
Pierce, Charles (B.) (cin): The Legend of Boggy Creek
Pierce, Charles (B.) (dir): Boggy Creek II-And the Legend And the Legend Continues; The Evictors; The Legend of Boggy Creek; The Norsemen; The Town That Dreaded Sundown
Pierce, Charles B. (wri): Boggy Creek II-And the Legend Continues; The Evictors; The Legend of Boggy Creek; The Norsemen
Pierce, Darryl (act): Waxwork II: Lost in Time
Pierce, David (act): Vampire's Kiss
Pierce, David Hyde (act, b. 1959): Addams Family Values; A Bug's Life; Wolf
Pierce, Denney (act): The Lawnmower Man
Pierce, Harvey (act): Deadtime Stories
Pierce, James (act): Tarzan and the Golden Lion
Pierce, Jill (act): Cyborg Cop II
Pierce, Julie (act): Outbreak
Pierce, Kathi (act): School Spirit
Pierce, Linda (act): Black Rainbow; The Handmaid's Tale; Web of Deceit
Pierce, Maggie (act): Tales of Terror

Pierce, Norman (GB act): *The Crimes of Stephen Hawke; The Demon Barber of Fleet Street; Sexton Blake and the Hooded Terror; Special Edition*
Pierce, Norman (USA act): *Dr. Dracula*
Pierce, Pattie (act): *Deadly Messages*
Pierce, Preston (act): *Angels' Wild Women*
Pierce, Richard (act): *Basket Case*
Pierce, Ronald (act): see Ely, Ron
Pierce, Scott (wri): *A Nightmare On Elm Street 4: The Dream Master*
Pierce, Stack (act): *I Saw What You Did (1988); Psychic Killer; Trader Horn (1973); WarGames*
Pierce, Tiana (act): *Mother's Day*
Pierce, Tony (act): *Trancers III: Deth Lives*
Pierce-Roberts, Tony (cin): *The Cold Room; The Dark Half; Splitting Heirs*
Piercy, Perry (act): *Dark of the Night; Night of the Red Hunter*
Pierdel, Andre (cin): *Traitement de Choc*
Pierfederici, Antonio (act): *La Maschera del Demonio*
Pierlot, Francis (act, 1885-1955): *The Accused (1948); The Catman of Paris; Crime Doctor's Manhunt; The Hidden Eye; Just Off Broadway; The Man With a Cloak; Philo Vance's Gamble; The Prisoner of Zenda (1952)*
Pieroni, Ania (act): *The House by the Cemetery; Inferno (1979); Tenebrae*
Pieroni, Donna (act): *Edward Scissorhands*
Pierotti, Piero (dir): *Ercole Contro Roma; Pirate and the Slave Girl; Pirate of the Black Hawk; Terror of the Red Mask*
Pierotti, Piero (wri): *Gli Invasori; Maciste al Inferno; Planets Against Us; Roma Contra Roma*
Pierpoint, Eric (act): *Alien Nation: Body and Soul; Alien Nation: Dark Horizon; Alien Nation: Millennium; Alien Nation: The Enemy Within; Forever Young; Invaders from Mars (1986)*
Pierre, Carlos (act): *Deadfall*
Pierre, Curtis (act): *Angel Heart*
Pierre, Marie-Helene (act): *Dr. Jekyll and Ms. Hyde*
Pierre, Olivier (act): *Dreamchild; Morons from Outer Space; The Return of Sherlock Holmes (1986)*
Pierreux, Jacqueline (act): *Cet Homme est Dangereux; I Tre Volti della Paura*
Pierro, Marina (act): *Behind Convent Walls*
Piers, Walter (act): *The Man from Scotland Yard; The Rosary; The Wickham Mystery*
Pierse, Sarah (act): *The Navigator: An Odyssey Across Time*
Pierson, Carl L. (wri): *The Mysterious Island (1929)*
Pierson, Eric (act): *Candyman: Farewell to the Flesh*
Pieters, Barbara (act): *Re-Animator*
Pietrobon, Massimo (act): *Sodom and Gomorrah*
Pietropinto, Angela (act): *Thinner*
Pietrosi, Antonia (act): *Satyricon*
Pietruski, Ryszard (act): *Bariera*
Pietschmann, Rainer (act): *Making Contact*
Pietschner, Tom (act): *Scalpel*
Piga, Aldo (mus): *L'Amante del Vampiri; Cinque Tombe per un Medium; L'Ultima Preda del Vampiro*
Piggot, Ian (act): *Kadoyng*
Piggott, Tempe (act): *The Black Pirate; Bride of Frankenstein; Dr. Jekyll and Mr. Hyde (1932)*
Pigot, Louis (act): *Sei Donne per l'Assassino*
Pigott-Smith, Tim(othy) (act): *Clash of the Titans; Dead Man's Folly; The Hunchback of Notre Dame (1982)*
Pike, Anita (act): *Charlie Chan In City In Darkness*
Pike, Bernard (act): *Skullduggery*
Pike, Dennis (cin): *Starship Invasions*
Pike, Don (act): *The Octagon*
Pike, Hy (act): *Vamp*
Pike, (J.) Kelvin (cin): *Apprentice to Murder; Warning Sign*
Pike, John (act): *One Wish Too Many; A Woman's Temptation*
Pike, Karen (act): *Phobia*
Pike, Nicholas (mus): *Attack of the 50-Foot Woman (1993); C.H.U.D. II; Critters 2: The Main Course; I'm Dangerous Tonight; Sleepwalkers; Virtual Obsession*
Pike, Vanessa (act): *The Mangler*
Pilafian, Peter (cin): *The Eiger Sanction*
Pilato, Joe (act): *Day of the Dead*
Pilavin, Barbara (act): *Frightmare (1983)*
Pilbeam, Nova (act, b. 1919): *Counterblast; The Man Who Knew Too Much (1934); The Three Weird Sisters; Young and Innocent*
Pilcher, Richard (act): *Serial Mom*
Pileggi, Mitch (act): *Dangerous Touch; Legion of Fire: Killer Ants; Night Visions; Return of the Living Dead, Part II; Shocker; The X-Files*
Pilgrim, George (act): *Tammy and the T-Rex*
Pilkington, Bill (act): *The Mind of Mr. Soames*
Pillar, Michael (wri): *Star Trek: Insurrection*
Pillars, Jeffrey (act): *Mr. Destiny*
Pilloud, Rod (act): *The Haunting of Sarah Hardy*
Pillow, Mark (act): *Superman IV: The Quest for Peace*
Pillsbury, Garth (act): *The Loch Ness Horror; Mistress of the Apes*
Pillsbury, Sam (dir): *Into the Badlands; Thrill*
Pillsbury, Sam (wri): *The Quiet Earth*
Pilmark, Soren (act): *The Kingdom*
Pilon, Daniel (act): *Plague; Scanners III: The Takeover; Starship Invasions*
Pilon, Donald (act): *City On Fire; Secret Weapons; The Uncanny*
Pilotto, Camillo (act): *Il Ladro di Venezia*
Piltz, George (act): *Daughter of the Jungle*
Pilu, Francois-Gabriel-Marie (act): see Perier, Francois
Pim, Alfred (act): *Fury at Smugglers' Bay*
Pimental, Hugo (act): *Pyro*
Pina, Lionel (act): *The Fan*
Pinal, Silvia (act): *El Angel Exterminador; Viridiana*
Pinchot, Bronson (act, b. 1959): *Amazing Stories; Babes In Toyland (1997); Quest for Camelot; Second Sight*
Pinckney, Jackson "Rock" (act): *Cyborg (1989)*
Pinder, Donna (act): *The Final Terror*
Pine, Granville Whitelaw (act): see Pine, Robert
Pine, Phillip (E.) (act, b. 1925): *Brainstorm (1965); The Clone Master; The Lost Missile; Murder by Contract; The Phantom from 10,000 Leagues; Project X (1967); The Set-Up (1949)*
Pine, Robert (act, b. 1941, nee Granville Whitelaw Pine): *Are You Lonesome Tonight? The Brotherhood of the Bell; Empire of the Ants; Munster, Go Home!; The Mysterious Two*
Pine, William (dir): *Swamp Fire*
Pinelli, Tullio (wri, b. 1908): *8 1/2; Giulietta degli Spiriti; Il Miracolo*
Pinero, Sir Arthur Wing (wri, 1855-1934): *The Enchanted Cottage (1924 & 1945)*
Pinero, Fred (act): *Death Curse of Tartu*
Pini, Giovanna (act): *Demons 2*
Pink, Sidney (W.) (dir): *Journey to the Seventh Planet*
Pink, Sid(ney) (W.) (wri): *The Angry Red Planet; Journey to the Seventh Planet; Pyro; Reptilicus*
Pinkard, Fred (act): *Fugitive from the Empire*
Pinke, Janice (act): *Funeral Home*
Pinkett, Jada (act, b. 1971): *Demon Knight; The Nutty Professor (1996); Scream 2*
Pinkham, Phineas T. (wri): *Invasion of the Girl Snatchers*
Pinkley, Diane (act): *Anguish*
Pinkley, Georgie (act): *Anguish*
Pinkney, John (wri): *Thirst*
Pinkney, Lyn (act): *Journey to the Unknown*
Pinkstone, Suzanne (act): *No Blade of Grass*
Pinkus, Lulu (act): *Mad Max; Thirst*
Pinner, Dick (act): *Monster from the Ocean Floor*
Pinner, Steven (act): *Link*
Pinon, Dominique (act): *Alien Resurrection; The City of Lost Children*
Pinori, Joseph (cin): *Alien Contamination*
Pinoteau, Claude (dir): *Le Silencieux*
Pinsent, Gordon (act): *Babar: The Movie; Colossus: The Forbin Project; Pippi Longstocking; A Vow to Kill*
Pinsent, Leah King (act): *April Fool's Day*
Pinsker, Seth (dir & wri): *The Hidden II*
Pinsky, Susan (act): *Beyond Dream's Door*
Pintauro, Danny (act, b. 1976): *Cujo; Timestalkers*
Pinter, Harold (act, b. 1930): *The Servant*
Pinter, Harold (wri, b. 1930): *The Comfort of Strangers; The Handmaid's Tale; The Quiller Memorandum; The Servant*
Pinthus, Jerri (act): *The Dungeonmaster*
Pintoff, Ernest (dir): *Blade (1973); Human Feelings*
Pintoff, Ernest (wri): *Blade (1973)*
Pinus, Luba (act): *Zombie Island Massacre*
Pinvidic, Margot (act): *The Stepfather*
Pinza, Carla (act): *The Believers*
Pio, Elith (act): *Blade af Satans Bog; Haxan*
Piontek, Klaus (act): *Held for Questioning*
Pious, Minerva (act): *Joe Macbeth; Pinocchio In Outer Space*
Piovani, Nicola (mus): *Fiorile; Kaos*
Piper, Brett (dir): *A Nymphoid Barbarian In Dinosaur Hell; They Bite*
Piper, Brett (wri): *A Nymphoid Barbarian In Dinosaur Hell; Raiders of the Living Dead*
Piper, Diana (act): *The Three Stooges Meet Hercules*
Piper, Evelyn (wri): *Bunny Lake Is Missing; The Nanny*
Piper, Frederick (act, b. 1902): *Catacombs (1964); Cosh Boy; Dead Lucky; Escape Route; Evidence In Concrete; Fiddlers Three; The Frightened City; Hunted (1952); Jamaica Inn (1939); The Man In the Road; The Monster of Highgate Ponds; Murder On Monday; My Brother's Keeper; The October Man; Return of a Stranger (1962); Ricochet; Sabotage; Warn That Man; What a Carve Up!*
Piper, Kelly (act): *Maniac (1980); Rawhead Rex*
Piper, Randy (act): *The Dungeonmaster*
Piper, Roddy (act): *Hell Comes to Frogtown; Immortal Combat; Sci-Fighters; They Live*
Piper, Ryan (act): *A Nymphoid Barbarian In Dinosaur Hell*
Piper, Sally (act): *A Nightmare On Elm Street 3: Dream Warriors*
Piperno, J. Henry (dir): *Ambush In Leopard Street*
Piperno, J. Henry (wri): *Enter Inspector Duval*
Pipkin, Al (act): *Jaws 3-D*
Pipoly, Daniel (act): *Lord of the Flies (1990)*
Piporro (act): *La Nave de los Monstruos*
Piquat, Roger (act): *The Count of Monte Cristo (1954)*
Piquer, Francisco (act): *Sound of Horror*
Piquer, Juan (dir & wri): *Supersonic Man; Where Time Began; Viaje al Centro de la Tierra*
Pirandello, Luigi (wri, 1867-1936): *As You Desire Me; Kaos*
Piranha, Floyd (act): *Redneck Zombies*
Pirie, David (wri): *The Woman In White (1998)*
Pirie, Marie (act): *An American Christmas Carol*
Pirkle, Joan (act): *RoboCop*
Pirkle, Mac (act): *King Kong Lives*
Pirnie, Alex (act): *A Nymphoid Barbarian In Dinosaur Hell*
Piro, Joseph (act): *Pumpkinhead*
Piros, Joanna (act): *Unforgettable*
Pirosh, Robert (wri, 1910-1989): *I Married a Witch*
Pirrie, Bruce (act): *The Pink Chiquitas*
Pirro, Mark (act): *A Polish Vampire In Burbank*
Pirro, Mark (dir): *Curse of the Queerwolf; Deathrow Gameshow; A Polish Vampire In Burbank*
Pirro, Mark (wri): *Deathrow Gameshow; A Polish Vampire In Burbank*
Pisana, Jennifer (act): *The Long Kiss Goodnight*
Pisano, Eddie (act): *It Came Upon the Midnight Clear*
Piscopo, Joe (act, b. 1951): *Dead Heat; King Kong (1976)*
Pisier, Marie-France (act, b. 1944): *The Prize of Peril; Trans-Europe Express*
Pistilli, Luigi (act): *Cadaveri Eccellenti; Twitch of the Death Nerve*
Pistoni, Franco (act): *The Barbarians (1987)*
Pisu, Mario (act): *8 1/2; Giulietta degli Spiriti*
Pitagora, Paolo (act): *Psychout for Murder*
Pitcairn, Jack (act): *In the Palace of the King*
Pitfarkin, Clyde (act): *White of the Eye*
Pithart, Aura (act): *The Boy Who Could Fly*
Pithey, Wensley (act): *The Boys; Guilt Is My Shadow; Kill Me Tomorrow; Lady In the Fog; Men of Sherwood Forest; One of Our Dinosaurs Is Missing; The Saint and the Brave Goose*
Pitillo, Maria (act): *Godzilla (1998)*
Pitimac, Cynara (act): *The Pink Chiquitas*
Pitoeff, Sacha (act): *L'Annee Derniere a Marienbad; Catch Me a Spy; Inferno (1979); La Poupee*
Pitofsky, Peter (act): *House*
Pitoniak, Anne (act): *Sister, Sister*
Pitt, Brad (act, b. 1963): *Cool World; Cutting Class; Interview With the Vampire; Meet Joe Black; Seven; Seven Years In Tibet; 12 Monkeys*
Pitt, Charles (act): *Bog*
Pitt, Chris (act): *The Lair of the White Worm*
Pitt, Fred (act): *Jane Shore (1915)*
Pitt, George Dibdin (wri): *Sweeney Todd*
Pitt, Ingrid (act, b. 1943, nee Natasha Petrovana): *Countess Dracula; The House That Dripped Blood; The Omegans; Sound of Horror; Transmutations; The Vampire Lovers; The Wicker Man*
Pitt, John (wri): *The Assistant*
Pitta, Elsie (act): *Electra (1961)*
Pittack, Robert (cin): *Queen of the Amazons (1947); The Vampire's Ghost*
Pitt-Chatham, C. (act): *The Resident Patient*
Pittman, Bruce (dir): *The Haunting of Hamilton High; Kurt Vonnegut's 'Harrison Bergeron'*
Pittman, Montgomery (wri): *Tarzan and the Lost Safari*
Pittman, Tom (act): *The Aliens Are Coming; Invasion of the Bee Girls*
Pittock, Michael (wri): *Where the Bullets Fly*
Pittoru, Fabio (wri): *The Night Evelyn Came Out of the Grave*
Pitts, Cary (J.) (act): *Outbreak; Rattlers*
Pitts, Clay (mus): *I Drink Your Blood*
Pitts Jr., Oscar (act): *Shadow Conspiracy*
Pitts, ZaSu (act, 1898-1963): *Forty Naughty Girls; Francis; Francis Joins the WACs; The Gazebo; The Plot Thickens; Secrets of the Night; Strangers of the Evening*
Pitzele, Robert (act): *Re-Animator*
Pitzer, Marilyn (act): *Black Magic Woman*
Pivar, Ben (wri): *The Leech Woman*
Piven, Byrne (act): *Creator; Pandora's Clock*
Piven, Jeremy (act): *Dr. Jekyll and Ms. Hyde; Kiss the Girls; 12:01*
Pizer, Larry (cin): *The Clairvoyant (1985); Mannequin Two: On the Move; Our Mother's House; Phantom of the Opera (1983); Phantom of the Paradise; Svengali (1983); Timerider; Too Scared to Scream*
Pizzuti, Riccardo (act): *Battle of the Amazons*
Place, Lou (act): *Swamp Women*
Place, Mary Kay (act): *Explorers; Modern Problems*
Place, Patricia (act): *Outbreak; Prey of the Chameleon*
Place, Shelli (act): *Party Line*
Plachy, Jiri (act): *Cisaruv Pekar, Pekaruv Cisar*
Plaissetty, Rene (dir): *The Yellow Claw*
Plakas, Demetra (act): *Serial Mom*
Plakias, Nick (act): *U.F.O.: Target Earth*
Plana, Antonio (act): *La Corona Negra*
Plana, Tony (act): *Nightmares (1983); Primal Fear*
Planck, Robert (cin): *Above Suspicion; The Bat Whispers; The Canterville Ghost (1944); Eyes In the Night; The Man In the Iron Mask (1939); The Three Musketeers (1948)*
Planden, Karen (act): *Black Roses*
Planer, Franz (E.) (cin, 1894-1963): *Alraune (1928); The Chase; Criss Cross; The Face Behind the Mask; The 5000 Fingers of Dr. T; Meet Boston Blackie; 99 River Street; Once Upon a Time (1944); One Touch of Venus; The Scarf; 20,000 Leagues Under the Sea (1954)*
Planer, Nigel (act): *Brazil; Yellowbeard*
Plank, Scott (act): *Dying to Remember*
Plant, A. Brian (act): *Robin Hood Outlawed*
Plant, Pamela (act): *The Tell-Tale Heart (1960)*
Plante, Don (act): *The Green Slime*
Plate, Bret (wri): *Superstition*
Platen, Karl (act): *Doctor Mabuse; M (1931)*
Plato, Dana (act, b. 1964): *Beyond the Bermuda Triangle; Return to Boggy Creek*
Plato, Joseph (act): *Fatal Passion*
Platt, David (act): *Blind Date; The Children*
Platt, Edward C. (act, 1916-1974): *Atlantis, the Lost Continent; Black Zoo; Cape Fear (1961); Cult of the Cobra; Omar Khayyam; Shock Treatment (1964); The Tattered Dress; The Unguarded Moment*
Platt, Howard (T.) (act): *The Cat from Outer Space; Westworld*
Platt, Marc (act, b. 1913): *Down to Earth*
Platt, Oliver (act): *Dr. Dolittle (1998); Flatliners; The Three Musketeers (1993); The Temp; A Time to Kill (1996)*
Platt, Ruth (act): *Murders In the Rue Morgue (1971)*
Platt, Victor (act): *Deadly Nightshade; Dollars for Sale; Man Detained; Partners In Crime (1961); Playback*
Platts, Diana (act): *The Pink Chiquitas*
Plavee, Dr. Josef (act): *Invisible Adversaries*
Playdon, Paul (wri): *Escape*
Player, Susie (act): *Invasion of the Bee Girls*
Players Special Effects (cin): *Crash and Burn*
Playfair, Nigel (act): *Crime on the Hill; Princess Clementina*
Playten, Alice (act, b. 1947): *Felix the Cat: The Movie; Heavy Metal; Legend*
Plaza, Begona (act): *Maid to Order; Timestalkers*
Plaza, Terisa (act): *Grim Prairie Tales*
Pleace, Wayne (act): *Howling III*
Pleasence, Angela (act): *A Christmas Carol (1984); From Beyond the Grave; The Godsend; Hitler: The Last Ten Days; Symptoms*
Pleasence, Donald (act, 1919-1995): *Alone In the Dark; The Black Windmill; Blood Relatives; Buried Alive (1989); A Choice of Weapons; Circus of Horrors; Computercide; The Corsican Brothers (1985); The Count of Monte Cristo (1975); Cul-de-Sac; Deathline; The Devil's Men; The Devonsville Terror; Dr.*

Crippen; Dracula (1979); Escape to Witch Mountain (1975); Eye of the Devil; Fantastic Voyage; Final Eye; The Flesh and the Fiends; Frankenstein's Great Aunt Tillie; From Beyond the Grave; Gold of the Amazon Women; Halloween; Halloween II; Halloween 4: The Return of Michael Myers; Halloween 5: The Revenge of Michael Myers; Halloween 6: The Origin of Michael Myers; Halloween: The Curse of Michael Myers; The Hands of Orlac (1959); Hell Is a City; The House of the Damned (1974); The House of Usher (1988); I Don't Want to Be Born; Innocent Bystanders; Into the Darkness; The Jerusalem File; Journey Into Fear (1975); The Man Inside; Matchless; Mister Freedom; The Monster Club; The Mutations; Night Creature; The Night of the Generals; 1984 (1955); Oh, God!; Phantom of Death; Phenomena; The Pied Piper (1971); Prince of Darkness; The Puma Man; The Shakedown; Spettri; Tales That Witness Madness; Ten Little Indians (1989); Terror In the Aisles; THX 1138; Tomorrow Never Comes; The Two-Headed Spy; The Uncanny; Warrior Queen; Warriors of the Wasteland; What a Carve Up!; The Wind of Change; You Only Live Twice

Plebani, Alberto (act): *Giulietta degli Spiriti; The Minotaur*

Plemiannikow, Roger Vadim (dir & wri): see Vadim, Roger

Pleshette, John (act): *Deadly Game; The Kid With the Broken Halo*

Pleshette, Suzanne (act, b. 1937): *The Birds; Blackbeard's Ghost; Fantasies; Oh, God! Book II; The Power (1967); The Shaggy D.A.; A Stranger Waits; Target: Harry*

Plessner, Amotz (mus): *Perfect Alibi*

Plimpton, Martha (act, b. 1970): *Daybreak; The Goonies; Josh and S.A.M.*

Plimpton, Shelley (act): *Glen and Randa*

Plisetskaya, Maya (act, b. 1925): *The Blue Bird (1976)*

Plomley, Roy (act): *Double Confession*

Plomley, Roy (wri): *Dr. Morelle-The Case of the Missing Heiress*

Plone, Allen (dir): *Night Screams*

Ploski, Joe (act): *Dr. Goldfoot and the Bikini Machine*

Plotkin, Ken (cin): *Beyond Evil*

Plotnikov, Boris (act): *The Savage Hunt of King Stakh*

Plotnikov, V. (act): *Shinel (1926)*

Plowden, Piers (R.C.) (act): *Full Eclipse; Waxwork II: Lost In Time*

Plowman, Jon (act): *Absolution*

Plowman, Melinda (act): *Billy the Kid vs. Dracula*

Plowman, Michael Richard (mus): *Trucks*

Plowright, Hilda (act): *36 Hours (1965)*

Plowright, Joan (act, b. 1929): *Brimstone & Treacle; Jane Eyre (1996); 101 Dalmatians (1996); The Scarlet Letter (1995); Time Without Pity*

Ployardt, John (act): *The Adventures of Ichabod and Mr. Toad*

Plues, George (act): *My Cousin Rachel*

Plumb, Edward (mus): *Bambi; Woman Who Came Back*

Plumb, Elizabeth (act): *The Psycho Lover*

Plumb, Hay (act): *The Demon Dog; Faust (1911); Hawkeye, King of the Castle; The Heat Wave (1911); Rachel's Sin*

Plumb, Hay (dir): *Aladdin: or, A Lad Out; CinderElfred; Curfew Must Not Ring Tonight; The Dead Heart; Deadlock (1931); The Fairies' Revenge; George Barnwell, the London Apprentice; A Ghostly Affair; Ghosts (1912); Hamlet (1913); Hawkeye, Jill and the Old Fiddle; King of the Castle; Highwayman Hal; King Robert of Sicily; The Magic Glass; The Man Who Wasn't; Mr. Meek's Nightmare; The Of-Course-I-Can Brothers; That Mysterious Fez; Things We Want to Know; Two Brothers and a Spy*

Plume, John (act): *The Fast Kill*

Plumeri, Terry (mus): *Dangerous Touch; Sometimes They Come Back*

Plummer, Amanda (act, b. 1957): *Freejack; Freeway; Made In Heaven; Needful Things; Nostradamus; The Prophecy (1995)*

Plummer, Christopher (act, b. 1927): *An American Tail; Babes In Toyland (1997); Dial M for Murder (1981); The Disappearance; Dolores Claiborne; Dreamscape; Eyewitness (1981); Firehead; A Ghost In Monte Carlo; Kurt Vonnegut's Harrison Bergeron; Light Years; The Man Who Would Be King; Mindfield; Murder by Decree; The Night of the Generals; Nobody Runs Forever; Ordeal by Innocence; Prototype; Red Blooded American Girl; Somewhere In Time; The Spiral Staircase (1975); Star Crash; Star Trek VI: The Undiscovered Country; 12 Monkeys; Wolf*

Plummer, Glenn (act): *Strange Days*

Plummer, Peter (dir): *Junket 89*

Plummer, Rose (act): *Possessed (1947)*

Plummer, Terrence/Terry (act): *Batman (1989); Deathline; Jekyll and Hyde*

Plunkett, Patricia (act, b. 1928): *Escort for Hire; The Flesh Is Weak; For Them That Trespass; Murder Without Crime*

Plympton, George (H.) (wri): *The Deadly Ray from Mars; Devil Goddess; Peril from the Planet Mongo; The Phantom Creeps; Purple Death from Outer Space; Zombies of Mora Tau*

Plytas, Steve (act): *Batman (1989); The Moon-Spinners; The Pursuers*

Pniewski, Michael (act): *Remote Control (1988)*

Pochat, Werner (act): *The Cat O' Nine Tails*

Pochet, Alex (act): *Beat the Devil*

Pochna, John (act): *The Bermuda Triangle*

Pochron, Jon Conrad (act): *Wheels of Terror*

Pocino, Benito (act): *Anguish*

Pockett, Christine (act): *The Vengeance of She*

Pockriss, Lee (mus): *The Phantom Tollbooth*

Podbrey, Alison (act): *The Peanut Butter Solution*

Podesser, Virginia (act): *The Kidnapping of the President*

Podesta, Rossana (act, b. 1934): *La Freccia d'Oro; Fury of the Pagans; Helen of Troy (1955); Hercules (1983); Raw Wind In Eden; The Seven Dwarfs to the Rescue; Sodom and Gomorrah; Ulysses; La Vergine di Norimberga*

Podewell, Cathy (act): *Earth Angel; Night of the Demons*

Podewell, Les (act): *Blink*

Podhora, Roman (act): *Night Visitors; Quarantine*

Podobed, Porfiri (act): *Luch Smerti*

Podorozhny, Alexander (act): *Zvenigora*

Poduvski, Jeff (act): *Blood Diner*

Poe, Amos (dir): *Dead Weekend*

Poe, Edgar Allan (wri, 1809-1849): *Annabel Lee; The Avenging Conscience; Berenice; The Black Cat (1934, 1965 & 1980); Buried Alive (1989); La Chute de la Maison Usher; The City Under the Sea; La Danza Macabra; Dr. Tarr's Torture Dungeon; The Fall of the House of Usher (1950, 1958, 1982 & 1988); La Fin du Monde; Haunting Fear; The Haunting of Morella; Histoires Extraordinaires; Horror; House of Usher (1960 & 1998); El Jorobado de la Morgue; The Living Coffin; Living Dead (1932); Lunatics In Power; Manfish; The Masque of the Red Death (1964 & 1989 {2}); Master of Horror; The Mummy Lives; The Murders In the Rue Morgue (1932, 1971 & 1986); The Mystery of Marie Roget; The Oblong Box; The Oval Portrait; Phantom of the Rue Morgue; The Pit (1962); The Pit and the Pendulum (1913, 1961 & 1990); Prelude; The Premature Burial; The Raven (1915, 1935, 1948, 1953 & 1963); Revenge In the House of Usher; Die Schlangengrube und das Pendel; Spirits of the Dead; Der Student von Prag (1913); Le Systeme du Docteur Goudron et du Professeur Plume; Tales of Terror; The Tell-Tale Heart (1934, 1941, 1953 {2} & 1960); The Tomb of Ligeia; Two Evil Eyes*

Poe, Harlan Cary (act): *Stigma*

Poe, James (wri, b. 1923): *Around the World In 80 Days; The Bedford Incident*

Poe, Rudger (dir): *Monster High*

Poelvoorde, Benoit (act, dir & wri): *Man Bites Dog*

Poerio, Adelina (act): *Don't Look Now*

Poff, Lon (act): *Dante's Inferno (1924); The Iron Mask*

Pogany, Gabor (cin): *Bluebeard (1972); Dr. Faustus; Top Secret (1978)*

Pogersdorff, Wilhelm (wri): *Chariots of the Gods*

Pogge, Roberto (act): *The Fish Men*

Poggi, Alessandro (act): *Tentacles*

Poggi, Fernando/Nando (act): *The Adventures of Hercules; Jason and the Argonauts*

Poggi, Grace (act): *The Snake Pit (1948); Sorry, Wrong Number (1948)*

Poggi, Lisa Ann (act): *Obsessed (1992)*

Poggi, Nando (act): see Poggi, Fernando/Nando

Poggi, Ottavio (wri): *Nefertite, Regina del Nilo; Rage of the Buccaneers*

Poggiali, Fabio (act): *Demons 2*

Pogostin, S. Lee (wri): *Nightmare Honeymoon*

Pogson, Kathryn (act): *Brazil; The Company of Wolves*

Pogue, Charles Edward (wri): *D.O.A. (1988); Dragonheart; The Fly (1986); Hands of a Murderer; Kull the Conqueror; Psycho III*

Pogue, John (wri): *U.S. Marshals*

Pogue, Ken(neth) (act): *An American Christmas Carol; Dead of Winter; Final Descent; The Neptune Factor; Still Not Quite Human; Virus (1980)*

Pogue, Thomas (act): *After the Thin Man*

Pohl, Klaus (act): *Die Frau im Mond; Das Testament des Dr. Mabuse*

Pohler, Joseph C. (act): see Pollar, Gene

Pohlmann, Eric (act, b. 1913): *Across the Bridge; Cairo; Carry On Screaming; Carry On Spying; The Counterfeit Plan; The Devil's Agent; Dr. Syn-Alias the Scarecrow; The Gelignite Gang; The Glass Tomb; Highly Dangerous; The High Terrace; Hot Enough for June; House of Secrets; The House of the Seven Hawks; I Accuse (1958); Interpol; Life Is a Circus; The Man Inside; The Man Who Couldn't Walk; Mark of the Phoenix; Night Train to Paris; Paris Express; A Prize of Gold; Thirty-Six Hours (1954); Three Crooked Men; Tiffany Jones; Venetian Bird; Visa to Canton; Where the Spies Are*

Pohtamo, Anne Marie (act): *Wolfen*

Poindexter (act): *Return from Witch Mountain*

Poindexter, Jerris L. (act): *Slam Dance*

Pointer, Muriel (act): *Where the Rainbow Ends*

Pointer, Priscilla (act): *Amazing Stories: The Movie VI; Blue Velvet; Carrie; C.H.U.D. II; Death Takes a Holiday (1971); Disturbed; The Flash; Fugitive from the Empire; The Magic Bubble; The Mysterious Two; A Nightmare On Elm Street 3: Dream Warriors; Rumpelstiltskin (1987); Twilight Zone*

Poire, Jean-Marie (dir): *The Visitors (1993)*

Poire, Jean-Marie (wri): *Dracula, Pere et Fils; The Visitors (1993)*

Poirier, Anne Claire (dir): *A Scream from Silence*

Poitier, Sidney (act, b. 1924): *The Bedford Incident*

Poitier, Sidney (dir, b. 1924): *Ghost Dad*

Pojar, Bretislav (cin, b. 1923): *Cisaruv Slavik*

Pojar, Bretislav (dir, b. 1923): *Pernikova Chaloupka*

Poklekowski, Ruth (act): *Making Contact*

Pol, Talitha (act): *Return from the Ashes; We Shall See*

Pola, Claude (wri): *Avalanche*

Pola, Eddie (act): *Catch as Catch Can*

Polack, Fernando S. (act): *The Mummy's Revenge*

Polack, James (mus): *Willy McBean and His Magic Machine*

Polak, Jindrich (dir): *Ikaria XB1; Rocket to Nowhere*

Polak, Jindrich (wri): *Ikaria XB1*

Polakof, James (dir): *Satan's Mistress*

Polan, Lou (act): *You Never Can Tell*

Polan, Nini (act): *Cuento de Hadas*

Poland, Cliff(ord) (cin): *Around the World Under the Sea; Mission Mars; Stanley*

Poland, Joseph (wri): *The Adventures of Captain Marvel; Captain Mephisto and the Transformation Machine; Dick Tracy vs. Crime, Inc.; Dr. Satan's Robot; Nyoka and the Lost Secrets of Hippocrates; Spy Smasher Returns*

Poland, Simon (act): *Alien from L.A.*

Polani, Anna Maria (act): *Maciste e la Regina di Samar*

Polanski, Roman (act, b. 1933): *Dracula (1974); The Fearless Vampire Killers or: Pardon Me, But Your Teeth Are In My Neck; The Magic Christian; The Tenant*

Polanski, Roman (dir, b. 1933): *Cul-de-Sac; The Fearless Vampire Killers or: Pardon Me, But Your Teeth Are In My Neck; Macbeth (1971); Repulsion; Rosemary's Baby; The Tenant*

Polanski, Roman (wri, b. 1933): *Aimez-Vous les Femmes?; Cul-de-Sac; The Fearless Vampire Killers or: Pardon Me, But Your Teeth Are In My Neck; Macbeth (1971); Repulsion; Rosemary's Baby; The Tenant*

Polder, Dutch (act): *The Tomb*

Poledouris, Basil (mus): *Alfred Hitchcock Presents; Amazons (1984); Cherry 2000; Conan the Barbarian; Conan the Destroyer; Flesh & Blood; The Hunt for Red October; The Jungle Book (1994); Red Dawn; RoboCop; RoboCop 3; Serial Mom; Spellbinder; Starship Troopers; Tintorera...Bloody Waters*

Polesello, Franca (act): *Tarzana, the Wild Girl*

Poletto, Piero (cin): *C'era una Volta*

Polevitskaya, Yelena (act): *The Queen of Spades (1960)*

Polglase, Van Nest (cin): *The Hunchback of Notre Dame (1939)*

Poli, Maurice (act): *Sandokan the Great*

Poli, Mimo (act): *Beat the Devil*

Police, The (mus): *Copycat*

Polinsky, Alexander (act): *Pumpkinhead II: Blood Wings*

Polis, Joel (act): *Dark Angel (1996)*

Polito, Gene (cin): *Colossus: The Forbin Project; Futureworld; The Phantom of Hollywood; Westworld*

Polito, Jon (act): *The Clairvoyant (1985); The Crow (1994); Fluke; Highlander; Remo Williams: The Adventure Begins; The Shaggy Dog (1994)*

Polito, Sol (act): *Blankman*

Polito, Sol (cin, 1892-1960): *The Adventures of Robin Hood; Arsenic and Old Lace; Cloak and Dagger (1946); The Haunted House (1929); The House of Horror (1929); Madame DuBarry (1934); The Mind Reader; Seven Footprints to Satan; Sorry, Wrong Number (1948)*

Politoff, Haydee (act): *Gran Amore del Conde Dracula; The Human Factor*

Polizos, Vic (act): *Condor; Eraser; Graveyard Shift (1990); Night of the Creeps*

Polk, Alexander (act): *Fright Night II*

Polk, Oscar (act): *Green Pastures*

Pollack, Anne (act): *Piranha II: The Spawning*

Pollack, Sydney (act, b. 1934): *Death Becomes Her; Eyes Wide Shut*

Pollack, Sydney (dir, b. 1934): *Castle Keep; 3 Days of the Condor*

Pollak, Cheryl (act): *My Best Friend Is a Vampire; Night Life (1989, USA)*

Pollak, George (act): *Inn of the Damned*

Pollak, Kevin (act): *The Usual Suspects; Willow*

Pollar, Gene (act, nee Joseph C. Pohler): *The Return of Tarzan*

Pollard, Alexander (act): *The Monster Maker (1943)*

Pollard, E.C. (wri): *Collision*

Pollard, Frank (act): *The Adventures of Dick Turpin-The King of Highwayman; The Adventures of Dick Turpin-200 Guineas Reward, Dead or Alive*

Pollard, Harry (dir & wri, 1883-1934): *The Devil's Assistant*

Pollard, Hugh (act): *Hansel and Gretel*

Pollard, Michael J. (act, b. 1939): *American Gothic; The Arrival (1990); Dick Tracy (1990); I Come In Peace; The Odyssey; Riders of the Storm; Scrooged; Skeeter; Sleepaway Camp 3: Teenage Wasteland; Split Second (1992)*

Pollard, Paul (cin): *The Satan Bug*

Pollard, Snub (act, 1886-1962, nee Harold Frazer): *The Clutching Hand; Man of a Thousand Faces*

Pollatschek, Susanne (act): *The Great Mouse Detective*

Pollet, Jean-Daniel (dir & wri, b. 1936): *Le Horla (1967)*

Polletin, Luciana (act): *Knives of the Avenger*

Pollett, Albert (act): *Charlie Chan In City In Darkness; For Heaven's Sake*

Pollexfen, Jack (dir, b. 1918): *Indestructible Man*

Pollexfen, Jack (wri, b. 1918): *Captain Kidd and the Slave Girl; Captive Women; Daughter of Dr. Jekyll; Indestructible Man; The Lady In the Iron Mask; The Man from Planet X; Monstrosity; The Neanderthal Man; Port Sinister; Return to Treasure Island; The Son of Dr. Jekyll; Son of Sinbad*

Polley, Sarah (act): *The Adventures of Baron Munchausen (1989); Babar: The Movie*

Pollini, Francis (wri): *Pretty Maids All In a Row*

Pollock, Aubrey (act): *Member of the Jury; Passenger to London*

Pollock, Channing (act): *Judex*

Pollock, Dee (act): *Beware, My Lovely; Carousel; Embassy; It Grows On Trees*

Pollock, Ellen (act): *Bedelia; The Golden Link; Horror Hospital; The Hypnotist (1957); The Long Knife; Master Spy (1963); Midnight (1931); Shadow of Death (1939); Who Killed the Cat?; The Wicked Lady*

Pollock, Gene (wri): *The Incredibly Strange Creatures Who Stopped Living and Became Mixed-Up Zombies; The Thrill Killers*

Pollock, George (act): *Those Dear Departed*

Pollock, George (dir, b. 1907): *Kill or Cure; Murder Ahoy; Murder at the Gallop; Murder Most Foul; Murder She Said; Stranger In Town (1957); Ten Little Indians (1965)*

Pollock, Louis (wri, b. 1904): *The Gamma People*

Pollock, Robert (wri): *Loophole*

Pollock, Wendy (act): *Jekyll and Hyde*

Polman, Jeffrey (wri): *Grave Secrets*

Polo, Lauri (act): *Vampire On Bikini Beach*

Polo, Teri (act): *The Arrival (1996); House of Frankenstein 1997; The Phantom of the Opera (1990)*

Polonsky, Abraham (wri, b. 1910): *Avalanche Express; Golden Earrings*

Polonsky, Alan (act): *Electric Dreams; Slipstream*

Polop, Francisco Lara (dir): Murder Mansion
Polotnikov, Nikolai (act): Devyat'dney Odnogo Goda
Polselli, Renato (dir): L'Amante del Vampiri; Il Vampiro dell'Opera
Polselli, Renato (wri): L'Amante del Vampiri
Polsky, Abe (wri): The Baby
Poltermann, Barry (dir & wri): The Unearthing
Poluski, Sam T. (act): The Jovial Fluid
Polytnsev, Dmitri (act): The Package
Pombo, Amanda (act): Raising Cain
Pomeranc, Max (act): Fluke
Pomerantz, Earl (act): Cannibal Girls
Pomerantz, Jeff (act): City Killer; Retribution (1988)
Pomeroy, Ada (act): La Figlia di Frankenstein
Pomeroy, John (dir): Dublin Nightmare
Pomeroy, William (act): The Frighteners
Pomes, Don (act): Deathmoon
Pomiesczykov, V. (wri): The Heavens Call
Pommerol, Lieut. (act): Queenie of the Circus
Pompa, George (act): The Lightning Incident
Pon, Lon (act): The Iron Mask
Pon, Patrick (act): The Resurrected
Ponazecki, Joe (act): The Cradle Will Fall; Man On a Swing
Poncin, Marcel (act): Saadia; So Long at the Fair
Pondal, Mary Paz (act): Tristana
Ponicsan, Daryl (wri): The Enemy Within
Pons, Marliza (act): The Mummy and the Curse of the Jackals
Ponsova, Y. (act): Shinel (1965)
Pont, Theo (act): The Lift
Ponte, Maria Luisa (act): Amador; Not On Your Life!; La Venganza de Don Mendo
Ponti, Marco (act): Vendetta for the Saint
Ponti, Sal (wri): Doctor Death: Seeker of Souls
Ponto, Erich (act): The Third Man
Ponton, Yvan (act): Scanners II: The New Order
Pontoppidan, Clara (act): Blade af Satans Bog; Haxan
Ponza, Geno (act): Killer Klowns from Outer Space
Ponzini, Antony (act): Gray Lady Down
Ponzio, John (act): The Dark Half
Ponzlov, Frederick (act): Full Eclipse
Pool, Ann Mary (act): The Mummy's Revenge
Pool, Robert Roy (wri): Outbreak
Poole, Arthur (act): The Female Swindler; The Girl Who Wrecked His Home; The Green Terror; The Phantom Picture
Poole, Dalton (act): D.A.R.Y.L.
Poole, Duane (wri): Chomps; A Face to Die For; I've Been Waiting for You; Praying Mantis; Sunstroke
Poole, Jackie (act): Dr. Jekyll and Sister Hyde
Poole, Michael (wri): The Stolen Plans (1952)
Poole, Roy (act): Experiment In Terror; A Stranger Is Watching
Pooley, Olaf (act): The Assassination Bureau; The Corpse; The Gamma People; Highly Dangerous; Naked Evil; Top Secret (1952)
Pooley, Olaf (wri): The Corpse; The Godsend
Poore, Richard (act): The Assistant
Pop, Iggy (act): The Crow: City of Angels; Hardware; Tank Girl
Pope, Bill (cin): Army of Darkness; Darkman (1990); Fire In the Sky (1993)
Pope, Brian (act): Twice Upon a Time
Pope, Caroline (act): The Lair of the White Worm
Pope, Conrad (mus): Project Metalbeast: DNA Overload
Pope, Dick (cin): The Reflecting Skin
Pope, J. Lamont (act): Running Against Time
Pope, Kim (act): Penetration
Pope, Peggy (act): Once Bitten
Pope, Thomas (wri): Hammett
Pope, Tim (dir): The Crow: City of Angels
Pope, Tim (wri): Don't Look in the Basement; The Manitou
Pope, Tony (act): Who Framed Roger Rabbit
Popescu, Mircea (dir): Viaggio Immaginario
Popescu, Peter (wri): Last Wave
Popkin, Leo (dir): The Well
Popkova, Oxana (act): The Saint
Popov, Oleg (act): The Blue Bird (1976)
Popovich, George (act): Wild Thing
Popovich, Pavel (act): Stellar Brothers-From the Kremlin to the Cosmos
Popp, Peter (act): Troubled Waters (1936)
Poppe, Nils (act, b. 1908): The Devil's Eye; Det Sjunde Inseglet
Poppel, Marc (act): Christine; Night of the Comet; Separate Lives
Poppen, Eric (wri): Virtual Assassin
Poppick, Eric (act): Heart and Souls; Single White Female
Popplewell, Jack (wri): Tread Softly Stranger
Popplewell, Randy (act): Creature; The Dungeonmaster

Pops (act): Vamp
Popwell, Johnny (act): Freejack
Popwell Sr., Johnny (act): Mutant
Popwell, Wade (act): Blood Waters of Dr. Z
Porath, Gideon (cin): Christmas Every Day
Porayko, Chris (act): The Little Match Girl (1987)
Porayko, David (act): The Little Match Girl (1987)
Porayko, Scott (act): The Little Match Girl (1987)
Porcaro, Joleen (act): Scared to Death (1980)
Porcasi, Paul (act, b. 1880): Charlie Chan In Egypt; The Florentine Dagger; Svengali (1931); Trouble for Two
Porcelli, Claudia (act): The Boogey Man
Poree, Anita (act): Targets
Porel, Marc (act): The Psychic
Porrett, Susan (act): The Company of Wolves; The Saint
Porretta, Matthew (act): Robin Hood: Men In Tights
Port, Debra (act): The Exorcist III
Port, George (act): The Frighteners
Portacio, Tony (act): Brazil
Portalupi, Piero (cin): Carthage In Flames
Portela, Manuel (act): Beverly Hills Bodysnatchers
Portell, Petula (act): Dr. Jekyll and Sister Hyde
Porten, Henny (act, 1888-1960): Anna Boleyn
Porteous, Peter (act): Lifeforce; Octopussy; Psyche 59; Venom (1982)
Porter, Andrew (act): Road Kill USA
Porter, Arthur Gould (act): Houdini (1953)
Porter, Beth (act): Cat and Mouse (1974); The Naked Witch
Porter, Bobby (act): Battle for the Planet of the Apes; Day of the Animals; Night of the Comet
Porter, Brett (act): Firehead
Porter, Caleb (act): Guy Fawkes and the Gunpowder Plot; Kismet (1914)
Porter, Cole (mus, 1893-1964): Evil Under the Sun
Porter, Dan (act): Making Contact
Porter, Debby/Debbie (act): Brainstorm (1983); Twilight Zone
Porter, Don (act, 1912-1997): Danger Woman; The Legend of Lizzie Borden; Night Monster; She-Wolf of London; Who Done It? (1942)
Porter, Edwin S. (cin, 1869-1941): The Dream of a Rarebit Fiend
Porter, Edwin S. (dir, 1869-1941): Alice's Adventures In Wonderland (1910); The Count of Monte Cristo (1912); The Dream of a Rarebit Fiend; Rescued from an Eagle's Nest; A Trip to Mars
Porter, Eric (act, 1928-1995): Hands of the Ripper; Hitler: The Last Ten Days; Kaleidoscope; The Spider and the Fly (1949); The 39 Steps (1978); Uncharted Seas
Porter, Heath (act): Stay Awake
Porter, Janet (act): Anguish
Porter, Janine (act): Secrets of the Phantom Caverns
Porter, Jean (act): One Million B.C.
Porter, Jon (cin): Nothing But Trouble
Porter, Julio (wri): The Saint In the Wax Museum
Porter, LuLu (act): The Brass Bottle (1964)
Porter, Marguerite (act): The Magic Toyshop
Porter, Nyree Dawn (act): Death In Small Doses (1973); From Beyond the Grave; The House That Dripped Blood; Jane Eyre (1970); Man at the Carlton Tower; Sentenced for Life
Porter, Richard Lee (act): The Deadly Spawn
Porter, Robert (act): Queen of Blood; Wonder Woman
Porter, Todd (act): Earthbound (1981)
Porter, William A. (act): When the Bough Breaks
Portes, Alison (act): The Squeeze
Portillo, Adolpho/A. Lopez (wri): El Baron del Terror; La Cabeza Viviente; Santa Claus (1959)
Portillo, Adolpho Torres (wri): Little Red Riding Hood vs. the Monsters; Pacto Diabolico; Las Vampiras (1969)
Portillo, Rafael (Lopez) (dir): La Momia; La Momia Contra el Robot Humano
Portillo, Rose (act): Exorcist II: The Heretic
Portman, Eric (act, 1903-1969): Assignment to Kill; The Bedford Incident; Child In the House; Corridor of Mirrors; The Crimes of Stephen Hawke; Daybreak; Deadfall; Dear Murderer; Escape to Danger; 49th Parallel; The Golden Mask; The Man Who Finally Died; Maria Marten: or, The Murder In the Red Barn (1935); The Mark of Cain; The Naked Edge; The Spider and the Fly (1949); The Spy With a Cold Nose; Wanted for Murder; West 11
Portman, Natalie (act): Mars Attacks!; Star Wars: Episode I-The Phantom Menace

Portman, Rachel (mus): The Adventures of Pinocchio (1996); Beauty and the Beast: The Enchanted Christmas
Portney, Charlotte (act): Frankenstein's Daughter (1958)
Portnow, Richard (act): Heart and Souls
Portser, Mary (act): Ed Wood
Portugese, Gladys (act): It's Alive III: Island of the Alive
Posco, Alfred (dir): The Magic Voyage of Sinbad
Posey, Matthew (act): I Come In Peace
Posey, Parker (act): Dead Connection
Posey, Stephen L./Steve (cin): Blood Song; Friday the 13th-Part V: A New Beginning; Hellhole; The Slumber Party Massacre
Posner, Bill (dir): Teen-Age Strangler
Posner, Steven (wri): Beyond the Universe
Pospisil, Eric (act): Unforgettable
Possnebacher, Hans (act): Das Schloss
Posson, Jeff (act): I Was a Zombie for the F.B.I.
Post, Angela (act): The Phantom Empire
Post, Guy Bates (act): Trouble for Two
Post, Markie (act): Appointment for a Killing; Dog's Best Friend; I've Been Waiting for You; Visitors of the Night
Post, Mike (mus): Captain America II; Dr. Scorpion
Post, Ted (dir, b. 1918): The Baby; Beneath the Planet of the Apes; Dr. Cook's Garden; Do Not Fold, Spindle or Mutilate; Night Slaves; Sandcastles
Post Jr., William (act, 1901-1989): The Black Camel; Sherlock Holmes and the Secret Weapon
Posta, Adrienne (act): Some Girls Do
Postal, Charles (act): The Unknown Terror
Poster, Steve(n) (cin): Blood Beach; The Boy Who Could Fly; The Cradle Will Fall; Dead and Buried; The Mysterious Two; Once You Meet a Stranger; Rocketman (1997); Roswell
Poster, Thomas W. (act): Watchers II
Postlethwaite, Pete(r) (act, b. 1945): Alice In Wonderland (1999); Dragonheart; Hamlet (1990); James and the Giant Peach; The Lost World: Jurassic Park; Treasure Island (1990); The Usual Suspects
Postnikov, Michail N. (act): Milczaca Gwiazda
Poston, Dick (wri): Blood of Ghastly Horror
Poston, Tiffanie (act): Adventures In Dinosaur City
Poston, Tom (act, b. 1927): The Old Dark House (1963); Zotz!
Post Production Associates (mus): Octaman
Potanah, Ruy (act): Os Deuses e os Mortos
Potechina, Lydia (act): Doctor Mabuse
Potel, Victor (act): The Millerson Case
Potenza, Vadia (act): Star Trek III: The Search for Spock
Potocki, Jan (wri): Rekopis Znaleziony w Saragossie
Potter, Beatrix (wri, 1866-1943): Peter Rabbit and the Tales of Beatrix Potter
Potter, Bertie (act): The Doll's Revenge; The Professor's Antigravitational Fluid
Potter, Charlie (act): The Witches (1990)
Potter, Chip (act): Ssssss
Potter, Dennis (wri): Brimstone & Treacle; Dreamchild; Gorky Park; Track 29
Potter, Doobie (act): Offerings
Potter, Gertie (act): Cinderella (1907 & 1913); The Doll's Revenge; The Ghosts' Holiday; The Nursemaid's Dream; The Pets' Tea Party; Snatched from a Terrible Death; That Fatal Sneeze; A Tramp's Dream of Wealth
Potter, Gillie (act): Death at Broadcasting House
Potter, Henry C. (dir, 1904-1977): Hellzapoppin
Potter, Hetty (act): The Pirate Ship; Prehistoric Peeps; The Tramp's Dream (1906)
Potter, Jerry (act): Misery
Potter, Madeleine (act): Hello Again; The Suicide Club (1988); Two Evil Eyes
Potter, Martin (act): The Big Sleep (1978); Craze; Satan's Slave; Satyricon; Twinsanity
Potter, Nicole (act): Street Trash
Potter, Sally (dir & wri): Orlando
Potter, Terry (act): Bad Taste
Potter, Tiffany (act): Demon Seed
Potterton, Gerald (dir): Heavy Metal
Pottier, Richard (dir): David and Goliath
Potts, Annie (act): Ghostbusters; Ghostbusters II; Her Deadly Rival; It Came Upon the Midnight Clear; The Man Who Fell to Earth (1987); Toy Story
Potts, Cliff (act): The Groundstar Conspiracy; Live Again, Die Again; Silent Running
Potts, Daniel (act): Greystoke: The Legend of Tarzan, Lord of the Apes
Potts, Faith (act): 12 Monkeys
Potts, Rayette (act): Offerings
Potts, Wallace (dir): Psycho Cop
Potvin, Frank (act): Alien High

Potworowska, Mimi (act): Mary Reilly; Mission: Impossible
Pouchie (act): Lo Strano Caso della Signora Ward
Poudevigne, Gregory (act): RoboCop
Pouget, Ely (act): Death Machine; Endless Descent; Lawnmower Man 2: Beyond Cyberspace
Pough, Rusty (act): Flight of the Navigator
Poujouly, Georges (act, b. 1940): Diabolique (1955); Jeux Interdits; Treasure of Bengal
Pouliot, Anne (act): Distortions
Poullair, Patricia (act): The Jewel of the Nile
Poulsen, William Anthony (act): Another Thin Man
Poulter, Lorna (act): The Falls
Poulton, A.G. (act): Collision
Poulton, Charles (act): The Loudwater Mystery; The Temptation of Carlton Earle
Poulton, Mabel (act): Moonbeam Magic; The Silent House; Terror On Tiptoe
Pound, Reginald (wri): Troubled Waters (1936)
Pound, Toots (act): Svengali (1954)
Pounder, CCH (act): Aladdin and the King of Thieves; Demon Knight; Lifepod; Netforce; Psycho IV: The Beginning; RoboCop 3; Sliver; White Dwarf
Pourmand, Mansour (dir): Zipperface
Pousette, Lena (act): Blood Beach
Pouyet, Eugene (act): The Conquering Power
Povill, Jon (wri): Total Recall
Powder, Steve (mus): Piranha II: The Spawning
Powell, Addison (act): Doctor Franken; 3 Days of the Condor
Powell, Alisa (act): Satan's Cheerleaders
Powell, Andrew (mus): Ladyhawke
Powell, Bellenden (act): Troubled Waters (1936)
Powell, Brittney (act): Dragonworld
Powell, Cari (act): Ghostriders
Powell, Charles (act): Screamers (1996)
Powell, Clifton (act): Deep Rising; Phantoms
Powell, Clive (act): Children of the Damned
Powell, Cynthia (act): An American Werewolf In London
Powell, David (act): The Green Goddess (1923); Missing Millions
Powell, Derek (act): The Great Anarchist Mystery
Powell, Dick (act, 1904-1963): Cornered; Cry Danger; It Happened Tomorrow; A Midsummer Night's Dream (1935); Murder, My Sweet; Pitfall; To the Ends of the Earth; You Never Can Tell
Powell, Dick (dir, 1904-1963): Split Second (1953)
Powell, Dinny (act): Superman II
Powell, Eddie (act): The Mummy's Shroud
Powell, Edith (act): The Keeper
Powell, Estehan Louis (act): Powder
Powell, (F.) Amos (wri): Curse of the Stone Hand; Demonoid; Tower of London (1962)
Powell, Frank (dir): Jane Shore (1911)
Powell, Fred (act): The Grip of Iron
Powell, Gwyneth (act): The Face of Darkness; Loophole
Powell, Jane (act, b. 1928): Enchanted Island
Powell, Jimmy (act): Time Flyer
Powell, Joe (act): Rearview Mirror
Powell, June (act): The Flesh and the Fiends; Tangier Assignment
Powell, Karen (act): Lady In White
Powell, Kati (act): Just Before Dawn (1980)
Powell, Lee (act): The Deadly Ray from Mars; Peril from the Planet Mongo; Purple Death from Outer Space; The Torpedo of Doom
Powell, Lester (wri): Black Widow (1951); Lady In the Fog
Powell, Lovelady (act): The Possession of Joel Delaney
Powell, Marcus (act): Metamorphosis: The Alien Factor; Wombling Free
Powell, Michael (act, 1905-1990): Peeping Tom
Powell, Michael (dir, 1905-1990): Black Narcissus; The Boy Who Turned Yellow; The Brown Wallet; C.O.D.; The Elusive Pimpernel (1950); The Fire Raisers; 49th Parallel; The Man Behind the Mask (1936); A Matter of Life and Death; Peeping Tom; The Phantom Light; The Spy In Black; The Star Reporter; The Thief of Bagdad (1940)
Powell, Michael (wri, 1905-1990): Black Narcissus; The Elusive Pimpernel (1950); The Fire Raisers; A Matter of Life and Death
Powell, Nosher (act): The Legend of Spider Forest
Powell, [illegible] ([illegible]): [illegible] The Human Factor
Powell, Petsye (act): Jekyll and Hyde...Together Again
Powell, Pip (act): Forty Winks
Powell, Randy (act): Deadly Dust

Powell, Reg (mus): Forbidden Zone: Alien Abduction; Ghost Writer; I Was a Teenage Sex Mutant; Pet Shop; Test Tube Teens from the Year 2000
Powell, Richard (act): Charlie Chan at the Opera
Powell, Richard (wri): My Gun Is Quick
Powell, Robert (act, b. 1944): The Asphyx; Asylum (1972); Frankenstein (1984); Harlequin; The Hunchback of Notre Dame (1982); The Mystery of Edwin Drood (1993); Secrets of the Phantom Caverns; Survivor (1980); The 39 Steps (1978); Tommy
Powell, Simon (dir): Harlequin
Powell, Stephanie (cin): Powder
Powell, Tim (act): Secrets of the Phantom Caverns
Powell, Violet (wri): The Girl In the Flat
Powell, William (act, 1892-1984): After the Thin Man; Aloma of the South Seas (1926); Another Thin Man; The Benson Murder Case; The Canary Murder Case; The Greene Murder Case; The Kennel Murder Case; Mr. Peabody and the Mermaid; Shadow of the Thin Man; Sherlock Holmes (1922); Song of the Thin Man; Star of Midnight; Take One False Step; The Thin Man; The Thin Man Goes Home; The Treasure of Lost Canyon
Powells, Victoria (act): Miracle Mile
Power, Chad (act): The Sitter
Power, Derry (act): Rawhead Rex; Warlords of the Deep
Power, Don (cin): Roller Blade Warriors: Taken by Force
Power, Edward (act): Empire of the Ants
Power, Hartley (act, 1894-1966): Alibi (1942); The Armchair Detective; Dead of Night (1945); Jury's Evidence; Living Dangerously; Murder Will Out (1939); The Return of the Frog
Power, John (act): Bulldog Drummond Escapes; The Grip of Iron
Power, John (dir): The Tommyknockers
Power, Madge (wri): The Invisible Fear
Power, Paul (act): The Adventures of Robin Hood; The Underwater City
Power, Robert (act): Final Eye
Power, Ronald (act): The Bruce Partington Plans; The Grip of Iron
Power, Sandra (act): The Nanny
Power, Taryn (act): The Count of Monte Cristo (1975); The Sea Serpent; Sinbad and the Eye of the Tiger
Power, Terri (act): The Silencers (1995)
Power (Sr.), Tyrone (act): The Lone Wolf (1924)
Power, Tyrone (act, 1914-1958): The Black Rose; The Black Swan; The House in the Square; The Luck of the Irish; Marie Antoinette (1938); The Mark of Zorro (1940); Nightmare Alley; Witness for the Prosecution
Power Jr., Tyrone (act, b. 1959): Cocoon; Cocoon: The Return
Power, Udana (act): Demon and the Mummy
Powers, Alexandra (act): Cast a Deadly Spell
Powers, Beverly (act): Invasion of the Bee Girls
Powers, Bruce (act): Horror of the Blood Monsters
Powers, Caroline Capers (act): The Oracle (1985)
Powers, David (act): The Fiendish Plot of Dr. Fu Manchu
Powers, Don (cin): The Intruder Within
Powers, Hubert (act): Glen and Randa
Powers, Jon (act): Sampa
Powers, Mala (act, b. 1921): City Beneath the Sea (1952); The Colossus of New York; Daddy's Gone A-Hunting; Death In Small Doses (1957); Doomsday Machine; Flight of the Lost Balloon; Man On the Prowl; The Unknown Terror
Powers, Marie (act): The Medium (1951)
Powers, Pamela (act): Cavegirl (1985)
Powers, Richard (act, b. 1904): Dick Tracy's Dilemma; Dig That Uranium!; The Jungle Woman; Port of 40 Thieves; Red Planet Mars
Powers, Stefanie (act, b. 1942, nee Stefania Federkievicz): The Astral Factor; Crescendo; Ellery Queen: Don't Look Behind You; Experiment In Terror; Fanatic (1965); The Invisible Strangler; Sweet, Sweet Rachel
Powers, Stephen (act): The Swarm; Twinkle, Twinle, Killer Kane
Powers, Teri (act): Galaxina
Powers, Tom (GB act): Aladdin: or, A Lad Out; The Basilisk; Be Sure Your Sins; Cinder-Elfred; Dr. Fenton's Ordeal; His Great Opportunity; The Hunchback (1914); In the Shadow of Big Ben; Morphia, the Death Drug; The Passing of a Soul; The Schemers: or, The Jewels of Hate; The Terror of the Air; The Unseen Witness
Powers, Tom (USA act): The Blue Dahlia; Destination Moon; Donovan's Brain; Double Indemnity (1944); Scared Stiff (1953); The Steel Trap; They Won't Believe Me; U.F.O.
Powers, Tom (wri): Aladdin: or, A Lad Out; Morphia, the Death Drug
Powledge, Dave (act): Leprechaun 2
Powley, Bryan (act): The Harbour Lights; Love from a Stranger (1937)
Poyner, Jim (act): Bug
Poynter, David (act): I Come In Peace
Poynter, Guy Kingsley (act): Floods of Fear; The Girl Hunters
Poyner, Roy (cin): Secret Rites; The Sexplorer
Pozenko, Yegor (act): The Saint
Pozharskaya, A. (act): Pikovaya Dama (1910)
Pozner, Vladimir (wri): The Conspirators; The Dark Mirror (1946)
Pozzi, Moana (act): Escape from the Bronx
Prada, Jose Maria (act): Amador
Prada, Vittorio (act): Il Vampiro dell'Opera
Pradier, Perrette (act): The Burning Court
Prado, Francisco (act): The Formula
Prado, Lilla (act): Cumbres Borrascosas
Prado, Lucia (act): Slugs
Prador, Irene (act): The Devil's Daffodil; Lost; No Orchids for Miss Blandish; The Snorkel; To the Devil a Daughter
Praed, Michael (act): Nightflyers; Robin Hood and the Sorcerer; Robin Hood: The Swords of Wayland; To Die For II: Son of Darkness; Writer's Block
Prager, Annie (act): The Last Man On Planet Earth
Prager, Stanley (dir): The Bang-Bang Kid
Praid, Mark (act): The Black Windmill
Prance, Janet Mary (act): 13 Frightened Girls
Prange, Laurie (act): The Dark Secret of Harvest Home; The Incredible Hulk, Part 2
Prasch-Grevenberg, Auguste (act): Doctor Mabuse
Praskins, Leonard (wri, b. 1902): Gorilla at Large; It Grows On Trees
Prather, Joan (act, b. 1950): The Devil's Rain
Prather, Maurice (cin): Carnival of Souls (1962)
Prather, Ronald (act): Kiss of the Tarantula
Prati, Pamela (act): The Adventures of Hercules
Pratt, Alan (act): Frankenhooker
Pratt Jr., Charles (wri): The Initiation
Pratt, Deborah (act): Spacehunter: Adventures In the Forbidden Zone
Pratt, Jane (act): The Boogey Man
Pratt, Judson (act): The Barefoot Executive; I Confess; Monster On the Campus
Pratt, Michael/Mike (act): Assassin (1973); A Dandy In Aspic; Face of a Stranger; Repulsion; Sitting Target; Twinsanity; The Vault of Horror
Pratt, Norma (act): The Toxic Avenger
Pratt, Purnell (B.) (act): The Casino Murder Case; The Gorilla (1931); A Night of Mystery (1937); A Shriek In the Night
Pratt, Roger (cin): Batman (1989); Black Angel (1980); Brazil; Mary Shelley's 'Frankenstein'; The Sender; 12 Monkeys
Pratt, Theodore (wri): The Incredible Mr. Limpet
Pratt, William Henry (act): see Karloff, Boris
Pravda, George (act): The Cold Room; Dracula (1973); Frankenstein Must Be Destroyed; Hide and Seek; Hot Enough for June; The Kremlin Letter; Person Unknown; Playback; Screamer; Taste of Excitement; Where the Spies Are
Pravda, Hana-Maria (act): And Soon the Darkness; The Kremlin Letter
Praxis Film Works (cin): Fortress
Pray for Rain (mus): Pretty Poison (1996); The Three Lives of Karen
Prebble, John (wri): Mysterious Island (1961)
Prechtel, Volker (act): The Name of the Rose
Preddy, Robby (act): Web of Deceit
Preece, Mike (act): Skullduggery
Preece, Tim (act): Brimstone & Treacle; Crossplot
Pregadio, Roberto (mus): The Invincible Barbarian
Preidel, Peter (act): The Village of the Damned (1960)
Preiss, Wolfgang (act): The Boys from Brazil; Cave of the Living Dead; The Formula; Der Henker von London; In the Steel Net of Dr. Mabuse; The Invisible Dr. Mabuse; Mistress of the World (1959); Il Mulino delle Donne di Pietra; The Secret of Dr. Mabuse; Die Tausend Augen des Dr. Mabuse; The Testament of Dr. Mabuse (1960)
Preisser, June (act, b. 1920): Murder In the Blue Room
Prejean, Albert (act, 1893-1979): Le Fantome du Moulin Rouge; L'Or du Cristobal; Paris Qui Dort; Les Trois Mousquetaires
Prell, Karen (act): Labyrinth (1986)
Prembudd, Penjit (act): Vice Versa (1988)
Preminger, Otto (act, 1906-1986): The Hobbit
Preminger, Otto (dir, 1906-1986): Angel Face; Bunny Lake Is Missing; Laura; River of No Return; The Thirteenth Letter
Prendergast, Gerard (act): Time Walker
Prendergast, Shaun (act): Mary Shelley's 'Frankenstein'
Prendergast, Tessa (act): Manfish
Prendes, Luis (act): Alien Predators; Mighty Ursus; Los Muertos No Perdonan; El Principe Encadenado; Pyro; Tuareg, the Desert Warrior
Prentice, Derek (act): Richard III (1955)
Prentice, Ernie (act): Susie Q
Prentice, Jordan (act): Howard the Duck
Prentiss, Ann (act): My Stepmother Is an Alien
Prentiss, David (wri): Gallery of Horror; Journey to the Center of Time; The Mighty Gorga
Prentiss, Ed (act): The Barefoot Executive; Project X (1967)
Prentiss, Paula (act, b. 1939, nee Paula Ragusa): Saturday the 14th; The Stepford Wives
Prentiss, Robert (act): Dangerous Touch; I Come In Peace
Prerost, Phillip (act): The Package
Prescod, Pearl (act): Naked Evil
Prescott, Elsa (act): Peter Ibbetson
Prescott, Guy (act): The Hypnotic Eye; Pharaoh's Curse; The Unearthly
Prescott, Kerrigan (act): Fiend Without a Face
Prescott, Norm (wri): Pinocchio In Outer Space
Presle, Micheline (act, b. 1922, nee Micheline Chassagne): Adventures of Captain Fabian; L'Assassino; Blind Date (1959); Demoniac; Les Derniers Jours de Pompeii; Le Diable et les Dix Commandements; La Nuit Fantastique; Peau d'Ane; Sins of Pompeii
Presnell, Harve (act, b. 1933): Blood Bath (1975); Fargo; Tidal Wave: No Escape
Presnell Jr., Robert (wri, b. 1914): Man in the Attic (1953); Ritual of Evil; Wink of an Eye
Presnell, Sherry (act): Willard
Press, Laura (act): The Pit (1983)
Press, Marvin (act): The Treasure of Lost Canyon
Pressburger, Emeric (dir, 1902-1988): Black Narcissus; The Elusive Pimpernel (1950); A Matter of Life and Death
Pressburger, Emeric (wri, 1902-1988): Black Narcissus; The Boy Who Turned Yellow; The Elusive Pimpernel (1950); 49th Parallel; A Matter of Life and Death; The Spy In Black; Wanted for Murder
Presser, Antonia (act): Fire & Sword
Pressfield, Steven (wri): Freejack; King Kong Lives; Separate Lives
Pressman, David (act): Stargate
Pressman, Lawrence (act, b. 1939): Cry for the Strangers; The Hellstrom Chronicle; The Man from Atlantis; The Uninvited (1996)
Pressman, Michael (dir, b. 1950): Haunted by Her Past; Teenage Mutant Ninja Turtles II: The Secret of the Ooze; To Gillian On Her 37th Birthday
Presson, Jason (act): Explorers; Gremlins 2: The New Batch; Invitation to Hell; Lady In White
Presson, Ron (act): Uninvited (1987)
Prestia, Shirley (act): Pandemonium; Species
Preston, Alan (act): Liquid Sky
Preston, Cyndy (act): Pin
Preston, David (wri): Spacehunter: Adventures In the Forbidden Zone; The Vindicator
Preston, Don (mus): Android; The Being; Blood Diner
Preston, Douglas (wri): The Relic
Preston, Duncan (act): Scandalous
Preston, Gaylene (dir & wri): Dark of the Night
Preston, Hayter (wri): Anything to Declare?
Preston, J.A. (act): Body Heat; Narrow Margin (1990); The Plutonium Incident; Remo Williams: The Adventure Begins
Preston, Kelly (act, b. 1963): Amazon Women On the Moon; Christine; From Dusk Till Dawn; Jack Frost 91998); Love at Stake; Mrs. Munck; Spacecamp; Spellbinder; Twins
Preston, Mike (act): Joe & the Colonel; Metalstorm: The Destruction of Jared Syn; The Road Warrior
Preston Jr., Richard (wri): The Silencers (1995)
Preston, Robert (act, 1918-1987, nee Robert Preston Messervey): Cloudburst; The Last Starfighter; This Gun for Hire (1942); Whispering Smith
Preston, Rose (act): Eyes of Fire
Preston, Roy (wri): The Naked Zoo
Preston, Trevor (wri): Night Hair Child; Slayground
Preston, Wayde (act): Captain America (1992)
Preston, William (act): The Exorcist III
Prete, Alessandro (act): Escape from the Bronx
Prete, Giancarlo (act): The Black Belly of the Tarantula; Ladyhawke; Satanik
Pretten, Philip (act): The Kiss (1988)
Pretty, Violet (act): see Heywood, Anne
Pretty Maids (mus): Demons (1985)
Preuss, Ruben (dir): Almost Dead; Dead On Sight
Prevert, Jacques (wri, 1900-1977): The Crime of Monsieur Lange; The Hunchback of Notre Dame (1957); Le Quai des Brumes
Prevert, Pierre (act, 1906-1988): L'Age d'Or
Previn, Andre (mus, b. 1929): Cause for Alarm!; Dead Ringer; Goodbye Charlie; It's Always Fair Weather; Rollerball; Scene of the Crime
Previn, Charles (mus): And Then There Were None; The Boys from Syracuse; Green Hell; Hellzapoppin; The House of the Seven Gables; Lady In the Morgue; Man-Made Monster; The Missing Guest; Saboteur; Sherlock Holmes and the Voice of Terror; Sherlock Holmes In Washington; Tower of London (1939); Who Done It? (1942); The Wolf Man (1941)
Prevost, Francoise (act): Comment Qu'ella Est!; Johnny Hamlet; The Murder Clinic; Payroll; Spirits of the Dead
Prewitt, Eunice (act): Fatal Attraction
Prewitt, Hal (act): I Was a Zombie for the F.B.I.
Prey, Margo (act): Troll II
Prezzo, Lupe (act): Die Tausend Augen des Dr. Mabuse
Price, Allan (act): Body Parts (1991); Cannibal Girls
Price, Barry (act): 12 Monkeys
Price, Bernard (act): The Hyena of London
Price, Bert (act): Quarantine
Price, Dan (wri): The Crawlers
Price, Daria (wri): Dawn of the Mummy; The Nesting
Price, David (F.) (dir): Children of the Corn II: The Final Sacrifice; Dr. Jekyll and Ms. Hyde; To Die For II: Son of Darkness
Price, David (F.) (wri): Dr. Jekyll and Ms. Hyde
Price, Dennis (act, 1915-1973, nee Dennistoun Franklyn John Rose-Price): Alice's Adventures In Wonderland (1972); The Bad Lord Byron; Curse of Simba; Dear Murderer; The Earth Dies Screaming; The Echo Murders; Fortune Is a Woman; The Frightened Bride; The Haunted House of Horror; A High Wind In Jamaica; Horror Hospital; Horror of Frankenstein; The Horror of It All; The House In the Square; A Jolly Bad Fellow; Kill or Cure; Kind Hearts and Coronets; The Magic Christian; Murder at 3 AM; Murder Most Foul; Murder Without Crime; Noose for a Lady; Paroxysmus; Piccadilly Third Stop; A Place of One's Own; Port Afrique; Pulp; Son of Dracula (1974); Ten Little Indians (1965); Theater of Blood; Those Fantastic Flying Fools; Time Is My Enemy; Tower of Evil; Twins of Evil; What a Carve Up!
Price, Dilys (act): Blue Blood
Price, Doug (act): Wild Thing
Price, Evadne (wri): Blondes for Danger; The Phantom Light; Silver Top; Wolf's Clothing (1936)
Price, George S. (mus): Guyana, Cult of the Damned
Price, Gertrude (act): The Grip of Iron
Price, Hal (act): The Devil Bat; The Lone Wolf Returns (1935)
Price, Harriet (act): Watchers II
Price, Herbert (wri): A Cottage On Dartmoor
Price, Ian (act): The Quatermass Conclusion
Price, Isabel (act): Unforgettable
Price, Jeffrey (wri): Who Framed Roger Rabbit
Price, Jim (act): To Die For II: Son of Darkness
Price, Joe (act): Attack of the Killer Tomatoes
Price, Karen (act): Swamp Thing
Price, Kenny L. (act): Doom Asylum
Price, Lindsay (act): Plymouth
Price, Lorin E. (act): Night of the Zombies (1981)
Price, Marc (act): Killer Tomatoes Eat France; Trick or Treat
Price, Mary (act): The Creeping Terror
Price, Nancy (act): Belphegor the Mountebank; Dead Man's Shoes; The Lyons Mail; The Speckled Band (1931); The Three Weird Sisters
Price, Noel (act): I Was a Zombie for the F.B.I.
Price, Peggy (act): The Pack
Price, Penny (act): Captain Kronos: Vampire Hunter
Price, Roger (act, b. 1920): The Cat from Outer Space
Price, Roland (cin): The Bride and the Beast; The Lost City
Price, Stanley (act): Cyclotrode X; Dick Tracy vs. Crime, Inc.; Slaves of the Invisible Monster
Price, Stanley (wri): I Don't Want to Be Born

Price, Sue (act): *Nemesis 2; Nemesis 3: Time Lapse*
Price, Therese (act): *To Die For II: Son of Darkness*
Price, Victoria (act): *Edward Scissorhands*
Price, Vincent (act, 1911-1993): *The Abominable Dr. Phibes; Adventures of Captain Fabian; Bagdad; The Baron of Arizona; The Bat (1959); Blood Bath at the House of Death; The Bribe; Casanova's Big Night; Champagne for Caesar; The City Under the Sea; The Comedy of Terrors; Confessions of an Opium Eater; Cry of the Banshee; Dangerous Mission; Dead Heat; Devil's Triangle; Diary of a Madman; Dr. Goldfoot and the Bikini Machine; Dr. Goldfoot and the Girl Bombs; Dr. Phibes Rises Again; Dragonwyck; Edward Scissorhands; Escapes; The Fly (1958); The Great Mouse Detective; Green Hell; The Haunted Palace (1963); House of 1,000 Dolls; House of the Long Shadows; The House of the Seven Gables; House of Usher (1960); House of Wax; House On Haunted Hill(1958); The Invisible Man Returns; It's Not the Size That Counts; Journey Into Fear (1975); The Last Man On Earth; Laura; Leave Her to Heaven; Madhouse; The Mad Magician; The Masque of the Red Death (1964); Master of the World; The Monster Club; Moss Rose; Naked Terror; Nefertite, Regina del Nilo; The Oblong Box; The Offspring; Once Upon a Midnight Scary; The Pit and the Pendulum (1961); Rage of the Buccaneers; The Raven (1963); Return of the Fly; Scream and Scream Again; Shock (1946); Son of Sinbad; The Story of Mankind; Taboos of the World; Tales of Terror; Theater of Blood; The Three Musketeers (1948); The Tingler; The Tomb of Ligeia; Tower of London (1939 & 1962); 2267 A.D.-When the Sleeper Wakes (unfinished); Twice-Told Tales; The Web; While the City Sleeps; Witch-Finder General*
Price, Walt(er) (act): *Beyond and Back; Sugar Hill*
Prichard, Hesketh (wri): *Don Q, Son of Zorro*
Prichard, Kate (wri): *Don Q, Son of Zorro*
Prichard, Robert (act): *Alien Space Avenger; Class of Nuke 'em High; The Toxic Avenger*
Prichard, Ted (act): *King Kong Lives*
Prickett, Maudie (act, 1913-1976): *The Gnome-Mobile; North by Northwest*
Prickett, Oliver (act): *Castle In the Desert*
Priddy, Nancy (act): *The Aliens Are Coming; Jaws of Satan*
Pride, Tad (cin): *Fortress*
Pridelle, Claire (act): *The Dead Heart; Diamond Cut Diamond; Faust (1911)*
Priest, Dan (act): *Moon of the Wolf; Rattlers*
Priest, Natalie (act, 1919-1987): *The Wrong Man*
Priest, Pat (act): *The Incredible 2-Headed Transplant; Some Call It Loving*
Priestley, J.B. (act, 1894-1984): *They Came to a City*
Priestley, J.B. (wri, 1894-1984): *An Inspector Calls; Jamaica Inn (1939); Last Holiday; The Old Dark House (1932 & 1963); They Came to a City*
Priestley, Jack (cin): *The First Deadly Sin; No Way to Treat a Lady*
Priestley, Jason (act): *Eye of the Beholder (1999); Watchers*
Priestley, Tom (cin): *Dr. Jekyll and Ms. Hyde; Lovestruck; Tales from the Crypt Presents Bordello of Blood*
Prieto, Antonio (act): *The Three Swords of Zorro*
Prieto, Aurore (act): *Docteur Petiot*
Prieto, Margot (act): *Faustina*
Prigunov, Lev (act): *The Saint*
Prikopsky, Jaro (act): *The Howling: New Moon Rising*
Prima, Louis (act): *The Jungle Book (1967)*
Primo (act): *Bad Moon*
Primus, Barry (act, b. 1938): *Autopsy; Spacecamp*
Prince the Wonder Dog (act): *Without a Clue*
Prince, Arthur (act): *Spiritualism Exposed (1926)*
Prince, Hansford (act): *Copycat*
Prince, Harold (dir, b. 1928): *Something for Everyone*
Prince, Jonathan (act): *Halloween II*
Prince, Jonathan (wri): *18 Again!*
prince, Karim (act): *National Lampoon's Men In White*
Prince, Michael (act): *The Haunted (1991); Midnight Lace (1981)*
Prince, Patrick (cin): *Scared to Death (1980)*
Prince, Robert/Bob (mus): *Charlie Chan: Happiness Is a Warm Clue; Gargoyles; Scream, Pretty Peggy; Squirm; The Strange and Deadly Occurrence*
Prince, Ron (act): *Amazons (1984)*
Prince, Taylor (act): *Empire of Ash III*
Prince, William (act, b. 1913): *Blade (1973); The Cat from Outer Space; City In Fear; Dead Reckoning; Family Plot; Macabre (1958); Secret of Treasure Mountain; Spontaneous Combustion; The Stepford Wives; Vice Versa (1988)*
Princi, Mark (wri): *Great White*
Principal, Victoria (act, b. 1945): *Beyond Obsession; Earthquake; Fantasy Island; The Naked Ape; Seduction: Three Tales from the 'Inner Sanctum'*
Prine, Andrew (act, b. 1936): *Amityville II: The Possession; Barn of the Naked Dead; Crypt of the Living Dead; The Dark Dancer; Demon and the Mummy; Eliminators; The Evil; Grizzly; Mind Over Murder; Night Slaves; Shadow Men; Simon, King of the Witches; The Town That Dreaded Sundown; V; Wonder Woman*
Prines, Mark (act): *Boarding House*
Pring, Gerald (act): *Dark Eyes of London*
Pringle, Aileen (act, 1895-1989, nee Aileen Bisbee): *Convicted; In the Palace of the King; Jane Eyre (1934); Murder at Midnight; The Mystic; The Phantom of Crestwood*
Pringle, Angela (act): *On a Clear Day You Can See Forever*
Pringle, Bryan (act): *Brazil; Haunted Honeymoon (1986); Jabberwocky; Snow White: A Tale of Terror; Vengeance*
Pringle, Byron (act): *Berserk*
Pringle, Joan (act): *Eyes of Terror; J.D.'s Revenge; Visions of Murder*
Prins, Kees (act): *The Lift*
Prinsloo, Sandra (act): *Claws*
Printz, John (act): *White Zombie*
Prinz, Isabel (act): *Slugs*
Prinze Jr., Freddie (act, b. 1976): *I Know What You Did Last Summer; I Still Know What You Did Last Summer; To Gillian on Her 37th Birthday; Wing Commander*
Prinzi, Frank (cin): *Night of the Living Dead (1990)*
Prinzi, Franz (cin): *Sleepwalk*
Prioli, Angelo (act): *Miracle In Milan*
Prior, Allan (wri): *King Solomon's Treasure*
Prior, Charles (act): *Dr. Caligari*
Prior, David A. (dir): *Bio-Force I; Final Sanction; Future Zone; The Lost Platoon; Mardi Gras for the Devil*
Prior, David A. (wri): *Bio-Force I; Final Sanction; Mardi Gras for the Devil; Raw Nerve*
Prior, Herbert (act): *The Man from Downing Street*
Prior, James (act): *To Let*
Prior, Matthew (act): *Circle of Deceit*
Prior, Stephen (act): *Time Flyer*
Prior, Ted (act): *Bio-Force I; Final Sanction; Future Zone; Possessed by the Night; Raw Nerve; Sledgehammer; Surf Nazis Must Die*
Priore, Hal (act): *Jack's Wife*
Prisco, Albert (act): *Monte Cristo*
Pritchard, Bonnie (act): *Time Chasers*
Pritchard, Hilary (act): *Haunted Palace (1949); The Vandergilt Diamond Mystery*
Pritchard, Josephine (act): *Change Partners*
Pritchard, Michael (act): *Ewoks: The Battle for Endor; Light Blast*
Pritchard, Stanton (act): *Revenge of the Virgins*
Pritchett, Paula (act): *Chappaqua*
Prival, Lucien (act): *Bride of Frankenstein; The Falcon's Alibi; In the Next Room; The Last of the Lone Wolf; Mr. Wong, Detective; Panama Menace; The Peacock Fan; The Sphinx (1933); The White Goddess*
Private Stock Effects Inc. (cin): *Strange Invaders*
Prizio, Diane (act): *The Horror of Party Beach*
Probyn, Brian (cin): *Frankenstein and the Monster from Hell; Innocent Bystanders; Inn of the Damned; The Jerusalem File; The Satanic Rites of Dracula; Straight On Till Morning*
Prochnau, William (wri): *By Dawn's Early Light*
Prochnow, Jurgen (act, b. 1941): *D.N.A.; Dune; In the Mouth of Madness; Judge Dredd; The Keep; Robin Hood (1991); The Seventh Sign; Terminus; Twin Peaks: Fire Walk With Me; Wing Commander*
Prociv, Dawn (act): *The Haunting of Sarah Hardy*
Proclemer, Anna (act): *A Quiet Place to Kill*
Procter, Maurice (wri): *The Diamond; Hell Is a City*
[illegible]
Proctor, Phil(ip) (act): *J-Men Forever!; Lobster Man from Mars; A Safe Place*
Prodromides, Jean (mus): *Et Mourir de Plaisir; Spirits of the Dead*
Profes, Anton (mus): *Embezzled Heaven*
Proft, Pat (act): *Modern Problems*
Proia, Gianni (dir): *World by Night No. 2*
Proietti, Biagio (wri): *The Black Cat (1980)*
Proietti, Luigi (act): *The Sex Machine; Who Is Killing the Great Chefs of Europe?*
Proietti, Stefano (act): *Amarcord*
Project Unlimited, Inc. (cin): *Around the World Under the Sea*
Prokhorova, Olga (act): *Project: Genesis*
Prokop, Paul (act): *The Velvet Vampire*
Prokop, Spencer (act): *RoboCop*
Pronto, Joe (act): *Garden of the Dead*
Pronzini, Bill (wri): *Tails You Live, Heads You're Dead*
Proom, Adele (act): *Killer Klowns from Outer Space*
Prophet, Melisa (act): *Looker; Time Walker*
Props, Babette (act): *Weird Science*
Proser, Chip (wri): *Iceman; Innerspace*
Prosky, John (act): *The Nutty Professor (1996)*
Prosky, Robert (act, b. 1930): *Christine; From the Dead of Night; Gremlins 2: The New Batch; The Keep; Miracle On 34th Street (1994); The Scarlet Letter (1995); World War III*
Prosperi, Federico (wri): *Curse II: The Bite*
Prosperi, Franco (wri): *Ercole al Centro della Terra; La Ragazza Che Sapeva Troppo*
Prosperi, Giorgio (wri): *Romolo e Remo*
Prosser, Don (act): *Just Imagine*
Protat, Francois (cin): *Brainscan; Johnny Mnemonic; The Kiss (1988); Tails You Live, Heads You're Dead; Tomorrow Never Comes*
Protazanov, Yakov/Jacob (dir, 1881-1945): *Aelita; Pikovaya Dama (1916)*
Protheroe, Brian (act): *Superman (1978)*
Proudlock, Roger (wri): *Panic at Madam Tussaud's*
Proudman, Dave (act): *Inn of the Damned*
Prouse, Peter (act): *The Man Who Fell to Earth (1976); Nightwing*
Prout, Victor (act): *Boundary House*
Prouty, Jed (act): *The Gracie Allen Murder Case; The Lone Wolf Keeps a Date*
Proval, David (act, b. 1943): *Innocent Blood; The Monster Squad; The Phantom (1996); The Relic; Romeo Is Bleeding; Vice Versa (1988); Wizards*
Provencher, Dylan (act): *Earthquake In New York*
Provine, Dorothy (act, b. 1937): *The Bonnie Parker Story; Kiss the Girls and Make Them Die; One Spy Too Many; The 30 Foot Bride of Candy Rock*
Provor, Frank (cin): *The Magic Voyage of Sinbad*
Provost, Jon (act, b. 1950): *The Computer Wore Tennis Shoes (1970)*
Provost, Keith (act): *Quarantine*
Provost, Richard (act): *Switch (1991)*
Prowse, Andrew (dir): *Demonstone*
Prowse, David/Dave (act): *Casino Royale; A Clockwork Orange; The Empire Strikes Back; Frankenstein and the Monster from Hell; Jabberwocky; The People That Time Forgot; Return of the Jedi; Star Wars; Vampire Circus*
Prowse, Juliet (act, 1936-1996): *Who Killed Teddy Bear?*
Proyas, Alex (dir): *The Crow (1994); Dark City*
Proyas, Alex (wri): *Dark City*
Pruce, Peter (wri): *Rasputin (1996)*
Prucnal, Anna (act): *La Citta delle Donne; Sweet Movie*
Pruett, Harold (act): *Precious Find; Spellcaster; Summer Camp Nightmare*
Pruett, Harrison (act): *The Nosferatu Diaries: Embrace of the Vampire*
Pruett, Winston (act): *Welcome to Arrow Beach*
Pruitt, James (act): *Always*
Prulhiere, Timi (act): *The Last Man On Planet Earth*
Pruna, Andy (act): *Mas Alla de la Aventura*
Prus, Boleslaw (wri): *Faraon*
Prussing, Louise (act): *The Woman In White (1929)*
Prutting, Stephen (act): *Not of This World*
Pryce, Craig (dir): *The Dark (1994); Revenge of the Radioactive Reporter*
Pryce, Edythe (wri): *Wednesday's Luck*
Pryce, Jonathan (act, b. 1947): *The Adventures of Baron Munchausen (1989); Brazil; Deadly Advice; The Doctor and the Devils; Freddie as F.R.O.7; Haunted Honeymoon (1986); Loophole; Murder Is Easy; Something Wicked This Way Comes; Tomorrow Never Dies; A Troll In Central Park*
Prymek, Jiri (act): *Valerie and Her Week of Wonders*
Pryor, Ainslie (act): *The Last Hunt*
Pryor, Christine (act): *The Adding Machine*
Pryor, Liz (act): *Gremlins 2: The New Batch*
Pryor, Maureen (act): *The Black Windmill; Life for Ruth; The Secret Place*
Pryor, Nicholas (act, b. 1935): *Amazons (1984); Brain Dead; Damien-Omen II; Dark Angel (1996); Love Can Be Murder; Man On a Swing; Pacific Heights; The Plutonium Incident; Sliver*
Pryor, Richard (act, b. 1940): *The Busy Body; The Muppet Movie; Some Call It Loving; Superman III; Wild In the Streets; The Wiz*
Pryor, Roger (act, 1902-1974): *Identity Unknown; The Lone Wolf Meets a Lady; The Man They Could Not Hang; The Man With Nine Lives; Panama Menace*
Pryse, Hugh (act): *Dark Secret; Port of Escape; Three Cases of Murder*
Pryssir, Geof (wri): *The Magic Bubble*
Pryzbylski, Frank (act): *Midnight (1980)*
Ptushko, Alexander (dir): *Ilya Mourometz; Novyi Gulliver*
Ptushko, Alexander (wri): *Novyi Gulliver*
Pucci, Robert (wri): *The Spider and the Fly (1994)*
Puccio, Nicholas A. (act): *Shadow Conspiracy*
Pudney, Alan (cin): *Double Exposure (1977); Slaughter High*
Pudney, John (wri): *The Net*
Pudovkin, Vsevolod (act, 1893-1953): *Luch Smerti*
Pudovkin, Vsevolod (dir, 1893-1953): *Mekhanikha Golovnovo Mozga*
Pudovkin, Vsevolod (wri, 1893-1953): *Luch Smerti; Mekhanikha Golovnovo Mozga*
Puente, Jesus (act): *Behind the Mask of Zorro; The Cobra; Ellay el Miedo; Hatchet for a Honeymoon; Marta*
Puerto, Carlos (wri): *Where Time Began; Viaje al Centro de la Tierra*
Puffy, Charles (act): *The Man Who Laughs (1928); Mockery; The Private Life of Helen of Troy*
Pugeat, Jack (act): *The Last of Sheila*
Pugh, Carmel (act): *Street Trash*
Pugh, David (act): *Burke and Hare*
Pugh, Rhys (act): *Zarkorr! The Invader*
Pugh, Robert (act): *Inseminoid*
Pugh, Willard (act): *The Guyver; The Hills Have Eyes II; Puppet Master 5; RoboCop 2*
Pughe, George (act): *East of Piccadilly; False Evidence; The Limping Man (1936)*
Pugilese, Al (act): *Philadelphia Experiment II*
Pugin, Bill (act): *Congo*
Puglia, Frank (act, 1892-1975): *Ali Baba and the Forty Thieves (1943); Bagdad; The Bandits of Corsica; Bulldog Drummond's Revenge; Casanova's Big Night; Charlie Chan In City In Darkness; Charlie Chan In Panama; The Fatal Hour (1940); The Jungle Book (1942); The Lost Moment; The Man Who Laughs (1928); Phantom of the Opera (1943); Secret Agent of Japan; The Sword of Ali Baba; Tarzan's Desert Mystery; 20 Million Miles to Earth*
Pugliese, Al (act): *The Annihilator*
Pugsley, Don(ald) (act): *Watchers II; When the Bough Breaks*
Pugsley, William (wri): *Dracula vs. Frankenstein*
Pulaski, Frank (act): *The Saracen Blade*
Pulci, Antonio (act): *Manhattan Baby*
Pulieri, Giuseppe (wri): *Deborah*
Pulliam, Keshia Knight (act, b. 1979): *A Connecticut Yankee In King Arthur's Court (1989); The Little Match Girl (1987)*
Pulling, Norah (wri): *One Wish Too Many*
Pullman, Bill (act): *Brain Dead; Casper; Independence Day; Malice; The Serpent and the Rainbow; Spaceballs*
Pully, B.S. (act): *Myra Breckinridge*
Pullman, Jack (wri): *The Executioner; Jane Eyre (1970); Kiss the Girls and Make Them Die*
Pulone, Gianni (act): *Demons of the Dead*
Punay, Rito (act): *Dangerous Money*
Punt, Shane (act): *The Clan of the Cave Bear*
Punzalan, Bruno (act): *Beast of Blood; Moro Witch Doctor; The Omegans; Wonder Women*
Punzo, Patrizia (act): *Rorret*
Pupa, Piccola (act): *The Ghost In the Invisible Bikini*
Pupillo, Massimo (dir): *Il Boia Scarlatto*
Puppo, Romano (act): *Escape from the Bronx; The Great Alligator*
Purcell, Dick (act, 1908-1944): *King of the Zombies; Mystery House; The Mystery of the 13th Guest; Nancy Drew, Detective; The Phantom Killer*
Purcell, [illegible] *Murder Ring; The Invisible Woman (1941)*
Purcell, Lee (act, b. 1947): *The Incredible Hulk Returns; Necromancy; Space Rage; Stranger In Our House*

Purcell, Noel (act, b. 1900): *The Crimson Pirate; Grand National Night; The Key; Mad About Men; Man In the Moon (1960); Moby Dick (1956); The Running Man (1963); Sinful Davey; Svengali (1954)*
Purcell, Robert (act): *Mark of the Gorilla*
Purcell, Roy (act): *The Deadly Females; Paris Express*
Purchase, Bruce (act): *Macbeth (1971); The Quatermass Conclusion; The Zany Adventures of Robin Hood*
Purcil, Karen (act): *Bad Ronald*
Purdee, Nathan (act): *Fire and Ice*
Purdell, Reginald (act): *Busman's Honeymoon; Candles at Nine; Crime On the Hill; The Dark Stairway; A Man About the House; The Missing People; A Night In Montmartre; Q Planes*
Purdell, Reginald (wri): *The Dark Tower (1943)*
Purdie, Robert (act): *Jane Shore (1915)*
Purdom, Edmund (act, b. 1926): *After the Fall of New York; Ator: The Fighting Eagle; El Castello dell'Orrore; Don't Open Till Christmas; Endless Descent; Fury of the Pagans; Last of the Vikings; The Man Who Laughs (1965); Moment of Danger; Nefertite, Regina del Nilo; Nights of Rasputin; Pieces; Strange Intruder*
Purdom, Edmund (dir, b. 1926): *Don't Open Till Christmas*
Purdom, Tita (act): *Jane Eyre (1957)*
Purdy-Gordon, Carolyn (act): *Dolls; Fortress; From Beyond; Re-Animator*
Purgason, Howard (act): *The Slumber Party Massacre*
Puri, Amrish (act): *Indiana Jones and the Temple of Doom*
Puri, Carlo (act): *The Count of Monte Cristo (1975)*
Puri, Jill (act): *Mighty Joe Young (1998)*
Puri, Om (act): *The Ghost and the Darkness; Wolf*
Purl, Linda (act, b. 1955): *Dark Mansions; In Self Defense; Visiting Hours; Web of Deceit*
Purrer, Ursula (act & dir): *Flaming Ears*
Purry, Lester (act): *Trauma (1993)*
Pursall, David (wri): *The Alphabet Murders; Kill or Cure; Murder Ahoy; Murder Most Foul; Murder She Said; The Secret Partner; The Southern Star; Tomorrow Never Comes*
Purvis, Jack (act): *The Adventures of Baron Munchausen (1989); Brazil; The Empire Strikes Back; Return of the Jedi; Star Wars; Time Bandits; Wombling Free*
Purwin, Alan (act): *Outbreak*
Puryear, Tony (wri): *Eraser*
Pusey, Arthur (act): *The Barton Mystery (1920); Moonbeam Magic; The Other Person; The Silent House*
Pushkin, Aleksander Sergeevich (wri, 1799-1837): *Morozko; Pikovaya Dama (1910 & 1916); The Queen of Spades (1937, 1948, 1960 & 1966)*
Pushman, Terrence (act): *Young Frankenstein*
Pustil, Jeff (act): *Def Con 4; Tails You Live, Heads You're Dead*
Putch, John (act): *Appointment for a Killing; Curfew; Jaws 3-D; Something Is Out There; Star Trek: Generations*
Puteska, Rudy (act): *It Came from Beneath the Sea*
Puthili, Asha (act): *Savages*
Putnam, Jock (act): *The Crawling Hand*
Putnam, Nina Wilcox (wri): *The Mummy (1932)*
Putt, Robert (act): *Hawk the Slayer; Treasure Island (1990)*
Puttnam, Alexander (act): *Sredni Vashtar*
Puttnam, Patsy (act): *The Pied Piper (1971)*
Puvanai, Nat (act): *Crocodile*
Puzo, Mario (wri, b. 1920): *Earthquake; Superman (1978); Superman II*
Puzynski, Wojciech (act): *Wielka, Wielka I Najwieksza*
Pyke, Hy (act): *Halloween Night; Nightmare In Blood; Spawn of the Slithis*
Pyke, Monty (act): *Lemora, the Lady Dracula*
Pylant, Ira (act): *I Was a Zombie for the F.B.I.*
Pyle, Denver (act, 1920-1997): *Escape to Witch Mountain (1975); The Flying Saucer (1950); Mara of the Wilderness; Please Murder Me; Return from Witch Mountain; Terrified (1963); Who Fears the Devil?*
Pyle, Howard (wri): *The Black Shield of Falworth*
Pym, Walter (act): *Patrick; Thirst*
Pyne, Daniel (wri): *Pacific Heights*
Pyne, Joe (act): *Mother Goose A Go-Go*
Pyne, Natasha (act): *The Devil-Ship Pirates; Madhouse; One of Our Dinosaurs Is Missing; Who Killed the Cat?*
Pyott, Keith (act): *Beautiful Stranger; I Accuse (1958); Masquerade; The Pirates of Blood River; The Village of the Damned (1960)*
Pyper-Ferguson, John (act): *The Warlord: Battle for the Galaxy*
Pytka, Joe (dir): *Space Jam*
Pyun, Albert (F.) (dir, b. 1956): *Alien from L.A.; Arcade; Brain Smasher...A Love Story; Captain America (1992); Cyborg (1989); Deceit (1993); Dollman; Heatseeker; Knights; Nemesis; Nemesis 3: Time Lapse; Radioactive Dreams; The Sword and the Sorcerer*
Pyun, Albert (F.) (wri, b. 1956): *Alien from L.A.; Knights; Nemesis 3: Time Lapse; Radioactive Dreams; The Sword and the Sorcerer*

Qing, Xu (act): *Life On a String*
Quabius, Faith (act): *Soylent Green*
Quackenboss, Bab (act): *I Was a Zombie for the F.B.I.*
Quackenbush, Larry (act): *Mutant; Scalpel*
Quade, John (act): *And You Thought Your Parents Were Weird; Planet Earth*
Quadflieg, Will (act): *Faust (1963); Lola Montes*
Quadros, Stephen (act): *Auntie Lee's Meat Pies; Dr. Caligari; Shock 'em Dead*
Quaglia, Pier Ana (act): *La Maldicion de los Karnsteins*
Quaid, David (L.) (cin): *Gold of the Amazon Women; Pretty Poison (1968); Santa Claus Conquers the Martians; The Swimmer*
Quaid, Dennis (act, b. 1954): *Are You In the House Alone?; Caveman (1981); D.O.A. (1988); Dragonheart; Dreamscape; Innerspace; Jaws 3-D; Wilder Napalm*
Quaid, Randy (act, b. 1953): *Frankenstein (1993); Freaked; Heartbeeps; Independence Day; Last Rites (1998); Martians Go Home; Of Mice and Men (1981); Parents; Purgatory; Targets; The Wraith*
Qualen, John (act, b. 1908, nee John Oleson): *All That Money Can Buy; Arabian Nights (1942); Captain Kidd; Charlie Chan In Paris; Dark Waters; The Fugitive (1947); Hans Christian Andersen; The Jungle Book (1942); Meet Nero Wolfe; Out of the Fog (1941); 7 Faces of Dr. Lao; Song of Scheherazade; Terror In the Haunted House*
Qualls, John (act): *Attack of the Killer Tomatoes*
Qualtinger, Helmut (act): *The Name of the Rose; Das Schloss*
Quan, Donald (mus): *The Cyber-Stalking*
Quan, Ke Huy (act): *The Goonies; Indiana Jones and the Temple of Doom*
Quandour, Mohy (dir & wri): *The Spectre of Edgar Allan Poe*
Quaranta, Lidia (act): *Cabiria*
Quarmby, John (act): *Arthur the King; A Christmas Carol (1984)*
Quarrier, Iain (act): *Cul-de-Sac; The Fearless Vampire Killers or: Pardon Me, But Your Teeth Are In My Neck; One Plus One; Separation*
Quarry, Robert (act): *Agent for H.A.R.M.; Alienator; Count Yorga, Vampire; Cyclone; The Deathmaster; Dr. Phibes Rises Again; Evil Spirits; Haunting Fear; Madhouse; The Phantom Empire; The Return of Count Yorga; Sugar Hill; Teenage Exorcist; Warlords*
Quarshie, Hugh (act): *Baby: Secret of the Lost Legend; The Church; Highlander; Nightbreed*
Quartararo, Gaetano (act): *Satanik; Il Trionfo di Ercole*
Quartermaine, Charles (act): *The Bishop Murder Case; The Face at the Window (1920); The Thirteenth Chair (1929)*
Quartermaine, Leon (act): *Dark World*
Quasimodo, Maria (Cumari) (act): *Demons of the Dead; Pulp; She (1983)*
Quatermass, Martin (wri): *Prince of Darkness*
Quatro, Michael (mus): *The Child*
Quattrini, Marisa (act): *L'Ultima Preda del Vampiro*
Quayle, Anna (act, b. 1937): *Casino Royale; Chitty Chitty Bang Bang; The Seven-Per-Cent Solution*
Quayle, (Sir) Anthony (act, 1913-1989): *Dial M for Murder (1981); Great Expectations (1974); Hamlet (1948); Holocaust 2000; Mackenna's Gold; The Man Who Wouldn't Talk; Murder by Decree; Operation Crossbow; A Study In Terror; Tarzan's Greatest Adventure;The Wrong Man*
Quayle, Jerry (act): *File It Under Fear*
Queant, Gilles (act): *L'Annee Derniere a Marienbad*
Quedens, Eunice (act): see Arden, Eve
Queen (mus): *Highlander*
Queen Kong (act): *Deathstalker II: Duel of the Titans*
Queen, Elizabeth (act): *Tomb of Torture*
Queen, Ellery (wri): *Close Call for Ellery Queen; Desperate Chance for Ellery Queen; Ellery Queen; Ellery Queen and the Murder Ring; Ellery Queen and the Perfect Crime; Ellery Queen: Don't Look Behind You; Ellery Queen, Master Detective; Ellery Queen's Penthouse Mystery; Enemy Agents Meet Ellery Queen; The Mandarin Mystery; The Spanish Cape Mystery; A Study In Terror*
Queen, Ron (act): *Nail Gun Massacre*
Queenan, D.J. (act): *Raiders of the Living Dead*
Queeney, Jerry (act): *Tarzan In Manhattan*
Quenet, Yvonne (act): *Secrets of Sex*
Quennell, Peter (wri): *The Bad Lord Byron*
Quentin, John (act): *King Solomon's Treasure*
Quentin, Patrick (wri): *Black Widow (1954); The Strange Awakening*
Quentin, Shirley (act): *The Temptress (1949)*
Quesada, Milo (act): *Cauldron of Blood; La Decima Vittima; La Ragazza Che Sapeva Troppo*
Quest, Ginger (act): *Vegas In Space*
Queste, John (dir): *Loophole*
Questel, Mae (act, 1908-1998): *It's Only Money; Who Framed Roger Rabbit*
Questi, Giulio (dir): *Plucked*
Queyant, Gilles (act): *Night Without Stars*
Quezada, Jose Elias Moreno y Cesareo (act): *Santa Claus (1959); Survive!*
Quezada, Roberto (cin): *The Unseen (1981)*
Quibell, Linda (act): *The Clan of the Cave Bear*
Quick, Diana (act): *The Big Sleep (1978); Nostradamus; Ordeal by Innocence; Phantom of the Opera (1983)*
Quick, Eldon (act): *Doc Savage, the Man of Bronze*
Quick, Karen (act): *House of Whipcord*
Quigley (act): *976-EVIL*
Quigley, Charles (act): *Charlie Chan's Secret; Cyclotrode X; Larceny In Her Heart;The Saint In Palm Springs; Three On a Ticket*
Quigley, Don (act): *The Purple Rose of Cairo*
Quigley, Gerry (act): *Millennium; Trilogy of Terror II*
Quigley, Godfrey (act, 1923-1994): *A Clockwork Orange; Daleks' Invasion Earth 2150 A.D.; Dead Man's Evidence*
Quigley, Jane (act): see Alexander, Jane
Quigley, Juanita (act): *Devil Doll (1936); The Man Who Reclaimed His Head*
Quigley, Lee (act): *Superman (1978)*
Quigley, Linnea (act): *Creepozoids; Dr. Alien; Graduation Day; The Guyver; Hollywood Chainsaw Hookers; Jack-O; Nightmare Sisters; Night of the Demons; Pumpkinhead II: Blood Wings; Sorority Babes In the Slimeball Bowl-O-Rama;Witchtrap*
Quigley, May (act): *Gremlins 2: The New Batch; Repossessed*
Quigley, Rita (act): *The Trap*
Quijada, Alfonso (act): *Timecop*
Quill, Michael (act): *The Warlord: Battle for the Galaxy*
Quill, Timothy Patrick (act): *Army of Darkness*
Quillan, Eddie (act, 1907-1990): *The Darker Side of Terror; Dark Streets of Cairo; The Ghost and Mr. Chicken; Kid Glove Killer; The Mandarin Mystery; The Strongest Man In the World*
Quilley, Denis (act): *The Black Windmill; Evil Under the Sun; Murder On the Orient Express; Where the Spies Are*
Quilligan, Veronica (act): *Liszt O' Mania; Robin and Marian*
Quilter, David (act): *The Secret Life of Ian Fleming*
Quilter, Robert (act): *Inn of the Damned*
Quimby, Steve (act): *Steps from Hell*
Quin, John (wri): *Shadow of Death (1939)*
Quine, Richard (act, 1920-1989): *The Clay Pigeon*
Quine, Richard (dir, 1920-1989): *Bell, Book and Candle; Oh Dad Poor Dad, Mamma's Hung You In the Closet and I'm Feelin' So Sad; Paris When It Sizzles; The Prisoner of Zenda (1979); Siren of Bagdad; W*
Quine, Tom (act): *How to Stuff a Wild Bikini*
Quinlan, Ed (act): *Fright Night II; Maid to Order*
Quinlan, Jim (wri): *Michael*
Quinlan, Joe (cin): *Metalstorm: The Destruction of Jared-Syn*
Quinlan, Kathleen (act, b. 1954): *Apollo 13; Blackout (1985); Event Horizon; Nightmare In Blood; Perfect Alibi; Strays; Twilight Zone; Warning Sign; Where Have All the People Gone?; Wild Thing*
Quinlan, Richard (cin): *Buried Secrets*
Quinlan, Siobhan (act): *In the Devil's Garden*
Quinlivan, Joe (cin): *Beyond Evil; Schizoid (1980)*
Quinn, Aidan (act, b. 1959): *Blink; Crusoe; The Handmaid's Tale; Haunted (1996); In Dreams; Mary Shelley's 'Frankenstein'; Practical Magic*
Quinn, Aileen (act): *The Frog Prince (1988)*
Quinn, Alberta (act): *Secrets of the Phantom Caverns*
Quinn, Annette (act): *Switch (1991)*
Quinn, Anthony (act, b. 1915): *Angels of Darkness; The Black Swan; Bulldog Drummond In Africa; City Beneath the Sea (1952); Daughter of Shanghai; East of Sumatra; The Ghost Breakers; Ghosts Can't Do It; A High Wind In Jamaica; The Hunchback of Notre Dame (1957); The Island of Lost Men; The Long Wait; The Magus; Mask of the Avenger; Portrait In Black; Sinbad the Sailor; Television Spy; Ulysses*
Quinn, Barbara (act): *The Clairvoyant (1985); He Knows You're Alone; Squirm*
Quinn, Bill (act): *Dark Intruder; Dark Mirror (1984); Dead and Buried; Dead Men Tell No Tales (1971); The Magician (1973); Satan's School for Girls; Star Trek V: The Final Frontier; Twilight Zone*
Quinn, Brendan (act): *Never-Never Land*
Quinn, Brian (cin): *Class of Nuke 'em High*
Quinn, Catherine (act): *Nothing But Trouble*
Quinn, Daniel (act): *Scanner Cop; Scanners: The Showdown*
Quinn, Declan (cin): *Freddy's Dead: The Final Nightmare; The Kill-Off*
Quinn, Dermot (wri): *Golden Ivory*
Quinn, Derry (wri): *Operation Crossbow; Rag Doll; The Trygon Factor*
Quinn, Duncan (act): *Echoes*
Quinn, Francesco (act): *The Dark Dancer; Dead Certain*
Quinn, Glenn (act): *Dr. Giggles*
Quinn, J.C. (act): *The Abyss; All-American Murder; Buried Alive II; Maximum Overdrive; Megaville; The Prophecy (1995); Twisted*
Quinn, James W. (act): *Witchboard; Witchtrap*
Quinn, Jeanette (act): *The Neanderthal Man*
Quinn, Joe (act): *Pretty Maids All In a Row*
Quinn, John (dir): *Cheerleader Camp*
Quinn, Louis (act, 1915-1988): *Birds Do It*
Quinn, Martha (act): *Bad Channels; Chopper Chicks In Zombietown*
Quinn, Michael (act): *Return of the Jedi*
Quinn, Millie (act): *Getting Lucky*
Quinn, Patricia (act): *Hawk the Slayer; The Rocky Horror Picture Show; Shock Treatment! (1981); Witching Time/ The Silent Scream*
Quinn, Tandra (act): *Mesa of Lost Women*
Quinn, Teddy (act): *Necromancy*
Quinn, Theresa (act): *Secrets of the Phantom Caverns*
Quinn, Tom (act): *Shadow Conspiracy*
Quinn, Tony (act): *Booby Trap; The Great Van Robbery; The Man Without a Body; The Saint Meets the Tiger; Shadow of a Man; The Trunk; Undercover Girl (1958)*
Quintana, Elvira (act): *The Curse of the Doll People*
Quintano, Gene (wri): *Allan Quatermain and the Lost City of Gold; King Solomon's Mines (1985); Treasure of the Four Crowns*
Quintavalle, Umberto P. (act): *Salo, o le Centoventi Giornate di Sodoma*
Quinten, Christopher (act): *RoboCop 2*
Quintero, Joe (act): *Jacob's Ladder*
Quinteros, Lorenzo (act): *Man Facing Southeast*
Quinton, Everett (act): *Hello Again*
Quiria, Virginia (act): *To All a Goodnight*
Quirk, Kathy (act): *Trauma (1993)*
Quiroga, Maria Casares (act): see Casares, Maria
Quiroga, Nelida (act): *Marta*
Quiroule, Pierre (wri): *Sexton Blake and the Hooded Terror*
Quitak, Oscar (act): *The Accursed; Blood Bath at the House of Death; Brazil; The Revenge of Frankenstein*
Quitero, M. (mus): *La Corona Negra*
Quivers, Robin (act): *Deadly Web*
Quon, J.B. (act): *Not of This World*
Quon, Marianne (act): *Charlie Chan In the Secret Service*

Raab, Gilles (act): *Perceval*
Raabjerg, Birgitte (act): *The Kingdom*
Raaen, John (act): *The Punisher*
Raaf, Vici (act): *Champagne for Caesar*
Raaj, Jagdish (act): *Tarzan Goes to India*
Raasch, Amy (act): *Hellmaster*

Rabal, Francisco (act, b. 1925): Belle de Jour; City of the Walking Dead; Exorcism's Daughter; The Tempter (1973); Viridiana
Rabal, Teresa (act): Viridiana
Rabasa, Ruben (act): The Unholy
Rabb, Joel (act): Vampire On Bikini Beach
Rabbett, Martin (act): Allan Quatermain and the Lost City of Gold
Rabe, Florence (act): see Bates, Florence
Rabella, Francesc (act): Anguish
Rabenalt, Arthur Maria (dir): Alraune (1952)
Rabett, Catherine (act): Roger Corman's Frankenstein Unbound
Rabey, Brian (act): Alien High
Rabier, Jean (cin, b. 1927): Banana Peel; Blood Relatives; Le Boucher; Les Parapluies de Cherbourg; La Rupture; Le Scandale
Rabiere, Richard (act): Happy Birthday to Me
Rabin, Jack (cin): Back from the Dead; The Beast of Hollow Mountain; Behemoth, the Sea Monster; Cat-Women of the Moon; Daughter of Dr. Jekyll; Death Race 2000; Flight to Mars; Invasion U.S.A.; The Neanderthal Man; The Night of the Hunter (1955); Pharaoh's Curse; Port Sinister; Queen of Outer Space; Rocketship X-M; The Unknown Terror; Unknown World; The Viking Women and the Sea Serpent; World Without End
Rabin, Jack (wri): Cat-Women of the Moon
Rabin, Trevor (mus): Armageddon
Rabinowitsh, Stuart (mus): The Video Dead
Rabinowitz, Harry (act): Electric Dreams
Rabito, Diana (act): Hipnosis
Racca, Claudio (cin): Deborah
Racette, Francine (act): The Disappearance; Quatro Mosche di Velluto Gris
Rachell, Carol (act): Popdown
Rachins, Alan (act): Heart Condition; Star Quest (1994); The Stepsister; Time Walker
Rachtman, Karyn (mus): Timecop
Racimo, Voctoria (act): The Day of the Dolphin; Prophecy (1979); Search for the Gods
Racine, Christian (cin): Alien High
Racine, Diane (act): Spellbinder
Racine, Roger (cin): Seizure; Zombie Nightmare
Racini, Peter (act): The Toxic Avenger
Rack, Tom (act): Secret Weapons; Wild Thing
Rackin, Martin (wri, 1918-1976): Long John Silver
Rackley, Luther (act): The Last Dinosaur
Rackman, Steve (act): Escape 2000; Howling III
Rad, Youri (act): Zombies Lake
Radburn, Veronica (act): The Ghastly Ones
Radcliffe, Karen (act): D.O.A. (1988); RoboCop; When the Bough Breaks
Radcliffe, Violet (act): Aladdin and His Wonderful Lamp
Radd, Ronald (act, 1929-1976): The Camp On Blood Island; The Kremlin Letter; Murder In Mind; The Offence; The Spiral Staircase (1975); Where the Spies Are
Raddatz, Carl (act): Das Madchen Rosemarie
Rademaker, Claudia (act): Lady Terminator
Rademakers, Fons (act, b. 1920): Daughters of Darkness
Rademakers, Fons (dir, b. 1920): Because of the Cats
Rader, Jack (act): Gray Lady Down; Outbreak
Rader, Peter (dir): Escape to Witch Mountain (1995); Grandma's House
Rader, Peter (wri): Escape to Witch Mountain (1995); Waterworld
Radford, Basil (act, 1897-1952): Dead of Night (1945); Gestapo; The Girl In the News; Jamaica Inn (1939); The Lady Vanishes (1938); Stop Press Girl; Young and Innocent
Radford, Lynne (act): 1984 (1984)
Radford, Michael (dir & wri): 1984 (1984)
Radford, Natalie (act): The Android Affair; Tomcat: Dangerous Desires
Radin, Oscar (mus): Mad Love
Raditschnig, Herbert (cin): The Outing
Radlauer, Dan (mus): Phoenix the Warrior
Radley, Frederick (act): The Quatermass Conclusion
Radner, Gilda (act, 1946-1989): Haunted Honeymoon (1986)
Radnitz, Robert (wri): Wink of an Eye
Rado, Ivan J. (act): Fugitive from the Empire; Puppet Master II; Subspecies
Radom, John (act): Mother's Day
Radomski, Eric (dir): Batman: Mask of the Phantasm
Radzikowska, E. (act): Wielka, Wielka I Najwieksza
Radzins, Elza (act): Korol Lir
Rae, Cassidy (act): [illegible]
Rae, Charlotte (act, b. 1926): The Worst Witch
Rae, Icilma (act): Fatal Fingers
Rae, James (act): Zombie Nightmare
Rae, Jere Lea (act): The Eliminator
Rae, John (act): Baffled!; The Big Chance; Fahrenheit 451; Fragment of Fear; Quatermass II
Rae, Katrina (act): Romeo Is Bleeding
Rae, Michael (dir): Laserblast
Rae, Stephen (act): Color Him Dead
Rae, Ted (act): Night of the Creeps
Rae, Ted (cin): Night of the Comet
Raebeck, Wendy (act): Shock Treatment! (1981)
Rafat, Ismat (act): Sphinx (1981)
Rafelson, Bob (dir, b. 1935): Black Widow (1987)
Raff, Karen (act): Killer Klowns from Outer Space
Raffanini, Piccio (dir): Obsession: A Taste for Fear
Raffael, Erika (act): The Big Switch; Man of Violence
Rafferty, Chips (act, 1909-1971, nee John Goffage): Skullduggery
Rafferty, Frances (act, b. 1922): The Hidden Eye; Lady at Midnight; Money Madness
Rafferty, Jean (act): I Lunghi Capelli della Morte
Rafferty, Kevin (dir): The Atomic Cafe
Rafferty, Pierce (dir): The Atomic Cafe
Rafferty, Wendell (act): Sling Blade
Raffill, Stewart (dir): The Ice Pirates; Mac and Me; Mannequin Two: On the Move; The Philadelphia Experiment; Tammy and the T-Rex
Raffill, Stewart (wri): The Ice Pirates; Mac and Me; Tammy and the T-Rex
Raffin, Deborah (act, b. 1953): Dance of the Dwarfs; Demon (1976); Last Video and Testament; Mind Over Murder; Scanners II: The New Order; The Sentinel; Sparkling Cyanide
Raffles (animal act): The Barefoot Executive
Raffo, John (wri): The Relic
Rafols, Mingo (act): Anguish
Raft, George (act, 1895-1980): Around the World In 80 Days; Background to Danger; Black Widow (1954); Casino Royale; Five Golden Dragons; Hammersmith Is Out; Intrigue; I'll Get You; Jet Over the Atlantic; Nocturne
Ragalyi, Elemer (cin): The Hunchback (1997); A Kid In King Arthur's Court; A Knight In Camelot; Ms. Scrooge; Never Talk to Strangers; The Phantom of the Opera (1989); Trilogy of Terror II
Ragan, Jim (act): The Cremators
Ragan, Mike (act): The Claw Monsters
Ragaway, Connie Hunter (act): Something Evil
Raghaven, G. (act): Tarzan Goes to India
Raghet, Ozzie (act): El Castello dell'Orrore
Ragin, Dave (cin): Behind That Curtain
Ragin, John S. (act): Earthquake
Raglan, James (act): Celia; Dick Barton Strikes Back; The Last Hour; Red Aces; Whispering Smith Hits London
Raglan, Robert (act): The Big Chance; Catch Me a Spy; The Child and the Killer; Child's Play (1954); The Haunted House of Horror; Hidden Homicide; High Jump; Information Received; Innocent Meeting; No Safety Ahead; Prehistoric Women (1966); Subterfuge; 23 Paces to Baker Street; Web of Suspicion; Where the Spies Are; A Woman's Temptation
Ragland, Rags (act, 1905-1946): The Canterville Ghost (1944)
Ragland, Robert O. (mus): Brainwaves; The Fear (1994); Grizzly; Mansion of the Doomed; Q; Shadow of Death (1983); The Supernaturals; The Thing With Two Heads
Ragno, Joseph (act): Daylight
Ragozzini, Ed (dir): Sasquatch, the Legend of Bigfoot
Ragsdale, Emily Y. (act): The Gifted One
Ragsdale, Tex (wri): Moontrap
Ragsdale, William (act): Frankenstein: The College Years; Fright Night; Fright Night II; Mannequin Two: On the Move
Ragusa, Angelo (act): The Barbarians (1987)
Ragusa, Paula (act): see Prentiss, Paula
Rahl, Mady (act): The White Spider
Rahlmann, Reed Kirk (act): Howard the Duck
Raho, (H)umi (act): Gli Orrori del Castello di Noremberga; Satanik
Raho, Umberto (act): Aladdin (1987); The Night Evelyn Came Out of the Grave; The Secret of Seagull Island; Lo Spettro; L'Uccello delle Piume di Cristallo
Raia, Cali (act): Invasion (1965)
Raider-Wexler, Victor (act): Netforce
Raiford, Robert (act): The Handmaid's Tale
Raikes, Robert (act): Alibi Rendered; Links of Justice; Quatermass II
Railsback, Steve (act, b. 1948): Alligator II: The Mutation; Barb Wire; Blue Monkey; Deadly Intent; Distortions; The Eliminators; Escape 2000 (1983); Forever; Lifeforce; Nukie; Scissors; Sunstroke; Trick or Treats
Railton, John (act): Hamlet (1969)
Raimbourg, Andre (act): see Bourvil
Raimbourg, Lucien (act): The Devil's Nightmare
Raimi, Ivan (act): Army of Darkness
Raimi, Ivan (wri): Army of Darkness; Darkman (1990)
Raimi, Sam (act, b. 1959): Body Bags; The Flintstones; Galaxis
Raimi, Sam (dir, b. 1959): Army of Darkness; Darkman (1990); The Evil Dead; Evil Dead 2: Dead by Dawn; Mantis
Raimi, Sam (wri, b. 1959): Army of Darkness; Darkman (1990); Darkman II: The Return of Durant; The Evil Dead; Evil Dead 2: Dead by Dawn
Raimi, Sonia (act): Tuck Everlasting
Raimi, Theodore (act): Army of Darkness; Darkman (1990); Evil Dead 2: Dead by Dawn; Shocker
Raimu (act, 1883-1946, nee Jules Muraire): Les Inconnus dans la Maison
Rain, Douglas (act): Oedipus Rex (1956); 2001: A Space Odyssey; 2010
Rain, Jeramie (act): The Last House On the Left
Rainbow, Joaquin (act): Wolfen
Raine, Jack (act, 1896-1979): The Clairvoyant (1934); Dangerous Ground; The Ghoul (1933); Just William's Luck; The October Man
Raine, Marcel (act): Forces Occultes
Raine, Norman Reilly (act, 1895-1971): Captain Kidd
Raine, Norman Reilly (wri, 1895-1971): The Adventures of Robin Hood; M (1950)
Raine, Patricia (act): It Happened In Soho; Pandora and the Flying Dutchman; Vice Versa (1947)
Rainer, John (act): Blue Blood
Raines, Cristina (act, b. 1953): Nightmares (1983); The Sentinel
Raines, Ella (act, 1921-1988, nee Ella Wallace Rains Old): Enter Arsene Lupin; The Man In the Road; Phantom Lady; The Suspect; The Web
Raines, Frances (act): Breeders; The Mutilator (1985)
Rainey, Ford (act): The Cellar (1989); Halloween II; A Howling In the Woods; The Naked Zoo; Strange New World
Rainey, Jamie (act): Clarence
Rainger, Ralph (mus): International House
Rainier, Patricia (act): Cocoon: The Return
Rains, Claude (act, 1889-1967): The Adventures of Robin Hood; Angel On My Shoulder (1946); The Clairvoyant (1934); Here Comes Mr. Jordan; The Invisible Man (1933); The Lost World (1960); The Man Who Reclaimed His Head; The Mystery of Edwin Drood (1935); Notorious (1946); Paris Express; Phantom of the Opera (1943); Il Planeta degli Uomini Spenti; The Unsuspected;Where Danger Lives; The Wolf Man (1941)
Rains, Fred (act): Aladdin In Pearlies; The Batallion Shot; The Burglar's Misfortune; The Harlequinade (1910); Her Greatest Performance; Jones' Nightmare; Lieutenant Daring and the Ship's Mascot
Rains, Fred (dir): Aladdin In Pearlies; The Burglar's Misfortune; The Harlequinade (1910); His Duty; Jones' Nightmare
Rains, Jessica (act): Scream, Pretty Peggy; Sleeper
Rains, Robert (act): I Lunghi Capelli della Morte
Rainsford, Rupert (act): The Mystery of Edwin Drood (1993)
Rainville, Paul (act): Clarence
Rairdon, Wally (act): The Devil Bat
Raitt, Bonnie (mus): Heart Condition
Rak, Kati (act): Daughter of Darkness (1990)
Rakerd, Cliff (act): Fargo
Raki, Laya (act): The Nylon Noose
Rakoff, Alvin (dir): City On Fire; Crossplot; Death Ship; King Solomon's Treasure; Long Distance; Passport to Shame
Raksa, Pola (act): Rekopis Znaleziony w Saragossie
Raksanyi, Gellert (act): Phantom of the Opera (1983)
Raksin, David (mus, b. 1912): The Day After; Kind Lady (1951); Laura; The Man With a Cloak; The Next Voice You Hear; The Secret Life of Walter Mitty; What's the Matter With Helen?
Raksin, Ruby (mus): Valley of the Dragons
Raleigh, Cecil (wri): The King's Minister
Raleigh, Saba (act): The Blue Bird (1910); Desire
Raley, Ron (wri): Edge of Sanity
Ralli, Giovanna (act): The Coed Murders; Deadfall
Ralls, Lee (act): Edward Scissorhands
Ralph, Hanna (act): Faust (1926); Die Nibelungen
Ralph, Jessie (act, 1864-1944): After the Thin Man; The Blue Bird (1940); The Garden Murder Case; The Mark of the Vampire (1935); Les Miserables (1935); Murder at the Vanities
Ralph, Ken (act): Empire of Ash III
Ralph, Louis (act): The Ghost Train (1927)
Ralph, Sheryl Lee (act): The Flintstones; Oliver & Company; Witch Hunt
Ralston, Esther (act, b. 1902): By Candlelight; A Kiss for Cinderella; Peter Pan (1924)
Ralston, Gilbert A. (wri, b. 1912): Ben; Willard
Ralston, Hal (act): Hell Night
Ralston, Ken (cin): The Golden Child; Return of the Jedi; Star Trek IV: The Voyage Home
Ralston, Marcia (act): Fly-Away Baby; Sh! The Octopus
Ralston, Teri (act): Neon Maniacs
Ralston, Vera (Hruba) (act, b. 1921): Accused of Murder; Fair Wind to Java; The Lady and the Monster; The Man Who Died Twice; Murder In the Music Hall; A Perilous Journey
Ramage, Cecil (act): Kind Hearts and Coronets; King of the Damned; On Secret Service; The Secret of Stamboul; The Strangler (1932)
Ramakrishna (act): The Jungle
Raman, Gordon (act): The Headless Eyes
Ramanathan, G. (mus): The Jungle
Ramart, Yusef (act): The Queen of Spades (1948)
Rambal, Enrique (act): El Angel Exterminador; El Hombre y el Monstruo
Rambaldi, Carlo (cin): Possession (1981)
Rambaldi, Vittoria (dir): Primal Rage
Rambeau, Marjorie (act, 1889-1970): Man of a Thousand Faces
Ramberg, Sterling (act): Revenge of the Teenage Vixens from Outer Space
Rambo, Dack (act, 1941-1994): Good Against Evil; Nightmare Honeymoon; The Spring; Ultra Warrior
Rameau, Emil (act): Gaslight (1944)
Ramer, Henry (act): Change of Mind; Screamers (1996); Starship Invasions; Welcome to Blood City
Ramer, Summer (act): Strange Behavior
Rametta, Guido (act): The Last Wave
Ramey, Betty (act): Prince of Darkness
Ramin, Sid (mus): Miracle On 34th Street (1973)
Ramirez, Carlos (act): Alien Predators
Ramirez, Efrem (act): Tammy and the T-Rex
Ramirez, J.J. (act): Flesh-Eating Mothers
Ramirez, Jose (act): Making Mr. Right
Ramirez, Juan (A.) (act): Chain Reaction (1996); Child's Play (1988); The Fugitive (1993); In the Company of Darkness; The Package
Ramirez, Judy (act): Phoenix the Warrior
Ramirez, Leo (act): Doomsday Machine
Ramirez, Raul (act): Circle of Death
Ramirez, Ray (act): The Brother from Another Planet
Ramis, Harold (act, b. 1944): Ghostbusters; Ghostbusters II; Heavy Metal
Ramis, Harold (dir, b. 1944): Groundhog Day; Multiplicity
Ramis, Harold (wri, b. 1944): Ghostbusters; Ghostbusters II; Groundhog Day
Ramon, Gordon (act): The Headless Eyes
Ramone, Phil (mus): The Mind Snatchers
Ramos, Kim (act): Beyond Atlantis; Twilight People
Ramos, Loyda (act): Hellhole
Ramos, Sophie (act): Lost Prophet
Rampling, Charlotte (act, b. 1946): Angel Heart; Asylum (1972); Caravan to Vaccares; D.O.A. (1988); Farewell, My Lovely; He Died With His Eyes Open; Mascara; The Night Porter; Orca; Sherlock Holmes In New York; Target: Harry; Zardoz
Ramrus, Al (wri): The Darker Side of Terror; The Island of Dr. Moreau (1977); Strange New World
Ramsay, Anne (Elizabeth) (act): Critters 4; Murder of Innocence; Perfect Alibi
Ramsay, Bruce (act): Curdled; Hellraiser: Bloodline
Ramsay, Errol J. (act): Starship Invasions
Ramsay, Nelson (act): Her Greatest Performance; [illegible]
Ramsay, Remak (act): Simon
Ramsay, Robin (act): 20th Century Oz
Ramsbottom, John (act): Kill and Kill Again
Ramsden, Dennis (act): Kadoyng; Whose Johnny

Ramsden, John (act): *The Howling: New Moon Rising*
Ramsden, Sybil (act): *The Howling: New Moon Rising*
Ramsen, Allan (wri): *Island of Terror*
Ramsen, Bobby (act): *It's Alive III: Island of the Alive; A Return to Salem's Lot*
Ramsey, Alicia (wri): *The Secret Kingdom; Silent Evidence*
Ramsey, Anne (act, 1929-1988): *Deadly Friend; Dr. Hackenstein; The Goonies; Love at Stake*
Ramsey, Anne Elizabeth (act): *Something Is Out There*
Ramsey, Bruce (act): *Hellraiser 4: Bloodline*
Ramsey, David (act): *The Nutty Professor (1996); Sanctuary of Fear*
Ramsey, George (act): *Congo Crossing*
Ramsey, Gordon (act): *A Return to Salem's Lot*
Ramsey, J. Nelson (act): *The House of Peril*
Ramsey, Jeff (act): *Firestarter*
Ramsey, John (wri): *Where the Rainbow Ends*
Ramsey, Logan (act, b. 1921): *The Beast Within; What's the Matter With Helen?*
Ramsey, Robert (act): *Sitting Target*
Ramsey, Robert (wri): *Destiny Turns On the Radio*
Ramsey, Steven (cin): *Nomads*
Ramsey, Thea (act): *Maniac (1934)*
Ramsey, Ward (act): *Cape Fear (1961); Dinosaurus!*
Ramsoondar, Leon Darnell (act): *Wild Thing*
Ramsower, Staci Linn (act): *Tank Girl*
Ramunni (act): *The Bogey Man*
Ramus, Doreen (act): *Quarantine*
Ranalli, Anna (act): *Perseus the Invincible*
Rancer, Sid (act): *Wolfman (1979)*
Ranchi, Federica (act): *Maciste-The Mighty; Son of Samson; La Vendetta di Ercole; Women of Devil's Island*
Rancourt, Jules (act): *Le Spectre Vert*
Rancourt, Renee (act): *Beyond the Door III*
Rand, Ayn (wri, 1905-1982): *Love Letters*
Rand, Edwin (act): *Tarantula*
Rand, Michael (act): *Meet Boston Blackie*
Rand, Patrick (dir): *Mom*
Rand, Sally (act): *The Road to Yesterday*
Randall, Ann (act): *Doomsday Voyage*
Randall, Anne (act): *Hell's Bloody Devils; Westworld*
Randall, Bob (act): see Livingston, Bob
Randall, Bob (wri): *The Fan; Zorro, the Gay Blade*
Randall, Chris (act): *The Right Hand of the Devil*
Randall, David (act): *The Road to Hong Kong*
Randall, Dick (act): *Slaughter High*
Randall, Dick (wri): *La Figlia di Frankenstein; Pieces*
Randall, Ethan (act): *Evolver*
Randall, Frank (act): *The Pleydell Mystery*
Randall, George (act): *Scalps*
Randall, Jacqueline (act): *Blood Beach*
Randall, John (act): *Blood Diner*
Randall, Kathleen (act): *Praying Mantis*
Randall, Meg (act): *Criss Cross*
Randall, Monica (act): *Witches' Mountain*
Randall, Stacie (act): *The Companion (1994); Dream a Little Dream 2; Trancers 4: Jack of Swords; Trancers 5: Sudden Deth*
Randall, Stephanie (act): *Prehistoric Women (1966)*
Randall, Stuart (act): *Captive Women; Indestructible Man; This Is My Love*
Randall, Sue (act): *Desk Set*
Randall, Tony (act, b. 1920, nee Leonard Rosenberg): *The Alphabet Murders; The Brass Bottle (1964); Gremlins 2: The New Batch; Hello Down There; I Spy, You Spy; The Littlest Angel (1969); My Little Pony; Our Man In Marrakesh; 7 Faces of Dr. Lao*
Randall, Walter (act): *The Hand (1960); The Hands of Orlac (1959); Tiffany Jones*
Randall, Zoe (act): *Curse III: Blood Sacrifice*
Randel, Tony (dir): *Amityville 1992: It's About Time; Children of the Night; Hellbound: Hellraiser II; Rattled; Ticks*
Randell, Ron (act, b. 1920): *Bulldog Drummond at Bay (1947); Bulldog Drummond Strikes Back (1947); Captive Women; The Girl In Black Stockings; The Girl On the Pier; Gold for the Caesars; The Hostage (1956); The Lone Wolf and His Lady; The Loves of Carmen (1948); Most Dangerous Man Alive; Omoo Omoo, The Shark God; The She-Creature; The Strange Case of Dr. Manning; Tyrant of the Sea*
Randeniya, Ravindra (act): *The God King*
Randian (act): *Freaks*
Randing, Ric (act): *Splatter University*
Randle, Betsy (act): *Guess Who's Coming for Christmas?*
Randle, Kevin D. (wri): *Roswell*
Randle, Theresa (act): *Heart Condition; Maid to Order; Space Jam; Spawn*
Randles, Bob (mus): *Metamorphoses*
Randol, George (act): *Green Pastures*
Randolf, Anders (act): *The Black Pirate; The Love Flower; Buried Treasure; Seven Keys to Baldpate (1925); Sherlock Holmes (1922); The Viking*
Randolf, Gary (act): *The Green Slime*
Randolph, Beverly (act): *The Return of the Living Dead (1985)*
Randolph, Bill (act): *Friday the 13th-Part 2*
Randolph, Chase (act): *Flight of the Navigator*
Randolph, Donald (act): *The Adventures of Hajji Baba; The Deadly Mantis; The Mad Magician; The Purple Mask; Rogues of Sherwood Forest; Son of Sinbad*
Randolph, Ed (act): *Dr. Heckyl & Mr. Hype; La Sorella di Satan*
Randolph, Elsie (act, b. 1904): *Frenzy; The Quatermass Conclusion; Rich and Strange*
Randolph, Henry (act): *The Brain Eaters*
Randolph, Isabel (act, 1889-1973): *The Missing Corpse*
Randolph, Jane (act, b. 1919): *Abbott and Costello Meet Frankenstein; Cat People (1942); Curse of the Cat People; The Falcon's Brother; The Falcon Strikes Back; Highways by Night; Open Secret; T-Men*
Randolph, John (act): *Conquest of the Planet of the Apes; Crosscurrent; Earthquake; Escape from the Planet of the Apes; Heaven Can Wait (1978); The Hotel Manor Inn; King Kong (1976); Nero Wolfe; The New, Original Wonder Woman; Pretty Poison (1968); Seconds*
Randolph, Josh (act): *The Blob (1958)*
Randolph, Lillian (act, 1915-1980): *Gildersleeve's Ghost; Hush...Hush, Sweet Charlotte; Magic*
Randolph, Scott (act): *Exterminator II*
Randolph, Windsor Taylor (act): *Amazons (1986)*
Random, Bob (act): *Village of the Giants*
Random, Robert (act): *Time Walker; Vampire at Midnight*
Randone, Salvo (act): *La Decima Vittima; Satyricon; Spirits of the Dead*
Rands, Della (act): *The Sky Bike*
Ranco, Harry (act): *The Old Gardener*
Raney, Janet (act): *Deadly Messages*
Ranft, Joe (act): *The Brave Little Toaster*
Ranft, Joe (wri): *The Brave Little Toaster; The Rescuers Down Under*
Ranft, John (wri): *The Brave Little Toaster*
Ranger, Mike (act): *Dracula Sucks*
Rangno, Terry (act): *The Little Savage*
Rania, Estrellita (act): *Pretty Maids All In a Row*
Ranieri, Massimo (act): *Death Rage; The Light at the Edge of the World*
Ranin, Saara (act): *The Kremlin Letter*
Rank, Claude (wri): *Nick Carter et le Trefle Rouge*
Rank, Ursula (act): *The Million Eyes of Sumuru*
Rankin, Arthur (act): *The Lone Wolf Returns (1935); Meet Nero Wolfe*
Rankin Jr., Arthur (dir): *The Flight of Dragons; The Hobbit*
Rankin Jr., Arthur (wri): *The Bermuda Depths; The Ivory Ape*
Rankin, Claire (act): *Escape Clause*
Rankin, Steve (act): *Storm of the Century*
Rannania, Edmond (act): *Embassy*
Rannow, Jerry (act): *The Wizard of Mars*
Ransenthaler, Peter (act): see Carsten, Peter
Ransley, Peter (wri): *The Hawk*
Ransom, Tim (act): *Outbreak*
Ransome, Prunella (act): *The Secret of Seagull Island*
Ransome, Sydney Lewis (act): *The Queen Mother; Still Waters Run Deep*
Ranson, Glen (act): *The Lucifer Complex*
Ranta, Richard (act): *I Was a Zombie for the F.B.I.*
Ranucci, Renato (act): see Rascel, Renato
Ranzi, Galatea (act): *Fiorile*
Rao, Krishna (dir & wri): *Crossworlds*
Rao, Raman (wri): *Crossworlds*
Rao, Ryan (act): *Evil Altar*
Raoul, Dale (act): *The Lawnmower Man; Netforce*
Rapagna, Anna (act): *Future Force*
Rapaport, Michael (act): *Point of No Retutn*
Rapgof, I. ("Count Amori") (wri): *Sonka Zolotaya Ruchka*
Raphael, John Nathaniel (wri): *Peter Ibbetson*
Raphaelson, Samson (wri, b. 1896): *Heaven Can Wait (1942); Suspicion (1941)*
Rapley, John (act): *Jane and the Lost City*
Rapoport, I.C. (wri): *To Kill a Clown*
Raposo, Joe (mus, 1937-1989): *The Great Muppet Caper; The Possession of Joel Delaney; Savages*
Rapp, Anthony (act): *Grave Secrets; Twister*
Rapp, Carl (act): *A Witch Without a Broom*
Rapp, Michael (mus): *Girlfriend from Hell*
Rapp, Paul (dir): *The Curious Female*
Rapp, Steve (act): *Wavelength*
Rappaport, David (act, 1951-1990): *Amazing Stories: The Movie VI; The Bride (1985); Sword of the Valiant; Time Bandits*
Rappaport, Ezra D. (wri): *Deja Vu; Harry and the Hendersons*
Rappaport, Sheeri (act): *Little Witches*
Rappazzo, Carmela (act): *Outbreak*
Rapper, Irving (dir, b. 1898): *Another Man's Poison; The Miracle (1959)*
Rappoport, Herbert (wri): *Die Herrin von Atlantis*
Raquello, Edward (act): *Calling Philo Vance; Charlie Chan at Monte Carlo; Torchy Gets Her Man*
Rarawa, Biu (act): *Avengers of the Reef*
Rasberry, James (act): *I Was a Zombie for the F.B.I.*
Rasberry, Robin (act): *Empire of Ash III*
Rasca, Nonong (cin): *Daughters of Satan; The Thirsty Dead*
Rascel, Renato (act, b. 1912, nee Renato Ranucci): *Destination Fury; L'Ours; Tempi Duri per i Vampiri*
Rasche, David (act): *Bigfoot: The Unforgettable Encounter; Dead Weekend; Out There; Sanctuary of Fear; Wicked Stepmother*
Raschig, Krafft (act): *Die Buchse der Pandora*
Rascovich, Mark (wri): *The Bedford Incident*
Rashovich, Gordon (act): *Dead Again*
Raskin, Alan (dir): *The Ghost and Mr. Chicken*
Raskin, Jay (dir): *I Married a Vampire*
Rasmussen, Eric (mus): *Scalps*
Rasp, Fritz (act): *Die Frau im Mond; The Hand of the Gallows; Metropolis (1926); Schatten, eine Nachtliche Halluzination; Spione*
Raspberry, Larry (act): *I Was a Zombie for the F.B.I.*
Rassimov, Ivan (act): *Blue Movie Blackmail; Demons of the Dead; Eaten Alive (1980); The Humanoid; Shock (1978); Spasmo; Lo Strano Caso della Signora Ward; La Strega In Amore*
Rassimov, Rada (act): *The Cat O' Nine Tails; Gli Orrori del Castello di Noremberga*
Rastattar, Wendy (act): *Midnight Offerings; Spawn of the Slithis*
Rasulala, Thalmus (act, 1935-1991): *The Bermuda Triangle; Blacula; Mom and Dad Save the World; The Package*
Rasumny, Jay (act): *To All a Goodnight*
Rasumny, Mikhail (act, 1890-1956): *The Unseen (1945)*
Ratchford, Jeremy (act): *Generation X; Short Circuit 2*
Ratcliff, Karum (act): *The Toxic Avenger, Part II*
Ratcliff, Sandy (act): *The Last Days of Man On Earth*
Ratckiffe, E.J. (act): *The Black Pirate*
Rath, Eral (cin): *Gargoyles; Miracle On 34th Street (1973)*
Rathbone, Basil (act, 1892-1967): *Above Suspicion; The Adventuresm of Ichabod and Mr. Toad; The Adventures of Sherlock Holmes (1939); Autopsia de un Fantasma; The Bishop Murder Case; The Black Cat (1941); The Black Sleep; Casanova's Big Night; The Comedy of Terrors; Crazy House (1943); Dressed to Kill (1946); Fingers at the Window; The Ghost In the Invisible Bikini; Gill-Woman; The Great Mouse Detective; Hillbillys In a Haunted House; The Hound of the Baskervilles (1939); The House of Fear (1945); House of Menace; The Last Days of Pompeii (1935); Love from a Stranger (1937); The Mad Doctor; The Magic Sword (1962); The Mark of Zorro (1940); Paris Calling; The Pearl of Death; Planeta Bura; Pursuit to Algiers; Queen of Blood; The Scarlet Claw; Sherlock Holmes and the Secret Weapon; Sherlock Holmes and the Voice of Terror; Sherlock Holmes Faces Death; Sherlock Holmes In Washington; Son of Frankenstein; Spider Woman; Tales of Terror; Terror by Night; Tower of London (1939); Two Before Zero; The Woman In Green*
Rathbone, Marion (act): *Richard III (1911)*
Rathbone, Mary (act): *Oh Heavenly Dog*
Rathbone, Nigel (act): *No Blade of Grass*
Rathburn, Eldon (mus): *The Universe*
Rathgeber, Ralph (act): see Meeker, Ralph
Rathje, Gustav (cin): *M (1931)*
Rathmell, John (wri): *Darkest Africa; The Lost Jungle; Radio Ranch; Sharad of Atlantis*
Rathony, Akos (V.) (dir): *Cave of the Living Dead; The Devil's Daffodil*
Ratib, Ahmed (act): *Dawn of the Mummy*
Ratib, Gamil (act): *To Commit a Murder*
Ratkiewicz, Eugene (act): *Midnight (1980)*
Ratliff, Erick (act): *The Stepford Children*
Ratliff, Garette (Patrick) (act): *Arachnophobia; Captain America (1992)*
Ratner, Bill (act): *Explorers*
Ratoff, Gregory (act, 1897-1960): *Abdullah's Harem; My Daughter Joy*
Ratoff, Gregory (dir, 1897-1960): *Black Magic (1949); The Corsican Brothers (1941); Lancer Spy; Moss Rose; My Daughter Joy*
Ratray, Devin (act): *Little Monsters*
Ratray, Peter (act): *The Love Statue*
Rattay, Wayne (act): *The Wizard of Gore*
Rattee, Paul (act): *Killer's Moon*
Rattigan, Terence (wri, 1911-1977): *The Sound Barrier*
Rattner, Larry (wri): *Halloween 4: The Return of Michael Myers*
Rattray, Heather (act): *Basket Case 2*
Ratzenberger, John (act, b. 1947): *Arabian Adventure; A Bug's Life; Dog's Best Friend; The Empire Strikes Back; Goliath Awaits; House II: The Second Story; Motel Hell; Outland; Superman (1978); Timestalkers; Toy Story II; Warlords of the Deep of the Deep*
Rau, Andrea (act): *Daughters of Darkness*
Rau, Jim (act): *The Wizard of Gore*
Rau, Umberto (act): *The Last Man On Earth*
Rauch, Earl Mac (wri): *The Adventures of Buckaroo Banzai*
Rauch, Siegfried (act): *Alien Contamination*
Raudkivi, Janus (act): *The Capture of Bigfoot*
Raugalis, John (cin): *Igor and the Lunatics*
Rauh, Stanley (wri): *Dressed to Kill (1941); Michael Shayne, Private Detective; Sleepers West*
Rausch, Don (act): *Red Alert*
Ravaioli, Isarco (act): *L'Amante del Vampiri; Satanik*
Ravalec, Blanche (act): *Moonraker*
Ravel, Jean (cin): *La Jetee*
Ravel, Maurice Joseph (mus, 1875-1937): *Le Horla (1967)*
Ravell, Graeme (mus): *Child's Play 2*
Raven, Elsa (act): *The Amityville Horror; Back to the Future; Creator; Twilight Zone*
Raven, Harry (act): *The Incredible Petrified World*
Raven, Max (dir): *The Abomination*
Raven, Mike (act): *Crucible of Terror; Disciple of Death; I, Monster; Lust for a Vampire*
Raven, Simon (wri): *Doctors Wear Scarlet*
Raven, Terry (act): *The Monster of Highgate Ponds*
Ravencroft, Thurl (act): *The Brave Little Toaster; The Brave Little Toaster Goes to Mars*
Ravenel, Florence (act): *The Twonky*
Raven-Symone (act): *Dr. Dolittle (1998); Zenon: Girl of the 21st Century*
Ravet (act): *The Passion of Joan of Arc*
Ravez, Romona (act): *The Devil's Hand (1961)*
Ravich, Rand (wri): *Candyman: Farewell to the Flesh*
Ravick, Tom (act): *Beyond the Time Barrier*
Ravinder (act): *Greystoke: The Legend of Tarzan, Lord of the Apes*
Rawi, Ousama (cin): *The Black Windmill; The Human Factor; Pulp*
Rawi, Ousama (dir): *The Housekeeper*
Rawle, Jeff (act): *A Hitch In Time*
Rawle, Jeff (wri): *The Young Poisoner's Handbook*
Rawley, James (act): *The Creature Walks Among Us*
Rawlings, Harriet (act): *Zombie Island Massacre*
Rawlings, Margaret (act): *Hands of the Ripper; Jekyll and Hyde*
Rawlings, Richard (L.) (cin): *Fantasies; Final Eye*
Rawlins, Eston (act): *The Ivory Ape*
Rawlins, Grace (act): *The Ivory Ape*
Rawlins, John (dir, b. 1902): *Arabian Nights (1942); Dick Tracy Meets Gruesome; Dick Tracy's Dilemma; The Great Impersonation (1942); The Missing Guest; Sherlock Holmes and the Voice of Terror; Sudan*
Rawlins, Lester (act): *They Might Be Giants*
Rawlinson, A.R. (wri): *The Black Rider; Celia; Cloak Without Dagger; Dark Secret; The Face at the Window (1939); Gaolbreak (1962); Gaslight (1940); King Solomon's Mines (1937); The Man Who Knew Too Much (1934);Menace (1934); Paul Temple's Triumph; Scarlet Thread; Sexton Blake and the Hooded Terror*
Rawlinson, Bill (act): *The Being*
Rawlinson, Brian (act): *Blind Terror*

Rawlinson, Gerald (act): *Alf's Carpet; The Callbox Mystery; Creeping Shadows; The Man at Six; The Old Man; The Silent House*
Rawlinson, Herbert (act, 1885-1953): *Blake of Scotland Yard; Nabonga; The Panther's Claw; Peril from the Planet Mongo; Purple Death from Outer Space; Torchy Gets Her Man*
Rawlinson, Howard (act): *Are You Dying Young Man?*
Rawls, Hardy (act): *Bates Motel*
Rawls, Lou (act): *Angel, Angel, Down We Go*
Rawnsley, Atherton (cin): *The Invincible Barbarian*
Rawnsley, Ben (act): *Timestalkers*
Rawson, Clayton (wri): *The Man Who Wouldn't Die*
Rawson, Stratton (wri): *Tuck Everlasting*
Rawsthorne, Alan (mus, 1905-1971): *Pandora and the Flying Dutchman*
Raxel, Antonio (act): *El Vampiro Sangriento*
Ray, A. (dir): *For Mother's Sake*
Ray, Albert (dir): *A Shriek In the Night; The Thirteenth Guest*
Ray, Albert (wri): *Charlie Chan In Reno*
Ray, Aldo (act, 1926-1991, nee Aldo DaRe): *Biohazard (1985); Bog; Death Dimension; Evils of the Night; Frankenstein's Great Aunt Tillie; Human Experiments; The Lucifer Complex; Mongrel; I Moschettiere del Mare; Nightfall (1956); Nightmare In the Sun; Nightstalker (1979); The Power (1967); Psychic Killer; The Secret of NIMH; Shock 'em Dead; Star Slammer*
Ray, Allen (act): *The Velvet Touch*
Ray, Allene (act): *The House Without a Key*
Ray, Andrew (act, b. 1939): *La Figlia di Frankenstein; Gideon's Day; Great Expectations (1974); Tarzana, the Wild Girl; The Yellow Balloon*
Ray, Bert (wri): *How to Make a Doll*
Ray, Billy (wri): *Color of Night; Volcano*
Ray, Bingham (act): *Shocker*
Ray, Christopher (cin): *The Alien Within*
Ray, Danny (act): *Halloween 4: The Return of Michael Myers*
Ray, Frankie (act): *Invasion of the Star Creatures*
Ray, Fred Olen (dir): *Alienator; Alien Dead; Attack of the 60 Foot Centerfold; Bad Girls from Mars; Beverly Hills Vamp; Biohazard (1985); Cyclone; Deep Space; Dinosaur Island (1994); Evil Toons; Haunting Fear; Hollywood Chainsaw Hookers; Inner Sanctum (1991); Inner Sanctum 2 It Fell from the Sky; Mind Twister; The Phantom Empire; Possessed by the Night; Scalps; Star Slammer; The Tomb; Warlords*
Ray, Fred Olen (wri): *Deep Space; It Fell from the Sky; The Phantom Empire; Scalps*
Ray, Gerald (act): *Witches' Brew*
Ray, Jacqueline (act): *Beyond the Universe*
Ray, James (act): *Charlie Chan and the Curse of the Dragon Queen*
Ray, Jesse (act): *Scream Dream*
Ray, Joey (act): *The Big Clock; The Saint In Palm Springs; The Steel Trap*
Ray, Leslie (wri): *My Demon Lover*
Ray, Man (dir & wri): *Dreams That Money Can Buy*
Ray, Marc B. (dir): *Scream Bloody Murder*
Ray, Michel (act, b. 1945): *The Space Children*
Ray, Mona (act): *Li'l Abner (1940)*
Ray, Nicholas (dir, 1911-1979): *Johnny Guitar; On Dangerous Ground*
Ray, Obee (cin): *Boarding House*
Ray, Phil (act): *Dangerous Fingers; Mr. Reeder In Room 13; Sexton Blake and he Bearded Doctor*
Ray, Philip (act): *Before I Wake; Date at Midnight; Devil Doll (1963); Frankenstein Created Woman; The Man Who Made Diamonds; Panic (1963); The Perfect Crime*
Ray, Raymond (act): *The Curse of Frankenstein*
Ray, Rene (act): *Once In a New Moon; The Passing of the Third Floor Back (1935); The Return of the Frog; The Secret Agent (1936); They Made Me a Fugitive; The Vicious Circle (1957)*
Ray, Rene (wri): *The Strange World of Planet X*
Ray, Robyn (act): *Piranha (1978)*
Ray, Satyajit (dir & wri, 1921-1992): *Devi; Paras Pathar*
Ray, Ted (act, b. 1909, nee Charles Olden): *Elstree Calling*
Ray, Terry (act): see Drew, Ellen
Ray, Tim (act): *Premonition (1972); Pretty Maids All In a Row*
Ray, Tim (mus): *Premonition (1972)*
Rayan, Andrew (cin): *Goliathon*
[illegible] *Man*
Raybourne, Richard (act): *Wild Thing*
Rayburn, Bill (act): *The Boogey Man*
Rayburn, Jeff (act): *The Dungeonmaster*
Raye, Carol (act): *While I Live*
Raye, Martha (act, 1916-1994, nee Margie Yvonne Reed): *Alice In Wonderland (1985); The Boys from Syracuse; Hellzapoppin*
Rayer, Maud (act): *The Murders In the Rue Morgue (1986)*
Rayfiel, David (wri): *Castle Keep; Deathwatch (1980); 3 Days of the Condor*
Rayfield, Heather (act): *Secrets of the Phantom Caverns*
Rayhall, Tom (act): *Howard the Duck*
Raymon, Marilyn (act): *Twinkle, Twinkle, Killer Kane*
Raymon, Sam (act): *Ganja and Hess*
Raymond, Alan (cin): *Glen and Randa*
Raymond, Alex (wri): *Flash Gordon (1980)*
Raymond, Barry (act): *The Ipcress File*
Raymond, Bill (act): *The Crow (1994); 12 Monkeys*
Raymond, Butch (act): *Flight of the Navigator*
Raymond, Candy (act): *The Plumber*
Raymond, Charles (act): *Don Q and the Artist; Don Q-How He Outwitted Don Luis; Don Q-How He Treated the Parole of Gevil Hay; Hamlet (1912); Lieutenant Daring and the Dancing Girl; Lieutenant Daring and the Labour Riots; Lieutenant Daring and the Plans of the Minefields; The Planter's Daughter*
Raymond, Charles (1990s act): *The First Power*
Raymond, Charles (dir): *The Adventures of Dick Turpin-A Deadly Foe, A Pack of Hounds, and Some Merry Monks; The Adventures of Dick Turpin-The Gunpowder Plot; The Adventures of Dick Turpin-The King of Highwaymen; The Adventures of Dick Turpin-200 Guineas Reward, Dead or Alive; Britain's Secret Treaty; The Cabby's Dream; The Counterfeiters; The Diamond Thieves; Dick Turpin's Last Ride to York; Dick Turpin's Ride to York (1913, B&C/Walturdaw); The Gambler's Nightmare; The Great Anarchist Mystery; The Great Cheque Fraud; Hamlet (1912); Her Rival's Necklace; The Jailbird: or, The Bishop and the Convict; Ju-Jitsu to the Rescue; The Kaiser's Spies; The Kidnapped Child; Lieutenant Daring and the Labour Riots; The Love of a Gypsy; The Mystery of the Diamond Belt; Queenie of the Circus; Robin Hood Outlawed; Spiritualism Exposed (1913); The Stolen Heirlooms; The Thornton Jewel Mystery; True Till Death; When Other Lips*
Raymond, Charles (wri): *Britain's Secret Treaty; The Counterfeiters; The Great Cheque Fraud; The Kaiser's Spies; The Mystery of the Diamond Belt; Spiritualism Exposed (1913)*
Raymond, Cyril (act, b. 1897): *Condemned to Death; Don't Talk to Strange Men; The Frightened Lady (1932); The Ghost Train (1931); The Lure; The Man Outside (1933); Night Train to Paris; The Shadow (1933); The Spy In Black; The Tunnel; Wuthering Heights (1920)*
Raymond, Derek (wri): see Cook, Robin
Raymond, Ernest (wri): *For Them That Trespass*
Raymond, Gary (act, b. 1935): *The Hunchback of Notre Dame (1965); Jason and the Argonauts; Suddenly Last Summer; Traitor's Gate*
Raymond, Gene (act, b. 1908, nee Raymond Guion): *Assigned to Danger; The Hanged Man; The Locket*
Raymond, George (act): *Starship Invasions*
Raymond, Guy (act): *4D Man; The Reluctant Astronaut*
Raymond, Jack (GB act): *Creatures of Clay; The English Rose; In the Shadow of Big Ben; On the Brink of the Precipice; Retribution (1913)*
Raymond, Jack (USA act): *Nightmare Alley*
Raymond, Jack (dir, 1886-1953): *The Frog; The Mind of Mr. Reeder; The Missing People; The Speckled Band (1931); The Spirit of the Heath; When Knights Were Bold (1936)*
Raymond, Jim (act): *Code Name: Minus One; The Man With the Power*
Raymond, Lee (act): *She Freak*
Raymond, Lina (act): *The Dark Secret of Harvest Home; Embryo*
Raymond, Marc (act): *Earthbound (1981)*
Raymond, Paula (act, b. 1928, nee Paula Ramona Wright): *The Bandits of Corsica; The Beast from 20,000 Fathoms; Blood of Dracula's Castle; The Flight That Disappeared; Hand of Death*
Raymond, Robin (act): *Beyond a Reasonable Doubt; Congo Crossing; Ellery Queen: Don't Look Behind You; Girls In Chains*
Raymond, Ronnie (act): *Murder She Said*
Raymond, Roy (act): *Boadicea; Lorna Doone (1920); Love In the Welsh Hills; The Mystery of the Silent Death*
Raymond, Sid (act): *Fright (1957); The Funhouse (1981); Making Mr. Right*
Raymond, Suzanna (act): *Peter Rabbit and the Tales of Beatrix Potter*
Rayne, Stephen (act): *Hawk the Slayer*
Rayner, Barnabus (wri): *The Dumb Man of Manchester*
Rayner, Christine (act): *A Garret In Bohemia; Queen of My Heart*
Rayner, Minnie (act): *Faust (1922); Gaslight (1940); The Man at Six; The Missing Rembrandt; Murder at the Inn; Silver Blaze (1937); The Sleeping Cardinal; The Triumph of Sherlock Holmes*
Raynham, Fred (act): *Boadicea; Blake the Lawbreaker; The Clue of the Second Goblet; The Great Office Mystery; The Hound of the Baskervilles (1921); The Sign of Four (1923)*
Raynor, Sheila (act): *A Clockwork Orange; Demons of the Mind; Monster of Terror; October Moth; The Omen*
Raynor, Timothy L. (act): *Final Exam*
Raynor, William/Bill (wri): *Francis In the Haunted House; Killers from Space; Phantom from Space; Prisoners of the Casbah; Target Earth*
Raynr, David (act): *Project X (1987)*
Raysses, Michael (act): *When the Bough Breaks*
Raz, Kavi (act): *Warning Sign*
Razutis, Al (cin): *The Keeper*
Rea, Charles (act): *The Ipcress File*
Rea, F.T. (act): *Shadow Conspiracy*
Rea, John Huntington (act): see Ridgely, John
Rea, Peggy (act): *Nothing But the Truth; What's the Matter With Helen?*
Rea, Stephen (act): *The Company of Wolves; The Doctor and the Devils; In Dreams; Interview With the Vampire*
Reach, John (act): *Lizzie*
Read, Brooks (act): *Eye of the Alien*
Read, Darryl (act): *Uncharted Seas*
Read, Donald (act): *Murder by Rope*
Read, Fred (act): *Forty Winks*
Read Jr., J. Parker (dir): *The Lone Wolf's Daughter (1919)*
Read, James (act): *The Initiation; Web of Deceit; When the Dark Man Calls*
Read, Jan (wri): *First Men In the Moon (1964); Grip of the Strangler; Jason and the Argonauts*
Read, John (cin): *Doppelganger (1969)*
Read, Margaret (act): *Kiss of the Vampire*
Read, Melanie (dir): *Trial Run*
Read, Peter (act): *The Mutagen*
Readdy, Ava (act): *When Time Ran Out*
Reade, Charles (wri): *The Lyons Mail*
Reade, Frank (act): *The Beetle*
Reade, Gil (act): *Escapes*
Reade, Nicki (act): *Return of the Jedi*
Reading, Bertice (act): *Little Shop of Horrors (1986)*
Reading, Donna (act): *Subterfuge*
Readman, Andrew (act): *101 Dalmatians (1996)*
Ready, Jerry (act): *Threads*
Ready, Rodger (act): *Curse of the Swamp Creature*
Ready, Roger (act): *Mars Needs Women*
Reagan, Maureen (act): *Death Takes a Holiday (1971)*
Reagan, Michael (act): *Cyclone*
Reagan, Nell (act): *Kiss Daddy Goodbye*
Reagan, Patrick (dir): *Kiss Daddy Goodbye*
Reagan III, Patrick (act): *Kiss Daddy Goodbye*
Reagan, Ronald (act, b. 1912): *Bedtime for Bonzo; Murder In the Air (1940); Night Unto Night; Nine Lives Are Not Enough*
Reale, Joseph/Joe (act): *Tarantulas: The Deadly Cargo; When a Stranger Calls*
Reamon, Tommy (act): *The Ultimate Impostor*
Rearden, Brad (act): *The Alien's Return; Silent Scream (1979)*
Reardon, Dennis (wri): *The Mind Snatchers*
Reardon, J.J. (act): *Secrets In the Attic*
Reardon, James (act): *To Let*
Reardon, James (dir): *Shadow of Evil (1921); To Let*
Reardon, Mildred (act): *Male and Female*
Reardon, Robert (act): *The Mail Van Murder*
Reason, Rex (act, b. 1928): *The Creature Walks Among Us; Lady Godiva; Salome (1953); Storm Over Tibet; This Island Earth*
Reason, Rhodes (act, b. 1930). *King Kong Escapes; Voodoo Island*
Reasoner, Harry (act, b. 1923): *V*
Reate, J.L. (act): *The Golden Child*
Reaves, Michael (wri): *Full Eclipse*
Rebalra, J. Carrara (wri): *El C*[illegible]
Rebane, Angel (act): *Rana: The Legend of Shadow Lake*
Rebane, Bill (act): *Monster A Go-Go*
Rebane, Bill (dir): *The Alpha Incident; The Capture of Bigfoot; The Giant Spider Invasion; Monster A Go-Go; Rana: The Legend of Shadow Lake*
Rebane, Bill (wri): *The Capture of Bigfoot; Monster A Go-Go*
Rebane, Randolph (act): *The Capture of Bigfoot*
Rebar, Alex (act): *The Incredible Melting Man*
Rebar, Alex (wri): *To All a Goodnight*
Rebel, Bernard (act): *The Curse of the Mummy's Tomb; Little Red Monkey; Mark of the Phoenix*
Reber, Fred (act): *Empire of Ash III*
Rebhorn, James (R.) (act): *The Game; He Knows You're Alone; Independence Day; Plymouth*
Rebla, Albert (act): *Forty Winks*
Rebstock, Gary (act): *The Monster Squad*
Recasner, Ron (act): *When the Bough Breaks*
Recchi, Vinicio (act): *Warriors of the Wasteland*
Recklin, Ruth (act): *Superwheels*
Rector, Jeff (act): *Dinosaur Valley Girls; Galaxis*
Rector, Jerry (act): *Uninvited (1993); Vampire's Kiss*
Red Norvo and Trio (act & mus): *Screaming Mimi*
Red, Eric (dir): *Bad Moon; Body Parts (1991)*
Red, Eric (wri): *Body Parts (1991); The Hitcher; Near Dark*
Red, Taia (act): *Body Parts (1991)*
Redanty, Marisa (act): *Spellbinder*
Redd, Mary-Robin (act): *Mirrors*
Redd, Richard (act): *Mr. Sycamore*
Reddemann, Manfred (act): *Hauser's Memory*
Redden, Leslie (act): *The Warlord: Battle for the Galaxy*
Reddick, Jerome (act): *Angel Heart*
Redding, Donald (act): *To Die For II: Son of Darkness*
Reddington, Ian (act): *Highlander*
Reddy, Brian (act): *Dante's Peak; Outbreak; Primal Fear*
Reddy, Don (cin): *Oh Heavenly Dog*
Reddy, Helen (act, b. 1942): *Pete's Dragon*
Reddy, Teddy (act): *The Ghost and the Darkness*
Redeker, Quinn (act): *Code Name: Minus One; The Three Stooges Meet Hercules*
Redfern, Anne (act): *Deadtime Stories*
Redfield, Dennis (act): *Dead and Buried; Deadly Messages; The Midnight Hour; Pulse; Space Rage*
Redfield, William (act, 1927-1976): *Conquest of Space; Fantastic Voyage*
Redford, Brian (act): *Cannibal Ferox; Ironmaster; Make Them Die Slowly*
Redford, H.E.D. (act): *Beyond and Back; Earthbound (1981); The Fall of the House of Usher (1982); Hangar 18; The Legend of Sleepy Hollow*
Redford, Ian (act): *Sleepwalker (1975)*
Redford, J.A.C. (mus): *A Kid In King Arthur's Court; Web of Deceit*
Redford, Robert (act, b. 1937): *3 Days of the Condor*
Redgrave, Corin (act, b. 1939): *The Deadly Affair; Excalibur; The Magus; The Woman In White (1998)*
Redgrave, Jemma (act): *Dream Demon*
Redgrave, Lynn (act, b. 1943): *The Bad Seed (1985); The Deadly Affair; Midnight (1989); Toothless; What Ever Happened to Baby Jane? (1991)*
Redgrave, (Sir), Michael (act, 1908-1985): *Assignment K; Dead of Night (1945); The Green Scarf; The Innocents; The Lady Vanishes (1938); Mr. Arkadin; 1984 (1955); The Secret Agent (1936); Secret Beyond the Door; Thunder Rock; Time Without Pity; Twinsanity*
Redgrave, Vanessa (act, b. 1937): *Agatha; Bear Island; Blow-Up; Camelot; Deep Impact; The Devils; Mission: Impossible; Murder On the Orient Express; Orpheus Descending; The Seven-Per-Cent Solution; They; Un Tranquillo Posto di Campagna; The Trojan Women; What Ever Happened to Baby Jane? (1991)*
Redick, Cecil (act): *The Cremators*
Reding, Juli (act): *Pattern for Murder; Tormented (1960); Why Must I Die?*
Redlin, Robert (wri): *After Dark, My Sweet*
Redman, Frank (cin): *Dick Tracy (1945); Dick Tracy Meets Gruesome; Dick Tracy's Dilemma; The Falcon In Danger; The Falcon In Mexico; The Falcon's Adventure; The Falcon's Alibi; The Saint In New York; The Saint Strikes Back; The Saint Takes Over; You'll Find Out*
Redman, Joyce (act): *Les Miserables (1978)*
Redmond Jr., Harry (cin): *Angel On My Shoulder (1946); Gog; The Last Days of Pompeii (1935); Riders to the Stars*
Redmond, Liam (act, b. 1913): *Daughter of Darkness (1948); The Diplomatic Corpse; The Ghost and Mr. Chicken; The Glass Tomb; High Treason (1951); Night of the D*[illegible]

(1957); No Trees In the Street; The Sky Bike; 23 Paces to Baker Street
Redmond, Marge (act): *Family Plot*
Redmond, Moira (act): *Jigsaw; Kill or Cure; Limbo Line; Marriage of Convenience; Nightmare (1963); Partners In Crime (1961); Pit of Darkness; The Share Out; Sign It Death; Violent Moment*
Redmond, Siobhan (act): *Mary Shelley's 'Frankenstein'*
Redon, Jean (wri): *Les Yeux sans Visage*
Redondo, Emiliano (act): *Treasure of the Four Crowns; Where Time Began*
Redpath, Ralph (act): *Mutant*
Redwine, Timothy (act): *Mystery Monsters!*
Redwing, Rodd (act, 1904-1971): *Creature from the Black Lagoon; The Flame Barrier; The Mole People; The Naked Jungle*
Redwood, John Hnery (act): *Werewolf of Washington*
Redwood, Manning (act): *Orpheus Descending; Outland; The Shining; Shock Treatment! (1981); A View to a Kill*
Reece, Ronald (act): *Funeral Home*
Reed, Alan (act): *Lady and the Tramp; The Man Called Flintstone; 1,001 Arabian Nights (1959)*
Reed, Alan (wri): *Creature*
Reed, Art(hur) (cin): *The Corpse Vanishes; Drums of Jeopardy (1931)*
Reed, Barbara (act): *Behind the Mask (1946); The Missing Lady; The Shadow Returns*
Reed, Bob (act): *As In Days of Yore; Through the Ages; When Clubs Were Clubs*
Reed, Bruce (act): *Fade to Black*
Reed, Bunny (act): *Theater of Blood*
Reed, (Sir) Carol (dir, 1906-1976): *The Fallen Idol; Gestapo; The Girl In the News; The Key; A Kid for Two Farthings; The Running Man (1963); The Third Man*
Reed, Charlie (act): *How to Stuff a Wild Bikini*
Reed, Christopher (wri): *The 6th Man*
Reed, David (act): *Murder Is My Business*
Reed, Dolores (act): *Invasion of the Star Creatures*
Reed, Donna (act, 1921-1986, nee Donna Mullenger): *Deadly Lessons; Eyes In the Night; It's a Wonderful Life; The Picture of Dorian Gray (1945); Raiders of the Seven Seas; Shadow of the Thin Man; Three Hours to Kill; The Whole Truth*
Reed, Enid R. (act): *Melody of Death*
Reed, Florence (act): *Great Expectations (1934)*
Reed, Geoffrey (act): *Macbeth (1971)*
Reed, George (act): *Green Pastures; Out of the Night*
Reed, Guy (act): *Wizards of the Lost Kingdom*
Reed, Hetty Langford (wri): *Queen of My Heart*
Reed, Isobel (act): see Elsom, Isobel
Reed, Jack (act): *The Dungeonmaster*
Reed, James (dir): *Tarzana, the Wild Girl*
Reed, Jerald (act): *So Sad About Gloria*
Reed, Joel M. (act): *Night of the Zombies (1981)*
Reed, Joel M. (dir): *Blood Bath (1975); Bloodsucking Freaks; The Incredible Torture Show; Night of the Zombies (1981)*
Reed, Joel M. (wri): *Blood Bath (1975); The Incredible Torture Show; Night of the Zombies (1981)*
Reed, Jordan (act): *Dr. Cook's Garden*
Reed, Julian (act): *Clarence*
Reed, Katherine (wri): *Lorna Doone (1922)*
Reed, Kesha (act): *Flatliners*
Reed, Langford (dir): *The Temptation of Joseph*
Reed, Langford (wri): *The Absent-Minded Professor (1907); The Angel of the Ward; Ib and Little Christina; A Knight Errant; The Martyrdom of Thomas A Becket; The Old Favourite and the Ugly Golliwog; An Overdose of Love Potion; The Pied Piper (1907); Robin Hood and His Merry Men; Saved by the Telegraph Code; The Tempest (1908); The Temptation of Joseph; The Water Babies: or, The Little Chimney Sweep; When the Man In the Moon Seeks a Wife*
Reed, Larry (act): *World of the Depraved*
Reed, Les (mus): *Creepshow 2*
Reed, Lewis (wri): *Tarzan and the Great River*
Reed, Libby (act): *Secrets of the Phantom Caverns*
Reed, Luther (wri, 1888-1961): *Young Diana*
Reed, Lydia (act): *The Vampire (1957)*
Reed, Margie Yvonne (act): see Raye, Martha
Reed, Marshall (act, 1917-1980): *Madman of Mandoras; The Night the World Exploded; Radar Secret Service; Till Death*
Reed, Maxwell (act, b. 1920): *Before I Wake; The Brain Machine; The Dark Man (1951); Daughter of Darkness (1948); Dear Murderer; Flame of Araby; Helen of Troy (1955); Picture Mommy Dead; Wall of Death (1952)*
Reed, Michael (cin): *The Devil-Ship Pirates; Diamonds On Wheels; Dracula, Prince of Darkness; The Fiction-Makers; The Gorgon; The Groundstar Conspiracy; Loophole; On Her Majesty's Secret Service; Prehistoric Women (1966); Rasputin, the Mad Monk*
Reed, Mike (act): *The Adding Machine*
Reed, Moira (act): *The Fatal Hour (1937)*
Reed, Morton (wri): *Space Rage*
Reed, Myrtle (act): *The Eyes of Annie Jones; The Slipper and the Rose*
Reed, Oliver (act, b. 1938): *The Adventures of Baron Munchausen (1989); The Assassination Bureau; The Big Sleep (1978); Blue Blood; The Brigand of Kandahar; The Brood; Burnt Offerings; Captain Clegg; Condorman; The Curse of the Werewolf; La Dame dans l'Auto Avec des Lunettes et un Fusil; The Damned; The Devils; Dr. Heckyl & Mr. Hype; A Ghost In Monte Carlo; Gor; The House of Usher (1988); Liszt O' Mania; Paranoiac; The Pirates of Blood River; The Pit and the Pendulum 1990); The Return of the Musketeers; Royal Flash; The Scarlet Blade; Severed Ties; The Shuttered Room; Sitting Target; Spasms; Sword of Sherwood Forest; Ten Little Indians (1974); The Three Musketeers (1974); Tommy; Tomorrow Never Comes; Treasure Island (1990); The Two Faces of Dr. Jekyll; Venom (1982); Z.P.G.*
Reed, Pam (act): *Tuck Everlasting*
Reed, Pamela (act, b. 1949): *The Clan of the Cave Bear; Eyewitness (1981); Junior (1994)*
Reed, Penelope (act): *Amazons (1986)*
Reed, Peyton (dir): *The Computer Wore Tennis Shoes (1995)*
Reed, Philip (act, b. 1908): *Aloma of the South Seas (1941); Big Town After Dark; British Agent; Her Sister's Secret; Song of Scheherazade; Song of the Thin Man; The Tattered Dress; Unknown Island*
Reed, Rachel (act): *Midnight Tease*
Reed, Ralph (act): *Not of This Earth (1957)*
Reed, Rex (act, b. 1940): *Myra Breckinridge; Superman (1978)*
Reed, Ricky Addison (act): *A Return to Salem's Lot*
Reed, Robert (act, 1932-1992): *Bloodlust!; Haunts of the Very Rich; Journey Into Darkness, Mandrake*
Reed, Roland D. (dir): *The House of Secrets (1937)*
Reed, Shanna (act): *Alien Avengers; Rattled; Remember Me; The Sister-In-Law*
Reed, Susanne (act): *The Sitter*
Reed, Suzanne (act): *Beyond the Bermuda Triangle; Up from the Depths*
Reed, Timothy Davis (act): *Not of This World*
Reed, Tom (wri): *Calling Philo Vance; The Florentine Dagger; Moss Rose; The Murders In the Rue Morgue (1932)*
Reed, Tracy (act): *Casino Royale; The Deadly Females; Devils of Darkness; Dr. Strangelove: or, How I Learned to Stop Worrying and Love the Bomb; Hammerhead; Journey to Midnight; The Main Chance; Maroc 7; Percy; Top Secret (1978)*
Reed, Walter (act): *The Destructors; Flying Disc Man from Mars; How to Make a Monster; Macumba Love; Missile Monsters; Mystery In Mexico; Superman and the Mole Men*
Reed, William (act): *Necropolis*
Reede, Rosemarie (act): *Curse of the Crimson Altar*
Reedy, James (cin): *Edward Scissorhands*
Reeh, Robert (act): *Rocket Attack U.S.A.*
Reems, Harry (act, b. 1947, nee Herbert Streicher): *The Amazing Dr. Jekyll; Case of the Full Moon Murders; Penetration*
Rees, Angharad (act): *Baffled!; Catch Me a Spy; The Curse of King Tut's Tomb; Hands of the Ripper; Moments; Once the Killing Starts*
Rees, Betty Ann (act): *The Deathmaster; Sugar Hill*
Rees, Christine (act): *The Vampire (1957)*
Rees, Donough (act): *Starship*
Rees, Edward (act): *They Came from Beyond Space*
Rees, Graham (act): *The Satanic Rites of Dracula*
Rees, Hubert (act): *Agatha; Blue Blood*
Rees, Jed (act): *Fear (1996)*
Rees, Jerry (dir & wri): *The Brave Little Toaster*
Rees, John (act): *Impact; A Prize of Arms; The Quiller Memorandum; Raiders of the Lost Ark; The Shout*
Rees, Llewellyn (act): *The Double; The House On Marsh Road*
Rees, Roger (act): *A Christmas Carol (1984); Teen Agent*
Rees, Yvette (act): *Curse of the Fly; Thirst; Troubled Waters (1964); Witchcraft (1964)*
Reese, Chris (wri): *Ghost Dad*
Reese, Della (act, b. 1931): *Psychic Killer*
Reese, Jeffrey (act): *The Dark (1979)*
Reese, Michelle (act): *The Night Stalker (1987); Switch (1991)*
Reese, Tom (act, b. 1930): *Ellery Queen; Murderers' Row; Vanishing Point (1971)*
Reese, William (cin): *The Kennel Murder Case; The Maltese Falcon (1931)*
Reeve, Ada (act): *They Came to a City*
Reeve, Christopher (act, b. 1952): *Death Dreams; Gray Lady Down; Mortal Sins; Rear Window (1998); Somewhere In Time; Superman (1978); Superman II; Superman III; Superman IV: The Quest for Peace; Village of the Damned (1995)*
Reeve, Christopher (wri, b. 1952): *Superman IV: The Quest for Peace*
Reeve, Geoffrey (dir): *Caravan to Vaccares; Puppet On a Chain*
Reeve, Leonard (dir & wri): *No Haunt for a Gentleman*
Reeves, Arthur B. (wri): *The Clutching Hand*
Reeves, Bob (act): *Dick Tracy (1945)*
Reeves, George (act, 1914-1959, nee George Besselo): *Blue, White and Perfect; Calling Philo Vance; Dead Men Tell; Jungle Goddess; Jungle Jim; The Mutineers; Samson and Delilah; Superman (1948); Superman and the Mole Men; Superman's Perils*
Reeves, J. Harold (act): *Just Imagine*
Reeves, Keanu (act, b. 1964): *Babes In Toyland (1986); Bill & Ted's Bogus Journey; Bill & Ted's Excellent Adventure; Bram Stoker's 'Dracula'; Chain Reaction (1996); Devil's Advocate; Freaked; Johnny Mnemonic; The Matrix; Young Again*
Reeves, (P.) Kynaston (act, b. 1893): *Bedelia; The Crimson Candle; Dark World; Dead Men Are Dangerous; The Echo Murders; Family Doctor; Fiend Without a Face; Four Sided Triangle; Hide and Seek; The Lodger (1932); Murder In Reverse; The Private Life of Sherlock Holmes; Puppets of Fate; The Shadow of the Cat; The Sign of Four (1932); Top Secret (1952); The Twenty Questions Murder; Vice Versa (1947)*
Reeves, Matt (dir): *Future Shock*
Reeves, Michael (dir, 1944-1969): *The Sorcerers; La Sorella di Satan; Witch-Finder General*
Reeves, Michael (wri, 1944-1969): *The Sorcerers; Witch-Finder General*
Reeves, Michael (1990s wri): *Batman: Mask of the Phantasm*
Reeves, Pat (act): *The Giant Gila Monster*
Reeves, Perrey (act): *Child's Play 3; Escape to Witch Mountain (1995); Plymouth*
Reeves, Philip (act): *The Goddess of Love*
Reeves, Richard (act): *Billy the Kid vs. Dracula; Target Earth; Tarzan's Hidden Jungle*
Reeves, Scott (act): *Friday the 13th, Part VIII-Jason Takes Manhattan*
Reeves, Steve (act, b. 1926): *Agi Murad, il Diavolo Bianco; The Avenger; La Battaglia di Maratona; Ercole e la Regina di Lidia; Il Figlio di Spartacus; Hercules (1957); The Last Days of Pompeii (1959); La Leggendi di Enea; Sandokan the Great; Il Terror dei Barberi; The Thief of Bagdad (1960); The Trojan Horse*
Reeves, Theodore (wri, 1910-1973): *Devotion*
Reeves, Walter (act): *Samson*
Reeves-Smith, H. (act): *The Return of Sherlock Holmes (1929)*
Reevis, Steve(n) (act): *Fargo; Grim Prairie Tales*
Reformina, Raul (act): *Strange Days*
Regalbuto, Joe (act, b. 1949): *Amazing Stories: The Movie V; Beyond Obsession; Bodily Harm; Invitation to Hell; Schizoid (1980); The Sword and the Sorcerer; Writer's Block*
Regan, Charles (act): *Werewolf of Washington*
Regan, Jayne (act): *Mr. Moto's Gamble; Thank You, Mr. Moto*
Regan, Pat(rick C.) (mus): *Leatherface: Texas Chainsaw Massacre III; Stepfather II; Stepfather III: Father's Day; Tales from the Darkside*
Regan, Paul (act): *The Devil's Cargo*
Regas, George (act): *Arrest Bulldog Drummond; Bulldog Drummond Strikes Back (1934); The Cat and the Canary (1939); Charlie Chan On Broadway; Mr. Moto Takes a Chance; Torchy Blane In Panama*
Regas, Pedro (act): *Madman of Mandoras*
Regehr, Duncan (act): *The Banker; Goliath Awaits; The Haunting of Lisa; The Monster Squad; Timemaster; Zorro: The Legend Begins*
Reger, Tammy (act): *Slugs*
Reggiani, Aldo (act): *The Cat O' Nine Tails*
Reggiani, Serge (act, b. 1922, nee Reggio Emilia): *Cat and Mouse (1978); Doulos-The Finger Man; I Hired a Contract Killer; Les Miserables (1957)*
Regin, Nadja (act): *Downfall; From Russia With Love; The Fur Collar; Goldfinger; The Man Without a Body; Number Six; Solo for Sparrow*
Regina, Paul (act): *The Awakening of Candra; Sharon's Secret*
Regine (act): *The Seven-Per-Cent Solution*
Regnier, Charles (act): *The Invisible Terror; The Secret Ways; A Study In Terror*
Regnoli, Piero (dir): *L'Ultima Preda del Vampiro*
Regnoli, Piero (wri): *Burial Ground; City of the Walking Dead; Deborah; L'Ultima Preda del Vampiro; I Vampiri*
Rego, Patricia (act): *The Bermuda Depths*
Regueiro, Antonio (act): *Anguish*
Regueiro, Francisco (wri): *Amador*
Reguli, Christina (act): *Web of Deceit*
Reg Wale Four, The (act): *Murder Reported*
Rehnolds, Lette (act): *Haunts*
Rehwaldt, Frank (wri): *Deadbolt*
Reich, Hans Leo (act): *Metropolis (1926)*
Reicher, Frank (act, 1875-1965): *Black Waters; Dr. Cyclops; The Florentine Dagger; Gildersleeve's Ghost; House of Frankenstein; House of Menace; The Invisible Ray; The Jade Mask; King Kong (1933); Mata Hari (1932); The Mummy's Ghost; The Mummy's Tomb; Murder On a Bridle Path; The Mystery of Marie Roget; Nazi Agent; Night Monster; Return of the Terror; Samson and Delilah; The Secret Life of Walter Mitty; Secret of the Chateau; Son of Kong; The Strange Mr. Gregory; Torchy Gets Her Man*
Reicher, Hedwig (act): *The Leopard Lady*
Reichert, Kittens (act): *The Scarlet Letter (1917)*
Reichert, Nancy (act): *Poor Devil*
Reichert, Tanya (act): *Perfect Little Angels*
Reichert, Wynn (act): *Sorority Girls and the Creature from Hell*
Reichman, Larry (act): *Nightbeast*
Reichmeister, Mimi (act): *Little Witches*
Reichow, Otto (act): *Above Suspicion; Back from the Dead; 36 Hours (1965)*
Reid, Alastair (dir): *The Night Digger; Something to Hide*
Reid, Alastair (wri): *Something to Hide*
Reid, Beryl (act, b. 1910): *Are You Dying Young Man?; The Assassination Bureau; The Doctor and the Devils; Dr. Phibes Rises Again; Psychomania (1972); Yellowbeard*
Reid, Bradley (act): *Nightfall (1988)*
Reid, Carl Benton (act, 1894-1973): *Lorna Doone (1951); Tarzan's Fight for Life; The Underwater City*
Reid, Don Brit (act): *The Magician (1973)*
Reid, Dorothy (wri): *Footsteps In the Fog*
Reid, Ella (act): *Caged Heat!*
Reid, Elliott (act, b. 1920): *The Absent-Minded Professor (1961); Son of Flubber; Vicki; The Whip Hand*
Reid, Frances (act): *The Andromeda Strain; Seconds*
Reid, Greg (act): *Re-Animator*
Reid, Houston (act): *Mutants In Paradise*
Reid, Kate (act, b. 1930): *The Andromeda Strain; Death Ship; Deceived; Double Negative; Plague*
Reid, Kathy (act): *Happy Birthday to Me*
Reid, Margot (act): *Color Me Dead*
Reid, Mary (act): *Amazon Women On the Moon; The Clan of the Cave Bear; Party Line*
Reid, Max (dir): *Wild Thing*
Reid, Michael Earl (act): *Army of Darkness*
Reid, Milton (act): *Arabian Adventure; Berserk; The Blood On Satan's Claw; Captain Clegg; Deadlier Than the Male; Dr. Phibes Rises Again; No. 1 of the Secret Service; The People That Time Forgot; The Spy Who Loved Me; Target: Harry; Terror (1979); The Terror of the Tongs; The Wonders of Aladdin*
Reid, Patricia (act): see Stanley, Kim
Reid, Ric (act): *The Little Match Girl (1987)*
Reid, Roger (act): *Cat People (1982)*
Reid, Rupert (act): *Meteorites!*
Reid, Sheila (act): *Brazil*
Reid, Steve (act): *Surf Nazis Must Die*
Reid, Tara (act): *A Return to Salem's Lot; What We Did That Night*
Reid, Tim (act, b. 1944): *It (1990)*
Reid, Trevor (act): *How to Murder a Rich Uncle Marriage of Convenience; Murder Reported; Satellite In the Sky; Walk a Tightrope; Zombie Island Massacre*
Reid, Wallace (act, 1890-1923): *Adam's Rib*
Reide, Sheldon (act): *Mother's Day*
Reider, Marcia (act): *Earthbound (1981)*
Reid-Harris, Barbara (act): *Secret Weapons*
Reidy, John (act): *The Toxic Avenger, Part II*

Reiff, Ethan (wri): *Demon Knight*
Reigle, James (wri): *Android*
Reigrod, Jon (act): *Witches' Brew*
Reilly, Andrew (act): *Liszt O' Mania*
Reilly, Charles Nelson (act, b. 1931): *Babes In Toyland (1997); A Troll In Central Park*
Reilly, John C. (act): *Dolores Claiborne*
Reilly, Robert (act): *Frankenstein Meets the Space Monster*
Reilly, Sean (act): *Phantom of the Mall: Eric's Revenge*
Reilly, Tom (act): *Slaughterhouse Rock*
Reilly, William (wri): *Mortal Thoughts*
Reiman, Eric (act): *Long John Silver*
Reimbold, Bill (act): *Raiders of the Lost Ark*
Reimers, Ed (act): *The Barefoot Executive*
Reimers, Nadine (act): *Evilspeak*
Reindel, Carl (act): *The Andromeda Strain*
Reineke, Gary (act): *Hitler's Daughter; The Kidnapping of the President; Millennium; Peter Benchley's 'Creature'; Rituals*
Reiner, Anna (wri): *Thunder Rock*
Reiner, Carl (act, b. 1922): *The Gazebo; The Man With Two Brains; Oh, God!; The Spirit of 76*
Reiner, Carl (dir, b. 1922): *All of Me; The Man With Two Brains; Oh, God!*
Reiner, Estelle (act): *The Man With Two Brains*
Reiner, Ivan (wri): *I Criminali della Galassia; The Green Slime*
Reiner, Jean (act): *Soultaker*
Reiner, Jeffrey (dir): *Blood and Concrete*
Reiner, Lucas (dir): *The Spirit of 76*
Reiner, Maxine (act): *Charlie Chan at the Circus*
Reiner, Richard (act): *Vampire On Bikini Beach*
Reiner, Rob (act, b. 1945): *The Spirit of 76*
Reiner, Rob (dir, b. 1945): *Misery; The Princess Bride*
Reiner, Thomas (act): *Sei Donne per l'Assassino*
Reiner, Tracy (act): *Apollo 13; Masque of the Red Death (1989)*
Reinert, Al (dir): *For All Mankind*
Reinert, Al (wri): *Apollo 13*
Reingold, Herb (act): *Distortions*
Reingold, Melanie (act): *Distortions*
Reingold, Warren (act): *Distortions*
Reinhard, Arthur (act): *Metropolis (1926)*
Reinhardt, Betty (wri): *Laura*
Reinhardt, John (wri): *Mr. Moto In Danger Island*
Reinhardt, Max (dir, 1873-1943): *A Midsummer Night's Dream (1935)*
Reinhardt, Max (wri, 1873-1943): *The Miracle (1959); Sumurun*
Reinhardt, Ray (act): *Cardiac Arrest; The Guardian; Something Is Out There; Time After Time; Visions of Murder*
Reinhardt, Sarah hale (act): *Seven*
Reinhardt, Wolfgang (wri): *Hitler: The Last Ten Days*
Reinhart, Alice (act): *Horror Express*
Reinhart, John (wri): *Tower of Terror*
Reinhold, Judge (act, b. 1956): *Black Magic (1992); Dad, the Angel & Me; Gremlins; Netforce; Pandemonium; The Santa Clause; Special Report: Journey to Mars; Vice Versa (1988)*
Reiniger, Lotte (dir, 1899-1981): *Aschenputtel; Dream Circus (unfinished); The Frog Prince (1954 & 1961); Die Goldene Gans (infinished); The Magic Horse; The Sleeping Beauty (1954); Snow White and Rose Red; The Three Wishes (1954); Thumbelina (1955)*
Reiniger, Scott H. (act): *Dawn of the Dead; Knightriders*
Reinking, Ann (act, b. 1947): *All That Jazz*
Reinl, Harald (dir): *Chariots of the Gods?; Forger of London; The Hand of the Gallows; In the Steel Net of Dr. Mabuse; The Invisible Dr. Mabuse; Die Schlangengrube und das Pendel; Treasure of Silver Lake*
Reino, Leonard (act): *Primal Scream*
Reis, Irving G. (cin): *Forbidden Planet*
Reis, Irving (dir, 1906-1953): *A Date With the Falcon; The Falcon Takes Over; The Gay Falcon*
Reis, Kurt (act): *Short Circuit 2*
Reis, Vivian (act): *Change of Mind; Curtains*
Reis, Whitney (act): *The Hidden*
Reisch, G. (wri): *Milczaca Gwiazda*
Reisch, Walter (dir, 1902-1983): *Song of Scheherazade*
Reisch, Walter (wri, 1902-1983): *F.P. 1 Antwortet Nicht; Journey to the Center of the Earth (1959); Song of Scheherazade*
Reischl, Geri (act): *The Brotherhood of Satan; I Dismember Mama*
Reisenfeld, Hugo (mus, b. 1883): *Tabu; Tarzan's Revenge*
Reiser, Clutch (mus): *Brain Damage*
Reiser, Hans (act): *The Story of the Dr. Lummel*

Reiser, Paul (act, b. 1956): *Aliens*
Reisman Jr., Philip H. (wri): *Short Walk to Daylight; A Very Missing Person*
Reisner, Charles (F.) (dir, 1887-1962): *The Cobra Strikes; Lost In a Harem*
Reisser, Dora (act): *Who Was Maddox?*
Reiswig, Isaac (act): *Phenomenon*
Reisz, Karel (dir, b. 1926): *Night Must Fall (1964)*
Reit, Ursula (act): *Willy Wonka and the Chocolate Factory*
Reitano, Tony (act): *Murder of Innocence*
Reiter, Bill (act): *The Haunting Passion*
Reith, Antonia/Tonie (act): *Eugene Aram; A Message from Mars (1913)*
Reith, Tonie (act): see Reith, Antonia/Tonie
Reitherman, Bruce (act): *The Jungle Book (1967)*
Reitherman, Wolf(gang) (dir): *The Aristocats; The Jungle Book (1967); 101 Dalmatians (1960); The Rescuers; Robin Hood (1973); Sleeping Beauty (1959); The Sword In the Stone*
Reitman, Catherine (act): *Ghostbusters II*
Reitman, Ivan (dir): *Cannibal Girls; Ghostbusters; Ghostbusters II; Junior (1994); Twins*
Reitman, Ivan (mus): *Rabid*
Reitman, Jason (act): *Ghostbusters II*
Reitz, Ric (act): *Web of Deceit*
Reitzen, Jack (act): *Appointment With Murder; Captain Kidd and the Slave Girl; The Naked Jungle*
Reiver, Harry (wri): *The Lone Wolf's Daughter (1929)*
Reizenstein, Franz (mus): *Circus of Horrors; The Mummy (1959)*
Rekert, Winston (act): *Eternal Evil; Moonlight Becomes You*
Relis, Harry (wri): *Captain Sinbad*
Relph, Emma (act): *The Witches (1990)*
Relph, Michael (wri, b. 1915): *The Assassination Bureau; Man In the Moon (1960); The Man Who Haunted Himself; A Place to Go; Woman of Straw*
Relph, Phyllis (act): *The Lights O' London*
Remar, James (act): *Blink; The Clan of the Cave Bear; Deadlock; Inferno (1998); Miracle On 34th Street (1994); Night Visions; The Phantom (1996); The Surgeon; Tales from the Darkside*
Remarque, Erich Maria (wri, 1898-1970): *The Last Ten Days of Adolf Hitler*
Remberg, Erika (act): *Candidate for Murder; Cave of the Living Dead; Circus of Horrors*
Remick, Jim (act): *Secrets of the Phantom Caverns*
Remick, Lee (act, 1935-1991): *Experiment In Terror; The Medusa Touch; No Way to Treat a Lady; The Omen; Rearview Mirror; The Running Man (1963); The Vision*
Remiddi, Patricia (act): *Il Mostro dell'Isola*
Remo, Andrew (dir & wri): *King Tut-Ankh-Amen's Eighth Wife*
Remsen, Bert (act): *Curfew; Dead Ringer; Dick Tracy (1990); Evil Spirits; Lies; Moon Pilot; Peacemaker (1990); Remote Control (1988); Sundown: The Vampire In Retreat; Tarantulas: The Deadly Cargo; Terrorvision*
Remsen, Guy (act): *Lies; Pretty Maids All In a Row*
Remsen, Kerry (act): *Ghoulies II; Pumpkinhead*
Remus, Lynn (act): *Body Parts (1991)*
Remus, Romola (act, d. 1987): *The Wizard of Oz (1910)*
Remy, Albert (act): *La Poursuite*
Remy, Helene (act): *L'Amante del Vampiri; Last of the Vikings*
Remy, Jacques (wri): *The Spy Is a Girl*
Remy, Maurice (act): *Forces Occultes*
Remy, Ronald (act): *The Blood Drinkers; Mad Doctor of Blood Island*
Renaday, Pete (act): *The Cat from Outer Space*
Renaldo, Duncan (act, 1904-1980): *The Bridge of San Luis Rey (1929); Jungle Gold; Panama Menace; Trader Horn (1931)*
Renaldo, Tito (act): *Ride the Pink Horse*
Renard, Colette (act): *La Poursuite*
Renard, David (act): *The Stepmother*
Renard, Emily (act): *Just Imagine*
Renard, Louis Miehe (act): *Journey to the Seventh Planet*
Renard, Maurice (wri): *Hands of a Stranger; The Hands of Orlac (1959); Mad Love; Orlacs Haende*
Renato, Paracchi (act): *Scream of the Demon Lover*
Renault, Georges (act, 1893-1969): *The Catman of Paris; Charlie Chan at Monte Carlo; East of Borneo; The Invisible Ray; Mr. Moto's Last Warning; The Son of Monte Cristo; Spy Smasher Returns*

Renay, Liz (act): *Blackenstein; A Date With Death; Day of the Nightmare; The Thrill Killers*
Rendel, Robert (act): *The Dark Stairway; Death at Broadcasting House; The Hound of the Baskervilles (1931); The Spy In Black*
Rendelstein, Les (wri): *Private Parts*
Renderer, Scott (act): *Poison (1990)*
Rene, Norman (dir): *Prelude to a Kiss*
Rene, Yves (act): *The Brother from Another Planet*
Reneau, Robert (wri): *Demolition Man*
Renella, Pat (act): *Moonchild*
Renevant, Georges (act): *Scotland Yard (1930); Le Spectre Vert*
Renfree, Gary (act): *Empire of Ash III*
Renfrey, Debra (act): *Empire of Ash III*
Renfrey, Derek (act): *Empire of Ash III*
Renfroe, Molly (act): *The Dark Half*
Renfurm, Arline (act): *Gebroken Spiegels*
Renick, Rachel (act): *Cocoon: The Return*
Renier, David (act): *Barracuda*
Renier, Yves (act): *Le Comte de Monte Cristo*
Renkov, N. (cin): *Novyi Gulliver*
Renn, Charles (act): *Santa Claus Conquers the Martians*
Renn, Grace (act): *Jurassic Women*
Renna, Patrick (act): *Beanstalk; Sometimes They Come Back...Again*
Rennahan, Ray (cin, 1896-1980): *At Sword's Point; A Connecticut Yankee In King Arthur's Court (1949); Doctor X; Flight to Tangier; I Love a Mystery (1966); Lady In the Dark; Mystery of the Wax Museum; The Three Caballeros; Whispering Smith*
Rennard, Deborah (act): *Land of Doom*
Renner, Michael (act): *Grim Prairie Tales*
Rennhofer, Linda (act): *Starship Invasions*
Rennie, Callum Keith (act): *Timecop; Unforgettable*
Rennie, Guy (act): *Invasion of the Body Snatchers (1956)*
Rennie, Hilary (act): *The Dragon of Pendragon Castle*
Rennie, James (act, d. 1965): *The Lash*
Rennie, Maggie (act): *Mark of the Devil (1985)*
Rennie, Michael (act, 1909-1971): *Assignment Terror; The Black Rose; Cyborg 2087; The Day the Earth Stood Still; Dracula vs. Frankenstein; 5 Fingers; The House In the Square; The Last Generation; The Lost World (1960); Les Miserables (1952); Omar Khayyam; The Power (1967); Subterfuge; The Thirteenth Letter; Tower of Terror; The Young, the Evil, and the Savage*
Rennison, Colleen (act): *Unforgettable*
Reno, Jean (act): *Le Dernier Combat; La Femme Nikita; Godzilla (1998); Mission: Impossible; The Visitors (1993)*
Reno, Jeff (wri): *Meet Joe Black*
Reno, John (act): *Black Magic Woman; Bloodspell; Dead of Night (1987)*
Renoir, Claude (cin, b. 1913): *Barbarella; La Dame dans l'Auto Avec des Lunettes et un Fusil; Et Mourir de Plaisir; The Green Glove; The Serpent (1973); Les Sorcieres de Salem; Spirits of the Dead; The Spy Who Loved Me*
Renoir, Jean (act, 1894-1979): *The Rules of the Game*
Renoir, Jean (dir, 1894-1979): *The Crime of Monsieur Lange; The Rules of the Game; Le Testament du Dr. Cordelier; Toni*
Renoir, Jean (wri, 1894-1979): *The Crime of Monsieur Lange; Le Testament du Dr. Cordelier; Toni*
Renoir, Leon (act): *Il Ladro di Venezia*
Renoir, Rita (act): *Red Desert*
Renoir, Sylvie (act): *Fantastic Planet*
Renom, Gaby (act): *Night of the Zombies (1983)*
Renoudet, Pete (act): *The Barefoot Executive; The Computer Wore Tennis Shoes (1970); The $1,000,000 Duck*
Renouf, Philip (act): *Brigadier Gerard*
Renton, David (act): *The Neptune Factor*
Rentoul, Patience (act): *No Haunt for a Gentleman*
Renwick, David W. (cin): *Fiend (1980)*
Renzetti, Joe (mus): *Basket Case 2; Child's Play (1988); Dead & Buried; The Exterminator; Frankenhooker; Poltergeist III; Through the Magic Pyramid*
Renzi, Eva (act): *Funeral In Berlin; Taste of Excitement; L'Uccello dalle Piume di Cristallo; Why Would Anyone Want to Kill a Nice Girl Like You?*
Renzi, Maggie (act): *The Brother from Another Planet*

Renzulli, Frank (act): *The Hidden; Warlock*
Renzullo, Mario (act): *Junket 89*
Repp, Pierre (act): *La Poursuite*
Repp, Stafford (act, 1918-1974): *Batman (1966)*
Requierme, Ana (act): *The Last Man On Planet Earth*
Requeiro, Francisco (dir): *Amador*
Requena, Manuel (act): *El Otro Fu-Manchu*
Reri (act): *Tabu*
Rescher, Dee Dee (act): *Communion; Once Bitten*
Rescher, Gayne (cin): *Angel On My Shoulder (1980); The Day After*
Reshovsky, Marc (cin): *Teen Witch*
Resines, Antonio (act): *Accion Mutante*
Resino, Andres (act): *Murder Mansion; La Noche de Walpurgis*
Resnais, Alain (dir & wri, b. 1922): *L'Annee Derniere a Marienbad*
Resnick, Judith (act): *Carnival of Blood*
Resnick, Ken (act): *The Silencers (1995)*
Resnick, Patricia (wri): *Quintet; Second Sight*
Resnick, Scott (act): *Class of Nuke 'em High, Part 2: Subhumanoid Meltdown*
Resnik, Gershon (act): *The Kidnapping of the President*
Resnikoff, Marta (act): *Nightlife (1989, USA-Mex)*
Resnikoff, Robert (dir & wri): *The First Power*
Ressel, Frank (act): *Tarzana, the Wild Girl*
Ressler, Scott (cin): *The Alien Within; Hollywood Chainsaw Hookers*
Resther, Jodie (act): *Wild Thing*
Reta, William (act): *Amazons (1986)*
Retford, Ella (act): *Poison Pen; Shadow of the Past*
Rethwisch, Gus (act): *House II: The Second Story; The Running Man (1987)*
Rettew, Michael (act): *Grim Prairie Tales*
Rettig, Tom(my) (act, 1941-1996): *The 5000 Fingers of Dr. T; For Heaven's Sake; The Lost Empire; River of No Return*
Retzer, Raul (act): *The Invisible Terror; 2069: A Sex Odyssey*
Reuben, Gloria (act): *Dead Air; Timecop*
Reubens, Paul (act, b. 1952): *Batman Returns; Beauty and the Beast: The Enchanted Christmas; Buffy the Vampire Slayer; Dr. Dolittle (1998); The Nightmare Before Christmas; Pandemonium*
Reuber-Staier, Eva (act): *The Slipper and the Rose*
Reumert, Poul (act): *Haxan*
Reuter, Marga (act): *Der Januskopf*
Reutermann, Wolf Rudiger (act): *The Cold Room*
Revan, Zeev (act): *The Jerusalem File*
Reve, Gerard (wri): *The Fourth Man*
Reveke, Rick (act): *Wonder Women*
Revel, Jean-Marie (act): *Les Enfants Terribles*
Revelins, Maria (act): *Secret Weapons*
Revell, Graeme (act): *The Crow (1994)*
Revell, Graeme (mus): *Boxing Helena; Child's Play 2; The Craft; The Crow: City of Angels; Dead Calm; The Crush; From Dusk Till Dawn; Ghost In the Machine; The Hand That Rocks the Cradle; Mighty Morphin Power Rangers; No Escape (1994); Psycho IV: The Beginning; The Saint; Spawn; Spontaneous Combustion; Strange Days; Tank Girl; Until the End of the World*
Revene, Larry (cin): *Deranged (1987)*
Revere, Anne (act, 1903-1990): *The Devil Commands; Dragonwyck; The Falcon Takes Over; Secret Beyond the Door; The Thin Man Goes Home*
Revere, Dorothy (act): *The Black Camel*
Reves, Martha/Marta (act): *Future Women; El Secreto del Doctor Orlof*
Revier, Dorothy (act, b. 1904): *By Candlelight; The Iron Mask*
Revier, Harry (dir, b. 1889): *Jungle Trail of the Son of Tarzan; The Lost City*
Revill, Clive (act, b. 1930): *The Assassination Bureau; The Black Windmill; Bunny Lake Is Missing; C.H.U.D. II; The Double Man; Dracula: Dead and Loving It; The Empire Strikes Back; Fathom; The Great Houdinis; The Headless Ghost; Kaleidoscope; The Legend of Hell House; The Little Prince; Modesty Blaise; Nobody Runs Forever; One of Our Dinosaurs Is Missing; The Private Life of Sherlock Holmes; Rumpelstiltskin (1987); She's Dressed to Kill; Zorro, the Gay Blade*
Reville, Alma (wri, 1900-1982): *The Lady Vanishes (1938); Murder; Number 17; The Paradine Case; The Passing of the Third Floor Back (1935); Rich and Strange; The Ring; Sabotage; The Secret Agent (1936); Shadow of a Doubt (1943 & 1991); Suspicion (1941); The 39 Steps (1935 & 1959); Young and Innocent*

Revilli, Vanna (act): *The Devil's Men*
Revivo, Marc (act): *Ed Wood*
Rex, Bert (act): *The Counterfeiters; The Great Cheque Fraud; The Stolen Heirlooms; The Thornton Jewel Mystery*
Rex, Jack (act): *Black Devils of Kali*
Rex, Roberta (act): *Children of the Damned*
Rey, Alejandro (act, 1930-1987): *Satan's Triangle; The Stepmother; Stunts Umlimited; The Swarm; Terrorvision; Twinkle, Twinkle, Killer Kane*
Rey, Antonia (act): *Jacob's Ladder*
Rey, Barbara (act): *Horror of the Zombies*
Rey, Bruno (act): *Sorceress (1982)*
Rey, Carl (act): *Graduation Day*
Rey, Edith (wri): *Spacehunter: Adventures In the Forbidden Zone; The Vindicator*
Rey, Fernando (act, 1917-1994): *Cadaveri Eccellenti; La Cara del Terror; Cartes sur Table; The Discreet Charm of the Bourgeoisie; Faustina; Goliath Against the Giants; The Knight of the Dragon; The Last Days of Pompeii (1959); The Light at the Edge of the World; Night Fiend; Quintet; The Running Man (1963); Tristana; Two Mafia Guys Vs. Goldginger; Viridiana*
Rey, Jose (act): *Deep Red (1994)*
Rey, Mariano (act): *Crypt of the Living Dead*
Rey, Rosa (act): *Secret Beyond the Door; Secret of the Incas*
Rey, Rubina (act): *The Grim Reaper*
Reybaz, Andre (act): *Le Golem (1966)*
Rey-Coquais, Cyrille (dir): *Georgette Meunier*
Reye, Nicolas (cin): *Creature of the Walking Dead*
Reyer, Walter (act): *Journey to the Lost City*
Reyes, Chito (act): *Daughters of Satan*
Reyes Jr., Ernie (act): *Red Sonja*
Reyes, Jose' Truchado (wri): *Exterminators of the Year 3000*
Reyes, Julian (act): *Alligator II: The Mutation*
Reyes, Pia (act): *Forbidden Zone: Alien Abduction*
Reyes, Richard (act): *RoboCop 2*
Reyes, Stanley J. (act): *Obsession (1976)*
Reyes, Theresa (act): *Dance of the Dwarfs*
Reyett, Ravinder Singh (act): *Octopussy*
Reyher, Ferdinand 9wri): *The World, the Flesh and the Devil*
Reynal, Madeleine (act): *Dr. Caligari*
Reynalds, Christopher (act): *The Night Digger*
Reynaud, Emile (dir, 1844-1918): *Clown et Ses Chiens; Guillaume Tell; Pauvre Pierrot*
Reynaud, Janine (act): *Kiss Me, Monster; Necronomicon; Sadist Erotica*
Reynolds, Abigail (act): *Mary Shelley's 'Frankenstein'*
Reynolds, Adeline DeWalt (act, 1862-1961): *Son of Dracula (1943); Witness to Murder*
Reynolds, Alan (act): *The Beginning of the End; Cape Fear (1961); Earth vs. the Flying Saucers; Tobor the Great*
Reynolds, Ben (cin): *Queen Kelly; The Scarlet Drop*
Reynolds, Bill (act): *Party Line*
Reynolds, Brian J. (cin): *What We Did That Night*
Reynolds, Buddy (act): *Cocoon: The Return*
Reynolds, Burke (act): *The Mummy and the Curse of the Jackals*
Reynolds, Burt (act, b. 1936): *All Dogs Go to Heaven; Frankenstein and Me; The Maddening; Operation C.I.A.; Skullduggery; Universal Soldier III: Unfinished Business*
Reynolds, Charles (act): *Wolfman (1979)*
Reynolds, Christopher (act, dir & wri): *Offerings*
Reynolds, Clarke (wri): *The Viking Queen*
Reynolds, Craig (act): *The Fatal Hour (1940); Just Before Dawn (1946); The Mystery of Mr. Wong; Smart Blonde*
Reynolds, Debbie (act, b. 1932, nee Mary Frances Reynolds): *Charlotte's Web; The Gazebo; Goodbye Charlie; What's the Matter With Helen?*
Reynolds, E. Vivian (act): *Her Greatest Performance*
Reynolds, Evelyn (act): *Terror In the Wax Museum*
Reynolds, Frederick (wri): *Dr. Sin Fang*
Reynolds, Gene (act): *Down Three Dark Streets*
Reynolds, Harriet (act): *The Secret Life of Ian Fleming*
Reynolds, Helene (act): *Blue, White and Perfect; Heaven Can Wait (1943); The Man Who Wouldn't Die*
Reynolds, Hilary (act): *High Spirits; The Outcasts*
Reynolds, James Ellis (act): *Jacob's Ladder*
Reynolds, Jay (act): *The Reincarnate*
Reynolds, Joan H. (act): *The Wraith*
Reynolds, John (act): *Manos, the Hands of Fate*
Reynolds, Jonathan (wri): *My Stepmother Is an Alien*
Reynolds, Joseph M. (act): *Dr. Black Mr. Hyde*
Reynolds, Judy (act): *Empire of Ash III*
Reynolds, Kathryn (act): *Trilogy of Terror*
Reynolds, Katie (act): *The Secret World of Polly Flynt*
Reynolds, Kevin (dir): *Amazing Stories: The Movie VI; Robin Hood: Prince of Thieves; Waterworld*
Reynolds, Kevin (wri): *Red Dawn*
Reynolds, Kristina (act): *Wolfman (1979)*
Reynolds, Larry (act): *Change of Mind; My Bloody Valentine; Virus (1980); Welcome to Blood City; When Michael Calls*
Reynolds, Lissa (act): *Secrets In the Attic*
Reynolds, Marjorie (act, 1916-1997, nee Marjorie Goodspeed): *Doomed to Die; The Fatal Hour (1940); Heaven Only Knows; Ministry of Fear; Mr. Wong In Chinatown; Mystery Plane; No Holds Barred; The Time of Their Lives*
Reynolds, Mary Frances (act): see Reynolds, Debbie
Reynolds, Michael (J.) (act): *Bear Island; The Kidnapping of the President; Millennium; The Neptune Factor; Plague; Sorry, Wrong Number (1989)*
Reynolds, Milan (act): *Strange Days*
Reynolds, Ollie (act): *The Legend of the Wolf Woman*
Reynolds, Patrick (act, b. 1953): *Eliminators*
Reynolds, Paul (act): *Little Shop of Horrors (1986); Slipstream*
Reynolds, Peter (act, b. 1926, nee Peter Horrocks): *The Bank Raiders; Black 13; The Breaking Point (1961); Daleks' Invasion Earth 2150 A.D.; Devil Girl from Mars; Gaolbreak (1962); Guilt Is My Shadow; The Hands of Orlac (1959); The Man Who Couldn't Walk; The Painted Smile; A Question of Suspense; West 11; Wrong Number*
Reynolds, Quentin (act): *Golden Earrings*
Reynolds, Robert (act): *Daughter of Darkness (1990)*
Reynolds, Rolf (act): *Xtro II: The Second Encounter*
Reynolds, Ryan (act): *Sabrina the Teenage Witch*
Reynolds, Sheldon (dir & wri, b. 1923): *Assignment to Kill; Foreign Intrigue*
Reynolds, Simon (act): *Gate II*
Reynolds, Tom (GB act): *Birds of Prey; The Lyons Mail; She (1925)*
Reynolds, Tom (USA act): *Fright (1957)*
Reynolds, Ursi (dir): *Ganjasaurus Rex*
Reynolds, Vera (act, 1899-1962): *The Monster Walks; The Road to Yesterday; Tangled Destinies*
Reynolds, Vickilyn (act): *Addams Family Values*
Reynolds, Willa (act): *Surf Nazis Must Die*
Reynolds, William (act): *Cult of the Cobra; Francis Goes to West Point; The Land Unknown; Son of Ali Baba; The Thing That Couldn't Die*
Reynolds-Long, Peter (dir): *The Hound of London*
Reynoldson, Rondel (act): *Unforgettable*
Reynoso, Jorge (act): *Robbers of the Sacred Mountain*
Rhames, Ving (act, b. 1961): *Body Count; Jacob's Ladder; Mission: Impossible; The People Under the Stairs*
Rhazis, Phoebus (act): *Electra (1961)*
Rhea, Bunny (act): *Cape Fear (1961)*
Rheaume, Dana (cin): *The Alien's Return*
Rheaume, Dell (cin): *Invasion of the Body Snatchers (1978)*
Rhema (act): *Voyage of the Rock Aliens*
Rhey, Ashlie (act): *Midnight Tease*
Rho, Angela (act): *Behind the Mask of Zorro; Ercole Contro i Figli del Sole*
Rho, Stella (act): *The Demon Barber of Fleet Street; Maria Marten: or, The Murder In the Red Barn (1935)*
Rhoades, Arthur S. (cin): *The Animal World*
Rhoades, Barbara (act, b. 1947): *The Great Houdinis; Scream, Blacula, Scream*
Rhoades, Michael (act): *Storm of the Century*
Rhoda, Sybil (act): *Boadicea; Downhill*
Rhodes, Andrew (act): *Runaway (1984)*
Rhodes, Bobby (act): *Demons 2; Endgame; The Great Alligator; Hercules (1983)*
Rhodes, Christopher (act): *Gorgo*
Rhodes, Cynthia (act): *Curse of the Crystal Eye; Runaway (1984)*
Rhodes, Donnelly (act): *Beyond Obsession; Big & Hairy; Change of Mind; The Neptune Factor; Oh Heavenly Dog; Our Man Flint: Dead On Target; Roswell: The Aliens Attack*
Rhodes, Earl (act): *Dark Places; The Medusa Touch; Young Sherlock Holmes*
Rhodes, Ebby (act): *Voodoo Heartbeat*
Rhodes, Erik (act, 1906-1990): *Charlie Chan In Paris; The Mysterious Mr. Moto; Special Investigator*
Rhodes, Esther (act): *The Ringer (1928)*
Rhodes, Grandon (act): *Born to Kill; Earth vs. the Flying Saucers; The Lost Volcano; Revenge of the Creature; Ride the Pink Horse; Secret of the Incas; Too Many Winners; The 27th Day*
Rhodes, Hari (act): *Conquest of the Planet of the Apes; Donor; Earth II; The Lost Missile; Matt Helm; Mirage (1965); The Satan Bug; Shock Corridor*
Rhodes, Harry (act): *Coma*
Rhodes, Jennifer (act): *Ghost Fever; Night Creature*
Rhodes, Jerry (act): *Barracuda*
Rhodes, Jordan (act): *The Night Stalker (1971); The Terminal Man; Wonder Woman*
Rhodes, Julie (act): *Slaughterhouse Rock*
Rhodes, Kenny (act): *The Munsters' Revenge*
Rhodes, Lee (act): *From Hell It Came*
Rhodes, Marjorie/Margery (act, b. 1902): *Escape to Danger; Footsteps In the Fog; Gideon's Day; The Girl On the Pier; Hands of the Ripper; Poison Pen; Uncle Silas; The Yellow Balloon*
Rhodes, Michael (act): *The Attic*
Rhodes, Michael (dir): *Visions of Murder*
Rhodes, Percy (act): *Hamlet (1913)*
Rhodes, Richard (act): *King Kong Lives*
Rhodes, Rick (act): *Barracuda*
Rhodimer, Carolyn (act): *The Witchmaker*
Rhomm, Patrice (wri): *The Devil's Nightmare*
Rhone, Kim (act): *Demons 2*
Rhouma, Gypsy (act): *Alf's Button (1930)*
Rhu, Andrea (act): *Ercole Contro i Figli del Sole*
Rhubarb the Cat (animal act): *The Comedy of Terrors*
Rhue, Madlyn (act, b. 1934): *Crackle of Death; Fantasies; Poor Devil*
Rhymer, Don (wri): *Under Wraps*
Rhyne, John Thomas (act): *Twister*
Rhys, Jean (wri): *Wide Sargasso Sea*
Rhys, Phillip (act): *Zenon: Girl of the 21st Century*
Rhys-Davies, John (act): *Aladdin and the King of Thieves; The Black Windmill; Body Armor; Cyborg Cop; Firewalker; The Gifted One; The Goddess of Love; Indiana Jones and the Last Crusade; In the Shadow of Kilimanjaro; King Solomon's Mines (1985); The Little Match Girl (1987); The Lost World (1993); Marquis de Sade; Raiders of the Lost Ark; Return to the Lost World; Ring of the Musketeers; Robot In the family; Sphinx (1981); Sunset Grill; Sword of the Valiant; The Trial of the Incredible Hulk; The Unnamable II*
Riad (act): *The Monster Squad*
Riano, Renie (act, d. 1971): *Mr. Moto In Danger Island; Nancy Drew and the Hidden Staircase; Nancy Drew, Detective; Nancy Drew, Troubleshooter*
Riba, Diego (act): *Evil Clutch*
Riba, Monserrat (act): *Hatchet for a Honeymoon*
Ribas, Joaquin (act): *Anguish*
Ribeiro, Alfonso (act): *Ticks*
Ribeiro, Joe (act): *Steel Dawn*
Ribera, Daniel (wri): *Behind the Mask of Zorro*
Ribero, Enrico (act): *Le Sang d'un Poete*
Riblett, Chris (act): *Midnight (1980)*
Ribman, Ronald (wri): *The Angel Levine*
Ricard, Adrian (act): *Dr. Black Mr. Hyde; The Man With Two Brains*
Ricardo, Diana (act): *Supergirl (1984)*
Ricardo, Diane (act): *Scream for Help*
Riccardi, Tony (act): *Princess Warrior*
Riccardini, Michele (act): *Ulysses*
Riccardo, Rick (act): *The Man Who Fell to Earth (1976)*
Riccelli, Carlos Alberto (act): *The Dolphin*
Ricci, Bill (act): *Don't Go In the House*
Ricci, Christina (act, b. 1980): *The Addams Family; Addams Family Values; Casper*
Ricci, Debra (wri): *Alien from L.A.*
Ricci, Mark (act): *Night of the Living Dead (1968)*
Ricci, Nora (act): *The Night Porter*
Ricci, Paolo (act): *Spara Forte, Piu Forte...Non Capisco*
Ricci, Paolo (cin): *The Black Cat (1980); Ironmaster*
Ricci, R.J. (act): *Night of the Living Dead (1968)*
Ricci, Richard (act): *Night of the Living Dead (1968)*
Ricci, Rudy (wri): *The Return of the Living Dead (1985)*
Ricci, Teodoro (dir, a.k.a. Anthony Richmond): *The Sharks' Cave*
Ricci, Tonino (dir): *Rush*
Ricciardi, William (act): *As You Desire Me*
Rice, Alfred (act): *Cinque Tombe per un Medium*
Rice, Anne (wri): *Exit to Eden; Interview With the Vampire*
Rice, Bill (dir): *The Vineyard*
Rice, Brett (act): *Edward Scissorhands; Matinee*
Rice, Craig (wri): *The Falcon In Danger; The Falcon's Brother*
Rice, Diana (act): *Barney's Great Adventure*
Rice, Dick (act): *Wolfman (1979)*
Rice, Elmer (wri, 1892-1967): *The Adding Machine; Dream Girl*
Rice, Florence (act, 1906-1974): *The Ghost and the Guest; Miracles for Sale; Mr. District Attorney; Phantom Raiders*
Rice, Frank (act): *The Gore-Gore Girls; Red Signals*
Rice, George (act): see O'Hanlon, George
Rice, Gigi (act): *Deadly Web*
Rice, Jack (act): *Crashing Las Vegas*
Rice, Jeff (wri): *Crackle of Death; Demon and the Mummy; The Night Stalker (1971); The Night Strangler*
Rice, Joan (act, b. 1930): *Blackmailed; Blonde Bait; Horror of Frankenstein; The Long Knife; Payroll; The Steel Key; The Story of Robin Hood*
Rice, Joel S. (act): *Final Exam*
Rice, John (act): *Ed Wood; Midnight (1980)*
Rice, John C. (act): *The Kiss (1896)*
Rice, John (wri): *Curiosity Kills*
Rice, Lee (act): *Howling III; Mad Max Beyond Thunderdome*
Rice, Milt (cin): *Damnation Alley; Flight to Mars; Gargoyles; Invasion of the Body Snatchers (1956); The Magic Sword (1962); Queen of Outer Space; World Without End*
Rice, Ron (dir, 1935-1964): *The Queen of Sheba Meets the Atom Man*
Rice, Tim (mus, b. 1944): *The Fan; The Lion King*
Rice, Warren (act): *Arachnophobia*
Rich, Adam (act, b. 1968): *The Devil and Max Devlin*
Rich, Allan (act): *The Entity; Fugitive from the Empire; Highlander 2: The Quickening; Joe & the Colonel*
Rich, Bernie (act): *Sabu and the Magic Ring*
Rich, Claude (act): *The Burning Court; La Mariee etait en Noir*
Rich, David Lowell (dir, b. 1923): *Adventures of the Queen; Brock's Last Case; Eye of the Cat; Have Rocket, Will Travel; The Horror at 37,000 Feet; The Mask of Sheba; Satan's School for Girls*
Rich, Dick (act): *Dressed to Kill (1941); The Neanderthal Man*
Rich, Doris (act): *Santa Claus Conquers the Martians*
Rich, Dorothy (act): *Student Bodies*
Rich, Eli (act): *Murderlust*
Rich, Irene (act, b. 1897): *Held for Murder*
Rich, Monica (act): *Night of Dark Shadows*
Rich, Richard (dir): *The Black Cauldron; The Fox and the Hound; The Swan Princess; The Swan Princess: Mystery of the Enchanted Treasure*
Rich, Richard (wri): *The Swan Princess*
Rich, Royce (act): *Hello Again*
Rich, Shirley (act): *Hello Again*
Rich, Tim (act): *The Haunted (1991)*
Rich, Vernon (act): *I've Lived Before; The War of the Worlds*
Rich, Vivian (act): *Enchantment*
Richard, Dawn (act): *I Was a Teenage Werewolf*
Richard, Edmond (cin): *The Discreet Charm of the Bourgeoisie*
Richard, Eric (act): *The Final Conflict; Venom (1982)*
Richard, Frieda (act): *Faust (1926)*
Richard, Jean (act): *Rope Around the Neck*
Richard, Jean-Louis (wri, b. 1927): *Fahrenheit 451; La Mariee etait en Noir; Mata Hari, Agent H21*
Richard, Jef (dir): *Berserker*
Ri'chard, Robert (act): *In His Father's Shoes*
Richard, Wendy (act): *No Blade of Grass*
Richarde, Tessa (act): *Cat People (1982)*
Richards, Addison (act, 1887-1964): *Betrayal from the East; Bewitched (1944); Call Northside 777; Charlie Chan In Panama; Close Call for Ellery Queen; The Flight That Disappeared; The Gracie Allen Murder Case; The Lone Wolf Strikes; The Millerson Case; Mr. Moto's Gamble; The Mummy's Curse; Nick Carter, Master Detective; Secret Agent of Japan; The Shanghai Cobra; Smart Blonde; Spellbound (1945); Strange Confession; The Walking Dead*
Richards, Ann (act, b. 1918): *Love from a Stranger (1947); Love Letters; Sorry, Wrong Number (1948)*

Richards, Ariana (act): *Disaster In Time; Jurassic Park; Tremors*

Richards, Arleigh (act): *Jacob's Ladder*

Richards, Aubrey (act): *The Curse of the Golem; Endless Night; The Ipcress File; The Man Who Haunted Himself*

Richards, Bethany (act): *Eve of Destruction*

Richards, Billie (act): *Willy McBean and His Magic Machine*

Richards, Brian (act): *Look What's Happened to Rosemary's Baby; Scream of the Wolf*

Richards, Burt (act): *Barracuda*

Richards, Cass (act): *The Hideous Sun Demon*

Richards, Cicely (act): *Trilby (1914)*

Richards, David (act): *Mr. Horatio Knibbles*

Richards, Dean (act): *Island of Blood; Red Blooded American Girl*

Richards, Denise (act): *Starship Troopers; Tammy and the T-Rex*

Richards, Dick (dir): *Death Valley; Farewell, My Lovely*

Richards, Elwyn (wri): *Sisters of Death*

Richards, Evan (act): *Altered States; Mute Witness; Society; Twilight Zone*

Richards, Frances (act): *The Living Ghost (1942)*

Richards, Frank (act): *Appointment With Murder; Before I Hang; Prisoners of the Casbah; The Scarf; Spy Chasers*

Richards, George (act): *The Bermuda Depths*

Richards, Gordon (act, b. 1893): *Flight to Nowhere; Larceny In Her Heart; 13 Lead Soldiers; White Pongo*

Richards, Grant (act, 1916-1963): *The Four Skulls of Jonathan Drake; Just Off Broadway; A Night of Mystery (1937)*

Richards, Gwil(l) (act): *It's Alive (1974); The Monster Squad; Motel Hell*

Richards, Jack L. (cin): *The Beast Within; Through Naked Eyes*

Richards, Jason (act): *Night of the Living Dead (1968); Trick or Treats*

Richards, Jeff (act, nee Richard Mansfield Taylor) (act): *Island of Lost Women; It's a Dog's Life; The Secret of the Purple Reef*

Richards, Jennifer (act): *Terrorvision*

Richards, Kathie (act): *The Dark (1979)*

Richards, Keith (act): *Queen of the Amazons (1947); The Snow Creature*

Richards, Kent (mus): *Zombie High*

Richards, Kim (act, b. 1964): *Devil Dog: The Hound of Hell; Escape to Witch Mountain (1975); Return from Witch Mountain*

Richards, Kurt (act): see Kidd, Jonathan

Richards, Kyle (act): *Curfew; Halloween; The Watcher In the Woods*

Richards, Lisa (Blake) (act): *Heaven Can Wait (1978); Return (1985); Silent Night, Bloody Night*

Richards, Lorrie (act): *The Magic Sword (1962); Trauma (1963)*

Richards, Mark Daly (act): *The Jewel of the Nile*

Richards, Michael (act): *Coneheads; Transylvania 6-5000*

Richards, Paul (act, 1924-1974): *Beneath the Planet of the Apes; Phantom of the Rue Morgue; The Tribe; The Unknown Terror*

Richards, Paula (act): *Night of the Living Dead (1968)*

Richards, Peggy (act): *The Stolen Sacrifice; The Wheel of Death*

Richards, Pennington (dir): *Stormy Crossing*

Richards, Sal (act): *Eyes of Laura Mars*

Richards, Silvia (wri): *Possessed (1947); Secret Beyond the Door*

Richards, Sindee Ann (act): *The Fool Killer*

Richards, Stony (act): *The Boogey Man*

Richards, Susan (act): *The Haunting; I Don't Want to Be Born; Journey to Midnight; The Rocking Horse Winner; The Village of the Damned (1960)*

Richards, Ted (act): *Street Fighter II: The Animated Movie*

Richards, Terry (act): *Raiders of the Lost Ark; Red Sonja*

Richards, Tom (act): *The Cursed Mountain Mystery*

Richards, Tony (act): *The Dungeonmaster*

Richardson, Barb (act): *Starship Invasions*

Richardson, Belle (act): *Alien High*

Richardson, Charles (act): *Satellite In the Sky*

Richardson, Cliff (act): *Zeppelin*

Richardson, Don (act): *The Pink Chiquitas*

Richardson, Doreen (act): *Mother's Day*

Richardson, Duncan (act): *The Glass Web*

Richardson, Frank(land A.) (dir): *The Black Tulip (1921); The Howard Case; The River House Ghost*

Richardson, Frank A. (wri): *The Man Who Made Diamonds*

Richardson, Ian (act): *Brazil; Dark City; The Fourth Protocol; The Hound Of The Baskervilles (1982); The Persecution and Assassination of Jean-Paul Marat as Performed by the Inmates of the Asylum of Charenton Under the Direction of the Marquis de Sade; The Phantom of the Opera (1990); The Sign of Four (1983)*

Richardson, Isis (act): *Phoenix the Warrior*

Richardson, Jack (act): *The Adventures of Robin Hood; Torchy Plays With Dynamite*

Richardson, James (act): *Meteor*

Richardson, Jay (act): *The Alien Within; Attack of the 60 Foot Centerfold; Bad Girls from Mars; The Channeler; Death Row Diner; Haunting Fear; Hollywood Chainsaw Hookers; The Newlydeads; Slashdance; Teenage Exorcist*

Richardson, Joely (act): *Event Horizon; Loch Ness; 101 Dalmatians (1996)*

Richardson, John (act, b. 1936): *Eyeball; Frankenstein 1980; La Maschera del Demonio; On a Clear Day You Can See Forever; One Million Years B.C.; She (1965); Torso; The Vengeance of She; War of the Planets*

Richardson, John (cin): *Aliens; Ladyhawke; The Living Daylights; Superman (1978); A View to a Kill; Warlords of the Deep*

Richardson, John (dir): see Merino, J.L.

Richardson, John (act, b. 1926): *The Believers; The Exorcist III; The Fly II*

Richardson, Lillie (act): *The Fugitive (1993); The Lightning Incident*

Richardson, Mark (dir): *Robot In the Family*

Richardson, Michael (act): *Earthquake*

Richardson, Mike (wri): *Timecop*

Richardson, Miles (act): *The Return of Sherlock Holmes (1986)*

Richardson, Miranda (act, b. 1958): *After Pilkington; Alice In Wonderland (1999); Merlin (1998); El Mono Loco; Transmutations*

Richardson, Natasha (act): *The Comfort of Strangers; Gothic; The Handmaid's Tale; Past Midnight*

Richardson, Patty (act): *Christmas Evil*

Richardson, Peter (act): *The Brother from Another Planet*

Richardson, (Sir) Ralph (act, 1902-1983): *Alice's Adventures In Wonderland (1972); The Bed-Sitting Room; Bulldog Jack; Dragonslayer; The Fallen Idol; Frankenstein: The True Story; The Ghoul (1933); Greystoke: The Legend of Tarzan, Lord of the Apes; The Man Who Could Work Miracles; Murder On Monday; The Return of Bulldog Drummond; Richard III (1955); Rollerball; The Sound Barrier; Tales from the Crypt (1971); Things to Come; Time Bandits; Watership Down; Who Slew Auntie Roo?; Woman of Straw; The Wrong Box*

Richardson, (Sir) Ralph (dir, 1902-1983): *Murder On Monday*

Richardson, Robert (act): *Pranks*

Richardson, Salli (act): *Gargoyles, The Movie: The Heroes Awaken*

Richardson, Sy (act): *Bad Dreams; Dead Man Walking; Repo Man; They Live*

Richardson, Tony (dir, 1928-1991): *Hamlet (1969); The Loved One; Mademoiselle; The Phantom of the Opera (1990)*

Richardson, Virgil (act): *Tarzan's Deadly Silence*

Riche, Paul (dir): *Forces Occultes*

Richeret, Nick (act): *The Man In the Iron Mask (1997)*

Richert, Ted (act): *Eyes of a Stranger; The Final Countdown; Piranha II: The Spawning*

Richert, William (dir & wri): *Winter Kills*

Richey, Don (act): *Once Bitten*

Richfield, Edwin (act): *The Adventures of Hal 5; The Black Rider; The Brain Machine; The Break; The Camp On Blood Island; Diamonds On Wheels; The Face of Fu Manchu; Find the Lady; Model for Murder; No Trees In the Street; Quatermass and the Pit; Quatermass II; The Secret of Blood Island; X...The Unknown*

Richie, Don (act): *Princess Warrior*

Richings, Julian (act): *Clarence*

Richler, Mordecai (wri): *Jacob Two-Two and the Hooded Fang*

Richman, Caryn (act): *Sleepstalker*

Richman, Charles (act): *Blondes at Work; Torchy Runs for Mayor*

Richman, Josh (act): *Fright Night II*

Richman, Marian (act): *Gog*

Richman, Peter (Mark) (act, b. 1927): *Agent for H.A.R.M.; City Killer; Dark Intruder; Friday the 13th, Part VIII-Jason Takes Manhattan; Judgment Day; FBI Factor; Dynasty; Roger (act): Pinocchio (1978)*

Richmond, Anthony (dir & wri): *Deja Vu*

Richmond, Anthony (B.)/Tony (cin): *Candyman; Don't Look Now; Madame Sin; The Man Who Fell to Earth (1976); Midnight's Child; Tales from the Hood; Vampira*

Richmond, Bill (wri): *The Nutty Professor (1963 & 1996)*

Richmond, Branscombe (act): *Deathmoon; Death Ring; The Hidden; Nemesis; Snow Kill; Star Trek III: The Search for Spock*

Richmond, Dennis (act): *Copycat*

Richmond, Doyle (act): *Orpheus Descending*

Richmond, Fiona (act): *The House On Straw Hill*

Richmond, Irene (act): *Dr. Terror's House of Horrors (1964); Nightmare (1963); Vengeance*

Richmond, John (act): *The Quatermass Conclusion*

Richmond, Kane (act, 1906-1973, nee Frederick W. Bowditch): *Behind the Mask (1946); Charlie Chan In Panama; Charlie Chan In Reno; Devil Diamond; The Lost City; The Missing Lady; Murder Over New York; Passkey to Danger; The Shadow Returns; Spy Smasher Returns; The Tiger Woman; Traffic In Crime*

Richmond, Ken (mus): *It Happened at Lake Wood Manor*

Richmond, Leo C. (act): *Daughter of the Jungle*

Richmond, Ralph (act): *Phantasm*

Richmond, Robin (act): *Murder at the Windmill*

Richmond, Steven (act): *Phantom of the Paradise*

Richmond, Susan (act): *Crow Hollow*

Richmond, Tom (cin): *Chopping Mall; Hard Rock Zombies; Nightmare On the 13th Floor*

Richmond, Tony (cin): see Richmond, Anthony (B.)/Tony

Richmond, Warner (act): *The Lost Jungle; Radio Ranch*

Richter, Daniel (act): *2001: A Space Odyssey*

Richter, Deborah (act): *Cyborg (1989)*

Richter, Hans (dir, 1888-1976): *Dreams That Money Can Buy; Vormittagsspuk*

Richter, Hans (wri, 1888-1976): *Dreams That Money Can Buy*

Richter, Mordecai (wri): *Jacob Two-Two and the Hooded Fang*

Richter, Paul (act, 1896-1962): *Doctor Mabuse; Die Nibelungen*

Richter, W.D. (dir): *The Adventures of Buckaroo Banzai; Late for Dinner*

Richter, W.D. (wri): *Big Trouble In Little China; Dracula (1979); Invasion of the Body Snatchers (1978); Needful Things*

Richwood, Patrick (act): *Frankenstein: The College Years*

Rick, Pat (act): *The Silence of the Hams*

Rickard, Dick (wri): *Snow White and the Seven Dwarfs*

Rickert, Leslie (act): *Explorers*

Ricketts, Helen (act): see Carter, Helena

Ricketts, Tom (act): *After the Thin Man; Bulldog Drummond (1929); Secrets of the Night; Trouble for Two*

Rickles, Don (act, b. 1926): *Innocent Blood; Pajama Party; Quest for Camelot; Toy Story; X—The Man With the X-Ray Eyes*

Rickman, Alan (act): *I Was a Teenage Zombie; Rasputin (1996); Robin Hood: Prince of Thieves; Shock! Shock! Shock!*

Rickman, Allen (act): *Flesh-Eating Mothers*

Rickman, Allen Lewis (act): *Metamorphosis: The Alien Factor*

Rickman, Catherine (act): *Grizzly*

Ricksen, Lucille (act): *Behind the Curtain (1924)*

Rico, Mona (act): *Zorro Rides Again*

Rico, Tony (act): *The Night of the Claw*

Riddell, James (dir): *Discipline*

Riddell, James (act): *Discipline; The Strange Case of Mr. Todmorden*

Riddell, Lyndsay (act): *The Magic Bubble*

Ridder, Nancy Ann (act): *Scream*

Riddick, J.L. (act): *Just Imagine*

Riddle, Hal (act): *Dr. Goldfoot and the Bikini Machine*

Riddle, K.K. (act): *Blood of Ghastly Horror*

Riddle, Nelson (mus, 1921-1995): *Batman (1966); Guyana, Cult of the Damned; Paris When It Sizzles*

Riddle, Scott (act): *Hologram Man*

Riddoch, Billy (act): *Shallow Grave*

Ridenour, David (act): *Spawn of the Slithis*

Rideout, Herbert (wri): *Cinderella (1913)*

Ridge, Francesca J. (act): *Angel Heart*

Ridgely, John (act, 1909-1968, nee John Huntington Rea): *Arsenic and Old Lace; The Big Sleep (1946); Blondes at Work; Cry Wolf (1947); The Invisible Menace; The Lost*

Volcano; Nancy Drew and the Hidden Staircase; Possessed (1947); Sealed Verdict; Torchy Blane In Panama; Torchy Gets Her Man; Torchy Plays With Dynamite; Torchy Runs for Mayor

Ridgely, Robert (act, 1931-1997): *The Nine Lives of Fritz the Cat; Robin Hood: Men In Tights*

Ridges, Stanley (C.) (act, 1892-1951): *Black Friday; Eyes In the Night; The File On Thelma Jordan; Mr. District Attorney; Nick Carter, Master Detective; Possessed (1947); The Suspect; Tarzan Triumphs*

Ridgeway, Freddie (act): *Follow the Hunter*

Ridgeway, Fritzi (act): *The Fatal 30*

Ridgeway, Suzanne (act): *From Hell It Came*

Ridgley, Robert (act): *The Nine Lives of Fritz the Cat*

Ridgwell, George (act, 1870-1935): *The Crime at Blossoms*

Ridgwell, George (dir, 1870-1935): *The Amazing Partnership; The Crimson Circle (1922); The Pointing Finger (1922); The Sword of Damocles*

Ridgwell, George (wri, 1870-1935): *The Sword of Damocles*

Ridings, Richard (act): *Erik the Viking*

Ridler, Anne (act): *The Camp On Blood Island*

Ridley, Arnold (act): *A Place to Die; A Stolen Face*

Ridley, Arnold (wri): *The Ghost Train (1927, 1931 & 1941); The Interrupted Journey; Meet Mr. Lucifer; The Warren Case; Who Killed the Cat?*

Ridley, Emma (act): *Return to Oz*

Ridley, Judith (act): *Night of the Living Dead (1968)*

Ridley, Julie (act): *Rearview Mirror*

Ridley, Philip (dir & wri): *The Reflecting Skin*

Ridley, Roy (wri): *Bedelia*

Ridout, William (act): *The Swordsman*

Ridoux, Serge (act): *The Murders In the Rue Morgue (1986)*

Ridste, Frances (act): see Landis, Carole

Riedel, Guy (wri): *Sometimes They Come Back...Again*

Riefenstahl, Leni (act & dir, b. 1902): *Das Blaue Licht*

Riegel, Cindy (act): *Dr. Heckyl & Mr. Hype*

Rieger, August (wri): *The Vampire Happening*

Riegert, Peter (act, b. 1947): *The Mask (1994); The Runestone*

Riehle, Richard (act): *Dominion; The Fugitive (1993); Of Mice and Men (1992); Prelude to a Kiss; Terminal*

Riehm, Sebastian (act): *Making Contact*

Rienits, Rex (wri): *Noose for a Lady*

Riento, Virgilio (act): *Miracle In Milan*

Riese, Felicia (act): see Roc, Patricia

Riesner, Dean (dir): *Bill and Coo*

Riesner, Dean (wri): *Play Misty for Me*

Rietty, Robert (act): *The Crooked Road; Gulliver's Travels (1977); Never Say Never Again; The Omen; The Scarlet Blade; Time to Remember*

Rietty, Victor (act): *Mr. H.C. Andersen*

Riffany, Linda (act): *The Brotherhood of Satan*

Rifkin, Adam (act & dir): *The Dark Backward*

Rifkin, Ron (act): *Silent Running; Wolf*

Rigali, Nino (act): *Raiders of the Living Dead*

Rigamonte, Robert (act): *Outbreak*

Rigano, Evi (act): *La Decima Vittima*

Rigaud, Jorge/George/Georges (act): *Carlota; The Colossus of Rhodes; Demons of the Dead; Ella y el Miedo; Eyeball; Horror Express; Leonor; A Lizard In a Woman's Skin; Marta*

Rigaud, Jorge (dir): *The Living Dead at Manchester Morgue*

Rigby, Arthur (act): *Crossroads to Crime*

Rigby, David (act): *The Pink Chiquitas*

Rigby, Edward (act, 1879-1951): *The Blue Bird (1910); Circle of Danger; Double Confession; The Fatal Hour (1937); Lorna Doone (1934); Murder In Reverse; Poison Pen; The Three Weird Sisters; Went the day Well?; Young and Innocent*

Rigby, Gordon (wri): *The Millerson Case*

Rigby, L.G. (wri): *The Monkey Talks*

Rigby, Ray (wri): *Operation Crossbow*

Rigby, Terence (act): *Watership Down*

Rigg, Carl (act): *The Body Stealers; Cry of the Banshee; Lifeforce; The Oblong Box; Toomorrow*

Rigg, Diana (act, b. 1938): *The Assassination Bureau; Evil Under the Sun; The Great Muppet Caper; The Haunting of Helen Walker; On Her Majesty's Secret Service; The Avengers; A Good Man In Africa; A Midsummer Night's Dream; The Worst Witch*

Riggan, Marshall (wri): *So Sad About Gloria*

Riggins, Nikki (act): *Scream Dream*

Riggins, Terrence (act): *Return of the Living Dead, Part II*

Riggio, Jerry (act): *Madman of Mandoras; Man-Eater of Kumaon*
Riggs & Trust (mus): *Heavy Metal*
Riggs, Alisha (act): *The Toxic Avenger*
Riggs, Bobby (act): *The Ultimate Impostor*
Riggs, Daphne (act): *The Private Life of Sherlock Holmes*
Riggs, Lynn (wri): *Sherlock Holmes and the Voice of Terror*
Riggs, Mary Elizabeth (act): see Brent, Evelyn
Riggs, Seth (act): *What Ever Happened to Aunt Alice?*
Rignault, Alexandre (act): *L'Eternel Retour; Les Sorcieres de Salem; Les Yeux sans Visage*
Rigney, Daniel (act): *The Island of Dr. Moreau (1996)*
Rigutini, Rosario (act): *Inferno (1979)*
Rijin, Brad (act): *A Return to Salem's Lot; Special Effects*
Rijxman, Lineke (act): *Gebroken Spiegels*
Riker, Robin (act): *Christmas Every Day; Stepmonster*
Riklis, M. (act): *Fake-Out*
Riley, Miss (act): *10 Rillington Place*
Riley, Bus (act): *Robin Cook's 'Mortal Fear'*
Riley, Claire (act): *Brainscan; Night Visitors*
Riley, Coleen (act): *Deadly Blessing*
Riley, Doris (act): *The Bermuda Depths*
Riley, Doug (mus): *Cannibal Girls*
Riley, Elaine (act): *The Big Clock; The Falcon Out West*
Riley, Gary (John) (act): *Back to the Future; Fear (1996)*
Riley, George (act): *The Day Mars Invaded Earth*
Riley, Jack (act): *Attack of the Killer Tomatoes; C.H.U.D. II*
Riley, Jan (act): *La Sorella di Satan*
Riley, Janet (act): *The Search for Bridey Murphy*
Riley, John (wri): *Princess Warrior*
Riley, Joseph (act): *Burnt Offerings*
Riley, Karma Insen (act): *The Handmaid's Tale*
Riley, Lauri (act): *It's Alive III: Island of the Alive*
Riley, Margaret (act): *The Toxic Avenger*
Riley, Miss (act): *10 Rillington Place*
Riley, Penny (act): *Maroc 7*
Riley, Rex (act): *Mind Over Murder*
Riley, Skip (act): *Fugitive from the Empire*
Riley, Steve (act): *Beyond and Back*
Riley, Steve (cin): *Eve of Destruction*
Riley, William (act): *The Incredible Hulk Returns*
Rilla, Walter (act, 1895-1980): *At the Villa Rose (1939); Cairo; Death Drums Along the River; Dr. Mabuse vs. Scotland Yard; The Face of Fu Manchu; Frozen Alive; The Gamma People; The Green Buddha; My Daughter Joy; The Scarlet Pimpernel (1934); The Secret Ways; Shadow of the Eagle; State Secret; The Testament of Dr. Mabuse (1960); Track the Man Down; Venetian Bird; Victim Five; The Wonderful World of the Brothers Grimm*
Rilla, Wolf (dir, b. 1920): *The Black Rider; Cairo; Noose for a Lady; Piccadilly Third Stop; The Village of the Damned (1960); Witness In the Dark*
Rilla, Wolf (wri, b. 1920): *The Village of the Damned (1960 & 1995)*
Rimmer, Jean (act): *The Deadly Females*
Rimmer, Shane (act): *Arabian Adventure; Baffled!; Crusoe; Dr. Strangelove: or, How I Learned to Stop Worrying and Love the Bomb; Dreamchild; The Human Factor; The Hunger; A Kiss Before Dying (1991); Morons from Outer Space; The People That Time Forgot; The Return of Sherlock Holmes (1986); Rollerball; The Spy Who Loved Me; Superman II; Superman III; Thunderbirds Are Go; Thunderbird 6; Warlords of the Deep*
Rimmington, Noelle (act): *Macbeth (1971)*
Rimmon, Eyal (act): *Waxwork II: Lost In Time*
Rimoldi, A. (act): *Atoll K*
Rimsky-Korsakov, Nikolai Andreevich (mus, 1844-1908): *The Magic Voyage of Sinbad*
Rinaldi, Antonio (cin): *Diabolik; Terrore Nello Spazio*
Rinaldi, Joe (wri): *Alice In Wonderland (1951); Babes In Toyland (1961); Peter Pan (1953)*
Rinaldo, Frederic (I.) (wri): *Abbott and Costello Meet Frankenstein; The Black Cat (1941); Crazy House (1943); Hold That Ghost; The Invisible Woman (1941)*
Rinder, Laurin (act): *Blood Beach*
Rinder, Laurin (mus): *New Year's Evil*
Rinehart, Mary Roberts (wri, 1876-1958): *The Bat (1926 & 1959); The Bat Whispers; 23 1/2 Hours Leave*
Ring, Cy(ril) (act): *Boston Blackie Goes Hollywood; I Wake Up Screaming*
Ring, John (act): *Too Scared to Scream*
Ringa, Charles (act): *Ghost Warrior*
Ringell, Alfredo (dir): *The Magic Bubble*
Ringell, Deborah Taper (dir): *The Magic Bubble*
Ringham, John (act): *Woof!; Woof Too! A Girl and Her Dog*
Ringhaver, Sanna (act): *Blood Waters of Dr. Z*
Ringkamp, B. Jonathan (wri): *The Clairvoyant (1985)*
Ringwald, Molly (act, b. 1968): *King Lear (1987); Spacehunter: Adventures In the Forbidden Zone; The Stand; Twice Upon a Time*
Ringwald, Monika (act): *The Sexplorer*
Rinna, Lisa (act): *Nick Fury: Agent of Shield; Robot Wars*
Rinter, Joe (act): see Penner, Joe
Rintoul, David (act): *The Hunchback of Notre Dame (1977); Legend of the Werewolf*
Rio, Nicole (act): *Sorority House Massacre; Visitants; The Zero Boys*
Riojas, Juan A. (act): *Virtuosity*
Rionda, Sasha (act): *Total Recall*
Riordan, Daniel (act): *The Adventures of Captain Zoom in Outer Space; Ed Wood*
Riordan, Irene (act): see Ryan, Irene
Riordan, Joan (act): *Web of Deceit*
Riordan, Joel McGinnis (act, d. 1982): *Boarding House*
Riordan, Marjorie (act): *Pursuit to Algiers; Three Strangers*
Riordan, Robert (act): *The Destructors*
Rios, Lalo (act): *City Beneath the Sea (1952); Touch of Evil*
Rios, Raquel (act): *Watchers II*
Rioseco, Carmela (act): *Turn Back the Clock*
Riparetti, Tony (mus): *Knights; Nemesis 3: Time Lapse*
Ripley, Arthur (dir, 1895-1961): *Atlantis (1948); The Chase*
Ripley, Corey (act): *Phoenix the Warrior*
Ripley, Fay (act): *Mute Witness*
Ripley, Heather (act): *Chitty Chitty Bang Bang*
Ripoli, Pablo (cin): *Tombs of the Blind Dead*
Ripp, Sir Lawrence (act): *The Alpha Incident*
Ripper, Michael (act, b. 1925): *Brides of Dracula; The Camp On Blood Island; Captain Clegg; The Creeping Flesh; The Curse of the Mummy's Tomb; The Curse of the Werewolf; Dead Lucky; The Deadly Bees; The Devil-Ship Pirates; Dracula Has Risen from the Grave; Girly; Jackpot; Journey Into Darkness; Legend of the Werewolf; The Man Who Could Cheat Death; Moon Zero Two; The Mummy (1959); The Mummy's Shroud; 1984 (1955); Old Mother Riley's Jungle Treasure; The Phantom of the Opera (1962); The Pirates of Blood River; The Plague of the Zombies; A Prize of Arms; Quatermass II; The Reptile; The Revenge of Frankenstein; Richard III (1955); Sammy's Super T-Shirt; The Scarlet Blade; Scars of Dracula; The Secret of Blood Island; Taste the Blood of Dracula; Torture Garden; The Ugly Duckling; Uncharted Seas; Where the Bullets Fly; X...The Unknown; Your Witness*
Rippert, Otto (dir & wri): *Homunculus*
Rippon, Todd (act): *The Frighteners*
Ripps, Lenny (wri): *Frankenweenie*
Rippy, Carol (act): *Moon 44*
Rippy, Leon (act): *The Arrival (1996); Eye of the Storm; King Kong Lives; Moon 44; Stargate; Track 29; Universal Soldier*
Rippy, Rodney Allen (act): *Oh, God! Book II*
Riquelme, Antonio (act): *La Torre de los Siete Jorobados*
Riquelme, Carlos (act): *Bring Me the Vampire; El Ladron de Cadaveres; A Woman's Devotion*
Riquelme, Carlos (dir): *Bring Me the Vampire*
Riquier, Georges (act): *Mata Hari, Agent H21*
Risbourg, Dominique (act): *A View to a Kill*
Risch, Peter (D.) (act): *Ghoulies; Something Wicked This Way Comes*
Risdon, Elizabeth (act, 1887-1958, nee Elizabeth Evans): *Beautiful Jim; The Courage of a Coward; Crime and Punishment (1935, USA); Full Confession; Grip (1915); Her Luck In London; London's Yellow Peril; Maria Marten: or, The Murder In the Red Barn (1913); Mexican Spitfire Sees a Ghost; The Princess of Happy Chance; The Suicide Club (1914); Weird Woman*
Risi, Paolo (act): *The Barbarians (1987)*
Risk, Victoria (act): *A Reflection of Fear*
Riskin, Robert (wri, 1897-1955): *Half Angel; Lost Horizon (1937); The Thin Man Goes Home*
Risley, Ann (act): *Simon*
Rispal, Jacques (act): *Aimez-Vous les Femmes?*
Riss, Dan (act): *Operation Secret; Riders to the Stars*
Risser, Wee (cin): *The Giant Gila Monster*
Rissi, Michael (dir): *Soultaker*
Risso, Roberto (act): *Revenge of the Pirates; The Seven Dwarfs to the Rescue*
Rissone, Francesco (act): *Miracle In Milan*
Rist, Robbie (act): *Through the Magic Pyramid*
Ristau, Raymond (act): *Street Trash*
Ristic, Suzanne (act): *Watchers*
"Rita" (wri): *My Lord Conceit; The Pointing Finger (1922 & 1933)*
Ritch, David (act): *Spookies; Strangers' Meeting*
Ritch, Steven (act): *City of Fear (1959); Valley of the Headhunters; The Werewolf (1955)*
Ritchard, Cyril (act, b. 1896): *Blackmail (1929); The Hobbit*
Ritchie, Clint (act): *A Force of One; The St. Valentine's Day Massacre*
Ritchie, Joanne (act): *Frankenhooker*
Ritchie, Joe (act): *The Big Sleep (1978)*
Ritchie, June (act, b. 1938): *Hunted (1973); The Mouse On the Moon*
Ritchie, Lionel (act): *The Preacher's Wife*
Ritchie, Michael (dir, b. 1938): *The Golden Child; The Island; A Simple Wish*
Ritchie, Stan (act): *Invasion of the Body Snatchers (1978); Nightmare In Blood*
Ritelis, Viktors (dir): *The Corpse*
Riter, Kristen (act): *Student Bodies*
Ritschel, Elke (act): *The Handmaids Tale*
Ritt, Martin (dir, 1913-1990): *The Spy Who Came In from the Cold*
Rittau, Gunther (cin, 1897-1971): *F.P. 1 Antwortet Nicht; Gold (German-speaking version); Metropolis (1926); Die Nibelungen*
Ritter, Brent (act): *Curse of the Blue Lights*
Ritter, Joe (wri): *The Toxic Avenger*
Ritter, John (act, b. 1948): *Americathon; The Barefoot Executive; The Colony (1995); The Flight of Dragons; It (1990); The Night That Panicked America; The Other (1972); Sling Blade; Stay Tuned*
Ritter, Magdalena (act): *Nostradamus*
Ritter, Thelma (act, 1905-1969): *Call Northside 777; Miracle On 34th Street (1947); Rear Window (1954)*
Ritvo, Rosemary (wri): *Alice, Sweet Alice*
Ritz Brothers, The (act): *The Gorilla (1939); The Three Musketeers (1939)*
Ritz, Joan (act): *Flying from Justice; The Harbour Lights; In the Ranks; The Romany Rye; Royal Love*
Riva, Emmanuele (act, b. 1927): *Thomas l'Imposteur*
Rival, Ross (act): *Wonder Women*
Rivalta, Giorgio (dir): *La Leggendi di Enea*
Rivas, Andy (act): *Vamp*
Rivas, Carlos (act): *The Beast of Hollow Mountain; The Black Scorpion (1957); Madman of Mandoras; The Miracle (1959); The White Orchid*
Rive, Patricia (act): *The Dogfighters*
Rivelli, Luisa (act): *Treasure of the Petrified Forest*
Rivera, Cheyenne (act): *The Octagon*
Rivera, Chita (act): *Once Upon a Brothers Grimm*
Rivera, Greg (act): *The Norsemen*
Rivera, Janice (act): *Mars Attacks!*
Rivera, Luis/Louis (act): *House of 1,000 Dolls; Murders In the Rue Morgue (1971)*
Rivera, Michael (act): *Def by Temptation*
Rivera, Mike (act): *The Norsemen*
Rivera, Ricardo (act): *The Blood Drinkers*
Rivera, Roberto G. (act): *The Curse of the Doll People*
Rivera, Stella (act): *Eyes of a Stranger*
Rivero, Carlos (act): *The Naked Jungle; Secret of the Incas*
Rivero, Enrique (act): *Le Sang d'un Poete*
Rivero, Jorge/George (act): *Conquest; The Sin of Adam and Eve*
Rivero, Julian (act): *Amazon Quest; The Falcon In Mexico*
Rivers, Joan (act, b. 1933): *The Muppets Take Manhattan; Serial Mom; Spaceballs; The Swimmer*
Rivers, Leslie Ann (act): *Kidnapped Co-Ed*
Rivers, Linda (act): *Curse of the Vampires*
Rivers, Michael (act): *The Fury of the Wolfman*
Rivers, Victor (act): *Black Magic Woman; Twin Peaks: Fire Walk With Me*
Rivers, Wayne (act): *Mr. Moto's Last Warning*
Rives, Robbie (act): *Shadowzone*
Rivette, Jacques (cin, b. 1928): *Berenice*
Riviere, Caroline (act): *The Perverse Countess*
Riviere, George(s) (act): *The Accident; Agent 383/Passport to Hell; Antinea, l'Amante della Citta Sepolta; La Danza Macabra; La Vergine di Norimberga*
Riviere, Jean-Marie (act): *Le Saint Mene la Dance*
Rivo, Phil (act): *The Toxic Avenger, Part II*
Rix, Colin (act): *Eye of the Needle; The Medusa Touch*
Rizley, Kent (act): *Endangered Species*
Rizzi, Gene (act): *The Saint In Palm Springs*
Rizzo, Alfredo (act): *Seven Slaves Against the World; L'Ultima Preda del Vampiro*
Rizzo, Carlo (act): *Deported*
Rizzo, Giacomo (act): *Dracula Blows His Cool*
Rizzo, Gianni (act): *Mission Stardust; Triumph of the Ten Gladiators*
Roa, Joaquin (act): *La Venganza de Don Mendo; Viridiana*
Roach, Bert (act): *Another Thin Man; Dr. Renault's Secret; The Falcon Out West; The Last Warning (1929); Liliom (1930); The Man In the Iron Mask (1939); Mr. Moto's Last Warning; The Murders In the Rue Morgue (1932); Think Fast, Mr. Moto; The Thin Man*
Roach, Chris (dir): *The 13th Floor*
Roach, Claudette (act): *The Haunted (1991); Millennium; Short Circuit 2*
Roach, Daryl (act): *Spacecamp; Watchers 3*
Roach, Frank R. (act): *Heart Condition*
Roach (Sr.), Hal (dir, 1892-1992): *Captain Fury; One Million B.C.; Turnabout*
Roach Jr., Hal (dir): *One Million B.C.*
Roach, Jennifer (act): *Wicked Stepmother*
Roach, Lesley (act): *Mr. Horatio Knibbles*
Roach, Neil (cin): *Donor; Fear Stalk; Tempting Fate*
Roach, Pat (act): *Clash of the Titans; Conan the Destroyer; Indiana Jones and the Temple of Doom; Never Say Never Again; Raiders of the Lost Ark; Red Sonja; Robin Hood: Prince of Thieves; The Spaceman and King Arthur; Willow; The Zany Adventures of Robin Hood*
Roach, Rickey (act): *Black Devil Doll from Hell*
Roache, Paul (act): *Trancers II: The Return of Jack Deth*
Road, Mike (act): *Destination Inner Space*
Roald, Glen (act): *Timecop*
Roan, Shula (act): *Sinthia: The Devil's Doll*
Roanne, Andre (act): *What Price Murder*
Roark, Garland (wri): *Fair Wind to Java*
Roark, Robert (act): *Killers from Space; Target Earth*
Roarke, Adam (act, 1937-1996): *Cyborg 2087; Dangerous Touch; Frogs; Psych-Out*
Roarke, John (act): *The Silence of the Hams*
Roat, Richard (act): *Heart and Souls; Westworld*
Robak, Alain (dir & wri): *The Evil Within*
Robards Sr., Jason (act, 1892-1963): *Bedlam; Charlie Chan Carries On; Desperate; The Falcon's Adventure; The Falcon's Alibi; The Fatal Hour (1940); A Game of Death; Isle of the Dead (1945); Mystery Plane; Strange Adventure*
Robards Jr., Jason (act, b. 1922): *Black Rainbow; A Boy and His Dog; The Day After; Dream a Little Dream; The Enemy Within; The Legend of the Lone Ranger; Mr. Sycamore; Murders In the Rue Morgue (1971); The St. Valentine's Day Massacre; Something Wicked This Way Comes; The Trial (1992)*
Robards III, Jason (act): *They Live*
Robards, Willis (act): *The Three Musketeers (1921)*
Robb, David (act): *The Deceivers; Paint Me a Murder; The Swordsman*
Robbe-Grillet, Alain (act & dir, b. 1917): *L'Annee Derniere a Marienbad; Trans-Europe Express*
Robbe-Grillet, Catherine (act): *Trans-Europe Express*
Robbie, Christopher (act): *Sudden Terror; Where Has Poor Mickey Gone?*
Robbins, Adele (act): *Blink*
Robbins, Brian (act): *Cellar Dweller; C.H.U.D. II*
Robbins, Christmas (act): *The Demon Lover*
Robbins, Cindy (act): *I Was a Teenage Werewolf*
Robbins, Clarence Aaron "Tod" (wri): *Freaks; The Unholy Three (1925 & 1930)*
Robbins, Dan (act): *The Suicide Club (1988)*
Robbins, Deanna (act): *Final Exam*
Robbins, Derek (dir & wri): *The Sex Victims*
Robbins, Dick (wri): *Chomps*
Robbins, Eva (act): *The Adventures of Hercules; Hercules (1983); Mascara*
Robbins, Gale (act, 1924-1980): *Between Midnight and Dawn; Double Jeopardy; Mr. Hex*
Robbins, Garry (act): *Humongous; Short Circuit 2*
Robbins, Glenn L. (act): *Cocoon: The Return*
Robbins, Herb (act): *The Doll Squad; Invasion of the Bee Girls*
Robbins, Jacqueline (act): *The Reflecting Skin*
Robbins, James (act): *Lady In the Morgue*
Robbins, Jane (act): *First Knight*
Robbins, Jane Marla (act): *Arachnophobia; Werewolf of Washington*
Robbins, Jenny (act): *Clegg*

Robbins, Joyce (act): *The Reflecting Skin*
Robbins, Kate (act): *Don't Look Down*
Robbins, Logan (act): *Casper: A Spirited Beginning*
Robbins, Matthew (dir): *Amazing Stories: The Movie VI*; **Batteries Not Included*; *Dragonslayer*
Robbins, Matthew (wri): **Batteries Not Included*; *Dragonslayer*; *Warning Sign*
Robbins, Michael (act): *Dead Man's Chest*; *The Great Muppet Caper*; *The Saint and the Brave Goose*; *Zeppelin*
Robbins, Peter (act): *Moment to Moment*
Robbins, Rex (act): *Simon*; *Vampire's Kiss*
Robbins, Tacey (act): *Blood of Ghastly Horror*
Robbins, Tim (act): *Erik the Viking*; *Howard the Duck*; *Jacob's Ladder*
Robbins, Tom (act): *Made In Heaven*
Robby the Robot (act): *Forbidden Planet*; *The Invisible Boy*; *The Phantom Empire*
Robe, Mike (dir): *Final Descent*; *Summer of Fear*
Robeling, Albin (act): *Nightmare Alley*
Rober, Richard (act): *Call Northside 777*; *The File On Thelma Jordan*; *I Married a Communist*; *The Well*
Roberson, Chuck (act): *Shock Corridor*
Roberson, James W. (dir): *Superstition*
Roberson, Philip A. (act): *Project X* (1987)
Robert, Guy (mus): *Perceval*
Robert, Jacques (wri): *Quelqu'un Derriere la Porte*; *To Commit a Murder*
Robert, Jason (act): *Alien High*
Robert, Marie-Christine (act): *The Phantom of the Opera* (1990)
Robert, Vincent (dir): *The Fear* (1994)
Roberts, Adelle (act): *Boston Blackie's Rendezvous*; *Just Before Dawn* (1946); *The Notorious Lone Wolf*
Roberts, Al (act): *Strange Invaders*
Roberts, Alan (act): *Dinosaurus!*
Roberts, Alice (act): *Die Buchse der Pandora*
Roberts, Allan (mus): *Down to Earth*
Roberts, Allene (act): *Panther Island*; *The Red House*
Roberts, Arnold (act): *Timestalkers*
Roberts, Art (act): *Brenda Starr* (1976)
Roberts, Arthur (act): *The Bermuda Triangle*; *The Bride* (1973); *Chopping Mall*; *Not of This Earth* (1988)
Roberts, Beatrice (act): *Mars Attacks the World*
Roberts, Ben (wri, b. 1916): *Green Fire*; *The Legend of the Lone Ranger*; *Man of a Thousand Faces*; *Midnight Lace* (1960); *Portrait In Black*
Roberts, Betty (act): *I Was a Zombie for the F.B.I.*
Roberts, Beverly (act, b. 1914): *Buried Alive* (1940); *West of Shanghai*
Roberts, Bruce (mus): *Daylight*
Roberts, Bump (act): *Nightbeast*
Roberts, Charles (act): *Enter Inspector Duval*
Roberts, Chris (dir & wri): *Wing Commander*
Roberts, Christian (act): *The Anniversary*; *The Mind of Mr. Soames*; *The Twisted Nerve*
Roberts, Claude (act): *Distortions*
Roberts, Clete (act): *Time After Time*
Roberts, Conrad (act): *Firepower*; *The Serpent and the Rainbow*
Roberts, Dave (act): *Blow Out*; *Torchy Runs for Mayor*
Roberts, Davis (act): *Demon and the Mummy*; *Demon Seed*; *Westworld*
Roberts, Deborah (dir): *Frankenstein General Hospital*
Roberts, Des (act): *Guess What Happened to Count Dracula*
Roberts, Desmond (act): *Gaol Break* (1936); *Grip of the Strangler*
Roberts, Doris (act, b. 1930): *Blood bath* (1975); *The Honeymoon Killers*; *It Happened One Christmas*
Roberts, Doug (act): *Serial Mom*
Roberts, Edith (act, 1899-1935): *Seven Keys to Baldpate* (1925); *The Taxi Mystery*
Roberts, Eliza (act): *The Nature of the Beast*
Roberts, Eric (act, b. 1956): *The Ambulance*; *The Cable Guy*; *Dark Angel* (1996); *Doctor Who*; *Final Analysis*; *The Glass Cage* (1996); *The Grave*; *Love Is a Gun*; *The Nature of the Beast*; *The Odyssey*; *Past Perfect*; *Power 98*; *Runaway Train*; *Sensation* (1994)
Roberts, Evelyn (act): *The Feathered Serpent* (1934); *The Green Scarf*; *The Midas Touch*; *The Return of the Scarlet Pimpernel*
Roberts, Ewan (act): *Baffled!*; *The Day of the Triffids*; *Five to One*; *Hostile Witness*; *The Internecine Project*; *The Lady Killers* (1956); *The Man In the White Suit*; *Night of the Demon* (1957); *The Partner*; *The Traitors*
Roberts, Florence (act, 1860-1940): *Babes In Toyland* (1934); *Les Miserables* (1935)
Roberts, Frank (act): *Praying Mantis*

Roberts, Glenn (act): *The Crater Lake Monster*
Roberts, Harry (dir): *The Barton Mystery* (1920)
Roberts, Ian (act): *Jane and the Lost City*
Roberts, Irmin (cin): *Conquest of Space*; *The War of the Worlds*
Roberts, Ivor (act): *Murder Is Easy*; *Without a Clue*
Roberts, J.H. (act): *Alf's Button Afloat*; *Alibi* (1931); *The Dark Tower* (1943); *The Door With Seven Locks* (1940); *The Ghosts of Berkeley Square*; *Juggernaut*; *Young and Innocent*
Roberts, Jack (act): *Dick Tracy Returns*
Roberts, Jackye (act): *Mannequin Two: On the Move*
Roberts, Jamie (act): *Lifeforce*
Roberts, Jason (act): *Claws*
Roberts Jr., Jay (act): *Aftershock*; *Warlords*
Roberts, Jeremy (act): *The Mask* (1994); *The People Under the Stairs*
Roberts, Jessica (act): *Jacob's Ladder*
Roberts, Jonathan (wri): *The Hunchback of Notre Dame* (1996); *The Lion King*; *Once Bitten*
Roberts, Judith (wri): *Simply Irresistible*
Roberts, Judith Anna (act): *Eraserhead*
Roberts, Julia (act, b. 1967): *Flatliners*; *Mary Reilly*
Roberts, Kane (act): *Shocker*
Roberts, Ken (act): *Fatal Pulse*; *The Great Land of Small*; *Wild Thing*
Roberts, Kim (act): *Don't Go In the House*
Roberts, Larry (act): *Lady and the Tramp*
Roberts, Lee (act): *Missile to the Moon*
Roberts, Lynne (act, b. 1922): *Behind City Lights*; *Dick Tracy Returns*; *Dr. Renault's Secret*; *The Ghost That Walks Alone*; *Hunt the Man Down*; *The Inner Circle*; *The Phantom Speaks*; *Port Sinister*; *Secret Service Investigator*
Roberts, M. (act): *Blind Date*
Roberts, Marguerite (wri): *The Bribe*; *Rampage*
Roberts, Marty (act): *Alien Space Avenger*
Roberts, Meade (wri): *Danger Route*
Roberts, Michael D. (act): *The Ice Pirates*; *Sleepstalker*
Roberts, Nancy (act): *Black Narcissus*; *Cosh Boy*; *The Devil's Profession*; *Signals In The Night*; *Superman III*
Roberts, Neil (act): *Nick Fury: Agent of Shield*
Roberts, Pascale (act): *The Peking Blonde*
Roberts, Pernell (act, b. 1930): *The Adventures of Nick Carter*; *Donor*
Roberts, Rachel (act, 1927-1980): *Baffled!*; *Charlie Chan and the Curse of the Dragon Queen*; *Great Expectations* (1974); *The Limping Man* (1953); *Murder On the Orient Express*; *Picnic at Hanging Rock*; *When a Stranger Calls*
Roberts, Ralph (act, b. 1922): *Killer's Kiss*
Roberts, Randolph (act): *Logan's Run*
Roberts, Randy (act): *Wicked, Wicked*
Roberts, Randy (cin): *Hammett*
Roberts, Ray (act): *It Fell from the Sky*
Roberts, Renee (act): *What Became of Jack and Jill*
Roberts, Rick (act): *Love and Human Remains*
Roberts, Roxanne (act): *The Fugitive* (1993)
Roberts, Roy (act, 1900-1975): *The Brasher Doubloon*; *Circumstantial Evidence*; *He Walked by Night*; *House of Wax*; *The Man with a Cloak*; *Nightmare Alley*; *Second Chance*; *The Strongest Man In the World*; *The Underwater City*
Roberts, Scott (wri): *Riders of the Storm*
Roberts, Sherry (act): *Mars Needs Women*
Roberts, Stanley (wri): *Who Done It?* (1942)
Roberts, Stephen/Steve(n) (act): *Brainstorm* (1965); *Diary of a Madman*; *Doomsday Machine*; *Gog*; *Terrified* (1963); *The Twonky*
Roberts, Tanya (act, b. 1956): *The Beastmaster*; *Inner Sanctum* (1991); *Sheena*; *Tourist Trap*; *A View to a Kill*
Roberts, Ted Jan (act): *The Power Within* (1995)
Roberts, Teresa (act): *I Was a Zombie for the F.B.I.*
Roberts, Tessa (act): *The Assistant*
Roberts, Thayer (act): *The Chinese Ring*; *This Is Not a Test*
Roberts, Theodore (act, 1861-1928): *Male and Female*
Roberts, Tony (act, b. 1939): *Amityville 3-D*; *18 Again!*; *The $1,000,000 Duck*; *Popcorn*; *Switch* (1991)
Roberts, Tracey (act): *Sideshow*
Roberts, Tracy (act): *Matinee*
Roberts, William (wri): *The Legend of the Lone Ranger*; *The Wonderful World of the Brothers Grimm*
Roberts, Wink (act): *The Day It Came to Earth*; *Legion of Fire: Killer Ants*

Roberts, Wyn (act): *Picnic at Hanging Rock*
Roberts, Yvonne (act): *Twin Peaks: Fire Walk With Me*
Robertshaw, Jerrold (act, 1866-1941): *Downhill*; *The Girl Who Didn't Care*; *She* (1925); *The Wandering Jew* (1923)
Robertson, Anthony (act): *Dr. Caligari*
Robertson, Blair (wri): *Agent for H.A.R.M.*; *The Slime People*
Robertson, Bob (act): *The Plutonium Incident*
Robertson, Christopher (dir): *Roger Corman's 'Frankenstein Unbound'*
Robertson, Cliff (act, b. 1925): *Brainstorm* (1983); *Charly*; *Dominique*; *Escape from L.A.*; *Man On a Swing*; *Masquerade*; *Obsession* (1976); *3 days of the Condor*
Robertson, Dale (act, b. 1923): *Son of Sinbad*
Robertson, David (act): *Attack of the Swamp Creature*
Robertson, David M. (dir): *Firebird 2015 A.D.*
Robertson, Dennis (act): *Dark Night of the Scarecrow*
Robertson, Doug (dir): *HauntedWeen*
Robertson, E. Arnot (wri): *Four Frightened People*
Robertson, Eric N. (mus): *Millennium*
Robertson, Francoise (act): *Alien High*
Robertson, George R. (act): *Hitler's Daughter*
Robertson, H. MacLeod (wri): *The Boy Who Never Was*; *Electric Eskimo*; *Sammy's Super T-Shirt*
Robertson, Harry (mus & wri): *Hawk the Slayer*; *Jane and the Lost City*; *Prisoners of the Lost Universe*
Robertson, Heilan (act): *Mad Max Beyond Thunderdome*
Robertson, James (act): *Mad Max Beyond Thunderdome*
Robertson, Jenny (act): *Notorious* (1992)
Robertson, John S. (dir, 1878-1964): *Dr. Jekyll and Mr. Hyde* (1920, Famous Players/Para); *The Enchanted Cottage* (1924); *Perpetua*; *The Phantom of Paris* (1931)
Robertson, John Wylie (act): see Watson, Wylie
Robertson, Joseph F. (dir): *Auntie Lee's Meat Pies*
Robertson, Kim (act): *Nightbreed*
Robertson, Kimmy (act): *Beauty and the Beast* (1991); *Honey, I Shrunk the Kids*; *Leprechaun 2*
Robertson, Laura (act): *End of the World* (1977)
Robertson, Lynn (act): *End of the World* (1977)
Robertson, Malcolm (act): *The Last Wave*
Robertson, Margaret (act): *The Vulture* (1966)
Robertson, Myles (act): *Prisoners of the Lost Universe*
Robertson, Nina (act): *Nightbreed*
Robertson, R.J. (act): *The Haunting of Morella*
Robertson, R.J. (wri): *Forbidden World*; *The Haunting of Morella*; *Not of This Earth* (1988)
Robertson, Sandy (act): *Avalanche*
Robertson, Struan (act): *The Devil's Gift*
Robertson, Tim (act): *The Cars That Ate Paris*; *The Time Guardian*
Robertson, Willard (act, 1886-1948): *Background to Danger*; *Dante's Inferno* (1935); *Doctor X*; *Supernatural* (1933); *Torchy Gets Her Man*
Robertson, William (act): *Dark August*
Robertson, Rev. William Preston (act): *Blood Simple*
Robeson, Kenneth (wri): see Dent, Lester
Robeson, Paul (act, 1898-1976): *King Solomon's Mines* (1937)
Robey (act): *The Quilt of Hathor*
Robey, George (act, 1869-1954, nee George Edward Wade): *Chu Chin Chow* (1934); *The Prehistoric Man* (1924)
Robey, George (wri, 1869-1954): *The Prehistoric Man* (1924)
Robie, Earl (act): *My Cousin Rachel*
Robie, Wendy (act): *The Dentist II*; *The People Under the Stairs*
Robillard, Kim (act): *Always*; *Project X* (1987)
Robin, Dany (act, b. 1927): *Rope Around the Neck*; *Topaz*
Robin, Diane (act): *The Relic*; *Retribution* (1988); *RoboCop*
Robin, Georges (dir & wri): *Mini Weekend*
Robin, Jacques (cin): *The Killing Game*; *Traitement de Choc*
Robin, Leo (mus): *International House*
Robin, Les (act): *Blood Diner*
Robin, Michael (act): *The Death of Mario Ricci*
Robin, Walt (act): *Mistress of the Apes*
Robinson, Dale (act): *Billion Dollar Brain*
Robinette, Nancy (act): *Serial Mom*

Robins, Herb (act): *The Funhouse* (1981); *The Worm Eaters*
Robins, Herb (dir & wri): *The Worm Eaters*
Robins, Jessie (act): *The Black Windmill*; *The Fearless Vampire Killers or: Pardon Me, But Your Teeth Are In My Neck*
Robins, John (wri): *Death Ship*
Robins, Lisa (act): *Philadelphia Experiment II*
Robins, Mikul (act): *Weird Science*
Robins, Oliver (act): *Don't Go to Sleep*; *Poltergeist II: The Other Side*
Robins, Phyllis (act): *They Made Me a Fugitive*
Robins, Sam (wri): *The Corpse Vanishes*
Robins, Sheila (act): *The Village of the Damned* (1960)
Robins, Toby (act): *For Your Eyes Only*; *Game for Three Losers*; *Licensed to Love and Kill*; *The Naked Runner*; *Scandalous*
Robinson, Aemilia (act): *The Haunting of Lisa*
Robinson, Alexia (act): *The Nutty Professor* (1996); *Total Recall*
Robinson Jr., Andre (act): *The Brother from Another Planet*
Robinson, Andrew (act): *Child's Play 3*; *Hellraiser*; *Into the Badlands*; *Pumpkinhead II: Blood Wings*; *The Puppet Masters*; *Trancers III: Deth Lives*
Robinson, Ann (act): *Midnight Movie Massacre*; *The War of the Worlds*
Robinson, Bartlett (act): *Sleeper*
Robinson, Betty Lou (act): *The Clone Master*
Robinson, Brian (act): *Grizzly*
Robinson, Bruce (act): *Beyond and Back*; *Tam Lin*
Robinson, Bruce (dir): *Jennifer 8*
Robinson, Bruce (wri): *In Dreams*; *Jennifer 8*
Robinson, Bumper (act): *Enemy Mine*; *Generation X*; *The Spirit*
Robinson, C. Jack (act): *Outbreak*
Robinson, Casey (wri): *While the City Sleeps*
Robinson, Charles (Knox) (act): *The Brotherhood of Satan*; *Ferde-Lance*; *The Screaming Woman*; *The Six Million Dollar Man*; *So Evil, My Sister*; *Sugar Hill*
Robinson, Charlie (act): *Gray Lady Down*
Robinson, Chris(topher) (act, b. 1938): *Beast from Haunted Cave*; *Diary of a High School Bride*; *Stanley*
Robinson, Claudia (act): *The Unholy*; *Wide Sargasso Sea*
Robinson, Daisy (act): *Rip Van Winkle* (1921)
Robinson, Dan (act): *Empire of Ash III*
Robinson, Dar (act): *Cyclone*; *Vamp*
Robinson, David (act): *The People Under the Stairs*
Robinson, Dennis (act): *The Haunting of Hamilton High*
Robinson, Dewey (act): *Cheaters at Play*; *The Chinese Cat*; *A Midsummer Night's Dream* (1935)
Robinson, Doug (act): *Enemy Mine*; *Outland*
Robinson, Douglas (act): *Diamonds On Wheels*; *Jason and the Argonauts*; *Licensed to Love and Kill*; *Piccadilly Third Stop*
Robinson, Edward G. (act, 1893-1973, nee Emmanuel Goldenberg): *Confessions of a Nazi Spy*; *Double Indemnity* (1944); *Flesh and Fantasy*; *The Glass Web*; *Illegal*; *Key Largo*; *Mackenna's Gold*; *My Daughter Joy*; *Night Has a Thousand Eyes*; *Nightmare* (1956); *The Peking Blonde*; *The Red House*; *Soylent Green*; *The Woman In the Window*
Robinson Jr., Edward G. (act): *Invasion U.S.A.*
Robinson, Elizabeth (act): *Black Magic Woman*; *Dr. Black Mr. Hyde*
Robinson, Ernie (act): *Brainstorm* (1983)
Robinson, Frances (act): *Dr. Jekyll and Mr. Hyde* (1941); *The Invisible Man Returns*; *The Last Warning* (1938); *The Lone Wolf Keeps a Date*; *Tower of London* (1939)
Robinson, Frank M. (wri, b. 1926): *The Power* (1967)
Robinson, Gardew (act): *A Connecticut Yankee In King Arthur's Court* (1989)
Robinson, Gary (mus): *The Devil-Ship Pirates*
Robinson, Geoff (act): *Quarantine*
Robinson, George (cin): *Abbott and Costello Meet Dr. Jekyll and Mr. Hyde*; *Abbott and Costello Meet the Invisible Man*; *Abbott and Costello Meet the Mummy*; *Ali Baba and the Forty Thieves* (1943); *Captive Wild Woman*; *The Cat Creeps* (1946); *The Challenge*; *Cobra Woman*; *Destiny* (1944); *Dracula's Daughter*; *The Falcon Takes Over*; *Francis In the Haunted House*; *Frankenstein Meets the Wolf Man*; *Great Expectations* (1934); *The Ghost of Frankenstein* (1942); *Gypsy Wildcat*; *House of Dracula*; *House of Frankenstein*; *The Invisible Ray*; *Jack and the Beanstalk* (1952); *The Mummy's Tomb*; *The Night Key*; *Son of Dracula* (1943); *Son of Frankenstein*; *The Spider Woman Strikes Back*

of Monte Cristo; Sudan; Tarantula; 13 Lead Soldiers; Tower of London (1939)
Robinson, Glen (cin): Amityville II: The Possession; Logan's Run; The Night of the Claw
Robinson, Harriet (act): White Angel
Robinson, Harry (mus): The Boy Who Never Was; Countess Dracula; Demons of the Mind; Electric Eskimo; The Flying Sorceror; The Ghoul (1974); The Glitterball; A Hitch In Time; The House In Nightmare Park; Legend of the Werewolf; Lust for a Vampire; The Oblong Box; Sammy's Super T-Shirt; There Goes the Bride; Twins of Evil; Where's Johnny
Robinson, Henry Ford (act): Zapped!
Robinson, Holly (act): Howard the Duck
Robinson, J. Peter (mus): Are You Lonesome Tonight?; Bates Motel; The Believers; Buried Secrets; Don't Look Now; Encino Man; Gargantua; The Gate; Generation X; The Gifted One; The Kiss (1988); The Lightning Incident; Return of the Living Dead, Part II; Vampire In Brooklyn; Wes Craven Presents Mind Ripper; Wes Craven's New Nightmare; With a Vengeance; The Wraith
Robinson, Jack A. (wri): Tarzan's Deadly Silence
Robinson, James (act): Demons of Ludlow
Robinson, James (wri): Cyber Bandits
Robinson, Jay (act, b.1930): Bram Stoker's 'Dracula'; Dying to Remember; The Sword and the Sorcerer
Robinson, Jo Ann (act): Scalps
Robinson, Joe (act): Beyond and Back; Diamonds Are Forever; Diamonds On Wheels; A Kid for Two Farthings; The Strange Awakening; The Tartar Invasion; Taur the Mighty; Thor and the Amazons; The Two Faces of Dr. Jekyll
Robinson, Joel (act): The Fugitive (1993)
Robinson, John (act): Ghost Ship (1952); Nothing But the Night; The Scarab Murder Case
Robinson, Judy (act): House of Whipcord
Robinson, Larry (mus): Tales from the Hood
Robinson, Lenna (act): The Hidden
Robinson, Les (act): Congo
Robinson, Mabel (act): The Wiz
Robinson, Madeleine (act, b. 1916, nee Madeleine Svoboda): I Married a Shadow; Leda; Mission to Venice; The Trial
Robinson, Matt (wri): The Possession of Joel Delaney
Robinson, Max (act): Earthbound (1981); Hangar 18
Robinson, McKinlay (act): The Pink Chiquitas; The Spirit
Robinson, Michael (act): The Frighteners
Robinson, Michael (dir): Deadly Sins
Robinson, Milton (act): The Power (1980)
Robinson, Norman (act): Kill and Kill Again
Robinson, Ocie (act): Hangar 18
Robinson, Patrick (act): Empire of Ash III
Robinson, Percy (wri): Wanted for Murder
Robinson, Pete (act): Freaks
Robinson, Pete(r Manning) (mus): Beyond Obsession; The Maddening; Night of the Hunter (1991); Once You Meet a Stranger; The Presence; Radioactive Dreams; Sometimes They Come Back...Again; What Ever Happened to Baby Jane? (1991)
Robinson, Phil Alden (wri): All of Me
Robinson, Ralph (cin): The Night of the Claw
Robinson, Randy (cin): The Final Terror
Robinson, Richard (act): Return of the Jedi
Robinson, Richard (wri): Kingdom of the Spiders; Piranha (1978)
Robinson, Roger (act): Meteor
Robinson, Ron (act): Angels In the Endzone
Robinson, Ruth (act): The Lone Wolf In Paris; The Search for Bridey Murphy; Torchy Plays With Dynamite; The Walking Dead
Robinson, Spike (act): Boston Blackie
Robinson, Steve (act): Cinque Tombe per un Medium
Robinson, Sugar Ray 9act, b. 1921): City Beneath the Sea (1970)
Robinson, Ted (dir): Those Dear Departed
Robinson, Tina (act): Arthur the King; Octopussy
Robison, Arthur (dir, 1886-1935): A Night of Horror; Schatten, eine Nachtliche Halluzination; Der Student von Prag (1935)
Robison, Karin (act): Twin Peaks: Fire Walk With Me
Robison, Mary Jeanette (act): see Robson, May
Robledo, Rafael H. (act): Darkman (1990)
Robles, German (act): El Ataud del Vampiro; El Baron del Terror; Blood of Nostradamus; La Cabeza Viviente; La Maldicion de Nostradamus; Nostradamus y el Destructor de Monstruos; Nostradamus y el Genio de la Tinieblas; El Vampiro
Robles, Renato (act): The Blood Drinkers
Robles, Richard (act): The Hunger
Robles, Rudy (act): Jungle Goddess; Omoo Omoo, the Shark God
Robotham, George (act): Alien Nation; The Goonies; The Prisoner of Zenda (1979); Savage Mutiny
Robsahm, Margrete (act): La Danza Macabra
Robson, Flora (act, 1902-1984): Alice's Adventures In Wonderland (1972); Are You Dying Young Man?; Black Narcissus; Clash of the Titans; Dominique; Eye of the Devil; Fragment of Fear; The Frightened Bride; Les Miserables (1978); Murder at the Gallop; Poison Pen; The Shuttered Room; Wuthering Heights (1939)
Robson, Karen (act): Picnic at Hanging Rock
Robson, Linda (act): Junket 89
Robson, Mark (dir, 1913-1978): Avalanche Express; Bedlam; Daddy's Gone A-Hunting; Earthquake; Ghost Ship (1943); Isle of the Dead (1945); The Seventh Victim
Robson, May (act, 1858-1942, nee Mary Jeanette Robison): Alice In Wonderland (1933)
Robson, Michael (wri): Holocaust 2000; The 39 Steps (1978); The Water Babies
Robson, Roberta (act): Point of Terror
Robson, Victor (act): The Golden Web
Robson, W. (wri): The Land Unknown
Robson, Wayne (act): Dead of Winter; Heads; Pippi Longstocking
Robson, Zuleika (act): Revenge (1971, GB)
Robusti, Guido (mus): Robin Hood and the Pirates
Roc, Lionel (act): Lemmy pour les Dames
Roc, Patricia (act, b. 1918, nee Felicia Riese): Bluebeard's Ten Honeymoons; Cartouche (1957); Circle of Danger; The Gaunt Stranger; The House In the Woods; The Hypnotist (1957); The Missing People; The Perfect Woman; Three Silent Men
Rocca, Daniela (act): Caltiki, il Mostro Immortale; La Regina delle Amazzoni
Rocchi, Luigina (act): Arabian Nights (1974); Il Montagna di Dio Cannibale
Rocchi, Marina (act): Yor, the Hunter from the Future
Rocchietta, Isabella (act): Roger Corman's 'Frankenstein Unbound'
Rocco, Alex (act, b. 1936): Blood Mania; Boris and Natasha; Dream a Little Dream; The Entity; Herbie Goes Bananas; Motor Psycho; Return to Horror High; Robin Cook's 'Harmful Intent'; The Spy Within; Stanley
Rocco, Antonio (act): Alice, Sweet Alice
Rocco, Lyla (act): L'Ultima Preda del Vampiro
Rocco, Marc (dir & wri): Dream a Little Dream
Rocco, Tony (act): Star Trek
Rocco, Tymm (mus): Zombie High
Roccos, Cleo (act): Blood Bath at the House of Death
Roccuzzo, Mario (act): The Clone Master; Condor; Retribution (1988); Wonder Woman
Rocha, Glauber (dir, 1938-1981, nee Victoria da Conquista): Terra em Transe
Roche (cin): L'Inhumaine
Roche, Brogan (act): The Craft
Roche, Eamonn (act): The Mask (1994)
Roche, Eugene (act, b. 1928): The Ghost of Flight 401; Oh, God! You Devil; The Possessed (1977); Roswell; The Sitter; Slaughterhouse-Five; They Might Be Giants; W
Roche, Jim (act): The Silence of the Lambs
Roche, John (act): Don Juan (1927); The Return of Peter Grimm (1926); The Unholy Night
Roche, Marcel (act): I Married a Shadow
Roche, Nichola (act): Return to Oz
Rochefort, Jean (act): Birgitt Haas Must Be Killed; Who Is Killing the Great Chefs of Europe?
Rochelle, Claire (act): Another Thin Man; Blonde for a Day
Rochelle, Robin (act): Sorority Babes In the Slimeball Bowl-O-Rama
Rochester (act): see Anderson, Eddie "Rochester"
Rochetti, Dante (act): The Man Who Saw Tomorrow
Rock, Berna (act): Operation Atlantis
Rock, Blossom (act): She-Devil (1957)
Rock, C.V. (wri): Cave of the Living Dead
Rock, Charles (act): The Black Spot; The Cage; Called Back; The Chinese Puzzle; A Christmas Carol (1914); The Firm of Girdlestone; The King's Minister; The King's Outcast; The Man In the Attic (1915); Rupert of Hentzau (1915); The Sons of Satan; Trilby (1914); Vice Versa (1916); Whoso Diggeth a Pit
Rock, Chris (act, b. 1966): Coneheads; Dr. Dolittle (1998)
Rock, Kevin (wri): Howling VI: The Freaks; Philadelphia Experiment II; Warlock: The Armageddon
Rock III, Monte (act): 2000 Years Later
Rock, Philip (wri): The Extraordinary Seaman; Most Dangerous Man Alive
Rock, Tony (act): The Devil's Hand (1961)
Rockas, Angelique/Anjelique (act): Outland; The Witches (1990)
Rockenbaygh, Zane (act): Lord of the Flies (1990)
Rocket, Charles (act): Earth Girls Are Easy; Hocus Pocus
Rockett, Sam (act): Stormy Crossing
Rockhold, Steve (act): Killer Klowns from Outer Space
Rockwell, Ed (act): Just Imagine
Rockwell, Rick (act): Killer Tomatoes Strike Back; Return of the Killer Tomatoes
Rockwell, Robert (act, b. 1925): Federal Agent at Large; Perfect Alibi; The Red Menace; The War of the Worlds
Rockwell, Sam (act): Clownhouse; Teenage Mutant Ninja Turtles
Rockwood, Roy (wri): African Treasure; Bomba and the Elephant Stampede; Bomba and the Hidden City; Bomba, the Jungle Boy; The Golden Idol; Killer Leopard; The Lion Hunters; Lord of the Jungle; The Lost Volcano; Panther Island; Safari Drums
Rodann, Ziva (act): Giants of Thessaly; Macumba Love; Pharaoh's Curse; The Private Lives of Adam and Eve; The Story of Mankind
Roddam, Franc (dir): The Bride (1985); Moby Dick (1998)
Roddam, Franc (wri): Moby Dick (1998)
Roddan, Allison (act): Monsieur Verdoux
Roddenberry, Dawn (act): Pretty Maids All In a Row
Roddenberry, Gene (wri, 1921-1991): Planet Earth; Pretty Maids All In a Row; The Questor Tapes; Spectre (1977); Star Trek; Star Trek II: The Wrath of Khan; Star Trek III: The Search for Spock; Star Trek IV: The Voyage Home; Star Trek V: The Final Frontier; Star Trek VI: The Undiscovered Country; Star Trek: Generations
Roddick, John (wri): Death Trap (1962); The Double; Double Exposure (1954); The Partner; Payment In Kind; Return to Sender; The Rivals
Roden, John (act): The Pirates of Blood River
Roden, Molly (act): Charlie Chan and the Curse of the Dragon Queen; Witness for the Prosecution
Rodenheaver, Sir (act): Blood Diner
Roderer, Walter (act): Superwheels
Roderick, George (act): Operation Third Form
Roderick, Olga (act, b. 1871, nee Jane Barnell): Freaks
Rodger, Claire (act): The Kiss (1988); Wild Thing
Rodger, Strewan (act): Who Is Killing the Great Chefs of Europe?
Rodgers, Anton (act): The Fourth Protocol; The Man Who Haunted Himself; Murder With Mirrors; Scrooge (1970)
Rodgers, Edgar (dir): Love and War In Toyland; The Nightmare of the Glad-Eye Twins
Rodgers, Gaby (act, b. 1928): Kiss Me Deadly
Rodgers, Ilona (act): Night of the Red Hunter
Rodgers, Marilyn (act): Patrick
Rodgers, Mark (wri): Let's Kill Uncle
Rodgers, Mary (wri): The Devil and Max Devlin; Freaky Friday (1976)
Rodgers, Mic (act): Point of No Return
Rodgers, Nile (mus): Earth Girls Are Easy
Rodgers, Pam (act): Dr. Goldfoot and the Bikini Machine
Rodgers, Philip (act): Anguish
Rodgers, Richard (mus, 1902-1979): The Boys from Syracuse; I Married an Angel; Love Me Tonight
Rodgers, Richard (wri, 1902-1981): Carousel; Cinderella (1997)
Rodgers, Sondra (act): The Hidden Eye
Rodgers, Tee (act): Project X (1987)
Rodine, Alex (act): Colossus: The Forbin Project; Futureworld; The Nude Bomb
Rodion, John (act): Tower of London (1939)
Rodionov, Alexei (cin): Orlando
Rodman, Howard (wri, 1920-1985): One of Our Spies Is Missing; The Rage: Carrie 2; Smile, Jenny, You're Dead
Rodman, Nancy (act): Chosen Survivors
Rodney, Jack (act): The Devil-Ship Pirates; The Share Out
Rodney, John (act): Pursued
Rodrigo, Roberto (act): Diabolique (1955)
Rodrigue, Madeleine (act): Paris Qui Dort
Rodrigues, Percy (act): The Astral Factor; Deadly Blessing; Galaxina; Genesis II; Hugo the Hippo; Rhinoceros (1974); Shadow of Death (1983); Treachery and Greed On the Planet of the Apes
Rodriguez, Agustin (act): Generation X; Strange Days
Rodroguez, Celia (act): The Blood Drinkers
Rodriguez, Charles (act): The Wiz
Rodriguez, Emilio (act): Deadfall
Rodriguez, Eva (act): Wolf
Rodriguez, Henrich (wri): El Vampiro
Rodriguez, Irma (act): Doctor of Doom
Rodriguez, Ismael (dir): Autopsia de un Fantasma; The Beast of Hollow Mountain
Rodriguez, Lucy (act): Species
Rodriguez, Marco (act): The Crow (1994)
Rodriguez, Maria Rosa (act): Aimez-Vous les Femmes?
Rodriguez, Mario Alberto (act): Macario
Rodriguez, Patricia (act): Alien High
Rodriguez, Roberto (dir): The Faculty; From Dusk Till Dawn; Little Red Riding Hood vs. the Monsters; The Queen's Swordsman
Rodriguez, Roberto (wri): The Queen's Swordsman
Rodriguez, Rosa M. (act): The Blood Spattered Bride
Rodrique, Madeleine (act): Paris Qui Dort
Rodway, Norman (act): Ambush In Leopard Street; Appointment With a Killer; Murder In Eden; The Penthouse (1967); A Question of Suspense
Roe, Channon (act): Buried Secrets
Roe, Guy (cin): Behind Locked Doors; Gojira; Target Earth
Roe, Matt (act): Puppet Master
Roe, Patricia (act): Tattoo
Roe, Willy (dir): The Playbirds
Roebuck, Daniel (act): Cavegirl (1985); The Cold Equations; The Fugitive (1993); Project X 1987); Terror Eyes (1987)
Roebuck, Tiny (act): Torchy Plays With Dynamite
Roeca, Sam (wri): Sabu and the Magic Ring
Roedel, John (act): The Alien's Return
Roedel, Mary Ann (act): The Alien's Return
Roeder, Peggy (act): In the Company of Darkness; Vice Versa (1988)
Roeg, Nicolas (cin, b. 1928): Fahrenheit 451; The Masque of the Red Death (1964); Victim Five
Roeg, Nicolas (dir, b. 1928): Cold Heaven; Don't Look Now; The Man Who Fell to Earth (1976); Performance; Track 29; The Witches (1990)
Roeg, Nicolas (wri, b. 1928): Death Drums Along the River; A Prize of Arms
Roemheld, Heinz (Eric) (mus, 1901-1985): The Black Cat (1934); Down to Earth; Heaven Only Knows; The Lady from Shanghai; The Monster That Challenged the World
Roerick, William (act, 1912-1995): The Day of the Dolphin; Not ofThis Earth (1957); The Wasp Woman (1959)
Roeyes, Maurice (act): Judge Dredd
Roffey, Jack (wri): Hostile Witness
Roffman, Julian (dir): The Mask (1961)
Rogan, Beth (act): Compelled; Innocent Meeting; Mysterious Island (1961)
Rogan, Josh (wri): Twilight Zone
Rogan, Michael (act): Doom Asylum
Rogel, Leonard (act): Werewolves On Wheels
Rogell, Albert S. (dir, 1901-1988): Before I Wake; The Black Cat (1941); Cyclone Cavalier; Heaven Only Knows; The Last Warning (1938); Li'l Abner (1940); The Lone Wolf In Paris; The Lone Wolf's Daughter (1929); Song of India
Rogers, Amanda (act): The Lightning Incident
Rogers, Anne (act): Sparkling Cyanide
Rogers, Anthony (act): Camelot; Tommy Tricker and the Stamp Traveller
Rogers, Barry (act): Secrets of the Phantom Caverns
Rogers, Bill (act): A Taste of Blood
Rogers, Carl (act): Capture That Capsule!
Rogers, Charles (act): Sorceress (1982)
Rogers, Charles "Buddy" (act): Mexican Spitfire Sees a Ghost
Rogers, Charles (dir): Babes In Toyland (1934)
Rogers, Charles (wri): A Chump at Oxford
Rogers, Connie (act): The Mutilator (1985)
Rogers, Elizabeth (act): Something Evil
Rogers, Eric (mus): Carry On Screaming; Carry On Spying; In the Devil's Garden; Meet Mr. Lucifer; Quest for Love; Revenge (1971, GB)
Rogers, Erica (act): The Horror of It All; The Rivals
Rogers, Gerald (act): The Adventures of Robin Hood; Arrest Bulldog Drummond; Bulldog Drummond's Secret Police
Rogers, Gil (act): The Children
Rogers, Ginger (act, 1911-1995, nee Virginia Katherine McMath): Black Widow (1954);

Lady In the Dark; Monkey Business; A Shriek In the Night; Star of Midnight; The Thirteenth Guest
Rogers, Holly (act): *The Punisher*
Rogers, Howard Emmett (wri): *Calling Bulldog Drummond; Eyes In the Night; The Hour of 13; The Mystery of Mr. X*
Rogers, Jane Jordan (act): *Mr. Horatio Knibbles*
Rogers, Jean (act): *Charlie Chan In Panama; Mars Attacks the World; The Night Key; Spaceship to the Unknown; Strange Mr. Gregory*
Rogers, Jean Scott (wri): *Doctor of Seven Dials*
Rogers, Jeffrey (act): *Friday the 13th-Part 3*
Rogers, John (act): *Arrest Bulldog Drummond; Behind That Curtain; Bulldog Drummond Comes Back; Charlie Chan at the Race Track; Charlie Chan Carries On; Charlie Chan In London; Les Miserables (1952); The Mysterious Mr. Moto; Think Fast, Mr. Moto; The Undying Monster*
Rogers, John (1990s act): *Teenage Mutant Ninja Turtles*
Rogers, Keri (act): *Flight of the Navigator*
Rogers, Larry (act): *Doctor Death: Seeker of Souls*
Rogers, Leo (cin): *Fiend Without a Face; Grip of the Strangler*
Rogers, Lesley (act): *The Fan*
Rogers, Linda (act): *The Comedy of Terrors*
Rogers, Liz (act): *The Return of Count Yorga*
Rogers, Liza (act): *Mini Weekend*
Rogers, Lorraine (act): *Psychomania (1964)*
Rogers, Maclean (dir): *The Crime at Blossoms; Dark Secret; The Feathered Serpent (1934); Mark of the Phoenix; Miracles Do Happen; Old Mother Riley's Jungle Treasure; Noddy In Toyland; Paul Temple Returns; Paul Temple's Triumph*
Rogers, Maclean (wri): *The Feathered Serpent (1934)*
Rogers, Maggie (act): *The Ghastly Ones*
Rogers, Malcolm (act): *The Deathshead Vampire*
Rogers, Marilyn (act): *Ladybug, Ladybug*
Rogers, Michael (act): *Mission: Impossible*
Rogers, Michael (wri): *Killer Fish*
Rogers, Mimi (act, b. 1956): *Deadlock; Hider In the House; A Kiss to Die For; Lost In Space; Reflections In the Dark; Virtual Obsession*
Rogers, Mitch (act): *Eyes of Fire*
Rogers, Mitzi (act): *Night of the Prowler*
Rogers, Nancy (act): *Vampire On Bikini Beach*
Rogers, Paul (act, b. 1917): *He Who Rides a Tiger; Life for Ruth; The Mark; Svengali (1954); The Third Secret*
Rogers, Peter (wri): *Dear Murderer*
Rogers, Reg (act): *Primal Fear*
Rogers, Rosemary (act): *Limbo Line*
Rogers, Roswell (wri): *Charley and the Angel; The $1,000,000 Duck*
Rogers, Roxanne (act): *976-EVIL*
Rogers, Ruth (act): *Arrest Bulldog Drummond*
Rogers, Sally (act): *While I Live*
Rogers, Sheila (act): *Jekyll and Hyde...Together Again*
Rogers, Stephen (act): *Stowaway to the Moon*
Rogers, Stuart (act): *Vamp*
Rogers, Stuart Edmond (act): *The Incredible Melting Man*
Rogers, Tristan (act): *The Flesh and Blood Show; The Rescuers Down Under*
Rogers, Wayne (act, b. 1933): *I Dream of Jeannie: Fifteen Years Later; It Happened One Christmas; The November Plan*
Rogers, Wayne (wri): *Astro Zombies*
Rogers, Will (act, 1879-1935): *A Connecticut Yankee; The Headless Horseman*
Rogerson, Maida (act): *Millennium*
Roguemore, Cliff (dir): *Devil's Son-In-Law*
Rohde, Juliet (act): *Hellhole*
Rohland, Leslie L. (act): *Halloween 4: The Return of Michael Myers*
Rohm, Maria (act, b. 1949): *The Blood of Fu Manchu; City of Fear (1965); Count Dracula; Dorian Gray; Eugenie...The Story of Her Journey Into Perversion; The Face of Eve; Five Golden Dragons; Future Women; House of 1,000 Dolls; Island of Despair; Marquis de Sade: Justine; The Million Eyes of Sumuru; Night of the Blood Monsters; Paroxysmus; Ten Little Indians (1974); Treasure Island (1971); The Vengeance of Fu Manchu*
Rohmer, Eric (act, b. 1920): *Berenice*
Rohmer, Eric (dir & wri, b. 1920): *Berenice; Perceval*
Rohmer, Patrice (act): *Phantom of the Paradise*
Rohmer, Sax (wri, 1883-1959): *The Blood of Fu Manchu; The Brides of Fu Manchu; The Castle of Fu Manchu; Daughter of the Dragon; Drums of Fu Manchu; The Face of Fu Manchu; The Fiendish Plot of Dr. Fu Manchu; Fu Manchu; The Mask of Fu Manchu; The Million Eyes of Sumuru; The Mysterious Dr. Fu Manchu; El Otro Fu Manchu; The Return of Dr. Fu Manchu; The Vengeance of Fu Manchu; The Yellow Claw*
Rohner, Clayton (act): *April Fool's Day; Destroyer; I, Madman; Naked Souls; Nightwish; The Relic; Snow Kill*
Rohr, Tony (act): *High Spirits; Jamaica Inn (1985)*
Roisman, Harper (act): *Ed and His Dead Mother*
Roizman, Owen (cin): *The Addams Family; The Exorcist; The Stepford Wives; 3 Days of the Condor*
Roja, Victoria Merida (act): *Robin and Marian*
Rojas, Carmen (act): *Doctor?? Coppelius!!*
Rojas, Emmanuel I. (cin): *Terror Is a Man*
Rojas, Julio (cin): *Los Muertos No Perdonan*
Rojas, Mini (cin): *Eues of a Stranger*
Rojo, Daniel (act): *Lady In White*
Rojo, Ethel (act): *Mi Adorable Esclava*
Rojo, Gustavo (act): *The Miracle (1959); No Survivors, Please; Parsifal; The Valley of Gwangi; A Witch Without a Broom*
Rojo, Helena (act): *Mary, Mary, Bloody Mary*
Rojo, Jaime (act): *The Refrigerator*
Rojo, Max (act): *Twilight People*
Rojo, Mercedes (act): *Cauldron of Blood*
Rojo, Molino (act): *Perseus the Invincible*
Rojo, Ruben/Rueben (act): *El Baron del Terror; Cauldron of Blood; Neutron vs. the Maniac; The Saint In the Wax Museum; A Thousand and One Nights (1968)*
Roker, Roxie (act): *The Bermuda Triangle*
Roland, Gilbert (act, 1905-1994, nee Luis Antonio Damaso de Alonso): *Around the World In 80 Days; Beneath the 12-Mile Reef; Captain Kidd; The Diamond Queen; Enemy Agents Meet Ellery Queen; Johnny Hamlet; The Mark of Zorro (1974)*
Roland Jr., Glenn R. (cin): *Blood Pen*
Roland, Gyl (act): *Barn of the Naked Dead; Warlock*
Roland, Jeanne (act): *The Curse of the Mummy's Tomb*
Roland, John (act): *Eyewitness (1981)*
Roland, Jurgen (dir): *The Green Archer; The Red Circle (1960)*
Rolando, Maria Luisa (act): *L'Amante del Vampiri*
Rolant, Arlena (act): *Angel Heart*
Rolapp, Thomas Cross (act): *Return (1985)*
Rolden, Emma (act): *La Momia Contra el Robot Humano*
Roley, Sutton (dir): *Chosen Survivors; How to Steal the World; The Loves of Dracula; Satan's Triangle; Sweet, Sweet Rachel; World of Dracula*
Rolf, Erik/Eric (act): *The Chance of a Lifetime; A Close Call for Boston Blackie; Eyes In the Night; Song of the South; U-Boat Prisoner*
Rolf, Tom (wri): *The Resurrection of Zachary Wheeler*
Rolfe, Alan (act): *Dilemma; Peeping Tom*
Rolfe, Charles (act): *Dear Murderer; Tower of Terror*
Rolfe, E.A. (wri): *The Scarf*
Rolfe, Guy (act, b. 1915): *The Alphabet Murders; —And Now the Screaming Starts!; The Dark Angel (1991); Dolls; Mr. Sardonicus; Portrait from Life; Puppet Master III: Toulon's Revenge; Puppet Master 4; Puppet Master 5; Snow White and the Three Stooges; The Spider and the Fly (1949); The Stranglers of Bombay; Uncle Silas; The Veils of Bagdad*
Rolfe, Lalla (act): *The Henderson Monster*
Rolfe, Sam (wri, 1924-1993): *The Mask of Sheba; Matt Helm; They Call It Murder*
Rolffes, Kirsten (act): *The Kingdom*
Rolfing, Tom (act): *He Knows You're Alone*
Rolike, Hank (act): *Something Is Out There*
Roling, Marcus (wri): *Class of Nuke 'em High, Part 2: Subhumanoid Meltdown*
Roll, Grant (act): *The Music of the Spheres*
Roll, Phillip (wri): *The Adventures of Robinson Crusoe (1952)*
Roll, Woody (act): *Pranks*
Rolland, Henri (act): *Paris Qui Dort*
Rollett, Raymond (act): *The Angel Who Pawned Her Harp; The Golden Rabbit; Men of Sherwood Forest; Return of a Stranger (1962); Supersonic Saucer; They Can't Hang Me*
Rollin, Jean (act): *Zombies Lake*
Rollin, Jean (dir): *Vierges et Vampires*
Rolling Stones, The (act & mus): *One Plus One*
Rollings, Gordon (act): *The Bed-Sitting Room; Blood Bath at the House of Death; Captain Clegg; Jabberwocky; Superman II; Superman III*
Rollins, Henry (act): *Johnny Mnemonic; Lost Highway*
Rollins, Oneida (act): *Jaws 2*
Rolston, Mark (act): *Daylight; Eraser; RoboCop 2; [illegible] Cop*
Rolt, Tobias (act): *Mata Hari (1985)*
Roma, Jess (act): *The Blood Drinkers*
Romagnoli, Mario (act): *Satyricon*
Romain, Yvonne (act): *The Brigand of Kandahar; Captain Clegg; Circus of Horrors; The Curse of the Werewolf; Devil Doll (1963); The Frightened City; The Last of Sheila; Return to Sender; Smokescreen*
Romaine, John (act): *The Kidnapping of the President*
Romaine, Katherine (act): *Metamorphosis: The Alien Factor*
Roman, Candy (act): *El Amor Brujo (1986)*
Roman, Frank (act): *Watchers II*
Roman, J.P. (act): *Remo Williams: The Adventure Begins*
Roman, Leticia (act): *La Ragazza Che Sapeva Troppo; The Spy In the Green Hat*
Roman, Murray (act): *2000 Years Later*
Roman, Paul Reid (act): *Mind Over Murder*
Roman, Phil (dir): *Tom and Jerry: The Movie*
Roman, Ric (act): *Appointment In Honduras; Lizzie; Up In Smoke*
Roman, Ruth (act, b. 1925): *The Baby; Day of the Animals; Down Three Dark Streets; Echoes; Five Steps to Danger; Impulse! (1974); The Killing Kind; Lightning Strikes Twice; Strangers On a Train; The Window*
Roman, Susan (act): *Heavy Metal; Rabid*
Romance, Viviane (act, b. 1912, nee Pauline Ronacher Ortmanns): *Carmen (1942); Liliom (1933); Nada*
Romancito, Richard (act): *Nightwing*
Romanelli, Carla (act): *Steppenwolf*
Romanis, George (mus): *She's Dressed to Kill*
Romano, Andy (act): *Eraser; The Fugitive (1993); How to Stuff a Wild Bikini; Return to Horror High; Sergeant Deadhead the Astronut!; Welcome to Arrow Beach*
Romano, Carlos (act): *Amityville 3-D; The Octagon; Yellowbeard*
Romano, Frank (act): *Fake-Out*
Romano, John (wri): *Dark Angel (1996)*
Romano, Maria (act): *Caged Women (1984)*
Romano, Renato (act): *Dorian Gray; L'Uccello delle Piume di Cristallo*
Romano, Rino (act): *The Club (1994)*
Romano, Tony (act): *Beyond and Back*
Romanoff, Ara (act): *Troma's War*
Romanoff, Constantine (act): *The Private Life of Helen of Troy*
Romans, Pierre (act): *Docteur Petiot*
Romantowska, Anna (act): *Przesluchanie*
Romanus, Richard (act): *Ghost of a Chance (1987); Giving Up the Ghost; Gold of the Amazon Women; Heavy Metal; Pandemonium; Point of No Return; Wizards*
Romanus, Robert (act): *Pulse; The Resurrected*
Romaors, Cherie (act): *The Malibu Beach Vampires*
Romashin, Anatoly (act): *Rasputin (1985)*
Romauldi, John (act): *Galaxis*
Romay, Lina (act): *Barbed Wire Dolls; Jack the Ripper (1979); The Perverse Countess*
Rome, Stewart (act): *The American Heiress; Behind the Curtain; Be Sure Your Sins; The Breaking Point (1914); The Bronze Idol; The Case of Lady Camber; The Chimes; The Cobweb; The Confession (1915); Creatures of Clay; The Cry of the Captive; The Dance of Death (1938); Dr. Fenton's Ordeal; Face to Face; The Girl In the Flat; A Grain of Sand; The Grand Babylon Hotel; The Grip of Ambition; The Guest of the Evening; The Incorruptible Crown; Jill and the Old Fiddle; Justice; The Last Hour; The Man Behind "The Times"; The Man With the Scar; A Moment of Darkness; The Quarry Mystery; The Schemers: or, The Jewels of Hate; The Squeaker (1937); The Stress of Circumstance; The Terror of the Air; The Tragedy of Basil Grieve*
Rome, Sydne (act, b. 1947): *Some Girls Do*
Rome, Tina (act): *The Baron of Arizona*
Romeo, Ina (act): *Outbreak; Remote Control (1988)*
Romer, Piet (act): *The Lift*
Romero, Blanquita (act): *Creature from the Haunted Sea*
Romero, Carlos (act): *Demon and the Mummy; Soylent Green*
Romero, Cesar (act, 1907-1994): *Around the World In 80 Days; Batman (1966); British Agent; Charlie Chan at Treasure Island; The Computer Wore Tennis Shoes (1970); F.B.I. Girl; Judgment Day; The Jungle; Lady In the Fog; The Last Generation; Latitude Zero; Lost Continent (1951); Now You See Him, Now You Don't; Prisoners of the Casbah; Sergeant Deadhead the Astronut!; The Spectre of Edgar Allan Poe; The Story of Mankind; Street of Shadows; The Strongest Man In the World; Target: Harry; The Thin Man; Two On a Guillotine; Warlock Moon*
Romero, Chabela (act): *Doctor of Doom*
Romero, Christina (act): *The Dark Half*
Romero, Eddie (dir): *Beast of Blood; Beast of the Yellow Night; Beyond Atlantis; Brides of Blood; Mad Doctor of Blood Island; Moro Witch Doctor; Twilight People; Woman Hunt*
Romero, Eddie (wri): *Beast of Blood; Beast of the Yellow Night; Moro Witch Doctor; The Scavengers; Twilight People*
Romero, George A. (act, b. 1940): *Martin*
Romero, George A. (cin, b. 1940): *Jack's Wife; Night of the Living Dead (1968)*
Romero, George (A.) (dir, b. 1940): *Code Name Trixie; Creepshow; The Dark Half; Dawn of the Dead; Day of the Dead; Jack's Wife; Knightriders; Martin; Monkey Shines; Night of the Living Dead (1968); Two Evil Eyes*
Romero, George (A.) (wri, b. 1940): *Creepshow 2; The Dark Half; Dawn of the Dead; Day of the Dead; Jack's Wife; Knightriders; Martin; Night of the Living Dead (1968 & 1990); Tales from the Darkside; Two Evil Eyes*
Romero, Joanelle (act): *Parasite*
Romero, Liz (act): *Wheels of Terror*
Romero, Ned (act): *Children of the Corn II: The Final Sacrifice*
Romero, Ramon (wri): *City Beneath the Sea (1952)*
Romero, Tina (act): *Sisters of Satan*
Romine, Roseanne (act): *Phantom of the Paradise*
Romitelli, Sante (Maria) (mus): *Hatchet for a Honeymoon; Yeti*
Romito, Vic (act): *The Golden Blade*
Romm, Mikhail (dir & wri, 1901-1971): *Devyat'dney Odnogo Goda*
Romney, E. (act): *Signals In the Night*
Romney, Edana (act, b. 1919): *Alibi (1942); Corridor of Mirrors; East of Piccadilly*
Romney, Edana (wri, b. 1919): *Corridor of Mirrors*
Romo, John (act): *Dead Women In Lingerie*
Romoff, Wood (act): *The Vampire (1957)*
Romoli, Gianini (wri): *Cemetery Man; Trauma (1993)*
Romy (act): *Vengeance of the Zombies*
Ron, Tiny (act): *Alien Nation: The Enemy Within*
Rona, Jeff (mus): *Netforce*
Ronald, Babs (act): *A Man's Shadow*
Ronald, James (wri): *The Suspect*
Ronald, Tom (act): *Lorna Doone (1920)*
Ronalds, Lolita (act): *Watchers 3*
Ronan, Danny (act): *Nightmare (1981)*
Ronane, John (act): *The Spiral Staircase (1975)*
Ronay, Edina (act): *He Who Rides a Tiger; Night Train to Paris; Our Mother's House; Prehistoric Women (1966); A Study In Terror; The Swordsman*
Ronay, Esther (dir): *Rapunzel Let Down Your Hair*
Ronay, Gabriel (wri): *Countess Dracula*
Ronco, Neil (act): *The Final Countdown*
Rondard, Patrice (wri): *Shadow of Evil (1964)*
Rondeau, Charles R. (dir): *The Devil's Partner; The Girl In Lover's Lane; The Threat (1960)*
Rondell, Ronald R. (act): *My Best Friend Is a Vampire*
Rondi, Brunello (dir, b. 1924): *Il Demonio*
Rondi, Brunello (wri, b. 1924): *La Citta delle Donne; 8 1/2; Giulietta degli Spiriti*
Rondinaro, Steve (act): *Making Mr. Right*
Ronee, Helena (act): *On Her Majesty's Secret Service*
Ronell, Ann (mus): *One Touch of Venus*
Ronet, Maurice (act, 1927-1983): *Amador; The Deadly Trap; Frantic; Lucrezia Borgia (1952); Le Scandale; La Sorciere; Sphinx (1981)*
Rons, John (mus): *Blood and Lace*
Ronson, Peter (act): *Journey to the Center of the Earth (1959)*
Rooff, Paul (wri): *The English Rose*
Rook, Charles Rowe (act): *Blood Beach*
Rook, Fiona (act): *Threads*
Rook, Roger (act): *Death Race 2000; The Lawnmower Man*
Rooke, Arthur (act): *The Blackmailers; For All Eternity; God's Clay; The Third Witness; The Wheel of Death*
Rooke, Arthur (dir): *For All Eternity; God's Clay*
Rooke, Arthur (wri): *God's Clay*
[illegible] (act): *High Treason (1929)*
Rooker, Francis (cin): *The Omegans*
Rooker, Michael (act, b. 1955): *Bram Stoker's 'Shadowbuilder'; The Dark Half*
Rooks, Conrad (act): *Chappaqua*

Rooks, Conrad (dir & wri): *Chappaqua; Siddhartha*
Roon, Roger (act): *Wheels of Terror*
Rooney, Anne (act): *Graveyard Shift (1990)*
Rooney, Brian (act): *The Punisher*
Rooney, Gary (act): *Trancers II: The Return of Jack Deth*
Rooney, John Francis (act): *Shamus*
Rooney, Mickey (act, b. 1920, nee Joe Yule Jr., a.k.a. Mickey McGuire): *Arabian Adventure; The Atomic Kid; B.J. Lang Presents; Babe: Pig In the City; Bon Baisers de Hong Kong; The Care Bears Movie; Il Diavolo Innamorato; The Domino Principle; Erik the Viking; Everything's Ducky; The Extraordinary Seaman; The Fox and the Hound; Francis In the Haunted House; How to Stuff a Wild Bikini; It Came Upon the Midnight Clear; Journey Back to Oz; Little Nemo: Adventures In Slumberland; The Lost Jungle; A Midsummer Night's Dream (1935); Pete's Dragon; Platinum High School; The Private Lives of Adam and Eve; Pulp; Silent Night, Deadly Night 5: The Toymaker; 24 Hours to Kill*
Rooney, Mickey (dir, b. 1920): *The Private Lives of Adam and Eve*
Rooney, Tim (act): *Village of the Giants*
Rooney, Wallace (act): *The Exorcist*
Roope, Fay (act): *The Atomic Kid; The Day the Earth Stood Still*
Roos, Casper (act): *Deadtime Stories*
Roos, Don (wri): *Diabolique (1996); Single White Female*
Roosa, Jimmy (mus): *Blood of Ghastly Horror*
Roosa, Stuart A. (act): *For All Mankind*
Roose, Lesley (act): *The Mutations (1985)*
Roose, Thorkild (act): *Vredens Dag*
Roosevelt, Buddy (act): *Dick Tracy (1937); Lost Planet Airmen; Shadow of the Thin Man*
Roost, Gary (act): *Erik the Viking*
Root, Amanda (act): *Jane Eyre (1995)*
Root, Lynn (wri): *Cabin In the Sky; A Date With the Falcon; The Falcon Takes Over; The Gay Falcon; The Saint In London; The Saint Takes Over*
Root, Nancy (act): *The Private Lives of Adam and Eve*
Root, Stephen (act): *Ghost (1990); The Lottery; Monkey Shines; Pandora's Clock*
Root, Wells (dir): *The Bold Caballero*
Rootes, Minor (act): *Graveyard Shift (1990)*
Ropelewski, Tom (wri): *The Kiss (1988)*
Roper, Brian (act): *The Girl On the Pier; Just William's Luck*
Roper, Gil (act): *Basket Case 3: The Progeny*
Roper, Tony (act): *The Wicker Man*
Roperto, Andrew (act): *Deadly Friend*
Ropes, Bradford (wri): *The Time of Their Lives*
Roppelt, Marty (act): *The Dark Half*
Roquemore, Henry (act): *The Gracie Allen Murder Case; Meet Nero Wolfe; The Saint In Palm Springs*
Roquette, Susanne (act): *The Vengeance of Fu Manchu*
Roquevert, Noel (act): *A Dog, a Mouse and a Sputnik; A Toi de Faire, Mignonne; Diabolique (1955); La Main du Diable*
Rorke, Hayden (act, 1911-1987): *The Barefoot Executive; Francis Goes to the Races; I Dream of Jeannie: Fifteen Years Later; The Legend of Lizzie Borden; Midnight Lace (1960); The Night Walker; Project Moonbase; When Worlds Collide*
Rory, Rossana (act): *Robin Hood and the Pirates*
Rosa, Alex (act): *Eyewitness (1981)*
Rosa, Bernardo (act): *Steps from Hell*
Rosa, Silvia (act): *Demons 2*
Rosado, Ronnie (act): *Making Mr. Right*
Rosales, Fernando (act): *Dr. Tarr's Torture Dungeon*
Rosales, Lina (act): *Goliath Against the Giants*
Rosales, Thomas/Tom/Tommy (act): *RoboCop 2; Space Rage; The Sword and the Sorcerer*
Rosamond, Clinton (act): *Green Pastures*
Rosander, Oscar (act): *Sexton Blake, Gambler*
Rosar, Annie (act): *Embezzled Heaven*
Rosario, Raymond (act): *Vice Versa (1988)*
Rosas, Misty (act): *Congo*
Rosari, Ana Maria (act): *Twitch of the Death Nerve*
Rosati, Faliero (dir): *High Frequency*
Rosati, Giuliano (act): *Warriors of the Wasteland*
Rosato, Lucio (act): *The Barbarians (1987)*
Rosato, Mary Lou (act): *Brenda Starr (1992)*
Rosato, Tony (act): *City of Shadows*
Rosay, Francoise (act, 1891-1974, nee Francoise Bandy de Naleche): *L'Auberge Rouge; The Full Treatment; Halfway House; Seven Deadly Sins; The Thirteenth Letter*
Rosborough, Patty (act): *Jacob's Ladder*
Roscoe, Alan (act): *The Death Kiss; Seven Keys to Baldpate (1929)*
Roscoe, Barbara (act): *The Ipcress File*
Rose, Alan (act): *Red Blooded American Girl*
Rose, Bernard (act & wri): *Candyman*
Rose, Bernard (dir): *Candyman; Paperhouse*
Rose, Bianca (act): *Alfred Hitchcock Presents; Shadow of a Doubt (1991)*
Rose, Calvin (act): *Look What's Happened to Rosemary's Baby*
Rose, Cleo (act): *The House Across the Lake*
Rose, Clifford (act): *The Cold Room; The Persecution and Assassination of Jean-Paul Marat as Performed by the Inmates of the Asylum of Charenton Under the Direction of the Marquis de Sade*
Rose, David (act): *And Women Shall Weep; The Headless Ghost*
Rose, Deborah (act): *The Bone Yard*
Rose, Deseree (act): *Blood Diner*
Rose, Diana (act): *The Seduction*
Rose, Edward (wri): *The Prisoner of Zenda (1915); Under the Red Robe (1915 & 1937)*
Rose, Felissa (act): *Sleepaway Camp*
Rose, Gabrielle (act): *The Stepfather; Timecop*
Rose, George (act, b. 1920): *Cat and Mouse (1958); Jack the Ripper (1958); The Flesh and the Fiends; Track the Man Down*
Rose, Greg (act): *Re-Animator*
Rose, Harry (act): *Simon, King of the Witches*
Rose, Herman A. (dir): *Target Earth*
Rose, Jack (wri, b. 1911): *The Great Muppet Caper*
Rose, Jackson (cin): *Behind the Curtain (1924); The Lost Zeppelin; Philo Vance Returns; Philo Vance's Gamble; Philo Vance's Secret Mission*
Rose, Jamie (act): *Chopper Chicks In Zombietown; Just Before Dawn (1980); Terminal*
Rose, Jane (act): *Halloween With the Addams Family*
Rose, Jeremy (mus): *Deathline*
Rose, Joel (wri): *Dead Weekend*
Rose, John C. (wri, b. 1905): *The Incredible Mr. Limpet*
Rose, Kari (act): *Slugs*
Rose, Laurie (act): *Woman Hunt*
Rose, Louisa (wri): *Sisters*
Rose, Mickey (dir & wri): *Student Bodies*
Rose, Nicky (act): *Gremlins 2: The New Batch*
Rose, Norman (act): *Pinocchio In Outer Space; The Telephone Book*
Rose, Phil (act): *Robin Hood: The Swords of Wayland; Threads*
Rose, Ralph (wri): *Let's Scare Jessica to Death*
Rose, Reginald (wri, b. 1921): *The Man In the Net*
Rose, Reva (act): *The Nine Lives of Fritz the Cat*
Rose, Robin Pearson (act): *Full Eclipse; Killer In the Mirror*
Rose, Ruth (wri): *King Kong (1933); The Last Days of Pompeii (1935); Mighty Joe Young (1949); She (1935); Son of Kong*
Rose, Sherrie (act): *Demon Knight; New Crime City: Los Angeles 2020*
Rose, Stanley (act): *Death Goes to School*
Rose, Stewart (act): *Koroshi*
Rose, Thomas (act): *Phantom Raiders*
Rose, Tim (act): *Howard the Duck; Return of the Jedi; Return to Oz*
Rose, Wally (act): *Octaman*
Rose, Wayne (cin): *Gremlins 2: The New Batch; The Night of the Claw*
Rose, William (wri, 1918-1987): *El Castello dell'Orrore; The Lady Killers (1956); My Daughter Joy*
Rosebrook, Jeb (wri): *The Black Hole; Miracle On 34th Street (1973)*
Rosebury, Paul (act): *The Quatermass Conclusion*
Roseen, Irene (act): *Phantasm III: Lord of the Dead*
Roselle, Rita (act): *The Black Camel*
Roselli, Lauren (act): *The Silence of the Lambs*
Roseman, Ben (act): *Night Tide*
Roseman, Edward (act): *The House of Secrets (1929)*
Roseman, Howard (wri): *Isn't It Shocking?*
Roseman, Ralph (act): *The Blob (1958)*
Rose Marie, (Baby) (act, b. 1925): *Bridge Across Time; International House; Witchboard*
Rosemond, Clinton (act): *Cabin In the Sky*
Rosemont, Romy (act): *Congo; Shadow of a Doubt (1991)*
Rosemore, Terrence (act): *Candyman: Farewell to the Flesh*
Rosen, Al (wri): *Troubled Waters (1964)*
Rosen, Alan (wri): *A Dangerous Affair*
Rosen, Barry (dir): *Devil's Express*
Rosen, Elisabeth (act): *Murder In a Small Town*
Rosen, Herschel (act): *Vampire's Kiss*
Rosen, Lance (act): *Child of Darkness, Child of Light; Tomorrow's Child*
Rosen, Martin (dir & wri): *Watership Down*
Rosen, Milton (mus): *The Challenge; Dressed to Kill (1946); Sudan; Terror by Night; 13 Lead Soldiers; The Time of Their Lives*
Rosen, Neal (act): *Flesh-Eating Mothers*
Rosen, Phil(ip) (dir, 1888-1951): *Black Magic (1944); Charlie Chan In the Secret Service; The Chinese Cat; The Jade Mask; The Phantom Broadcast; Phantom of Chinatown; The Red Dragon (1945); Return of the Ape Man; The Scarlet Clue; The Sphinx (1933); Spooks Run Wild; The Strange Mr. Gregory*
Rosen, Sam (wri): *The Phantom Tollbooth*
Rosenbaum, Henry (wri): *The Dunwich Horror*
Rosenbaum, Joel (mus): *The Outing*
Rosenberg, Alan (act): *After Midnight; Freaky Friday (1995); Giving Up the Ghost; Miracle Mile; White of the Eye; Witch Hunt*
Rosenberg, Arthur (act): *Captain America II*
Rosenberg, C.A. (wri): *Maniac (1980)*
Rosenberg, Frank P. (wri): *Gray Lady Down*
Rosenberg, Ilan (cin): *Turbo: A Power Rangers Movie*
Rosenberg, Ina (act): see Balin, Ina
Rosenberg, Laurel (act): *I, Desire*
Rosenberg, Leonard (act): see Randall, Tony
Rosenberg, Marc (wri): *Encounter at Raven's Gate*
Rosenberg, Philip (wri): *Murder of Innocence*
Rosenberg, Saturday (act): *Encounter at Raven's Gate*
Rosenberg, Scott (wri): *Disturbing Behavior*
Rosenberg, Stephen (act): *Jacob Two-Two and the Hooded Fang*
Rosenberg, Stuart (dir, b. 1928): *The Amityville Horror; Asylum for a Spy*
Rosenblat, Barbara (act): *Little Shop of Horrors (1986)*
Rosenblatt, Gary (act): *Class of Nuke 'em High*
Rosenblatt, Martin (act): see Martin, Ross
Rosenbloom, Maxie (act, 1904-1976): *The Boogie Man Will Get You; Ghost Crazy; I Married a Monster from Outer Space; Mr. Moto's Gamble; The Spy In the Green Hat*
Rosener, George (act): *Doctor X*
Rosengren, Clive (act): *Ed Wood; Something Is Out There*
Rosenka, Evelyn (act): *Anguish*
Rosenkranz, Tommy (act): *Time Flyer*
Rosenman, Leonard (mus, b. 1924): *Battle for the Planet of the Apes; Beneath the Planet of the Apes; The Car; The Cat Creature; Countdown; Fantastic Voyage; The Lord of the Rings; Mrs. Munck; The Possessed (1977); Prophecy (1979); Race With the Devil; RoboCop 2; Sherlock Holmes In New York; Star Trek IV: The Voyage Home*
Rosenthal (wri): *Dracula Blows His Cool*
Rosenthal, Alan (act): *Starship Invasions*
Rosenthal, Clara (act): *The Projectionist*
Rosenthal, Elliot (mus): *A Time to Kill (1996)*
Rosenthal, Harry (act): *The Big Clock*
Rosenthal, Joe (dir): *Hiawatha (1903); The Love of a Romany Lass; One of the Bulldog Breed*
Rosenthal, Laurence (mus): *Clash of the Titans; Death at Love House; The House That Wouldn't Die; How Awful About Allan; The Island of Dr. Moreau (1977); Meteor; Revenge of the Stepford Wives; Satan's School for Girls*
Rosenthal, Lyova (act): see Grant, Lee
Rosenthal, Mark (wri): *The Jewel of the Nile; Sometimes They Come Back; Star Trek VI: The Undiscovered Country; Superman IV: The Quest for Peace*
Rosenthal, Rick (dir): *Halloween II*
Rosenthal, Robert J. (dir & wri): *Zapped!*
Rosenthal, Ron (act): *Black Rainbow*
Rosenwald, Francis (wri): *The Leech Woman*
Rose-Price, Dennistoun Franklyn John (act): see Price, Dennis
Roser, Robert (act): *Serial Mom*
Roshal, G. (dir): *Song of Abai*
Roshal, Grigori (wri): *Novyi Gulliver*
Rosher, Charles (cin, 1885-1974): *The Cat Creature; Kismet (1944); Nightwing; Pretty Maids All In a Row; Song of the Thin Man*
Rosher Jr., Charles (cin): *Heartbeeps; Hex*
Rosi, Francesco (dir, b. 1922): *Cadaveri Eccellenti; C'era una Volta; Chronicle of a Death Foretold; The Mattei Affair*
Rosi, Francesco (wri, b. 1922): *Cadaveri Eccellenti; C'era una Volta; The Mattei Affair*
Rosi, G.V. (act & wri): *The Pierrot's Romance*
Rosi, Stelvio (act, a.k.a. Stanley Cooper): *La Orgia de los Muertos*
Rosich, Steve (act): *Offerings*
Rosing, Bodil (act): *The Bishop Murder Case; The Return of Peter Grimm (1926)*
Rositani, Frank (act): *Outbreak*
Rositto, Alonzo (act): *Seven Footprints to Satan*
Roskilly, Charles (act): *Batman (1989)*
Rosley, Adrian (act): *The Walking Dead*
Rosling, Tara (act): *Escape Clause*
Rosman, Mark (dir): *Evolver; The House On Sorority Row; Time Flyer*
Rosman, Mark (wri): *The House On Sorority Row; Time Flyer*
Rosmer, Milton (act, 1881-1971): *The Amazing Partnership; The Chinese Puzzle; The Golden Web; High Treason (1929); The Man Without a Soul; The Mystery of a Hansom Cab; The Phantom Light; Still Waters Run Deep; Wuthering Heights (1920)*
Rosmer, Milton (dir, 1881-1971): *The Secret of the Loch (1934)*
Rosmer, Milton (wri, 1881-1971): *The Golden Web*
Rosner, Larraine Blanc (act): *Hellhole*
Rosner, Rock (wri): *Panic In the Skies!*
Rosny Sr., J.H. (wri): *Quest for Fire*
Roson, Manuel (act): *No Exit*
Ross, Alan (act): *Rana: The Legend of Shadow Lake*
Ross, Alec (act): *Traitor's Gate*
Ross, Alex (act): *The Package*
Ross, Annabel (wri): *The Velvet Touch*
Ross, Annie (GB act): *Straight On Till Morning*
Ross, Annie (USA act): *Basket Case 2; Basket Case 3: The Progeny; Superman III; Witchery*
Ross, Anthony (act): *Between Midnight and Dawn*
Ross, Arnie (act): *Flight of the Navigator; Piranha II: The Spawning*
Ross, Arthur (A.) (wri): *Creature from the Black Lagoon; The Creature Walks Among Us; Satan's School for Girls; The 30 Foot Bride of Candy Rock; The Three Worlds of Gulliver*
Ross, Benjamin (dir & wri): *The Young Poisoner's Handbook*
Ross, Betsy King (act): *Radio Ranch*
Ross, Beverly (act): *Bloodshed; The Coming; Crazed*
Ross, Brian (L.) (wri): *Dying to Remember; Pretty Poison (1996)*
Ross, Charles (wri): *The Mad Butcher*
Ross, Chelcie (act): *Bill & Ted's Bogus Journey; Chain Reaction (1996); Keep My Grave Open; The Package*
Ross, David (act): *Mary Reilly*
Ross, Debby Lynn (act): *Night of the Comet*
Ross, Dev (wri): *The Land Before Time II: The Great Valley Adventure; The Land Before Time III: The Time of the Great Giving; The Land Before Time IV: Journey Through the Mists*
Ross, Diana (act, b. 1944): *The Wiz*
Ross, Don (act): *Poor Devil; Trancers; Walk the Dark Street*
Ross, Edward (dir): *Psychout for Murder*
Ross, Franc (act): *Amityville Dollhouse*
Ross, Fred (act): *The Angry Red Planet*
Ross, Gary (dir): *Pleasantville*
Ross, Gary (wri): *Big*
Ross, Gaylen (act): *Creepshow; Dawn of the Dead; Madman*
Ross, Gene (act): *Alfred Hitchcock Presents; Encounter With the Unknown; The Goonies; Halloween 4: The Return of Michael Myers; Keep My Grave Open*
Ross, Gordon (act): *Attack of the Killer Tomatoes*
Ross, Harry (act): *The Woman Eater*
Ross, Hector (act): *The Fur Collar; The Man With the Twisted Lip; The Material Witness; Ring of Spies; The Steel Key*
Ross, Herbert (act): *The Man at Six*
Ross, Herbert (dir, b. 1927): *The Last of Sheila; The Seven-Per-Cent Solution*
Ross, Howard (act): *Marta; The New Gladiators*
Ross, Hugh (act): *Nightbreed*
Ross, J. McLaren (wri): *The Key Man; The Strange Awakening*
Ross, Jane (act): *Rocket Attack U.S.A.*
Ross, Janet (act): *The King's Daughter; The Princess of Happy Chance; When Knights Were Bold (1916)*
Ross, Jerry (mus): *Damn Yankees*
Ross, Jo (act): *Morons from Outer Space*
Ross, Joanna (act): *Captain Kronos: Vampire Hunter*
Ross, Joe (E.) (act): *Human Feelings; Kingdom of the Spiders; The Love Bug*
Ross, John (act): *Ed Wood*
Ross, Justin (act): *The Fan*
Ross, Katharine (act, b. 1943): *The Final Countdown; Games; The Legacy; The Stepford Wives; The Swarm*
Ross, Katherine (act): *Blood Pen*
Ross, Keith (act): see Keith, Ian
Ross, Kelly (wri): *Dead Men Tell No Tales (1971)*

Ross, Kimberly (act): *The Last Starfighter; Pumpkinhead*
Ross, Lanny (act): *Gulliver's Travels (1939)*
Ross, Larry (act): *The Funhouse (1981)*
Ross, Lenore (act): *The Monster In the Basement*
Ross, Liz (act): *End of the World (1977)*
Ross, Liza (act): *Batman (1989)*
Ross, Lynne (act): *Outer Touch*
Ross, Marion (act, b. 1928): *Colossus: The Forbin Project; Lizzie; Midnight Offerings; Secret of the Incas*
Ross, Matthew (act): *A Deadly Vision; 12 Monkeys*
Ross, Merrie Lynn (act): *Class of '84; The Lucifer Complex*
Ross, Michael/Mike (act): *Attack of the 50-Foot Woman (1958); Bowery to Bagdad; Captain Kidd and the Slave Girl; D.O.A. (1949); Ghost Chasers; I Saw What You Did (1988); Tarzan and the She-Devil*
Ross, Mickey (act): *Flesh-Eating Mothers*
Ross, Milton (act): *The False Faces; The Feathered Serpent (1948)*
Ross, Myrna (act): *How to Stuff a Wild Bikini; 2000 Years Later*
Ross, Neil (act): *Dick Tracy (1990); Explorers*
Ross, Oriel (act): *Pimpernel Smith*
Ross, Pamela (act): *Sorority House Massacre*
Ross, Paul (wri): *Beyond Evil; Journey Into Beyond*
Ross, Phillip (act): *The Private Life of Sherlock Holmes*
Ross, Red (act): *Samson and the Mighty Challenge; The Son of Hercules In the Land of Darkness*
Ross, Ricco/Rico (act): *Aliens; Mission: Impossible; The Return of Sherlock Holmes (1986); Slipstream*
Ross, Robert (act): *Gold of the Amazon Women; The Invisible Maniac*
Ross Jr., Robert (act): *The Invisible Maniac*
Ross, Ron (act): *Battle Beyond the Stars (1980)*
Ross, Rose (act): *Mother's Day*
Ross, Ruthey (act): *Phantom of the Paradise*
Ross, Sammy (act): *The War Lord*
Ross, Sandi (act): *Ms. Scrooge*
Ross, Shavar (act): *Friday the 13th-Part V: A New Beginning*
Ross, Sherri (act): *Starship Invasions*
Ross, Shirley (act, 1909-1975): *Mind Killer; Night Vision*
Ross, Stan (act): *Dr. Heckyl & Mr. Hype; The Private Eyes (1980)*
Ross, Stanley (act): *Sleeper*
Ross, Stanley Ralph (wri): *The New, Original Wonder Woman*
Ross, Steve (act): *The Clone Master*
Ross, Steven (act): *Maid to Order*
Ross, Ted (act): *Amityville II: The Possession; The Wiz*
Ross, Terrence G. (act): *Rabid*
Ross, Terry Ann (act): *Cry Terror!; The Three Faces of Eve*
Ross, Thomas W. (act): *The Saint's Double Trouble*
Ross, Tiny (act): *Time Bandits*
Ross, Tony (act): *Santa Claus Conquers the Martians*
Ross, William (act): *The Green Slime; The Last Dinosaur; The War In Space*
Ross, William (mus): *Thumbelina (1994)*
Rossall, Kerry (act): *They Live*
Rosse, Adele (act): *I, Desire*
Rosse, Eric (act): *Night Visions*
Rossellini, Isabella (act, b. 1952): *Blue Velvet; Death Becomes Her; Merlin (1998); The Odyssey*
Rossellini, Raffaella (act): *The Witches' Black Sabbath*
Rossellini, Renzo (mus): *The Queen of Babylon; Teodora, Imperatrice di Bisanzio*
Rossellini, Roberto (dir & wri, 1906-1977): *Il Miracolo*
Rossen, Carol (act): *The Fury; The Ghost of Flight 401; Revenge (1971, USA); The Stepford Wives*
Rossen, Robert (dir, 1908-1966): *Lilith*
Rossen, Robert (wri, 1908-1966): *Lilith; Out of the Fog (1941)*
Rossen, Steven (wri): *A Choice of Weapons*
Rosser, Ed (act): *Grendel, Grendel, Grendel*
Rossett, Alan (act): *Notorious (1992)*
Rossetti, Franco (wri): *Romolo e Remo*
Rossi, Fausto (cin): *Battle of the Amazons*
Rossi, Leo (act): *Bio-Force I; Halloween II; Maniac Cop 2*
Rossi, Luigi (act): *Amarcord*
Rossi, Robert (act): *The Last of Sheila*
Rossi, Salvatore (act): *Kaos*
Rossi, Sandro (act): *Slaughter Hotel (1972)*
Rossi, Sergio (act): *The Eyes Behind the Stars*
Rossi, Steve (act): *The Last of the Secret Agents?*

Rossi-Drago, Eleonora/Eleonore (act, b. 1925, nee Palmina Omiccioli): *The Bible; Carpet of Horror; David and Goliath; Il Disco Volante; Dorian Gray; Hipnosis; I Pirati di Capri; The Red Hand; Sword of the Conqueror*
Rossilli, Paul (act): *Bridge Across Time; The Haunting Passion; Star Trek VI: The Undiscovered Country*
Rossington, Norman (act, b. 1928): *Deathline; Digby-The Biggest Dog In the World; House of the Long Shadows; Negatives; The Prisoner of Zenda (1979); The Wrong Box*
Rossini, Gabriel (wri): *Ironmaster*
Rossini, Gioacchino (mus, 1792-1868): *Stories from a Flying Trunk*
Rossini, Jan (act): *Cry of the Banshee; When Dinosaurs Ruled the Earth*
Rossini, Renato (act): *Il Trionfo di Ercole*
Rossio, Terry (wri): *Aladdin (1992); Little Monsters; The Puppet Masters*
Rossi-Stuart, Giacomo (act, a.k.a. Jack Stuart): *Blue Movie Blackmail; Caltiki, il Mostro Immortale; Death Comes from Space; Death Smiles On a Murderer; I Diavoli della Spazio; The Glass Sphinx; Knives of the Avenger; The Last Man On Earth; La Leggendi di Enea; Macabre (1980); The Night Evelyn Came Out of the Grave; Operazione Paura; Planet On the Prowl; Revenge of the Gladiators; Sodom and Gomorrah; Zorro (1975)*
Rossiter, Leonard (act, 1926-1984): *Deadfall; Deadlier Than the Male; A Jolly Bad Fellow; Otley; 2001: A Space Odyssey; The Witches (1966); The Wrong Box*
Rossitto, ("Little") Angelo (act): *The Baron of Arizona; Brain of Blood; Carousel; The Clones; The Corpse Vanishes; Dracula vs. Frankenstein; Galaxina; Invasion of the Saucer Men; Jungle Moon Men; Mesa of Lost Women; Mr. Wong In Chinatown; The Offspring; Seven Footprints to Satan; Something Wicked This Way Comes; Spooks Run Wild; The Story of Mankind; Terrified (1963)*
Ross-Norris, Vicki (act): *Shadow Conspiracy*
Rosso, Enrica (act): *Rorret*
Rosso, Pierro (act): *The Last of Sheila*
Rossomme, Richard (act): *Matinee*
Rosson, Edward (cin): *Love at First Bite*
Rosson, Harold/Hal (cin, 1895-1988): *The Bad Seed (1956); Buried Treasure; The Ghost Goes West; Kongo; The Man Who Could Work Miracles; The Scarlet Pimpernel (1934); Tarzan the Ape Man (1932); Three Wise Fools; Treasure Island (1934); Trent's Last Case (1929); Ulysses; The Wizard of Oz (1939)*
Rosson, Richard (dir, 1894-1953): *The Wizard*
Rossovich, Rick (act): *Black Scorpion (1995); Cover Me; Fatally Yours; Legend of the Lost Tomb; New Crime City: Los Angeles 2020; Paint It Black; Spellbinder; Streets of Fire; The Terminator; Warning Sign*
Rossovich, Rick (dir): *New Crime City: Los Angeles 2020*
Rossovich, Tim (act): *Fake-Out; Looker; Trick or Treats*
Rossummoen, Sverre (act): *The Witches (1990)*
Rostaine, H.L. (wri): *Revenge In the House of Usher*
Rosten, Leo (wri, 1908-1997): *The Conspirators; Lured; The Velvet Touch*
Roster, David (act): *Invasion of the Girl Snatchers*
Rostoff, Leonid (act): *Colossus: The Forbin Project*
Rostran, Bryan (act): *Top Secret (1978)*
Roswell, Maggie (act): *Fire and Ice*
Roszyk, Greg "B.D." (act): *The Fear (1994)*
Rota, Carlo (act): *Murder In a Small Town*
Rota, Nino (mus, 1911-1979): *Amarcord; Death On the Nile; 8 1/2; Giulietta degli Spiriti; Obsession (1949); I Pirati di Capri; The Reluctant Saint; Satyricon; Lo Sceicco Bianco; Spara Forte, Piu Forte...Non Capisco; Spirits of the Dead; Venetian Bird*
Rotblatt, Dan (wri): *Phoenix the Warrior*
Rotblatt, Janet (act): *The Craft; Heart and Souls*
Rote, Edward (act): *Eraser*
Rote, Kyle (act): *Werewolf of Washington*
Roth, Adam (mus): *The Refrigerator*
Roth, Andrea (act): *The Club (1994); Crossworlds; Seedpeople*
Roth, Alanna (act): *The Dungeonmaster*
Roth, Allison (act): *Grave Secrets*
Roth, Andrea (act): *Seedpeople*
Roth, [illegible]
Roth, Chris (act): *Roller Blade Warriors: Taken by Force*
Roth, Cy (dir & wri, b. 1912): *Fire Maidens of Outer Space*

Roth, Eric (wri): *The Postman (1997)*
Roth, Gene (act, 1903-1976, nee Gene Stutenroth): *Attack of the Giant Leeches; The Baron of Arizona; Charlie Chan In the Secret Service; A Game of Death; Ghost of Zorro; Lady Godiva; Prince Valiant (1954); Red Planet Mars; The Shanghai Cobra; She Demons; The Spider (1958); Spider Woman; The Three Stooges Meet Hercules; Tormented (1960); Twice-Told Tales; Zombies of Mora Tau*
Roth, George (act): *Batman (1989); Nightbreed*
Roth, Ivan E. (act): *Blue Monkey; Night of the Comet; Night of the Creeps*
Roth, Jerry (act): *Werewolf of Washington*
Roth, Joan (act): *Luther the Geek*
Roth, Joanna (act): *Mary Shelley's 'Frankenstein'; Snow White: A Tale of Terror*
Roth, Johnny (act): *The Bride and the Beast*
Roth, Kathryn (act): *Web of Deceit*
Roth, Lillian (act, 1910-1980, nee Lillian Rutstein): *Alice, Sweet Alice*
Roth, Martha (act): *The Black Pirates; El Hombre y el Monstruo*
Roth, Matt (act): *Blink*
Roth, Michele/Michelle (act): *Night Visions; Not of This World; Retribution (1988)*
Roth, Nathan (act): *Witches' Brew*
Roth, Paul Edwin (act): *Confess, Dr. Corda*
Roth, Philip (wri, b. 1933): *Portnoy's Complaint*
Roth, Phillip J. (dir & wri): *A.P.E.X.; Digital Man; Prototype X29A*
Roth, Ray (act): *Wild Thing*
Roth, Richard (act): *Young Frankenstein*
Roth, Robert J. (dir): *The Man Who Fell to Earth (1987)*
Roth, Stan (act): *I, Madman*
Roth, Stephanie (act): *Escape Clause*
Roth, Tim (act): *Murder With Mirrors*
Roth, William (act): *Funeral Home*
Rotha, Paul (dir, b. 1907): *Cat and Mouse (1958)*
Rotha, Paul (wri, b. 1907): *Cat and Mouse (1958); The Lodger (1932)*
Rotha, Wanda (act): *Hamlet (1960); Saadia*
Rothberg, Jeff (wri): *Bogus; A Simple Wish*
Rothchild, Rebecca (act): *The Mummy and the Curse of the Jackals*
Rothenberg, Susan (act): *Silent Night, Bloody Night*
Rotheray, Rosemary (act): *The Tell-Tale Heart (1960)*
Rothman, Conrad (cin): *Witches' Brew*
Rothman, John (act): *Copycat; Hello Again; Rear Window (1998)*
Rothman, Randy (act): *Sorceress (1982)*
Rothman, Stephanie (dir): *Blood Bath (1966); Terminal Island; The Velvet Vampire*
Rothman, Stephanie (wri): *Beyond Atlantis; Blood Bath (1966); Terminal Island; The Velvet Vampire*
Rothmann, Conrad C. (cin): *Thirst*
Rotholz, Ronnie (act): *Santa Claus Conquers the Martians*
Rothrock, Cynthia (act): *Tiger Claws*
Rothschild, Dorothy (wri): see Parker, Dorothy
Rothschild, Gerry (act): *Always*
Rothstein, Richard (dir): *Bates Motel*
Rothstein, Richard (wri): *Bates Motel; Death Valley; The Gifted One; Human Experiments; Invitation to Hell; Universal Soldier*
Rothwell, Alan (act): *Zeppelin*
Rothwell, Michael (act): *Fragment of Fear*
Rothwell, Robert (act): *Now You See Him, Now You Don't*
Rothwell, Talbot (wri): *Carry On Screaming; Carry On Spying*
Rotsler, William (dir): *Mantis In Lace*
Rotter, Fritz (wri): *Alraune (1952)*
Rotter, Sylvia (act): *The Secret Life of Ian Fleming*
Rottlander, Yella (act): *The Scarlet Letter (1972)*
Rotundo, Nick (wri): *The Pink Chiquitas*
Rotunno, Giuseppe (cin, b. 1926): *The Adventures of Baron Munchausen (1989); All That Jazz; Amarcord; The Bible; La Citta delle Donne; Haunted Summer; On the Beach; Red Sonja; Satyricon; Spirits of the Dead; Wolf*
Roubicek, George (act): *The Bedford Incident; Billion Dollar Brain; Blind Date (1959)*
Rouffio, Jacques (wri): *Le Trio Infernal*
Rougas, Michael (act): *I Was a Teenage Werewolf; A Nightmare On Elm Street 3: Dream Warriors; Star Trek*
Rougerie, Jean (act): *The Phantom of the Opera (1990); The Prize of Peril; A View to a Kill*
Rougeul, Jean (act): *8 1/2*
Roughwood, Owen (act): *The Queen Mother; Under the Red Robe (1915)*

Rouleau, Raymond (act, dir & wri, b. 1904): *Les Sorcieres de Salem*
Roumanoff, Anne (act): *The Phantom of the Opera (1990)*
Roundebush, William (act): *Barracuda*
Rounds, David (act): *The Coming*
Rounds, Tahmus (act): *Copycat*
Roundtree, Danita (act): *Mutants In Paradise*
Roundtree, Richard (act, b. 1942): *Amityville: A New Generation; Earthquake; Embassy; The Fifth Missile; George of the Jungle; Maniac Cop; Mind Twister; Party Line; Q; Seven; Steel; Theodore Rex*
Rounseville, Robert (act): *Carousel*
Roupe, Larry (act): *Beyond and Back*
Rourke, Mickey (act): *Angel Heart; Body Heat; City In Fear; Fade to Black*
Rouse, Mitch (act): *In the Company of Darkness*
Rouse, Russell (dir, 1913-1987): *The Thief (1952); The Well*
Rouse, Russell (wri, 1913-1987): *Color Me Dead; D.O.A. (1949 & 1988); The Thief (1952); The Well*
Rousseau, Gerry (act): *Quarantine*
Rousseau, Pierre (act): *Nick Carter et le Trefle Rouge*
Roussel, Elvera (act): *The Cradle Will Fall*
Roussel, Gilbert (dir): *Women's Prison Massacre*
Roussel, Simone (act): see Morgan, Michele
Rousselot, Philippe (cin): *Interview With the Vampire; Mary Reilly*
Roussillon, Jean-Paul (act): *He Died With His Eyes Open*
Roussimoff, Ari (act): *Frankenhooker*
Routledge, Alison (act): *The Bridge to Nowhere; The Quiet Earth*
Routledge, Patricia (act): *The Curse of King Tut's Tomb; Egghead's Robot*
Rouve, Pierre (dir & wri): *Stranger in the House (1967)*
Rouvel, Catherine (act): *Landru; La Rupture*
Roux, Jacques (act): *The List of Adrian Messenger*
Roux, Tony (act): *Charlie Chan at the Opera*
Rovere, Patrizia Della (act): *Ercole e la Regina di Lidia*
Roveri, Ermanno (act): *The Magic World of Topo Gigio*
Rovira-Beleta (dir): *El Amor Brujo (1972)*
Row, Alexander (dir): *Cinderella (1961); Jack Frost*
Row, Alexander (wri): *Cinderella (1961)*
Rowan, Dan (act): *The Maltese Bippy*
Rowan, Don (act): *Buried Alive (1940); The Deadly Ray from Mars; Nancy Drew and the Hidden Staircase; Peril from the Planet Mongo; Purple Death from Outer Space*
Rowan, Dorothy (act): *The Man Who Stayed at Home*
Rowan, Dorothy (wri): *Dangerous Ground*
Rowan, Gay (act): *Revenge of the Stepford Wives*
Rowan, June (act): *Party Line*
Rowan, Kelly (act): *Candyman: Farewell to the Flesh*
Rowan, Sue (act): *The Amazing Dr. Jekyll*
Rowatt, Graham (act): *Darkman II: The Return of Durant*
Rowbotham, Bill (act): see Owen, Bill
Rowbottom, Jo (act): *The Laughing Girl Murder; The Liquidator*
Rowden, William Courtenay/W.C. (wri): *Les Miserables (1922); The Prisoner of Zenda (1915); Rupert of Hentzau (1915); Scrooge (1922); Trilby (1922)*
Rowe, Arthur (wri): *Crackle of Death; Demon and the Mummy; The Devil's Men; Zeppelin*
Rowe, Brad (act): *Purgatory*
Rowe, Charles (act): *Midnight Lace (1981)*
Rowe, Douglas (act): *Critters 2: The Main Course; Writer's Block*
Rowe, Earl (act): *The Blob (1958)*
Rowe, Frances (act): *The Teckman Mystery; They Came to a City*
Rowe, Frank (cin): *A Boy and His Dog*
Rowe, Freddie (wri): *Howling IV; Howling V: The Rebirth*
Rowe, George (act): *Mermaids of Tiburon*
Rowe, Greg (act): *The Last Wave*
Rowe, Guy (cin): *Amazon Quest*
Rowe, Hahn (mus): *Clean, Shaven*
Rowe, Hansford (act): *Amazons (1984); Dante's Peak; The First Power; Simon; V*
Rowe, Jack (act): *Flesh Gordon*
Rowe, Leanne (act): *Jane Eyre (1996)*
Rowe, Nevan (act): *Sleeping Dogs (1977)*
Rowe, Nicholas (act): *Young Sherlock Holmes*
Rowe, Nicholas (wri): *Jane Shore (1908, 1911 & 1915)*
Rowe, Patrick (act): *Howling III; Spacehunter: Adventures In the Forbidden Zone*
Rowe, Ryan (wri): *The Computer Wore Tennis Shoes (1995)*

Rowe, Shawne (act): Dead Connection; Jack's Back
Rowe, Stephen (act): Cybertracker 2; The Silencers (1995)
Rowe, T. (wri): Les Titans
Rowe, Tom (wri): The Green Slime; The Light at the Edge of the World; Tarzan, the Ape Man (1981)
Rowe, Vern (act): Pandemonium; The Shaggy D.A.
Rowell, Shannon (act): King Kong Lives
Rowell, Victoria (act): Barb Wire; Full Eclipse
Rowland, Betty (act): The World's Greatest Sinner
Rowland, Beverly (Booth) (act): Beyond and Back; Earthbound (1981); Halloween 4: The Return of Michael Myers
Rowland, Eva (act): The Lifeguardsman
Rowland, Henry (act): Diamonds Are Forever; Paris After Dark; Return to Treasure Island; 36 Hours (1965); Zorro, the Avenger
Rowland, Leesa (act): Class of Nuke 'em High, Part 2: Subhumanoid Meltdown
Rowland, Oscar (act): Beyond and Back; Earthbound (1981)
Rowland, Roy (dir, b. 1910): The 5000 Fingers of Dr. T; The Girl Hunters; The Sea Pirate; Scene of the Crime; Witness to Murder
Rowland, Roy (wri, b. 1910): The Girl Hunters
Rowland, William (dir, b. 1900): Flight to Nowhere
Rowlands, Anthony (act): Secrets of Sex
Rowlands, Art (act): The Black Pearl
Rowlands, David (act): Electric Eskimo
Rowlands, Lady (act): Dr. Strange
Rowlands, Patsy (act): Alice's Adventures In Wonderland (1972); Sammy's Super T-Shirt; Vengeance
Rowlatt, Michael (act): Outer Touch
Rowley, Bill (act): The Nesting
Rowley, Nic (mus): The Quatermass Conclusion
Rowley, Peter (act): Those Dear Departed
Rowse, Amanda (act): Secrets In the Attic
Rowse, Hugh (act): King Solomon's Treasure
Rox, Robbie (act): Clarence; Escape Clause
Rox, Roy (act): Glen and Randa
Roy, Bill (act): Beyond the Living
Roy, Deep (act): Disturbed; Howling VI: The Freaks, Licensed to Love and Kill; The Resurrected; Return of the Jedi; Return to Oz; Starship
Roy, Diana (act): The Invincible Barbarian
Roy, Edward (act): Millennium
Roy, Gary (act): The Norsemen
Roy, Esperanza (act): Nightmare Hotel
Roy, Gloria (act): Charlie Chan at the Race Track; Charlie Chan In Egypt; Charlie Chan's Greatest Case; Charlie Chan's Secret; Mr. Moto In Danger Island; Mr. Moto Takes a Chance
Roy, James (act): Martin
Roy, Lise (act): The Corsican Brothers (1985)
Roy, Raymond (act): Targets
Roy, Thomas (act): 12 Monkeys
Royal Ballet Co. (act): Peter Rabbit and the Tales of Beatrix Potter
Royal, Charles F. (wri): Tarzan and the Green Goddess
Royale, Allan (act): Welcome to Blood City
Royan, Yves (act): Vous Pegez?
Royce, Christiane (act): El Castello dell'Orrore
Royce, Dixie Lynn (act): Nightmares (1983)
Royce, Julian (act): The Frightened Lady (1932); Honour In Pawn; Iron Justice
Royce, Lionel (act): Charlie Chan In Panama; Panama Menace; The Son of Monte Cristo; White Pongo
Royce, Paul (act): Hello Again
Royce, Riza (act): The Bat (1959)
Royde, Beverly (act): Just Imagine
Roye, Phillip (act): Dr. Black Mr. Hyde
Roylance, Pamela (act): The Slumber Party Massacre
Royle, Selena (act, 1904-1983): Main Street After Dark; Robot Monster
Royle, William (act): Mr. Wong In Chinatown; Peril from the Planet Mongo; Purple Death from Outer Space
Royston, D.J. (act): Sling Blade
Royston, Gerald (act): Buttons; The Fish and the Ring
Royston, Harry (act): At the Foot of the Scaffold; The Bronze Idol; The Codicil; The Coiner's Den; The Curtain; A Double Life (1912); The Forsaken; Held for Ransom; His Evil Genius; The Hunchback (1914); Justice; The Mill Girl; A Night of Peril; On the Brink of the Precipice; Partners In Crime (1913); Paying the Penalty; The Promise; Rachel's Sin; Retribution (1913); The Silence of Richard Wilton; The Silver Lining; The Terror of the Air; Tried In the Fire; Winning His Stripes
Royston, Marie (act): Children of the Forest
Royston, Roy (act): Children of the Forest; Mr. Wu (1919); The Plague of the Zombies
Royval, Carlos (act): Witches' Brew
Rozakis, Gregory (act): Abduction
Rozanski, Gary (act): Street Trash
Rozema, Patricia (dir): White Room
Rozin, Spela (act): The Son of Hercules In the Land of Darkness
Rozos, Laura (act): Blind Date
Rozsa, Miklos (mus, 1907-1995): Criss Cross; Dark Waters; Double Indemnity (1944); A Double Life (1947); Eye of the Needle; Five Graves to Cairo; The Golden Voyage of Sinbad; The Jungle Book (1942); Knights of the Round Table; Last Embrace; The Lost Weekend; The Man In Half Moon Street; The Power (1967); The Private Life of Sherlock Holmes; The Red House; Secret Beyond the Door; Sodom and Gomorrah; Song of Scheherazade; Spellbound (1945); The Spy In Black; The Strange Love of Martha Ivers; The Thief of Bagdad (1940); Time After Time; A Woman's Vengeance; The World, the Flesh and the Devil
Rozycki, Christopher (act): The Saint
Ru, Kahli (act): Mizpah: or, Love's Sacrifice
Ruan, Javier (act): They Call Him Marcado
Ruane, Clare (act): The Quatermass Conclusion
Ruane, John (dir): Death In Brunswick; That Eye, the Sky
Ruano, Cesar Gonzalez (act): Mi Adorable Esclava
Ruanova, Alfred(o) (wri): Los Automatas de la Muerte; La Maldicion de Nostradamus; Nostradamus y el Destructor de Monstruos; Orlak, el Infierno de Frankenstein
Rub, Christian (act, 1887-1956): Dracula's Daughter; The Jungle Woman; Murder On a Bridle Path; Peter Ibbetson; Pinocchio (1940); Strange Confession
Ruban, Al (act): Swamp Thing
Rubbo, Michael (dir & wri): The Peanut Butter Solution
Rubell, Maria (act): 976-EVIL
Ruben, Albert (wri): City In Fear
Ruben, Andy (wri): Dance of the Damned
Ruben, J. Walter (dir, 1899-1942): The Phantom of Crestwood; Trouble for Two
Ruben, J. Walter (wri, 1899-1942): The Phantom of Crestwood
Ruben, Joseph (dir): Dreamscape; The Good Son; The Stepfather
Ruben, Joseph (wri): Dreamscape
Ruben, Katt Shea (act): Barbarian Queen
Ruben, Katt Shea (dir): Dance of the Damned; Poison Ivy (1992)
Ruben, Michael (act): I Was a Teenage Zombie
Ruben, Paul (act): Necropolis
Ruben, Tom (act): Dance of the Damned
Rubenfeld, Nik (dir): Alien Private Eye
Rubens, Marybeth (act): Firebird 2015 A.D.; Prom Night
Rubens, Percival (dir): The Demon (1981); Survival Zone; Sweet Murder
Rubens, Percival (wri): The Demon (1981)
Rubenstein, Arthur (mus): Dead Man's Island
Rubenstein, David Paul (act): Street Trash
Rubenstein, Phil (act): Elvira, Mistress of the Dark; Ghost Warrior; RoboCop 2
Rubes, Anthony Dean (act): The Amityville Curse
Rubes, Jan (act): The Amityville Curse; Blood Relations; Dead of Winter; Deceived; The Kiss (1988)
Rubes, Susan (Douglas) (act): Haunted by Her Past; Last Bride of Salem
Rubey, Lucille (act): Jungle Trail of the Son of Tarzan
Rubie, Les (act): Funeral Home; Spasms
Rubin, Alec (act): Killer's Kiss
Rubin, Benny (act, b. 1899): The Ghost In the Invisible Bikini; The Shaggy D.A.; Up In Smoke
Rubin, Bruce (Joel) (wri): Brainstorm (1983); Deadly Friend; Deep Impact; Ghost (1990); Jacob's Ladder; Zapped!
Rubin, Cayda (act): Storm of the Century
Rubin, Charles (act): Invasion of the Girl Snatchers
Rubin, Daniel F./Danny (wri): Groundhog Day
Rubin, Glynn (act): Nightwing; When Time Ran Out
Rubin, Jennifer (act): Bad Dreams; The Crush; Full Eclipse; Little Witches; A Nightmare On Elm Street 3: Dream Warriors; Screamers (1996); Wasp Woman (1995)
Rubin, John Gould (act): Dead Again
Rubin, Koya Yair (act): The Jerusalem File
Rubin, Lance (mus): The Death of the Incredible Hulk; Dr. Heckyl & Mr. Hype; Happy Birthday to Me; The Incredible Hulk Returns
Rubin, Mann (wri): Brainstorm (1965); The First Deadly Sin
Rubin, Manny (wri): Walk a Tightrope
Rubin, Michael (act): I Was a Teenage Zombie
Rubin, Murray (act): Doctor Mordrid; I, Madman
Rubin, Sam (act): Wes Craven's New Nightmare
Rubin, Sondra (act): Ghost (1990)
Rubin, Talya (act): Alien High; The Kiss (1988)
Rubin, Zarya (act): Alien High
Rubinchink, Valery (dir & wri): The Savage Hunt of King Stakh
Rubineck, Saul (act): Agency; The Android Affair; Death Ship; Sanctuary of Fear; Synapse
Rubinfeld, Eddie (act): Haunts
Rubinfeld, Michele (act): Haunts
Rubinfeld, Norm (act): Haunts
Rubinfeld, Sandy (act): Haunts
Rubini, Giulia (act): David and Goliath; Rage of the Buccaneers
Rubini, Michel (mus): The Haunting of Sarah Hardy; The Hunger; Nemesis; Not Quite Human II; Secrets of the Phantom Caverns; Too Good to Be True
Rubini, Sergio (cin): Dawn of the Mummy
Rubinov, V. (wri): Sonka Zolotaya Ruchka
Rubinow, John (act): Death Dreams
Rubins, Marybeth (act): Prom Night
Rubinskis, Wolf (act): Los Automatas de la Muerte; Extranos Caminos; El Ladron de Cadaveres; Neutron Battles the Karate Assassins; Neutron, el Enmascarado Negro; Neutron Traps the Invisible Killers; Neutron vs. the Amazing Dr. Caronte; Neutron vs. the Maniac
Rubinstein, Arthur B. (mus): It Came Upon the Midnight Clear; Wargames
Rubinstein, Donald (mus): Knightriders; Martin
Rubinstein, John (act, b. 1946): The Boys from Brazil; The Car; A Howling In the Woods; She's Dressed to Kill; Something Evil; Whispering Death
Rubinstein, Ora (act): Altered States
Rubinstein, Zelda (act): Anguish; Little Witches; Poltergeist; Poltergeist II: The Other Side; Poltergeisy III; Teen Witch
Rubio, Ben (act): Daughters of Satan
Rubio, Jose (act): Behind the Mask of Zorro; Goliath Against the Giants; El Secreto del Doctor Orlof
Rubio, Maria (act): Monstroid
Rubio, Pablo Alvarez (act): Dracula (1931, Spanish-speaking version)
Ruby, Harry (act): The Story of Mankind
Ruby, Herman (wri): The Gorilla (1931)
Ruby, Irving B. (cin): The Man from Beyond
Ruchaud, Frederique (act): Au Coeur de la Vie
Ruck, Alan (act): Star Trek: Generations; Twister
Rucker, Barbara (act): The Stepford Wives
Rucker, Bo (act): Superman (1978)
Rucker, Charles (act): Screams of a Winter Night
Rucker, Christiane (act): Die Schlangengrube und das Pendel
Rucker, Dennis (act): A Very Missing Person; You'll Like My Mother
Rucker, G. (wri): Milczaca Gwiazda
Rucker, Hanna (act): Das Kalte Herz
Rucker, Steve (mus): Creature; Dawn of the Mummy; Little Nemo: Adventures In Slumberland; 976-EVIL
Rudall, Nicholas (act): Chain Reaction (1996)
Rudd, Paul Stephen (act): Halloween: The Curse of Michael Myers
Rudder, Michael (act): Dr. Jekyll and Ms. Hyde
Ruddock, John (act): The Fallen Idol; The Laughing Lady; Treasure at the Mill; Under Capricorn; Wanted for Murder
Ruddy, Albert S. (wri): Megaforce
Ruddy, Joshua (act): Harry and the Hendersons
Rude, Dick (act): Night of the Comet; Repo Man
Rudel, Roger (act): Le Boucher; Nick Carter et le Trefle Rouge
Rudelstein, John (act): The Malibu Beach Vampires
Rudin, Andrew (mus): Satyricon
Rudin, Herman (act): Beauty and the Beast (1962)
Rudin, Stuart (act): The Silence of the Lambs
Rudkin, David (act): A TV dante: cantos I-VIII
Rudley, Herbert (act, b. 1911): The Black Sleep
Rudling, John (act): The Lady Killers (1956); The Man In the White Suit
Rudnaya, Natalya (act): Yolanta
Rudnick, Abraham (act): Fake-Out
Rudnick, Charles (cin): Nightmare In Blood
Rudnick, Paul (wri): Addams Family Values
Rudnick, Steve (wri): The Santa Clause; Space Jam
Rudnik, Oleg (act): 2010
Rudnitsky, Mark (wri): Class of Nuke 'em High
Rudolph, Alan (dir, b. 1943): Barn of the Naked Dead; Endangered Species; Made In Heaven; Mortal Thoughts; Premonition (1972); Remember My Name
Rudolph, Alan (wri, b. 1943): Endangered Species; Premonition (1972); Remember My Name
Rudolph, Helmut (act): Der Verlorene
Rudolph, Johanna (act): Due to an Act of God
Rudolph, Joyce (act): Endangered Species; Premonition (1972)
Rudolph, Lansa (act): Der Januskopf
Rudolph, Oscar (dir): Rocket Man (1954)
Rudoy, Joshua (act): Amazing Stories: The Movie V; Flatliners
Rudrud, Kristin (act): Fargo
Rudy, Reed (act): Zapped Again
Rue, Ed (act): Some Call It Loving
Rueber-Staier, Eve/Eva (act): For Your Eyes Only; Octopussy; The Spy Who Loved Me
Rueckert, Carla (wri): Invasion of the Girl Snatchers
Rueckert, James (act): Invasion of the Girl Snatchers
Ruehl, Mercedes (act, b. 1948): Big
Rueprecht, Albert (act): The Fifth Musketeer
Rueting, Barbara (act): Operation Crossbow; The Phantom of Soho; The Squeaker (1965)
Ruettiger, Rudy (act): In the Company of Darkness
Ruff, Stephen (act): The McGuffin
Ruffalo, Mark (act): Houdini (1998)
Ruffin, Don (act): Sometimes They Come Back
Ruffing, Jack (act): Midnight (1980)
Ruffini, Claudio (act): Super Fuzz
Ruffner, Benjamin (wri): Halloween 4: The Return of Michael Myers
Ruffo, Eleonora (act): Ercole al Centro della Terra; Queen of Sheba; Star Pilot; La Vendetta di Ercole
Rufus (act): The Tenant
Ruge, Steven (act): The Silencers (1995)
Ruggeri, Alessio (act): Spara Forte, Piu Forte...Non Capisco
Ruggeri, Osvaldo (act): Scenes from a Murder
Ruggieri, Francoise (act): Seconds
Ruggiero, Allelon (act): Thinner
Ruggiero, Bob (act): The Man Who Saw Tomorrow
Ruggles, Charles/Charlie (act, 1892-1970): Alice In Wonderland (1933); The Invisible Woman (1941); Love Me Tonight; Murders In the Zoo; Son of Flubber
Ruggles, Wesley (dir, 1889-1972): Condemned
Ruginis, Vyto (act): Last Gasp; Phenomenon
Rugoff, Edward (wri): Mannequin; Mannequin Two: On the Move
Ruhl, Michel (act): Nick Carter et le Trefle Rouge
Ruhl, William (act): Dark Alibi; The Shanghai Chest
Ruhmann, Heinz (act, b. 1902): It Happened In Broad Daylight; Die Leuchter des Kaisers; Man Who Walked Through the Wall
Ruick, Barbara (act, 1931-1974): Carousel
Ruimy, Randi (act): The Mask (1994)
Ruiz, Emilio (cin): Slugs
Ruiz, Juan Carlos (act): They Call Him Marcado
Ruiz, Maria (act): Witchcraft 2: The Temptress
Ruiz, Raul (dir & wri): City of Pirates
Ruiz-Anchia, Juan (cin): The Adventures of Pinocchio (1996); The Jungle Book (1994)
Rule, Beverly C./B.C. (dir & wri): The Invisible Web; One Hour Past Midnight
Rule, Gary (act): Lord of the Flies (1990)
Rule, Janice (act, b. 1931): The Ambushers; Bell, Book and Candle; The Devil and Miss Sarah; The Swimmer; A Woman's Devotion
Rule, Mercedes (act): Twisted
Rule, Timothy (act): Deadtime Stories
Ruleman, Mark (act): I Was a Zombie for the F.B.I.
Rulfs, Helen (act): see Vinson, Helen
Rullo, Cynthia (act): Cavegirl (1985)
Rumann, Siegfried Albon (act): see Ruman(n), Sig
Ruman, Sig (act, 1884-1967, nee Siegfried Albon Rumann): The Bold Caballero; Enemy Agents Meet Ellery Queen; Houdini (1953); House of Frankenstein; It Happened Tomorrow; Lancer Spy; The Last of the Secret Agents?; The Saint In New York; Spy Chasers; Tarzan Triumphs; Thank You, Mr. Moto; Think Fast, Mr. Moto; 36 Hours (1965); Way...Way Out
Rumbold, Jonathan (wri): The Creeping Flesh
Rumm, Ute (act): The Fifth Musketeer
Runacre, Jenny (act): The Lady Vanishes (1979); The Last Days of Man On Earth; The Passenger; Spectre (1977); The Witches (1990)
Rundell, Steve (cin): The Silencers (1995)

Rundell, Sylvia (act): Mars Needs Women
Rundle, Cis (act): Dark Mirror (1984)
Runningfox, Joseph (act): To Save a Child
Runte, Terry (wri): Super Mario Bros.
Runyard, Michael/Mike (act): Covenant; Point of No Return
Runyon, Jennifer (act): Carnosaur; 18 Again!; Ghostbusters; To All a Goodnight
Rupe, Carmen (act): Stalking Laura
Rupp, Jacob (act): Timecop
Rupp, Sieghart (act): Dead Pigeon On Beethoven Street
Ruppert, Charles (act): see Drake, Charles
Ruprecht, David (act): Jekyll and Hyde...Together Again
Ruric, Peter (wri): The Black Cat (1934)
Ruscio, Al (act): The Silence of the Hams
Ruscio, Elizabeth (act): Hider In the House
Rusconi, Jane (wri): Hush
Rush, Barbara (act, b. 1927): The Black Shield of Falworth; The Eyes of Charles Sand; It Came from Outer Space; Moon of the Wolf; Prince of Pirates; Strategy of Terror; Web of Deceit; When Worlds Collide
Rush, Deborah (act): The Purple Rose of Cairo
Rush, Dennis (act): Man of a Thousand Faces
Rush, Dick (act): After the Thin Man; The Benson Murder Case; Bulldog Drummond's Secret Police
Rush, Elizabeth (act): Invasion of the Girl Snatchers
Rush, Geoffrey (act): The House On Haunted Hill (1999); Les Miserables (1998)
Rush, Jordan (wri): Never Talk to Strangers
Rush, Richard (act, b. 1929): Distortions
Rush, Richard (dir, b. 1929): Color of Night; A Man Called Dagger; Psych-Out
Rush, Richard (wri, b. 1929): Color of Night
Rush, Robert Lee (act): Dressed to Kill (1980)
Rush, Sarah (act): Battlestar Galactica; Dr. Strange; The Nude Bomb
Rushe, George (act): The Ivory Ape
Rusher, Sara (act): Wes Craven's New Nightmare
Rushing, Brad (cin): National Lampoon's Men In White
Rushing, Jerry (act): Dogs of Hell; Final Exam; Mutant
Rushmore, Karen (act): Too Scared to Scream
Rushton, Jared (act): Big; Honey, I Shrunk the Kids; Lady In White; Pet Sematary Two
Rushton, Kevin (act): Darkman II: The Return of Durant; Never Talk to Strangers
Rushton, Toby (act): Never-Never Land
Rushton, William (act): The Magic Shop
Rusic, Rita (act): Russicum
Rusich, Stellina (act): Unforgettable
Rusk, John (act): Poltergeist III
Ruskin, Harry (wri, b. 1894): The Girl In the Kremlin; The Hidden Eye; Lady Godiva; Lost In a Harem; Miracles for Sale
Ruskin, Joseph (act): Captain America (1978); Cyber-Tracker; Diary of a Madman; Dr. Scorpion; The Man Who Wasn't There; The Munsters' Revenge; The Sword and the Sorcerer
Ruskin, Sheila (act): Who Is Killing the Great Chefs of Europe?
Ruskin, Shimen (act): Donovan's Brain
Rusler, Robert (act): A Nightmare On Elm Street, Part 2: Freddy's Revenge; Sometimes They Come Back; Vamp; Weird Science
Rusoff, Gary (wri): The Evictors
Rusoff, Lou (wri, d. 1963): Alakazam the Great; Cat Girl; Day the World Ended (1955); The Ghost of Dragstrip Hollow; Girls In Prison; It Conquered the World; The Phantom from 10,000 Leagues; The She-Creature
Russ, Debbie (act): The Flying Sorceror
Russ, Martin (act): The Sand Castle
Russ, Tim (act): Dead Connection; Eve of Destruction; Journey to the Center of the Earth (1993); Star Trek: Generations; Timestalkers
Russ, William (act): Dead of Winter; Traces of Red; The Unholy
Russe, Dan (act): The Incredibly Strange Creatures Who Stopped Living and Became Mixed-Up Zombies
Russek, Jorge (act): Zorro, the Gay Blade
Russel, Del (act): From Beyond
Russel, Tony (act): Behind the Mask of Zorro; I Criminali della Galassia; The Deadly Diaphanoids; Knights of Terror; Secret of the Sphinx; Sword of Damascus
Russell, Anna (act): Kill or Cure
Russell, Anthony (act): Ed Wood
Russell, Autumn (act): Zombies of Mora Tau
Russell, Bertha (act): It Happened Here
Russell, Betsy (act): Cheerleader Camp
Russell, Billy (act): Gestapo; I Start Counting; The Man In the White Suit; Negatives
Russell, Bing (act): Billy the Kid vs. Dracula; The Computer Wore Tennis Shoes (1970); Dick Tracy (1990); A Taste of Evil
Russell, Brian (act): Copycat
Russell, Carlton L. (act): Twin Peaks: Fire Walk With Me
Russell, Charles (act): Inner Sanctum (1949)
Russell, Charles/Chuck (dir): The Blob (1988); Eraser; The Mask (1994); A Nightmare On Elm Street 3: Dream Warriors
Russell, Chuck (wri): The Blob (1988); Dreamscape; A Nightmare On Elm Street 3: Dream Warriors
Russell, Connie (act): Nightmare (1956)
Russell, Corrinne (act): Highlander
Russell, Don (act): Dungeons of Horror; The Sadist
Russell, Elizabeth (act): Bedlam; Cat People (1942); The Corpse Vanishes; Curse of the Cat People; A Date With the Falcon; The Seventh Victim; Weird Woman
Russell, Evan (act): Without a Clue
Russell, Franz (act): Change of Mind
Russell, Gail (act, 1924-1961): Lady In the Dark; Night Has a Thousand Eyes; Song of India; The Tattered Dress; The Uninvited (1944); The Unseen (1945)
Russell, Geoffrey (act): The God King; Murder by Decree
Russell, Gordon (wri): House of Dark Shadows
Russell, Harriet (act): The Crime of Dr. Crespi
Russell, Harry (act): Starship Invasions
Russell, Henry (mus): Five
Russell, Ian (act): Haunted Palace (1949)
Russell, Iris (act): Downfall; Spell of Evil
Russell, Jack (act): Maid to Order
Russell, Jack (cin): The Beast from 20,000 Fathoms
Russell, Jackie (GB act): The Lair of the White Worm
Russell, Jackie (USA act): The Screaming Woman
Russell, James (act): The Batallion Shot; A Cry In the Night (1915); The Eleventh Hour (1916); Lieutenant Daring and the Stolen Invention; The Man Who Forgot; Signals In the Night
Russell, Jane (act, b. 1921): The Road to Bali
Russell, Janet (act): Operation C.I.A.
Russell, Jeff (act): Full Eclipse
Russell, John (act, 1921-1991): Fair Wind to Java; Somewhere In the Night
Russell, John (C.) (act): Sorority House Massacre
Russell (Jr.), John (L.) (cin): The Cabinet of Caligari; Indestructible Man; Invasion U.S.A.; Macbeth (1947); The Man from Planet X; Psycho (1960); Tobor the Great
Russell, Johnny (act): The Blue Bird (1940)
Russell, Karen (act): Dead Certain; Dick Tracy (1990)
Russell, Kathleen (act): The Antique Brooch
Russell, Ken (dir, b. 1927): Altered States; Billion Dollar Brain; The Devils; Gothic; The Lair of the White Worm; Liszt O' Mania; Tommy
Russell, Ken (wri, b. 1927): The Devils; The Lair of the White Worm; Liszt O' Mania; Tommy
Russell, Keri (act, b. 1976): Honey, I Blew Up the Kid; The Lottery
Russell, Kimberly (act): Ghost Dad
Russell, Kurt (act, b. 1951): The Barefoot Executive; Big Trouble In Little China; Charley and the Angel; The Computer Wore Tennis Shoes (1970); Escape from L.A.; Escape from New York; The Fox and the Hound; Now You See Him, Now You Don't; Search for the Gods; Soldier; Stargate; The Strongest Man In the World; The Thing (1982)
Russell, Kurt (wri, b. 1951): Escape from L.A.
Russell, Lewis J. (act): The Lost Weekend
Russell, Lisa Ann (act): A.P.E.X.
Russell, Marigold (act): Stranger from Venus
Russell, Mike (act): Not Quite Human II
Russell, Neil (act): The $1,000,000 Duck; Now You See Him, Now You Don't
Russell, Nipsey (act, b. 1924): The Wiz
Russell, Paula (act): Amazons (1984)
Russell, Ray (wri): Chamber of Horrors (1966); The Horror of It All; Incubus (1982); Mr. Sardonicus; The Premature Burial; X—The Man With the X-Ray Eyes; Zotz!
Russell, Robert (GB act): Bedazzled; Double Exposure (1977); Sitting target; Sudden Terror; Witch-Finder General
Russell, Robert (USA act): The Clutching Hand
Russell, Rosalind (act, 1911-1976): The [illegible] (1937); Oh Dad Poor Dad, Mamma's Hung You In the Closet and I'm Feelin' So Sad; Trouble for Two; The Velvet Touch
Russell, Roy (act): Richard III (1955)
Russell, Roy (wri): The Witches and the Grinnygog
Russell, Stefene (act): Plan 10 from Outer Space
Russell, Suzanne (act): Curtains
Russell, Tanya (act): Hellhole
Russell, Theresa (act, b. 1957): Black Widow (1987); Cold Heaven; Once You Meet a Stranger; The Spy Within; Track 29
Russell, Tina (act): Penetration
Russell, Victoria (act): Tommy
Russell, Violet (act): A Prehistoric Love Story
Russell, Vy (wri): Indestructible Man; Monstrosity
Russell, Ward (cin): Lawnmower Man 2: Beyond Cyberspace; The X-Files
Russell, William (GB act): The Adventures of Hal 5; The Big Chance; Return to Sender; The Share Out; Superman (1978); Terror (1979)
Russell, William (USA act): Boston Blackie; The Kill-Off
Russell-Tavernan, Mara (act): Castle Sinister (1948)
Russo, Dina (act): School Spirit
Russo, Gaetano (act): Ladyhawke
Russo, Gianni (act, b. 1943): Laserblast
Russo, Gus (mus): Basket Case; Brain Damage
Russo, Irwin (act): Saturday the 14th
Russo, James (act, b. 1953): Cold Heaven; A Kiss Before Dying (1991); The Postman (1997); The Secretary; A Stranger Is Watching; Trauma (1993)
Russo, Jodean (act): Revenge of the Virgins
Russo, John (A.) (dir, b. 1939): The Majorettes; Midnight (1980); Midnight 2: Sex Death, and Videotape
Russo, John (A.) (wri, b. 1939): The Majorettes; Midnight (1980); Night of the Living Dead (1968 & 1990); The Return of the Living Dead (1985); Voodoo Dawn
Russo, Matt (act): Superman (1978)
Russo, Michael/Mike (act): Demonic Toys; The Toxic Avenger
Russo, Raymond (act): Midnight (1980)
Russo, Rene (act): Freejack; Mr. Destiny; Outbreak
Russo, Tom (cin): Scared to Death (1980)
Russom, Leon (act): Alien Nation: Body and Soul; No Way Out; Silver Bullet; Star Trek VI: The Undiscovered Country
Russon, Stanley (act): Beyond and Back
Rust, Allan (act): Philadelphia Experiment II
Rust, John (dir): The Smurfs and the Magic Flute
Rust, Richard (act): Homicidal; I Escaped from Devil's Island
Rustam, Mardi (dir): Evils of the Night
Rustam, Mardi (wri): Eaten Alive! (1976); Evils of the Night
Rustichelli, Carlo (mus): Antinea, l'Amante della Citta Sepolta; The Conquest of Mycenae; The Minotaur; Sei Donne per l'Assassino; Sword of the Conqueror
Ruth, Rebecca (act): Total Recall
Rutherford, Ann (act, b. 1924): The Adventures of Don Juan; Bermuda Mystery; A Christmas Carol (1938); The Happy Land; The Madonna's Secret; The Secret Life of Walter Mitty; The Slipper and the Rose
Rutherford, Cedric (wri): Wild Women of Wongo
Rutherford, Holly (act): Zapped!
Rutherford, Jeremy (act): Junior (1986)
Rutherford, Kelly (act, b. 1968): Buried Secrets; Phantom of the Mall: Eric's Revenge
Rutherford, Margaret (act, 1892-1972): The Alphabet Murders; Blithe Spirits; Mad About Men; Miranda; The Mouse On the Moon; Murder Ahoy; Murder at the Gallop; Murder Most Foul; Murder She Said
Rutherford, Maxwell (act): The Whispering
Rutherford, Michael (mus): The Shout
Rutherford, Montagu (act): Hamlet (1913)
Rutherford, Paris (mus): Crucible of Terror
Rutland, Barbara (act): The Queen Mother
Rutland, John (act): Calculated Risk; Memoirs of a Survivor
Rutledge, Warren (act): Secrets of the Phantom Caverns
Rutstein, Lillian (act): see Roth, Lillian
Rutstein, Sonia (mus): Igor and the Lunatics
Rutt, Todd (dir): Shock! Shock! Shock!
Ruttan, Susan (act): Bad Dreams; Bay Coven
Ruttenberg, Joseph (cin, 1898-1983): Brigadoon; Cause for Alarm!; Dr. Jekyll and Mr. Hyde (1941); Gaslight (1944); Green Mansions; Kind Lady (1951); On Borrowed Time; The Prisoner of Zenda (1952)
Ruttenberg, Neil (wri): Deathstalker II: Duel of the Titans; Magic Island; Prehysteria 3
Rutter, Anne (act): Murder Motel
Rutter, John (act): Virus (1980)
Rutter, Maureen (act): No Blade of Grass
Rutter, Owen (wri): Once In a New Moon
Rutter, Peta (act): Strange Behavior
Ruttmann, Walter (cin, 1887-1941): Die Nibelungen
Ruud, Michael (act): Beyond and Back; Earthbound (1981); The Fall of the House of Usher (1982); Halloween 4: The Return of Michael Myers; Hangar 18; The Legend of Sleepy Hollow; The Time Machine (1978)
Ruud, Sif (act): Ansiktet
Ruxton, Richard (act): The Galaxy Invader; Nightbeast
Ruymen, Ann (act): Private Parts
Ruysdael, Basil (act, 1888-1960): Half Angel; Pearl of the South Pacific; Prince Valiant (1954); The Scarf
Ruzzolini, Giuseppe (cin): Arabian Nights (1974); Firestarter; Treasure of the Four Crowns
Ryabchikov, Yevgeni (wri): Stellar Brothers-From the Kremlin to the Cosmos
Ryals, Patrick (act): The Hand That Rocks the Cradle
Ryan, Adam (act): The Rescuers Down Under
Ryan, Andrew (cin): Goliathon
Ryan, Bridgit (act): The Stand
Ryan, Christopher (act): Santa Claus (1985)
Ryan, Deborah (act): The Initiation of Sarah; Kiss Meets the Phantom of the Park
Ryan, Dick (act, 1897-1969): For Heaven's Sake
Ryan, Don (wri): Devil's Island; Fly-Away Baby; Smart Blonde
Ryan, Edmon (act): Dark Eyes of London; Mystery Street; The Playground
Ryan, Elverez (act): The Pink Chiquita
Ryan, Fran (act): Amazing Stories: The Movie V; Eyes of Fire; Suture
Ryan, Frank P. (act): Gremlins 2: The New Batch
Ryan, George Peter (act): Eat and Run
Ryan, Irene (act, 1906-1973, nee Irene Riordan): Blackbeard the Pirate; Bonzo Goes to College; Half Angel; Mighty Joe Young (1949)
Ryan, James (act): Kill and Kill Again; Kill or Be Killed; Space Mutiny
Ryan, Janna (act): Warriors of the Wasteland
Ryan, John (GB act): Persecution
Ryan, John (P.) (USA act): American Cyborg; Steel Warrior; Batman: Mask of the Phantasm; City of Shadows; Class of 1999; Futureworld; It Lives Again; It's Alive (1974); Runaway Train
Ryan, John Joseph (act): see Lord, Jack
Ryan, Joseph R. (act): Primal Fear
Ryan, Kathleen (act, b. 1922): Sail Into Danger; The Sound of Fury; The Yellow Balloon
Ryan, Ken (act): Def Con 4; The Long Kiss Goodnight; Popcorn
Ryan, Leslie (act): Night of the Creeps
Ryan, Linda (act): Mind Over Murder
Ryan, Madge (act): A Clockwork Orange; Endless Night; Frenzy; I Start Counting; The Lady Vanishes (1979); The Strange Affair; Who Is Killing the Great Chefs of Europe?; Witness In the Dark; Yellow Dog
Ryan, Mark (act): The Corsican Brothers (1985); First Knight
Ryan, Marlene (act): The Devil's Gift
Ryan, Mary (act): The Outcasts; Rawhead Rex
Ryan, Meg (act, b. 1961): Amityville 3-D; Anastasia; City of Angels; D.O.A. (1988); Innerspace; Prelude to a Kiss
Ryan, Michael (M.) (act): Body Heat; Remo Williams: The Adventure Begins; Slayground; The Strangler (1963)
Ryan, Mitch (act): A Reflection of Fear
Ryan, Mitchell (act): Deadly Game; A Face to Die For; Halloween: The Curse of Michael Myers; Judge Dredd; Liar Liar; Northstar; Of Mice and Men (1981); A Reflection of Fear
Ryan, Nancy (act): Pandemonium
Ryan, Natasha (act): The Amityville Horror; The Day Time Ended; The Entity; Good Against Evil; Kingdom of the Spiders
Ryan, Paddy (act): An American Werewolf In London
Ryan Jr., Pat (act): The Toxic Avenger
Ryan, Patricia (act): Soho Incident
Ryan, Patrick (act): Child of Darkness, Child of Light
Ryan, Paul (act): Charlie Chan and the Curse of the Dragon Queen
Ryan, Paul (cin): A Passion to Kill
Ryan, Philip (act): Hands of the Ripper
Ryan, R. L. (act): [illegible] and Run; Street Trash
Ryan, Remy (act): RoboCop 3
Ryan, Robert (act, 1913-1973): Berlin Express; Beware, My Lovely; The Boy With Green Hair; The Busy Body; Captain Nemo and the

Underwater City; Caught (1948); City Beneath the Sea (1952); The Crooked Road; Crossfire; I Married a Communist; Inferno (1953); On Dangerous Ground; The Secret Fury; The Set-Up (1949)
Ryan, Ron (act): Windows
Ryan, Sean B. (act): Puppet Master II
Ryan, Sheila (act, 1921-1975): A-Haunting We Will Go; Caged Fury; The Cobra Strikes; Dead Men Tell; Dressed to Kill (1941); Fingerprints Don't Lie; Jungle Manhunt; The Lone Wolf In Mexico; Mask of the Dragon; Philo Vance's Secret Mission
Ryan, Stephanie (act): Frankenhooker
Ryan, Steve (act): D.A.R.Y.L.
Ryan, Taylor (act): Mata Hari (1985)
Ryan, Thomas (act): Body Count (1987); The Relic; Wolfen
Ryan, Tim (act, d. 1956): Dark Alibi; Detective Kitty O'Day; Ghost Crazy; The Golden Eye; Hold That Line; The Shanghai Chest; The Sky Dragon
Ryan, Tim (1990s act): The Lightning Incident
Ryan, Tim (wri): The Boys from Brooklyn; Ghost Crazy; Jalopy; The Mystery of the 13th Guest; No Holds Barred; Spook Busters
Ryan, Will (act): An American Tail; The Land Before Time; Thumbelina (1994)
Ryane, Jenafor (act): Unforgettable
Rybowski, Sheldon (act): Prom Night
Rycerz, Dan (act): It's Alive III: Island of the Alive
Rydall, Derek (act): Phantom of the Mall: Eric's Revenge; Popcorn
Rydbeck, Whitney (act): Battle Beyond the Stars (1980); Murder of Innocence; Sleeper
Rydeberg, Georg (act): Vargtimmen
Rydell, Charles (act): The Sand Castle
Rydell, Christopher (act): Trauma (1993)
Ryder, Alfred (act): Escape to Witch Mountain (1975); Probe; T-Men; W
Ryder, Amy (act): Candyman: Farewell to the Flesh
Ryder, Dana (act): Forever Evil
Ryder, Eddie (act): The Man In the Santa Claus Suit
Ryder, Gerard (act): Venom (1982)
Ryder, Mark (mus): Trancers; Trancers II: The Return of Jack Deth
Ryder, Michael (act): Troma's War
Ryder, Paul (wri): Information Received; A Matter of Choice; A Prize of Arms; The Strange World of Planet X
Ryder, Winona (act, b. 1971): Alien Resurrection; Beetlejuice; Bram Stoker's 'Dracula' The Crucible (1996); Edward Scissorhands; Heathers; Lost Souls (1999)
Rydman, Sture (dir & wri): The Return (1973, GB)
Rydon, Rick/Ryck (act): The Child and the Killer; Dead Man's Evidence; Double Exposure (1954); Satellite In the Sky
Rye, Ann (act): Don't Look Now
Rye, Isabella (act): S*H*E (1980)
Rye, Michael (act): Hands of a Stranger
Rye, Stellan (dir): Der Student von Prag (1913)
Ryea, Tom (cin): V
Ryecart, Patrick (act): Arthur the King
Ryerson, Ann (act): Friday the 13th, Part VI: Jason Lives
Ryerson, Florence (wri): The Canary Murder Case; The Casino Murder Case; Drums of Jeopardy (1931); The Mysterious Dr. Fu Manchu; The Return of Dr. Fu Manchu; The Wizard of Oz (1939)
Rylance, Mark (act): The McGuffin; Prospero's Books
Rylander, Eric (cin): The Hidden; Nothing But Trouble
Ryle, Lawrence (act): Houdini (1953)
Ryley, J.H. (act): Hamlet (1913)
Rymal, Reggie (act): House of Wax
Rynearson, Marjorie (act): RoboCop
Ryon, Rex (act): Jack's Back; The Man In the Iron Mask (1997)
Ryshpan, Howard (act): Rabid
Ryu, Daisuke (act): Ran
Ryu, Tomoe (wri): Inn of Evil
Ryuoka, Shin (act): Kwaidan
Ryusaki, Bill M. (act): Point of No Return

Saachiko (act): Gremlins 2: The New Batch
Saad, Margit (act) The Criminal; Hi, Here's Eddie; Playback
Saad, Robert (cin): Cannibal Girls; Shivers
Saalman, Raelyn (act): Attack of the 60 Foot Centerfold
Saan, Miel (act): Confessions of an Opium Eater
Saarinen, Eric (cin): The Hills Have Eyes
Saavedra, Frank (act): The Blood Drinkers
Sabag, Fabio (act): Killer Fish
Sabath, Bernadette (act): The Clan of the Cave Bear
Sabatini, Rafael (wri, 1875-1950): The Black Swan; Bluff; Fortunes of Captain Blood
Sabato (Jr.), Antonio (act, b. 1972): Escape from the Bronx; Man With Icy Eyes; Thrill; War of the Robots
Sabato, Bo (act): Noon Maniacs
Sabben-Clare, J.W. (wri): The Lure
Sabel, Eugene (act): The Blob (1958)
Sabella, Ernie (act): Fright Night II; The Lion King; The Lion King II: Simba's Pride
Sabin, Robert C. (act): Slime City
Sabine, Winifred (act): Frankenstein and the Monster from Hell
Sabino, Ellen (act): Mannequin Two: On the Move
Sabo, Joseph (wri): Pinocchio (1940)
Sabo, Timothy E. (wri): Project Metalbeast: DNA Overload
Sabrina (act): The Ice House
Sabu (act, 1924-1963, nee Sabu Dastagir): Arabian Nights (1942); Black Narcissus; Cobra Woman; The Drum; Elephant Boy; Jaguar; The Jungle Book (1942); Jungle Hell; Man-Eater of Kumaon; Mistress of the World (1959); Rampage; Sabu and the Magic Ring; Savage Drums; Song of India; Tangier; The Thief of Bagdad (1940); Treasure of Bengal; White Savage
Sabu, Paul (mus): Hard Rock Zombies
Sabucci, Stefania (act): Making Contact
Sacchari, Micki (act): Empire of Ash III
Sacchetti, Bob (act): Raiders of the Living Dead
Sacchetti, Dardano/Danny (wri): The Cat O' Nine Tails; Demons (1985); Demons 2; Exterminators of the Year 3000; The Gates of Hell; Ironmaster; Manhattan Baby
Sacchi, Robert (act): Pulp
Saccio, Thomas (act): The Fan
Sacdalan, Felipe J. (cin): The Blood Drinkers; Moro Witch Doctor
Sacha, Jean (dir): Cet Homme est Dangereux
Sacha, Orlando (act): Crime Zone; No Exit
Sacher, Toby (wri): Blood Mania
Sachs, Adrianne (act): RoboCop
Sachs, Alice (act): Fear No Evil (1981)
Sachs, Andrew (act): Frightmare (1974); Hitler: The Last Ten Days; House of Mortal Sin; Robin Hood Junior (1975)
Sachs, Beryl (wri): Radar Secret Service
Sachs, Leonard (act): Behemoth, the Sea Monster; The Door In the Wall; The Dover Road Mystery; Face In the Night; The Gamma People; Konga; The Man Who Wouldn't Talk; Men of Sherwood Forest; Number Six; Pit of Darkness; The Secret of Stamboul; Seven Thunders; A Taste of Fear
Sachs, Robin (act): Vampire Circus
Sachs, Stephen (act): Pranks
Sachs, William (dir): The Force Beyond; Galaxina; The Incredible Melting Man
Sachs, William (wri): Galaxina; The Incredible Melting Man
Sachse, Salli (act): Dr. Goldfoot and the Bikini Machine; The Ghost In the Invisible Bikini; The Million Eyes of Sumuru; Sergeant Deadhead the Astronut!; The Trip
Sacket, Joseph (act): The Worm Eaters
Sackheim, Daniel (dir): The Lottery
Sackheim, Jerry (wri): The Black Castle; The Boy and the Pirates; The Strange Door
Sackler, Howard (dir, 1930-1982): A Midsummer Night's Dream (1959)
Sackler, Howard (wri, 1930-1982): Gray Lady Down; Jaws 2; A Midsummer Night's Dream (1959)
Sacks, Michael (act): The Amityville Horror; Interface; Slaughterhouse-Five; Starflight: The Plane That Couldn't Land
Sacripanti, Humbert (act): Il Ladro di Venezia
Sacristan, Gregorio (wri): Sound of Horror
Sada, Yutaka (act): High and Low
Sader, Alan (act): King Kong Lives
Sadleir, Michael (wri): Fanny by Gaslight
Sadler, Andrea (act): Alien High
Sadler, Avril (act): The Hand of Night
Sadler, Bill (act): Project X (1987)
Sadler, Nicholas (act): Sometimes They Come Back; Twister
Sadler, Tracy Anne (act): The Bermuda Depths
Sadler, William (act): Bill & Ted's Bogus Journey; Demon Knight; Freaked; Rocketman (1997); Solo; Tales from the Crypt (1989)
Sadler, Winifred (act): The Man In Motley; The Rocks of Valpre
Sadoff, Fred (act): Dead Men Tell No Tales (1971); The Poseidon Adventure; The Questor Tapes; The Terminal Man
Sadusk, Maureen (act): Knightriders
Saebisch, Karl Georg (act): The Red Circle (1960)
Saeta, Eddie (dir): Doctor Death: Seeker of Souls
Safan, Craig (mus): Alfred Hitchcock Presents; Fade to Black; Lady Beware; The Last Starfighter; A Nightmare On Elm Street 4: The Dream Master; Nightmares (1983); Remo Williams: The Adventure Begins; Timestalkers; Warning Sign
Safarova, Ludmila (act): Howling II
Saffold, Tony (act): Trauma (1993)
Saffran, Michael (act): Slaughter High
Safrankova, Libuse (act): Three Nuts for Cinderella
Sagal, Boris (dir, 1923-1981): Dial M for Murder (1981); Hauser's Memory; The Helicopter Spies; Night Gallery; The Omega Man; Sherlock Holmes In New York
Sagal, Joey (act): The Hidden
Sagal, Katey (act, b. 1956): Maid to Order
Sagal, Liz (act): Howard the Duck
Sagan, Carl (wri, 1934-1996): Contact
Sagan, Francoise (wri, b. 1935): Landru
Sagar, Anthony (act): Carry On Screaming; The Offence
Sagarbarria, Schorber (act): Equalizer 2000
Sagawa, Kaziro (cin): The Last Dinosaur
Sage, Helen (act): Teenagers from Outer Space
Sage, Willard (act): Colossus: The Forbin Project; It's a Dog's Life
Sagebrecht, Marianne (act, b. 1945): Dust Devil
Sager, Carole Bayer (mus, b. 1946): The Devil and Max Devlin
Sager, Lyn Marie (act): Fire In the Sky (1993)
Sager, Ray (act): The Gruesome Twosome; The Wizard of Gore
Sagoes, Ken(neth) (act): A Nightmare On Elm Street 3: Dream Warriors; Project X (1987)
Sahag, John (act): Eyes of Laura Mars
Sahagun, Elena (act): Teenage Exorcist
Sahara, Kenji (act): Destroy All Monsters; Ghidrah, the Three-Headed Monster; Godzilla's Revenge; Godzilla vs. Mothra; The H-Man; King Kong vs. Godzilla; Mothra; The Mysterians; The War of the Gargantuas; Yog-Monster from Space
Sahl, Michael (mus): Blood Bath (1975)
Sahl, Mort (act, b. 1926): Johnny Cool
Saia, Anna (act): The Black Belly of the Tarantula
Saidy, Fred (wri): Finian's Rainbow
Saied, Baher (act): Dawn of the Mummy
Saiger, Susan (act): Eating Raoul
Saiko, Jonnie (act): Roller Blade Warriors: Taken by Force
Saint, Eva Marie (act, b. 1924): The Curse of King Tut's Tomb; North by Northwest; 36 Hours (1965)
Saint, H.F. (wri): Memoirs of an Invisible Man
Saint, Jan (act): Frankenhooker; Jacob's Ladder
St. Angel, Michael (act): Black Zoo; The Brighton Strangler; The Falcon Out West
St. Angelo, Bob (act): The Adventures of Robin Hood
St. Audrie, Stella (act): Rupert of Hentzau (1915)
St. Clair, Arthur (wri): The Mask of Dijon; Philo Vance's Gamble; Shadow of Terror
St. Clair, David (act): Lord of the Flies (1963)
St. Clair, Elizabeth (act): Welcome to Arrow Beach
St. Clair, Joan (act): Paris Express
St. Clair, Malcolm (dir, 1897-1952): The Canary Murder Case; Crack-Up; Remote Control (1930)
St. Clair, Michael (act): A Reflection of Fear; Skullduggery
St. Clair, Michael/Mike (wri): The Body Stealers; Mission Mars
St. Clair, Wynne (act): Fairyland
St. Claire, Bonwitt (act): The Clone Master
St. Claire, Suzette (act): The Slipper and the Rose
St. Claire, Taylor (act): The Naked Detective
St. Cyr, Lili (act, 1918-1999): Son of Sinbad
St. David, Martyn (act): Vice Versa (1988)
St. Denis, Madelon (wri): The Death Kiss
Saint-Denis, Michel (act): The Secret Agent (1936)
Sainte-Marie, Diane (act): Gremlins 2: The New Batch
Sainteye, Louis (act): Jeux Interdits
St. George, Clement (act): The Bermuda Triangle; Time After Time
St. George, Lady Georgina (act): The Witch of the Welsh Mountains
St. George, Phillip (act): Rocket Attack U.S.A.
St. Gerard, Michael (act): Replikator: Cloned to Kill
St. Ivanyi, Andra (act): The Outing
St. Jacques, Raymond (act, 1930-1990): Change of Mind; Dark Mansions; Search for the Gods; They Live; Voodoo Dawn
St. Jacques, Sterling (act): Eyes of Laura Mars
St. James, David (act): Monolith
St. James, Howard (cin): Strays
St. James, Jon (mus): Cavegirl (1985)
St. James, Malinda (act): Beyond and Back
St. James, Scott (act): Bates Motel
Saint James, Susan (act, b. 1946, nee Susan Miller): Love at First Bite
St. John, Al (act, 1893-1963): Face In the Fog (1935); His Brother's Ghost
St. John, Austin (act): Turbo: A Power Rangers Movie
St. John, Betta (act, b. 1929, nee Betty Streidler): Alias John Preston; City of the Dead; Dangerous Mission; Doctor of Seven Dials; The Saracen Blade; The Snorkel; Tarzan and the Lost Safari; Tarzan the Magnificent
St. John, Bill (act): The Ghost of Dragstrip Hollow
St. John, Billy (act): The Outing
Saint John, Brigitte (act): The Emerald of Artatama
St. John, Bronwyn (act): Getting Lucky; Lunatic
St. John, Dorothy (act): Topsy's Dream of Toyland
St. John, Howard (act, 1905-1974): Counterspy Meets Scotland Yard; Illegal; Li'l Abner (1959); Shockproof; Strait-Jacket; Strangers On a Train
St. John, Jill (act, b. 1940, nee Jill Oppenheim): Brenda Starr (1976); The Concrete Jungle (1982); Diamonds Are Forever; The King's Pirate; The Liquidator; The Lost World (1960); Out There; Sitting Target
St. John, Kathleen (act): The Quatermass Conclusion
St. John, Marco (act): Cat People (1982); Friday the 13th-Part V: A New Beginning; The Mind Snatchers (1963); The Package
St. John, Michelle (act): Pocahontas
St. John, N.G. (wri): Ms. 45
St. John, Nicholas (wri): The Addiction; The Body Snatchers; Driller Killer; Ms. 45
Saint John, Tony (act): 7 Doors of Death
St. Joseph, Ellis (wri): Flesh and Fantasy
Saint-Just, Eric (act): Oasis of the Zombies
Saint Macary, Xavier (act): Confidentially Yours
St. Martin, Mary Eugenia (act): Bring Me the Vampire
St. Maur, Adele (act): The Invisible Ray
St. Michaels, Michael (act): The Video Dead
St. Paule, Irma (act): The Bride In Black; Thinner; 12 Monkeys
Saint-Peter, Lucille (act): Brain Damage
Saint Peter, Mary (act): Psychophobia
St. Pierre, Dave (act): Unforgettable
St. Pierre, Monique (act): Motel Hell
St. Polis, John (act): Death from a Distance; In the Next Room; Kismet (1930); Mr. Wong, Detective; The Phantom of the Opera (1925); The Return of Peter Grimm (1926)
Saintsbury, H.A. (act): The Valley of Fear (1916)
Saint Simon, Lucile (act): The Hands of Orlac (1959)
Sainz, Tina (act): The Saga of the Draculas
Saire, Rebecca (act): The Quatermass Conclusion
Saire, Warren (act): The Monster Club
Saito, Bill (act): The Wrecking Crew
Saito, James (act): Covenant; Teenage Mutant Ninja Turtles
Saito, Noritake (act): Yog-Monster from Space
Saito, Takao (cin): Ran
Saizis, Vincent (cin): Ravagers
Sajbel, Michael O. (wri): Superstition
Sakabe, Osamu (act): Mr. Destiny
Sakai, Sachio (act): Godzilla's Revenge; Gojira
Sakai, Wakako (act): Inn of Evil
Sakall, S.Z. (act, 1884-1955): Wonder Man
Sakamoto, Dennis (act): Eyewitness (1981)
Sakamoto, Ryuichi (mus): The Handmaid's Tale
Sakata, Harold (act, 1920-1982): Death Dimension; Dimension 5; Goldfinger; Impulse! (1974)
Sakelaris, Anastasia (act): Alien Avengers
Saker, Annie (act): The Lifeguardsman
Saki (wri, 1870-1916): Sredni Vashtar
Saks, Matthew (act): Outbreak
Sakurai, Koro (act): Mothra
Sala, Gregorio (act): Track of the Moon Beast
Sala, Henry (dir): Nightmare Weekend
Sala, Luisa (act): El Secreto del Doctor Orlof
Sala, Vittorio (dir, b. 1918): Berlino Appuntamento per le Spie; L'Intrigo; La Regina della Amazzoni
Salamaa, Elsa (act): Gorky Park
Salaman, Chloe (act): Dragonslayer
Salaman, Toby (act): The Corsican Brothers (1985)
Salamanca, J.R. (wri): Lilith

Salamon, Franco (act): *Exterminators of the Year 3000*

Saland, Ellen (act): *The Amityville Horror*

Salas, Pierre L. (wri): *Curse of the Vampires*

Salatore, Bruce (act): *Shock Chamber*

Salaverri, Enrique Cahen (dir): *Carlota*

Salayan, Vic (act): *Daughters of Satan*

Salazar, Abel (act): *El Ataud del Vampiro; El Baron del Terror; La Cabeza Viviente; El Hombre y el Monstruo; La Maldicion de la Llorona; El Vampiro*

Salazar, Abel (wri): *Wrestling Women vs. the Aztec Mummy*

Salazar, Alfred(o) (wri): *Doctor of Doom; H.G. Wells' The New Invisible Man; El Hombre y el Monstruo; La Momia Contra el Robot Humano*

Salazar, George (act): *The Lightning Incident*

Salazar, Jorge Emilio (act): *Tiempo de Morir*

Salce, Luciano (dir, b. 1922): *Slalom*

Salcedo, Felisa (act): *The Blood Drinkers*

Salcedo, Paquito (act): *The Blood Drinkers; Curse of the Vampires; Daughters of Satan*

Saldana, Ramon (act): *Brenda Starr (1992)*

Saldanha, Raul Faustino (act): *The Boys from Brazil*

Sale, Chic (act): *Treasure Island (1934)*

Sale, Fred (act): *A Midsummer Night's Dream (1935)*

Sale, Richard (dir, b. 1911): *Half Angel*

Sale, Virginia (act, 1899-1992): *Moby Dick (1930); Think Fast, Mr. Moto; The Thin Man Goes Home; Topper (1937)*

Saleh, Eva (act): *Savages*

Salem, Kario (act): *Savage; Through the Magic Pyramid*

Salem, Lionel (act): *L'Age d'Or*

Salem, Pamela (act): *Never Say Never Again; The Secret of Seagull Island*

Salemme, Lina (act): *Demons 2*

Salenger, Meredith (act): *Dream a Little Dream; The Kiss (1988); Village of the Damned (1995)*

Salerno Jr., Charles (cin): *Bewitched (1944)*

Salerno, Enrico (act): *The Man In the Iron Mask (1962); Siege of Syracuse; L'Uccello delle Piume di Cristallo*

Salerno, Maria (act): *Ercole alla Conquista della Atlantide*

Salerno, Randy (act): *Primal Fear*

Salerno, Shane (wri): *Armageddon*

Salerno, Signor N. (act): *The Midnight Girl*

Sales, Gary (wri): *Madman*

Sales, Soupy (act, b. 1926, nee Milton Hines): *Birds Do It*

Salew, John (act): *The Bad Lord Byron; Bedelia; Counterblast; Dark Secret; Dead Men Are Dangerous; Father Brown; The Impersonator; Kind Hearts and Coronets; Murder In Reverse; Mystery Junction; No Highway In the Sky; The Saint Meets the Tiger; The Shakedown; Three Cases of Murder; Time Flies (1944); Wanted for Murder*

Salfrank, Herman (cin): *Der Mude Tod*

Salgari, Emilio (wri): *Black Devils of Kali; Carthage In Flames*

Salimar, Alfred (wri): *La Casa del Terror*

Salin, Kari (act): *Terminal Justice*

Salinas, Chucho (act): *Doctor of Doom*

Salinas, Jone (act): *A Man About the House*

Salinger, Diane (act): *Batman Returns; The Butcher's Wife; Creature; The Magic Bubble*

Salinger, Matt (act): *Captain America (1992)*

Salisbury, Frances (act): *The Wiz*

Salkow, Sidney (dir, b. 1909): *Bulldog Drummond at Bay (1947); The Last Man On Earth; The Lone Wolf Keeps a Date; The Lone Wolf Meets a Lady; The Lone Wolf Strikes; The Lone Wolf Takes a Chance; The Murder Game; Raiders of the Seven Seas; Shadow of the Eagle; Twice-Told Tales*

Salkow, Sidney (wri, b. 1909): *The Lone Wolf Keeps a Date; The Lone Wolf Takes a Chance*

Salles, Elvira (act): *Anguish*

Sallis, Peter (act, b. 1921): *Clash by Night; The Curse of the Werewolf; Frankenstein: The True Story; Full Circle; The Mouse On the Moon; The Night Digger; Scream and Scream Again; Taste the Blood of Dracula; The Third Secret; Who Is Killing the Great Chefs of Europe?; Wuthering Heights (1970)*

Sallis, Zoe (act): *The Bible*

Salloum, Kelly (act): *Once Bitten*

Salmi, Albert (act, 1928-1990): *The Ambushers; The Coming; Dragonslayer; Empire of the Ants; Escape from the Planet of the Apes; Superstition*

Salminen, Timo (cin): *I Hired a Contract Killer*

Salmon, Peter (act): *Jabberwocky*

Salmonova, Lyda (act): *Der Golem (1914); The Golem: How He Came Into the World; Der Student von Prag (1913)*

Salome, Tony (act): *Demon Knight*

Salomon, Amnon (cin): *The Mangler*

Salomon, Mikael/Michael (cin): *The Abyss; Always; Arachnophobia*

Salomons, Jean-Pierre (act): see Aumont, Jean-Pierre

Salonaga, Lea (act): *Mulan*

Salort, Michael (act): *Gremlins 2: The New Batch*

Salsberg, Gerry (act): *Phobia*

Salsbury, Colgate (act): *Serial Mom*

Salsedo, Frank S. (act): *Magic In the Water*

Salt, Jennifer (act, b. 1944): *Gargoyles; Sisters*

Salt, John (wri): *The Witness*

Salt, Waldo (wri, 1914-1987): *The Flame and the Arrow; M (1950)*

Saltamerenda, Louis (act): *Il Ladro di Venezia*

Salten, Felix (wri, 1869-1945): *Bambi; The Shaggy D.A.; The Shaggy Dog (1959 & 1994)*

Salter, Hans/H.J. (mus, b. 1896): *Frankenstein Meets the Wolf Man; The Frozen Ghost; The Great Impersonation (1942); Hold That Ghost; House of Frankenstein; House of Horrors (1946); Invisible Agent; The Invisible Man's Revenge; Man-Eater of Kumaon; The Man In the Net; Raw Wind In Eden; Sherlock Holmes Faces Death; Sign of the Pagan; Son of Dracula (1943); Spider Woman; The Strange Death of Adolf Hitler; The Web; You Never Can Tell*

Salter, Ivor (act): *Dog Eat Dog; House of Whipcord; Tiffany Jones*

Salter, Nicholas (act): *Don't Look Now*

Salt-n-Pepa (act): *Stay Tuned*

Saltzman, Avery (act): *Haunted by Her Past*

Saltzman, David (wri): *Mrs. Santa Claus*

Salva, Victor (dir): *Clownhouse; The Nature of the Beast; Powder*

Salva, Victor (wri): *The Nature of the Beast; Powder*

Salvador, Jaime (dir): *Pacto Diabolico; La Senora Muerte*

Salvati, Sergio (cin): *The Black Cat (1980); Cellar Dweller; Crawlspace; The Gates of Hell; Ghoulies II; The House by the Cemetery; Puppet Master; Zombie*

Salvatore, Enrico (act): *Terror of Rome Against the Son of Hercules; L'Ultima Preda del Vampiro*

Salvatori, Renato (act, 1933-1988): *Cadaveri Eccellenti; The Light at the Edge of the World*

Salvi, Emimmo (dir): *Vulcan, Son of Jupiter*

Salvi, Emimmo (wri): *David and Goliath; Il Gigante di Metropolis; The Tartars; Il Terror dei Barberi; Treasure of the Petrified Forest*

Salvin, Pedro (act): *Memories of Murder*

Salvini, Alexander (wri): *Monte Cristo*

Salvioni, Giorgio (wri): *La Decima Vittima*

Salvo, John (act): *Dawn of the Mummy*

Saly, Julie (act): *The Craving*

Salzedo, Leonard (mus): *Before I Wake; The Glass Tomb; The Revenge of Frankenstein*

Salzer, Albert J. (act): *Women and Bloody Terror*

Salzman, Bernard (cin): *The Android Affair*

Sam (animal act): *The Corpse*

Samaha, John (act): *The Punisher*

Samain, David (act): *Oh Heavenly Dog*

Samaniegos, Ramon (act): see Novarro, Ramon

Samarina, Yelena (act): *Amador; House of 1,000 Dolls; The Scarlet Letter (1972)*

Samarine, Valerie (act): *La Noche de Walpurgis*

Samaritani, Giovanni (act): *The McGuffin*

Samberg, Isaac (act): *The Dybbuk*

Sambrell, Aldo (act): *The Golden Voyage of Sinbad; The Light at the Edge of the World; Monstroid; Treasure Island (1971); Voodoo Black Exorcist*

Samek, Bonita (act): *Cavegirl (1985)*

Samel, Udo (act): *Kondom des Grauens*

Samer, Arlene (wri): *Peggy Sue Got Married*

Sammeth, Barbara (act): *The Devil's Daughter (1972); The Mad Room*

Samms, Emma (act, b. 1961): *Arabian Adventure; A Connecticut Yankee In King Arthur's Court (1989); Goliath Awaits; Robin Cook's Harmful Intent; Star Quest (1994)*

Samoilovich, Leon (act): *The Package*

Sampietro, Ines Isabella (act): see Miranda, Isa

Samples, Candy (act): *Flesh Gordon*

Samples, William (act): *Watchers*

Sampson, Daniel (act): *Starship Invasions*

Sampson, Darlce (act): *Grim Prairie Tales*

Sampson, Don Re' (act): *Appointment for a Killing; Halloween 4: The Return of Michael Myers; Robin Cook's 'Mortal Fear'*

Sampson, Elena (act): *The Thirsty Dead*

Sampson, Josie (act): *The Night of the Dark Shadows*

Sampson, Lummi (act): *Grim Prairie Tales*

Sampson, Robert (act): *The Arrival (1996); The Dark Side of the Moon; The Gates of Hell; Re-Animator; Robot Jox*

Sampson, Ruth (act): *A Cornish Romance*

Sampson, Samsochi (act): *Grim Prairie Tales*

Sampson, Teddy (act): *Bits of Life*

Sampson, Will (act, 1933-1987): *Firewalker; Orca; Poltergeist II: The Other Side*

Samson, David (act): *Polyester*

Samson, Ivan (act): *The March Hare; Paul Temple's Triumph*

Samuda, Jackie (act): *The Mutagen; Shock Chamber*

Samuel, Emily (act): *Shocker*

Samuel, Jackie (act): *Blink*

Samuel, Joanne (act): *Alison's Birthday; Chilling (1981); Mad Max*

Samuel, Marc (act): *Notorious (1992)*

Samuell, A.W. (act): *The Resurrection of Zachary Wheeler*

Samuels, Carol (act): *Targets*

Samuels, Lester (wri): *The Long Wait*

Samuels, Louise (act): *A Polish Vampire In Burbank*

Samuels, Miriam (act): see Karlin, Miriam

Samuels, Ted (cin): *The Asphyx; Daleks' Invasion Earth 2150 A.D.; Dr. Who and the Daleks; The Tomb of Ligeia*

Samuelson, G.B. (dir): *Buttons; The Callbox Mystery; The Wickham Mystery*

Sanada, Hiroyuki (act): *Message from Space*

Sanager, Ray (act): *Grim Prairie Tales*

Sanchez, Adan (act): *Into the Badlands*

Sanchez, Fernando (cin): *Night of the Sorcerers*

Sanchez, Francisco (cin): *House of Doom (1973); Master Stroke; The Mummy's Revenge*

Sanchez, Joanna (act): *Wolf*

Sanchez, Leon (cin): *The Bees; Tintorera...Bloody Waters*

Sanchez, Melisa (act): *Getting Lucky; Princess Warrior*

Sanchez, Pedro (act): *Johnny Hamlet*

Sancho, Ferdinand (act): *Voodoo Black Exorcist*

Sancho, Fernando (act): *Goliath Against the Giants*

Sancrotti, Ezio (act): *Scream of the Demon Lover*

Sand, Barbara (act): *Silent Night, Bloody Night*

Sand, Carlton (wri): *The Millerson Case*

Sand, Paul (act): *Justin Case; The Legend of Sleepy Hollow; Once Upon a Brothers Grimm; Teen Wolf Too*

Sanda, Dominique (act, b. 1948, nee Dominique Varaigne): *Damnation Alley; Steppenwolf; Without Apparent Motive*

Sande, Angel (act): *Squirm*

Sande, Walter (act, 1908-1971): *After Midnight With Boston Blackie; Alias Boston Blackie; A Blueprint for Murder; Boston Blackie Goes Hollywood; The Chance of a Lifetime; Confessions of Boston Blackie; Invaders from Mars (1953); The Jungle Girl; The Navy vs. the Night Monsters; Nocturne; Red Planet Mars; The Spider (1945); The Steel Trap; The War of the Worlds*

Sandefur, Dale (wri): *Ghost Town*

Sandefur, Duke (wri): *The Phantom of the Opera (1989)*

Sander, Otto (act): *Wings of Desire*

Sanderford, John (act): *The Alchemist; Fantasies; Looker*

Sanders, Albert (act): *Piranha II: The Spawning*

Sanders, Alex (act): *Secret Rites*

Sanders, Anita (act): *La Decima Vittima*

Sanders, Beverly (act): *Look What's Happened to Rosemary's Baby; Love at First Bite; Magic*

Sanders, Butch (act): *Trick or Treats*

Sanders, Byron (act): *The Flesh Eaters*

Sanders, Cornelia (act): *Damien-Omen II*

Sanders, Damon (act): *The Time Guardian*

Sanders, Denis (dir): see Sanders, (R.) Denis

Sanders, Dex Elliott (act): *Strange Days*

Sanders, Douglas (act): *Sorceress (1982)*

Sanders, Elizabeth (act): *Batman Forever; It's Alive III: Island of the Alive*

Sanders, George (act, 1906-1972): *Assignment Paris; The Black Swan; Bluebeard's Ten Honeymoons; The Body Stealers; Cairo; Confessions of a Nazi Spy; A Date With the Falcon; Doomwatch; Endless Night; The Falcon's Brother; The Falcon Takes Over; Foreign Correspondent; From the Earth to the Moon; Future Women; The Gay Falcon; The Ghost and Mrs. Muir; Green Hell; Hangover Square; The House of the Seven Gables; In Search of the Castaways; The Kremlin Letter; Lancer Spy; The Last Voyage; The Lodger (1944); Lured; The Man Who Could Work Miracles; Mr. Moto's Last Warning; Paris After Dark; The Picture of Dorian Gray (1945); Psychomania (1972); The Quiller Memorandum; Rage In Heaven; Rebecca; Rio 70; The Saint In London; The Saint In Palm Springs; The Saint's Double Trouble; The Saint Strikes Back; The Saint Takes Over; Samson and Delilah; The Son of Monte Cristo; Things*

---

to Come; The Village of the Damned (1960); While the City Sleeps; The Whole Truth; Witness to Murder; World by Night No. 2

Sanders, George (wri): *The Stranger Came Home*

Sanders, Henry G. (act): *Deadly Messages; Endangered Species; The Man Who Fell to Earth (1987)*

Sanders, Hugh (act): *The Glass Web; The Great Rupert; Panic In Year Zero; Scared Stiff (1953)*

Sanders, Irene (act): *The Final Terror*

Sanders, Jay O. (act, b. 1953): *Daylight; Kiss the Girls; Mr. Destiny; My Boyfriend's Back; Three Wishes (1995)*

Sanders, Lamar (wri): *The Kirlian Witness*

Sanders, Lawrence (wri): *The First Deadly Sin*

Sanders, Lugene (act): *Tormented (1960)*

Sanders, Neara (act): *Flesh and Fantasy*

Sanders, Paul Austin (act): *Dark Universe*

Sanders, (R.) Denis (dir, 1929-1987): *Crime and Punishment, U.S.A.; Invasion of the Bee Girls; The Night of the Hunter (1955); Shock Treatment (1964)*

Sanders, Richard (act, b. 1940): *Good Against Evil; Neon City; The Nude Bomb*

Sanders, Robert (act): *Frogs*

Sanders, Sam (act): *Blink; Poltergeist III*

Sanders, Sandy (act): *Missile Monsters; The Norsemen; Phantom from Space*

Sanders, Scott (act): *Murder In Reverse*

Sanders, Selga (act): *Princess Warrior*

Sanders, Shepard (act): *Freeway Maniac*

Sanders, Stuart (act): *Mr. H.C. Andersen*

Sanders, Tami (act): *Halloween 4: The Return of Michael Myers*

Sanders, Terry (dir, b. 1931): *Crime and Punishment, U.S.A.*

Sanders, Thomas (act): see Conway, Tom

Sanders-Brahms, Helma (dir): *No Mercy, No Future*

Sanderson, Challis (dir): *Faust (1922); The Scarlet Letter (1922)*

Sanderson, Joan (act): *The Great Muppet Caper*

Sanderson, Martyn (act): *Trial Run*

Sanderson, Paul (act): *Charlie Chan and the Curse of the Dragon Queen*

Sanderson, William (act): *Blade Runner; Mirror, Mirror; Mirror, Mirror 2: Raven Dance; Phoenix (1995); Sometimes They Come Back*

Sandford, Christopher (act): *Die Screaming, Marianne; Vampira*

Sandford, David (act): *Fair Game (1985)*

Sandford, John (act): *Secrets of the Phantom Caverns*

Sandford, Stanley (J.) (act): *The Iron Mask; Modern Times*

Sandford, Tiny (act): *Modern Times*

Sandground, Maurice (dir): *As In Days of Yore*

Sandick, Molly (act): *The Handmaid's Tale*

Sandiford, Hadley (act): *Shock Chamber*

Sandin, Will (act): *Halloween*

Sandkuhler, Steve (act): *Nightbeast*

Sandler, Adam (act): *Coneheads*

Sandler, Allan (act): *Beyond the Universe*

Sandler, Barry (wri): *All-American Murder; Mirror Crack'd*

Sandler, Robert (wri): *Cannibal Girls*

Sandman, Lee (act): *Super Fuzz*

Sandor, Anna (wri): *Tarzan In Manhattan*

Sandor, Gregory (cin): *Sisters*

Sandor, Steve (act): *Fire and Ice; Stryker; Twinkle, Twinkle, Killer Kane*

Sandoval, Antony (act): *Heartless*

Sandoval, Michael/Miguel (act): *Howard the Duck; Jurassic Park; Repo Man*

Sandoz, Dolores (act): *The Night of the Claw*

Sandoz, Maurice (wri): *The Maze*

Sandrelli, Stefania (act, b. 1946): *The Black Belly of the Tarantula*

Sandri, Gya (act): *Hercules, the Avenger*

Sandrine (act): *Gli Amori di Ercole*

Sandrock, Adele (act): *Doctor Mabuse*

Sands, Andrew (act): *Surf Nazis Must Die*

Sands, Anita (act): *Diary of a High School Bride*

Sands, Billy (act): *The Munsters' Revenge*

Sands, Bobby (act): *Vampire On Bikini Beach*

Sands, Dick (act): *Phantom from Space*

Sands, Hugh (act): *Mad Max Beyond Thunderdome*

Sands, Julu (act, b. 1927): *Aladdin and His Lamp*

Sands, Johnny (act): *U-238 and the Witch Doctor*

Sands, Julian (act): *Arachnophobia; Boxing Helena; Gothic; Leaving Las Vegas; Phantom of the Opera (1998); Tale of a Vampire; The Turn of the Screw; Vibes; Warlock; Warlock: The Armageddon; Witch Hunt*

Sands, Leslie (act): *The Clue of the New Pin (1961); Danger Route; The Deadly Affair; Death Trap (1962); Life for Ruth*
Sands, Leslie (wri): *Another Man's Poison*
Sands, Marion (act): *Mad Max Beyond Thunderdome*
Sands, Peggy (act): *Phoenix the Warrior*
Sands, Ran (act): *Blood Screams*
Sands, Red (act): *Deathstalker II: Duel of the Titans*
Sands, Sheila (act): *Subterfuge*
Sands, Sompote (dir): *Crocodile*
Sands, Tommy (act, b. 1937): *Babes In Toyland (1961)*
Sandulescu, Jacques (act): *They Might Be Giants; Vampire's Kiss*
Sandweiss, Ellen (act): *The Evil Dead*
Sandy the Dog (animal act): *Watchers*
Sandy, Gary (act, b. 1945): *Troll; Unlikely Angel*
Sandys, Karl (act): *Mother's Day*
Saner, Cengiz (act): *Sphinx (1981)*
Sanford, Blaine (mus): *The Magnetic Monster*
Sanford, Christopher (act): *The Kremlin Letter*
Sanford, Donald S. (wri): *Ravagers*
Sanford, Erskine (act): *Angel On My Shoulder (1946); The Lady from Shanghai; Macbeth (1947); Ministry of Fear; Possessed (1947); Spellbound (1945)*
Sanford, Garwin (act): *The Death of the Incredible Hulk; Quarantine; Unforgettable*
Sanford, Gerald (wri): *The Stranger*
Sanford, Isabel (act): *Love at First Bite*
Sanford, Jason (act): *Pumpkinhead II: Blood Wings*
Sanford, Ralph (act): *Blondes at Work; A Night for Crime; Torchy Plays With Dynamite; Up In Smoke*
Sanford, Terry (wri): *It Happened In Soho*
Sanforth, Clifford (dir): *Murder by Television*
Sangarmano, Angelo (wri): *Maciste e la Regina di Samar*
Sanger, Edward (act): see Herbert, Holmes
Sanger, Jonathan (act): *Flight of the Navigator*
Sanger, Jonathan (dir): *Obsessed (1992)*
San Giacomo, Laura (act, b. 1961): *The Apocalypse; The Stand*
Sangster, Alfred (act): *The Third Clue*
Sangster, Jimmy (dir, b. 1925): *Fear In the Night (1972); Horror of Frankenstein; Lust for a Vampire*
Sangster, Jimmy (wri, b. 1925, a.k.a. John Sansom): *The Anniversary; Blood of the Vampire; Brides of Dracula; Crescendo; The Criminal; The Curse of Frankenstein; Deadlier Than the Male; The Devil and Max Devlin; The Devil-Ship Pirates; Dracula, Prince of Darkness; Face of a Stranger; Fear In the Night (1972); Good Against Evil; The Hell-Fire Club; Horror of Dracula; Horror of Frankenstein; Hysteria!; Intent to Kill; Jack the Ripper (1958); The Legacy; Maniac (1963); The Man Who Could Cheat Death; The Mummy (1959); The Nanny; Nightmare (1963); No Place to Hide (1981); Once Upon a Spy; Paranoiac; Phobia; The Revenge of Frankenstein; Scream, Pretty Peggy; The Snorkel; A Taste of Evil; A Taste of Fear; The Terror of the Tongs; To Have and to Hold; Traitor's Gate; The Trollenberg Terror; Who Slew Auntie Roo?; X...The Unknown*
Sangster, Ortega (act): *Glen and Randa*
Sanguineau, Frank (act): *Firepower*
Sanguino, Victoria Hernendez (act): *Robin and Marian*
Sanipoli, Vittorio (act): *Sword of the Conqueror*
Sanjo, Mina (act): *Roller Blade Warriors: Taken by Force*
San Juan, Christina (act): *Alien Predators*
San Juan, Manuel (cin): *A Thousand and One Nights (1968)*
San Juan, Olga (act, b. 1927): *One Touch of Venus*
Sanjust, Filippo (wri, a.k.a. Philip Just): *Caltiki, il Mostro Immortale; The Thief of Baghdad (1960)*
Sank, Lesley (act): *Deadtime Stories*
Sank, Leslie A. (act): *Single White Female*
San Marco, Maria (act): *Sleep, My Love*
San Martin, Conrado (act): *The Awful Dr. Orlof; The Colossus of Rhodes; Faustina*
Sansom, John (wri): see Sangster, Jimmy
Sansom, Ken (act): *The Clone Master*
Sansom, Robert (act): *Before I Wake; Hour of Decision*
Sansone, Patricia (act): *Candyman: Farewell to the Flesh*
Sansone, Paul (act): *Street Trash; Vampire's Kiss*
Santacroce, Mary Nell (act): *Mutant; The Night of the Hunter (1991); The Private Eyes (1980); Rearview Mirror*
Santamaran, Erick (dir): *Decoy for Terror; Playgirl Killer*
Santamaria, Miguel (act): *Dr. Tarr's Torture Dungeon*
Santana, Jose (act): **Batteries Not Included*
Santangelo, Melody (act): *Rhinoceros (1974)*
Santanon, (Enano) (act): *The Fear Chamber; Isle of the Snake People; The Queen's Swordsman*
Santean, Antonio (dir): *The Glass Cage (1961)*
Santell, Alfred (dir, 1895-1981): *Aloma of the South Seas (1941); Beyond the Blue Horizon; The Gorilla (1927); The Hairy Ape*
Santiago, Cirio H. (dir): *Demon of Paradise; Dune Warriors; Equalizer 2000; Future Hunters; Raiders of the Sun; Stryker; The Vampire Girls*
Santiago, Cleofe (act): *Forever Evil*
Santiago, Luis (cin): *Alien Warrior*
Santiago, Renoly (act): *Daylight*
Santiago, Rubin (act): *A Taste for Flesh and Blood*
Santiago, Stephen (act): *Street Trash*
Santiago-Hudson, Ruben (act): *Devil's Advocate; Rear Window (1998)*
Santini, John (act): *Seven*
Santisteban, Alfonso (mus): *The Mummy's Revenge*
Santo (act): *Ghost of the Strangler; Grave Robbers; Saint and the Blue Demon vs. Dracula and the Wolf Man; Saint and the Blue Demon vs. the Monsters; The Saint and the Treasure of Dracula; The Saint Faces Black Magic; The Saint In the Revenge of the Vampire Women; The Saint In the Vengeance of the Mummy; The Saint In the Wax Museum; The Saint vs. Capulina; The Saint vs. Frankenstein's Daughter; The Saint vs. the Blue Demon In Atlantis; The Saint vs. the Zombies; Santo and the Hotel of Death; Santo Attacks the Witches; El Santo Contra las Vampiras; Santo vs. Baron Brakola; Santo vs. the King of Crime; Suicide Mission; The Vampire and Sex; The Work of Death*
Santo, Linda (act): *Phoenix the Warrior*
Santo, Vincent (act): *2000 Maniacs*
Santoni, Espartaco (act): *Exorcism's Daughter; House of Exorcism; Night Fiend*
Santoni, Reni (act): *Dr. Dolittle (1998); The Package*
Santoro, Dean (act): *The Man from Atlantis; Slaughter*
Santos, Burt (act): *Die Sister, Die!*
Santos, Gaston (act): *The Living Coffin; Misterios del Ultratumba; Swamp of the Lost Souls*
Santos, Jeorge (act): *The Omegans*
Santos, Marcia (act): *Waxwork II: Lost In Time*
Santostefano, Damon (dir): *Severed Ties*
Santschi, Tom (act, 1878-1931): *Faust (1909)*
Sanucci, Frank (mus): *The Living Ghost (1942)*
Sanvido, Guy (act): *Change of Mind*
Sanville, Michael (act): *Dreams Come True*
Sanvitale, Giuseppe (act): *Satyricon*
Sanz, Alberto (act): *The Trojan Women*
Sanz, Carlos (act): *The Package*
Sanz, Francisco (act): *Tombs of the Blind Dead*
Sanz, Javier (act): *A Midsummer Night's Dream (1985)*
Sapara, Ade (act): *Crusoe*
Saperstein, David (dir): *Beyond the Stars*
Saperstein, David (wri): *Cocoon; Cocoon: The Return*
Sapin, Louis (wri): *Torticola Contre Frankensberg*
Sapinsley, Alvin (act): *Sherlock Holmes In New York*
Sapinsley, Alvin (wri): *Moon of the Wolf; Sherlock Holmes In New York*
Sapountzakis, Themi (act): *The Fan*
Sapper (wri, 1888-1937, nee H.C. McNeile): *Arrest Bulldog Drummond; Bulldog Drummond (1923 & 1929); Bulldog Drummond at Bay (1937 & 1947); Bulldog Drummond Comes Back; Bulldog Drummond Escapes; Bulldog Drummond In Africa; Bulldog Drummond's Bride; Bulldog Drummond's Peril; Bulldog Drummond's Revenge; Bulldog Drummond's Secret Police; Bulldog Drummond's Third Round; Bulldog Drummond Strikes Back (1934 & 1947); Bulldog Jack; Calling Bulldog Drummond; The Challenge; Deadlier Than the Male; The Return of Bulldog Drummond; Some Girls Do; Temple Tower; 13 Lead Soldiers*
Saputo, Vicki (act): *The Devil's Gift*
Sara, Mia (act, b. 1967): *Apprentice to Murder; Caroline at Midnight; Daughter of Darkness (1990); Legend; The Maddening; Timecop; 20,000 Leagues Under the Sea (1997, ABC-TV); Undertow*
Sarabia, Ric (act): *The Quilt of Hathor; Short Circuit 2; Sorry, Wrong Number (1989)*
Saraceni, Ivan Jean (act): *The Bride (1973)*
Sarafian, Deran (dir): *Alien Predators; Interzone; Road Flower; The Road Killers; To Die For*
Sarafian, Deran (wri): *Alien Predators*
Sarafian, Richard (C.) (act, b. 1927): *Road Flower; To Die For*
Sarafian, Richard (C.) (dir, b. 1927): *Fragment of Fear; Shadow On the Land; Vanishing Point (1971)*
Sarafian, Tedi (wri): *Road Flower; The Road Killers; Tank Girl*
Sarandon, Chris (act, b. 1942): *Child's Play (1988); Collision Course (1992); Dean R. Koontz' Whispers; Fright Night; The Nightmare Before Christmas; The Princess Bride; The Resurrected; The Sentinel; Tales from the Crypt Presents Bordello of Blood; Temptress (1995); Terminal Justice; When the Dark Man Calls*
Sarandon, Susan (act, b. 1946): *The Hunger; James and the Giant Peach; The Rocky Horror Picture Show; The Witches of Eastwick*
Sarantsev, Yurie (act): *Planeta Bura*
Sarapo, Theo (act): *Judex*
Sarchet, Kate (act): *The Man With Two Brains*
Sarchielli, Massimo (act): *Castle Freak; Fragment of Fear; Giulietta degli Spiriti; Ladyhawke; The McGuffin*
Sarcinello Sr., Frank (act): *Death Row Diner*
Sardansky, Nick (act): *Deathstalker II: Duel of the Titans*
Sarde, Philippe (mus): *Eve of Destruction; Ghost Story (1981); I Married a Shadow; Lancelot du Lac; Lord of the Flies (1990); The Manhattan Project; Quest for Fire; The Tenant*
Sardelli, Nelson (act): *Fake-Out; Myra Breckinridge*
Sardou, Victorien (wri): *A Night of Mystery (1928)*
Sarecky, Barney (wri): *The Ape Man; Darkest Africa*
Sarelle, Leilani (act): *Neon Maniacs*
Sarfati, Maurice (act): *The Hunchback of Notre Dame (1957)*
Sarfoh, Anthony (act): *Baby: Secret of the Lost Legend*
Sargent, Alvin (wri): *Bogus; Gambit*
Sargent, Bob(by) (act): *Alien Nation; Endangered Species; Piranha (1978)*
Sargent, Dick (act): *Acting On Impulse; Body Count (1987)*
Sargent, John (act): *Eugene Aram*
Sargent, Joseph/Joe (dir, b. 1925): *Colossus: The Forbin Project; Crime and Punishment (1998); The Immortal; Jaws: The Revenge; Nightmares (1983); The Night That Panicked America; One Spy Too Many; The Spy In the Green Hat; Tomorrow's Child*
Sargent, Lew (act): *Tarzan and the Green Goddess*
Sargent, Richard/Dick (act, 1933-1994, nee Richard Cox): *The Beast with a Million Eyes; The Clonus Horror; Fantasy Island; The Ghost and Mr. Chicken; The Groundstar Conspiracy; The Stepfather; Tanya's Island; Teen Witch*
Sargent, William (act): *The Immortal*
Sargenti, Marina (dir): *Child of Darkness, Child of Light; Mirror, Mirror*
Saric, H. (cin): *Cave of the Living Dead*
Saric, Ivan (act): *Fugitive from the Empire; The Howling*
Sarin, Vic (dir): *Cold Comfort*
Sarkar, Kali (act): *Devi*
Sarkar, Sam (act): *Friday the 13th, Part VIII-Jason Takes Manhattan*
Sarkissian, Sos (act): *Solaris*
Sarl, Sidney (act): *The Girl Who Took the Wring Turning*
Sarne, Michael (dir & wri): *Myra Breckinridge*
Sarne, Mike (act): *Moment of Decision; A Place to Go*
Sarner, Alexander (act): *The Chinese Puzzle*
Sarno, John (act): *Gold of the Amazon Women*
Sarno, Jonathan (dir & wri): *The Kirlian Witness*
Saro, Oscar (act): *Dr. Tarr's Torture Dungeon*
Sarony, Leslie (act): *Game for Three Losers; Noddy In Toyland*
Sarossy, Michael (act): *Werewolf of Washington*
Sarossy, Paul (cin): *Love and Human Remains*
Sarrasin, Donna (act): *Dr. Jekyll and Ms. Hyde; Witchboard: The Possession*
Sarrazin, Michael (act, b. 1940): *Double Negative; Earthquake In New York; Eye of the Cat; Franken-stein: The True Story; The Groundstar Conspiracy; Mascara; Midnight In Saint Petersburg; The Reincarnation of Peter Proud; The Seduction*
Sarruf, Alexander (act): see D'Arcy, Alex
Sartain, Gailard (act): *Endangered Species; Ernest Saves Christmas; Wishman*
Sartarelli, Marcello (Wri): *Roma Contra Roma*
Sartene, Jean (wri): *The Grip (1913)*
Sartov, Hendrick (cin): *One Exciting Night*
Sartre, Jean-Paul (wri, 1905-1980): *No Exit*
Sasaki, George (act): *Varan the Unbelievable*
Sasaki, Katsuhiko (act): *Godzilla vs. Megalon; Terror of Mechagodzilla*
Sasaki, Nozomu (act): *Akira*
Sasaki, Toshiyuki (act): *The House Where Evil Dwells*
Sasakibara, Yasushi (cin): *The Mystery of Rampo*
Sasdy, Peter (dir): *Countess Dracula; Doomwatch; Hands of the Ripper; I Don't Want to Be Born; Journey Into Darkness; King Arthur, the Young Warlord; Nothing But the Night; Taste the Blood of Dracula; Welcome to Blood City*
Sasdy, Peter (wri): *Countess Dracula*
Saslavsky, Luis (dir, b. 1906): *La Corona Negra; Demoniac*
Sass, Edward (act): *In the Ranks*
Sass, J.W. (act): *The Toxic Avenger, Part II*
Sass, Jeffrey W. (wri): *Class of Nuke 'em High, Part 2: Subhumanoid Meltdown*
Sassaman, Nicole (act): *Witchcraft 5: Dance With the Devil*
Sassard, Jacqueline (act): *Les Titans*
Sassin, Richard (act): *Night of the Creeps*
Sasso, Enrico (cin): *Satanik*
Sasso, Maria Chara (act): *Demons 2*
Sasso, Ugo (act): *David and Goliath*
Sassone, Francis "Oley" (dir): *Future Shock*
Sassone, Michael (act): *In the Company of Darkness*
Sassover, Nate (mus): *The Telephone Book*
Sasway, Joe (act): *The Crater Lake Monster*
Satake, Hiroyuki (act): *Mothra*
Satana, Kim (act): *The Human Duplicators*
Satana, Tura (act): *Astro Zombies; The Doll Squad; Faster, Pussycat! Kill! Kill!*
Satch, Makogo (act): *Samurai Pirate*
Satlof, Ron (dir): *Deadly Dust; Joe & the Colonel*
Sato, Hajime (dir): *Body Snatcher from Hell; Terror from Beneath the Sea*
Sato, Junya (dir): *The Bullet Train*
Sato, Katsuyuki (act): *The Toxic Avenger, Part II*
Sato, Kei (act): *Godzilla 1985; Inn of Evil; Kwaidan; Live Today, Die Tomorrow; Onibaba*
Sato, Makata (act): *Message from Space*
Sato, Masanori (act): *The Toxic Avenger, Part II*
Sato, Masaru (mus): *The H-Man; Throne of Blood*
Sato, Mitsuru (act): *The H-Man*
Sato, Sachiko (act): *Virus (1980)*
Sato, Shimako (dir & wri): *Tale of a Vampire*
Sato, Tomomi (act): *Body Snatcher from Hell*
Satoh, Kimio (act): *Popcorn*
Sattels, Barry (act): *Dawn of the Mummy*
Satterfield, Paul (act): *Arena (1989)*
Sattler, Ernst (act): *Confess, Dr. Corda*
Satton, Lon (act): *Live and Let Die*
Sauber, Thomas J. (act): *Impulse (1984)*
Saucier, Jason (act): *The Crawlers*
Sauer, Joseph (act): see Sawyer, Joseph/Joe
Saukko, Beverly (act): *Blood Song*
Saul, Beverly Jean (act): see Tyler, Beverly
Saul, John (wri): *Cry for the Strangers*
Saul, Oscar (wri, b. 1912): *Once Upon a Time (1944); The Silencers (1966); Woman In Hiding*
Saulsberry, Rodney (act): *The Philadelphia Experiment; Tarzan In Manhattan*
Saum, Cliff (act): *Torchy Gets Her Man; Torchy Plays With Dynamite*
Saunders, Basil (act): *Widow Twan-Kee*
Saunders, Charles (dir, b. 1904): *Black Orchid; Danger by My Side; Dangerous Afternoon; Dark Interval; Death of an Angel; The End of the Line; Find the Lady; The Gentle Trap; The Golden Link; Jungle Street; Kill Her Gently; Murder Reported; Naked Fury; The Woman Eater*
Saunders, Charles (wri, b. 1904): *Amazons (1986); The Man Without a Body*
Saunders, Donald (act): *Funeral Home*
Saunders, Enid (act): *Superman III*
Saunders, Ervin (act): *Brain of Blood*
Saunders, George A. (act): *Naked Evil*
Saunders, George (wri): *Scanner Cop*
Saunders, Gil (wri): *The Case of the Smiling Widow*
Saunders, Gloria (act): *Captive Women; Prisoners of the Casbah*
Saunders, J. Jay (act): *Salvage; Someone's Watching Me!; Tammy and the T-Rex*
Saunders, Joe (act): *Dark Star*
Saunders, John L. (act): *Moontrap*
Saunders, Lanna (act): *Body Heat*
Saunders, Lew (act): *Demonoid*
Saunders, Linda (act): *Blood Bath (1966); Mara of the Wilderness*
Saunders, Lois (act): *Scream*

Saunders, Lori (act): *Blood Bath (1966); So Sad About Gloria*
Saunders, Nancy (act): *Crime Doctor; The Lone Wolf In London; The Millerson Case*
Saunders, Pamela (act): *Alien Warrior*
Saunders, Shepard (act): *Witches' Brew*
Saunders, Stuart (act): *Horrors of the Black Museum; Licensed to Kill; Man Accused; Nothing But the Night; Octopussy; Scandalous; The Trollenberg Terror; Witness In the Dark*
Saunders, Tom (act): *Tainted Image*
Saunders, William G./W.G. (act): *The Failure; The Man Who Stayed at Home; The Prehistoric Man (1924); Widow Twan-Kee*
Saura, Carlos (dir & wri, b. 1932): *El Amor Brujo (1986)*
Saura, Marina (act): *Flesh & Blood*
Sautet, Claude (wri, b. 1924): *Banana Peel; Les Yeux sans Visage*
Sautoy, Carmen (act): *The Man With the Golden Gun*
Sauvajon, Marc-Gilbert (wri): *A Toi de Faire, Migonne; Comment Qu'ella Est! Lemmy pour les Dames*
Sauve, Steven (mus): *The Mutagen*
Savadier, Russell (act): *Outlaw of Gor; Steel Dawn*
Savage, Ann (act, b. 1921): *After Midnight With Boston Blackie; Apology for Murder; Detour; One Dangerous Night; Passport to Suez; Pygmy Island; Scared Stiff (1945); The Spider (1945); The Unwritten Code*
Savage, Archie (act): *Assignment-Outer Space*
Savage, Ben (act): *Little Monsters; She Woke Up*
Savage, Booth (act): *Curtains*
Savage, Brad (act): *Red Dawn; Return from Witch Mountain; Salem's Lot*
Savage, Charles E. (wri): *Panic In the City*
Savage, Colette (act): *The Brave Little Toaster*
Savage, Cynthia (act): *Wes Craven's New Nightmare*
Savage, Derek (dir): *The Meateater*
Savage, Fred (act, b. 1976): *The Boy Who Could Fly; Little Monsters; The Princess Bride; Vice Versa (1988)*
Savage, John (act): *Carnosaur 2; The Killing Kind; Killing Obsession; Lost Souls (1998); Markus 4*
Savage, Ken (act): *The Creeping Terror*
Savage, Matthew (act): *Without a Clue*
Savage, Nellie (act): *The Sorrows of Satan (1925)*
Savage, Nick (act): *Fright Night*
Savage, Paul (act): *The Night the World Exploded*
Savage, Tracie (act): *Friday the 13th-Part 3*
Savage, Vic (act): *The Creeping Terror*
Savagnone, Giuseppe (mus): *David and Goliath*
Saval, Dany (act): *Atomic Agent; Moon Pilot*
Savalas, Candace (act): *Alice In Wonderland (1985)*
Savalas, George (act): *Alice In Wonderland (1985); Fake-Out*
Savalas, Telly (act, 1924-1994): *Alice In Wonderland (1985); The Assassination Bureau; Beyond the Poseidon Adventure; Cape Fear (1961); Capricorn One; The Diamond Mercenaries; Fake-Out; GoBots: Battle of the Rock Lords; Horror Express; House of Exorcism; Johnny Cool; The Karate Killers; Mackenna's Gold; Mind Twister; The Muppet Movie; On Her Majesty's Secret Service; Pretty Maids All In a Row; Scenes from a Murder*
Savant, Doug (act, b. 1964): *Godzilla (1998); Maniac Cop 3: Badge of Silence; Paint It Black; Terminal; Trick or Treat*
Savarino, Janet (act): *Phantom of the Paradise*
Savarino, Jean (act): *Phantom of the Paradise*
Savath, Phil (act): *The Haunting Passion*
Savelle, Bradley (act): *Judge Dredd*
Savident, John (act): *A Choice of Weapons; A Clockwork Orange; Hitler: The Last Ten Days; Otley; The Wicked Lady*
Savides, Harris (act): *Seven*
Savidge, Jennifer (act): *Pandora's Clock; True Crime*
Savignac, Jean-Paul (dir & wri): *Nick Carter et le Trefle Rouge*
Saville, David (act): *The Big Sleep (1978)*
Saville, De Sacia (act): *Jungle Trail of the Son of Tarzan*
Saville, Edith (act): *Forging Ahead*
Saville, Ken (act): *Dark of the Night*
Saville, Malcolm (wri): *Treasure at the Mill*
Saville, Philip (act): *The Betrayal (1958); The Great Van Robbery; The Mirror and Markheim; The Night of the Full Moon; On [illegible] Crooked Men*
Saville, Philip (dir): *Shadey*
Saville, Victor (dir, 1897-1979): *Calling Bulldog Drummond; Dark Journey; I Was a Spy; The Long Wait*
Saville, W. (wri): *Kind Hearts Are More Than Coronets; The Mystic Mat*
Saville, William (act): *The Rocks of valpre*
Savina, Carlo (mus): *House of Exorcism; Hunters of the Golden Cobra*
Savini, Tom (act): *Creepshow; Creepshow 2; Effects; From Dusk Till Dawn; Heartstopper; Knightriders; Maniac (1980); Martin; Mr. Stitch; The Ripper (1985)*
Savini, Tom (cin): *Martin; The Prowler*
Savini, Tom (dir): *Night of the Living Dead (1990)*
Savio, Dan (act): *Deathstalker II: Duel of the Titans*
Saviola, Camille (act): *Addams Family Values; Nightlife (1989, USA-Mex)*
Savitsky, Sam (act): *Arrest Bulldog Drummond*
Savoie, Paul (act): *A Scream from Silence*
Savory, Gerald (wri): *Urge to Kill; Young and Innocent*
Savoy, Suzanne (act): *The Cellar (1989); I Come In Peace*
Sawa, Devon (act, b. 1979): *Casper; Night of the Twisters*
Sawada, Kenji (act): *Deaths In Tokimeki*
Sawaguchi, Yasuko (act): *Godzilla 1985*
Sawalha, Nadim (act): *The Awakening; Sinbad and the Eye of the Tiger; Sphinx (1981); The Spy Who Loved Me*
Sawara, Kenji (act): *Atragon; Rodan, the Flying Monster*
Sawaya, Amy (act): *The Man Who Fell to Earth (1987)*
Sawaya, George (act): *The Black Sleep; The Devil's Rain; Hands of a Stranger; Moon of the Wolf*
Sawicki, Mark (act & cin): *The Strangeness*
Sawtell, Paul (mus, b. 1906): *The Animal World; Black Magic (1949); The Black Scorpion (1957); Crime Doctor's Warning; Dick Tracy Meets Gruesome; Dick Tracy's Dilemma; Five Weeks In a Balloon; The Fly (1958); A Game of Death; The Gay Falcon; Ghost Diver; Gildersleeve's Ghost; Jack the Giant Killer; Kronos (1957); The Lost World (1960); Motor Psycho; Return of the Fly; Return to Treasure Island; She-Devil (1957); The Story of Mankind; Tarzan and the Amazons; Tarzan and the She-Devil; Tarzan's Desert Mystery; Tarzan's Hidden Jungle; Tarzan's Savage Fury; Tarzan Triumphs; Voyage to the Bottom of the Sea; Weird Woman*
Sawyer, David (act): *Children of the Night (1992)*
Sawyer, Joseph/Joe (act, 1907-1982, nee Joseph Sauer): *A Double Life (1947); Gilda; It Came from Outer Space; The Killing; Special Investigator; Tarzan's Desert Mystery; Tarzan's Revenge; The Walking Dead*
Sawyer, Linwood (wri): *Alien Space Avenger*
Sawyer, Ted (act): *Time Flyer*
Sawyer, Toni (act): *The Stepford Children*
Swyer, Tony (wri): *Die Sister, Die!*
Sawyer-Young, Kat (act): *Moon 44*
Sax, Arline (act): *The Glass Cage (1961)*
Sax, Gary (act): *Heart Condition*
Sax, Geoffrey (dir): *Doctor Who*
Saxby, Lily (act): *The Dungeon of Death; The Port of Missing Women; The Underworld of London; Vice and Virtue: or, The Tempters of London*
Saxe, Templar (act): *Devil's Angel*
Saxer, Walter (act): *El Castello dell'Orrore*
Saxon (mus): *Demons (1985)*
Saxon, Aaron (act): *The Raven (1963); The Undead*
Saxon, James (act): *The Nesting*
Saxon, John (act, b. 1935, nee Carmen Orrico): *Aftershock; The Arrival (1990); The Baby Doll Murders; Battle Beyond the Stars (1980); The Bees; Beyond Evil; Blood Beach; Blood Salvage; Cannibal In the Streets; From Dusk Till Dawn; Hellmaster; Killing Obsession; Night Caller from Outer Space; A Nightmare On Elm Street; A Nightmare On Elm Street 3: Dream Warriors; Planet Earth; Portrait In Black; Prisoners of the Lost Universe; Queen of Blood; La Ragazza Che Sapeva Troppo; Scorpion With Two Tails; Sette la Morte; Silent Night, Evil Night; Strange New World; Strange Shadows In an Empty Room; Tenebrae; The Unguarded Moment; Wes Craven's New Nightmare*
Saxon, Leif (wri): *Egghead's Robot*
Saxon, Peter (wri): *Scream and Scream Again*
Saxon, Rebecca (act): *The Silence of the Lambs*
Saxon, Rolf (act): *Mission: Impossible*
Saxon, Vin (act): *Rat Pfink & Boo Boo*
Saxon-Snell, H. (act): *The Clue of the New Pin (1929); Murder at the Inn; Once In a New Moon; The Return of Bulldog Drummond*
Saxton, John (C.) (wri): *Blackout (1978); Class of '84; Happy Birthday to Me*
Sayadian, Stephen (dir & wri): *Dr. Caligari*
Sayce, Charlotte (act): *Who Slew Auntie Roo?*
Sayer, Diane (act): *The Strangler (1963)*
Sayer, Jay (act): *The Viking Women and the Sea Serpent; War of the Satellites*
Sayer, Philip (act): *Arthur the King; The Hunger; Slayground; Xtro*
Sayers, Dorothy L. (wri, 1893-1957): *Busman's Honeymoon; The Silent Passenger*
Sayers, Jo Ann (act): *The Man With Nine Lives*
Sayers, Michael (wri): *Casino Royale*
Sayle, Alexei (act): *The Bride (1985); Gorky Park*
Sayles, Francis (act): *Satan Met a Lady*
Sayles, John (act, b. 1950): *The Brother from Another Planet; Matinee*
Sayles, John (dir, b. 1950): *The Brother from Another Planet; The Secret of Roan Inish*
Sayles, John (wri, b. 1950): *Alligator (1981); Battle Beyond the Stars (1980); The Brother from Another Planet; The Clan of the Cave Bear; The Howling; Piranha (1978 & 1995); Wild Thing*
Saylor, Dennis (act): *Earthbound (1981); Snow Kill*
Saylor, Katie A. (act): *Invasion of the Bee Girls*
Saylor, Syd (act, 1895-1962): *The Crawling Hand; Kelly of the Secret Service; The Lost Jungle; Mr. Moto's Gamble; Time to Kill (1942)*
Saynor, Charles (act): *Cloudburst*
Saynor, Ian (act): *Dreamhouse (1981)*
Sayre, George W./Wallace (wri): *The Man They Could Not Hang; The Shanghai Cobra; Untamed Women*
Sayre, Jeffrey (act): *Possessed (1947); Torchy Runs for Mayor*
Saysanasky, Siluck (act): *The Peanut Butter Solution*
Sazanov, A. (wri): *The Heavens Call*
Sazarino, Dan (act): *Who?*
Sbarge, Raphael (act): *Babes In Toyland (1997); Carnosaur; Deadly Web; The Hidden II; Miracle Mile; My Science Project*
Sbocker, Emily (act): *Mad Max Beyond Thunderdome*
Sbragia, Giancarlo (act): *Death Rage; War Gods of Babylon*
Sbragia, Mattia (act): *Dial Help*
Scacchi, Greta (act): *The Odyssey; Rasputin (1996)*
Scaccia, Mario (act): *L'Anticristo; Robin Hood and the Pirates*
Scace, Norman (act): *Act of Murder (1964); Infamous Conduct*
Scaddan, Harry W. (act): *O.H.M.S.*
Scaddan, Joan (act): *London by Night (1913)*
Scagnetti, Bruno (act): *Amarcord*
Scaife, Edward/Ted (cin, b. 1912): *An Inspector Calls; A Kid for Two Farthings; The Kremlin Letter; The Liquidator; Murder On Monday; Night of the Demon (1957); The Ringer (1952); Sitting Target; Tarzan's Greatest Adventure; Tarzan the Magnificent; The Two-Headed Spy; The Water Babies*
Scala, Dominico (cin): *Colossus and the Headhunters*
Scala, Gaetano (act): *The Conquest of Mycenae*
Scala, Gia (act, b. 1936, nee Giovanna Scoglio): *I Aim at the Stars; The Price of Fear; Triumph of Robin Hood; The 2-Headed Spy*
Scaldati, Franco (act): *Kaos*
Scales, Prunella (act): *The Boys from Brazil; Freddie as F.R.0.7; The Hound Of The Baskervilles (1978); The Wicked Lady; Wolf*
Scalia, Jack (act, b. 1951): *Amazons (1984); Dark Breed; Donor; Endless Descent; The Silencers (1995); Storybook; Tall, Dark and Deadly; T-Force; With a Vengeance*
Scalici, Jack (act): *Caveman (1981); Something Is Out There*
Scallon, Brenda (act): *The Outcasts*
Scalso, Jack (act): *The Nest of the Cuckoo Birds*
Scammell, David (act): *Revenge of the Radioactive Reporter*
Scammell, Terence (act): *The Mephisto Waltz*
Scandi, Josephine (act): *Slaughter High*
Scanlan, Jerry (act): *Heaven Can Wait (1978)*
Scanlan, Joseph (L.) (dir): *I Still Dream of Jeannie; Our Man Flint: Dead On Target*
Scanlon, John (act): *Lovespell*
[illegible] *Man; The Night the World Exploded; Screaming Mimi; The Tattered Dress*
Scarabelli, Michele (act): *Alien Nation: Body and Soul; Alien Nation: Dark Horizon; Alien Nation: Millennium; Alien Nation: The Enemy Within; The Colony (1995); Deadbolt*
Scarano, Christopher (act): *Blood Song*
Scarano, Tecla (act): *Spara Forte, Piu Forte...Non Capisco*
Scarber, Sam (act): *Eraser; Shocker*
Scarborough, John (act): *Jekyll and Hyde*
Scardamaglia, Elio (dir, a.k.a. Michael Hamilton): *The Murder Clinic*
Scardamaglia, Francesco (wri): *Johnny Hamlet; Maciste, l'Eroe Piu Grande del Mondo*
Scardino, Don (act): *He Knows You're Alone; Squirm*
Scardino, Hal (act): *The Indian In the Cupboard*
Scardon, Paul (act): *The Shanghai Chest*
Scarfe, Alan (act): *Cauchemares*
Scarlatti, Alessandro (mus): *El Angel Exterminador*
Scarmuzza, Christina (act): *Man Facing Southeast*
Scarpa, Renato (act): *Don't Look Now*
Scarpelli (wri): *OK, Nero!*
Scarpelli, Umberto (dir): *Il Gigante di Metropolis*
Scarpelli, Umberto (wri): *David and Goliath*
Scarritt, Hunt (act): *Candyman: Farewell to the Flesh*
Scarroll, David (act): *Scalpel*
Scarry, Rick (act): *Addams Family Values; Ghost In the Machine*
Scarwid, Diana (act): *Brenda Starr (1992); Night of the Hunter (1991); The Possessed (1977); Psycho III; Strange Invaders*
Scattini, Luigi (dir): *The Glass Sphinx*
Scavolini, Romano (dir & wri): *Nightmare (1981)*
Scega, V. (dir): *Samson*
Scelfo, Leonora (act): *Scream*
Scelza, Jetta (act): *Dark Night of the Scarecrow*
Scer, Nancy (act): *Survival 1990*
Schaal, Richard (act): *Once Bitten; Slaughterhouse-Five*
Schaal, Wendy (act): **Batteries Not Included; The 'Burbs; Creature; Innerspace; Out There*
Schable, Robert (act): *Bella Donna (1923); Sherlock Holmes (1922)*
Schacht, Franne (act & wri): *Laserblast*
Schacht, Mary Ann (act): *Igor and the Lunatics*
Schacht, Sam (act): *Doctor Franken*
Schachter, Felice (act): *Zapped!*
Schadrack, Chris (act): *I Was a Zombie for the F.B.I.*
Schadt, Rachel (act): *Seven*
Schaech, Johnathon (act, b. 1969): *Houdini (1998); Hush*
Schaedler, Gary (cin): *Edward Scissorhands*
Schaefer, Armand (dir): *The Lost Jungle*
Schaefer, Craig (act): *Night of the Creeps*
Schaefer, Hal (mus): *The Amsterdam Kill*
Schaefer, Joshua (act): *True Crime*
Schaefer, Laura (act): *Catacombs (1989); Curse IV: The Ultimate Sacrifice; Ghost Town*
Schaefer, Robert (wri): *The Lone Ranger and the Lost City of Gold*
Schaefer, Natalie (act, 1901-1991): *Casanova's Big Night; Caught (1948); I'm Dangerous Tonight; Repeat Performance; Secret Beyond the Door; The Snake Pit (1948)*
Schaeffer, Francis (dir): *Headhunter; Wired to Kill*
Schaeffer, Mary (act): *Maxim Xul*
Schafer, John Clayton (act): *Dead Connection*
Schafer, Martin (cin): *An Unsuitable Job for a Woman*
Schaff, Leo (act): *The Fan*
Schaffer, Glenn (act): *Santa Claus Conquers the Martians*
Schaffner, Franklin J. (act & wri, 1920-1989): *The Boys from Brazil; The Double Man; Planet of the Apes; Sphinx (1981)*
Schaffner, Franklin (dir, 1920-1989): *The War Lord*
Schallerova, Jaroslava (act): *Valerie and Her Week of Wonders*
Schallert, William (act, b. 1922): *Captive Women; Colossus: The Forbin Project; The Computer Wore Tennis Shoes (1970); Cry Terror!; Escape; The Girl In the Kremlin; Gog; Hangar 18; The Incredible Shrinking Man; Innerspace; The Man from Planet X; Port Sinister; Storm Over Tibet; The Story of Mankind; The Strongest Man In the World; Sword of Venus; The Tattered Dress; Through Naked Eyes; Tobor the Great; Twilight Zone*
Schanley, Tom (act): *Heartless; The Return of the Six Million Dollar Man and the Bionic Woman*
Schanz, Heidi (act): *Seven; Virtuosity*
Schanzer, Karl (act): *Dementia 13*
Schanzer, Karl (wri): *Invasion Sinitestra*
Scharf, Alan (act): *Attack of the Killer Tomatoes*

Scharf, Walter (mus): Ben; Buccaneer's Girl; Cinderfella; It's Only Money; The Lady and the Monster; Midnight Offerings; The Nutty Professor (1963); Woman Who Came Back
Scharff, Lester (act): Secrets of the Lone Wolf
Scharn, Hal (act): The Crater Lake Monster
Schatz, Austin (act): The Mutagen
Schauer, Von (act): Attack of the Killer Tomatoes
Schauffler, Florence (act): The Goddess of Love; Pumpkinhead
Schayer, Richard (wri, b. 1882): The Bandits of Corsica; Lancelot and Guinevere; The Mummy (1932); Trader Horn (1931)
Scheckwitz, Al (act): Donor
Schedeen, Ann (act): Embryo; Exo-Man; Praying Mantis
Scheele, John (cin): My Science Project
Scheer, Cherie (act): The Henderson Monster
Scheerer, Robert (dir): It Happened at Lake Wood Manor; Poor Devil
Scheff, Michael (wri): Topper (1979)
Scheffer, Dick (act): The Lift
Scheibel, Ian (act): Android
Scheider, Roy (R.) (act, b. 1935): All That Jazz; The Curse of the Living Corpse; The French Conspiracy; Jaws; Jaws 2; Last Embrace; Marathon Man; Romeo Is Bleeding; Still of the Night; 2010; The White Raven
Schein, Loren (act): Microwave Massacre
Scheirer, Clay (cin): Timecop
Scheitz, Clemens (act): Nodferatu, the Vampyre
Scheley, Linda (act): The Monolith Monsters
Schell, Carl (act): Lycanthropus
Schell, Catherine (von) (act): Amsterdam Affair; The Black Windmill; Gulliver's Travels (1977); Look Back In Darkness; Madame Sin; Moon Zero Two; On Her Majesty's Secret Service; The Prisoner of Zenda (1979); Traitor's Gate
Schell, Maria (act, b. 1926): Island of Despair; The Maek; Night of the Blood Monster; 99 Women; Superman (1978)
Schell, Maximilian (act, b. 1930): Avalanche Express; The Black Hole; The Deadly Affair; Deep Impact; Hamlet (1960); Krakatoa-East of Java; The Phantom of the Opera (1983); The Reluctant Saint; Return from the Ashes; Das Schloss; Topkapi
Schell, Ronnie (act): The Cat from Outer Space; The Devil and Max Devlin; Jetsons: The Movie; Love at First Bite; The Shaggy D.A.
Schell, Tom (act): Death Row Diner
Schellenberg, August (act): Bear Island; Heavy Metal
Schellerup, Henning (cin): The Bermuda Triangle; Beyond and Back; Kiss of the Tarantula;
Silent Night, Deadly Night
Schellerup, Henning (dir): The Legend of Sleepy Hollow; The Time Machine (1978)
Schellhardt, Mary Kate (act): Apollo 13
Schembri, Julian (act): Revenge of the Teenage Vixens from Outer Space
Schemmel, Sandy (act): Dark Side of Midnight
Schenck, Earl (act): Buried Treasure; Salome (1922)
Schenck, George (dir): Superbeast
Schenck, George (wri): Deathmoon; Dying to Remember; Escape 2000; Futureworld; It Came Upon the Midnight Clear; The Phantom of Hollywood; Superbeast
Schenkel, Carl (dir): Bay Coven; Out of Order; The Surgeon; Tarzan and the Lost City
Schenkkan, Robert (act): Sanctuary of Fear
Schenplugova, Olga (act): The Fifth Horseman Is Fear
Schepisi, Fred (dir): Iceman
Schepps, Shawn (wri): Encino Man
Scherbakov, Yevgeny (act): The Blue Bird (1976)
Scherer, Gene (act): Re-Animator
Scherer, Glenn (act): Cocoon: The Return; Rana: The Legend of Shadow Lake
Scherlis, Michael J. (act): Slaughterhouse Rock
Schermuly, Ralf (act): The Ape Creature
Scherr, Kenneth (act): Surf Nazis Must Die
Scherrer, Paul (act): Children of the Corn II: The Final Sacrifice; Running Against Time
Schertzinger, Victor (dir, 1888-1941): The Return of Peter Grimm (1926); Strange Justice
Scherzer, Gary (act): Blood Diner
Scheuermann, Thilo (act): Making Contact
Schiaffino, Rosanna (act, b. 1939): Blood On His Sword; The Minotaur; The Red Dragon (1965); Sette Contro la Morte; La Strega in Amore
Schiano, Natasha (act): The Boogey Man
Schiavelli, Vincent (act): The Alien's Return; Batman Returns; Escape to Witch Mountain (1995); Ghost (1990); Lord of Illusions; Lurking Fear; Mr. Frost
Schibli, Paul (dir): The Nutcracker Prince
Schick, Ben (act): The Goddess of Love
Schickel, Erika (act): The Toxic Avenger, Part II
Schickele, Peter (mus): Silent Running
Schidor, Dieter (act): The Formula; Terminus
Schiegel, Kurt (act): Starship Invasions
Schierbeck, Poul (mus): Vredens Dag
Schierl, Angela Hans (act & dir): Flaming Ears
Schiff, Richard (act): The Arrival (1996); Dr. Dolittle (1998); Ghost In the Machine; The Lost World: Jurassic Park; Seven
Schiff, Sara (wri): Lord of the Flies (1990)
Schiff, Steve (mus): Waxwork II: Lost In Time
Schiffer, Michael (wri): The Peacemaker (1997)
Schiffler, Carrie (act): The Edge of Hell
Schiffman, Suzanne (wri): Confidentially Yours
Schifrin, Lalo (mus, b. 1932): The Amityville Horror; Amityville II: The Possession; The Aquarians; The Beguiled; Blindfold; Bridge Across Time; The Cat from Outer Space; Caveman (1981); Class of '84; Day of the Animals; Earth II; Eye of the Cat; Les Felins; Forgotten City of the Planet of the Apes; The Fourth Protocol; Good Against Evil; The Hellstrom Chronicle; I Deal In Danger; The Liquidator; Loophole; The Manitou; Man On a Swing; The Mask of Sheba; Murderers' Row; The Neptune Factor; The Nude Bomb; Pretty Maids All In a Row; The President's Analyst; Rage; Return from Witch Mountain; Rollercoaster; The Seduction; Starflight: The Plane That Couldn't Land; A Stranger Is Watching; THX 1138; The Venetian Affair; Way...Way Out
Schildkraut, Joseph (act, 1895-1964): Lancer Spy; The Man In the Iron Mask (1939); Marie Antoinette (1938); Mr. Moto Takes a Vacation; Phantom Raiders; The Road to Yesterday; The Tell-Tale Heart (1941); The Three Musketeers (1939); The Wandering Jew (1920)
Schildkraut, Rudolf (act): The Wandering Jew (1920)
Schillaci, Barbara (act): Switch (1991)
Schiller, Danny (act): Erik the Viking
Schiller, Dorothy (act): Capture That Capsule!
Schiller, Fanny (act): The Black Scorpion (1957); A Woman's Devotion
Schiller, Fred (wri): Boston Blackie's Rendezvous
Schiller, Frederick (act): The Accursed; Lady of Vengeance; The Trollenberg Terror; Who Done It? (1956)
Schiller, Norbert (act): Frankenstein (1970); The Return of Dracula; Sign of the Pagan; Young Frankenstein
Schiller, Wilton (wri): Captain America II
Schilling, Gus (act, 1908-1957): The Lady from Shanghai; Macbeth (1947)
Schilling, Vivian (act): Future Shock; Soultaker; Terror Eyes (1987)
Schilling, Vivian (wri): Soultaker
Schilling, William (G.) (act): The Island; White of the Eye
Schilsky, Austin (act): see Trevor, Austin
Schinasi, Gina (act): Uninvited (1987)
Schiott, Jorgen (act): Vampire's Kiss
Schipa, Carlos (act): Appointment With Murder
Schipek, Dietmar (dir): Flaming Ears
Schiraldi, Vittorio (dir): Fangs
Schirmer, Bill (cin): The Flash; Fugitive from the Empire
Schittenheim, Gisela Eve (act): see Helm, Brigitte
Schitzoff, Friedrich (act): Supergirl (1971)
Schjelderup, Gerik (act): State Secret
Schlarth, Sharon (act): Dead as a Doorman; Eat and Run
Schlatter, Charlie (act): All-American Murder; 18 Again!
Schlegel, Margarete (act): Der Januskopf
Schlesinger, John (dir, b. 1926): The Believers; Marathon Man; Pacific Heights; The Starfish
Schlesinger, John (wri, b. 1926): The Starfish
Schlesinger, Otto (act): A Taste of Blood
Schlesinger, Susan (act): The Starfish
Schlessinger, Renate (act): Night of the Zombies (1981)
Schletz, Elke (act): see Sommer, Elke
Schlick, Frederick (wri): Tarzan and the Trappers
Schliessler, Tobias (A.) (cin): Candyman: Farewell to the Flesh; Child of Darkness, Child of Light; Quarantine; Them (1996); Volcano: Fire On the Mountain; Writer's Block
Schlitzie (act, b. 1892): Freaks
Schloemp, Petrus (cin): Hauser's Memory; Who?
Schlondorff, Volker (dir, b. 1939): A Degree of Murder; The Handmaid's Tale; Der Junge Torless
Schlondorff, Volker (wri, b. 1939): A Degree of Murder; Der Junge Torless
Schloss, Zander (act): Repo Man
Schloss, Zander (mus): Space Rage
Schmale, Dan (act): Fatal Exposure
Schmalle, Loren (act): Witchcraft 7: Judgement Hour
Schmaus, Albert J. (act): Martin
Schmaus, Lillian (act): Martin
Schmerling, John (act): The Deadly Spawn
Schmid, Helmut (act): The Naked Woman and Satan; The Testament of Dr. Mabuse (1960)
Schmidhauser, Hannes (act): The Invisible Terror
Schmidt (dir): Order and Disorder
Schmidt, Arne L. (wri): Chain Reaction (1996)
Schmidt, Arnold (wri): Deja Vu
Schmidt, Brick (act): Blood Diner
Schmidt, Donald R. (wri): Roswell
Schmidt, Folkert (act): I Come In Peace
Schmidt, Gerhard (wri): Hipnosis
Schmidt, Helmut (act): A Prize of Arms
Schmidt, Kai (act): Mockery
Schmidt, Kendall (mus): Neon Maniacs
Schmidt, Marlene (act): The Stepmother
Schmidt, Marlene (wri): The Fifth Floor; Mortuary
Schmidt, Paul (act): The Playground
Schmidt, Ron(n) (cin): Beastmaster 2: Through the Portal of Time; Bloodspell; Dead of Night (1987); Lord of Illusions; Philadelphia Experiment II
Schmidt, Ronald (wri): A.P.E.X.; Digital Man
Schmidt, Stan (act): Kill and Kill Again
Schmidt, Stephen (wri): La Isla de la Muerte
Schmidt, Walter Roeber (wri): Monstroid
Schmidt, Wayne (wri): The Day Time Ended
Schmidt, Wendy (act): The Pit (1983)
Schmidtke, Ned (act): The Relic
Schmidtner, Christiana (act): The Giant Spider Invasion; Scream, Pretty Peggy
Schmidt-Reitwein, Joerg (cin): Nosferatu, the Vampyre
Schminke, Eleonore (act): Jonathan
Schmit, Dan (cin): Cyborg 2: Glass Shadow
Schmitt, Fred (act): Mutants In Paradise
Schmitt, Harrison H. (act): For All Mankind
Schmitz, Peter (act): Fargo
Schmitz, Sybille (act): F.P. 1 Antwortet Nicht
Schmitzburger, Paul (act): The Slipper and the Rose
Schmoeller, David (act): The Arrival (1990)
Schmoeller, David (dir): The Arrival (1990); Catacombs (1989); Crawlspace; Curse IV: The Ultimate Sacrifice; Netherworld; Puppet Master; The Seduction; Tourist Trap
Schmoeller, David (wri): The Arrival (1990); Crawlspace; The Day Time Ended; Ghost Town; The Seduction; Tourist Trap
Schmoll, Benjamin (act): Julie Darling
Schnabel, Stefan (act): Blood Bath (1975); Houdini (1953); The Secret Ways; The 27th Day
Schnall, Peter (cin): The Mutilator (1985)
Schnarre, Monika (act): Waxwork II: Lost In Time
Schneck, Stephen (wri): Welcome to Blood City
Schnee, Charles (wri, 1918-1962): The Next Voice You Hear
Schnee, Thelma (wri): The Colossus of New York; Father Brown
Schneeberger, Hans (cin): Das Blaue Licht
Schneevoight, George (cin): Blade af Satans Bog
Schneid, Scott J. (wri): Phantom of the Mall: Eric's Revenge
Schneider, Andrew (act): The Incredible 2-Headed Transplant
Schneider, Andrew (wri): Alien Nation: Dark Horizon; Alien Nation: The Enemy Within
Schneider, Barry (wri): Ruby
Schneider, Bonnie (act): Murderlust
Schneider, Carol (act): Jacob's Ladder
Schneider, Charles (act): Zarkorr! The Invader
Schneider, Daniele (act): Secret Weapons; Virus (1980)
Schneider, David (act): Mission: Impossible; The Saint
Schneider, Edith (act): The Quiller Memorandum
Schneider, Gary (act): Class of Nuke 'em High; The Toxic Avenger
Schneider, Guenther (act): see Arnold, Edward
Schneider/Snider, Helmut (act): Captain Sinbad; Kemek
Schneider, John (act, b. 1954): The Curse; Night of the Twisters
Schneider, John A. (act): Serial Mom
Schneider, Kurt (act): see Earles, Harry
Schneider, Maria (act): Jane Eyre (1996); Mama Dracula; The Passenger
Schneider, Mark (act): Ghostbusters II; The Premonition (1975)
Schneider, Marliese K. (act): Species
Schneider, Rob (act, b. 1964): The Adventures of Pinocchio (1996); Judge Dredd
Schneider, Romy (act, 1938-1982, nee Rosemarie Albach-Retty): Angel On Wheels; Deathwatch (1980); The Inquisitor; Otley; The Trial; Le Trio Infernal
Schneider, Vic (act): Frankenstein Island
Schneiderman, Al (act): Werewolf of Washington
Schneiderman, George (cin): Boston Blackie; Charlie Chan Carries On; Scotland Yard (1930)
Schnell, Gitt (act): Nosferatu, eine Symphonie des Grauens
Schnitzer, Gerald (wri): Bowery at Midnight; The Corpse Vanishes
Schnitzer, Robert Allen (dir & wri): The Premonition (1975)
Schnitzler, Arthur (wri): Eyes Wide Shut
Schockley, Bill (act): RoboCop
Schoedsack, Ernest B. (dir, b. 1893): Dr. Cyclops; King Kong (1933); The Last Days of Pompeii (1935); Mighty Joe Young (1949); The Most Dangerous Game; Son of Kong
Schoelen, Jill (act): Babes In Toyland (1986); Chiller; Curse II: The Bite; Cutting Class; The Phantom of the Opera (1989); Popcorn; The Stepfather; When a Stranger Calls Back
Schoenberg, Steven (wri): Alien Warrior
Schoene, Reiner (act): The Eiger Sanction; The Handmaid's Tale
Schoener, Ingeborg (act): El Invencible Hombre Invisible; Mark of the Devil (1972)
Schoenfeld, Bernard (C.) (wri): The Magic Sword (1962); Phantom Lady; The Space Children
Schoenherr, Dietmar (act): The Monster of London (1964); Secret Agent 077-Operation Hong Kong; Victim Five
Schoeny, Jeffrey (act): The Last Man On Planet Earth
Schoettle, Jane (act): Short Circuit 2
Schofield, Annabel (act): Body Armor; Solar Crisis
Schofield, David (act): An American Werewolf In London; Jekyll and Hyde
Schofield, John (act): The Secret Adventures of Tom Thumb
Schofield, Johnnie (act): Murder On Monday; The Perfect Woman; The Shop at Sly Corner; While I Live
Schofield, Katharine/Katherine (act): The Carnation Killer; Lifeforce
Schofield, Meriel (act): Mary Shelley's 'Frankenstein'
Schofield, Paul (wri): Boston Blackie
Scholefield, Alan (wri): Venom (1982)
Scholes, Kim (mus): The Nesting
Scholl, Art (act): Time Flyer
Scholtz, Eva (act): The Black Abbot (1963)
Scholz-Conway, John (dir): Once the Killing Starts
Schomaker, Fred (act): Street Trash
Schombing, Jason (Scott) (act): I Still Dream of Jeannie; Timecop
Schon, Kyra (act, b. 1957): Night of the Living Dead (1968)
Schon, Margaret (act): Die Nibelungen
Schonblum, Terry (act): Rabid
Schone, Reiner (act): Babylon 5: In the Beginning
Schonemann, Emile (cin): Aelita; Die Spinnen
Schoner, Inge (act): The Mystery of Thug Island
Schonherr, Dietmar (act): Victim Five
Schooley, Robert (wri): Aladdin and the King of Thieves
Schoolfield, Jeff (cin): The Eiger Sanction
Schoolnik, Skip (dir): Hide and Go Shriek
Schoonover, Gloria Jean (act): see Jean, Gloria
Schoorel, Lex (act): Modesty Blaise
Schoppert, Bill (act): Lord of the Flies (1990)
Schorr, Mike (cin): Dead Connection
Schott, Bob (act): Future Hunters; Vamp
Schott, Dale (dir): Care Bears Movie II: A New Generation
Schow, David J. (wri): Critters 4; Leatherface: Texas Chainsaw Massacre III
Schown, Fanny (act): see Shore, Dinah
Schrader, Barry (mus): Galaxy of Terror
Schrader, Paul (dir, b. 1946): Cat People (1982); The Comfort of Strangers; Touch; Witch Hunt
Schrader, Paul (wri, b. 1946): Obsession (1976); Touch
Schrage, Lisa (act): The Food of the Gods, Part II; The Haunting of Hamilton High
Schrager, Rudy (mus): Fear In the Night (1947); Sleep, My Love
Schram, Bitty (act): Caught (1996)
Schramm, Karla (act): Jungle Trail of the Son of Tarzan
Schrank, Joseph (wri): Cabin In the Sky
Schreck, Max (act): Am Rande der Welt; Nosferatu, Eine Symphonie des Grauens
Schreck, Vicki (act): Freaky Friday (1976)

Scott, Linda (Gaye) (act): *Hammersmith Is Out; Westworld*
Scott, Lisa Marie (act): *The Glass Cage (1996)*
Scott, Lizabeth (act, b. 1922, nee Emma Matzo): *Dead Reckoning; Pitfall; Pulp; Scared Stiff (1953); A Stolen Face; The Weapon*
Scott, Lloyd (act): *Night of the Red Hunter*
Scott, Lorri (act): *Doomsday Machine*
Scott, Margaretta (act, b. 1912): *Counterblast; Crescendo; Fanny by Gaslight; The Girl In the News; The Last Man to Hang?; The Return of the Scarlet Pimpernel; Things to Come; A Woman Possessed*
Scott, Mark (act): *Killers from Space*
Scott, Martha (act, b. 1914): *Charlotte's Web; The Devil's Daughter (1972); Summer Girl*
Scott, Mary (act): *Philo Vance Returns*
Scott, Michael (cin): *Roger Corman's 'Frankenstein Unbound'*
Scott, Michael (dir): *Like Father, Like Santa; Sharon's Secret*
Scott, Michele (act): *Evil of Frankenstein*
Scott, Mike (act): *Red Alert*
Scott, Millicent (act): *Curse of the Crimson Altar*
Scott, Morton (mus): *Secrets of Scotland Yard*
Scott, Nathan (mus): *X-15*
Scott, Oz (dir): *Bride of Boogedy*
Scott, Patricia (act): *To Commit a Murder*
Scott, Peter Graham (dir, b. 1923): *Account Rendered; The Big Chance; Breakout; Captain Clegg; The Headless Ghost; Panic at Madam Tussaud's; Subterfuge*
Scott, Peter Graham (wri, b. 1923): *Panic at Madam Tussaud's*
Scott, Phil (act): *Bulldog Drummond's Third Round*
Scott, Phillip (mus): *Those Dear Departed*
Scott, Pippa (act): *Bad Ronald; Demon and the Mummy*
Scott, Randolph (act, 1898-1987, nee Randolph Crane): *Captain Kidd; Home, Sweet Homicide; Murders In the Zoo; Paris Calling; She (1935); Supernatural (1933)*
Scott, Randolph (child act): *The Capture of Bigfoot*
Scott, Ray (cin): *The Night of the Claw*
Scott, Richard S. (act): *Solar Crisis*
Scott, Ridley (dir, b. 1939): *Alien; Blade Runner; Legend*
Scott, Robert (dir & wri): *The Video Dead*
Scott, Robert (E.) (act): *A Close Call for Boston Blackie; Crime Doctor's Courage; Exposed; The Notorious Lone Wolf; One Mysterious Night; Shadowed; The Unknown (1946)*
Scott, Roger (act): *It Came Upon the Midnight Clear; Repossessed*
Scott, Ron (act): *Mars Needs Women*
Scott, Ronald Joshua (act): *The Relic*
Scott, Sandra (act): *The Housekeeper*
Scott, Sandu (act): *Family Doctor*
Scott, Sherman (dir): see Newfield, Sam
Scott, Sherman (wri): *Bad Girls from Mars; Haunting Fear; Inner Sanctum 2*
Scott, Sherry (act): *Satan's Mistress*
Scott, Simon (act): *The Couch; I've Lived Before; Man of a Thousand Faces; Moon Pilot*
Scott, Stephen (act): *The Flesh and the Fiends*
Scott, Susan (act): *Demons of the Dead; Emanuelle e gli Ultimi Cannibali*
Scott, Sydna (act): *Mr. Sycamore*
Scott, T.J. (act): *The Pink Chiquitas*
Scott, T.J. (dir): *TC 2000; Young Hercules*
Scott, T.J. (wri): *TC 2000*
Scott, Talmedge (act): *Shock Waves*
Scott, Terry (act): *A Ghost of a Chance (1968); Murder Most Foul*
Scott, Thomas (act): *Motor Psycho*
Scott, Thurman (act): *Werewolf of Washington*
Scott, Timothy (act): *Love Me Deadly; Nightmares (1983); Vanishing Point (1971)*
Scott, Tom (act): *The Green Slime; Herbie Goes Bananas; Werewolf of Washington*
Scott, Tom (mus): *Conquest of the Planet of the Apes; Final Notice*
Scott, Tom Everett (act): *An American Werewolf In Paris*
Scott, Tony (dir): *The Hunger*
Scott, Victoria (act): *Blades*
Scott, Wallace (act): *Tarzan and the Huntress*
Scott, Walter (act): *Mr. Sycamore*
Scott, Will (wri): *Creeping Shadows; The Limping Man (1936)*
Scott, William (act): *Dante's Inferno (1924)*
Scott, Zachary (act, 1914-1965): *Appointment In Honduras; Danger Signal; Guilty Bystander; It's Only Money; Lightning Strikes Twice; Man In the Shadow; The Mask of Dimitrios; Ruthless; Shadow On the Wall*
Scottane, Liliane (act): *The Camp On Blood Island; The Headless Ghost*
Scott-Elder, B. (wri): *Blind Man's Bluff (1936)*
Scott-Gatty, Alex (act): *Hamlet (1913)*
Scotti, Allen (act): *Virtuosity*
Scotti, Andrea (act): *Gli Amori di Ercole; Atom Age Vampire; Ercole Contro i Figli del Sole; The Legend of the Wolf Woman*
Scotti, Vito (act): *Conquest of Space; Halloween With the Addams Family; Herbie Goes Bananas; Herbie Rides Again; Master of the World; The Nude Bomb; Sabaka*
Scotton, Myrtle (act): *Phantasm*
Scott-Paget, John (act): *The Hound of London*
Scott-Taylor, Jonathan (act): *Damien-Omen II*
Scott-Thomas, Kristin (act): *Mission: Impossible; Richard III (1995)*
Scott-Wilson, Marloe (act): *Kill and Kill Again*
Scotty, Alf (act): *What the?*
Scougall, Adam (act): *Mad Max Beyond Thunderdome*
Scoular, Angela (act): *Casino Royale; On Her Majesty's Secret Service*
Scoular, Christopher (act): *An American Werewolf In London*
Scourby, Alexander (act, 1913-1985): *The Executioner; The Shaggy Dog (1959); Sign of the Pagan; The Stuff*
Scranton, Peter (act): *Spacecamp*
Scratuglia, Ivan (act): *La Strega In Amore*
Screaming Mad George (cin): *Curse II: The Bite*
Screaming Mad George (dir): *The Guyver*
Screech, S.A. (wri): *The Magic Glass*
Scriba, Mik (act): *The Package*
Scribner, Don (act): *Slave Girls from Beyond Infinity*
Scribner, George (dir): *Oliver & Company*
Scribner, Ronnie (act): *Salem's Lot*
Scrimm, Angus (act): *The Lost Empire; Mindwarp (1990); Phantasm; Phantasm II; Phantasm III: Lord of the Dead; Subspecies*
Scriven, Anthony Boyd (act): *Dressed to Kill (1980)*
Scroggins, Bobbie (act): *The Woman In Question*
Scroggins, Helen (act): *Vampire's Kiss*
Scroggins, Renee (act): *Vampire's Kiss*
Scroggins, Valerie Jean (act): *Vampire's Kiss*
Scrutton, Daphne (act): see Anderson, Daphne
Scudamore, Margaret (act): *Double Alibi; The Vengeance of the Air*
Scuddamore, Simon (act): *Slaughter High*
Scudder, Billy (act): *The Alchemist*
Scully, David (act): *The Hand That Rocks the Cradle*
Scully, Rick (act): *The Cars That Ate Paris*
Scully, Samantha (act): *Silent Night, Deadly Night III*
Scully, Sean (act): *Dr. Syn-Alias the Scarecrow; Hunted In Holland*
Scully, Terry (act): *The Asphyx; Captain Clegg; Night After Night After Night; Twinsanity*
Scully, William J. (dir): *Annabel Lee*
Scurfield, Matthew (act): *Raiders of the Lost Ark*
Sdruscia, Carolina (act): *Kemek*
Seabourne, Peter (dir & wri): *Countdown to Danger*
Seabrook, William (wri, 1887-1945): *White Zombie*
Seabury, Forrest (act): *The Drums of Jeopardy (1923)*
Seabury, Inez (act): *The Invisible Ray*
Seabury, Warren (act): *Pretty Maids All In a Row*
Seacat, Sandra (dir): *In the Spirit*
Seacombe, Dorothy (act): *The Yellow Mask*
Seager, Vanya (act): *Xtro*
Seago, Sandra (act): *I Was a Zombie for the F.B.I.*
Seagram, Lisa (act): *2000 Years Later*
Seagrave, Jocelyn (act): *Assault On Dome 4*
Seagren, Bob (act): *The Return of the Six Million Dollar Man and the Bionic Woman*
Seagrove, Jenny (act): *Deadly Game (1991); The Guardian; Mark of the Devil (1985); Sherlock Holmes and the Incident at Victoria Falls*
Seal, Elizabeth (act): *Vampire Circus*
Seal, Peter (act): *Above Suspicion*
Seale, Douglas (act): *Ernest Saves Christmas; Ghostbusters II; Haunted by Her Past; Mr. Destiny*
Seale, John (cin): *City of Angels; The Hitcher*
Seales, Franklyn (act, 1952-1990): *Star Trek*
Sealey, Scott (act): *The Boy Who Cried Werewolf*
Seals Jr., Frank (act): *The Silence of the Lambs*
Seaman, Jack (wri): *Project Moonbase*
Seaman, Milton (act): *The Purple Rose of Cairo*
Seaman, Peter (wri): *Who Framed Roger Rabbit*
Seaman, Rick (act): *Endangered Species*
Seaman, Rick (wri): *Chain Reaction (1996)*
Seaman, Robert (cin): *Killer In the Mirror*
"Seamark" (wri): *Murder In Reverse*
Seamens, Sueanne (act): *The Majorettes*
Seamon, Ed (act): *The Rosary Murders*
Seamon, Pamela (act): *White of the Eye*
Sear, Walter E. (mus): *The Oracle (1985)*
Searcy, Nick (act): *The Fugitive (1993)*
Searle, Francis (dir, b. 1905): *Celia; Cloudburst; Dead Man's Evidence; Freedom to Die; Gaolbreak (1962); The Man In Black; The Marked One; Murder at Site Three; Night of the Prowler; Talk of the Devil; Things Happen at Night; Undercover Girl (1958); Whispering Smith Hits London*
Searle, Francis (wri, b. 1905): *Celia; Cloudburst; Talk of the Devil*
Searle, Humphrey (mus): *The Abominable Snowman of the Himalayas; The Haunting*
Searle, Jackie (act): *Great Expectations (1934); Murder On the Blackboard*
Searle, Kamuela C. (act): *Jungle Trail of the Son of Tarzan*
Searle, Sam (act): *Male and Female*
Searle, Thomas/Tom (act): *Surf Nazis Must Die; They Live*
Searles, Frank (wri): *Countdown*
Searles, Jefferson Dudley (act): *The Invisible Boy*
Sears, Ann (act): *Cat and Mouse (1958); Lady of Vengeance; Man Detained; Tales from the Crypt (1971); The Unstoppable Man; Vengeance*
Sears, Fjanet (act): *Escape Clause*
Sears, Fred (act): *Boston Blackie's Chinese Venture; The Lone Wolf and His Lady*
Sears, Fred F. (dir, 1913-1957): *Cell 2455, Death Row; Crash Landing; Down to Earth; Earth vs. the Flying Saucers; The 49th Man; The Giant Claw; The Night the World Exploded; The Werewolf (1955)*
Sears, Heather (act, b. 1935): *Black Torment; Great Expectations (1974); The Phantom of the Opera (1962)*
Sears, Ian (act): *Electric Eskimo*
Sears, Ted (wri): *Alice In Wonderland (1951); Pinocchio (1940); Snow White and the Seven Dwarfs*
Sears, Zelda (act): *The Bishop Murder Case*
Sears, Zenas (act): *The Legend of Blood Mountain*
Seastrom (orig. Sjostrom), Victor (dir, 1879-1960): *He Who Gets Slapped; The Phantom Chariot; The Scarlet Letter (1926); The Tower of Lies; Under the Red Robe (1937)*
Seastrom, Victor (wri, 1879-1960): *He Who Gets Slapped*
Seaton, Arthur (act): *The Ghost Goes West; The Howard Case*
Seaton, George (dir, 1911-1979): *For Heaven's Sake; Miracle On 34th Street (1947); 36 Hours (1965)*
Seaton, George (wri, 1911-1979): *For Heaven's Sake; Miracle On 34th Street (1947 & 1994); 36 Hours (1965)*
Seavy, George (act): *Raiders of the Living Dead*
Seaward, Carolyn (act): *Octopussy*
Seaward, Sydney (act): *The Flaw (1933); The Yellow Claw*
Seawright, Roy (cin): *One Million B.C.*
Seay, James (act): *The Amazing Colossal Man; The Beginning of the End; Captain Kidd and the Slave Girl; The Day the Earth Stood Still; The Destructors; Enemy Agents Meet Ellery Queen; Phantom from Space; Return to Treasure Island; Secret Beyond the Door; The Son of Monte Cristo; The Threat (1960); Time to Kill (1942); Voodoo Tiger*
Sebaldt, Christian (cin): *The Adventures of Galgameth; Casper: A Spirited Beginning*
Sebaldt, Maria (act): *Hi, Here's Eddie*
Sebastian, Beverly (act): *Rocktober Blood*
Sebastian, Don (act): *Super Fuzz*
Sebastian, Dorothy (act, 1904-1957): *The Unholy Night*
Sebastian, Ferd (dir): *Rocktober Blood*
Sebastian, John (dir & wri): *Planeta Bura*
Sebastian, Kristina (act): *Cyborg (1989)*
Sebastian, Sharon (act): *Eve of Destruction*
Sebelius, Gregg (dir): *Sampa*
Seberg, Jean (act, 1938-1979): *Cat and Mouse (1974); The French Conspiracy; Lilith; Moment to Moment; The Mouse That Roared*
Sebesky, Don (mus): *The Rosary Murders*
Seca, Pedro Munos (wri): *La Venganza de Don Mendo*
Secchy, Tony (cin): *Secret Agent Superdragon*
Seccia, Cesare (wri): *The Colossus of Rhodes; Goliath Against the Giants*
Sechan, Edmond (cin, b. 1919): *L'Ours; The Red Balloon*
Sechan, Edmond (dir & wri, b. 1919): *L'Ours*
Seckel, Bill (cin): *The Night of the Claw*
Secombe, Andrew (act): *I Don't Want to Be Born*
Secombe, Harry (act, b. 1921): *The Bed-Sitting Room; Jet Storm; Svengali (1954)*
Secor, Chuck (act): *Neon Maniacs*
Secor, Kyle (act): *Beauty's Revenge; Late for Dinner; Mind Games*
Secora, Michael (act): *Trancers II: The Return of Jack Deth*
Secrist, Larry (cin): *Haunts*
Seda, Jon (act): *Primal Fear; 12 Monkeys*
Sedaka, Neil (act): *Decoy for Terror*
Sedaka, Neil (mus): *Playgirl Killer*
Sedan, Rolfe/Rolphe (act): *The Iron Mask; Phantom of the Rue Morgue; The Thin Man*
Sedat, Sibilla (act): *Satyricon*
Seddon, Jack (wri): *The Alphabet Murders; Kill or Cure; Murder Ahoy; Murder Most Foul; Murder She Said; The Secret Partner; The Southern Star; Tomorrow Never Comes*
Seddon, Margaret (act): *Through the Dark*
Seder, Rufus Butler (act, dir & wri): *Screamplay*
Sedgwick, Edward (dir): *Beware, Spooks!; The Gladiator*
Sedgwick, Katrina (act): *The Last Wave*
Sedgwick, Kyra (act): *Heart and Souls; Phenomenon*
Sedgwick, Paulita (act): *Savages*
Sedgwick, Robert (act): *Tales from the Darkside*
Sedley, Henry (act): *The Ghost Talks*
Sedwick, Shannon (act): *Blood Simple*
Sedykh, Natalya (act): *Jack Frost*
Seeber, Guido (cin): *Geheimnisse einer Seele; Der Golem (1914); Der Student von Prag (1913)*
Seeberg, Ian (wri): *The Companion (1994)*
Seebohm, Alison (act): *The Servant*
Seefield, Kai S. (act): *The Night Porter*
Seegar, Miriam (act): *Seven Keys to Baldpate (1929); Strangers of the Evening; When Knights Were Bold (1929)*
Seegar, Sara (act): *Mr. Reeder In Room 13*
Seeger, Mindy (act): *976-EVIL*
Seekins, Scott M. (act): *Fire In the Sky (1993)*
Seel, Charles (act): *Duel; I Was a Teenage Frankenstein; Lady In a Cage; Ssssss; Westworld*
Seeley Jr., E.S. (wri): *The Hideous Sun Demon*
Seeley, Eileen (act): *Creature; A Dangerous Affair*
Seeley, John (mus): *The Hideous Sun Demon*
Seeley, S.K. (dir): *Amazon Quest*
Seely, Charlotte (act): *Spookies*
Seely, Joe (act): *A Nightmare On Elm Street 5: The Dream Child*
Seely, Tim (act): *Agatha*
Seff, Manuel/Manny (wri): *The Falcon's Alibi; Trouble for Two*
Sefton, Mr. (act): *The Harper Mystery*
Sefton, Ernest (act): *The Body Vanishes; Dr. Sin Fang; Double Alibi; The Fatal Hour (1937); The Third Clue; Wolf's Clothing (1936)*
Segal, Francine (act): *Cat People (1982)*
Segal, George (act, b. 1936): *The Babysitter (1995); The Black Bird (1975); The Cable Guy; The Cold Room; Houdini (1998); No Way to Treat a Lady; The Quiller Memorandum; Rollercoaster; The St. Valentine's Day Massacre; The Southern Star; The Terminal Man; Who Is Killing the Great Chefs of Europe?; The Zany Adventures of Robin Hood*
Segal, Gilles (act): *Ils Appellent Ca un Accident; Topkapi*
Segal, Harry (act): *Agatha*
Segal, Jeffrey (act): *The Traitors*
Segal, John (act): *Inseminoid; Slaughter High*
Segal, Jonathan (act): *Exo-Man; The Man With the Power*
Segal, Josh (act): *Scared Stiff (1987)*
Segal, McNally (act): *Nightbreed*
Segal, Michael (act): *The Black Windmill; Nothing But the Night; The Prisoner of Zenda (1979); Rentadick*
Segal, Michael Ryan (act): *12 Monkeys*
Segal, Misha (mus): *The Phantom of the Opera (1989)*
Segal, Nena (act): *The Refrigerator*
Segal, Nick (act): *Chopping Mall; School Spirit*
Segal, Susan (act): *The Last Man On Planet Earth*
Segal, Zohra (act): *Tales That Witness Madness; The Vengeance of She*
Segale, Gianna (act): *Love Slaves of the Amazons*
Segall, Bernardo (act): *Moon of the Wolf*
Segall, Bernardo (mus): *Night Slaves*
Segall, Don (act & wri): *The Goddess of Love*
Segall, Harry (wri, b. 1897): *Angel On My Shoulder (1946); For Heaven's Sake; Heaven Can Wait (1978); Here Comes Mr. Jordan; The Lone Wolf Strikes*
Segall, Pamela (act): *After Midnight; Gate II*

Segall, Stuart (dir): Drive-In Massacre
Segar, Max (act): The Goonies
Segawa, Hiroshi (cin): Suna No Onna
Segovia, Elena (act): Hundra
Segri, Aldo (wri): The Nights of Lucretia Borgia
Segura, Jaime (act): Flesh & Blood
Segura, Santiago (act, b. 1965): Accion Mutante; El Dia de la Bestia; Solo Se Muere Dos Veces
Sehres, Bill (act): Cavegirl (1985)
Seibel, Lynn (act): Zapped!
Seibel, Mary (act): The Package
Seidel, Lea (act): I Aim at the Stars
Seidel, Mary (act): Blink
Seidel, Tim (act): Ghost Rider (1943)
Seidel, Tom(my) (act): Charlie Chan In City In Darkness; Dick Tracy Returns
Seidelman, Arthur Allan/A. (dir): Dying to Remember; Echoes; Hercules In New York; Trapped In Space
Seidelman, Michael (act): Making Mr. Right
Seidelman, Susan (dir): Making Mr. Right
Seiden, Raymond (act): The Toxic Avenger, Part II
Seidman, Sara (act): The Handmaid's Tale
Seidner, Justin (act): RoboCop 2
Seigner, Francoise (act): L'Enfant Sauvage
Seiler, Lew(is) (dir, 1891-1964): Charlie Chan In Paris; The Ghost Talks; Murder In the Air (1940); Operation Secret; The Smiling Ghost
Seiler, Neil (act): Captain Kronos: Vampire Hunter
Seiller, Phyllis (act): see Brooks, Phyllis
Seiter, William (A.) (dir, 1891-1964): Make Haste to Live; One Touch of Venus
Seitz, David (act): Mutants In Paradise
Seitz, Debra (act): Alien Nation
Seitz, George (B.) (dir, 1880-1944): Drums of Jeopardy (1931); House of Menace; Midnight Mystery; Night Beat; Shadow of Doubt; Sky Murder; The 13th Chair (1937); Treason; Widow In Scarlet
Seitz, Guido (act): Making Contact
Seitz, John (act): The Prowler (1981)
Seitz, John (F.) (cin, b. 1892): The Big Clock; The Conquering Power; Desert Legion; Five Graves to Cairo; In the Next Room; Invaders from Mars (1953); Island of Lost Women; Kismet (1930); The Lost Weekend; The Magician (1926); The Man In the Net; Murder Will Out (1930); Night Has a Thousand Eyes; The Prisoner of Zenda (1922); Sunset Boulevard; Trifling Women; The Unseen (1945); When Worlds Collide
Setiz, Ryan (act): Brainwaves; Shadow of Death (1983)
Seka (act): Dracula Sucks
Sekaryongo (act): King Solomon's Mines (1949)
Sekawa, Hiroshi (cin): Tanin No Kao
Sekely, Steve (dir, 1899-1979, nee Istvan Szekely): Blonde Savage; The Day of the Triffids; Revenge of the Zombies (1943)
Sekers, Alan (dir): The Arp Statue
Seki, Isao (wri): Live Today, Die Tomorrow
Sekia, Mamiya (act): The Last Dinosaur
Sekigushi, Ginzo (act): Suna No Onna
Sekine, Tsutomu (act): Erik the Viking; The Toxic Avenger, Part II
Sekizawa, Shinichi (wri): Atragon; Battle In Outer Space; Dogora, the Space Monster; Ghidrah, the Three-Headed Monster; Godzilla's Revenge; Godzilla vs. Mothra; Latitude Zero; Mothra; The Secret of the Telegian; Son of Godzilla
Sekka, Johnny (act): Babylon 5: The Gathering; Charlie Chan and the Curse of the Dragon Queen; Doctors Wear Scarlet; The Southern Star; Woman of Straw
Sekulovich, Mladen (act): see Malden, Karl
Selander, Lesley (dir, 1903-1979): The Catman of Paris; The Fatal Witness; Flight to Mars; The Lone Ranger and the Lost City of Gold; The Sky Dragon; The Vampire's Ghost
Selayah, Akushula (act): Tarzan, the Ape Man (1981)
Selbie, Evelyn (act): The Mysterious Dr. Fu Manchu; The Return of Dr. Fu Manchu
Selbst, Irving (act): Winter Kills
Selburg, David (act): Species
Selby, Anthony (act): The City Under the Sea
Selby, Charles (wri): London by Night (1913)
Selby, David (act, b. 1941): Doctor Franken; Night of Dark Shadows
Selby, Nicholas (act): Macbeth (1971); Mata Hari (1985)
Selby, Sarah (act, 1906-1980): Moon Pilot; Tower of London (1962); Trapped by Boston Blackie
Selby, Tony (act): Witch-Finder General
Seldon, Tom [illegible]
Seldes, Marian (act): Crime and Punishment, U.S.A.

Seldon, Barbara (act): Deadtime Stories
Seldon-Truss, Leslie (dir & wri): Fetters of Fear
Self, William (act): The Thing from Another World
Selick, Henry (dir): James and the Giant Peach; The Nightmare Before Christmas
Selinsky, Wladimir (mus): Something Evil
Selk, George (act): The Vampire (1957)
Selkirk, Jamie (act): Dead Alive
Selko, Warren (act): Beverly Hills Bodysnatchers
Sell, Jack M. (cin, dir & wri): The Psychotronic Man
Sellajaah, Akushla (act): Il Montagna di Dio Cannibale
Selland, Marie (act): Invasion of the Body Snatchers (1956)
Sellars, Elizabeth (act, b. 1923): Cloudburst; A Ghost In Monte Carlo; Guilt Is My Shadow; Hunted (1952); Jet Storm; The Last Man to Hang?; The Mummy's Shroud; Never Let Go; Three Cases of Murder
Sellars, Peter (act): King Lear (1987)
Sellars, Randolph (cin): Prey of the Chameleon
Sellecca, Connie (act, b. 1955): The Bermuda Depths; Captain America II; A Dangerous Affair; Doomsday Rock; She's Dressed to Kill; Turn Back the Clock
Selleck, Tom (act, b. 1945): Coma; Daughters of Satan; Myra Breckinridge; Runaway (1984); Terminal Island
Sellers, Alan (act): The Curse of the Golem
Sellers, Arthur (act & wri): Modern Problems
Sellers, Leslie (act): Alien High
Sellers, Mary (act): The Crawlers
Sellers, Peter (act, 1925-1980): Alice's Adventures In Wonderland (1972); Casino Royale; Dr. Strangelove: or, How I Learned to Stop Worrying and Love the Bomb; The Fiendish Plot of Dr. Fu Manchu; The Lady Killers (1956); The Magic Christian; The Mouse That Roared; Murder by Death; Never let Go; The Prisoner of Zenda (1979); The Road to Hong Kong; Tom Thumb; The Wrong Box
Sellers, Peter (wri, 1925-1980): The Magic Christian
Sellers, Sabrina (act): El Barbaro; Conquest
Sellers, Victoria (act): Warlords
Sellier Jr., Charles E. (dir): Silent Night, Deadly Night
Sellon, Charles (A.) (act): Bulldog Drummond (1929); The Casino Murder Case; The Monster (1925)
Selmier, Dean (act): The Blood Spattered Bride; Murders In the Rue Morgue (1971)
Selten, Morton (act, 1860-1940, nee Morton Stubbs): Dark World; The Ghost Goes West; Juggernaut; Once In a New Moon; The Thief of Bagdad (1940)
Seltzer, David (wri): Damien-Omen II; The Final Conflict; The Hellstrom Chronicle; The Omen; Prophecy (1979)
Seltzer, Dov (mus): The Mummy Lives
Selway, George (act): Maroc 7
Selwyn, Clarissa (act): The Brass Bottle (1923); The Grit of a Dandy
Selwyn, Edgar (dir): The Mystery of Mr. X
Selzer, Milton (act): Blood and Lace; Capricorn One; The Evil
Selznick, Arna (dir): The Care Bears Movie
Selznick, David O. (wri, 1902-1965): The Paradine Case
Semand, Britt (act): Horror of the Blood Monsters
Sembera, Tricia (act): The Ivory Ape
Semels, Harry (act): The Chance of a Lifetime
Sementsov, Mady (act): Humanoid Woman
Seminara, George (act): I Was a Teenage Zombie
Semitjof, Wladimir (wri): The Invisible Terror
Semler, Dean (cin): Dead Calm; Razorback; The Road Warrior; Super Mario Bros.; Waterworld
Semochenko, Irina (act): Devotion
Semon, Larry (act & dir, 1889-1928): The Wizard of Oz (1925)
Sempere, Francisco (cin): Amador; Cauldron of Blood; Hipnosis
Semple Jr., Lorenzo (wri): Batman (1966); Daddy's Gone A-Hunting; Fathom; Flash Gordon (1980); King Kong (1976); Never Say Never Again; Pretty Poison (1968 & 1996); Rearview Mirror; Sheena; 3 Days of the Condor
Semprun, Jorge (wri): L'Aveu; The French Conspiracy
Sen, Bachoo (act): Towers Open Fire
Senac, Herman (act): Blood Diner
Senatore, Paolo (act): Diario Segreto da un Carcere Femminile
Senda, Koreya (act): Battle In Outer Space; The H-Man
[illegible] Easy
Sendin, Ashleigh (act): The Demon (1981)

Sendry, Al(bert) (mus, b. 1921): Bloody Wednesday
Seneca, Joe (act): Amazing Stories: The Movie; V; The Blob (1988); Tarzan In Manhattan
Senelka, Peter (dir): Teen Alien
Senensky, Ralph (dir): Death Cruise
Senftleben, Gunther (cin): Brainwashed; Captain Sinbad
Sengoku, Noriko (act): Kwaidan
Sengotta, Will (act): Fear (1996)
Senior, Gilbert (act): Skullduggery
Senju, Akira (mus): The Mystery of Rampo
Sens-Cazenave, A. (wri): Cauchemares
Sentis, Ivonne (act): Where Time Began
Sentman, David (act): The Green Slime
Sen Yung, Victor (act, 1915-1980): Betrayal from the East; Castle In the Desert; Charlie Chan at the Wax Museum; Charlie Chan at Treasure Island; Charlie Chan In Honolulu; Charlie Chan In Panama; Charlie Chan In Reno; Charlie Chan In Rio; Charlie Chan's Murder Cruise; The Chinese Ring; Confessions of an Opium Eater; Dangerous Money; Dead Men Tell; The Docks of New Orleans; The Feathered Serpent (1948); The Golden Eye; Murder Over New York; Secret Agent of Japan; Shadows Over Chinatown; The Shanghai Chest; She Demons; The Trap
Senzy, Arthur (act): The Craft
Seoane, Jose Maria (act): Behind the Mask of Zorro
Septien, Al (wri): Leprechaun 2; Sleepstalker
Sequi, Mario (dir): The Cobra
Sera, Ian (act): Mystery On Monster Island; Pieces
Serafin, Enzo (cin): Gli Amori di Ercole; The Medium (1951); The Mysterious Island of Captain Nemo; Raw Wind In Eden
Serafine, Frank (mus): Nightfall (1988)
Seragnoli, Oreste (act): My Cousin Rachel
Serandrei, Mario (wri): La Maschera del Demonio
Serano, Manuel (act): Beat the Devil
Serasinghe, Irangani (act): The God King
Serato, Massimo (act, b. 1917): Gli Amori di Ercole; Challenge of the Gladiators; I Criminali della Galassia; David and Goliath; La Decima Vittima; Don't Look Now; Goliath, the Rebel Slave; Hipnosis; Il Ladro di Venezia; The Lion of Thebes; Pirate and the Slave Girl; Queen of the Pirates; Terror of the Red Mask; Tyrant of Lydia Against the Son of Hercules
Seray, Bernard (act): Night of the Zombies (1983)
Serbedzija, Lucija (act): The Saint
Serbedzija, Rade (act): The Saint
Serbegia, Rade (act): Mighty Joe Young (1998)
Serena (act): Dracula Sucks
Serenda, John (mus): Empire of Ash III
Serene, Douglas (act): Martin
Serene, Jeanne (act): Martin
Seresin, Michael (cin): Angel Heart
Sergei, Ivan (act): Mother, May I Sleep with Danger?; Star Command
Sergent, Dan (act): Shock Chamber
Sergeyev, Konstantin (dir & wri): The Sleeping Beauty (1965, Russ)
Serio, Frank (act): Runaway (1984)
Serio, Renato (mus): Alone In the Dark
Serling, Rod (act, 1924-1975): Encounter With the Unknown; The Outer Space Connection
Serling, Rod (wri, 1924-1975): Night Gallery; Planet of the Apes; Seven Days In May; Time Travelers (1976); A Town Has Turned to Dust
Sermet, Ozen (mus): Tarzan and the Jungle Boy
Serna, Assumpta (act): The Craft; Desvio al Paraiso; Nostradamus
Serna, Gil (act): Buck Rogers In the 25th Century
Serna, Monica (act): Dr. Tarr's Torture Dungeon
Serna, Pepe (act): The Adventures of Buckaroo Banzai; A Force of One; Red Dawn
Sernas, Jacques (act, b. 1925): Il Figlio di Spartacus; Helen of Troy (1955); Maciste Contre il Vampiro; The Nights of Lucretia Borgia; Romolo e Remo; Sign of the Gladiator
Seroff, Muni (act): Charlie Chan In the Secret Service
Seros, Alexander (wri): Point of No Return
Serpe, Pamela (act): Dr. Black Mr. Hyde
Serra, Alessandro (act): Ladyhawke
Serra, Deborah (wri): Snow White: A Tale of Terror
Serra, Eric (mus): The Fifth Element; Goldeneye
Serra, Gianna (act): The Glass Sphinx; Our Man Flint
Serra, Ray(mond) (act): The Silence of the Hams; Teenage Mutant Ninja Turtles; Wolfen
Serrador, Narciso (Ibanez) (dir): The House That Screamed; Island of the Damned
Serrador, Pastor (act): El Secreto del Doctor Orloff
Serrano, Carlos (dir): Parsifal
Serrano, Dominique (act): Trauma (1993)

Serrano, Louis (act): Love Slaves of the Amazons
Serrano, Nestor (act): Brenda Starr (1992); Daylight
Serrano, Rosario (act): Night Watch (1973)
Serrano, Sandy (act): Zapped!
Serrat, John (act): The Strange Awakening
Serrault, Michel (act, b. 1927): Buffet Froid; Diabolique (1955); Docteur Petiot; The Hatter's Ghost; He Died With His Eyes Open; The Inquisitor
Serre, Catherine (act): Moonraker
Serre, Henri (act): Mr. Frost
Serre, Josephine (act): Jane Eyre (1996)
Serret, John (act): Night Crossing; Return from the Ashes; Sword of the Valiant; A Taste of Fear; Two Wives at One Wedding
Sersen, Fred (cin, 1890-1962): The Blue Bird (1940); Call Northside 777; The Day the Earth Stood Still; Dragonwyck; Heaven Can Wait (1942); It Happens Every Spring; Jane Eyre (1944); The Lodger (1944); Nightmare Alley; Shock (1946); The Snake Pit (1948)
Servais, Jean (act, 1910-1976): Agent of Doom; The Corsican Brothers (1960); The Devil's Nightmare; The Gentle Art of Murder; The Lebanese Mission
Serve, Alain (act): Perceval
Server, Eric (act): Dr. Scorpion; Dogs; Slaughter
Servera, Maria Cristina (act): 13 Frightened Girls
Servess, Mary (act): The Lone Wolf Keeps a Date
Sessa, Alex (dir): Amazons (1986); Stormquest
Sessak, Hilde (act): The Ape Creature
Sesselman, Sabrina (act): Information Received; Die Turmit den Sieben Schlossern
Sessions, Almira (act, 1889-1974): The Bishop's Wife; The Boston Strangler; Monsieur Verdoux; Rosemary's Baby; Willard; Woman Who Came Back
Sessions, Bob (act): Little Shop of Horrors (1986); Nightbreed
Sesta, Hilary (act): The Black Windmill; Murder by Decree
Setala, Minna (act): Empire of Ash III
Setbon, Philippe (dir): Mr. Frost
Seth, Roshan (act): Indiana Jones and the Temple of Doom; Slipstream
Sethe, Harry (act): To All a Goodnight
Seton, Anya (wri, 1904-1990): Dragonwyck
Seton, Bruce (act, 1909-1969): Ambush In Leopard Street; Blackmailed; Dead Man's Evidence; The Demon Barber of Fleet Street; Freedom to Die; The Frightened City; Gorgo; Hidden Homicide; Love from a Stranger (1937); Miracles Do Happen; Paul Temple's Triumph; Undercover Girl (1958); Violent Moment
Seton, Violet (act): Devotion
Settlelen, Peter (act): Mark of the Devil (1985)
Settle, Matthew (act): A Deadly Vision; I Still Know What You Did Last Summer
Setton, Maxwell (act): The Golden Mask
Sety, Gerard (act): Aimez-Vous les Femmes?
Seurat, Denis (act): Moonraker
Seuss, Dr. (wri, 1904-1991, nee Theodor Seuss Geisel): The 5000 Fingers of Dr. T; How the Grinch Stole Christmas
Seven, Johnny (act): The Destructors
Sever, Stane (act): Cave of the Living Dead
Severance, Joan (act, b. 1958): Black Scorpion (1995); In Dark Places; The Runestone; The White Raven
Severe, Peggy (act): Angel Heart
Severeid, Susanne (act): Don't Answer the Phone!; Howling IV
Severn, Billy (act): The Enchanted Forest
Severn, Cliff (act): They Live In Fear
Severn, Maida (act): The Unseen (1981)
Severne, Mary Ann (act): Possession (1973)
Sevi, Mark (wri): Scanners: The Showdown
Sevier, Coy (act): My Best Friend Is a Vampire; The Outing
Sevilla, Carmen (act): Babes In Bagdad
Sevilla, Ninon (act): Cry of the Bewitched
Sevy, Brad "Cat" (act): The Flash
Seward, Billie (act): Charlie Chan at Treasure Island
Seward, Edmond (wri): Spook Busters
Sewards, Terence (act): Captain Kronos: Vampire Hunter
Sewell, George (act): Diamonds On Wheels; Doppleganger (1969); Get Carter; The Haunted House of Horror; Kaleidoscope; Mark of the Devil (1985); Robbery; The Vengeance of She
Sewell, Rufus (act): Dark City; Hamlet (1996)
Sewell, Vernon (dir, b. 1903): Burke and Hare; [illegible] The Deathshead Vampire; Ghost Keeper; Ghost Ship (1952); The Ghosts of Berkeley Square; House of Mystery (1961); The Man In the Back Seat; A Matter of Choice; The Medium

(1934); Soho Incident; Strongroom; Urge to Kill; The Wind of Change; Wrong Number

Sewell, Vernon (wri, b. 1903): *Ghost Ship (1952); House of Mystery (1961); A Matter of Choice; The Medium (1934)*

Sexton, Gary (act): *WarGames*

Sexton, Ryan (act): *The Toxic Avenger*

Sexton, Sandra (act): *Curse II: The Bite*

Sexton, Tobe (act): *Offerings*

Seyfi, Riza (wri): *Drakula Istanbulda*

Seyler, Athene (act, 1889-1990, nee Athene Hannen): *How to Murder a Rich Uncle; I Thank a Fool; Night of the Demon (1957); The Private Life of Don Juan; The Queen of Spades (1948); The Saint In London; Scrooge (1935); Sensation (1937); Visa to Canton*

Seymour, Anna (act): *Threads*

Seymour, Anne (act, 1909-1988): *Angel On My Shoulder (1980); Blindfold; Chiller; Mirage (1965); Never-Never Land; Trancers*

Seymour, Carolyn (act): *Condor; Congo; Midnight Cabaret; Mistress of Paradise; The Return of the Man from U.N.C.L.E.; The Ruling Class; Yellow Dog; Zorro, The Gay Blade*

Seymour, Charles (act): *The Great Anarchist Mystery*

Seymour, Dan (act, 1915-1982): *Abbott and Costello Meet the Mummy; Beyond a Reasonable Doubt; Escape to Witch Mountain (1975); Intrigue (1947); Key Largo; Philo Vance's Gamble; Return of the Fly; Second Chance; Undersea Girl (1958); Watusi*

Seymour, Dorin (act): *Eraser; The Oracle (1985)*

Seymour, Henry (wri): *Craze*

Seymour, James (wri): *The Ghosts of Berkeley Square; The Saint Meets the Tiger*

Seymour, Jane (act, b. 1951, nee Jane Frankenberg): *Are You Lonesome Tonight?; Battlestar Galactica; Dark Mirror (1984); Frankenstein: The True Story; The Haunting Passion; Jamaica Inn (1985); Live and Let Die; Oh Heavenly Dog; Phantom of the Opera (1983); Praying Mantis; Quest for Camelot; The Scarlet Pimpernel (1982); Sinbad and the Eye of the Tiger; Somewhere In Time; Sunstroke*

Seymour, Jeff (act, dir & wri): *Rave Review*

Seymour, Madeleine (act): *The House of Peril; No Escape (1934)*

Seymour, Ralph (act): *Ghoulies; Just Before Dawn (1980); Killer Party; The Relic*

Seymour, Sheldon (act): *Monster A Go-Go*

Seymour, Sheldon (mus): see Lewis, Herschell Gordon

Seymour, Susan (act): *Wild Thing*

Seyn, Seyna (act): *Giulietta degli Spiriti*

Seyrig, Delphine (act, 1932-1990): *L'Annee Derniere a Marienbad; The Black Windmill; Daughters of Darkness; The Discreet Charm of the Bourgeoisie; Mister Freedom; Peau d'Ane*

Seyrig, Francis (mus): *L'Annee Derniere a Marienbad*

Sferrazza, Mark (act): *Street Trash*

Sfinnias, Yanni (act): *Vampire's Kiss*

Sgarro, Nicholas (dir): *The Man With the Power*

Sguassro, Carlo (act): *Funeral Home*

Shackelford, Dan (act): *Deadly Blessing*

Shackelford, Ted (act, b. 1947): *Dying to Remember; The Spider and the Fly (1994)*

Shackleton, Michael (dir): *Survivor (1987)*

Shacklock, Harry (act): *The Fast Kill*

Shadix, Glenn (act): *Beetlejuice; Demolition Man; Heathers; Meet the Applegates; Nightlife (1989, USA-Mex); The Nightmare Before Christmas; Sleepwalkers*

Shadow (mus): *New Year's Evil*

Shadow, John (wri): *Pieces*

Shadows, The (mus): *The Boys*

Shadyac, Tom (dir & wri): *Liar Liar; The Nutty Professor (1996)*

Shaefer, A. (wri): *Radio Ranch*

Shaefer, Steve (act): *Fargo*

Shaeffer, David (act): *Mission: Impossible*

Shaeffer, Karl (act): *Killer Klowns from Outer Space*

Shaenwise, Lenore (act): *The Brotherhood of Satan*

Shafer, Bobby Ray (act): *Psycho Cop 2*

Shafer, Robert (act): *Damn Yankees*

Shaff, Edmund L. (act): *Ed Wood*

Shaffer, Anthony (wri): *Absolution; Death on the Nile; Evil Under the Sun; Frenzy; Sleuth; Whodunit; The Wicker Man*

Shaffer, Marie (act): *Jane Eyre (1921)*

Shaffer, Paul (act): *Hercules (1997); Light Years*

Shaffer, Todd (act): *Friday the 13th, Part VIII-Jason Takes Manhattan*

Shafto, Robert (act): *Sabu and the Magic Ring*

Shagan, Steve (wri): *The Formula; Nightwing; Primal Fear*

Shah, Dhiru (act): *Watchers II*

Shah, Kiran (act): *Jekyll and Hyde; Legend; The People That Time Forgot; Raiders of the Lost Ark*

Shah, Krishna (dir): *Hard Rock Zombies*

Shaheen, Frank (act): *The Offspring*

Shaheen, Nancy (act): *The Offspring*

Shail, Gary (act): *Jekyll and Hyde; Shock Treatment! (1981)*

Shaiman, Marc (act): *Heart and Souls*

Shaiman, Marc (mus): *The Addams Family; Addams Family Values; Bogus; Heart and Souls; Misery*

Shain, Harvey (act): *Planet of Dinosaurs*

Shairp, Mordaunt (wri): *The Crime at Blossoms; Dark Secret*

Shakar, Martin (act): *The Children*

Shakespeare, John (mus): *Killer's Moon; The Sexplorer*

Shakespeare, William (wri, 1564-1616): *The Boys from Syracuse; Le Duel d'Hamlet; Forbidden Planet; Hamlet (1907, 1912, 1913, 1914, 1915, 1920, 1948, 1960, 1964, 1969, 1990 & 1996); Johnny Hamlet; Korol Lir; King Lear (1970 & 1987); Macbeth (1909, 1911, 1916, 1922, 1947 & 1971); A Midsummer Night's Dream (1935, 1959, 1985 & 1999); Prospero's Books; Ran; Richard III (1908, 1911, 1955 & 1995); Shakespeare's Tragedy, King Lear; Strange Illusion; The Tempest (1905, 1908, 1980 & 1998); Tromeo and Juliet*

Shakoor, Jill (act): *Barracuda*

Shakti (act): *The Golden Child*

Shakurov, Sergei (act): *Parad Planyet*

Shale, Kerry (act): *Little Shop of Horrors (1986)*

Shalet, Diane (act): *Do Not Fold, Spindle or Mutilate*

Shalhoub, Tony (act): *Addams Family Values*

Shalikar, Daniel (act): *Honey, I Blew Up the Kid*

Shalikar, Joshua (act): *Honey, I Blew Up the Kid*

Shalita, Nelson (act): *Congo*

Shallo, Karen (act): *Hello Again; Mortal Thoughts*

Shalom, Rainbow (act): *Once Bitten*

Shalroub, Maechel (act): see Sharif, Omar

Shamata, Charles/Chuck (act): *Change of Mind; The Devil and Max Devlin; Escape Clause; The House by the Lake; Scanners; Starcrossed; Stone Cold Dead; Welcome to Blood City*

Shamroy, Leon (cin, 1901-1974): *The Adventures of Sherlock Holmes (1939); The Black Swan; Desk Set; The Glass-Bottom Boat; The Great Gambini; Leave Her to Heaven; Planet of the Apes; Snow White and the Three Stooges*

Shamshak, Sam (act): *To All a Goodnight*

Shamsi, Mohammed (act): *The Man Who Would Be King*

Shan, Rezza (act): *They Live*

Shand, Ian (dir): *Kadoyng*

Shandel, Pia (act): *Shadow of the Hawk*

Shandling, Garry (act): *Dr. Dolittle (1998)*

Shandor (act): *One Dark Night*

Shane (act): *The Arrival (1996)*

Shane, Gene (act): *The Velvet Vampire*

Shane, Maxwell (dir, b. 1905-1983): *Fear In the Night (1947); Nightmare (1956)*

Shane, Maxwell (wri, b. 1905-1983): *Fear In the Night (1947); The Mummy's Hand; Nightmare (1956); One Body Too Many*

Shane, Sara (act): *Sign of the Pagan; Tarzan's Greatest Adventure; Three Bad Sisters*

Shane, Tamara (act): *Mr. Arkadin*

Shaner, John (act): *A Bucket of Blood (1959); The Darker Side of Terror; The Little Shop of Horrors (1960)*

Shaner, John Herman (wri): *The Darker Side of Terror; The Island of Dr. Moreau (1977)*

Shaner, Madeleine (act): *The Darker Side of Terror*

Shaner, Michael (act): *Crime Zone; Purgatory*

Shank, Gregg (act): *The Day Mars Invaded Earth*

Shankar, Ravi (act, b. 1920): *Chappaqua*

Shankar, Ravi (mus, b. 1920): *Chappaqua; Charly; Paras Pathar*

Shankel, Philip (act): *Zombies of Mora Tau*

Shankley, Amelia (act): *Dreamchild*

Shanklin, Douglas Alan (act): *Star Trek III: The Search for Spock*

Shanklin, Ray (mus): *Heavy Traffic*

Shanks, Don (act): *Sweet Sixteen*

Shanley, Debi (act): *Delirium*

Shanley, John Patrick (wri): *Congo; We're Back! A Dinosaur's Story*

Shanley, Kenneth (act): *Koroshi*

Shanne, Peter (act): *Short Circuit 2*

Shannon, Al (act): *The Drifter*

Shannon, Frank (act): *The Adventurous Blonde; Blondes at Work; The Deadly Ray from Mars; Mars Attacks the World; Peril from the Planet Mongo; Purple Death from Outer Space; Spaceship to the Unknown; Torchy Blane In Chinatown; Torchy Blane In Panama; Torchy Gets Her Man; Torchy Plays With Dynamite; Torchy Runs for Mayor*

Shannon, Frank (dir): *The Invincible Barbarian*

Shannon, Glenn (act): *Midnight (1980)*

Shannon, Harry (act, 1890-1964): *The Falcon Takes Over; The Lady from Shanghai; The Mummy's Ghost; The Red House; The Saint In Palm Springs; The Scarf; Where Danger Lives; Witness to Murder*

Shannon, Jamie (act): *Millennium*

Shannon, Johnny (act): *Performance*

Shannon, Michael/Mike J./Jay (act): *Assassin (1973); Future Cop; Little Shop of Horrors (1986); Murder by Moonlight; Never-Never Land; Superman II*

Shannon, Molly (act): *The Phantom of the Opera (1989)*

Shannon, Noel (act): *The Girl In the Flat*

Shannon, Peggy (act, 1907-1941): *Deluge*

Shannon, Richard (act): *Houdini (1953); The Space Children*

Shannon, Robert T. (wri): *Unknown Island*

Shannon, Russell (act): *The Darker Side of Terror*

Shaoul, Jack (dir & wri): *Robot In the Family*

Shapcott, Megan (act): *Howling III*

Shaphren, Brent (act): *The Fugitive (1993); Poltergeist III*

Shapiro, Alan (dir): *The Crush*

Shapiro, Barry (act): *The Toxic Avenger*

Shapiro, Beverly (act): *Bloodeaters; Toxic Zombies*

Shapiro, David (mus): *Hell Comes to Frogtown*

Shapiro, Elisha (act): *Waxwork II: Lost In Time*

Shapiro, Harold (act): *Beverly Hills Bodysnatchers*

Shapiro, J. David (wri): *Robin Hood: Men In Tights*

Shapiro, Jodi (act): *Surf Nazis Must Die*

Shapiro, Josif (dir): *The Sleeping Beauty (1965, Russ)*

Shapiro, Ken (dir & wri, b. 1943): *Modern Problems*

Shapiro, Michael (dir): *Max Q: Emergency Landing*

Shapiro, Paul (dir): *Heads; What We Did That Night*

Shapiro, Ron (act): *Attack of the Killer Tomatoes*

Shapiro, Stanley (wri): *Running Against Time*

Shapiro, Susan (dir): *Rapunzel Let Down Your Hair*

Shapiro, Ted (mus): *Bloodeaters; Toxic Zombies*

Shaps, Cyril (act): *Avalanche Express; Erik the Viking; The Kremlin Letter; Passport to Shame; The Pursuers; Return of a Stranger (1962); The Spaceman and King Arthur; The Spy Who Loved Me; Tennis Court*

Shari, Bonnie (act): *The Brain That Wouldn't Die*

Sharian, John (act): *Death Machine*

Sharif, Marcia (act): *Zombies Lake*

Sharif, Omar (act, b. 1933, nee Maechel Shalroub): *The Burglars; C'era una Volta; Eaters of the Dead; Gulliver's Travels (1996); Mackenna's Gold; The Mysterious Island of Captain Nemo; The Night of the Generals; Oh Heavenly Dog; S*H*E (1980); Top Secret! (1984)*

Shark, David (act): *Soultaker*

Sharkey, Billy Ray (act): *After Midnight; WarGames*

Sharkey, Joe (act): *Picking Up the Pieces*

Sharkey, Ray (act, 1953-1993): *Hellhole; The Rain Killer*

Sharland, Gus (act): *Forging Ahead*

Sharma, Madhau (act): *The Awakening*

Sharma, Romesh (act): *Siddhartha*

Sharman, James/Jim (dir & wri): *The Rocky Horror Picture Show; Shock Treatment! (1981)*

Sharman, Jane (act): *Talk of the Devil*

Sharman, Maisie (wri): *Death Goes to School*

Sharon, Bo (act): *The Puppet Masters*

Sharon, William (act): *Experiment In Terror*

Sharp, Alan (wri): *Damnation Alley; Night Moves*

Sharp, Anne (act): *Blind Spot (1958); The Trollenberg Terror*

Sharp, Anthony (act): *A Clockwork Orange; The Clue of the Silver Key; Die Screaming, Marianne; House of Mortal Sin; Invasion (1965); Never Say Never Again; No Blade of Grass; One of Our Dinosaurs Is Missing*

Sharp, Danielle (act): *Howling III*

Sharp, Don (dir, b. 1922): *The Adventures of Hal 5; Bear Island; The Brides of Fu Manchu; Curse of the Fly; Dark Places; The Devil-Ship Pirates; The Face of Fu Manchu; Guardian of the Abyss; Kiss of the Vampire; Our Man In Marrakesh; The Professionals; Psychomania (1972); Puppet On a Chain; Rasputin, the Mad Monk; Secrets of the Phantom Caverns; Taste of Excitement; The 39 Steps (1978); Those Fantastic Flying Fools; Witchcraft (1964)*

Sharp, Don (wri, b. 1922): *The Adventures of Hal 5; Bear Island; Child's Play (1954); Puppet On a Chain; Taste of Excitement*

Sharp, Henry (cin): *Alice In Wonderland (1933); The Black Pirate; Don Q, Son of Zorro; The Iron Mask; Lorna Doone (1922); The Man In Half Moon Street; Ministry of Fear; The Mysterious Doctor; Woman Who Came Back*

Sharp, Ian (dir): *The Corsican Brothers (1985)*

Sharp, John (act): *—And Now the Screaming Starts!; The Bride (1985); A Christmas Carol (1984); The Fiendish Plot of Dr. Fu Manchu; The Golden Rabbit; The Savage Curse; Top Secret! (1984); The Wicker Man*

Sharp, John Gerrard (wri): *The Runaway (1964)*

Sharp, Jon (act): *Covenant*

Sharp, Leonard (act): *The Hangman Waits; The Lady Killers (1956); Maria Marten: or, The Murder In the Red Barn (1935)*

Sharp, Margery (wri): *The Rescuers; The Rescuers Down Under*

Sharp, Marie (act): *Cafe Flesh*

Sharp, Nikki (act): *The Little Match Girl (1987)*

Sharp, Rachel (act): *Teen Wolf Too*

Sharp, Richard D. (act): *Mission: Impossible*

Sharp, Sandra (act): *Are You In the House Alone?*

Sharp, Sara Jennifer (act): *The Hand That Rocks Cradle*

Sharp, Ted (act): *Just Imagine*

Sharp, Thom J. (act): *Body Heat; Repossessed*

Sharpe, Albert (act): *Darby O'Gill and the Little People; Portrait of Jennie; The Return of October; You Never Can Tell*

Sharpe, Alex (act): *Please Murder Me*

Sharpe, Anthony (act): *A Clockwork Orange; Gawain and the Green Knight*

Sharpe, Bernard (act): *Otley*

Sharpe, Cornelia (act): *The Reincarnation of Peter Proud; S*H*E (1980); Venom (1982)*

Sharpe, David/Dave (act): *Desert Legion; Dick Tracy Returns; The Falcon's Adventure; The Veils of Bagdad*

Sharpe, Edith (act): *Cash On Demand; Cloudburst*

Sharpe, Karen (act): *The Jungle Girl*

Sharpe, Lester (act): *Amazon Quest; The Flying Saucer (1950); The Mummy's Ghost; The Strange Death of Adolf Hitler; Time to Kill (1942)*

Sharpe, Richard (act): *Lifeforce*

Sharples, Dick (wri): *The Golden Rabbit*

Sharpsteen, Ben (dir): *Dumbo; Fantasia; Pinocchio (1940)*

Sharrett, Michael (act): *Deadly Friend*

Sharvell-Martin, Michael (act): *Frightmare (1974); Kadoyng*

Shas, Krishna (dir & wri): *Hard Rock Zombies*

Shatner, Melanie (act): *Bloodstone: Subspecies II; Cthulhu Mansion; The First Power; Star Trek V: The Final Frontier; Syngenor*

Shatner, William (act, b. 1931): *The Babysitter; Bill & Ted's Bogus Journey; Dead Man's Island; The Devil's Rain; The Horror at 37,000 Feet; The Hound Of The Baskervilles (1972); Impulse! (1974); Incubus (1965); The Kidnapping of the President; Kingdom of the Spiders; The People; Prisoner of Zenda, Inc.; Sole Survivor (1970); Star Trek; Star Trek II: The Wrath of Khan; Star Trek III: The Search for Spock; Star Trek IV: The Voyage Home; Star Trek V: The Final Frontier; Star Trek VI: The Undiscovered Country; Star Trek: Generations; TekWar; Visiting Hours*

Shatner, William (dir & wri, b. 1931): *Star Trek V: The Final Frontier*

Shattuck, Shari (act): *Arena (1989); Desert Warrior; The Goddess of Love; Naked Cage; The Spring; Uninvited (1987)*

Shatynski, Steve (act): *Always*

Shaughnessy, Alfred (dir): *Cat Girl; The Impersonator; Suspended Alibi*

Shaughnessy, Alfred (wri): *Crescendo; The Flesh and Blood Show; The Hostage (1956); The Impersonator; Tiffany Jones*

Shaughnessy, Mickey (act, 1920-1985): *The Burglar; Conquest of Space; Primal Scream; Sex Kittens Go to College*

Shavelson, Melville (dir, b. 1917): *The Great Houdinis*

Shaver, Helen (act): *The Amityville Horror; The Believers; The Craft; The Land Before Time;*

Starship Invasions; Tree of Hands; Tremors II: Aftershocks
Shaw, Adriana (act): Altered States; The Tribe
Shaw, Al (act): The Gracie Allen Murder Case
Shaw, Alona (act): Cyborg Cop
Shaw, Anabel (act): Bulldog Drummond Strikes Back (1947); Killer at Large; Secret Beyond the Door; Shock (1946)
Shaw, Andrew (act): Dead Connection
Shaw, Andy (act): Primal Fear
Shaw, Anthony (GB act): How to Murder a Rich Uncle
Shaw, Anthony (USA act): He Knows You're Alone
Shaw, Barbara (act): No Haunt for a Gentleman
Shaw, Barnaby (act): Vampire Circus
Shaw, Barnett (act): Mars Needs Women
Shaw, Beatrice (act): The Quatermass Conclusion
Shaw, Bill (act): Ghostriders
Shaw, Bob (act): Time After Time
Shaw, Bobbi (act): The Ghost In the Invisible Bikini; How to Stuff a Wild Bikini; Pajama Party; Sergeant Deadhead the Astronut!
Shaw, C. Montague (act): Destination Saturn; Dick Tracy vs. Crime, Inc.; Dr. Satan's Robot; Mr. Moto's Last Warning; Sherlock Holmes (1932)
Shaw, Charles K. (wri): Death Is a Number
Shaw, Chris (act & dir): Split (1990)
Shaw, Christine (act): Clue of the Twisted Candle
Shaw, Crystal (act): The Alien Within; Hard Rock Zombies; Laser Moon
Shaw, Curtis (act): Trancers II: The Return of Jack Deth
Shaw, David (wri): The Man Inside; Take One False Step
Shaw, Denis (act): The Candlelight Murder; The Curse of the Werewolf; The Great Van Robbery; House of Blackmail; Innocent Meeting; Jack the Ripper (1958); Links of Justice; Moment of Indiscretion; The Mummy (1959); No Safety Ahead; Passport to Shame; The Pirates of Blood River; Seven Thunders; The Viking; A Wpman Possessed; The Viking Queen; Who Done It? (1956)
Shaw, Elizabeth Lloyd (act): Fire and Ice
Shaw, Ellen (act): Space Master X-7
Shaw, Fiona (act): The Avengers; Jane Eyre (1996); Super Mario Bros.
Shaw, Francis (mus): Paint Me a Murder
Shaw, Fred (act): Beyond the Poseidon Adventure
Shaw, George Bernard (wri, 1856-1950): Androcles and the Lion
Shaw, George Newman (mus): Kidnapped Co-Ed
Shaw, Harold (dir): The Ashes of Revenge; A Christmas Carol (1914); The Firm of Girdlestone; A Garret In Bohemia; The King's Minister; The Ring and the Rajah; Trilby (1914); The Two Roads
Shaw, Harold (wri): A Christmas Carol (1914)
Shaw, Helen (act): Twilight Zone; Wicked Stepmother
Shaw, Henry G. (act): The Call of the Drum
Shaw, Ian (mus): Warrior Queen
Shaw, Irwin (wri, 1913-1984): Out of the Fog (1941); Take One False Step; Ulysses
Shaw, Jack (act): Dick Barton, Special Agent
Shaw, Jackie (act): Offerings
Shaw, James (act): The Wiz
Shaw, Janet (act): The Adventures of Robin Hood; Dark Alibi; Prehistoric Women (1950); The Scarlet Clue; Shadow of a Doubt (1943); Torchy Blane In Chinatown
Shaw, Jenifer (act): The Hound of the Baskervilles (1972)
Shaw, Joseph (act): The Brood; Change of Mind
Shaw, Julie (act): The Big Switch
Shaw, Kris (act): House of Secrets (1993)
Shaw, Larry (dir): Donor; Don't Look Down; Robin Cook's 'Mortal Fear'; The Uninvited (1996)
Shaw, Lewis (act): Flat No. 3; Strange Evidence
Shaw, Lou (wri): The Bat People; Crypt of the Living Dead
Shaw, Martha (act): WarGames
Shaw, Martin (act): The Golden Voyage of Sinbad; Macbeth (1971); The Scarlet Pimpernel (1999)
Shaw, Mary Ellen (act): Phantasm
Shaw, Maxwell (act): The Man Inside; The Oblong Box
Shaw, Michael (act): Number Six; The Strangers
Shaw, Montague (act): Behind That Curtain; Charlie Chan In London; Charlie Chan's Murder Cruise
Shaw, Natalie (act): Summer of Fear
Shaw, Paula (act): Communion
Shaw, Philip (wri): Tarzana, the Wild Girl
Shaw, Reta (act): Escape to Witch Mountain (1975); The Ghost and Mr. Chicken; Mary Poppins
Shaw, Richard (act): Compelled; First Man Into Space; Hidden Homicide; The Hour of 13; The Man Who Couldn't Walk; Partners In Crime (1961)
Shaw, Robert (act, 1928-1978): Avalanche Express; Black Sunday (1977); The Deep; From Russia With Love; Jaws; The Lavender Hill Mob; A Reflection of Fear; Robin and Marian; Tomorrow at Ten
Shaw, Roderick (act): Vampire Circus
Shaw, Roland (mus): The Secret of My Success; Straight on Till Morning
Shaw, Sebastian (act, b. 1905): Bulldog Sees It Through; East of Piccadilly; It Happened Here; Return of the Jedi; The Spy In Black; The Squeaker (1937); Three Silent Men
Shaw, Stan (act): Cutthroat Island; Daylight; Fear (1990); Lifepod; The Monster Squad; Runaway (1984)
Shaw, Steve (act): Child of Glass; Howling III; The Zero Boys
Shaw, Steve(n) (cin): Pandora's Clock; The Stepford Children; Visions of Murder; The Zero Boys
Shaw, Susan (act, 1929-1978, nee Patsy Sloots): Blonde Blackmailer; Chain of Events; The Diplomatic Corpse; Fire Maidens of Outer Space; Pool of London; Sitting Target; The Time Is My Enemy; Wall of Death (1952); The Woman In Question
Shaw, Tina (act): The Lair of the White Worm
Shaw, Tom (act): Twinkle, Twinkle, Killer Kane
Shaw, Vanessa (act): Horror Hospital
Shaw, Victoria (act, b. 1935, nee Jeanette Elphick): I Aim at the Stars; To Trap a Spy; Westworld
Shaw, Vinessa (act): Hocus Pocus
Shaw, Winifred (act, b. 1910): The Gift of Gab; Satan Met a Lady; Smart Blonde
Shawlee, Joan (act, b. 1929): Bowery to Bagdad; Conquest of Space; Dead Men Tell No Tales (1971); Francis Joins the WACs; House of Horrors (1946); Prehistoric Women (1950); The Reluctant Astronaut; The St. Valentine's Day Massacre; Willard
Shawn, Dick (act, 1929-1987, nee Richard Schulefand): Love at First Bite; Maid to Order; Way...Way Out; The Wizard of Baghdad
Shawn, Eric (act): Gremlins 2: The New Batch
Shawn, Shirley (act): The Lost Missile
Shawn, Wallace (act, b. 1943): The Magic Bubble; Mom and Dad Save the World; My Favorite Martian; Nice Girls Don't Explode; The Princess Bride; Simon; Strange Invaders; Toy Story
Shay, Diane (act): Dr. Tarr's Torture Dungeon
Shay, John (act): The Missing Corpse; The Shanghai Chest
Shay, Mildred (act): Little Shop of Horrors (1986)
Shay, William E. (act): The Lone Wolf (1917)
Shaye, Lin (act): Critters; Critters 2: The Main Course; The Hidden; Jekyll and Hyde...Together Again; The Nature of the Beast; A Nightmare On Elm Street; Slam Dance; Wes Craven's New Nightmare
Shaye, Robert (act): Wes Craven's New Nightmare
Shayne, Arnie (act): Red Alert
Shayne, Bob (wri): The Return of Sherlock Holmes (1986)
Shayne, Edith (act): Buried Treasure
Shayne, Konstantin (act): Escape In the Fog; The Falcon In Hollywood; Five Graves to Cairo; Vertigo
Shayne, Linda (act): Humanoids from the Deep; The Lost Empire; Purple People Eater
Shayne, Robert (act, 1900-1992, nee Robert Shaen Dawe): The Barefoot Executive; Behind the Mask (1946); Eyes of the Jungle; The Face of Marble; The Giant Claw; How to Make a Monster; Indestructible Man; Jungle Captive; Kronos (1957); The Neanderthal Man; Spook Chasers; Teenage Cave Man; The Threat (1949); Three Strangers; Tobor the Great; War of the Satellites
Shayne, Ruell (act): The Giant Claw
Shayne, Sharon (act): Blood Bath (1975)
Shayne, Tamara (act, 1923-1983): The Snake Pit (1948)
She, Elizabeth (act): Howling V: The Rebirth; The Howling: New Moon Rising
Shea, Eric (act): The Poseidon Adventure
Shea, Gloria (act): The Last Days of Pompeii (1935)
Shea, Jack (act): A Nightmare On Elm Street; A Nightmare On Elm Street 3: Dream Warriors; Satan's Satellites
Shea, Jack (dir): The Monitors
Shea, James K. (dir): Planet of Dinosaurs
Shea, Joe (act): Pandemonium
Shea, Joey (act): We're Back! A Dinosaur's Story
Shea, John (act, b. 1954): Freejack; Honey, I Blew Up the Kid; Light Years; Notorious (1992)
Shea, Karin Mary (act): Time After Time
Shea, Mike (cin): The Horrible House On the Hill
Shea, Robert (act): Lord of the Flies (1990)
Shea, Tom (act): Friday the 13th-Part 2; Somewhere Tomorrow
Shean, Darcy (act): Cocoon: The Return; Don't Go In the House
Shear, Barry (dir, 1920-1979): Ellery Queen: Don't Look Behind You; The Karate Killers; Night Gallery; Short Walk to Daylight; The Todd Killings; Wild In the Streets
Shear, Barry (wri, 1920-1979): Madame Sin
Shear, Melissa (act): Repossessed
Shear, Pearl (act): Doctor Mordrid
Shear, Rhonda (act): Galaxina
Sheard, Michael (act): The Empire Strikes Back
Shearer, Harry (act, b. 1943): Blood and Concrete; Godzilla (1998); My Stepmother Is an Alien
Shearer, Jack (act): Visions of Murder
Shearer, Johnetta (act): Copycat
Shearer, Moira (act, b. 1926): Peeping Tom
Shearer, Norma (act, 1904-1983): He Who Gets Slapped; Marie Antoinette (1938); The Tower of Lies
Shearin, John (act): Alfred Hitchcock Presents
Shearing, Joseph (wri): The Mark of Cain
Shearman, Alan (act): Vice Versa (1988)
Shearman, Roger (cin): A Force of One
Shearmur, Ed(ward) (mus): Demon Knight; The Hunchback (1997); Species II
Shebbeare, Norma (act): 10 Rillington Place
Shebuyeva, Y. (act): Pikovaya Dama (1916)
Sheckley, Robert (wri, b. 1928): Condorman; La Decima Vittima; Freejack
Sheean, Vincent (wri): Foreign Correspondent
Sheedy, Ally (act, b. 1962): Buried Alive II; Deadly Lessons; Fear (1990); The Fury Within; The Haunting of Seacliff Inn; Maid to Order; Man's Best Friend; Short Circuit; WarGames
Sheehan, Gladys (act): Rawhead Rex
Sheehan, John (act): Kismet (1930); Smart Blonde; Torchy Plays With Dynamite
Sheehan, Michael (act): The Swarm
Sheehan, Percy Poore (wri): The Hunchback of Notre Dame (1923); The Lost City
Sheehy, Allison (act): Invader
Sheekman, Arthur (wri, b. 1901): Dream Girl; Roman Scandals
Sheeler, Mark (act, b. 1923): From Hell It Came
Sheen, Al (act): The Blue Bird (1940)
Sheen, Charlie (act, b. 1965): The Arrival (1996); Red Dawn; Shadow Conspiracy; The Three Musketeers (1993); The Wraith
Sheen, David (act): The Disappearance of Nora
Sheen, Martin (act, b. 1940, nee Ramon Estevez): The Believers; Beyond the Stars; The Dead Zone; The Final Countdown; Firestarter; Grey Knight; The Little Girl Who Lives Down the Lane; Loophole; Project: Alf; Pursuit (1972); Rage; River of Souls; Roswell; Shadow Conspiracy; Spawn; Voyage of Terror; When the Bough Breaks
Sheen, Michael (act): Mary Reilly
Sheen, Ruth (act): The Young Poisoner's Handbook
Sheen, Simon (wri): The Adventures of Galgameth
Sheers, Susan (act): Tiffany Jones
Sheff, Stanley (act): Waxwork II: Lost In Time
Sheffer, Craig (act, b. 1960): Bloodknot; Eye of the Storm; Fire In the Sky (1993); The Grave; Nightbreed; Road Flower; The Road Killers; Voyage of the Rock Aliens
Sheffield, Billy (act): The Boy With Green Hair
Sheffield, David (wri): The Nutty Professor (1996)
Sheffield, Johnny (act, b. 1931): African Treasure; Bomba and the Elephant Stampede; Bomba and the Hidden City; Bomba, the Jungle Boy; The Golden Idol; The Jungle Girl; Killer Leopard; The Lion Hunters; Lord of the Jungle; The Lost Volcano; Panther Island; Safari Drums; Tarzan and the Amazons; Tarzan and the Huntress; Tarzan and the Leopard Woman; Tarzan Finds a Son!; Tarzan's Desert Mystery; Tarzan's New York Adventure; [illegible] Triumphs
Sheffield, Raye (act): The Darker Side of Terror; Final Eye
Sheffield, Reginald (act, 1901-1957): The Adventures of Robin Hood; Charlie Chan In London; Devotion; Eyes In the Night; Second Chance; The Story of Mankind; Three Strangers; 23 Paces to Baker Street
Sheffler, Marc (act): The Last House On the Left
Shefter, Bert (mus, b. 1904): Curse of the Fly; Ghost Diver; Kronos (1957); Motor Psycho; Return of the Fly; She-Devil (1957); Voyage to the Bottom of the Sea
Sheil, Ruth (act): The Mirror and Markheim
Sheiner, David (act): The Darker Side of Terror; One Spy Too Many
Shekles, Gail (act): see Stevens, Craig
Shelby, Nicole (act): Terror In the Wax Museum
Shelden, Jana (act): The Sender
Sheldon, Caroline (act): The Damned
Sheldon, David (wri): Grizzly
Sheldon, Gene (act): Babes In Toyland (1961); The Sign of Zorro (1960)
Sheldon, Jack (act): Freaky Friday (1976)
Sheldon, Jana (act): The Shining
Sheldon, Lorell (act): The Missing Corpse
Sheldon, Louis (act): Blind Date
Sheldon, Lynette (act): The Incredible Torture Show
Sheldon, Nancy (act): The Mummy and the Curse of the Jackals
Sheldon, Sidney (wri, b. 1917): I Dream of Jeannie: Fifteen Years Later; I Still Dream of Jeannie
Sheldon, Suzanne (act): Kismet (1914)
Sheldon, Valerie (act): Berserker
Sheldon, Walter J. (wri): The Manster
Shelford, Tom (act): The Adventures of Dick Turpin-200 Guineas Reward, Dead or Alive
Shell, Ray (act): The McGuffin
Shell, Tom (act): Dinosaur Island (1994); Surf Nazis Must Die; Teenage Exorcist; The Zero Boys
Shellabarger, Kalei (act): The Invisible Maniac
Shellen, Stephen (act): Amazons (1984); American Gothic; Dr. Jekyll and Ms. Hyde; The Stepfather; Still Life
Shelley, Adrienne (act): Road Flower
Shelley, Barbara (act, b. 1937): Blind Corner; Blood of the Vampire; Bobbikins; The Camp On Blood Island; Cat Girl; The Dark Angel (1991); Deadly Record; Death Trap (1962); Dracula, Prince of Darkness; End of the Line; Ghost Story (1975); The Gorgon; Maigret; Man In the Dark (1965); Murder at Site Three; Quatermass and the Pit; Rasputin, the Mad Monk; The Secret of Blood Island; The Shadow of the Cat; The Solitary Child; The Village of the Damned (1960)
Shelley, Carole (act): The Aristocats; Robin Hood (1973)
Shelley, Dave (act): Code Name: Minus One
Shelley, George (act): Forty Naughty Girls
Shelley, Joshua (dir): The Perils of Pauline
Shelley, Mary W. (wri, 1797-1851): The Bride (1985); Bride of Frankenstein; The Curse of Frankenstein; Doctor Franken; Frankenstein (1910, 1931, 1973, 1974, 1984 & 1993); Frankenstein: The True Story; Horror of Frankenstein; Life Without Soul; Mary Shelley's 'Frankenstein;' Roger Corman's 'Frankenstein Unbound;' Terror of Frankenstein
Shelley, Norman (act): Death In the Hand; Gulliver's Travels (1977); The Man Without a Body; Otley; They Came to a City
Shelley, Paul (act): Macbeth (1971)
Shelley, Robert (cin): The Visitor
Shelly, Adrienne (act): Hexed; The Road Killers
Shelly, John (act): Anguish
Shelton, Abigail (act): Human Feelings
Shelton, Anne (act): King Arthur Was a Gentleman
Shelton, Charles F. (wri): Deadtime Stories
Shelton, Deborah (act): Blind Vision; Blood Tide; Body Double; Hunk; Mysterious Island of Beautiful Women; Perfect Victims; Plughead Rewired: Circuitry Man II; Nemesis; Silk Degrees
Shelton, Don (act): Invasion of the Saucer Men; Mystery Street; Them! (1954)
Shelton, John (act, 1917-1972): A-Haunting We Will Go; The Time of Their Lives; Whispering Ghosts
Shelton, Marc P. (act): The Relic
Shelton, Marla (act): The Lone Wolf Meets a Lady
Shelton, Marley (act): Warriors of Virtue
Shelton, Sloane (act): All That Jazz; Orpheus Descending
Shelton, Toby (dir): The Return of Jafar
Shelton, Thomas (act): Shadow Conspiracy
Shelton, William R. (wri): Stowaway to the Moon
Shelyne, Carole (act): Dark August

Shemanski, Anita (act): *Anguish*
Shemayme, John A. (act): *Prophecy* (1979)
Shemayme, Steve (act): *Prophecy* (1979)
Shen, Chan (act): *Legend of the Seven Golden Vampires*
Shenar, Paul (act): *Code Name: Minus One; Dark Mansions; Dream Lover; The Night That Panicked America*
Shendal, Margaret (act): *The Supernaturals*
Shenderey, Dee (act): *Burke and Hare*
Shendrikova, Valentina (act): *Korol Lir*
Shendt (act): *Vampire at Midnight*
Sheng, Lu (act): *Infra-Man*
Shengold, Nina (wri): *Earth Angel*
Shenkman, Ben (act): *Eraser*
Shenna, Leila (act): *Moonraker*
Shenton, Thomas (act): *The Tell-Tale Heart* (1934)
Shep (animal act): *Follow the Hunter*
Shepard, Court (act): *Space Master X-7*
Shepard, Elaine (act): *Darkest Africa; The Falcon In Danger*
Shepard, Hilary (act): *Peacemaker* (1990); *Scanner Cop; Turbo: A Power Rangers Movie*
Shepard, Jan (act): *Attack of the Giant Leeches*
Shepard, Jewel (act): *Caged Heat II: Stripped of Freedom; The Return of the Living Dead* (1985); *Scanners: The Showdown*
Shepard, Linda (act): *Flesh Gordon*
Shepard, Patty (act): *La Noche de Walpurgis; El Retorno de la Walpurgis; Witches' Mountain*
Shepard, Richard (act): *Simon, King of the Witches*
Shepard, Richmond (act): *Vampire at Midnight*
Shepard, Sam (act, b. 1943): *Purgatory*
Shepard, Shelby (act): *Class of Nuke 'em High, Part 2: Subhumanoid Meltdown*
Shepard, Sonny (act): *The Crater Lake Monster*
Sheperd, Jean (act): *Thunder Rock*
Sheperd, Karen (act): *Cyborg 2: Glass Shadow*
Shephard, William (act): *Death Race 2000; Phantom of the Paradise*
Shepherd, Albert (act): *The Anniversary*
Shepherd, Amanda (act): *Hocus Pocus*
Shepherd, Baby (act): *I Hear You Calling Me*
Shepherd, Barbara B. (act): *The Cradle Will Fall*
Shepherd, Claire (act): *The Girl In a Swing*
Shepherd, Chaz Lamar (act): *The Nutty Professor* (1996)
Shepherd, Cybill (act, b. 1950): *The Alien's Return; Chances Are; The Lady Vanishes* (1979)
Shepherd, Elizabeth (act): *Blind Corner; Damien-Omen II; Double Negative; The Kidnapping of the President; Man In the Dark* (1965); *The Tomb of Ligeia*
Shepherd, Horace (dir): *Death Is a Number; A Tale of Tails*
Shepherd, Jack (act): *No Escape* (1994); *Something to Hide*
Shepherd, Jessica (act): *Fargo*
Shepherd, John (act): *Friday the 13th-Part V: A New Beginning*
Shepherd, Sally (act): *The House of Fear* (1945); *The Snake Pit* (1948); *The Woman In Green*
Shepherd, Suzanne (act): *Jacob's Ladder*
Shepley, Michael (act): *Bella Donna* (1934); *Gideon's Day; Mr. Denning Drives North; Murder On Monday; A Place of One's Own; The Shot In the Dark; Tangled Evidence; The Triumph of Sherlock Holmes*
Shepodd, Jon (act): *Deep Freeze*
Sheppard, Anthony (act): *Mr. Horatio Knibbles*
Sheppard, Anthony (wri): *Talk of the Devil*
Sheppard, Delia (act): *Haunting Fear; Mirror Images; Night Rhythms; Witchcraft 2: The Temptress*
Sheppard, Kim (act): *Trancers*
Sheppard, Morgan (act): *Hawk the Slayer; The Keep; Paint Me a Murder; The Persecution and Assassination of Jean-Paul Marat as Performed by the Inmates of the Asylum of Charenton Under the Direction of the Marquis de Sade*
Sheppard, Patty (act): *Crypt of the Living Dead; Slugs; The Werewolf vs. the Vampire Woman*
Sheppard, Paula (E.) (act): *Alice, Sweet Alice; Liquid Sky*
Sheppard, W. Morgan (act): *Elvira, Mistress of the Dark; Needful Things; Sometimes They Come Back...Again*
Shepperd, John (act): see Strudwick, Shepperd
Sheppo, Nelson G. (act): *The Capture of Bigfoot*
Shepridge, John C. (wri): *Rapture*
Sher, Anthony/Antony (act): *Erik the Viking; Shadey; Superman II; The Young Poisoner's Handbook*
Sher, Jack (dir & wri, 1913-1988): *The Three Worlds of Gulliver*

Sherayko, Peter (act): *Tarzan In Manhattan; Warlock*
Sherbanee, Maurice (act): *Mausoleum; The Six Million Dollar Man*
Sherdeman, Ted (wri, 1910-1987): *Latitude Zero; Them!* (1954)
Shergood, Adrian (act): *Murder Motel*
Sheridan, Ann (act, 1915-1967, nee Clara Lou Sheridan): *Appointment In Honduras; Murder at the Vanities; Mystery House; Woman On the Run*
Sheridan, Bob (wri): *Dinosaur Island* (1994)
Sheridan, Cecil (act): *The Viking Queen*
Sheridan, Clara Lou (act): see Sheridan, Ann
Sheridan, Dani (act): *On Her Majesty's Secret Service; The Sorcerers*
Sheridan, Dinah (act, b. 1920): *Dark Secret; The Hills of Donegal; The Mirror Crack'd; Murder In Reverse; No Trace; Paul Temple's Triumph; The Sound Barrier*
Sheridan, Frank (act): *One Exciting Night; The Spanish Cape Mystery*
Sheridan, Jamey (act): *The Stand*
Sheridan, Liz (act): *Jekyll and Hyde...Together Again; School Spirit*
Sheridan, Margaret (act): *The Diamond; The Thing from Another World*
Sheridan, Nicolette (act, b. 1963): *Dark Mansions; Dead Man's Folly*
Sheridan, Richard (act): *The Secret of Roan Inish*
Sheridan, Robert (act): *Werewolf of Washington*
Sheridan, Rondell (act): *Deadtime Stories*
Sheridan, Susan (act): *The Black Cauldron*
Sheriff Jr., Sidney (act): *The Brother from Another Planet*
Sherlock, Charles (act): *The Scarlet Clue*
Sherlock, Jay (act): *The Being*
Sherlock, Jerry (wri): *Charlie Chan and the Curse of the Dragon Queen*
Sherman, Alan (act): *Dreamchild*
Sherman, Ann (act): *The Murder Clinic*
Sherman, Arthur (act): *The Punisher*
Sherman, Bob (act): *Haunters of the Deep; Little Shop of Horrors* (1986); *The Spy Who Loved Me*
Sherman, David (wri): *Frankenstein and Me*
Sherman, Editta (act): *Ms. 45*
Sherman, Ellen (act): *Dr. Tarr's Torture Dungeon*
Sherman, Fred (act): *Space Master X-7*
Sherman, Gary (A.) (dir): *Dead and Buried; Deathline; The Mysterious Two; Poltergeist III*
Sherman, Gary (wri): *Deathline; The Mysterious Two; Phobia; Poltergeist III*
Sherman, George (dir, 1908-1991): *The Bandit of Sherwood Forest; Crime Doctor's Courage; The Lady and the Monster; Larceny; Secret of the Whistler; Son of Robin Hood; Spy Hunt; The Veils of Bagdad; The Wizard of Baghdad*
Sherman, Hiram (act): *Oh Dad Poor Dad, Mamma's Hung You In the Closet and I'm Feelin' So Sad*
Sherman, Howard (act): *Day of the Dead*
Sherman, Jan-Michael (wri): *Kiss Meets the Phantom of the Park*
Sherman, John (wri): *Face In the Night; Jackpot*
Sherman, Kerry (act): *Eyes of Fire; Satan's Cheerleaders*
Sherman, Laurie (act): *She* (1983)
Sherman, Lowell (act, 1885-1934): *The Face In the Fog* (1922); *Midnight Mystery*
Sherman, Marianne (act): *Mark of the Devil* (1985)
Sherman, Orville (act): *The Brain Eaters; Pretty Maids All In a Row; Scream of the Wolf; Westworld*
Sherman, Richard M. (mus, b. 1928): *Bedknobs and Broomsticks; Charlotte's Web; Chitty Chitty Bang Bang; Mary Poppins; The Monkey's Uncle; The Slipper and the Rose*
Sherman, Richard M. (wri, b. 1928): *The Slipper and the Rose*
Sherman, Robert (act): *Children Shouldn't Play With Dead Things; Lost Souls* (1998)
Sherman, Robert B. (mus, b. 1925): *Bedknobs and Broomsticks; Charlotte's Web; Chitty Chitty Bang Bang; Mary Poppins; The Monkey's Uncle; The Slipper and the Rose*
Sherman, Robert B. (wri, b. 1925): *The Slipper and the Rose*
Sherman, Samuel M. (dir): *Raiders of the Living Dead*
Sherman, Samuel M. (wri): *Blood of Ghastly Horror; Brain of Blood; Dracula vs. Frankenstein; Raiders of the Living Dead*
Sherman, Stanford (wri): *The Ice Pirates; Krull; The Man Who Wasn't There*
Sherman, Steven (act): *Earthbound* (1981)
Sherman, Vincent (dir, b. 1906): *The Adventures of Don Juan; The Return of Dr. X*

Sherman, Wendy (act): *The Man With Two Brains*
Shermer, Carol (act): *Repossessed*
Shermis, Boyd (cin): *Storm of the Century*
Sherpac, Rose (act): *Anguish*
Sherr, Francis (act): *The Diabolical Invention*
Sherrard, Tudor (act): *Seven*
Sherrier, Julian (act): *The Road to Hong Kong; Stopover Forever*
Sherriff, R.C. (wri, b. 1896): *The Invisible Man* (1933); *Murder On Monday; No Highway In the Sky; The Old Dark House* (1932)
Sherrill, Babbette (act): *Death Curse of Tartu*
Sherrill, David (act): *The Wraith*
Sherrill, Louise (act): *Blood and Lace*
Sherrin, Ned (act): *Orlando*
Sherry, Craighall (act): *Spione*
Sherry, Diane (act): *Pretty Maids All In a Row; Superman* (1978)
Sherry, Edna (wri): *Sudden Fear*
Sherry, Gordon (dir): *Ysani the Priestess*
Sherry, Gordon (wri): *Black Limelight*
Sherry, John B. (wri): *The Beguiled*
Sherwin, Chief (act): *The Being*
Sherwin, Derrick (act): *Accidental Death; The Clue of the Silver Key; Payment In Kind; Position of Trust; The Vengeance of She*
Sherwin, Louis (wri): *The Eleventh Hour* (1923)
Sherwood, Anthony (act): *Deadbolt; Terror Train; Wild Thing*
Sherwood, David (wri): *Curse of the Crystal Eye; Steel Dawn*
Sherwood, Gale (act): *Blonde Savage*
Sherwood, George (act): *Missile Monsters*
Sherwood, Hal (wri): *The Ghastly Ones*
Sherwood, John (dir): *The Creature Walks Among Us; The Monolith Monsters*
Sherwood, Josephine (act): see Hull, Josephine
Sherwood, Lydia (act): *Midnight at Madame Tussaud's*
Sherwood, Madeleine (act): see Thornton-Sherwood, Madeleine
Sherwood, Robert E. (wri, 1896-1955): *The Bishop's Wife; The Ghost Goes West; The Preacher's Wife; Rebecca; Roman Scandals; The Scarlet Pimpernel* (1934)
Sherwood, Robin (act): *Love Butcher; Tourist Trap*
Sherwood, Tony (act): *Scanners*
Sherwood, William (act): *Dublin Nightmare; Horror of Dracula; The Man Without a Body*
Sherwood, Yorke (act): *Bulldog Drummond Strikes Back* (1934); *Devotion; Temple Tower; 23 Paces to Baker Street*
Shevelove, Burt (wri, 1915-1982): *The Wrong Box*
Shew, Edward Spencer (wri): *Hands of the Ripper*
Sheybal, Vladek (act, b. 1933): *Avalanche Express; Billion Dollar Brain; Casino Royale; Deadfall; From Russia With Love; Gulliver's Travels* (1977); *Innocent Bystanders; The Lady Vanishes* (1979); *Limbo Line; Puppet On a Chain; Red Dawn; Return from the Ashes*
Shiba, Kazuo (act): *Son of Godzilla*
Shibaki, Toshio (act): *Godzilla vs. the Smog Monster*
Shibata, George (act): *Around the World Under the Sea*
Shideler, Carol (act): *Blind Date*
Shiel, Matthew Phipps (wri, 1865-1947): *The World, the Flesh and the Devil*
Shields, Arthur (act, 1896-1970): *Above Suspicion; Daughter of Dr. Jekyll; Dr. Renault's Secret; Enchanted Island; The Gay Falcon; Lady Godiva; The Picture of Dorian Gray* (1945); *Seven Keys to Baldpate* (1947); *Three Strangers; The Verdict* (1946); *World for Ransom*
Shields, Bob J. (act): *Barracuda*
Shields, Brooke (act, b. 1965): *Alice, Sweet Alice; Brenda Starr* (1992); *Freaked; Freeway; The Seventh Floor; Stalking Laura*
Shields, Carrie (act): *Making Contact*
Shields, Frank (dir): *Fatal Sky; Project: Alien*
Shields, John (act): *The Octagon*
Shields, John Barton (act): *Blood Diner*
Shields, Nicholas (act): *The Hearse; Time After Time*
Shields, Sonny (act): *Friday the 13th-Part V: A New Beginning*
Shields, Tammy (act): *Making Contact*
Shields, Tim (wri): *The Last Shot You Hear*
Shields, William (act): see Fitzgerald, Barry
Shiff, Stanley (dir): *Lobster Man from Mars*
Shifrin, Su (act): *Superman* (1978)
Shigeta, James (act, b. 1933): *Lost Horizon* (1973); *Matt Helm; The Questor Tapes; Space Marines; Tomorrow's Child*
Shill, Ned (act): *Long John Silver*
Shilling, Marion (act): *The Clutching Hand*

Shillo, Michael (act): *No Way Out; The Whole Truth*
Shiloa, Yoseph (act): *American Cyborg: Steel Warrior*
Shils, Edward (act): *It's Alive III: Island of the Alive; A Return to Salem's Lot*
Shilton, Peter (act): *Equalizer 2000*
Shima, Koji (dir): *Uchujin Tokyo No Arawaru*
Shima, Yvonne (act): *Dr. No*
Shimada, Teru (act): *Mr. Moto's Last Warning; One Spy Too Many; Revolt of the Zombies; The Snow Creature; You Only Live Twice*
Shimatsu, Derick (act): *Varan the Unbelievable*
Shimerman, Armin (act): *Arena* (1989); *The Hitcher*
Shimkus, Joanna (act): *Boom*
Shimoda, Yuki (act, 1921-1981): *The Octagon*
Shimono, Sab (act): *Suture*
Shimura, Takashi (act, 1905-1982): *Ghidrah, the Three-Headed Monster; Gojira; High and Low; Kwaidan; Mothra; The Mysterians; Throne of Blood; Tora No 0 0 Fumu Otokotachi*
Shinas, Sofia (act): *The Crow* (1994)
Shindo, Kaneto (dir, b. 1912): *Kuroneko; Live Today, Die Tomorrow; Onibaba*
Shindo, Kaneto (wri, b. 1912): *Kuroneko; Live Today, Die Tomorrow; Onibaba; Yoru No Tsuzumi*
Shine, Andy (act): *Richard III* (1955)
Shine, Bill(y) (act): see Shine, William/Bill(y)
Shine, Wilfred (act): *The Bells* (1931); *The Hound Of The Baskervilles* (1931); *The Last Hour*
Shine, William/Bill(y) (act, b. 1911): *The Diplomatic Corpse; The House in the Woods; Jack the Ripper* (1958); *The Last Hour; The Man Inside; The McGuffin; Old Mother Riley's Jungle Treasure; Richard III* (1955); *The Scarlet Pimpernel* (1934); *The Sky Bike; Vice Versa* (1947); *Wanted for Murder; The Yellow Mask; Young and Innocent*
Shiner, Ronald (act, 1903-1966): *The Black Tulip* (1937); *Bulldog Sees It Through; The Case of the Frightened Lady; I Killed the Count; King Arthur Was a Gentleman; The Mind of Mr. Reeder; The Missing People*
Shinew, Leonard (act): *Freejack*
Shingler, Helen (act): *Family Doctor*
Shink, Joseph M. (wri): *Blood Song*
Shinn, Margaret (act): *House of the Black Death*
Shino, Hiroko (act): *Murder In the Doll House*
Shinoburyu (act): *The Toxic Avenger, Part II*
Shiomi, Sue (act): *Message from Space*
Shipler, Craig (act): *Beyond and Back*
Shipman, Barry (wri, b. 1912): *The Deadly Ray from Mars; Dick Tracy* (1937); *Dick Tracy Returns; Dick Tracy's G-Men; Eyes of the Jungle; Peril from the Planet Mongo; Purple Death from Outer Space; The Torpedo of Doom*
Shipow, Emanuel (act): *The Tomb*
Shipp, John Wesley (act, b. 1955): *Deadly Web; The Flash; The Flash 2: Revenge of the Trickster; The Neverending Story II: The Next Chapter*
Shipp, Mary (act): *Jennifer* (1953)
Shippy, Kenneth Robert (act): *Crawlspace*
Shirakawa, Yumi (act): *The H-Man; The Mysterians; Rodan, the Flying Monster; The Secret of the Telegian*
Shiraki, Maya (act): *The Toxic Avenger, Part II*
Shire, David (mus): *The Companion* (1994); *Farewell, My Lovely; Killer Bees; Ms. Scrooge; Oh, God! You Devil; Rear Window* (1998); *Return to Oz; Short Circuit; Time Flyer; The Tribe; 2010; Vice Versa* (1988)
Shire, Talia (act, b. 1946, a.k.a. Talia Coppola): *Cold Heaven; Gas-s-s-s!; The Dunwich Horror; Hyper Sapien: People from Another Star; Murderer's Keep; Prophecy* (1979); *Windows*
Shires, Spencer (act): *The Sky Bike*
Shirin, Moti (act): *The Little Drummer Girl*
Shirk, Adam Hull (wri): *The Ape* (1940); *The House of Mystery* (1931)
Shirley, Aleisa (act): *Spacehunter: Adventures In the Forbidden Zone; Sweet Sixteen*
Shirley, Anne (act, b. 1918, nee Dawn Paris, a.k.a. Dawn O'Day): *All That Money Can Buy; Liliom* (1930); *Murder, My Sweet; Rasputin and the Empress*
Shirley, Arthur (wri): *The Grip of Iron; Her Life In London; The King of Crime; The Lifeguardsman*
Shirley, Bill (act): *Abbott and Costello Meet Captain Kidd; Sleeping Beauty* (1959)
Shirley, Clinton Austin (act): *RoboCop 2*
Shirley, Joseph (act): *Neon Maniacs*
Shirley, Mercedes (act): *Human Experiments*
Shirley, Peg (act): *The Return of Count Yorga*
Shirley, Stanla (act): *Dead of Night* (1987)
Shirow, Masamune (wri): *Ghost In the Shell*

Shirriff, Cathie (act): *Murder In Space; Star Trek III: The Search for Spock; Vampira*
Shirvani, Kristy (act): *Addams Family Values*
Shist, Joel (cin): *Timecop*
Shlasinger, Zev (wri): *Flesh-Eating Mothers*
Shmuger, Marc (wri): *Dead of Winter*
Shneider, Natasha (act): *2010*
Shneiderov, Vladimir (dir): *Zolotoye Ozero*
Shnitke, Alfred (mus): *Rasputin (1985)*
Shock, Donna (act): *The Alien Within*
Shockley, Stephanie (act): *Howling V: The Rebirth*
Shockley, William (act): *Howling V: The Rebirth; Switch (1991)*
Shoemaker, Ann (act, 1891-1978): *Above Suspicion; Ellery Queen, Master Detective; House by the River*
Shoemaker, Emily (wri): *Circumstances Unknown*
Shoemaker, Joshua L. (act): *Serial Mom*
Shohan, Naomi (act): *Vamp*
Sholder, Jack (dir): *Alone In the Dark; By Dawn's Early Light; Generation X; The Hidden; A Nightmare On Elm Street, Part 2: Freddy's Revenge; 12:01*
Sholder, Jack (wri): *Alone In the Dark*
Sholem, Lee (dir, b. 1900): *Cannibal Attack; Doomsday Machine; Hell Ship Mutiny; Jungle Man-Eaters; Pharaoh's Curse; Superman and the Mole Men; Tarzan's Magic Fountain; Tobor the Great*
Sholto, Pamela (act): *Hellraiser*
Shone, Moira (act): *Spasms*
Shonteff, Lindsay (dir): *Clegg; Curse of Simba; Devil Doll (1963); The Fast Kill; The Killing Edge; Licensed to Kill; Licensed to Love and Kill; The Million Eyes of Sumuru; No. 1 of the Secret Service; Spy Story; The Swordsman*
Shonteff, Lindsay (wri): *Licensed to Kill*
Shoob, Michael (wri): *Parasite*
Shook, Warner (act): *Knightriders*
Shoop, Pamela (Susan) (act): *Empire of the Ants; Halloween II*
Shoptesse, Joel (act): *Grim Prairie Tales*
Shor, Dan (act): *Bill & Ted's Excellent Adventure; Solar Crisis; Strange Behavior; Strange Invaders*
Shor, Sol (wri): *The Adventures of Captain Marvel; Cyclotrode X; Daughter of the Jungle; Dick Tracy Returns; Dick Tracy's G-Men; Dr. Satan's Robot; Lost Planet Airmen; Savage Mutiny; The Torpedo of Doom*
Shore, Dick (act): *End of the World (1977)*
Shore, Dinah (act, 1917-1994, nee Fanny Schown): *Oh, God!*
Shore, Howard (mus): *Big; The Brood; Crash (1996); Dead Ringers; Ed Wood; The Fly (1986); A Kiss Before Dying (1991); Prelude to a Kiss; Scanners; Seven; The Silence of the Lambs; Single White Female; Videodrome*
Shore, James (act): *Mutants In Paradise*
Shore, Pauly (act, b. 1968): *Bio-Dome; Casper: A Spirited Beginning; 18 Again!; Encino Man; Phantom of the Mall: Eric's Revenge*
Shore, Richard (cin): *Night of Dark Shadows*
Shore, Roberta (act): *The Shaggy Dog (1959)*
Shore, Sammy (act): *Fake-Out*
Shores, Lynn (dir): *Charlie Chan at the Wax Museum*
Shorr, Richard (dir & wri): *Witches' Brew*
Short, Bernardette (act): *An Unsuitable Job for a Woman*
Short, Don (cin): *The Eleventh Hour (1923)*
Short, Dorothy (act): *Daughter of the Tong; Spooks Run Wild*
Short, Florence (act): *The Enchanted Cottage (1924); The Love Flower*
Short, Gertrude (act): *Blackie's Redemption; Bulldog Drummond (1929); Son of Kong; The Thin Man*
Short, James (act): *Eraser*
Short, Jean (act): *The Fatal Night*
Short, John (act): *Maximum Overdrive*
Short, Lew (act): *The Black Pearl*
Short, Martin (act, b. 1951): *Alice In Wonderland (1999); Innerspace; Mars Attacks!; Merlin (1998); The Pebble and the Penguin; Really Weird Tales; A Simple Wish; We're Back! A Dinosaur's Story*
Short, Robert (act): *Cocoon: The Return; Scared to Death (1980)*
Short, Robert (wri): *Programmed to Kill; Scared to Death (1980)*
Short, Robin (act): *The Baron of Arizona*
Short, William Michael (act): *Ed Wood*
Shorte, Dino (act): *Midnight Offerings; Project X (1987)*
Shorter, Ken (act): *Dragonslayer*
Shorthouse, Tom (act): *The Resurrected*
Shostakovich, Dmitri (mus, 1906-1975): *Korol Lir*
Shostrom, Mark (cin): *From Beyond*
Shotola, Ron (act): *The Outing*
Shotter, Ralph Champion (act): see Michael, Ralph
Shotter, Winifred (act): *Candles at Nine*
Shou, Robin (act): *Mortal Kombat; Mortal Kombat: Annihilation*
Shout, Chris (act): *The Pink Chiquitas*
Shout, Jason (act): *The Pink Chiquitas*
Shovlin, Joseph Kenneth (act): see Whalen, Michael
Show, Grant (act): *Pretty Poison (1996)*
Showacre, David (act): *Cat People (1982)*
Shower, Kathy (act): *Cyber-Chic; Frankenstein General Hospital*
Shpetner, Stanley (wri): *The Bonnie Parker Story*
Shragge, Lawrence (mus): *Firebird 2015 A.D.*
Shrake, Bud (wri): *Nightwing*
Shrapnel, John (act): *101 Dalmatians (1996)*
Shreve, Evelyn (act): *The Blood Drinkers*
Shrieve, Michael (mus): *Return (1985)*
Shrimpton, Jean (act): *Privilege*
Shriner, Kin (act): *The Crying Child; Cyberzone*
Shriner, Wil (act): *Amazing Stories: The Movie VI; Time Trackers*
Shroyer, Sonny (act): *The Devil and Max Devlin*
Shroyer, Stephanie (act): *Alien Nation*
Shryack, Dennis (wri): *The Car*
Shubert, Eddie (act): *Satan Met a Lady*
Shubert, Lynn (wri): *The Loch Ness Horror*
Shue, Elizabeth (act, b. 1963): *Back to the Future, Part III; Heart and Souls; Link; The Saint; The Trigger Effect*
Shuford, Stephanie (act): *Dreams Come True*
Shuftan, Eugen (cin): see Schufftan/Shuftan, Eugen
Shull, Jerry (act): *The Phantom Empire*
Shull, John Kenton (act): *Bates Motel*
Shull, Richard B. (act, b. 1929): *Heartbeeps; The Pack; Splash; Ssssss*
Shuman, Barbara (act): *Fiend (1980)*
Shuman, David (act): *Robot In the Family*
Shuman, Felix (act): *Damien-Omen II*
Shuman, Jimmy (act): *Asterix In Britain*
Shuman, Mort (act): *The Little Girl Who Lives Down the Lane*
Shumway, Lee (act): *The Bat (1926); Charlie Chan at the Opera; The Lone Wolf Returns (1935); Mr. Moto In Danger Island; The Mysterious Mr. Wong*
Shusett, Ronald (wri): *Alien; Aliens; Alien 3; Dead and Buried; The Final Terror; Freejack; King Kong Lives; Phobia; Total Recall; W*
Shuster, Rick (act): *Eraser*
Shutan, Jan (act): *Dracula's Dog*
Shute, Nevil (wri, 1899-1960): *No Highway In the Sky; On the Beach*
Shute, Valerie (act): *In the Devil's Garden*
Shutt, Tim (act): *Mutants In Paradise*
Shutta, Ethel (act): *The Playground*
Shuttleworth, Bobby (act): *Secrets of the Phantom Caverns*
Shuttleworth, Daryl (act): *Ebenezer; Millennium*
Shuttleworth, Debbie (act): *Secrets of the Phantom Caverns*
Shuttleworth, Marie (act): *Secrets of the Phantom Caverns*
Shu-yi, Tsen (act): *Infra-Man*
Shvorin, A. (act): *The Heavens Call*
Shydner, Ritch (act): *C.H.U.D. II; The Man Who Fell to Earth (1987)*
Shyman, James (dir & wri): *Slashdance*
Siani, Ed (act): *Capture That Capsule!*
Siani, Sabrina (act): *Ator: The Fighting Eagle; Conquest; The Invincible Barbarian; 2020 Texas Gladiators*
Sibbald, Tony (act): *Mark of the Devil (1985); The Quatermass Conclusion; Scream for Help; Superman II*
Sibbett, Jane (act): *The Resurrected*
Siberry, Michael (act): *Teen Agent*
Sibert, Roderick Spencer (act): *The Wiz*
Sibirskaia, Nadia (act): *The Crime of Monsieur Lange; Menilmontant*
Sibley, Lucy (act): *The Murdock Trial*
Sibley, Miss (act): *The Harper Mystery*
Sicari, Joseph R. (act): *A Gnome Named Gnorm; Night School*
Sichel, John (dir): *The Savage Curse; Spell of Evil*
Sickner, William (A.) (cin): *Bomba and the Hidden City; Bomba, the Jungle Boy; The Chinese Ring; Dangerous Money; Dark Alibi; The Docks of New Orleans; The Falcon In San Francisco; The Feathered Serpent (1948); The Golden Eye; The Mummy's Ghost; Panther Island; Peril from the Planet Mongo; The Phantom Creeps; Purple Death from Outer Space; The Scarlet Clue; Shadows Over Chinatown; The Shanghai Chest; The Sky Dragon*
Sicoly, Michael (act): *Memories of Murder*
Sidaway, Marlene (act): *The Magic Toyshop*
Siddall, Cory (act): *The Music of the Spheres*
Siddall, Teddi (act): *Tomorrow's Child*
Sidelnikov, N. (mus): *Shinel (1965)*
Sidley, Robert (act): *The Resurrected*
Sidney, Ann (act): *Performance*
Sidney, D.J. (act): *Shock Waves*
Sidney, George (dir, b. 1911): *The Three Musketeers (1948)*
Sidney, Jon (act): *The Day After Halloween*
Sidney, Scott (dir): *Tarzan of the Apes*
Sidney, Sylvia (act, b. 1910, nee Sophia Kosow): *Beetlejuice; Damien-Omen II; Death at Love House; Demon (1976); Do Not Fold, Spindle or Mutilate; Hammett; Love from a Stranger (1947); Mars Attacks!; The Miracle Man (1932); Les Miserables (1952); Sabotage; Snowbeast*
Sie, James (act): *Chain Reaction (1996)*
Sieber, Matyas (mus): *Animal Farm (1954); Chase a Crooked Shadow*
Siebert, Charles (act, b. 1938): *Blue Sunshine; Coma; The Incredible Hulk; Tarantulas: The Deadly Cargo; Topper (1979)*
Siederman, Paul (act): *Deranged (1987)*
Siedow, Jim (act): *Red Alert; The Texas Chainsaw Massacre; The Texas Chainsaw Massacre 2*
Sief, Percy (act): *Victim Five*
Siegal, Donna (act): *Martin*
Siegel, Barbara (act): *Werewolf of Washington*
Siegel, Barry (wri): *Windows*
Siegel, Bernard (act): *Laugh, Clown, Laugh; The Phantom of the Opera (1925)*
Siegel, Charles (act): *It (1990)*
Siegel, Cornelius (cin): *Nosferatu, the Vampyre*
Siegel, David (dir & wri): *Suture*
Siegel, Don(ald) (act, 1912-1991): *Invasion of the Body Snatchers (1978); Play Misty for Me*
Siegel, Don(ald) (dir, 1912-1991): *The Beguiled; The Black Windmill; The Hanged Man; Invasion of the Body Snatchers (1956); The Lineup; Night Unto Night; Private Hell 36; The Verdict (1946)*
Siegel, Lionel E. (wri): *Exo-Man; The Ultimate Impostor*
Siegel, Mark (act): *The Crater Lake Monster*
Siegel, Michael (act): *Killer Klowns from Outer Space*
Siegel, Richard (wri): *Stay Tuned*
Siegfried, John (act): *Trader Horn (1973)*
Siegler, Al(len G.) (cin): *The Black Room; The Devil Commands; The Lone Wolf In Mexico; The Lone Wolf Spy Hunt; Through the Dark; Unknown World*
Siegler, Marc (act): *Repossessed*
Siegler, Marc (wri): *Galaxy of Terror*
Siegler, Mark (act): *The Hidden; Roller Blade Warriors: Taken by Force*
Siegmann, George (act): *The Avenging Conscience; The Cat and the Canary (1927); The Man Who Laughs (1928); Monte Cristo; The Three Musketeers (1921)*
Sieman, Frank (act): *The Curse of the Golem*
Siemaszko, Casey (act): *Amazing Stories; Back to the Future, Part II; Black Scorpion (1995); Of Mice and Men (1992); Painted Heart; Storm of the Century*
Siemaszko, Nina (act): *Sawbones*
Sienko, Kinga (act): *Wielka, Wielka I Najwieksza*
Sierck, Detlef (dir): see Sirk, Douglas
Sierra, Gregory (act): *Beneath the Planet of the Apes; The Clones; Code Name: Dancer; Donor; Honey, I Blew Up the Kids; The Prisoner of Zenda (1979); Something Is Out There; The Towering Inferno*
Sierra, Sara Lopez (act): *Caveman (1981)*
Sieveking, Lance (wri): *The Third Clue*
Sievernich, Chris (act): *Chinese Boxes*
Siff, Helen Infield (act): *Earth Girls Are Easy*
Sigel, Lisa (act): *Deadly Game*
Sigley, Marjorie L. (wri): *Never-Never Land*
Signor, Tari (act): *A Deadly Vision*
Signorelli, James (dir): *Elvira, Mistress of the Dark*
Signorelli, Tom (act): *Alice, Sweet Alice; The Bride In Black; Dick Tracy (1990); Robot In the Family*
Signoret, Simone (act, 1921-1985, nee Simone-Henriette-Charlotte Kaminker): *L'Aveu; The Deadly Affair; Diabolique (1955); Games; Mister Freedom; La Mort en Ce Jardin; The Sleeping Car Murders; Les Sorcieres de Salem*
Siguineau, Frank (act): *An American Werewolf In London*
Sigurdsson, Hylnur (act): *The Flintstones*
Sigurdsson, Marino (act): *The Flintstones*
Sihol, Caroline (act): *Confidentially Yours*
Sikking, James (B.) (act, b. 1934): *The Astronaut; Bay Coven; Daddy's Gone A-Hunting; Morons from Outer Space; Narrow Margin (1990); Outland; Scorpio; Seduced by Evil; Star Trek III: The Search for Spock; The Terminal Man; Too Good to Be True*
Silas, Sean (wri): *A Vow to Kill*
Silberg, Tusse (act): *The Company of Wolves; Flight to Berlin; Gorky Park; The Saint*
Silberling, Brad (dir, b. 1963): *Casper; City of Angels*
Silbersher, Marvin (act): *The Immortal*
Silcock, Robert (act): *The Plutonium Incident*
Silenti, Vira (act): *Son of Samson; The Witch's Curse*
Siletti, Mario (act): *My Cousin Rachel; Teodora, Imperatrice di Bisanzio*
Siliotto, Carlo (mus): *Fluke*
Silju, Erik (act): *The Island at the Top of the World*
Silke, James R. (wri): *The Barbarians (1987); King Solomon's Mines (1985)*
Silkosky, Ronald (wri): *The Dunwich Horror*
Sill, Douglas (act): *Justin Case*
Silla, Felix (act): *The Black Bird (1975); The Brood; Buck Rogers In the 25th Century; Demon Seed; Halloween With the Addams Family; Ssssss*
Sillas, Karen (act): *The Beast (1996)*
Silliman, Maureen (act): *Sanctuary of Fear*
Silliphant, Robert (act & wri): *The Incredibly Strange Creatures Who Stopped Living and Became Mixed-Up Zombies*
Silliphant, Stirling (wri, 1918-1996): *Charly; Circle of Iron; The Lineup; Nightfall (1956); The Poseidon Adventure; The Swarm; The Towering Inferno; The Village of the Damned (1960 & 1995)*
Sills, Milton (act, 1882-1930): *Adam's Rib*
Silo, Susan (act): *Once Upon a Forest*
Silva, Carmen (act): *House of Exorcism*
Silva, David (act): *Dr. Tarr's Torture Dungeon; Sisters of Satan*
Silva, Franco (act): *Le Comte de Monte Cristo*
Silva, Frank (act): *Twin Peaks: Fire Walk With Me*
Silva, Henry (act, b. 1928): *Allan Quatermain and the Lost City of Gold; Alligator (1981); Amazon Women On the Moon; Assassination; Black Noon; Buck Rogers In the 25th Century; Chained Heat; Cinderfella; Dick Tracy (1990); Escape from the Bronx; Green Mansions; Johnny Cool; The Manchurian Candidate; Manhunt In Milan; Matchless; Megaforce; Possessed by the Night; The Return of Mr. Moto; The Silence of the Hams; Thirst; Virus (1980)*
Silva, Jimmy (act): *Shriek of the Mutilated*
Silva, Kathy (act): *Soylent Green*
Silva, Maria (act): *The Mummy's Revenge; El Retorno de la Walpurgis*
Silva, Rita (act): *The Invincible Barbarian*
Silva, Simone (act): *The Golden Mask; Street of Shadows*
Silvain, Eugene (act): *The Passion of Joan of Arc*
Silvani, Alana (act): *Switch (1991)*
Silvani, Aldo (act): *Beat the Devil; Il Ladro di Venezia; Sodom and Gomorrah*
Silvani, Jole (act): *La Citta delle Donne*
Silveira, Ruth (act): *Once Bitten*
Silver, Alain Joel (act): *Cyborg 2: Glass Shadow*
Silver, Amanda (wri): *The Hand That Rocks the Cradle; The Relic*
Silver, Andrew (dir & wri): *Return (1985)*
Silver, Borah (act): *Elves*
Silver, Christine (act): *Mystery Junction; The Pleydell Mystery; Room to Let*
Silver, Dolores (act): *The Howling: New Moon Rising*
Silver, Elaine (act): *The Flintstones*
Silver, Erik (act): *House*
Silver, Fawn (act): *Orgy of the Dead (1965); Terror In the Jungle*
Silver, Fred (act): *Just Imagine*
Silver, George (act): *The Mirror Crack'd*
Silver, Joe (act, 1922-1989): *Rabid; Rhinoceros (1974); Shivers*
Silver, Kitty (act): *The Island of Dr. Moreau (1996)*
Silver, Leon (act): *The Lifetaker*
Silver, Marc (act): *Deadly Messages; I, Desire; Motel Hell*
Silver, Mark (act): *House*
Silver, Melanie (act): *The Flintstones*
Silver, Michael (act): *Jason Goes to Hell: The Final Friday*
Silver, Michael Bushman (act): [illegible]
Silver, Nancey (wri): *Christmas Every Day*
Silver, Norm (act): *Asteroid*
Silver, Pat (wri): *Paint Me a Murder; The Wizard of Baghdad*

Silver, Raphael D. (dir): *The Legend of the Wolf Woman*
Silver, Robert (act): *Devil In the Flesh; Eat and Run*
Silver, Ron (act): *The Arrival (1996); Eat and Run; The Beneficiary; The Entity; Lifepod; Oh, God! You Devil; The Return of the World's Greatest Detective; Shadow Zone: The Undead Express; Silent Rage; Timecop; The White Raven*
Silver, Ron (dir): *Lifepod*
Silvera, Frank (act, 1914-1970): *Crime and Punishment, U.S.A.; Fear and Desire; Killer's Kiss; The St. Valentine's Day Massacre*
Silverback, Michael (act): *To the Ends of Time*
Silverberg, Robert (wri): *Amanda and the Alien*
Silverblatt, Howard (act): see Da Silva, Howard
Silverbrand, David (act): *Outbreak*
Silverheels, Jay (act, 1917-1980): *The Feathered Serpent (1948); The Lone Ranger; The Lone Ranger and the Lost City of Gold*
Silverkleit, David (act): *The Bees*
Silverlake, Arthur (act): see Lake, Arthur
Silverman, Bob (act): see Silverman, Robert/Bob
Silverman, David Michael (act): *Copycat*
Silverman, Jim (act): *Waxwork II: Lost In Time*
Silverman, Jonathan (act, b. 1966): *Death Becomes Her; 12:01*
Silverman, Julie (act): *Heart Condition*
Silverman, N. Paul (act): *The Carrier*
Silverman, Robert/Bob (act): *The Brood; Prom Night; Rabid; Scanners*
Silverman, Stanley (mus): *Eyewitness (1981); Simon*
Silvernail, Clarke (wri): *Behind That Curtain*
Silvernail, Karen (act): *The Toxic Avenger, Part II*
Silvers, Candace (act): *My Science Project*
Silvers, Louis (mus): *The House of Horror (1929)*
Silvers, Nancey (wri): *Dog's Best Friend*
Silvers, Phil (act, 1912-1985, nee Philip Silversmith): *Just Off Broadway; The Strongest Man In the World; There Goes the Bride; A Thousand and One Nights (1945)*
Silvers, Sid (wri, b. 1908): *The Gorilla (1939)*
Silversmith, Philip (act): see Silvers, Phil
Silverstein, Elizabeth (act): *Howling V: The Rebirth*
Silverstein, Elliot (dir, b. 1927): *The Car; Nightmare Honeymoon*
Silverstein, Elliott (act): *Blood Song*
Silverstone, Alicia (act, b. 1976): *The Babysitter (1995); Batman and Robin; The Crush; Hideaway; True Crime*
Silverthorn, Richard Jay (act): *Fear No Evil (1981)*
Silverton, Dorothy (wri): *Terror Out of the Sky*
Silvestre, Flor (act): *They Call Him Marcado*
Silvestre, Armando (act): *Los Automatas de la Muerte; Doctor of Doom; Neutron, el Enmascarado Negro; Night of the Bloody Apes; The White Orchid; Wrestling Women vs. the Aztec Mummy*
Silvestri, Alan (mus): *The Abyss; Back to the Future; Back to the Future, Part II; Back to the Future, Part III; Cat's Eye; The Clan of the Cave Bear; Contact; Death Becomes Her; Eraser; Ferngully: The Last Rain Forest; Flight of the Navigator; Judge Dredd; The Long Kiss Goodnight; Mac and Me; My Stepmother Is an Alien; Practical Magic; Predator; Predator 2; Romancing the Stone; Super Mario Bros.; Tales from the Crypt (1989); Volcano; Who Framed Roger Rabbit*
Silvestri, Larry (act): *Tales from the Darkside*
Silvestri, Umberto (act): *Teodora, Imperatrice di Bisanzio; Ulysses*
Silvey, Susie (act): *The Playbirds*
Silvia, David (act): *El Baron del Terror*
Sim, Alastair (act, 1900-1976): *Alf's Button Afloat; Green for Danger; The Green Man; An Inspector Calls; Law and Disorder; The Man In the Mirror; Royal Flash; The Ruling Class; Scrooge (1951); The Squeaker (1937); Stage Fright (1950); Strange Experiment; The Terror (1938); Troubled Waters (1936)*
Sim, Gerald (act): *Dr. Jekyll and Sister Hyde; Dr. Phibes Rises Again; Frenzy; Kadoyng; The Murder Game; Once the Killing Starts; Paint Me a Murder; Seance On a Wet Afternoon; The Slipper and the Rose; The Wrong Box*
Sim, Matthew (act): *Without a Clue*
Sim, Sheila (act, b. 1922): *Pandora and the Flying Dutchman*
Simandl, Louis A. (dir & wri): *Empire of Ash III*
Simcoe, Benjamin (wri): *Bomb In the High Street*
Simcox, Tom (act): *Grim Prairie Tales*
Simek, Vasek C. (act): *Dead Again; Ed Wood*
Simenez, Jose Luis (act): *El Vampiro*
Simenon, Georges (wri, 1903-1989): *The Hatter's Ghost; Les Inconnus dans la Maison; Paris Express; Stranger In the House (1967)*
Simeone, Gustavo (act): *Satanik*
Simi (act): *Tarzan Goes to India*
Similuk, Peter (act): *The Hideous Sun Demon*
Simmerman, James (act): *The Being*
Simmons, Allene (act): *Time Walker*
Simmons, Bob (act): *Fury at Smugglers' Bay*
Simmons, Chelan (act): *It (1990)*
Simmons, Clarence (act): *Just Imagine*
Simmons, Dick (act): *Lady In the Dark; Rear Window (1954)*
Simmons, Dion (act): *Jacob's Ladder*
Simmons, Floyd (act): *The Deadly Mantis*
Simmons, Gary (act): *Haunters of the Deep*
Simmons, Gene (act, b. 1949): *Kiss Meets the Phantom of the Park; Runaway (1984); Trick or Treat*
Simmons, George (act): *The Swarm*
Simmons, Grace (act): *Assassin (1986)*
Simmons, Guy (act): *The Dungeonmaster*
Simmons, Jean (act, b. 1929): *Affair With a Stranger; Androcles and the Lion; Angel Face; Black Narcissus; Cage of Gold; The Dain Curse; Dominique; Footsteps In the Fog; Great Expectations (1946); Hamlet (1948); Meet Sexton Blake; Mr. Sycamore; So Long at the Fair; Uncle Silas*
Simmons, Kevin (act): *Street Trash*
Simmons, Maude (act): *Portrait of Jennie*
Simmons, Mike (act): *The Crater Lake Monster*
Simmons, Monica (act): *The Night Brings Charlie*
Simmons, Pat (1950s act): *The Giant Gila Monster*
Simmons, Pat (1980s act): *My Science Project*
Simmons, Redbeard (wri): *Meet the Applegates*
Simmons, Richard (act): *The Resurrection of Zachary Wheeler*
Simmons, Richard Alan (dir): *Fear No Evil (1969)*
Simmons, Richard Alan (wri): *Congo Crossing; Fear No Evil (1969); Ritual of Evil*
Simmons, Stan (act): *Curse of the Fly; Kiss of the Vampire*
Simmons, Thom (act): *In the Company of Darkness*
Simmons, Thomas G. (act): *The Fugitive (1993)*
Simmons, Tasha (act): *Susie Q*
Simmons, Trish (act): *Lady Beware*
Simms, Al (mus): *Alakazam the Great*
Simms, Ginny (act): *You'll Find Out*
Simms, Hilda (act): *Black Widow (1954)*
Simms, Jay (wri): *Creation of the Humanoids; The Giant Gila Monster; The Killer Shrews; Panic In Year Zero; The Resurrection of Zachary Wheeler*
Simms, Leslie (act): *Blood Mania; Point of Terror*
Simms, Michael David (act): *Alien Nation*
Simms, Tasha (act): *Memories of Murder*
Simon, Adam (dir & wri): *Brain Dead; Carnosaur*
Simon, Alex (wri): *Piranha (1995); Suspect Device*
Simon, Carly (mus, b. 1944): *The Spy Who Loved Me*
Simon, Francois (act): see Simon, Michel
Simon, Gunther (act): *Milczaca Gwiazda*
Simon, J. Piquer/J.P. (dir): *Cthulhu Mansion; Endless Descent; Mystery On Monster Island; Pieces; Slugs*
Simon, J.P. (wri): *Cthulhu Mansion; Endless Descent*
Simon, Joe (wri): *Captain America (1978 & 1992); Captain America II*
Simon, Josette (act): *Bridge of Time*
Simon, Lynda (act): *Scalpel*
Simon, Marty (mus): *I Worship His Shadow; Scanners II: The New Order*
Simon, Mayo (wri): *Futureworld; The Man from Atlantis; Marooned; Phase IV*
Simon, Michel (act, 1895-1975, nee Francois Simon): *La Beaute du Diable; Le Diable et les Dix Commandements; It Happened in Broad Daylight; The Naked Woman and Satan; The Passion of Joan of Arc; Poison (1951); Le Quai des Brumes; Saadia*
Simon, Michelle (act): *The Erotic Adventures of Zorro*
Simon, Neil (wri, b. 1927): *Murder by Death*
Simon, Peter (act): *The Cradle Will Fall*
Simon, Robert (F.) (act): *The Chinese Web; Face of Fire; Roogie's Bump; The Wizard of Baghdad*
Simon, S.J. (wri): *The Ghosts of Berkeley Square*
Simon, Simone (act, b. 1914): *All That Money Can Buy; Cat People (1942); Curse of the Cat People*
Simon, Stephen Kenyatta (act): *Angel Heart*
Simon, S. Sylvan (dir, 1910-1951): *The Cockeyed Miracle*
Simonds, David (act): *The Refrigerator*
Simonds Jr., P.K. (act & wri): *Beverly Hills Bodysnatchers*
Simone, Lisa (act): *The Giant Gila Monster; Missile to the Moon*
Simone, Mike (act): *The Pink Chiquitas*
Simoneau, Yves (dir): *Intensity*
Simonelli, George A. (act): *Repossessed*
Simonelli, Giorgio (dir): *Robin Hood and the Pirates; Ursus In the Land of Fire*
Simonelli, Giorgio (wri): *Tomb of Torture*
Simonelli, Giovanni (wri): *Goliath Against the Giants; Seven Deaths In the Cat's Eye*
Simonett, Ted (act): *Sorry, Wrong Number (1989)*
Simonetti, Claudio (mus): *Conquest; Demons (1985)*
Simonetti, Enrico (mus): *Macumba Love*
Simonin, Albert (wri): *Le Saint Mene la Dance*
Simons, Frank (act): *Time Flyer*
Simons, John (act): *The Son of Hercules In the Land of Darkness*
Simons, Robyn (act): *Memories of Murder*
Simonsen, William (act): *The Curse of Bigfoot*
Simonson, Theodore/Ted (wri): *The Blob (1958); 4D Man*
Simotes, Tony (act): *Alien Nation; Maid to Order*
Simoun, A.R. (wri): *The Serpent and the Rainbow*
Simoun, Henri (wri): *Exo-Man; The Six Milion Dollar Man*
Simovic, Tomislav (mus): *Sedmi Kontinent*
Simper, Robert (act): *Howling III; Mad Max Beyond Thunderdome; The Punisher*
Simper, Roy (cin): *Not Guilty; One Deadly Owner; A Place to Die; Possession (1973); Spell of Evil*
Simpkins, Danny (act): *The Handmaid's Tale*
Simpkins, Deboeah (act): *I Was A Zombie for the F.B.I.*
Simpson, Alan (wri): *The Spy With a Cold Nose*
Simpson, Brock (act): *The Haunting of Hamilton High; Prom Night; Prom Night IV: Deliver Us from Evil*
Simpson, Byron (wri): *The Rescuers Down Under*
Simpson, Christopher George (act): *Ed Wood*
Simpson, Denis (act): *Spasms*
Simpson, Dick (act): *Mars Needs Women*
Simpson, Edward (wri): *The Mind of Mr. Soames*
Simpson, Frank (act): *Remo Williams: The Adventure Begins*
Simpson, Freddie Marie (act): *Popcorn*
Simpson, Geoffrey (cin): *The Navigator: An Odyssey Across Time*
Simpson, George (wri): *The Disappearance of Flight 412*
Simpson, Georgina (act): *Otley*
Simpson, Gillian (act): *A Witch Without a Broom*
Simpson, Harold (wri): *The Phantom Picture; Santa Claus (1912)*
Simpson, Helen (wri): *Murder; Sabotage; Under Capricorn*
Simpson, Ivan (F.) (act): *The Adventures of Robin Hood; Charlie Chan's Greatest Case; The Green Goddess (1923 & 1929); The Hound of the Baskervilles (1939); The Invisible Man Returns; A Kiss for Cinderella; The Mark of the Vampire (1935); The Mystery of Mr. X; A Night of Mystery (1937); The Phantom of Crestwood; Trouble for Two*
Simpson, Jay (act): *Erik the Viking*
Simpson, Jim (act): *Werewolf of Washington*
Simpson, John (act): *Night of the Living Dead (1968)*
Simpson, Jonathan (act): *Star Trek V: The Final Frontier*
Simpson, Marianne (act): *My Best Friend Is a Vampire*
Simpson, Michael (act): *Fortress*
Simpson, Michael A. (dir): *Sleepaway Camp 2: Unhappy Campers; Sleepaway Camp 3. Teenage Wasteland*
Simpson, Mickey (act, 1913-1985): *The Boys from Brooklyn; The Falcon Takes Over; The Lone Ranger; Prince Valiant (1954); Tarzan and the Huntress; World Without End*
Simpson, Napoleon (act): *The Mummy's Curse*
Simpson, Noelle (act): *Blind Date*
Simpson, Norma (act): see Marsh, Carol(e)
Simpson, O.J. (act, b. 1947): *Capricorn One; The Cassandra Crossing; The Diamond Mercenaries; Firepower; The Towering Inferno*
Simpson, Peggy (act): *The 39 Steps (1935)*
Simpson, Raymond E. (act): *Sugar Hill*
Simpson, Ronald (act): *Last Holiday*
Simpson, Russell (act, b. 1880): *The Millerson Case*
Simpson, Sandy (act): *Goliath Awaits*
Simpson, Susan Eileen (act): *Ed Wood*
Simpson, Teresa (act): *The Edge of Hell; The Toxic Avenger*
Sims, George R. (dir): *Lady Letmere's Jewellery*
Sims, George R. (wri): *The English Rose; The Harbour Lights; In the Ranks; Lady Letmere's Jewellery; The Lights O' London; The Romany Rye*
Sims, Greg H. (wri): *Return to Horror High*
Sims, Halle (act): *Tuck Everlasting*
Sims, Jackson (act): *The Kill-Off*
Sims, Joan (act, b. 1930): *The Canterville Ghost (1996); Carry On Screaming; Colonel March Investigates; Meet Mr. Lucifer; One of Our Dinosaurs Is Missing; Passport to Shame*
Sims, Robin (act): *The Channeler*
Sims, Sylvia (act): *Hostile Witness*
Sims, Warwick (act): *Goliath Awaits; The Man With Two Brains*
Sinatra, Christina (act): *Fantasy Island*
Sinatra, Frank (act, 1915-1998): *Around the World In 80 Days; Cool World; The First Deadly Sin; The List of Adrian Messenger; The Manchurian Candidate; The Naked Runner; The Road to Hong Kong; Suddenly; Who Framed Roger Rabbit*
Sinatra Jr., Frank (mus): *Beach Girls and the Monster*
Sinatra, Nancy (act, b. 1940): *The Ghost In the Invisible Bikini; The Last of the Secret Agents?*
Sinatra, Richard (act): *Beast from Haunted Cave*
Sinbad (act, b. 1956): *Coneheads; The Meteor Man*
Sinclair, Alan (act): *Flesh Gordon*
Sinclair, Andrew (dir): *Blue Blood*
Sinclair, Andrew (wri): *Blue Blood; Tennis Court*
Sinclair, Annette (act): *Hide and Go Shriek*
Sinclair, Arthur (act): *King Solomon's Mines (1937)*
Sinclair, Baby Simon (act): *Hamlet (1990)*
Sinclair, Charles (wri): *Chase a Crooked Shadow; The Green Slime*
Sinclair, Edward (act): *The Bells (1931); Tower of Terror*
Sinclair, Elizabeth (act): *The Wicker Man*
Sinclair, Eric (act): *The Missing Corpse; Sparkling Cyanide; War of the Satellites*
Sinclair, Hugh (act, 1903-1962): *Alibi (1942); Circle of Danger; Corridor of Mirrors; No Trace; The Rocking Horse Winner; The Saint Meets the Tiger; The Saint's Vacation*
Sinclair, Irene (wri): *One Exciting Night*
Sinclair, Jill (act): *Howling II*
Sinclair, John Gordon (act): *Erik the Viking*
Sinclair, Joshua (wri): *The Golden Lady*
Sinclair, Lisa (act): *Dead Connection*
Sinclair, M. (act): *Old St. Paul's*
Sinclair, Madge (act): *The Lion King*
Sinclair, Pamela (act): *Hamlet (1990)*
Sinclair, Patricia (act): *The Strange World of Planet X*
Sinclair, Peggy (act): *The Savage Curse; Tennis Court*
Sinclair, Peter (act): *In the Wake of a Stranger; Invasion (1965); Web of Suspicion*
Sinclair, Peter (cin): *Notorious (1992); Outer Touch*
Sinclair, Ronald (act): *A Christmas Carol (1938); Tower of London (1939)*
Sinclair, Stephen (wri): *Dead Alive*
Sinclair, Toni (act): *—And Now the Screaming Starts!*
Sinclair, Upton (wri, 1878-1968): *The Gnome-Mobile*
Sinclaire, Crystin (act): *Ruby*
Sindell, Saul (act): *The Eliminator*
Sinden, Donald (act, b. 1923): *The Canterville Ghost (1996); The Island at the Top of the World; Mad About Men; Mix Me a Person; Rentadick*
Sinden, Leon (act): *Rentadick*
Sinden, Marc (act): *The Wicked Lady*
Sing, Chan (act): *The Amsterdam Kill*
Sing, Wong (act): *Man Beast*
Singer, Alexander (dir, b. 1932): *Psyche 59; Time Travelers (1976)*
Singer, Bryan (dir): *The Usual Suspects*
Singer, Campbell (act, b. 1909): *Cage of Gold; Dick Barton at Bay; Flat Two; The Girl On the Pier; The Hands of Orlac (1959); Lady In the Fog; The Man With the Twisted Lip; Murder on Monday; No Trees In the Street; The Ringer (1952); The Yellow Balloon*
Singer, Isaac Bashevis (wri): *Aaron's Magic Village*

Singer, John(ny) (act): The Dark Man (1951); The Demon Barber of Fleet Street; Haunted Palace (1949)
Singer, Leon (act): Dr. Tarr's Torture Dungeon
Singer, Linda (act): Junior (1986); Zombie Nightmare
Singer, Lori (act, b. 1962): Sunset Grill; Warlock
Singer, Marc (act): The Beastmaster; Beastmaster 2: Through the Portal of Time; Beastmaster III: The Eye of Braxus; The Berlin Conspiracy; Cyberzone; Deadly Game (1991); Dead Space; Forgotten City of the Planet of the Apes; High Desert Kill; Silk Degrees; The Two Worlds of Jennie Logan; V; Victim of Desire; Watchers II
Singer, Norm (act): Beyond Dream's Door
Singer, Ray (act): Prisoners of the Casbah
Singer, Ray (wri): The Maltese Bippy
Singer, Raymond (act): The Entity
Singer, Reuben (act): The Questor Tapes
Singer, Ritchie (act): Encounter at Raven's Gate; Those Dear Departed
Singer, S. Edward (act): Ms. 45
Singer, Steve (act): Ms. 45
Singh, Amrik (act): Siddhartha
Singh, Raj (act): Indiana Jones and the Temple of Doom
Singh, Shogwan (act): The Bride and the Beast
Singleton, Doris (act): Deadly Messages
Singleton, Eleva (act): Copycat
Singleton, Gay (act): Yellow Dog
Singleton, Joe (act): Secrets of the Night
Singleton, Keith (act): Student Bodies
Singleton, Mark (act): Compelled; Enter Inspector Duval; Gang War; Night of the Prowler; Sentenced for Life
Singleton, Penny (act, b. 1912, nee Dorothy McNulty): After the Thin Man; Jetsons: The Movie
Singleton, Ralph S. (dir): Graveyard Shift (1990)
Sinise, Gary (act, b. 1956): Apollo 13; Impostor; Of Mice and Men (1992); Snake Eyes; The Stand
Sinise, Gary (dir, b. 1956): Of Mice and Men (1992)
Sinkys, Albert (act): Ms. 45
Sinutko, Shane (act): The Shaggy D.A.
Sioberg, Gunnar (act): The Devil's Eye
Siodmak, Curt (act, b. 1902): Metropolis (1926)
Siodmak, Curt (dir, b. 1902): Bride of the Gorilla; Curucu, Beast of the Amazon; The Devil's Messenger; Love Slaves of the Amazons; The Magnetic Monster
Siodmak, Curt/Kurt (wri, b. 1902): The Ape (1940); The Beast With Five Fingers; Black Friday; Bride of the Gorilla; The Climax; Creature With the Atom Brain; Curucu, Beast of the Amazon; The Devil's Messenger; Donovan's Brain; Earth vs. the Flying Saucers; F.P. 1 Antwortet Nicht; Frankenstein Meets the Wolf Man; Hauser's Memory; House of Frankenstein; Invisible Agent; The Invisible Man Returns; The Invisible Woman (1941); I Walked With a Zombie; The Lady and the Monster; Love Slaves of the Amazons; The Magnetic Monster; The Naked Woman and Satan; The Return of Monte Cristo; Riders to the Stars; Son of Dracula (1943); Tarzan's Magic Fountain; The Tunnel; Vengeance; The Wolf Man (1941)
Siodmak, Robert (dir, 1900-1973): Cobra Woman; The Crimson Pirate; Criss Cross; The Dark Mirror (1946); Deported; The Devil Strikes at Night; Phantom Lady; Son of Dracula (1943); The Spiral Staircase (1946); The Suspect; Ultimatum
Sipes, Glen (act): Destination Inner Space
Sira, Gurdial (act): Octopussy
Sira, Puneet (act): Arabian Adventure
Siren, Pehr-Olof (act): The Kremlin Letter
Siriaque (act): King Solomon's Mines (1949)
Siriani, Nancy (act): Ghoul School
Sirico, Tony (act): Romeo Is Bleeding
Sirk, Douglas (dir, 1900-1987, nee Detlaf Sierck): Atlantis (1948); Lured; Mystery Submarine; Shockproof; Sign of the Pagan; Sleep, My Love
Sir Lancelot (act): Curse of the Cat People; Ghost Ship (1943); I Walked With a Zombie; The Unknown Terror; Zombies On Broadway
Sirlin, Arnie (cin): C.H.U.D. II
Sirokhtin, I. (dir): Lunnyi Kamen
Sirola, Joe (act, b. 1930): Seizure
Siron, Eleanor (act): Wonder Women
Sirtis, Marina (act, b. 1955): Blind Date; Gargoyles, the Movie: The Heroes Awaken; Star Trek: First Contact; Star Trek: Generations; Star Trek: Insurrection; Waxwork II: Lost In Time
Sisnett, Le Roy (act): Strange Behavior
Sissel, Sandi (cin): Barney's Great Adventure; Dad, the Angel & Me; The Flash; Full Eclipse; In the Company of Darkness; The People Under the Stairs; Toothless
Sissons, Kimber (act): Phantom of the Mall: Eric's Revenge; The Silence of the Hams
Sistare, Anna Maria (act): Appointment for a Killing
Sisti, Michelan (act): Teenage Mutant Ninja Turtles
Sisto, Jeremy (act): The Crew; Hideaway; The Shaggy Dog (1994)
Sisto, Rocco (act): Eraser; Innocent Blood; Red Riding Hood; Scream for Help
Sisty, Frank (act): Deathstalker II: Duel of the Titans
Sitka, Emil (act): Private Eyes (1953); The Three Stooges In Orbit; The Three Stooges Meet Hercules
Sitwell, Osbert (wri): A Place of One's Own
Siu-Tung, Ching (dir): A Chinese Ghost Story II; A Terra-Cotta Warrior
Sivertsen, Mark (act): Howling V: The Rebirth
Six, Sean (act): Alien Nation: Body and Soul; Alien Nation: Dark Horizon; Alien Nation: Millennium; Alien Nation: The Enemy Within
Sizemore, Tom (act, b. 1961): Heart and Souls; The Relic; Strange Days
Sizova, Alla (act): The Sleeping Beauty (1965, Russ)
Sjoberg, Alf (dir, 1903-1980): Hets
Sjoberg, Karen (act): The Jar
Sjoberg, Kurt (act): Dracula Sucks
Sjoblom, Ulla (act): Ansiktet
Sjogren, John (dir): The Mosaic Project
Sjoke, Eva (act): see Bartok, Eva
Sjoman, Vilgot (dir & wri, b. 1924): I Am Curious (Yellow)
Sjostedt, Sture (act): Mother's Day
Sjostrom, Rik (wri): I Vampiri
Sjostrom, Victor (David) (act, 1879-1960): Smultronstallet
Sjostrom, Victor (dir): see Seastrom, Victor
Skaaren, Warren (wri, 1946-1990): Batman (1989); Beetlejuice
Skaff, George (act): Exorcist II: The Heretic; Frogs; The Incredible Petrified World; Man Beast; Soneone's Watching Me!; Wavelength
Skaggs, James/Jimmie F. (act): Backlash: Oblivion 2; Ghost Town; Puppet Master
Skaggs, Norm (act): Shadow of a Doubt (1991)
Skahill, Don William (act): Fargo
Skala, Lilia (act): Charly; Probe
Skall, William V. (cin, 1897-1976): Rope
Skalnik, Michelle (act): Hideaway
Skarke, Peter (act): Howling II
Skarreso, Karin (act): House of 1,000 Dolls
Skarsgard, Stellan (act): The Hunt for Red October; Insomnia (1998)
Skarstedt, Vance (wri): The Slime People
Skarvellis, Jack (act): The Rats Are Coming! The Werewolves Are Here!
Skay, Brigitte (act): Alien Women; Twitch of the Death Nerve; Zeta One
Skeaping, Colin (act): Return to Oz; Superman (1978)
Skeen, Charlie (act): The Hidden
Skein, Farmer (act): Fatal Fingers
Skelly, Jack (act): The Dark Half
Skelton, Maxine (act): Macbeth (1971)
Skelton, Red (act, b. 1913, nee Richard Skelton): Around the World In 80 Days
Skelton, Richard (act): see Skelton, Red
Skerritt, Tom (act, b. 1933): Alien; Calendar Girl Murders; Contact; A Dangerous Summer; The Dead Zone; The Devil's Rain; Maid to Order; Poison Ivy (1992); Poltergeist III; Spacecamp
Skersick, Susan (act): The Green Slime
Sketchley, Anne (act): The Pink Chiquitas
Sketchly, Les (act): 23 Paces to Baker Street
Skewes, Michael (J.) (act): The Package; Rana: The Legend of Shadow Lake
Ski, Maria (act): The Sexplorer
Skie, Shawn (act): Lord of the Flies (1990)
Skikne, Larushka Mischa (act & dir): see Harvey, Laurence
Skiles, Marlin (mus, b. 1906): Crashing Las Vegas; The Disembodied; Flight to Mars; Gilda; Hold That Hypnotist; The Hypnotic Eye; The Maze; Queen of Outer Space; The Resurrection of Zachary Wheeler; Safari Drums; Space Monster; Spy Chasers; The Strangler (1963)
Skillen, Nancy (act): Bridge Across Time
Skillman, Viletta (act): Clownhouse
Skilton, Gerry (act): Howling III
Skinner, Allen (act): I Was a Teen-Age Mummy
Skinner, Anita (act): Sole Survivor
Skinner, Colin (act): The Hound of London
Skinner, Cornelia Otis (act, 1901-1979): The Swimmer; The Uninvited (1944)
Skinner, Frank (mus, b. 1898): Abbott and Costello Meet Frankenstein; Arabian Nights (1942); Bedtime for Bonzo; Black Angel (1946); Bonzo Goes to College; Desert Legion; Francis; Francis Goes to the Races; Harvey; It Grows On Trees; Midnight Lace (1960); A Night In Paradise; Pillow of Death; Portrait In Black; Ride the Pink Horse; Saboteur; Sherlock Holmes and the Secret Weapon; Sherlock Holmes In Washington; Sign of the Pagan; Son of Frankenstein; The Tattered Dress; White Savage; Who Done It? (1942)
Skinner, Keith (act): Mademoiselle; The Slipper and the Rose
Skinner, Kisha (act): Jacob's Ladder
Skinner, Otis (act): Kismet (1920 & 1930)
Skinner, T.B. (act): The Wiz
Skinner-Garter, Corinne (act): The Godsend
Skinta, George (act): Bates Motel
Skipp, John (wri): A Nightmare On Elm Street 5: The Dream Child
Skipper, Max (act): Howling III
Skipper, Pat (act): Demolition Man
Skipworth, Alison (act, 1875-1952, nee Alison Groom): Alice In Wonderland (1933); The Casino Murder Case; Outward Bound; Satan Met a Lady
Skjoldbjaerg, Erik (dir): Insomnia (1998)
Sklair, Sam (mus): The Orchard End Murder
Sklar, Al (act): Attack of the Killer Tomatoes
Sklarey, Seth (act): Children Shouldn't Play With Dead Things
Sklover, Carl (act): Appointment With Murder
Skoda, Albin (act): The Last Ten Days of Adolf Hitler
Skodis, Bob (act): Nightlife (1989, USA-Mex)
Skolimowski, Jerzy (act, b. 1938): Mars Attacks!
Skolimowski, Jerzy (dir & wri, b. 1938): Bariera; The Shout
Skomarovsky, Vladimir (act): 2010
Skorobogatov, Masha (act): The Silence of the Lambs
Skot-Hansen, Mogens (wri): Vredens Dag
Skouras, Costas (act): The Devil's Men
Skousen, Kevin (act): The Hand That Rocks the Cradle
Skye, Ione (act, b. 1970): Stranded
Skye, Raven (act): The Toxic Avenger, Part II
Skylar, Don (act): Blood Pen
Skyhorse, Paul (act): Wolfen
Slack, Ben(jamin) (act): Man On a Swing; Piranha (1995); Silent Night, Deadly Night 4: Initiation; Society
Slade, Demian (act): Radioactive Dreams
Slade, Jon (C.) (act): Black Magic Woman; 976-EVIL; Slam Dance
Slade, Mark (act): The Astral Factor; Voyage to the Bottom of the Sea
Slade, Max Elliott (act): Apollo 13
Slagle, Charly (act): Twisted
Slama, Mark (act): Shocker
Slaney, Ivor (mus): Death Ship; Lady In the Fog; Murder by Proxy; Prey (1978); The Saint's Return; Terror (1979)
Slate, Henry (act): The Cat from Outer Space; Herbie Goes Bananas; The Shaggy D.A.
Slate, Jeremy (act, b. 1925): Crosscurrent; Dead Pit; The Lawnmower Man; Stowaway to the Moon; Stranger In Our House
Slate, Lane (wri): The Car; Isn't It Shocking?; The Strange and Deadly Occurrence; The Tribe
Slater, Barney (wri, b. 1923): Gorilla at Large; It Grows On Trees
Slater, Blair (act): Zenon: Girl of the 21st Century
Slater, Christian (act, b. 1969): Beyond the Stars; Ferngully: The Last Rain Forest; Heathers; Interview With the Vampire; The Name of the Rose; Robin Hood: Prince of Thieves; Star Trek VI: The Undiscovered Country; Tales from the Darkside; Twisted
Slater, Debbie (act): Popdown
Slater, Helen (act, b. 1964): Betrayal of the Dove; Supergirl (1984); 12:01
Slater, Jack (act): Remote Control (1988)
Slater, Jennifer (act): Violent Women
Slater, John (act): The Flanagan Boy; Murder In Reverse; A Place to Go; The Ringer (1952); The Saint Meets the Tiger; Violent Playground; Went the Day Well?
Slater, Ryan (act): The Babysitter (1995)
Slater, Suzanne (act): Mind Twister
Slater, Suzee (act): Chopping Mall
Slatter, Chris (dir): The Project
Slattery, James (act): see Darling, Candy
Slattery, John (act): Eraser
Slattery, Page (act): Cape Fear (1961)
Slattery, Richard X. (act, 1925-1997): Wonder Woman
Slatzer, Robert F. (dir & wri, b. 1927): Big Foot
Slaughter, N. Carter (act): see Slaughter, Tod
Slaughter, Tod (act, 1885-1956, nee N. Carter Slaughter): Crimes at the Dark House; The Crimes of Stephen Hawke; The Demon Barber of Fleet Street; The Face at the Window (1939); A Ghost for Sale; The Greed of William Hart; Maria Marten: or, The Murder In the Red Barn (1935); Murder at Scotland Yard; Murder at the Grange; Sexton Blake and the Hooded Terror
Slavica (act): Dracula Sucks
Slavin, George (F.) (wri, b. 1916): Rocket Man (1954); Son of Robin Hood
Slavin, Millie (act): Forever Young; Revenge of the Stepford Wives; Summer Girl
Slavin, Randall (act): Generation X; Primal Fear
Slavin, Slick (act): The Bride and the Beast
Slavin, Susan (act): Black Zoo
Slavinsky, Yevgeni (cin): Pikovaya Dama (1916)
Slaymaker, Rocky (act): Distortions
Slayton, Bobby (act): Ed Wood; The Shaggy Dog (1994)
Sleap, Steve (act): Howard the Duck
Sledge, John (dir): The Invisible Avenger
Sledge, Tommy (act): Lobster Man from Mars
Sledmere, Peter (act): Night of the Red Hunter
Sleep, Wayne (act): Peter Rabbit and the Tales of Beatrix Potter
Sleep'n'Eat (act): see Best, Willie
Sleet, Jackson (act): Project X (1987)
Slesar, Henry (wri, b. 1927): Alfred Hitchcock Presents; The Eyes of Annie Jones; The Maddening; Murders In the Rue Morgue (1971); Terror from the Year 5,000; Two On a Guillotine
Slezak, Walter (act, 1902-1983): Bedtime for Bonzo; Born to Kill; Cornered; Doctor?? Coppelius!!; Lifeboat; The Miracle (1959); Sinbad the Sailor; The Spanish Main; Spy Hunt; Treasure Island (1971); 24 Hours to Kill; The Wonderful World of the Brothers Grimm
Slider, Dan (mus): Uninvited (1987)
Sloan, Bill (act): Treasure Island (1990)
Sloan, Chuck (act): Total Recall
Sloan, David (act): The Hideous Sun Demon
Sloan, Gary (act): Witchcraft (1988)
Sloan, Holly Goldberg (wri): Angels In the Outfield (1994)
Sloan, Michael (wri): Assassin (1973); Bionic Showdown: The Six Million Dollar Man and the Bionic Woman; Earthquake In New York; Moments; The Return of the Man from U.N.C.L.E.; The Return of the Six Million Dollar Man and the Bionic Woman
Sloan, Ron (act): Friday the 13th-Part V: A New Beginning
Sloane, Bart (cin): 4D Man
Sloane, Everett (act, 1909-1965): Journey Into Fear (1942); The Lady from Shanghai
Sloane, John (act): The Last Train
Sloane, Michael (wri): The Day the Screaming Stopped; Hunted (1973)
Sloane, Olive (act, 1896-1963): The Frightened Bride; The Golden Link; The House On Marsh Road; The Howard Case; The Last Man to Hang?; The Man In the Road; Meet Mr. Lucifer; The Price of Silence; Seven Days to Noon; Thunder Rock; Tower of Terror; Under Capricorn; Wrong Number
Sloane, Rick (dir): Visitants
Sloane, William (wri, b. 1906): The Devil Commands
Slobbe, Frank (act): Dark of the Night
Slocombe, Douglas (cin, b. 1913): Boom; Cage of Gold; Circus of Horrors; Dead of Night (1945); Fathom; The Fearless Vampire Killers: or Pardon Me, But Your Teeth Are In My Neck; A High Wind In Jamaica; Indiana Jones and the Last Crusade; Indiana Jones and the Temple of Doom; Kind Hearts and Coronets; The Lady Vanishes (1979); The Lavender Hill Mob; The Maids; The Man In the White Suit; The Mark; Never Say Never Again; Raiders of the Lost Ark; The Return (1973, GB); Robbery; Rollerball; The Servant; A Taste of Fear; The Third Secret
Sloman, Edward (dir): The Lost Zeppelin; Murder by the Clock
Sloman, Roger (act): The Monster Club
Slonisco, Federico/Frederick (cin): Ator: The Fighting Eagle; Endgame
Sloots, Patsy (act): see Shaw, Susan
[illegible]
Slowe, Georgia (act): The Company of Wolves
Sloyan, James (act): Xanadu
Sluizer, George (dir): The Vanishing (1988 & 1993)

Sluka, Christopher (act): *Vampire's Kiss*
Slutsky, Susan (act): *The Toxic Avenger, Part II*
Slyter, Fred (act): *The Ultimate Warrior*
Smacchi, Sergio (act): *Super Fuzz*
Smader, David (act): *The Jerusalem File*
Smale, Gail (act): *The Horrible House On the Hill*
Small, Bob (act): *Eyes of a Stranger*
Small, Edgar (act): *Alien Nation; The Kindred*
Small, George (mus): *Last Rites (1980)*
Small, Jerome (wri): *Twilight People*
Small, Marya (act): *Fade to Black; Sleeper; Zapped!*
Small, Merrya (act): *Puppet Master*
Small, Michael (mus): *Audrey Rose; Black Widow (1987); Jaws: The Revenge; The Lathe of Heaven; Marathon Man; The Stepford Wives*
Small, Peg (act): *Orpheus Descending*
Small, Richard B. (act): *The Black Bird (1975)*
Small, Robert (act): *Flight of the Navigator*
Small, Stanley (act): *The Body Snatchers*
Small, Sylvia (act): *The Body Snatchers*
Smalley, Ben (act): *The House of the Dead*
Smalley, Peter (wri): *Dead End Drive-In*
Smalley, Phillips (act): *The Taxi Mystery*
Smallman, Amy (act): *Virtuosity*
Smart, Dee (act): *Blackwater Trail*
Smart, Jean (act): *Project X (1987)*
Smart, Jonathan (act): *The Lawnmower Man*
Smart, Patsy (act): *Baffled!; Electric Dreams; Great Expectations (1974); The Legacy; The Tell-Tale Heart (1960)*
Smart, Ralph (wri, b. 1908): *Alf's Button Afloat; The Phantom Light*
Smart, Rebecca (act): *Doom Runners*
Smart, Robert (mus): *Time Runner*
Smart, Roy (act): *Bedknobs and Broomsticks*
Smart, Sarah (act): *Woof Too! A Girl and Her Dog; Woof Again! Why Me?*
Smart, Tony (act): *The Fifth Musketeer*
Smead, Lillie (act): *The Old Gardener*
Smeaton, Bruce (mus): *The Cars That Ate Paris; Iceman; Picnic at Hanging Rock*
Smedley, Richard (act): *Brain of Blood; Blood of Ghastly Horror*
Smedley, Robert (act): *Children Shouldn't Play With Dead Things*
Smeeton, Phil (act): *Judge Dredd*
Smekalova, Hana (act): see Marly, Florence
Smerczak, Ron (act): *House of Whipcord; Prisoners of the Lost Universe*
Smethurst, Jack (act): *The Main Chance; Night After Night After Night*
Smethurst, William (wri): *Robin Hood Junior (1975)*
Smiar, Brian (act): *Running Against Time*
Smich, John (mus): *The Magic Voyage of Sinbad*
Smid, Daniel (act): *The Kremlin Letter*
Smight, John/Jack (dir, b. 1926): *Damnation Alley; Double Indemnity (1973); Frankenstein: The True Story; The Illustrated Man; Kaleidoscope; No Way to Treat a Lady; The Screaming Woman; Strategy of Terror*
Smika, Gina (act): *The Sword and the Sorcerer*
Smildsin, Kurt (act): *Matinee*
Smiles, Finch (act): see Finch-Smiles, Frank
Smiley, Des (act): *The Resurrected*
Smiley, Don (act): *The Incredibly Strange Creatures Who Stopped Living and Became Mixed-Up Zombies*
Smiley, Joseph (act): *The Face In the Fog (1922); Seven Keys to baldpate (1917)*
Smiley, Joseph W. (dir): *Life Without Soul*
Smiley, Pril (mus): *The Premonition (1975)*
Smillie, Bill (act): *When Time Ran Out*
Smilie, Jim (act): *Murder On the Midnight Express*
Smillie, Bill (act): *Piranha (1978)*
Smilowitz, Josh (act): *Mother's Day*
Smith, A. Thomas (act): *Invader*
Smith, Adam (act): *The Saint*
Smith, Alexis (act, 1921-1993, nee Gladys Smith): *The Decision of Christopher Blake; The Horn Blows at Midnight; The Little Girl Who Lives Down the Lane; The Smiling Ghost; Split Second (1953); The Two Mrs. Carrolls; Undercover Girl (1950); The Woman In White (1948)*
Smith, Alice H. (act): *After the Thin Man*
Smith, Allison (act): *Jason Goes to Hell: The Final Friday*
Smith, Andrea (act): *The Private Lives of Adam and Eve*
Smith, Anna Nicole (act, b. 1967): *Skyscraper*
Smith, Art (act, 1899-1973): *Caught (1948); Mr. Peabody and the Mermaid; The Next Voice You Hear; Ride the Pink Horse; The Sound of Fury; T-Men*
Smith, Art (1990s act): *Warlock*
Smith, Arthur (mus): *Wolfman (1979)*
Smith, B.A. (act): *Narrow Margin (1990)*
Smith, Bill (1940s act): *The Thin Man Goes Home*
Smith, Bill (1980s act): *Mother's Day*
Smith, Bob (act): *The Lair of the White Worm*
Smith, Brandon (act): *Dean Koontz' 'Mr. Murder'; I Come In Peace; Powder; RoboCop 2*
Smith, Brenda (act): *Mr. Sycamore*
Smith, Brian (act): *Feet of Clay; The Rivals; The Village of the Damned (1960)*
Smith, Brian C. (act): *Cocoon: The Return*
Smith, Brittany Alyse (act): *Pinocchio's Revenge*
Smith, Brooke (act): *The Silence of the Lambs*
Smith, Bryan "Travis" (act): *Waxwork II: Lost In Time*
Smith, Bubba (act): *Gremlins 2: The New Batch; The Silence of the Hams*
Smith, Burnal "Custus" (act): *Skullduggery*
Smith, Butterball (act): *Stanley*
Smith, C. Aubrey (act, 1863-1948): *And Then There Were None; Another Thin Man; Beyond Tomorrow; Birds of Prey; Bulldog Drummond Strikes Back (1934); Dr. Jekyll and Mr. Hyde (1941); The Face at the Window (1920); Flesh and Fantasy; The Florentine Dagger; Love Me Tonight; The Phantom of Paris (1931); The Prisoner of Zenda (1937); Rebecca; Secrets of Scotland Yard; Scotland Yard Investigator; The Shuttle of Life; Trader Horn (1931); The Tunnel*
Smith, Carole (act): *Fantasies*
Smith, Caroline (act): *Buck Rogers In the 25th Century*
Smith, Cedric (act): *Millennium; Witchboard: The Possession*
Smith, Chad (act): *The Package*
Smith, Charles (act, b. 1920): *Henry Aldrich Haunts a House; Nancy Drew, Reporter*
Smith, Charles Edward (act): *The Hidden*
Smith, Charles Martin (act, b. 1955): *The Beast (1996); Boris and Natasha; Herbie Goes Bananas; Perfect Alibi; Roswell; Starman*
Smith, Charles Martin (dir): *Boris and Natasha; Trick or Treat*
Smith, Cheryl ("Rainbeaux") (act): *Laserblast; Lemora, the Lady Dracula; Phantom of the Paradise*
Smith, Chief Tug (act): *Superman (1978)*
Smith, Clarence (act): *Just Imagine*
Smith, Clive (dir): *Pippi Longstocking*
Smith, Clive (mus): *Liquid Sky*
Smith, Colby (act): *Dead and Buried; The Final Countdown*
Smith, Constance (act, b. 1929): *Man In the Attic (1953); Murder at the Windmill; The Perfect Woman; Room to Let; The Thirteenth Letter*
Smith, Cotter (act): *Bridge of Time; Cameron's Closet; Lady Beware; Lifeform; Midnight's Child; Remember Me*
Smith, Craig (act): *Bad Taste*
Smith, Craig (cin): *Solar Crisis*
Smith, Curt (act): *Dead Connection*
Smith, Cyril (act, 1892-1963): *The Angel Who Pawned Her Harp; The Black Abbot (1934); Bulldog Jack; Dark Journey; The Dark Man (1951); The Echo Murders; The Frog; The Interrupted Journey; I Was a Spy; Law and Disorder; The Lost Hours; Meet Sexton Blake; Mother Riley Meets the Vampire; Old St. Paul's; The Return of the Frog; The Rocking Horse Winner; A Stolen Face; Svengali (1954); They Made Me a Fugitive; The Tunnel; Vice Versa (1947)*
Smith, Danielle (act): *White of the Eye*
Smith, David (GB act): *Never-Never Land*
Smith, David (USA act): *Metalstorm: The Destruction of Jared-Syn*
Smith, David Anthony (act): *Judgment Day*
Smith, Dawn (act): *Ellery Queen*
Smith, Dawn Eisler (act): *Impulse (1984)*
Smith, Dean (act): *Scream of the Wolf; Timestalkers*
Smith, Debra (act): *Midnight (1980)*
Smith Jr., Delos V. (act): *The Pack*
Smith, Dennis (act): *Howling IV*
Smith, Derek (act): *The Carnation Killer; Recluse; Screamer*
Smith, Dick (cin): *Tales from the Darkside*
Smith, Dodie (wri): *101 Dalmatians (1960 & 1996); The Uninvited (1944)*
Smith, Don (act): *Razorback*
Smith, Doug (act): *Death Ship*
Smith, Douglas (cin): *Independence Day*
Smith, Doyle (cin): *Perfect Alibi*
Smith, Earle (wri): *The Legend of Boggy Creek; The Town That Dreaded Sundown*
Smith, Ebbe Roe (act): *Pandemonium*
Smith Jr., Eddie (Bo) "Ed" (act): *The Fugitive (1993); The Package*
Smith, Elbert (act): *The Blob (1958); 4D Man*
Smith, (Lady) Eleanor (wri): *The Man In Grey*
Smith, Ella Mae (act): *Night of the Living Dead (1968)*
Smith, Elliot (act): *Making Contact*
Smith, Elsa (act): *—And Now the Screaming Starts!*
Smith, Emanuel (act): *Monstroid; The Resurrection of Zachary Wheeler*
Smith, Emily (act): *Dr. Dracula*
Smith, Emmett E. (act): *Voodoo Woman*
Smith, Erle O. (dir & wri): *Terrors*
Smith Jr., Erle (act): *Terrors*
Smith, Ernest (act): *Just Imagine*
Smith, Ernest (cin): *The Man from Downing Street; Tarzan and the Green Goddess*
Smith, Ernie (act): *Wizards of the Lost Kingdom*
Smith, Eve (act): *The Bad Seed (1985); Elvira, Mistress of the Dark; It Came Upon the Midnight Clear; Romancing the Stone; Wicked Stepmother*
Smith, Evelyne (act): *Night of the Creeps*
Smith, Evert (act): *Mr. Sycamore*
Smith, F. Percy (dir): *Bewildering Transformations; Chemical Portraiture; Transformations (1914)*
Smith, F. Percy (wri): *Bewildering Transformations*
Smith, Fabiana (act): *Amazons (1986)*
Smith, Frank (act): *The Cape Canaveral Monsters*
Smith, Frank Leon (wri): *The House Without a Key*
Smith, Frazer (act): *Electric Dreams*
Smith, Frazier (act): *Repossessed*
Smith, Frederick E. (wri): *Devil Doll (1963)*
Smith, G. Michael (act): *Offerings*
Smith, Garnett (act): *Laboratory*
Smith, Gary (act): *Attack of the Killer Tomatoes; Mr. Horatio Knibbles*
Smith, George Albert/G.A. (dir, 1864-1959): *Aladdin and the Wonderful Lamp; The Amazons' March and Evolutions; Animated Clown Portrait; As Seen Through a Telescope; Cinderella and the Fairy Godmother; The Conjurer; The Corsican Brothers (1897); Dick Whittington; Dorothy's Dream; Faust and Mephistopheles; The Haunted Castle (1897); The Haunted Picture Gallery; The Inexhaustible Cab; Making Sausages; Mary Jane's Mishap: or, Don't Fool with the Paraffin; The Mesmerist (1898); Mother Goose Nursery Rhymes; Photographing a Ghost; Santa Claus (1898); X-Rays*
Smith, Gilbert (act): *Warning Sign*
Smith, Gladys (act): see Smith, Alexis
Smith, Gladys Mary (act): see Pickford, Mary
Smith, Glenn (cin): *Nightmare In Wax*
Smith, Graham (act): *Terrors*
Smith, Gregory (act): *The Adventures of Captain Zoom In Outer Space; Shadow Zone: My Teacher Ate My Homework; Small Soldiers; Zenon: Girl of the 21st Century*
Smith, Gregory Edward (act): *Spellbreaker: Secret of the Leprechauns*
Smith, Hal (act, 1916-1994): *The Ghost and Mr. Chicken; Here Come the Littles; The $1,000,000 Duck; The Three Stooges Meet Hercules*
Smith, Hal (wri): *It Came from Beneath the Sea*
Smith, Hank (act): *Street Fighter II: The Animated Movie*
Smith, Harold Jacob (wri): *Enchanted Island*
Smith, Harry (act): *The Man In Grey*
Smith, Heather (act): *The Pink Chiquitas*
Smith, Hillary Bailey (act): *Love Potion No. 9*
Smith, Howard (act): *Call Northside 777; Face of Fire; I Bury the Living*
Smith, Howard Ellis (wri): *Think Fast, Mr. Moto*
Smith, Hubert (wri): *Night Creature*
Smith, Hugh (act): *Invasion of the Girl Snatchers*
Smith, Ian (act): *Body Melt; Child's Play (1954)*
Smith, Ilan-Michael (act): *Journey to the Center of the Earth (1989)*
Smith, J. Augustus (act): *Drums O'Voodoo*
Smith, J. Louis (act): *Shadow of the Thin Man*
Smith, Jack (act, 1932-1989): *Blonde Cobra; The Iliac Passion*
Smith, Jack (act): *The Barefoot Executive; The Phantom Creeps; Silent Night, Bloody Night*
Smith, Jack (dir): *The Lady Luna(tic)'s Hat; Living Statues; Love versus Science; The Magic Box; Suspected: or, The Mysterious Lodger*
Smith Jr., Jack (act): *The China Syndrome*
Smith, Jaclyn (act, b. 1948): *Deja Vu; Free Fall; Love Can Be Murder; The Night They Saved Christmas; Probe*
Smith, Jaime Renee (act): *Children of the Corn IV*
Smith, James (act): *Watchers II*
Smith, James Ellison (act): see Ellison, James
Smith, James H. (act): *Neon Maniacs*
Smith, Jamie (act): *Killer's Kiss*
Smith, Jamie Renee (act): *Dante's Peak*
Smith, Janet M. (wri): *The Dragon of Pendragon Castle*
Smith, Jay (act): *Cocoon: The Return; The Haunting of Hamilton High*
Smith, Jayne (act): *R.O.T.O.R.*
Smith, Jeff (wri): *Monster A Go-Go*
Smith, Jim (act): *The Resurrected*
Smith, Jody (act): *Dream a Little Dream*
Smith, John (act, 1931-1995, nee Robert E. Van Orden): *Island of Lost Women; Women of Pitcairn Island*
Smith, John W. (act): *Star Crystal*
Smith, Johnny L. (act): *The Body Snatchers*
Smith, Karen (act): *Freaky Friday (1976)*
Smith, Kavan (act): *Escape from Mars*
Smith, Keith (act): *The Body Snatchers; Face of a Stranger*
Smith, Kenneth L. (act): *Jungle Moon Men*
Smith, Kent (act, 1907-1985): *Assignment to Kill; The Balcony; The Cat Creature; Cat People (1942); Die Sister, Die!; The Disappearance of Flight 412; Games; The Garden Murder Case; Hitler's Children; How Awful About Allan; The Last Child; Lost Horizon (1973); Moon Pilot; The Mugger; The Night Stalker (1971); Probe; The Spiral Staircase (1946); This Side of the Law*
Smith, Kevin (act): *Young Hercules*
Smith, Kurtwood (act): *Boxing Helena; The Crush; Deadly Messages; Dead On Sight; Fortress; RoboCop; Star Trek VI: The Undiscovered Country*
Smith, Lane (act): *Amazing Stories: The Movie V; Bridge Across Time; Dark Night of the Scarecrow; Man On a Swing; Prison (1988); Red Dawn; The Spy Within*
Smith, Leon (act): *Distortions*
Smith, Leonard (cin): *Devil Doll (1936); Tarzan Escapes*
Smith, Lewis (act): *The Adventures of Buckaroo Banzai; The Final Terror; The Heavenly Kid; The Man Who Fell to Earth (1987)*
Smith, Lily (act): *The Toxic Avenger, Part II*
Smith, Lionel Mark (act): *Galaxina*
Smith, Liz (act): *Agatha; Alice In Wonderland (1999); Apartment Zero; A Christmas Carol (1984); The Fan; High Spirits*
Smith, Lois (act, b. 1930): *Fatal Attraction; Twisted; Twister*
Smith, Loring (act): *Shadow of the Thin Man*
Smith, L'Ronald (act): *Blood Diner*
Smith, Lydia (act): *King Kong Lives*
Smith, Maddy (act): *Taste the Blood of Dracula*
Smith, Madeline (act): *The Amazing Mr. Blunden; Frankenstein and the Monster from Hell; Live and Let Die; Tam Lin; Theater of Blood; The Vampire Lovers*
Smith, Madolyn (act, b. 1958): *All of Me; 2010*
Smith, Maggie (act, b. 1934): *Clash of the Titans; Curtain Call; Death On the Nile; Evil Under the Sun; Murder by Death; Nowhere to Go; Richard III (1995)*
Smith, Maggie Jean (act): *Gold of the Amazon Women*
Smith, Malcolm (act): *Nightbreed*
Smith, Marc (act): *The Final Conflict; Slaughter High*
Smith, Maria (act): *The Incredible Shrinking Woman*
Smith, Marion Owen (act): *Memoirs of a Survivor*
Smith, Marisa (act): *The Brother from Another Planet*
Smith, Marjorie (act): *Who Is Killing the Great Chefs of Europe?*
Smith, Mark (act): *Blood Diner; Kiss of the Tarantula*
Smith, Mark (wri): *El Castello dell'Orrore*
Smith, Mark Allen (wri): *Robin Hood (1991)*
Smith, Martin Cruz (wri): *Gorky Park; Nightwing*
Smith, Mary (act): *Jaws: The Revenge*
Smith, Mary Louise (act): *Charlie Chan at the Opera*
Smith, Mel (act): *Morons from Outer Space; The Princess Bride; Slayground*
Smith, Mel (wri): *Morons from Outer Space*
Smith, Melanie (act): *The Baby Doll Murders; Night Hunter; Trancers III: Deth Lives*
Smith, Michelle (act): *Virtuosity*
Smith, Mitchell (wri): *A Choice of Weapons*
Smith, Mittie (act): *Time Flyer*
Smith, Mona (act): see Barrie, Mona
Smith, Muriel (act): *The Chimes*
Smith, Murray (Can act): *Rabid*
Smith, Murray (USA act): *Just Imagine*

Smith, Murray (wri): *Bear Island; The Day the Screaming Stopped; Die Screaming, Marianne*
Smith, Myron (act): *The Toxic Avenger, Part II*
Smith, Noel (dir): *Torchy Plays With Dynamite*
Smith, Norman (act): *The Amazing Transparent Man*
Smith, Oliver (act): *Hellbound: Hellraiser II; Hellraiser*
Smith, Oscar (act): *The Canary Murder Case; Night of Terror (1933)*
Smith, Paul (act): *The Deadly Mantis; Dune; Now You See Him, Now You Don't; Pieces; Red Sonja; Terminal Entry*
Smith, Paul (mus, 1906-1985): *Moon Pilot; Pinocchio (1940); The Shaggy Dog (1959); Snow White and the Seven Dwarfs; The Three Lives of Thomasina; 20,000 Leagues Under the Sea (1954)*
Smith, Paul Gerard (wri): *The Boys from Syracuse*
Smith, Paul L. (act): *Haunted Honeymoon (1986); Ten Little Indians (1989)*
Smith, Penny (act): *The Clan of the Cave Bear*
Smith, Peter (act): *Embassy; Quarantine; The Quiet Earth*
Smith, Phillip (act): *Night of the Living Dead (1968)*
Smith, Putter (act): *Diamonds Are Forever*
Smith, Queenie (act, 1898-1978): *The Great Rupert; Hold That Hypnotist; Sleep, My Love; The Snake Pit (1948)*
Smith, Rainbeaux (act): *Caged Heat!; The Incredible Melting Man*
Smith, Ray (act): *Look Back In Darkness*
Smith, Rebecca Dianna (act): *Nightmare Honeymoon*
Smith, Reid "Chip" (act): *Blood Mania*
Smith, Rex (act, b. 1956): *A Passion to Kill; Transformations (1989); The Trial of the Incredible Hulk*
Smith, Richard Dana (wri): *The Dentist II*
Smith, Robert (GB wri): *Xtro*
Smith, Robert (USA wri): *Invasion U.S.A.; Platinum High School; Sudden Fear*
Smith, Robin (act): *Lunar Cop*
Smith, Robert Weston (act): see Wolfman Jack
Smith, Roger (act, b. 1932): *Crash Landing; Man of a Thousand Faces*
Smith, Roger (1980s & 1990s act): *The Being; Tales from the Hood*
Smith, Ronald (act): *Terrors*
Smith, Roosevelt (act): *Prophecy (1979)*
Smith, Roy Allen (dir): *The Land Before Time II: The Great Valley Adventure; The Land Before Time III: The Time of the Great Giving; The Land Before Time IV: Journey Through the Mists*
Smith, Russell W. (act): *Strange Days*
Smith, Ryan (act): *Mary Shelley's 'Frankenstein'*
Smith, S.J. (wri): *Silent Night, Deadly Night 4: Initiation*
Smith, Scott (act): *Stargate*
Smith, Sean (wri): *The Dogfighters*
Smith, Sebastian (act): *Museum Mystery; Prehistoric Peeps; The Tramp's Dream (1906)*
Smith, Mrs. (Sebastian) (act): *Prehistoric Peeps*
Smith, Seth (act): *Shadow of a Doubt (1991)*
Smith, Sharon (act): *Nightmare (1981)*
Smith, Shawn (act): *It!—The Terror from Beyond Space; The Land Unknown; World Without End*
Smith, Shawnee (act, b. 1968): *The Blob (1988); Carnival of Souls (1998); I Saw What You Did (1988); The Stand; Twice Upon a Time*
Smith, Shelley (act): *The Phoenix (1981); This House Possessed*
Smith, Shelley (wri): *The Running Man (1963)*
Smith, Shirley W. (wri): *It Happens Every Spring*
Smith, Stephanie (act): *Copycat*
Smith, Stephanie Ann (act): *Under Lock and Key*
Smith, Stephen (cin): *Slayground*
Smith, Steven Brian (act): *Slaughterhouse Rock*
Smith, Sukie (act): *The Witches (1990)*
Smith, Suzanna (act): *Warrior Queen*
Smith, Sydney (act): *The Great Gold Robbery*
Smith, Symba (act): *Once You Meet a Stranger*
Smith, T. Ryder (act): *Brainscan*
Smith, Tammy L. (act): *Dante's Peak*
Smith, Taran Noah (act, b. 1984): *Ebbie; Little Bigfoot 2: The Journey Home*
Smith, Tasha (act): *Max Q: Emergency Landing*
Smith, Terri Susan (act): *Basket Case*
Smith, Thaddeus (act): *Psycho II; Road Games*
Smith, Thorne (wri, 1892-1934): *I Married a Witch; Night Life of the Gods; Topper (1937 & 1979); Topper Returns; Topper Takes a Trip; Turnabout*
Smith, Tom (act): *The Outing*
Smith, Tony (act): *Blood Diner*
Smith, Tracy (act): *Endangered Species*
Smith, (Chief) Tug (act): *Superman (1978)*
Smith, Tyler (act): *Raiders of the Living Dead*
Smith, Valarian (act): *Mistress of Paradise*
Smith, Valentine (act): *The Toxic Avenger, Part II*
Smith, Victor (act): *Wolfman (1979)*
Smith, Vincent (act): *Rawhead Rex*
Smith, Wallace (wri): *Bulldog Drummond (1929); The Lost Squadron*
Smith, Walter (act): see Robinson, Sugar Ray
Smith, Wayne (act): *Mr. Sycamore*
Smith, Web (act): *Capture That Capsule!*
Smith, Webb (wri): *Pinocchio (1940); Snow White and the Seven Dwarfs*
Smith, Wendell (act): *The Haunting of Hamilton High*
Smith, Will (act, b. 1968): *Independence Day; Men In Black*
Smith, Willetta (act): *Prisoners of the Casbah*
Smith, William (act): *Conan the Barbarian; Crackle of Death; Empire of Ash III; Evil Altar; Forgotten City of the Planet of the Apes; Grave of the Vampire; Hell Comes to Frogtown; Invasion of the Bee Girls; Maniac Cop; Memorial Valley Massacre; Red Dawn; The Ultimate Warrior*
Smith Jr., William Massie (act): *Mutants In Paradise*
Smith, Willie E. (act): *The Legend of Boggy Creek*
Smith, Willy (cin): *Amazons (1986)*
Smith, Wilson (act): *Cameron's Closet*
Smith, Yeardley (act): *Maximum Overdrive; We're Back! A Dinosaur's Story*
Smithee, Alan (dir): *Hellraiser 4: Bloodline; Picking Up the Pieces; Solar Crisis*
Smithee, Alan (wri): *The Horror Show*
Smithers, William/Bill (act): *The Brotherhood of the Bell; Deathsport*
Smith-Marriott, Hugh (act): *Diagnosis: Murder*
Smiths, The (mus): *Demons 2*
Smith-Sands, Lindsey (act): *Child of Darkness, Child of Light*
Smitrovich, Bill (act): *Bodily Harm; Dean Koontz' 'Mr. Murder'*
Smits, Jimmy (act, b. 1955): *The Believers; Switch (1991); The Tommyknockers*
Smits, Sonja (act): *The Pit (1983); Videodrome*
Smogghe, Andre (act): *Sky Above Heaven*
Smoktonovsky, Innokenty (act, 1925-1994): *Crime and Punishment (1975); Devyat'dney Odnogo Goda*
Smolek, Jeff (act): *Matinee*
Smolinski, Aaron (act): *Superman (1978)*
Smolinski, Adam (act): *Don't Look Down*
Smolka, Ken (act): *In Self Defense*
Smollen, Bradley J. (wri): *The Man from Downing Street*
Smook, Jan (act): *The Exorcist III*
Smoot, Fred (act): *Beware! The Blob*
Smoot, Reed (cin): *The Wraith*
Smothers, Loren (act): *Always*
Smothers, Tom (act, b. 1937): *Pandemonium; There Goes the Bride*
Smrzik, Igor (act): *Howling II*
Smurl, Jack (wri): *The Haunted (1991)*
Smurl, Janet (wri): *The Haunted (1991)*
Smyj, Brian (act): *Shadow Conspiracy*
Smyrner, Ann(e) (act): *The Black Cobra; House of 1,000 Dolls; Journey to the Seventh Planet; Legacy of Horror (1964); Mission Stardust; Reptilicus; Victim Five*
Smythe, James (act): *Frankenhooker*
Smythe, Karen (act): *The Nest; School Spirit*
Smythe, Sally (act): *Return of the Living Dead, Part II*
Smythe, Vernon (act): *The Curse of the Mummy's Tomb*
Snagge, John (act): *The Magic Christian*
Snay, Tim (act): *Stalking Laura*
Sneagle, Brian (act): *Deranged (1974)*
Snegoff, Gregory (act): *Fist of the North Star; Ladyhawke; Misery; My Neighbor Totoro; She (1983)*
Sneider, Gerti (act): *2069: A Sex Odyssey*
Snell, Anthony (act): *Hour of Decision; The Sound Barrier*
Snell, Bernice (act): *Just Imagine*
Snell, David (act): *Q; Stalking Laura*
Snell, David (mus): *The Hidden Eye; Lady In the Lake; Lost In a Harem; Song of the Thin Man; Tarzan's New York Adventure; Tarzan's Secret Treasure; The Thin Man Goes Home*
Snell, Earle (wri): *Torchy Plays With Dynamite; Torchy Runs for Mayor*
Snell, Harold (act): *Eugene Aram*
Snell, James (act): *The Godsend*
Snell, Kenneth (act): *Charlie Chan and the Curse of the Dragon Queen*
Snell, Patsy (act): *Captain Nemo and the Underwater City*
Snell, Shelley (act): *Premonition (1972)*
Snell, T.J. (act): *Neon Maniacs*
Sneller, Jeffery (M.) (wri): *In the Shadow of Kilimanjaro; Kingdom of the Spiders*
Snider, Andrew (act): *The Stepfather*
Snider, Bill (act): *The Swarm*
Snider, Helmut (act): see Schneider, Helmut
Snider, Norman (wri): *Body Parts (1991); Dead Ringers*
Snider, William (act): *Project X (1987)*
Snipes, Wesley (act, b. 1962): *Blade (1998); Demolition Man; U.S. Marshals*
Snively, Robert (act): *Someone's Watching Me!*
Snodgrass, Melinda M. (wri): *Star Command; Trapped In Space*
Snodgress, Carrie (act, b. 1946): *The Attic; Death Benefit; The Fury; Trick or Treats*
Snoijink, Liz (act): *The Lift*
Snow, Dan (act): *The Toxic Avenger; The Toxic Avenger, Part II*
Snow, David (act): *Pranks*
Snow, Elvira (act): *Freaks*
Snow, G.A. (wri): *The Phantom Thief*
Snow, Jack T. (act): *Heaven Can Wait (1978)*
Snow, Jenny Lee (act): *Freaks*
Snow, Marguerite (act, 1889-1958): *Dr. Jekyll and Mr. Hyde (1912); She (1911)*
Snow, Mark (mus): *Disturbing Behavior; Dolly Dearest; Ernest Saves Christmas; I Dream of Jeannie: Fifteen Years Later; Jake Speed; Summer of Fear; 20,000 Leagues Under the Sea (1997, ABC-TV); The X-Files*
Snow, Norman (act): *The Last Starfighter*
Snow, Pia (act): *Cafe Flesh*
Snow, Victoria (act): *Millennium*
Snowden, Eric (act): *Jungle Gents*
Snowden, Leigh (act, 1932-1982): *The Creature Walks Among Us; Francis In the Navy; I've Lived Before; Kiss Me Deadly*
Snowden, Roger (act): *Gulliver's Travels (1977)*
Snyder, (Arlen) Dean (act): *Night School; No Place to Hide (1981); Prison (1988); Scalpel; Wheels of Terror*
Snyder, Drew (act): *Night School; Space Raiders; Separate Lives; Wargames*
Snyder, Eric (act): *Blood Diner*
Snyder, Howard (wri): *Abbott and Costello Meet the Killer*
Snyder, Jack (dir & wri): *Fatal Exam*
Snyder, John (act): *Eraser; Tattoo*
Snyder, Michael (act): *Star Trek IV: The Voyage Home*
Snyder, Moriah Shining Dove (act): *The Prophecy (1995)*
Snyder, Nancy (act): *The Kirlian Witness*
Snyder, Sammy (act): *Tomorrow Never Comes*
Snyder, Sandy (act): *Murder-In-Law*
Snyder, Stuart (act): *Silent Night, Deadly Night III*
Snyder, Suzanne (act): *Killer Klowns from Outer Space; Night of the Creeps; Retribution (1988); Return of the Living Dead, Part II; Weird Science*
Snyder, Suzy (act): *Remo Williams: The Adventure Begins*
Snyder, William (E.) (cin): *The Bandit of Sherwood Forest; Beyond a Reasonable Doubt; Blackbeard the Pirate; Creature from the Black Lagoon; The $1,000,000 Duck; Moon Pilot; The Return of October; Second Chance; Son of Sinbad; Tarzan and the Trappers; Tarzan's Fight for Life; White Savage*
Snyders, Sammy (act): *An American Christmas Carol; The Pit (1983)*
Snyders, Virginia (act): *Never-Never Land*
Soall, Terence (act): *The Legend of Spider Forest*
Soans, Robin (act): *Absolution*
Soavi, Michele (act): *Phenomena*
Soavi, Michele/Michael (dir): *Cemetery Man; The Church; The Devil's Daughter (1995); La Setta; Stagefright (1987)*
Sobel, Barry (act): *Martians Go Home*
Sobel, Curt (mus): *Alien Nation; Cast a Deadly Spell*
Sobel, Mark (dir): *Storm Chasers: Revenge of the Twister*
Sobers, Gary (act): *Junket 89*
Sobieski, Carol (wri, 1939-1990): *Reflections of Murder*
Soblosky, Perry (act): *Captain Kronos: Vampire Hunter*
Sobolevski, Piotr (act): *Shinel (1926)*
Soboloff, Arnold (act): *The Cat from Outer Space*
Sobolov, David (act): *Unforgettable*
Sobotka, Bohumil (wri): *Do You Keep a Lion at Home?*
Sobotka, Ruth (act): *Killer's Kiss*
Socas, Maria (act): *Deathstalker II: Duel of the Titans; The Warrior and the Sorceress; Wizards of the Lost Kingdom*
Socher, Cheryl (act): *Twilight Zone*
Socher, Hylton (act): *The Beginning of the End*
Soder, Rolf (act): *The Island at the Top of the World*
Soderbergh, Steven (act, dir): *Schizopolis*
Soderbergh, Steven (wri): *Nightwatch (1998); Schizopolis*
Soderling, Walter (act): *Confessions of Boston Blackie; The Falcon In Hollywood; The Gracie Allen Murder Case*
Soeteman, Gerard (wri): *Flesh & Blood; The Fourth Man*
Sofaer, Abraham (act, b. 1896): *Captain Sinbad; Dual Alibi; The Ghosts of Berkeley Square; The House Opposite (1931); Journey to the Center of Time; A Matter of Life and Death; The Naked Jungle; Omar Khayyam; Pandora and the Flying Dutchman; The Story of Mankind; Twice-Told Tales; The Wandering Jew (1933)*
Soffer, Roger (wri): *Kazaam*
Sofia, Vinicio (act): *Il Ladro di Venezia*
Sohl, Jerry (wri, b. 1913): *Curse of the Crimson Altar; Monster of Terror*
Sohnker, Hans (act): *The Phantom of Soho; Valley of Fear (1964)*
S.O.I.S. Co. (cin): *Revenge In the House of Usher*
Soisson, Joel (dir): *Maniac Cop 3: Badge of Silence*
Soisson, Joel (wri): *The Supernaturals; Trick or Treat*
Sojak, Notari (act): *Destroy All Monsters*
Sojin, (Kamiyama/K.) (act): *The Bat (1926); The Chinese Parrot; The Road to Mandalay; The Sea Beast; Seven Footprints to Satan; The Thief of Bagdad (1924); The Unholy Night*
Sokoloff, Harvey (act): *Clarence*
Sokoloff, Marla (act, b. 1980): *True Crime*
Sokoloff, Vladimir (act, 1889-1962): *The Baron of Arizona; Beyond the Time Barrier; Cloak and Dagger (1946); The Conspirators; Istanbul; I Was a Teenage Werewolf; Mr. Sardonicus; Monster from Green Hell; Sabu and the Magic Ring; West of Shanghai*
Sokolova, Natasha (act): *The Spider and the Fly (1949)*
Sokolow, Alec (dir): *Frankenstein Sings*
Sokolow, Alec (wri): *Toy Story*
Sokolowska, Anna (dir & wri): *Wielka, Wielka I Najwieksza*
Sola, Jose (mus): *Pyro*
Solano, Rosalio (cin): *El Ataud del Vampiro; I Escaped from Devil's Island*
Solar, Silvia (act): *Eyeball; Hi, Here's Eddie; La Maldicion de la Bestia*
Solares, Gilberto Martinez (dir & wri): *La Casa del Terror*
Solares, Raul/Raoul Martinez (cin): *El Hombre y el Monstruo; La Invasion de los Vampiros; Swamp of the Lost Souls*
Solari, Suzanne (act): *Roller Blade Warriors: Taken by Force*
Solaro, Gianni (act): *Sword of Damascus*
Solbelli, Olga (act): *Gli Amori di Ercole; Teodora, Imperatrice di Bisanzio*
Solberg, Steven (act): *Luminous Procuress*
Soldani, Charles (act): *Daughter of the Jungle*
Soldati, Mario (dir, b. 1906): *OK, Nero!; Il Sogno di Zorro; The Stranger's Hand*
Soldo, Chris (act(: *Winter Kills*
Sole, Alfred (dir): *Alice, Sweet Alice; Pandemonium; Tanya's Island*
Sole, Alfred (wri): *Alice, Sweet Alice*
Soler, Andres (act): *Flying Saucers*
Soler, Domingo (act): *Blood of Nostradamus; La Maldicion de la Llorona; La Maldicion de Nostradamus; Nostradamus y el Destructor de Monstruos; Nostradamus y el Genio de la Tinieblas*
Soler, Ivette (act): *Popcorn*
Soler, Juan A. (act): *The Mummy's Revenge*
Soler, Julian (dir): *Flying Saucers*
Soler, Mercedes (act): *El Vampiro*
Soler, Vicente (act): *Tristana*
Soles, P.J. (act): *Alienator; Blood Bath (1975); Carrie; Halloween; Little Bigfoot; Out There; The Possessed (1977)*
Soles, Paul (act): *Willy McBean and His Magic Machine*
Soles, Steven (mus): *Destiny Turns On the Radio; Silent Night, Deadly Night III*
Solfizi, Loredana (act): *La Citta delle Donne*
Soli, Christine (act): *Offerings*
Solimine, Chris (wri): *The Odyssey*
Solinas, Giovanni (act): *Seven Dwarfs to the Rescue*
Solis, Charito (act): *Buddha*

Solis, Leonard (cin): Amazons (1986); Deathstalker II: Duel of the Titans; Wizards of the Lost Kingdom
Solis, Martha "Guera" (act): Doctor of Doom
Solitari, Bruno B. (act): Kemek
Solito, Samuel R. (act): Night of the Living Dead (1968)
Solleville, Marie Clair (wri): Orgasmo
Sollima, Sergio (wri): Goliath Against the Giants; Requiem for a Secret Agent
Solntseva, Yulia (act, b. 1901): Aelita
Sologne, Madeleine (act): L'Eternel Retour
Soloman, Emma (act): The Punisher
Solomin, Juri (act): The Red Tent
Solomon, Bruce (act): Children Shouldn't Play With Dead Things; Night of the Creeps
Solomon, Carol (act): The Dungeonmaster
Solomon, Charles (act): The Channler; Witchcraft 2: The Temptress; Witchcraft 3: The Kiss of Death; Witchcraft 4: The Virgin Heart
Solomon, David (wri): Amazons (1984)
Solomon, Ed(ward) (wri): Bill & Ted's Bogus Journey; Bill & Ted's Excellent Adventure; Mom and Dad Save the World; Super Mario Bros.
Solomon, Elliot (mus): Black Roses
Solomon, Jonny (act): Vampire at Midnight
Solomon III, King (act): Trader Horn (1973)
Solomon, Shirley (act): Starship Invasions
Solon, Ewen (act, b. 1923): Account Rendered; The Curse of the Werewolf; The Hound of the Baskervilles (1959); Infamous Conduct; Jack the Ripper (1958); 1984 (1955); The Spaceman and King Arthur; The Terror of the Tongs; Valley of the Eagles; The Wicked Lady
Solonitsyn, Anatoly (act): Solaris
Solorio, Sofia (act): Dr. Tarr's Torture Dungeon
Solotoff, Rocky (cin): An American Tail
Soloviev, Yuri (act): The Sleeping Beauty (1965, Russ)
Solovyov, L. (wri): Shinel (1965)
Solow, Bruce (act): Eyes of Fire
Solow, Eugene (wri): League of Frightened Men; Of Mice and Men (1939); Return of the Terror
Solowicz, Dick (act): Sometimes They Come Back
Solvay, Paul (dir): The Devil's Wedding Night
Solway, Larry (act): The Brood
Somack, Jack (act): Blood Bath (1975)
Soman, Claude (wri): Ashes
Somer, Yanti (act): Reactor; War of the Planets
Somerfield, Helga (act): 24 Hours to Kill
Somers, Connie (act): The People of the Rocks
Somers, Dalton (dir): The People of the Rocks
Somers, Esther (act): Portrait of Jennie; The Snake Pit (1948)
Somers, Julian (act): Fatal Journey; Hunted (1952)
Somers, Julie (act): Death of an Angel
Somers, Kristi (act): Hell Comes to Frogtown; Return to Horror High
Somers, Paul (wri): The Desperate Man
Somers, Suzanne (act, b. 1946): Devil's Food; It Happened at Lake Wood Manor; Lovestruck; Seduced by Evil; Serial Mom
Somers-Clarke, Constance (act): Gipsy Hate
Somerville, Jimmy (act): Orlando
Somerville, Roy (wri): Jungle Trail of the Son of Tarzan
Sommer, Elke (act, b. 1940, nee Elke Schletz): The Astral Factor; Deadlier Than the Male; House of Exorcism; The Invisible Strangler; It's Not the Size That Counts; Gli Orrori del Castello di Noremberga; Percy; The Prisoner of Zenda (1979); Probe; Severed Ties; Ten Little Indians (1974); The Venetian Affair; The Wrecking Crew; Zeppelin
Sommer, Josef (act): Bionic Showdown: The Six Million Dollar Man and the Bionic Woman; D.A.R.Y.L.; Doctor Franken; Dracula's Widow; The Enemy Within; The Henderson Monster; Iceman; Malice; Man On a Swing; The Rosary Murders; Sparkling Cyanide; Still of the Night; Strange Days; Target
Sommer, Robert (act): Daylight
Sommerfeld, Helga (act): The Phantom of Soho
Sommers, April (act): Death Dimension
Sommers, Joanie (act): Everything's Ducky
Sommers, Russell (act): Lifeforce
Sommers, Stephen (dir): Deep Rising; The Jungle Book (1994); The Mummy (1999)
Sommers, Stephen (wri): Deep Rising; The Jungle Book (1994)
Sommerset, Pat (act): Bulldog Drummond Escapes; Bulldog Drummond Strikes Back (1934); The Lone Wolf Returns (1935)
Sommerville, Ian (act): Towers Open Fire
Somrack, Danny (act): Slaughterhouse Rock
Sondergaard, Gale (act, 1899-1985): The Black Cat (1941); The Blue Bird (1940); The Cat and the Canary (1939); The Cat Creature; The Climax; Echoes; Enemy Agents Meet Ellery Queen; Enter Arsene Lupin; Gypsy Wildcat; The Invisible Man's Revenge; Maid of Salem; The Mark of Zorro (1940); A Night In Paradise; Paris Calling; Spider Woman; The Spider Woman Strikes Back; The Strange Death of Adolf Hitler; The Time of Their Lives
Sondheim, Stephen (wri): The Last of Sheila
Sonego, Rudolpho (wri): Il Disco Volante
Song, Lim Bun (act): The Fiendish Plot of Dr. Fu Manchu
Song, Magie (act): Dr. Caligari
Song, Tamela (act): Silent Night, Deadly Night III
Song-Ki, Ahn (act): Gesom E Kako Shipta; Village In the Mist
Sonka, Anne (act): The Giant Gila Monster
Sonnenfeld, Barry (act, b. 1953): Addams Family Values
Sonnenfeld, Barry (cin, b. 1953): Big; Blood Simple; Misery
Sonnenfeld, Barry (dir, b. 1953): The Addams Family; Addams Family Values; Men In Black
Sonnex, Johanna (act): Stories from a Flying Trunk
Sonoma (mus): Satan's Cheerleaders
Sonoi, Keisuke (act): The X from Outer Space
Sont, Gerry (act): Chilling (1981)
Sony Pictures Imageworks (cin): Wolf
Sonye, Michael (D.) (act): The Phantom Empire; Roller Blade Warriors: Taken by Force; Surf Nazis Must Die; The Tomb
Sonye, Michael (wri): Blood Diner
Soo, David (act): Quarantine
Soo, Jack (act, 1915-1979): Return from Witch Mountain
Soo, Papillon Soo (act): A View to a Kill
Sood, Surgit (act): No Blade of Grass
Sood, Veena (act): Memories of Murder; Timecop
Sookdeo, Diana (act): Wild Thing
Soong, Anita (act): Experiment In Terror
Soo Soo, Papillon (act): A View to a Kill
Sopanen, Jeri (cin): The Bermuda Depths
Soper, Mark (act): Phenomenon
Soper, Mike (act): Blood Rage
Sophocles (wri, 496?-406 B.C.): Antigone; Edipo Re; Electra (1961); Oedipus Rex (1956 & 1967)
Sopkiw, Michael (act): After the Fall of New York; Blastfighter
Soraya (act): She (1965)
Sorbo, Kevin (act): Kull the Conqueror
Sorcey, Juliet (act): Communion
Sordi, Alberto (act, b. 1925): And Suddenly It's Murder; Il Disco Volante; Lo Sceicco Bianco
Soreen, Ann (act): The Black Tulip (1937)
Sorel, Agnes (act): Window to Paris
Sorel, George (act): Son of the Thin Man
Sorel, Jean (act, b. 1934, nee Jean de Rochbrune): Belle de Jour; Hipnosis; A Lizard In a Woman's Skin; The Man Who Laughs (1965); A Quiet Place to Kill; Trader Horn (1973)
Sorel, Louise (act): Charlie Chan: Happiness Is a Warm Clue; The Loves of Dracula; The Mark of Zorro (1974); Rona Jaffe's Mazes and Monsters; World of Dracula
Sorel, Sonia (act): Blonde for a Day; Bluebeard (1944); Captain Kidd and the Slave Girl
Sorel, Theodore/Ted (act): Basket Case 2; Doctor Franken; From Beyond
Soremekun, Koi (act): What We Did That Night
Sorensen, Carl (cin): Flesh-Eating Mothers
Sorensen, Eva (act): The Incredible 2-Headed Transplant
Sorensen, Paul (act): Escape to Witch Mountain (1975); The Resurrection of Zachary Wheeler; Sherlock Holmes In New York; Star Trek III: The Search for Spock
Sorensen, Rick (act): The Cat from Outer Space
Sorensen, Sam (mus): Party Line
Sorenson, Bob (act): The Lightning Incident
Sorenson, Fred (act): Raiders of the Lost Ark
Sorenson, Heidi (act): Fright Night
Sorenson, Linda (act): Dean R. Koontz' 'Whispers'; Our Man Flint: Dead On Target; Stone Cold Dead
Sorenson, Peter (act): Sampa
Sorenson, Ricki(e)/Rick(y) (act): The Cat from Outer Space; Man of a Thousand Faces; The Sword In the Stone; Tarzan and the Trappers; Tarzan's Fight for Life
Sorent, Sylvia (act): La Danza Macabra
Soreny, Eve (act): Assignment to Kill
Soresi, Jon (act): Batman (1989)
Soria, Mario (act): Operation Kid Brother
Soriano, Antonio (cin): The Servants of Twilight
Soriano, Charo (act): Gran Amore del Conde Dracula
Sorina, Alexandra (act): Orlacs Haende
Sorkin, Aaron (wri): Malice
Sorley, Edward (act): Bulldog Drummond's Third Round; The Pied Piper of Hamelin; The Sword of Damocles
Soroca, Karen (act): To Die For II: Son of Darkness
Sorrel, George (act): Charlie Chan In Monte Carlo; Charlie Chan In City In Darkness
Sorrell, Cindy (wri): Black Roses
Sorrell, Karen (act): The Mysterious Mr. Moto
Sorrell, Rozlyn (act): A Nightmare On Elm Street 3: Dream Warriors
Sorrells, Bill (act): The Clone Master; Heaven Can Wait (1978); The Howling; Witches' Brew
Sorrentino, Richard (act): Werewolf of Washington
Sorrentino, Robert (cin): Day of the Animals
Sorrentino, Spike (act): Attack of the Killer Tomatoes
Sortman, Robin (act): The Strangeness
Sorvino, Mira (act, b. 1970): Mimic
Sorvino, Paul (act, b. 1939): Chiller; The Day of the Dolphin; Dick Tracy (1990); Escape Clause; Houdini (1998); I, the Jury (1982); Oh, God!; The Rocketeer; The Stuff
Sorya, Francoise (act): see Aimee, Anouk
Sos, Laszlo (act): Phantom of the Opera (1983)
Sosa, Elizabeth (act): Mirrors
Sosa, Guillermo Bravo (act): Run for the Sun
Sosman, Pipo (act): Babes In Toyland (1986)
Sosna, David (act): Point of No Return
Sosso, Pietro (act): The Last of the Lone Wolf; Rip Van Winkle (1921)
Sotello, Dimas (act): Secret of the Incas
Soter, Rena (act): Nightmare Street
Sothern, Ann (act, b. 1909, nee Harriette Lake): The Blue Gardenia; The Killing Kind; Lady In a Cage; The Manitou; Shadow On the Wall
Sothern, Dean (act): Halloween With the Addams Family
Soto, Fernando (act): La Invasion de los Vampiros
Soto, Hugo (act): Man Facing Southeast; Time to Come
Soto, Jose (act): Wolf
Soto, Talisa (act, b. 1967): Licence to Kill (1989); Mortal Kombat; Mortal Kombat: Annihilation; Vampirella (1996)
Sotos, Jim (dir): Sweet Sixteen
Sottelo, Willie (act): The Horror from Beyond
Sottile, Michael (act): Outbreak
Souchon, Alain (act): One Deadly Summer
Soucie, Kath (act): Space Jam
Soucy, Hector (act): Conquest of the Planet of the Apes
Souder, Dennis (act): The Toxic Avenger
Souder, Larry (act): King Kong Lives
Soul, David (act, b. 1943): The Bride In Black; The Disappearance of Flight 412; The Fifth Missile; Salem's Lot; Through Naked Eyes; World War III
Soule, Olan (act): The Atomic City; The Destructors; The Shaggy D.A.
Sousa, John Philip (mus, 1854-1932): Doc Savage, the Man of Bronze
Souster, Tim (mus): Slugs
Soutar, Andrew (wri): The Black Night; I Hear You Calling Me
Soutar, Farren (act): The Black Abbot (1934)
Soutendijk, Rene(e) (act): The Cold Room; Eve of Destruction; The Fourth Man; Grave Secrets; Out of Order
South, Leonard J. (cin): Family Plot; Scream, Pretty Peggy
Southard, Harry (act): The House of Secrets (1929)
Southcott, Fleet (cin): The House That Wouldn't Die; How Awful About Allan
Southcott, Tim (cin): Satan's School for Girls
Souther, John David/J.D. (act): Always; Purgatory
Southerland, Joe (mus): The Day It Came to Earth
Southern, Eve (act): The Haunted House (1929)
Southern, Fred (act): Eugene Aram
Southern, Terry (wri, 1924-1995): Barbarella; Dr. Strangelove: or, How I Learned to Stop Worrying and Love the Bomb; The Loved One; The Magic Christian
Southon, Mike (cin): Gothic; A Kiss Before Dying (1991); Paperhouse; The Secret Life of Ian Fleming; Snow White: A Tale of Terror
Southwell, Gilbert (dir): A Child's Dream of Christmas; Detective Ferris; Father's Coat to the Rescue; The Submarine Plans
Soutten, Ben (act): The Crimes of Stephen Hawke; The Demon Barber of Fleet Street; The Mystery of the Mary Celeste; The Sign of Four (1932); Under the Red Robe (1937)
Souvestre, Pierre (wri): Fantomas (1913); Fantomas Contro Scotland Yard
Souza, Emory (act): The Evil
Sova, Peter (cin): Late for Dinner
Soviak, George (act): Demonoid; End of the World (1977)
Soviero, Donaldo (act): Martin
Sowards, Jack (wri): Death Cruise
Sowerby, Jane (act): The Pink Chiquitas
Sowle, Diana (act): Willy Wonka and the Chocolate Factory
Sozansky, John (act): Martin
Spaak, Agnes (act): Baraka X-77; El Secreto del Doctor Orlof
Spaak, Catherine (act, b. 1945): The Cat O' Nine Tails; Le Trou
Spaak, Charles (wri, 1903-1975): The Burning Court; Cartouche (1962)
Spaccatini, Antonino (act): Amarcord
Space, Arthur (act, 1908-1983): African Treasure; The Bat People; The Claw Monsters; The Cockeyed Miracle; The Folks at Red Wolf Inn; The Lone Wolf and His Lady; Mansion of the Doomed; The Red House; The Swarm; Target Earth; 20 Million Miles to Earth
Spacek, Sissy (act, b. 1949): Carrie
Spacey, Kevin (act): Doomsday Gun; Outbreak; Seven; A Time to Kill (1996); The Usual Suspects
Spade, David (act): Coneheads; Senseless (1998)
Spader, James (act, b. 1960): Crash (1996); Curtain Call; Jack's Back; Mannequin; Starcrossed; Stargate; Wolf
Spadero, Thom (act): Dead of Night (1987)
Spadola, Pasquale (act): Kaos
Spadorcia, Enrico (wri): Robin Hood and the Pirates
Spagnoli, Alberto (cin): The Adventures of Hercules; Hercules (1983); Killer Fish
Spagnuolo, Billy (act): Maniac (1980)
Spagnuolo, Denise (act): Maniac (1980)
Spagnuolo, Diana (act): Maniac (1980)
Spain, Delbert (act): The Unnamable
Spain, Fay (act, 1932-1983): The Abductors; Ercole alla Conquista della Atlantide; Flight to Fury; The Naked Zoo; The Private Lives of Adam and Eve
Spain, Susan (act): Lunatic
Spalding, Ernest (act): Love In the Welsh Hills
Spalding, Harry (wri): Curse of the Fly; The Day Mars Invaded Earth; House of the Damned (1962); The Murder Game; Spaceflight IC-1; Witchcraft (1964)
Spalding, Ken (act): Dimension 5
Spalding, Kim (act): It!—The Terror from Beyond Space
Spall, Tim(othy) (act): The Bride (1985); Crusoe; Dream Demon; Gothic
Spalla, Ermino (act): Miracle In Milan
Spalla, Ignazio (act): Spara Forte, Piu Forte...Non Capisco
Spang, Laurette (act): Battlestar Galactica
Spangler, Dick (act): Conquest of the Planet of the Apes; The Seventh Sign
Spangler, Scott Bailey (act): My Science Project
Spano, Joe (act): Primal Fear; Warlock Moon
Spano, Roberto (wri): El Castello dell'Orrore
Spano, Vincent (act): Creator; High Frequency
Spanoghe, Ali (act): Blind Date
Spanos, E. (act): Blind Date
Spany, Joe (act): Warlock Moon
Sparber, Hershel (act): King Kong Lives
Spargo, Sheree (act): The Lightning Incident
Sparkes, Sybil (act): The Grit of a Dandy
Sparkle, Susan (act): The Amazing Dr. Jekyll
Sparkman, Jim (act): Always
Sparks (mus): Rollercoaster
Sparks, Cheryl (act): Silent Running
Sparks, Don (act): Reflections of Murder
Sparks, Donita (act): Serial Mom
Sparks, Frank (act): Jaws 2
Sparks, Mel (act): Surf Nazis Must Die
Sparks, Ned (act, 1883-1957): Alias the Lone Wolf; Alice In Wonderland (1933); The Canary Murder Case; Seven Keys to Baldpate (1925)
Sparks, Richard (act): The Toxic Avenger, Part II
Sparkuhl, Theodor (cin, 1894-1945): Among the Living; Anna Boleyn; Die Augen der Mumie Ma; Carmen (1918); Madame DuBarry (1919); Die Puppe; The Remarkable Andrew; Sumurun
Sparr, Robert (dir): Once You Kiss a Stranger
Sparrow, Sharolyn (act): The Pink Chiquitas
Sparrow, Walter (act): Dr. Terror's House of Horrors (1964); Robin Hood: Prince of Thieves
Sparv, Camilla (act, b. 1943): America 3000; Assignment K; Mackenna's Gold; Murderers' Row; Nobody Runs Forever; Survival Zone
Spatz, Linda (act): Kiss of the Tarantula

Spaulding, George L. (act): *The Chinese Ring; The Golden Eye*
Spaulding, Thomas (cin): *The Blob (1958)*
Spaull, Colin (act): *Nodddy In Toyland*
Speakman, Jeff (act): *Escape from Atlantis; Slaughterhouse Rock; Timelock*
Spear, Bernard (act): *Bedazzled; Gulliver's Travels (1977); Wombling Free*
Spear, David (mus): *The Creature Wasn't Nice; Fear No Evil (1981); Kiss Daddy Goodbye*
Spear, Eric (mus): *Ghost Ship (1952); Street of Shadows*
Spear, Susie (act): *Dante's Peak*
Spearman, Frank H. (wri): *Whispering Smith*
Spearman, Janet (act): *Secrets of Sex*
Spears, Diana (act): *The Devil's Hand (1961)*
Spears, Steve J. (act & wri): *Those Dear Departed*
Speary, Phil (act): *The Attic*
Specht, Beth (act): *Billion Dollar Threat*
Specht, (Georges) (cin): *L'Atlantide (1920); L'Inhumaine*
Specht, Karen (act): *Billion Dollar Threat*
Specht, Lisa (act): *The First Power*
Specht, Robert (wri): *The Immortal; Night Slaves*
Speck, Jan (act): *Modern Problems; Pandemonium; Point of No Return*
Specter, Don (act): *Mr. Sycamore*
Spector, Craig (wri): *A Nightmare On Elm Street 5: The Dream Child; Volcano: Fire On the Mountain*
Speechley, David (wri): *Outer Touch*
Speed, Carol (act): *Abby*
Speed, Jacqui (act): *Cauldron of Blood*
Speelmans, Herman (act): *F.P. 1 Antwortet Nicht*
Speer, Charlotte (act): *Planet of Dinosaurs*
Speer, Martin (act): *The Dark Ride; Exo-Man; The Hills Have Eyes; Killer's Delight*
Speer, W. Harold (dir): *Xmas Greeting Film*
Speer, Walter (dir): *The Motor Bandits*
Speeth, Christopher (dir & wri): *Malatesta's Carnival*
Speight, Johnny (wri): *Privilege*
Speights, Leslie (act): *One Dark Night*
Speir, Dona (act): *Fit to Kill; Hard Hunted*
Speirs, Gordon (act): *Alien High*
Speizer, Andres (act): *Tombs of the Blind Dead*
Spell, Karen (act): *Cyborg (1989)*
Spelling, Aaron (act): *Black Widow (1954); Vicki*
Spelling, Daniel (act): *Dr. Black Mr. Hyde; The Night God Screamed*
Spelling, Tori (act): *Awake to Danger; Mother, May I Sleep with Danger?*
Spellos, Peter (act): *Dinosaur Island (1994)*
Spelman, Sharon (act): *The Stepford Children*
Spelson, Peter (act & wri): *The Psychotronic Man*
Spelvin, Georgina (act): *High Priestess of Sexual Witchcraft; I Spit On Your Corpse*
Spence, Bruce (act): *The Cars That Ate Paris; Moby Dick (1998); The Road Warrior; 20th Century Oz*
Spence, Grayce (act): *She's Dressed to Kill*
Spence, Mindy (act): *Wheels of Terror; Seduced by Evil*
Spence, Norm (act): *Trilogy of Terror II*
Spence, Ralph (wri): *The Gorilla (1927, 1931 & 1939); King Solomon's Mines (1937)*
Spenceley, Peter (wri): *The Creeping Flesh*
Spencer, Alan (dir & wri): *Hexed*
Spencer, Alexandra (act): *Without a Clue*
Spencer, Barbara (act): *Just Before Dawn (1980)*
Spencer, Benton (dir): *The Club (1994)*
Spencer, Brenton (cin): *Blue Monkey*
Spencer, Bud (act): *Aladdin (1987); Quatro Mosche di Velluto Gris; The Sheriff and the Satellite Kid*
Spencer, Cleon (act): *Superman II*
Spencer, Derek (wri): *The Return of Swamp Thing*
Spencer, Douglas (act): *The Big Clock; Houdini (1953); Monkey Business; River of No Return; The Thing from Another World; This Island Earth; The Three Faces of Eve*
Spencer, Frank (mus): *Cloudburst*
Spencer, Gladys (act): *Psyche 59*
Spencer, James Lawrence (cin): *Magic Island*
Spencer, John (act): *Echoes; WarGames*
Spencer, Marian (act): *Doctor of Seven Dials; Intimate Relations; Seance On a Wet Afternoon; Spellbound (1941); The Three Worlds of Gulliver*
Spencer, Marv (act): *The Killing Edge*
Spencer, Penny (act): *Countdown to Danger; The Playbirds*
Spencer, Sally-Jane (act): *The Anniversary*
Spencer, Tracie (mus): *A Connecticut Yankee In King Arthur's Court (1989)*
Spencer, Valerie (act): *Blink*
Spencer, William (cin): *Countdown; The Mephisto Waltz*
Spender, Elizabeth (act): *Brazil*
Spendler, Emily (act): *The Meateater*
Spenser, David (act): *Battle Beneath the Earth; The Earth Dies Screaming; The Stranglers of Bombay*
Spenser, Jeremy (act, b. 1937): *Fahrenheit 451; He Who Rides a Tiger; The Spider and the Fly (1949); Vengeance*
Spenser, Lou (act): *Lady Beware*
Spensley, Philip (act): *Deadbolt; Oh Heavenly Dog*
Spentzos, Sophia (act): *Victim Five*
Spera, Andrea (act): *Demons 2*
Spera, Robert (dir): *Witchcraft (1988)*
Sperber, Milo (act): *Billion Dollar Brain*
Sperber, Wende Jo (act): *Back to the Future*
Sperdakos, George (act): *Exo-Man*
Sperling, David (cin): *Bloodeaters; The Boogey Man; Street Trash; Toxic Zombies*
Speyer, Erica (act): *The Sand Castle*
Speziali, Renato (act): *Marte, Dio della Guerra*
Spheeris, Penelope (dir): *Senseless (1998)*
Spicer, Bernard (wri): *Ambush In Leopard Street*
Spicer, Bryan (dir): *Mighty Morphin Power Rangers*
Spicer, Jerry (act): *Peacemaker (1990); Witchcraft 6: The Devil's Mistress*
Spicer, Tessa (act): *Flash Gordon (1980)*
Spicer, Venetia (act): *Flash Gordon (1980)*
Spiegel, Barbara (act): *Glen and Randa; Werewolf of Washington*
Spiegel, Bernard (act): *The Phantom of the Opera (1990)*
Spiegel, Dennis (mus): *Zorro: The Legend Begins*
Spiegel, Harry (act): *Darkman II: The Return of Durant*
Spiegel, Scott (act): *Darkman (1990); The Dead Next Door*
Spiegel, Scott (dir): *Intruder (1988)*
Spiegel, Scott (wri): *Evil Dead 2: Dead by Dawn*
Spiegel, Victor (mus): *Dolls*
Spiegelgass, Leonard (wri, 1909-1985): *The Boys from Syracuse; Mystery Street*
Spielberg, Anne (wri): *Big; Christine; Winter Kills*
Spileberg, David (act): *Christine; The Henderson Monster*
Spielberg, Steven (act, b. 1947): *Something Evil*
Spielberg, Steven (dir, b. 1947): *Always; Amazing Stories; Amazing Stories II; Close Encounters of the Third Kind; Duel; E.T.-The Extra-Terrestrial; Indiana Jones and the Last Crusade; Indiana Jones and the Temple of Doom; Jaws; Jurassic Park; L.A. 2017; The Lost World: Jurassic Park; Minority Report; Night Gallery; Raiders of the Lost Ark; Something Evil; Twilight Zone*
Spielberg, Steven (wri, b. 1947): *Close Encounters of the Third Kind; The Goonies; Poltergeist*
Spier, Riva (act): *Ghost Keeper; Rabid; Syngenor*
Spier, William (wri): *Tam Lin*
Spiers, Elliott (act): *Paperhouse*
Spiers, Ros (act): *The Man from Hong Kong*
Spies, Adrian (wri, 1920-1998): *Hauser's Memory; The Scorpio Letters*
Spiker, Ray (act): *Prince Valiant (1954)*
Spila, Otello (cin): *Dorian Gray*
Spillane, Mickey (act, b. 1918, nee Frank Morrison): *The Girl Hunters; Ring of Fear*
Spillane, Mickey (wri, b. 1918): *The Girl Hunters; I, the Jury (1953 & 1982); Kiss Me Deadly; The Long Wait; Margin for Murder; My Gun Is Quick*
Spillman, Harry (act): *Code Name Trixie*
Spilsbury, Klinton (act): *The Legend of the Lone Ranger*
Spina, Harold (mus): *Everything's Ducky*
Spina, Maria Grazia (act): *Tiger of the Seven Seas; Zorro Contro Maciste*
Spinak, Larry (act): *Return to Horror High; Vamp*
Spinalli, S.J. (act): *Copycat*
Spindler, Vlado (act): *Arthur the King*
Spinell, Joe (act): *The First Deadly Sin; The Last Horror Film; Maniac (1980); Star Crash; Twinkle, Twinkle, Killer Kane; Winter Kills*
Spinell, Joe (wri): *Maniac (1980)*
Spinella, Stephen (act): *Virtuosity*
Spiner, Brent (act, b. 1955): *Independence Day; Phenomenon; Star Trek: First Contact; Star Trek: Generations; Star Trek: Insurrection*
Spinetti, Victor (act, b. 1933): *Digby-The Biggest Dog In the World; The Little Prince; The Princess and the Goblin*
Spink, George (act): *A Message from Mars (1921)*
Spinks, James (act): *Damien-Omen II*
Spinner, Anthony (wri): *The Lottery*
Spinner, Jennifer (act): *Vampire's Kiss*
Spinner, Marilyn (act): *Queen of the Jungle*
Spinola, Lanfranco (act): *Il Montagna di Dio Cannibale*
Spinotti, Dante (cin): *Blink; The Comfort of Strangers*
Spira, Camilla (act): *Das Testament des Dr. Mabuse*
Spira, Francoise (act): *L'Annee Derniere a Marienbad*
Spirit, Hugh (act): *Return of the Jedi*
Spirson, Leslie Lehr (wri): *Heartless*
Spitz, Joyce (act): *Embryo*
Spitzley, Nathaniel (act): *Arachnophobia*
Spivack, Melodee (act): *Fist of the North Star*
Spivak, Gloria (act): *Carnival of Blood*
Spivy, (Mme.) (act, 1906-1971): *The Fugitive Kind; The Manchurian Candidate*
Spoliansky.Spolianski, Mischa/Michael (mus, b. 1898): *Hitler: The Last Ten Days; King Solomon's Mines (1937); The Man Who Could Work Miracles; The Private Life of Don Juan; Wanted for Murder*
Spollos, Peter (act): *The Guyver*
Sponholtz, Kuno (act): *Night of the Zombies (1981)*
Spooner, Judy (act): *The Private Life of Sherlock Holmes*
Spooner, Tina (act): *The Private Life of Sherlock Holmes*
Sporleder, Gregory (act): *Twister*
Sposito, Carletto (act): *Teodora, Imperatrice di Bisanzio*
Spot the Urbanora Dog (animal act): *The Stolen Airship Plans*
Spotnitz, Frank (wri): *The X-Files*
Spottiswoode, Roger (dir): *Terror Train*
Sprackling, Simon (dir): *Funny Man*
Spradlin, G.D. (act): *Ed Wood; The Formula; The Long Kiss Goodnight*
Spradling, Charles/Charlie (act): *Bad Channels; Puppet Master II; To Sleep With a Vampire*
Spraggon, Peter (act): *Killer's Moon*
Sprague, W.E. (wri): *Motor Psycho*
Spratley, Tom (act): *The Man With Two Brains*
Spratling, Tony (cin): *Edge of Sanity; The Man Who Haunted Himself*
Spraysberry, Robert (mus): *Bodily Harm; A Passion to Kill*
Sprigg, Stanhope (wri): *The Murder of Squire Jeffrey; Paul Sleuth and the Mystic Seven; Paul Sleuth, Crime Investigator: The Burglary Syndicate; Paul Sleuth-The Mystery of the Astorian Crown Prince*
Spriggs, Elizabeth (avct): *Alice In Wonderland (1999); The Cold Room; An Unsuitable Job for a Woman; Work Is a Four Letter Word*
Spring, Helen (act): *Willard*
Springer, Gary (act, b. 1954): *Jaws 2*
Springer Jr., John (act): *When Time Ran Out*
Springfield, Rick (act, b. 1949): *Battlestar Galactica; Nick Knight*
Springfield, Rick (mus, b. 1949): *Demons (1985)*
Springfield, Wayne (act): *Android*
Springford, Ruth (act): *The Changeling*
Springsteen, Pamela (act): *My Science Project; Sleepaway Camp 2: Unhappy Campers; Sleepaway Camp 3: Teenage Wasteland*
Springsteen, R.G. (dir, b. 1904): *I Cover the Underworld; The Red Menace; Secret Venture; Track the Man Down*
Sprink, Cynthia (act): *Neon Maniacs*
Sprinkle, James (act): *Mutants In Paradise*
Sprinkle, Larry (act): *King Kong Lives*
Sprogoe, Ove (act): *Crazy Paradise; Journey to the Seventh Planet*
Sprotte, Bert (act): *The Private Life of Helen of Troy*
Sproule, Peter (act): *Terror (1979)*
Sproule, Scott (act): *Species*
Spruance, Don (act): *This Is Not a Test*
Spry, Robin (act): *Kings and Desperate Men*
Spurgeon, Charles (cin): *Oh Dad Poor Dad, Mamma's Hung You In the Closet and I'm Feelin' So Sad*
Spurin-Calleja, Joseph (act): see Calleia, Joseph
Spurlock, Carl (act): *Secrets of the Phantom Caverns*
Spurlock, Shelley (act): *Bad Ronald; Cocoon: The Return*
Spurr, Sandra (act): *Hunted In Holland*
Spurrier, Jill (act): *The Naked Cell*
Squier, Lucita (wri): *Bits of Life*
Squignoll, Tim (act): *Princess Warrior*
Squire, Anthony (dir & wri): *Mr. Selkie*
Squire, David (act): *Memoirs of a Survivor*
Squire, Janie (act): *Piranha (1978)*
Squire, Ronald (act, 1886-1958, nee Ronald Squirl): *Around the World In 80 Days; A Christmas Carol (1938); Footsteps In the Fog; My Cousin Rachel; No Highway In the Sky; The Rocking Horse Winner*
Squire, William (act): *A Challenge for Robin Hood; The 39 Steps (1978)*
Squires, Chris (cin): *True Crime*
Squires, Scott (cin): *Dragonheart*
Squirl, Ronald (act): see Squire, Ronald
Squitieri, Pasquale (dir): *Russicum*
Srivilai, Krung (act): *S.T.A.B.*
Staal, Herta (act): *The Dancing Heart*
Staats, Robert (act): *The Projectionist*
Stabans, Abraham (act): *Dr. Tarr's Torture Dungeon*
Stabler, Robert W. (act): *Anatomy of a Psycho*
Stacey, Bill (act): *Road Games*
Stacey, Eddie (act): *Hawk the Slayer; Prey (1978)*
Stacey, Eric (act): *It Came Upon the Midnight Clear*
Stacey, Paul (act): *The Young Poisoner's Handbook*
Stacey, Violet (act): *Spiritualism Exposed (1913)*
Stach, Virginia (act): *Murders In the Rue Morgue (1971)*
Stack, Elizabeth (act): *The Initiation of Sarah; Murder On Flight 502*
Stack, Guenther (act): *The Glass Cell*
Stack, Robert (act, b. 1919): *Adventures of the Queen; Asylum for a Spy; Bwana Devil; The Caretakers; The Last Voyage; Murder On Flight 502; The Strange and Deadly Occurrence*
Stack, Tim (act): *The Brave Little Toaster*
Stack, Timothy (act): *I, Desire; Justin Case*
Stack, William (act): *Charlie Chan's Greatest Case; The Girl from Downing Street*
Stackelberg, Catharina (wri): *Pippi Longstocking*
Stackleborg, Gene (wri): *The Man Outside (1967)*
Stacy, Chris (act): *Matinee; Mr. Destiny*
Stacy, James (act, b. 1937): *Double Exposure; Ordeak; Something Wicked This Way Comes*
Stacy, John (act): *The Big Game; The Headless Ghost; Il Planeta degli Uomini Spenti; La Ragazza Che Sapeva Troppo; Revenge of the Dead (1984); Yeti*
Stacy, Michelle (act): *Day of the Animals; Demon Seed; Logan's Run; The Rescuers*
Stacy, Neil (act): *The Quatermass Conclusion*
Stader, Jim(my) (act): *Beyond the Poseidon Adventure; Forgotten City of the Planet of the Apes*
Stader, Paul (act): *Beyond the Poseidon Adventure; Ghost Diver; Satan's Satellites*
Stader Jr., Paul (act): *It's Alive III: Island of the Alive*
Stader, Peter (act): *Beyond the Poseidon Adventure*
Stadlen, Lewis J. (act, b. 1947): *Savages*
Stadler, Maria (act): *The Naked Woman and Satan*
Stadner, Suzan (act): *Return of the Living Dead, Part II*
Staff, Kathy (act): *Mary Reilly*
Staffa, Laura (act): *The Outing*
Staffell, Charles (cin): *The Man Who Haunted Himself*
Stafford, Ann (act): *Keep My Grave Open*
Stafford, Baird (act): *Nightmare (1981)*
Stafford, Brendan (J.) (cin): *Koroshi; The Man Without a Body; Vendetta for the Saint*
Stafford, Frederic(k) (act, b. 1928): *Formula C-12/Beirut; The Legend of the Wolf Woman; OSS 117-Mission for a Killer; Topaz*
Stafford, Gino (wri): *Il Gigante di Metropolis*
Stafford, Jim (act): *E.S.P.*
Stafford, Nancy (act): *Deadly Invasion: The Killer Bee Nightmare*
Stafford, Tamara (act): *The Hills Have Eyes II*
Stagg, Bima (wri): *Survivor (1987)*
Stagnard, Carola (act): *Tenebrae*
Stagni, Ferruccio (act): *Ulysses*
Stahelski, Chad (act): *Nemesis 2*
Stahl, Andrew (act): *Mr. Destiny; Rearview Mirror*
Stahl, Jerry (wri): *Dr. Caligari*
Stahl, John M. (dir, 1886-1950): *Leave Her to Heaven*
Stahl (Jr.), Jorge/George (cin): *The Beast of Hollow Mountain; Enchanted Island; The Little Savage; A Woman's Devotion*
Stahl, Lisa (act): *Heart Condition*
Stahl, Nick (act): *Disturbing Behavior*
Stahl, Richard (act): *Beware! The Blob; Good Against Evil*
Stahl, William (act): [illegible]
Stahl, Willy (mus): *Nabonga*
Stahl-Nachbaur, Ernst (act): *M (1931)*

Stainer, Leslie Howard (act): see Howard, Leslie

Stainer-Hutchins, Michael (cin): *The Devil Rides Out*

Stainton, Michael (act): *Jekyll and Hyde*

Stainton, Philip (act): *The Elusive Pimpernel (1950); The Lady Killers (1956); Moby Dick (1956); Who Done It? (1956)*

Stait, Brent (act): *Intensity; I Still Dream of Jeannie; Roswell: The Aliens Attack*

Stakis, Stassia (act): *Fake-Out*

Staley, Charity (act): *Alien Space Avenger*

Staley, James (act): *The Night They Saved Christmas; Robot Wars; The Stepford Children*

Staley, Joan (act): *Cape Fear (1961); The Ghost and Mr. Chicken; Johnny Cool; Valley of the Dragons*

Staley, Marilyn (act): *It's Alive III: Island of the Alive; The Stuff*

Stalker, Gary (act): *Dark of the Night*

Stalker-Mason, Liz (act): *Prom Night*

Stallich, Jan (cin): *Cisaruv Pekar, Pekaruv Cisar; Le Golem (1936)*

Stallings, Laurence (wri, 1894-1968): *The Jungle Book (1942)*

Stallone, Frank (act): *Fear (1988); The Masque of the Red Death (1989, 21st Century); The Pink Chiquitas; Ten Little Indians (1989)*

Stallone, Frank (wri): *The Pink Chiquitas*

Stallone, Sage (act): *Daylight; Fatally Yours*

Stallone, Sylvester (act, b. 1946): *Antz; Daylight; Death Race 2000; Demolition Man; Judge Dredd*

Stamatin, Andy (act): *The Toxic Avenger*

Stamboulieh, Anthony (act): *Eyewitness (1970); Sudden Terror*

Stamos, John (act, b. 1963): *Alice In Wonderland (1985)*

Stamp, John (act): *—And Now the Screaming Starts!*

Stamp, Terence (act, b. 1940): *Alien Nation; The Collector; The Company of Wolves; Link; The Mind of Mr. Soames; Modesty Blaise; Mystery On Monster Island; Spirits of the Dead; Superman (1978); Superman II; Teorema; The Thief of Baghdad (1978)*

Stampe, Will (act): *Dr. Jekyll and Sister Hyde; The Flying Sorceror; The Main Chance; Rentadick*

Stamper, Dave (mus): *Such Men Are Dangerous*

Stamper, Larry (wri): *Wild Thing*

Stamper, Pope (act): *Ghosts (1914); The Stickpin*

Stamp-Taylor, Enid (act): *Alibi (1942); Blind Man's Bluff (1936); The Feathered Serpent (1934)*

Stander, Lionel (act, 1908-1994): *The Black Bird (1975); Call Northside 777; The Cassandra Crossing; Cul-de-Sac; A Dandy In Aspic; League of Frightened Men; The Loved One; Meet Nero Wolfe; Pulp; Treasure Island (1971); Wicked Stepmother; Zenabel*

Standeven, Guy (act): *The Road to Hong Kong*

Standford, Donald (wri): *A Taste of Blood*

Stanford, Nathania (act): *The Lost World (1993)*

Standifer, Glenn (act): *Wargames*

Standing, Dorothy (act): see Hammond, Kay

Standing, Sir Guy (act, 1873-1937): *Bulldog Drummond Escapes; Death Takes a Holiday (1934); The Double Door*

Standing, Joan (act): *Dracula (1931, English-speaking version)*

Standing, John (act, b. 1934): *Gulliver's Travels (1996); The Legacy; Nightflyers; The Psychopath (1965); Torture Garden; The Woman In White (1998)*

Standing, Percy Darrell (act): *Life Without Soul*

Standing, Wyndham (act): *Bulldog Drummond's Secret Police; Counter-Espionage; The Son of Monte Cristo; A Study in Scarlet (1933)*

Standjofski, Harry (act): *Wild Thing*

Stanec, Dagmar (act): *Bram Stoker's 'Dracula'*

Stanfill, Joseph (act): *Blood Song*

Stanford, Don (wri): *Monster A Go-Go*

Stanford, Evelyn (act): *I Was a Zombie for the F.B.I.*

Stanford, Jeremy (act): *Watchers II; Watchers 3*

Stanford, Robert (act): *Passport to Suez*

Stang, Arnold (act, b. 1925): *Alakazam the Great; Ghost Dad; Hello Down There; Hercules In New York; Pinocchio In Outer Space; The Wonderful World of the Brothers Grimm*

Stang, Jack (act): *Ring of Fear*

Stange, Hugh (wri): *The Black Camel*

Stanger, Hugo (L.) (act): *Beetlejuice; Impulse (1984); The Seventh Sign; Time Walker*

Stango, Jan (act): *The Flash*

Stanhope, Warren (act): *The Bedford Incident; Curse of the Fly*

Staniford, Reg (act): *No Blade of Grass*

Stanislas (mus): *Biggles: Adventures In Time*

Stanislaus, Louis (act): *Dick Turpin's Ride to York*

Stanlee, Claudia (act): *They Live*

Stanley, Alvah (act): *The Sword and the Sorcerer*

Stanley, Charles (act): *23 Paces to Baker Street*

Stanley, Diane (act): *Planet of the Apes*

Stanley, Edwin (act): *Charlie Chan In Panama; Dick Tracy (1937); The Mandarin Mystery; The Missing Guest; Mr. Moto In Danger Island; Mr. Moto's Gamble; The Phantom Creeps*

Stanley, Eric (act): *The Silver Greyhound (1932)*

Stanley, Erika (act): *Nightmare In Blood*

Stanley, Erle (act): *The River House Ghost*

Stanley, Florence (act): *The Day of the Dolphin*

Stanley, Forrest (act): *The Cat and the Canary (1927); Through the Dark; Young Diana*

Stanley, Frank (W.) (cin): *Cry for the Strangers; Dark Mirror (1984); The Eiger Sanction*

Stanley, George (act): *The Man from Downing Street; The Spider (1958); Tormented (1960)*

Stanley, John (dir & wri): *Nightmare In Blood*

Stanley, Kim (act, b. 1921, nee Patricia Reid): *Seance On a Wet Afternoon*

Stanley, Lauren (act): *Mac and Me*

Stanley, Paul (act): *Kiss Meets the Phantom of the Park*

Stanley, Paul (dir): *Sole Survivor (1970); The Ultimate Impostor*

Stanley, Phyllis (act): *The Black Sleep*

Stanley, Ralph (mus): *Unknown Island*

Stanley, Rebecca (act): *Eyes of Fire*

Stanley, Richard (dir): *Dust Devil; Hardware*

Stanley, Richard (wri): *Dust Devil; Hardware; The Island of Dr. Moreau (1996)*

Stanley, (S.) Victor (act): *The Ghost Camera; Puppets of Fate; Whispering Tongues*

Stanmore, B. (act): *A Message from Mars (1913)*

Stanmore, Frank (act): *Chamber of Horrors (1929); Faust (1923); His Reformation; The House On the Marsh; The House Opposite (1931); The Man Without a Soul; Marzipan of the Shapes; The Old Man; Tut-Tut and His Terrible Tomb; What a Night!*

Stannard, Don (act): *Dick Barton at Bay; Dick Barton, Detective; Dick Barton, Special Agent; Dick Barton Strikes Back*

Stannard, Eliot (act): *Grip (1915)*

Stannard, Eliot (dir): *The Courage of a Coward; Fatal Fingers*

Stannard, Eliot (wri): *Beautiful Jim; The Bells (1923); Champagne; The Courage of a Coward; Downhill; Fatal Fingers; Flames; Grip (1915); Her Luck In London; Hutch Stirs 'em Up; Lady Audley's Secret (1920); The Lodger (1926); London's Yellow Peril; Lucrezia Borgia: or, Plaything of Power; The Mystery of a Hansom Cab; Scrooge (1923); The Silver Bridge; A Smart Set; The Woman Who Was Nothing; Wuthering Heights (1920)*

Stannett, Ron (cin): *Circle of Deceit*

Stansbury, Hope (act): *The Rats Are Coming! The Werewolves Are Here!*

Stansfield, Claire (act): *Sensation (1994); Wes Craven Presents Mind Ripper*

Stanton, Arch (act): *Deathstalker II: Duel of the Titans*

Stanton, Barry (act): *Demons of the Mind; King Lear (1970)*

Stanton, Bryan (act): *Stranger In the House (1967)*

Stanton, Dan (act): *Gremlins 2: The New Batch*

Stanton, Dane (wri): *The Answer; Still Waters Run Deep*

Stanton, Don (act): *Gremlins 2: The New Batch*

Stanton, Ernie (act): *The Adventures of Robin Hood; Bulldog Drummond Escapes; Mr. Wong In Chinatown*

Stanton, Harry (act): *Secret of the Incas; What's the Matter With Helen?*

Stanton, Harry Dean (act, b. 1926): *Alien; The Care Bears Movie; Christine; Deathwatch (1980); Dream a Little Dream; Escape from New York; Farewell, My Lovely; The Hostage (1966); Never Talk to Strangers; One Magic Christmas; Red Dawn; Repo Man; Slam Dance; Twin Peaks: Fire Walk With Me; UFOria*

Stanton, Helene (act): *Jungle Moon Men; The Phantom from 10,000 Leagues*

Stanton, Joe (act): *Mother's Day*

Stanton, Maria (act): *Dr. Jekyll and Ms. Hyde*

Stanton, Paul (act): *Charlie Chan at the Circus; Cry Wolf (1947)*

Stanton, Penny (act): *Short Circuit*

Stanton, Robert (act): *Voodoo Blood Bath*

Stanton, Sylvia (act): *Carousel*

Stanton, Val (act): *The Adventures of Robin Hood*

Stanton, Valerie (act): *Mini Weekend*

Stanton, Will (act): *Devil's Island*

Stanton, Will (wri): *Charley and the Angel*

Stanton-Miranda (act): *The Silence of the Lambs*

Stanwood, Donald A. (wri): *The Memory of Eva Ryker*

Stanwyck, Barbara (act, 1907-1990, nee Ruby Stevens): *Crime of Passion; Cry Wolf (1947); Double Indemnity (1944); Flesh and Fantasy; The House That Wouldn't Die; Lady of Burlesque; The Man With a Cloak; Night Nurse; The Night Walker; Sorry, Wrong Number (1948); The Strange Love of Martha Ivers; A Taste of Evil; The Two Mrs. Carrolls; Witness to Murder*

Stany, Jacques (act): *Terror of Rome Against the Son of Hercules; Il Trionfo di Ercole*

Stapel, Huub (act): *The Lift*

Stapf, Greta (act): *Time Walker*

Stapler, Robin (act): *Black Roses*

Staples, Arthur (act): *Mr. Meek's Nightmare*

Staples, Paul (cin): *Nomads*

Staples, Robert (cin): *The Night of the Claw*

Staples, Sheryl (act): *The Stepford Children*

Stapleton, Dan (act): *Voodoo Blood Bath*

Stapleton, James (act): *Hands of a Stranger*

Stapleton, Jay (wri): *Heads*

Stapleton, Jean (act, b. 1923): *Damn Yankees; Dead Man's Folly; Michael; Something Wild*

Stapleton, Maureen (act, b. 1925): *Cocoon; Cocoon: The Return; The Cosmic Eye; Doin' Time On Planet Earth; The Fan; The Fugitive Kind; Made In Heaven*

Stapleton, Nicola (act): *Hansel and Gretel*

Stapleton, Oliver (cin): *Earth Girls Are Easy*

Stapley, Maitland (act): *Rip Van Winkle (1914)*

Stapley, Richard (act): *The Challenge (1960); Jungle Man-Eaters; The Strange Door*

Stapp, Marjorie (act): *Daughter of Dr. Jekyll; Indestructible Man; Kronos (1957); The Monster That Challenged the World; Port Sinister*

Stapp, Philip (wri): *Animal Farm (1954)*

Star, Darren (wri): *Teen Agent*

Star, Fredro (act): *The Addiction*

Starewicz, Wladyslaw (dir, 1882-1965): *Le Roman de Renard*

Starita, Barbara (act): *The Alien's Return*

Starita, Michael R. (act): *The Alien's Return*

Stark, Anthony (wri): *The Dogfighters*

Stark, Arthur (act): *The Green Slime*

Stark, Don (act): *Evilspeak*

Stark, Graham (act, b. 1922): *Blood Bath at the House of Death; A Ghost of a Chance (1968); Gulliver's Travels (1977); Hawk the Slayer; Jane and the Lost City; Lancelot and Guinevere; The Laughing Girl Murder; The Magic Christian; The Mouse On the Moon; The Prisoner of Zenda (1979); Superman III; There Goes the Bride; Those Fantastic Flying Fools; Where's Johnny; The Wrong Box*

Stark, Harriet L. (act): *Slugs*

Stark, Jonathan (act): *Fright Night; House II: The Second Story; Project X (1987)*

Stark, Koo (act): *Electric Dreams; The Rocky Horror Picture Show*

Stark, Richard (wri): *Slayground*

Stark, Timothy (act): *Frankenstein (1993)*

Stark, Wilbur (wri): *Vampire Circus*

Starke, Anthony (act): *18 Again!; Inferno (1998); Repossessed; Return of the Killer Tomatoes*

Starke, Pauline (act, 1900-1977): *A Connecticut Yankee In King Arthur's Court (1921); Dante's Inferno (1924); In the Palace of the King; The Viking*

Starkes, Jaison (wri): *J.D.'s Revenge*

Stark-Gesettenbaur, Gustl (act): *Die Frau im Mond*

Starks, Michael D. (act): *The Nutty Professor (1996)*

Starling, Lynn (wri): *The Cat and the Canary (1939); The Climax*

Staron, Debi (act): *The Toxic Avenger, Part II*

Starr, Adam (act): *Looker; Vampire (1979)*

Starr, Beau (act): *Dead Air; Halloween 4: The Return of Michael Myers; Halloween 5: The Revenge of Michael Myers; Never Talk to Strangers*

Starr, Ben (wri): *The Busy Body; Our Man Flint; The Spirit Is Willing*

Starr, Don (act): *Night of the Lepus*

Starr, Freddie (act): *The Squeeze*

Starr, James A. (wri): *In the Next Room*

Starr, Michael (act): *Evil Stalks This House*

Starr, Mike (act): *Ed Wood; Freejack; King Kong Lives; Mardi Gras for the Devil; Murder In a Small Town*

Starr, Pat (act): *Arthur the King; Dreamchild; Judge Dredd; Mission: Impossible; Outland*

Starr, Ringo (act, b. 1940): *Alice In Wonderland (1985); Caveman (1981); Liszt O' Mania; The Magic Christian; Son of Dracula (1974)*

Starr, Robert (act): *Alien Nation; The Last Starfighter*

Starr, Ron (act): *This Is Not a Test*

Starr, Texas (act): *Orgy of the Dead (1965)*

Starrett, Charles (act, 1904-1986): *Green Eyes; Jungle Bride; The Mask of Fu Manchu*

Starrett, Jack (act): *Angels from Hell; Nightwish*

Starrett, Jack (dir): *Race With the Devil*

Starrett, Jennifer (act): *Frightmare (1983)*

Star-Shemah (act): *Wes Craven's New Nightmare*

Staskel, James (act): *Nothing But Trouble*

Stass, Herbert (act): *The Invisible Terror*

Stassino, Paul (act): *Echo of Barbara; The Magus; Man Detained; Moment of Danger; The Moon-Spinners; The Stranglers of Bombay; Thunderball; A Touch of the Other; The Verdict (1964); Where the Spies Are*

Stather, Frank (dir & wri): *The Fatal Formula*

Statheros, Elena (act): *Switch (1991)*

Statler, Jennifer (act): *Violent Women*

Statler, Marjorie (act): *She (1925)*

Staub, Peter W. (act): *Superwheels*

Staub, Ralph (dir): *The Mandarin Mystery*

Staunton, Ann (act): *Philo Vance Returns; The Vampire (1957)*

Staunton, Imelda (act): *Deadly Advice*

Staunton, Kim (act): *The Brother from Another Planet*

Stavin, Mary (act): *Arthur the King; House; Howling V: The Rebirth; Octopussy; A View to a Kill*

Stavin, William (act): *Howling V: The Rebirth*

Stavrakis, Taso N. (cin): *He Knows You're Alone*

Stavrou, Ari(s) (cin): *The Devil's Men; The Next One*

Stawicki, Jerzy (cin): *Profesor Zazul*

Stawicki, Jerzy (dir & wri): *Profesor Zazul; Przyjaciel*

Stay, Richard (act): *Halloween 4: The Return of Michael Myers*

Stayner, Michael (act): *Billion Dollar Brain*

Stead, John (act): *The Long Kiss Goodnight*

Steadman, Alison (act): *The Adventures of Baron Munchausen (1989)*

Steadman, Bob (cin): *Slaughter*

Steadman, Ian (act): *Jane and the Lost City; Prisoners of the Lost Universe*

Steadman, John (act): *Dark Night of the Scarecrow; Fade to Black; The Hills Have Eyes; Sherlock Holmes In New York*

Steadman, Robert (cin): *Calendar Girl Murders; Lifepod; Roswell: The Aliens Attack; She Woke Up; Terror In the Shadows; Treasure Island (1990)*

Steadman, Vera (act): *The Clutching Hand*

Steafel, Sheila (act): *Blood Bath at the House of Death; Catch Me a Spy; Digby-The Biggest Dog In the World; Otley; Quatermass and the Pit; Woof!*

Steakley, John (wri): *Vampires (1998)*

Stearns, Denise (act): *To All a Goodnight*

Stearns, Louis (act): *Annabel Lee*

Stearns, Michael (act): *Battle for the Planet of the Apes*

Stearns, Michael (mus): *Temptress (1995)*

Stearns, Speed (act): *Metalstorm: The Destruction of Jared-Syn*

Stears, John (cin): *Chitty Chitty Bang Bang; Goldfinger; Haunted Honeymoon (1986); Theater of Blood; Thunderball*

Stebel, Sidney L. (wri): *Mirrors*

Steck, Jim (act): *Electric Dreams*

Steckel, Leonard (act): *The Secret of the Black Trunk*

Steckler, Ray Dennis (dir): *The Hollywood Strangler Meets the Skid Row Slasher; The Incredibly Strange Creatures Who Stopped Living and Became Mixed-Up Zombies; The Lemon Grove Kids Meet the Monsters; Rat Pfink & Boo Boo; Sinthia: The Devil's Doll; The Thrill Killers*

Steckler, Ray Dennis (wri): *The Thrill Killers*

Steedman, Tony (act): *Bill & Ted's Excellent Adventure; Gawain and the Green Knight; Paint Me a Murder; The Return of Sherlock Holmes (1986); The 39 Steps (1978); The Zany Adventures of Robin Hood*

Steeger, Ingrid (act): *The Erotic Adventures of the Three Musketeers*

Steel, Alan (act, nee Sergio Ciani): *Ercole Contro Roma; Hercules and the Masked Rider; Hercules and the Treasure of the Incas; Lost Treasure of the Aztecs; Maciste e la Regina di Samar; Samson; Samson and the Mighty Challenge; The Three Avengers; Zorro Contro Maciste*

Steel, Amy (act): *April Fool's Day; Friday the 13th—Part 2; What Ever Happened to Baby Jane? (1991)*

Steel, Andrew (act): *Philadelphia Experiment II*

Steel, Anthony (act, b. 1920): *Another Man's Poison; 48 Hours to Live; A Matter of Choice; The Mirror Crack'd; The Monster Club; Tiger of the Seven Seas; Valerie*
Steel, Rod (act): *The Thing With Two Heads*
Steele, Barbara (act, b. 1937): *Amante d'Oltretomba; Un Angelo per Satan; Caged Heat!; Cinque Tombe per un Medium; Curse of the Crimson Altar; La Danza Macabra; 8 1/2; Der Junge Torless; I Lunghi Capelli della Morte; La Maschera del Demonio; The Monocle; Piranha (1978); The Pit and the Pendulum (1961); Raptus; La Sanglante Sorciere; Sapphire; Shivers; Silent Scream (1979); La Sorella di Satan; Lo Spettro*
Steele, Bob (act, 1907-1988, nee Robert Bradbury): *The Atomic Submarine; The Big Sleep (1946); Giant from the Unknown; Nightmare Honeymoon; Of Mice and Men (1939); Revenge of the Zombies (1943)*
Steele, Brian (act): *Peter Benchley's 'Creature'*
Steele, Cynthia (act): *Spellbinder*
Steele, Don (act): *Death Race 2000; Kiss Meets the Phantom of the Park*
Steele, Freddie (act): *Black Angel (1946)*
Steele, Geoffrey (act): *Terror by Night*
Steele, George "The Animal" (act): *Ed Wood*
Steele, Jimmy (act): *Madman*
Steele, Karen (act): *Cyborg 2087*
Steele, Lee (act): *The Nesting*
Steele, Mike (act): *The Bat (1959); The Lost Missile*
Steele, Pippa (act): *Lust for a Vampire; Stranger In the House (1967); The Vampire Lovers*
Steele, Tom (act): *Cyclotrode X; Lost Planet Airmen; Missile Monsters; Sakima and the Masked Marvel; Satan's Satellites*
Steele, Tommy (act, b. 1936): *Finian's Rainbow; Kill Me Tomorrow*
Steele, Vernon (act): *Bulldog Drummond Strikes Back (1934); The Lone Wolf In London*
Steeley, Derek (act): *Werewolf of Washington*
Steelman, Sabrina (act): *The King's Avenger*
Steelsmith, Mary (act): *Death Valley; Weird Science*
Steely, Ann (act): see O'Donnell, Cathy
Steely, Jack (cin): *The Incredible 2-Headed Transplant; The Thing With Two Heads*
Steen, Bodil (act): *Crazy Paradise*
Steen, Irving (act): *The Fall of the House of Usher (1950)*
Steen, Jessica (act): *The Housekeeper; Still Life*
Steen, Kristin (act): *Silent Night, Bloody Night*
Steen, Mike (act): *Crack in the World*
Steenburgen, Mary (act, b. 1953): *Back to the Future, Part III; The Butcher's Wife; Dead of Winter; Gulliver's Travels (1996); Noah's Ark (1999); One Magic Christmas; Powder; Time After Time*
Steensland, David (dir): *Escapes*
Steer, Caroline (act): *The Rocking Horse Winner*
Steerman, A. Harding (act): *Bluff; The Elusive Pimpernel (1919); Iron Justice*
Steers, Glenn (act): *Raiders of the Living Dead*
Steers, Larry (act): *The Docks of New Orleans; Trouble for Two; White Pongo*
Stefan, Marina (act): *Shriek of the Mutilated*
Stefanelli, Benito (act): *Battle of the Amazons; Ironmaster*
Stefanelli, Marco (act): *Battle of the Amazons*
Stefani, Francesco (dir): *Das Singende Ringende Baumchen*
Stefani, Michael (act): *Trancers*
Stefanich, Mark (act): *The Good Son*
Stefano, Joe (act): *The UFO Incident*
Stefano, Joseph (wri): *Eye of the Cat; Home for the Holidays; The Kindred; Live Again, Die Again; The Magician (1973); The Naked Edge; Psycho (1960); Psycho IV: The Beginning; Revenge (1971, USA)*
Stefano, Kathleen (act): *Copycat; Killer Klowns from Outer Space*
Steffan, Mark (act): *The Sword and the Sorcerer*
Steffe, Michael (cin): *Timecop*
Steffen, Anthony (act): *Killer Fish; The Night Evelyn Came Out of the Grave; Savage Island*
Steffen, Sirry (act): *The Crawling Hand*
Stegani, Giorgio (wri): *Il Mulino delle Donne di Pietra; The Trojan Horse*
Steger, Fredric (act): *Cloudburst*
Stegers, Bernice (act): *La Citta delle Donne; Frozen Terror; Xtro*
Stegger, Karl (act): *Crazy Paradise*
Stegman, Jon (act): *Spacecamp*
Stehli, Edgar (act): *Atlantis, the Lost Continent; 4D Man; Seconds*
Stehnova, Jana (act): *The Deserter and the Nomads*
Steiger, Rod (act, b. 1925): *American Gothic; The Amityville Horror; Cry Terror!; The Illustrated Man; The Kindred; The Loved One; The Mark; Mars Attacks!; The Neighbor; No Way to Treat a Lady; Out There; 13 West Street*
Steiger, Vanessa (act): *The Grim Reaper*
Stein, Andrew (mus): *Deathsport*
Stein, Ben (act, b. 1944): *Casper; Ghostbusters II; National Lampoon's Men In White*
Stein, Benjamin J. (act): *The Mask (1994)*
Stein, Chris (mus): *Polyester*
Stein, Darren (dir & wri): *Jawbreaker*
Stein, David (act): *The Amityville Curse*
Stein, Elliott (act): *Batman (1989); Secrets of Sex*
Stein, Elliott (wri): *Secrets of Sex*
Stein, Franz (act): *M (1931)*
Stein, George (act): see Stone, George E.
Stein, Heidi (act): *Fortress*
Stein, Herbert (mus): *I've Lived Before*
Stein, Herman (mus): *Let's Kill Uncle; The Unguarded Moment*
Stein, Kerry (act): *Witches' Brew*
Stein, Lotte (act): *The Climax*
Stein, Paul (dir, 1891-1952): *Black Limelight; Counterblast; The Laughing Lady; Poison Pen; The Saint Meets the Tiger; The Twenty Questions Murder*
Stein, Peter (cin): *C.H.U.D.; Ernest Saves Christmas; Friday the 13th-Part 2; Graveyard Shift (1990); Night Visions; Pet Sematary*
Stein, Rob (act): *My Bloody Valentine*
Stein, Ron (act): *Forgotten City of the Planet of the Apes*
Stein, Ronald (mus, b. 1930): *Atlas; Attack of the Crab Monsters; Attack of the 50-Foot Woman (1958); Dementia 13; Dinosaurus!; The Ghost of Dragstrip Hollow; The Haunted Palace (1963); Invasion of the Saucer Men; It Conquered the World; Not of This Earth (1957); The Premature Burial; The Terror (1963); The Undead; The Underwater City*
Stein, Sam(my) (act): *The Lost Patrol (1934); The Veils of Bagdad*
Steinbach, Victor (act): *2010*
Steinbeck, John (wri, 1902-1968): *Lifeboat; Of Mice and Men (1939, 1981 & 1992)*
Steinbeck, Muriel (act): *Long John Silver*
Steinberg, David (act, b. 1942): *Fearless Frank; Willow*
Steinberg, Elsy (act): see Stewart, Elaine
Steinberg, Robert Martin (act): *Single White Female*
Steinberg, Stewart (act): *The Island*
Steindler, Maureen (act): *Poltergeist III*
Steiner, Anastasia (act): *Dr. Caligari*
Steiner, Fred (mus): *Run for the Sun*
Steiner, John (act): *Ark of the Sun God; Hunters of the Golden Cobra; I Don't Want to Be Born; The Persecution and Assassination of Jean-Paul Marat as Performed by the Inmates of the Asylum of Charenton Under the Direction of the Marquis de Sade; Shock (1978); Sinbad and the Seven Seas; Tenebrae; Yor, the Hunter from the Future*
Steiner, Marcel (act): *From Beyond the Grave*
Steiner, Max (mus, 1888-1971): *The Adventures of Don Juan; Arsenic and Old Lace; The Beast With Five Fingers; The Big Sleep (1946); Cloak and Dagger (1946); The Decision of Christopher Blake; Helen of Troy (1955); Key Largo; King Kong (1933); Lightning Strikes Twice; The Lost Patrol (1934); The Most Dangerous Game; The Penguin Pool Murder; The Phantom of Crestwood; Pursued; She (1935); Son of Kong; The Three Musketeers (1935); Two On a Guillotine; The Woman In White (1948)*
Steiner, Sherry (act): *Asylum of Satan; Demon (1976)*
Steiner, William (cin): *The Window*
Steinert, Anni (act): *Lycanthropus*
Steinfeld, Jake (act): *Home Sweet Home; Repossessed*
Steinke, Brad (act): *Appointment for a Killing*
Steinke, Hans (act): *Island of Lost Souls*
Steinmann, Danny (dir & wri): *Friday the 13th-Part V: A New Beginning*
Steinmetz, Dennis (dir): *Halloween With the Addams Family*
Steinmetz, Richard (act): *Skyscraper*
Steinruck, Albert (act): *The Golem: How He Came Into the World*
Steinsland, Kristin (act): *The Witches (1990)*
Steis, William (act): *Demon of Paradise; Equalizer 2000; Raiders of the Sun*
Stelfox, Shirley (act): *Corruption; 1984 (1984)*
Stell, Frank (act): *The Astral Factor*
Stella, Antoinette (act): *The Loves of Dracula; World of Dracula*
Stellari, Gian (mus): *Robin Hood and the Pirates*
Steller, Carolyn (act): *The Horrible House On the Hill*
Stelli, Jean (dir): *L'Or du Cristobal*
Stelling, William (act): *13 Lead Soldiers*
Stelter, Jim (act): *I Was a Zombie for the F.B.I.*
Stelzer, Peter A. (act): *Bates Motel*
Stemmle, Robert A./R.A. (wri): *Confess, Dr. Corda; Der Henker von London; Das Testament des Dr. Mabuse (1962)*
Stempel, Bruno (cin): *Dangerous Touch*
Sten, Anna (act, b. 1908, nee Anyushka Stenski): *Exile Express*
Stenberg, Brigitta (act): *Raiders of the Sun*
Stenberg, William (act): *The Mysterious Monsters*
Stenbock-Fermor, A. (wri): *Milczaca Gwiazda*
Stenborg, Helen (act): *Dr. Cook's Garden*
Stengel, Christian (wri): *Crime and Punishment (1935, Fr)*
Stengel, Leni (act): *Cracked Nuts (1931)*
Stengler, Mack (cin): *The Ape Man; Bowery at Midnight; The Living Ghost (1942)*
Steno (dir, 1914-1988): *I Moschettiere del Mare; One Night of Fame; Psycosissimo*
Steno (wri, 1914-1988): *OK, Nero!*
Stensgaard, Yutte (act): *Alien Women; Burke and Hare; Lust for a Vampire; Zeta One*
Stenski, Anyushka (act): see Sten, Anna
Stensland, Inger (act): see Stevens, Inger
Stenstrom, David (act): *Project X (1987)*
Stensvold, Alan (cin): *Cyborg 2087; The Destructors; Dimension 5; Please Murder Me; Tarzan and the Trappers*
Stenta, Dick (act): *End of the World (1977)*
Stepak, Lorne (act): *Phobia*
Stepanek, Elisabeth (act): *No Mercy, No Future*
Stepanek, Karel (act, b. 1899): *The Accursed; City Beneath the Sea (1952); Counterblast; Devil Doll (1963); Escape to Danger; The Fallen Idol; The File of the Golden Goose; The Frozen Dead; I Aim at the Stars; Licensed to Kill; The Man In the Road; Operation Crossbow; Secret Venture; State Secret*
Stepanek, Zdenek (act): *Cisaruv Pekar; Pekaruv Cisar; Ikaria XB1*
Stepashkin, Vadim (act): *The Saint*
Stephane, Nicole (act): *Les Enfants Terribles*
Stephani, Frederick (dir): *Spaceship to the Unknown*
Stephano, Tony (act): *The Reincarnation of Peter Proud*
Stephen, A.C. (dir): *Orgy of the Dead*
Stephen, Dan(iel) (act): *2020 Texas Gladiators; Warriors of the Wasteland*
Stephen, Jim (act): *The Monster Squad*
Stephen, Karen (act): *Happy Birthday to Me*
Stephen, Susan (act, b. 1931): *Golden Ivory; The House Across the Lake; Return of a Stranger (1962); A Stolen Face*
Stephens, Ann (act): *Your Witness*
Stephens, Bee (act): *Just Imagine*
Stephens, Duncan (act): *Raiders of the Living Dead*
Stephens, Frank (act): *The Docks of New Orleans*
Stephens, Harvey (act, 1901-1986): *The Bat (1959); Diary of a Madman; Lady In the Dark; Maid of Salem; A Night of Mystery (1937); The Omen*
Stephens, Heather (act): *Dante's Peak*
Stephens, James (act): *The Mysterious Two*
Stephens, John M. (cin): *Fer-de-Lance; Probe*
Stephens, Laraine (act): *The Adventures of Nick Carter; Matt Helm; The Screaming Woman*
Stephens, Martin (act, b. 1949): *The Hell-Fire Club; The Innocents; The Village of the Damned (1960); The Witches (1966); The Witness*
Stephens, Mike (act): *Popcorn*
Stephens, Nancy (act): *Halloween; Halloween II; The Magician (1973)*
Stephens, Peter (act): *Kill Her Gently*
Stephens, R. david (act): *The First Power*
Stephens, Robert (act, b. 1931): *Afraid of the Dark; The Asphyx; The Private Life of Sherlock Holmes; The Shout; Wings of Fame*
Stephens, Roy (act): *Dr. Strangelove: or, How I Learned to Stop Worrying and Love the Bomb*
Stephens, Sally (act): *A Place to Die*
Stephens, William (wri): *Jungle Goddess*
Stephenson, Ben (act): *Stalking Laura*
Stephenson, Carl (wri): *The Naked Jungle*
Stephenson, Charles Alan (act): *Ed Wood*
Stephenson, Craig (act): *Beyond and Back*
Stephenson, Denise (act): *Gotham*
Stephenson, Dennis (act): *Zombie Island Massacre*
Stephenson, Geoffrey (cin): *The Bride (1973); Howling II*
Stephenson, Henry (act, 1871-1956): *The Adventures of Sherlock Holmes (1939); The* [illegible] *of Mr. X; The Return of Monte Cristo; Secrets of Scotland Yard; Tarzan and the Amazons*
Stephenson, James (act, 1888-1941): *Calling Philo Vance; Confessions of a Nazi Spy; Dangerous Fingers; The Dark Stairway; Devil's Island; The Man Who Made Diamonds; Murder In the Air (1940); Nancy Drew, Detective; The Perfect Crime; Torchy Blane In Chinatown*
Stephenson, John (act): *Charlotte's Web; The Hobbit*
Stephenson, John (dir): *Animal Farm (1999)*
Stephenson, Mark Kinsey (act): *The Unnamable; The Unnamable II*
Stephenson, Michael (act): *Beyond Darkness; Troll II*
Stephenson, Pamela (act): *Blood Bath at the House of Death; The Day the Screaming Stopped; Superman III; Those Dear Departed*
Stephenson, Robert (act): *Seven*
Stephenson, Sheila (act): *How to Stuff a Wild Bikini*
Stepkanova, Jana (act): *The Death of Tarzan*
Stepp, Alan (act): *The Outing*
Steppat, Ilse (act, 1917-1969): *The Invisible Terror; On Her Majesty's Secret Service*
Sterckx, Pierre (wri): *Mama Dracula*
Stering, Amy (act): *Praying Mantis*
Sterke, Jeanette (act): *The Double; Moments*
Sterland, John (act): *Batman (1989); The Return of Sherlock Holmes (1986)*
Sterler, Hermione (act): *Golden Earrings*
Sterling, Bruce (act): *In the Palace of the King*
Sterling, Dick (act): *Barracuda*
Sterling, Ford (act, 1883-1939, nee George F. Stitch): *Alice In Wonderland (1933); The Brass Bottle (1923); He Who Gets Slapped; Kismet (1930)*
Sterling, Jan (act, b. 1923, nee Jane Sterling Adriance): *Appointment With Danger; Mystery Street; 1984 (1955); Split Second (1953)*
Sterling, Lesli Kay (act): *Forbidden Games (1995)*
Sterling, Maury (act): *Outbreak*
Sterling, Philip (act): *Audrey Rose; The Death of the Incredible Hulk; Dr. Scorpion; Dr. Strange; The November Plan*
Sterling, Robert (act, b. 1917, nee Robert Sterling Hart): *Armored Car Robbery; Voyage to the Bottom of the Sea*
Sterling, Tisha (act): *Betrayal (1974); The Coming; The Killer Inside Me; The Name of the Game Is Kill; Night Slaves; Village of the Giants*
Sterling, William (act): *Doomed to Die*
Sterling, William (dir & wri): *Alice's Adventures In Wonderland (1972)*
Sterman, Bruce (act): *Zombie Island Massacre*
Stern, Alex (wri): *Dead and Buried*
Stern, Daniel (act): *C.H.U.D.; D.O.A. (1988); Frankenweenie; Leviathan; Little Monsters*
Stern, David (wri): *Francis; Francis Covers the Big Town; Francis Goes to the Races; Francis Goes to West Point; Francis In the Haunted House; Francis In the Navy; Francis Joins the WACs; Swamp Women*
Stern, Eric (act): *Garden of the Dead; Love Butcher*
Stern, Erik (act): *Love Butcher; Wargames*
Stern, Jamie (act): *Assassin (1986)*
Stern, Jon (act): *The Toxic Avenger, Part II*
Stern, Joshua Michael (wri): *Amityville Dollhouse*
Stern, Kate (act): *Communion*
Stern, Leonard B. (wri): *The Nude Bomb*
Stern, Otto (act): *Hauser's Memory*
Stern, Philip Van Doren (wri): *It's a Wonderful Life*
Stern, Sandor (dir): *Assassin (1986); Pin; Web of Deceit*
Stern, Sandor (wri): *The Amityville Horror; Assassin (1986); Red Alert; Secret Weapons; Shark Kill; The Strange and Deadly Occurrence; Web of Deceit; Where Have All the People Gone?*
Stern, Steven H./Hilliard (dir): *The Devil and Max Devlin; Final Notice; The Ghost of Flight 401; Murder In Space; Not Quite Human; Rolling Vengeance; Rona Jaffe's Mazes and Monsters*
Stern, Stewart (act): *Fright Night*
Stern, Theodore (mus): *The Worm Eaters*
Stern, Tim (act): *Santa Claus (1985)*
Stern, Tom (act): *Angels from Hell; The Entity; Freaked*
Stern, Tom (dir & wri): *Freaked*
Stern, Tom (dir): *Freaked*
Sterndale, Martin (act): *Jungle Street*
Sterndale-Bennett, Joan (act): *No Haunt for a* [illegible]
Sterne, David (act): *Sinbad and the Eye of the Tiger; Venom (1982)*
Sterne, George F. (act): *Ed Wood*

Sterne, Gordon (act): *The Adding Machine; An American Werewolf In London; The Child and the Killer; The Fur Collar; Highlander; The Vulture* (1966)

Sterne, Morgan (act): *Ellery Queen: Don't Look Behind You; No Exit*

Sternhagen, Frances (act, b. 1930): *Communion; Misery; Outland; Prototype; Raising Cain; She Woke Up*

Sternlieb, Toby (act): *To All a Goodnight*

Sternlight, Mel (cin): *The Angry Red Planet*

Sterringa, Wiske (act): *The Lift*

Sterroll, Gertrude (act): *Lorna Doone* (1920); *The Shadow Between*

Stetson, Lee (act): *Return* (1985)

Steuart, David (act): *Eclipse* (1977)

Steuer, Max (wri): *The Committee*

Steuer, Monica (act): *Total Recall*

Stevan, Robyn (act): *The Little Match Girl* (1987); *The Stepfather*

Steven, Carl (act): *Honey, I Shrunk the Kids; Star Trek III: The Search for Spock*

Stevenin, Jean-Francois (act): *Flight to Berlin*

Stevens, Alex (act): *The Projectionist; Scanners; Silent Night, Bloody Night*

Stevens, Andrew (act, b. 1955): *Day of the Animals; The Fury; Munchie; Munchie Strikes Back; Red Blooded American Girl; Scared Stiff* (1987); *Scorned; The Seduction; The Terror Within; The Terror Within II; Topper* (1979)

Stevens, Andrew (dir, b. 1955): *The Terror Within II; Virtual Combat*

Stevens, Angela (act): *Creature With the Atom Brain; Devil Goddess; Savage Mutiny*

Stevens, Arnold (dir): *Attack of the Swamp Creature*

Stevens, Art (dir): *The Fox and the Hound; The Rescuers*

Stevens, Art (wri): *The Fox and the Hound*

Stevens, Bard (act): *Bug*

Stevens, Brian (act): *Secrets of the Phantom Caverns*

Stevens, Brinke (act): *Bad Girls from Mars; Grandma's House; Haunting Fear; Nightmare Sisters; Slavegirls from Beyond Infinity; The Slumber Party Massacre; Sorority Babes In the Slimeball Bowl-O-Rama; Teenage Exorcist; Warlords*

Stevens, Brinke (wri): *Teenage Exorcist*

Stevens, Casey (act): *Prom Night*

Stevens, Charles (act): *The Black Pirate; Don Q, Son of Zorro; Eyes of the Jungle; The Feathered Serpent* (1948); *The Iron Mask; Killer Leopard; The Mark of Zorro* (1920); *The Mummy's Curse; The Mysterious Dr. Fu Manchu; Savage Mutiny; Thank You, Mr. Moto; The Thief of Bagdad* (1924); *The Three Musketeers* (1921)

Stevens, Connie (act, b. 1938, nee Concetta Ann Ingolia): *The Last Generation; The Littlest Angel* (1969); *Two On a Guillotine; Way...Way Out*

Stevens, Constance (act): see Gray, Sally

Stevens, Craig (act, b. 1918, nee Gail Shekles): *Abbott and Costello Meet Dr. Jekyll and Mr. Hyde; Condor; The Deadly Mantis; The Hidden Hand; Killer Bees; Limbo Line; Murder Without Tears; Night Unto Night*

Stevens, Damion (act): *Running Against Time*

Stevens, Dana (wri): *Blink; City of Angels*

Stevens, Dave (wri): *The Rocketeer*

Stevens, David (wri): *Crime and Punishment* (1998)

Stevens, Dodie (act): *Alakazam the Great*

Stevens, Dorinda (act): *The Gentle Trap; The Golden Link; Horrors of the Black Museum; Night Train to Paris; Night Without Pity; The Shakedown; The Undesirable Neighbour; The Verdict* (1964)

Stevens, Edmond (wri): *Mother, May I Sleep with Danger?; Night of the Hunter* (1991)

Stevens, Edwin (act): *The Lone Wolf's Daughter* (1919)

Stevens, Eilene/Eileen (act): *Attack of the 50-Foot Woman* (1958); *Invasion of the Body Snatchers* (1956)

Stevens, Fisher (act, b. 1963): *The Brother from Another Planet; My Science Project; Short Circuit; Short Circuit 2; Super Mario Bros.*

Stevens, Fran (act): *Silent Night, Bloody Night*

Stevens, G. Wesley (act): *Fake-Out*

Stevens, George (act): *Witchery*

Stevens, Helena (act): *The Adding Machine; Highlander*

Stevens, Inger (act, 1935-1970, nee Inger Stensland): *Cry Terror!; The Mask of Sheba; The World, the Flesh and the Devil*

Stevens, Jack (act): *Howling VI: The Freaks*

Stevens, Jacques (act): *The Hound Of The Baskervilles* (1978)

Stevens, James (mus): *They Came from Beyond Space*

Stevens, Jean (act): *The Missing Juror*

Stevens, John (cin): *Blacula*

Stevens, Johnny (act): see Brodie, Steve

Stevens, Jon (wri): *Cyborg Cop II*

Stevens, K.T. (act, b. 1919, nee Gloria Wood): *Jungle Hell; Missile to the Moon*

Stevens, Kay (act): *Jaws 3-D*

Stevens, Ken (act): *Return to Oz*

Stevens, Kimberly (act): *Evil Obsession*

Stevens, Landers (act): *Charlie Chan's Secret; The Lone Wolf Spy Hunt*

Stevens, Lauder (act): *The Gorilla* (1931)

Stevens, Leslie (dir, b. 1924): *I Love a Mystery* (1966); *Incubus* (1965); *Private Property*

Stevens, Leslie (wri, b. 1924): *The Aquarians; Buck Rogers In the 25th Century; Code Name: Minus One; Fer-de-Lance; I Love a Mystery* (1966); *Incubus* (1965); *Private Property; Probe; Sheena; The War Lord*

Stevens, Marc (act): *High Priestess of Sexual Witchcraft; Penetration*

Stevens, Mark (act, b. 1922, nee Richard Stevens): *Between Midnight and Dawn; Escape from Hell; Frozen Alive; The Lost Hours; September Storm; The Snake Pit* (1948); *The Street With No Name*

Stevens, Marya (act): *Queen of Outer Space*

Stevens, Michael Edward (act): *Moby Dick* (1998)

Stevens, Monica (act): *Journey to the Center of Time*

Stevens, Morgan (act): *Survival Zone*

Stevens, Morton (mus): *Alice In Wonderland* (1985); *Poor Devil; Time Travelers* (1976)

Stevens, Onslow (act, 1902-1977, nee Onslow Ford Stevenson): *Angel On My Shoulder* (1946); *Bomba, the Jungle Boy; The Couch; The Creeper* (1948); *Follow the Hunter; House of Dracula; Mark of the Gorilla; The Monster and the Girl; Night Has a Thousand Eyes; The Secret of the Blue Room; Them!* (1954); *The Three Musketeers* (1935)

Stevens, Paul (act): *Battle for the Planet of the Apes; The Mask* (1961); *Rage*

Stevens, Rachel (act): *Desk Set*

Stevens, Reginald (act): *The Mystery of a London Flat*

Stevens, Richard (act): see Stevens, Mark

Stevens, Rise (act): *Journey Back to Oz*

Stevens, Robbie (act): *Mary Reilly*

Stevens, Robert (act): *The Millerson Case*

Stevens, Robert (M.) (cin): *The 'Burbs; Serial Mom*

Stevens, Robert (dir): *Change of Mind; I Thank a Fool*

Stevens, Robert C. (act): *Heaven Can Wait* (1978)

Stevens, Rock (act): *Challenge of the Gladiators; Ercole i Tiranni di Babilonia; Giant of Evil Island; Goliath at the Conquest of Damascus*

Stevens, Ronald Smokey (act): *The Wiz*

Stevens, Ronnie (act): *Morons from Outer Space; Some Girls Do*

Stevens, Rory (act): *Carrie*

Stevens, Roy (act): *Superman* (1978)

Stevens, Ruby (act): see Stanwyck, Barbara

Stevens, Stella (act, b. 1936, nee Estelle Eggleston): *Amazons* (1984); *Arnold; Chained Heat; Cruise Into Terror; The Granny; Li'l Abner* (1959); *The Mad Room; The Manitou; Mom; Monster In the Closet; The New, Original Wonder Woman; The Nutty Professor* (1963); *The Poseidon Adventure; The Secret of My Success; The Silencers* (1966); *Space Hunter; The Terror Within II; Virtual Combat; Wacko*

Stevens, Thomas Terry Hoar (act): see Terry-Thomas

Stevens, Tony (act): *Sorceress* (1982)

Stevens, Vi (act): *Serena*

Stevens, Wade (act): *Nightwing*

Stevens, Warren (act, b. 1928): *The Amazing Captain Nemo; Cyborg 2087; Forbidden Planet; Gorilla at Large; Intent to Kill; On the Threshold of Space; The Price of Fear*

Stevens, Warren A. (act): *Leprechaun 2*

Stevens, William (act): *Gargoyles*

Stevenson, Al (act): *Critters 2: The Main Course*

Stevenson, Alexandra (act): *Prehistoric Women* (1966)

Stevenson, Bill (act): *The 'Burbs; Child's Play 2; Outbreak*

Stevenson, Burton Egbert (wri): *In the Next Room*

Stevenson, Charles (act): *The Mysterious Dr. Fu Manchu*

Stevenson Jr., Charles C. (act): *Beverly Hills Bodysnatchers; Ed Wood*

Stevenson, Dandy (act): *King Kong Lives*

Stevenson, Deborah (act): *The Entity*

Stevenson, Doug (act): *Iced*

Stevenson (Jr.), Houseley/Housely (act, b. 1879): *The Atomic City; The Challenge* (1960); *Somewhere In the Night; Take One False Step; The War of the Worlds*

Stevenson, Margot (act): *Calling Philo Vance*

Stevenson, McLean (act, 1929-1996): *The Cat from Outer Space*

Stevenson, Onslow Ford (act): see Stevens, Onslow

Stevenson, Parker (act, b. 1953): *Are You Lonesome Tonight?; Not of This Earth* (1995); *Official Denial; This House Possessed*

Stevenson, Phil (act): *Killer's Kiss*

Stevenson, Richard (act): *The House of Secrets* (1929)

Stevenson, Rick (dir & wri): *Magic In the Water*

Stevenson, Robert (act): *Follow the Hunter*

Stevenson, Robert (dir, 1905-1986): *The Absent-Minded Professor* (1961); *Bedknobs and Broomsticks; Blackbeard's Ghost; Darby O'Gill and the Little People; The Gnome-Mobile; I Married a Communist; In Search of the Castaways; The Island at the Top of the World; Jane Eyre* (1944); *King Solomon's Mines* (1937); *The Love Bug; The Man Who Changed His Mind; Mary Poppins; The Misadventures of Merlin Jones; The Monkey's Uncle; One of Our Dinosaurs Is Missing; The Shaggy D.A.; Son of Flubber*

Stevenson, Robert (wri, 1905-1986): *F.P. 1 Antwortet Nicht; The Ringer* (1931)

Stevenson, Robert Louis (wri, 1850-1894): *Adventure Island; The Body Snatcher* (1945); *The Bottle Imp; Dr. Heckyl & Mr. Hype; Doctor Jekyll* (1964); *Dr. Jekyll and Mr. Hyde* (1908, 1910, 1912, 1913 {2}, 1919, 1920 {2}, 1925, 1932, 1939 & 1941); *Dr. Jekyll and Ms. Hyde; Dr. Jekyll and Sister Hyde; Dr. Jekyll's Hide; Il Dottor Jekyll; The Duality of Man; Edge of Sanity; Horrible Hyde; I, Monster; Der Januskopf; Jekyll and Hyde; Jekyll and Hyde...Together Again; Living Dead* (1932); *Long John Silver; The Man and the Beast; The Mirror and Markheim; My Friend, Dr. Jekyll; The Nutty Professor* (1963 & 1996); *The Strange Door; The Suicide Club* (1914 & 1988); *Le Testament du Dr. Cordelier; Treasure Island* (1920, 1934, 1950, 1971, 1976 & 1990); *The Treasure of Lost Canyon; Trouble for Two; The Two Faces of Dr. Jekyll; The Ugly Duckling; When Quackel Did Hyde; The Wrong Box*

Stevenson, Tom (act): *The Beginning or the End?; Counter-Espionage; The Lone Wolf In London*

Stevenson, Venetia (act): *City of the Dead; Island of Lost Women; Jet Over the Atlantic*

Steward, Don (cin): *Land of the Pharaohs; The Thing from Another World; What Ever Happened to Baby Jane?* (1962)

Steward, Ernest (cin): *The Assassin* (1952); *Dark Places; Deadlier Than the Male; The Face of Fu Manchu; Hot Enough for June; Quest for Love; Some Girls Do; Ten Little Indians* (1965); *The 39 Steps* (1959); *Venetian Bird*

Stewart, Alan (L.) (dir): *Ghostriders*

Stewart, Alexandra (act, b. 1939): *Agency; Because of the Cats; Black Moon* (1975); *Kemek; La Mariee etait en Noir; Maroc 7; Mickey One; Phobia; Tarzan the Magnificent; The Uncanny; Zeppelin*

Stewart, Amy (act): *Trucks*

Stewart, Anita (act): *The Invisible Fear*

Stewart, Athole (act, 1879-1940): *The Clairvoyant* (1934); *Dr. Syn; I Killed the Count; Poison Pen; The Speckled Band* (1931); *The Spy In Black*

Stewart, Bill (act): *Morons from Outer Space; 101 Dalmatians* (1996)

Stewart, Bobby (act): *Bambi*

Stewart, Brad (act): *Empire of Ash III*

Stewart, Bruce (wri): *The Hand of Night*

Stewart, Cassie (act): *Dolls*

Stewart, Catherine Mary (act): *The Annihilator; The Last Starfighter; Murder by the Book; Nightflyers; Night of the Comet; Out of Annie's Past; World Gone Wild*

Stewart, Charles (act): *War of the Colossal Beast*

Stewart, Charlotte (act): *Dark Angel: The Ascent; Eraserhead; Tremors*

Stewart, Dean (act): *The Resurrection of Zachary Wheeler*

Stewart, Dick (act): *The Glass Web*

Stewart, Don (cin): *Rocketship X-M*

Stewart, Donald (act, b. 1935): *No Highway In the Sky*

Stewart, Donald (wri): *Deathsport; The Hunt for Red October*

Stewart, Donald Ogden (wri, 1894-1980): *Keeper of the Flame; Marie Antoinette* (1938); *Moment of Danger*

Stewart, Douglas (act): *The Mysterious Mr. Nicholson*

Stewart, Douglas Day (wri): *The Scarlet Letter* (1995)

Stewart, Elaine (act, b. 1929, nee Elsy Steinberg): *The Adventures of Hajji Baba; Brigadoon; Most Dangerous Man Alive; The Tattered Dress*

Stewart, Eleanor (act): *The Torpedo of Doom*

Stewart, Evelyn (act): see Galli, Ida

Stewart, Ewan (act): *Flight to Berlin*

Stewart, Frank (act): *Galactic Gigolo*

Stewart, Fred Mustard (wri, b. 1932): *The Mephisto Waltz*

Stewart, French (act, b. 1964): *Magic Island; Stargate*

Stewart, George (act): *So Sad About Gloria*

Stewart, Hamilton (act): *The Silver Greyhound* (1919)

Stewart, Jack (act): *Hunted* (1952); *The Pirates of Blood River; Strongroom; The Three Lives of Thomasina*

Stewart, Jackie (act): *Sling Blade*

Stewart, James (act, 1908-1997): *After the Thin Man; An American Tail: Fievel Goes West; Bell, Book and Candle; The Big Sleep* (1978); *Call Northside 777; Harvey; It's a Wonderful Life; The Man Who Knew Too Much* (1956); *No Highway In the Sky; Rear Window* (1954); *Rope; Vertigo*

Stewart, James LaBlache (act): see Granger, Stewart

Stewart, Jamie (act): *Sling Blade*

Stewart, Jay (act): *Explorers*

Stewart, Jean (act): *Getting Lucky*

Stewart, Jean-Pierre (act): *Notorious* (1992)

Stewart, John (act): *Who?*

Stewart, John (dir): *Hidden Obsession*

Stewart, John Michael (act): *Neon Maniacs*

Stewart, Johna (act): *The Adventures of Galgameth; Young Hercules*

Stewart, Jon (act): *The Faculty*

Stewart, Kay (act): *The Screaming Woman*

Stewart, Larry (dir, 1929-1997): *The Initiation*

Stewart, Lawrence/Larry (act): *The Invisible Ray; Thief of Damascus*

Stewart, Lynn (act): *Elvira, Mistress of the Dark*

Stewart, Lynne Marie (act): *Pandemonium*

Stewart, Malcolm (act): *Timecop*

Stewart, Margie (act): *The Falcon In Hollywood; Gildersleeve's Ghost*

Stewart, Marianne (act): *Back from the Dead; Hush...Hush, Sweet Charlotte*

Stewart, Martin (cin): *Night of the Red Hunter*

Stewart, Mary (wri, b. 1916): *The Moon-Spinners*

Stewart, Maurice (act): *Death Curse of Tartu*

Stewart, Megan (act): *Flatliners*

Stewart, Mel (act): *Bride of Re-Animator; Dead Heat; The Invisible Woman* (1983)

Stewart, Michael (wri): *Eye of the Storm*

Stewart, Nick (act): *Phantom of the Jungle*

Stewart, Nicodemus (act): *Gildersleeve's Ghost*

Stewart, Nils Allen (act): *The Mask* (1994)

Stewart, Patrick (act, b. 1940): *The Canterville Ghost* (1996); *Dune; Excalibur; Lifeforce; Moby Dick* (1998); *The Pagemaster; The Prince of Egypt; Star Trek: First Contact; Star Trek: Generations; Star Trek: Insurrection*

Stewart, Paul (act, 1908-1986): *Appointment With Danger; City Beneath the Sea* (1970); *Kiss Me Deadly; The Window*

Stewart, Paul (1990s act): *Brainscan*

Stewart, Paul (cin): *Mutant*

Stewart, Paula (act): *Kemek*

Stewart, Peg (act): *The Boogens; The Fall of the House of Usher* (1982); *The Time Machine* (1978)

Stewart, Peggie (act): *The Vampire's Ghost*

Stewart, Peggy (act, b. 1923): *Beyond Evil; Terror In the Wax Museum*

Stewart, Peter (dir): see Newfield, Sam

Stewart, Randall (act): *Anguish*

Stewart, Ray (act): *Space Raiders*

Stewart, Richard (act): *Watch Me When I Kill*

Stewart, Rick (act): *A Nymphoid Barbarian In Dinosaur Hell*

Stewart, Robert (Banks) (wri): *Backfire!; Danger Route; Downfall; Marriage of Convenience; Never Mention Murder; Partners In Crime* (1961); *Playback; The Sinister Man; Vengeance*

Stewart, Rob(in) (act): *Digby-The Biggest Dog In the World; The Haunted House of Horror; Legend of the Seven Golden Vampires*

Stewart, Roy (1920s act): *The Viking*

Stewart, Roy (act): Live and Let Die; One Plus One; Twins of Evil
Stewart, Sally (act): Dangerous Fingers; The Lady Vanishes (1938)
Stewart, Sam (act): The Projectionist
Stewart, Scott (act): Sling Blade
Stewart, Sophie (act, b. 1909): Devil Girl from Mars; The Man Who Could Work Miracles; Maria Marten: or, The Murder In the Red Barn (1935); The Return of the Scarlet Pimpernel; Things to Come; Uncle Silas; Under the Red Robe (1937)
Stewart, Susan (act): Mantis In Lace
Stewart, Sylvester (act): Trick or Treats
Stewart, Thomas A. (act): Jaws 2
Stewart, Tom (act): Marooned
Stewart, Tonea (act): The Body Snatchers; Mistress of Paradise
Stewart, Trish (act): Mansion of the Doomed; Salvage; Time Travelers (1976)
Stewart, W. Alonzo (act): Angel Heart
Stewart, Yvonne (act): Satan's Sadists
Stewert, Evelyn (act): The Psychic
Steyn, Jack (cin): Bay Coven
Sthare, Ingrid (act): Sometimes They Come Back...Again
Stibich, John T. (act): Vice Versa (1988)
Stickney, Dorothy (act): Murder at the Vanities; The Uninvited (1944)
Stidder, Ted (act): The Haunting Passion
Stiers, David Ogden (act, b. 1942): The Bad Seed (1985); Beauty and the Beast (1991); Creator; Final Notice; The Hunchback of Notre Dame (1996); Magic; Oh, God!; Past Tense; Pocahontas; Pocahontas II; Journey to a New World; THX 1138
Stifter, Magnus (act): Der Januskopf
Stiglitz, Hugo (act): City of the Walking Dead; Guyana, Cult of the Damned; The Night of a Thousand Cats; Robinson Crusoe and the Tiger; Survive!; Tintorera ...Bloody Waters
Stiles, Leslie (wri): The Polar Star
Stiles, Victor (act): Santa Claus Conquers the Martians
Stiliadis, Nicolas (cin): The Pink Chiquitas
Still, Summer (act): Web of Deceit
Stille, Robin (act): The Slumber Party Massacre
Stiller, Amy (act): Vampire's Kiss
Stiller, Ben (act & dir): The Cable Guy
Stiller, Jerry (act, b. 1929): The McGuffin
Stiller, Mauritz (dir & wri, 1883-1928): Herr Arnes Pengar (1919); The Story of Gosta Berling
Stilles, Michelle (act): The Howling: New Moon Rising
Stillin, Marie (act): Nightscream; The Stepfather
Stillwagon, Arick (act): Night of the Creeps
Stilwell, Diane (act): Earth Girls Are Easy
Stimely, Brett (act): Bloodstone
Stimpson, Viola Kate (act): The Alchemist; Graduation Day
Stimson, Ken (act): Spawn of the Slithis
Stine, Clifford (cin): Abbott and Costello Go to Mars; Abbott and Costello Meet the Mummy; The Brass Bottle (1964); East of Sumatra; I've Lived Before; It Came from Outer Space; The Land Unknown; The Mole People; The Monolith Monsters; Step Down to Terror; Tarantula; This Island Earth
Stine, Harold (E.) (cin): The Busy Body; The Couch; The Incredible Mr. Limpet; Mighty Joe Young (1949); The Night Walker; The Poseidon Adventure; Project X (1967); The Spirit Is Willing
Stine, R.L. (wri): Superstitious
Sting (act, b. 1951, nee Gordon Sumner): The Adventures of Baron Munchausen (1989); The Bride (1985); Brimstone & Treacle; Dune
Sting (mus, b. 1951): Brimstone & Treacle
Stinson, John (act): Creature; The Hand (1981); Scared to Death (1980)
Stiny, Herbert (act): Dracula Blows His Cool
Stipo, Donna-Marie (act): The Toxic Avenger
Stirber, John (cin): Red Sonja
Stirdivant, Marc (wri): Condorman
Stirk, Cathy (act): The Punisher
Stirling, Charles (act): Atlas
Stirling, Helen (act): The Secret of Seagull Island
Stirling, Joseph (dir): Cloak Without Dagger
Stirling, Linda (act): Captain Mephisto and the Transformation Machine; Cyclotrode X; Invisible Informer; Jungle Gold; The Madonna's Secret; Mysterious Mr. Valentine
Stirling, Pamela (act): The Echo Murders; Return from the Ashes
Stitch, George F. (act): see Sterling, Ford
Stitt, Alexander (dir): Grendel, Grendel Grendel
Stitzel, Robert (wri): Brainstorm (1983)
Stobaeus, John (act): The Toxic Avenger
Stobart, Ed (act): Judge Dredd
Stobie, Richard (act): Witches' Brew
Stock, Alan (act): Frightmare (1983); Time Walker
Stock, Barbara (act): I, Desire; Wizards of the Lost Kingdom
Stock, Jennifer (act): Shriek of the Mutilated
Stock, Mark (dir): Midnight Movie Massacre
Stock, Michael (act): The Golden Lady
Stock, Nigel (act, b. 1919): The Mirror Crack'd; Never Let Go; The Night of the Generals; To Have and To Hold; Uncharted Seas; Yellowbeard; Young Sherlock Holmes
Stock, Ralph (wri): Gypsy Wildcat
Stockdale, Carl(ton) (act): The Black Pearl; The Fatal 30; Revolt of the Zombies; The Vampire Bat
Stocker, John (act): The Kidnapping of the President
Stocker, Steven (act): Bobbikins
Stocker, Walter (act): Madman of Mandoras
Stocker, Walter (dir): Till Death
Stockfeld, Betty (act): The Man Who Changed His Name
Stockham, William (act): Forever Evil
Stocklin, Tania (dir): Georgette Meunier
Stockman, Boyd (act): The Alligator People; Radar Secret Service
Stockman, Paul (act): Dr. Blood's Coffin
Stock-Poynton, Amy (act): Beanstalk; Bill & Ted's Bogus Journey
Stockton, Kevin (act): The Wiz
Stockton, Rose (act): Fargo
Stockwell, Dean (act, b. 1936): The Adventures of Nick Carter; The Arnelo Affair; Blue Velvet; The Boy With Green Hair; Dune; The Dunwich Horror; Home, Sweet Homicide; Limit Up; Naked Souls; Psych-Out; Song of the Thin Man; The Sweet Scent of Death; The Time Guardian; Werewolf of Washington
Stockwell, Guy (act, b. 1937): Blindfold; The Coming; The Disappearance of Flight 412; Grotesque; It's Alive (1974); The Monitors; The Three Swords of Zorro; The War Lord
Stockwell, Harry (act): Satan's Triangle; Werewolf of Washington
Stockwell, John (act, b. 1961): Christine; My Science Project; The Nurse; Radioactive Dreams
Stoddard, Gene (cin): The Night of the Claw
Stoddard, Malcolm (act): The Godsend; Tree of Hands
Stoddard, Marie (act): To Catch a Thief
Stoddard, Ray (act): Dick Tracy (1990)
Stoddard, William (wri): Zombie Island Massacre
Stoeber, Orville (mus): Let's Scare Jessica to Death
Stoeckel, Liz (act): Steps from Hell
Stohl, Hank (act): Satan's Triangle
Stoiber, Edmund (act): Witches' Brew
Stoker, Austin (act): Abby; Battle for the Planet of the Apes; Code Name: Minus One; Horror High; The Man With the Power; Time Walker; Uninvited (1987)
Stoker, Bram (wri, 1847-1912): The Awakening; Blood from the Mummy's Tomb; Bram Stoker's Dracula; Bram Stoker's 'Shadowbuilder'; Bram Stoker's 'The Mummy'; Burial of the Rats; Count Dracula; Dracula (1931, 1973, 1974 & 1979); Dracula's Daughter; Drakula; Horror of Dracula; The Lair of the White Worm; Nosferatu, eine Symphonie des Grauens; Nosferatu, the Vampyre
Stoker, Cliff (act): Graveyard Shift (1987)
Stoker, Sylvia (act): Threads
Stokes, Al (act): Green Pastures
Stokes, Angela (act): Def by Temptation
Stokes, Barry (act): Enemy Mine; Hawk the Slayer; Outer Touch; Prey (1978)
Stokes, George (act): Ravagers
Stokes, John (cin): Alien Cargo; Chameleon; The Fury Within; Gargantua; Meteorites!
Stokey, Susan (act): The Phantom Empire; The Power (1980); The Tomb
Stikie, Mike (act): Jacob's Ladder
Stolar, Edward (act): The Magic Voyage of Sinbad
Stole, Mink (act): Multiple Maniacs; Polyester; Serial Mom
Stoler, Shirley (act, 1928-1999): Frankenhooker; The Honeymoon Killers
Stoll, George (mus, b. 1905): Cabin In the Sky
Stoll, Gunther (act): The Castle of Fu Manchu; The Hunchback of Soho
Stollery, David (act): Jack and the Beanstalk (1952)
Stoloff, Ben(jamin) (dir, 1895-1960): The Hidden Hand; The Mysterious Doctor; Night of Terror (1933)
Stoloff, M.W./Morris (mus, 1893-1980): After Midnight With Boston Blackie; The Bandit of Sherwood Forest; Blind Alley; Boston Blackie Goes Hollywood; The Chance of a Lifetime; Counter-Espionage; The Face Behind the Mask; The 5000 Fingers of Dr. T; Gilda; Here Comes Mr. Jordan; The Lone Wolf Keeps a Date; The Lone Wolf Spy Hunt; One Dangerous Night; Passport to Suez; The Return of the Vampire; Rogues of Sherwood Forest; Secrets of the Lone Wolf
Stoloff, Victor (wri): She-Gods of Shark Reef
Stolow, Henry (act): Enemy Mine
Stoltz, Eric (act, b. 1960): Anaconda; Fluke; The Fly II; Haunted Summer; The Heart of Justice; The Prophecy (1995); Sister, Sister
Stolz, Clarissa (act): Locker 69
Stolz, Robert (mus): It Happened Tomorrow
Stolzemberg, Elke (act): Hundra
Stone, Andrew (L.) (dir & wri, b. 1902): A Blueprint for Murder; Cry Terror!; Hell's Headquarters; Julie; The Last Voyage; The Night Holds Terror; Ring of Fire; The Secret of My Success; The Steel Trap
Stone, Andy (act): Look What's Happened to Rosemary's Baby
Stone, Annette (act): White Zombie
Stone, Arthur (act): Charlie Chan In Egypt
Stone, Bernard (act): The Main Chance
Stone, Christopher (act, 1940-1995): Cujo; Dying to Remember; The Howling; Love Me Deadly
Stone, Christopher L. (mus): Galaxis; Phantasm III: Lord of the Dead; The Munsters' Scary Little Christmas; Prison (1988); Ticks
Stone, David (wri): Hide and Seek
Stone, Dee Wallace (act): see Wallace (Stone), Dee
Stone, Doris (act): Charlie Chan In London
Stone, Dorothy (act): Revolt of the Zombies
Stone, Doug (act): Shock Chamber
Stone, Ed (act): Dante's Peak; Species
Stone, Eric (act): Black Zoo; First Knight
Stone, Ezra (act, b. 1917): The Munsters' Revenge; A Very Missing Person
Stone, Fred (act): Dracula (1973)
Stone, Gene (cin): Nabonga
Stone, George (cin): The Mad Monster
Stone, George E. (act, 1903-1967, nee George Stein): The Adventurous Blonde; After Midnight With Boston Blackie; Alias Boston Blackie; Boston Blackie and the Law; Boston Blackie Booked On Suspicion; Boston Blackie Goes Hollywood; Boston Blackie's Appointment With Death; Boston Blackie's Rendezvous; The Chance of a Lifetime; A Close Call for Boston Blackie; Confessions of Boston Blackie; The Dragon Murder Case; The Face Behind the Mask; Island of Doomed Men; Jungle Hell; Mr. Moto's Gamble; One Mysterious Night; The Phantom of Crestwood; The Phantom Thief; Scared Stiff (1945); Secret of the Chateau; The Story of Mankind; Trapped by Boston Blackie; The Vampire Bat
Stone, Greg (act): Dangerous Touch
Stone, Gus (act): Endgame
Stone, Hank (act): Philadelphia Experiment II
Stone, Harold J. (act, b. 1911): The Invisible Boy; The St. Valentine's Day Massacre; The Wrong Man; X—The Man With the X-Ray Eyes
Stone, Ivory (act): Blackenstein
Stone, J.D. (act): Murder of Innocence; Ticks
Stone, James (F.) (act): Black Widow (1954); The Glass Web
Stone, Janice (act): The Giant Gila Monster
Stone, Jeffrey (act): The Girl In the Kremlin; The Thing That Couldn't Die
Stone, Jeffrey (wri): Unearthly Stranger
Stone, Jesse (act): Ernest Saves Christmas
Stone, John (act): Colonel Bogey; In the Devil's Garden; Moment of Indiscretion; The Unseeing Eye
Stone, John (wri): Passport to Suez
Stone, Laurie (mus): Official Denial
Stone, Leonard (act): A Man Called Dagger; Once Upon a Spy; Soylent Green; Willy Wonka and the Chocolate Factory
Stone, Les (act): Dark of the Night
Stone, Lewis (act, 1879-1953): Angels In the Outfield (1951); The Lost World (1925); Mata Hari (1932); The Mystery of Mr. X; The Phantom of Paris (1931); The Prisoner of Zenda (1922 & 1952); The Private Life of Helen of Troy; Talk About a Stranger; The 13th Chair (1937); Three Wise Fools; Treasure Island (1934); Trifling Women
Stone, Madison (act): Evil Toons
Stone, Marianne (act): Berserk; Carry On Screaming; Craze; The Creeping Flesh; The Curse of the Mummy's Tomb; [illegible] of Diana; In the Devil's Garden; Night of the Prowler; No Trees In the Street; Paranoiac; Passport to Treason; Penny Gold; Person Unknown; Quatermass II; Sammy's Super T-Shirt; Scrooge (1970); Spaceways; Tower of Evil; Troubled Waters (1964); The Vault of Horror; Who Slew Auntie Roo?
Stone, Matthew (wri): Destiny Turns On the Radio
Stone, Merritt (act): The Magic Sword (1962); Port Sinister; The Spider (1958); Tormented (1960)
Stone, Michael (act): Eraser
Stone, Milburn (act, 1905-1980): The Atomic City; Captive Wild Women; The Frozen Ghost; Invaders from Mars (1953); The Jungle Woman; The Mad Ghoul; Mystery Plane; Nick Carter, Master Detective; Phantom Lady; The Port of Missing Girls; Second Chance; Sherlock Holmes Faces Death; The Sky Dragon; Strange Confession; The Thirteenth Man
Stone, Noreen (wri): Brenda Starr (1992)
Stone, Norman (act): Death Magic
Stone, Norman (dir): The Vision
Stone, Oliver (act, b. 1946): The Hand (1981)
Stone, Oliver (dir, b. 1946): The Hand (1981); Seizure
Stone, Oliver (wri, b. 1946): Conan the Barbarian; The Hand (1981); Seizure
Stone, Paddy (act): Scrooge (1970)
Stone, Peter (wri): Mirage (1965); Who Is Killing the Great Chefs of Europe?
Stone, Philip (act): A Clockwork Orange; Flash Gordon (1980); Fragment of Fear; Hitler: The Last Ten Days; Indiana Jones and the Temple of Doom; The Medusa Touch; Never Mention Murder; Phantom of the Opera (1983); Quest for Love; The Shining; Unearthly Stranger
Stone, Rhesa Reagan (act): The Handmaid's Tale
Stone, Ric (act): Grendel, Grendel, Grendel
Stone, Richard (mus): Pumpkinhead
Stone, Ron (act): The Outing
Stone, Roy (act): The Big Switch
Stone, Sharon (act, b. 1958): Allan Quatermain and the Lost City of Gold; Antz; Beyond the Stars; Calendar Girl Murders; Deadly Blessing; Diabolique (1996); King Solomon's Mines (1985); Scissors; Sliver; Sphere; Total Recall
Stone, Simon (act): Making Contact
Stone, Stephanie Ann (act): Bridge Across Time
Stone, Teresa (act): Blood Diner
Stone, Uta (act): How to Stuff a Wild Bikini
Stone, Virginia (dir): Evil In the Deep
Stonefish, George (act): Wolfen
Stoneground (act): Dracula A.D. 1972
Stoneham (Jr.), John (act): Haunted by Her Past; Hitler's Daughter; Millennium; Phobia; The Pit (1983)
Stoneham Sr., John (act): Body Parts (1991)
Stoner, Ahmad (act): Full Eclipse
Stoner, Joy (act): I Was a Teenage Frankenstein
Stoner, Sherri (act): Deadly Messages; Impulse (1984)
Stones, Sherri (wri): Casper
Stones, Tad (dir): The Return of Jafar
Stoney, Heather (act): Deathline
Stoney, Jack (act): The Falcon's Alibi; Mr. Moto In Danger Island
Stoner, Kevin (act): Cash on Demand; The Deathshead Vampire; How to Murder a Rich Uncle; The Man Who Was Nobody; On the Run (1963); Ordeal by Innocence; The Quatermass Conclusion; Return of a Stranger (1962)
Stoner, Lynda (act): Escape 2000
Stoops, Ronald R. (act): The Final Countdown
Stoor, M. (act): Wielka, Wielka I Najwieksza
Stopkewich, Lynne (dir & wri): Kissed
Stoppa, Paolo/Paul (act, 1906-1988): La Beaute du Diable; Il Ladro di Venezia; Miracle In Milan
Stoppard, Tom (wri): Brazil
Stoppelmoor, Cheryl Jean (act): Satan's School for Girls
Stoppi, Franca (act): Buried Alive (1981)
Storaro, Vittorio (cin, b. 1940): Agatha; Ladyhawke; L'Uccello delle Piume di Cristallo
Storch, Larry (act, b. 1923): Fake-Out; The Flight of Dragons; The Monitors; The Silence of the Hams; Sweet Sixteen; Without Warning (1980); The Woman Hunter
Storer, Suzanne (act): Never-Never Land
Storey, Edith (act, b. 1892): The Dust of Egypt
Storey, Fred (wri): Rip Van Winkle (1914)
Storey, Howard (act): The Little Match Girl (1987)
Storey, John (act): Eye of the Storm; Stargate
Storey, June (act): The Lone Wolf Takes a Chance; The Snake Pit (1948)
Storey, Lynn (act): The Little Shop of Horrors (1960)
Storey, Ray (act): It Came from Beneath the Sea

Storke, Adam (act): *Death Becomes Her; Highway to Hell; Lifepod; The Phantom of the Opera (1990); The Stand*
Storm, Anthony (act): *Once Bitten*
Storm, Casey (act): *Once Bitten*
Storm, Debi (act): *The Brotherhood of Satan*
Storm, Esben (dir): *Deadly*
Storm, Gale (act, b. 1921, nee Josephine Cottle): *Between Midnight and Dawn; Lure of the Islands; Revenge of the Zombies (1943)*
Storm, Howard (dir): *Once Bitten*
Storm, James/Jim (act): *Night of Dark Shadows; Scream of the Wolf; Trilogy of Terror*
Storm, Lesley (wri): *Alibi (1942); Discipline; East of Piccadilly; The Ringer (1952)*
Storm, Morty (act): *Street Trash*
Storm, Tempest (act): *World of the Depraved*
Storm, Theodor (wri): *Chronik von Grieshuus*
Storm, Wayne (act): *The Phoenix (1981); Time After Time*
Stormare, Peter (act): *Armageddon; Fargo; The Lost World: Jurassic Park; Purgatory*
Stormer, Aaron (act): *Matinee*
Storms, Kirsten (act): *Zenon: Girl of the 21st Century*
Storr, catherine (wri): *Paperhouse*
Storr, Otto (act): *The Naked Woman and Satan*
Storrie, Kelly (act): *Constable Smith and the Magic Baton; Constable Smith In Trouble Again; Constable Smith On the Warpath*
Storry, Malcolm (act): *The Princess Bride*
Storvick, Tom (cin): *I Still Dream of Jeannie*
Storvik, Tim (cin): *Timecop*
Story, David (act): *The Ice House*
Story, Jack Trevor (wri): *Mix Me a Person; The Trouble With Harry*
Story, Robert (act): *The Ice House*
Story-Gofton, E. (act): *The Other Person*
Stossel, Ludwig (act, 1883-1973): *Above Suspicion; The Beginning or the End?; Bluebeard (1944); The Climax; Cloak and Dagger (1946); From the Earth to the Moon; The Great Impersonation (1942); House of Dracula; The Strange Death of Adolf Hitler; Temptation (1946); The White Goddess; Who Done It? (1942)*
Stotes, Ben (act): *Popcorn*
Stothart, Herbert P. (mus, 1884-1949): *After the Thin Man; A Guy Named Joe; Kismet (1944); Marie Antoinette (1938); The Picture of Dorian Gray (1945); Rasputin and the Empress; The Three Musketeers (1948); Treasure Island (1934)*
Stott, Judith (act): *Night of the Eagle*
Stott, Walter (mus): *Captain Nemo and the Underwater City*
Stouffer, Larry N. (dir): *Horror High*
Stout, Archie (J.) (cin, b. 1886): *The Benson Murder Case; Captain Kidd; Darkened Rooms; Dark Waters; It Happened Tomorrow; Mystery Plane; The Return of Dr. Fu Manchu; Tarzan and the Amazons; Tarzan and the Huntress*
Stout, Don (act): *Shock Waves*
Stout, Rex (wri, 1886-1975): *League of Frightened Men; Meet Nero Wolfe; Nero Wolfe*
Stovall, Ted (mus): *The Boy Who Cried Werewolf*
Stovall, Tom (act): *The Food of the Gods*
Stover, Armon (act): *Killer Klowns from Outer Space*
Stover, George (act): *Attack of the 60 Foot Centerfold; Fiend (1980); The Galaxy Invader; Nightbeast; Polyester*
Stover, Lois (act): *Forever Evil*
Stovin, Jerry (act): *Solo for Sparrow*
Stovitz, Ken (act): *Blue Velvet*
Stow, Percy (dir): *The Absent-Minded Professor (1907); Alice In Wonderland (1903); Attempted Murder In a Railway Train; Beauty and the Beast (1905); The Black Triangles; Cock-a-Doodle-Doo; The Convict and the Curate; Electrical House-Building; The Electric Leg; Electric Transformation; Father's Baby Boy; Gigantic Marionettes; A Glass of Goat's Milk; The Glutton's Nightmare; The Horse That Ate the Baby; Ib and Little Christina; It's Love That Makes the World Go Round; The Jealous Doll: or, The Frustrated Elopement; Lieutenant Rose and the Boxers; Lieutenant Rose and the Chinese Pirates; Lieutenant Rose and the Foreign Spy; Lieutenant Rose and the Gun-Runners; Lieutenant Rose and the Hidden Treasure; Lieutenant Rose and the Moorish Pirates; Lieutenant Rose and the Patent Aeroplane; Lieutenant Rose and the Royal Visit; Lieutenant Rose and the Sealed Orders; Lieutenant Rose and the Stolen Code; Lieutenant Rose and the Stolen Ship; Lieutenant Rose and the Train Wreckers; The Martyrdom of Thomas a Becket; The Mistletoe Bough; A Modern Dick Whittington; The Old Favourite and the Ugly Golliwog; Only One Girl: or, A Boom In Sausages; An Overdose of Love Potion; The Pied Piper (1907); The Professor's Strength Tablets; Robin Hood and His Merry Men; Saved by the Telegraph Code; She Must Have Swallowed It; The Tempest (1908); That Eternal Ping-Pong; The Truth Will Out; The Unclean World: The Suburban-Bunkum Microbe-Guyoscope; The Water Babies: or, The Little Chimney Sweep; When the Man In the Moon Seeks a Wife*
Stowe, Madeleine (act, b. 1958): *Amazons (1984); Blink; 12 Monkeys*
Stowell, Dan (act): *Boston Blackie Booked On Suspicion; Boston Blackie's Rendezvous*
Stowitts (act): *The Magician (1926)*
Stoyanov, Michael (act): *Freaked*
Stoycoff, Michael (act): *She Demons*
Strachocki, Janusz (act): *O Dwoch Takich Co Ukradli Ksiezyc*
Straczynski, J. Michael (wri): *Babylon 5: A Call to Arms; Babylon 5: The Gathering; River of Souls; Thirdspace: A Babylon 5 Adventure*
Stradi, Anne (act): *The House of Usher (1988)*
Stradling (Sr.), Harry (cin, 1910-1970): *Androcles and the Lion; Angel Face; The Corsican Brothers (1941); Dark Journey; Hans Christian Andersen; Helen of Troy (1955); Jamaica Inn (1939); Johnny Guitar; Moment to Moment; Nazi Agent; On a Clear Day You Can See Forver;The Picture of Dorian Gray (1945); Suspicion (1941)*
Stradling Jr., Harry (cin): *Damnation Alley; The Mad Room; Prophecy (1979)*
Stradner, Rose (act): *Blind Alley*
Stradvec, Michael (act): *Sometimes They Come Back...Again*
Strahan, Ruth P. (act): *Body Heat*
Strahl, Erwin (act): *The Invisible Terror*
Straight, Beatrice (act, b. 1918): *The Borrowers (1973); Chiller; The Dain Curse; Deceived; The Formula; Poltergeist*
Strain, Jim (wri): *Jumanji*
Strain, Julie (act): *Blonde Heaven; Midnight Confessions; Night Rhythms; Psycho Cop 2; Victim of Desire; Witchcraft 4: Virgin Heart*
Strait, Ralph (act): *Halloween III: Season of the Witch*
Straker, Peter (act): *Morons from Outer Space*
Strand, Maud (act): *Somewhere In Time*
Strandin, Ebon (act): *Blade af Satans Bog*
Strandmark, Erik (act): *Det Sjunde Inseglet*
Strang, Harry (act): *Charlie Chan at the Opera; Charlie Chan In Shanghai; Charlie Chan's Murder Cruise; Dick Tracy (1945); The Greene Murder Case; Mr. Moto In Danger Island; Mr. Moto Takes a Vacation; Phantom from Space*
Strang, Rose (act): *The Sexplorer*
Strange, Billy (mus): *De Sade*
Strange, Derrick (act): *Revenge of the Radioactive Reporter*
Strange, Glenn (act, 1899-1974): *Abbott and Costello Meet Frankenstein; The Black Raven; House of Dracula; House of Frankenstein; The Mad Monster; The Master Minds (1949); Master Minds (1950); The Monster Maker (1943); The Veils of Bagdad*
Strange, Julian (act): *Night Crossing*
Strange, Mark (act): *Isabel*
Strange, Philip (act): *Behind That Curtain; No Escape (1934); The Unholy Night*
Strange, Richard (act): *Batman (1989); Robin Hood: Prince of Thieves*
Strange, Robert (act): *The Mad Monster; The Saint Strikes Back; The Walking Dead*
Strange, Sarah (act): *Hideaway*
Strange, Valerie L. (act): *Scalpel*
Strange, Walter (cin): *Appointment With Murder; The Devil's Cargo*
Strangio, Frank (mus): *Dead End Drive-In*
Stranks, Alan (wri): *Dick Barton, Special Agent*
Strano, Carl (act): *Space Rage*
Strano, Michael (act): *Flight of the Navigator*
Strans, Kurt (act): *Forever Evil*
Stransky, Charles (act): *Ghost In the Machine*
Strasberg, Ivan (cin): *No. 1 of the Secret Service*
Strasberg, Lee (act): *The Cassandra Crossing*
Strasberg, Susan (act, b. 1938): *Bloody Birthday; Frankenstein (1973); Hauser's Memory; The Manitou; The Name of the Game Is Kill; Psych-Out; Rollercoaster; Rona Jaffe's Mazes and Monsters; So Evil, My Sister; Sweet Sixteen; A Taste of Fear; The Trip; Who Fears the Devil?*
Strasser, Michael (act): *Bride of Re-Animator; Timestalkers*
Strasser, Robin (act): *The Bride (1973)*
Strasser, Shirlee (act): *Jack's Wife*
Strassman, Marcia (act, b. 1948): *And You Thought Your Parents Were Weird; Brave New World (1980); Brenda Starr (1976); Haunted by Her Past; Honey, I Blew Up the Kid; Honey, I Shrunk the Kids*
Strate, Walter (dir): *Violated*
Stratford, Peter (act): *The Day After Halloween*
Stratford Jr., Willie (act): *The Bone Yard*
Strathairn, David (act): *The Brother from Another Planet; Dolores Claiborne; Iceman*
Strathan, Ida (act): *With Human Instinct*
Strathern, Lloyd (wri): *Roller Blade Warriors: Taken by Force*
Stratten, Dorothy (act, 1960-1980): *Galaxina*
Stratton, Arthur (act): *The Crime at Blossoms; The Man at Six; The Ringer (1931); The Silent House*
Stratton, Charles (act): *Munchies; Summer Camp Nightmare*
Stratton, Gil (act): *The Cat from Outer Space*
Stratton, Hank (act): *Demonwarp; The Man Who Fell to Earth (1987)*
Stratton, Inger (act): *The Naked Runner; The Playground*
Stratton, Jan (act): *Hellhole; She Woke Up*
Stratton, John (GB act, b. 1925): *Frankenstein and the Monster from Hell; Strangler's Web*
Stratton, John (USA act): *Terror from the Year 5,000*
Stratton, Julia (act): *The Man With Two Heads*
Stratton, Patrick (act): *Offerings*
Stratz, Rudolf (wri): *Schloss Vogelod*
Straub, John (act): *Project Moonbase*
Straub, Peter (wri): *Full Circle; Ghost Story (1981)*
Strausbaugh, Ken (act): *Total Recall*
Strauss, Guy (act): *The Good Son*
Strauss, Johann (mus, 1804-1849): *2001: A Space Odyssey*
Strauss, Malcolm (dir): *Salome (1923)*
Strauss, Peter (act, b. 1947): *Angel On My Shoulder (1980); Flight of Black Angel; Spacehunter: I*
Strauss, Richard (mus, 1864-1949): *2001: A Space Odyssey*
Strauss, Robert (act, b. 1913): *The Atomic Kid; 4D Man; Li'l Abner (1959); September Storm*
Stravinsky, Igor (mus, 1882-1971): *The Balcony; Dream Circus (unfinished)*
Straw, Jack (act): *The 30 Foot Bride of Candy Rock*
Strawberry Alarm Clock (mus): *Psych-Out*
Strawberry, Mary (act): *Blood and Lace*
Strawn, Arthur (wri): *The Black Room; Flight to Mars; The Man Who Lived Twice*
Strawther, Larry (wri): *Without a Clue*
Strayer, Frank (dir, 1891-1964): *Condemned to Live; The Ghost Walks; The Monster Walks; Murder at Midnight; Seeds of Destruction; Tangled Destinies; The Vampire Bat*
Strebel, Monica (act): *Slaughter Hotel (1972)*
Streep, Meryl (act, b. 1949): *Death Becomes Her; Still of the Night*
Street, George (act): *The Flesh and the Fiends; Pimpernel Smith*
Streeter, Coolidge (wri): *The Man from Beyond*
Streicher, Herbert (act): see Reems, Harry
Streidler, Betty (act): see St. John, Betta
Streiner, Russ(ell) (act): *The Majorettes; Night of the Living Dead (1968)*
Streiner, Russell (wri): *The Return of the Living Dead (1985)*
Streisand, Barbra (act, b. 1942): *On a Clear Day You Can See Forever*
Streisand, Barbra (mus, b. 1942): *Eyes of Laura Mars*
Streisin, Dorothy (act): *Kemek*
Strelich, Thomas (wri): *Out There*
Strelioff, Pat(ricia) (act): *Black Roses; The Quilt of Hathor*
Strenge, Walter (cin): *Cry Terror!*
Stretch, Gary (act): *Dead Connection*
Stribling, Melissa (act): *Crow Hollow; Crucible of Terror; Horror of Dracula; Journey Into Darkness; The League of Gentlemen; Murder Reported; Noose for a Lady; The Secret Partner*
Stribolt, Oscar (act): *Haxan*
Strick, Joseph (dir, b. 1923): *The Balcony*
Strick, Wesley (wri): *Arachnophobia; Cape Fear (1991); The Saint; Wolf*
Strickland, Bob (act): *Flight of the Navigator*
Strickland, Gail (act): *Ellery Queen; Hyper Sapien: People from Another Star; Lies; Starflight: The Plane That Couldn't Land*
Strickland, Mabel (act): *Willie's Dream*
Stricklen, Jerry (act): *The House of Seven Corpses*
Stricklyn, Ray (act, b. 1930): *The Lost World (1960); The Return of Dracula*
Strickson, Mark (act): *A Christmas Carol (1984)*
Stride, John (act): *Macbeth (1971); Oh Heavenly Dog; The Omen; Something to Hide*
Stride, Karen (act): *The Vampire Girls*
Strieb, Hal (act): *Maxim Xul*
Strieber, Whitley (wri): *Communion; The Hunger; Wolfen*
Striglos, Bill (act): *Heavy Traffic; Tarantulas: The Deadly Cargo*
Striker, Joseph (act): *The House of Secrets (1929)*
Strimling, Gene (act): *Always*
Strimpell, Stephen (act): *A Stranger Is Watching*
Strindberg, Anita (act): *L'Anticristo; Diario Segreto da un Carcere Femminile; Women In Cell Block 7*
Strindberg, Goran (cin, b. 1917): *The Devil's Wanton*
Stringer, Lewis (act): *Trunk Crime*
Stringer, Michael (act): *Trick or Treats*
Stringer, Nick (act): *The Shout*
Stringer, (R.) Michael (cin): *Demonwarp; The Eliminator*
Stringer, Sheila (act): *The Legend of Blood Mountain*
Stringer, Wayne (act): *Trick or Treats*
Stritch, Elaine (act, b. 1926): *Cocoon: The Return; The Scarlet Hour; The Spiral Staircase (1975); Who Killed Teddy Bear?*
Strizhenov, Oleg (act): *The Queen of Spades (1960)*
Strobel, Al (act): *Child of Darkness, Child of Light; Twin Peaks: Fire Walk With Me*
Strobel, Frank (mus): *The Young Poisoner's Handbook*
Strobel, John (act): *Escape from New York*
Strock, Herbert L. (dir, b. 1918): *Blood of Dracula; The Crawling Hand; The Devil's Messenger; Gog; How to Make a Monster; I Was a Teenage Frankenstein; Monstroid; Witches' Brew*
Strock, Herbert L. (wri, b. 1918): *The Crawling Hand; Monstroid*
Strock, Raymond L. (wri): *Larceny In Her Heart*
Strode, Woody (act, 1914-1994): *African Treasure; Bride of the Gorilla; City Beneath the Sea (1952); The Final Executioner; Jungle Gents; Kingdom of the Spiders; The Last Voyage; Manhunt In Milan; Ravagers; Tarzan's Deadly Silence; Tarzan's Fight for Life; Tarzan's Three Challenges*
Stroele, H.W. (act): *Mr. Moto's Last Warning*
Stroh, Heidi (act): *Sei Donne per l'Assassino*
Strohm, Roy (act): *Just Imagine*
Strohsahl Jr., George H. (act): *The Final Countdown*
Stroll, Edson (act): *Snow White and the Three Stooges; The Three Stooges In Orbit*
Strom, Florence (act): *Return of the Fly*
Strom, Olaf (act): *Metropolis (1926)*
Stromberg, William R. (dir & wri): *The Crater Lake Monster*
Stromboli (act): *The Bride (1985)*
Stronach, Tami (act): *The Neverending Story*
Strong, Austin (wri): *Three Wise Fools*
Strong, Brenda (act): *The Craft; Island City*
Strong, Charles (wri): *Dr. Cyclops*
Strong, Dennis (act): *Stone Cold Dead*
Strong, Gwynneth (act): *Dark Water; Nothing But the Night*
Strong, James Lyle (act): *The Force On Thunder Mountain*
Strong, Jim (act): *Beyond and Back*
Strong, Leonard (act): *The Atomic City; Cult of the Cobra; The Naked Jungle; Scared Stiff (1953)*
Strong, Michael (act): *Crackle of Death; Life, Liberty and Pursuit On the Planet of the Apes*
Strong, Porter (act): *One Exciting Night*
Strong, Rider (act): *Benefit of the Doubt*
Strong, Sidney (act): *The Devil's Profession*
Strong, Steve(n) (act): *Looker; Tarzan, the Ape Man (1981)*
Strongheart (animal act): *The Return of Boston Blackie*
Strongshield, Cyrus (act): *The Norsemen*
Stroock, Geraldine (act): see Brooks, Geraldine
Stroppa, Dino (act): *Bog*
Stross, Raymond (wri): *The Very Edge*
Strother, Fred (act): *12 Monkeys*
Stroud, Don (act, b. 1943): *The Amityville Horror; Carnosaur 2; The Deadly Dream; Explosion; Games; The House by the Lake; The Killer Inside Me; Licence to Kill (1989); National Lampoon's Men In White; Sweet Sixteen; Twisted Justice*
Stroud, Duke (act): *Children of the Corn III: Urban Sacrifice*
Stroud, Trey (act): *The Initiation*
Stroup Sr., Wendell (act): *Getting Lucky*
Strouse, Nicholas (act): *Doin' Time On Planet Earth*

Stroyberg, Annette (act): see Vadim, Annette
Stroyberg, Camilla (act): *Et Mourir de Plaisir*
Strozzi, Tito (act): *Cave of the Living Dead*
Strozier, Henry (act): *Shadow Conspiracy*
Strube, Cordelia (act): *Millennium*
Struble, Blair Nicole (act): *The Handmaid's Tale*
Struchkova, Raisa (act): *Cinderella (1961)*
Strudwick, Shepperd (act, 1907-1983, a.k.a. John Shepperd): *Beyond a Reasonable Doubt; Dr. Renault's Secret; The Loves of Edgar Allan Poe; The Monitors; Psychomania (1964); The Reckless Moment; Strange Triangle*
Strueby, Katherine (wri): *Forbidden; The Shop at Sly Corner*
Strummer, Joe (mus): *When Pigs Fly*
Strus, George (act): *Silent Night, Bloody Night*
Struss, Karl (cin, 1887-1982): *The Alligator People; Aloma of the South Seas (1941); Atlantis (1948); Dr. Jekyll and Mr. Hyde (1932); The Fly (1958); Four Frightened People; Girl Missing; Heaven Only Knows; Island of Lost Souls; Journey Into Fear (1942); Kronos (1957); Mesa of Lost Women; Rocketship X-M; Tarzan and the Leopard Woman; Tarzan and the She-Devil; Tarzan's Magic Fountain; Tarzan's Peril; Tarzan's Savage Fury*
Struthers, Sally (act, b. 1948): *Alice In Wonderland (1985); The Great Houdinis*
Strutin, Stuart (wri): *Class of Nuke 'em High*
Strutton, William (wri): *Assignment K*
Struycken, Carel (act): *The Addams Family; Addams Family Values; Backlash: Oblivion 2; Ewoks: The Battle for Endor; Journey to the Center of the Earth (1993); Oblivion; Out There; The Prey (1980); The Servants of Twilight; The Witches of Eastwick*
Strydom, Adriaan (mus): *Survivor (1987)*
Stryker, Amy (act): *Impulse (1984)*
Stryker, Dan (act): *To All a Goodnight*
Stryker, Jonathan (dir): *Curtains*
Strzalskowski, Henry (act): *Equalizer 2000*
Stuart, Aimee (wri): *Fanny by Gaslight; The Wicked Lady*
Stuart, Alan (act): *Superman II*
Stuart, Alexander (wri): *Ordeal by Innocence*
Stuart, Arlen (act): *Ben*
Stuart, Blanche Irwin (act): *Jacob's Ladder*
Stuart, Brian (dir): *Sorceress (1982)*
Stuart, Cassie (act): *Ordeal by Innocence; Slayground*
Stuart, Chad (act): *The Jungle Book (1967)*
Stuart, Donald (act): *Devotion; The Invisible Man (1933); The Undying Monster*
Stuart, Donald (wri): *The Man Outside (1933); The Shadow (1933)*
Stuart, Eleanor (act): *Oedipus Rex (1956)*
Stuart, Eva (act): *The Cloister and the Woman*
Stuart, Ewan (act): *A Distant Scream*
Stuart, Gloria (act, b. 1909, nee Gloria Stuart Finch): *The Gift of Gab; The Invisible Man (1933); The Old Dark House (1932); The Prisoner of Shark Island; Roman Scandals; The Secret of the Blue Room; The Three Musketeers (1939); The Whistler*
Stuart, Ian A. (wri): *The Pit (1983)*
Stuart, Jack (act): see Rossi-Stuart, Giacomo
Stuart, James R. (act): *Reactor; War of the Robots*
Stuart, Jason (act): *The Lost Empire*
Stuart, Jeanne (act): *Bella Donna (1934); Creeping Shadows; The Shadow (1933)*
Stuart, Jeb (wri): *The Fugitive (1993); Leviathan*
Stuart, John (GB act, 1898-1979): *Alias John Preston; Bella Donna (1934); The Black Abbot (1934); Blackmail (1929); Blood of the Vampire; Candles at Nine; Chain of Events; The Claydon Treasure Mystery; The Crossroads Gallows; Danger by My Side; Elstree Calling; Escape from Broadmoor (1948); Four Sided Triangle; The Hound of the Baskervilles (1931); House of Darkness; Man On the Run; Men of Sherwood Forest; Midnight (1931); Mr. Denning Drives North; The Mummy (1959); Number 17; Old Mother Riley's Ghosts; Paranoiac; The Pointing Finger; Quatermass II; The Revenge of Frankenstein; The Ringer (1952); Royal Flash; The Scarlet Blade; The Secret Man; Superman (1978); The Unseeing Eye; The Village of the Damned (1960); The Wandering Jew (1933)*
Stuart, John (USA act): *Shadowzone*
Stuart, John "Easton" (act): *The Man With Two Brains*
Stuart, Josephine (act): *The Straw Man*
Stuart, Kathie (act): *Intensity*
Stuart, Kathleen (act): *Just William's Luck*
Stuart, Katie (act): *Atomic Dog*
Stuart, Laird (act): *RoboCop*
Stuart, Madge (act): *The Crimson Circle (1922); The Elusive Pimpernel (1919)*
Stuart, Margaret (act): *Digby-The Biggest Dog In the World*
Stuart, Martin (act): *Rip Van Winkle (1914)*
Stuart, Mel (dir): *Brenda Starr (1976); Willy Wonka and the Chocolate Factory*
Stuart, Nicholas (act): *The Adding Machine*
Stuart, Nick (act, 1903-1973): *Killer Ape*
Stuart, Norman (act): *Arnold; Battlestar Galactica; Star Trek*
Stuart, Nuba (act): *Naked Evil*
Stuart, Paul (act): *Kiss Me Deadly*
Stuart, Randy (act): *The Incredible Shrinking Man*
Stuart, Ross (act): *Arms of the Avenger*
Stuart, St. John (act): *The Gamma People*
Stuart, Sir Simeon (act): *The Crimson Circle (1922); The Face at the Window (1920); The Shadow Between*
Stuart, Suzanne (act): *Scream, Baby, Scream*
Stubblefield, Tom (act): *Secrets of the Phantom Caverns*
Stubbs, Dave (act): *Empire of Ash III*
Stubbs, Harry (act): *Frankenstein Meets the Wolf Man; The Invisible Man (1933); The Invisible Man Returns; The Mummy's Hand; The Spanish Cape Mystery*
Stubbs, Imogen (act): *Erik the Viking*
Stubbs, Levi (act): *Little Shop of Horrors (1986)*
Stubbs, Morton (act): see Selten, Morton
Stubbs, Una (act): *Penny Gold; The Water Babies*
Stubing, Solvy (act): *Battle of the Amazons*
Stuckmeyer, John (wri): *The Sword and the Sorcerer*
Stucky, Lisa (act): *Princess Warrior*
Studenkova, Zdena (act): *Beauty and the Beast (1985)*
Studer, Carl (J.) (act): *Les Felins; Quelqu'un Derriere la Porte*
Studi, Wes (act): *The Killing Jar*
Study, Lomax (act): *Wonder Woman*
Stuhmer, Hank (act): *Nightbeast*
Stumar, Charles (cin): *The Mummy (1932); The Raven (1935); Werewolf of London*
Stumar, John (cin): *The Lone Wolf Takes a Chance; The Return of the Vampire*
Stumpf, Randy (act): *Are You In the House Alone?*
Stunnenberg, Coby (act): *Gebroken Spiegels*
Sturgeon, Scott (wri): *Asteroid*
Sturgeon, Theodore (wri, 1918-1985): *Killdozer*
Sturgeon, William (act): *The Nutty Professor (1996)*
Sturgeon, Wina (act): *Exo-Man*
Sturges, Eddie (act): *The Phantom of Crestwood*
Sturges, Jeff (mus): *Hellhole*
Sturges, John (dir, 1910-1992): *Kind Lady (1951); Marooned; Mystery Street; The Satan Bug; Shadowed*
Sturges, Pat (act): *Turn Back the Clock*
Sturges, Preston (wri): *Virtual Obsession*
Sturges, Shannon (act): *Convict 762; Tornado!*
Sturgess, Olive (act): *The Raven (1963)*
Sturgess, Peter (act): *Funeral Home*
Sturgess, Rosie (act): *Thirst*
Sturgis, Edwin (act): *Seven Keys to Baldpate (1925)*
Sturgis, Gary Anthony (act): *Virtuosity*
Sturkie, Dan (act): *Dr. Heckyl & Mr. Hype*
Sturlin, Ross (act): *Night of the Blood-Beast*
Sturm, Hans (act): *The Golem: How He Came Into the World*
Sturm, Steve (act): *Mother's Day*
Sturridge, Charles (dir): *Gulliver's Travels (1996)*
Sturridge, Thomas (act): *Gulliver's Travels (1996)*
Sturtevant, Jimmy (act): *Hell Night*
Sturz, Usa (act): *Howard the Duck*
Stutenroth, Gene (act): see Roth, Gene
Stutfield, Rupert (act): *What's Bred...Comes Out In the Flesh*
Stuthman, Fred (act): *Firepower; The Private Eyes (1980)*
Stuto, Darlene (act): *Ms. 45*
Stutt, David (act): *Threads*
Stutz, Birgit (act): *Making Contact*
Stuyck, Pieter (act): *Superman (1978)*
Style, Michael (wri): *The Vampire Lovers*
Styler, Trudie (act): *Fair Game (1988)*
Styles, Edwin (act): *The Full Treatment; Top Secret (1952)*
Styncromb, David (act): *The Offspring*
Su, Charline (act): *Seven*
Suande, Bill (wri): *Terror On the Beach*
Suarez, Bobby (dir): *Warriors of the Apocalypse*
Suarez, Emma (act): *La Ardilla Roja*
Suarez, Gonzalo (dir): *El Extrano Caso del Dr. Fausto*
Suarez, Jose (act): *Baraka X-77; Carthage In Flames; Slave Girls of Sheba*
Suarez, Luis (act): *Monstroid*
Subert, Gaston (act): *Mission: Impossible*
Subiela, Eliseo (dir): *Man Facing Southeast*
Subkoff, Tara (act): *Freeway; When the Bough Breaks*
Subor, Michel (act): *The Queen of Spades (1966); Topaz*
Subotsky, Milton (wri, b. 1921): *At the Earth's Core; City of the Dead; Daleks' Invasion Earth 2150 A.D.; Dr. Terror's House of Horrors (1964); Dr. Who and the Daleks; I, Monster; The Skull; Tales from the Crypt (1971); They Came from Beyond Space; The Vault of Horror*
Sucher, Henry (wri, b. 1900): *Captive Wild Woman; The Frozen Ghost; The Jungle Woman; The Mummy's Ghost; The Mummy's Tomb*
Suchet, David (act): *Greystoke: The Legend of Tarzan, Lord of the Apes; Harry and the Hendersons; The Hunchback of Notre Dame (1982); The Little Drummer Girl; A Perfect Murder; Thirteen at Dinner; Wing Commander*
Suckmann, Erich (act): *The Last Ten Days of Adolf Hitler*
Suddeth, Greg (wri): *Pet Shop; Prehysteria*
Suddeth, Skipp (act): *Eraser; Mutants In Paradise*
Sudina, Marina (act): *Mute Witness*
Sudlow, Susie (act): *Ark of the Sun God*
Sudrow, Penelope (act): *A Nightmare On Elm Street 3: Dream Warriors*
Sudzin, Jeffrey (act): *Remote Control (1988); The Wraith*
Suedo, Julie (act): *The Dance of Death (1938); Dark Eyes of London; The Dream Doctor; Widow Twan-Kee*
Suergiu, Kathy (act): *Eyes of a Stranger*
Sues, Alan (act): *Oh Heavenly Dog*
Sufrin, Lawrence (act): *Street Trash*
Suga, Toshiro (act): *Moonraker*
Sugai, Kin (act): *Kwaidan*
Sugarman, Fred (act): *Wheels of Terror*
Sugarman, Sparky (mus): *Cinderella 2000*
Sugg, Penny (act): *Color Me Dead*
Suggs, Steven (act): *The Gifted One*
Sugimura, Haruko (act): *Kwaidan*
Sugiura, Naoki (act): *Deaths In Tokimeki*
Sugiyama, Kenji (cin): *Alakazam the Great*
Sugiyama, Tadayuki (act): *The Toxic Avenger, Part II*
Suhosky, Robert (wri): *The House Where Evil Dwells*
Suhrstedt, Tim(othy) (cin): *Android; Bill & Ted's Excellent Adventure; Critters; Forbidden World; Mannequin; Remote Control (1988); Space Rage; Teen Wolf; To Gillian On Her 37th Birthday*
Suin, Charles (cin): *Mr. Peek-A-Boo*
Sujata (act): *Desert Legion; The Diamond Queen; Fair Wind to Java; Salome (1953)*
Suki, M. (act): *Il Montagna di Dio Cannibale*
Sukman, Harry (mus): *Around the World Under the Sea; Gog; Planet Earth; Riders to the Stars; Sabu and the Magic Ring; Salem's Lot; Someone's Watching Me!*
Sukowa, Barbara (act): *Johnny Mnemonic; Lost Souls (1998)*
Sullivan, Barry (act, 1912-1994, nee Patrick Barry): *Cause for Alarm!; Earthquake; Framed; How to Steal the World; The Human Factor; The Immortal; Julie; Lady In the Dark; L.A. 2017; The Magician (1973); My Blood Runs Cold; Night Gallery; Oh, God!; Pyro; Queen Bee; Suspense; Terrore Nello Spazio*
Sullivan, Bonnie (act): *Revenge of the Stepford Wives*
Sullivan, Brad (act): *Ghost Story (1981); The Island; Orpheus Descending*
Sullivan, Brian (cin): *Wish Upon a Star*
Sullivan, Brick (act): *Undersea Girl*
Sullivan, C. Gardner (wri): *The Gracie Allen Murder Case*
Sullivan, Charles/Charlie (act): *Boston Blackie Goes Hollywood; The Shanghai Chest; Torchy Plays With Dynamite*
Sullivan, Chris (act): *Lifeforce*
Sullivan, D.J. (act): *Attack of the Killer Tomatoes; Look What's Happened to Rosemary's Baby; Return of the Killer Tomatoes*
Sullivan, Didi (act): see Perego, Didi
Sullivan, Don (act): *The Giant Gila Monster; The Monster of Piedras Blancas; Teenage Zombies*
Sullivan, Ed (act, 1902-1974): *The Last of the Secret Agents?*
Sullivan, Edward (act): *Mr. H.C. Andersen*
Sullivan, Elizabeth (act): see Lanchester, Elsa
Sullivan, Elliott (act, 1907-1974): *Cat and Mouse (1974); Fear Is the Key; The Saint's Double Trouble*
Sullivan, Francis L. (act, 1903-1956): *Chu Chin Chow (1934); The Drum; Drums of Tahiti; Fiddlers Three; F.P. 1 Antwortet Nicht; The Gables Mystery; Great Expectations (1934 & 1946); The Laughing Lady; The Limping Man (1936); The Missing Rembrandt; The Mystery of Edwin Drood (1935); Pimpernel Smith; The Return of Bulldog Drummond; Sabotage; The Stickpin; Take My Life; The Wandering Jew (1933)*
Sullivan, Frank (act): see Sully, Frank
Sullivan, George (act): *Halloween 4: The Return of Michael Myers*
Sullivan, Greg (act): *Metamorphosis: The Alien Factor*
Sullivan, Haley (act): *The Last of the Lone Wolf*
Sullivan, Hugh (act): *The Persecution and Assassination of Jean-Paul Marat as Performed by the Inmates of the Asylum of Charenton Under the Direction of the Marquis de Sade*
Sullivan, Ian (act): *The Clone Master*
Sullivan, J. Christopher (act, b. 1932): *Critters 2: The Main Course; Ghost (1990)*
Sullivan, Jean (act): *Squirm*
Sullivan, Jenny (act): *The Other (1972); V*
Sullivan, Jim (act): *Yeti*
Sullivan, John E. (cin): *Eraser*
Sullivan, Justin (act): *Scream*
Sullivan, Kate (act): *Pulp*
Sullivan, Kim (act): *Mad Max*
Sullivan, Liam (act): *Final Eye; The Magic Sword (1962); Secrets of the Phantom Caverns*
Sullivan, Marie (act): *Elvira, Mistress of the Dark*
Sullivan, Mary (act): *Humongous*
Sullivan, Michael (act): *Madman*
Sullivan, Mike (act): *Piranha (1978)*
Sullivan, Nancy (act): *The Last Man On Planet Earth*
Sullivan, Owen (act): *Damien-Omen II*
Sullivan, Rob (act): *Pandemonium*
Sullivan, Sean (act): *Change of Mind; The Dead Zone; Gang War; 2001: A Space Odyssey*
Sullivan, Sean Gregory (act): *Howling VI: The Freaks*
Sullivan, Sheila (act): *Houston, We've Got a Problem; A Name for Evil*
Sullivan, Susan (act, b. 1944): *City In Fear; The Dark Ride; The Incredible Hulk; Killer's Delight; Our Man Flint: Dead On Target*
Sullivan, Susan J. (act): *Star Trek*
Sullivan, William/Billy (act): *Murder by Television*
Sully, Frank (act, b. 1910, nee Frank Sullivan): *Another Thin Man; Boston Blackie and the Law; Boston Blackie Booked On Suspicion; Boston Blackie's Chinese Venture; Boston Blackie's Rendezvous; A Close Call for Boston Blackie; Crime Doctor's Manhunt; The Ghost That Walks Alone; Jungle Moon Men; One Dangerous Night; The Phantom Thief; Trapped by Boston Blackie*
Sully, Robert (act): *Love Letters*
Sulochana (act): *The Jungle*
Sultan, Arne (wri): *The Nude Bomb; Poor Devil*
Sul-te-wan, Mme. (act): *Maid of Salem; Queen Kelly; Torchy Plays With Dynamite*
Sulzberger, Cyrus L. (wri): *The Playground*
Sumac, Yma (act, b. 1927): *Omar Khayyam; Secret of the Incas*
Summer, Donna (mus): *Daylight; The Deep*
Summer, Herbert (act): *Night of the Living Dead (1968)*
Summerfield, Eleanor (act, b. 1921): *The Black Glove; Man On the Run; Murder by Proxy; The Running Man (1963); Take My Life; Top Secret (1952); The Watcher In the Woods*
Summerfield, Joan (act): see Kent, Jean
Summerland, Augusta (act): see Harrison, Linda
Summerland, Katy (act): *The Puppet Masters*
Summers, Bob (mus): *Beyond and Back; The Boogens; Earthbound (1981); Guyana, Cult of the Damned; The Legend of Sleepy Hollow; One Dark Night*
Summers, Bunny (act): *From Beyond; Merlin's Shop of Mystical Wonders; Re-Animator*
Summers, Deen (act): *Phantom of the Paradise*
Summers, Dorothy (act): *No Haunt for a Gentleman*
Summers, Hope (act): *The Couch; The Ghost and Mr. Chicken; Homicidal; The Return of Dracula; Rosemary's Baby*
Summers, James (act): *Prehistoric Women (1950)*
Summers, Jeremy (act): *Avalanche*
Summers, Jeremy (dir, b. 1931): *The Face of Eve; Five Golden Dragons; House of 1,000*

Dolls; Sammy's Super T-Shirt; The Vengeance of Fu Manchu
Summers, Jill (act): Agatha
Summers, Leonora (act, 1898-1976): The Sea Beast
Summers, Leslie (act): Dr. Goldfoot and the Bikini Machine
Summers, Lorie (act): X—The Man With the X-Ray Eyes
Summers, Neil (act): Dick Tracy (1990); RoboCop
Summers, Walter (dir, b. 1896): At the Villa Rose (1939); Chamber of Horrors (1929); Dark Eyes of London; The House Opposite (1931); The Limping Man (1936); The Lost Patrol (1929); The Return of Bulldog Drummond; The Warren Case
Summers, Walter (wri, b. 1896): Black Limelight; Chamber of Horrors (1929); Dark Eyes of London; The House Opposite (1931); The Limping Man (1936); The Lost Patrol (1929); The Return of Bulldog Drummond; She (1925); The Warren Case
Summers, Yale (act): The Amazing Captain Nemo
Summerscale, Frank (act): Children of the Damned
Summerville, George J. (act): see Summerville, Slim
Summerville, Irene Scase (act): The Toxic Avenger, Part II
Summerville, Slim (act, 1892-1946, nee George J. Summerville): Charlie Chan In Reno; The Chinese Parrot; The Last Warning (1929)
Sumner, David (act): Out of the Fog (1962); Touch of Death
Sumner, Geoffrey (act): Cul-de-Sac; The Dark Man (1951); Dark Secret; Law and Disorder; There Goes the Bride; Top Secret (1952)
Sumner, Gordon (act): see Sting
Sumner, John (act): The Frighteners
Sumner, Olympia (act): The Adventures of Dick Turpin-The Gunpowder Plot
Sumner, Peter (act): Color Me Dead
Sumpter, Donald (act): The Black Panther; Night After Night After Night
Sun, Leland (act): Jekyll and Hyde...Together Again
Sunazuka, Hideo (act): Ebirah, Horror of the Deep
Sundance, Roy (act): The Toxic Avenger, Part II
Sundbert, Clinton (act, b. 1919): Mr. Peabody and the Mermaid; Song of the Thin Man; The Wonderful World of the Brothers Grimm
Sunde, Myron (act): Just Imagine
Sunderland, Janet (act): Honey, I Shrunk the Kids
Sunders, Lon (act): Pumpkinhead II: Blood Wings
Sundfor, Paul (mus): Attack of the Killer Tomatoes
Sundin, Michael (act): Return to Oz
Sundquist, Gerry (act): The Black Panther; Don't Open Till Christmas; The Hunchback of Notre Dame (1982)
Sundquist, Jerry (act): Blind Date
Sundstrom, Neal (dir): Howling V: The Rebirth
Sung, Elizabeth (Fong) (act): Cyborg 2: Glass Shadow; Death Ring; The Puppet Masters
Sung, Michael (act): Varan the Unbelievable
Sung-Kuen, Moon (act): Gesom E Kako Shipta
Sunseri, Jack A. (dir): The Chilling (1989)
Sunshine, Jerry (act): Valley of the Dragons
Sunter, Irene (act): The Wicker Man
Supiran, Ricky (act): Space Rage
Supor Jr., Joe (act): The Toxic Avenger
Suprenant, Jennifer (act): Halloween With the Addams Family
Surdez, George (wri): Desert Legion
Surensky, D. (cin): Jack Frost
Suriani, Cristina (act): Horror Rises from the Tomb; The Saga of the Draculas
Surina, Daniela (act): The Dead Are Alive
Surkin, Eddie (Etan) (cin): Deadly Messages; Single White Female; To Die For
Surman, John (act): Without a Clue
Surnow, Joel (wri): Ring of the Musketeers
Surovy, Nicolas (act): Doctor Franken; Forever Young; 12:01
Surow, Robert (act): The Magic Voyage of Sinbad
Surratt, Harold (act): Shadow Conspiracy
Surtees, Alan (act): The Adding Machine; Erik the Viking; Eye of the Needle
Surtees, Bruce (cin): The Beguiled; Conquest of the Planet of the Apes; Murder In a Small Town; Play Misty for Me; Psycho III; White Dog
Surtees, Robert L. (cin, 1906-1985): The Collector; Dr. Dolittle (1967); King Solomon's Mines (1949); Kisses for My President; Lost Horizon (1973); The Other (1972); The Satan Bug
Surtees, Sven (act): Octopussy
Survinski, Rege (cin): Jack's Wife
Survinski, Regis J. (act): Martin
Survinski, Vincent D. (act): Martin
Susands, Patrick (act): The Strangler (1932)
Suschitzky, Peter (cin): Crash (1996); Dead Ringers; It Happened Here; Krull; Liszt O' Mania; The Man In the Iron Mask (1998); Mars Attacks!; The Pied Piper (1971); Privilege; The Rocky Horror Picture Show
Suschitzky, Wolfgang (cin, b. 1912): Moments; The Oracle (1952); Something to Hide; Theater of Blood; The Vengeance of She
Susi, Carol Ann (act): Crackle of Death; Donor
Suska, Almanta (act): Hunters of the Golden Cobra
Suskin, Mitch (cin): Cocoon
Susman, Todd (act): Bodily Harm
Suso, Henry (dir & wri): Deathsport
Sussex, C.L. (act): It's Alive III: Island of the Alive
Susskind, David (act): Simon
Susskind, Steve (act): Star Trek V: The Final Frontier
Sussman, Bruce (mus): The Pebble and the Penguin; Thumbelina (1994)
Sustr, Miro (act): Howling II
Sutch, Herbert (act): One Exciting Night
Sutcliff, Rosemary (wri): Gawain and the Green Knight; Ghost Story (1975); Sword of the Valiant
Sutcliffe, Clare (act): I Start Counting
Sutcliffe, Irene (act): Agatha
Sutcliffe, Peter (wri): Dolly Dearest
Suter, Andrea (act): The Toxic Avenger
Sutherd, Dick (act): Melody of Death
Sutherland, (A.) Edward (dir, 1897-1973): Beyond Tomorrow; The Boys from Syracuse; International House; The Invisible Woman (1941); Murders In the Zoo; Nine Lives Are Not Enough
Sutherland, Catherine (act): Turbo: A Power Rangers Movie
Sutherland, Dick (act): Don Juan (1927); The Road to Yesterday
Sutherland, Donald (act, b. 1934): Apprentice to Murder; Bear Island; The Bedford Incident; Benefit of the Doubt; Billion Dollar Brain; Blood Relatives; Buffy the Slayer; Castle of the Living Dead; The Disappearance; Dr. Terror's House of Horrors (1964); Don't Look Now; Eye of the Needle; Fallen; Fanatic (1965); Instinct; Invasion of the Body Snatchers (1978); Lady Ice; The Lifeforce Experiment; Murder by Decree; Ordeal by Innocence; Outbreak; The Puppet Masters; The Rosary Murders; Shadow Conspiracy; Time to Kill (1996); Virus (1999)
Sutherland, Evelyn Greenleaf (wri): The Road to Yesterday
Sutherland, Frank (act): Scouts to the Rescue
Sutherland, Mrs. (Frank) (act): Scouts to the Rescue
Sutherland, Grant (act): The Spy In Black
Sutherland, Hal (dir): Journey Back to Oz; Pinocchio and the Emperor of the Night
Sutherland, Ian (wri): Rituals
Sutherland, John (act): Bambi; Jack's Back
Sutherland, Keith (act): Happy Birthday to Me
Sutherland, Kiefer (act, b. 1966): Amazing Stories; Dark City; Flatliners; Freeway; The Lost Boys; The Nutcracker Prince; The Three Musketeers (1993); Twin Peaks: Fire Walk With Me; The Vanishing (1993)
Sutherland, Kristine (act): Honey, I Shrunk the Kids
Sutherland, Victor (act): Donovan's Brain
Sutorius, James (act): Prototype
Sutter, Randy (act): Remote Control (1988)
Suttles, Jennifer (act): The Initiation
Suttles, John (act): Mutants In Paradise
Suttles, M. Darnell (act): Congo
Sutton, Carlos (act): Mata Hari (1985)
Sutton, Carol (act): Candyman: Farewell to the Flesh; Mirrors; The Savage Bees
Sutton, Delores (act): Tales from the Darkside
Sutton, Dudley (act, b. 1933): The Big Sleep (1978); The Boys; Brimstone & Treacle; Crossplot; The Devils; Diamonds On Wheels; Great Expectations (1974); The London Connection; Madame Sin; No. 1 of the Secret Service; Orlando; The Playbirds
Sutton, Emma (act): Sword of the Valiant
Sutton, Frank (act, 1923-1974): The Satan Bug
Sutton, Gertrude (act): Son of Kong
Sutton, Grady (act, 1906-1995): Myra Breckinridge; Philo Vance's Gamble; Whispering Ghosts
Sutton, Jacqui (act): Deadly Game
Sutton, John (act, 1908-1963): Adventures of Casanova; The Adventures of Robin Hood; Arrest Bulldog Drummond; Bagdad; The Bat (1959); Bride of Vengeance; Bulldog Drummond's Bride; Bulldog Drummond's Revenge; East of Sumatra; The Invisible Man Returns; Jane Eyre (1944); The Lady In the Iron Mask; Murder Over New York; My Cousin Rachel; Return of the Fly; Thief of Damascus; The Three Musketeers (1948); Tower of London (1939)
Sutton, Kay (act): The Saint In New York
Sutton, Larry (act): The Toxic Avenger
Sutton, Lori (act): A Polish Vampire In Burbank
Sutton, Raymond (act): Planet Earth
Suwanatat, Sulaleewan (act): Vice Versa (1988)
Suzman, Janet (act, b. 1939): The Black Windmill; The Zany Adventures of Robin Hood
Suzuki, Kazumasa (act): The Toxic Avenger, Part II
Suzuki, Mizuho (act): Godzilla 1985
Suzuki, Pat (act, b. 1931): Skullduggery
Suzuki, Toyoaki (act): Gojira
Svankmajer, Jan (dir & wri): Alice
Svanoe, Bill (wri): Seduced by Evil
Svashenko, Semyon (act): Zvenigora
Svatek, Peter (dir): Sci-Fighters; Witchboard: The Possession
Svedin, Ray (cin): Misery
Svedlund, Doris (act): The Devil's Wanton
Svehla, Dick (act): Nightbeast
Svehla, Gary (act): Nightbeast
Svenson, Bo (act, b. 1941): Beyond the Door III; Butcher, Baker (Nightmare Maker); Curse II: The Bite; Deep Space; Frankenstein (1973); Gold of the Amazon Women; Heartless; Primal Rage; Snowbeast; Steel Frontier; Virus (1980); Wizards of the Lost Kingdom
Sverak, Jan (dir): Accumulator 1
Sverak, Zdenek (act): Accumulator 1
Sverre, Johan (act): The Witches (1990)
Svetlov, B. (act): Sonka Zolotaya Ruchka
Svierkier, Anna (act): Vredens Dag
Svoboda, Madeleine (act): see Robinson, Madeleine
Swaby, Paul (act): Little Shop of Horrors (1986)
Swackhammer, E.W. (dir): Are You Lonesome Tonight?; Bridge Across Time; The Dain Curse; Death at Love House; Vampire (1979)
Swaffer, Hannen (act): Death at Broadcasting House; Spellbound (1941)
Swaffer, Mignon (act): A Yell of a Night
Swafford, Ken (act): The Black Bird (1975)
Swafford, Mary (act): King Kong Lives
Swailes, Gary (act): Vamp
Swain, Bobby Lee (act): Shocker
Swain, Brian (act): The Being
Swain, Caskey (act): Friday the 13th-Part V: A New Beginning
Swain, Dwight V. (wri): Stark Fear
Swain, Howard (act): Miracle Mile
Swain, Jack (cin): Are You In the House Alone?
Swain, James W. (act): Secrets of the Phantom Caverns
Swain, Mack (act): His Prehistoric Past; The Last Warning (1929); Mockery
Swain, Michael (act): Joe & the Colonel
Swain, Stacey (act): Cavegirl (1985)
Swalve, Darwyn (act): Deadly Reactor
Swan, Don (dir): Gore-Met Zombie Chef from Hell
Swan, Joye (act): D.O.A. (1988)
Swan, Kitty (act): House of 1,000 Dolls
Swan, Robert (act): Doomsday Machine; From Hell It Came
Swan, William (act): Lady In a Cage; The Monster That Challenged the World
Swank, Hilary (act, b. 1974): Buffy the Vampire Slayer; Sometimes They Come Back...Again
Swann, Dale (act): Demon Knight; The Gifted One; Gremlins 2: The New Batch
Swann, Kim (act): Serial Mom
Swann, Robert (act): The Creeping Flesh; Girly; The Witches and the Grinnygog
Swanson, Brenda (act): Dead Connection; Prototype X29A; Scanners: The Showdown
Swanson, Erik (act): Slugs
Swanson, Forrest (act): To All a Goodnight
Swanson, Gary (act): The Guardian
Swanson, Gloria (act, 1899-1983, nee Josephine May Swenson): Killer Bees; Male and Female; Queen Kelly; Sunset Boulevard
Swanson, Greg (act): Terror Train
Swanson, Jack (act): Ernest Saves Christmas
Swanson, Jackie (act): It's Alive III: Island of the Alive; Oblivion
Swanson, Jandi (act): Pumpkinhead
Swanson, Jeff (act): Gremlins 2: The New Batch
Swanson, Kristy (act, b. 1970): Buffy the Vampire Slayer; Deadly Friend; Flowers In the Attic; Highway to Hell; Mannequin Two: On the Move; The Phantom (1996)
Swanson, Larry (act): Scream, Baby, Scream
Swanson, Logan (wri): The Last Man On Earth
Swanson, Maureen (act): Knights of the Round Table; The Malpas Mystery
Swanson, Rochelle (act): Cyberzone; Hungry for You
Swanson, Scott (act): It (1990)
Swanson, Sterling (act): Dogs; Don't Be Afraid of the Dark; Slaughter
Swanstrom, Karin (act): The Story of Gosta Berling
Swanton, Harold (wri): Alfred Hitchcock Presents; Appointment With Murder
Swanwick, Peter (act): The Desperate Man; Lady In the Fog; Murder Reported; No Haunt for a Gentleman; The Trunk
Swart, Fred (act): Creatures the World Forgot
Swart, Rufus (act): Cyborg Cop; Dust Devil; The House of Usher (1988)
Swartz, Andrea (act): The Pit (1983)
Swartz, Charles (S.) (wri): Terminal Island; The Velvet Vampire
Swartz, Kelley (act): The Headless Eyes
Swartz, Tony (act): Battlestar Galactica; Fugitive from the Empire; The UFO Incident
Swatek, Martha (act): Jaws 2
Swaybill, Roger E. (wri): The Lathe of Heaven
Swayze, Don (act): Appointment for a Killing; Death Ring; Joe & the Colonel
Swayze, Patrick (act, b. 1952): Ghost (1990); Red Dawn; Steel Dawn; Three Wishes (1995)
Swearington, Bill (act): Elvira, Mistress of the Dark
Sweeney, Bob (act): It Grows On Trees; Marnie; Moon Pilot; Son of Flubber
Sweeney, D.B. (act): Blue Desert; Fire In the Sky (1993); Spawn
Sweeney, George (act): Without a Clue
Sweeney, James R. (act): Nightmare On the 13th Floor
Sweeney, Julia (act): Coneheads; Gremlins 2: The New Batch; Honey, I Blew Up the Kid
Sweeney, Mary (act): Invasion of the Bee Girls
Sweeney, Matt (cin): The Goonies
Sweeney, Maureen (act): The Squeeze
Sweeney, Pepper (act): Running Against Time
Sweeney, Terry (wri): Love at Stake
Sweeney, Warren (act): Running Against Time
Sweeny, Ann (act): The Incredible Melting Man
Sweeny, Ed Charles (act): Destination Inner Space
Sweet, Blanche (act, 1895-1986, nee Sarah Blanche Sweet): The Avenging Conscience; In the Palace of the King; The Lesser Evil; The Woman In White (1929)
Sweet, Dolph (act, 1920-1985): Colossus: The Forbin Project; Deathmoon; Fear Is the Key; Finian's Rainbow; Heaven Can Wait (1978); Sisters; The Swimmer; The Telephone Book
Sweet, Gary (act): Stage Fright (1983)
Sweet, Sarah Blanche (act): see Sweet, Blanche
Sweet, Shane (act): Murder of Innocence
Sweete, Barbara Willis (act): Bigfoot: The Unforgettable Encounter
Sweitzer, Rod (act): The Invisible Maniac; The Malibu Beach Vampires
Swenning, William (cin): I Dismember Mama
Swenson, Charles (dir): The Mouse and His Child; Twice Upon a Time
Swenson, Inga (act, b. 1934): Bay Coven; Earth II
Swenson, Josephine May (act): see Swanson, Gloria
Swenson, Karl (act, 1908-1978): The Birds; A Howling In the Woods; Seconds; The Sword In the Stone; Vanishing Point (1971)
Swenson, Swen (act): What's the Matter With Helen?
Swerdlow, Kevin B. (act): Blink
Swerdlow, Tommy (act): Child's Play (1988); Howard the Duck
Swerling, Jo (wri, b. 1894): Behind the Mask (1932); Dirigible; It's a Wonderful Life; Leave Her to Heaven; Lifeboat
Swetland, William (act): Mirrors
Swetlow, Joel (act): The Warlord: Battle for the Galaxy
Swicegood, T.L.P. (wri): The Undertaker and His Pals
Swick, Ron (act): Tuck Everlasting
Swickard, Charles (dir): The Three Musketeers (1916)
Swickard, Josef (act): Dante's Inferno (1924); Don Juan (1927); The Lost City; The Wizard of Oz (1925)
Swicord, Robin (wri): Practical Magic
Swidereka, Eva (act): Blood Diner
Swift, Clive (act): Deathline; Excalibur; Frenzy

Swift, David (act): The Black Panther; The Internecine Project
Swift, Francine (act): Vamp
Swift, Hazel (wri): The Flying Sorceror
Swift, Jessica (act): Rapunzel Let Down Your Hair; Zardoz
Swift, Joan (act): Brainstorm (1965)
Swift, Jonathan (wri, 1667-1745): Le Dernier Voyage de Gulliver (unfinished); Gulliver's Travels (1939, 1977 & 1996); Gulliver's Travels Beyond the Moon; Laputa: Castle In the Sky; Novyi Gulliver; The Three Worlds of Gulliver; Les Voyages de Gulliver
Swift, Susan (act): Audrey Rose; The Coming; Halloween: The Curse of Michael Myers
Swiggert Jr., John L. (act): For All Mankind
Swim, David (act): The Boogey Man
Swinburne, Mercia (act): Alibi (1931)
Swinburne, Nora (act, b. 1902, nee Elinore Swinburne Johnson): Alf's Button (1930); The Bad Lord Byron; Fanny by Gaslight; Helen of Troy (1955); The Man In Grey; My Daughter Joy; The Strange Awakening; A Voice Said Goodnight
Swindells, John (act): In the Devil's Garden
Swing, Catherine (act): Darkman II: The Return of Durant
Swingle, Ward (mus): Aimez-Vous les Femmes?
Swingler, Richard (act): Twilight Zone
Swinley, Ion (act): The Barton Mystery (1932); Trilby (1914)
Swinson, Howard (act): The Return of Sherlock Holmes (1986)
Swinstead, Joan (act): Wolf's Clothing (1936)
Swinton, Tilde (act): Orlando
Swit, Loretta (act): Race With the Devil
Switz, Reggie (act): The Troubles of a Hypochondriac
Switzer, Carl (act): Cause for Alarm!; Dig That Uranium!; Track of the Cat
Switzer, Michael (dir): The Lightning Incident; Nothing But the Truth; Remember Me; Stalking Laura; Unlikely Angel; With a Vengeance
Switzer, Ron (dir): Science Crazed
Swofford, Ken (act): The Andromeda Strain; Black Roses; Captain America II; The Stepford Children
Swon, John (act): Charlie Chan Carries On
Swope, Topo (act): Pretty Maids All In a Row
Swope, Tracy Brooks (act): Inner Sanctum 2; The Ultimate Impostor
Swords, Travis (act): Godzilla 1985; Project X (1987)
Swoyer, Ann Myrtle (act): see Walker, Nancy
Sydes, Carol (act): Cape Fear (1961)
Sydney, Aurele (act): The Green Terror
Sydney, Basil (act, 1894-1968): Around the World In 80 Days; Blind Man's Bluff (1936); Hamlet (1948); The Hands of Orlac (1959); Salome (1953); The Third Clue; The Three Worlds of Gulliver; Treasure Island (1950); The Tunnel; Went the Day Well?; White Lilac
Sydney, Derek (act): Carry On Spying; Evidence In Concrete; The Mail Van Murder; The Trollenberg Terror; The Witness
Sydney, Edward (act): A Fight for Life; The Wrecker of Lives
Sydney, R. (wri): Blood Relatives
Sydney, Susan (act): No Blade of Grass
Sydow, Dia (act): House of the Living Dead
Sykes, Brenda (act): Pretty Maids All In a Row
Sykes, Eric (act, b. 1924): Kill or Cure; The Liquidator; Splitting Heirs; The Spy With a Cold Nose; Theater of Blood; UFOs Are Coming Wednesday
Sykes, Greg (act): Killer Klowns from Outer Space
Sykes, Kim (act): Single White Female
Sykes, Percival H.T. (wri): An Affair of Honour
Sykes, Peter (dir): The Committee; Demons of the Mind; The House In Nightmare Park; The Legend of Spider Forest; To the Devil a Daughter
Sykes, Peter (wri): The Committee
Sylbert, Lulu (act): Strange Behavior; Strange Invaders
Sylva, Marguerita (act): The Seventh Victim
Sylva, Vesta (act): Maria Marten (1928); Where the Rainbow Ends
Sylvain (act): The Southern Star
Sylvani, Gladys (act): At the Eleventh Hour; The Coiner's Den; The Deception (1912); Jim of the Mounted Police; Rachel's Sin; A Woman's Wit
Sylver, Kim (act): Maid to Order
Sylvers, Jeremy (act): Child's Play 3
Sylvester, Charles (act): The Thief of Bagdad (1924)
Sylvester, Harold (act): Space Rage
Sylvester, John (wri): The Echo Murders
Sylvester, Jules (act): Bram Stoker's 'Dracula'
Sylvester, Julian (act): Project X (1987)
Sylvester, Kate (act): The Sign of the Cross
Sylvester, William (act, b. 1922): Blind Corner; Devil Doll (1963); Devils of Darkness; Don't Be Afraid of the Dark; Dublin Nightmare; Gorgo; The Hand of Night; Heaven Can Wait (1978); House of Blackmail; Incident at Midnight; Information Received; Man In the Dark (1965); Offbeat; Ring of Spies; The Stranger Came Home; 2001: A Space Odyssey; Whirlpool (1959); The Yellow Balloon
Sylvestre, Phil (act): House of Usher (1960)
Sylvie (act, 1883-1970): Ulysses
Symington, Donald (act): Sanctuary of Fear; Wolfen
Symonds, Robert (act, b. 1926): C.H.U.D. II; Gray Lady Down; Mandroid; Rumpelstiltskin (1987); Superstition
Symons, Julian (wri): Counterspy
Symons, R.F. (act): Brigadier Gerard
Sympson, Tony (act): House of Whipcord; Jabberwocky; Sexton Blake and the Bearded Doctor; Sexton Blake and the Hooded Terror; Sexton Blake and the Mademoiselle; Tiffany Jones
Syms, Sylvia (act, b. 1934): Asylum (1972); The Birthday Present; Danger Route; The Fiction-Makers; Give Us Tomorrow; No Trees In the Street; Operation Crossbow; There Goes the Bride
Syrewicz, Stanislas (mus): The Lair of the White Worm
Syson, Michael (wri): Fear In the Night (1972)
Syte the Fool (act): Mutants In Paradise
Syvret, Michaeline (act): Oh Heavenly Dog
Szabo, Desiree (act): Alice In Wonderland (1985)
Szabo, Laszlo (act): Alphaville, une Etrange Aventure de Lemmy Caution; L'Aveu
Szabo, Todd "Shred" (act): Bloodspell
Szapoloska, Grazyna (act): Lebewohl Fremde
Szarabajka, Keith (act): Nightlife (1989, USA-Mex); Simon; Warning Sign
Szatler, Renata (act): Howling V: The Rebirth
Szczepkowski, A. (act): Wielka, Wielka I Najwieksza
Szczerbic, Joanna (act): Bariera
Szeibert, Joseph "Simon" (act): Twin Peaks: Fire Walk With Me
Szekely, Istvan (dir): see Sekely, Steve
Szekores, Clare (act): The Turn of the Screw
Szigeti, Cynthia (act): 976-EVIL
Szilayyi, Peter (cin): Daughter of Darkness (1990)
Szmanda, Ray (act): The Alpha Incident
Szollosi, Tom (wri): Snow White: A Tale of Terror
Szu, Shih (act): Legend of the Seven Golden Vampires
Szubanski, Magda (act): Babe; Babe: Pig In the City
Szulzinger, Boris (dir): Jungle Burger; Mama Dracula
Szulzinger, Boris (wri): Mama Dracula
Szurgot, Ryan (act): Cocoon: The Return
Szwarc, Jeannot (dir, b. 1937): Bug; The Devil's Daughter (1972); Jaws 2; The Murders In the Rue Morgue (1986); Night of Terror (1972); Santa Claus (1985); Somewhere In Time; Supergirl (1984)
Szymanski, Bernard (act): The Haunting of Sarah Hardy
Szymkovicz, Gloria (act): Don't Go In the House

T, Mr. (act): Freaked
Taafe, Alice (act): see Terry, Alice
Taav, Michael (dir): Painted Heart
Tab, Joe (act): Electra (1995)
Taba, Therese (act): Baby: Secret of the Lost Legend
Tabakin, Ralph (act): Sphere
Tabakin, Tari (act): The Deathmaster
Tabban, Diane (act): The Blob (1958)
Tabet, Andre (wri): Nights of Rasputin
Tabet, Georges (act): The Green Glove
Tabet, Hedda (act): Gebroken Spiegels
Tabet, Sylvio (dir): Beastmaster 2: Through the Portal of Time
Tabler, Dempsey (act): Jungle Trail of the Son of Tarzan
Tabler, Jon (act): The Mosaic Project
Tablian, Vic (act): Raiders of the Lost Ark; Sphinx (1981)
Taboada, Carlos/Charles (E.) (wri): La Maldicion de Nostradamus; Nostradamus y el Destructor de Monstruos; Orlak, el Infierno de Frankenstein
Tabor, David (act): The Nesting
Tabor, Eron (act): I Spit On Your Grave
Tabor, Margaret (wri): Nightmare Street
Tabori, George (wri): I Confess; No Exit; Secret Ceremony
Tabori, Katrina (act): Shadow Conspiracy
Tabori, Kristoffer (act, b. 1952): Brave New World (1980)
Tabori, Paul (wri, b. 1908): Alias John Preston; Four Sided Triangle; The Malpas Mystery; Mantrap; Morning Call; Spaceways; Strip Tease Murder; Valley of the Eagles
Taborsky, Miroslav (act): Snow White: A Tale of Terror
Tabrizi, Davood A. (mus): The Navigator: An Odyssey Across Time
Tackechi, Toyoko (act): The Manster
Taczanowski, Hubert (cin): The Young Poisoner's Handbook
Taeger, Ralph (act, b. 1936): X-15
Tafler, Jean (act): The Deadly Spawn
Tafler, Sydney (act, 1916-1979): Assassin for Hire; The Bank Raiders; Berserk; Blind Man's Bluff (1952); Booby Trap; The Counterfeit Plan; Dial 999 (1955); Fire Maidens of Outer Space; The Floating Dutchman; The Glass Tomb; Guilty?; Interpol; A Kid for Two Farthings; The Lavender Hill Mob; The Long Arm; Melody of Hate; Mystery Junction; The Saint's Return; Scarlet Thread; Secret People; The Spy Who Loved Me; The Surgeon's Knife; Venetian Bird; Wide Boy
Tafoya, Al (act): Fade to Black
Taft, Andrew (act): Lord of the Flies (1990)
Taft, Edward (act): Lord of the Flies (1990)
Taft, Jerry (act): It's Alive (1974)
Taft, Ronald (act): Blood and Lace
Taft, Sara (act): Tower of London (1962)
Taftazani, Amid (act): The Drum
Tafur, Robert (act): Evilspeak; Secret of the Incas
Tafuri, Sara (act): La Citta delle Donne
Tagawa, Cary-Hiroyuki (act): Mortal Kombat; Nemesis; Netforce; Not of This World; The Phantom (1996); Spellbinder
Tager, Aron (act): Dr. Jekyll and Ms. Hyde
Taggart, Ben (act): Alias Boston Blackie; Before I Hang; The Gracie Allen Murder Case; The Lone Wolf Takes a Chance; Man-Made Monster; One Mysterious Night; Peril from the Planet Mongo; Purple Death from Outer Space; The Thin Man
Taggart, Brian (wri): Child of Darkness, Child of Light; The Mark of Zorro (1974); Of Unknown Origin; Omen IV: The Awakening; Poltergeist III; The Spell; Trucks; Visiting Hours; What Ever Happened to Baby Jane?(1991)
Taggart, Pita (act): Splash, Too
Taggart, Rita (act): The China Syndrome; The Horror Show
Taggart, Tom (wri): Gog
Taggert, Hal (act): Desk Set; The Monster That Challenged the World
Taggert, Jimmy Medina (act): Tarzan In Manhattan
Taglavini, Ferruccio (act): One Night of Fame
Tagliabue, Andrea (act): Sodom and Gomorrah
Tagoe, Eddie (act): Baby: Secret of the Lost Legend; The Boy Who Never Was; Raiders of the Lost Ark; Top Secret! (1984); Who Is Killing the Great Chefs of Europe?
Tagore, Rabindranath (wri, 1861-1941): Devi
Tagore, Sharmila (act): Devi
Taguchi, Tomoroh (act): Iron Man
Taha, Fadi (act): La Captive du Desert
Taichi, Kiwako (act): Kuroneko
Tainguy, Lucien (cin): Le Voyage dans la Lune
Tait, Don (wri): Herbie Goes Bananas; The Shaggy D.A.; The Spaceman and King Arthur
Taj (mus): Deadtime Stories
Tajima, Reiko (act): Godzilla vs. the Bionic Monster
Tajima, Yoshibumi (act): Godzilla's Revenge; Mothra; Rodan, the Flying Monster
Tajo, Italo (act): Faust and the Devil
Taka, Miko (act): Judge Dee and the Monastery Murder; The Power (1967)
Takacs, Maria (act): City of Fear (1965)
Takacs, Tibor (dir): The Gate; Gate II; I, Madman; 984: Prisoner of the Future; Sabrina the Teenage Witch
Takada, Koji (wri): Virus (1980)
Takada, Minoru (act): Atomic Rulers of the World; Battle In Outer Space
Takada, Miwa (act): Majin, Monster of Terror
Takada, Terry (act): Deathmoon
Takagi, Hiroshi (act): Mothra
Takahashi, Atsuko (act): Yog-Monster from Space
Takahashi, Choei (act): Lake of Dracula
Takahashi, Fumi (wri): Attack of the Monsters; Gammera, the Invincible; Gammera vs. Barugon; Gammera vs. Guiron; Gammera vs. Gyaos; Gammera vs. Jiger; Gammera vs. Viras; Gammera vs.Zigra; Return of the Giant Monsters
Takahashi, Hidenori (act): The Toxic Avenger, Part II
Takahashi, Masay (act): Body Snatcher from Hell
Takahashi, Mitsumi (act): Wild Thing
Takahashi, Osahide (act): Lake of Dracula
Takahashi, Wes Ford (cin): The Frighteners
Takahisa, Susumu (wri): Fist of the North Star
Takakjian, Glenn (dir & wri): Metamorphosis: The Alien Factor
Takakura, Ken (act): The Bullet Train
Takakuwa, T./Tsutomu (act): Gammera vs. Jiger; Gammera vs. Monster X
Takamoto, Iwao (dir): Charlotte's Web
Takano, Mak (act): Contact
Takara, Mitzuko (act): Sodom and Gomorrah
Takarada, Akira (act): Chusingura (1963); Ebirah, Horror of the Deep; Godzilla vs.Mothra; Gojira; Half-Human; King Kong Escapes; Latitude Zero; Monster Zero
Takase, Kyoshi (act): Chu Chin Chow (1934); Midnight (1931); The Silent House; The Yellow Claw
Takashi (dir & wri): Metamorphoses
Takashima, Kaku (act): Lake of Dracula
Takashima, Masahiro (act): Gunhed
Takashima, Minoru (act): Godzilla On Monster Island
Takashima, Tadao (act): Atragon; Frankenstein vs. the Giant Devil Fish; King Kong vs. Godzilla; Son of Godzilla
Takatsuka, Toru (act): Gammera vs. Viras
Takayama, Yukiko (wri): The Terror of Godzilla; Terror of Mechagodzilla
Takeda, Tetsuya (act): Godzilla 1985
Takei, George (act): Backlash: Oblivion 2; Oblivion; Star Trek; Star Trek II: The Wrath of Khan; Star Trek III: The Search for Spock; Star Trek IV: The Voyage Home; Star Trek V: The Final Frontier; Star Trek VI: The Undiscovered Country
Takemitsu, Toru (mus): Inn of Evil; Kwaidan; Ran; Suna No Onna; Tanin No Kao
Takenaka, Naoto (act): The Mystery of Rampo
Takeshi (act): Johnny Mnemonic
Takigawa, Yumi (act): Virus (1980)
Takimoto, Takeshi (act): The Toxic Avenger, Part II
Takizawa, Osamu (act): Kwaidan
Takuma, Shin (act): Godzilla 1985
Talalay, Rachel (act): Android
Talalay, Rachel (dir): Freddy's Dead: The Final Nightmare; Ghost In the Machine
Talalay, Rachel (wri): Freddy's Dead: The Final Nightmare
Talarowski, Joe (act): Student Bodies
Talazac, Odette (act): The Crime of Monsieur Lange; Le Sang d'un Poete
Talbert, John (act): Blood of Ghastly Horror
Talbot, Bud (wri): Case of the Full Moon Murders
Talbot, Irvin (mus): The Search for Bridey Murphy
Talbot, Ken(neth) (cin): Battle Beneath the Earth; Countess Dracula; Doomwatch; The Girl Hunters; Hands of the Ripper; I Don't Want to Be Born;Journey Into Darkness; Journey to Midnight; Journey to the Unknown; Maroc 7; Nothing But the Night; Persecution
Talbot, Lyle (act, 1901-1996, nee Lysle Hollywood): African Treasure; Appointment With Murder; Atom Man vs. Superman; Captain Kidd and the Slave Girl; Champagne for Caesar; City of Fear (1959); The Devil's Cargo; The Dragon Murder Case; The Falcon Out West; Fury of the Congo; Glen or Glenda?; Highway 13; Jungle Manhunt; Mesa of Lost Women; Murder Is My Business; The Mutineers; A Night for Crime; One Body Too Many; Plan 9 from Outer Space; Return of the Terror; The Scarf; A Shriek In the Night; The Sky Dragon; Sudden Danger; The Thirteenth Guest; Tobor the Great; Untamed Women; The Vicious Circle (1948)
Talbot, Michael (act): Carrie
Talbot, Nita (act, b. 1930): Amityville 1992: It's About Time; Chained Heat; The Concrete Jungle (1982); Frightmare (1983); Night of the the Claw; Puppet Master II; They Call It Murder
Talbot, Paul (dir): Freakshow
Talbot, Roger (act): The Playground
Talbot, Rowland (wri): Allan Field's Warning; Beneath the Mask; Brigadier Gerard; A
Brother's Atonement; By His Father's Orders; The Debt of Gambling; The Devil's Bondman; A Double Life (1913); For All Eternity; The Eccentric Uncle's Will; The German Spy Peril; The Girl Who Didn't Care; The Great Bullion Robbery; His Honour at Stake; His Sister's Honour; In London's Toils; In the Hands of the

London Crooks; In the Toils of the Blackmailer; Jane Shore (1915); London by Night (1913); Ora Pro Nobis; The Passions of Men; The Picture of Dorian Gray (1916); Polly the Girl Scout and
the Jewel Thieves; The Price of Deception; The Rogues of London; Royal Love; Satan's Amazon; The Strange Case of Philip Kent; The Trail of the Fatal Ruby; The Tube of Death; When Paths Diverge; The Woman Who Dared
Talbot, Susan (act): *A Witch Without a Broom*
Talbott, Gloria (act): *The Cyclops; Daughter of Dr. Jekyll; I Married a Monster from Outer Space; The Leech Woman*
Talbott, Hudson (wri): *We're Back! A Dinosaur's Story*
Talfrey, Hira (act): *The Curse of the Werewolf*
Talgorn, Frederic (mus): *Edge of Sanity; Fortress; Robot Jox*
Taliaferro, Hal (act, b. 1895): *The Man With Nine Lives*
Taliaferro, Mabel (act, 1887-1979): *Alice In Wonderland (1920); Cinderella (1911, Selig)*
Tallas, Greg (dir): *Cataclysm*
Tallas, Gregg (R.) (dir): *Atlantis (1948); Prehistoric Women (1950)*
Tallas, Gregg (R.) (wri): *Prehistoric Women (1950); Sound of Horror*
Talley, Adrianne (act): *Secrets of the Phantom Caverns*
Talley, Belinda (act): *Secrets of the Phantom Caverns*
Talley, Brent (act): *Secrets of the Phantom Caverns*
Tallichet, Margaret (act, 1914-1991): *Stranger On the Third Floor*
Tallman, Chester (act): *The Saint In Palm Springs*
Tallman, Patricia (act): *Army of Darkness; Babylon 5: The Gathering; Knightriders; Night of*
the Living Dead (1990); Thirdspace: A Babylon 5 Adventure
Tallman, Robert (wri): *The Devil's Cargo*
Talltree, Luana (act): *Angels from Hell*
Tally, Ted (wri): *The Silence of the Lambs*
Talmadge, Richard (act): *Laughing at Danger*
Talmadge, Richard (dir, 1892-1981, nee Sylvester Metzetti): *Casino Royale; Project Moonbase*
Talmadge, Victor (act): *Copycat*
Talman, Lloyd (act): *Robin Hood (1922)*
Talman, William (act): *Hell On Devil's Island; The Hitch-Hiker; I Married a Communist*
Talman, William (wri): *I've Lived Before*
Talton, Alix (act): *The Deadly Mantis; The Man Who Knew Too Much (1956)*
Talus, Pamela (act): *Stanley*
Tamahori, Lee (dir): *The Edge*
Tamai, Masao (cin): *Gojira*
Tamara (act): *Hundra*
Tamarin, Paul (act): *The Bedford Incident; Billion Dollar Brain; Dr. Strangelove: or, How I Learned to Stop Worrying and Love the Bomb*
Tamarov, Dimitri (act): *The Kremlin Letter*
Tamba (animal act): *Jungle Manhunt; Voodoo Tiger*
Tamba, Tetsuro (act, b. 1929): *Harakiri; Kwaidan; Message from Space; The Submersion of Japan; You Only Live Twice*
Tamberlani, Carlo (act): *The Colossus of Rhodes; The Last Days of Pompeii (1959); The Lion of Thebes; The Minotaur; Parsifal; Samson; Son of Samson; The Trojan Horse*
Tamberlani, Ferdinand (act): *Il Ladro di Venezia*
Tamberlani, Nando (act): *Last of the Vikings; Maciste e la Regina di Samar; The Trojan Horse*
Tambini, Catherine (act): *The Boogey Man*
Tamblyn, Eddie (act): *Charlie Chan at the Opera*
Tamblyn, Russ (act, b. 1934): *Aftershock; Attack of the 60 Foot Centerfold; Cyclone; Dracula vs. Frankenstein; The Female Bunch; The Haunting; Invisible Mom; The Last Hunt; Necromancer: Satan's Servant; The Phantom Empire; Samson and Delilah; Satan's Sadists; Tom Thumb; The War of the Gargantuas; The Wonderful World of the Brothers Grimm*
Tambor, Jeffrey (act, b. 1944): *The Awakening of Candra; Brenda Starr (1992); Dr. Dolittle (1998); The Man Who Wasn't There; Meet Jor Black; Saturday the 14th*
Tamburella, P.W. (dir & wri): *The Seven Dwarfs to the Rescue*
Tamburi, Jenny (act): *Duario Segreto da un Carcere Femminile; The Psychic; Women In Cell Block 7*
Tamburrelli, Karla (act): *Forever Young; Nothing But Trouble*
Tamburro, Charles/Chuck (act): *Avalanche; The Long Kiss Goodnight; Outbreak; Seven*
Tamburro, Michael (act): *Outbreak; Virtuosity*
Tamerlis, Zoe (act): *Ms. 45; Special Effects*
Tamiroff, Akim (act, 1899-1972): *Alphaville, une Etrange Aventure de Lemmy Caution; The Bacchantes; Black Magic (1949); The Black Sleep; The Blue Panther; The Bridge of San Luis Rey (1944); The Corsican Brothers (1941); Desert Legion; Five Graves to Cairo; Gabriel Over the White House; The Great Gambini; The Liquidator; Marquis de Sade: Justine; Mr. Arkadin; The Reluctant Saint; The Tartar Invasion; Topkapi; The Trial; La Tulipe Noire; The Vulture (1966)*
Tamiya, Jiro (act): *Yellow Dog*
Tamm, Mary (act): *Tales That Witness Madness*
Tammes, Fred(eric) (cin): *Caravan to Vaccares; Survivor (1987)*
Tammi, Tom (act): *Blood Bath (1975)*
Tamura, Tamutsu (act): *Suna No Onna*
Tan, John (act): *The Fiendish Plot of Dr. Fu Manchu*
Tan, Philip (act): *Batman (1989); The Fiendish Plot of Dr. Fu Manchu; Return to Oz; Transmutations*
Tana, Leni (act): *She Demons*
Tanaka, Ken (act): *Godzilla 1985*
Tanaka, Kenzo (act): *Kwaidan*
Tanaka, Kinuyo (act, 1909-1977): *Ugetsu Monogatari*
Tanaka, Kunie (act): *Kwaidan*
Tanaka, Shigeo (dir): *Gammera vs. Barugon*
Tanaka, Tom (act): *Contact*
Tanaka, Tomoyuki (wri): *Godzilla 1985*
Tanaka, Prof. Toru (act): *Darkman (1990); Deadly Game; The Running Man (1987)*
Tanchuck, Nat(haniel) (wri): *Chained for Life; The Shuttered Room*
Tancred, Anthony (act): *Britannia Mews*
Tandy, Jessica (act, 1909-1994): **Batteries Not Included; The Birds; Cocoon; Cocoon: The Return; Dragonwyck; Murder In the Family; Still of the Night; A Woman's Vengeance*
Tanelah, A. Maana (act): *Scream Bloody Murder*
Tanet, Ronald (act): *Crypt of Dark Secrets*
Tangerine Dream (mus): *City of Shadows; Firestarter; The Keep; Legend; Miracle Mile; Near*
Dark; Strange Behavior; Wavelength
Tang-Hua-Ta (act): *Milczaca Gwiazda*
Tani, Akira (act): *Kwaidan*
Tani, Yoko (act, b. 1932): *Agent 255/Desperate Mission; Invasion (1965); Koroshi; Maciste alla Corte del Gran Khan; Milczaca Gwiazda; The Partner; Piccadilly Third Stop; The Secret of Dr. Mabuse; The Tartar Invasion*
Tani, Yukio (act): *Ju-Jitsu to the Rescue*
Taniguchi, Senkichi (dir): *Samurai Pirate*
Tanin, Eleanore (act): *The Werewolf (1955)*
Tannen, Bill (act): see Tannen, William/Bill
Tannen, Charles (act): *Gorilla at Large; The Monster That Challenged the World; Think Fast, Mr. Moto; Voyage to the Bottom of the Sea*
Tannen, Julius (act, 1880-1965): *House of Frankenstein*
Tannen, Steve (act): *Endangered Species; The Nest*
Tannen, William/Bill (act, 1911-1976): *Captain Kidd and the Slave Girl; Devil Goddess; Eyes of the Jungle; The Golden Idol; Jungle Jim; Jungle Jim In the Forbidden Land; Nazi Agent; Pygmy Island; Raiders of the Seven Seas; Talk About a Stranger*
Tannenbaum, Max-Gerard (dir): see Oury, Gerard
Tanner, Clay (act): *Race With the Devil*
Tanner, Gordon (act): *Caravan to Vaccares; Dr. Strangelove: or, How I Learned to Stop Worrying and Love the Bomb; On the Run (1958); The Return of Mr. Moto*
Tanner, Jeff (act): *12 Monkeys*
Tanner, Joy (act): *Prom Night IV: Deliver Us from Evil*
Tanner, Larry (act): *Mars Needs Women*
Tanner, Stella (act): *Jane Eyre (1970); Otley*
Tanney, Savant (act): *Switch*
Tanogashira, Yasuhiro (act): *The Toxic Avenger, Part II*
Tanous, Mark (act): *The Demon (1981)*
Tansey, Charles (act): *The Resurrection of Zachary Wheeler*
Tansley, Derek (act): *Curse of the Crimson Altar; Hide and Seek; Mr. Selkie; The Servant*
Tansman, Alexander (mus): *Flesh and Fantasy*
Tansy (act): *Return to Oz*
Tanura, Philip (cin, b. 1909): *Alias Boston Blackie; Bulldog Drummond at Bay (1947); Confessions of Boston Blackie; Counter Espionage; Crime Doctor's Gamble; Crime Doctor's Manhunt; The Flying Saucer (1950); Just Before Dawn (1946); The Lone Wolf and His Lady; The Millerson Case; Trapped by Boston Blackie*
Tanzania, Warhawk (act): *Devil's Express*
Tanzi, Mario (act): *Blink*
Tanzilli, Josiane (act): *Amarcord*
Tapia, Amanda (act): *Grim Prairie Tales*
Tapia, Jesse (act): *Grim Prairie Tales*
Tapia, Kathy (act): *Repossessed*
Tapia, Mecedes (act): *Grim Prairie Tales*
Tapley, Colin (act): *Barbados Quest; The Black Room;Blood of the Vampire; Bulldog Drummond Escapes; Cloudburst; Compelled; The Diamond; Gang War; Innocent Meeting; Late Night Final; Little Red Monkey; Man Accused; A Night of Mystery (1937); Night Train for Inverness; Noose for a Lady; Paranoiac; Peter Ibbetson; Samson and Delilah; The Steel Key; Stranger In Town (1957); Strongroom; 3 Steps to the Gallows; Wide Boy*
Taplitz, Daniel (dir): *Nightlife (1989, USA-Mex)*
Taplitz, Daniel (wri): *Black Magic (1992); Nightlife (1989, USA-Mex)*
Tapp, Jimmy (act): *Of Unknown Origin*
Tappert, Horst (act): *The Ape Creature*
Tapping, Sydney (act): see Fairbrother, Sydney
Taradash, Daniel (wri, b. 1913): *Bell, Book and Candle; Castle Keep; Don't Bother to Knock*
Taraman, Gary (act): *Beyond the Poseidon Adventure*
Taran, George (cin): *The Diabolical Invention*
Tarantik, Jiri (cin): *Baron Prasil*
Tarantina, Brian (act): *Jacob's Ladder*
Tarantini, Tom (act): *The Nature of the Beast; Powder*
Tarantino, Quentin (act, b. 1963): *Destiny Turns On the Radio; From Dusk Till Dawn; King Lear (1987)*
Tarantino, Quentin (wri, b. 1963): *From Dusk Till Dawn*
Tarascio, Enzo (act): *The Dead Are Alive*
Taratorkin, Georgi (act): *Crime and Punishment (1970)*
Tarbes, J.J. (cin): *Blackout (1978)*
Tarbes, Monique (act): *How to Destroy the Reputation of the Greatest Secret Agent; Secret Agent (1974)*
Tarbuck, Barbara (act): *The Death of the Incredible Hulk*
Tarkington, Rockne (act): *Beware! The Blob; The Intruder Within*
Tarkovsky, Andrei (dir, 1932-1986): *My Name Is Ivan; Solaris; Stalker*
Tarkovsky, Andrei (wri, 1932-1986):*Solaris*
Tarloff, Frank (wri): *The Double Man*
Tarlov, Mark (dir): *Simply Irresistible*
Tarlton, Alan (act): *Golden Ivory*
Tarn, Michael (act): *A Clockwork Orange*
Tarp, Lotte (act): *Morianna*
Tarpley, Candece (act): *Ganja and Hess*
Tarrant, Gage (act): *RoboCop 2*
Tarrant, John (act): *Starship*
Tarrare, Daniel (act): *Perceval*
Tarses, Jay (act): *Teen Wolf*
Tarses, Jay (wri): *The Great Muppet Caper; The Muppets Take Manhattan*
Tarso, Ignacio Lopez (act):*Macario*
Tartan, Jim (act): *Dark Night of the Scarecrow*
Tartar, Mara (act): *The Mummy's Hand*
Tarter, Dale (act): *The Magician (1973)*
Tarver, Leonard (act): *The Beast With a Million Eyes*
Tarver, Milt (act): *Beverly Hills Bodysnatchers; Running Against Time; Total Recall*
Tarver, Tony (act): *Hamlet (1948)*
Tarvers, Jim (act): *Jack and the Beanstalk (1917)*
Tarzan (animal act): *When Pigs Fly*
Tasco, Rai (act): *Dr. Black Mr. Hyde; Planet Earth*
Tash, Max (dir): *The Adventures of Captain Zoom In Outer Space*
Tash, Steven (act): *Christine; Ghostbusters*
Tashlin, Frank (dir, 1913-1972): *The Alphabet Murders; Cinderfella; The Glass-Bottom Boat; It's Only Money*
Tashlin, Frank (wri, 1913-1972): *Cinderfella; One Touch of Venus*
Tashman, Lilyan (act, 1899-1934): *Bulldog Drummond (1929); The Cat Creeps (1930); The Lone Wolf's Daughter (1929); Murder by the Clock*
Task, Maggie (act): *A Stranger Is Watching*
Tasker, Robert (wri): *Doctor X*
Tasna, Rolf (act): *The Dragon's Blood*
Tass, Art (act): *Wizards of the Lost Kingdom*
Tassinaro, Ron (act): *Raiders of the Living Dead*
Tassoni, Coralina Cataldi (act): *Demons 2; Evil Clutch; Terror at the Opera*
Tassoni, Mark (act): *Child of Darkness, Child of Light*
Tata, Joe E. (act): *Terminal; Terror Out of the Sky*
Tataku, Susumu (wri): *Body Snatcher from Hell*
Tatar, Kate (act): *Mad Max Beyond Thunderdome*
Tataranowicz, Tom (dir): *Bravestarr—The Movie*
Tatarsky, Jack (act): *Glen and Randa*
Tate, Dale (act): *Attack of the 50-Foot Woman (1958); The Brain from Planet Arous*
Tate, Dwight (act): *Glen and Randa*
Tate, Jacques (act): *The Invisible Woman (1983)*
Tate, John (act): *On the Beach*
Tate, Larenz (act): *The Postman (1997)*
Tate, Laura (act): *Dead Space; Subspecies*
Tate, Lincoln (act): *Battle of the Amazons; Grotesque*
Tate, Nick (act): *Licensed to Love and Kill*
Tate, Reginald (act): *Dark Journey; Escape Route; The Man Behind the Mask (1936); Noose;*
The Phantom Light; Poison Pen; The Riverside Murder; Secret People; The Story of Robin Hood; Tangled Evidence; Too Dangerous to Live; Uncle Silas; Whispering Tongues
Tate, Sharon (act, 1943-1969): *Eye of the Devil; The Fearless Vampire Killers or: Pardon Me,But Your Teeth Are In My Neck; The Wrecking Crew*
Tati, Jacques (act, 1907-1982, nee Jacques Tatischeff): *Sylvia and the Phantom*
Tatischeff, Jacques (act): see Tati, Jacques
Tattersall, David (cin): *Theodore Rex*
Tattersall, Gale (cin): *Dark Water; Hideaway; Virtuosity*
Tatton, Rosamund (act): *The Cloister and the Woman*
Tatum, Bradford (act): *Powder*
Tatum, Jean(ne) (act): *The Astounding She-Monster; The Ghost of Dragstrip Hollow*
Tatum, Judy (act): *Witchboard*
Tatum, Roy (act): *A Kiss to Die For; Rearview Mirror*
Taube, Sven-Bertil (act): *Guilt*
Taubes, Frank (wri): *The Mask (1961)*
Taulbee, Harold (act): *Poltergeist III*
Taurog, Norman (dir, 1899-1981): *The Beginning or the End?; Dr. Goldfoot and the Bikini Machine; Sergeant Deadhead the Astronut!; Visit to a Small Planet*
Tausek, Bryant (act): *Deadtime Stories*
Tausik, David (dir): *Haunted Symphony*
Taussig, Frank Hart (wri): *Giant from the Unknown*
Tavares, Fernanda (act): *Secret Weapons*
Tavares-Finson, Cindy (act): *Popcorn*
Tavella, Dino (wri): *Il Mostro di Venezia*
Tavera, Michael (mus): *The Land Before Time II: The Great Valley Adventure; The Land Before Time III: The Time of the Great Giving; The Land Before Time IV: Journey Through the Mists; The Land Before Time V: The Mysterious Island*
Tavernier, Albert (act): *The Man from Beyond*
Tavernier, Bertrand (dir & wri, b. 1941): *Deathwatch (1980)*
Taviani, Paolo (dir & wri): *Fiorile; Kaos*
Taviani, Vittorio (dir & wri): *Fiorile; Kaos*
Tavier, Vincent (wri): *Man Bites Dog*
Tavin, Erin (act): *The Craft*
Tavis, Norman (act): *Oh Heavenly Dog*
Tawara, Hitomi (act): *The Toxic Avenger, Part II*
Tawfik, Magged (act): *A Story of Tutankhamun*
Taxier, Arthur (act): *Alfred Hitchcock Presents*
Tayback, Tom (act): *The Hidden II*
Tayback, Vic (act, 1930-1990): *All Dogs Go to Heaven; Beverly Hills Bodysnatchers; Blood and Lace; Mansion of the Doomed; Murderer's Keep; The Mysterious Two; The Shaggy D.A.; Through the Magic Pyramid*
Taye-Loren, Carolyn (act): *Witchcraft 5: Dance With the Devil*
Tayir, Andre (act): *Ravagers*
Taylor, Al (act): *The Haunting of Sarah Hardy*
Taylor, Al(fred) (cin): *Killer Klowns from Outer Space; Mutant*
Taylor, Alice (act): *The Woman Who Wouldn't Die (1965)*
Taylor, Alma (act, 1895-1974): *Aladdin: or, A Lad Out; Alf's Button (1920); The American Heiress; Anna the Adventuress; The Basilisk; Be Sure Your Sins; Blind Fate; Boundary House; The Cobweb; Curfew Must Not Ring Tonight; Deadlock (1931); The Grand Babylon Hotel; His Great Opportunity; In the Shadow of Big Ben; Jill and the Old Fiddle; Justice; King Robert of Sicily; The*

Kleptomaniac; Lost; The Man Who Stayed at Home; The Mill Girl; A Moment of Darkness; Morphia, the Death Drug; The Mystery of Mr. Marks; Partners In Crime (1913); The Passing of a Soul; Paying the Penalty; The Schemers: or, The Jewels of Hate; The Shadow of Egypt; The Tinted Venus; Tried In the Fire; Winning His Stripes

Taylor, Amy (act): *Haunters of the Deep*

Taylor, Anita (act): *Student Bodies*

Taylor, Benedict (act): *The Corsican Brothers (1985);Thirteen at Dinner; The Watcher In the Woods*

Taylor, Bernard (wri): *The Godsend*

Taylor, Bill (act): *The Fog; The Pit (1983)*

Taylor, Bill (cin): *Dark Star; Roger Corman's 'Frankenstein Unbound'*

Taylor, Bill (mus): *Dark Star*

Taylor, Brian (act): *Haunted by Her Past*

Taylor, Bruce (act): *Dead as a Doorman*

Taylor, Bruce A. (wri): *The Annihilator; Inferno (1998)*

Taylor, Buck (act): *Timestalkers*

Taylor, Carli (act): *Charlie Chan In London*

Taylor, Chad (act): *Miracle Mile*

Taylor, Chris (act): *The Mask (1994)*

Taylor, Christine (act): *The Craft*

Taylor, Clarisse/Clarice (act): *Change of Mind; Play Misty for Me*

Taylor, Corey Joshua (act):*Eraser*

Taylor, Courtney (act): *The Companion (1994); Cover Me; Prom Night III: The Last Kiss; Tracks of a Killer*

Taylor, Curtis (act): *Hellhole; Mr. Sycamore*

Taylor, Dan (cin): *Metamorphosis: The Alien Factor*

Taylor, Darien (act): *The Body Snatchers*

Taylor, Deborah (act): *The Brother from Another Planet; Haunted by Her Past*

Taylor, Dendrie (Allyn) (act): *Night Visions; Shocker; Species; Star Trek: Generations*

Taylor, Denise (act): *Barracuda*

Taylor, Dixie (act): *Red Alert*

Taylor, Don (act, 1920-1999): *Love Slaves of the Amazons; Men of Sherwood Forest; Song of the Thin Man*

Taylor, Don (dir, 1920-1999): *Damien-Omen II; Escape from the Planet of the Apes; Everything's Ducky; The Final Countdown; Ghost of a Chance (1987); The Island of Dr. Moreau (1977); Secret Weapons*

Taylor, Donald (dir): *The Night of the Full Moon; The Straw Man*

Taylor, Donald (wri): *The Devil's Daffodil; The Night of the Full Moon; The Straw Man*

Taylor, Donald Dexter (act): *The Red Dragon (1945)*

Taylor, Dub (act, 1907-1994): *Back to the Future, Part III; Burnt Offerings; Creature from Black Lake; The Rescuers; Them! (1954)*

Taylor, Dwight (wri, 1902-1986): *I Wake Up Screaming; The Thin Man Goes Home*

Taylor, Dyanna (cin): *Eat and Run*

Taylor, Elaine (act): *The Anniversary; Casino Royale*

Taylor, Elizabeth (act, b. 1932): *The Blue Bird (1976); Boom; Dr. Faustus; The Flintstones; Hammersmith Is Out; Jane Eyre (1944); The Mirror Crack'd; Night Watch (1973); Reflections In a Golden Eye; Secret Ceremony; Suddenly Last Summer; Winter Kills*

Taylor, Elsie (act): *Macbeth (1971)*

Taylor, Eric (wri): *The Black Cat (1941); Black Friday; Close Call for Ellery Queen; Crime Doctor's Courage; Crime Doctor's Manhunt; Crime Doctor's Strangest Case; Crime Doctor's Warning; Desperate Chance for Ellery Queen; Dick Tracy (1945); Dick Tracy Meets Gruesome; Ellery Queen and the Murder Ring; Ellery Queen and the Perfect Crime; Ellery Queen, Master Detective; Ellery Queen's Penthouse Mystery; Enemy Agents Meet Ellery Queen; The Ghost of Frankenstein; Just Before Dawn (1946); Lady In the Morgue; Phantom of the Opera (1943);Shadows In the Night; Son of Dracula (1943); The Whistler; The White Goddess*

Taylor, Estelle (act, 1899-1958): *Don Juan (1927); Liliom (1930); Monte Cristo; Where East Is East*

Taylor, Femi (act): *Return of the Jedi*

Taylor, Ferris (act): *The Docks of New Orleans; The Saint In Palm Springs*

Taylor, Forrest (act): *Cyclotrode X; Face In the Fog (1935); Forbidden Jungle; The Golden Eye; Kelly of the Secret Service*

Taylor, Fran (act): *Dream a Little Dream*

Taylor, Francis (mus): *2020 Texas Gladiators*

Taylor, Fred (act): *Terror from the Year 5,000*

Taylor, Gary (act): *Empire of Ash III*

Taylor, George (act): *After the Thin Man*

Taylor, Gil (dir & wri): *Dr. Frankenstein On Campus*

Taylor, Gilbert (cin, b. 1914): *The Bedford Incident; Cul-de-Sac; Dracula (1979); Dr. Strangelove: or, How I Learned to Stop Worrying and Love the Bomb; Flash Gordon (1980); Frenzy; The Full Treatment; High Treason (1951); Macbeth (1971); The Omen; Repulsion; Seven Days to Noon; Star Wars; Venom (1982); Work Is a Four Letter Word; The Yellow Balloon; Yield to the Night*

Taylor, Gin (act): *Mirrors*

Taylor, Grant (act): *Long John Silver; On the Beach; Quatermass and the Pit*

Taylor, Greg (wri): *Jumanji*

Taylor, Hillman (wri): *Zontar: The Thing from Venus*

Taylor, Holland (act, b. 1943): *Awake to Danger; George of the Jungle; The Jewel of the Nile; Romancing the Stone; The Truman Show*

Taylor, J.O. (cin): *Alias the Lone Wolf; King Kong (1933); The Lone Wolf Returns (1926); Son of Kong*

Taylor, Jack (act): *Carry On Spying; Count Dracula; Dr. Jekyll y el Hombre Lobo; Eugenie...The Story of Her Journey Into Perversion; Horror of the Zombies; The Mummy's Revenge; Necronomicon; Night of the Sorcerers; La Orgia Nocturna de los Vampiros; Paranoiac; Pieces; Shadow of a Man; Stormy Crossing; The Trollenberg Terror; Where Time Began*

Taylor, Jackie (act): *Satan's Sadists*

Taylor, James (act):*Morons from Outer Space*

Taylor, Jana (act): *Dreamscape*

Taylor, Jeannine (act): *Friday the 13th (1980)*

Taylor, Jennifer Joan (act):*Fright Night II; In the Company of Darkness*

Taylor, Joan (act): *Earth vs. the Flying Saucers; Girls In Prison; Omar Khayyam; 20 Million Miles to Earth*

Taylor, Joanne (act): *Blood Diner*

Taylor, John (act): *The Fiendish Plot of Dr. Fu Manchu; The Seventh Sign*

Taylor, Josh (act): *Separate Lives*

Taylor, Joyce (act): *Atlantis, the Lost Continent; Beauty and the Beast (1962); Beyond a Reasonable Doubt; Ring of Fire; 13 Frightened Girls; Twice-Told Tales*

Taylor, Jud (dir): *City In Fear; The Disappearance of Flight 401; Future Cop; Revenge (1971, USA); Search for the Gods*

Taylor, Karl (act): *Twisted*

Taylor, Kelli (act): *The Club (1994)*

Taylor, Kenneth (wri): *Beyond This Place*

Taylor, Kent (act, 1907-1987, nee Louis Weiss): *Angels' Wild Women; Blood of Ghastly Horror; Brain of Blood; Brides of Blood; The Crawling Hand; The Crimson Key; Dangerous Millions; The Day Mars Invaded Earth; Deadline for Murder; Death Takes a Holiday (1934); The Gracie Allen Murder Case; Half-Past Midnight; Hell's Bloody Devils; House of Horrors (1946); I Spit On Your Corpse; The Mighty Gorga; The Phantom from 10,000 Leagues; The Phantom of Hollywood; Satan's Sadists; Secret Venture; Seeds of Destruction; Track the Man Down; White Woman*

Taylor, Kevin (act): *Enemy Mine*

Taylor, Kimberly (act): *Frankenhooker*

Taylor, Kit (act): *Cassandra; Chilling (1981); In the Devil's Garden; Long John Silver*

Taylor Sr., Lance (act): *Blacula; Frogs*

Taylor, Larry (act): *—And Now the Screaming Starts!; Crosstrap; The Girl Hunters; Kil 1; Prisoners of the Lost Universe*

Taylor, Lauren-Marie (act): *Friday the 13th-Part 2; Neighbors*

Taylor, Lawrence Edmund/L.E. (wri): *Bulldog Drummond Strikes Back (1947); Philo Vance's Gamble; Philo Vance's Secret Mission*

Taylor, Lee (act): *The Haunting Passion; Quarantine*

Taylor, Leo (act): *Meteories!*

Taylor, Lindsay (act): *Hard to Die*

Taylor, Lili (act): *The Addiction*

Taylor, Lisa (act): *Eyes of Laura Mars; Lady In White*

Taylor, Lynne (act): *Life for Ruth*

Taylor, Malcolm (act): see McDowell, Malcolm

Taylor, Malcolm (dir): *Murder Motel*

Taylor, Marina (act): *Lurkers*

Taylor, Marjorie (act): *The Crimes of Stephen Hawke;The Face at the Window (1939); Miracles Do Happen; Silver Top*

Taylor, Mark (act): *Angel Heart*

Taylor, Mark L. (act): *Alfred Hitchcock Presents; Arachnophobia; Honey, I Shrunk the Kids*

Taylor, Marlon (act): *It (1990)*

Taylor, Martha (act): *Manhattan Baby*

Taylor, Mary (act): *Class of Nuke 'em High*

Taylor, Merle Ann (act): *Dr. Heckyl & Mr. Hype*

Taylor, Meshach (act): *Damien-Omen II; Double, Double,Toil and Trouble; Explorers; The Howling; Mannequin; Mannequin Two: On the Move; Ultra Warrior; Warning Sign*

Taylor, Michelle (act): *Supergirl (1984)*

Taylor, Mimi (act): *Peril from the Planet Mongo; Purple Death from Outer Space*

Taylor, Patti (act): *Gog*

Taylor, Pauline (act): *A Clockwork Orange*

Taylor, Peter (act): *The Village of the Damned (1960)*

Taylor, Philip John (wri): *I'm Dangerous Tonight*

Taylor, Ray (dir, 1888-1952): *The Deadly Ray from Mars; Dick Tracy (1937); Peril from the Planet Mongo; Purple Death from Outer Space*

Taylor, Regina (act): *Spirit Lost*

Taylor, Renee (act): *Forever*

Taylor, Rex (wri): *Dick Tracy Returns; Dick Tracy's G-Men; The Mandarin Mystery*

Taylor, Richard (mus): *The Intimate Stranger; Zex*

Taylor, Richard Mansfield (act): see Richards, Jeff

Taylor, Rip (act): *Amazon Women On the Moon; Calendar Girl Murders; The Silence of the Hams*

Taylor, Robert (act, 1911-1969, nee Spangler Arlington Brough): *The Bribe; The Glass Sphinx; The House of the Seven Hawks;Knights of the Round Table; The Last Hunt; The Night Walker*

Taylor, Robert (1980s act): *Something Is Out There*

Taylor, Robert (dir): *The Nine Lives of Fritz the Cat*

Taylor, Roberta (act): *Frankenstein (1984); The Witches (1990)*

Taylor, Rochelle (act): *Murderlust*

Taylor, Rocky (act): *—And Now the Screaming Starts!;Batman (1989); The Slipper and the Rose*

Taylor, Rod (act, b. 1930): *The Birds; Germicide; The Glass-Bottom Boat; The Liquidator; Long John Silver; Nobody Runs Forever; 101 Dalmatians (1961); La Regina delle Amazzoni; Step Down to Terror; 36 Hours (1965); The Time Machine (1960); Trader Horn (1973); The Warlord: Battle for the Galaxy; World Without End*

Taylor, Roderick (wri): *The Annihilator; Inferno (1998)*

Taylor, Roger D. (act): *Secrets of the Phantom Caverns*

Taylor, Ron (act): *Heart Condition*

Taylor, Ronnie (cin): *Popcorn*

Taylor, Rosemary (act): *Peter Rabbit and the Tales of Beatrix Potter*

Taylor, Russi (act): *Jetsons: The Movie; Who Framed Roger Rabbit*

Taylor, S.E.V. (dir & wri): *The Lone Wolf (1924)*

Taylor, Samuel (W.) (wri, 1895-1958): *The Absent-Minded Professor (1961); Bait; Son of Flubber; Topaz; Vertigo*

Taylor, Sharon (act): *Attack of the Killer Tomatoes*

Taylor, Shaun (act): *The Pink Chiquitas*

Taylor, Shaw (act): *The Medusa Touch*

Taylor, Siobhan (act): *The Damned*

Taylor, Stan (cin): *Earth Angel*

Taylor, Susan (act): *I Was a Zombie for the F.B.I.*

Taylor, Tamara (act): *Senseless (1998)*

Taylor, Tom (act): *Dark Night of the Scarecrow*

Taylor, Tom (wri): *Still Waters Run Deep*

Taylor, Totti Truman (act): *Chitty Chitty Bang Bang; A Woman Possessed*

Taylor, Tyrone (act): *Redneck Zombies*

Taylor, Valerie (act): *Baffled!; Berkeley Square; Faces In the Dark; Repulsion; Went the Day Well?; What a Carve Up!*

Taylor, Valerie (wri): *Take My Life*

Taylor, Vaughn (act, 1910-1983): *Dark Intruder; Francis Goes to the Races; The Power (1967); Psycho (1960); Screaming Mimi; The Wizard of Baghdad*

Taylor, Vida (act): *Clash of the Titans*

Taylor, W. (cin): *Animal Farm (1954)*

Taylor, Wally (act): *The Golden Child; Night of the Creeps; Peacemaker (1990); When a Stranger Calls*

Taylor, William B. (act): *Twilight Zone*

Taylor, Willis (act): *Empire of Ash III*

Taylor, Wilton (act): *Blackie's Redemption; The Cave Girl (1921); Outside the Law*

Taylor-Allan, Lee (act): *Stargate*

Taylor-Gordon, Hannah (act): *Mary Shelley's 'Frankenstein'*

Taylor-Young, Leigh (act, b. 1944): *The Jagged Edge; Looker; Soylent Green*

Tayma, Masamitsu (act): *Mothra*

Tayman, Robert (act): *House of Whipcord; Moon Zero Two; Vampire Circus*

Tazaki, Jun (act): *Atragon; Destroy All Monsters;Ebirah, Horror of the Deep; Gorath; Kwaidan; The War of the Gargantuas*

Tazewell, Charles (wri): *The Littlest Angel (1969)*

Tchaikovsky, Petr Ilich (mus, 1840-1893): *Dracula (1931, English-speaking version); The Sleeping Beauty (1965, Russ)*

Tchakalova, Ludmilla (act):*The Stolen Plans (1952)*

Tchendei, I. (wri): *The Shadows of Forgotten Ancestors*

Tcherina, Ludmilla (act): *Mata Hari's Daughter; Parsifal; Sign of the Pagan; Sins of Rome*

Tcherina, Pierre (wri): *Asterix In Britain*

Tchikine, Kostia (cin): *Johnny the Giant Killer*

Tead, Phil (act): *Follow the Hunter*

Teagarden, Beth (act): *The Stuff*

Teagardin, Phyllis (act): *The Cabinet of Caligari*

Teague, Anthony (act): *The Barefoot Executive*

Teague, George J. (cin): *Behind Locked Doors*

Teague, Lewis (dir): *Alligator (1981); Cat's Eye; Collision Course (1992); Cujo; Deadlock; The Jewel of the Nile*

Teague, Marshall (act): *The Colony (1995)*

Teague, Raoul (act): *Chilling (1981)*

Teakle, Spencer (act): *Cover Girl Killer; The Gentle Trap*

Teal, Ray (act, 1902-1976): *The Bandit of Sherwood Forest; Captain Kidd; The Chance of a Lifetime; Shadow of the Thin Man; The Thin Man Goes Home*

Teal, Sonne (act): *La Poupee*

Teale, Owen (act): *The Hawk; Robin Hood (1991)*

Teare, Shanna L. (act): *Waxwork II: Lost In Time*

Tearle, Conway (act, 1882-1938, nee Frederick Levy): *Bella Donna (1923); Held for Murder; The Lost Zeppelin; The Mystic*

Tearle, David (act): *The Case of the Old Rope Man;The Green Goddess (1929)*

Tearle, (Sir) Godfrey (act, 1884-1953): *The Beginning or the End?; The Fool; Puppets of Fate; The 39 Steps (1935)*

Teasdale, Veree (act, b. 1897): *A Midsummer Night's Dream (1935); Roman Scandals; Topper Takes a Trip; Turnabout*

Tebar, Juan (wri): *Ceremonia Sangrienta; The House That Screamed*

Tedesco, Paola (act): *Battle of the Amazons*

Ted Lewis and His Orchestra (act & mus): *Hold That Ghost*

Tedrow, Irene (act): *Empire of the Ants; Just Before Dawn (1946); Live Again, Die Again; The Two Worlds of Jennie Logan*

Tee, Elsa (act): *Death In High Heels*

Teed, G.H. (wri): *The Clue of the Second Goblet; Sexton Blake and the Mademoiselle*

Teed, Jill (act): *Peter Benchley's 'Creature'*

Teefy, Maureen (act): *Supergirl (1984)*

Teegarden, Byron (act): *Attack of the Killer Tomatoes*

Teele, Margot (act): *The Human Duplicators*

Teer, Barbara Ann (act): *The Angel Levine*

Teesdale, Carol (act): *Runaway*

Teeth (mus): *Boarding House*

Teetsel, Frederic (mus): *Adventures In Dinosaur City; The Haunting of Morella*

Tefkin, Blair (act): *Fright Night II; V*

Teich, Aarin (act): *Bloodspell; Dead of Night (1987)*

Teichman, Edith (act): *The Green Archer*

Teifer, Gregory (wri): *The Amsterdam Kill*

Teigh, Lila (act): *Poor Devil*

Teinowitz, Harry (act): *The Package*

Teissier, Elizabeth (act): *Castle Keep*

Teitsort, John (act): *Echoes*

Teixeira, Virgilio (act): *La Cara del Terror; Ella y el Miedo; The 7th Voyage of Sinbad*

Tejada, Raquel (act): see Welch, Raquel

Tejada-Flores, Miguel (wri): *Atomic Dog; Fright Night II; Screamers (1996); Tails You Live, Heads You're Dead*

Teje, Tora (act): *Haxan*

Tekase, Kyoshi (act): *Deadlock (1931)*

Telaak, William (wri): *The Phantom Planet*

Telezynska, Isabella/Izabella (act): *Pandemonium; To the Devil a Daughter*

Telfer, James (act): *Apartment Zero*

Telfer, (Robert) Frank (act): Arachnophobia; The Stuff; Wicked Stepmother
Telford, Frank (dir): The Bamboo Saucer
Telford, Frank (wri): Hello Down There
Telford, Robert (act): The House of the Dead
Tellegen, Mike (act): The Gracie Allen Murder Case
Teller, Ira (wri): Silent Night, Bloody Night
Teller, Iza (act): Billion Dollar Brain; The Devils
Tellini, P. (wri): Atoll K
Tellone, Rita (act): Eyes of Laura Mars
Temperance Seven (act): The Wrong Box
Tempest, Mary (act): An American Werewolf In London
Temple, Eileen (act): A Message from Mars (1913)
Temple, Fay (act): The Devil's Bondman; The Mystery of a Hansom Cab; Strategy
Temple, Kate (act): The Tempest (1980)
Temple, Loretta (act): The Boy Who Cried Werewolf
Temple, Shirley (act, b. 1928): The Blue Bird (1940)
Temple, Wilfred (act): The Yellow Mask
Temple, William A. (act): The Nature of the Beast
Temple, William F. (wri, b. 1914): Four Sided Triangle
Templeman, Harcourt (dir): The Bells (1931)
Temple-Smith, John (wri): Black Orchid; Home to Danger; One Way Out; Profile; The Viking Queen
Temple-Smith, Maurice (wri): Profile
Templeton, Mrs. (act): Wuthering Heights (1920)
Templeton, Charles (wri): The Kidnapping of the President
Templeton, Beatrix (act): Bleak House; The Princess of Happy Chance
Templeton, Joyce (act): For All Eternity; Whosoever Shall Offend
Templeton, William (P.) (wri): Double Confession; 1984 (1955)
Tenalia, Aimee (act): The Night Brings Charlie
Tenaya (act): The Manitou
Tenbrooke, Harry (act): Seven Footprints to Satan
Tendeter, Kay (act): The Fall of the House of Usher (1950)
Tengende, Oliver (act): King Solomon's Mines (1985)
Tennant, Andy (dir): Ever After: A Cinderella Story
Tennant, Barbara (act): Robin Hood (1912)
Tennant, Frank (act): Flying from Justice; The Harper Mystery; In the Ranks; The Murdock Trial; A Rogue's Wife; The Romany Rye; Royal Love; The Story of the Rosary; What's Bred...Comes Out In the Flesh
Tennant, Pauline (act): The Queen of Spades (1948)
Tennant, Victoria (act, b. 1951): All of Me; Dean R. Koontz' 'Whispers'; Flowers In the Attic;The Handmaid's Tale; Inseminoid; Maigret; Sphinx (1981)
Tenney, Del (dir): The Curse of the Living Corpse; The Horror of Party Beach; Voodoo Blood Bath
Tenney, Del (wri): The Curse of the Living Corpse; Voodoo Blood Bath
Tenney, Dennis Michael (mus): Leprechaun 3; Night of the Demons; Peacemaker (1990); Witchboard;Witchboard 2: The Devil's Doorway
Tenney, Jon (act, b. 1963): Night Visions; The Phantom (1996)
Tenney, Kevin S. (dir): The Cellar (1989); Night of the Demons; Peacemaker (1990); Witchboard; Witchboard 2: The Devil's Doorway; Witchtrap
Tenney, Kevin S. (wri): Peacemaker (1990); Witchboard;Witchboard 2: The Devil's Doorway; Witchboard: The Possession
Tennyson, Alfred (wri, 1850-1892): The Lady of Shallot
Tennyson, Walter (dir): Alibi Inn; The Body Vanishes; The Ghost Walks (1935)
Tenser, Mark (wri): The Hearse
Tenser, Tony (wri): Mini Weekend
Tensi, Francesco (act): Ghosts-Italian Style; Sodom and Gomorrah
Tenzer, Bert (dir & wri): 2000 Years Later
Teodoro, Mario (act): Dance of the Dwarfs
Tepper, Craig (wri): Double Jeopardy
Tepper, Kirby (act): Miracle Mile
Ter, Angel (act): Supersonic Man
Teran, Manuel (cin): Zorro: The Legend Begins
Terao, Akira (act): Ran
Terechova, Margareta (act): The Blue Bird (1976)
Terene, Mark (act): Millennium
Tergesen, Lee (act): Alien High
Terhune, Bob (act): Grim Prairie Tales; Prophecy (1979)
Terizzi, Carla (act): La Citta delle Donne
Terlesky, John (act): Chopping Mall; Deathstalker II: The Duel of the Titans
Termo, Leonard (act): Ed Wood; Midnight Cabaret
Teroda, Kazuo (dir): Aladdin and the King of Thieves
Terr, Mischa (act): The Nasty Rabbit
Terr, Mischa (mus): King Dinosaur
Terraine, Molly (act): The Firm of Girdlestone
Terranova, Tiffany (act): Mutants In Paradise
Terree, Agi (act): Beyond the Universe
Terrell, John Canada (act):Def by Temptation
Terrell, Ken(neth) (act): Attack of the 50-Foot Woman (1958); The Brain from Planet Arous; Dick Tracy's G-Men; Indestructible Man; Master of the World; Port Sinister; Return to Treasure Island; Sabu and the Magic Ring
Terrell, Steve (act): Invasion of the Saucer Men
Terrell, Yolande (act): The Tell-Tale Heart (1934); They Drive by Night
Terrence, John (act): The Alien Within
Terrington, Kit (act): The Door In the Wall; The Secret of the Forest
Terris, Malcolm (act): Mata Hari (1985); Slayground
Terrot, Charles (wri): The Angel Who Pawned Her Harp
Terry, Alice (act, 1899-1987, nee Alice Taafe): The Conquering Power; The Magician (1926); The Prisoner of Zenda (1922)
Terry, Carol (act): Bog; The Lucifer Complex
Terry, Diane (act): Time Walker
Terry, Dick (act): Phantom of Chinatown
Terry, Don (act): Drums of the Congo; Sherlock Holmes In Washington; White Savage; Who Killed Gail Preston?
Terry, Edward (act): The Children; Luther the Geek
Terry, Edward (wri): The Children
Terry, Ellen (act): Her Greatest Performance
Terry, Gay Partington (wri): The Toxic Avenger, Part II; The Toxic Avenger, Part III: The Last Temptation of Toxie
Terry, Harry (act): The Face at the Window (1939); I'm an Explosive; The Ring; The Unholy Quest
Terry, Hazel (act): Kill or Cure; The Servant
Terry, Herbie (act): Falling Fire
Terry, James (act): Spaceflight IC-1
Terry, John (act): Hawk the Slayer; Of Mice and Men (1992); Reflections In the Dark; The Resurrected; Seduction: There Goes the Bride; Three Tales from the 'Inner Sanctum'
Terry, Jonathon (act): The Return of the Living Dead (1985); Return of the Living Dead, Part II
Terry, Joy (act): The Neanderthal Man
Terry, June Ellen (act): Jane Eyre (1921)
Terry, Karen (act): No Blade of Grass
Terry, Kim (act): Slugs
Terry, Martin (act): The Sorcerers
Terry, Nigel (act): Deja Vu; Excalibur; The Hunchback (1997)
Terry, Paul (act): James and the Giant Peach
Terry, Peter (act): The Dead Next Door
Terry, Phillip (act, b. 1909): Born to Kill; The Leech Woman; The Lost Weekend; The Monster and the Girl; The Navy vs. the Night Monsters; On Borrowed Time; Seven Keys to Baldpate (1947)
Terry, Robert/Bob (act): Blake of Scotland Yard; Dick Tracy Returns
Terry, Ruth (act): Hand of Death
Terry, Sheila (act): Murder On a Bridle Path; The Sphinx (1933)
Terry, William (act): Behind City Lights; Strangers In the Night
Terry-Lewis, Mabel (act): Jamaica Inn (1939); The Scarlet Pimpernel (1934); The Squeaker (1937); They Came to a City
Terry-Thomas (act, 1911-1990, nee Thomas Terry Hoar Stevens): The Abominable Dr. Phibes; Diabolik; Dr. Phibes Rises Again; The Green Man; The Hound Of The Baskervilles (1978); I Love a Mystery (1966); Kill or Cure; Kiss the Girls and Make Them Die; The Mouse On the Moon; Munster, Go Home!; Our Man In Marrakesh; The Perils of Pauline; Robin Hood (1973); Those Fantastic Flying Fools; Tom Thumb; 2000 Years Later; The Vault of Horror; The Wonderful World of the Brothers Grimm
Tershman, Michael E. (cin): Her Deadly Rival
Ter Stagge, Johanna (act): The Vanishing (1988)
Terwilliger, George (wri): Pocomania
Terzano, Ubaldo (cin, a.k.a. David Hamilton): La Frusta e il Corpo; La Maschera del Demonio; La Ragazza Che Sapeva Troppo; Sei Donne per l'Assassino; I Tre Volti della Paura
Terzo, Venus (act): It (1990)
Tesarz, Jan (act): Krotki Film O Zabijaniu
Tesco, Nicky (act): I Hired a Contract Killer
Tesh, John (act, b. 1952): Shocker
Teshigahara, Hiroshi (dir, b. 1927): Suna No Onna; Tanin No Kao
Tesich, Steve (wri): Eyewitness (1981)
Teslof, Jeanne (act): The Wacky World of Dr. Morgus
Tessari, Duccio (dir, b. 1926): La Morte Risale a Ieri Sera; Per Amore...Per Magia; Les Titans; Zorro (1975)
Tessari, Duccio (wri, b. 1926): Carthage In Flames; Ercole al Centro della Terra; Ercole alla Conquista della Atlantide; The Last Days of Pompeii (1959); Maciste alla Corte del Gran Khan; Maciste Contre il Vampiro; Per Amore...Per Magia;Romolo e Remo; Les Titans
Tessari, Fiorenza (act): Phenomena
Tessier, Elisabeth (act): The Blood Rose
Tessier, Laurence (act): The Grip of Iron
Tessier, Robert/Bob (act, 1934-1990): Billion Dollar Threat; The Deep; Doc Savage, the Man of Bronze; Future Force; The Lost Empire; Nightwish; Star Crash; The Sword and the Sorcerer
Tester, Desmond (act, b. 1919): The Drum; Sabotage
Testi, Fabio (act): Nada; S*H*E (1980); The Uranium Conspiracy
Testory, Francois (act): A Midsummer Night's Dream (1985)
Testory, Marcus (act): The Cyber-Stalking
Tetley, Graeme (wri): Dark of the Night
Tetley, Walter (act): Tower of London (1939)
Tetrick, Bob (act): The Spider (1958); War of the Colossal Beast
Tetzel, Joan (act, b. 1924): The Paradine Case
Tetzlaff, Ted (cin, b. 1903): Arrest Bulldog Drummond; The Enchanted Cottage (1945); I Married a Witch; The Mad Doctor; Notorious (1946)
Tetzlaff, Ted (dir, b. 1903): Son of Sinbad; Time Bomb; The Treasure of Lost Canyon; Under the Gun; The Window
Teuber, Andreas (act): Dr. Faustus
Teves, Pamela (act): The Fourth Man
Tevis, Peter (mus): Flesh Gordon
Tevis, Walter (wri, b. 1928): The Man Who Fell to Earth (1976 & 1987)
Tevos, Herbert (dir & wri): Mesa of Lost Women
Tew, Sharon K. (act): Cyborg (1989)
Tewes, Lauren (act): Eyes of a Stranger
TeWiata, Beryl (act): Strange Behavior
Te Wiata, Inia (act): In Search of the Castaways
Tewson, Josephine (act): The Hound of the Baskervilles (1978)
Texera, Leo (act): The Bad Lord Byron
Texiere, Jacob (act): Blade af Satans Bog
Texter, Gilda (act): Vanishing Point (1971)
Tey, Josephine (wri): Young and Innocent
Teynac, Maurice (act): Night Without Stars; The Reluctant Spy
Tezuka, Katsumi (act): Mothra
Tezuka, Osamu (wri): Alakazam the Great
Tezuka, Yasutaka (act): The Toxic Avenger, Part II
Thacker, Russ (act, b. 1946):Savages
Thackery, Bud (cin, b. 1903): Cyclotrode X; Strategy of Terror
Thackery, Frank (cin): Chiller
Thal, Eric (act): The Puppet Masters
Thalasso, Arthur (act): Secrets of the Night
Thalken, Meg (act): Poltergeist III
Thall, Benj (act): The Haunted (1991); The Puppet Masters; Repossessed
Thamar, Tilda (act): The Master Plan
Thanassoulis, Panos (act): Singapore Sling
Thanisch, Jennifer (act): Dark Places
Thatcher, Heather (act): Altar Chains; First Men In the Moon (1919); Flesh and Fantasy; Gaslight (1944); The Green Terror; The Hour of 13; The Private Life of Don Juan; The Undying Monster
Thatcher, Torin (act, 1905-1981): Blackbeard the Pirate; The Black Shield of Falworth; Brenda Starr (1976); The Crimson Pirate; Great Expectations (1946); Helen of Troy (1955); Houdini (1953); Istanbul; Jack the Giant Killer; Lady Godiva; Law and Disorder; The Man Who Could Work Miracles; The Miracle (1959); Sabotage; The 7th Voyage of Sinbad; The Spy In Black;Witness for the Prosecution; Young and Innocent
Thauven, Tatiana (act): Anguish
Thaw, John (act): Dead Man's Chest; Dr. Phibes Rises Again; Five to One
Thaw, Laura (act): The Keeper
Thawley, Tod (act): Terminal Justice
Thawnton, Tony (act): Curse of Simba
Thaxter, Phyllis (act, b. 1921): Bewitched (1944); Operation Secret; Superman (1978)
Thayer, Brynn (act): Ghost of a Chance (1987)
Thayer, Lorna (act): The Aliens Are Coming; The Beast With a Million Eyes; Dead Men Tell No Tales (1971); Jennifer (1953); Rhinoceros (1974)
Thayer, Meg (act): Omega Cop
Thayer, Michael (act): Planet of Dinosaurs
Thayer, Tiffany (wri): Strangers of the Evening
Theatre du Chatelet, Ballerinas of the (act): Le Voyage dans la Lune
Thebus, Mary Ann (act): Blink
Theby, Rosemary (act): Boston Blackie's Little Pal; Secrets of the Night
Thedford, Marcello (act): Daylight
Theel, Lynn (act): Humanoids from the Deep; Without Warning (1980)
Theibaud, Jim (act): 976-EVIL
Theil, Karlheinz (act): Shock Chamber
Theilade, Nini (act): A Midsummer Night's Dream (1935)
Their, Mechtild (act): Homunculus
Theirse, Darryl (act): The Warlord: Battle for the Galaxy
Theis, Herbert V. (cin): The Omegans
Theison, Rolf (act): The Strangeness
Theiss, Manuella (act): Barn of the Naked Dead
Theiss, Richard H. (mus): The Loch Ness Horror
Thelman, Joseph (act): Night of the Sorcerers; Tombs of the Blind Dead
Themmen, Paris (act): Willy Wonka and the Chocolate Factory
Then, Tony (act): The Swordsman
Theodorakis, Mikis (mus, b. 1925): The Day the Fish Came Out; Electra (1961); The Shadow of the Cat; The Trojan Women
Theodore, (Brother) (act): The 'Burbs; The Hobbit; The Invisible Kid; Nocturna, Granddaughter of Dracula; The Return of the King
Theodore, Ralph (act): Confessions of Boston Blackie
Theodore, Stag (act): For Your Eyes Only
Theoren, Robert (wri): My Daughter Joy
Theorer, Gerard (act): Millennium
Theriault, Robin (act): To All a Goodnight
Theron, Charlize (act, b. 1975): Devil's Advocate; Mighty Joe Young (1998)
Theroux, Earl (act): The Nature of the Beast
Thesiger, Ernest (act, 1879-1961): Ashes; The Bad Lord Byron; Bride of Frankenstein; Father Brown; The Ghosts of Berkeley Square; The Ghoul (1933); Last Holiday; The Man In the White Suit; The Man Who Could Work Miracles; Meet Mr. Lucifer; The Old Dark House (1932); A Place of One's Own; Portrait from Life; Scrooge (1951); They Drive by Night; Who Done It? (1956)
Thew, Harvey (wri): The Mad Genius; Supernatural (1933)
Thew, Manora (act): Arsene Lupin; At the Villa Rose (1920); Honour in Pawn; Mr. Lyndon at Liberty; The Polar Star; Ultus and the Three-Button Mystery
Thewlis, David (act): Afraid of the Dark; Dragonheart; The Island of Dr. Moreau (1996); James and the Giant Peach; Seven Years In Tibet
T'hezan, Helia (act): The Phantom of the Opera (1990)
Thibault, Carl (act): The Monster Squad
Thibault, Debi (act): Galactic Gigolo; Psychos In Love
Thibeau, Jack (act): Alfred Hitchcock Presents; The Hitcher; Ms. 45; Warning Sign
Thiberghian, Jerome (act): Brainscan; Scanners
Thicke, Alan (act, b. 1947): And You Thought Your Parents Were Weird; Calendar Girl Murders; Stepmonster; Not Quite Human II; Still Not Quite Human
Thiele, Myriam (act): Making Contact
Thiele, Rolf (dir, 1918-1982): Grimm's Fairy Tales for Adults; Das Madchen Rosemarie
Thiele, Rolf (wri, 1918-1982): Grimm's Fairy Tales for Adults
Thiele, William (dir, 1890-1975): The Madonna's Secret; Tarzan's Desert Mystery; Tarzan Triumphs
Thieltges, Gary (cin): Eating Raoul; Retribution (1988)
Thierry, Richard (cin): I Lunghi Capelli della Morte
Thiessen, Tiffani-Amber (act, b. 1974): Buried Secrets
Thigpen, M.D., Corbett H. (wri): The Three Faces of Eve
Thigpen, Kevin (act): 12 Monkeys
Thigpen, Lynne (act): Hello Again; Pretty Poison (1996)

Thimig, Helen (act): Cloak and Dagger (1946); Cry Wolf (1947); Isle of the Dead (1945); The Locket
Thinnes, Roy (act, b. 1938): Alien High; Black Noon; Doppelganger (1969); The Horror at 37,000 Feet; The Norliss Tapes; The Other Man; Rush Week; Satan's School for Girls; Terminal; Whispering Death
Thirard, Armand (cin, b. 1899): Atoll K; Diabolique (1955); La Main du Diable; Le Salaire de la Peur
Thirloway, Greg (act): Zenon: Girl of the 21st Century
Third Ear Band, The (mus): Macbeth (1971)
Thirtle, Robert (act): Return to Oz
33 1/3 (mus): Boarding House
Thoeren, Robert (wri): Temptation (1946)
Thom, Harold (act): Invasion of the Girl Snatchers
Thom, Robert (dir): Angel, Angel, Down We Go
Thom, Robert (wri): Angel, Angel, Down We Go; Death Race 2000; Wild In the Streets
Thoma, Maralyn (wri): Killer's Delight
Thoma, Michael (act): Treasure Island (1990)
Thomas, Alfred (act): Tarzana, the Wild Girl
Thomas, Ali (act): Rain Without Thunder
Thomas, Amy Brandon (act): The Cry for Justice; The English Rose; Murder
Thomas, Andre (cin): Corridor of Mirrors; Torticola Contre Frankensberg
Thomas, Annika (act): Fortress
Thomas, Anthony (act): The Brother from Another Planet
Thomas, Basil (wri): Stop Press Girl
Thomas, Benny (act): Toomorrow
Thomas, Bernard B. (act): Pillow of Death
Thomas, Betty (dir, b. 1949): Dr. Dolittle (1998)
Thomas, Bill (act): Contact
Thomas, Christopher (mus): There's Nothing Out There
Thomas, Clarence (act): Shock Waves
Thomas, Craig (act): Star Trek
Thomas, Damien (act): Sinbad and the Eye of the Tiger; Tiffany Jones; Twins of Evil
Thomas, Daniel (act): The Ivory Ape
Thomas, Danny (act): Journey Back to Oz
Thomas, Dave (act): Boris and Natasha; Coneheads; Love at Stake; Pippi Longstocking
Thomas, David Jean (act): A.P.E.X.
Thomas, Della (act): Dr. Black Mr. Hyde
Thomas, Diane (wri): Always; The Jewel of the Nile; Romancing the Stone
Thomas, Doris (act): The Demons (1974)
Thomas, Drew (act): Akira
Thomas, Duane (act): Dr. Heckyl & Mr. Hype
Thomas, Dylan (wri, 1914-1953): The Doctor and the Devils; The Three Weird Sisters
Thomas, E. Leslie (act): The Brain from Planet Arous
Thomas, Ed (act): The Saint In Palm Springs
Thomas, Edward (cin): New Year's Evil
Thomas, Edward (mus): Willy McBean and His Magic Machine
Thomas, Elton (act): see Fairbanks Sr., Douglas
Thomas, Elton (wri): The Iron Mask
Thomas, Evan (act): Arrest Bulldog Drummond; The Hound Of The Baskervilles (1939)
Thomas, Frank (M.) (act): Desperate Chance for Ellery Queen; Forty Naughty Girls
Thomas, Frankie (act): Nancy Drew and the Hidden Staircase; Nancy Drew, Detective; Nancy Drew, Reporter; Nancy Drew, Troubleshooter
Thomas, Freyda (act): The Haunted (1991)
Thomas, George (act): Alien High
Thomas, Gerald (dir, b. 1920): Carry On Screaming; Carry On Spying; Chain of Events; The Solitary Child; The Vicious Circle (1957)
Thomas, Gretchen (act): I Was A Teenage Frankenstein
Thomas, Gwen (act): Phobia
Thomas, Harding (act): Ora Pro Nobis; St. Elmo
Thomas, Heather (act, b. 1957): Cyclone; Hidden Obsession; Red Blooded American Girl; Zapped!
Thomas, Henry (act, b. 1971): Beyond Obsession; Bombshell; Cloak and Dagger (1984); E.T.-The Extra-Terrestrial; Fire In the Sky (1993); Moby Dick (1998); Psycho IV: The Beginning; The Quest
Thomas, Hilary (act): The Fury
Thomas, Huw (act): First Men In the Moon (1964)
Thomas, Ian (mus): Bloodknot
Thomas, Jack W. (wri): Embryo
Thomas, James E./Jim (wri): Predator; Predator 2
Thomas, Jameson (act, 1892-1939): Charlie Chan In Egypt; Chu Chin Chow (1923); Convicted; Elstree Calling; High Treason (1929); Jane Eyre (1934); League of Frightened Men
Thomas, Jay (act): Encino Woman
Thomas, Jerry (dir): The Green Hornet
Thomas, John (act): The Lone Wolf Returns (1935)
Thomas, John (cin): Freeway; Shadow of the Hawk; Timecop
Thomas, John (C.) (wri): Predator; Predator 2
Thomas, John Joseph (act): Blood Beach
Thomas, Jonathan Taylor (act, b. 1981): The Adventures of Pinocchio (1996); The Lion King
Thomas, Kejo (act): Dr. Black Mr. Hyde
Thomas, Ken (act): Mars Attacks!
Thomas, Kristin Scott (act): Gulliver's Travels (1996); The Secret Life of Ian Fleming
Thomas, Larri (act): Curucu, Beast of the Amazon
Thomas, Larry (act): Night Ripper
Thomas, Lee (wri): Doctor Franken
Thomas, Leslie (act): Tormented (1960)
Thomas, Lionel (mus): Dracula Sucks
Thomas, Lisa (act): One Million Years B.C.
Thomas, Llewelyn (act): The Boogey Man
Thomas, Lyn (act): Arson for Hire; Space Master X-7
Thomas, Mark (act): The Final Countdown
Thomas, Marlo (act, b. 1943): In the Spirit; It Happened One Christmas
Thomas, Melody (act): The Beguiled; The Fury; Piranha (1978)
Thomas, Michael (wri): The Hunger; Ladyhawke; The McGuffin
Thomas, Michelle Rene (act): Midnight In Saint Petersburg
Thomas, Mickey (act): Dream a Little Dream
Thomas, Neville (act): King Solomon's Mines (1985)
Thomas, Patrick (act): Perfect Alibi
Thomas, Paul (act): Dracula Sucks; Secrets of the Phantom Caverns
Thomas, Peter (act): Tales from the Crypt (1971)
Thomas, Peter (mus): The Ape Creature; The Trygon Factor
Thomas, Philip M. (act): Stigma
Thomas, Queenie (act): Faust (1923); Her Redemption; Tut-Tut and His Terrible Tomb
Thomas, R.L. (dir): Apprentice to Murder
Thomas, Rachel (act, 1904-1995): Catacombs (1964)
Thomas, Ralph (dir, b. 1915): Deadlier Than the Male; Hot Enough for June; It's Not the Size That Counts; Mad About Men; Nobody Runs Forever; Percy; Quest for Love; Some Girls Do; The 39 Steps (1959); Venetian Bird
Thomas, Raymond Anthony (act): Jacob's Ladder
Thomas, Richard (act, b. 1951): Battle Beyond the Stars (1980); Big & Hairy; It (1990); Stalking Laura; The Todd Killings; You'll Like My Mother
Thomas, Robert (act): The Long Kiss Goodnight
Thomas, Robin (act): Amityville Dollhouse; Color Me Perfect; From the Dead of Night; Haunted by Her Past; Halloweentown; Memories of Murder; Svengali (1983)
Thomas, Rohn (act): The Dark Half
Thomas, Ron (act): Night Screams
Thomas, Ross (wri): Hammett
Thomas, Roy (act): Angel Heart
Thomas, Roy (wri): Conan the Destroyer; Fire and Ice
Thomas, Scott (act): Lost In Time
Thomas, Sharon (act): Star Trek III: The Search for Spock; Wheels of Terror
Thomas, Sian (act): Erik the Viking
Thomas, Tabetha (act): Edward Scissorhands
Thomas, Theodore (act): Timecop
Thomas, Timothy (act): Wolf
Thomas, Tressa (act): Flatliners
Thomas, Trevor (act): Inseminoid; Sheena; Transmutations
Thomas, Ty (act): Surf Nazis Must Die
Thomas, Victor (mus): The Adventures of Pinocchio (1996)
Thomas, Virginia (act): The Private Life of Helen of Troy
Thomas, William C. (dir, b. 1903): Big Town After Dark
Thomas, Yvonne (act): Spiritualism Exposed (1926)
Thomason, Donna (act): Stalking Laura
Thomason, Harry (dir): The Day It Came to Earth; Encounter with the Unknown; So Sad About Gloria
Thomason, Mark (act): Contact
Thomerson, Jack (act): Nemesis
Thomerson, Tim (act): Bad Channels; Cherry 2000; Die Watching; Dollman; Dollman vs. Demonic Toys; Dominion; Fade to Black; The Flash; Heatseeker; The Incredible Hulk Returns; Jekyll and Hyde...Together Again; Near Dark; Nemesis; Nemesis 3: Time Lapse; Remember My Name; Trancers; Trancers II: The Return of Jack Deth; Trancers III: Sudden Deth; Trancers 4: Jack of Swords; Trancers 5: Deth Lives; Zone Troopers
Thompson, Ada (act): see Merchant, Vivien
Thompson, Alina (act): Dead Cold
Thompson, Andrea (act): Doin' Time On Planet Earth
Thompson, Bill (act): Alice In Wonderland (1951); The Aristocats; Lady and the Tramp; Peter Pan (1953)
Thompson, Blanche (act): The Dungeon
Thompson, Blue (act): The Abomination
Thompson, Bob (act): The Giant Gila Monster
Thompson, Brett (dir): Adventures In Dinosaur City
Thompson, Brian (act): Alien Nation; Doctor Mordrid; Fright Night II; Dragonheart; Miracle Mile; Moon 44; Mortal Kombat: Annihilation; Nightwish; Star Trek: Generations
Thompson, Brit (act): Virtuosity
Thompson, Bud (act): Glen and Randa
Thompson, Carlos (act, b. 1916): Mistress of the World (1959); Raw Wind In Eden
Thompson, Caroline (wri): The Addams Family; Edward Scissorhands; The Nightmare Before Christmas
Thompson, Carolyn (act): Three On a Meathook
Thompson, Charles (act): Teenage Cave Man
Thompson, Cindy Ann (act): Cavegirl (1985)
Thompson, Cynthia (act): Not of This Earth (1988)
Thompson, Deborah (act): Flatliners
Thompson, Derek (act): Ghost (1990)
Thompson, Don (act): Battle Beyond the Stars (1980)
Thompson, Donald G. (wri): The Evil; Superstition
Thimpson, Elizabeth (act): The Car
Thompson, Emma (act, b. 1959): The Crucible (1996); Dead Again; Junior
Thompson, Emmalee (act): The Last Man On Planet Earth
Thompson, Eric (act): Dougal and the Blue Cat
Thompson, Estelle Merle O'Brien (act): see Oberon, Merle
Thompson, Fred Dalton (act): The Hunt for Red October; No Way Out
Thompson, Galen (act): The Evil
Thompson, Gary Scott (wri): Split Second (1992)
Thompson, Gordon (act): The Intruder (1981); Virus (1980)
Thompson, H.A.R. (cin): No Blade of Grass
Thompson, Harlan (wri): The Ghost Talks
Thompson, Heather (act): Jaws: The Revenge
Thompson, Helen (act): The Bloodless Vampire
Thompson, Henry (act): The Secret of the Moor
Thompson, Hilarie (act): Hex
Thompson, Hilary (act): Cruise Into Terror
Thompson, Howard (wri): The Glitterball
Thompson, Hugh (act): The Altar Stairs; Queen of the Sea
Thompson, Ian (act): Madhouse
Thompson, J. Lee (dir, b. 1914): Battle for the Planet of the Apes; Cape Fear (1961); Conquest of the Planet of the Apes; Eye of the Devil; Firewalker; Happy Birthday to Me; I Aim at the Stars; King Solomon's Mines (1985); Mackenna's Gold; Murder Without Crime; No Trees In the Street; The Reincarnation of Peter Proud; Return from the Ashes; The Yellow Balloon; Yield to the Night
Thompson, J. Lee (wri, b. 1914): East of Piccadilly; For Them That Trespass; Murder Without Crime; The Yellow Balloon
Thompson, Jack (act, b. 1940): Flesh & Blood
Thompson, James B. (act): Gunbed
Thompson, Jamie (cin): Cyborg 2: Glass Shadow; Grave Secrets
Thompson, Jeanne (act): Abbott and Costello Go to Mars
Thompson, Jeffrey (act): Shadow Conspiracy; Wolfen
Thompson, Jim (wri): After Dark, My Sweet; The Killer Inside Me
Thompson, Jimmy (GB act): The Whole Truth
Thompson, Jimmy (USA act): Forbidden Planet
Thompson, Jody (act): Perfect Little Angels
Thompson, John (act): The Merry Men of Sherwood
Thompson, John Jenner (act): see Dall, John
Thompson, Joy (act): Prom Night
Thompson, Kenneth (act): Just Imagine
Thompson, Kenneth (wri): The Fall of the House of Usher (1950)
Thompson, Kevin (act): Blade Runner; The Ewok Adventure; Night of the Creeps; Weird Science
Thompson, Lea (act, b. 1961): Back to the Future; Back to the Future, Part II; Back to the Future, Part III; Howard the Duck; Jaws 3-D; Red Dawn; Spacecamp
Thompson, Leslie (act): Arnold; Terror In the Wax Museum
Thompson, Linda (act): RoboCop 2
Thompson, Marc Anthony (act): Slam Dance
Thompson, Mark (act): Jason Goes to Hell: The Final Friday
Thompson, Marshall (act, 1925-1992): Around the World Under the Sea; Bog; The Cockeyed Miracle; Cruise Into Terror; Cult of the Cobra; Dial 1119; The Fall of the House of Usher (1958); Fiend Without a Face; First Man Into Space; Flight of the Lost Balloon; The Formula; It!—The Terror from Beyond Space; Mystery Street; The Secret Man; White Dog
Thompson, Martin (act): Mr. Destiny
Thompson, Matt (act): D.O.A. (1988)
Thompson, Melvin (act): Killer Klowns from Outer Space
Thompson, Neil (act): Mad Max; Modern Problems
Thompson, Paul (act): The Disembodied; Jungle Man-Eaters; Valley of the Headhunters
Thompson, Peter (Euro act): Kemek; Twins of Evil
Thompson, Peter (USA act): A Double Life (1947)
Thompson, Ray (act): Jungle Trail of the Son of Tarzan
Thompson, Phyllis (act): Heavy Traffic
Thompson, Raymond (act): Superman (1978)
Thompson, Richard (cin): Weird Science
Thompson, Richard S. (mus): The Eliminator
Thompson, Rick (act): Empire of Ash III
Thompson, Rob (wri): Ratboy
Thompson, Robert (act): Patrick; Road Games; Thirst
Thompson, Robert E. (wri): Brave New World (1980); The Hound Of The Baskervilles (1972)
Thompson, Ross (act): The Chain Reaction (1980)
Thompson, Scott (act): Future Shock; Millennium; Popcorn
Thompson, Shawn Alex (act): Heads
Thompson, Slim (act): Green Pastures
Thompson, Stewart (act): The Odyssey
Thompson, Susanna (act): Bermuda Triangle (1996)
Thompson, Terry (act): Blood Diner
Thompson, Tia (act): The Horrible House On the Hill
Thompson, "Tiger" (act): Earthbound (1981); The Legend of Sleepy Hollow
Thompson, Wesley (act): Amazons (1984); Casper
Thompson, William (C.) (cin): The Astounding She-Monster; Bride of the Monster; Glen or Glenda?; The Golden Mistress; Plan 9 from Outer Space
Thompson-Carlin, Deborah (act): Prison Planet
Thomsen, Gregg (act): Soultaker
Thomsen, Richard (act): Twisted
Thomsett, Sally (act): Straw Dogs
Thomson, Alex (cin): Alien 3; The Cat and the Canary (1978); Date With an Angel; Deathline; Demolition Man; Dr. Phibes Rises Again; Electric Dreams; Excalibur; Fear Is the Key; Hamlet (1996); High Spirits; The Keep; Legend; Leviathan; Mr. Destiny; The Night Digger; The Scarlet Letter (1995); Wings of Fame
Thomson, Anna (act): Blood Run; The Crow (1994)
Thomson, Beatrix (act): The Story of Shirley Yorke
Thomson, Brian (wri): Shock Treatment! (1981)
Thomson, Chris (dir): Meteorites!; Trucks
Thomson, Davidson (act): Jacob's Ladder
Thomson, Gordon (act): Explosion; Starship Invasions
Thomson, Helen (act): Bloodmoon (1990)
Thomson, Kenneth (act): Held for Murder
Thomson, Kim (act): Hands of a Murderer; Jekyll and Hyde
Thomson, Margaret (dir): Child's Play (1954)
Thomson, Marsh (act): Operation C.I.A.
Thomson, R.H. (act): An American Christmas Carol
Thomson, Rosalyn (act): Edward Scissorhands
Thomson, Scott (act): Frightmare (1983); Ghoulies; Parasite; Twister
Thoolen, Gerard (act): The Lift; Prospero's Books

Thor (mus): Zombie Nightmare
Thor, Cameron (act): Jurassic Park
Thor, Jerome (act, b. 1920): House of the Black Death; Mr. Sycamore
Thor, Jon-Mikl (act): The Edge of Hell; Zombie Nightmare
Thor, Jon-Mikl (wri): The Edge of Hell
Thor, Larry (act): The Amazing Colossal Man
Thorburn, June (act, 1931-1967): Escort for Hire; Fury at Smugglers' Bay; Master Spy (1963); The Price of Silence; The Scarlet Blade; The Three Worlds of Gulliver; Tom Thumb; Transatlantic
Thordsen, Kelly (act, 1916-1978): Charley and the Angel; Invasion of the Saucer Men; The Misadventures of Merlin Jones; Now You See Him, Now You Don't
Thoren, Ernest (wri): An Act of Murder (1948)
Thorley, Ken (act): The Adventures of Galgameth; Ghost In the Machine
Thorn, Ray (act): The Incredible 2-Headed Transplant
Thorn, Ronald Scott (wri): The Full Treatment
Thornberg, Betty (act): see Hutton, Betty
Thornbury, Bill (act): Phantasm; Phantasm III: Lord of the Dead
Thorndike, Oliver (act): Bulldog Drummond at Bay (1947)
Thorndike, Russell (act): The Bells (1923); Fiddlers Three; Lucrezia Borgia: or, Plaything of Power; Macbeth (1922); Puppets of Fate; Richard III (1955); The Roof; Scrooge (1923); The Shot In the Dark; Whispering Tongues
Thorndike, (Dame) Sybil (act, 1882-1976): Britannia Mews; Esmeralda; Jane Shore (1922); Jet Storm; Macbeth (1922); The Scarlet Letter (1922); Stage Fright (1950)
Thorndyke, Russell (wri): Captain Clegg; Dr. Syn; Dr. Syn-Alias the Scarecrow
Thorne, Angela (act): Yellow Dog
Thorne, Anthony (wri): The Bad Lord Byron; So Long at the Fair
Thorne, Dyanne (act): Hellhole; Point of Terror
Thorne, E.P. (wri): Three Silent Men
Thorne, Gary (act): The Depraved
Thorne, Guy (wri): The Disappearance of the Judge
Thorne, Ken(neth) (mus): Arabian Adventure; The Bed-Sitting Room; Escape Clause;The House Where Evil Dwells; The Hunchback of Notre Dame (1982); The Magic Christian; The Return of Sherlock Holmes (1986); Royal Flash; Sunset Grill; Superman II; Superman III
Thorne, Mike (mus): Memoirs of a Survivor
Thorne, Regina (act): Pacto Diabolico; La Senora Muerte
Thorne, Richard (act): For Heaven's Sake
Thorne, Stephen (act): Kadoyng; Runaway (1984)
Thorne, Tracy (act): The Exorcist III
Thorne-Smith, Courtney (act): Beauty's Revenge
Thornhill, Mark (act): Secrets of the Phantom Caverns
Thornley, Sophia (act): The Hound of London
Thornley, Steven (wri): Hangar 18
Thornton, Ann (act): Arthur the King
Thornton, Billy Bob (act, b. 1955): Armageddon; Chopper Chicks In Zombietown; Out There; Sling Blade
Thornton, Billy Bob (dir & wri, b. 1955): Sling Blade
Thornton, Christopher (act): Watchers II
Thornton, Cyril (act): The Adventures of Robin Hood; The Thin Man
Thornton, Edward (act): My Lord Conceit
Thornton, Evans (act): Night of the Lepus
Thornton, F. Martin (act): The Tempter (1913)
Thornton, F. Martin (dir): The Fish and the Ring; In Gollywog Land; In the Days of Robin Hood; The Iron Stair (1920); Jane Shore (1915); Love and War In Toyland; Melody of Death; Mephisto; My Lord Conceit; The New Adventures of Baron Munchausen; Santa Claus (1912); The Second Penalty; The Splendid Coward; The Tempter (1913)
Thornton, F. Martin (wri): The Iron Stair (1920); My Lord Conceit
Thornton, Frank (act): The Bed-Sitting Room; Carry On Screaming; Digby-The Biggest Dog In the World; The Murder Game; The Private Life of Sherlock Holmes; Radio Cab Murder; The Tell-Tale Heart (1960); The Tomb of Ligeia; Vampira
Thornton, John (act): Plymouth
Thornton, Lou (act): Wes Craven's New Nightmare
Thornton, Peter (act): Theater of Blood
Thornton, Ralph (wri): Blood of Dracula; I Was a Teenage Werewolf
Thornton, Ron (wri): Hypernauts
Thornton, Sigrid (act): The Day After Halloween; Trapped In Space
Thornton-Sherwood, Madeleine (act, b. 1926): The Changeling; Haunted by Her Past
Thorp, Richard (act): Lancelot and Guinevere
Thorpe, Dickie (act): Lieutenant Daring and the Plans of the Minefields
Thorpe, George (act): Daughter of Darkness (1948)
Thorpe, Gordon (act): The Bridge of San Luis Rey (1929); The Iron Mask
Thorpe, Harry (cin): Rupert of Hentzau (1923)
Thorpe, Jerry (dir, b. 1930): Crosscurrent; The Possessed (1977); Smile, Jenny, You're Dead; The Venetian Affair
Thorpe, Madge (act): The Adventures of Dick Turpin-The King of Highwaymen
Thorpe, Richard (dir, 1896-1991, nee Rollo Smolt Thorpe): Above Suspicion; The House of the Seven Hawks; Knights of the Round Table; Night Must Fall (1937); The Prisoner of Zenda (1952); The Scorpio Letters; Secret of the Chateau; The Tartars; Tarzan Escapes; Tarzan Finds a Son!; Tarzan's New York Adventure; Tarzan's Secret Treasure; The Thin Man Goes Home
Thorpe, Rose H. (wri): Curfew Must Not Ring Tonight; Curfew Shall Not Ring Tonight
Thorpe, Ted (act): Savage Mutiny
Thorpe-Bates, Peggy (act): The Saint and the Brave Goose
Thorsen, Sven (act): Cyborg 2: Glass Shadow
Thorson, Linda (act): Curtains
Thorson, Russ(ell) (act): Half-Human; My Blood Runs Cold; Night Slaves; Please Murder Me; The Screaming Woman; 36 Hours (1965); Two On a Guillotine
Thourlby, William (act): The Creeping Terror; Destination Inner Space
Thrasher, Sunny Besen (act): The Care Bears Movie
Three Eddies, The (act): Elstree Calling
Threlt, Maggie (act): Dimension 5
Thring, Frank (act): Howling III; The Man from Hong Kong
Throne, Malachi (act): Eat and Run
Thulin, Ingrid (act, b. 1929): Ansiktet; The Cassandra Crossing; Foreign Intrigue; Return from the Ashes; Smultronstallet; Tystnaden;Vargtimmen
Thunder, Rino (act): Wolfen
Thunderbolt, C.J. (act): Mr. Moto Takes a Chance
Thundercloud, Chief (act): The Falcon Out West
Thunderwolf (act): Dead Connection; Nemesis
Thunhurst, Bill (act): Jack's Wife
Thurber, James (wri, 1894-1961): The Secret Life of Walter Mitty
Thurseon, Debbie (act): The Prey (1980)
Thurman, Betsy (act): Ganja and Hess
Thurman, Beverly (act): The Giant Gila Monster
Thurman, Bill(y) (act): Creature from Black Lake; Curse of the Swamp Creature; In the Year 2889; It's Alive! (1968); Mars Needs Women; Mountaintop Motel Massacre; Night Fright; Zontar: The Thing from Venus
Thurman, Uma (act, b. 1970): The Adventures of Baron Munchausen (1989); The Avengers; Batman and Robin; Gattaca; Jennifer 8; Les Miserables (1998); Robin Hood (1991)
Thurmond, Lin (act): Santa Claus Conquers the Martians
Thurn-Taxis, Alexis (dir): A Night for Crime
Thursby, David/Dave (act): The Adventures of Robin Hood; Bulldog Drummond at Bay (1947); Devotion; The Undying Monster
Thursfield, Sophie (act): The Girl In a Swing
Thurston, Carol (act): The Conspirators; The Hypnotic Eye; Killer Ape; Swamp Fire;Women of Pitcairn Island
Thurston, E. Temple (wri): The Wandering Jew (1933)
Thurston, Harry (act): And Then There Were None
Thurston, Pepper (act): Invasion of the Girl Snatchers
Thurston, Robert (act): I Still Dream of Jeannie
Thurston, Sammy (act): Hellhole
Thurston, Ted (act): The Man In the Santa Claus Suit
Thynne, Alexander (wri): Blue Blood
Thyssen, Greta (act): Journey to the Seventh Planet; Terror Is a Man
Tibbetts, Martha (act): Meet Nero Wolfe
Tibbles, George (wri): Halloween With the Addams Family; Munster, Go Home!
Tiberghien, Jerome (act): City On Fire; Happy Birthday to Me; Oh Heavenly Dog; Rabid; Secret Weapons
Tichenor, Edna (act): London After Midnight
Tichy, Gerard (act): La Cara del Terror; Gladiators Seven; Hatchet for a Honeymoon; Horror; Master Stroke; The Mysterious Island of Captain Nemo; La Orgia de los Muertos; Pieces; The Sea Serpent; Superargo vs. Diabolicus
Tickle, Frank (act): The Bank Messenger Mystery; Twin Faces
Tickner, Clive (cin): The Inside Man; Loch Ness; The Puppet Masters; Split Second (1992)
Tickner, French (act): The Death of the Incredible Hulk
Tickner, Royston (act): Diamonds On Wheels
Tickner, Shane (act): Mad Max Beyond Thunderdome
Tico, Randy (mus): Ghosts Can't Do It
Ticotin, Rachel (act, b. 1959): Total Recall
Tidy, Frank (cin): The Butcher's Wife; Chain Reaction (1996); Hitler's Daughter; The Package; Slipstream; Sorry, Wrong Number (1989); Spacehunter: Adventures In the Forbidden Zone
Tidyman, Ernest (wri, 1928-1984): A Force of One
Tieche, Gary (cin): Amanda and the Alien; Out There
Tiemeyer, Hans (act): Spy In the Sky
Tieri, Arnoldo (act): The Man Who Wagged His Tail
Tiernan, Andrew (act): Snow White: A Tale of Terror
Tiernate, Anumwat (act): Vice Versa (1988)
Tierney, Gene (act, 1920-1991): Black Widow (1954); Las Cuatro Noches de la Luna Llena; Daughter of the Mind; Dragonwyck; The Ghost and Mrs. Muir; Heaven Can Wait (1942); Laura; Leave Her to Heaven
Tierney, Jacob (act): Josh and S.A.M.
Tierney, Jerry (act): see Brady, Scott
Tierney, Lawrence (act, b. 1919): Anduction; Born to Kill; The Devil Thumbs a Ride; The Female Jungle; Ghost Ship (1943); The Horror Show; Kill or Be Killed (1950); Midnight (1980); Naked Evil; The Offspring; Silver Bullet; Step by Step
Tierney, Malcolm (act): The Medusa Touch; The Saint
Tierney, Maura (act, b. 1965): Dead Women In Lingerie; Instinct; Liar Liar; Primal Fear; The Temp
Tierney, Shawn (act): Curse II: The Bite
Tierney, Terrence (act): Beverly Hills Bodysnatchers
Tiersten, Jonathan (act): Sleepaway Camp
Tiezzi, Augusto (cin): The Conquest of Mycenae
Tiffany (act): Jetsons: The Movie
Tigar, Kenneth (act): The Babysitter; Creator; 18 Again!; Phantasm II; Primal Fear
Tigerman, Gary (act): Pretty Maids All In a Row
Tighe, Karen (act): The Deadly Spawn
Tighe, Kevin (act): Escape to Witch Mountain (1995)
Tignor, Tammie M. (act): Student Bodies
Tigrett, Isaac (act): Nothing But Trouble
Tik (act): Xtro
Tikhomirov, Roman (dir): Queen of Spades (1960)
Til, Roger (act): Stargate; 12 to the Moon; Valley of the Dragons
Tilbury, Zeffie (act, 1863-1945): After the Thin Man; Arrest Bulldog Drummond; Bulldog Drummond Escapes; Bulldog Drummond's Peril; Charlie Chan Carries On; The Last Days of Pompeii (1935); Mystery Liner; The Mystery of Edwin Drood (1935); Werewolf of London
Tilden, Lawrence (act): La Figlia di Frankenstein
Tilden, Leif (act): Teenage Mutant Ninja Turtles
Tilden, Peter (act): Shocker
Tilghman, Robin (act): He Knows You're Alone
Till, Eric (dir, b. 1929): An American Christmas Carol; Clarence
Till, Jenny (act): A Challenge for Robin Hood; No.1 of the Secret Service; Theatre of Death
Till, Justine (act): An American Christmas Carol
Till, Tilde (act): Cinque Tombe per un Medium
Tillach, Allison (act): Mutants In Paradise
Tillach, Lynne (act): Mutants In Paradise
Tillar, Jack (mus): Alligator II: The Mutation; The Man Who Saw Tomorrow
Tilldon-Davis, Diana (act): Howling IV
Tiller, Nadja (act, b. 1929): The Burning Court; The Dead Are Alive; Killer Spy; Das Madchen Rosemarie
Tiller, Stephen (act): The Saint; Without a Clue
Tilles, Faye (act): The Galaxy Invader
Tilley, Frank (dir): The Pied Piper of Hamelin
Tilley, Patrick (wri): The Legacy; The People That Time Forgot; Wuthering Heights (1970)
Tillinger, John (act): Hello Again
Tillitt, James (act): Hellbound: Hellraiser II
Tillman, Fritz (act): Confess, Dr. Corda
Tillman, Mike (act): The Alien's Return; Uninvited (1987)
Tillmanns, R.L. (dir): Witchcraft III: The Kiss of Death
Tillotson, Johnny (act): The Fat Spy
Tilly, Jennifer (act): Bride of Chucky; Heads; High Spirits; Liar Liar; The Nosferatu Diaries: Embrace of the Vampire; Remote Control (1988)
Tilly, Meg (act, b. 1960): The Body Snatchers; The Girl In a Swing; Impulse (1984); One Dark Night; Psycho II
Tilsely, Reg (mus): The Haunted House of Horror
Tilsey, Vincent (wri): The Hunchback of Notre Dame (1965)
Tilson-Chowne, C. (act): The Loudwater Mystery
Tilton, Charlene (act, b. 1958): The Fall of the House of Usher (1982); The Silence of the Hams
Tilton, Connie (act): The Haunting; When Dinosaurs Ruled the Earth
Tilton, Miles (act): Premonition (1972)
Tilvern, Alan (act): The Bespoke Overcoat; Chase a Crooked Shadow; Danger by My Side; The Frozen Dead; Little Shop of Horrors (1986); The Malpas Mystery; Rasputin, the Mad Monk; Superman (1978)
Tim, Tany (act): Crocodile
Timbes, Graham (act): Jack's Back
Timko, Johnny (act): Prophecy (1979); Weird Science
Timm, Bruce W. (dir): Batman: Mask of the Phantasm
Timm, Doug (mus): The Man Who Fell to Earth (1987); Nightflyers
Timm, Marjorie May (act): Charlie Chan at the Opera
Timmerman, Diane (act): The Package
Timmins, Cali (act): Spacehunter: Adventures In the Forbidden Zone
Timmons, Lori (act): Happy Birthday to Me
Timms, Stanley (act): Ms. 45
Timoney, Mary (act): The Cradle Will Fall
Timp, Coby (act): The Lift
Tindall, Hilary (act): Yellow Dog
Tindall, Loren (act, 1920-1973): Francis; Power of the Whistler
Tinder, Paul (act): The Goddess of Love
Tingwell, Charles (act, b. 1924): Bobbikins; Dracula, Prince of Darkness; Endplay; Murder Ahoy; Murder at the Gallop; Murder Most Foul; Murder She Said; Nobody Runs Forever; The Secret of Blood Island; Tarzan the Magnificent; Thunderbirds Are Go
Tingwell, Virginia (act): Tam Lin
Tinling, James (dir, 1889-1955): Charlie Chan In Shanghai; Mr Moto's Gamble; Tales of Robin Hood
Tinling, Therese Xavier (act): The Hand That Rocks the Cradle
Tinnell, Robert (act): Surf Nazis Must Die
Tinnell, Robert (dir): Frankenstein and Me
Tinney, Lloyd (act): The Resurrected
Tino, Mike (act): Vampire at Midnight
Tinsley, Jack (act): 4D Man
Tin Tan (act): La Casa del Terror; El Fantasma de la Opereta; Gregorio and His Angel
Tinti, Gabriele (act): Caged Women (1984); Emanuelle e gli Ultimi Cannibali; House of Exorcism; The Mysterious Island of Captain Nemo; Passager de la Pluie; The Secret of Seagull Island; Sodom and Gomorrah
Tintle, David (act): Jaws 2
Tinyanov, Yuri (act & wri): Shinel (1926)
Tiny Tim (act, 1932-1996): Blood Harvest
Tiomkin, Dmitri (mus, 1894-1979): The Adventures of Hajji Baba; Alice In Wonderland (1933); Angel Face; Angel On My Shoulder (1946); The Bridge of San Luis Rey (1944); The Casino Murder Case; Champagne for Caesar; The Corsican Brothers (1941); The Dark Mirror (1946); Dial M for Murder (1954); D.O.A. (1949); It's a Wonderful Life; The Lady In the Iron Mask; Land of the Pharaohs; Lost Horizon (1937); Mackenna's Gold; Peking Express; Portrait of Jennie; Shadow of a Doubt (1943); The Steel Trap; Strangers On a Train; Tarzan and the Mermaids; The Thing from Another World
Tippett, Phil (cin): RoboCop 2; Three Wishes (1995)
Tippit, Wayne (act): Running Against Time
Tipple, Gordon (act): Time Runner
Tippo, Patti (act): Ed Wood
Tipton, Brian (cin): Nothing But Trouble
Tipton, George Aliceson (mus): The Demon Murder Case; Red Alert
Tirard, Ann (act): The Full Treatment; Memoirs of a Survivor; Perfect Friday; Recluse; The Witches (1990)

Tirelli, Jaime (act): The Brother from Another Planet
Tirl, George (cin): The Initiation; Steel Dawn
Tisdall, Billy (act): Mad Max
Tissier, Jean (act): The Hunchback of Notre Dame (1957)
Titheradge, Dion (wri): Dangerous Ground
Titheradge, Madge (act): Brigadier Gerard; The Woman Who Was Nothing
Titmuss, Phyllis (act): The Recoil (1922)
Tittell-Brune, Fanny (act): Iron Justice
Tittinger, Greg (wri): Beyond the Living
Tittle, Bently (act): Dark Universe
Tittle, La Donna (act): The Relic
Titus, Chris (act): Killer Klowns from Outer Space
Titus, Eve (wri): The Great Mouse Detective
Tjernberg, Ove (act): Morianna
Tkaczyk, Jan (cin): Bezludna Planeta
T'Kaye, Eileen (act): Magic In the Mirror
To, Johnny (dir): The Heroic Trio
Toal, Maureen (act): A Guy Called Caesar; Otley
Tobey, Ken(neth) (act): The Beast from 20,000 Fathoms; Ben; Cry Terror!; Down Three Dark Streets; Ghost Writer; Gremlins; Gremlins 2: The New Batch; Homebodies; Honey, I Blew Up the Kid; The Howling; Innerspace; It Came from Beneath the Sea; The Lost Empire; Rage; Ring of Fear; The Search for Bridey Murphy; Single White Female; Stark Fear; Strange Invaders; The Thing from Another World; 20 Million Miles to Earth; The Vampire (1957); X-15
Tobey, Robert (cin): Space Monster
Tobias, George (act, 1901-1980): Between Two Worlds; The Hunchback of Notre Dame (1939); The Magic Carpet; Nightmare In the Sun; The Night Strangler; Out of the Fog (1941); The Set-Up (1949); Sinbad the Sailor; The Tattered Dress
Tobias, Oliver (act): Arabian Adventure; The God King; King Arthur, the Young Warlord; Last Video and Testament; Mata Hari (1985); Terror from Within; The Wicked Lady
Tobin, Bud (wri): The Playbirds
Tobin, Dan (act, 1909-1982): The Big Clock; Black Limelight; Herbie Rides Again; The Velvet Touch
Tobin, Genevieve (act, b. 1904): The Great Gambini; The Man In the Mirror
Tobin, Katharine (act): The Bad Seed (1985)
Tobin, Matthew (act): The Telephone Book
Tobin, Niall (act): Lovespell; Rawhead Rex
Tobin, Roy (act): Just Imagine
Tobisch, Lotte (act): The Last Ten Days of Adolf Hitler
Tobolowsky, Stephen (act): Deadlock; Dr. Jekyll and Ms. Hyde; Groundhog Day; Josh and S.A.M.; Keep My Grave Open; Memoirs of an Invisible Man; Night Visitors; The Philadelphia Experiment; Single White Female
Toby, Doug (act): Red Dawn
Tobyansen, John (act): When a Stranger Calls
Tocci, Bruno (act): Robin Hood and the Pirates
Tocci, Chigo (act): The Secret of Seagull Island
Toch, (Dr.) Ernst (mus, 1887-1964): The Cat and the Canary (1939); Dr. Cyclops; The Ghost Breakers; Ladies In Retirement; Peter Ibbetson; The Unseen (1945)
Tochi, Brian (act): The Octagon; The Omega Man
Tock, Louis (act): The Diabolical Invention
Tod, Malcolm (act): The Bruce Partington Planes; The Crimson Circle (1922); Hutch Stirs 'em Up
Todd, Ann (GB act, b. 1909): Beware, My Brethren; Daybreak; The Fiend (1972); The Ghost Train (1931); The Green Scarf; Madeleine; The McGuffin; The Paradine Case; Poison Pen; The Return of Bulldog Drummond; So Evil My Love; The Sound Barrier;
The Squeaker (1937); A Taste of Fear; Things to Come; Time Without Pity
Todd, Ann (USA act, b. 1932, nee Ann Todd Mayfield): The Lion Hunters
Todd, Antonio (act): The Fear (1994); Shadow Conspiracy
Todd, Arthur (L.) (cin): The Adventurous Blonde; The Brass Bottle (1923); The Florentine Dagger; Torchy Gets Her Man; Torchy Plays With Dynamite
Todd, Beverly (act): The Ghost of Flight 401
Todd, Bob (act): Digby-The Biggest Dog In the World; The Flying Sorceror; Scars of Dracula; Superman III
Todd, Erica (act): Covenant
Todd, George (act): Creature of the Walking Dead

Todd, James (act): Charlie Chan's Chance; Francis;The Lone Wolf and His Lady; The Luck of the Irish; Trapped
Todd, Johanne (act): Android
Todd, Larry (cin): Dr. Dracula
Todd, Lisa (act): Blood Hook; The Devil's Rain; The Doll Squad; Woman Hunt
Todd, Lola (act): The Bells (1926)
Todd, Mabel (act): The Ghost and the Guest
Todd, Michael (act): Neon Maniacs; Puppet Master II
Todd, Rachel (act): The Hidden
Todd, Richard (act, b. 1919): Asylum (1972); The Big Sleep (1978); The Boys; Chase a Crooked Shadow; Death Drums Along the River; Dorian Gray; For Them That Trespass; The Gentle Art of Murder; House of the Long Shadows; Intent to Kill; The Interrupted Journey; Lightning Strikes Twice; Marie Antoinette (1953); Never Let Go; Not Guilty; No. 1 of the Secret Service; Operation Crossbow; Stage Fright (1950); The Story of Robin Hood; Subterfuge; Venetian Bird; The Very Edge
Todd, Russell (act, b. 1960): Chopping Mall; Friday the 13th-Part 2; He Knows You're Alone;Sweet Murder
Todd, Ryan (act): A Dangerous Affair; First Knight
Todd, Sally (act): Frankenstein's Daughter (1958); The Unearthly; The Viking Women and the Sea Serpent
Todd, Thelma (act, 1906-1935): The Haunted House (1929); The House of Horror (1929); The Maltese Falcon (1931); Seven Footprints to Satan
Todd, Toni (act): Philo Vance's Gamble; Philo Vance's Secret Mission
Todd, Tony (act): Babylon 5: A Call to Arms; Beastmaster III: The Eye of Braxus; Bram Stoker's 'Shadowbuilder'; The Bride In Black; Candyman; Candyman: Farewell to the Flesh; The Crow (1994); Night of the Living Dead (1990); Them (1996); Voodoo Dawn; Wishmaster
Todesco, Anita (act): Morgan the Pirate
Toeche-Mittler, Karin (act): L'Annee Derniere a Marienbad
Toes, Malcolm (act): No Blade of Grass
Tofflemire, Anne (act): Howard the Duck
Toffolo, Lino (act): When Women Had Tails
Togin, Chotaro (act): Godzilla's Revenge
Tognazzi, Ugo (act, 1922-1990): Barbarella; La Donna Scimmia; Majstori i Margarita; My Friend, Dr. Jekyll; Psycosissimo
Toguri, David (act): Koroshi
Tohill, Tamara (act): Test Tube Teens from the Year 2000
Toji, Marcus (act): Toothless
Tok (act): Xtro
Tokar, Norman (dir, 1920-1979): The Cat from Outer Space
Tokuda, Marilyn (act): The Jitters
Tokunaga, Reiko (act): Time of the Apes
Tokunaga, Tom (cin): The Package
Tokunda, Marilyn (act): Xanadu
Tokuno, Dean (act): Poltergeist III
Tol, Henriette (act): Gebroken Spiegels; A Question of Silence
Tolan, Kathleen (act): The Rosary Murders
Tolan, Michael (act): All That Jazz; Hiawatha (1952)
Toland, Gregg (cin, 1904-1948): The Bishop's Wife; Bulldog Drummond (1929); Condemned (1929); Mad Love; Les Miserables (1935); Roman Scandals; Wuthering Heights (1939)
Tolbert, Berlinda (act): A Connecticut Yankee In King Arthur's Court (1989); Dangerous Touch
Tolces, Todd (act): The Haunting of Sarah Hardy
Tolden, Michael (act): Curse of the Swamp Creature
Toledo, Fabiola (act): Demons (1985)
Toledo, Jose (act): Nightwing
Toler, Sidney (act, 1875-1947): Black Magic (1944); Castle In the Desert; Charlie Chan at the Wax Museum; Charlie Chan at Treasure Island; Charlie Chan In City In Darkness; Charlie Chan In Honolulu; Charlie Chan In Panama; Charlie Chan In Reno; Charlie Chan In Rio; Charlie Chan In the Secret Service; Charlie Chan's Murder Cruise; The Chinese Cat; Dangerous Money; Dark Alibi; Dead Men Tell; The Jade Mask; King of the Jungle; Murder Over New York; The Red Dragon (1965); The Scarlet Clue; Shadows Over Chinatown; The Trap; White Savage
Toles-Bey, John (act): Extreme Measures; The Nature of the Beast
Toley, Guy (act): Congo

Tolkan, James (act, b. 1931): Back to the Future, Part II; Dick Tracy (1990); Iceman; Masters of the Universe; Nightmares (1983); They Might Be Giants; War Games; Werewolf of Washington; Wolfen
Tolkien, J.R.R. (wri, 1892-1973): The Hobbit; The Lord of the Rings; The Return of the King
Tolkin, Mel (wri): The Last of the Secret Agents?
Tolkin, Michael (wri): Deep Impact
Tolkin, Stephen (wri): Captain America (1992); Dean Koontz' 'Mr. Murder'; Intensity
Toll, John (cin): Jack
Toll, Judy (act): The Brave Little Toaster
Tollaire, August (act): The Monkey Talks
Tolnas, Gunnar (act): Himmelskibet
Tolnay, Akos (wri): The Avenging Hand (1936); Elephant Boy; Return of a Stranger
Tolo, Marilu' (act, b. 1948): Messalina Against the Son of Hercules; Sleep of Death; Terror of Rome Against the Son of Hercules; Il Trionfo di Ercole
Tolsky, Susan (act): Charley and the Angel; Pretty Maids All In a Row
Tolstoy, Alexei (wri, 1828-1910): Aelita; I Tre Volti della Paura
Tolstoy, Leo (wri): Agi Murad, il Diavolo Bianco
Tolubeyev, Y. (act): Shinel (1965)
Tolzac, Jean (act): Revenge In the House of Usher
Tom, Alonso Mendez (act): Chac
Tom, David (act): Stay Tuned; Stepfather III: Father's Day
Tom Jr., Layne (act): Charlie Chan at the Olympics; Charlie Chan In Honolulu; Charlie Chan's Murder Cruise
Toma, Michael (act): Winter Kills
Tomack, David (act): The Spider (1958)
Tomack, Sid (act): Boston Blackie's Chinese Venture; Crime Doctor's Diary
Tomaino, Titti (act): La Ragazza Che Sapeva Troppo
Tomalin, O'Brien (wri): Slaughter
Tomanoczy, Winona (act): Glen and Randa
Tomanovich, Dara (act): Bio-Dome
Tomarken, Peter (act): Heaven Can Wait (1978)
Tomasino, Jeana (act): The Capture of Bigfoot; Looker
Tombes, Andrew (act, b. 1891): Charlie Chan at the Olympics; Close Call for Ellery Queen; Phantom Lady
Tombragel, Maurice (wri):Boston Blackie's Chinese Venture; The Creeper (1948); Horror Island; The Lone Wolf In Mexico; Moon Pilot; Trapped by Boston Blackie
Tomecko, John (act): Project Moonbase
Tomei, Lisa (wri): Godzilla 1985
Tomek, Eric (wri): Alien Contamination
Tomelty, Frances (act): The Medusa Touch
Tomelty, Joseph (act, b. 1910): Black Torment; Devil Girl from Mars; Hell Is a City; A Kid for Two Farthings; Lancelot and Guinevere; Life Is a Circus; Meet Mr. Lucifer; Moby Dick (1956); The Oracle (1952); A Prize of Gold; The Sound Barrier; Timeslip;Tread Softly Stranger
Tomioka, Mike (cin): War of the Wizards
Tomioka, Mototaka (cin): Terror of Mechagodzilla
Tomita, Tamlyn (act): Babylon 5: The Gathering; The Killing Jar; The last Man On Planet Earth
Tomlin, Lily (act, b. 1939): All of Me; The Incredible Shrinking Woman
Tomlinson, D. Geoff (act): Agatha
Tomlinson, David (act, b. 1917): Bedknobs and Broomsticks; Bon Baisers de Hong Kong; Calling Bulldog Drummond; The City Under the Sea; Dominique; The Fiendish Plot of Dr. Fu Manchu; The Liquidator; The Love Bug; Mary Poppins; Miranda; My Brother's Keeper; Pimpernel Smith; Sleeping Car to Trieste; So Long at the Fair; The Water Babies; Wombling Free
Tomlinson, Lionel (dir): Death In High Heels; Who Killed Van Loon?
Tomlinson, Michael (act): Jacob's Ladder; The Package
Tomney, Ed (mus): When the Bough Breaks
Tomotake, Masanori (act): Kwaidan
Tompkins, Andrew (act): The Wicker Man
Tompkins, Angel (act, b. 1942): Amazon Women On the Moon; The Bees; Naked Cage; Probe
Tompkins, Darlene (act): Beyond the Time Barrier
Toms, Bernard (wri): The Strange Affair
Tondo, Jerry [illegible] Chan [illegible]
Tone, Franchot (act, 1906-1968): Dark Waters; Five Graves to Cairo; Gabriel Over the White House; Mickey One; Nobody Runs Forever; Phantom Lady

Toner, Bessie (act): Tarzan of the Apes
Toner, Tom (act): The Return of Count Yorga
Tong, Kaity (act): Wolf
Tong, Kam (act): Dimension 5; This Is My Love
Tong, Sam (act): Think Fast, Mr. Moto
Tonge, Assheton (act): A Christmas Carol (1914)
Tonge, Philip (act): House of Wax; Invisible Invaders; Macabre (1958); Miracle On 34th Street (1947); Track of the Cat; Witness for the Prosecution
Tongolele (act): Isle of the Snake People
Tonietti, Anna (act): Spirits of the Dead
Toniolo, Edoardo (act): Gladiators Seven
Tonna, Elliot (act): Getting Lucky
Tonoyama, Taiji (act): Onibaba
Tonsing, Evan (act): The House of the Dead
Tonti, Aldo (cin, b. 1910): The Count of Monte Cristo (1975);Kali-Yug, la Dea della Vendetta; Kiss the Girls and Make Them Die; Il Mistero del Tempio Indiano; Reflections In a Golden Eye
Tontini, Renato (act): I Vampiri
Tony Coca Cola & the Roosters (act & mus): Driller Killer
Tooker, William (H.) (act): The Lone Wolf (1924); Murder by Television; The Scarlet Letter (1926)
Toolan, Rebecca (act): Hideaway
Toomay, Tim (act): Beverly Hills Bodysnatchers
Toomey, Jerry (act): The Swarm
Toomey, Regis (act, 1898-1991): Betryal from the East; The Big Sleep (1946); The Bishop's Wife; The Boy With Green Hair; Chomps; The Invisible Menace; The Lone Wolf Takes a Chance; Mighty Joe Young (1949); Murder by the Clock; Murder In the Blue Room; Murder On the Blackboard; One Frightened Night; Out of the Night;The Phantom Creeps; Phantom Lady; The Phantom of Hollywood; Spellbound (1945); Strange Adventure; Strange Illusion; The Thirteenth Hour (1947); Voyage to the Bottom of the Sea
Toomey, Sam (act): Howling III
Toomin, Melissa (act): The Initiation
Toone, Geoffrey (act): Captain Sinbad; Dr. Crippen; Dr. Who and the Daleks; Echo of Diana;
Luck of the Navy; Murder at Site Three; Poison Pen; Personal and Confidential; Queer Cargo; The
Terror of the Tongs
Toone, Jim (act): The Final Countdown
Toor, Ravinder (act): Fear (1996)
Toothman, Lisa (act): Hard Rock Zombies; Roller Blade Warriors: Taken by Force; Witchcraft III: The Kiss of Death
Tootoosis, Gordon (act): Pocahontas
Topa, John (act): Red Planet Mars
Topart, Jean (act): Fantastic Planet; Le Testament du Dr. Cordelier
Topham, Rhet (wri): 976-EVIL; Trick or Treat
Topic, Velibor (act): The Saint
Topol (act, b. 1935, nee Chaim Topol): Flash Gordon (1980); For Your Eyes Only
Topor, Roland (act): Nosferatu, the Vampyre; Sweet Movie
Topor, Roland (wri): Fantastic Planet; The Tenant
Topper, Burt (dir): Diary of a High School Bride; The Strangler (1963)
Topper, Burt (wri): Diary of a High School Bride
Topper, J.C. (act): Wizards of the Lost Kingdom
Torbet, Bruce (act): Street Trash
Torbet, Bruce (cin): Basket Case; Brain Damage
Torchia, Ron (act): Wild Thing
Torchio, Deborah (act): Flatliners
Torday, Terry (act): Arthur the King; Tower of Screaming Virgins
Tordoff, John (act): Robin Hood: Prince of Thieves; Stories from a Flying Trunk; Without a Clue
Torell, Robin (act): Galaxina
Toren, Heller (act): Five to One; The Liquidator
Toren, Marta (act, 1926-1957): Assignment—Paris; Deported; Illegal Entry; Mystery Submarine; Paris Express; Spy Hunt
Toreno, Juan (act): Meet Nero Wolfe
Torey, Hal (act): Invisible Invaders; The Spider (1958); War of the Colossal Beast
Torgerson, Skip (act): Raiders of the Seven Seas
Torgeson, Sonia (act): Teenagers from Outer Space
Torgl, Mark (act): The Toxic Avenger
Torgov, Sarah (act): American Gothic
Torhonen, Lauri (act): Gorky Park
Toriel, Caprice (act): Murder by Contract
[illegible]
Torme, Mel (act, b. 1925): The Fearmakers; Ghost Catchers;The Private Lives of Adam and Eve

Torme, Tracy (wri): *Fire In the Sky (1993); Spellbinder*
Torn, Anthony (act): *Wicked Stepmother*
Torn, Danae (act): *Writer's Block*
Torn, Rip (act, b. 1931, nee Elmore Torn): *The Beastmaster; By Dawn's Early Light; Coma; Dolly Dearest; Hercules (1997); The Man Who Fell to Earth (1976); Men In Black; One Spy Too Many; RoboCop 3; Senseless (1998); A Stranger Is Watching*
Tornatore, Joe (dir): *Curse of the Crystal Eye; Grotesque*
Tornbech, Svend (act): *The Story of Gosta Berling*
Tornborg, Kay (act): *Who?*
Torne, Regina (act): *The Big Cube*
Toro, Antonio (wri): *Amityville: A New Generation*
Torppe, Danil (act): *The Return of the Six Million Dollar Man and the Bionic Woman*
Torre, Frank (cin): *Salem's Lot*
Torrence, David (act, 1880-1942): *Charlie Chan In London; The Drums of Jeopardy (1923); Jane Eyre (1934); The Mask of Fu Manchu; The Mystic; Scotland Yard (1930); Sherlock Holmes (1922)*
Torrence, Ernest (act, 1878-1933): *The Brass Bottle (1923); The Bridge of San Luis Rey (1929);The Hunchback of Notre Dame (1923); Peter Pan (1924); Sherlock Holmes (1932); The Unholy Night*
Torres, Alicia (act): *El Otro Fu-Manchu*
Torres, Cristina (act): *Hundra*
Torres, Gabriel (cin): *Chosen Survivors; The Mask of Sheba*
Torres, Gina (act): *Dark Angel (1996); Mantis*
Torres, Joan (wri): *Blacula; Scream, Blacula, Scream*
Torres, Liz (act): *Storm Chasers: Revenge of the Twister*
Torres, Lola (act): *The Last Days of Pompeii (1959)*
Torres, Raquel (act): *The Bridge of San Luis Rey (1929)*
Torres, Rosanna (act): *The Pink Chiquitas*
Torrey, Joe (act): *Tales from the Hood*
Torrey, Michael (act): *The Cradle Will Fall*
Torrey, Nuria (act): *The Emerald of Artatama*
Torriani, Aimee (act): *To Catch a Thief*
Torricella, Edoardo (act): *Giulietta degli Spiriti*
Tors, Ivan (wri, 1916-1983): *Gog; The Magnetic Monster; Storm Over Tibet*
Torstensdotter, Elsa Viveca (act): see Lindfors, Viveca
Tortora, Oz (act): *The First Power*
Tortosa, Silvia (act): *Horror Express; When the Screaming Stops*
Torvay, Jose (act): *The Hitch-Hiker; Mystery In Mexico; A Woman's Devotion*
Toscano, Bruce (dir): *The Jar*
Tosi, Arturo (act): *Seven Dwarfs to the Rescue*
Tosi, Domenico (act): *Seven Dwarfs to the Rescue*
Tosi, Luigi (act): *Black Devils of Kali; David and Goliath; Treasure of Bengal*
Tosi, Maria (act): *Il Ladro di Venezia*
Tosi, Mario (cin): *Carrie; Frogs; Reflections of Murder; Some Call It Loving*
Toso, Otello (act): *Planets Against Us*
Tossbert, Robert (act): *Prototype X29A*
Tot, Amerigo (act): *Pulp*
Toth, Frank (act): *Twilight Zone*
Totheroh, Dan (wri): *All That Money Can Buy; The Count of Monte Cristo (1934); Roogie's Bump*
Totheroh, Roland/Rollie (cin): *Modern Times; Monsieur Verdoux*
Totman, Wellyn (wri): *One Frightened Night*
Toto (mus): *Dune*
Toto, Ecce Homo (act): *King Solomon's Mines (1937)*
Totten, Robert (act): *Trauma (1963)*
Tottenham, Merle (act): *Dead Men Are Dangerous; The Invisible Man (1933); Night Club Queen; Night Must Fall (1937); Room to Let*
Totter, Audrey (act, b. 1918): *Alias Nick Beal; The Beginning or the End?; The Cockeyed Miracle; F.B.I. Girl; Ghost Diver; Lady In the Lake; Main Street After Dark; Man In the Dark (1953); The Set-Up (1949); The Unsuspected*
Tottman, Jayne (act): *Superman (1978)*
Touceda, Enrique (wri): *Creature of Destruction*
Tougas, Bert (cin): *Escape Clause*
Tough, Michael (act): *Prom Night; Virus (1980)*
Touliatos, George (act): *Firebird 2015 A.D.; Firepower; Gladiator Cop: The Swordsman 2; Mortal Sins; Prom Night; Robbers of the Sacred Mountain; Stone Cold Dead; Tracks of a Killer; Virus (1980)*
Toumanova, Tamara (act, 1917-1996): *The Private Life of Sherlock Holmes; Torn Curtain*
Toura, Rokuhiro (act): *Live Today, Die Tomorrow*
Tourane, Jean (dir): *The Secret of Magic Island*
Tourneur, Andree (act): *The Conquering Power*
Tourneur, Jacques (dir, 1904-1977): *Anne of the Indies; Appointment In Honduras; La Battaglia di Maratona; Berlin Express; Cat People (1942); Circle of Danger; The City Under the Sea; The Comedy of Terrors; The Fearmakers; The Flame and the Arrow; I Walked With a Zombie; The Leopard Man; Nick Carter, Master Detective; Nightfall (1956); Night of the Demon (1957); Out of the Past (1947); Phantom Raiders*
Tourneur, Maurice (dir, 1876-1961, nee Maurice Thomas): *Aloma of the South Seas (1926);The Blue Bird (1918); The Brass Bottle (1923); Koenigsmark; Lorna Doone (1922); La Main du Diable; The Mysterious Island (1929); Le Systeme du Docteur Goudron et du Professeur Plume; Treasure Island (1920); Trilby (1915);While Paris Sleeps*
Tourneur, Maurice (wri, 1876-1961): *Lorna Doone (1922)*
Tournier, Jean (cin): *The Fiendish Plot of Dr. Fu Manchu; Moonraker*
Tourret, Pat (wri): *Tiffany Jones*
Tours, Frank (mus): *Beyond Tomorrow; The Villain Still Pursued Her*
Toussaint, Beth (act): *The Presence*
Toussaint, Lorraine (act): *Point of No Return*
Toussaint, Steve (act): *Judge Dredd*
Tova, Teresa (act): *Curtains*
Tovar, Lupita (act): *Crime Doctor's Courage; Dracula (1931, Spanish-speaking version); Green Hell*
Tover, Leo (cin, 1902-1964): *A Blueprint for Murder; The Day the Earth Stood Still; Journey to the Center of the Earth (1959); The Lost Squadron; Murder at the Vanities; The Snake Pit (1948)*
Tovey, Arthur (act): *Willard*
Tovey, George (act): *Frenzy*
Tovey, Roberta (act): *Are You Dying Young Man?; Daleks' Invasion Earth 2150 A.D.;Dr. Who and the Daleks; A High Wind In Jamaica; Operation Third Form; Touch of Death*
Tovoli, Luciano (cin): *The Passenger; Single White Female; Suspiria; Tenebrae*
Towb, Harry (act): *Digby-The Biggest Dog In theWorld; Murder at Site Three*
Towe, Darden (act): *Mutants In Paradise*
Tower, Lorena (act): *Night of the Sorcerers*
Tower, Richard (cin): *Doctor X*
Tower, Wade (act): *The Ripper (1985)*
Towers, Constance (act): *The Relic; Shock Corridor*
Towers, Harry Alan (wri): see Welbeck, Peter
Towers, Robert (act): *Masters of the Universe; Switch (1991); Terrified (1963)*
Towey, John Madden (act): *The Invisible Kid*
Towles, Tom (act): *The Borrower; Fortress; Night of the Living Dead (1990); The Pit and the Pendulum (1990)*
Towne, Aline (act): *Gog; Retik, the Moon Menace; Satan's Satellites; Slaves of the Invisible Monster; The Steel Trap*
Towne, Robert (wri): *Last Woman On Earth; Mission: Impossible; The Tomb of Ligeia*
Towne, Roger (wri): *Sword of the Valiant*
Towne, Rosella (act): *Blondes at Work*
Townes, Colin (mus): *Hands of a Murderer*
Townes, Harry (act): *Operation Manhunt; Screaming Mimi; Strategy of Terror; The Warrior and the Sorceress*
Townley, Houghton (wri): *The Splendid Coward*
Townley, Jack (wri, b. 1897): *Crashing Las Vegas; The Disembodied; Up In Smoke*
Townley, Jon (cin): *Virtuosity*
Townley, Toke (act): *Bang! You're Dead; Men of Sherwood Forest; Scars of Dracula*
Towns, Colin (mus): *Daughter of Darkness (1990); Full Circle; The Puppet Masters; Rawhead Rex; Slayground; Vampire's Kiss*
Townsend, Barbara (act): *The Annihilator*
Townsend, Bud (dir): *The Folks at Red Wolf Inn; Nightmare In Wax*
Townsend, Casey (act): *Who Killed Teddy Bear?*
Townsend, Genevieve (act): *The Secret Kingdom*
Townsend, H. (act): *The Red-Headed League*
Townsend, Jill (act): *The Awakening; The Seven-Per-Cent Solution; Sitting Target*
Townsend, Jim (act): *Night of the Creeps*
Townsend, Leo (wri, b. 1908): *How to Stuff a Wild Bikini; Morning Call*
Townsend, Primi (act): *Schizo (1977)*
Townsend, Robert (act, b. 1957): *The Meteor Man; Ratboy; Streets of Fire*
Townsend, Robert (dir & wri, b. 1957): *The Meteor Man*
Townsend (Jr.), Vince (M./Monroe) (act): *The Alligator People; Jungle Man-Eaters; Maid to Order; Valley of the Headhunters; Weird Science*
Townshend, Marchioness of (wri): *Behind the Scenes; The Family Solicitor; The House of Mystery (1913); A Strong Man's Love; When East Meets West*
Townshend, Pete (act & wri): *Tommy*
Townsley, Herman (S.) (cin): *The Angry Red Planet; House On Haunted Hill (1958); The Mask (1961)*
Toy, Ah (act): *Blackie's Redemption*
Toy, Alan (act): *Black Magic Woman; Dead Connection*
Toye, Wendy (dir, b. 1917): *The Stranger Left No Card; The Teckman Mystery; Three Cases of Murder*
Toyne, gabriel (act): *The Curse of the Wraydons*
Toyokawa, Etshushi (act): *Angel Dust*
Tozer, J.R. (act): *The Answer; The Black Night; The Brass Bottle (1914); The Call of the Drum; The Greek Interpreter*
Tozer, Stephen (act): *Trial Run*
Tozere, Fred (act): *Nancy Drew and the Hidden Staircase*
Tozzi, Fausto (act): *In the Steel Net of Dr. Mabuse; Knives of the Avenger; The Night of the Great Attack; The Red Cloak; Scheherazade; The Wonders of Aladdin*
Trace, Christopher (act): *Urge to Kill*
Tracey, Ian (act): *The Keeper; Timcecop*
Tracey, Matt (act): *Sometimes They Come Back...Again*
Tracey, Tabbetha (act): *Eyes of a Stranger*
Trachta, Jeff (act): *Night Eyes...Fatal Passion*
Tracy, Brooke (act): *Twisted*
Tracy, Emily (act): *Lady In White*
Tracy, Kim (act): *The Girl Hunters; Konga*
Tracy, Lee (act, 1898-1968): *Betryal from the East; Doctor X; Liliom (1930)*
Tracy, Lynn (act): *Night of the Demon (1957)*
Tracy, Margaret (wri): *White of the Eye*
Tracy, Marlene (act): *I Dismember Mama*
Tracy, Spencer (act, 1900-1967): *Dante's Inferno (1935); Desk Set; Dr. Jekyll and Mr. Hyde (1941);A Guy Named Joe; Keeper of the Flame*
Tracy, Tony (act): *Flight of the Navigator*
Traeger, Rick (act): *Bedknobs and Broomsticks; The Destructors*
Trafficante, Mara (wri): *Deadbolt*
Trager, Solomon (act): *To All a Goodnight*
Traill, Armitage (wri): *The Thirteenth Guest*
Traill, George (act): *Wuthering Heights (1920)*
Train, Jack (act): *Catacombs (1964); Colonel Bogey; King Arthur Was a Gentleman; The Twenty Questions Murder*
Trainor, Mary Ellen (act): *Congo; A Face to Die For; Ghostbusters II; The Goonies; The Monster Squad; Romancing the Stone; Tales from the Crypt (1989)*
Trainor, Saxon (act): *Magic In the Mirror*
Traister, Andrew (act): *Zontar: The Thing from Venus*
Trakas, George (act): *Silent Night, Bloody Night*
Trammell, Sam (act): *The Hotel Manor Inn*
Trampe, Ray (wri): *Destination Saturn*
Tranche, Andre (wri): *A Lizard In a Woman's Skin*
Trane, Reuben (cin): *Shock Waves*
Trani, Maurizio (cin): *Witchery*
Trankina, Vince (act): *Death Race 2000*
Tranquilli, Silvano (act): *The Black Belly of the Tarantula; Spara Forte, Piu Forte...Non Capisco*
Trantow, Cordula (act): *Das Schloss*
Trapp, Roger (act): *Aimez Vous les Femmes?*
Trathen, Edward (act): *Slugs*
Trauberg, Leonid (dir, b. 1902): *Shinel (1926)*
Trautman, Allan (act): *Return of the Living Dead, Part II*
Travanti, Dan(iel J.) (act, b. 1940): *The Love War; Megaville; Millennium; Wasp Woman (1995); Who Killed Teddy Bear?*
Travelstead, Ted (act): *Children of the Corn II: The Final Sacrifice*
Traven, Bruno (wri): *Macario*
Travers, Alfred (dir): *Dual Alibi; The Primitives; Solution by Phone*
Travers, Alfred (wri): *Dual Alibi; The Primitives*
Travers, Ben (wri): *Thark; Uncle Silas*
Travers, Beverly (act): *Missing Millions*
Travers, Bill (act, 1922-1994): *Counterspy; Footsteps In the Fog; Gorgo; Mantrap; Street of Shadows*
Travers, Constance (act): *White Lilac*
Travers, Henry (act, 1874-1965, nee Travers Heagerty): *Death Takes a Holiday (1934); The Invisible Man (1933); None Shall Escape; On Borrowed Time; Shadow of a Doubt (1943)*
Travers, Lana (act): *The Deadly Females*
Travers, Linden (act, b. 1913, nee Florence Lindon-Travers): *The Bad Lord Byron; Double Alibi;The Ghost Train (1941); The Lady Vanishes (1938); The Missing Million; No Orchids for Miss Blandish; The Terror (1938); Wednesday's Luck*
Travers, Marisa (act): *Frankenstein 1980*
Travers, P.L. (wri, 1900-1996): *Mary Poppins*
Travers, Roy (act): *The Blue Bird (1910); A Brother's Atonement; A Double Life (1913); The House of Peril; In London's Toils; In the Hands of the London Crooks; Jane Shore (1915); The Lights O' London; London by Night (1913); Moonbeam Magic; The Mystery of the Silent Death; The Price of Deception; The Rogues of London; The Splendid Coward; When Paths Diverge*
Travers, Susan (act): *The Abominable Dr. Phibes; The Mind Snatchers; Out of the Fog (1962); Peeping Tom; The SnakeWoman*
Traverso, Susana (act): *Barbarian Queen*
Travesi, Rafael G. (wri): *El Santo Contra las Vampiras*
Traviglio, Leonardo (act): *Top Secret (1978)*
Travis, Henry (act): *The Brain from Planet Arous*
Travis, June (act): *The Gladiator; Monster A Go-Go*
Travis, Kylie (act): *Retroactive*
Travis, Lisa (act): *Trick or Treats*
Travis, Mark (act): *Moonchild*
Travis, Nancy (act, b. 1961): *Bogus; Destiny Turns On the Radio; Fluke; The Vanishing (1993)*
Travis, Rashell (act): *Trick or Treats*
Travis, Richard (act, b. 1913, nee William Justice): *Big Town After Dark; Blonde Bait; Cyborg 2087; Danger Zone; Fingerprints Don't Lie; Mask of the Dragon; Missile to the Moon; Pier 23*
Travis, Ron (act): *Dreamchild; Hellbound: Hellraiser II; Outland; Scandalous; The Sender*
Travis, Stacey (act): *Earth Girls Are Easy; Hardware; Suspect Device*
Travis, Tony (act): *Flesh Gordon 2: Flesh Gordon Meets the Cosmic Cheerleaders; Ghost Warrior*
Travnicek, Pavel (act): *Three Nuts for Cinderella*
Travolta, Ellen (act): *Are You In the House Alone?; Human Experiments*
Travolta, Joey (act): *Amazon Women On the Moon; Ghost Writer; Snow Kill*
Travolta, John (act, b. 1954): *Blow Out; Boris and Natasha; Carrie; The Devil's Rain; Michael; Phenomenon*
Travolta, Margaret (act): *In the Company of Darkness*
Traxler, Stephen (dir & wri): *Spawn of the Slithis*
Traylor, David (act): *She (1983)*
Traylor, Susan (act): *Lord of Illusions*
Traylor, William (act): *The Adventures of Buckaroo Banzai; The Man With Two Brains; S*H*E (1980)*
Traynor, Robert (act): *Body Heat; Psycho II*
Treacher, Arthur (act, 1894-1975): *Mary Poppins; A Midsummer Night's Dream (1935); Satan Met a Lady; Slave Girl*
Treacy, Emerson (act): *The Prowler (1951)*
Treacy, John (act): *Capture That Capsule!*
Treadway, Patrick (act): *The Video Dead*
Treadwell, Laura (act): *Nightmare Alley*
Treas, Terri (act): *Alien Nation: Body and Soul; Alien Nation: Dark Horizon; Alien Nation: Millennium; Alien Nation: The Enemy Within; Deathstalker III: Warriors from Hell; House IV; The Nest; Nightmare On the 13th Floor; Roger Corman's Frankenstein Unbound; The Terror Within*
Trebicka, Jirina (act): *Mission: Impossible*
Trebor, Robert (act): *Making Mr. Right; My Demon Lover*
Tree, David (act): *Don't Look Now; The Drum; Knight Without Armour; Q Planes; The Return of the Scarlet Pimpernel*
Tree, Dorothy (act, b. 1909): *Charlie Chan In City In Darkness; Crime Doctor; The Dragon Murder Case; Four Hours to Kill; The Mystery of Mr. Wong; Nazi Agent; Sky Murder*
Tree, Sir Henry Beerbohm (act): *Macbeth (1916)*
Tree, Sir Herbert (act): *Trilby (1914)*
Tree, Lady (act): *The Man Who Could Work Miracles; Still Waters Run Deep*

Tree, Madge (act): The Abbey Grange; The House of Peril; The House On the Marsh; St. Elmo; The Silver Bridge
Treen, Mary (act, 1907-1989): I Married a Monster from Outer Space; Maid of Salem
Tregaskis, Richard (wri): Fair Wind to Java
Tregloan, Peter (act): Grim
Trego, Ann (act): The Greed of William Hart
Treitman, Seymour (act): So Sad About Gloria
Trejean, Guy (act): I Married a Shadow; The Serpent (1973)
Trejo, Danny (act, b. 1944): Anaconda; From Dusk Till Dawn; The Hidden; Runaway Train
Trelawney, E. (act): Riches and Rogues
Trell, Max (wri): The Last Man to Hang?; 16 Fathoms Deep
Trelour, Di (act): Mad Max
Tremayne, Les (act, b. 1913): The Angry Red Planet; Creature of Destruction; Fangs; Francis Goes to West Point; It Grows On Trees; The Monolith Monsters; The Monster of Piedras Blancas; The Slime People; The Unguarded Moment; The War of the Worlds
Tremblay, Kay (act): Oh Heavenly Dog
Trenaman, John (act): Hamlet (1969)
Trenas, Tote (cin): Alien Predators
Trenchard-Smith, Brian (dir): Atomic Dog; Dead End Drive-In; Doomsday Rock; Escape Clause; Escape 2000; Leprechaun 3; The Man from Hong Kong; Official Denial; Out of the Body; Voyage of Terror
Trend, Jean (act): Doomwatch
Trenk, William (act): The Strange Death of Adolf Hitler
Trent, Anthony (act): Mini Weekend
Trent, Jack (act): The Chinese Parrot
Trent, John (act): The Great Gabbo; Mystery Plane
Trent, John (dir, b. 1935): The Only Way Out Is Dead
Trent, Lee (act): The Falcon Out West
Trent, Ruth (act): Weekend of Fear
Trentham, Barbara (act): Deathmoon; The Possession of Joel Delaney; Rollerball
Tress, Jessica (act): The Zero Boys
Tressler, Dieter (act): Gli Orrori del Castello di Noremberga
Tressler, Dori (act): To All a Goodnight
Trestini, Giorgio (act): Don't Look Now
Treu, Blair (dir): Wish Upon a Star
Treu, Wolfgang (cin): The Little Drummer Girl; Das Schloss
Treuting, Stephen (act): Offerings
Trevallion, M. (act): The Mysterious Mechanical Toy
Trevanian (wri, b. 1929): The Eiger Sanction
Trevarthen, Noel (act): Backfire!; Corruption; The Curse of the Golem; Escort for Hire; Great Expectations (1974); The Material Witness; To Have and To Hold; The Vengeance of Fu Manchu
Treveiller, Robert (act): Her Deadly Rival
Trevelyan, Hilda (act): The 39 Steps (1935); The Tunnel
Trever, Howard (act): Girly
Treves, Frederick (act): Paper Mask
Treville, Georges (act & dir): The Beryl Coronet; The Copper Beeches; The Musgrave Ritual (1912); The Mystery of Boscombe Vale; The Reigate Squires (1912); Silver Blaze (1912); The Speckled Band (1912); The Stolen Papers
Treville, Roger (act): The Green Glove; Mr. Peek-A-Boo
Trevina, David (act): Diagnosis: Murder; 1984 (1984)
Trevino, Jesus Salvador (dir): Thirdspace: A Babylon 5 Adventure
Trevino, Jorge/George (act): The Beast of Hollow Mountain; Ghost Diver; The White Orchid
Trevino, Vic (act): Beastmaster 2: Through the Portal of Time
Trevlac, John (act): see Calvert, John
Trevor, Ann(e) (act): Maria Marten: or, The Murder In the Red Barn (1935); Wuthering Heights (1920)
Trevor, Austin (act, 1897-1978, nee Austin Schilsky): Alibi (1931); The Alphabet Murders; Dark Journey; The Day the Earth Caught Fire; Death at Broadcasting House; Father Brown; Gestapo; Horrors of the Black Museum; Inside the Room; Knight Without Armour; Konga; Law and Disorder; Never Back Losers; A Night In Montmartre; On Secret Service; Sabotage; The Silent Passenger; So Long at the Fair
Trevor, Claire (act, b. 1909, nee Claire Wemlinger): Born to Kill; Dante's Inferno (1935); Key Largo; Murder, My Sweet; The Velvet Touch
Trevor, Edward (act): Charlie Chan's Secret
Trevor, Elleston (wri): Mantrap
Trevor, Hugh (act): Midnight Mystery
Trevor, Jack (act): Champagne; Geheimnisse einer Seele; A Voice Said Goodnight
Trevor, Norman (act): Jane Eyre (1921); The Wizard
Trevor, Spencer (act): Alf's Button (1930); The Lifeguardsman; The Return of Bulldog Drummond; The Star Reporter
TRF Music Libraries (mus): Lost Prophet
Triana, Jorge Ali (dir): Tiempo de Morir
Triandade, Rogerio (act): Vampire's Kiss
Trice, Judy Pryor (act): Sling Blade
Trice, Marguerite Gwynne (act): see Gwynne, Anne
Trichter, Judd (act): Stanley's Dragon
Trickett, Vicki (act): The Cabinet of Caligari; The Three Stooges Meet Hercules
Triesault, Ivan (act, 1902-1980): The Amazing Transparent Man Batman (1966); Crime Doctor's Manhunt; Cry of the Werewolf; Desert Legion; Golden Earrings; Notorious (1946); The Return of Monte Cristo; The Strange Death of Adolf Hitler
Trieste, Leopoldo (act): Don't Look Now; Pulp; Spara Forte, Piu Forte...Non Capisco
Trigg, Margaret (act): R.O.T.O.R.
Trigger, Sarah (act): Bill & Ted's Bogus Journey; Destiny Turns On the Radio; Pet Sematary Two
Trikonis, Gus (dir): Dance of the Swarfs; The Darker Side of Terror; The Evil; She's Dressed to Kill
Trilling, Zoe (act): Tobe Hooper's Night Terrors
Trim, Ron (act): Return of the Killer Tomatoes
Trimble, Larry (act): The Murdock Trial
Trimble, Larry (dir): Alone In London; The Harper Mystery; The Murdock Trial
Trimble, Larry (wri): The Harper Mystery
Trimble, Lawrence (act): Superman (1978)
Trimboli, Robert (act): Deadtime Stories
Trimingham, Ernest A. (act): The Adventures of Dick Turpin-The King of Highwaymen; TheAdventures of Dick Turpin-200 Guineas Reward, Dead or Alive; Where the Rainbow Ends
Trinder, Tommy (act, 1909-1989): Fiddlers Three
Trinidad, Arsenio "Sonny" (act): Darkman (1990); Neon City
Trinka, Paul (act): Faster, Pussycat! Kill! Kill!
Trintignant, Jean-Louis (act, b. 1930): Act of Aggression; Antinea,l'Amante della Citta Sepolta; The City of Lost Children; Confidentially Yours; The French Conspiracy; Mata Hari, Agent H21; Plucked; The Sleeping Car Murders; Spotlight On Murder;Trans-Europe Express; Without Apparent Motive
Trintignant, Marie (act): Wings of Fame
Triolo, Lori (act): Intensity
Tripod, Irene (act): The House of Peril; Marzipan of the Shapes
Tripp, Ellen (act): Invasion of the Girl Snatchers
Tripp, Louis (act): The Gate; Gate II
Tripp, Paul (act): The Christmas That Almost Wasn't; The Sleeping Beauty (1965, W. Ger)
Trippel, Dieter R. (act): Eraser
Tripplehorn, Jeanne (act, b. 1963): Waterworld
Triscari, Filomena (act): Body Heat
Triska, Jon (act): 2010
Tristan, Dorothy (act): The Incredible Hulk, Part 2; Isn't It Shocking?; Man On a Swing
Tristram, Una (act): The Bandit's Daughter; A Daughter of Satan (1914); The Fairy Bottle; The Masked Smuggler; The Sixth Commandment; The Thief (192);The Vengeance of Daniel Whidden; The Wrecker of Lives
Tritonz, The (mus): The Edge of Hell
Trivas, Victor (dir & wri, 1896-1970): The Naked Woman and Satan
Trizers, Bryan (dir): Psi Factor
Trmal (cin): Do You Keep a Lion at Home?
Trnka, Jiri (dir, 1912-1969): Cisaruv Slavik; Kyberneticka Babicka
Trnka, Jiri (wri, 1912-1969): Kyberneticka Babicka
Trnka Puppets, The (act): see Jiri Trnka Puppets
Trocchi, Alexander (act): Towers Open Fire
Troiano, Domenic (mus): Let Me Call You Sweetheart; Remember Me
Troiano, William (G.) (cin): The Devil's Messenger; Horror of the Blood Monsters; The Mummy and the Curse of the Jackals; The Slime People
Troisio, Antonio (wri): Murder Mansion
Trolley, Leonard (act): In the Shadow of Kilimanjaro
Troncatty, Ron (act): Running Against Time
Troncone, Marilee (act): Legacy of Horror
Tronson, Robert (dir, b. 1924): Man at the Carlton Tower; Man Detained; Never Back Losers; Number Six; On the Run (1963); Ring of Spies; The Traitors
Trooper, Margot (act): Hipnosis; The Mysterious Magician; Traitor's Gate
Troost, Ernest (mus): The Canterville Ghost (1996); Dead Heat; Tremors
Trosper, Elizabeth (act): Shadows Run Black
Trosper, Guy (wri): Eyes In the Night; The Spy Who Came In from the Cold
Trotiner, Glen (act): Freejack
Trott, Judi (act): Robin Hood: The Swords of Wayland
Trotta, Ed(ward) (act): I'm Dangerous Tonight; Liar Liar
Trotter, Charles (L.) (act): Forever Evil; Student Bodies
Trotter, Kate (act): Clarence; The Quilt of Hathor
Trotter, Laura (act): City of the Walking Dead; Miami Golem; Rush
Troughton, Patrick (act, b. 1920): The Black Knight; Black Torment; Frankenstein and the Monster from Hell; The Gorgon; Hamlet (1948); A Hitch In Time; The Insect Play; Jason and the Argonauts; The Omen; The Phantom of the Opera (1962); Richard III (1955); Scars of Dracula; Sinbad and the Eye of the Tiger; Treasure Island (1950); The Viking Queen; The Woman With No Name
Troum, Kenn (act): Teenage Mutant Ninja Turtles
Troupe, Al (act): Microwave Massacre
Trousdale, Gary (dir): Beauty and the Beast (1991); The Hunchback of Notre Dame (1996)
Trout, Dink (act): Alice In Wonderland (1951)
Troutsouvas, Sam (act): Ghost (1990)
Troutt, Terry (act): The Attic
Trouville, Beatrice (act): The Temptation of Carlton Earle
Trovajoli, Armando (mus): Atom Age Vampire; Il Gigante di Metropolis
Trow, Alan M. (cin): Monolith
Trow, Bob (act): Jack's Wife
Trow, George Swift (wri): Savages
Trowbridge, Andrea (act): The House In the Woods
Trowbridge, Charles (act, 1882-1967): The Beginning or the End?; Blue,White and Perfect; Dressed to Kill (1941); The Fatal Hour (1940); The Garden Murder Case; The House of the Seven Gables; The Invisible Menace; Mad Love;The Man They Could Not Hang; The Man with Nine Lives; The Mummy's Hand; Nancy Drew, Detective; The Red Dragon (1945); Shock (1946); The Son of Monte Cristo; Tarzan and the Huntress;Valley of the Zombies
Trowe, Jose Chavez (act): The Bees; Demonoid; Run for the Sun
Troy, April (act): Phantom of the Paradise
Troy, Hector (act): Eyes of Laura Mars
Troy, Louise (act): Ghostbusters II
Troyan, Maurice (act): The Magic Voyage of Sinbad
Troyer, Debra (act): The Philadelphia Experiment
Truax, Bill (act): Horror High
Truax, John (act): The Curse of the Undead
Trubshawe, Michael (act, d. 1985): Bedazzled; A Dandy In Aspic; Gideon's Day; I Accuse (1958); The Lavender Hill Mob; The Magic Christian; The Mouse On the Moon
Truchado, Jose (act): The Glass Sphinx
Truchon, Isabelle (act): Deadbolt
Trudeau, Margaret (act): Kings and Desperate Men
True, Garrison (act): Day of the Animals
True, Rachel (act): The Craft; The Nosferatu Diaries: Embrace of the Vampire
Trueblood, Guerdon (wri): Amazons (1984); It Happened at Lake Wood Manor; Jaws 3-D; The Love War; The Savage Bees; Sole Survivor (1970); Tarantulas: The Deadly Cargo; Terror Out of the Sky
Truesdell, June (wri): The Accused (1949)
Truett, Richard (act): The Odyssey
Truex, Ernest (act, 1890-1973): A Night In Paradise
Truex, Philip (act): The Trouble With Harry
Truffaut, Francois (act, 1932-1984): Close Encounters of the Third Kind; L'Enfant Sauvage
Truffaut, Francois (dir & wri, 1932- 1984): Confidentially Yours; L'Enfant Sauvage; Fahrenheit 451; La Marieeetait en Noir; Mata Hari, Agent H21
Truffitt, Nigel (act): Howling V: The Rebirth
Trujillo, Raoul (act): Highlander: The Final Dimension; Scanners II: The New Order
Trujillo, Valentin (act): Scanners II: The New Order
Truman, Michael (dir, 1916-1974): Girl In the Headlines; Koroshi
Truman, Ralph (act, b. 1900): The Bells (1931); Beyond This Place; The Case of Gabriel Perry; The Crimson Circle (1936); The Interrupted Journey; The Laughing Lady; The Long Arm; The Man Who Knew Too Much (1956); The Perfect Flaw; The Saint In London; The Silent Passenger; The Spaniard's Curse; Treasure Island (1950); Under the Red Robe (1937)
Truman, Tim (mus): Deadly Game; In the Company of Darkness
Trumbo, Dalton (wri, 1905-1976): Always; A Guy Named Joe; The Lone Wolf Strikes; The Prowler (1951);The Remarkable Andrew
Trumbo, Karen (act): Child of Darkness, Child of Light
Trumbull, Brad (act): The Right Hand of the Devil
Trumbull, Douglas (cin): Close Encounters of the Third Kind; Star Trek; 2001: A Space Odyssey
Trumbull, Douglas (dir): Brainstorm (1983); Silent Running
Trumper, Herbert (act): The Adventures of Dick Turpin-The Gunpowder Plot; The Adventures of Dick Turpin-The King of Highwaymen; The Angel of the Ward
Trumpette, Francoise (act): The Corsican Brothers (1985)
Trundy, Natalie (act): Battle for the Planet of the Apes; Beneath the Planet of the Apes; Conquest of the Planet of the Apes; Escape from the Planet of the Apes
Truscott, John (act): The Ivory Ape
Truscott-Jones, Reginald (act & dir): see Milland, Ray
Truss, Seldon (wri): The Long Knife
Trussell, Ann (cin): Time Walker
Trussell, Hal (cin): One Dark Night
Trustman, Alan R. (wri): Lady Ice
Trustman, Susan (act): Dr. Jekyll and Ms. Hyde
Truti, Gabriele (act): Women's Prison Massacre
Trutner, Kirk (act): Dante's Peak
Tryoler, William (act): The Phantom of the Opera (1925)
Tryon, Glenn (act): Tangled Destinies
Tryon, Helene (act): Wolfman (1979)
Tryon, Tom (act, 1926-1991): Color Me Dead; The Fall of the House of Usher (1958); I Married a Monster from Outer Space; Moon Pilot; The Scarlet Hour
Tryon, Thomas/Tom (wri, 1926-1991): The Dark Secret of Harvest Home; The Other (1972)
Trytel, W.L. (mus): Scrooge (1935); The Triumph of Sherlock Holmes
Tsamchoe, Lhakpa (act): Seven Years In Tibet
Tsangarides, Christopher (act): Memoirs of a Survivor
Tsangas, Christos (act): Iphigenia
Tschechowa, Olga (act): Schloss Vogelod
Tschernisch, Sergei (act): Colossus: The Forbin Project
Tschernow, A. (mus): Planeta Bura
Tschetter, Dean (wri): Picking Up the Pieces
Tschetwerikoff, Konstantin (cin): F.P. 1 Antwortet Nicht; Die Frauim Mond
Tse, Mariko (act): The Flash
Tseretelly, Nikolai (act): Aelita
Tsien, Marie (act): The 27th Day
Tso, Yee Jee (act): Doctor Who
Tsu, Irene (act, b. 1943): Judge Dee and the Monastery Murder; How to Stuff a Wild Bikini; Women of the Prehistoric Planet
Tsubouchi, David (act): Videodrome
Tsubouchi, Kinko (act): The Golden Child
Tsuburaya, Eiji (cin, 1902-1978): Atragon; Battle In Outer Space; Destroy All Monsters; Dogora,the Space Monster; Frankenstein vs. the Giant Devil Fish; Ghidrah, the Three-Headed Monster; Godzilla Raids Again; Godzilla's Revenge; Godzilla vs. Mothra; Gojira; Gorath; Latitude Zero; King Kong Escapes; King Kong vs. Godzilla; Mantango; Monster Zero; Mothra; The Mysterians; Rodan, the Flying Monster; Samurai Pirate
Tsuchiya, Yoshio (act): Battle In Outer Space; Destroy All Monsters; The Human Vapor;Yog-Monster from Space
Tsuda, Mitsuo (act): Mothra
Tsui, Roland (act): Outbreak
Tsukada, Wataru (act): The Toxic Avenger, Part II
Tsukamoto, Shinya (act, dir & wri): Iron Man

Tsukasa, Yoko (act, b. 1934): Chusingura (1963)
Tsukerman, Slava (dir & mus): Liquid Sky
Tsukimiya, Otomie (act): Kwaidan
Tsurumaru, Mitsuhiko (act): Kwaidan
Tsuruta, Koji (act): The Secret of the Telegian; Secret Scrolls-Parts I & II
Tsushima, Toshiaki (mus): The Green Slime; The War In Space
Tsutsumi, Yasuhisa (act): Mothra
Tu, Lily (act): Revenge of the Zombies (1981)
Tu, Poulet (act): The Face of Fu Manchu
Tubb, Mike (cin): Rocket Attack U.S.A.
Tubbs, William (act): Le Salaire de la Peur
Tubert, Marcelo (act): Leprechaun 3; Tremors 2: Aftershocks
Tubin, Rita (act): The Creeping Terror
Tucci, Michael (act): Pandemonium
Tucci, Stanley (act): Monkey Shines; Prelude to a Kiss
Tucek, Sarabeth (act): Flatliners
Tucherer, Eugene (dir): The Spy Is a Girl
Tuchinski, W. (wri): El Cuerpo del Lito
Tuchner, Michael (dir): Awake to Danger; Fear Is the Key; The Hunchback of Notre Dame (1982)
Tuck, Jessica (act): Batman Forever; Lifepod
Tucker, Alan (act): Burke and Hare
Tucker, Ann (act): To All a Goodnight
Tucker, Burnell (act): The Empire Strikes Back; Flash Gordon (1980); Lifeforce; Scream for Help; The Shining; Superman (1978)
Tucker, Chris (act): The Fifth Element
Tucker, Duane (act): Charlie Chan and the Curse of the Dragon Queen; Phantasm III: Lord of the Dead
Tucker, Forrest (act, 1919-1986): The Abominable Snowman of the Himalayas; Boston Blackie Goes Hollywood; Counter-Espionage; Counterplot; Dangerous Business; Finger Man; Keeper of the Flame; The Strange World of Planet X;Timestalkers; The Trollenberg Terror
Tucker, Gail (act): Offerings
Tucker, George (dir): The Miracle Man (1919)
Tucker, George Loane/L. (dir, 1881-1921): Arsene Lupin; The Black Spot; The Cage; Called Back; The Game of Liberty; The Man Without a Soul; On His majesty's Service; The Prisoner of Zenda (1915); Rupert of Hentzau (1915); The Sons of Satan
Tucker, George L. (wri, 1881-1921): The Man Without a Soul
Tucker, Gil (act): Mad Max
Tucker, Harland (act): Charlie Chan at the Opera; The Invisible Menace; The Lone Wolf Strikes
Tucker, Hubert (act): Deadly Strangers; Jamaica Inn (1985); The Return of Sherlock Holmes (1986)
Tucker, Jack (act): Firefight
Tucker, James (act): Lost Prophet
Tucker, James (dir & wri): Lunatic; Steps from Hell
Tucker, Jerry (act): Dick Tracy Returns
Tucker, Larry (act): Shock Corridor
Tucker, Lillian (act): The Cave Girl (1921)
Tucker, Martin (act): Death Screams
Tucker, Michael (act, b. 1944): Eyes of Laura Mars; In the Nick of Time; Vampire (1979)
Tucker, Nana (act): The Sentinel
Tucker, Ondrea (act): Lunatic
Tucker, Phil (dir): The Cape Canaveral Monsters; Robot Monster
Tucker, Phil (wri): The Cape Canaveral Monsters
Tucker, Richard (act, 1869-1942): The Bat Whispers; The Benson Murder Case; The Black Camel;Convicted; The Eleventh Hour (1923); The Plot Thickens; The Unholy Night
Tucker, Rocky (act): Lunatic; Steps from Hell
Tucker, Steven (act): Lost Prophet
Tucker, Teddy (act): The Deep
Tuckett, Rita (act): Storm of the Century
Tudor, Christine (act): The Eliminator
Tudor, F.C.S. (dir & wri): The Devil's Profession
Tudor, Jennifer (act): Hamlet (1969)
Tudor, Pamela (act): Treasure of the Petrified Forest
Tudor, Ray (act): The Flesh Eaters
Tuerpe, Paul (act): Eve of Destruction; The Goonies; Ladyhawke; Superman (1978)
Tuesday, Ruby (act): She-Devils on Wheels
Tufano, Brian (cin): Dreamscape; Murder Is Easy
Tufeld, Dick (act): Lost In Space
Tufts, Bowen Charleston (act): see Tufts, Sonny
Tufts, Sonny (act, 1911-1970, nee Bowen Charleston Tufts): Cat-Women of the Moon; Run for the Hills; Serpent Island
Tugend, Harry (wri, 1898-1989): Ali Baba Goes to Town
Tugnett, Christopher (act): The Pink Chiquitas
Tula (act): For Your Eyes Only
Tull, Debbie (act): Happy Birthday to Me
Tull, Patrick (act): Murder Motel
Tulley, Paul (act): Meteor
Tulli, Marco (act): Beat the Devil; Robin Hood and the Pirates; The Shadow of Zorro;The Wonders of Aladdin
Tullis Jr., Dan (act): The First Power
Tulloch, Mandy (act): Robin Hood Junior (1975)
Tully, Brian (act): Captain Kronos: Vampire Hunter; The Flesh and Blood Show
Tully, George (act): The Woman Who Was Nothing
Tully, John (wri): Dublin Nightmare; Faces In the Dark; In the Wake of a Stranger; The Man from Nowhere; Mr. Selkie
Tully, Montgomery (dir, b. 1904): Battle Beneath the Earth; Boy With a Flute; The Case of the River Morgue; The Case of the Smiling Widow; Clash by Night; The Counterfeit Plan; The Crossroad Gallows; Dead Lucky; Destination Death; Dial 999 (1955); The Diamond; The Diplomatic Corpse; The Glass Tomb; The House On Marsh Road; The Hypnotist (1957); Inside Information; Jackpot; The Key Man; Late Night Final; The Lonely House; The Long Knife; Man Accused; Man In the Shadow; The Man Who Was Nobody; Man With a Gun; Master Spy (1963); Murder In Reverse; Night Crossing; No Road Back; Out of the Fog (1962); Person Unknown; The Price of Silence; Print of Death; The Silent Witness (1954); The Strange Awakening; The Terrornauts; The Third Alibi; Thirty-Six Hours (1954); Two Wives at One Wedding; Wall of Death (1956); The White Cliffs Mystery; Who Killed the Cat?; Zex
Tully, Montgomery (wri, b. 1904): Boy With a Flute; The Case of the River Morgue; Clash by Night; Dial 999 (1955); The Hypnotist (1957); Jackpot; Master Spy (1963); Late Night Final; Murder In Reverse; No Road Back; Out of the Fog (1962); The Third Alibi; Thirty-Six Hours (1954); Wall of Death (1956); Who Killed the Cat?
Tully, Richard Walton (wri): Trilby (1923)
Tully, Susan (act): Never-Never Land
Tully, Tom (act, 1902-1982): Intrigue (1947); Lady In the Lake; The Unseen (1945)
Tumiati, Gualtiero (act): Ulysses
Tunberg, Karl (wri): I Thank a Fool
Tung, Ching Siu (dir): A Chinese Ghost Story
Tunnicliffe, Reg (act): The Food of the Gods
Tun Tun (act): Chamber of Horrors (1966)
Tunick, Irve (wri): Lady of Vengeance
Tunney, Robin (act): The Craft; Encino Man
Tupou, Manu (act): The Extraordinary Seaman
Tupper, Tristam (wri): The Night Key
Tupu, Larney (act): The Punisher
Tura, James (act): Rocket Attack U.S.A.
Turbide, Elizabeth (act): Wild Thing
Turbide, Manon (act): Alien High
Turco, Paige (act): Teenage Mutant Ninja Turtles II:The Secret of the Ooze
Turco, Paolo (act): Top Secret (1978)
Tureck, Shari (act): The Pink Chiquitas
Turenne, Louis (act): Eat and Run
Turgeon, Peter (act): The Possession of Joel Delaney
Turich, Felipe (act): Fer-de-Lance; Jesse James Meets Frankenstein's Daughter
Turich, Rosa (act): Jesse James Meets Frankenstein's Daughter
Turilli, Max (act): Zone Troopers
Turk, Danilo (act): Cave of the Living Dead
Turk, Larry (act): 976-EVIL
Turk, R. (cin): Animal Farm (1954)
Turkel, Ann (act): The Cassandra Crossing; Deep Space; The Fear (1994); Humanoids from the Deep; Matt Helm; 99 and 44/100% Dead; Ravagers
Turkel, Joseph/Joe (act): Blade Runner; The Bonnie Parker Story; The Boy and the Pirates; Cycle Psycho; Dark Side of the Moon; The Killing; The Shining; Tormented (1960); Village of the Giants
Turko, Jun (act): Dance of the Dwarfs
Turko, Rosemarie (dir & wri): The Dungeonmaster
Turley, Ed (act): Road Games
Turley, Jack (wri): Empire of the Ants; Terror On the 40th Floor
Turley, James Austin (act): The Swarm
Turley, Linda (act): Dead and Buried
Turman, Glynn (act): Gremlins; J.D.'s Revenge
Turnbull, John (act): The Black Abbot (1934); Black Mask; Daybreak; Dead Men Are Dangerous; The Gaunt Stranger; The Girl In the Flat; The Hangman Waits; The Iron Stair (1933); The Limping Man (1936); Line Engaged; The Man at Six; The Man Outside (1933); Murder On the Second Floor; Once In a New Moon; The Passing of the Third Floor Back (1935); Passing Shadows; A Place of One's Own; Puppets of Fate; The Scarlet Pimpernel (1934); Sexton Blake and the Bearded Doctor; The Shadow
(1933); Silver Blaze (1937); Spies of the Air; Tangled Evidence; The Terror (1938); The 39 Steps (1935); Three Silent Men; A Voice Said Goodnight; Warn London; The Wickham Mystery
Turnbull, Ray (act): Mad Max Beyond Thunderdome
Turnbull, Tom (cin): The Cyber-Stalking
Turner, Anna (act): The Last Man to Hang?; Lost; Urge to Kill
Turner, Arnold (act): Too Good to Be True
Turner, B.J. (act): Night Angel
Turner, Barbara (act): The Monster from Green Hell; Wink of an Eye
Turner, Bonnie (wri): Coneheads
Turner, Brad (dir): Roswell: The Aliens Attack
Turner, Bruce (cin): The Quilt of Hathor
Turner, Cedric (act): Falling Fire
Turner, Chester (dir): Black Devil Doll from Hell
Turner, Claramae (act): Carousel
Turner, Clive (act): Howling IV; Howling V: The Rebirth; The Howling: New Moon Rising
Turner, Clive (dir): Howling IV; Howling V: The Rebirth; The Howling: New Moon Rising
Turner, Clice (wri): Howling IV; Howling V: The Rebirth; The Howling: New Moon Rising
Turner, Colin (wri): King Solomon's Treasure
Turner, Dave (act): Tomorrow's Child
Turner, Dean (act): Embassy
Turner, Dean (dir): Valley of Blood
Turner, Ed (wri): Ernest Saves Christmas
Turner, Elise (act): The Zero Boys
Turner, Elizabeth (1930s act): Just Imagine
Turner, Elizabeth (1970s act): Beyond the Door
Turner, Florence (act, 1885-1946): Alone In London; The Chinese Parrot; The Harper Mystery; The Murdock Trial; Richard III (1908)
Turner, Frances (act): Back from the Dead
Turner, Frank C. (act): The Fly II; It (1990); Watchers
Turner, Frantz (act): Solar Crisis
Turner, Gail (act): Don't Go In the House
Turner, George (act): The English Rose; Forging Ahead; A Safe Affair; Twin Faces
Turner, Janine (act): The Ambulance; Circle of Deceit; Monkey Shines
Turner, Jim (act): Joe's Apartment; The Lost Boys
Turner, John (act, b. 1932): L'Amante del Vampiri; Behemoth, the Sea Monster; Black Torment; Captain Nemo and the Underwater City; A Place to Die; The Slipper and the Rose
Turner, John Hastings (wri): Blind Spot (1932); The Ghoul (1933); Murder at Monte Carlo; The Silver Greyhound (1932); A
Voice Said Goodnight
Turner, Joseph (act): Valley of Blood
Turner, Julia Jean Frances Mildred (act): see Turner, Lana
Turner, June (act): Deathline
Turner, Kathleen (act, b. 1954): Body Heat; The Jewel of the Nile; The Man With Two Brains; Peggy Sue Got Married; Romancing the Stone; Serial Mom; A Simple Wish; Who Framed Roger Rabbit
Turner, Lana (act, 1920-1995, nee Julia Jean Frances Mildred Turner): The Big Cube; Dr. Jekyll and Mr. Hyde (1941); Persecution;Portrait In Black; The Three Musketeers (1948); Witches' Brew
Turner, Larry (act): The Pit and the Pendulum (1961)
Turner, Maidel (act): The Raven (1935)
Turner, Michelle (act): Dead Alive
Turner, Peter (act): The Day the Screaming Stopped; The Tempest (1980)
Turner, Richard (act): Shadow Conspiracy
Turner, Robert Brooks (act):The Sound Barrier
Turner, Simon (act): The Big Sleep (1978)
Turner, Stephen (act): The Final Conflict
Turner, Ted (act): Starship Invasions
Turner, Teddy (act): Dracula (1979)
Turner, Terry (wri): Coneheads
Turner, Tierre (act): The Horrible House On the Hill
Turner, Tim (act): The Crossroad Gallows; Grip of the Strangler; Jackpot; The Night of the Full Moon; Police Dog; Print of Death
Turner, Tina (act, b. 1939, nee Anna Mae Bullock): Mad Max Beyond Thunderdome; Tommy
Turner, Tina (mus, b. 1939): Goldeneye
Turner, Vickery (act): The Bermuda Triangle; The Mind of Mr. Soames
Turner, Wendy (act): The Spider's Web
Turner, William (act): Reflections of Murder; Scream of the Butterfly
Turner, Yolande (act): Limbo Line
Turney, Prof. Alan (wri): Yellow Dog
Turney, Catherine (wri): Back from the Dead; Cry Wolf (1947)
Turney, Jim (act): Secrets of the Phantom Caverns
Turney, Michael (act): Teenage Mutant Ninja Turtles
Turney, Nadyne (act): Sweet Kill
Turpin, Ben (act, 1874-1940): Cracked Nuts (1931)
Turpin, Gerry (cin, b. 1930): The Last of Sheila; Seance On a Wet Afternoon; What Became of Jack and Jill; The Wrong Box
Turquand, Todd (act): Burnt Offerings
Turtletaub, Jon (dir): Phenomenon
Turturro, Aida (act): Junior (1994)
Turturro, John (act, b. 1957): Being Human; Exterminator II
Turturro, Nicholas (act, b. 1962): Shadow Conspiracy
Tusell, Felix (wri): Eyeball
Tusher, Betty (wri): Psych-Out
Tushingham, Aisha (act): The Housekeeper
Tushingham, Rita (act, b. 1942): The Bed-Sitting Room; The Housekeeper; The Human Factor; A Place to Go Straight On Till Morning
Tuson, Thelma (act): Chu Chin Chow (1934)
Tutain, Roland (act): The Rules of the Game
Tutin, Alexander (act): The Saint
Tutin, Dorothy (act, b. 1930): Murder with Mirrors
Tuttle, Frank W. (dir, 1892-1956): The Benson Murder Case; A Cry In the Night (1956); The Greene Murder Case; Island of Lost Women; Puritan Passions; Roman Scandals; The Studio Murder Mystery; Suspense; This Gun for Hire (1942)
Tuttle, Frank W. (wri, 1892-1963): Puritan Passions
Tuttle, Lurene (act, 1906-1986): The Clonus Horror; Don't Bother to Knock; The Ghost and Mr. Chicken; The Glass Slipper; Human Experiments; It Came Upon the Midnight Clear; Live Again, Die Again; Macbeth (1947); The Manitou; Niagara; Nightmare In the Sun; Psycho (1960); The Whip Hand
Tuttle, Tex (act): Raiders of the Living Dead
Tutto, Ray D. (act): see Williams, Robin
Tuuli, Eya (act): Castle Keep
Twain, Mark (wri, 1835-1910): A Connecticut Yankee; A Connecticut Yankee In King Arthur's Court (1921, 1949 & 1989); A Kid In King Arthur's Court; A Knight In Camelot; The Mysterious Stranger; The Spaceman and King Arthur
Twain, Michael (act): Beyond the Universe
Tweddell, Frank (act): Carousel
Tweed, Barbette (act): It Came Upon the Midnight Clear
Tweed, Frank (act): Puritan Passions
Tweed, Frederic (wri): Gabriel Over the White House
Tweed, Shannon (act, b. 1957): Cold Sweat; The Dark Dancer; Electra (1995); Of Unknown Origin; Possessed by the Night; Stormy Nights; Twisted Justice; Victim of Desire
Tweed, Terry (act): Night Rhythms; The Reincarnate
Tweedlie, Molly (act): The Mutations
Twelvetrees, Helen (act, 1908-1958, nee Helen Jurgens): The Cat Creeps (1930); The Ghost Talks; The Spanish Cape Mystery
Twenlow, Mabel (act): The Man With the Magnetic Eyes; Special Edition
Twigg, Jenny (act): Holocaust 2000
Twiggy (act, b. 1949, nee Lesley Hornby): Body Bags; The Doctor and the Devils; There Goes the Bride; W
Twinn, Chris (act): Dragonslayer
Twist, Derek (dir): Family Doctor; Police Dog
Twist, Derek (wri): Family Doctor; Murder Will Out (1939); Police Dog; They Drive by Night
Twist, John (wri): Helen of Troy (1955); Operation Secret; The Saint Strikes Back;
Sinbad the Sailor
Twitchell, Archie (act): Charlie Chan In the Wax Museum
Twitchell, Tifni (act): Communion

Twitty, Conway (act): *Platinum High School; Sex Kittens Go to College*
Two Eagle, Dale (act): *Neighbors*
Twofeathers, Bill (act): *The Norsemen*
Twogood, Mark (act): *Neon Maniacs*
Twohy, D.T. (wri): *Critters 2: The Main Course; Warlock*
Twohy, David (dir): *The Arrival (1996); Disaster In Time*
Twohy, David (N.) (wri): *The Arrival (1996); Disaster In Time; The Fugitive (1993); Warlock: The Armageddon; Waterworld*
Twohy, Dick (act): *Capture That Capsule!*
Twomey, Anne (act): *Deadly Friend; Orpheus Descending; Rear Window (1998)*
Twomey, Janell (act): *The Octagon*
Twyford, Cyril (wri): *The House of the Arrow (1930); The Missing Rembrandt; The Sleeping Cardinal; The Triumph of Sherlock Holmes*
Tydor, Jonathan (wri): *Dead Connection; I Come In Peace*
Tye, Allison (act): *The Pit (1983)*
Tyler, Beverly (act, b. 1928, nee Beverly Jean Saul): *The Beginning or the End?; Voodoo Island*
Tyler, Cary (act): *Darkman (1990)*
Tyler, Cindy (act): *Magic Spectacles*
Tyler, Grant (act): *Daughter of Darkness (1948)*
Tyler, Harry (act): *After the Thin Man; The Glass Web; The Gracie Allen Murder Case; Witness to Murder; Woman Who Came Back*
Tyler, Ian (act): *Highlander*
Tyler, Jeff (act): *Neon Maniacs*
Tyler, Lelah (act): *Charlie Chan In the Secret Service*
Tyler, Leon (act): *The Ghost of Dragstrip Hollow; The Monkey's Uncle*
Tyler, Liv (act): *Armageddon*
Tyler, Richard (act): *The Atomic Submarine*
Tyler, Stephen (dir): *The Last Slumber Party*
Tyler, Steve (act): *Into the Badlands*
Tyler, Steven Gregory (act): *To Save a Child*
Tyler, Tom (act, 1903-1954, nee William Burns): *The Adventures of Captain Marvel; The Golden Eye; The Mummy's Hand*
Tylo, Michael (act): *Zorro: The Legend Begins*
Tylor, Christopher James (act): *Wicked Stepmother*
Tynan, Brandon (act): *The Lone Wolf Spy Hunt; Nancy Drew, Detective*
Tynan, Kathleen (wri, 1937-1995): *Agatha*
Tynan, Kenneth (wri, 1927-1980): *Macbeth (1971); Nowhere to Go*
Tyndale, Kate (act): *A Message from Mars (1913)*
Tyne, George (act): *Call Northside 777; The Lone Wolf and His Lady; They Won't Believe Me*
Tyner, Amanda (act): *Offerings*
Tyner, Charles (act): *Deadly Messages; Evilspeak; Family Plot; Pulse*
Tynes, Danita (act): *The Pink Chiquitas*
Tyng, Christopher (mus): *Kazaam*
Tyre, William Elijah (act): *Street Trash*
Tyree, Mary (act): *Kiss of the Tarantula*
Tyrell, Steve (mus): *The Night Stalker (1987)*
Tyrrell, Dick (act): *A Child, a Wand and a Wish*
Tyrrell, Geoffrey (act): *Cat Girl; The Flesh and the Fiends*
Tyrrell, Gerrard (act): *Maria Marten: or, The Murder In the Red Barn (1935)*
Tyrrell, John (act): *Boston Blackie Goes Hollywood; Boston Blackie's Rendezvous; The Lone Wolf Spy Hunt; The Man They Could Not Hang; Meet Boston Blackie; One Mysterious Night*
Tyrrell, Susan (act, b. 1946): *Butcher, Baker (Nightmare Maker); The Demolitionist; Fire and Ice; Flesh & Blood; Forbidden Zone; The Killer Inside Me; Midnight Lace (1981); The Offspring; Powder*
Tyson, Cathy (act): *The Serpent and the Rainbow*
Tyson, Cicely (act, b. 1933): *The Blue Bird (1976); Bridge of Time; House of Secrets (1993); Ms. Scrooge*
Tyson, Pamala (act): *Seven*
Tyson, Richard (act): *The Glass Cage (1996)*
Tyszkiewicz, Beata (act): *Rekopis Znaleziony w Saragossie*
Tyzack, Margaret (act): *A Clockwork Orange; The Corsican Brothers (1985); The Legacy; The Quatermass Conclusion; Ring of Spies; 2001: A Space Odyssey*
Tzadock, Arnon (act): *Programmed to Kill*
Tzavellas, George (dir): *Antigone*
Tzelniker, Meier (act, b. 1894): *Jungle Street; Last Holiday; The Sorcerers; The Teckman Mystery*
Tzipine, Georges (mus): *Black Devils of Kali*
Tzudiker, Rob/Bob (act): *The Golden Child; Total Recall*
Tzudiker, Bob (wri): *The Hunchback of Notre Dame (1996)*

Uala, Joe (act): *Strange Days*
Ubach, Alanna (act): *Freeway; Virtuosity*
Uberti, Anny Delli (act): *La Vergine di Norimberga*
Uchida, Wally (act): *Ghost Warrior*
Uchiyama, Jiiko (act): *The Toxic Avenger, Part II*
Udal, Vicky (act): *Talk of the Devil*
Udenio, Fabiana (act): *Bride of Re-Animator; RoboCop 2*
Uderzo, Alberto (wri): *Asterix In Britain*
Udoff, Yale (wri): *Eve of Destruction*
Udvarnoky, Chris (act): *The Other (1972)*
Udvarnoky, Martin (act): *The Other (1972)*
Udy, Claudia (act): *Edge of Sanity; The Pink Chiquitas*
Udy, Helene (act): *My Bloody Valentine; Nightflyers; Sweet Murder*
Ueda, Akinari (wri): *Ugetsu Monogatari*
Ueda, Kichijiro/K. (act): *Gammera vs. Gyaos; Return of the Giant Monsters*
Ueda, Masaharu (cin): *Ran*
Uehara, Akira (cin): *Gammera vs. Zigra*
Uehara, Ken (act): *Atragon; Mothra*
Ueki, Hitoshi (act): *The Crazy Family*
Ugarte, Julian (act): *Demons of the Dead*
Uhden, Vance (wri): *The Devil's Jest*
Uhl, Paul (cin): *The Love War*
Uhlen, Gisela (act): *The Indian Scarf*
Uhlen, Susanne (act): *Killer With a Silk Scarf*
Uhler, Eric (act): *It Came Upon the Midnight Clear*
Uhry, Ghislain (wri): *Black Moon (1975)*
Ujlaky, Denes (act): *Phantom of the Opera (1983)*
Ukmar, Bruno (act): *Terror of Rome Against the Son of Hercules*
Ukmar, Franco/Frank (act): *Battle of the Amazons; Endgame*
Ukonu, A.E. (act): *The Disembodied*
Ukovich, Milena (act): *Dracula (1974)*
Ulfik, Rick (mus): *Street Trash*
Ulius, Betty (wri): *Psych-Out*
Ullman, Dan(iel) (wri, b. 1920): *Man Afraid; The Maze; Mysterious Island (1961)*
Ullman, Elwood (wri, 1903-1985): *The Bowery Boys Meet the Monsters; Bowery to Bagdad; Dig That Uranium!; Dr. Goldfoot and the Bikini Machine; The Ghost In the Invisible Bikini; Jungle Gents; Paris Playboys; Private Eyes (1953); Snow White and the Three Stooges; Spook Chasers; The Three Stooges In Orbit; The Three Stooges Meet Hercules*
Ullman, Tracey (act, b. 1961): *Robin Hood: Men In Tights*
Ullman Jr., William A. (wri): *Buried Alive (1940)*
Ullmann, Liv (act, b. 1939): *Leonor; Lost Horizon (1973); The Night Visitor; Persona; Vargtimmen*
Ulloa, Alejandro (cin): *Exterminators of the Year 3000; Horror Express*
Ulloa, Alessandro (cin): *Goliath Against the Giants; Horror; Mi Adorable Esclava; El Principe Encadenado*
Ulman (Sr.), Douglas Elton (act & dir): see Fairbanks (Sr.), Douglas
Ulman Jr., Douglas Elton (act): see Fairbanks Jr., Douglas
Ulmer, Edgar G. (dir, 1904-1972): *The Amazing Transparent Man; Antinea, l'Amante della Citta Sepolta; Babes In Bagdad; Beyond the Time Barrier; The Black Cat (1934); Bluebeard (1944); Daughter of Dr. Jekyll; Detour; Girls In Chains; The Man from Planet X; Out of the Night; I Pirati di Capri; Ruthless; Sette Contro la Morte; Strange Illusion; The Wife of Monte Cristo*
Ulmer, Edgar G. (wri, 1904-1972): *Antinea, l'Amante della Citta Sepolta*
Ulmer, Jonathan (act): *Strange Invaders*
Ulric, Lenore (act, 1892-1970): *Temptation (1946)*
Ulrich, Frederick R. (wri): *Phantom of the Mall: Eric's Revenge*
Ulrich, Kim Johnston (act): *Rumpelstiltskin (1996)*
Ulrich, Kurt (wri): *Der Raecher*
Ulrich, Ronald (act): *Cannibal Girls*
Ulrich, Skeet (act, b. 1969): *The Craft; Scream; Touch*
Ulstad, Ron (act): *Nothing But Trouble*
Ultimate Effects (cin): *Pumpkinhead II: Blood Wings*
Ultra Violet (act): *Savages; Simon, King of the Witches; The Telephone Book*

Umbach, Martin (act): *The Neverending Story II: The Next Chapter*
Umbers, Margaret (act): *The Bridge to Nowhere; Dark of the Night; Death Warmed Up*
Umburg, Werner (act): *Murders In the Rue Morgue (1971)*
Umeda, Tomoko (act): *Godzilla On Monster Island*
Umemiya, Tatsuya (act): *The Final War*
Umena, Monica (act): *Demons 2*
Umetsu, Yasuomi (dir): *Robot Carnival*
Umile, Marc (act): *Mutant Hunt*
Umland, Ken (act): *Scanners*
Umlauf, Ellen (act): *Dracula Blows His Cool; Wings of Fame*
Umstadter, David (act): *Silent Night, Deadly Night III*
Underdown, Edward (act, b. 1908): *Beat the Devil; The Camp On Blood Island; The Dark Man (1951); The Day the Earth Caught Fire; Digby-The Biggest Dog In the World; Dr. Crippen; Dr. Terror's House of Horrors (1964); The Hand of Night; Information Received; Locker 69; The Magic Christian; Man On the Run; The October Man; Recoil (1953); Street of Shadows; The Third Alibi; Thunderball; Traitor's Gate; The Two-Headed Spy; The Voice of Merrill; The Warren Case; Woman of Straw; The Woman With No Name*
Underwood, Cathy (act): *The Secret Life of Ian Fleming*
Underwood, David (act): *Asteroid*
Underwood, Ian (mus): *Fugitive from the Empire*
Underwood, Jay (act): *The Boy Who Could Fly; The Invisible Kid; Not Quite Human; Not Quite Human II; Sleepstalker; Star Command; Still Not QuiteHuman; To Die For II: Son of Darkness*
Underwood, Ron (dir): *Heart and Souls; Mighty Joe Young (1998); Tremors*
Underwood, Ron (wri): *Tremors*
Unett, Marjorie (act): *Strategy*
Ung, Tom (act): *Think Fast, Mr. Moto*
Ungaro, Francesca (act): *Sei Donne per l'Assassino*
Ungaro, Nestore (dir & wri): *The Secret of Seagull Island*
Unger, Bertil (act): *The Lucifer Complex*
Unger, Deborah (Kara) (act): *Crash (1996); The Game; Highlander: The Final Dimension*
Unger, Gladys (wri): *Great Expectations (1934); A Night of Mystery (1937)*
Unger, Gustof (act): *The Lucifer Complex*
Unger, Joe (act): *Leatherface: Texas Chainsaw Massacre III; Pumpkinhead II: Blood Wings*
Unger, Matt (wri): *Class of Nuke 'em High, Part 2: Subhumanoid Meltdown*
Ungerman, William (act): *Twin Peaks: Fire Walk With Me*
Uno, Jukichi (act): *Onibaba*
Uno, Koji (act): *Mothra*
Uno, Michael Tishiyuko (dir): *Buried Secrets*
Unsain, Joseph (wri): *Creature of the Walking Dead*
Unsinn, Joe (cin): *Goliath Awaits*
Unson, Vic (act): *Twilight People*
Unsworth, Geoffrey (cin, 1914-1980): *Alice's Adventures In Wonderland (1972); The Assassination Bureau; The Internecine Project; The Magic Christian; Murder On the Orient Express; Oh Dad Poor Dad, Mamma's Hung You In the Closet and I'm Feelin' So Sad; Royal Flash; The Spider and the Fly (1949); The Story of Robin Hood; Superman (1978); Superman II; Tiger In the Smoke; 2001: A Space Odyssey; Voices; Zardoz*
Unterkircher, Hans (act): *Der Letzte Mann*
Unveragh, Adrian (act): *The Body Snatchers*
Unwin Stanley (act): *Chitty Chitty Bang Bang*
Upcher, Peter (act): *Faust (1923); Tut-Tut and His Terrible Tomb*
Updike, John (wri, b. 1932): *The Witches of Eastwick*
Upton, Morgan (act): *It Happened One Christmas; Nightmare In Blood; Time Flyer*
Upton, Nick (act): *The Secret Adventures of Tom Thumb*
Uraneff, Vadim (act): *The Sea Beast*
Urbahns, Paul (act): *Invasion of the Girl Snatchers*
Urbanski, Paul (act): *The Carrier*
Urbini, Pier Luigi (mus): *L'Ultima Preda del Vampiro*
Urbisaglia, Serse (cin): *Sodom and Gomorrah*
Ure, Mary (act, 1933-1975): *The Mind Benders (1963); A Reflection of Fear*
Urecal, Minerva (act, 1896-1966): *The Ape Man; The Bridge of San Luis Rey (1944); Ghost Crazy; Ghosts On the Loose; The Living Ghost (1942); The Lost Moment; Master Minds (1950); 7 Faces of Dr. Lao; Shadow of a Doubt (1943); Sudden Danger; Take One False Step; The Trap*
Urena, Fabio (act): *The Puppet Masters*
Urich, Christian (act): *Lost Prophet*
Urich, Robert (act, b. 1947): *Endangered Species; Final Descent; The Ice Pirates; In a Stranger's Hand; Invitation to Hell; Killdozer; Murder by Night; Young Again*
Uris, Leon (wri, b. 1924): *Topaz*
Urquhart, Gordon (wri): *The Brain Eaters*
Urquhart, Mollie/Molly (act): *The Black Windmill; Digby-The Biggest Dog In the World; House of Mystery (1961); Yield to the Night*
Urquhart, Robert (act, b. 1922): *The Break; Children of the Full Moon; The Curse of Frankenstein; Danger Tomorrow; Golden Ivory; The House of the Arrow (1953); Knights of the Round Table; Limbo Line; Murder at the Gallop; Paul Temple Returns; Tread Softly; You Can't Escape*
Urreta, Alice (mus): *Isle of the Snake People*
Urruty, Natalia (wri): *Moebius*
Ursin, David (act): *Critters 2: The Main Course; Killer in the Mirror; Solar Crisis*
Ursitti, Susan (act): *Teen Wolf; Zapped!*
Urstein, Laura (act): *Once Bitten*
Urueta, Chano (dir): *El Baron del Terror; La Cabeza Viviente; El Espejo de la Bruja*
Uruf, George (act): *The Green Slime*
Urzi, Saro (act): *Beat the Devil; Revenge of the Pirates*
Use, Ondine (act): *The Love Statue*
Usher (act, b. 1979): *The Faculty*
Usher, Guy (act): *After the Thin Man; Charlie Chan at the Opera; Destination Saturn; The Devil Bat; Doomed to Die; Mr. Wong In Chinatown; The Penguin Pool Murder; The Spanish Cape Mystery*
Usher, Vickie (act): *The Toxic Avenger*
Uslar, A. (act): *Blind Date*
Ussachevsky, Vladimir (mus): *No Exit*
Ussing, Olaf (act): *Vredens Dag*
Ustinov, Pavla (act): *Charlie Chan and the Curse of the Dragon Queen; The Thief of Baghdad (1978)*
Ustinov, Peter (act, b. 1921): *Alice In Wonderland (1999); Blackbeard's Ghost; Charlie Chan and the Curse of the Dragon Queen; Dead Man's Folly; Death On the Nile; Evil Under the Sun; The Great Muppet Caper; Grendel, Grendel, Grendel; Hammersmith Is Out; Logan's Run; Lola Montes; The Man Who Wagged His Tail; The Mouse and His Child; One of Our Dinosaurs Is Missing; The Phoenix and the Magic Carpet; Robin Hood (1973); The Thief of Baghdad (1978); Thirteen at Dinner; Topkapi*
Ustinov, Peter (dir, b. 1921): *Hammersmith Is Out; Vice Versa (1947)*
Ustinov, Peter (wri, b. 1921): *Vice Versa (1947)*
Ustinov, Tamara (act): *Blood from the Mummy's Tomb; The Blood On Satan's Claw*
Utay, William (act): *Bodily Harm; Species*
Utley, Scott (act): *Covenant*
Utsui, Ken (act): *Atomic Rulers of the World; Evil Brain from Outer Space; Gammera vs. Zigra*
Utt, Kenneth (act): *The Silence of the Lambs*
Uva, Angela (act): *Trick or Treats*
Uva, David (act): *Trick or Treats*
Uvarova, Y. (act): *Portret Doriana Greya*
Uzzell, Corene (act): *Seven Keys to Baldpate (1917)*

Vabbel, Marc (act): *What Price Murder*
Vacano, Jost (cin): *The Neverending Story; RoboCop; Total Recall*
Vaccarello, Andrea (act): *The Initiation*
Vaccaro, Brenda (act, b. 1939): *Capricorn One; The First Deadly Sin; The House by the Lake; Masque of the Red Death (1989, 21st Century); Supergirl (1984); Ten Little Indians (1989); Zorro, the Gay Blade*
Vacchiann, Carmen (act): *Empire of Ash III*
Vachell, Horace Annesley/H.A. (wri): *The Case of Lady Camber; The House of Peril; The Story of Shirley Yorke*
Vacio, Natividad (act): *The Man With Two Brains*
Vadaszffy, Zsolt (act): *The Ipcress File*
Vadim, Annette (act, nee Annette Stroyberg): *Agent of Doom; Et Mourir de Plaisir*
Vadim, Roger (dir, b. 1928, nee Roger Vadim Plemiannikow): *Barbarella; Et Mourir de Plaisir; Pretty Maids All In a Row; Spirits of the Dead; Le Vice et la Vertu*
Vadim, Roger (wri, b. 1928): *Barbarella; Blackmailed; Et Mourir de Plaisir*
Vadis, Dan (act): *Hercules and the Ten Avengers; Samson and the Seven Challenges; The Son of*

Hercules In the Land of Darkness; Il Trionfo di Ercole; Triumph of the Ten Gladiators
Vadnay, Laszlo (wri): *Flesh and Fantasy; The Great Rupert; Way...Way Out*
Vaeoso, Henry (act): *Night of the Red Hunter*
Vaessen, Eric (act): *The Ape Creature*
Vagenende, Mme. (act): *The Black Windmill*
Vague, Vera (act): see Allen, Barbara (Jo)
Vahanian, Marc (act): *The Amityville Horror*
Vaicik, Stella (act): *Vivce Versa (1988)*
Vail, Justina (act): *Carnosaur 3: Primal Species; Naked Souls*
Vail, Myrtle (act): *The Little Shop of Horrors (1960)*
Vail, Tina (act): *Wes Craven's New Nightmare*
Vail, William (act): *The Texas Chainsaw Massacre*
Vailati, Bruno (dir): *La Battaglia di Maratona*
Vailati, Bruno (wri): *La Battaglia di Maratona; The Thief of Baghdad (1960)*
Vaile, David (act): *Simon, King of the Witches*
Vailland, Roger (wri): *Et Mourir de Plaisir*
Vails, Michael J. (act): *I Was a Zombie for the F.B.I.*
Vajda, Ernest (wri, 1887-1954): *Marie Antoinette (1938); A Night of Mystery (1928); Such Men Are Dangerous*
Vajda, Ladislas (dir, 1905-1965): *The Man Who Wagged His Tail; The Woman With No Name*
Vajda, Ladislas (wri, 1905-1965): *The Woman With No Name*
Vajda, Laszlo (wri): *Die Herrin von Atlantis*
Valade, Paul (act): *Deadbolt*
Valandrey, Charlotte (act): *Orlando*
Valbel, Henri (act): *Forces Occultes*
Valbiro, Anthony (act): *Spookies*
Valcauda, Armando (cin): *Hercules (1983)*
Valcke, Serge-Henri (act): *The Lift*
Valdemar, Carlos (wri): *Guyana, Cult of the Damned*
Valderi, Xenia (act): *Red Desert*
Valdes, Mario (act): *Neon Maniacs*
Valdes, Paloma (act): *La Venganza de Don Mendo*
Valdez, Daniel (act): *The China Syndrome*
Valdez, Eric F. (act): *The Octagon*
Valdez, Esteban (act): *Caveman (1981)*
Valdez, Mario (act): *The Octagon*
Valdis, Sigrid (act): *Our Man Flint*
Valduga, Ena (act): *The Invisible Terror*
Vale, Douglas (act): *Bloodspell*
Vale, Martin (wri): *The Two Mrs. Carrolls*
Vale, Nina (act): *Cornered*
Vale, Rita (act): *The Thief (1952)*
Vale, Virginia (act): *Panama Menace*
Valencia, Mathew (act): *Lawnmower Man 2: Beyond Cyberspace*
Valencia, Vance (act): *Contact; I, Madman*
Valente, Pasquale (act): *Demons 2*
Valente, Victor (act): *The Eyes Behind the Stars*
Valenti, Mark (wri): *Like Father, Like Santa*
Valentin, Albert (wri): *Terror of Rome Against the Son of Hercules*
Valentin, Mirko (act): *Castle of the Living Dead; La Vergine di Norimberga*
Valentine, A.J. (act): *Flight of the Lost Balloon*
Valentine, Anthony (act): *The Girl On the Pier; The Monster Club; Murder Is Easy; Performance; Robin Hood and the Sorcerer; To the Devil a Daughter; Tower of Evil*
Valentine, Barbara (act): *Horrors of Spider Island*
Valentine, Chris (act): *The People*
Valentine, Cindy (act): *The Pink Chiquitas*
Valentine, Elizabeth (act): *Kiss of the Vampire*
Valentine, John (act): *The Lost Patrol (1929)*
Valentine, Joseph (cin, 1900-1949, nee Giuseppe Valentino): *The Boys from Syracuse; Hold That Ghost; Possessed (1947); Rope, Saboteur; Shadow of a Doubt (1943); Sleep, My Love; The Wolf Man (1941)*
Valentine, Karen (act, b. 1947): *The Power Within (1995); Return to Fantasy Island*
Valentine, Kim (act): *Grandma's House*
Valentine, Nancy (act): *The Black Castle; Night Slaves*
Valentine, Paul (act): *The Man Who Saw Tomorrow; Out of the Past (1947)*
Valentine, Scott (act, b. 1958): *Carnosaur 3: Primal Species; Deadtime Stories; Mars; My Demon Lover; Object of Obsession; Out of Annie's Past; Till the End of the Night; To Sleep With a Vampire; The Unborn II*
Valentine, Stephanie (act): *The People*
Valentine, Steve (act): *Mars Attacks!*
Valentine, Val (wri): *Alf's Secret; Elstree Calling; Forbidden; Fortune Is a Woman; Mother Riley Meets the Vampire; Old Mother Riley's Jungle Treasure; Rich and Strange; The Ringer (1952); They Can't Hang Me; This Was a Woman; The Yellow Mask*
Valentino, Giuseppe (cin): see Valentine, Joseph
Valentino, Rudolph (act, 1895-1926): *The Conquering Power*
Valenza, Tasia (act): *Sometimes They Come Back*
Valera, Dominique (act): *Terminus*
Valere, Simone (act): *La Beaute du Diable*
Valerie, Babs (act): *Ashes*
Valerie, Jeanne (act): *Nick Carter et le Trefle Rouge*
Valerie, Joan (act, d. 1983): *Charlie Chan at the Wax Museum; Just Off Broadway; Michael Shayne, Private Detective; Murder Over New York*
Valery, Ann(e) (act): *Kind Hearts and Coronets; One Way Out; Stop Press Girl*
Valim, Mark (act): *Phenomenon*
Valin, Jonathan (wri): *Final Notice*
Valiquette, Rick (act): *The Clan of the Cave Bear*
Valk, Frederick (act, 1901-1956): *Dead of Night (1945); The Flanagan Boy; Gestapo; Hotel Reserve; Latin Quarter; The Patient Vanishes; Secret Venture; Thunder Rock; Top Secret (1952)*
Vallacher, Kitty (act): *Grave of the Vampire*
Vallance, Louise (act): *Robbers of the Sacred Mountain*
Valle, Richard (act): *La Isla de la Muerte*
Vallee, Marcel (act): *Paris Qui Dort*
Vallee, Rudy (act, 1901-1986): *International House*
Valles, Carlos (act): *Endgame*
Valley, Micele (act): *Singapore Sling*
Valli, (Alida) (act, b. 1921, nee Alida Maria Altenburger): *L'Anticristo; The Cassandra Crossing; Edipo Re; House of Exorcism; Inferno (1979); The Paradine Case; The Stranger's Hand; Suspiria; The Third Man; Les Yeux sans Visage*
Valli, Romolo (act, 1924-1980): *Boom; Holocaust 2000*
Valli, Virginia (act, 1895-1968): *The Lost Zeppelin; The Shock (1923)*
Vallier, Helene (act): *Saadia*
Valliere, Archie (act): *Jaws 3-D*
Vallin, Rick (act): *Bowery to Bagdad; Captive Girl; Dangerous Money; Ghosts On the Loose; The Golden Idol; Jungle Manhunt; The Panther's Claw; Secrets of a Sorority Girl; Strange Fascination; Voodoo Tiger*
Vallis, Jane (act): *Picnic at Hanging Rock*
Vallis, Robert/Bob (act): *The Amazing Partnership; The Greek Interpreter; The Hound of the Baskervilles (1921); The Man With the Twisted Lip (1921); Melody of Death*
Vallon, Michael (act): *Black Widow (1954)*
Vallone, Raf (act, b. 1916): *The Adventures of Mandrin; Amanti d'Oltretomba; Don Juan's Night of Love; The Girl In Room 2A; The Human Factor; Kiss the Girls and Make Them Die; The Kremlin Letter; La Morte Risale a Ieri Sera; Obsession (1954); A Thousand and One Nights (1968)*
Vallone, Saverio (act): *The Grim Reaper*
Vallot, keith (act): *Lunatic*
Valmont, Bullet (act): *The Mask (1994)*
Valmont, Jean (act): *Fantastic Planet*
Valmont, Vera (act): *La Maldicion de los Karnsteins; September Storm*
Valmour, Martin (act): *Queenie of the Circus*
Valmy, Andre (act): *Le Saint Mene la Dance*
Valoie, Connie (act): *The Creeping Terror*
Valois, Valerie (act): *Scanners III: The Takeover*
Valori, Bice (act): *Hercules In the Vale of Woe*
Valverda, Rafael (act): *Loves of Carmen (1927)*
Valverde, Maximo (act): *Night Fiend; The Sharks' Cave*
Valverde, Mike (act): *The Lawnmower Man*
Vampira (act, b. 1922, nee Maila Nurmi): *The Magic Sword (1962); Night of the Ghouls; Plan 9 from Outer Space; Sex Kittens Go to College*
Van, Alex (act): *Web of Deceit*
Van, Beatrice (wri): *Night of Terror (1933)*
Van, Bobby (act, 1933-1980): *Doomsday Machine; Lost Horizon (1973); The Navy vs. the Night Monsters*
Van, Frankie (act): *The Curse of the Undead*
Van Allsburg, Chris (wri): *Jumanji*
van Ammelrooy, Willeke (act): *The Lift; My Nights With Susan, Sandra, Olga and Julie*
Van Ark, Joan (act, b. 1943): *Frogs; The Last Dinosaur; Tainted Blood; When the Dark Man Calls*
Van Atta, Lee (act): *Dick Tracy (1937)*
Van Avery, Dale (wri): *The Murders In the Rue Morgue (1932)*
van Beers, Stanley (act): *Before I Wake; Late Night Final; The Man Without a Body; The Quatermass Experiment*
Van Berg, Detlef (act): *Dracula Sucks*
Van Bergen, Ingrid (act): *The Devil's Daffodil; Der Raecher*
Van Bergen, Lewis (act): *The Relic; Space Rage*
Vanbrugh, Irene (act): *Knight Without Armour*
Van Burek, Nicolas (act): *Clarence*
Van Buren, Ned (cin): *The Headless Horseman*
Van Camp, Lenore (act): *Sleepstalker*
Van Camp, Paul (act): *The Monster Squad*
Vance, Brenda (act): *Night Shadow*
Vance, Courtney B. (act, b. 1960): *The Hunt for Red October; The Preacher's Wife*
Vance, Danitra (act): *Limit Up*
Vance, Dennis (act): *Shadow of the Eagle*
Vance, Don (act): *The Groundstar Conspiracy*
Vance, Jim (act): *Blood Cult*
Vance, John Holbrook (wri): *Bad Ronald*
Vance, Joseph Louis (wri): *Alias the Lone Wolf; Cheaters at Play; Counter-Espionage; The False Faces; The Last of the Lone Wolf; The Lone Wolf (1917 & 1924); The Lone Wolf and His Lady; The Lone Wolf In London; The Lone Wolf In Mexico; The Lone Wolf In Paris; The Lone Wolf Keeps a Date; The Lone Wolf Meets a Lady; The Lone Wolf Returns (1926 & 1935); The Lone Wolf's Daughter (1919 & 1929); The Lone Wolf Spy Hunt; The Lone Wolf Strikes; The Lone Wolf Takes a Chance; The Notorious Lone Wolf; One Dangerous Night; Passport to Suez; Secrets of the Lone Wolf*
Vance, Leigh (wri): *And Women Shall Weep; The Black Windmill; Crossplot; Dr. Crippen; The Flesh Is Weak; The Frightened City; Piccadilly Third Stop; The Shakedown; Witness In the Dark*
Vance, Lucille (act): *Bowery at Midnight*
Vance, Vivian (act, 1912-1979): *The Great Houdinis; The Secret Fury*
Van Cleef, Lee (act, 1925-1989): *The Bandits of Corsica; The Beast from 20,000 Fathoms; Escape from New York; It Conquered the World; The Octagon; Private Eyes (1953)*
Van Cleef, Stephen (act): *Def by Temptation*
Van Dalsem, Michael (act): *The Bermuda Triangle*
van Dalsum, Josine (act): *The Lift*
Van Dam, Gwen (act): *Star Trek: Generations*
Van Damme, Jean-Claude (act, b. 1960): *Cyborg (1989); Timecop; Universal Soldier*
Van Day, David (act): *Screamtime*
Vandell, Ed (act): *Wicked Stepmother*
Van den Bergh, Gert (act): *Victim Five*
Van Den Bogaerd, Derek (act): see Bogarde, Dirk
Van Den Houten, Devvie (act): *What's the Matter With Helen?*
Vander, Musetta (act): *Backlash: Oblivion 2; Monolith; Project Shadowchaser III*
Vanderbosch, Alfred (dir): *The Lonely Road*
Van Der Byl, Dutch (cin): *Dark Mirror (1984)*
Van Der Byl, Philip (act): *Prisoners of the Lost Universe*
Van Der Byl, Vincent (act): *King Solomon's Mines (1985)*
Vandercook, John W. (wri): *Mr. Moto In Danger Island*
Van Der Enden, Edward (cin): *Daughters of Darkness*
Van der Gragt, Hans (act): *My Nights With Susan, Sandra, Olga and Julie*
Vandergrift III, Charles (act): *It's Alive III: Island of the Alive*
Vandergrift, Monte (act): *The Kennel Murder Case; The Mandarin Mystery; The Phantom Creeps*
Vanderkloot, Victoria (act): *The Fan*
van der Linden, Paul (cin): *King Solomon's Treasure*
van der Made, Guus (act): *The Fourth Man*
Van Derman, Carol (act): *Noose*
Vandernoot, Alexandra (act): *Highlander: The Gathering*
Vanderpump, Lisa (act): *Killer's Moon*
VanderPyl, Jean (act, 1920-1999): *The Flintstones; Jetsons: The Movie*
Vanders, Warren (act): *The Bermuda Triangle; The Tribe*
Van Der Stolk, Pieter (act): *Howling II*
Van Der Veer, Gregory (cin): *Metalstorm: The Destruction of Jared-Syn*
Van Der Veer, Willard (cin): *The Crawling Hand*
Van Der Velde, Nadine (act): *After Midnight; Critters; Munchies*
van der Vlis, Diana (act): *The Girl In Black Stockings; Lovespell; X—The Man With the X-Ray Eyes*
Van de Sande, Theo (cin): *Body Parts (1991); The First Power; Miracle Mile; Volcano*
Van Deter, Tonia (act): *How to Stuff a Wild Bikini*
Van Devere, Trish (act, b. 1943): *The Changeling; The Day of the Dolphin; The Hearse*
Van Dien, Casper (act): *Beastmaster III: The Eye of Braxus; Nightscream; Starship Troopers; Tarzan and the Lost City*
Van Dine, S.S. (wri, 1888-1939, nee Willard Huntingdon Wright): *The Benson Murder Case; The Bishop Murder Case; Calling Philo Vance; The Canary Murder Case; The Casino Murder Case; The Dragon Murder Case; The Garden Murder Case; The Gracie Allen Murder Case; The Greene Murder Case; The Kennel Murder Case; A Night of Mystery (1937); Philo Vance Returns; Philo Vance's Gamble; Philo Vance's Secret Mission; The Scarab Murder Case*
Vandis, Titos (act): *The Exorcist; Satan's Triangle*
Van Dolsen, Foy (act): *Horror Island*
Van Doorn, Trudy (act): *Quest for Love*
Van Doren, Mamie (act, b. 1933, nee Joan Lucille Olander): *Francis Joins the WACs; The Girl In Black Stockings; The Navy vs. the Night Monsters; The Private Lives of Adam and Eve; Sex Kittens Go to College; Voyage to a Prehistoric Planet*
Van Dorn, Mildred (act): *Liliom (1930)*
Van Dreelen, John (act): *Beyond the Time Barrier; The Big Game; The Clone Master; Covenant; The Formula; The Leech Woman; Lost Horizon (1973); 13 Ghosts; The Ultimate Impostor; The Wizard of Baghdad*
Vandross, Luther (act): *The Meteor Man*
Van Druten, John (wri, 1901-1957): *Bell, Book and Candle; Night Must Fall (1937)*
van Dungen, Fritz (act): see Dorn, Philip
Van Dusen, Granville (act): *Dr. Scorpion*
Van Dycke, Tom (wri): *The Man Who Lived Twice*
Van Dyke, Barry (act): *It Happened at Lake Wood Manor*
Van Dyke, Bonnie (act): *The Bat People; Scream of the Wolf*
Van Dyke, Dick (act, b. 1925): *Chitty Chitty Bang Bang; Dick Tracy (1990); Ghost of a Chance (1987); Mary Poppins*
Van Dyke, Sandee (act): *Murder of Innocence*
Van Dyke, Tom (wri): *Murder at Monte Carlo*
Van Dyke (II), W.S. (dir, 1887-1943): *After the Thin Man; I Married an Angel; Marie Antoinette (1938); Rage In Heaven; Shadow of the Thin Man; Tarzan the Ape Man (1932); The Thin Man; Trader Horn (1931)*
Vane, Amy (act): *Secret Cinema*
Vane, Charles (act): *Caught In His Own Net; The Cobweb; Face to Face; The Failure; The Golden Dawn; The Grand Babylon Hotel; The Lyons Mail; The Man Behind "The Times"; The Murder of Squire Jeffrey; Paul Sleuth and the Mystic Seven; Paul Sleuth, Crime Investigator: The Burglary Syndicate; Paul Sleuth-The Mystery of the Astorian Crown Prince; The Polar Star; Queen of My Heart; Royal Love; The Story of the Rosary; The Wheel of Death; Whosoever Shall Offend*
Vane, Norman Thaddeus (dir): *Frightmare (1983); Midnight (1989)*
Vane, Norman Thaddeus (wri): *Frightmare (1983); Midnight (1989); Shadow of the Hawk*
Vane, Sutton (wri, 1888-1963): *Between Two Worlds; Outward Bound*
Vanel, Charles (act, 1885-1989): *Cadaveri Eccellenti; Diabolique (1955), The Mask of the Gorilla; La Mort en Ce Jardin; La Nuit de la Revanche; L'Or du Cristobal; La Poursuite; Le Salaire de la Peur; To Catch a Thief*
Van Endres, Joe (act): *It Came Upon the Midnight Clear*
Van Enger, Charles (cin, b. 1890): *Abbott and Costello Meet Frankenstein; Abbott and Costello Meet the Killer; Africa Screams; The Boys from Brooklyn; Bride of the Gorilla; Crazy House (1943); The Magnetic Monster; Night Monster; The Phantom of the Opera (1925); Salome (1922); Sherlock Holmes Faces Death; Spider Woman; The Time of Their Lives; Who Done It? (1942)*
Van Eps, Worster (act): see Parker, Willard
Van Ess, Connie (act): *Stigma*
Van Evera, Jack (act): *Funeral Home; My Bloody Valentine*
Van Every, Dale (wri): *Trader Horn (1931)*
Van Eyck, Peter (act, 1913-1969): *Assignment to Kill; The Devil's Agent; Dr. Mabuse vs. Scotland Yard; Five Graves to Cairo; The Glass Tower; High Season for Spies; Das Madchen Rosemarie; Mr. Arkadin; Requiem for a Secret Agent; Run for the Sun; Le Salaire de la Peur; The Secret of Dr. Mabuse; The Snorkel; The Spy Who Came In from the Cold; Station*

Six-Sahara; Tarzan's Hidden Jungle; Die Tausend Augen des Dr. Mabuse; Vengeance
Van Eyssen, John (act, b. 1923): Account Rendered; The Accursed; Blind date (1959); Four Sided Triangle; Horror of Dracula; Marriage of Convenience; Men of Sherwood Forest; Moment of Indiscretion; Partners In Crime (1961); Quatermass II; Three Steps In the Dark; The Whole Truth
Van Fleet, Jo (act, b. 1922): Satan's School for Girls; The Tenant
Van Fleet, Richard (act): Ben; The Magician (1973)
Vangelis (mus, b. 1943): Blade Runner
van Groningen, Ger (act): The Lift
Van Gulick, Robert (wri): Judge Dee and the Monastery Murder
Van Gysegham, Andre (act): Face In the Night; The Limping Man (1953); The Pied Piper (1971)
Van Haden, Andres (act): Cheaters at Play
Van Haren, Roger (act): The Pit (1983)
Van Hartingsveld, Lo (act): Nosferatu, the Vampyre
Van Hawley, Norman (act): The Manster
van Heemstra, Edda Hepburn (act): see Hepburn, Audrey
Van Heerden, Marcel (act): Steel Dawn
Van Hensbergen, Lo (act): Amsterdam Affair
van Hentenryk, Kevin (act): Basket Case; Basket Case 2; Basket Case 3: The Progeny
Van Highland, Gwen (act): Mother's Day
Van Hoose, Jeffrey (act): Addams Family Values
Van Horn, Donald (act): Tales from the Darkside
Van Horn, Emil (act): The Ape Man
Van Horn, Maya (act): Nightfall (1956)
Van Husen, Dan (act): Nosferatu, the Vampyre
Vanity (act): Highlander: The Gathering; Memories of Murder; Neon City
Vankaast, Anthony (act): Strange Behaviour
Vanke, Elena (act): Cinderella (1961)
Van Koghbe, Elliot (act): Boarding House
Van Lamsweerde, Pino (dir): Asterix In Britain
Van Lenhoff, Vincent (act): Beverly Hills Bodysnatchers
Van Lidth, Erland (act): Alone In the Dark; The Running Man (1987)
Van Lingen, Thor (act): Return of the Living Dead, Part II
Vanlint, Derek (cin): Alien; Dragonslayer
Vanloo, Rolf E. (wri): Gold
van Loon, Hendrik (wri, 1882-1944): The Story of Mankind
van Loon, Larry (cin): Scalps
Van Lusil, Jan (wri): Traitor Spy
van Mello, Luk (act): The Lift
Van Meter, Harry L. (act): The Hunchback of Notre Dame (1923)
Vann, Jay (wri): Tarzan's Revenge
Vanna, Nina (act): Lucrezia Borgia: or, Plaything of Power; The Man Without Desire; Scrooge (1923)
Vanner, Sue (act): The Spy Who Loved Me
Van Ness, Jon (act): End of the World (1977); Hospital Massacre; Tourist Trap
Vanni, Massimo (act): Escape from the Bronx
Vanni, Renata (act): Lady In White
Vanni, Robert (act): The Psychotronic Man
Vannicola, Joanne (act): Love and Human Remains
Van Norden, Peter (act): The Stand
Vannucchi, Luigi (act): The Red Tent
Van Nutter, Rik (act): Assignment-Outer Space; Thunderball
Van Nuys, Ed (act): Always
Vanoni, Ornella (act): Romolo e Remo
Van Oostrum, Kees (cin): The Gifted One; Separate Lives; Thinner
Van Orden, Robert E. (act): see Smith, John
Van Orman, Gary (act): Rattlers
Van Ost, Valerie (act): Corruption; The Satanic Rites of Dracula
Van Pallandt, Nina (act): The Sword and the Sorcerer
Van Parys, Georges (mus, 1902-1970): L'Age d'Or; Diabolique (1955); Madame DuBarry (1954); Mr. Peek-a-Boo; Nathalie, Agent Secret
Van Patten, Dick (act, b. 1928): Charly; Freaky Friday (1976); The Midnight Hour; Psychomania (1964); The Shaggy D.A.; Soylent Green; Spaceballs; The Strongest Man In the World; Westworld
Van Patten, Jim(my) (act): Freaky Friday (1976); Toy Story
Van Patten, Joyce (act, b. 1934): The Demon Murder Case; The Haunted (1991); Monkey Shines; The Stranger Within
Van Patten, Nels (act): Ghost Writer; Grotesque
Van Patten, Patricia (act): Herbie Goes Bananas
Van Patten, Timothy (act): Class of '84; Curse IV: The Ultimate Sacrifice; Zone Troopers
Van Patten, Vincent (act, b. 1958): Charley and the Angel; Hell Night
Van Peebles, Mario (act, b. 1957): Exterminator II; Full Eclipse; Highlander: The Final Dimension; Jaws: The Revenge; Solo
Van Pernis, Mona (act): The Ripper (1985)
Van Ravenswaay, Susan (act): Strange Behavior
Van Rees, Iris (wri): Target...Earth?
Van Rees, Joost (dir): Target...Earth?
Van Riel, Greg (act): Rabid
Van Rodgers, Joe (wri): Brain of Blood
Van Ronkel, Rip (wri): Beautiful Stranger; Destination Moon
Van Rooten, Luis (act, 1906-1973): The Big Clock; Boston Blackie's Chinese Venture; Curse of the Faceless Man; The Gentleman from Nowhere
Van Rooyen, Alex (act): Because of the Cats
Van Scott, Glory (act): The Wiz
Van Selst, Will (act): Amsterdam Affair
Van Sickel, Dale (act): Cyclotrode X; Duel; Lost Planet Airmen; Missile Monsters; Satan's Satellites
VanSickler, John (act): The Resurrection of Zachary Wheeler
Van Sloan, Edward (act, 1882-1964): Before I Hang; Behind the Mask (1932); The Black Room; The Crime of Dr. Crespi; The Death Kiss; Death Takes a Holiday (1934); Deluge; Dracula (1931, English-speaking version); Dracula's Daughter; Frankenstein (1931); The Last Days of Pompeii (1935); The Mask of Dijon; The Mummy (1932); The Phantom Creeps
Van Spall, Richard (act): Nightbreed
Vanterpool, Freda T. (act): The Deathmaster
Van't Hoff, Anke (act): Gebroken Spiegels
Van Tongreen, John (mus): Peter Benchley's 'Creature'
Van Trees, James (cin): Angel On My Shoulder (1946); The Green Goddess (1929); The Lone Wolf's Daughter (1929)
Van Valkenburg, Eric (act): The Fan
Can Valkenburgh, Deborah (act): Streets of Fire
Van Vooren, Monique (act, b. 1925): Fearless Frank; Frankenstein (1974); Tarzan and the She-Devil
Van Voorhees, Yvette (act): Xanadu
Van Warmerdam, Alex (act & dir): Der Noorderlingen
van Wijk, Carola Gijsbers (act): The Lift
Van Winkle, Joseph (wri): Dark Places
Van Winkle, Marsha (act): Party Line
Vanya (act): For Your Eyes Only
Van Zandt, Billy (act): Jaws 2; Star Trek
Van Zandt, Ned (act): The Presence
Van Zandt, Phil(ip) (act, 1904-1958): Between Midnight and Dawn; The Big Clock; Boston Blackie's Rendezvous; Ghost Chasers; Gog; House of Frankenstein; Invisible Agent; The Lone Wolf and His Lady; Man of a Thousand Faces; Prisoners of the Casbah; The Shanghai Chest; Son of Ali Baba; Sudan; Tarzan's Desert Mystery; Tarzan Triumphs; Thief of Damascus; The 27th Day; Where Danger Lives
Van Zeebroeck, Bruno (cin): Not of This World
Van Zyl, Dee Dee (act): The Hand That Rocks the Cradle
Varaigne, Dominique (act): see Sanda, Dominique
Varconi, Victor (act, 1896-1976, nee Mihaly Varkonyi): The Atomic Submarine; The Black Camel; The Man Who Turned to Stone; Menace (1934); Mr. Moto Takes a Vacation; Samson and Delilah
Varconi, Victor (wri, 1896-1976): Menace (1934)
Varden, Evelyn (act, 1895-1958): The Bad Seed (1956); The Night of the Hunter (1955)
Varden, Norma (act, b. 1898): Dr. Dolittle (1967); Les Miserables (1952); Scotland Yard (1941); Strangers On a Train; 13 Frightened Girls; Witness for the Prosecution
Vardi, Mirella (act): Blind Date
Varela Jr., Alfredo (wri): Creature of the Walking Dead
Varela, Amanda (act): The Falcon's Brother
Varela, Jesus (act): Parsifal
Varela, Yolanda (act): La Casa del Terror
Varelli, Alfredo (act): Siege of Syracuse
Varennes, Andre (act): La Main du Diable
Varennes, Jacques (act): Diabolique (1955); Orphee
Varese, Francesco (cin): Lost In the Bermuda Triangle
[illegible] (act): Bride of the Gorilla; Space Master X-7
Varga, Richie (act): Eraser
Vargas, Catherine (act): Phoenix the Warrior
Vargas, Daniele (act): Caltiki, il Mostro Immortale; Ercole Contro Roma; Revenge of the Gladiators; Sodom and Gomorrah; Spirits of the Dead
Vargas, Henry (cin): The Unholy
Vargas, Jean (act): The Slumber Party Massacre
Vargas, John (act): Seduced by Evil
Vargas, Manuela (act): A Midsummer Night's Dream (1985)
Vargas, Valentina (act): Hellraiser: Bloodline; The Name of the Rose
Vari, Giovanni (act): Robin Hood and the Pirates
Vari, Giuseppe (dir): Roma Contra Roma
Varick, Alfred (act): see Drayton, Alfred
Varis, Kelly (act): Gammera vs. Jiger
Varkonyi, Mihaly (act): see Varconi, Victor
Varley, Ann (act): The Nesting
Varley, Beatrice (act, b. 1896): Bang! You're Dead; Bedelia; The Black Rider; Death Goes to School; Echo of Barbara; Horrors of the Black Museum; The Man In Grey; My Brother's Keeper; Night Without Pity; Paul Temple's Triumph; Send for Paul Temple; She Shall Have Murder; The Surgeon's Knife; Tiger In the Smoke; The Upturned Glass; Young and Innocent
Varley, John (act): Meet Sexton Blake
Varley, John (wri): Millennium
Varnadow, Peggy (act): see Dow, Peggy
Varnals, Wendy (act): Corruption
Varnel, Marcel (dir, 1894-1947): Alf's Button Afloat; Chandu the Magician; The Ghost at St. Michael's; King Arthur Was a Gentleman
Varnel, Max (dir): The Child and the Killer; Enter Inspector Duval; The Great Van Robbery; Links of Justice; Moment of Indiscretion; Murder In Eden; No Safety Ahead; A Question of Suspense; Return of a Stranger (1962); The Rivals; Sentenced for Life; Web of Suspicion; A Woman Possessed
Varner, Mike (cin): The Day It Came to Earth
Varney, Jim (act): Ernest Saves Christmas; Ernest Scared Stupid; Slam Dunk Ernest; Toy Story; Wilder Napalm
Varney, Robert (act): The Swarm
Varnick, Neil T. (wri): The Mummy's Tomb
Varno, Martin (wri): Night of the Blood-Beast
Varno, Roland (act): As You Desire Me; Flight to Nowhere; My Name Is Julia Ross; The Return of the Vampire
Varriani, Emilio (cin): Gli Orrori del Castello di Norembega
Vars, Henry (mus): House of the Damned (1962)
Varsami, Maria (act): Nostradamus
Varsi, Diane (act, 1938-1992): The People; Wild In the Streets
Vartan, Michael (act): Fiorile
Varyagin, A. (act): Sonka Zolotaya Ruchka
Vasallo, Carlos (wri): Conquest
Vasarykova, Magda (act): Na Komete
Vasaturo, Bill (act): Twisted
Vasayova, Emilie (act): Ikaria XB1
Vas Dias, Thelma (act): The Lady Vanishes (1938)
Vash, Karl (cin): M (1931)
Vasicek, Karel (act): Order and Disorder
Vasova, Marie (act): Cisaruv Pekar, Pekaruv Cisar
Vasquez, Erica Vega (act): Grim Prairie Tales
Vasquez, Jessica Vega (act): Grim Prairie Tales
Vasquez, Peter Mark (act): Fire In the Sky (1993); Point of No Return; Sleepstalker
Vasquez, Roberta (act): Hard Hunted
Vasquez, Romeo (act): Curse of the Vampires
Vass, Alexandro (act): Spawn of the Slithis
Vassallo, Rita (act): Trauma (1993)
Vasseur, Didier (mus): Blackout (1978)
Vassey, Liz (act): The Adventures of Captain Zoom In Outer Space
Vasut, Marek (act): Mission: Impossible
Vater, Erwin (act): Metropolis (1926)
Vaucher, Suzanna (act): Deadtime Stories
Vaughan, Bernard (act): The Cloister and the Woman; The Valley of Fear (1916)
Vaughan, Betty (act): Neon Maniacs
Vaughan, David (act): Killer's Kiss
Vaughan, Dennis (act): Zorro: The Legend Begins
Vaughan, Dorothy (act): After the Thin Man; The Ape (1940)
Vaughan, Gillian (act): And Women Shall Weep
Vaughan, Gwyneth (act): The Man from Yesterday (1949); Things Happen at Night
Vaughan, Jimmy (act): The Woman Eater
Vaughan, Kathleen (act): Belphegor the Mountebank; The Crimson Circle (1922); The Face at the Window (1920); The Last Hour; The Prince and the Beggarmaid
Vaughan, Martin (act): Picnic at Hanging Rock
Vaughan, Mollie (act): The Vultures of London
Vaughan, Paris (act): Buffy the Vampire Slayer
Vaughan, Paul (act): Threads
Vaughan, Peter (act, b. 1923): Brazil; The Devil's Agent; The Eyes Have It; Eyewitness (1970); Fanatic (1965); Hammerhead; Haunted Honeymoon (1986); Jamaica Inn (1985); The Man Outside (1967); The Naked Runner; The Pied Piper (1971); The Return (1973, GB); Sapphire; Smokescreen; Straw Dogs; Sudden Terror; Symptoms; Taste of Excitement; Time Bandits; The Village of the Damned (1960); Why Would Anyone Want to Kill a Nice Girl Like You?
Vaughan, Rees (act): The Playground
Vaughn, Delane (act): Strange Days
Vaughn, Grady (act): The Giant Gila Monster
Vaughn, Hilda (act): Charlie Chan at the Opera; Charlie Chan at the Wax Museum; The Phantom of Crestwood
Vaughn, Jerry (act): Lies
Vaughn, Judson (act): Web of Deceit
Vaughn, Kerry (act): Prehistoric Women (1950)
Vaughn, Ned (act): The Hunt for Red October; Max Q: Emergency Landing; Nightscream; Secrets of the Phantom Caverns
Vaughn, Robert (act, b. 1932): Battle Beyond the Stars (1980); The Caretakers; C.H.U.D. II; City In Fear; Demon Seed; Doctor Franken; Escape to Witch Mountain (1995); Fantasies; Hangar 18; The Helicopter Spies; How to Steal the World; Joe's Apartment; The Karate Killers; The Lucifer Complex; The Mind of Mr. Soames; One of Our Spies Is Missing; One Spy Too Many; The Return of the Man from U.N.C.L.E.; The Spy In the Green Hat; The Spy With My Face; Starship Invasions;Superman III; Teenage Cave Man; To Trap a Spy; The Towering Inferno; Transylvania Twist; The Venetian Affair; Virtual Obsession; Virus (1980); The Woman Hunter
Vaughn, Vince (act): The Lost World: Jurassic Park; Psycho (1998)
Vaughn, William (act): Condemned (1929)
Vaughter, Marcus (act): Nightmare Sisters; Visitants
Vauthier, Jean (wri): Les Abysses
Vautier, Sydney (act): A Bid for Fortune; The Wraith of the Tomb
Vaverka, Anton (act): The Phantom of the Opera (1925); Secrets of the Night
Vavitch, Michael (act): The Bridge of San Luis Rey (1929)
Vawter, Ron (act, b. 1948): Plymouth; The Silence of the Lambs
Vazak, P.H. (wri): Greystoke: The Legend of Tarzan, Lord of the Apes
Vaz Dias, Selma (act): Bluebeard's Ten Honeymoons; Cat Girl; The Flanagan Boy; Night Plane to Amsterdam; Strangers' Meeting; The Tell-Tale Heart (1960)
Vasquez, Laura (act): The Beast (1996)
Vazquez, Jose Luis Lopez (act): Not On Your Life!
Vazzoler, Chandra (act): Ator: The Fighting Eagle
Vea, Katena (act): see Victor, Katherine
Veadov, Alex (act): Contact
Veazie, Carol (act): Crackle of Death; Signpost to Murder
Vecchietti, Alberto (wri): Il Mostro dell'Isola
Vecchio, Sal (act): Ruby
Vechialli, Paul (wri): Nick Carter et le Trefle Rouge
Vedder, Will(iam) (act): World Without End; You Never Can Tell
Veeder, Deeann (act): Carnage
Veerman, Hans (act): Flesh & Blood; The Fourth Man; The Lift
Veevers, Wally (cin, d. 1983): The Day of the Triffids; The Keep; Satellite In the Sky; Sodom and Gomorrah; Superman (1978); 2001: A Space Odyssey
Vega, Alexa (act): Netforce; Twister
Vegh, Joseph (dir): Katharsis
Vehr, Nicholas (act): Above Suspicion
Veidt, Conrad (act, 1892-1943, nee Conrad Weidt): Above Suspicion; Bella Donna (1934); Cesare Borgia; Dark Journey; F.P. 1 Antwortet Nicht; I Was a Spy; Der Januskopf; Das Kabinett des Dr. Caligari; King of the Damned; Lucrezia Borgia (1922); The Man Who Laughs (1928); Nazi Agent; Orlacs Haende; The Passing of the Third Floor Back (1935); Rasputin (1930); Satanas; The Spy In Black; Der Student von Prag (1926); The Thief of Bagdad (1940); Under the Red Robe (1937); [illegible] Wandering Jew (1933)
Veiller, Anthony (wri, 1903-1965): The List of Adrian Messenger; Red Planet Mars
Veiller, Bayard (act): Red Planet Mars

Veiller, Bayard (wri): The Thirteenth Chair (1929)
Veilliux, Robert E. (act): Neon Maniacs
Veiness, Amy (act): The Saint Meets the Tiger
Veitch, Anthony Scott (wri): Night of the Blood Monster
Vejar, Harry J. (act): Invasion of the Body Snatchers (1956)
Vejar, Mike (dir): Babylon 5: A Call to Arms
Vejrazka, Vitezlan (act): The Devil's Trap
Velarde, Mike (mus): Horror of the Blood Monsters
Velarde, Teresa (act): Outbreak; The People Under the Stairs
Velasco, Gary (act): Nothing But Trouble
Velasco, Nemia (act): Moro Witch Doctor
Velasco, Ramiro (act): Body Heat
Velasquez, Vicky (act): The Blood Drinkers
Velazquez, Esther (act): Amazons (1986)
Velazquez, Lorena (act): Doctor of Doom; La Nave de los Monstruos; The Saint vs. the Zombies; El Santo Contra las Vampiras; Wrestling Women vs. the Aztec Mummy
Velazquez, Teresa (act): The Night of a Thousand Cats
Veletti, Rosa (act): M (1931)
Velez, Eddie (act, b. 1958): A Passion to Kill; The Presence; Repo Man
Velez, Josephine (act): Dracula (1931, English-speaking version)
Velez, Lupe (act, 1909-1944): Kongo; Mexican Spitfire Sees a Ghost; Where East Is East
Velez, Raul (act): Street Trash
Velia, Tania (act): Missile to the Moon; Queen of Outer Space
Veljohnson, Reginald (act): The Bride In Black; Remo Williams: The Adventure Begins
Vella, David (act): Thirst
Vella, John (act): Sting of Death
Vella, Marlow (act): The Pink Chiquitas
Vellani, Zul (act): Siddhartha
Veltman, Charles (act): Revenge of the Virgins
Venable, David (wri): Fortress
Venable, Evelyn (act, b. 1913): Death Takes a Holiday (1934); The Double Door; Pinocchio (1940)
Venable, Sarah (act): Martin
Venantini, Luca (act): Aladdin (1987); Exterminators of the Year 3000
Venantini, Venantino (act): The Adventures of Hercules; Cannibal Ferox; Exterminators of the Year 3000; Ladyhawke; Seven Deaths In the Cat's Eye
Venard, Shirley (act): Satan's Touch
Vendell, Veronique (act): Barbarella; The Night of the Generals; Victim Five
Vendig, Peggy (act): The Checkered Flag
Venegas, Arturo (act): The Secret Life of Ian Fleming
Veness, Amy (act): The Angelus; Blanche Fury; Fanny by Gaslight; Lorna Doone (1934); Madeleine; The Man In Grey; My Brother's Keeper; The Woman With No Name
Venetos, Father George J. (act): Killer In the Mirror
Veninger, Ingrid (act): The Gate
Venitskaya, Valia (act): A Romance of Wastdale
Vennera, Chick (act): The Terror Within II
Venora, Diane (act): Eaters of the Dead; Three Wishes (1995); Wolfen
Ventantonio, John (act): Private Parts
Ventham, Wanda (act): Captain Kronos: Vampire Hunter; Death Is a Woman; The Deathshead Vampire
Ventigmilia, Carlos (cin): 20 Million Miles to Earth
Ventola, Anthony (act): Class of Nuke 'em High
Ventress, Connie (act): Stalking Laura
Ventriss, Jenny (act): A Stranger Is Watching
Ventura, Angelo (act): Beyond Atlantis; Twilight People
Ventura, Cheryl (act): Silent Night, Deadly Night III
Ventura, Clyde (act): Bury Me an Angel; Poor Devil
Ventura, Jesse "The Body" (act, b. 1951): Abraxas, Guardian of the Universe; Demolition Man; Predator; Repossessed; The Running Man (1987)
Ventura, Lino (act, 1918-1987, nee Angelo Borrini): Cadavera Eccellenti; Le Deuxieme Souffle; Le Diable et les Dix Commandements; Escape to Nowhere; The Great Manhunt (1974); The Great Spy Chase; The Inquisitor; The Mask of the Gorilla; The Medusa Touch; Mistress of the World (1959); Le Silencieux
Ventura, Viviane/Vivienne (act): Battle Beneath the Earth; A High Wind In Jamaica; Return from the Ashes
Venture, Richard (act): The Dark Secret of Harvest Home; Looker; Man On a Swing
Venturiello, Massimo (act): Rorret
Venturini, Edward (dir): The Headless Horseman
Venturini, Mark (act): Friday the 13th-Part V: A New Beginning
Venturini, Sandra (act): The Adventures of Hercules
Venturoli, Vittorio (act): La Strega In Amore
Venus, Brenda (act): Deathsport; The Eiger Sanction
Venuti, Christopher G. (act): Bloodspell
Vera, Racquel (act): Dance of the Dwarfs
Vera, Victoria (act): Monster Dog
Vera-Ellen (act): Wonder Man
Verbit, Helen (act): The New, Original Wonder Woman;The Return of the World's Greatest Detective
Verbitzky, Alejandro (wri): El Ladron de Cadaveres
Verbois, Jack (act): I Come In Peace
Verbrugge, Jacques (act): Hunted In Holland
Vercoe, Stephen (act): Knights of the Round Table
Vercors (wri, 1902-1991, nee Jean Bruller): Skullduggery
Vercoutere, Marcel (cin): The Exorcist; Search for the Gods
Verde, Dino (wri): Tempi Duri per i Vampiri
Verdetti, Salvatore (act): Arabian Nights (1974)
Verdi, Francis M. (act): The House of Secrets (1929)
Verdin, Octavia (act): The Secret Life of Ian Fleming
Verdon, Gwen (act, b. 1925): Cocoon; Cocoon: The Return; Damn Yankees
verDorn, Jerry (act): The Cradle Will Fall
Verducci, Pat (dir & wri): True Crime
Verdugo, Elena (act, b. 1926): Day of the Nightmare; The Frozen Ghost; House of Frankenstein; The Lost Tribe; The Lost Volcano; The Sky Dragon; Snow Dog; Song of Scheherazade; Thief of Damascus
Verdugo, Paul (act): Beverly Hills Bodysnatchers
Vere, Miss (act): The Thornton Jewel Mystery
Verea, John (act): Full Eclipse
Verebes, Ernest (act): The Ghost Train (1927)
Verebes, Erno (act, b. 1904): The Big Clock; The Climax; Houdini (1953); The Strange Death of Adolf Hitler
Vereen, Ben (act, b. 1946): All That Jazz; Gas-s-s-s!; Once Upon a Forest
Veres, Jim (act): I, Desire
Vergara, Luis Enrique (wri): Invasion Sinitestra
Vergelin, Jose (wri): The Devil's Gift
Verges, Betty (act): Dracula Blows His Cool
Verges, Flamma (act): The Human Factor
Verhaeghe, Victor (act): Dead Dudes In the House
Verhagen, Jean (act): see Hagen, Jean
Verheiden, Mark (wri): The Mask (1994); Timecop
Verhoeven, Paul (dir, b. 1939): Flesh & Blood; The Fourth Man; The Hollow Man; Das Kalte Herz; RoboCop; Starship Troopers; Total Recall
Verhoeven, Paul (wri, b. 1939): Flesh & Blood
Verica, Tom (act): Lost In the Bermuda Triangle
Verkade, Edward (act): The Black Tulip (1921)
Verlakis, Niklos (act): The Devil's Men
Verley, Renaud (act): A Bell from Hell
Verlin, Melanie (act): Midnight (1980)
Vermilyea, Harold (act, 1889-1958): The Big Clock; Sorry, Wrong Number (1948)
Verna, Antonyia (act): Surf Nazis Must Die
Vernac, Denise (act): Alraune (1952); The Mask of Dijon
Vernan, Ron (act): Once Bitten
Vernay, Robert (dir): The Count of Monte Cristo (1955)
Verne, Bob (act): Cavegirl (1985)
Verne, Jules (wri, 1828-1905): The Airship Destroyer; Around the World In 80 Days; Captain Nemo and the Underwater City; Deux Cent Mille Lieues Sous les Mers; The Diabolical Invention; Five Weeks In a Balloon; From the Earth to the Moon; In Search of the Castaways; Journey to the Center of the Earth (1959, 1989 & 1993); The Light at the Edge of the World; Master of the World; Mysterious Island (1929 & 1961); Mystery On Monster Island; Na Komete; The Southern Star; Those Fantastic Flying Fools; 20,000 Leagues Under the Sea (1916, USA; 1954 & 1997 {2 TVMs}); Valley of the Dragons; Les Vingt Mille Leaues Sur les Mers; Viaje al Centro de la Tierra; Where Time Began
Verne, Kaaren (act, 1915-1968, nee Ingabor Katrine Klinckerfuss): The Great Impersonation (1942); Sherlock Holmes and the Secret Weapon; Sky Murder; Ten Days In Paris
Vernell, Carl (act): Flesh and Fantasy
Vernengo, Ines (act): Man Facing Southeast
Verner, Anthony (act): At the Earth's Core; The Black Windmill
Verner, Gerald (wri): Meet Mr. Callaghan; Noose for a Lady; Tread Softly
Verner, Lois (act): Nancy Drew, Reporter
Verneuil, Henri (dir, b. 1920, nee Achod Malakian): The Burglars; The Night Caller; The Serpent (1973); What Price Murder
Verneuil, Henri (wri, b. 1920): The Serpent (1973); What Price Murder
Verney, Anthony (wri): The Limping Man (1953)
Verney, Guy (act): The Floating Dutchman
Verno, Jerry (act): Anything to Declare?; The Chinese Bungalow; The Demon Barber of Fleet Street; The Gables Mystery; The Perfect Woman; A Place to Go; Queer Cargo; Sensation (1937); The 39 Steps (1935); Young and Innocent
Vernon, Anne (act, b. 1925, nee Edith Vignaud): Les Parapluies de Cherbourg; Time Bomb
Vernon, Charles (act): The Foreman's Treachery; The Stolen Plans (1914)
Vernon, Charles (dir): Bernardo's Confession; From Scotland Yard
Vernon, Don (act): Macbeth (1971)
Vernon, Dorothy (act): Flat No. 3; The House of Silence
Vernon, Doug (act): Attack of the Killer Tomatoes
Vernon, Gabor (act): Dracula (1979); Octopussy
Vernon, Glen (act): The Annihilator
Vernon, Glenn (act): Bedlam; I Bury the Living
Vernon, Harry (wri): Mr. Wu (1919 & 1927)
Vernon, Harvey (act): Nightmare On the 13th Floor
Vernon, Howard (act): Adventures of Captain Fabian; Alphaville, une Etrange Aventure de Lemmy Caution; The Awful Dr. Orlof; The Blood Rose; The Diabolical Dr. Z; Dr. Orloff's Invisible Horror; The Invisible Dead; La Mome Vert-de-Gris; Necronomicon; Night of the Blood Monster; Operation Double Cross; The Perverse Countess; Revenge In the House of Usher; The Secret Ways; Die Tausend Augen des Dr. Mabuse; Virgin Among the Living Dead; Zombies Lake
Vernon, Irene (act): The Mystery of the Old Mill; The Sound of Fury; The Stolen Airship Plans; When Paths Diverge
Vernon, Jackie (act, 1924-1987): Amazon Women On the Moon; Demon and the Mummy; Microwave Massacre; The Monitors
Vernon, James Michael (wri): Encounter at Raven's Gate
Vernon, James Nugent (act): Class of Nuke 'em High
Vernon, John (act, b. 1932): The Black Windmill; Blue Monkey; Cat and Mouse (1974); Chained Heat; Curtains; Fear Is the Key; Heavy Metal; Herbie Goes Bananas; Killer Klowns from Outer Space; Matt Helm; The Questor Tapes; Sweet Movie; Topaz; The Uncanny; W
Vernon, Kate (act): Bloodknot; Dangerous Touch; House of Secrets (1993); The Sister-In-Law
Vernon, Lou (act): On the Beach
Vernon, Maurice (wri): Mr. Wu (1919 & 1927)
Vernon, Peter (act): Bridge Across Time
Vernon, Richard (act, b. 1907): Accidental Death; Cash On Demand; Clue of the Twisted Candle; Evil Under the Sun; Goldfinger; Hot Enough for June; Oh Heavenly Dog; Sammy's Super T-Shirt; The Satanic Rites of Dracula; The Secret of My Success; The Servant; The Share Out; The Tomb of Ligeia; The Village of the Damned (1960)
Vernon, Richard (dir & wri): Street of Shadows
Vernon, Valerie (act): The Glass Tomb; Gog
Vernon, Wally (act, 1914-1970): Charlie Chan at Treasure Island; Charlie Chan In Panama; The Gorilla (1939)
Vernov, Gennadi (act): Planeta Bura
Vero, Joseph (act): Street Trash
Verrecchia, Albert (mus): Deborah
Verrell, Cec (act): Death Dreams; Hell Comes to Frogtown; Mad at the Moon; Runaway (1984)
Versini, Marie (act): The Brides of Fu Manchu; Temple of the White Elephants
Versois, Odile (act, 1930-1980, nee Militza de Poliakoff-Baidarov): Cartouche (1962); Passport to Shame
Vertisya, Lucille (act): The Magic Voyage of Sinbad
Vertlieb, Steve (act): Fiend (1980)
Verushka (act): Blow-Up; The Bride (1985)
Verveen, Arie (act): Caught (1996)
Veryan, Nora (act): Spiritism
Verzier, Rene (cin): City On Fire; Deadly Eyes; Death Ship; The Little Girl Who Lives Down the Lane; Of Unknown Origin; Rabid; Rituals; Wild Thing
Veselov, Nikolai (act): The Saint
Ve Sota, Bruno (act, 1922-1976): Attack of the Giant Leeches; Bait; A Bucket of Blood (1959); Creature of the Walking Dead; Dementia; The Devil's Hand (1961); The Female Jungle; The Haunted Palace (1963); Invasion of the Star Creatures; A Man Called Dagger; Night Tide; Something Evil; The Undead; War of the Satellites; The Wasp Woman (1959)
Ve Sota, Bruno (dir, 1922-1976): The Brain Eaters; The Female Jungle; Invasion of the Star Creatures
Ve Sota, Bruno (wri, 1922-1976): The Female Jungle
Vessel, (H)Edy (act): Psycosissimo; Sword of the Conqueror; The Thief of Baghdad (1960); The Trojan Horse
Vesterhalt, Max (act): For Your Eyes Only
Vetri, Victoria (act, a.k.a. Angela Dorian): Invasion of the Bee Girls; Rosemary's Baby; When Dinosaurs Ruled the Earth
Vetterly, Beatrice (act): Blind Date
Veugelers, Marijke (act): Gebroken Spiegels
Vezarian, Ross (act): The Keeper
Viadas, Juan (act): Accion Mutante
Vialla, A. (act): L'Auberge Rouge
Vianello, Maria Teresa (act): Raptus
Vianello, Raimondo (act): Psycosissimo
Vianna, Wilson (act): Curucu, Beast of the Amazon; Love Slaves of the Amazons
Vibart, Henry (act): The Bargain; Behind the Curtain; The Beryl Coronet (1921); Creatures of Clay; The Crimson Circle (1922); Dr. Fenton's Ordeal; The Grand Babylon Hotel; High Treason (1929); The Incorruptible Crown; In the Shadow of Big Ben; A Kiss for Cinderella; The Nightbirds of London; The Passing of a Soul; Princess Clementina; The Schemers: or, The Jewels of Hate; The Stress of Circumstance; The Terror of the Air
Vibert, Marcel (act): Forces Occultes
Vibert, Ronan (act): The Scarlet Pimpernel (1999)
Vicari, Clem (mus): Mother's Day
Vicario, Renato (act): Il Mostro dell'Isola
Vicary, Renee (act): Hellhole
Vich, V. (cin): Faust and the Devil; Le Golem (1936)
Vichi, Gerry (act): Windows
Vick, Helen (act): School Spirit
Vick, John (act): The Fog
Vickerman, Michael (wri): Warriors of Virtue
Vickers, Lindsay (dir): The Lake
Vickers, Martha (act, 1925-1971, a.k.a. Martha MacVicar): The Big Sleep (1946); The Burglar; Captive Wild Woman; The Falcon In Mexico; Ruthless
Vickers, Michael/Mike (mus): At the Earth's Core; Dracula A.D. 1972; Warlords of the Deep
Vickers, Philip (act): The Whole Truth
Vickers, Roy (wri): False Evidence; The Girl In the News; A Question of Suspense
Vickers, Yvette (act): Attack of the 50-Foot Woman (1958); Attack of the Giant Leeches; The Dead Don't Die; Evil Spirits; What's the Matter With Helen?
Vickery, John (act): Dr. Giggles; Fist of the North Star
Vico, Coleen (act): The Devil's Hand (1961)
Vico, Maria (act): Hundra; Night Fiend
Vico, Mario (act): Ella y el Miedo
Vicquery, Jean-Claude (cin): Terminus
Victor, barry (wri): Cyborg 3
Victor, Charles (act, 1896-1965): Calling Bulldog Drummond; Dial 999 (1955); East of Piccadilly; The Elusive Pimpernel (1950); Escape to Danger; Eyewitness (1956); Fear In the Night (1947); 49th Parallel; The Frightened Man; The Girl On the Pier; Meet Mr. Lucifer; The Missing Million; The Pit and the Pendulum (1961); Police Dog; Port Sinister; The Ringer (1952); The Saint Meets the Tiger; The Saint's Return; They Met In the Dark; Tiger In the Smoke; While I Live; The Woman In Question
Victor, Gloria (act): Invasion of the Star Creatures
Victor, Henry (act, 1898-1945): Blue, White and Perfect; The Crimson Circle (1922); Freaks; King of the Zombies; The King's Romance; The Mummy (1932); Murder at Monte Carlo; Nick Carter, Master Detective; Pra Pro Nobis; The Picture of Dorian Gray (1916); The Scotland Yard Mystery; The Secret Voice; She (1925)
Victor, Herbert (wri): Bedelia
Victor, James (act): Zorro: The Legend Begins

Victor, Katherine (act, a.k.a. Katena Vea): *The Cape Canaveral Monsters; Creature of the Walking Dead; Curse of the Stone Hand; House of the Black Death; Mesa of Lost Women; Teenage Zombies; The Wild World of Batwoman*
Victor, Kathrin (act): *Frankenstein Island*
Victor, Mark (wri): *Cool World; Poltergeist; Poltergeist II: The Other Side*
Victor, Paula (act): *The Entity*
Victoria, Vesta (act): *The Dance of Death (1938)*
Victory, Fiona (act): *Return to Oz*
Vida, Piero (act): *The Night Porter*
Vidal, Gil (act): *La Maldicion de la Bestia*
Vidal, Gore (act, b. 1925): *Gattaca; Shadow Conspiracy*
Vidal, Gore (wri, b. 1925): *I Accuse (1958); Myra Breckinridge; The Scapegoat; Suddenly Last Summer; Visit to a Small Planet*
Vidal, Henri (act, 1919-1959): *Angel On Wheels; What Price Murder*
Vidal, Maria (act): *Once Bitten*
Vidal, Pedro (act): *Anguish*
Vidale, Thea (act): *Dr. Jekyll and Ms. Hyde*
Vidalie, Albert (wri): *Torticola Contre Frankensberg*
Vidette, John (dir & wri): *Doomsday Voyage*
Vidgeon, Robin (cin): *The Fly II; Hellbound: Hellraiser II; Nightbreed; Parents*
Vidler, Julia (act): *Double Exposure (1977)*
Vidler, Steven (act): *Encounter at Raven's Gate*
Vidler, Susan (act): *The Woman In White (1998)*
Vidmark, Robert (act): *Battle of the Amazons*
Vidon, Henry (act): *Behemoth, the Sea Monster; Blood of the Vampire; The Key Man; Return from the Ashes; The Snorkel*
Vidor, Charles (dir, 1900-1959): *Blind Alley; The Double Door; Gilda; The Great Gambini; Hans Christian Andersen; Ladies In Retirement; The Loves of Carmen (1948)*
Vidor, John (act): *Brainstorm (1983); My Science Project*
Vidor, King (dir, 1895-1982): *Lightning Strikes Twice*
Vidosa, Christian (act): *Falling Fire*
Vidotto, Mira (act): *Lo Strano Caso della Signora Ward*
Vidov, Oleg (act): *The Red Mantle*
Vidovic, Peter (act): *The Saint*
Viela, Michael (act): *Waxwork II: Lost In Time*
Vieluf, Vince (act): *An American Werewolf In Paris*
Viera, Abidah (act): *Black Magic Woman*
Vieria, Asia (act): *Omen IV: The Awakening*
Vierny, Sacha (cin, b. 1919): *Aimez-Vous les Femmes?; L'Annee Derniere a Marienbad; Belle de Jour; Prospero's Books*
Viertel, Berthold (dir): *The Passing of the Third Floor Back (1935)*
Viertel, Berthold (wri): *Schloss Vogelod*
Viertel, Jack (wri): *Delusion*
Viertel, Peter (wri): *Saboteur*
Viespi, Alexander (act): see Cord, Alex
Viet, Howard (act): *The Witchmaker*
Vieyra, Emilio (dir): *The Curious Dr. Humpp*
Vig, Tommy (mus): *The Kid With the Broken Halo; Sweet Sixteen*
Vigarito, Tom (act): *The Toxic Avenger, Part II*
Vigden, Cheryl (act): *A Ghost of a Chance (1968)*
Vigil, Helen (act): *The Temple of Venus*
Vignaud, Edith (act): see Vernon, Anne
Vignola, Robert (dir): *The Scarlet Letter (1934); The Vampire (1913, USA); Young Diana*
Vignon, Jean-Paul (act): *Perfect Alibi*
Vigny, Benno (wri): *Der Verlorene*
Vigoda, Abe (act, b. 1921): *Batman: Mask of the Phantasm*
Vigran, Herb (act): *Bedtime for Bonzo; Charlotte's Web; The Shaggy D.A.; The Vampire (1957)*
Viharo, George (act): *The Evil*
Viharo, Robert (act): *The Evil; The Night Stalker (1987)*
Vila, Camilo (dir): *The Unholy*
Vila, Felix (dir): *Devil Woman*
Vila Jr., Tony (act): *Cocoon: The Return*
Vilanch, Bruce (act): *The Ice Pirates*
Vilar, Antonio (act): *El Principe Encadenado*
Vilars, Felix (dir): *Devil Woman*
Vilasini (act): *The Bogey Man*
Vilers, Vania (act): *Caravan to Vaccares*
Vilfrid, Jacques (wri): *Les Femmes s'en Balancent*
Villa, Carlos (mus): *Mystery On Monster Island*
Villa, Franco (cin): *Slaughter Hotel (1972)*
Villain-Marais, Jean (act): see Marais, Jean
Villani, Mike (act): *Return of the Killer Tomatoes*
Villard, Dimitri (act): *Time Walker*
Villard, Dimitri (wri): *Once Bitten*
Villard, Frank (act, b. 1917, nee Francois Drouineau): *Guilty?; Mata Hari, Agent H21*
Villard, Tom (act, 1954-1994): *Parasite; Popcorn*
Villarias, Carlos (act): *El Cuerpo del Lito; Dracula (1931, Spanish-speaking version)*
Villarreai, Julio (act): *The Beast of Hollow Mountain*
Villasante, Jose (act): *La Maldicion de los Karnsteins*
Villasenor, Christopher (act): *Ghostbusters II*
Villasenor, Leopoldo (cin): *Guyana, Cult of the Damned*
Ville, Paul (act): *L'Enfant Sauvage*
Villechaize, Herve (act, 1943-1993): *Fantasy Island; Forbidden Zone; Malatesta's Carnival; The Man With the Golden Gun; Return to Fantasy Island; Seizure*
Villela, Michael (act): *Gotham; The Slumber Party Massacre*
Villella, Ferdinando (act): *Amarcord*
Villemaire, James (act): *Gate II; Matinee*
Villena, Fernando (act): *Terrore Nello Spazio*
Villena, Francisco (act): *Treasure of the Four Crowns*
Villeneuve, Dale (act): *Unforgettable*
Villers, Dan (act): *Revenge In the House of Usher*
Villers, James (act): *Girl In the Headlines*
Villiers, Caroline (act): *Captain Kronos: Vampire Hunter*
Villiers, Charles (act): *Schlock*
Villiers, Christopher (act): *First Knight; Top Secret! (1984)*
Villiers, David (dir): *Candidate for Murder*
Villiers, James (act, b. 1930): *The Alphabet Murders; The Amazing Mr. Blunden; Asylum (1972); Blood from the Mummy's Tomb; The Clue of the New Pin (1961); The Damned; For Your Eyes Only; Murder at the Gallop; The Nanny; Otley; Repulsion; The Ruling Class; The Scarlet Pimpernel (1982); Some Girls Do; Spectre (1977); The Wrong Box*
Villiers, Kenneth (act): *Things to Come*
Villiers, Mavis (act): *Cat and Mouse (1974); Double Alibi; The Haunting; Straight On Till Morning; Suddenly Last Summer; Too Many Detectives*
Villis, Marjorie (act): *Further Exploits of Sexton Blake-The Mystery of the S.S. Olympic; Love In the Welsh Hills; The Silver Greyhound (1919)*
Vilven, Stanley (act): *Dark Secret*
Vince, Charles (act): *The Professionals*
Vince, Eugene (act): *The Green Slime*
Vince, Nicholas (act): *Hellbound: Hellraiser II; Hellraiser; Nightbreed*
Vince, Pruitt Taylor (act): *Angel Heart; Fear (1990); Jacob's Ladder*
Vincenot, Louis (act): *Werewolf of London*
Vincent, Alex (act): *Child's Play (1988); Child's Play 2*
Vincent, Allen (act): *Mystery of the Wax Museum*
Vincent, Allen (wri): *The Face Behind the Mask*
Vincent, Amy (cin): *Jawbreaker*
Vincent, Chuck (dir): *Deranged (1987); Warrior Queen; Wildest Dreams*
Vincent, Dan (act): *Battle Beyond the Stars (1980)*
Vincent, Frank (act): *Mortal Thoughts; Netforce*
Vincent, Glen (act): *Repossessed; Sorority Girls and the Creature from Hell*
Vincent, Jan-Michael (act, b. 1944): *Alienator; The Alien's Return; Damnation Alley; Demonstone; Haunting Fear; Hidden Obsession; Ice Cream Man; Jurasic Women; Raw Nerve; Sandcastles; Shadow of the Hawk; Tarzan In Manhattan; Xtro II: The Second Encounter*
Vincent, Julie (act): *A Scream from Silence*
Vincent, June (act): *Black Angel (1946); The Challenge; The Climax; The Creeper (1948); The Lone Wolf and His Lady; Trapped by Boston Blackie; Zamba*
Vincent, Karl (act): *Shocker*
Vincent, Larry "Seymour" (act): *Doctor Death: Seeker of Souls; The Incredible 2-Headed Transplant; The Witchmaker*
Vincent, Lawrence (act): *The Hotel Manor Inn*
Vincent, Leslie (act): *Pursuit to Algiers*
Vincent, Mike (act): *The Norsemen*
Vincent, Millard (act): *Torchy Runs for Mayor*
Vincent, Patrick (act): *The Deadly Trap*
Vincent, Phillip (act): *OSA*
Vincent, Romo (act): *Hurricane Island; The Naked Jungle; Sergeant Deadhead the Astronut!*
Vincent, Ron (act): *The Chilling (1989)*
Vincent, Virginia (act): *The Baby; Crackle of Death; The Hills Have Eyes; The Hills Have Eyes II; Invitation to Hell; The $1,000,000 Duck; Night Slaves; The Return of Dracula*
Vincent, Yves (act): *Sins of Rome*
Vincent, Zachary (act): *The Alien's Return*
Vincente, Roy (act): *The Monster of Highgate Ponds*
Vincenzoni, Luciano (wri): *Orca*
Vinciguerra, Caroline (act): *Stalking Laura*
Vincioni, Jim (act): *Boarding House*
Vincz, Melanie (act): *The Lost Empire*
Vincze, Ernest (cin): *Biggles: Adventures In Time*
Vindeni, Dino (wri): *Voodoo*
Viner, Edward (act): *When Paths Diverge*
Viner, Michael (act): *The Thing With Two Heads*
Vines, Michael (wri): *American Gothic; Dance of the Dwarfs*
Ving, Lee (act): *Alfred Hitchcock Presents; Grave Secrets; Streets of Fire*
Vingelli, Nino (act): *The Black Belly of the Tarantula; Spara Forte, Piu Forte...Non Capisco*
Vinicombe, Walter (act): see Patch, Wally
Vining, Dan (wri): *Her Deadly Rival*
Vinklarek (cin): *Do You Keep a Lion at Home?*
Vinnichenko, Leeza (act): *Too Good to Be True*
Vinovich, Steve (act): *Mannequin; The Swan Princess*
Vinson, Gary (act): *The Munsters' Revenge*
Vinson, Helen (act, b. 1905, nee Helen Rulfs): *The Kennel Murder Case; King of the Damned; The Lady and the Monster; The Thin Man Goes Home; The Tunnel*
Vinson, Robert (act): *Piranha (1978)*
Vint, Alan (act): *Earthquake*
Vint, Bill (act): *A Howling In the Woods*
Vint, Jesse (act): *Blood Pen; Bug; Deathsport; Deep Red (1994); Earthquake; Forbidden World; I Come In Peace; Reflections of Murder; Silent Running; Welcome to Arrow Beach*
Vint, Kelly (act): *Stargate*
Vintas, Gustav (act): *And You Thought Your Parents Were Weird; Midnight (1989); Tales from the Crypt (1989); Vampire at Midnight*
Violent Femmes (mus): *I Was a Teenage Zombie*
Vipond, Neil (act): *Bay Coven; Phobia*
Virlogeux, Henri (act): *Le Saint Prend l'Affut*
Virly, Joan (act): *Revenge In the House of Usher*
Virten, Anastasia (act): *The Amphibian Man*
Virzinskaya, M. (act): *The Amphibian Man*
Visaroff, Michael (act): *Charlie Chan at the Wax Museum; Flight to Nowhere; The House of Horror (1929); The Mark of the Vampire (1935); The Son of Monte Cristo*
Visconti, Luchino (dir, b. 1906): *El Mono Loco*
Visedo, Maria Jesus (act): *Hundra*
Visitor, Nana (act): *The Spirit*
Visviki, Agatha (act): *Blind Date*
Vitale, Alex (act): *Beyond the Door III; Urban Warriors*
Vitale, Anthony (act): *The Norsemen*
Vitale, Antonella (act): *Terror at the Opera*
Vitale, Fred (act): *F.B.I. Code 98*
Vitale, Joseph (act, b. 1905): *A Connecticut Yankee In King Arthur's Court (1949); The Falcon In Mexico; Gildersleeve's Ghost; The Lost Tribe; Zombies On Broadway*
Vitale, Milly (act, b. 1938): *The Black Devil (1963); The Flesh Is Weak; Revenge of the Pirates*
Vitales, Iliany (act): *Dance of the Dwarfs*
Vitali, Juan (act): *Apartment Zero*
Vitali, Leon (act): *Blue Movie Blackmail; Terror of Frankenstein*
Vitarelli, Joseph (mus): *Nothing But the Truth*
Viterelli, Joe (act): *Eraser*
Vitold, Michel (act): *L'Aveu; Judex; Le Testament du Dr. Cordelier*
Vitte, Ray (act): *A Force of One; The Man In the Santa Claus Suit*
Vittes, Louis (wri): *The Eyes of Annie Jones; I Married a Monster from Outer Space*
Vittet, Judith (act): *The City of Lost Children*
Vitti, Monica (act, b. 1931, nee Maria Luisa Ciociarelli): *Il Disco Volante; Modesty Blaise; Red Desert*
Vitti, Ralph (act): see Dante, Michael
Vittori, Vittorio (act): *Satyricon*
Vitzin, George (act): *The Blue Bird (1976)*
Viva (act): *Forbidden Zone; For Your Eyes Only*
Vivaldi, Antonio (mus, 1675-1743): *L'Enfant Sauvage; Les Enfants Terribles*
Vivaldi, Giana (act): *Operazione Paura*
Vivaldi, Laura (act): *Lipstick*
Vivani, Augusto (cin): *Gli Amori di Ercole*
Vivarelli, Piero (act & dir): *Satanik*
Vives, May (act): *Anguish*
Vivian, April (act): *Discipline*
Vivian, Bette (act): *The Legend of Spider Forest*
Vivian, Dean (act): *Stalking Laura*
Vivian, James (act): *Counterspy*
Vivian, Percival (act): *Prince Valiant (1954)*
Vivian, Sidney (act): *The Key*
Viviani, Sonia (act): *The Adventures of Hercules; City of the Walking Dead*
Viviano, Sal (act): *Black Roses; The Jitters*
Vivien, Sidney (act): *Subterfuge*
Vivio, Marco (act): *Demons 2*
Vizbor, Juri (act): *The Red Tent*
Vize, Tom (act): *Poor Devil*
Vlad, Alessio (mus): *Jane Eyre (1996)*
Vlad, Roman (mus): *Hipnosis; I Vampiri*
Vlady, Marina (act, b. 1937, nee Marina de Poliakoff-Baidaroff): *Don't Tempt the Devil; The Double Agents; Enough Rope; The Games of the Countess Dolingen of Gratz; La Nuit des Espions; La Sorciere; The Thief of Baghdad (1978)*
Vlahos, Sam (act): *The Flash*
Vlasek, June (act): see Lang, June
Voe, Sandra (act): *Agatha; Erik the Viking*
Vogan, Emmett (act): *Blue, White and Perfect; A Close Call for Boston Blackie; Cyclotrode X; Dangerous Money; The Docks of New Orleans; Fly-Away Baby; The Lady Confesses; The Mummy's Ghost; The Mummy's Tomb; The Sky Dragon; Tobor the Great; Woman Who Came Back*
Vogeding, Frederick/Fredrik/Fred (act): *The Black Room; Charlie Chan at the Olympics; Charlie Chan In City In Darkness; Charlie Chan In Shanghai; The Great Impersonation (1942); Mr. Moto Takes a Chance; Murder On the Blackboard; The Mysterious Mr. Moto; Think Fast, Mr. Moto*
Vogel, Darlene (act): *Back to the Future, Part II*
Vogel, Debbie (act): *Fiend (1980)*
Vogel, Jesse (dir): *The Adventures of Pinocchio*
Vogel, Klaus (wri): *Virgin Witch*
Vogel, Paul C. (cin, 1899-1975): *Angels In the Outfield (1951); The Gazebo; It's a Dog's Life; Lady In the Lake; The Magic Sword (1962); Signpost to Murder; The Time Machine (1960); Village of the Giants; The Wonderful World of the Brothers Grimm*
Vogel, Peter (act): *The Phantom of Soho*
Vogel, Robert (act): *Basket Case*
Vogel, Tony (act): *Black Angel (1980); The Final Conflict; Mission: Impossible; Raiders of the Lost Ark*
Vogel, Vikki (act): *The Keeper*
Vogel, Virgil (W.) (dir): *Condor; The Land Unknown; The Mole People; Rymdinvasion i Lappland; The Sword of Ali Baba*
Vogelsang, Judith (dir): *Heartless*
Voges, Danie (act): *Prisoners of the Lost Universe*
Vogler, Rudiger (act): *Until the End of the World*
Vogt, Carl (act): see Calhern, Louis
Vogt, Charles-Hans (act): *Das Singende Ringende Baumchen*
Vogt, K.T. (act): *The Puppet Masters*
Vogt, Peter (act): *The Silencers (1995)*
Vohrer, Alfred (dir): *The Ape Creature; Creature With the Blue Hand; The Indian Scarf; The Inn On the River; The Mysterious Magician; The Squeaker (1965); Die Toten Augen von London; Die Tur mit den Sieben Schlossern*
Vohs, Joan (act, b. 1931): *Terror at Midnight*
Voight, Jill (act): *Friday the 13th-Part 2*
Voight, Jon (act, b. 1938): *Anaconda; Fearless Frank; Mission: Impossible; Noah's Ark (1999); Runaway Train*
Voigt, Dustin (act): *Them (1996)*
Voigtlander, Ted (cin): *The Bad Seed (1985); Night of the Lepus; Sparkling Cyanide*
Voikov, Zandor (act): *Dracula vs. Frankenstein*
Voit, Mieczyslaw (act): *Matka Joanna od Aniolow*
Vojya (cin): *Do You Keep a Lion at Home?*
Voland, Herbert (act): *The Munsters' Revenge*
Volante, Gian Maria (act, b. 1933): *Chronicle of a Death Foretold; The Death of Mario Ricci; The French Conspiracy; The Mattei Affair; La Strega In Amore; The Witch (1966)*
Volante, Vicki (act): *Angels' Wild Women; Blood of Dracula's Castle; Brain of Blood; Hell's Bloody Devils; Horror of the Blood Monsters*
Volchek, Galina (act): *Korol Lir*
Vold, Ingrid (act): *To Sleep With a Vampire*
Volgeman, Karl H. (wri): *Mission Stardust*
Volk, Paul G. (dir): *Steel Frontier*
Volk, Stephen (wri): *Gothic; The Guardian; The Kiss (1988)*
Volkov, Alexander (act): *Portret Doriana Greya*
Vollmoeller, Karl (wri, 1878-1948): *The Miracle (1959)*
Volonto, Claudio (act): *Twitch of the Death Nerve*
Voloshin, Julian (act): *Aladdin (1987)*
Volpe, Fred(erick) (act): *Altar Chains; The Lifeguardsman*
Volpi, Franco (act, 1921-1997): *Romolo e Remo*
Volpin, M. (wri): *Jack Frost*
Volz, Nedra (act): *Earth Girls Are Easy; The Silence of the Hams*
Volz, Wolfgang (act): *Funeral In Berlin*

von Alten, Ferdinand (act): *Der Student von Prag (1926)*
von Alten, Theodore (act): *Champagne*
Von Baky, Josef/Joseph (dir): *Die Avonturen von Baron Munchausen; Confess, Dr. Corda; The Strange Countess*
von Balieff, Olga (act): *Das Wachsfigurenkabinett*
Von Bargen, Daniel (act): *Inferno (1998); Lord of Illusions; The Silence of the Lambs; Thinner*
Von Blank, Christiane/Christina (act): *The Dead Are Alive; Virgin Among the Living Dead*
von Borsody, Hans (act): *The Invisible Terror*
von Brincken, William/Wilhelm (act): *Bulldog Drummond In Africa; Counter-Espionage; Hidden Enemy; International Crime; Queen Kelly; Thank You, Mr. Moto*
Von Daniken, Erich (wri): *Chariots of the Gods?*
von Deek, Wilhelm (act): *L'Annee Derniere a Marienbad*
von Detten, Erik (act, b. 1982): *Christmas Every Day; Escape to Witch Mountain (1995); Toy Story*
Von Dohlen, Lenny (act): *Blind Vision; Dracula's Widow; Electric Dreams; Jennifer 8; Love Kills; Twin Peaks: Fire Walk With Me*
von Eltz, Theodore (act): *Blondes at Work; The Cat Creeps (1930); The Devil's Cargo; Ellery Queen's Penthouse Mystery; Kismet (1930); The Son of Monte Cristo; Strangers of the Evening; The Westland Case*
von Francois, Hardy (act): *Nosferatu, eine Symphonie des Grauens*
von Frankenstein, Clement (act): *The Haunting of Morella*
von Friedl, Loni (act): *The Blood of Fu Manchu; Doppelganger (1969)*
Von Fritsch, Gunther (dir): *Curse of the Cat People*
von Furstenberg, Tatiana (act): *Bram Stoker's 'Dracula'*
von Gerkan, Betty (act): see Hughes, Kathleen
von Gerlach, Arthur (dir): *Chronik von Grieshuus*
von Griffensteinbrunner, Heinz-Gergesmuller (act): *Supergirl (1971)*
von Harbou, Thea (wri, 1888-1954): *Chronik von Grieshuus; Doctor Mabuse; Die Frau im Mond; Journey to the Lost City; M (1931); Metropolis (1926); Der Mude Tod; Die Nibelungen; Phantom (1922); Spione; Der Steinerne Reiter; Das Testament des Dr. Mabuse*
von Hauser, Paul (act): *Demons of Ludlow*
von Herkomer, Hubert (act & wri): *The White Witch*
von Herkomer, Hubert (dir): *The Grit of a Dandy; The White Witch*
von Herkomer, Siegfried (wri): *The Grit of a Dandy*
von Hofmannstahl, Hugo (wri): *Das Fremde Madchen*
von Homburg, Wilhelm (act): *Eye of the Storm; Ghostbusters II; The Package; The Silence of the Hams; The Wrecking Crew*
von Jansky, Ladi (cin): *Dr. Caligari*
von Koch, Erland (mus): *The Devil's Wanton*
Von Kotze, John (cin): *The Vengeance of Fu Manchu*
von Krogh, Britta (act): *Stopover Forever*
Von Leer, Hunter (act): *Halloween II*
von Losch, Maria Magdalena Dietrich (act): see Dietrich, Marlene
von Meyerinck, Hubert (act): *The Ape Creature*
von Morhart, Hans (act): *Spy Smasher Returns*
Vonn, Veola (act): *Charlie Chan In City In Darkness; Phantom of the Rue Morgue; Spy Chasers; The 30 Foot Bride of Candy Rock*
Vonnegut Jr., Kurt (wri, b. 1922): *Slaughterhouse-Five*
von Ornsteiner, Joel (act): *Robot Holocaust; Slashdance*
von Palleske, Heidi (act): *Blind Fear; Dead Ringers; Falling Fire*
Von Schab, Oskar (act): *Jonathan*
von Schell, Catherina (act): see Schell, Catherine
Von Schellerdorf, Heinrich (act): *Rawhead Rex*
Von Scherler, Sasha (act): *The Man In the Santa Claus Suit*
von Schlettow, Hans Adalbert (act): *Doctor Mabuse; Die Nibelungen*
Von Schreiber, Shawn (act): *A Stranger Is Watching*
von Seyffertitz, Gustav (act, 1863-1943): *The Bat Whispers; The Bells (1926); The Canary Murder Case; Don Juan (1927); The Face In the Fog (1922); The Lone Wolf (1924); The Lone Wolf Returns (1926); Murder On a Bridle Path; Murder On the Blackboard; Mystery Liner; The Penguin Pool Murder; Rasputin and the Empress; Shanghai Express; She (1935); Sherlock Holmes (1922); Son of Frankenstein; The Wizard*
von Sternberg, Josef (dir, 1894-1969): *Crime and Punishment (1935, USA); Shanghai Express*
Von Sternberg, Nicholas (cin): *Ghost Writer; I Was a Teenage Sex Mutant; Slaughterhouse Rock; Tourist Trap; Uninvited (1987)*
von Stroheim, Erich (act, 1885-1957): *Alraune (1952); As You Desire Me; The Crime of Dr. Crespi; Five Graves to Cairo; The Great Gabbo; The Lady and the Monster; The Lost Squadron; The Mask of Dijon; Menaces; Scotland Yard Investigator; Sunset Boulevard; Ultimatum; Under Secret Orders*
von Stroheim, Erich (dir, 1885-1957): *Queen Kelly*
von Stroheim, Erich (wri, 1885-1957): *Devil Doll (1936); Queen Kelly*
von Sydow, Max (act, b. 1929): *Ansiktet; Cadaveri Eccellenti; Conan the Barbarian; Deathwatch (1980); Dreamscape; Dune; Embassy; The Exorcist; Exorcist II: The Heretic; Flash Gordon (1980); Judge Dredd; A Kiss Before Dying (1991); The Kremlin Letter; Needful Things; Never Say Never Again; The Night Visitor; The Quiller Memorandum; Det Sjunde Inseglet; Smultronstallet; Steppenwolf; 3 Days of the Condor; Through a Glass Darkly; The Ultimate Warrior; Until the End of the World; Vargtimmen; What Dreams May Come; Woman of Terror*
von Teuffen, Hatz (act): *The Flying Saucer (1950)*
Von Treuberg, Franz (act): *House of Exorcism*
von Trier, Lars (act): *The Element of Crime*
von Trier, Lars (dir & wri): *The Element of Crime; The Kingdom*
von Twardowski, Hans (Heinz) (act): *Genuine; Das Kabinett des Dr. Caligari; The Strange Death of Adolf Hitler*
von Vietinghoff, Jochen (act): *Chinese Boxes*
Von Voorhees, Victoria (act): *Time Walker*
von Walter, Hertha (act): *M (1931); Number Seventeen (1928); Spione*
von Wangenheim, Gustav (act): *Die Frau im Mond; Nosferatu, eine Symphonie des Grauens; Der Steinerne Reiter*
Von Watts, Hamilton (act): *The Nutty Professor (1996)*
Von Wernherr, Otto (act): *Liquid Sky; The Package*
von Weyrauch, Hubertus (act): *No Mercy, No Future*
von Wright, Victor (act): *The Tomb*
von Zell, Harry (act, 1906-1981): *For Heaven's Sake*
Von Zerneck, Danielle (act): *Appointment for a Killing; My Science Project*
Von Zerneck Jr., Frank (act): *Invitation to Hell*
von Zerneck, Peter (act, 1908-1992): *Goliath Awaits*
Vool, Herbert (act): *Happy Birthday to Me*
Voorhees, Debbisue (act): *Friday the 13th—Part V: A New Beginning*
Vopelka, Derrick (act): *Endless Descent*
Vorgan, Gigi (act): *Alfred Hitchcock Presents; Caveman (1981); Jaws 2*
Vorhaus, Bernard (dir, b. 1898): *The Amazing Mr. X; Crime On the Hill; Dark World; The Ghost Camera; Night Club Queen; Ten Minute Alibi*
Vorhaus, Bernard (wri, b. 1898): *Crime On the Hill*
Voris, Cyrus (wri): *Demon Knight*
Vorkapich, Edward (cin): *Face of Fire*
Vorkov, Zandor (act): *Brain of Blood*
Voros, Glen (act): *Bog*
Vorsel, Niels (wri): *The Element of Crime*
Vosburgh, Alfred (act): *Enchantment*
Vosburgh, Tilly (act): *Erik the Viking*
Voska, Vaclav (act): *Beauty and the Beast (1985); Murder Czech Style*
Voskanian, Robert (dir): *The Child*
Voskovec, George (act, 1905-1981): *The Boston Strangler; Man On a Swing; Somewhere In Time; The Spy Who Came In from the Cold; The 27th Day*
Vosloo, Arnold (act): *Darkman II: The Return of Durant; Darkman III: Die Darkman Die; Diary of a Serial Killer; Steel Dawn*
Vosper, Frank (act): *Koenigsmark; The Man Who Knew Too Much (1934); The Secret of Stamboul; Spy of Napoleon; Strange Evidence*
Vosper, Frank (wri): *Love from a Stranger (1937); Murder On the Second Floor; On Secret Service*
Vosper, John (act): *The Magnetic Monster*
Vosper, Margery (wri): *Alfred Hitchcock Presents*
Voss, Kurt (wri): *Dangerous Touch*
Voss, Philip (act): *Frankenstein and the Monster from Hell*
Voss, V.I. (wri): *Voodoo Woman*
Vossler, Robert (act): *Murder Reported*
Vossoughi, Behrouz (act): *Sphinx (1981); Time Walker*
Votocek, Otakar (dir): *Wings of Fame*
Votrian, Ralph (act): *The Invisible Boy*
Voutsinas, Andreas (act): *Spirits of the Dead*
Voyagis, Yorgo (act): *The Little Drummer Girl; Running Delilah*
Voyce, Jonathan (act): *The Gifted One*
Vozoff, Lorinne (act): *Impulse (1984); Too Good to Be True*
Vraa, Sanna (act): *Flatliners*
Vrana, Vlasta (act): *Brainscan; Happy Birthday to Me; The Kiss (1988); Midnight In Saint Petersburg; Rabid; Scanners II: The New Order; Secret Weapons*
Vreeken, Ron (act): *The Island of Dr. Moreau (1996)*
VreNon, Taunie (act): *Mutant Hunt; Switch (1991)*
Vroom, Siem (act): *The Lift*
Vrooman, Spencer (act): *Casper; Pet Shop*
Vrstala, Jiri (act): *Ikaria XB1; Rocket to Nowhere*
Vrus, Iris (act): *Sedmi Kontinent*
Vu, Stephanie (act): *Secrets In the Attic*
Vuattoux, Rene G. (cin): *Le Saint Mene la Dance*
Vuco, Olivera (act): *Mark of the Devil (1972)*
Vucotich, Milena (act): *Giulietta degli Spiriti*
Vujisic, Pavle (act): *Majstori i Margarita*
Vujovic, Vladimir (act): see Auclair, Michel
Vukotic, Bisera (act): *Castle Keep*
Vukotic, Dusan (dir, b. 1927): *Abrakadabra; Astromati; Kravna Na Mjesecu; Nestasni Robot; Sedmi Kontinent*
Vukotic, Dusan (wri, b. 1927): *Kravna Na Mjesecu*
Vukusic, Tom (act): *Arthur the King*
Vulchanov, Rangel (dir): *Esop*
Vuletic, Jenny (act): *Howling III*
Vulpiani, Mario (cin): *Castle Freak*
Vultaggio, Lisa (act): *Mortal Sins*
Vundla, Ka (act): *In the Shadow of Kilimanjaro*
Vuolo, Tito (act): *Between Midnight and Dawn; The Bishop's Wife; Shadow of the Thin Man; Sorry, Wrong Number (1948); 20 Million Miles to Earth*
Vuynovich, Lydia (act): *Fiend (1980)*
Vye, Murvyn (act, 1913-1976): *The Boy and the Pirates; A Connecticut Yankee In King Arthur's Court (1949); Golden Earrings; Pearl of the South Pacific; River of No Return; The Road to Bali; Voodoo Island*
Vylars, C. (wri): *House of Mystery (1961)*
Vyner, Margaret (act): *The Cavalier of the Streets; The Patient Vanishes; Sensation (1937)*
Vyvyan, Jack (act): *The Howard Case*

Wachink, Dobi (act): *La Captive du Desert*
Wachsmann, Franz (mus): see Waxman, Franz
Wacks, Jonathan (dir): *Ed and His Dead Mother*
Wada, Keinosuke (act): *Onna Kyuketsuki*
Waddell, Gary (act): *Stir; 20th Century Oz*
Waddell, Jody (act): *Freejack*
Waddell, Justine (act): *The Woman In White (1998)*
Waddell, Karen (act): *Conundrum*
Wadden, W.F. (act): *Xtro II: The Second Encounter*
Waddington, Patrick (act): *The Black Tulip (1937); The Clouded Crystal; Family Doctor*
Waddington, Rona (act): *Secret Weapons*
Waddington, Steve (act): *Don't Get Me Started; Tarzan and the Lost City*
Waddy, Gyle (act): *The Wiz*
Wade, Adam (act): *Phantom of the Paradise*
Wade, Bessie (act): *The Velvet Touch*
Wade, Christopher (act): *Mind Killer*
Wade, Kay (act): *Fake-Out*
Wade, Kevin (wri): *Junior (1994); Meet Joe Black*
Wade, Lindy (act): *All That Money Can Buy*
Wade, Michael (act): *The Monster of Highgate Ponds*
Wade, Monroe (act): *The Horror of Party Beach*
Wade, Roy (cin): *Charlotte's Web*
Wade, Russell (act): *The Body Snatcher (1945); The Falcon In Danger; A Game of Death; Ghost Ship (1943); Shoot to Kill (1947)*
Wade, Stuart (act): *Monster from the Ocean Floor; Teenage Monster*
Wade, Tim (act): *Deadly Messages*
Wademant, Annette (wri): *What Price Murder*
Wadkins, Melanie (act): *So Sad About Gloria*
Wadleigh, Michael (act, dir & wri, b. 1941): *Wolfen*
Wadsack, Richard H. (wri): *Screams of a Winter Night*
Wadsworth, Henry (act, 1902-1974): *The Mark of the Vampire (1935); The Thin Man*
Waegner, Eva (act): *Paradisio*
Wage, Julie (act): *I Was a Zombie for the F.B.I.*
Wagenheim, Charles (act, 1894-1979): *Beauty and the Beast (1962); Calling Dr. Death; Charlie Chan at the Wax Museum; Man-Eater of Kumaon; Meet Boston Blackie*
Wager, Anthony (act): *Great Expectations (1946); The Hijackers; Night Caller from Outer Space; Night of the Prowler*
Wager, Walter (wri): *Twilight's Last Gleaming*
Wagerman, Seth (act): *It Came Upon the Midnight Clear*
Wages, William (cin): *Love Potion No. 9; Purgatory; Robin Cook's 'Mortal Fear'*
Waggner, George (dir, b. 1894): *The Climax; Horror Island; Man-Made Monster; The Mystery of Marie Roget; Mystery Plane; South of Tahiti; Tangier; The Wolf Man (1941)*
Waggoner, Lyle (act, b. 1935): *Cyber-Chic; Dead Women In Lingerie; Dream a Little Evil; Journey to the Center of Time; Love Me Deadly; The New, Original Wonder Woman; Wizards of the Demon Sword*
Wagner, Adrian (mus): *Eclipse (1977)*
Wagner, Bruce (act): *I, Madman; Night Visions; Shocker*
Wagner, Bruce (wri): *A Nightmare On Elm Street 3: Dream Warriors*
Wagner, Carla Jean (wri): *Alien Cargo; Murder by Moonlight*
Wagner, Chuck (act): *America 3000*
Wagner, David (act): *Pet Shop*
Wagner, Fernando (act): *Tarzan and the Mermaids*
Wagner, Frank (act): *Alien Nation*
Wagner, Fritz Arno (cin, 1889-1958): *Chronik von Grieshuus; M (1931); Der Mude Tod; Nosferatu, eine Symphonie des Grauens; Schatten, eine Nachtliche Halluzination; Schloss Vogelod; Spione; Das Testament des Dr. Mabuse*
Wagner, Jack (act, 1896-1965): *Nancy Drew, Reporter*
Wagner, Jack (act, b. 1959): *Trapped In Space*
Wagner, Jane (wri): *The Incredible Shrinking Woman*
Wagner, Jefferson (act): *Monolith*
Wagner, Lindsay (act, b. 1949): *Bionic Ever After?; Bionic Showdown: The Six Million Dollar Man and the Bionic Woman; The Bionic Woman; From the Dead of Night; The Return of the Six Million Dollar Man and the Bionic Woman; She Woke Up; The Two Worlds of Jennie Logan; Voyage of Terror; Young Again*
Wagner, Lou (act): *The Adventures of Galgameth; Beneath the Planet of the Apes; Conquest of the Planet of the Apes; Mirrors; Planet of the Apes; The UFO Incident*
Wagner, Mary (act): *To All a Goodnight*
Wagner, Max (act): *Charlie Chan In Shanghai; The Gracie Allen Murder Case; Invaders from Mars (1953); The Lost Jungle; Mr. Moto In Danger Island; Possessed (1947); Smart Blonde*
Wagner, Michael Dan (act): *Tremors*
Wagner, Natasha Gregson (act): *Lost Highway; Wes Craven Presents Mind Ripper*
Wagner, Richard (mus, 1813-1883): *The Flying Dutchman*
Wagner, Robert (act, b. 1930): *Beneath the 12-Mile Reef; City Beneath the Sun (1970); Crosscurrent; Death at Love House; A Kiss Before Dying (1956); Madame Sin; Prince Valiant (1954); This Gun for Hire (1991); The Towering Inferno*
Wagner, Roy (H.) (cin): *A Nightmare On Elm Street 3: Dream Warriors; Return to Horror High; Witchboard*
Wagner, Sidney (cin): *Cabin In the Sky; A Christmas Carol (1938); Tarzan's New York Adventure*
Wagner, Terry (act): *Midnight Offerings*
Wagner, Thomas (act): *Alien Nation; The Drifter*
Wagner, Wende/Wendy (act): *Destination Inner Space; Rosemary's Baby*
Wagner, Wilhelm Richard (wri, 1813-1883): *Parsifal*
Wagstaff, Elsie (act): *Celia; The Dark Tower (1943); Frankenstein and the Monster from Hell; A Place to Die; The Snake Woman*
Wahl, Corinne (act): *Equalizer 2000*
Wahl, Evelyn (act): *Jungle Siren*
Wahlberg, Donnie (act): *Purgatory*
Wahlberg, Mark (act, b. 1971): *Fear (1996)*
Wahloo, Per (wri): *Morianna*
Wahlstrom, Chris (act): *I Am Curious (Yellow)*
Wahlund, Torsten (act): *The Island at the Top of the World*

Wahrman, Diane (act): Terror In the Wax Museum
Wai, Lau Koon (dir): Mr. Vampire; Mr. Vampire II; Mr. Vampire III; Mr. Vampire IV
Wain, Charles (mus): The Last Wave
Wain, Edward (act): Creature from the Haunted Sea; Last Woman On Earth
Wainwright, James (act): Killdozer; Warlords of the 21st Century
Wainwright, John (wri): The Inquisitor
Wainwright, Michael (act): Zapped!
Wainwright, Richard (wri): The Secret of Stamboul
Wainwright, Rupert (act): Dreamchild
Waisbren, Brad (act): A Polish Vampire In Burbank
Waisglass, Elaine (wri): The Housekeeper
Waite, Malcolm (act): The Monkey Talks
Waite, Ralph (act, b. 1928): Crash and Burn; Red Alert
Waite, Ric (cin): The Initiation of Sarah; Red Alert; Red Dawn; Revenge of the Stepford Wives
Waites, Thomas G. (act): The Clan of the Cave Bear
Waithe, Herbert (act): Robinson Crusoe (1927)
Waitresses, The (mus): I Was a Teenage Zombie
Waits, Tom (act): Bram Stoker's 'Dracula'
Waizman, Max (act): Dick Tracy vs. Crime, Inc.
Wajda, Andrzej (dir, b. 1926): Samson
Wajnberg, Alexander (act): Mama Dracula
Wajnberg, Marc-Henri (wri): Mama Dracula
Wakabayashi, Akiko (act): Dogora, the Space Monster; You Only Live Twice
Wakamatsu, Akira (act): Mothra
Wakamatsu, Takeshi (act): Angel Dust
Wakayama, Setsuko (act): Godzilla Raids Again
Wakayama, Tomisaburo (act): Phoenix (1978)
Wakefield, David (act): Bates Motel
Wakefield, Hugh (act, b. 1888): Blithe Spirit; The Crime at Blossoms; The Crimson Circle (1936); The Limping Man (1936); The Man They Could Not Arrest; The Man Who Knew Too Much (1934); No Highway In the Sky; Sorry You've Been Troubled
Wakeford, Kent (cin): Doctor Death: Seeker of Souls
Wakeham, Deborah (act): Northstar
Wakeman, Jay (act): Night of the Creeps
Wakeman, Rick (act): Liszt O' Mania
Wakeman, Rick (mus): The Burning; Creepshow 2; Liszt O' Mania; Midnight In Saint Petersburg; She (1983)
Walacinski, Adam (mus): O Dwoch Takich Co Ukradli Ksiezyc
Walas, Chris (dir): The Fly II
Walberg, Garry (act): The Immortal; The Spirit
Walbridge, John (wri): Alice In Wonderland (1951)
Walbrook, Anton (act, 1900-1968, nee Adolph Wilhelm Wohlbruck): 49th Parallel; Gaslight (1940); I Accuse (1958); Lola Montes; The Queen of Spades (1948); The Rat; Der Student von Prag (1935)
Walburn, Raymond (act, 1887-1969): The Count of Monte Cristo (1934); The Lone Wolf Returns (1935)
Walch, Ernst (act): Curse of the Stone Hand
Walcott, Arthur (act): The Amazing Partnership; The Bells (1923); The Loudwater Mystery; The Mystery of a Hansom Cab; The Other Person; The Shadow of Egypt; The Tiger of San Pedro; The Woman of the Iron Bracelets
Walcott, George (act): The Mandarin Mystery
Walcott, Gregory (act): Code Name: Minus One; Ed Wood; The Eiger Sanction; House II: The Second Story; Plan 9 from Outer Space
Walcutt, John (act): Return (1985); The Seventh Sign; Virtuosity
Wald, John (act): Nightmare Alley
Wald, Jerry (wri, 1912-1962): Out of the Fog (1941)
Wald, Malvin (wri): Behind Locked Doors; The Legend of Sleepy Hollow; Paroxysmus
Wald, Robert (act): The Prey (1980)
Walden, Barbara (act): The Private Lives of Adam and Eve
Walden, Chris (mus): A Deadly Vision
Walden, Diana (act): Phantom of the Paradise
Walden, Regina (act): Electric Dreams
Walden, Robert (act): Audrey Rose; Blue Sunshine; Capricorn One; Murderer's Keep; Rage
Walden, Susan (act): The Possessed (1977)
Walden, W.G. Snuffy (mus): The Stand
Walder, Ernest (act): The Quiller Memorandum
Waldhorn, Gary (act): Zeppelin
Waldis, Otto (act, 1905-1974): Attack of the 50-Foot Woman (1958); Bagdad; Berlin Express; The Black Castle; Prince Valiant (1954); Unknown World
Waldman, Grant Austin (dir): The Channeler; Teenage Exorcist
Waldman, Marian (act): Deranged (1974); Phobia; Silent Night, Evil Night; When Michael Calls
Waldo, Janet (act): The Gracie Allen Murder Case; Once Upon a Forest
Waldock, Denis (wri): Miranda
Waldon, Regina (act): The Fog
Waldren, Peter (act): Eat and Run
Waldrige, Harold (act): The Death Kiss
Waldron (Sr.), Charles (act): The Big Sleep (1946); Crime and Punishment (1935, USA); The Great Impersonation (1935, USA); On Borrowed Time; The Son of Monte Cristo; Stranger On the Third Floor
Waldron, John (act): Captain America II
Waldron, Tom (wri): Morning Call
Wale, Henry (act): see Oscar, Henry
Wale, Terry (act): Infamous Conduct
Walen, Niels (mus): The Glass Cell
Wales, Ethel (act): The Gladiator; The Monster (1925)
Wales, William (wri): Amityville 3-D
Walford, Ann (act); The Gold Express
Walken, Christopher (act, b. 1943): The Addiction; All-American Murder; Antz; Batman Returns; Brainstorm (1983); The Comfort of Strangers; Communion; The Dead Zone; Last Embrace; The Mind Snatchers; The Prophecy II; Puss In Boots; The Sentinel; Touch; A View to a Kill
Walken, Georgianne (act): Brainstorm (1983)
Walker, Ally (act): Eye of the Storm; Kazaam; Universal Soldier; When the Bough Breaks
Walker, Andrew/Andy (act): Running Against Time; Seven
Walker, Andrew Kevin (wri): Brainscan; Hideaway; Seven
Walker, Ann (act): Remote Control (1988)
Walker, Arnetia (act): Cast a Deadly Spell
Walker, Bill (act): see Walker, William/Bill
Walker, Bill (mus): Bog
Walker, Blanche (act): The House of Peril
Walker, Brian (act): Blind Date
Walker, Bruce (act): Dick Barton Strikes Back
Walker, Bruce (wri): Cosh Boy
Walker, Carolyn (act): 12 Monkeys
Walker, Charles (act): Covenant
Walker, Charlotte (act, 1878-1958): The Lone Wolf (1924); The Midnight Girl; The Savage
Walker, Cheryl (act): Identity Unknown; Larceny In Her Heart; Murder Is My Business; Three On a Ticket
Walker, Chris (act): Desire; The Man Without Desire
Walker, Clint (act, b. 1927, a.k.a. Jett Norman): Deadly Harvest; Hysterical; Jungle Gents; Killdozer; Mysterious Island of Beautiful Women; Scream of the Wolf; Snowbeast
Walker, Dorian (dir): Teen Witch
Walker, Edmund (act): see Kemp, Jeremy
Walker, Ellie Wood (act): Targets
Walker, Eric (act, b. 1970): And You Thought Your Parents Were Weird; The Ewok Adventure; Ewoks: The Battle for Endor
Walker, Fiona (act): The Asphyx
Walker, Gene (act): End of the World (1977); Lizzie
Walker, Gloria (act): —And Now the Screaming Starts!; Satan's Slave
Walker, Greg (act): Gargoyles
Walker, Hal (dir, 1896-1956): The Road to Bali; The Road to Utopia
Walker, Helen (act, 1921-1968): Call Northside 777; The Man In Half Moon Street; Nightmare Alley
Walker, Ian (wri): The Body Vanishes
Walker, Jack David (act): The Guardian
Walker, James (act): 1984 (1984)
Walker, Jayne (act): I Was a Teen-Age Mummy
Walker, Jeff (act): The Reflecting Skin
Walker, Jimmie (act): Frankenstein Sings; The Guyver
Walker, John (act): Vampire's Kiss
Walker, Johnny (act): Heart Condition
Walker, Joseph/Joe (cin, 1893-1985): The Dark Past; Here Comes Mr. Jordan; It's a Wonderful Life; Lost Horizon (1937); Midnight Mystery; Submarine; Tarzan and the Golden Lion; The Velvet Touch
Walker, Joyce (act): Howling II
Walker, Judy (act): Blood Beach
Walker, Kathryn (act): D.A.R.Y.L.; Neighbors
Walker, Keith (act): The Goonies
Walker, Ken(neth) (mus): The Deadly Spawn
Walker, Kim (act): Deadly Weapon; Heathers
Walker, Laura (act): The Norwood Builder
Walker, Lillias (act): What Became of Jack and Jill
Walker, Liza (act): El Mono Loco
Walker, Lou (act): Brainstorm (1983); Rearview Mirror
Walker, Maggie (act): Scream and Die!
Walker, Marcy (act): Midnight's Child; Terror In the Shadows
Walker, Mark (act): The Neptune Factor; Rabid
Walker, Martin (act): Black 13; The Drum; The Flying Fool; Sensation (1937); Silver Blaze (1937)
Walker, Matthew (act): Child's Play 3; I'm Dangerous Tonight; Nightmare Street
Walker, Michael (act): Thinner
Walker, Miss (act): The Hound Of The Baskervilles (1921)
Walker, Nancy (act, 1922-1992, nee Ann Myrtle Swoyer): Human Feelings; Murder by Death
Walker, Nella (act): The Beginning or the End?; Four Frightened People; The Locket; The Saint Strikes Back; The Saint Takes Over; Seven Keys to Baldpate (1929)
Walker, Norman (dir): Dangerous Ground; The Flaw (1933); Forging Ahead
Walker, Paul (act): Monster In the Closet; Programmed to Kill; Tammy and the T-Rex
Walker, Peggy Walton (act): Pumpkinhead
Walker, Pete(r) (GB act): The Flesh and Blood Show; House of Whipcord
Walker, Peter (USA act): OSA; Strange Behavior; W
Walker, Pete(r) (dir): The Big Switch; The Day the Screaming Stopped; Die Screaming, Marianne; The Flesh and Blood Show; Frightmare (1974); House of Mortal Sin; House of the Long Shadows; House of Whipcord; Man of Violence; Schizo (1977); Tiffany Jones
Walker, Pete(r) (wri): The Big Switch; Frightmare (1974); House of Mortal Sin; House of Whipcord; Man of Violence; Tiffany Jones
Walker, Polly (act): Lorna Doone (1990); Sliver
Walker, Ray (act, 1904-1980): The Beast With Five Fingers; Dark Alibi; The Dark Hour; Mr. Moto In Danger Island; Secret of the Whistler; The Unsuspected
Walker, Robert (1930s act): The Clutching Hand
Walker (Sr.), Robert (act, 1918-1951): The Beginning or the End?; One Touch of Venus; Strangers On a Train
Walker Jr., Robert (act, b. 1941): Beware! The Blob; The Devonsville Terror; Evil Town; The Face of Eve; Hex; The Spectre of Edgar Allan Poe; Warlock Moon
Walker, Rock (A.) (act): The Alien's Return; Endangered Species; Gargoyles; Ghost Warrior; Weird Science
Walker, Rudolph (act): 10 Rillington Place
Walker, Scott (act): Human Feelings; The Muppet Movie; Orca
Walker, Shirley (act): Angel Heart
Walker, Shirley (mus): The Adventures of Captain Zoom In Outer Space; Asteroid; Batman: Mask of the Phantasm; The Dungeonmaster; The Flash; Ghoulies; Memoirs of an Invisible Man
Walker, Sydney (act): Prelude to a Kiss; Shadow of a Doubt (1991)
Walker, Stuart (dir, 1890-1940): Great Expectations (1934); The Mystery of Edwin Drood (1935); Werewolf of London; White Woman
Walker, Syd (act): I Killed the Count; Old Bill Through the Ages
Walker, Terry (act): The Invisible Ghost; Voodoo Man
Walker, Tracye (act): The Outing
Walker, Vernon L./Verne (cin, 1894-1948): All That Money Can Buy; Genius at Work; Gildersleeve's Ghost; King Kong (1933); The Last Days of Pompeii (1935); Murder, My Sweet; Robin Hood Jr.; Son of Kong; The Spiral Staircase (1946); Suspicion (1941)
Walker, Wally (act): The Docks of New Orleans
Walker, Will (act): Deathsport
Walker, William/Bill (act): Dimension 5; The Golden Eye; Hush...Hush, Sweet Charlotte; Jamaica Run; Killer Leopard; The Mask (1961)
Walker, Zena (act): Change Partners; Danger Tomorrow; Girl In the Headlines; The Last Shot You Hear; The Marked One; Murder In Mind; The Traitors, Troubled Waters 91964)
Wall, Geraldine (act, 1913-1970): Black Magic (1944); Black Widow (1954)
Wall, Jean (act): Frantic
Wall, John (dir): Potter of the Yard; Too Many Detectives
Wall, Max (act, 1908-1990): Chitty Chitty Bang Bang; The Hound Of The Baskervilles (1978); Jabberwocky; One of Our Dinosaurs Is Missing
Wall, Nichols (act): I Was a Zombie for the F.B.I.
Wall, Tony (act): Asylum (1972); Licensed to Kill; Tales from the Crypt (1971)
Wallace, Art (wri): Dr. Cook's Garden; Forgotten City of the Planet of the Apes; She Waits
Wallace, Basil (act): Deadlock
Wallace, Bill (act): The Fear (1994); A Force of One
Wallace, Brian (act): Peeping Tom
Wallace, Bryan Edgar (wri): The Clairvoyant (1934); The Flying Squad (1940); The Frightened Lady (1932); The Jewel; The Mind of Mr. Reeder; The Missing Million; The Phantom of Soho; The Secret of Dr. Mabuse; The Squeaker (1937); White Face
Wallace, Chris (act): Don't Answer the Phone!; New Year's Evil
Wallace, Connie (act): The Raven (1963)
Wallace, David (act): The Babysitter; Humongous; Mortuary; Rona Jaffe's Mazes and Monsters
Wallace (Stone), Dee (act): Alligator II: The Mutation; Critters; Cujo; E.T.-The Extra-Terrestrial; The Frighteners; The Hills Have Eyes; The Howling; I'm Dangerous Tonight; Invisible Mom; Legend of the White Horse; The Phoenix and the Magic Carpet; Popcorn; The Stepford Wives; Temptress (1995); Witness to the Execution
Wallace, Donald K. (act): Night of the Zombies (1981)
Wallace, Doug (wri): Sensation (1994)
Wallace, E.F. (act): The Story of the Rosary
Wallace, Earl (wri): Curse of the Black Widow
Wallace, Edgar (dir, 1875-1932): Red Aces; The Squeaker (1930)
Wallace, Edgar (wri, 1875-1932): Accidental Death; Attempt to Kill; Backfire!; Candidate for Murder; Carpet of Horror; The Case of the Frightened Lady; The Clue of the New Pin (1929 & 1961); The Clue of the Silver Key; Clue of the Twisted Candle; The Crimson Circle (1922 & 1936); The Curse of the Hidden Vault; Curse of the Yellow Snake; Dark Eyes of London; Death Trap (1962); The Devil's Daffodil; The Door With Seven Locks (1940); The Double; Downfall; Death Drums Along the River; Face of a Stranger; The Feathered Serpent (1934); Five to One; Flat Two; Forger of London; The Fourth Square; The Frightened Lady (1932); The Frog; The Gaunt Stranger; The Green Terror; The Hand of the Gallows; Der Henker von London; The Hound of the Baskervilles (1931); Incident at Midnight; The Indian Scarf; The Inn On Dartmoor; The Inn On the River; The Invisible Terror; King Kong (1933); King Kong Lives; Legacy of Horror (1964); Locker 69; The Main Chance; The Malpas Mystery; Man at the Carlton Tower; Man Detained; The Man They Could Not Arrest; The Man Who Changed His Name; The Man Who Was Nobody; Marriage of Convenience; Melody of Death; The Menace (1932); The Mind of Mr. Reeder; The Missing People; Mr. Reeder In Room 13; The Mysterious Magician; Never Back Losers; Never Mention Murder; Number Six; The Old Man; On the Run (1963); The Partner; Partners In Crime (1961); Playback; Der Raecher; Red Aces; The Red Circle (1929 & 1960); The Red Hand; The Return of the Frog; Return of the Terror; Return to Sender; Ricochet; The Ringer (1928, 1931 & 1952); The Rivals; The Secret of the Black Trunk; Secret of the Red Orchid; The Set-Up (1963); The Share Out; The Sinister Man; Solo for Sparrow; The Squeaker (1930, 1937 & 1965); The Strange Countess; The Terror (1928 & 1938); Time to Remember; To Have and To Hold; Die Toten Augen von London; Traitor's Gate; Die Tur mit den Sieben Schlossern; The Verdict (1964); We Shall See; Who Was Maddox?; The Yellow Mask
Wallace, Elizabeth (GB act): The Night of the Full Moon
Wallace, Elizabeth (USA act): The Bees; Final Eye
Wallace, Enrique (cin): La Momia Contra El Robot Humano
Wallace, Franck (mus): Lo Spettro
Wallace, Gary (act): The Jar
Wallace, Gavin (act): Eclipse (1977)
Wallace, Geoffrey (act): They Came from Beyond Space
Wallace, George (act): Forbidden Planet; Retik, the Moon Menace
Wallace, George D. (act): The Haunted (1991)
Wallace, Bill (act): The Velvet Touch
Wallace, Hedger (act): The Creeping Flesh; Tales from the Crypt (1971); The Witness

Wallace, Helen (act): Back from the Dead; Francis In the Haunted House; Jack the Giant Killer
Wallace, Henry (cin): Doctor of Doom
Wallace, Ian (act): Assassin for Hire; Tom Thumb
Wallace, Inez (wri): I Walked with a Zombie
Wallace, Irving (wri, b. 1916): Desert Legion
Wallace, J.T. (act): Terrorgram
Wallace, Jean (act, 1923-1990, nee Jean Wallasek): Lancelot and Guinevere; No Blade of Grass; Star of India; Storm Fear
Wallace, Jerry (act): Friday the 13th-Part 2
Wallace, John (act): The Black Pirate
Wallace, Julie T. (act): The Living Daylights
Wallace, Lee (act): Batman (1989); World War III
Wallace, Marcia (act): Teen Witch
Wallace, Morgan (act): Charlie Chan at the Olympics; Dante's Inferno (1935); Dick Tracy (1945); Ellery Queen, Master Detective; The Falcon's Alibi; The House of Secrets (1937); Lady In the Morgue; The Maltese Falcon (1931); Mr. Moto Takes a Vacation; Murder On a Honeymoon; The Mystery of Mr. Wong; One Exciting Night
Wallace, Oliver (mus): The Adventures of Ichabod and Mr. Toas; Alice In Wonderland (1951); Darby O'Gill and the Little People; Dumbo; Peter Pan (1953)
Wallace, Parnum (act): Our Mother's House
Wallace, Randall (dir): The Man In the Iron Mask (1998)
Wallace, Randall (wri): Dark Angel; The Man In the Iron Mask (1998)
Wallace, Richard (cin): Creature of the Walking Dead
Wallace, Richard (dir): Framed; Sinbad the Sailor
Wallace, Rick (dir): Dad, the Angel & Me
Wallace, Ruby Ann (act): see Dee, Ruby
Wallace, Stephen (dir): Stir
Wallace, Tim (act): Nomads
Wallace, Tommy Lee (dir): Fright Night II; Halloween III: Season of the Witch; It (1990); Once You Meet a Stranger; The Presence; Witness to the Execution
Wallace, Tommy Lee (wri): Amityville II: The Possession; Fright Night II; Halloween III: Season of the Witch; It (1990)
Wallace, Trevor (wri): Journey Into Fear (1975)
Wallach, Eli (act, b. 1915): The Angel Levine; Circle of Iron; A Cold Night's Death; The Deep; The Domino Principle; Firepower; Kisses for My President; The Lineup; Mackenna's Gold; The Moon-Spinners; The Sentinel; Winter Kills
Wallack, Edwin (act): The Hunchback of Notre Dame (1923)
Wallack, Kathryn (wri): Sabrina the Teenage Witch
Wallasek, Jean (act): see Wallace, Jean
Wallen, Sherry (act): Mannequin Two: On the Move
Waller, Anthony (dir): An American Werewolf In Paris
Waller, David (act): Perfect Friday; Work Is a Four Letter Word
Waller, Eddy (act): Meet Nero Wolfe; The Millerson Case; Nightmare Alley
Waller, Fred (cin): Puritan Passions
Waller, (J.) Wallett (act): A Cornish Romance; A Tragedy of the Cornish Coast
Waller, (J.) Wallett (dir): A Message from Mars (1913); The Smugglers' Cave; A Vagabond's Revenge
Waller, (J.) Wallett (wri): A Message from Mars (1913)
Waller, Lewis (act): Brigadier Gerard
Waller, Philip (act): The Stepford Children
Waller, Rani (act): Flame In the Heather; Murder In the family; Murder Tomorrow
Wallerstein, Herb (dir): Snowbeast
Walley, Deborah (act): The Bubble; Dr. Goldfoot and the Bikini Machine; The Ghost In the Invisible Bikini; Sergeant Deadhead the Astronut!; The Severed Arm
Walley, Moira (act): Runaway (1984)
Walley, Norma (act): The Crimson Circle (1922)
Wallin, Peter (mus): The Visitors (1989)
Walling, Chris (cin): Solo
Walling, Jonathan (act): Student Bodies
Walling, Mike (act): Scandalous
Walling, Richard (act): The Return of Peter Grimm (1926)
Walling, Will(iam) (act): Kismet (1930); The Temple of Venus
Wallis, Bertram (act): The Wandering Jew (1933)
Wallis, Bill (act): Brazil; The Canterville Ghost (1986); Jamaica Inn (1985); The Orchard End Murder; The Secret Life of Ian Fleming
Wallis, Francis (act): Someone at the Top of the Stairs
Wallis, J.H. (wri): The Woman In the Window
Wallis, Jacquie (act): Kiss of the Vampire
Wallis, Peter (act): Dracula (1979)
Wallis, Shani (act, b. 1941): Arnold; Terror In the Wax Museum
Wallner, Herman (act): Kiss of the Tarantula
Wallner, Martha (act): Das Schloss
Wallner, Max (wri): Premiere
Wallop, Douglass (wri, b. 1920): Damn Yankees
Walls, H. Michael (act): 12 Monkeys
Walls, Kevin Patrick (act): Scream
Walls, Tom (act, 1883-1949): Halfway House; The Interrupted Journey; Strange Boarders; Thark; They Met In the dark; While I Live
Walls, Tom (dir, 1883-1949): Thark
Walmsley, Anna (act): The Revenge of Frankenstein
Walper, Cicely (act): The Brotherhood of Satan
Walpole, Hugh (wri, 1884-1941): House of Menace; Kind Lady (1951)
Walravens, Jean-Paul (dir): Jungle Burger
Walsch, John (act): Def Con 4
Walsh, Bill (wri): The Absent-Minded Professor (1961); Bedknobs and Broomsticks; Blackbeard's Ghost; Flubber; Herbie Rides Again; The Love Bug; Mary Poppins; The Misadventures of Merlin Jones; One of Our Dinosaurs Is Missing; The Shaggy Dog (1959 & 1994); Son of Flubber
Walsh, Brigid Conley (act): Quest of the Delta Knights
Walsh, Christopher (act): Endgame
Walsh, Dale (act): Tarzan's New Adventure
Walsh, Dan (act): Attack of the Killer Tomatoes
Walsh, David M. (cin): Murder by Death; My Science Project; Sleeper
Walsh, Dennis C. (act): Killer Klowns from Outer Space
Walsh, Dermot (act, b. 1924): At the Stroke of Nine; The Blue Parrot; Bond of Fear; The Breaking Point (1961); Chain of Events; Counterspy; The Flesh and the Fiends; The Floating Dutchman; The Frightened Man; Ghost Ship (1952); The Hideout; Infamous Conduct; Journey to the Unknown; The Mark of Cain; The Night of the Full Moon; Out of the Shadow; Shoot to Kill (1961); The Straw Man; The Tell-Tale Heart (1960); Torment (1949); The Trunk; The Wicked Lady; The Witness; A Woman of Mystery
Walsh, Dick (act): Tormented (1960)
Walsh, Dylan (act): Congo
Walsh, Edward (act): Count Yorga, Vampire; Crypt of the Living Dead; The Return of Count Yorga
Walsh, Fiona (act): Arachnophobia
Walsh, Fran(ces) (wri): Dead Alive; The Frighteners; Meet the Feebles
Walsh, Gerry (act): Rawhead Rex
Walsh, Gwynyth (act): Blue Monkey; The Crush; Star Trek: Generations; Zenon: Girl of the 21st Century
Walsh, J.T. (act, 1944-1998): The Babysitter (1995); The Little Death; Miracle On 34th Street (1994); Narrow Margin (1990); Needful Things; Pleasantville; Sling Blade
Walsh, Jessie Joe (act): Notorious (1992)
Walsh, Joey (act): Hans Christian Andersen
Walsh, John (act): Amazons (1984); Body Parts (1991)
Walsh, John D. (act): The Midnight Girl
Walsh, Johnny (act): Wild Women of Wongo
Walsh, Judy (act): Cannibal Attack; Second Chance
Walsh, Kathleen (act): Summer of Fear
Walsh, Kay (act, b. 1914): Cast a Dark Shadow; The Chinese Bungalow; Dr. Syn-Alias the Scarecrow; He Who Rides a Tiger; Hunted (1952); Journey to the Unknown; Last Holiday; The Mind of Mr. Reeder; The Missing People; The October Man; The Ruling Class; Scrooge (1970); The Secret of Stamboul; Stage Fright (1950); A Study In Terror; Taste of Excitement; Vice Versa (1947); The Witches (1966)
Walsh, Kay (wri): Great Expectations (1946)
Walsh, Leigh (act): Barracuda
Walsh, Lelia (act): Mara of the Wilderness
Walsh, M. Emmet (act, b. 1935): Blade Runner; Blood Simple; Critters; Escape from the Planet of the Apes; The Flash; Harry and the Hendersons; The Lottery; National Lampoon's Men In White; Portraits of a Killer; Red Alert; Scandalous; Sundown: The Vampire In Retreat; They Might Be Giants; Wilder Napalm
Walsh, Matthew Jason (act): Midnight 2: Sex, Death, and Videotape
Walsh, Pat (act): My Bloody Valentine
Walsh, Percy (act): The Case of Gabriel Perry; Checkmate; Dick Barton at Bay; Pimpernel Smith; Traitor Spy
Walsh, Percy (wri): Chin Chin Chinaman
Walsh, Raoul (dir, 1887-1981): Background to Danger; Blackbeard the Pirate; The Horn Blows at Midnight; Lost and Found On a South Sea Island; Loves of Carmen (1927); The Monkey Talks; Pursued; The Serpent (1916); The Thief of Bagdad (1924); Women of All Nations
Walsh, Raoul (wri, 1887-1981): The Serpent (1916)
Walsh, Raymond (act): Eraserhead
Walsh, Rob (mus): Blood Song; Nightbeast
Walsh, Robin (act): Midnight (1980)
Walsh, Sally (act): The Curse of Frankenstein
Walsh, Sharon (act): The Incredibly Strange Creatures Who Stopped Living and Became Mixed-Up Zombies
Walsh, Stuart (act): Mara of the Wilderness
Walsh, Sydney (act): Homewrecker; To Die For
Walsh, Terry (act): Jekyll and Hyde
Walsh, Tricia (act): Terror (1979)
Walsh, Wendy (act): The Mask (1994)
Walshe, Pat (act): The Wizard of Oz (1939)
Walsky, Oryan (act): Into the Badlands
Walston, Ray (act, b. 1918): Blood Salvage; Damn Yankees; The Fall of the House of Usher (1982); Galaxy of Terror; The Kid With the Broken Halo; My Favorite Martian; Of Mice and Men (1992); Popcorn; Project: Alf; Saturday the 14th Strikes Back; The Stand
Walter, Eugene (act): The Black Belly of the Tarantula
Walter, Harry (act): The Black Tulip (1921)
Walter, Jerry (act): Invasion of the Body Snatchers (1978); Nightmare In Blood
Walter, Jessica (act, b. 1940): Dr. Strange; Doomsday Rock; Ghost In the Machine; Home for the Holidays; The Immortal; Killer In the Mirror; Lilith; Play Misty for Me; She's Dressed to Kill; Temptress (1995); They Call It Murder; Vampire (1979)
Walter, Jules (act): The Boy Who Never Was
Walter, Linda Lee (act): Maniac (1980)
Walter, Mariane (act): The Toolbox Murders
Walter, Mary (act): The Blood Drinkers; Curse of the Vampires
Walter, Michael (S.) (act): Neon Maniacs; Serial Mom
Walter, Mike (act): Metalstorm: The Destruction of Jared-Syn
Walter, Olive (act): The Blue Bird (1910)
Walter, Perla (act): Chiller; Maid to Order; The Man With Two Brains
Walter, Rosa (act): The Ghost Train (1927)
Walter, Dr. Sidney (act): The Mysterious Monsters
Walter, Tracey (act, b. 1942): Batman (1989); The Companion (1994); Conan the Destroyer; Cyborg 2: Glass Shadow; Destiny Turns On the Radio; The Hand (1981); Not of This World; Out of the Dark; Repo Man; The Silence of the Lambs; Timerider; Timestalkers
Walter, Wilfrid (act): Dark Eyes of London
Walters, Anthony (act): A Christmas Carol (1984)
Walters, Bernice (act): The Beggar Girl's Wedding
Walters, Bessie (act): The Female Swindler
Walters, Charles (dir, 1911-1982): The Glass Slipper
Walters, Don (act): The Incredible Melting Man
Walters, Dorothy (act): A Kiss for Cinderella
Walters, Hal (act): Come Into My Parlour; Death On the Set; The Perfect Flaw; The River House Ghost; Sabotage; They Came by Night; The Vulture (1937)
Walters, Happy (mus): Mighty Morphin Power Rangers
Walters, Hugh (act): Brimstone & Treacle
Walters, Justin (act): The Curse of the Werewolf
Walters, Laurie (act): The People; Warlock Moon
Walters, Luana (act): The Corpse Vanishes; Girls In Prison; The She-Creature
Walters, Mary (act): The Thirsty Dead
Walters, Melora (act): Ed Wood; Eraser; Twice Upon a Time
Walters, Nancy (act): Monster On the Campus
Walters, Rock (act): Laserblast
Walters, Susan (1940s act): Shoot to Kill (1947)
Walters, Susan (1990s act): I Married a Monster
Walters, Thorley (act, b. 1913): The Adventures of Sherlock Holmes' Smarter Brother; The Birthday Present; Dracula, Prince of Darkness; The Earth Dies Screaming; Frankenstein Created Woman; Frankenstein Must Be Destroyed; A Lady Mislaid; The Last Shot You Hear; The Little Drummer Girl; The Man Who Haunted Himself; Murder She Said; The People That Time Forgot; The Phantom of the Opera (1962); The Psychopath (1965); Ring of Spies; Sherlock Holmes and the Deadly Necklace; The Sign of Four (1983); Trog; Trunk Crime; The Twisted Nerve; Valley of Fear (1964); Vampire Circus; Who Done It? (1956); The Wrong Box; You Can't Escape
Walthall, Henry B. (act, 1878-1936): The Avenging Conscience; The Bridge of San Luis Rey (1929); Chandu the Magician; The Confession (1920); Dante's Inferno (1935); Devil Doll (1936); The False Faces; The Garden Murder Case; London After Midnight; The Raven (1915); The Road to Mandalay; The Scarlet Letter (1926 & 1934); Temple Tower
Walthall, Romy (act): The Howling: New Moon Rising
Walther, Jurg (cin): Blood Diner
Waltman, Alan (act): The Clan of the Cave Bear
Walton, Bryn (mus): Secret Lives
Walton, Douglas (act): Bride of Frankenstein; Charlie Chan In London; Dick Tracy vs. Cueball; The Garden Murder Case; The Lost Patrol (1934); Murder, My Sweet; The Picture of Dorian Gray (1945); The Secret of Madame Blanche
Walton, Emma (act): Switch (1991)
Walton, Fred (dir): Alfred Hitchcock Presents; April Fool's Day; Dead Air; Homewrecker; I Saw What You Did (1988); The Rosary Murders; The Stepford Husbands; When a Stranger Calls; When a Stranger Calls Back
Walton, Fred (wri): Alfred Hitchcock Presents; The Rosary Murders; When a Stranger Calls; When a Stranger Calls Back
Walton, Harry (cin): Dark Star
Walton, Herbert C. (act): The Angel Who Pawned Her Harp; Britannia Mews; Time Bomb
Walton, J. (dir): see Losey, Joseph
Walton, Janie (act): Alice In Wonderland (1985)
Walton, Jeffrey (mus): Attack of the 60 Foot Centerfold; Dark Universe
Walton, Peggy (act): What's the Matter With Helen?
Walton, Sunni (act): Donor
Walton, Travis (act & wri): Fire In the Sky (1993)
Walton, Sir William (mus, b. 1902): Hamlet (1948); Richard III (1955)
Waltz, Christoph (act): Fire & Sword
Waltz, Lisa (act): Lifepod; Pet Sematary Two
Waltz, Patrick (act): Queen of Outer Space
Waltzer, Jack (act): Werewolf of Washington
Walwin, Kent (wri): Biggles: Adventures In Time
Wama, Wim (act): Gebroken Spiegels
Wambu, Oke (act): The Hunger
Wanaguru, Dudley (act): Il Montagna di Dio Cannibale
Wanamaker, Sam (act, 1919-1993): Cat and Mouse (1974); The Criminal; Danger Route; The Day the Fish Came Out; Death On the Nile; Mr. Denning Drives North; Running Against Time; The Secret; The Spiral Staircase (1975); The Spy Who Came In from the Cold; Superman IV: The Quest for Peace
Wanamaker, Sam (dir, 1919-1993): The Executioner; The File of the Golden Goose; Sinbad and the Eye of the Tiger
Wang, George (act): The Big Game; La Decima Vittima
Wang, James/Jimmy (act): Charlie Chan's Chance; Charlie Chan's Courage
Wang, Luoyong (act): Daylight
Wang, Richard (act): The Chinese Ring
Wang, Steve (dir): The Guyver; Guyver 2: Dark Hero
Wang, Wayne (dir): Slam Dance
Wang Yu, Jimmy (act): The Man from Hong Kong
Wanka, Rolf (act): Captain Sinbad
Wannberg, Ken (mus): Of Unknown Origin; The Philadelphia Experiment
Waram, Percy (act): Ministry of Fear
Waratum, Ram (act): Vice Versa (1988)
Warbeck, David (act, b. 1941): Ark of the Sun God; The Black Cat (1980); Craze; Formula for a Murder; Hunters of the Golden Cobra; Miami Golem; Only a Scream Away; Panic (1983); 7 Doors of Death; Trog; Twins of Evil
Warburton, E.A. (act): The Blue Bird (1910)
Warburton, John (act, 1903-1981): Charlie Chan's Greatest Case; City Beneath the Sea (1952); East of Sumatra; A Study In Scarlet (1933); Tarzan and the Huntress

Warburton, Valeria (act): *Starship Invasions*
Warchol, Grzegorz (dir): *I Like Bats*
Ward, Al (act): *The Cremators*
Ward, Al C. (wri): *Please Murder Me*
Ward, Albert (dir): *The Female Swindler; The Girl Who Wrecked His Home; The Phantom Picture; The Pleydell Mystery; Queen of My Heart; Queen of the Wicked; When Woman Hates*
Ward, Albert (wri): *The Girl Who Wrecked His Home; The Phantom Picture; The Pleydell Mystery; Queen of the Wicked; When Woman Hates*
Ward, Aleardo (act): *Spirits of the Dead*
Ward, Alonzo (act): *Jaws 3-D*
Ward, Amelita (act): *The Dark Mirror (1946); The Falcon and the Co-Eds; The Falcon In Danger; Gildersleeve's Ghost; Jungle Captive*
Ward, Bert (act): *Agatha*
Ward, Bethany (act): *The Haunting of Sarah Hardy*
Ward, Bill (act): *A Place to Die*
Ward, Burt (act, b. 1945): *Batman (1966); Cyber-Chic*
Ward, Cecil (act): *The Lifeguardsman; The Second Stain; The Shuttle of Life*
Ward, Chancer (act): *The Bat Whispers*
Ward, Christy (act): *Sling Blade*
Ward, David (act): *Hotel Reserve*
Ward, Dervis (act): *Gorgo; The Vengeance of She*
Ward, Edmund (wri): *Amsterdam Affair; Twinsanity*
Ward, Edward (mus): *After the Thin Man; Ali Baba and the Forty Thieves (1943); Another Thin Man; The Climax; Cobra Woman; Great Expectations (1934); Gypsy Wildcat; House of Menace; Night Must Fall (1937); Phantom of the Opera (1943); The Son of Monte Cristo*
Ward, Felix (act): *Spookies*
Ward, Fred (act): *Cast a Deadly Spell; Chain Reaction (1996); Remo Williams: The Adventure Begins; Timerider; Tremors; Tremors 2: Aftershocks; UFOria*
Ward, Georgina (act): *The Man Who Finally Died*
Ward, James "Skip" (act): *The Mad Room; Myra Breckinridge; The Nutty Professor (1963); Voyage to the Bottom of the Sea*
Ward, Janet (act): *Night Moves*
Ward, Jay (wri): *George of the Jungle*
Ward, Jeff (act): *Angel Heart*
Ward, Jeffrey L. (act): *Dante's Peak*
Ward, Joan (act): *No Blade of Grass*
Ward, John (act): *Dream a Little Dream; Space Master X-7*
Ward, John D. (act): *Teenage Mutant Ninja Turtles*
Ward, Jomarie (act): *Pretty Maids All In a Row*
Ward, Jonathan (act): *Ferngully: The Last Rain Forest; Mac and Me*
Ward, Julian (wri): *Dangerous Voyage*
Ward, Katherine (act): *Son of Kong*
Ward, Kelly (wri): *Once Upon a Forest*
Ward, Lalla (act): *Vampire Circus*
Ward, Larry (act): *Deathhead Virgin; Macabre (1980)*
Ward, Lesley (act): *An American Werewolf In London*
Ward, Luci (wri): *The Frozen Ghost; The Night the World Exploded*
Ward, Lyman (act): *Alfred Hitchcock Presents; Creature; A Nightmare On Elm Street, Part 2: Freddy's Revenge; Perfect Victims; The Phoenix (1981); Sleepwalkers*
Ward, Mackenzie (act): *Dark Secret*
Ward, Marion (wri): *The Man Who Laughs (1928)*
Ward, Mark (act): *A Ghost of a Chance (1968)*
Ward, Mary Jane (wri): *The Snake Pit (1948)*
Ward, Megan (act): *Amityville 1992: It's About Time; Arcade; Crash and Burn; Don't Look Down; Encino Man; Freaked; Joe's Apartment; Trancers II: The Return of Jack Deth; Trancers III: Deth Lives*
Ward, Merlin (act): *Are You Dying Young Man?*
Ward, Michael (act, b. 1915): *Carry On Screaming; Frankenstein and the Monster from Hell; The Frightened Man; No Trace; Sleeping Car to Trieste; Tread Softly; Where the Bullets Fly*
Ward, Mike (act): *The Mutagen*
Ward, Nick (act): *Dead Alive*
Ward, Olivia (act): *Ghostbusters II*
Ward, Pamela (act): *Hellhole; School Spirit*
Ward, Peggy (act): *Sergeant Deadhead the Astronut!*
Ward, Penelope Dudley (act): *The Case of the Frightened Lady*
Ward, Polly (act): *Alf's Button (1930); Bulldog Sees It Through*

Ward, Rachel (act): *After Dark, My Sweet; Black Magic (1992); Double Jeopardy; The Final Terror; Night School; Wide Sargasso Sea*
Ward, Robert (act): *The Brotherhood of Satan; Death Dreams; Strait-Jacket*
Ward, Robin (act): *Dr. Frankenstein On Campus*
Ward, Roger (act): *Escape 2000; Mad Max; The Man from Hong Kong*
Ward, Ronald (act): *Alibi (1931); Escape to Danger; The Man Behind the Mask (1936); My Daughter Joy; The Passing of the Third Floor Back (1935); Strange Experiment; The Straw Man; They Met In the Dark*
Ward, Sandy (act): *Cujo; The Velvet Vampire*
Ward, Sela (act, b. 1957): *Child of Darkness, Child of Light; Double Jeopardy; The Fugitive (1993); The Haunting of Sarah Hardy; Hello Again*
Ward, Simon (act, b. 1941): *The Corsican Brothers (1985); Deadly Strangers; Dominique; Dracula (1973); Frankenstein Must Be Destroyed; Hitler: The Last Ten Days; Holocaust 2000; I Start Counting; The Monster Club; Quest for Love; Supergirl (1984); The Three Musketeers (1974)*
Ward, Skip (act): see Ward, James "Skip"
Ward, Sophie (act): *Full Circle; The Hunger; Return to Oz; Waxwork II: Lost In Time; Young Sherlock Holmes*
Ward, Terry (act): *Praying Mantis*
Ward, Tony (act): *Color Me Dead*
Ward, Trevor (act): *My Cousin Rachel*
Ward, Valerie (act): *Dear Murderer*
Ward, Vincent (dir): *The Navigator: An Odyssey Across Time; What Dreams May Come*
Ward, Vincent (wri): *Alien 3; The Navigator: An Odyssey Across Time*
Ward, Wally (act): *The Invisible Kid; Weird Science*
Ward, Warwick (act): *Belphegor the Mountebank; Birds of Prey; Blind Spot (1932); Bulldog Drummond (1923); The Callbox Mystery; Deadlock (1931); F.P. 1 Antwortet Nicht; The Golden Dawn; Maria Marten (1928); Sorry You've Been Troubled; Wuthering Heights (1920); The Yellow Mask*
Ward, Wayne "Crescendo" (act): *Earth Girls Are Easy*
Ward, William Ashley (act): *Rearview Mirror*
Ward, Zack (act): *The Club (1994)*
Warda, Arne (act): *Blood of Ghastly Horror*
Warde, Anthony (act): *The Atomic City; The Chinese Cat; Dark Alibi; Destination Saturn; Dick Tracy vs. Crime, Inc.; Houdini (1953); The Man Who Knew Too Much (1956); Mr. Moto Takes a Vacation; Raiders of the Seven Seas; Rear Window (1954); Sombra the Spider Woman; The Thin Man Goes Home*
Warde, George Edward (act): see Robey, George
Warde, Harlan (act): *Cry Terror!; Donovan's Brain; Operation Secret*
Warde, Shirley (act): *The Devil Commands*
Warden, Florence (wri): *The House On the Marsh*
Warden, Hugh (act): *Galaxina*
Warden, Jack (act, b. 1920): *Alice In Wonderland (1985); Beyond the Poseidon Adventure; Blindfold; Death On the Nile; The Great Muppet Caper; Guilty as Sin; Heaven Can Wait (1978); Topper (1979)*
Warden, Judith (wri): *Wall of Death (1956)*
Ward-Freeman, Cassandra (act): *Teenage Mutant Ninja Turtles*
Ward-Lewis, Colin (act): *Threads*
Wardlow, John (act): *The Clan of the Cave Bear*
Wardlow, Keith (act): *The Clan of the Cave Bear; Watchers*
Wardwell, Geoffrey (act): *Crimes at the Dark House; What Happened Then?*
War Eagle, John (act): *Search for the Gods*
Ware, Clyde (wri): *The Spy With My Face*
Ware, Derek (act): *Give Us Tomorrow; The Primitives*
Ware, Eric (act): *Web of Deceit*
Ware, Graham (act): *Inn of the Damned*
Ware, Harlan (act): *The Monster That Challenged the World*
Ware, Helen (act): *Secret of the Chateau*
Ware, Herta (act): *Alien Nation: Millennium; Amazing Stories: The Movie V; Cocoon; Cocoon: The Return; Critters 2: The Main Course; Dr. Heckyl & Mr. Hype; Slam Dance; Species*
Ware, Howard (act): *The Giant Gila Monster*
Ware, Irene (act): *Chandu the Magician; The Dark Hour; Federal Agent; The Raven (1935); Rendezvous at Midnight; Six Hours to Live*
Ware, Jeff(rey) (act): *Thinner; Wolfen*
Ware, Marie (act): *The Fugitive (1993)*
Ware, Mary (act): *Secrets of a Sorority Girl*
Ware, Midge (act): *Untamed Women*

Ware, Peter (act): *Asteroid; Howling IV*
Wareing, Lesley (act): *The Mind of Mr. Reeder; The Terror (1938)*
Wareth, Ahmed Abdel (act): *Sphinx (1981)*
Waretini, Piripi (act): *Moby Dick (1998)*
Warfield, Chris (act): *Diary of a Madman*
Warfield, Emily (act): *Beyond Obsession*
Warfield, Marsha (act, b. 1954): *Doomsday Rock*
Warfield, Natalie (act): *The House Without a Key*
Warford, Jack (act): *Dr. Heckyl & Mr. Hype; The Little Shop of Horrors (1960)*
Warhol, Andy (act, 1928-1987): *The Iliac Passion*
Warhol, Andy (dir, 1928-1987): *Batman Dracula; Outer and Inner Space; Tarzan and Jane Regained Sort Of*
Waring, Kate (act): *White of the Eye*
Waring, Todd (act): *Splash, Too*
Wark, Virginia (act): *Mad Max Beyond Thunderdome*
Warkentin, Thomas (wri): *Heavy Metal*
Warkol, Jordan Blake (act): *The Shaggy Dog (1994)*
Warlock, Bill(y) (act): *Halloween II; Panic In the Skies!; Society*
Warlock, Fred (act): *101 Dalmatians (1961)*
Warlock, Richard/Dick (act): *The Cat from Outer Space; Firestarter; Halloween II; Halloween III: Season of the Witch; Pumpkinhead; Remote Control (1988); Uninvited (1987)*
Warmington, S.J. (act): *Sabotage; A Smart Set*
Warner, Amy (act): *The Last Man On Planet Earth*
Warner, Bob (act): *Funeral Home; Starship Invasions*
Warner, Brian (cin): *Spasms*
Warner, David (act, b. 1941): *Beastmaster III: The Eye of Braxus; Body Bags; Cast a Deadly Spell; A Christmas Carol (1984); The Company of Wolves; The Deadly Affair; The Disappearance; Final Equinox; Frankenstein (1984); From Beyond the Grave; Grave Secrets; Houdini (1998); Ice Cream Man; Inner Sanctum 2; In the Mouth of Madness; The Island; The Lost World (1993); The Man With Two Brains; Mortal Passions; My Best Friend Is a Vampire; Naked Souls; Necronomicon: Book of the Dead; Nightwing; The Omen; Perfect Friday; Quest of the Delta Knights; Rasputin (1996); Return to the Lost World; Scream 2; The Secret Life of Ian Fleming; Star Trek V: The Final Frontier; Teenage Mutant Ninja Turtles II: The Secret of the Ooze; Star Trek VI: The Undiscovered Country; The 39 Steps (1978); Time After Time; Time Bandits; Tron; The Unnamable II; Waxwork; Work Is a Four Letter Word*
Warner, Douglas (wri): *The Informers*
Warner, Gary (act): *Lurkers*
Warner, H.B. (act, 1876-1958): *All That Money Can Buy; Arrest Bulldog Drummond; Bulldog Drummond In Africa; Bulldog Drummond's Bride; Bulldog Drummond's Secret Police; Charlie Chan's Chance; The Corsican Brothers (1941); Cross Examination; Ellery Queen and the Perfect Crime; The Garden Murder Case; The Gracie Allen Murder Case; The Green Goddess (1929); Hitler's Children; It's a Wonderful Life; Liliom (1930); Lost Horizon (1937); The Menace (1932); The Phantom of Crestwood; Savage Drums; Sunset Boulevard; Supernatural (1933); Topper Returns*
Warner, Jack (act, 1894-1981, nee Jack Waters): *Bang! You're Dead; Dear Murderer; Dominique; The Dummy Talks; Jigsaw; The Lady Killers (1956); My Brother's Keeper; The Quatermass Experiment; Scrooge (1951); Valley of the Eagles*
Warner, Jerry (wri): *The Cat Creeps (1946)*
Warner, John (act): *Professor Potter's Magic Potions; Without a Clue*
Warner, Julie (act): *Dean Koontz' 'Mr. Murder'; Flatliners; The Puppet Masters*
Warner, Paula (act): *Don't Answer the Phone!*
Warner, Richard (act): *Infamous Conduct; The Large Rope; The Mummy's Shroud; Never Back Losers; The Shadow of the Cat; The Share Out; The Strange World of Planet X; The Village of the Damned (1960)*
Warner, Rick (act): *Netforce; 12 Monkeys*
Warner, Robert (act): *Deranged (1974); Octaman; When Michael Calls*
Warner, Steven (act): *The Little Prince*
Warnock, Craig (act): *Time Bandits*
Warn-Pegg, Ann (act): *Deadly Sins*
Warr, Terry (mus): *Scream and Die!*
Warre, Michael (wri): *All Hallowe'en*
Warren, A.E. (act): *The Unholy Three (1925)*

Warren, Aimee (act): *Alien Nation: Body and Soul*
Warren, Allen R. (act): *Boarding House*
Warren, Barry (act): *The Devil-Ship Pirates; Do You Know This Voice?; Frankenstein Created Woman; Kiss of the Vampire*
Warren, Betty (act): *So Long at the Fair; They Met In the Dark; Tread Softly Stranger*
Warren, C. Denier (act): *The Adding Machine; The Body Vanishes; The Clairvoyant (1934); The Dragon of Pendragon Castle; Escort for Hire; House of Blackmail; Spy of Napoleon; Strange Boarders; The Treasure of Monte Cristo (1961); Who Killed John Savage?*
Warren, Charles Marquis (dir, b. 1912): *Back from the Dead; Flight to Tangier; The Unknown Terror*
Warren, Charles Marquis (wri, b. 1912): *Flight to Tangier*
Warren, Danielle (act): *Alien Nation: Body and Soul*
Warren, Deryn (dir): *Black Magic Woman; Bloodspell; Dead of Night (1987)*
Warren, Dodie (act): *The Destructors*
Warren, Dorothy (act): *The Man Without Desire*
Warren, Dwight (cin): *The Altar Stairs; The Shock (1923)*
Warren, E. Alyn/A. (act): *Devil Doll (1936); Outside the Law; Tarzan the Fearless*
Warren, Ed (wri): *The Haunted (1991)*
Warren, F. Brooke (wri): *The Face at the Window (1920, 1932 & 1939)*
Warren, Fran (act): *Abbott and Costello Meet Captain Kidd*
Warren, Frances (wri): *The Secret Voice*
Warren, Fred (act): *The Bells (1926); The Mysterious Mr. Wong; Revolt of the Zombies*
Warren, Gene (cin): *Atlantis, the Lost Continent; Dinosaurus!; The Power (1967); The Time Machine (1960); Who Fears the Devil?*
Warren Jr., Gene (cin): *Attack of the 50-Foot Woman (1993); The Beast (1996); Fright Night II; Lady In White; Nemesis*
Warren, Gene (wri): *Starflight: The Plane That Couldn't Land*
Warren, George (act): *The Final Countdown*
Warren, Gloria (act): *Dangerous Money*
Warren, Hal P. (act, dir & wri): *Manos, the Hands of Fate*
Warren, Helen (act): *The Curse of the Living Corpse*
Warren, Herbert (act): *The House of Secrets (1929)*
Warren, Jack (cin): *The Colossus of New York*
Warren, James (act): *Port Sinister*
Warren, Janet (act): *The Jade Mask; The Shanghai Cobra; The Twonky*
Warren, Jennifer (act): *Amazons (1984); The Intruder Within; Mutant; Night Moves; Shark Kill*
Warren, Jerry (dir): *Curse of the Stone Hand; Frankenstein Island; The Incredible Petrified World; Man Beast; Rymdinvasion i Lappland; Teenage Zombies; Terror of the Bloodhunters; The Wild World of Batwoman*
Warren, Jerry (wri): *The Wild World of Batwoman*
Warren, John (GB act): *Haunted Palace (1949); Up to His Tricks*
Warren, John (USA act): *Bride of the Monster*
Warren, John (wri): *Life Is a Circus*
Warren, John F. (cin): *Dark Intruder; Daughter of Dr. Jekyll; The Search for Bridey Murphy; Torn Curtain*
Warren, Joseph (dir): *Urban Warriors*
Warren, Karl (act): *12 Monkeys*
Warren, Katherine (act): *The Prowler (1951); Son of Ali Baba; The Steel Trap; Talk About a Stranger*
Warren, Ken (act): *Beyond Atlantis*
Warren, Kenneth J. (act): *The Boys; The Creeping Flesh; The Criminal; Demons of the Mind; Digby-The Biggest Dog In the World; Dr. Blood's Coffin; The Double Man; The Fiction-Makers; The Grand Junction Case; A High Wind In Jamaica; I, Monster; The Informers; The Invisible Asset; Strip Tease Murder; A Woman's Temptation*
Warren, Laurie (act): *Princess Warrior*
Warren, Lee (act): *The Alligator People*
Warren, Lesley Ann (act): *Color of Night*
Warren, Lori (act): *Twisted Justice*
Warren, Lorraine (wri): *The Haunted (1991)*
Warren, Low (wri): *Old St. Paul's*
Warren, Mark (act): *Secrets of the Phantom Caverns*
Warren, Mervyn (mus): *The Preacher's Wife*
Warren, Michael (act, b. 1946): *A Passion to Kill; Robin Cook's Invasion*

Warren, Norman J. (dir): Bloody New Year; Inseminoid; Outer Touch; Prey (1978); Satan's Slave; Terror (1979); Time Warp Terror
Warren, Pat (act): Eyes of A Stranger
Warren, Phil(ip) (act): The Falcon's Adventure; Flesh and Fantasy; The Gracie Allen Murder Case
Warren, Phyllis (act): The Weird Ones
Warren, Ruth (act): A Close Call for Boston Blackie
Warren, Sandra (act): Curtains
Warren, Steve (act): The Beginning of the End
Warren, Yvonne (act): Murder Reported
Warrender, Harold (act, 1903-1953): Intimate Relations; Pandora and the Flying Dutchman; The Six Men; Time Bomb; Under the Frozen Falls
Warrenton, Gil(bert) (cin): The Cat and the Canary (1927); The Flight That Disappeared; The Ghost of Dragstrip Hollow; The Man Who Laughs (1928); Master of the World; Mesa of Lost Women; Missing Millions; Panic In Year Zero; Secrets of the Night; The Spanish Cape Mystery; The Sphinx (1933)
Warrick, Ruth (act, b. 1915): The Corsican Brothers (1941); Guest In the House; Journey Into Fear (1942); Roogie's Bump; Song of the South
Warrilow, David (act): Simon
Warrington, Bill (cin): Quatermass II
Warrington, Don (act): Blood Bath at the House of Death
Warrington, Kenneth (act): Appointment With Crime; Death In High Heels; The Hangman Waits
Warrington, Neil (act): Further Exploits of Sexton Blake-The Mystery of the S.S. Olympic
Warry-Smith, Dan (act): Earthquake In New York; The Long Kiss Goodnight
Warshofsky, Fred (dir & wri): The Outer Space Connection
Warsk, Richard Bennett (act): Distortions
Warville, Lizzie (act): For Your Eyes Only
Warwick, Breck (act): Satan's Sadists
Warwick, Dionne (mus, b. 1941): The Seduction
Warwick, Ethel (act): The Man Outside (1933)
Warwick, Gina (act): The Haunted House of Horror
Warwick, James (act): The House of Lurking Death
Warwick, James (wri): Blind Alley
Warwick, John (act, b. 1905, nee John McIntosh Beattie): Bang! You're Dead; The Case of the Frightened Lady; Catch as Catch Can; Circumstantial Evidence (1952); Contraband Spain; The Crossroad Gallows; Dancing With Crime; Dangerous Voyage; Dead Men Are Dangerous; The Desperate Man; Double Alibi; Escape Route; The Face at the Window (1939); Horrors of the Black Museum; The Long Arm; The Mind of Mr. Reeder; The Missing Million; Murder at Site Three; The Mysterious Bullet; Never Look Back; Passenger to London; Pool of London; Print of Death; The Saint's Vacation; This Man Is News; Town On Trial; The Tyburn Case; While I Live
Warwick, Norman (act): Superman (1978)
Warwick, Norman (cin): The Abominable Dr. Phibes; The Creeping Flesh; Dr. Jekyll and Sister Hyde; The Godsend; The Last Days of Man on Earth; Tales from the Crypt (1971); Tales That Witness Madness; They Came from Beyond Space; Torture Garden
Warwick, Richard (act): The Bed-Sitting Room; Hamlet (1990); The Tempest (1980)
Warwick, Robert (act, 1978-1965, nee Robert Taylor Bien): The Adventures of Don Juan; The Adventures of Robin Hood; The Bold caballero; Charlie Chan at the Race Track; Charlie Chan's Greatest Case; Doctor X; The Dragon Murder Case; The Falcon's Adventure; Francis; I Married a Witch; Jamaica Run; Kismet (1944); Lady Godiva; Night Life of the Gods; Salome (1953); Sudan
Waserman, Kastle (act): Vampire On Bikini Beach
Wash, John (cin): Dark Star
Wash, John (dir & wri): Oxo-Omo-Ono
Washbourne, Mona (act, b. 1903): The Bed-Sitting Room; The Blue Bird (1976); Brides of Dracula; Cast a dark Shadow; Child's Play (1954); The Collector; Dark Interval; Fragment of Fear; The London Connection; Night Must Fall (1964); Stranger In Town (1957); What Became of Jack and Jill
Washbrook, Johnny (act): The Space Children
Washburn, Beverly (act): The Lone Ranger; Spider Baby
Washburn, Bryant (act, 1889-1963): Chandu; The Clutching Hand; The Falcon In Hollywood; The Falcon In Mexico; Nabonga; Night of Terror (1933); Rupert of Hentzau (1923); The Westland Case; The Wizard of Oz (1925)
Washburn, Charles (act): Skullduggery
Washburn, Deric (wri): Silent Running
Washburn, Don (act): Space Raiders
Washburn, Rick (act): Angel Heart
Washick, Jennifer (act): The Silencers (1995)
Washimo, Hikonari (act): Popcorn
Washington, Ada (act): The Last House On the Left
Washington, Denzel (act, b. 1955): Fallen; Heart Condition; The Preacher's Wife; Virtuosity
Washington, Erik (act): Dr. Black Mr. Hyde
Washington, Judy (act): Phantom of the Paradise
Washington, Kenneth (W.) (act): Tarzan's Deadly Silence; Westworld
Washington, Ned (mus): Pinocchio (1940)
Washington, Sharon (act): The Long Kiss Goodnight
Washington, Shirley (act): Wonder Women
Washington, Vernon (act): The Dark (1979); Friday the 13th-Part V: A New Beginning; The Last Starfighter
Washman, Kenneth (act): Weekend of Fear
Wasley, Andre (act): Jeux Interdits
Wass, Ted (act): The Canterville Ghost (1986); Oh, God! You Devil; Sheena
Wasserman, Allan (act): Big
Wasserman, Carl (act): Rabid
Wasserman, Jerry (act): Circle of Deceit; Quarantine
Wasserman, Lee (wri): Retribution (1988)
Wassil, Chuck (act): I Married a Monster from Outer Space
Wasson, Art (cin): The Angry Red Planet
Wasson, Craig (act, b. 1954): Body Double; Ghost Story (1981); Midnight Fear; A Nightmare On Elm Street 3: Dream Warriors; Schizoid (1980); The Sister-In-Law; Trapped In Space
Waszynsky, Michael (dir): The Dybbuk
Watanabe, Akira (cin): The Green Slime
Watanabe, Gedde (act): Gremlins 2: The New Batch; Perfect Alibi; The Spring; Vamp
Watanabe, Misako (act): Kwaidan
Watanabe, Toru (act): Ebirah, Horror of the Deep
Watanabe, Yukiko (act): Virus (1980)
Waterbury, Laura (act): Honey, I Shrunk the Kids
Waterfield, Bob (act): Jungle Manhunt
Waterhouse, Al (act): Quarantine
Waterhouse, Keith (wri): West 11
Waterhouse, Tracey (act): Nick Fury: Agent of Shield
Waterhouse, Winnifred (act): Quarantine
Waterland, Terry (act): Bear Island; My Bloody Valentine
Waterman, Al (act): Endgame
Waterman, Annie (act): Repossessed
Waterman, Arnold C. (act): Death Valley
Waterman, Dennis (act): Alice's Adventures In Wonderland (1972); The Eyes Have It; Fright (1971); Night Train for Inverness; The Pirates of Blood River; Scars of Dracula
Waterman, Felicity (act): Miracle Beach
Waterman, Ida (act): The Enchanted Cottage (1924)
Waterman, Willard (act, 1914-1995): Mystery Street
Watermeier, Steve (act): I Was a Zombie for the F.B.I.
Waters, Chastity (act): The Offspring
Waters, Daniel (wri): Batman Returns; Demolition Man; Heathers
Waters, Ed (wri): The Intruder Within
Waters, Ethel (act, 1900-1977): Cabin In the Sky
Waters, George (wri): Why Must I Die?
Waters Jr., Harry (act): Back to the Future, Part II
Waters, Jack (act): see Warner, Jack
Waters, Jan (act): Corruption; Touch of Death
Waters, John (act): Endplay
Waters, John (dir): Multiple Maniacs; Polyester; Serial Mom
Waters, John (wri): Polyester; Serial Mom
Waters, Mel (act): Prophecy (1979)
Waters, Naomi (act): The Perfect Flaw
Waters, Philip (Alan) (cin): Captain America (1992); Cyborg (1989)
Waters, Russell (act, b. 1908): Bomb In the High Street; Danger Tomorrow; Death of an Angel; The Devil Rides Out; Man In the Moon (1960); The Man In the White Suit; Marriage of Convenience; Mr. Denning Drives North; Obsession (1949); Saturday Island; Third Party Risk; The Trygon Factor; Turn the Key Softly; The Twisted Nerve; The Wicker Man
Waterston, Sam (act, b. 1940): Capricorn One; The Enemy Within; The Fifth Missile; Journey Into Fear (1975); Reflections of Murder; Savages; Serial Mom; Shadow Conspiracy; Warning Sign
Watford, Gwen(doline) (act): Do You Know This Voice?; The Fall of the House of Usher (1950); The Ghoul (1974); Taste the Blood of Dracula; The Very Edge
Watkin, David (cin, b. 1925): The Bed-Sitting Room; Bogus; The Devils; Hamlet (1990); Jane Eyre (1996); Mademoiselle; The Persecution and Assassination of Jean-Paul Marat as Performed by the Inmates of the Asylum of Charenton Under the Direction of the Marquis de Sade; Return to Oz; Robin and Marian; The Three Musketeers (1974); To the Devil a Daughter; Yellow Dog
Watkin, Ian (act): Dead Alive
Watkin, Lawrence (Edward) (wri): Darby O'Gill and the Little People; On Borrowed Time; The Story of Robin Hood; Treasure Island (1950)
Watkin, Pierre (act, 1894-1960): The Beginning of the End; The Chance of a Lifetime; Creature With the Atom Brain; Dead Man's Eyes; The Hunted (1948); The Jungle Woman; Murder Is My Business; Radar Secret Service; The Saint Takes Over; The Shanghai Chest; Swamp Fire; Trapped by Boston Blackie
Watkins, Art (act): Empire of Ash III
Watkins, James Louis (act): J.D.'s Revenge; Killer In the Mirror; Spellbinder
Watkins, Jim (act): The Magician (1973)
Watkins, John (L.) (act): Nightmare (1981)
Watkins, Linda (act, 1908-1976): Bad Ronald; Charlie Chan's Chance; Cheaters at Play; From Hell It Came
Watkins, Michael (act): Paint Me a Murder; Venom (1982)
Watkins, Michael (cin): Heart and Souls; Point of No Return
Watkins, Michelle (act): The Outing
Watkins, Peter (dir, b. 1935): The Gladiators; Privilege
Watkins, Shawn Edward (act): Matinee
Watkins, Sophie (act): The Frighteners
Watling, Dilys (act): Calculated Risk
Watling, Jack (act, b. 1923): The Birthday Present; Chain of Events; City After Midnight; Flat Two; Gideon's Day; The Golden Link; Links of Justice; Meet Mr. Lucifer; Mr. Arkadin; The Nanny; The Solitary Child; Under Capricorn; Who Was Maddox?
Watson, Adele (act): The Black Pearl
Watson, Alan (wri): Horror Hospital; Stone Cold Dead
Watson, Alberta (act): The Keep; Murder In Space; White of the Eye
Watson, Barry (act): Killing Mrs. Tingle
Watson, Bobby (act): see Watson, Robert/Bobby
Watson, Bobs (act, b. 1930): On Borrowed Time; What Ever Happened to Baby Jane? (1962)
Watson, Bruce (act): The Magician (1973)
Watson, Carlton (act): Short Circuit 2
Watson, Cavan (act): The Net
Watson, David (act): Beneath the Planet of the Apes
Watson, Debbie (act, b. 1949): Munster, Go Home!
Watson, Ernest (act): Angel Heart
Watson, Gary (act): Once the Killing Starts
Watson, Henrietta (act): The Brown Wallet; Collision; Creeping Shadows; The Pointing Finger; The Shot In the Dark
Watson, Henry (act): Unforgettable
Watson, Jack (act): Five to One; From Beyond the Grave; The Gorgon; King Arthur, the Young Warlord; Konga; The Man Who Was Nobody; Master Spy (1963); Night Caller from Outer Space; Out of the Fog (1962); Peeping Tom; Schizo (1977); The Strange Affair; Time to Remember; Tower of Evil; Treasure Island (1976)
Watson (Jr.), James (act): Killdozer
Watson, Jan (act): Dr. Goldfoot and the Bikini Machine
Watson, John (act): Booby Trap; Cat Girl; Vengeance
Watson, John (dir): Deathstalker
Watson, John (wri): A Gnome Named Gnorm; Robin Hood: Prince of Thieves
Watson, June (act): Murder Motel
Watson, Justice (act): Tower of London (1962)
Watson, Ken (act): Nothing But the Night
Watson, Lane (act): The Dark Mirror (1946)
Watson, Larry (act): The Adventures of Nick Carter
Watson, Lorraine (act): Slaughterhouse Rock
Watson, Lucille (act, 1879-1962): Footsteps In the Dark; Rage In Heaven; The Thin Man Goes Home
Watson, Margo (act): Snow Kill
Watson, Michael (act): Subspecies
Watson, Mills (act, b. 1941): Charley and the Angel; Cujo; The Incredible Hulk, Part 2
Watson, Minor (act, 1889-1965): Charlie Chan In Paris; Enemy Agents Meet Ellery Queen; The Falcon Out West; The Happy Land; Shadows In the Night; The Thin Man Goes Home
Watson, Mitch (act): Primal Rage
Watson, Moray (act): Find the Lady; Operation Crossbow; Quiller: Price of Violence
Watson, Muse (act): The Handmaid's Tale; I Still Know What You Did Last Summer
Watson, Ralph (act): The Anniversary
Watson, Reatha (act): see LaMarr, Barbara
Watson, Richard (act): La Sorella di Satan
Watson, Robert/Bobby (act, 1888-1965): The Adventurous Blonde; After the Thin Man; The Big Clock; The Devil Checks Up; The Story of Mankind
Watson, Roy (act): Wolf Blood
Watson, Tom (act): Haunters of the Deep
Watson, Violet (act): see Lyel, Viola
Watson, Virginia (act): Virtuosity
Watson, William (act): It's Alive III: Island of the Alive; The Sword and the Sorcerer
Watson, Woody (act): All-American Murder; I Come In Peace; Powder; RoboCop 2
Watson, Wylie (act, 1889-1966, nee John Wylie Robertson): Black Mask; Bulldog Sees It Through; Jamaica Inn (1939); Murder In Reverse; Queer Cargo; The Saint Meets the Tiger; Shadow of the Past; Things Happen at Night; The 39 Steps (1935); Your Witness
Watt, Harry (dir, b. 1906): Fiddlers Three
Watt, Sparky (act): The Hand (1981)
Watters, Fred (act): My Bloody Valentine
Watters, Mark (act): In the Shadow of Kilimanjaro
Watters, Mark (mus): Aladdin and the King of Thieves; Babes In Toyland (1997); The Pebble and the Penguin; The Return of Jafar
Watters, William (act, nee Arch Hall Sr.): Eegah!
Wattis, Richard (act, b. 1912): The Abominable Snowman of the Himalayas; The Alphabet Murders; Bunny Lake Is Missing; Carry On Spying; Casino Royale; Chitty Chitty Bang Bang; Diamonds On Wheels; Egghead's Robot; Eyewitness (1956); The Green Man; I Thank a Fool; The Liquidator; The Man Who Knew Too Much (1956); Mother Riley Meets the Vampire; Operation Crossbow; Tam Lin; Top Secret (1952); The Ugly Duckling
Watts, Charles (act): Dead Ringer; The Lone Ranger and the Lost City of Gold; The Man With a Cloak; Seven Days In May; Something Wild
Watts, Cliff (act): The Video Dead
Watts, Diane (act): The Blue Parrot
Watts, Elizabeth (act): Fright (1957)
Watts, Frank (cin): The Corsican Brothers (1985); D.A.R.Y.L.; Mark of the Devil (1985); Paint Me a Murder; Rearview Mirror; The Saint and the Brave Goose; Tennis Court
Watts, Freddie (act): The Angel Who Pawned Her Harp
Watts, Gwendolyn (act); Fanatic (1965)
Watts, James (act): The Lost Patrol (1929)
Watts, Jeanne (act): Memoirs of a Survivor
Watts, Lionel (act): Outward Bound
Watts, Lyonel (act): Strange Evidence
Watts, Marilyn (act): see Corday, Mara
Watts, Naomi (act): Bermuda Triangle (1996); Children of the Corn IV; Matinee; Tank Girl
Watts, Queenie (act): Schizo (1977)
Watts, Tom (dir): Abide With Me; The Angel of the Ward
Watts-Phillips, N. (act): Abide With Me; The Counterfeiters; For All Eternity
Waugh, Bruce D. (act): Raiders of the Living Dead
Waugh, Evelyn (wri, 1903-1966): The Loved One
Waugh, Fred (act): To Die For
Waugh, Hilary (wri): Jigsaw
Wave, Virginia (act): Man-Eater of Kumaon
Wavemaker (mus): The Tempest (1979)
Wawrzyniak, Kazimierz (cin): Wielka, Wielka I Najwieksza
Wax, Ruby (act): Shock Treatment! (1981)
Waxman, Al(bert S.) (act): Collision Course (1992); Double Negative; I Still Dream of Jeannie; Millennium; Spasms; When MichaelCalls
Waxman, Franz (mus, 1906-1967, nee Franz Wachsmann): Alias Nick Beal; Anne of the

Indies; Bride of Frankenstein; A Christmas Carol (1938); Cry Wolf (1947); Dark Passage; Devil Doll (1936); Dr. Jekyll and Mr. Hyde (1941); The Great Impersonation (1935); The Horn Blows at Midnight; The Invisible Ray; My Cousin Rachel; On Borrowed Time; The Paradine Case; Possessed (1947); Prince Valiant (1954); Rear Window (1954); Rebecca; Sorry, Wrong Number (1948); Sunset Boulevard; Suspicion (1941); This Is My Love; Trouble for Two; The Two Mrs. Carrolls; The Unsuspected

Waxman, Harry (cin, 1911-1984): The Anniversary; Are You Dying Young Man?; Blue Blood; The Day the Earth Caught Fire; Digby-The Biggest Dog In the World; Endless Night; Fury at Smugglers' Bay; Journey Into Fear (1975); Lancelot and Guinevere; Man In the Moon (1960); The Nanny; Night Hair Child; Sapphire; She (1965); The Trygon Factor; The Twisted Nerve; The Uncanny; Vampyres...Daughters of Dracula; The Wicker Man

Waxman, Stanley (act): Satan's Satellites

Way, Ann (act): Brazil; Endless Night; Haunted Honeymoon (1986)

Way, Eileen (act): Sphinx (1981); The Stranger Left No Card; Street of Shadows; Venetian Bird

Way, Guy (act): Invasion of the Body Snatchers (1956)

Way, Wendy (act): Phantasm III: Lord of the Dead

Wayans, Damon (act): Blankman; Earth Girls Are Easy

Wayans, Marlon (act, b. 1972): Batman Returns; Senseless (1998); The 6th Man

Wayborn, Kristina (act): Octopussy

Wayland, Len (act): Code Name: Minus One; Dead Men Tell No Tales (1971)

Waymon, Sam (mus): Ganja and Hess

Wayn, Peter (act): The Camp On Blood Island; The Woman Eater

Wayne, Billy (act): Charlie Chan at the Opera; Charlie Chan On Broadway; The Missing Guest

Wayne, David (act, 1913-1995, nee Wayne McKeekan): An American Christmas Carol; The Andromeda Strain; Ellery Queen; M (1950); Portrait of Jennie; The Three Faces of Eve

Wayne, Dennis (act): Echoes

Wayne, Dennis (wri): Satan's Sadists

Wayne, Dig (act): Judge Dredd

Wayne, Fredd (act): The Phantom of Hollywood

Wayne, Janice (act): The Coming

Wayne, John (act): Legend of the Lost

Wayne, Keith (act): Night of the Living Dead (1968)

Wayne, Ken (act): On the Beach; The Punisher; Solo for Sparrow

Wayne, Naunton (act, 1901-1970, nee Henry Wayne Davies): Circle of Danger; Dead of Night (1945); Double Confession; The Frightened Bride; Gestapo; Highly Dangerous; The Lady Vanishes (1938); Obsession (1949); Stop Press Girl

Wayne, Nina (act, b. 1943): The Night Strangler

Wayne, Patricia (act): Your Witness

Wayne, Patrick (act, b. 1939): Beyond Atlantis; The People That Time Forgot; Revenge (1986); Sinbad and the Eye of the Tiger; Sole Survivor (1970)

Wayne, Robert (act): Dick Tracy's G-Men

Wayne, Sarah (act): Magic In the water

Waynesmith, Gary (act): Slaughterhouse-Five

Wazaki, Toshiya (act): The X from Outer Space

Wead, Frank (wri, 1895-1947): The Beginning or the End?; The Great Impersonation (1935)

Wead, "Spig" (wri): Dirigible

Weakley, Brian (act): Eye of the Alien

Weary, A.C. (act): Secrets of the Phantom Caverns

Weaslen, Al (act): Mr. Moto's Last Warning

Weatherbee, Paul (act): The Toxic Avenger, Part II

Weatherly, Shawn (act): Amityville 1992: It's About Time; Party Line; Shadowzone

Weatherly, Michael (act): The Advanced Guard; Asteroid

Weatherly, Shawn (act): Mind Games (1989)

Weathers, Carl (act, b. 1948): The Bermuda Depths; Predator

Weathers, Philip (wri): No Road Back

Weatherwax, Ken (act): Halloween With the Addams Family

Weaver, Dennis (act, b. 1924): Don't Go to Sleep; Duel; Terror On the Beach; Way...Way Out; What's the Matter with Helen?

Weaver, Dennis (cin): Charlotte's Web

Weaver, Doodles (act, 1911-1983): Another Thin Man; The Birds; Bigfoot; Earthbound (1981); Ring of Fire; Topper (1937)

Weaver, Fritz (act, b. 1926): Black Sunday (1977); Creepshow; The Day of the Dolphin; Demon Seed; Fail-Safe; Jaws of Satan; The Legend of Lizzie Borden; The Maltese Bippy; Marathon Man; To Trap a Spy

Weaver, Jacki (act): Picnic at Hanging Rock

Weaver, Lee (act): Heaven Can Wait (1978); Heavy Traffic; Vanishing Point (1971)

Weaver, Lynn (act): The Shaman

Weaver, Malcolm (act): Raiders of the Lost Ark

Weaver, Marjorie (act, b. 1913): Charlie Chan's Murder Cruise; Just Off Broadway; The Man Who Wouldn't Die; Michael Shayne, Private Detective; Murder Over New York; Shadow of Suspicion

Weaver, Robert A. (wri): Night of Bloody Horror; Women and Bloody Terror

Weaver, Robin (act): The Muppet Christmas Carol

Weaver, Rose (act): The Gifted One; Lady In White

Weaver, Sigourney (act, b. 1949): Alien; Aliens; Alien 3; Alien Resurrection; Copycat; Eyewitness (1981); Ghostbusters; Ghostbusters II; Snow White: A Tale of Terror

Weaver, Vernon (act): Mad Max

Weavers, Mark (act): Legend of the Werewolf; Persecution

Weaving, Hugo (act): Babe

Webb, Alan (act, b. 1906): The Hunchback of Notre Dame (1982); King Lear (1970); The Third Secret

Webb, Bruce (act): The Fugitive (1993)

Webb, Bunty (act): Curtains

Webb, Cassandra (act): Starship

Webb, Charles (wri): Belphegor the Mountebank

Webb, Chloe (act): Heart Condition; Twins

Webb, Chris (act): Without a Clue

Webb, Christopher (act): Party Line

Webb, Christopher (wri): see Wibberley, Leonard

Webb, Clifton (act, 1891-1966, nee Webb Parmalee Hollenbeck): For Heaven's Sake; Laura

Webb, Danny (act): Alien 3

Webb, Denis (act): Death Is a Number; Mystery Junction

Webb, Des (act): The Empire Strikes Back

Webb, Dick (act): Faust (1922); The King's Romance; The Scarlet Letter (1922); The Story of the Rosary

Webb, Esmond (act): The Mind of Mr. Soames

Webb, Frank (act): The Computer Wore Tennis Shoes (1970)

Webb, Georgia Janelle (act): A Return to Salem's Lot

Webb, Gregory (act): Puppet Master II

Webb, Harry (act): The Underworld of London; Vice and Virtue: or, The Tempters of London

Webb, Jack (act, 1920-1982): Appointment With Danger; He Walked by Night; Red Nightmare; Sunset Boulevard

Webb, Jacklin (act): Of Unknown Origin

Webb, James (act): Frankenstein Island

Webb, James R. (wri, 1909-1974): Cape Fear (1961 & 1991); Operation Secret; Phantom of the Rue Morgue

Webb, Jim(my) (mus): The Last Unicorn; The Naked Ape

Webb, Laurie (wri): Double Alibi

Webb, Lewis (act): Zombies of Mora Tau

Webb, Mathea (act): Dying Game

Webb, Millard (dir, 1893-1935): The Sea Beast

Webb, Mitch (act): Nightbreed

Webb, Richard (act): Attack of the Mayan Mummy; Beware! The Blob; The Big Clock; A Connecticut Yankee In King Arthur's Court (1949); Night Has a Thousand Eyes; Out of the Past (1947); Prince Valiant (1954); The Remarkable Andrew; Slaves of the Invisible Monster; Time Travelers (1976)

Webb, Richard (cin): Poor Devil

Webb, Rita (act): Alien Women; Frenzy; The Hound Of The Baskervilles (1978); The London Connection; Venom (1982)

Webb, Robert (cin): Legend of the Witches

Webb, Robert D. (dir, b. 1903): Beneath the 12-Mile Reef; On the Threshold of Space; The Spider (1945)

Webb, Roger (mus): Burke and Hare; The Godsend

Webb, Roy (mus, b. 1888): At Sword's Point; Bedlam; The Body Snatcher (1945); Cat People (1942); Curse of the Cat People; Dick Tracy (1945); The Enchanted Cottage (1945); The Falcon Out West; The Falcon's Brother; Forty Naughty Girls; Hitler's Children; Houdini (1953); I Married a Witch; I Walked With a Zombie; The Last Days of Pompeii (1935); The Leopard Man; The Locket; Mighty Joe Young (1949); Murder, My Sweet; Notorious (1946); Operation Secret; Out of the Past 91947); The Saint In Palm Springs; Second Chance; The Seventh Victim; Sinbad the Sailor; The Spiral Staircase (1946); Split Second (1953); Stranger On the Third Floor; They Won't Believe Me; Welcome to Blood City; Where Danger Lives; The Window; Zombies On Broadway

Webb, T.K. (act): The Zero Boys

Webb, William (dir): Double Exposure (1977); Party Line

Webb, William (wri): Double Exposure (1977)

Webber, Andrew Lloyd (mus, b. 1948): The Phantom of the Opera (1999)

Webber, Diane (act): Ghost Diver; Mermaids of Tiburon; Sinthia: The Devil's Doll; The Witchmaker

Webber, George (cin): The House of Secrets (1929)

Webber, Margaret (act): The Starfish

Webber, Peggy (act): Macbeth (1947); The Screaming Skull; The Space Children; The Wrong Man

Webber, Richard (act): The Phantom Planet

Webber, Robert (act, 1924-1989): Assassin (1986); Don't Go to Sleep; Double Indemnity (1973); Hauser's Memory; Hysteria!; The Silencers (1966); Something Is Out There; Starflight: The Plane That Couldn't Land

Webber, Tim (cin): Merlin (1998)

Webber, Timothy (act): Ghost of a Chance (1987); Millennium; Terror Train

Weber, Andre (act): The Great Spy Chase

Weber, Ben (act): Twister

Weber, Billy (dir): Josh and S.A.M.

Weber, Fred (act): Dressed to Kill (1980)

Weber, Harvey (act): Return of the Killer Tomatoes

Weber, Herbert (act): Dick Tracy (1937)

Weber, Jake (act): Meet Joe Black

Weber, Lois (dir, 1882-1939): The Dumb Girl of Portici

Weber, Paul (act): Star Trek

Weber, Richard (act): 12 to the Moon

Weber, Rick (act): Space Rage

Weber, Steven (act, b. 1961): Dracula: Dead and Loving It; In the Company of Darkness; Single White Female; The Temp

Weber, Tania (act): Ulysses

Weber, Tom (act): Martin

Webling, Bob (wri): The Sign of Zorro (1960); Zorro, the Avenger

Webling, Peggy (wri): Boundary House; Frankenstein (1931)

Webster, Mr. (act): The Mysterious Mechanical Toy

Webster, Ben (act): Downhill; A Garret In Bohemia; 12-10; The Two Roads

Webster, Brett (cin): Scalps

Webster, Byron (act): The Nude Bomb; On a Clear Day You Can See Forever; Poor Devil; The Poseidon Adventure; Time After Time

Webster, D.J. (dir): Dark Side of the Moon

Webster, Derek (act): Stargate

Webster, Diana (act): Dr. Strange

Webster, Donald (act): The Green Shoes; Straw Dogs

Webster, Joy (act): The Curse of the Werewolf; Jungle Street; Shoot to Kill (1961); Stormy Crossing; The Two Faces of Dr. Jekyll; The Woman Eater

Webster, M. Coates (wri, b. 1906): The Brute Man; Jungle Captive; Strange Confession

Webster, Mary (act): Master of the World

Webster, Nicholas (dir): Mission Mars; Santa Claus Conquers the Martians

Webster, Paddy (act): Cat Girl

Webster, Patricia (act): How to Murder a Rich Uncle

Webster, Paul Francis (mus): The Stepmother

Webster, Tina (act): Miracle Mile

Webster, Tony (act): No Way Out

Webster-Brough, Jean (act): Spaceways

Wechsberg, Peter (dir & wri): Deafula

Wechsler, Jean (act): Jack's Wife

Weddell, Mimi (act): Last Rites (1980); The Purple Rose of Cairo; Student Bodies

Weddle, Tracy (act): Scared to Death (1980)

Weddle, Vernon (act): The Clone Master; Endangered Species; Oh, God! Book II

Wedgeworth, Ann (act): Made In Heaven; My Science Project; A Stranger Waits

Wedin, Maria (act): End of the World (1977)

Wedlock Jr., Hugh (wri): Abbott and Costello Meet the Killer

Weed, Don (cin): Damnation Alley

Weed, Frank (1910s act): Cinderella (1911, Selig)

Weed, Frank (1960s act): Death Curse of Tartu

Weekes, Harry (act): Prehistoric Peeps

Weeks, Art (act): Blood Diner

Weeks, Barbara (act): Cheaters at Play; Hell's Headquarters

Weeks, Howard (cin): The Man from Planet X

Weeks, James/Jimmie Ray (act): Eyewitness (1981); King Kong Lives

Weeks, Michelle (act): Little Shop of Horrors (1986)

Weeks, Stephen (dir): Gawain and the Green Knight; Ghost Story (1975); I, Monster; Sword of the Valiant

Weeks, Stephen (wri): Gawain and the Green Knight; Ghost Story (1975); Sword of the Valiant

Weeks, Terry Allen (act): I Was a Zombie for the F.B.I.

Weenick, Annabelle (act): Curse of the Swamp Creature; Deadly Blessing

Wegener, Paul (act, 1874-1948): Alraune (1928); Der Golem (1914); The Golem: How He Came Into the World; Der Golem und die Tanzerin; Living Dead (1932); Lucrezia Borgia (1922); The Magician (1926); Rubezahls Hochzeit; Der Student von Prag (1913); Sumurun; Svengali (1927); Das Weib des Pharao

Wegener, Paul (dir, 1874-1948): Der Golem (1914); The Golem: How He Came Into the World; Der Golem und die Tanzerin; Rubezahls Hochzeit; Svengali (1927)

Wegener, Paul (wri, 1874-1948): The Golem: How He Came Into the World; Der Golem und die Tanzerin; Rubezahls Hochzeit; Der Student von Prag (1913); Svengali (1927)

Wegier, Bella (act): see Darvi, Bella

Wehling, Bob (dir): Magic Spectacles

Wei, Lo (act): Call Him Mr. Shatter

Weibel, Peter (act): Invisible Adversaries

Weidler, Virginia (act, 1927-1968): The Lone Wolf Spy Hunt; Maid of Salem; Peter Ibbetson

Weidner, John (wri): Midnight Kiss

Weidt, Conrad (act): see Veidt, Conrad

Weigel, Herman (wri): The Neverending Story

Weigel, Paul (act): The Black Cat (1934); The Invisible Ray; The Vampire Bat

Weigel, Teri (act): Cheerleader Camp; Return of the Killer Tomatoes

Weigell, Arthur (wri): Her Heritage

Weighall, Ian (act): Bedknobs and Broomsticks

Weil, Richard (wri): The Mysterious Doctor; The Phantom Thief

Weil, Robert (act): The Fan; Rhinoceros (1974)

Weil, Samuel (dir): Class of Nuke 'em High; The Toxic Avenger

Weill, Claudia (dir, b. 1947): Giving Up the Ghost

Weill, Kurt (mus, 1900-1950): Lady In the Dark; One Touch of Venus

Weiller, Don Lee (act): Surf Nazis Must Die

Weiman, Rita (wri): Possessed (1947)

Weimann, Mathias (act): Das Blaue Licht

Wein, Dean (act): Heart Condition; Midnight Offerings; Revenge of the Stepford Wives

Wein, Joseph (cin): Cyborg Cop

Wein, Len (wri): Swamp Thing

Weinbach, Robert D. (wri): The Mutations

Weinbaum, Stanley G. (wri, 1900-1935): She-Devil (1957)

Weincke, Jan (cin): Dead of Winter; Hello Again

Weiner Family, The (act): Silent Night, Deadly Night III

Weiner, Andreana (act): Addams Family Values

Weiner, Mark (act): The Entity

Weinger, Scott (act): Aladdin (1992); Aladdin and the King of Thieves; The Return of Jafar; The Shaggy Dog (1994)

Weingrod, Herschel (wri): My Stepmother Is an Alien; Space Jam; Twins

Weingrod, Jerico (wri): My Stepmother Is an Alien

Weinman, Richard C. (wri): Pumpkinhead

Weinrib, Lenny/Lennie (act): Bedknobs and Broomsticks; Tales of Terror

Weinstein, Bob (wri): The Burning

Weinstein, Dave (act): Street Trash

Weinstein, David (act): Lord of the Flies (1990)

Weinstein, David (wri): Big Trouble In Little China

Weintraub, Carl (act): Sorry, Wrong Number (1989)

Weintraub, Cindy (act): Humanoids from the Deep; The Prowler (1981)

Weintraub, Fred (wri): A Choice of Weapons

Weintraub, Joseph (wri): Scalpel

Weintraub, William (act): 7 Surprizes

Weir, Helen (act): The Boy Who Turned Yellow

Weir, Ingrid (act): The Last Wave

Weir, Kyle (act): Secrets of the Phantom Caverns

Weir, Larry (mus): Teen Witch

Weir, Molly (act): Assassin (1973); Hands of the Ripper; Mr. Selkie; One of Our Dinosaurs Is

Missing; Scrooge (1970); The Silent Witness (1954)
Weir, Peter (dir, b. 1944): The Cars That Ate Paris; The Last Wave; Picnic at Hanging Rock; The Plumber; The Truman Show
Weir, Peter (wri, b. 1944): The Cars That Ate Paris; The Last Wave; The Plumber
Weir, Rickie (act): Terror In the Wax Museum
Weis, Don (dir, b. 1922): The Adventures of Hajji Baba; Crackle of Death; Demon and the Mummy; The Ghost In the Invisible Bikini; The King's Pirate; The Munsters' Revenge; Pajama Party
Weis, Heidelinde (act): The Man Outside (1967); Something for Everyone
Weis, Jack (dir, b. 1932): Crypt of Dark Secrets; Mardi Gras Massacre
Weisberg, Brenda (wri): The Lone Wolf In London; The Mad Ghoul; The Mummy's Ghost; Shadowed; Weird Woman
Weisburd, Dan E. (wri): Dinosaurus!
Weise, Ursula V. (act): Jack the Ripper (1979)
Weisenfreund, Muni (act): see Muni, Paul
Weiser, Shari (act): Babes In Toyland (1986)
Weiser, Stanley (wri): Project X (1987)
Weiser, Susan (act): Phantom of the Paradise
Weisman, A.T. (wri): The High Terrace
Weisman, David (wri): Dream a Little Dream 2
Weisman, Jessica (act): Amazons (1984)
Weisman, Matthew (wri): Teen Wolf; Teen Wolf Too
Weisman, Sam (dir): George of the Jungle
Weiss, Adrian (dir & wri): The Bride and the Beast
Weiss, Arthur (wri): Around the World Under the Sea
Weiss, Craig (cin): Legion of Fire: Killer Ants; Purgatory; Robin Cook's Invasion; Virtual Obsession
Weiss, David (act): The Toxic Avenger
Weiss, Ehrich (act): see Houdini, Harry
Weiss, Elliot (act): The Toxic Avenger, Part II
Weiss, Erick (act): The Fear (1994)
Weiss, Harry (act): The Punisher
Weiss, Helmuth (act): Frozen Alive
Weiss, Itzik (act): The Jerusalem File
Weiss, Janeen Ellen (act): Remote Control (1988)
Weiss, Jeff (act): Mr. Destiny
Weiss, Jiri (dir, b. 1913): Vrazda Po Cesku
Weiss, Joel (act): Congo
Weiss, Louis (act): see Taylor, Kent
Weiss, Lydia (act): Neon Maniacs
Weiss, Michael T. (act): Freeway; Howling IV; Remember Me
Weiss, Neil (act): The Zero Boys
Weiss, Peter (wri, 1916-1982): The Persecution and Assassination of Jean-Paul Marat as Performed by the Inmates of the Asylum of Charenton Under the Direction of the Marquis de Sade
Weiss, Robert K. (act): Nothing But Trouble
Weiss, Robert K. (dir): Amazon Women On the Moon
Weiss, Roberta (act): The Dead Zone
Weiss, Trudy (act): The Intruder (1981)
Weiss, William Christopher (act): The Toxic Avenger
Weiss, William Murray (act): Little Monsters
Weiss, Zohren (act): 101 Dalmatians (1996)
Weissbach, Herbert (act): De Sade
Weisse, Nikola (act): Jack the Ripper (1979)
Weisser, Morgan (act): Desvio al Paraiso
Weisser, Norbert (act): Adrenalin; Android; Arcade; Captain America (1992); Deceit; Heatseeker: Midnight Cabaret; Nemesis 3: Time Lapse; Omega Doom; Radioactive Dreams; Twilight Zone
Weissman, Jeffrey (act): Back to the Future, Part II; Twilight Zone
Weissmuller, Johnny (act, 1904-1984): Cannibal Attack; Captive Girl; Devil Goddess; Fury of the Congo; Jungle Jim; Jungle Jim In the Forbidden Land; Jungle Man-Eaters; Jungle Manhunt; Jungle Moon Men; Killer Ape; The Lost Tribe; Mark of the Gorilla; Pygmy Island; Savage Mutiny; Swamp Fire; Tarzan and His Mate; Tarzan and the Amazons; Tarzan and the Huntress; Tarzan and the Leopard Woman; Tarzan and the Mermaids; Tarzan Escapes; Tarzan Finds a Son!; Tarzan's Desert Mystery; Tarzan's New York Adventure; Tarzan's Secret Treasure; Tarzan the Ape Man (1932); Tarzan Triumphs; Valley of the Headhunters; Voodoo Tiger
Weissmuller Jr., Johnny (act): Ewoks: The Battle for Endor; Jungle Burger
Weist, Lucinda (act): The Silencers (1995)
Weisz, Rachel (act): Chain Reaction (1996); The Mummy (1999)
Weitz, Bruce (act, b. 1943): Prehysteria 3
Weitzenhoffer, Max (act): Wolf
Welbeck, Peter (wri, nee Harry Alan Towers): The Blood of Fu Manchu; The Brides of Fu Manchu; The Castle of Fu Manchu; Circus of Fear; City of Fear (1965); Count Dracula; Death Drums Along the River; Eugenie...The Story of Her Journey into Perversion; The Face of Eve; The Face of Fu Manchu; Five Golden Dragons; Future Women; House of 1,000 Dolls; Island of Despair; The Mangler; Midnight In Saint Petersburg; The Million Eyes of Sumuru; Night of the Blood Monster; Rio 70; Ten Little Indians (1965 & 1974); Those Fantastic Flying Fools; 24 Hours to Kill; The Vengeance of Fu Manchu; Victim Five; Warrior Queen
Welbourne, Charles S. (cin): Creature from the Black Lagoon; Manfish; Revenge of the Creature; The Three Stooges Meet Hercules
Welbourne, Scotty (cin): The Monster That Challenged the World
Welch, Bernie (act): Endangered Species
Welch, Ed (mus): Haunters of the Deep; The 39 Steps (1978)
Welch, Eddie (wri): The Gracie Allen Murder Case
Welch, Elizabeth (act): Alibi (1942); Arabian Adventure; Dead of Night (1945); Death at Broadcasting House; Fiddlers Three; The Tempest (1980)
Welch, Eric (act): Vamp
Welch, Frederic (act): Teenagers from Outer Space
Welch, Jackie (act): The Cradle Will Fall
Welch, James (act): When Knights Were Bold (1916)
Welch, Nelson (act): I, Madman; Killer in the Mirror
Welch, Noel (act): Dr. Dracula
Welch, Peter (act, b. 1922): The Secret of Blood Island
Welch, Raquel (act, b. 1942, nee Raquel Tejada): Bedazzled; Bluebeard (1972); Fantastic Voyage; Fathom; The Last of Sheila; The Magic Christian; Myra Breckinridge; One Million Years B.C.; Le Plus Vieux Metier du Monde; Spara Forte, Piu Forte...Non Capisco; Tainted Blood; The Three Musketeers (1974)
Welch, Richard C. (cin): Robin Cook's 'Mortal Fear'
Welch, Roger (act): Praying Mantis
Welch, Shannon (act): The Warlord: Battle for the Galaxy
Welch, Steven Kent (cin): Return of the Killer Tomatoes
Welch, Tahnee (act, b. 1961): Cocoon; Cocoon: The Return; Johnny 2.0; Sleeping Beauty (1986)
Welch, William (wri): The Brotherhood of Satan
Welchman, Harry (act): The House On the Marsh; The Lyons Mail; Mad About Men; Mr. Lyndon at Liberty; A Princess of the Blood; Three Cases of Murder
Welcker, Gertrud (act): Chronik von Grieshuus; Doctor Mabuse
Weld, Susan Ker (act): see Weld, Tuesday
Weld, Tuesday (act, b. 1943, nee Susan Ker Weld): Pretty Poison (1968); The Private Lives of Adam and Eve; Reflections of Murder; A Safe Place; Sex Kittens Go to College
Welden, Alex (cin): Invasion of the Saucer Men; Phantom from Space
Welden, Ben (act, b. 1901): Alibi Inn; Appointment With Murder; The Avenging Hand (1936); The Black Abbot (1934); Close Call for Ellery Queen; Death On the Set; Killers from Space; The Lone Wolf Spy Hunt; The Man Who Changed His Name; The Medium (1934); The Missing Rembrandt; Mr. Hex; The Mystery of the Mary Celeste; Puppets of Fate; The Saint In New York; Search for Danger; Shadows In the Night; Too Many Winners; Trapped by Boston Blackie; The Triumph of Sherlock Holmes
Welden, Michael (act): Dangerous Touch
Weldon, Alec (cin): Crack In the World
Weldon, Ann (act): The Incredible Hulk, Part 2
Weldon, Jess (act): The Thief of Bagdad (1924)
Weldon, Joan (act, b. 1933): Them! (1954)
Weldon, Meg (act): Poltergeist III
Weldon, Michael (act): The Hidden II
Weldon, Robert (act): Dead Men Tell
Weldon, Tim (act): The Illustrated Man
Welford, Nancy (act): A Safe Affair
Welker, Frank (act): Aladdin (1992); Aladdin and the King of Thieves; The Computer Wore Tennis Shoes (1970); Explorers; Gargoyles, the Movie: The Heroes Awaken; The Golden Child; The Land Before Time III: The Time of the Great Giving; Now You See Him, Now You Don't; The Pagemaster; Pinocchio and the Emperor of the Night; Pocahontas; The Rescuers Down Under; The Return of Jafar; Spacecamp; Species; Stargate; Zorro, the Gay Blade
Well, Karen (act): Burial Ground
Welland, Colin (act): The Secret Life of Ian Fleming; Straw Dogs
Welland, Paul (dir): Bernard and the Genie
Weller, Mary Louise (act): Blood Tide; The Evil; Once Upon a Spy
Weller, Michael (act): RoboCop 2
Weller, Peter (act): The Adventures of Buckaroo Banzai; Leviathan; Of Unknown Origin; RoboCop; RoboCop 2; Screamers (1996); Sunset Grill
Welles, Adam (act): La Figlia di Frankenstein
Welles, Christopher (act): Macbeth (1947)
Welles, Gretchen (act): The Gruesome Twosome
Welles, Gwen (act): A Safe Place
Welles, Jesse (act): A Stranger Waits
Welles, Laurence (act): Manhattan Baby
Welles, Mark (act): Wizards of the Lost Kingdom
Welles, Mel (act): Abbott and Costello Meet the Mummy; Attack of the Crab Monsters; Chopping Mall; Dr. Heckyl & Mr. Hype; Hold That Hypnotist; The Little Shop of Horrors (1960); La Sorella di Satan
Welles, Mel (dir): La Figlia di Frankenstein; La Isla de la Muerte
Welles, Merri (act): The Little Shop of Horrors (1960)
Welles, Orson (act, 1915-1985): Black Magic (1949); The Black Rose; Casino Royale; David and Goliath; It Happened One Christmas; Jane Eyre (1944); Journey Into Fear (1942); The Kremlin Letter; The Lady from Shanghai; Macbeth (1947); The Man Who Saw Tomorrow; Mr. Arkadin; Moby Dick (1956); The Muppet Movie; Necromancy; A Safe Place; The Satanist; The Southern Star; The Tartars; Ten Little Indians (1974); The Third Man; Three Cases of Murder; Treasure Island (1971); Trent's Last Case (1952); The Trial
Welles, Orson (dir, 1915-1985): The Lady from Shanghai; Macbeth (1947): Mr. Arkadin; The Trial
Welles, Orson (wri, 1915-1985): Journey Into Fear (1942); The Lady from Shanghai; Macbeth (1947); Mr. Arkadin; Monsieur Verdoux; Treasure Island (1971); The Trial
Welles, Steve (act): Puppet Master II; Solar Crisis
Welles, Terri (act): Looker
Welles, Tiny (act): Curse II: The Bite
Welles, Virginia (act): Francis In the Haunted House
Wellesley, Alfred (act): The Last Chance; Museum Mystery
Wellesley, Charles (act): The Lost World (1925)
Wellesley, George (wri): The Chinese Bungalow
Wellesley, Gordon (Wong) (wri): Dead Man's Evidence; Gestapo; The Green Scarf; Lorna Doone (1934); The Malpas Mystery; The March Hare; The Right to Live; Visa to Canton
Wellford, Christina (act): I Was a Zombie for the F.B.I.
Wellington, Anthony (act): Batman (1989)
Wellington, David (act): Neon Maniacs
Wellington, David (wri): Zombie Nightmare
Wellington, Larry (mus): The Gruesome Twosome; The Wizard of Gore
Wellington, Warwick (act): Rupert of Hentzau (1915)
Wellington-Lloyd, Helen (act): The Tempest (1980)
Wellins, Cori (act): Arachnophobia
Wellman, Harold (E.) (cin): The Animal World; Atlantis, the Lost Continent; The Invisible Boy; The Mask of Sheba; Watusi
Wellman, William A. (dir, 1896-1975): Lady of Burlesque; The Next Voice You Hear; Night Nurse; Track of the Cat
Wellman Jr., William (act): Curfew; It's Alive (1974); Macumba Love; The Puppet Masters
Wells, Aarika (act): Fantasies
Wells, Adrian (act): Spacecamp
Wells, Alan (act): The Beginning of the End; Cape Fear (1961)
Wells, Angie (act): A Ghost In Monte Carlo
Wells, Ann (act): Creature of the Walking Dead
Wells, Audrey (wri): George of the Jungle
Wells, Bdr. Billy (act): Concerning Mr. Martin; The Ring
Wekks, Brember (act): The Old Dark House (1932)
Wells, Carol (act): Lizzie
Wells, Carole (act): The House of Seven Corpses
Wells, Carrie (act): The Bad Seed (1985)
Wells, Claudia (act): Back to the Future
Wells, Conrad (cin): Behind That Curtain
Wells, Dan (act): Nightfall (1988)
Wells, Danny (act): The Man In the Santa Claus Suit; The Shaggy D.A.
Wells, David (act): Disaster In Time; The Guyver; Philadelphia Experiment II; Silent Night, Deadly Night 4: Initiation
Wells, Dawn (act): Return to Boggy Creek; The Town That Dreaded Sundown
Wells, Deering (act): Richard III (1955)
Wells, Dolores (act): The Time Travelers (1964)
Wells, Don (act): Around the World Under the Sea
Wells, Elaine (act): Kill Her Gently
Wells, Eric Briant (act): Fortress; The Goonies; The Puppet Masters
Wells, Frank (wri): Supersonic Saucer
Wells, George (wri, b. 1909): Angels In the Outfield (1951); The Gazebo
Wells, H.G. (wri, 1866-1946): The Airship Destroyer; Code Name: Minus One; Dead of Night (1945); The Door In the Wall; Empire of the Ants; First Men In the Moon (1919 & 1964); The Food of the Gods; The Food of the Gods II; H.G. Wells' 'The New Invisible Man;' Invisible Agent; The Invisible Man (1933 & 1975); The Invisible Man's Revenge; The Island of Dr. Moreau (1977 & 1996); Island of Lost Souls; The Magic Shop; The Man Who Could Work Miracles; The Night That Panicked America; The Shape of Things to Come (1979); Things to Come; The Time Machine (1960 & 1978); 2267 A.D.-When the Sleeper Wakes (unfinished); Village of the Giants; The War of the Worlds
Wells, Hubert (act): Bram Stoker's Dracula
Wells, Ingeborg (act): Across the Bridge; Child's Play (1954); Death Is a Number; Double Exposure (1954); House of Blackmail; Port of Escape
Wells, J.C. (act): Beyond the Living
Wells, Jacqueline (act): see Bishop, Julie
Wells, Janet (act): Strange Behavior
Wells, Jerrold (act): Candidate for Murder; The Element of Crime; Frankenstein and the Monster from Hell; Gawain and the Green Knight; Maniac (1963); Masquerade; The Pirates of Blood River; Playback; Time Bandits; The Vault of Horror
Wells, Jesse (act): The Return of Count Yorga; Wizards
Wells, John (act): For Your Eyes Only; Greystoke: The Legend of Tarzan, Lord of the Apes; Rentadick
Wells, John (wri): Rentadick
Wells, Julia Elizabeth (act): see Andrews, Julie
Wells, Mary (act): Howard the Duck
Wells, Patrick (act): Child's Play (1954)
Wells, Ralph C. (wri): The Pied Piper of Hamelin
Wells, Simon (dir): An American Tail: Fievel Goes West; The Prince of Egypt; We're Back! A Dinosaur's Story
Wells, Ted (act): Hard Rock Zombies
Wells, Terry (act): Lord of the Flies (1990)
Wells, Tico (act): The Relic; Universal Soldier
Wells, Tracy (act): Mirror, Mirror 2: Raven Dance
Wells, Vernon (act): Circuitry Man; Fortress; Innerspace; Plughead Rewired: Circuitry Man II; The Road Warrior; 2002: Rape of Eden; Weird Science
Wells, Veronica (act): Boom; The Secret of Seagull Island
Welsbacher, Dick (act): The Attic; When the Bough Breaks
Welsford, Christine (act): Murder at the Windmill
Welsh, Fred (act): Howling III
Welsh, Jane (act): The Bells (1931); The Case of the River Morgue; Condemned to Death; The Dragon of Pendragon Castle; Fatal Journey; Just William's Luck; The Missing Rembrandt; The Sleeping Cardinal; Whispering Tongues
Welsh, Janet (act): The Dungeonmaster
Welsh, John (act): The Birthday Present; Confession (1955); The Counterfeit Plan; An Inspector Calls; It Came Upon the Midnight Clear; Konga; Krull; The Man In the Road; Man In the Shadow; The Man Who Haunted Himself; The Man Who Wouldn't Talk; Nightmare (1963); The Norsemen; The Pied Piper (1971); Rasputin, the Mad Monk; The Revenge of Frankenstein; The Square Mile Murder; A Story of Tutankhamun; Subterfuge; The Surgeon's Knife; The 39 Steps (1978); Yellow Dog
Welsh, Jonathan (act): City On Fire; Hitler's Daughter; Starship Invasions
Welsh, Kenneth (act): Escape Clause; Hideaway; Of Unknown Origin; Phobia; Portraits of a Killer; The Spider and the Fly (1994); A Stranger Waits; Timecop

Welsh, Margaret (act): *Shadow of a Doubt (1991)*
Welsh, Scott (act): *Bits of Life*
Welsh, Thomas (wri): *Ultus, the Man from the Dead*
Welsh, William (act): *The Shock (1923); 20,000 Leagues Under the Sea (1916, USA)*
Welt, Jan (act): *Werewolf of Washington*
Welter, Ariadne/Ariadna (act): *El Ataud del Vampiro; El Baron del Terror; The Devil's Hand (1961); 100 Cries of Terror; The Queen's Swordsman; El Vampiro*
Welter, Blanca Rosa (act): see Christian, Linda
Weltman, Stu (act): *The Tomb*
Welton, Danny (act): *Terrified (1963)*
Wemble, Deanna (act): *Twisted*
Wemlinger, Claire (act): see Trevor, Claire
Wemyss, Ann (act): *Strange Experiment*
Wen, Ming-Na (act, b. 1963): *Mulan; Star Quest (1994); Tempting Fate*
Wenckus, Philip (act): *The Prey (1980)*
Wendel, David (act): *The Monster Squad*
Wendel, Lara (act): *Ghosthouse; Tenebrae*
Wendell, Howard (act): *The Four Skulls of Jonathan Drake; My Blood Runs Cold; Prince Valiant (1954)*
Wenders, Wim (dir, b. 1945): *Hammettl The Scarlet Letter (1972); Until the End of the World; Wings of Desire*
Wenders, Wim (wri, b. 1945): *Until the End of the World; Wings of Desire*
Wendhausen, Fritz (dir): *Der Sohn der Hagar; Der Steinerne Reiter*
Wendkos, Paul (dir, b. 1923): *The Awakening of Candra; The Bad Seed (1985); The Brotherhood of the Bell; The Burglar; Good Against Evil; Haunts of the Very Rich; The Legend of Lizzie Borden; The Mephisto Waltz; Terror On the Beach*
Wendl, Alan J. (act): *Serial Mom*
Wendorff, Leola (act): *The Little Shop of Horrors (1960)*
Wendstrom, Harold (cin): *The Face In the Fog (1922); The Lost Patrol (1934); Young Diana*
Wendt, Bettina (act): *Vice Versa (1988)*
Wendt, George (act, b. 1948): *Alice In Wonderland (1999); Alien Avengers; Alien Avengers II; Dreamscape; Forever Young; House; Jekyll and Hyde...Together Again*
Wendy, Barbara (act): *Horror Hospital*
Wenger, Allan (act): *Roujin Z*
Wenger, Brahm (mus): *Voyage of Terror*
Wenger, Cliff (cin): *Burnt Offerings; The Golden Child; The Island; Rearview Mirror; Reflections of Murder*
Wengraf, John (act, 1896-1974): *The Disembodied; 5 Fingers; Gog; The Return of Dracula; 12 to the Moon; U-Boat Prisoner*
Wenham, Jane (act): *An Inspector Calls; The Teckman Mystery*
Wenk, Richard (dir & wri): *Vamp*
Wenland, Burt(on) (act): *Africa Screams; Killer Ape; Killers from Space; Phantom from Space*
Wenneman, Klaus (act): *Out of Order*
Wenner, Leslie (act): *The Wizard of Baghdad*
Wennerstrom, Leif (act): *Deadtime Stories*
Wentworth, Chantal (act): *Blink*
Wentworth, John (act): *The Invisible Asset; The Last Shot You Hear*
Wentworth, Martha (act): *Daughter of Dr. Jekyll; The Sword In the Stone*
Wentworth, Robin (act): *Nothing But the Night; The Stateless Man*
Wentworth, Scott (act): *Free Fall*
Wentz, Kip (act): *Poltergeist III*
Wentz, Lawrence T. (act): *Congo*
Wentzel (cin): *La Folie du Docteur Tube*
Wentzel, Chris (act): *The Hidden*
Wenzel, Mark (act): *Return of the Killer Tomatoes*
Wenzlaff, George (act): see Winslow, George "Foghorn"
Wepper, Fritz (act): *Le Dernier Combat*
Werb, Mike (wri): *Darkman III: Die darkman Die; The Mask (1994)*
Werdin, Egon (cin): *Making Contact*
Werfel, Franz (wri, 1890-1945): *Embezzled Heaven*
Werich, Jan (act): *Assignment K; Baron Prasil; Cisaruv Pekar, Pekaruv Cisar*
Werker, Alfred (L.) (dir, b. 1896): *The Adventures of Sherlock Holmes (1939); A-Haunting We Will Go; He Walked by Night; Repeat Performance; Shock (1946); Whispering Ghosts*
Werkmeister, Hans (dir): *Algol*
Werle, Barbara (act): *Krakatoa-East of Java; Seconds*
Werle, Keith (act): *Night of the Creeps*
Werle, Lars Johan (mus): *Persona*
Werlin, Mark (wri): *A Face to Die For*
Werlin, Marvin (wri): *A Face to Die For*
Werndorff, Oscar M. (dir): *The Bells (1931)*
Werner, Gabriel (act): *L'Annee Derniere a Marienbad*
Werner, Ilse (act): *Die Avonturen von Baron Munchhausen*
Werner, Jenny (act): *The Third Man*
Werner, Karen (act): *The Mysterious Two*
Werner, Oskar (act, 1922-1984, nee O. Josef Bschliessmayer): *Fahrenheit 451; The Last Ten Days of Adolf Hitler; Lola Montes; The Spy Who Came In from the Cold*
Werner, Peter (dir): *Tempting Fate*
Werner, Robert (act): *The Fifth Musketeer*
Werner, Roy (act): *The Nutty Professor (1996)*
Wernicke, Otto (act): *Das Testament des Dr. Mabuse*
Wernli, Wendy (act): *Laserblast*
Werschkul, Gordon M. (act): see Scott, Gordon
Wert, Doug (act): *Haunted Symphony; Roswell; Wasp Woman (1995)*
Wertheimer, Joe (act): *Happy Birthday to Me*
Wertimer, Ned (act): *Chiller; The Pack; Santa Claus Conquers the Martians*
Werzanski, Yossi (act): *The Jerusalem File*
Wescoatt, Rusty (act): *Captive Girl; Pygmy Island; The Three Stooges Meet Hercules*
Wescott, Don (act): *Fargo*
Weske, Brian (act): *The Big Switch; Jungle Street; Just William's Luck; Night Without Pity; No Safety Ahead; Panic (1963)*
Weske, Victor (act): *Tower of Terror*
Wesley, John (act): *Jack's Back; Nothing But Trouble; Timestalkers*
Wesley, Kassie (act): *Evil Dead 2: Dead by Dawn*
Wessel, Richard/Dick (act, 1912-1965): *Blackbeard the Pirate; Bowery to Bagdad; Dick Tracy vs. Cueball; Enemy Agents Meet Ellery Queen; The Scarf*
Wesson, Dick (act): *Destination Moon*
Wesson, Dick (wri): *Change of Mind*
Wesson, Eileen (act): *They Live; Zarkorr! The Invader*
Wesson, Jessica (act): *Casper*
West, Adam (act, b. 1934): *Batman (1966); Doin' Time On Planet Earth; The Eyes of Charles Sand; Mara of the Wilderness; Maxim Xul; Omega Cop; One Dark Night; Poor Devil; Robinson Crusoe On Mars; Zombie Nightmare*
West, Anita (act): *Impact*
West, Billy (act): *Joe's Apartment; Space Jam*
West, Borge (act): *The Force On Thunder Mountain*
West, Brian (cin): *Blood Bath at the House of Death; A Distant Scream; Murder With Mirrors; Never-Never Land*
West, Buck (act): *To All a Goodnight*
West, Chandra (act): *A Face to Die For; Puppet Master 5; Universal Soldier III: Unfinished Business*
West, Charles (act): *The House Without a Key; The Road to Yesterday*
West, Christopher (act): *Stargate*
West, Claudine (wri): *Marie Antoinette (1938); On Borrowed Time*
West, Con (wri): *The Dummy Talks; Miracles Do Happen; Old Mother Riley's Ghosts*
West, Del (act): *The Navy vs. the Night Monsters*
West, Don (act): *Copycat*
West, Dottie (act): *Aurora Encounter*
West, Elliot (wri): *The Fearmakers*
West, Ford (act): *Sherlock Jr.*
West, Fred(erick E.) (cin): *Invasion of the Saucer Men; It Conquered the World; The She-Creature; Terror In the Haunted House*
West, George (act): *The Tower*
West, Geraldine (act): *Hush...Hush, Sweet Charlotte*
West, Gregory (act): *The Surgeon*
West, H.E. (act): *Night Tide*
West, H. St. Barbe (act): *Condemned to Death; The Vultures of London*
West, Henry (act): *Dr. Tarr's Torture Dungeon*
West, James (mus): *The Crater Lake Monster*
West, Jeremy (act): *Catacombs (1989); Curse IV: The Ultimate Sacrifice; Howling VI: The Freaks; The Ice Pirates*
West, John Stuart (act): *Night of the Comet*
West, Joseph (wri): *The Fatal Hour (1940); Man-Made Monster; Phantom of Chinatown*
West, Julian (act): *Vampyr*
West, Kevin (E.) (act): *Bio-Dome; Monolith*
West, Kit (cin): *Moon Zero Two; Some Girls Do; Young Sherlock Holmes*
West, Lillian (act): *The Fatal 30; Where Danger Lives*
West, Lockwood (act): *Celia; Game for Three Losers; The Satanic Rites of Dracula*
West, Mae (act, 1893-1980): *Myra Breckinridge*
West, Margaret St. Barbe (act): *Urge to Kill*
West, Mariano Nunez (mus): *Moebius*
West, Mark (act): *Transmutations*
West, Martin (act): *Family Plot; Hellhole*
West, Morris L. (wri): *The Crooked Road*
West, Norma (act): *Spaceflight IC-1*
West, Parker (act): *Lemora, the Lady Dracula*
West, Peggy (act): *The Haunting of Sarah Hardy*
West, R. Harley (act): *The Crimson Triangle; Her Life In London; The Vultures of London*
West, R. Harley (dir): *Crime and the Penalty*
West, Red (act): *Prey of the Chameleon*
West, Roland (dir, 1887-1952): *The Bat (1926); The Bat Whispers; The Monster (1925)*
West, Roland (wri, 1887-1952): *The Bat Whispers*
West, Samuel B. (wri): *Captain Sinbad*
West, Shannon (act): *Flesh Gordon*
West, Stephen (act): *The Hand That Rocks the Cradle*
West, Timothy (act): *Agatha; Hitler: The Last Ten Days; Murder Is Easy; The 39 Steps (1978); The Twisted Nerve*
West, Walter (act): *A Bold Adventuress*
West, Walter (dir): *The Answer; A Bold Adventuress; By the Hand of a Brother; The Case of Lady Camber; The Loudwater Mystery; Maria Marten (1928); The Mystery of a London Flat; Sweeney Todd; The Ware Case; We Do Believe In Ghosts*
West, Walter (wri): *A Bold Adventuress; The Loudwater Mystery*
Westaway, Simon (act): *Alien Cargo*
Westberg, David (act): *The Curious Female*
Westbrook, Darryl (act): *The Hideous Sun Demon*
Westbrook, John (act): *The Masque of the Red Death (1964); A Prize of Arms; The Tomb of Ligeia*
Westbrook, Wendi (act): *Under Lock and Key*
Westbury, Ken (cin): *Hands of a Murderer*
Westcott, Genevieve (act): *The Frighteners*
Westcott, Helen (act, b. 1929, nee Myrthas Helen Hickman): *Abbott and Costello Meet Dr. Jekyll and Mr. Hyde; The Battles of Chief Pontiac; Homicide; The Invisible Avenger; A Midsummer Night's Dream (1935); Monster On the Campus; 13 Lead Soldiers*
Westcott, Netta (act): *In His Grip*
Westcott, Rusty (act): *The Snow Creature*
Westcott, Wendy (act): *Child's Play (1954)*
Westenskow, Mike (act): *The Stand*
Wester, Peter (cin): *I Am Curious (Yellow)*
Westerby, Robert (wri, 1909-1968): *Beautiful Stranger; Before I Wake; The Devil's Agent; Dr. Syn-Alias the Scarecrow; The Golden Mask; Soho Incident; The Spider and the Fly (1949); The Surgeon's Knife; The Three Lives of Thomasina; Town On Trial*
Westerfield, James (act, 1913-1971): *Homicidal; Jungle Heat; The Shaggy Dog (1959)*
Westerholm, Tracy (act): *Xtro II: The Second Encounter*
Westfield, Michael (act): *Zotz!*
Westgate, Murray (act): *Change of Mind; Happy Birthday to Me; The Kidnapping of the President; Last Bride of Salem; Rituals*
Westheimer Co. (cin): *The President's Analyst*
Westheimer, Dr. Ruth (act): *Electric Dreams*
Westlake, Donald (E.) (wri): *The Busy Body; The Stepfather; Stepfather II; Stepfather III: Father's Day*
Westlake, Dorothy (wri): *The Hound Of The Baskervilles (1921)*
Westlake, Eva (act): *At the Villa Rose (1920); The Barton Mystery (1920); Rupert of Hentzau (1915)*
Westlake, Nigel (mus): *Babe; Babe: Pig In the City*
Westley, Helen (act, 1879-1942): *Death Takes a Holiday (1934); The Smiling Ghost*
Westley, Peter (act): *The Falls*
Westman, Nydia (act, 1911-1970): *Bulldog Drummond's Peril; Bulldog Drummond's Revenge; The Cat and the Canary (1939); The Invisible Ray; King of the Jungle; The Reluctant Astronaut; The Remarkable Andrew; The Velvet Touch*
Westman, Tony (cin): *Needful Things*
Westmoreland, James (act): *Don't Answer the Phone!*
Westmoreland, Robert/Bob (act): *The Island; Ravagers*
Westo, Ernie (act): *Mike Murphy's Dream of Love and Riches; Mike Murphy's Dream of the Wild West; The Misadventures of Mike Murphy; The Strength That Failed; Through the Ages; When Clubs Were Clubs*
Weston, Armand (dir & wri): *The Nesting*
Weston, Bill (act): *A Choice of Weapons; Krull*
Weston, Charles (act): *Detective Finn: or, In the Heart of London; The Doctor's Crime; The King of Seven Dials; Self-Accused; Vice and Virtue: or, The Tempters of London*
Weston, Charles (dir): *The Bishop's Silence; The Broken Chisel; Detective Finn: or, In the Heart of London; The Dungeon of Death; The Hand at the Window; The King of Seven Dials; Lieutenant Daring and the Mystery of Room 41; The Master Crook; The Master Spy (1914); My Son; The Port of Missing Women; Riches and Rogues; Self-Accused; Through the Clouds; The Underworld of London; Vice and Virtue: or, The Tempters of London; What a Woman Will Do; What Men Will Do; Wife of a Thief*
Weston, Charles (wri): *Detective Finn: or, In the Heart of London; Self-Accused; Through the Clouds; Vice and Virtue: or, The Tempters of London*
Weston, David (act, b. 1938): *The Masque of the Red Death (1964); Quest for Love; Witchcraft (1964)*
Weston, Debora (act): *Nightbreed; The Return of Sherlock Holmes (1986)*
Weston, Ellen (act): *Miracle On 34th Street (1973); The Questor Tapes; Revenge of the Stepford Wives*
Weston, Eric (dir & wri): *Evilspeak*
Weston, Garnett (wri): *Blackmail (1929); Bulldog Drummond In Africa; Bulldog Drummond's Bride; Bulldog Drummond's Secret Police; Supernatural (1933); White Zombie*
Weston, Graham (act): *A Place to Die*
Weston, Harold (act): *The Smugglers' Cave*
Weston, Harold (dir): *The Black Night; The Call of the Drum; Honour In Pawn; The Mystery of a Hansom Cab; Strategy*
Weston, Harold (wri): *The Black Night; The Call of the Drum; Double Alibi; Honour In Pawn; The Smugglers' Cave; Strategy*
Weston, Jack (act, b. 1926): *I Love a Mystery (1966); The Incredible Mr. Limpet; It's Only Money; Short Circuit 2*
Weston, Jeff (act): *Demonic Toys; Puppet Master II; The Silence of the Hams*
Weston, Leslie (act): *Corridor of Mirrors; Two for danger*
Weston, Paul (act): *Robin Hood: Prince of Thieves; Roger Corman's 'Frankenstein Unbound'; The Satanic Rites of Dracula*
Weston, Stan (act): *The Power (1980); Torment (1986)*
Weston, Steve (act): *When Michael Calls*
Weston, William (act): *The Black Bird (1926)*
Westover, Clyde C. (wri): *The Man from Downing Street*
Westrick, Bobby (act): *Goblin*
Westwood, Patrick (act): *The Pit and the Pendulum (1961)*
Westwood, Russell (act): *Soho Incident*
Westy, Peter (act): *Who Framed Roger Rabbit*
Wetanson, Burt (wri): *American Gothic*
Wetherell, M.A. (act, dir & wri): *Robinson Crusoe (1927)*
Wetherell, Virginia (act): *The Big Switch; A Clockwork Orange; Curse of the Crimson Altar; Demons of the Mind; Disciple of Death; Dr. Jekyll and Sister Hyde; Dracula (1973); Man of Violence; The Partner; Ricochet*
Wetherwax, Michael (mus): *Midnight (1989); Sorority House Massacre*
Wetmore, Judy (act): *Terror In the Wax Museum*
Wetson, Dave (act): *Empire of Ash III*
Wettig, Patricia (act, b. 1951): *Nothing But the Truth*
Wetzel, Kristina (act): *Zombie Island Massacre*
Wetzl, Fulvio (dir & wri): *Rorret*
Wexel, Shane (act): *The Exorcist III*
Wexler, Haskell (cin, b. 1923): *The Loved One; The Rich Man's Wife; The Secret of Roan Inish*
Wexler, Paul (act): *The Bowery Boys Meet the Monsters*
Wexler, Richard (act): *Werewolf of Washington*
Wexley, John (wri): *Footsteps In the Dark*
Weyand, Ron(ald) (act): *Man On a Swing; Svengali (1983); They Might Be Giants*
Weyher, Ruth (act): *Geheimnisse einer Seele; Schatten, eine Nächtliche Halluzination*
Weyland, Len (act): *Dead Men Tell No Tales (1971)*
Weyland, Tom (act): *People Who Own the Dark*
Weyman, Stanley (wri): *Under the Red Robe (1915 & 1937)*
Weyson, Samantha (act): *Mr. Selkie*
Whale, James (dir, 1896-1957): *Bride of Frankenstein; By Candlelight; Frankenstein*

(1931); Green Hell; The Invisible Man (1933); The Man In the Iron Mask (1939); The Old Dark House (1932)
Whalen, Arleen (act): *Castle In the Desert*
Whalen, Fred L. (act): *The Cat from Outer Space*
Whalen, Michael (act, 1902-1974, nee Joseph Kenneth Shovlin): *Ellery Queen, Master Detective; Highway 13; Missile to the Moon; Omoo Omoo, the Shark God; The Phantom from 10,000 Leagues*
Whalen, Sean (act): *The People Under the Stairs; Tammy and the T-Rex*
Whalen, Tom (act): *Moontrap*
Whaley, Andrew (act): *King Solomon's Mines (1985)*
Whaley, Frank (act): *Little Monsters; Retroactive*
Whaley, Joseph (wri): *Bodily Harm*
Whaley, Michael (act): *Running Against Time; Twice Upon a Time*
Whalin, Justin (act): *Child's Play 3; Murder of Innocence; Serial Mom; Susie Q*
Whalley, Joanne (act): *A Christmas Carol (1984); Kill Me Again; A TV Dante: Cantos I-VIII; Willow*
Whalley, Norma (act): *The Golden Pince-Nez; The Mystery of Mr. Bernard Brown; Yellow Face*
Wharmby, Tony (dir): *Seduced by Evil; Sorry, Wrong Number (1989)*
Wharton, Anne (act): *Heartbeeps*
Whatham, Claude (dir): *Murder Elite; Murder Is Easy*
Whealy, Blake (act): *Blink*
Wheat, Jim (dir): *After Midnight; Ewoks: The Battle for Endor; Lies*
Wheat, Jim (wri): *The Alien's Return; Ewoks: The Battle for Endor; The Fly II; Free Fall; Lies; Rattled; Silent Scream (1979); The Stepford Husbands*
Wheat, Ken (dir): *After Midnight; Ewoks: The Battle for Endor; Lies*
Wheat, Ken (wri): *The Alien's Return; Ewoks: The Battle for Endor; The Fly II; Free Fall; Lies; Rattled; Silent Scream (1979); The Stepford Husbands*
Wheatcroft, Stanhope (act): *Laughing at Danger*
Wheatley, Alan (act, b. 1907): *Appointment With Crime; Clash by Night; Corridor of Mirrors; Counterblast; The Diamond; Home to Danger; The House Across the Lake; A Jolly Bad Fellow; The Limping Man (1953); Master Spy (1963); The Shadow of the Cat; Sleeping Car to Trieste; Spaceways; Tomorrow at Ten; Whispering Smith Hits London*
Wheatley, Blane (act): *The Unnamable*
Wheatley, Catharine (act): *A Polish Vampire In Burbank*
Wheatley, David (dir): *The Magic Toyshop*
Wheatley, Dennis (wri, 1897-1977): *The Devil Rides Out; The Satanist; The Spy In White; To the Devil a Daughter; Uncharted Seas*
Wheatley, Thomas (act): *The Living Daylights*
Wheaton, Amy (act): *The Curse*
Wheaton, Julie (act): *Rana: The Legend of Shadow Lake*
Wheaton, Wil (act, b. 1972): *The Curse; The Last Starfighter; The Man Who Fell to Earth (1987); Mr. Stitch*
Whedon, John (wri, 1905-1991): *The Island at the Top of the World*
Whedon, Joss (wri): *Alien Resurrection; Buffy the Vampire Slayer; Toy Story*
Wheeland, Waldron (wri): *The Omegans*
Wheeldon, Barbara (act): *Funeral Home*
Wheeler, Adair (act): *Strange Behavior*
Wheeler, Bert (act, 1895-1968): *Cracked Nuts (1931)*
Wheeler, Charles (F.) (cin): *Bad Ronald; The Barefoot Executive; The Cat from Outer Space; Charley and the Angel; Condorman; Freaky Friday (1976); She Waits; Silent Running*
Wheeler, Ed (act): *Daylight; Thinner*
Wheeler, Gregory (act): *Asteroid*
Wheeler, H. (act): *The Greek Interpreter*
Wheeler, Harvey (wri): *Fail-Safe*
Wheeler, Jane (act): *The Neighbor*
Wheeler, Joseph (act): *Satyricon*
Wheeler, Margaret (act): *The Brotherhood of Satan; Twilight Zone*
Wheeler, Paul (wri): *Caravan to Vaccares; The Legacy; Puppet On a Chain*
Wheeler, R. (wri): *Atoll K*
Wheeler, Rene (wri, b. 1912): *Teodora, Imperatrice di Bisanzio*
Wheeler, Rick (act): *Outbreak*
Wheeler, Skip (act): *Graveyard Shift (1990)*
Wheeler-Nicholson, Dana (act): *Circuitry Man; The Little Drummer Girl*
Wheels, Helen (act): *The Toxic Avenger, Part II*
Whelan, Albert (act): *Matinee Idol*
Whelan, Arleen (act): *Women of Pitcairn Island*
Whelan, Jeremy (act): *Blades*
Whelan, Julia (act): *Christmas Every Day*
Whelan, Richard (act): *The Neptune Factor*
Whelan, Robert (act): *Superman (1978)*
Whelan, Tim (dir, 1893-1957): *The Mad Doctor; Q Planes; Ten Days In Paris; The Thief of Bagdad (1940); This Was a Woman; When Knights Were Bold (1929)*
Whelan, Tim (wri, 1893-1957): *When Knights Were Bold (1929)*
Whelchel, Jerilou (act): *The Mysterious Monsters*
Whelehan, William J. (act): *Damien-Omen II*
Whelen, Christopher (mus): *The Face of Fu Manchu*
Wherry, Daniel (act): *The Voice of Merrill*
Whibley, Alan (cin): *Excalibur; Paperhouse; The Secret Life of Ian Fleming; Venom (1982)*
Whibley, Burnell (mus): *No Blade of Grass*
Whicker, Alan (act): *The Magic Christian*
Whifler, Graeme (wri): *Dr. Giggles*
Whiley, Manning (act): *Consider Your Verdict; The Dummy Talks; The Flying Squad (1940); The Ghost at St. Michael's; Meet Sexton Blake; Pimpernel Smith; The Saint's Vacation; The Shop at Sly Corner; Trunk Crime; Uncle Silas*
Whinery, Webster (act): *Angel Heart; Remo Williams: The Adventure Begins*
Whinnery, Barbara (act): *Crawlspace*
Whipp, Joseph (act): *Amazons (1986); Chiller; The Hidden; Midnight Lace (1981); Scream*
Whipper, Leigh (act): *The Hidden Eye; Of Mice and Men (1939)*
Whipple, Sam (act): *Jekyll and Hyde...Together Again*
Whirry, Shannon (act): *Dangerous Prey; The Granny; Mirror Images II; Omega Doom; Private Obsession*
Whisenhunt, Larry (act): *Silent Running*
Whitaker, Albic (act): *Flight of the Navigator*
Whitaker, Charles (act): *The Mad Monster*
Whitaker, Christina (act): *Naked Cage; Vampire at Midnight*
Whitaker, David (mus): *Dr. Jekyll and Sister Hyde; Dominique; The Playbirds; Psychomania (1972); Scream and Scream Again; Sudden Terror; The Sword and the Sorcerer; Vampira; Vampire Circus*
Whitaker, David (wri): *Subterfuge*
Whitaker, Duane (act): *Tales from the Hood*
Whitaker, Dwayne (act): *Leatherface: Texas Chainsaw Massacre III*
Whitaker, Forest (act, b. 1961): *Amazing Stories: The Movie VI; The Body Snatchers; The Enemy Within; Phenomenon; Species*
Whitaker, Johnny (act, b. 1959): *The Littlest Angel (1969); Something Evil*
Whitaker, Richard (act): *The Hidden*
Whitaker, Rod (wri): *The Eiger Sanction*
Whitaker, William (act): *The Clone Master*
Whitburn, Denis (wri): *The Cursed Mountain Mystery*
Whitby, Arthur (act): *Princess Clementina*
Whitchurch, Philip (act): *Blue Ice*
Whitcomb, Ian (act): *Contact*
Whitcraft, Elizabeth (act): *Angel Heart*
Whitcutt, Mike (cin): *Only a Scream Away*
White, Al (act): *A Fire In the Sky (1978)*
White, Alan (act): *A Lady Mislaid; Seven Keys*
White, Alice (act, 1904-1983): *The Gift of Gab; Murder at Midnight; The Private Life of Helen of Troy; Secret of the Chateau*
White, Angela (act): *Face In the Night; The Man Inside*
White, Barbara (act): *This Was a Woman*
White, Bart (act): *HauntedWeen*
White, Bernie (act): *Body Count (1987); Killing Obsession*
White, Brad (wri): *Superstition*
White, Bruce (act): *Dark Water; Repo Man*
White, Bryan (act): *Quest for Camelot*
White, Carol (act, b. 1941): *Daddy's Gone A-Hunting; Gaolbreak (1962); The Man In the Back Seat; Never Let Go; The Playground; Prehistoric Women (1966); The Squeeze*
White, Carole Ita (act): *Hellhole*
White, Cathy (act): *Those Dear Departed*
White, Charlene (act): *The Hidden*
White, Chris (act): *Nightbeast*
White, Chrissie (act, b. 1894): *At the Foot of the Scaffold; The Bargain; The Basilisk; Behind the Curtain; The Breaking Point (1914); Broken Threads; The Confession (1915); The Curtain; The Deception (1912); Dr. Fenton'sOrdeal; Dr. Trimball's Verdict; Face to Face; The Failure; Gipsy Nan; A Grain of Sand; Held for Ransom; The Incorruptible Crown; The Jewel Thieves; The Man Behind "The Times"; The Man Who Stayed at Home; The Man With the Scar; The Nightbirds of London; The Promise; The Red Light; The Unseen Witness; Wildflower*
White, Christine (act): *Macabre (1958)*
White, Daisy (act): *Curtains*
White, Dan (act): *Attack of the Giant Leeches; Beyond the Bermuda Triangle; The Last Hunt; Voodoo Man*
White, Daniel (mus): *Amador; The Blood of Fu Manchu; Future Women; Revenge In the House of Usher; Zombies Lake*
White, David (act, 1916-1990): *Spider-Man*
White, Deborah (act): *The Return of the Six Million Dollar Man and the Bionic Woman*
White, Deloy (act): *The Bees*
White, Donna (act): *Deathmoon*
White, Dorothy (act): *Get Carter*
White, Doug (cin): *The Alchemist*
White, E.B. (wri): *Charlotte's Web*
White, Earl (act): *Nemesis 2*
White, Elaine (act): *Fiend (1980)*
White, Ethel Lina (wri): *Alfred Hitchcock Presents; The Lady Vanishes (1938 & 1979); The Spiral Staircase (1946 & 1975); The Unseen (1945)*
White, Frances (act): *Screamer*
White, George (dir): *My Gun Is Quick*
White, Gregg (act): *Invasion of the Bee Girls*
White, Gregory (act): *The Sitter*
White, H. Fisher (act): *The Triumph of the Scarlet Pimpernel*
White, Harriet (act): *La Frusta e il Corpo; The Murder Clinic; Rapture; Raptus; Sei Donne per l'Assassino; Lo Spettro*
White, Harrison (act): *Doom Asylum; Seven*
White, Huey (act): *The Thin Man*
White, J.B. (act): *Gotham*
White, J.B. (wri): *The Beast (1996)*
White, J. Fisher (act): *Betrayal (1932); The Man Who Made Diamonds; Under the Red Robe (1937); What Happened Then?*
White, Jacqueline (act): *Crossfire; Mystery In Mexico; The Narrow Margin (1952); Seven Keys to Baldpate (1947)*
White, James Gordon (wri): *Big Foot; The Incredible 2-Headed Transplant; The Thing With Two Heads*
White, Jan (act): *Jack's Wife*
White, Jason (act): *Dragonslayer*
White, Jennifer (act): *The Murder Game*
White, Jeremy (act): *More Deadly Than the Male*
White, Jesse (act, 1917-1997, nee Jesse Wiedenfeld): *The Bad Seed (1956); Bedtime for Bonzo; The Cat from Outer Space; Francis Goes to the Races; The Ghost In the Invisible Bikini; Harvey; It's Only Money; Matinee; Monster In the Closet; Pajama Party; The Reluctant Astronaut; The Spirit Is Willing; Witness to Murder*
White, Jim (cin): *The Day of the Dolphin*
White, John (Euro act): *Tentacles*
White, John (USA act): *Secrets of the Phantom Caverns*
White, John Sylvester (act): *The Legend of Sleepy Hollow*
White, Jo Mullin (act): *The Rosary Murders*
White, Jon Manchip (wri): *The Camp On Blood Island; Crack In the World; Naked Evil*
White, Joni Ruth (act): *Polyester*
White, Joseph (act): *Primal Scream*
White, Kathleen Elizabeth (act): see Wilson, Marie
White, Kenneth (act): *Chiller; Fire In the Sky (1993)*
White, Lee "Lasses" (act): *The Golden Eye*
White, Leo (act): *The Kennel Murder Case; The Thin Man*
White, Leonard (act): *At the Stroke of Nine; The Dark Man (1951)*
White, Les (act): *The Deadly Affair; Without a Clue*
White, Leslie T. (wri): *The Man They Could Not Hang*
White, Les(ter) (H.) (cin): *Beyond Tomorrow; Drums of Tahiti; The Hidden Eye; Invisible Agent; Lost In a Harem; The Monster That Challenged the World; Sherlock Holmes and the Secret Weapon; Sherlock Holmes In Washington; White Savage*
White, Linda Grabler (act): *The Keeper*
White, Lionel (wri): *The Killing*
White, Lucian (act): *Midnight (1980)*
White, Madge (act): *The Copper Beeches (1921)*
White, Marjorie (act): *The Black Camel; Charlie Chan Carries On; Just Imagine*
White, Meadows (act): *Ghost Ship (1952); The Twenty Questions Murder*
White, Merrill G. (dir & wri): *Ghost Diver*
White, Michael (act): *Goliath Awaits; The Toxic Avenger, Part II*
White, Michael Jai (act): *Spawn*
White, Michelle (act): *The Three Lives of Karen*
White, Myrna (act): *Freejack*
White, Nathan J. (dir): *The Carrier*
White, Noni (wri): *The Hunchback of Notre Dame (1996)*
White, Paddy (act): *The Keeper*
White, Patricia (act): see Barry, Patricia
White, Patrick (act): *Children of the Damned*
White, Paul (dir): *The Crimes of Stephen Hawke*
White, Paul (wri): *The House of Silence; Master Spy (1963)*
White, Pearl (act, 1889-1938): *Terreur*
White, Pete (act): *Brainscan*
White, Pete (cin): *The Eiger Sanction*
White, Peter (act): *Terror of Rome Against the Son of Hercules*
White, Preston (act): *Shock Waves*
White, R. Meadows (act): *Fiend Without a Face*
White, Richard (act): *Beauty and the Beast (1991)*
White, Robb (wri): *Homicidal; House On Haunted Hill (1958); Macabre (1958); 13 Ghosts; The Tingler*
White, Robertson (wri): *The Adventurous Blonde; Charlie Chan's Murder Cruise; Dick Tracy Meets Gruesome; Lady In the Morgue; The Westland Case*
White, Robynne (act): *Street Trash*
White, Ron (act): *Guilty as Sin; Screamers (1996)*
White, Rosina (act): *Prehistoric Peeps*
White, Roy (act): *The Premonition (1975)*
White, Ruth (act, 1914-1969): *Charly*
White, S. Frank (act): *Sandcastles*
White, Sanford (wri): *Mantis In Lace*
White, Sarah (act): *Return to Oz*
White, Sebastian (act): *I Come In Peace*
White, Sheila (act): *The Spaceman and King Arthur*
White, Shirley (wri): *Tarzan's Savage Fury*
White, Slappy (act): *Amazon Women On the Moon*
White, Stephen (wri): *Barney's Great Adventure*
White, Steve (dir): *Amityville Dollhouse*
White, Stuart (act): *The Devil's Gift*
White, T.H. (wri, 1906-1964): *Camelot; The Sword In the Stone*
White, Ted (act): *Demonoid; The Hidden*
White, Terry (act): *Spacecamp*
White, Tom (act): *In the Company of Darkness*
White, Valerie (act): *The Blue Parrot; Halfway House*
White, Vanna (act, b. 1957): *The Goddess of Love; Graduation Day; Midnight Offerings*
White, Warren (act): *Targets*
White, Will J. (act): *Westworld*
White, William (act): *Terror of the Bloodhunters*
White, William B. (act): *Charlotte's Web*
Whitecloud, John P. (act): *Poltergeist II: The Other Side*
White Eagle, Charles (act): *Altered States*
Whitehead, Geoffrey (act): *—And Now the Screaming Starts!*
Whitehead, Graham (act): *My Bloody Valentine*
Whitehead, Joe (act): *The Jade Mask; The Sky Dragon*
Whitehead, Michael (act): *Alien High*
Whitehead, O.Z. (act): *Beware, My Lovely; Panic In Year Zero; The Scarf*
Whitehead, Paxton (act): *Boris and Natasha; Child of Darkness, Child of Light; My Boyfriend's Back*
Whitehead, Robert (act): *Bridge of Time*
Whitehill, Lou (wri): *Wonder Women*
Whitelaw, Billie (act, b. 1932): *The Adding Machine; Bobbikins; Breakout; The Dark Crystal; Deadly Advice; The Devil's Agent; The Flesh and the Fiends; Freddie as F.R.O.7; Frenzy; Hell Is a City; Jamaica Inn (1985); Jane Eyre (1996); Lorna Doone (1990); Merlin (1998); Murder Elite; Night Watch (1973); The Omen; Payroll; Shadey; Slayground; The Twisted Nerve; An Unsuitable Job for a Woman; The Water Babies*
Whitelaw, David (wri): *The Roof*
Whiteley, Annette (act): *Black Torment; The Devil-Ship Pirates*
Whiteley, Arkie (act): *Razorback; The Secret Life of Ian Fleming*
Whiteley, Jon (act, b. 1945): *Hunted (1952); The Spanish Gardener; The Weapon*
Whiteman, Frank (act): *I Dismember Mama*
Whiteman, George (act): *King Kong (1976)*
Whiteman, Peter (act): *La Figlia di Frankenstein*
Whiteman, Russ (act): *I Was a Teenage Frankenstein; Zotz!*
Whitemore, Hugh (wri): *The Blue Bird (1976); Jane Eyre (1996)*
Whitestone, Steve (wri): *The Pebble and the Penguin*
Whitfield, Anne (act): *The Six Million Dollar Man*
Whitfield, June (act): *The Spy With a Cold Nose*

Whitfield, Lynn (act): *Jaws: The Revenge*

Whitfield, Robert (act): *African Treasure*

Whitfield, Smoki (act): *Bomba and the Hidden City; Bomba, the Jungle Boy; The Golden Idol; Jungle Goddess; Killer Leopard; The Lion Hunters; Panther Island; Safari Drums*

Whitford, Bradley (act): *Dead as a Doorman; Nothing But the Truth*

Whitford, Peter (act): *Dead End Drive-In*

Whiting, Barbara (act): *Beware, My Lovely*

Whiting, John (wri): *The Devils*

Whiting, Leonard (act, b. 1951): *Frankenstein: The True Story*

Whiting, Margaret (act): *The Informers; Sinbad and the Eye of the Tiger*

Whiting, Peter (act): *Psychomania (1972)*

Whiting, Robyn (act): *The Erotic Adventures of Zorro*

Whitley, Crane (act): *Crime Doctor's Diary; Spy Smasher Returns*

Whitley, Kent (act): *Atlas*

Whitley, Richard (wri): *Pandemonium*

Whitley, William (cin): *Jungle Manhunt; Savage Mutiny; Tarzan's Hidden Jungle*

Whitlock, Albert (cin): *Dune; Dracula (1979); Earthquake; Ghost Story (1981); Greystoke: The Legend of Tarzan, Lord of the Apes; Heartbeeps; The Island; The Prisoner of Zenda (1979); The Questor Tapes; The Sentinel; The Thing (1982); The Wiz*

Whitlock Jr., Isiah (act): *Gremlins 2: The New Batch*

Whitlock, Lloyd (act): *The Lone Wolf Returns (1935); The Lost Jungle; Tangled Destinies*

Whitlow, Jill (act): *Night of the Creeps; Twice Dead; Weird Science*

Whitman, David (act): *Tam Lin*

Whitman, Ernest (act): *Blonde Savage; Green Pastures*

Whitman, Jack (cin): *Deathmoon; I Dream of Jeannie: Fifteen Years Later*

Whitman, Kari (act): *Phantom of the Mall: Eric's Revenge*

Whitman, Parker (act): *The Haunted (1991); Total Recall*

Whitman, Peter (act): *Dreamchild; Little Shop of Horrors (1986); Morons from Outer Space; Scandalous; Superman II*

Whitman, Stuart (act, b. 1928): *Call Him Mr. Shatter; The Cat Creature; City Beneath the Sea (1970); Deadly Reactor; Demonoid; Eaten Alive! (1976); The Girl In Black Stockings; Guyana, Cult of the Damned; The Last Generation; The Mark; The Monster Club; Night of the Lepus; Omega Cop; The Only Way Out Is Dead; Revenge (1971, USA); Ruby; Shock Treatment (1964);Signpost to Murder; Strange Shadows In an Empty Room; Welcome to Arrow Beach; When Worlds Collide; The Woman Hunter*

Whitman, Walt (act): *The Mark of Zorro (1920); The Three Musketeers (1916)*

Whitmire, Steve (act): *The Dark Crystal; Labyrinth (1986)*

Whitmore (Sr.), James (act, b. 1920): *Face of Fire; The First Deadly Sin; The Next Voice You Hear; Planet of the Apes; The Relic; Shadow In the Sky; Them! (1954)*

Whitmore Jr., James (act):*Human Feelings; A Force of One*

Whitmore, Stanford (wri): *The Dark (1979); The Eyes of Charles Sand; Hammersmith Is Out; The Hanged Man*

Whitney, Ann (act): *The Fugitive (1993)*

Whitney, Bob (act): *Hand of Death*

Whitney, Chris (act): *The Incredible Melting Man*

Whitney, Claire (act, 1890-1969): *The Mummy's Ghost*

Whitney, Grace Lee (act, b. 1930): *Star Trek*

Whitney, Helene (act): *The Hunchback of Notre Dame (1939); The Saint's Double Trouble*

Whitney, Iris (act): *Eyewitness (1981)*

Whitney, John (act): *Fog Island*

Whitney, Michael (act): *There Goes the Bride*

Whitney, Peter (act, 1916-1972, nee Peter King Engle): *The Brute Man; Gorilla at Large; Nine Lives Are Not Enough; The Notorious Lone Wolf; The Sword of Ali Baba; Three Strangers; The Wonderful World of the Brothers Grimm*

Whitney, Taylor (act): *Curse of the Queerwolf*

Whiton, James (wri): *The Abominable Dr. Phibes; Dr. Phibes Rises Again*

Whitrow, Benjamin (act): *Brimstone & Treacle; The Saint*

Whitson, Garson (mus): *Wonder Woman*

Whitson, Frank (act): *Boston Blackie's Little Pal*

Whittaker-Jones, Paul (act, b. 1900): *[...] (1973); Candidate for Murder; Dr. Jekyll and*

Sister Hyde; The Masque of the Red Death (1964); Wrong Number

Whittaker, Charles E. (wri): *The Man Who Laughs (1928); The Savage*

Whittaker, Ian (act): *Cosh Boy; The Revenge of Frankenstein*

Whittaker, James (1930's wri): *The Last of the Lone Wolf*

Whittaker, James (1980's wri): *Gray Lady Down; Megaforce*

Whittaker, Slim (act): *The Clutching Hand; The Falcon Out West*

Whittaker, Stephen (act): *Bury Me an Angel*

Whitten, Claude (act): *Dick Turpin's Ride to York*

Whitten, Leslie H. (wri): *Moon of the Wolf*

Whitten, Norman (act): *Alice In Wonderland (1903)*

Whitten, Norman (dir): *In the Days of Saint Patrick*

Whitten, Vernon (act): *In the Days of Saint Patrick*

Whitthorne, Paul (act): *Critters 4*

Whitting, Robin (act): *Prison Girls*

Whittingham, Jack (wri, b. 1910): *The Birthday Present; Cage of Gold; Counterblast; Escape to Danger; Hunted (1952); The Laughing Lady; Never Say Never Again; Pool of London; Q Planes; Thunderball*

Whittinghill, Dick (act): *Moon Pilot*

Whittington, Gene (act): *Escape from the Planet of the Apes; Psycho II*

Whittington, Jessy (act): *Forever Evil*

Whittington, Valerie (act): *Ordeal by Innocence*

Whittle, Annie (act): *Trial Run*

Whitton, Chuck (cin): *Phoenix the Warrior*

Whitton, Kim (act): *Phoenix the Warrior*

Whitton, Margaret (act, b. 1950): *Little Monsters*

Whitton, William (act): *Lemora, the Lady Dracula; The Mummy and the Curse of the Jackals*

Whitty, (Dame) May (act, 1865-1948): *Devotion; Flesh and Fantasy; Gaslight (1944); The Lady Vanishes (1938); My Name Is Julia Ross; Night Must Fall (1937); The Return of October; Suspicion (1941); The 13th Chair (1937)*

Whitty, Susan (act): *The Toxic Avenger, Part II*

Whitworth, Dean (act): *King Kong Lives*

Whitworth, James (act): *The Hills Have Eyes; Planet of Dinosaurs*

Who, The (mus & wri): *Tommy*

Who, Gary (act): *Fair Game (1985)*

Who, Wendy (act): *The Keeper*

Whorf, Richard (act, 1906-1966): *Champagne for Caesar; The Hidden Eye; Keeper of the Flame; Love from a Stranger (1947)*

Whybrow, Arthur (act): *Xtro*

Whybrow, Roy (cin): *The Legend of Spider Forest; Sphinx (1981)*

Whyle, James (act): *Steel Dawn*

Whyte, Laura (act): *Scalpel*

Whyte, Patrick (act): *The Hideous Sun Demon*

Whyte, Ron (wri): *The Mind Snatchers*

Wiard, William (dir): *Deadly Lessons; Fantasies*

Wiatrak, Ken (cin): *Slavegirls from Beyond Infinity*

Wiazemsky, Anne (act): *One Plus One; Teorema*

Wibberley, Leonard (wri, 1915-1983, a.k.a. Leonard Holton, Patrick O'Connor & Chris-topher Webb): *The Mouse On the Moon; The Mouse That Roared*

Wick, Charles (wri): *Snow White and the Three Stooges*

Wick, Leslie Ann (act): *Revenge of the Living Zombies*

Wick, Norma (act): *Hideaway*

Wick, Norma Jean (act): *Circle of Deceit*

Wickenburg, Kim (act): *Revenge of the Teenage Vixens from Outer Space*

Wicker, David (act): *Metamorphosis*

Wickert, Tony (act): *The Painted Smile*

Wickes, David (dir & wri): *Frankenstein (1993); Jekyll and Hyde*

Wickes, Mary (act, 1916-1995): *The Decision of Christopher Blake; The Hunchback of Notre Dame (1996); The Spirit Is Willing; Who Done It? (1942)*

Wicket, W.W. (wri): *The Seventh Sign; Spacecamp*

Wickham, Jeffrey (act): *Murder On the Midnight Express*

Wicking, Christopher (wri): *Blood from the Mummy's Tomb; Cry of the Banshee; Demons of the Mind; The Legend of Spider Forest; Murders In the Rue Morgue (1971); Scream and Scream Again; To the Devil a Daughter*

Wickman, Karl (act): *Darkman (1990)*

Wickman, Ray (act): *The Creeping Terror*

Wickremasinghe, Douglas (act): *The God King*

Wicks, Rebecca (act): *Jack-O'Lantern*

Wickware, Scott (act): *Escape Clause*

Wicky, Bernhard (act): *Deathwatch (1980); The Glass Cell*

Widdoes, Kathleen (act, b. 1939): *Charlie Chan: Happiness Is a Warm Clue; The Mephisto Waltz; Savages*

Widecrantz, Sven (act): *Primal Scream*

Widelitz, Stacy (mus): *Phantom of the Mall: Eric's Revenge; Return to Horror High*

Widelock, John (act): *Silent Scream (1979)*

Widen, Gregory (dir): *The Prophecy (1995)*

Widen, Gregory (wri): *Highlander; Highlander 2: The Quickening; Highlander: The Final Dimension; The Prophecy (1995)*

Widerberg, Bo (dir, 1930-1997): *Man On the Roof*

Widl, Susanne (act): *Invisible Adversaries*

Widmann, Ellen (act): *M (1931)*

Widmark, Richard (act, b. 1914): *Bear Island; The Bedford Incident; Brock's Last Case; Coma; The Domino Principle; Don't Bother to Knock; Murder On the Orient Express; A Prize of Gold; Rollercoaster; Run for the Sun; The Secret Ways; The Street With No Name; The Swarm; To the Devil a Daughter; Twilight's Last Gleaming*

Widom, Bud (act): *The Green Slime*

Wieand, Dick (act): *Friday the 13th-Part V: A New Beginning*

Wiebe, Lesley (act): *Empire of Ash III*

Wieczik, Barbara (act): *Confess, Dr. Corda*

Wiedenfeld, Jesse (act): see White, Jesse

Wieder, Anna Marie (act): *Hello Again*

Wiederhorn, Ken (dir): *Eyes of a Stranger; Return of the Living Dead, Part II; Shock Waves*

Wiedermann, Elena (act): *She (1983)*

Wieman, Bill (act): *Nightbeast*

Wiemer, Robert (dir): *Somewhere Tomorrow*

Wienand, Jannie (act): *The Demon (1981)*

Wiene, Robert (dir, 1881-1938): *Dr. Hallers; Genuine; Das Kabinett des Dr. Caligari; Orlacs Haende; Raskolnikov; Ultimatum*

Wiene, Robert (wri, 1881-1938): *Raskolnikov*

Wiener, Sabrina (act): *Pet Shop*

Wiesenfeld, Joe (wri): *A Knight In Camelot; 20,000 Leagues Under the Sea (1997, CBS-TV)*

Wiest, Dianne (act, b. 1948): *Edward Scissorhands; The Lost Boys; Practical Magic; The Purple Rose of Cairo*

Wiest, Heannine (act): *Turn Back the Clock*

Wieternik, Nora (act): *Flesh Gordon*

Wieth, Mogens (act): *The Man Who Knew Too Much (1956)*

Wifstrand, Naima (act): *Ansiktet; La Sorciere; Valley of the Eagles*

Wiggins, Chris (act): *An American Christmas Carol; Babar: The Movie; Murder by Decree; The Neptune Factor; The Quilt of Hathor; Virus (1980); Welcome to Blood City*

Wiggins, Jim/Jimmy (act): *The Bermuda Triangle; King Kong Lives*

Wiggins, Lillian (act): *The Black Cross Gang; Queen of the London Counterfeiters; The Water Rats of London; When London Sleeps*

Wiggins, Russell (G.) (act): *Nightfall (1988); The Screaming Woman*

Wight, Peter (act): *Jane Eyre (1997)*

Wightman, Dawna (act): *The Amityville Curse*

Wightman, Deby (act): *Howling III*

Wightman, Robert (act): *Impulse (1984); Stepfather III: Father's Day*

Wilbee, Codie Lucas (act): *The Reflecting Skin*

Wilbur, Crane (dir, 1887-1973): *The Bat (1959)*

Wilbur, Crane (wri, 1887-1973): *The Amazing Mr. X; The Bat (1959); House of Wax; The Invisible Menace; The Mad Magician; The Monster (1925); Mysterious Island (1961)*

Wilbur, George (act): *Beyond the Poseidon Adventure; The Clonus Horror; Ghostbusters II; Halloween: The Curse of Michael Myers; Virus (1980)*

Wilbur, George P. (act): *Eve of Destruction; Halloween 4: The Return of Michael Myers; Halloween: The Curse of Michael Myers; Remote Control (1988); Total Recall*

Wilbur, Jane (act): *End of the World (1977)*

Wilbur, Joe (cin): *Dirigible*

Wilburn, Ken (act): *I Was a Zombie for the F.B.I.*

Wilby, James (act): *Dreamchild; The Woman In White (1998)*

Wilcher, Daryl (act): *Freejack*

Wilcocks, Jack (act): *Queen of My Heart*

Wilcots, Joey (act): *Addams Family Values*

Wilcox, Joseph (cin): *Community Most Pleasant*

Wilcox, Collin (act): *Jaws 2; The Name of the Game is Kill*

Wilcox, Frank (act, 1907-1974): *The Beginning of the End; The Beginning or the End?; Earth vs. the Flying Saucers; The $1,000,000 Duck; Philo Vance Returns; Samson and Delilah; The Treasure of Lost Canyon*

Wilcox, Fred (McLeod) (dir, 1908-1964): *Forbidden Planet; Shadow In the Sky*

Wilcox, Herbert (dir, 1892-1977): *Chu Chin Chow (1923); The Man Who Wouldn't Talk; Trent's Last Case (1952); The Woman In White (1929)*

Wilcox, Herbert (wri, 1892-1977): *Chu Chin Chow (1923); When Knights Were Bold (1929); The Woman In White (1929)*

Wilcox, Jackson (act): *Under the Red Robe (1915)*

Wilcox, John (cin): *The Black Knight; Craze; Daleks' Invasion Earth 2150 A.D.; The Deadly Bees; Dr. Who and the Daleks; Evil of Frankenstein; The Ghoul (1974); Hysteria!; Legend of the Seven Golden Vampires; Legend of the Werewolf; Mr. Denning Drives North; The Mouse That Roared; Nightmare (1963); The Psychopath (1965); The Skull*

Wilcox, John (mus): *The Mouse That Roared*

Wilcox, Larry (act): *Deadly Lessons*

Wilcox, Lisa (act): *A Nightmare On Elm Street 4: The Dream Master; A Nightmare On Elm Street 5: The Dream Child*

Wilcox, Mary (act): *Beast of the Yellow Night; Love Me Deadly; Psychic Killer*

Wilcox, Robert (act, 1909-1955): *Buried Alive (1940); Doctor Satan's Robot; Island of Doomed Men; The Lone Wolf Strikes; The Man They Could Not Hang; The Unknown (1946)*

Wilcox, Shannon (act): *Seven*

Wilcox, Sheelah (act): *Twins of Evil*

Wilcoxon, Henry (act, 1905-1984): *A Connecticut Yankee In King Arthur's Court (1949); The Corsican Brothers (1941); Doomsday Machine; The Lone Wolf Takes a Chance; The Man Who Wouldn't Die; The Mysterious Mr. Moto; Samson and Delilah; Scotland Yard (1941); Sweet Sixteen; The Tribe; The Two Worlds of Jennie Logan; The War Lord*

Wild, Harry (J.) (cin): *Cornered; The Falcon's Adventure; Murder, My Sweet; Pitfall; The Saint In Palm Springs; Tarzan's Desert Mystery; Tarzan Triumphs; They Won't Believe Me*

Wild, Jack (act, b. 1953): *The Pied Piper (1971); Robin Hood: Prince of Thieves*

Wild, Janet (act): *The Fiend (1972)*

Wild, Katy (act): *The Deadly Bees; Dr. Terror's House of Horrors (1964); Evil of Frankenstein; On the Run (1963); They Came from Beyond Space*

Wild, Lois (act): *Sharad of Atlantis*

Wilde, Al (act): *Jaws 2*

Wilde, Andrew (act): *1984 (1984)*

Wilde, Barbie (act): *Hellbound: Hellraiser II*

Wilde, Bob (act): *Unforgettable*

Wilde, Brian (act): *Night of the Demon (1957); To the Devil a Daughter*

Wilde, Claudine (act): *The Cyber-Stalking*

Wilde, Colette (act): *Circus of Horrors; Clue of the Twisted Candle; The Day of theTriffids; House of Mystery (1961); Inside Information; Maroc 7; Night of the Prowler; The Professionals*

Wilde, Cornel (act, 1915-1989): *At Sword's Point; The Bandit of Sherwood Forest; The Fifth Musketeer; Gargoyles; Guest In the House; Lancelot and Guinevere; Leave Her to Heaven; The Norsemen; Omar Khayyam; Operation Secret; Saadia; Sharks' Treasure; Shockproof; Star of India; Storm Fear; A Thousand and One Nights (1945)*

Wilde, Cornel (dir, 1915-1989): *Lancelot and Guinevere; No Blade of Grass; Sharks' Treasure; Storm Fear*

Wilde, Cornel (wri, 1915-1989): *Sharks' Treasure*

Wilde, Edward (cin): *Vampire On Bikini Beach*

Wilde, Hagar (wri): *Guest In the House; Shadow of the Eagle; This Is My Love*

Wilde, Heather (act): *Counter-Espionage; The Undying Monster*

Wilde, Jeannette (act): *Dr. Jekyll and Sister Hyde*

Wilde, Lorna (act): *The Body Stealers*

Wilde, Marty (act): *Jet Storm*

Wilde, Oscar (wri, 1854-1900): *The Canterville Ghost (1944 & 1986); Dorian Gray; Flesh and Fantasy; A Modern Salome; The Picture of Dorian Gray (1916 & 1945); Dorian Gray's Salome (1922?); The Sins of Dorian Gray*

Wilde, Robert (act): *Are You Dying Young Man?*

Wilde, Thomas (act): *Space Master X-7*
Wilde, Wilbur (act): *Dead End Drive-In*
Wilder, Alan (act): *Child's Play (1988); Poltergeist III*
Wilder, Alec (act): *The Sand Castle*
Wilder, Billy (dir, b. 1906): *Five Graves to Cairo; The Lost Weekend; The Private Life of Sherlock Holmes; Sunset Boulevard; Witness for the Prosecution*
Wilder, Billy (wri, b. 1906): *Double Indemnity (1944); Five Graves to Cairo; The Private Life of Sherlock Holmes; Sunset Boulevard; Witness for the Prosecution*
Wilder, Cosmo (act): *The Toxic Avenger*
Wilder, Gene (act, b. 1938): *The Adventures of Sherlock Holmes' Smarter Brother; Alice In Wonderland (1999); Haunted Honeymoon (1986); The Little Prince; Murder In a Small Town; Rhinoceros (1974); Willy Wonka and the Chocolate Factory; Young Frankenstein*
Wilder, Gene (dir, b. 1938): *The Adventures of Sherlock Holmes' Smarter Brother; Haunted Honeymoon (1986)*
Wilder, Gene (wri, b. 1938): *The Adventures of Sherlock Holmes' Smarter Brother; Haunted Honeymoon (1986); Murder In a Small Town*
Wilder, Glen (act): *Logan's Run*
Wilder, James (act): *A Face to Die For; Prey of the Chameleon; Zombie High*
Wilder, John (act): *The Unguarded Moment*
Wilder, Myles (dir): *Spy In the Sky*
Wilder, Myles (wri): *Bluebeard's Ten Honeymoons; Fright (1957); Killers from Space; Manfish; Phantom from Space; The Snow Creature; Spy In the Sky*
Wilder, Nick (act): *Stargate*
Wilder, Thornton (wri, 1897-1975): *The Bridge of San Luis Rey (1929 & 1944); Shadow of a Doubt (1943 & 1991)*
Wilder, W. Lee (dir): *Bluebeard's Ten Honeymoons; Fright (1957); Killers from Space; Manfish; The Man Without a Body; The Omegans; Phantom from Space; The Snow Creature*
Wilder, Yvonne (act & wri): *The Return of Count Yorga*
Wildgen, Lee (act): *Prom Night*
Wilding, April (act): *Hands of the Ripper*
Wilding, Elisabetta (act): *La Strega in Amore*
Wilding, Michael (act, 1912-1979): *Cottage to Let; Frankenstein: The True Story; The Glass Slipper; The Naked Edge; Stage Fright (1950); Trent's Last Case (1952); Under Capricorn*
Wildman, Amanda (act): *The Demon (1981)*
Wildman, John (act): *Humongous*
Wildman, John Stuart (act): *Sorority Babes In the Slimeball Bowl-O-Rama*
Wildman, Valerie (act): *Inner Sanctum (1991); Mars Attacks!; Neon City*
Wildsmith, Dawn (act): *Alienator; Cyclone; Hollywood Chainsaw Hookers; The Phantom Empire; Surf Nazis Must Die; The Tomb; Warlords*
Wilenchick, Glen (act): *The Last Warning (1938)*
Wiles, Gordon (dir): *Charlie Chan's Secret*
Wiles, Mark (act): *The Norsemen*
Wiles, Michael Shamus (act): *Leatherface: Texas Chainsaw Massacre III; The Puppet Masters*
Wiles, Mike (act): *Vampire at Midnight*
Wiles, Bernard (wri): *Secrets In the Attic*
Wiley, Bill (act): *Mistress of Paradise*
Wiley, Ed(ward) (act): *The Canterville Ghost (1996); Highlander; The Hunger; Little Shop of Horrors (1986); Morons from Outer Space*
Wiley, Ethan (dir): *House II: The Second Story*
Wiley, Ethan (wri): *House; House II: The Second Story*
Wiley, Francis (act): *The Plague of the Zombies*
Wiley, Hugh (wri): *Doomed to Die; The Fatal Hour (1940); Mr. Wong, Detective; Mr. Wong In Chinatown; The Mystery of Mr. Wong; Phantom of Chinatown*
Wiley, Jan (act): *The Brute Man; Dick Tracy vs. Crime, Inc.; The Living Ghost (1942); She-Wolf of London*
Wiley, Jane K. (act): *Fade to Black*
Wiley, Laurel (act): *Test Tube Teens from the Year 2000*
Wiley, Meason (act): *Powder*
Wiley, Richard (act): *Alienator*
Wiley, Sharon (act): *The Private Lives of Adam and Eve*
Wilhelm, Kate (wri): *The Lookalike*
Wilhelm, Theodore (act): *Shoot to Kill (1961); The Stateless Man; The Trollenberg Terror*
Wilhelm, Wolfgang (wri): *Escape to Danger; Pimpernel Smith; The Saint Meets the Tiger; Secret People; Thunder Rock*
Wilhite, Dian (act): *Flesh Feast*
Wilhoite, Benji (act): *Web of Deceit*
Wilhoite, Kathleen (act): *Angel Heart; Brenda Starr (1992); Color of Night; Dream Demon; Fire In the Sky (1993); Witchboard*
Wilk, Harry (cin): *The Falcon Out West*
Wilke, Robert (J.) (act, b. 1913): *The Boy Who Cried Werewolf; The Catman of Paris; The Lone Ranger; The Resurrection of Zachary Wheeler; They Call It Murder; 20,000 Leagues Under the Sea (1954)*
Wilkerson, Bill (act): *Dr. Cyclops*
Wilkerson, Guy (act, 1901-1971): *The Haunted Palace (1963); Spooks Run Wild*
Wilkerson, Ralph (wri): *Beyond and Back*
Wilkes, Donna (act): *Blood Song; Grotesque; Jaws 2; Schizoid (1980)*
Wilkes, Elaine (act): *Killer Party*
Wilkes, Emily (act): *Starship Invasions*
Wilkes, Melissa (act): *The Boy Who Never Was*
Wilkey, Jim (act): *Dick Tracy (1990)*
Wilkins, Barbara (act): *The Flesh Eaters; I Saw What You Did (1965)*
Wilkins, Jeremy (act): *Curse of the Fly; Thunderbirds Are Go; Thunderbird 6*
Wilkins, Martin (act): *Bomba, the Jungle Boy; The Jungle Girl; Law of the Jungle; Voodoo Woman*
Wilkins, Mike (act): *Bridge Across Time*
Wilkinson, Albert (act): *Wombling Free*
Wilkinson, Arthur (mus): *The Perfect Woman*
Wilkinson, Charles (dir & wri): *Quarantine*
Wilkinson, Elizabeth (act): *A Taste of Blood*
Wilkinson, Geoffrey (act): *Treasure Island (1950)*
Wilkinson, Irving (act): *The Ivory Ape*
Wilkinson, June (act): *Frankenstein's Great Aunt Tillie; Macumba Love; The Private Lives of Adam and Eve*
Wilkinson, Katherine (act): *Venom (1982)*
Wilkinson, M. Scott (act): *Beyond and Back*
Wilkinson, Marc (mus): *The Blood On Satan's Claw; Enigma; The Fiendish Plot of Dr. Fu Manchu; The Quatermass Conclusion; The Return (1973, GB)*
Wilkinson, Roderick (wri): *Three Cases of Murder*
Wilkinson, Sam (act): *The Lost Patrol (1929); The Prince and the Beggarmaid; Troubled Waters (1936)*
Wilkinson, Scott (act): *Wish Upon a Star*
Wilkinson, Tom (act): *The Ghost and the Darkness; Paper Mask*
Wilkinson, Wallace (act): *Mutant*
Wilkof, Lee (act): *The Entity*
Wilks, Cindy (act): *The Exterminator*
Willamette, John (act): *Surf Nazis Must Die*
Willard, Bonnie Jane (act): *Rearview Mirror*
Willard, Edmund (act): *Dark Journey; King of the Damned; The Mystery of the Mary Celeste; A Night In Montmartre*
Willard, Fred (act, b. 1939): *Americathon; Prehysteria 3; Salem's Lot*
Willard, John (act): *Sherlock Holmes (1922)*
Willard, John (wri): *Black Waters; The Cat And the Canary (1927, 1939 & 1978); The Cat Creeps (1930); The Mask of Fu Manchu*
Willard, Sandra (wri): *Slaughterhouse Rock*
Willardson, Jeanne (act): *The Sinister Urge*
Willatt, Irvin (dir): *The False Faces*
Willcox, Jack (act): *Prison Planet*
Willcox, Toyah (act): *The Quatermass Conclusion; The Tempest (1980)*
Willens, Bill (act): *Brainstorm (1983)*
Willes, Jean (act, 1923-1989): *Abbott and Costello Go to Mars; Bowery to Bagdad; Chinatown at Midnight; Invasion of the Body Snatchers (1956); Jungle Jim In the Forbidden Land; The Man Who Turned to Stone*
Willes, Peter (act): *The Hound Of The Baskervilles (1939)*
Willey, Eddie (act): *The Houseboat Mystery*
Willey, Leonard (act): *The Adventures of Robin Hood*
Willhelm, John (mus): *Kidnapped Co-Ed*
William, George B. (act): *The Phantom of the Opera (1925)*
William, John (wri): *The Omega Man*
William, Leonard (dir): *The Anatomist*
William, Spencer (act): *Raptus*
William, Thomas (act): *Star Crystal*
William, Warren (act, 1896-1948, nee William Krech): *The Case of the Curious Bride; Counter-Espionage; The Dragon Murder Case; Fear (1946); The Gracie Allen Murder Case; The Lone Wolf Keeps a Date; The Lone Wolf Meets a Lady; The Lone Wolf Spy Hunt; The Lone Wolf Strikes; The Lone Wolf Takes a Chance; The Man In the Iron Mask (1939); The Mind Reader; One Dangerous Night; Out of the Night; Passport to Suez; Satan Met a Lady; Secrets of the Lone Wolf; Strange Illusion; The Wolf Man (1941)*
Williams, Aaron (act): *Chain Reaction (1996)*
Williams, Adam (act, b. 1927): *North by Northwest; The Space Children*
Williams, Afram Bill (act): *Flatliners*
Williams, Al (wri): *Arachnophobia*
Williams, Albert (act): *Jack and the Beanstalk (1924)*
Williams, Alistair (act): *Vengeance*
Williams, Allen (act): *Meteor*
Williams, Alva (act): *Jacob's Ladder*
Williams, Anson (dir): *All-American Murder*
Williams, Arnold (act): *Live and Let Die; Scream, Blacula, Scream*
Williams, Barbara (Can act): *Firebird 2015 A.D.; Watchers*
Williams, Barbara (USA act): *Bone Daddy; Forever Evil*
Williams, Ben (act): *The Curse of the Wraydons; The Demon Barber of Fleet Street; Dual Alibi; Flame In the Heather; The Man Without a Face; Nothing Venture; Old Mother Riley's Ghosts; Paul Temple Returns; The Saint Meets the Tiger; You Pay Your Money*
Williams, Ben Ames (wri, 1889-1953): *Leave Her to Heaven; Too Good to Be True*
Williams, Bert (act, dir & wri, b. 1922): *The Nest of the Cuckoo Birds*
Williams, Bill (act, 1915-1992, nee Bill MacWilliams): *The Body Snatcher (1945); The Clay Pigeon; Deadline at Dawn; A Fire In the Sky (1978); The Giant Spider Invasion; The Hairy Ape; Murder In the Blue Room; The Phantom of Hollywood; Spaceflight IC-1; Space Master X-7*
Williams, Billy "Sly" (act): *Voodoo Dawn*
Williams, Billy (cin): *Billion Dollar Brain; Dreamchild; The Magus; The Manhattan Project; The Mind of Mr. Soames; Night Watch (1973); Ordeal by Innocence; Saturn 3; Tam Lin*
Williams, Billy Dee (act, b. 1937): *Alien Intruder; Batman (1989); The Empire Strikes Back; Mask of Death; Return of the Jedi*
Williams, Bob (cin): *One Dark Night*
Williams, Bob (wri): *20 Million Miles to Earth*
Williams, Bransby (act & wri): *Bernardo's Confession; Scrooge (1928)*
Williams, Brett (act): *The Punisher*
Williams, Brock (dir): *I'm a Stranger*
Williams, Brock (wri): *Chin Chin Chinaman; Condemned to Death; Crime Unlimited; Dancing With Crime; The Dark Stairway; The Dark Tower (1943); Date With Disaster; The Gentle Trap; The Gilded Cage; The High Terrace; I'm a Stranger; Meet Mr. Callaghan; Meet Mr. Malcolm; Murder Will Out (1939); Naked Fury; The Night Won't Talk; The Painted Smile; A Place of One's Own; Q Planes; Rag Doll; Stormy Crossing; The Thirteenth Candle; Three Steps In the Dark; Two for Danger; Wolf's Clothing (1936)*
Williams, Brook (act): *Absolution; Hammersmith Is Out; The Medusa Touch; The Plague of the Zombies*
Williams, C. aBecket (wri): *A Yell of a Night*
Williams, C.D. (act): *Devil's Angel*
Williams, Cara (act, b. 1925, nee Bernice Kamiat): *The Happy Land; The Spider (1945)*
Williams, Carole (act): *One Spy Too Many*
Williams, Caroline (act): *Leprechaun 3; Stepfather II; The Texas Chainsaw Massacre 2*
Williams, Cedric (cin): *The Fatal Night*
Williams, Charles (act, b. 1898): *Blue, White and Perfect; Charlie Chan On Broadway; Mr. Moto's Gamble; The Thin Man; Time to Kill (1942)*
Williams, Charles (mus): *The Night Has Eyes*
Williams, Charles (wri): *Confidentially Yours; Dead Calm*
Williams, Cheri A. (act): *Ed Wood*
Williams, Chili (act): *Captive Women; The Falcon In Hollywood*
Williams, Chino (act): *It Came Upon the Midnight Clear; Weird Science*
Williams, Chris (act): *Outland*
Williams, Chuck (act): *Soultaker*
Williams, Cindy (act, b. 1947): *The Creature Wasn't Nice; Earth Angel; Gas-s-s-s!; The Killing Kind; The Stepford Husbands; UFOria*
Williams III, Clarence (act, b. 1940): *Last Rites (1998), Maniac Cop 2; Perfect Victims; The Silencers (1995); Tales from the Hood*
Williams Jr., Clarence (act): *Primal Fear*
Williams, Clark (act): *Secret of the Chateau; Werewolf of London*
Williams, Clondell (act): *Getting Lucky*
Williams, Cress (act): *Peter Benchley's 'Creature'*
Williams, Cynda (act): *Grey Knight; Spirit Lost*
Williams, D.J. (act): *The Crimes of Stephen Hawke; The Demon Barber of Fleet Street; Elephant Boy; The Fatal Hour (1937); The Ghost Train (1941); The House of Silence; Maria Marten: or, The Murder In the Red Barn (1935); Mr. Reeder In Room 13; The Pointing Finger; Scrooge (1935); The Secret of the Loch (1934)*
Williams, D.J. (dir): *The Shuttle of Life*
Williams, David (act): *Kadoyng*
Williams, David (wri): *The Two Worlds of Jennie Logan*
Williams, David C. (mus): *The Prophecy (1995)*
Williams, Derek (act): *Concerning Mr. Martin; The Crimson Candle*
Williams, Derek (cin, b. 1906): *The Ghost at St. Michael's*
Williams, Derek (dir & wri): *Hunted In Holland*
Williams, Dick Anthony (act, b. 1941): *Brave New World (1980); The Deep; Edward Scissorhands; Through Naked Eyes*
Williams, Don (act): *The Ghastly Ones*
Williams, Don S. (act): *The Stepfather*
Williams, Doug (act): *The Nutty Professor (1996)*
Williams, E.H. (act): *Betrayal (1932)*
Williams, Earle (act, 1880-1927): *The Man from Downing Street; Red Signals*
Williams, Edward (mus): *Unearthly Stranger*
Williams, Edy (act): *Bad Girls from Mars; Chained Heat; Dr. Alien Hellhole; I Was a Teenage Sex Mutant; The Last of the Secret Agents?*
Williams, Eileen (act): *The Housekeeper; Shock Chamber*
Williams, Ellis (act): *Alien Nation: Millennium; The Brother from Another Planet; Def by Temptation*
Williams, Elmo (dir, b. 1913): *Hell Ship Mutiny*
Williams, Emlyn (act, 1905-1987): *Another Man's Poison; Beyond This Place; Dead Men Tell No Tales (1938); Eye of the Devil; The Frightened Lady (1932); The Girl In the News; I Accuse (1958); Jamaica Inn (1939); The Scarf; They Drive by Night*
Williams, Emlyn (wri, 1905-1987): *Dead Men Tell No Tales (1938); The Man Who Knew Too Much (1934); Night Must Fall (1937 & 1964); Time Without Pity*
Williams, Eric (1910s act): *Hamlet (1914)*
Williams, Eric (act): *Blood Diner*
Williams, Eric Bransby (act): *The Secret Kingdom; When Knights Were Bold (1929)*
Williams, Ernest (act): *Forever Evil*
Williams, Esther (act, b. 1923): *A Guy Named Joe; Raw Wind In Eden; The Unguarded Moment*
Williams, Eugene (act): *Evolver*
Williams, Finty (act): *The Mystery of Edwin Drood (1993)*
Williams, Florine (wri): *The Man from Downing Street*
Williams, Frank (act): *Company of Fools; Countdown to Danger; Jabberwocky; Oh Heavenly Dog; One of Our Dinosaurs Is Missing*
Williams, Fred(erick) (act): *Count Dracula; Giulietta degli Spiriti; The Nibelungs (1966)*
Williams, Freeman (act): *Forever Evil*
Williams, G. Mac (cin): *The Clairvoyant (1934)*
Williams, Gerald M. (cin): *Getting Lucky*
Williams, Gordon (wri): *Straw Dogs*
Williams, Grant (act, 1930-1985): *Brain of Blood; The Couch; Doomsday Machine; The Incredible Shrinking Man; The Leech Woman; The Monolith Monsters*
Williams, Guinn (act, 1899-1962): *Liliom (1930); Lure of the Islands; The Phantom (1931); The Phantom Broadcast*
Williams, Guy (act, 1924-1989): *Bonzo Goes to College; Captain Sinbad; I Was a Teenage Werewolf; The Sign of Zorro (1960); Zorro, the Avenger*
Williams, Gwen (act): *The Secret of the Moor; A Smart Set*
Williams, Gwyneth (act): *Empire of Ash III*
Williams, Harcourt (act, 1880-1957): *Around the World In 80 Days; Cage of Gold; For Them That Trespass; Hamlet (1948); The Late Edwina Black; Time Bomb; Under Capricorn; Vice Versa (1947); Your Witness*
Williams, Harland (act): *Rocketman (1997)*
Williams, Harry (act): *Train Ride to Hollywood*
Williams Jr., Harry (act): *The Toxic Avenger, Part II*
Williams, Harry M. (act): *The China Syndrome*
Williams, Heathcote (act): *The Odyssey; Orlando; Slipstream; The Tempest (1980)*
Williams, Howard (act): *Quatermass II*
Williams, Hugh (act, 1904-1969): *After Dark; Dark Eyes of London; The Dark Stairway; Dead Men Tell No Tales (1938); Dr. Faustus; The Jewel; The Man Behind the*

Mask (1936); A Night In Montmartre; The Perfect Crime; Premiere; Take My Life; White Face; Wuthering Heights (1939)
Williams, Ian Patrick (act): Bad Channels; Bloodmoon (1990); Dolls; Not of This World; Re-Animator; Terrorvision
Williams, Ivory (act): Green Pastures
Williams, J.B. (dir): The Tell-Tale Heart (1953, GB)
Williams, J.B. (wri): A Man About the House; The Tell-Tale Heart (1953, GB)
Williams, Jack (act): African Treasure; Billy the Kid vs. Dracula
Williams, Jack Eric (mus):Nightmare (1981)
Williams, Jason (act): Flesh Gordon; Time Walker; Vampire at Midnight
Williams, Jason (wri): Time Walker
Williams, Jeff (act): The Brotherhood of Satan; The Haunting of Sarah Hardy
Williams, Jill (act): Sentenced for Life
Williams, Jim (act): Island of Blood; The Newlydeads
Williams, JoBeth (act, b. 1949): The Day After; Endangered Species; Poltergeist; Poltergeist II: The Other Side; Switch (1991)
Williams, Joe (act & mus, b. 1918): Cinderfella
Williams, John (act, b. 1903): Dial M for Murder (1954); The Hound Of The Baskervilles (1972); Kind Lady (1951); Midnight Lace (1960); The Swarm; To Catch a Thief; Visit to a Small Planet; Witness for the Prosecution; A Woman's Vengeance
Williams, John (mus, b. 1932): Always; Black Sunday (1977); Close Encounters of the Third Kind; Daddy's Gone A-Hunting; Dracula (1979); Earthquake; The Eiger Sanction; The Empire Strikes Back; E.T.-The Extra-Terrestrial; Family Plot; The Fury; Heartbeeps; Images; Indiana Jones and the Last Crusade; Indiana Jones and the Temple of Doom; Jane Eyre (1970); Jaws; Jaws 2; Jaws: The Revenge; Jurassic Park; The Lost World: Jurassic Park; The Poseidon Adventure; Quintet; Raiders of the Lost Ark; Return of the Jedi; The Screaming Woman; Spacecamp; Star Wars; Superman (1978); Superman II; Superman IV: The Quest for Peace; The Towering Inferno; The Witches of Eastwick
Williams, John Timothy (act): Timestalkers
Williams, John Warner (act): Black Magic Woman
Williams, Johnny (act): The Mask (1994); Ritual of Evil; Victim of Desire
Williams, Johnny (mus): The Secret Ways
Williams, Joseph (mus): The Nosferatu Diaries: Embrace of the Vampire
Williams, Joyce (act): The Keeper; Pretty Maids All In a Row; Soylent Green
Williams, Justin (act): Dante's Peak
Williams, Kelli (act): Lifepod; Zapped Again
Williams, Ken (mus): Perfect Little Angels; Storm Chasers: Revenge of the Twister
Williams, Kenneth (act, 1926-1988): Carry On Screaming; Carry On Spying; The Hound of the Baskervilles (1978); Trent's Last Case (1952)
Williams, Kent (act): Time After Time; WarGames
Williams, Kevin (act): Making Mr. Right
Williams, Kit (act): The Damned; Koroshi
Williams, Kuumba (act): see Williams, Sylvia "Kuumba"
Williams, Larry (act): Nancy Drew, Reporter; Torchy Blane In Panama; Torchy Plays With Dynamite; Torchy Runs for Mayor
Williams, Larry B. (wri): Spacecamp
Williams, Leon (act): Doctor Death: Seeker of Souls
Williams, Les (act): The Mutagen
Williams, Lionel (act): Red Blooded American Girl
Williams, Lori (act): Faster, Pussycat! Kill! Kill!
Williams, Lottie (act): Nancy Drew, Detective
Williams, Louis Sheldon (act): Our Mother's House
Williams, Lyman (act): Supernatural (1933)
Williams, Mac F. (act): Beverly Hills Bodysnatchers
Williams, Mack (act): Cape Fear (1961); The Monster That Challenged the World
Williams, Mark (act): The Borrowers (1998); 101 Dalmatians (1996)
Williams, Mary Parker (act): Wish Upon a Star
Williams, Maston (act): The Lost Jungle
Williams, Maud (act): Flying from Justice
Williams, Meadow (act): The Mask (1994)
Williams, Melanie F. (act):Chiller
Williams, Michael (act): Enigma; Murder by Night; The Persecution and Assassination of Jean-Paul Marat as Performed by the Inmates of the Asylum of Charenton Under the Direction of the Marquis de Sade
Williams, Michelle (act): Halloween H20; Species; Timemaster
Williams, Moses (act): Outbreak
Williams, Myrna (act): see Loy, Myrna
Williams, Myrna (act): The Toxic Avenger
Williams, Nat (act): Ator: The Fighting Eagle; Endgame
Williams, Natalie (act): Forever Evil
Williams, Natasha (act): A Connecticut Yankee In King Arthur's Court (1989)
Williams, Norman (act): Secret People
Williams, Norman (cin): The Million Eyes of Sumuru
Williams III, Norman Neale (act): see Kincaid, Aron
Williams, Olivia (act): The Postman (1997)
Williams, Pat (GB act): The Unwritten Law
Williams, Pat (USA act): Don't Go In the House
Williams, Pat(rick) (mus): All of Me; Charlie Chan and the Curse of the Dragon Queen; Hex; In the Spirit; A Knight In Camelot; The Magician (1973); The Man With the Power; Ssssss; Tomorrow's Child
Williams, Paul (act, b. 1940): Battle for the Planet of the Apes; The Loved One; The Muppet Movie; The Night They Saved Christmas; Phantom of the Paradise; Solar Crisis; Stone Cold Dead
Williams, Paul (mus, b. 1940): Agatha; The Muppet Movie; The Night They Saved Christmas; Phantom of the Paradise
Williams, Pega (act): Mad Max Beyond Thunderdome
Williams, Percy (act): London After Midnight; The Unholy Three (1925)
Williams, Peter (act): Footsteps In the Fog; Gammera vs. Viras; Richard III (1955); The Straw Man; Two Letter Alibi
Williams, Phaeder (act): Empire of Ash III
Williams, Philip (act): Clarence; Trilogy of Terror II
Williams, Polly (act): The Slipper and the Rose
Williams, R.J. (act): The Night They Saved Christmas
Williams, Rex (act): Above Suspicion
Williams, Rhoda (act): Cinderella (1950); Space Master X-7
Williams, Rhys (act, 1897-1969): The Black Shield of Falworth; Kiss Tomorrow Goodbye; Lightning Strikes Twice; Man In the Attic (1953); Midnight Lace (1960); Les Miserables (1952); Our Man Flint; Skullduggery; The Spiral Staircase (1946); Tyrant of the Sea
Williams, Richard (act): The Child and the Killer; The Final Conflict; Who Framed Roger Rabbit
Williams, Rick (mus): The Changeling
Williams, Robert (B.) (act): The Bat (1959); Boston Blackie Booked On Suspicion; Boston Blackie's Rendezvous; One Mysterious Night; Revenge of the Creature; The Unguarded Moment; The White Goddess
Williams, Robert H. (act): The Lone Wolf and His Lady
Williams, Robert (wri): Escape 2000
Williams, Robin (act, b. 1952, a.k.a. Ray D. Tutto): The Adventures of Baron Munchausen (1989); Aladdin (1992); Aladdin and the King of Thieves; Andrew Martin; Being Human; Dead Again; Ferngully: The Last Rain Forest; Flubber; Hamlet (1996); Hook; Jack; Jumanji; The Secret Agent (1996); What Dreams May Come
Williams, Roger (GB act):Meet Mr. Callaghan
Williams, Roger (USA act): The Clutching Hand
Williams, Rosemary (act): How to Stuff a Wild Bikini
Williams, Rush (act): The Curse of the Undead
Williams, Ryan (act): Tales from the Hood
Williams, Sam (act): Headhunter; King Solomon's Mines (1985); King Solomon's Treasure
Williams, Samm-Art (act): Blood Simple
Williams, Sammy (act): Demon (1976)
Williams, Samuel Ross (act): The Jewel of the Nile
Williams, Sharon (act): Don't Look Now
Williams, Simon (act): The Blood on Satan's Claw; The Fiendish Plot of Dr. Fu Manchu; Jabberwocky; The Prisoner of Zenda (1979); The Return of the Man from U.N.C.L.E.; The Uncanny
Williams Jr., Spencer (act & wri): Blood of Jesus; Son of Ingagi
Williams Jr., Spencer (dir): Blood of Jesus
Williams, Spice (act): The Guyver; Star Trek V: The Final Frontier; Uninvited (1987)
Williams, Stephanie (act): The Fan
Williams, Stephen (dir): Shadow Zone: The Undead Express
Williams, Steve "Spaz" (cin): Spawn
Williams, Steven (act): Deep Red (1994); House; Jason Goes to Hell: The Final Friday; Northstar; Twilight Zone
Williams, Sumner (act): On Dangerous Ground
Williams, Sundra Jean (act): Def by Temptation
Williams, Sylvia "Kuumba" (act): Mirrors; Obsession (1976); The Savage Bees
Williams, Tarah (act): Mad Max Beyond Thunderdome
Williams, Ted (act): The Wiz
Williams, Tennessee (wri, 1911-1983): Boom; The Fugitive Kind; Orpheus Descending; Suddenly Last Summer
Williams, Thomas (act): The Premonition (1975)
Williams, Tiger (act): Earthquake
Williams, Tony (act): Alien Warrior
Williams, Tony (dir & wri): Next of Kin
Williams, Treat (act, b. 1948): Dead Heat; Deep Rising; The Phantom (1996); Russicum
Williams, Trudel (act): Vamp
Williams, Van (act): The Caretakers; The Green Hornet
Williams, Vanessa (L.) (act, b. 1963): Candyman; Eraser; Futuresport; The Odyssey
Williams, Walter (act): La Decima Vittima; The Secret of Seagull Island; Top Secret (1978)
Williams, Wendy (act): Feet of Clay
Williams, Wilfred (E.) (act): Serial Mom; 12 Monkeys
Williams, William B. (cin): Deluge
Williams, Yolanda (act): RoboCop
Williams, Zach/Zack (act): Jungle Goddess; Son of Ingagi
Williamson, Alister (act): The Abominable Dr. Phibes; Evil of Frankenstein; Murder On the Midnight Express; The Oblong Box; The Return of Mr. Moto
Williamson, Cecil H. (dir & wri): Hi-Jack
Williamson, Cindy (act): Boarding House
Williamson, David (act): Moon 44
Williamson, Dean (act): Threads
Williamson, Don (act): Terror In the Wax Museum
Williamson, Florence (act): The Ayah's Revenge
Williamson, Fred (act, b. 1938): Deadly Intent; From Dusk Till Dawn; The New Gladiators; New York Ripper; Warriors of the Wasteland
Williamson, Jake (act): The Swan Princess: Escape from Castle Mountain
Williamson, James (dir): The Ayah's Revenge; The Brigand's Daughter; The Clown Barber; An Eclipse of the Moon; The Elixir of Life; An Evildoer's Sad End; Gabriel Grub the Surly Sexton; Harlequinade-What They Found In the Laundry Basket; An Interesting Story; The Little Match Seller; The Magic Extinguisher; The Marvellous Hair Restorer; The Professor's Great Discovery; The Puzzled Bather and His Animated Clothes; Remorse; Saved by a Dream (1909); The Tower of London (1909)
Williamson, Jo (act): Terror In the Wax Museum
Williamson, Kevin (act, b. 1965): Scream 2
Williamson, Kevin (dir, b. 1965): Killing Mrs. Tingle
Williamson, Kevin (wri, b. 1965): The Faculty; I Know What You Did Last Summer; Killing Mrs. Tingle; Scream; Scream 2
Williamson, Laird (act): Tarantulas: The Deadly Cargo
Williamson, Lambert (mus): The Adding Machine
Williamson, Malcolm (mus): Crescendo; Nothing But the Night; Watership Down
Williamson, Mykel T./Mykelti (act, b. 1960): The First Power; Miracle Mile; Species II; Streets of Fire
Williamson, Nicol (act, b. 1939): Black Widow (1987); Excalibur; The Exorcist III; Hamlet (1969); Inadmissable Evidence; The Jerusalem File; Return to Oz; Robin and Marian; The Seven-Per-Cent Solution; Spawn; Venom (1982)
Williamson, Paul (act): Return to Sender; Venom (1982)
Williamson, Simon (act): Return of the Jedi
Williamson, Tony (wri): Night Watch (1973)
Willie Tee & The Wild Magnolias (act & mus): Mirrors
Willims, Allen (act): The Two Worlds of Jennie Logan
Willing, George (act): The Count of Monte Cristo (1975)
Willing, Nick (dir): Alice In Wonderland (1999)
Willingham, Dale (act): Frogs
Willingham, Ken (act): Cavegirl (1985)
Willingham, Noble (act): Fire In the Sky (1993); The Howling; Of Mice and Men (1992); Where Have All the People Gone?
Willis, Miss (act): Black Peter
Willis, Austin (act): Death Takes a Holiday (1971); Goldfinger; I Aim at the Stars; The Mouse That Roared
Willis, Bruce (act, b. 1955): Armageddon; Color of Night; Death Becomes Her; The Fifth Element; Mortal Thoughts; 12 Monkeys
Willis, Cooper (act): The Mystery of Edwin Drood (1909)
Willis, Donald (act): The Hidden; The Incredible Hulk Returns
Willis, F. McGrew (wri): The Man In the Mirror; Premiere
Willis, Gary (act): The House of the Dead
Willis, Gordon (cin): Malice; The Purple Rose of Cairo; Windows
Willis, Gordon (dir): Windows
Willis, Horton (act): The Dark (1979)
Willis, Hubert (act): The Abbey Grange; Altar Chains; The Beryl Coronet (1921); Black Peter; The Boscombe Valley Mystery (1922); The Bruce Partington Plans; A Case of Identity; Charles Augustus Milverton; The Copper Beeches (1921); The Devil's Foot; The Dying Detective; The Empty House; The Golden Pince-Nez; The Greek Interpreter; The Hound of the Baskervilles (1921); The King's Daughter; Lady Audley's Secret (1920); The Lion's Cubs; The Man In Motley; The Man In the Attic (1915); The Man Without a Soul; The Man With the Twisted Lip (1921); A Message from Mars (1913); The Musgrave Ritual (1922); The Naval Treaty; The Noble Bachelor; The Norwood Builder; The Priory School; The Red Circle (1922); The Red-Headed League; The Reigate Squires (1922); The Resident Patient; A Scandal In Bohemia; The Second Stain; The Six Napoleons; The Solitary Cyclist; The Stockbroker's Clerk; The Tiger of San Pedro; Yellow Face
Willis, Mrs. (Hubert) (act): Black Peter
Willis, Jack (act): I Come In Peace
Willis, Jack (cin): Siege of the Saxons
Willis, Jerome (act): Lifeforce; The Magus; Siege of the Saxons; Yellow Dog
Willis, Lee (wri): Woman Who Came Back
Willis, Marlene (act): Attack of the Puppet People
Willis, Matt (act): Blonde Savage; Invisible Agent; The Mysterious Doctor; The Return of the Vampire; Saboteur
Willis, Norman (act): The Falcon Out West; The Living Ghost (1942); Voodoo Woman
Willis, Penelope (act): Mind Over Murder
Willis, Ronnie (act): Strange Days
Willis, Stanley (dir): The Haunted Man
Willis, Suzanna (act): The Monster Club
Willis, Ted (wri): Burnt Evidence; The Large Rope; No Trees In the Street
Willis, W.G. (wri): Jane Shore (1915)
Willis-Burch, Sherry (act): Final Exam; Killer Party
Willit, E. Hunter (wri): Psych-Out
Willits, Adam (act): Mad Max Beyond Thunderdome
Willits, Daniel (act): Mad Max Beyond Thunderdome
Willm, Pierre-Richard (act): The Count of Monte Cristo (1955)
Willman, Noel (act, 1918-1988): Across the Bridge; Androcles and the Lion; The Criminal; Kiss of the Vampire; The Man Who Knew Too Much (1956); The Net; Never Let Go; The Reptile; The Vengeance of She
Willmas, James (act): Beware, My Lovely
Willmer, Catherine (act): The Devils; An Inspector Calls; Madhouse
Willock, Dave (act): The Barefoot Executive; Hush...Hush, Sweet Charlotte; It Came from Outer Space; Now You See Him, Now You Don't; Queen of Outer Space; Revenge of the Creature; Spellbound (1945); What Ever Happened to Baby Jane? (1962)
Willock, Margaret (act): The Strange and Deadly Occurrence
Willoughby, Anna (act): Macbeth (1971)
Willoughby, George (act): Valley of the Eagles
Willoughby, Leueen (act): The Final Conflict; Superman (1978); Superman II
Willoughby, Lewis (act): Bluff; Trapped by the Mormons
Willoughby, Lewis (dir): The Secret of the Moor
Willows, Alec (act): Gotham
Willrich, Randolph (act): Alice, Sweet Alice; Doctor Franken
Wills, Annika (act): Candidate for Murder
Wills, Chill (act, 1902-1978): Francis Joins the WACs; Leave Her to Heaven; Sky Murder; Tarzan's New York Adventure

Wills, Drusilla (act): *The Black Abbot (1934); The Lodger (1932); Night Club Queen*
Wills, Henry (act): *Beyond the Poseidon Adventure; Night of the Lepus*
Wills, Sherrie (act): *The Exorcist III*
Wills, Terry (act): *Deadly Messages; Once Bitten*
Willson, Gwen (act): *Black Magic Woman*
Willson, Paul (act): *The Devonsville Terror; My Best Friend Is a Vampire; 976-EVIL; The Pack; Shadow of Death (1983)*
Wilmer, Catherine (act): *Game for Three Losers*
Wilmer, Douglas (act, b. 1920): *The Adventures of Sherlock Holmes' Smarter Brother; The Brides of Fu Manchu; The Golden Voyage of Sinbad; Hammerhead; Jason and the Argonauts; Men of Sherwood Forest; Octopussy; Passport to Treason; Richard III (1955); Sword of the Valiant; The Vampire Lovers; The Vengeance of Fu Manchu*
Wilmer, Geoffrey (act): *The Cry for Justice; The Musgrave Ritual (1922)*
Wilmore, Duncan (act): *Project X (1987); WarGames*
Wilmot, David (act): *The Tale of Sweeney Todd*
Wilmot, Gerry (act): *Candles at Nine*
Wilmot, Ivan (act): *Dial 999; Passenger to London; Twin Faces*
Wilmot, Ronan (act): *Rawhead Rex*
Wilms, Andre (act): *Torment (1993)*
Wilms, Dominique (act): *Les Femmes s'en Balancent; La Mome Vert-de-Gris*
Wilner, Ann (act): *Bride of the Monster*
Wilsey, Eric (act): *Fire In the Sky (1993)*
Wilsey, Pamela (act): *Contact*
Wilsey, Shannon (act): *The Invisible Maniac*
Wilshin, Sunday (act): *Champagne; Collision; Hutch Stirs 'em Up; Murder by Rope*
Wilson, Ajita (act): *Savage Island*
Wilson, Albert (cin): *The Lone Wolf (1924)*
Wilson, Andy (act): *2000 Maniacs*
Wilson, Anthony (wri): *Final Eye; Future Cop; The Night That Panicked America*
Wilson, Barbara (Euro act): *The Murder Clinic; Rymdinvasion i Lappland*
Wilson, Barbara (USA act): *Blood of Dracula; The Man Who Turned to Stone*
Wilson, Barry M. (cin): *Twice Upon a Time*
Wilson, Brad (act): *Grotesque*
Wilson, Brian (act): *How to Stuff a Wild Bikini*
Wilson, Bridgette (act): *I Know What You Did last Summer; Mortal Kombat; Sweet Evil; Virtual Obsession*
Wilson, Cal (act): *Battle for the Planet of the Apes*
Wilson, Candy (act): *The Sin of Adam and Eve*
Wilson, Carey (wri): *Gabriel Over the White House; He Who Gets Slapped; Murder at the Vanities; The Private Life of Helen of Troy*
Wilson, Charles (act): *The Adventurous Blonde; Blonde for a Day; The Dragon Murder Case; Dressed to Kill (1941); Four Hours to Kill; The Kennel Murder Case; Larceny In Her Heart; The Return of Dr. X; Satan Met a Lady; Shadows In the Night*
Wilson, Cheryl (act): *Unforgettable*
Wilson, Cheryl-Ann (act): *Cellar Dweller*
Wilson, Christopher (act): *No Blade of Grass*
Wilson, Clarence (H.) (act): *One Frightened Night; The Penguin Pool Murder; Son of Kong; The Westland Case*
Wilson, Colin (wri): *Lifeforce*
Wilson, Corey (act): *The Fear (1994)*
Wilson, Cynthia Ann (act): *Ed Wood*
Wilson, Cynthia-Gail (act): *Deadly Messages*
Wilson, Dale (act): *Doomsday Rock; I Still Dream of Jeannie; The Stepfather; Watchers*
Wilson, Dana (act): *Wild Women*
Wilson, David (act): *Gray Lady Down*
Wilson, Demond (act, b. 1946): *Full Moon High*
Wilson, Dennis (mus): *The Accursed*
Wilson, Dick (act): *Diary of a Madman*
Wilson, Don (Can act): *Empire of Ash III*
Wilson, Don (USA act, b. 1901): *The Chase; Niagara*
Wilson, Don "The Dragon" (act): *Cyber-Tracker; Cybertracker 2; Futurekick; Night Hunter; Virtual Combat*
Wilson, Donald (wri): *The Keeper; Three Cases of Murder*
Wilson, Donald B. (wri): *Under the Frozen Falls*
Wilson, Dorothy (act): *Before Dawn; The Last Days of Pompeii (1935)*
Wilson, Elizabeth (GB act): *The Man from Scotland Yard*
Wilson, Elizabeth (USA act): *The Addams Family; The Believers; The Birds; The Day of the Dolphin; The Incredible Shrinking Woman; Man On a Swing; Raw Wind In Eden; Sanctuary of Fear*
Wilson, Eric (act): *Appointment With Murder; Counter-Espionage; The Docks of New Orleans*
Wilson, F. Paul (wri): *The Keep*
Wilson, F. Stewart (act): *Invasion of the Bee Girls*
Wilson, Flip (act, 1933-1998): *Pinocchio (1976)*
Wilson, Frank (Austral act): *Patrick*
Wilson, Frank (GB act): *Cinderella (1907); Face to Face; Faust (1911); His Evil Genius*
Wilson, Frank (USA act): *Green Pastures*
Wilson, Frank (dir): *Behind the Curtain; Bertie's Book of Magic; Billiard's Mad; The Breaking Point (1914); The Bridge Destroyer; The Bronze Idol; The Coiner's Den; The Confession (1915); Creatures of Clay; The Cry of the Captive; A Deal With the Devil; Dr. Fenton's Ordeal; Dr. Trimball's Verdict; Face to Face; A Grain of Sand; The Grand Babylon Hotel; The Grip of Ambition; The Guest of the Evening; The Heat Wave (1911); Held for Ransom; His Evil Genius; The House Opposite (1917); How Billy Kept His Word; The Hunchback (1914); The Incorruptible Crown; In the Shadow of Big Ben; The Jewel Thieves Outwitted; Justice; The Lunatics at Liberty; A Lunatic Expected; The Man Behind "The Times"; A Man of Mystery; The Man With the Scar; A New Aladdin; The Night Bell; The Nightbirds of London; The Postman (1910); A Present from India; The Prodigal's Return; Retribution (1913); The Schemers: or, The Jewels of Hate; A Silent Witness (1913); Something Like a Bag; The Terror of the Air; A Touch of Hydrophobia; The Tragedy of Basil Grieve; The Unseen Witness; Winning His Stripes*
Wilson, Frank (wri): *Under the Frozen Falls*
Wilson, Gene (act): *The Resurrection of Zachary Wheeler*
Wilson, George (Euro act): *C'era una Volta; The Conspiracy of Torture*
Wilson, George (USA act): *Attack of the Killer Tomatoes*
Wilson, Gerald (wri): *Firepower*
Wilson, Glenni (act): *I Was a Zombie for the F.B.I.*
Wilson Jr., Gordon (wri): *La Danza Macabra; Horror*
Wilson, Gwenda (act): *Dangerous Afternoon*
Wilson, Harry (act): *Frankenstein's Daughter (1958)*
Wilson, Henry (act): *The Sign of Four (1923)*
Wilson, Howard (act): *The Lost Patrol (1934); Think Fast, Mr. Moto*
Wilson, Ian (act): *The Day of the Triffids; How to Murder a Rich Uncle; The Phantom of the Opera (1962); The Unholy Quest; The Wicker Man*
Wilson, Ian (cin): *Captain Kronos: Vampire Hunter; Erik the Viking; Fright (1971); Gawain and the Green Knight; The House In Nightmare Park; The Quatermass Conclusion*
Wilson, J. Donald (wri): *The Whistler*
Wilson, Jack (act): *Single White Female*
Wilson, James (cin): *Invasion (1965)*
Wilson, James L. (dir): *Screams of a Winter Night*
Wilson, Janis (act): *The Strange Love of Martha Ivers*
Wilson, Jeannie (act): *The Devil and Max Devlin*
Wilson, Jim (act): *Jaws 2*
Wilson, John (wri): *Look What's Happened to Rosemary's Baby*
Wilson, Joi (act): *Creepozoids*
Wilson, Josephine (act): *The Dark Tower (1943)*
Wilson, Kara (act): *Jane Eyre (1970)*
Wilson, Kathy (act): *Jaws 2*
Wilson, Kristin (act): *Dr. Dolittle (1998)*
Wilson, Lambert (act, b. 1959): *Frankenstein (1993)*
Wilson, Larry (wri): *The Addams Family; Beetlejuice*
Wilson, Lenny (act): *Primal Fear*
Wilson, Lewis (act): *A Place to Die; Wild Women*
Wilson, Lisa (act): *The Unnamable*
Wilson, Lisle (act): *The Incredible Melting Man*
Wilson, Lois (act, 1894-1988): *Alias the Lone Wolf; Bella Donna (1923); Deluge; The Dumb Girl of Portici*
Wilson, Lynn (act): *Happy Birthday to Me*
Wilson, Mak (act): *Little Shop of Horrors (1986); Return to Oz*
Wilson, Manning (act): *The Hands of Orlac (1959); The Set-Up (1963); Tales from the Crypt (1971)*
Wilson, Mara (act, b. 1987): *Miracle on 34th Street (1994); A Simple Wish*
Wilson, Marie (act, 1916-1972, nee Kathleen Elizabeth White): *Babes In Toyland (1934); Fabulous Joe; Flying Blind; The Invisible Menace; Satan Met a Lady; The Story of Mankind*
Wilson, Mark Bryan (act): *The Nutty Professor (1996)*
Wilson, Maurice J. (wri): *Clash by Night; Guilty?; Jackpot; The House On Marsh Road; Master Spy (1963); The Price of Silence; The Third Alibi; Who Killed the Cat?*
Wilson, Michael (act): *The Monsters Christmas*
Wilson, Michael (G.) (wri, 1914-1978): *5 Fingers; For Your Eyes Only; It's a Wonderful Life; Licence to Kill (1989); The Living Daylights; Octopussy; Planet of the Apes; A View to a Kill*
Wilson, Michele (act): *Appointment for a Killing*
Wilson, Neil (act): *A Clockwork Orange; Dr. Jekyll and Sister Hyde; The Lady Killers (1956)*
Wilson, Norm (act): *They Live*
Wilson, O.D. (act): *Cyborg (1989)*
Wilson, Owen (act): *Anaconda*
Wilson, Patricia (act): *Demon Seed; The Nutty Professor (1996); Stranger In Our House*
Wilson, Paul (act): *Terror In the Wax Museum*
Wilson, Paul (cin): *For Your Eyes Only*
Wilson, Ralph (act): *It Happened Here*
Wilson, Reagan (act): *Blood Mania*
Wilson, Rex (dir): *Ora Pro Nobis; St. Elmo*
Wilson, Rex (wri): *St. Elmo*
Wilson, Richard (act): *Gulliver's Travels (1996); Koroshi; Professor Potter's Magic Potions*
Wilson, Richard (dir & wri, b. 1915): *Raw Wind In Eden*
Wilson, Rick (act): *Beyond the Poseidon Adventure*
Wilson, Rita (act): *The Day It Came to Earth*
Wilson, Robert Brian (act): *Silent Night, Deadly Night*
Wilson, Rod (act): *Darkman II: The Return of Durant*
Wilson, Ronald (act): *Quatermass II*
Wilson, Ross (mus): *20th Century Oz*
Wilson, Roy Alan (act): *The Outing*
Wilson, S.S. (dir): *Tremors 2: Aftershocks*
Wilson, S.S. (wri): **Batteries Not Included; Ghost Dad; Heart and Souls; Short Circuit; Short Circuit 2; Tremors; Tremors 2: Aftershocks*
Wilson, Scott (act, b. 1942): *Castle Keep; The Exorcist III; Twinkle, Twinkle, Killer Kane*
Wilson, Serretta (act): *Psychomania (1972); Tower of Evil*
Wilson, Sheree J. (act): *Hellbound; Past Tense*
Wilson, Stanley (mus): *Dark Intruder; Daughter of the Jungle; Missile Monsters; Satan's Satellites*
Wilson, Stuart (act): *Crossworlds; Exit to Eden; No Escape (1994); The Prisoner of Zenda (1979)*
Wilson, Sue (act): *Creatures the World Forgot*
Wilson, Terry (act): *Westworld*
Wilson, Theodore (act, 1944-1991): *Maid to Order*
Wilson, Thick (act): *The Dark Crystal; The Mirror Crack'd*
Wilson, Thomas F./Tom (act): *April Fool's Day; Back to the Future; Back to the Future, Part II; Back to the Future, Part III; National Lampoon's 'Men In White'*
Wilson, Tom (act): *Secrets of the Night*
Wilson, Trey (act, 1948-1989): *Twins; The Vampire Girls*
Wilson, W. Cronin (act): *Red Aces; The Squeaker (1930)*
Wilson, Warren (wri): *Hellzapoppin*
Wilson, Zoey (act): *The Handmaid's Tale*
Wilson-White, Lance (act): *Tidal Wave: No Escape*
Wilson-Wilson, Beverly (act): *The Outing*
Wilton, Ann(e) (act): *Dead Men Tell No Tales (1938); Fanny by Gaslight; Richard III (1955)*
Wilton, Eric (act): *After the Thin Man; Meet Nero Wolfe; Mr. Moto's Last Warning*
Wilton, Penelope (act): *The Borrowers (1993)*
Wilton, Robb (act): *The Silent Passenger*
Wilton, Robert (act): *The Secret of the Loch (1934)*
Wiltrup, Aage (cin): *Journey to the Seventh Planet; Reptilicus*
Wiltse, David (wri): *Revenge of the Stepford Wives*
Wiltshear, Ed (act): *Starship Invasions*
Wiltshire, Maurice (wri): *My Brother's Keeper*
Wiltshire, Richard (act): *Child of Darkness, Child ofLight; The Haunting of Sarah Hardy*
Wiltsie, Melissa (act): *Hawk the Slayer; Little Shop ofHorrors (1986); Superman II*
Wilz, Walter (act): *The Secret Ways*
Wiman, Dwight (act): *Puritan Passions*
Wimbury, David (wri): *Prey (1978)*
Wimbush, Mary (act): *Fragment of Fear; Vampire Circus*
Wimby, Julius (act): *Scalpel*
Wimmer, Brian (act): *Blue Flame; Late for Dinner; The Maddening; Tank Girl*
Wimmer, Kurt (wri): *The Neighbor; Relative Fear; Sphere*
Wimperis, Arthur (wri, 1874-1953): *Calling Bulldog Drummond; Dark Journey; The Drum; Knight Without Armour; The Man They Could Not Arrest; Q Planes; The Return of the Scarlet Pimpernel; The Scarlet Pimpernel (1934); Under the Red Robe (1937)*
Wimpy, Rex(ford) (cin): *Devotion; The Reluctant Astronaut*
Winans, Del (act): *Fiend (1980)*
Winans, Sam (mus): *Doomsday Rock; Ghost Writer; I Was a Teenage Sex Mutant*
Winarsky, Jan (act): *Echoes*
Winburn, James R. (dir): *Evil Altar*
Winburn, Jim (act): *Charlie Chan and the Curse of the Dragon Queen*
Winbush, Camille (act): *Eraser*
Winbush, Leroy (act): *Bog*
Wincelberg, Simon (wri): *On the Threshold of Space*
Wincenty, Richard (cin): *The Cyber-Stalking*
Wincer, Simon (dir): *D.A.R.Y.L.; The Day After Halloween; The Phantom (1996)*
Winch, Barry (act): *Tommy*
Winch, Evelyn (wri): *The Girl In the Flat*
Winch, Reginald/Reggie (act): *The Man from Nowhere; Sammy's Super T-Shirt*
Winchell, Gerald (cin): *Bog*
Winchell, Paul (act): *The Aristocats; The Fox and the Hound*
Winchell, Walter (act, 1897-1972): *Wild In the Streets*
Winchester, Anna-Maria (act): *The Chain Reaction (1980)*
Winchester, Edie (act): *Secrets of the Phantom Caverns*
Winchester, Maud (act): *Bram Stoker's 'Dracula'*
Winchester, Stephanic (act): *Secrets of the Phantom Caverns*
Winckler, Robert (act): *Mr. Moto Takes a Vacation*
Wincott, Geoffrey (act): *Dick Barton, Special Agent*
Wincott, Jeff (act): *Prom Night*
Wincott, Michael (act): *An American Christmas Carol; The Crow (1994); Curtains; Robin Hood: Prince of Thieves; Romeo Is Bleeding; Strange Days; The Three Musketeers (1993)*
Windburn, Jim (act): *Halloween*
Winder, Michael (wri): *Welcome to Blood City*
Windermere, Fred (dir): *The Taxi Mystery*
Windheim, Marek (act): *Charlie Chan In City In Darkness; The Lone Wolf Spy Hunt*
Winding, Andrea (cin): *Le Trio Infernal*
Winding, Victor (act): *Frightmare (1974); House of Mortal Sin; The Medusa Touch; Schizo (1977)*
Windmill Girls, The (act): *Murder at the Windmill*
Windom, Stephen (cin): *The Postman (1997)*
Windom, William (act, b. 1923): *Attack of the 50-Foot Woman (1993); Children of the Corn IV; Committed; Escape; Escape from the Planet of the Apes; The Mephisto Waltz; Now You See Him, Now You Don't; Pinocchio and the Emperor of the Night; Pursuit (1972); Space Rage; A Taste of Evil*
Windon, Stephen (cin): *The Postman (1997)*
Windsor, Allen (act): *The Incredible Petrified World*
Windsor, Barbara (act, b. 1937): *Carry On Spying; Chitty Chitty Bang Bang; Death Trap (1962); A Study In Terror; Too Hot to Handle*
Windsor, Chris (dir): *Big Meat Eater*
Windsor, Claire (act, 1897-1972): *Rupert of Hentzau (1923)*
Windsor, Frank (act): *Assassin (1973); The London Connection; Who Is Killing the Great Chefs of Europe?*
Windsor, Marie (act, b. 1924, nee Emily Marie Bertelson): *Abbott and Costello Meet the Mummy; Cat-Women of the Moon; Chamber of Horrors (1966); The Day Mars Invaded Earth; Freaky Friday (1976); The Girl In Black Stockings; Hurricane Island; Island Women; Joe & the Colonel; The Jungle; The Killing; The Narrow Margin (1952); Salem's Lot; The Sniper; Song of the Thin Man; The Story of Mankind; Swamp Women*
Windsor, Romy (act): *The House of Usher (1988); Howling IV*
Windsor, Tammy (act): *The Little Shop of Horrors (1960)*

Windsor, Tod (act): *Sergeant Deadhead the Astronut!*

Windtree, Daniel (act): *The People Under the Stairs*

Windust, Penelope (act): *Ghost Town; Tarantulas: The Deadly Cargo; V*

Winer, Harry (dir): *Spacecamp*

Winer, Richard (dir & wri): *Devil's Triangle*

Wines, Carol (act): *Kismet (1930)*

Winfield, Dave (act): *The Last Home Run*

Winfield, Gilbert (act): *Fiend Without a Face; On the Run (1958)*

Winfield, Paul (act, b. 1941): *Damnation Alley; The Horror at 37,000 Feet; Mars Attacks!; The Serpent and the Rainbow; Star Trek II: The Wrath of Khan; The Terminator; Twilight's Last Gleaming; White Dog; White Dwarf*

Winford, Mary (act): *The Crater Lake Monster*

Winfrey, Jonathan (dir): *Black Scorpion (1995)*

Winfrey, Oprah (act, b. 1954): *Beloved*

Wing, Anna (act): *Full Circle; The Godsend; The Hound Of The Baskervilles (1978); The Witches and the Grinnygog; Xtro*

Wing, Lara (act): *Shanks*

Wing, Leslie (act): *Asteroid; The Dungeonmaster; The Frighteners; Ghost Warrior; Retribution (1988)*

Wing, Virginia (act): *Jekyll and Hyde...Together Again*

Wing, Ward (act): *The Conquering Power*

Wing, William E. (wri): *Tarzan and the Golden Lion*

Wing, Mrs. Wong (act): *Mr. Wu (1927)*

Wingard, Tim (act): *The Offspring*

Wingate, Eugenie (act): *Scream, Baby, Scream*

Winger, Debra (act, b. 1955): *Black Widow (1987); Made In Heaven; Wilder Napalm*

Wingert, Sally (act): *Fargo*

Wingreen, Jason (act): *The Dunwich Horror; The Man With the Power; Oh, God! You Devil; The Terminal Man*

Wingren, Cliff (cin): *Grave of the Vampire*

Wingrove, Ian (cin): *At the Earth's Core; Edge of Sanity; The People That Time Forgot; Return to Oz*

Wingrove, James (act): *Mad Max Beyond Thunderdome*

Wings (cin): *Bog*

Wings (mus): *Live and Let Die; Oh Heavenly Dog*

Winham, Francine (dir): *Rapunzel Let Down Your Hair*

Winick, Gary (dir): *Curfew*

Winkelspecht, Micah (act): *Addams Family Values; Casper*

Winker, James R. (act): *Witches' Brew*

Winkler, Bill (act): *The Fear (1994)*

Winkler, Charles (dir): *Disturbed*

Winkler, Gary (act): *Deathline*

Winkler, Henry (act, b. 1945): *An American Christmas Carol*

Winkler, Mel (act): *Full Eclipse*

Winkler, Suzanne (act): *Deathline*

Winkless, Jeff (act): *The Nest*

Winkless, Terence H. (dir): *The Berlin Conspiracy; The Nest*

Winkless, Terence H. (wri): *The Howling*

Winley, Robert (act): *I Saw What You Did (1988)*

Winmill, Sammie (act): *The Pied Piper (1971)*

Winn, Claude (act): *Detective Daring and the Thames Coiners*

Winn, Godfrey (act): *Eyewitness (1956)*

Winn, Kitty (act, b. 1944): *The Exorcist; Exorcist II: The Heretic; The House That Wouldn't Die; Mirrors; They Might Be Giants*

Winn, Stanley W. (act): *The Premonition (1975)*

Winne, Robert (act): see Hutton, Robert

Winner, Howard (cin): *Birds Do It*

Winner, Jeffrey (act): *Alice In Wonderland (1985)*

Winner, Michael (dir, b. 1936): *The Big Sleep (1978); Firepower; The Nightcomers; Out of the Shadow; Scorpio; Scream for Help; The Sentinel; Shoot to Kill (1961); West 11; The Wicked Lady*

Winner, Michael (wri, b. 1936): *The Beast Must Die; The Big Sleep (1978); The Sentinel; Shoot to Kill (1961)*

Winner, Vic (act): *Gran Amore del Conde Drácula; Horror Rises from the Tomb; El Jorobado de la Morgue; Vengeance of the Zombies*

Winnicka, Lucina (act): *Matka Joanna od Aniolow; Milczaca Gwiazda*

Winnicki, Joanna (act): see Lucy...

Winning, David (dir): *Turbo: A Power Rangers Movie*

Winninger, Charles (act, 1884-1969): *Beyond Tomorrow; Flesh and Fantasy; Night Nurse*

Winningham, Mare (act): *Made In Heaven; Miracle Mile*

Winslet, Kate (act, b. 1975): *Hamlet (1996); A Kid In King Arthur's Court*

Winslow, Bonnie (act): *Just Imagine*

Winslow, Dick (act): *Francis In the Haunted House*

Winslow, Dicky (dir): *The Assassination of the King and Queen of Servia; The Corsican Brothers (1902); Little Jim: or, The Cottage Was a Thatched One; Maria Martin: or, The Murder at the Red Barn*

Winslow, Dicky (wri): *The Corsican Brothers (1902); Little Jim: or, The Cottage Was a Thatched One; Maria Martin: or, The Murder at the Red Barn*

Winslow, George "Foghorn" (act, b. 1946, nee George Wenzlaff): *Monkey Business; Rocket Man (1954)*

Winslow, Michael (act): *TAG: The Assassination Game*

Winslow, Moira (act): *The Demon (1981)*

Winslowe, Dick (act): *Embryo*

Winslowe, Paula (act): *Bambi*

Winsor, Lisa (act): *Mutants In Paradise*

Winston, Bruce (act): *Alf's Button (1930); Alf's Button Afloat; Latin Quarter; The Thief of Bagdad (1940)*

Winston, Chuck (act): *The Silencers (1995)*

Winston, Colleen (act): *Watchers*

Winston, Helen(e) (act): *A Boy and His Dog; The Brotherhood of Satan; Heavy Traffic; Port Sinister; The Shaggy D.A.; Tobor the Great; What's the Matter With Helen?; The Witchmaker*

Winston, Irene (act): *Rear Window (1954)*

Winston, Janelle (act): *Maniac (1980)*

Winston, Jimmy (act): *No Blade of Grass*

Winston, Matt (act): *Wes Craven's New Nightmare*

Winston, Norman (act): *This Is Not a Test*

Winston, Raymond (act): *War of the Colossal Beast*

Winston, Richard (act): *Princess Warrior*

Winston, Robert (act): *The Horror from Beyond*

Winston, Stan (dir): *A Gnome Named Gnorm; Pumpkinhead*

Winston, Stan (wri): *Pumpkinhead*

Winston, Steve (act): *The Falcon Out West*

Winter, Alex(ander) (act): *Bill & Ted's Bogus Journey; Bill & Ted's Excellent Adventure; Haunted Summer; The Lost Boys*

Winter, Alex (dir & wri): *Freaked*

Winter, A'Ryen (act): *Boarding House*

Winter, Bootles (act): *Beautiful Jim*

Winter, Cherry (act): *The Shadow Between*

Winter, Donna (act): *The Toxic Avenger*

Winter, Donovan (act): *The Awakening Hour*

Winter, Donovan (dir): *The Awakening Hour; The Deadly Females; Give Us Tomorrow; The Trunk*

Winter, Donovan (wri): *The Awakening; Bullet from the Past; The Deadly Females; Give Us Tomorrow; The Trunk*

Winter, Edgar (mus): *Netherworld*

Winter, Heinz (act): *The Fifth Musketeer*

Winter, Jessie (act): *Murder In the Family*

Winter, John Strange (wri): *Beautiful Jim; Grip (1915)*

Winter, Keith (wri): *Above Suspicion; Devotion*

Winter, Lex (act): *The Vampire Girls*

Winter, Marion (act): *Superwheels*

Winter, Pauline (act): *The Ipcress File*

Winter, Phillip (act): *Rebecca*

Winter, Vincent (act, b. 1947): *Beyond This Place; Gorgo; The Three Lives of Thomasina*

Winter-Blossom (act): *The Thief of Bagdad (1924)*

Wintergate, John (dir): *Boarding House*

Wintermaier, Monic (act): *Making Contact*

Winterman, Frank (act): *Grave of the Vampire*

Winters, Anthony (act): *Gremlins 2: The New Batch*

Winters, Bernie (act): *Dollars for Sale*

Winters, D.D. (act): *Tanya's Island; Terror Train*

Winters, David (dir): *The Last Horror Film; Space Mutiny*

Winters, Deborah (act): *Blue Sunshine; The Outing; Tarantulas: The Deadly Cargo*

Winters, Holle K. (act): *Motor Psycho*

Winters, Jonathan (act, b. 1925): *Alakazam the Great; Alice In Wonderland (1985); The Flintstones; The Loved One; Oh Dad Poor Dad, Mamma's Hung You In the Closet and I'm Feelin' So Sad; The Shadow (1994)*

Winters, Kristoffer Ryan (act): *Contact*

Winters, Leslie (act): *The Mysterious Dr. Fu Manchu; Seven Footprints to Satan*

Winters, Loren (act): *Freeway Maniac*

Winters, Michael (act): *Pandora's Clock*

Winters, Nathan Forrest (act): *Clownhouse*

Winters, Patricia (act): *Cocoon: The Return*

Winters, Paul (dir): *Freeway Maniac*

Winters, Peter M. (wri): *Salome (1922)*

Winters, Roland (act, 1904-1989): *Abbott and Costello Meet the Killer; Between Midnight and Dawn; The Chinese Ring; The Docks of New Orleans; Everything's Ducky; The Feathered Serpent (1948); The Golden Eye; Miracle On 34th Street (1973); The Return of October; The Shanghai Chest; The Sky Dragon*

Winters, Shelley (act, b. 1922, nee Shirley Schrift): *The Adventures of Nick Carter; Alice In Wonderland (1985); The Balcony; City On Fire; Deja Vu; The Devil's Daughter (1972); A Double Life (1947); The Initiation of Sarah; Journey Into Fear (1975); Larceny; The Mad Room; Mrs. Munck; The Night of the Hunter (1955); Pete's Dragon; The Poseidon Adventure; Purple People Eater; Revenge (1971, USA); The Silence of the Hams; Something to Hide; Take One False Step; The Tenant; Tentacles; A Thousand and One Nights (1945); The Visitor; What's the Matter With Helen?; Who Slew Auntie Roo?; Wild In the Streets; Woman of Terror*

Winters, Stacy (act): *Raiders from Beneath the Sea*

Winters, Time (act): *The Adventures of Galgameth; Disaster In Time; Gremlins 2: The New Batch; Thinner*

Winters, Tony (act): *Virtuosity*

Wintersole, William (Richard) (act): *Coma; Seconds*

Winterstein, Richard (act): *Mind Over Murder*

Winther, Karen (act): *Haxan*

Winthrop, Christine (act): *Salome (1923)*

Winton, Colleen (act): *Watchers*

Winton, Jane (act): *The Bridge of San Luis Rey (1929); Don Juan (1927); In the Next Room; The Monkey Talks*

Winwood, Estelle (act, 1883-1984, nee Estelle Goodwin): *The Cabinet of Caligari; Camelot; Darby O'Gill and the Little People; Dead Ringer; Games; The Glass Slipper; The Magic Sword (1962); Murder by Death; 23 Paces to Baker Street*

Winz, Cher (mus): *Star Crash*

Wirag, James (wri): *The Psychotronic Man*

Wirries, Jim (act): *White of the Eye*

Wirth, Billy (act): *The Body Snatchers; The Final Mission; The Lost Boys; Space Marines; Venus Rising*

Wirth, Peter (act): *Mutants In Paradise*

Wirth, Sandra (act): *Missile to the Moon*

Wirtz, Aad (act): *The Falls*

Wisbar, Franck/Frank (dir & wri, 1899-1967): *Devil Bat's Daughter; Strangler of the Swamp*

Wisberg, Aubrey (wri, 1911-1990): *After Midnight With Boston Blackie; Captain Kidd and the Slave Girl; Captive Women; Counter-Espionage; I Diavoli della Spazio; The Falcon's Adventure; Hercules In New York; Just Before Dawn (1946); The Lady In the Iron Mask; The Man from Planet X; Mission Mars; The Neanderthal Man; Port Sinister; Return to Treasure Island; Son of Sinbad*

Wisberg, Claude (act): *The Adventures of Robin Hood; Torchy Runs for Mayor*

Wisch, Allen (act): *Trick or Treats*

Wischnewski, Siegfried (act): *The Nibelungs (1966)*

Wisden, Robert (act): *Circle of Deceit*

Wisden, Robert Charles (act): *Firebird 2015 A.D.*

Wise, Ashton (act): *Tales from the Darkside*

Wise, David (wri): *Beastmaster III: The Eye of Braxus*

Wise, Gary (act): *Fatal Exposure*

Wise, Greg (act, b. 1966): *House of Frankenstein 1997*

Wise, Herbert (dir): *To Have and To Hold*

Wise, Kirk (dir): *Beauty and the Beast (1991); The Hunchback of Notre Dame (1996)*

Wise, Michael (act): *The First Power*

Wise, Ray (act): *Cat People (1982); Condor; Endless Descent; Grey Knight; Powder; RoboCop; Sunstroke; Swamp Thing; Twin Peaks: Fire Walk With Me*

Wise, Robert (dir, b. 1914): *The Andromeda Strain; Audrey Rose; The Body Snatcher (1945); Born to Kill; Curse of the Cat People; The Day the Earth Stood Still; A Game of Death: The Haunting; Helen of Troy (1955); Mystery In Mexico; The Set-Up (1949); Star Trek*

Wiseman, Don (act): *The Bermuda Triangle; Red Alert*

Wiseman, Joseph (act, b. 1919): *Buck Rogers In the 25th Century; Dr. No; Journey Into Fear (1975); The Mask of Sheba; Les Miserables (1952); Pursuit (1972)*

Wiseman, Michael (act): *Spirit of the Night*

Wiser, Linda (act): *The Incredible Hulk, Part 2*

Wishart, Louis (act): *Inn of the Damned*

Wisher, William (wri): *Eaters of the Dead; Judge Dredd; Terminator 2: Judgment Day*

Wishman, Doris (dir): *Nude On the Moon*

Wisley, Michael (act): *Shadow of a Doubt (1991)*

Wisniewski, Andreas (act): *Gothic; The Living Daylights; Mission: Impossible*

Witham, Gene (act): *Grizzly; The Offspring*

Witherell, Joe (act): *Frightmare (1983)*

Withers, Googie (act, b. 1917): *Accused (1936); Bulldog Sees It Through; Busman's Honeymoon; Crime Over London; Dark World; Dead of Night (1945); Hamlet (1948); The Lady Vanishes (1938); Miranda; Port of Escape; Strange Boarders; They Came to a City*

Withers, Grant (act, 1904-1959): *Daughter of the Tong; Doomed to Die; Fair Wind to Java; The Fatal Hour (1940); Lady Godiva; Mr. Wong, Detective; Mr. Wong In Chinatown; The Mystery of Mr. Wong; Phantom of Chinatown; The Vampire's Ghost*

Withers, Isabel (act): *Possessed (1947)*

Withers, Jane (act): *Danger Street; Faces In the Fog*

Withers, Margaret (act): *City After Midnight; The Flying Scot; Murder On Monday*

Witherspoon, Cora (act, 1890-1957): *Charlie Chan's Murder Cruise; Marie Antoinette (1938)*

Witherspoon, Dane (act): *Asteroid; Seedpeople*

Witherspoon, John (act): *Killer Tomatoes Strike Back; Vampire In Brooklyn*

Witherspoon, Reese (act, b. 1976): *Fear (1996); Freeway; Pleasantville*

Withrow, Glenn (act): *Nightflyers; Sweet Sixteen*

Witken, Jacof (act): *Children of the Full Moon*

Witker, Kristi (act): *Gremlins 2: The New Batch*

Witkiewicz, Stanislaw (wri): *In an Old Manor House*

Witkin, Jacob (act): *Arabian Adventure; Matinee*

Witkin, Stephen (wri): *Lovestruck*

Witney, Michael (act, 1931-1983): *W*

Witney, William (dir, b. 1915): *The Adventures of Captain Marvel; The Bonnie Parker Story; Cyclotrode X; Dick Tracy Returns; Dick Tracy's G-Men; Dick Tracy vs. Crime, Inc.; Doctor Satan's Robot; Drums of Fu Manchu; I Escaped from Devil's Island; Lost Island of Kioga; Master of the World; Nyoka and the Lost Secrets of Hippocrates; Spy Smasher Returns; The Torpedo of Doom*

Witschge, Cor (act): *The Lift*

Witt, Alicia (act): *Fun; Urban Legend*

Witt, Alicia Roanne (act): *Dune; Urban Legend*

Witt, Dan (act): *Oh Heavenly Dog*

Witt, Eileen (act): *Asteroid*

Witt, Howard (act): *Bride of Boogedy; Revenge of the Stepford Wives*

Witt, Kathryn (act): *Demon of Paradise; Looker*

Witt, Michael (act): *Earthbound (1981); The Legend of Sleepy Hollow*

Witt, Rameon (act): *Alien Warrior*

Witt, William (act): *Torment (1986)*

Witte, Heinrich (act): *Nosferatu, eine Symphonie des Grauens*

Witter, Karen (act): *Midnight (1989); Popcorn; The Vineyard*

Witthans, Robert (act): *Deathmoon*

Witting, Steve (act): *Batman Returns*

Witting, Wigand (act): *Due to an Act of God*

Wittman, Malcolm (act): *Red Alert*

Witty, Christopher (act): *The Damned; Masquerade*

Witty, John (act): *Moment of Indiscretion; Solution by Phone; The Vault of Horror*

Wix, Florence (act): *The Gracie Allen Murder Case; The Missing Guest; The Return of Boston Blackie*

Wixted, Kevin (act): *Magic In the Mirror*

Wixted, Michael-James (act): *Where Have All the People Gone?*

Wizard Works (cin): *The Phantom Empire*

Wladon, Jean (act): *One Million Years B.C.*

Wodoslowsky, Stefan (act): *Mindfield*

Wodson, Elaine (act): *The Angel Who Pawned Her Harp*

Woehrle, John (act): *It's Alive III: Island of the Alive*

Woelfel, Jay (dir): *Beyond Dream's Door*

Woelfel, Jill (act): *Angels' Wild Women*

Woeller, David (act): *Glen and Randa*

Woerner, Carl (act): *Night of the Zombies (1981)*

Woertz, Greg (act): *Waxwork II: Lost In Time*

Woeste, Peter L. (cin): *Mindfield*

Wohl, David (act): *Chillers; D.A.R.Y.L.; Switch (1991)*

Wohlbruck, Adolph Anton Wilhelm (act): see Walbrook, Anton
Wohlfahrt, Waldemar (act): El Vampiro de la Utopista
Wohrman, Bill (act): Cocoon: The Return
Wohrman, Scott (act): Barracuda
Woinsky, Marc (act): Amazons (1986)
Wojciechowski, Michael G. (cin): Sleepstalker
Wojno, Stanley (act): Scalpel
Wolande, Gene (act): RoboCop; Tidal Wave: No Escape
Wolberg, Joe (act): Anguish
Wolcott, Abigail (act): Hellgate
Wolcott, Alexander (act): The Gift of Gab
Wolcott, James L. (dir): Wild Women of Wongo
Wolcott, Jann Arrington (wri): Seduced by Evil
Wolcott, Ona (act): see Munson, Ona
Wolders, Suzanne (act): Kemek
Wolf, Christopher (act): Test Tube Teens from the Year 2000
Wolf, Debra (act): Blood Diner
Wolf, Fred (dir): The Mouse and His Child; The Point
Wolf, Gary K. (wri): Who Framed Roger Rabbit
Wolf, Harry L. (cin): The Munsters' Revenge; The Nude Bomb
Wolf, Kelly (act): Graveyard Shift (1990)
Wolf, Leslie (act): The Trouble With Harry
Wolf, Marc/Mark (D.) (cin): Monstroid; The Phantom Empire
Wolf, Rita (act): Slipstream
Wolfe, Bud (act): Cyclotrode X
Wolfe, David (act): The Scarf
Wolfe, Diana (act): The Man Who Fell to Earth (1987)
Wolfe, Digby (wri): Bond of Fear
Wolfe, Ian (act, 1896-1992): Amazing Stories: The Movie V; Bedlam; The Brighton Strangler; Creator; The Devil's Daughter (1972); Diary of a Madman; Dick Tracy (1990); Dressed to Kill (1946); The Falcon's Adventure; Flesh and Fantasy; Games; Homebodies; Houdini (1953); The Invisible Man's Revenge; League of Frightened Men; The Lost World (1960); Mad Love; Mr. Sycamore; The Notorious Lone Wolf; On Borrowed Time; The Pearl of Death; The Raven (1935); Secret Agent of Japan; The Terminal Man; THX 1138; Witness for the Prosecution; The Wonderful World of the Brothers Grimm; Zombies On Broadway
Wolfe, Jason (act): The Reflecting Skin
Wolfe, Jim (act): Chillers, The Fan, Strangest Dreams: Invasion of the Space Preachers
Wolfe, Kedric (act): Dr. Heckyl & Mr. Hype; Up from the Depths
Wolfe, Rose (act): Nightbeast
Wolfe, Stuart (act): The Cold Room
Wolff, Ed(ward) (act): The Colossus of New York; The Phantom Creeps
Wolff, Frank (act, 1924-1971): Atlas; Beast from Haunted Cave; Il Demonio; The Wasp Woman (1959); When Women Had Tails
Wolff, Harald (act): Les Parapluies de Cherbourg
Wolff, Lothar (wri): Animal Farm (1954)
Wolff, Michael (mus): Dark Angel (1996)
Wolff, Tristan (act): The Silencers (1995)
Wolfington, Iggie (act): Hex
Wolfit, (Sir) Donald (act, 1902-1968): The Accursed; Blood of the Vampire; Checkmate; Death at Broadcasting House; Dr. Crippen; Guilty?; The Hands of Orlac (1959); The House of the Seven Hawks; I Accuse (1958); The Man In the Road; A Man On the Beach; The Mark; A Prize of Gold; The Ringer (1952); Satellite In the Sky; Sexton Blake and the Bearded Doctor; The Silent Passenger; Svengali (1954)
Wolfman Jack (act, 1938-1995, nee Robert Weston Smith): Midnight (1989); The Midnight Hour; Motel Hell
Wolfman, Wendy (act): Poltergeist III
Wolfski, Dariusz (cin): A Perfect Murder
Wolfson, P.J. (wri): Mad Love
Wolgers, Beppe (act): Dunderklumpen
Wolheim, Louis (act, 1880-1931): Condemned; Dr. Jekyll and Mr. Hyde (1920, Famous Players/ Para); The Face In the Fog (1922); Sherlock Holmes (1922)
Wolinsky, Marcos (act): Deathstalker II: Duel of the Titans
Wolk, Andrew (act): The Toxic Avenger, Part II
Wolk, Andy (dir): Traces of Red
Wolk, Michael (wri): Innocent Blood
Wolke, Steve (cin): The Hidden
Wolkind, Jenny (wri): Brenda Starr (1992)
Wolkkovicz, Emily (act): Horror
Wollaston, Nicholas (wri): Eclipse (1977)
Wollen, Peter (wri): The Passenger
Wollter, Sven (act): Man on the Roof
Wolos-Fonteno, David (act): Eraser
Wolski, Dariusz (cin): Nightfall (1988); Romeo Is Bleeding
Wolter, Ralf (act): Dracula Blows his Cool
Wolter, U. (wri): I Aim at the Stars
Wolveridge, Carol (act): 1984 (1955)
Womack, Steve (wri): Volcano: Fire On the Mountain
Womble, Andre (act): Change of Mind
Womble, Bill (act): The Alien's Return
Wonacott, Edna May (act): Shadow of a Doubt (1943)
Wong, Anna May (act, 1907-1961): Bits of Life; The Chinese Parrot; Chu Chin Chow (1934); Daughter of Shanghai; Daughter of the Dragon; Ellery Queen's Penthouse Mystery; Elstree Calling; The Island of Lost Men; Mr. Wu (1927); Peter Pan (1924); Portrait in Black; Shanghai Express; A Study In Scarlet (1933); The Thief of Bagdad(1924)
Wong, Anthony (act): The Heroic Trio
Wong, Arthur (act): Confessions of an Opium Eater; One Spy Too Many
Wong, B.D. (act): Jurassic Park; Mulan; Seven Years In Tibet
Wong, (Barbara) Jean (act): The Chinese Ring; The Golden Eye; The Red Dragon (1945); The Trap
Wong, Bruce (act): The Mystery of Mr. Wong; Time to Kill (1942)
Wong, Diana (act): Death In High Heels
Wong, Elaine (act): Inn of the Damned
Wong, Harry D.K. (act): Heaven Can Wait (1978)
Wong, Iris (act): Charlie Chan In Reno; Charlie Chan In Rio; Mr. Moto Takes a Vacation
Wong, Jadine (act): I Drink Your Blood; Mr. Moto Takes a Vacation
Wong, Kai (act): Charlie Chan and the Curse of the Dragon Queen
Wong, Kimmy (act): Eyewitness (1981)
Wong, Michael (act): The Vineyard
Wong, Michelle (act): Switch (1991)
Wong, Phillip (act): Watchers
Wong, R. (act): Invasion of the Body Snatchers (1978)
Wong, Russell (act): The Prophecy II
Wong, Steve (act): Arena (1989)
Wong, Sylvia (act): Street Trash
Wong, Victor (1930s act): King Kong (1933); Mr. Moto Takes a Vacation; Son of Kong
Wong, Victor (1970s & 1980s act): Big Trouble In Little China; The Golden Child; Prince of Darkness; Tremors
Wong, Vincent (act): Batman (1989); Little Shop of Horrors (1986)
Wontner, Arthur (act, 1875-1960): Blanche Fury; Condemned to Death; The Elusive Pimpernel (1950); Line Engaged; The Missing Rembrandt; The Sign of Four (1932); Silver Blaze (1937); The Sleeping Cardinal; The Terror (1938); Three Cases of Murder; The Triumph of Sherlock Holmes
Woo, James Wing (act): Marathon Man
Wood, Alfred (act): The Batallion Shot
Wood, Andy (act): Ghost Warrior
Wood, Annabella (act): Bloodthirsty Butchers; Scream and Die!
Wood, Annie (act): Cellblock Sisters: Banished Behind Bars
Wood, Barbara Alyn (act): Repossessed
Wood, Bari (wri): Dead Ringers
Wood, Bonnie (act): Scream
Wood, Brian (cin): Edward Scissorhands
Wood, Charles (wri): The Bed-Sitting Room
Wood, Christopher (wri): Remo Williams: The Adventure Begins; The Spy Who Loved Me
Wood, Clement (wri): Barbarella
Wood, Clive (act): The Crucifer of Blood; Treasure Island (1990)
Wood, Cynthia (act): Strange New World
Wood, Cyrus (wri): Dante's Inferno (1924)
Wood, David (act): Brainstorm (1983); Tales That Witness Madness
Wood, David (cin): Edward Scissorhands
Wood, David King (act): Men of Sherwood Forest; The Quatermass Experiment; The Stranger Came Home
Wood, Douglas (act): Boston Blackie Booked On Suspicion; Dracula's Daughter; Great Expectations (1934)
Wood, Drew (act):—And Now the Screaming Starts!
Wood Jr., Edward D. (act, d. 1978): Glen or Glenda?
Wood Jr., Edward D. (dir, d. 1978): Bride of the Monster; Glen or Glenda?; Night of the Ghouls; Plan 9 from Outer Space; The Sinister Urge
Wood Jr., Edward D. (wri, d. 1978): The Bride and the Beast; Bride of the Monster; Glen or Glenda?; Night of the Ghouls; Orgy of the Dead (1965); Plan 9 from Outer Space; The Sinister Urge
Wood, Elijah (act, b. 1981): Deep Impact; The Faculty; Forever Young; The Good Son
Wood, Forrest (act): Soylent Green; The War Lord
Wood, Freeman (act): The Lone Wolf Returns (1926)
Wood, Gary (act): Hungry for You
Wood, Gloria (act): see Stevens, K.T.
Wood, Grace (act): Mr. Wong, Detective
Wood, Haydn (act): Lifeforce
Wood, Helen (act): Charlie Chan at the Race Track; Crack-Up
Wood, Howarth (act): Golden Ivory
Wood, Jake (act): Flesh & Blood
Wood, James (dir): Dr. Jekyll's Dungeon of Death
Wood, Jane (act): The Witches and the Grinnygog
Wood, Janet (act): Fangs; The Folks at Red Wolf Inn
Wood, Jeane (act): Back from the Dead; Sorority Girl (1957)
Wood (Morgan), Joan Wentworth (wri): The Callbox Mystery
Wood, John (GB act): The Avengers; The Case of Gabriel Perry; Jane Eyre (1996); Ladyhawke; Luck of the Navy; Orlando; Rasputin (1996); Richard III (1995); A Stolen Face
Wood, John (USA act): The Purple Rose of Cairo; Wargames
Wood, John (E.) (USA act): The Last Days of Pompeii (1935); The Naked Jungle; U-Boat Prisoner
Wood, John Lisbon (act): Darkman (1990); Kiss Meets the Phantom of the Park
Wood, Julie (act): Peter Rabbit and the Tales of Beatrix Potter
Wood, Ken (act, nee Giovanni Cianfriglia): Superargo e i Giganti Senza Volto; Superargo vs. Diabolicus
Wood, Lana (act): Captain America II; Diamonds Are Forever; Satan's Mistress
Wood, Marjorie (act): Nightmare Alley
Wood, Mary Laura (act): Black Orchid; Escort for Hire; The Ghost Train Murder; The High Terrace; Hour of Decision; The Man Inside; Mantrap; Stranger In Town (1957); Valley of the Eagles
Wood, Michael/Mike (cin): Edward Scissorhands; Firestarter; Innerspace; Mad Max Beyond Thunderdome; Poltergeist; Wheels of Terror
Wood, Mikaela (act): The Three Swords of Zorro
Wood, Milton (act): Phantom of the Jungle
Wood, Myrna (act): The Resurrection of Zachary Wheeler
Wood, Nancy (act): Scandalous
Wood, Natalie (act, 1938-1981, nee Natasha Gurdin): Brainstorm (1983); A Cry In The Night (1956); The Ghost and Mrs. Muir; The Happy Land; The Memory of Eva Ryker; Meteor; Miracle On 34th Street (1947)
Wood, Oliver (cin): Bill & Ted's Bogus Journey; Don't Go In the House; The Honeymoon Killers; Neon Maniacs
Wood, Peggy (act, 1894-1978): Dream Girl
Wood, Peggy Ann (act): A Place to Die
Wood, Raven (act & wri): Ysani the Priestess
Wood, Rebecca (act): Barbarian Queen II (The Empress Strikes Back); Switch (1991)
Wood, Richard (cin): The Night They Saved Christmas
Wood, Robert (act): How to Make a Doll
Wood, Sam B. (act): The Safe (1930)
Wood, Sam (dir): The Next Corner
Wood, Thomas (act): Blood Feast; A Taste of Blood; 2000 Maniacs
Wood, Tom (act): The Fugitive (1993); Slaughterhouse-Five; U.S. Marshals
Wood, Ursula (act): The Starfish
Wood, Victor (act): My Cousin Rachel
Wood, Virginia (act): The Destructors
Wood, Wallace (act): Romeo Is Bleeding
Wood, Walter (act): Lies
Wood, William (wri): City Killer; Haunts of the Very Rich
Wood, Wilson (act): Black Widow (1954); Satan's Satellites
Woodard, Alfre (act): Gulliver's Travels (1996); Heart and Souls; Primal Fear; Remember My Name; Scrooged; Special Report: Journey to Mars; Star Trek: First Contact
Woodard, Don (act): Spellbinder
Woodard, Jimmy (act): Graveyard Shift (1990)
Woodbine, Bokeem (act): Freeway
Woodbridge, Bill (act): Monolith
Woodbridge, George (act, b. 1907): Blanche Fury; Cloudburst; The Curse of the Werewolf; Diamonds On Wheels; Doomwatch; Double Confession; Dracula, Prince of Darkness; The Fallen Idol; The Flanagan Boy; The Flesh and the Fiends; The Green Buddha; Horror of Dracula; An Inspector Calls; Out of the Fog (1962); A Place of One's Own; The Reptile; The Revenge of Frankenstein; Richard III (1955); Son of Robin Hood; Third Party Risk; Tower of Terror; What a Carve Up!
Woodburn, Eric (act): The Innocents
Woodbury, Joan (act, 1915-1989): Boston Blackie's Chinese Venture; Charlie Chan on Broadway; The Chinese Cat; Confessions of Boston Blackie; Forty Naughty Girls; King of the Zombies; The Living Ghost (1942); Phantom Killer; The Time Travelers (1964); The Whistler
Woodbury, Judith (act): The Nutty Professor (1996)
Woodbury, Woody (act): Beyond the Bermuda Triangle
Woodcock, John (act): Empire of Ash III; Skullduggery
Woodcroft, Todd (act): Superman II
Woode, Margo (act): Somewhere In the Night
Woodell, Barbara (act): The Baron of Arizona
Woodell, Pat (act): Twilight People
Wooden, Christopher (wri): Dinosaur Island (1994)
Woodfield, Gitta (wri): The Hypnotic Eye
Woodfield, William (Read) (wri): Earth II; The Hypnotic Eye; Satan's Triangle
Woodfork, Ray (act): Remo Williams: The Adventure Begins
Woodhead, Lydia M. (act):Scalpel
Woodington, Albie (act): First Knight
Woodland, Lauren (act): Alien Nation: Body and Soul; Alien Nation: Dark Horizon; Alien Nation: Millennium; Alien Nation: The Enemy Within
Woodlawn, Holly (act, b. 1947, nee Harold Ajzenberg): Broken Goddess
Woodley, Chris (Allen) (act): Pretty Maids All In a Row; The Velvet Vampire
Woodman, Pardoe (act): Desire; The Mystery of Mr. Bernard Brown
Woodnutt, John (act): Lifeforce
Woodridge, John (mus): Rx Murder
Woodruff, Largo (act): The Funhouse (1981)
Woodruff Jr., Tom (act): The Monster Squad; Pumpkinhead
Woodruff, Zola (act): The Fairy Doll
Woods, Alma (act): Strange Behavior
Woods, Arthur (dir); Busman's Honeymoon; Dangerous Medicine; The Dark Stairway; The Nursemaid Who Disappeared; On Secret Service; They Drive by Night
Woods, Arthur (wri): On Secret Service
Woods, Aubrey (act, b. 1928): The Abominable Dr. Phibes; The Greed of William Hart; The Queen of Spades (1948); Willy Wonka and the Chocolate Factory; Wuthering Heights (1970); Z.P.G.
Woods, Barbara Alyn (act): Circuitry Man
Woods, Bill (act): Maniac (1934)
Woods Jr., Bill (act): Alien Nation
Woods, Daniel (act): Forever Evil
Woods, Denise (act): Don't Go In the House
Woods, Donald (act, b. 1904): The Beast from 20,000 Fathoms; The Black Doll; The Bridge of San Luis Rey (1944); Charlie Chan On Broadway; Charlie Chan's Courage; Dimension 5; The Florentine Dagger; The Lost Volcano; 13 Ghosts; Wonder Man
Woods, Dusty (act): Phoenix the Warrior
Woods, Eddie (act): Tarzan the Fearless
Woods, Elizabeth (act): To Die For II: Son of Darkness
Woods, Emily (act): Enemy Mine
Woods, Genia (act): Battle of the Amazons
Woods, George J. (act): Bates Motel
Woods, Grant (act): The Silencers (1966)
Woods, Harry (act): Mr. Moto In Danger Island
Woods, Harry Lewis (act): The Viking
Woods, Ilene (act): Cinderella (1950)
Woods, Jack (act & dir): Equinox
Woods, Jack (wri): Beware! The Blob; Equinox
Woods, James (act, b. 1947): Cat's Eye; Contact; Eyewitness (1981); Hercules (1997); Night Moves; Vampires (1998); Videodrome
Woods, Kara (act): Christmas Every Day
Woods, Leon (act): The Tommyknockers
Woods, Lesley (act): Bad Ronald; Don't Be Afraid of the Dark; The Uninvited (1996)
Woods, Lotta (wri): The Iron Mask; Robin Hood (1922)
Woods, Mark (dir): Witchcraft 2: The Temptress
Woods, Michael (act): The Haunting of Sarah Hardy; Lady Beware; Omen IV: The Awakening; Sparkling Cyanide
Woods, Middleton (act): The Curse of Frankenstein

Woods, Ren (act, b. 1958): *The Brother from Another Planet; Xanadu*
Woods, Richard (wri): *Endangered Species*
Woods, Robert (act): *The Perverse Countess*
Woods, Robert S. (act): *Fantasies*
Wiids, Rosane (act): *Boarding House*
Wood-Sharke, Rebecca (act): *Friday the 13th-Part V: A New Beginning*
Wood-Sims, Stella (act): *The Silver Bridge*
Woodson, Julie (act): *The Bermuda Depths*
Woodson, William (act): *Escape from the Planet of the Apes*
Woodthorpe, Peter (act): *A Christmas Carol (1984); Evil of Frankenstein; The Hunchback of Notre Dame (1965); Hysteria!; The Mirror Crack'd; The Odyssey; The Skull*
Woodville, A. Caton (act): *Ultus, the Man from the Dead*
Woodville, Catherine (act): *The Brigand of Kandahar; The Clue of the New Pin (1961); The Crooked Road; The Informers; Underworld Informers*
Woodville, Katharine/Kate (act): *The Aquarians; Fear No Evil (1969); Whispering Death*
Woodvine, John (act): *An American Werewolf In London; The Devils; Dragonworld; Murder With Mirrors*
Woodward, Bob (act): *Radar Secret Service*
Woodward, Edward (act, b. 1930): *Arthur the King; A Christmas Carol (1984); Deadly Advice; Doctors Wear Scarlet; The File of the Golden Goose; Gulliver's Travels (1996); Hands of a Murderer; Hunted (1973); Sitting Target; The Wicker Man*
Woodward, Joanne (act, b. 1931): *The Fugitive Kind; A Kiss Before Dying (1956); They Might Be Giants; Signpost to Murder; The Three Faces of Eve*
Woodward, Lawrence (act): *The Punisher*
Woodward, Morgan (act): *Battle Beyond the Stars (1980); Treachery and Greed On the Planet of the Apes; The Sword of Ali Baba*
Woodward, Morgan (wri): *The Devil's Bedroom*
Woodward, Patti (act): see Darwell, Jane
Woodward, Peter (act): *Babylon 5: A Call to Arms*
Woodward, Tim (act): *The Dark Angel (1991)*
Woodward, Tina (act): *Mr. Sardonicus*
Woodworth, Andrew (act): *The Computer Wore Tennis Shoes (1995); Ghost In the Machine*
Woody, Dave (wri): *Return to Boggy Creek*
Woodyatt, Adam (act): *The Witches and the Grinnygog*
Wooland, Norman (act, b. 1910): *The Flesh Is Weak; Guilty?; Hamlet (1948); Life for Ruth; Madeleine; The Master Plan; Night Train for Inverness; No Road Back; The Projected Man; Richard III (1955); The Ringer (1952)*
Woolcott, Alexander (wri): *The Dark Tower (1943)*
Wooldridge, Susan (act): *Dead Man's Folly; Frankenstein (1984); The Shout*
Wooley, Sheb (act): *Purple People Eater*
Woolf, Bill (act): *The Shanghai Chest*
Woolf, Charles (act): *Elvira, Mistress of the Dark*
Woolf, Edgar (Allan) (wri): *The Casino Murder Case; The Mask of Fu Manchu; The Wizard of Oz (1939)*
Woolf, Frank (act): *The Prince and the Beggarmaid*
Woolf, Gabriel (act): *Knights of the Round Table*
Woolf, Harry (act): *Maid to Order*
Woolf, Henry (act): *The Bed-Sitting Room; Gorky Park; The Hound Of The Baskervilles (1978); The Ruling Class; Superman III*
Woolf, Jack (cin): *Daughter of the Mind; Dead Men Tell No Tales (1971); Good Against Evil; Killer Bees; The Mark of Zorro (1974)*
Woolf, James (act): *Billion Dollar Brain*
Woolf, Vicki (act): *Hands of the Ripper*
Woolf, Victor (act): *Frankenstein and the Monster from Hell*
Woolf, Virginia (wri, 1882-1941): *Orlando*
Woolfe, Betty (act): *Murder by Decree*
Woolfenden, Guy (mus): *Work Is a Four Letter Word*
Woolgar, Jack (act): *Deathline; Gawain and the Green Knight; Hammerhead*
Woollen, Susan (act): *The Return of the Six Million Dollar Man and the Bionic Woman*
Woolley, Edgar Montillion (act): see Woolley, Monty
Woolley, Monty (act, 1888-1963, nee Edgar Montillion Woolley): *The Bishop's Wife*
Woolman, Harry (cin): *Dr. Black Mr. Hyde; Earthbound (1981); End of the World (1977); The Fall of the House of Usher (1982); The Incredible Melting Man; The Mummy and the Curse of the Jackals; The Slime People; The Time Machine (1978); The Unseen (1981)*

Woolnough, Jeff (dir): *Lost Souls (1998)*
Woolrich, Cornell (wri): *Black Angel (1946); The Chase; I'm Dangerous Tonight; I Married a Shadow; The Leopard Man; Night Has a Thousand Eyes; Rear Window (1954 & 1998); The Window*
Woolridge, Karen (act): *Haunted by Her Past*
Woolridge, Susan (act): *Afraid of the dark*
Woolsey, Brent (act): *Timecop*
Woolsey, Douglas (cin): *A Matter of Life and Death*
Woolsey, Ralph (cin): *The Pack*
Woolsey, Robert (act, 1889-1938): *Cracked Nuts (1931)*
Woolvett, Jaimz (act): *The Dark (1994)*
Woon, Basil (wri): *The Perfect Crime; Two for Danger*
Wooton, Sarita (act): *Wuthering Heights (1939)*
Wootten, Rosemary (wri): *Persecution*
Wopat, Tom (act, b. 1950): *Meteorites!*
Worcester, Alec (act): *At the Eleventh Hour; At the Foot of the Scaffold; Blind Fate; The Book; The Coiner's Den; Curfew Must Not Ring Tonight; The Deception (1912); Dr. Trimball's Verdict; George Barnwell; His Evil Genius; Justice; King Robert of Sicily; The Legend of King Cophetua; The Man Behind the Mask (1914); Paying the Penalty; The Prodigal's Return; The Promise; The Red Light; The Silence of Richard Wilton; Tried In the Fire; Two Brothers and a Spy; A Woman's Wit*
Worden, Hank (act, 1901-1992, nee Norton Earl Worden): *Black Noon; The Man With a Cloak*
Worden, Hank (1990s act): *Space Rage*
Worden, Norton Earl (act): see Worden, Hank
Wordsworth, Richard (act): *The Camp On Blood Island; The Curse of the Werewolf; The Quatermass Experiment; The Revenge of Frankenstein; Time Without Pity*
Worell, Herta (act): *Dracula Blows His Cool*
Workman, Jimmy (act): *The Addams Family; Addams Family Values*
Workman, Lindsay (act): *Westworld*
World, Al (dir): *The Son of Hercules In the Land of Darkness*
World, Christina (act): *The Golden Lady*
Worley, Billy (act): *Strange Days*
Worley, Jo Anne (act, b. 1927): *Beauty and the Beast (1991); The Shaggy D.A.; Through the Magic Pyramid*
Worlock, Frederic(k) (act, b. 1886): *The Black Swan; Dr. Jekyll and Mr. Hyde (1941); Dressed to Kill (1946); The Fatal Witness; Hangover Square; Kismet (1914); The Lodger (1944); The Lone Wolf In London; Love from a Stranger (1947); Miracles for Sale; Murder Over New York; 101 Dalmatians (1961); Passport to Suez; Pursuit to Algiers; Secrets of Scotland Yard; Sherlock Holmes Faces Death; She-Wolf of London; Terror by Night; The Woman In Green*
Wormald, S. (dir): *Lady Candale's Diamonds; A Lively Skeleton; A Mechanical Husband; The Next of Kin (1908); The Peril of the Fleet*
Wormser, Richard (wri): *The Phantom Thief*
Woronov, Mary (act, b. 1943): *Acting On Impulse; Chopping Mall; Death Race 2000; Dick Tracy (1990); Eating Eating Raoul; Heartbeeps; Hellhole; Kemek; The Movie House Massacre; The Munsters' Scary Little Christmas; Night of the Comet; Nomads; Seizure; Silent Night, Bloody Night; Terrorvision; Warlock; Watchers II*
Worrall, Bruce (cin): *Circumstances Unknown*
Worrall, Letchmere (wri): *The Man Who Stayed at Home*
Worrall, Max (act): *Mad Max Beyond Thunderdome*
Worsley, Joyce (act): *Signpost to Murder*
Worsley, Wallace (dir): *A Blind Bargain; The Hunchback of Notre Dame (1923); The Penalty*
Worsnop, Wilfrid (act): see Lawson, Wilfrid
Worth, Alison (act): *Arthur the King; For Your Eyes Only; Octopussy*
Worth, Brian (act, b. 1914): *Assignment Redhead; Barbados Quest; The Boy Who Turned Yellow; Breakaway; Dead Lucky; An Inspector Calls; Last Holiday; Moment of Danger; On Her Majesty's Secret Service; Peeping Tom; Scrooge (1951); The Terror of the Tongs*
Worth, Constance (act): *Boston Blackie Goes Hollywood; Crime Doctor; Crime Doctor's Strangest Case; Criminals Within; Love In the Welsh Hills; Meet Boston Blackie*
Worth, David (act): *Meet Boston Blackie*
Worth, David (cin): *The Night They Saved Christmas*

Worth, David (dir & wri): *Warriors of the Wasteland*
Worth, Frank (mus): *Bride of the Monster*
Worth, Harry J. (act): *The Amazing Partnership; Charles Augustus Milverton; The Crimson Circle (1922); Through Stormy Waters*
Worth, Irene (act): *Eyewitness (1981); King Lear (1970); The Scapegoat; Secret People*
Worth, Lillian (act): *Crooked Alley*
Worth, Lothrop (B.) (cin): *Billy the Kid vs. Dracula; Gog; I Was a Teenage Frankenstein*
Worth, Martin (wri): *A Distant Scream*
Worth, Nicholas (act): *Blood and Concrete; Dark Angel: The Ascent; Darkman (1990); Don't Answer the Phone!; Hell Comes to Frogtown; Invitation to Hell; No Way Out; Swamp Thing*
Worth, Stan V. (mus): *The House of the Dead*
Worthen, Jenna (act): *Deadly Blessing*
Worthing, Helen Lee (act): *Don Juan (1927)*
Worthington, Rick (act): *Empire of Ash III*
Worthington, William (act): *The Green Goddess (1923); The Return of Boston Blackie*
Worthy, Angela (act): *Vampire at Midnight*
Worthy, Athena (act): *Dance of the Damned*
Woshner, Lawrence (act): *Lady Beware*
Woster, Eric (wri): *Star Crystal*
Wouterse, Jack (act): *Der Noorderlingen*
Wouterson, Loes (act): *Der Noorderlingen*
Wowchuck, Harry (act): *The Entity*
Woxholt, Egil (cin): *Captain Nemo and the Underwater City; Koroshi; On Her Majesty's Secret Service*
Woxholt, Greta (act): see Gynt, Greta
Woyt, Jim (act): *The Toxic Avenger, Part II*
Wozniak, Tadeusz (act): *O Dwoch Takich Co Ukradli Ksiezyc*
Woznicki, Paul (mus): *Fiend (1980)*
Wragge, Martin (wri): *Survivor (1987)*
Wrangell, Basil (dir): *Philo Vance's Gamble*
Wrangler, Greg (act): *Barbarian Queen II (The Empress Strikes Back); The Mummy Lives*
Wray, Ardel (wri): *The Falcon and the Co-Eds; Isle of the Dead (1945); I Walked With a Zombie; The Leopard Man*
Wray, Dean (act): *Circle of Deceit*
Wray, Fay (act, b. 1907): *Black Moon (1934); Bulldog Jack; The Clairvoyant (1934); Crime of Passion; Dirigible; Doctor X; King Kong (1933); The Most Dangerous Game; Mystery of the Wax Museum; Queen Bee; The Vampire Bat; When Knights Were Bold (1936)*
Wray, Jackie (act): *The Tower*
Wray, John (act, 1888-1940): *The Cat and the Canary (1939); The Death Kiss; Doctor X; Miss Pinkerton*
Wreford, John (act): *Maroc 7; The Mutations*
Wren, Clare (act): *Steel and Lace*
Wren, Doug (act): *Bad Taste*
Wren, Richard (act): *Electric Eskimo; The Wicker Man*
Wrenn, Trevor (cin): *Scream and Die!; Symptoms*
Wrentz, Lawrence T. (act): *The Silence of the Lambs*
Wrestler, Philip (wri): *Crosstrap*
Wrigg, Anne (act): *Haunted Palace (1949)*
Wright, Alex (act): *Vengeance Is Mine*
Wright, Amy (act): *The Amityville Horror; Deceived; Robot In the Family; The Scarlet Letter (1995)*
Wright, Angus (act): *First Knight; Mary Shelley's 'Frankenstein'*
Wright, Ben (act): *Arnold; The Little Mermaid; My Blood Runs Cold; 101 Dalmatians (1961); Pharaoh's Curse; Prince Valiant (1954); Probe; Terror In the Wax Museum; 23 Paces to Baker Street*
Wright, Betty Ren (wri): *Secrets In the Attic*
Wright, Bruce (act): *Battlestar Galactica; Fire In the Sky (1993); I, Desire; Twister*
Wright, Clarence (act): *Dual Alibi; A Place of One's Own*
Wright Jr., Cobina (act): *Charlie Chan In Rio*
Wright, Cowley (act): *The Rocks of Valpre*
Wright, David Grant (act): *Writer's Block*
Wright, Debbie (act): *Cavegirl (1985)*
Wright, Doug (act): *The Toxic Avenger, Part II*
Wright, Ed (act): *When a Stranger Calls*
Wright, Ethel (act): *The Enchanted Cottage (1924)*
Wright, Fanny (act): *Chamber of Horrors (1929); Come Into My Parlour; The Rat*
Wright, Fred (act): *The Grand Babylon Hotel; The Norwood Builder*
Wright, Gary (mus): *Endangered Species*
Wright, Haidee (act): *Strange Evidence*
Wright, Humbert (act): *Bulldog*
Wright, Herbert J. (wri): *Shadow of the Hawk; Through the Magic Pyramid*

Wright, Howard (act): *The Spider (1958); War of the Colossal Beast*
Wright, Hugh E. (act): *Scrooge (1935); The Shot In the Dark*
Wright, Humberston (act): *Alf's Button (1930); Boadicea; The English Rose; God's Clay; High Treason (1929); The Rocks of Valpre; The Sign of Four (1923); Trapped by the London Sharks*
Wright, J. Madison (act): *The Warlord: Battle for the Galaxy*
Wright, Janet (act): *American Gothic*
Wright, Jay (act): *The Boogey Man*
Wright, Jenny (act): *I, Madman; The Lawnmower Man; Near Dark*
Wright, Jenny Lee (act): *Madhouse; The Slipper and the Rose*
Wright, Judith (act): *Brenda Starr (1976)*
Wright, Julia (act): *Dr. Jekyll and Sister Hyde*
Wright, Ken (act): *Prince of Darkness*
Wright, Larry (act): *The Nest of the Cuckoo Birds*
Wright, Laura (act): *The Gables Mystery*
Wright, Lenore (wri): *Grave Secrets*
Wright, Louise (act): *When a Stranger Calls*
Wright, Maggie (act): *Rasputin, the Mad Monk; Twins of Evil*
Wright, Marbeth (act): *Just Imagine*
Wright, Marcella (act): *La Orgia de los Muertos*
Wright, Marie (act): *Gaslight (1940); Murder; Sexton Blake and the Hooded Terror; Silver Top*
Wright, Mary Catherine (act): *Heart Condition*
Wright, Matthew (act): *High Spirits*
Wright, Max (act): *All That Jazz; Simon; The Stand*
Wright, Michael (act): *V*
Wright, N'Bushe (act): *Blade*
Wright, Patrick (act): *Frightmare (1983); Graduation Day; Project X (1967); Track of the Moon Beast*
Wright, Paula (act): *Virgin Witch*
Wright, Paula Ramona (act): see Raymond, Paula
Wright (Penn), Robin (act, b. 1966): *The Princess Bride*
Wright, Ron (act): *Capture That Capsule!*
Wright, Roy (act): *The Devil's Hand (1961)*
Wright, S. Fowler (wri, b. 1874): *Deluge*
Wright, Samuel E. (act): *The Little Mermaid*
Wright, Steve (act): *Runaway (1984)*
Wright, Steven (act): *Babe: Pig In the City; Sledgehammer; The Swan Princess*
Wright, Teresa (act, b. 1918): *Flood; Pursued; The Search for Bridey Murphy; Shadow of a Doubt (1943); Somewhere In Time; The Steel Trap; Track of the Cat*
Wright, Terry (act): *Once the Killing Starts*
Wright, Thomas Julian/T.J. (act): *Deadly Game (1991)*
Wright, Thomas J. (dir): *Deadly Game (1991); Highlander: The Gathering; Snow Kill*
Wright, Tom (act): *The Brother from Another Planet; Past Midnight; Tales from the Hood*
Wright, Tommy (GB act): *Mary Shelley's 'Frankenstein'*
Wright, Tommy (USA act): *Dr. Caligari*
Wright, Tony (GB act, b. 1925): *Attempt to Kill; The Creeping Flesh; Faces In the Dark; The Flanagan Boy; The House On Marsh Road; In the Wake of a Stranger; The Liquidator; Seven Thunders; The Spaniard's Curse; Tiger In the Smoke*
Wright, Tony (USA act): *The Offspring*
Wright, Tonya (act): *Mad Max Beyond Thunderdome*
Wright, Wayne (act): *Primal Fear*
Wright, Wendell (W.) (act): *Condor; The Howling; Jack's Back*
Wright, Willard Huntingdon (wri): see Van Dine, S.S.
Wright, Will(iam) (act, b. 1891): *The Beginning or the End?; Boston Blackie Goes Hollywood; Cape Fear (1961); Daughter of the Jungle; Escape In the Fog; The Mask of Dijon; Niagara; One Mysterious Night; Philo Vance Returns; Shadow of the Thin Man; The 30 Foot Bride of Candy Rock*
Wright, Z (act): *Def by Temptation*
Wrighton, Mr. (act): *The Harper Mystery*
Wrightson, Berni(e) (wri): *Heavy Metal; Swamp Thing*
Wrigley, Ben (act): *Bedknobs and Broomsticks*
Wrixon, Maris (act): *The Ape (1940); British Intelligence; The Face of Marble; Footsteps In the Dark; Highway 13; White Pongo*
Wroe, Trudy (act): *Beyond a Reasonable Doubt; The Pink Chiquitas*
Wrona, Gloria (act): *Midnight Lace (1960)*
Wrubel, Allie (mus): *Midnight Lace (1960)*
Wu, Humphle (act): *Ellery Queen and the Perfect Crime; Mr. Moto Takes a Vacation*
Wu, Vivian (act): *The Guyver*

Wuhl, Robert (act, b. 1952): *Batman (1989); Dr. Jekyll and Ms. Hyde; Tales from the Crypt (1989)*
Wuhrer, Kari (act): *Anaconda; Beastmaster 2: Through the Portal of Time; An Occasional Hell; Thinner*
Wul, Stefan (wri): *Fantastic Planet*
Wulff, Kai (act): *Night of the Zombies (1981); Twilight Zone*
Wunderlee, Frank (act): *One Exciting Night*
Wunderlich, Melinda (act): *Laserblast*
Wupperman, Francis (act): see Morgan, Frank
Wupperman, Ralph (act): see Morgan, Ralph
Wurlitzer, Rudolph (wri): *Glen and Randa*
Wussow, Klausjuergen (act): *The Green Archer; The Red Circle (1960)*
Wuttig, Heinz Oskar (wri): *Die Tausend Augen des Dr. Mabuse*
Wyashiro, Niki (act): *Matango*
Wyatt Jr., Allen (act): *Avalanche*
Wyatt, Dale (act): *From Beyond; Ghoulies II; Snow White: A Tale of Terror; Troll*
Wyatt, Eustace (act): *Journey Into Fear (1942)*
Wyatt, Jane (act, b. 1912): *Amityville: The Evil Escapes; Great Expectations (1934); House by the River; Lost Horizon (1937); Pitfall; Star Trek IV: The Voyage Home*
Wyatt, Len (act): *Happy Birthday to Me*
Wyatt, Obel (act): *Mothra*
Wyatt, Steve (act): *The Silence of the Lambs*
Wyatt, Tessa (act): *Are You Dying Young Man?; Spy Story*
Wycherly, Margaret (act, 1881-1956): *The Keeper of the Flame; The Man With a Cloak; The Thirteenth Chair (1929)*
Wyckoff, Alvin (cin): *The Lost Jungle*
Wyckoff, Robert (cin): *Mara of the Wilderness*
Wylie, John (act): *Robot In the Family*
Wycliff, Chris(topher) (act): *My Best Friend Is a Vampire; The Outing*
Wycoff, Leon (act): see Ames, Leon
Wyenn, Than (act): *The Beginning of the End; Black Sunday (1977); The Boy and the Pirates; Ellery Queen: Don't Look Behind You; The Invisible Boy*
Wyer, Reg(inald) (cin): *The Brigand of Kandahar; Devils of Darkness; Four Sided Triangle; Island of Terror; Night of the Eagle; Spaceways; Unearthly Stranger*
Wyerch, Harold (act): *Empire of Ash III*
Wyeth, Katya (act): *A Clockwork Orange; Hands of the Ripper; No. 1 of the Secret Service; Straight on Till Morning; Twins of Evil*
Wylde, Derna (act): *Planet of Dinosaurs*
Wylde, Tony (act): *Museum Mystery*
Wyldeck, Martin (act): *Die Screaming, Marianne; The Hypnotist (1957); Night Must Fall (1964); The Oblong Box; The Return of Mr. Moto; Spell of Evil; Tiffany Jones; Timeslip*
Wyler, Ellie (act): *Midnight (1980)*
Wyler, Richard (act): *Future Women; High Jump; Rio 70*
Wyler, William (dir, 1902-1981): *The Collector; Wuthering Heights (1939)*
Wyles, J. David (ri): *Arthur the King*
Wylie, Adam (act): *Under Wraps*
Wylie, Frank (act): *Macbeth (1971); Not Guilty*
Wylie, Pat (act): *End of the World (1977)*
Wylie, Philip (wri, 1902-1971): *Charlie Chan In Reno; Island of Lost Souls; King of the Jungle; L.A. 2017; Murders In the Zoo; When Worlds Collide*
Wyllie, Meg (act): *The Tribe*
Wylton, Tim (act): *Blue Blood*
Wyman, Bill (mus): *Phenomena*
Wyman, Dan (mus): *The Alien's Return; Hell Night; The Lawnmower Man; Without Warning (1980)*
Wyman, Frank (wri): *A Touch of the Other*
Wyman, Jane (act, b. 1914, nee Sarah Jane Fulks): *The Body Disappears; Crime by Night; The Lost Weekend; Smart Blonde; The Spy Ring; Stage Fright (1950); Torchy Plays With Dynamite*
Wyman, John (act): *Arabian Adventure; For Your Eyes Only*
Wymark, Patrick (act, 1926-1970, nee Patrick Cheeseman): *The Blood On Satan's Claw; The Criminal; Dr. Syn-Alias the Scarecrow; Doppelganger (1969); Operation Crossbow; The Psychopath (1965); Repulsion; Secret of Blood Island; The Skull; West 11; Witch-Finder General*
Wymark, Tristram (act): *The Cold Room*
Wymer, Patty (act): *The Witchmaker*
Wymore, Patrice (act, b. 1927): *Chamber of Horrors (1966)*
Wynands, Dan (act): *Eraser*
Wynant, H.M. (act): *Code Name: Minus One; Conquest of the Planet of the Apes; Earthbound (1981); Hangar 18*
Wyn-Davies, Charles (act): *Mary Shelley's 'Frankenstein'*
Wyndham, Anthea (act): *Position of Trust*
Wyndham, Dennis (act): *Dancing With Crime; The Face at the Window (1932); Gipsy Blood; Lorna Doone (1920); The Man They Could Not Arrest; Men of Sherwood Forest; Old Mother Riley's Ghosts; The Stolen Necklace*
Wyndham, Joan (act): *Juggernaut*
Wyndham, John (act): *Strange Behaviour*
Wyndham, John (wri, 1903-1969): *The Day of the Triffids; Quest for Love; The Village of the Damned (1960 & 1995)*
Wyndham, Robert (act): *Dead of Night (1945); Who Killed Van Loo?*
Wyndham, Ruby (act): *In the Ranks*
Wyndham, Victoria (act): *Terror In the Shadows*
Wyndham-Lewis, D.B. (wri): *The Man Who Knew Too Much (1934 & 1956)*
Wyner, George (act): *Deadly Messages; Dogs; Slaughter; Spaceballs*
Wyner, Joel (act): *The Club (1994)*
Wyngarde, Peter (act): *Flash Gordon (1980); The Innocents; Night of the Eagle*
Wynn, Ed (act, 1886-1966, nee Isaiah Edwin Leopold): *The Absent-Minded Professor (1961); Alice In Wonderland (1951); Cinderfella; The Gnome-Mobile; Mary Poppins; Son of Flubber*
Wynn, George (act): *The Monkey's Paw (1923); Scrooge (1922); Trapped by the Mormons*
Wynn, John (act): *Late Night Final*
Wynn, John (cin): *Witchery*
Wynn, Joseph (act): *Change of Mind*
Wynn, Keenan (act, 1916-1986, nee Frank Leopold): *The Absent-Minded Professor (1961); Angels In the Outfield (1951); Around the World Under the Sea; Billion Dollar Threat; B.J. Lang Presents; The Clonus Horror; The Cockeyed Miracle; The Dark (1979); Demon and the Mummy; The Devil's Rain; Dr. Strangelove: or, How I Learned to Stop Worrying and Love the Bomb; Finian's Rainbow; The Glass Slipper; Hyper Sapien: People from Another Star; Hysterical; The Internecine Project; The Killer Inside Me; Kind Lady (1951); Laserblast; The Last Unicorn; The Lucifer Complex; Mackenna's Gold; Man With Icy Eyes; The Monitors; Nightmare In the Sun; No Place to Hide (1956); Orca; Piranha (1978); Pretty Maids All In a Row; The Return of the Man from U.N.C.L.E.; The Shaggy D.A.; Song of the Thin Man; Son of Flubber; The Three Musketeers (1948); Wavelength*
Wynn, Kitty (act): *Mirrors*
Wynn, Manny (cin): *The Mind Snatchers (1963)*
Wynn, May (act, b. 1930, nee Donna Lee Hickey): *The Unknown Terror*
Wynn, Ned (act): *How to Stuff a Wild Bikini*
Wynn, Ned (wri): *Don't Go to Sleep*
Wynn, Robert (dir): *The Resurrection of Zachary Wheeler*
Wynn, Tracy Keenan (wri): *The Deep*
Wynn, Zoe (act): *The Angelus; Catch as Catch Can*
Wynne, Bert (act): *The Game of Liberty; The Polar Star; When Knights Were Bold(1916)*
Wynne, Christopher (act): *Remote Control (1988)*
Wynne, Daphne (act): *Fairyland*
Wynne, Gilbert (act): *Clegg; Night After Night After Night*
Wynne, Herbert/Bert (dir): *Belphegor the Mountebank; A Night of Magic; A Safe Affair*
Wynne, Jeff (wri): *Storm Chasers: Revenge of the Twister*
Wynne, Michael (act): *Nothing But the Night; A Place to Go; Rag Doll; The Road to Hong Kong*
Wynne, Wayne (act): *Attack of the Killer Tomatoes*
Wynne-Simmons, Robert (dir): *The Outcasts*
Wynne-Simmons, Robert (wri): *The Blood On Satan's Claw; The Outcasts*
Wynorski, Jim (dir): *Chopping Mall; Deathstalker II: Duel of the Titans; Dinosaur Island (1994); Hard to Die; The Haunting of Morella; The Lost Empire; Munchie; Not of This Earth (1988); The Return of Swamp Thing; Sorority House Massacre 2; Victim of Desire*
Wynorski, Jim (wri): *Chopping Mall; Deathstalker II: Duel of the Titans; Forbidden World; The Lost Empire; Not of This Earth (1988); Sorceress (1982)*
Wynter, Ben (act): *Welcome II the Terrordome*
Wynter, Dagmar (act): see Wynter, Dana
Wynter, Dana (act, b. 1930, nee Dagmar Wynter): *Colonel March Investigates; The Crimson Pirate; Invasion of the Body Snatchers (1956); The List of Adrian Messenger; The Questor Tapes*
Wynter, Mark (act): *The Haunted House of Horror; Superman (1978)*
Wynter, Paul (act): *Molemen Against the Son of Hercules*
Wynters, Charlotte (act): *Desperate Chance for Ellery Queen; Ellery Queen and the Murder Ring; The Falcon's Brother; Nancy Drew, Troubleshooter; Smart Blonde*
Wynters, Sharyn (act): *Westworld*
Wynyard, Diana (act, 1906-1964, nee Dorothy Isobel Cox): *Gaslight (1940); On the Night of the Fire; Rasputin and the Empress*
Wyrauch, Howard (act): *Tuck Everlasting*
Wyse, Linda (act): *So Sad About Gloria*
Wyss, Amanda (act): *Black Magic Woman; A Nightmare On Elm Street; Shakma; To Die For; To Die For II: Son of Darkness*
Wyss, Megan (act): *Night Screams*
Xavier, Nelson (act): *Os Deuses e os Mortos*
Xenofontov, Alexander (wri): *The Amphibian Man*
Xuereb, Emmanuel (act): *Grim*
Yablans, Irwin (wri): *Prison (1988)*
Yablans, Mickey (act): *Halloween; Prison (1988)*
Yablonsky, Yabo (dir & wri): *B.J. Lang Presents*
Yabuku, Reuben (act): *Moontrap*
Yachigusa, Kaoru (act): *The Human Vapor*
Yaconelli, Frank (act): *Death Takes a Holiday (1934); Dr. Cyclops*
Yaconelli, Steve (cin): *The Phantom of the Opera (1990)*
Yaconelli, Zacharias/Zachary/Z. (act): *Amazon Quest; The Baron of Arizona; Secret of the Incas*
Yaeckel, Louis (act): *Just Imagine*
Yaeger, Donna (act): *Slaughter High*
Yaffe, Ben (act): *Werewolf of Washington*
Yagher, Jeff (act): *Bionic Showdown: The Six Million Dollar Man and the Bionic Woman*
Yagher, Kevin (cin): *Retribution (1988)*
Yagi, James (act): *King Kong vs. Godzilla*
Yahiro, Fuji (wri): *Buddha*
Yakin, Boaz (wri): *The Punisher*
Yakmazaki, Kazuo (dir): *A Wind Named Amnesia*
Yakub, Michael (dir): *The Shaman*
Yakunina, Valentina (act): *Mission: Impossible*
Yale, Stan (act): *Monolith; Watchers II*
Yallop, Julia (act): *The Bees*
Yama, Michael (act): *The Hidden*
Yama, Yachuco (act): *Operation Kid Brother*
Yamada, Akira (act): *Mothra*
Yamada, Gerald (act): *The Street Fighter*
Yamada, Isuzu (act, b. 1917): *Throne of Blood*
Tamada, Kazuo (cin): *Chusingura (1963)*
Yamada, Minosuke (act): *The Mysterians; Rodan, the Flying Monster*
Yamada, Sora (act): *The Toxic Avenger, Part II*
Yamagata, Isao (act): *Uchujin Tokyo No Arawaru*
Yamaguchi, Akira (act): *Godzilla vs. Hedora; Godzilla vs. the Smog Monster*
Yamaguchi, Tetsuya (dir): *The Magic Serpent*
Tamaguchi, Toshimi (act): *The Toxic Avenger, Part II*
Yamaki, Kenji (act): *The Punisher*
Yamamoto, Fujiko (act): *Buddha*
Yamamoto, Kei (act): *The Bullet Train; Inn of Evil*
Yamamoto, Michio (dir): *Lake of Dracula; The Vampire Doll*
Yamamoto, Ren (act): *Gojira*
Yamamoto, Shugoro (wri): *Inn of Evil*
Yamamoto, Yasushi (act): *Mothra*
Yamamoto, Yoko (act): *Gappa, the Triphibian Monster*
Yamanak, Ichiro (act): *The Toxic Avenger, Part II*
Yamanaka, Lisa (act): *Babar: The Movie*
Yamanouchi, Al (act): *Endgame*
Yamaoka, Otto (act): *The Benson Murder Case; The Black Camel*
Yamasawa, Yoshikazu (cin): *The Green Slime*
Yamashita, Tadashi (act): *The Octagon*
Yamazak, Iwao (wri): *Gappa, the Triphibian Monster*
Yamazaki, Kiyoshi (act): *Red Sonja*
Yamazaki, Tsutomu (act): *High and Low*
Yamazuki, Masayuki (act): *The Final Countdown*
Yana (act): *Interpol*
Yancey, Johnathan (act): *The Outing*
Yancy, Emily (act): *Blacula; Poor Devil; The Sword and the Sorcerer*
Yang, Ginny (act): *The Brother from Another Planet*
Yang, William (act): *Howling III*
Yanagisawa, Shinichi (act): *The X from Outer Space*
Yanilou (act): *The Hands of Orlac (1959)*
Yank, Big (act): *Fire and Ice*
Yannatos, Michael (act): *The Next One*
Yanne, Jean (act, b. 1933): *Le Boucher; Le Paltoquet*
Yanni, Rosanna (act): *Gran Amore del Conde Dracula; El Jorobado de la Morgue; Kiss Me, Monster; Sadist Erotica*
Yano, Sen (act): *Suna No Onna*
Yanova, Varvara (act): *Portret Doriana Greya*
Yanover, Ron(ald) (wri): *Cyborg 2: Glass Shadow; The Jungle Book (1994)*
Yanovsky, Zal (act): *Heavy Metal*
Yanse, Jean (act): *Le Saint Prend l'Affut*
Yapp, Tommy (act): *The Brides of Fu Manchu; Koroshi*
Yaranko, Adam (act): *Quarantine*
Yarbo, Lillian (act): *The Gracie Allen Murder Case*
Yarborough, Barton (act): *The Devil's Mask; The Ghost of Frankenstein; I Love a Mystery (1945); The Red Dragon (1945)*
Yarborough, Glen (act): *The Return of the King*
Yarborough, Valerie (act): *Serial Mom*
Yarbrough, Bill (act): *Wheels of Terror*
Yarbrough, Glenn (mus): *The Hobbit*
Yarbrough, Jean (dir, b. 1900): *The Brute Man; The Challenge; Crashing Las Vegas; The Creeper (1948); The Devil Bat; Hillbillys In a Haunted House; House of Horrors (1946); Jack and the Beanstalk (1952); King of the Zombies; Law of the Jungle; Lure of the Islands; Master Minds (1950); The Mutineers; Panama Menace; She-Wolf of London; Women of Pitcairn Island*
Yarde, Margaret (act): *Crimes at the Dark House; The Face at the Window (1939); Matineeldol; Scrooge (1935)*
Yardley, David (cin): *Razorback*
Yardley, Stephen (act): *Slayground*
Yared, Gabriel (mus): *City of Angels; Light Years*
Yari, Bob (dir): *Mind Games (1989)*
Yarlett, Claire (act): *Blackout (1995)*
Yarna, Nicole (act): *Popdown*
Yarnall, Bob (act): *Revenge of the Teenage Vixens from Outer Space*
Yarnall, Celeste (act): *Around the World Under the Sea; Beast of Blood; The Face of Eve; The Velvet Vampire*
Yarnell, Sally (act): *The Black Sleep*
Yaru, Marina (act): *Spirits of the Dead*
Yarussi, Daniel (cin): *The Coming; Graduation Day; Vampire at Midnight*
Yarza, Rosita (act): *Behind the Mask of Zorro; El Otro Fu-Manchu*
Yasbeck, Amy (act, b. 1963): *Dracula: Dead and Loving It; House II: The Second Story; The Mask (1994); Splash, Too*
Yashima, Momo (act): *Charlie Chan and the Curse of the Dragon Queen; Star Trek*
Yasuda, Kimiyoshi (dir): *Majin, Monster of Terror*
Yasumi, Toshio/T. (wri): *Chusingura (1963); The Final War*
Yasuoka, Rikiya (act): *The Toxic Avenger, Part II*
Yasutake, Patti (act): *Star Trek: Generations*
Yates, Art (act): *Empire of Ash III*
Yates, Cassie (act, b. 1951): *The Evil; The Haunted (1991); Of Mice and Men (1981)*
Yates, George Worthington (wri, b. 1901): *Attack of the Puppet People; Earth vs. the Flying Saucers; The Falcon In Mexico; The Flame Barrier; Frankenstein—1970; It Came from Beneath the Sea; The Saracen Blade; Space Master X-7; The Spanish Main; The Spider (1958); Them! (1954); Tormented; War of the Colossal Beast*
Yates, Jeremiah (act): *The Toxic Avenger, Part II*
Yates, John (act): *Simon, King of the Witches*
Yates, Marjorie (act): *The Black Panther; The Glitterball; Legend of the Werewolf*
Yates, Maud (act): *God's Clay; The Green Terror; In London's Toils; Jane Shore (1915); The Rogues of London; Trapped by the London Sharks*
Yates, Norman (act): *In the Grip of Death; The Prisoner of Zenda (1915)*
Yates, Paul (act): *The Frighteners; I Was a Zombie for the F.B.I.*
Yates, Pauline (act): *Never Mention Murder*
Yates, Peter (dir, b. 1929): *The Deep; Eyewitness (1981); Koroshi; Krull; Robbery*
Yates, Peter (wri, b. 1929): *Robbery*
Yates, William R. (wri): *Diamonds On Wheels*
Yaungsri, Prakit (act): *Night Creature*
Yawitz, Paul (wri, b. 1905): *Alias Boston Blackie; The Black Scorpion (1957); Boston Blackie Booked On Suspicion; Boston Blackie Goes Hollywood; The Chance of a Lifetime; A*

Close Call for Boston Blackie; Confessions of Boston Blackie; The Falcon's Alibi; One Mysterious Night
Yawnick, Fred (cin): *The Coming*
Ya Ying, Liu (act): *Shatter*
Yazaki, Tomonori (act): *Godzilla's Revenge*
Ybarra, Ramon (act): *Street Trash*
Yea, Helena (act): *Memories of Murder*
Yeager, Biff (act): *The Annihilator; Edward Scissorhands; Ed Wood; Human Feelings; Repo Man; School Spirit*
Yeager, Caroline (act): *The Sins of Dorian Gray*
Yeager, Steve (act): *Polyester*
Yeagher, Kevin (dir): *Hellraiser 4: Bloodline*
Yea-Min, Lee (act): *Village In the Mist*
Yeary, Lee (act): *Strait-Jacket*
Yeaworth Jr., Irvin S./Shortess (dir): *The Blob (1958); Dinosaurus!; 4D Man*
Yeaworth, Jean (wri): *Dinosaurus!*
Yedidia, Mario (act): *Under Wraps; Warriors of Virtue*
Yee, Dewi (act): *Charlie Chan and the Curse of the Dragon Queen*
Yee, Kelvin Han (act): *Copycat*
Yee, Stuart W. (act): *Copycat*
Yeldham, Peter (wri): *The Liquidator; Our Man In Marrakesh; Ten Little Indians (1965); 24 Hours to Kill; Victim Five*
Yellen, Gaye (act): *Night of Bloody Horror*
Yellen, Peter (act): *Driller Killer; Ms. 45*
Yellen, Sherman (wri): *Great Expectations (1974); Phantom of the Opera (1983)*
Yelling, Cavanaugh (act): *Web of Deceit*
Yelten, Jack (wri): *Ali Baba Goes to Town*
Yelton, Duke (wri): *Hillbillys In a Haunted House*
Yemelianov, Vladimir/V. (act): *Korol Lir; Planeta Bura*
Yen, Ann (act): *Prince of Darkness*
Yench, John (act): *The Omegans*
Yeoh, Michelle (act): *The Heroic Trio; Tomorrow Never Dies*
Yeoman, Robert (D.) (cin): *Dead Heat; Past Midnight*
Yepes, Jose (act): *The Mummy's Revenge*
Yerby, Frank (wri, 1916-1992): *The Saracen Blade*
Yeretzian, George (act): *Just Imagine*
Yergin, Irving (wri): *The Murder Game*
Yesko, Jeff (act): *I, Madman; Killer Klowns from Outer Space; School Spirit; Time Walker*
Yesso, Don (act): *Hocus Pocus*
Yetta (act): *Earth Girls Are Easy*
Yetter, William (act): *Above Suspicion; Counter-Espionage*
Yeun, Kelly (act): *Quarantine*
Yeung, Bob (act): *TC 2000*
Yezhkina, A. (act): *Shinel (1965)*
Yiasomi, George (act): *King Kong Lives; Young Indiana Jones: Travels with Father*
Yilmaz, Mechmed (act): *Moon 44*
Yimou, Zhang (act): *A Terra-Cotta Warrior*
Ying, Liu Ya (act): *Call Him Mr. Shatter*
Ying, Pai (act): *A Touch of Zen*
Ying, Qu (act): *Warriors of Virtue*
Yip, David (act): *Indiana Jones and the Temple of Doom; The Quatermass Conclusion; A View to a Kill*
Yniguez, Richard (act): *Shark Kill; Stalking Laura; World War III*
Yoakam, Dwight (act, b. 1956): *Roswell*
Yocum, Barbie (act): *Offerings*
Yoder, Aly (act): *The Resurrection of Zachary Wheeler*
Yoder, Mike (act): *Surf Nazis Must Die*
Yohn, Erica (act): *An American Tail: Fievel Goes West; Good Against Evil*
Yohnka, Merritt (act): *Timestalkers; Watchers II*
Yoke-Moon, Lee (act): *Children of the Damned*
Yonenaka, Ted (act): *Vampire On Bikini Beach*
Yong, Liu Ka (act): *Call Him Mr. Shatter*
Yordan, Philip (wri, b. 1913): *The Black Book; Bloody Wednesday; The Chase; The Day of the Triffids; Houdini (1953); Joe Macbeth; Johnny Guitar; The Naked Jungle; Suspense; The Unholy; Woman Who Came Back*
York, Andrew (wri): *Danger Route*
York, Cecil Morton (act): *First Men In the Moon (1919); Flying from Justice; The Golden Pince-Nez; In His Grip; Lorna Doone (1920); Old Bill Through the Ages; Trapped by the Mormons; Wuthering Heights (1920)*
York, Francine (act): *Curse of the Swamp Creature; The Doll Squad; Flood; I Love a Mystery (1966); Space Monster; Time Travelers (1976)*
York, Gerald (act): *It's Alive (1974); Simon, King of the Witches*
York, Jeff (act): *Fear In the Night (1947)*
York, John J. (act): *Closer and Closer; Night of the Creeps*
York, Michael (act, b. 1942): *Dark Mansions; Great Expectations (1974); The Island of Dr. Moreau (1977); A Knight In Camelot; Logan's Run; Lost Horizon (1973); Murder On the Orient Express; Not of This Earth (1995); Perfect Little Angels; Phantom of Death; Phantom of the Opera (1983); Return of the Musketeers; Something for Everyone; The Strange Affair; The Three Musketeers (1974); Wide Sargasso Sea; Zeppelin*
York, Roy (act): *Hamlet (1990)*
York, Susannah (act, b. 1942): *The Awakening; A Christmas Carol (1984); Images; Jane Eyre (1970); Just Ask for Diamond; Kaleidoscope; Loophole; The Maids; The Shout; Superman (1978); Superman II; Yellowbeard*
York, W. Allen (act): *It's Alive (1974)*
York, Wayne (act): *Runaway (1984)*
Yorke, Carol Gabriel (act): *Ghost In the Machine*
Yorke, Doris (act): *The Flaw (1955)*
Yorke, Duke (act): *Alias Boston Blackie; Island of Lost Souls*
Yorke, Edith (act): *The Phantom of the Opera (1925); Seven Keys to Baldpate (1925 & 1929)*
Yorke, Tracey (act): *The Big Switch*
Yorku, Harry (act): *Vice Versa (1988)*
Yorston, David (act): *The Green Slime; The Neptune Factor; Superman (1978)*
Yoshida, Hiroaki (dir & wri): *Twilight of the Cockroaches*
Yoshida, Teruo (act): *Body Snatcher from Hell*
Yoshida, Tetsuo (wri): *Majin, Monster of Terror; The Return of Giant Majin*
Yoshimura, Jitsuko (act): *Onibaba*
Yoshioka, Adele (act): *Charlie Chan: Happiness Is a Warm Clue*
Yoshkin, Nicolai (act): see Kosleck, Martin
Yost, David (act): *Mighty Morphin Power Rangers*
Yost, Dorothy (wri): *Murder On a Bridle Path*
Yost, Herbert (act): *Edgar Allan Poe*
Yost, Jason Harold (act): *Mighty Morphin Power Rangers*
Yost, Larry (wri): *Homebodies*
Yost, Norma (act): *Cape Fear (1961)*
Yost, Robert M. (wri): *Dante's Inferno (1935)*
Yothers, Cory "Bumpers" (act): *Dreamscape*
Youmans, William (act): *The Little Match Girl (1987)*
Young, Alan (act, b. 1919, nee Angus Young): *Androcles and the Lion; The Cat from Outer Space; Earth Angel; The Great Mouse Detective; The Time Machine (1960); Tom Thumb*
Young, Alice (act): *Princess Clementina*
Young, Angus (act): see Young, Alan
Young, Anita (act): *Peter Rabbit and the Tales of Beatrix Potter*
Young, Arthur (act, 1898-1959): *The Gelignite Gang; An Inspector Calls; Stranger from Venus*
Young, Ben (act): *Westworld*
Young, Benny (act): *Funny Man*
Young, Bill (act): *Escape 2000*
Young, Bob (mus): *Color Me Dead; Inn of the Damned*
Young, Brendan (act): *Mad Max*
Young, Brogan (act): *Virtuosity*
Young, Bruce (A.) (act): *Blink; Phenomenon; She Woke Up; What Ever Happened to Baby Jane? (1991)*
Young, Buck (act): *Look What's Happened to Rosemary's Baby; Tarzan In Manhattan*
Young, Burt (act, b. 1940, a.k.a. John Harris): *Amityville II: The Possession; Blood Beach; Carnival of Blood; Twilight's Last Gleaming*
Young, Cameron (act): *My Science Project*
Young, Carleton (act, 1907-1971): *Beyond a Reasonable Doubt; Cry Terror!; The Day the Earth Stood Still; Destination Saturn; Dick Tracy (1937); Phantom of the Jungle; Prince Valiant (1954); The Steel Trap; 20,000 Leagues Under the Sea (1954)*
Young, Carroll (wri, b. 1908): *Bomba and the Hidden City; Cannibal Attack; Captive Girl; Fury of the Congo; The Jungle; Killer Ape; Lost Continent (1951); Mark of the Gorilla; Pygmy Island; She-Devil (1957); Tarzan and the Mermaids; Tarzan and the She-Devil; Tarzan's Desert Mystery; Tarzan Triumphs*
Young, Charles W. (act): *Darkman (1990)*
Young, Chris (act): *Warlock: The Armageddon*
Young, Chris(topher) (mus): *Copycat; The Dark Half; Def Con 4; Flowers In the Attic; The Fly II; Hellbound: Hellraiser II; Hellraiser; Hush; Invaders from Mars (1986); Jennifer 8; A Nightmare On Elm Street, Part 2: Freddy's Revenge; The Power (1980); Pranks; Species; Tales from the Hood; Torment (1986); Trick or Treat; Unforgettable; Virtuosity; Wizards of the Lost Kingdom*
Young, Clara Kimball (act, 1890-1960): *Chandu; The Savage Woman; Trilby (1915)*
Young, Clarence Upson (wri): *Night Monster; The Plot Thickens; The Strange Case of Dr. Rx; Time to Kill (1942)*
Young, Clarissa (act): *The Godsend*
Young, Cleo (act): *Silent Night, Bloody Night*
Young, Clifton (act): *Dark Passage; Possessed (1947)*
Young, Clint (act): *Mind Over Murder; Time Walker*
Young, Dalene (wri): *The Plutonium Incident*
Young, Darren (act): *Cavegirl (1985)*
Young, David (GB act): *Sammy's Super T-Shirt*
Young, David (USA act): *Mary, Mary, Bloody Mary; Nightbreed; Poor Devil*
Young, De De (act): *Seconds*
Young, Denise (act): *The Bone Yard*
Young, Dey (act): *The Gifted One; Not Quite Human II; The Serpent and the Rainbow; Shadow Conspiracy; Spontaneous Combustion; Strange Behavior; Strange Invaders*
Young, Donald/Donnie (act): *Starship Invasions; Strange Days*
Young, Dov (act): *Wavelength*
Young, Eric (act): *Invasion (1965); The Sinister Man*
Young, Ernest F. (act): *The Mysterious Mr. Wong*
Young, Felicity (act): *Cover Girl Killer; Freedom to Die; The Gentle Trap; Out of the Shadow*
Young, Francis Brett (wri): *A Man About the House*
Young, Frederick/Freddie A. (cin, b. 1902): *The Asphyx; Bedelia; The Blue Bird (1976); The Deadly Affair; 49th Parallel; Gideon's Day; Gorgo; Great Expectations (1974); I Accuse (1958); Knights of the Round Table; Sword of the Valiant; Time Bomb; Treasure Island (1950); You Only Live Twice*
Young, Gary (act): *The Nude Bomb*
Young, Gig (act, 1913-1978, nee Byron Barr): *Deborah; Desk Set; Double Indemnity (1944); Hunt the Man Down; Love Letters; Pitfall; Sherlock Holmes In New York; The Shuttered Room; Spectre (1977); The Three Musketeers (1948); The Woman In White (1948)*
Young, Gladys (act): *One Wish Too Many*
Young, Gretchen (act): see Young, Loretta
Young, Harold (dir, b. 1897): *The Frozen Ghost; Jungle Captive; The Mummy's Tomb; Roogie's Bump; The Scarlet Pimpernel (1934)*
Young, Harrison (act): *Waxwork II: Lost In Time*
Young, Howard Irving (wri): *The Crimson Circle (1936); Midnight Mystery; The Secret of Stamboul; Time Flies (1944)*
Young, Ivan (act): *The Return of Dracula*
Young, J. Arthur (act): *The Living Ghost (1942)*
Young, James (act): *The Thing from Another World; Trilby (1915)*
Young, James (dir): *The Bells (1926); The Devil (1921); Trilby (1923)*
Young, James (wri): *The Bells (1926)*
Young, Jeremy (act): *Sudden Terror*
Young, Jimmy (act): *Otley*
Young, Joan (act): *Blood from the Mummy's Tomb; Child's Play (1954); The Fallen Idol; Mystery Junction; Suddenly Last Summer; Things Happen at Night; Vice Versa (1947)*
Young, John (act): *Black Angel (1980); Monty Python and the Holy Grail; The Wicker Man*
Young, John Sacret (wri): *The Possessed (1977)*
Young, Jordan (act): *Serial Mom*
Young, Karen (act): *Daylight; Jaws: The Revenge*
Young, Kendal (wri): *In the Devil's Garden*
Young, Keone (act): *Alien Nation; Beverly Hills Bodysnatchers; Eyewitness (1981); Fear (1990)*
Young, Leonard (mus): *No. 1 of the Secret Service*
Young, Les (cin): *Satan's Slave; The Swordsman; Terror (1979)*
Young, Les (wri): *Terror (1979)*
Young, Lilani (act): *Koroshi*
Young, Lois (act): *The Unseen (1981)*
Young, Loretta (act, b. 1913, nee Gretchen Young): *The Accused (1949); The Bishop's Wife; Bulldog Drummond Strikes Back (1934); Cause for Alarm!; Half Angel; Kismet (1930); Laugh, Clown, Laugh*
Young, Mark (wri): *Once Upon a Forest*
Young, Marlana (act): *Strange Days*
Young, Mary (Euro act): *The Murder Clinic*
Young, Mary (USA act): *The Lost Weekend; This Is My Love*
Young, Moira (wri): *Terror (1979)*
Young, Nathaniel (act): *Street Trash*
Young, Ned (act): *Seconds*
Young, Nedrick (act): *Captain Scarlett; Dead Men Walk*
Young, Nedrick (wri): *Shadow On the Land*
Young, Neil (act): *The Island of Dr. Moreau (1996); Made In Heaven*
Young, Otis (act, b. 1932): *Blood Beach; The Capture of Bigfoot; The Clones*
Young, Patrick (act): *Millennium*
Young, Paul (act): *Mad Max*
Young, Peter (wri): *The Fox and the Hound*
Young, Polly Ann (act): *The Invisible Ghost; Mystery Plane*
Young, Ray (act): *Blood of Dracula's Castle; Blue Sunshine*
Young, Raymond (act): *The Deadly Females; Death of an Angel; Destination Death; The Flesh and Blood Show; The Project; Scream and Die!; The 39 Steps (1978); Venetian Bird*
Young, Ric(hard) (act): *Assassin (1986); Cyborg 2: Glass Shadow; Friday the 13th—Part V: A New Beginning; Indiana Jones and the Last Crusade; Indiana Jones and the Temple of Doom*
Young, Robbin (act): *For Your Eyes Only*
Young, Robert (act, 1907-1998): *The Black Camel; The Canterville Ghost (1944); Crossfire; The Enchanted Cottage (1945); Miracles for Sale; The Secret Agent (1936); Secret of the Incas; They Won't Believe Me*
Young, Robert (Malcolm) (dir): *Doomsday Gun; Jane Eyre (1997); Splitting Heirs; Trauma (1963); Vampire Circus; The Worst Witch*
Young, (Robert) Malcolm (wri): *The Crawling Hand; Escape to Witch Mountain (1975); The Ghost of Flight 401; Sparkling Cyanide; Starflight: The Plane That Couldn't Land; Trauma (1963)*
Young, Robert Terry (act): *Brainstorm (1983)*
Young, Roger (dir): *A Knight In Camelot*
Young, Roger (wri): *Final Descent; Robin Cook's 'Mortal Fear'*
Young, Roland (act, 1887-1953): *Ali Baba Goes to Town; And Then There Were None; The Bishop Murder Case; King Solomon's Mines (1937); The Man Who Could Work Miracles; Sherlock Holmes (1922); Topper (1937); Topper Returns; Topper Takes a Trip; The Unholy Night*
Young, Ron (act): *Strange Days*
Young Jr., Russell James (act): *Eyes of Fire*
Young, Sallee Sunshine (act): *Pandemonium*
Young, sara (act): *The Nature of the Beast*
Young, Sean (act, b. 1960): *Baby: Secret of the Lost Legend; Blade Runner; Dr. Jekyll and Ms. Hyde; Dune; Forever; The Invader (1996); A Kiss Before Dying (1991); Mirage (1995); No Way Out; Witness to the Execution*
Young, Skip (act, 1929-1993): *The Spider (1958)*
Young, Starlina (act): *Def by Temptation*
Young, Stephen (act, b. 1939, nee Stephen Levy): *Deadline; The Mask of Sheba; Rage; Soylent Green*
Young, Steven (act): *The Toxic Avenger, Part II*
Young, Tammany (act): *Bits of Life*
Young, Terence (dir, 1915-1994): *Corridor of Mirrors; Dr. No; The Frightened Bride; From Russia With Love; Safari; Thunderball; Too Hot to Handle; Valley of the Eagles*
Young, Terence (wri, 1915-1994): *The Bad Lord Byron; On the Night of the Fire; Valley of the Eagles*
Young, Tony (act): *Guyana, Cult of the Damned*
Young, Tony (dir): *Hidden Homicide; Port of Escape*
Young, Tony (wri): *Hidden Homicide; Port of Escape*
Young, Trudy (act): *The Reincarnate*
Young, Victor (act): *Escape Clause; I Still Dream of Jeannie*
Young, Victor (mus, 1900-1956): *The Accused (1949); Around the World In 80 Days; Beyond the Blue Horizon; The Big Clock; Blackbeard the Pirate; The Blue Dahlia; A Connecticut Yankee In King Arthur's Court (1949); Dream Girl; Fair Wind to Java; Golden Earrings; Johnny Guitar; Love Letters; Maid of Salem; Ministry of Fear; Night Has a Thousand Eyes; Omar Khayyam; Samson and Delilah; Son of Sinbad; The Uninvited (1944)*
Young, W. (act): *Prehistoric People*
Young, Waldemar (wri, 1890-1938): *The Black Bird (1926); Island of Lost Souls; London After Midnight; Love Me Tonight; The Miracle Man (1932); The Mystic; Peter Ibbetson; The Unholy Three (1925); The Unknown (1927)*
Young, Walter (act): *The Adventurous Blonde*
Young, Warwick (act): *Alien Cargo*

Young, William Allen (act): The Day After; Stalking Laura
Young, Yvonne (act): Nightmare In Blood
Youngblood, Rob (act): Twice Upon a Time
Youngdeer, James (dir): The Black Cross Gang; Lieutenant Daring, RN, and the Water Rats; Queen of the London Counterfeiters; The Water Rats of London
Youngdeer, James (wri): The Black Cross Gang; Lieutenant Daring, RN, and the Water Rats; The Water Rats of London
Younger, Henry (wri): The Curse of the Mummy's Tomb; Prehistoric Women (1966)
Younger, Jack (act): Dinosaurus!; Hand of Death
Youngfellow, Barrie (act): It Came Upon the Midnight Clear; Nightmare In Blood; Vampire (1979)
Younggren, Gerald (act): The Lost Boys
Youngman, Gary (dir): Dead as a Doorman
Youngman, Henny (act, 1906-1998): Amazon Women On the Moon; The Gore-Gore Girls; Mother Goose A Go-Go
Youngren, Janis (act): Starship Invasions
Youngs, Gail (act): Alfred Hitchcock Presents; Timestalkers
Youngs, Jim (act): Cyborg 2: Glass Shadow; Skeeter
Younkins, Jerry (dir & wri): The Demon Lover
Youssov, Vadim (cin): Solaris
Youstos, Harry (act): The Alpha Incident; The Capture of Bigfoot
Yowlachie, Chief (act): The Scarlet Letter (1926)
Yrigoyen, Joe (act): The Prisoner of Zenda (1979)
Yu, Albert (dir): Devil Woman
Yu, Chin (act): Cloak Without Dagger
Yu, Ju (act): Teenage Mutant Ninja Turtles
Yu, Linda (act): Primal Fear
Yu, Ronny (dir): Bride of Chucky; Warriors of Virtue
Yuasa, Noriaki (dir): Attack of the Monsters; Gammera, the Invincible; Gammera vs. Guiron; Gammera vs. Gyaos; Gammera vs. Jiger; Gammera vs. Viras; Gammera vs. Zigra; The Return of the Giant Monsters
Yubero, Manuel Lopez (wri): Amador
Yu-Ching, Liu (act): Tarzan and the Golden Lion
Yuen, Galen (act): Cyborg 2: Glass Shadow
Yui, Masayuki (act): Ran
Yuill, Jimmy (act): Mary Shelley's 'Frankenstein'; Paper Mask
Yuk, Henry (act): Eyewitness (1981)
Yule, Ian (act): The Big Game
Yule Jr., Joe (act): see Rooney, Mickey
Yule, John (act): The Flesh and Blood Show; Frightmare (1974); House of Mortal Sin
Yulin, Harris (act): Bad Dreams; The Believers; Cutthroat Island; Ghostbusters II; Loch Ness; Multiplicity; Narrow Margin (1990); Night Moves
Yu Ling, Barbara (act): Hardware; The Satanic Rites of Dracula
Yumi, Raoru (act): Phoenix (1978)
Yung, Liu Chia (act): Legend of the Seven Golden Vampires
Yun-Hee, Chong (act): Village In the Mist
Yunker, Peter (act): Memories of Murder
Yunus, Tariq (act): The Deceivers
Yurevsky, Y. (dir): Sonka Zolotaya Ruchka
Yuricich, Richard (cin): Brainstorm (1983)
Yurka, Blanche (act, 1887-1974): At Sword's Point; The Bridge of San Luis Rey (1944); Cry of the Werewolf; Ellery Queen and the Murder Ring; One Body Too Many
Yuro, Dominique (act): The Outing
Yuro, Robert (act): Crackle of Death
Yurtik, Yuri (wri): Zvenigora
Yuseph, Johnny (act): Mothra
Yusolfsky, J. Gary (act): see Lockwood, Gary
Yuspeh, Ira (mus): 7 Doors of Death
Yuspeh, Mitch (mus): 7 Doors of Death
Yuval, Peter (dir): Firehead
Yuzna, Brian (dir): Bride of Re-Animator; The Dentist II; Necronomicon: Book of the Dead; Silent Night, Deadly Night 4: Initiation; Society
Yuzna, Brian (wri): From Beyond; Honey, I Blew Up the Kid; Honey, I Shrunk the Kids; Silent Night, Deadly Night 4: Initiation
Yuzna, Conan (act): Silent Night, Deadly Night 4: Initiation
Z, Bunki (act): The Kindred
Zaaglol, Saad (act): A Story of Tutankhamun
Zabala, Elsa (act): Amador; Hundra
Zabala, Jose Maria (dir): The Fury of the Wolfman
Zabel, Bruce (wri): Official Denial
Zaborin, Lila (act): Blood Orgy of the She-Devils
Zabka, William (act): The Power Within (1995)
Zabriskie, Grace (act): Child's Play 2; The Crew; Ferngully: The Last Rain Forest; Houdini (1998); Megaville; The Private Eyes (1980); The Servants of Twilight; Twin Peaks: Fire Walk With Me
Zacapa, Daniel (act): Phenomenon; Seven
Zacarias, Miguel (dir): The Sin of Adam and Eve
Zach, Debra (act): RoboCop
Zacha, William T./W.T. (act & wri): The Ultimate Impostor
Zacharias, Alfred (dir & wri): The Bees; Demonoid
Zacharias, Steve (act): The Kremlin Letter
Zachary, Justin (act): To All a Goodnight
Zache, Bob (act): White of the Eye
Zacherle, John (act): Frankenhooker
Zachmanoglou, Nike (act): Ms. 45; Trick or Treats
Zack, Roman (act): Street Trash
Zada, Aamy (act): Two Evil Eyes
Zada, Ramy (act): After Midnight; The Judas Project
Zadora, Pia (act, b. 1956): Fake-Out; Santa Claus Conquers the Martians; Voyage of the Rock Aliens
Zagaria, Anita (act): Zone Troopers
Zagarino, Frank (Anthony) (act): Armstrong; Cyborg Cop III; Barbarian Queen; Orion's Key; Project: Shadowchasher; Project Shadowchaser III; Waxwork II: Lost In Time
Zagon, Marty (act): Metalstorm: The Destruction of Jared-Syn
Zagot, Bill (act): Shock Chamber
Zahlava, Bruce (cin): Blood Diner
Zahler, Gordon (mus): Plan 9 from Outer Space
Zahler, Lee (mus): Crime Doctor; Ellery Queen and the Murder Ring; Ellery Queen and the Perfect Crime; Queen of the Amazons (1947)
Zahner, Sigrid K. (act): Primal Fear
Zahorsky, Bohus (act): Baron Prasil
Zahrn, Will (act): The Package
Zaichenko, Pyotr (act): Parad Planyet
Zaigue, Robert (act): Witches' Brew
Zajac, Mathew (act): Transmutations
Zajdman, Monica (act): Oh Heavenly Dog
Zajonc, Robert "Bobby Z" (act): Arachnophobia; Outbreak; Shadow Conspiracy
Zak (animal act): Brainscan
Zakharov, Rostislav (dir & wri): Cinderella (1961)
Zalata, Jane (act): The Diabolical Invention
Zalewska, Halina (act): I Lunghi Capelli della Morte; Triumph of the Ten Gladiators
Zallian, Steven (wri): Mission: Impossible
Zaloom, George (act): Psycho IV: The Beginning
Zaloom, George (wri): Encino Man
Zaloom, Joe (act): Echoes
Zamacona, Jorge (wri): World Gone Wild
Zamecki, Richard (act): Forever Evil
Zammi, Alfredo (act): Colossus and the Headhunters
Zammit, Eddie (act): The Dungeonmaster
Zamora, Del (act): Repo Man; RoboCop
Zampa, Luigi (dir, 1905-1991): The Flower In His Mouth; His Last 12 Hours
Zamperla, Nazzareno (act): Il Trionfo di Ercole
Zampi, Mario (dir, 1903-1963): The Fatal Night; Shadow of the Past; Top Secret (1952)
Zampi, Mario (wri, 1903-1963): Shadow of the Past
Zamuto, Elliot (act): The Legend of the Wolf Woman
Zanchi, Kenneth (act): Wes Craven's New Nightmare
Zander, Peter (act): The Return of Mr. Moto
Zane, Bartine (act): Galaxina
Zane, Billy (act, b. 1966): Back to the Future; Back to the Future, Part II; Blood and Concrete; Critters; Dead Calm; Demon Knight; Megaville; Orlando; The Phantom (1996); Pocahontas II: Journey to a New World; Reflections In the Dark; The Silence of the Hams
Zane, Lisa (act): Freddy's Dead: The Final Nightmare; Her Deadly Rival; The Nurse; Terrified (1995)
Zane, Milton (act): Eyewitness (1981)
Zangwill, Israel (wri): The Verdict (1946)
Zanin, Bruno (act): Amarcord
Zann, Lenore (act): Def Con 4; Happy Birthday to Me; Return (1985)
Zanolli, Angelo (act): Maciste-The Mighty; Morgan the Pirate; Son of Samson; The Witch's Curse
Zanotto, Juan (wri): Yor, the Hunter from the Future
Zanuck, Darryl F. (wri, 1902-1979): Wolf's Clothing (1927)
Zanville, Bernard (act): see Clark, Dane
Zany, Bob (act): Repossessed
Zapata, Carmen (act): Point of No Return; There Goes the Bride; W
Zapata, Mike (act): Voodoo Heartbeat
Zapien, Danny (act): Nightwing
Zapp, Kelly (act): Wavelength
Zappa, Frank (mus): The World's Greatest Sinner
Zappa, Moon (act): Heartstopper; Nightmares (1983); The Spirit of 76
Zappala, Joseph (mus): Swords of the Space Ark
Zappata, Janet (act): Dangerous Touch
Zappia, Robert (wri): Halloween H20
Zapponi, Bernardino (wri): La Citta delle Donne; Profundo Rosso; Satyricon; Spirits of the Dead
Zara (act): On Her Majesty's Secret Service
Zaran, Nick (act): Tiffany Jones
Zarchi, Meir (dir & wri): I Spit On Your Grave
Zardi, Dominique (act): La Rupture
Zardi, Federico (wri): The Trojan Horse
Zaremba, John (act, 1909-1986): Earth vs. the Flying Saucers; Frankenstein's Daughter (1958); Herbie Rides Again; The Legend of Lizzie Borden; The Magnetic Monster; Return to Fantasy Island; The Time Machine (1978); 20 Million Miles to Earth
Zaremby, Justin (act): The Hand That Rocks the Cradle
Zareschi, Elena (act): Ulysses
Zaro, Jose (act): El Castillo de la Bofetadas
Zarou, Elias (act): The Spider and the Fly (1994)
Zarov, Elias (act): The Kidnapping of the President
Zarro, Joe (act): The Toxic Avenger
Zarro, Ric (cin): The Warlord: Battle for the Galaxy
Zarro, Ron (cin): The Warlord: Battle for the Galaxy
Zarvade, Nestor (act): El Vampiro Acecha
Zaslov, Alan (dir): The Return of Jafar
Zaslow, Michael (act, 1944-1998): Meteor
Zatovic, Milos (act): The Groundstar Conspiracy
Zavadsky, Yuri (act): Aelita
Zavaglia, Lawrence (act): Ms. 45
Zavattini, Cesare (wri, 1902-1989): Il Cappotto; His Last 12 Hours; Miracle In Milan
Zavelyov, Boris (cin): Zvenigora
Zavitz, Lee (cin): Bride of the Gorilla; Captain Kidd; Destination Moon; From the Earth to the Moon; The Snow Creature
Zavod, Allan (mus): Communion; Howling III; Martians Go Home; The Time Guardian
Zaza, Munair (act): Popcorn
Zaza, Paul (J.) (mus): The Club (1994); Curtains; The Haunting of Hamilton High; The Housekeeper; Murder by Decree; My Bloody Valentine; The Pink Chiquitas; Popcorn; Prom Night
Zbonek, Edwin (dir): Der Henker von London; The Monster of London
Z'Dar, Robert (act): Beastmaster 2: Through the Portal of Time; Evil Altar; Final Sanction; Frogtown II; A Gnome Named Gnorm; Maniac Cop; Maniac Cop 2; Maniac Cop 3: Badge of Silence; The Night Stalker (1987); Soultaker
Zebro, Lisa (act): Dr. Heckyl & Mr. Hype
Zebulon, Michael (act): Heart and Souls
Zecca, Ferdinand (act, 1864-1947): Les Sept Chateaux du Diable; Une Tempete dans une Chambre a Coucher
Zecca, Ferdinand (dir, 1864-1947): Ali Baba et les 400 Voleurs; La Conquete de l'Air; Le Sept Chateaux du Diable; Une Tempete dans une Chambre a Coucher
Zecca, Ferdinand (wri, 1864-1947): Ali Baba et les 400 Voleurs; La Conquete de l'Air
Zecevic, Paul W. (act): Cameron's Closet
Zee, Eleanor (act): Blood Beach
Zeeman, George E. (act): Oh Heavenly Dog
Zeff, Ilene Cara (act): Nightfall (1988)
Zeffirelli, Franco (dir, b. 1923): Hamlet (1990); Jane Eyre (1996)
Zeffirelli, Franco (wri, b. 1923): Jane Eyre (1996)
Zeglio, Primo (dir): Mission Stardust; Revenge of the Pirates
Zeglio, Primo (wri): Sword of the Conqueror
Zehetgruber, Rudolf (dir): Superwheels
Zeigler, Jesse (act): Matinee
Zeigler, Ted (act): The Devil and Max Devlin
Zeilinski, Rafal (act & dir): Spellcaster
Zeimann, Sonja (act): De Sade
Zeisberger, Ingmar (act): The Strangler of Blackmoor Castle
Zeisler, Alfred (dir): Crime Over London; Fear (1946); Schuss im Morgengrauen
Zeitlin, Denny (mus): Invasion of the Body Snatchers (1978)
Zeitlin, Erica (act): My Best Friend Is a Vampire
Zeitlin, Lawrence (wri): Paradisio
Zelaya, Don (act): Amazon Quest
Zelazny, Roger (wri, 1937-1995): Damnation Alley
Zelenovic, Srdjan (act): Frankenstein (1974)
Zeller, Gary (cin): Scanners
Zeller, Wolfgang (mus): Vampyr
Zellner, Alan (act): I Was a Zombie for the F.B.I.
Zellner, Arthur J. (wri): A Message from Mars (1921)
Zellweger, Renee (act, b. 1969): Return of the Texas Chainsaw Massacre
Zelnik, Fred (dir): I Killed the Count
Zelnik, Jerzy (act): Faraon
Zelouf, Susan (wri): Curse II: The Bite
Zeltser, Yuri (dir): Eye of the Storm
Zeltser, Yuri (wri): Bad Dreams; Eye of the Storm
Zeman, Karel (dir & wri, b. 1910): Baron Prasil; Cesta Do Praveku; The Diabolical Invention; Na Komete; War of the Fools
Zeman, Richard (act): Brainscan
Zemarel, Jamie (act): Nightbeast
Zemeckis, Alex (act): Contact
Zemeckis, Robert (dir, b. 1952): Amazing Stories; Back to the Future; Back to the Future, Part II; Back to the Future, Part III; Contact; Death Becomes Her; Romancing the Stone; Tales from the Crypt (1989); What Lies Beneath; Who Framed Roger Rabbit
Zemeckis, Robert (wri, b. 1952): Back to the Future; Back to the Future, Part III; Tales from the Crypt Presents Bordello of Blood
Zenda, John (act): Halloween II; Invitation to Hell
Zendar, Fred (act): Beyond the Poseidon Adventure
Zenon, Michael (act): Rituals
Zenor, Suzanne (act): The Baby
Zens, Will (dir & wri, b. 1920): Capture That Capsule!
Zentall, Kate (act): Once Bitten
Zentz, Martin (act): Lord of the Flies (1990)
Zepeda, Gerardo (act): Caveman (1981); Dr. Tarr's Torture Dungeon
Zepeda, Jorge (act): Amityville 3-D; The Arrival (1996)
Zerbe, Anthony (act): Asteroid; Child of Glass; The Dead Zone; Farewell, My Lovely; The First Deadly Sin; The Hound of the Baskervilles (1972); Kiss Meets the Phantom of the Park; Licence to Kill (1989); The Omega Man; The Return of the Man from U.N.C.L.E.; Star Trek: Insurrection; Steel Dawn; To Save a Child
Zerbe, Maylon (act): Forever Evil
Zerbinati, Luigi (act): Satyricon
Zerby, Kim (act): see Darby, Kim
Zerna, Gene (act): Dr. Caligari
Zernecke, Linda (act): Through the Magic Pyramid
Zertuche, Kinta (wri): The Wasp Woman (1959)
Zetlin, Barry (act): Beverly Hills Bodysnatchers
Zetlin, Barry (dir & wri): The Dogfighters
Zetterling, Mai (act, 1925-1994): The Bad Lord Byron; Blackmailed; Faces In the Dark; The Frightened Bride; Hets; Jet Storm; The Man Who Finally Died; Offbeat; Piccadilly Third Stop; Portrait from Life; A Prize of Gold; The Ringer (1952); The Witches (1990)
Zharikov, Ye (act): My Name Is Ivan
Zharkov, Alexei (act): Parad Planyet
Zheimo, Anna (act): Shinel (1926)
Zheliabuzhsky, Yuri (cin): Aelita
Zheliabuzhsky, Yuri (dir): Morozko
Zheljazkova, Binka (dir): Privarzaniat Balon
Zhengyuan, Zhang (act): Life On a String
Zhivago, Stacia (act): Sorority House Massacre 2
Zhongyuan, Liu (act): Life On a String
Zhonov, Georgi (act): Planeta Bura
Zlchy, Theodore (dir): Night Without Pity
Zido, Janis (act): The House On Sorority Row
Ziegler, Anne (act): Faust (1936); The Laughing Lady
Ziegler, Ernest (act): Willy Wonka and the Chocolate Factory
Ziegler, Karen (act): see Black, Karen
Ziehl, Joan (act): The Telephone Book
Ziehm, Howard (dir): Flesh Gordon; Flesh Gordon 2: Flesh Gordon Meets the Cosmic Cheerleaders
Ziehm, Howard (cin): Flesh Gordon
Ziehm, Judy (act): Flesh Gordon
Zielinski, Jerzy (cin): Powder
Zielinski, Rafal (dir): Fun
Ziemann, Sonja (act): The Secret Ways
Zien, Chip (act): Hello Again; Howard the Duck
Zierold, Jan (act): Making Contact
Ziesing, Lucinda (act): The Boogey Man

Ziffren, Lester (wri): *Charlie Chan In Panama; Charlie Chan In Rio; Charlie Chan's Murder Cruise; Murder Over New York*

Zigmond, Jerry (wri): *The She-Creature*

Ziller, Paul (dir): *Panic In the Skies!; Pledge Night*

Zima, Madeline (act): *The Hand That Rocks the Cradle*

Zima, Yvonne (act, b. 1989): *Christmas Every Day; The Long Kiss Goodnight*

Zimbalist, Al (cin): *Cat-Women of the Moon*

Zimbalist, Al (wri): *Cat-Women of the Moon; King Dinosaur*

Zimbalist, Donald (wri): *Valley of the Dragons*

Zimbalist Jr., Efrem (act, b. 1923): *Batman: Mask of the Phantasm; Terror Out of the Sky; Zorro: The Legend Begins*

Zimbalist, Stephanie (act, b. 1956): *The Awakening; The Babysitter; Tomorrow's Child*

Zimbo (animal act): *The Man Who Laughs (1928)*

Zimeas, John (act): *House of Usher (1960)*

Zimm, Maurice (wri): *Creature from the Black Lagoon*

Zimmel, Harv (wri): *Snow Kill*

Zimmer, Hans (mus): *The Borrowers (1998); The Lion King; Pacific Heights; Paperhouse; The Peacemaker (1997); Point of No Return; The Prince of Egypt; The Zero Boys*

Zimmer, Kim (act, b. 1955): *Body Heat*

Zimmer, Pierre (act): *Le Deuxieme Souffle; Le Silencieux*

Zimmer, Sonia (act): *Prom Night*

Zimmerman, Alex (act): *Ghostbusters II*

Zimmerman, Bruce (act): *The Toxic Avenger*

Zimmerman, Jack (act): *The Pit (1983)*

Zimmerman, Joey (act): *Halloweentown*

Zimmerman, Ken (act): *I Was a Zombie for the F.B.I.*

Zimmerman, Matt (act): *Thunderbirds Are Go; Thunderbird 6*

Zimmerman, Natalie (act): *Murder of Innocence*

Zimmerman, Patric (act): *Jetsons: The Movie*

Zimmerman, Vernon (dir): *Fade to Black*

Zimmerman, Vernon (wri): *Fade to Black; Hex; Teen Witch*

Zimmerman, Victor (act): *The Great Impersonation (1942); Peril from the Planet Mongo; Purple Death from Outer Space*

Zimmern, Terri (act): *The Manster*

Zimmers, Don (mus): *Screams of a Winter Night*

Zindel, Paul (wri): *Alice In Wonderland (1985); Babes In Toyland (1986); A Connecticut Yankee In King Arthur's Court (1989)*

Zink, Chuck (act): *Mission Mars*

Zink, Ralph Spencer (wri): *The Invisible Menace*

Zinnemann, Fred (dir, 1907-1997): *Eyes In the Night; Kid Glove Killer*

Zinner, Peter (mus): *King Kong vs. Godzilla*

Zinny, Karl (act): *Demons (1985)*

Zinny, Victoria (act): *Beyond the Door III; Viridiana*

Zipp, William (act): *Future Force*

Zippel, David (mus): *Hercules (1997)*

Zipson, Alan (act): *The Abominable Dr. Phibes*

Ziskie, Dan (act): *Twisted*

Ziskin, Joel (wri): *Mata Hari (1985)*

Zitner, Alan (act): *Fortress*

Zito, Joseph (dir): *Abduction; Friday the 13th-The Final Chapter; The Prowler (1981)*

Zito, Robin (act): *Fake-Out*

Zittel, Zygmunt (act): *Matka Joanna od Aniolow*

Zittrer, Carl (mus): *Children Shouldn't Play With Dead Things; Deranged (1974); Murder by Decree; Prom Night; Silent Night, Evil Night*

Zitzermann, Bernard (cin): *I Married a Shadow*

Zivojinovic, Bata (act): *Majstori i Margarita*

Ziyad II, Seifullah (act): *The Silence of the Hams*

Zlotoff, Lee David (dir): *Plymouth*

Zlotoff, Lee (David) (wri): *Link; Plymouth*

Zmed, Adrian (act): *The Final Terror; Storm Chasers: Revenge of the Twister*

Zobda, France (act): *Sheena*

Zobel, Richard (act): *To Sleep With a Vampire*

Zobian, Mark (act): *Dead Dudes In the House*

Zohar, Rita (act): *From the Dead of Night; Lady In White*

Zoll, Marika (act): *The Dungeonmaster*

Zolotin, Adam (act): *Dog's Best Friend; Jack; Storm of the Century*

Zombies, The (act & mus): *Bunny Lake Is Missing*

Zomina, Sonia (act): *Eyes of a Stranger; The Funhouse (1981)*

Zondag, Dick (dir): *We're Back! A Dinosaur's Story*

Zondag, Ralph (dir): *We're Back! A Dinosaur's Story*

Zongwan, Wei (act): *Buddha's Lock*

Zoofoot (act): *Redneck Zombies*

Zoppe, James (act): *Getting Lucky*

Zorich, Louis (act): *They Might Be Giants*

Zorn, Eric (wri): *Murder of Innocence*

Zorn, Gunther (act): *Making Contact*

Zorn, John (mus): *Funny Games*

Zounds Jr., Archibald (wri): *La Vendetta di Ercole*

Zovia, Allan (mus): *Fatal Sky*

Zoykic, Lydia (act): *The Saint*

Zozaya, Paloma (act): *Dr. Tarr's Torture Dungeon*

Zsigmond, Vilmos/William (cin, b. 1930): *Blood of Ghastly Horror; Blow Out; Close Encounters of the Third Kind; The Ghost and the Darkness; Horror of the Blood Monsters; Images; The Monitors; The Nasty Rabbit; Obsession (1976); The Sadist; Sliver; The Time Travelers (1964); Winter Kills; The Witches of Eastwick*

Zsigmond, William (cin): see Zsigmond, Vilmos/William

Zsombolyai, Janos (cin): *Return (1985)*

Zuanelli, Umberto (act): *La Citta delle Donne*

Zuanic, Rod (act): *Mad Max Beyond Thunderdome*

Zuber, Marc (act): *Robin Hood: Prince of Thieves; The Satanic Rites of Dracula*

Zubiaga, Antonio (act): *Dr. Tarr's Torture Dungeon*

Zubizarreta, Arrate (act): *Hundra*

Zubkov, Valentin (act): *My Name Is Ivan*

Zucco, George (act, 1886-1960): *The Adventures of Sherlock Holmes (1939); After the Thin Man; Arrest Bulldog Drummond; The Black Raven; The Black Swan; The Cat and the Canary (1939); Charlie Chan In Honolulu; Confidential Agent; Dark Streets of Cairo; Dead Men Walk; Dr. Renault's Secret; Ellery Queen and the Murder Ring; The Flying Serpent; Fog Island; House of Frankenstein; The Hunchback of Notre Dame (1939); I Love a Mystery (1945); London by Night (1937); Lured; The Mad Ghoul; The Mad Monster; The Man Who Could Work Miracles; Marie Antoinette (1938); The Monster and the Girl; Moss Rose; The Mummy's Ghost; The Mummy's Hand; The Mummy's Tomb; The Rare Book Murders; Return of the Ape Man; The Roof; Scared to Death (1947); Shadows In the Night; Sherlock Holmes In Washington; Sudan; Tarzan and the Mermaids; Topper Returns; Voodoo Man; What Happened Then?*

Zuck, Alexandra (act): see Dee, Sandra

Zucker, Bob (act): *First Knight*

Zucker, Burt (act): *First Knight*

Zucker, Charlotte (act): *First Knight; Ghost (1990)*

Zucker, David (dir & wri): *Top Secret! (1984)*

Zucker, Frank (cin): *The Man from Beyond*

Zucker, Jerry (dir): *First Knight; Ghost (1990); Top Secret! (1984)*

Zucker, Jerry (wri): *Top Secret! (1984)*

Zucker, Kate (act): *First Knight*

Zucker, Miriam (act): *Street Trash*

Zucker, Ralph (dir): *Cinque Tombe per un Medium*

Zucker, Ralph (wri): *The Devil's Wedding Night*

Zuckerman, Alex(ander) (act): *The Exorcist III; Freaked*

Zuckerman, Buck (act & wri): see Henry, Buck

Zuckerman, George (wri): *Spy Hunt; The Tattered Dress*

Zuckerman, Steve (mus): *Spawn of the Slithis*

Zuckert, William/Bill (act, 1920-1997): *Devil Dog: The Hound of Hell; Ellery Queen: Don't Look Behind You; Hangar 18; Killer in the Mirror; Shock Corridor; The Time Machine (1978)*

Zuckmann, Eric (act): *I Aim at the Stars*

Zuelke, Mark (act): *Sinful Intrigue*

Zugsmith, Albert (dir, b. 1910): *Confessions of an Opium Eater; Dog Eat Dog; On Her Bed of Roses; The Private Lives of Adam and Eve; Sex Kittens Go to College*

Zugsmith, Albert (wri, b. 1910): *On Her Bed of Roses*

Zukor, Frank (cin): *The Midnight Girl*

Zulawski, Andrzej (dir & wri): *Possession (1981)*

Zully, Stewart J. (act): *Wolf*

Zuniga, Daphne (act): *The Fly II; The Initiation; Pandora's Clock; Prey of the Chameleon; Spaceballs*

Zurakowska, Dianik (act): *Cauldron of Blood*

Zuri, Jahi J.J. (act): *Nemesis 2*

Zurk, Steve (act): *Biohazard: The Alien Force; Matinee*

Zurli, Guido (dir): *The Mad Butcher*

Zussin, Victoria (act): *The Purple Rose of Cairo*

Zutaut, Brad (act): *Girlfriend from Hell*

Zweig, Stefan (wri, 1881-1942): *Brainwashed*

Zweigler, Mark (act): *Poltergeist III*

Zwerling, Darrell (act): *Doc Savage, the Man of Bronze; The Ultimate Warrior*

Zwick, Joel (dir): *Second Sight*

Zynda, Henry (act): *Spy Smasher Returns*

Zynda, Tom (act): *I Was a Zombie for the F.B.I.*

Film Chronology

1896

Dix Chapeaux en 60 Secondes - *Fr*
The Egg-Laying Man - *GB*
The Fakir - *Fr*
Guillaume Tell - *Fr*
The Kiss - *USA*
Le Manoir du Diable - *Fr*
The Mysterious Paper - *Fr*
The Mysterious Rabbit - *GB*
Une Nuit Terrible - *Fr*
Un Petit Diable - *Fr*
Rip Van Winkle - *USA*
Seance de Prestidigitation - *Fr*
Tom Old Boot - *Fr*
The Vanishing Lady - *Fr*

1897

L'Auberge Ensorcelee - *Fr*
Le Cabinet de Mephistopheles - *Fr*
Le Cauchemar - *Fr*
Le Chateau Hante - *Fr*
La Cigale et la Fourmi - *Fr*
The Corsican Brothers - *GB*
D. Devant, Conjurer - *Fr*
L'Execution d'un Espion - *Fr*
Faust and Marguerite - *Fr*
Hail Britannia - *GB*
L'Hallucination de l'Alchemiste - *Fr*
The Joyful Skeleton - *Fr*
The Laboratory of Mephistophles - *Fr*
Making Sausages - *GB*
Le Magnetiseur - *Fr*
Professor Garland the Conjurer - *GB*
The Vanishing Lady - *GB*
X-Rays - *GB*

1898

The Adventures of William Tell - *Fr*
Animated Clown Portrait - *GB*
Cinderella and the Fairy Godmother - *GB*
La Caverne Maudite - *Fr*
The Clown Barber - *GB*
Creations Spontanees - *Fr*
The Damnation of Faust - *Fr*
Disaster, Launching of HMS Albion - *GB*
Faust and Mephistophles - *GB*
Fencing Contest from 'The Three Musketeers' - *GB*
The Four Troublesome Heads - *Fr*
The Haunted Cave - *Fr*
L'Homme dans la Lune - *Fr*
Illusions Fantasmagoriques - *Fr*
Le Magicien - *Fr*
Magie Diabolique - *Fr*
The Mesmerist - *GB*
Photographing a Ghost - *GB*
Pygmalion et Galatee - *Fr*
Le Reve d'Artiste - *Fr*
Le Reve du Pauvre - *Fr*
Santa Claus - *GB*
Santa Claus and the Children - *GB*
The Temptation of St. Anthony - *Fr*
The Triple Lady - *Fr*

1899

Aladdin and the Wonderful Lamp - *GB*
The Awakening of Chrysis - *Fr*
Cendrillon - *Fr*
Le Chevalier Mystere - *Fr*
Cleopatre - *Fr*
La Cremation - *Fr*
La Danse de Feu - *Fr*
Le Diable au Couvent - *Fr*
Dick Whittington - *GB*
Evocation Spirite - *Fr*
The Haunted Picture Gallery - *GB*
L'Impressioniste Fin de Siecle - *Fr*
The Inexhaustible Cab - *GB*
The Lightning Change Artist - *GB*
Le Miroir de Cagliostro - *Fr*
The Miser's Doom - *GB*
Neptune et Amphitrite - *Fr*
La Pierre Philosophale - *Fr*
Le Portrait Mysterieux - *Fr*
Le Spectre - *Fr*
La Statue de Neige - *Fr*
Upside Down: or, The Human Flies - *GB*
The Would-Be Conjurer - *GB*

1900

As Seen Through the Eyes of a Telescope - *GB*
Chinese Magic - *GB*
The Clown and the Enchanted Candle - *GB*
Clown and the Policeman - *GB*

The Conjurer - *GB*
The Conjurer and the Boer - *GB*
Coppelia ou la Poupee Animee - *Fr*
Le Deshabille Impossible - *Fr*
Le Duel d'Hamlet - *Fr*
Le Fou Assassin - *Fr*
The Gunpowder Plot - *GB*
L'Illusioniste Double et la Tete Vivante - *Fr*
Jeanne d'Arc - *Fr*
The Last Days of Pompeii - *GB*
Living Statues - *GB*
Le Livre Magique - *Fr*
Le Malade Hydrophobe - *Fr*
Les Miracles du Brahmane - *Fr*
The One Man Band - *Fr*
Le Repas Fantastique - *Fr*
Le Reve de Noel - *Fr*
Le Reve du Rajah ou la Foret Enchantée - *Fr*
Les Sept Peches Capitaux - *Fr*
Sherlock Holmes Baffled - *USA*
Le Sorcier, le Prince et le Bon Genie - *Fr*
Spiritisme Abracadabrant - *Fr*
Topsy-Turvy Villa - *GB*
Les Trois Bacchantes - *Fr*
The Up-to-Date Conjurer - *GB*
The White Slave - *USA*

1901

Ali Baba et les 400 Voleurs- *Fr*
Artistic Creation - *Fr*
Barbe-Bleue - *Fr*
The Brahmin and the Butterfly - *Fr*
Le Chapeau a Surprises - *Fr*
The Cheese Mites: or, Lilliputians in a London Restaurant - *GB*
La Conquete de l'Air - *Fr*
The Devil in the Studio - *GB*
Dislocation Mysterieuse - *Fr*
Dolly's Toys - *GB*
The Drunkard's Conversion - *GB*
The Elixir of Life - *GB*
Excelsior! - *Fr*
The Famous Illusion of Kolta - *GB*
La Fontaine Sacree ou la Vengeance de Boudha - *Fr*
The Glutton's Nightmare - *GB*
Guguste et Belzebuth - *Fr*
Harlequinade—What They Found in the Laundry Basket - *GB*
The Haunted Curiosity Shop - *GB*
L'Homme aux Cent Trucs - *Fr*
The Indian Chief and the Seidlitz - *GB*
The Magic Extinguisher - *GB*
The Magician's Cavern - *Fr*
The Magic Sword: or, A Mediaeval Mystery -*GB*
The Marvellous Hair Restorer - *GB*
Off to Bloomington Asylum - *Fr*
Ora Pro Nobis: or, The Poor Orphan's Last Prayer - *GB*
An Over-Incubated Baby - *GB*
Le Petit Chaperon Rouge - *Fr*
La Phrenologie Burlesque - *Fr*
The Puzzled Bather and His Animated Clothes - *GB*
Scrooge: or, Marley's Ghost - *GB*
Le Temple de la Magie - *Fr*
La Tour Maudite - *Fr*
Undressing Extraordinary: or, The Troubles of a Tired Traveller - *GB*
The Waif and the Wizard: or, The Home Made Happy - *GB*
William Tell (R. W. Paul) *GB*
William Tell - (Warwick Trading Co.) - *GB*

1902

The Amazons' March and Evolutions - *GB*
L'Armoire des Freres Davenport - *Fr*
Les Aventures de Robinson Crusoe - *Fr*
Le Bataillon Elastique - *Fr*
La Clownesse Fantome - *Fr*
The Corsican Brothers - *GB*
La Danseuse Microscopique - *Fr*
Le Diable Geant ou le Miracle de la Madonne - *Fr*
The Dwarf and the Giant - *Fr*
The Enchanted Cup - *GB*
L'Equilibre Impossible - *Fr*
The Eruption of Mont-Pele - *Fr*
The Extraordinary Waiter - *GB*
A Father's Vengeance - *GB*
Father Thames' Temperance Cure - *GB*
La Femme Volante - *Fr*
Frankenstein's Trestle - *USA*
L'Homme-Mouche - *Fr*

The Hotel Mystery - *GB*
Une Indigestion - *GB*
Little Jim: or, The Cottage Was a Thatched One - *GB*
The Maniac's Guillotine - *GB*
The Man with the Rubber Head - *Fr*
Maria Martin: or, The Murder at the Red Barn - *Fr*
Mother Goose Nursery Rhymes - *GB*
Le Reve du Pariah - *Fr*
That Eternal Ping-Pong - *GB*
Les Tresors de Satan - *Fr*
Le Voyage dans la Lune - *Fr*
Les Voyages de Gulliver - *Fr*
The Wild Man of Borneo - *GB*

1903

Adventurous Voyage of 'The Arctic' - *GB*
Alice in Wonderland - *GB*
The Assassination of the King and Queen of Servia - *GB*
Le Chaudron Infernal - *Fr*
Cheese Mites - *GB*
Le Corbeille Enchantée - *Fr*
David Devant, Conjurer - *GB*
Dorothy's Dream - *GB*
The Effects of Too Much Scotch - *GB*
The Enchanted Well - *Fr*
L'Enchanteur Alcofrisbas - *Fr*
An Evil-Doer's Sad End - *GB*
An Extraordinary Cab Accident - *GB*
Extraordinary Illusions - *Fr*
Faust aux Enfers - *Fr*
Les Filles du Diable - *Fr*
La Flamme Merveilleuse - *Fr*
La Guirlande Merveilleuse - *Fr*
The Infernal Cakewalk- *Fr*
Jack et Jim - *Fr*
King of Coins - *GB*
La Lanterne Magique - *Fr*
The magical Box - *Fr*
The Marvelous Syringe - *GB*
Mary Jane's Mishap: or, Don't Fool with the Paraffin - *GB*
Le Melomane - *Fr*
Le Monstre - *Fr*
Les Mousquetaires de la Reine - *Fr*
The Mysterious Mechanical Toy - *GB*
L'Oracle de Delphes - *Fr*
A Photographic Episode - *GB*
Pocket Boxers - *GB*
Le Portrait Spirite - *Fr*
Remorse - *GB*
Le Reve du Maitre de Ballet - *Fr*
Le Revenant - *Fr*
Rip Van Winkle - *GB*
Le Royaume des Fees - *Fr*
Le Sorcier - *Fr*
La Statue Animee - *Fr*
A Substantial Ghost - *GB*
Tom Tight et Dum Dum - *Fr*
Le Tonnerre de Jupiter - *Fr*

1904

Les Apparitions Fugitives - *Fr*
Le Coffre Enchante - *Fr*
Les Costumes Animes - *Fr*
Daisy's Adventures in the Land of Chrysanthemums - *GB*
La Dame Fantome - *Fr*
Damnation of Doctor Faust - *Fr*
Le Diner Impossible - *Fr*
Dr. Cut'emup - *GB*
The Enchanted Toymaker - *GB*
For the Hand of a Princess - *GB*
Gabriel Grub the Surly Sexton - *GB*
The Haunted Scene Painter - *GB*
An Interesting Story - *GB*
Jap the Giant Killer - *GB*
The Jonah Man: or, The Traveller Bewitched - *GB*
Le Juif Errant - *Fr*
The Kidnapped Child - *GB*
Le Merveilleux Eventail Vivant - *Fr*
Un Miracle sous l'Inquisition - *Fr*
Mr. Mosenstein - *GB*
The Mistletoe Bough - *GB*
The Music Hall Manager's Dilemma - *GB*
The Pierrot's Romance - *GB*
Un Peu de Feu, S.V.P. - *Fr*
Le Reve de l'Horloger - *Fr*
Revenge! - *GB*
Le Rosier Miraculeux - *Fr*
La Sirene - *Fr*
Siva, l'Invisible - *Fr*

The Slavey's Dream - *GB*
Sorcellerie Culinaire - *Fr*
Tchin-Chao, the Chinese Conjurer - *Fr*
Les Transmutations Imperceptibles - *Fr*
Up to His Tricks - *GB*
Le Voyage a Travers l'Impossible - *Fr*

1905

The Adventures of Sherlock Holmes - *USA*
L'Ange de Noel - *Fr*
The Babes in the Wood - *GB*
Beauty and the Beast - *GB*
Les Cartes Vivantes - *Fr*
La Chaise a Porteurs Enchantee - *Fr*
A Christmas Card: or, The Story of Three Homes - *GB*
Le Compositeur Toque - *GB*
The Dancer's Dream - *GB*
Le Diable Noir - *Fr*
Doings in Dolly Land - *GB*
An Eccentric Burglary - *GB*
An Eclipse of the Moon - *GB*
The Electric Goose - *GB*
The Freak Barber - *GB*
Goaded to Anarchy - *GB*
La Grotte aux Surprises - *Fr*
L'Ile de Calypso: Ulysse et Polypheme - *Fr*
La Legende de Rip Van Winkle - *Fr*
Le Menuet Lilliputien - *Fr*
A Mesmerian Experiment - *Fr*
Natural Laws Reversed - *GB*
The Night Before Christmas - *USA*
Le Palais des Mille et Une Nuits - *Fr*
Le Phenix ou le Coffret de Cristal - *Fr*
The Pierrot and the Devil's Dice - *GB*
Prehistoric Peeps - *GB*
Shamus O'Brien: or, Saved from the Scaffold - *GB*
Le Systeme du Docteur Sonflamort - *Fr*
Table Turning - *GB*
The Tempest - *GB*
La Tour de Londres et les Dernieres Moments d'Anne Boleyn - *Fr*
The Visions of an Opium Smoker - *GB*

1906

The Cabby's Dream - *GB*
The Coming of Santa Claus - *GB*
The Conjurer's Pupil - *GB*
Cupid and the Widow - *GB*
Le Dirigeable Fantastique ou le Cauchemar d'un Inventeur - *Fr*
The Dream of a Rarebit Fiend - *USA*
The Eccentric Thief - *GB*
The Fairy Godmother - *GB*
Le Fantome d'Alger - *Fr*
Les 400 Farces du Diable - *Fr*
The Gambler's Nightmare - *GB*
The Hand of the Artist - *GB*
The Horse That Ate the Baby - *GB*
How to Make Time Fly - *GB*
The Impossible Lovers - *GB*
Les Incendiaires - *Fr*
Introductions Extraordinary - *GB*
Jack le Ramoneur - *Fr*
Just in Time - *GB*
Lady Audley's Secret - *GB*
The Little Conjurer - *GB*
A Lively Quarter Day - *GB*
The Madman's Fate - *GB*
The Magic Bottle - *GB*
The Magic Ring - *GB*
La Magie a Travers les Ages - *Fr*
The Medium Exposed - *GB*
The Motor Valet - *GB*
The Mysterious Retort - *Fr*
The Pirate Ship - *GB*
Punch and Judy - *Fr*
The Puzzle Maniac - *GB*
The ? Motorist - *GB*
Soap Bubbles - *GB*
The Tramp's Dream - *GB*
The Vacuum Cleaner Nightmare - *GB*
A Visit to a Spiritualist - *GB*
The Witch - *GB*
The World's Wizard - *GB*

1907

The Absent-Minded Professor - *GB*
The Apple of Discord - *GB*
The Bewildering Cabinet - *Fr*
The Brigand's Daughter - *GB*
Le Carton Fantastique - *Fr*
Comedy Cartoons - *GB*
The Chef's Revenge - *GB*

983

Cinderella - GB
The Cook's Dream - GB
Delerium in a Studio - Fr
Deux Cent Mille Lieues sous les Mers - Fr
Diablo Nightmare - GB
The Dodger's Dodged - GB
The Doll's Revenge - GB
Dreamland Adventures - GB
Drink - GB
The Eclipse - Fr
The Fatal Hand - GB
Les Fromages Automobiles - Fr
The Ghosts' Holiday - GB
The Green Dragon - GB
Hair Restorer - GB
Hamlet - Fr
Hanky Panky Cards - GB
The Haunted Bedroom - GB
Her Rival's Necklace - GB
A Knight Errant - GB
The Madman's Bride - GB
The Mad Monkey - GB
A Modern Galatea - GB
My Lady's Revenge - GB
Never Complain to Your Laundress - GB
La Nouvelle Peine de Mort - Fr
Oh That Molar! - GB
An Overdose of Love Potion - GB
The Pied Piper - GB
The Power of the Sultan - USA
The Red Spectre - Fr
Rescued from an Eagle's Nest - USA
Le Reve de Shakespeare - Fr
The Ride of the Valkyries - GB
Satan en Prison - Fr
Sister Mary Jane's Top Note - GB
The Sorcerer's Scissors - GB
That Fatal Sneeze - GB
A Tramp's Dream of Wealth - GB
True Till Death - GB
Le Tunnel sous la Manche ou le Cauchemar Franco-Anglais - Fr
The Viking's Bride - GB
The Waif and the Statue - GB
The Water Babies: or, The Little Chimney Sweep - GB
When the Devil Drives - GB
Willie's Magic Wand - GB
The Witch Kiss - Fr

1908
An Angelic Servant - Fr
Animated Matches - GB
The Assassination of the Duc de Guise - Fr
Les Aventures de Don Quichotte - Fr
The Burglar and the Clock - GB
La Cuisine de l'Ogre - Fr
The Devil and the Cornet - GB
The Devil's Bargain - GB
Dr. Jekyll and Mr. Hyde - USA
Don Quixote's Dream - GB
Dreams of Toyland - GB
The Drunkard's Dream - GB
The Dumb Man of Manchester - GB
The Fairy's Sword - GB
A Faithless Sword - GB
Le Fakir de Singapoure - Fr
Fantasmagorie - Fr
La Fontaine Merveilleuse - Fr
La Genie de Feu - Fr
Grandmother's Story - Fr
The Great Salome Dance - GB
The Greedy Girl - GB
The Hands of a Wizard - GB
The Harmless Lunatic's Escape - GB
How the Artful Dodger Secured a Meal - GB
In the Land of Nod - GB
The Invisible Button - GB
Jane Shore - GB
The Knight of Black Art - Fr
The Lady Luna(tic)'s Hat - GB
The Lightning Postcard Artist - GB
Long-Distance Wireless Photography - Fr
The Lost Handkerchief - GB
The Love of a Gypsy - GB
Lunatics in Power - USA
The Magical Box - GB
The Magic Garden - GB
The Man and His Bottle - GB
The Man and the Latchkey - GB
The Man Who Learned to Fly - GB
Mechanical Legs - GB
Nick Carter - USA
Nick Carter—Bandits in Evening Dress - USA
The Nursemaid's Dream - GB
The Old Favourite and the Ugly Golliwog - GB
Oriental Black Art - Fr
[illegible] - GB
The Phantom Ship - GB
La Poupee Vivante - Fr
The Prehistoric Man - Fr

The Prehistoric Man - GB
The Professor's Antigravitational Fluid - GB
The Professor's Great Discovery - GB
A Quick-Change Mesmerist - GB
The Red Barn Crime: or, Maria Martin - GB
Le Reve d'un Fumeur d'Opium - Fr
Richard III - USA
Robin Hood and His Merry Men - GB
The Scarlet Letter - USA
Snatched from a Terrible Death - GB
The Tempest - GB
Les Torches Humaines - Fr
The Tricky Convict: or, The Magic Cap - GB
Gli Ultimi Giorni di Pompei - It
Vengeance is Mine - GB
The Waif's Christmas - GB
Weary Willie Steals a Fish - GB
When the Man in the Moon Seeks a Wife - GB

1909
An Absorbing Tale - GB
The Airship Destroyer - GB
Animated Cotton - GB
The Bewitched Manor House - Fr
Bobby Wideawake - GB
Cinderella Up-to-Date - Fr
The Convict's Dream - GB
The Council of Three - GB
The Devil (Biograph) - USA
The Devil (Edison) - USA
Drowsy Dick's Dream - GB
Edgar Allan Poe - USA
The Electric Servant - GB
Electric Transformation - GB
The Faithful Clock - GB
The Fatal Appetiser - GB
Father's Baby Boy - GB
From Servant Girl to Duchess - GB
Gertie the Dinosaur - USA
A Glass of Goat's Milk - GB
Her Lover's Honour - GB
How I Cooked Peary's Record - GB
Hypnotic Suggestion - GB
Hypnotist's Revenge - Fr
Invisibility - GB
The Invisible Dog - GB
The Jealous Doll: or, The Frustrated Elopement - GB
The Kidnapped King - GB
The Life of Moses - USA
Little Jim - GB
Little Nemo - USA
The Lost Memory - GB
The Love of a Hunchback - GB
Love versus Science - GB
Macbeth - It
The Magic Carpet - GB
The Miser's Fate - GB
Mistaken Identity - GB
Monty Learns to Swim - GB
The Mummy and King Rameses - Fr
The Mystery of Edwin Drood - GB
Nick Carter in Danger - USA
Nick Carter—Sleeping Pills - USA
The Peril of the Fleet - GB
A Prince of Khyber - GB
Professor Puddenhead's Patents—The Aerocab and Vacuum Provider - GB
Professor Puddenhead's Patents—The Electric Enlarger - GB
The Professor's Dream - GB
The Professor's Strength Tablets - GB
The Professor's Twirly-Whirly Cigarettes - GB
Richelieu, or The Cardinal's Conspiracy - USA
Salome Mad - GB
Saved by a Dream - GB
Scouts to the Rescue - GB
Sexton Blake - GB
Shakespeare's Tragedy, King Lear - GB
Sherlock Holmes - Den
The Sleepwalker - GB
Sooty Sketches - GB
Suspected: or, The Mysterious Lodger - GB
Le Systeme du Docteur Goudron et du Professeur Plume - Fr
The Tale of the Ark - GB
The Tower of London - GB
I Tre Moschettieri - It
The Trial of Abraham's Faith - GB
Turning the Tables - GB
The Wizard's Walking Stick - GB
The Wrong Cab - GB
Zillah, a Story of Gipsy Life - GB

1910
The Aerial Submarine - GB
The Airtight Safe - GB
Alice's Adventures in Wonderland - USA
The Bewitched Boxing Gloves - GB
The Blue Bird - GB
La Caduta di Troia - It

Ching-Ching's Revenge - GB
Cock-a-Doodle-Doo - GB
The Detective in Peril - GB
Dr. Brian Pellie, Thief and Coiner - GB
Dr. Jekyll and Mr. Hyde - Den
The Duality of Man - GB
The Electric Vitalizer - GB
Embroidery Extraordinary - GB
Erratic Power - GB
Faust - GB
Frankenstein - USA
The Freezing Mixture - GB
Galathee - Fr
The Harlequinade - GB
The Hindoo's Treachery - GB
L'Homme aux Mille Inventions - Fr
Hot Pickles - GB
Les Illusions Fantaisistes - Fr
Invigorating Electricity - GB
Jewel Thieves Run to Earth by Sexton Blake - GB
A Lively Skeleton - GB
Le Locataire Diabolique - Fr
Lucrezia Borgia - It
A Lunatic Expected - GB
A Mechanical Husband - GB
The Mechanical Mary Anne - GB
Mr. Poorluck's Dream - GB
Mr. Tubby's Triumph - GB
A Modern Love Potion - GB
Le Mousquetaire de la Reine - Fr
Moveite, a New Hustling Powder - GB
Nick Carter as an Acrobat - USA
Only One Girl: or, A Boom in Sausages - GB
Le Papillon Fantastique - Fr
Pikovaya Dama - Russ
Professor Piecan's Discovery - GB
The Queen of the May - GB
Rip Van Winkle - USA
Le Roi des Mediums - Fr
The Sculptor's Dream - GB
Le Secret du Medecin - Fr
Sleepy Sam's Awakening - GB
A Thrilling Story - GB
The Toymaker's Dream - GB
A Trip to Mars - USA
Vice Versa - GB
Wanted, a Mummy - GB
The Wizard of Oz - USA
A Woman's Treachery - GB

1911
The Advantages of Hypnotism - GB
The Aerial Anarchists - GB
The Automatic Motorist - GB
A Bag of Monkey Nuts - GB
Brown Bewitched - GB
Buffalo Bill on the Brain - GB
The Cap of Invisibility - GB
A Case for Sherlock Holmes - GB
Cinderella (Selig) - USA
Cinderella (Thanhouser) - USA
Dandy Dick of Bishopsgate - GB
The Demon Dog - GB
Dr. Brian Pellie and the Bank Robbery - GB
Dr. Brian Pellie and the Baronet's Bride - GB
The Faith Healer - GB
The Fakir's Fan - GB
A False Friend - GB
Faust - GB
The Foreign Spy - GB
Giles Has His Fortune Told - GB
Gipsy Nan - GB
Les Hallucinations du Baron de Munchausen - Fr
Have It Out, My Boy, Have It Out! - GB
The Heat Wave - GB
His Conscience - GB
How a Mosquito Operates - USA
The Hunchback - GB
Jane Shore - GB
Jim of the Mounted Police - GB
Jones' Nightmare - GB
A Juvenile Hypnotist - GB
The King's Peril - GB
Kitty in Dreamland - GB
Little Lady Lafayette - GB
Little Red Riding Hood - GB
The Lobster Nightmare - GB
The Lunatic at Liberty - GB
Macbeth - GB
The Magic Ring - GB
The Man Who Kept Silent - GB
Mischievous Puck - GB
The Modern Pygmalion and Galatea - GB
The Mummy - USA
Mystic Manipulations - GB
Nick Carter—The Mystery of the White Bed - USA
Notre Dame de Paris - Fr
Pharos the Wonder Worker - GB
The Pirates of 1920 - GB

The Prehistoric Man - GB
A Present from India - GB
Princess Clementina - GB
Rachel's Sin - GB
Richard III - GB
Right is Might - GB
Satan—or, The Drama of Humanity - It
The Scarlet Letter - USA
Scroggins Goes in for Chemistry and Discovers a Marvellous Powder - GB
Scroggins Has His Fortune Told - GB
She - USA
Through Fire to Fortune - GB
Topsy's Dream of Toyland - GB
A Touch of Hydrophobia - GB
A Tragedy of the Olden Times - GB
A Very Powerful Voice - GB
A Village Tragedy - GB
With Mask and Pistol - GB
The Wizard and the Brigands - GB
Xmas Greeting Film - GB

1912
The Adventures of Dick Turpin—The Gunpowder Plot - GB
The Adventures of Dick Turpin—The King of the Highwaymen - GB
A la Conquete du Pole - Fr
Aladdin in Pearlies - GB
Animated Toys - GB
At the Eleventh Hour - GB
The Avaricious Monk - GB
Bertie's Book of Magic - GB
The Beryl Coronet - GB
Bewildering Transformations - GB
Billiards Mad - GB
Card Manipulations - GB
The Cat's Cup Final - GB
Children of the Forest - GB
A Child's Dream of Christmas - GB
A Chinaman's First Day in London - GB
Cinderella - GB
Cinderella: or, The Glass Slipper - Fr
Clever Egg Conjuring - GB
The Conjuring Tramps - GB
The Conjurer as a Good Samaritan - GB
Constable Smith and the Magic Baton - GB
Constable Smith in Trouble Again - GB
Constable Smith on the Warpath - GB
The Copper Beeches - GB
The Count of Monte Cristo - USA
The Crystal Gazer - GB
Danse Vampiresque - Den
Dante's Inferno - It
The Deception - GB
Detective Ferris - GB
Dr. Brian Pellie and the Spanish Grandees - GB
Dr. Brian Pellie Escapes from Prison - GB
Dr. Jekyll and Mr. Hyde - USA
Dream Paintings - GB
An Eccentric Sportsman - GB
Electrical House-Building - GB
The Electric Belt - GB
The Electric Legs - GB
The Eye of the Idol - GB
The Fairy Doll - GB
Father's Forty Winks - GB
The Flooded Mine - GB
The Forced Confession - GB
Ghosts - GB
The Great Anarchist Mystery - GB
The Great Tiger Ruby - GB
Hamlet - GB
The Harvest of Sin - GB
The Heart of a Woman - GB
The Herncrake Witch - GB
His Honour at Stake - GB
In Fairyland - GB
The Irony of Fate - GB
Jack and the Fairies - GB
Japanese Magic - GB
The Jester's Joke - GB
The Joker's Mistake - GB
King Robert of Sicily - GB
Kleptomania Tablets - GB
The Lady of Shallot - GB
The Land of the Nursery Rhymes - GB
The Legend of King Cophetua - GB
The Lesser Evil - USA
A Letter to the Princess - GB
The Lonely Inn - GB
Lorna Doone - GB
Love Patches - GB
A Man of Mystery - GB
Man's Genesis - USA
The Masked Smuggler - GB
Mephisto - GB
Mirth and Mystery - GB
The Missing Tiara - GB
Modelling Extraordinary - GB

A Modern Mystery - *GB*
The Mummy - *GB*
The Musgrave Ritual - *GB*
The Mystery of Boscombe Vale - *GB*
The Mystic Ring - *GB*
Nan in Fairyland - *GB*
Never Again, Never! - *GB*
A New Aladdin - *GB*
A Night of Peril - *GB*
Not in These - *GB*
Old Mother Hubbard - *GB*
Overcharged - *GB*
The Palace of Mystery - *GB*
Paul Sleuth, Crime Investigator: The Burglary Syndicate -*GB*
Pygmalion and Galatea - *GB*
The Rajah's Revenge - *GB*
The Reigate Squires - *GB*
Robin Hood - *USA*
Robin Hood Outlawed - *GB*
Santa Claus - *GB*
Sexton Blake v. Baron Kettler - *GB*
She Must Have Swallowed *It* - *GB*
A Shock-ing Complaint - *GB*
Silver Blaze - *GB*
The Sleeping Beauty - *GB*
A Smoky Story - *GB*
The Smuggler's Revenge - *GB*
The Speckled Band - *GB*
Sports in Moggyland - *GB*
The Stolen Airship Plans - *GB*
The Stolen Papers - *GB*
The Submarine Plans - *GB*
Ten Little Nigger Boys - *GB*
The Trail of the Fatal Ruby - *GB*
Vampyrn - *Swed*
The Vengeance of Daniel Whidden - *GB*
The Vengeance of Egypt - *Fr*
While the Cook Slept - *GB*
William Drake, Thief - *GB*
The Witch of the Welsh Mountains - *GB*

1913

Der Andere - Ger
Atlantis - Ger
At the Foot of the Scaffold - *GB*
Balaoo - *Fr*
Belinda's Dream - *GB*
Bewitched Matches - *Fr*
Black and White - *GB*
Bumbles' Diminisher - *GB*
Cinderella - *GB*
The Cloister and the Woman - *GB*
Crime at the Mill - *GB*
The Daughter of Romany - *GB*
A Daughter of Satan - *USA*
Daydreams - *GB*
Dick Turpin's Ride to York - *GB*
Dicke Turpin's Ride to Yorke - *GB*
Dr. Brian Pellie and the Wedding Gifts - *GB*
Dr. Jekyll and Mr. Hyde - *GB*
Dr. Jekyll and Mr. Hyde - *USA*
Dr. Trimball's Verdict - *GB*
The Fairies' Revenge - *GB*
The Fairy Bottle - *GB*
Fantomas - *Fr*
The Fate of a King - *GB*
The Fish and the Ring - *GB*
For East is East - *GB*
The Foreign Spy - *GB*
The Foundling - *GB*
Das Fremde Madchen - Ger
Gigantic Marionettes - *GB*
Gipsy Hate - *GB*
Guy Fawkes and the Gunpowder Plot - *GB*
Hamlet - *GB*
The Harper Mystery - *GB*
Det Hemmelighedsfulde X - Den
Here We Are Again - *GB*
Highwayman Hal - *GB*
His Wonderful Lamp - *GB*
The House of Mystery - *GB*
In Prehistoric Days - *USA*
In the days of Robin Hood - *GB*
In the Dead Man's Room - *GB*
In the Toils of the Blackmailer - *GB*
The Isle of the Dead - Den
It's Love That Makes the World Go Round - *GB*
The Jovial Fluid - *GB*
Larks in Toyland - *GB*
Liquid Love - *GB*
Little Micky the Mesmerist - *GB*
London by Night - *GB*
The Long Ago - *USA*
Love and War in Toyland - *GB*
Maria Marten: or, The Murder in the Red Barn - *GB*
A Message from Mars - *GB*
Mifanwy—A Tragedy - *GB*
The Misadventures of Mike Murphy - *GB*
Mother Gets the Wrong Tonic - *GB*
The Murder of Squire Jeffrey - *GB*
The Mystic Mat - *GB*

The Mystic Moonstone - *GB*
A Newsboy's Christmas Dream - *GB*
The Nightmare of the Glad-Eye Twins - *GB*
The Of-Course-I-Can Brothers - *GB*
An Old Toymaker's Dream - *GB*
Once Upon a Time - *GB*
On the Brink of the Precipice - *GB*
Partners in Crime - *GB*
The Passions of Men - *GB*
Pimple's Inferno - *GB*
The Pit and the Pendulum - *USA*
Popsy Wopsy - *GB*
Professor Hoskin's Patent Hustler - *GB*
The Rejuvenation of Dan - *GB*
Satan - *GB*
The Scarlet Letter - *GB*
The Scarlet Letter - *USA*
Scrooge - *GB*
Secret Service - *GB*
Snatched from Death - *GB*
Spiritualism Exposed - *GB*
The Star and Crescent - *GB*
Der Student von Prag - Ger
The Tempter - *GB*
Through the Clouds - *GB*
Time Flies - *GB*
The Tramp's Dream - *GB*
The Tube of Death - *GB*
Gli Ultimi Giorni di Pompei - *It*
The Vampire - *GB*
The Vampire - *USA*
The Werewolf - *USA*
The White Witch - *GB*
Willie's Dream of Mick Squinter - *GB*
A Woman's Hate - *GB*

1914

The Adventures of a Football - *GB*
Aladdin: or, A Lad Out - *GB*
The Antique Brooch - *GB*
The Avenging Conscience - *USA*
The Basilisk - *GB*
Beautiful Jim - *GB*
Bernardo's Confession - *GB*
The Bishop's Silence - *GB*
The Black Cross Gang - *GB*
The Black Spot - *GB*
The Bloodstained Shoe - *GB*
The Brass Bottle - *GB*
The Breaking Point - *GB*
The Bridge Destroyer - *GB*
The Bronze Idol - *GB*
The Cage - *GB*
Called Back - *GB*
The Chimes - *GB*
A Chinese Vengeance - *GB*
A Christmas Carol - *GB*
Cinder-Elfred - *GB*
The Corner House Burglary - *GB*
Creatures of Clay - *GB*
The Cry of the Captive - *GB*
The Curtain - *GB*
A Daughter of Satan - *GB*
The Dead Heart - *GB*
The Desert Island - *GB*
Detective Daring and the Thames Coiners - *GB*
Detective Finn and the Foreign Spies - *GB*
Detective Finn: or, In the Heart of London - *GB*
Diamond Cut Diamond - *GB*
Dr. Fenton's Ordeal - *GB*
Dr. Paxton's Last Crime - *GB*
The Doctor's Crime - *GB*
The Electric Doll - *GB*
Eugene Aram - *GB*
The Fakir's Spell - *GB*
The False Wireless - *GB*
The Family Solicitor - *GB*
Fear of the Hangman - *GB*
For Love and the Crown - *GB*
The German Spy Peril - *GB*
A Ghostly Affair - *GB*
Ghosts - *GB*
The Gloves of Ptames - *GB*
Der Golem - Ger
The Great German North Sea Tunnel - *GB*
The Great Spy Raid - *GB*
The Grit of a Dandy - *GB*
Guarding Britain's Secrets - *GB*
The Guest of the Evening - *GB*
The Gypsy's Curse - *GB*
A Hair-Raising Episode in One Splash - *GB*
The Harbour Lights - *GB*
Henpeck's Nightmare - *GB*
The Hidden Witness - *GB*
His Just Desserts - *GB*
His Prehistoric Past - *USA*
His Sister's Honour - *GB*
The Houseboat Mystery - *GB*
The Humpty Dumpty's Circus - *GB*
In the Grip of Spies - *GB*
In the Shadow of Big Ben - *GB*

Jollyboy's Dream - *GB*
Justice - *GB*
The Kaiser's Dream -*GB*
The Kaiser's Spies - *GB*
The King of Crime - *GB*
The King of Seven Dials - *GB*
The King's Minister - *GB*
The King's Romance - *GB*
Kismet - *GB*
The Kiss of Clay - *GB*
Lieutenant Daring, Aerial Scout - *GB*
Lieutenant Daring and the Stolen Invention - *GB*
Lieutenant Pimple and the Stolen Submarine - *GB*
The Lights O' London - *GB*
The Little Match Girl - *GB*
The Live Wire - *GB*
A London Mystery - *GB*
London's Underworld - *GB*
Love and Magic - *GB*
Love Spots - *GB*
Magical Mysteries - *GB*
The Magic Glass - *GB*
Magic Squares - *GB*
The Man Behind the Mask - *GB*
The Man with a Scar - *GB*
Marjory's Goldfish - *GB*
The Master Crook Outwitted by a Child - *GB*
The Master Crook Turns Detective - *GB*
A Merry Night - *GB*
Mike Murphy's Dream of Love and Riches - *GB*
Mike Murphy's Dream of the Wild West - *GB*
Mr. Meek's Nightmare - *GB*
Morphia, the Death Drug - *GB*
The Murdock Trial - *GB*
The Mystery of Mr. Marks - *GB*
The Mystery of the Diamond Belt - *GB*
The Mystery of the Old Mill - *GB*
Neptune's Daughter - *USA*
The Night Bell - *GB*
Old St. Paul's - *GB*
The Opium Cigarettes - *GB*
The Patchwork Girl of Oz - *USA*
Paul Sleuth and the Mystic Seven - *GB*
Pearls of Death - *GB*
The People of the Rocks - *GB*
The Phantom of the Brain - *GB*
Pimple and Galatea - *GB*
A Price on His Head - *GB*
The Primeval Test - *USA*
The Prisoner of Zenda - *USA*
The Pursuit of Venus - *GB*
The Quarry Mystery - *GB*
Queenie of the Circus - *GB*
Queen of the London Counterfeiters - *GB*
The Rajah's Tiara - *GB*
The Ring and the Rajah - *GB*
The Ring That Wasn't - *GB*
Rip Van Winkle - *GB*
Saved by a Dream - *GB*
The Schemers: or, The Jewels of Hate - *GB*
The Second Penalty - *GB*
A Secret Life - *GB*
The Secret of the Air - *GB*
Self-Accused - *GB*
The Shirker's Nightmare - *GB*
The Showman's Dream - *GB*
The Sins of Harvey Clare - *GB*
The Smugglers' Cave - *GB*
Some Fish! - *GB*
The Sorrows of Selina - *GB*
Spirits - Den
Sports in Toyland - *GB*
The Spy - *GB*
The Stolen Masterpiece - *GB*
The Stolen Plans - *GB*
The Story of a Cross - *GB*
The Strength That Failed - *GB*
The Stress of Circumstance - *GB*
A Study in Scarlet - *GB*
The Suicide Club - *GB*
Swanker and the Witch's Curse - *GB*
Swanker Meets His Girl - *GB*
The Tangram - *GB*
Temptation - *GB*
The Temptation of Joseph - *GB*
The Terror of the Air - *GB*
That Mysterious Fez - *GB*
Thelma: or, Saved from the Sea - *GB*
Through the Ages - *GB*
Tigris - *It*
To Save the King - *GB*
The Tragedy of Basil Grieve - *GB*
Transformations - *GB*
The Tricky Stick - *GB*
Trilby - *GB*
The Unseen Witness - *GB*
The Vampire's Tower - *USA*
The Vengeance of the Air - *GB*
Wake Up!: or, A Dream of Tomorrow - *GB*
When London Sleeps - *GB*
The Wrecker of Lives - *GB*

1915

Adventures of Willie Woodbine and Lightning Harry—A Joyride to the Cannibal Islands - *GB*
The Airman's Children - *GB*
Aladdin - *GB*
Alone in London - *GB*
And Then He Woke Up - *GB*
The Angel of the Ward - *GB*
The Arab's Curse - *GB*
The Ashes of Revenge - *GB*
The Beggar Girl's Wedding - *GB*
Behind the Curtain - *GB*
Beneath the Mask - *GB*
The Blackmailers - *GB*
A Bold Adventuress - *GB*
Buttons - *GB*
By the Hand of a Brother - *GB*
The Cakes of Khandipore - *GB*
The Charm That Charmed - *GB*
The Chimney's Secret - *USA*
The Club of Pharos - *GB*
The Clue of the Cigar Band - *GB*
The Confession - *GB*
The Counterfeiters - *GB*
The Crimson Triangle - *GB*
A Cry in the Night - *GB*
Darkest London: or, The Dancer's Romance - *GB*
A Devil of a Honeymoon - *GB*
The Devil's Bondman - *GB*
The Devil's Profession - *GB*
The Devil to Pay - *GB*
The Dungeon of Death - *GB*
The Dustman's Nightmare - *GB*
The Dust of Egypt - *USA*
The Fatal Formula - *GB*
Fetters of Fear - *GB*
A Fight for Life - *GB*
The Firm of Girdlestone - *GB*
A Fluke in the 'Fluence - *GB*
Flying from Justice - *GB*
La Folie du Docteur Tube - *Fr*
From Scotland Yard - *GB*
A Garret in Bohemia - *GB*
The Girl Who Took the Wrong Turn - *GB*
The Great Cheque Fraud - *GB*
Hamlet - *GB*
The Hand at the Window - *GB*
The Harlequinade - *GB*
The Haunting of Silas P. Gould - *GB*
Hawkeye, King of the Castle - *GB*
Heba the Snake Woman - *GB*
Her Fatal Hand - *GB*
Her Life in London - *GB*
His Phantom Burglar - *GB*
Horrible Hyde - *USA*
Humoty Dumpty R.A. - *GB*
The Incorruptible Crown - *GB*
Iron Justice - *GB*
The Ivory Hand - *GB*
Jane Shore - *GB*
Jim the Scorpion - *GB*
The Kweer Kuss - *GB*
Life without Soul - *USA*
The Lion's Cubs - *GB*
The Live Mummy - *GB*
London Nighthawks - *GB*
London's Yellow Peril - *GB*
Maciste - *It*
The Man in the Attic - *GB*
The Man Who Stayed at Home - *GB*
The Man Who Wasn't - *GB*
The Man with the Scar - *GB*
The Master of Merripit - *GB*
The Mesmerist - *GB*
Mizpah: or, Love's Sacrifice - *GB*
The Monkey's Paw - *GB*
Monty's Monocle - *GB*
The Moonstone - *USA*
The Mysteries of London - *GB*
The Mystery of a Hansom Cab - *GB*
The Mystery of a London Flat - *GB*
The New Adventures of Baron Munchausen - *GB*
The New Governess - *GB*
Nick Carter and the Black-Coated Thieves - *USA*
The Octopus Gang - *GB*
Pawns of Mars - *USA*
The Port of Missing Women - *GB*
Portret Doriana Greya - *Russ*
A Prehistoric Love Story - *GB*
The Prisoner of Zenda - *GB*
Quicksands of Life - *GB*
The Raven - *USA*
The Rogues of London - *GB*
The Romany Rye - *GB*
Royal Love - *GB*
Rupert of Hentzau - *GB*
Ruskin's Agony(?) - *GB*
Selina-Ella - *GB*
The Seventh Word - *GB*
Sexton Pimple - *GB*

Slavers of the Thames - *GB*
The Sons of Satan - *GB*
Spoof for Oof - *GB*
The Stolen Heirlooms - *GB*
Strategy - *GB*
The Striped Stocking Gang - *GB*
A Study in Skarlit - *GB*
The Tell-Tale Globe - *GB*
Things We Want to Know - *GB*
The Thornton Jewel Mystery - *GB*
Trilby - *USA*
The Troubles of a Hypochondriac - *GB*
The Two Roads - *GB*
The Underworld of London - *GB*
A Vagabond's Revenge - *GB*
The Vampire's Clutch - *USA*
Vice and Virtue: or, The Tempters of London - *GB*
Well I'm— - *GB*
What The? - *GB*
When Clubs Were Clubs - *GB*
When East Meets West - *GB*
Which is Witch? - *GB*
Whoso Diggeth a Pit - *GB*
The Woman Who Dared - *GB*
The World's Worst Wizard - *GB*
The Wraith of the Tomb - *GB*

1916

Abide with Me - *GB*
Altar Chains - *GB*
The Answer - *GB*
Arsene Lupin - *GB*
The Black Circle Gang - *GB*
The Black Night - *GB*
Black Orchids - *USA*
The Black Triangles - *GB*
Boots from Bootle - *GB*
The Cellar of Death - *GB*
The Charlatan - *GB*
Crime and the Penalty - *GB*
Daphne and the Pirate - *USA*
Daughter of the Gods - *USA*
A Deal with the Devil - *GB*
A Deuce of a Girl - *GB*
The Devil's Assistant - *USA*
The Dumb Girl of Portici - *USA*
The Eleventh Hour - *GB*
Enchantment - *USA*
The Enemy Amongst Us - *GB*
England's Future Safeguard - *GB*
Face to Face - *GB*
Fairyland - *GB*
Fatal Fingers - *GB*
The Five Wishes - *GB*
The Flying Torpedo - *USA*
The Game of Liberty - *GB*
The Girl Who Didn't Care - *GB*
The Girl Who Wrecked His Home - *GB*
The Grand Babylon Hotel - *GB*
Her Greatest Performance - *GB*
Homunculus - *Ger*
Honour in Pawn - *GB*
In the Hands of the Spoilers - *GB*
Into the Light - *GB*
Joey's Dream - *GB*
Judgement - *GB*
The King's Daughter - *GB*
The Lifeguardsman - *GB*
London's Enemies - *GB*
The Lyons Mail - *GB*
The Man in Motley - *GB*
The Man Who Forgot - *GB*
The Man without a Soul - *GB*
Mike and the Miser - *GB*
A Night of Horror - *Ger*
Only a Room-er - *GB*
On the Carpet - *GB*
Paste - *GB*
The Phantom Picture - *GB*
The Picture of Dorian Gray - *GB*
Pikovaya Dama - *Russ*
Pimple's Midsummer Night's Dream - *GB*
The Pleydell Mystery - *GB*
The Portrait of Dolly Grey - *GB*
The Price He Paid - *GB*
The Princess of Happy Chance - *GB*
A Princess of the Blood - *GB*
The Queen Mother - *GB*
Queen of the Wicked - *GB*
Rays That Erase - *GB*
Retribution - *GB*
Rubezahls Hochzeit - *Ger*
The Scarecrow - *GB*
A Shattered Idyll - *GB*
She - *GB*
Sonka Zolotaya Ruchka - *Russ*
Still Waters Run Deep - *GB*
The Stolen Sacrifice - *GB*
The Strange Case of Philip Kent - *GB*
Tanks - *GB*
The Terrible 'Tec - *GB*

Too Much Sausage - *GB*
Tragedy at Holly Cottage - *GB*
Trapped by the London Sharks - *GB*
The Valley of Fear - *GB*
A Vampire Out of Work - *USA*
Vice Versa - *GB*
Les Vingt Mille Leaues sous les Mers - *Fr*
Wand-erful Will - *GB*
What's Bred...Comes Out in the Flesh - *GB*
The Wheel of Death - *GB*
When Knights Were Bold - *GB*
When Woman Hates - *GB*
Yogi - *Ger*

1917

Aladdin and His Wonderful Lamp - *USA*
All Clear: No Need to Take Cover - *GB*
The American Heiress - *GB*
As in Days of Yore - *GB*
Asthore - *GB*
The Bottle Imp - *USA*
The Cobweb - *GB*
The Dinosaur and the Missing Link - *USA*
The Failure - *GB*
Flames - *GB*
The Flower of Doom - *USA*
For All Eternity - *GB*
Der Golem und die Tanzerin - *Ger*
A Grain of Sand - *GB*
Himmelskibet - *Den*
The Hound Of The Baskervilles - *Ger*
The House Opposite - *GB*
Jack and the Beanstalk - *USA*
The Jury of Fate - *USA*
The Lone Wolf - *USA*
The Man Behind "The Times" - *GB*
Ora Pro Nobis - *GB*
Queen of My Heart - *GB*
Salome - *USA*
The Scarlet Letter - *USA*
Seven Keys to Baldpate - *USA*
She - *USA*
Sirens of the Sea - *USA*
Snow White - *USA*
The Sorrows of Satan - *GB*
The Third Witness - *GB*
The Ware Case - *GB*
The Woman Who Was Nothing - *GB*

1918

Die Augen der Mumie Ma - *Ger*
The Blue Bird - *USA*
Boston Blackie's Little Pal - *USA*
Boundary House - *GB*
Carmen - *Ger*
The Eyes of Mystery - *USA*
The Ghost of Slumber Mountain - *USA*
The Girl from Downing Street - *GB*
J'Accuse - *Fr*
Million B.C. - *USA*
Les Miserables - *USA*
The Passing of the Third Floor Back - *GB*
Queen of the Sea - *USA*
Revenge - *USA*
Romance of Tarzan - *USA*
Roses of Picardy - *GB*
The Savage Woman - *USA*
The Sinking of the Lusitania - *USA*
Tarzan of the Apes - *USA*

1919

The Arc - *Ger*
The Beetle - *GB*
Blackie's Redemption - *USA*
Blade at Satans Bog - *Den*
The Case of a Doped Actress - *GB*
The Chinese Puzzle - *GB*
The Cry for Justice - *GB*
The Devil's Locksmith - *Austria*
The Disappearance of the Judge - *GB*
Dr. Jekyll and Mr. Hyde - *USA*
A Dreamland Frolic - *GB*
The Elusive Pimpernel - *GB*
The False Faces - *USA*
First Men in the Moon - *GB*
The Further Exploits of Sexton Blake—The Mystery of the S.S. Olympic - *GB*
God's Clay - *GB*
The Green Terror - *GB*
Her Heritage - *GB*
Herr Arnes Pengar - *Swed*
Die Herrin der Welt - *Ger*
I Hear You Calling Me - *GB*
Das Kabinett des Dr. Caligari - *Ger*
The Lone Wolf's Daughter - *USA*
Lucrezia Borgia - *It*
Madame DuBarry - *Ger*
Male and Female - *USA*
The Miracle Man - *USA*
Mr. Wu - *GB*
The Necklace of Death - *Ger*

The Polar Star - *GB*
Die Puppe - *Ger*
The Rocks of Valpre - *GB*
The Sands of Time - *GB*
Satanas - *Ger*
The Secret of the Moor - *GB*
The Silver Greyhound - *GB*
A Smart Set - *GB*
Die Spinne - *Ger*
To Let - *GB*
12-10 - *GB*
23 1/2 Hours Leave - *USA*
Whosoever Shall Offend - *GB*

1920

Alf's Button - *GB*
Algol - *Ger*
Anna Boleyn - *Ger*
L'Atlantide - *Fr*
At the Villa Rose - *GB*
The Barton Mystery - *GB*
The Black Spider - *GB*
The Case of Lady Camber - *GB*
Desire - *GB*
Dr. Jekyll and Mr. Hyde (Famous Players/Par) - *USA*
Dr. Jekyll and Mr. Hyde (Arrow) - *USA*
The English Rose - *GB*
The Face at the Window - *GB*
Forty Winks - *GB*
Genuine - *Ger*
The Golden Web - *GB*
The Golem: How He Came into the World - *Ger*
The Grip of Iron - *GB*
Hamlet - *Ger*
Haunted Spooks - *USA*
Haxan - *Swed*
The House on the Marsh - *GB*
Der Januskopf - *Ger*
Labyrinth des Grauens - *Ger*
Lady Audley's Secret - *GB*
Lorna Doone - *GB*
A Man's Shadow - *GB*
The Mark of Zorro - *USA*
Marzipan of the Shapes - *GB*
Le Mort du Soleil - *Fr*
One Hour Before Dawn - *USA*
The Penalty - *USA*
The Return of Tarzan - *USA*
The Scarlet Letter - *USA*
The Shadow Between - *GB*
The Shuttle of Life - *GB*
The Silver Bridge - *GB*
Sumurun - *Ger*
The Sword of Damocles - *GB*
Terror Island - *USA*
Die Teufelsanbeter - *Ger*
Through Stormy Waters - *GB*
Treasure Island - *USA*
Trent's Last Case - *GB*
The Twin Pawns - *USA*
The Vampire - *USA*
When Quackel Did Hyde - *USA*
The Woman of the Iron Bracelets - *GB*
Wuthering Heights - *GB*
The Yellow Claw - *GB*

1921

The Amazing Partnership - *GB*
Annabel Lee - *USA*
The Bargain - *GB*
Bits of Life - *USA*
The Black Tulip - *GB*
Blood Money - *GB*
Bluff - *GB*
Buried Treasure - *USA*
The Cave Girl - *USA*
A Connecticut Yankee in King Arthur's Court - *USA*
The Devil - *USA*
Drakula - *Hung*
The Fatal 30 - *USA*
The Golden Dawn - *GB*
The Haunted House - *USA*
The Hound Of The Baskervilles - *GB*
The Invisible Fear - *USA*
The Invisible Web - *USA*
Jane Eyre - *USA*
The Loudwater Mystery - *GB*
Love in the Welsh Hills - *GB*
A Message from Mars - *USA*
Der Mude Tod - *Ger*
My Lord Conceit - *GB*
The Mystery of Mr. Bernard Brown - *GB*
Nick Carter - *GB*
The Other Person - *GB*
Outside the Law - *USA*
Rip Van Winkle - *USA*
Schloss Vögelöd - *Ger*
Shadow of Evil - *GB*
The Spirit of the Heath - *GB*

The Three Musketeers - *USA*
The Tinted Venus - *GB*
Les Trois Mousquetaires - *Fr*
Das Weib des Pharao - *Ger*
Where the Rainbow Ends - *GB*

1922
The Altar Stairs - *USA*
Aschenputtel - *Ger*
A Blind Bargain - *USA*
The Conquering Power - *USA*
The Crimson Circle - *GB*
Devil's Angel - *USA*
Doctor Mabuse - *Ger*
Don Juan et Faust - *Fr*
The Dungeon - *USA*
Esmeralda - *GB*
The Face in the Fog - *USA*
Faust - *GB*
The Headless Horseman - *USA*
The House of Peril - *GB*
Lorna Doone - *USA*
Lucrezia Borgia - *Ger*
Macbeth - *GB*
The Man from Beyond - *USA*
The Man from Downing Street - *USA*
Melody of Death - *GB*
Les Miserables - *GB*
Missing Millions - *USA*
Monte Cristo - *USA*
Nosferatu, eine Symphonie des Grauens - *Ger*
One Exciting Night - *USA*
Phantom - *Ger*
The Prisoner of Zenda - *USA*
Robin Hood - *USA*
Salome - *USA*
Samson and Dalila - *Austria*
The Scarlet Letter - *GB*
Schatten, eine Nachtliche Halluzination - *Ger*
Scrooge - *GB*
Sherlock Holmes - *USA*
Silent Evidence - *GB*
Trifling Women - *USA*
Trilby - *GB*
Der Verlorene Schuh - *Ger*
Eine Versunkene Welt - *Austria*
Young Diana - *USA*

1923
Adam's Rib - *USA*
Bella Donna - *USA*
The Bells - *GB*
Boston Blackie - *USA*
The Brass Bottle - *USA*
Bulldog Drummond - *GB*
Chronik von Grieshuus - *Ger*
Chu Chin Chow - *GB-Ger*
Crooked Alley - *USA*
The Dancer of the Nile - *USA*
The Drums of Jeopardy - *USA*
The Eleventh Hour - *USA*
Evolution - *USA*
Faust - *GB*
Finger Prints - *USA*
The Flying Dutchman - *USA*
The Ghost of Tolston's Manor - *USA*
The Green Goddess - *USA*
The Hunchback of Notre Dame - *USA*
Hutch Stirs 'em Up - *GB*
L'Inhumaine - *Fr*
In the Palace of the King - *USA*
Jungle Trail of the Son of Tarzan - *USA*
King Tut-Ankh-Amen's Eighth Wife - *USA*
Le Loup-Garou - *Fr*
Lucrezia Borgia: or, Plaything of Power - *GB*
The Man without Desire - *GB*
The Monkey's Paw - *GB*
Paris Qui Dort - *Fr*
Puritan Passions - *USA*
Raskolnikov - *Ger*
Robin Hood Jr. - *USA*
Rupert of Hentzau - *USA*
St. Elmo - *GB*
Scrooge - *GB*
The Shimmy Sheik - *GB*
The Shock - *USA*
The Sign of Four - *GB*
Der Steinerne Reiter - *Ger*
The Temple of Venus - *USA*
The Three Musketeers - *Russ*
Trilby - *USA*
Tut-Tut and His Terrible Tomb - *GB*
The Way - *GB*
While Paris Sleeps - *USA*
Widow Twan-Kee - *GB*

1924
Aelita - *Russ*
Behind the Curtain - *USA*
Dante's Inferno - *USA*
The Enchanted Cottage - *USA*

Le Fantome du Moulin Rouge - *Fr*
He Who Gets Slapped - *USA*
Jack and the Beanstalk - *USA*
Der Letzte Mann - *Ger*
The Lone Wolf - *USA*
Mezhplanetnaya Revolutsiya - *Russ*
Moonbeam Magic - *GB*
Morozko - *Russ*
The Mystery Film - *GB*
Die Nibelungen - *Ger*
Old Bill Through the Ages - *GB*
One Hour Past Midnight - *USA*
Orlacs Haende - *Austria*
Peter Pan - *USA*
The Prehistoric Man - *GB*
Robin Hood's Men - *GB*
Romance of the Nile - *USA*
Sherlock Jr. - *USA*
The Silent Watcher - *USA*
The Story of Gosta Berling - *Swed*
Terreur - *Fr*
The Thief of Bagdad - *USA*
Through the Dark - *USA*
Le Voyage Imaginaire - *Fr*
Das Wachsfigurenkabinett - *Ger*

1925
Arabella - *Ger*
Bulldog Drummond's Third Round - *GB*
Dr. Jekyll and Mr. Hyde - *USA*
Don Q, Son of Zorro - *USA*
The Hidden Menace - *USA*
The Lost World - *USA*
Luch Smerti - *Russ*
The Midnight Girl - *USA*
Les Miserables - *Fr*
The Monster - *USA*
The Mystic - *USA*
The Phantom of the Opera - *USA*
The Road to Yesterday - *USA*
The Secret Kingdom - *GB*
Secrets of the Night - *USA*
Seven Keys to Baldpate - *USA*
She - *GB-Ger*
The Sorrows of Satan - *USA*
The Tower of Lies - *USA*
The Unholy Three - *USA*
The Wizard of Oz - *USA*
Wunder der Schopfung - *Ger*

1926
The Bat - *USA*
The Bells - *USA*
The Black Bird - *USA*
The Black Pirate - *USA*
Boadicea - *GB*
La Coquille et le Clergyman - *Fr*
Faust - *Ger*
Geheimnisse einer Seele - *Ger*
The Gypsy Romance - *USA*
The House without a Key - *USA*
A Kiss for Cinderella - *USA*
The Lodger - *GB*
London After Midnight - *USA*
The Lone Wolf Returns - *USA*
Machiste in Hell - *It*
The Magician - *USA*
Mekhanikha Golovnovo Mozga - *Russ*
Metropolis - *Ger*
The Pied Piper of Hamelin - *GB*
The Return of Peter Grimm - *USA*
The Road to Mandalay - *USA*
The Savage - *USA*
The Scarlet Letter - *USA*
The Sea Beast - *USA*
Shinel - *Russ*
Spiritualism Exposed - *GB*
Der Student von Prag - *Ger*

1927
Alias the Lone Wolf - *USA*
Am Rande der Welt - *Ger*
The Cat and the Canary - *USA*
The Chinese Parrot - *USA*
La Chute de la Maison Usher - *Fr*
Don Juan - *USA*
Downhill - *USA*
The Ghost Train - *GB*
La Glace a Trois Faces - *Fr*
The Gorilla - *USA*
Loves of Carmen - *USA*
Mr. Wu - *USA*
Mockery - *USA*
The Monkey Talks - *USA*
Perils of the Jungle - *USA*
Prelude - *GB*
The Private Life of Helen of Troy - *USA*
The Return of Boston Blackie - *USA*
The Ring - *GB*
Robinson Crusoe - *GB*
Der Sohn der Hagar - *Ger*

Spione - *Ger*
Svengali - *Ger*
Tarzan and the Golden Lion - *USA*
The Thirteenth Hour - *USA*
The Unknown - *USA*
The Wizard - *USA*
Wolf's Clothing - *USA*
Zvenigora - *Russ*

1928
Alraune - *Ger*
The Black Pearl - *USA*
Blake, the Lawbreaker - *GB*
Cagliostro - *Ger*
Champagne - *GB*
Un Chien Andalou - *Fr*
The Clue of the Second Goblet - *GB*
Die Frau im Mond - *Ger*
The Great Office Mystery - *GB*
Laugh, Clown, Laugh - *USA*
The Leopard Lady - *USA*
The Man Who Laughs - *USA*
Maria Marten - *GB*
The Mystery of the Silent Death - *GB*
A Night of Mystery - *USA*
The Ringer - *GB*
Scrooge - *GB*
Sexton Blake, Gambler - *GB*
Silken Threads - *GB*
Sweeney Todd - *GB*
The Terror - *USA*
The Triumph of the Scarlet Pimpernel - *GB*
Vormittagsspuk - *Ger*
West of Zanzibar - *USA*
Where East is West - *USA*

1929
Alf's Carpet - *GB*
Behind That Curtain - *USA*
Blackmail - *GB*
Black Waters - *GB*
The Bridge of San Luis Rey - *USA*
Bulldog Drummond - *USA*
The Canary Murder Case - *USA*
Chamber of Horrors - *GB*
The Clue of the New Pin - *GB*
Condemned - *USA*
Darkened Rooms - *USA*
The Devil Bear - *USA*
The Ghost Talks - *USA*
The Glittering Sword - *GB*
The Great Gabbo - *USA*
The Greene Murder Case - *USA*
The Green Goddess - *USA*
The Haunted House - *USA*
High Treason - *GB*
The Hound Of The Baskervilles - *Ger*
The House of Horror - *USA*
The House of Secrets - *USA*
The Iron Mask - *USA*
The Last Warning - *USA*
The Lone Wolf's Daughter - *USA*
The Lost Patrol - *GB*
The Lost Zeppelin - *USA*
The Mysterious Dr. Fu Manchu - *USA*
The Mysterious Island - *USA*
Red Aces - *GB*
The Red Circle - *Ger*
The Return of Sherlock Holmes - *USA*
St. George and the Dragon - *GB*
Seven Footprints to Satan - *USA*
The Silent House - *GB*
The Studio Murder Mystery - *USA*
The Thirteenth Chair - *USA*
Trent's Last Case - *USA*
The Unholy Night - *USA*
When Knights Were Bold - *GB*
The Woman in White - *GB*

1930
L'Age d'Or - *Sp*
Alf's Button - *GB*
Alraune - *Ger*
Ashes - *GB*
The Benson Murder Case - *USA*
Birds of Prey - *GB*
The Bishop Murder Case - *USA*
The Cat Creeps - *USA*
El Cuerpo del Lito - *USA*
Dr. Hallers - *Ger*
Elstree Calling - *GB*
La Fin du Monde - *Fr*
The House of the Arrow - *GB*
In the Next Room - *USA*
Just Imagine - *USA*
Kismet - *USA*
The Last Hour - *GB*
The Last of the Lone Wolf - *USA*
Liliom - *USA*
Midnight Mystery - *USA*
Moby Dick - *USA*

Murder - *GB*
Murder Will Out - *USA*
Outward Bound - *USA*
Rasputin - *GB*
Remote Control - *USA*
The Return of Dr. Fu Manchu - *USA*
Le Sang d'un Poete - *Fr*
Scotland Yard - *USA*
Seven Keys to Baldpate - *USA*
Le Spectre Vert - *USA*
The Squeaker - *GB*
Such Men are Dangerous - *USA*
Temple Tower - *USA*
Terrors - *GB*
The Unholy Three - *USA*
The Yellow Mask - *GB*

1931
Alibi - *GB*
The Bat Whispers - *USA*
The Bells - *GB*
The Black Camel - *USA*
Das Blaue Licht - *Ger*
Charlie Chan Carries On - *USA*
A Connecticut Yankee - *USA*
Cracked Nuts - *USA*
Creation (unfinished) - *USA*
Creeping Shadows - *GB*
Daughter of the Dragon - *USA*
Dirigible - *USA*
Dracula (2 versions) - *USA*
Die Dreizehn Koffer des Herrn O.F. - *Ger*
Drums of Jeopardy - *USA*
Evolution - *USA*
Frankenstein - *USA*
The Ghost Train - *USA*
Gipsy Blood - *GB*
The Gorilla - *USA*
The Hound Of The Baskervilles - *GB*
The House of Mystery - *USA*
The House Opposite - *GB*
Kongo - *USA*
The Lash - *USA*
M - *Ger*
The Mad Genius - *USA*
The Maltese Falcon - *USA*
The Man at Six - *GB*
The Man They Could Not Arrest - *GB*
Midnight - *USA*
Murder by the Clock - *USA*
Le Mystere de la Chambre Jaune - *Fr*
The Old Man - *GB*
Rich and Strange - *GB*
The Ringer - *GB*
The Sleeping Cardinal - *GB*
The Speckled Band - *GB*
Svengali - *USA*
Tabu - *USA*
Vampyr - *Ger-Fr*
What a Night! - *GB*
The Wickham Mystery - *GB*
Women of All Nations - *USA*

1932
After Dark - *GB*
Alias the Doctor - *USA*
As You Desire Me - *USA*
The Barton Mystery - *GB*
Behind the Mask - *USA*
The Callbox Mystery - *GB*
Castle Sinister - *GB*
Chandu the Magician - *USA*
Charlie Chan's Chance - *USA*
Cheaters at Play - *USA*
Chushingura - *Jap*
Condemned to Death - *GB*
Dr. Jekyll and Mr. Hyde - *USA*
Dr. Jekyll's Hide - *USA*
Doctor X - *USA*
The Face at the Window - *GB*
Freaks - *USA*
The Frightened Lady - *GB*
Die Herrin von Atlantis - *Ger*
Island of Lost Souls - *USA*
Living Dead - *Ger*
The Lodger - *GB*
The Lost Squadron - *USA*
Love Me Tonight - *USA*
The Mask of Fu Manchu - *USA*
Mata Hari - *USA*
The Menace - *USA*
Mensch ohne Namen - *Ger*
The Merry Men of Sherwood - *GB*
The Miracle Man - *USA*
The Missing Rembrandt - *GB*
Miss Pinkerton - *USA*
The Monster Walks - *USA*
The Most Dangerous Game - *USA*
The Mummy - *USA*
Murder at Covent Garden - *GB*
The Murders in the Rue Morgue - *USA*

Number 17 - GB
The Old Dark House - USA
The Penguin Pool Murder - USA
The Phantom of Crestwood - USA
Rasputin and the Empress - USA
The River House Ghost - GB
Shanghai Express - USA
Sherlock Holmes - USA
The Sign of Four - GB
The Silver Greyhound - GB
The Spider - USA
Strange Adventure - USA
The Strangler - GB
Tarzan the Ape Man - USA
Das Testament des Dr. Mabuse - Ger
Thark - GB
The Thirteenth Guest - USA
A Voice Said Goodnight - GB
White Zombie - USA
Widow in Scarlet - USA
A Yell of a Night - GB

1933

Alice in Wonderland - USA
Before Dawn - USA
Berkeley Square - USA
Charlie Chan's Greatest Case - USA
The Crime at Blossoms - GB
Crime on the Hill - GB
The Death Kiss - USA
Deluge - USA
A Dickensian Fantasy - GB
Eyes of Fate - GB
The Flaw - GB
F.P. 1 Antwortet Nicht - GB-Ger
Forging Ahead - GB
Gabriel Over the White House - USA
The Ghost Camera- GB
The Ghoul - GB
I'm an Explosive - GB
International House - USA
The Invisible Man - USA
An Invisible Man Goes on the Town - Ger
I Was a Spy - GB
The Kennel Murder Case - USA
King Kong - USA
King of the Jungle - USA
Liliom - Fr
The Lure - GB
The Man Outside - GB
The Mind Reader - USA
Murders in the Zoo - USA
Mystery of the Wax Museum - USA
Nagana - USA
Night of Terror - USA
On Secret Service - GB
The Pointing Finger - GB
Puppets of Fate - GB
Roman Scandals - USA
Schuss im Morgengrauen - Ger
The Secret of Madame Blanche - USA
The Secret of the Blue Room - USA
The Shadow - GB
The Shot in the Dark - GB
Son of Kong - USA
The Sphinx - USA
The Stickpin - GB
The Stolen Necklace - GB
Strange Evidence - GB
A Study in Scarlet - USA
Supernatural - USA
A Tale of Tails - GB
Tarzan the Fearless - USA
The Thirteenth Candle - GB
Treason - USA
The Vampire Bat - USA
The Wandering Jew - GB
White Woman - USA

1934

Babes in Toyland - USA
Bella Donna - GB
The Best Man Wins - USA
The Black Abbot - GB
The Black Cat - USA
Black Moon - USA
British Agent - USA
Bulldog Drummond Strikes Back - USA
The Case of the Howling Dog - USA
Chandu - USA
Charlie Chan in London - USA
Charlie Chan's Courage - USA
Chu Chin Chow - GB
The Clairvoyant - GB
The Count of Monte Cristo - USA
The Crimson Candle - GB
Dangerous Ground - GB
Death at Broadcasting House - GB
Death Takes a Holiday - USA
The Double Door - USA
The Dragon Murder Case - USA

The Feathered Serpent - GB
Flat No. 3 - GB
Four Frightened People - USA
The Ghost Walks - USA
The Gift of Gab - USA
The Girl in the Flat - GB
Gold (2 versions) - Ger
Great Expectations - SA
Green Eyes - USA
Jane Eyre - USA
Lost in the Stratosphere - USA
The Lost Jungle - USA
The Lost Patrol - USA
Madame DuBarry - USA
Madame Spy - USA
The Man Who Changed His Name - GB
The Man Who Knew Too Much - GB
The Medium - GB
Menace - GB
Murder at the Inn - GB
Murder at the Vanities - USA
Murder on the Blackboard - USA
The Mystery of Mr. X - USA
No Escape - GB
Novyi Gulliver - Russ
Passing Shadows - GB
The Phantom of the Convent - Mex
The Private Life of Don Juan - GB
The Return of Bulldog Drummond - GB
The Return of Peter Grimm - USA
The Return of the Terror - USA
The Scarlet Letter - USA
The Scarlet Pimpernel - GB
The Scotland Yard Mystery - GB
Secret of the Chateau - USA
The Secret of the Loch - GB
Tangled Evidence - GB
Tarzan and His Mate - USA
The Tell-Tale Heart - GB
The Thin Man - USA
The Third Clue - GB
Treasure Island - USA
The Unholy Quest - GB
The Warren Case - GB
Whispering Tongues - GB
Wishes - GB
Ysani the Priestess - GB

1935

The Black Room - USA
Bride of Frankenstein - USA
Bulldog Jack - GB
The Case of the Curious Bride - USA
The Casino Murder Case - USA
Charlie Chan in Egypt - USA
Charlie Chan in Paris - USA
Charlie Chan in Shanghai - USA
Condemned to Live - USA
Crime and Punishment - USA
The Crime of Dr. Crespi - USA
Dante's Inferno - USA
Dark World - GB
Death from a Distance - USA
Discipline - GB
Face in the Fog - USA
The Florentine Dagger - USA
The Ghost Goes West - GB
The Ghost Walks - GB
The Great Impersonation - USA
House of Menace - USA
Inside the Room - GB
The Invisible Ray - USA
The Last Days of Pompeii - USA
The Lone Wolf Returns - USA
The Lost City - USA
Lunnyi Kamen - Russ
Mad Love - USA
The Man Who Reclaimed His Head - USA
Maria Marten: or, The Murder in the Red Barn - GB
The Mark of the Vampire - USA
A Midsummer Night's Dream - USA
Les Miserables - USA
Murder at Monte Carlo - GB
Murder by Television - USA
Murder on a Honeymoon - USA
The Mysterious Mr. Wong - USA
The Mystery of Edwin Drood - USA
The Mystery of the Mary Celeste - GB
Night Life of the Gods - USA
Once in a New Moon - GB
One Frightened Night - USA
The Passing of the Third Floor Back - GB
Peter Ibbetson - USA
The Phantom Light - GB
Radio Ranch - USA
The Raven - USA
Return In the Night - USA
Scrooge - GB
Sexton Blake and the Bearded Doctor - GB
Sexton Blake and the Mademoiselle - GB

She - USA
The Silent Passenger - GB
The Strange Case of Mr. Todmorden - GB
Der Student von Prag - Ger
Tarzan's New Adventure - USA
The 39 Steps - GB
The Triumph of Sherlock Holmes - GB
The Tunnel - GB
Werewolf of London - USA
White Lilac - GB
Zolotoye Ozero - Russ

1936

After the Thin Man - USA
The Birth of the Robot - GB
Blake of Scotland Yard - USA
Blind Man's Bluff - GB
The Bold Caballero - USA
Charlie Chan at the Circus - USA
Charlie Chan at the Opera - USA
Charlie Chan at the Race Track - USA
Charlie Chan's Secret - USA
The Clutching Hand - USA
Crack-Up - USA
The Crimes of Stephen Hawke - GB
The Crimson Circle - GB
The Dark Hour - USA
The Demon Barber of Fleet Street - GB
Devil Doll - USA
Dracula's Daughter - USA
The Dream Doctor - GB
Faust - GB
The Garden Murder Case - USA
Green Pastures - USA
The Howard Case - GB
Juggernaut - GB
Die Leuchter des Kaisers - Austria
The Limping Man - GB
The Man Behind the Mask - GB
The Man in the Mirror - GB
The Man Who Changed His Mind - GB
The Man Who Could Work Miracles - GB
The Man Who Lived Twice - USA
Meet Nero Wolfe - USA
Midnight at Madame Tussaud's - GB
Modern Times - USA
Murder by Rope - GB
Murder on a Bridle Path - USA
The Plot Thickens - USA
The Preview Murder Mystery - USA
Revolt of the Zombies - USA
Sabotage - GB
Satan Met a Lady - USA
The Scarab Murder Case - GB
The Secret Agent - GB
The Secret of Stamboul - GB
Someone at the Door - GB
Tarzan Escapes - USA
Things to Come - GB
The Walking Dead - USA
When Knights Were Bold - GB
Wolf's Clothing - GB

1937

The Adventurous Blonde - USA
Ali Baba Goes to Town - USA
The Black Tulip - GB
Bulldog Drummond at Bay - GB
Bulldog Drummond Comes Back - USA
Bulldog Drummond Escapes - USA
Bulldog Drummond's Revenge - USA
Charlie Chan at Monte Carlo - USA
Charlie Chan at the Olympics - USA
Charlie Chan on Broadway - USA
Dangerous Fingers - GB
Dark Journey - GB
Daughter of Shanghai - USA
Dick Tracy - USA
Dr. Sin Fang - GB
Dr. Syn - GB
Double Alibi - GB
Elephant Boy - GB
The Fatal Hour - GB
Fly-Away Baby - USA
Forty Naughty Girls - USA
The Frog - GB
The Girl from Scotland Yard - USA
The Great Gambini - USA
J'Accuse - Fr
King Solomon's Mines - GB
Knight without Armour - GB
Lancer Spy - USA
League of Frightened Men - USA
London by Night - USA
Lost Horizon - USA
Love from a Stranger - GB
The Man Who Made Diamonds - GB
Museum Mystery - GB
The Flight That ... - USA
Night Must Fall - USA

A Night of Mystery - USA
Passenger to London - GB
The Perfect Crime - GB
The Prisoner of Zenda - USA
The Queen of Spades - Fr
The Rare Book Murders - USA
The Return of the Scarlet Pimpernel - GB
Secret Lives - GB
Sh! The Octopus - USA
Silver Blaze - GB
Smart Blonde - USA
The Squeaker - GB
Strange Experiment - GB
Tarzan's Revenge - USA
Thank You, Mr. Moto - USA
The 13th Chair - USA
Topper - USA
Under Secret Orders - GB
The Vulture - GB
The Westland Case - USA
Young and Innocent - GB

1938

The Adventures of Robin Hood - USA
Aladdin's Lantern - USA
Alf's Button Afloat - GB
The Barefoot Boy - USA
The Black Doll - USA
Black Limelight - GB
Blondes at Work - USA
Bulldog Drummond in Africa - USA
Bulldog Drummond's Peril - USA
Charlie Chan in Honolulu - USA
A Christmas Carol - USA
The Claydon Treasure Mystery - GB
The Dance of Death - GB
The Dark Stairway - GB
Dick Tracy Returns - USA
The Drum - GB
The Gables Mystery - GB
The Gaunt Stranger - GB
The Gladiator - USA
The Invisible Menace - USA
Lady in the Morgue - USA
The Lady Vanishes - GB
The Last Warning - USA
Lion Man - USA
The Lone Wolf in Paris - USA
Marie Antoinette - USA
Mars Attacks the World - USA
Miracles Do Happen - GB
The Missing Guest - USA
Mr. Moto's Gamble - USA
Mr. Moto Takes a Chance - USA
Mr. Moto Takes a Vacation - USA
Mr. Reeder in Room 13 - GB
Mr. Wong, Detective - USA
Mysterious Mr. Wong - USA
Nancy Drew, Detective - USA
Rasputin - Fr
The Return of the Frog - GB
The Saint in New York - USA
Sexton Blake and the Hooded Terror - GB
The Spy Ring - USA
Tarzan and the Green Goddess - USA
The Terror - GB
Torchy Blane in Panama - USA
Torchy Gets Her Man - USA

1939

The Adventures of Sherlock Holmes - USA
Another Thin Man - USA
Arrest Bulldog Drummond - USA
At the Villa Rose - GB
Beware, Spooks! - USA
Blind Alley - USA
The Body Vanishes - GB
Bulldog Drummond's Bride - USA
Bulldog Drummond's Secret Police - USA
The Cat and the Canary - USA
Charlie Chan at Treasure Island - USA
Charlie Chan in City in Darkness - USA
Charlie Chan in Reno - USA
A Chump at Oxford - USA
Dark Eyes of London - GB
Dead Men are Dangerous - GB
Devjani - India
Dick Tracy's G-Men - USA
Dr. Cyclops - USA
Dr. Jekyll and Mr. Hyde - USA
Exile Express - USA
The Face at the Window - GB
The Gorilla - USA
The Gracie Allen Murder Case - USA
Gulliver's Travels - USA
The Hound Of The Baskervilles - USA
House of Fear - USA
The Hunchback of Notre Dame - USA
I Killed the Count - GB
I Met ... - GB
The Island of Lost Men - USA

Jamaica Inn - *GB*
The Lone Wolf Spy Hunt - *USA*
The Man in the Iron Mask - *USA*
The Man They Could Not Hang - *USA*
The Midas Touch - *GB*
The Mind of Mr. Reeder - *GB*
Miracles for Sale - *USA*
The Missing People - *GB*
Mrs. Pym of Scotland Yard - *GB*
Mr. Moto in Danger Island - *USA*
Mr. Moto's Last Warning - *USA*
Mr. Wong in Chinatown - *USA*
The Mystery of Mr. Wong - *USA*
Mystery of the White Room - *USA*
Mystery Plane - *USA*
Nancy Drew and the Hidden Staircase - *USA*
Nancy Drew, Reporter - *USA*
Nancy Drew, Troubleshooter - *USA*
Nick Carter, Master Detective - *USA*
Of Mice and Men - *USA*
On Borrowed Time - *USA*
L'Or du Cristobal - *Fr*
The Phantom Creeps - *USA*
Pocomania - *USA*
Poison Pen - *GB*
The Return of Dr. X - *USA*
The Rules of the Game - *Fr*
The Saint in London - *GB*
The Saint Strikes Back - *GB*
Shadow of Death - *GB*
Son of Frankenstein - *USA*
The Spider - *USA*
The Spy in Black - *GB*
Tarzan Finds a Son! - *USA*
Television Spy - *USA*
The Three Musketeers - *USA*
Topper Takes a Trip - *USA*
Torchy Blane in Chinatown - *USA*
Torchy Plays with Dynamite - *USA*
Torchy Runs for Mayor - *USA*
Tower of London - *USA*
Trunk Crime - *GB*
The War Eagle (unfinished) - *USA*
The Wizard of Oz - *USA*
Wuthering Heights - *USA*

1940

The Ape - *USA*
Before I Hang - *USA*
Beyond Tomorrow - *USA*
Black Friday - *USA*
The Blue Bird - *USA*
The Boys from Syracuse - *USA*
British Intelligence - *USA*
Bulldog Sees It Through - *GB*
Buried Alive - *USA*
Busman's Honeymoon - *GB*
Calling Philo Vance - *USA*
The Case of the Frightened Lady - *GB*
Charlie Chan at the Wax Museum - *USA*
Charlie Chan in Panama - *USA*
Charlie Chan's Murder Cruise - *USA*
Crimes at the Dark House - *GB*
Dark Streets of Cairo - *USA*
Devil's Island - *USA*
Doomed to Die - *USA*
The Door with Seven Locks - *GB*
Earthbound - *USA*
Ellery Queen, Master Detective - *USA*
The Fatal Hour - *USA*
Foreign Correspondent - *USA*
Gaslight - *GB*
Gestapo - *GB*
The Ghost Breakers - *USA*
The Ghost Creeps - *USA*
The Girl in the News - *GB*
Green Hell - *USA*
The House of the Arrow - *GB*
The House of the Seven Gables - *USA*
Invisible Killer - *USA*
The Invisible Man Returns - *USA*
Island of Doomed Men - *USA*
Isle of Destiny - *USA*
Law and Disorder - *GB*
L'il Abner - *USA*
The Lone Wolf Meets a Lady - *USA*
The Lone Wolf Strikes - *USA*
The Mad Doctor - *USA*
The Man with Nine Lives - *USA*
The Mark of Zorro - *USA*
Michael Shayne, Private Detective - *USA*
The Mummy's Hand - *USA*
Murder in the Air - *USA*
Murder over New York - *USA*
Mystery Sea Raider - *USA*
One Million B.C. - *USA*
Phantom Raider - *USA*
Rebecca - *USA*
The Saint's Double Trouble - *USA*
The Saint Takes Over - *USA*
Sky Murder - *USA*

Son of Ingagi - *USA*
The Son of Monte Cristo - *USA*
Strangers on the Third Floor - *USA*
The Thief of Bagdad - *GB*
The Thirteenth Instant - *GB*
Three Silent Men - *GB*
The Villain Still Pursued Her - *USA*
You'll Find Out - *USA*
Zanzibar - *USA*

1941

All That Money Can Buy - *USA*
Among the Living - *USA*
The Black Cat - *USA*
Blue, White and Perfect - *USA*
The Body Disappears - *USA*
Charlie Chan in Rio - *USA*
Confessions of Boston Blackie - *USA*
The Corsican Brothers - *USA*
Cracked Nuts - *USA*
A Date with the Falcon - *USA*
Dead Men Tell - *USA*
The Devil Bat - *USA*
The Devil Checks Up - *GB*
The Devil Commands - *USA*
Dick Tracy vs. Crime, Inc. - *USA*
Dr. Jekyll and Mr. Hyde - *USA*
Dressed to Kill - *USA*
East of Piccadilly - *GB*
Ellery Queen and the Murder Ring - *USA*
Ellery Queen and the Perfect Crime - *USA*
Ellery Queen's Penthouse Mystery - *USA*
The Face Behind the Mask - *USA*
49th Parallel - *GB*
The Gay Falcon - *USA*
The Ghost at St. Michael's - *GB*
The Ghost of Frankenstein - *USA*
The Ghost Train - *GB*
Hellzapoppin - *USA*
Here Comes Mr. Jordan - *USA*
Hold That Ghost - *USA*
Horror Island - *USA*
The Invisible Ghost - *USA*
The Invisible Woman - *USA*
I Wake Up Screaming - *USA*
Jungle Man - *USA*
King of the Zombies - *USA*
Ladies in Retirement - *USA*
The Lone Wolf Keeps a Date - *USA*
The Lone Wolf Takes a Chance - *USA*
The Mad Doctor of Market Street - *USA*
La Main du Diable - *Fr*
The Maltese Falcon - *USA*
Man-Made Monster - *USA*
Meet Boston Blackie - *USA*
The Monster and the Girl - *USA*
Old Mother Riley's Ghosts - *GB*
Out of the Fog - *USA*
Paris Calling - *USA*
The Patient Vanishes - *GB*
Phantom of Chinatown - *USA*
Pimpernel Smith - *GB*
The Remarkable Andrew - *USA*
The Saint in Palm Springs - *USA*
The Saint Meets the Tiger - *GB*
The Saint's Vacation - *GB*
Scotland Yard - *USA*
Secrets of the Lone Wolf - *USA*
Shadow of the Thin Man - *USA*
Sleepers West - *USA*
The Smiling Ghost - *USA*
Spellbound - *GB*
Spooks Run Wild - *USA*
Suspicion - *USA*
Tarzan's Secret Treasure - *USA*
The Tell-Tale Heart - *USA*
Topper Returns - *USA*
Tower of Terror - *GB*
The Wolf Man - *USA*

1942

A-Haunting We Will Go - *USA*
Alias Boston Blackie - *USA*
Alibi - *GB*
Arabian Nights - *USA*
Beyond the Blue Horizon - *USA*
Black Dragons - *USA*
The Black Swan - *USA*
The Boogie Man Will Get You - *USA*
Boston Blackie Goes Hollywood - *USA*
Bowery at Midnight - *USA*
Cabin in the Sky - *USA*
Carmen - *Fr*
Castle in the Desert - *USA*
Cat People - *USA*
Close Call for Ellery Queen - *USA*
The Corpse Vanishes - *USA*
Counter-Espionage - *USA*
Desperate Chance for Ellery Queen - *USA*
Dr. Renault's Secret - *USA*
Drums of the Congo - *USA*

L'Eternel Retour - *Fr*
Eyes in the Night - *USA*
Eyes of the Underworld - *USA*
The Falcon's Brother - *USA*
The Falcon Takes Over - *USA*
Fingers at the Window - *USA*
The Great Impersonation - *USA*
Gwangi (unfinished) - *USA*
Heaven Can Wait - *USA*
The Hidden Hand - *USA*
I Married an Angel - *USA*
I Married a Witch - *USA*
Les Inconnus dans la Maison - *Fr*
Invisible Agent - *USA*
Journey into Fear - *USA*
The Jungle Book - *USA*
Jungle Siren - *USA*
Just Off Broadway - *USA*
King Arthur Was a Gentleman - *GB*
The Living Ghost - *USA*
London Blackout Murders - *USA*
The Loves of Edgar Allan Poe - *USA*
The Mad Monster - *USA*
The Man Who Wouldn't Die - *USA*
The Mummy's Tomb - *USA*
The Mystery of Marie Roget - *USA*
Nazi Agent - *USA*
The Night Has Eyes - *GB*
Night Monster - *USA*
La Nuit Fantastique - *Fr*
The Phantom Killer - *USA*
Prisoner of Mars - *USA*
Saboteur - *USA*
Secret Agent of Japan - *USA*
Sherlock Holmes and the Secret Weapon - *USA*
Sherlock Holmes and the Voice of Terror - *USA*
Sherlock Holmes in Washington - *USA*
S.O.S. Coast Guard - *USA*
The Strange Case of Dr. Rx - *USA*
Tarzan's New York Adventure - *USA*
Thunder Rock - *GB*
Time to Kill - *USA*
The Undying Monster - *USA*
Les Visiteurs du Soir - *Fr*
Whispering Ghosts - *USA*
Who Done It? - *USA*

1943

Above Suspicion - *USA*
After Midnight with Boston Blackie - *USA*
Ali Baba and the Forty Thieves - *USA*
The Ape Man - *USA*
Die Avonturen von Baron Munchausen - *Ger*
Background to Danger - *USA*
Le Baron Fantome - *Fr*
The Black Raven - *USA*
Calling Dr. Death - *USA*
Captive Wild Woman - *USA*
The Chance of a Lifetime - *USA*
Cobra Woman - *USA*
Le Corbeau - *Fr*
The Count of Monte Cristo - *Fr*
Crazy House - *USA*
Crime Doctor - *USA*
Crime Doctor's Strangest Case - *USA*
The Dark Tower - *USA*
Dead Men Walk - *USA*
Dr. Terror's House of Horrors - *USA*
The Dummy Talks - *GB*
Escape to Danger - *GB*
The Falcon and the Co-Eds - *USA*
The Falcon in Danger - *USA*
The Falcon Strikes Back - *USA*
Flesh and Fantasy - *USA*
Forces Occultes - *Fr*
Frankenstein Meets the Wolf Man - *USA*
The Ghost and the Guest - *USA*
Ghost Catchers - *USA*
Ghost Ship - *USA*
Ghosts on the Loose - *USA*
A Guy Named Joe - *USA*
The Happy Land - *USA*
Henry Aldrich Haunts a House - *USA*
I Walked with a Zombie - *USA*
Lady of Burlesque - *USA*
The Leopard Man - *USA*
The Mad Ghoul - *USA*
The Man in Grey - *GB*
Les Miserables - *It*
The Monster Maker - *USA*
The Mysterious Doctor - *USA*
The Mystery of the 13th Guest - *USA*
A Night of Adventure - *USA*
One Dangerous Night - *USA*
Passport to Suez - *USA*
Phantom of the Opera - *USA*
The Return of the Vampire - *USA*
Revenge of the Zombies - *USA*
The Seventh Victim - *USA*
Shadow of a Doubt - *USA*
Sherlock Holmes Faces Death - *USA*

Son of Dracula - *USA*
The Strange Death of Adolf Hitler - *USA*
Tarzan's Desert Mystery - *USA*
Tarzan Triumphs - *USA*
Vredens Dag - *Den*
White Savage - *USA*

1944

Address Unknown - *USA*
Arsenic and Old Lace - *USA*
Bermuda Mystery - *USA*
Between Two Worlds - *USA*
Bewitched - *USA*
Black Magic - *USA*
The Black Parachute - *USA*
Bluebeard - *USA*
Boston Blackie's Appointment with Death - *USA*
The Bridge of San Luis Rey - *USA*
Call of the Jungle - *USA*
Candles at Nine - *GB*
The Canterville Ghost - *USA*
Charlie Chan in the Secret Service - *USA*
The Chinese Cat - *USA*
The Climax - *USA*
The Conspirators - *USA*
Crime by Night - *USA*
Crime Doctor's Courage - *USA*
Cry of the Werewolf - *USA*
Curse of the Cat People - *USA*
Dark Waters - *USA*
Dead Man's Eyes - *USA*
Destiny - *USA*
Detective Kitty O'Day - *USA*
Enter Arsene Lupin - *USA*
Faces in the Fog - *USA*
The Falcon in Hollywood - *USA*
The Falcon in Mexico - *USA*
The Falcon Out West - *USA*
Fanny by Gaslight - *GB*
Fiddlers Three - *GB*
The Frozen Ghost - *USA*
Gaslight - *USA*
Ghost Crazy - *USA*
The Ghost That Walks Alone - *USA*
Gildersleeve's Ghost - *USA*
The Girl in the Case - *USA*
Guest in the House - *USA*
Gypsy Wildcat - *USA*
The Hairy Ape - *USA*
Halfway House - *GB*
Hets - *Swed*
House of Frankenstein - *USA*
The Invisible Man's Revenge - *USA*
It Happened Tomorrow - *USA*
Jane Eyre - *USA*
The Jungle Woman - *USA*
Kismet - *USA*
The Lady and the Monster - *USA*
Lady in the Dark - *USA*
Lady in the Death House - *USA*
Laura - *USA*
Lifeboat - *USA*
The Lodger - *USA*
Lost in a Harem - *USA*
The Man from Scotland Yard - *USA*
The Man in Half Moon Street - *USA*
The Mask of Dimitrios - *USA*
Meet Sexton Blake - *GB*
Ministry of Fear - *USA*
The Missing Juror - *USA*
The Mummy's Ghost - *USA*
Murder, My Sweet - *USA*
Nabonga - *USA*
A Night of Magic - *GB*
Once Upon a Time - *USA*
One Body Too Many - *USA*
One Mysterious Night - *USA*
The Pearl of Death - *USA*
Phantom Lady - *USA*
Port of 40 Thieves - *USA*
Return of the Ape Man - *USA*
The Scarlet Claw - *USA*
Secrets of Scotland Yard - *USA*
Seven Doors to Death - *USA*
Shadow of Suspicion - *USA*
Shadows in the Night - *USA*
Shake Hands with Murder - *USA*
Soul of a Monster - *USA*
Spider Woman - *US*
Strangers in the Night - *USA*
The Sultan's Daughter - *USA*
The Suspect - *USA*
They Came to a City - *GB*
They Live in Fear - *USA*
The Thin Man Goes Home - *USA*
Time Flies - *GB*
La Torre de los Siete Jorobados - *Sp*
U-Boat Prisoner - *USA*
The Uninvited - *USA*
The Unwritten Code - *USA*
Voodoo Man - *USA*

Weird Woman - *USA*
The Whistler - *USA*
The Woman in the Window - *USA*

1945

Adventures of Kitty O'Day - *USA*
And Then There Were None - *USA*
Apology for Murder - *USA*
Behind City Lights - *USA*
Black Market Babies - *USA*
Blithe Spirit - *GB*
The Body Snatcher - *USA*
Boston Blackie Booked on Suspicion - *USA*
Boston Blackie's Rendezvous - *USA*
The Brighton Strangler - *USA*
Captain Kidd - *USA*
El Castillo de las Bofetadas - *Sp*
Circumstantial Evidence - *USA*
Cornered - *USA*
Crime Doctor's Warning - *USA*
The Crimson Canary - *USA*
Dangerous Intruders - *USA*
Danger Signal - *USA*
Dead of Night - *GB*
Detour - *USA*
Dick Tracy, Detective - *USA*
The Echo Murders - *GB*
The Enchanted Cottage - *USA*
The Enchanted Forest - *USA*
Escape in the Fog - *USA*
The Falcon in San Francisco - *USA*
The Fatal Witness - *USA*
Fog Island - *USA*
Follow That Woman - *USA*
A Game of Death - *USA*
Hangover Square - *USA*
The Hidden Eye - *USA*
The Horn Blows at Midnight - *USA*
House of Dracula - *USA*
The House of Fear - *USA*
Identity Unknown - *USA*
I Love a Mystery - *USA*
Isle of the Dead - *USA*
The Jade Mask - *USA*
Jungle Captive - *USA*
The Lady Confesses - *USA*
Leave Her to Heaven - *USA*
The Lost Weekend - *USA*
Love Letters - *USA*
Main Street After Dark - *USA*
The Missing Corpse - *USA*
The Mummy's Curse - *USA*
Murder in Reverse - *GB*
Murder in the Blue Room - *USA*
El Otro Fu-Manchu - *Sp*
Out of the Night - *USA*
The Phantom Speaks - *USA*
The Picture of Dorian Gray - *USA*
Pillow of Death - *USA*
A Place of One's Own - *GB*
Power of the Whistler - *USA*
Pursuit to Algiers - *USA*
The Red Dragon - *USA*
Return of the Vikings - *GB*
The Road to Utopia - *USA*
Scared Stiff - *USA*
The Scarlet Clue - *USA*
Scotland Yard Investigator - *USA*
Shadow of Terror - *USA*
The Shanghai Cobra - *USA*
Song of Abai - *Russ*
Spellbound - *USA*
The Spider - *USA*
Strange Confession - *USA*
Strangler of the Swamp - *USA*
Sudan - *USA*
Tarzan and the Amazons - *USA*
A Thousand and One Nights - *USA*
The Tiger Woman - US
The Unseen - *USA*
The Vampire's Ghost - *USA*
Voice of the Whistler - *USA*
White Pongo - *USA*
The Woman in Green - *USA*
Woman Who Came Back - *USA*
Zombies on Broadway - *USA*

1946

Accomplice - *USA*
Angel on My Shoulder - *USA*
The Bandit of Sherwood Forest - *USA*
The Beast with Five Fingers - *USA*
Bedelia - *GB*
Bedlam - *USA*
Behind the Mask - *USA*
La Belle et la Bete - *Fr*
Below the Deadline - *USA*
The Big Sleep - *USA*
Black Angel - *USA*
Blonde for a Day - *USA*
Boston Blackie and the Law - *USA*

The Brute Man - *USA*
The Cat Creeps - *USA*
The Catman of Paris - *USA*
The Chase - *USA*
Cloak and Dagger - *USA*
A Close Call for Boston Blackie - *USA*
The Cockeyed Miracle - *USA*
Crime Doctor's Manhunt - *USA*
Dangerous Business - *USA*
Dangerous Millions - *USA*
Dangerous Money - *USA*
Danger Woman - *USA*
Dark Alibi - *USA*
The Dark Mirror - *USA*
Deadline for Murder - *USA*
Dear Murderer - *GB*
Decoy - *USA*
Devil Bat's Daughter - *USA*
Devil Monster - *USA*
The Devil's Mask - *USA*
Devotion - *USA*
Dick Tracy vs. Cueball - *USA*
Dragonwyck - *USA*
Dreams That Money Can Buy - *USA*
Dressed to Kill - *USA*
The Face of Marble - *USA*
The Falcon's Adventure - *USA*
The Falcon's Alibi - *USA*
Fear - *USA*
Flight to Nowhere - *USA*
The Flying Serpent - *USA*
The French Key - *USA*
Genius at Work - *USA*
Gilda - *USA*
The Glass Alibi - *USA*
Great Expectations - *GB*
Green for Danger - *GB*
Her Sister's Secret - *USA*
His Brother's Ghost - *USA*
Home, Sweet Homicide - *USA*
House of Horrors - *USA*
The Inner Circle - *USA*
Invisible Informer - *USA*
It's a Wonderful Life - *USA*
Just Before Dawn - *USA*
Lady in the Lake - *USA*
Larceny in Her Heart - *USA*
The Laughing Lady - *GB*
The Locket - *USA*
Mark of the Whistler - *USA*
The Mask of Dijon - *USA*
A Matter of Life and Death - *GB*
The Missing Lady - *USA*
Mr. Hex - *USA*
Murder in the Music Hall - *USA*
Murder is My Business - *USA*
The Mysterious Intruder - *USA*
Mysterious Mr. Valentine - *USA*
A Night in Paradise - *USA*
Notorious - *USA*
The Notorious Lone Wolf - *USA*
Passkey to Danger - *USA*
The Phantom Thief - *USA*
The Return of Monte Cristo - *USA*
Secrets of a Sorority Girl - *USA*
Shadowed - *USA*
Shadow of a Woman - *USA*
The Shadow Returns - *USA*
Shadows over Chinatown - *USA*
She-Wolf of London - *USA*
Shock - *USA*
Sinbad the Sailor - *USA*
So Dark the Night - *USA*
Somewhere in the Night - *USA*
The Spider Woman Strikes Back - *USA*
The Spiral Staircase - *USA*
Spook Busters - *USA*
Step by Step - *USA*
Strange Mr. Gregory - *USA*
Strange Triangle - *USA*
Suspense - *USA*
Swamp Fire - *USA*
Tarzan and the Leopard Woman - *USA*
Temptation - *USA*
Terror by Night - *USA*
They Made Me a Killer - *USA*
Three Strangers - *USA*
Three Wise Fools - *USA*
The Time of Their Lives - *USA*
Traffic in Crime - *USA*
The Truth About Murder - *USA*
Undercover Woman - *USA*
The Unknown - *USA*
Valley of the Zombies - *USA*
The Verdict - *USA*
Wanted for Murder - *GB*
The Wife of Monte Cristo - *USA*

1947

Adventure Island - *USA*
L'Aigle a Deux Tetes - *Fr*

The Beginning or the End? - *USA*
Big Town After Dark - *USA*
Bill and Coo - *USA*
The Bishop's Wife - *USA*
Blackmail - *USA*
Black Narcissus - *GB*
Blind Spot - *USA*
Blonde Savage - *USA*
Born to Kill - *USA*
The Brasher Doubloon - *USA*
Bulldog Drummond at Bay - *USA*
Bulldog Drummond Strikes Back - *USA*
Bury Me Dead - *USA*
The Chinese Ring - *USA*
The Crimson Key - *USA*
Cry Wolf - *USA*
Danger Street - *USA*
Dark Delusion - *USA*
Desperate - *USA*
The Devil Thumbs a Ride - *USA*
Dick Tracy Meets Gruesome - *USA*
Dick Tracy's Dilemma - *USA*
A Double Life - *USA*
Down to Earth - *USA*
Dual Alibi - *GB*
Exposed - *USA*
Fabulous Joe - *USA*
Fear in the Night - *USA*
Framed - *USA*
The Fugitive - *USA*
The Ghost and Mrs. Muir - *USA*
The Ghost Goes Wild - *USA*
The Ghosts of Berkeley Square - *GB*
Golden Earrings - *USA*
The Guilty - *USA*
The Hangman Waits - *GB*
The Hat Box Mystery - *USA*
Heaven Only Knows - *USA*
The Hills of Donegal - *GB*
In Self Defense - *USA*
Intrigue - *USA*
The Invisible Wall - *USA*
Just William's Luck - *GB*
Key Witness - *USA*
Killer at Large - *USA*
The Lady from Shanghai - *USA*
The Lone Wolf in London - *USA*
The Lone Wolf in Mexico - *USA*
The Lost Moment - *USA*
Love from a Stranger - *USA*
Lured - *USA*
Macbeth - *USA*
A Man About the House - *GB*
The Millerson Case - *USA*
Miracle on 34th Street - *USA*
Miranda - *GB*
Moss Rose - *USA*
The Mysterious Mr. Nicholson - *GB*
Nightmare Alley - *USA*
Night Unto Night - *USA*
The October Man - *GB*
La Otra - *Mex*
The Paradine Case - *USA*
Philo Vance Returns - *UA*
Philo Vance's Gamble -*USA*
Philo Vance's Secret Mssion - *USA*
Pirates of Monterey -*USA*
Possessed - *USA*
Pursued - *USA*
Queen of the Amazons - *USA*
The Red House - *USA*
Repeat Performance - *USA*
Ride the Pink Horse - *USA*
Scared to Death - *USA*
The Secret Life of Walter Mitty - *USA*
The Secret of the Whistler - *USA*
Seven Keys to Baldpate - *USA*
Shoot to Kill - *USA*
The Shop at Sly Corner - *GB*
Slave Girl - *USA*
Song of Scheherazade - *USA*
Song of the Thin Man - *USA*
Take My Life - *GB*
Tarzan and the Huntress - *USA*
They Made Me a Fugitive - *GB*
The Thirteenth Hour - *USA*
Three on a Ticket - *USA*
Too Many Winners - *USA*
The Trap - *USA*
The 12th Hour - *USA*
The Two Mrs. Carrolls - *USA*
Uncle Silas - *GB*
The Unsuspected - *USA*
Vice Versa - *GB*
Violence - *USA*
The Web - *USA*
Web of Danger - *USA*
The Bp Dullum In Shuuu - *GB*
While I Live - *GB*
The White Gorilla - *USA*

1948

Abbott and Costello Meet Frankenstein - *USA*
The Accused - *USA*
An Act of Murder - *USA*
Adventures of Casanova - *USA*
The Amazing Mr. X - *USA*
Appointment with Murder - *USA*
The Argyle Secrets - *USA*
Assigned to Danger - *USA*
Atlantis - *USA*
The Bad Lord Byron - *GB*
Bad Sister - *GB*
Behind Locked Doors - *USA*
Berlin Express - *USA*
The Big Clock - *USA*
The Boy with Green Hair - *USA*
Castle Sinister - *GB*
Caught - *USA*
The Challenge - *USA*
Cisaruv Slavik - *Czech*
The Clouded Crystal - *GB*
The Cobra Strikes - *USA*
Colonel Bogey - *GB*
Corridor of Mirrors - *GB*
Counterblast - *GB*
The Creeper - *USA*
Crime Doctor's Gamble - *USA*
Daughter of Darkness - *GB*
Death in the Hand - *GB*
The Decision of Christopher Blake - *USA*
Les Derniers Jours de Pompeii - *Fr*
The Devil's Cargo - *USA*
The Devil's Wanton - *Swed*
Dick Barton, Detective - *GB*
Dick Barton, Special Agent - *GB*
The Docks of New Orleans - *USA*
Dream Girl - *USA*
Escape from Broadmoor - *GB*
The Fallen Idol - *GB*
The Fatal Night - *GB*
Faust and the Devil - *It*
The Feathered Serpent - *USA*
For You I Die - *USA*
The Gentleman from Nowhere - *USA*
The Golden Eye - *USA*
The Greed of William Hart - *GB*
Half-Past Midnight - *USA*
Hamlet - *GB*
Histoires Extraordinaires - *Fr*
House of Darkness - *GB*
The Hunted - *USA*
It Happened in Soho - *GB*
Jungle Goddess - *USA*
Jungle Jim - *USA*
Kiss the Blood Off My Hands - *USA*
Lady at Midnight - *USA*
Larceny - *USA*
Let's Live Agan - *USA*
The Luck of the Irish - *USA*
Man-Eater of Kumaon - *USA*
The Mark of Cain - *GB*
Il Miracolo - *It*
Mr. Peabody and the Mermaid - *USA*
Money Madness - *USA*
Mystery in Mexico - *USA*
Night Comes Too Soon - *GB*
Night Has a Thousand Eyes - *USA*
Noose - *GB*
One Night of Fame - *Fr*
One Touch of Venus - *USA*
Open Secret - *USA*
Out of the Storm - *USA*
Panic at Madam Tussaud's - *GB*
Les Parents Terribles - *Fr*
Perilous Waters - *USA*
A Piece of Cake - *GB*
Pitfall - *USA*
Portrait from Life - *GB*
Port Said - *USA*
The Prince of Thieves - *USA*
The Queen of Spades - *GB*
The Raven - *USA*
The Return of October - *USA*
The Return of the Whistler - *USA*
Rope - *USA*
Sealed Verdict - *USA*
Secret Beyond the Door - *USA*
Secret Service Investigator - *USA*
The Shanghai Chest - *USA*
16 Fathoms Deep - *USA*
Sleeping Car to Trieste - *GB*
Sleep, My Love - *USA*
Smuggler's Cove - *USA*
The Snake Pit - *USA*
So Evil My Love- *USA*
Sorry, Wrong Number - *USA*
State Department—File 649 - *USA*
Strange Gamble - *USA*
Sword of the Avenger - *USA*
Tarzan and the Mermaids - *USA*

Things Happen at Night - *GB*
13 Lead Soldiers - *USA*
The Three Musketeers - *USA*
The Three Weird Sisters - *GB*
To the Ends of the Earth - *USA*
Trapped by Boston Blackie - *USA*
Unknown Island - *USA*
The Velvet Touch - *USA*
Vicious Circle - *USA*
The Woman in White - *USA*

1949
Abbott and Costello Meet the Killer - *USA*
The Adventures of Don Juan - *USA*
Africa Screams - *USA*
Alias Nick Beal - *USA*
Amazon Quest - *USA*
Bagdad - *USA*
The Baron of Arizona - *USA*
The Black Book - *USA*
Black Magic - *USA*
Black Midnight - *USA*
Bomba, the Jungle Boy - *USA*
Boston Blackie's Chinese Venture - *USA*
The Bribe - *USA*
Bride of Vengeance - *USA*
Celia - *GB*
A Connecticut Yankee in King Arthur's Court - *USA*
Il Comte Ugolino - *It*
Crime Doctor's Diary - *USA*
Dark Secret - *GB*
Daughter of the Jungle - *USA*
D.O.A. - *USA*
The Devil's Henchman - *USA*
Dick Barton Strikes Back - *GB*
Follow Me Quietly - *USA*
Forbidden - *GB*
The Forbidden Street - *USA*
For Them That Trespass - *GB*
Haunted Palace - *GB*
Highway 13 - *USA*
Homicide - *USA*
Homicide for Three - *USA*
I Cheated the Law - *USA*
Illegal Entry - *USA*
Incident - *USA*
Inner Sanctum - *USA*
The Interrupted Journey - *GB*
It Happens Every Spring - *USA*
Kind Hearts and Coronets - *GB*
King Solomon's Mines - *USA*
The Lone Wolf and His Lady - *USA*
The Lost Tribe - *USA*
Man on the Run - *GB*
The Master Minds - *USA*
Mighty Joe Young - *USA*
Murder at the Windmill - *GB*
The Mutineers - *USA*
Obsession - *GB*
The Perfect Woman - *GB*
I Pirati di Capri - *It*
Portrait of Jennie - *USA*
Post Office Investigator - *USA*
Project X - *USA*
The Red Menace - *USA*
The Rocking Horse Wnner - *GB*
Room to Let - *GB*
Samson and Delilah - *USA*
Scene of the Crime - *USA*
Search for Danger - *USA*
Secret of St. Ives - *USA*
The Set-Up - *USA*
Shickproof - *USA*
The Sky Dragon - *USA*
Song of India - *USA*
Special Agent - *USA*
The Spider and the Fly - *GB*
Stop Press Girl - *GB*
Take One False Step - *USA*
Tarzan's Magic Fountain - *USA*
The Third Man - *GB*
The Threat - *USA*
Torment - *GB*
Trapped - *USA*
Treasure of Monte Cristo - *USA*
Under Capricorn - *USA*
Whispering Smith - *USA*
The Window - *USA*
Zamba - *USA*

1950
Alice in Wonderland - *GB*
Armored Car Robbery - *USA*
Atoll K - *It-Fr*
Atom Man vs. Superman - *USA*
La Beauté du Diable - *It-Fr*
Between Midnight and Dawn - *USA*
The Black Rose - *GB*
Bomba and the Hidden City - *USA*
Buccaneer's Girl - *USA*

Cage of Gold - *GB*
Captive Girl - *USA*
Chained for Life - *USA*
Champagne for Caesar - *USA*
Chinatown at Midnight - *USA*
La Corona Negra - *Sp*
Cry Murder - *USA*
Dark Interval - *GB*
David Harding, Counterspy - *USA*
Deported - *USA*
Destination Moon - *USA*
Destination Murder - *USA*
Dick Barton at Bay - *GB*
Double Confession - *GB*
The Dragon of Pendragon Castle - *GB*
The Elusive Pimpernel - *GB*
Les Enfants Terribles - *Fr*
The Fall of the House of Usher - *GB*
Federal Agent at Large - *USA*
The Flying Saucer - *USA*
Forbidden Jungle - *USA*
For Heaven's Sake - *USA*
Fortunes of Captain Blood - *USA*
Francis - *USA*
The Great Rupert - *USA*
Guilt is My Shadow - *GB*
Guilty Bystander - *USA*
Harvey - *USA*
Highly Dangerous - *GB*
His Last 12 Hours - *It*
Jungle Stampede - *USA*
Killer Shark - *USA*
Kill or Be Killed - *USA*
Last Holiday - *GB*
Last of the Buccaneers - *USA*
The Lost Volcano - *USA*
Love and Poison - *It*
M - *USA*
The Man in Black - *GB*
Mark of the Gorilla - *USA*
Mary Ryan, Detective - *USA*
Master Minds - *USA*
Mr. Drake's Duck - *GB*
Mr. H.C. Andersen - *GB*
Murder without Crime - *GB*
My Daughter Joy - *GB*
Mystery Street - *USA*
The Next Voice You Hear - *USA*
No Trace - *GB*
On the Isle of Samoa - *USA*
Orphee - *Fr*
Panther Island - *USA*
Paul Temple's Triumph - *GB*
Prehistoric Women - *USA*
Pygmy Island - *USA*
Radar Secret Service - *USA*
Rapture - *GB*
Rocket Attack U.S.A. - *USA*
Rocketship X-M - *USA*
Rogues of Sherwood Forest - *USA*
The Scarf - *USA*
Seven Days to Noon - *GB*
Shadow of the Eagle - *GB*
Shadow of the Past - *GB*
Shadow on the Wall - *USA*
She Shall Have Murder - *GB*
Sideshow - *USA*
Snow Dog - *USA*
So Long at the Fair - *GB*
Spy Hunt - *USA*
Stage Fright - *GB*
State Secret - *GB*
Sunset Boulevard - *USA*
Superman's Perils - *USA*
Sylvia and the Phantom - *Fr*
Tarzan and the Slave Girl - *USA*
The Tattooed Stranger - *USA*
This Side of the Law - *USA*
Treasure Island - *USA*
The Twenty Questions Murder - *GB*
Two Lost Worlds - *USA*
Tyrant of the Sea - *USA*
Undercover Girl - *USA*
Vendetta - *USA*
La Villa dei Mostri - *It*
Where Danger Lives - *USA*
Woman in Hiding - *USA*
The Woman in Question - *GB*
Woman on the Run - *USA*
The Woman with No Name - *GB*
Your Witness - *GB*

1951
Abbott and Costello Meet the Invisible Man - *USA*
Adventures of Captain Fabian - *USA*
Angels in the Outfield - *USA*
Appointment with Danger - *USA*
At Sword's Point - *USA*
L'Auberge Rouge - *Fr*
Babes in Bagdad - *USA-Sp*
Bedtime for Bonzo - *USA*

Blackmailed - *GB*
Bomba and the Elephant Stampede - *USA*
Bride of the Gorilla - *USA*
Calling Bulldog Drummond - *GB*
Chain of Circumstance - *USA*
Circle of Danger - *GB*
Cisaruv Pekar, Pekaruv Cisar - *Czech*
Cloudburst - *GB*
Counterspy Meets Scotland Yard - *USA*
Cry Danger - *USA*
Cuento de Hadas - *Sp*
Danger Zone - *USA*
The Dark Man - *GB*
The Day the Earth Stood Still - *USA*
Death is a Number - *GB*
Double Crossbones - *USA*
F.B.I. Girl - *USA*
Fingerprints Don't Lie - *USA*
Five - *USA*
Flight to Mars - *USA*
Francis Goes to the Races - *USA*
Fury of the Congo - *USA*
Ghost Chasers - *USA*
The Girl on the Bridge - *USA*
Gypsy Fury - *USA*
Half Angel - *USA*
High Treason - *GB*
The House in the Square - *USA*
Hurricane Island - *USA*
Insurance Investigator - *USA*
I Was a Communist for the F.B.I. - *USA*
Jungle Headhunters - *USA*
Jungle Manhunt - *USA*
Jungle of Chang - *USA*
Kind Lady - *USA*
Il Ladro di Venezia - *It*
The Late Edwina Black - *GB*
The Lavender Hill Mob - *GB*
Lightning Strikes Twice - *USA*
The Lion Hunters - *USA*
Lost Continent - *USA*
Lost Planet Airmen - *USA*
The Magic Carpet - *USA*
The Man from Planet X - *USA*
The Man in the White Suit - *GB*
The Man with a Cloak - *USA*
The Man with My Face - *USA*
The Man with the Twisted Lip - *GB*
Mask of the Avenger - *USA*
Mask of the Dragon - *USA*
The Medium - *It*
Miracle in Milan - *It*
Missing Women - *USA*
Mr. Denning Drives North - *GB*
Mr. Peek-A-Boo - *Fr*
Mother Riley Meets the Vampire - *GB*
Murder on Monday - *GB*
Mystery Junction - *GB*
Night into Morning - *USA*
Night without Stars - *GB*
OK, Nero! - *It*
Old Mother Riley's Junge Treasure - *GB*
Pandora and the Flying Dutchman - *GB*
Parsifal - *Sp*
Peking Express - *USA*
Pickup - *USA*
Pier 23 - *USA*
Poison - *USA*
Pool of London - *GB*
The Prowler - *USA*
Savage Drums - *USA*
Scarlet Thread - *GB*
Scrooge - *GB*
Secrets of Monte Carlo - *USA*
Smuggler's Gold - *USA*
Smuggler's Island - *USA*
The Son of Dr. Jekyll - *USA*
The Sound Barrier - *GB*
Storm Bound - *It*
Storm Over Tibet - *USA*
The Strange Door - *USA*
Strangers on a Train - *USA*
Superman and the Mole Men - *USA*
The Sword of Monte Cristo - *USA*
Tales of Robin Hood - *USA*
Tarazan's Peril - *USA*
The Thing from Another World - *USA*
The Thirteenth Letter - *USA*
The Treasure of Lost Canyon - *USA*
Unknown World - *USA*
Valley of the Eagles - *GB*
Der Verlorene - *W. Ger*
When Worlds Collide - *USA*
You Never Can Tell - *USA*

1952
Abbott and Costello Meet Captain Kidd - *USA*
African Treasure - *USA*
Aladdin and His Lamp - *USA*
Alraune - *W. Ger*
Androcles and the Lion - *USA*

Another Man's Poison - *GB*
Assignment—Paris - *USA*
Astrologie - *Fr*
The Atomic City - *USA*
Les Aventures Extraordinaires de Jules Verne - *Fr*
The Battles of Chief Pontiac - *USA*
Beware, My Lovely - *USA*
Blackbeard the Pirate - *USA*
The Black Castle - *USA*
Bonzo Goes to College - *USA*
The Boys from Brooklyn - *USA*
Captain Pirate - *USA*
Captive Women - *USA*
City Beneath the Sea - *USA*
Confidence Girl - *USA*
The Crimson Pirate - *GB*
Crow Hollow - *GB*
Death of an Angel - *GB*
Don't Bother to Knock - *USA*
The 5000 Fingers of Dr. T - *USA*
Flame of Araby - *USA*
Francis Goes to West Point - *USA*
The Frightened Bride - *GB*
A Ghost for Sale - *GB*
Ghost Ship - *GB*
The Green Glove - *USA*
Hiawatha - *USA*
Hold That Line - *USA*
The Hour of 13 - *GB*
Hunted - *GB*
It Grows on Trees - *USA*
Jack and the Beanstalk - *USA*
Jeux Interdits - *Fr*
The Jungle - *USA*
The Jungle Girl - *USA*
Jungle Jim in the Forbidden Land - *USA*
Lady in the Fog - *GB*
The Lady in the Iron Mask - *USA*
Last Train from Bombay - *USA*
The Lost Hours - *GB*
Lucrezia Borgia - *Fr*
Mesa of Lost Women - *USA*
Les Miserables - *USA*
Monkey Business - *USA*
Murder at Scotland Yard - *GB*
Murder at the Grange - *GB*
Mutiny - *USA*
My Cousin Rachel - *USA*
The Net - *GB*
No Haunt for a Gentleman - *GB*
No Holds Barred - *USA*
On Dangerous Ground - *USA*
Operation Secret - *USA*
The Oracle - *GB*
Paris Express - *GB*
Paul Temple Returns - *GB*
Pirate Submarine - *USA*
The Prisoner of Zenda - *USA*
Ramar and the Burning Barrier - *USA*
Ramar and the Deadly Females - *USA*
Ramar and the Jungle Secrets - *USA*
Ramar and the Savage Challengers - *USA*
Ramar and the Unknown Terror - *USA*
Ramar of the Jungle - *USA*
Ramar's Mission to India - *USA*
Red Planet Mars - *USA*
The Resurrected Monster - *Mex*
The Ringer - *GB*
The Road to Bali - *USA*
Saturday Island - *GB*
Lo Sceicco Bianco - *It*
Seeds of Destruction - *USA*
Il Segreto delle Tre Punte - *It*
Shadow in the Sky - *USA*
The Singing Princess - *GB*
The Sniper - *USA*
Son of Ali Baba - *USA*
The Starfish - *GB*
The Steel Key - *GB*
The Steel Trap - *USA*
A Stolen Face - *GB*
The Story of Robin Hood - *GB*
Strange Fascination - *USA*
Sudden Fear - *USA*
Talk About a Stranger - *USA*
Tarzan's Savage Fury - *USA*
The Thief - *USA*
Thief of Damascus - *USA*
Top Secret - *GB*
Torticola Contre Frankensberg - *Fr*
Tread Softly - *GB*
Trent's Last Case - *GB*
Tromba, the Tiger Man - *USA*
Untamed Women - *USA*
Venetian Bird - *GB*
The Voice of Merrill - *GB*
Voodoo Tiger - *USA*
Wall of Death - *GB*
The War of the Worlds - *USA*
Whispering Smith Hits London - *GB*
Woman in the Dark - *USA*

The Yellow Balloon - *GB*

<u>1953</u>

Abbott and Costello Go to Mars - *USA*
Abbott and Costello Meet Dr. Jekyll and
Mr. Hyde - *USA*
Affair with a Stranger - *USA*
All Hallowe'en - *GB*
The Bandits of Corsica - *USA*
The Beast from 20,000 Fathoms - *USA*
Beat the Devil - *GB*
Black Butterflies - *Mex*
Black Orchid - *GB*
Black 13 - *USA*
A Blueprint for Murder - *USA*
Bwana Devil - *USA*
The Candlelight Murder - *GB*
Capt. John Smith and Pocahontas - *USA*
Captain Scarlett - *USA*
Cat-Women of the Moon - *USA*
Colonel March Investigates - *GB*
Colonel March of Scotland Yard - *GB*
Cosh Boy - *GB*
Counterspy - *GB*
Cumbres Borrascosas - *Sp*
Death Goes to School - *GB*
Desert Legion - *USA*
The Diamond Queen - *USA*
Donovan's Brain - *USA*
Dragon's Gold - *USA*
Drakula Istanbulda - *Turk*
Eyes of the Jungle - *USA*
Fair Wind to Java - *USA*
Fangs of the Arctic - *USA*
Fear and Desire - *USA*
The Flanagan Boy - *GB*
Four Sided Triangle - *GB*
Francis Covers the Big Town - *USA*
The Girl on the Pier - *GB*
The Glass Web - *USA*
Glen or Glenda? - *USA*
The Golden Blade - *USA*
Grand National Night - *GB*
The Gypsy Moon - *USA*
Houdini - *USA*
House of Blackmail - *GB*
House of the Arrow - *GB*
House of Wax - *USA*
I Confess - *USA*
Intimate Relations - *GB*
Invaders from Mars - *USA*
Invasion U.S.A. - *USA*
It Came from Outer Space - *USA*
I, the Jury - *USA*
I'll Get You - *USA*
Jalopy - *USA*
Jamaica Run - *USA*
Jennifer - *USA*
Johnny the Giant Killer - *Fr*
Killer Ape - *USA*
The Limping Man - *GB*
The Love of Three Queens - *It*
The Magnetic Monster - *USA*
Man in Hiding - *GB*
Man in the Attic - *USA*
Man in the Dark - *USA*
Marie Antoinette - *Fr*
The Maze - *USA*
Meet Mr. Lucifer - *GB*
La Mome Vert-de-Gris - *Fr*
Il Mostro dell'Isola - *It*
Murder without Tears - *USA*
The Neanderthal Man - *USA*
Niagara - *USA*
Noose for a Lady - *GB*
One Girl's Confession - *USA*
Orient Express - *W. Ger*
A Perilous Journey - *USA*
Perils of the Jungle - *USA*
Phantom from Space - *USA*
Phantom of the Rue Morgue - *USA*
Port Sinister - *USA*
Prince of Pirates - *USA*
Prisoners of the Casbah - *USA*
Private Eyes - *USA*
Project Moonbase - *USA*
Raiders of the Seven Seas - *USA*
The Raven - *GB*
Robot Monster - *USA*
Run for the Hills - *USA*
Safari Drums - *USA*
The Saint's Return - *GB*
La Salaire de la Peur - *Fr*
Salome - *USA*
Savage Mutiny - *USA*
Scared Stiff - *USA*
Second Chance - *USA*
Seven Deadly Sins - *It-Fr*
Sins of Jezebel - *USA*
Siren of Bagdad - *USA*

Slaves of Babylon - *USA*
Spaceways - *GB*
Split Second - *USA*
The Stranger Left No Card - *GB*
Stranger on the Prowl - *USA*
The Straw Man - *GB*
Street of Shadows - *GB*
Sword of Venus - *USA*
Tangier Incident - *USA*
Tarzan and the She-Devil - *USA*
The Tell-Tale Heart - *GB*
The Tell-Tale Heart - *USA*
Teodora, Imperatrice di Bisanzio - *It*
Thy Neighbor's Wife - *USA*
Treasure of Bengal - *It*
Turn the Key Softly - *GB*
The Twonky - *USA*
Ugetsu Monogatari - *Jap*
Valley of the Headhunters - *USA*
The Veils of Bagdad - *USA*
The White Goddess - *USA*

<u>1954</u>

The Adventures of Hajji Baba - *USA*
Affairs of Messalina - *It*
Ali-Baba et les Quarante Voleurs - *Fr*
The Angel Who Pawned Her Harp - *GB*
Animal Farm - *GB*
The Atomic Kid - *USA*
Bait - *USA*
Berenice - *Fr*
Beyond the Moon - *USA*
The Black Glove - *USA*
The Black Knight - *GB*
The Black Pirates - *USA*
The Black Rider - *GB*
The Black Shield of Falworth - *USA*
Black Widow - *USA*
The Bowery Boys Meet the Monsters - *USA*
Bowery to Bagdad - *USA*
Cannibal Attack - *USA*
Captain Kidd and the Slave Girl - *USA*
Cesta Do Praveku - *Czech*
Child's Play - *GB*
The Cold Sun - *USA*
The Crash of Moons - *USA*
Creature from the Black Lagoon - *USA*
Dangerous Mission - *USA*
Devil Girl from Mars - *GB*
Dial M for Murder - *USA*
The Diamond - *GB*
Down Three Dark Streets - *USA*
Duel in Space - *USA*
Duel in the Jungle - *USA*
Fatal Journey - *GB*
Les Femmes s'en Balancent - *Fr*
Follow the Hunter - *USA*
Francis Joins the WACs - *USA*
Gog - *USA*
Gojira - *Jap*
The Golden Idol - *USA*
Golden Ivory - *GB*
The Golden Link - *GB*
The Golden Mask - *GB*
The Golden Mistress - *USA*
Gorilla at Large - *USA*
The Green Buddha - *GB*
The Green Scarf - *GB*
Herr Arnes Pengar - *Swed*
The House Across the Lake - *GB*
An Inspector Calls - *GB*
Jivaro - *USA*
Jungle Gents - *USA*
Jungle Man-Eaters - *USA*
Killer Leopard - *USA*
Killers from Space - *USA*
King Dinosaur - *USA*
Knights of the Round Table - *GB*
Long John Silver - *Austra*
The Long Wait - *USA*
Mad About Men - *GB*
Madame DuBarry - *Fr*
The Mad Magician - *USA*
Make Haste to Live - *USA*
Manhunt in Space - *USA*
Mata Hari's Daughter - *It*
Men of Sherwood Forest - *GB*
The Mirror and Markheim - *GB*
Monster from the Ocean Floor - *USA*
Naked Alibi - *USA*
The Naked Jungle - *USA*
The Night of the Full Moon - *GB*
Obsession - *Fr*
Operation Manhunt - *USA*
Paid to Kill - *USA*
Paris Playboys - *USA*
Pod Gwiazda Frygijska - *Pol*
Prince Valiant - *USA*
The Queen of Babylon - *It*
Queen of Sheba - *It*
A Race for Life - *USA*

Rear Window - *USA*
Return to Treasure Island - *USA*
Riders to the Stars - *USA*
Ring of Fear - *USA*
River of No Return - *USA*
Rocket Man - *USA*
Roogie's Bump - *USA*
Saadia - *USA*
The Saracen Blade - *USA*
The Scarlet Spear - *USA*
Secret of the Incas - *USA*
Security Risk - *USA*
Serpent Island - *USA*
The She-Wolf - *It*
Shield for Murder - *USA*
Sins of Rome - *It*
The Snow Creature - *USA*
Solution by Phone - *GB*
The Stranger Came Home - *GB*
Stranger from Venus - *GB*
The Stranger's Hand - *GB*
Svengali - *GB*
Target Earth - *USA*
The Teckman Mystery - *GB*
Terror Ship - *USA*
Them! - *USA*
Thirty-Six Hours - *GB*
This is My Love - *USA*
Three Hours to Kill - *USA*
The Three Wishes - *GB*
Time is My Enemy - *GB*
Tobor the Great - *USA*
20,000 Leagues Under the Sea - *USA*
Ulysses - *It*
Violated - *USA*
The White Orchid - *USA*
Witness to Murder - *USA*

<u>1955</u>

Abbott and Costello Meet the Mummy - *USA*
African Manhunt - *USA*
Alias John Preston - *GB*
Barbados Quest - *GB*
The Beast with a Million Eyes - *USA*
Before I Wake - *GB*
The Bespoke Overcoat - *GB*
Betrayed Women - *USA*
Black Devils of Kali - *It*
The Brain Machine - *GB*
Cell 2455, Death Row - *USA*
City of Shadows - *USA*
Conquest of Space - *USA*
Creature with the Atom Brain - *USA*
The Crooked Web - *USA*
Cult of the Cobra - *USA*
Day the World Ended - *USA*
Dementia - *USA*
Devil Goddess - *USA*
Diabolique - *Fr*
Dig That Uranium! - *USA*
Don Juan's Night of Love - *It*
Double Jeopardy - *USA*
The Female Jungle - *USA*
The Finger Man - *USA*
Flying Saucers - *Mex*
Footsteps in the Fog - *GB*
Francis in the Navy - *USA*
The Glass Slipper - *USA*
The Glass Tomb - *GB*
Godzilla Raids Again - *Jap*
Hell's Island - *USA*
Hold Back Tomorrow - *USA*
I Cover the Underworld - *USA*
The Intruder - *GB*
It Came from Beneath the Sea - *USA*
It's a Dog's Life - *USA*
It's Always Fair Weather - *USA*
Jungle Moon Men - *USA*
Das Kalte Herz - *E. Ger*
A Kid for Two Farthings - *GB*
Killer's Kiss - *USA*
King Robot (unfinished) - *USA*
Kiss Me Deadly - *USA*
Lady Godiva - *USA*
Land of the Pharaohs - *USA*
The Last Hunt - *USA*
The Last Musketeer - *Fr*
The Last Ten Days of Adolf Hitler - *Austria*
A Life at Stake - *USA*
Little Red Monkey - *GB*
Lola Montes - *GB*
Lord of the Jungle - *USA*
Man Beast - *USA*
Mr. Arkadin - *GB-Sp*
Murder by Proxy - *GB*
Murder is My Beat - *USA*
The Night Holds Terror - *USA*
The Night of the Hunter - *USA*
1001 GB
Pearl of the South Pacific - *USA*
Phantom of the Jungle - *USA*

Pirates of Tripoli - *USA*
The Purple Mask - *USA*
The Quatermass Experiment - *GB*
Revenge of the Creature - *USA*
Richard III - *GB*
Sabaka - *USA*
Savage Princess - *India*
Secret Venture - *GB*
Shadow of a Man - *GB*
Sins of Pompeii - *It*
Son of Sinbad - *USA*
La Sorciere - *Fr-Swed*
Spy Chasers - *USA*
Sudden Danger - *USA*
Tarantula - *USA*
Tarzan's Hidden Jungle - *USA*
They Can't Hang Me - *GB*
This Island Earth - *USA*
Three Cases of Murder - *GB*
Thumbelina - *GB*
Thunder Over Sangoland - *USA*
Timeslip - *GB*
To Catch a Thief - *USA*
Track the Man Down - *GB*
The Trouble with Harry - *USA*
The Werewolf - *USA*

<u>1956</u>

Abdullah's Harem - *USA*
Accused of Murder - *USA*
Adam and Eve - *Mex*
The Animal World - *USA*
Around the World in 80 Days - *USA*
The Bad Seed - *USA*
The Beast of Hollow Mountain - *USA*
Beyond a Reasonable Doubt - *USA*
The Black Sleep - *USA*
Blonde Bait - *USA*
Bride of the Monster - *USA*
Calling Homicide - *USA*
Carousel - *USA*
Cloak Without Dagger - *GB*
Congo Crossin - *USA*
Crashing Las Vegas - *USA*
The Creature Walks Among Us - *USA*
A Cry in the Night - *USA*
The Curse o Frankenstein - *GB*
Curucu, Best of the Amazon - *USA*
Dark Ventre - *USA*
The Deadliest Sin - *USA*
The Deadly Mantis - *USA*
Don Juan - *W. Ger*
The Door in the Wall - *GB*
Dracos - *Greece*
Earth vs. the Flying Saucers - *USA*
Find the Lady - *GB*
Fire Maidens of Outer Space - *GB*
Forbidden Planet - *USA*
Foreign Intrigue - *USA*
Francis in the Haunted House - *USA*
The Gamma People - *GB*
Girls in Prison - *USA*
The Golden Demon - *Jap*
The Green Man - *GB*
I've Lived Before - *USA*
Ilya Mourometz - *Russ*
The Incredible Shrinking Man - *USA*
Indestructible Man - *USA*
The Intimate Stranger - *GB*
Invasion of the Body Snatchers - *USA*
The Invisible Boy - *USA*
It Conquered the World - *USA*
Jaguar - *USA*
Julie - *USA*
Jungle Hell - *USA*
The Killer is Loose - *USA*
The Killing - *USA*
El Ladron de Cadaveres - *Mex*
The Lady Killers - *GB*
The Last Man to Hang? - *GB*
The Lebanese Mission - *Fr*
The Living Idol - *USA-Mex*
Lock Up Your Daughters - *USA*
The Lone Ranger - *USA*
Macumba - *USA*
Manfish - *USA*
The Man in the Road - *GB*
The Man Who Knew Too Much - *USA*
The March Hare - *GB*
Moby Dick - *USA*
The Mole Peole - *USA*
La Mort en Le Jardin - *Fr*
The Naked Gun - *USA*
Nestasni Robot - *Yugo*
Nightfall - *USA*
Nightmare - *USA*
No Place to Hide - *USA*
Oedipus Rex - *Can*
On the Threshold of Space - *USA*
Passport to Treason - *GB*

Person Unknown - GB
The Phantom from 10,000 Leagues - USA
Please Murder Me - USA
Postmark for Danger - USA
The Price of Fear - USA
Quatermass II - GB
The Red Balloon - Fr
A Rocket from Calabuch - Sp
Rodan, the Flying Monster - Jap
Run for the Sun - USA
Satellite in the Sky - GB
The Search for Bridey Murphy - USA
The Secret of the Forest - GB
Secret of Treasure Mountain - USA
Shadow of Fear - USA
The She-Creature - USA
The Snow Was Black - Fr
Soho Incident - GB
Spy for Germany - W. Ger
Star of India - USA
Storm Fear - USA
Strange Intruder - USA
S - USA
Supersonic Saucer - GB
Swamp Women - USA
Terror at Midnight - USA
Three Bad Sisters - USA
23 Paces to Baker Street - USA
U.F.O. - USA
The Undead - USA
The Unguarded Moment - USA
I Vampiri - It
El Vampiro Acecha - Argent
Voodoo Island - USA
Vous Pegez? - Fr
Walk the Dark Street - USA
While the City Sleeps - USA
Who Done It? - GB
A Woman's Devotion - USA
Women of Pitcairn Island - USA
World Without End - USA
X...The Unknown - GB

1957
The Abominable Snowman of the Himalayas - GB
Abrakadabra - Yugo
The Amazing Colossal Man - USA
Un Amour de Poche - Fr
Angels of Darkness - It
The Astounding She-Monster - USA
Attack of the Crab Monsters - USA
At the Stroke of Nine - GB
Back from the Dead - USA
The Beginning of the End - USA
The Black Scorpion - USA
Blood of Dracula - USA
The Bride and the Beast - USA
The Burglar - USA
Cartouche - GB
Cat Girl - GB
Chain of Evidence - USA
Chase a Crooked Shadow - GB
The Crimes of Stephen Hawke - GB
The Cyclops - USA
Daughter of Dr. Jekyll - USA
Demoniac - Fr
Desk Set - USA
The Devil Strikes at Night - W. Ger
The Diabolical Invention - Czech
The Disembodied - USA
The End of the Line - GB
Five Steps to Danger - USA
Footsteps in the Night - USA
Frantic - Fr
Fright - USA
Ghost Diver - USA
The Giant Claw - USA
The Girl in Black Stockings - USA
The Girl in the Kremlin - USA
The Glass Tower - W. Ger
Grip of the Strangler - GB
Half-Human - Jap
Hell on Devil's Island - USA
Hell Ship Mutiny - USA
Hercules - It
Hidden Fear - USA
Hold That Hypnotist - USA
Hour of Decision - GB
The House in the Woods - GB
How to Murder a Rich Uncle - GB
The Hunchback of Notre Dame - It-Fr
The Hypnotist - GB
I Bury the Living - USA
Invasion of the Saucer Men - USA
The Invisible Avenger - USA
I Was a Teenage Frankenstein - USA
I Was a Teenage Werewolf - USA
Jane Eyre - USA
Jungle Heat - USA
The Key Man - GB
Kill Her Gently - GB

Kill Me Tomorrow - GB
Kronos - USA
Lady of Vengeance - GB
The Land Unknown - USA
Legend of the Lost - USA
Lizzie - USA
Love Slaves of the Amazons - USA
A Man Escaped - Fr
Man in the Shadow - GB
Man of a Thousand Face - USA
Man on the Prowl - US
The Man Who Turned to Stone - USA
The Man Who Wagged His Tail - It-Sp
The Man Without a Body - GB
Mark of the Phoenix - GB
Les Miserables - Fr
La Momia - Mex
The Monolith Monsters - USA
The Monster from Green Hell - USA
The Monster That Challenged the World - USA
Murder Reported - GB
My Gun is Quick - USA
The Mysterians - Jap
Night of the Demon - GB
The Night the World Exploded - USA
Not of This Earth - USA
Omar Khayyam - USA
Pharaoh's Curse - USA
The Revenge of Frankenstein - GB
Rocket to Nowhere - Czech
Sabu and the Magic Ring - USA
The Secret of the Loch - GB
Seven Thunders - USA
The Shadow on the Window - USA
She Demons - USA
She-Devil - USA
She-Gods of Shark Reef - USA
Det Sjunde Inseglet - Swed
Smultronstallet - Swed
Les Sorcieres de Salem - Fr
Speaking of Murder - Fr
Spook Chasers - USA
The Story of Mankind - USA
Suspended Alibi - GB
Tarzan and the Lost Safari - GB
The Tattered Dress - USA
Teenage Monster - USA
Teenage Zombies - USA
The Three Faces of Eve - USA
Throne of Blood - Jap
Treasure at the Mill - GB
The Trollenberg Terror - GB
20 Million Miles to Earth - USA
The 27th Day - USA
Uchujin Tokyo No Arawaru - Jap
Undersea Girl - USA
The Unearthly - USA
The Unknown Terror - USA
Up in Smoke - USA
Valerie - USA
The Vampire - USA
El Vampiro - Mex
The Vicious Circle - GB
The Viking Women and the Sea Serpent - USA
Vodoo Woman - USA
What Price Murder - Fr
Witness for the Prosecution - USA
The Wrong Man - USA
Zombies of Mora Tau - USA

1958
The Accursed - GB
The Adventures of Hal 5 - GB
Ansiktet - Swed
Appointment with a Shadow - USA
El Ataud del Vampiro - Mex
Attack of the 50-Foot Woman - USA
Attack of the Puppet People - USA
Bell, Book and Candle - USA
Black Orpheus - Fr-Brz
The Blob - USA
Blood of the Vampire - GB
The Bonnie Parker Story - USA
The Brain Eaters - USA
The Brain from Planet Arous - USA
The Camp on Blood Island - GB
The Colossus of New York - USA
The Cosmic Man - USA
Crash Landing - USA
Crime and Punishment - Fr
The Crossroad Gallows - GB
The Cry Baby Killer - USA
Cry Terror! - USA
Curse of the Faceless Man - USA
Damn Yankees - USA
The Dancing Heart - W. Ger
Deep Freeze - USA
The Diplomatic Corpse - GB
Doctor of Seven Dials - GB
Edge of Fury - USA
Enchanted Island - USA

The Fall of the House of Usher - USA
Family Doctor - GB
Faustina - Sp
The Fearmakers - USA
Fiend Without a Face - GB
First Man into Space - GB
The Flame Barrier - USA
Floods of Fear - GB
The Fly - USA
Flying Disc Man from Mars - USA
Frankenstein—1970 - USA
Frankenstein's Daughter - USA
From Hell It Came - USA
From the Earth to the Moon - USA
Giant from the Unknown - USA
Gideon's Day - GB
Hi, Here's Eddie - W. Ger
El Hombre y el Monstruo - Mex
Horror of Dracula - GB
House on Haunted Hill - USA
How to Make a Monster - USA
I Accuse - GB
I Married a Monster from Outer Space - USA
Island Women - USA
It!—The Terror from Beyond Space - USA
Jack the Ripper - GB
The Key - USA
A Lady Mislaid - GB
Liane, das Madchen aus dem Urwald - W. Ger
Lie is a Circus - USA
Links of Justice - GB
The Living Coffin - Mex
The Lone Ranger and the Lost City of Gold - USA
The Lost Missile - USA-Can
Macabre - USA
The Man Inside - GB
The Man Upstairs - GB
The Man Who Died Twice - USA
Menace in the Night - GB
Missile Monsters - USA
Missile to the Moon - USA
Misterios del Ultratumba - Mex
The Monster of Piedras Blancas - USA
Monster on the Campus - USA
The Mugger - USA
Murder by Contract - USA
Night of the Blood-Beast - USA
Noddy in Toyland - GB
Paras Pathar - India
Queen of Outer Space - USA
The Return of Dracula - USA
Rymdinvasion i Lappland - USA-Swed
Satan's Satellites - USA
Screaming Mimi - USA
The Screaming Skull - USA
The Secret Man - GB
The 7th Voyage of Sinbad - USA
Das Singende Ringende Baumchen - E. Ger
The Snorkel - GB
The Solitary Child - GB
Son of Robin Hood - GB
The Space Children - USA
Space Master X-7 - USA
The Spaniard's Curse - GB
The Spider - USA
Spy in the Sky - GB
Step Down to Terror - USA
The Strange Awakening - GB
The Strange Case of Dr. Manning - GB
The Strange World of Planet X - GB
Street of Darkness - USA
Tarzan and the Trappers - USA
Tarzan's Fight for Life - USA
Teenage Cave Man - USA
Terror from the Year 5,000 - USA
Terror in the Haunted House - USA
Le Testament d'Orphee - Fr
The Thing That Couldn't Die - USA
Tom Thumb - USA-GB
The Two-Headed Spy - GB
Undercover Girl - GB
Vertigo - USA
War of the Colossal Beast - USA
Watusi - USA
Wild Women of Wongo - USA
Wink of an Eye - USA
A Woman of Mystery - GB
The World, the Flesh and the Devil - USA
Yoru No Tsuzumi - Jap
Zex - GB

1959
Agent of Doom - USA
The Alligator People - USA
The Angry Red Planet - USA
Arson for Hire - USA
Atomic Agent - Fr
The Atomic Submarine - USA
Attack of the Giant Leeches - USA
Attack of the Jungle Women - USA
The Bat - USA

La Battaglia di Maratona - It
Beast from Haunted Cave - USA
Behemoth, the Sea Monster - GB
Beyond the Time Barrier - USA
Beyond This Place - GB
Bobbikins - GB
A Bucket of Blood - USA
La Cabeza Viviente - Mex
Caltiki, il Mostro Immortale - It
Carlota - Sp
Carthage in Flames - It
La Casa del Terror - Mex
City After Midnight - USA
Counterplot - USA
Crime and Punishment, U.S.A. - USA
Curse of the Stone Hand - Mex
The Curse of the Undead - USA
Darby O'Gill and the Little People - USA
A Date with Death - USA
David and Goliath - It
Deadly Record - GB
Death Comes from Space - W. Ger-It
The Devil's Messenger - Swed
Diary of a High School Bride - USA
Embezzled Heaven - Austria
Ercole e la Regina di Lidia - It-Fr
Face of Fire - USA-Swed
El Fantasma de la Opereta - Mex
The Flesh and the Fiends - GB
Forbidden Island - USA
48 Hours to Live - Swed
4D Man - USA
The Four Skulls of Jonathan Drake - USA
The Fugitive Kind - USA
The Gazebo - USA
The Ghost of Dragstrip Hollow - USA
The Ghost Train Murder - GB
The Giant Gila Monster - USA
Green Mansions - USA
The Hands of Orlac - GB-Fr
Have Rocket, Will Travel - USA
The Headless Ghost - GB
The Heavens Call - Russ
Hidden Homicide - GB
The Hideous Sun Demon - USA
The H-Man - Jap
Horrors of the Black Museum - GB
The Hound Of The Baskervilles - GB
The Hypnotic Eye - USA
The Incredible Petrified World - USA
Intent to Kill - USA
Invisible Invaders - USA
Island of Lost Women - USA
Journey to the Center of the Earth - USA
Journey to the Lost City - W. Ger-It-Fr
The Killer Shrews - USA
The Last Days of Pompeii - It-Sp
Leda - Fr
L'il Abner - USA
The Little Savage - USA
The Lonely Sex - USA
Long Distance - GB-W. Ger
Lost Treasure of the Aztecs - It
The Man in the Net - USA
The Man Who Could Cheat Death - GB
A Midsummer Night's Dream - Czech
Milczaca Gwiazda - Pol-E. Ger
The Miracle - USA
Mistress of the World - It-Fr-W. Ger
Model for Murder - GB
La Momia Contra el Robot Humano - Mex
The Mouse That Roared - GB
The Mummy - GB
Murder at Site Three - GB
Nathalie, Agent Secret - Fr
Night of the Ghouls - USA
Night Train for Inverness - GB
North by Northwest - USA
On the Beach - USA
Peeping Tom - GB
The Phantom of the Red House - Mex
Plan 9 from Outer Space - USA
Return of the Fly - USA
Sampa - Fin-Russ
Santa Claus - Mex
Sapphire - GB
The Scavengers - USA
The Shaggy Dog - USA
Siege of Syracuse - It
The Sinister Urge - USA
Spiritism - Mex
The Spy is a Girl - Fr
The Stranglers of Bombay - GB
Suddenly Last Summer - USA-GB
Tarzan's Greatest Adventure - GB
Tarzan, the Ape Man - USA
Teenagers from Outer Space - USA
Tempi Duri per i Vampiri - It
Il Terror dei Barberi - It
Terror is a Man - USA
The 30 Foot Bride of Candy Rock - USA

The 39 Steps - *GB*
The Tingler - *USA*
The Ugly Duckling - *GB*
The Unseeing Eye - *GB*
The Wasp Woman - *USA*
Web of Suspicion - *GB*
Witness in the Dark - *GB*
The Woman Eater - *GB*
Les Yeux sans Visage - *It-Fr*
The Young Captives - *USA*
Zorro Rides Again - *USA*

1960

The Adventures of Mandrin - *It*
Ali Baba and the Sacred Crown - *It*
The Amazing Transparent Man - *USA*
Gli Amori di Ercole - *It-Fr*
Antinea, l'Amante della Citta Sepolta - *It-Fr*
Assignment—Outer Space - *It*
Atlas - *USA*
Atom Age Vampire - *It-Fr*
Battle in Outer Space - *Jap*
Blood of Nostradamus - *Mex*
Bluebeard's Ten Honeymoons - *GB*
The Boy and the Pirates - *USA*
Brainwashed - *W. Ger*
Brides of Dracula - *GB*
Cage of Evil - *USA*
La Calavera Negra - *Mex*
The Cape Canaveral Monsters - *USA*
Cinderfella - *USA*
Circle of Death - *Mex*
Circus of Horrors - *GB*
City of the Dead - *GB*
Clue of the Twisted Candle - *GB*
Colossus and the Headhunters - *It*
Colossus and the Huns - *It*
Colossus of the Arena - *It*
Comment Qu'ella Est! - *Fr*
Le Comte de Monte Cristo - *Fr*
The Conquest of Mycenae - *It-Fr*
The Corsican Brothers - *Fr*
Cover Girl Killer - *GB*
Cry of the Bewitched - *Mex*
Danger Tomorrow - *GB*
Date at Midnight - *GB*
The Dead One - *USA*
Le Dernier Voyage de Gulliver (unfinished) - *Fr*
The Devil May Well Laugh - *Switz*
The Devil's Eye - *Swed*
Dinosaurus! - *It*
Doctor of Doom - *Mex*
The Enchanted Sword - *Sp*
Escape from Terror - *USA*
Et Mourir de Plaisir - *It-Fr*
Faces in the Dark - *GB*
Fellowship of the Frog - *W. Ger*
The Final War - *Jap*
The Full Treatment - *GB*
Giants of Thessaly - *It*
The Golden Falcon - *It*
Gorgo - *GB*
Hamlet - *W. Ger*
The Hand - *GB*
The Hand of the Gallows - *W. Ger*
Hercules and the Masked Rider - *It*
Hercules and the Treasure of the Incas - *It*
H.G. Wells' The New Invisible Man - *Mex*
Horrors of Spider Island - *W. Ger*
House of Usher - *USA*
The House on Marsh Road - *GB*
The Human Vapor - *Jap*
I Aim at the Stars - *USA*
The Insect Play - *GB*
It Happened in Broad Daylight - *Switz*
Knights of the Teutonic Order - *Pol*
The Last Train - *GB*
Last Woman on Earth - *USA*
The Leech Woman - *USA*
Lipstick - *It*
Little Red Riding Hood vs. the Monsters - *Mex*
The Little Shop of Horrors - *USA*
The Littlest Angel - *Mex*
The Lost World - *USA*
Maciste al Inferno - *It*
Macumba Love - *USA*
La Maldicion de Nostradamus - *Mex*
The Malpas Mystery - *GB*
Man in the Moon - *GB*
The Man Who Was Nobody - *GB*
La Maschera del Demonio - *It*
The Masked Conqueror - *It*
Mask of the Musketeers - *It*
Master of Horror - *Argent*
Midnight Lace - *USA*
Morgan the Pirate - *It*
Il Mulino delle Donne di Pietra - *It-Fr*
El Mundo de los Vampiros - *Mex*
Nights of Rasputin - *It-Fr*
Nostradamus y el Genio de la Tinieblas - *Mex*
October Moth - *GB*

101 Dalmations - *USA*
Orlak, el Infierno de Frankenstein - *Mex*
Pirate of the Black Hawk - *It*
Il Planeta degli Uomini Spenti - *It*
Platinum High School - *USA*
Portrait in Black - *USA*
The Private Lives of Adam and Eve - *USA*
Private Property - *USA*
Psycho - *USA*
The Queen of Spades - *Russ*
Queen of the Pirates - *It*
Queen of the Seas - *It*
The Queen's Swordsman - *Mex*
Der Raecher - *W. Ger*
The Red Circle - *W. Ger*
The Red Hand - *W. Ger*
La Regina della Amazzoni - *It*
Revak, lo Schiavo di Cartagine - *It*
Revenge of Ursus - *It*
Ring of Terror - *USA*
Robin Hood and the Pirates - *It*
Samson - *It*
Samson Against the Sheik - *It*
El Santo Contra las Vampiras - *Mex*
The Secret Mark of d'Artagnan - *It*
The Secret of the Purple Reef - *USA*
The Secret of the Telegian - *Jap*
September Storm - *USA*
Sex Kittens Go to College - *USA*
The Shakedown - *GB*
The Sign of Zorro - *USA*
The Snake Woman - *GB*
The Snow Queen - *Russ*
Son of Samson - *It-Fr-Yugo*
Spider's Web - *GB*
The Strangler of Blackmoor Castle - *W. Ger*
Sword of Sherwood Forest - *GB*
The Tartar Invasion - *It-Fr*
The Tartars - *It*
Tarzan the Magnificent - *GB*
Die Tausend Augen des Dr. Mabuse - *W. Ger-It-Fr*
The Tell-Tale Heart - *GB*
Tenemos 18 Anos - *Sp*
Terror of the Black Mask - *It*
The Testament of Dr. Mabuse - *W. Ger*
The Thief of Bagdad - *It-Fr*
13 Ghosts - *USA*
Thor and the Amazons - *It*
The Threat - *USA*
Three Came to Kill - *USA*
Three Murderesses - *Fr*
The Three Worlds of Gulliver - *GB*
The Time Machine - *USA*
Tormented - *USA*
Die Toten Augen von London - *W. Ger*
12 to the Moon - *USA*
The Two Faces of Dr. Jekyll - *GB*
L'Ultima Preda del Vampiro - *It*
Untamed Mistress - *USA*
Urge to Kill - *GB*
La Vendetta di Ercole - *It*
La Vergine di Roma - *It*
The Village of the Damned - *GB*
Violent Women - *USA*
Visit to a Small Planet - *USA*
Why Must I Die? - *USA*
The Wizard of Baghdad - *USA*
Women of Devil's Island - *Fr*

1961

The Absent-Minded Profesor - *USA*
Alakazam the Great - *Jap*
L'Amante del Vampiri - *It*
The Anatomist - *GB*
Anatomy of a Psycho - *USA*
Angel on Wheels - *Fr*
L'Annee Derniere a Marienbad - *Fr*
Antigone - *Greece*
L'Assassino - *It*
Atlantis, the Lost Continent - *USA*
Atlas in the Land of Cyclops - *It*
Attempt to Kill - *GB*
The Awful Dr. Orlof - *Fr-Sp*
Babes in Toyland - *USA*
The Bacchantes - *It*
The Bad Flower - *S. Korea*
El Baron del Terror - *Mex*
Baron Prasil - *Czech*
The Beast of Yucca Flats - *USA*
Bloodlust! - *USA*
Blood on His Sword - *Fr*
The Burning Court - *It-Fr-W. Ger*
Cape Fear - *USA*
Capture That Capsule! - *USA*
Cash on Demand - *GB*
Cinderella - *Russ*
The Clue of the New Pin - *GB*
The Clue of the Silver Key - *GB*
The Colossus of Rhodes - *It*
Confess, Dr. Corda - *W. Ger*
Creature from the Haunted Sea - *USA*

The Curse of the Doll People - *Mex*
The Curse of the Werewolf - *GB*
The Damned - *GB*
The Day the Earth Caught Fire - *GB*
The Devil's Hand - *USA*
Devyat'dney Odnogo Goda - *Russ*
Il Disco Volante - *It*
Dr. Blood's Coffin - *GB*
A Dog, a Mouse and a Sputnik - *Fr*
Electra - *Greece*
Ercole al Centro della Terra - *It*
Ercole alla Conquista della Atlantide - *It-Fr*
El Espejo de la Bruja - *Mex*
Everything's Ducky - *USA*
Flight of the Lost Balloon - *USA*
The Flight That Disappeared - *USA*
The Frightened City - *GB*
Fury at Smugglers' Bay - *GB*
Il Gigante di Metropolis - *It*
The Glass Cage - *GB*
Goliath Against the Giants - *It-Sp*
The Green Archer - *W. Ger*
Homicidal - *USA*
House of Mystery - *GB*
The Incredible Face of Dr. B - *Mex*
The Innocents - *GB*
In Search of the Castaways - *GB*
In the Steel Net of Dr. Mabuse - *W. Ger*
The Invisible Dr. Mabuse - *W. Ger*
Jack the Giant Killer - *USA*
Journey to the Seventh Planet - *USA-Swed*
The King's Avenger - *Fr*
Konga - *GB*
La leggendi di Enea - *It-Fr*
Macario - *Mex*
Maciste alla Corte del Gran Khan - *It*
Maciste Contre il Vampiro - *It*
Magic Spectacles - *It*
Man at the Carlton Tower - *GB*
Man Detained - *GB*
The Man of the First Century - *Czech*
The Mask - *Can*
Master of the World - *USA*
Matka Joanna od Aniolow - *Pol*
Mighty Ursus - *It-Sp*
The Minotaur - *It*
Mr. Sardonicus - *USA*
The Monster of Highgate Ponds - *GB*
Most Dangerous Man Alive - *USA*
Mothra - *Jap*
Murder in Eden - *GB*
Murder She Said - *GB*
My Friend, Dr. Jekyll - *It*
Mysterious Island - *GB*
The Naked Edge - *GB*
Naked Terror - *USA*
The Naked Woman and Satan - *W. Ger*
Neutron vs. the Death Robots - *Mex*
Neutron vs. the Maniac - *Mex*
The Nights of Lucretia Borgia - *It*
The Phantom Planet - *USA*
The Pirates of Blood River - *GB*
The Pit and the Pendulum - *USA*
Planets Against Us - *It-Fr*
El Principe Encadenado - *Sp*
The Red Cloak - *It*
Reptilicus - *Den*
Roland the Mighty - *It*
Romolo e Remo - *It*
Romulus and the Sabines - *It*
The Saint in the Wax Museum - *Mex*
Le Saint Mene la Dance - *Fr*
The Sand Castle - *USA*
Santo and the Hotel of Death - *Mex*
The Shadow of the Cat - *GB*
Shoot to Kill - *GB*
The Sinister Man - *GB*
Slave Girls of Sheba - *It*
Snow White and the Three Stooges - *USA*
Something Wild - *USA*
The Strange Countess - *W. Ger*
Sword of the Conqueror - *It*
A Taste of Fear - *GB*
Taur the Mighty - *It*
The Terror of the Tongs - *GB*
Le Testament du Dr. Cordelier - *Fr*
Thigh Line Lyre Triangular - *USA*
Through a Glass Darkly - *Swed*
The Treasure of Monte Cristo - *GB*
The Trojan Horse - *It-Fr*
The Trunk - *GB*
The Underwater City - *USA*
Ursus nella Valle dei Leoni - *It*
Valley of the Dragons - *USA*
Il Vampiro dell'Opera - *It*
Voyage to the Bottom of the Sea - *USA*
What a Carve Up! - *GB*
The Wonders of Aladdin - *USA-It*
Wycieczka w Kosmos - *Pol*
X-15 - *USA*

1962

The Accident - *GB*
El Angel Exterminador - *Mex*
Ape Man of the Jungle - *It*
Au Coeur de la Vie - *Fr*
Beauty and the Beast - *USA*
Behind the Mask of Zorro - *It-Sp*
Bezludna Planeta - *Pol*
Black Panther of Ratana - *W. Ger*
The Brain That Wouldn't Die - *USA*
The Cabinet of Caligari - *USA*
Candidate for Murder - *GB*
Captain Clegg - *GB*
Carnival of Souls - *USA*
Carpet of Horror - *W. Ger*
Cartes sur Table - *Sp-Fr*
Cartouche - *Fr*
El Castillo de los Monstruos - *Mex*
Confessions of an Opium Eater - *USA*
The Couch - *USA*
La Creation du Monde - *Fr*
Creation of the Humanoids - *USA*
Danger by My Side - *GB*
Death Trap - *GB*
Devi - *India*
The Devil's Agent - *GB-W. Ger*
The Devil's Daffodil - *GB*
The Devil's Partner - *USA*
Le Diable et les Dix Commandements - *It-Fr*
Diary of a Madman - *USA*
Dr. Crippen - *GB*
Dr. No - *GB*
Dog Star Man (Part I) - *USA*
The Double Agents - *Fr*
Duel at the Rio Grande - *It*
Dungeons of Horror - *USA*
Eegah! - *USA*
Experiment in Terror - *USA*
Il Figlio di Spartacus - *It*
Fire Monsters vs. the Son of Hercules - *It*
Five Weeks in a Balloon - *USA*
La Freccia d'Oro - *It*
Fury of Achilles - *It*
The Gentle Art of Murder - *Fr*
The Golden Rabbit - *GB*
Gold for the Caesars - *It*
Gorath - *Jap*
Hand of Death - *USA*
Hands of a Stranger - *USA*
Harakiri - *Jap*
Hercules Against the Barbarian - *It*
Hercules in the Vale of Woe - *It*
Hercules vs. Ulysses - *It*
House of the Damned - *USA*
House on Bare Mountain - *USA*
Information Received - *GB*
La Invasion de los Vampiros - *Mex*
Invasion of the Neptune Men - *Jap*
Invasion of the Star Creatures - *USA*
It's Only Money - *USA*
La Jetee - *Fr*
Karate, the Hand of Death - *USA*
Kill or Cure - *GB*
King Kong vs. Godzilla - *Jap*
Kiss of the Vampire - *GB*
Knights of Terror - *It*
Labirynt - *Pol*
Ladies' Man - *Fr*
Lancelot and Guinevere - *GB*
Landru - *Fr*
Last of the Vikings - *It*
Life for Ruth - *GB*
The Littlest Warror - *Jap*
Locker 69 - *GB*
The Macabre Path - *Mex*
Maciste, l'Ero Piu Grande del Mondo - *It*
The Magic Sword - *USA*
The Magic Voyage of Sinbad - *Yugo*
La maldicion de la Llorona - *Mex*
The Manchurian Candidate - *USA*
Maniac - *GB*
The Man in The Iron Mask - *Fr*
The Manster - *GB-Jap*
The Man Who Finally Died - *GB*
Marte, Dio della Guerra - *It*
The Masked Man Against the Pirates - *Sp*
Mermaids of Tiburon - *USA*
Mi Adorable Esclava - *Sp*
Molemen Against the Son of Hercules - *It*
The Monster in the Basement - *USA*
Moon Pilot - *USA*
The Murdering Mite - *Jap*
My Name is Ivan - *Russ*
Nefertite, Regina del Nilo - *It*
Neutron Battles the Karate Assassins - *Mex*
Night of the Eagle - *GB*
No Exit - *USA*
Nostradamus y el Destructor de Monstruos - *Mex*
Number Six - *GB*
O Dwoch Takich co Ukradli Ksiezyc - *Pol*

Omicron - It
Out of the Fog - GB
Panic in Year Zero - USA
Paradisio - GB
Perseus the Invincible - It
The Phantom of the Opera - GB
The Pirate and the Slave Girl - It
The Pit - GB
Planeta Bura - Russ
Playback - GB
La Poupee - Fr
The Premature Burial - USA
The Prisoner of the Iron Mask - It
Profesor Zazul - Pol
Psycosissimo - It
La Ragazza Che Sapeva Troppo - It
Rage of the Buccaneers - It
Raptus - It
The Reluctant Saint - It
Return from the Beyond - Mex
Return of a Stranger - GB
The Road to Hong Kong - GB
The Saint vs. the Zombies - Mex
Santo vs. the King of Crime - Mex
The Secret of Dr. Mabuse - W. Ger-It-Fr
The Secret of the Black Trunk - W. Ger
Secret of the Red Orchid - W. Ger
Senseless - USA
The Seventh Sword - It-Sp
The Shadow of Zorro - Sp
Slave Queen of Babylon - It
The Slime People - USA
Son of Hercules in the Land of Fire - It
Space Demon - USA
Lo Spettro - It
La Strage dei Vampiri - It
Swamp of the Lost Souls - Mex
Sword of Damascus - It
Tales of Terror - USA
Tarzan Goes to India - GB
Terror of the Bloodhunters - USA
13 West Street - USA
This is Not a Test - USA
The Three Stooges in Orbit - USA
The Three Stooges Meet Hercules - USA
Les Titans - It-Fr
Tower of London - USA
Triumph of Robin Hood - It
Die Tur mit den Sieben Schlossern - W. Ger
Two Before Zero - USA
Ulysses Against the Son of Hercules - It
Varan the Unbelievable - USA-Jap
La Venganza de Don Mendo - Sp
Vengeance - GB-W. Ger
The Very Edge - GB
Le Vice et la Vertu - Fr
The Wacky World of Dr. Morgus - USA
War Gods of Babylon - It
The Weird Ones - USA
What Ever Happened to Baby Jane? - USA
Who Stole the Body? - Fr
Wielka, Wielka I Najwiksza - Pol
The Wonderful World of the Brothers Grimm - USA
The World's Greatest Sinner - USA
Zotz! - USA

1963

Les Abysses - Fr
Ali Baba and the Seven Saracens - It
Arms of the Avenger - It
Astromati - Yugo
A Toi de Faire, Migonne - Fr
Attack of the Mayan Mummy - Mex
The Balcony - USA
Beast of Babylon Against the Son of Hercules - It-Fr
The Birds - USA
The Black Abbot - W. Ger
The Black Evil - It
Black Zoo - USA
Blonde Cobra - USA
Blood Feast - USA
Buddha - Jap
Call Me Bwana - GB
Captain Sinbad - W. Ger
La Cara del Terror - Sp
The Caretakers - USA
Castle of the Living Dead - Fr
The Checkered Flag - USA
Children of the Damned - GB
Chushingura - Jap
Clash by Night - GB
The Comedy of Terrors - USA
The Crawling Hand - USA
Creature of the Walking Dead - USA
Curse of the Yellow Snake - W. Ger
Dangerous Agent - Fr
The Day Mars Invaded Earth - USA
The Day of the Triffids - GB
Dementia 13 - USA-GB

Il Demonio - It
Devil Doll - GB
The Devil's Castle - Turk
The Devil-Ship Pirates - GB
Diane the Zebra Woman - USA
Dr. Strangelove: or, How I Learned to Stop Worrying and Love the Bomb - GB
Dr. Syn—Alias the Scarecrow - GB
Dog Eat Dog - USA-W. Ger-It
Dogora, the Space Monster - Jap
Dog Star Man (Part II) - USA
The Doll - Swed
The Double - GB
Do You Keep a Lion at Home? - Czech
The Dragon's Blood - It
Drums of Africa - USA
8 1/2 - It
Ella y el Miedo - Sp
Ercole Contro i Figli del Sole - It-Sp
The Eyes of Annie Jones - GB
Faust - W. Ger
Flaming Creatures - USA
From Russia with Love - GB
La Frusta e il Corpo - I
The Ghost of Elisha Doom - Yugo
The Girl Hunters - GB
Goldstein - It
Goliath, the Rebel Slave - It
The Haunted Palace - USA
The Haunting - GB
The Hell-Fire Club - GB
Der Henker von London - W. Ger
Hercules of the Desert - It
Hercules—Prisoner of Evil - It
Hercules, Samson and Ulysses - It
Hide and Seek - GB
High and Low - Jap
Hipnosis - Sp-W. Ger-It
Horror - It-Sp
The Horror of Party Beach - USA
Hot Enough for June - GB
Ikaria XB1 - Czech
Incident at Midnight - GB
The Incredibly Strange Creatures Who Stopped Living and Became Mixed-Up Zombies - USA
The Indian Scarf - W. Ger
Invasione - It
The Invisible Terror - W. Ger
I Was a Teen-Age Mummy - USA
Jason and the Argonauts - GB
Johnny Cool - USA
Judex - It-Fr
Kali-Yug, la Dea della Vendetta - It
Katharsis - It
Killer Spy - Fr
A Killing Success - Fr
Kyberneticka Babicka - Yugo
Ladybug, Ladybug - USA
Lady in a Cage - USA
The List of Adrian Messenger - USA-GB
Lord of the Flies - GB
Lycanthropus - It-Austria
Madman of Mandoras - USA
La Maldicion de los Karnsteins - It-Sp
The Man in the Moonlight Mask - Jap
Master Spy - GB
Matango - Jap
The Mind Benders - GB
Mission to Venice - Fr
Monstrosity - USA
The Mouse on the Moon - GB
Los Muertos No Perdonan - Sp
Murder at the Gallop - GB
Murder on the Campus - GB
Die Nashorner - W. Ger
La Nave de los Monstruos - Mex
Neutron, el Enmascarado Negro - Mex
Neutron vs. the Amazing Dr. Caronte - Mex
Niebezpieczenstwo - Pol
Nightmare - GB
Nightmare in the Sun - USA
Night Tide - USA
No Survivors, Please - W. Ger
Not on Your Life! - Sp
The Nutty Professor - USA
The Nylon Noose - W. Ger
The Old Dark House - GB
Operation Atlantis - It
L'Ours - Fr
Paranoiac - GB
Paris When It Sizzles - USA
The Phantom of Soho - W. Ger
La Poursuite - Fr
La Prima Donna - Fr
Przyjaciel - Pol
Pyro - It
The Queen of Sheba Meets the Atom Man (unfinished) - USA
Rampage - USA
The Raven - USA
The Right Hand of the Devil - USA

Ring of Spies - GB
Roma Contro Roma - It
The Sadist - USA
Samson and the Sea Beasts - It
The Scarlet Blade - GB
Scheherazade - Fr
Secret of the Sphinx - Fr
The Servant - GB
Shock Corridor - USA
Siege of the Saxons - GB
Sins of Babylon - It
Sodom and Gomorrah - It-Fr
Sonny's Flight to the Moon - W. Ger
Son of Flubber - USA
Stark Fear - USA
Stellar Brothers—From the Kremlin to the Cosmos - Russ
The Strangler - USA
Tarzan and Jane Regained Sort Of - USA
Tarzan's Three Challenges - USA
Temple of the White Elephants - It
The Temptress and the Monk - Jap
Terrified - USA
The Terror - USA
Terror of Rome Against the Son of Hercules - It-Fr
13 Frightened Girls - USA
The Three Lives of Thomasina - GB
The Three Swords of Zorro - It-Sp
Tomb of Torture - It
Trauma - USA
I Tre Volti della Paura - It
The Trial - Fr
Triumph of the Son of Hercules - It
La Tulipe Noire - Fr
Twice-Told Tales - USA
Tyrant of Lydia Against the Son of Hercules - It
Tystnaden - Swed
Unearthly Stranger - GB
Vengeance of the Three Musketeers - Fr
La Vergine di Norimberga - It
Viaggio Immaginario - Ruman
Vulcan, Son of Jupiter - It
The White Spider - W. Ger
Wild is My Love - USA
Woman of Straw - GB
Wrestling Women vs. the Aztec Mummy - Mex
X—The Man with the X-Ray Eyes - USA

1964

Act of Murder - GB
Adventurer of Tortuga - It
Agent 383/Passport to Hell - It
Agent 255/Desperate Mission - Jap
Aimez-Vous les Femmes? - It-Fr
The Amphibian Man - Russ
Atlas Against the Czar - It
Atomic Rulers of the World - Jap
Atragon - Jap
Batman Dracula - USA
Beach Girls and the Monster - USA
The Black Cobra - W. Ger
Black Torment - GB
The Brass Bottle - USA
Carry on Spying - GB
Castle of Terrors - GB
Catacombs - GB
Cave of the Living Dead - W. Ger
Challenge of the Gladiators - It
Code Name: Tiger - Fr
Conqueror of Atlantis - It
Crack in the World - GB
The Creeping Terror - USA
Las Cuatro Noches de la Luna Llena - Sp
Curse of Simba - GB
Curse of the Fly - GB
The Curse of the Hidden Vault - W. Ger
The Curse of the Living Corpse - USA
The Curse of the Mummy's Tomb - GB
La Danza Macabra - GB-It
Dead Ringer - USA
The Demon from Devil's Lake - USA
Devil of the Desert Against the Son of Hercules - It
The Devil's Bedroom - USA
Devils of Darkness - GB
The Devil's Trap - Czech
The Diabolical Axe - Mex
Doctor Jekyll - It
Dr. Mabuse vs. Scotland Yard - W. Ger
Dr. Terror's House of Horrors - GB
Dog Star Man (Parts III & IV) - USA
La Donna Scimmia - It
Don't Tempt the Devil - Fr
Downfall - GB
The Earth Dies Screaming - GB
Ercole Contro i Tiranni di Babilonia - It
Ercole Contro Roma - It-Fr
Evil Brain from Outer Space - Jap

Evil of Frankenstein - GB
Fail-Safe - USA
Fantomas Contro Scotland Yard - It-Fr
Les Felins - Fr
First Men in the Moon - GB
The Flesh Eaters - USA
Frozen Alive - GB-W. Ger
FX 18, Secret Agent - Fr
Giant of Evil Island - It
Gladiators Seven - It
Godzilla vs. Mothra - Jap
Goldfinger - GB
Goliath at the Conquest of Damascus - It
Goodbye Charlie - USA
The Gorgon - GB
Hamlet - Russ
The Hanged Man - USA
Hercules and the Ten Avengers - It
Hercules, the Avenger - It
Honeymoon of Horror - USA
The Horror of It All - USA
The Human Duplicators - USA
Hush...Hush, Sweet Charlotte - USA
The Hyena of London - It
Hysteria! - GB
The Incredible Mr. Limpet - USA
The Inn on Dartmoor - W. Ger
L'Intrigo - It
El Invencible Hombre Invisible - It-Sp-W. Ger
The Invincible Brothers Maciste - It
It Happened Here - GB
Kindar the Invulnerable - It
Kisses for My President - USA
Kiss Me Quick - USA
Kwaidan - Jap
The Last Man on Earth - USA-It
Legacy of Horror - W. Ger
Lilith - USA
The Lion of Thebes - It-Fr
The Lost Face - Czech
The Love Statue - USA
Maciste in King Solomon's Mines - It-Fr
Maciste alla Corte della Zar - It
Maciste e la Regina di Samar - It-Fr
Majin, Monster of Terror - Jap
Le Manoir Maudit - Fr
Man Who Walked Through the Wall - W. Ger
Mara of the Wilderness - USA
Marnie - USA
Mary Poppins - USA
The Mask of the Gorilla - Fr
The Masque of the Red Death - USA-GB
Masquerade - GB
Mata Hari, Agent H21 - Fr
Messalina Against the Son of Hercules - It
The Misadventures of Merlin Jones - USA
The Model Murder Case - GB
Mondo Balordo - It
The Monkey's Uncle - USA
The Monocle - Fr
The Monster of London - W. Ger
The Moon-Spinners - GB
Moro Witch Doctor - USA-Phil
Murder Most Foul - GB
Mutiny in Outer Space - USA
The Mystery of Thug Island - It
The Nasty Rabbit - USA
Neutron Traps the Invisible Killers - Mex
Never Mention Murder - GB
Nick Carter Va Tout Casser - Fr
Night Must Fall - GB
The Night of the Great Attack - It
The Night Walker - USA
None But the Lonely Spy - It
Olga's Girls - USA
Onibaba - Jap
Operation Crossbow - GB
Order and Disorder - Czech
Pajama Party - USA
Les Parapluies de Cherbourg - Fr
Pattern for Murder - W. Ger
Psyche 59 - GB
Psychomania - USA
Red Desert - It
Rekopis Znaleziony w Saragossie - Pol
Revenge of the Black Eagle - It
Robinson Crusoe on Mars - USA
Rope Around the Neck - Fr
Samson and the Mighty Challenge - It
Samson and the Seven Challenges - It
Sandokan Against the Leopard of Sarawak - It
Sandokan Fights Back - It
Sandokan the Great - It-Fr-Sp
La Sanglante Sorciere - It-Fr
Santa Claus Conquers the Martians - USA
Santo Attacks the Witches - Mex
The Satan Bug - USA
Seance on a Wet Afternoon - GB
Secret Agent 077—Operation Hong Kong - W. Ger
The Secret Door - GB

El Secreto del Dr. Orlof - *Sp-Austria*
The Secret of Blood Island - *GB*
The Secret of Magic Island - *Fr*
The Secrets of Dracula - *Phil*
Sei Donne per l'Assassino - *It*
Sette Contro la Morte - *It*
Seven days in May - *USA*
7 Faces of Dr. Lao - *USA*
7 Surprizes - *Can*
The Seventh Juror - *Fr*
Shadow of Evil - *It-Fr*
The Shadows of Forgotten Ancestors - *Russ*
Shell Shock - *USA*
Sherlock Holmes and the Deadly
Necklace - *W. Ger*
Shock Treatment - *USA*
The Son of Hercules in the Land of Darkness - *It*
Space Monster - *USA*
The Spy I Love - *Fr*
Strait-Jacket - *USA*
Suna No Onna - *Jap*
Teen-Age Strangler - *USA*
Temple of a Thousand Lights - *It*
The Third Secret - *GB*
The Three Avengers - *It*
The Thrill Killers - *USA*
The Time Travelers - *USA*
The Tomb of Ligeia - *USA-GB*
Topkapi - *It*
Treasure of the Petrified Forest - *It*
The Triumph of Hercules - *It-Fr*
Two on a Guillotine - *USA*
2000 Maniacs - *USA*
Valley of Fear - *W. Ger*
Le Vampire de Dusseldorf - *Fr*
Victim Five - *GB-W. Ger*
Voodoo Blood Bath - *USA*
War of the Fools - *Czech*
Where Has Poor Mickey Gone? - *GB*
Witchcraft - *GB*
The Witch House - *Mex*
The Wizard of Mars - *USA*
Yolanta - *Russ*
Zorro Contro Maciste - *It*

1965
Adventure at the Center of the Earth - *Mex*
Agent for H.A.R.M. - *USA*
The Alphabet Murders - *GB*
Alphaville, une Etrange Aventure de Lemmy
Caution - *Fr*
Amador - *Sp-Fr*
Amanti d'Oltretomba - *It*
Banana Peel - *Fr*
The Beast That Killed Women - *USA*
The Bedford Incident - *USA-GB*
Berlino Appuntamento per le Spie - *It*
Billy the Kid vs. Dracula - *USA*
Birds Do It - *USA*
The Black Cat - *USA*
The Bloodless Vampire - *USA*
The Blue Panther - *Fr*
Il Boia Scarlatto - *It*
The Boy Cried Murder - *GB*
Brainstorm - *USA*
The Brigand of Kandahar - *GB*
Bring Me the Vampire - *Mex*
La Brulure de Mille Soleils - *Fr*
Bunny Lake is Missing - *USA-GB*
Cinque Tombe per un Medium - *It*
Circus of Fear - *GB*
The City Under the Sea - *GB*
Code Name: Jaguar - *Fr*
The Collector - *USA-GB*
Color Me Blood Red - *USA*
Crazy Paradise - *Den*
Cul-de-Sac - *GB*
Dark Intruder - *USA*
Day of the Nightmare - *USA*
The Deadly Ray from Mars - *USA*
Dead Man's Chest - *GB*
La Decima Vittima - *It-Fr*
The Defilers - *USA*
Destination Saturn - *USA*
The Diabolical Dr. Z - *Sp-Fr-W. Ger*
I Diavoli della Spazio - *It*
Dr. Goldfoot and the Bikini Machine - *USA*
Dr. Who and the Daleks - *GB*
Les Escargots - *Fr*
The Eye Creatures - *USA*
Eye of the Alien - *Uruguay*
Eye of the Devil - *GB*
El Fabricante de Monstruos - *Sp*
The Face of Fu Manchu - *GB*
Fanatic - *GB*
Faraon - *Pol*
Faster, Pussycat! Kill! Kill! - *USA*
The D___ _____ - *USA*
Frankenstein Meets the Space Monster - *USA*
Gammera, the Invincible - *USA-Jap*
Gappa, the Triphibian Monster - *Jap*

Ghidrah, the Three-Headed Monster - *Jap*
Ghost of the Stranger - *Mex*
Giulietta degli Spiriti - *It*
Hercules and the Princess of Troy - *USA*
The Hidden Face - *GB*
A High Wind in Jamaica - *GB*
The Horror from Beyond - *USA*
House of the Black Death - *USA*
How to Stuff a Wild Bikini - *USA*
The Hunchback of Notre Dame - *GB*
Incubus - *USA*
Insomnia - *Fr*
Interpol Code 8 - *Jap*
Invasion - *GB*
The Ipcress File - *GB*
I Saw What You Did - *USA*
I Spy, You Spy - *GB*
Jack Frost - *Russ*
Killers Are Challenged - *It*
Knives of the Avenger - *It*
The Legend of Blood Montain - *USA*
Licensed to Kill - *GB*
La Loba - *Mex*
The Loved One - *USA*
I Lunghi Capelli della Morte - *It*
The Magic Weaver - *Russ*
Man in the Dark - *GB*
The Man Who Laughs - *It*
M.M.M. 83 - *It*
Modesty Blaise - *GB*
Moment to Moment - *USA*
Monster A-Go-Go - *USA*
Monster of Terror - *GB*
The Moon - *Russ*
Morianna - *Swed*
Il Mostro di Venezia - *It*
My Blood Runs Cold - *USA*
The Mysterious Magician - *W. Ger*
The Nanny - *GB*
The Navy vs. the Night Monsters - *USA*
The Nest of the Cuckoo Birds - *USA*
Nick Carter et le Trefle Rouge - *Fr*
100 Cries of Terror - *Mex*
Operation Double Cross - *Fr*
Operation Solo - *W. Ger*
L'Or du Duc - *Fr*
Orgy of the Dead - *USA*
OSS 117—Mission for a Killer - *It-Fr*
Our Man Flint - *USA*
The Overcoat - *Russ*
Peril from the Planet Mongo - *USA*
Un Peu de Votre Sang - *Fr*
The Plague of the Zombies - *GB*
Playgirl Killer - *Can*
The Playground - *USA*
Portrait in Terror - *USA*
The Psychopath - *GB*
Purple Death from Outer Space - *USA*
Raiders from Beneath the Sea - *USA*
Red Dragon - *It-W. Ger*
Repulsion - *GB*
Requiem for a Secret Agent - *It*
Return from the Ashes - *GB*
The Return of Mr. Moto - *GB*
Revenge of the Gladiators - *It-Fr*
Samurai Pirate - *Jap*
Santo vs. Baron Brakola - *Mex*
Scream of the Butterfly - *USA*
Secret Agent Fireball - *It*
The Secret of My Success - *GB*
Sergeant Deadhead the Astronaut! - *USA*
The Seven Dwarfs to the Rescue - *It*
She - *GB*
The Skull - *GB*
Sky Above Heaven - *It-Fr*
Slalom - *It*
The Sleeping Beauty - *Russ*
The Sleeping Car Murders - *Fr*
Snow White - *W. Ger*
La Sorella di Satan - *It*
Sound of Horror - *Sp*
Spaceflight IC-1 - *GB*
Spaceship to the Unknown - *USA*
Spider Baby - *USA*
The Spy Strikes Silently - *It*
The Spy Who Came in from the Cold - *GB*
The Squeaker - *W. Ger*
Steps Towards the Mont - *Ruman*
Strangler's Web - *GB*
A Study in Terror - *GB*
The Sword of Ali Baba - *USA*
Taboos of the World - *It*
Tell Me Whom to Kill - *Fr*
Ten Little Indians - *GB*
Terrore Nello Spazio - *It-Sp*
Theatre of Death - *GB*
Thomas l'Imposteur - *Fr*
Thunderball - *GB*
24 Hours to Kill - *GB*
Two Mafia Guys vs. Goldginger - *It*

Underworld Informers - *GB*
Village of the Giants - *USA*
The Violence of Desire - *It*
Where the Spies Are - *GB*
Who Killed Teddy Bear? - *USA*
Wild, Wild Planet - *It*
Willy McBean and His Magic Machine - *Jap*
The Witches Attack - *Mex*
The Woman Who Wouldn't Die - *USA*
Women of the Prehistoric Planet - *US*
World by Night No. 2 - *It*

1966
The Adventures of Captain Marvel - *USA*
An Affair of State - *W. Ger*
Allures - *USA*
Un Angelo per Satan - *It*
Around the World Under the Sea - *USA*
Baraka X-77 - *Fr*
Bariera - *Pol*
Batman - *USA*
The Becket Affair - *It*
The Bible - *USA-It*
Blood Bath - *USA*
The Blood Drinkers - *Phil*
The Blue Demon - *Mex*
The Brides of Fu Manchu - *GB*
The Busy Body - *USA*
Captain Mephisto and the Transformation
Machine - *USA*
Carry on Screaming - *GB*
Castle of Evil - *USA*
Chamber of Horrors - *USA*
Chappaqua - *USA*
The Christmas That Almost Wasn't - *USA-It*
Cinderella - *Mex*
The Claw Monsters - *USA*
Curse of the Swamp Creature - *USA*
Cyborg 2087 - *USA*
Cyclotrode X - *USA*
Daleks' Invasion Earth 2150 A.D. - *GB*
Darkest Africa - *USA*
The Deadly Affair - *GB*
The Deadly Bees - *GB*
The Deadly Diaphanoids - *It*
Death Curse of Tartu - *USA*
Death is a Woman - *GB*
Destination Inner Space - *USA*
Il Diavolo Innamorato - *It*
Dimension 5 - *USA*
Dinosaur Island - *Mex*
Doctor?? Coppelius!! - *Sp*
Dr. Goldfoot and the Girl Bombs - *USA-It*
Dr. Satan - *Mex*
Doctor Satan's Robots - *USA*
Dracula, Prince of Darkness - *GB*
Ebirah, Horror of the Deep - *Jap*
Enough Rope - *Fr*
Fahrenheit 451 - *GB-Fr*
Fantastic Voyage - *USA*
The Fat Spy - *USA*
Five Golden Dragons - *GB-Hong Kong*
Formula C-12/Beirut - *W. Ger*
Frankenstein Created Woman - *GB*
Frankenstein vs. the Giant Devil Fish - *Jap*
The Frozen Dead - *GB*
Funeral in Berlin - *GB*
Galaxie - *USA*
Gallery of Horror - *USA*
Gammera vs. Barugon - *Jap*
The Ghost and Mr. Chicken - *USA*
The Ghost in the Invisible Bikini - *USA*
The Gnome-Mobile - *USA*
Le Golem - *Fr*
Grave Robbers - *Mex*
The Great Spy Chase - *Fr*
Gregorio and His Angel - *Mex*
The Gruesome Twosome - *USA*
Gulliver's Travels Beyond the Moon - *Jap*
The Hand - *Czech*
The Hand of Night - *GB*
Hold On! - *USA*
The Hostage - *USA*
I Deal in Danger - *USA*
I Love a Mystery - *USA*
The Inauguration of the Pleasure Dome - *USA*
In Like Flint - *USA*
La Isla de la Muerte - *Sp-W. Ger*
Island of Terror - *GB*
James Tont: Operation Goldsinger - *W. Ger*
Jesse James Meets Frankenstein's Daughter - *USA*
Der Junge Torless - *Fr-W. Ger*
Jungle Gold - *USA*
Kiss Kiss, Kill Kill - *W. Ger*
The Last of the Secret Agents? - *USA*
The Lemon Grove Kids Meet the Monsters - *USA*
Let's Kill Uncle - *USA*
Lightning Bolt - *It-Sp*
The Liquidator - *GB*
Lost Island of Kioga - *USA*
Madam White Snake - *Nat'list China*

Magic Lotus Lantern - *Red China*
The Magic Serpent - *Jap*
The Man Called Flintstone - *USA*
Manos, the Hands of Fate - *USA*
Maroc 7 - *GB*
Matchless - *It*
The Million Eyes of Sumuru - *GB*
Mother Goose A Go-Go - *USA*
The Mummy's Shroud - *GB*
Munster, Go Home! - *USA*
The Murder Clinic - *It-Fr*
Murderers' Row - *USA*
Naked Evil - *GB*
Nattmara - *Swed*
The Nibelungs - *W. Ger*
Night Caller from Outer Space - *GB*
The Night of the Generals - *GB-Fr*
Nyoka and the Lost Secrets of Hippocrates - *USA*
Oh Dad Poor Dad, Mamma's Hung You in
the Closet and I'm Feelin' So Sad - *USA*
One Million Years B.C. - *GB*
One of Our Spies is Missing - *USA*
One Spy Too Many - *USA*
On Her Bed of Roses - *USA*
Operation Counterspy - *Fr*
Operazione Paura - *It*
Our Man in Marrakesh - *GB*
The Peacock Princess - *Red China*
The Persecution and Assassination of Jean-
Paul Marat as Performed by the Inmates of
the Asylum of Charenton Under the
Direction of the Marquis de Sade - *GB*
Persona - *Swed*
Picture Mommy Dead - *USA*
Planet on the Prowl - *It*
Prehistoric Women - *GB*
Privilege - *GB*
The Projected Man - *GB*
Queen of Blood - *USA*
The Queen of Spades - *Fr*
The Quiller Memorandum - *GB*
Rasputin, the Mad Monk - *GB*
Rat Pfink & Boo Boo - *USA*
Relativity - *USA*
The Reluctant Astronaut - *USA*
The Reptile - *GB*
Retik, the Moon Menace - *USA*
The Return of Giant Majin - *Jap*
Return of the Giant Monsters - *Jap*
Run, Psycho, Run - *It*
Le Saint Prend l'Affut - *Fr*
Sakima and the Masked Marvel - *USA*
Salto - *Pol*
Le Scandale - *Fr*
The Scorpio Letters - *USA*
Seconds - *USA*
Secret Agent Superdragon - *It-Fr-W. Ger*
Sedmi Kontinent - *Czech-Yugo*
Sharad of Atlantis - *USA*
The Silencers - *USA*
Slaves of the Invisible Monster - *USA*
Sombra, the Spider Woman - *USA*
Spara Forte, Piu Forte...Non Capisco - *It*
The Spirit is Willing - *USA*
Spy Smasher Returns - *USA*
The Spy with a Cold Nose - *GB*
The Spy with My Face - *USA*
Star Pilot - *It*
Sting of Death - *USA*
Strangler of the Tower - *W. Ger*
La Strega in Amore - *It*
Superargo vs. Diabolicus - *It*
A Target for Killing - *W. Ger*
Tarzan and the Valley of Gold - *USA-Switz*
Terra em Transe - *Brz*
Terror Beneath the Sea - *Jap*
The Terrornauts - *GB*
They Came from Beyond Space - *GB*
Thunderbirds Are Go - *GB*
To Commit a Murder - *Fr*
Torn Curtain - *USA*
The Torpedo of Doom - *USA*
To Trap a Spy - *USA*
Trans-Europe Express - *Fr*
The Trygon Factor - *GB*
Uproar in Heaven - *Red China*
U-238 and the Witch Doctor - *USA*
The Viking Queen - *GB*
The Vulture - *GB*
The War of the Gargantuas - *Jap*
Way...Way Out - *USA*
Weekend of Fear - *USA*
Where the Bullets Fly - *GB*
Who Killed the Cat? - *GB*
The Wild World of Batwoman - *USA*
The Witches - *GB*
A Witch Without a Broom - *Sp*
The Wrong Box - *GB*
The X from Outer Space - *Jap*
Zontar: The Thing from Venus - *USA*

1967

Aladdin and His Magic Lamp - *Russ*
The Ambushers - *USA*
The Anniversary - *GB*
Assassination - *It*
Assignment K - *GB*
Assignment to Kill - *USA*
Asylum for a Spy - *USA*
Autopsia de un Fantasma - *Mex*
The Bang-Bang Kid - *It*
Batman Fights Dracula - *Phil*
Battle Beneath the Earth - *GB*
Bat Woman - *Mex*
Bedazzled - *GB*
Belle de Jour - *Fr*
Billion Dollar Brain - *GB*
Blackbeard's Ghost - *USA*
The Bubble - *USA*
Camelot - *USA*
Casino Royale - *GB*
C'Era una Volta - *It-Fr*
A Challenge for Robin Hood - *GB*
The Cobra - *It-Sp*
Countdown - *USA*
Creature with the Blue Hand - *W. Ger*
The Curse of the Golem - *GB*
A Dandy in Aspic - *GB*
Danger Route - *GB*
The Day the Fish Came Out - *GB-Greece*
Deadlier Than the Male - *GB*
Deathwatch - *USA*
A Degree of Murder - *W. Ger*
Diabolically Yours - *Fr*
Diabolik - *It-Fr*
Dr. Dolittle - *USA*
Dr. Satan and Black Magic - *Mex*
The Double Man - *GB*
Edipo Re - *It*
The Emerald of Artatama - *Sp-W. Ger*
The Empire of Dracula - *Mex*
End of August at the Hotel Ozone - *Czech*
Fathom - *USA*
Faust XX - *It*
The Fearless Vampire Killers or: Pardon Me,
But Your Teeth Are in My Neck - *GB*
The Fiction-Makers - *GB*
The Fifth Horseman is Fear - *Czech*
Games - *USA*
Gammera vs. Gyaos - *Jap*
Ghosts—Italian Style - *It*
The Glass Sphinx - *Egypt-It-Sp*
Godzilla's Revenge - *Jap*
High Season for Spies - *W. Ger*
Hillbillys in a Haunted House - *USA*
Le Horla - *Fr*
House of 1,000 Dolls - *GB-W. Ger-Sp*
The Hunchback of Soho - *W. Ger*
I Am Curious (Yellow) - *Swed*
I Killed Rasputin - *Fr*
The Iliac Passion - *USA*
Italian Secret Service - *It*
Journey to the Center of Time - *USA*
The Karate Killers - *USA*
Killer with a Silk Scarf - *W. Ger*
The Killing Game - *Fr*
Kiss the Girls and Make Them Die - *USA-It*
Koroshi - *GB*
The Man Outside - *GB*
Master Stroke - *USA*
Monster Zero - *Jap*
Muha - *Yugo*
The Night of the Big Heat - *GB*
No Way to Treat a Lady - *USA*
L'Ombre dans la Glace - *Fr*
Operation Kid Brother - *It*
Our Mother's House - *GB*
The Penthouse - *GB*
Per Amore...Per Magia - *It*
The Perils of Pauline - *USA*
Le Plus Vieux Metier du Monde - *Fr-W.
Ger-It*
The Power - *USA*
The President's Analyst - *USA*
Privarzaniat Balon - *Bulg*
Project X - *USA*
Putiat Kam Pleadite - *Bulg*
Quatermass and the Pit - *GB*
The Red Mantle - *Swed-Den-Ice*
Reflections in a Golden Eye - *USA*
The St. Valentine's Day Massacre - *USA*
Die Schlangengrube und das Pendel - *W. Ger*
She Freak - *USA*
The Shuttered Room - *GB*
The Sky Bike - *GB*
The Sorcerers - *GB*
The Spy in the Green Hat - *USA*
Spy Today, Die Tomorrow - *W. Ger*
Stranger in the House - *GB*
Strategy of Terror - *USA*
Superargo e i Giganti Senza Volto - *It-Sp*
The Swimmer - *USA*

Talk of the Devil - *GB*
Tanin No Kao - *Jap*
Tarzan and the Great River - *USA*
A Taste of Blood - *USA*
Those Fantastic Flying Fools - *USA-GB*
Torture Garden - *USA*
The Trip - *USA*
2267 A.D.—When the Sleeper Wakes
(unfinished) - *USA*
The Undertaker and His Pals - *USA*
Vargtimmen - *Swed*
The Venetian Affair - *USA*
The Vengeance of Fu Manchu - *GB*
Vrazda Po Cesku - *Czech*
What on Earth? - *Can*
Yongary, Monster from the Deep - *Jap-Korean*
You Only Live Twice - *GB*

1968

The Adding Machine - *USA*
The Andromeda Nebula - *Russ*
The Ape Creature - *W. Ger*
Artists in the Circus Tent/Perplexed - *W. Ger*
Astro Zombies - *USA*
Attack of the Monsters - *Jap*
The Bamboo Saucer - *USA*
Barbarella - *It-Fr*
Berserk - *GB*
The Blood of Fu Manchu - *GB*
The Boston Strangler - *USA*
Brides of Blood - *Phil*
The Cage of Stone - *Fr*
Castle Keep - *USA*
Charly - *USA*
Chitty Chitty Bang Bang - *GB*
Corruption - *GB*
Creature of Destruction - *USA*
The Cremator - *Czech*
Curse of the Crimson Altar - *GB*
The Deathshead Vampire - *GB*
Destroy All Monsters - *Jap*
The Destructors - *USA*
The Devil Rides Out - *GB*
Dr. Faustus - *GB*
Dracula Has Risen from the Grave - *GB*
Dracula Meets the Outer Space Chicks - *USA*
Esop - *Bulg-Czech*
The Exotic Ones - *USA*
The Extraordinary Seaman - *USA*
The Face of Eve - *GB-Sp*
The Fear Chamber - *USA-Mex*
Gammera vs. Viras - *Jap*
A Ghost of a Chance - *USA*
The Giant's Three Golden Hairs - *W. Ger*
The Green Slime - *USA-Jap*
The Haunted House of Horror - *GB*
The Helicopter Spies - *USA*
Hello Down There - *USA*
House of Evil - *USA-Mex*
How to Make a Doll - *USA*
How to Steal the World - *USA*
In the Year 2889 - *USA*
Invasion Siniestra - *USA-Mex*
Isabel - *Can*
Isabell, a Dream - *It*
Island of Despair - *Sp*
Isle of the Snake People - *USA-Mex*
I, the Justice - *Czech*
It's Alive! - *USA*
Its Name Was Robert - *Russ*
Journey into Darkness - *GB*
King Kong Escapes - *Jap*
Kiss Me, Monster - *Sp*
Kong Island - *Sp*
Kuroneko - *Jap*
Limbo Line - *GB*
The Love Bug - *USA*
Mad Monster Party - *USA*
The Mad Room - *USA*
The Magus - *GB*
A Man Called Dagger - *USA*
Mantis in Lace - *USA*
La Mariee etait en Noir - *Fr*
Mars Needs Women - *USA*
Mission Mars - *USA*
Mission Stardust - *It-W. Ger-Sp*
The Name of the Game is Kill - *USA*
Necronomicon - *W. Ger*
Negatives - *GB*
Night Fright - *USA*
Night of the Bloody Apes - *Mex*
Night of the Living Dead - *USA*
Las Noches del Hombre Lobo - *Sp-Fr*
The Omegans - *USA*
Operation: Lovebirds - *Den*
Orgasmo - *It-Fr*
OSS 117—Double Agent - *It-Fr*
Otley - *GB*
Pacto Diabolico - *Mex*
Panic in the City - *USA*
The Phantom Tollbooth - *USA*

Planet of the Apes - *USA*
Please, Don't Joke with Martians - *Fr*
Pretty Poison - *USA*
The Profound Desire of the Gods - *Jap*
Psych-Out - *USA*
Relax, Freddie - *Den*
Rosemary's Baby - *USA*
The Saint in the Revenge of the Vampire
Women - *Mex*
The Saint vs. the Blue Demon in Atlantis - *Mex*
Das Schloss - *W. Ger*
Secret Ceremony - *GB*
Secret Scrolls: Parts I & II - *Jap*
La Senora Muerte - *Mex*
Shadow on the Land - *USA*
She-Devils on Wheels - *USA*
Something Weird - *USA*
Son of Godzilla - *Jap*
Subterfuge - *GB*
Targets - *USA*
Tarzan and the Jungle Boy - *USA-Switz*
They Ran for Their Lives - *USA*
A Thousand and One Nights - *It-Sp*
Thunderbird 6 - *GB*
THX 1138 4EB - *USA*
Un Tranquillo Posto di Campagna - *It*
The Twisted Nerve - *GB*
2001: A Space Odyssey - *USA-GB*
2000 Years Later - *USA*
Uncharted Seas - *GB*
Upior - *Pol*
The Vampire and Sex - *Mex*
Vendetta for the Saint - *GB*
Voyage into Space - *Jap*
Voyage to a Prehistoric Planet - *USA*
Wild in the Streets - *USA*
Witch-Finder General - *GB*
The Wizard of Gore - *USA*
Work is a Four Letter Word - *GB*

1969

The Adventures of Ulysses - *It*
Angel, Angel, Down We Go - *USA*
The Assassination Bureau - *GB*
The Assistant - *GB*
The Bed-Sitting Room - *GB*
The Big Cube - *USA-Mex*
Blood of Dracula's Castle - *USA*
The Blood Rose - *Fr*
Body Snatcher from Hell - *Jap*
The Body Stealers - *GB*
Le Boucher - *It-Fr*
Captain Nemo and the Underwater City - *GB*
Change of Mind - *USA*
Chariots of the Gods? - *W. Ger*
Clegg - *GB*
Color Me Dead - *Austral*
Crescendo - *GB*
The Curious Female - *USA*
Daddy's Gone A-Hunting - *USA*
Daughter of the Mind - *USA*
Death May Be Your Santa Claus - *GB*
De Sade - *USA-W. Ger*
Doppelganger - *GB*
Dracula (The Dirty Old Man) - *USA*
Dracula vs. Frankenstein - *USA*
The Dunwich Horror - *USA*
Eugenie...The Story of Her Journey into
Perversion - *GB-Sp-W. Ger*
El Extrano Caso del Dr. Fausto - *Sp*
Eye of the Cat - *USA*
Fangs of the Living Dead - *It-Sp*
Fearless Frank - *USA*
Fear No Evil - *USA*
The Female Bunch - *USA*
Fireball Jungle - *USA*
Fragment of Fear - *GB*
Frankenstein Must Be Destroyed - *GB*
Gammera vs. Guiron - *Jap*
Gammera vs. Monster X - *Jap*
Genii - *Czech*
The Ghastly Ones - *USA*
Gill-Woman - *It*
Hamlet - *GB*
Hatchet for a Honeymoon - *It-Sp*
Honeycomb - *Sp*
Horror of the Blood Monsters - *USA-Phil*
Ice - *USA*
The Ice House - *USA*
The Illustrated Man - *USA*
The Image - *GB*
The Immortal - *USA*
Invasion - *Argent*
I Start Counting - *GB*
Journey to Midnight - *GB*
Journey to the Unknown - *GB*
Latitude Zero - *USA-Jap*
The Littlest Angel - *USA*
Mad Doctor of Blood Island - *USA-Phil*
The Magic Christian - *GB*
The Maltese Bippy - *USA*

Marooned - *USA*
Marquis de Sade: Justine - *It-Sp*
Men of Action Meet the Women of Drakula - *Phil*
The Mighty Gorga - *USA*
Mister Freedom - *Fr*
The Monitors - *USA*
Moon Zero Two - *GB*
The Mummy and the Curse of the Jackals - *USA*
Night Gallery - *USA*
Nightmare in Wax - *USA*
Night of Bloody Horror - *USA*
The Oblong Box - *GB*
On Her Majesty's Secret Service - *GB*
Paroxysmus - *Sp*
Plucked - *It-Fr*
A Quiet Place to Kill - *It-Sp*
The Red Tent - *It-Russ*
Ritual of Evil - *USA*
Robinson Crusoe and the Tiger - *Mex*
Satanik - *It*
Satan's Sadists - *USA*
Satyricon - *It*
Scream, Baby, Scream - *USA*
Some Girls Do - *GB*
The Southern Star - *GB-Fr*
Space-Thing - *USA*
Spirits of the Dead - *It-Fr*
Target: Harry - *USA*
Taste the Blood of Dracula - *GB*
They Call It Murder - *USA*
Topaz - *USA*
Torture Dungeon - *USA*
L'Uccello delle Piume di Cristallo - *It*
The Valley of Gwangi - *USA*
Las Vampiras - *Mex*
The Vatican Affair - *It*
What Ever Happened to Aunt Alice? - *USA*
Why Would Anyone Want to Kill a Nice
Girl Like You? - *GB*
The Witchmaker *USA*
The Work of Death - *Mex*
The Wrecking Crew - *USA*
Zenabel - *It*
Zeta One - *GB*

1970

And Soon the Darkness - *GB*
The Angel Levine - *USA*
The Aquarians - *USA*
Are You Dying, Young Man? - *GB*
Assignment Terror - *W. Ger-It-Sp*
Beast of Blood - *Phil*
Beast of the Yellow Night - *Phil*
The Beguiled - *USA*
Beneath the Planet of the Apes - *USA*
The Blood on Satan's Claw - *GB*
Bloodthirsty Butchers - *USA*
The Brotherhood of Satan - *USA*
The Brotherhood of the Bell - *USA*
Carnival of Blood - *USA*
The Castle of Fu Manchu - *GB-W. Ger*
City Beneath the Sea - *USA*
Colossus: The Forbin Project - *USA*
The Computer Wore Tennis Shoes - *USA*
The Corpse - *GB*
Count Dracula - *GB-Sp*
Countess Dracula - *GB*
Count Yorga, Vampire - *USA*
Creatures the World Forgot - *GB*
Crime and Punishment - *Russ*
Crosscurrent - *USA*
Crowhaven Farm - *USA*
Cry of the Banshee - *GB*
Curse of the Vampires - *Phil*
Daughters of Darkness - *Belg-Fr-W. Ger-It*
Decoy for Terror - *Can*
Os Deuses e os Mortos - *Yugo-W. Ger-It*
Die Screaming, Marianne - *GB*
Dr. Frankenstein on Campus - *Can*
Doctors Wear Scarlet - *GB*
Dorian Gray - *It-Licht-W. Ger*
Dracula's Vampire Lust - *Switz*
Egghead's Robot - *GB*
L'Enfant Sauvage - *Fr*
Equinox - *USA*
Five Dolls for an August Moon - *It*
Flesh Feast - *USA*
The Fury of the Wolfman - *Sp*
Gammera vs. Jiger - *Jap*
Gas-s-s-s! - *USA*
Grimm's Fairy Tales for Adults - *W. Ger*
Guess What Happened to Count Dracula - *USA*
Hauder's Memory - *USA*
Hell's Bloody Devils - *USA*
Hercules in New York - *USA*
The Honeymoon Killers - *USA*
Horror of Frankenstein - *GB*
Horror Rises from the Tomb - *Sp*
House of Dark Shadows - *USA*
The House That Dripped Blood - *GB*
The House That Screamed - *Sp*

The House That Wouldn't Die - *USA*
How Awful About Allan - *USA*
I Drink Your Blood - *USA*
I, Monster - *GB*
Is This Trip Really Necessary? - *USA*
Jane Eyre - *GB*
Jonathan - *W. Ger*
Kemek - *It*
King Lear - *GB-Den*
The Kremlin Letter - *USA*
Legend of the Witches - *GB*
The Love War - *USA*
Lust for a Vampire - *GB*
Macunaima - *Brz*
The Man Who Haunted Himself - *GB*
The Mask of Sheba - *USA*
The Mind of Mr. Soames - *GB*
La Morte Risale a Ieri Sera - *It*
Murder Mansion - *Sp*
Myra Breckinridge - *USA*
The Naked Zoo - *USA*
Na Komete - *Czech*
Night of the Sorcerers - *Sp*
Night of the Witches - *USA*
Night Slaves - *USA*
The Night Visitor - *Swed*
No Blade of Grass - *GB*
La Noche de Walpurgis - *Sp-W. Ger*
On a Clear Day You Can See Forever - *USA*
The Only Way Out is Dead - *Can*
The Other Man - *USA*
Peau d'Ane - *Fr*
The Private Life of Sherlock Holmes - *GB*
The Projectionist - *USA*
The Psycho Lover - *USA*
Red Alert - *USA*
Rio 70 - *Sp-W. Ger-USA*
The Saint and the Blue Demon vs. the Monsters - *Mex*
Scars of Dracula - *GB*
Scream and Scream Again - *GB*
Scrooge - *GB*
Secrets of Sex - *GB*
Skullduggery - *USA*
Sole Survivor - *USA*
Lo Strano Caso della Signora Ward - *It-Sp*
Sudden Terror - *GB*
Tarzan's Deadly Silence - *USA*
Toomorrow - *GB*
Tristana - *Sp-Fr*
Trog - *GB*
Twinsanity - *GB*
The Vampire Lovers - *GB*
El Vampiro de la Utopista - *Sp*
Virgin Witch - *GB*
Whirlpool - *Den*
Willard - *USA*
Witches' Mountain - *Sp*
Women and Bloody Terror - *USA*
Wuthering Heights - *GB*
Yog—Monster from Space - *Jap*

<u>1971</u>
The Abominable Dr. Phibes - *GB*
The Andromeda Strain - *USA*
The Astronaut - *USA*
Avengers of the Reef - *Austral*
B.J. Lang Presents - *USA*
The Barefoot Executive - *USA*
Bedknobs and Broomsticks - *USA*
Beware! The Blob - *USA*
Black Noon - *USA*
Blind Terror - *GB*
Blood and Lace - *USA*
Blood from the Mummy's Tomb - *GB*
Blood Mania - *USA*
Blood of Ghastly Horror - *USA*
The Body Beneath - *USA*
Brain of Blood - *USA*
Case of the Full Moon Murders - *USA*
Catch Me a Spy - *GB-Fr*
The Cat O' Nine Tails - *It*
Cauldron of Blood - *USA-Sp*
Charlie Chan: Happiness is a Warm Clue - *USA*
Chelsea Bird - *GB*
A Clockwork Orange - *GB*
The Corpse Grinders - *USA*
Les Cousines - *Fr*
Daredevil - *USA*
The Deadly Dream - *USA*
The Deadly Trap - *Fr*
Dead Men Tell No Tales - *USA*
Death by Invitation - *USA*
Death Takes a Holiday - *USA*
The Devil and Miss Sarah - *USA*
The Devils - *GB*
The Devil's Nightmare - *Belg-It*
Diary of a [illegible] - *GB*
Dr. Cook's Garden - *USA*
Dr. Jekyll and Sister Hyde - *GB*
Dr. Jekyll y el Hombre Lobo - *Sp*

Do Not Fold, Spindle or Mutilate - *USA*
Dracula A.D. 1972 - *GB*
Earth II - *USA*
Ellery Queen: Don't Look Behind You - *USA*
The Erotic Adventures of the Three Musketeers - *W. Ger*
Escape - *USA*
Escape from the Planet of the Apes - *USA*
Faustine et le Bel Ete - *Fr*
La Figlia di Frankenstein - *It*
Fright - *GB*
Gammera vs. Zigra - *Jap*
Gentlemen, I Have Killed Einstein - *Czech*
Glen and Randa - *USA*
Godzilla vs. the Smog Monster - *Jap*
The Gore-Gore Girls - *USA*
Guru, the Mad Monk - *USA*
Hands of the Ripper - *GB*
The Hellstrom Chronicle - *USA*
House of Madness - *Mex*
A Howling in the Woods - *USA*
The Incredible 2-Headed Transplant - *USA*
Inn of Evil - *Jap*
In the Devil's Garden - *GB*
Invasion of the Blood Farmers - *USA*
Korol Lir - *Russ*
L.A. 2017 - *USA*
Lake of Dracula - *Jap*
The Last Child - *USA*
The Last Generation *USA*
Let's Scare Jessica to Death - *USA*
The Light at the Edge of the World - *USA-Sp-Licht*
A Lizard in a Woman's Skin - *It-Fr-Sp*
Macbeth - *GB*
Man with Icy Eyes - *It*
Marta - *It-Sp*
The Mephisto Waltz - *USA*
Murders in the Rue Morgue - *USA-Sp*
Necrophagus - *Sp*
The Nightcomers - *GB*
The Night Digger - *GB*
The Night God Screamed - *USA*
Night of Dark Shadows - *USA*
The Night Stalker - *USA*
Octaman - *USA*
The Omega Man - *USA*
Orfeo - *USA*
The People - *USA*
Percy - *GB*
Peter Rabbit and the Tales of Beatrix Potter - *GB*
The Pied Piper - *GB*
Play Misty for Me - *USA*
Point of Terror - *USA*
Quelqu'un Derriere la Porte - *It-Fr*
Quest for Love - *GB*
A Reflection of Fear - *USA*
The Reincarnate - *Can*
The Resurrection of Zachary Wheeler - *USA*
The Return of Count Yorga - *USA*
Revenge - *GB*
Revenge - *USA*
The Saint in the Vengeance of the Mummy - *Mex*
The Saint vs. Capulina - *Mex*
The Saint vs. Frankenstein's Daughter - *Mex*
Scream of the Demon Lover - *It-Sp*
The Shoemaker and the Elves - *W. Ger*
Silent Running - *USA*
Simon, King of the Witches - *USA*
Six Penguins - *Bulg*
Suicide Mission - *Mex*
Supergirl - *W. Ger*
Sweet, Sweet Rachel - *USA*
Tales from the Crypt - *GB*
A Taste of Evil - *USA*
10 Rillington Place - *GB*
They Might Be Giants - *USA*
THX 1138 - *USA*
The Touch of Satan - *USA*
Treasure Island - *GB-W. Ger-Sp-Fr*
The Trojan Women - *GB-Sp*
Twins of Evil - *GB*
Vampire Circus - *GB*
The Vampire Happening - *W. Ger*
Vanishing Point - *USA*
The Velvet Vampire - *USA*
Werewolves on Wheels - *USA*
What's the Matter with Helen? - *USA*
Whispering Death - *USA*
Who Slew Auntie Roo? - *GB*
Willy Wonka and the Chocolate Factory - *USA*
Zeppelin - *GB*
Z.P.G. *USA GB*

<u>1972</u>
The Adventures of Nick Carter - *USA*
Alabama's Ghost - *USA*
Alice's Adventures in Wonderland - *GB*
The Amazing Mr. Blunden - *GB*
El Amor Brujo - *Sp*
Angels' Wild Women - *USA*

The Asphyx - *GB*
Asylum - *GB*
Asylum of Satan - *USA*
Baffled! - *GB*
Ben - *USA*
Beware, My Brethren - *GB*
Big Foot - *USA*
The Big Game - *USA*
The Black Belly of the Tarantula - *It*
The Black Harbest of Countess Dracula - *It*
Blacula - *USA*
Blood Orgy of the She-Devils - *USA*
The Blood Spattered Bride - *Sp*
Bluebeard - *It*
The Boy Who Turned Yellow - *GB*
The Burglars - *Fr*
Burke and Hare - *GB*
Bury Me an Angel - *USA*
Cannibal Girls - *Can*
Ceremonia Sangriena - *It-Sp*
Children Shouldn't Play with Dead Things - *USA*
Conquest of the Planet of the Apes - *USA*
The Creeping Flesh - *GB*
The Cremators - *USA*
Crucible of Terror - *GB*
Crypt of the Living Dead - *USA*
Daughters of Satan - *USA*
The Dead Are Alive - *It*
Dear, Dead Delilah - *USA*
Deathdream - *Can*
Deathline - *GB*
The Deathmaster - *USA*
Demons of the Mind - *GB*
The Devil's Daughter - *USA*
The Devil's Wedding Night - *Sp*
The Devil's Women - *Mex*
Disciple of Death - *GB*
The Discreet Charm of the Bourgeoisie - *Fr*
Dr. Phibes Rises Again - *USA*
Doomsday Machine - *USA*
Doomwatch - *GB*
Dot and the Kangaroo - *Austral*
Embassy - *GB*
Endless Night - *GB*
The Eyes Behind the Stars - *It*
The Eyes of Charles Sand - *USA*
Fear in the Night - *GB*
Fear is the Key - *GB*
The Fiend - *GB*
The Flesh and Blood Show - *GB*
The Folks at Red Wolf Inn - *USA*
Frankenstein 1980 - *It*
Frenzy - *GB*
Frogs - *USA*
Garden of the Dead - *USA*
Gargoyles - *USA*
Gran Amore del Conde Dracula - *Sp*
The Groundstar Conspiracy - *USA*
Hammersmith is Out - *USA*
Haunts of the Very Rich - *USA*
Home for the Holidays - *USA*
Horror Express - *GB-Sp*
The Hound Of The Baskervilles - *USA-GB*
I Love You, I Kill You - *W. Ger*
Images - *GB*
In Search of Dracula - *Swed*
Jack's Wife - *USA*
The Jerusalem File - *USA*
Johnny Hamlet - *It*
El Jorobado de la Morgue - *Sp*
Kadoyng - *GB*
Kiss of the Tarantula - *USA*
The Last House on the Left - *USA*
The Legend of Boggy Creek - *USA*
Live Today, Die Tomorrow - *Jap*
Love Me Deadly - *USA*
Luminous Procuress - *USA*
Madame Sin - *USA-GB*
The Mad Butcher - *It*
The Man and the Beast - *Mex*
Manhattan Baby - *It*
The Man with Two Heads - *USA-GB*
Mark of the Devil - *GB-W. Ger*
The Mind Snatchers - *GB-W. Ger*
Mister, You Are a Widower - *Czech*
Moon of the Wolf - *USA*
Moonwalk One - *USA*
Necromancy - *USA*
Neither the Sea Nor the Sand - *USA*
The Night Evelyn Came Out of the Grave - *It*
Night Hair Child - *GB*
The Night of a Thousand Cats - *Mex*
Night of Terror - *USA*
Night of the Blood Monster - *Sp-W. Ger-It*
Night of the Cobra Woman - *USA*
Night of the Lepus - *USA*
The Night Strangler - *USA*
Nothing But the Night - *GB*
Now You See Him, Now You Don't - *USA*
La Orgia de los Muertos - *Sp*
Gli Orrori del Castello di Nuremberga - *It*

The Other - *USA*
Please Don't Eat My Mother - *USA*
Poor Devil - *USA*
Portnoy's Complaint - *USA*
The Poseidon Adventure - *USA*
The Possession of Joel Delaney - *USA*
Premonition - *USA*
Private Parts - *USA*
Probe - *USA*
Psychomania - *GB*
Pursuit - *USA*
Quatro Mosche di Velluto Gris - *It-Fr*
Rage - *USA*
The Rats Are Coming! The Werewolves Are Here! - *USA*
Rebellion de las Muertas - *Mex*
Rentadick - *GB*
The Ruling Class - *GB*
The Saga of the Draculas - *Sp*
Saint and the Blue Demon vs. Dracula and the Wolf Man - *Mex*
The Saint Faces Black Magic - *Mex*
Sandcastles - *USA*
Savages - *USA*
The Scarlet Letter - *W. Ger*
Schlock - *USA*
Scream Bloody Murder - *USA*
The Screaming Woman - *USA*
Secret Rites - *GB*
Seven Deaths in the Cat's Eye - *It-Fr-W. Ger*
She Waits - *USA*
Short Walk to Daylight - *USA*
Slaughter Hotel - *It*
Slaughterhouse-Five - *USA*
Sleuth - *GB*
Solaris - *Russ*
Something Evil - *USA*
The Spectre of Edgar Allan Poe - *USA*
Stanley - *USA*
Stigma - *USA*
Straight On Till Morning - *GB*
Superbeast - *Phil*
Superzan and the Space Boy - *Mex*
Sweet Kill - *USA*
Tam Lin - *GB*
The Thing with Two Heads - *USA*
To Kill a Clown - *USA*
Tombs of the Blind Dead - *Sp-Port*
Tower of Evil - *GB*
Traitement de Choc - *It-Fr*
Tup, Tup - *Yugo*
Twilight People - *Phil*
Twitch of the Death Nerve - *It*
The Vampire Doll - *Jap*
Vengeance of the Zombies - *Sp*
A Very Missing Person - *USA*
Vierges et Vampires - *Fr*
Voodoo Heartbeat - *USA*
Web of the Spider - *It*
What Became of Jack and Jill - *GB*
When Michael Calls - *USA*
The Woman Hunter - *USA*
The Wonderful Land of Oz - *USA*
You'll Like My Mother - *USA*

<u>1973</u>
The Alien Oro - *Can*
Amarcord - *It-Fr*
Anatomy of Terror - *USA*
And Now the Screaming Starts! - *GB*
The Arena - *USA*
Assassin - *GB*
El Ataque de los Muertos sin Ojos - *Sp*
Battle for the Planet of the Apes - *USA*
Battle of the Amazons - *It-Sp*
The Beginning - *Can*
Beyond Atlantis - *Phil*
Blackenstein - *USA*
Blade - *USA*
Blood Harvest - *USA*
The Borrowers - *USA*
The Boy Who Cried Werewolf - *USA*
The Bride - *Can*
Brock's Last Case - *USA*
Broken Goddess - *USA*
The Carnation Killer - *GB*
El Castello dell'Orrore - *It*
The Cat Creature - *USA*
Charley and the Angel - *USA*
The Clones - *USA*
Code Name Trixie - *USA*
A Cold Night's Death - *USA*
Craze - *GB*
Dark Places - *GB*
Death in Small Doses - *GB*
Death Smiles on a Murderer - *W. Ger-It*
Digby—The Biggest Dog in the World - *GB*
Doctor Death: Seeker of Souls - *USA*
The Doll Squad - *USA*
Don't Be Afraid of the Dark - *USA*
Don't Look in the Basement - *USA*

Don't Look Now - GB-It
Dracula - USA-Can
Dying Room Only - USA
Encounter with the Unknown - USA
The Exorcist - USA
Fantastic Planet - Fr-Czech
File It Under Fear - GB
Frankenstein and the Monster from Hell - GB
Frankenstein: The True Story - USA-GB
From Beyond the Grave - GB
Future Women - Phil
Ganja and Hess - USA
Gawain and the Green Knight - GB
Genesis II - USA
Godzilla vs. Megalon - Jap
Hans Christian Andersen's Magic Adventure - Sp
Happy Mother's Day, Love George - USA
Hex - USA
Hitler: The Last Ten Days - GB-It
The Horror at 37,000 Feet - USA
Horror Hospital - GB
The House in Nightmare Park - GB
House of Doom - Sp
The House of Seven Corpses - USA
House of the Living Dead - S. Afr
I Dismember Mama - USA
Invasion of the Bee Girls - USA
Invasion of the Girl Snatchers - USA
Isn't It Shocking? - USA
Killdozer - USA
The Killing Kind - USA
The Laughing Girl Murder - GB
Legacy of Blood - USA
Legacy of Satan - USA
The Legend of Hell House - GB
Live and Let Die - GB
Lost Horizon - USA
The Mad Bomber - USA
The Magician - USA
Malatesta's Carnival - USA
Miracle on 34th Street - USA
The Mummy's Revenge - Sp
Murder in Mind - GB
The Mutations - GB
The Naked Ape - USA
The Neptune Factor - Can
Nightmare Honeymoon - USA
Nightmare Hotel - S
Night Watch - GB
The Norliss Tapes - USA
Les Nuits Rouges - Fr
One Deadly Owner - GB
La Orgia Nocturna de los Vampiros - Sp
The Owl and the Lemming - Can
Phase IV - GB
Possession - USA
The Princess and the Pearls - Czech
The Psychopath - GB
The Return - Can
The Return - GB
Sadist Erotica - W. Ger-Sp
The Satanic Rites of Dracula - GB
Satan's School for Girls - USA
Scream and Die! - GB
Scream, Blacula, Scream - USA
Scream, Pretty Peggy - USA
The Serpent - It-Fr-W. Ger
Sign It Death - GB
Silent Night, Bloody Night - USA
Sisters - USA
The Six Million Dollar Man - USA
Sleeper - USA
Some Call It Loving - USA
Someone at the Top of the Stairs - GB
Soylent Green - USA
Spell of Evil - GB
Sssssss - USA
The Stranger - USA
Superchick - USA
Sweet Movie - Fr-Can-W. Ger
Tales That Witness Madness - GB
Terminal Island - USA
Terror in the Wax Museum - USA
Terror on the Beach - USA
Theater of Blood - GB
Three Nuts for Cinderella - Czech
Three on a Meathook - USA
The Vault of Horror - GB
Voices - GB
Voyage to the Outer Planets - USA
W - USA
Wedding in Blood - Fr
Werewolf of Washington - USA
Westworld - USA
When Women Had Tails - It
When the Screaming Stops - Sp
Who? - GB
Who Fears the Devil? - USA
Wicked, Wicked - USA
The Wicker Man - GB
The Worm Eaters - USA

Zardoz - GB

1974

Abby - USA
Anticristo - It
Apartment on the Thirteenth Floor - Sp
Arnold - USA
Back to the Planet of the Apes - USA
Bad Ronald - USA
The Bat People - USA
The Beast - Fr
The Beast Must Die - GB
A Bell from Hell - Sp
Betrayal - USA
The Black Windmill - GB
Blood! - USA
Blue Blood - GB
Caged Heat! - USA
Call Him Mr. Shatter - GB-Hong Kong
Captain Kronos: Vampire Hunter - GB
Caravan to Vaccares - GB-Fr
Catastrophe 1999: The Prophecies of Nostradamus - Jap
Chosen Survivors- USA
Color Him Dead - GB
Come Out, Come Out, Wherever You Are - GB
Contes Immoraux - Fr
Crackle of Death - USA
The Day of the Dolphin - USA
Deadly Strangers - GB
Dead People - USA
Death Cruise - USA
Deborah - It
Demon Witch Child - Sp
Deranged - Can
The Disappearance of Flight 412 - USA
Dracula - USA-It-W. Ger
Dunderklumpen - Swed
Earthquake - USA
Exorcism's Daughter - Sp
The Eyes Have It - GB
Farewell to the Planet of the Apes - USA
Fer-de-Lance - USA
Flesh Gordon - USA
Forgotten City of the Planet of the Apes - USA
Frankenstein - USA-It-W. Ger
Frightmare - GB
The Ghoul - GB
Girl on a Broom - Czech
Godzilla vs. Gigan - Jap
Godzilla vs. the Bionic Monster - Jap
The Golden Voyage of Sinbad - GB
Grave of the Vampire - USA
Great Expectations - USA-GB
The Great Manhunt - It
The Green Hornet - USA
Homebodies - USA
Horror High - USA
Horror of the Zombies - Sp
The House of the Damned - GB-Sp
House of Whipcord - GB
The House on Skull Mountain - USA
Houston, We've Got a Problem - USA
Impulse! - USA
Inn of the Damned - Austral
Invasion from Inner Earth - Can
The Island at the Top of the World - USA
It's Alive! - USA
Killer Bees - USA
Killer with Two Faces - GB
Last Bride of Salem - USA
The Last Days of Man on Earth - GB
The Legend of Spider Forest - GB
Legend of the Seven Golden Vampires - GB-Hong Kong
Lemora, the Lady Dracula - USA
Life, Liberty and Pursuit on the Planet of the Apes - USA
The Little Prince - GB
Live Again, Die Again - USA
The Living Dead at the Manchester Morgue - Fr-Sp
Madhouse - GB
Man on a Swing - USA
The Man with the Golden Gun - GB
Mark of the Devil II - GB-W. Ger
The Mark of Zorro - USA
Moments - GB
Moonchild - USA
Murder is a One-Act Play - GB
Murder Motel - GB
Murder on the Orient Express - GB
The Mysterious Island of Captain Nemo - Fr-Sp
The Night Porter - It
99 and 44/100% Dead - USA
Not Guilty - GB
Once the Killing Starts - GB
Only a Scream Away - GB
Persecution - GB
The Phantom of Hollywood - USA
Phantom of the Paradise - USA

Planet Earth - USA
The Questor Tapes - USA
Reflections of Murder - USA
The Reincarnation of Peter Proud - USA
Rhinoceros - USA
The Savage Curse - GB
Screamer - GB
Scream of the Wolf - USA
Secret Agent - Fr
Seeds of Evil - USA
Seizure - Can
Shanks - USA
Shark Kill - USA
Shriek of the Mutilated - USA
Silent Night, Evil Night - Can
Smile, Jenny, You're Dead - USA
Son of Dracula - GB
Stoner - Hong Kong
The Strange and Deadly Occurrence - USA
The Stranger Within - USA
The Strongest Man in the World - USA
The Submersion of Japan - Jap
Sugar Hill - USA
Tender Dracula - Fr
Ten Little Indians - GB-Sp
The Terminal Man - USA
Terror on the 40th Floor - USA
The Texas Chainsaw Massacre - USA
The Three Musketeers - GB
Tommy - GB
Torso - It
The Towering Inferno - USA
Treachery and Greed on the Planet of the Apes - USA
The Tribe - USA
Le Trio Infernal - Fr
2069: A Sex Odyssey - W. Ger
U.F.O.: Target Earth - USA
Vampira - GB
Voodoo Black Exorcist - Sp
Welcome to Arrow Beach - USA
Where Have All the People Gone? - USA
Where's Johnny - GB
Wonder Woman - USA
Young Frankenstein - USA

1975

Act of Aggression - Fr
Adventures of the Queen - USA
Appointment with a Killer - USA
Barbed Wire Dolls - W. Ger
Beyond the Bermuda Triangle - USA
Beyond the Door - USA-It
The Black Bird - USA
Black Moon - Fr-W. Ger
Blood Bath - USA
Blood Pen - USA
Blood Waters of Dr. Z - USA
Bon Baisers de Hong Kong - Fr
A Boy and His Dog - USA
Bug - USA
The Count of Monte Cristo - GB
The Cursed Medallion - GB-It
The Curse of Bigfoot - USA
Dark Star - USA
The Dead Don't Die - USA
Deafula - USA
Death Race 2000 - USA
Demon and the Mummy - USA
Devil's Express - USA
The Devil's Rain - USA
Devil's Web - GB
Diagnosis: Murder - GB
Dial a Deadly Number - GB
Doc Savage, the Man of Bronze - USA
Dr. Tarr's Torture Dungeon - Mex
The Eiger Sanction - USA
Ellery Queen - USA
Escape to Witch Mountain - USA
Espy - Jap
Les Experiences Erotiques de Frankenstein - Fr
Farewell, My Lovely - USA
The Flying Sorcerer - GB
Ghost Story - GB
Haunts - USA
Holy Wednesday - USA
The Horrible House on the Hill - USA
House of Exorcism - It
House of Mortal Sin - GB
The Human Factor - GB-It
I Don't Want to Be Born - GB
If It's a Man, Hang Up - GB
Infra-Man - Hong Kong
The Invisible Man - USA
It's Not the Size That Counts - GB
Jaws - USA
Journey into Fear - Can
Lancelot du Lac - Fr
The Land That Time Forgot - GB
The Legend of Lizzie Borden - USA
Legend of the Werewolf - GB

Liszt O' Mania - GB
Logan's Run - GB
Look Back in Darkness - GB
Lord Shango - USA
Love Butcher - USA
The Man Who Would Be King - USA
Mary, Mary, Bloody Mary - Mex
Matt Helm - USA
Melody of Hate - GB
Mirror of Deception - GB
Mr. Sycamore - USA
Monty Python and the Holy Grail - GB
Murder on Flight 502 - USA
Murder on the Last Night Train - It
Murder on the Midnight Express - GB
The New, Original Wonder Woman - USA
The Next Victim - USA
The Night Caller - Fr
Night of the Seagulls - Sp
The Night That Panicked America - USA
Nurse Will Make It Better - USA
One of Our Dinosaurs is Missing - USA
The Outer Space Connection - USA
People Who Own the Dark - Sp
Picnic at Hanging Rock - Austral
A Place to Die - GB
The Premonition - USA
Psychic Killer - USA
Quiller: Price of Violence - GB
Race with the Devil - USA
Robin Hood Junior - GB
The Rocky Horror Picture Show - GB
Rollerball - GB
Royal Flash - GB
Satan's Triangle - USA
Search for the Gods - USA
The Sex Machine - It
The Sexplorer - GB
Shivers - Can
Sleepwalker - GB
Snuff - It
So Sad About Gloria - USA
Spermula - Fr
The Spiral Staircase - GB
The Stepford Wives - USA
A Story of Tutankhamun - GB
Srowaway to the Moon - USA
Strange New World - USA
Superbug - W. Ger
Terror from Within - GB
Terror of Frankenstein - Swed-Ire
The Terror of Godzilla - Jap
The Thirsty Dead - USA
3 Days of the Condor - USA
To the Devil a Daughter - GB-W. Ger
Trilogy of Terror - USA
The UFO Incident - USA
The Ultimate Warrior - USA
Vampyres...Daughters of Dracula - GB
Warlock Moon - USA
When Women Lost Their Tails - It
Zorro - It-Fr

1976

The Adventures of Sherlock Holmes' Smarter Brother - GB
The Amazing Dr. Jekyll - USA
A*P*E* - USA
At the Earth's Core - GB
Barn of the Naked Dead - USA
Barracuda - USA
Beyond Belief - USA
The Blue Bird - USA-Russ
Brenda Starr - USA
Burnt Offerings - USA
Cannibal - It
Carrie - USA
The Cars That Ate Paris - Austral
Code Name: Minus One - USA
The Conspiracy of Torture - It
Creature from Black Lake - USA
Day of the Animals - USA
The Deadly Females - GB
Deadly Harvest - Can
Death at Love House - USA
Demon - USA
The Demon Lover - USA
The Devil's Men - GB
Devil's Web - USA
Devil Woman - Phil
Dr. Black Mr. Hyde - USA
Drive-In Massacre - USA
Eaten Alive! - USA
Embryo - USA
The Face of Darkness - GB
Family Plot - USA
Flood - USA
The Flower in His Mouth - It
The Food of the Gods - USA
Future Cop - USA
Futureworld - USA

The Giant Spider Invasion - USA
The Girl in Room 2A - It
The Great Houdinis - USA
Grizzly - USA
Island of the Damned - Sp
J.D.'s Revenge - USA
Jack and the Beanstalk - Jap
The Keeper - Can
The Killer Inside Me - USA
King Kong - USA
King Solomon's Treasure - Can
Look What's Happened to Rosemary's Baby -USA
The Maids - GB
La Maldicion de la Bestia - Sp
The Man from Nowhere - GB
Man on the Roof - Swed
Mansion of the Doomed - USA
The Man Who Fell to Earth - GB
Marathon Man - USA
Martin - USA
Mirrors - USA
Murder by Death - USA
The Mysterious Monsters - USA
Obsession - USA
Oh, God! - USA
The Omen - USA
Penetration - It
Pinocchio - USA
Profundo Rosso - It
Rabid - Can
The Return of the World's Greatest
Detective - USA
Robin and Marian - USA
The Satanist - GB
Satan's Slaves - GB
The Savage Bees - USA
Scalpel - USA
The Sentinel - USA
The Seven-Per-Cent Solution - USA
Shadow of the Hawk - Can
The Shaggy D.A. - USA
Sherlock Holmes in New York - USA
Shock Waves - USA
The Slipper and the Rose - GB
Spasmo - It
The Spy Who Loved Me - GB
Squirm - USA
Superbug, Super Agent - W. Ger
Survive! - Mex
Symptoms - GB
The Tenant - Fr
Time Travelers - USA
Treasure Island - USA-GB

1977
Alice, Sweet Alice - It
The Alpha Incident - USA
The Amazing World of Psychic Phenomena -USA
Audrey Rose - USA
Black Sunday - USA
The Car - USA
Cauchemares - Can
The Child - USA
Cinderella 2000 - USA
Close Encounters of the Third Kind - USA
The Crater Lake Monster - USA
Curse of the Black Widow - USA
Damnation Alley - USA
The Day It Came to Earth - USA
Dead of Night - USA
Death Rage - It
Death Ride - USA
The Deep - USA
Demon Seed - USA
Demons of the Dead - It
Dr. Dracula - USA
Eclipse - GB
Empire of the Ants - USA
End of the World - USA
Eraserhead - USA
Evil in the Deep - USA
Exo-Man - USA
Exorcist II: The Heretic - USA
Fantasy Island - USA
Final Eye - USA
The Force on Thunder Mountain - USA
The Glitterball - GB
Godzilla on Monster Island - Jap
Goliathon - Hong Kong
Good Against Evil - USA
Gulliver's Travels - GB
Halloween with the Addams Family - USA
Herbie Goes to Monte Carlo - USA
The Hills Have Eyes - USA
The Hobbit - USA-Jap
The House by the Lake - Can
The Hunchback of Notre Dame - GB
The Incredible Hulk - USA
The Incredible Hulk, Part 2 - USA
The Incredible Melting Man - USA
Iphigenia - Greece

The Island of Dr. Moreau - USA
I Spit on Your Grave - USA
It Happened at Lake Wood Manor - USA
It Happened One Christmas - USA
Jabberwocky - GB
Jacob Two-Two and the Hooded Fang - Can
Journey into Beyond - USA
Kingdom of the Spiders - USA
The Last Dinosaur - USA
Last House on Dead End Street - USA
The Last Wave - Austral
The Legend of the Wolf Woman - Sp
The Little Girl Who Lives Down the Lane - USA
The Long, Dark Night - USA
Lost in Time - USA
The Man from Atlantis - USA
The Man with the Power - USA
Meat Cleaver Massacre - USA
My Brother Has Bad Dreams - USA
Mysteries from Beyond Earth - USA
Nero Wolfe - Austral
The New House on the Left - It
Night Creature - USA-Thai
Night Fiend - Sp
Orca - USA
Overlords of the UFO - USA
The People That Time Forgot - GB
Pete's Dragon - USA
The Possessed - USA
The Psychic - It
Return to Boggy Creek - USA
Rollercoaster - USA
Ruby - USA
Satan's Cheerleaders - USA
Schizo - GB
Sinbad and the Eye of the Tiger - USA
Snowbeast - USA
Spectre - GB
The Spell - USA
Spider-Man - USA
Starship Invasions - Can
Star Wars - USA
The Strange Possession of Mrs. Oliver - USA
Strange Shadows in an Empty Room - It-Can
Suspiria - It
Swords of the Space Ark - Jap
Tarantulas: The Deadly Cargo - USA
Tentacles - It
Tintorera...Bloody Waters - GB-Mex
The Tormented - It
The Town That Dreaded Sundown - USA
Track of the Moon Beast - USA
20th Century Oz - GB
The Uncanny - GB
Viage al Centro de la Tierra - Sp
Violette Noziere - Fr-Can
Welcome to Blood City - GB
Woman of Terror - USA-It
Yeti - It

1978
The Amazing Captain Nemo - USA
Amuck - It
Are You in the House Alone? - USA
Attack of the Killer Tomatoes - USA
Autopsy - It-Sp
Avalanche - USA
The Bees - USA-Mex
The Bermuda Depths - USA
Beyond and Back - USA
Beyond the Living - USA
The Big Sleep - GB
Blackout - Fr-Can
Blue Sunshine - USA
The Boys from Brazil - USA
Capricorn One - USA
Captain America - USA
The Cat and the Canary - GB
The Cat from Outer Space - USA
Child of Glass - USA
The Chinese Web - USA
Circle of Iron - GB
The Clone Master - USA
Coma - USA
Con Caper/Curse of Rava - USA
Cruise into Terror - USA
Damien—Omen II - USA
The Dark Secret of Harvest Home - USA
The Day the Screaming Stopped - GB
The Day Time Ended - Sp
Deadly Dust - USA
Dear Detective - Fr
Deathmoon - USA
Death on the Nile - GB
Deathsport - USA
Devil Dog: The Hound of Hell - USA
Dr. Scorpion - USA
Dr. Strange - USA
Dracula's Dog - USA
The Evil - USA
Evil of Dracula - Jap

Eyeball - It
Eyes of Laura Mars - USA
A Fire in the Sky - USA
The Fish Men - It
The Force Beyond - USA
Full Circle - GB-Can
The Fury - USA
Future Women - Sp-Brz
The Ghost of Flight 401 - USA
Heaven Can Wait - USA
Hitler's Son - W. Ger
Holocaust 2000 - GB-It
The Hound Of The Baskervilles - GB
Human Feelings - USA
The Incredible Torture Show - USA
The Initiation of Sarah - USA
Invasion of the Body Snatchers - USA
It Lives Again - USA
Jaws 2 - USA
Jennifer - USA
Killer's Moon - GB
The Kirlian Witness - USA
Kiss Meets the Phantom of the Park - USA
The Lake - USA
Laserblast - USA
The Legacy - GB
Legacy of Horror - USA
The Lord of the Rings - USA
Magic - USA
The Manitou - USA
The Medusa Touch - GB-Fr
Message from Space - Jap
Metamorphoses - Jap
Monstroid - USA
Nightbeast - USA
Nightmare in Blood - USA
The Norsemen - USA
No. 1 of the Secret Service - GB
Patrick - Austral
Perceval - Fr
Piranha - USA
Plague - Can
Planet of Dinosaurs - USA
The Playbirds - GB
The Plumber - Austral
Prey - GB
The Quatermass Conclusion - GB
The Redeemer - USA
Return from Witch Mountain - USA
Return to Fantasy Island - USA
Rituals - Can
Saraba Uchu Senkan Yamato - Jap
Sasquatch, the Legend of Bigfoot - USA
Satan's Mistress - USA
Scalawag Bunch - It
Shock - It
Sisters of Death - USA
Someone's Watching Me! - USA
Spawn of the Slithis - USA
Stranger in Our House - USA
Superman - USA
Superwheels - W. Ger
The Swarm - USA
Terror of Mechagodzilla - Jap
Terror Out of the Sky - USA
The Thief of Baghdad - USA-GB
The 39 Steps - USA
The Time Machine - USA
The Toolbox Murders - USA
Top Secret - USA
The Uranium Conspiracy - It
The Vampire Girls - Phil
Vampirella (unfinished) - GB
The War in Space - Jap
Warlords of the Deep - GB
War of the Planets - It
Watership Down - GB
Where Time Began - Sp
The Wiz - USA
Wombling Free - GB

1979
Agatha - GB
Alien - USA
All That Jazz - USA
An American Christmas Carol - USA
Americathon - USA
The Amityville Horror - USA
Arabian Adventure - GB
Battlestar Galactica - USA
Beyond the Poseidon Aventure - USA
Billion Dollar Threat - USA
The Black Hole - USA
The Brood - Can
Buck Rogers in the 25th Century - USA
Captain America II - USA
The Capture of Bigfoot - USA
The Cauldron of Death - It
The China Syndrome - USA
Chomps - USA
City on Fire - Can

The Clonus Horror - USA
Crocodile - Hong Kong
The Dark - USA
The Darker Side of Terror - USA
Dawn of the Dead - USA
Dominique - USA
Don't Go in the House - USA
Dracula - GB
Dracula, Pere et Fils - Fr
Driller Killer - USA
Electric Eskimo - GB
The Evictors - USA
The Fabulous Baron Munchausen - Fr
The Fifth Musketeer - GB
The Godsend - GB
Gold of the Amazon Women - USA
Halloween - USA
A Hitch in Time - GB
Human Experiments - USA
The Humanoid - It
Inferno - It
It Fell from the Sky - USA
Jack the Ripper - W. Ger-Switz
Killer Fish - USA-It-Brz
The Lady Vanishes - GB
Last Embrace - USA
The Legend of Sleepy Hollow - USA
Licensed to Love and Kill - GB
The London Connection - GB
Love at First Bite - USA
The Loves of Dracula - USA
The Lucifer Complex - USA
Mad Max - Austral
The Mafu Cage - USA
Mandrake - USA
The Man in the Santa Claus Suit - USA
Meteor - USA
Mind over Murder - USA
Les Miserables - Jap
Mr. Selkie - GB
Il Montagna di Dio Cannibale - It
Moonraker - GB
Murder by Decree - GB-Can
Murder in the Doll House - Jap
Nightwing - USA
Nocturna, Granddaughter of Dracula - USA
Nosferatu, the Vampyre - W. Ger
Outer Touch - GB
Panic - GB
Phantasm - USA
The Prisoner of Zenda - GB
Prophecy - USA
Queen of the Cannibals - It
Quintet - USA
Ravagers - USA
Salem's Lot - USA
Salvage - USA
Sanctuary of Fear - USA
Screams of a Winter Night - USA
The Shape of Things to Come - Can
She's Dressed to Kill - USA
The Sheriff and the Satellite Kid - It
The Shout - GB
Silent Scream - USA
Sleep of Death - Swed
The Spaceman and King Arthur - GB
Stalker - Russ
Star Crash - It
Star Trek - USA
Stories from a Flying Trunk - GB
Supersonic Man - Sp
Terror - GB
Thirst - Austral
Time After Time - USA
Toby and the Koala Bear - Austral
Topper - USA
Tourist Trap - USA
The Two Worlds of Jennie Logan - USA
The Ultimate Impostor - USA
Up from the Depths - Phil
A Vacation in Hell - USA
Vampire - USA
The Visitor - USA-It
The Water Babies - USA
When a Stranger Calls - USA
Witches' Brew - USA

1980
The Aliens Are Coming - USA
The Alien's Return - USA
Altered States - USA
Angel on My Shoulder - USA
The Attic - USA
The Awakening - GB
The Babysitter - USA
Battle Beyond the Stars - USA
Bear Island - USA-GB-Can
Black Angel - GB
The Black Out - It
Blood Beach - USA
Bloodeaters - USA

The Bogey Man - *India*
The Boogeyman - *USA*
The Boy Who Never Was - *GB*
Brave New World - *USA*
Burial Ground - *It*
The Chain Reaction - *Austral*
The Changeling - *Can*
Charlie Boy/The Thirteenth Reunion - *GB*
The Children - *USA*
The Coming - *USA*
The Craving - *Sp*
Cry Wolf - *GB*
The Curse of King Tut's Tomb - *USA*
Dark Water - *GB*
The Day After Halloween - *Austral*
Death Ship - *GB-Can*
Doctor Franken - *USA*
Dr. Heckyll & Mr. Hype - *USA*
Don't Answer the Phone! - *USA*
Dressed to Kill - *USA*
Eaten Alive - *It*
Effects - *USA*
The Eliminator - *USA*
The Empire Strikes Back - *USA*
Fade to Black - *USA*
Fiend - *USA*
The Fiendish Plot of Dr. Fu Manchu - *GB*
The Fifth Floor - *USA*
The Final Countdown - *USA*
Flash Gordon - *GB*
The Fog - *USA*
A Force of One - *USA*
Friday the 13th - *USA*
Friday the 13th...The Orphan - *USA*
Galaxina - *USA*
Guardian of Hell - *It*
Guyana, Cult of the Damned - *Mex-Panama-Sp*
Hangar 18 - *USA*
Harlequin - *Austral*
Hawk the Slayer - *GB*
The Hearse - *USA*
He Knows You're Alone - *USA*
The Henderson Monster - *USA*
Herbie Goes Bananas - *USA*
The House of the Dead - *USA*
The House That Bled to Death/Growing Pains - *GB*
Humanoids from the Deep - *USA*
The Incredible Voyage of Stingray - *GB*
The Island - *USA*
The Ivory Ape - *USA*
Just Before Dawn - *USA*
The Kidnapping of the President - *Can*
Last Rites - *USA*
The Lathe of Heaven - *USA*
Macabre - *It*
Mama Dracula - *Fr-Belg*
Maniac - *USA*
Mas Alla de la Aventure - *Argent*
The Memory of Eva Ryker - *USA*
Midnight - *USA*
The Mirror Crack'd - *GB*
Mistress of the Apes - *USA*
The Monster Club - *GB*
Motel Hell - *USA*
Mother's Day - *USA*
My Bloody Valentine - *USA*
Mystery Island - *Austral*
New Year's Evil - *USA*
The Nude Bomb - *USA*
The Octagon - *USA*
Oh, God! Book II - *USA*
Oh Heavenly Dog - *USA*
Once Upon a Spy - *USA*
Phobia - *Can*
The Phoenix - *Hong Kong*
The Plutonium Incident - *Can*
The Power - *USA*
The Prey - *USA*
Prom Night - *Can*
The Psychotronic Man - *USA*
The Puma Man - *It*
Rana: The Legend of Shadow Lake - *USA*
The Return of the King - *USA*
Revenge of the Stepford Wives - *USA*
The Saint and the Brave Goose - *GB*
Saturn 3 - *GB*
Scanners - *Can*
Scared to Death - *USA*
Schizoid - *USA*
S*H*E - *USA-W. Ger-It*
The Shining - *USA-GB*
Simon - *USA*
Somewhere in Time - *USA*
Stone Cold Dead - *Can*
Strange Behaviour - *GB*
The Strangers - *It*
Stunts Unlimited - *USA*
Tanya's Island - *Can*
Target...Earth? - *USA*
The Tempest - *GB*

Terror Train - *USA*
Thunderbirds to the Rescue - *GB*
To All a Goodnight - *USA*
Toxic Zombies - *USA*
Twinkle, Twinkle, Killer Kane - *USA*
Virus - *Jap-Can*
The Watcher in the Woods - *GB*
When Time Ran Out - *USA*
Windows - *USA*
Witching Time/The Silent Scream - *GB*
Without Warning - *Can*
Xanadu - *USA*
Zombie - *It*
Zombies Lake - *Sp-Fr*

1981
Alien Contamination - *It*
Alligator - *USA*
An American Werewolf in London - *GB*
The Baby - *USA*
The Best of Sex and Violence - *USA*
Beyond the Universe - *USA*
Blow Out - *USA*
The Boogens - *USA*
Boogeyman II - *USA*
Castle Rock - *Can*
Caveman - *USA*
Charlie Chan and the Curse of the Dragon Queen - *USA*
Chilling - *Austral*
City of Women - *It*
Clash of the Titans - *GB*
Condorman - *USA*
The Creature Wasn't Nice - *USA*
Dark Night of the Scarecrow - *USA*
Dawn of the Mummy - *It-Egypt*
Dead and Buried - *USA*
Deadly Blessing - *USA*
Delusion - *USA*
The Demon - *GB*
Demonoid - *USA*
The Devil and Max Devlin - *USA*
Dial M for Murder - *USA*
The Disappearance - *Can*
Dot and Santa Claus - *Austral*
Dragonslayer - *GB*
Earthbound - *USA*
Escape from New York - *USA*
Evil Stalks This House - *Can*
Excalibur - *GB*
Eyes of a Stranger - *USA*
The Fan - *USA*
Fear No Evil - *USA*
The Final Conflict - *USA*
Final Exam - *USA*
Firebird 2015 A.D. - *Can*
For Your Eyes Only - *GB*
Frankenstein Island - *USA*
Friday the 13th—Part 2 - *USA*
Fugitive from the Empire - *USA*
The Funhouse - *USA*
Galaxy of Terror - *USA*
The Games of the Countess Dolingen of Gratz - *Fr*
Ghost Story - *USA*
Goliath Awaits - *USA*
Graduation Day - *USA*
The Great Alligator - *It*
The Grim Reaper - *It*
Halloween II - *USA*
The Hand - *USA*
Happy Birthday to Me - *Can*
Heartbeeps - *USA*
Heavy Metal - *USA*
Hell Night - *USA*
House of Death - *USA*
The Howling - *USA*
Humanoid Woman - *Russ*
Humongous - *Can*
The Incredible Shrinking Woman - *USA*
Inseminoid - *USA*
The Intruder - *Can*
The Intruder Within - *USA*
Jaws of Satan - *USA*
Knightriders - *USA*
The Last Chase - *USA*
The Legend of the Lone Ranger - *USA*
Looker - *USA*
The Man Who Saw Tomorrow - *USA*
Memoirs of a Survivor - *GB*
Midnight Lace - *USA*
Midnight Offerings - *USA*
Miss Morison's Ghosts - *GB*
Mistress of Paradise - *USA*
Modern Problems - *USA*
The Monsters Christmas - *New Zeal*
The Monsters' Revenge - *USA*
Ms. 45 - *USA*
Mystery on Monster Island - *USA-Sp*
Neighbors - *USA*
The Nesting - *USA*

Never-Never Land - *GB*
The Next One - *USA-Greece*
Nightmare - *USA*
Night of the Zombies - *USA*
Night School - *USA*
No Place to Hide - *USA*
Of Mice and Men - *USA*
The Orchard End Murder - *GB*
Outland - *USA*
The Phoenix - *USA*
Polyester - *USA*
Possession - *Fr-W. Ger*
Pranks - *USA*
The Prowler - *USA*
Quest for Fire - *Fr-Can*
Raiders of the Lost Ark - *USA*
Revenge of the Humanoids - *Fr*
Road Games - *Austral*
The Road Warrior - *Austral*
Samurai Reincarnation - *Jap*
The Secret of Seagull Island - *GB*
Shock Treatment! - *GB*
Sphinx - *USA*
Sredni Vashtar - *GB*
Strange Behavior - *New Zeal*
Student Bodies - *USA*
Super Fuzz - *USA-It*
Superman II - *USA*
Tarzan, the Ape Man - *USA*
Tattoo - *USA*
This House Possessed - *USA*
Through the Magic Pyramid - *USA*
Thunderbirds in Outer Space - *GB*
Time Bandits - *GB*
Tuck Everlasting - *USA*
The Unseen - *USA*
Wolfen - *USA*
Zorro, the Gay Blade - *USA*

1982
Alone in the Dark - *USA*
Amityville II: The Possession - *USA*
The Atomic Cafe - *USA*
The Beastmaster - *USA*
The Beast Within - *USA*
Blade Runner - *USA*
Blood Bath at the House of Death - *GB*
Blood Song - *USA*
Boarding House - *USA*
The Burning - *USA*
Butcher, Baker (Nightmare Maker) - *USA*
Cannibal in the Streets - *It*
Captain Scarlet vs. the Mysterons - *GB*
Cat People - *USA*
A Christmas Carol - *Austral*
Chronopolis - *Fr*
Class of '84 - *Can*
Computercide - *USA*
Conan the Barbarian - *USA*
Creepshow - *USA*
Cry for the Strangers - *USA*
The Dark Crystal - *USA*
The Dead and the Deadly - *Hong Kong*
Death Valley - *USA*
Demon - *GB-Greece*
Dr. Jekyll's Dungeon of Death - *USA*
Don't Go to Sleep - *USA*
Endangered Species - *USA*
E.T.—The Extra-Terrestrial - *USA*
Evilspeak - *USA*
Evil Under the Sun - *GB*
The Fall of the House of Usher - *USA*
Fantasies - *USA*
Fire & Sword- *W. Ger-Ire*
Forbidden World - *USA*
Friday the 13th—Part 3 - *USA*
Full Moon High - *USA*
Funeral Home - *Can*
Great White - *It*
Halloween III: Season of the Witch - *USA*
Hospital Massacre - *USA*
The Hound Of The Baskervilles - *GB*
House of the Long Shadows - *USA*
The House Where Evil Dwells - *GB-Jap*
The House with the Dark Staircase - *It*
The Hunchback of Notre Dame - *GB*
Hunters of the Golden Cobra - *It*
I, Desire - *USA*
I, the Jury - *USA*
Incubus - *Can*
Jekyll and Hyde...Together Again - *USA*
Julie Darling - *Can-W. Ger*
The Kid with the Broken Halo - *USA*
Kiss Daddy Goodbye - *USA*
Liquid Sky - *USA*
The Loch Ness Horror - *USA*
Madman - *USA*
The Magic Shop - *GB*
Megaforce - *USA*
Moon Madness - *Fr*

Murder is Easy - *GB*
The Mysterious Stranger - *W. Ger*
The Mysterious Two - *USA*
The Night of the Claw - *USA*
Pandemonium - *USA*
Parasite - *USA*
Poltergeist - *USA*
Psychophobia - *W. Ger*
Q - *USA*
Robbers of the Sacred Mountain - *Can*
Rona Jaffe's Mazes and Monsters - *USA*
Saturday the 14th - *USA*
The Savage Hunt of King Stakh - *Russ*
The Scarlet Pimpernel - *USA*
The Secret of NIMH - *USA*
The Seduction - *USA*
The Sender - *GB*
Silent Rage - *USA*
The Slayer - *USA*
The Slumber Party Massacre - *USA*
Sorceress - *USA-Mex*
Spasms - *Can*
Star Trek II: The Wrath of Khan - *USA*
Still of the Night - *USA*
A Stranger is Watching - *USA*
Swamp Thing - *USA*
Sweet Sixteen - *USA*
The Sword and the Sorcerer - *USA*
The Thing - *USA*
The Throne of Fire - *It*
Timerider - *USA*
Time Walker - *USA*
Tomorrow's Child - *USA*
Too Scared to Scream - *USA*
Trick or Treats - *USA*
Tron - *USA*
Venom - *GB*
Visiting Hours - *Can*
Wavelength - *USA*
World War III - *USA*
Xtro - *GB*
Zapped! - *USA*

1983
The Adventures of Young Robin Hood - *GB*
Amityville 3-D - *USA*
Ator: The Fighting Eagle - *USA-It*
Automan - *USA*
The Awakening of Candra - *USA*
Basket Case - *USA*
The Being - *USA*
Bells - *Can*
Beyond Evil - *USA*
A Blade in the Dark - *It*
Blood Link - *It*
Bloodshed - *USA*
Blood Simple - *USA*
Bog - *USA*
Brainstorm - *USA*
Christine - *USA*
City of the Walking Dead - *It-Sp*
The Cradle Will Fall - *USA*
Cujo - *USA*
Curtains - *Can*
Dance of the Dwarfs - *USA*
The Day After - *USA*
Deadly Eyes - *Can*
Deadly Lessons - *USA*
The Dead Zone - *Can*
Deathstalker - *USA-Mex*
The Demon Murder Case - *USA*
Le Dernier Combat - *Fr*
The Devonsville Terror - *USA*
The Dragon That Wasn't...Or Was He? - *Neth*
Echoes - *USA*
The Entity - *USA*
Escape 2000 - *Austral*
The Evil Dead - *USA*
Eyes of Fire - *USA*
Frightmare - *USA*
The Gates of Hell - *It*
The Haunting Passion - *USA*
Hercules - *It*
The House by the Cemetery - *It*
The House on Sorority Row - *USA*
Hundra - *It-Sp*
The Hunger - *USA*
Iceman - *USA*
The Invisible Woman - *USA*
Ironmaster - *USA-It-Fr*
Jaws 3-D - *USA*
The Keep - *USA*
Krull - *USA*
Legend of the Dinosaurs - *Jap*
The Lift - *Belg*
The Lost Empire - *USA*
Lovespell - *Ire*
The Man Who Wasn't There - *USA*
The Man with Two Brains - *USA*
Mausoleum - *USA*
Meanwhile on a Distant Planet - *GB*

Metalstorm: The Destruction of Jared-Syn - *USA*
Mortuary - *USA*
Mutant - *USA*
Never Say Never Again - *GB*
Next of Kin - *GB*
Nightmares - *USA*
Night of the Zombies - *It-Sp*
Octopussy - *GB*
Of Unknown Origin - *Can*
One Dark Night - *USA*
Panic - *It*
Phantom of the Opera - *GB-Hung*
Pieces - *Sp*
Piranha II: The Spawning - *USA-It*
The Pit - *Can*
Prisoners of the Lost Universe - *GB*
Professor Potter's Magic Potions - *GB*
Prototype - *USA*
Psycho II - *USA*
Razorback - *Austral*
Return of the Jedi - *USA*
The Return of the Man from U.N.C.L.E. - *USA*
Scalps - *USA*
Screamtime - *GB*
7 Doors of Death - *It*
Shadow of Death - *USA*
She - *USA-It*
The Sign of Four - *GB*
The Sins of Dorian Gray - *USA*
Slaughter - *USA*
The Smurfs and the Magic Flute - *Belg-Fr*
Something Wicked This Way Comes - *USA*
Somewhere Tomorrow - *USA*
Spacehunter: Adventures in the Forbidden Zone - *Can*
Space Raiders - *USA*
Sparkling Cyanide - *USA*
Splatter - *USA*
Starflight: The Plane That Couldn't Land - *USA*
Strange Invaders - *New Zeal*
The Strangeness - *USA*
Summer Girl - *USA*
Superman III - *USA*
Svengali - *USA*
Sword of the Valiant - *GB*
Tenebrae - *It*
The Tower - *Can*
Twilight Zone - *USA*
V - *USA*
Videodrome - *Can*
Village in the Mist - *S. Korea*
Warriors of the Wasteland - *It*
The Witches and the Grinnygog - *GB*
The Wizard of Oz - *Jap*
Yor, the Hunter from the Future - *Turk-It*
Zu: Warriors of the Magic Mountain - *Hong Kong*

1984

The Adventures of Buckaroo Banzai - *USA*
All of Me - *USA*
Amazons - *USA*
Android - *USA*
Ator, the Blademaster - *USA-It*
Biohazard - *USA*
Blastfighter - *It*
Blind Date - *GB-Greece*
Body Double - *USA*
Brazil - *GB*
The Brother from Another Planet - *USA*
Children of the Corn - *USA*
A Christmas Carol - *USA-GB*
C.H.U.D. - *USA*
Cloak and Dagger - *USA*
The Cold Room - *GB*
Conan the Destroyer - *USA*
Conquest - *It*
Creature - *USA*
Dark Mirror - *USA*
Death Warmed Up - *New Zeal*
The Devil's Gift - *USA*
Don't Open Till Christmas - *GB*
Dreamscape - *USA*
Dune - *USA*
Electric Dreams - *GB*
The Enchantress - *Greece*
Endgame - *It*
Evils of the Night - *USA*
The Ewok Adventure - *USA*
Exterminators of the Year 3000 - *It-Sp*
Eyes of the Evil Dead - *It*
The Final Terror - *USA*
Firestarter - *USA*
The Fourth Man - *Belg*
Frankenstein - *GB*
Friday the 13th—The Final Chapter - *USA*
Ghostbusters - *USA*
Ghost Warrior - *USA*
Gremlins - *USA*
Greystoke: The Legend of Tarzan, Lord of the Apes - *GB*

Howling II - *GB-USA*
The Ice Pirates - *USA*
Impulse - *USA*
Indiana Jones and the Temple of Doom - *USA*
The Initiation - *USA*
Invitation to Hell - *USA*
It Came Upon the Midnight Clear - *USA*
I Was a Zombie for the F.B.I. - *USA*
The Last Starfighter - *USA*
Masks of Death - *GB*
The Music of the Spheres - *Can*
The Neverending Story - *W. Ger*
Night of the Comet - *USA*
The Night They Saved Christmas - *USA*
1984 - *GB*
Oh, God! You Devil! - *USA*
Out of Order - *W. Ger*
The Philadelphia Experiment - *USA*
A Polish Vampire in Burbank - *USA*
Professor Potter's Problem - *GB*
Radioactive Dreams - *USA*
Rainbow Brite and the Star Stealer - *Jap*
Rattlers - *USA*
Revenge of the Dead - *It*
Robin Hood and the Sorcerer - *GB*
Robin Hood: The Swords of Wayland - *GB*
Romancing the Stone - *USA*
Runaway - *USA*
Sarah's House - *Pol*
Secrets of the Phantom Caverns - *USA*
Sheena - *USA*
Shock Chamber - *Can*
Silent Night, Deadly Night - *USA*
Special Effects - *USA*
Splash - *USA*
Starman - *USA*
Star Trek III: The Search for Spock - *USA*
Supergirl - *USA-GB*
Survival 1990 - *Can*
The Terminator - *USA*
Terror in the Aisles - *USA*
Threads - *GB-Austral*
Top Secret! - *GB*
The Toxic Avenger - *USA*
Trancers - *USA*
Tuareg, the Desert Warrior - *It*
2020 Texas Gladiators - *USA-It*
2010 - *USA*
Unico in the Island of Magic - *Jap*
The Zany Adventures of Robin Hood - *USA-GB*
Zombie Island Massacre - *USA*

1985

The Adventures of Hercules - *USA-It*
After the Fall of New York - *It-Fr*
The Alchemist - *USA*
Alfred Hitchcock Presents - *USA*
Alice in Wonderland - *USA*
Alien Warrior - *Can*
And the Wall Came Tumbling Down - *GB*
Arthur the King - *GB*
Baby: Secret of the Lost Legend - *USA*
Back to the Future - *USA*
The Bad Seed - *USA*
Beauty and the Beast - *Czech*
Black Carrion - *GB*
Boggy Creek II—The Legend Continues - *USA*
Breeders - *USA*
The Bride - *GB*
Bridge Across Time - *USA*
Cat's Eye - *USA*
Cave Girl - *USA*
Child's Play - *GB*
Chiller - *USA*
The Clairvoyant - *USA*
Cocoon - *USA*
The Company of Wolves - *GB*
Covenant - *USA*
Creator - *USA*
Dark of the Night - *New Zeal*
D.A.R.Y.L. - *USA*
Day of the Dead - *USA*
Deadly Messages - *USA*
Def Con 4 - *USA*
Deja Vu - *GB*
Demons - *It*
A Distant Scream - *GB*
The Doctor and the Devils - *GB*
Dot and Keeto - *Austral*
Dreamchild - *GB*
The Dungeonmaster - *USA*
Enemy Mine - *USA-W. Ger*
Escape from the Bronx - *It*
Ewoks: The Battle for Endor - *USA*
Explorers - *USA*
Flesh & Blood - *USA-Sp*
Friday the 13th-Part V: A New Beginning - *USA*
Fright Night - *USA*
The Galaxy Invader - *USA*
Ghoulies - *USA*
Godzilla 1985 - *Jap*

The Goonies - *USA*
Hard Rock Zombies - *USA*
Haunters of the Deep - *GB*
The Heavenly Kid - *USA*
Hellhole - *USA*
Here Come the Littles - *Fr*
I Dream of Jeannie: Fifteen Years Later - *USA*
Igor and the Lunatics - *USA*
In Possession - *GB*
The Invincible Barbarian - *USA-It*
Jamaica Inn - *GB*
The Jewel of the Nile - *USA*
Joe & the Colonel - *USA*
King Solomon's Mines - *USA*
Ladyhawke - *GB-It*
Last Video and Testament - *GB*
Lifeforce - *USA*
Mad Max Beyond Thunderdome - *Austral*
Making Contact - *W. Ger*
Mark of the Devil - *GB*
Mata Hari - *GB*
The McGuffin - *GB*
The Midnight Hour - *USA*
A Midsummer Night's Dream - *GB-Sp*
Murder with Mirrors - *GB*
The Mutilator - *USA*
My Science Project - *USA*
A Nightmare on Elm Street - *USA*
A Nightmare on Elm Street, Part 2: Freddy's Revenge - *USA*
Nomads - *USA*
Odin: Photon Space Sailor Starlight - *USA*
Once Bitten - *USA*
One Magic Christmas - *USA-Can*
The Oracle - *USA*
Paint Me a Murder - *GB*
Phenomena - *It*
Pray for Death - *GB*
The Quiet Earth - *New Zeal*
Ran - *Jap*
Rasputin - *Russ*
Re-Animator - *USA*
Red Ocean - *USA*
Red Sonja - *GB-It*
Remo Williams: The Adventure Begins - *USA*
Return - *USA*
The Return of the Living Dead - *USA*
Return to Oz - *USA-GB*
Revenge in the House of Usher - *Sp-Fr*
Revenge of the Teenage Vixens from Outer Space - *USA*
Santa Claus - *USA*
School Spirit - *USA*
The Secret of the Sword - *USA*
Secret Weapons - *USA*
Silver Bullet - *USA*
Slaughter High - *USA*
Space Rage - *USA*
Starcrossed - *USA*
Star Crystal - *USA*
The Stuff - *USA*
Superstition - *USA*
The Sweet Scent of Death - *GB*
Teen Wolf - *USA*
Tennis Court - *GB*
Time Flyer - *USA*
The Tomb - *USA*
Transmutations - *GB*
Transylvania 6-5000 - *USA*
Twisted - *USA*
Vampire Hunter D - *USA*
A View to a Kill - *GB*
Warning Sign - *USA*
Weird Science - *USA*
The Wind in the Willows - *USA*
Wizards of the Lost Kingdom - *USA-Argent*
Wolfman - *USA*
World of Dracula - *USA*
Young Sherlock Holmes - *GB*

1986

The Adventures of the American Rabbit - *USA*
Aliens - *USA*
Amazons - *USA-Mex*
America 3000 - *USA*
El Amor Brujo - *Sp*
The Annihilator - *USA*
April Fool's Day - *USA*
Assassin - *USA*
Aurora Encounter - *USA*
Babes in Toyland - *USA-W. Ger*
Biggles: Adventures in Time - *GB*
Big Trouble in Little China - *USA*
The Blue Lightning - *USA*
Blue Velvet - *USA*
The Boy Who Could Fly - *USA*
The Canonville Ghost - *USA*
Chopping Mall - *USA*
The Clan of the Cave Bear - *USA*
Class of Nuke 'em High - *USA*

Condor - *USA*
Crawlspace - *USA-It*
The Crazy Family - *Jap*
Critters - *USA*
Dark Mansions - *USA*
Dead End Drive-In - *Austral*
Deadly Friend - *USA*
Dead Man's Folly - *USA-GB*
Dolls - *USA-It*
Dot and the Whale - *Austral*
Dream Lover - *USA*
Easy Prey - *USA*
Eat and Run - *USA*
Eliminators - *USA-Sp*
The Elm-Chanted Forest - *USA*
The Fifth Missile - *USA*
Firewalker - *USA*
Flight of the Navigator - *USA*
The Fly - *Can*
Friday the 13th, Part VI: Jason Lives - *USA*
From Beyond - *USA*
Fugitive Alien - *Jap*
The Golden Child - *USA*
Haunted Honeymoon - *USA*
The Haunted School - *Austral*
Highlander - *USA-GB*
The Hills Have Eyes II - *USA*
The Hitcher - *USA*
House - *USA*
The Housekeeper - *Can*
Howard the Duck - *USA*
Hyper Sapien: People from Another Star - *USA*
In the Shadow of Kilimanjaro - *USA*
Invaders from Mars - *USA*
It's Alive III: Island of the Alive - *USA*
Jake Speed - *USA*
Killer in the Mirror - *USA*
Killer Party - *USA*
King Kong Lives - *USA*
Labyrinth - *USA-GB*
Legend - *USA*
Link - *GB*
Little Shop of Horrors - *USA-GB*
The Majorettes - *USA*
The Manhattan Project - *USA*
Maximum Overdrive - *USA*
Mr. Vampire - *Hong Kong*
Mr. Vampire II - *Hong Kong*
Morons from Outer Space - *GB*
Mountaintop Motel Massacre - *USA*
The Murders in the Rue Morgue - *USA-GB-Fr*
The Name of the Rose - *W. Ger-It-Fr*
Neon Maniacs - *USA*
Night of the Creeps - *USA*
Northstar - *USA*
The Phantom Empire - *USA*
The Pink Chiquitas - *Can*
Poltergeist II: The Other Side - *USA*
Psycho III - *USA*
The Quest - *USA*
Raiders of the Living Dead - *USA*
Ratboy - *USA*
The Return of Sherlock Holmes - *USA-GB*
Short Circuit - *USA*
Sinbad - *USA-It*
Sleeping Beauty - *USA-Ire*
Solarbabies - *USA*
Sorority House Massacre - *USA*
Spacecamp - *USA*
Spookies - *USA*
Star Trek IV: The Voyage Home - *USA*
The Stepfather - *Can*
The Supernaturals - *USA*
Terrorvision - *USA*
The Texas Chainsaw Massacre 2 - *USA*
Torment - *USA*
Trick or Treat - *USA*
Troll - *USA-It*
UFOria - *USA*
Vamp - *USA*
Vampires in Havana - *Cuba*
The Vindicator - *Can*
Warrior Queen - *GB*
When the Wind Blows - *GB*
The Worst Witch - *USA*
The Wraith - *USA*
Young Again - *USA*
The Zero Boys - *USA*
Zone Troopers - *USA-It*

1987

Aladdin - *It*
Alien High - *Can*
Alien Predators - *USA*
Allan Quatermain and the Lost City of Gold - *USA*
Amazon Women on the Moon - *USA*
Angel Heart - *USA*
Bates Motel - *USA*
*Batteries Not Included - *USA*
Bay Coven - *USA*
The Believers - *USA*

Black Widow - *USA*
Blood Diner - *USA*
Blood Hook - *USA*
Bloody New Year - *GB*
Blue Monkey - *Can*
Brain Damage - *USA*
The Brave Little Toaster - *USA*
Bride of Boogedy - *USA*
Buddha's Lock - *Hong Kong-Red China*
Cameron's Closet - *USA*
Cassandra - *USA*
A Chinese Ghost Story - *Hong Kong*
Creepozoids - *USA*
Creepshow 2 - *USA*
The Curse - *USA*
Cyclone - *USA*
Date with an Angel - *USA*
Dead of Night - *USA*
Dead of Winter - *USA*
Deadtime Stories - *USA*
Deathrow Gameshow - *USA*
Deathstalker II: Duel of the Titans - *USA*
Deranged - *USA*
Distortions - *USA*
The Dolphin - *Brz*
Doom Asylum - *USA*
The Edge of Hell - *Can*
Equalizer 2000 - *USA-Phil*
Eternal Evil - *USA-Can*
Evil Dead 2: Dead by Dawn - *USA*
Flowers in the Attic - *USA*
Forever Evil - *USA*
The Garbage Pail Kids - *USA*
The Gate - *Can*
Ghost Fever - *USA*
Ghost of a Chance - *USA*
Gothic - *GB*
Graveyard Shift - *Can*
Hansel and Gretel - *USA*
Harry and the Hendersons - *USA*
Haunted by Her Past - *USA*
The Haunting of Hamilton High - *Can*
Hello Again - *USA*
The Hidden - *USA*
House II: The Second Story - *USA*
Howling III - *Austral*
Hunter's Blood - *USA*
I Married a Vampire - *USA*
Innerspace - *USA*
Iron Warrior...The Legend! - *It*
I Was a Teenage Zombie - *USA*
Jane and the Lost City - *GB*
Jaws: The Revenge - *USA*
Killer Klowns from Outer Space - *USA*
The Kindred - *USA*
Lady Beware - *USA*
The Lamp - *USA*
The Last Slumber Party - *USA*
The Little Match Girl - *USA*
The Living Daylights - *GB*
The Lost Boys - *USA*
Love at Stake - *USA*
Lurkers - *USA*
Made in Heaven - *USA*
The Magic Snowman - *USA-Yugo*
Maid to Order - *USA*
Making Mr. Right - *USA*
Man Facing Southeast - *Argent*
Mannequin - *USA*
The Man Who Fell to Earth - *USA*
Masters of the Universe - *USA*
Miami Golem - *It*
Mind Killer - *USA*
Mr. Vampire III - *Hong Kong*
Monster in the Closet - *USA*
The Monster Squad - *USA*
Moon in Scorpio - *USA*
Munchies - *USA*
Mutant Hunt - *USA*
My Demon Lover - *USA*
Near Dark - *USA*
New York Ripper - *It*
Nightflyers - *USA*
A Nightmare on Elm Street 3: Dream Warriors - *USA*
The Night Stalker - *USA*
No Way Out - *USA*
The Offspring - *USA*
The Outing - *USA*
Pinocchio and the Emperor of the Night - *USA*
Predator - *USA*
Primal Scream - *USA*
Prince of Darkness - *USA*
The Princess Bride - *USA*
Programmed to Kill - *USA*
Project X - *USA*
Psycho Girls - *Can*
Psychos in Love - *USA*
Rawhead Rex - *GB*
Red Riding Hood - *USA*
Rest in Pieces - *USA*

The Return of the Six Million Dollar Man and the Bionic Woman - *USA*
Return to Horror High - *USA*
A Return to Salem's Lot - *USA*
RoboCop - *USA*
Rolling Vengeance - *USA*
Rumpelstiltskin - *USA*
The Running Man - *USA*
Scared Stiff - *USA*
Screamplay - *USA*
The Secret World of Polly Flynt - *GB*
Silent Night, Deadly Night, Part II - *USA*
Sister, Sister - *USA*
Slaughterhouse Rock - *USA*
Slavegirls from Beyond Infinity - *USA*
Sleepwalk - *W. Ger*
Slumber Party Massacre II - *USA*
Spaceballs - *USA*
Spettri - *It*
The Spirit - *USA*
Steel Dawn - *USA*
The Stepford Children - *USA*
The Story of Snow White - *USA*
Street Trash - *USA*
Superman IV: The Quest for Peace - *USA*
Surf Nazis Must Die - *USA*
Survivor - *USA*
Teen Wolf Too - *USA*
Those Dear Departed - *Austral*
Time of the Apes - *Jap*
Timestalkers - *USA*
Time Warp Terror - *GB*
Twisted Nightmare - *USA*
Uninvited - *USA*
Vampire at Midnight - *USA*
The Video Dead - *USA*
Warriors of the Wind - *Jap*
White of the Eye - *USA*
Wild Thing - *Can*
Witchboard - *USA*
The Witches of Eastwick - *USA*
The Young Magician - *Can-Pol*
Zombie High - *Can*
Zombie Nightmare - *USA*

1988

Alice - *Czech*
Alice Through the Looking Glass - *USA*
Alien Nation - *USA*
American Gothic - *GB*
Anguish - *Sp*
Apprentice to Murder - *USA*
Bad Dreams - *USA*
Bad Taste - *New Zeal*
Beetlejuice - *USA*
Big - *USA*
The Blob - *USA*
Blood Relations - *Can*
Bloodspell - *USA*
Boris and Natasha - *USA*
The Brain - *USA*
Bravestarr—The Movie - *USA*
Cannibal Campout - *USA*
Cellar Dweller - *USA-It*
Cherry 2000 - *USA*
Child's Play - *USA*
Critters 2: The Main Course - *USA*
Dance of the Damned - *USA*
Dark Age - *Austral*
Dead Heat - *USA*
Deadly Dreams - *USA*
Deadly Intent - *USA*
Deadly Obsession - *USA*
Dead Man Walking - *USA*
D.O.A. - *USA*
Dead Ringers - *Can*
Death Row Diner - *USA*
Deathstalker III: Warriors from Hell - *USA*
Deep Space - *USA*
Demons 2 - *It*
Demonwarp - *USA*
Destroyer - *USA*
Dr. Hackenstein - *USA*
Doin' Time on Planet Earth - *USA*
Dracula's Widow - *USA*
The Drifter - *USA*
18 Again! - *USA*
Elvira, Mistress of the Dark - *USA*
Ernest Saves Christmas - *USA*
Fair Game - *It*
Flesh-Eating Mothers - *USA*
14 Going on 30 - *USA*
Freeway Maniac - *USA*
Friday the 13th, Part VII-The New Blood - *USA*
The Frog Prince - *USA*
Galactic Gigolo - *USA*
Ghosthouse - *It*
Ghostriders - *USA*
Ghost Town - *USA*
Ghoulies II - *USA-It*
The Goddess of Love - *USA*

Gor - *It*
Gotham - *Can*
Grotesque - *USA*
Halloween 4: The Return of Michael Myers - *USA*
Haunted Summer - *USA*
Hellbent - *USA*
Hellbound: Hellraiser II - *GB*
Hell Comes to Frogtown - *USA*
High Spirits - *USA*
Hollywood Chainsaw Hookers - *USA*
Howling IV - *Austral*
The Incredible Hulk Returns - *USA*
The Invisible Kid - *USA*
I Saw What You Did - *USA*
Jack's Back - *USA*
Justin Case - *USA*
The Kiss - *Can*
Lady in White - *USA*
Ladykillers - *USA*
The Lair of the White Worm - *GB*
Light Years - *Fr*
Mac and Me - *USA*
Maniac Cop - *USA*
The Man with Three Coffins - *S. Korea*
Miracle Mile - *USA*
Missing Link - *USA*
Mr. Vampire IV - *Hong Kong*
Monkey Shines - *USA*
The Mutagen - *Can*
Mutants in Paradise - *USA*
My Best Friend is a Vampire - *USA*
My Stepmother is an Alien - *USA*
The Nest - *USA*
Nightfall - *Fr*
Nightmare at Noon - *USA*
A Nightmare on Elm Street 4: The Dream Master - *USA*
Night of the Demons - *USA*
Not of this Earth - *USA*
Paperhose - *GB*
Party Line - *USA*
Phantasm II - *USA*
Phantom of the Mall: Eric's Revenge - *USA*
Phoenix the Warrior - *USA*
Poltergeist III - *USA*
Prime Evil - *USA*
Prison - *USA*
Pulse - *USA*
Pumpkinhead - *USA*
Purple People Eater - *USA*
Puss in Boots - *USA*
The Quilt of Hathor - *USA*
Redneck Zombies - *USA*
The Rejuvenator - *USA*
Remote Control - *USA*
Retribution - *USA*
Return of the Killer Tomatoes - *USA*
Return of the Living Dead, Part II - *USA*
Riders of the Storm - *USA*
Saturday the 14th Strikes Back - *USA*
Scrooged - *USA*
The Serpent and the Rainbow - *USA*
The Seventh Sign - *USA*
Short Circuit 2 - *USA*
Slime City - *USA*
Slugs - *Sp*
Something is Out There - *USA-Austral*
Sorority Babes in the Slimeball Bowl-O-Rama - *USA*
Spellbinder - *USA*
Splash, Too - *USA*
Stranded - *USA*
The Suicide Club - *USA*
Terror at the Opera - *It*
They Live - *USA*
Tommy Tricker and the Stamp Traveller - *Can*
Too Good to be True - *USA*
Top Kids - *W. Ger*
Troma's War - *USA*
Twice Dead - *USA*
The Unholy - *USA*
The Unnamable - *USA*
Vampire on Bikini Beach - *USA*
A Very Old Man with Enormous Wings - *Sp*
Vibes - *USA*
Vice Versa - *USA*
Watchers - *Can*
Waxwork - *USA*
Whisper Kill - *USA*
Who Framed Roger Rabbit - *USA*
Wicked Stepmother - *USA*
Willow - *USA*
Witchcraft - *USA*
The Witches' Black Sabbath - *It*
Without a Clue - *GB*
World Gone Wild - *USA*

1989

The Abyss - *USA*
The Adventures of Baron Munchausen - *GB*
After Midnight - *USA*

Akira - *Jap*
Alien Seed - *USA*
Always - *USA*
Amityville: The Evil Escapes - *USA*
Arena - *USA*
Back to the Future, Part II - *USA*
The Banker - *USA*
Batman - *USA*
Beverly Hills Bodysnatchers - *USA*
Beyond the Stars - *USA*
Bill & Ted's Excellent Adventure - *USA*
Black Rainbow - *GB*
Black Roses - *USA*
Blades - *USA*
Blind Fear - *Can*
The Borrower - *USA*
The 'Burbs - *US*
The Cellar - *USA*
Chances Are - *USA*
C.H.U.D. II - *USA*
Clownhouse - *USA*
Communion - *USA*
A Connecticut Yankee in King Arthur's Court - *USA*
Crime Zone - *USA*
Curse II: The Bite - *USA*
Cyber Chic - *USA*
Cyborg - *USA*
Dead Calm - *Austral*
Deepstar Six - *USA*
Dr. Caligari - *USA*
Dr. M - *Ger-Fr*
Dream a Little Dream - *USA*
Earth Girls Are Easy - *USA*
Edge of Sanity - *GB-Hung*
Empire of Ash III - *Can*
Endless Descent - *USA-Sp*
Erik the Viking - *GB*
Evil Below - *USA*
Fear Stalk - *USA*
The Fly II - *USA*
The Food of the Gods, Part II - *Can*
Friday the 13th, Part VIII—Jason Takes Manhattan - *USA*
Fright Night II - *USA*
From the Dead of Night - *USA*
Future Hunters - *USA*
Ghostbusters II - *USA*
The Gifted One - *USA*
Girlfriend from Hell - *USA*
The Girl in a Swing - *GD*
A Gnome Named Gnorm - *USA*
Halloween 5: The Revenge of Michael Myers - *USA*
The Haunting of Sarah Hardy - *USA*
Honey, I Shrunk the Kids - *USA*
The Horror Show - *USA*
Howling V: The Rebirth - *GB-Hung*
I, Madman - *USA*
Indiana Jones and the Last Crusade - *USA*
I Was a Teenage Sex Mutant - *USA*
Journey to the Center of the Earth - *GB*
Katy Meets the Aliens - *USA*
Laputa: Castle in the Sky - *Jap*
Leviathan - *USA*
Licence to Kill - *USA*
Little Monsters - *USA*
Lobster Man from Mars - *USA*
Lords of the Deep - *USA*
Masque of the Red Death - *USA* (Roger Corman/New World)
Masque of the Red Death - *USA* (21st Century)
Me and Him - *W. Ger*
Midnight - *USA*
Millennium - *Can*
Monster High - *USA*
Moontrap - *USA*
Murder by Moonlight - *GB*
My Mom's a Werewolf - *USA*
The Navigator: An Odyssey Across Time - *New Zeal*
Necromancer: Satan's Servant - *USA*
Nick Knight - *USA*
Night Life - *USA*
Nightlife - *USA-Mex*
A Nightmare on Elm Street 5: The Dream Child - *USA*
Nightmare Sisters - *USA*
Night of the Red Hunter - *New Zeal*
976-Evil - *USA*
Obsession: A Taste for Fear - *It*
Offerings - *USA*
Outlaw of Gor - *It*
Out of the Dark - *USA*
Parents - *USA*
The Penthouse - *USA*
Pet Sematary - *USA*
The Phantom of the Opera - *USA-GB*
Princess Warrior - *USA*
Prom Night III: The Last Kiss - *Can*

The Punisher - *Austral*
Puppet Master - *USA*
Quarantine - *Can*
Repossessed - *USA*
The Return of Swamp Thing - *USA*
Rising Storm - *USA*
Roller Blade Warriors: Taken by Force - *USA*
Rorret - *It*
Second Sight - *USA*
Shocker - *USA*
Silent Night, Deadly Night III - *USA*
Slipstream - *GB*
Sorry, Wrong Number - *USA*
Star Trek V: The Final Frontier - *USA*
Stepfather II - *Can*
Stuff Stephanie in the Incinerator - *USA*
Tarzan in Manhattan - *USA*
Teen Witch - *USA*
Ten Little Indians - *GB*
The Terror Within - *USA*
The Time Guardian - *Austral*
Time Trackers - *USA*
To Die For - *USA*
The Toxic Avenger, Part II - *USA*
The Toxic Avenger, Part III: The Last Temptation of Toxie - *USA*
Transformations - *USA*
Transylvania Twist - *USA*
The Trial of the Incredible Hulk - *USA*
Turn Back the Clock - *USA*
Twilight of the Cockroaches - *Jap*
The Understudy: Graveyard Shift II - *Can*
Vampire's Kiss - *USA*
The Visitors - *Swed*
Witchery - *It*
Witchtrap - *USA*
Zapped Again - *USA*

1990
The Ambulance - *USA*
Arachnophobia - *USA*
Back to the Future, Part III - *USA*
Basket Case 2 - *USA*
Beyond the Door III - *USA*
The Black Cat - *USA*
Blind Vision - *USA*
Blood and Concrete -*USA*
The Blood of Heroes - *USA*
The Boy from Andromeda - *USA*
Brain Dead - *USA*
Buried Alive - *USA*
La Captive du Desert - *Fr*
Child's Play 2 - *USA*
A Chinese Ghost Story II - *Hong Kong*
Circuitry Man - *USA*
Clarence - *Can-New Zeal*
Class of 1999 - *USA*
Collision Course - *USA*
Crash and Burn - *USA*
Cutting Class - *USA*
Cyber Chic -*USA*
Darkman - *USA*
Daughter of Darkness - *GB-Hung*
Dean R. Koontz' Whispers - *USA*
Def by Temptation - *USA*
Demon Wind - *USA*
Dick Tracy - *USA*
Disturbed - *USA*
Docteur Petiot - *Fr*
Donor - *USA*
Edward Scissorhands - *USA*
Encounter at Raven's Gate - *Austral*
Evil Spirits - *USA*
The Exorcist III - *USA*
Fatal Sky - *USA-Austral-Yugo*
Fear - *USA*
Fertilize the Blaspheming Bombshell! - *USA*
Firehead - *USA*
The First Power - *USA*
The Flash - *USA*
Flatliners - *USA*
For All Mankind - *USA*
Frankenhooker - *USA*
Frostbiter: Wrath of the Wendigo - *USA*
Future Zone - *USA*
The German Chainsaw Massacre - *Ger*
Getting Lucky - *USA*
Ghost - *USA*
Ghost Dad - *USA*
A Ghost in Monte Carlo - *GB*
Ghosts Can't Do It - *USA*
Ghost Writer - *USA*
The Gift - *GB*
Grave Secrets - *USA*
Graveyard Shift - *USA*
Gremlins 2: The New Batch - *USA*
Grim Prairie Tales - *USA*
The Guardian - *USA*
Guess Who's Coming for Christmas? - *USA*
Hamlet - *It*

The Handmaid's Tale - *USA*
Hands of a Murderer - *GB*
Hardware - *GB*
The Haunting of Morella - *USA*
Headhunter - *USA*
Heart Condition - *USA*
Hitler's Daughter - *USA-Can*
I'm Dangerous Tonight - *USA*
I Come in Peace - *USA*
I Hired a Contract Killer - *Fin-Swed*
In the Spirit - *USA*
It - *USA*
Jacob's Ladder - *USA*
Jekyll and Hyde - *USA-GB*
Jetsons: The Movie - *USA*
Leatherface: Texas Chainsaw Massacre III - *USA*
Lord of the Flies - *USA*
Maniac Cop 2 - *USA*
Martians Go Home - *USA*
Megaville - *USA*
Memories of Murder - *USA*
Meridian - *USA*
Metamorphosis: The Alien Factor - *USA*
Midnight Movie Massacre - *USA*
Mindwarp - *USA*
Mirror, Mirror - *USA*
Misery - *USA*
Mr. Destiny - *USA*
Mr. Frost - *GB-Fr*
Mom - *USA*
A Mom for Christmas - *USA*
El Mono Loco - *Sp*
Moon 44 - *USA-W. Ger*
Mother Goose Rock 'n' Rhyme - *USA*
Narrow Margin - *USA*
Night Angel - *USA*
Nightbreed - *USA-GB*
Nightmare on the 13th Floor - *USA*
Night of the Living Dead - *USA*
Night Visions - *USA*
Nudist Colony of the Dead - *USA*
Nukie - *USA*
The Nutcracker Prince - *Can*
Orpheus Descending - *USA*
Pacific Heights - *USA*
Peacemaker - *USA*
The Phantom of the Opera - *USA-GB*
The Pit and the Pendulum - *USA*
Poison - *USA*
Predator 2 - *USA*
Psycho IV: The Beginning - *USA*
Puppet Master II - *USA*
Quest for the Mighty Sword - *It*
The Rain Killer - *USA*
Red Blooded American Girl - *USA*
RoboCop 2 - *USA*
Robot Jox - *USA*
Rockula - *USA*
Roger Corman's 'Frankenstein Unbound' - *USA*
Running Against Time - *USA*
The Secret Life of Ian Fleming - *USA-GB*
Shadowzone - *USA*
Shakma - *USA*
Silent Night, Deadly Night 4: Initiation - *USA*
Sinbad and the Seven Seas - *It*
Singapore Sling - *Greece*
The Sleeping Car - *USA*
Slumber Party Massacre 3 - *USA*
Solar Crisis - *USA-Jap*
Sorority Girls and the Creature from Hell - *USA*
Soultaker - *USA*
Strangest Dreams: Invasion of the Space Preachers - *USA*
Subspecies - *USA*
Sundown: The Vampire in Retreat - *USA*
Syngenor - *USA*
Tales from the Darkside - *USA*
Teenage Mutant Ninja Turtles - *USA*
A Terra-Cotta Warrior - *Hong Kong-Can*
Total Recall - *USA*
Treasure Island - *USA-GB*
Tremors - *USA*
Two Evil Eyes - *It*
UFOs Are Coming Wednesday - *Russ*
Vampyre - *USA*
Voodoo Dawn - *USA*
Watchers II - *USA*
Wheels of Terror - *USA*
White Room - *GB-Can*
Witchboard 2: The Devil's Doorway - *USA*
The Witches - *GB*
The Witching of Ben Wagner - *USA*
Woof! - *GD*
Zorro: The Legend Begins - *USA*

1991
Mummy? ... - *Can*
The ... Family - *USA*
Afraid of the Dark - *GB-Fr*
The Alien Within - *USA*
And You Thought Your Parents Were Weird *USA*

Angels - *GB*
Barbarian Queen II (The Empress Strikes Back) - *USA*
Beastmaster 2: Through the Portal of Time - *USA*
Beauty and the Beast - *USA*
The Berlin Conspiracy - *USA*
Bernard and the Genie - *GB*
Bill & Ted's Bogus Journey - *USA*
Black Magic Mansion - *GB*
Body Parts - *USA*
Bride of Re-Animator - *USA*
Brother Future - *USA*
The Butcher's Wife - *USA*
Cape Fear - *USA*
Cast a Deadly Spell - *USA*
Child of Darkness, Child of Light - *USA*
Child's Play 3 - *USA*
Chopper Chicks in Zombietown - *USA*
Class of Nuke 'em High, Part 2: Subhumanoid Meltdown - *USA*
Class of Nuke 'em High 3: The Good, the Bad and the Subhumanoid - *USA*
Committed - *USA*
Curse III: Blood Sacrifice - *USA*
The Dark Backward - *USA*
Dead Again - *USA*
Dead Dudes in the House - *USA*
Deadly Game - *USA*
Dead Space - *USA*
Death Dreams - *USA*
Deceived - *USA*
Dollman - *USA*
Dolly Dearest - *USA*
Dream a Little Evil - *USA*
Drop Dead Fred - *USA*
Earth Angel - *USA*
Ernest Scared Stupid - *USA*
Eve of Destruction - *USA*
Evil Toons - *USA*
Fist of the North Star - *Jap*
Flaming Ears - *Austria*
Frankenstein: The College Years - *USA*
Fraternity Demon - *USA*
Freddy's Dead: The Final Nightmare - *USA*
Gawin - *Fr*
Godzilla vs. King Ghidora - *Jap*
The Haunted - *USA*
Haunting Fear - *USA*
Highlander 2: The Quickening - *GB*
Hook - *USA*
House IV - *USA*
Howling VI: The Freaks - *USA*
L'Ile au Tresor - *USA-Fr*
In Between - *USA*
Inner Sanctum - *USA*
Into the Badlands - *USA*
I Still Dream of Jeannie - *USA*
Kafka - *USA-Fr*
Kill, Kill, Overkill - *USA*
Late for Dinner - *USA*
The Lightning Incident - *USA*
The Magic Riddle - *USA*
Mannequin Two: On the Move - *USA*
Meet the Applegates - *USA*
Mirror Images - *USA*
Mortal Thoughts - *USA*
Naked Lunch - *GB-Can*
Neon City - *Can*
The Neverending Story II: The Next Chapter - *Ger*
Night of the Hunter - *USA*
976-Evil II: The Astral Factor - *USA*
Nothing But Trouble - *US*
Not of This World - *USA*
A Nymphoid Barbarian in Dinosaur Hell - *USA*
Omen IV: The Awakening - *USA*
Pale Blood - *USA*
The People Under the Stairs - *USA*
Picking Up the Pieces - *USA*
Plymouth - *USA*
Popcorn - *USA-Jamaica*
Prom Night IV: Deliver Us from Evil - *Can*
Prospero's Books - *GB*
Puppet Master III: Toulon's Revenge - *USA*
The Rapture - *USA*
Raw Nerve - *USA*
The Reflecting Skin - *Can*
The Returning - *USA*
Robin Hood - *USA-GB*
Robin Hood: Prince of Thieves - *USA*
Robot Carnival - *Jap*
The Rocketeer - *USA*
Scanners II: The New Order - *Can*
Scissors - *USA*
Sebastian Star Bear: First Mission - *USA*
The Servants of Twilight - *USA*
La Sema - *Ir*
Shadow of a Doubt - *USA*
The Silence of the Lambs - *USA*
Silent Motive - *USA*
Silent Night, Deadly Night 5: The

Toymaker - *USA*
The Sitter - *USA*
Sometimes They Come Back - *USA*
Spellcaster - *USA*
The Spirit of '76 - *USA*
Star Trek VI: The Undiscovered Country - *USA*
Stepfather III: Father's Day - *USA*
Strays - *USA*
Suburban Commando - *USA*
Switch - *USA*
Teenage Mutant Ninja Turtles II: The Secret of the Ooze - *USA*
Teen Agent - *USA*
Terminator 2: Judgment Day - *USA*
The Terror Within II - *USA*
Tetsuo II: Bodyhammer - *Jap*
A Time to Die - *USA*
To Die For II: Son of Darkness - *USA*
To Save a Child - *USA*
Trancers II: The Return of Jack Deth - *USA*
Tribulation 99: Alien Anomalies Under America - *USA*
The Unborn - *USA*
Until the End of the World - *W. Ger-Fr-Austral*
Vegas in Space - *USA*
Warlock - *USA*
Waxwork II: Lost in Time - *USA*
What Ever Happened to Baby Jane? - *USA*
White Light - *Can*
Witchcraft III: The Kiss of Death - *USA*
Wizards of the Demon Sword - *USA*
Woof Too!: A Girl and Her Dog - *GB*
Writer's Block - *USA*
Xtro II: The Second Encounter - *USA*
You're Driving Me Crazy - *USA*

1992
Adventures in Dinosaur City - *USA*
Aladdin - *USA*
Alien 3 - *USA*
All-American Murder - *USA*
Amityville 1992: It's About Time - *USA*
As in Heaven - *Ice*
The Baby Doll Murders - *USA*
Bad Channels - *USA*
Basket Case 3: The Progeny - *USA*
Batman Returns - *USA*
Benny's Video - *Austria*
Black Magic - *USA*
Blink of an Eye - *USA*
Body Language - *USA*
Braindead - *New Zeal*
Bram Stoker's 'Dracula' - *USA*
Brenda Starr - *USA*
Candyman - *USA*
Captain America - *USA*
Children of the Night - *USA*
Confessions of a Serial Killer - *USA*
Cool World - *USA*
Critters 3 - *USA*
Critters 4 - *USA*
Curse IV: The Ultimate Sacrifice - *USA*
Dead Alive - *New Zeal*
Deadly Rivals - *USA*
Death Becomes Her - *USA*
Death Ring - *USA*
Demonic Toys - *USA*
Desire and Hell at Sunset Motel - *USA*
The Diamond Fleece - *USA*
Disaster in Time - *USA*
Dr. Giggles - *USA*
Doctor Mordrid - *USA*
Doppleganger: The Evil Within - *USA*
Dune Warriors - *USA*
Encino Man - *USA*
Eyes of the Beholder - *USA*
The Fear Inside - *USA*
Final Analysis - *USA*
Final Judgment - *USA*
Forever Young - *USA*
Freddie as F.R.O.7. - *GB*
Freejack - *USA*
Gate II - *USA*
Godzilla vs. Biollante - *Jap*
The Guyver - *USA*
The Hand That Rocks the Cradle - *USA*
Hard Hunted - *USA*
The Hawk - *GB*
Hellraiser III: Hell on Earth - *GB*
Highway to Hell - *USA*
Homewrecker - *USA*
Honey, I Blew Up the Kid - *USA*
Illusions - *USA*
Immortal Sins - *USA*
Innocent Blood - *USA*
Iron Maze - *Jap*
Jack Be Nimble - *New Zeal*
Jennifer 8 - *USA*
Knight Moves - *USA*
Ladykiller - *USA*

Landslide - *USA*
The Lawnmower Man - *USA*
Liquid Dreams - *USA*
Little Nemo: Adventures in Slumberland - *Jap*
Lost Prophet - *USA*
Love Can be Murder - *USA*
Love Potion No. 9 - *USA*
The Magic Bubble - *USA*
Memoirs of an Invisible Man - *USA*
Miracle Beach - *USA*
Mom and Dad Save the World - *USA*
Moon Warriors - *Hong Kong*
Mortal Sins - *USA*
Munchie -*USA*
Nemesis -*USA*
Netherworld - *USA*
Night and the City - *USA*
Night Rhythms - *USA*
Notorious - *USA*
Of Mice and Men - *USA*
Orlando - *GB-It-Fr-Russ-Neth*
The Paint Job - *USA*
Pet Sematary Two - *USA*
Play Nice - *USA*
Prelude to a Kiss - *USA*
The Premonition - *Swed*
The Presence - *USA*
Prey of the Chameleon - *USA*
Project: Shadowchaser - *USA*
Prototype X29A - *USA*
Psychic - *USA*
Quiet Killer - *USA*
Raising Cain - *USA*
The Refrigerator - *USA*
The Resurrected - *USA*
The Runestone - *USA*
Scanners III: The Takeover - *Can*
Schramm - *Ger*
Seduction: Three Tales from the 'Inner
Sanctum' - *USA*
Seedpeople - *USA*
Severed Ties - *USA*
Shadowhunter - *USA*
Single White Female - *USA*
Sleepwalkers - *USA*
Sorority House Massacre 2 -*USA*
Split Second - *USA*
Stay Tuned - *USA*
The Swordsman - *USA*
Tale of a Vampire - *GB-Jap*
There's Nothing Out There - *USA*
Tiger Claws - *USA*
Time Runner - *USA*
Traces of Red - *USA*
Trancers III: Deth Lives - *USA*
The Trial - *GB*
Troll II - *USA*
Twin Peaks: Fire Walk with Me - *USA*
Ultraviolet - *USA*
Universal Soldier - *USA-Ger*
Whispers in the Dark - *USA*
The Wicked City - *Jap*
Woof Again! Why Me? - *GB*
Wuthering Heights - *GB*

1993
Accion Mutante - *Sp*
Acting on Impulse - *USA*
Addams Family Values - *USA*
Alferd Packer: The Musical - *USA*
Alien Intruder - *USA*
Almost Dead - *USA*
Amityville: A New Generation - *USA*
Arcade - *USA*
Arctic Blue - *USA*
Army of Darkness - *USA*
Attack of the 50-Foot Woman - *USA*
Batman: Mask of the Phantasm - *USA*
Beach Babes from Beyond - *USA*
Bedevil - *Austral*
Betrayal of the Dove - *USA*
Bloodlust: Subspecies III - *USA*
Bloodstone: Subspecies II - *USA*
Blue Ice - *USA*
Body Bags - *USA*
Body Melt - *Austral*
Body Shot - *USA*
The Body Snatchers - *USA*
Boxing Helena - *USA*
Brain Smasher...A Love Story - *USA*
Cannibal! The Musical - *USA*
Careful - *Can*
Carnosaur - *USA*
Caroline at Midnight - *USA*
Children of the Corn II: The Final Sacrifice - *USA*
Class of 1999 II: The Substitute - *USA*
Cold Sweat - *USA*
Coneheads - *USA*
The Crawlers - *USA*
Cronos - *Mex*
The Crush - *USA*

Cyborg Cop - *USA*
Cyborg 2: Glass Shadow - *USA*
The Dark Half - *USA*
Dark Universe - *USA*
Daybreak - *USA*
Dead Connection - *USA*
Deadly Advice - *GB*
Dead On - *USA*
Demolition Man - *USA*
Demon City Shinjuku - *Jap*
Die Watching - *USA*
Dinosaur Island - *USA*
The Disappearance of Nora - *USA*
Dollman vs. Demonic Toys - *USA*
Dracula Rising - *USA*
Dust Devil - *USA*
Ed and His Dead Mother - *USA*
8-Man After - *Jap*
The Final Mission - *USA*
Fiorile - *It*
Fire in the Sky - *USA*
Fit to Kill - *USA*
Forever - *USA*
Fortress - *USA-Austral*
Frankenstein - *USA-GB*
Freaked - *USA*
Frogtown II - *USA*
The Fugitive - *USA*
Full Eclipse - *USA*
Future Shock - *USA*
Ghost in the Machine - *USA*
The Good Son - *USA*
Grey Knight - *USA*
Groundhog Day - *USA*
Hard to Die - *USA*
Hear No Evil - *USA*
Heart and Souls - *USA*
Hellbound - *USA*
Hellmaster - *USA*
Hexed - *USA*
The Hidden II - *USA*
Hidden Fears - *USA*
Hidden Obsession - *USA*
Hocus Pocus - *USA*
A House in the Hills - *USA*
House of Secrets - *USA*
In the Company of Darkness - *USA*
Invisible: The Chronicles of Benjamin
Knight - *USA*
Jason Goes to Hell: The Final Friday - *USA*
Jonny's Golden Quest - *USA*
The Judas Project - *USA*
Jurassic Park - *USA*
A Kiss to Die For - *USA*
Knights - *USA*
Last Action Hero - *USA*
Leprechaun - *USA*
Lifepod - *USA*
The Lipstick Camera - *USA*
Love and Human Remains - *Can*
Mandroid - *USA*
Man's Best Friend - *USA*
Mardi Gras for the Devil - *USA*
Matinee - *USA*
Merlin - *USA*
The Meteor Man - *USA*
Midnight Edition - *USA*
Midnight Kiss - *USA*
Mirror, Mirror 2: Raven Dance - *USA*
Monica's Journey - *Austria*
Monolith - *USA*
Mother's Boys- *USA*
My Boyfriend's Back - *USA*
The Mystery of Edwin Drood - *GB*
Necronomicon - *USA*
Needful Things - *USA*
The Nightmare Before Christmas - *USA*
Night Owl - *USA*
Official Denial - *USA*
Phantasm III: Lord of the Dead - *USA*
Philadelphia Experiment II - *USA*
Praying Mantis - *USA*
Prehysteria - *USA*
Pumpkinhead II: Blood Wings - *USA*
Puppet Master 4 - *USA*
Red Sleep - *USA*
Remote - *USA*
Return of the Living Dead III - *USA*
Road Flower - *USA*
Robin Cook's 'Harmful Intent' - *USA*
Robin Hood: Men in Tights - *USA*
RoboCop 3 - *USA*
Robot Wars - *USA*
Sankofa - *USA-Ger-Ghana-Burkina Faso*
Scanner Cop - *USA*
The Secret Adventures of Tom Thumb - *GB*
Secrets in the Attic - *USA*
Sex and the Single Alien - *USA*
Sins of the Night - *USA*
Sliver - *USA*
Snapdragon - *USA*

Stepmonster - *USA*
Super Mario Bros. - *USA*
Tainted Blood - *USA*
TC 2000 - *USA*
Teenage Catgirls in Heat - *USA*
Teenage Mutant Ninja Turtles III - *USA*
The Temp - *USA*
Teresa's Tattoo - *USA*
Test Tube Teens from the Year 2000 - *USA*
They - *USA*
The Three Musketeers - *USA*
Ticks - *USA*
To Catch a Yeti - *USA*
Tomcat: Dangerous Desires - *USA*
Trancers 4: Jack of Swords - *USA*
Trauma - *It*
12:01 - *USA*
Under Investigation - *USA*
The Unnamable II - *USA*
The Vanishing - *USA*
The Visitors - *Fr*
Voyage - *It-GB-Malta*
Warlock: The Armageddon - *USA*
We're Back! A Dinosaur's Story - *USA*
When a Stranger Calls Back - *USA*
When the Bough Breaks - *USA*
White Angel - *GB*
Wide Sargasso Sea - *USA*
Wilder Napalm - *USA*
Wishman - *USA*
Witch Academy - *USA*
Witchboard 2: The Devil's Doorway - *USA*
Zipperface - *USA*

1994
Accumulator 1 - *Czech*
American Cyborg: Steel Warrior - *USA*
Angels in the Outfield - *USA*
A.P.E.X. - *USA*
Armed and Deadly - *USA*
Automatic - *USA*
Bandit Queen - *Ind-GB*
Beanstalk - *USA*
Beyond Bedlam - *USA*
The Birds II: Land's End - *USA*
Blankman - *USA*
Blink - *USA*
Brainscan - *USA*
A Brilliant Disguise - *USA*
Caged Heat II: Stripped of Freedom - *USA*
Cassan: Robot Hunter - *USA*
Charlie's Ghost Story - *USA*
Circuitry Man II: Plughead Rewired - *USA*
The Club - *USA*
Color of Night - *USA*
The Companion - *USA*
Confessions of a Sorority Girl - *USA*
The Conspiracy of Fear - *USA*
Criminal Passion - *USA*
The Crow - *USA*
Cyber-Tracker - *USA*
Cyborg Cop II - *USA*
The Dark - *USA*
Dark Angel: The Ascent - *USA*
Dark Reflection - *USA*
Dead Air - *USA*
Dead Beat - *USA*
Deep Red - *USA*
Demon Keeper - *USA*
Don't Get Me Started - *GB-Ger*
Doomsday Gun - *USA*
Dragonworld - *GB*
Dream a Little Dream 2 - *USA*
Ed Wood - *USA*
The Enemy Within - *USA*
Exit to Eden - *USA*
Eyes of Terror - *USA*
Eyes of the Serpent - *USA*
Fantastic Four - *USA*
Faust - *Czech*
The Fear - *USA*
The Final Mission - *USA*
Flinch - *USA*
The Flintstones - *USA*
The Force - *USA*
From Beijing with Love - *Hong Kong*
Ghoulies IV - *USA*
Girls in Prison - *USA*
Ground Zero - *USA*
Guinevere - *USA*
Guyver 2: Dark Hero - *USA*
The Haunting of Seacliff Inn - *USA*
Heads - *USA*
Hologram Man - *USA*
Immortal Combat - *USA*
Inner Sanctum 2 - *USA*
Interview with the Vampire - *USA*
Island City - *USA*
The Jungle Book - *USA*
Junior - *USA*
Lady in Waiting - *USA*

Leprechaun 2 - *USA*
The Lifeforce Experiment - *GB-Can*
The Lion King - *USA*
Love is a Gun - *USA*
Lurking Fear - *GB*
The Maddening - *USA*
Mantis - *USA*
Mary Shelley's 'Frankenstein' - *GB*
The Mask - *USA*
Midnight Tease - *USA*
Miracle on 34th Street - *USA*
Mirror Images II - *USA*
Munchie Strikes Back - *USA*
Nemesis 2 - *USA*
The Neverending Story III: Escape from
Fantasia - *Ger*
New Crime City: Los Angeles 2020 - *USA*
Night of the Archer - *USA*
Night of the Demons 2 - *USA*
Nightscare - *USA*
No Escape - *USA*
Nostradamus - *GB-Ger*
Oblivion - *USA*
The Pagemaster - *USA*
The Paperboy - *USA*
Past Tense - *USA*
Perfect Alibi - *USA*
Pet Shop - *USA*
Possessed by the Night - *USA*
Prehysteria! 2 - *USA*
Probable Cause - *USA*
Project: Metalbeast - *USA*
Psycho Cop 2 - *USA*
Puppet Master 5 - *USA*
The Puppet Masters - *USA*
Rave Review - *USA*
La Reine Margot - *It-Fr-Ger*
Ring of the Musketeers - *USA*
Romeo is Bleeding - *USA*
Roswell - *USA*
Running Delilah - *USA*
The Santa Clause - *USA*
Scanners: The Showdown - *Can*
Scorned - *USA*
Seduced by Evil - *USA*
Sensation - *USA*
Scrial Mom - *USA*
Seventh Floor - *Austral*
71 Fragments of a Chronology of Chance -
Austria-Ger
The Shadow - *USA*
Shallow Grave - *GB*
Shattered Image - *USA*
Shrunken Heads - *USA*
The Silence of the Hams - *It*
Silk Degrees - *USA*
Sister My Sister - *GB*
Skeeter - *USA*
The Soft Kill - *USA*
Sorceress - *USA*
Stalked - *USA*
Stargate - *USA-Ger*
Star Trek: Generations - *USA*
Surviving the Game - *USA*
Suture - *USA*
The Swan Princess - *USA*
T-Force - *USA*
That Eye, the Sky - *Austral*
Thumbelina - *USA*
Till the End of Night - *USA*
Timecop - *USA*
Trancers 5: Sudden Deth - *USA*
Treacherous - *USA*
A Troll in Central Park - *USA*
2002: Rape of Eden - *USA*
The Unborn II - *USA*
Visions of Murder - *USA*
Watchers III - *USA*
Welcome II the Terrordome - *USA*
Wes Craven's New Nightmare - *USA*
The Whispering - *USA*
The Wings of Honneamise - *Jap*
Witch Hunt - *USA*
Witness to the Execution - *USA*
Wolf - *USA*
Woof Returns! A Kid's Best Friend - *GB*

1995
The Addiction - *USA*
The Adventures of Captain Zoom in Outer
Space - *USA*
Alien Terminator - *USA*
Amanda and the Alien - *USA*
The Android Affair - *USA*
Apollo 13 - *USA*
Attack of the 60 Foot Centerfold - *USA*
At the Midnight Hour - *GB*
The Babysitter - *USA*
Batman Forever - *USA*
Bio-Force I - *USA*
Blackout - *USA*

Blonde Heaven - *USA*
Bloodknot - *USA*
Blood Run - *USA*
Bodily Harm - *USA*
Bullet to Beijing - *GB*
Candyman: Farewell to the Flesh - *USA*
Carnosaur 2 - *USA*
Casper - *USA*
Castle Freak - *USA*
Cave Girl Island - *USA*
Cellblock Sisters: Banished Behind Bars - *USA*
Children of the Corn III: Urban Sacrifice - *USA*
The City of Lost Children - *Fr*
Congo - *USA*
The Convent - *GB-Port-Fr*
Copycat - *USA*
The Courtyard - *USA*
The Crew - *USA*
Cutthroat Island - *USA*
Cybertracker 2 - *USA*
Cyberzone - *USA*
Cyborg Cop III - *USA*
Cyborg 3 - *USA*
Dad, the Angel & Me - *USA*
The Dark Dancer - *USA*
Darkman II: The Return of Durant - *USA*
Darkman III: Die Darkman Die - *USA*
Deadly Invasion: The Killer Bee Nightmare -*USA*
Deadly Love - *USA*
Dead Weekend - *USA*
Death Machine - *USA*
The Demolitionist - *USA*
Demon Knight - *USA*
The Devil's Daughter - *USA*
Digital Man - *USA*
Dinosaur Valley Girls - *USA*
Dr. Jekyll and Ms. Hyde - *USA*
Dolores Claiborne - *USA*
Dominion - *USA*
Dracula: Dead and Loving *It* - *USA*
Dream Man - *USA*
Ebbie - *USA*
Electra - *USA*
First Knight - *USA*
Fluke - *USA*
Forbidden Games - *USA*
Galaxis - *USA*
Godzilla vs. Destroyer - *Jap*
Goldeneye - *USA-GB*
The Granny - *USA*
Gulliver's Travels - *USA*
Halloween 6: The Origin of Michael Myers - *USA*
Halloween: The Curse of Michael Myers - *USA*
The Haunting of Helen Walker - *USA*
Heatseeker - *USA*
Hellraiser: Bloodline - *GB*
Here Come the Munsters - *USA*
Hideaway - *USA*
Highlander: The Final Dimension - *Can-Fr-GB*
The Howling: New Moon Rising - *Austral*
Ice Cream Man - *USA*
The Indian in the Cupboard - *USA*
In the Mouth of Madness - *USA*
Jack-O'Lantern - *USA*
Jade - *USA*
Johnny Mnemonic - *USA*
Judge Dredd - *USA*
Jumanji - *USA*
Jurassic Women - *USA*
A Kid in King Arthur's Court - *USA*
Kids of the Round Table - *USA*
The Kingdom - *Den*
Kurt Vonnegut's 'Harrison Bergeron' - *USA*
Last Gasp - *USA*
Leprechaun 3 - *USA*
Lord of Illusions - *USA*
Lunar Cop - *USA*
Magic in the Water - *USA*
Magic Island - *USA*
The Mangler - *USA*
The Man in the Attic - *USA*
Mighty Morphin Power Rangers - *USA*
Les Miserables - *Fr*
Mrs. Munck - *USA*
Mortal Kombat - *USA*
The Mummy Lives - *USA*
Nadja - *USA*
The Nature of the Beast - *USA*
Nemesis 3: Time Lapse - *USA*
Never Talk to Strangers - *USA*
The Nosferatu Diaries: Embrace of the Vampire - *USA*
Nothing But the Truth - *USA*
Not of This Earth - *USA*
Omega Doom - *USA*

Outbreak - *USA*
Out of Annie's Past - *USA*
Out There - *USA*
Piranha - *USA*
Powder - *USA*
The Power Within - *USA*
Private Obsession - *USA*
Project: Metalbeast, DNA Overload - *USA*
Project Shadowchaser III - *USA*
The Prophecy - *USA*
Proteus - *USA*
Rage - *USA*
Reflections in the Dark - *USA*
Relative Fear - *Can*
Remember Me - *USA*
Return of the Texas Chainsaw Massacre - *USA*
Richard III - *GB*
The Scarlet Letter - *USA*
The Secret of Roan Inish - *USA*
Serial Killer - *USA*
Serpent's Lair - *USA*
Seven - *USA*
The Silencers - *USA*
Sinful Intrigue - *USA*
The Sister-in-Law - *USA*
Sleepstalker - *USA*
The Song Spinner - *USA*
Species - *USA*
Stanley's Dragon - *USA*
Steel Frontier - *USA*
Storybook - *USA*
Strange Days - *USA*
Susie Q - *USA*
Tails You Live, Heads You're Dead - *USA*
Tales from the Hood - *USA*
Tall, Dark and Deadly - *USA*
Tank Girl - *USA*
Temptress - *USA*
Terminal Justice - *USA*
Three Wishes - *USA*
Timemaster - *USA*
Tobe Hooper's Night Terrors - *USA*
Toy Story - *USA*
Tunnel Vision - *Austral*
12 Monkeys - *USA*
Under Lock and Key - *USA*
Vampire in Brooklyn - *USA*
Victim of Desire - *USA*
Village of the Damned - *USA*
Virtual Combat - *USA*
Virtuosity - *USA*
Visitors of the Night - *USA*
Voodoo - *USA*
A Vow to a Kill - *USA*
Waterworld - *USA*
Wes Craven Presents Mind Ripper - *USA*
When the Dark Man Calls - *USA*
White Dwarf - *USA*
Widow's Kiss - *USA*
Wish Me Luck - *USA*
Witchboard: The Possession - *USA*
Young Indiana Jones and the Attack of the Hawkmen - *USA*

1996
Adrenalin - *USA*
The Adventures of Pinocchio - *USA*
Alien Avengers - *USA*
Alien Nation: Body and Soul - *USA*
Alien Nation: Millennium - *USA*
Alien Nation: The Enemy Within - *USA*
Alien Nation: The Udara Legacy - *USA*
Angel Dust - *Jap*
The Arrival - *USA*
Bad Moon - *USA*
Barb Wire - *USA*
The Beast - *USA*
Beastmaster III: The Eye of Braxus - *USA*
Bermuda Triangle - *USA*
Bio-Dome - *USA*
Blood & Donuts - *Can*
Bloodhounds - *USA*
Bogus - *USA*
Buried Secrets - *USA*
The Cable Guy - *USA*
Cemetery Man - *It-Fr*
Chain Reaction - *USA*
Christmas Every Day - *USA*
Closer and Closer - *USA*
The Cold Equations - *USA*
Color Me Perfect - *USA*
Conundrum - *USA*
The Craft - *USA*
Crash - *Can*
Crossworlds - *USA*

The Crow: City of Angels - *USA*
The Crucible - *USA*
The Crying Child - *USA*
Curdled - *USA*
Dark Angel - *USA*
Dark Breed - *USA*
Daylight - *USA*
Deadly Web - *USA*
Dead Man's Island - *USA*
Death Benefit - *USA*
Death Game - *USA*
The Dentist - *USA*
Devil's Advocate - *USA*
Devil's Food - *USA*
Diabolique - *USA*
D.N.A. - *USA*
Doctor Who - *USA*
Dragonheart - *USA*
Encino Woman - *USA*
Eraser - *USA*
Escape from L.A. - *USA*
Evolver - *USA*
The Ex - *USA*
Extreme Measures - *USA*
A Face to Die For - *USA*
Fargo - *USA*
Fear - *USA*
Frankenstein and Me - *Can*
Freeway - *USA*
The Frighteners - *USA*
From Dusk Till dawn - *USA*
Generation X - *USA*
The Ghost and the Darkness - *USA*
Ghost in the Shell - *Jap*
The Grave - *USA*
Gulliver's Travels - *USA*
Hamlet - *USA*
Haunted - *GB*
The Haunting of Lisa - *USA*
House of the Damned - *USA*
Human Timebomb - *USA*
The Hunchback of Notre Dame - *USA*
Independence Day - *USA*
Infernal Affairs - *USA*
Inhumanoid - *USA*
The Island of Dr. Moreau - *USA*
It Came from Outer Space II - *USA*
Jack - *USA*
James and the Giant Peach - *USA*
Jane Eyre - *GB-It*
Joe's Apartment - *USA*
Kazaam - *USA*
Last Exit to Earth - *USA*
Lawnmower Man 2: Beyond Cyberspace - *USA*
Lifeform - *USA*
The Limbic Region - *USA*
Loch Ness - *GB*
The Long Kiss Goodnight - *GB*
The Lottery - *USA*
The Machine - *USA*
Magic Hunter - *GB-Hung*
Marquis de Sade - *USA*
Mars Attacks! - *USA*
Mary Reilly - *USA-GB*
Mask of Death - *USA*
Michael - *USA*
Mission: Impossible - *USA*
Mrs. Santa Claus - *USA*
Mother, May I Sleep with Danger? - *USA*
Multiplicity - *USA*
The Munsters' Scary Little Christmas - *USA*
Mystery Science Theater 3000: The Movie - *USA*
Naked Souls - *USA*
Night Visitors - *USA*
The Nutty Professor - *USA*
Once You Meet a Stranger - *USA*
101 Dalmations - *USA*
Pandora's Clock - *USA*
Past Perfect - *USA*
The Phantom - *USA*
Phenomenon - *USA*
Pinocchio's Revenge - *USA*
The Preacher's Wife - *USA*
Pretty Poison - *USA*
Primal Fear - *USA*
Prisoner of Zenda, Inc. - *USA*
Project: Alf - *USA*
Prophet - *USA*
Rasputin - *USA*
Rattled - *USA*
The Rich Man's Wife - *USA*
Rumpelstiltskin - *USA*
Sabrina the Teenage Witch - *USA*
Scream - *USA*
Screamers - *Can*
The Secret Agent - *GB*
Shadow Warriors - *USA*

Shadow Zone: The Undead Express - *USA*
Snow White in the Black Forest - *USA*
Solo - *USA*
Sometimes They Come Back...Again - *USA*
Space Jam - *USA*
Space Marines - *USA*
Special Report: Journey to Mars - *USA*
Star Command - *USA*
Star Trek: First Contact - *USA*
The Stepford Husbands - *USA*
Summer of Fear - *USA*
Superstitious - *USA*
The Surgeon - *USA*
Synapse - *USA*
Tales from the Crypt Presents Bordello of Blood - *USA*
Terminal - *USA*
Them - *USA*
Theodore Rex - *USA*
Thinner - *USA*
A Time to Kill - *USA*
To Gillian on Her 37th Birthday - *USA*
Tornado! - *USA*
To the Ends of Time - *GB*
Tracks of a Killer - *USA*
Tremors 2: Aftershocks - *USA*
Trilogy of Terror II - *USA*
Twister - *USA*
Undertow - *USA*
Unforgettable - *USA*
The Uninvited - *USA*
Unlikely Angel - *USA*
Vampirella - *USA*
When Pigs Fly - *USA*
Whiskers - *USA*
Yesterday's Target - *USA*
Young Indiana Jones: Travels with Father - *USA*

1997
Alien Resurrection - *USA*
Amityville: Dollhouse - *USA*
Anaconda - *USA*
The Apocalypse - *USA*
Asteroid - *USA*
Batman and Robin - *USA*
Beauty and the Beast: The Enchanted Christmas - *USA*
Bridge of Time - *USA*
Buried Alive II - *USA*
Casper the Friendly Ghost: A Spirited Beginning - *USA*
Contact - *USA*
Dante's Peak - *USA*
A Deadly Vision - *USA*
The Fifth Element - *USA-Fr*
George of the Jungle - *USA*
Head Above Water - *USA*
Hercules - *USA*
Hercules and Xena—The Animated Movie: The Battle for Mount Olympus - *USA*
Honey, We Shrunk Ourselves - *USA*
The Hotel Manor Inn - *USA*
The Hunchback - *USA*
In His Father's Shoes - *USA*
Kissed - *Can*
Leapin' Leprechauns - *USA*
Liar Liar - *USA*
Lost Highway - *USA*
The Lost World: Jurassic Park - *USA*
The Mask of Zorro - *USA*
Men in Black - *USA*
Moebius - *Arg*
Nightscream - *USA*
The Odyssey - *USA*
Precious Find - *USA*
The Relic - *USA*
Robin Cook's 'Invasion' - *USA*
The Saint - *USA*
Schizopolis - *USA*
Scream II - *USA*
The Second Jungle Book: Mowgli and Baloo *USA*
Seven Years in Tibet - *USA*
A Simple Wish - *USA*
The 6th Man - *USA*
Sling Blade - *USA*
Starship Troopers - *USA*
Tidal Wave: No Escape - *USA*
Tomorrow Never Dies - *USA-GB*
Touch - *USA*
Toy Story II - *USA*
Tromeo and Juliet - *USA*
Turbo: A Power Rangers Movie - *USA-Jap*
20,000 Leagues Under the Sea - *USA* (ABC-TV)
20,000 Leagues Under the Sea - *USA* (CBS-TV)
Underworld - *USA*
Volcano - *USA*
Volcano: Fire on the Mountain - *USA*

Literature Appendix

Source	Adaptation
The A.B.C. Murders (*Agatha Christie*)	The Alphabet Murders
"The Adaptive Ultimate" (*Stanley G. Weinbaum*)	She-Devil
The Admirable Crichton (*James M. Barrie*)	Male and Female
"The Adventure of the Empty House" (*Sir Arthur Conan Doyle*)	The Woman in Green
"The Adventure of the Five Orange Pips" (*Sir Arthur Conan Doyle*)	The House of Fear (1945)
After the Funeral (*Agatha Christie*)	Murder at the Gallop
Airing in a Closed Carriage (*Joseph Shearing*)	The Mark of Cain
"Air Raid" (*John Varley*)	Millennium
Alf's Button (*W.A. Darlington*)	Alf's Button Afloat
The Alien (*L.P. Davies*)	The Groundstar Conspiracy
Allan Quatermain (*H. Rider Haggard*)	King Solomon's Treasure
All on a Summer's Day (*John Garden*)	Double Confession
Alter Ego (*Arch Oboler*)	Bewitched
Always (*Trevor Meldal-Johnsen*)	Deja Vu
Ammie, Come Home (*Barbara Michaels*)	The House That Wouldn't Die
Among the Dead (*Pierre Boileau & Thomas Narcejac*)	Vertigo
And Then There Were None (*Agatha Christie*)	Five Dolls for an August Moon; Ten Little Indians (1965, 1974 & 1989)
Angels of Doom (*Leslie Charteris*)	The Saint Strikes Back
Angel Street (*Patrick Hamilton*)	Gaslight (1940 & 1944)
"Annabel Lee" (*Edgar Allan Poe*)	The Avenging Conscience
Anne Pedersdotter (*Wiers Jensen*)	Vredens Dag
"An Answer in Grand Larceny" (*Jack Boyle*)	Missing Millions
Appointment with Fear (*Roy Huggins*)	State Secret
"Ashenden" (*Somerset Maugham*)	The Secret Agent (1936)
The Aspern Papers (*Henry James*)	The Lost Moment
"Assassination Bureau, Ltd." (*Jack London & Robert Fish*)	The Assassination Bureau
The Assize of the Dying (*Edith Pargiter*)	The Spaniard's Curse
Astronauci (*Stanislaw Lem*)	Milczaca Gwiazda
Aura (*Carlos Fuentes*)	La Strega in Amore
Ayesha: The Return of She (*H. Rider Haggard*)	The Vengeance of She
Balaoo (*Gaston Leroux*)	The Wizard
"The Ballad of Tam Lin" (*Robert Burns*)	Tam Lin
"The Basement Room" (*Graham Greene*)	The Fallen Idol
Before the Fact (*Francis Iles*)	Suspicion
Beggar My Neighbor (*Arthur Ridley*)	Meet Mr. Lucifer
Behind That Curtain (*Earl Derr Biggers*)	Charlie Chan's Chance
Bella Donna (*Robert Hichens*)	Temptation (1946)
"The Benediction" (*Christopher Crowe*)	Nightmares (1983)
Benighted (*J.B. Priestley*)	The Old Dark House (1932 & 1963)
Berkeley Square (*John L. Balderston*)	The House in the Square
The Berlin Memorandum (*Len Deighton*)	Funeral in Berlin
"The Best Laid Plans of a Man in Love" (*Edgar Wallace*)	Candidate for Murder
Bid Time Return (*Richard Matheson*)	Somewhere in Time
The Big Ben Mystery (*Israel Zangwill*)	The Verdict
The Big Clock (*Kenneth Fearing*)	No Way Out
The Bird's Nest (*Shirley Jackson*)	Lizzie
Birthday (*Lazlo Bus-Fekete*)	Heaven Can Wait (1942)
"The Bishop of Battle" (*Christopher Crowe*)	Nightmares (1983)
The Bishop's Wife (*Robert Nathan*)	The Preacher's Wife
Black Alibi (*Cornell Woolrich*)	The Leopard Man
"The Black Cat" (*Edgar Allan Poe*)	Living Dead (1932); Tales of Terror
The Black Gang (*Sapper*)	The Return of Bulldog Drummond
The Black Path of Fear (*Cornell Woolrich*)	The Chase
The Blazing Launch Murder (*Rex Hardinge*)	Sexton Blake and the Bearded Doctor
The Body Snatchers (*Jack Finney*)	Invasion of the Body Snatchers (1956 & 1978)
Bombe Sur Table (*Claude Rank*)	Nick Carter et le Trefle Rouge
"Bottle Baby" (*Henry Slesar*)	Terror from the Year 5,000
"The Brides of Countess Dracula" (*Ralph Zucker & Ian Danby*)	The Devil's Wedding Night
Die Bruder Grimm (*Dr. Hermann Gerstner*)	The Wonderful World of the Brothers Grimm
The Brute (*Guy des Cars*)	The Green Scarf
Bulldog Drummond Again (*Sapper*)	Bulldog Drummond Escapes
Bulldog Drummond and the Oriental Mind (*Sapper*)	Bulldog Drummond's Bride
Burn, Witch, Burn (*A. Merritt*)	Devil Doll (1936)
Cabal (*Clive Barker*)	Nightbreed
Call for the Dead (*John Le Carre*)	The Deadly Affair
"A Can of Beans" (*Billy Wilder & Charles Brackett*)	Sunset Boulevard
Captain Grant's Children (*Jules Verne*)	In Search of the Castaways
Career of a Comet (*Jules Verne*)	Valley of the Dragons
Carmen (*Georges Bizet*)	Gipsy Blood
Carmilla (*J. Sheridan LeFanu*)	The Blood Spattered Bride; Et Mourir de Plaisir; Lust for a Vampire; La Maldicion de los Karnsteins; Twins of Evil; The Vampire Lovers; Vampyr
The Carry Cot (*Alexander Thynne*)	Blue Blood
"The Case of Charles Dexter Ward" (*H.P. Lovecraft*)	The Haunted Palace (1963); The Resurrected
The Case of Mr. Pelham (*Anthony Armstrong*)	The Man Who Haunted Himself
The Case of the Frightened Lady (*Edgar Wallace*)	The Frightened Lady
The Case of the Stolen Dispatches (*Anthony Parsons*)	Meet Sexton Blake
The Case of the Three Weird Sisters (*Charlotte Armstrong*)	The Three Weird Sisters
"The Cask of Amontillado" (*Edgar Allan Poe*)	Histoires Extraordinaires; Master of Horror; Tales of Terror
"Casting the Runes" (*Montague R. James*)	Night of the Demon (1957)
Castle Minerva (*Victor Canning*)	Masquerade
The Cat and the Canary (*John Willard*)	The Cat Creeps (1930)
Cat of Many Tails (*Ellery Queen*)	Ellery Queen: Don't Look Behind You
The Challenge (*Sapper*)	Bulldog Drummond in Africa
"Charles August Milverton" (*Sir Arthur Conan Doyle*)	The Missing Rembrandt
Charlie and the Chocolate Factory (*Roald Dahl*)	Willy Wonka and the Chocolate Factory
The Chase of the Golden Plate (*Jacques Futrelle*)	The Man Behind the Mask (1936)
"Chickamauga" (*Ambrose Bierce*)	Au Coeur de la Vie
Children! Children! (*Jack Horrigan*)	Twisted
The Children of Light (*H.L. Lawrence*)	The Damned
The Chinese Orange Mystery (*Ellery Queen*)	The Mandarin Mystery
The Chinese Parrot (*Earl Derr Biggers*)	Charlie Chan's Courage
Chink in the Armour (*Marie Belloc Lowndes*)	The House of Peril
Choice Cuts (*Pierre Boileau & Thomas Narcejac*)	Body Parts
A Christmas Carol (*Charles Dickens*)	An American Christmas Carol; A Dickensian Fantasy; Ebbie; Scrooge (1913, 1922, 1928, 1935, 1951 & 1970); Scrooge: or, Marley's Ghost; Scrooged
Christopher Syn (*Russell Thorndike & William Buchanan*)	Dr. Syn—Alias the Scarecrow
"Cinderella" (*Charles Perrault*)	Cinderella and the Fairy Godmother; Cinderfella; The Glass Slipper; The Slipper and the Rose; Three Nuts for Cinderella; Der Verlorene Schuh
The Circular Staircase (*Mary Roberts Rinehart*)	The Bat (1926 & 1959); The Bat Whispers
The Circus of Dr. Lao (*Charles G. Finney*)	7 Faces of Dr. Lao
"The City in the Sea" (*Edgar Allan Poe*)	The City Under the Sea
Clean Break (*Lionel White*)	The Killing
"The Cloak" (*Nikolai Gogol*)	The Bespoke Overcoat
"The Cloak" (*Robert Bloch*)	The House That Dripped Blood
The Clock (*Cicely Frazer-Simpson*)	The Fatal Hour (1937)
"The Cobbler and the Elves" (*Brothers Grimm*)	The Wonderful World of the Brothers Grimm
A Coffin for Dimitrios (*Eric Ambler*)	The Mask of Dimitrios
Colossus (*D.F. Jones*)	Colossus: The Forbin Project
"The Colour Out of Space" (*H.P. Lovecraft*)	The Curse; Monster of Terror
The Comedy of Errors (*William Shakespeare*)	The Boys from Syracuse
Come to Mother	Live Again, Die Again
Commissioner X (*Bert F. Island*)	Kiss Kiss, Kill Kill
Condemned to Devil's Island (*Blair Niles*)	Condemned
Confessions of an English Opium Eater (*Thomas De Quincey*)	Confessions of an Opium Eater
Conjure Wife (*Fritz Leiber*)	Night of the Eagle; Weird Woman; Witches' Brew
A Connecticut Yankee in King Arthur's Court (*Mark Twain*)	A Kid in King Arthur's Court; The Spaceman and King Arthur
"The Conversation of Eiros and Charmion" (*Edgar Allan Poe*)	La Fin du Monde
A Convict Has Escaped (*Jackson Budd*)	They Made Me a Fugitive
The Corsican Brothers (*Alexander Dumas*)	The Bandits of Corsica
Counterspy Express (*A.S. Fleischman*)	Spy in the Sky
The Count of Monte Cristo (*Alexander Dumas*)	Monte Cristo
The Creaking Chair (*Lawrence Meynell*)	Street of Shadows
The Creature (*Nigel Kneale*)	The Abominable Snowman of the Himalayas
Crime and Punishment (*Dostoevski*)	Crime and Punishment, U.S.A.; Fear (1946); Raskolnikov
Crime at Blossoms (*Mordaunt Shairp*)	Dark Secret
Crime is My Business (*W. Howard Baker*)	Murder at Site Three
Criss Cross Code (*Julian Symons*)	Counterspy
The Crossing (*Jim Flanagan*)	The Haunting of Sarah Hardy
The Crucible (*Arthur Miller*)	Les Sorcieres de Salem
The Curse of Capistrano (*Johnston McCulley*)	The Mark of Zorro (1920, 1940 & 1974); The Mask of Zorro; The Sign of Zorro; Zorro (1975); Zorro, the Gay Blade; Zorro: The Legend Begins
Cyborg (*Martin Caidin*)	Bionic Showdown: The Six Million Dollar Man and the Bionic Woman; The Return of the Six Million Dollar Man and the Bionic Woman; The Six Million Dollar Man
"Cycle of the Werewolf" (*Stephen King*)	Silver Bullet
The D.A. Draws a Circle (*Erle Stanley Gardner*)	They Call It Murder
The Daffodil Mystery (*Edgar Wallace*)	The Devil's Daffodil
"Dancing Men" (*Sir Arthur Conan Doyle*)	Sherlock Holmes and the Secret Weapon
"The Dancing Princess" (*Brothers Grimm*)	The Wonderful World of the Brothers Grimm
The Dark Chase (*David Goodis*)	Nightfall (1956)
Dark Eyes of London (*Edgar Wallace*)	Die Toten Augen von London
David Golder (*Irene Nemirowsky*)	My Daughter Joy
"The Day It All Happened, Baby"	Wild in the Streets
Day of the Arrow (*Philip Loraine*)	Eye of the Devil
The Dead Don't Care (*Jonathan Latimer*)	The Last Warning (1938)
Deadlock (*Leslie Sands*)	Another Man's Poison
The Dead Take No Bows (*Richard Burke*)	Dressed to Kill (1941)
Dear Evelyn (*Dale Eunson & Hagar Wilde*)	Guest in the House
A Debt Discharged (*Edgar Wallace*)	Man Detained
The Deeds of Dr. Deadcert (*Joan Fleming*)	Family Doctor
Demon Caravan (*Georges Surdez*)	Desert Legion
D'entre les Morts (*Pierre Boileau & Thomas Narcejac*)	Vertigo
Department K (*Hartley Howard*)	Assignment K
"The Devil and Daniel Webster" (*Stephen Vincent Benet*)	All That Money Can Buy
Devilday (*Angus Hall*)	Madhouse
"The Diminishing Draft" (*Waldemar Kaempffert*)	Un Amour de Poche
The Disoriented Man (*Peter Saxon*)	Scream and Scream Again
Dividend on Death (*Brett Halliday*)	Michael Shayne, Private Detective
La Divina Comedia (*Dante*)	Il Conte Ugolino; Dante's Inferno (1912 & 1924)
Do Androids Dream of Electric Sheep? (*Philip K. Dick*)	Blade Runner

Work (Author)	Film Adaptation
Liliom (Ferenc Molnar)	Carousel
The Limping Man (Will Scott)	Creeping Shadows
"Little Ida" (Hans Christian Andersen)	Stories from a Flying Trunk
"The Little Match Girl" (Hans Christian Andersen)	The Little Match Seller; Stories from a Flying Trunk
The Lizard's Tail (Marc Brandel)	The Hand (1981)
The Lodger (Marie Belloc Lowndes)	Man in the Attic (1953)
The Lone House Mystery (Edgar Wallace)	Attempt to Kill
The Lone Wolf's Daughter (Joseph Louis Vance)	The Lone Wolf Spy Hunt
"The Long Rain" (Ray Bradbury)	The Illustrated Man
"Lord Saville's Crime" (Oscar Wilde)	Flesh and Fantasy
Lost Moon (Jim Lovell & Jeffrey Kluger)	Apollo 13
The Lost Ones (Ian Cameron)	The Island at the Top of the World
"Lot" (Ward Moore)	Panic in Year Zero
"Lot's Daughter" (Ward Moore)	Panic in Year Zero
Love Kills (Dan Greenburg)	A Deadly Vision
Lucky Star (Owen Rutter)	Once in a New Moon
"Lucy Comes to Stay" (Robert Bloch)	Asylum
Macbeth (William Shakespeare)	Throne of Blood
Machiste in Hell	The Witch's Curse
The Magic Island (William Seabrook)	White Zombie
The Magnificent Andrew (Dalton Trumbo)	The Remarkable Andrew
Make Room! Make Room! (Harry Harrison)	Soylent Green
The Maltese Falcon (Dashiell Hammett)	The Black Bird (1975); Satan Met a Lady
The Man (Mel Dinelli)	Beware, My Lovely
A Man about a Dog (Alec Coppel)	Obsession (1949)
The Man at Six (Jack Celestin & Jack de Leon)	The Gables Mystery
The Man at the Carlton (Edgar Wallace)	Man at the Carlton Tower
Man Hunt (Vernon Clancey)	Dangerous Fingers
The Man in Half Moon Street (Barre Lyndon)	The Man Who Could Cheat Death
The Man in the Iron Mask (Alexander Dumas)	The Fifth Musketeer; The Iron Mask
"Mannikins of Horror" (Robert Bloch)	Asylum
"The Man Who Collected Poe" (Robert Bloch)	Torture Garden
The Man Who Couldn't Sleep (Charles Eric Maine)	Zex
Marianne Dreams (Catherine Storr)	Paperhouse
Mary Ann (Alex Karmel)	Something Wild
Master Crook (Bruce Walker)	Cosh Boy
Master of the Hounds (Algis Budrys)	To Kill a Clown
Mathilda Shouted Fire (Janet Green)	Midnight Lace (1960 & 1981)
Mazes and Monsters (Rona Jaffe)	Rona Jaffe's Mazes and Monsters
Meet a Body (Frank Launder & Sidney Gilliat)	The Green Man
Meet the Tiger (Leslie Charteris)	The Saint Meets the Tiger
Memoires d'un Medecin (Alexander Dumas)	Black Magic (1949)
Men of Iron (Howard Pyle)	The Black Shield of Falworth
The Meter Man (C. Scott Forbes)	The Penthouse (1967)
"Method for Murder" (Robert Bloch)	The House That Dripped Blood
"Metzengerstein" (Edgar Allan Poe)	Spirits of the Dead
"The Middle Toe of the Right Foot" (Ambrose Bierce)	The Return (1973, GB)
The Midwich Cuckoos (John Wyndham)	The Village of the Damned (1960 & 1995)
The Million Pound Day (Leslie Charteris)	The Saint in London
The Mills of God (Ernst Lothar)	An Act of Murder (1948)
The Mind of Mr. Reeder (Edgar Wallace)	The Missing People
Mister Moto's Last Warning (John P. Marquand)	The Mysterious Mr. Moto
Mrs. Christopher (Elizabeth Myers)	Blackmailed
Mrs. McGinty's Dead (Agatha Christie)	Murder Most Foul
Mrs. White (Margaret Tracy)	White of the Eye
Moby Dick (Herman Melville)	The Sea Beast
"The Mocking Bird" (Ambrose Bierce)	Au Coeur de la Vie
Monkey Planet (Pierre Boulle)	Planet of the Apes
"The Monkey's Paw" (W.W. Jacobs)	Deathdream
"The Monster" (Stephen Crane)	Face of Fire
"Morella" (Edgar Allan Poe)	The Haunting of Morella; Tales of Terror
Le Mort D'Arthur (Sir Thomas Malory)	Excalibur; Knights of the Round Table
"The Most Dangerous Game" (Richard Connell)	Bloodlust!; A Game of Death; Run for the Sun
The Mouse Who Wouldn't Play Ball (Anthony Gilbert)	Candles at Nine
Murder at Shinglestrand (Paul Capon)	Hidden Homicide
Murder for the Millions (Robert Chapman)	Murder Reported
Murder in Amityville (Hans Holzer)	Amityville II: The Possession
Murder in Mayfair (Frederic Goldsmith)	Hour of Decision
Murder on the Calais Coach (Agatha Christie)	Murder on the Orient Express
"The Murders in the Rue Morgue" (Edgar Allan Poe)	Phantom of the Rue Morgue
My Client Curley (Norman Corwin)	Once Upon a Time (1944)
Mystery of Caversham Square (Pierre Quiroule)	Sexton Blake and the Hooded Terror
Mystery of the Dead Police (Philip MacDonald)	The Hour of 13
The Nanny (Dan Greenburg)	The Guardian
The Necromancers (Robert Benson)	Spellbound (1941)
Nest in a Falling Tree (Joy Crowley)	The Night Digger
"Never Bet the Devil Your Head" (Edgar Allan Poe)	Spirits of the Dead
Nevskii Prospekt (Nikolai Gogol)	Shinel
The Night Callers (Frank Crisp)	Night Caller from Outer Space
Night Mail (Henry Holt)	The Spider (1939)
Nightmare [1947] (William Irish)	Fear in the Night
Nightmare [1965] (Anne Blaisdell)	Fanatic
"Night of the Rat" (Jeffrey Bloom)	Nightmares (1983)
Night of Wenceslas (Lionel Davidson)	Hot Enough for June
"Nobody's House" (A.M. Burrage)	The Return (1973, GB)
No Coffin for the Corpse (Clayton Rawson)	The Man Who Wouldn't Die
No Hard Feelings (Frederick Nebel)	Smart Blonde
None Came Back (Curt Neumann)	Rocketship X-M
No Nightingales (S.J. Simon & Caryl Brahms)	The Ghosts of Berkeley Square
Nos Deux Consciences (Paul Anthelme)	I Confess
Notre Dame de Paris (Victor Hugo)	Esmeralda; The Hunchback (1997); The Hunchback of Notre Dame (1923, 1939, 1957, 1965, 1977, 1982 & 1996)
The Obi (Jon Manchip White)	Naked Evil
"An Occurrence at Owl Creek Bridge" (Ambrose Bierce)	Au Coeur de la Vie
The Octave of Claudius (Barry Pain)	A Blind Bargain
The Odyssey (Homer)	The Adventures of Ulysses; L'Ile de Calypso: Ulysse et Polypheme; Ulysses
Oedipus at Colonus (Sophocles)	Edipo Re
Oedipus Rex (Sophocles)	Edipo Re
Off on a Comet (Jules Verne)	Na Komete; Valley of the Dragons
Oms en Serie (Stefan Wul)	Fantastic Planet
The Once and Future King (T.H. White)	Camelot
Once Off Guard (J.H. Wallis)	The Woman in the Window
"One Night of 21 Hours" (Renato Pestriniero)	Terrore Nello Spazio
Operation Terror (The Gordons)	Experiment in Terror
Orpheus Descending (Tennessee Williams)	The Fugitive Kind
The Other One (Catherine Turney)	Back from the Dead
Our Two Consciences (Paul Anthelme)	I Confess
Out of the Dark (Ursula Curtiss)	I Saw What You Did (1965 & 1988)
The Outsiders (A.E. Marton)	The Glass Tomb
Outward Bound (Sutton Vane)	Between Two Worlds
Ozma of Oz (L. Frank Baum)	Return to Oz
Panther's Moon (Victor Canning)	Spy Hunt
The Paper Chase (John McNally)	The Wickham Mystery
Paradigm Red (Harold King)	Red Alert
Paradise Lost (John Milton)	Satan—or, The Drama of Humanity
Les Parents Terribles (Jean Cocteau)	Intimate Relations
Passport to Oblivion (James Leasor)	Where the Spies Are
The Password to Larkspur Lane (Carolyn Keene)	Nancy Drew, Detective
Path to Savagery (Robert Edmond Alter)	Ravagers
"Patrol" (Philip MacDonald)	The Lost Patrol (1929 & 1934)
Pay the Piper (Peter Howard [Howard Koch])	The Intimate Stranger
Peabody's Mermaid (Guy & Constance Jones)	Mr. Peabody and the Mermaid
The Peaceful Inn (Denis Ogden & T.E.B. Clarke)	Halfway House
Peacock's Feather (George S. Hellman)	A Night in Paradise
The Penal Colony (Richard Herley)	No Escape (1994)
Personal History (Vincent Sheean)	Foreign Correspondent
The Pickwick Papers (Charles Dickens)	Gabriel Grub the Surly Sexton
The Picture of Dorian Gray (Oscar Wilde)	Dorian Gray; The Sins of Dorian Gray
"The Pit and the Pendulum" (Edgar Allan Poe)	The Avenging Conscience; Blood Demon
Pity My Simplicity (Chris Massie)	Love Letters
Planet of the Dead (Stanislaw Lem)	Milczaca Gwiazda
Poison (Claude & Alice Askew)	The Pleydell Mystery
The Poltergeist (Frank Harvey)	Things Happen at Night
"Prelude to Murder" (Walter C. Brown)	The House in the Woods
"The Premature Burial" (Edgar Allan Poe)	The Crime of Dr. Crespi; Haunting Fear; The Living Coffin; Prelude
"Prey" (Richard Matheson)	Trilogy of Terror
"A Problem in Larceny" (Jack Boyle)	Missing Millions
Prometheus Bound (Aeschylus)	The Iliac Passion
Psycho (Robert Bloch)	Bates Motel
The Puppet Masters (Robert A. Heinlein)	The Brain Eaters
The Purple Cloud (Matthew Phipps Shiel)	The World, the Flesh and the Devil
"The Purple Hieroglyph" (Will F. Jenkins)	Murder Will Out (1930)
Puzzle for Fiends (Patrick Quentin)	The Strange Awakening
Query ("Seamark")	Murder in Reverse
Questi Fantasmi (Eduardo De Filippo)	Ghosts—Italian Style
The Raiders (Samuel Crockett)	The Secret of the Loch (1957)
The Rainbird Pattern (Victor Canning)	Family Plot
Random Quest (John Wyndham)	Quest for Love
"Rapaccini's Daughter" (Nathaniel Hawthorne)	Twice-Told Tales
Ratman's Notebooks (Stephen Gilbert)	Willard
The Rats (James Herbert)	Deadly Eyes
The Ravine (Kendal Young)	In the Devil's Garden
Red Alert (Peter Bryant)	Dr. Strangelove: or, How I Learned to Stop Worrying and Love the Bomb
The Return of Bulldog Drummond (Sapper)	Bulldog Drummond's Revenge
Rhinoceros (Eugene Ionesco)	Die Nashorner
Rich is the Treasure (Maurice Procter)	The Diamond
Ride the Pink Horse (Dorothy B. Hughes)	The Hanged Man
The Ringer (Edgar Wallace)	The Gaunt Stranger
The Ring of the Nibelung	Die Nibelungen
"Rip Van Winkle" (Washington Irving)	La Legende de Rip Van Winkle
Rita	The Pointing Finger
"The Rival Dummy" (Ben Hecht)	The Great Gabbo
Robinson Crusoe (Daniel Defoe)	Robinson Crusoe and the Tiger; Robinson Crusoe on Mars
Robur, the Conqueror (Jules Verne)	Master of the World
Rocketship Galileo (Robert A. Heinlein)	Destination Moon
"Room 40, O.B." (Denison Clift)	Secrets of Scotland Yard
Room 13 (Edgar Wallace)	Mr. Reeder in Room 13
The Royal Game (Stefan Zweig)	Brainwashed
The Ruthless Ones (Laurence Moody)	What Became of Jack and Jill
The Saint in Miami (Leslie Charteris)	Le Saint Mene la Dance
Sardonicus (Ray Russell)	Mr. Sardonicus
The Scarecrow (Percy MacKaye)	Puritan Passions

1009

Song Appendix

Song	Film
"Acapulco"	EVE OF DESTRUCTION
"Addicted to Love"	WRAITH, THE
"After All These Years"	TOM THUMB
"Ain't Got You"	VAMPIRE ON BIKINI BEACH
"All for Love"	LURED
"All Gone"	SERVANT, THE
"All I Ever Need is You"	POLISH VAMPIRE IN BURBANK, A
"All I Know for Sure"	WAVELENGTH
"All in Your Mind"	BLOOD SONG
"All Noshed Out"	BEVERLY HILLS BODYSNATCHERS
"All Over You"	DEF BY TEMPTATION
"All Talk"	RADIOACTIVE DREAMS
"All Time High"	OCTOPUSSY
"Alone in Love"	GRAVEYARD SHIFT (1987)
"Alone in the Night"	RETURN OF THE LIVING DEAD, PART II
"Always"	TO DIE FOR
"Always Let Him Know"	CHILLING
"Amado Mio"	GILDA
"American Dream"	VAMPIRE AT MIDNIGHT
"Amor"	SCHOOL SPIRIT
"And Something Ends"	DEATH OF THE INCREDIBLE HULK, THE
"Angela"	DAY AFTER HALLOWEEN, THE
"Angel Eyes"	JENNIFER (1953)
"Angel is Love, An"	BARBARELLA
"Angel of Death"	GREMLINS 2: THE NEW BATCH
"Animal Attraction"	EARTH GIRLS ARE EASY
"Another Goodbye"	VAMPIRE AT MIDNIGHT
"Another Side of Me"	LEGACY, THE
"Are You a Dream?"	TOM THUMB
"Armies of the Night"	FRIGHT NIGHT
"Arrow Through Me"	OH HEAVENLY DOG
"Atmospheric Fragments"	MUTANTS IN PARADISE
"Aurora"	HOLD THAT GHOST
"Ay Si Si"	BLOOD DINER
"Baby Let's Make Love"	BLOOD DINER
"Baby Lied"	NEON MANIACS
"Back Home"	ELIMINATOR, THE
"Back in Business"	DICK TRACY (1990)
"Bad Blood Slam Dance"	MY BEST FRIEND IS A VAMPIRE
"Bad Case of Lovin' You"	RETURN OF THE LIVING DEAD, PART II
"Bad Hangover Everyday I Stay in Love with You"	SCHOOL SPIRIT
"Bad Mistake"	WRAITH, THE
"Bargain with the Devil"	BEYOND THE DOOR
"Be A Lion"	WIZ, THE
"Beautiful Dreamer"	MIGHTY JOE YOUNG
"Believe in Yourself"	WIZ, THE
"Benson Arizona"	DARK STAR
"Better Off Dead"	FEAR, THE (1994)
"Beware the Caribbean"	MANFISH
"Big Fish"	MANFISH
"Birth of the Sandman"	SLEEPSTALKER
"Blackout"	MUTANTS IN PARADISE
"Black Peter"	FEAR, THE (1994)
"Black Queen's Beads"	BARBARELLA
"Blind Alley"	SPELLBINDER
"Bloodstone"	'BURBS, THE
"Blue Night Shadow"	ONCE BITTEN
"Blue to Black"	SLEEPSTALKER
"Body Builder"	TOXIC AVENGER, THE
"Body Heat"	PHANTON OF THE MALL: ERIC'S REVENGE
"Body Talk"	TOXIC AVENGER, THE
"Body to Body"	EARTH GIRLS ARE EASY
"Bomp Me"	ZAPPED!
"Boozers are Losers"	ENDANGERED SPECIES
"Boppin' Tonight"	FRIGHT NIGHT
"Boss of the Block"	BROTHER FROM ANOTHER PLANET, THE
"Boy and a Girl, A"	SCHOOL SPIRIT
"Boy are U Ready"	GETTING LUCKY
"Boys and the Babies, The"	BLINK
"Brain in a Jar"	NIGHTMARE SISTERS
"Brand New Day, A"	WIZ, THE
"Brand New Girl"	EARTH GIRLS ARE EASY
"Brave New Dance"	C.H.U.D. II
"Bright Eyes"	WATERSHIP DOWN
"Broken Dream"	FRIDAY THE 13TH, PART VIII—JASON TAKES MANHATTAN
"Broken Man"	TERROR TRAIN
"Bud the Chud"	C.H.U.D. II
"Burning My Heart Out"	BROTHER FROM ANOTHER PLANET, THE
"Candyman"	WILLY WONKA AND THE CHOCOLATE FACTORY
"Can't Get Much Closer"	GETTING LUCKY
"Can't Let Go"	TO DIE FOR
"Can't We Start Over"	CHILLING
"Captain Coke"	BEWARE! THE BLOB
"Carousel World"	CARNIVAL OF BLOOD
"Castle in Spain"	BABES IN TOYLAND (1961)
"Caught in a Web of Love"	TO DIE FOR II: SON OF DARKNESS
"'Cause I'm a Blond"	EARTH GIRLS ARE EASY
"C'est Moi"	CAMELOT
"Challenge, The"	EDGE OF HELL, THE
"Chase, The"	TOXIC AVENGER, THE
"Che Sera Sera"	MAN WHO KNEW TOO MUCH, THE (1956)
"Choice You Made, The"	NEON MANIACS
"Christmas All Over the World"	SANTA CLAUS (1985)
"Clapping Song, The"	FLATLINERS
"Climbing Up"	KING SOLOMON'S MINES (1937)
"Close Enough for Love"	AGATHA
"Come Back to Me"	ON A CLEAR DAY YOU CAN SEE FOREVER
"Come Love Me Again"	ATTIC, THE
"Come to Me"	FRIGHT NIGHT II
"Coming Back for More"	MY BEST FRIEND IS A VAMPIRE
"Contact"	GRAVEYARD SHIFT (1987)
"Corn Rigs"	WICKER MAN, THE
"Country Rain"	HUMAN EXPERIMENTS
"Crazy in the Night"	VICE VERSA (1988)
"Crazy Over You"	BLOOD DINER
"Cross My Heart"	CONNECTICUT YANKEE IN KING ARTHUR'S COURT, A (1989)
"Cry Little Sister"	LOST BOYS, THE
"Crystal Hearts"	CYBORG 2: GLASS SHADOW
"Cute"	CINDERFELLA
"Cutting Loose"	CHILLING
"Daddy-Bird"	FRANKENSTEIN'S DAUGHTER
"Daddy's Gonna Boogie Tonight"	RADIOACTIVE DREAMS
"Dance Magic"	LABYRINTH (1986)
"Dance of Victory"	JUST IMAGINE
"Dancing Doll"	TO DIE FOR
"Dancing Mary"	NOMADS
"Dancing Shoes"	TOM THUMB
"Danger"	EDGE OF HELL, THE
"Danger Boy"	TOMB, THE
"Danger Danger"	CHILLING
"Dangerous Eyes"	OH, GOD! YOU DEVIL
"Darkest Side of the Night"	FRIDAY THE 13TH, PART VIII—JASON TAKES MANHATTAN
"Day in the Life of a Fool, A"	BLACK ORPHEUS
"Death Knell"	CELLAR DWELLER
"Death Song, The"	THOSE DEAR DEPARTED
"Dedication"	SCHOOL SPIRIT
"Deep Inside Your Love"	FLY II, THE
"Deep in the Jungle"	WEIRD SCIENCE
"Defiance"	DANCE OF THE DWARFS
"Desert Rain"	MONOLITH
"Dinero"	BROTHER FROM ANOTHER PLANET, THE
"Ding Dong, the Witch is Dead"	WIZARD OF OZ, THE (1939)
"Dizzy Tonite"	VIDEO DEAD, THE
"Doin' Those Things You Do"	SCHOOL SPIRIT
"Don is Alive!, The"	BEVERLY HILLS BODYSNATCHERS
"Don't Ever Go Away"	CARNIVAL OF BLOOD
"Don't Follow Me"	MY BEST FRIEND IS A VAMPIRE
"Don't Turn Away"	HOWARD THE DUCK
"Don't Wait"	PHANTOM OF THE MALL: ERIC'S REVENGE
"Do the Right Thing"	PEOPLE UNDER THE STAIRS, THE
"Do the Zombie Stomp"	HORROR OF PARTY BEACH, THE
"Doubleback"	BACK TO THE FUTURE, PART II
"Down in Louisiana"	ATTACK OF THE 50-FOOT WOMAN (1993)
"Down in the Meadow"	RIVER OF NO RETURN
"Dream of Romance"	LILIOM (1930)
"Dreams to Remember"	DREAM A LITTLE DREAM
"Dress to Kill"	DREAM A LITTLE DREAM
"Drinking Song, The"	JUST IMAGINE
"Drop Kick Me Jesus"	TREMORS
"Ease on Down the Road"	WIZ, THE
"Easy Money"	PHANTOM OF THE MALL: ERIC'S REVENGE
"Eat Raw Meat"	FLESH-EATING MOTHERS
"Eat You Alive"	RADIOACTIVE DREAMS
"Eeny, Meeny, Miney, Mo"	I WAS A TEENAGE WEREWOLF
"Enemy Lines"	TO DIE FOR II: SON OF DARKNESS
"Energy"	EDGE OF HELL, THE
"Enough Is Never Enough"	WHEN THE BOUGH BREAKS
"Eternal Woman"	SHE (1983)
"Everybody Get Some"	BLOOD DINER
"Every Now and Then"	GREAT GABBO, THE
"Every Step of the Way"	GOTHAM
"(Everything I Do) I Do It for You"	ROBIN HOOD: PRINCE OF THIEVES
"Evil Dream"	Q
"Exits and Truck Stops"	CREATURE FROM BLACK LAKE
"Face to Face"	DEF BY TEMPTATION; ONCE BITTEN
"Fade to Black"	PROM NIGHT
"Fall Break"	MUTILATOR, THE
"Falling"	MONOLITH
"Fear, Flesh and Blood"	FEAR, THE (1994)

"'59 Volvo"	BLOOD DINER
"Fire Doesn't Burn"	DEVIL'S GIFT, THE
"Fits Like a Glove"	GETTING LUCKY
"5 O'Clock World"	SWEET SIXTEEN
"Flesh"	ALIEN WARRIOR
"Flesh & Fire"	MONOLITH
"Flesh to Flesh"	RETURN OF THE LIVING DEAD, PART II
"Floretta"	BABES IN TOYLAND (1961)
"Fly Away"	FIFTH FLOOR, THE
"Follow Me"	CAMELOT
"Fool"	DEF BY TEMPTATION
"Forest of No Return, The"	BABES IN TOYLAND (1961)
"For Love"	C.H.U.D. II
"For You I'd Die"	TO DIE FOR
"Freedom Sings"	SOLAR CRISIS
"Free Fall"	PUMPKINHEAD II: BLOOD WINGS
"Frodo of the Nine Fingers, and the Ring of Doom"	RETURN OF THE KING, THE
"Funky Love"	TERROR TRAIN
"Future's So Bright, I Gotta Wear Shades, The"	DREAM A LITTLE DREAM; MY BEST FRIEND IS A VAMPIRE
"Galaxy Glue"	INCREDIBLE SHRINKING WOMAN, THE
"Gamblin'"	ELIMINATOR, THE
"Gangster Rock"	GRADUATION DAY
"Gently Johnny"	WICKER MAN, THE
"Geronimo"	GHOST IN THE INVISIBLE BIKINI, THE
"Getaway"	BROTHER FROM ANOTHER PLANET, THE
"Get Dead"	MIDNIGHT HOUR, THE
"Get It Right"	VAMPIRE AT MIDNIGHT
"Ghoul in School, The"	LYCANTHROPUS
"Girl from Rio, The"	FUTURE WOMEN
"Give It Up"	FRIGHT NIGHT
"Give Me Love"	DR. TERROR'S HOUSE OF HORRORS
"Go Away"	PUMPKINHEAD II: BLOOD WINGS
"God Bless Us Every One"	CHRISTMAS CAROL, A (1984)
"Goodbye"	MANFISH
"Goodbye, Little Yellow Bird"	PICTURE OF DORIAN GRAY, THE (1945)
"Good Man in a Bad Time"	FRIGHT NIGHT
"Good Time Lady"	CHILLING
"Go to Sleep"	BABES IN TOYLAND (1961)
"Got to Believe in Magic"	ZAPPED!
"Got to Have It"	EVE OF DESTRUCTION
"Graduation Day Blues"	GRADUATION DAY
"Gravity"	COCOON
"Greatest Adventure, The"	HOBBIT, THE
"Green Side of the Mountain"	KINGDOM OF THE SPIDERS
"Greet the Teacher"	RETURN TO HORROR HIGH
"Ground You Walk On, The"	EARTH GIRLS ARE EASY
"Guantanamera"	PUMPKINHEAD II: BLOOD WINGS
"Guilty Pleasures"	RADIOACTIVE DREAMS
"Guys Like Girls"	C.H.U.D. II
"Hands Off"	ONCE BITTEN
"Hard to Believe"	MY SCIENCE PROJECT
"Hard to Find"	UNINVITED (1987)
"Have a Heart"	HEART CONDITION
"Heads Will Turn"	EDGE OF HELL, THE
"Hearse Burnin' Rubber"	BEVERLY HILLS BODYSNATCHERS
"Heart"	DAMN YANKEES
"Heartbeat Getting Stronger"	MY BEST FRIEND IS A VAMPIRE
"Heart of a Working Man"	TREMORS
"Heart of Darkness"	PHANTOM OF THE MALL: ERIC'S REVENGE
"Hearts, Not Diamonds"	FAN, THE
"Hearts vs. Heads"	WRAITH, THE
"Heaven in Paradise"	BLOOD DINER
"He Isn't You"	ON A CLEAR DAY YOU CAN SEE FOR-EVER
"He's the Wizard"	WIZ, THE
"Here Comes Mr. Fun Hog"	SCHOOL SPIRIT
"Here Come the Gravedigger"	FEAR, THE (1994)
"Here in Darkness"	SORORITY BABES IN THE SLIMEBALL BOWL-A-RAMA
"He'll Be There"	DR. JEKYLL AND SISTER HYDE
"Hey, Hey, Hey, and a Hi Ho"	ANGEL, ANGEL, DOWN WE GO
"Hey Party Girl"	SORORITY BABES IN THE SLIMEBALL BOWL-A-RAMA
"Hey, There's a Bikini in My Casket"	BEVERLY HILLS BODY-SNATCHERS
"High Priest of Love"	RETURN OF THE LIVING DEAD, PART II
"Hit and Run"	MY SCIENCE PROJECT
"Hit Me"	EARTH GIRLS ARE EASY
"Hold Me"	THREE FACES OF EVE, THE
"Hold On Blue Eyes"	WRAITH, THE
"Hold the Light"	ALIEN WARRIOR
"Hole in One"	GETTING LUCKY
"Home"	WIZ, THE
"Homeboy"	BROTHER FROM ANOTHER PLANET, THE
"Hot for You Tonight"	SCHOOL SPIRIT
"Howling Chicken"	HOWLING, THE
"How Long"	SWEET SIXTEEN
"How to Handle a Woman"	CAMELOT
"Hunger City"	HOWARD THE DUCK
"Hungry for Me Again"	DEF BY TEMPTATION
"Hushabye Mountain"	CHITTY CHITTY BANG BANG
"Hyde's Got Nothing to Hide"	JEKYLL AND HYDE...TOGETHER AGAIN
"I Ain't What You Need"	PUMPKINHEAD II: BLOOD WINGS
"I'm a Hungry Man"	C.H.U.D. II
"I'm Alive"	XANADU
"I'm Dangerous"	ZOMBIE NIGHTMARE
"I'm Gonna File My Claim"	RIVER OF NO RETURN
"I'm Laughing"	GREAT GABBO, THE
"I'm On My Way"	HOWARD THE DUCK
"I'm Ready"	GREMLINS 2: THE NEW BATCH
"I'm Restless"	STARCROSSED
"I'm the Man"	RETURN OF THE LIVING DEAD, PART II
"I Am the Words, You Are the Melody"	JUST IMAGINE
"I Can't Do the Sum"	BABES IN TOYLAND (1961)
"I Can't Stop"	WHEN THE BOUGH BREAKS
"I Can Still Shine"	MAID TO ORDER
"I Cry"	SLEEPSTALKER
"I Don't Want to Be Alone Tonight"	NEON MANIACS
"If Ever I Would Leave You"	CAMELOT
"If I Loved You"	CAROUSEL
"If I Only Had a Brain"	WIZARD OF OZ, THE (1939)
"If It Was Only Up to Me"	OH, GOD! YOU DEVIL
"If My Love is Blind"	SPELLBINDER
"I Give It All to You"	LOST HORIZON (1973)
"I Hate People"	SCROOGE (1970)
"I've Written a Letter to Daddy"	WHAT EVER HAPPENED TO BABY JANE? (1962)
"I Hear the Back Beat"	PRINCESS WARRIOR
"I Like 'em Big and Stupid"	EARTH GIRLS ARE EASY
"I Loved You Once in Silence"	CAMELOT
"I Love the Night Life"	LOVE AT FIRST BITE
"In and Out"	DEF BY TEMPTATION
"In a Sexy Mood"	DEF BY TEMPTATION
"Incense, Peppermint"	PSYCH-OUT
"I Need an Alibi"	PHANTOM OF THE MALL: ERIC'S REVENGE
"I Need You"	SINS OF DORIAN GRAY, THE
"Inner Manipulations"	PRESIDENT'S ANALYST, THE
"Insulated Man"	BLINK
"In These Hard Times"	STUDY IN TERROR, A
"Into the Mystic"	DREAM A LITTLE DREAM
"I Saw a Light"	HENDERSON MONSTER, THE
"Is There a Phantom in the Mall?"	PHANTOM OF THE MALL: ERIC'S REVENGE
"Is This What Feeling Gets?"	WIZ, THE
"It Don't Come Cheap"	HOWARD THE DUCK
"I Think We're Alone Now"	MOTHER'S DAY
"It's a Cowboy Lovin' Night"	TREMORS
"It's Raining Dreams"	BEYOND TOMORROW
"It's So Easy Not to Try"	RETURN OF THE KING, THE
"It's Still Love"	PUMPKINHEAD II: BLOOD WINGS
"It's the End of the World As We Know It (And I Feel Fine)"	DREAM A LITTLE DREAM
"It's the Night Again"	HE KNOWS YOU'RE ALONE
"It's This Love"	TOXIC AVENGER, THE
"It's You Who Said It"	TO DIE FOR
"I Want More"	SCHOOL SPIRIT
"I Want You"	STEPFATHER, THE
"I'll Be There"	TOO SCARED TO SCREAM
"I'll Never Tie You Down"	HE KNOWS YOU'RE ALONE
"I Will Wait for You"	PARAPLUIES DE CHERBOURG, LES
"I Wonder What the King is Doing Tonight"	CAMELOT
"J.J. Blues"	FRIDAY THE 13TH, PART VIII—JASON TAKES MANHATTAN
"Jawbreaker"	PRINCESS WARRIOR
"Jenny"	LADY IN THE DARK
"Jerusalem Ridge"	BLINK
"Jubilation T. Cornpone"	LI'L ABNER (1959)
"June is Bustin' Out All Over"	CAROUSEL
"Just a Whisper Away"	BABES IN TOYLAND (1961)
"Just for Fun"	ZAPPED!
"Just Like You (Theme from PUMPKINHEAD II)"	PUMPKINHEAD II: BLOOD WINGS
"Just One Kiss"	ONCE BITTEN
"Key, The"	CHILLING
"Kick Around"	ROLLER BLADE WARRIORS: TAKEN BY FORCE
"Kick Around Me"	TOMB, THE
"Killer, The"	GRADUATION DAY
"Kinda Insane"	BEVERLY HILLS BODYSNATCHERS
"King and Queen of Hearts"	ZAPPED!
"King of the Streets"	ALIEN WARRIOR
"Kiss"	NIAGARA
"Kiss Me Where It Hurts"	SCHOOL SPIRIT
"Kiss My Stinky White Ass"	DESTROYER
"Kukuana"	KING SOLOMON'S MINES (1937)
"Ladybird"	FRIGHT (1971)
"Lament"	OMAR KHAYYAM
"Laying Down the Law"	LOST BOYS, THE
"Lay It on the Line"	TOXIC AVENGER, THE
"Laziest Gal in Town, The"	STAGE FRIGHT

"Leave My Monkey Alone"	TARZAN IN MANHATTAN
"Leave Tomorrow 'till It Comes"	RETURN OF THE KING, THE
"Let Me Be a People"	CINDERFELLA
"Let Me Give You Money"	BLOOD DINER
"Let's Fall Apart Together Tonight"	Q
"Let's Stay Young Forever"	DOWN TO EARTH
"Let's Take a Drive to Beverly Hills"	BEVERLY HILLS BODY-SNATCHERS
"Let's Talk"	FRIGHT NIGHT
"Lies"	ROLLER BLADE WARRIORS: TAKEN BY FORCE
"Life is a Precious Thing"	ASSASSINATION BUREAU, THE
"Lisa"	REAR WINDOW
"Little Lucille"	MUTANTS IN PARADISE
"Live Alone and Like It"	DICK TRACY (1990)
"Live It Up"	EDGE OF HELL, THE
"Living in the City"	FRIDAY THE 13TH, PART VIII—JASON TAKES MANHATTAN
"Living on the Edge"	VAMPIRE ON BIKINI BEACH
"Livin' on the Brink"	LUCIFER COMPLEX, THE
"Loaded with Love"	VAMPIRE ON BIKINI BEACH
"Locked in a Cage"	'BURBS, THE
"Lock, Stock and Teardrops"	FLY II, THE
"Long Summer"	ELIMINATOR, THE
"Look for a Star"	CIRCUS OF HORRORS
"Looking for Clues"	RETURN OF THE LIVING DEAD, PART II
"Look of Love, The"	CASINO ROYALE
"Lost Incas"	BLOOD DINER
"Lost in Love Again"	ELIMINATOR, THE
"Lost in the Shadows"	LOST BOYS, THE
"Love Attack"	TO DIE FOR II: SON OF DARKNESS
"Love Came for Me"	SPLASH
"Love Changes Everything"	GETTING LUCKY
"Love Handgrenade"	FRANKENHOOKER
"Love is Love"	ELECTRIC DREAMS
"Love Me Till I Die"	PROM NIGHT
"Lover's Language"	ELIMINATOR, THE
"Love's Hiding Place"	SEDUCTION, THE
"Love Shriek"	SHRIEK OF THE MUTILATED
"Loves of Omar Khayyam, The"	OMAR KHAYYAM
"Love Will Make Your Mind Go Wild"	BLOOD DINER
"Love with All the Trimmings"	ON A CLEAR DAY YOU CAN SEE FOREVER
"Love Won't Be"	BLINK
"Lucky Strike"	GRADUATION DAY
"Lusty Month of May, The"	CAMELOT
"Machine"	'BURBS, THE
"Madam's Song, The"	SEVEN-PER-CENT SOLUTION, THE
"Maggy"	I COME IN PEACE
"Magic"	XANADU
"Make Some Noise"	'BURBS, THE
"Make the Music Pretty"	GHOST IN THE INVISIBLE BIKINI, THE
"Makin' Up for Lost Time"	INITIATION, THE
"Man for Me"	RETURN TO HORROR HIGH
"Man in the Mask, The"	LEGEND OF THE LONE RANGER, THE
"Man Talk"	C.H.U.D. II
"Man Turned Inside Out"	SLAUGHTERHOUSE ROCK
"March of the Monsters"	GODZILLA'S REVENGE
"March of the Toys"	BABES IN TOYLAND (1961)
"Master Dancer"	CELLAR DWELLER
"Matter of the Heart"	WRAITH, THE
"Maybe It's Love"	EDGE OF HELL, THE
"Me and My Rhythm Box"	LIQUID SKY
"Melinda"	ON A CLEAR DAY YOU CAN SEE FOREVER
"Melissa"	SWEET SIXTEEN
"Method to My Madness"	WEIRD SCIENCE
"Midnight"	TO DIE FOR II: SON OF DARKNESS
"Midnight Again"	MIDNIGHT (1980)
"Midnight Kiss"	VAMPIRE AT MIDNIGHT
"Mimi"	LOVE ME TONIGHT
"Mind Benders"	ALIEN HIGH
"Mindmaker Song, The"	ATTACK OF THE KILLER TOMATOES
"Miracles"	MIRACLE ON 34TH STREET (1973)
"Misery"	MONOLITH
"Molly Malone"	PREMATURE BURIAL, THE
"Monsters"	FLESH-EATING MOTHERS
"Moon's a Window to Heaven, The"	STAR TREK V: THE FINAL FRONTIER
"Moonlight Music"	EVERYTHING'S DUCKY
"Morning After, The"	POSEIDON ADVENTURE, THE
"Mother Lover"	ANGEL, ANGEL, DOWN WE GO
"Mothers Ought to Tell Their Daughters"	JUST IMAGINE
"Move"	DICK TRACY (1990)
"My Baby's Back"	POLISH VAMPIRE IN BURBANK, A
"My Boy, Bill"	CAROUSEL
"My Friend the Doctor"	DR. DOLITTLE
"My Heroine"	WHEN THE BOUGH BREAKS
"My Lonely Life"	CARA DEL TERROR, LA
"My Love is Like a Red, Red Rose"	JOURNEY TO THE CENTER OF THE EARTH (1959)
"My Mind's Made Up"	MY SCIENCE PROJECT
"My Spirit Runs Free"	CAPTURE OF BIGFOOT, THE
"My Star"	EWOKS: THE BATTLE FOR ENDOR
"Mystery Baby"	CELLAR DWELLER
"Mystery Lover"	HE KNOWS YOU'RE ALONE
"Natural, Natural Baby"	BEGINNING OF THE END, THE
"Nature Boy"	BOY WITH GREEN HAIR, THE
"Nearer to Morning"	C.H.U.D. II
"Nervous and Shakey"	WEIRD SCIENCE
"Never, Never Wed"	JUST IMAGINE
"Never Say No"	FRANKENHOOKER
"Never Surrender"	WRAITH, THE
"Never Swat a Fly"	JUST IMAGINE
"Never Turn Away"	DREAM A LITTLE DREAM
"Next Train Out, The"	BLOOD OF DRACULA'S CASTLE
"Nicole"	TRANSMUTATIONS
"Night Has Many Eyes, The"	NIGHT WATCH
"Nightmare"	RADIOACTIVE DREAMS
"Night on the Town, A"	ECHOES
"Nobody Does It Better"	SPY WHO LOVED ME, THE
"No More Lonely Days"	WAVELENGTH
"No More Tears"	MISSION MARS
"Nothing at All"	TOXIC AVENGER, THE
"Nothing Changes"	CELLAR DWELLER
"Nothing's Gonna Stop Us Now"	MANNEQUIN
"Nothing That is Possible"	CYBORG 2: GLASS SHADOW
"Not Me"	INITIATION, THE
"Oedipus Rex"	THOSE DEAR DEPARTED
"Old Bamboo, The"	CHITTY CHITTY BANG BANG
"Old Man Moon"	TOPPER (1937)
"On a Mission"	DEF BY TEMPTATION
"Once a Year Night"	MAN IN THE SANTA CLAUS SUIT, THE
"One Dream at a Time"	SVENGALI (1983)
"One for All and All for One"	SATAN'S CHEERLEADERS
"One for All, All for One"	IRON MASK, THE
"One More Try"	UNINVITED (1987)
"One Silver Dollar"	RIVER OF NO RETURN
"One Way or Another"	MY BEST FRIEND IS A VAMPIRE
"Only One, The"	SLAUGHTERHOUSE ROCK
"Only Roses for You"	DEVIL'S GIFT, THE
"Open My Eyes"	MAD ROOM, THE
"Open Your Eyes and Dream"	MIRACLE ON 34TH STREET (1973)
"Orion"	ELIMINATOR, THE
"Orlop Piano"	SOLAR CRISIS
"Out for the Kill"	ZOMBIE NIGHTMARE
"Out on the Run"	STARCROSSED
"Over the Rainbow"	WIZARD OF OZ, THE (1939)
"Pandora's Box"	FRANKENHOOKER
"Part of You"	SLAUGHTERHOUSE ROCK
"Party Town"	FLATLINERS
"Pass Away"	MUTANTS IN PARADISE
"Peaceful Verde Valley"	KINGDOM OF THE SPIDERS
"People Have More Fun Than Anyone"	DOWN TO EARTH
"Personality"	ROAD TO UTOPIA, THE
"Planet of Love"	PUNISHER, THE
"Poor Albert"	I DISMEMBER MAMA
"Popcorn"	SHRIEK OF THE MUTILATED
"Power Love"	WRAITH, THE
"Power of Love, The"	BACK TO THE FUTURE
"Power of the Night"	CRITTERS
"Power of Your Suggestion"	MY BEST FRIEND IS A VAMPIRE
"Private Joy"	WEIRD SCIENCE
"Promised Land"	BROTHER FROM ANOTHER PLANET, THE
"Psychedelic Man"	RADIOACTIVE DREAMS
"Puberty Love"	ATTACK OF THE KILLER TOMATOES
"Pull Up to the Bumper"	TARZAN IN MANHATTAN
"Put on Your Hi-Heels"	PRINCESS WARRIOR
"Put the Blame on Mame"	GILDA
"Putting the Night on Hold"	BLOOD DINER
"Questa O Quella"	'BURBS, THE
"Question Me an Answer"	LOST HORIZON (1973)
"Reach Out and Rock Somebody"	TO DIE FOR II: SON OF DARKNESS
"Read to Break"	ALIEN WARRIOR
"Ready or Not"	ZAPPED!
"Real Me, The"	VENGEANCE OF FU MANCHU, THE
"Rebel Yell"	WRAITH, THE
"Rebirth"	ZOMBIE NIGHTMARE
"Red Hot"	MUTANTS IN PARADISE
"Reefer Man"	INTERNATIONAL HOUSE
"Relax"	BODY DOUBLE
"Remarkable Woman, A"	FAN, THE
"Rescue Me"	SHE (1983)
"Return to Paradise"	OH HEAVENLY DOG
"Right or Wrong"	MARTA
"Right Way, The"	PUMPKINHEAD II: BLOOD WINGS
"Road Leads to Nowhere, The"	LAST HOUSE ON THE LEFT, THE
"Roads"	RETURN OF THE KING, THE
"Rock Me All Night"	NEON MANIACS
"Rock Myself to Sleep"	FRIGHT NIGHT
"Rocky Mountain Waltz"	HOWLING, THE
"Romance of Elmer Stremingway, The"	JUST IMAGINE
"Round and Round"	EVE OF DESTRUCTION

"Rumanian Folk Dance"	TO DIE FOR II: SON OF DARKNESS
"Runaway"	VAMPIRE ON BIKINI BEACH
"Runaway Blues"	SON OF KONG
"Run Between the Raindrops"	STEPFATHER, THE
"Running"	PHANTOM OF THE MALL: ERIC'S REVENGE
"Safe Beneath the Water"	CHILLING
"Same Man I Was Before"	MY BEST FRIEND IS A VAMPIRE
"Saturday Nite Rockers"	TOMB, THE
"Save Me Tonight"	FRIGHT NIGHT
"S.O.S."	SWEET SIXTEEN
"Save the Earth"	GODZILLA VS. THE SMOG MONSTER
"Savior"	ROLLER BLADE WARRIORS: TAKEN BY FORCE
"Say This to Me"	FRIDAY THE 13TH, PART VIII—JASON TAKES MANHATTAN
"Scary Movies"	RETURN TO HORROR HIGH
"Scream in the Night"	SHE (1983)
"Scream Machine"	MY BEST FRIEND IS A VAMPIRE
"Scream of Angels"	WRAITH, THE
"Seasons of Love"	UNINVITED (1987)
"Seaweed"	NIGHT TIDE
"Second Wind"	EVE OF DESTRUCTION
"Secret Loser"	WRAITH, THE
"Seli"	MISSION STARDUST
"Sensual One, The"	PHANTOM OF THE MALL: ERIC'S REVENGE
"Sensuous Tiger"	CAPTURE OF BIGFOOT, THE
"Set Me Free"	SLAUGHTERHOUSE ROCK
"Set the Night to Music"	VICE VERSA (1988)
"Seven at Once"	GOODBYE CHARLIE
"Sex and the Single Man"	DEF BY TEMPTATION
"Sex is a Weapon"	MY BEST FRIEND IS A VAMPIRE
"Shake It Out"	BLOOD DINER
"Shame on You"	PHANTOM OF THE MALL: ERIC'S REVENGE
"She's a Fire"	RADIOACTIVE DREAMS
"She's a Siren"	PUMPKINHEAD II: BLOOD WINGS
"She Makes Me Crazy"	ONCE BITTEN
"She'll Burn You"	RADIOACTIVE DREAMS
"Shock Value"	MUTANTS IN PARADISE
"Shoot the Moon"	ZAPPED!
"Show Me Your Spine"	ROBOCOP
"Simon Bar Sinister"	NEW YEAR'S EVIL
"Simple Joys of Maidenhood, The"	CAMELOT
"Single Life for Me"	ROLLER BLADE WARRIORS: TAKEN BY FORCE
"Siren's Song"	SPELLBINDER
"Situation"	GREMLINS 2: THE NEW BATCH
"Sleep Baby Sleep"	SLEEPSTALKER
"Sleeping Beauty"	STEPFATHER, THE
"Sling Shot"	GREMLINS 2: THE NEW BATCH
"Slowly He Sank into the Sea"	BABES IN TOYLAND (1961)
"Small Things"	RETURN OF THE KING, THE
"Smokin' in the Boys Room"	WRAITH, THE
"Smooth & Cool"	ALIEN WARRIOR
"Somebody Stop This Madness"	EMBASSY
"Something Called Love"	GAZEBO, THE
"Something Evil, Something Dangerous"	HOWLING IV
"Somewhere In Between"	CHINA SYNDROME, THE
"Song for Guy"	OH HEAVENLY DOG
"Sooner or Later (I Always Get My Man)"	DICK TRACY (1990)
"Sorority Sister Succubus"	NIGHTMARE SISTERS
"Souls Not for Sale"	PUMPKINHEAD II: BLOOD WINGS
"Sound of 'Goodbye,' The"	HOUSE OF THE DEAD, THE
"Spacehopper"	RETURN OF THE LIVING DEAD, PART II
"Sparrow"	STANLEY
"Speak Low When You Speak Love"	ONE TOUCH OF VENUS
"Special Date"	FRANKENSTEIN'S DAUGHTER
"Stalker's Rocker"	FRIDAY THE 13TH, PART VIII—JASON TAKES MANHATTAN
"Stand Tall"	ATTACK OF THE 50-FOOT WOMAN (1993)
"Stand Up and Fight"	GHOST IN THE INVISIBLE BIKINI, THE
"Star Spangled Baby"	ZAPPED!
"Start a New World"	STANLEY
"Start the Day"	BEN
"Steal Your Thunder"	EDGE OF HELL, THE
"Stella by Starlight"	UNINVITED, THE (1944)
"Steppin' Right"	VAMPIRE AT MIDNIGHT
"Stop Following Me"	INITIATION, THE
"Stop Talking about Us"	ONCE BITTEN
"Strange Pursuit"	HIDEOUS SUN DEMON, THE
"Stranger, The"	ELIMINATOR, THE
"Strangers"	NOMADS
"Strike"	FRIDAY THE 13TH, PART VIII—JASON TAKES MANHATTAN
"String Quartet in G"	UNINVITED (1987)
"String Trio in D"	SCHOOL SPIRIT
"Stud Party"	BLOOD DINER
"Suburbia"	FLESH-EATING MOTHERS
"Sucker"	VAMPIRE ON BIKINI BEACH
"Summer of Love"	EARTH GIRLS ARE EASY
"Sun in My Eyes"	TAM LIN
"Surfomatic 2000"	BEVERLY HILLS BODYSNATCHERS
"Suspension"	BUCK ROGERS IN THE 25TH CENTURY
"Sweet Innocence"	MONOLITH
"Sweet Nothing"	SORCERERS, THE
"Tailspin"	ECHOES
"Take My Heart"	OMAR KHAYYAM
"Talented Shoes, The"	TOM THUMB
"Talk to the Animals"	DR. DOLITTLE
"Tamara's Bio Project"	FRIDAY THE 13TH, PART VIII—JASON TAKES MANHATTAN
"Taste of Latin, A"	PUMPKINHEAD II: BLOOD WINGS
"Tell-Tale Harp, The"	NIGHT TIDE
"Temper Tantrum"	NEW YEAR'S EVIL
"Tesla Girls"	WEIRD SCIENCE
"Texas Flash"	INITIATION, THE
"Thank You Very Much"	SCROOGE (1970)
"Theme for Valerie"	CHILLING
"There Goes That Song Again"	STRAIT-JACKET
"There's No One in My Heart But You"	JUNGLE GOD-DESS
"There's Something About an Old-Fashioned Girl"	JUST IMAGINE
"Thief Song"	LILIOM (1930)
"Things I Treasure"	KINGDOM OF THE SPIDERS
"This Is the Beat"	BEVERLY HILLS BODYSNATCHERS
"This Power of Ours"	ZAPPED!
"Those Were the Days"	WRAITH, THE
"Those Were the Good Old Days"	DAMN YANKEES
"Throb"	EARTH GIRLS ARE EASY
"Thumbs Up"	I COME IN PEACE
"Ticket, The"	ATTIC, THE
"Tickin' of the Clock"	RADIOACTIVE DREAMS
"Time Goes By"	MR. SYCAMORE
"Time of Our Lives"	FIVE GOLDEN DRAGONS
"Time Out of Mind"	ECHOES
"Time Runs Wild"	DREAM A LITTLE DREAM
"Today, Tonight and Tomorrow"	SO SAD ABOUT GLORIA
"Together in Electric Dreams"	ELECTRIC DREAMS
"Tomato Stomp"	ATTACK OF THE KILLER TOMATOES
"Tomorrow is a Foreign Land"	BIG GAME, THE
"Tonight"	PHANTOM OF THE MALL: ERIC'S REVENGE
"Too Bad You're Crazy"	APRIL FOOL'S DAY
"Too Many Nights"	ATTACK OF THE 50-FOOT WOMAN (1993)
"Toot Sweets"	CHITTY CHITTY BANG BANG
"Torment"	SCREAM, BLACULA, SCREAM
"Torn and Tattered"	TO DIE FOR
"Touch Me One More Time"	DARK MIRROR (1984)
"Touch Me Tonight"	I COME IN PEACE
"Toxic Lover"	TOXIC AVENGER, PART II, THE
"Toyland"	BABES IN TOYLAND (1961)
"Transfer Station Blue"	RETURN (1985)
"Treat Me"	NEON MANIACS
"Truly Scrmptious"	CHITTY CHITTY BANG BANG
"Trust No Man"	FEAR, THE (1994)
"Tryin to Kill a Saturday Night"	ZAPPED!
"Try Me"	TOMB, THE
"Try to Run"	MUTANTS IN PARADISE
"Turn Away"	RADIOACTIVE DREAMS
"Turn It On"	WEIRD SCIENCE
"Turn Out the Light"	CHILLING
"Turn to Me"	TOXIC AVENGER, PART II, THE
"Twila Star"	PUMPKINHEAD II: BLOOD WINGS
"Twisted"	TOMB, THE
"Two Marys"	WHEN THE BOUGH BREAKS
"Two People in the World"	BROTHER FROM ANOTHER PLANET, THE
"Tyranny"	TO DIE FOR
"Ugly"	I COME IN PEACE
"Underground"	LABYRINTH (1986)
"Underneath the Mango Tree"	DR. NO
"Updike's Theme"	ZAPPED!
"Up There"	UNNAMABLE, THE
"Vernon's Theme"	HORROR HIGH
"Vicious Minds"	PUNISHER, THE
"View from the Window"	RETURN (1985)
"Voo Doo Stew"	PRINCESS WARRIOR
"Wake Up Call"	WRAITH, THE
"Walk with Me"	BOG
"Waltzing Matilda"	ON THE BEACH
"Wanted Man"	WEIRD SCIENCE
"War"	SHE (1983)
"Warmer Than a Whisper"	ROAD TO HONG KONG, THE
"Warm Side of the Door, The"	SILENT NIGHT, DEADLY NIGHT
"Was a Time"	SOLAR CRISIS
"We're Off to See the Wizard"	WIZARD OF OZ, THE (1939)
"We Are Survivors"	SURVIVOR
"Wednesday's Child"	QUILLER MEMORANDUM, THE
"We Don't Need Another Hero"	MAD MAX BEYOND THUNDERDOME
"We Hate You"	NEON MANIACS
"We Have All the Time in the World"	ON HER MAJESTY'S SECRET SERVICE
"We Live to Rock"	EDGE OF HELL, THE
"We May Never Love Like This Again"	TOWERING INFERNO, THE

BOSTON BLACKIE:

Boston Blackie's Little Pal, 1918, Metro. <u>W</u>: Bert Lytell;
Blackie's Redemption, 1919, Metro. <u>W</u>: Bert Lytell;
Missing Millions, 1922, Para. <u>W</u>: David Powell;
The Face in the Fog, 1922, Para. <u>W</u>: Lionel Barrymore;
Boston Blackie, 1923, Fox. <u>W</u>: William Russell;
Crooked Alley, 1923, Univ. <u>W</u>: Thomas Carrigan;
Through the Dark, 1924, Goldwyn. <u>W</u>: Forrest Stanley;
The Return of Boston Blackie, 1927, Chadwick. <u>W</u>: Raymond Glenn; *Meet Boston Blackie*, 1941, Col. <u>W</u>: Chester Morris;
Confessions of Boston Blackie, 1941, Col. <u>W</u>: Chester Morris;
Alias Boston Blackie, 1942, Col. <u>W</u>: Chester Morris; *Boston Blackie Goes Hollywood*, 1942, Col. <u>W</u>: Chester Morris;
After Midnight with Boston Blackie, 1943, Col. <u>W</u>: Chester Morris;
The Chance of a Lifetime, 1943, Col. <u>W</u>: Chester Morris;
One Mysterious Night, 1944, Col. <u>W</u>: Chester Morris; *Boston Blackie Booked on Suspicion*, 1945, Col. <u>W</u>: Chester Morris;
Boston Blackie's Rendezvous, 1945, Col. <u>W</u>: Chester Morris;
A Close Call for Boston Blackie, 1946, Col. <u>W</u>: Chester Morris; *The Phantom Thief*, 1946, Col. <u>W</u>: Chester Morris;
Boston Blackie and the Law, 1946, Col. <u>W</u>: Chester Morris;
Trapped by Boston Blackie, 1948, Col. <u>W</u>: Chester Morris;
Boston Blackie's Chinese Venture, 1949, Col. <u>W</u>: Chester Morris

BULLDOG DRUMMOND:

Bulldog Drummond, 1923, Astra-Nat'l. <u>W</u>: Carlyle Blackwell;
Bulldog Drummond's Third Round, 1925, Astra-Nat'l. <u>W</u>: Jack Buchanan;
Bulldog Drummond, 1929, UA. <u>W</u>: Ronald Colman;
Temple Tower, 1930, Fox. <u>W</u>: Kenneth MacKenna;
Bulldog Drummond Strikes Back, 1934, UA. <u>W</u>: Ronald Colman;
The Return of Bulldog Drummond, 1934, BIP-Wardour. <u>W</u>: Ralph Richardson;
Bulldog Jack, 1935, Gaumont British. <u>W</u>: Athole Fleming;
Bulldog Drummond Escapes, 1937, Para. <u>W</u>: Ray Milland;
Bulldog Drummond at Bay, 1937, Rep. <u>W</u>: John Lodge;
Bulldog Drummond Comes Back, 1937, Para. <u>W</u>: John Howard;
Bulldog Drummond's Revenge, 1937, Para. <u>W</u>: John Howard;
Bulldog Drummond's Peril, 1938, Para. <u>W</u>: John Howard;
Bulldog Drummond in Africa, 1938, Para. <u>W</u>: John Howard;
Bulldog Drummond's Secret Police, 1939, Para. <u>W</u>: John Howard;
Bulldog Drummond's Bride, 1939, Para. <u>W</u>: John Howard;
Arrest Bulldog Drummond, 1939, Para. <u>W</u>: John Howard;
Bulldog Drummond at Bay, 1947, Col. <u>W</u>: Ron Randell;
Bulldog Drummond Strikes Back, 1947, Col. <u>W</u>: Ron Randell;
The Challenge, 1948, 20th-Fox. <u>W</u>: Tom Conway;
13 Lead Soldiers, 1948, 20th-Fox. <u>W</u>: Tom Conway; *Calling Bulldog Drummond*, 1951, MGM. <u>W</u>: Walter Pidgeon;
Deadlier Than the Male, 1967, Rank/Univ. <u>W</u>: Richard Johnson;
Some Girls Do, 1969, Rank. <u>W</u>: Richard Johnson

CHARLIE CHAN:

The House Without a Key, 1926, Pathe (serial). <u>W</u>: George Kuwa;
The Chinese Parrot, 1927, Univ. <u>W</u>: K. Sojin;
Behind That Curtain, 1929, Fox. <u>W</u>: E.L. Park;
Charlie Chan Carries On, 1931, Fox. <u>W</u>: Warner Oland;
The Black Camel, 1931, Fox. <u>W</u>: Warner Oland;
Charlie Chan's Chance, 1932, Fox. <u>W</u>: Warner Oland;
Charlie Chan's Greatest Case, 1933, Fox. <u>W</u>: Warner Oland;
Charlie Chan's Courage, 1934, Fox. <u>W</u>: Warner Oland;
Chan in London, 1934, Fox. <u>W</u>: Warner Oland;
Charlie Chan in Paris, 1935, Fox. <u>W</u>: Warner Oland;
Charlie Chan in Egypt, 1935, Fox. <u>W</u>: Warner Oland;
Charlie Chan in Shanghai, 1935, Fox. <u>W</u>: Warner Oland;
Charlie Chan's Secret, 1936, 20th-Fox. <u>W</u>: Warner Oland;
Charlie Chan at the Circus, 1936, 20th-Fox. <u>W</u>: Warner Oland;
Charlie Chan at the Race Track, 1936, 20th-Fox. <u>W</u>: Warner Oland;
Charlie Chan at the Opera, 1936, 20th-Fox. <u>W</u>: Warner Oland;
Charlie Chan at the Olympics, 1937, 20th-Fox. <u>W</u>: Warner Oland;
Charlie Chan on Broadway, 1937, 20th-Fox. <u>W</u>: Warner Oland;
Charlie Chan at Monte Carlo, 1937, 20th-Fox. <u>W</u>: Warner Oland;
Charlie Chan in Honolulu, 1938, 20th-Fox. <u>W</u>: Sidney Toler;
Charlie Chan in Reno, 1939, 20th-Fox. <u>W</u>: Sidney Toler;
Charlie Chan at Treasure Island, 1939, 20th-Fox. <u>W</u>: Sidney Toler;
Charlie Chan in City in Darkness, 1939, 20th-Fox. <u>W</u>: Sidney Toler;
Charlie Chan in Panama, 1940, 20th-Fox. <u>W</u>: Sidney Toler;
Charlie Chan's Murder Cruise, 1940, 20th-Fox. <u>W</u>: Sidney Toler;
Charlie Chan at the Wax Museum, 1940, 20th-Fox. <u>W</u>: Sidney Toler;
Murder Over New York, 1940, 20th-Fox. <u>W</u>: Sidney Toler;
Dead Men Tell, 1941, 20th-Fox. <u>W</u>: Sidney Toler;
Charlie Chan in Rio, 1941, 20th-Fox. <u>W</u>: Sidney Toler;
Castle in the Desert, 1942, 20th-Fox. <u>W</u>: Sidney Toler;
Charlie Chan in the Secret Service, 1944, Mono. <u>W</u>: Sidney Toler;
The Chinese Cat, 1944, Mono. <u>W</u>: Sidney Toler;
Black Magic, 1944, Mono. <u>W</u>: Sidney Toler;
The Jade Mask, 1945, Mono. <u>W</u>: Sidney Toler;
The Scarlet Clue, 1945, Mono. <u>W</u>: Sidney Toler;

The Shanghai Cobra, 1945, Mono. <u>W</u>: Sidney Toler;
The Red Dragon, 1945, Mono. <u>W</u>: Sidney Toler;
Dark Alibi, 1946, Mono. <u>W</u>: Sidney Toler;
Shadows Over Chinatown, 1946, Mono. <u>W</u>: Sidney Toler;
Dangerous Money, 1946, Mono. <u>W</u>: Sidney Toler;
The Trap, 1947, Mono. <u>W</u>: Sidney Toler;
The Chinese Ring, 1947, Mono. <u>W</u>: Roland Winters;
The Docks of New Orleans, 1948, Mono. <u>W</u>: Roland Winters;
The Shanghai Chest, 1948, Mono. <u>W</u>: Roland Winters;
The Golden Eye, 1948, Mono. <u>W</u>: Roland Winters;
The Feathered Serpent, 1948, Mono. <u>W</u>: Roland Winters;
Sky Dragon, 1949, Mono. <u>W</u>: Roland Winters;
Charlie Chan: Happiness is a Warm Clue, 1971, Univ. <u>W</u>: Ross Martin;
Charlie Chan and the Curse of the Dragon Queen, 1981, American Cinema. <u>W</u>: Peter Ustinov;

CRIME DOCTOR:

Crime Doctor, 1943, Col. <u>W</u>: Warner Baxter;
Crime Doctor's Strangest Case, 1943, Col. <u>W</u>: Warner Baxter;
Shadows in the Night, 1944, Col. <u>W</u>: Warner Baxter;
Crime Doctor's Courage, 1945, Col. <u>W</u>: Warner Baxter;
Crime Doctor's Warning, 1945, Col. <u>W</u>: Warner Baxter;
Crime Doctor's Manhunt, 1946, Col. <u>W</u>: Warner Baxter;
Just Before Dawn, 1946, Col. <u>W</u>: Warner Baxter;
The Millerson Case, 1947, Col. <u>W</u>: Warner Baxter;
Crime Doctor's Gamble, 1947, Col. <u>W</u>: Warner Baxter;
Crime Doctor's Diary, 1949, Col. <u>W</u>: Warner Baxter

DICK TRACY:

Dick Tracy, 1937, Rep (serial). <u>W</u>: Ralph Byrd;
Dick Tracy Returns, 1938, Rep (serial). <u>W</u>: Ralph Byrd;
Dick Tracy's G-Men, 1939, Rep (serial). <u>W</u>: Ralph Byrd;
Dick Tracy vs. Crime, Inc., 1941, Rep (serial). <u>W</u>: Ralph Byrd;
Dick Tracy, 1945, RKO. <u>W</u>: Morgan Conway;
Dick Tracy vs. Cueball, 1946, RKO. <u>W</u>: Morgan Conway;
Dick Tracy's Dilemma, 1947, RKO. <u>W</u>: Ralph Byrd;
Dick Tracy Meets Gruesome, 1947, RKO. <u>W</u>: Ralph Byrd;
Dick Tracy, 1990, Touchstone. <u>W</u>: Warren Beatty

ELLERY QUEEN:

The Spanish Cape Mystery, 1935, Rep. <u>W</u>: Donald Cook;
The Mandarin Mystery, 1936, Rep. <u>W</u>: Eddie Quillan;
Ellery Queen, Master Detective, 1940, Col. <u>W</u>: Ralph Bellamy;
Ellery Queen's Penthouse Mystery, 1941, Col. <u>W</u>: Ralph Bellamy;
Ellery Queen and the Perfect Crime, 1941, Col. <u>W</u>: Ralph Bellamy;
Ellery Queen and the Murder Ring, 1941, Col. <u>W</u>: Ralph Bellamy;
Close Call for Ellery Queen, 1942, Col. <u>W</u>: William Gargan;
Desperate Chance for Ellery Queen, 1942, Col. <u>W</u>: William Gargan;
Enemy Agents Meet Ellery Queen, 1942, Col. <u>W</u>: William Gargan;
Ellery Queen: Don't Look Behind You, 1971, Univ/ABC-TV. <u>W</u>: Peter Lawford;
Ellery Queen, 1975, Univ/ABC-TV. <u>W</u>: Jim Hutton

THE FALCON:

The Gay Falcon, 1941, RKO. <u>W</u>: George Sanders;
A Date with the Falcon, 1941, RKO. <u>W</u>: George Sanders;
The Falcon Takes Over, 1942, RKO. <u>W</u>: George Sanders;
The Falcon's Brother, 1942, RKO. <u>W</u>: George Sanders;
The Falcon Strikes Back, 1943, RKO. <u>W</u>: Tom Conway;
The Falcon in Danger, 1943, RKO. <u>W</u>: Tom Conway;
The Falcon and the Co-Eds, 1943, RKO. <u>W</u>: Tom Conway;
The Falcon Out West, 1944, RKO. <u>W</u>: Tom Conway;
The Falcon in Mexico, 1944, RKO. <u>W</u>: Tom Conway;
The Falcon in Hollywood, 1944, RKO. <u>W</u>: Tom Conway;
The Falcon in San Francisco, 1945, RKO. <u>W</u>: Tom Conway;
The Falcon's Alibi, 1946, RKO. <u>W</u>: Tom Conway;
The Falcon's Adventure, 1946, RKO. <u>W</u>: Tom Conway;
The Devil's Cargo, 1948, Film Classics. <u>W</u>: John Calvert;
Appointment with Murder, 1948, Film Classics. <u>W</u>: John Calvert;
Search for Danger, 1949, Film Classics. <u>W</u>: John Calvert

HILDEGARDE WITHERS:

The Penguin Pool Murder, 1932, RKO. <u>W</u>: Edna May Oliver;
Murder on the Blackboard, 1934, RKO. <u>W</u>: Edna May Oliver;
Murder on a Honeymoon, 1935, RKO. <u>W</u>: Edna May Oliver;
Murder on a Bridle Path, 1936, RKO. <u>W</u>: Helen Broderick;
The Plot Thickens, 1936, RKO. <u>W</u>: ZaSu Pitts;
Forty Naughty Girls, 1937, RKO. <u>W</u>: ZaSu Pitts;
A Very Missing Person, 1972, Univ/ABC-TV. <u>W</u>: Eve Arden

THE LONE WOLF:

The Lone Wolf, 1917, Selznick. <u>W</u>: Bert Lytell;
The False Faces, 1919, Para-Artcraft. <u>W</u>: Henry B. Walthall;
The Lone Wolf's Daughter, 1919, W.W. Hodkinson. <u>W</u>: Bertram Grassby;
The Lone Wolf, 1924, Assoc. Exhibitors. <u>W</u>: Jack Holt;
The Lone Wolf Returns, 1926, Col. <u>W</u>: Bert Lytell;

Alias the Lone Wolf, 1927, Col. <u>W</u>: Bert Lytell;
The Lone Wolf's Daughter, 1929, Col. <u>W</u>: Bert Lytell;
The Last of the Lone Wolf, 1930, Col. <u>W</u>: Bert Lytell;
Cheaters at Play, 1932, Fox. <u>W</u>: Thomas Meighan;
The Lone Wolf Returns, 1935, Col. <u>W</u>: Melvyn Douglas;
The Lone Wolf in Paris, 1938, Col. <u>W</u>: Francis Lederer;
The Lone Wolf Spy Hunt, 1939, Col. <u>W</u>: Warren William;
The Lone Wolf Strikes, 1940, Col. <u>W</u>: Warren William;
The Lone Wolf Meets a Lady, 1940, Col. <u>W</u>: Warren William;
The Lone Wolf Takes a Chance, 1941, Col. <u>W</u>: Warren William;
The Lone Wolf Keeps a Date, 1941, Col. <u>W</u>: Warren William;
Secrets of the Lone Wolf, 1941, Col. <u>W</u>: Warren William;
Counter-Espionage, 1942, Col. <u>W</u>: Warren William; *One Dangerous Night*, 1943, Col. <u>W</u>: Warren William;
Passport to Suez, 1943, Col. <u>W</u>: Warren William;
The Notorious Lone Wolf, 1946, Col. <u>W</u>: Gerald Mohr;
The Lone Wolf in London, 1947, Col. <u>W</u>: Gerald Mohr;
The Lone Wolf in Mexico, 1947, Col. <u>W</u>: Gerald Mohr;
The Lone Wolf and His Lady, 1949, Col. <u>W</u>: Ron Randell

MICHAEL SHAYNE:

Michael Shayne, Private Detective, 1940, 20th-Fox. <u>W</u>: Lloyd Nolan;
Sleepers West, 1941, 20th-Fox. <u>W</u>: Lloyd Nolan;
Dressed to Kill, 1941, 20th-Fox. <u>W</u>: Lloyd Nolan;
Blue, White and Perfect, 1941, 20th-Fox. <u>W</u>: Lloyd Nolan;
The Man Who Wouldn't Die, 1942, 20th-Fox. <u>W</u>: Lloyd Nolan;
Just Off Broadway, 1942, 20th-Fox. <u>W</u>: Lloyd Nolan;
Time to Kill, 1942, 20th-Fox. <u>W</u>: Lloyd Nolan;
Murder is My Business, 1946, PRC. <u>W</u>: Hugh Beaumont;
Larceny in Her Heart, 1946, PRC. <u>W</u>: Hugh Beaumont;
Blonde for a Day, 1946, PRC. <u>W</u>: Hugh Beaumont;
Three on a Ticket, 1947, PRC. <u>W</u>: Hugh Beaumont;
Too Many Winners, 1947, PRC. <u>W</u>: Hugh Beaumont

MR. MOTO:

Think Fast, Mr. Moto, 1937, 20th-Fox. <u>W</u>: Peter Lorre;
Thank You, Mr. Moto, 1937, 20th-Fox. <u>W</u>: Peter Lorre;
Mr. Moto's Gamble, 1938, 20th-Fox. <u>W</u>: Peter Lorre;
Mr. Moto Takes a Chance, 1938, 20th-Fox. <u>W</u>: Peter Lorre;
The Mysterious Mr. Moto, 1938, 20th-Fox. <u>W</u>: Peter Lorre;
Mr. Moto's Last Warning, 1939, 20th-Fox. <u>W</u>: Peter Lorre;
Mr. Moto in Danger Island, 1939, 20th-Fox. <u>W</u>: Peter Lorre;
Mr. Moto Takes a Vacation, 1939, 20th-Fox. <u>W</u>: Peter Lorre;
The Return of Mr. Moto, 1965, 20th-Fox. <u>W</u>: Henry Silva

MR. WONG:

Mr. Wong, Detective, 1938, Mono. <u>W</u>: Boris Karloff;
The Mystery of Mr. Wong, 1939, Mono. <u>W</u>: Boris Karloff;
Mr. Wong in Chinatown, 1939, Mono. <u>W</u>: Boris Karloff;
The Fatal Hour, 1940, Mono. <u>W</u>: Boris Karloff;
Doomed to Die, 1940, Mono. <u>W</u>: Boris Karloff;
Phantom of Chinatown, 1941, Mono. <u>W</u>: Keye Luke

THE SAINT:

The Saint in New York, 1938, RKO. <u>W</u>: Louis Hayward;
The Saint Strikes Back, 1939, RKO. <u>W</u>: George Sanders;
The Saint in London, 1939, RKO. <u>W</u>: George Sanders;
The Saint's Double Trouble, 1940, RKO. <u>W</u>: George Sanders;
The Saint Takes Over, 1940, RKO. <u>W</u>: George Sanders;
The Saint in Palm Springs, 1941, RKO. <u>W</u>: George Sanders;
The Saint's Vacation, 1941, RKO. <u>W</u>: Hugh Sinclair;
The Saint Meets the Tiger, 1943, Rep. <u>W</u>: Hugh Sinclair;
The Saint's Girl Friday, 1954, RKO. <u>W</u>: Louis Hayward;
Le Saint Mene la Dance, 1961, Films du Cyclope. <u>W</u>: Felix Marten;
Le Saint Prend l'Affut, 1966, SNC/Intermondia. <u>W</u>: Jean Marais;
The Fiction-Makers, 1967, ITC. <u>W</u>: Roger Moore;
Vendetta for the Saint, 1968, ITC. <u>W</u>: Roger Moore;
The Saint, 1997, Para. <u>W</u>: Val Kilmer

THE THIN MAN:

The Thin Man, 1934, MGM. <u>W</u>: William Powell;
After the Thin Man, 1936, MGM. <u>W</u>: William Powell;
Another Thin Man, 1939, MGM. <u>W</u>: William Powell;
Shadow of the Thin Man, 1941, MGM. <u>W</u>: William Powell;
The Thin Man Goes Home, 1944, MGM. <u>W</u>: William Powell;
Song of the Thin Man, 1947, MGM. <u>W</u>: William Powell

TORCHY BLANE:

Smart Blonde, 1937, WB. <u>W</u>: Glenda Farrell;
Fly-Away Baby, 1937, WB. <u>W</u>: Glenda Farrell;
The Adventurous Blonde, 1937, WB. <u>W</u>: Glenda Farrell;
Blondes at Work, 1938, WB. <u>W</u>: Glenda Farrell;
Torchy Blane in Panama, 1938, WB. <u>W</u>: Lola Lane;
Torchy Gets Her Man, 1938, WB. <u>W</u>: Glenda Farrell;
Torchy Blane in Chinatown, 1939, WB. <u>W</u>: Glenda Farrell;
Torchy Runs for Mayor, 1939, WB. <u>W</u>: Glenda Farrell;
Torchy Plays with Dynamite, 1939, WB. <u>W</u>: Jane Wyman